Stanley Gibbons
STAMP CATALOGUE

PART 1

British Commonwealth 1992/93

Including post-independence issues of
Ireland, Fiji and South Africa

Ninety-fifth edition

VOLUME 2
Countries J to Z

Stanley Gibbons Publications Ltd
London and Ringwood

By Appointment to Her Majesty The Queen
Stanley Gibbons Ltd, London
Philatelists

Published by **Stanley Gibbons Publications Ltd**
Editorial, Sales Offices and Distribution Centre:
5 Parkside, Christchurch Road, Ringwood,
Hants BH24 3SH.

ISBN: 0-85259-329-5

Item No. 2812 (92/3)

Text assembled by Black Bear Press Limited, Cambridge

Made and Printed in Great Britain by William Clowes Limited, Beccles, Suffolk

Preface to the 1992/93 Edition

REORGANIZATION AND REVIVAL

The long-anticipated point when this catalogue could no longer be produced as a single volume was reached with the publication of the 1992 edition. It was then clear to us that the *Part 1* had become physically difficult to use, due to its weight and bulk, and there were other associated problems such as the visibility of the text in columns next to the binding edge.

Plans for this eventuality had already been made. Regular readers may remember the questionnaire included with the 1987 edition and further soundings were taken subsequently. A detailed analysis of the options available to us was given in the January 1992 issue of *Gibbons Stamp Monthly*. After careful consideration of these it was decided that an alphabetical split, of the type which had worked successfully for *Stamps of the World* since 1983, was the best alternative.

It is our firm intention that the division into two volumes will provide easier handling without losing too much of the convenience of a single volume. To achieve this two further innovations, previewed in the preface last year, have been introduced. Readers will now find all issues for a particular country or territory listed under its current name. For example, stamps inscribed "BASUTOLAND" are now included, with their successors, under "LESOTHO" and those of "NORTHERN RHODESIA" precede those for "ZAMBIA". In almost all instances the catalogue and illustration numbers already run-on and there are obvious advantages in having issues listed consecutively. The other alteration is that stamps for previously separate colonies which subsequently united to form a federation are now listed before the issues for the larger country, rather than in alphabetical sequence. The Australian colonies now appear before Australia, the Canadian provinces before Canada and the various territories which combined to form South Africa are listed in the catalogue under "S". Full details of all these relocations will be found in the boxed panel on page xvi.

As the two volumes of the *Part 1* will be available separately it is our intention that each volume will be self-contained. Considerable progress towards this has been made in this edition with the provision of further illustrations and the amendment of cross-references in Volume 2. It is hoped to complete the task in next year's catalogue.

The reorganization of *Part 1* has, to a certain extent, overshadowed important trends elsewhere. The review of prices in this volume shows a stamp market in a far more healthy condition than has been the case for a number of years. There are other pointers to renewed interest in the hobby. Attendance figures for exhibitions and stamp fairs continue to rise, the flow of material for auction is improving and the more restrained approach of many postal administrations to the production of new issues have all combined to indicate that far brighter times are ahead.

PRICES

It is a relief to report that the era of widespread price reductions appears to have passed. With the exception of commemorative issues from the 1960s and 1970s, where levels are still depressed due to more than adequate stocks, increased demand, coupled with insufficient supplies, has caused prices to rise.

Trends visible in the 1992 edition continue. Some classic issues remain quiet, but rises from the later Queen Victoria issues onwards are substantial. Interest in the stamps of King George VI has grown to a point where there are even rises for some of the Omnibus sets and such movements have extended to the definitive issues of the present reign where some worthwhile increases occur for the first time in many years. Errors and varieties, as always, are still much sought-after, as are used examples of postage due issues.

The market in stamps from what is now **Malaysia** is still most active. There are considerable increases this year in the issues of the **Straits Settlements** and the trend has continued to the King George VI period both there and in the **Malayan States.** There are further rises amongst the issues for the **Japanese Occupation of Malaya** and the scarcer issues of **Labuan** continue to increase in value.

Elsewhere there is further evidence of the sustained demand for stamps from the classic period with many early **Ceylon** up in price and there is considerable activity amongst the **Uganda** "Missionaries".

A careful review, with the assistance of Mr. M. Bale, has been made of the **Palestine** issues from 1918 to 1922 and it is hoped that the new levels will more accurately reflect the current market for these stamps.

Interest in the **British Occupation of Mafia Island** continues unabated and the early overprints of **Zanzibar** have required more work to reflect the scarcity of these issues.

Recent auctions have provided a stimulus to **Transvaal** stamps and it is also interesting to note that the sometimes-neglected issues of **Turks and Caicos Islands** to 1893 have also had attention for this edition.

REVISIONS IN THIS EDITION

The task of listing chalk-surfaced paper varieties has been completed with work on the King George VI issues. Additional listings appear under **Leeward Islands, Malaya B.M.A., Mauritius, St. Kitts–Nevis, Seychelles** and **Sudan.**

A number of additional King George VI varieties have been added and the policy of improving the listings has been extended back to earlier issues with the inclusion of the malformed and repaired "S" flaw of the Queen Victoria Key Type (originally brought to our attention by Mr. P. O. Beale) and the King Edward VII dented frame ("Glover" flaw), both on **Seychelles,** and the split "A" on the King George V stamps of **St. Helena** and **Seychelles.**

Listings of butterflies and other insects in this edition have been revised to reflect the work of the Butterfly and Moth Stamp Society for our thematic catalogue *Collect Butterflies and Other Insects on Stamps.* It is worth noting that our listings of fauna and flora subjects often provide more accurate descriptions of species than the stamp captions.

Interest in the stamps of the **British West Indies** has been recently stimulated by the publication of Robson Lowe's long-awaited 6th volume of the *Encyclopaedia of British Empire Postage Stamps* which covers the issues of the Leeward Islands. The opportunity has been taken to revise the listing of these territories and additional information is now provided for **Leeward Islands, Montserrat** and the **St. Kitts–Nevis** group.

Jamaica. Further details are given for the 1916–17 War Tax overprints.

Malaysia—Labuan. The well-known variety showing the right foot omitted from the second Chinese character, which occurs on the 12c. value between 1879 and 1881, is now listed.

Mauritius. Issues to 1935 have been rewritten to provide a more chronological sequence for the earlier stamps, the consolidation of the Queen Victoria Crown CA watermark issues into two sets, one covering 1883 to 1894 and the other 1900 to 1905, and a better sequence for the later Key Types. Many additional dates are now quoted and these are reproduced, with permission, from Mr. Peter Ibbotson's impressive new handbook *The Postal History and Stamps of Mauritius.*

Morocco Agencies. Listings are now provided for unoverprinted Great Britain stamps used at the Tangier and Tetuan post offices between 1937 and 1949 based on information very kindly supplied by Mr. A. H. Bishop. It is hoped to provide prices for these stamps, some of which are believed to be scarce, in subsequent editions.

Namibia. In response to requests from collectors a third price column, for used singles of either inscription, has been added for the alternately- inscribed stamps of **South West Africa** between 1923 and 1949.

Palestine. A list of post offices outside Palestine which used E.E.F. issues between 1918 and 1920 is now provided, the information being reproduced, with permission, from *British Empire Campaigns and Occupations in the Near East 1914–1924* by John Firebrace.

St. Kitts–Nevis. Further King George VI flaws have been added.

Seychelles. A listing is now provided for the stamps of Mauritius used at the Victoria post office on the Seychelles between 1861 and 1890.

Singapore. The differences between the work of the two printers of the 1985 Insects definitives are now illustrated and listed. We are grateful to Mr. L. C. Stanway for making his research into these issues available to us.

South Africa. The **Orange Free State** Police Franks of 1896 to 1899 have now been included with the help of Mr. A. R. Allison of the Orange Free State Study Circle.

A third price column, for used singles of either inscription, has been added as appropriate to the listings for **South Africa** stamps between 1926 and 1951.

Considerable research into the status of No. D73 has concluded that, although this stamp may well have been printed, the lack of a confirmed example suggests that it was never issued. The entry has, in consequence, been deleted.

Sri Lanka. The listing of the **Ceylon** Official overprints has been revised with the help of Mr. A. P. Tonge of the Ceylon Study Circle.

Uganda. Discussions over a number of years have failed to produce any confirmed examples of Nos. 1, 3 and 5. These have been, consequently, deleted with the agreement of the East Africa Study Circle and the leading Expert Committees in this country.

Zimbabwe. The elusive 25c. on 10c. Postage Due surcharge of January 1990 finally makes its appearance in the catalogue and we are grateful to Mr. J. Barry of the Rhodesia Study Circle for providing the information on this stamp.

There are many other alterations elsewhere and, as always, we are most grateful to those collectors, dealers and postal administrations who continue to provide us with invaluable help in the improvement of the listings.

A final reminder. The two-volume *Part 1* catalogue to be published *next* year will be dated 1993, so the predating of editions, which has caused an increasing amount of confusion in recent years, will then be at an end.

David J. Aggersberg

Stanley Gibbons Holdings Plc Addresses

STANLEY GIBBONS LIMITED, STANLEY GIBBONS AUCTIONS LIMITED

399 Strand, London WC2R 0LX

Auction Room and Specialist Departments. Open Monday–Friday 9.30 a.m. to 5 p.m.

Shop. Open Monday 9.30 a.m. to 5.30 p.m., Tuesday–Friday 8.30 a.m. to 5.30 p.m. and Saturday 10 a.m. to 4 p.m.

Telephone 071 836 8444 and Fax 071 836 7342 for all departments.

STANLEY GIBBONS PUBLICATIONS LIMITED

5 Parkside, Christchurch Road, Ringwood, Hants BH24 3SH. Telephone 0425 472363 (24 hour answer phone service) and Fax 0425 470247.

Publications Shop (at above address). Open Monday–Friday 9.30 a.m. to 3.30 p.m.

Publications Mail Order. FREEPHONE 0800 611622 Monday–Friday 8.30 a.m. to 5.00 p.m.

STANLEY GIBBONS AUSTRALIA PTY LTD

P.O. Box 863J, Melbourne 3001, Australia. Telephone (01 0613) 670 3332 and Telex AA 37223.

STANLEY GIBBONS PUBLICATIONS LIMITED OVERSEAS REPRESENTATION

Stanley Gibbons Publications Ltd are represented overseas by the following sole distributors (*), main agents (**) or licensees (***).

Australia*

Lighthouse Philatelic (Aust.) Pty Ltd
PO Box 763
Strawberry Hills
New South Wales 2012
Australia

Belgium and Luxembourg**

Philac
Rue du Midi 48
Bruxelles
Belgium 1000

Canada*

Lighthouse Publications (Canada) Ltd
255 Duke Street
Montreal
Quebec
Canada H3C 2M2

Denmark**

Nordfrim
DK 5450
Otterup
Denmark

France*

Davo France SARL
25 Rue Monge
75005 Paris
France

Germany and Austria**

Leuchtturm Albenverlag
Paul Koch KG
Am Spakenberg 45
Postfach 1340
D-2054 Geesthacht
Germany

Ka-Be Briefmarkenalben-Verlag
Daimlerstrasse 15
Volkhardt GMBH
Goppingen
Germany

Hong Kong**

Po-on Stamp Service
GPO Box 2498
Hong Kong

Israel**

Capital Stamps
PO Box 3769
Jerusalem 91036
Israel

Italy*

Secrian Srl
Via Pantelleria 2
1-20156 Milano
Italy

Japan**

Japan Philatelic Co Ltd
PO Box 2
Suginami-Minami
Tokyo
Japan

Netherlands*

Davo Publications
PO Box 411
7400 AK Deventer
Netherlands

New Zealand*

Philatelic Distributors Ltd
PO Box 863
New Plymouth
New Zealand

Norway**

Wennergren Cappelen AS
Nedre Vollgate 4
PO Box 738
Sentrum N-0105
Oslo 1
Norway

Singapore***

Stanley Gibbons (Singapore) Pte Ltd
Raffles City
PO Box 1689
Singapore 9117
Republic of Singapore

South Africa

Stanley Gibbons (Pty) Ltd***
PO Box 930
Parklands
RSA 2121

Republic Coin and Stamp Accessories (Pty)**
PO Box 260325
Excom 2023
Johannesburg
RSA

Sweden*

Chr Winther Sorensen AB
Box 43
S-310 Knared
Sweden

Switzerland**

Phila Service
Burgstrasse 160
CH 4125 Riehen
Switzerland

USA*

Lighthouse Publications Inc
PO Box 705
274 Washington Avenue
Hackensack
New Jersey 07602-0705
USA

West Indies/Caribbean**

Hugh Dunphy
PO Box 413
Kingston 10
Jamaica
West Indies

Contents

Numbers Added or Changed

STAMPS ADDED

Excluding new issues which have appeared in Gibbons *Stamp Monthly* Supplements, the following are the Catalogue numbers of stamps listed in this edition for the first time.

Jamaica. 68d, 68eb

Kenya, Uganda and Tanganyika (British East Africa). 34b, 61a

Leeward Islands. 109a/ab, 110b, 111a, 112a, 113b

Lesotho. 948ea/eb, 948fa

Malaysia — Straits Settlements. 75b, 80c, 225ab
BMA Malaya. 1a, 2a, 4b, 6a, 8a, 12a, 12ba, 13a, 14a
Malaysia. 48a, 49a, 50a, 254a, 410b/ba, 411b, 424a, 430a, 431a, 447a
Negri Sembilan (Sungei Ujong). 36a, 38a, 43c
Negri Sembilan. 24a
Pahang. 18b, 31a
Perak. 105a
Selangor. 70ab, 71a
Labuan. 3a, 9a, 11d, 13c, 14a, 15d, 34f, 72c, 83eb, 85f, 90b, 121a
Sabah (North Borneo). 79b, 94ab, 204*a*, 344b, J6a, J14a

Maldive Islands. 213a

Malta. 103c, 334c, 337a

Mauritius. 245f, 259b/ba, 260b/ba, 261a, 263a, 488a

Montserrat. 7bb, O14a

Morocco Agencies. Z170/224

Namibia. 359ba, 524a, 558a

New Zealand. 605a, 720a, 1562a

Norfolk Island. 62a

Pakistan. O132, O135a, O136, O138/9

Papua New Guinea (New Guinea). 6a, 11e, 24ia, 24k, 64df, 64ea

Rhodesia. 106*b*, 106ca, 107, 107*b*/ba, 107ca, 114*b*

St. Helena. 85a, 86a

St. Kitts–Nevis — Nevis. F6a
St. Kitts–Nevis. 71bb, 73ba/bd, 74a, 74bb, 75c/ca, 76ab, 77ac, 77b/bc

St. Vincent. MS1136*a*

Seychelles. Z1/65, ZR1, 28a, 29a, 30a, 33a, 35a, 36a, 37b, 42b, 45b, 46a, 47a, 48a, 49a, 50a, 51a, 52a, 53a, 54a, 55a, 56a, 57a, 58a, 59a, 60a, 61a, 62a, 63a, 64a, 65a, 66a, 67a, 68a, 69a, 70a, 71a, 72a, 73b, 74a, 75a, 76a, 77a, 78a, 79a, 80a, 81b, 128c, 129c, 130c, 135a, 136ab, 137ac, 138ab, 138ad, 139ca, 140ab, 143*b*, 144a, 145ab, 238a, 378ba

Singapore. 491a, 492a, 493a, 494a, 495a, 496a, 497a, 498a

South Africa — Orange Free State. 117o, PF1/3
Transvaal. 11a, 14b, 99c, 105b, 171a, 227g
South Africa. 45a, 45ba, 388ab

South Arabian Federation — Kathiri State of Seiyun. 75a

Sri Lanka. 605c/d, 921b/c, O7a

Sudan. 3a, 4a, 37a, 38a, 39a, 40a, 41a, 42a, 43a, 44a, 44ba, 45a, 45ba, 46ba, 109a, O36a, O38a, O39a, O39ca, O40a

Swaziland. 475a

Transjordan. 39ba, 129b

Tristan da Cunha. D3a

Uganda. 93b

Vanuatu. F243a

Zambia. 86a, 520a

Zimbabwe. 61a, D33

CATALOGUE NUMBERS ALTERED

The table below is a cross-reference for those stamps, the Catalogue numbers of which have altered in this edition.

Old	New
Jamaica	
68*d*/da	68*e*/ea
69aa	69ab
Leeward Islands	
51*c*	51*d*
51*d*	51*c*
109*a*/ab	109*b*/ba
110*b*/*c*	110*ba*/*bb*
111*a*	111*ab*
112a	112ab
113*b*	113*c*
Malaysia — B.M.A. Malaya	
8*a*/*b*	8*b*/*c*
12*a*	12*b*
13a	13ab
Pahang	
18b/cb	18c/dc
Labuan	
83a	83ea
85a	85fa
85b	85db
90b/d	90c/e
93a	93ba
120a	120ba
121a	121b
Sabah (North Borneo)	
79b/c	79c/d
93c	93ab
102c	102ab
Maldive Islands	
1428/37	1437/45
Malta	
103c	103d
Mauritius	
26/34	36/44
35/42	26/32
43	34
44	33
45	35
46/7	54/5
48/55	46/53
69	70
70	69
74/5	78/b
101	102
102	104
103	110
104/8	112/16
110	103
111/12	105/6
113	109
114	111
115/20	117/21
125	101
126/7	107/8
128/31*a*	127/31
140	141
141	149
142/9	156/63
150	140
151/7	142/8
158/63	150/5
197	196*a*
207/8	209/10
209/11	212/15
212	217
213	219
214	220
215/a	227/a
216	231
216*a*/*b*	232*a*/*b*
217	232
218/23	236/41
224	222
225/7	242/4
228/9	207/8
230	211
231	216
232	218
233	219*a*
234	221
235/8*b*	223/6*b*
239/41*a*	228/30*a*
242/4*a*	233/5*a*
260*b*	260*c*
261*a*	261*b*
801/2	806/7
808	810
809	801
811/12	802/3
814	804
815	813
817	805
Montserrat	
O14a	O14b
Pakistan	
O132	O133
O133	O135
O134	O137
Rhodesia	
106	106*c*
106*b*	106
107	107*c*
115	114*c*
St. Kitts–Nevis — St. Christopher	
3	*Deleted*
7	*Deleted*
9/10	7/8
22	23
23	22
Nevis	
1	5a
2	6a
3	7a
4	8a
27	27*a*
27*a*	27
St. Kitts–Nevis	
19*b*	19*ab*
44a	*Deleted*
71*aa*/ab	71a/*ba*
74a/ab	74b/ba
77ac	77ad
Seychelles	
137*b*	137ab
138*b*	138ac
139*b*	139ab
139d	139cb
144*a*	144*b*
South Africa — Orange Free State	
136d	136ca
South Africa	
45*a*	45*b*
D73	*Deleted*
Sri Lanka	
6a	5a
329ca	*Deleted*
O7a	O7b
Sudan	
44*a*/*b*	44*b*/*c*
45*a*/*b*	45*b*/*c*
O39*a*/*b*	O39*b*/*c*
O40*a*/*b*	O40*b*/*c*
Trinidad and Tobago	
D26aa/b	D26a/ac
D28aa/b	D28a/ac
D31aa/b	D31a/ac
Uganda	
1	*Deleted*
3	*Deleted*
5	*Deleted*
Zambia	
629	631
630	635
631/40	637/46
D1b	D1ab
D3aa/b	D3a/ac
Zimbabwe	
D1/25	D8/32

Specialist Philatelic Societies

British Decimal Stamps Study Circle
Secretary—Mr. P. R. Daniels
70 Moor Park Close, Rainham, Gillingham, Kent ME8 8QT

Great Britain Philatelic Society
Membership Secretary—Mr. D. S. Glover
10 Rockwood Park, Saint Hill, East Grinstead, West Sussex RH19 4JX

Great Britain Decimal Stamp Book Study Circle
Membership Secretary—Mr. A. J. Wilkins
3 Buttermere Close, Brierley Hill, West Midlands DY5 3SD

Channel Islands Specialists Society
Membership Secretary—Mr. B. Cropp
17 Westlands Avenue, Huntercombe, Slough, Berkshire SL1 6AG

Ascension Study Circle
Secretary—Dr. R. C. F. Baker
Greys, Tower Road, Whitstable, Kent CT5 2ER

Bechuanalands and Botswana Society
Secretary—Mr. M. George
P.O. Box 108, St. Albans, Hertfordshire AL1 3AD

Belize Philatelic Study Circle
Secretary—Mr. C. R. Gambill
730 Collingswood, Corpus Christi, Texas 78412, U.S.A.

Bermuda Collectors Society
Secretary—Mr. T. J. McMahon
Nash Road, Purdy Station, N.Y. 10578, U.S.A.

Bermuda High (Keyplates)
Editor—Mr. R. W. Dickgiesser
P.O. Box 475, Derby, CT 06418, U.S.A.

British Caribbean Philatelic Study Group
Overseas Director—Mr. R. V. Swarbrick
The Four Winds, 919 Uppingham Road, Bushby, Leicestershire LE7 9RR

British Society of Australian Philately
Secretary—Mr. T. R. Finlayson
86 Clarence Road, Fleet, Hampshire GU13 9RS

British West Indies Study Circle
Secretary—Mr. M. Wilson
Timbers, Chequers Road, Tharston, Norwich, Norfolk NR15 2YA

Burma Philatelic Study Circle
Secretary—Mr. A. Meech
7208-91 Avenue, Edmonton, Alberta, Canada T6B 0R8

Canadian Philatelic Society of Great Britain
Secretary—Mr. B. T. Stalker
Glaramara, Parc Bryn Coch, Upper Bryn Coch, Mold, Clwyd

Ceylon Study Circle
Secretary—Mr. R.W.P. Frost
42 Lonsdale Road, Cannington, Bridgwater, Somerset TA5 2JS

Cyprus Study Circle
Secretary—Dr. R. I. Watson
Hill Cottage, Slinfold, West Sussex RH13 7SN

East Africa Study Circle
Secretary—Mr. R. Dunstan
Chantry Court, 1 The Close, Warminster, Wiltshire BA12 9AL

Falklands Islands Study Group
Membership Secretary—Mr. D. W. A. Jeffery
38 Bradstock Road, Stoneleigh, Epsom, Surrey KT17 2LH

Gibraltar Philatelic Society
Honorary Secretary—Mr. M. Ramagge
P.O. Box 270, Gibraltar

Gibraltar Study Circle
Membership Secretary—Mr. B. M. Walker
21 Orchard Street, Aberdeen AB2 3DA

Great Britain Overprints Society
Membership Secretary—Mr. A. H. Bishop
The Coach House, Ridgemount Road, Sunningdale, Berkshire SL5 9RL

Greater Southern Africa Philatelic Society
Representative—Mr. A. H. Murray
Erlesdene Garden Cottage, Greenwalk, Bowdon, Altrincham, Cheshire WA14 2SL

Hong Kong Study Circle
Membership Secretary—Mr. P. V. Ball
37 Hart Court, Newcastle-under-Lyme, Staffordshire ST5 2AL

Indian Ocean Study Circle (Western Islands)
Secretary—Mrs. D. J. Hopson
Field Acre, Hoe Benham, Newbury, Berkshire RG16 8PD

India Study Circle
Secretary—Dr. W. Fincham
10 Vallis Way, London W13 0DD

Irish Philatelic Circle
General Secretary—Mr. P. J. Wood
21 Loftus Road, London W12 7EH

King George V Silver Jubilee Study Circle
Secretary—Mr. N. Levinge
11 Broadway, Northampton NN1 4SF

King George VI Collectors Society
Secretary—Mr. F. R. Lockyer, OBE
24 Stourwood Road, Southbourne, Bournemouth, Dorset BH6 3QP

Malaya Study Group
Membership Secretary—Mr. D. Moon
Holly Cottage, Barrows Road, Cheddar, Somerset BS27 3BD

Malta Study Circle
Membership Secretary—Mr. D. Ward
40 Kingsman Road, Stanford-le-Hope, Essex SS17 0JW

New Zealand Society of Great Britain
General Secretary—Mrs. M. Frankcom
Queens House, 34a Tarrant Street, Arundel, West Sussex BN18 9DJ

Orange Free State Study Circle
Secretary—Mr. J. R. Stroud
28 Oxford Street, Burnham-on-Sea, Somerset TA8 1LQ

Pacific Islands Study Circle of Great Britain
Honorary Secretary—Mr. J. D. Ray
24 Woodvale Avenue, London SE25 4AE

Papuan Philatelic Society
Secretary—Mr. G. Amedro
45A Main Street, Gorebridge, Midlothian EH23 4BX

Pitcairn Islands Study Group (U.K.)
Honorary Secretary—Mr. A. B. Mears
Ragnall Cottge, Ragnall Lane, Walkley Wood, Nailsworth, Stroud, Gloucestershire GL6 0RX

Rhodesian Study Circle
Membership Secretary—Miss B. J. R. Lashbrook
25 Exe View, Exminster, Devon EX6 8AL

St. Helena, Ascension and Tristan da Cunha Philatelic Society
Secretary—Mrs. V. W. Finne
P.O. Box 366, Calpella, California 95418, U.S.A.

Sarawak Specialists Society
Secretary—Dr. J. Higgins
The Stone House, Grimston Road, South Wootton, Kings Lynn, Norfolk PE30 3NR

South African Collectors' Society
General Secretary—Mr. W. A. Page
138 Chastilian Road, Dartford, Kent DA1 3LG

Sudan Study Group
Secretary—Mr. J. W. Scott
Bemerton, Lingfield Road, East Grinstead, West Sussex RH19 2EJ

Tonga and Tin Can Mail Study Circle
Secretary—Mr. T. Jackson
121 Mullingar Ct. 1A, Schaumburg, IL60193-3258, U.S.A.

Transvaal Study Circle
Secretary—Mr. J. Woolgar
132 Dale Street, Chatham, Kent ME4 6QH

West Africa Study Circle
Secretary—Mr. J. Powell
7 Pebble Moor, Edlesborough, Dunstable, Bedfordshire LU6 2HZ

General Philatelic Information

and Guidelines to the Scope of the Part 1 (British Commonwealth) Catalogue

The notes which follow seek to reflect current practice in compiling the Part 1 (British Commonwealth) Catalogue.

It scarcely needs emphasising that the *Stanley Gibbons Stamp Catalogue* has a very long history and that the vast quantity of information it contains has been carefully built up by successive generations through the work of countless individuals. Philately itself is never static and the Catalogue has evolved and developed during this long time-span. Thus, while these notes are important for today's criteria, they may be less precise the further back in the listings one travels. They are not intended to inaugurate some unwanted series of piecemeal alterations in a widely respected work, but it does seem to us useful that Catalogue users know as exactly as possible the policies currently in operation.

PRICES

The prices quoted in this Catalogue are the estimated selling prices of Stanley Gibbons Ltd at the time of publication. They are, *unless it is specifically stated otherwise*, for examples in fine condition for the issue concerned. Superb examples are worth more; those of a lower quality considerably less.

All prices are subject to change without prior notice and Stanley Gibbons Ltd may from time to time offer stamps below catalogue price. Individual low value stamps sold at 399, Strand are liable to an additional handling charge.

No guarantee is given to supply all stamps priced, since it is not possible to keep every catalogued item in stock. Commemorative issues may, at times, only be available in complete sets and not as individual values.

Quotation of prices. The prices in the left-hand column are for unused stamps and those in the right-hand column are for used.

A dagger (†) denotes that the item listed does not exist in that condition and a blank, or dash, that it exists, or may exist, but no market price is known.

Prices are expressed in pounds and pence sterling. One pound comprises 100 pence (£1 = 100p).

The method of notation is as follows: pence in numerals (e.g. 10 denotes ten pence); pound and pence, up to £100, in numerals (e.g. 4·25 denotes four pounds and twenty-five pence); prices above £100 expressed in whole pounds with the "£" sign shown.

Unused stamps. Great Britain and Commonwealth: the prices for unused stamps of Queen Victoria to King George V are for lightly hinged examples. Unused prices for King Edward VIII to Queen Elizabeth II issues are for unmounted mint.

Some stamps from the King George VI period are often difficult to find in unmounted mint condition. In such instances we would expect that collectors would need to pay a high proportion of the price quoted to obtain mounted mint examples. Generally speaking lightly mounted mint stamps from this reign, issued before 1945, are in considerable demand.

Mounted mint stamps from the reign of Queen Elizabeth II are frequently available at lower prices than those quoted for the stamps unmounted.

Used stamps. The used prices are normally for stamps postally used but may be for stamps cancelled-to-order where this practice exists.

A pen-cancellation on early issues can sometimes correctly denote postal use. Instances are individually noted in the Catalogue in explanation of the used price given.

Prices quoted for bisects on cover or on large piece are for those dated during the period officially authorised.

Stamps not sold unused to the public (e.g. some official stamps) are priced used only.

The use of "unified" designs, that is stamps inscribed for both postal and fiscal purposes, results in a number of stamps of very high face value. In some instances these may not have been primarily intended for postal purposes, but if they are so inscribed we include them. We only price such items used, however, where there is evidence of normal postal usage.

Cover prices. To assist collectors, cover prices are quoted for issues up to 1945 at the beginning of each country.

The system gives a general guide in the form of a factor by which the corresponding used price of the loose stamp should be multiplied when found in fine average condition on cover.

Care is needed in applying the factors and they relate to a cover which bears a single of the denomination listed; strips and blocks would need individual valuation outside the scope. If more than one denomination is present the most highly priced attracts the multiplier and the remainder are priced at the simple figure for used singles in arriving at a total.

The cover should be of non-philatelic origin, bearing the correct postal rate for the period and distance involved and cancelled with the markings normal to the offices concerned. Purely philatelic items have a cover value only slightly greater than the catalogue value for the corresponding used stamps. This applies generally to those high-value stamps used philatelically rather than in the normal course of commerce. Low-value stamps, e.g. $\frac{1}{4}$d. and $\frac{1}{2}$d., are desirable when used as a single rate on cover and merit an increase in "multiplier" value.

First-day covers in the period up to 1945 are not within the scope of the system and the multiplier should not be used. As a special category of philatelic usage, with wide variations in valuation according to scarcity, they require separate treatment.

Oversized covers, difficult to accommodate on an album page, should be reckoned as worth little more than the corresponding value of the used stamps. The condition of a cover affects its value. Except for "wreck covers", serious damage or soiling reduce the value where the postal markings and stamps are ordinary ones. Conversely, visual appeal adds to the value and this can include freshness of appearance, important addresses, old-fashioned but legible hand-writing, historic town-names, etc.

The multipliers are a base on which further value would be added to take account of the cover's postal historical importance in demonstrating such things as unusual, scarce or emergency cancels, interesting routes, significant postal markings, combination usage, the development of postal rates, and so on.

For *Great Britain*, rather than multiplication factors, the cover price is shown as a third column, following the prices for unused and used stamps. It will be extended beyond King Edward VII in subsequent editions.

Minimum price. The minimum price quoted is ten pence. This represents a handling charge rather than a basis for valuing common stamps, for which the 10p price should not be reckoned automatically, since it covers a variation in real scarcity.

Set prices. Set prices are generally for one of each value, excluding shades and varieties, but including major colour changes. Where there are alternative shades, etc., the cheapest is usually included. The number of stamps in the set is always stated for clarity. The mint prices for sets containing *se-tenant* pieces are based on the prices quoted for such combinations, and not on those for the individual stamps.

Specimen stamps. The pricing of these items is explained under that heading.

Repricing. Collectors will be aware that the market factors of supply and demand directly influence the prices quoted in this Catalogue. Whatever the scarcity of a particular stamp, if there is no one in the market who wishes to buy it it cannot be expected to achieve a high price. Conversely, the same item actively sought by numerous potential buyers may cause the price to rise.

All the prices in this Catalogue are examined during the preparation of each new edition by expert staff of Stanley Gibbons and repriced as necessary. They take many factors into account, including supply and demand, and are in close touch with the international stamp market and the auction world.

Commonwealth cover prices and advice on postal history material originally provided by Edward B. Proud.

GUARANTEE

All stamps are guaranteed genuine originals in the following terms:

If not as described, and returned by the purchaser, we undertake to refund the price paid to us in the original transaction. If any stamp is certified as genuine by the Expert Committee of the Royal Philatelic Society, London, or by B.P.A. Expertising Ltd, the purchaser shall not be entitled to make any claim against us for any error, omission or mistake in such certificate.

Consumers' statutory rights are not affected by the above guarantee.

The recognised Expert Committees in this country are those of the Royal Philatelic Society, 41 Devonshire Place, London W1N 1PE, and B.P.A. Expertising Ltd, P.O. Box 137, Leatherhead, Surrey KT22 0RG. They do not undertake valuations under any circumstances and fees are payable for their services.

THE CATALOGUE IN GENERAL

Contents. The Catalogue is confined to adhesive postage stamps, including miniature sheets. For particular categories the rules are:

(*a*) Revenue (fiscal) stamps or telegraph stamps are listed only where they have been expressly authorised for postal duty.

(*b*) Stamps issued only precancelled are included, but normally issued stamps available additionally with precancel have no separate precancel listing unless the face value is changed.

(*c*) Stamps prepared for use but not issued, hitherto accorded full listing, are nowadays footnoted with a price (where possible).

(*d*) Bisects (trisects, etc.) are only listed where such usage was officially authorised.

(*e*) Stamps issued only on first day covers or in presentation packs and not available separately are not listed but may be priced in a footnote.

(*f*) New printings are only included in this Catalogue where they show a major philatelic variety, such as a change in shade, watermark or paper. Further details of modern new printings, including changes in imprint dates, are given in the *Two Reigns Catalogue* series. (Details for the relevant areas are also given in *Collect Channel Islands and Isle of Man Stamps*.)

(*g*) Official and unofficial reprints are dealt with by footnote.

(*h*) Stamps from imperforate printings of modern issues which also occur perforated are covered by footnotes, but are listed where widely available for postal use.

Exclusions. The following are excluded: (*a*) non-postal revenue or fiscal stamps; (*b*) postage stamps used fiscally; (*c*) local carriage labels and private local issues; (*d*) telegraph stamps; (*e*) bogus or phantom stamps; (*f*) railway or airline letter fee stamps, bus or road transport company labels; (*g*) cut-outs; (*h*) all types of non-postal labels and souvenirs; (*i*) documentary labels for the postal service, e.g. registration, recorded delivery, airmail etiquettes, etc.; (*j*) privately applied embellishments to official issues and privately commissioned items generally; (*k*) stamps for training postal officers.

Full listing. "Full listing" confers our recognition and implies allotting a catalogue number and (wherever possible) a price quotation.

In judging status for inclusion in the catalogue broad considerations are applied to stamps. They must be issued by a legitimate postal authority, recognised by the government concerned, and must be adhesives valid for proper postal use in the class of service for which they are inscribed. Stamps, with the exception of such categories as postage dues and officials, must be available to the general public, at face value, in reasonable quantities without any artificial restrictions being imposed on their distribution.

We record as abbreviated Appendix entries, without catalogue numbers or prices, stamps from countries which either persist in having far more issues than can be justified by postal need or have failed to maintain control over their distribution so that they have not been available to the public in reasonable quantities at face value. Miniature sheets and imperforate stamps are not mentioned in these entries.

The publishers of this catalogue have observed, with concern, the proliferation of "artificial" stamp-issuing territories. On several occasions this has resulted in separately inscribed issues for various component parts of otherwise united states or territories.

Stanley Gibbons Publications Ltd have decided that where such circumstances occur, they will not, in the future, list these items in the SG catalogue without first satisfying themselves that the stamps represent a genuine political, historical or postal division within the country concerned. Any such issues which do not fulfil this stipulation will be recorded in the Catalogue Appendix only.

For errors and varieties the criterion is legitimate (albeit inadvertent) sale through a postal administration in the normal course of business. Details of provenance are always important; printers' waste and fraudulently manufactured material is excluded.

Certificates. In assessing unlisted items due weight is given to Certificates from recognised Expert Committees and, where appropriate, we will usually ask to see them.

New issues. New issues are listed regularly in the Catalogue Supplement published in *Gibbons Stamp Monthly,* whence they are consolidated into the next available edition of the Catalogue.

Date of issue. Where local issue dates differ from dates of release by agencies, "date of issue" is the local date. Fortuitous stray usage before the officially intended date is disregarded in listing. For ease of reference, the Catalogue displays in the top corner the date of issue of the first set listed on each page.

Catalogue numbers. Stamps of each country are catalogued chronologically by date of issue. Subsidiary classes are placed at the end of the country, as separate lists, with a distinguishing letter prefix to the catalogue number, e.g. D for postage due, O for official and E for express delivery stamps.

The catalogue number appears in the extreme left column. The boldface Type numbers in the next column are merely cross-references to illustrations. Catalogue numbers in the *Gibbons Stamp Monthly* Supplement are provisional only and may need to be altered when the lists are consolidated. For the numbering of miniature sheets and sheetlets *see* section below.

Once published in the Catalogue, numbers are changed as little as possible; really serious renumbering is reserved for the occasions when a complete country or an entire issue is being rewritten. The edition first affected includes cross-reference tables of old and new numbers.

Our catalogue numbers are universally recognised in specifying stamps and as a hallmark of status.

Illustrations. Stamps are illustrated at three-quarters linear size. Stamps not illustrated are the same size and format as the value shown, unless otherwise indicated. Stamps issued only as miniature sheets have the stamp alone illustrated but sheet size is also quoted. Overprints, surcharges and watermarks are normally actual size. Illustrations of varieties are often enlarged to show the detail.

Designers. Designers' names are quoted where known, though space precludes naming every individual concerned in the production of a set. In particular, photographers supplying material are usually named only where they also make an active contribution in the design stage; posed photographs of reigning monarchs are, however, an exception to this rule.

CONTACTING THE CATALOGUE EDITOR

The editor is always interested in hearing from people who have new information which will improve or correct the Catalogue. As a general rule he must see and examine the actual stamps before they can be considered for listing; photographs or photocopies are insufficient evidence.

Submissions should be made in writing to the Catalogue Editor, Stanley Gibbons Publications Ltd. at the Ringwood office. The cost of return postage for items submitted is appreciated, and this should include the registration fee if required.

Where information is solicited purely for the benefit of the enquirer, the editor cannot undertake to reply if the answer is already contained in these published notes or if return postage is omitted. Written communications are greatly preferred to enquiries by telephone and the editor regrets that he or his staff cannot see personal callers without a prior appointment being made. Correspondence may be subject to delay during the production period of each new edition.

The editor welcomes close contact with study circles and is interested, too, in finding reliable local correspondents who will verify and supplement official information in countries where this is deficient.

We regret we do not give opinions as to the genuineness of stamps, nor do we identify stamps or number them by our Catalogue.

TECHNICAL MATTERS

The meanings of the technical terms used in the catalogue will be found in our *Philatelic Terms Illustrated* (3rd edition), (*price £7.50 plus postage and packing charge*).

References below to "more specialised" listings are to be taken to indicate, as appropriate, the Stanley Gibbons *Great Britain Specialised Catalogue* in 5 volumes; the *Great Britain, Australia* or *New Zealand Concise Catalogues* and (for Commonwealth stamps from 1937) the *Two Reigns Stamp Catalogue* series.

1. Printing

Printing errors. Errors in printing are of major interest to the Catalogue. Authenticated items meriting consideration would include: background, centre or frame inverted or omitted; centre or subject transposed; error of colour; error or omission of value; double prints and impressions; printed both sides; and so on. Designs *tête-bêche,* whether intentionally or by accident, are listable. *Se-tenant* arrangements of stamps are recognised in the listings or footnotes. Gutter pairs (a pair of stamps separated by blank margin) are not included in this volume. Colours only partially omitted are not listed. Stamps with embossing omitted and (for Commonwealth countries) stamps printed on the gummed side are reserved for our more specialised listings.

Printing varieties. Listing is accorded to major changes in the printing base which lead to completely new types. In recess-printing this could be a design re-engraved; in photogravure or photolithography a screen altered in whole or in part. It can also encompass flat-bed and rotary printing if the results are readily distinguishable.

To be considered at all, varieties must be constant.

Early stamps, produced by primitive methods, were prone to numerous imperfections: the lists reflect this, recognising re-entries, retouches, broken frames, misshapen letters, and so on. Printing technology has, however, radically improved over the years, during which time photogravure and lithography have become predominant. Varieties nowadays are more in the nature of flaws and these, being too specialised for this general catalogue, are almost always outside the scope. The development of our range of specialised catalogues allows us now to list those items which have philatelic significance in their appropriate volume.

In no catalogue, however, do we list such items as: dry prints, kiss prints, doctor-blade flaws, colour shifts or registration flaws (unless they lead to the complete omission of a colour from an individual stamp), lithographic ring flaws, and so on. Neither do we recognise fortuitous happenings like paper creases or confetti flaws.

Overprints (and surcharges). Overprints of different types qualify for separate listing. These include overprints in different colours; overprints from different printing processes such as litho and typo; overprints in totally different typefaces, etc. Major errors in machine-printed overprints are important and listable. They include: overprint inverted or omitted; overprint double (treble, etc.); overprint diagonal; overprint double, one inverted; pairs with one overprint omitted, e.g. from a radical shift to an adjoining stamp; error of colour; error of type fount; letters inverted or omitted, etc. If the overprint is handstamped, few of these would qualify and a distinction is drawn. We continue, however, to list pairs of stamps where one has a handstamped overprint and the other has not.

Varieties occurring in overprints will often take the form of broken letters, slight differences in spacing, rising spaces, etc. Only the most important would be considered for footnote mention.

Sheet positions. If space permits we quote sheet positions of listed varieties and authenticated data is solicited for this purpose.

De La Rue plates. The Catalogue classifies the general plates used by De La Rue for printing British Colonial stamps as follows:

VICTORIAN KEY TYPE

Die I

1. The ball of decoration on the second point of the crown appears as a dark mass of lines.
2. Dark vertical shading separates the front hair from the bun.
3. The vertical line of colour outlining the front of the throat stops at the sixth line of shading on the neck.

4. The white space in the coil of the hair above the curl is roughly the shape of a pin's head.

Die II

1. There are very few lines of colour in the ball and it appears almost white.
2. A white vertical strand of hair appears in place of the dark shading.
3. The line stops at the eighth line of shading.
4. The white space is oblong, with a line of colour partially dividing it at the left end.

Plates numbered 1 and 2 are both Die I. Plates 3 and 4 are Die II.

GEORGIAN KEY TYPE

Die I

A. The second (thick) line below the name of the country is cut slanting, conforming roughly to the shape of the crown on each side.
B. The labels of solid colour bearing the words "POSTAGE" and "& REVENUE" are square at the inner top corners.
C. There is a projecting "bud" on the outer spiral of the ornament in each of the lower corners.

Die II

A. The second line is cut vertically on each side of the crown.
B. The labels curve inwards at the top.
C. There is no "bud" in this position.

Unless otherwise stated in the lists, all stamps with watermark Multiple Crown CA (w **8**) are Die I while those with watermark Multiple Crown Script CA (w **9**) are Die II. The Georgian Die II was introduced in April 1921 and was used for Plates 10 to 22 and 26 to 28. Plates 23 to 25 were made from Die I by mistake.

2. Paper

All stamps listed are deemed to be on "ordinary" paper of the wove type and white in colour; only departures from this are normally mentioned.

Types. Where classification so requires we distinguish such other types of paper as, for example, vertically and horizontally laid; wove and laid bâtonné; card(board); carton; cartridge; glazed; granite; native; pelure; porous; quadrillé; ribbed; rice; and silk thread.

Wove paper

Laid paper

Granite paper

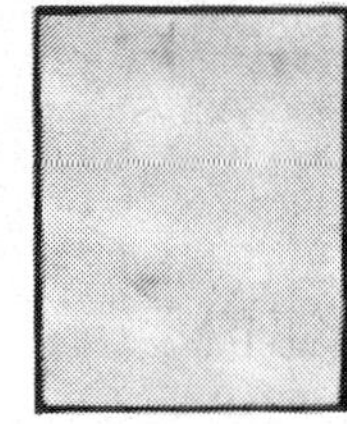
Quadrillé paper

Burelé band

The various makeshifts for normal paper are listed as appropriate. The varieties of double paper and joined paper are recognised. The security device of a printed burelé band on the back of a stamp, as in early Queensland, qualifies for listing.

Descriptive terms. The fact that a paper is handmade (and thus probably of uneven thickness) is mentioned where necessary. Such descriptive terms as "hard" and "soft"; "smooth" and 'rough"; "thick", "medium" and "thin" are applied where there is philatelic merit in classifying papers. We do not, for example, even in more specialised listings, classify paper thicknesses in the Wilding and Machin definitives of Great Britain. Weight standards for the paper apply to complete reels only, so that differences on individual stamps are acceptable to the printer provided the reel conforms overall.

Coloured, very white and toned papers. A coloured paper is one that is coloured right through (front and back of the stamp). In the Catalogue the colour of the paper is given in *italics,* thus:

black/*rose* = black design on rose paper.

Papers have been made specially white in recent years by, for example, a very heavy coating of chalk. We do not classify shades of whiteness of paper as distinct varieties. There does exist, however, a type of paper from early days called toned. This is off-white, often brownish or buffish, but it cannot be assigned any definite colour. A toning effect brought on by climate, incorrect storage or gum staining is disregarded here, as this was not the state of the paper when issued.

Modern developments. Two modern developments also affect the listings: printing on self-adhesive paper and the use of metallic foils. For self-adhesive stamps *see* under "Gum", below. Care should be taken not to damage the embossing on stamps impressed on metallic foils, such as Sierra Leone 1965–67, by subjecting the album pages to undue pressure. The possibility of faked "missing gold heads" is noted at the appropriate places in the listing of modern Great Britain.

"Ordinary" and "Chalk-surfaced" papers. The availability of many postage stamps for revenue purposes made necessary some safeguard against the illegitimate re-use of stamps with removable cancellations. This was at first secured by using fugitive inks and later by printing on chalk-surfaced paper, both of which made it difficult to remove any form of obliteration without also damaging the stamp design.

This catalogue now lists these chalk-surfaced paper varieties from their introduction in 1905. Where no indication is given, the paper is "ordinary".

Our chalk-surfaced paper is specifically one which shows a black mark when touched with a silver wire. The paper used during the Second World War for high values, as in Bermuda, the Leeward Islands, etc., was thinly coated with some kind of surfacing which does not react to silver and is therefore regarded (and listed) as "ordinary". Stamps on chalk-surfaced paper can easily lose this coating through immersion in water.

Another paper introduced during the War as a substitute for chalk-surfaced is rather thick, very white and glossy and shows little or no watermark, nor does it show a black line when touched with silver. In the Bahamas high values this paper might be mistaken for the chalk-surfaced (which is thinner and poorer-looking) but for the silver test.

Glazed paper. In 1969 the Crown Agents introduced a new general-purpose paper for use in conjunction with all current printing processes. It generally has a marked glossy surface but the degree varies according to the process used, being more marked in recess-printing stamps. As it does not respond to the silver test this presents a further test where previous printings were on chalky paper. A change of paper to the glazed variety merits separate listing.

Green and yellow papers. Issues of the First World War and immediate postwar period occur on green and yellow papers and these are given separate Catalogue listing. The original coloured papers (coloured throughout) gave way to surface-coloured papers, the stamps having "white backs"; other stamps show one colour on the front and a different one at the back. Because of the numerous variations a grouping of colours is adopted as follows:

YELLOW PAPERS

(1) The original *yellow* paper (throughout), usually bright in colour. The gum is often sparse, of harsh consistency and dull-looking.

(2) The *white backs.*

(3) A bright *lemon* paper. The colour must have a pronounced greenish tinge, different from the "yellow" in (1). As a rule, the gum on stamps using this lemon paper is plentiful, smooth and shiny, and the watermark shows distinctly. Care is needed with stamps printed in green on yellow paper (1) as it may appear that the paper is this lemon.

(4) An *orange-buff* paper. The colour must have a distinct brownish tinge. It is not to be confused with a muddy yellow (1) nor the misleading appearance (on the surface) of stamps printed in red on yellow paper where an engraved plate has been insufficiently wiped.

(5) A *pale yellow* paper that has a creamy tone to the yellow.

GREEN PAPERS

(6) The original "green" paper, varying considerably through shades of *blue-green* and *yellow-green,* the front and back sometimes differing.

(7) The *white backs.*

(8) A paper blue-green on the surface with *pale olive* back. The back must be markedly paler than the front and this and the pronounced olive tinge to the back distinguish it from (6).

(9) Paper with a vivid green surface, commonly called *emerald-green*; it has the olive back of (8).

(10) Paper with *emerald-green* both back and front.

3. Perforation and Rouletting

Perforation gauge. The gauge of a perforation is the number of holes in a length of 2 cm. For correct classification the size of the holes (large or small) may need to be distinguished; in a few cases the actual number of holes on each edge of the stamp needs to be quoted.

Measurement. The Gibbons *Instanta* gauge is the standard for measuring perforations. The stamp is viewed against a dark background with the transparent gauge put on top of it. Though the gauge measures to decimal accuracy, perforations read from it are generally quoted in the Catalogue to the nearest half. For example:

Just over perf 12¾ to just under 13¼	= perf 13
Perf 13¼ exactly, rounded up	= perf 13½
Just over perf 13¼ to just under 13¾	= perf 13½
Perf 13¾ exactly, rounded up	= perf 14

However, where classification depends on it, actual quarter-perforations are quoted.

Notation. Where no perforation is quoted for an issue it is imperforate. Perforations are usually abbreviated (and spoken) as follows, though sometimes they may be spelled out for clarity. This notation for rectangular stamps (the majority) applies to diamond shapes if "top" is read as the edge to the top right.

P 14: perforated alike on all sides (read: "perf 14").

P 14 × 15: the first figure refers to top and bottom, the second to left and right sides (read: "perf 14 by 15"). This is a compound perforation. For an upright triangular stamp the first figure refers to the two sloping sides and second to the base. In inverted triangulars the base is first and the second figure refers to the sloping sides.

P 14–15: perforation measuring anything between 14 and 15: the holes are irregularly spaced, thus the gauge may vary along a single line or even along a single edge of the stamp (read: "perf 14 to 15").

P 14 *irregular*: perforated 14 from a worn perforator, giving badly aligned holes irregularly spaced (read: "irregular perf 14").

P comp(ound) 14 × 15: two gauges in use but not necessarily on opposite sides of the stamp. It could be one side in one gauge and three in the other; or two adjacent sides with the same gauge. (Read: "perf compound of 14 and 15".) For three gauges or more, abbreviated as "*P* 14, 14½, 15 *or compound*" for example.

P 14, 14½: perforated approximately 14¼ (read: "perf 14 or 14½"). It does *not* mean two stamps, one perf 14 and the other perf 14½. This obsolescent notation is gradually being replaced in the Catalogue.

Imperf: imperforate (not perforated).

Imperf × *P* 14: imperforate at top and bottom and perf 14 at sides.

Perf × imperf

P 14 × *imperf*: perf 14 at top and bottom and imperforate at sides.

Such headings as "*P* 13 × 14 (*vert*) and *P* 14 × 13 (*horiz*)" indicate which perforations apply to which stamp format—vertical or horizontal.

Some stamps are additionally perforated so that a label or tab is detachable; others have been perforated suitably for use as two halves. Listings are normally for whole stamps, unless stated otherwise.

Other terms. Perforation almost always gives circular holes; where other shapes have been used they are specified, e.g. square holes; lozenge perf. Interrupted perfs are brought about by the omission of pins at regular intervals. Perforations merely simulated by being printed as part of the design are of course ignored. With few exceptions, privately applied perforations are not listed.

In the nineteenth century perforations are often described as clean cut (clean, sharply incised holes), intermediate or rough (rough holes, imperfectly cut, often the result of blunt pins).

Perforation errors and varieties. Authenticated errors, where a stamp normally perforated is accidentally issued imperforate, are listed provided no traces of perforation (blind holes or indentations) remain. They must be provided as pairs, both stamps wholly imperforate, and are only priced in that form.

In Great Britain, numerous of these part-perforated stamps have arisen from the introduction of the Jumelle Press. This has a rotary perforator with rows of pins on one drum engaging with holes on another. Engagement is only gradual when the perforating unit is started up or stopped, giving rise to perforations "fading out", a variety mentioned above as not listed.

Stamps imperforate between stamp and sheet margin are not listed in this catalogue, but such errors on Great Britain stamps will be found in the *Great Britain Specialised Catalogue*.

Pairs described as "imperforate between" have the line of perforations between the two stamps omitted.

Imperf between (*horiz pair*): a horizontal pair of stamps with perfs all around the edges but none between the stamps.

Imperf between (*vert pair*): a vertical pair of stamps with perfs all around the edges but none between the stamps.

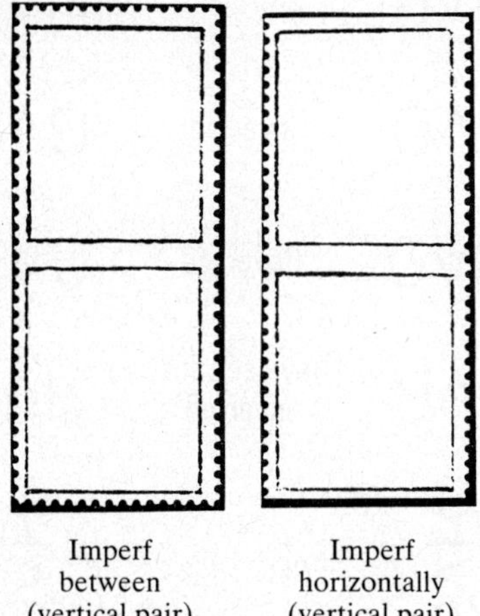

Imperf between (vertical pair) — Imperf horizontally (vertical pair)

Where several of the rows have escaped perforation the resulting varieties are listable. Thus:

Imperf vert (*horiz pair*): a horizontal pair of stamps perforated top and bottom; all three vertical directions are imperf—the two outer edges and between the stamps.

Imperf horiz (*vert pair*): a vertical pair perforated at left and right edges; all three horizontal directions are imperf—the top, bottom and between the stamps.

Straight edges. Large sheets cut up before issue to post offices can cause stamps with straight edges, i.e. imperf on one side or on two sides at right angles. They are not usually listable in this condition and are worth less than corresponding stamps properly perforated all round. This does not, however, apply to certain stamps, mainly from coils and booklets, where straight edges on various sides are the manufacturing norm affecting every stamp. The listings and notes make clear which sides are correctly imperf.

Malfunction. Varieties of double, misplaced or partial perforation caused by error or machine malfunction are not listable, neither are freaks, such as perforations placed diagonally from paper folds, nor missing holes caused by broken pins.

Centering. Well-centred stamps have designs surrounded by equal opposite margins. Where this condition affects the price the fact is stated.

Types of perforating. Where necessary for classification, perforation types are distinguished. These include:

Line perforation from one line of pins punching single rows of holes at a time.

Comb perforation from pins disposed across the sheet in comb formation, punching out holes at three sides of the stamp a row at a time.

Harrow perforation applied to a whole pane or sheet at one stroke.

Rotary perforation from toothed wheels operating across a sheet, then crosswise.

Sewing-machine perforation. The resultant condition, clean-cut or rough, is distinguished where required.

Pin-perforation is the commonly applied term for pin-roulette in which, instead of being punched out, round holes are pricked by sharp-pointed pins and no paper is removed.

Mixed perforation occurs when stamps with defective perforations are re-perforated in a different gauge.

Punctured stamps. Perforation holes can be punched into the face of the stamp. Patterns of small holes, often in the shape of initial letters, are privately applied devices against pilferage. These "perfins" are outside the scope except for Australia, Papua and Sudan where they were used as official stamps by the national administration. Identification devices, when officially inspired, are listed or noted; they can be shapes, or letters or words formed from holes, sometimes converting one class of stamp into another.

Rouletting. In rouletting the paper is cut, for ease of separation, but none is removed. The gauge is measured, when needed, as for perforations. Traditional French terms descriptive of the type of cut are often used and types include:

Arc roulette (*percé en arc*). Cuts are minute, spaced arcs, each roughly a semicircle.

Cross roulette (*percé en croix*). Cuts are tiny diagonal crosses.

Line roulette (*percé en ligne* or *en ligne droite*). Short straight cuts parallel to the frame of the stamp. The commonest basic roulette. Where not further described, "roulette" means this type.

Rouletted in colour or *coloured roulette* (*percé en lignes colorées* or *en lignes de couleur*). Cuts with coloured edges, arising from notched rule inked simultaneously with the printing plate.

Saw-tooth roulette (*percé en scie*). Cuts applied zigzag fashion to resemble the teeth of a saw.

Serpentine roulette (*percé en serpentin*). Cuts as sharply wavy lines.

Zigzag roulette (*percé en zigzags*). Short straight cuts at angles in alternate directions, producing sharp points on separation. U.S. usage favours "serrate(d) roulette" for this type.

Pin-roulette (originally *percé en points* and now *perforés trous d'epingle*) is commonly called pin-perforation in English.

4. Gum

All stamps listed are assumed to have gum of some kind; if they were issued without gum this is stated. Original gum (o.g.) means that which was present on the stamp as issued to the public. Deleterious climates and the presence of certain chemicals can cause gum to crack and, with early stamps, even make the paper deteriorate. Unscrupulous fakers are adept in removing it and regumming the stamp to meet the unreasoning demand often made for "full o.g." in cases where such a thing is virtually impossible.

The gum normally used on stamps has been gum arabic until the late 1960s when synthetic adhesives were introduced. Harrison and Sons Ltd for instance use *polyvinyl alcohol,* known to philatelists as PVA. This is almost invisible except for a slight yellowish tinge which was incorporated to make it possible to see that the stamps have been gummed. It has advantages in hot countries, as stamps do not curl and sheets are less likely to stick together. Gum arabic and PVA are not distinguished in the lists except that where a stamp exists with both forms this is indicated in footnotes. Our more specialised catalogues provide separate listing of gums for Great Britain.

Self-adhesive stamps are issued on backing paper, from which they are peeled before affixing to mail. Unused examples are priced as for backing paper intact, in which condition they are recommended to be kept. Used examples are best collected on cover or on piece.

5. Watermarks

Stamps are on unwatermarked paper except where the heading to the set says otherwise.

Detection. Watermarks are detected for Catalogue description by one of four methods: (1) holding stamps to the light; (2) laying stamps face down on a dark background; (3) adding a few drops of petroleum ether 40/60 to the stamp laid face down in a watermark tray; (4) by use of the Morley-Bright Detector, or other equipment, which work by revealing the thinning of the paper at the watermark (Note that petroleum ether is highly inflammable in use and can damage photogravure stamps.)

Listable types. Stamps occurring on both watermarked and unwatermarked papers are different types and both receive full listing.

Single watermarks (devices occurring once on every stamp) can be modified in size and shape as between different issues; the types are noted but not usually separately listed. Fortuitous absence of watermark from a single stamp or its gross displacement would not be listable.

To overcome registration difficulties the device may be repeated at close intervals (a *multiple watermark*), single stamps thus showing parts of several devices. Similarly, a large *sheet watermark* (or *all-over watermark*) covering numerous stamps can be used. We give informative notes and illustrations for them. The designs may be such that numbers of stamps in the sheet automatically lack watermark: this is not a listable variety. Multiple and all-over watermarks sometimes undergo modifications, but if the various types are difficult to distinguish from single stamps notes are given but not separate listings.

Papermakers' watermarks are noted where known but not listed separately, since most stamps in the sheet will lack them. Sheet watermarks which are nothing more than officially adopted papermakers' watermarks are, however, given normal listing.

Marginal watermarks, falling outside the pane of stamps, are ignored except where misplacement caused the adjoining row to be affected, in which case they are footnoted.

Watermark errors and varieties. Watermark errors are recognised as of major importance. They comprise stamps intended to be on unwatermarked paper but issued watermarked by mistake, or stamps printed on paper with the wrong watermark. Watermark varieties, on the other hand, such as broken or deformed bits on the dandy roll, are not listable.

Watermark positions. The diagram shows how watermark position is described in the Catalogue. Paper has a side intended for printing and watermarks are usually impressed so that they read normally when looked through from that printed side. However, since philatelists customarily detect watermarks by looking at the back of the stamp the watermark diagram also makes clear what is actually seen.

Illustrations in the Catalogue are of watermarks in normal positions (from the front of the stamps) and are actual size where possible.

Differences in watermark position are collectable as distinct varieties. In this Catalogue, however, only normal and sideways watermarks are listed (and "sideways inverted" is treated as "sideways"). Inverted and reversed watermarks have always been outside its scope: in the early days of flat-bed printing sheets of watermarked paper were fed indiscriminately through the press and the resulting watermark positions had no particular philatelic significance. Similarly, the special make-up of sheets for booklets can in some cases give equal quantities of normal and inverted watermarks.

Collectors are reminded that inverted and reversed watermarks are listed in the *Great Britain Specialised Catalogue, Great Britain, Australia* or *New Zealand Concise Catalogues* and (for Commonwealth stamps from 1937) in the *Two Reigns Catalogue* series.

Where a watermark comes indiscriminately in various positions our policy is to cover this by a general note: we do not give separate listings because the watermark position in these circumstances has no particular philatelic importance. There is a general note of this sort in modern Cyprus, for example. Issues printed since 1962 by Aspioti-Elka occur with the vertical stamps having the watermark normal or inverted, while horizontal stamps are likewise found with the watermark reading upwards or downwards.

AS DESCRIBED (Read through front of stamp)		AS SEEN DURING WATERMARK DETECTION (Stamp face down and back examined)
GvR	Normal	
	Inverted	
	Reversed	GvR
	Reversed and inverted	
GvR	Sideways	
GvR	Sideways inverted	

Standard types of watermark. Some watermarks have been used generally for various British possessions rather than exclusively for a single colony. To avoid repetition the Catalogue classifies 17 general types, as under, with references in the headings throughout the listings being given either in words or in the form "*W* w **14**" (meaning "watermark type w **14**"). In those cases where watermark illustrations appear in the listings themselves, the respective reference reads, for example, *W* **153**, thus indicating that the watermark will be found in the normal sequence of illustrations as (type) **153**.

The general types are as follows, with an example of each quoted.

W	*Description*	*Example*
w **1**	Large Star	St. Helena No. 1
w **2**	Small Star	Turks Is. No. 4
w **3**	Broad (pointed) Star	Grenada No. 24
w **4**	Crown (over) CC, small stamp	Antigua No. 13
w **5**	Crown (over) CC, large stamp	Antigua No. 31
w **6**	Crown (over) CA, small stamp	Antigua No. 21
w **7**	Crown CA (CA over Crown), large stamp	Sierra Leone No. 54
w **8**	Multiple Crown CA	Antigua No. 41
w **9**	Multiple Crown Script CA	Seychelles No. 158
w **9*a***	do. Error	Seychelles No. 158a
w **9*b***	do. Error	Seychelles No. 158b
w **10**	V over Crown	N.S.W. No. 327
w **11**	Crown over A	N.S.W. No. 347
w **12**	Multiple St. Edward's Crown Block CA	Antigua No. 149
w **13**	Multiple PTM	Johore No. 166
w **14**	Multiple Crown CA Diagonal	Antigua No. 426
w **15**	Multiple POST OFFICE	Kiribati No. 141
w **16**	Multiple Crown Script CA Diagonal	Ascension No. 376
w **17**	Multiple CARTOR	Brunei No. 357

CC in these watermarks is an abbreviation for "Crown Colonies" and CA for "Crown Agents". Watermarks w **1**, w **2** and w **3** are on stamps printed by Perkins, Bacon; w **4** onwards on stamps from De La Rue and other printers.

w **1**
Large Star

w **2**
Small Star

w **3**
Broad (pointed) Star

Watermark w **1**, *Large Star,* measures 15 to 16 mm across the star from point to point and about 27 mm from centre to centre vertically between stars in the sheet. It was made for long stamps like Ceylon 1857 and St. Helena 1856.

Watermark w **2**, *Small Star,* is of similar design but measures 12 to 13½ mm from point to point and 24 mm from centre to centre vertically. It was for use with ordinary-size stamps such as Grenada 1863–71.

When the Large Star watermark was used with the smaller stamps it only occasionally comes in the centre of the paper. It is frequently so misplaced as to show portions of two stars above and below and this eccentricity will very often help in determining the watermark.

Watermark w **3**, *Broad (pointed) Star*, resembles w **1** but the points are broader.

w **4**
Crown (over) CC

w **5**
Crown (over) CC

Two *Crown (over) CC* watermarks were used: w **4** was for stamps of ordinary size and w **5** for those of larger size.

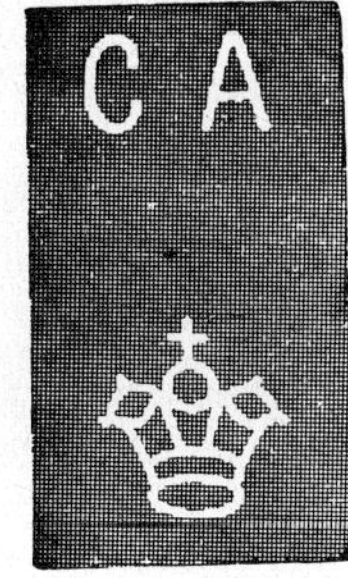

w **6**
Crown (over) CA

w **7**
CA over Crown

Two watermarks of *Crown CA* type were used, w **6** being for stamps of ordinary size. The other, w **7**, is properly described as *CA over Crown*. It was specially made for paper on which it was intended to print long fiscal stamps: that some were used postally accounts for the appearance of w **7** in the Catalogue. The watermark occupies twice the space of the ordinary Crown CA watermark, w **6**. Stamps of normal size printed on paper with w **7** watermark show it *sideways*; it takes a horizontal pair of stamps to show the entire watermark.

w **8**
Multiple Crown CA

w **9**
Multiple Crown Script CA

Multiple watermarks began in 1904 with w **8**, *Multiple Crown CA*, changed from 1921 to w **9**, *Multiple Crown Script CA*. On stamps of ordinary size portions of two or three watermarks appear and on the large-sized stamps a greater number can be observed. The change to letters in script character with w **9** was accompanied by a Crown of distinctly different shape.

w **9***a*: Error,
Crown missing

w **9***b*: Error,
St. Edward's Crown

The *Multiple Crown Script CA* watermark, w **9**, is known with two errors recurring among the 1950–52 printings of several territories. In the first a crown has fallen away from the dandy-roll that impresses the watermark into the paper pulp. It gives w **9***a*, *Crown missing*, but this omission has been found in both "Crown only" (*illustrated*) and "Crown CA" rows. The resulting faulty paper was used for Seychelles, Johore and the postage due stamps of nine colonies.

When the omission was noticed a second mishap occurred, which was to insert a wrong crown in the space, giving w **9***b*, *St. Edward's Crown*. This produced varieties in Bahamas, St. Kitts-Nevis and Singapore and the incorrect crown likewise occurs in "Crown only" and "Crown CA" rows.

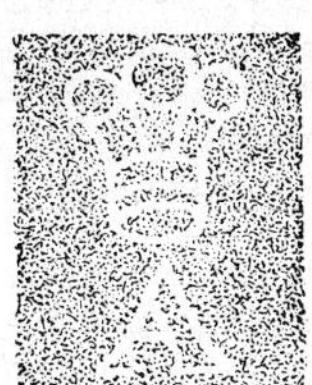

w **10**
V over Crown

w **11**
Crown over A

Resuming the general types, two watermarks found in issues of several Australian States are: w **10**, *V over Crown*, and w **11**, *Crown over A*.

w **12**
Multiple St. Edward's Crown Block CA

The *Multiple St. Edward's Crown Block CA* watermark, w **12**, was introduced in 1957 and besides the change in the Crown (from that used in *Multiple Crown Script CA*, w **9**) the letters reverted to block capitals. The new watermark began to appear sideways in 1966 and these stamps are generally listed as separate sets.

w **13**
Multiple PTM

The watermark w **13**, *Multiple PTM*, was introduced for new Malayan issues in November 1961.

w **14**
Multiple Crown CA Diagonal

By 1974 the two dandy-rolls (the "upright" and the "sideways") for w **12** were wearing out; the Crown Agents therefore discontinued using the sideways-watermark one and retained the other only as a stand-by. A new dandy-roll with the pattern of w **14**, *Multiple Crown CA Diagonal*, was introduced and first saw use with some Churchill Centenary issues.

The new watermark has the design arranged in gradually spiralling rows. It is improved in design to allow smooth passage over the paper (the gaps between letters and rows had caused jolts in previous dandy-rolls) and the sharp corners and angles, where fibres used to accumulate, have been eliminated by rounding.

This watermark has no "normal" sideways position amongst the different printers using it. To avoid confusion our more specialised listings do not rely on such terms as "sideways inverted" but describe the direction in which the watermark points.

w **15**
Multiple POST OFFICE

During 1981 w **15**, *Multiple POST OFFICE*, was introduced for certain issues prepared by Philatelists Ltd, acting for various countries in the Indian Ocean, Pacific and West Indies.

w **16**
Multiple Crown Script CA Diagonal

A new Crown Agents watermark was introduced during 1985, w **16**, *Multiple Crown Script CA Diagonal*. This was very similar to the previous w **14**, but showed "CA" in script rather than block letters. It was first used on the omnibus series of stamps commemorating the Life and Times of Queen Elizabeth the Queen Mother.

w **17**
Multiple CARTOR

Watermark w **17**, *Multiple CARTOR*, was used from 1985 for issues printed by this French firm for countries which did not normally use the Crown Agents watermark.

In recent years the use of watermarks has, to a small extent, been superseded by fluorescent security markings. These are often more visible from the reverse of the stamp (Cook Islands from 1970 onwards), but have occurred printed over the design (Hong Kong Nos. 415/30). In 1982 the Crown Agents introduced a new stock paper, without watermark, known as "C-Kurity" on which a fluorescent pattern of blue rosettes is visible on the reverse, beneath the gum. This paper was used for issues from Gambia and Norfolk Island.

6. Colours

Stamps in two or three colours have these named in order of appearance, from the centre moving outwards. Four colours or more are usually listed as multicoloured.

In compound colour names the second is the predominant one, thus:

orange-red = a red tending towards orange;

red-orange = an orange containing more red than usual.

Standard colours used. The 200 colours most used for stamp identification are given in the Stanley Gibbons Stamp Colour Key. The Catalogue has used the Stamp Colour Key as standard for describing new issues for some years. The names are also introduced as lists are rewritten, though exceptions are made for those early issues where traditional names have become universally established.

Determining colours. When comparing actual stamps with colour samples in the Stamp Colour Key, view in a good north daylight (or its best substitute: fluorescent "colour-matching" light). Sunshine is not recommended. Choose a solid portion of the stamp design; if available, marginal markings such as solid bars of colour or colour check dots are helpful. Shading lines in the design can be misleading as they appear lighter than solid colour. Postmarked portions of a stamp appear darker than normal. If more than one colour is present, mask off the extraneous ones as the eye tends to mix them.

Errors of colour. Major colour errors in stamps or overprints which qualify for listing are: wrong colours; one colour inverted in relation to the rest; albinos (colourless impressions), where these have Expert Committee certificates; colours completely omitted, but only on unused stamps (if found on used stamps the information is footnoted) and with good credentials, missing colours being frequently faked.

Colours only partially omitted are not recognised. Colour shifts, however spectacular, are not listed.

Shades. Shades in philately refer to variations in the intensity of a colour or the presence of differing amounts of other colours. They are particularly significant when they can be linked to specific printings. In general, shades need to be quite marked to fall within the scope of this Catalogue; it does not favour nowadays listing the often numerous shades of a stamp, but chooses a single applicable colour name which will indicate particular groups of outstanding shades. Furthermore, the listings refer to colours as issued: they may deteriorate into something different through the passage of time.

Modern colour printing by lithography is prone to marked differences of shade, even within a single run, and variations can occur within the same sheet. Such shades are not listed.

Aniline colours. An aniline colour meant originally one derived from coal-tar; it now refers more widely to colour of a particular brightness suffused on the surface of a stamp and showing through clearly on the back.

Colours of overprints and surcharges. All overprints and surcharges are in black unless stated otherwise in the heading or after the description of the stamp.

7. Specimen Stamps

Originally, stamps overprinted SPECIMEN were circulated to postmasters or kept in official records, but after the establishment of the Universal Postal Union supplies were sent to Berne for distribution to the postal administrations of member countries.

During the period 1884 to 1928 most of the stamps of British Crown Colonies required for this purpose were overprinted SPECIMEN in various shapes and sizes by their printers from typeset formes. Some locally produced provisionals were handstamped locally, as were sets prepared for presentation. From 1928 stamps were punched with holes forming the word SPECIMEN, each firm of printers using a different machine or machines. From 1948 the stamps supplied for U.P.U. distribution were no longer punctured.

Stamps of some other Commonwealth territories were overprinted or handstamped locally, while stamps of Great Britain and those overprinted for use in overseas postal agencies (mostly of the higher denominations) bore SPECIMEN overprints and handstamps applied by the Inland Revenue or the Post Office.

SPECIMEN SPECIMEN

De La Rue & Co. Ltd.

SPECIMEN. SPECIMEN.

Bradbury, Wilkinson & Co. Ltd.

SPECIMEN SPECIMEN

Waterlow & Sons Ltd.

SPECIMEN SPECIMEN SPECIMEN

Great Britain overprints

Some of the commoner types of overprints or punctures are illustrated here. Collectors are warned that dangerous forgeries of the punctured type exist.

The *Part* 1 (*British Commonwealth*) *Catalogue* records those Specimen overprints or perforations intended for distribution by the U.P.U. to member countries. In addition the Specimen overprints of Australia and its dependent territories, which were sold to collectors by the Post Office, are also included.

All other Specimens are outside the scope of this volume. The *Two Reigns Catalogue* series contains details of modern Specimen overprints issued for publicity purposes.

Specimens are not quoted in Great Britain as they are fully listed in the Stanley Gibbons *Great Britain Specialised Catalogue*.

In specifying type of specimen for individual high-value stamps, "H/S" means handstamped, "Optd" is overprinted and "Perf" is punctured. Some sets occur mixed, e.g. "Optd/Perf". If unspecified, the type is apparent from the date or it is the same as for the lower values quoted as a set.

Prices. Prices for stamps up to £1 are quoted in sets; higher values are priced singly after the colours, thus "(S. £20)". Where specimens exist in more than one type the price quoted is for the cheapest. Specimen stamps have rarely survived even as pairs; these and strips of three, four or five are worth considerably more than singles.

8. Luminescence

Machines which sort mail electronically have been introduced in recent years. In consequence some countries have issued stamps on fluorescent or phosphorescent papers, while others have marked their stamps with phosphor bands.

The various papers can only be distinguished by ultraviolet lamps emitting particular wavelengths. They are separately listed only when the stamps have some other means of distinguishing them, visible without the use of these lamps. Where this is not so, the papers are recorded in footnotes or headings.

For this Catalogue we do not consider it appropriate that collectors be compelled to have use of an ultraviolet lamp before being able to identify stamps by our listings. Some experience will also be found necessary in interpreting the results given by ultraviolet. Collectors using the lamps, nevertheless, should exercise great care in their use as exposure to their light is extremely dangerous to the eyes.

Phosphor bands are listable, since they are visible to the naked eye (by holding stamps at an angle to the light and looking along them, the bands appear dark). Stamps existing with and without phosphor bands or with differing numbers of bands are given separate listings. Varieties such as double bands, bands omitted, misplaced or printed on the back are not listed.

Detailed descriptions appear at appropriate places in the listings in explanation of luminescent papers; *see*, for example, Australia above No. 308, Canada above Nos. 472 and 611, Cook Is. above No. 249, etc.

For Great Britain, where since 1959 phosphors have played a prominent and intricate part in stamp issues, the main notes above Nos. 599, 723 and after the Decimal Machin issue (No. X841 onwards) should be studied, as well as the footnotes to individual listings where appropriate. In general the classification is as follows.

Stamps with *phosphor bands* are those where a separate cylinder applies the phosphor after the stamps are printed. Issues with "all-over" phosphor have the "band" covering the entire stamp. Parts of the stamp covered by phosphor bands, or the entire surface for "all-over" phosphor versions, appear matt. Stamps on *phosphorised paper* have the phosphor added to the paper coating before the stamps are printed. Issues on this paper have a completely shiny surface.

Further particularisation of phosphor—their methods of printing and the colours they exhibit under ultraviolet—is outside the scope. The more specialised listings should be consulted for this information.

9. Coil Stamps

Stamps issued only in coil form are given full listing. If stamps are issued in both sheets and coils the coil stamps are listed separately only where there is some feature (e.g. perforation or watermark sideways) by which singles can be distinguished. Coil strips containing different stamps *se-tenant* are also listed.

Coil join pairs are too random and too easily faked to permit of listing; similarly ignored are coil stamps which have accidentally suffered an extra row of perforations from the claw mechanism in a malfunctioning vending machine.

10. Booklet Stamps

Stamp booklets are outside the scope of this Catalogue.

Single stamps from booklets are listed if they are distinguishable in some way (such as watermark or perforation) from similar sheet stamps.

Booklet panes are listed where they contain stamps of different denominations *se-tenant*, where stamp-size labels are included, or where such panes are otherwise identifiable. Booklet panes are placed in the listing under the lowest denomination present.

Particular perforations (straight edges) are covered by appropriate notes.

11. Miniature Sheets and Sheetlets

We distinguish between "miniature sheets" and "sheetlets" and this affects the catalogue numbering. An item in sheet form that is postally valid, containing a single stamp, pair, block or set of stamps, with wide, inscribed and/or decorative margins, is a *miniature sheet* if it is sold at post offices as an indivisible entity. As such the Catalogue allots a single **MS** number and describes what stamps make it up. (*See* Great Britain 1978 Historic Buildings, No. **MS**1058, as an example.) The *sheetlet* or *small sheet* differs in that the individual stamps are intended to be purchased separately for postal purposes. For sheetlets, all the component postage stamps are numbered individually and the composition explained in a footnote. (The 1978 Christmas Island Christmas sheetlet, Nos. 99/107, is an example.) Note that the definitions refer to post office sale—not how items may be subsequently offered by stamp dealers.

Production as sheetlets is a modern marketing development chosen by postal administrations to interest collectors in purchasing the item complete; if he has done so he should, as with all *se-tenant* arrangements, keep the sheetlet intact in his collection.

The Catalogue will in future no longer give full listing to designs, originally issued in normal sheets, which subsequently appear in sheetlets showing changes of colour, perforation, printing process or face value. Such stamps will be covered by footnotes.

12. Forgeries and Fakes

Forgeries. Where space permits, notes are considered if they can give a concise description that will permit unequivocal detection of a forgery. Generalised warnings, lacking detail, are not nowadays inserted, since their value to the collector is problematic.

Fakes. Unwitting fakes are numerous, particularly "new shades" which are colour changelings brought about by exposure to sunlight, soaking in water contaminated with dyes from adherent paper, contact with oil and dirt from a pocketbook, and so on. Fraudulent operators, in addition, can offer to arrange: removal of hinge marks; repairs of thins on white or coloured papers; replacement of missing margins or perforations; reperforating in true or false gauges; removal of fiscal cancellations; rejoining of severed pairs, strips and blocks; and (a major hazard) regumming. Collectors can only be urged to purchase from reputable sources and to insist upon Expert Committee certification where there is any kind of doubt.

The Catalogue can consider footnotes about fakes where these are specific enough to assist in detection.

1935 SILVER JUBILEE CROWN COLONY ISSUE

The Crown Colony Windsor Castle design by Harold Fleury is, surely, one of the most impressive produced in the 20th-century and its reproduction in the recess process by three of the leading stamp-printing firms of the era has provided a subject for philatelic research which has yet to be exhausted.

Each of the three, Bradbury, Wilkinson & Co. and Waterlow and Sons, who both produced fifteen issues, together with De La Rue & Co. who printed fourteen, used a series of vignette (centre) plates coupled with individual frame plates for each value. All were taken from dies made by Waterlow. Several worthwhile varieties exist on the frame plates, but most interest has been concentrated on the centre plates, each of which was used to print a considerable number of different stamps.

Sheets printed by Bradbury, Wilkinson were without printed plate numbers, but research has now identified eleven centre plates which were probably used in permanent pairings. A twelfth plate awaits confirmation. Stamps from some of these centre plates have revealed a number of prominent plate flaws, the most famous of which, the extra flagstaff, has been eagerly sought by collectors for many years.

Extra flagstaff (Plate 1" R. 9/1)

Short extra flagstaff (Plate "2" R. 2/1)

Lightning conductor (Plate "3" R. 2/5)

Flagstaff on right-hand turret (Plate "5" R. 7/1)

Double flagstaff (Plate "6" R. 5/2)

De La Rue sheets were initially printed with plate numbers, but in many instances these were subsequently trimmed off. Surviving examples do, however, enable a positive identification of six centre plates, 2A, 2B, (2A), (2B), 4 and 4/ to be made. The evidence of sheet markings and plate flaws clearly demonstrates that there were two different pairs of plates numbered 2A 2B. The second pair is designated (2A) (2B) by specialist collectors to avoid further confusion. The number of major plate flaws is not so great as on the Bradbury, Wilkinson sheets, but four examples are included in the catalogue.

Diagonal line by turret (Plate 2A R. 10/2)

Dot to left of chapel (Plate 2B R. 8/3)

Dot by flagstaff (Plate 4 R. 8/4)

Dash by turret (Plate 4/ R. 3/6)

Much less is known concerning the Waterlow centre plate system as the sheets did not show plate numbers. Ten individual plates have, so far, been identified and it is believed that these were used in pairs. The two versions of the kite and log flaw from plate "2" show that this plate exists in two states.

Kite and vertical log (Plate "2A" R. 10/6)

Kite and horizontal log (Plate "2B" R. 10/6)

Abbreviations

Printers

A.B.N. Co	American Bank Note Co, New York.
A. & M.	Alden & Mowbray Ltd, Oxford.
Ashton-Potter	Ashton-Potter Ltd, Toronto.
Aspioti-Elka (Aspiotis)	Aspioti-Elka, Greece.
B.A.B.N.	British American Bank Note Co, Ottawa.
B.D.T.	B.D.T. International Security Printing Ltd, Dublin, Ireland.
B.W.	Bradbury Wilkinson & Co, Ltd.
Cartor	Cartor S.A., L'Aigle, France
C.B.N.	Canadian Bank Note Co, Ottawa.
Continental B.N. Co	Continental Bank Note Co.
Courvoisier	Imprimerie Courvoisier S.A., La-Chaux-de-Fonds, Switzerland.
D.L.R.	De La Rue & Co, Ltd, London, and (from 1961) Bogota, Colombia.
Edila	Editions de l'Aubetin, S.A.
Enschedé	Joh. Enschedé en Zonen, Haarlem, Netherlands.
Format	Format International Security Printers, Ltd, London.
Harrison	Harrison & Sons, Ltd, London
Heraclio Fournier	Heraclio Fournier S.A., Vitoria, Spain.
J.W.	John Waddington Security Print Ltd., Leeds
P.B.	Perkins Bacon Ltd, London.
Questa	Questa Colour Security Printers, Ltd., London
Ueberreuter	Ueberreuter (incorporating Bruder Rosenbaum), Korneuburg, Austria.
Walsall	Walsall Security Printers, Ltd.
Waterlow	Waterlow & Sons, Ltd, London.

General Abbreviations

Alph	Alphabet
Anniv	Anniversary
Comp	Compound (perforation)
Des	Designer; designed
Diag	Diagonal; diagonally
Eng	Engraver; engraved
F.C.	Fiscal Cancellation
H/S	Handstamped
Horiz	Horizontal; horizontally
Imp, Imperf	Imperforate
Inscr	Inscribed
L	Left
Litho	Lithographed
mm	Millimetres
MS	Miniature sheet
N.Y.	New York
Opt(d)	Overprint(ed)
P or P-c	Pen-cancelled
P, Pf or Perf	Perforated
Photo	Photogravure
Pl	Plate
Pr	Pair
Ptd	Printed
Ptg	Printing
R	Right
R.	Row
Recess	Recess-printed
Roto	Rotogravure
Roul	Rouletted
S	Specimen (overprint)
Surch	Surcharge(d)
T.C.	Telegraph Cancellation
T	Type
Typo	Typographed
Un	Unused
Us	Used
Vert	Vertical; vertically
W or wmk	Watermark
Wmk s	Watermark sideways

(†)=Does not exist.

(—) (or blank price column)=Exists, or may exist, but no market price is known.

/ between colours means "on" and the colour following is that of the paper on which the stamp is printed.

Colours of Stamps

Bl (blue); blk (black); brn (brown); car, carm (carmine); choc (chocolate); clar (claret); emer (emerald); grn (green); ind (indigo); mag (magenta); mar (maroon); mult (multicoloured); mve (mauve); ol (olive); orge (orange); pk (pink); pur (purple); scar (scarlet); sep (sepia); turq (turquoise); ultram (ultramarine); verm (vermilion); vio (violet); yell (yellow).

Colour of Overprints and Surcharges

(B.) = blue, (Blk.) = black, (Br.) = brown, (C.) = carmine, (G.) = green, (Mag.) = magenta, (Mve.) = mauve, (Ol.) = olive, (O.) = orange, (P.) = purple, (Pk.) = pink, (R.)=red, (Sil.) = silver, (V.) = violet, (Vm.) or (Verm.) = vermilion, (W.) = white, (Y.) = yellow.

Arabic Numerals

As in the case of European figures, the details of the Arabic numerals vary in different stamp designs, but they should be readily recognised with the aid of this illustration.

٠	١	٢	٣	٤	٥	٦	٧	٨	٩
0	1	2	3	4	5	6	7	8	9

COUNTRIES RELOCATED IN THIS EDITION

Aden *see* SOUTH ARABIAN FEDERATION
Aden Protectorate States *see* SOUTH ARABIAN FEDERATION
Basutoland *see* LESOTHO
Bechuanaland *see* BOTSWANA
British Columbia & Vancouver Island *see* CANADA
British East Africa *see* KENYA, UGANDA AND TANGANYIKA
British Guiana *see* GUYANA
British Honduras *see* BELIZE
Cape of Good Hope *see* SOUTH AFRICA
Ceylon *see* SRI LANKA
Gilbert Islands *see* KIRIBATI
Gold Coast *see* GHANA
Griqualand West *see* SOUTH AFRICA
Labuan *see* MALAYSIA
Lagos *see* NIGERIA
Natal *see* SOUTH AFRICA
New Brunswick *see* CANADA
Newfoundland *see* CANADA
New Guinea *see* PAPUA NEW GUINEA
New Hebrides *see* VANUATU
New Republic *see* SOUTH AFRICA
New South Wales *see* AUSTRALIA
Niger Coast Protectorate *see* NIGERIA
Niger Company Territories *see* NIGERIA
North Borneo *see* MALAYSIA
Northern Nigeria *see* NIGERIA
Northern Rhodesia *see* ZAMBIA
Nova Scotia *see* CANADA
Nyasaland *see* MALAWI
Orange Free State *see* SOUTH AFRICA
Papua (British New Guinea) *see* PAPUA NEW GUINEA
Prince Edward Island *see* CANADA
Queensland *see* AUSTRALIA
Rhodesia (from No. 351) *see* ZIMBABWE
Sabah *see* MALAYSIA
Sarawak *see* MALAYSIA
South Australia *see* AUSTRALIA
Southern Nigeria *see* NIGERIA
Southern Rhodesia *see* ZIMBABWE
South West Africa *see* NAMIBIA
Stellaland *see* BOTSWANA
Tanganyika *see* TANZANIA
Tasmania *see* AUSTRALIA
Transvaal *see* SOUTH AFRICA
Victoria *see* AUSTRALIA
Western Australia *see* AUSTRALIA
Zanzibar *see* TANZANIA
Zululand *see* SOUTH AFRICA

Stanley Gibbons Stamp Catalogue
Complete List of Parts

1 British Commonwealth
(Annual in two volumes)

2 Austria & Hungary (4th edition, 1988)
Austria, Bosnia & Herzegovina, U.N. (Vienna), Hungary

3 Balkans (3rd edition, 1987)
Albania, Bulgaria, Greece & Islands, Rumania, Yugoslavia

4 Benelux (3rd edition, 1988)
Belgium & Colonies, Netherlands & Colonies, Luxembourg

5 Czechoslovakia & Poland (4th edition, 1991)
Czechoslovakia, Bohemia & Moravia, Slovakia, Poland

6 France (3rd edition, 1987)
France, Colonies, Post Offices, Andorra, Monaco

7 Germany (4th edition, 1992)
Germany, States, Colonies, Post Offices

8 Italy & Switzerland (3rd edition, 1986)
Italy & Colonies, Fiume, San Marino, Vatican City, Trieste, Liechtenstein, Switzerland, U.N. (Geneva)

9 Portugal & Spain (3rd edition, 1991)
Andorra, Portugal & Colonies, Spain & Colonies

10 Russia (4th edition, 1991)
Russia, Baltic States, Mongolia, Tuva

11 Scandinavia (3rd edition, 1988)
Aland Island, Denmark, Faroe Islands, Finland, Greenland, Iceland, Norway, Sweden

12 Africa since Independence A-E (2nd edition, 1983)
Algeria, Angola, Benin, Bophuthatswana, Burundi, Cameroun, Cape Verde, Central African Republic, Chad, Comoro Islands, Congo, Djibouti, Equatorial Guinea, Ethiopia

13 Africa since Independence F-M (1st edition, 1981)
Gabon, Guinea, Guinea-Bissau, Ivory Coast, Liberia, Libya, Malagasy Republic, Mali, Mauritania, Morocco, Mozambique

14 Africa since Independence N-Z (1st edition, 1981)
Niger Republic, Rwanda, St. Thomas & Prince, Senegal, Somalia, Sudan, Togo, Transkei, Tunisia, Upper Volta, Venda, Zaire

15 Central America (2nd edition, 1984)
Costa Rica, Cuba, Dominican Republic, El Salvador, Guatemala, Haiti, Honduras, Mexico, Nicaragua, Panama

16 Central Asia (2nd edition, 1983)
Afghanistan, Iran, Turkey

17 China (4th edition, 1989)
China, Taiwan, Tibet, Foreign P.O.s

18 Japan & Korea (3rd edition, 1992)
Japan, Ryukyus, Korean Empire, South Korea, North Korea

19 Middle East (4th edition, 1990)
Bahrain, Egypt, Iraq, Israel, Jordan, Kuwait, Lebanon, Oman, Qatar, Saudi Arabia, Syria, U.A.E., Yemen A.R., Yemen P.D.R.

20 South America (3rd edition, 1989)
Argentina, Bolivia, Brazil, Chile, Colombia, Ecuador, Paraguay, Peru, Surinam, Uruguay, Venezuela

21 South-East Asia (2nd edition, 1985)
Bhutan, Burma, Indonesia, Kampuchea, Laos, Nepal, Philippines, Thailand, Vietnam

22 United States (3rd edition, 1990)
U.S. & Possessions, Canal Zone, Marshall Islands, Micronesia, Palau, U.N. (New York, Geneva, Vienna)

GREAT BRITAIN SPECIALISED CATALOGUES

Volume 1 **Queen Victoria** (10th edition, 1992)
Volume 2 **King Edward VII to King George VI** (8th edition, 1989)
Volume 3 **Queen Elizabeth II Pre-decimal Issues** (8th edition, 1990)
Volume 4 **Queen Elizabeth II Decimal Definitive Issues** (6th edition, 1991)
Volume 5 **Queen Elizabeth II Decimal Special Issues** (2nd edition, 1991)

THEMATIC CATALOGUES

Collect Birds on Stamps (3rd edition forthcoming)
Collect Mammals on Stamps (1st edition, 1986)
Collect Railways on Stamps (2nd edition, 1990)
Collect Ships on Stamps (2nd edition forthcoming)
Collect Fungi on Stamps (1st edition, 1991)
Collect Butterflies and Other Insects on Stamps (1st edition, 1991)
Collect Chess on Stamps (forthcoming)
Collect Aircraft on Stamps (forthcoming)

Stanley Gibbons

GREAT BRITAIN ALBUMS

The World-famous WINDSOR – now in three volumes and available in a choice of styles.
Popular with collectors since 1925, the Windsor is our most detailed Great Britain album with spaces for all those special items such as se-tenant strips and panes, sideways watermarks and shades, as well as all the definitives, special issues, postage dues, officials, regionals and Channel Islands Occupation issues.
The superb quality leaves provide spaces for every stamp while on the facing page is an illustrated catalogue giving details and SG catalogue numbers for easy reference.
All new Windsor Albums come with a free sheet of self-adhesive Album Titles which includes volume number stickers for those collections which have already expanded past Volume 3.

THE WINDSOR POPULAR
Housed in a handsome spring-back binder in deep green or red. Annual supplements.
Item 5240 Volume 1 1840–1970
Item 5242 Volume 2 1970–1981
Item 5428 Volume 3 1982–date

WINDSOR SOVEREIGN
Bound in tan leather-finish PVC ring binder with a matching slipcase, this luxury 22-ring binder is the perfect setting for that special GB collection.
Item 5244 Volume 1 1840–1970
Item 5246 Volume 2 1970–1981
Item 5483 Volume 3 1982–date
Blank leaves, headed 'GREAT BRITAIN' and suitable for both Windsor Popular and Sovereign Albums are available for those 'special' items not provided for on the printed pages (Item 0322).

For further details visit your favourite stamp shop or write to:
Stanley Gibbons Publications Ltd.,
5 Parkside, Christchurch Road,
Ringwood, Hampshire BH24 3SH.
Telephone 0425 472363

The Stanley Gibbons Great Britain One Country Album
Ideal for the straightforward GB collection. Housed in a padded leather-finish, maroon, PVC binder each stamp is illustrated and identified by its Stanley Gibbons catalogue number for ease of use. In two volumes. Complete with Self-adhesive Album Title sheet.
Item 5250 Volume 1 1840–1970
Item 5252 Volume 2 1970–date

NOTE:
These are the *ONLY* Great Britain Albums which identify each space by its Stanley Gibbons catalogue number.

THE KING GEORGE VI ALBUM

Stanley Gibbons proudly present a superb reprint of the prestigious King George VI Stamp Album.
Attractively bound in rich red buckram with matching head and tail bands and gold blocked on the front and spine, it is presented in a matching library slip case.
The pages are of superior quality cream cartridge interleaved throughout with glassine and fully guarded to allow for expansion. They are attractively laid out and written up to provide the perfect setting for a straightforward collection of this popular period and include spaces for watermark changes, officials, postage dues and express and special delivery issues.

Item 3419 **King George VI Stamp Album**

THE NEW IMPERIAL ALBUM

Another old favourite reprinted and reintroduced by popular demand!
The two-volume New Imperial, successor to the Imperial Album first published in 1873, provides spaces for the stamps of the British Empire, Egypt and Iraq, from SG 1 up to the end of the reign of King George V (1840 to mid-1936).
Provision is made for major variations of watermark, perforation and shade as well as postage dues, officials, special delivery stamps etc. Pages are attractively laid out in traditional style with spaces for stamps on the right hand page and, on the facing leaf, an illustrated catalogue for easy identification.
The New Imperial is bound in red buckram and gold blocked on the front and spine. The superior quality cartridge leaves are fully guarded to allow for expansion. Boxed.

Item 3275 **New Imperial Album** (two volume set)

Please note that neither of these albums is designed to be used with hingeless mounts.

For further details visit your favourite stamp shop or write to:
Stanley Gibbons Publications Ltd.,
5 Parkside, Christchurch Road, Ringwood, Hampshire BH24 3SH. **Telephone 0425 472363**

Select Bibliography

The literature on British Commonwealth stamps is vast, but works are often difficult to obtain once they are out of print. The selection of books below has been made on the basis of authority together with availability to the general reader, either as new or secondhand. Very specialised studies, and those covering aspects of postal history to which there are no references in the catalogue, have been excluded.

The following abbreviations are used to denote publishers:
CRL–Christie's Robson Lowe; HH–Harry Hayes; PB–Proud Bailey Co. Ltd.; PC–Philip Cockrill; RPSL–Royal Philatelic Society, London; SG–Stanley Gibbons Ltd.

Where no publisher is quoted, the book is published by its author.

GENERAL. *Encyclopaedia of British Empire Postage Stamps. Vols 1–6.* Edited Robson Lowe. (CRL, 1951–1991)

The Commemorative Stamps of the British Commonwealth. H.D.S. Haverbeck. (Faber, 1955)

Specimen Stamps of the Crown Colonies 1857–1948. Marcus Samuel. (RPSL, 1976 and 1984 Supplement)

U.P.U. Specimen Stamps. J. Bendon. (1988)

Silver Jubilee of King George V Stamps Handbook. A.J. Ainscough. (Ainwheel Developments, 1985)

The Printings of King George VI Colonial Stamps. W.J.W. Potter & Lt-Col R.C.M. Shelton. (1952)

King George VI Large Key Type Stamps of Bermuda, Leeward Islands, Nyasaland. R.W. Dickgiesser and E.P. Yendall. (Triad Publications, 1985)

GREAT BRITAIN. For extensive bibliographies see *G.B. Specialised Catalogues. Vols 1–5.*

Channel Islands. *Stamps and Postal History of the Channel Islands.* W. Newport. (Heineman, 1972)

ADEN. *The Postal History of British Aden 1839–67.* Major R.W. Pratt (PB, 1985)

ASCENSION. *Ascension. The Stamps and Postal History.* J.H. Attwood. (CRL, 1981)

BAHAMAS. *The Postage Stamps and Postal History of the Bahamas.* H.G.D. Gisburn. (SG, 1950)

BARBADOS. *The Stamps of Barbados.* E.A. Bayley. (1989)

BASUTOLAND. *The Cancellations and Postal Markings of Basutoland/Lesotho Post Offices.* A.H. Scott. (Collectors Mail Auctions (Pty) Ltd, 1980)

BATUM. *British Occupation of Batum.* P.T. Ashford. (1989)

BRITISH EAST AFRICA. *British East Africa. The Stamps and Postal Stationery.* J. Minns. (RPSL, 1982 and 1990 Supplement)

BRITISH GUIANA. *The Postage Stamps and Postal History of British Guiana.* W.A. Townsend and F.G. Howe. (RPSL, 1970)

BRITISH OCCUPATION OF GERMAN COLONIES. *G.R.I.* R.M. Gibbs. (CRL, 1989)

BRITISH POSTAL AGENCIES IN EASTERN ARABIA. *The Postal Agencies in Eastern Arabia and the Gulf.* N. Donaldson. (HH, 1975)

BRITISH WEST AFRICA. *The Postal History and Handstamps of British West Africa.* C. McCaig. (CRL, 1978)

BRUNEI. *Brunei. The Definitive Issues and Postal Cancellations to 1974.* E. Thorndike. (PC, 1983)

BURMA. *Burma Postal History.* G. Davis and D. Martin. (CRL, 1971 and 1987 Supplement)

CANADA. *Stamps of British North America.* F. Jarrett. (Quarterman Publications Inc, 1975)

The Postage Stamps and Postal History of Canada. W.S. Boggs. (Quarterman Publications Inc, 1974)

The Edward VII Issue of Canada. G.C. Marler. (National Postal Museum, Canada, 1975)

The Admiral Issue of Canada. G.C. Marler. (American Philatelic Society, 1982)

CAPE OF GOOD HOPE. *Postmarks of the Cape of Good Hope.* R. Goldblatt. (Reijger Publishers (Pty) Ltd, 1984)

CAYMAN ISLANDS. *The Postal History of the Cayman Islands.* T.E. Giraldi and P.P. McCann. (Triad Publications, 1989)

COCOS (KEELING) ISLANDS. *Cocos (Keeling) Islands. A Philatelic and Postal History to 1979.* P. Collas & J. Hill. (B. & K. Philatelic Publishing, 1991)

COOK ISLANDS. *The Early Cook Islands Post Office.* A.R. Burge. (Hawthorn Press, 1978)

CYPRUS. *Cyprus 1353–1986.* W. Castle. (CRL, 3rd edition, 1987)

FALKLAND ISLANDS. *The Postage Stamps of the Falkland Islands and Dependencies.* B.S.H. Grant. (SG, 1952)

The De La Rue Definitives of the Falkland Islands 1901–29. J.P. Bunt. (1986)

The Falkland Islands. Printings of the Pictorial Issue of 1938–49. C.E. Glass. (CRL, 1979)

FIJI. *The Postal History of Fiji 1911–1952.* J.G. Rodger. (Pacific Islands Study Circle, 1991)

GAMBIA. *The Stamps and Postal History of the Gambia.* Edited J.O. Andrew. (CRL, 1985)

GIBRALTAR. *Posted in Gibraltar.* W. Hine-Haycock. (CRL, 1978)

HONG KONG. *The Philatelic History of Hong Kong. Vol 1.* (Hong Kong Study Circle, 1984)

Cancellations of the Treaty Ports of Hong Kong. H. Schoenfeld. (1988)

INDIA. *India Used Abroad.* V.S. Dastur. (Mysore Philatelics, 1982)

A Handbook on Gwalior Postal History and Stamps. V.K. Gupta. (1980)

LABUAN. *A Concise Guide to the Queen Issues of Labuan.* R. Price.

MALAYSIA. *The Postal History of British Malaya. Vols 1–3.* E.B. Proud. (PB, 1982–84)

The Postage Stamps of Federated Malay States. W.A. Reeves. (Malaya Study Group, 1978)

MALTA. *Malta. The Postal History and Postage Stamps.* Edited R.E. Martin. (CRL, 1980 and 1985 Supplement)

MAURITIUS. *The Postal History and Stamps of Mauritius.* P. Ibbotson. (RPSL, 1991)

MOROCCO AGENCIES. *British Post Offices and Agencies in Morocco 1857–1907 and Local Posts 1891–1914.* R.K. Clough. (Gibraltar Study Circle, 1984).

NEWFOUNDLAND. *The Postage Stamps and Postal History of Newfoundland.* W.S. Boggs. (Quarterman Publications, 1975)

NEW SOUTH WALES. *The Postal History of New South Wales 1788–1901.* Edited J.S. White. (Philatelic Assoc of New South Wales, 1988)

NEW ZEALAND. *The Postage Stamps of New Zealand. Vols I–VII.* (Royal Philatelic Society of New Zealand, 1939–88)

The Postal History and Postage Stamps of the Tokelau/Union Islands. A.H. Burgess. (Pacific Islands Study Circle, 1977)

NORTH BORNEO. *The Stamps and Postal History of North Borneo. Parts 1–3.* L.H. Shipman and P.K. Cassells. (Sarawak Specialists Society, 1976–88)

ORANGE FREE STATE. *Stamps of the Orange Free State. Parts 1–3.* G.D. Buckley & W.B. Marriott. (Orange Free State Study Circle, 1967–80)

PAPUA. *The Postal History of British New Guinea and Papua 1885–1942.* R. Lee. (CRL, 1983)

RHODESIA. *Mashonaland. A Postal History 1890–96.* A. Drysdall and D. Collis (CRL, 1990)

Rhodesia. A Postal History. R.C. Smith. (1967 and 1970 Supplement)

ST. HELENA. *St. Helena. Postal History and Stamps.* E. Hibbert. (CRL, 1979)

SAMOA. *A Postal History of the Samoan Islands (Parts I and II).* Edited R. Burge. (Royal Philatelic Society of New Zealand, 1987–89)

SARAWAK. *The Stamps and Postal History of Sarawak.* W.A. Forrester-Wood. (Sarawak Specialists Society, 1959 & 1970 Supplement)

Sarawak: The Issues of 1871 and 1875. W. Batty-Smith & W. Watterson.

SIERRA LEONE. *The Postal Service of Sierra Leone.* P.O. Beale. (RPSL, 1988)

SOLOMON ISLANDS. *British Solomon Islands Protectorate. Its Postage Stamps and Postal History.* H.G.D. Gisburn. (T. Sanders (Philatelist) Ltd., 1956)

SOUTH AUSTRALIA. *The Departmental Stamps of South Australia.* A.R. Butler. (RPSL, 1978)

SOUTH WEST AFRICA. *The Overprinted Stamps of South West Africa to 1930.* N. Becker. (Philatelic Holdings (Pty) Ltd, 1990)

SUDAN. *Sudan. The Stamps and Postal Stationery of 1867 to 1970.* E.C.W. Stagg. (HH, 1977)

TANGANYIKA. *The Postal History of Tanganyika. 1915–1961.* E.B. Proud. (PB, 1989)

TASMANIA. *Stamps and Postal History of Tasmania.* W.E. Tinsley. (RPSL, 1986)

The Pictorial Stamps of Tasmania 1899–1912. K.E. Lancaster. (Royal Philatelic Society of Victoria, 1986)

TRANSVAAL. *Transvaal Philately.* Edited I.B. Mathews. (Reijger Publishers (Pty) Ltd, 1986)

TRISTAN DA CUNHA. *The History and Postal History of Tristan da Cunha.* G. Crabb. (1980)

TURKS AND CAICOS ISLANDS. *Turks Islands and Caicos Islands to 1950.* J.J. Challis. (Roses Caribbean Philatelic Society, 1983)

TUVALU. *Tuvalu. A Philatelic Handbook.* M. Forand. (Tuvalu Philatelic Society, 1982)

VICTORIA. *The Stamps of Victoria.* G. Kellow. (B. & K. Philatelic Publishing, 1990)

WESTERN AUSTRALIA. *Western Australia. The Stamps and Postal History.* Edited M. Hamilton and B. Pope. (Western Australia Study Group, 1979)

Postage Stamps and Postal History of Western Australia. Vols 1–3. M. Juhl. (1981–83)

STANLEY GIBBONS STAMP CATALOGUE

Part 1: BRITISH COMMONWEALTH

VOLUME 2: COUNTRIES J TO Z

95th EDITION—1992/93

Jamaica

Records show that the first local Postmaster for Jamaica on a regular basis was appointed as early as 1671, although a reasonably organised service did not evolve until 1687–8. In the early years of the 18th century overseas mail was carried by the British packets, but between 1704 and 1711 this service was run on a commercial basis by Edmund Dummer. Following the collapse of the Dummer scheme Jamaica was virtually without a Post Office until 1720 and it was not until 1755 that overseas mail was again carried by British packets.

The stamps of Great Britain were used on the island from 8 May 1858 to August 1860. Although there had been much friction between the local inhabitants and the British G.P.O. it was not until 1 August 1860 that the Jamaica authorities assumed responsibility for the postal service.

KINGSTON

Z 1

Stamps of GREAT BRITAIN *cancelled* "A 01" *as Type* Z **1**.

1858 *to* **1860.**

Z1	1d. rose-red (1857), *perf* 16	£170
Z2	1d. rose-red (1857), *perf* 14	25·00
Z4	4d. rose (1857)	35·00
Z5	6d. lilac (1856)	35·00
Z6	1s. green (1856)	70·00

Z 2

Stamps of GREAT BRITAIN *cancelled* "A 01" *as Type* Z **2**.

1859 *to* **1860.**

Z 7	1d. rose-red (1857), *perf* 14	£160
Z 9	4d. rose (1857)	35·00
Z10	6d. lilac (1856)	35·00
Z11	1s. green (1856)	£225

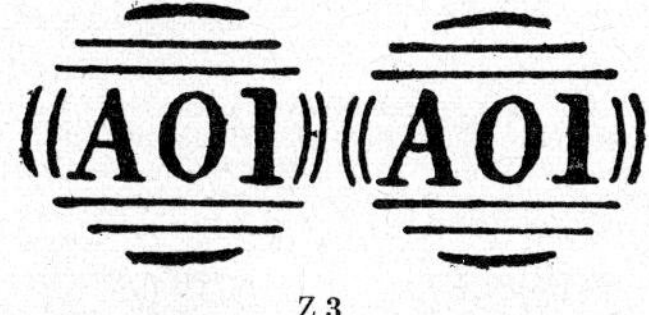

Z 3

Stamps of GREAT BRITAIN *cancelled* "A 01" *as Type* Z **1**.

1859 *to* **1860.**

Z12	1d. rose-red (1857), *perf* 14	£200
Z14	4d. rose (1857)	£120
	a. Thick glazed paper	£400
Z15	6d. lilac (1856)	£120
Z16	1s. green (1856)	

Cancellation "A 01" was later used by the London, Foreign Branch Office.

OTHER JAMAICA POST OFFICES

British stamps were issued to several District post offices between 8 May 1858 and 1 March 1859 (i.e. before the Obliterators A 27–A 78 were issued). These can only be distinguished (off the cover) when they have the Town's date-stamp on them. They are worth about three times the price of those with an obliteration number.

Stamps of GREAT BRITAIN *cancelled* "A 27" *to* "A 78" *as Type* Z **1**

1859 *to* **1860.**

"A 27". ALEXANDRIA

Z17	1d. rose-red (1857), *perf* 14	£425
Z17*a*	2d. blue (1855) Large Crown, *perf* 14 (Plate 6)	£475
Z18	4d. rose (1857)	£160
Z19	6d. lilac (1856)	£375

"A 28". ANNOTTO BAY

Z20	1d. rose-red (1857), *perf* 14	£300
Z21	4d. rose (1857)	70·00
Z22	6d. lilac (1856)	£225

"A 29". BATH

Z23	1d. rose-red (1857), *perf* 14	£120
Z24	4d. rose (1857)	85·00
Z25	6d. lilac (1856)	£400

"A 30". BLACK RIVER

Z26	1d. rose-red (1857), *perf* 14	£120
Z27	4d. rose (1857)	50·00
Z28	6d. lilac (1856)	£120

"A 31". BROWN'S TOWN

Z29	1d. rose-red (1857), *perf* 14	£160
Z30	4d. rose (1857)	£160
Z31	6d. lilac (1856)	£160

"A 32". BUFF BAY

Z32	1d. rose-red (1857), *perf* 14	£120
Z33	4d. rose (1857)	£150
Z34	6d. lilac (1856)	£120

"A 33". CHAPLETON

Z35	1d. rose-red (1857), *perf* 14	£160
Z36	4d. rose (1857)	95·00
Z37	6d. lilac (1856)	£160

"A 34". CLAREMONT

Z38	1d. rose-red (1857), *perf* 14	£300
Z39	4d. rose (1857)	£150
Z40	6d. lilac (1856)	£300

"A 35". CLARENDON
(Near Four Paths)

Z41	1d. rose-red (1857), *perf* 14	£250
Z42	4d. rose (1857)	£100
Z43	6d. lilac (1856)	£160

"A 36". DRY HARBOUR

Z44	1d. rose-red (1857), *perf* 14	£375
Z45	4d. rose (1857)	£300
Z46	6d. lilac (1856)	£250

"A 37". DUNCANS

Z47	1d. rose-red (1857), *perf* 14	
Z48	4d. rose (1857)	£375
Z49	6d. lilac (1856)	£250

"A 38". EWARTON

A 38 was sent out to EWARTON but it is believed that this office was closed towards the end of 1858 before it arrived as no genuine used specimens have been found on British stamps.

"A 39". FALMOUTH

Z53	1d. rose-red (1857), *perf* 14	75·00
Z54	4d. rose (1857)	35·00
Z55	6d. lilac (1856)	55·00
Z56	1s. green (1856)	£425

"A 40". FLINT RIVER
(Near Hopewell)

Z57	1d. rose-red (1857), *perf* 14	£150
Z58	4d. rose (1857)	£100
Z59	6d. lilac (1856)	£150
Z60	1s. green (1856)	£425

"A 41". GAYLE

Z61	1d. rose-red (1857), *perf* 14	£450
Z62	4d. rose (1857)	£120
Z63	6d. lilac (1856)	£130
Z64	1s. green (1856)	£170

"A 42". GOLDEN SPRING
(Near Stony Hill)

Z65	1d. rose-red (1857), *perf* 14	£170
Z66	4d. rose (1857)	£150
Z67	6d. lilac (1856)	£400
Z68	1s. green (1856)	£425

"A 43". GORDON TOWN

Z69	1d. rose-red (1857), *perf* 14	
Z70	4d. rose (1857)	
Z71	6d. lilac (1856)	£450

"A 44". GOSHEN
(Near Santa Cruz)

Z72	1d. rose-red (1857), *perf* 14	£120
Z73	4d. rose (1857)	£110
Z74	6d. lilac (1856)	50·00

"A 45". GRANGE HILL

Z75	1d. rose-red (1857), *perf* 14	£150
Z76	4d. rose (1857)	38·00
Z77	6d. lilac (1856)	55·00
Z77*a*	1s. green (1856)	£375

"A 46". GREEN ISLAND

Z78	1d. rose-red (1857), *perf* 14	£300
Z79	4d. rose (1857)	£150
Z80	6d. lilac (1856)	£250
Z81	1s. green (1856)	£425

"A 47". HIGHGATE

Z82	1d. rose-red (1857), *perf* 14	£170
Z83	4d. rose (1857)	£110
Z84	6d. lilac (1856)	£170

"A 48". HOPE BAY

Z85	1d. rose-red (1857), *perf* 14	£400
Z86	4d. rose (1857)	£150
Z87	6d. lilac (1856)	£400

"A 49". LILLIPUT
(Near Balaclava)

Z88	1d. rose-red (1857), *perf* 14	£150
Z89	4d. rose (1857)	£150
Z90	6d. lilac (1856)	75·00

"A 50". LITTLE RIVER

A 50 was sent out for use at LITTLE RIVER, but it is believed that this office closed late in 1858, before the obliterator could be issued. No specimen has yet been found used on British stamps.

"A 51". LUCEA

Z91	1d. rose-red (1857), *perf* 14	£225
Z92	4d. rose (1857)	48·00
Z93	6d. lilac (1856)	£150

"A 52". MANCHIONEAL

Z94	1d. rose-red (1857), *perf* 14	£300
Z95	4d. rose (1857)	£160
Z96	6d. lilac (1856)	

"A 53". MANDEVILLE

Z97	1d. rose-red (1857), *perf* 14	£160
Z98	4d. rose (1857)	50·00
Z99	6d. lilac (1856)	£140

"A 54". MAY HILL
(Near Spur Tree)

Z100	1d. rose-red (1857), *perf* 14	75·00
Z101	4d. rose (1857)	75·00
Z102	6d. lilac (1856)	50·00

"A 55". MILE GULLY

Z103	1d. rose-red (1857), *perf* 14	£250
Z104	4d. rose (1857)	£150
Z105	6d. lilac (1856)	£150

"A 56". MONEAGUE

Z106	1d. rose-red (1857), *perf* 14	£150
Z107	4d. rose (1857)	£190
Z108	6d. lilac (1856)	£400

"A 57". MONTEGO BAY

Z109	1d. rose-red (1857), *perf* 14	£160
Z110	4d. rose (1857)	40·00
Z111	6d. lilac (1856)	50·00
Z112	1s. green (1856)	£425

"A 58". MONTPELIER

Z113	1d. rose-red (1857), *perf* 14	
Z114	4d. rose (1857)	
Z115	6d. lilac (1856)	£650

"A 59". MORANT BAY

Z116	1d. rose-red (1857), *perf* 14	£300
Z117	4d. rose (1857)	50·00
Z118	6d. lilac (1856)	50·00

"A 60". OCHO RIOS

Z119	1d. rose-red (1857), *perf* 14	
Z120	4d. rose (1857)	75·00
Z121	6d. lilac (1856)	£140

"A 61". OLD HARBOUR

Z122	1d. rose-red (1857), *perf* 14	£150
Z123	4d. rose (1857)	£110
Z124	6d. lilac (1856)	£110

"A 62". PLANTAIN GARDEN RIVER
(Near Golden Grove)

Z125	1d. rose-red (1857), *perf* 14	£110
Z126	4d. rose (1857)	80·00
Z127	6d. lilac (1856)	£110

"A 63". PEAR TREE GROVE

No genuine specimen of A 63 has been found on a British stamp.

"A 64". PORT ANTONIO

Z131	1d. rose-red (1857), *perf* 14	£375
Z132	4d. rose (1857)	£225
Z133	6d. lilac (1856)	£225

"A 65". PORT MORANT

Z134	1d. rose-red (1857), *perf* 14	£225
Z135	4d. rose (1857)	85·00
Z136	6d. lilac (1856)	£225

"A 66". PORT MARIA

Z137	1d. rose-red (1857), *perf* 14	£150
Z138	4d. rose (1857)	55·00
Z139	6d. lilac (1856)	£225

"A 67". PORT ROYAL

Z140	1d. rose-red (1857), *perf* 14	£300
Z140*a*	2d. blue (1858) (plate 9)	
Z141	4d. rose (1857)	£300
Z142	6d. lilac (1856)	£300

"A 68". PORUS

Z143	1d. rose-red (1857), *perf* 14	£150
Z144	4d. rose (1857)	70·00
Z145	6d. lilac (1856)	£300

"A 69". RAMBLE

Z146	1d. rose-red (1857), *perf* 14	£150
Z147	4d. rose (1857)	£150
	a. Thick glazed paper	£400
Z149	6d. lilac (1856)	£225

"A 70". RIO BUENO

Z150	1d. rose-red (1857), *perf* 14	
Z151	4d. rose (1857)	£130
Z152	6d. lilac (1856)	85·00

"A 71". RODNEY HALL
(Now called Linstead)

Z153	1d. rose-red (1857), *perf* 14	£120
Z154	4d. rose (1857)	80·00
Z155	6d. lilac (1856)	£110

"A 72". SAINT DAVID
(Now called Yallahs)

Z156	1d. rose-red (1857), *perf* 14	£150
Z157	4d. rose (1857)	£300
Z158	6d. lilac (1856)	

"A 73". ST. ANN'S BAY

Z159	1d. rose-red (1857), *perf* 14	£150
Z160	4d. rose (1857)	75·00
Z161	6d. lilac (1856)	£150

"A 74". SALT GUT
(Near Oracabessa)

Z162	1d. rose-red (1857), *perf* 14	£140
Z163	4d. rose (1857)	
Z164	6d. lilac (1856)	£150

"A 75". SAVANNA-LA-MAR

Z165	1d. rose-red (1857), *perf* 14	50·00
Z166	4d. rose (1857)	40·00
Z167	6d. lilac (1856)	£150
Z168	1s. green (1856)	£375

"A 76". SPANISH TOWN

Z169	1d. rose-red (1857), *perf* 14	85·00
Z170	4d. rose (1857)	40·00
Z171	6d. lilac (1856)	85·00
Z172	1s. green (1856)	£250

"A 77". STEWART TOWN

Z173	1d. rose-red (1857), *perf* 14	£400
Z174	4d. rose (1857)	£250
Z175	6d. lilac (1856)	£150

"A 78". VERE
(Now called Alley)

Z176	1d. rose-red (1857), *perf* 14	£225
Z177	4d. rose (1857)	75·00
Z178	6d. lilac (1856)	50·00
Z179	1s. green (1856)	£425

The use of British stamps in Jamaica after August 1860 for civilian mail was unauthorised by the P.M.G. of Great Britain.

PRICES FOR STAMPS ON COVER

Nos. 1/6	*from* × 4
Nos. 7/15	*from* × 6
Nos. 16/26	*from* × 8
Nos. 27/9	*from* × 6
No. 30	*from* × 5
Nos. 31/2	*from* × 15
Nos. 33/6	*from* × 5
Nos. 37/56	*from* × 3
No. 57	*from* × 4
Nos. 58/67	*from* × 3
Nos. 68/77	*from* × 6
Nos. 78/89	*from* × 3
Nos. 90/103	*from* × 4
Nos. 104/7	*from* × 5
Nos. 108/17	*from* × 3
Nos. 118/20	*from* × 5
Nos. 121/33*a*	*from* × 4
Nos. 134/40	*from* × 8
Nos. F1/9	*from* × 3
Nos. O1/5	*from* × 30

CROWN COLONY

PRINTERS. Until 1923, all the stamps of Jamaica were typographed by De La Rue & Co, Ltd, London, *unless otherwise stated.*

The official dates of issue are given, where known, but where definite information is not available the dates are those of earliest known use, etc.

CONDITION. Mint or fine used specimens of stamps with the pineapple watermark are rarely met with and are worth considerably more than our prices which are for stamps in average condition. Inferior specimens can be supplied at much lower prices.

1

2

3

4

5

6

7

A

1860 (23 Nov)–**63.** *W* **7.** *P* 14.

1	1	1d. pale blue	60·00	15·00
		a. Pale greenish blue	65·00	19·00
		b. Blue	50·00	12·00
		c. Deep blue	95·00	28·00
		d. Bisected (½d.) (11.61) (on cover)	†	£650
2	2	2d. rose	£190	45·00
		a. Deep rose	£120	45·00
3	3	3d. green (10.9.63)	£130	25·00
4	4	4d. brown-orange	£200	35·00
		a. Red-orange	£200	22·00
5	5	6d. dull lilac	£180	18·00
		a. Grey-purple	£275	32·00
		b. Deep purple	£800	40·00
6	6	1s. yellow-brown	£450	23·00
		a. Purple-brown	£500	23·00
		b. Dull brown	£180	27·00
		c. "$" for "S" in "SHILLING" (A)	£1600	£600

The diagonal bisection of the 1d. was authorized by a P.O. notice dated 20 November 1861. Specimens are only of value when on original envelope or wrapper. The authority was withdrawn as from 1 December 1872. Fakes are frequently met with. Other bisections were unauthorized.

The so-called "dollar variety" of the 1s. occurs once in each sheet of stamps in all shades and in later colours, etc, on the second stamp in the second row of the left upper pane. The prices quoted above are for the dull brown shade, the prices for the other shades being proportionate to their normal value.

All values except the 3d. are known imperf, mint only.

There are two types of watermark in the 3d. and 1s., one being short and squat and the other elongated.

8

9

10

1870–83. *Wmk Crown CC.* (*a*) *P* 14.

7	8	½d. claret (29.10.72)	12·00	3·50
		a. Deep claret (1883)	13·00	3·50
8	1	1d. blue (4.73)	45·00	75
		a. Deep blue	48·00	1·50
9	2	2d. rose (4.70)	48·00	70
		a. Deep rose	70·00	85
10	3	3d. green (1.70)	90·00	7·00
11	4	4d. brown-orange (1872)	£150	9·00
		a. Red-orange	£350	6·00
12	5	6d. mauve (10.3.71)	48·00	5·50
13	6	1s. dull-brown (*to deep*) (23.2.73)	25·00	8·50
		a. "$" for "S" in "SHILLING" (A)	£1100	£600
		(*b*) *P* 12½		
14	9	2s. Venetian red (27.8.75)	40·00	15·00
15	10	5s. lilac (27.8.75)	90·00	£120
7/15		*Set of* 9	£450	£140

The ½d., 1d., 4d., 2s. and 5s. are known imperforate.

1883–97. *Wmk Crown CA. P* 14.

16	8	½d. yellow-green (1885)	2·25	30
		a. Green	80	10
17	1	1d. blue (1884)	£350	4·50
18		1d. rose (*to deep*) (3.3.85)	48·00	75
		a. Carmine	22·00	50
19	2	2d. rose (*to deep*) (17.3.84)	£150	3·75
20		2d. grey (1885)	55·00	1·25
		a. Slate	40·00	50
21	3	3d. sage-green (1886)	4·00	85
		a. Pale olive-green	2·50	1·00
22	4	4d. red-orange* (9.3.83)	£350	19·00
		a. Red-brown (*shades*)	2·00	35
23	5	6d. deep yellow (4.10.90)	16·00	6·00
		a. Orange-yellow	4·00	3·50
24	6	1s. brown (*to deep*) (3.97)	5·00	4·50
		a. "$" for "S" in "SHILLING" (A)	£850	£450
		b. Chocolate	15·00	11·00
25	9	2s. Venetian red (1897)	27·00	17·00
26	10	5s. lilac (1897)	48·00	48·00
16/26		*Set of* 11	£550	80·00
16, 18, 20, 21, 22 and 23 Optd "Specimen"		*Set of* 6	£450	

*No. 22 is the same colour as No. 11*a*.

The 1d. carmine, 2d. slate, and 2s. are known imperf. All values to the 6d. inclusive are known perf 12. These are proofs.

NEW INFORMATION

The editor is always interested to correspond with people who have new information that will improve or correct the Catalogue.

11

TWO PENCE
HALF-PENNY
(12)

1889–91. *Value tablet in second colour. Wmk Crown CA. P* 14.

27	11	1d. purple and mauve (8.3.89)	2·25	10
28		2d. green (8.3.89)	17·00	3·50
		a. Deep green (*brown gum*)	4·50	6·00
29		2½d. dull purple and blue (25.2.91)	4·50	40
27/9		*Set of* 3	10·00	3·50
27/9 Optd "Specimen"		*Set of* 3	£100	

A very wide range of shades may be found in the 1d. The headplate was printed in many shades of purple, and the duty-plate in various shades of mauve and purple and also in carmine, etc. There are fewer shades for the other values and they are not so pronounced.

1890 (4(?) June). *No.* 22*a surch with T* **12** *by C. Vendyres, Kingston.*

30	4	2½d. on 4d. red-brown	27·00	8·50
		a. Spacing between lines of surch 1½ mm	32·00	17·00
		b. Surch double	£325	£225
		c. "PFNNY" for "PENNY"	75·00	65·00
		ca. Ditto and broken "K" for "Y"	£130	£110

This provisional was issued pending receipt of No. 29 which is listed above for convenience of reference.

Three settings exist. (1) Ten varieties arranged in a single vertical row and repeated six times in the pane. (2) Twelve varieties, in two horizontal rows of six, repeated five times, alternate rows show 1 and 1½ mm spacing between lines of surcharge. (3) Three varieties, arranged horizontally and repeated twenty times. All these settings can be reconstructed by examination of the spacing and relative position of the words of the surcharge and of the broken letters, etc, which are numerous.

A variety reading "PFNNK", with the "K" unbroken, is a forgery. Varieties c. and ca. may be found in the double surcharge.

Surcharges misplaced either horizontally or vertically are met with, the normal position being central at the foot of the stamp with "HALF-PENNY" covering the old value.

13 Llandovery Falls, Jamaica (photo by Dr. J. Johnston)

14 Arms of Jamaica

(Recess D.L.R.)

1900–1. *Wmk Crown CC* (*sideways*). *P* 14.

31	13	1d. red (1.5.00)	1·00	10
32		1d. slate-black and red (25.9.01)	1·75	10
		a. Blued paper	£110	£100
		b. Imperf between (pair)	£5500	
31/32 Optd "Specimen"		*Set of* 2	£130	

Many shades exist of both centre and frame of the bi-coloured 1d. which was, of course, printed from two plates and the design shows minor differences from that of the 1d. red which was printed from a single plate.

(Typo D.L.R.)

1903–4. *Wmk Crown CA. P* 14.

33	14	½d. grey and dull green (16.11.03)	1·50	10
		a. "SER.ET" for "SERVIET"	40·00	45·00
34		1d. grey and carmine (24.2.04)	1·50	10
		a. "SER.ET" for "SERVIET"	32·00	35·00
35		2½d. grey and ultramarine (16.11.03)	2·00	30
		a. "SER.ET" for "SERVIET"	60·00	70·00
36		5d. grey and yellow (1.3.04)	12·00	23·00
		a. "SER.ET" for "SERVIET"	£600	£700
33/6		*Set of* 4	15·00	23·00
33/6 Optd "Specimen"		*Set of* 4	75·00	

The "SER.ET" variety occurs once in each sheet of stamps on the second stamp in the fourth row of the left upper pane.

The centres of the above and later bi-coloured stamps in the Arms type vary in colour from grey to grey-black.

15 Arms type redrawn 16

1905–11. *Wmk Mult Crown CA. P* 14 (*a*) *Arms types. Chalk-surfaced paper.*

37	14	½d. grey and dull green (24.11.05)	5·50	20
		a. "SER.ET" for "SERVIET"	32·00	32·00
38	15	½d. yell-grn (*ordinary paper*) (8.11.06)	5·50	40
		a. Dull green	3·75	20
		b. Deep green	3·75	20
39	14	1d. grey and carmine (20.11.05)	17·00	25
40	16	1d. carmine (*ordinary paper*) (1.10.06)	1·25	10
41	14	2½d. grey and ultramarine (12.11.07)	2·75	1·00
42		2½d. pale ultramarine (*ordinary paper*) (21.9.10)	2·50	1·25
		a. Deep ultramarine	2·50	1·75
43		5d. grey and orange-yellow (24.4.07)	32·00	38·00
		a. "SER.ET" for "SERVIET"	£800	£900
44		6d. dull and bright purple (18.8.11)	11·00	12·00
45		5s. grey and violet (11.05)	40·00	30·00
37/45		*Set of* 9	£100	75·00
38, 40, 42, 44, 45 Optd "Specimen"		*Set of* 5	£130	

See note below No. 36 concerning grey centres.

(b) Queen Victoria types. Ordinary paper

46 **3** 3d. olive-green (15.5.05) .. .. 6·00 1·50
a. Sage-green (1907) .. .. .. 5·00 1·25
47 3d. purple/*yellow* (10.3.10) .. .. 4·25 2·50
a. Chalk-surfaced paper. *Pale purple/yellow* (11.7.10) .. .. .. 2·00 1·40
48 **4** 4d. red-brown (6.6.08) .. .. .. 70·00 38·00
49 4d. black/*yellow* (*chalk-surfaced paper*) (21.9.10) .. .. 7·00 25·00
50 4d. red/*yellow* (3.10.11) .. .. 1·50 5·00
51 **5** 6d. dull orange (27.6.06) .. .. 15·00 22·00
a. Golden yellow (9.09) .. .. 22·00 30·00
52 6d. lilac (19.11.09) .. .. .. 20·00 20·00
a. Chalk-surfaced paper. *Purple* (7.10) 7·00 11·00
53 **6** 1s. brown (11.06) .. .. .. 16·00 11·00
a. Deep brown .. .. .. 27·00 15·00
b. "$" for "S" in "SHILLING" (A) .. £900 £900
54 1s. black/*green* (*chalk-surfaced paper*) (21.9.10) .. .. 3·50 8·50
a. "$" for "S" in "SHILLING" (A) .. £800 £1000
55 **9** 2s. Venetian red (11.08) .. .. 90·00 £120
56 2s. purple/*blue* (*chalk-surfaced paper*) (21.9.10) .. .. 6·00 3·50
46/56 .. .. *Set of* 11 £190 £225
47, 49, 50, 52, 54, 56 Optd "Specimen" *Set of* 6 £170

17

18

(T **17/18** typo D.L.R.)

1911 (3 Feb). *Wmk Mult Crown CA. P* 14.
57 **17** 2d. grey (Optd S. £35) .. .. .. 1·75 13·00

1912–20. *Wmk Mult Crown CA. Chalk-surfaced paper* (*3d. to 5s.*). *P* 14.
58 **18** 1d. carmine-red (5.12.12) 45 10
a. Scarlet (1916) 30 15
59 1½d. brown-orange (13.7.16) .. .. 1·00 15
a. Yellow-orange .. .. .. 7·00 1·00
b. Wmk sideways .. .. .. † £1300
60 2d. grey (2.8.12) .. .. .. 90 1·75
a. Slate-grey .. .. .. 1·00 3·00
61 2½d. blue (13.2.13) 60 15
a. Deep bright blue 65 45
62 3d. purple/*yellow* (6.3.12) 40 45
a. White back (2.4.13) 55 40
b. On lemon (25.9.16) (Optd S. £32) .. 3·50 1·25
63 4d. black and red/*yellow* (4.4.13) .. 50 1·50
a. White back (7.5.14) .. .. 50 3·00
b. On lemon (1916) (Optd S. £32) .. 17·00 17·00
c. On pale yellow (1919) .. .. 22·00 13·00
64 6d. dull and bright purple (14.11.12) .. 4·00 8·50
a. Dull purple and bright mauve (1915) 70 1·00
b. Dull purple & bright magenta (1920) 2·00 2·25
65 1s. black/*green* (2.8.12) .. .. 2·25 2·00
a. White back (4.1.15) .. .. 70 3·50
b. On blue-green, olive back (1920) .. 2·25 4·00
66 2s. purple and bright blue/*blue* (10.1.19) 9·50 17·00
67 5s. green and red/*yellow* (5.9.19) .. 35·00 55·00
a. On pale yellow .. .. .. 45·00 60·00
b. On orange-buff £100 £130
58/67 .. .. *Set of* 10 45·00 70·00
58/67 Optd "Specimen" .. .. *Set of* 10 £190

For the ½d. and 6d. with Script wmk see Nos. 89*a*/90.

The paper of No. 67 is a bright yellow and the gum rough and dull. No. 67*a* is on practically the normal creamy "pale yellow" paper, and the gum is smooth and shiny. The paper of No. 67*b* approaches the "coffee" colour of the true "orange-buff", and the colours of both head and frame are paler, the latter being of a carmine tone.

RED CROSS LABELS. A voluntary organization, the Jamaica War Stamp League later the Jamaica Patriotic Stamp League, was founded in November 1915 by Mr. Lewis Ashenheim, a Kingston solicitor. The aims of the League were to support the British Red Cross, collect funds for the purchase of aircraft for the Royal Flying Corps and the relief of Polish Jews.

One fund-raising method used was the sale, from 1 December 1915, of ½d. charity labels. These labels, which were available from post offices, depicted a bi-plane above a cross and were printed in red by Dennison Manufacturing Company, Framingham, U.S.A., the stamps being perforated 12 except for those along the edges of the sheet which have one side imperforate.

From 22 December 1915 supplies of the labels were overprinted "JAMAICA" in red, the colour of this overprint being changed to black from 15 January 1916. Copies sold from 11 March 1916 carried an additional "Half-Penny" surcharge, also in black.

Such labels had no postal validity when used by the general public, but, by special order of the Governor, were accepted for the payment of postage on the League's official mail. To obtain this concession the envelopes were to be inscribed "Red Cross Business" or "Jamaica Patriotic Stamp League" and the labels used endorsed with Mr. Ashenheim's signature. Such covers are rare.

WAR STAMP. (19) | WAR STAMP. (20) | WAR STAMP. (21)

(T **19/21** optd locally)

1916 (1 Apr–Sept). *Optd with T* **19**.
68 **15** ½d. yellow-green 10 35
a. No stop after "STAMP" (R. 18/2) .. 7·50 17·00
b. Opt double .. .. 95·00 95·00
c. Opt inverted .. .. 80·00 90·00
d. Space between "W" and "A" (R. 20/1) 7·50 17·00
e. Blue-green 10 50
ea. No stop after "STAMP" (R. 3/11 or 11/1) .. .. 7·50 17·00
eb. Space between "W" and "A" (R. 20/1) 7·50 17·00

69 **18** 3d. purple/*yellow* (white back) .. .. 3·50 13·00
a. On lemon (6.16) .. .. .. 1·00 13·00
ab. No stop after "STAMP" (R. 8/6 or 9/6) 20·00 55·00
b. On pale yellow (9.16) .. .. 3·50 16·00

Minor varieties: ½d. (i) Small "P"; (ii) "WARISTAMP" (raised quad between words); (iii) Two stops after "STAMP". 3d. "WARISTAMP". There were several settings of the overprint used for each value. Where two positions are quoted for a variety these did not occur on the same sheet.

NOTE. The above and succeeding stamps with "WAR STAMP" overprint were issued for payment of a special war tax on letters and postcards or on parcels. Ordinary unoverprinted stamps could also be used for this purpose.

1916 (Sept–Dec). *Optd with T* **20**.
70 **15** ½d. blue-green (*shades*) (2.10.16) .. 10 30
a. No stop after "STAMP" (R. 5/7) .. 9·00 24·00
b. Opt omitted (in pair with normal) .. £650 £550
c. "R" inserted by hand (R. 11/10) .. £375 £300
71 **18** 1½d. orange (1.9.16) 10 15
aa. Wmk sideways .. .. .. — £1200
a. No stop after "STAMP" (R. 4/12, 8/6, 10/10, 11/1, 18/12, 19/12) .. .. 5·00 5·50
b. "S" in "STAMP" omitted (R. 6/12) (Dec) .. .. 90·00 £100
c. "S" inserted by hand £250
d. "R" in "WAR" omitted (R. 1/10) .. £500 £425
e. "R" inserted by hand £350 £300
f. Inverted "d" for "P" £150 £120
72 3d. purple/*lemon* (2.10.16) 25 90
aa. Opt inverted £375
a. No stop after "STAMP" (R. 5/7) .. 19·00 40·00
b. "S" in "STAMP" omitted (R. 6/12) (Dec) £275 £225
c. "S" inserted by hand £180 £180
d. "S" inserted inverted £275 £225
e. On yellow (12.16) .. .. .. 6·00 9·00
ea. "S" in "STAMP" omitted (R. 6/12) .. £350 £250
eb. "S" inserted by hand £275 £180
ec. "S" inserted inverted £325 £225

Minor varieties, such as raised quads, small stop, double stop, spaced letters and letters of different sizes, also exist in this overprint. The setting was altered several times.

1917 (March). *Optd with T* **21**.
73 **15** ½d. blue-green (*shades*) (25.3.17) .. 10 20
a. No stop after "STAMP" (R. 2/5, 8/11, 8/12) .. .. 7·50 17·00
b. Stop inserted and "P" impressed a second time (R. 7/6) £140
c. Optd on back only .. .. .. 95·00
d. Opt inverted .. .. .. 9·00 23·00
74 **18** 1½d. orange (3.3.17) 10 10
aa. Wmk sideways .. .. .. — £1300
a. No stop after "STAMP" (R. 2/5, 8/11, 8/12) .. .. 7·50 15·00
b. Stop inserted and "P" impressed a second time (R. 7/6) £190
c. Opt double .. .. 80·00 85·00
d. Opt inverted .. .. .. 80·00 75·00
75 3d. purple/*yellow* (3.3.17) 15 30
a. No stop after "STAMP" (R. 2/5, 8/11, 8/12) .. .. 13·00 22·00
b. Stop inserted and "P" impressed a second time (R. 7/6) £170
c. Opt inverted £140
d. Opt sideways (reading up) £300
da. Opt omitted (in horiz pair with No. 75d) £1600

No. 75da shows the left-hand stamp as No. 75d and the right-hand stamp without overprint.

There are numerous minor varieties in this overprint with the setting being altered several times.

WAR STAMP
(22)

1919 (4 Oct). *Optd with T* **22** *by D.L.R.*
76 **15** ½d. green (R.) 10 15
77 **18** 3d. purple/*yellow* (R.) .. .. .. 1·25 3·00
a. Pale purple/buff (R.) .. .. 65 1·25
b. Deep purple/buff (R.) .. .. 4·25 6·00
76/7 Optd "Specimen" .. .. *Set of* 2 70·00

We list the most distinct variations in the 3d. The buff tone of the paper varies considerably in depth.

23 Jamaica Exhibition 1891

24 Arawak Woman preparing Cassava

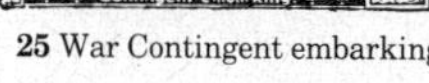
25 War Contingent embarking

26 King's House, Spanish Town

Re-entry. Nos. 80a, 93a

The greater part of the design is re-entered, the hull showing in very solid colour and the people appear very blurred. There are also minor re-entries on stamps above (R. 7/4 and 6/4).

27 Return of War Contingent

A B

28 Landing of Columbus

29 Cathedral, Spanish Town

34

(Typo (½d., 1d.), recess (others) D.L.R.)

1919–21. *T* **23/29**, **34** *and similar vert designs. Wmk Mult Crown CA* (*sideways on 1d., 1½d. and 10s.*). *Chalk-surfaced paper* (*½d., 1d.*). *P* 14.
78 **23** ½d. green and olive-green (12.11.20) .. 40 30
79 **24** 1d. carmine and orange (3.10.21) .. 1·75 90
80 **25** 1½d. green (*shades*) (4.7.19) 25 35
a. Major re-entry (R. 8/4) .. .. 60·00
81 **26** 2d. indigo and green (18.2.21) .. 80 2·50
82 **27** 2½d. deep blue and blue (A) (18.2.21) .. 11·00 3·00
a. Blue-black and deep blue (A) .. 70 90
83 **28** 3d. myrtle-green and blue (8.4.21) .. 1·50 80
84 **29** 4d. brown and deep green (21.2.21) .. 2·50 6·50
85 – 1s. orange-yell & red-orge (10.12.20) 3·75 4·50
a. Frame inverted £18000 £13000
86 – 2s. light blue and brown (10.12.20) .. 13·00 22·00
87 – 3s. violet-blue and orange (10.12.20) .. 20·00 48·00
88 – 5s. blue and yellow-orange (15.4.21) .. 48·00 48·00
a. Blue and pale dull orange .. 45·00 48·00
89 **34** 10s. myrtle-green (6.5.20) .. .. 75·00 £140
78/89 .. .. .. *Set of* 12 £140 £250
78/89 Optd "Specimen" .. .. *Set of* 12 £250

Designs: *Vert*—1s. Statue of Queen Victoria, Kingston; 2s. Admiral Rodney Memorial; 3s. Sir Charles Metcalfe Monument; 5s. Jamaican scenery.

The 2½d. of the above series showed the Union Jack at left, incorrectly, as indicated in illustration A. In the issue on paper with Script wmk the design was corrected (Illustration B).

A 6d. stamp showing the reading of the Declaration of Freedom from Slavery in 1836 was prepared and sent out in April 1921, but for political reasons was not issued and the stock was destroyed. Copies overprinted "Specimen" are known on both the Mult CA and Script CA papers, and are worth £500 each. Price without "Specimen" on Script CA £14000.

"Bow" flaw (R.18/12)

1921 (21 Oct)–**27**. *Wmk Mult Script CA. Chalk-surfaced paper (6d.). P* 14.
89*a* **18** ½d. green (Optd S. £45) (3.11.27) .. 20 10
ab. Bow flaw .. .. 22·00
90 6d. dull pur & brt magenta (Optd S. £35) 5·50 3·00

35 "POSTAGE & REVENUE" added

36 Port Royal in 1853

(Printing as before; the 6d. recess-printed)

1921–29. *As Nos.* 78/89. *Wmk Mult Script CA* (*sideways on* 1d. *and* 1½d.). *Chalk-surfaced paper* (½d., 1d.). *P* 14.
91 **23** ½d. green and olive-green (5.2.22) .. 50 15
a. Green and deep olive-green .. 25 10
92 **35** 1d. carmine and orange (5.12.22) .. 1·50 10
93 **25** 1½d. green (*shades*) (2.2.21) 30 15
a. Major re-entry (R. 8/4) .. .. 60·00
94 **26** 2d. indigo and green (4.11.21) .. .. 3·00 30
a. Indigo and grey-green (1925) .. 3·50 35
95 **27** 2½d. deep blue and blue (B) (4.11.21) .. 5·50 90
a. Dull blue and blue (B) .. .. 6·00 45
96 **28** 3d. myrtle-green and blue (6.3.22) .. 1·50 30
a. Green and pale blue 40 15
97 **29** 4d. brown and deep green (5.12.21) .. 45 15
a. Chocolate and dull green 40 15
98 **36** 6d. black and blue (5.12.22) .. .. 10·00 85
a. Grey and dull blue .. .. .. 6·50 60
99 – 1s. orange and red-orange (4.11.21) .. 1·40 65
a. Orange-yellow and brown-orange .. 60 15
100 – 2s. light blue and brown (5.2.22) .. 2·50 35
101 – 3s. violet-blue and orange (23.8.21) .. 6·50 9·50
102 – 5s. blue and yellow-brown (8.11.23) .. 24·00 25·00
a. Blue and pale dull orange .. .. 50·00 55·00
b. Blue and yellow-orange (1927) .. 22·00 22·00
c. Blue and pale bistre-brown (1929) .. 22·00 22·00
103 **34** 10s. myrtle-green (March (?) 1922) .. 48·00 60·00
91/103 .. .. *Set of* 13 85·00 85·00
91/103 Optd "Specimen" .. .. *Set of* 13 £250

The frame of No. 102*a* is the same colour as that of No. 88*a*.

The designs of all values of the pictorial series, with the exception of the 5s. and 10s. (which originated with the Governor, Sir Leslie Probyn), were selected by Mr. F. C. Cundall, F.S.A. The 1d. and 5s. were drawn by Miss Cundall, the 3d. by Mrs. Cundall, and the 10s. by De La Rue & Co. The 6d. is from a lithograph. The other designs are from photographs, the frames of all being the work of Miss Cundall and Miss Wood.

37

38

39

(Centres from photos by Miss V. F. Taylor. Frames des F. C. Cundall, F.S.A., and drawn by Miss Cundall. Recess B.W.)

1923 (1 Nov). *Child Welfare. Wmk Mult Script CA. P* 12.
104 **37** ½d. +½d. black and green .. .. 60 3·00
105 **38** 1d. +½d. black and scarlet .. .. 1·50 10·00
106 **39** 2½d. +½d. black and blue .. .. 7·00 18·00
104/6 .. .. *Set of* 3 8·00 28·00
104/6 Optd "Specimen" .. .. *Set of* 3 £120

Sold at a premium of ½d. for the Child Welfare League, these stamps were on sale annually from 1 November to 31 January, until 31 January 1927, when their sale ceased, the remainders being destroyed on 21 February 1927.

40

41

42

Die I Die II

(Recess D.L.R.)

1929–32. *Wmk Mult Script CA. P* 14.
108 **40** 1d. scarlet (Die I) 40 10
a. Die II (1932) 50 10
109 **41** 1½d. chocolate 40 15
110 **42** 9d. maroon .. .. 2·50 1·00
108/10 .. .. *Set of* 3 3·00 1·10
108/10 Perf "Specimen" .. .. *Set of* 3 75·00

In Die I the shading below JAMAICA is formed of thickened parallel lines, and in Die II of diagonal cross-hatching.

43 Coco Palms at Don Christopher's Cove

44 Wag Water River, St. Andrew

45 Priestman's River, Portland

(Dies eng and recess Waterlow)

1932. *Wmk Mult Script CA* (*sideways on* 2d. *and* 2½d.). *P* 12½.
111 **43** 2d. black and green (late 1932) .. 4·25 1·25
a. Imperf between (vert pair) £5000
112 **44** 2½d. turquoise-blue & ultram (5.3.32) .. 80 70
a. Imperf between (vert pair) £6000 £6000
113 **45** 6d. grey-black and purple (2.32) .. 3·75 1·25
111/13 .. .. *Set of* 3 8·00 3·00
111/13 Perf "Specimen" .. .. *Set of* 3 75·00

46 Windsor Castle.

(Des H. Fleury. Recess B.W.)

1935 (6 May). *Silver Jubilee. Wmk Mult Script CA. P* 11×12.
114 **46** 1d. deep blue and scarlet 20 15
d. Flagstaff on right-hand turret .. 42·00
115 1½d. ultramarine and grey-black .. 35 35
a. Extra flagstaff .. .. .. 75·00 £100
b. Short extra flagstaff .. .. 55·00
c. Lightning conductor .. .. 50·00
116 6d. green and indigo .. .. .. 3·00 5·00
a. Extra flagstaff £190 £200
b. Short extra flagstaff £130
c. Lightning conductor £110
117 1s. slate and purple .. .. .. 3·00 5·00
a. Extra flagstaff £275 £350
b. Short extra flagstaff £170
c. Lightning conductor £150
114/17 .. .. *Set of* 4 6·00 9·50
114/17 Perf "Specimen" .. .. *Set of* 4 75·00

For illustrations of plate varieties see Omnibus section following Zimbabwe.

47 King George VI and Queen Elizabeth

(Des and recess D.L.R.)

1937 (12 May). *Coronation. Wmk Mult Script CA. P* 14.
118 **47** 1d. scarlet 30 15
119 1½d. grey-black 50 30
120 2½d. bright blue .. .. 1·10 70
118/20 .. .. *Set of* 3 1·60 1·00
118/20 Perf "Specimen" .. .. *Set of* 3 55·00

48 King George VI

49 Coco Palms at Don Christopher's Cove

50 Bananas

51 Citrus Grove

52 Kingston Harbour

53 Sugar Industry

54 Bamboo Walk

55 King George VI

56 Tobacco Growing and Cigar Making

Repaired chimney (Plate 1 R. 11/1)

(Recess D.L.R. (T **48**, 5s. and 10s.), Waterlow (others))

1938–52. *T* **48/56** *and as Nos.* 88, 112/13, *but with inset portrait of King George VI, as in T* **49**. *Wmk Mult Script CA. P* 13½×14 (½*d.*, 1*d.*, 1½*d.*), 14 (5*s.*, 10*s.*) *or* 12½ (*others*).
121 **48** ½d. blue-green (10.10.38) 20 10
a. Wmk sideways .. .. .. † £2500
121*b* ½d. orange (25.10.51) 20 30
122 1d. scarlet (10.10.38) 10 10
122*a* 1d. blue-green (25.10.51) 30 10
123 1½d. brown (10.10.38) 10 10
124 **49** 2d. grey and green 10 30
a. Perf 13×13½ 35 30
b. Perf 12½×13 (1951) 50 20
125 **44** 2½d. greenish blue and ultramarine .. 1·25 90
126 **50** 3d. ultramarine and green 40 40
126*a* 3d. greenish blue and ultram (15.8.49) 1·25 85
126*b* 3d. green and scarlet (1.7.52) .. 80 20
127 **51** 4d. brown and green 15 10
128 **45** 6d. grey and purple 60 30
a. Perf 13½×13 (10.10.50) 60 10
129 **52** 9d. lake 15 15
130 **53** 1s. green and purple-brown .. .. 1·00 10
a. Repaired chimney .. .. £130 70·00
131 **54** 2s. blue and chocolate .. .. 7·00 60
132 – 5s. slate-blue and yellow-orange .. 7·50 2·00
a. Perf 14, line (1941) £2250 £130
b. Perf 13 (24.10.49) .. .. 6·00 3·00
ba. Blue and orange (10.10.50) .. 4·00 2·75
133 **55** 10s. myrtle-green .. .. .. 11·00 7·00
aa. Perf 13 (10.10.50) .. .. 8·50 5·00
133*a* **56** £1 chocolate and violet (15.8.49) .. 24·00 26·00
121/33*a* .. .. *Set of* 18 45·00 32·00
121/33 Perf "Specimen" .. .. *Set of* 13 £180

No. 132a shows the emergency use of a line perforation machine, giving an irregular gauge of 14–14.15, after the De La Rue works were damaged in December 1940. The normal comb measures 13.8×13.7.

PRICES OF SETS

Set prices are given for many issues, generally those containing three stamps or more. Definitive sets include one of each value or major colour change, but do not cover different perforations, die types or minor shades. Where a choice is possible the set prices are based on the cheapest versions of the stamps included in the listings.

SELF-GOVERNMENT

57 Courthouse, Falmouth

58 King Charles II and King George VI

59 Institute of Jamaica

(Recess Waterlow)

1945 (20 Aug)–**46**. *New Constitution. T* **57/9** *and similar designs. Wmk Mult Script CA. P* 12½.

134	**57**	1½d. sepia	15	15
		a. Perf 12½×13 (1946)	1·25	30
135	**58**	2d. green	3·25	70
		a. Perf 12½×13 (1945)	15	30
136	**59**	3d. ultramarine	15	20
		a. Perf 13 (1946)	70	1·10
137	–	4½d. slate	15	25
		a. Perf 13 (1946)	70	90
138	–	2s. red-brown	25	40
139	–	5s. indigo	50	70
140	**59**	10s. green	70	1·25
134/40		*Set of* 7	1·75	3·25
134/40 Perf "Specimen"		*Set of* 7	£140	

Designs: *Vert* (*as T* **57**)—2s. "Labour and Learning". *Horiz* (*as T* **59**)—4½d. House of Assembly; 5s. Scroll, flag and King George VI.

60 Houses of Parliament, London

(Des and recess D.L.R.)

1946 (14 Oct). *Victory. Wmk Mult Script CA. P* 13½×14.

141	**60**	1½d. purple-brown	55	10
		a. Perf 13½	30	40
142		3d. blue	55	45
		a. Perf 13½	30	2·00
141/2 Perf "Specimen"		*Set of* 2	48·00	

61

62

King George VI and Queen Elizabeth

(Des and photo Waterlow (T **61**). Design recess, name typo B.W. (T **62**))

1948 (1 Dec). *Royal Silver Wedding. Wmk Mult Script CA.*

143	**61**	1½d. red-brown (*p* 14×15)	30	10
144	**62**	£1 scarlet (*p* 11½×11)	23·00	42·00

63 Hermes, Globe and Forms of Transport

64 Hemispheres, Aeroplane and Steamer

65 Hermes and Globe

66 U.P.U. Monument

(Recess Waterlow (T **63**, **66**). Design recess, name typo B.W. (T **64/5**))

1949 (10 Oct). *75th Anniv of Universal Postal Union. Wmk Mult Script CA.*

145	**63**	1½d. red-brown (*p* 13½–14)	25	15
146	**64**	2d. deep blue-green (*p* 11×11½)	45	90
147	**65**	3d. deep blue (*p* 11×11½)	45	70
148	**66**	6d. purple (*p* 13½–14)	55	1·25
145/8		*Set of* 4	1·50	2·75

67 Arms of University

68 Princess Alice

(Recess Waterlow)

1951 (16 Feb). *Inauguration of B.W.I. University College. Wmk Mult Script CA. P* 14×14½.

149	**67**	2d. black and red-brown	30	20
150	**68**	6d. grey-black and purple	35	20

69 Scout Badge and Map of Caribbean

70 Scout Badge and Map of Jamaica

(Litho B.W.)

1952 (5 Mar). *First Caribbean Scout Jamboree. Wmk Mult Script CA. P* 13½×13 (*2d.*) *or* 13×13½ (*6d.*).

151	**69**	2d. blue, apple-green and black	15	10
152	**70**	6d. yellow-green, carmine-red and black	15	30

71 Queen Elizabeth II

72 Coco Palms at Don Christopher's Cove

(Des and eng B.W. Recess D.L.R.)

1953 (2 June). *Coronation. Wmk Mult Script CA. P* 13½×13.

153	**71**	2d. black and deep yellow-green	10	10

(Recess Waterlow)

1953 (25 Nov). *Royal Visit. Wmk Mult Script CA. P* 12½×13.

154	**72**	2d. grey-black and green	10	10

73 Man-o'-War at Port Royal

(Recess D.L.R.)

1955 (10 May). *Tercentenary Issue. T* **73** *and similar horiz designs. Wmk Mult Script CA. P* 12½.

155		2d. black and olive-green	20	10
156		2½d. black and deep bright blue	15	35
157		3d. black and claret	15	30
158		6d. black and carmine-red	20	20
155/8		*Set of* 4	65	80

Designs:—2½d. Old Montego Bay; 3d. Old Kingston; 6d. Proclamation of Abolition of Slavery, 1838.

74 Palms

75 Mahoe

76 Blue Mountain Peak

77 Arms of Jamaica

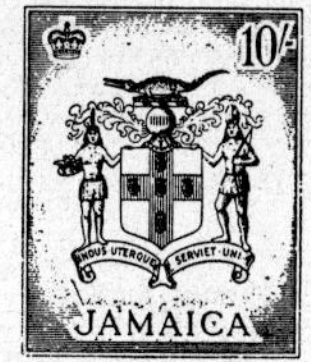

78 Arms of Jamaica

(Recess B.W. (T **77/8**), D.L.R. (others))

1956 (1 May)–**58**. *T* **74/8** *and similar designs. Wmk Mult Script CA. P* 13 (*½d to 6d.*), 13½ (*8d. to 2s.*) *or* 11½ (*3s. to £1*).

159	**74**	½d. black and deep orange-red	10	10
160	–	1d. black and emerald	10	10
161	–	2d. black and carmine-red (2.8.56)	10	10
162	–	2½d. black and deep bright blue (2.8.56)	15	40
163	**75**	3d. emerald and red-brown (17.12.56)	15	10
164	–	4d. bronze-green and blue (17.12.56)	15	10
165	–	5d. scarlet and bronze-green (17.12.56)	20	1·00
166	–	6d. black and deep rose-red (3.9.56)	1·25	10
167	**76**	8d. ultramarine & red-orge (15.11.56)	15	10
168	–	1s. yellow-green and blue (15.11.56)	30	10
169	–	1s. 6d. ultram & reddish pur (15.11.56)	30	10
170	–	2s. blue and bronze-green (15.11.56)	1·50	75
		a. *Grey-blue & bronze-green* (24.4.58)	2·50	85
171	**77**	3s. black and blue (2.8.56)	50	70
172		5s. black and carmine-red (15.8.56)	1·00	1·25
173	**78**	10s. black and blue-green (15.8.56)	10·00	5·50
174		£1 black and purple (15.8.56)	16·00	5·50
159/74		*Set of* 16	29·00	14·00

Designs: *Vert* (*as T* **74/5**)—1d. Sugar Cane; 2d. Pineapples; 2½d. Bananas; 4d. Breadfruit; 5d. Ackee; 6d. Streamertail. *Horiz* (*as T* **76**)—1s. Royal Botanic Gardens, Hope; 1s. 6d. Rafting on the Rio Grande; 2s. Fort Charles.

79 Federation Map

(Recess B.W.)

1958 (22 Apr). *Inauguration of British Caribbean Federation. W w* **12**. *P* 11½×11.

175	**79**	2d. deep green	35	10
176		5d. blue	60	1·25
177		6d. scarlet	60	30
175/7		*Set of* 3	1·40	1·50

81 "Britannia" flying over *City of Berlin*, 1860

83 1s. Stamps of 1860 and 1956

(Recess Waterlow)

1960 (4 Jan). *Stamp Centenary. T* **81**, **83** *and similar design. W w* **12**. *P* 13 × 13½ (*1s.*) *or* 13½ × 14 (*others*).

178		2d. blue and reddish purple	35	10
179		6d. carmine and olive-green	40	10
180		1s. red-brown, yellow-green and blue	40	15
178/80		*Set of* 3	1·00	30

Design: *As T* **81**—6d. Postal mule-cart and motor-van.

INDEPENDENT

1
9
6
2
INDEPENDENCE
(84)

1
9
6
2
INDEPENDENCE
1962
(85)

86 Military Bugler and Map

(Des V. Whiteley. Photo D.L.R. (2, 4d., 1s. 6d., 5s.))

1962 (8 Aug)–**63**. *Independence.*

(*a*) *Nos.* 159/60, 162, 171, 173/4 *optd as T* **84** *and Nos.* 163, 165/8, 170 *optd with T* **85**

181 **74** ½d. black and deep orange-red .. 10 50
182 – 1d. black and emerald 10 10
183 – 2½d. black and deep bright blue .. 10 85
184 **75** 3d. emerald and red-brown 10 10
185 – 5d. scarlet and bronze-green 15 60
186 – 6d. black and deep rose-red 75 10
187 **76** 8d. ultram & red-orge (opt at upper left) 15 10
a. Opt at lower left (17.9.63?) .. 15 15
188 – 1s. yellow-green and blue 15 10
189 – 2s. blue and bronze-green 80 80
a. Dp blue & dp bronze-green (20.8.63) 1·75 90
190 **77** 3s. black and blue .. .. .. 90 1·50
191 **78** 10s. black and blue-green .. .. 2·00 4·00
192 £1 black and purple .. .. .. 2·75 5·50

(*b*) *Horiz designs as T* **86.** *W* w **12.** *P* 13

193 2d. multicoloured 15 10
194 4d. multicoloured 15 10
195 1s. 6d. black and red 65 85
196 5s. multicoloured .. .. 1·25 2·00
181/96 .. .. *Set of* 16 9·00 15·00

Designs:—2, 4d. Type **86**; 1s. 6d. Gordon House and banner; 5s. Map, factories and fruit.

For these overprints on stamps watermarked w **12** see Nos. 205/13.

89 Kingston Seal, Weightlifting, Boxing, Football and Cycling

93 Farmer and Crops

(Photo Harrison)

1962 (11 Aug). *Ninth Central American and Caribbean Games, Kingston. T* **89** *and similar horiz designs. W* w **12.** *P* 14½ × 14.

197 1d. sepia and carmine-red 10 10
198 6d. sepia and greenish blue 10 10
199 8d. sepia and bistre 10 10
200 2s. multicoloured 25 40
197/200 .. .. *Set of* 4 45 50

Designs:—6d. Kingston seal, diving, sailing, swimming and water polo; 8d. Kingston seal, pole-vaulting, javelin throwing, discus throwing, relay-racing and hurdling; 2s. Kingston coat of arms and athlete.

An imperf miniature sheet exists, but this was never available at face value or at any post office.

(Des M. Goaman. Litho D.L.R.)

1963 (4 June). *Freedom from Hunger. P* 12½.

201 **93** 1d. multicoloured 15 10
202 8d. multicoloured 50 20

94 Red Cross Emblem

95 Carole Joan Crawford ("Miss World 1963")

(Des V. Whiteley. Litho B.W.)

1963 (4 Sept). *Red Cross Centenary. W* w **12.** *P* 13½.

203 **94** 2d. red and black 15 10
204 1s. 6d. red and blue 40 65

1963–64. *As Nos.* 181/90, *but wmk* w **12.**

205 **74** ½d. black & deep orange-red (3.12.63*) 10 15
206 – 1d. black and emerald (3.4.64) .. 10 15
207 – 2½d. black and deep bright blue (3.4.64) 25 90
208 **75** 3d. emerald and red-brown (17.12.63*) 15 15
209 – 5d. scarlet and bronze-green (3.4.64) .. 30 1·50
210 **76** 8d. ultramarine and red-orange (3.4.64) 20 55
211 – 1s. yellow-green and blue (21.12.63*) 35 75
212 – 2s. dp blue & dp bronze-green (3.4.64) 60 2·50
213 **77** 3s. black and blue (5.2.64) .. .. 2·00 7·50
205/13 .. .. *Set of* 9 3·50 12·50

The overprint on the 8d., 1s. and 2s. is at lower left, the others are as before.

*These are the earliest known dates recorded in Jamaica.

(Des and photo D.L.R.)

1964 (14 Feb–25 May). *"Miss World 1963" Commemoration. P* 13.

214 **95** 3d. multicoloured 10 10
215 1s. multicoloured 10 10
216 1s. 6d. multicoloured 15 20
214/16 .. .. *Set of* 3 30 30
MS216*a* 153×101 mm. Nos. 214/16. Imperf (25.5.64) .. .. 80 1·50

96 *Lignum Vitae*

97 Blue Mahoe

103 Gypsum Industry

109 Arms of Jamaica

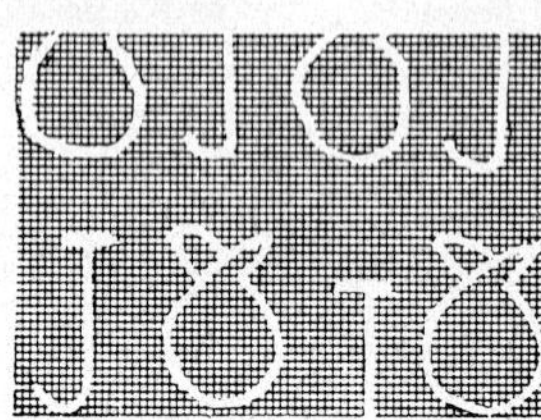

111 Multiple "J" and Pineapple

(Des V. Whiteley. Photo Harrison)

1964 (4 May)–**68.** *T* **96/7, 103, 109** *and similar designs. W* **111.** *P* 14½ (1*d.*, 2*d.*, 2½*d.*, 6*d.*, 8*d.*), 14×14½ (1½*d.*, 3*d.*, 4*d.*, 10*s.*), 14½×14 (9*d.*, 1*s.*, 3*s.*, 5*s.*, £1) *or* 13½×14½ (1*s.* 6*d.*, 2*s.*).

217 1d. violet-blue, dp green & lt brn (*shades*) 10 10
218 1½d. multicoloured 15 10
219 2d. red, yellow and grey-green 15 10
220 2½d. multicoloured 60 60
221 3d. yellow, black and emerald 15 10
222 4d. ochre and violet 35 10
223 6d. multicoloured .. .. .. 1·75 10
a. Blue omitted .. .. .. 35·00
b. Value omitted .. .. ..
224 8d. mult (yellowish green background) .. 1·25 60
a. Red (beak) omitted .. .. 75·00
b. Greyish green background (16.7.68) 3·25 2·25
225 9d. blue and yellow-bistre 45 10
226 1s. black and light brown 20 10
a. Light brown omitted £150
ab. Value only omitted .. ..
b. Black omitted £350
ba. "NATIONAL STADIUM" etc omitted £400
227 1s. 6d. black, light blue and buff .. 75 15
228 2s. red-brown, black and light blue .. 1·25 15
229 3s. blue and dull green .. .. 1·00 80
a. Perf 13½×14½ 35 65
230 5s. black, ochre and blue .. .. 1·10 50
231 10s. multicoloured .. .. .. 1·25 1·00
a. Blue ("JAMAICA", etc) omitted .. £170
232 £1 multicoloured .. .. .. 1·50 1·00
217/32 .. .. *Set of* 16 10·00 4·25

Designs: *Horiz.* (*As T* **96**)—1½d. Ackee; 2½d. Land shells; 3d. National flag over Jamaica; 4d. *Murex antillarum*; 6d. *Papilio homerus*; 8d. Streamertail. *As T* **103**—1s. National Stadium; 1s. 6d. Palisadoes International Airport; 2s. Bauxite mining; 3s. Blue Marlin (sport fishing); 5s. Exploration of sunken city, Port Royal; £1 Queen Elizabeth II and national flag.

No. 223b. Two left half sheets are known with the black printing shifted downwards to such an extent that the value is omitted from the top row.

Nos. 226a/ab came from a sheet on which the two bottom rows had the colour omitted with the next row showing it missing from the lower third of the stamps.

A similar sheet, but with the colour missing from the top two rows and part of the third produced Nos 226b/ba.

112 Scout Belt

113 Globe, Scout Hat and Scarf

114 Scout Badge and Alligator

(Photo Harrison)

1964 (27 Aug). *Sixth Inter-American Scout Conference, Kingston. W* **111.** *P* 14 (1*s.*) *or* 14½ × 14 (*others*).

233 **112** 3d. red, black and pink 10 10
234 **113** 8d. bright blue, olive and black .. 10 20
235 **114** 1s. gold, deep blue and light blue .. 15 20
233/5 .. .. *Set of* 3 30 35

115 Gordon House, Kingston

118 Eleanor Roosevelt

(Des V. Whiteley. Photo Harrison)

1964 (16 Nov). *Tenth Commonwealth Parliamentary Conference, Kingston. T* **115** *and similar horiz designs. W* **111.** *P* 14½ × 14.

236 3d. black and yellow-green 10 10
237 6d. black and carmine-red 10 10
238 1s. 6d. black and bright blue 15 20
236/8 .. .. *Set of* 3 30 30

Designs:—6d. Headquarters House, Kingston; 1s. 6d. House of Assembly, Spanish Town.

(Des V. Whiteley. Photo Harrison)

1964 (10 Dec). *16th Anniv of Declaration of Human Rights. W* **111.** *P* 14½ × 14.

239 **118** 1s. black, red and light green 10 10

119 Guides' Emblem on Map

120 Guide Emblems

(Photo Harrison)

1965 (17 May). *Golden Jubilee of Jamaica Girl Guides Association. W* **111** (*sideways on* 3*d.*). *P* 14 × 14½ (3*d.*) *or* 14 (1*s.*).

240 **119** 3d. yellow, green and light blue .. 10 10
241 **120** 1s. yellow, black and apple-green .. 20 20

121 Uniform Cap

122 Flag-bearer and Drummer

(Photo Harrison)

1965 (23 Aug). *Salvation Army Centenary. W* **111.** *P* 14 × 14½ (3*d.*) *or* 14½ × 14 (1*s.* 6*d.*).

242 **121** 3d. multicoloured 10 10
243 **122** 1s. 6d. multicoloured 25 25

123 Paul Bogle, William Gordon and Morant Bay Court House

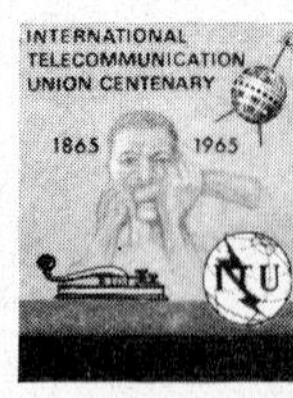

124 Abeng-blower, "Telstar", Morse Key and I.T.U. Emblem

(Photo Enschedé)

1965 (29 Dec). *Centenary of Morant Bay Rebellion. No wmk. P* 14 × 13.

244 **123** 3d. light brown, ultramarine and black 10 10
245 1s. 6d. lt brown, yellow-green & black 10 10
246 3s. light brown, rose and black .. 20 30
244/6 .. .. *Set of* 3 35 40

(Photo Harrison)

1965 (29 Dec). *I.T.U. Centenary. W* **111.** *P* 14 × 14½.

247 **124** 1s. black, grey-blue and red 40 15

ROYAL VISIT
MARCH 1966

(125)

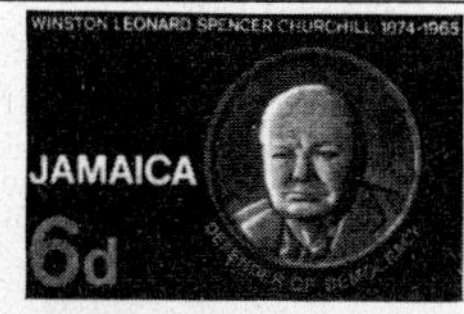

126 Sir Winston Churchill

1966 (3 Mar). *Royal Visit. Nos.* 221, 223, 226/7 *optd with T* **125**.

248 3d. yellow, black and emerald 15 10
249 6d. multicoloured 70 10
250 1s. black and light brown 55 10
251 1s. 6d. black, light blue and buff 70 60
248/51 . . . . *Set of* 4 1·75 65

(Des Jennifer Toombs. Photo Harrison)

1966 (18 April). *Churchill Commemoration. W* **111**. *P* 14.

252 **126** 6d. black and olive-green 35 20
253 1s. bistre-brown and deep violet-blue . . 65 70

127 Statue of Athlete and Flags **131** Bolivar's Statue and Flags of Jamaica and Venezuela

(Des V. Whiteley. Photo Harrison)

1966 (4 Aug). *Eighth British Empire and Commonwealth Games. T* **127** *and similar horiz designs. W* **111**. *P* 14½ × 14.

254 3d. multicoloured 10 10
255 6d. multicoloured 10 10
256 1s. multicoloured 10 10
257 3s. bright gold and deep blue 20 35
a. Dull gold and deep blue . .
254/7 . . . . *Set of* 4 35 45
MS258 128×103 mm. Nos. 254/7. Imperf . . 4·25 7·00

Designs:—6d. Racing cyclists; 1s. National Stadium, Kingston; 3s. Games emblem.

No. **MS**258 has been seen with the whole printing inverted except for the brown background.

(Des and photo Harrison)

1966 (5 Dec). 150*th Anniv of "Jamaica Letter". W* **111**. *P* 14 × 15.

259 **131** 8d. multicoloured 10 10

132 Jamaican Pavilion **133** Sir Donald Sangster (Prime Minister)

(Des V. Whiteley. Photo Harrison)

1967 (28 Apr). *World Fair, Montreal. W* **111**. *P* 14½.

260 **132** 6d. multicoloured 10 10
261 1s. multicoloured 10 10

(Des and photo Enschedé)

1967 (28 Aug). *Sangster Memorial Issue. P* 13½.

262 **133** 3d. multicoloured 10 10
263 1s. 6d. multicoloured 10 10

134 Traffic Duty

135 Personnel of the Force

(Des V. Whiteley. Photo Enschedé)

1967 (28 Nov). *Centenary of the Constabulary Force. T* **134/5** *and similar horiz design. Multicoloured. W* **111**. *P* 13½ × 14.

264 3d. Type **134** 10 10
a. Wmk sideways 40 45
265 1s. Type **135** 15 10
266 1s. 6d. Badge and Constables of 1867 and 1967 (*as T* **134**) 20 20
264/6 . . . . *Set of* 3 40 30

136 Wicket-keeping **137** Sir Alexander and Lady Bustamante

(Des V. Whiteley. Photo Harrison)

1968 (8 Feb). *M.C.C.'s West Indian Tour. T* **136** *and similar vert designs. Multicoloured. W* **111** (*sideways*). *P* 14.

267 6d. Type **136** 20 30
a. Horiz strip of 3. Nos. 267/9 . . . . 1·50
268 6d. Batting 20 30
269 6d. Bowling 20 30
267/9 . . . . *Set of* 3 55 80

Nos. 267/9 were issued in small sheets of 9 comprising three *se-tenant* strips as No. 267a.

Nos. 267/9 exist on PVA gum as well as on gum arabic.

(Des and photo Harrison)

1968 (23 May). *Labour Day. W* **111**. *P* 14.

270 **137** 3d. rose and black 10 10
271 1s. olive and black 10 10

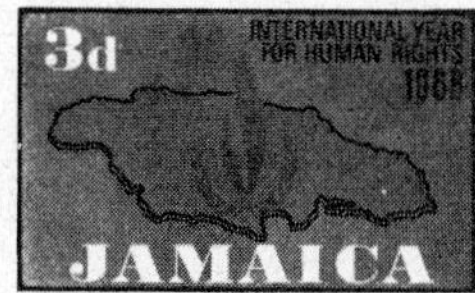

138 Human Rights Emblem over Map of Jamaica

(Photo Harrison)

1968 (3 Dec). *Human Rights Year. T* **138** *and similar multi-coloured designs. W* **111**. *P* 14.

272 3d. Type **138** 10 10
a. Gold (flame) omitted . . . . . . 90·00
273 1s. Hands cupping Human Rights emblem (*vert*) 10 10
274 3s. Jamaican holding "Human Rights" . . 20 25
a. Gold (flame) omitted £100
272/4 . . . . *Set of* 3 35 30

Three designs, showing 3d. Bowls of Grain, 1s. Abacus, 3s. Hands in Prayer, were prepared but not issued (*Price for set of 3 mint* £100).

141 ILO Emblem

142 Nurse, and Children being weighed and measured

(Des V. Whiteley. Litho Format)

1969 (23 May). 50*th Anniv of International Labour Organization. P* 14.

275 **141** 6d. orange-yellow and blackish brown 10 10
276 3s. bright emerald and blackish brown 20 30

(Des and photo Harrison)

1969 (30 May). 20*th Anniv of W.H.O. T* **142** *and similar designs. W* **111**. *P* 14.

277 6d. grey, brown and orange 10 10
278 1s. black, sepia and blue-green 10 10
279 3s. grey-black, brown and pale bright blue 20 30
277/9 . . . . *Set of* 3 30 35

Designs: *Horiz*—1s. Malaria eradication. *Vert*—3s. Trainee nurse.

(New Currency. 100 cents = 1 dollar)

C-DAY
8th September
1969
1c

(145)

146 "The Adoration of the Kings" (detail, Foppa)

1969 (8 Sept). *Decimal currency. Nos.* 217, 219, 221/3 *and* 225/32 *surch as T* **145**. *Sterling values unobliterated except* 1 *c. to* 4 *c. and* 8 *c.*

280 1 c. on 1d. violet-blue, dp green & lt brown . . 10 10
281 2 c. on 2d. red, yellow and grey-green . . 10 10
282 3 c. on 3d. yellow, black and emerald . . 10 10
283 4 c. on 4d. ochre and violet 45 10
a. "8t" of "8th" omitted (R. 10/1) . . . . 25·00
284 5 c. on 6d. multicoloured 80 10
a. Blue omitted . . . . 35·00
285 8 c. on 9d. blue and yellow-bistre 10 10
286 10 c. on 1s. black and light brown 10 10
287 15 c. on 1s. 6d. black, light blue and buff . . 30 60
288 20 c. on 2s. red-brown, black and light blue 1·00 55
a. "8th" omitted . . . .
289 30 c. on 3s. blue and dull green . . . . 1·50 2·00
290 50 c. on 5s. black, ochre and blue . . . . 1·25 2·00
291 $1 on 10s. multicoloured . . . . . . 1·50 3·25
292 $2 on £1 multicoloured . . . . . . 1·50 6·00
280/92 . . . . *Set of* 13 7·50 13·00

No. 281 exists with PVA gum as well as gum arabic.

Unlike the positional No. 283a the similar variety on the 20 c. on 2s. was caused by a paper fold.

(Des J. Cooter. Litho D.L.R.)

1969 (25 Oct). *Christmas. Paintings. T* **146** *and similar vert designs. Multicoloured. W* **111**. *P* 13.

293 2 c. Type **146** 10 10
294 5 c. "Madonna, Child and St. John" (Raphael) 10 10
295 8 c. "The Adoration of the Kings" (detail, Dosso Dossi) 15 10
293/5 . . . . *Set of* 3 25 25

149 Half Penny, 1869 **151** George William Gordon

(Des G. Drummond. Litho P.B.)

1969 (27 Oct). *Centenary of First Jamaican Coins. T* **149** *and similar horiz design. W* **111**. *P* 12½.

296 3 c. silver, black and mauve 15 25
b. Wmk sideways 20 20
297 15 c. silver, black and light emerald 10 10

Design:—15 c. One penny, 1869.

(Des G. Vasarhelyi. Litho Enschedé)

1970 (11 Mar). *National Heroes. T* **151** *and similar vert designs. Multicoloured. P* 12 × 12½.

298 1 c. Type **151** 10 10
a. Yellow (from flags) omitted £180
299 3 c. Sir Alexander Bustamante 10 10
300 5 c. Norman Manley 10 10
301 10 c. Marcus Garvey 15 10
302 15 c. Paul Bogle 20 15
298/302 . . . . *Set of* 5 40 30

156 "Christ appearing to St. Peter" (Carracci)

2c

(159)

(Des G. Drummond. Photo Enschedé)

1970 (23 Mar). *Easter. T* **156** *and similar vert designs. Multi-coloured. W* **111**. *P* 12 × 12½.

303 3 c. Type **156** 10 10
304 10 c. "Christ Crucified" (Antonello da Messina) 10 10
305 20 c. Easter Lily 20 25
303/5 . . . . *Set of* 3 30 30

1970 (16 July). *No.* 219 *surch with T* **159**.

306 2 c. on 2d. red, yellow and grey-green . . 15 20

160 *Lignum Vitae* **161** Cable Ship *Dacia*

1970 (7 Sept–2 Nov). *Decimal Currency. Designs as Nos.* 217/32 *but inscr as T* **160** *in new currency. W* **111** (*sideways on* 2, 4, 15, 20 *c. and* $1). *P* 14½ (1, 5 c.), 14 × 14½ (4 c., $1), 13½ × 14½ (15, 20 *c.*) *or* 14½ × 14 (*others*).

307 1 c. violet-blue, deep green & lt brown .. 40 40
308 2 c. red, yellow and grey-green (as 2d.) .. 15 10
309 3 c. yellow, black and emerald (as 3d.) .. 15 10
310 4 c. ochre and violet (as 4d.) 65 10
311 5 c. multicoloured (as 6d.) .. .. .. 2·25 10
312 8 c. blue and yellow-bistre (as 9d.) 20 10
a. Wmk sideways 40 45
313 10 c. black and light brown (as 1s.) 20 10
314 15 c. black, light blue and buff (as 1s. 6d.) (2.11) 80 60
315 20 c. red-brown, black & lt blue (as 2s.) (2.11) 1·00 1·00
316 30 c. blue and dull green (as 3s.) (2.11) .. 1·25 1·25
317 50 c. black, ochre and blue (as 5s.) (2.11) .. 1·25 2·50
318 $1 multicoloured (as 10s.) (2.11) .. .. 1·25 2·50
319 $2 multicoloured (as £1) (2.11) .. .. 1·50 2·75
307/19 .. .. *Set of* 13 10·00 10·50

(Des G. Drummond. Litho J.W.)

1970 (12 Oct). *Centenary of Telegraph Service. T* **161** *and similar horiz designs. W* **111** (*sideways*). *P* 14½ × 14.

320 3 c. yellow, red and black 15 10
321 10 c. black and turquoise 20 10
322 50 c. multicoloured .. .. 50 1·00
320/2 .. .. *Set of* 3 75 1·10

Designs:—10 c. Bright's cable gear aboard *Dacia*; 50 c. Morse key and chart.

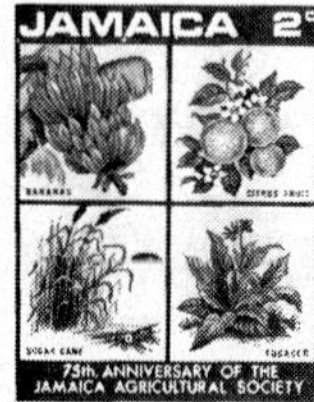

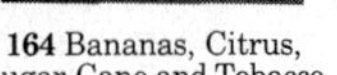

164 Bananas, Citrus, Sugar-Cane and Tobacco

165 *The Projector* (1845)

(Des G. Drummond. Litho Questa)

1970 (2 Nov). *75th Anniv of Jamaican Agricultural Society. W* **111**. *P* 14.

323 **164** 2 c. multicoloured 10 30
324 10 c. multicoloured 20 10

(Des V. Whiteley. Litho Format)

1970 (21 Nov). *125th Anniv of Jamaican Railways. T* **165** *and similar horiz designs. Multicoloured. W* **111** (*sideways*). *P* 13½.

325 3 c. Type **165** 25 10
326 15 c. Steam locomotive No. 54 (1944) .. 70 30
327 50 c. Diesel locomotive No. 102 (1967) .. 1·75 2·00
325/7 .. .. *Set of* 3 2·40 2·25

168 Church of St. Jago de la Vega

169 Henry Morgan and Ships

(Des R. Granger Barrett. Litho J.W.)

1971 (22 Feb). *Centenary of Disestablishment of the Church of England in Jamaica. T* **168** *and similar vert design. Multicoloured. W* **111**. *P* 14½.

328 3 c. Type **168** 10 10
329 10 c. Type **168** 10 10
330 20 c. Type **168** 15 25
331 30 c. Emblem of Church of England in Jamaica 20 45
328/31 .. .. *Set of* 4 35 70

(Des J.W. Litho Questa)

1971 (10 May). *Pirates and Buccaneers. T* **169** *and similar horiz designs. Multicoloured. W* **111** (*sideways*). *P* 14.

332 3 c. Type **169** 30 10
333 15 c. Mary Read, Anne Bonny and trial pamphlet 55 15
334 30 c. Pirate schooner attacking merchantman 1·10 1·25
332/4 .. .. *Set of* 3 1·75 1·40

PRICES OF SETS

Set prices are given for many issues, generally those containing three stamps or more. Definitive sets include one of each value or major colour change, but do not cover different perforations, die types or minor shades. Where a choice is possible the set prices are based on the cheapest versions of the stamps included in the listings.

170 1s. Stamp of 1919 with Frame Inverted

171 Satellite and Dish Aerial

(Des Jennifer Toombs. Litho J.W.)

1971 (30 Oct). *Tercentenary of Post Office Establishment. T* **170** *and similar designs. W* **111** (*sideways, except* 50 *c.*). *P* 13½.

335 3 c. black and lake 10 10
336 5 c. grey-black and bright green 10 10
337 8 c. black and violet 15 10
338 10 c. brown, black and indigo 15 10
339 20 c. multicoloured 25 35
340 50 c. ochre, black and slate 45 80
335/40 .. .. *Set of* 6 1·00 1·25

Designs: *Horiz*—3 c. Dummer packet letter, 1705; 5 c. Pre-stamp inland letter, 1793; 8 c. Harbour St. P.O., Kingston, 1820; 10 c. Modern stamp and cancellation; 20 c. British stamps used in Jamaica, 1859.

(Des Cable & Wireless Ltd. Litho J.W.)

1972 (17 Feb). *Opening of Jamaican Earth Satellite Station. W* **111**. *P* 14 × 13½.

341 **171** 3 c. multicoloured 15 10
342 15 c. multicoloured 20 15
343 50 c. multicoloured .. .. .. 55 1·25
341/3 .. .. *Set of* 3 80 1·25

172 Causeway, Kingston Harbour

173 Air Jamaica Hostess and Aircraft

(Des J.W. Litho Format)

1972 (17 Apr–2 Oct). *Multicoloured designs as T* **172** (1 *to* 6 *c.*) *or* **173** (8 *c. to* $2). *W* **111** (*sideways on horiz designs*). *P* 14½ × 14 (1, 2 *c.*), 14 × 14½ (3, 4, 5, 6 *c.*) *or* 13½ (*others*).

344 1 c. Pimento (*vert*) (5.6) 10 10
345 2 c. Red Ginger (*vert*) (5.6) 10 10
346 3 c. Bauxite Industry (5.6) 10 10
347 4 c. Type **172** 10 10
348 5 c. Oil Refinery (5.6) 10 10
349 6 c. Senate Building, University of the West Indies (5.6) 10 10
350 8 c. National Stadium (5.6) 10 10
351 9 c. Devon House (5.6) 10 10
352 10 c. Type **173** 10 10
353 15 c. Old Iron Bridge, Spanish Town (*vert*) (2.10) 55 10
354 20 c. College of Arts, Science and Technology (2.10) 30 15
355 30 c. Dunn's River Falls (*vert*) (2.10) 35 15
356 50 c. River rafting (5.6) 60 40
357 $1 Jamaica House (2.10) 75 65
358 $2 Kings House (2.10) .. .. .. 1·00 1·25
344/58 .. .. *Set of* 15 3·50 2·75

TENTH
ANNIVERSARY
INDEPENDENCE
1962-1972
(**174**)

175 Arms of Kingston

1972 (8 Aug). *Tenth Anniv of Independence. Nos.* 346, 352 *and* 356 *optd as T* **174**.

359 3 c. Bauxite Industry 10 10
360 10 c. Type **173** 10 10
361 50 c. River rafting .. .. 40 1·25
359/61 .. .. *Set of* 3 45 1·25

(Des R. Granger Barrett. Litho J.W.)

1972 (4 Dec). *Centenary of Kingston as Capital. W* **111** (*sideways on* 50 *c.*). *P* 13½ × 14 (5 *and* 30 *c.*) *or* 14 × 13½ (50 *c.*).

362 **175** 5 c. multicoloured 10 10
363 30 c. multicoloured 20 25
364 – 50 c. multicoloured 40 75
362/4 .. .. *Set of* 3 60 1·00

The 50 c. is as T **175**, but horiz.

176 Small Indian Mongoose on Map

(Des R. Granger Barrett. Litho Questa)

1973 (9 Apr). *Centenary of Introduction of the Mongoose. T* **176** *and similar horiz designs. W* **111** (*sideways*). *P* 14 × 14½.

365 8 c. light apple-green, yellow-green and black 10 10
366 40 c. light cobalt, light blue and black .. 25 50
367 60 c. salmon-pink, brownish salmon & black 50 1·00
365/7 .. .. *Set of* 3 75 1·40
MS368 165 × 95 mm. Nos. 365/7 .. .. 1·50 3·00

Designs:—40 c. Mongoose and rat; 60 c. Mongoose and chicken.

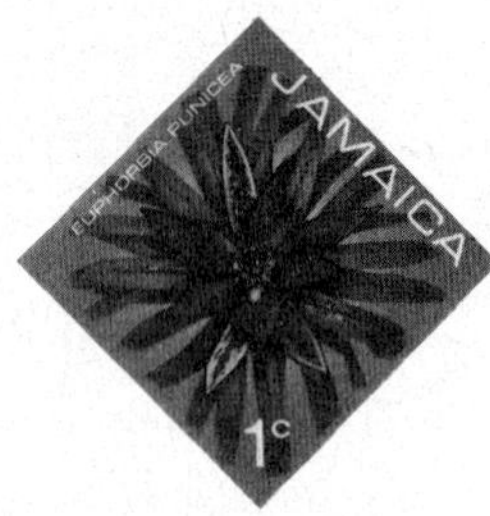

177 *Euphorbia punicea*

(Des Sylvia Goaman. Litho Questa)

1973 (9 July). *Flora. T* **177** *and similar diamond-shaped designs. Multicoloured. W* **111**. *P* 14.

369 1 c. Type **177** 10 10
370 6 c. *Hylocereus triangularis* 15 10
371 9 c. *Columnea argentea* 15 10
372 15 c. *Portlandia grandiflora* 25 15
373 30 c. *Samyda pubescens* 50 60
374 50 c. *Cordia sebestena* .. .. 80 1·25
369/74 .. .. *Set of* 6 1·75 2·00

178 *Broughtonia sanguinea*

(Des Sylvia Goaman. Litho B.W.)

1973 (8 Oct). *Orchids. T* **178** *and similar multicoloured designs. W* **111** (*sideways*) *on* 5 *c.*, $1). *P* 14×13½ (5 *c.*, $1) *or* 13½×14 (*others*).

375 5 c. Type **178** 40 10
376 10 c. *Arpophyllum jamaicense* (*vert*) .. 50 10
377 20 c. *Oncidium pulchellum* (*vert*) .. .. 1·25 25
378 $1 *Brassia maculata* .. .. .. 2·75 2·75
375/8 .. .. *Set of* 4 4·50 2·75
MS379 161×95 mm. Nos. 375/8. Wmk sideways. P 12 .. .. 4·00 4·00

179 *Mary*, 1808–15

180 "Journeys"

(Des J. Cooter. Litho J.W.)

1974 (8 Apr). *Mail Packet Boats. T* **179** *and similar horiz designs. Multicoloured. W* **111** (*sideways on Nos.* 380/3, *upright on* **MS**384). *P* 13½ (5 *c.*, 50 *c.*) *or* 14 (*others*).

380 5 c. Type **179** 20 10
a. Perf 14 .. .. 3·00 2·25
381 10 c. *Queensbury*, 1814–27 .. .. .. 25 10
382 15 c. *Sheldrake*, 1829–34 .. .. .. 45 40
383 50 c. *Thames*, 1842 .. .. 1·75 2·25
380/3 .. .. *Set of* 4 2·40 2·50
MS384 133 × 159 mm. Nos. 380/4. P 13½ (*sold at* 90 *c.*) .. .. 3·25 4·50

(Des R. Granger Barrett. Litho Questa)

1974 (1 Aug). *National Dance Theatre Company. T* **180** *and similar vert designs showing dance-works. Multicoloured. W* **111**. *P* 13½.

385 5 c. Type **180** 10 10
386 10 c. "Jamaican Promenade" 10 10
387 30 c. "Jamaican Promenade" 25 30
388 50 c. "Misa Criolla" 45 80
385/8 .. .. *Set of* 4 70 1·10
MS389 161 × 102 mm. Nos. 385/8 (*sold at* $1) .. 1·50 2·25

181 U.P.U. Emblem and Globe

(Des V. Whiteley. Litho J.W.)

1974 (9 Oct). *Centenary of Universal Postal Union*. W **111** (*sideways*). P 14.
390 **181** 5 c. multicoloured 10 10
391 9 c. multicoloured 10 10
392 50 c. multicoloured 35 80
390/2 .. .. *Set of* 3 50 80

182 Senate Building and Sir Hugh Wooding

183 Commonwealth Symbol

(Des R. Granger Barrett. Litho Questa)

1975 (13 Jan). *25th Anniv of University of West Indies*. T **182** *and similar horiz design. Multicoloured*. W **111** (*sideways*). P 14.
393 5 c. Type **182** 10 10
394 10 c. University Chapel and H.R.H. Princess Alice 10 10
395 30 c. Type **182** 15 25
396 50 c. As 10 c. 30 60
393/6 .. .. *Set of* 4 50 80

(Des C. Abbott. Litho Questa)

1975 (29 Apr). *Heads of Commonwealth Conference*. T **183** *and similar square designs. Multicoloured*. W **111**. P 13½.
397 5 c. Type **183** 10 10
398 10 c. Jamaican coat of arms 10 10
399 30 c. Dove of Peace 15 30
400 50 c. Jamaican flag 30 80
397/400 .. .. *Set of* 4 50 1·10

184 *Eurytides marcellinus*

185 Koo Koo or Actor Boy

(Des J. Cooter. Litho Questa)

1975 (25 Aug). *Butterflies* (*1st series*). T **184** *and similar vert designs showing the family Papilionidae. Multicoloured*. W **111**. P 14.
401 10 c. Type **184** 55 20
402 20 c. *Papilio thoas* .. .. 1·10 1·10
403 25 c. *Papilo thersites* .. .. 1·25 1·60
404 30 c. *Papilo homerus* .. .. 1·40 2·00
401/4 .. .. *Set of* 4 4·00 4·50
MS405 134×179 mm. Nos. 401/4 (*sold at* 95 *c.*) 5·00 7·00
See also Nos. 429/33 and 443/47.

(Des C. Abbott. Litho J.W.)

1975 (3 Nov). *Christmas*. T **185** *and similar vert designs showing Belisario prints of* "*John Canoe*" (*Christmas*) *Festival* (*1st series*). *Multicoloured*. W **111**. P 14.
406 8 c. Type **185** 10 10
407 10 c. Red Set-girls 10 10
408 20 c. French Set-girls 15 15
409 50 c. Jaw-bone or House John Canoe 35 70
406/9 .. .. *Set of* 4 55 90
MS410 138 × 141 mm. Nos. 406/9. P 13½ (*sold at* $1) .. .. 1·50 2·75
See also Nos. 421/**MS**424.

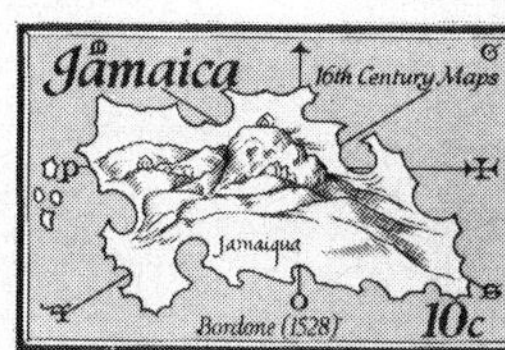

186 Bordone Map, 1528

(Des L. Curtis. Litho Questa)

1976 (12 Mar). *16th Century Maps of Jamaica*. T **186** *and similar horiz designs*. W **111** (*sideways*). P 13½.
411 10 c. brown, light stone and light vermilion 20 10
412 20 c. multicoloured 35 25
413 30 c. multicoloured 60 75
414 50 c. multicoloured .. .. 85 1·25
411/14 .. .. *Set of* 4 1·75 2·10
Designs—20 c. Porcacchi map, 1576; 30 c. DeBry map, 1594; 50 c. Langenes map, 1598.
See also Nos. 425/8.

187 Olympic Rings

(Des Sir H. McDonald: adapted V. Whiteley Studio. Litho Walsall)

1976 (14 June). *Olympic Games, Montreal*. W **111** (*sideways*). P 13½.
415 **187** 10 c. multicoloured 10 10
416 20 c. multicoloured 15 15
417 25 c. multicoloured 15 20
418 50 c. multicoloured 30 90
415/18 .. .. *Set of* 4 60 1·25

187a Map of the Caribbean

(Des PAD Studio. Litho Questa)

1976 (9 Aug). *West Indian Victory in World Cricket Cup*. T **187a** *and similar design. No wmk*. P 14.
419 10 c. multicoloured 40 40
420 25 c. black and magenta .. .. 85 1·25
Design: *Vert*—25 c. Prudential Cup.

(Des C. Abbott. Litho J.W.)

1976 (8 Nov). *Christmas. Belisario Prints* (*2nd series*). *Multicoloured designs as* T **185**. W **111**. P 13½.
421 10 c. Queen of the set-girls 10 10
422 20 c. Band of the Jaw-bone John Canoe .. 15 10
423 50 c. Koo Koo (actor-boy) 30 50
421/3 .. .. *Set of* 3 40 60
MS424 110 × 140 mm. Nos. 421/3. P 14 × 14½ (*sold at* 90 *c.*) .. .. 70 2·00

(Des L. Curtis. Litho J.W.)

1977 (28 Feb). *17th Century Maps of Jamaica. Designs as* T **186**. W **111** (*sideways*). P 13.
425 9 c. multicoloured 30 10
426 10 c. multicoloured 30 10
427 25 c. grey-black, pale blue and bright blue .. 70 60
428 40 c. grey-black, light turquoise and grey-blue 80 85
425/8 .. .. *Set of* 4 1·90 1·40
Designs:—9 c. Hickeringill map, 1661; 10 c. Ogilby map, 1671; 25 c. Visscher map, 1680; 40 c. Thornton map, 1689.

(Des J. Cooter. Litho J.W.)

1977 (9 May). *Butterflies* (*2nd series*). *Multicoloured designs as* T **184** *showing the families Nymphalidae and Pieridae*. W **111**. P 13½.
429 10 c. *Eurema elathea* 35 10
430 20 c. *Dynamine egaea* 75 55
431 25 c. *Chlosyne pantoni* .. .. 1·00 1·25
432 40 c. *Hypolimnas misippus* .. .. 1·50 2·00
429/32 .. .. *Set of* 4 3·25 3·50
MS433 139×120 mm. Nos. 429/32. P 14½ (*sold at* $1.05) .. .. 4·50 7·00

188 Map, Scout Emblem and Streamertail

189 Trumpeter

(Des Daphne Padden. Litho Questa)

1977 (5 Aug). *Sixth Caribbean Jamboree, Jamaica. Multicoloured; background colours given*. W **111** (*sideways*). P 13½.
434 **188** 10 c. new blue 20 10
435 20 c. light yellow-green 40 15
436 25 c. orange 45 20
437 50 c. light magenta .. .. 75 1·10
434/7 .. .. *Set of* 4 1·60 1·25

(Des C. Abbott. Litho Questa)

1977 (19 Dec). *50th Anniv of Jamaica Military Band*. T **189** *and similar multicoloured designs*. W **111** (*sideways on horiz designs*). P 14.
438 9 c. Type **189** 15 10
439 10 c. Clarinet players 15 10
440 20 c. Two kettle drummers (*vert*) 40 35
441 25 c. Cellist and trumpeter (*vert*) 55 65
438/41 .. .. *Set of* 4 1·10 1·00
MS442 120 × 137 mm. Nos. 438/41. Wmk sideways (*sold at* 75 *c.*) .. .. 2·50 3·75

(Des J. Cooter. Litho Walsall)

1978 (17 Apr). *Butterflies* (*3rd series*). *Multicoloured designs as* T **184**. W **111**. P 14.
443 10 c. *Callophrys crethona* 25 10
444 20 c. *Siproeta stelenes* 50 20
445 25 c. *Urbanus proteus* 65 35
446 50 c. *Anaea troglodyta* .. .. 1·40 1·60
443/6 .. .. *Set of* 4 2·50 2·00
MS447 100×125 mm. Nos. 443/6 (*sold at* $1.15) 2·50 3·25
a. Error. Imperf £180

190 Half-figure with Canopy

191 Norman Manley (statue)

(Des J. Cooter. Litho J.W.)

1978 (10 July). *Arawak Artefacts* (*1st series*). T **190** *and similar vert designs*. W **111**. P 13½ × 13.
448 10 c. deep brown, yellow and black 10 10
449 20 c. deep brown, mauve and black 10 10
450 50 c. deep brown, apple-green and black .. 30 35
448/50 .. .. *Set of* 3 40 45
MS451 135 × 90 mm. Nos. 448/50. P 14 (*sold at* 90 *c.*) .. .. 60 1·00
Designs:—20 c. Standing figure; 50 c. Birdman.
See also Nos. 479/83.

(Des and litho J.W.)

1978 (25 Sept). *24th Commonwealth Parliamentary Conference*. T **191** *and similar vert designs. Multicoloured*. W **111**. P 13.
452 10 c. Type **191** 10 10
453 20 c. Sir Alexander Bustamante (statue) .. 10 10
454 25 c. City of Kingston Crest 15 15
455 40 c. Gordon House Chamber, House of Representatives 25 35
452/5 .. .. *Set of* 4 50 60

192 Band and Banner

193 "Negro Aroused" (sculpture by Edna Manley)

(Des V. Whiteley. Litho J.W.)

1978 (4 Dec). *Christmas. Centenary of Salvation Army*. T **192** *and similar horiz designs. Multicoloured*. W **111** (*sideways*). P 14.
456 10 c. Type **192** 20 10
457 20 c. Trumpeter 25 10
458 25 c. Banner 25 20
459 50 c. William Booth (founder) .. .. .. 40 1·00
456/9 .. .. *Set of* 4 1·00 1·25

(Des G. Hutchins. Litho J.W.)

1978 (11 Dec). *International Anti-Apartheid Year*. W **111**. P 13.
460 **193** 10 c. multicoloured 10 10

194 Tennis, Montego Bay

195 Arms and Map of Jamaica

(Des and litho Harrison ($5). Des Walsall. Litho J.W. (others))

1979 (15 Jan)–**84.** *Vert designs as T* **194**, *and T* **195.** *Multi-coloured. White ordinary paper* (15, 65, 75 *c*., $5) *or cream chalk-surfaced paper* (*others*). *W* **111** (*sideways on* $5). *P* 14½ × 14 ($5) *or* 13½ (*others*).

461 1 c. Type **194** (26.11.79) 30 30
462 2 c. Golf, Tryall, Hanover (26.11.79) 40 40
a. White ordinary paper (8.84) 75 75
463 4 c. Horse riding, Negril Beach (26.11.79) .. 15 20
a. White ordinary paper (8.84) 75 75
464 5 c. Old waterwheel, Tryall, Hanover (26.11.79) 15 10
a. White ordinary paper (27.8.82) 35 30
465 6 c. Fern Gully, Ocho Rios (26.11.79) .. 15 10
466 7 c. Dunn's River Falls, Ocho Rios (26.11.79) 15 10
467 8 c. Jamaican Tody (bird) (28.4.80) 40 20
468 10 c. Jamaican Mango (bird) (28.4.80) .. 40 10
a. White ordinary paper (27.8.82) 60 20
469 12 c. Yellow-billed Amazon (28.4.80) 40 20
470 15 c. Streamertail (bird) (28.4.80) .. 55 10
471 35 c. White-chinned Thrush (28.4.80) .. 55 10
472 50 c. Jamaican Woodpecker (28.4.80) 70 15
473 65 c. Rafting, Martha Brae Trelawny (28.4.80) 30 20
474 75 c. Blue Marlin Fleet, Port Antonio (28.4.80) 30 20
475 $1 Scuba Diving, Ocho Rios (28.4.80) .. 30 30
a. White ordinary paper (27.8.82) 60 60
476 $2 Sailing boats, Montego Bay (28.4.80) .. 50 35
a. White ordinary paper (27.8.82) 90 90
477 $5 Type **195** .. .. 1·00 1·60
461/77 .. .. *Set of* 17 6·00 4·25

TENTH
ANNIVERSARY
AIR JAMAICA
1st APRIL 1979

(**196**)

197 Grinding Stone, *circa* 400 BC.

1979 (2 Apr). *10th Anniv of Air Jamaica. No.* 352 *optd with T* **196.**

478 10 c. Type **173** 10 20

(Des D. Bowen. Litho Questa)

1979 (23 Apr). *Arawak Artefacts* (*2nd series*). *T* **197** *and similar multicoloured designs. W* **111** (*sideways on* 10, 20 *and* 25 *c*.). *P* 14.

479 5 c. Type **197** 10 10
480 10 c. Stone implements, *c*. 500 AD (*horiz*) .. 10 10
481 20 c. Cooking pot, *c*. 300 AD (*horiz*) 10 15
482 25 c. Serving boat, *c*. 300 AD (*horiz*) 15 20
483 50 c. Storage jar fragment, *c*. 300 AD 25 35
479/83 .. .. *Set of* 5 55 70

198 1962 1s. 6d. Independence Commemorative Stamp

(Des J.W. from a local design by J. Mahfood. Litho Walsall)

1979 (13 Aug). *Death Centenary of Sir Rowland Hill. T* **198** *and similar horiz designs showing stamps and Sir Rowland Hill. W* **111** (*sideways*). *P* 14.

484 10 c. black, scarlet-vermilion & brt scarlet .. 10 10
485 20 c. orange-yellow and yellowish brown .. 15 15
486 25 c. mauve and blue 20 20
487 50 c. multicoloured 30 40
484/7 .. .. *Set of* 4 65 70
MS488 146 × 94 mm. No. 485 (*sold at* 30 *c*.) .. 30 45

Designs:—20 c. 1920 1s. with frame inverted; 25 c. 1860 6d.; 50 c. 1968 3d. Human Rights Year commemorative.

199 Group of Children

(Des J.W. Litho Harrison)

1979 (1 Oct). *Christmas. International Year of the Child. T* **199** *and similar multicoloured designs. W* **111** (*sideways on* 10, 25 *and* 50 *c*.). *P* 14.

489 10 c. Type **199** 10 10
490 20 c. Doll (*vert*) 10 10
491 25 c. "The Family" (painting by child) .. 15 15
492 50 c. "House on the Hill" (painting by child) .. 25 40
489/92 .. .. *Set of* 4 50 60

NEW INFORMATION

The editor is always interested to correspond with people who have new information that will improve or correct the Catalogue.

200 Date Tree Hall, 1886 (original home of Institute)

(Des G. Drummond. Litho Walsall)

1980 (25 Feb). *Centenary of Institute of Jamaica. T* **200** *and similar multicoloured designs. W* **111** (*sideways on* 5, 15 *and* 50 *c*.). *P* 13½.

493 5 c. Type **200** 10 10
494 15 c. Institute building, 1980 .. .. .. 15 10
495 35 c. Microfilm reader (*vert*) 20 20
496 50 c. Hawksbill Turtle and Green Turtle .. 30 25
497 75 c. Jamaican Owl (*vert*) 75 50
493/7 .. .. *Set of* 5 1·40 1·00

201 Don Quarrie (200 Metres, 1976)

(Des BG Studio. Litho Walsall)

1980 (21 July). *Olympic Games, Moscow. Jamaican Olympic Athletics Gold Medal Winners. T* **201** *and similar horiz designs. Multicoloured. W* **111** (*sideways*). *P* 13.

498 15 c. Type **201** 15 10
499 35 c. Arthur Wint (4 × 400 Metres Relay, 1952) 25 30
a. Horiz strip of 4. Nos. 499/502 90
500 35 c. Leslie Laing (4 × 400 Metres Relay, 1952) 25 30
501 35 c. Herbert McKenley (4 × 400 Metres Relay, 1952) 25 30
502 35 c. George Rhoden (4 × 400 Metres Relay, 1952) 25 30
498/502 .. .. *Set of* 5 90 1·10

Nos. 499/502 were printed together, *se-tenant*, in horizontal strips of 4 throughout the sheet.

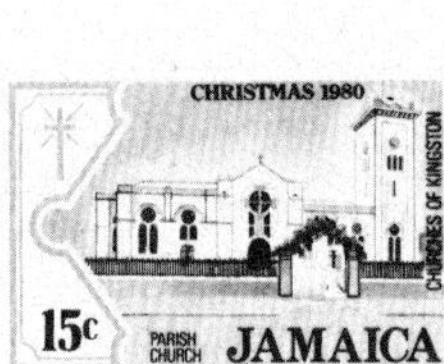

202 Parish Church

203 Blood Cup Sponge

(Des J.W. Litho Harrison)

1980 (24 Nov). *Christmas. Churches* (*1st series*). *T* **202** *and similar horiz designs. Multicoloured. W* **111** (*sideways*). *P* 14.

503 15 c. Type **202** 10 10
504 20 c. Coke Memorial Church 10 10
505 25 c. Church of the Redeemer 15 10
506 $5 Holy Trinity Cathedral .. .. .. 1·00 2·00
503/6 .. .. *Set of* 4 1·10 2·10
MS507 120 × 139 mm. Nos. 503/6. P 14½ (*sold at* $5.70) .. .. 1·75 3·00

See also Nos. 537/40 and 570/2.

(Des J. Mahfood. Litho Walsall)

1981 (27 Feb). *Marine Life* (*1st series*). *T* **203** *and similar multi-coloured designs. W* **111** (*sideways on* 45 *and* 75 *c*.). *P* 14.

508 20 c. Type **203** 15 10
509 45 c. Tube Sponge (*horiz*) 25 30
510 60 c. Black Coral 35 40
511 75 c. Tyre Reef (*horiz*) 40 55
508/11 .. .. *Set of* 4 1·00 1·25

See also Nos. 541/5.

204 Brown's Hutia (or Indian Coney)

205 White Orchid

(Des D. Bowen. Litho Questa)

1981 (25 May). *Brown's Hutia* (*or Indian Coney*). *T* **204** *and similar horiz designs. Multicoloured. W* **111**. *P* 14.

512 20 c. Hutia facing right 15 20
a. Horiz strip of 4. Nos. 512/15 55
513 20 c. Type **204** 15 20
514 20 c. Hutia facing left and eating 15 20
515 20 c. Hutia family 15 20
512/15 .. .. *Set of* 4 55 70

Nos. 512/15 were printed together, *se-tenant*, in horizontal strips of 4 throughout the sheet.

(Des J.W. Litho Format)

1981 (29 July). *Royal Wedding. T* **205** *and similar vert designs. Multicoloured. W w* **14** (*sideways*). *P* 13½ ($5) *or* 15 (*others*).

516 20 c. Type **205** 20 10
a. Perf 15 × 14½ 25 25
ab. Booklet pane. Nos. 516a/19a .. .. 3·50
517 45 c. Royal Coach 35 20
a. Perf 15 × 14½ 50 50
518 60 c. Prince Charles and Lady Diana Spencer 50 30
a. Perf 15 × 14½ 60 60
519 $5 St. James' Palace .. .. .. 1·00 1·50
a. Perf 15 × 14½ .. .. 2·50 3·50
516/19 .. .. *Set of* 4 1·75 1·90
MS520 98 × 85 mm. No. 519. Wmk upright. P 13½ 1·90 2·40

Nos. 516/18 also exist perforated 13½ (*price for set of* 3 £2.25 *mint or used*) from additional sheetlets of 5 stamps and one label. No. 519 exists from both normal sheets and sheetlets.

Nos. 516a/19a are from $6.25 stamp booklets.

206 Blind Man at Work

207 W.F.D. Emblem on 1964 1½d. Definitive

(Des G. Vasarhelyi. Litho J.W.)

1981 (14 Sept). *International Year for Disabled Persons. T* **206** *and similar horiz designs. Multicoloured. W* **111** (*sideways*). *P* 13.

521 20 c. Type **206** 15 15
522 45 c. Painting with the mouth 40 40
523 60 c. Deaf student communicating with sign language 50 50
524 $1.50, Basketball players .. .. .. 1·25 1·25
521/4 .. .. *Set of* 4 2·10 2·10

(Des J. Mahfood. Litho J.W.)

1981 (16 Oct). *World Food Day. Stamps on Stamps. T* **207** *and similar designs showing W.F.D. emblems on various definitives. W* **111** (*sideways on* 20 *c*., $2 *and* $4). *P* 13.

525 20 c. multicoloured 30 15
526 45 c. black, rose and orange 60 40
527 $2 black, violet-blue and green .. .. 1·75 1·40
528 $4 black, green and light brown .. .. 3·00 2·50
525/8 .. .. *Set of* 4 5·00 4·00

Designs: *Vert as T* **207**—45 c. 1922 1d. (40 × 26 *mm*.).—$2 As 1938 3d. but with W.F.D. emblem replacing King's head; $4 As 1938 1s. but with W.F.D. emblem replacing King's head.

Nos. 525/8 were so designed that the face values obliterated those on the stamps depicted.

208 "Survival" (song title)

209 Webb Memorial Baptist Church

(Litho Format)

1981 (20 Oct). *Bob Marley* (*musician*) *Commemoration. T* **208** *and similar vert designs inscribed with song titles. In black and vermilion* ($5.25) *or multicoloured* (*others*). *W w* **14** (*sideways*). *P* 15.

529 1 c. Type **208** 10 10
530 2 c. "Exodus" 10 10
531 3 c. "Is this Love" 10 10
532 15 c. "Coming in from the Cold"* 40 15
533 20 c. "Positive Vibration"† 50 20
534 60 c. "War" .. .. 1·25 1·00
535 $3 "Could you be Loved" .. .. .. 6·50 5·00
529/35 .. .. *Set of* 7 8·00 6·00
MS536 134 × 110 mm. $5.25, Bob Marley (wmk upright) .. .. 6·00 4·75

*Part of initial "C" of song title inscription does not show on the design.

†Incorrectly inscribed "OSITIVE VIBRATION".

(Des J.W. Litho Questa)

1981 (11 Dec). *Christmas. Churches* (*2nd series*). *T* **209** *and similar horiz designs. Multicoloured. W* **111** (*sideways*). *P* 14.

537 10 c. Type **209** 10 10
538 45 c. Church of God in Jamaica 30 15
539 $5 Bryce United Church .. .. .. 2·25 2·50
537/9 .. .. *Set of* 3 2·40 2·50
MS540 120 × 168 mm. Nos. 537/9 (wmk upright). P 12 .. .. 3·50 3·25

210 Gorgonian Coral

211 Cub Scout

(Des J. Mahfood; adapted PAD Studio. Litho Questa)

1982 (22 Feb). *Marine Life* (2nd series). *T* **210** *and similar multi-coloured designs.* W **111** (*sideways on* 45, 60, 75 *c. and* $3). *P* 14.

541 20 c. Type **210** .. 25 10
542 45 c. Hard Sponge and diver (*horiz*) .. 45 25
543 60 c. American Manatee (*horiz*) .. 60 40
544 75 c. Plume Worm (*horiz*) .. 70 50
545 $3 Coral Banded Shrimp (*horiz*) .. 2·00 1·60
541/5 .. *Set of* 5 3·50 2·50

(Des L. Curtis. Litho J.W.)

1982 (12 July). *75th Anniv of Boy Scout Movement. T* **211** *and similar vert designs. Multicoloured.* W **111**. *P* 13½ × 13.

546 20 c. Type **211** .. 40 15
547 45 c. Scout camp .. 75 35
548 60 c. "Out of Many, One People" .. 95 45
549 $2 Lord Baden-Powell .. 1·75 1·50
546/9 .. *Set of* 4 3·50 2·25
MS550 80 × 130 mm. Nos. 546/9 .. 3·50 4·00

212 *Lignum vitae* (national flower)

ROYAL BABY
21.6.82
(**212***a*)

(Des R. Sauer. Litho Questa)

1982 (30 Aug). *21st Birthday of Princess of Wales. T* **212** *and similar vert designs.* W **111**. *P* 14½ × 14.

551 20 c. Type **212** .. 20 20
a. Booklet pane. Nos. 551/3 .. 1·00
552 45 c. Carriage ride .. 35 35
553 60 c. Wedding .. 50 50
554 75 c. *Saxifraga longifolia* .. 70 70
a. Booklet pane. Nos. 554/6 .. 3·00
555 $2 Princess of Wales .. 1·25 1·50
556 $3 *Viola gracilis major* .. 1·50 2·00
551/6 .. *Set of* 6 4·00 4·75
MS557 106 × 75 mm. $5 Honeymoon photograph 2·50 3·00

Nos. 554 and 556 were printed in small sheets of 6 including one *se-tenant*, stamp-size, label. The other values were printed in sheets of 40.

1982 (13 Sept). *Birth of Prince William of Wales. Nos.* 551/7 *optd with T* **212***a*.

558 20 c. Type **212** .. 20 20
a. Booklet pane. Nos. 558/60 .. 1·00
559 45 c. Carriage ride .. 35 35
560 60 c. Wedding .. 50 50
561 75 c. *Saxifraga longifolia* .. 70 70
a. Booklet pane. Nos. 561/3 .. 3·00
562 $2 Princess of Wales .. 1·25 1·50
563 $3 *Viola gracilis major* .. 1·50 2·00
558/63 .. *Set of* 6 4·00 4·75
MS564 106 × 75 mm. $5 Honeymoon photograph 2·75 3·50

213 Prey Captured **214** Queen Elizabeth II

(Des N. Arlott. Litho Questa)

1982 (25 Oct). *Jamaican Birds* (1st series). *Jamaican Lizard Cuckoo. T* **213** *and similar vert designs. Multicoloured.* W **111**. *P* 14½.

565 $1 Type **213** .. 80 80
a. Horiz strip of 5. Nos. 565/9 .. 3·50
566 $1 Searching for prey .. 80 80
567 $1 Calling prior to prey search .. 80 80
568 $1 Adult landing .. 80 80
569 $1 Adult flying in .. 80 80
565/9 .. *Set of* 5 3·50 3·50

Nos. 565/9 were printed in horizontal *se-tenant* strips of 5 throughout the sheet.

See also Nos. 642/5 and 707/10.

(Des and litho J.W.)

1982 (8 Dec). *Christmas. Churches* (3rd series). *Horiz designs as T* **209**. *Multicoloured.* W **111** (*sideways*). *P* 13.

570 20 c. United Pentecostal Church .. 15 10
571 45 c. Disciples of Christ Church .. 30 25
572 75 c. Open Bible Church .. 55 70
570/2 .. *Set of* 3 90 95

(Des D. Miller. Litho Walsall)

1983 (14 Feb). *Royal Visit. T* **214** *and similar vert design. Multi-coloured.* W **111**. *P* 14.

573 $2 Type **214** .. 2·50 2·00
574 $3 Coat of Arms .. 3·50 2·75

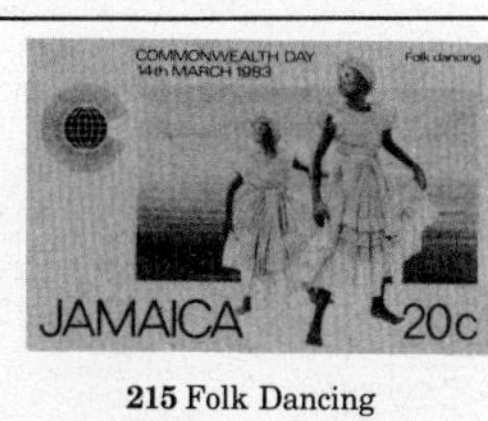

215 Folk Dancing

(Des Walsall. Litho Format)

1983 (14 Mar). *Commonwealth Day. T* **215** *and similar horiz designs. Multicoloured.* W **111** (*sideways*). *P* 14.

575 20 c. Type **215** .. 15 15
576 45 c. Bauxite mining .. 35 35
577 75 c. World map showing position of Jamaica 45 45
578 $2 Coat of arms and family .. 1·25 1·40
575/8 .. *Set of* 4 2·00 2·10

216 General Cargo Ship at Wharf

217 Norman Manley and Sir Alexander Bustamante

(Des A. Theobald. Litho Format)

1983 (17 Mar). *25th Anniv of International Maritime Organization. T* **216** *and similar horiz designs. Multicoloured. P* 14.

579 15 c. Type **216** .. 65 20
580 20 c. *Veendam* (cruise liner) at Kingston .. 90 25
581 45 c. Container ship entering port .. 1·25 65
582 $1 Tanker passing International Seabed Headquarters Building .. 2·25 2·50
579/82 .. *Set of* 4 4·50 3·25

(Des D. Miller. Litho Harrison)

1983 (25 July). *21st Anniv of Independence.* W **111**. *P* 14.

583 **217** 15 c. multicoloured .. 15 15
584 20 c. multicoloured .. 15 20
585 45 c. multicoloured .. 30 40
583/5 .. *Set of* 3 55 70

218 Ship-to-Shore Radio

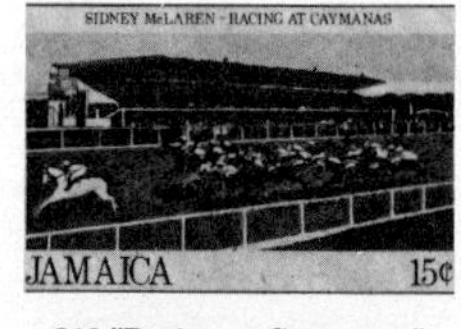

219 "Racing at Caymanas" (Sidney Mclaren)

(Des Walsall. Litho Harrison)

1983 (18 Oct). *World Communications Year. T* **218** *and similar horiz designs. Multicoloured.* W **111** (*sideways*). *P* 14.

586 20 c. Type **218** .. 15 15
587 45 c. Postal services .. 35 40
588 75 c. Telephone communications .. 55 1·00
589 $1 T.V. via satellite .. 75 1·50
586/9 .. *Set of* 4 1·50 2·75

(Des D. Miller. Litho J.W.)

1983 (12 Dec). *Christmas. Paintings. T* **219** *and similar multi-coloured designs.* W **111** (*sideways on* 15 *c.,* 20 *c.*). *P* 13 × 13½ (15 *c.,* 20 *c.*) *or* 13½ × 13 (*others*).

590 15 c. Type **219** .. 10 10
591 20 c. "Seated Figures" (Karl Parboosingh) .. 10 10
592 75 c. "The Petitioner" (Henry Daley) (*vert*) .. 30 25
593 $2 "Banana Plantation" (John Dunkley) (*vert*) .. 70 1·00
590/3 .. *Set of* 4 1·00 1·25

220 Sir Alexander Bustamante

221 "D.H. 60G Gipsy Moth" Seaplane

(Des D. Miller. Litho Questa)

1984 (24 Feb). *Birth Centenary of Sir Alexander Bustamante. T* **220** *and similar vert design. Multicoloured.* W **111**. *P* 14.

594 20 c. Type **220** .. 30 40
a. Horiz pair. Nos. 594/5 .. 60 80
595 20 c. Birthplace, Blenheim .. 30 40

Nos. 594/5 were printed together, *se-tenant*, in horizontal pairs throughout the sheet.

(Des A. Theobald. Litho Questa)

1984 (11 June). *Seaplanes and Flying Boats. T* **221** *and similar horiz designs. Multicoloured.* W **111** (*sideways*). *P* 14.

596 25 c. Type **221** .. 55 15
597 55 c. Consolidated "Commodore" flying boat .. 75 45
598 $1.50, Sikorsky "S-38" flying boat .. 1·50 1·75
599 $3 Sikorsky "S-40" flying boat .. 2·00 2·25
596/9 .. *Set of* 4 4·25 4·25

222 Cycling

5c

223

(Des G. Vasarhelyi. Litho J.W.)

1984 (11 July). *Olympic Games, Los Angeles. T* **222** *and similar horiz designs. Multicoloured.* W **111** (*sideways*). *P* 14.

600 25 c. Type **222** .. 10 10
601 55 c. Relay running .. 20 25
602 $1.50, Start of race .. 60 1·00
603 $3 Finish of race .. 1·10 1·75
600/3 .. *Set of* 4 1·75 2·75
MS604 135 × 105 mm. Nos. 600/3 (*sold at* $5.40). P 13 × 13½ .. 1·90 2·75

1984 (7 Aug). *Nos.* 465 *and* 469 *surch as T* **223**.

605 5 c. on 6 c. Fern Gully, Ocho Rios .. 10 15
606 10 c. on 12 c. Yellow-billed Amazon .. 30 25

224 Head of Jamaican Boa Snake

(Des I. Loe. Litho Questa)

1984 (22 Oct). *Jamaican Boa Snake. T* **224** *and similar horiz designs. Multicoloured.* W **111** (*sideways*). *P* 14½.

607 25 c. Type **224** .. 30 15
608 55 c. Boa snake on branch over stream .. 50 45
609 70 c. Snake with young .. 60 65
610 $1 Snake on log .. 70 80
607/10 .. *Set of* 4 1·90 1·90
MS611 133 × 97 mm. As Nos. 607/10 but without W.W.F. emblem (*sold at* $2.60) .. 1·75 1·75

225 *Enterprise* (1845)

226 "Accompong Madonna" (Namba Roy)

(Des D. Hartley-Marjoram. Litho Enschedé)

1984 (16 Nov). *Railway Locomotives* (1st series). *T* **225** *and similar horiz designs. Multicoloured.* W **111** (*sideways*). *P* 13½ × 13.

612 25 c. Type **225** .. 50 15
613 55 c. Tank locomotive (1880) .. 70 50
614 $1.50, Kitson-Meyer tank locomotive (1904) 1·00 1·25
615 $3 Super-heated locomotive (1916) .. 1·75 2·00
612/15 .. *Set of* 4 3·50 3·50

See also Nos. 634/7.

(Des G. Vasarhelyi. Litho Harrison)

1984 (6 Dec). *Christmas. Sculptures. T* **226** *and similar vert designs. Multicoloured.* W **111**. *P* 14.

616 20 c. Type **226** .. 20 10
617 25 c. "Head" (Alvin Marriott) .. 25 10
618 55 c. "Moon" (Edna Manley) .. 50 40
619 $1.50, "All Women are Five Women" (Mallica Reynolds (Kapo)) .. 1·00 1·50
616/19 .. *Set of* 4 1·75 1·90

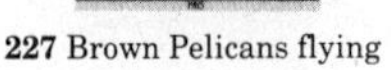

227 Brown Pelicans flying

228 The Queen Mother at Belfast University

(Des N. Arlott. Litho Walsall)

1985 (15 Apr). *Birth Bicentenary of John J. Audubon (ornithologist). Brown Pelican. T* **227** *and similar vert designs. Multicoloured. W* **111**. *P* 13½×13.

620	20 c. Type **227**. .	40	10
621	55 c. Diving for fish . .	55	30
622	$2 Young pelican taking food from adult . .	1·00	1·00
623	$5 "Brown Pelican" (John J. Audubon) . .	1·50	2·25
620/3	*Set of* 4	3·00	3·25
MS624	100×100 mm. Nos. 620/3 (*sold at* $7.85)	3·00	3·50

(Des A. Theobald ($5), C. Abbott (others). Litho Questa)

1985 (7 June). *Life and Times of Queen Elizabeth the Queen Mother. T* **228** *and similar vert designs. Multicoloured. W* **111**. *P* 14½×14.

625	25 c. With photograph album, 1963 . .	10	10
626	55 c. With Prince Charles at Garter Ceremony, Windsor Castle, 1983 . .	15	15
627	$1.50, Type **228** . .	35	40
628	$3 With Prince Henry at his christening (from photo by Lord Snowdon) . .	65	70
625/8	*Set of* 4	1·10	1·25
MS629	91×74 mm. $5 With the Queen, Prince Philip and Princess Anne at Ascot. Wmk sideways	1·25	1·40

229 Maps and Emblems

(Des D. Miller. Litho Harrison)

1985 (30 July). *International Youth Year and 5th Pan-American Scout Jamboree. W* **111** (*sideways*). *P* 14.

630	**229**	25 c. multicoloured	10	10
631		55 c. multicoloured	15	15
632		70 c. multicoloured	20	20
633		$4 multicoloured	90	1·10
630/3		*Set of* 4	1·25	1·40

(Des D. Hartley. Litho Harrison)

1985 (30 Sept). *Railway Locomotives (2nd series). Horiz designs as T* **225**. *Multicoloured. W* **111** (*sideways*). *P* 14.

634	25 c. Baldwin locomotive No. 16	45	10
635	55 c. Rogers locomotive	70	15
636	$1.50, Locomotive *The Projector*	1·00	75
637	$4 Diesel locomotive No. 102	1·75	1·75
634/7	*Set of* 4	3·50	2·50

230 "The Old Settlement" (Ralph Campbell)

230a Princess Elizabeth and Princess Margaret, 1939

(Litho Format)

1985 (9 Dec). *Christmas. Jamaican Paintings. T* **230** *and similar multicoloured designs. W* **111** (*sideways on* 20, 75 *c.*). *P* 14.

638	20 c. Type **230**. .	10	10
639	55 c. "The Vendor" (Albert Huie) (*vert*)	15	15
640	75 c. "Road Menders" (Gaston Tabois)	15	20
641	$4 "Woman, must I not be about my Father's business?" (Carl Abrahams) (*vert*)	90	95
638/41	*Set of* 4	1·10	1·25

(Des N. Arlott. Litho B.D.T.)

1986 (10 Feb). *Jamaican Birds (2nd series). Vert designs as T* **213**. *Multicoloured. W* **111**. *P* 14.

642	25 c. Chestnut-bellied Cuckoo	40	10
643	55 c. Jamaican Becard	55	30
644	$1.50, White-eyed Thrush . .	70	1·00
645	$5 Rufous-tailed Flycatcher	1·60	2·75
642/5	*Set of* 4	3·00	3·75

(Des A. Theobald. Litho Harrison)

1986 (21 Apr). *60th Birthday of Queen Elizabeth II. T* **230a** *and similar vert designs. Multicoloured. W* **111**. *P* 14½×14.

646	20 c. Type **230a**	10	10
647	25 c. With Prince Charles and Prince Andrew, 1962	10	10
648	70 c. Queen visiting War Memorial, Montego Bay, 1983	15	25
649	$3 On state visit to Luxembourg, 1976 . .	65	90
650	$5 At Crown Agents Head Office, London, 1983 . .	1·25	1·75
646/50	*Set of* 5	1·90	2·75

231 Bustamante Children's Hospital

231a Prince Andrew and Miss Sarah Ferguson, Ascot, 1985

(Des D. Miller. Litho Questa)

1986 (19 May). *"Ameripex '86" International Stamp Exhibition, Chicago. T* **231** *and similar vert designs. Multicoloured. W* **111**. *P* 14½×14.

651	25 c. Type **231**. .	20	10
652	55 c. Air Jamaica jet airliner and map of holiday resorts . .	25	15
653	$3 Norman Manley Law School . .	1·00	1·10
654	$5 Bauxite and agricultural exports	3·00	3·00
651/4	*Set of* 4	4·00	4·00
MS655	85×106 mm. Nos. 651/4 (*sold at* $8.90) . .	4·00	4·00

(Des D. Miller. Litho Walsall)

1986 (23 July). *Royal Wedding. T* **231a** *and similar square design. Multicoloured. W* **111**. *P* 14½×14.

656	20 c. Type **231a**	15	10
657	$5 Prince Andrew making speech, Fredericton, Canada, 1985	1·40	1·50

232 Richard "Shrimpy" Clarke

5c

(**233**)

(Des G. Vasarhelyi. Litho Questa)

1986 (27 Oct). *Jamaican Boxing Champions. T* **232** *and similar vert designs. Multicoloured. W* **111**. *P* 14.

658	45 c. Type **232**. .	20	15
659	70 c. Michael McCallum	30	20
660	$2 Trevor Berbick . .	70	55
661	$4 Richard "Shrimpy" Clarke, Michael McCallum and Trevor Berbick	1·25	1·25
658/61	*Set of* 4	2·25	1·90

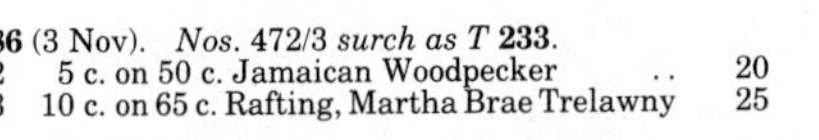

1986 (3 Nov). *Nos. 472/3 surch as T* **233**.

662	5 c. on 50 c. Jamaican Woodpecker	20	25
663	10 c. on 65 c. Rafting, Martha Brae Trelawny	25	25

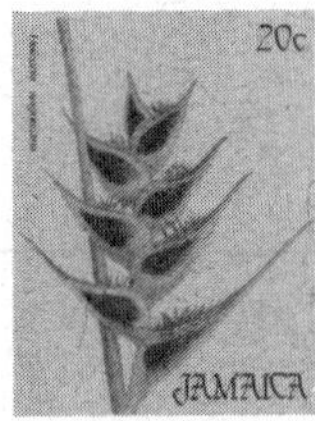

234 *Heliconia wagneriana*

235 Crown Cone

(Des Annette Robinson. Litho B.D.T.)

1986 (1 Dec). *Christmas. Flowers (1st series). T* **234** *and similar multicoloured designs. W* **111** (*sideways on* 25 *c.*, $5). *P* 13½.

664	20 c. Type **234**. .	10	10
665	25 c. *Heliconia psittacorum* (*horiz*) . .	10	10
666	55 c. *Heliconia rostrata*	20	30
667	$5 *Strelitzia reginae* (*horiz*)	1·60	2·75
664/7	*Set of* 4	1·75	2·75

See also Nos. 703/6 and 739/42.

(Des A. Riley. Litho Format)

1987 (23 Feb). *Sea Shells. T* **235** *and similar vert designs. Multicoloured. W* **111**. *P* 15.

668	35 c. Type **235**. .	20	10
669	75 c. Measled Cowrie . .	30	20
670	$1 Trumpet Triton . .	40	40
671	$5 Rooster Tail Conch	1·40	1·75
668/71	*Set of* 4	2·10	2·25

COVER PRICES

Cover factors are quoted at the beginning of each country for most issues to 1945. An explanation of the system can be found on page x. The factors quoted do not, however, apply to philatelic covers.

236 Norman Manley

237 Arms of Jamaica

(Des C. Slania (1 c. to 90 c.). Litho Enschedé)

1987 (18 May)–**91**. *Vert portraits as T* **236** *and T* **237**. *W* **111** (*sideways on* $1 *to* $50). *Cream paper* (2 *c. to* 9 *c.* (*Nos.* 673A/80A)). *P* 12½×13 (1 *to* 90 *c.*) *or* 13×13½ ($1 *to* $50).
A. *Without imprint.* B. *With imprint date at foot.*

			A		B	
672	**236**	1 c. scarlet and pale pink	10	10	†	
673		2 c. brt carm & pale rose-pk	10	10	†	
674		3 c. yellow-ol & pale stone	10	10	†	
675		4 c. myrtle-grn & pale grn	10	10	†	
676		5 c. slate-blue and pale bluish grey	10	10	10	10
677		6 c. dull ultramarine and pale lavender-grey	10	10	†	
678		7 c. reddish vio & pale mve	10	10	†	
679		8 c. dp mag & pale rose-pk	10	10	†	
680		9 c. olive-sepia & pale brn	10	10	†	
681	–	10 c. dp rose-red & pale pink	10	10	†	
682	–	20 c. reddish orange & flesh	15	10	10	10
683	–	30 c. brt green & pale green	10	10	†	
684	–	40 c. dp turquoise-green & pale turquoise-green . .	15	10	10	10
685	–	50 c. grey-ol & pale ol-grey	15	10	10	10
686	–	60 c. brt blue & pale azure	10	10	†	
687	–	70 c. bluish violet & pale vio	10	10	†	
688	–	80 c. reddish violet and pale rose-lilac	10	10	†	
689		90 c. light reddish brown and pale grey-brown . .	10	10	†	
690	**237**	$1 olive-sepia and cream	10	15	10	15
691		$2 bright orange & cream	15	20	†	
692		$5 brown-ol & pale stone	35	40	†	
693		$10 dp turquoise-blue & pale azure . .	70	75	†	
693*c*		$25 bluish violet and pale lavender	†		1·75	1·90
693*d*		$50 deep mauve and pale rose-lilac	†		3·50	3·75
672A/93A		*Set of* 22	2·10	2·25		
676B/93*d*B		*Set of* 7			5·00	5·50

Designs:—10 c. to 90 c. Sir Alexander Bustamante.

Dates of issue: 18.5.87, Nos. 672A/93A; 6.6.88, Nos. 676B, 682B; 12.2.91, Nos. 684B, 685B; 6.6.91, No. 690B; 9.10.91, Nos. 693*c*B, 693*d*B.

No. 682B exists with different imprint dates beneath the design.

238 Jamaican Flag and Coast at Sunset

239 Marcus Garvey

(Des D. Miller. Litho Walsall)

1987 (27 July). *25th Anniv of Independence. T* **238** *and similar multicoloured design. W* **111** (*sideways on* 70 *c.*). *P* 14.

694	55 c. Type **238**. .	40	30
695	70 c. Jamaican flag and inscription (*horiz*) . .	50	60

(Des D. Miller. Litho Walsall)

1987 (17 Aug). *Birth Centenary of Marcus Garvey (founder of Universal Negro Improvement Association). T* **239** *and similar vert design, both black, emerald and lemon. W* **111**. *P* 14.

696	25 c. Type **239**. .	30	40
	a. Horiz pair. Nos. 696/7 . .	60	80
697	25 c. Statue of Marcus Garvey	30	40

Nos. 696/7 were printed together, *se-tenant*, in horizontal pairs throughout the sheet.

240 Salvation Army School for the Blind

241 Hibiscus Hybrid

(Des L. Curtis. Litho Walsall)

1987 (8 Oct). *Centenary of Salvation Army in Jamaica. T* **240** *and similar horiz designs. Multicoloured. W* **111** (*sideways*). *P* 13×13½.

698	25 c. Type **240**. .	30	10
699	55 c. Col. Mary Booth and Bramwell Booth Memorial Hall . .	45	20

700 $3 Welfare Service lorry, 1929 .. .. 1·25 1·25
701 $5 Col. Abram Davey and S.S. *Alene*, 1887 2·00 2·25
698/701 .. .. *Set of* 4 3·50 3·50
MS702 100×80 mm. Nos. 698/701 (*sold at* $8.90) 3·50 3·75

(Des Annette Robinson. Litho Harrison)

1987 (30 Nov). *Christmas. Flowers* (2*nd series*). *T* **241** *and similar vert designs. Multicoloured. W* **111**. *P* $14^1/_2$×14.
703 20 c. Type **241**.. .. .. 10 10
704 25 c. *Hibiscus elatus* 10 10
705 $4 *Hibiscus cannabinus* 90 95
706 $5 *Hibiscus rosasinensis* .. .. .. 1·25 1·40
703/6 .. .. *Set of* 4 2·00 2·25

242 Chestnut-bellied Cuckoo, Black-billed Parrot and Jamaican Euphonia

243 Blue Whales

(Des N. Arlott. Litho Walsall)

1988 (22 Jan). *Jamaican Birds* (3*rd series*). *T* **242** *and similar vert designs. Multicoloured. W* **111**. *P* 14.
707 45 c. Type **242**.. .. .. 50 50
a. Horiz pair. Nos. 707/8 .. .. .. 1·00 1·00
708 45 c. Jamaican White-eyed Vireo, Rufous-throated Solitaire and Yellow-crowned Elaenia 50 50
709 $5 Snowy Plover, Little Blue Heron and Great White Heron .. .. 2·00 2·00
a. Horiz pair. Nos. 709/10.. .. .. 4·00 4·00
710 $5 Common Stilt, Snowy Egret and Black-crowned Night Heron .. .. .. 2·00 2·00
707/10 .. .. *Set of* 4 4·50 4·50
The two designs of each value were printed together, *se-tenant*, in horizontal pairs throughout the sheets, each pair forming a composite design.

(Des A. Riley. Litho Harrison)

1988 (14 Apr). *Marine Mammals. T* **243** *and similar horiz designs. Multicoloured. W* **111** (*sideways*). *P* 14.
711 20 c. Type **243** 40 15
712 25 c. Gervais's Whales 40 15
713 55 c. Killer Whales 60 20
714 $5 Common Dolphins .. .. 2·50 2·00
711/14 .. .. *Set of* 4 3·50 2·25

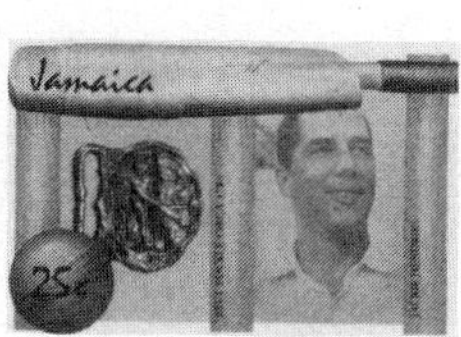

243a Jackie Hendriks

244 Jamaican Red Cross Workers with Ambulance

(Des D. Hartley. Litho Walsall)

1988 (6 June). *West Indian Cricket. T* **243a** *and similar horiz designs, each showing portrait, cricket equipment and early belt buckle. Multicoloured. W* **111** (*sideways*). *P* 14.
715 25 c. Type **243a** 30 10
716 55 c. George Headley 55 20
717 $2 Michael Holding .. .. 1·25 85
718 $3 R. K. Nunes .. .. 1·50 1·25
719 $4 Allan Rae .. .. 1·75 1·50
715/19 .. .. *Set of* 5 4·75 3·50

(Des S. Noon. Litho Walsall)

1988 (8 Aug). 125*th Anniv of International Red Cross. T* **244** *and similar vert design. Multicoloured. W* **111**. *P* $14^1/_2$ × 14.
720 55 c. Type **244** 30 20
721 $5 Henri Dunant (founder) in field hospital .. .. 1·40 1·40

245 Boxing

(Des P. Broadbent. Litho B.D.T.)

1988 (24 Aug). *Olympic Games, Seoul. T* **245** *and similar horiz designs. Multicoloured. W* **111** (*sideways*). *P* 14.
722 25 c. Type **245** 10 10
723 45 c. Cycling 10 10
724 $4 Athletics 85 90
725 $5 Hurdling .. .. 1·00 1·10
722/5 .. .. *Set of* 4 1·75 2·00
MS726 127 × 87 mm. Nos. 722/5 (*sold at* $9.90) 2·10 2·25

246 Bobsled Team Members and Logo

(Des D. Miller. Litho B.D.T.)

1988 (4 Nov). *Jamaican Olympic Bobsled Team. T* **246** *and similar horiz designs. Multicoloured. W* **111** (*sideways*). *P* 14.
727 25 c. Type **246** 10 30
a. Horiz pair. Nos. 727/8 .. .. 15 60
728 25 c. Two-man bobsled 10 30
729 $5 Bobsled team members (*different*) and logo .. .. 1·00 1·50
a. Horiz pair. Nos. 729/30 .. .. 2·00 3·00
730 $5 Four-man bobsled .. .. .. 1·00 1·50
727/30 .. .. *Set of* 4 1·90 3·25
Nos. 727/8 and 729/30 were printed together, *se-tenant*, in horizontal pairs throughout the sheets.

+25c

HURRICANE GILBERT RELIEF FUND

(**247**)

1988 (11 Nov). *Hurricane Gilbert Relief Fund. Nos.* 722/5 *surch as T* **247** *by Format. A. In red. B. In black.*

		A		B	
731	25 c. + 25 c. Type **245** ..	10	15	10	15
732	45 c. + 45 c. Cycling ..	20	25	20	25
733	$4 + $4 Athletics ..	1·75	1·90	1·75	1·90
734	$5 + $5 Hurdling ..	2·10	2·25	2·10	2·25
731/4	.. .. *Set of* 4	3·75	4·00	3·75	4·00

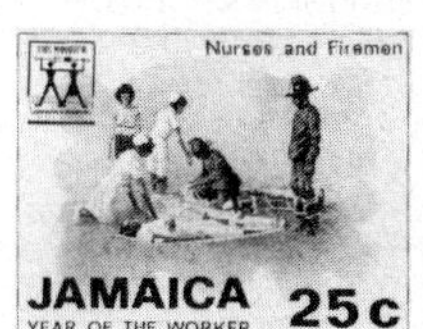

248 Nurses and Firemen

(Des S. Noon. Litho Format)

1988 (24 Nov). *Year of the Worker. T* **248** *and similar horiz designs. Multicoloured. W* **111** (*sideways*). *P* 14.
735 25 c. Type **248** 20 10
736 55 c. Woodcarver 25 20
737 $3 Textile workers .. .. 1·00 1·25
738 $5 Workers on fish farm .. .. .. 1·40 1·50
735/8 .. .. *Set of* 4 2·50 2·75

(Des Annette Robinson. Litho Format)

1988 (15 Dec). *Christmas. Flowers* (3*rd series*). *Multicoloured designs as T* **241**. *W* **111** (*sideways on* 55 *c.*, $4). *P* 14.
739 25 c. *Euphorbia pulcherrima* 10 10
740 55 c. *Spathodea campanulata* (*horiz*) .. 15 15
741 $3 *Hylocereus triangularis* 75 80
742 $4 *Broughtonia sanguinea* (*horiz*) .. 85 90
739/42 .. .. *Set of* 4 1·60 1·75

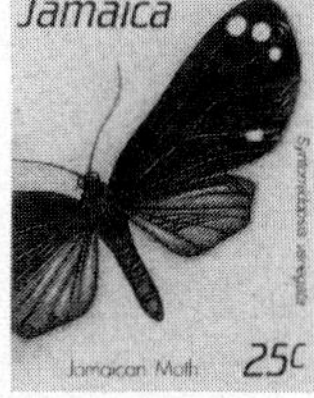

249 Old York Castle School

250 *Syntomidopsis variegata*

(Des A. Theobald. Litho B.D.T.)

1989 (19 Jan). *Bicentenary of Methodist Church in Jamaica. T* **249** *and similar horiz designs. W* **111** (*sideways*). *P* $13^1/_2$.
743 25 c. black and bright blue 10 10
744 45 c. black and rosine 15 10
745 $5 black and yellow-green .. .. .. 1·25 1·50
743/5 .. .. *Set of* 3 1·25 1·50
Designs:—45 c. Revd. Thomas Coke and Parade Chapel, Kingston; $5 Father Hugh Sherlock and St. John's Church.

(Des I. Loe. Litho B.D.T.)

1989 (30 Aug). *Jamaican Moths* (1*st series*). *T* **250** *and similar vert designs. Multicoloured. W* **111**. *P* 14×$13^1/_2$.
746 25 c. Type **250** 30 10
747 55 c. *Himantoides perkinsae* 40 15
748 $3 *Arctia nigriplaga* .. .. .. 1·10 1·10
749 $5 *Sthenognatha toddi* .. .. .. 1·50 1·75
746/9 .. .. *Set of* 4 3·00 2·75
See also Nos. 758/61 and 790/3.

Jamaica 45c
1915 1990
75th Anniversary of Guiding in Jamaica

251 Arawak Fisherman with Catch

252 Girl Guide

(Des Josephine Martin. Litho Cartor, France)

1989 (22 Dec). 500*th Anniv of Discovery of America by Columbus* (1992) (1*st issue*). *T* **251** *and similar vert designs. Multicoloured. W* **111**. *P* $13^1/_2$.
750 25 c. Type **251** 20 10
751 70 c. Arawak man smoking 40 30
752 $5 King Ferdinand and Queen Isabella inspecting caravels .. .. .. 1·75 2·00
753 $10 Columbus with chart .. .. .. 3·00 3·25
750/3 .. .. *Set of* 4 4·75 5·00
MS754 150×200 mm. Nos. 750/3. Wmk sideways. P $12^1/_2$ (*sold at* $16.15) .. .. 4·25 4·50
No. **MS**754 also exists imperforate from a limited printing used in Presentation Packs.
See also Nos. 774/9 and 802/7.

(Des J. Sayer. Litho B.D.T.)

1990 (28 June). 75*th Anniv of Girl Guide Movement in Jamaica. T* **252** *and similar vert designs. Multicoloured. W* **111** (*inverted on* $5). *P* 14.
755 45 c. Type **252** 30 15
756 55 c. Guide leader 35 15
757 $5 Brownie, guide and ranger .. .. 2·00 2·25
755/7 .. .. *Set of* 3 2·40 2·25

(Des I. Loe. Litho B.D.T.)

1990 (12 Sept). *Jamaican Moths* (2*nd series*). *Vert designs as T* **250**. *Multicoloured. W* **111**. *P* 14×$13^1/_2$.
758 25 c. *Eunomia rubripunctata* 20 10
759 55 c. *Perigonia jamaicensis* 30 15
760 $4 *Uraga haemorrhoa* .. .. .. 1·00 1·10
761 $5 *Empyreuma pugione* .. .. .. 1·10 1·25
758/61 .. .. *Set of* 4 2·40 2·40

(**253**)

254 Teaching English

1990 (12 Sept). *"EXPO 90" International Garden and Greenery Exhibition, Osaka. Nos.* 758/61 *optd with T* **253**.
762 25 c. *Eunomia rubripunctata* 20 10
763 55 c. *Perigonia jamaicensis* 30 15
764 $4 *Uraga haemorrhoa* .. .. .. 1·00 1·10
765 $5 *Empyreuma pugione* .. .. .. 1·10 1·25
762/5 .. .. *Set of* 4 2·40 2·40

(Des G. Vasarhelyi. Litho B.D.T.)

1990 (10 Oct). *International Literacy Year. T* **254** *and similar horiz design. Multicoloured. W* **111** (*sideways*). *P* 14.
766 55 c. Type **254** 20 10
767 $5 Teaching maths .. .. 1·50 1·50

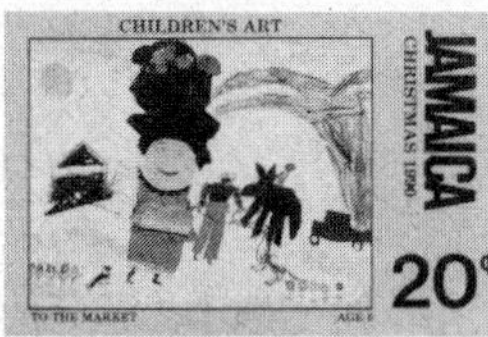

255 "To the Market"

(Adapted J. Mahfood and D. Miller. Litho Walsall)

1990 (7 Dec). *Christmas. Children's Paintings. T* **255** *and similar multicoloured designs. W* **111** (*sideways on horiz designs*). *P* 14×$13^1/_2$ ($5) *or* $13^1/_2$×14 (*others*).
768 20 c. Type **255** 10 10
769 25 c. "House and Garden" 10 10
770 55 c. "Jack and Jill" 15 15
771 70 c. "Market" 15 15
772 $1.50, "Lonely" 40 45
773 $5 "Market Woman" (*vert*) .. .. 1·25 1·25
768/73 .. .. *Set of* 6 1·90 1·90

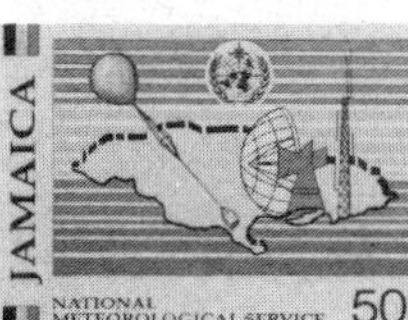

256 Map of First Voyage, 1492

257 Weather Balloon, Dish Aerial and Map of Jamaica.

(Des Josephine Martin. Litho Questa)

1990 (19 Dec). *500th Anniv of Discovery of America by Columbus* (1992) (*2nd issue*). *T* **256** *and similar horiz designs. Multicoloured. W* **111** (*sideways*). *P* 14.

774 25 c. Type **256** 10 10
775 45 c. Map of second voyage, 1493 .. .. .. 10 10
776 $5 Map of third voyage, 1498 .. .. .. 1·00 1·10
777 $10 Map of fourth voyage, 1502 .. .. .. 1·90 2·10
774/7 .. .. *Set of* 4 2·75 3·00
MS778 126×99 mm. 25, 45 c., $5, $10 Composite map of Caribbean showing routes of voyages .. 3·00 3·25
MS779 148×207 mm. Nos. 774/7. Imperf .. 3·00 3·25

Unlike the imperforate version of No. **MS**754, No. **MS**779 was freely available at face value.

(Adapted G. Vasarhelyi. Litho B.D.T.)

1991 (20 May). *11th World Meteorological Congress, Kingston. W* **111** (*sideways*). *P* 14.

780 **257** 50 c. multicoloured 15 10
781 $10 multicoloured .. .. 1·00 1·10

258 Bust of Mary Seacole

259 Jamaican Iguana

(Des Jennifer Toombs. Litho B.D.T.)

1991 (24 June). *International Council of Nurses Meeting of National Representatives. T* **258** *and similar horiz designs. W* **111** (*sideways*). *P* 13½.

782 50 c. multicoloured 15 10
783 $1.10, multicoloured 20 20
MS784 89×60 mm. $8 agate, pale orange-brown and yellow-ochre (*sold at* $8.20) 85 95

Designs:—$1.10, Mary Seacole House; $8 Hospital at Scutari, 1854.

(Des I. Loe. Litho Cartor)

1991 (29 July). *50th Anniv of Natural History Society of Jamaica. Jamaican Iguana. T* **259** *and similar vert designs. Multicoloured. W* **111**. *P* 13.

785 $1.10, Type **259** 15 15
a. Horiz strip of 5. Nos. 785/9 60
786 $1.10, Head of iguana looking right .. 15 15
787 $1.10, Iguana climbing 15 15
788 $1.10, Iguana on rock looking left .. 15 15
789 $1.10, Close-up of iguana's head .. 15 15
785/9 .. .. *Set of* 5 60 60

Nos. 785/9 were printed together, *se-tenant*, in horizontal strips of 5 throughout the sheet.

(Des I. Loe. Litho B.D.T.)

1991 (12 Aug). *Jamaican Moths* (*3rd series*). *Multicoloured designs as T* **250**. *W* **111**. *P* 14×13½.

790 50 c. *Urania sloanus* 15 10
791 $1.10, *Phoenicoprocta jamaicensis* .. 20 15
792 $1.40, *Horama grotei* 25 20
793 $8 *Amplypterus gannascus* 90 95
790/3 .. .. *Set of* 4 1·40 1·25

(260)

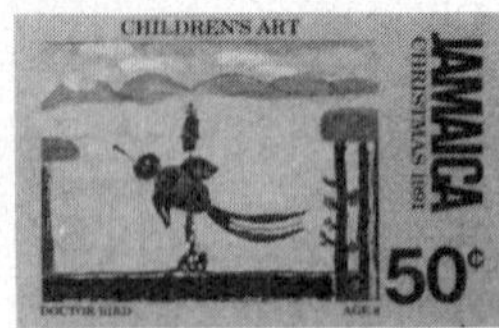

261 "Doctor Bird"

1991 (23 Sept). *"Philanippon '91" International Stamp Exhibition, Tokyo. Nos. 790/3 optd with T* **260**.

794 50 c. *Urania sloanus* 15 10
795 $1.10, *Phoenicoprocta jamaicensis* .. 20 15
796 $1.40, *Horama grotei* 25 20
797 $8 *Amplypterus gannascus* 90 95
794/7 .. .. *Set of* 4 1·40 1·25

(Litho Enschedé)

1991 (27 Nov). *Christmas. Children's Paintings. T* **261** *and similar horiz designs. Multicoloured. W* **111** (*sideways*). *P* 14×15.

798 50 c. Type **261** 15 10
799 $1.10, "Road scene" 20 15
800 $5 "Children and house" 50 55
801 $10 "Cows grazing" .. .. .. 95 1·00
798/801 .. .. *Set of* 4 1·60 1·60

262 Indians threatening Ships

263 Compasses and Square Symbol

(Des Josephine Martin. Litho B.D.T.)

1991 (16 Dec). *500th Anniv of Discovery of America by Columbus* (1992) (*3rd issue*). *T* **262** *and similar horiz designs. Multicoloured. W* **111** (*sideways*). *P* 13½.

802 50 c. Type **262** 10 10
803 $1.10, Spaniards setting dog on Indians .. 10 15
804 $1.40, Indian with gift of pineapple .. 10 15
805 $25 Columbus describes Jamaica with crumpled paper .. .. .. 1·75 1·90
802/5 .. .. *Set of* 4 1·90 2·10
MS806 125×102 mm. Nos. 802/5 (*sold at* $28.20) 2·00 2·10
MS807 210×150 mm. Nos. 802/5. Imperf .. 2·00 2·10

(Litho Cartor)

1992 (1 May). *250th Anniv of First Provisional Grand Master of English Freemasonry in Jamaica. T* **263** *and similar vert designs. Multicoloured. W* **111**. *P* 13½.

808 50 c. Type **263** 10 10
809 $1.10, Symbol in stained glass window .. 10 10
810 $1.40, Compasses and square on book .. 10 10
811 $25 Eye in triangle symbol .. .. 1·75 2·00
808/11 .. .. *Set of* 4 1·75 1·90
MS812 140×80 mm. Nos. 808/11 (*sold at* $28.50) 2·00 2·10

POSTAL FISCALS

Revenue stamps were authorised for postal use by Post Office notice of 12 October 1887.

CONDITION. The note at the beginning also applies to Nos. F1/6.

F 1

(Typo D.L.R.)

1865–71 (Issued). *P* 14. (*a*) *Wmk Pineapple* (*T* **7**).

F1 **F 1** 1d. rose (1865) .. .. 70·00 90·00
a. Imperf (pair) £400

(*b*) *Wmk Crown CC*

F2 **F 1** 1d. rose (1868) .. .. 50·00 50·00

(*c*) *Wmk CA over Crown* (*Type* w **7** *sideways, covering two stamps*)

F3 **F 1** 1d. rose (1870 or 1871) .. .. .. 17·00 7·00
a. Imperf .. ..

F 2

F 3

(Typo D.L.R.)

1855–74 (Issued). *Glazed paper. P* 14. (*a*) *No wmk.*

F4 **F 2** 1½d. blue/*blue* (1857) .. .. .. 45·00 45·00
a. Imperf (1855) .. .. ..
b. Blue on white .. .. .. 50·00 55·00
F5 3d. purple/*blue* (1857) .. .. .. 42·00 50·00
a. Imperf (1855) .. .. ..
b. Purple on lilac (1857) .. .. 42·00 50·00
ba. Imperf (1855) .. .. ..
c. Purple on white (1857) .. .. 50·00 50·00

(*b*) *Wmk Crown CC*

F6 **F 2** 3d. purple/*lilac* (1874) .. .. .. 8·50 13·00

All the above stamps *imperf* are exceedingly rare postally used.

1858 (1 Jan). (Issued). *No wmk. P* 15½ × 15.

F7 **F 3** 1s. rose/*bluish* .. .. 65·00 70·00
F8 5s. lilac/*bluish* £325 £375
F9 10s. green/*bluish* £375 £425

Telegraph stamps were also used postally, but no authority was given for such use.

OFFICIAL STAMPS

OFFICIAL **OFFICIAL**

(O 1) (O 2)

1890 (1 April). *No.* 16 *optd with Type* O **1** *by C. Vendryes, Kingston.*

(*a*) "OFFICIAL" 17 *to* 17½ *mm long*

O1 **8** ½d. green .. .. 5·00 1·00
a. "O" omitted £450
b. One "I" omitted .. .. ..
c. Both "I"s omitted £500 £500
d. "L" omitted .. .. .. — £550
e. Opt inverted .. .. .. 65·00 70·00
f. Opt double .. .. .. 65·00 70·00
g. Opt. double, one inverted £325 £325
h. Opt double, one vertical £550
j. Pair, overprints *tête-bêche* .. ..

(*b*) "OFFICIAL" 15 *to* 16 *mm long*

O2 **8** ½d. green .. .. 22·00 22·00
a. Opt double £500

There were four (or possibly five) settings of this overprint, all but one being of the longer type. There are numerous minor varieties, due to broken type, etc. (*e.g.* a broken "E" used for "F").

Stamps with the 17–17½ mm opt were reissued in 1894 during a temporary shortage of No. O3.

1890–1. *Optd with Type* O **2** *by D.L.R. Wmk Crown CA. P* 14.

O3 **8** ½d. green (1891) .. .. .. 3·25 15
O4 **11** 1d. rose (1.4.90) .. .. .. 3·25 40
O5 2d. grey (1.4.90) .. .. .. 3·75 1·00
O3/5 .. .. *Set of* 3 9·25 1·40
O3/5 Optd "Specimen" .. .. *Set of* 3 £100

PRICES OF SETS

Set prices are given for many issues, generally those containing three stamps or more. Definitive sets include one of each value or major colour change, but do not cover different perforations, die types or minor shades. Where a choice is possible the set prices are based on the cheapest versions of the stamps included in the listings.

Jordan *see* Transjordan

Kenya

INDEPENDENT

1 Cattle Ranching

2 Wood-carving

3 National Assembly

(Des V. Whiteley. Photo Harrison)

1963 (12 Dec). *Independence. T* **1/3** *and similar designs. P* 14 × 15 *(small designs) or* 14½ *(others).*

1	5 c. brown, deep blue, green and bistre	10	30
2	10 c. brown	10	10
3	15 c. magenta	45	10
4	20 c. black and yellow-green	15	10
5	30 c. black and yellow	15	10
6	40 c. brown and light blue	15	20
7	50 c. crimson, black and green	15	10
8	65 c. deep turquoise-green and yellow	55	65
9	1 s. multicoloured	20	10
10	1 s. 30, brown, black and yellow-green	1·75	10
11	2 s. multicoloured	50	30
12	5 s. brown, ultramarine and yellow-green	1·25	40
13	10 s. brown and deep blue	6·50	1·75
14	20 s. black and rose	5·50	4·50
1/14	*Set of* 14	16·00	7·50

Designs: *As T* 1/2—15 c. Heavy industry; 20 c. Timber industry; 30 c. Jomo Kenyatta and Mt Kenya; 40 c. Fishing industry; 50 c. Kenya flag; 65 c. Pyrethrum industry. *As T* 3—1 s. 30, Tourism (Treetops Hotel); 2 s. Coffee industry; 5 s. Tea industry; 10 s. Mombasa Port; 20 s. Royal College, Nairobi.

The 10 c. was produced in coils of 1000 in addition to normal sheets.

REPUBLIC

4 Cockerel

(Des M. Goaman. Photo J. Enschedé)

1964 (12 Dec). *Inauguration of Republic T* **4** *and similar vert designs. Multicoloured. P* 13 × 12½.

15	15 c. Type **4**	20	15
16	30 c. President Kenyatta	25	10
17	50 c. Lion	35	10
18	1 s. 30, Hartlaub's Turaco	2·50	50
19	2 s. 50, Nandi flame	2·00	3·75
15/19	*Set of* 5	4·50	4·00

5 Thomson's Gazelle

6 Sable Antelope

7 Greater Kudu

(Des Rena Fennessy. Photo Harrison)

1966 (12 Dec)–**71**. *Various designs as T* **5/7**. *Chalk-surfaced paper. P* 14 × 14½ *(5 c. to 70 c.) or* 14½ *(others).*

20	5 c. orange, black and sepia	15	20
21	10 c. black and apple-green	10	10
	a. Glazed, ordinary paper (13.7.71)	70	1·00
22	15 c. black and orange	10	10
	a. Glazed, ordinary paper (13.7.71)	70	80
23	20 c. ochre, black and blue	10	15
	a. Glazed, ordinary paper (22.1.71)	1·00	1·25
24	30 c. Prussian blue, blue and black	10	10
25	40 c. black and yellow-brown	40	30
	a. Glazed, ordinary paper (19.2.71)	1·00	1·25
26	50 c. black and red-orange	40	10
	a. Glazed, ordinary paper (19.2.71)	9·00	1·50
27	65 c. black and light green	1·25	2·00
28	70 c. black and claret (15.9.69)	2·25	1·25
	a. Glazed, ordinary paper (19.2.71)	10·00	8·00
29	1 s. olive-brown, black and slate-blue	20	10
	a. Glazed, ordinary paper (22.1.71)	1·25	70
30	1 s. 30, indigo, light olive-green and black	2·50	20
31	1 s. 50, black, orange-brown and dull sage-green (15.9.69)	2·00	2·00
	a. Glazed, ordinary paper (22.1.71)	4·00	6·00
32	2 s. 50, yellow, black and olive-brown	2·50	1·25
	a. Glazed, ordinary paper (22.1.71)	4·00	6·50
33	5 s. yellow, black and emerald	1·00	70
	a. Glazed, ordinary paper (22.1.71)	4·00	7·00
34	10 s. yellow-ochre, black and red-brown	2·50	2·00
35	20 s. yellow-ochre, yellow-orange, blk & gold	7·50	8·50
20/35	*Set of* 16	21·00	16·00
21a/33a	*Set of* 10	32·00	30·00

Designs: *As T* 5/6—15 c. Aardvark ("Ant Bear"); 20 c. Lesser Bushbaby; 30 c. Warthog; 40 c. Common Zebra; 50 c. African Buffalo; 65 c. Black Rhinoceros; 70 c. Ostrich. *As T* 7—1 s. 30, African Elephant; 1 s. 50, Bat-eared Fox; 2 s. 50, Cheetah; 5 s. Savanna Monkey ("Vervet Monkey"); 10 s. Giant Ground Pangolin; 20 s. Lion.

On chalk-surfaced paper, all values except 30 c., 50 c. and 2 s. 50 exist with PVA gum as well as gum arabic but the 70 c. and 1 s. 50 exist with PVA gum only. The stamps on glazed, ordinary paper exist with PVA gum only.

Nos. 21 and 26 exist in coils constructed from normal sheets.

8 Rose Dawn

9 Rock Shell

2/-

(10)

50 c. A. Inscr "*Janthina globosa*".
B. Inscr "*Janthina janthina*".

70 c. C. Inscr "*Nautilus pompileus*".
D. Inscr "*Nautilus pompilius*".

(Des Rena Fennessy. Photo Harrison)

1971 (15 Dec)–**74**. *T* **8/9** *and similar vert designs showing sea-shells. Multicoloured. (a) Size as T* **8**. *P* 14½ × 14.

36	5 c. Type **8**	10	30
37	10 c. Bishop's Cap (yellow-green background)	10	10
	a. Olive-green background (21.1.74)	40	10
38	15 c. Strawberry Shell	15	10
39	20 c. Black Prince	15	10
40	30 c. Mermaid's Ear	20	10
41	40 c. Top Shell	20	10
42	50 c. Violet Shell (A)	30	10
43	50 c. Violet Shell (B) (21.1.74)	8·50	1·25
44	60 c. Cameo	30	45
45	70 c. Pearly Nautilus (C)	45	1·50
46	70 c. Pearly Nautilus (D) (21.1.74)	8·50	4·50
	(b) Size as T **9**. *P* 14		
47	1 s. Type **9** (yellow-buff background)	30	10
	a. Buff background (21.1.74)	20	10
48	1 s. 50, Triton	60	10
49	2 s. 50, Neptune's Trumpet	80	10
50	5 s. Turban Shell (pale ol-yell background)	1·25	10
	a. Pale olive-bistre background (13.6.73)	1·00	10
51	10 s. Cloth of Gold	3·25	15
52	20 s. Spider Shell (grey background)	6·00	75
	a. Bluish slate background (12.9.73)	3·75	35
36/52	*Set of* 17	25·00	8·00

1975 (17 Nov). *Nos. 48/9 and 52 surch as T* **10**.

53	2 s. on 1 s. 50, Triton	3·50	2·50
54	3 s. on 2 s. 50, Neptune's Trumpet	9·50	15·00
55	40 s. on 20 s. Spider Shell	6·00	11·00
53/5	*Set of* 3	16·00	26·00

The surcharge on No. 55 does not have a dot beneath the stroke following the face value.

For commemorative stamps, issued between 1964 and 1976, inscribed "UGANDA KENYA TANGANYIKA AND ZANZIBAR" (or "TANZANIA UGANDA KENYA") see under KENYA, UGANDA AND TANGANYIKA.

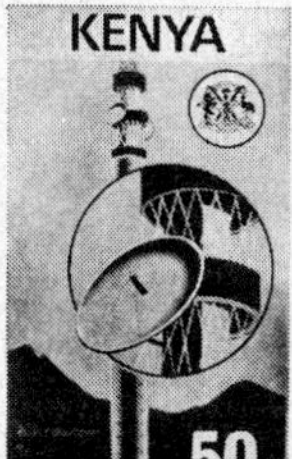

11 Microwave Tower

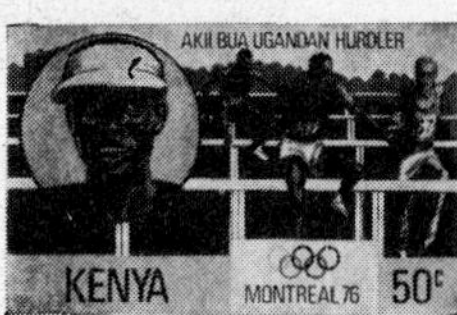

12 Akii Bua, Ugandan Hurdler

(Des H. Nickelsen. Litho Format)

1976 (15 Apr). *Telecommunications Development. T* **11** *and similar multicoloured designs. P* 14.

56	50 c. Type **11**	10	10
57	1 s. Cordless switchboard *(horiz)*	10	10
58	2 s. Telephones	20	30
59	3 s. Message Switching Centre *(horiz)*	25	45
56/9	*Set of* 4	55	75
MS60	120 × 120 mm. Nos. 56/9. Imperf	2·00	2·25

Nos. 56/7 and 59 exist imperforate from stock dispersed by the liquidator of Format International Security Printers Ltd.

(Des Beryl Moore. Litho Format)

1976 (7 July*). *Olympic Games, Montreal. T* **12** *and similar horiz designs. Multicoloured. P* 14½.

61	50 c. Type **12**	10	10
62	1 s. Filbert Bayi, Tanzanian runner	15	10
63	2 s. Steve Muchoki, Kenyan boxer	45	35
64	3 s. Olympic flame and East African flags	60	50
61/4	*Set of* 4	1·10	85
MS65	129 × 154 mm. Nos. 61/4. P 13	6·50	6·50

*This is the local date of issue; the Crown Agents released the stamps two days earlier.

Nos. 61 and 63 exist imperforate from stock dispersed by the liquidator of Format Internationl Security Printers Ltd.

13 Diesel Train, Tanzania–Zambia Railway

14 Nile Perch

(Des H. Moghul. Litho Format)

1976 (4 Oct). *Railway Transport. T* **13** *and similar horiz designs. Multicoloured. P* 14½.

66	50 c. Type **13**	35	10
67	1 s. Nile Bridge, Uganda	60	15
68	2 s. Nakuru Station, Kenya	2·25	1·25
69	3 s. Class "A" steam locomotive, 1896	2·50	1·75
66/9	*Set of* 4	5·00	3·00
MS70	154 × 103 mm. Nos. 66/9. P 13	8·00	8·00

Nos. 66/8 and **MS**70 exist imperforate from stock dispersed by the liquidator of Format International Security Printers Ltd.

(Des Adrienne Kennaway. Litho Format)

1977 (10 Jan). *Game Fish of East Africa. T* **14** *and similar vert designs. Multicoloured. P* 14*.

71	50 c. Type **14**	20	10
72	1 s. Tilapia	30	10
73	3 s. Sailfish	1·60	90
74	5 s. Black Marlin	1·90	1·25
71/4	*Set of* 4	3·50	2·00
MS75	153 × 129 mm. Nos. 71/4	9·00	4·00

*On No. **MS**75 the right-hand side of the 5 s. value is perforated 13½.

15 Maasai Manyatta (village), Kenya

(Des Rena Fennessy. Litho Questa)

1977 (15 Jan). *Second World Black and African Festival of Arts and Culture, Nigeria. T* **15** *and similar horiz designs. Multicoloured. P* 13½.

76	50 c. Type **15**	15	10
77	1 s. "Heartbeat of Africa" (Ugandan dancers)	25	10
78	2 s. Makonde sculpture, Tanzania	1·25	1·25
79	3 s. "Early Man and Technology" (skinning hippopotamus)	1·50	1·75
76/9	*Set of* 4	2·75	2·75
MS80	132 × 109 mm. Nos. 76/9	4·75	4·75

16 Rally-car and Villagers

(Litho Questa)

1977 (5 Apr). *25th Anniv of Safari Rally. T* **16** *and similar horiz designs. Multicoloured. P* 14.

81	50 c. Type **16**	20	10
82	1 s. President Kenyatta starting rally	30	10
83	2 s. Car fording river	70	1·00
84	5 s. Car and elephants	1·25	1·75
81/4	*Set of* 4	2·25	2·50
MS85	126 × 93 mm. Nos. 81/4	4·00	5·00

17 Canon Kivebulaya

(Des Beryl Moore. Litho Questa)

1977 (30 June). *Centenary of Ugandan Church. T* **17** *and similar horiz designs. Multicoloured. P* 14 × 13½.

86	50 c. Type **17**	10	10
87	1 s. Modern Namirembe Cathedral	10	10
88	2 s. The first Cathedral	30	45
89	5 s. Early congregation, Kigezi	50	85
86/9	*Set of* 4	85	1·25
MS90	126 × 94 mm. Nos. 86/9	1·75	3·00

18 Sagana Royal Lodge, Nyeri, 1952

(Des G. Vasarhelyi (50s.), J. Cooter (others). Litho Questa)

1977 (20 July). *Silver Jubilee. T* **18** *and similar multicoloured designs. P* 13½.

91	2 s. Type **18**	30	30
92	5 s. Treetops Hotel (*vert*)	65	65
93	10 s. Queen Elizabeth and President Kenyatta	90	1·25
94	15 s. Royal visit, 1972	1·25	1·75
91/4	*Set of* 4	2·75	3·50
MS95	Two sheets: (a) 140 × 60 mm, No. 94; (b) 152 × 127 mm, 50 s. Queen and Prince Philip in Treetops Hotel *Set of* 2	4·00	4·50

19 Pancake Tortoise

(Des Rena Fennessy. Litho Questa)

1977 (26 Sept). *Endangered Species. T* **19** *and similar horiz designs. Multicoloured. P* 14.

96	50 c. Type **19**	30	10
97	1 s. Nile Crocodile	40	10
98	2 s. Hunter's Hartebeest	1·40	75
99	3 s. Red Colobus	1·75	1·00
100	5 s. Dugong	2·00	1·50
96/100	*Set of* 5	5·25	3·00
MS101	127 × 101 mm. Nos. 97/100	7·00	8·00

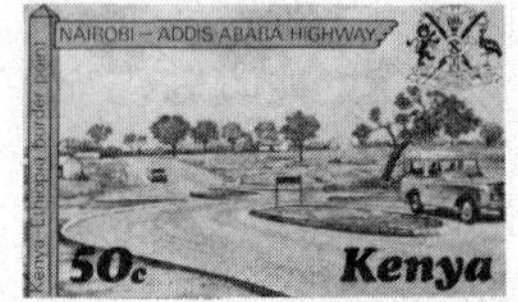

20 Kenya–Ethiopia Border Point

(Litho Questa)

1977 (10 Nov). *Nairobi–Addis Ababa Highway. T* **20** *and similar horiz designs. Multicoloured. P* 14.

102	50 c. Type **20**	15	10
103	1 s. Archer's Post	20	10
104	2 s. Thika Flyover	75	60
105	5 s. Marsabit Game Lodge	1·75	1·50
102/5	*Set of* 4	2·50	2·00
MS106	144 × 91 mm. Nos. 102/5	3·75	5·00

21 Gypsum **22** Amethyst

(Des Rena Fennessy. Photo Harrison)

1977 (10 Dec*). *Minerals. Multicoloured designs.*

(*a*) *Vert as T* **21.** *P* 14½ × 14

107	10 c. Type **21**	75	20
108	20 c. Trona	1·00	20
109	30 c. Kyanite	1·10	20
110	40 c. Amazonite	1·10	10
111	50 c. Galena	1·10	10
112	70 c. Silicified wood	1·40	30
113	80 c. Fluorite	1·40	30

(*b*) *Horiz as T* **22.** *P* 14

114	1 s. Type **22**	1·40	10
	a. Gold (face value and inscr) omitted		
115	1 s. 50, Agate	1·75	20
	a. Gold (face vaue and inscr) omitted		
116	2 s. Tourmaline	1·75	20
	a. Gold (face value and inscr) omitted		
117	3 s. Aquamarine	1·75	45
118	5 s. Rhodolite Garnet	1·75	80
119	10 s. Sapphire	2·00	1·75
120	20 s. Ruby	5·00	2·75
121	40 s. Green Grossular Garnet	11·00	12·00
107/21	*Set of* 15	30·00	17·00

*This is the local issue date. The stamps were released in London on 9 December.

23 Joe Kadenge (Kenya) and Forwards

(Des H. Moghul. Litho Questa)

1978 (10 Apr). *World Cup Football Championship, Argentina. T* **23** *and similar horiz designs showing footballers. Multicoloured. P* 14 × 13½.

122	50 c. Type **23**	10	10
123	1 s. Mohamed Chuma (Tanzania) and Cup presentation	10	10
124	2 s. Omari Kidevu (Zanzibar) and goalmouth scene	40	60
125	3 s. Polly Ouma (Uganda) and three forwards	50	85
122/5	*Set of* 4	1·00	1·40
MS126	136 × 81 mm. Nos. 122/5	2·75	3·00

24 Boxing

(Des H. Moghul. Photo Heraclio Fournier)

1978 (17 July). *Commonwealth Games, Edmonton. T* **24** *and similar horiz designs. Multicoloured. P* 13 × 14.

127	50 c. Type **24**	15	10
128	1 s. Welcoming Olympic Games Team, 1968	20	10
129	3 s. Javelin throwing	60	80
130	5 s. President Kenyatta admiring boxer's trophy	75	1·25
127/30	*Set of* 4	1·50	2·00

25 "Overloading is Dangerous"

(Litho Walsall)

1978 (18 Sept). *Road Safety. T* **25** *and similar horiz designs. Multicoloured. P* 13½.

131	50 c. Type **25**	35	10
132	1 s. "Speed does not pay"	50	20
133	1 s. 50, "Ignoring Traffic Signs may cause death"	65	40
134	2 s. "Slow down at School Crossing"	90	80
135	3 s. "Never cross a continuous line"	1·10	1·25
136	5 s. "Approach Railway Level Crossing with extreme caution"	1·75	2·00
131/6	*Set of* 6	4·75	4·25

26 President Kenyatta at Mass Rally, 1963 **27** Freedom Fighters, Namibia

(Des Beryl Moore. Litho J.W.)

1978 (16 Oct). *Kenyatta Day. T* **26** *and similar horiz designs. Multicoloured. P* 14.

137	50 c. "Harambee Water Project"	15	10
138	1 s. Handing over of Independence Instruments, 1963	25	10
139	2 s. Type **26**	45	30
140	3 s. "Harambee, 15 Great Years"	70	55
141	5 s. "Struggle for Independence, 1952"	90	80
137/41	*Set of* 5	2·25	1·60

(Des L. Curtis. Litho Questa)

1978 (11 Dec*). *International Anti-Apartheid Year. T* **27** *and similar horiz designs. P* 14 × 14½.

142	50 c. multicoloured	20	10
143	1 s. black and cobalt	25	10
144	2 s. multicoloured	60	30
145	3 s. multicoloured	80	55
146	5 s. multicoloured	90	80
142/6	*Set of* 5	2·50	1·60

Designs:—1 s. International seminar on apartheid, racial discrimination and colonialism in South Africa; 2 s. Steve Biko's tombstone; 3 s. Nelson Mandela; 5 s. Bishop Lamont.

*This is the local date of issue; the Crown Agents released the stamps the previous day.

28 Children Playing

(Des Beryl Moore. Litho Walsall)

1979 (5 Feb). *International Year of the Child. T* **28** *and similar horiz designs. Multicoloured. P* 13½ × 14.

147	50 c. Type **28**	15	10
148	2 s. Child fishing	40	40
149	3 s. Children singing and dancing	60	60
150	5 s. Children working with camels	85	85
147/50	*Set of* 4	1·75	1·75

29 "The Lion and the Jewel" **30** Blind Telephone Operator

(Des Beryl Moore. Litho Enschedé)

1979 (6 Apr). *Kenya National Theatre. T* **29** *and similar horiz designs. Multicoloured. P* 13 × 13½.

151	50 c. Type **29**	15	10
152	1 s. Scene from "Utisi"	20	10
153	2 s. "Entertainment past and present" (programmes from past productions)	35	30
154	3 s. Kenya National Theatre	50	45
155	5 s. Nairobi City Players production of "Genesis"	90	75
151/5	*Set of* 5	1·90	1·50

(Litho Harrison)

1979 (29 June*). *50th Anniv of Salvation Army Social Services. T* **30** *and similar multicoloured designs. P* 13½ × 13 (50 c., 1s.) *or* 13 × 13½ (*others*).

156	50 c. Type **30**	30	10
157	1 s. Care for the Aged	30	10
158	3 s. Village polytechnic (*horiz*)	85	70
159	5 s. Vocational training (*horiz*)	1·10	1·10
156/9	*Set of* 4	2·25	1·75

*This is the local date of issue; the Crown Agents released the stamps on 4 June.

MINIMUM PRICE

The minimum price quote is 10p which represents a handling charge rather than a basis for valuing common stamps. For further notes about prices see introductory pages.

31 "Father of the Nation" (Kenyatta's funeral procession)   32 British East Africa Company 1890 1 a. Stamp

(Des H. Moghul. Litho Questa)

1979 (21 Aug*). *1st Death Anniv of President Kenyatta. T* **31** *and similar vert designs. Multicoloured. P* 13½ × 14.
160 50 c. Type **31** 10 10
161 1 s. "First President of Kenya" (Kenyatta receiving independence) 15 10
162 3 s. "Kenyatta the politician" (speaking at rally) 35 45
163 5 s. "A true son of Kenya" (Kenyatta as a boy carpenter) 60 85
160/3 .. .. *Set of* 4 1·00 1·25
*This is the local date of issue; the Crown Agents did not release the stamps until 29 August.

(Des J.W. Litho Harrison)

1979 (27 Nov). *Death Centenary of Sir Rowland Hill. T* **32** *and similar vert designs showing stamps. P* 14 × 14½.
164 50 c. multicoloured 15 10
165 1 s. multicoloured 15 10
166 2 s. black, magenta and yellow-ochre 30 40
167 5 s. multicoloured .. .. 60 1·00
164/7 .. .. *Set of* 4 1·10 1·40
Designs:—1 s. Kenya, Uganda and Tanganyika 1935 1 s.; 2 s. Penny Black; 5 s. 1964 Inauguration of Republic 2 s. 50, commemorative.

33 Roads, Globe and Conference Emblem

(Des H. Moghul. Litho Questa)

1980 (10 Jan). *I.R.F. (International Road Federation) African Highway Conference, Nairobi. T* **33** *and similar horiz designs. Multicoloured. P* 14 × 13½.
168 50 c. Type **33** 10 10
169 1 s. New weighbridge, Athi River 15 10
170 3 s. New Nyali Bridge, Mombasa 40 75
171 5 s. Highway to Jomo Kenyatta International Airport .. .. 70 1·25
168/71 .. .. *Set of* 4 1·25 2·00

34 Mobile Unit in action, Masailand   35 Statue of Sir Rowland Hill

(Des Beryl Moore. Litho Questa)

1980 (20 Mar). *Flying Doctor Service. T* **34** *and similar multi-coloured designs. P* 14½.
172 50 c. Type **34** 10 10
173 1 s. Donkey transport to Turkana airstrip (*vert*) 15 10
174 3 s. Surgical team in action at outstation (*vert*) 50 90
175 5 s. Emergency airlift from North Eastern Province .. .. 80 1·40
172/5 .. .. *Set of* 4 1·40 2·25
MS176 146 × 133 mm. Nos. 172/5 .. .. .. 1·50 2·50

(Des J.W. Litho Questa)

1980 (6 May). *"London 1980" International Stamp Exhibition. P* 14.
177 **35** 25 s. multicoloured .. .. .. 1·50 2·50
MS178 114×101 mm. No. 177 .. .. .. 1·60 2·75

36 Pope John Paul II   37 *Taeniura lymma*

(Des Sister Frances Randal. Litho Italian Govt Ptg Works, Rome)

1980 (8 May). *Papal Visit. T* **36** *and similar multicoloured designs. P* 13.
179 50 c. Type **36** 30 10
180 1 s. Pope John Paul II, cathedral and coat of arms (*vert*) 40 10
181 5 s. Pope John Paul II, Papal and Kenyan flags on dove symbol (*vert*) 85 70
182 10 s. President Moi, Pope John Paul II and map of Africa .. .. 1·40 1·40
179/82 .. .. *Set of* 4 2·75 2·00

(Des Adrienne Kennaway. Litho Harrison)

1980 (27 June). *Marine Life. T* **37** *and similar vert designs. Multicoloured. P* 14.
183 50 c. Type **37** 20 10
184 2 s. *Amphiprion allardi* 65 50
185 3 s. *Chromodoris quadricolor* 80 80
186 5 s. *Eretmochelys imbricata* .. .. .. 1·25 1·25
183/6 .. .. *Set of* 4 2·50 2·40

38 National Archives

(Des A. Odhuno; adapted L. Curtis. Litho Questa)

1980 (9 Oct). *Historic Buildings. T* **38** *and similar horiz designs. Multicoloured. P* 14.
187 50 c. Type **38** 10 10
188 1 s. Provincial Commissioner's Office, Nairobi 15 10
189 1 s. 50, Nairobi House 20 20
190 2 s. Norfolk Hotel 25 50
191 3 s. McMillan Library 35 65
192 5 s. Kipande House .. .. 55 1·00
187/92 .. .. *Set of* 6 1·40 2·25

39 "Disabled Enjoys Affection"

(Des H. Moghul. Litho Enschedé)

1981 (10 Feb). *International Year for Disabled Persons. T* **39** *and similar horiz designs. Multicoloured. P* 14 × 13.
193 50 c. Type **39** 15 10
194 1 s. President Moi presenting Kenyan flag to Disabled Olympic Games team captain 20 10
195 3 s. Blind people climbing Mount Kenya, 1975 .. .. 55 65
196 5 s. Disabled artist at work .. .. 85 1·00
193/6 .. .. *Set of* 4 1·60 1·60

40 Longonot Complex

(Des H. Moghul. Litho Harrison)

1981 (15 Apr). *Satellite Communications. T* **40** *and similar horiz designs. Multicoloured. P* 14 × 14½.
197 50 c. Type **40** 15 10
198 2 s. "Intelsat V" 50 35
199 3 s. "Longonot I" 60 55
200 5 s. "Longonot II" 85 85
197/200 .. .. *Set of* 4 1·90 1·60

41 Kenyatta Conference Centre   42 St. Paul's Cathedral

(Des L. Curtis. Litho Questa (**MS**206) or J.W. (others))

1981 (17 June*). *O.A.U. (Organisation of African Unity) Summit Conference, Nairobi. T* **41** *and similar horiz designs in black, bistre-yellow and new blue* (1s.) *or multicoloured (others). P* 13½.
201 50 c. Type **41** 15 10
202 1 s. "Panaftel" earth stations 20 10
203 3 s. Parliament Building 40 40
204 5 s. Jomo Kenyatta International Airport .. 65 65
205 10 s. O.A.U. flag .. .. 1·00 1·00
201/5 .. .. *Set of* 5 2·25 2·00
MS206 110 × 110 mm. No. 205. P 14½ × 14 .. 1·10 1·50
*This is the local date of issue; the Crown Agents did not release the stamps until 24 June.

(Des A. Theobald. Litho Questa)

1981 (29 July). *Royal Wedding. T* **42** *and similar vert designs. Multicoloured. P* 14.
207 50 c. Prince Charles and President Daniel Arap Moi 15 10
208 3 s. Type **42** 25 20
209 5 s. Royal Yacht *Britannia* 40 35
210 10 s. Prince Charles on safari in Kenya 55 70
207/10 .. .. *Set of* 4 1·25 1·25
MS211 85×102 mm. 25 s. Prince Charles and Lady Diana Spencer .. .. 1·40 1·60
Nos. 207/10 also exist perforated 12 (*price for set of* 4 £1.75 *mint or used*) from additional sheetlets of five stamps and one label.
Insufficient supplies of No. **MS**211 were received by 29 July for a full distribution, but subsequently the miniature sheet was freely available.

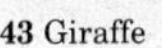

43 Giraffe   44 "Technical Development"

(Des Rena Fennessy. Litho Questa)

1981 (31 Aug). *Rare Animals. T* **43** *and similar vert designs. Multicoloured. P* 14½.
212 50 c. Type **43** 15 10
213 2 s. Bongo 35 20
214 5 s. Roan Antelope 70 55
215 10 s. Agile Mangabey .. .. 1·25 1·10
212/15 .. .. *Set of* 4 2·25 1·75

(Des H. Moghul, adapted L. Curtis. Litho Questa)

1981 (16 Oct). *World Food Day. T* **44** *and similar vert designs. Multicoloured. P* 14.
216 50 c. Type **44** 10 10
217 1 s. "Mwea rice projects" 15 10
218 2 s. "Irrigation schemes" 30 25
219 5 s. "Breeding livestock" 60 70
216/19 .. .. *Set of* 4 1·00 90

45 Kamba   46 *Australopithecus boisei*

(Des Adrienne Kennaway. Litho Harrison)

1981 (18 Dec). *Ceremonial Costumes (1st series). T* **45** *and similar vert designs. Multicoloured. P* 14½ × 13½.
220 50 c. Type **45** 25 10
221 1 s. Turkana 30 10
222 2 s. Giriama 65 25
223 3 s. Masai 90 40
224 5 s. Luo .. .. 1·25 85
220/4 .. .. *Set of* 5 3·00 1·40
See also Nos. 329/33, 413/17 and 515/19.

(Des Adrienne Kennaway. Litho Format)

1982 (19 Jan). *"Origins of Mankind". Skulls. T* **46** *and similar horiz designs. Multicoloured. P* 13½ × 14.

225	50 c. Type **46**	65	10
226	2 s. *Homo erectus*	1·50	55
227	3 s. *Homo habilis*	1·90	1·25
228	5 s. *Proconsul africanus*	2·75	2·50
225/8	*Set of* 4	6·25	4·00

47 Tree-planting

(Des L. Curtis. Litho Harrison)

1982 (9 June). *75th Anniv of Boy Scout Movement (Nos.* 229, 231, 233 *and* 235) *and 60th Anniv of Girl Guide Movement (Nos.* 230, 232, 234 *and* 236). *T* **47** *and similar horiz designs. Multicoloured. P* 14½.

229	70 c. Type **47**	40	30
	a. Horiz pair. Nos. 229/30	80	60
230	70 c. Paying homage	40	30
231	3 s. 50, "Be Prepared"	90	70
	a. Horiz pair. Nos. 231/2	1·75	1·40
232	3 s. 50, "International Friendship"	90	70
233	5 s. Helping disabled	1·10	1·25
	a. Horiz pair. Nos. 233/4	2·10	2·50
234	5 s. Community service	1·10	1·25
235	6 s. 50, Paxtu Cottage (Lord Baden-Powell's home)	1·50	1·75
	a. Horiz pair. Nos. 235/6	3·00	3·50
236	6 s. 50, Lady Baden-Powell	1·50	1·75
229/36	*Set of* 8	7·00	7·25
MS237	112 × 112 mm. Nos. 229, 231, 233 and 235	3·00	3·00

The two designs of each value were printed together, *se-tenant*, in horizontal pairs throughout the sheet.

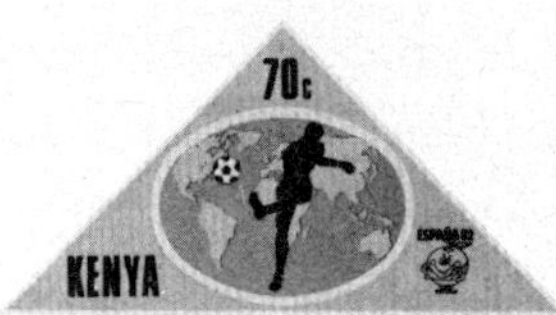

48 Footballer displaying Shooting Skill

(Des local artist. Litho Harrison)

1982 (5 July). *World Cup Football Championships, Spain. T* **48** *and similar triangular designs showing footballers silhouetted against world map. Multicoloured. P* 12½.

238	70 c. Type **48**	75	30
239	3 s. 50, Heading	1·40	1·25
240	5 s. Goalkeeping	2·00	2·00
241	10 s. Dribbling	3·00	3·25
238/41	*Set of* 4	6·50	6·25
MS242	101 × 76 mm. 20 s. Tackling. P 13 × 14	3·50	3·50

49 Cattle Judging — **50** Micro-wave Radio System — (51)

(Des H. Moghul. Litho Harrison)

1982 (28 Sept). *80th Anniv of Agricultural Society of Kenya. T* **49** *and similar vert designs. Multicoloured. P* 14½.

243	70 c. Type **49**	50	10
244	2 s. 50, Farm machinery	1·25	1·00
245	3 s. 50, Musical ride	1·50	1·50
246	6 s. 50, Agricultural Society emblem	2·00	2·25
243/6	*Set of* 4	4·75	4·25

(Des H. Moghul. Photo Courvoisier)

1982 (21 Oct). *I.T.U. Plenipotentiary Conference, Nairobi. T* **50** *and similar vert designs. Multicoloured. P* 11½.

247	70 c. Type **50**	40	10
248	3 s. 50, Sea-to-shore service link	1·00	1·25
249	5 s. Rural telecommunications system	1·50	2·00
250	6 s. 50, I.T.U. emblem	1·90	2·50
247/50	*Set of* 4	4·25	5·25

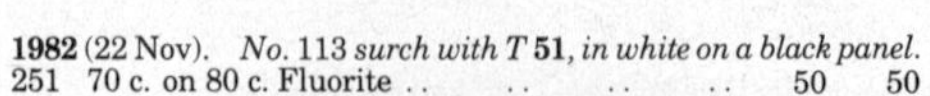

1982 (22 Nov). *No.* 113 *surch with T* **51**, *in white on a black panel.*

251	70 c. on 80 c. Fluorite	50	50

52 Container Cranes

(Des R. Vigurs. Litho Questa)

1983 (20 Jan). *5th Anniv of Kenya Ports Authority. T* **52** *and similar horiz designs. P* 14.

252	70 c. Type **52**	50	10
253	2 s. Port by night	1·25	1·00
254	3 s. 50, Container cranes (*different*)	1·75	1·75
255	5 s. Map of Mombasa Port	2·00	2·50
252/5	*Set of* 4	5·00	4·75
MS256	125 × 85 mm. Nos. 252/5	5·00	6·00

53 Shada Zambarau — **54** Waridi Kikuba

(Des Rena Fennessy. Photo Harrison)

1983 (15 Feb)–**85**. *Flowers. Multicoloured.*

(*a*) *Vert designs as T* **53**. *P* 14½ × 14

257	10 c. Type **53**	30	15
258	20 c. Kilua Kingulima	45	15
259	30 c. Mwalika Mwiya	45	15
260	40 c. Ziyungi Buluu	45	15
261	50 c. Kilua Habashia	45	15
262	70 c. Chanuo Kato	50	15
262*a*	80 c. As 40 c. (7.8.85)	1·50	30
262*b*	1 s. Waridi Kikuba (5.8.85*)	1·50	30

(*b*) *Vert designs as T* **54**. *P* 14

263	1 s. Type **54**	45	15
264	1 s. 50, Mshomoro Mtambazi	65	30
265	2 s. Papatuo Boti	65	30
266	2 s. 50, Tumba Mboni	1·00	30
266*a*	3 s. Mkuku Mrembo (12.8.85)	2·25	1·00
267	3 s. 50, Mtongo Mbeja	1·00	70
	a. Gold (inscr and face value) omitted		
267*b*	4 s. Mnukia Muuma (7.8.85)	2·25	2·00
268	5 s. Nyungu Chepuo	1·00	60
268*a*	7 s. Mlua Miba (7.8.85)	2·75	3·00
269	10 s. Muafunili	1·50	1·75
270	20 s. Mbake Nyanza	2·25	2·50
271	40 s. Njuga Pagwa	4·00	6·00
257/71	*Set of* 20	23·00	18·00

*Earliest known postmark date.

55 Coffee Plucking — **56** Examining Parcels

(Des C. Fernandes. Litho Harrison)

1983 (14 Mar). *Commonwealth Day. T* **55** *and similar multicoloured designs. P* 14 × 14½ (70 c., 2 s.) *or* 14½ × 14 (*others*).

272	70 c. Type **55**	10	10
273	2 s. President Daniel Arap Moi	15	20
274	5 s. Satellite view of Earth (*horiz*)	45	45
275	10 s. Masai dance (*horiz*)	90	1·00
272/5	*Set of* 4	1·40	1·50

(Des H. Moghul. Litho Harrison)

1983 (11 May). *30th Anniv of Customs Co-operation Council. T* **56** *and similar vert designs. Multicoloured. P* 14.

276	70 c. Type **56**	15	10
277	2 s. 50, Customs Headquarters, Mombasa	35	25
278	3 s. 50, Customs Council Headquarters, Brussels	45	35
279	10 s. Customs patrol boat	1·40	1·40
276/9	*Set of* 4	2·10	1·90

57 Communications via Satellite — **58** Ships in Kilindini Harbour

(Litho Harrison)

1983 (4 July). *World Communications Year. T* **57** *and similar multicoloured designs. P* 14 × 14½ (70 c., 2 s. 50) *or* 14½ × 14 (*others*).

280	70 c. Type **57**	45	10
281	2 s. 50, "Telephone and Postal Services"	1·00	1·00
282	3 s. 50, Communications by sea and air (*horiz*)	1·40	1·60
283	5 s. Road and rail communications (*horiz*)	1·75	2·00
280/3	*Set of* 4	4·25	4·25

(Litho Harrison)

1983 (22 Sept). *25th Anniv of Intergovernmental Maritime Organization. T* **58** *and similar horiz designs. Multicoloured. P* 14.

284	70 c. Type **58**	65	10
285	2 s. 50, Life-saving devices	1·25	1·00
286	3 s. 50, Mombasa container terminal	1·75	1·40
287	10 s. Marine park	2·50	2·75
284/7	*Set of* 4	5·50	4·75

59 President Moi signing Visitors' Book

(Litho Harrison)

1983 (31 Oct). *29th Commonwealth Parliamentary Conference. T* **59** *and similar multicoloured designs. P* 14.

288	70 c. Type **59**	20	10
289	2 s. 50, Parliament building, Nairobi (*vert*)	45	35
290	5 s. State opening of Parliament (*vert*)	85	60
288/90	*Set of* 3	1·40	90
MS291	122 × 141 mm. Nos. 288/90	1·50	2·25

60 Kenyan and British Flags

(Des A. Theobald. Litho Harrison)

1983 (10 Nov). *Royal Visit. T* **60** *and similar horiz designs. Multicoloured. P* 14.

292	70 c. Type **60**	40	10
293	3 s. 50, Sagana State Lodge	1·25	45
294	5 s. Treetops Hotel	1·75	80
295	10 s. Queen Elizabeth II and President Moi	2·75	2·50
292/5	*Set of* 4	5·50	3·50
MS296	126 × 100 mm. 25 s. Designs as Nos. 292/5, but without face values. Imperf	2·50	3·50

61 President Moi — **62** White-backed Night Heron

(Des and litho Harrison)

1983 (9 Dec). *20th Anniv of Independence. T* **61** *and similar horiz designs. Multicoloured. P* 14½.

297	70 c. Type **61**	10	10
298	2 s. President Moi planting tree	20	20
299	3 s. 50, Kenyan flag and emblem	35	35
300	5 s. School milk scheme	50	50
301	10 s. People of Kenya	1·00	1·10
297/301	*Set of* 5	1·90	2·00
MS302	126 × 93 mm. 25 s. Designs as Nos. 297 and 299/301, but without face values. Imperf	1·75	2·75

(Des Agnes Odero. Litho Harrison)

1984 (6 Feb). *Rare Birds of Kenya. T* **62** *and similar vert designs. Multicoloured. P* 14½ × 13½.

303	70 c. Type **62**	90	20
304	2 s. 50, Quail Plover	1·50	1·40
305	3 s. 50, Taita Olive Thrush	1·75	1·60
306	5 s. Mufumbiri Shrike ("Yellow Gonolek")	2·00	2·00
307	10 s. White-winged Apalis	2·75	3·50
303/7	*Set of* 5	8·00	8·00

NEW INFORMATION

The editor is always interested to correspond with people who have new information that will improve or correct the Catalogue.

63 Radar Tower

64 Running

(Des C. Fernandes. Litho Harrison)

1984 (2 Apr). *40th Anniv of International Civil Aviation Organization. T* **63** *and similar multicoloured designs. P* 14.
308 70 c. Type **63** 10 10
309 2 s. 50, Kenya School of Aviation (*horiz*) .. 30 30
310 3 s. 50, Aircraft taking off from Moi airport (*horiz*) 40 45
311 5 s. Air traffic control centre 55 60
308/11 .. .. *Set of* 4 1·25 1·25

(Des and litho Harrison)

1984 (21 May). *Olympic Games, Los Angeles. T* **64** *and similar horiz designs. P* 14½.
312 70 c. black, bright yellow-green and bronze-green 20 10
313 2 s. 50, black, bright magenta and reddish violet 45 25
314 5 s. black, pale turquoise-blue and steel blue 90 55
315 10 s. black, bistre-yellow and brown .. .. 1·75 1·25
312/15 .. .. *Set of* 4 3·00 1·90
MS316 130 × 121 mm. 25 s. Designs as Nos. 312/15 but without face values. Imperf .. .. 2·50 3·00
Designs:—2 s. 50, Hurdling; 5 s. Boxing; 10 s. Hockey.

65 Conference and Kenya Library Association Logos

66 Doves and Cross

(Des and litho Harrison)

1984 (28 June). *50th Conference of the International Federation of Library Associations. T* **65** *and similar horiz designs. Multicoloured. P* 14½.
317 70 c. Type **65** 10 10
318 3 s. 50, Mobile library 40 50
319 5 s. Adult library 55 70
320 10 s. Children's library .. .. 1·00 1·50
317/20 .. .. *Set of* 4 1·75 2·50

(Des K. Bisley. Litho Harrison)

1984 (23 Aug). *4th World Conference on Religion and Peace. T* **66** *and similar vert designs, each showing a different central symbol. Multicoloured. P* 14½.
321 70 c. Type **66** 30 10
322 2 s. 50, Arabic inscription .. .. 80 1·00
323 3 s. 50, Peace emblem .. .. 1·10 1·25
324 6 s. 50, Star and Crescent .. .. 1·60 2·00
321/4 .. .. *Set of* 4 3·50 3·75

67 Export Year Logo

68 Knight and Nyayo National Stadium

(Litho Harrison)

1984 (1 Oct). *Kenya Export Year. T* **67** *and similar multicoloured designs. P* 14½.
325 70 c. Type **67** 30 10
326 3 s. 50, Forklift truck with air cargo (*horiz*) 1·25 1·25
327 5 s. Loading ship's cargo .. .. 1·75 1·75
328 10 s. Kenyan products (*horiz*) .. .. .. 2·50 3·25
325/8 .. .. *Set of* 4 5·25 5·75

(Litho Harrison)

1984 (5 Nov). *Ceremonial Costumes (2nd series). Vert designs as T* **45**. *Multicoloured. P* 14½ × 13½.
329 70 c. Luhya 40 15
330 2 s. Kikuyu .. .. 1·00 90
331 3 s. 50, Pokomo .. .. 1·40 1·25
332 5 s. Nandi .. .. 1·75 1·75
333 10 s. Rendile .. .. 2·50 3·25
329/33 .. .. *Set of* 5 6·50 6·50

(Litho Harrison)

1984 (21 Dec). *60th Anniv of World Chess Federation. T* **68** *and similar horiz designs. Multicoloured. P* 14½.
334 70 c. Type **68** 70 20
335 2 s. 50, Rook and Fort Jesus .. .. .. 1·25 1·00
336 3 s. 50, Bishop and National Monument .. 1·75 1·40
337 5 s. Queen and Parliament Building .. .. 2·00 2·00
338 10 s. King and Nyayo Fountain .. .. .. 2·75 3·25
334/8 .. .. *Set of* 5 7·50 7·00

69 Cooking with Wood-burning Stove and Charcoal Fire

(Des H. Moghul. Litho J.W.)

1985 (22 Jan). *Energy Conservation. T* **69** *and similar horiz designs. Multicoloured. P* 13½.
339 70 c. Type **69** 15 10
340 2 s. Solar energy panel on roof 35 40
341 3 s. 50, Production of gas from cow dung .. 55 75
342 10 s. Ploughing with oxen .. .. 1·25 2·25
339/42 .. .. *Set of* 4 2·10 3·25
MS343 110 × 85 mm. 20 s. Designs as Nos. 339/42, but without face values .. .. .. 2·25 2·50

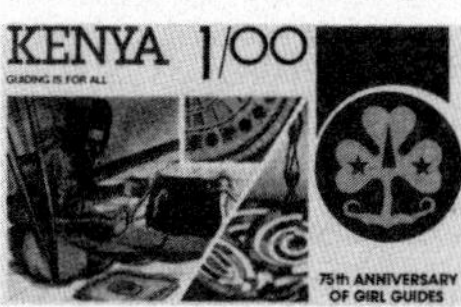

70 Crippled Girl Guide making Table-mat

(Litho J.W.)

1985 (27 Mar). *75th Anniv of Girl Guide Movement. T* **70** *and similar horiz designs. Multicoloured. P* 13½.
344 1 s. Type **70** 40 15
345 3 s. Girl Guides doing community service .. 1·00 75
346 5 s. Lady Olave Baden-Powell (founder) .. 1·60 1·40
347 7 s. Girl Guides gardening .. .. 2·00 2·25
344/7 .. .. *Set of* 4 4·50 4·00

71 Stylised Figures and Globe

72 Man with Malaria

(Des and litho Harrison)

1985 (8 May). *World Red Cross Day. T* **71** *and similar horiz designs. P* 14½.
348 1 s. black and rosine 40 15
349 4 s. multicoloured .. .. 1·40 1·25
350 5 s. multicoloured .. .. 1·60 1·40
351 7 s. multicoloured .. .. 2·25 2·25
348/51 .. .. *Set of* 4 5·00 4·50
Designs:—4 s. First aid team; 5 s. Hearts containing crosses ("Blood Donation"); 7 s. Cornucopia ("Famine Relief").

(Des H. Moghul. Litho Harrison)

1985 (25 June). *7th International Congress of Protozoology, Nairobi. T* **72** *and similar vert designs. Multicoloured. P* 14½.
352 1 s. Type **72** 45 15
353 3 s. Child with Leishmaniasis .. .. .. 1·60 1·10
354 5 s. Cow with Trypanosomiasis .. .. .. 2·00 1·40
355 7 s. Dog with Babesiosis .. .. 2·50 2·25
352/5 .. .. *Set of* 4 6·00 4·50

73 Repairing Water Pipes

74 The Last Supper

(Des J. Tobula and Harrison. Litho Harrison)

1985 (15 July). *United Nations Women's Decade Conference. T* **73** *and similar vert designs. Multicoloured. P* 14½.
356 1 s. Type **73** 10 10
357 3 s. Traditional food preparation 40 35
358 5 s. Basket-weaving 60 55
359 7 s. Dressmaking 75 70
356/9 .. .. *Set of* 4 1·60 1·50

(Des Eucharistic Congress Secretariat. Litho J.W.)

1985 (17 Aug*). *43rd International Eucharistic Congress, Nairobi. T* **74** *and similar horiz designs. Multicoloured. P* 13½.
360 1 s. Type **74** 35 10
361 3 s. Village family ("The Eucharist and the Christian Family") .. .. 1·00 65
362 5 s. Congress altar, Uhuru Park .. .. .. 1·25 95
363 7 s. St. Peter Claver's Church, Nairobi .. 1·75 1·75
360/3 .. .. *Set of* 4 4·00 3·00
MS364 117 × 80 mm. 25 s. Pope John Paul II .. 3·50 3·50
* This is the local date of issue. The Crown Agents released the stamps on 15 August and this date also appears on first day covers serviced by Kenya Posts and Telecommunications Corporation.

75 Black Rhinoceros

(Des Rena Fennessy. Litho Harrison)

1985 (10 Dec). *Endangered Animals. T* **75** *and similar horiz designs. Multicoloured. P* 14½.
365 1 s. Type **75** 60 20
366 3 s. Cheetah .. .. 1·50 1·25
367 5 s. De Brazza's Monkey .. .. 2·00 1·75
368 10 s. Grevy's Zebra .. .. 3·00 3·50
365/8 .. .. *Set of* 4 6·50 6·00
MS369 129 × 122 mm. 25 s. Endangered species (122 × 114 *mm*). Imperf .. .. 4·00 4·00

76 *Borassus aethiopum*

77 Dove and U.N. Logo (from poster)

(Des Rena Fennessy. Litho Questa)

1986 (24 Jan). *Indigenous Trees. T* **76** *and similar horiz designs. Multicoloured. P* 14½.
370 1 s. Type **76** 40 15
371 3 s. *Acacia xanthophloea* .. .. 1·25 1·25
372 5 s. *Ficus natalensis* .. .. 1·90 2·00
373 7 s. *Spathodea nilotica* .. .. 2·40 3·00
370/3 .. .. *Set of* 4 5·50 5·75
MS374 117 × 96 mm. 25 s. Landscape with trees (109 × 90 *mm*). Imperf .. .. 3·25 4·00

(Des Advertising Link. Litho Questa)

1986 (30 Apr*). *International Peace Year. T* **77** *and similar multicoloured designs. P* 14½.
375 1 s. Type **77** 15 10
376 3 s. U.N. General Assembly (*horiz*) 45 40
377 7 s. Nuclear explosion .. .. 1·00 85
378 10 s. Quotation from Wall of Isaiah, U.N. Building, New York (*horiz*) .. .. 1·40 1·25
375/8 .. .. *Set of* 4 2·75 2·25
*This is the local date of issue. The Crown Agents released the stamps on 17 April and this date also appears on first day covers serviced by Kenya Posts and Telecommunications Corporation.

78 Dribbling the Ball

79 Rural Post Office and Telephone

(Des C. Fernandes. Litho Harrison)

1986 (8 May). *World Cup Football Championship, Mexico. T* **78** *and similar multicoloured designs. P* 14½.
379 1 s. Type **78** 40 15
380 3 s. Scoring from a penalty .. .. 1·00 55
381 5 s. Tackling .. .. 1·75 1·25
382 7 s. Cup winners .. .. 2·25 2·00
383 10 s. Heading the ball .. .. 2·75 2·75
379/83 .. .. *Set of* 5 7·50 6·00
MS384 110 × 86 mm. 30 s. Harambee Stars football team (102 × 78 *mm*). Imperf .. .. 3·25 3·75

(Des H. Moghul. Litho Cartor, France)

1986 (11 June). *"Expo '86" World Fair, Vancouver. T* **79** *and similar horiz designs. Multicoloured. P* 13½ × 13.
385 1 s. Type **79** 40 15
386 3 s. Container depot, Embakasi .. .. .. 1·25 85
387 5 s. Aircraft landing at game park airstrip .. 1·75 1·25
388 7 s. Container ship .. .. 2·00 2·00
389 10 s. Transporting produce to market .. .. 2·50 2·75
385/9 .. .. *Set of* 5 7·00 6·25

On 15 July 1986 Kenya was scheduled to release a set of five stamps, 1, 3, 4, 7 and 10 s., for the Commonwealth Games at Edinburgh. A political decision was taken at the last moment not to issue the stamps, but this instruction did not reach some of the sub-post offices until the morning of 15 July. About two hundred stamps, mainly the 1 s. value, were sold by these sub-post offices before the instruction arrived. Examples of the 1 s. exist used on commercial mail from Kenyatta College sub-post office from 17 July 1986 onwards.

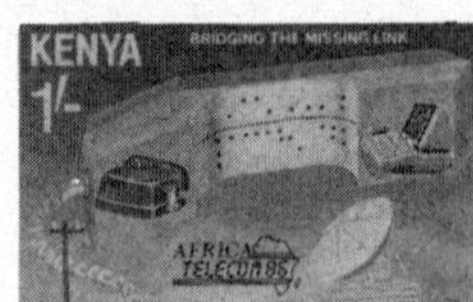

80 Telephone, Computer and Dish Aerial

(Des H. Moghul. Litho Harrison)

1986 (16 Sept). *African Telecommunications. T* **80** *and similar horiz designs. Multicoloured. P* 14½.

390 1 s. Type **80** 25 10
391 3 s. Telephones of 1876, 1936 and 1986 .. 60 40
392 5 s. Dish aerial, satellite, telephones and map of Africa 85 85
393 7 s. Kenyan manufacture of telecommunications equipment .. .. 1·10 1·25
390/3 .. .. *Set of* 4 2·50 2·25

81 Mashua **82** The Nativity

(Des Mukund Arts. Litho Mardon Printers Ltd, Zimbabwe)

1986 (30 Oct). *Dhows of Kenya. T* **81** *and similar horiz designs. Multicoloured. P* 14½.

394 1 s. Type **81** 45 20
395 3 s. Mtepe .. .. 1·25 1·00
396 5 s. Dau La Mwao .. .. 1·75 1·50
397 10 s. Jahazi .. .. 2·50 3·00
394/7 .. .. *Set of* 4 5·50 5·00
MS398 118 × 80 mm. 25 s. Lamu dhow and map of Indian Ocean .. .. 4·00 4·50

(Des Mukund Arts. Photo Courvoisier)

1986 (5 Dec). *Christmas. T* **82** *and similar multicoloured designs. Granite paper. P* 11½.

399 1 s. Type **82** 20 10
400 3 s. Shepherd and sheep 60 45
401 5 s. Angel and slogan "LOVE PEACE UNITY" (*horiz*) .. .. 1·00 75
402 7 s. The Magi riding camels (*horiz*) .. .. 1·25 1·40
399/402 .. .. *Set of* 4 2·75 2·40

83 Immunization **84** Akamba Woodcarvers

(Des Judith D'Inca. Litho Harrison)

1987 (6 Jan). *40th Anniv of United Nations Children's Fund. T* **83** *and similar vert designs. Multicoloured. P* 14.

403 1 s. Type **83** 20 10
404 3 s. Food and nutrition 45 35
405 4 s. Oral rehydration therapy 60 45
406 5 s. Family planning 75 60
407 10 s. Female literacy .. .. 1·25 1·25
403/7 .. .. *Set of* 5 3·00 2·50

(Des C. Fernandes. Litho Questa)

1987 (25 Mar). *Tourism. T* **84** *and similar horiz designs. Multicoloured. P* 14½.

408 1 s. Type **84** 30 10
409 3 s. Tourists on beach 85 70
410 5 s. Tourist and guide at view point .. 1·25 1·25
411 7 s. Pride of lions .. .. 1·75 2·00
408/11 .. .. *Set of* 4 3·75 3·50
MS412 118 × 81 mm. 30 s. Geysers .. .. 4·25 5·00

(Des Mukund Arts. Litho Harrison)

1987 (20 May). *Ceremonial Costumes* (3rd series). *Vert designs as T* **45**. *Multicoloured. P* 14½ × 13½.

413 1 s. Embu 10 10
414 3 s. Kisii 25 30
415 5 s. Samburu 40 60
416 7 s. Taita 60 80
417 10 s. Boran .. .. 80 1·10
413/17 .. .. *Set of* 5 1·90 2·50

85 Telecommunications by Satellite **86** Volleyball

(Des Mukund Arts. Litho Harrison)

1987 (1 July). *10th Anniv of Kenya Posts and Telecommunications Corporation. T* **85** *and similar triangular designs. Multicoloured. P* 13½.

418 1 s. Type **85** 10 15
419 3 s. Rural post office, Kajiado 20 35
420 4 s. Awarding trophy, Welfare Sports .. 30 45
421 5 s. Village and telephone box 35 50
422 7 s. Speedpost labels and outline map of Kenya 50 70
418/22 .. .. *Set of* 5 1·25 2·00
MS423 110 × 80 mm. 25 s. Corporation flag .. 1·75 1·90

Nos. 418/22 were each printed as horizontal *tête-bêche* pairs within the sheet.

(Des C. Fernandes. Litho D.L.R.)

1987 (5 Aug). *4th All-Africa Games, Nairobi. T* **86** *and similar multicoloured designs. P* 14½ × 14.

424 1 s. Type **86** 10 10
425 3 s. Cycling 20 30
426 4 s. Boxing 30 40
427 5 s. Swimming 35 45
428 7 s. Steeplechasing 50 75
424/8 .. .. *Set of* 5 1·25 1·75
MS429 117 × 80 mm. 30 s. Kasarani Sports Complex (*horiz*). P 14 × 14½ .. .. 2·10 2·25

87 *Aloe volkensii*

(Des Advertising Link. Litho Cartor, France)

1987 (10 Nov). *Medicinal Herbs. T* **87** *and similar vert designs. Multicoloured. P* 13½ × 14.

430 1 s. Type **87** 15 10
431 3 s. *Cassia didymobotrya* 40 40
432 5 s. *Erythrina abyssinica* 65 65
433 7 s. *Adenium obesum* .. .. .. 85 1·00
434 10 s. Herbalist's clinic .. .. .. 1·25 1·50
430/4 .. .. *Set of* 5 3·00 3·25

88 *Epamera sidus* **89** *Papilio rex*

(Des Rena Fennessy. Photo Harrison)

1988 (15 Feb)–**90**. *Butterflies. Multicoloured.*

(*a*) *Vert designs as T* **88**. *P* 15 × 14

434*a* 10 c. *Cyrestis camillus* (1.9.89) 10 10
435 20 c. Type **88** 10 10
436 40 c. *Cynthia cardui* 10 10
437 50 c. *Colotis evippe* 10 10
438 70 c. *Precis westermanni* 10 10
439 80 c. *Colias electo* 10 10
440 1 s. *Eronia leda* 10 10
440*a* 1 s. 50, *Papilio dardanus* (18.5.90) .. 10 10

(*b*) *Vert designs as T* **89**. *P* 14½

441 2 s. Type **89** 10 10
442 2 s. 50, *Colotis phisadia* 10 15
443 3 s. *Papilio desmondi* 10 15
444 3 s. 50, *Papilio demodocus* 15 20
445 4 s. *Papilio phorcas* 15 20
446 5 s. *Charaxes druceanus* 20 25
447 7 s. *Cymothoe teita* 30 35
448 10 s. *Charaxes zoolina* 40 45
449 20 s. *Papilio dardanus* 80 85
450 40 s. *Charaxes cithaeron* .. .. .. 1·60 1·75
434*a*/50 .. .. *Set of* 18 3·75 4·25

Examples of the 1 s. value were used in error at Kisumu from 2 February 1988.

90 Samburu Lodge and Crocodiles

(Des Advertising Link. Litho Questa)

1988 (31 May). *Kenyan Game Lodges. T* **90** *and similar horiz designs. Multicoloured. P* 14½.

451 1 s. Type **90** 20 10
452 3 s. Naro Moru River Lodge and rock climbing 55 35
453 4 s. Mara Serena Lodge and zebra with foal 65 50
454 5 s. Voi Safari Lodge and buffalo 70 60
455 7 s. Kilimanjaro Buffalo Lodge and giraffes 85 75
456 10 s. Meru Mulika Lodge and rhinoceroses 1·10 90
451/6 .. .. *Set of* 6 3·50 2·75

91 Athletes and Stadium, Commonwealth Games, Brisbane, 1982

(Des D. Ashby. Litho Harrison)

1988 (10 June). *"Expo '88" World Fair, Brisbane, and Bicentenary of Australian Settlement. T* **91** *and similar horiz designs. Multicoloured. P* 14½.

457 1 s. Type **91** 15 10
458 3 s. Flying Doctor Service aircraft 40 35
459 4 s. H.M.S. *Sirius* (frigate), 1788 .. .. 45 40
460 5 s. Ostrich and emu 55 50
461 7 s. Queen Elizabeth II, President Arap Moi of Kenya and Prime Minister Hawke of Australia 70 80
457/61 .. .. *Set of* 5 2·00 1·90
MS462 117×80 mm. 30 s. Entrance to Kenya Pavilion .. .. 1·90 2·00

92 W.H.O. Logo and Slogan **93** Handball

(Des Mukund Arts. Litho National Printing & Packaging, Zimbabwe)

1988 (1 July). *40th Anniv of World Health Organization. T* **92** *and similar horiz designs. P* 14½.

463 1 s. greenish blue, gold and ultramarine .. 20 10
464 3 s. multicoloured 50 40
465 5 s. multicoloured 70 60
466 7 s. multicoloured .. .. 1·00 90
463/6 .. .. *Set of* 4 2·25 1·75

Designs:—3 s. Mother with young son and nutritious food; 5 s. Giving oral vaccine to baby; 7 s. Village women drawing clean water from pump.

(Des H. Moghul. Litho D.L.R.)

1988 (1 Aug). *Olympic Games, Seoul. T* **93** *and similar vert designs. Multicoloured. P* 14½×14.

467 1 s. Type **93** 10 10
468 3 s. Judo 25 25
469 5 s. Weightlifting 35 35
470 7 s. Javelin 50 50
471 10 s. Relay racing 65 65
467/71 .. .. *Set of* 5 1·60 1·60
MS472 110×78 mm. 30 s. Tennis .. .. 1·90 2·00

94 Calabashes **95** Pres. Arap Moi taking Oath, 1978

(Des Mukund Arts. Litho D.L.R.)

1988 (20 Sept). *Kenyan Material Culture. T* **94** *and similar multicoloured designs. P* 14½×14 (*vert*) *or* 14×14½ (*horiz*).

473 1 s. Type **94** 10 10
474 3 s. Milk gourds 20 25

475 5 s. Cooking pots (*horiz*) 30 35
476 7 s. Winnowing trays (*horiz*) 45 50
477 10 s. Reed baskets (*horiz*) 60 65
473/7 . . . . *Set of* 5 1·40 1·60
MS478 118×80 mm. 25 s. Gourds, calabash and horn (*horiz*) . . . . 1·50 1·60

(Des Mukund Arts. Litho Harrison)

1988 (13 Oct). 10*th Anniv of "Nyayo" Era. T* **95** *and similar horiz designs. Multicoloured. P* 13½×14½.
479 1 s. Type **95** 20 10
480 3 s. Building soil conservation barrier . . 50 40
481 3 s. 50, Passengers boarding bus 50 40
482 4 s. Metalwork shop 60 60
483 5 s. Moi University, Eldoret 70 70
484 7 s. Aerial view of hospital . . . . 90 1·00
485 10 s. Pres. Arap Moi and Mrs. Thatcher at Kapsabet Telephone Exchange . . 1·75 1·90
479/85 . . . . *Set of* 7 4·75 4·50

96 Kenya Flag

(Des Mukund Arts. Photo Courvoisier)

1988 (9 Dec). 25*th Anniv of Independence. T* **96** *and similar horiz designs. Multicoloured. Granite paper. P* 11½.
486 1 s. Type **96** 15 10
487 3 s. Coffee picking 35 35
488 5 s. Proposed Kenya Posts and Telecommunications Headquarters building . . 60 60
489 7 s. Kenya Airways *Harambee Star* "A310-300" Airbus 80 80
490 10 s. New diesel locomotive No. 9401 . . 1·10 1·25
486/90 . . . . *Set of* 5 2·75 2·75

97 Gedi Ruins, Malindi

(Des Mukund Arts. Litho National Printing & Packaging, Zimbabwe)

1989 (15 Mar). *Historic Monuments. T* **97** *and similar multicoloured designs. P* 14½.
491 1 s. 20, Type **97** 15 10
492 3 s. 40, Vasco Da Gama Pillar, Malindi (*vert*) 30 30
493 4 s. 40, Ishiakani Monument, Kiunga . . 40 40
494 5 s. 50, Fort Jesus, Mombasa 50 50
495 7 s. 70, She Burnan Omwe, Lamu (*vert*) . . 65 70
491/5 . . . . *Set of* 5 1·75 1·75

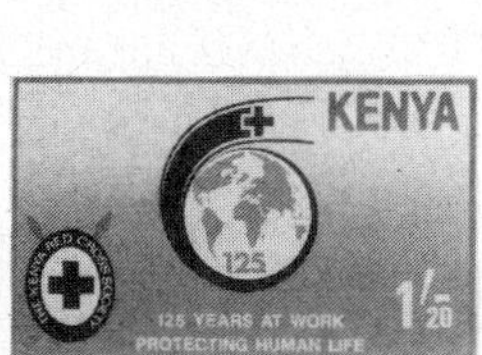

98 125th Anniversary and Kenya Red Cross Logos

99 Female Giraffe and Calf

(Des H. Moghul. Litho Cartor, France)

1989 (8 May). 125*th Anniv of International Red Cross. T* **98** *and similar horiz designs. Multicoloured. P* 14×13½.
496 1 s. 20, Type **98** 15 10
497 3 s. 40, Red Cross workers with car crash victim 30 30
498 4 s. 40, Disaster relief team distributing blankets 40 40
499 5 s. 50, Henri Dunant (founder) 50 50
500 7 s. 70, Blood donor 65 70
496/500 . . . . *Set of* 5 1·75 1·75

(Des Doreen McGuinness. Litho Walsall)

1989 (12 July). *Reticulated Giraffe. T* **99** *and similar vert designs. Multicoloured. P* 14½.
501 1 s. 20, Type **99** 30 15
502 3 s. 40, Giraffe drinking 65 65
503 4 s. 40, Two giraffes 80 80
504 5 s. 50, Giraffe feeding . . . . . . 1·00 1·25
501/4 . . . . *Set of* 4 2·50 2·50
MS505 80×110 mm. 30 s. Designs as Nos. 501/4, but without face values . . . . . . 3·00 3·00
Designs from No. **MS**505 are without the Worldwide Fund for Nature logo.

ALTERED CATALOGUE NUMBERS

Any Catalogue numbers altered from the last edition are shown as a list in the introductory pages.

100 *Pleurotus sajor-ceju*

101 Independence Monuments

(Des Dvora Bochman. Litho Questa)

1989 (6 Sept). *Mushrooms. T* **100** *and similar vert designs. Multicoloured. P* 14½.
506 1 s. 20, Type **100** 30 15
507 3 s. 40, *Agaricus bisporus* 50 40
508 4 s. 40, *Agaricus bisporus* (*different*) . . 70 65
509 5 s. 50, *Termitomyces schimperi* 90 90
510 7 s. 70, *Lentinus edodes* . . . . . . 1·40 1·50
506/10 . . . . *Set of* 5 3·50 3·25

(Des Conference and Exhibitions Secretariat, Nairobi. Litho Cartor, France)

1989 (9 Nov). *Birth Centenary of Jawaharlal Nehru (Indian statesman). T* **101** *and similar vert designs. Multicoloured. P* 13½×14.
511 1 s. 20, Type **101** 30 15
512 3 s. 40, Nehru with graduates and open book 60 50
513 5 s. 50, Jawaharlal Nehru 80 70
514 7 s. 70, Industrial complex and cogwheels 1·25 1·25
511/14 . . . . *Set of* 4 2·75 2·40

(Des Mukund Arts. Litho Harrison)

1989 (20 Dec). *Ceremonial Costumes* (4*th series*). *Vert designs as T* **45**. *Multicoloured. P* 14½×13½.
515 1 s. 20, Kipsigis 25 15
516 3 s. 40, Rabai 55 50
517 5 s. 50, Duruma 75 70
518 7 s. 70, Kuria . . . . 1·10 1·25
519 10 s. Bajuni . . . . 1·50 1·60
515/19 . . . . *Set of* 5 3·75 3·75

102 EMS Speedpost Letters and Parcel

(Des Conference & Exhibitions Secretariat Ltd, Nairobi. Litho Cartor, France)

1990 (23 Mar). 10*th Anniv of Pan African Postal Union. T* **101** *and similar multicoloured designs. P* 14×13½ (*horiz*) *or* 13½×14 (*vert*).
520 1 s. 20, Type **102** 15 10
521 3 s. 40, Mail runner 30 30
522 5 s. 50, Mandera Post Office 50 50
523 7 s. 70, EMS Speedpost Letters and globe (*vert*) 70 80
524 10 s. P.A.P.U. logo (*vert*) 80 90
520/4 . . . . *Set of* 5 2·25 2·40

103 "Stamp King" with Tweezers and Magnifying Glass

104 Moi Golden Cup

(Des D. Miller. Photo Courvoisier)

1990 (27 Apr). *"Stamp World London 90" International Stamp Exhibition. T* **103** *and similar horiz designs. Granite paper. P* 11½.
525 1 s. 50, multicoloured 15 10
526 4 s. 50, multicoloured 40 35
527 6 s. 50, black, bright carmine and azure . . 45 60
528 9 s. multicoloured . . . . 70 1·00
525/8 . . . . *Set of* 4 1·50 1·90
MS529 113×77 mm. Nos. 525/8 . . . . 2·00 2·50
Designs:—4 s. 50, Penny Black and Kenya Stamp Bureau postmark; 6 s. 50, Early British cancellations; 9 s. Ronald Ngala Street Post Office, Nairobi.

(Litho Harrison)

1990 (21 May). *World Cup Football Championship, Italy. Trophies. T* **104** *and similar vert designs. Multicoloured. P* 14½.
530 1 s. 50, Type **104** 20 10
531 4 s. 50, East and Central Africa Challenge Cup 50 50
532 6 s. 50, East and Central Africa Club Championship Cup 70 70
533 9 s. World Cup . . . . 1·00 1·25
530/3 . . . . *Set of* 4 2·25 2·25

105 K.A.N.U. Flag

(Des Mukund Arts. Litho Harrison)

1990 (11 June). 50*th Anniv of Kenya African National Union. T* **105** *and similar horiz designs. Multicoloured. P* 14½.
534 1 s. 50, Type **105** 15 10
535 2 s. 50, Nyayo Monument 15 15
536 4 s. 50, Party Headquarters 35 35
537 5 s. Jomo Kenyatta (founder) 40 40
538 6 s. 50, President Arap Moi 50 60
539 9 s. President Moi addressing rally . . 70 80
540 10 s. Queue of voters . . . . 80 1·00
534/40 . . . . *Set of* 7 2·75 3·00

106 Desktop Computer

(Litho Questa)

1990 (12 July). 125*th Anniv of International Telecommunications Union. T* **106** *and similar horiz designs. Multicoloured. P* 14½.
541 1 s. 50, Type **106** 15 10
542 4 s. 50, Telephone switchboard assembly, Gilgil 35 35
543 6 s. 50, "125 YEARS" 45 65
544 9 s. Urban and rural telecommunications 70 1·00
541/4 . . . . *Set of* 4 1·50 1·90

107 Queen Mother at British Museum, 1988

108 Queen Elizabeth at Hospital Garden Party, 1947

(Des D. Miller. Litho Questa)

1990 (4 Aug). 90*th Birthday of Queen Elizabeth the Queen Mother. P* 14×15 (10 *s.*) *or* 14½ (40 *s.*).
545 **107** 10 s. multicoloured 80 80
546 **108** 40 s. black and brown-olive . . . . 2·75 2·75

109 Kenya 1988 2 s. Definitive

110 Adult Literacy Class

(Des D. Miller. Litho D.L.R.)

1990 (5 Sept). *Centenary of Postage Stamps in Kenya. T* **109** *and similar vert designs. Multicoloured. P* 14×14½.
547 1 s. 50, Type **109** 15 10
548 4 s. 50, East Africa and Uganda 1903 1 a. 35 35
549 6 s. 50, British East Africa Co 1890 ½ a. optd on G.B. 1d. 50 50
550 9 s. Kenya and Uganda 1922 20 c. 75 75
551 20 s. Kenya, Uganda, Tanzania 1971 2 s. 50, Railway commemorative . . . . 1·25 1·50
547/51 . . . . *Set of* 5 2·75 3·00

(Des H. Moghul. Litho Cartor, France)

1990 (30 Nov). *International Literacy Year. T* **110** *and similar vert designs. Multicoloured. P* 13½×14.
552 1 s. 50, Type **110** 15 10
553 4 s. 50, Teaching by radio 35 35
554 6 s. 50, Technical training 55 60
555 9 s. International Literacy Year logo . . 85 90
552/5 . . . . *Set of* 4 1·60 1·60

111 National Flag

(Des H. Moghul. Litho Cartor)

1991 (29 Nov). *Olympic Games, Barcelona* (1992). *T* **111** *and similar horiz designs. Multicoloured. P* 14×13½.

556	2 s. Type **111**	15	10
557	6 s. Basketball	35	35
558	7 s. Hockey	45	45
559	8 s. 50, Table tennis	55	55
560	11 s. Boxing	65	65
556/60	*Set of* 5	2·00	1·90

112 Queen and Prince Philip with Pres. Moi

113 Symbolic Man and Pointing Finger

(Des D. Miller. Litho Cartor)

1992 (6 Feb). *40th Anniv of Queen Elizabeth II's Accession. T* **112** *and similar horiz designs. Multicoloured. P* 14×13½.

561	3 s. Type **112**	10	10
562	8 s. Storks in tree	30	35
563	11 s. Treetops Hotel	45	50
564	14 s. Three portraits of Queen Elizabeth	60	65
565	40 s. Queen Elizabeth II	1·60	1·75
561/5	*Set of* 5	2·75	3·00

(Des H. Mogul. Litho Cartor)

1992 (31 Jan). *AIDS Day. T* **113** *and similar vert designs. Multicoloured. P* 13½×14.

566	2 s. Type **113**	10	10
567	6 s. Victim and drugs	20	25
568	8 s. 50, Male and female symbols	30	35
569	11 s. Symbolic figure and hypodermic syringe	45	50
566/9	*Set of* 4	95	1·10

POSTAGE DUE STAMPS

The Postage Due stamps of Kenya, Uganda and Tanganyika were used in Kenya until 2 January 1967.

D 3

(Litho D.L.R.)

1967 (3 Jan)–**70**. *Chalk-surfaced paper. P* 14×13½.

D13	D 3	5 c. scarlet	15	1·75
		a. Perf 14. Ordinary paper. *Dull scarlet* (16.12.69)	30	2·75
D14		10 c. green	20	1·75
		a. Perf 14. Ordinary paper (16.12.69)	45	2·75
D15		20 c. blue	60	2·00
		a. Perf 14. Ordinary paper. *Deep blue* (16.12.69)	45	3·25
D16		30 c. brown	70	2·50
		a. Perf 14. Ordinary paper. *Light red-brown* (16.12.69)	60	4·50
D17		40 c. bright purple	65	4·00
		a. Perf 14. Ordinary paper. *Pale bright purple* (16.12.69)	55	6·50
D18		1 s. bright orange	1·75	5·50
		a. Perf 14. Ordinary paper. *Dull bright orange* (18.2.70)	1·00	8·00
D13/18		*Set of* 6	3·50	16·00
D13a/18a		*Set of* 6	3·00	25·00

1971 (13 July)–**73**. *P* 14 × 15. (*a*) *Chalk-surfaced paper* (13.7.71).

D19	D 3	10 c. green	4·50	5·50
D20		20 c. deep dull blue	5·50	6·50
D21		30 c. red-brown	6·00	7·00
D22		1 s. dull bright orange	8·50	20·00
D19/22		*Set of* 4	22·00	35·00

(*b*) *Glazed, ordinary paper* (20.2.73)

D23	D 3	5 c. bright scarlet	1·25	3·25
D24		10 c. dull yellow-green	1·25	3·25
D25		20 c. deep blue	1·00	3·50
D27		40 c. bright purple	90	4·75
D28		1 s. bright orange	1·25	8·50
D23/8		*Set of* 5	5·00	21·00

1973 (12 Dec). *Glazed, ordinary paper. P* 15.

D29	D 3	5 c. red	30	2·50
D30		10 c. emerald	30	2·50
D31		20 c. deep blue	30	3·00
D32		30 c. red-brown	30	3·50
D33		40 c. bright purple	2·75	5·50
D34		1 s. bright orange	95	7·50
D29/34		*Set of* 6	4·50	22·00

1979 (27 Mar). *Chalk-surfaced paper. P* 14.

D35	D 3	10 c. bright emerald	65	2·25
D36		20 c. deep dull blue	1·40	2·75
D37		30 c. dull red-brown	80	2·25
D38		40 c. bright reddish purple	1·50	3·50
D39		80 c. dull red	70	2·00
D40		1 s. bright reddish orange	70	2·25
D35/40		*Set of* 6	5·25	13·50

1983 (Dec). *W w* **14**. *P* 14.

D41	D 3	10 c. yellowish green	10	10
D42		20 c. deep blue	10	10
D43		40 c. bright purple	3·00	3·50
D41/3		*Set of* 3	3·00	3·50

(Litho Harrison)

1985 (7 Aug)–**87**. *Ordinary paper. P* 14½ × 14.

D44	D 3	30 c. red-brown (9.1.87)	10	10
D45		40 c. bright magenta (9.1.87)	10	10
D46		80 c. dull vermilion (9.1.87)	10	10
D47		1 s. bright orange (1986)	10	10
D48		2 s. violet	10	10
D44/8		*Set of* 5	25	30

No. D47 was issued by the Crown Agents with Nos. D44/6, but was available in Kenya by November 1986.

OFFICIAL STAMPS

Intended for use on official correspondence of the Kenya Government only but there is no evidence that they were so used.

OFFICIAL

(O 4)

(15 c. 30 c. opt typo; others in photogravure)

1964 (1 Oct). *Nos.* 1/5 *and* 7 *optd with Type* O 4.

O21	5 c. brown, deep blue, green and bistre	10
O22	10 c. brown	10
O23	15 c. magenta	40
O24	20 c. black and yellow-green	20
O25	30 c. black and yellow	30
O26	50 c. crimson, black and green	1·75
O21/26	*Set of* 6	2·50

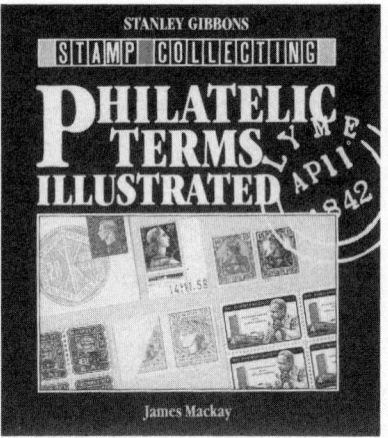

Kenya, Uganda and Tanganyika (Tanzania)

BRITISH EAST AFRICA

The area which became British East Africa had been part of the domain of the Zanzibari Sultans since 1794. In 1887 the administration of the province was granted to the British East Africa Association, incorporated as the Imperial British East Africa Company the following year.

Company post offices were established at Lamu and Mombasa in May 1890, British mails having been previously sent via the Indian post office on Zanzibar, opened in 1875.

A German postal agency opened at Lamu on 22 November 1888 and continued to operate until 31 March 1891, using German stamps. These can be identified by the "LAMU/OSTAFRIKA" cancellations and are listed under German East Africa in our *Part 7 (Germany)* catalogue.

PRICES FOR STAMPS ON COVER

Nos. 1/3	*from* × 6
Nos. 4/19	*from* × 20
Nos. 20/6	*from* × 3
Nos. 27/8	*from* × 6
Nos. 29/30	*from* × 12
Nos. 31/2	*from* × 4
Nos. 33/47	*from* × 10
No. 48	*from* × 12
Nos. 49/63	*from* × 10
No. 64	*from* × 8
Nos. 65/79	*from* × 15
Nos. 80/91	*from* × 8
Nos. 92/6	*from* × 12
Nos. 97/9	—

BRITISH EAST AFRICA COMPANY ADMINISTRATION

BRITISH EAST AFRICA COMPANY
HALF ANNA
(1)

BRITISH EAST AFRICA COMPANY
1 ANNA
(2)

(Surch D.L.R.)

1890 (May). *Stamps of Great Britain (Queen Victoria) surch as T 1 or 2 (1 a. and 4 a.).*

1	**57**	½ a. on 1d. deep purple	£325	£200
2	**73**	1 a. on 2d. green and carmine	£400	£275
3	**78**	4 a. on 5d. dull purple and blue	£450	£275

A copy of the ½ a. with the short crossbar of "F" in "HALF" omitted exists in the Royal Collection but is the only known example.

Stamps of INDIA were used in British East Africa between late July and September 1890 being postmarked "MOMBASA" or "LAMU".

3

4

5 ANNAS.
(5)

(Litho B.W.)

1890 (14 Oct)–**94**. *P* 14.

4	**3**	½ a. dull brown	2·00	2·50
		a. Imperf (pair)	£550	£400
		b. Deep brown (9.93)	70	2·00
		ba. Imperf (pair)	£500	£350
		bb. Imperf between (horiz pair)	£1500	£750
		bc. Imperf between (vert pair)	£600	£450
		c. Pale brown (12.94)	1·00	2·00
5		1 a. blue-green	3·00	3·50
		aa. "ANL" (broken "D") (R.6/3)	£225	£250
		a. Imperf (pair)	£650	£425
		ab. "ANL" (broken "D") (R.6/3)	£4750	
		b. Deep blue-green (12.94)	75	
		ba. Imperf (pair)	£650	£425
6		2 a. vermilion	2·75	3·25
		a. Imperf (pair)	£950	£450
7		2½ a. black/*yellow-buff* (7.91)	42·00	14·00
		a. Black/pale buff (7.92)	40·00	4·00
		b. Black/bright yellow (9.93)	3·75	3·25
		bb. Imperf (pair)	£600	£400
		bc. Imperf between (horiz pair)	£550	£400
		bd. Imperf between (vert pair)	£750	£450
8		3 a. black/*dull red* (2.91)	6·00	9·00
		a. Black/bright red (9.93)	1·25	2·00
		ab. Imperf (pair)	£550	£375
		ac. Imperf between (horiz pair)	£600	£375
		ad. Imperf between (vert pair)	£450	£350
9		4 a. yellow-brown	2·50	4·50
		a. Imperf (pair)	£1100	£475
10		4 a. grey (*imperf*)	£1200	£1400
11	**3**	4½ a. dull violet (2.91)	25·00	13·00
		a. Brown-purple (9.93)	2·50	12·00
		ab. Imperf (pair)	£800	£375
		ac. Imperf between (horiz pair)	£1200	£1200
		ad. Imperf between (vert pair)	£550	£425
12		8 a. blue	5·50	6·50
		a. Imperf (pair)	£1500	£500
13		8 a. grey	£250	£225
14		1 r. carmine	6·00	9·00
		a. Imperf (pair)	£2250	£550
15		1 r. grey	£225	£225
16	**4**	2 r. brick-red	11·00	15·00
17		3 r. slate-purple	8·00	18·00
18		4 r. ultramarine	12·00	24·00
19		5 r. grey-green	30·00	45·00
4/19		*Set of* 15 (*perf*)	£500	£500

For the 5 a. and 7½ a. see Nos. 29/30.

The paper of Nos. 7, 7*a*, 7*b*, 8 and 8*a* is coloured on the surface only.

Printings of 1890/92 are on thin paper having the outer margins of the sheets imperf and bearing sheet watermark "PURE LINEN WOVE BANK" and "W. C. S. & Co." in a monogram, the trademark of the makers, Messrs. William Collins, Sons & Co.

1893/94 printings are on thicker coarser paper with outer margins perforated through the selvedge and without watermark. Single specimens cannot always be distinguished by lack of watermark alone. Exceptions are the 1893 printings of the 2½ a. and 3 a. which were on Wiggins Teape paper showing a sheet watermark of "1011" in figures 1 centimetre high.

Nos. 7 (coloured through) and 16/19 on thick unwatermarked paper are from a special printing made for presentation purposes.

The printings of the 4 a., 8 a. and 1 r. values in grey were intended for fiscal purposes, but in the event, were made available for postal use.

Forgeries of the 4 a., 8 a., 1 r., grey and 2 to 5 r. exist. The latter are common and can be distinguished by the scroll above "LIGHT" where there are five vertical lines of shading in the forgeries and seven in the genuine stamps. Forged cancellations exist on the commoner stamps. Beware of "imperf" stamps made by trimming margins of stamps from marginal rows.

1891. *Mombasa Provisionals*. (*a*) *New value handstamped in dull violet, and manuscript initials in black.*

20	**3**	"½ Anna' on 2 a. vermilion ("A.D.") (January)	£2500	£750
		a. "½ Anna" double	—	£2750
21		"1 Anna' on 4 a. brown ("A.B.") (February)	£4500	£1200

(*b*) *Manuscript value and initials in black*

22	**3**	"½ Anna" on 2 a. vermilion ("A.D.") (January)	—	£950
		a. Error. "½ Annas" ("A.D.")		
23		"½ Anna" on 2 a. vermilion ("A.B.") (February)	£2500	£650
		a. Error. "½ Annas" ("A.B.")	—	£850
24		"½ Anna" on 3 a. black/*dull red* ("A.B.") (May)	£3250	£900
25		"1 Anna" on 3 a. black/*dull red* ("V.H.M.") (June)	£3250	£850
26		"1 Anna" on 4 a. brown ("A.B.") (March)	£2500	£800

A.D. = Andrew Dick, Chief Accountant.
A.B. = Archibald Brown, Cashier of the Company.
V.H.M. = Victor H. Mackenzie, Bank Manager.

(Surch B.W.)

1894 (1 Nov). *Surch as T* **5**.

27	**3**	5 a. on 8 a. blue	50·00	70·00
28		7½ a. on 1 r. carmine	50·00	70·00
27/28 Handstamped "Specimen"		*Set of* 2	90·00	

Forgeries exist.

1894 (Dec). *No wmk. P* 14.

29	**3**	5 a. black/*grey-blue*	1·25	9·50
30		7½ a. black	1·25	9·50
29/30 Handstamped "Specimen"		*Set of* 2	75·00	

These two stamps have "LD" after "COMPANY" in the inscription.

The paper of No. 29 is coloured on the surface only.

1895 (Feb.). *Surch with manuscript value and initials* ("T.E.C.R.").

31	**3**	"½ anna" on 3 a. black/*dull red* (19.2)	£180	45·00
32		"1 anna" on 3 a. black/*dull red* (22.2)	£2250	£1100

T.E.C.R. = T. E. C. Remington, Postmaster at Mombasa.

The Company experienced considerable financial problems during 1894 with the result that the British Government agreed to assume the administration of the territory, as a protectorate, on 1 July 1895.

IMPERIAL ADMINISTRATION

BRITISH EAST AFRICA
(6)

2½
(7)

(Handstamped at Mombasa)

1895 (1 July). *Handstamped with T* **6**.

33	**3**	½ a. deep brown	55·00	20·00
		a. Pale brown	65·00	30·00
		b. Double	£250	£250
34		1 a. blue-green	60·00	60·00
		a. Double	£250	£250
		b. "ANL" (broken "D") (R. 6/3)		
35		2 a. vermilion	£110	85·00
		a. Double	£300	£300
36		2½ a. black/*bright yellow*	90·00	48·00
		a. Double	£300	£275
37		3 a. black/*dull red*	42·00	35·00
38		4 a. yellow-brown	38·00	35·00
		a. Double	£275	£275
39		4½ a. dull violet	£100	80·00
		a. Double	£375	£375
		b. Brown-purple	£650	£550
		ba. Double	£1200	£1100
40	**3**	5 a. black/*grey-blue*	£120	90·00
		a. Double	£550	£550
		b. Inverted	†	£2000
41		7½ a. black	75·00	75·00
		a. Double	£350	£350
42		8 a. blue	75·00	65·00
		a. Double	£375	£375
		b. Inverted	£1800	
43		1 r. carmine	42·00	42·00
		a. Double	£300	£325
44	**4**	2 r. brick-red	£180	£180
45		3 r. slate-purple	£110	£100
		a. Double	£600	£600
		b. Inverted		
46		4 r. ultramarine	£110	£100
		a. Double	£600	£600
47		5 r. grey-green	£250	£225
		a. Double	£900	£900
33/47		*Set of* 15	£1200	£1100

Forgeries exist.

1895 (1 Oct). *No.* 39 *surch locally with T* **7**.

48	**3**	2½ a. on 4½ a. dull violet (R.)	75·00	60·00
		a. Opt (T **6**) double	£550	£500

British East Africa
(8)

British East Africa
(9)

SETTING OF TYPE **8**. This consisted of 120 impressions in 10 horizontal rows of 12 stamps. This matched the size of the pane for all the Indian issues to 1 r. with the exception of the 6 a. The sheets of this value contained four panes, each 8 × 10, which meant that the outer vertical margins also received the overprint.

The setting of Type **9** is not known.

Although only the one setting was used for the low values it is known that some of the overprint errors occurred, or were corrected, during the course of the various printings.

(Overprinted at the offices of *The Zanzibar Gazette*)

1895 (11 Nov)–**96**. *Stamps of India (Queen Victoria) optd with T* **8** *or* **9** (2 *r. to* 5 *r.*).

49	**23**	½ a. deep green	3·00	3·00
		a. "Britlsh" for "British"	£1800	£1600
		b. "Br1tish" for "British" (R. 10/12)	£200	
		c. "Afr1ca" for "Africa" (R. 1/11)	£200	
		d. Opt double, one albino	£350	
50	**25**	1 a. plum	2·75	3·25
		a. "Britlsh" for "British"	£2250	£1300
		b. "Br1tish" for "British" (R. 10/12)	£200	
		c. "Afr1ca" for "Africa" (R. 1/11)	£200	
51	**26**	1½ a. sepia (23.11.95)	3·75	3·00
		a. "Br1tish" for "British" (R. 10/12)	£250	
		b. "Afr1ca" for "Africa" (R. 1/11)	£250	
52	**27**	2 a. ultramarine	3·25	2·50
		a. "Britlsh" for "British"	£1500	
		b. "Br1tish" for "British" (R. 10/12)	£200	£200
		c. "Afr1ca" for "Africa" (R. 1/11)	£200	£200
53	**36**	2½ a. green	5·00	2·50
		a. "Biitish" for "British"	£3250	
		b. "Bpitish" for "British"	£3250	
		c. "Britlsh" for "British"	†	£1400
		d. "Eas" for "East" (R. 2/12)	£700	£900
		e. "Br1tish" for "British" (R. 10/12)	£275	£250
		f. "Afr1ca" for "Africa" (R. 1/11)	£275	
54	**28**	3 a. brown-orange (18.12.95)	7·50	8·00
		a. "Br1tish" for "British" (R. 10/12)	£300	£300
		b. "Afr1ca" for "Africa" (R. 1/11)	£300	
55	**29**	4 a. olive-green (18.12.95)	20·00	15·00
		a. Slate-green	18·00	15·00
		b. "Br1tish" for "British" (R. 10/12)	£350	£350
		c. "Afr1ca" for "Africa" (R. 1/11)	£350	
56	**21**	6 a. pale brown (18.12.95)	22·00	27·00
		a. "Br1tish" for "British" (R. 10/8)	£425	
		b. "Afr1ca" for "Africa" (R. 1/7)	£425	
		c. Opt double, one albino	£750	
57	**31**	8 a. dull mauve (18.12.95)	45·00	48·00
		a. "Br1tish" for "British" (R. 10/12)	£475	
		b. "Afr1ca" for "Africa" (R. 1/11)	£475	
		c. Magenta (1896)	28·00	35·00
		ca. "Br1tish" for "British" (R.10/12)	£425	
		cb. "Afr1ca" for "Africa" (R. 1/11)	£425	
		cc. Inverted "a" for "t" of "East" (R. 2/12)	†	£2500
58	**32**	12 a. purple/*red* (18.12.95)	19·00	26·00
		a. "Br1tish" for "British" (R.10/12)	£425	£425
		b. "Afr1ca" for "Africa" (R.1/11)	£425	
59	**33**	1 r. slate (18.12.95)	45·00	48·00
		a. "Br1tish" for "British" (R.10/12)	£650	
		b. "Afr1ca" for "Africa" (R.1/11)	£650	
60	**37**	1 r. green and carmine (1896)	26·00	40·00
		a. Inverted "a" for "t" of "East" (R.2/12)	£2250	
		b. "Br1tish" for "British" (R.10/12)	£450	
		c. "Afr1ca" for "Africa" (R.1/11)	£450	
		d. Opt double, one sideways	£300	£475
61	**38**	2 r. carmine & yellow-brown (18.12.95)	48·00	75·00
		a. "B" handstamped		
62		3 r. brown and green (18.12.95)	60·00	85·00
63		5 r. ultramarine and violet (18.12.95)	75·00	95·00
		a. Opt double	£1800	
		b. "B" handstamped	£1300	£1300
49/63		*Set of* 15	£300	£400

The 2½ a. is known on cover used on 31 October but was probably from a trial printing released in error.

The relative horizontal positions of the three lines of the overprint vary considerably but the distance vertically between the lines of the overprint is constant.

In both the "Br1tish" and "Afr1ca" errors the figure one is in a smaller type size.

There are other varieties, such as inverted "s" in "British", wide and narrow "B", and inverted "V" for "A" in "Africa" (R.1/1 and R.6/7).

During the overprinting of the 2 r. and 5 r. the "B" of "British" sometimes failed to print so that only traces of the letter appeared. It was replaced by a handstamped "B" which is often out of alignment with the rest of the overprint. The handstamp is known double. The variety may also exist on the 3 r.

The 2, 3 and 5 r., normally overprinted in larger type than the lower values, are also known with a smaller overprint, for use as specimen stamps for the U.P.U. These were not issued for postal purposes (*Price* £375 *un. per set*). The lower values were reprinted at the same time using similar type to the original overprint.

Forgeries exist.

2½ (10)

11

1895 (20 Dec). *No. 51 surch locally with T* **10** *in bright red.*
64 **26** 2½ on 1½ a. sepia .. .. 38·00 32·00
a. Inverted "1" in fraction (R.5/7, 10/7) £475 £475
b. "Brltish" for "British" (R.10/12) .. £650
c. "Afrlca" for "Africa" (R.1/11) .. £650

The setting of Type **10** was in 5 horizontal rows of 12 stamps, repeated twice for each pane.

No. 51 also exists surcharged with T **12, 13** and **14** in *brown-red*. These stamps were sent to the Postal Union authorities at Berne, but were never issued to the public (*Price unused*: T **12** £55, T **13** £120, T **14** £85).

(Recess D.L.R.)

1896 (26 May)–**1901**. *Wmk Crown CA. P* 14.
65 **11** ½ a. yellow-green 85 45
66 1 a. carmine-rose .. .. 1·60 30
a. Bright rose-red .. .. .. 1·50 30
b. Rosine (1901) .. .. .. 16·00 2·50
67 2 a. chocolate .. .. 1·50 2·75
68 2½ a. deep blue .. .. 4·50 1·10
a. Violet-blue .. .. .. 5·00 1·40
b. Inverted "S" (R.1/1) .. .. 60·00 40·00
69 3 a. grey .. .. 2·50 4·75
70 4 a. deep green .. .. 5·50 2·50
71 4½ a. orange-yellow .. .. .. 3·75 7·50
72 5 a. yellow-bistre .. .. .. 7·50 4·00
73 7½ a. mauve .. .. 5·00 16·00
74 8 a. grey-olive .. .. 2·50 4·50
75 1 r. pale dull blue .. .. .. 22·00 17·00
a. Ultramarine .. .. .. 26·00 20·00
76 2 r. orange .. .. 50·00 24·00
77 3 r. deep violet .. .. .. 50·00 27·00
78 4 r. carmine-lake .. .. .. 50·00 48·00
79 5 r. sepia .. .. 50·00 40·00
a. Thin "U" in "RUPEES" (R.3/2) .. £1000 £1000
65/79 .. .. *Set of* 15 £225 £150
65/79 Optd "Specimen" .. .. *Set of* 15 £275

(Overprinted at the offices of *The Zanzibar Gazette*)

1897 (2 Jan). *Stamps of Zanzibar (1896 issue) optd with T* **8**. *Wmk Single Rosette.*
80 **13** ½ a. green and red .. .. .. 35·00 35·00
81 1 a. indigo and red .. .. .. 60·00 60·00
82 2 a. red-brown and red .. .. .. 25·00 20·00
83 4½ a. orange and red .. .. .. 32·00 25·00
84 5 a. bistre and red .. .. .. 35·00 28·00
a. "Bri" for "British" .. .. .. † £850
85 7½ a. mauve and red .. .. .. 38·00 35·00
a. "Bri" for "British" £850
80/85 .. .. *Set of* 6 £200 £180

Nos. 84a and 85a appear to have occurred when the type was obscured during part of the overprinting.

The above six stamps exist with an overprint similar to T **8** but normally showing a stop after "Africa". These overprints (in red on the 1 a.) were made officially to supply the U.P.U. However, the stop does not always show. Pieces are known showing overprints with and without stop *se-tenant* (including the red overprint on the 1 a.).

Stamps of Zanzibar, wmk. "Multiple Rosettes" and overprinted with T **8** are forgeries.

2½ (12) 2½ (13) 2½ (14)

SETTING OF TYPES 12/14. The setting of 60 (6×10) contained 26 examples of Type **12**, 10 of Type **13** and **24** of Type **14**.

1897 (2 Jan). *Nos. 157 and 162 of Zanzibar optd with T* **8** *and further surch locally, in red.*
86 **12** 2½ on 1 a. indigo and red .. .. 70·00 50·00
b. Opt Type **8** double £4000
87 **13** 2½ on 1 a. indigo and red .. .. £130 90·00
88 **14** 2½ on 1 a. indigo and red .. .. 75·00 55·00
a. Opt Type **8** double £4500
89 **12** 2½ on 3 a. grey and red .. .. 65·00 48·00
90 **13** 2½ on 3 a. grey and red .. .. £120 85·00
91 **14** 2½ on 3 a. grey and red .. .. 70·00 50·00
86/91 .. .. *Set of* 6 £450 £325

Both the notes after No. 85 also apply here.

A special printing for U.P.U. requirements was made with the 2½ surcharge on the 1 a. and 3 a. stamps overprinted as T **8** but *with stop* after "Africa". It also included a "2" over "1" error in T **14**.

15

(Recess D.L.R.)

1897 (Nov)–**1903**. *Wmk Crown CC. P* 14.
92 **15** 1 r. grey-blue .. .. 28·00 25·00
a. Dull blue (1901) .. .. .. 24·00 17·00
b. Bright ultramarine (1903) .. .. £100 80·00
93 2 r. orange .. .. 48·00 48·00
94 3 r. deep violet .. .. 48·00 65·00
95 4 r. carmine £110 £140
96 5 r. deep sepia £110 £150
97 10 r. yellow-bistre (S. £60) £150 £225
98 20 r. pale green (S. £125) £550 £1000
99 50 r. mauve (S. £250) £1800 £2750
92/96 Optd "Specimen" .. .. *Set of* 5 £180

On 1 April 1901 the postal administrations of British East Africa and Uganda were merged. Subsequent issues were inscribed "EAST AFRICA AND UGANDA PROTECTORATES".

EAST AFRICA AND UGANDA PROTECTORATES

For earlier issues see BRITISH EAST AFRICA and UGANDA.

For the issues of the Mandated Territory of Tanganyika and the war-time issues that preceded them, see TANGANYIKA.

PRICES FOR STAMPS ON COVER TO 1945	
Nos. 1/43	*from* × 3
Nos. 44/75	*from* × 2
Nos. 76/95	*from* × 3
Nos. 96/105	—
Nos. 110/23	*from* × 2
Nos. 124/7	*from* × 3
Nos. 128/30	*from* × 5
Nos. 131/54	*from* × 3
Nos. D1/12	*from* × 8

PRINTERS. All the stamps issued between 1903 and 1927 were typographed by De La Rue & Co. Ltd, London.

USED HIGH VALUES. Beware of cleaned fiscally cancelled copies with faked postmarks.

1

2

1903 (24 July)–**04**. *P* 14. (*a*) *Wmk Crown CA.*
1 ½ a. green (16.2.04) .. .. .. 1·60 4·50
2 1 a. grey and red .. .. .. 1·75 30
3 2 a. dull and bright purple (24.7.03) .. 6·00 2·50
4 2½ a. blue .. .. 12·00 32·00
5 3 a. brown-purple and green .. .. 15·00 28·00
6 4 a. grey-green and black .. .. 11·00 14·00
7 5 a. grey and orange-brown .. .. 18·00 35·00
8 8 a. grey and pale blue .. .. .. 18·00 28·00

(*b*) *Wmk Crown CC. Ordinary paper*
9 **2** 1 r. green .. .. 13·00 35·00
a. Chalk-surfaced paper .. .. 18·00 42·00
10 2 r. dull and bright purple .. .. 45·00 48·00
11 3 r. grey-green and black .. .. 60·00 90·00
12 4 r. grey and emerald-green .. .. 75·00 £100
13 5 r. grey and red .. .. .. 75·00 £110
14 10 r. grey and ultramarine £120 £160
a. Chalk-surfaced paper £140 £170
15 20 r. grey and stone (Optd S. £120) .. £450 £600
16 50 r. grey and red-brown (Optd S. £250) £1100 £1400
1/13 .. .. *Set of* 13 £300 £450
1/14 Optd "Specimen" .. .. *Set of* 14 £250

1904–07. *Wmk Mult Crown CA. Ordinary paper* (½ *a. to* 8 *a.*) *or chalk-surfaced paper* (1 *r. to* 50 *r.*).
17 **1** ½ a. grey-green .. .. .. 3·50 80
a. Chalk-surfaced paper .. .. 3·00 1·00
18 1 a. grey and red .. .. .. 2·75 20
a. Chalk-surfaced paper .. .. 2·50 20
19 2 a. dull and bright purple .. .. 3·00 90
a. Chalk-surfaced paper .. .. 2·50 1·00
20 2½ a. blue .. .. 13·00 24·00
21 2½ a. ultramarine and blue .. .. 7·50 16·00
22 3 a. brown-purple and green .. .. 3·75 15·00
a. Chalk-surfaced paper .. .. 3·75 16·00
23 4 a. grey-green and black .. .. 7·50 12·00
a. Chalk-surfaced paper .. .. 7·50 15·00
24 5 a. grey and orange-brown .. .. 7·50 14·00
a. Chalk-surfaced paper .. .. 6·50 18·00
25 8 a. grey and pale blue .. .. 7·00 8·00
a. Chalk-surfaced paper .. .. 7·00 9·00
26 **2** 1 r. green (1907) .. .. .. 26·00 50·00
27 2 r. dull and bright purple (1906) .. 30·00 45·00
28 3 r. grey-green and black (1907) .. 45·00 80·00
29 4 r. grey and emerald-green (1907) .. 48·00 £100
30 5 r. grey and red (1907) .. .. 50·00 80·00
31 10 r. grey and ultramarine (1907) .. £120 £150
32 20 r. grey and stone (1907) £500 £650
33 50 r. grey and red-brown (1907) .. £1300 £1600
17/30 .. .. *Set of* 13 £200 £375

(New Currency. 100 cents = 1 rupee)

1907–08. *Wmk Mult Crown CA. Chalk-surfaced paper* (10, 12, 25, 50, 75 *c.*). *P* 14.
34 **1** 1 c. brown (1908) 30 15
35 3 c. grey-green .. .. .. 3·00 25
a. Blue-green .. .. .. 4·50 2·00
36 **1** 6 c. red .. .. 2·75 10
37 10 c. lilac and pale olive .. .. 9·00 8·50
38 12 c. dull and bright purple .. .. 4·25 2·75
39 15 c. bright blue .. .. .. 9·50 8·50
40 25 c. grey-green and black .. .. 3·75 6·50
41 50 c. grey-green and orange-brown .. 6·50 12·00
42 75 c. grey and pale blue (1908) .. 4·50 20·00
34/42 .. .. *Set of* 9 40·00 55·00
34/42 Optd "Specimen" .. .. *Set of* 9 £180

Original

Redrawn

1910. *T* **1** *redrawn. Printed from a single plate. Wmk Mult Crown CA. P* 14.
43 6 c. red .. .. 4·00 20

In the redrawn type a fine white line has been cut around the value tablets and above the name tablet separating the latter from the leaves above, EAST AFRICA AND UGANDA is in shorter and thicker letters and PROTECTORATES in taller letters than in No. 36.

3

4

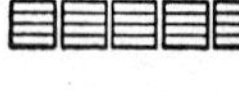

4 cents (5)

1912–21. *Wmk Mult Crown CA. Chalk-surfaced paper* (25 *c. to* 500 *r.*). *P* 14.
44 **3** 1 c. black 20 55
45 3 c. green .. .. 2·00 25
a. Deep blue-green (1917) .. .. 2·75 65
46 6 c. red 50 15
a. Scarlet (1917) .. .. .. 9·00 1·00
47 10 c. yellow-orange .. .. .. 2·00 20
a. Orange (1921) .. .. .. 6·00 1·25
48 12 c. slate-grey .. .. .. 2·75 50
49 15 c. bright blue .. .. .. 2·75 55
50 25 c. black and red/*yellow* 45 90
a. White back (5.14) (Optd S. £25) .. 50 2·25
b. On lemon (1916) (Optd S. £25) .. 8·50 9·50
c. On orange-buff (1921) .. .. 24·00 10·50
d. On pale yellow (1921) .. .. 6·50 3·25
51 50 c. black and lilac .. .. .. 1·50 80
52 75 c. black/*green* .. .. .. 1·50 11·00
a. White back (5.14) (Optd S. £25) .. 90 8·50
b. On blue-grn, ol back (Optd S. £25) 6·00 3·75
c. On emerald, olive back (1919) .. 38·00 85·00
d. On emerald back (1921) .. .. 10·00 23·00
53 **4** 1 r. black/*green* .. .. .. 1·75 3·25
a. On emerald back (1919) .. .. 5·00 27·00
54 2 r. red and black/*blue* .. .. 20·00 28·00
55 3 r. violet and green .. .. .. 20·00 42·00
56 4 r. red and green/*yellow* .. .. 42·00 80·00
a. On pale yellow .. .. .. 65·00 95·00
57 5 r. blue and dull purple .. .. 42·00 85·00
58 10 r. red and green/*green* .. .. 75·00 £120
59 20 r. black and purple/*red* £250 £250
60 20 r. purple and blue/*blue* (1918) .. £225 £225
61 50 r. carmine and green (Optd S. £160) £600 £600
a. Ordinary paper. *Dull rose-red and dull greyish green* £700 £700
62 100 r. purple & black/*red* (Optd S. £300) £2750 £1800
63 500 r. green & red/*green* (Optd S. £650) £12000
44/58 .. .. *Set of* 15 £190 £325
44/60 Optd "Specimen" .. .. *Set of* 17 £500

For values in this series overprinted "G.E.A." (German East Africa) see Tanganyika Nos. 45/62.

1919 (7 Apr). *T* **3** *surch with T* **5** *by the Swift Press, Nairobi.*
64 4 c. on 6 c. scarlet (*shades*) 20 15
a. Bars omitted .. .. .. 25·00 38·00
b. Surch double .. .. .. 90·00 £110
c. Surch inverted £150 £180
d. Pair, one without surch £450 £475
64 H/S "Specimen" .. .. 55·00

1921–22. *Wmk Mult Script CA. Chalk-surfaced paper* (50 *c. to* 50 *r.*). *P* 14.
65 **3** 1 c. black 35 70
66 3 c. green .. .. 1·25 3·50
a. Blue-green .. .. .. 6·50 7·00
67 6 c. carmine-red .. .. .. 1·25 3·75
68 10 c. orange (12.21) .. .. .. 3·75 30
69 12 c. slate-grey .. .. .. 3·25 30·00
70 15 c. bright blue .. .. .. 3·25 10·00
71 50 c. black and dull purple .. .. 9·50 45·00
72 **4** 2 r. red and black/*blue* .. .. 45·00 90·00
73 3 r. violet and green .. .. .. 75·00 £120
74 5 r. blue and dull purple .. .. 80·00 £140
75 50 r. carmine and green (Optd S. £225) .. £1900 £2750
65/74 .. .. *Set of* 10 £200 £400
65/74 Optd "Specimen" .. .. *Set of* 10 £225

For values in this series overprinted "G.E.A." see Tanganyika Nos. 63/73.

MINIMUM PRICE

The minimum price quote is 10p which represents a handling charge rather than a basis for valuing common stamps. For further notes about prices see introductory pages.

KENYA AND UGANDA

(New Currency. 100 cents = 1 shilling)

On 23 July 1920 Kenya became a Crown Colony with the exception of the coastal strip, previously part of the Sultan of Zanzibar's territories, which remained a protectorate.

6 7

1922 (1 Nov)–**27**. *Wmk Script CA. P* 14.

(*a*) *Wmk upright. Ordinary paper*

76 **6** 1 c. pale brown 60 70
a. *Deep brown* (1923) .. .. 1·25 2·25
77 5 c. dull violet .. .. 2·00 30
a. *Bright violet* .. .. 2·75 90
78 5 c. green (1927) .. .. 2·00 10
79 10 c. green .. .. 1·25 10
80 10 c. black (5.27) .. .. 1·75 10
81 12 c. jet-black .. .. 5·00 26·00
a. *Grey-black* .. .. 1·50 19·00
82 15 c. rose-carmine 80 10
83 20 c. dull orange-yellow .. .. 2·50 10
a. *Bright orange* .. .. 2·75 10
84 30 c. ultramarine .. .. 1·25 20
85 50 c. grey .. .. 1·75 10
86 75 c. olive .. .. 2·25 7·50

(*b*) *Wmk sideways. Chalk-surfaced paper*

87 **7** 1 s. green .. .. 2·75 2·00
88 2 s. dull purple .. .. 7·50 7·00
89 2 s. 50 c. brown (1.10.25) .. .. 18·00 60·00
90 3 s. brownish grey .. .. 15·00 6·00
a. *Jet-black* .. .. 28·00 26·00
91 4 s. grey (1.10.25) .. .. 18·00 60·00
92 5 s. carmine-red .. .. 22·00 18·00
93 7 s. 50 c. orange-yellow (1.10.25) .. 60·00 £130
94 10 s. bright blue .. .. 48·00 48·00
95 £1 black and orange £140 £190
96 £2 green and purple (1.10.25) (S. £120) £700
97 £3 purple and yellow (1.10.25) (S. £140) £850
98 £4 black & magenta (1.10.25) (S. £180) £1400
99 £5 black and blue (S. £225) .. £1800
100 £10 black and green (S. £275) .. £7500
101 £20 red and green (1.10.25) (S. £450) £12000
102 £25 black and red (S. £475) .. £13000
103 £50 black and brown (S. £550) .. £17000
104 £75 purple and grey (1.10.25) (S. £650) £32000
105 £100 red and black (1.10.25) (S. £700) £35000
76/95 .. .. *Set of* 20 £325 £475
76/95 Optd "Specimen" .. *Set of* 20 £475

Specimen copies of Nos. 96/105 are all overprinted.

KENYA, UGANDA AND TANGANYIKA

The postal administrations of Kenya, Tanganyika and Uganda were amalgamated on 1 January 1933. On the independence of the three territories the combined administration became the East African Posts and Telecommunications Corporation.

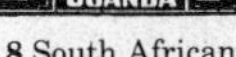

8 South African Crowned Cranes

9 Dhow on Lake Victoria

10 Lion

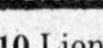

11 Kilimanjaro

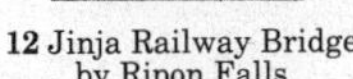

12 Jinja Railway Bridge by Ripon Falls

13 Mt. Kenya

14 Lake Naivasha

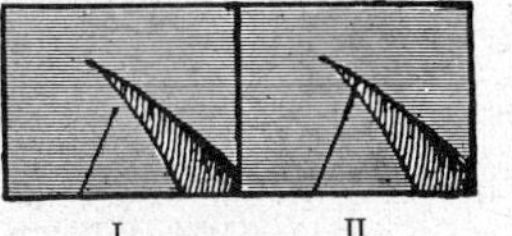

I II

(Des 1 c., 20 c., 10 s., R. C. Luck, 10 c., £1, A. Ross, 15 c., 2 s., G. Gill Holmes, 30 c., 5 s., R. N. Ambasana. 65 c., L. R. Cutts. T **10** typo, remainder recess D.L.R.).

1935 (1 May)–**36**. *Wmk Mult Script CA. Chalk-surfaced paper* (10 *c.*, £1). *P* 12×13 (**10**), 14 (**9** *and* **14**) *and* 13 (*remainder*).

110 **8** 1 c. black and red-brown 15 50
111 **9** 5 c. black and green (I) 40 15
a. Rope joined to sail (II) (1937) .. 12·00 3·00
b. Perf 13×12 (I) (1936) £400 £110
ba. Rope joined to sail (II) (1937) .. £350 85·00
112 **10** 10 c. black and yellow .. .. 2·25 15
113 **11** 15 c. black and scarlet 75 10
114 **8** 20 c. black and orange 85 10
115 **12** 30 c. black and blue 80 80
116 **9** 50 c. bright purple and black (I) .. 75 10
117 **13** 65 c. black and brown .. .. 90 2·00
118 **14** 1 s. black and green 75 35
a. Perf 13×12 (1936) .. .. £850 80·00
119 **11** 2 s. lake and purple .. .. 4·25 3·50
120 **14** 3 s. blue and black .. .. 5·00 13·00
a. Perf 13×12 (1936) £1400
121 **12** 5 s. black and carmine .. .. 15·00 23·00
122 **8** 10 s. purple and blue .. .. 40·00 48·00
123 **10** £1 black and red £120 £130
110/23 .. .. *Set of* 14 £170 £200
110/23 Perf "Specimen" .. *Set of* 14 £225

Line through "0" of 1910 (R.4/2)

1935 (6 May). *Silver Jubilee. As Nos.* 114/17 *of Jamaica, but ptd by D.L.R. P* 13½×14.

124 20 c. light blue and olive-green 35 10
h. Dot by flagstaff .. .. 35·00
i. Dash by turret .. .. 35·00
125 30 c. brown and deep blue .. .. 2·00 1·50
f. Diagonal line by turret .. .. 75·00
g. Dot to left of chapel .. .. 80·00
i. Dash by turret .. .. 80·00
126 65 c. green and indigo .. .. 1·75 2·00
f. Diagonal line by turret .. .. 70·00
g. Dot to left of chapel .. .. 75·00
127 1 s. slate and purple .. .. 2·00 1·40
f. Diagonal line by turret .. .. 75·00
l. Line through "0" of 1910 .. .. 70·00
124/7 .. .. *Set of* 4 5·50 4·50
124/7 Perf "Specimen" .. *Set of* 4 95·00

For illustrations of the other plate varieties see Omnibus section following Zimbabwe.

1937 (12 May). *Coronation. As Nos.* 118/20 *of Jamaica.*

128 5 c. green 25 10
129 20 c. orange 55 15
130 30 c. bright blue 85 85
128/30 .. .. *Set of* 3 1·50 1·00
128/30 Perf "Specimen" .. *Set of* 3 60·00

15 Dhow on Lake Victoria

Retouch on 1 c. (Pl 2, R. 9/6)

Retouch on 10 c. and 1s. (Pl 7B, R. 5/10 and 6/7)

With dot

Dot removed

In the 50 c., on Frame-plate 3, the dot was removed by retouching on all but five stamps (R.5/2, 6/1, 7/2, 7/4, and 9/1). In addition, other stamps show traces of the dot where the retouching was not completely effective.

PERFORATIONS. In this issue, to aid identification, the perforations are indicated to the nearest quarter.

(T **10** typo, others recess D.L.R.)

1938 (11 Apr)–**54**. *As T* **8** *to* **14** (*but with portrait of King George VI in place of King George V, as in T* **15**). *Wmk Mult Script CA. Chalk-surfaced paper* (£1).

131 **8** 1 c. black & red-brown (*p* 13¼) (2.5.38) 50 30
a. Perf 13¼×13¾. *Black and chocbrown* (1942) 10 35
ab. Retouched value tablet .. .. 42·00 42·00
ac. Black & dp chocolate-brown (1946) 80 65
ad. Ditto. Retouched tablet .. .. 42·00 42·00
ae. Black and red-brown (26.9.51) .. 35 70
132 **15** 5 c. black and green (II) (*p* 13×11¾) .. 55 10
133 5 c. reddish brn & orange (*p* 13×11¾) (1.6.49) .. .. 35 1·50
a. Perf 13×12½ (14.6.50) .. .. 50 1·50
134 **14** 10 c. red-brn & orge (*p* 13×11¾) (2.5.38) 40 10
a. Perf 14 (22.4.41) .. .. 65·00 6·00
135 10 c. black and green (*p* 13×11¾) (1.6.49) 20 20
a. Mountain retouch .. .. 50·00 16·00
b. Perf 13×12½ (14.6.50) 60 10
136 10 c. brown and grey (*p* 13×12½) (1.4.52) 35 20
137 **11** 15 c. black and rose-red (*p* 13¼) (2.5.38) 2·50 15
a. Perf 13¾×13¼ (2.43) .. .. 1·25 2·00
138 15 c. black & green (*p* 13¾×13¼) (1.4.52) 60 1·25
139 **8** 20 c. black and orange (*p* 13¼) (2.5.38) 18·00 15
a. Perf 14 (19.5.41) .. .. 38·00 1·50
b. Perf 13¼×13¾ (25.2.42) .. .. 1·75 10
ba. Deep black and deep orange (8.51) 3·00 30
140 **15** 25 c. blk & carm-red (*p* 13×12½) (1.4.52) 1·25 80
141 **12** 30 c. black and dull vio-bl (*p* 13¼) (2.5.38) 32·00 40
a. Perf 14 (3.7.41) .. .. £110 11·00
b. Perf 13¼×13¾ (9.42) 40 10
142 30 c. dull purple and brown (*p* 13¼×13¾) (1.4.52) 55 10
143 **8** 40 c. black & blue (*p* 13¼×13¾) (1.4.52) 1·25 1·50
144 **15** 50 c. purple & blk (II) (*p* 13×11¾) (2.5.38) 5·00 20
a. Rope not joined to sail (I) (R. 2/5) .. £180 £150
b. Dull claret and black (29.7.47) .. 4·50 70
c. Brown-purple and black (4.48) .. 5·50 70
d. Reddish purple and black (28.4.49) 6·00 40
e. Ditto. Perf 13×12½ (10.49) .. 2·50 30
ea. Dot removed (14.6.50) .. .. 9·00 20
eb. Ditto. In pair, with normal .. .. £170 70·00
145 **14** 1 s. black & yellowish brn (*p* 13×11¾) (2.5.38) .. .. 1·50 10
a. Black and brown (9.42) .. .. 1·75 30
ab. Mountain retouch (7.49) .. .. £120 55·00
b. Perf 13×12½ (10.49) .. .. 2·00 20
ba. Deep black and brown (*clearer impression*) (14.6.50) .. .. 1·75 40
146 **11** 2 s. lake-brn & brn-pur (*p* 13¼) (2.5.38) 80·00 1·50
a. Perf 14 (1941) .. .. 55·00 8·50
b. Perf 13¾×13¼ (24.2.44) .. .. 5·50 10
147 **14** 3 s. dull ultramarine & blk (*p* 13×11¾) (2.5.38) .. .. 20·00 1·10
a. Deep violet-blue and black (29.7.47) 22·00 2·75
b. Ditto. Perf 13×12½ (14.6.50) .. 10·00 90
148 **12** 5 s. black and carmine (*p* 13¼) (2.5.38) £110 7·00
a. Perf 14 (1941) .. .. 18·00 1·25
b. Perf 13¼×13¾ (24.2.44) .. .. 10·00 30
149 **8** 10 s. purple and blue (*p* 13¼) (2.5.38) .. £110 16·00
a. Perf 14. *Reddish purple & bl* (1941) 42·00 20·00
b. Perf 13¼×13¾ (24.2.44) .. .. 15·00 2·50
150 **10** £1 black and red (*p* 11¾×13) (12.10.38) £200 80·00
a. Perf 14 (1941) .. .. 12·00 11·00
ab. Ordinary paper (24.2.44) .. .. 10·00 11·00
b. Perf 12½ (21.1.54) .. .. 10·00 20·00
131/150ab (*cheapest*) .. .. *Set of* 20 55·00 18·00
131/150 Perf "Specimen" .. *Set of* 13 £300

The first printing of the 50 c. utilised the King George V centre plate on which each impression had been individually corrected to show the rope joined to sail. R.2/5 was missed, however, and this continued to show Type I until replaced by a new printing in September 1938.

Stamps perf 14, together with Nos. 131a, 137a, 139b, 141b, 146b, 148b and 149b, are known as "Blitz perfs", the differences in perforation being the result of air raid damage to the De La Rue works in which the perforators normally used were destroyed. Where dates of issue are quoted for these stamps they represent earliest known postmark dates.

10c
KENYA
TANGANYIKA
UGANDA

(16)

A screw head in the surcharging forme appears as a crescent moon (R. 20/4)

1941 (1 July)–**42**. *Pictorial Stamps of South Africa variously surch as T* **16** *by Government Printer, Pretoria. Inscr alternately in English and Afrikaans.*

Unused pair *Used pair*

151 5 c. on 1d. grey and carmine (No. 56) .. 60 1·50
152 10 c. on 3d. ultramarine (No. 59) .. .. 1·00 2·75
153 20 c. on 6d. green and vermilion (No. 61*a*) .. 60 1·75
154 70 c. on 1s. brown and chalky blue (No. 62) (20.4.42) .. .. 4·50 4·00
a. Crescent moon flaw .. .. 50·00
151/4 .. .. *Set of* 4 *pairs* 6·00 9·00
151/4 Handstamped "Specimen" *Set of* 4 *pairs* £180

1946 (11 Nov). *Victory. As Nos.* 141/2 *of Jamaica.*

Unused *Used*

155 20 c. red-orange 10 10
156 30 c. blue 10 10
155/6 Perf "Specimen" .. *Set of* 2 50·00

Examples of Nos. 155/6 were prereleased at Lindi on 15 October 1946.

1948 (1 Dec). *Royal Silver Wedding. As Nos.* 143/4 *of Jamaica.*

157 20 c. orange 15 10
158 £1 scarlet .. .. 30·00 35·00

1949 (10 Oct). *75th Anniv of Universal Postal Union. As Nos. 145/8 of Jamaica.*

159		20 c. red-orange	15	10
160		30 c. deep blue	40	25
161		50 c. grey	40	10
162		1 s. red-brown	75	40
159/62		*Set of* 4	1·50	70

17 Lake Naivasha

(Recess D.L.R.)

1952 (1 Feb). *Visit of Princess Elizabeth and Duke of Edinburgh. Wmk Mult Script CA. P* 13 × 12½.

163	**17**	10 c. black and green	10	30
164		1 s. black and brown	20	1·75

1953 (2 June). *Coronation. As No.* 153 *of Jamaica.*

165		20 c. black and red-orange	15	10

1954 (28 Apr). *Royal Visit. As No.* 171 *but inscr* "ROYAL VISIT 1954" *below portrait.*

166		30 c. black and deep ultramarine	10	15

18 Owen Falls Dam

19 Giraffe

20 Royal Lodge, Sagana

21 Queen Elizabeth II

(Des G. Gill Holmes (10, 50 c.), H. Grieme (15 c., 1 s. 30, 5 s.), R. McLellan Sim (10 s.), De La Rue (65 c., 2 s., £1), O.C. Meronti (others). Recess D.L.R.)

1954 (1 June)–**59**. *Designs as T* **18/21**. *Wmk Mult Script CA. P* 13 (£1); *others,* 12½ × 13 (*vert*) *or* 13 × 12½ (*horiz*).

167		5 c. black and deep brown	10	10
		a. Vignette inverted	†	£12000
168		10 c. carmine-red	40	10
169		15 c. black and light blue (28.3.58)	45	30
		a. Redrawn. Stop below "c" of "15 c" (29.4.59)	45	10
170		20 c. black and orange	30	10
		a. Imperf (pair)	£475	£550
171		30 c. black and deep ultramarine	35	10
		a. Vignette inverted	†	£10000
172		40 c. bistre-brown (28.3.58)	2·50	40
173		50 c. reddish purple	20	10
		a. Claret (23.1.57)	20	10
174		65 c. bluish green & brown-purple (1.12.55)	2·50	50
175		1 s. black and claret	30	10
176		1 s. 30, orange and deep lilac (1.12.55)	4·00	10
177		2 s. black and green	1·50	20
		a. Black and bronze-green (19.4.56)	2·50	45
178		5 s. black and orange	4·25	60
179		10 s. black and deep ultramarine	10·00	1·50
180		£1 brown-red and black	15·00	6·50
		a. Venetian red and black (19.4.56)	27·00	8·50
167/80		*Set of* 14	38·00	9·00

Designs: *Vert as T* **18/19**—5, 30 c. Type **18**; 10, 50 c. Type **19**; 20, 40 c., 1 s. Lion. *Horiz as T* **20**—15 c., 1 s. 30, 5 s. African Elephants; 65 c., 2 s. Kilimanjaro.

Only one example of No. 167a and two of No. 171a have been found, all being used.

25 Map of E. Africa showing Lakes

(Recess Waterlow)

1958 (30 July). *Centenary of Discovery of Lakes Tanganyika and Victoria by Burton and Speke. W w* **12**. *P* 12½.

181	**25**	40 c. blue and deep green	20	15
182		1 s. 30 c. green and violet	30	70

26 Sisal

27 Cotton

28 Mt Kenya and Giant Plants

29 Queen Elizabeth II

(Des M. Goaman. Photo (5 c. to 65 c.), recess (others) D.L.R.)

1960 (1 Oct). *Designs as T* **26/9**. *W w* **12**. *P* 15 × 14 (5 *c. to* 65 *c.*), 13 (20 *s.*) *or* 14 (*others*).

183		5 c. Prussian blue	10	10
184		10 c. yellow-green	10	10
185		15 c. dull purple	15	10
186		20 c. magenta	10	10
187		25 c. bronze-green	2·00	55
188		30 c. vermilion	10	10
189		40 c. greenish blue	15	10
190		50 c. slate-violet	15	10
191		65 c. yellow-olive	30	45
192		1 s. deep reddish violet and reddish purple	40	10
193		1 s. 30, chocolate and brown-red	1·00	10
194		2 s. deep grey-blue and greenish blue	1·00	15
195		2 s. 50, olive-green and deep bluish green	2·00	1·50
196		5 s. rose-red and purple	3·25	45
197		10 s. blackish green and olive-green	4·25	2·50
		a. Imperf (pair)	£180	
198		20 s. violet-blue and lake	11·00	9·00
183/198		*Set of* 16	23·00	14·00

Designs: *Vert as T* **26/7**—15 c. Coffee; 20 c. Blue Wildebeest; 25 c. Ostrich; 30 c. Thomson's Gazelle; 40 c. Manta Ray; 50 c. Common Zebra; 65 c. Cheetah. *Horiz as T* **28**—1 s. 30, Murchison Falls and Hippopotamus; 2 s. Mt Kilimanjaro and Giraffe; 2 s. 50, Candelabra Tree and Black Rhinoceros; 5 s. Crater Lake and Mountains of the Moon; 10 s. Ngorongoro Crater and African Buffalo.

The 10 c. and 50 c. exist in coils with the designs slightly shorter in height, a wider horizontal gutter every eleven stamps and, in the case of the 10 c. only, printed with a coarser 200 screen instead of the normal 250. (*Price for* 10 c. 10*p. unused.*) Plate 2 of 30 c. shows coarser 200 screen. (*Price* 25*p. unused.*)

30 Land Tillage

(Des V. Whiteley. Photo Harrison)

1963 (21 Mar). *Freedom from Hunger. T* **30** *and similar horiz design. P* 14½.

199	**30**	15 c. blue and yellow-olive	10	10
200	–	30 c. red-brown and yellow	20	10
201	**30**	50 c. blue and orange-brown	30	10
202	–	1 s. 30, red-brown and light blue	55	90
199/202		*Set of* 4	1·00	1·10

Design:—30 c., 1 s. 30, African with Corncob.

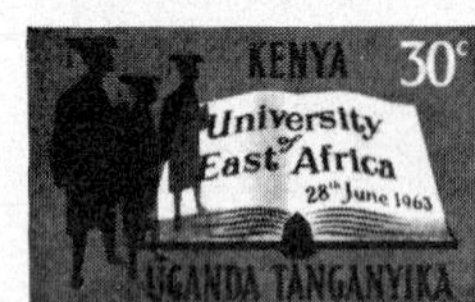

31 Scholars and Open Book

(Photo Harrison)

1963 (28 June). *Founding of East African University. P* 14½.

203	**31**	30 c. lake, violet, black and greenish blue	10	10
204		1 s. 30, lake, blue, red & lt yellow-brown	10	10

32 Red Cross Emblem

(Des V. Whiteley. Photo Harrison)

1963 (2 Sept). *Centenary of Red Cross. P* 14½.

205	**32**	30 c. red and blue	75	10
206		50 c. red and yellow-brown	1·00	35

PRINTERS. All the following stamps were printed in photogravure by Harrison, *unless otherwise stated.*

33 Chrysanthemum Emblems **34**

35 East African "Flags"

(Des V. Whiteley)

1964 (21 Oct). *Olympic Games. Tokyo. P* 14½.

207	**33**	30 c. yellow and reddish violet	10	10
208	**34**	50 c. deep reddish violet and yellow	10	10
209	**35**	1 s. 30, orange-yellow, dp green & lt blue	15	10
210		2 s. 50, magenta, deep violet-blue & lt bl	25	60
207/10		*Set of* 4	45	70

KENYA, UGANDA AND TANZANIA

The following stamps were issued by the East African Postal Administration for use in Uganda, Kenya and Tanzania, excluding Zanzibar.

36 Rally Badge

37 Cars *en route*

1965 (15 Apr*). *13th East African Safari Rally. P* 14.

211	**36**	30 c. black, yellow and turquoise	10	10
212		50 c. black, yellow and brown	10	10
		a. Imperf (pair)		
213	**37**	1 s. 30, dp bluish green, yell-ochre & blue	20	10
214		2 s. 50, dp bluish green, brn-red & lt blue	30	65
211/14		*Set of* 4	60	80

*This is the local release date. The Crown Agents in London issued the stamps the previous day.

38 I.T.U. Emblem and Symbols

1965 (17 May). *I.T.U. Centenary. P* 14½.

215	**38**	30 c. gold, chocolate and magenta	10	10
216		50 c. gold, chocolate and grey	15	10
217		1 s. 30, gold, chocolate and blue	30	10
218		2 s. 50, gold, chocolate & turquoise-grn	55	80
215/18		*Set of* 4	1·00	1·00

39 I.C.Y. Emblem

1965 (4 Aug). *International Co-operation Year. P* 14½ × 14.

219	**39**	30 c. deep bluish green and gold	10	10
220		50 c. black and gold	15	10
221		1 s. 30, ultramarine and gold	30	10
222		2 s. 50, carmine-red and gold	75	1·75
219/22		*Set of* 4	1·25	1·75

40 Game Park Lodge, Tanzania

(Des Rena Fennessy)

1966 (4 Apr). *Tourism. T* **40** *and similar horiz designs. Multi-coloured. P* 14½.

223	30 c. Type **40**	15	10
224	50 c. Murchison Falls, Uganda	40	10
	a. Blue omitted	£170	
225	1 s. 30, Lesser Flamingoes, Lake Nakuru, Kenya	1·50	20
226	2 s. 50, Deep Sea Fishing, Tanzania.. ..	1·50	1·40
223/6	.. .. *Set of* 4	3·25	1·60

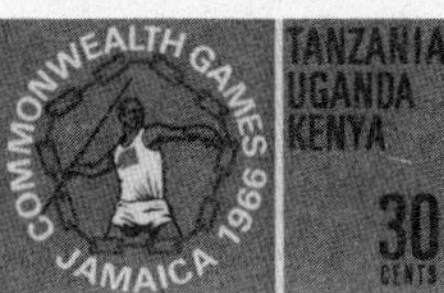

41 Games Emblem

(Des Harrison)

1966 (2 Aug). *Eighth British Empire and Commonwealth Games Jamaica. P* 14½.

227	**41**	30 c. black, gold, turq-green & grey ..	10	10
228		50 c. black, gold, cobalt and cerise ..	10	10
229		1 s. 30, blk, gold, rosine & dp bluish grn	15	10
230		2 s. 50, black, gold, lake and ultramarine	30	55
227/30		.. .. *Set of* 4	55	60

42 U.N.E.S.C.O. Emblem

(Des Harrison)

1966 (3 Oct). *20th Anniv of U.N.E.S.C.O. P* 14½ × 14.

231	**42**	30 c. black, emerald and red	25	10
232		50 c. black, emerald and light brown ..	30	10
233		1 s. 30, black, emerald and grey ..	75	15
234		2 s. 50, black, emerald and yellow ..	1·40	1·25
231/4		.. .. *Set of* 4	2·40	1·25

43 D.H. "Dragon Rapide"

(Des R. Granger Barrett)

1967 (23 Jan). *21st Anniv of East African Airways. T* **43** *and similar horiz designs. P* 14½.

235	30 c. slate-violet, greenish blue & myrtle-grn	30	10
236	50 c. multicoloured	40	10
	a. Red omitted	£150	
237	1 s. 30, multicoloured	85	15
238	2 s. 50, multicoloured	1·25	1·75
235/8	.. .. *Set of* 4	2·50	1·90

Designs:—50 c. "Super VC-10"; 1 s. 30, "Comet 4"; 2 s. 50, "F-27 Friendship".

44 Pillar Tomb **45** Rock Painting

(Des Rena Fennessy)

1967 (2 May). *Archaeological Relics. T* **44/5** *and similar designs. P* 14½.

239	30 c. ochre, black and deep reddish purple ..	15	10
240	50 c. orange-red, black and greyish brown ..	40	10
241	1 s. 30, black, greenish, yellow and deep yellow-green	75	10
242	2 s. 50, black, ochre and brown-red	1·10	1·25
239/42	.. .. *Set of* 4	2·25	1·40

Designs:—1 s. 30, Clay head; 2 s. 50, Proconsul skull.

48 Unified Symbols of Kenya, Tanzania, and Uganda

(Des Rena Fennessy)

1967 (1 Dec). *Foundation of East African Community. P* 14½ × 14.

243	**48**	5 s. gold, black and grey	40	1·00

49 Mountaineering

(Des Rena Fennessy)

1968 (4 Mar). *Mountains of East Africa. T* **49** *and similar horiz designs. Multicoloured. P* 14.

244	30 c. Type **49**	10	10
245	50 c. Mount Kenya	15	10
246	1 s. 30, Mount Kilimanjaro	30	10
247	2 s. 50, Ruwenzori Mountains	55	1·00
244/7	.. .. *Set of* 4	1·00	1·10

50 Family and Rural Hospital

(Des Rena Fennessy. Litho D.L.R.)

1968 (13 May). *20th Anniv of World Health Organization. T* **50** *and similar horiz designs. P* 13½.

248	30 c. deep yellow-green, lilac and chocolate ..	10	10
249	50 c. slate-lilac, lilac and black	10	10
250	1 s. 30, yellow-brown, lilac and chocolate ..	15	10
251	2 s. 50, grey, black and reddish lilac.. ..	25	60
248/51	.. .. *Set of* 4	50	75

Designs:—50 c. Family and nurse; 1 s. 30, Family and micro-scope; 2 s. 50, Family and hypodermic syringe.

51 Olympic Stadium, Mexico City

(Des V. Whiteley)

1968 (14 Oct). *Olympic Games, Mexico. T* **51** *and similar designs. P* 14.

252	30 c. light green and black	10	10
253	50 c. black and blue-green	10	10
254	1 s. 30, carmine-red, black and grey.. ..	15	10
255	2 s. 50, blackish brown and yellow-brown ..	25	60
252/5	.. .. *Set of* 4	50	75

Designs: *Horiz*—50 c. High-diving boards; 1 s. 30, Running tracks. *Vert*—2 s. 50, Boxing ring.

52 M.V. *Umoja*

(Des A. Grosart)

1969 (20 Jan). *Water Transport. T* **52** *and similar horiz designs. P* 14.

256	30 c. deep blue, light blue and slate-grey ..	15	10
	a. Slate-grey omitted	32·00	
257	50 c. multicoloured	20	10
258	1 s. 30, bronze-grn, greenish blue & blue ..	45	15
259	2 s. 50, red-orange, dp blue & pale blue ..	1·00	1·50
256/9	.. .. *Set of* 4	1·60	1·75

Designs:—50 c. S.S. *Harambee*; 1 s. 30, M.V. *Victoria*; 2 s. 50, *St. Michael*.

53 I.L.O. Emblem and Agriculture **54** Pope Paul VI and Ruwenzori Mountains

(Des Rena Fennessy)

1969 (14 Apr). *50th Anniv of International Labour Organization. T* **53** *and similar horiz designs. P* 14.

260	30 c. black, green and greenish yellow ..	10	10
261	50 c. black, plum, cerise and rose	10	10
262	1 s. 30, black, orange-brown & yellow-orange	10	10
263	2 s. 50, black, ultramarine & turquoise-blue	20	30
260/3	.. .. *Set of* 4	35	40

Designs:—50 c. I.L.O. emblem and building work; 1 s. 30, I.L.O. emblem and factory workers; 2 s. 50, I.L.O. emblem and shipping.

(Des Harrison)

1969 (31 July). *Visit of Pope Paul VI to Uganda. P* 14.

264	**54**	30 c. black, gold and royal blue	15	10
265		70 c. black, gold and claret	20	10
266		1 s. 50, black, gold and deep blue	30	20
267		2 s. 50, black, gold and violet	45	75
264/7		.. .. *Set of* 4	1·00	95

55 Euphorbia Tree shaped as Africa and Emblem **56** Marimba

(Des Rena Fennessy. Litho B.W.)

1969 (8 Dec). *Fifth Anniv of African Development Bank. P* 13½.

268	**55**	30 c. dp bluish green, gold & blue-green	10	10
269		70 c. dp bluish green, gold & reddish pur	15	10
270		1 s. 50, dp bluish grn, gold & lt turq-bl	20	10
271		2 s. 50, dp bluish grn, gold & orge-brn	25	35
268/71		.. .. *Set of* 4	55	45

(Des Rena Fennessy. Litho B.W.)

1970 (16 Feb). *Musical Instruments. T* **56** *and similar horiz designs. P* 11 × 12.

272	30 c. buff, yellow-brown and bistre-brown ..	15	10
273	70 c. olive-green, yellow-brown and yellow ..	20	10
274	1 s. 50, chocolate and yellow..	40	10
275	2 s. 50, salmon, yellow and chocolate ..	60	60
272/5	.. .. *Set of* 4	1·25	70

Designs:—70 c. Amadinda; 1 s. 50, Nzomari; 2 s. 50, Adeudeu.

57 Satellite Earth Station **58** Athlete

(Des V. Whiteley. Litho J.W.)

1970 (18 May). *Inauguration of East African Satellite Earth Station. T* **57** *and similar horiz designs. P* 14½ × 14.

276	30 c. multicoloured	10	10
277	70 c. multicoloured	15	10
278	1 s. 50, black, slate-violet and pale orange ..	20	10
279	2 s. 50, multicoloured	45	60
276/9	.. .. *Set of* 4	75	70

Designs:—70 c. Transmitter in daytime; 1 s. 50, Transmitter at night; 2 s. 50, Earth and satellite.

(Des Rena Fennessy. Litho Walsall)

1970 (13 July). *Ninth Commonwealth Games. P* 14 × 14½.

280	**58**	30 c. orange-brown and black	10	10
281		70 c. olive-green and black	10	10
282		1 s. 50, slate-lilac and black	10	10
283		2 s. 50, turquoise-blue and black ..	20	40
280/3		.. .. *Set of* 4	35	50

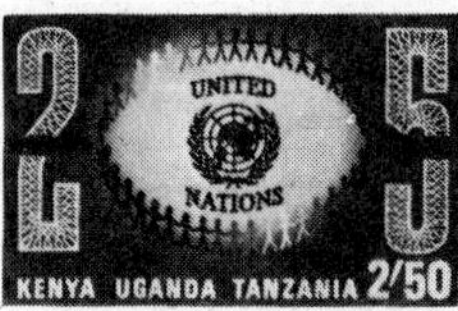

59 "25" and U.N. Emblem

(Des Rena Fennessy)

1970 (19 Oct). *25th Anniv of United Nations. P* 14½.

284	**59**	30 c. multicoloured	10	10
285		70 c. multicoloured	10	10
286		1 s. 50, multicoloured	20	10
287		2 s. 50, multicoloured	45	80
284/7		.. .. *Set of* 4	70	90

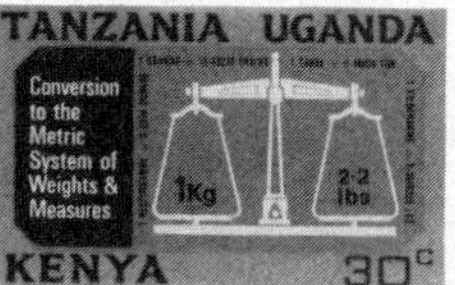

60 Balance and Weight Equivalents

(Des and litho J.W.)

1971 (4 Jan). *Conversion to Metric System. T* **60** *and similar horiz designs. Multicoloured. P* 14½ × 14.

288	30 c. Type **60**	10	10
289	70 c. Fahrenheit and Centigrade Thermometers	10	10
290	1 s. 50, Petrol Pump and Liquid Capacities	15	10
291	2 s. 50, Surveyors and Land Measures	35	65
288/91	*Set of* 4	60	70

61 Class "11" Locomotive

(Des Rena Fennessy)

1971 (5 Apr). *Railway Transport. T* **61** *and similar horiz designs. Multicoloured. P* 14.

292	30 c. Type **61**	35	10
293	70 c. Class "90" locomotive	55	10
294	1 s. 50, Class "59" locomotive	1·25	50
295	2 s. 50, Class "30" locomotive	2·25	2·75
292/5	*Set of* 4	4·00	3·00
MS296	120 × 88 mm. Nos. 292/5	6·50	9·00

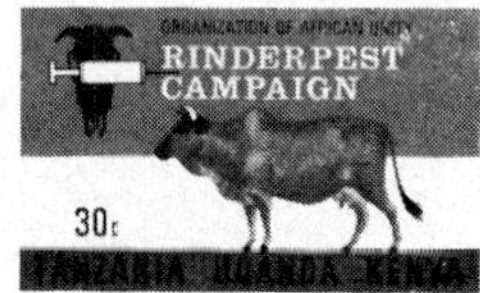

62 Syringe and Cow

(Des Rena Fennessy. Litho)

1971 (5 July). *O.A.U. Rinderpest Campaign. T* **62** *and similar horiz design. P* 14.

297	**62**	30 c. black, pale yell-brn & pale yell-grn	10	10
298	–	70 c. black, pale slate-blue & pale yell-brn	10	10
299	**62**	1 s. 50, black, plum & pale yellow-brn	15	10
300	–	2 s. 50, black, brown-red & pale yell-brn	25	50
297/300		*Set of* 4	45	60

Design:—70 c., 2 s. 50, As T **62**, but with bull facing right.

63 Livingstone meets Stanley

(Des and litho J.W.)

1971 (28 Oct). *Centenary of Livingstone and Stanley meeting at Ujiji. P* 13½ × 14.

301	**63**	5 s. multicoloured	30	75

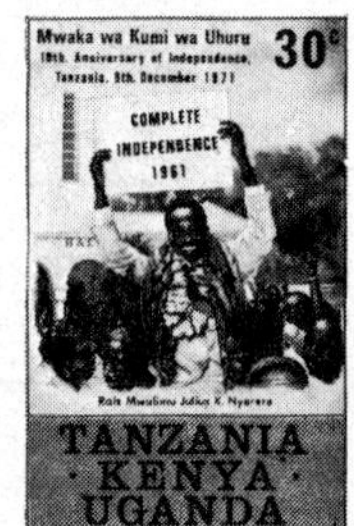

64 President Nyerere and Supporters

(Des G. Drummond. Litho J.W.)

1971 (9 Dec). *Tenth Anniv of Tanzanian Independence. T* **64** *and similar horiz designs. Multicoloured. P* 13½.

302	30 c. Type **64**	10	10
303	70 c. Ujamaa village	10	10
304	1 s. 50, Dar es Salaam University	20	20
305	2 s. 50, Kilimanjaro airport	55	1·40
302/5	*Set of* 4	80	1·50

65 Flags and Trade Fair Emblem

(Des Trade Fair Publicity Agents. Litho Questa)

1972 (23 Feb). *All-Africa Trade Fair. P* 13½ × 14.

306	**65**	30 c. multicoloured	10	10
307		70 c. multicoloured	10	10
308		1 s. 50, multicoloured	10	10
309		2 s. 50, multicoloured	25	55
306/9		*Set of* 4	40	60

66 Child with Cup

(Des Rena Fennessy. Litho Questa)

1972 (24 Apr). *25th Anniv of UNICEF. T* **66** *and similar horiz designs. Multicoloured. P* 14 × 14½.

310	30 c. Type **66**	10	10
311	70 c. Children with ball	10	10
312	1 s. 50, Child at blackboard	10	10
313	2 s. 50, Child and tractor	25	50
310/13	*Set of* 4	35	60

67 Hurdling

(Des G. Vasarhelyi. Litho J.W.)

1972 (28 Aug). *Olympic Games, Munich. T* **67** *and similar horiz designs. Multicoloured. P* 14.

314	40 c. Type **67**	10	10
315	70 c. Running	10	10
316	1 s. 50, Boxing	20	10
317	2 s. 50, Hockey	30	1·00
314/17	*Set of* 4	60	1·10
MS318	131 × 98 mm. Nos. 314/17	3·25	5·50

68 Kobs

(Des G. Drummond. Litho D.L.R.)

1972 (9 Oct). *Tenth Anniv of Ugandan Independence. T* **68** *and similar horiz designs. Multicoloured. P* 14.

319	40 c. Type **68**	20	10
320	70 c. Conference Centre	20	10
321	1 s. 50, Makerere University	45	20
322	2 s. 50, Coat of Arms	85	1·50
319/22	*Set of* 4	1·50	1·60
MS323	132 × 120 mm. Nos. 319/22. P 13 × 14	2·75	3·50

69 Community Flag

(Des Rena Fennessy. Litho)

1972 (1 Dec). *Fifth Anniv of East African Community. P* 14½ × 14.

324	**69**	5 s. multicoloured	75	1·25

70 Run-of-the-wind Anemometer

71 "Learning by Serving"

(Des P. Powell. Litho)

1973 (1 Mar*). *I.M.O./W.M.O. Centenary. T* **70** *and similar multicoloured designs. P* 14½.

325	40 c. Type **70**	10	10
326	70 c. Weather balloon (*vert*)	15	10
327	1 s. 50, Meteorological rocket	25	15
328	2 s. 50, Satellite receiving aerial	55	1·25
325/8	*Set of* 4	90	1·40

No. 325 exists with country name at foot instead of at top, and also with country name omitted (or with imprint or plate numbers in lieu). These are because of faulty registration of the perforation comb.

*This is the local release date. The Crown Agents in London did not place the stamps on sale until 5 March.

(Des Rena Fennessy. Litho)

1973 (16 July). *24th World Scout Conference, Nairobi. T* **71** *and similar vert designs. P* 14.

329	40 c. multicoloured	15	10
330	70 c. Venetian red, reddish violet and black	20	10
331	1 s. 50, cobalt, reddish violet and black	45	30
332	2 s. 50, multicoloured	1·00	1·75
329/32	*Set of* 4	1·60	2·00

Designs:—70 c. Baden-Powell's grave, Nyeri; 1 s. 50, World Scout emblem; 2 s. 50, Lord Baden-Powell.

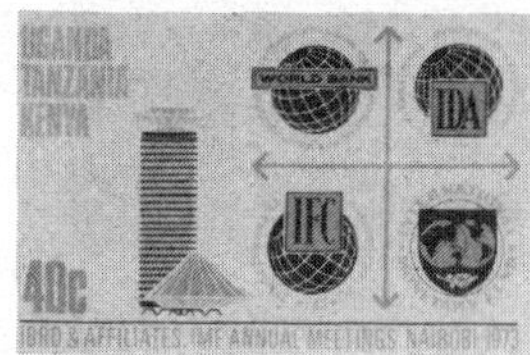

72 Kenyatta Conference Centre

(Des Marketing Communications Ltd, Nairobi; adapted J. Cooter. Litho D.L.R.)

1973 (29 Sept*). *I.M.F./World Bank Conference. T* **72** *and similar designs. P* 13½ × 14 (1 s. 50) *or* 14 × 13½ (*others*).

333	40 c. sage-green, light greenish grey & black	10	10
334	70 c. orange-brown, greenish grey and black	10	10
335	1 s. 50, multicoloured	25	35
336	2 s. 50, orange, greenish grey and black	35	90
333/6	*Set of* 4	65	1·25
MS337	166 × 141 mm. Nos. 333/6. Imperf	1·40	2·50

Designs:—Nos. 334/6 show different arrangements of Bank emblems and the Conference Centre, the 1 s. 50 being vertical.

*This is the local release date. The Crown Agents in London issued the stamps on 24 September.

73 Police Dog-handler

74 Tea Factory

(Des C. Abbott. Litho Questa)

1973 (24 Oct)–**74**. *50th Anniv of Interpol. T* **73** *and similar vert designs. P* 14.

338	40 c. yellow, blue and black	40	10
339	70 c. turquoise-green, orange-yellow & black	70	15
340	1 s. 50, light violet, yellow and black	1·25	90
341	2 s. 50, light yellow-green, red-orange and black (I)	3·50	4·50
342	2 s. 50, light yellow-green, red-orange, and black (II) (25.2.74)	3·50	4·50
338/42	*Set of* 5	8·50	9·00

Designs:—70 c. East African Policeman; 1 s. 50, Interpol emblem; 2 s. 50, Interpol H.Q.

Nos. 341/2. Type I inscribed "St. Clans"; Type II corrected to "St. Cloud".

(Des G. Drummond. Litho Enschedé)

1973 (12 Dec). *10th Anniv of Kenya's Independence. T* **74** *and similar horiz designs. Multicoloured. P* 13 × 13½.

343	40 c. Type **74**	10	10
344	70 c. Kenyatta Hospital	10	10
345	1 s. 50, Nairobi Airport	30	20
346	2 s. 50, Kindaruma hydro-electric scheme	65	1·50
343/6	*Set of* 4	1·00	1·60

75 Party H.Q.

(Des PAD Studio. Litho D.L.R.)

1974 (12 Jan). *Tenth Anniv of Zanzibar's Revolution. T* **75** *and similar horiz designs. Multicoloured. P* 13½.

347	40 c. Type **75**	10	10
348	70 c. Housing scheme	10	10
349	1 s. 50, Colour T.V.	30	20
350	2 s. 50, Amaan Stadium	65	1·50
347/50	*Set of* 4	1·00	1·60

76 "Symbol of Union"

(Des Jennifer Toombs. Litho Questa)

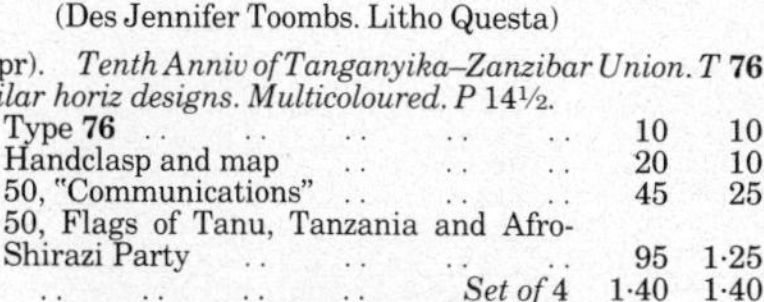

1974 (26 Apr). *Tenth Anniv of Tanganyika–Zanzibar Union. T* **76** *and similar horiz designs. Multicoloured. P* 14½.

351	40 c. Type **76**	10	10
352	70 c. Handclasp and map	20	10
353	1 s. 50, "Communications"	45	25
354	2 s. 50, Flags of Tanu, Tanzania and Afro-Shirazi Party	95	1·25
351/4	*Set of* 4	1·40	1·40

77 East African Family ("Stability of the Home")

(Des locally; adapted PAD Studio. Litho)

1974 (15 July). *17th Social Welfare Conference, Nairobi. T* **77** *and similar horiz designs. P* 14½.

355	40 c. greenish yellow, lake-brown and black	10	10
356	70 c. multicoloured	10	10
357	1 s. 50, olive-green, yellow-green and black	20	30
358	2 s. 50, light rose, reddish violet and black	45	1·50
355/8	*Set of* 4	70	1·75

Designs:—70 c. Dawn and drummer (U.N. Second Development Plan); 1 s. 50, Agricultural scene (Rural Development Plan); 2 s. 50, Transport and telephone ("Communications").

78 New Postal H.Q., Kampala

(Des Rena Fennessy. Litho)

1974 (9 Oct). *Centenary of Universal Postal Union. T* **78** *and similar horiz designs. Multicoloured. P* 14½.

359	40 c. Type **78**	10	10
360	70 c. Mail-train and post-van	15	10
361	1 s. 50, U.P.U. Building, Berne	15	15
362	2 s. 50, Loading mail into "VC-10"	30	80
359/62	*Set of* 4	60	95

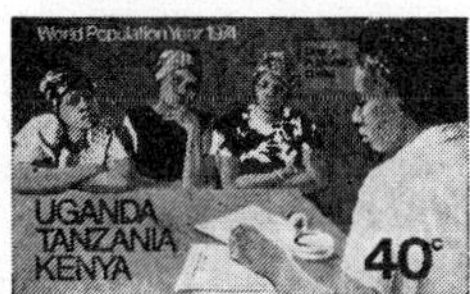

79 Family-planning Clinic

(Des C. Abbott. Litho)

1974 (16 Dec). *World Population Year. T* **79** *and similar horiz designs. P* 14.

363	40 c. multicoloured	10	10
364	70 c. deep reddish violet and scarlet	10	10
365	1 s. 50, multicoloured	15	15
366	2 s. 50, apple-green, blue-green & bluish blk	30	90
363/6	*Set of* 4	55	1·00

Designs:—70 c. "Tug of war"; 1 s. 50, Population "scales"; 2 s. 50, W.P.Y. emblem.

80 Seronera Wild-Life Lodge, Tanzania

(Des R. Granger Barrett. Litho)

1975 (26 Feb*). *East Africa Game Lodges. T* **80** *and similar horiz designs. Multicoloured. P* 14.

367	40 c. Type **80**	15	10
368	70 c. Mweya Safari Lodge, Uganda	20	10
369	1 s. 50, "Ark"—Aberdare Forest Lodge, Kenya	35	30
370	2 s. 50, Paraa Safari Lodge, Uganda	80	2·00
367/70	*Set of* 4	1·40	2·25

*This is the local release date. The Crown Agents in London issued the stamps on 24 February.

PRICES OF SETS

Set prices are given for many issues, generally those containing three stamps or more. Definitive sets include one of each value or major colour change, but do not cover different perforations, die types or minor shades. Where a choice is possible the set prices are based on the cheapest versions of the stamps included in the listings.

81 Kitana (wooden comb), Bajun of Kenya **82** International Airport, Entebbe

(Des Mrs. Gombe of the E.A.P.T.; adapted C. Abbott. Litho Questa)

1975 (5 May). *African Arts. T* **81** *and similar vert designs. Multicoloured. P* 13½.

371	50 c. Type **81**	10	10
372	1 s. Earring, Chaga of Tanzania	15	10
373	2 s. Okoco (armlet), Acholi of Uganda	30	35
374	3 s. Kitete (Kamba gourd), Kenya	70	95
371/4	*Set of* 4	1·10	1·25

(Des PAD Studio. Litho State Ptg Wks, Warsaw)

1975 (28 July). *O.A.U. Summit Conference, Kampala. T* **82** *and similar multicoloured designs. P* 11.

375	50 c. Type **82**	10	10
376	1 s. Map of Africa and flag (*vert*)	10	10
377	2 s. Nile Hotel, Kampala	25	65
378	3 s. Martyrs' Shrine, Namugongo (*vert*)	35	1·25
375/8	*Set of* 4	70	1·90

83 Ahmed ("Presidential" Elephant) **84** Maasai Manyatta (village), Kenya

(Des locally. Litho State Ptg Wks, Warsaw)

1975 (11 Sept). *Rare Animals. T* **83** *and similar vert designs. Multicoloured. P* 11.

379	50 c. Type **83**	40	10
380	1 s. Albino buffalo	40	10
381	2 s. Ahmed in grounds of National Museum	1·25	1·50
382	3 s. Abbott's Duiker	1·25	2·25
379/82	*Set of* 4	3·00	3·50

(Des Rena Fennessy. Litho Questa)

1975 (3 Nov). *Second World Black and African Festival of Arts and Culture, Nigeria* (1977). *T* **84** *and similar horiz designs. Multicoloured. P* 13½ × 14.

383	50 c. Type **84**	15	10
384	1 s. "Heartbeat of Africa" (Ugandan dancers)	15	10
385	2 s. Makonde sculpture, Tanzania	45	65
386	3 s. "Early Man and Technology" (skinning hippopotamus)	75	1·10
383/6	*Set of* 4	1·40	1·75

For similar stamps see Nos. 76/80 of Kenya and the corresponding issues of Tanzania and Uganda.

85 Fokker "Friendship" at Nairobi Airport

(Des local artist. Litho State Security Ptg Wks, Warsaw)

1976 (2 Jan). *30th Anniv of East African Airways. T* **85** *and similar triangular designs. Multicoloured. P* 11½.

387	50 c. Type **85**	55	20
	a. Black (aircraft) and blue omitted	†	£550
388	1 s. "DC 9" at Kilimanjaro Airport	65	20
389	2 s. Super "VC 10" at Entebbe Airport	2·00	2·00
390	3 s. East African Airways Crest	2·50	2·50
387/90	*Set of* 4	5·00	4·50

Two black plates were used for each of Nos. 387/9: one for the frame and the other for the centre. No. 387a, three used copies of which are known, has the printing from the blue and centre black plates omitted.

Further commemorative issues were released during 1976–78, using common designs, but inscribed for one republic only. These are listed under KENYA, TANZANIA, or UGANDA.

Co-operation between the postal services of the three member countries virtually ceased after 30 June 1977, the postal services of Kenya, Tanzania and Uganda then operating independently.

OFFICIAL STAMPS

For use on official correspondence of the Tanganyika Government.

OFFICIAL

(O 1)

1959 (1 July). *Nos.* 167/71, 173 *and* 175/80 *optd as Type* O **1**.

O 1	5 c. black and deep brown	10	10
O 2	10 c. carmine-red	10	10
O 3	15 c. black and light blue (No. 169a)	10	10
O 4	20 c. black and orange	10	10
	a. Opt double	—	£500
O 5	30 c. black and deep ultramarine	10	10
O 6	50 c. reddish purple	10	10
O 7	1 s. black and claret	15	10
O 8	1 s. 30, orange and deep lilac	65	30
O 9	2 s. black and bronze-green	85	50
O10	5 s. black and orange	2·00	1·25
O11	10 s. black and deep ultramarine	2·00	2·50
O12	£1 brown-red and black	6·00	10·00
O1/12	*Set of* 12	11·00	13·50

The 30 c., 50 c. and 1 s. exist with overprint double, but with the two impressions almost coincident.

OFFICIAL **OFFICIAL**

(O 2) (O 3)

1960 (18 Oct). *Nos.* 183/6, 188, 190, 192 *and* 196 *optd with Type* O **2** (*cents values*) *or* O **3**.

O13	5 c. Prussian blue	10	15
O14	10 c. yellow-green	10	10
O15	15 c. dull purple	10	15
O16	20 c. magenta	10	10
O17	30 c. vermilion	10	10
O18	50 c. slate-violet	30	15
O19	1 s. deep reddish violet and reddish purple	30	10
O20	5 s. rose-red and purple	4·00	65
O13/20	*Set of* 8	4·50	1·10

POSTAGE DUE STAMPS

D 1 D 2

(Typo Waterlow)

1928–33. *Wmk Mult Script CA. P* 15 × 14.

D1 D **1**	5 c. violet	1·25	25
D2	10 c. vermilion	1·25	15
D3	20 c. yellow-green	1·25	2·50
D4	30 c. brown (1931)	7·50	7·50
D5	40 c. dull blue	4·75	11·00
D6	1 s. grey-green (1933)	32·00	48·00
D1/6	*Set of* 6	42·00	65·00
D1/6 Optd/Perf "Specimen"	*Set of* 6	£100	

(Typo D.L.R.)

1935 (1 May)–**60**. *Wmk Mult Script CA. P* 14.

D 7 D **2**	5 c. violet	1·25	40
D 8	10 c. scarlet	30	10
D 9	20 c. green	40	15
D10	30 c. brown	60	50
	a. Bistre-brown (19.7.60)	2·00	3·00
D11	40 c. ultramarine	1·50	3·00
D12	1 s. grey	10·00	17·00
D7/12	*Set of* 6	12·50	19·00
D7/12 Perf "Specimen"	*Set of* 6	75·00	

Kiribati

(*formerly* Gilbert Islands)

GILBERT ISLANDS

On 1 January 1976, the Gilbert Islands and Tuvalu (Ellice Islands) became separate Crown Colonies.

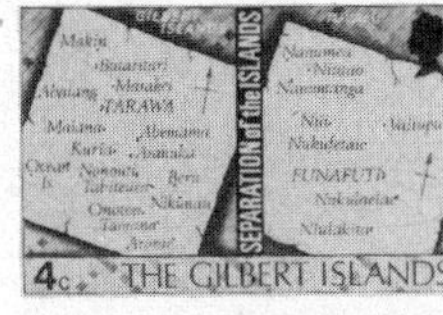

THE GILBERT ISLANDS

1 Charts of Gilbert Islands and Tuvalu (formerly Ellice) Islands (**2**)

(Des J. Cooter. Litho Questa)

1976 (2 Jan). *Separation of the Islands. T* **1** *and similar horiz design. Multicoloured. W w* **14** (*sideways*). *P* 14.

1	4 c. Type **1**	50	75
2	35 c. Maps of Tarawa and Funafuti	1·25	2·00

1976 (2 Jan). *Nos.* 173/86 *of Gilbert & Ellice Is optd as T* **2**.

(*a*) *W w* **12** (*sideways on Nos.* 5/7 *and* 9/10)

3	1 c. Cutting toddy (R.)	25	20
4	2 c. Lagoon fishing (R.)	50	75
5	2 c. Lagoon fishing (*wmk sideways*) (R.)	50	30
6	3 c. Cleaning pandanus leaves (R.)	17·00	22·00
7	4 c. Casting nets (R.)	30	50

8 20 c. Beating a pandanus leaf (R.) † £100
9 20 c. Beating a pandanus leaf (*wmk sideways*) (R.) 5·00 3·25
10 25 c. Loading copra 40·00 50·00
 a. Opt double (Blk. + R.) £250
10*b* 50 c. Local handicrafts £700 £800

(*b*) W w **14** (*sideways on* 3, 5, 20, 25 *and* 35 *c.*; *inverted on others*)
11 1 c. Cutting toddy (R.) 20 30
12 3 c. Cleaning pandanus leaves (R.) 40 50
13 5 c. Gilbertese canoe (R.) 50 50
14 6 c. De-husking coconuts 50 60
15 8 c. Weaving pandanus fronds (R.) 50 60
16 10 c. Weaving a basket 50 60
17 15 c. Tiger Shark 1·50 1·25
18 20 c. Beating a pandanus leaf (R.) 1·50 90
19 25 c. Loading copra 2·00 1·25
20 35 c. Fishing at night (Gold) 2·00 1·75
21 50 c. Local handicrafts 2·50 2·75
22 $1 Weaving coconut screens (R.) 8·00 9·00
 a. Opt double £275
3, 4, 7 *and* 12/22 *Set of* 14 19·00 19·00

3 M.V. *Teraaka*

(Des J. Cooter. Litho Questa)

1976 (1 July). *Horiz designs as T* **3**. *Multicoloured*. W w **14** (*sideways*). *P* 14.
23 1 c. Type **3** 20 15
24 3 c. M.V. *Tautunu* 30 20
25 4 c. Moorish Idol 30 20
26 5 c. Hibiscus 30 20
27 6 c. Eastern Reef Heron 35 30
28 7 c. Tarawa Cathedral 30 30
29 8 c. Frangipani 30 30
30 10 c. Maneaba building 30 30
31 12 c. Betio Harbour 45 45
32 15 c. Evening scene 55 45
33 20 c. Marakei Atoll 35 35
34 35 c. Tangintebu Chapel 35 40
35 40 c. Flamboyant tree 40 45
36 50 c. *Hypolimnas bolina* (butterfly) 2·25 1·75
37 $1 Ferry *Tabakea* 2·00 2·50
38 $2 National flag 2·25 2·75
23/38 *Set of* 16 9·50 10·00

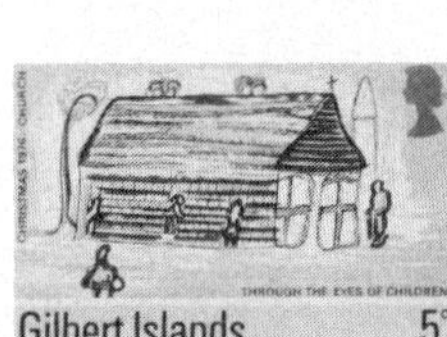

4 Church

5 Porcupine Fish Helmet

(Des P. Powell. Litho Questa)

1976 (15 Sept). *Christmas. Children's Drawings. T* **4** *and similar multicoloured designs*. W w **14** (*sideways on* 5 *and* 35 *c.*). *P* 14.
39 5 c. Type **4** 35 15
40 15 c. Feasting (*vert*) 50 15
41 20 c. Maneaba (*vert*) 55 30
42 35 c. Dancing 70 45
39/42 *Set of* 4 1·90 95

(Des J. Cooter. Litho J.W.)

1976 (6 Dec). *Artefacts. T* **5** *and similar vert designs. Multicoloured*. W w **14**. *P* 13.
43 5 c. Type **5** 35 15
44 15 c. Shark's Teeth Dagger 50 35
45 20 c. Fighting Gauntlet 55 40
46 35 c. Coconut Body Armour 70 55
43/6 *Set of* 4 1·90 1·25
MS47 140 × 130 mm. Nos. 43/6. P 14 10·00 14·00

6 Queen in Coronation Robes

7 Commodore Byron and H.M.S. *Dolphin*

(Des J. Cooter. Litho Questa)

1977 (7 Feb). *Silver Jubilee. T* **6** *and similar vert designs. Multicoloured*. W w **14**. *P* 14.
48 8 c. Prince Charles' visit, 1970 15 10
49 20 c. Prince Philip's visit, 1959 20 15
50 40 c. Type **6** 30 35
48/50 *Set of* 3 60 55

(Des J. Cooter. Litho Questa)

1977 (1 June). *Explorers. T* **7** *and similar horiz designs. Multicoloured*. W w **14** (*sideways*). *P* 14.
51 5 c. Type **7** 1·00 1·50
52 15 c. Capt. Fanning and *Betsey* 1·50 2·75
53 20 c. Admiral Bellingshausen and *Vostok* 2·00 3·25
54 35 c. Capt. Wilkes and *Vincennes* 3·50 5·75
51/4 *Set of* 4 7·00 12·00

8 H.M.S. *Resolution* and H.M.S. *Discovery*

9 Emblem and Island Scene

(Des J. Cooter. Litho Questa)

1977 (12 Sept). *Christmas and Bicentenary of Capt. Cook's Discovery of Christmas Is. T* **8** *and similar multicoloured designs*. W w **14** (*sideways on* 15 *and* 40 *c.*). *P* 14.
55 8 c. Type **8** 55 10
56 15 c. Logbook entry (*horiz*) 70 15
57 20 c. Capt. Cook 85 20
58 40 c. Landing party (*horiz*) 1·75 60
55/8 *Set of* 4 3·50 95
MS59 140 × 140 mm. Nos. 55/8. Wmk sideways 10·00 12·00

(Des J. Cooter. Litho J.W.)

1977 (5 Dec). *50th Anniv of Scouting in the Gilbert Is. T* **9** *and similar multicoloured designs*. W w **14** (*sideways on* 15 *and* 20 *c.*). *P* 13.
60 8 c. Type **9** 20 10
61 15 c. Patrol meeting (*horiz*) 30 20
62 20 c. Mat making (*horiz*) 40 20
63 40 c. Canoeing 50 55
60/3 *Set of* 4 1·25 95

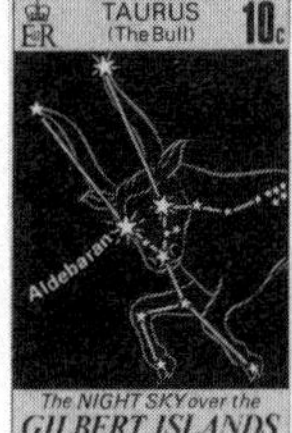

10 Taurus (The Bull)

11 Unicorn of Scotland

(Des J. Cooter. Litho Questa)

1978 (20 Feb). *Night Sky over the Gilbert Is. T* **10** *and similar vert designs*. W w **14**. *P* 14.
64 10 c. black and light new blue 20 15
65 20 c. black and light rose-red 30 30
66 25 c. black and sage-green 35 35
67 45 c. black and orange 50 60
64/7 *Set of* 4 1·25 1·25
Designs:—20 c. Canis Major (the Great Dog); 25 c. Scorpio (the Scorpion); 45 c. Orion (the Giant Warrior).

(Des C. Abbott. Litho Questa)

1978 (21 Apr). *25th Anniv of Coronation. T* **11** *and similar vert designs*. *P* 15.
68 45 c. green, bluish violet and silver 30 40
 a. Sheetlet. Nos. 68/70 × 2 1·60
69 45 c. multicoloured 30 40
70 45 c. green, bluish violet and silver 30 40
68/70 *Set of* 3 80 1·10
Designs:—No. 68, Type **11**; No. 69, Queen Elizabeth II; No. 70, Great Frigate Bird.
Nos. 68/70 were printed together in small sheets of 6, containing two *se-tenant* strips of 3, with horizontal gutter margin between.

12 Birds in Flight to Tarawa

(Des local artists; adapted G. Hutchins. Litho Enschedé)

1978 (5 June). *25th Anniv of Return of King George V School to Tarawa. T* **12** *and similar horiz designs. Multicoloured*. W w **14** (*sideways*). *P* 14 × 13.
71 10 c. Type **12** 10 10
72 20 c. Tarawa, Abemama and school badge 20 20
73 25 c. Rejoicing islanders 20 20
74 45 c. King George V School on Tarawa and Abemama 35 35
71/4 *Set of* 4 75 75

13 "Te Kaue ni Maie"

14 H.M.S. *Endeavour*

(Des W. Walsh. Litho J.W.)

1978 (25 Sept). *Christmas. Kaue (traditional head decorations). T* **13** *and similar horiz designs. Multicoloured*. W w **14** (*sideways*). *P* 14.
75 10 c. Type **13** 15 10
76 20 c. "Te Itera" 20 15
77 25 c. "Te Bau" 25 20
78 45 c. "Te Tai" 35 30
75/8 *Set of* 4 85 65
MS79 149 × 99 mm. Nos. 75/8. P 13 × 13½ 1·75 4·50

(Des and litho (45 c. also embossed) Walsall)

1979 (22 Feb*). *Bicentenary of Captain Cook's Voyages, 1768–79. T* **14** *and similar vert designs*. *P* 11.
80 10 c. multicoloured 25 15
81 20 c. multicoloured 40 30
82 25 c. black, light green and pale lilac 50 45
83 45 c. multicoloured 75 80
80/3 *Set of* 4 1·75 1·50
Designs:—20 c. Green Turtle; 25 c. Quadrant; 45 c. Flaxman/Wedgwood medallion of Captain Cook.
*This was the local issue date; the stamps were released in London on 15 January.

The Gilbert Islands achieved independence on 12 July 1979 and were renamed Kiribati.

KIRIBATI

INDEPENDENT

15 Kiribati Flag

(Des G. Drummond. Litho Questa)

1979 (12 July). *Independence. T* **15** *and similar horiz design. Multicoloured*. W w **14** (*sideways*). *P* 14.
84 10 c. Type **15** 10 20
85 45 c. Houses of Parliament and Maneaba ni Maungatabu (House of Assembly) 30 50

16 M.V. *Teraaka* (training ship)

17 Gilbert and Ellice Islands 1911 ½d. Stamp

(Des J. Cooter. Litho Questa)

1979 (12 July)–**80**. *Horiz designs as T* **16**. *Multicoloured*. W w **14** (*sideways*). *P* 14.
86 1 c. Type **16** 10 10
87 3 c. M.V. *Tautunu* (inter-island freighter) 10 10
88 5 c. Hibiscus 10 10
89 7 c. Catholic Cathedral, Tarawa 10 10
90 10 c. Maneaba, Bikenibeu 10 10
91 12 c. Betio Harbour 15 15
92 15 c. Eastern Reef Heron 35 20
93 20 c. Flamboyant Tree 20 20
94 25 c. Moorish Idol (fish) 30 30
95 30 c. Frangipani 25 25
96 35 c. G.I.P.C. Chapel, Tangintebu 25 25
97 50 c. *Hypolimnas bolina* (butterfly) 75 55
98 $1 *Tabakea* (Tarawa Lagoon ferry) 70 75
99 $2 Evening scene 80 1·00
99*a* $5 National flag (27.8.80) 5·00 7·50
86/99*a* *Set of* 15 8·00 10·50
See also Nos. 121/35.

(Des J.W. Litho Questa)

1979 (27 Sept). *Death Centenary of Sir Rowland Hill. T* **17** *and similar vert designs showing stamps. Multicoloured*. W w **14**. *P* 14.
100 10 c. Type **17** 10 10
101 20 c. Gilbert and Ellice Islands 1956 2s. 6d. definitive 15 20
102 25 c. Great Britain 1902 2s. 6d. 15 20
103 45 c. Gilbert and Ellice Islands 1924 10s. 25 35
100/3 *Set of* 4 60 75
MS104 113 × 110 mm. Nos. 100/3 75 85

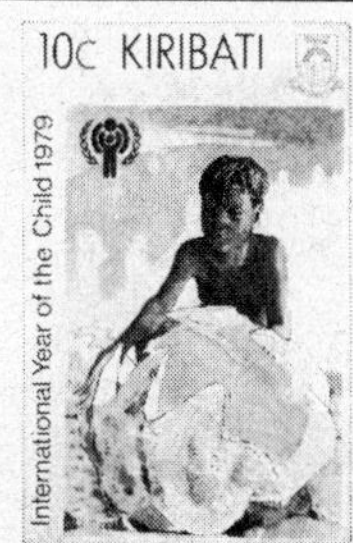

18 Boy with Clam Shell

(Des D. Bowen. Litho Enschedé)

1979 (28 Nov). *International Year of the Child. T* **18** *and similar multicoloured designs. W w* **14** *(sideways on 20 c.). P* 13 × 13½ (20 c.) *or* 13½ × 13 *(others).*

105	10 c. Type **18**	10	10
106	20 c. Child climbing coconut tree (*horiz*)	10	10
107	45 c. Girl reading	15	20
108	$1 Child in costume	30	50
105/8	*Set of* 4	55	75

19 Downrange Station, Christmas Island

(Des J. Cooter. Litho Format)

1980 (20 Feb). *Satellite Tracking. T* **19** *and similar multicoloured designs. P* 14½.

109	25 c. Type **19**	10	10
110	45 c. Map of South Pacific showing trajectory of Experimental Communications Satellite	15	15
111	$1 Rocket launch, Tanegashima, Japan (*vert*)	30	35
109/11	*Set of* 3	50	55

20 T.S. *Teraaka*

(Litho Format)

1980 (30 Apr). *"London 1980" International Stamp Exhibition. T* **20** *and similar horiz designs. Multicoloured. P* 14½.

112	12 c. Type **20**	10	10
113	25 c. Loading Air Tungaru aeroplane, Bonriki Airport	10	10
114	30 c. Radio Operator	15	10
115	$1 Bairiki Post Office	30	35
112/15	*Set of* 4	50	50
MS116	139 × 116 mm. Nos. 112/15. P 14 ×14½	55	75

Nos. 112/15 were each printed in sheets of 12 containing *se-tenant* stamp-size labels in positions 4 and 6.

21 *Achaea janata*

(Des J. Cooter. Litho Questa)

1980 (27 Aug). *Moths. T* **21** *and similar horiz designs. Multicoloured. P* 14.

117	12 c. Type **21**	15	10
118	25 c. *Ethmia nigroapicella*	20	15
119	30 c. *Utetheisa pulchelloides*	20	15
120	50 c. *Anua coronata*	25	25
117/20	*Set of* 4	70	60

1980 (27 Aug)–**81**. *As Nos.* 86/99*a but no wmk.*

121	1 c. Type **16** (4.81)	10	20
122	3 c. M.V. *Tautunu* (inter-island freighter) (6.1.81)	10	20
123	5 c. Hibiscus	10	15
124	7 c. Catholic Cathedral, Tarawa	10	15
125	10 c. Maneaba, Bikenibeu (19.11.80)	10	15
126	12 c. Betio Harbour (11.12.80)	15	20
127	15 c. Eastern Reef Heron (11.12.80)	35	30
128	20 c. Flamboyant Tree (6.1.81)	20	40
129	25 c. Moorish Idol (19.11.80)	25	30
130	30 c. Frangipani (4.81)	25	40
131	35 c. G.I.P.C. Chapel, Tangintebu (4.81)	25	40
132	50 c. *Hypolimnas bolina elliciana* (butterfly) (4.81)	75	85
133	$1 *Tabakea* (Tarawa Lagoon ferry) (11.12.80)	90	1·75
134	$2 Evening scene (11.12.80)	1·40	2·50
135	$5 National flag (11.12.80)	3·00	5·50
121/35	*Set of* 15	7·00	12·00

22 Captain Cook Hotel, Christmas Island

(Des J. Cooter. Litho Format)

1980 (19 Nov). *Development. T* **22** *and similar horiz designs. Multicoloured. P* 13½ × 14.

136	10 c. Type **22**	10	10
137	20 c. Sports Stadium	10	10
138	25 c. International Airport, Bonriki	15	10
139	35 c. National Library and Archives	15	10
140	$1 Otintai Hotel	30	40
136/40	*Set of* 5	65	65

23 *Acalypha godseffiana*

(Des J. Cooter. Litho Format)

1981 (18 Feb). *Flowers. T* **23** *and similar vert designs. Multicoloured. W w* **15**. *P* 14 × 13½.

141	12 c. Type **23**	10	10
142	30 c. *Hibiscus schizopetalus*	15	15
143	35 c. *Calotropis gigantea*	15	15
144	50 c. *Euphorbia pulcherrima*	20	20
141/4	*Set of* 4	55	55

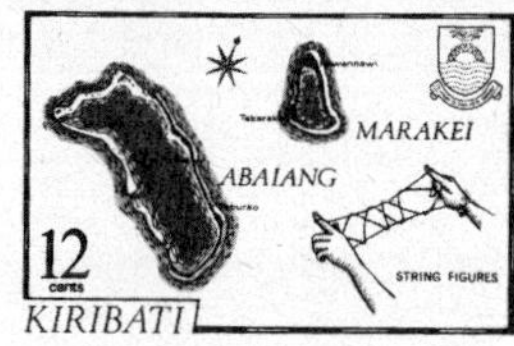

25 Maps of Abaiang and Marakei, and String Figures

(Des J. Cooter. Litho Format)

1981 (6 May). *Island Maps* (1*st series*). *T* **25** *and similar horiz designs. Multicoloured. W w* **15** *(sideways). P* 13½ × 14.

145	12 c. Type **25**	15	10
146	30 c. Maps of Little Makin and Butaritari, and village house	25	10
147	35 c. Map of Maiana, and coral road	30	15
148	$1 Map of Christmas Island, and Captain Cook's H.M.S. *Resolution*	90	75
145/8	*Set of* 4	1·40	1·00

See also Nos. 201/4, 215/18, 237/40, 256/60 and 270/3.

26 *Katherine*

27 Prince Charles and Lady Diana Spencer

(Des D. Shults. Litho Questa)

1981 (29 July–26 Nov). *Royal Wedding. Horiz designs as T* **26**, *showing Royal Yachts, and T* **27**. *Multicoloured.* (a) *W w* **15**. *P* 14.

149	12 c. Type **26**	15	15
	a. Sheetlet. No. 149 × 6 and No. 150	1·00	
150	12 c. Type **27**	30	30
151	50 c. *Osborne*	45	45
	a. Sheetlet No. 151 × 6 and No. 152	3·00	
152	50 c. Type **27**	75	75
153	$2 *Britannia*	75	1·00
	a. Sheetlet. No. 153 × 6 and No. 154	6·00	
154	$2 Type **27**	2·00	3·00
149/154	*Set of* 6	4·00	5·00
MS155	120 × 109 mm. $1.20, Type **27**. Wmk sideways. P 12 (26 Nov)	2·00	2·25

(b) *Booklet stamps. No wmk. P* 12 (26 Nov)

156	12 c. Type **26**	15	15
	a. Booklet pane. No. 156 × 4	60	
157	50 c. Type **27**	75	80
	a. Booklet pane. No. 157 × 2	1·50	

Nos. 49/54 were printed in sheetlets of seven stamps of the same face value, each containing six of the "Royal Yacht" design and one as Type **27**.

Nos. 156/7 come from $1.96 stamp booklets.

28 Tuna Bait Breeding Centre, Bonriki Fish Farm

(Des G. Drummond. Litho Questa)

1981 (19 Nov). *Tuna Fishing Industry. T* **28** *and similar horiz designs. Multicoloured. W w* **15**. *P* 14.

158	12 c. Type **28**	15	10
159	30 c. Tuna fishing	25	20
160	35 c. Cold storage, Betio	25	25
161	50 c. Government Tuna Fishing Vessel *Nei Manganibuka*	50	50
158/61	*Set of* 4	1·00	95
MS162	134 × 99 mm. Nos. 158/61. Wmk sideways	1·25	1·40

29 Pomarine Skua

(Des G. Drummond. Litho Questa)

1982 (18 Feb)–**85**. *Birds. Multicoloured designs as T* **29**. *P* 14.

163	1 c. Type **29**	15	15
164	2 c. Mallard	15	15
165	4 c. White-winged Petrel	20	20
166	5 c. Blue-faced Booby	20	20
167	7 c. Friendly Quail Dove	20	20
168	8 c. Common Shoveler	20	20
169	12 c. Polynesian Reed Warbler	20	20
170	15 c. American Golden Plover	25	25
171	20 c. Eastern Reef Heron	30	30
171*a*	25 c. Common Noddy (31.1.83)	1·50	1·00
172	30 c. Brown Booby	30	30
173	35 c. Audubon's Shearwater	30	35
174	40 c. White-throated Storm Petrel (*vert*)	35	40
175	50 c. Bristle-thighed Curlew (*vert*)	40	45
175*a*	55 c. White Tern (*inscr* "Fairy Tern") (*vert*) (19.11.85)	4·00	4·00
176	$1 Kuhl's Lory (*vert*)	85	90
177	$2 Long-tailed Koel (*vert*)	1·60	1·75
178	$5 Great Frigate Bird (*vert*)	4·25	4·50
163/78	*Set of* 18	14·00	14·00

30 De Havilland "DH114 (Heron)" **31** Mary of Teck, Princess of Wales, 1893

(Des G. Drummond. Litho Format)

1982 (18 Feb). *Inauguration of Air Tungaru Airline. T* **30** *and similar horiz designs. Multicoloured. W w* **15** *(sideways). P* 14.

179	12 c. Type **30**	10	10
180	30 c. Britten-Norman "Trislander"	20	20
181	35 c. Casa "212 (Aviocar)"	25	25
182	50 c. Boeing "727"	35	35
179/82	*Set of* 4	75	75

(Des D. Shults and J. Cooter. Litho Format)

1982 (19 May). *21st Birthday of Princess of Wales. T* **31** *and similar vert designs. Multicoloured. W w* **15**. *P* 13½ × 14.

183	12 c. Type **31**	10	10
184	50 c. Coat of Arms of Mary of Teck	30	30
185	$1 Diana, Princess of Wales	50	50
183/5	*Set of* 3	75	75

The 12 c. design is incorrectly dated; Mary of Teck became Princess of Wales in 1901.

1982 (14 July). *Birth of Prince William of Wales. Nos.* 183/5 *optd with T* **19** *of St. Kitts.*

186	12 c. Type **31**	15	15
187	50 c. Coat of arms of Mary of Teck	35	35
	a. Opt inverted	14·00	
188	$1 Diana, Princess of Wales	55	55
186/8	*Set of* 3	95	95

32 First Aid Practice

(Des J. Cooter. Litho Format)

1982 (12 Aug). *75th Anniv of Boy Scout Movement. T* **32** *and similar horiz designs. Multicoloured.* W w **15** (*sideways*). P 13½ × 14.

189 12 c. Type **32** 15 15
190 25 c. Boat repairs 30 30
191 30 c. On parade 35 35
192 50 c. Gilbert Islands 1977 8 c. Scouting stamp and "75" 60 60
189/92 .. .. *Set of* 4 1·25 1·25

33 Queen and Duke of Edinburgh with Local Dancer

(Des PAD Studio. Litho Walsall)

1982 (23 Oct). *Royal Visit. T* **33** *and similar horiz designs. Multicoloured.* W w **15** (*sideways*). P 14.

193 12 c. Type **33** 15 15
194 25 c. Queen, Duke of Edinburgh and outrigger canoe 20 20
195 35 c. New Philatelic Bureau building 30 30
193/5 .. .. *Set of* 3 60 60
MS196 88 × 76 mm. 50 c. Queen Elizabeth II .. 60 60

On No. **MS**196 the captions on the map for the islands of Teraina and Tabuaeren have been transposed.

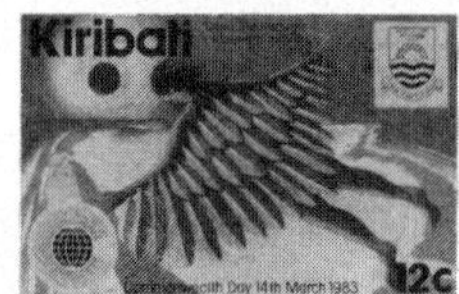

34 "Obaia, The Feathered" (Kiribati legend)

(Des J.W. Litho Format)

1983 (14 Mar). *Commonwealth Day. T* **34** *and similar horiz designs. Multicoloured.* W w **15** (*sideways*). P 14.

197 12 c. Type **34** 15 10
198 30 c. Robert Louis Stevenson Hotel, Abemama 20 20
199 50 c. Container ship off Betio 25 25
200 $1 Map of Kiribati 45 65
197/200 .. .. *Set of* 4 95 1·10

(Des J. Cooter. Litho Format)

1983 (19 May). *Island Maps* (*2nd series*). *Multicoloured designs as T* **25**. W w **15** (*sideways on* 12 *and* 25 c.). P 13½ × 14 (*horiz*) or 14 × 13½ (*vert*).

201 12 c. Beru, Nikunau and canoe 20 20
202 25 c. Abemama, Aranuka, Kuria and fish .. 30 30
203 35 c. Nonouti and reef fishing (*vert*) 40 40
204 50 c. Tarawa and House of Assembly (*vert*) .. 60 55
201/4 .. .. *Set of* 4 1·40 1·25

35 Collecting Coconuts

(Des G. Drummond. Litho Questa)

1983 (8 Aug). *Copra Industry. T* **35** *and similar horiz designs. Multicoloured.* W w **15**. P 14.

205 12 c. Type **35** 25 20
206 25 c. Selecting coconuts for copra 45 35
207 30 c. Removing husks 50 40
208 35 c. Drying copra 55 45
209 50 c. Loading copra at Betio 65 55
205/9 .. .. *Set of* 5 2·25 1·75

36 War Memorials

(Des J. Cooter. Litho Format)

1983 (17 Nov). *40th Anniv of Battle of Tarawa. T* **36** *and similar horiz designs. Multicoloured.* W w **15** (*sideways*). P 14.

210 12 c. Type **36** 20 20
211 30 c. Maps of Tarawa and Pacific Ocean .. 45 40
212 35 c. Gun emplacement 50 45
213 50 c. Modern and war-time landscapes .. 75 65
214 $1 Aircraft carrier U.S.S. *Tarawa* .. .. 1·25 1·10
210/14 .. .. *Set of* 5 2·75 2·50

(Des J. Cooter. Litho Format)

1984 (14 Feb). *Island Maps* (*3rd series*). *Multicoloured designs as T* **25**. W w **15** (*sideways*). P 13½ × 14.

215 12 c. Teraina and Captain Fanning's ship *Betsey*, 1798 .. .. 40 15
216 30 c. Nikumaroro and Hawksbill Turtle .. 70 35
217 35 c. Kanton and local postmark 80 40
218 50 c. Banaba and Flying Fish .. .. .. 1·10 55
215/18 .. .. *Set of* 4 2·75 1·25

37 Tug *Riki*

(Des J. Cooter. Litho J.W.)

1984 (9 May). *Kiribati Shipping Corporation. T* **37** *and similar horiz designs. Multicoloured.* W w **15** (*sideways*). P 14.

219 12 c. Type **37** 25 15
220 35 c. Ferry *Nei Nimanoa* 45 35
221 50 c. Ferry *Nei Tebaa* 75 60
222 $1 Cargo ship *Nei Momi* .. .. .. 1·25 1·10
219/22 .. .. *Set of* 4 2·40 2·00
MS223 115 × 98 mm. Nos. 219/222. P 13 × 13½ 2·75 3·50

38 Water and Sewage Schemes

(Des J. Cooter. Litho Format)

1984 (21 Aug). *"Ausipex" International Stamp Exhibition, Melbourne. T* **38** *and similar horiz designs. Multicoloured.* W w **15** (*sideways*). P 13½ × 14.

224 12 c. Type **38** 25 15
225 30 c. *Nouamake* (game fishing boat) 50 30
226 35 c. Overseas training schemes 60 40
227 50 c. International communications link .. 75 55
224/7 .. .. *Set of* 4 1·90 1·25

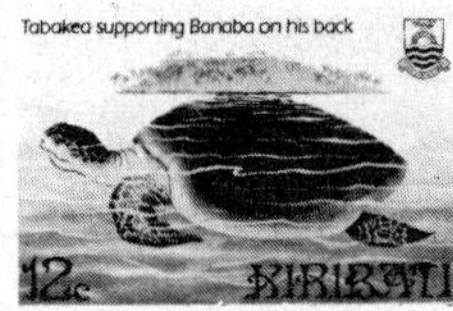

39 "Tabakea supporting Banaba"

(Des Jennifer Toombs. Litho Format)

1984 (21 Nov). *Kiribati Legends* (*1st series*). *T* **39** *and similar horiz designs. Multicoloured.* W w **15** (*sideways*). P 14.

228 12 c. Type **39** 20 20
229 30 c. "Nakaa, Judge of the Dead" 35 35
230 35 c. "Naareau and Dragonfly" 45 45
231 50 c. "Whistling Ghosts" 55 55
228/31 .. .. *Set of* 4 1·40 1·40

See also Nos. 245/8.

40 Tang

(Des G. Drummond. Litho Questa)

1985 (19 Feb). *Reef Fishes. T* **40** *and similar horiz designs. Multicoloured.* W w **15**. P 14.

232 12 c. Type **40** 60 25
233 25 c. White-barred Triggerfish .. .. .. 1·00 55
234 35 c. Surgeon Fish .. .. 1·25 70
235 80 c. Squirrel Fish .. .. 2·00 1·75
232/5 .. .. *Set of* 4 4·25 3·00
MS236 140 × 107 mm. Nos. 232/5. Wmk sideways 4·25 3·25

(Des J. Cooter. Litho J.W.)

1985 (9 May). *Island Maps* (*4th series*). *Horiz designs as T* **25**. *Multicoloured.* W w **15** (*sideways*). P 13½.

237 12 c. Tabuaeran and Great Frigate Bird .. 55 15
238 35 c. Rawaki and germinating coconuts .. 85 40
239 50 c. Arorae and Xanthid Crab .. .. 1·10 55
240 $1 Tamana and fish hook .. .. .. 1·75 1·00
237/40 .. .. *Set of* 4 3·75 2·00

41 Youths playing Football on Beach

(Des R. Stokes. Litho Cambec Press, Melbourne)

1985 (5 Aug). *International Youth Year. T* **41** *and similar multicoloured designs.* P 13½.

241 15 c. Type **41** 60 35
242 35 c. Logos of I.Y.Y. and Kiribati Youth Year .. .. 1·00 90
243 40 c. Girl preparing food (*vert*) .. .. .. 1·10 1·00
244 55 c. Map illustrating Kiribati's youth exchange links .. .. 1·40 1·40
241/4 .. .. *Set of* 4 3·75 3·25

(Des Jennifer Toombs. Litho Questa)

1985 (19 Nov). *Kiribati Legends* (*2nd series*). *Horiz designs as T* **39**. *Multicoloured.* P 14.

245 15 c. "Nang Kineia and the Tickling Ghosts" 50 30
246 35 c. "Auriaria and Tituabine" 85 75
247 40 c. "The first coming of Babai at Arorae" .. 1·00 1·00
248 55 c. "Riiki and the Milky Way" .. .. .. 1·25 1·50
245/8 .. .. *Set of* 4 3·25 3·25

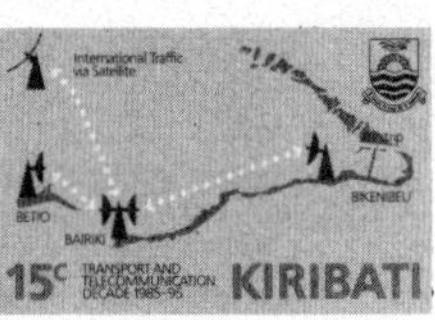

42 Map showing Telecommunications Satellite Link

(Litho Walsall)

1985 (9 Dec). *Transport and Telecommunications Decade* (*1st issue*). *T* **42** *and similar horiz design. Multicoloured.* P 14.

249 15 c. Type **42** 70 55
250 40 c. M.V. *Moanaraoi* (Tarawa-Suva service) 1·40 1·50

See also Nos. 268/9, 293/4 and 314/15.

(Des A. Theobald. Litho Questa)

1986 (21 Apr). *60th Birthday of Queen Elizabeth II. Vert designs as T* **230a** *of Jamaica. Multicoloured.* P 14½×14.

251 15 c. Princess Elizabeth in Girl Guide uniform, Windsor Castle, 1938 .. .. .. 15 15
252 35 c. At Trooping the Colour, 1980 .. .. 30 35
253 40 c. With Duke of Edinburgh in Kiribati, 1982 .. .. 35 40
254 55 c. At banquet, Austrian Embassy, London, 1966 .. .. 50 60
255 $1 At Crown Agents Head Office, London, 1983 .. .. 90 1·25
251/5 .. .. *Set of* 5 2·00 2·50

(Des J. Cooter. Litho Questa)

1986 (17 June). *Island Maps* (*5th series*). *Horiz designs as T* **25**. *Multicoloured.* P 13½ × 14.

256 15 c. Manra and Coconut Crab 70 35
257 30 c. Birnie and McKean Islands and cowrie shells .. .. 1·25 80
258 35 c. Orona and Red-footed Booby .. .. 1·40 1·00
259 40 c. Malden Island and whaling ship, 1844 .. 1·50 1·50
260 55 c. Vostok, Flint and Caroline Islands and *Vostok*, 1820 .. .. 1·75 2·00
256/60 .. .. *Set of* 5 6·00 5·00

43 *Lepidodactylus lugubris* — **44** Maps of Australia and Kiribati

(Des G. Drummond. Litho Questa)

1986 (26 Aug). *Geckos. T* **43** *and similar horiz designs. Multicoloured.* P 14.

261 15 c. Type **43** 75 35
262 35 c. *Gehyra mutilata* .. .. 1·25 90
263 40 c. *Hemidactylus frenatus* .. .. .. 1·40 1·25
264 55 c. *Gehyra oceanica* .. .. 1·90 2·00
261/4 .. .. *Set of* 4 4·75 4·00

(Des D. Miller. Litho Format)

1986 (29 Dec). *America's Cup Yachting Championship. T* **44** *and similar vert designs. Multicoloured. P* 13½×14.

265 15 c. Type **44** 20 30
a. Horiz strip of 3. Nos. 265/7 .. .. 1·75
266 55 c. America's Cup and map of course .. 50 75
267 $1.50, *Australia II* (1983 winner) .. .. 1·25 1·50
265/7 .. .. *Set of* 3 1·75 2·25

Nos. 265/7 were printed together, *se-tenant*, in horizontal strips of 3 throughout the sheet with the $1.50 at left and the 15 c. at centre of each strip.

40TH WEDDING ANNIVERSARY

45 Freighter *Moamoa* (**45***a*)

(Des and litho Questa)

1987 (31 Mar). *Transport and Telecommunications Decade (2nd issue). T* **45** *and similar horiz design. Multicoloured. P* 13½×14.

268 30 c. Type **45** .. .. 1·00 1·00
269 55 c. Telephone switchboard and automatic exchange .. .. 1·75 1·75

(Des J. Cooter. Litho Format)

1987 (22 Sept). *Island Maps (6th series). Multicoloured designs as T* **25**, *but vert. P* 14×13½.

270 15 c. Starbuck and Red-tailed Tropic Bird .. 40 25
271 30 c. Enderbury and White Tern 60 45
272 55 c. Tabiteuea and Pandanus Tree 85 70
273 $1 Onotoa and okai (house) .. .. 1·50 1·50
270/3 .. .. *Set of* 4 3·00 2·50

Nos. 271/3 exist imperforate from stock dispersed by the liquidator of Format International Security Printers Ltd.

(Des G. Drummond. Litho Format)

1987 (27 Oct). *Skinks. Horiz designs as T* **43**. *Multicoloured. P* 15.

274 15 c. *Emoia nigra* 30 25
275 35 c. *Cryptoblepharus sp.* 55 45
276 40 c. *Emoia cyanura* 60 50
277 $1 *Lipinia noctua* .. .. 1·40 1·40
274/7 .. .. *Set of* 4 2·50 2·40
MS278 130×114 mm. Nos. 274/7 .. .. 3·00 3·50

Nos. 274/8 exist imperforate from stock dispersed by the liquidator of Format International Security Printers Ltd.

1987 (30 Nov). *Royal Ruby Wedding. Nos. 251/5 optd with T* **45***a in silver.*

279 15 c. Princess Elizabeth in Girl Guide uniform, Windsor Castle, 1938 .. .. 15 15
280 35 c. At Trooping the Colour, 1980 .. .. 30 35
281 40 c. With Duke of Edinburgh in Kiribati, 1982 .. .. 35 45
282 55 c. At banquet, Austrian Embassy, London, 1966 .. .. 50 60
283 $1 At Crown Agents Head Office, London, 1983 .. .. 90 1·25
279/83 .. .. *Set of* 5 2·00 2·50

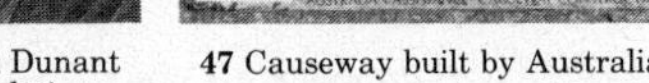

46 Henri Dunant (founder) 47 Causeway built by Australia

(Des A. Theobald. Litho Questa)

1988 (9 May). *125th Anniv of International Red Cross. T* **46** *and similar vert designs. Multicoloured. P* 14½×14.

284 15 c. Type **46** 25 20
285 35 c. Red Cross workers in Independence parade, 1979 .. .. 45 45
286 40 c. Red Cross workers with patient .. 55 55
287 55 c. Gilbert & Ellice Islands 1970 British Red Cross Centenary 10 c. stamp .. 65 70
284/7 .. .. *Set of* 4 1·60 1·60

(Des CPE Australia Ltd ($2), D. Miller (others). Litho CPE Australia Ltd, Melbourne ($2), Format (others))

1988 (30 July). *Bicentenary of Australian Settlement and "Sydpex '88" National Stamp Exhibition, Sydney. T* **47** *and similar horiz designs. Multicoloured. P* 14½.

288 15 c. Type **47** 25 20
289 35 c. Capt. Cook and Pacific map 60 50
290 $1 Obverse of Australian $10 Bicentenary banknote .. .. 1·25 1·25
a. Horiz pair. Nos. 290/1 .. .. 2·50 2·50
291 $1 Reverse of $10 Bicentenary banknote 1·25 1·25
288/91 .. .. *Set of* 4 3·00 3·00
MS292 95 × 76 mm. $2 *Logistic Ace* (container ship) (37 × 26 *mm*). P 13½ × 14 .. .. 1·90 2·50

Nos. 290/1 were printed together, *se-tenant*, in horizontal pairs throughout the sheet.

No. **MS**292 also commemorates the 150th anniversary of the first screw-driven steamship.

48 Manual Telephone Exchange and Map of Kiritimati

(Des A. Theobald. Litho Questa)

1988 (28 Dec). *Transport and Communications Decade (3rd issue). T* **48** *and similar horiz design. Multicoloured. W* w **14** *(sideways). P* 14.

293 35 c. Type **48** 50 50
294 45 c. Betio–Bairiki Causeway 60 60

49 *Hound* (brigantine), 1835 50 Eastern Reef Heron

(Des E. Nisbet. Litho Questa)

1989 (26 May). *Nautical History (1st series). T* **49** *and similar horiz designs. Multicoloured. W* w **16** *(sideways). P* 14½.

295 15 c. Type **49** 55 30
296 30 c. *Phantom* (brig), 1854 .. .. .. 80 60
297 40 c. H.M.S. *Alacrity* (schooner), 1873 .. 90 80
298 $1 *Charles W. Morgan* (whaling ship), 1851 .. .. 2·00 2·00
295/8 .. .. *Set of* 4 3·75 3·25

See also Nos. 343/7.

(Des D. Johnstone. Litho Questa)

1989 (28 June). *Birds with Young. T* **50** *and similar vert designs. Multicoloured. W* w **16**. *P* 14½.

299 15 c. Type **50** 35 35
a. Vert pair. Nos. 299/300 .. .. 70 70
300 15 c. Eastern Reef Heron chicks in nest .. 35 35
301 $1 White-tailed Tropic Bird .. .. 1·50 1·75
a. Vert pair. Nos. 301/2 .. .. 3·00 3·50
302 $1 Young White-tailed Tropic Bird .. 1·50 1·75
299/302 .. .. *Set of* 4 3·25 3·75

Nos. 299/300 and 301/2 were each printed together, *se-tenant*, in vertical pairs throughout the sheets, each pair forming a composite design.

51 House of Assembly 51*a* "Apollo 10" on Launch Gantry

(Des D. Miller. Litho Cartor, France)

1989 (12 July). *10th Anniv of Independence. T* **51** *and similar vert design. Multicoloured. W* w **16** *(inverted). P* 13½×14.

303 15 c. Type **51** 25 25
304 $1 Constitution .. .. 1·25 1·25

(Des A. Theobald ($2.50), D. Miller (others). Litho Questa)

1989 (20 July). *20th Anniv of First Manned Landing on Moon. T* **51***a and similar multicoloured designs. W* w **16** *(sideways on 50, 60 c.) P* 14×13½ *(20, 75 c.) or* 14 *(others).*

305 20 c. Type **51***a* 30 30
306 50 c. Crew of "Apollo 10" (30×30 *mm*) .. 70 70
307 60 c. "Apollo 10" emblem (30×30 *mm*) .. 80 80
308 75 c. "Apollo 10" splashdown, Hawaii .. 95 95
305/8 .. .. *Set of* 4 2·50 2·50
MS309 82×100 mm. $2.50, "Apollo 11" command module in lunar orbit. P 14×13½ .. .. 3·25 3·75

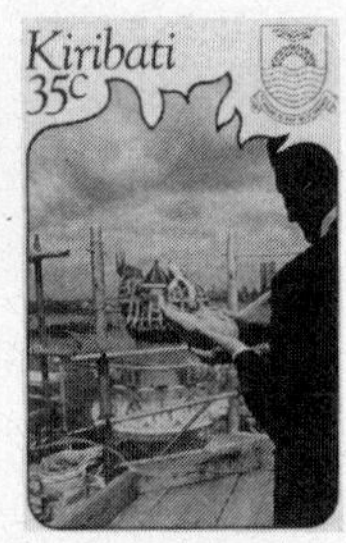

51*b* Gilbert and Ellice Islands, 1949 75th Anniv of U.P.U. 3d. Stamp 51*c* Examining Fragment of Statue

(Des D. Miller. Litho Walsall)

1989 (7 Aug*). *"Philexfrance 89" International Stamp Exhibition, Paris, and "World Stamp Expo '89", Washington (1st issue). Sheet* 104×86 *mm. W* w **16**. *P* 14×13½.

MS310 51*b* $2 multicoloured .. .. 2·25 2·75

*This is the local date of issue. The agents, Caphco Ltd, placed stocks on sale in London and Paris from 7 July.

(Des D. Miller, adapted Walsall. Litho Walsall)

1989 (25 Sept). *"Philexfrance 89" International Stamp Exhibition, Paris, and "World Stamp Expo '89", Washington (2nd issue). T* **51***c and similar vert designs, showing Statue of Liberty. Multicoloured. W* w **14**. *P* 14×13½.

311 35 c. Type **51***c* 45 55
a. Sheetlet. Nos. 311/13 .. .. 1·25
312 35 c. Workman drilling Statue 45 55
313 35 c. Surveyor with drawing 45 55
311/13 .. .. *Set of* 3 1·25 1·50

Nos. 311/13 were printed, *se-tenant*, in sheetlets of 3.

52 Telecommunications Centre (53)

(Des L. Curtis. Litho Questa)

1989 (16 Oct). *Transport and Communications Decade (4th issue). T* **52** *and similar horiz design. Multicoloured. W* w **16** *(sideways). P* 14.

314 30 c. Type **52** 75 75
315 75 c. *Mataburo* (inter-island freighter) .. 1·50 1·50

1989 (21 Oct). *"Melbourne Stampshow '89". Nos. 301/2 optd with T* **53**.

316 $1 White-tailed Tropic Bird .. .. 1·50 1·75
a. Vert pair. Nos. 316/17 .. .. 3·00 3·50
317 $1 Young White-tailed Tropic Bird .. 1·50 1·75

54 Virgin and Child (detail, "The Adoration of the Holy Child" (Denys Calvert)) 55 Gilbert and Ellice Islands 1912 1d. and G.B. Twopence Blue Stamps

(Des D. Miller. Litho Questa)

1989 (1 Dec). *Christmas. T* **54** *and similar vert designs showing paintings. Multicoloured. W* w **16**. *P* 14.

318 10 c. Type **53** 20 15
319 15 c. "The Adoration of the Holy Child" (Denys Calvert) 30 25
320 55 c. "The Holy Family and St. Elizabeth" (Rubens) 85 70
321 $1 "Madonna with Child and Maria Magdalena" (School of Correggio) .. 1·75 2·00
318/21 .. .. *Set of* 4 2·75 2·75

(Des D. Miller. Litho Questa)

1990 (1 May). *150th Anniv of the Penny Black and "Stamp World London 90" International Stamp Exhibition. T* **55** *and similar horiz designs. Multicoloured. W* w **16** *(sideways). P* 14.

322 15 c. Type **55** 30 20
323 50 c. Gilbert and Ellice Islands 1911 ½d. and G.B. Penny Black 75 65
324 60 c. Kiribati 1982 1 c. bird and G.B. 1870 ½d. 85 85
325 $1 Gilbert Islands 1976 1 c. ship and G.B. 1841 1d. red-brown .. .. 1·40 1·60
322/5 .. .. *Set of* 4 3·00 3·00

56 Blue-barred Orange Parrotfish

(Des G. Drummond. Litho Questa)

1990 (12 July). *Fishes. T* **56** *and similar horiz designs. Multicoloured. W w* **14** *(sideways). P* 14.

326	1 c. Type **56**	10	10
327	5 c. Honeycomb Rock Cod	10	10
328	10 c. Blue-fin Jack	10	15
329	15 c. Paddle Tail Snapper	15	20
330	20 c. Variegated Emperor	20	25
331	25 c. Rainbow Runner	25	30
332	30 c. Black-saddled Coral Trout	25	30
333	35 c. Great Barracuda	30	35
334	40 c. Convict Surgeonfish	35	40
335	50 c. Violet Squirrelfish	45	50
336	60 c. Freckled Hawkfish	55	60
337	75 c. Pennant Coralfish	70	75
338	$1 Yellow and Blue Sea Perch	90	95
339	$2 Pacific Sailfish	1·90	2·00
340	$5 Whitetip Reef Shark	4·50	4·75
326/40	*Set of* 15	9·75	10·50

For 23 c. value watermarked w **16** (sideways) see No. 356.

(Des D. Miller. Litho Questa)

1990 (4 Aug). *90th Birthday of Queen Elizabeth the Queen Mother. Vert designs as T* **107** *(75 c.) or* **108** *($2) of Kenya. W w* **16**. *P* 14×15 *(75 c.) or* 14½ *($2).*

341	75 c. multicoloured	1·00	75
342	$2 brownish black and myrtle-green	2·25	2·50

Designs:—75 c. Queen Elizabeth the Queen Mother; $2 King George VI and Queen Elizabeth with air raid victim, London, 1940.

(Des E. Nisbet. Litho Questa)

1990 (5 Nov). *Nautical History (2nd series). Horiz designs as T* **49**. *Multicoloured. W w* **16** *(sideways). P* 14½.

343	15 c. *Herald* (whaling ship), 1851	30	20
344	50 c. *Belle* (barque), 1849	65	60
345	60 c. *Supply* (schooner), 1851	75	80
346	75 c. *Triton* (whaling ship), 1848	90	1·00
343/6	*Set of* 4	2·40	2·40
MS347	95×75 mm. $2 *Charlotte* (convict transport), 1789	2·75	3·25

57 Manta Ray **58** Queen Elizabeth II

(Des G. Drummond. Litho Questa)

1991 (17 Jan). *Endangered Fishes. T* **57** *and similar horiz designs. Multicoloured. W w* **14** *(sideways). P* 14.

348	15 c. Type **57**	30	20
349	20 c. Manta Ray (*different*)	30	25
350	30 c. Whale Shark	50	50
351	35 c. Whale Shark (*different*)	50	60
348/51	*Set of* 4	1·40	1·40

1991 (30 Apr). *Horiz design as Nos.* 326/40, *but W w* **16** *(sideways). P* 14.

356	23 c. Bennett's Pufferfish	20	25

(Des D. Miller. Litho Questa)

1991 (17 June). *65th Birthday of Queen Elizabeth II and 70th Birthday of Prince Philip. T* **58** *and similar vert design. Multicoloured. W w* **16** *(sideways). P* 14½×14.

366	65 c. Type **58**	1·00	1·00
	a. Horiz pair. Nos. 366/7 separated by label	2·00	2·00
367	70 c. Prince Philip in R.A.F. uniform	1·00	1·00

Nos. 366/7 were printed together, *se-tenant*, in sheetlets of 10 (2×5) with designs alternating and the vertical rows separated by inscribed labels.

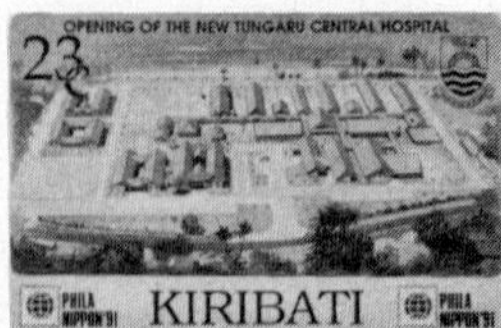

59 Aerial View of Hospital

(Des G. Vasarhelyi. Litho Questa)

1991 (16 Nov). *"Philanippon '91" International Stamp Exhibition, Tokyo, and Opening of Tungaru Central Hospital. T* **59** *and similar horiz designs. Multicoloured. W w* **16** *(sideways). P* 13½×14.

368	23 c. Type **59**	30	30
369	50 c. Traditional dancers	60	60
370	60 c. Hospital entrance	70	70
371	75 c. Foundation stone and plaques	95	95
368/71	*Set of* 4	2·25	2·25
MS372	125×83 mm. $5 Casualty on trolley and ambulance	5·25	5·50

60 Mother and Child

(Des G. Vasarhelyi. Litho Questa)

1991 (2 Dec). *Christmas. T* **60** *and similar horiz designs. Multicoloured. W w* **14** *(sideways). P* 14.

373	23 c. Type **60**	30	30
374	50 c. The Holy Family in Pacific setting	65	65
375	60 c. The Holy Family in traditional setting	75	75
376	75 c. Adoration of the Shepherds	1·00	1·00
373/6	*Set of* 4	2·40	2·40

(Des D. Miller. Litho Questa)

1992 (6 Feb). *40th Anniv of Queen Elizabeth II's Accession. Horiz designs as T* **112** *of Kenya. W w* **14** *(sideways). P* 14.

377	23 c. Kiribati village	20	25
378	30 c. Lagoon at sunset	30	35
379	50 c. Tarawa waterfront	45	50
380	60 c. Three portraits of Queen Elizabeth	55	60
381	75 c. Queen Elizabeth II	70	75
377/81	*Set of* 5	2·00	2·25

POSTAGE DUE STAMPS

D **1** Kiribati Coat of Arms

(Litho Format)

1981 (27 Aug). *P* 14.

D1	D **1**	1 c. black and magenta	10	10
D2		2 c. black and greenish blue	10	10
D3		5 c. black and bright green	10	10
D4		10 c. black and chestnut	10	15
D5		20 c. black and bright blue	20	25
D6		30 c. black and brown-ochre	25	30
D7		40 c. black and purple	35	40
D8		50 c. black and deep blue-green	45	50
D9		$1 black and orange-red	90	95
D1/9		*Set of* 9	2·10	2·40

Nos. D1/9 exist imperforate from stock dispersed by the liquidator of Format International Security Printers Ltd.

OFFICIAL STAMPS

O.K.G.S. (O **1**) **O.K.G.S.** (O **2**)

1981 (May). *Optd with Type* O **1**. A. *On Nos.* 86, 90/3, 95 *and* 97/9*a*, *W w* **14** *(sideways)*. B. *On Nos.* 121/35. *No wmk.*

		A		B	
O 1	1 c. Type **16**	2·25	2·50	10	10
O 2	3 c. M.V. *Tautunu* (inter-island freighter)	†		10	10
O 3	5 c. Hibiscus	†		10	10
O 4	7 c. Catholic Cathedral, Tarawa	†		10	10
O 5	10 c. Maneaba, Bikenibeu	14·00	14·00	10	10
	a. Opt double	†		15·00	—
O 6	12 c. Betio Harbour	3·25	3·25	15	15
O 7	15 c. Reef Egret	12·00	12·00	15	20
O 8	20 c. Flamboyant Tree	10·00	10·00	20	25
O 9	25 c. Moorish Idol	†		25	30
O10	30 c. Frangipani	7·00	7·00	30	35
	a. Opt double	†		20·00	—
O11	35 c. G.I.P.C. Chapel, Tangintebu	†		35	40
O12	50 c. *Hypolimnas bolina* (butterfly)	5·00	5·00	50	55
	a. Opt double	†		60·00	—
	b. Opt inverted	†		60·00	—
O13	$1 *Tabakea* (Tarawa Lagoon ferry)	9·00	9·00	1·00	1·00
O14	$2 Evening scene	12·00	12·00	2·00	2·25
	a. Opt double	†		£110	—
O15	$5 National flag	3·75	3·75	4·00	4·25
	a. Opt inverted	£150	—	†	
O1A/15A	*Set of* 10	70·00	70·00		
O1B/15B	*Set of* 15			8·00	9·00

1983. *Nos.* 86, 90/3, 95, 97/9 *and* 131 *optd with Type* O **2**.

O16	1 c. Type **16**	3·50	3·50
O17	10 c. Maneaba, Bikenibeu	11·00	8·00
O18	12 c. Betio Harbour	4·00	4·00
O19	15 c. Eastern Reef Heron	13·00	13·00
O20	20 c. Flamboyant Tree	6·50	6·50
O21	30 c. Frangipani	8·00	5·00
O21*a*	35 c. G.I.P.C. Chapel, Tangintebu	†	—
O22	50 c. *Hypolimnas bolina elliciana* (butterfly)	5·50	4·00
O23	$1 *Tabakea* (Tarawa Lagoon ferry)	10·00	8·00
O24	$2 Evening scene	16·00	10·00

1983 (28 June). *Nos.* 169, 172/3, 175 *and* 177 *optd with Type* O **2**.

O25	12 c. Polynesian Reed Warbler	40	30
O26	30 c. Brown Booby	70	50
O27	35 c. Audubon's Shearwater	80	60
O28	50 c. Bristle-thighed Curlew	1·00	80
O29	$2 Long-tailed Koel	3·00	2·75
O25/9	*Set of* 5	5·50	4·50

Kuwait

Kuwait, an independent Arab shaikhdom since 1756, placed itself under British protection in 1899 to counter the spread of Ottoman influence in the Arabian Gulf.

The first, somewhat limited, postal service, via Bushire, commenced with the appointment of a Political Agent to Kuwait in August 1904. Because of diplomatic problems this system continued until 21 January 1915 when a regular Indian post office was established.

Limited supplies of Indian stamps were used by the Political Agency postal service, but these became available to the general public from 21 January 1915. Stamps seen postally used from Kuwait before 1923 are usually ½ a., 1 a., 1 r. or 5 r. values, with the occasional Official issue. Much more common are values to 15 r., both postage and Official, used telegraphically.

Before 1910 the name of the shaikhdom was spelt "KOWEIT" and this spelling appears on various circular postmarks used between 1915 and 1923. The more modern version of the name was first used for a postal cancellation in 1923.

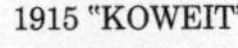
1915 "KOWEIT"

1923 "KUWAIT"

On 1 August 1921 responsibility for the Kuwait postal service passed to the Iraq Post Office, but later it reverted to Indian administration some time before 1929.

PRICES FOR STAMPS ON COVER TO 1945	
Nos. 1/15	*from* × 5
Nos. 16/29	*from* × 3
Nos. 31/51	*from* × 2
Nos. 52/63	*from* × 4
Nos. O1/27	*from* × 10

USED HIGH VALUES. It is necessary to emphasize that used prices quoted for high value stamps are for postally used examples.

KUWAIT (1) KUWAIT (2)

1923 (1 Apr)–**24**. *Stamps of India (King George V), optd with T* **1** *or* **2** *(rupee values, 15½ mm). Star wmk. P* 14.

No.	Type	Description	Unused	Used
1	**56**	½ a. green	60	2·50
		a. Opt double	£180	
		b. Vert pair, one without opt	£400	
2	**57**	1 a. chocolate	1·25	1·25
		a. Opt double	£200	
		b. Opt omitted (lower stamp of vert pair)	£650	
3	**58**	1½ a. chocolate (A)	1·00	4·00
4	**59**	2 a. violet	1·25	50
		a. Bright purple		
5	**61**	2 a. 6 p. ultramarine	1·75	7·50
6	**62**	3 a. orange-brown	3·75	15·00
7		3 a. ultramarine (1924)	9·00	1·50
8	**63**	4 a. deep olive	7·00	20·00
		a. Olive-green		
9	**64**	6 a. yellow-bistre	8·50	13·00
10	**65**	8 a. purple	8·00	23·00
		a. Mauve		
11	**66**	12 a. claret	14·00	25·00
12	**67**	1 r. brown and green	14·00	11·00
		a. Red-brown and blue-green	18·00	15·00
13		2 r. carmine and yellow-brown	40·00	90·00
14		5 r. ultramarine and violet	80·00	£200
15		10 r. green and scarlet	£120	£450
1/15		*Set of* 15	£275	£750

Essays of the overprint using the obsolete spelling "KOWEIT" were prepared in 1923 and can be found on the original 14 values of the postage stamps and on the 13 stamps of the Official series. (*Price per set of* 27 *unused* £19000).

Nos. 1/4 and 6/7 are all known with inverted overprint. It is doubtful if such errors were actually sold at the Kuwait Post Office, although some are known on registered or ordinary covers.

From 22 April 1929 the post office in Kuwait was again placed under the control of the Iraq Mandate postal administration.

KUWAIT (3) KUWAIT (4)

1929–37. *Stamps of India (King George V, Nasik printing), optd with T* **3** *or* **4** *(rupee values). Mult Star wmk. P* 14.

No.	Type	Description	Unused	Used
16	**56**	½ a. green	1·00	1·25
16*a*	**79**	½ a. green (1934)	4·50	60
17	**57**	1 a. chocolate	7·00	1·25
17*a*	**81**	1 a. chocolate (1934)	4·50	40
18	**70**	2 a. purple	1·25	40
19		2 a. vermilion	23·00	60·00
19*a*	**59**	2 a. vermilion (1934)	15·00	5·00
19*b*		2 a. vermilion (*small die*) (1937)	2·75	1·60
20	**62**	3 a. bright blue	2·75	1·25
21		3 a. carmine	5·50	4·00
22	**71**	4 a. sage-green	25·00	60·00
22*a*	**63**	4 a. sage-green (1934)	5·00	8·00
22*b*	**64**	6 a. bistre (1937)	17·00	30·00
23	**65**	8 a. reddish purple	9·00	13·00
24	**66**	12 a. claret (1933)	18·00	35·00
25	**67**	1 r. chocolate and green	10·00	22·00
		a. Extended 'T'	£180	
26		2 r. carmine and orange	10·00	50·00
		a. Extended 'T'	£200	
27		5 r. ultramarine and purple (1937)	70·00	£180
		a. Extended 'T'	£325	
28		10 r. green and scarlet (1934)	£160	£350
		a. Extended 'T'	£650	
29		15 r. blue and olive (1937)	£450	£700
		a. Extended 'T'	£900	
16/29		*Set of* 20	£750	£1300

The 'T' of 'KUWAIT' shows a ¾ mm downward extension on R. 3/2, lower left pane.

1933 (Feb)–**34**. *Air. Stamps of India optd as T* **2** (16½ *mm*).

No.	Type	Description	Unused	Used
31	**72**	2 a. deep blue-green	11·00	20·00
32		3 a. blue	1·25	2·00
		a. Stamp doubly printed	£850	£650
33		4 a. drab	£100	£200
34		6 a. bistre (2.34)	1·25	4·00
31/4		*Set of* 4	£100	£200

1939. *Nos.* 247/8, 251, 253, 255/63 *of India optd with T* **3** *or* **4** *(rupee values).*

No.	Type	Description	Unused	Used
36	**91**	½ a. red-brown	6·00	75
38		1 a. carmine	6·00	75
39	**92**	2 a. vermilion	6·00	1·50
41	–	3 a. yellow-green	4·75	1·25
43	–	4 a. brown	21·00	8·00
44	–	6 a. turquoise-green	20·00	6·00
45	–	8 a. slate-violet	25·00	24·00
46	–	12 a. lake	22·00	24·00
47	**93**	1 r. grey and red-brown	3·75	1·90
		a. Extended 'T'	£190	
48		2 r. purple and brown	3·75	7·50
		a. Extended 'T'	£190	
49		5 r. green and blue	12·00	15·00
		a. Extended 'T'	£300	
50		10 r. purple and claret	60·00	60·00
		a. Opt double	£300	
		b. Extended 'T'	£425	
51		15 r. brown and green	85·00	£140
		a. Extended 'T'	£600	
36/51		*Set of* 13	£250	£250

On later printings the extended 'T' variety was corrected in two stages.

> Following the rebellion in Iraq control of the Kuwait postal service was assumed by the Indian authorities.
> Unoverprinted stamps of INDIA were used in Kuwait between 1941 and 1945.

1945. *Stamps of India (King George VI, on white background) optd with T* **3**.

No.	Type	Description	Unused	Used
52	**100*a***	3 p. slate	70	1·25
53		½ a. purple	70	1·00
54		9 p. green	70	4·25
55		1 a. carmine	70	70
56	**101**	1½ a. dull violet	70	3·00
57		2 a. vermilion	80	1·00
58		3 a. bright violet	70	1·50
59		3½ a. bright blue	2·50	2·00
60	**102**	4 a. brown	70	1·00
60*a*		6 a. turquoise-green	11·00	8·50
61		8 a. slate-violet	2·00	80
62		12 a. lake	4·00	1·50
63	**103**	14 a. purple	6·00	11·00
52/63		*Set of* 13	28·00	35·00

Following a short period of Pakistani control, from August 1947 the Kuwait postal service passed to British administration on 1 April 1948.

KUWAIT 1 ANNA (5) KUWAIT 5 RUPEES (6)

NOTE. From 1948 onwards, for stamps with similar surcharges, but without name of country, see British Postal Agencies in Eastern Arabia.

1948 (1 Apr)–**49**. *Stamps of Great Britain (K.G. VI), surch as T* **5** *or* **6** *(rupee values).*

No.	Type	Description	Unused	Used
64	**128**	½ a. on ½d. pale green	10	30
65		1 a. on 1d. pale scarlet	10	30
66		1½ a. on 1½d. pale red-brown	10	30
67		2 a. on 2d. pale orange	10	30
68		2½ a. on 2½d. light ultramarine	10	40
69		3 a. on 3d. pale violet	10	10
		a. Pair, one surch albino		
70	**129**	6 a. on 6d. purple	15	10
71	**130**	1 r. on 1s. bistre-brown	25	40
72	**131**	2 r. on 2s. 6d. yellow-green	70	2·00
73		5 r. on 5s. red	1·50	4·00
73*a*	**132**	10 r. on 10s. ultramarine (4.7.49)	30·00	6·00
64/73*a*		*Set of* 11	30·00	13·00

KUWAIT 2½ ANNAS (7) KUWAIT 15 RUPEES (8)

1948 (26 Apr). *Royal Silver Wedding. Nos.* 493/4 *of Great Britain surch with T* **7** *or* **8**.

No.	Type	Description	Unused	Used
74	**137**	2½ a. on 2½d. ultramarine	30	15
75	**138**	15 r. on £1 blue	30·00	27·00
		a. Short bars (R.3/4)	£120	

No. 75a has the bars cancelling the original face value 3 mm long instead of the 3½ mm of the normal surcharge.

1948 (29 July). *Olympic Games. Nos.* 495/8 *of Great Britain surch as T* **7**, *but in one line* (6 *a.*) *or two lines (others).*

No.	Type	Description	Unused	Used
76	**139**	2½ a. on 2½d. ultramarine	55	80
77	**140**	3 a. on 3d. violet	55	90
78	**141**	6 a. on 6d. bright purple	80	1·25
79	**142**	1 r. on 1s. brown	85	1·25
76/9		*Set of* 4	2·50	3·75

1949 (10 Oct). *75th Anniv of U.P.U. Nos.* 499/502 *of Great Britain surch* "KUWAIT" *and new values.*

No.	Type	Description	Unused	Used
80	**143**	2½ a. on 2½d. ultramarine	40	40
81	**144**	3 a. on 3d. violet	65	55
82	**145**	6 a. on 6d. bright purple	80	55
83	**146**	1 r. on 1s. brown	1·25	50
80/3		*Set of* 4	2·75	1·75

KUWAIT 2 RUPEES Type I — KUWAIT 2 RUPEES Type II (8*a*)

KUWAIT 10 RUPEES Type I — KUWAIT 10 RUPEES Type II (8*b*)

2 r. Type I	Type-set surcharge. "2" level with "RUPEES". Surcharge sharp.
Type II.	Plate-printed surcharge. "2" raised. Surcharge worn.
10 r. Type I.	Type-set surcharge. "1" and "O" spaced. Surcharge sharp and clean.
Type II.	Plate-printed surcharge. "1" and "O" closer together. Surcharge appears heavy and worn, see especially "A", "R" and "P".

KUWAIT Extra bar in centre (R. 7/2) — KUWAIT Extra bar at top (R. 2/2)

1950 (2 Oct)–**54**. *Nos.* 503/11 *of Great Britain surch as T* **5** *or* **8*a/b*** *(rupee values).*

No.	Type	Description	Unused	Used
84	**128**	½ a. on ½d. pale orange (3.5.51)	15	1·00
85		1 a. on 1d. light ultramarine (3.5.51)	15	50
86		1½ a. on 1½d. pale green (3.5.51)	15	2·00
87		2 a. on 2d. pale red-brown (3.5.51)	15	35
88		2½ a. on 2½d. pale scarlet (3.5.51)	20	70
89	**129**	4 a. on 4d. light ultramarine	20	25
90	**147**	2 r. on 2s. 6d. yellow-green (I) (3.5.51)	11·00	4·25
		a. Extra bar in centre	£225	£225
		b. Type II surch (1954)	£160	42·00
91	**148**	5 r. on 5s. red (3.5.51)	14·00	5·00
		a. Extra bar at top	£180	£180
92	**149**	10 r. on 10s. ultramarine (I) (3.5.51)	26·00	5·50
		a. Type II surch (1953)	£180	50·00
84/92		*Set of* 9	45·00	17·00

No. 92a is known with surch spaced 10 mm apart instead of 9 mm.

1952 (10 Dec)–**54**. *Stamps of Great Britain (Queen Elizabeth II). Wmk Tudor Crown, surch as T* **5** *(in two lines only on 2½ and 6 a.).*

No.	Type	Description	Unused	Used
93	**154**	½ a. on ½d. orange-red (31.8.53)	15	10
94		1 a. on 1d. ultramarine (31.8.53)	15	10
95		1½ a. on 1½d. green	15	10
96		2 a. on 2d. red-brown (31.8.53)	35	10
97	**155**	2½ a. on 2½d. carmine-red	15	10
98		3 a. on 3d. deep lilac (B.) (18.1.54)	40	10
99	**156**	4 a. on 4d. ultramarine (2.11.53)	1·25	45
100	**157**	6 a. on 6d. reddish purple (18.1.54)	85	10
101	**160**	12 a. on 1s. 3d. green (2.11.53)	4·50	1·75
102	**159**	1 r. on 1s. 6d. grey-blue (2.11.53)	4·50	10
93/102		*Set of* 10	11·00	2·25

1953 (3 June). *Coronation. Stamps of Great Britain surch* "KUWAIT" *and new values.*

No.	Type	Description	Unused	Used
103	**161**	2½ a. on 2½d. carmine-red	2·25	75
104	**162**	4 a. on 4d. ultramarine	3·00	80
105	**163**	12 a. on 1s. 3d. deep yellow-green	4·00	2·00
106	**164**	1 r. on 1s. 6d. deep grey-blue	4·00	80
103/6		*Set of* 4	12·00	4·00

KUWAIT 2 RUPEES I

KUWAIT 2 RUPEES II

(9)

KUWAIT 5 RUPEES I

KUWAIT 5 RUPEES II

(10)

KUWAIT 10 RUPEES I

KUWAIT 10 RUPEES II

(11)

Type I (**9/11**). Type-set overprints. Bold (generally thicker) letters with sharp corners and straight edges. Bars close together and usually slightly longer than in Type II.

Type II (**9/11**). Plate-printed overprints. Thinner letters, rounder corners and rough edges. Bars wider apart.

1955–57. *Nos. 536/8 of Great Britain surch.*

No.	Type	Description	I (23.9.55) Unused	I Used	II (10.10.57) Unused	II Used
107	**166**	2 r. on 2s. 6d. black-brown	5·00	1·00	55·00	7·00
108	**167**	5 r. on 5s. rose-red	7·00	3·25	85·00	26·00
109	**168**	10 r. on 10s. ultramarine	8·00	4·00	£140	90·00
107/9		*Set of* 3	18·00	7·50	£250	£110

1956. *Stamps of Great Britain (Queen Elizabeth II). Wmk St. Edward's Crown, surch as T* **5** *(in two lines only on 2½ and 6 a.).*

No.	Type	Description	Unused	Used
110	**154**	½ a. on ½d. orange-red	10	10
111		1 a. on 1d. ultramarine	30	15
112		1½ a. on 1½d. green	15	10
113		2 a. on 2d. red-brown	15	10
114	**155**	2½ a. on 2½d. carmine-red	30	20
116	**156**	4 a. on 4d. ultramarine	4·75	1·00
117	**157**	6 a. on 6d. reddish purple	1·75	20
118	**160**	12 a. on 1s. 3d. green	9·50	4·00
119	**159**	1 r. on 1s. 6d. grey-blue	1·75	10
110/19		*Set of* 9	17·00	5·00

(New Currency. 100 naye paise = 1 rupee)

KUWAIT NP 1 NP **(12)**

KUWAIT 3 NP NP **(13)**

KUWAIT 75 NP **(14)**

1957 (1 June)–**58**. *Stamps of Great Britain (Queen Elizabeth II). W* **165**, *St. Edward's Crown, surch as T* **12** (1, 15, 25, 40, 50 *n.p.*), **14** (75 *n.p.*) *or* **13** *(others).*

No.	Type	Description	Unused	Used
120	**157**	1 n.p. on 5d. brown	10	40
121	**154**	3 n.p. on ½d. orange-red	30	65
122		6 n.p. on 1d. ultramarine	30	65
123		9 n.p. on 1½d. green	30	40
124		12 n.p. on 2d. light red-brown	30	50
125	**155**	15 n.p. on 2½d. carmine-red (Type I)	30	10
		a. Type II (11.58)	28·00	48·00
126		20 n.p. on 3d. deep lilac (B.)	30	10
127	**156**	25 n.p. on 4d. ultramarine	1·50	2·25
128	**157**	40 n.p. on 6d. reddish purple	65	10
129	**158**	50 n.p. on 9d. bronze-green	4·25	2·75
130	**160**	75 n.p. on 1s. 3d. green	4·25	3·25
120/30		*Set of* 11	11·00	10·00

15 Shaikh Abdullah as-Salim as-Sabah

(Recess D.L.R.)

1958 (1 Feb). *P* 12½.

No.	Type	Description	Unused	Used
131	**35**	5 n.p. bluish green	30	10
132		10 n.p. rose-red	35	10
136		40 n.p. maroon	75	20
131/6		*Set of* 3	1·25	30

Nos. 131/6 were only valid for internal use in Kuwait prior to 1 February 1959. Further values were added to this series following the closure of the British Agency Post Offices on 31 January 1959. Responsibility of the postal service then passed to the Kuwait Government and later issues are listed in Part 19 (*Middle East*) of this catalogue.

OFFICIAL STAMPS

KUWAIT SERVICE (O 1)

KUWAIT SERVICE (O 2)

1923–24. *Stamps of India (King George V), optd with Type* O **1** *or* O **2** *(rupee values, 15½–16 mm). Star Wmk. P* 14.

No.	Type	Description	Unused	Used
O 1	**56**	½ a. green	35	11·00
		a. Opt double, one albino	75·00	
O 2	**57**	1 a. chocolate	40	6·00
		a. Opt double, one albino	75·00	
O 3	**58**	1½ a. chocolate (A)	1·00	16·00
O 4	**59**	2 a. violet	3·00	14·00
		a. Bright purple		
O 5	**61**	2 a. 6p. ultramarine	2·50	27·00
O 6	**62**	3 a. orange-brown	3·25	40·00
O 7		3 a. ultramarine (1924)	3·00	27·00
O 8	**63**	4 a. olive-green	3·00	38·00
O 9	**65**	8 a. purple	4·50	38·00
		a. Mauve		
O10	**67**	1 r. brown and green	10·00	65·00
		a. Opt double, one albino	75·00	
O11		2 r. carmine and yellow-brown	16·00	95·00
O12		5 r. ultramarine and violet	48·00	£225
		a. Opt double, one albino	£120	
O13		10 r. green and scarlet	90·00	£350
O14		15 r. blue and olive	£150	£475
O1/14		*Set of* 14	£300	£1300

1929–33. *Stamps of India (Nasik printing) optd as Types* O **1** *(spaced 10 mm) or* O **2** *(14½ mm × 19–20 mm wide). Mult Star wmk. P* 14.

No.	Type	Description	Unused	Used
O16	**57**	1 a. chocolate	1·25	16·00
O17	**70**	2 a. purple	45·00	£100
O19	**62**	3 a. blue	1·60	22·00
O20	**71**	4 a. sage-green	4·25	55·00
O21	**65**	8 a. reddish purple	3·25	60·00
O22	**66**	12 a. claret	17·00	95·00
O23	**67**	1 r. chocolate and green	4·00	£110
O24		2 r. carmine and orange	7·00	£170
O25		5 r. ultramarine and purple	25·00	£375
O26		10 r. green and scarlet	50·00	£550
O27		15 r. blue and olive	£110	£950
O16/27		*Set of* 11	£225	£2250

Labuan
see Malaysia

Lagos
see Nigeria

PRICES OF SETS

Set prices are given for many issues, generally those containing three stamps or more. Definitive sets include one of each value or major colour change, but do not cover different perforations, die types or minor shades. Where a choice is possible the set prices are based on the cheapest versions of the stamps included in the listings.

Leeward Islands

The Federal Colony of the Leeward Islands was constituted in 1871 formalising links between Antigua, British Virgin Islands, Dominica, Montserrat and St. Kitts-Nevis which stretched back to the 1670s. Issues for the individual islands were superseded by those inscribed "LEEWARD ISLANDS", but were in concurrent use with them from 1903. Dominica was transferred to the Windward Islands on 31 December 1939.

PRICES FOR STAMPS ON COVER TO 1945	
Nos. 1/8	*from* × 10
Nos. 9/16	*from* × 12
Nos. 17/19	*from* × 8
Nos. 20/8	*from* × 5
Nos. 29/35	*from* × 4
Nos. 36/45	*from* × 5
Nos. 46/57	*from* × 4
Nos. 58/87	*from* × 5
Nos. 88/91	*from* × 6
Nos. 92/4	*from* × 10
Nos. 95/114	*from* × 5

PRINTERS. All the stamps of Leeward Islands were typographed by De La Rue & Co, Ltd, London, *except where otherwise stated.*

1

2

1890 (31 Oct). *Name and value in second colour. Wmk Crown CA. P* 14.

No.	Type	Description	Unused	Used
1	**1**	½d. dull mauve and green	1·00	40
2		1d. dull mauve and rose	1·25	10
3		2½d. dull mauve and blue	2·75	15
4		4d. dull mauve and orange	2·75	7·00
5		6d. dull mauve and brown	5·00	6·50
6		7d. dull mauve and slate	1·75	9·00
7	**2**	1s. green and carmine	11·00	27·00
8		5s. green and blue	£130	£225
1/8		*Set of* 8	£140	£250
1/8 Optd "Specimen"		*Set of* 8	£200	

The colours of this issue are fugitive.

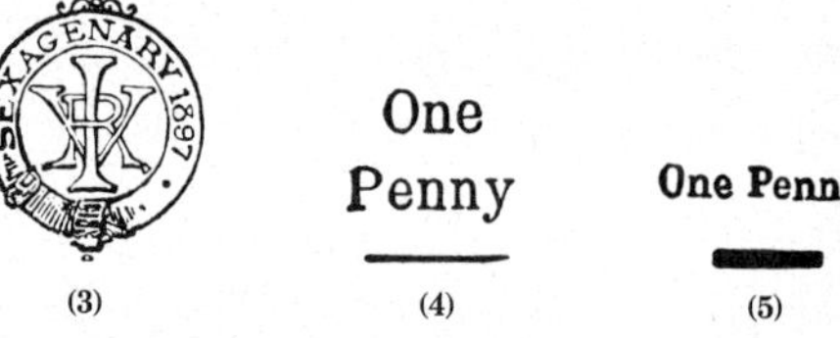

(3) (4) (5)

1897 (22 July). *Queen Victoria's Diamond Jubilee. Handstamped with T* **3**.

No.	Type	Description	Unused	Used
9	**1**	½d. dull mauve and green	2·50	8·00
		a. Opt double	£1200	
10		1d. dull mauve and rose	3·25	8·50
		a. Opt double	£1000	
		b. Opt triple	£3250	
11		2½d. dull mauve and blue	3·50	8·50
		a. Opt double	£1200	
12		4d. dull mauve and orange	24·00	55·00
		a. Opt double	£1200	
13		6d. dull mauve and brown	40·00	75·00
		a. Opt double	£1400	
14		7d. dull mauve and slate	45·00	75·00
		a. Opt double	£1400	
15	**2**	1s. green and carmine	£120	£190
		a. Opt double	£1800	
16		5s. green and blue	£650	£950
		a. Opt double	£5000	
9/16		*Set of* 8	£800	£1200

Beware of forgeries.

1902 (11 Aug.) *Nos. 4/6 surch.*

No.	Type	Description	Unused	Used
17	**4**	1d. on 4d. dull mauve and orange	80	3·75
		a. Pair, one with tall narrow "O" in "One"	27·00	55·00
		b. Surch double		
18		1d. on 6d. dull mauve and brown	90	4·50
		a. Pair, one with tall narrow "O" in "One"	40·00	60·00
19	**5**	1d. on 7d. dull mauve and slate	90	3·25
17/19		*Set of* 3	2·40	10·50

The tall narrow "O" variety occurred on R. 1/1, 5/3, 5/5 and 7/4.

6

7

8

Wide "A" (R.6/1 of left pane)

Dropped "R" (R.1/1 of left pane)

1902 (1 Sept–Oct). *Wmk Crown CA. P* 14.

20 **6** ½d. dull purple and green .. .. 1·00 40
21 1d. dull purple and carmine .. .. 2·25 10
22 **7** 2d. dull purple and ochre (Oct) .. .. 2·25 4·00
23 **6** 2½d. dull purple and ultramarine .. .. 1·25 1·25
a. Wide "A" in "LEEWARD" £120 £120
24 **7** 3d. dull purple and black (Oct) .. .. 1·00 5·00
25 **6** 6d. dull purple and brown .. .. 1·00 6·00
26 **8** 1s. green and carmine .. .. .. 1·75 12·00
a. Dropped "R" in "LEEWARD" £130
27 **7** 2s. 6d. green and black (Oct) .. .. 20·00 45·00
28 **8** 5s. green and blue (Oct) .. .. 32·00 50·00
20/8 .. .. .. *Set of* 9 55·00 £110
20/8 Optd "Specimen" .. .. *Set of* 9 £130

1905 (Apr)–**08**. *Wmk Mult Crown CA. Ordinary paper* (½d., 3d.) *or chalk-surfaced paper* (*others*).

29 **6** ½d. dull purple and green (2.06) .. 80 1·75
a. Chalk-surfaced paper (25.7.08) .. 2·00 3·00
30 1d. dull purple and carmine (29.8.06) .. 2·75 70
31 **7** 2d. dull purple and ochre (25.7.08) .. 2·75 8·50
32 **6** 2½d. dull purple and ultramarine (23.7.06) 24·00 24·00
a. Wide "A" in "LEEWARD" £275 £275
33 **7** 3d. dull purple and black .. .. 6·00 22·00
a. Chalk-surfaced paper (18.4.08) .. 12·00 30·00
34 **6** 6d. dull purple and brown (15.7.08) .. 22·00 45·00
35 **8** 1s. green and carmine (15.7.08) .. 28·00 55·00
29/35 .. .. .. *Set of* 7 75·00 £140

1907 (14 Apr)–**11**. *Wmk Mult Crown CA. Chalk-surfaced paper* (3d. *to* 5s.). *P* 14.

36 **7** ¼d. brown ((7.8.09) 35 75
37 **6** ½d. dull green 85 65
38 1d. bright red (7.07) .. .. .. 1·50 35
a. Rose-carmine .. .. .. 14·00 70
39 **7** 2d. grey (3.8.11) .. .. .. 1·00 6·50
40 **6** 2½d. bright blue (5.07) .. .. 1·40 2·50
a. Wide "A" in "LEEWARD" £130 £130
41 **7** 3d. purple/*yellow* (28.10.10) .. .. 1·00 4·25
42 **6** 6d. dull and bright purple (3.8.11) .. 3·00 5·50
43 **8** 1s. black/*green* (3.8.11) .. .. 2·75 14·00
44 **7** 2s. 6d. black and red/*blue* (15.9.11) .. 28·00 42·00
45 **8** 5s. green and red/*yellow* (21.11.10) .. 28·00 48·00
36/45 .. .. .. *Set of* 10 60·00 £110
36/45 Optd "Specimen" .. .. *Set of* 10 £170

10

11

12

13

1912 (23 Oct)–**22**. *Wmk Mult Crown CA. Chalk-surfaced paper* (3d. *to* 5s.). *P* 14.

46 **10** ¼d. brown 40 20
a. Pale brown (1916) 50 45
47 **11** ½d. yellow-green (12.12) .. .. .. 1·25 50
a. Deep green (1916) .. .. .. 1·25 50
48 1d. carmine-red 75 20
a. Bright scarlet (1915) .. .. .. 1·25 30
49 **10** 2d. slate-grey (9.1.13) .. .. .. 70 1·40
50 **11** 2½d. bright blue .. .. 2·75 7·00
a. Deep bright blue .. .. .. 3·50 4·00
51 **10** 3d. purple/*yellow* (9.1.13) .. .. .. 40 5·00
a. White back (Optd S. £35) (11.13) .. 32·00 55·00
b. On lemon (1916) .. .. .. 1·25 11·00
c. On pale yellow (Optd S. £30) (1920) 23·00 40·00
d. On orange-buff (1920) .. .. 80 5·00
52 4d. black and red/*pale yellow* (Die II) (12.5.22) .. .. 70 12·00
53 **11** 6d. dull and bright purple (9.1.13) .. 1·00 6·00
54 **12** 1s. black/*green* (9.1.13) .. .. 1·00 4·50
a. White back (Optd S. £35) (11.13) .. 23·00 35·00
b. On blue-green, olive back (Optd S. £35) (1914) .. .. .. 90 5·50
55 **10** 2s. purple and blue/*blue* (Die II) (12.5.22) 3·00 20·00
56 2s. 6d. black and red/*blue* (11.13) .. 11·00 25·00
57 **12** 5s. green and red/*yellow* (9.14) .. .. 20·00 55·00
a. White back (Optd S. £40) (11.13) .. 30·00 48·00
b. On lemon (1916) .. .. .. 10·00 40·00
c. On orange-buff (1920) .. .. 65·00 £110
46/57 .. .. .. *Set of* 12 28·00 £110
46/57 Optd "Specimen" .. .. *Set of* 12 £225

HIGH VALUE KEY TYPES. The reign of King Edward VII saw the appearance of the first in a new series of "key type" designs, initially on the issues of Malaya—Straits Settlements and Nyasaland, to be used for high value denominations where a smaller design was felt to be inappropriate. The system was extended during the reign of King George V, using the portrait as Leeward Islands Type **13**, to cover Bermuda, Ceylon, Leeward Islands, Malaya—Straits Settlements, Malta and Nyasaland. A number of these territories continued to use the key type concept for high value King George VI stamps and one, Leeward Islands, for stamps of Queen Elizabeth II.

In each instance the King George V issues were printed in sheets of 60 (12×5) on various coloured papers. The system utilised a common "head" plate used with individual "duty" plates which printed the territory name and face value.

Two major plate flaws occur on the King George V head plate: the break on scroll on R. 1/12 and the broken crown and scroll on R. 2/12. Both of these occur in different states, having been repaired and then damaged once again, perhaps on several occasions. The prices quoted in the listings are for examples approximately as illustrated.

Break in scroll (R. 1/12)

Broken crown and scroll (R. 2/12)

1921 (Oct)–**32**. *Wmk Mult Script CA or Mult Crown CA* (£1). *Chalk-surfaced paper* (3d. *to* £1). *P* 14.

(*a*) *Die* II (1921–29)

58 **10** ¼d. brown (1.4.22) 45 70
59 **11** ½d. blue-green 30 20
60 1d. carmine-red 30 10
61 1d. bright violet (21.8.22) 30 20
62 1d. bright scarlet (1929) 60 30
63 **10** 1½d. carmine-red (10.9.26) 50 45
64 1½d. red-brown (1929) 30 10
65 2d. slate-grey (6.22) 50 25
66 **11** 2½d. orange-yellow (22.9.23) .. .. 3·75 27·00
67 2½d. bright blue (1.3.27) 75 30
68 **10** 3d. light ultramarine (22.9.23) .. .. 2·00 16·00
a. Deep ultramarine .. .. .. 23·00 40·00
69 3d. purple/*yellow* (1.7.27) .. .. 40 3·75
70 4d. black and red/*pale yellow* (2.24) .. 1·25 11·00
71 5d. dull purple and olive-green (12.5.22) 50 4·25
72 **11** 6d. dull and bright purple (17.7.23) .. 7·00 20·00
73 **12** 1s. black/*emerald* (17.7.23) .. .. 1·25 5·50
74 **10** 2s. purple and blue/*blue* (12.5.22) .. 16·00 35·00
a. Red-purple and blue/blue (1926) .. 7·00 30·00
75 2s. 6d. black and red/*blue* (17.7.23) .. 6·50 22·00
76 3s. bright green and violet (12.5.22) .. 8·00 22·00
77 4s. black and red (12.5.22) .. .. 8·00 32·00
78 **12** 5s. green and red/*pale yellow* (17.7.23) 28·00 48·00
79 **13** 10s. green and red/*green* (1928) .. 48·00 70·00
a. Break in scroll £140
b. Broken crown and scroll £140
80 £1 purple and black/*red* (1928) .. £225 £250
a. Break in scroll £375
b. Broken crown and scroll £375
58/80 .. .. .. *Set of* 22 £300 £450
58/80 Optd/Perf "Specimen" .. *Set of* 23 £550

(*b*) *Reversion to Die* I (*Plate* 23) (1931–32)

81 **10** ¼d. brown .. .. 60 6·00
82 **11** ½d. blue-green (1931) .. .. .. 4·75 15·00
83 1d. bright scarlet .. .. .. 2·50 10
84 **10** 1½d. red-brown .. .. .. 1·50 1·75
85 **11** 2½d. bright blue .. .. 3·50 3·50
86 6d. dull and bright purple .. .. 11·00 38·00
87 **12** 1s. black/*emerald* .. .. .. 22·00 35·00
81/7 .. .. *Set of* 7 42·00 90·00

1935 (6 May). *Silver Jubilee. As Nos.* 114/17 *of Jamaica, but printed by Waterlow. P* 11×12.

88 1d. deep blue and scarlet 75 40
89 1½d. ultramarine and grey 85 60
90 2½d. brown and deep blue .. .. .. 1·25 2·50
91 1s. slate and purple .. .. 5·00 9·00
j. Kite and vertical log .. .. .. 85·00
k. Kite and horizontal log .. .. .. 90·00
88/91 .. .. *Set of* 4 7·00 11·00
88/91 Perf "Specimen" .. .. *Set of* 4 75·00

For illustrations of plate varieties see Omnibus section following Zimbabwe.

1937 (12 May). *Coronation. As Nos.* 118/20 *of Jamaica.*

92 1d. scarlet 30 15
93 1½d. buff 30 25
94 2½d. bright blue 30 35
92/4 .. .. *Set of* 3 80 65
92/4 Perf "Specimen .. .. *Set of* 3 55·00

14

15

(Die A)

(Die B)

In Die B the figure "1" has a broader top and more projecting serif.

"D I" shaved at foot 1d. R. 7/3 of left pane (all ptgs between Sept 1947 and July 1949. 1s. R. 9/6 of right pane (1st ptg only))

Broken second "E" in "LEEWARD" (R. 4/1 of right pane) (Pl. 3 ptgs from December 1943 until corrected in June 1949)

Broken lower right scroll (R. 5/12. 1942 ptgs only)

Gash in chin (R. 2/5. 1942 ptgs only)

1938 (25 Nov)–**51**. *T* **14** (*and similar type, but shaded value tablet*, ½d., 1d., 2½d., 6d.) *and* **15** (10s., £1). *Chalk-surfaced paper* (3d. *to* £1). *P* 14.

(*a*) *Wmk Mult Script CA*

95 ¼d. brown 10 15
a. Chalk-surfaced paper. *Dp brn* (13.6.49) 10 15
96 ½d. emerald 15 15
97 ½d. slate-grey (*chalk-surfaced paper*) (1.7.49) 30 10
98 1d. scarlet (Die A) .. .. .. 5·50 80
99 1d. scarlet (*shades*) (Die B) (1940) .. 60 30
a. "D I" flaw (9.47) .. .. .. 60·00
b. Carmine (9.42) .. .. .. 50 2·75
c. Red (13.9.48) .. .. .. 1·75 1·25
ca. "D I" flaw .. .. 70·00
100 1d. blue-green (*chalk-surfaced paper*) (1.7.49) 55 10
a. "D I" flaw .. .. 60·00
101 1½d. chestnut 20 15
102 1½d. yellow-orange and black (*chalk-surfaced paper*) (1.7.49) 50 10
103 2d. olive-grey 15 10
a. Slate-grey (11.42) .. .. .. 3·75 2·75
104 2d. scarlet (*chalk-surfaced paper*) (1.7.49) 1·40 15
a. Vermilion (24.10.51) .. .. .. 8·00 6·00
105 2½d. bright blue .. .. 3·50 85
a. Light bright blue (11.42) 40 20
106 2½d. black and purple (*chalk-surfaced paper*) (1.7.49) 55 10
107 3d. orange .. .. 30·00 1·60
a. Ordinary paper. *Pale orange* (11.42) 30 40
108 3d. bright blue (1.7.49) 65 10
109 6d. deep dull purple and bright purple .. 9·00 3·25
a. Ordinary paper (8.42) .. .. .. 2·00 1·50
ab. Broken "E" .. .. 80·00
b. Purple and deep magenta (9.47) .. 1·25 1·00
ba. Broken "E" .. .. 70·00

110 1s. black/*emerald* .. .. .. 5·00 1·25
a. "D I" flaw £120
b. Ordinary paper (3.42) .. .. 1·25 35
ba. Grey and black/emerald (8.42) .. 18·00 1·75
bb. Black and grey/emerald (11.42) .. 90·00 10·00
111 2s. reddish purple and blue/*blue* .. 12·00 1·25
a. Ordinary paper (3.42) .. .. 7·50 55
ab. Deep purple and blue/blue (29.9.47) .. 5·00 90
112 5s. green and red/*yellow* .. .. 22·00 14·00
a. Ordinary paper (12.43) .. .. 18·00 11·00
ab. Broken "E" £180
b. Bright green and red/yellow (24.10.51) 25·00 14·00
113 10s. bluish green and deep red/*green* .. £130 90·00
a. Ordinary paper. *Pale green and dull red/green* (26.6.44*) £200 £150
ae. Broken lower right scroll £1200
b. Ordinary paper. *Green and red/green* (22.2.45*) .. .. .. 80·00 38·00
c. Ordinary paper. *Deep green and deep vermilion/green* (17.7.48*) .. .. 75·00 50·00

(*b*) *Wmk Mult Crown CA*

114 £1 brown-purple and black/*red* £200 £160
a. Purple and black/carmine (3.42) .. 60·00 32·00
ae. Broken lower right scroll £600 £325
af. Gash in chin £400
b. Brown-purple & blk/salmon (3.12.43) 24·00 20·00
c. Perf 13. *Violet & black/scar* (13.12.51) 27·00 30·00
ca. Wmk sideways £2500
95/114*b* .. .. .. *Set of* 19 £120 65·00
95/114 Perf "Specimen" .. *Set of* 13 £375

* Dates quoted for Nos. 113a/c are earliest known postmark dates. No. 113a was despatched to the Leeward Islands in March 1942, No. 113b in December 1943 and No. 113c in June 1944.

Nos. 96, 98/9 and 99b exist in coils constructed from normal sheets.

1946 (1 Nov). *Victory. As Nos.* 141/2 *of Jamaica.*
115 1½d. brown 15 10
116 3d. red-orange 15 10
115/16 Perf "Specimen" .. .. *Set of* 2 50·00

1949 (2 Jan). *Royal Silver Wedding. As Nos.* 143/4 *of Jamaica.*
117 2½d. ultramarine 10 10
118 5s. green .. .. 3·75 2·50

1949 (10 Oct). *75th Anniv of Universal Postal Union. As Nos.* 145/8 *of Jamaica.*
119 2½d. blue-black 15 10
120 3d. deep blue 40 40
121 6d. magenta 40 30
122 1s. blue-green 45 30
119/22 .. .. *Set of* 4 1·25 1·00

1951 (16 Feb). *Inauguration of B.W.I. University College. As Nos.* 149/50 *of Jamaica.*
123 3 c. orange and black 15 15
124 12 c. rose-carmine and reddish violet 30 15

1953 (2 June). *Coronation. As No.* 153 *of Jamaica.*
125 3 c. black and green 10 35

16 Queen Elizabeth II **17**

1954. (22 Feb). *Chalk-surfaced paper. Wmk Mult Script CA. P* 14 (*T* **16**) *or* 13 (*T* **17**)
126 **16** ½ c. brown 10 10
127 1 c. grey 10 10
128 2 c. green 10 10
129 3 c. yellow-orange and black 10 10
130 4 c. rose-red 10 10
131 5 c. black and brown-purple 30 10
132 6 c. yellow-orange 30 10
133 8 c. ultramarine 70 10
134 12 c. dull and reddish purple 70 10
135 24 c. black and green 70 10
136 48 c. dull purple and ultramarine .. 4·50 2·75
137 60 c. brown and green .. .. .. 4·50 2·00
138 $1.20, yellow-green and rose-red .. 3·75 2·75
139 **17** $2.40, bluish green and red .. .. 4·00 5·00
140 $4.80, brown-purple and black .. 4·50 6·50
126/40 .. .. *Set of* 15 22·00 17·00

The 3 c., 4 c., 6 c., 8 c., 24 c., 48 c., 60 c. and $1.20 have their value tablets unshaded.

The stamps of Leeward Islands were withdrawn and invalidated on 1 July 1956 when the federal colony was dissolved.

Lesotho

(*formerly* Basutoland)

BASUTOLAND

Stamps of CAPE OF GOOD HOPE were used in Basutoland from about 1876, initially cancelled by upright oval with framed number type postmarks of that colony. Cancellation numbers known to have been used in Basutoland are 133 (Quthing), 156 (Mafeteng), 210 (Mohaleshoek), 277 (Morija), 281 (Maseru), 317 (Thlotse Heights) and 688 (Teyateyaneng).

From 1910 until 1933 the stamps of SOUTH AFRICA were in use. Stamps of the Union provinces are also known used in Basutoland during the early years of this period and can also be found cancelled-to-order during 1932–33.

The following post offices and postal agencies existed in Basutoland before December 1933. Stamps of Cape of Good Hope or South Africa with recognisable postmarks from them are worth a premium. For a few of the smaller offices or agencies there are, as yet, no actual examples recorded. Dates given are those generally accepted as the year in which the office was first opened.

Bokong (1931)
Butha Buthe (1907)
Jonathan's (1927)
Khabos (1927)
Khetisas (1930)
Khukhune (1933)
Kolonyama (1914)
Kueneng (1914)
Leribe (1890)
Mafeteng (1874)
Majara (1912)
Makhoa (1932)
Makoalis (1927)
Mamathes (1919)
Mapoteng (1925)
Marakabeis (1932)
Maseru (1872)
Maseru Rail (1915?)
Mashai (1929)
Matsaile (1930)
Mekading (1914)
Mofokas (1915)
Mohaleshoek (1873)
Mokhotlong (1921)
Morija (1884)
Motsekuoa (1915)
Mount Morosi (1918)
Mphotos (1914)
Peka (1908)
Phamong (1932)
Pitseng (1921)
Qachasnek (1895)
Qalo (1923?)
Quthing (1882)
Rankakalas (1933)
Roma Mission (1913)
Sebapala (1930)
Seforong (1924)
Sehlabathebe (1921)
Sekake (1931)
Teyateyaneng (1886)
Thaba Bosigo (1913)
Thabana Morena (1922)
Thabaneng (1914)
Thaba Tseka (1929)
Thlotse Heights (1872)
Tsepo (1923)
Tsoelike (1927)
Tsoloane (1918)

For further details of the postal history of Basutoland see *The Cancellations and Postal Markings of Basutoland/Lesotho* by A. H. Scott, published by Collectors Mail Auctions (Pty) Ltd, Cape Town, from which the above has been, with permission, extracted.

PRICES FOR STAMPS ON COVER TO 1945

Nos. 1/19	*from* × 5
Nos. 11/14	*from* × 6
Nos. 15/17	*from* × 10
Nos. 18/28	*from* × 6
Nos. 29/31	*from* × 10
Nos. O1/4	*from* × 4
Nos. D1/2	*from* × 25

CROWN COLONY

1 King George V, Nile Crocodile and Mountains   **2** King George VI, Nile Crocodile and Mountains

(Recess Waterlow)

1933 (1 Dec). *Wmk Mult Script CA. P* 12½.
1 **1** ½d. emerald 60 75
2 1d. scarlet 60 35
3 2d. bright purple 70 35
4 3d. bright blue 70 60
5 4d. grey .. .. 2·50 6·50
6 6d. orange-yellow .. .. .. 3·00 1·50
7 1s. red-orange .. .. .. 3·75 4·50
8 2s. 6d. sepia .. .. .. 20·00 40·00
9 5s. violet .. .. .. 42·00 60·00
10 10s. olive-green £100 £110
1/10 .. .. .. *Set of* 10 £150 £190
1/10 Perf "Specimen" .. .. *Set of* 10 £250

1935 (4 May). *Silver Jubilee. As Nos.* 114/17 *of Jamaica, but ptd by D.L.R. P* 13½×14.
11 1d. deep blue and carmine 45 25
12 2d. ultramarine and grey 55 75
f. Diagonal line by turret .. .. 40·00
g. Dot to left of chapel .. .. 40·00
13 3d. brown and deep blue .. .. 3·25 1·00
g. Dot to left of chapel .. .. 65·00
h. Dot by flagstaff .. .. 65·00
14 6d. slate and purple .. .. .. 3·75 1·25
g. Dot to left of chapel .. .. 75·00
h. Dot by flagstaff .. .. .. 75·00
i. Dash by turret .. .. .. 75·00
11/14 .. .. .. *Set of* 4 7·25 3·00
11/14 Perf "Specimen" .. *Set of* 4 75·00

For illustrations of plate varieties see Omnibus section following Zimbabwe.

1937 (12 May). *Coronation. As Nos.* 118/20 *of Jamaica. P* 14.
15 1d. scarlet 35 10
16 2d. bright purple 40 55
17 3d. bright blue 65 75
15/17 .. .. .. *Set of* 3 1·25 1·10
15/17 Perf "Specimen" .. *Set of* 3 55·00

Tower flaw (R. 2/4)

(Recess Waterlow)

1938 (1 Apr). *Wmk Mult Script CA. P* 12½.
18 **2** ½d. green 20 30
19 1d. scarlet 40 15
a. Tower flaw .. .. .. 45·00
20 1½d. light blue 40 30
21 2d. bright purple 30 30
22 3d. bright blue 30 50
23 4d. grey .. .. 1·25 2·00
24 6d. orange-yellow 40 50
25 1s. red-orange 40 45
26 2s. 6d. sepia .. .. .. 7·00 5·00
27 5s. violet .. .. .. 16·00 8·50
28 10s. olive-green .. .. .. 16·00 15·00
18/28 .. .. .. *Set of* 11 38·00 30·00
18/28 Perf "Specimen" .. *Set of* 11 £180

Basutoland
(3)

1945 (3 Dec). *Victory. Stamps of South Africa, optd with T* **3**, *inscr alternately in English and Afrikaans.*

			Un. pair	Used pair
29	**55**	1d. brown and carmine	20	25
30	**56**	2d. slate-blue and violet	20	30
31	**57**	3d. deep blue and blue	20	50
29/31		.. .. .. *Set of 3 pairs*	55	95

4 King George VI   **5** King George VI and Queen Elizabeth

6 Queen Elizabeth II as Princess, and Princess Margaret

7 The Royal Family

(Recess Waterlow)

1947 (17 Feb). *Royal Visit. Wmk Mult Script CA. P* 12½.
32 **4** 1d. scarlet 10 10
33 **5** 2d. green 10 10
34 **6** 3d. ultramarine 10 10
35 **7** 1s. mauve 10 10
32/5 .. .. *Set of* 4 35 30
32/5 Perf "Specimen" .. .. *Set of* 4 80·00

1948 (1 Dec). *Royal Silver Wedding. As Nos.* 143/4 *of Jamaica.*
36 1½d. ultramarine 20 10
37 10s. grey-olive .. .. 27·00 22·00

1949 (10 Oct). *75th Anniv of Universal Postal Union. As Nos.* 145/8 *of Jamaica.*
38 1½d. blue 30 25
39 3d. deep blue .. .. 1·10 50
40 6d. orange .. .. 1·25 70
41 1s. red-brown .. .. 1·25 80
38/41 .. .. *Set of* 4 3·50 2·00

1953 (3 June). *Coronation. As No.* 153 *of Jamaica.*
42 2d. black and reddish purple 10 20

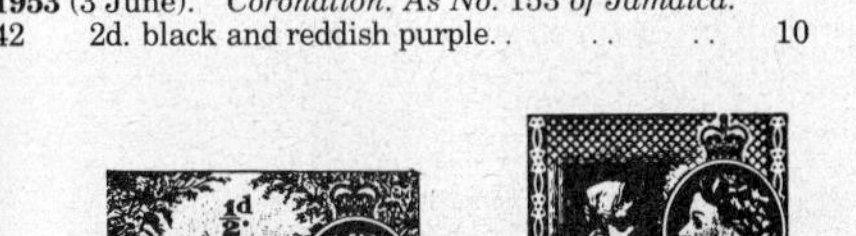

8 Qiloane **9** Mohair (Shearing Angora Goats)

(Recess D.L.R.)

1954 (18 Oct)–**58**. *Designs as T* **8/9**. *Wmk Mult Script CA. P* 11½ (*10s.*) *or* 13½ (*others*).

43 ½d. grey-black and sepia 10 10
44 1d. grey-black and bluish green 10 10
45 2d. deep bright blue and orange 60 10
46 3d. yellow-green and deep rose-red 80 10
a. Yellow-green and rose (27.11.58) . . 1·40 25
47 4½d. indigo and deep ultramarine 70 15
48 6d. chestnut and deep grey-green . . . . 1·25 10
49 1s. bronze-green and purple . . . . 1·25 20
50 1s. 3d. brown and turquoise-green . . . . 7·50 3·50
51 2s. 6d. deep ultramarine and crimson . . 5·50 5·50
a. Brt ultram & crimson-lake (27.11.58) 15·00 10·00
52 5s. black and carmine-red . . . . 4·75 8·50
53 10s. black and maroon . . . . 16·00 20·00
43/53 . . . . *Set of* 11 35·00 35·00

Designs: *Horiz as T* **8**—1d. Orange River; 2d Mosuto horseman; 3d. Basuto household; 4½d. Maletsunyane Falls; 6d. Herd-boy with Lesiba. 1s. Pastoral scene; 1s. 3d. Aeroplane over Lancers' Gap; 2s. 6d. Old Fort Leribe; 5s. Mission Cave House.

½d. ■ (**19**)

20 "Chief Moshoeshoe I" (engraving by Delangle)

1959 (1 Aug). *No. 45 surch with T* **19**, *by South African Govt Ptr, Pretoria.*
54 ½d. on 2d. deep bright blue and orange . . 10 10

(Des from drawings by James Walton. Recess Waterlow)

1959 (15 Dec). *Basutoland National Council. T* **20** *and similar vert designs. W* w **12**. *P* 13 × 13½.
55 3d. black and yellow-olive 15 10
56 1s. carmine and yellow-green 20 10
57 1s. 3d. ultramarine and red-orange 35 25
55/7 . . . . *Set of* 3 65 35

Designs:—1s. Council house; 1s. 3d. Mosuto horseman.

(New Currency. 100 cents = 1 rand)

½c. (**23**) 1c. (**24**) 2c (**25**)

2½c (I) 2½c (II) 3½c (I) 3½c (II)

5c (I) 5c (II) 10c (I) 10c (II)

12½c (I) 12½c (II) 50c (I) 50c (II)

25c (I) 25c (II) 25c (III)

R1 (I) R1 (II) R1 (III)

1961 (14 Feb). *Nos. 43/53 surch with T* **23** (½ *c.*), **24** (1 *c.*) *or as T* **25** (*others*) *by South African Govt Printer, Pretoria*

58 ½ c. on ½d. grey-black and sepia 10 10
a. Surch double £225
59 1 c. on 1d. grey-black and bluish green . . 10 10
60 2 c. on 2d. deep bright blue and orange . . 10 10
a. Surch inverted . . . . 90·00
61 2½ c. on 3d. yellow-green and rose (Type I) . . 10 10
a. Type II 10 10
b. Type II inverted . . . . — £900
62 3½ c. on 4½d. indigo & deep ultram (Type I) . . 10 10
a. Type II . . . . 2·00 2·50
63 5 c. on 6d. chestnut & dp grey-green (Type I) 10 10
a. Type II 15 10
64 10 c. on 1s. bronze-green and purple (Type I) . . 10 10
a. Type II . . . . 55·00 55·00
65 12½ c. on 1s. 3d. brown & turq-green (Type I) . . 15 20
a. Type II 20 10
66 25 c. on 2s. 6d. bright ultramarine and crimson-lake (Type I) 15 30
a. Type II . . . . 17·00 7·00
b. Type III 25 50
67 50 c. on 5s. black and carmine-red (Type I) . . 1·75 2·50
a. Type II . . . . 90 1·25
68 1 r. on 10s. black and maroon (Type I) . . 18·00 3·75
a. Type II . . . . 8·50 18·00
b. Type III . . . . 2·50 3·50
58/68b . . . . *Set of* 11 4·00 4·75

There were two printings of the 2½ c. Type II, differing in the position of the surcharge on the stamps.

Examples of the 2 c. surcharge are known in a fount similar to Type **24**.

26 Basuto Household **27** Protein Foods

(Recess D.L.R.)

1961–63. *As Nos. 43/53 but values in cents as in T* **26**. *Wmk Mult Script CA. P* 13½ *or* 11½ (1 *r.*).

69 ½ c. grey-black and sepia (as ½d.) (25.9.62) 10 15
a. Imperf (pair) £180
70 1 c. grey-blk & bluish grn (as 1d.) (25.9.62) 10 30
71 2 c. dp brt blue & orange (as 2d.) (25.9.62) 50 85
72 2½ c. yellow-green & deep rose-red (14.2.61) 60 10
a. Pale yellow-green & rose-red (22.5.62) 1·00 15
73 3½ c. indigo & dp ultram (as 4½d.) (25.9.62) 30 80
74 5 c. chestnut and deep grey-green (as 6d.) (10.8.62) 30 35
75 10 c. bronze-green & pur (as 1s.) (22.10.62) 20 20
76 12½ c. brown and turquoise-green (as 1s. 3d.) (17.12.62) . . . . . . 7·50 6·00
77 25 c. deep ultramarine and crimson (as 2s. 6d.) (25.9.62) . . . . 2·50 6·00
78 50 c. black & carmine-red (as 5s.) (22.10.62) 4·50 7·00
79 1 r. black and maroon (as 10s.) (4.2.63) . . 13·00 8·50
a. Black and light maroon (16.12.63) . . 15·00 12·00
69/79 . . . . *Set of* 11 27·00 27·00

(Des M. Goaman. Photo Harrison)

1963 (4 June). *Freedom from Hunger. W* w **12**. *P* 14×14½.
80 **27** 12½ c. reddish violet 40 15

1963 (2 Sept). *Red Cross Centenary. As Nos. 203/4 of Jamaica.*
81 2½ c. red and black 20 10
82 12½ c. red and blue 60 50

1964. *As Nos. 70, 72, 74, 76 and 78, but W* w **12**.
84 1 c. grey-black and bluish green (11.8.64) . . 10 20
86 2½ c. pale yellow-green and rose-red (10.3.64) 15 15
88 5 c. chestnut and deep grey-green (10.11.64) 30 40
90 12½ c. brown and turquoise-green (10.11.64) . . 2·25 1·50
92 50 c. black and carmine-red (29.9.64) . . . . 6·75 10·00
84/92 . . . . *Set of* 5 8·50 11·00

SELF-GOVERNMENT

28 Mosotho Woman and Child **29** Maseru Border Post

1965 (10 May). *New Constitution. T* **28/9** *and similar horiz designs. Multicoloured. W* w **12**. *P* 14×13½.
94 2½ c. Type **28** 10 10
95 3½ c. Type **29** 15 10
96 5 c. Mountain scene 15 10
97 12½ c. Legislative Buildings 25 30
94/7 . . . . *Set of* 4 60 55

30 I.T.U. Emblem **31** I.C.Y. Emblem

(Des M. Goaman. Litho Enschedé)

1965 (17 May). *I.T.U. Centenary. W* w **12**. *P* 11×11½.
98 **30** 1 c. orange-red and bright purple . . 15 10
99 20 c. light blue and orange-brown . . 35 30

(Des V. Whiteley. Litho Harrison)

1965 (25 Oct). *International Co-operation Year. W* w **12**. *P* 14½.
100 **31** ½ c. reddish purple & turquoise-green 10 10
101 12½ c. deep bluish green and lavender 45 35

32 Sir Winston Churchill and St. Paul's Cathedral in Wartime

(Des Jennifer Toombs. Photo Harrison)

1966 (24 Jan). *Churchill Commemoration. Printed in black, cerise, gold and background in colours stated. W* w **12**. *P* 14.
102 **32** 1 c. new blue 15 25
103 2½ c. deep green 40 10
104 10 c. brown 60 25
105 22½ c. bluish violet 80 50
102/5 . . . . *Set of* 4 1·75 1·00

Basutoland attained independence on 4 October 1966 as the Kingdom of Lesotho.

LESOTHO

INDEPENDENT KINGDOM

33 Moshoeshoe I and Moshoeshoe II

(Des and photo Harrison)

1966 (4 Oct). *Independence. P* 12½×13.
106 **33** 2½ c. light brown, black and red . . 10 10
107 5 c. light brown, black and new blue . . 10 10
108 10 c. light brown, black and emerald . . 15 10
109 20 c. light brown, black & bright purple 20 10
106/9 . . . . *Set of* 4 45 20

LESOTHO (**34**)

35 "Education Culture and Science"

1966 (1 Nov). *Stamps of Basutoland optd as T* **34**. *A. Nos. 69/71 and 73/9 (Script CA wmk). B. Nos. 84/96 and unissud 1 r. (wmk* w **12**).

		A		B	
110	½ c. grey-black and sepia . .	10	10	†	
111	1 c. grey-blk and bluish grn	10	10	10	10
112	2 c. deep bright blue & orange	40	10	†	
113	2½ c. pale yell-grn & rose-red . .	†		20	10
114	3½ c. ind & dp ultram	30	10	†	
115	5 c. chestnut & dp grey-grn . .	20	10	20	10
116	10 c. bronze-green and purple	20	10	†	
117	12½ c. brown & turq-green . .	2·25	35	30	20
118	25 c. deep ultram & crimson . .	40	20	†	
119	50 c. black and carmine-red . .	1·00	65	80	50
120	1 r. black and maroon . .	1·00	1·75	1·00	75
	a. "LSEOTHO"	60·00	—	40·00	—
	b. Opt double	80·00	—	†	
	ba. Ditto. "LSEOTHO" . .	—	—	†	
110A/120A	. . . . *Set of* 10	5·25	3·00		
111B/120B	. . . . *Set of* 6			2·25	1·40

(Des V. Whiteley. Litho D.L.R.)

1966 (1 Dec). *20th Anniv of U.N.E.S.C.O. P* 14½ × 14.
121 **35** 2½ c. orange-yellow and emerald-green 10 10
122 5 c. light green and olive 15 10
123 12½ c. light blue and red 35 10
124 25 c. red-orange and deep greenish blue 60 25
121/4 . . . . *Set of* 4 1·10 40

36 Maize **37** Moshoeshoe II

(Des and photo Harrison)

1967 (1 Apr). *Designs as T* **36/7**. *No wmk. P* 14½×13½ (2 *r.*) *or* 13½×14½ (*others*).

125	½ c. bluish green and light bluish violet ..	10	10
126	1 c. sepia and rose-red	10	10
127	2 c. orange-yellow and light green ..	10	10
128	2½ c. black and ochre	10	10
129	3½ c. chalky blue and yellow	10	10
130	5 c. bistre and new blue	10	10
131	10 c. yellow-brown and bluish grey ..	10	10
132	12½ c. black and red-orange	20	10
133	25 c. black and bright blue	55	20
134	50 c. black, new blue and turquoise ..	4·50	45
135	1 r. multicoloured	1·25	75
136	2 r. black, gold and magenta	1·50	1·75
125/36	.. .. *Set of* 12	7·50	3·00

Designs: *Horiz as T* **36**—1 c. Cattle; 2 c. Agaves (wrongly inscr "Aloes"); 2½ c. Basotho Hat; 3½ c. Merino Sheep ("Wool"); 5 c. Basotho Pony; 10 c. Wheat; 12½ c. Angora Goat ("Mohair"); 25 c. Maletsunyane Falls; 50 c. Diamonds; 1 r. Arms of Lesotho.

See also Nos. 147/59 and 191/203.

46 Students and University

(Des V. Whiteley. Photo Harrison)

1967 (7 Apr). *First Conferment of University Degrees. P* 14 × 14½.

137 **46**	1 c. sepia, ultram & light yellow-orange	10	10
138	2½ c. sepia, ultram & light greenish blue	10	10
139	12½ c. sepia, ultramarine and rose ..	10	10
140	25 c. sepia, ultramarine and light violet	15	10
137/40	.. .. *Set of* 4	30	15

47 Statue of Moshoeshoe I

(Des and photo Harrison)

1967 (4 Oct). *First Anniv of Independence. T* **47** *and similar triangular designs. P* 14½ × 14.

141	2½ c. black and light yellow-green	10	10
142	12½ c. multicoloured	25	10
143	25 c. black, green and light ochre	35	15
141/3	.. .. *Set of* 3	65	25

Designs:—12½ c. Lesotho flag; 25 c. Crocodile (national emblem).

50 Lord Baden-Powell and Scout Saluting

(Des V. Whiteley. Photo Harrison)

1967 (1 Nov). *60th Anniv of Scout Movement. P* 14 × 14½.

144 **50**	15 c. multicoloured	15	10

51 W.H.O. Emblem and World Map

(Des G. Vasarhelyi. Photo Harrison)

1968 (7 Apr). *20th Anniv of World Health Organization. T* **51** *and similar horiz design. P* 14 × 14½.

145	2½ c. blue, gold and carmine-red	15	10
	a. Gold (emblem) omitted		
146	25 c. multicoloured	35	10

Design:—25 c. Nurse and child.

ALTERED CATALOGUE NUMBERS

Any Catalogue numbers altered from the last edition are shown as a list in the introductory pages.

53 Basotho Hat

54 Sorghum

1968–69. *As Nos.* 125/36 *and T* **54**, *but wmk* **53** (*sideways on* 2 *r.*).

147	½ c. bluish green & lt bluish vio (26.11.68)	10	10
	a. Blue-green and violet (30.9.69) ..	40	40
148	1 c. sepia and rose-red (26.11.68) ..	10	10
149	2 c. orange-yellow & lt green (26.11.68)	10	10
	a. Orange-yellow & yell-grn (30.9.69)	30	30
150	2½ c. black and ochre (21.10.68) ..	15	10
	a. Black and yellow-ochre (30.9.69) ..	30	30
151	3 c. chocolate, green & yell-brn (1.8.68)	15	15
152	3½ c. chalky blue and yellow (26.11.68) ..	15	10
153	5 c. bistre and new blue (22.7.68) ..	30	10
154	10 c. yell-brn & pale bluish grey (26.11.68)	15	10
155	12½ c. black and red-orange (30.9.69) ..	60	35
156	25 c. black and bright blue (30.9.69) ..	1·25	1·00
157	50 c. black, new blue & turquoise (30.9.69)	6·50	1·50
158	1 r. multicoloured (26.11.68)	3·50	3·00
159	2 r. black, gold and magenta (30.9.69) ..	16·00	14·00
147/59	.. .. *Set of* 13	26·00	18·00

55 Running Hunters

(Des Jennifer Toombs. Photo Harrison)

1968 (1 Nov). *Rock Paintings. T* **55** *and similar designs. W* **53** (*sideways on* 5 *c.*, 15 *c.*). *P* 14 × 14½ (5 *c.*, 15 *c.*) *or* 14½ × 14 (*others*).

160	3 c. yellow-brown, lt blue-green & blackish green	15	10
161	3½ c. greenish yellow, yellow-olive and sepia	20	10
162	5 c. Venetian red, yell-ochre & blackish brn	25	10
163	10 c. yellow, rose and deep maroon.. ..	35	10
164	15 c. light buff, pale olive-yell & blackish brn	65	25
165	20 c. yellow-grn, greenish yellow & blackish brown	75	35
166	25 c. yellow, orange-brown and black ..	90	50
160/6	.. .. *Set of* 7	2·75	1·25

Designs: *Horiz*—3½ c. Baboons; 10 c. Archers; 20 c. Eland; 25 c. Hunting scene. *Vert*—5 c. Javelin throwing; 15 c. Blue Cranes.

62 Queen Elizabeth II Hospital

(Des C. R. Househam and G. Drummond. Litho P.B.)

1969 (11 Mar). *Centenary of Maseru (capital). T* **62** *and similar horiz designs. Multicoloured. W* **53** (*sideways*). *P* 14 × 13½.

167	2½ c. Type **62**	10	10
168	10 c. Lesotho Radio Station..	10	10
169	12½ c. Leabua Jonathan Airport	10	10
170	25 c. Royal Palace	15	15
167/70	.. .. *Set of* 4	30	20

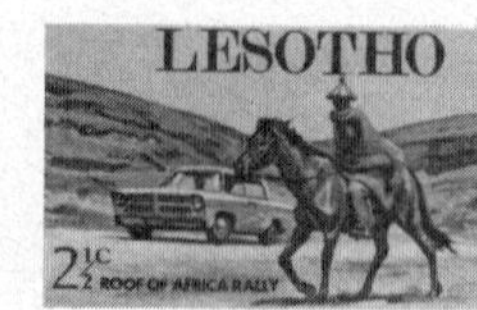

66 Rally Car passing Mosotho Horseman

(Des P. Wheeler. Photo Harrison)

1969 (26 Sept). *Roof of Africa Car Rally. T* **66** *and similar horiz designs. W* **53**. *P* 14.

171	2½ c. yellow, mauve and plum	10	10
172	12½ c. cobalt, greenish yellow and olive-grey	15	10
173	15 c. blue, black and mauve	15	10
174	20 c. black, red and yellow	15	10
171/4	.. .. *Set of* 4	45	30

Designs:—12½ c. Rally car on mountain road; 15 c. Chequered flags and mountain scenery; 20 c. Map of rally route and Rally Trophy.

71 Gryponyx and Footprints

75 Moshoeshoe I, when a Young Man

(Des Jennifer Toombs. Photo Harrison)

1970 (5 Jan). *Prehistoric Footprints (1st series). T* **71** *and similar designs. W* **53** (*sideways*). *P* 14 × 14½ (3 *c.*) *or* 14½ × 14 (*others*).

175	3 c. pale brown, yellow-brown and sepia ..	25	20
176	5 c. dull purple, pink and sepia	35	30
177	10 c. pale yellow, black, and sepia	50	35
178	15 c. olive-yellow, black and sepia	75	1·00
179	25 c. cobalt and black	1·75	2·00
175/9	.. .. *Set of* 5	3·25	3·50

Designs: (60 × 23 *mm*)—3 c. Dinosaur footprints at Moyeni. (40 × 24 *mm*)—10 c. Plateosauravus and footprints; 15 c. Tritylodon and footprints; 25 c. Massospondylus and footprints.

See also Nos. 596/8.

(Des G. Vasarhelyi. Litho D.L.R.)

1970 (11 Mar). *Death Centenary of King Moshoeshoe I. T* **75** *and similar vert design. W* **53**. *P* 13½.

180	2½ c. pale green and magenta	10	10
181	25 c. pale blue and chesnut..	15	10

Design:—25 c. Moshoeshoe I as an old man.

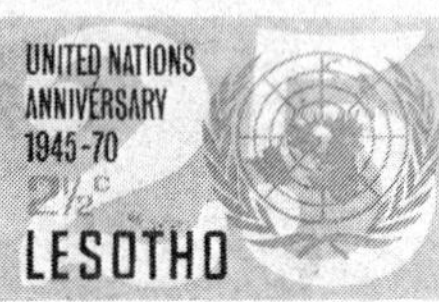

77 U.N. Emblem and "25"

1970 (26 June). *25th Anniv of United Nations. T* **77** *and similar horiz designs. W* **53** (*sideways*). *P* 14½ × 14.

182	2½ c. light pink, light blue and maroon ..	10	10
183	10 c. multicoloured	10	10
184	12½ c. brown-red, cobalt and drab	10	10
185	25 c. multicoloured	15	10
182/5	.. .. *Set of* 4	20	20

Designs:— 10 c. U.N. Building; 12½ c. "People of the World"; 25 c. Symbolic dove.

78 Basotho Hat Gift Shop, Maseru

(Des G. Drummond. Litho Questa)

1970 (27 Oct). *Tourism. T* **78** *and similar horiz designs. Multicoloured. W* **53** (*sideways*). *P* 14.

186	2½ c. Type **78**	10	10
187	5 c. Trout fishing	20	10
188	10 c. Pony trekking..	25	10
189	12½ c. Skiing	45	10
190	20 c. Holiday Inn, Maseru	45	50
186/90	.. .. *Set of* 5	1·25	70

79 Maize

80 Lammergeier

(Des Harrison. Litho Questa)

1971 (4 Jan–1 Apr). *As Nos.* 147/58 *but in new format omitting portrait of Moshoeshoe II, as in T* **79**. 4 *c. and* 2 *r. in new designs. W* **53** (*sideways except* 2 *r.*). *P* 14.

191	½ c. blue-green and light bluish violet ..	10	10
192	1 c. brown and orange-red..	10	10
193	2 c. yellow and green	10	10
194	2½ c. black, olive-green and yellow-ochre ..	10	10
195	3 c. brown, green and yellow-ochre ..	10	10
196	3½ c. indigo and yellow	10	10
196*a*	4 c. multicoloured (1.4.71)..	20	10
197	5 c. yellow-brown and pale blue	15	10
198	10 c. orange-brown and grey-blue	15	10
199	12½ c. chocolate and yellow-orange	25	30
200	25 c. slate and pale bright blue	60	40
201	50 c. black, pale blue and turquoise-green ..	4·50	2·25
202	1 r. multicoloured	2·75	2·25
203	2 r. yellow-brown and ultramarine ..	2·75	3·00
191/203	.. .. *Set of* 14	10·50	8·00

Designs: *Horiz*—4 c. National flag. *Vert*—2 r. Statue of Moshoeshoe I.

For 2 r. value without watermark see No. 401.

(Des R. Granger Barrett. Litho J.W.)

1971 (1 Mar). *Birds. T* **80** *and similar vert designs. Multicoloured. W* **53.** *P* 14.

204 2½ c. Type **80** .. .. 1·25 10
205 5 c. Bald Ibis .. .. 2·00 90
206 10 c. Rufous Rockjumper .. .. 2·75 1·25
207 12½ c. Blue Bustard .. .. 3·25 1·40
208 15 c. Painted Snipe .. .. 4·00 2·50
209 20 c. Golden-breasted Bunting .. .. .. 4·00 2·50
210 25 c. Ground Woodpecker .. .. 4·25 2·75
204/10 .. .. *Set of* 7 19·00 10·00

81 Lionel Collett Dam

(Des G. Drummond. Litho J.W.)

1971 (15 July). *Soil Conservation. T* **81** *and similar horiz designs. Multicoloured. W* **53** *(sideways). P* 14.

211 4 c. Type **81** 10 10
212 10 c. Contour ridges 10 10
213 15 c. Earth dams 25 10
214 25 c. Beaver dams 35 35
211/14 .. .. *Set of* 4 70 50

82 Diamond Mining

(Des J.W. Litho Questa)

1971 (4 Oct). *Development. T* **82** *and similar horiz designs. Multicoloured. W* **53** *(sideways). P* 14.

215 4 c. Type **82** 40 10
216 10 c. Pottery 25 10
217 15 c. Weaving 35 15
218 20 c. Construction 45 30
215/18 .. .. *Set of* 4 1·40 50

83 Mail Cart

84 Sprinting

(Des D. B. Picton-Phillips. Litho Questa)

1972 (3 Jan). *Post Office Centenary. T* **83** *and similar designs. W* **53** *(sideways on* 5, 10 *and* 20 *c.). P* 14 × 13½ *(*15 *c.) or* 13½ × 14 *(others).*

219 5 c. pale pink and black 15 10
220 10 c. multicoloured 15 10
221 15 c. pale drab, light blue and black 30 15
222 20 c. multicoloured 45 70
219/22 .. .. *Set of* 4 95 80

Designs: *Horiz*—10 c. Postal bus; 20 c. Maseru P.O. *Vert*—15 c. Cape of Good Hope 4d. stamp of 1876.

(Des J. W. Litho Questa)

1972 (1 Sept). *Olympic Games. Munich. T* **84** *and similar vert designs. Multicoloured. W* **53.** *P* 14.

223 4 c. Type **84** 10 10
224 10 c. Shot putting 15 10
225 15 c. Hurdling 20 10
226 25 c. Long-jumping 30 20
223/6 .. .. *Set of* 4 60 35

85 "Adoration of the Shepherds" (Matthias Stomer)

(Des and litho J.W.)

1972 (1 Dec). *Christmas. W* **53** *(sideways). P* 14.

227 **85** 4 c. multicoloured 10 10
228 10 c. multicoloured 10 10
229 25 c. multicoloured 15 20
227/9 .. .. *Set of* 3 30 30

O.A.U.
10th Anniversary
Freedom in Unity

86 W.H.O. Emblem (**87**)

(Des. J. Cooter. Litho Questa)

1973 (7 Apr). *25th Anniv of W.H.O. W* **53** *(sideways). P* 13½.

230 **86** 20 c. greenish blue and yellow 20 15

1973 (25 May). *Tenth Anniv of O.A.U. Nos.* 194 *and* 196*a*/8 *optd with T* **87** *by Govt Printer, Maseru.*

231 2½ c. black, olive-green and yellow-ochre .. 10 10
232 4 c. multicoloured 10 10
a. Horiz pair, one without opt £150
233 5 c. yellow-brown and pale blue 10 10
234 10 c. orange-brown and grey-blue 15 15
231/4 .. .. *Set of* 4 35 35

88 Basotho Hat and W.F.P. Emblem

(Des locally; adapted J. Cooter. Litho Format)

1973 (1 June). *Tenth Anniv of World Food Programme. T* **88** *and similar horiz designs. Multicoloured. W* **53** *(sideways). P* 13½.

235 4 c. Type **88** 10 10
236 15 c. School feeding 20 15
237 20 c. Infant feeding 20 20
a. Imperf (pair) .. ..
238 25 c. "Food for Work" 25 25
235/8 .. .. *Set of* 4 65 60

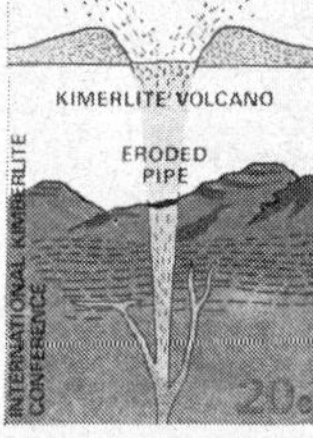

89 *Aeropetes tulbaghia* **90** Kimberlite Volcano

(Des A. McLeod; artwork G. Drummond. Litho Questa)

1973 (3 Sept). *Butterflies. T* **89** *and similar horiz designs. Multicoloured. W* **53** *(sideways). P* 14.

239 4 c. Type **89** 30 10
240 5 c. *Papilio demodocus* 40 25
241 10 c. *Cynthia cardui* 80 50
242 15 c. *Precis hierta* .. .. 1·10 1·00
243 20 c. *Precis oenone* .. .. 1·10 1·00
244 25 c. *Danaus chrysippus* .. .. .. 1·60 1·75
245 30 c. *Colotis evenina* .. .. 1·90 2·00
239/45 .. .. *Set of* 7 6·50 6·00

(Des PAD Studio. Litho Questa)

1973 (1 Oct). *International Kimberlite Conference. T* **90** *and similar multicoloured designs. W* **53** *(sideways on* 10 *and* 15 *c.). P* 13½.

246 10 c. Map of diamond mines (*horiz*) 90 50
247 15 c. Kimberlite-diamond rock (*horiz*) .. 1·10 1·00
248 20 c. Type **90** .. .. 1·40 1·50
249 30 c. Diamond prospecting .. .. .. 2·25 3·00
246/9 .. .. *Set of* 4 5·00 5·50

Type **90** is incorrectly inscribed "KIMERLITE VOLCANO".

91 "Health" **92** Open Book and Wreath

(Des R. Granger Barrett. Litho Questa)

1974 (18 Feb). *Youth and Development. T* **91** *and similar horiz designs. Multicoloured. W* **53** *(sideways). P* 13½.

250 4 c. Type **91** 10 10
251 10 c. "Education" 10 10
252 20 c. "Agriculture" 15 10
253 25 c. "Industry" 25 20
254 30 c. "Service" 30 25
250/4 .. .. *Set of* 5 75 55

(Des PAD Studio. Litho Questa)

1974 (7 Apr). *Tenth Anniv of U.B.L.S. T* **92** *and similar vert designs. Multicoloured. W* **53.** *P* 14.

255 10 c. Type **92** 10 10
256 15 c. Flags, mortar-board and scroll 10 10
257 20 c. Map of Africa 15 10
258 25 c. King Moshoeshoe II capping a graduate 15 15
255/8 .. .. *Set of* 4 40 30

93 Senqunyane River Bridge, Marakabei

(Des J. Cooter. Litho Questa)

1974 (26 June). *Rivers and Bridges. T* **93** *and similar horiz designs. Multicoloured. W* **53** *(sideways). P* 14½.

259 4 c. Type **93** 10 10
260 5 c. Tsoelike River and bridge 10 10
261 10 c. Makhaleng River Bridge 20 10
262 15 c. Seaka Bridge, Orange/Senqu River .. 35 35
263 20 c. Masianokeng Bridge, Phuthiatsana River 40 40
264 25 c. Mahobong Bridge, Hlotse River 45 45
259/64 .. .. *Set of* 6 1·50 1·25

94 U.P.U. Emblem

(Des R. Granger Barrett. Litho Enschedé)

1974 (6 Sept). *Centenary of Universal Postal Union. T* **94** *and similar horiz designs. W* **53** *(sideways). P* 13½ × 13.

265 4 c. light emerald and black 10 10
266 10 c. orange, greenish yellow and black .. 10 10
267 15 c. multicoloured 15 15
268 20 c. multicoloured 20 20
265/8 .. .. *Set of* 4 45 40

Designs:—10 c. Map of air-mail routes; 15 c. Post Office H.Q., Maseru; 20 c. Horseman taking rural mail.

On No. 266 the inscriptions for the airstrips at Makhotlong and Mohlanapeng were transposed in error.

95 Siege of Thaba-Bosiu

(Des Jennifer Toombs. Litho Enschedé)

1974 (25 Nov). *150th Anniv of Establishment of Thaba-Bosiu as Capital. T* **95** *and similar multicoloured designs. W* **53** *(sideways on* 4 *and* 5 *c.). P* 12½ × 12 *(*4 *and* 5 *c.) or* 12 × 12½ *(others).*

269 4 c. Type **95** 10 10
270 5 c. The wreath-laying 10 10
271 10 c. Moshoeshoe I (*vert*) 25 10
272 20 c. Makoanyane, the warrior (*vert*) 65 30
269/72 .. .. *Set of* 4 1·00 40

96 Mamokhorong

(Des PAD Studio. Litho Questa)

1975 (25 Jan). *Basotho Musical Instruments. T* **96** *and similar horiz designs. Multicoloured. W* **53** *(sideways). P* 14.

273 4 c. Type **96** 10 10
274 10 c. Lesiba 10 10
275 15 c. Setolotolo 15 20
276 20 c. Meropa 15 20
273/6 .. .. *Set of* 4 40 45
MS277 108 × 92 mm. Nos. 273/6 .. .. .. 1·25 2·00

97 Horseman in Rock Archway **98** Morena Moshoeshoe I

(Des J. Cooter. Litho Questa)

1975 (15 Apr). *Sehlabathebe National Park. T* **97** *and similar horiz designs. Multicoloured.* W **53** (*sideways*). *P* 14.
278 4 c. Type **97** 15 10
279 5 c. Mountain view through arch 15 10
280 15 c. Antelope by stream 35 30
281 20 c. Mountains and lake 40 35
282 25 c. Tourists by frozen waterfall 50 50
278/82 *Set of* 5 1·40 1·10

(Des G. Vasarhelyi. Litho Questa)

1975 (10 Sept). *Leaders of Lesotho. T* **98** *and similar vert designs.* W **53**. *P* 14.
283 3 c. black and light blue 10 10
284 4 c. black and light mauve 10 10
285 5 c. black and pink 10 10
286 6 c. black and light grey-brown 10 10
287 10 c. black and light claret 10 10
288 15 c. black and light orange-red 20 20
289 20 c. black and dull green 25 30
290 25 c. black and azure 25 40
283/90 *Set of* 8 1·00 1·10
Designs:—4 c. King Moshoeshoe II; 5 c. Morena Letsie I; 6 c. Morena Lerotholi; 10 c. Morena Letsie II; 15 c. Morena Griffith; 20 c. Morena Seeiso Griffith Lerotholi; 25 c. Mofumahali Mantsebo Seeiso, O.B.E.
The 25 c. also commemorates International Women's Year.

99 Mokhibo Dance

(Des PAD Studio. Litho Questa)

1975 (17 Dec). *Traditional Dances. T* **99** *and similar horiz designs. Multicoloured.* W **53** (*sideways*). *P* 14 × 14½.
291 4 c. Type **99** 10 10
292 10 c. Ndlamo 10 10
293 15 c. Baleseli 25 30
294 20 c. Mohobelo 30 35
291/4 *Set of* 4 60 65
MS295 111 × 100 mm. Nos. 291/94 2·50 2·50

100 Enrolment

(Des L. Curtis. Litho Questa)

1976 (20 Feb). *25th Anniv of the Lesotho Red Cross. T* **100** *and similar horiz designs. Multicoloured.* W **53** (*sideways*). *P* 14.
296 4 c. Type **100** 35 10
297 10 c. Medical aid 50 10
298 15 c. Rural service 95 45
299 25 c. Relief supplies 1·25 55
296/9 *Set of* 4 2·75 1·00

101 Tapestry **102** Football

(Des V. Whiteley Studio. Litho Format)

1976 (2 June). *Multicoloured designs as T* **101**. W **53** (*sideways on* 2 *to* 50 *c.*). *P* 14.
300 2 c. Type **101** 10 10
301 3 c. Mosotho horseman 20 10
302 4 c. Map of Lesotho 35 10
303 5 c. Lesotho Brown diamond 55 10
304 10 c. Lesotho Bank 30 10
305 15 c. Lesotho and O.A.U. flags 65 20
306 25 c. Sehlabathebe National Park 80 35
307 40 c. Pottery 95 50
308 50 c. Prehistoric rock art 1·50 90
309 1 r. King Moshoeshoe II (*vert*) 1·40 1·75
300/309 *Set of* 10 6·00 3·50
For 25 c., 40 c. and 50 c. values on unwatermarked paper, see Nos. 398/400.

(Des P. Powell. Litho Questa)

1976 (9 Aug). *Olympic Games, Montreal. T* **102** *and similar vert designs. Multicoloured.* W **53**. *P* 14.
310 4 c. Type **102** 10 10
311 10 c. Weightlifting 10 10
312 15 c. Boxing 15 10
313 25 c. Throwing the discus 30 25
310/13 *Set of* 4 55 40

103 "Rising Sun" **104** Telephones, 1876 and 1976

(Des L. Curtis. Litho Questa)

1976 (4 Oct). *Tenth Anniv of Independence. T* **103** *and similar vert designs. Multicoloured.* W **53**. *P* 14.
314 4 c. Type **103** 10 10
315 10 c. Open gates 10 10
316 15 c. Broken chains 30 10
317 25 c. Aeroplane over hotel 40 25
314/17 *Set of* 4 80 35

(Des and litho J.W.)

1976 (6 Dec). *Telephone Centenary. T* **104** *and similar horiz designs. Multicoloured.* W **53** (*sideways*). *P* 13.
318 4 c. Type **104** 10 10
319 10 c. Early handset and telephone-user, 1976 10 10
320 15 c. Wall telephone and telephone exchange 15 15
321 25 c. Stick telephone and Alexander Graham Bell 30 40
318/21 *Set of* 4 55 55

105 *Aloe striatula* **106** Large-toothed Rock Hyrax

(Des D. Findlay. Litho Walsall)

1977 (14 Feb). *Aloes and Succulents. T* **105** *and similar vert designs. Multicoloured.* W **53** (*inverted*). *P* 14.
322 3 c. Type **105** 20 10
323 4 c. *Aloe aristata* 25 10
324 5 c. *Kniphofia caulescens* 30 10
325 10 c. *Euphorbia pulvinata* 45 10
326 15 c. *Aloe saponaria* 80 40
327 20 c. *Caralluma lutea* 1·10 65
328 25 c. *Aloe polyphylla* 1·60 90
322/8 *Set of* 7 4·25 2·00

(Des D. Findlay. Litho Questa)

1977 (25 Apr). *Animals. T* **106** *and similar horiz designs. Multicoloured.* W **53** (*sideways*). *P* 14.
329 4 c. Type **106** 20 10
330 5 c. Cape Porcupine 25 10
331 10 c. Zorilla (polecat) 40 10
332 15 c. Klipspringer 90 70
333 25 c. Chacma Baboon 1·40 1·10
329/33 *Set of* 5 2·75 1·75

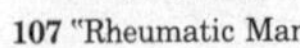

107 "Rheumatic Man" **108** *Barbus holubi*

(Des C. Abbott. Litho Questa)

1977 (4 July). *World Rheumatism Year. T* **107** *and similar vert designs showing the "Rheumatic Man".* W **53**. *P* 14.
334 4 c. yellow and red 10 10
335 10 c. new blue and deep blue 10 10
336 15 c. yellow and blue-green 25 10
337 25 c. orange-red and black 40 45
334/7 *Set of* 4 75 55
Designs:—10 c. Man surrounded by "pain"; 15 c. Man surrounded by "chain"; 25 c. Man supporting globe.

(Des D. Findlay. Litho Questa)

1977 (28 Sept). *Fish. T* **108** *and similar horiz designs. Multicoloured.* W **53** (*sideways*). *P* 14.
338 4 c. Type **108** 15 10
339 10 c. *Labeo capensis* 30 10
340 15 c. *Salmo gairdneri* 60 35
341 25 c. *Oreodaimon quathlambae* 85 60
338/41 *Set of* 4 1·75 1·00

(**109**) **110** Black and White Heads

1977 (7 Dec*). *No.* 198 *surch with T* **109** *by Govt Printer, Maseru.*
342 3 c. on 10 c. yellow-brown and pale bluish grey 1·25 80
*Earliest known date of use.

(Des Jennifer Toombs. Litho Walsall)

1977 (12 Dec). *Decade for Action to Combat Racism. T* **110** *and similar vert designs.* W **53**. *P* 14.
343 4 c. chocolate and mauve 10 10
344 10 c. chocolate and light new blue 10 10
345 15 c. chocolate and light orange 15 15
346 25 c. chocolate and light turquoise-green 25 25
343/6 *Set of* 4 55 45
Designs:—10 c. Jigsaw pieces; 15 c. Cogwheels; 25 c. Handshake.

(Des D. Findlay. Litho Questa)

1978 (13 Feb). *Flowers. Vert designs similar to T* **105**. *Multicoloured.* W **53**. *P* 14.
347 2 c. *Papaver aculeatum* 10 15
348 3 c. *Diascia integerrima* 10 15
349 4 c. *Helichrysum trilineatum* 10 10
350 5 c. *Zaluzianskya maritima* 10 10
351 10 c. *Gladiolus natalensis* 20 20
352 15 c. *Chironia krebsii* 30 30
353 25 c. *Wahlenbergia undulata* 50 90
354 40 c. *Brunsvigia radulosa* 85 1·75
347/54 *Set of* 8 2·00 3·25

111 Edward Jenner performing Vaccination **112** Tsoloane Falls

(Des G. Hutchins. Litho J.W.)

1978 (8 May). *Global Eradication of Smallpox. T* **111** *and similar vert design. Multicoloured.* W **53**. *P* 13.
355 5 c. Type **111** 10 10
356 25 c. Head of child and W.H.O. emblem 30 25

(Des Kobus De Beer Art Studio. Litho Questa)

1978 (28 July). *Waterfalls. T* **112** *and similar vert designs. Multicoloured.* W **53**. *P* 14.
357 4 c. Type **112** 15 10
358 10 c. Qiloane Falls 25 10
359 15 c. Tsoelikana Falls 45 25
360 25 c. Maletsunyane Falls 75 60
357/60 *Set of* 4 1·40 90

113 Wright *Flyer*, 1903 **114** *Orthetrum farinosum*

(Des L. Curtis. Litho Harrison)

1978 (9 Oct). *75th Anniv of Powered Flight. T* **113** *and similar horiz design.* W **53** (*sideways*). *P* 14½ × 14.
361 5 c. black, brown-ochre and new blue 10 10
362 25 c. multicoloured 30 20
Design:—25 c. Wilbur and Orville Wright.

(Des D. Findlay. Litho Questa)

1978 (18 Dec). *Insects. T* **114** *and similar vert designs. Multicoloured.* W **53**. *P* 14.
363 4 c. Type **114** 10 10
364 10 c. *Phymateus viridipes* 20 10
365 15 c. *Belonogaster lateritius* 30 20
366 25 c. *Sphodromantis gastrica* 50 45
363/6 *Set of* 4 1·00 70

115 Oudehout Branch in flower

116 Mampharoane

(Des D. Findlay. Litho Questa)

1979 (26 Mar). *Trees. T* **115** *and similar vert designs showing branches in flower. Multicoloured.* W **53**. P 14.

367	4 c. Type **115** ..	15	10
368	10 c. Wild Olive	20	10
369	15 c. Blinkblaar	35	60
370	25 c. Cape Holly	70	1·25
367/70	*Set of* 4	1·25	1·75

(New Currency. 100 lisente = 1(màloti)

(Des D. Findlay. Litho Questa)

1979 (1 June). *Reptiles. T* **116** *and similar horiz designs. Multicoloured.* P 14. A. *No wmk.* B. W **53** *(sideways).*

		A		B	
371	4 s. Type **116** ..	10	10	10	10
372	10 s. Qoaane	20	10	20	10
373	15 s. Leupa	30	35	30	60
374	25 s. Masumu	60	65	60	1·25
371/4 ..	*Set of* 4	1·10	1·00	1·10	1·75

117 Basutoland 1933 1d. Stamp

118 Detail of Painting "Children's Games" by Brueghel

(Des J.W. Litho Format)

1979 (22 Oct). *Death Centenary of Sir Rowland Hill. T* **117** *and similar vert designs showing stamps.* P 14.

375	4 s. multicoloured	10	10
376	15 s. multicoloured	30	20
377	25 s. black, yellow-orange and olive-bistre	40	30
375/7 ..	*Set of* 3	70	50
MS378	118 × 95 mm. 50 s. multicoloured	60	80

Designs:—15 s. Basutoland 1962 ½ c. definitive; 25 s. Penny Black; 50 s. 1972 15 c. Post Office Centenary commemorative.

(Des C. Abbott. Litho Questa)

1979 (10 Dec). *International Year of the Child. T* **118** *and similar vert designs showing details of the painting "Children's Games" by Brueghel.* W **53**. P 14.

379	4 s. multicoloured	10	10
380	10 s. multicoloured	10	10
381	15 s. multicoloured	15	15
379/81	*Set of* 3	30	30
MS382	113 × 88 mm. 25 s. multicoloured *(horiz)* (wmk sideways)	40	45

119 Beer Strainer, Broom and Mat

(Des Kobus de Beer Art Studio. Litho Walsall)

1980 (18 Feb). *Grasswork. T* **119** *and similar horiz designs. Multicoloured.* W **53** *(sideways).* P 14.

383	4 s. Type **119** ..	10	10
384	10 s. Winnowing Basket	10	10
385	15 s. Basotho Hat	20	15
386	25 s. Grain storage	35	25
383/6 ..	*Set of* 4	60	45

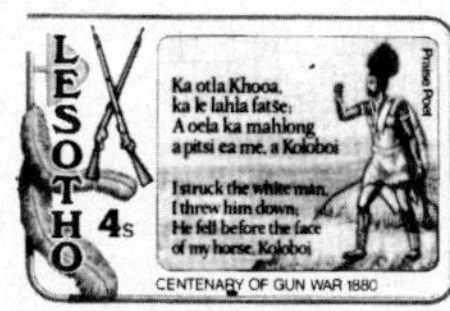

120 Praise Poet

(Des BG Studio. Litho Walsall)

1980 (6 May). *Centenary of Gun War. T* **120** *and similar horiz designs. Multicoloured.* P 14.

387	4 s. Type **120** ..	15	10
388	5 s. Lerotholi (commander of Basotho Army)	15	10
389	10 s. Ambush at Qalabane	20	10
390	15 s. Snider and Martini-Henry rifles	40	25
391	25 s. Map showing main areas of action	50	35
387/91	*Set of* 5	1·25	70

121 Olympic Flame, Flags and Kremlin

s
=

(122)

(Des G. Vasarhelyi. Litho Format)

1980 (20 Sept). *Olympic Games, Moscow. T* **121** *and similar horiz designs. Multicoloured.* P 14½.

392	25 s. Type **121** ..	25	25
	a. Horiz strip of 5. Nos. 392/6	1·10	
393	25 s. Doves, flame and flags	25	25
394	25 s. Football	25	25
395	25 s. Running	25	25
396	25 s. Opening ceremony	25	25
392/6 ..	*Set of* 5	1·10	1·10
MS397	110 × 85 mm. 1 m. 40, Ancient and modern athletes carrying Olympic torch	1·10	1·25

Nos. 392/6 were printed together, *se-tenant*, in horizontal strips of 5 throughout the sheet.

1980. *As Nos.* 203 *and* 306/8, *but without wmk.*

398	25 c. Sehlabathebe National Park	1·50	
399	40 c. Pottery	6·00	
400	50 c. Prehistoric rock art	6·00	6·00
401	2 r. Statue of Moshoeshoe I (yellow-brown and ultramarine)	2·50	4·50
398/401	*Set of* 4	14·50	

Two opt types of No. 409:

Type I. Cancelling bars centred on depth of "M1" (stamps surcharged in individual panes of 25 and from the righthand panes of those surcharged in sheets of 50 (2 panes 5 × 5)).

Type II. Lower cancelling bar aligns with foot of "M1" (stamps from lefthand panes of those surcharged in sheets of 50).

1980 (20 Oct)–**81**. *As Nos.* 300/5, 309 *and* 398/401 *surch as T* **122** *or with new figures of value* (5 *s.* (*No.* 410A), 6, 75 *s.*, 1 *and* 2 *m.*). A. *By typo (locally).* B. *By litho (London).*

(*a*) *W* **53** *(sideways on* 2, 3, 6, 10, 40, 50 *and* 75 *s.)*

		A		B	
402	2 s. on 2 c. Type **101** ..	10	10	10	10
403	3 s. on 3 c. Mosotho horseman	10	10	10	10
404	6 s. on 4 c. Map of Lesotho	10	10	10	10
	a. Surch double ..	†	—	†	
	b. Albino surch ..	†	—	†	
405	10 s. on 10 c. Lesotho Bank ..	80	10	5·00	5·50
405*a*	25 s. on 25 c. Sehlabathebe National Park ..	5·00	5·00	†	
406	40 s. on 40 c. Pottery ..	45	50	45	50
407	50 s. on 50 c. Prehistoric rock art ..	1·25	—	50	55
408	75 s. on 15 c. Lesotho and O.A.U. flags ..	70	75	†	
409	1 m. on 1 r. King Moshoeshoe II (I) (Sil.) ..	95	1·00	†	
	a. Surch double, one inverted ..	55·00	—	†	
	b. Opt Type II ..	3·75	4·00	†	

(*b*) *No wmk*

		A		B	
410	5 s. on 5 c. Lesotho Brown diamond ..	10	10	10	10
	a. Third surch (Basotho hat and "5 s.") double ..	—	—	†	
	b. Basotho hat and "5 s." surch albino ..	—	—	†	
	c. Basotho hat and "5 s." omitted ..	25·00	—	†	
	d. Second surch ("6 s." and bars) albino ..	28·00	—	†	
411	10 s. on 10 c. Lesotho Bank	†		10	10
412	25 s. on 25 c. Sehlabathebe National Park ..	25	30	25	30
	a. Surch double ..	20·00	—	†	
413	40 s. on 40 c. Pottery ..	5·00	5·00	†	
414	50 s. on 50 c. Prehistoric rock art	50	55	†	
415	75 s. on 15 c. Lesotho and O.A.U. flags ..	†		70	75
416	1 m. on 1 r. King Moshoeshoe II (Blk. and Sil.) ..	†		95	1·00
417	2 m. on 2 r. Statue of Moshoeshoe I ..	1·90	2·00	1·90	2·00
402/17 ..	*Set of* 12			4·50	4·75

No. 410A is a further surcharge on No. 410B. Initially sheets of No. 410B were locally surcharged "6 s.", but this was later obliterated by a Basotho hat emblem and a further "5 s." surcharge added, both in typography.

The surcharge on No. 416 is similar to that on No. 409 but has the cancelling bars printed in black and the new face value in silver.

On each value except the 5 s. and 1 m. stamps, the design of the surcharge on the local printing is identical to that on the London printing. Stamps from the local printing can easily be identified from those of the London printing as indentations are clearly visible on the reverse of stamps with the typographed surcharge.

It is believed that the local surcharges were not placed on general sale before 1 December 1980. No. 410A did not appear until 20 January 1981.

123 Beer Mug

124 Queen Elizabeth the Queen Mother and Prince Charles

(Des G. Vasarhelyi (No. **MS**422), Kobus de Beer Art Studio (others). Litho Format (No. **MS**422), Questa (others)).

1980 (20 Nov). *Pottery. T* **123** *and similar horiz designs. Multicoloured.* W **53** *(sideways).* P 14.

418	4 s. Type **123** ..	10	10
419	10 s. Beer brewing pot..	10	10
420	15 s. Water pot	15	15
421	25 s. Pot shapes	25	30
418/21	*Set of* 4	50	50
MS422	150 × 110 mm. 40 s. × 4 Wedgwood plaques of Prince Philip; Queen Elizabeth II; Prince Charles; Princess Anne *(each* 22 × 35 *mm).* P 14 × 14½	1·00	1·40

No. **MS**422 was issued to commemorate the 250th birth anniversary of Josiah Wedgwood.

(Des G. Vasarhelyi. Litho Format)

1980 (1 Dec). *80th Birthday of Queen Elizabeth the Queen Mother. T* **124** *and similar multicoloured designs.* P 14½.

423	5 s. Type **124** ..	25	25
	a. Horiz strip of 3. Nos. 423/5	1·60	
424	10 s. Queen Elizabeth the Queen Mother	30	30
425	1 m. Basutoland 1947 Royal Visit 2d. commemorative and flags (54 × 44 *mm*)	1·25	1·25
423/5 ..	*Set of* 3	1·60	1·60

Nos. 423/5 were printed together, *se-tenant*, in horizontal strips of 3 throughout small sheets of nine stamps.

125 Lesotho Evangelical Church, Morija

(Des G. Vasarhelyi. Litho Format (75 s., 1 m. 50), Harrison (others))

1980 (8 Dec). *Christmas. T* **125** *and similar horiz designs. Multicoloured. No wmk* (75 *s.*) *or* W **53** *(others).* P 14 × 14½.

426	4 s. Type **125** ..	10	10
427	15 s. St. Agnes' Anglican Church, Teyateyaneng	10	10
428	25 s. Cathedral of Our Lady of Victories, Maseru	15	10
429	75 s. University Chapel, Roma	45	50
426/9 ..	*Set of* 4	65	60
MS430	110 × 85 mm. 1 m. 50, Nativity scene (43 × 29 *mm*). No wmk. P 14½ ..	1·00	1·25

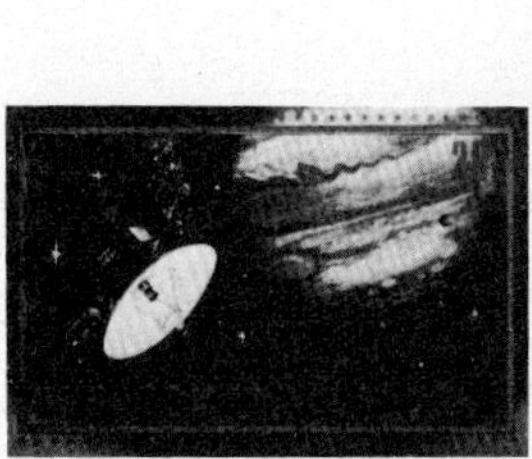
126 "Voyager" Satellite and Jupiter

127 Greater Kestrel

(Des G. Vasarhelyi. Litho Format)

1981 (15 Mar). *Space Exploration. T* **126** *and similar horiz designs. Multicoloured.* P 13½ × 14.

431	25 s. Type **126** ..	40	30
	a. Horiz strip of 5. Nos. 431/5	1·75	
432	25 s. "Voyager" and Saturn	40	30
433	25 s. "Voyager" passing Saturn	40	30
434	25 s. "Space Shuttle" releasing satellite	40	30
435	25 s. "Space Shuttle" launch ..	40	30
431/5 ..	*Set of* 5	1·75	1·40
MS436	111 × 85 mm. 1 m. 40, Saturn	1·75	1·50

Nos. 431/5 were printed together, *se-tenant*, in horizontal strips of 5 throughout the sheet.

(Des G. Vasarhelyi. Litho Format)

1981 (20 Apr–Dec). *Birds. Multicoloured designs as T* **127**. P 14½.

437	1 s. Type **127** ..	15	10
	a. Perf 13 (12.81)	40	30
438	2 s. Speckled Pigeon *(horiz)* ..	15	10
	a. Perf 13 (12.81)	55	30
439	3 s. South African Crowned Crane ..	20	10
440	5 s. Bokmakierie Shrike	20	10
	a. Perf 13 (12.81)	75	30
441	6 s. Cape Robin Chat..	30	10
442	7 s. Yellow Canary ..	30	10

443 10 s. Red-billed Pintail (*horiz*) 40 10
a. Perf 13 (12.81) 80 30
444 25 s. Malachite Kingfisher .. .. .. 1·00 15
445 40 s. Yellow-tufted Malachite Sunbird (*horiz*) 1·25 30
446 60 s. Cape Longclaw (*horiz*) .. .. .. 1·50 45
447 75 s. Hoopoe (*horiz*) .. .. 2·25 50
448 1 m. Red Bishop (*horiz*) .. .. .. 2·50 1·00
449 2 m. Egyptian Goose (*horiz*) .. .. .. 3·50 3·00
450 5 m. Lilac-breasted Roller (*horiz*) .. .. 6·00 7·00
437/50 .. .. *Set of* 14 18·00 11·50

Nos. 437/41 and 443 exist with different imprint dates below the designs.

Nos. 437/50 exist imperforate and as progressive proofs from stock dispersed by the liquidator of Format International Security Printers Ltd.

For these stamps watermarked w **14** see Nos. 500/13.

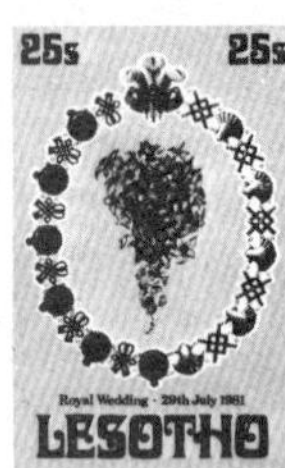

128 Wedding Bouquet from Lesotho

(Des J.W. Litho Format)

1981 (22 July). *Royal Wedding. T* **128** *and similar vert designs. Multicoloured. P* 14.

451 25 s. Type **128** 30 40
a. Booklet pane. No. 451 × 3 plus printed label 90
b. Booklet pane. Nos. 451/3 plus printed label .. .. 1·40
452 50 s. Prince Charles riding 55 75
a. Booklet pane. No. 452 × 3 plus printed label .. .. 1·60
453 75 s. Prince Charles and Lady Diana Spencer 75 1·00
a. Booklet pane. No. 453 × 3 plus printed label .. .. 2·25
451/3 .. .. *Set of* 3 1·40 1·90

Nos. 451/3 also exist imperforate from a restricted printing (*price for set of* 3 £6 *mint*).

Booklet panes Nos. 451a/3a exist part-perforated from stock dispersed by the liquidator of Format International Security Printers Ltd.

129 Prince Charles and Lady Diana Spencer

(Des G. Vasarhelyi. Litho Format)

1981 (5 Sept). *Royal Wedding* (*2nd issue*). *Sheet* 115 × 90 *mm. P* 14½.

MS454 **129** 1 m. 50, multicoloured .. .. 2·75 2·40

No. **MS**454 also exists imperforate from a restricted printing (*price* £5 *mint*).

130 "Santa planning his Annual Visit"

131 Duke of Edinburgh, Award Scheme Emblem and Flags

1981 (5 Oct). *Christmas. Paintings by Norman Rockwell* (*6 to* 60 *s.*) *or Botticelli* (1 *m.* 25). *T* **130** *and similar multicoloured designs. P* 13½.

455 6 s. Type **130** 20 10
456 10 s. "Santa reading his Mail" 30 10
457 15 s. "The Little Spooners" 35 15
458 20 s. "Raleigh Rockwell Travels" 45 20
459 25 s. "Ride 'em Cowboy" 55 25
460 60 s. "The Discovery" .. .. 1·00 75
455/60 .. .. *Set of* 6 2·50 1·40
MS461 111 × 85 mm. 1 m. 25, "Mystic Nativity" (48 × 31 *mm*). P 13½ × 14 .. .. .. 2·00 1·90

(Des G. Vasarhelyi. Litho Format)

1981 (5 Nov). *25th Anniv of Duke of Edinburgh Award Scheme. T* **131** *and similar multicoloured designs. P* 14½.

462 6 s. Type **131** 10 10
463 7 s. Tree planting 10 10
464 25 s. Gardening 30 30
465 40 s. Mountain climbing 50 50
466 75 s. Award Scheme emblem 85 85
462/6 .. .. *Set of* 5 1·75 1·75
MS467 111 × 85 mm. 1 m. 40, Duke of Edinburgh (45 × 30 *mm*) .. .. 1·60 1·60

132 Wild Cat

(Des G. Vasarhelyi. Litho Format)

1981 (16 Nov). *Wildlife. T* **132** *and similar multicoloured designs. P* 13½ (6, 25 *s.*) *or* 14½ (*others*).

468 6 s. Type **132** 15 10
469 20 s. Chacma Baboon (44 × 31 *mm*) 30 30
470 25 s. Eland 35 35
471 40 s. Cape Porcupine (44 × 31 *mm*) 60 60
472 50 s. Oribi (44 × 31 *mm*) 75 75
468/72 .. .. *Set of* 5 1·90 1·90
MS473 111 × 85 mm. 1 m. 50, Black-backed Jackal (47 × 31 *mm*). P 13½ × 14 .. .. 1·60 1·90

133 Scout Bugler

(Des G. Vasarhelyi. Litho Format)

1982 (5 Mar). *75th Anniv of Boy Scout Movement. T* **133** *and similar horiz designs. Multicoloured. P* 13½.

474 6 s. Type **133** 45 25
a. Booklet pane. Nos. 474/8 × 2 and **MS**479 8·50
475 30 s. Scouts hiking 70 50
476 40 s. Scout sketching 75 60
477 50 s. Scout with flag 80 65
478 75 s. Scouts saluting 90 80
474/8 .. .. *Set of* 5 3·25 2·50
MS479 117 × 92 mm. 1 m. 50, Lord Baden-Powell 2·00 2·50

134 Jules Rimet Trophy with Footballers and Flags of 1930 Finalists (Argentina and Uruguay)

(Des G. Vasarhelyi. Litho Format)

1982 (14 Apr). *World Cup Football Championship, Spain. T* **134** *and similar horiz designs showing World Football Cup with players and flags of countries in past finals* (*Nos.* 480/90). *Multicoloured. P* 14½.

480 15 s. Type **134** 20 20
a. Sheetlet. Nos. 480/91 .. .. .. 2·10
481 15 s. Jules Rimet Trophy with Czechoslovakia and Italy, 1934 .. .. 20 20
482 15 s. Jules Rimet Trophy with Hungary and Italy, 1938 .. .. 20 20
483 15 s. Jules Rimet Trophy with Brazil and Uruguay, 1950 .. .. 20 20
484 15 s. Jules Rimet Trophy with Hungary and West Germany, 1954 .. .. .. 20 20
485 15 s. Jules Rimet Trophy with Sweden and Brazil, 1958 .. .. 20 20
486 15 s. Jules Rimet Trophy with Czechoslovakia and Brazil, 1962 .. .. 20 20
487 15 s. Jules Rimet Trophy with West Germany and England, 1966 .. .. .. 20 20
488 15 s. Jules Rimet Trophy with Italy and Brazil, 1970 .. .. 20 20
489 15 s. World Cup with Holland and West Germany, 1974 .. .. 20 20
490 15 s. World Cup with Holland and Argentina, 1978 .. .. 20 20
491 15 s. World Cup and map of World on footballs 20 20
480/91 .. .. *Set of* 12 2·10 2·10
MS492 118 × 93 mm. 1 m. 25, Bernabeu Stadium, Madrid (47 × 35 *mm*). P 13½ .. .. 2·00 2·25

Nos. 480/91 were printed together, *se-tenant*, in a sheetlet of 12.

135 Portrait of George Washington

136 Lady Diana Spencer in Tetbury, May 1981

(Des G. Vasarhelyi. Litho Format)

1982 (7 June). *250th Birth Anniv of George Washington. T* **135** *and similar horiz designs. Multicoloured. P* 14 × 13½.

493 6 s. Type **135** 10 10
494 7 s. Washington with step-children and dog 10 10
495 10 s. Washington with Indian chief 15 10
496 25 s. Washington with troops 35 35
497 40 s. Washington arriving in New York .. 50 50
498 1 m. Washington on parade .. .. .. 1·25 1·25
493/8 .. .. *Set of* 6 2·25 2·25
MS499 117 × 92 mm. 1 m. 25, Washington crossing the Delaware .. .. 2·00 1·50

1982 (14 June). *As Nos.* 437/50 *but W* w **14** (*sideways on Nos.* 500, 502/5 *and* 507).

500 1 s. Type **127** 10 30
501 2 s. Speckled Pigeon (*horiz*) 10 30
502 3 s. South African Crowned Crane 10 30
503 5 s. Bokmakierie Shrike 10 10
504 6 s. Cape Robin Chat 10 10
505 7 s. Yellow Canary 10 10
506 10 s. Red-billed Pintail (*horiz*) 15 10
507 25 s. Malachite Kingfisher 35 30
508 40 s. Yellow-tufted Malachite Sunbird (*horiz*) 55 35
509 60 s. Cape Longclaw (*horiz*) 80 70
510 75 s. Hoopoe (*horiz*) .. .. 1·25 85
511 1 m. Red Bishop (*horiz*) .. .. .. 1·60 2·25
512 2 m. Egyptian Goose (*horiz*) .. .. .. 2·75 4·00
513 5 m. Lilac-breasted Roller (*horiz*) .. .. 5·50 10·00
500/13 .. .. *Set of* 14 12·00 18·00

(Des Jennifer Toombs. Litho Format)

1982 (1 July). *21st Birthday of Princess of Wales. T* **136** *and similar vert designs. Multicoloured. W* w **14**. A. *P* 13½. B. *P* 13½ × 14.

		A		B	
514	30 s. Lesotho coat of arms ..	50	50	30	30
515	50 s. Type **136**	45	50	75	80
516	75 s. Wedding picture at Buckingham Palace ..	75	80	70	70
517	1 m. Formal portrait	1·00	1·25	1·00	1·25
514/17	.. .. *Set of* 4	2·40	2·75	2·40	2·75

137 Mosotho reading Sesotho Bible

138 Birthday Greetings

(Des G. Vasarhelyi. Litho Format)

1982 (20 Aug). *Centenary of Sesotho Bible, T* **137** *and similar multicoloured designs. P* 14½.

518 6 s. Type **137** 10 10
a. Horiz strip of 3. Nos. 518/20 90
519 15 s. Sesotho Bible and Virgin Mary holding infant Jesus 20 20
520 1 m. Sesotho Bible and Cathedral (62 × 42 *mm*) 70 80
518/20 .. .. *Set of* 3 90 1·00

Nos. 518/20 were printed together, *se-tenant*, in horizontal strips of 3 throughout the sheet.

(Des G. Vasarhelyi. Litho Questa)

1982 (30 Sept). *Birth of Prince William of Wales. T* **138** *and similar vert design. Multicoloured. P* 14 × 13½.

521 6 s. Type **138** 15 15
a. Sheetlet. No. 521 and 522 × 5 .. .. 4·00
522 60 s. Princess Diana and Prince William of Wales 80 80

Nos. 521/2 come from sheetlets of 6 containing one 6 s. and five 60 s. stamps.

139 "A Partridge in a Pear Tree"

(Litho Format)

1982 (1 Dec). *Christmas. "The Twelve Days of Christmas". T* **139** *and similar horiz designs depicting Walt Disney cartoon characters. Multicoloured. P* 11.

523 2 s. Type **139** 10 10
a. Horiz pair. Nos. 523/4 .. .. .. 10 10
524 2 s. "Two turtle doves" 10 10
525 3 s. "Three French hens" 10 10
a. Horiz pair. Nos. 525/6 .. .. .. 10 10
526 3 s. "Four calling birds" 10 10
527 4 s. "Five golden rings" 10 10
a. Horiz pair. Nos. 527/8 .. .. .. 15 15
528 4 s. "Six geese a-laying" 10 10

529 75 s. "Seven swans a-swimming" .. .. .. 1·25 1·25
a. Horiz pair. Nos. 529/30 .. .. .. 2·50 2·50
530 75 s. "Eight maids a-milking".. .. .. .. 1·25 1·25
523/30 .. .. *Set of* 8 2·50 2·50
MS531 126 × 101 mm. 1 m. 50, "Nine ladies dancing, ten lords a-leaping, eleven pipers piping, twelve drummers drumming". P 13½ .. .. 1·75 2·00

Nos. 523/4, 525/6, 527/8 and 529/30 were each printed in horizontal *se-tenant* pairs throughout the sheet.

140 *Lepista caffrorum*

(Des G. Vasarhelyi. Litho Format)

1983 (11 Jan). *Fungi. T* **140** *and similar horiz designs. Multicoloured. P* 14½.
532 10 s. Type **140** 15 10
a. *Tête-bêche* (vert pair) 30 30
b. Booklet pane. Nos. 532/5 .. .. 2·50
c. Booklet pane. Nos. 532/3 55
533 30 s. *Broomeia congregata* 40 40
a. *Tête-bêche* (vert pair) 80 80
534 50 s. *Afroboletus luteolus* 85 85
a. *Tête-bêche* (vert pair) .. .. .. 1·60 1·60
535 75 s. *Lentinus tuber-regium* .. .. .. 1·40 1·40
a. *Tête-bêche* (vert pair) .. .. .. 2·75 2·75
532/5 .. .. *Set of* 4 2·50 2·50

Nos. 532/5 were each printed in sheets of 36 stamps plus 4 labels as the fourth horizontal row. The stamps in horizontal rows two, six, eight and ten were inverted, forming vertical *tête-bêche* pairs.

141 Ba-Leseli Dance

(Des J.W. Litho Format)

1983 (14 Mar). *Commonwealth Day. T* **141** *and similar multicoloured designs. P* 14½.
536 5 s. Type **141** 10 10
537 30 s. Tapestry weaving 35 40
538 60 s. Queen Elizabeth II (*vert*).. .. .. 70 85
539 75 s. King Moshoeshoe II (*vert*) .. .. .. 90 1·10
536/9 .. .. *Set of* 4 1·75 2·25

142 "Dancers in a Trance" (rock painting from Ntloana Tsoana)

(Des G. Drummond. Litho Format)

1983 (20 May). *Rock Paintings. T* **142** *and similar multicoloured designs. P* 14½.
540 6 s. Type **142** 15 10
541 25 s. "Baboons", Sehonghong 40 35
542 60 s. "Hunters attacking Mountain Reedbuck", Makhetha 90 95
543 75 s. "Eland", Lehaha la Likhomo .. .. 1·25 1·40
540/3 .. .. *Set of* 4 2·40 2·50
MS544 166 × 84 mm. Nos. 540/3 and 10 s. "Cattle herding", Sehonghong (52 × 52 *mm*) .. .. 2·40 3·00

143 Montgolfier Balloon, 1783

(Des J.W. Litho Format)

1983 (11 July). *Bicentenary of Manned Flight. T* **143** *and similar multicoloured designs. P* 14½.
545 7 s. Type **143** 15 10
a. Booklet pane. Nos. 545/8 .. .. 3·50
546 30 s. Wright brothers and *Flyer* 45 40
547 60 s. First airmail flight 80 75
548 1 m. "Concorde" .. .. 2·50 1·50
545/8 .. .. *Set of* 4 3·50 2·50
MS549 180 × 92 mm. Nos. 545/8 and 6 s. Dornier "228" of Lesotho Airways (60 × 60 *mm*) .. .. 3·25 2·75

144 Rev. Eugene Casalis

(Des G. Vasarhelyi. Litho Questa)

1983 (5 Sept). *150th Anniv of Arrival of the French Missionaries. T* **144** *and similar horiz designs. Multicoloured. P* 13½ × 14.
550 6 s. Type **144** 10 10
a. *Tête-bêche* (vert pair) 10 15
551 25 s. The founding of Morija 30 40
a. *Tête-bêche* (vert pair) 60 80
552 40 s. Baptism of Libe 50 70
a. *Tête-bêche* (vert pair) .. .. .. 1·00 1·40
553 75 s. Map of Lesotho .. .. 90 1·25
a. *Tête-bêche* (vert pair) .. .. .. 1·75 2·50
550/3 .. .. *Set of* 4 1·60 2·25

Nos. 550/3 were each issued in sheets of 20 containing two panes (2 × 5) separated by a vertical gutter. Within these sheets horizontal rows two and four are inverted forming *tête-bêche* vertical pairs.

145 Mickey Mouse and Pluto Greeted by Friends

(Litho Questa)

1983 (18 Oct). *Christmas. T* **145** *and similar horiz designs showing Disney cartoon characters in scenes from "Old Christmas" (Washington Irving's sketchbook). Multicoloured. P* 14×13½.
554 1 s. Type **145** 10 10
555 2 s. Donald Duck and Pluto 10 10
556 3 s. Donald Duck with Huey, Dewey and Louie 10 10
557 4 s. Goofy, Donald Duck and Mickey Mouse 10 10
558 5 s. Goofy holding turkey, Donald Duck and Mickey Mouse 10 10
559 6 s. Goofy and Mickey Mouse 10 10
560 75 s. Donald and Daisy Duck .. .. .. 1·50 70
561 1 m. Goofy and Clarabell .. .. .. 2·00 1·25
554/61 .. .. *Set of* 8 3·50 2·00
MS562 132 × 113 mm. 1 m. 75, Scrooge McDuck, Pluto and Donald Duck .. .. 3·00 2·00

14 *Danaus chrysippus*

(Des and litho Format)

1984 (20 Jan). *Butterflies. T* **146** *and similar horiz designs. Multicoloured. P* 14.
563 1 s. Type **146** 15 10
564 2 s. *Aeropetes tulbaghia* 15 10
565 3 s. *Colotis evenina* 20 10
566 4 s. *Precis oenone* 20 10
567 5 s. *Precis hierta* 20 10
568 6 s. *Catopsilia florella* 20 10
569 7 s. *Phalanta phalantha* 20 10
570 10 s. *Acraea stenobea* 30 10
571 15 s. *Cynthia cardui* 50 10
572 20 s. *Colotis subfasciatus* 60 10
573 30 s. *Charaxes jasius* 65 20
574 50 s. *Terias brigitta* 85 30
575 60 s. *Pontia helice* 95 35
576 75 s. *Colotis regina* .. .. 1·25 40
577 1 m. *Hypolimnas misippus* .. .. .. 1·50 70
578 5 m. *Papilio demodocus* .. .. .. 4·50 4·00
563/78 .. .. *Set of* 16 11·00 6·00

Nos. 563/73 and 576 exist imperforate and as progressive proofs from stock dispersed by the liquidator of Format International Security Printers Ltd.

147 "Thou Shalt not have Strange Gods before Me"

(Des G. Vasarhelyi. Litho Format)

1984 (30 Mar). *Easter. The Ten Commandments. T* **147** *and similar vert designs. Multicoloured. P* 13½ × 14.
579 20 s. Type **147** 30 25
a. Sheetlet. Nos. 579/88 .. .. .. 2·75
580 20 s. "Thou shalt not take the name of the Lord thy God in vain" 30 25
581 20 s. "Remember thou keep holy the Lord's Day" 30 25
582 20 s. "Honour thy father and mother" .. 30 25
583 20 s. "Thou shalt not kill" 30 25
584 20 s. "Thou shalt not commit adultery" .. 30 25
585 20 s. "Thou shalt not steal" 30 25
586 20 s. "Thou shalt not bear false witness against thy neighbour" 30 25
587 20 s. "Thou shalt not covet thy neighbour's wife" 30 25
588 20 s. "Thou shalt not covet thy neighbour's goods" 30 25
579/88 .. .. *Set of* 10 2·75 2·25
MS589 102 × 73 mm. 1 m. 50, Moses with Tablets (45 × 28 *mm*). P 14. .. .. 1·50 2·00

Nos. 579/88 were printed together in small sheets of 12 including 2 *se-tenant* stamp-size labels.

148 Torch Bearer

(Des G. Vasarhelyi. Litho Format)

1984 (3 May). *Olympic Games, Los Angeles. T* **148** *and similar horiz designs. Multicoloured. P* 13½ × 14.
590 10 s. Type **148** 10 10
591 30 s. Horse-riding 30 35
592 50 s. Swimming 50 55
593 75 s. Basketball 70 75
594 1 m. Running .. .. 95 1·10
590/4 .. .. *Set of* 5 2·25 2·50
MS595 101 × 72 mm. 1 m. 50, Olympic Flame and flags .. .. 1·50 2·00

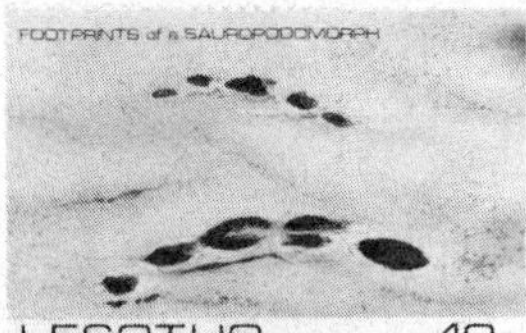

149 Sauropodomorph Footprints

(Des G. Drummond. Litho Format)

1984 (2 July). *Prehistoric Footprints (2nd series). T* **149** *and similar horiz designs. Multicoloured. P* 13½ × 14.
596 10 s. Type **149** 55 20
597 30 s. Lesothosaurus footprints .. .. 1·50 75
598 50 s. Footprint of carnivorous dinosaur .. 1·75 1·25
596/8 .. .. *Set of* 3 3·50 2·00

150 Wells Fargo Coach, 1852

(Des G. Vasarhelyi. Litho Format)

1984 (5 Sept). *"Ausipex" International Stamp Exhibition, Melbourne, and Bicentenary of First Mail Coach Run. T* **150** *and similar horiz designs. Multicoloured. P* 14.
599 6 s. Type **150** 10 10
a. Sheetlet. Nos. 599 × 4 and No. 603 .. 70
600 7 s. Basotho mail cart, *circa* 1900 .. .. 10 10
a. Sheetlet. No. 600 × 4 and No. 603 .. 80
601 10 s. Bath mail coach, 1784 .. .. .. 10 10
a. Sheetlet. No. 601 × 4 and No. 603 .. 90
602 30 s. Cobb coach, 1853.. .. .. .. 30 35
a. Sheetlet. No. 602 × 4 and No. 603 .. 1·60

603 50 s. Exhibition logo and Royal Exhibition Buildings, Melbourne (82 × 25 *mm*) .. 50 55
599/603 .. .. *Set of* 5 95 1·10
MS604. 147 × 98 mm. 1 m. 75, G.B. Penny Black, Basutoland 1934 "OFFICIAL" optd 6d. and Western Australia 1854 4d. with frame inverted (82 × 25 *mm*) .. .. 2·75 3·00

In addition to the listed sheetlets, Nos. 599/602 also exist in separate sheets of 50. No. 603 only comes from the sheetlets.

151 "The Orient Express" (1900)

(Des Walsall. Litho Format)

1984 (5 Nov). *Railways of the World. T* **151** *and similar horiz designs. Multicoloured. P* 14 × 13½.
605 6 s. Type **151** 40 10
606 15 s. German State Railways Class "05" No. 05001 (1935) 45 20
607 30 s. Caledonian Railway *Cardean* (1906) .. 70 35
608 60 s. Santa Fe "Super Chief" (1940) .. .. 1·25 65
609 1 m. L.N.E.R. "Flying Scotsman" (1934) .. 1·75 1·00
605/9 .. .. *Set of* 5 4·00 2·00
MS610 108 × 82 mm. 2 m. South African Railways "The Blue Train" (1972) .. .. 2·75 2·50

152 Eland Calf **153** Crown of Lesotho

(Des G. Drummond. Litho Format)

1984 (20 Dec). *Baby Animals. T* **152** *and similar horiz designs. Multicoloured. P* 14 × 13½ (1 *m.*) *or* 15 (*others*).
611 15 s. Type **152** 35 20
612 20 s. Young Chacma Baboons 40 25
613 30 s. Oribi calf 55 30
614 75 s. Young Natal Red Hares .. .. 1·25 75
615 1 m. Black-backed Jackal pups (46 × 27 *mm*) 1·50 1·25
611/15 .. .. *Set of* 5 3·50 2·50

(Des G. Vasarhelyi. Litho Format)

1985 (30 Jan). *Silver Jubilee of King Moshoeshoe II. T* **153** *and similar vert designs. Multicoloured. P* 15.
616 6 s. Type **153** 10 10
617 30 s. King Moshoeshoe in 1960 .. .. 20 25
618 75 s. King Moshoeshoe in traditional dress, 1985 .. .. 50 55
619 1 m. King Moshoeshoe in uniform, 1985 .. 70 75
616/19 .. .. *Set of* 4 1·25 1·50

154 Christ condemned to Death

(Des G. Vasarhelyi. Litho Format)

1985 (8 Mar). *Easter. The Stations of the Cross. T* **154** *and similar vert designs. Multicoloured. P* 11.
620 20 s. Type **154** 15 15
a. Sheetlet. Nos. 620/33 .. .. .. 1·75
621 20 s. Christ carrying the Cross 15 15
622 20 s. Falling for the first time 15 15
623 20 s. Christ meets Mary 15 15
624 20 s. Simon of Cyrene helping to carry the Cross 15 15
625 20 s. Veronica wiping the face of Christ .. 15 15
626 20 s. Christ falling a second time 15 15
627 20 s. Consoling the women of Jerusalem .. 15 15
628 20 s. Falling for the third time 15 15
629 20 s. Christ being stripped 15 15
630 20 s. Christ nailed to the Cross 15 15
631 20 s. Dying on the Cross 15 15
632 20 s. Christ taken down from the Cross .. 15 15
633 20 s. Christ being laid in the sepulchre .. 15 15
620/33 .. .. *Set of* 14 1·75 1·75
MS634 138 × 98 mm. 2 m. "The Crucifixion" (Mathias Grünewald). P 13½ × 14 .. .. 2·50 3·00

Nos. 620/33 were printed together, *se-tenant*, in a sheetlet of 14 stamps with one stamp-sized label which appears in the central position.

155 Duchess of York with Princess Elizabeth, 1931

(Des G. Vasarhelyi. Litho Format)

1985 (30 May). *Life and Times of Queen Elizabeth the Queen Mother. T* **155** *and similar multicoloured designs. P* 13½ × 14.
635 10 s. Type **155** 15 10
636 30 s. The Queen Mother in 1975 .. .. 50 50
637 60 s. Queen Mother with Queen Elizabeth and Princess Margaret, 1980 .. .. 80 80
638 2 m. Four generations of Royal Family at Prince Henry's christening, 1984 .. 3·00 3·00
635/8 .. .. *Set of* 4 4·00 4·00
MS639 139 × 98 mm. 2 m. Queen Elizabeth with the Princess of Wales and her children at Prince Henry's christening (37 × 50 *mm*) .. .. 2·75 2·75

156 B.M.W. "732i" **157** American Cliff Swallow

(Litho Format)

1985 (10 June). *Century of Motoring. T* **156** *and similar multicoloured designs. P* 14 × 13½.
640 6 s. Type **156** 25 15
641 10 s. Ford "Crown Victoria" 35 15
642 30 s. Mercedes-Benz "500SE" 75 50
643 90 s. Cadillac "Eldorado Biarritz" .. .. 2·00 2·00
644 2 m. Rolls-Royce "Silver Spirit" .. .. 3·00 3·25
640/4 .. .. *Set of* 5 5·75 5·50
MS645 139 × 98 mm. 2 m. Rolls-Royce "Silver Ghost Tourer", 1907 (37 × 50 *mm*). P 13½ × 14 .. 4·25 4·25

Nos. 640/5 exist imperforate from stock dispersed by the liquidator of Format International Security Printers Ltd.

(Litho Format)

1985 (5 Aug). *Birth Bicentenary of John J. Audubon (ornithologist). T* **157** *and similar multicoloured designs showing original paintings. P* 15.
646 5 s. Type **157** 30 15
647 6 s. Great Crested Grebe (*horiz*) 30 15
648 10 s. Vesper Sparrow (*horiz*) 45 15
649 30 s. Greenshank (*horiz*) .. .. .. 1·00 55
650 60 s. Stilt Sandpiper (*horiz*) .. .. 1·75 1·75
651 2 m. Glossy Ibis (*horiz*) .. .. .. 3·25 3·50
646/51 .. .. *Set of* 6 6·50 5·75

Nos. 646/51 were reissued in February 1986 in sheetlets containing five stamps and one label.

158 Two Youths Rock-climbing **159** U.N. (New York) 1951 1 c. Definitive and U.N. Flag

(Des Walsall. Litho Format)

1985 (26 Sept). *International Youth Year and 75th Anniv of Girl Guide Movement. T* **158** *and similar vert designs. Multicoloured. P* 15.
652 10 s. Type **158** 20 10
653 30 s. Young technician in hospital laboratory 50 40
654 75 s. Three guides on parade .. .. .. 1·00 90
655 2 m. Guide saluting .. .. 2·40 2·40
652/5 .. .. *Set of* 4 3·75 3·50
MS656 138 × 98 mm. 2 m. "Olave, Lady Baden-Powell" (Grace Wheatley) (37 × 50 *mm*). P 13½ × 14 .. .. 2·40 2·75

(Des G. Vasarhelyi. Litho Format)

1985 (15 Oct). *40th Anniv of United Nations Organization. T* **159** *and similar designs. P* 15.
657 10 s. multicoloured 25 10
658 30 s. multicoloured 60 35
659 50 s. multicoloured 95 65
660 2 m. black and bronze-green .. .. .. 5·00 3·25
657/60 .. .. *Set of* 4 6·25 4·00

Designs: *Vert*—30 s. Ha Sofonia Earth Satellite Station; 2 m. Maimonides (physician, philosopher and scholar). *Horiz*—50 s. Lesotho Airways aircraft at Maseru Airport.

160 Cosmos

160a Mrs. Jumbo and Baby Dumbo

(Des G. Drummond. Litho Format)

1985 (11 Nov). *Wild Flowers. T* **160** *and similar vert designs. Multicoloured. P* 15.
661 6 s. Type **160** 40 15
662 10 s. Small Agapanthus 55 15
663 30 s. Pink Witchweed .. .. 1·10 50
664 60 s. Small Iris .. .. 1·75 1·25
665 90 s. Wild Geranium or Cranesbill .. .. 2·40 2·00
666 1 m. Large Spotted Orchid .. .. .. 3·75 3·75
661/6 .. .. *Set of* 6 9·00 7·00

(Des Walt Disney Productions. Litho Questa)

1985 (2 Dec). *150th Birth Anniv of Mark Twain. T* **160a** *and similar vert designs showing Walt Disney cartoon characters illustrating various Mark Twain quotations. Multicoloured. P* 11.
667 6 s. Type **160a** 30 15
668 50 s. Uncle Scrooge and Goofy reading newspaper .. .. 1·00 60
669 90 s. Winnie the Pooh, Tigger, Piglet and Owl .. .. 1·50 1·10
670 1 m. 50, Goofy at ship's wheel .. .. 2·25 1·75
667/70 .. .. *Set of* 4 4·50 3·25
MS671 127 × 102 mm. 1 m. 25, Mickey Mouse as astronaut. P 13½ × 14 .. .. 3·00 2·00

No. 669 was printed in sheetlets of 8 stamps.

160b Donald Duck as the Tailor **161** Male Lammergeier on Watch

(Des Walt Disney Productions. Litho Format)

1985 (2 Dec). *Birth Bicentenaries of Grimm Brothers (folklorists). T* **160b** *and similar vert designs showing Walt Disney cartoon characters in scenes from "The Wishing Table". Multicoloured. P* 11.
672 10 s. Type **160b** 35 15
673 60 s. The second son (Dewey) with magic donkey and gold coins .. .. .. 1·25 75
674 75 s. The eldest son (Huey) with wishing table laden with food .. .. .. 1·50 90
675 1 m. The innkeeper stealing the third son's (Louie) magic cudgel .. .. .. 2·00 1·50
672/5 .. .. *Set of* 4 4·50 3·00
MS676 127 × 102 mm. 1 m. 50, The tailor and eldest son with wishing table. P 13½ × 14 .. 3·00 3·50

No. 673 was printed in sheetlets of 8 stamps.

(Des G. Drummond. Litho Format)

1986 (20 Jan). *Flora and Fauna of Lesotho. T* **161** *and similar vert designs. Multicoloured. P* 15.
677 7 s. Type **161** 60 15
678 9 s. Prickly Pear 60 15
679 12 s. Stapelia 60 15
680 15 s. Pair of Lammergeiers .. .. .. 1·50 35
681 35 s. Pig's Ears .. .. 1·10 50
682 50 s. Male Lammergeier in flight .. .. 2·50 1·60
683 1 m. Adult and juvenile Lammergeiers .. 3·50 3·50
684 2 m. Columnar cereus .. .. 3·75 4·00
677/84 .. .. *Set of* 8 13·00 9·25
MS685 125 × 106 mm. 2 m. Verreaux's Eagle .. 6·00 7·00

162 Two Players chasing Ball **162a** Galileo and 200-inch Hale Telescope at Mt Palomar Observatory, California

(Des Lori Anzalone. Litho Questa)

1986 (17 Mar). *World Cup Football Championship, Mexico. T* **162** *and similar vert designs. Multicoloured. P* 14.

686 35 s. Type **162** 90 40
687 50 s. Goalkeeper saving goal .. .. .. 1·25 90
688 1 m. Three players chasing ball .. .. 2·50 2·25
689 2 m. Two players competing for ball .. 4·00 4·00
686/9 .. .. *Set of* 4 7·75 6·75
MS690 104×74 mm. 3 m. Player heading ball .. 7·50 7·50

(Des W. Hanson. Litho Questa)

1986 (5 Apr). *Appearance of Halley's Comet. T* **162a** *and similar horiz designs. Multicoloured. P* 14.

691 9 s. Type **162a** 40 15
692 15 s. Halley's Comet and "Pioneer Venus 2" spacecraft 60 15
693 70 s. Halley's Comet of 684 A.D. (from Nuremberg Chronicle, 1493) .. .. 1·40 1·00
694 3 m. Comet and landing of William the Conqueror, 1066 .. .. 3·50 4·00
691/4 .. .. *Set of* 4 5·50 4·75
MS695 101×70 mm. 4 m. Halley's Comet over Lesotho .. .. 5·00 5·50

Nos. 691/3 show the face value followed by "S". Examples of these stamps without this currency abbreviation were prepared, but not issued.

163 International Year of the Child Gold Coin

163a Princess Elizabeth in Pantomime

(Litho Format)

1986 (Apr). *First Anniv of New Currency* (1980). *T* **163** *and similar horiz designs. Multicoloured. P* 13½×14.

696 30 s. Type **163** .. .. 6·50 5·50
a. Horiz strip of 5. Nos. 696/700 .. .. 30·00
697 30 s. Five maloti banknote .. .. .. 6·50 5·50
698 30 s. Fifty lisente coin .. .. .. 6·50 5·50
699 30 s. Ten maloti banknote .. .. .. 6·50 5·50
700 30 s. One sente coin .. .. 6·50 5·50
696/700 .. .. *Set of* 5 30·00 25·00

Nos. 696/700 were printed together, *se-tenant*, in horizontal strips of 5 throughout the sheet.

These stamps were prepared in 1980, but were not issued at that time. Due to increased postal rates a severe shortage of 30 s. stamps occurred in 1986 and Nos. 696/700 were sold for postal purposes from mid-April until early August.

(Des L. Nardo. Litho Questa)

1986 (21 Apr). *60th Birthday of Queen Elizabeth II. T* **163a** *and similar vert designs. P* 14.

701 90 s. black and yellow 60 60
702 1 m. multicoloured 65 65
703 2 m. multicoloured .. .. 1·40 1·40
701/3 .. .. *Set of* 3 2·40 2·40
MS704 119×85 mm. 4 m. black and grey-brown 3·00 3·50

Designs:— 1 m. Queen at Windsor Horse Show, 1971; 2 m. At Royal Festival Hall, 1971; 4 m. Princess Elizabeth in 1934.

163b Statue of Liberty and Bela Bartok (composer)

(Des J. Iskowitz. Litho Questa)

1986 (5 May). *Centenary of Statue of Liberty. T* **163b** *and similar horiz designs showing the Statue of Liberty and immigrants to the U.S.A. Multicoloured. P* 14.

705 15 s. Type **163b** 55 20
706 35 s. Felix Adler (philosopher) 65 30
707 1 m. Victor Herbert (composer) .. .. 2·25 1·50
708 3 m. David Niven (actor) .. .. .. 3·25 3·50
705/8 .. .. *Set of* 4 6·00 5·00
MS709 103×74 mm. 3 m. Statue of Liberty (*vert*) 4·00 4·25

163c Mickey Mouse and Goofy as Japanese Mail Runners

(Des Walt Disney Productions. Litho Format)

1986 (25 May). *"Ameripex" International Stamp Exhibition, Chicago. T* **163c** *and similar horiz designs showing Walt Disney cartoon characters delivering mail. Multicoloured. P* 11.

710 15 s. Type **163c** 30 20
711 35 s. Mickey Mouse and Pluto with mail sledge 55 30
712 1 m. Goofy as postman riding Harley-Davidson motorcycle .. .. 1·25 1·25
713 2 m. Donald Duck operating railway mail-bag apparatus .. .. 2·00 2·00
710/13 .. .. *Set of* 4 3·75 3·25
MS714 127×101 mm. 4 m. Goofy driving mail to aircraft. P 14×13½ .. .. 6·00 6·00

9s (164) 9s (165) 15s (166) 35s (167) 35s (167a)

35s Small "s"

Nos. 720a, 720ba, 721a, 721ca. Occurs eleven times in the sheet of 40 on R. 1/5, 1/6, 1/8, 1/9, 2/6, 2/7, 2/8, 3/5, 4/4, 4/6 and 4/8 for Nos. 720a and 720ba or R. 1/4, 2/4, 4/4, 5/4, 6/4, 7/1, 7/4, 9/1, 9/3, 10/1 and 10/2 for Nos. 721a and 721ca.

No. 728a. Occurs thirteen times in the sheet of 49 on R. 6/2 to 7 and on all positions in Row 7.

9s (168) 35s (169) 20s (170)

1986 (6 June)–**88**. *Various stamps surch* (a) *As T* **164/7a** *by Lesotho Ads, Maseru.* (i) *On Nos.* 440, 447, 500/1, 506/7 *and* 509.

715 9 s. on 10 s. Red-billed Pintail (*horiz*) (No. 506) (Type **164**) .. .. 1·25 1·25
a. Surch on No. 443 ("1982" imprint date) .. .. 2·25 2·25
b. Surch double .. .. † —
c. Surch double, one inverted .. .. † —
716 15 s. on 1 s. Type **127** (No. 500) (22.8.86) 4·00 3·00
a. Surch on No. 437 ("1982" imprint date) £110
b. Surch on No. 437a .. .. .. 5·00 6·00
717 15 s. on 2 s. Speckled Pigeon (*horiz*) (22.8.86) .. .. 4·00 4·50
a. Surch double .. .. 60·00
718 15 s. on 5 s. Bokmakierie Shrike ("1982" imprint date) (2.11.87) 40 35
719 15 s. on 60 s. Cape Longclaw (*horiz*) (No. 509) (22.8.86) 20 10
a. Surch on No. 446 .. .. 60 30
720 35 s. on 25 s. Malachite Kingfisher (No. 507) (9.87) .. .. 15·00 20·00
a. Small "s" .. .. 32·00 35·00
b. Surch on No. 444 .. .. .. 50·00 50·00
ba. Small "s" £100 £100
721 35 s. on 75 s. Hoopoe (*horiz*) (No. 447) (Type **167**) (9.87) .. .. 16·00 16·00
a. Small "s" .. .. 32·00 32·00
b. Surch double .. .. 55·00
c. Surch on No. 510 .. .. .. £110 95·00
ca. Small "s" £200
721*d* 35 s. on 75 s. Hoopoe (*horiz*) (No. 447) (Type **167a**) (1.88) .. .. 75·00

(ii) *On Nos.* 563/5, 567, 573 *and* 575/6

722 9 s. on 30 s. *Charaxes jasius* (Type **164**) (1.7.86) 15 10
a. Surch with Type **165** .. .. .. 6·50 4·50
ab. Surch double .. .. † —
723 9 s. on 60 s. *Pontia helice* (Type **165**) (1.7.86) .. .. 4·00 4·00
a. Surch double .. .. 50·00
b. Surch double, one inverted .. .. 50·00
724 15 s. on 1 s. Type **146** (25.6.86) .. .. 2·75 2·75
725 15 s. on 2 s. *Aeropetes tulbaghia* (25.6.86) 20 20
726 15 s. on 3 s. *Colotis evenina* (25.6.86) .. 20 20
727 15 s. on 5 s. *Precis hierta* (14.8.87) .. 20 20
a. Surch double .. .. 32·00
728 35 s. on 75 s. *Colotis regina* (15.8.86) .. 35 35
a. Small "s" .. .. 1·50 1·50

(b) *As T* **168/70** *by Epic Printers, Maseru.*
(i) *On Nos.* 440 *and* 444

729 9 s. on 5 s. Bokmakierie Shrike ("1982" imprint date) (30.12.87) 15 20
730 16 s. on 25 s. Malachite Kingfisher (No. 444) (3.88) .. .. 1·00 1·00
a. Surch on No. 507 .. .. £225
731 35 s. on 25 s. Malachite Kingfisher (No. 444) (15.12.87) 60 60
a. Surch on No. 507 .. .. 13·00 10·00

(ii) *On Nos.* 566 *and* 569

732 20 s. on 4 s. *Precis oenone* (30.12.87) .. 10 10
a. Surch double, one inverted .. .. 12·00 90·00
733 40 s. on 7 s. *Phalanta phalantha* (30.12.87) 15 20

(iii) *On No.* 722

734 3 s. on 9 s. on 30 s. *Charaxes jasius* (2.2.88) 15 15
a. Surch Type **164** double .. .. † —
735 7 s. on 9 s. on 30 s. *Charaxes jasius* (2.2.88) 25 25
715/35 .. .. *Set of* 21 45·00 50·00

NEW INFORMATION

The editor is always interested to correspond with people who have new information that will improve or correct the Catalogue.

170a Prince Andrew and Miss Sarah Ferguson

171 Basotho Pony and Rider

(Des D. Miller. Litho Questa)

1986 (23 July). *Royal Wedding. T* **170a** *and similar vert designs. Multicoloured. P* 14.

736 50 s. Type **170a** 40 40
737 1 m. Prince Andrew 70 70
738 3 m. Prince Andrew piloting helicopter .. 2·00 2·00
736/8 .. .. *Set of* 3 2·75 2·75
MS739 88×88 mm. 4 m. Prince Andrew and Miss Sarah Ferguson (*different*) .. .. .. 4·50 4·50

(Des B. Bundock. Litho Format)

1986 (3 Oct). *20th Anniv of Independence. T* **171** *and similar horiz designs. Multicoloured. P* 15.

740 9 s. Type **171** 25 10
741 15 s. Basotho woman spinning mohair .. 30 15
742 35 s. Crossing river by rowing boat 45 30
743 3 m. Thaba Tseka Post Office .. .. 2·40 2·50
740/3 .. .. *Set of* 4 3·00 2·75
MS744 109×78 mm. 4 m. King Moshoeshoe I .. 6·50 7·00

171a Chip n'Dale pulling Christmas Cracker

172 Rally Car

(Des Walt Disney Co. Litho Format)

1986 (4 Nov). *Christmas. T* **171a** *and similar vert designs showing Walt Disney cartoon characters. Multicoloured. P* 11.

745 15 s. Type **171a** 20 15
746 35 s. Mickey and Minnie Mouse 45 30
747 1 m. Pluto pulling Christmas taffy .. 1·00 90
748 2 m. Aunt Matilda baking .. .. .. 1·75 1·75
745/8 .. .. *Set of* 4 3·00 2·75
MS749 126×102 mm. 5 m. Huey and Dewey with gingerbread house. P 13½×14 .. .. .. 5·00 5·50

(Litho Questa)

1987 (28 Apr). *Roof of Africa Motor Rally. T* **172** *and similar vert designs. Multicoloured. P* 14.

750 9 s. Type **172** 10 10
751 15 s. Motorcyclist 15 10
752 35 s. Motorcyclist (*different*) 30 25
753 4 m. Rally car (*different*) .. .. .. 2·50 2·50
750/3 .. .. *Set of* 4 2·75 2·75

173 Lawn Tennis

174 Isaac Newton and Reflecting Telescope

(Des Y. Berry. Litho Questa)

1987 (29 May). *Olympic Games, Seoul* (1988) (*1st issue*). *T* **173** *and similar vert designs. Multicoloured. P* 14.

754 9 s. Type **173** 15 10
755 15 s. Judo 15 10
756 20 s. Athletics 20 15
757 35 s. Boxing 30 30
758 1 m. Diving 85 95
759 3 m. Ten-pin bowling .. .. 2·25 2·50
754/9 .. .. *Set of* 6 3·50 3·50
MS760 Two sheets, each 75×105 mm. (a) 2 m. Lawn tennis (*different*). (b) 4 m. Football *Set of* 2 *sheets* 3·25 3·75

Nos. 754/60 incorrectly show the Lesotho flag with white field and emblem at top right.

Similar stamps, with face values of 5, 10, 25, 40, 50 s., 3 m. 50 and a 4 m. miniature sheet showing the correct flag with white field and emblem at top left, were placed on philatelic sale from 30 November 1987. They were not, however, according to the Lesotho Philatelic Bureau, sold through post offices and agencies for postal purposes (*Price for set of* 6 £2.40, *mint; miniature sheet* £2.75 *mint*).

See also Nos. 838/42.

(Des Mary Walters. Litho Format)

1987 (30 June). *Great Scientific Discoveries. T* **174** *and similar horiz designs. Multicoloured. P* 15.
761 5 s. Type **174** 10 10
762 9 s. Alexander Graham Bell and first telephone 10 10
763 75 s. Robert Goddard and liquid fuel rocket .. 40 45
764 4 m. Chuck Yeager and "X-1" rocket plane .. 2·25 2·40
761/4 .. .. *Set of* 4 2·50 2·75
MS765 98×68 mm. 4 m. "Mariner 10" spacecraft 2·25 2·75

175 Grey Rhebuck

176 Scouts hiking

(Des G. Drummond. Litho Format)

1987 (14 Aug). *Flora and Fauna. T* **175** *and similar multicoloured designs. P* 15.
766 5 s. Type **175** 30 15
767 9 s. Cape Clawless Otter 30 15
768 15 s. Cape Grey Mongoose 40 20
769 20 s. Free State Daisy (*vert*) 45 20
770 35 s. River Bells (*vert*) 60 30
771 1 m. Turkey Flower (*vert*) .. .. .. 1·50 1·50
772 2 m. Sweet Briar (*vert*) .. .. .. 2·25 2·50
773 3 m. Mountain Reedbuck .. .. .. 2·75 3·00
766/73 .. .. *Set of* 8 7·75 7·25
MS774 114×98 mm. (a) 2 m. Pig-Lily (*vert*). (b) 4 m. Cape Wildebeest .. *Set of* 2 *sheets* 3·75 4·25

(Des Mary Walters. Litho Questa)

1987 (10 Sept). *World Scout Jamboree, Australia. T* **176** *and similar vert designs. Multicoloured. P* 14.
775 9 s. Type **176** 30 15
776 15 s. Scouts playing football 35 15
777 35 s. Kangaroos 45 30
778 75 s. Scout saluting 90 55
779 4 m. Australian scout windsurfing .. .. 3·00 3·00
775/9 .. .. *Set of* 5 4·50 3·75
MS780 96×66 mm. 4 m. Outline map and flag of Australia .. .. 3·00 3·50

177 Spotted Trunkfish and Columbus' Fleet

178 "Madonna and Child" (detail)

(Des I. MacLaury. Litho Questa)

1987 (14 Dec). *500th Anniv of Discovery of America by Columbus* (1992). *T* **177** *and similar horiz designs. Multicoloured. P* 14.
781 9 s. Type **177** 10 10
782 15 s. Green Turtle and ships 10 10
783 35 s. Columbus watching Common Dolphins from ship 20 25
784 5 m. White-tailed Tropic Bird and fleet at sea .. .. 2·75 3·00
781/4 .. .. *Set of* 4 2·75 3·00
MS785 105×76 mm. 4 m. *Santa Maria* and Cuban Amazon in flight .. .. 3·00 3·25
No. 782 is inscribed "Carribbean" in error.

(Litho Questa)

1987 (21 Dec). *Christmas. T* **178** *and similar vert designs showing religious paintings by Raphael. Multicoloured. P* 14.
786 9 s. Type **178** 20 10
787 15 s. "Marriage of the Virgin" 30 15
788 35 s. "Coronation of the Virgin" (detail) .. 55 30
789 90 s. "Madonna of the Chair" .. .. 1·25 1·25
786/9 .. .. *Set of* 4 2·10 1·60
MS790 75×100 mm. 3 m. "Madonna and Child enthroned with Five Saints" (detail) .. .. 2·25 2·50

179 Lesser Pied Kingfisher

40TH WEDDING ANNIVERSARY
H.M. QUEEN ELIZABETH II
H.R.H. THE DUKE OF EDINBURGH

(180)

(Des G. Drummond. Litho Format)

1988 (5 Apr). *Birds. T* **179** *and similar horiz designs. Multicoloured. Without printer's imprint. P* 15.
791 2 s. Type **179** 15 15
792 3 s. Three-banded Plover 15 15
793 5 s. Spur-winged Goose 15 15
794 10 s. Clapper Lark 15 15
795 12 s. Red-eyed Bulbul 30 15
796 16 s. Cape Weaver 30 15
797 20 s. Paradise Sparrow ("Red-headed Finch") 30 15
798 30 s. Mountain Chat 30 15
799 40 s. Stonechat 30 20
800 55 s. Pied Barbet 35 25
801 60 s. Cape Glossy Starling 40 30
802 75 s. Cape Sparrow 55 40
803 1 m. Cattle Egret 65 50
804 3 m. Giant Kingfisher .. .. .. 1·75 2·00
805 10 m. Helmet Guineafowl .. .. .. 5·50 6·00
791/805 .. .. *Set of* 15 10·00 9·75
For these stamps showing Questa imprint at bottom left see Nos. 887/99.

1988 (3 May)*. *Royal Ruby Wedding. Nos.* 701/4 *optd with T* **180** *in silver.*
806 90 s. black and yellow 35 40
807 1 m. multicoloured 40 45
808 2 m. multicoloured 80 85
806/8 .. .. *Set of* 3 1·40 1·50
MS809 119×85 mm. 4 m. black and grey-brown 1·60 1·75
*Nos. 806/9 were not available in Lesotho until the middle of 1990.

181 Mickey Mouse and Goofy outside Presidential Palace, Helsinki

(Des Walt Disney Co. Litho Questa)

1988 (2 June). *"Finlandia '88" International Stamp Exhibition, Helsinki. T* **181** *and similar horiz designs showing Walt Disney cartoon characters in Finland. Multicoloured. P* 14×13½.
810 1 s. Type **181** 10 10
811 2 s. Goofy and Mickey Mouse in sauna .. 10 10
812 3 s. Goofy and Mickey Mouse fishing in lake 10 10
813 4 s. Mickey and Minnie Mouse and Finlandia Hall, Helsinki 10 10
814 5 s. Mickey Mouse photographing Goofy at Sibelius Monument, Helsinki 10 10
815 10 s. Mickey Mouse and Goofy pony trekking 10 10
816 3 m. Goofy, Mickey and Minnie Mouse at Helsinki Olympic Stadium .. .. 1·25 1·40
817 5 m. Mickey Mouse and Goofy meeting Santa at Arctic Circle .. .. 2·00 2·10
810/17 .. .. *Set of* 8 3·25 3·50
MS818 Two sheets, each 127×102 mm. (a) 4 m. Mickey Mouse and nephew as Lapps. (b) 4 m. Daisy Duck, Goofy, Mickey and Minnie Mouse by fountain, Helsinki .. *Set of* 2 *sheets* 3·25 3·50

182 Pope John Paul II giving Communion

183 Large-toothed Rock Hyrax

(Litho Questa)

1988 (1 Sept). *Visit of Pope John Paul II. T* **182** *and similar multicoloured designs. P* 14.
819 55 s. Type **182** 20 25
820 2 m. Pope leading procession 80 85
821 3 m. Pope at airport .. .. 1·25 1·40
822 4 m. Pope John Paul II .. .. .. 1·60 1·75
819/22 .. .. *Set of* 4 3·50 3·75
MS823 98×79 mm. 5 m. Archbishop Morapeli (*horiz*) .. .. 2·00 2·10

(Des L. Watkins. Litho B.D.T.)

1988 (13 Oct). *Small Mammals of Lesotho. T* **183** *and similar vert designs. Multicoloured. P* 14.
824 16 s. Type **183** 10 10
825 40 s. Ratel and Honey Guide (bird) 15 20
826 75 s. Small-spotted Genet 30 35
827 3 m. Yellow Mongoose .. .. .. 1·25 1·40
824/7 .. .. *Set of* 4 1·60 1·75
MS828 110×78 mm. 4 m. Meerkat .. .. 1·60 1·75

184 "Birth of Venus" (detail) (Botticelli)

(Litho Questa)

1988 (17 Oct). *Famous Paintings. T* **184** *and similar vert designs. Multicoloured. P* 13½ × 14.
829 15 s. Type **184** 10 10
830 25 s. "View of Toledo" (El Greco) 10 15
831 40 s. "Maids of Honour" (detail) (Velasquez) 15 20
832 50 s. "The Fifer" (Manet) 20 25
833 55 s. "Starry Night" (detail) (Van Gogh) .. 20 25
834 75 s. "Prima Ballerina" (Degas) 30 35
835 2 m. "Bridge over Water Lilies" (Monet) .. 80 85
836 3 m. "Guernica" (detail) (Picasso) .. .. 1·25 1·40
829/36 .. .. *Set of* 8 2·75 3·25
MS837 Two sheets, each 110×95 mm. (a) 4 m. "The Presentation of the Virgin in the Temple" (Titian). (b) 4 m. "The Miracle of the Newborn Infant" (Titian) .. .. .. *Set of* 2 *sheets* 3·25 3·50

185 Wrestling

(Des J. Martin. Litho B.D.T.)

1988 (11 Nov). *Olympic Games, Seoul (2nd issue). T* **185** *and similar multicoloured designs. P* 14.
838 12 s. Type **185** 10 10
839 16 s. Show jumping (*vert*) 10 10
840 55 s. Shooting 20 25
841 3 m. 50, As 16 s. (*vert*) .. .. .. 1·40 1·50
838/41 .. .. *Set of* 4 1·50 1·60
MS842 108×77 mm. 4 m. Olympic flame (*vert*) .. 1·60 1·75

186 Yannick Noah and Eiffel Tower, Paris

186a "The Averoldi Polyptych" (detail) (Titian)

(Des J. McDaniels. Litho Questa)

1988 (18 Nov). *75th Anniv of International Tennis Federation. T* **186** *and similar multicoloured designs. P* 14.
843 12 s. Type **186** 10 10
844 20 s. Rod Laver and Sydney Harbour Bridge and Opera House 10 10
845 30 s. Ivan Lendl and Prague 10 15
846 65 s. Jimmy Connors and Tokyo (*vert*) .. 25 30
847 1 m. Arthur Ashe and Barcelona (*vert*) .. 40 45
848 1 m. 55, Althea Gibson and New York (*vert*) 60 65
849 2 m. Chris Evert and Vienna (*vert*) .. 80 85
850 2 m. 40, Boris Becker and Houses of Parliament, London (*vert*) .. 1·00 1·10
851 3 m. Martina Navratilova and Golden Gate Bridge, San Francisco .. .. 1·25 1·40
843/51 .. .. *Set of* 9 4·00 4·50
MS852 98×72 mm. 4 m. Steffi Graf and Berlin 1·60 1·75
No. 844 is inscribed "SIDNEY" in error.

(Litho Questa)

1988 (1 Dec). *Christmas. 500th Birth Anniv of Titian (artist). T* **186a** *and similar multicoloured designs. P* 13½×14.
853 12 s. Type **186a** 10 10
854 20 s. "Christ and the Adulteress" (detail) .. 10 10
855 35 s. "Christ and the Adulteress" (different detail) 15 20
856 45 s. "Angel of the Annunciation" 20 25
857 65 s. "Saint Dominic" 25 30
858 1 m. "The Vendramin Family" (detail) .. 40 45
859 2 m. "Mary Magdalen" 80 85
860 3 m. "The Tribute Money" .. .. .. 1·25 1·40
853/60 .. .. *Set of* 8 3·00 3·25
MS861 (a) 94 × 110 mm. 5 m. "Mater Dolorosa". P 13½ × 14. (b) 110 × 94 mm. 5 m. "Christ and the Woman taken in Adultery" (*horiz*). P 14 × 13½ .. .. .. *Set of* 2 *sheets* 4·00 4·25

187 Pilatus "PC-6 Turbo Porter"

(Des K. Gromell. Litho Questa)

1989 (30 Jan). *125th Anniv of International Red Cross. Aircraft. T* **187** *and similar multicoloured designs. P* 14.

862 12 s. Type **187** 10 10
863 20 s. Unloading medical supplies from Cessna "Caravan" 10 10
864 55 s. De Havilland "DHC-6 Otter" 20 25
865 3 m. Douglas "DC-3" .. .. .. 1·25 1·40
862/5 .. .. *Set of* 4 1·40 1·60
MS866 109×80 mm. 4 m. Red Cross logo and Douglas "DC-3" (*vert*) .. .. 1·60 1·75

187a "Dawn Mist at Mishima" (Hiroshige)

(Litho Questa)

1989 (19 June). *Japanese Art. Paintings by Hiroshige. T* **187a** *and similar horiz designs. Multicoloured. P* 14×13½.

867 12 s. Type **187a** 10 10
868 16 s. "Night Snow at Kambara" 10 10
869 20 s. "Wayside Inn at Mariko Station" .. 10 10
870 35 s. "Shower at Shono" 15 20
871 55 s. "Snowfall on the Kisokaido near Oi" .. 20 25
872 1 m. "Autumn Moon at Seba" 40 45
873 3 m. 20, "Evening Moon at Ryogoku Bridge" 1·25 1·40
874 5 m. "Cherry Blossoms at Arashiyama" .. 2·00 2·10
867/74 .. .. *Set of* 8 3·75 4·25
MS875 Two sheets, each 102×76 mm. (a) 4 m. "Listening to the Singing Insects at Dokanyama". (b) 4 m. "Moonlight, Nagakubo" *Set of* 2 *sheets* 3·25 3·50

Nos. 867/74 were each printed in sheetlets of 10 containing two horizontal strips of 5 stamps separated by printed labels commemorating Emperor Hirohito.

188 Mickey Mouse as General

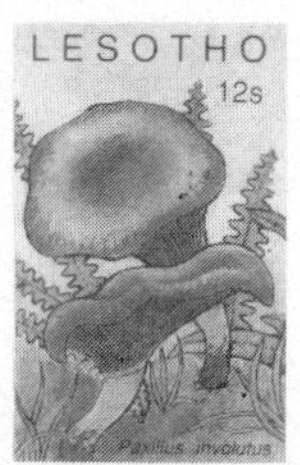

189 *Paxillus involutus*

(Des Walt Disney Company. Litho Questa)

1989 (10 July). *"Philexfrance 89" International Stamp Exhibition, Paris. T* **188** *and similar multicoloured designs showing Walt Disney cartoon characters in French military uniforms of the Revolutionary period. P* 13½×14.

876 1 s. Type **188** 10 10
877 2 s. Ludwig von Drake as infantryman .. 10 10
878 3 s. Goofy as grenadier 10 10
879 4 s. Horace Horsecollar as cavalryman .. 10 10
880 5 s. Pete as hussar 10 10
881 10 s. Donald Duck as marine 10 10
882 3 m. Gyro Gearloose as National Guard .. 1·25 1·40
883 5 m. Scrooge McDuck as admiral .. .. 2·00 2·10
876/83 .. .. *Set of* 8 3·25 3·50
MS884 Two sheets, each 127×102 mm. (a) 4 m. Mickey and Minnie Mouse as King Louis XVI and Marie Antoinette with Goofy as a National Guard (*horiz*). P 14×13½. (b) 4 m. Mickey Mouse as drummer. P 13½×14 .. *Set of* 2 *sheets* 3·25 3·50

No. 879 is inscribed "CALVARYMAN" in error.

(Litho Questa)

1989 (31 Aug)–**91**. *As Nos.* 793, 795/7 *and* 803/5, *but with printer's imprint at bottom left. P* 14.

887 5 s. Spur-winged Goose (18.1.90) .. 15 15
889 12 s. Red-eyed Bulbul 20 15
890 16 s. Cape Weaver (11.11.89) 25 20
891 20 s. Paradise Sparrow ("Red-headed Finch") (2.12.89) 25 20
897 1 m. Cattle Egret (1991) 65 60
898 3 m. Giant Kingfisher (1991) .. .. 1·75 2·00
899 10 m. Helmet Guineafowl (1991) .. .. 5·50 6·00
887/99 .. .. *Set of* 7 8·00 8·50

(Des S. Wood. Litho Questa)

1989 (8 Sept). *Fungi. T* **189** *and similar vert designs. Multicoloured. P* 14.

900 12 s. Type **189** 10 10
901 16 s. *Ganoderma applanatum* 10 10
902 55 s. *Suillus granulatus* 20 25
903 5 m. *Stereum hirsutum* .. .. .. 2·00 2·25
900/3 .. .. *Set of* 4 2·10 2·40
MS904 96×69 mm. 4 m. *Scleroderma flavidum* 1·60 1·75

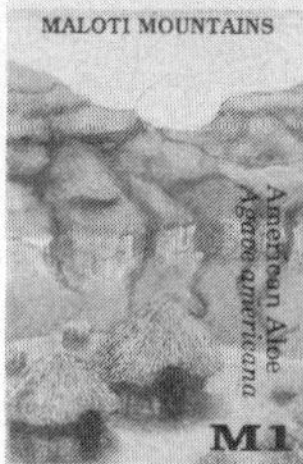

190 Sesotho Huts

191 Marsh Sandpiper

(Des S. Wood. Litho Questa)

1989 (18 Sept). *Maloti Mountains. T* **190** *and similar vert designs. Multicoloured. P* 14.

905 1 m. Type **190** 40 45
a. Horiz strip of 4. Nos. 905/8 .. .. 1·40
906 1 m. American Aloe and mountains .. 40 45
907 1 m. River valley with waterfall 40 45
908 1 m. Sesotho tribesman on ledge 40 45
905/8 .. .. *Set of* 4 1·40 1·60
MS909 86×117 mm. 4 m. Spiral Aloe .. .. 1·60 1·75

Nos. 905/8 were printed together, *se-tenant*, in horizontal strips of 4 throughout the sheet forming a composite design.

(Des Tracy Pedersen. Litho Questa)

1989 (18 Sept). *Migrant Birds. T* **191** *and similar multicoloured designs. P* 14.

910 12 s. Type **191** 10 10
911 65 s. Little Stint 25 30
912 1 m. Ringed Plover 40 45
913 4 m. Curlew Sandpiper .. .. .. 1·60 1·75
910/13 .. .. *Set of* 4 2·10 2·25
MS914 97×69 mm. 5 m. Ruff (*vert*) .. .. 2·00 2·10

192 Launch of "Apollo 11"

193 English Penny Post Paid Mark, 1680

(Des G. Welker. Litho Questa)

1989 (6 Nov). *20th Anniv of First Manned Landing on Moon. T* **192** *and similar multicoloured designs. P* 14.

915 12 s. Type **192** 10 10
916 16 s. Lunar module *Eagle* landing on Moon (*horiz*) 10 10
917 40 s. Neil Armstrong leaving *Eagle* .. 15 20
918 55 s. Edwin Aldrin on Moon (*horiz*) .. 20 25
919 1 m. Aldrin performing scientific experiment (*horiz*) 40 45
920 2 m. *Eagle* leaving Moon (*horiz*) 80 85
921 3 m. Command module *Columbia* in Moon orbit (*horiz*) .. .. 1·25 1·40
922 4 m. Command module on parachutes .. 1·60 1·75
915/22 .. .. *Set of* 8 4·00 4·50
MS923 81×111 mm. 5 m. Astronaut on Moon 2·00 2·10

(Des U. Purins. Litho B.D.T.)

1989 (17 Nov). *"World Stamp Expo '89" International Stamp Exhibition, Washington. Stamps and Postmarks. T* **193** *and similar horiz designs. P* 14.

924 75 s. brown-lake, black and stone 30 35
a. Sheetlet. Nos. 924/32 .. .. 2·40
925 75 s. black, grey and rosine 30 35
926 75 s. dull violet, black and cinnamon .. 30 35
927 75 s. red-brown, black and cinnamon .. 30 35
928 75 s. black and olive-yellow 30 35
929 75 s. multicoloured 30 35
930 75 s. black and bright brown-lilac 30 35
931 75 s. black, bright carmine and pale brown 30 35
932 75 s. brt carmine, black & greenish yellow 30 35
924/32 .. .. *Set of* 9 2·40 2·75

Designs:— No. 925, German postal seal and feather, 1807; 926, British Post Offices in Crete 1898 20 pa. stamp; 927, Bermuda 1848 Perot 1d. provisional; 928, U.S.A. Pony Express cancellation, 1860; 929, Finland 1856 5 k. stamp; 930, Fiji 1870 *Fiji Times* 1d. stamp, 1870; 931, Sweden newspaper wrapper handstamp, 1823; 932, Bhor 1879 ½ a. stamp.

Nos. 924/32 were printed together, *se-tenant*, in sheetlets of 9.

MINIMUM PRICE

The minimum price quote is 10p which represents a handling charge rather than a basis for valuing common stamps. For further notes about prices see introductory pages.

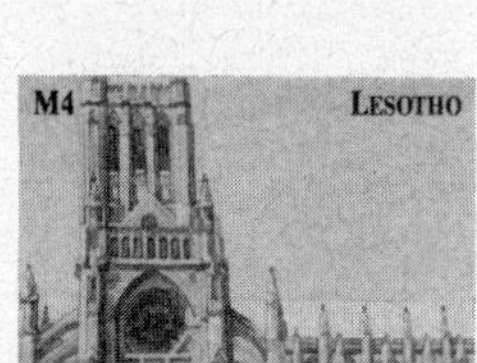

193a Cathedral Church of St. Peter and St. Paul, Washington

193b "The Immaculate Conception" (Velasquez)

(Des Design Element. Litho Questa)

1989 (17 Nov). *"World Stamp Expo '89" International Stamp Exhibition, Washington (2nd issue). Sheet* 78×61 *mm. P* 14.

MS933 **193a** 4 m. multicoloured .. .. 1·60 1·75

(Litho Questa)

1989 (18 Dec). *Christmas. Paintings by Velasquez. T* **193b** *and similar vert designs. Multicoloured. P* 14.

934 12 s. Type **193b** 10 10
935 20 s. "St. Anthony Abbot and St. Paul the Hermit" 10 10
936 35 s. "St. Thomas the Apostle" 15 20
937 55 s. "Christ in the House of Martha and Mary" 20 25
938 1 m. "St. John writing The Apocalypse on Patmos" 40 45
939 3 m. "The Virgin presenting the Chasuble to St. Ildephonsus" .. .. .. 1·25 1·40
940 4 m. "The Adoration of the Magi" .. .. 1·60 1·75
934/40 .. .. *Set of* 7 3·50 3·75
MS941 71×96 mm. 5 m. "The Coronation of the Virgin" .. .. 2·00 2·10

194 Scene from 1966 World Cup Final, England

(Des G. Vasarhelyi. Litho Questa)

1989 (27 Dec). *World Cup Football Championship, Italy. T* **194** *and similar horiz designs showing scenes from past finals. Multicoloured. P* 14.

942 12 s. Type **194** 10 10
943 16 s. 1970 final, Mexico 10 10
944 55 s. 1974 final, West Germany 20 25
945 5 m. 1982 final, Spain .. .. .. 2·00 2·10
942/5 .. .. *Set of* 4 2·10 2·25
MS946 106×85 mm. 4 m. Player's legs and symbolic football .. .. 1·60 1·75

16 s	16 s	16 s	16 s
(**195**)	(**196**)	Long bars (R. 6/3)	(**196a**)

1990 (22 Feb)–**91**. *Nos.* 795, 798/9 *and* 889 *surch with T* **195/6a** *by Lesotho Ads.*

947 16 s. on 12 s. Red-eyed Bulbul (No. 795) (T **195**) 25 15
948 16 s. on 12 s. Red-eyed Bulbul (No. 889) (T **196**) 20 30
a. Surch inverted .. .. .. 40·00
b. Surch double .. .. .. 60·00
c. Long bars .. ..
d. Surch with Type **195** .. .. ..
948*e* 16 s. on 30 s. Mountain Chat (No. 798) (T **196a**) (18.1.91) 10 10
eb. Lower bar omitted .. .. ..
948*f* 16 s. on 30 s. Mountain Chat (No. 798) (T **196a**) (18.1.91) 10 10
ea. Surch inverted .. .. ..
eb. Lower bar omitted .. .. ..
947/8*f* .. .. *Set of* 4 50 50

The lower cancelling bar is frequently completely omitted from Type **196a** on R. 4/4, although on occasions traces of it do remain.

197 *Byblia anvatara*

198 *Satyrium princeps*

(Des L. Nelson. Litho Questa)

1990 (26 Feb). *Butterflies. T* **197** *and similar vert designs. Multicoloured. P* 14.

949 12 s. Type **197** 10 10
950 16 s. *Cynthia cardui* 10 10
951 55 s. *Precis oenone* 20 25
952 65 s. *Pseudacraea boisduvali* 25 30
953 1 m. *Precis orithya* 40 45
954 2 m. *Precis sophia* 80 85
955 3 m. *Danaus chrysippus* .. .. .. 1·25 1·40
956 4 m. *Druryia antimachus* .. .. .. 1·60 1·75
949/56 .. .. *Set of* 8 4·25 4·50
MS957 105×70 mm. 5 m. *Papilio demodocus* .. 2·00 2·10

(Des B. Tear. Litho Questa)

1990 (12 Mar). *"EXPO 90" International Garden and Greenery Exhibition, Osaka. Local Orchids. T* **198** *and similar horiz designs. Multicoloured. P* 14.

958 12 s. Type **198** 10 10
959 16 s. *Huttonaea pulchra* 10 10
960 55 s. *Herschelia graminifolia* 20 25
961 1 m. *Ansellia gigantea* 40 45
962 1 m. 55, *Polystachya pubescens* 60 65
963 2 m. 40, *Penthea filicornis* .. .. .. 1·00 1·10
964 3 m. *Disperis capensis* .. .. .. 1·25 1·40
965 4 m. *Disa uniflora* .. .. 1·60 1·75
958/65 .. .. *Set of* 8 4·75 5·25
MS966 95×68 mm. 5 m. *Stenoglottis longifolia* 2·00 2·10

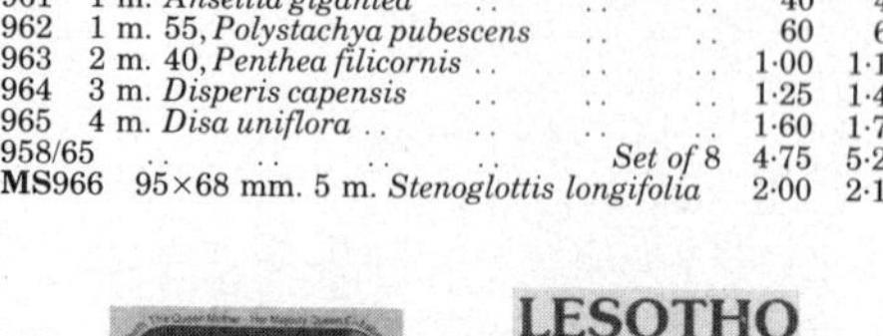

198a Lady Elizabeth Bowes-Lyon and Brother in Fancy Dress

199 King Moshoeshoe II and Prince Mohato wearing Seana-Marena Blankets

(Des Young Phillips Studio. Litho Questa)

1990 (5 July). *90th Birthday of Queen Elizabeth the Queen Mother. T* **198a** *and similar vert portraits, 1910–1919. P* 14.

967 1 m. 50, brownish black and bright magenta 60 65
a. Strip of 3. Nos. 967/9 .. .. .. 1·60
968 1 m. 50, brownish black and bright magenta 60 65
969 1 m. 50, brownish black and bright magenta 60 65
967/9 .. .. *Set of* 3 1·60 1·75
MS970 90×75 mm. 5 m. dull orange-brown, brownish black and bright magenta .. .. 2·00 2·10

Designs:—No. 967, Type **198a**; No. 968, Lady Elizabeth Bowes-Lyon in evening dress; No. 969, Lady Elizabeth Bowes-Lyon wearing hat; No. **MS**970, Lady Elizabeth Bowes-Lyon as a child.

Nos. 967/9 were printed together, horizontally and vertically *se-tenant*, in sheetlets of 9 (3×3).

(Litho B.D.T.)

1990 (17 Aug). *Traditional Blankets. T* **199** *and similar multicoloured designs. P* 14.

971 12 s. Type **199** 10 10
972 16 s. Prince Mohato wearing Seana-Marena blanket 10 10
973 1 m. Pope John Paul II wearing Seana-Marena blanket 40 45
974 3 m. Basotho horsemen wearing Matlama blankets .. .. 1·25 1·40
971/4 .. .. *Set of* 4 1·60 1·75
MS975 85×104 mm. 5 m. Pope John Paul II wearing hat and Seana-Marena blanket (*horiz*) 2·00 2·10

200 Filling Truck at No. 1 Quarry

201 Mother breastfeeding Baby

(Litho B.D.T.)

1990 (24 Aug). *Lesotho Highlands Water Project. T* **200** *and similar vert designs. Multicoloured. P* 14.

976 16 s. Type **200** 10 10
977 20 s. Tanker lorry on Pitseng–Malibamatso road 10 10
978 55 s. Piers for Malibamatso Bridge 20 25
979 2 m. Excavating Mphosong section of Pitseng–Malibamatso road 80 85
976/9 .. .. *Set of* 4 1·00 1·10
MS980 104×85 mm. 5 m. Sinking blasting boreholes on Pitseng–Malibamatso road .. 2·00 2·10

(Litho Questa)

1990 (26 Oct). *U.N.I.C.E.F. Child Survival Campaign. T* **201** *and similar vert designs. Multicoloured. P* 14.

981 12 s. Type **201** 10 10
982 55 s. Baby receiving oral rehydration therapy 20 25
983 1 m. Weight monitoring 40 45
981/3 .. .. *Set of* 3 60 70

202 Men's Triple Jump

203 "Virgin and Child" (detail, Rubens)

(Des B. Grout. Litho Questa)

1990 (5 Nov). *Olympic Games, Barcelona* (1992). *T* **202** *and similar multicoloured designs. P* 14.

984 16 s. Type **202** 10 10
985 55 s. Men's 200 metres race 20 25
986 1 m. Men's 5000 metres race 40 45
987 4 m. Show jumping .. .. .. 1·60 1·75
984/7 .. .. *Set of* 4 2·00 2·25
MS988 100×70 mm. 5 m. Olympic flame (*horiz*) 2·00 2·10

(Litho Questa)

1990 (5 Dec). *Christmas. Paintings by Rubens. T* **203** *and similar vert designs. Multicoloured. P* $13^1/_2$×14.

989 12 s. Type **203** 10 10
990 16 s. "Adoration of the Magi" (detail) .. 10 10
991 55 s. "Head of One of the Three Kings" .. 20 25
992 80 s. "Adoration of the Magi" (different detail) 35 40
993 1 m. "Virgin and Child" (different detail) .. 40 45
994 2 m. "Adoration of the Magi" (different detail) 80 85
995 3 m. "Virgin and Child" (different detail) .. 1·25 1·40
996 4 m. "Adoration of the Magi" (different detail) .. .. 1·60 1·75
989/96 .. .. *Set of* 8 4·25 4·75
MS997 71×100 mm. 5 m. "Assumption of the Virgin" (detail) .. .. 2·00 2·10

204 Mickey Mouse at Nagasaki Peace Park

(Des Walt Disney Company. Litho Questa)

1991 (10 June). *"Philanippon '91" International Stamp Exhibition, Tokyo. T* **204** *and similar horiz designs showing Walt Disney cartoon characters in Japan. Multicoloured. P* 14×$13^1/_2$.

998 20 s. Type **204** 10 10
999 30 s. Mickey Mouse on Kamakura Beach .. 10 15
1000 40 s. Mickey and Donald Duck with Bunraku puppet 15 20
1001 50 s. Mickey and Donald eating soba .. 20 25
1002 75 s. Mickey and Minnie Mouse at tea house 30 35
1003 1 m. Mickey running after bullet train .. 40 45
1004 3 m. Mickey Mouse with deer at Todaiji Temple, Nara .. .. .. 1·25 1·40
1005 4 m. Mickey and Minnie outside Imperial Palace .. .. 1·60 1·75
998/1005 .. .. *Set of* 8 3·75 4·25
MS1006 Two sheets, each 127×112 mm. (a) 5 m. Mickey Mouse skiing; (b) 5 m. Mickey and Minnie having a picnic .. .. *Set of* 2 *sheets* 4·00 4·25

205 Stewart Granger (*King Solomon's Mines*)

206 *Satyrus aello*

(Des R. Jung. Litho Questa)

1991 (20 June). *Famous Films with African Themes. T* **205** *and similar vert designs. Multicoloured. P* 14.

1007 12 s. Type **205** 10 10
1008 16 s. Johnny Weissmuller (*Tarzan the Ape Man*) 10 10
1009 30 s. Clark Gable with Grace Kelly (*Mogambo*) 10 15
1010 55 s. Sigourney Weaver and male gorilla (*Gorillas in the Mist*) 20 25
1011 70 s. Humphrey Bogart and Katharine Hepburn (*The African Queen*) .. 30 35
1012 1 m. John Wayne and capture of rhinoceros (*Hatari!*) 40 45
1013 2 m. Meryl Streep and light aircraft (*Out of Africa*) 80 85
1014 4 m. Arsenio Hall and Eddie Murphy (*Coming to America*) .. .. 1·60 1·75
1007/14 .. .. *Set of* 8 3·25 3·50
MS1015 108×77mm. 5 m. Elsa the lioness (*Born Free*) .. .. 2·00 2·10

(Des S. Heimann. Litho Cartor)

1991 (1 Aug). *Butterflies. T* **206** *and similar horiz designs. Multicoloured. P* $13^1/_2$.

1016 2 s. Type **205** 10 10
1017 3 s. *Erebia medusa* 10 10
1018 5 s. *Melanargia galathea* 10 10
1019 10 s. *Erebia aethiops* 10 10
1020 20 s. *Coenonympha pamphilus* 10 10
1021 25 s. *Pyrameis atalanta* 10 10
1022 30 s. *Charaxes jasius* 10 15
1023 40 s. *Colias palaeno* 15 20
1024 50 s. *Colias cliopatra* 20 25
1025 60 s. *Colias philodice* 25 30
1026 70 s. *Rhumni gonepterix* 30 35
1027 1 m. *Colias caesonia* 40 45
1028 2 m. *Pyrameis cardui* 80 85
1029 3 m. *Danaus chrysippus* .. .. .. 1·25 1·50
1030 10 m. *Apatura iris* .. .. .. 4·00 4·25
1016/30 .. .. *Set of* 15 8·00 9·00

207 Victim of Drug Abuse

208 Wattled Cranes

(Litho Cartor)

1991 (23 Sept). *"Say No To Drugs" Campaign. P* $13^1/_2$×14.

1031 **207** 16 s. multicoloured 10 10

(Litho Cartor)

1991 (10 Oct). *Southern Africa Development Co-ordination Conference Tourism Promotion. T* **208** *and similar horiz designs. Multicoloured. P* 14×$13^1/_2$.

1032 12 s. Type **208** 10 10
1033 16 s. Butterfly on flowers 10 10
1034 25 s. Zebra and tourist bus at Mukurub (former rock formation), Namibia .. 10 10
1032/4 .. .. *Set of* 3 30 30
MS1035 75×117 mm. 3 m. Basotho women in ceremonial dress. P 13×12 .. .. .. 1·25 1·50

209 De Gaulle in 1939

210 Prince and Princess of Wales

(Des D. Miller. Litho B.D.T.)

1991 (6 Dec). *Birth Centenary of Charles de Gaulle (French statesman). T* **209** *and similar vert designs. P* 14.

1036 20 s. black and lake-brown 10 10
1037 40 s. black and purple 15 20
1038 50 s. black and yellow-olive 20 25
1039 60 s. black and greenish blue 25 30
1040 4 m. black and dull vermilion .. .. 1·60 1·75
1036/40 .. .. *Set of* 5 2·25 2·50

Designs:—40 s. General De Gaulle as Free French leader; 50 s. De Gaulle as provisional President of France 1944–46; 60 s. Charles de Gaulle in 1958; 4 m. Pres. De Gaulle, 1969.

(Des D. Miller. Litho B.D.T.)

1991 (9 Dec). *10th Wedding Anniv of Prince and Princess of Wales. T* **210** *and similar horiz designs. Multicoloured. P* 14.

1041 50 s. Type **210** 20 25
1042 70 s. Prince Charles at polo and Princess Diana holding Prince Henry 30 35
1043 1 m. Prince Charles with Prince Henry and Princess Diana in evening dress .. 40 45
1044 3 m. Prince William and Prince Henry in school uniform .. .. .. 1·25 1·50
1041/4 .. .. *Set of* 4 2·10 2·50
MS1045 68×91 mm. 4 m. Portraits of Prince with Princess and sons .. .. .. 1·60 1·75

211 "St. Anne with Mary and the Child Jesus" (Dürer)

212 Mickey Mouse and Pluto pinning the Tail on the Donkey

(Litho Walsall)

1991 (13 Dec). *Christmas. Drawings by Albrecht Dürer. T* **211** *and similar vert designs. P* 12.

1046	20 s. black and bright magenta	10	10
1047	30 s. black and new blue	10	10
1048	50 s. black and yellowish green	20	25
1049	60 s. black and vermilion	25	30
1050	70 s. black and lemon	30	35
1051	1 m. black and orange	40	45
1052	2 m. black and bright purple	80	85
1053	4 m. black and ultramarine	1·60	1·75
1046/53	*Set of* 8	3·50	3·75
MS1054	Two sheets, each 102×127 mm. (a) 5 m. black and carmine-rose. (b) 5 m. black and cobalt. P 14 *Set of 2 sheets*	4·00	4·25

Designs:—30 s. "Mary on Grass Bench"; 50 s. "Mary with Crown of Stars"; 60 s. "Mary with Child beside Tree"; 70 s. "Mary with Child beside Wall"; 1 m. "Mary in Halo on Crescent Moon"; 2 m. "Mary breastfeeding Child"; 4 m. "Mary with Infant in Swaddling Clothes"; 5 m. (No. **MS**1054a) "The Birth of Christ"; 5 m. (No. **MS**1054b) "The Holy Family with Dragonfly".

(Des Walt Disney Co. Litho Questa)

1991 (16 Dec). *Children's Games. T* **212** *and similar vert designs showing Walt Disney cartoon characters. Multicoloured. P* 13½×14.

1055	20 s. Type **212**	10	10
1056	30 s. Mickey playing mancala	10	10
1057	40 s. Mickey rolling hoop	15	20
1058	50 s. Minnie Mouse hula-hooping	20	25
1059	70 s. Mickey and Pluto throwing a frisbee	30	35
1060	1 m. Donald Duck with a diabolo	40	45
1061	2 m. Donald's nephews playing marbles	80	85
1062	3 m. Donald with Rubik's cube	1·25	1·50
1055/62	*Set of* 8	3·00	3·50
MS1063	Two sheets, each 127×112 mm. (a) 5 m. Donald's and Mickey's nephews playing tug-of-war; (b) 5 m. Mickey and Donald mock fighting *Set of 2 sheets*	4·00	4·25

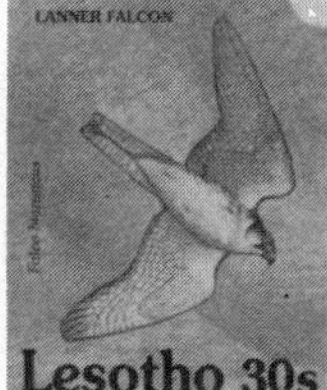

213 Lanner Falcon

(Des Tracy Pedersen. Litho Questa)

1992 (10 Feb). *Birds. T* **213** *and similar vert designs. Multicoloured. P* 14½×14.

1064	30 s. Type **213**	10	10
	a. Sheetlet. Nos. 1064/83	1·60	
1065	30 s. Bateleur	10	10
1066	30 s. Paradise Sparrow ("Red-headed Finch")	10	10
1067	30 s. Lesser Striped Swallow	10	10
1068	30 s. Alpine Swift	10	10
1069	30 s. Didric Cuckoo	10	10
1070	30 s. Yellow-tufted Malachite Sunbird	10	10
1071	30 s. Burchell's Gonolek ("Crimson-breasted Shrike")	10	10
1072	30 s. Pin-tailed Whydah	10	10
1073	30 s. Lilac-breasted Roller	10	10
1074	30 s. Black Korhaan	10	10
1075	30 s. Black-collared Barbet	10	10
1076	30 s. Secretary Bird	10	10
1077	30 s. Red-billed Quelea	10	10
1078	30 s. Red Bishop	10	10
1079	30 s. Ring-necked Dove	10	10
1080	30 s. Yellow Canary	10	10
1081	30 s. Cape Longclaw	10	10
1082	30 s. Cordon-bleu ("Blue Waxbill")	10	10
1083	30 s. Golden Bishop	10	10
1064/83	*Set of* 20	1·60	1·60

Nos. 1064/83 were printed together, *se-tenant*, as a sheetlet of 20 with the backgrounds forming a composite design.

OMNIBUS ISSUES

Details, together with prices for complete sets, of the various Omnibus issues from the 1935 Silver Jubilee series to date are included in a special section following Zimbabwe at the end of Volume 2.

OFFICIAL STAMPS

OFFICIAL

(O 1)

1934 (4 May). *Nos. 1/3 and 6 optd with Type* O **1**.

O1 1	½d. emerald	£2000	£2000
O2	1d. scarlet	£1300	£1000
O3	2d. bright purple	£750	£550
O4	6d. orange-yellow	£10000	£4500
O1/4	*Set of* 4	£13000	£7000

Collectors are advised to buy these stamps only from reliable sources. They were not sold to the public.

POSTAGE DUE STAMPS

D 1

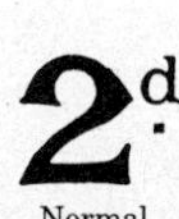

Normal

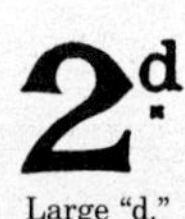

Large "d."
(R. 9/6, 10/6)

(Typo D.L.R.)

1933 (1 Dec)–**52.** *Wmk Mult Script CA. Ordinary paper. P* 14.

D1 D 1	1d. carmine	1·75	3·75
	a. *Scarlet* (1938)	24·00	27·00
	b. Chalk-surfaced paper. *Deep carmine* (24.10.51)	30	50
	ba. Error. Crown missing, W9*a*	85·00	
	bb. Error. St. Edward's Crown, W9*b*	48·00	
D2	2d. violet	3·75	6·00
	a. Chalk-surfaced paper (6.11.52)	30	1·00
	ab. Error. Crown missing, W9*a*	90·00	
	ac. Error. St. Edward's Crown, W9*a*	48·00	
	ad. Large "d"	4·50	
D1/2 Perf "Specimen"	*Set of* 2	42·00	

D 2

(Typo D.L.R.)

1956 (1 Dec). *Wmk Mult Script CA. P* 14.

D3 D 2	1d. carmine	15	1·50
D4	2d. deep reddish violet	15	2·00

5c 5c
(I) (II)

1961 (14 Feb). *Surch as T* **24**, *but without stop.*

D5 D 2	1 c. on 1d. carmine	10	25
D6	1 c. on 2d. deep reddish violet	10	25
D7	5 c. on 2d. deep reddish violet (Type I)	15	25
	a. Type II	15·00	38·00
D5/7	*Set of* 3	30	70

1961 (June). *No. D2a surch as T* **24** (*without stop*).

D8 D 1	5 c. on 2d. violet	1·50	5·50
	a. Error. Missing Crown, W9*a*	£950	
	b. Error. St. Edward's Crown, W9*b*	£225	
	c. Large "d"	15·00	

1964. *As No. D3/4 but values in cents and W* w **12** (*sideways on* 1 c.).

D9 D 2	1 c. carmine	1·25	4·75
D10	5 c. deep reddish violet	1·25	4·75

1966 (1 Nov). *Nos. D9/10 optd as T* **32** *but smaller.*

D11 D 2	1 c. carmine	20	60
	a. "LSEOTHO" (R.4/7)	25·00	
D12	5 c. deep reddish violet	20	90
	a. "LSEOTHO" (R.4/7)	45·00	

No. D11 exists with the overprint centred near the foot of the stamp (just above "POSTAGE DUE") (*price* £50 *mint*). It is believed that this comes from a proof sheet which was issued in the normal way. It contains the "LSEOTHO" error, which only occurred in the first printing.

D 1

D 2

(Litho B.W.)

1967 (18 Apr). *No wmk. P* 13½.

D13 D 1	1 c. blue	15	1·75
D14	2 c. brown-rose	15	2·00
D15	5 c. emerald	20	2·25
D13/15	*Set of* 3	45	5·50

1976 (30 Nov). *W* **53** (*sideways*). *P* 13½.

D17 D 1	2 c. rose-red	1·25	2·75
D18	5 c. emerald	1·50	3·25

(Des G. Vasarhelyi. Litho)

1986. *No wmk. P* 13×13½.

D19 D 2	2 s. light green	10	10
D20	5 s. new blue	10	10
D21	25 s. violet	10	10
D19/21	*Set of* 3	20	20

POSTAL FISCAL

In July 1961 the 10s. stamp, T **9**, surcharged "R1 Revenue", was used for postage at one post office at least, but such usage was officially unauthorised.

Appendix

The following stamps have either been issued in excess of postal needs, or have not been made available to the public in reasonable quantities at face value. Miniature sheets, imperforate stamps etc., are excluded from this section.

1981–83

15th Anniv of Independence. Classic Stamps of the World. 10 m. × 40, each embossed on gold foil.

Long Island

PRICES FOR STAMPS ON COVER

Most covers from Long Island are philatelic, but these are worth from ×2 (Nos. 1/3) or from ×6 (others).

The Turkish island of Chustan (or Keustan) in the Gulf of Smyrna was occupied by the Royal Navy during April 1916 and renamed Long Island.

The following stamps were provided by the Civil Administrator, Lieut-Cmdr H. Pirie-Gordon, for the postal service inaugurated on 7 May 1916.

(1)

2

1916 (7 May). *Turkish fiscal stamps surch by typewriter as in T* **1**. *No wmk. P* 12.

1 ½d. on 20 pa. green and buff (new value in red, remainder of surch in black) .. £2250 £4000
2 1d. on 10 pa. carmine and buff .. £2500 £4000
3 2½d. on 1 pi. violet and buff (R.) £2500 £4000
Quantities issued: ½d. 25; 1d. 20; 2½d. 25.

1916 (7 May). *Typewritten as T* **2** *in various colours of ribbon and carbon. Each stamp initialled by the Civil Administrator. No gum. Imperf.*

(*a*) *On pale green paper with horizontal grey lines. No wmk. Sheets of* 16 *or* 12 *with stamps initialled in red ink.*

4 ½d. black £500 £550
a. "G.R.I." double £1600
b. "7" for "&" .. ..
5 ½d. blue £500
a. "G.R.I." double £1600
b. "7" for "&" .. ..
6 ½d. mauve £475 £550
a. "G.R.I." double £1200
b. "7" for "&" £1500
Quantity issued: 140 in all.

(*b*) *On thin horiz laid paper with sheet wmk of* "SILVER LINEN" *in double-lined capitals. Sheets of* 20 *with stamps initialled in red ink.*

7 ½d. black £250 £300
a. "postage" for "Postage" £650
8 ½d. blue £300
b. "7" for "&" £650
9 ½d. mauve £160 £200
a. "postage" for "Postage" £550
b. "7" for "&" £550
10 1d. black £110 £200
a. "7" for "&" £475
b. "Rvevue" for "Revenue" £475
g. "Postegg" for "Postage" £475
11 1d. blue £140
a. "7" for "&" £550
c. "postage" for "Postage" £550
e. "G.R?I?" for "G.R.I." £800
f. "ONR" for "ONE" £550
12 1d. mauve £110 £200
a. "7" for "&" £550
b. "Rvevue" for "Revenue" £550
c. "postage" for "Postage" £550
e. "G.R?I?" for "G.R.I." .. .. .. † £800
f. "ONR" for "ONE" £550 £600
g. "Postegg" for "Postage" £550
13 1d. red £120 £180
a. "7" for "&" £475
c. "postage" for "Postage" £475
f. "ONR" for "ONE" £475 £650
14 2½d. black £475
15 2½d. blue £475 £550
16 2½d. mauve £425 £500
17 6d. black (inscr "SIX PENCE") £600 £600
b. Without red ink initials .. .. — £950
19 6d. mauve (inscr "SIX PENCE") £225 £300
a. "SIXPENCE" (one word) £600
20 1s. black £100 £200
a. "ISLANA" for "ISLAND" £425
b. "Postge" for "Postage" £550 £650
c. "Rebenue" for "Revenue" £550
21 1s. blue £375
22 1s. mauve £100 £200
a. "ISLANA" for "ISLAND" £450
b. "Postge" for "Postage" £450
c. "Rebenue" for "Revenue" £600
Quantities issued (all colours); ½d. 280; 1d. 1068; 2½d. 80; 6d. 100; 1s. 532.

(*c*) *On thin wove paper. No wmk. Sheets of* 24 *with stamps initialled in indelible pencil.*

23 ½d. black £160 £250
25 ½d. mauve £425
26 1d. black £170 £200
27 1d. red £900 £500
30 2d. black £140 £200
a. "ISTAD" for "ISLAND" £1200
b. Error. 1d. and 2d. *se-tenant* £1600
c. Initialled in red ink .. .. .. — £400
31 2d. mauve £140 £200
a. Error. 1d. and 2d. *se-tenant* £2000
32 2½d. black £250 £300
33 2½d. blue £700
34 2½d. mauve £425 £475
35 6d. black £140 £200
a. "Rvenne&" for "Revenue" £475
b. Error. 2d. and 6d. *se-tenant*, also ISLND" for "ISLAND" £1800 £1800
36 6d. blue £475
a. "Rvenne&" for "Revenue" £1300
b. Error. 2d. and 6d. *se-tenant*, also "ISLND" for "ISLAND" .. ..
Quantities issued (all colours); ½d. 144; 1d. 144; 2d. 288; 2½d. 144; 6d. 240.

TOP COPIES AND CARBONS. It is believed that the production sequence of the typewritten stamps was as follows:

Nos. 4/6 Three sheets of black top copies, two of 12 and one of 16
Three sheets of blue carbons, two of 12 and one of 16
Five sheets of mauve carbons, all of 12
Nos. 7/9 *Sheets of* 20
Three sheets of black top copies
Three sheets of blue carbons
Eight sheets of mauve carbons
Nos. 10/13 *Sheets of* 20
Eleven sheets of red top copies
Fifteen sheets of black carbons
Six sheets of blue carbons
Twenty-two sheets of mauve carbons
Nos. 14/16 *Sheets of* 20
One sheet of black top copies
One sheet of blue carbons
Two sheets of mauve carbons
Nos. 17/19 *Sheets of* 20
One sheet of black top copies
One sheet of blue carbons*
Three sheets of mauve carbons
Nos. 20/22 *Sheets of* 20
Five sheets of black top copies
Nine sheets of black carbons
Two sheets of blue carbons
Twelve sheets of mauve carbons
Nos. 23/5 *Sheets of* 24
One sheet of black top copies
Three sheets of black carbons
One sheet of blue carbons*
One sheet of mauve carbons
Nos. 26/9 *Sheets of* 24
One sheet of red top copies
Three sheets of black carbons
One sheet of blue carbons*
One sheet of mauve carbons*
Nos. 30/1 *Sheets of* 24
Two sheets of black top copies
Six sheets of black carbons (inc one as No. 30c)
Four sheets of mauve carbons
Nos. 32/4 *Sheets of* 24
One sheet of black top copies
Three sheets of black carbons
One sheet of blue carbons
One sheet of mauve carbons
Nos. 35/6 *Sheets of* 24
Two sheets of black top copies
Six sheets of black carbons
Two sheets of blue carbons

*These carbons are described in written records, but their existence has yet to be confirmed by actual examples.

Madagascar

PRICES FOR STAMPS ON COVER

Nos. 1/47	*from* × 5
Nos. 50/6	*from* × 20
Nos. 57/62	*from* × 30

BRITISH CONSULAR MAIL

After May 1883 mail from the British community at Antananarivo, the capital, was sent by runner to the British Consulate at Tamatave for forwarding via the French Post Office.

In March of the following year the British Vice-Consul at Antananarivo, Mr. W. C. Pickersgill, reorganised this service and issued stamps for use on both local and overseas mail. Such stamps were only gummed at one of the top corners. This was to facilitate their removal from overseas mail where they were replaced by Mauritius stamps (at Port Louis) or by French issues (at the Vice-Consulate) for transmission via Tamatave and Reunion. Local mail usually had the stamps removed also, being marked with a "PAID" or a Vice-Consular handstamp, although a few covers have survived intact.

CONDITION. Due to the type of paper used, stamps of the British Consular Mail are usually found with slight faults, especially thins. Our prices are for average examples, really fine stamps being worth a premium.

USED STAMPS. Postmarks are not usually found on these issues. Cancellations usually take the form of a manuscript line or cross in crayon, ink or pencil or as five parallel horizontal bars in black or red, approximately 15 mm long.

1

2

1884 (Mar). *Typo locally. Rouletted vertically in colour. No gum, except on one upper corner. With circular consular handstamp reading* "BRITISH VICE-CONSULATE ANTANANARIVO" *around Royal arms in black.*

(*a*) *Inscr* "LETTER".

1 **1** 6d. (½ oz) magenta £400 £425
a. Violet handstamp £1200
2 1s. (1 oz) magenta £375
3 1s. 6d. (1½ oz) magenta £375
4 2s. (2 oz) magenta £550

(*b*) *Inscr* "POSTAL PACKET"

5 **1** 1d. (1 oz) magenta £350 £300
a. Without handstamp £2000 £2000
6 2d. (2 oz) magenta £250 £250
7 3d. (3 oz) magenta £250 £225
8 4d. (1 oz amended in ms to "4 oz") magenta £600 £600
a. Without manuscript amendment .. £1600 £1600
ab. Violet handstamp £1000
ac. Without handstamp £2000 £2000

Nos. 1/8 were printed in horizontal strips of four, each strip containing two impressions of the setting. Each strip contained two stamps with normal stops after "B.C.M." and two with a hollow stop after "B" (1d., 2d., 3d., 4d., 6d. and 2s.) or after "M" (1s. and 1s. 6d.).

Several values are known with the handstamp either inverted or double.

1886. *Manuscript provisionals.*

(*a*) *No.* 2 *with* "SHILLING" *erased and* "PENNY" *written above in red ink*

9 **1** 1d. on 1s. (1 oz) magenta .. .. ..

(*b*) *No.* 2 *surch* "4½d." *and* "W.C.P." *in red ink with a line through the original value*

10 **1** 4½d. on 1s. (1 oz) magenta .. ..

1886. *As No.* 1, *but colour changed. Handstamped with circular* "BRITISH VICE-CONSULATE ANTANANARIVO" *in black.*

11 **1** 6d. (½ oz) rose-red £500 £450

1886. *As No.* 8, *but handstamped* "BRITISH CONSULAR MAIL ANTANANARIVO" *in black* (B) *or violet* (V)

		B		V	
12 **1**	4d. (1 oz) magenta	£1600	—	£2250	—

1886. *Typo locally. Rouletted vertically in colour. No gum, except on one upper corner.*

I. "POSTAGE" 29½ *mm long. Stops after* "POSTAGE" *and value*

(*a*) *Handstamped* "BRITISH VICE-CONSULATE ANTANANARIVO" *in black* (B) *or violet* (V)

		B		V	
14 **2**	1d. rose	£100	£120	£250	—
15	1½d. rose	£900	—	£600	—
16	2d. rose	£110	—	£275	—
17	3d. rose	£750	£750	£275	£275
18	4½d. rose	£700	£600	£275	£275
19	8d. rose	£1200	£1200	£1000	£1000
20	9d. rose	£2250	£2250	£900	—

(*b*) *Handstamped* "BRITISH CONSULAR MAIL ANTANANARIVO" *in black*

21 **2** 1d. rose .. .. 65·00
22 1½d. rose .. .. 65·00
23 2d. rose .. .. 75·00
24 3d. rose .. .. 80·00 85·00
a. Handstamp in red .. .. .. — £2500
25 4½d. rose .. .. 80·00 85·00
a. Handstamp in red .. .. .. — £2000
26 8d. rose .. .. 80·00
a. Handstamp in violet £1100
27 9d. rose .. .. 90·00 £100
a. Without handstamp £1600
b. Handstamp in violet £200

II. "POSTAGE" 29½ *mm long. No stops after* "POSTAGE" *or value*

(*a*) *Handstamped* "BRITISH VICE-CONSULATE ANTANANARIVO" *in violet*

28 **2** 1d. rose £750
29 1½d. rose £1000
30 3d. rose £1100
31 4½d. rose £1000
32 6d. rose £850

(*b*) *Handstamped* "BRITISH CONSULAR MAIL ANTANANARIVO" *in black* (B) *or violet* (V)

		B		V	
33	1d. rose	70·00	75·00	80·00	—
	a. Without handstamp ..	£1000			
34	1½d. rose	65·00	70·00	90·00	—
	a. Without handstamp ..	£1000			
35	2d. rose	65·00	70·00	£110	—

36 3d. rose .. .. .. 65·00 70·00 £110 —
a. Without handstamp .. £1200
37 4½d. rose .. .. .. 70·00 75·00 £110 —
a. Without handstamp .. £1300
38 6d. rose .. .. .. 70·00 75·00 £200 —
a. Without handstamp .. £1400

III. "POSTAGE" 24½ *mm long. No stop after* "POSTAGE", *but stop after value.*

(*a*) *Handstamped* "BRITISH VICE-CONSULATE ANTANANARIVO" *in violet*

39 2 4d. rose £400
40 8d. rose £500
41 1s. 6d. rose £1800
42 2s. rose £1300
a. Handstamp in black .. .. ..

(*b*) *Handstamped* "BRITISH CONSULAR MAIL ANTANANARIVO" *in black* (B) *or violet* (V)

B V

43 4d. rose .. .. .. £180 — £275 —
a. Without handstamp .. £1200
44 8d. rose .. .. .. £400 — £450 —
a. Without handstamp .. £1300
45 1s. rose .. .. .. £350 — £1000 —
a. Without handstamp .. £1300
46 1s. 6d. rose .. .. .. £350 — £1100 —
a. Without handstamp .. £1800
47 2s. rose .. .. .. £450 — £1200 —
a. Without handstamp .. £1800

The above were also printed in horizontal strips of four.

The stamps of the British Consular Mail were suppressed in 1887, but the postal service continued with the charges paid in cash.

BRITISH INLAND MAIL

In January 1895 the Malagasy government agreed that a syndicate of British merchants at Antananarivo, including the Vice-Consul, should operate an inland postal service during the war with France. Mail was sent by runner to the port of Vatomandry and forwarded via Durban where Natal stamps were added.

Nos. 50/62 were cancelled with dated circular postmarks inscribed "BRITISH MAIL".

4

5 Malagasy Runners

(Typeset London Missionary Society Press, Antananarivo)

1895 (Jan). *Rouletted in black.* (*a*) *Thick laid paper.*
50 4 4d. black .. .. 22·00 12·00
a. "FUOR" for "FOUR" .. .. .. — £650

(*b*) *In black on coloured wove paper*

51 4 1d. *blue-grey* .. .. 22·00 12·00
52 6d. *pale yellow* .. .. 22·00 12·00
53 8d. *salmon* .. .. 22·00 12·00
54 1s. *fawn* .. .. 35·00 12·00
55 2s. *bright rose* .. .. 35·00 14·00
a. Italic "2" at left .. .. .. £120 60·00
56 4s. *grey* .. .. 50·00 12·00
50/6 .. .. *Set of* 7 £180 75·00

There are six types of each value, printed in blocks of 6 (2×3) separated by gutters, four times on each sheet; the upper and lower blocks being *tête-bêche*.

Nos. 50a and 55a occur in the sixth position in their respective blocks. No. 50a was soon corrected.

(Typo John Haddon & Co, London)

1895 (Mar). *The inscription in the lower label varies for each value. P* 12.
57 5 2d. blue .. .. 5·00 20·00
a. Imperf between (pair) £400
58 4d. rose .. .. 5·00 20·00
a. Imperf between (pair) £250
59 6d. green .. .. 5·00 20·00
a. Imperf between (pair) £400
60 1s. slate-blue .. .. 6·50 26·00
a. Imperf between (pair) £400
61 2s. chocolate .. .. 7·00 30·00
a. Imperf between (pair) £400
62 4s. bright purple .. .. .. 10·00 40·00
a. Imperf between (pair) .. ..
57/62 .. .. *Set of* 6 35·00 £140

This post was suppressed when the French entered Antananarivo on 30 September 1895.

PRICES OF SETS

Set prices are given for many issues, generally those containing three stamps or more. Definitive sets include one of each value or major colour change, but do not cover different perforations, die types or minor shades. Where a choice is possible the set prices are based on the cheapest versions of the stamps included in the listings.

Malawi

(*formerly* Nyasaland)

PRICES FOR STAMPS ON COVER TO 1945

Nos. 1/9*a*	*from* × 15
Nos. 10/19	—
No. 20	*from* × 10
Nos. 21/6	*from* × 5
Nos. 27/31	—
Nos. 32/7	*from* × 6
Nos. 38/42	—
Nos. 43/7	*from* × 12
Nos. 48/52	—
No. 53	*from* × 15
No. 54	*from* × 2
No. 55	*from* × 4
Nos. 55*b*/7*a*	*from* × 7
Nos. 57*d*/63	*from* × 6
Nos. 64/71	—
Nos. 72/9	*from* × 5
Nos. 80/2	—
Nos. 83/95	*from* × 4
Nos. 96/9	—
Nos. 100/57	*from* × 2

By 1891 the territory west of Lake Nyasa was recognised as being under British protection and the southern, eastern and northern borders had been delineated with the Portuguese and German governments.

BRITISH CENTRAL AFRICA

A protectorate under the name "Nyassaland Districts" was declared on 14 May 1891, the title being changed to the "British Central Africa Protectorate" on 22 February 1893. Such a description had been in use for some time previously and the handwritten notice of 20 July 1891, announcing the introduction of postal services, described the area as "British Central Africa".

Until 1895 the British South Africa Company contributed to the revenues of the protectorate administration which, in return governed North-eastern Rhodesia. Stamps of the British South Africa Company overprinted "B.C.A.", in addition to use in British Central Africa, were issued to post offices at Fife, Fort Rosebery, Katwe, Johnston Falls, Rhodesia (later Kalungwisi) and Tanganyika (later Abercorn) in North-eastern Rhodesia from 1893 until 1899.

B.C.A. (1)

B.C.A. FOUR SHILLINGS. (2)

ONE PENNY. (3)

1891 (April)–**1895.** *Stamps of Rhodesia optd as T* 1. *P* 14, 14½.
1 1 1d. black .. .. 1·75 2·25
2 4 2d. sea-green and vermilion .. 1·75 2·50
a. Bisected (1d.) (on cover) (1895) .. † £1800
3 4d. reddish chestnut and black .. 1·50 3·75
4 1 6d. ultramarine .. .. 40·00 20·00
5 6d. deep blue .. .. 5·00 8·00
6 4 8d. rose-lake and ultramarine .. 12·00 28·00
6*a* 8d. red and ultramarine .. .. 23·00 45·00
7 1 1s. grey-brown .. .. 9·50 11·00
8 2s. vermilion .. .. 20·00 38·00
9 2s. 6d. grey-purple .. .. .. 42·00 60·00
9*a* 2s. 6d. lilac .. .. 50·00 60·00
10 4 3s. brown and green (1895) .. 45·00 48·00
11 4s. grey-black and vermilion (2.93) .. 45·00 70·00
12 1 5s. orange-yellow .. .. .. 45·00 60·00
13 10s. deep green .. .. 85·00 £110
14 2 £1 deep blue £425 £425
15 £2 rose-red £650
16 £5 sage-green £1200
17 £10 brown £2500
1/14 .. .. *Set of* 13 £600 £750

The overprint varies on values up to 10s. Sets may be made with *thin* or *thick* letters.

The bisected 2d, No. 2a, was authorised for use at Blantyre, Chiromo and Zomba in July and October 1895.

1892 (Aug)–**93.** *Stamps of Rhodesia surch as T* 2.
18 4 3s. on 4s. grey-black and vermilion (10.93) £300 £300
19 1 4s. on 5s. orange-yellow .. .. .. 70·00 80·00

1895. *No.* 2 *surch at Cape Town with T* 3.
20 4 1d. on 2d. sea-green and vermilion .. 6·00 25·00
a. Surch double £2750 £2000

Specimens are known with double surcharge, without stop after "PENNY". These are from a trial printing made at Blantyre, but it is believed that they were not issued to the public (*Price* £600 *un.*).

5 Arms of the Protectorate 6

(Des Sir Harry Johnston. Litho D.L.R.)

1895. *No wmk. P* 14.
21 5 1d. black .. .. 6·00 5·00
22 2d. black and green .. .. .. 13·00 11·00
23 4d. black and reddish buff .. .. 25·00 26·00
24 6d. black and blue .. .. .. 32·00 6·00
25 1s. black and rose .. .. .. 45·00 20·00
26 6 2s. 6d. black and bright magenta .. £110 £130
27 3s. black and yellow .. .. .. 70·00 29·00
28 5s. black and olive .. .. .. 90·00 95·00
29 £1 black and yellow-orange £650 £350
30 £10 black and orange-vermilion .. £3000 £2750
31 £25 black and blue-green £5500
21/8 .. .. *Set of* 8 £350 £275
21/9 Optd "Specimen" .. .. *Set of* 9 £375

Cancellations inscribed "BRITISH CENTRAL AFRICA" within a double-circle and with the name of a town across the centre or at foot were intended for use on stamps presented for the payment of the hut tax. Such marks can be found in black, violet or blue and are without date.

1896 (Feb). *Wmk Crown CA* (*T* 5) *or CC* (*sideways*) (*T* 6), *P* 14.
32 5 1d. black .. .. 3·00 4·50
33 2d. black and green .. .. .. 13·00 5·00
34 4d. black and orange-brown .. .. 15·00 17·00
35 6d. black and blue .. .. .. 12·00 9·00
36 1s. black and rose .. .. .. 17·00 10·00
37 6 2s. 6d. black and magenta .. .. 80·00 80·00
38 3s. black and yellow .. .. .. 60·00 32·00
39 5s. black and olive .. .. .. 80·00 90·00
40 £1 black and blue £650 £350
41 £10 black and orange (Optd S. £175) .. £3500 £2500
42 £25 black and green (Optd S. £325) .. £7500
32/9 .. .. *Set of* 8 £250 £200
32/40 Optd "Specimen" .. .. *Set of* 9 £375

7

8

(Typo D.L.R.)

1897 (Aug). *T* 7 (*wmk Crown CA*) *and* 8 (*wmk Crown CC*). *P* 14.
43 7 1d. black and ultramarine .. .. 1·00 60
44 2d. black and yellow .. .. .. 1·25 80
45 4d. black and carmine .. .. .. 5·00 1·50
46 6d. black and green .. .. .. 25·00 4·25
47 1s. black and dull purple .. .. 6·00 7·00
48 8 2s. 6d. black and ultramarine .. 35·00 38·00
49 3s. black and sea-green £160 £200
50 4s. black and carmine .. .. .. 50·00 70·00
50*a* 10s. black and olive-green .. .. 80·00 90·00
51 £1 black and dull purple £200 £140
52 £10 black and yellow (Optd S. £175) .. £2750 £1500
43/51 .. .. *Set of* 10 £500 £500
43/51 Optd "Specimen" .. .. *Set of* 10 £225

ONE PENNY (9)

10

1897 (31 Dec). *No.* 49 *surch with T* 9, *in red.*
53 8 1d. on 3s. black and sea-green .. .. 5·00 8·50
a. "PNNEY" (R. 4/2) £1300 £1300
b. "PENN" £750 £700
c. Surch double £450

No. 53b shows an albino impression of the "Y".

1898 (11 Mar). *Imperf.*

(*a*) *Setting I. The vertical frame lines of the stamps cross the space between the two rows of the sheet*

(i) *With the initials* "J.G." *or* "J.T.G." *on the back in black ink*
54 10 1d. vermilion and grey-blue .. .. — £450
a. Without the initials £1500
b. Without the initials and centre inverted £6000

(ii) *With a control number and letter or letters, printed in plain relief at the back*
55 10 1d. vermilion and grey-blue .. .. — £200

(*b*) *Setting II. The vertical frame lines do not cross the space between the rows except at the extreme ends of the sheet. Control as No.* 55.
55*b* 10 1d. vermilion and pale ultramarine .. — 40·00
c. Control on face .. .. .. — £3000
d. Centre omitted (vert pair with normal) £6500
56 1d. vermilion and deep ultramarine .. — 40·00
a. Without Control at back .. .. £1200 75·00
b. Control doubly impressed .. .. — £225

1898 (June). *Setting II. Control as No.* 55. *P* 12.
57 **10** 1d. vermilion and pale ultramarine .. £1300 14·00
57*a* 1d. vermilion and deep ultramarine .. — 14·00
ab. Without Control at back .. .. £1300 45·00
ac. Two different Controls on back .. — £400
ad. Control printed in black £1400

The two different settings of these stamps are each in 30 types, issued without gum.

1901. *Wmk Crown CA. P* 14.
57*d* **7** 1d. dull purple and carmine-rose .. 1·00 40
57*e* 4d. dull purple and olive-green .. .. 4·00 5·00
58 6d. dull purple and brown .. .. 3·50 3·00
57*d*/8 .. .. .. *Set of* 3 7·50 7·50
57*d*/58 Optd "Specimen" .. .. *Set of* 3 60·00

11

12

(Typo D.L.R.)

1903–4. *T* **11** (*Wmk Crown CA*) *and* **12** (*Wmk Crown CC*). *P* 14.
59 **11** 1d. grey and carmine .. .. .. 2·75 25
60 2d. dull and bright purple .. .. 3·25 1·00
61 4d. grey-green and black .. .. 2·50 5·00
62 6d. grey and reddish buff .. .. 2·50 2·00
62*a* 1s. grey and blue .. .. .. 2·50 6·50
63 **12** 2s. 6d. grey-green and green .. .. 25·00 35·00
64 4s. dull and bright purple .. .. 48·00 70·00
65 10s. grey-green and black .. .. 65·00 £110
66 £1 grey and carmine £180 £150
67 £10 grey and blue (Optd S. £200) .. £3500 £3250
59/66 .. .. .. *Set of* 9 £275 £325
59/66 Optd "Specimen" .. .. *Set of* 9 £275

1907. *Wmk Mult Crown CA. Chalk-surfaced paper. P* 14.
68 **11** 1d. grey and carmine .. .. .. 1·50 90
69 2d. dull and bright purple £8000
70 4d. grey-green and black £8000
71 6d. grey and reddish buff .. .. 26·00 35·00

Nos. 69/70 were not issued in Nyasaland.

NYASALAND PROTECTORATE

The title of the Protectorate was changed again from 6 July 1907.

13

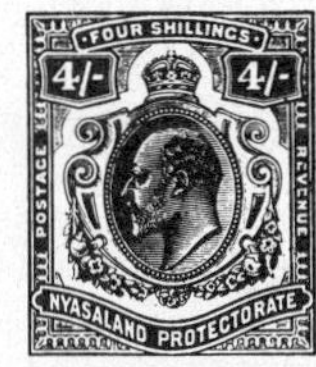

14

(Typo D.L.R.)

1908 (22 July). *P* 14. (*a*) *Wmk Crown CA. Chalk-surfaced paper.*
72 **13** 1s. black/*green* .. .. 1·40 5·50

(*b*) *Wmk Mult Crown CA. Ordinary paper* (½*d.*, 1*d.*) *or chalk-surfaced paper* (*others*).
73 **13** ½d. green 65 60
74 1d. carmine .. .. .. 1·00 20
75 3d. purple/*yellow* .. .. .. 1·00 2·25
76 4d. black and red/*yellow* .. .. 1·00 1·50
77 6d. dull purple and bright purple .. 3·75 6·00
78 **14** 2s. 6d. black and red/*blue* .. .. 32·00 55·00
79 4s. carmine and black .. .. .. 55·00 70·00
80 10s. green and red/*green* .. .. 70·00 £110
81 £1 purple and black/*red* £375 £425
82 £10 purple & ultramarine (Optd S. £450) £7000 £4250
72/81 .. .. .. *Set of* 10 £475 £600
72/81 Optd "Specimen" .. .. *Set of* 10 £400

15

16

1913 (1 Apr)–**19.** *Wmk Mult Crown CA. Ordinary paper* (½*d. to* 2½*d.*) *or chalk-surfaced paper* (*others*). *P* 14.
83 **15** ½d. green 50 60
84 ½d. blue-green (1918) 50 60
85 1d. carmine-red 75 60
86 1d. scarlet (1916) 55 45
87 2d. grey (1916) .. .. .. 1·25 60
88 2d. slate .. .. .. 2·50 1·00
89 2½d. bright blue .. .. .. 70 2·00
90 3d. purple/*yellow* (1914) .. .. 2·00 2·25
a. On pale yellow .. .. 2·50 6·50
91 4d. black and red/*yellow* (*shades*) .. 2·00 2·00
a. On pale yellow .. .. 3·75 7·00
92 6d. dull and bright purple .. .. 2·50 4·75
92*a* 6d. dull purple and bright violet .. 6·50 10·00
93 **15** 1s. black/*green* .. .. .. 1·75 4·75
a. On blue-green, olive back .. 2·00 1·50
b. On emerald back (Optd S. £35) .. 1·00 4·00
94 **16** 2s. 6d. black and red/*blue* .. .. 9·50 10·00
a. Break in scroll .. .. 65·00
b. Broken crown and scroll .. .. 65·00
95 4s. carmine and black .. .. 10·00 28·00
a. Break in scroll .. .. 85·00
b. Broken crown and scroll .. .. 85·00
96 10s. pale green and deep scarlet/*green* 48·00 70·00
a. Break in scroll £150
b. Broken crown and scroll £150
c. Green and deep scarlet/green (1919) 48·00 70·00
98 £1 purple and black/*red* £150 £140
a. Break in scroll £350
b. Broken crown and scroll £350
99 £10 purple & dull ultram (Optd S. £300) £3500
a. Purple and royal blue (1919) .. £2750 £1500
ab. Break in scroll .. ..
ac. Broken crown and scroll .. ..
83/98 .. .. .. *Set of* 12 £180 £200
83/98 Optd "Specimen" .. .. *Set of* 12 £350

For illustrations of the varieties on Nos. 94/9 see above Leeward Islands No. 58.

For stamps overprinted "N.F." see TANZANIA.

1921–30. *Wmk Mult Script CA. Ordinary paper* (½*d. to* 2*d.*) *or chalk-surfaced paper* (*others*). *P* 14.
100 **15** ½d. green 60 20
101 1d. carmine 50 25
102 1½d. orange .. .. .. 3·25 15·00
103 2d. grey 55 20
105 3d. purple/*pale yellow* .. .. 4·75 2·50
106 4d. black and red/*yellow* .. .. 2·50 4·25
107 6d. dull and bright purple .. .. 3·00 3·25
108 1s. black/*emerald* (1930) .. .. 5·50 6·50
109 2s. purple and blue/*blue* .. .. 9·00 10·00
a. Break in scroll .. .. 60·00
b. Broken crown and scroll .. .. 60·00
110 **16** 2s. 6d. black and red/*blue* (1924) .. 12·00 15·00
a. Break in scroll .. .. 70·00
b. Broken crown and scroll .. .. 70·00
111 4s. carmine and black .. .. 10·00 12·00
a. Break in scroll .. .. 75·00
b. Broken crown and scroll .. .. 75·00
112 5s. green and red/*yellow* (1929) .. 27·00 42·00
a. Break in scroll £110
b. Broken crown and scroll £110
113 10s. green and red/*pale emerald* (1926) 65·00 85·00
a. Break in scroll £180
b. Broken crown and scroll £180
c. Green and scarlet/emerald (1927) £225 £400
ca. Break in scroll £500
cb. Broken crown and scroll £500
100/13 .. .. .. *Set of* 13 £130 £160
100/13 Optd "Specimen" .. .. *Set of* 13 £325

For illustrations of the varieties on Nos. 109/13 see above Leeward Islands No. 58.

17 King George V and Symbol of the Protectorate

(Des Major H. E. Green. Recess Waterlow)

1934 (June)–**35.** *Wmk Mult Script CA. P* 12½.
114 **17** ½d. green 75 45
115 1d. brown 75 40
116 1½d. carmine .. .. .. 75 1·25
117 2d. pale grey .. .. .. 80 1·00
118 3d. blue .. .. .. 1·50 1·25
119 4d. bright magenta (20.5.35) .. .. 2·25 1·75
120 6d. violet .. .. .. 1·50 40
121 9d. olive-bistre (20.5.35) .. .. 2·50 8·50
122 1s. black and orange .. .. 2·50 5·50
114/22 .. .. .. *Set of* 9 12·00 18·00
114/22 Perf "Specimen" .. .. *Set of* 9 £120

1935 (6 May). *Silver Jubilee. As Nos.* 114/17 *of Jamaica, but ptd by Waterlow. P* 11×12.
123 1d. ultramarine and grey 65 45
j. Kite and vertical log .. .. 30·00
124 2d. green and indigo 70 45
125 3d. brown and deep blue .. .. 6·00 9·50
j. Kite and vertical log .. .. 80·00
126 1s. slate and purple .. .. .. 13·00 17·00
j. Kite and vertical log £120
123/6 .. .. .. *Set of* 4 18·00 25·00
123/6 Perf "Specimen" .. .. *Set of* 4 75·00

For illustration of plate variety see Omnibus section following Zimbabwe.

1937 (12 May). *Coronation. As Nos.* 118/20 *of Jamaica, but ptd by B.W. P* 11×11½.
127 ½d. green 30 20
128 1d. brown 55 20
129 2d. grey-black 55 40
127/9 .. .. .. *Set of* 3 1·25 70
127/9 Perf "Specimen" .. .. *Set of* 3 55·00

18 Symbol of the Protectorate

19

(T **18** recess Waterlow; T **19** typo D.L.R.)

1938 (1 Jan)–**44.** *Chalk-surfaced paper* (2*s. to* £1). *P* 12½ (*T* **18**) *or* 14 (*T* **19**). (*a*) *Wmk Mult Script CA*
130 **18** ½d. green 30 20
130*a* ½d. brown (12.12.42) 10 40
131 1d. brown 30 10
131*a* 1d. green (12.12.42) 10 10
132 1½d. carmine .. .. .. 55 2·25
132*a* 1½d. grey (12.12.42) .. .. .. 10 1·00
133 2d. grey 75 30
133*a* 2d. carmine (12.12.42) 10 20
134 3d. blue 10 10
135 4d. bright magenta 55 20
136 6d. violet 85 20
137 9d. olive-bistre .. .. .. 1·00 1·75
138 1s. black and orange .. .. 1·25 30
139 **19** 2s. purple and blue/*blue* .. .. 10·00 4·75
140 2s. 6d. black and red/*blue* .. .. 10·00 4·50
141 5s. pale green and red/*yellow* .. 38·00 14·00
a. Ordinary paper. *Green and red/ pale yellow* (3.44) .. .. 75·00 45·00
142 10s. emerald and deep red/*pale green* 38·00 18·00
a. Ordinary paper. *Bluish green and brown-red/pale green* (1.38) .. £225 85·00

(*b*) *Wmk Mult Crown CA*
143 **19** £1 purple and black/*red* .. .. 27·00 20·00
130/43 .. .. .. *Set of* 18 £120 60·00
130/43 Perf "Specimen" .. .. *Set of* 18 £600

No. 141a has a yellow surfacing often applied in horizontal lines giving the appearance of laid paper.

The printer's archives record the despatch of No. 142a to Nyasaland in January 1938, but no used examples have been reported before 1945.

21 King's African Rifles

20 Lake Nyasa

(Recess B.W.)

1945 (1 Sept). *T* **20**/**1** *and similar designs. Wmk Mult Script CA* (*sideways on horiz designs*). *P* 12.
144 ½d. black and chocolate 10 10
145 1d. black and emerald 10 40
146 1½d. black and grey-green 10 40
147 2d. black and scarlet 10 10
148 3d. black and light blue 10 20
149 4d. black and claret 50 35
150 6d. black and violet 75 15
151 9d. black and olive .. .. .. 60 2·00
152 1s. indigo and deep green 70 10
153 2s. emerald and maroon .. .. 3·25 3·25
154 2s. 6d. emerald and blue .. .. 4·25 2·50
155 5s. purple and blue .. .. .. 4·25 3·50
156 10s. claret and emerald .. .. 7·50 6·50
157 20s. scarlet and black .. .. 13·00 14·00
144/57 .. .. .. *Set of* 14 32·00 30·00
144/57 Perf "Specimen" .. .. *Set of* 14 £250

Designs: *Horiz*—1½d., 6d. Tea estate; 2d., 1s., 10s. Map of Nyasaland; 4d., 2s. 6d. Tobacco; 9d. Type **20**; 5s., 20s. Badge of Nyasaland. *Vert*—3d., 2s. Fishing Village.

1946 (16 Dec). *Victory. As Nos.* 141/2 *of Jamaica.*
158 1d. green 10 10
159 2d. red-orange 10 10
158/9 Perf "Specimen" .. .. *Set of* 2 50·00

26 Symbol of the Protectorate

27 Arms in 1891 and 1951

(Recess B.W.)

1947 (20 Oct). *Wmk Mult Script CA. P* 12.
160 **26** 1d. red-brown and yellow-green 20 10
160 Perf "Specimen" .. .. .. 45·00

1948 (15 Dec). *Royal Silver Wedding. As Nos.* 143/4 *of Jamaica.*
161 1d. green 15 10
162 10s. mauve .. .. .. 11·00 15·00

1949 (21 Nov). *75th Anniv of U.P.U. As Nos.* 145/8 *of Jamaica.*
163 1d. blue-green 30 15
164 3d. greenish blue .. .. .. 1·00 50
165 6d. purple .. .. .. 1·00 50
166 1s. ultramarine .. .. .. 1·00 50
163/6 .. .. .. *Set of* 4 3·00 1·50

(Des C. Twynam. Recess B.W.)

1951 (15 May). *Diamond Jubilee of Protectorate. Wmk Mult Script CA. P* 11 × 12.
167 **27** 2d. black and scarlet 50 30
168 3d. black and turquoise-blue 50 75
169 6d. black and violet 50 90
170 5s. black and indigo .. .. .. 1·10 5·00
167/70 .. .. .. *Set of* 4 2·40 6·25

28 Arms of Rhodesia and Nyasaland

29 Grading Cotton

(Recess Waterlow)

1953 (30 May). *Rhodes Centenary Exhibition. Wmk Mult Script CA. P 14×13½.*

171 **28**	6d. violet	10	15

1953 (2 June). *Coronation. As No. 153 of Jamaica, but ptd by B.W.*

172	2d. black and brown-orange	20	10

(Recess B.W.)

1953 (1 Sept)–**54**. *Designs previously used for King George VI issue, but with portrait of Queen Elizabeth II as in T* **29**. *Wmk Mult Script CA. P 12.*

173	½d. black and chocolate	10	55
	a. Perf 12 × 12½ (8.3.54)	10	40
174	1d. brown and bright green	30	10
175	1½d. black and deep grey-green	15	1·25
176	2d. black and yellow-orange	40	10
	a. Perf 12 × 12½ (8.3.54)	15	10
177	2½d. green and black	10	15
178	3d. black and scarlet	30	10
179	4½d. black and light blue	30	40
180	6d. black and violet	40	30
	a. Perf 12 × 12½ (8.3.54)	15	10
181	9d. black and deep olive	70	2·00
182	1s. deep blue and slate-green	35	10
183	2s. deep green and brown-red	2·00	2·75
184	2s. 6d. deep emerald and deep blue	2·75	4·00
185	5s. purple and Prussian blue	4·50	4·50
186	10s. carmine and deep emerald	4·00	7·00
187	20s. red and black	9·50	9·50
173a/87	*Set of* 15	22·00	29·00

Designs: *Horiz*—½d., 9d. Lake Nyasa; 1½d., 6d. Tea estate; 2d., 1s., 10s. Map of Nyasaland; 3d., 2s. 6d. Tobacco; 5s., 20s. Badge of Nyasaland. *Vert*—1d. Symbol of the protectorate; 4½d., 2s. Fishing village.

Stamps perf 12 × 12½ come from sheets comb-perforated 11.8 × 12.25. They were also issued in coils of 480 stamps made up from sheets.

For issues between 1954 and 1963, see RHODESIA AND NYASALAND.

30

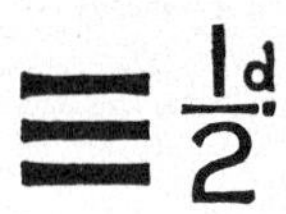

(31)

(Recess B.W.)

1963 (1 Nov). *Revenue stamps optd* "POSTAGE", *as in T* **30**, *or additionally surch as T* **31**. *P* 12.

188	½d. on 1d. greenish blue	20	15
189	1d. green	20	10
190	2d. scarlet	20	20
191	3d. blue	20	10
192	6d. brown-purple	20	10
193	9d. on 1s. cerise	30	25
194	1s. purple	35	10
195	2s. 6d. black	40	1·50
196	5s. chocolate	65	1·25
197	10s. yellow-olive	1·25	3·50
	a. Greenish olive	6·50	8·50
198	£1 deep violet	3·25	3·50
188/98	*Set of* 11	6·50	9·50

32 Mother and Child

33 Chambo (fish)

34 Tea Industry

35 Nyala

(Des V. Whiteley. Photo Harrison)

1964 (1 Jan). *Designs as T* **32/5**. *P* 14½.

199	½d. reddish violet	10	10
200	1d. black and green	10	10
201	2d. light red-brown	10	10
202	3d. red-brown, yellow-green & bistre-brown	10	10
203	4d. indigo and orange-yellow	20	20
204	6d. purple, yellow-green and light blue	30	10
205	1s. brown, turquoise-blue and pale yellow	15	10
206	1s. 3d. bronze-green and chestnut	90	10
207	2s. 6d. brown and blue	90	50
208	5s. blue, green, yellow and black	90	1·25
209	10s. green, orange-brown and black	1·50	3·00
210	£1 deep reddish purple and yellow	5·50	4·00
199/210	*Set of* 12	9·50	8·00

Designs: *As T* **32/3**—2d. Zebu Bull; 3d. Groundnuts; 4d. Fishing. *As T* **34**—1s. Timber; 1s. 3d. Turkish tobacco industry; 2s. 6d. Cotton industry; 5s. Monkey Bay, Lake Nyasa; 10s. Forestry, Afzelia.

Nyasaland attained independence on 5 July 1964 when the country was renamed Malawi.

MALAWI

INDEPENDENT

44 Dr. H. Banda (Prime Minister) and Independence Monument

(Des M. Goaman. Photo Harrison)

1964 (6 July). *Independence. T* **44** *and similar horiz designs. P* 14½.

211	3d. yellow-olive and deep sepia	10	10
212	6d. red, gold, blue, carmine and lake	10	10
213	1s. 3d. red, green, black and bluish violet	20	10
214	2s. 6d. multicoloured	30	35
	a. Blue omitted	£180	
211/14	*Set of* 4	50	45

Designs:—6d. Banda and rising sun. 1s. 3d. Banda and Malawi flag; 2s. 6d. Banda and Malawi coat of arms.

Six examples of No. 214a are known from the top horizontal row of an otherwise normal sheet.

48 Tung Tree

49 Christmas Star and Globe

(Des V. Whiteley. Photo Harrison)

1964 (6 July)–**65**. *As Nos. 199/210, but inscr* "MALAWI" *and T* **48** *(9d.). No wmk. P* 14½.

215	½d. reddish violet	10	35
216	1d. black and green	10	10
217	2d. light red-brown	10	10
218	3d. red-brown, yellow-green & bistre-brown	15	10
219	4d. black and orange-yellow	25	15
220	6d. bluish violet, yellow-green and light blue	40	10
221	9d. bistre-brown, green and yellow	30	15
222	1s. brown, turquoise-blue and pale yellow	25	10
223	1s. 3d. bronze-green and chestnut	50	40
224	2s. 6d. brown and blue	1·10	1·00
225	5s. blue, green, yellow and sepia	65	2·00
225*a*	5s. blue, green, yellow and sepia (1.6.65)	3·25	90
226	10s. green, orange-brown and black	1·50	2·00
227	£1 deep reddish purple and yellow	6·00	5·50
215/27	*Set of* 14	13·00	11·00

No. 225*a* is inscribed "LAKE MALAWI" instead of "LAKE NYASA".

See also Nos. 252/62.

(Des V. Whiteley. Photo Harrison)

1964 (1 Dec). *Christmas. P* 14½.

228 **49**	3d. blue-green and gold	10	10
	a. Gold (star) omitted	90·00	
229	6d. magenta and gold	10	10
230	1s. 3d. reddish violet and gold	10	10
231	2s. 6d. blue and gold	20	25
228/31	*Set of* 4	30	25
MS231*a*	83 × 126 mm. Nos. 228/31. Imperf	1·00	1·75

No. 228a comes from a sheet on which 41 examples had the gold colour omitted due to a paper fold.

50 Coins

(51)

(Des V. Whiteley. Photo Enschedé)

1965 (1 Mar). *Malawi's First Coinage. Coins in black and silver. P* 13½.

232 **50**	3d. green	10	10
233	9d. magenta	10	10
	a. Silver omitted	†	—
234	1s. 6d. purple	15	10
235	3s. blue	25	20
232/5	*Set of* 4	50	20
MS235*a*	126 × 104 mm. Nos. 232/5. Imperf	1·00	1·10

1965 (14 June). *Nos. 223/4 surch as T* **51**.

236	1s. 6d. on 1s. 3d. bronze-green and chestnut	10	10
237	3s. on 2s. 6d. brown and blue	20	20

On No. 237 "3/–" occurs below the bars.

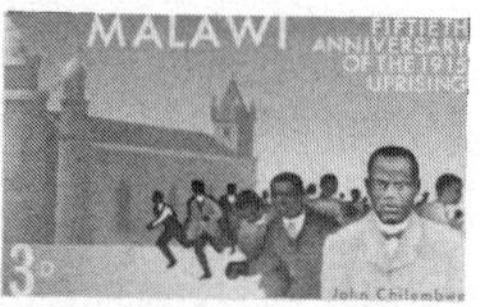

52 Chilembwe leading Rebels

(Des M. Goaman. Photo Harrison)

1965 (20 Aug). *50th Anniv of* 1915 *Rising. P* 14 × 14½.

238 **52**	3d. violet and light olive-green	10	10
239	9d. olive-brown and red-orange	10	10
240	1s. 6d. red-brown and grey-blue	10	10
241	3s. turquoise-green and slate-blue	15	15
238/41	*Set of* 4	30	20
MS241*a*	127 × 83 mm. Nos. 238/41	6·50	7·00

53 "Learning and Scholarship"

(Des H. E. Baxter. Photo Harrison)

1965 (6 Oct). *Opening of Malawi University. P* 14½.

242 **53**	3d. black and emerald	10	10
243	9d. black and magenta	10	10
244	1s. 6d. black and reddish violet	10	10
245	3s. black and blue	15	20
242/5	*Set of* 4	30	20
MS246	127 × 84 mm. Nos. 242/5	3·50	3·50

54 *Papilio ophidicephalus*

(Des V. Whiteley. Photo Enschedé)

1966 (15 Feb). *Malawi Butterflies. T* **54** *and similar horiz designs. Multicoloured. P* 13½.

247	4d. Type **54**	60	10
248	9d. *Papilio desmondi (magdae)*	85	10
249	1s. 6d. *Epamera handmani*	1·25	30
250	3s. *Amauris crawshayi*	2·50	3·00
247/50	*Set of* 4	4·75	3·00
MS251	130×100 mm. Nos. 247/50	15·00	11·00

55 Cockerels

56 Burley Tobacco

57 *Cyrestis camillus* (butterfly)

(New values des V. Whiteley (1s. 6d.), M. Goaman (£2). Photo Harrison)

1966–67. *As Nos. 215 etc. but* W **55** (*sideways on* ½*d.,* 2*d.*), *and new values and designs* (1*s.* 6*d.,* £2). *P* 14½.

No.	Type	Description	Unused	Used
252	–	½d. reddish violet (1.4.66)	10	10
253	–	1d. black and green (1.4.66)	15	10
254	–	2d. light red-brown (4.6.66)*	15	10
255	–	3d. red-brn, yell-grn & bis-brn (4.3.67)*	20	10
256	–	6d. bluish violet, yell-grn & lt bl (2.7.66)*	25	10
257	**48**	9d. bistre-brown, green & yell (5.12.66)*	35	10
258	–	1s. brown, turquoise-bl & pale yell (1.4.66)	25	10
259	**56**	1s. 6d. chocolate & yellow-grn (15.11.66)	30	10
260	–	5s. blue, green, yellow & sepia (6.10.66)*	7·50	2·00
261	–	10s. green, orange-brown & blk (6.10.66)*	17·00	12·00
262	**57**	£2 black, orange-yellow, pale yellow and slate-violet (7.9.66)	25·00	24·00
252/62		*Set of* 11	45·00	35·00

*These are local dates of issue. The Crown Agents, in London, did not distribute these printings until some time later.

No. 260 is inscribed "LAKE MALAWI".

The 2d. exists with both PVA gum and gum arabic.

58 British Central Africa 6d. Stamp of 1891

59 President Banda

(Des V. Whiteley. Photo Harrison)

1966 (4 May–10 June). *75th Anniv of Postal Services.* W **55**. *P* 14½.

No.	Type	Description	Unused	Used
263	**58**	4d. grey-blue and yellow-green	10	10
264		9d. grey-blue and claret	10	10
265		1s. 6d. grey-blue and reddish lilac	15	10
266		3s. grey-blue and new blue	25	30
263/6		*Set of* 4	45	35
MS267		83 × 127 mm. Nos. 263/6 (10 June)	4·25	3·25

REPUBLIC

(Des M. Goaman. Photo Harrison)

1966 (6 July). *Republic Day.* W **55**. *P* 14 × 14½.

No.	Type	Description	Unused	Used
268	**59**	4d. brown, silver and emerald	10	10
269		9d. brown, silver and magenta	10	10
270		1s. 6d. brown, silver and violet	10	10
271		3s. brown, silver and blue	15	15
268/71		*Set of* 4	30	20
MS272		83 × 127 mm. Nos. 268/71	1·75	2·25

60 Bethlehem

(Des and photo Harrison)

1966 (12 Oct). *Christmas.* W **55**. *P* 14½.

No.	Type	Description	Unused	Used
273	**60**	4d. myrtle-green and gold	10	10
274		9d. brown-purple and gold	10	10
275		1s. 6d. orange-red and gold	15	10
276		3s. blue and gold	40	50
273/6		*Set of* 4	65	55

61 *Ilala I*

(Des Mrs. H. Breggar. Photo Harrison)

1967 (4 Jan). *Lake Malawi Steamers. T* **61** *and similar horiz designs.* W **55**. *P* 14½.

No.	Description	Unused	Used
277	4d. black, yellow and bright green	20	10
	a. Yellow omitted		
278	9d. black, yellow and magenta	25	10
279	1s. 6d., black, red and violet	40	15
280	3s. black, red and bright blue	1·00	1·25
277/80	*Set of* 4	1·75	1·40

Designs:—9d. *Dove*; 1s. 6d. *Chauncy Maples I* (wrongly inscr "Chauncey"); 3s. *Gwendolen*.

62 Turquoise-gold Chichlid

(Des R. Granger Barrett. Photo Enschedé)

1967 (3 May). *Lake Malawi Chichlids. T* **62** *and similar horiz designs. Multicoloured.* W **55** (*sideways*). *P* 12½ × 12.

No.	Description	Unused	Used
281	4d. Type **62**	15	10
282	9d. Red Finned chichlid	20	10
283	1s. 6d. Zebra chichlid	30	10
284	3s. Golden chichlid	1·00	1·00
	a. Imperf (pair)	£140	
281/4	*Set of* 4	1·50	1·10

63 Rising Sun and Gearwheel

(Des Jennifer Toombs. Litho D.L.R.)

1967 (5 July). *Industrial Development. P* 13½ × 13.

No.	Type	Description	Unused	Used
285	**63**	4d. black and emerald	10	10
286		9d. black and carmine	10	10
287		1s. 6d. black and reddish violet	10	10
288		3s. black and bright blue	15	15
285/8		*Set of* 4	30	20
MS289		134 × 108 mm. Nos. 285/8	75	1·40

64 Mary and Joseph beside Crib

(Des Jennifer Toombs. Photo Harrison)

1967 (21 Nov–1 Dec). *Christmas.* W **55**. *P* 14 × 14½.

No.	Type	Description	Unused	Used
290	**64**	4d. royal blue and turquoise-green	10	10
291		9d. royal blue and light red	10	10
292		1s. 6d. royal blue and yellow	10	10
293		3s. royal blue and new blue	15	15
290/3		*Set of* 4	30	20
MS294		114 × 100 mm. Nos. 290/3. Wmk sideways. P 14 × 13½ (1 Dec)	1·00	2·50

65 *Calotropis procera*

(Des G. Drummond. Litho D.L.R.)

1968 (24 Apr). *Wild Flowers. T* **65** *and similar horiz designs. Multicoloured.* W **55** (*sideways*). *P* 13½ × 13.

No.	Description	Unused	Used
295	4d. Type **65**	15	10
296	9d. *Borreria dibrachiata*	15	10
297	1s. 6d. *Hibiscus rhodanthus*	15	10
298	3s. *Bidens pinnatipartita*	20	20
295/8	*Set of* 4	60	25
MS299	135 × 91 mm. Nos. 295/8	1·25	2·50

66 Saddleback Steam Locomotive, *Thistle* No. 1

(Des R. Granger Barrett. Photo Harrison)

1968 (24 July). *Malawi Locomotives. T* **66** *and similar horiz designs.* W **55**. *P* 14 × 14½.

No.	Description	Unused	Used
300	4d. grey-green, slate-blue and red	25	10
301	9d. red, slate-blue and myrtle-green	30	10
302	1s. 6d. multicoloured	55	15
303	3s. multicoloured	1·00	1·00
300/3	*Set of* 4	1·90	1·25
MS304	120 × 88 mm. Nos. 300/3. P 14½	3·00	5·50

Designs:—9d. Class "G" steam locomotive; 1s. 6d. Diesel locomotive *Zambesi*; 3s. Diesel railcar.

67 "The Nativity" (Piero della Francesca)

(Des and photo Harrison)

1968 (6 Nov). *Christmas. Paintings. T* **67** *and similar horiz designs. Multicoloured.* W **55** (*sideways on* 4*d.*). *P* 14 × 14½.

No.	Description	Unused	Used
305	4d. Type **67**	10	10
306	9d. "The Adoration of the Shepherds" (Murillo)	10	10
307	1s. 6d. "The Adoration of the Shepherds" (Reni)	10	10
308	3s. "Nativity with God the Father and Holy Ghost" (Pittoni)	15	10
305/8	*Set of* 4	30	20
MS309	115 × 101 mm. Nos. 305/8. P 14 × 13½	35	1·40

68 Scarlet-chested Sunbird

69 Nyasa Lovebird

70 Carmine Bee Eater

(Des V. Whiteley. Photo Harrison)

1968 (13 Nov). *Birds. T* **68/70** *and similar designs. Multicoloured.* W **55** (*sideways on* 1*d. to* 4*d. and* 3*s. to* £1). *P* 14½.

No.	Description	Unused	Used
310	1d. Type **68**	15	10
311	2d. Violet Starling	15	10
312	3d. White-browed Robin Chat	20	10
313	4d. Red-billed Fire Finch	35	30
	a. Red omitted		
314	6d. Type **69**	45	10
315	9d. Yellow-rumped Bishop	50	60
316	1s. Type **70**	60	15
317	1s. 6d. Grey-headed Bush Shrike	5·00	6·00
318	2s. Paradise Whydah	5·00	7·00
319	3s. African Paradise Flycatcher	4·50	3·75
320	5s. Bateleur	5·50	4·00
321	10s. Saddle-bill Stork	5·50	7·50
322	£1 Purple Heron	12·00	17·00
323	£2 Knysna Turaco	35·00	48·00
310/323	*Set of* 14	65·00	85·00

Sizes:—2d. to 4d. as T **68**; 9d. as T **69**; 1s. 6d., 2s., £2 as T **70**; 3s. to £1 as T **70** but vertical.

No. 310 exists in coils, constructed from normal sheets.

71 I.L.O. Emblem

(Des G. Drummond. Photo, emblem die-stamped Harrison)

1969 (5 Feb). *50th Anniv of the International Labour Organization.* W **55** (*sideways on No.* **MS**328). *P* 14.

No.	Type	Description	Unused	Used
324	**71**	4d. gold and myrtle-green	10	10
325		9d. gold and chocolate	10	10
326		1s. 6d. gold and blackish brown	10	10
327		3s. gold and indigo	15	15
324/7		*Set of* 4	30	20
MS328		127 × 89 mm. Nos. 324/7	2·25	6·50

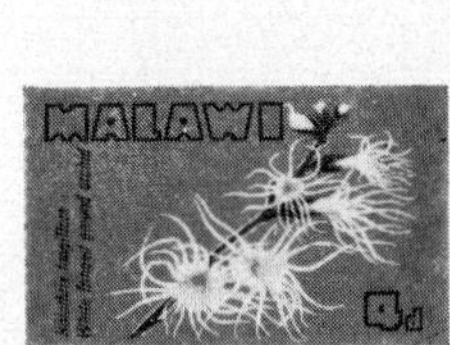

72 White-fringed Ground Orchid

73 African Development Bank Emblem

(Des J.W. Litho B.W.)

1969 (9 July). *Orchids of Malawi. T* **72** *and similar horiz designs. Multicoloured.* W **55**. *P* 13½ × 13.

No.	Description	Unused	Used
329	4d. Type **72**	15	10
330	9d. Red Ground orchid	20	10
331	1s. 6d. Leopard Tree orchid	30	10
332	3s. Blue Ground orchid	60	1·75
329/32	*Set of* 4	1·10	1·75
MS333	118 × 86 mm. Nos. 329/32	1·10	3·50

(Des G. Vasarhelyi. Litho D.L.R.)

1969 (10 Sept). *Fifth Anniv of African Development Bank.* W **55**. *P* 14.

No.	Type	Description	Unused	Used
334	**73**	4d. yellow, yellow-ochre and chocolate	10	10
335		9d. yellow, yellow-ochre & myrtle-green	10	10
336		1s. 6d. yellow, yell-ochre & blackish brn	10	10
337		3s. yellow, yellow-ochre and indigo	15	15
334/7		*Set of* 4	30	20
MS338		102 × 137 mm. Nos. 334/7	40	90

74 Dove over Bethlehem

75 *Zonocerus elegans* (grasshopper)

(Des Jennifer Toombs. Photo Harrison)

1969 (5 Nov). *Christmas. W* **55**. *P* 14½ × 14.
339 **74** 2d. black and olive-yellow 10 10
340 4d. black and deep turquoise 10 10
341 9d. black and scarlet 10 10
342 1s. 6d. black & deep bluish violet .. 10 10
343 3s. black and ultramarine 15 15
339/43 .. .. *Set of* 5 30 20
MS344 130 × 71 mm. Nos. 339/43 .. .. 1·00 1·75
a. Ultramarine (background of 3s.) omitted £400

(Des V. Whiteley. Litho Format)

1970 (4 Feb). *Insects of Malawi. T* **75** *and similar vert designs. Multicoloured. W* **55**. *P* 14.
345 4d. Type **75** 15 10
346 9d. *Mylabris dicincta* (beetle) 15 10
347 1s. 6d. *Henosepilachna elaterii* (ladybird) 20 10
348 3s. *Sphodromantis speculabunda* (mantid) 35 45
345/8 .. .. *Set of* 4 75 55
MS349 86×137 mm. Nos. 345/8 .. .. 1·25 2·25

Rand Easter Show
1970

(76)

1970 (18 Mar). *Rand Easter Show. No.* 317 *optd with T* **76**.
350 1s. 6d. multicoloured 15 80

77 Runner

(Des J. Cooter. Litho B.W.)

1970 (3 June). *Ninth British Commonwealth Games, Edinburgh. W* **55**. *P* 13.
351 **77** 4d. royal blue and blue-green 10 10
352 9d. royal blue and carmine 10 10
353 1s. 6d. royal blue and dull yellow .. 10 10
354 3s. royal blue and new blue 15 15
351/4 .. .. *Set of* 4 25 20
MS355 146 × 96 mm. Nos. 351/4 .. .. .. 55 90

(New Currency, 100 tambalas = 1 kwacha)

10t

(78)

79 *Aegocera trimeni*

1970 (2 Sept). *Decimal Currency. Nos.* 316 *and* 318 *surch as T* **78**.
356 10 t. on 1s. multicoloured 50 25
a. Surch double .. .. † —
357 20 t. on 2s. multicoloured .. .. .. 1·40 1·00

(Des R. Granger Barrett. Litho B.W.)

1970 (30 Sept). *Moths. T* **79** *and similar horiz designs. Multicoloured. W* **55**. *P* 11 × 11½.
358 4d. Type **79** 20 10
359 9d. *Faidherbia bauhiniae* 30 10
360 1s. 6d. *Parasa karschi* 50 10
361 3s. *Teracotona euprepia* .. .. 1·25 2·00
358/61 .. .. *Set of* 4 2·00 2·00
MS362 112×92 mm. Nos. 358/61 .. .. 3·75 4·50

80 Mother and Child

30t
Special United Kingdom Delivery Service

(81)

(Des Brother W. Meyer. Litho J.W.)

1970 (4 Nov). *Christmas. W* **55** *(sideways). P* 14.
363 **80** 2d. black and light yellow 10 10
364 4d. black and emerald 10 10
365 9d. black and orange-red 10 10
366 1s. 6d. black and light purple 10 10
367 3s. black and blue 15 15
363/7 .. .. *Set of* 5 25 25
MS368 166 × 100 mm. Nos. 363/7 .. .. 75 1·75

1971 (8 Feb). *No.* 319 *surch with T* **81**.
369 30 t. on 3s. multicoloured .. .. 20 1·75

No. 369 was issued for use on letters carried by an emergency airmail service from Malawi to Great Britain during the British postal strike. The fee of 30 t. was to cover the charge for delivery by a private service, and ordinary stamps to pay the normal airmail fee had to be affixed as well.

The strike ended on 8 March, when private delivery services were withdrawn.

82 Decimal Coinage and Cockerel

(Des V. Whiteley. Litho Format)

1971 (15 Feb). *Decimal Coinage. W* **55** *(sideways). P* 14.
370 **82** 3 t. multicoloured 10 10
371 8 t. multicoloured 10 10
372 15 t. multicoloured 15 10
373 30 t. multicoloured 25 30
370/3 .. .. *Set of* 4 45 35
MS374 140 × 101 mm. Nos. 370/73 .. .. 80 1·75

83 Greater Kudu

84 Eland

(Des and litho J.W.)

1971 (15 Feb)–**74**. *Decimal Currency. Antelopes. Vert designs as T* **83** *(1 t. to 8 t.), or T* **84** *(others). Multicoloured. W* **55** *(sideways on 1 t. to 8 t.). P* 13½ × 14 *(1 t to 8 t.) or* 14½ *(others).*
375 1 t. Type **83** 10 10
a. Coil stamp. P 14½×14 .. .. 15 30
b. Perf 14† (12.11.74) 45 45
376 2 t. Nyala 15 10
377 3 t. Mountain Reedbuck 20 10
a. Perf 14† (12.11.74) 65 65
378 5 t. Puku 40 10
a. Perf 14† (12.11.74) 65 80
379 8 t. Impala 45 10
380 10 t. Type **84** 60 10
381 15 t. Klipspringer .. .. .. 1·00 20
382 20 t. Suni .. .. 1·50 50
383 30 t. Roan Antelope .. .. .. 4·00 70
384 50 t. Waterbuck 90 65
385 1 k. Bushbuck .. .. 2·00 85
386 2 k. Red Forest Duiker .. .. .. 3·50 1·50
387 4 k. Common Duiker .. .. .. 19·00 17·00
375/87 .. .. *Set of* 13 30·00 19·00

No. 387 is incorrectly inscr "Gray Duiker".

† These actually gauge 14·2 × 14 instead of 13·7 × 14 and are line-perforated; in blocks they can easily be distinguished as in alternate rows across the sheet the horizontal perfs have two holes where they cross the vertical perfs; the watermark is also sideways inverted.

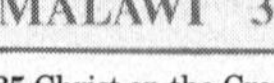

85 Christ on the Cross

87 *Holarrhena febrifuga*

(Des G. Drummond. Litho Questa)

1971 (7 Apr). *Easter. Details from Painting "The Small Passion" by Dürer. T* **85** *and similar vert design. W* **55**. *P* 13½.
388 3 t. black and green 10 10
a. Pair. Nos. 388/9 .. .. .. 10 10
389 3 t. black and green 10 10
390 8 t. black and orange-red 10 10
a. Pair. Nos. 390/1 .. .. .. 20 20
391 8 t. black and orange-red 10 10
392 15 t. black and violet 15 15
a. Pair. Nos. 392/3 .. .. .. 30 30
393 15 t. black and violet 15 15

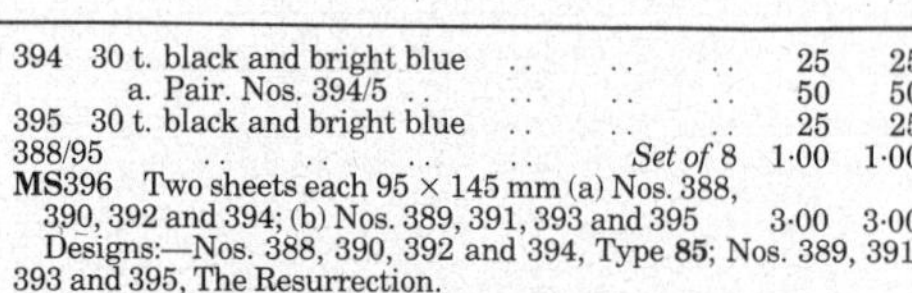

394 30 t. black and bright blue 25 25
a. Pair. Nos. 394/5 .. .. .. 50 50
395 30 t. black and bright blue 25 25
388/95 .. .. *Set of* 8 1·00 1·00
MS396 Two sheets each 95 × 145 mm (a) Nos. 388, 390, 392 and 394; (b) Nos. 389, 391, 393 and 395 3·00 3·00

Designs:—Nos. 388, 390, 392 and 394, Type **85**; Nos. 389, 391, 393 and 395, The Resurrection.

Nos. 388/9, 390/1, 392/3 and 394/5 were each printed together, *se-tenant*, in pairs throughout the sheet.

(Des G. Drummond. Litho J.W.)

1971 (14 July). *Flowering Shrubs and Trees. T* **87** *and similar vert designs. Multicoloured. W* **55**. *P* 14.
397 3 t. Type **87** 10 10
398 8 t. *Brachystegia spiciformis* 15 10
399 15 t. *Securidaca longepedunculata* 25 10
400 30 t. *Pterocarpus rotundifolius* 40 50
397/400 .. .. *Set of* 4 80 55
MS401 102 × 135 mm. Nos. 397/400 .. .. 1·25 2·00

88 Drum Major

89 "Madonna and Child" (William Dyce)

(Des J.W. Litho Questa)

1971 (5 Oct). *50th Anniv of Malawi Police Force. W* **55**. *P* 14 × 14½.
402 **88** 30 t. multicoloured .. .. .. 65 1·00

(Des J. Cooter. Litho Format)

1971 (10 Nov). *Christmas. T* **89** *and similar vert designs. Multicoloured. W* **55**. *P* 14½.
403 3 t. Type **89** 10 10
404 8 t. "The Holy Family" (M. Schöngauer) .. 15 10
405 15 t. "The Holy Family with St. John" (Raphael) 30 20
406 30 t. "The Holy Family" (Bronzino) 65 80
403/6 .. .. *Set of* 4 1·10 1·00
MS407 101 × 139 mm. Nos. 403/6 .. .. 1·40 2·50

90 Vickers "Viscount"

(Des R. Granger Barrett. Litho Questa)

1972 (9 Feb). *Air. Malawi Aircraft. T* **90** *and similar horiz designs. Multicoloured. W* **55** *(sideways). P* 13½.
408 3 t. Type **90** 25 10
409 8 t. Hawker Siddeley "748" 40 10
410 15 t. Britten-Norman "Islander" 65 30
411 30 t. B.A.C. "One-Eleven" .. .. .. 1·10 1·75
408/11 .. .. *Set of* 4 2·25 2·00
MS412 143 × 94 mm. Nos. 408/11 .. .. 7·50 5·50

91 Figures (Chencherere Hill)

92 Boxing

(Des R. Granger Barrett. Litho Format)

1972 (10 May). *Rock Paintings. T* **91** *and similar horiz designs. W* **55** *(sideways). P* 13½.
413 3 t. apple-green, grey-green and black .. 35 10
414 8 t. red, grey and black 45 10
415 15 t. multicoloured 70 30
416 30 t. multicoloured .. .. 1·00 1·00
413/16 .. .. *Set of* 4 2·25 1·25
MS417 121 × 97 mm. Nos. 413/16. P 15 .. .. 3·25 2·75

Designs:—8 t. Lizard and cat (Chencherere Hill); 15 t. Schematics (Diwa Hill); 30 t. Sun through rain (Mikolongwe Hill).

(Des local artist. Litho Harrison)

1972 (9 Aug). *Olympic Games, Munich. W* **55** *(sideways). P* 14 × 14½.
418 **92** 3 t. multicoloured 10 10
419 8 t. multicoloured 10 10
420 15 t. multicoloured 15 10
421 30 t. multicoloured 35 45
418/21 .. .. *Set of* 4 60 55
MS422 110 × 92 mm. Nos. 418/21. P 14 × 13½ .. 1·25 1·75

93 Arms of Malawi

94 "Adoration of the Kings" (Orcagna)

(Des G. Drummond. Litho Questa)

1972 (20 Oct). *Commonwealth Parliamentary Conference.* W **55**. P 13½.
423 **93** 15 t. multicoloured 30 35

(Des V. Whiteley. Litho Questa)

1972 (8 Nov). *Christmas. T* **94** *and similar vert designs. Multicoloured.* W **55**. P 14½ × 14.
424 3 t. Type **94** 10 10
425 8 t. "Madonna and Child Enthroned" (Florentine School) 10 10
426 15 t. "Virgin and Child" (Crivelli) 20 10
427 30 t. "Virgin and Child with St. Anne" (Flemish School) 45 70
424/7 .. .. *Set of* 4 70 80
MS428 95 × 121 mm. Nos. 424/7 .. .. .. 1·10 2·00

"**MALAŴI**". All issues from No. 429 onwards have a circumflex accent over the "W", to give the correct pronunciation of "Malavi".

95 *Charaxes bohemani*

(Des PAD Studio. Litho Questa)

1973 (7 Feb–5 Apr). *Butterflies. T* **95** *and similar horiz designs. Multicoloured.* W **55** (*sideways*). P 13½ × 14.
429 3 t. Type **95** 20 10
430 8 t. *Uranothauma crawshayi* 45 10
431 15 t. *Charaxes acuminatus* 65 30
432 30 t. *Amauris ansorgei* (inscr in error "EUPHAEDRA ZADDACHI") .. .. 3·00 6·00
433 30 t. *Amauris ansorgei* (inscr corrected) (5 Apr) .. .. 3·00 6·00
429/33 .. .. *Set of* 5 6·50 11·00
MS434 145×95 mm. Nos. 429/32 .. .. 7·00 11·50

96 Livingstone and Map

(Des J.W. Litho Format)

1973 (1 May). *Death Centenary of David Livingstone* (1st issue). W **55** (*sideways*). P 13½ × 14.
435 **96** 3 t. multicoloured 10 10
436 8 t. multicoloured 15 10
437 15 t. multicoloured 30 10
438 30 t. multicoloured 45 60
435/8 .. .. *Set of* 4 90 70
MS439 144 × 95 mm. Nos. 435/8 .. .. .. 90 1·50
See also Nos. 450/**MS**451.

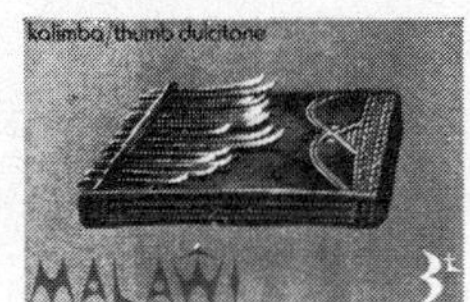

97 Thumb Dulcitone

(Des Jennifer Toombs. Litho Questa)

1973 (8 Aug). *Musical Instruments. T* **97** *and similar multicoloured designs.* W **55** (*sideways on* 8, 15 *t. and* **MS**444). P 14.
440 3 t. Type **97** 10 10
441 8 t. Hand zither (*vert*) 15 10
442 15 t. Hand drum (*vert*) 20 10
443 30 t. One-stringed fiddle 40 60
440/3 .. .. *Set of* 4 70 65
MS444 120 × 103 mm. Nos. 440/3 .. .. .. 2·25 2·00

98 The Magi

(Des J.W. Litho Format)

1973 (7 Nov). *Christmas.* W **55** (*sideways*). P 13½.
445 **98** 3 t. greenish blue, dp lilac & dull ultram 10 10
446 8 t. salmon-red, bluish lilac & red-brn 10 10
447 15 t. reddish mve, greenish bl & dp mve 15 10
448 30 t. orange-yell, bluish lilac & lt lake-brn 30 55
445/8 .. .. *Set of* 4 50 60
MS449 165 × 114 mm. Nos. 445/8 .. .. 75 1·40

99 Stained-glass Window, Livingstonia Mission

(Des PAD Studio. Litho Questa)

1973 (12 Dec). *Death Centenary of David Livingstone* (2nd issue). W **55** (*sideways*). P 13½.
450 **99** 50 t. multicoloured .. .. 45 1·00
MS451 71 × 77 mm. No. 450 .. .. .. 80 1·60

100 Largemouth Black Bass

(Des Sylvia Goaman. Litho Questa)

1974 (20 Feb). *35th Anniv of Malawi Angling Society. T* **100** *and similar horiz designs. Multicoloured.* W **55** (*sideways*). P 14.
452 3 t. Type **100** 20 10
453 8 t. Rainbow Trout 25 10
454 15 t. Lake Salmon 45 20
455 30 t. Tiger Fish 75 75
452/5 .. .. *Set of* 4 1·50 95
MS456 169 × 93 mm. Nos. 452/5 .. .. .. 1·50 1·60

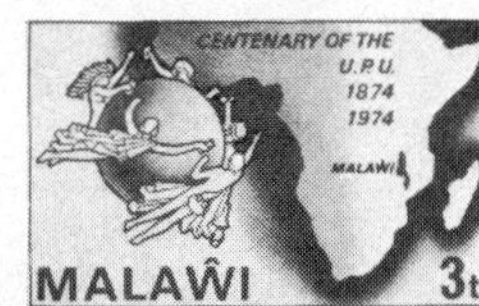

101 U.P.U. Monument and Map of Africa

(Des J. Cooter. Litho J.W.)

1974 (24 Apr). *Centenary of Universal Postal Union.* W **55** (*sideways*). P 13½ (Nos. 460/**MS**461) or 14½ × 14 (*others*).
457 **101** 3 t. green and ochre 10 10
a. Perf 13½ (pair) .. .. ..
458 8 t. red and ochre 10 10
459 15 t. violet and ochre 15 10
460 30 t. indigo and ochre 30 70
457/60 .. .. *Set of* 4 60 80
MS461 115 × 146 mm. Nos. 457/60 .. .. 65 1·75
a. Perf 14½ × 14 .. .. .. † —
No. 457a comes from normal sheets and not No. **MS**461. It can also be identified as a marginal single.

102 Capital Hill, Lilongwe

(Des PAD Studio. Litho Questa)

1974 (3 July). *Tenth Anniv of Independence.* W **55** (*sideways*). P 14.
462 **102** 3 t. multicoloured 10 10
463 8 t. multicoloured 10 10
464 15 t. multicoloured 10 10
465 30 t. multicoloured 25 35
462/5 .. .. *Set of* 4 40 40
MS466 120 × 86 mm. Nos. 462/5 .. .. .. 45 1·00

103 "Madonna of the Meadow" (Bellini)

104 Arms of Malawi

(Des Jennifer Toombs. Litho Enschedé)

1974 (4 Dec). *Christmas. T* **103** *and similar horiz designs. Multicoloured.* W **55** (*sideways*). P 13 × 13½.
467 3 t. Type **103** 10 10
468 8 t. "The Holy Family with Sts. John and Elizabeth" (Jordaens) 10 10
469 15 t. "The Nativity" (Pieter de Grebber) .. 15 10
470 30 t. "Adoration of the Shepherds" (Lorenzo di Credi) 30 50
467/70 .. .. *Set of* 4 50 50
MS471 163 × 107 mm. Nos. 467/70 .. .. 60 1·25

(Des and litho Harrison)

1975 (1 Feb)–**84**. *Coil stamps.* W **55** (*sideways*). P 14½×14.
472 **104** 1 t. deep blue 10 30
472*a* 5 t. bright carmine (20.9.84) 20 30

105 African Snipe 106 Spur-winged Goose

(Des J.W. Litho Questa)

1975 (19 Feb). *Birds. T* **105/6** *and similar multicoloured designs.* W **55** (*sideways on* 2, 3, 8, 50 *t.*, 1 *k.*, 4 *k.*). *White, ordinary paper.*

(*a*) *Size as T* **105**. P 13½ × 14 (1, 5 *t.*) *or* 14 × 13½ (*others*)
473 1 t. Type **105** 30 70
474 2 t. Double-banded Sandgrouse 50 60
475 3 t. Blue Quail .. .. 1·50 40
476 5 t. Bare-throated Francolin .. .. .. 3·00 35
477 8 t. Harlequin Quail .. .. 4·25 45

(*b*) *Size as T* **106**. P 14
478 10 t. Type **106** .. .. 7·50 50
479 15 t. Barrow's Bustard .. .. .. 3·50 1·75
480 20 t. Comb Duck .. .. 1·00 1·25
481 30 t. Helmet Guineafowl .. .. .. 1·25 70
482 50 t. African Pigmy Goose .. .. .. 2·00 1·60
483 1 k. Garganey .. .. 3·00 4·00
484 2 k. White-faced Whistling Duck .. .. 12·00 9·50
485 4 k. African Green Pigeon .. .. 13·00 16·00
473/85 .. .. *Set of* 13 48·00 35·00
See also Nos. 501/4

107 M.V. *Mpasa*

108 *Habenaria splendens*

(Des R. Granger Barrett. Litho J.W.)

1975 (12 Mar). *Ships of Lake Malawi* (1st series). *T* **107** *and similar horiz designs. Multicoloured.* W **55** (*sideways*). P 13½.
486 3 t. Type **107** 15 10
487 8 t. M.V. *Ilala II* 25 10
488 15 t. M.V. *Chauncy Maples II* 40 20
489 30 t. M.V. *Nkwazi* 65 80
486/9 .. .. *Set of* 4 1·25 1·00
MS490 105 × 142 mm. Nos. 486/9. P 14 .. .. 1·75 2·75
See also Nos. 728/32.

(Des Sylvia Goaman. Litho Questa)

1975 (6 June). *Malawi Orchids. T* **108** *and similar vert designs. Multicoloured.* W **55**. P 14.
491 3 t. Type **108** 15 10
492 10 t. *Eulophia cucullata* 25 10
493 20 t. *Disa welwitschii* 40 20
494 40 t. *Angraecum conchiferum* 70 85
491/4 .. .. *Set of* 4 1·40 1·00
MS495 127 × 111 mm. Nos. 491/4 .. .. .. 3·75 4·00

109 Thick-tailed Bushbaby

10th ACP
Ministerial
Conference
1975
(110)

(Des R. Granger Barrett. Litho Walsall)

1975 (3 Sept). *Malawi Animals. T* **109** *and similar vert designs. Multicoloured. W* **55** *(inverted). P* 14.
496 3 t. Type **109**.. .. .. 10 10
497 10 t. Leopard 35 10
498 20 t. Roan Antelope 55 30
499 40 t. Common Zebra .. .. 1·00 1·75
496/9 .. .. *Set of* 4 1·75 2·00
MS500 88 × 130 mm. Nos. 496/9. W **55** (sideways) 2·50 3·00

1975 (1 Oct). *As Nos.* 473 *etc, but no wmk. Toned, chalk-surfaced paper.*
501 3 t. Blue Quail .. .. 2·50 1·25
502 10 t. Type **106** .. .. 2·00 1·25
503 15 t. Barrow's Bustard .. .. 2·00 1·75
504 2 k. White-faced Whistling Duck .. .. 9·50 9·50
501/4 .. .. *Set of* 4 14·50 12·50
Nos. 505/13 vacant.

1975 (9 Dec). *Tenth Africa, Caribbean and Pacific Ministerial Conference. No.* 482 *optd with T* **110**.
514 50 t. African Pigmy Goose .. .. 75 1·10

111 "A Castle with the Adoration of the Magi"

112 Alexander Graham Bell

(Des PAD Studio. Litho J.W.)

1975 (12 Dec). *Christmas. T* **111** *and similar horiz designs showing religious medallions. Multicoloured. W* **55** *(sideways). P* 13 × 13½.
515 3 t. Type **111**.. .. .. 10 10
516 10 t. "The Nativity" 15 10
517 20 t. "The Adoration of the Magi" 20 10
518 40 t. "The Angel appearing to the Shepherds" 50 85
515/18 .. .. *Set of* 4 80 95
MS519 98 × 168 mm. Nos. 515/18. P 14 .. .. 1·50 2·75

(Des C. Abbott. Litho Questa)

1976 (24 Mar). *Centenary of the Telephone. W* **55**. *P* 14.
520 **112** 3 t. black and dull green 10 10
521 10 t. black and magenta.. .. .. 10 10
522 20 t. black and light reddish violet .. 20 10
523 40 t. black and bright blue 50 70
520/3 .. .. *Set of* 4 80 80
MS524 137 × 114 mm. Nos. 520/3 .. .. 1·10 1·75

113 President Banda

114 Bagnall Diesel Shunter

(Des PAD Studio. Litho J.W.)

1976 (2 July). *Tenth Anniv of the Republic. Multicoloured; frame colour given. W* **55**. *P* 13.
525 **113** 3 t. green 10 10
526 10 t. magenta 10 10
527 20 t. new blue 20 10
528 40 t. dull ultramarine 50 70
525/8 .. .. *Set of* 4 80 80
MS529 102 × 112 mm. Nos. 524/8. P 13½ .. 95 1·50

(Des G. Drummond. Litho Questa)

1976 (1 Oct). *Malawi Locomotives. T* **114** *and similar horiz designs. Multicoloured. W* **55** *(sideways). P* 14½ × 14.
530 3 t. Type **114**.. .. .. 15 10
531 10 t. "Shire" Class diesel locomotive .. 40 10
532 20 t. Nippon Sharyo diesel locomotive .. 80 45
533 40 t. Hunslet diesel locomotive .. .. 1·75 2·25
530/3 .. .. *Set of* 4 2·75 2·50
MS534 130 × 118 mm. Nos. 530/3 .. .. 2·75 3·50

Blantyre
Mission
Centenary
1876-1976
(115)

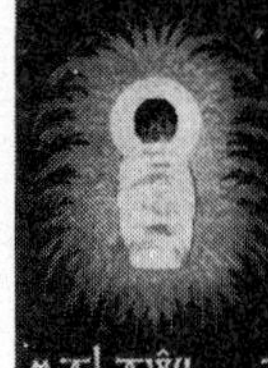

116 Child on Bed of Straw

1976 (22 Oct). *Centenary of Blantyre Mission. Nos.* 503 *and* 481 *optd with T* **115**.
535 15 t. Barrow's Bustard 55 70
536 30 t. Helmet Guineafowl .. .. .. 85 1·40

(Des Jennifer Toombs. Litho Walsall)

1976 (6 Dec). *Christmas. W* **55**. *P* 14.
537 **116** 3 t. multicoloured 10 10
538 10 t. multicoloured 10 10
539 20 t. multicoloured 20 10
540 40 t. multicoloured 40 60
537/40 .. .. *Set of* 4 70 70
MS541 135 × 95 mm. Nos. 537/40 .. .. 1·00 1·75

117 Man and Woman

118 Chileka Airport

(Des G. Hutchins. Litho Questa)

1977 (1 Apr). *Handicrafts. T* **117** *and similar multicoloured designs showing wood-carvings. W* **55** *(sideways on* 10 *and* 20 *t.). P* 14.
542 4 t. Type **117** 10 10
543 10 t. Elephant (*horiz*) 15 10
544 20 t. Rhino (*horiz*) 20 10
545 40 t. Deer 50 70
542/5 .. .. *Set of* 4 80 80
MS546 153 × 112 mm. Nos. 542/5. Wmk sideways 1·50 2·25

(Des Harrison. Litho Walsall)

1977 (12 July). *Transport. T* **118** *and similar horiz designs. Multicoloured. W* **55** *(sideways). P* 14½ × 14.
547 4 t. Type **118** 15 10
548 10 t. Blantyre-Lilongwe Road 25 10
549 20 t. M.V. *Ilala II* 80 30
550 40 t. Blantyre-Nacala rail line .. .. 1·50 1·40
547/50 .. .. *Set of* 4 2·40 1·60
MS551 127 × 83 mm. Nos. 547/50 .. .. 2·40 3·00

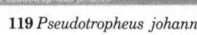

119 *Pseudotropheus johanni*

120 "Madonna and Child with St. Catherine and the Blessed Stefano Maconi" (Borgognone)

(Des R. Granger Barrett. Litho J.W.)

1977 (4 Oct). *Fish of Lake Malawi. T* **119** *and similar horiz designs. Multicoloured. P* 13½. *A. No wmk. B. W* **55** *(sideways).*

		A		B	
552 4 t. Type **119** ..	..	30	10	15	10
553 10 t. *Pseudotropheus livingstoni*		40	10	25	20
554 20 t. *Pseudotropheus zebra*	..	85	25	—	1·50
555 40 t. *Genyochromis mento*	..	95	95	95	95
552/5	*Set of* 4	2·25	1·25	†	
MS556 147 × 99 mm. Nos. 552/5. P 13		2·10	3·00	3·25	4·00

(Des G. Hutchins. Litho Enschedé)

1977 (21 Nov). *Christmas. T* **120** *and similar vert designs. Multicoloured; frame colours given. No wmk. P* 14 × 13½.
557 4 t. deep blue-green 10 10
558 10 t. light vermilion 10 10
559 20 t. dull violet 20 10
560 40 t. blue 50 70
557/60 .. .. *Set of* 4 80 80
MS561 150 × 116 mm. Nos. 557/60 .. .. 2·00 2·50
Designs:—10 t. "Madonna and Child with the Eternal Father and Angels" (Borgognone); 20 t. Bottigella altarpiece (detail, Foppa); 40 t. "Madonna of the Fountain" (van Eyck).

121 "Entry of Christ into Jerusalem" (Giotto)

122 Nyala

(Des G. Hutchins. Litho Cartor S.A., France)

1978 (1 Mar). *Easter T* **121** *and similar vert designs showing paintings by Giotto. Multicoloured. P* 12 × 12½.
562 4 t. Type **121** 10 10
563 10 t. "The Crucifixion" 10 10
564 20 t. "Descent from the Cross" 20 10
565 40 t. "Jesus appears before Mary" 40 55
562/5 .. .. *Set of* 4 70 70
MS566 150 × 99 mm. Nos. 562/5 .. .. .. 1·00 1·60

(Des G. Hutchins. Litho Enschedé)

1978 (1 June). *Wildlife. T* **122** *and similar multicoloured designs. P* 13½ × 13 (4, 40 *t.*) *or* 13 × 13½ (*others*).
567 4 t. Type **122**.. .. .. 25 10
568 10 t. Lion (*horiz*) 60 15
569 20 t. Common Zebra (*horiz*) 85 60
570 40 t. Mountain Reedbuck .. .. .. 1·40 2·00
567/70 .. .. *Set of* 4 2·75 2·50
MS571 173 × 113 mm. Nos. 567/70 .. .. 4·00 4·50

123 Malamulo Seventh Day Adventist Church

124 *Vanilla polylepis*

(Des and litho Walsall)

1978 (15 Nov). *Christmas. Churches. T* **123** *and similar horiz designs. Multicoloured. W* **55** *(sideways). P* 13½.
572 4 t. Type **123** 10 10
573 10 t. Likoma Cathedral 10 10
574 20 t. St. Michael's and All Angels', Blantyre .. 20 10
575 40 t. Zomba Catholic Cathedral 40 60
572/5 .. .. *Set of* 4 70 70
MS576 190 × 105 mm. Nos. 572/5 .. .. 70 1·50

(Des G. Drummond. Litho J.W.)

1979 (2 Jan). *Orchids. Vert designs as T* **124**. *Multicoloured. W* **55**. *P* 13½.
577 1 t. Type **124** 30 10
578 2 t. *Cirrhopetalum umbellatum* 30 10
579 5 t. *Calanthe natalensis* 30 10
580 7 t. *Ansellia gigantea* 30 10
581 8 t. *Tridactyle bicaudata* 30 10
582 10 t. *Acampe pachyglossa* 30 10
583 15 t. *Eulophia quartiniana* 40 15
584 20 t. *Cyrtorchis arcuata* (*variabilis*) 45 30
585 30 t. *Eulophia tricristata* 65 30
586 50 t. *Disa hamatopetala* 80 50
587 75 t. *Cynorchis glandulosa* .. .. .. 1·00 1·00
588 1 k. *Aerangis kotschyana* .. .. .. 1·40 80
589 1 k. 50, *Polystachya dendrobiiflora* .. .. 1·50 1·40
590 2 k. *Disa ornithantha*.. .. .. .. 1·75 1·60
591 4 k. *Cyrtorchis praetermissa* .. .. .. 3·00 3·50
577/91 .. .. *Set of* 15 11·50 9·00

125 Tsamba

126 Train crossing Viaduct

(Des L. Curtis. Litho Questa)

1979 (21 Jan). *National Tree Planting Day. T* **125** *and similar vert designs. Multicoloured. W* **55**. *P* 13½.
592 5 t. Type **125** 15 10
593 10 t. Mulanje Cedar 20 10
594 20 t. Mlombwa 30 20
595 40 t. Mbawa 60 75
592/5 .. .. *Set of* 4 1·10 95
MS596 118 × 153 mm. Nos. 592/5 .. .. 1·10 1·75

(Des J.W. Litho Questa)

1979 (17 Feb). *Opening of Salima-Lilongwe Railway. T* **126** *and similar horiz designs. Multicoloured. W* **55** *(sideways) (5 t.) or no wmk (others). P* 14½.

597 5 t. Type **126** 25 10
598 10 t. Diesel railcar at station 40 10
599 20 t. Train rounding bend 60 30
600 40 t. Diesel train passing through cutting .. 85 1·25
597/600 .. .. *Set of* 4 1·90 1·50
MS601 153 × 103 mm. Nos. 597/600. W **55** (sideways) .. .. 3·75 4·00

Examples of an unissued 4 t. value as Type **126** and of a miniature sheet containing this 4 t. value exist from supplies sent to Malawi before it was decided to increase the internal postage rate to 5 t.

127 Young Child

(Des BG Studio. Litho Questa)

1979 (10 July). *International Year of the Child. T* **127** *and similar horiz designs showing young children. Multicoloured; background colours given. W* **55** *(sideways). P* 13½.

602 5 t. green 10 10
603 10 t. red 10 10
604 20 t. mauve 20 10
605 40 t. blue 40 60
602/5 .. .. *Set of* 4 65 70

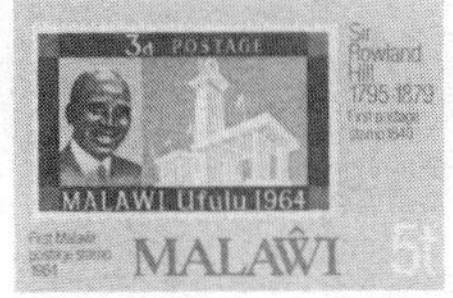

128 1964 3d. Independence Commemorative Stamp

(Des J.W. Litho Enschedé)

1979 (17 Sept). *Death Centenary of Sir Rowland Hill. T* **128** *and similar horiz designs showing 1964 Independence commemorative stamps. Multicoloured. W* **55** *(sideways). P* 13 × 13½.

606 5 t. Type **128** 10 10
607 10 t. 6d. value 10 10
608 20 t. 1s. 3d. value 20 10
609 40 t. 2s. 6d. value 35 60
606/9 .. .. *Set of* 4 65 70
MS610 163 × 108 mm. Nos. 606/9 .. .. 65 1·10

129 River Landscape

130 Limbe Rotary Club Emblem

(Des BG Studio. Litho Format)

1979 (15 Nov). *Christmas. T* **129** *and similar horiz designs showing landscapes. Multicoloured. W* **55** *(sideways). P* 13½ × 14.

611 5 t. Type **129** 10 10
612 10 t. Sunset 10 10
613 20 t. Forest and hill 25 10
614 40 t. Plain and mountain 50 50
611/14 .. .. *Set of* 4 85 65

(Des L. Curtis. Litho J.W.)

1980 (23 Feb). *75th Anniv of Rotary International. T* **130** *and similar vert designs. W* **55**. *P* 13½.

615 5 t. multicoloured 10 10
616 10 t. multicoloured 10 10
617 20 t. multicoloured 25 10
618 40 t. ultramarine and gold .. .. .. 60 1·40
615/18 .. .. *Set of* 4 95 1·50
MS619 105 × 144 mm. Nos. 615/18. P 14 × 14½. 1·40 1·75

Designs:—10 t. Blantyre Rotary Club pennant; 20 t. Lilongwe Rotary Club pennant; 40 t. Rotary International emblem.

131 Mangochi District Post Office

132 Agate Nodule

(Des C. Abbott. Litho Walsall)

1980 (6 May). *"London 1980" International Stamp Exhibition. T* **131** *and similar horiz designs. W* **55** *(sideways). P* 14½ × 14.

620 5 t. black and blue-green 10 10
621 10 t. black and vermilion 10 10
622 20 t. black and violet 15 10
623 1 k. black and deep blue .. .. .. 65 1·00
620/3 .. .. *Set of* 4 80 1·10
MS624 114 × 89 mm. Nos. 620/3 .. .. .. 2·00 2·25

Designs:—10 t. New Blantyre Sorting Office; 20 t. Mail Transfer Hut, Walala; 1 k. First Nyasaland Post Office, Chiromo.

(Des G. Drummond. Litho J.W.)

1980 (20 Aug). *Gemstones. T* **132** *and similar vert designs. Multicoloured. W* **55**. *P* 13.

625 5 t. Type **132** 30 10
626 10 t. Sunstone 45 10
627 20 t. Smoky Quartz 70 15
628 1 k. Kyanite crystal .. .. 2·25 2·00
625/8 .. .. *Set of* 4 3·25 2·00

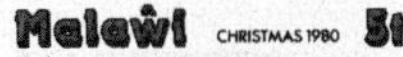

133 Elephants

134 Suni

(Des C. Abbott. Litho J.W.)

1980 (10 Nov). *Christmas. Children's Paintings. T* **133** *and similar horiz designs. Multicoloured. W* **55** *(sideways). P* 13.

629 5 t. Type **133** 10 10
630 10 t. Flowers 10 10
631 20 t. "Shire" class diesel train 20 10
632 1 k. Malachite Kingfisher .. .. .. 70 1·10
629/32 .. .. *Set of* 4 1·00 1·10

(Des G. Drummond. Litho Questa)

1981 (4 Feb). *Wildlife. T* **134** *and similar horiz designs. Multicoloured. W* **55** *(sideways). P* 14.

633 7 t. Type **134** 15 10
634 10 t. Blue Duiker 20 10
635 20 t. African Buffalo 30 15
636 1 k. Lichtenstein's Hartebeest .. .. .. 1·25 1·60
633/6 .. .. *Set of* 4 1·75 1·75

135 "Kanjedza II" Standard "A" Earth Station

(Des L. Curtis. Litho Harrison)

1981 (2 May). *International Communications. T* **135** *and similar horiz designs. Multicoloured. W* **55** *(sideways). P* 14½.

637 7 t. Type **135** 10 10
638 10 t. Blantyre International Gateway Exchange 15 10
639 20 t. "Kanjedza I" standard "B" earth station 25 15
640 1 k. "Satellite communications" .. .. 1·50 1·50
637/40 .. .. *Set of* 4 1·75 1·60
MS641 101 × 151 mm. Nos. 637/40 .. .. 2·00 2·75

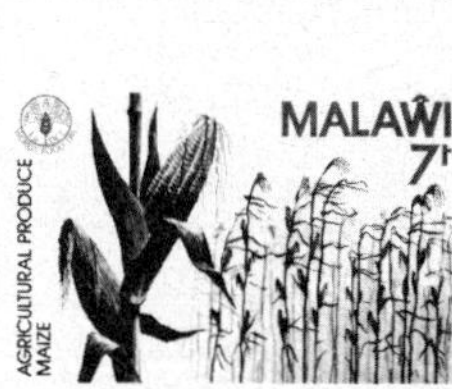

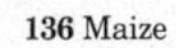

136 Maize

137 "The Adoration of the Shepherds" (Murillo)

(Des Jennifer Toombs. Litho Harrison)

1981 (11 Sept). *World Food Day. Agricultural Produce. T* **136** *and similar horiz designs. Multicoloured. W* **55** *(sideways). P* 14.

642 7 t. Type **136** 15 10
643 10 t. Rice 20 10
644 20 t. Finger-millet 30 20
645 1 k. Wheat .. .. 1·00 1·40
642/5 .. .. *Set of* 4 1·50 1·50

(Des BG Studio. Litho J.W.)

1981 (26 Nov). *Christmas. Paintings. T* **137** *and similar multicoloured designs. W* **55** *(sideways on 10 and 20 t.). P* 13½ × 13 *(7 t., 1 k.) or* 13 × 13½ *(others).*

646 7 t. Type **137** 15 10
647 10 t. "The Holy Family" (Lippi) (*horiz*) .. 20 10
648 20 t. "The Adoration of the Shepherds" (Louis le Nain) (*horiz*) 35 15
649 1 k. "The Virgin and Child, St. John the Baptist and an Angel" (Paolo Morando) 90 1·25
646/9 .. .. *Set of* 4 1·40 1·40

138 Impala Herd

(Des A. Theobald. Litho Harrison)

1982 (15 Mar). *National Parks. Wildlife. T* **138** *and similar horiz designs. Multicoloured. W* **55** *(sideways). P* 14½ × 14.

650 7 t. Type **138** 20 10
651 10 t. Lions 35 10
652 20 t. Greater Kudu 50 15
653 1 k. Greater Flamingoes .. .. .. 2·25 2·25
650/3 .. .. *Set of* 4 3·00 2·25

139 Kamuzu Academy

140 Attacker challenging Goalkeeper

(Des PAD Studio. Litho Questa)

1982 (1 July). *Kamuzu Academy. T* **139** *and similar horiz designs showing buildings. W* **55** *(sideways). P* 14½.

654 7 t. multicoloured 10 10
655 20 t. multicoloured 20 10
656 30 t. multicoloured 30 30
657 1 k. multicoloured .. .. 75 1·25
654/7 .. .. *Set of* 4 1·25 1·60

(Des and litho Harrison)

1982 (8 Sept). *World Cup Football Championship, Spain. T* **140** *and similar vert designs. Multicoloured. W* **55**. *P* 14 × 15.

658 7 t. Type **140** 35 10
659 20 t. FIFA World Cup trophy 70 40
660 30 t. Football stadium .. .. 90 1·00
658/60 .. .. *Set of* 3 1·75 1·40
MS661 80 × 59 mm. 1 k. Football .. .. .. 1·25 1·60

141 Blantyre War Memorial, St. Paul's Church

(Des W. Fenton. Litho Format)

1982 (5 Nov). *Remembrance Day. T* **141** *and similar horiz designs. Multicoloured. W* **55** *(sideways). P* 14½ × 14.

662 7 t. Type **141** 10 10
663 20 t. Zomba war memorial 15 10
664 30 t. Chichiri war memorial 20 30
665 1 k. Lilongwe war memorial .. .. .. 65 2·00
662/5 .. .. *Set of* 4 1·00 2·25

142 Kwacha International Conference Centre

143 "Christ and St. Peter"

(Des Walsall. Litho Format)

1983 (14 Mar). *Commonwealth Day. T* **142** *and similar horiz designs. Multicoloured.* W **55** *(sideways). P* 14.

666 7 t. Type **142** .. 10 10
667 20 t. Tea-picking, Mulanje .. 20 10
668 30 t. World map showing position of Malawi 30 30
669 1 k. President Dr. H. Kamuzu Banda .. 80 1·25
666/9 .. *Set of* 4 1·25 1·50

(Des C. Abbott. Litho Format)

1983 (4 Apr). *500th Birth Anniv of Raphael. Details from the cartoon for "The Miraculous Draught of Fishes" Tapestry. T* **143** *and similar multicoloured designs.* W **55** *(sideways on* 30 *t.). P* 14.

670 7 t. Type **143** .. 25 10
671 20 t. "Hauling in the Catch" .. 50 30
672 30 t. "Fishing Village" *(horiz)* .. 75 1·00
670/2 .. *Set of* 3 1·40 1·25
MS673 110 × 90 mm. 1 k. "Apostle" .. 1·10 1·25

144 Pair by Lake

145 Kamuzu International Airport

(Des N. Arlott. Litho Questa)

1983 (11 July). *African Fish Eagle. T* **144** *and similar vert designs. Multicoloured.* W **55**. *P* 14.

674 30 t. Type **144** .. 70 80
a. Horiz strip of 5. Nos. 674/8 .. 3·25
675 30 t. Making gull-like call .. 70 80
676 30 t. Diving on prey .. 70 80
677 30 t. Carrying fish .. 70 80
678 30 t. Feeding on catch .. 70 80
674/8 .. *Set of* 5 3·25 3·50

Nos. 674/8 were printed together, *se-tenant*, in horizontal strips of 5 throughout the sheet, the backgrounds of each design forming a composite picture of Lake Malawi.

(Des A. Theobald. Litho Questa)

1983 (31 Aug). *Bicentenary of Manned Flight. T* **145** *and similar horiz designs. Multicoloured.* W **55** *(sideways). P* 14.

679 7 t. Type **145** .. 10 10
680 20 t. Kamuzu International Airport *(different)* 25 15
681 30 t. BAC "One Eleven" .. 40 40
682 1 k. Flying boat at Cape Maclear .. 1·10 2·00
679/82 .. *Set of* 4 1·75 2·40
MS683 100 × 121 mm. Nos. 679/82 .. 2·00 3·50

146 *Clerodendrum myricoides*

147 *Melanochromis auratus*

(Des R. Reader. Litho J.W.)

1983 (1 Nov). *Christmas. Flowers. T* **146** *and similar vert designs. Multicoloured. P* 13 (20 *t.*) *or* 14 (*others*).

684 7 t. Type **146** .. 35 10
a. Perf 13 .. 15·00
685 20 t. *Gloriosa superba* .. 75 15
686 30 t. *Gladiolus laxiflorus* .. 1·00 40
687 1 k. *Aframomum angustifolium* .. 2·00 2·50
684/7 .. *Set of* 4 3·75 2·75

(Des L. Curtis. Litho Harrison)

1984 (2 Jan). *Fishes. T* **147** *and similar horiz designs. Multicoloured.* W **55** *(sideways). P* 14½ × 14.

688 1 t. Type **147** .. 10 15
689 2 t. *Haplochromis compressiceps* .. 15 20
690 5 t. *Labeotropheus fuelleborni* .. 20 20
691 7 t. *Pseudotropheus lombardoi* .. 20 10
692 8 t. Gold *Pseudotropheus zebra* .. 20 10
693 10 t. *Trematocranus jacobfreibergi* .. 20 10
694 15 t. *Melanochromis crabro* .. 30 10
695 20 t. Marbled *Pseudotropheus zebra* .. 30 10
696 30 t. *Labidochromis caeruleus* .. 40 20
697 40 t. *Haplochromis venustus* .. 60 30
698 50 t. *Aulonacara of* Thumbi .. 70 50
699 75 t. *Melanochromis vermivorus* .. 90 65
700 1 k. *Pseudotropheus zebra* .. 1·25 1·00
701 2 k. *Trematocranus spp.* .. 2·00 2·25
702 4 k. *Aulonacara of* Mbenje .. 2·75 4·00
688/702 .. *Set of* 15 9·25 9·75

Nos. 688 and 691/7 exist with different imprint dates at foot.

148 Smith's Red Hare

149 Running

(Des Garden Studios. Litho Format)

1984 (2 Feb). *Small Mammals. T* **148** *and similar horiz designs. Multicoloured.* W **55** *(sideways). P* 14.

703 7 t. Type **148** .. 30 10
704 20 t. Gambian Sun Squirrel .. 70 15
705 30 t. South African Hedgehog .. 1·00 50
706 1 k. Large-spotted Genet .. 2·25 3·25
703/6 .. *Set of* 4 3·75 3·75

(Des C. Collins. Litho Harrison)

1984 (1 June). *Olympic Games, Los Angeles. T* **149** *and similar vert designs. Multicoloured.* W **55** *(sideways). P* 14.

707 7 t. Type **149** .. 10 10
708 20 t. Boxing .. 25 15
709 30 t. Cycling .. 35 25
710 1 k. Long jumping .. 1·00 1·25
707/10 .. *Set of* 4 1·50 1·50
MS711 90 × 128 mm. Nos. 707/10. Wmk upright 1·50 2·75

150 *Euphaedra neophron*

151 "The Virgin and Child" (Duccio)

(Des and photo Courvoisier)

1984 (1 Aug). *Butterflies. T* **150** *and similar vert designs. Granite paper. P* 11½.

712 7 t. multicoloured .. 60 10
713 20 t. lemon, blackish brown and red .. 1·00 15
714 30 t. multicoloured .. 1·25 55
715 1 k. multicoloured .. 2·75 3·25
712/15 .. *Set of* 4 5·00 3·50

Designs:—20 t. *Papilio dardanus*; 30 t. *Antanartia schaeneia*; 1 k. *Spindasis nyassae.*

(Des C. Abbott. Litho Harrison)

1984 (22 Oct). *Christmas. Religious Paintings. T* **151** *and similar vert designs.* W **55**. *P* 14½.

716 7 t. Type **151** .. 30 10
717 20 t. "Madonna and Child" (Raphael) .. 75 15
718 30 t. "The Virgin and Child" (ascr to Lippi) .. 1·00 40
719 1 k. "The Wilton Diptych" .. 2·25 2·25
716/19 .. *Set of* 4 4·00 2·50

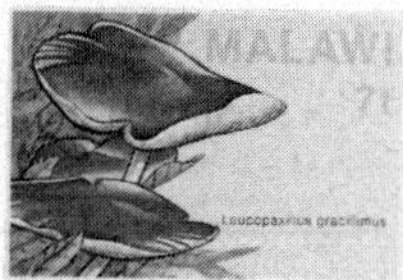

152 *Leucopaxillus gracillimus*

(Des A. Jardine. Litho Harrison)

1985 (23 Jan). *Fungi. T* **152** *and similar horiz designs. Multicoloured.* W **55** *(sideways). P* 14½ × 14.

720 7 t. Type **152** .. 60 10
721 20 t. *Limacella guttata* .. 1·25 25
722 30 t. *Termitomyces eurrhizus* .. 1·50 45
723 1 k. *Xerulina asprata* .. 2·50 3·25
720/3 .. *Set of* 4 5·25 3·50

153 Map showing Member States, and Lumberjack (Forestry)

(Des A. Theobald. Litho Harrison)

1985 (1 Apr). *5th Anniv of Southern African Development Co-ordination Conference. T* **153** *and similar horiz designs showing map and aspects of development.* W **55** *(sideways). P* 14.

724 7 t. black, yellowish green and pale green 40 10
725 15 t. black, scarlet-vermilion & salmon pink 60 15
726 20 t. blk, bright bluish violet & bright mauve 1·50 45
727 1 k. black, bright blue and cobalt .. 2·00 2·00
724/7 .. *Set of* 4 4·00 2·40

Designs:—15 t. Radio mast (Communications); 20 t. Diesel locomotive (Transport); 1 k. Trawler and net (Fishing).

154 M.V. *Ufulu*

155 Stierling's Woodpecker

(Des L. Curtis. Litho Cartor S.A., France)

1985 (3 June). *Ships of Lake Malawi (2nd series). T* **154** *and similar horiz designs. Multicoloured.* W **55** *(sideways). P* 13½ × 13.

728 7 t. Type **154** .. 55 10
729 15 t. M.V. *Chauncy Maples II* .. 1·00 15
730 20 t. M.V. *Mtendere* .. 1·25 30
731 1 k. M.V. *Ilala II* .. 3·00 3·00
728/31 .. *Set of* 4 5·25 3·25
MS732 120 × 84 mm. Nos. 728/31. P 13 × 12 .. 5·25 3·75

(Des M. Stringer. Litho Harrison)

1985 (1 Aug). *Birth Bicentenary of John J. Audubon (ornithologist). T* **155** *and similar vert designs. Multicoloured.* W **55**. *P* 14.

733 7 t. Type **155** .. 55 10
734 15 t. Lesser Seedcracker .. 1·00 20
735 20 t. East Coast Akelat .. 1·25 40
736 1 k. Boehm's Bee Eater .. 2·50 3·25
733/6 .. *Set of* 4 4·75 3·50
MS737 130 × 90 mm. Nos. 733/6. Wmk sideways .. 4·75 3·75

156 "The Virgin of Humility" (Jaime Serra)

157 Halley's Comet and Path of *Giotto* Spacecraft

(Photo Courvoisier)

1985 (14 Oct). *Christmas. Nativity Paintings. T* **156** *and similar vert designs. Multicoloured. Granite paper. P* 11½.

738 7 t. Type **156** .. 20 10
739 15 t. "The Adoration of the Magi" (Stefano da Zevio) .. 40 15
740 20 t. "Madonna and Child" (Gerard van Honthorst) .. 45 20
741 1 k. "Virgin of Zbraslav" (Master of Vissy Brod) .. 1·75 1·40
738/41 .. *Set of* 4 2·50 1·60

(Des N. Shewring. Litho Walsall)

1986 (10 Feb). *Appearance of Halley's Comet. T* **157** *and similar vert designs. Multicoloured.* W **55**. *P* 14½ × 14.

742 8 t. Type **157** .. 10 10
743 15 t. Halley's Comet above Earth .. 15 15
744 20 t. Comet and dish aerial, Malawi .. 20 20
745 1 k. *Giotto* spacecraft .. 85 1·00
742/5 .. *Set of* 4 1·10 1·25

158 Two Players competing for Ball

159 President Banda

(Des and photo Courvoisier)

1986 (26 May). *World Cup Football Championship, Mexico. T* **158** *and similar horiz designs. Multicoloured. Granite paper. P* 11½.

746 8 t. Type **158** .. 30 10
747 15 t. Goalkeeper saving goal .. 45 15
748 20 t. Two players competing for ball *(different)* .. 60 25
749 1 k. Player kicking ball .. 2·25 1·40
746/9 .. *Set of* 4 3·25 1·60
MS750 108 × 77 mm. Nos. 746/9 .. 5·50 5·50

(Des and litho Harrison)

1986 (30 June). *20th Anniv of the Republic. T* **159** *and similar vert designs. Multicoloured. P* 14.

751 8 t. Type **159** .. 30 30
752 15 t. National flag .. 40 15
753 20 t. Malawi coat of arms .. 45 25
754 1 k. Kamuzu Airport and emblem of national airline .. 1·50 1·25
751/4 .. *Set of* 4 2·40 1·75

It is reported that No. 751 was withdrawn locally five days after issue.

160 "Virgin and Child" (Botticelli)

161 Wattled Crane

(Des and photo Courvoisier)

1986 (15 Dec). *Christmas. T* **160** *and similar vert designs showing paintings. Multicoloured. Granite paper. P* 11½.

755 8 t. Type **160** .. 20 10
756 15 t. "Adoration of the Shepherds" (Guido Reni) .. 35 10
757 20 t. "Madonna of the Veil" (Carlo Dolci) .. 45 20
758 1 k. "Adoration of the Magi" (Jean Bourdichon) .. 2·00 1·40
755/8 .. *Set of* 4 2·75 1·60

(Des W. Oliver. Litho Walsall)

1987 (16 Feb)–**88**. *Wattled Crane. T* **161** *and similar horiz designs. Multicoloured. P* 14×14½. (*a*) *W* **55** (*sideways*).

759 8 t. Type **161** .. 40 10
760 15 t. Two cranes .. 65 15
761 20 t. Cranes at nest .. 80 30
762 75 t. Crane in lake .. 1·60 2·25
759/62 .. *Set of* 4 3·00 2·50

(*b*) *W* w **14** (*sideways*) (10.88)

763 8 t. Type **161** .. 40 10
764 15 t. Two cranes .. 65 15
765 20 t. Cranes at nest .. 80 20
766 75 t. Cranes in lake .. 1·40 1·75
763/6 .. *Set of* 4 3·00 2·00

162 Locomotive *Shamrock* No. 2, 1902

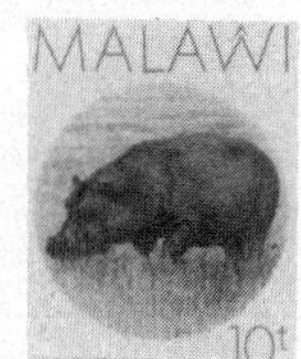

163 Hippopotamus grazing

(Des and litho Cartor S.A., France)

1987 (25 May). *Steam Locomotives. T* **162** *and similar horiz designs. Multicoloured. P* 14×13½.

767 10 t. Type **162** .. 50 10
768 25 t. "D" class, No. 8, 1914 .. 70 15
769 30 t. *Thistle* No. 1, 1902 .. 75 20
770 1 k. "Kitson" class, No. 6, 1903 .. 1·75 1·25
767/70 .. *Set of* 4 3·25 1·50

(Des and photo Courvoisier)

1987 (24 Aug). *Hippopotamus. T* **163** *and similar vert designs. Multicoloured. Granite paper. P* 12½.

771 10 t. Type **163** .. 30 10
772 25 t. Hippopotami in water .. 60 15
773 30 t. Female and calf in water .. 65 30
774 1 k. Hippopotami and egret .. 1·75 1·40
771/4 .. *Set of* 4 3·00 1·75
MS775 78×101 mm. Nos. 771/4 .. 3·00 3·00

164 *Stathmostelma spectabile*

165 Malawi and Staunton Knights

(Des and litho Harrison)

1987 (19 Oct). *Christmas. Wild Flowers. T* **164** *and similar vert designs. Multicoloured. P* 14.

776 10 t. Type **164** .. 25 10
777 25 t. *Pentanisia schweinfurthii* .. 50 15
778 30 t. *Chironia krebsii* .. 55 25
779 1 k. *Ochna macrocalyx* .. 1·75 1·10
776/9 .. *Set of* 4 2·75 1·40

(Des Jennifer Toombs. Litho Walsall)

1988 (8 Feb). *Chess. T* **165** *and similar vert designs showing local and Staunton chess pieces. Multicoloured. W* w **16**. *P* 14½×14.

780 15 t. Type **165** .. 50 15
781 35 t. Bishops .. 85 45
782 50 t. Rooks .. 1·25 80
783 2 k. Queens .. 3·00 3·25
780/3 .. *Set of* 4 5·00 4·25

166 High Jumping

167 Eastern Forest Scrub Warbler

(Des and litho Harrison)

1988 (13 June). *Olympic Games, Seoul. T* **166** *and similar vert designs. Multicoloured. P* 14.

784 15 t. Type **166** .. 20 10
785 35 t. Javelin throwing .. 35 20
786 50 t. Tennis .. 45 30
787 2 k. Shot-putting .. 1·40 1·25
784/7 .. *Set of* 4 2·25 1·75
MS788 91×121 mm. Nos. 784/7 .. 2·25 2·00

(Des N. Arlott (10 k.), Courvoisier (others). Litho Questa (10 k.) or photo Courvoisier (others))

1988 (25 July–3 Oct). *Birds. T* **167** *and similar vert designs. Multicoloured. W* w **14** *(sideways) (10 k.) or no wmk (others). Granite paper (1 t. to 4 k.). P* 15×14½ *(10 k.) or* 11½ *(others)*.

789 1 t. Type **167** .. 10 10
790 2 t. Yellow-throated Woodland Warbler .. 10 10
791 5 t. Moustached Green Tinkerbird .. 10 10
792 7 t. Waller's Red-winged Starling .. 10 10
793 8 t. Oriole-Finch .. 10 10
794 10 t. Starred Robin .. 10 10
795 15 t. Bar-tailed Trogon .. 10 10
796 20 t. Green-backed Twin-spot .. 10 10
797 30 t. African Grey Cuckoo Shrike .. 10 15
798 40 t. Black-fronted Bush Shrike .. 15 20
799 50 t. White-tailed Crested Flycatcher .. 20 25
800 75 t. Green Barbet .. 30 35
801 1 k. Lemon Dove ("Cinnamon Dove") .. 40 45
802 2 k. Silvery-cheeked Hornbill .. 80 85
803 4 k. Crowned Eagle .. 1·60 1·75
804 10 k. Anchieta's Sunbird (3 Oct) .. 4·25 4·50
789/804 .. *Set of* 16 7·50 8·00

167*a* Rebuilt Royal Exchange, 1844

168 "Madonna in the Church" (Jan van Eyck)

(Des D. Miller (15 t.), L. Curtis and D. Miller (35 t.), A. Theobald and D. Miller (50 t.), E. Nisbet and D. Miller (2 k.). Litho B.D.T.)

1988 (24 Oct). *300th Anniv of Lloyd's of London. T* **167***a and similar multicoloured designs. W* w **14** *(sideways on 35, 50 t.). P* 14.

805 15 t. Type **167***a* .. 20 10
806 35 t. Opening ceremony, Nkula Falls Hydro-electric Power Station .. 45 20
807 50 t. Air Malawi "1-11" airliner (*horiz*) .. 60 30
808 2 k. *Seawise University* (formerly *Queen Elizabeth*) on fire, Hong Kong, 1972 .. 1·90 1·90
805/8 .. *Set of* 4 2·75 2·25

(Des and litho Harrison)

1988 (28 Nov). *Christmas. T* **168** *and similar vert designs showing paintings. Multicoloured. P* 14.

809 15 t. Type **168** .. 20 10
810 35 t. "Virgin, Infant Jesus and St. Anna" (da Vinci) .. 35 20
811 50 t. "Virgin and Angels" (Cimabue) .. 45 40
812 2 k. "Virgin and Child" (Baldovinetti Apenio) .. 1·75 1·60
809/12 .. *Set of* 4 2·50 2·00

169 *Serranochromis robustus*

(Des and litho Harrison)

1989 (10 Apr). *50th Anniv of Malawi Angling Society. T* **169** *and similar horiz designs. Multicoloured. P* 14.

813 15 t. Type **169** .. 35 10
814 35 t. Lake Salmon .. 65 20
815 50 t. Yellow Fish .. 85 55
816 2 k. Tiger Fish .. 2·25 2·00
813/16 .. *Set of* 4 3·75 2·50

170 Independence Arch, Blantyre

(Des and litho Harrison)

1989 (26 June). *25th Anniv of Independence. T* **170** *and similar horiz designs. Multicoloured. P* 14.

817 15 t. Type **170** .. 20 10
818 35 t. Grain silos .. 35 20
819 50 t. Capital Hill, Lilongwe .. 50 45
820 2 k. Reserve Bank Headquarters .. 1·75 2·00
817/20 .. *Set of* 4 2·50 2·50

171 Blantyre Digital Telex Exchange

(Des and litho Harrison)

1989 (30 Oct). *25th Anniv of African Development Bank. T* **171** *and similar horiz designs. Multicoloured. P* 14.

821 15 t. Type **171** .. 20 10
822 40 t. Dzalanyama steer .. 40 20
823 50 t. Mikolongwe heifer .. 50 45
824 2 k. Zebu bull .. 1·75 2·00
821/4 .. *Set of* 4 2·50 2·50

172 Rural House with Verandah

(Des and litho Harrison)

1989 (1 Dec). *25th Anniv of Malawi–United Nations Co-operation. T* **172** *and similar horiz designs. Multicoloured. P* 14.

825 15 t. Type **172** .. 20 10
826 40 t. Rural house .. 40 20
827 50 t. Traditional hut and modern houses .. 50 45
828 2 k. Tea plantation .. 1·75 2·00
825/8 .. *Set of* 4 2·50 2·50

173 St. Michael and All Angels Church

(Des and litho Harrison)

1989 (15 Dec). *Christmas. Churches of Malawi. T* **173** *and similar horiz designs. Multicoloured. P* 14.

829 15 t. Type **173** .. 20 10
830 40 t. Catholic Cathedral, Limbe .. 40 20
831 50 t. C.C.A.P. Church, Nkhoma .. 50 45
832 2 k. Cathedral, Likoma Island .. 1·75 2·00
829/32 .. *Set of* 4 2·50 2·50

174 Ford "Sedan", 1915

175 Player heading Ball into Net

(Des and litho Cartor, France)

1990 (2 Apr). *Vintage Vehicles. T* **174** *and similar horiz designs. Multicoloured. P* 14×13½.

833 15 t. Type **174** .. 20 10
834 40 t. Two-seater Ford, 1915 .. 40 20
835 50 t. Ford pick-up, 1915 .. 50 40
836 2 k. Chevrolet bus, 1930 .. 1·50 1·60
833/6 .. *Set of* 4 2·40 2·00
MS837 120×85 mm. Nos. 833/6. P 13×12 .. 2·75 3·00

(Des and litho Questa)

1990 (14 June). *World Cup Football Championship, Italy. T* **175** *and similar vert designs. Multicoloured. P* 14.

838	15 t. Type **175**	20	10
839	40 t. Player tackling	40	20
840	50 t. Player scoring goal	50	35
841	2 k. World Cup	1·50	1·60
838/41	*Set of* 4	2·40	2·00
MS842	88×118 mm. Nos. 838/41	2·75	3·00

176 Anniversary Emblem on Map

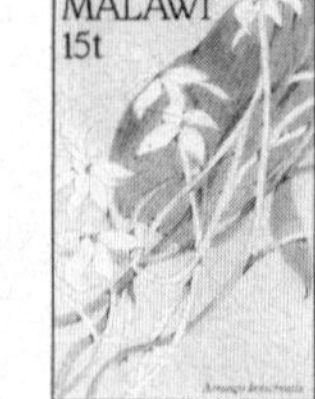

177 *Aerangis kotschyana*

(Des and litho Questa)

1990 (24 Aug). *Tenth Anniv of Southern Africa Development Co-ordination Conference. T* **176** *and similar horiz designs. Multicoloured. P* 14.

843	15 t. Type **176**	15	10
844	40 t. Chambo Fish	25	20
845	50 t. Cedar plantation	35	30
846	2 k. Male Nyala (antelope)	1·40	1·60
843/6	*Set of* 4	2·00	2·00
MS847	174×116 mm. Nos. 843/6	2·50	2·50

(Litho Cartor, France)

1990 (26 Nov). *Orchids. T* **177** *and similar vert designs. Multicoloured. P* 13½×14.

848	15 t. Type **177**	20	10
849	40 t. *Angraecum eburneum*	35	20
850	50 t. *Aerangis luteo-alba rhodostica*	45	30
851	2 k. *Cyrtorchis arcuata whytei*	1·50	1·50
848/51	*Set of* 4	2·25	1·90
MS852	85×120 mm. Nos. 848/51. P 12×13	2·50	2·50

178 "The Virgin and the Child Jesus" (Raphael)

179 Buffalo

(Litho Cartor, France)

1990 (7 Dec). *Christmas. Paintings by Raphael. T* **178** *and similar vert designs. Multicoloured. P* 13½×14.

853	15 t. Type **178**	15	10
854	40 t. "Transfiguration" (detail)	25	20
855	50 t. "St. Catherine of Alexandrie" (detail)	35	30
856	2 k. "Transfiguration"	1·40	1·50
853/6	*Set of* 4	2·00	1·90
MS857	85×120 mm. Nos. 853/6. P 12×13	2·50	2·50

(Litho Cartor)

1991 (23 Apr). *Wildlife. T* **179** *and similar horiz designs. Multicoloured. P* 14×13½.

858	20 t. Type **179**	15	10
859	60 t. Cheetah	40	35
860	75 t. Greater Kudu	50	40
861	2 k. Black Rhinoceros	1·25	1·40
858/61	*Set of* 4	2·10	2·00
MS862	120×85 mm. Nos. 858/61. P 13×12	2·10	2·10

180 Chiromo Post Office, 1891

181 Red Locust

(Litho Cartor)

1991 (2 July). *Centenary of Postal Services. T* **180** *and similar horiz designs. Multicoloured. P* 14×13½.

863	20 t. Type **180**	15	10
864	60 t. Re-constructed mail exchange hut at Walala	40	35
865	75 t. Mangochi post office	50	40
866	2 k. Satellite Earth station	1·25	1·40
863/6	*Set of* 4	2·10	2·00
MS867	119×83 mm. Nos. 863/6. P 13×12	2·25	2·25

(Litho Cartor)

1991 (21 Sept). *Insects. T* **181** *and similar vert designs. Multicoloured. P* 13½×14.

868	20 t. Type **181**	15	10
869	60 t. Weevil	40	35
870	75 t. Cotton Stainer Bug	50	40
871	2 k. Pollen Beetle	1·25	1·40
868/71	*Set of* 4	2·10	2·00

182 Child in Manger

(Litho Cartor)

1991 (26 Nov). *Christmas. T* **182** *and similar vert designs. Multicoloured. P* 13½×14.

872	20 t. Type **182**	10	10
873	60 t. Adoration of the Kings and Shepherds	25	30
874	75 t. Nativity	30	35
875	2 k. Virgin and Child	80	85
872/5	*Set of* 4	1·25	1·50

POSTAGE DUE STAMPS

D 1

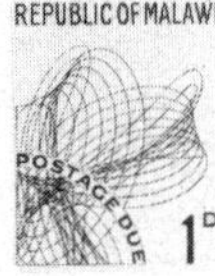

D 2

(Typo D.L.R.)

1950 (1 July). *Wmk Mult Script CA. P* 14.

D1	D 1	1d. scarlet	2·00	7·00
D2		2d. ultramarine	5·00	13·00
D3		3d. green	7·50	4·75
D4		4d. purple	12·00	30·00
D5		6d. yellow-orange	20·00	55·00
D1/5		*Set of* 5	42·00	£100

1967 (1 Sept). *W* **55**. *P* 11½.

D 6	D 2	1d. carmine	15	1·75
D 7		2d. sepia	20	1·75
D 8		4d. reddish violet	25	2·00
D 9		6d. blue	25	2·25
D10		8d. emerald	35	2·50
D11		1s. black	45	2·75
D6/11		*Set of* 6	1·50	11·50

1971 (5 Feb). *As Nos.* D6/11, *but values in tambalas. W* **55**. *P* 11½.

D12	D 2	2 t. greenish drab	20	1·75
D13		4 t. bright mauve	50	1·75
D14		6 t. royal blue	40	2·00
D15		8 t. dull green	45	2·00
D16		10 t. blackish brown	65	2·00
D12/16		*Set of* 5	2·00	8·50

(Litho Walsall)

1975–84. *Design redrawn, with circumflex accent over* "W" *of* "MALAWI". *P* 14. (a) *W* **55** (*sideways*).

D17	D 2	2 t. chestnut (15.9.75)	1·25	5·50
D18		2 t. brown (14.6.82)	10	10
D19		4 t. deep mauve (14.6.82)	10	10
D20		6 t. royal blue (9.84)	10	10
D21		8 t. green (9.84)	10	10
D22		10 t. black (14.6.82)	10	10
D17/22		*Set of* 6	1·40	5·50

(*b*) *No wmk*

D23	D 2	2 t. brown (19.10.77)	2·25	2·50
D24		4 t. mauve (19.10.77)	2·25	2·50
D25		8 t. green (15.12.78)	1·50	2·50
D26		10 t. brownish grey (19.10.77)	2·50	3·00
D23/6		*Set of* 4	7·75	9·50

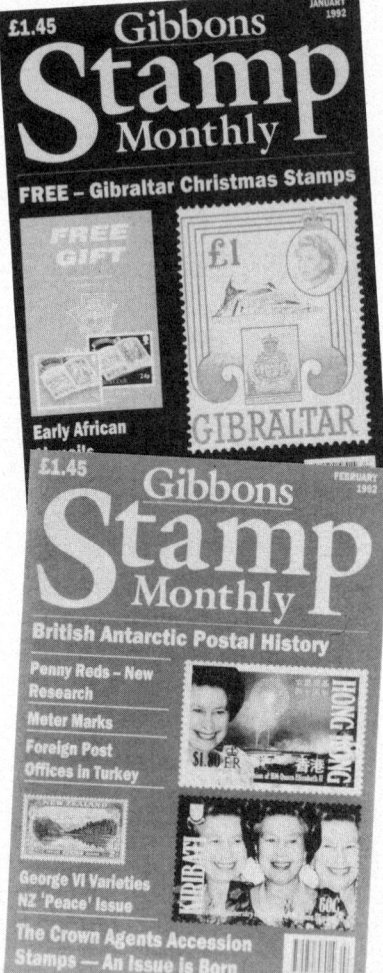

Malaysia

The Federation of Malaysia was set up on 16 September 1963, and consisted of the former Malayan Federation, the State of Singapore and the two former Crown Colonies in Borneo, Sabah (North Borneo) and Sarawak. Singapore left the federation to become an independent republic on 9 August 1965.

Malaysia now consists of thirteen States (11 in Peninsular Malaysia and two in Borneo), together with the Federal Territories of Kuala Lumpur and Labuan.

The philatelic history of the component parts of the federation is most complex. Under this heading are now listed previous issues made by the present States of the Federation.

The method adopted is to show the general issues for the area first, before dealing with the issues for the individual States. The section is divided as follows:

I. STRAITS SETTLEMENTS
II. FEDERATED MALAY STATES
III. MALAYAN POSTAL UNION
IV. MALAYA (BRITISH MILITARY ADMINISTRATION)
V. MALAYAN FEDERATION
VI. MALAYSIA
VII. MALAYAN STATES—Johore, Kedah, Kelantan, Malacca, Negri Sembilan (with Sungei Ujong), Pahang, Penang, Perak, Perlis, Selangor, Trengganu
VIII. JAPANESE OCCUPATION OF MALAYA
IX. THAI OCCUPATION OF MALAYA
X. LABUAN
XI. SABAH (NORTH BORNEO)
XII. JAPANESE OCCUPATION OF NORTH BORNEO
XIII. SARAWAK
XIV. JAPANESE OCCUPATION OF SARAWAK

I. STRAITS SETTLEMENTS

The three original Settlements, Malacca, Penang (with Province Wellesley) and Singapore (including Christmas Island and Cocos (Keeling) Islands) were formed into a Crown Colony during 1867. Labuan was attached to the colony in 1896, becoming the fourth Settlement in 1906.

The first known prestamp cover with postal markings from Penang (Prince of Wales Island) is dated March 1806 and from Malacca, under British civil administration, February 1841. The civil post office at Singapore opened on 1 February 1823.

The stamps of India were used at all three post offices from late in 1854 until the Straits Settlements became a separate colony on 1 September 1867.

The Indian stamps were initially cancelled by dumb obliterators and their use in the Straits Settlements can only be identified from complete covers. In 1856 cancellations of the standard Indian octagonal type were issued, numbered "B 109" for Malacca, "B 147" for Penang and "B 172" for Singapore.

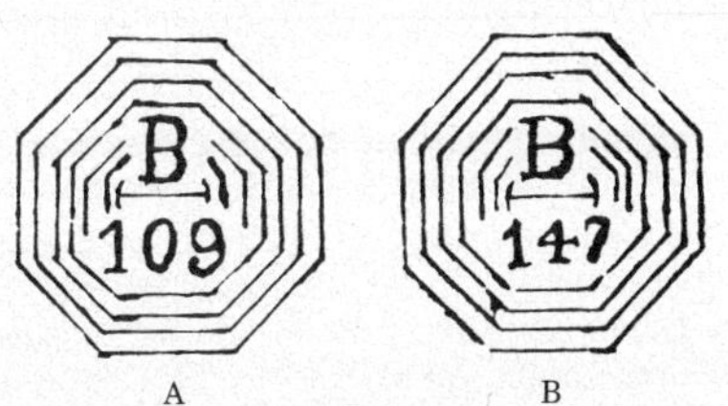

A B

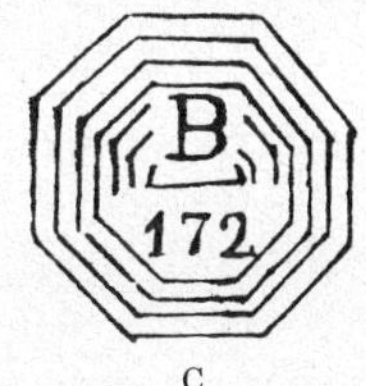

C

The Penang and Singapore octagonals were replaced by a duplex type, consisting of a double-ringed datestamp and a diamond-shaped obliterator containing the office number, in 1863 and 1865 respectively.

D

SINGAPORE AU 21 65 172

E

PRICES. Catalogue prices in this section are for stamps with clearly legible, if partial, examples of the postmarks.

MALACCA

Stamps of INDIA *cancelled with Type* A.

1854. (*Nos*. 2/34).
Z1 ½ a. blue (Die I) .. £500
Z2 1 a. red (Die I) .. £400
Z3 1 a. dull red (Die II) .. £450
Z4 2 a. green .. £700
Z5 4 a. blue and red (Head Die II) (*cut-to-shape*) .. £800

1855. (*Nos*. 35/6).
Z6 8 a. carmine (Die I)/*blue glazed* .. £120

1856–64. (*Nos*. 37/49).
Z7 ½ a. pale blue (Die I) .. 65·00
Z8 1 a. brown .. 55·00
Z9 2 a. yellow-buff .. 55·00
Z10 2 a. yellow .. 65·00
Z11 4 a. green .. £110
Z12 8 a. carmine (Die I) .. 80·00

1860. (*Nos*. 51/3).
Z13 8 p. purple/*bluish* .. £160
Z14 8 p. purple/*white* .. 80·00

1865. (*Nos*. 54/65).
Z15 4 a. green .. £100

PENANG

Stamps of INDIA *cancelled with Type* B.

1854. (*Nos*. 2/34).
Z20 ½ a. blue (Die I) .. 95·00
Z21 1 a. red (Die I) .. 75·00
Z22 2 a. green .. £110
Z23 4 a. blue and pale red (Head Die I) .. £600
Z24 4 a. blue and red (Head Die II) .. £650
Z25 4 a. blue and red (Head Die III) .. £550

1855. (*Nos*. 35/6).
Z26 4 a. black/*blue glazed* .. 26·00
Z27 8 a. carmine (Die I)/*blue glazed* .. 30·00
a. Bisected (4 a.) (1860) (on cover) .. £17000

1856–64. (*Nos*. 37/49).
Z28 ½ a. pale blue (Die I) .. 28·00
Z29 1 a. brown .. 18·00
Z30 2 a. dull pink .. 24·00
Z31 2 a. yellow-buff .. 22·00
Z32 2 a. yellow .. 22·00
Z33 2 a. orange .. 24·00
Z34 4 a. black .. 16·00
Z35 8 a. carmine (Die I) .. 22·00

1860. (*Nos*. 51/3).
Z36 8 p. purple/*white* .. 50·00

Stamps of INDIA *cancelled with Type* D.

1856–64. (*Nos*. 37/49).
Z40 1 a. brown .. 15·00
Z41 2 a. yellow .. 20·00
Z42 4 a. black .. 17·00
Z43 4 a. green .. 45·00
Z44 8 a. carmine (Die I) .. 19·00

1860. (*Nos*. 51/3).
Z45 8 p. purple/*white* .. 35·00
Z46 8 p. mauve .. 32·00

1865. (*Nos*. 54/65).
Z47 8 p. purple
Z48 1 a. deep brown .. 14·00
Z49 2 a. yellow .. 17·00
Z50 4 a. green .. 50·00
Z51 8 a. carmine (Die I)

1866–67. (*Nos*. 69/72).
Z52 4 a. green (Die I) .. 48·00

SINGAPORE

Stamps of INDIA *cancelled with Type* C.

1854. (*Nos*. 2/34).
Z60 ½ a. blue (Die I) .. 70·00
Z61 1 a. red (Die I) .. 60·00
Z62 1 a. dull red (Die II) .. 80·00
Z63 1 a. red (Die III) .. £400
Z64 2 a. green .. 65·00
a. Bisected (1 a.) (1857) (on cover)
Z65 4 a. blue and pale red (Head Die I) .. £500
Z66 4 a. blue and red (Head Die II) .. £550
Z67 4 a. blue and red (Head Die III) .. £450

1855. (*Nos*. 35/6).
Z68 4 a. black/*blue glazed* .. 16·00
a. Bisected (2 a.) (1859) (on cover) .. £4250
Z69 8 a. carmine/*blue glazed* .. 18·00
a. Bisected (4 a.) (1859) (on cover) .. £18000

1856–64. (*Nos*. 37/49).
Z70 ½ a. pale blue (Die I) .. 11·00
Z71 1 a. brown .. 12·00
a. Bisected (½ a.) (1859) (on cover) .. £17000
Z72 2 a. dull pink .. 18·00
Z73 2 a. yellow-buff .. 13·00
Z74 2 a. yellow .. 13·00
Z75 2 a. orange .. 15·00
Z76 4 a. black .. 11·00
a. Bisected diagonally (2 a.) (1859) (on cover) .. £6000
Z77 4 a. green .. 42·00
Z78 8 a. carmine (Die I) .. 14·00
a. Bisected (4 a.) (1859) (on cover) .. £17000

1860. (*Nos*. 51/3).
Z79 8 p. purple/*bluish* .. £140
Z80 8 p. purple/*white* .. 24·00
a. Bisected diagonally (4 p.) (1862) (on cover) £18000
Z81 8 p. mauve .. 24·00

1865. (*Nos*. 54/65).
Z82 ½ a. blue (Die I) .. 12·00
Z83 8 p. purple .. 42·00
Z84 1 a. deep brown .. 11·00
Z85 2 a. yellow .. 13·00
Z86 2 a. orange .. 13·00
Z87 4 a. green .. 42·00
Z88 8 a. carmine (Die I) .. £150

1866–67. (*Nos*. 69/72).
Z89 4 a. green (Die I) .. 40·00
Z90 6 a. 8 p. slate .. 55·00

OFFICIAL STAMPS

1866–67. (*Nos*. O6/14).
Z91 ½ a. pale blue .. 95·00
Z92 2 a. yellow .. £180

Stamps of INDIA *cancelled with Type* E.

1856–64. (*Nos*. 37/49).
Z100 1 a. brown .. £130
Z101 2 a. yellow .. £160
Z102 4 a. black .. £160
Z103 8 a. carmine (Die I) .. £160

1860. (*Nos*. 51/3).
Z104 8 p. purple/*white* .. £160

1865. (*Nos*. 54/65).
Z105 2 a. yellow .. £130
Z106 2 a. orange .. £130
Z107 4 a. green .. £170

PRICES FOR STAMPS ON COVER

Nos. 1/9	*from* × 10
Nos. 11/19	*from* × 8
Nos. 20/47	*from* × 7
Nos. 48/9	*from* × 10
Nos. 50/71	*from* × 5
No. 72	—
Nos. 73/8	*from* × 6
No. 80	*from* × 10
Nos. 82/5	*from* × 5
Nos. 86/7	*from* × 10
Nos. 88/94	*from* × 5
Nos. 95/105	*from* × 6
Nos. 106/9	*from* × 10
Nos. 110/21	*from* × 5
No. 122	—
Nos. 123/6	*from* × 4
Nos. 127/38	*from* × 3
Nos. 139/40	—
Nos. 141/51	*from* × 12
Nos. 152/67	*from* × 3
Nos. 168/9	—
Nos. 193/212	*from* × 3
Nos. 213/15	—
Nos. 216/17	*from* × 10
Nos. 218/40*a*	*from* × 3
Nos. 240*b*/*d*	—
Nos. 241/55	*from* × 15
Nos. 256/9	*from* × 4
Nos. 260/98	*from* × 3
Nos. D1/6	*from* × 20

PRINTERS. All Straits Settlements issues were printed in typography by De La Rue & Co, Ltd, London, *unless otherwise stated.*

THREE-HALF-CENTS (1) 32 CENTS (2)

1867 (1 Sept). *Stamps of India surch as T* **1** *or* **2** (24 c., 32 c.) *by De La Rue. Wmk Elephant's Head. P* 14.

1	**11**	1½ c. on ½ a. blue (Die I) (R.)	55·00	£150
2		2 c. on 1 a. brown (R.)	55·00	50·00
3		3 c. on 1 a. brown (B.)	60·00	55·00
4		4 c. on 1 a. brown (Bk.)	£120	£150
5		6 c. on 2 a. yellow (P.)	£250	£150
6		8 c. on 2 a. yellow (G.)	75·00	30·00

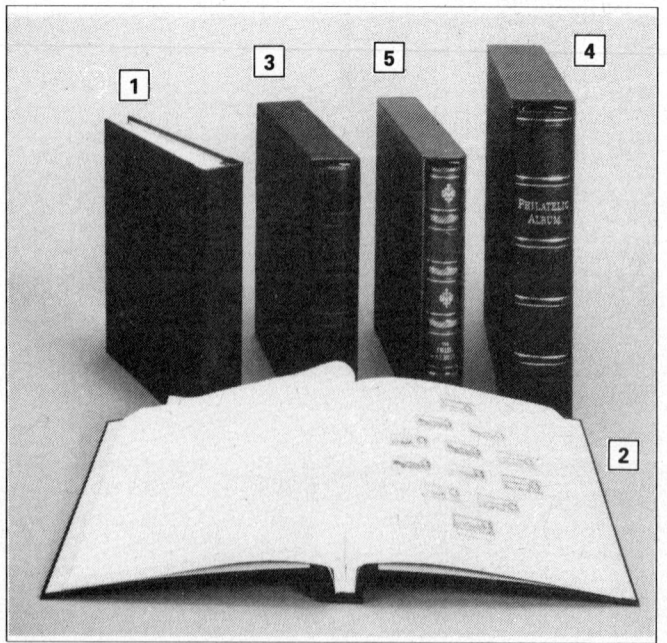

7 17 12 c. on 4 a. green (R.) £350 £180
a. Surch double £650
8 11 24 c. on 8 a. rose (Die II) (B.) .. .. £160 60·00
9 32 c. on 2 a. yellow (Bk.) .. .. .. £160 60·00

The 32 c. was re-issued for postal use in 1884.
No. 7a is only known unused.

1869 (?). *No.* 1 *with* "THREE HALF" *deleted and* "2" *written above, in black manuscript.*
10 2 on 1½ c. on ½ a. blue £4000 £2500

This stamp has been known from very early days and was apparently used at Penang, but nothing is known of its history.

5 6 7

8 9

1867 (Dec)–**72**. *Wmk Crown CC. P* 14. *Ornaments in corners differ for each value.*
11 5 2 c. brown (6.68) .. .. .. 13·00 1·75
a. Yellow-brown .. .. .. 14·00 1·75
b. Deep brown .. .. .. 42·00 7·50
12 4 c. rose (7.68) .. .. .. 20·00 4·00
a. Deep rose .. .. .. 26·00 4·75
13 6 c. dull lilac (1.68) .. .. .. 48·00 10·00
a. Bright lilac .. .. .. 48·00 10·00
14 6 8 c. orange-yellow .. .. .. 70·00 5·50
a. Orange .. .. .. 70·00 7·00
15 12 c. blue .. .. .. 60·00 4·50
a. Ultramarine .. .. .. 60·00 7·50
16 7 24 c. blue-green .. .. .. 65·00 3·50
a. Yellow-green .. .. .. 95·00 18·00
17 8 30 c. claret (12.72) .. .. .. 85·00 7·00
18 9 32 c. pale red .. .. .. £225 55·00
19 96 c. grey .. .. .. £150 27·00
a. Perf 12½ (6.71) £1100 £225

Five Cents. (10) Seven Cents. (11)

1879 (May). *Nos.* 14*a and* 18 *surch with T* **10** *and* **11**.
20 6 5 c. on 8 c. orange .. .. .. 55·00 80·00
a. No stop after "Cents" £400 £425
b. "F i" spaced £425 £450
21 9 7 c. on 32 c. pale red .. .. 60·00 70·00
a. No stop after "Cents" £500 £550

The no stop error occured once in the setting.

10 cents. (12)

10 (*a*) 10 (*b*) 10 (*c*) 10 (*d*)
10 (*e*) 10 (*f*) 10 (*g*) 10 (*h*)
10 (*i*) 10 (*j*) 10 (*jj*) 10 (*k*) 10 (*l*)

(*a*) "1" thin curved serif and thin foot, "0" narrow.
(*b*) "1" thick curved serif and thick foot; "0" broad. Both numerals heavy.
(*c*) "1" as (*a*); "0" as (*b*)
(*d*) "1" as (*a*) but thicker; "0" as (*a*)
(*e*) As (*a*) but sides of "0" thicker.
(*f*) "1" as (*d*); "0" as (*e*)
(*g*) As (*a*) but "0" narrower.
(*h*) "1" thin, curved serif and thick foot; "0" as (*g*)
(*i*) "1" as (*b*); "0" as (*a*)
(*j*) "1" as (*d*); "0" as (*g*) but raised.
(*jj*) "1" as (*a*) but shorter, and with shorter serif and thicker foot; "0" as (*g*) but level with "1".
(*k*) "1" as (*jj*); "0" as (*d*)
(*l*) "1" straight serif; "0" as (*d*).

1880 (Mar). *No.* 17 *surch with T* **12** (*showing numerals* (*a*) *to* (*jj*)).
22 10 c. on 30 c. claret (*a*) .. .. .. £100 45·00
23 10 c. on 30 c. claret (*b*) .. .. .. 95·00 40·00
24 10 c. on 30 c. claret (*c*) £1000 £250
25 10 c. on 30 c. claret (*d*) .. .. .. £450 95·00
26 10 c. on 30 c. claret (*e*) £1700 £425
27 10 c. on 30 c. claret (*f*) £1700 £425
28 10 c. on 30 c. claret (*g*) £600 £180
29 10 c. on 30 c. claret (*h*) £1700 £425
30 10 c. on 30 c. claret (*i*) £1700 £425
31 10 c. on 30 c. claret (*j*) £1700 £425
32 10 c. on 30 c. claret (*jj*) £1700 £425

Nos. 22/32 come from the same setting of 60 (6 × 10) containing twenty examples of No. 22 (R.1/1-2, 1/4, 1/6, 2/1-6, 3/1, 3/3, 3/5, 4/1, 4/3-4, 10/1, 10/3-5), twenty-two of No. 23 (R.4/1, 5/1-6, 6/1-6, 7/1, 8/2-4, 9/1-5), six of No. 25 (R.1/5, 3/2, 3/4, 4/2, 4/5, 10/2), four of No. 28 (R.7/2-5), two of No. 24 (R.9/6, 10/6) and one each of Nos. 26 (R.3/2), 27 (R.1/3), 29 (R.7/6), 30 (R.8/1), 31 (R.8/6) and 32 (R.8/5).

No. 23 is known with large stop after "cents" and also with stop low.

1880 (April). *No.* 17 *surch as T* **12**, *but without "cents.", showing numerals* (*a*) *to* (*c*), (*g*), (*j*), (*k*) *and* (*l*).
33 10 on 30 c. claret (*a*) .. .. .. 70·00 35·00
34 10 on 30 c. claret (*b*) .. .. .. 80·00 40·00
35 10 on 30 c. claret (*c*) £250 £100
36 10 on 30 c. claret (*g*) £550 £225
37 10 on 30 c. claret (*i*) £1200 £550
38 10 on 30 c. claret (*k*) £1200 £550
39 10 on 30 c. claret (*l*) £1200 £550

Nos. 33/9 were surcharged from an amended setting of 60 (6×10) of which only 58 positions have been identified. Of those known No. 33 occurs on twenty-four (R. 6/1-6, 7/1-6, 8/1-6, 9/1-2, 9/6, 10/1-3, No. 34 on twenty (R. 1/2-6, 2/2-6, 3/1-6, 4/3-5, 5/6) No. 35 on eight (R. 2/1, 4/2, 4/6, 5/1-5). No. 36 on three (R. 9/3-5) and Nos. 37 (R. 10/6), 38 (R. 10/4) and 39 (R. 10/5) on one each.

The first and fourth positions in the first vertical column have not been identified. A single example of the Royal Collection shows the "1" as (*b*) and "0" as (*g*) which may come from one of these positions, but this has not been confirmed.

5 cents. (13) 5 cents. (14) 5 cents. (15)

1880 (Aug). *No.* 14*a surch with T* **13** *to* **15**.
41 13 5 c. on 8 c. orange .. .. .. 65·00 80·00
42 14 5 c. on 8 c. orange .. .. .. 55·00 70·00
43 15 5 c. on 8 c. orange £180 £225

Surcharged in a setting of 60 (6 × 10) with T **13** on rows one to four, T **14** on rows five to nine and T **15** on row ten.

10 cents. (16) 5 cents. (17)

1880–81. *Nos.* 13, 15/*a and* 17 *surch with T* **16**.
44 10 c. on 6 c. lilac (11.81) .. .. .. 30·00 6·00
a. Surch double .. .. .. — £1200
45 10 c. on 12 c. ultramarine (1.81) .. .. 38·00 16·00
a. Blue .. .. .. 26·00 9·00
46 10 c. on 30 c. claret (12.80) .. .. £150 60·00

A second printing of the 10 c. on 6 c. has the surcharge heavier and the "10" usually more to the left or right of "cents".

1882 (Jan). *No.* 12 *surch with T* **17**.
47 5 c. on 4 c. rose £160 £180

18 19

1882 (Jan). *Wmk Crown CC. P* 14.
48 18 5 c. purple-brown .. .. .. 65·00 65·00
49 19 10 c. slate (Optd S. £170) .. .. £180 55·00

1882. *Wmk Crown CA. P* 14.
50 5 2 c. brown (Aug) .. .. .. £180 25·00
51 4 c. rose (April) .. .. .. 85·00 4·00
52 6 8 c. orange (Sept) .. .. .. 2·00 35
53 19 10 c. slate (Oct) .. .. .. 2·00 50

For the 4 c. in deep carmine see No. 98.

TWO CENTS 20*a* "S" wide — TWO CENTS 20*b* "E" and "S" wide — TWO CENTS 20*c* "N" wide

TWO CENTS 20*d* All letters narrow — TWO CENTS 20*e* "EN" and "S" wide — TWO CENTS 20*f* "E" wide

1883 (Apr). *Nos.* 52 *and* 18 *surch with T* **20***a*/*f*.
54 20*a* 2 c. on 8 c. orange .. .. .. 80·00 65·00
55 20*b* 2 c. on 8 c. orange .. .. .. 80·00 65·00
56 20*c* 2 c. on 8 c. orange .. .. .. 80·00 65·00
57 20*d* 2 c. on 8 c. orange .. .. .. 60·00 45·00
a. Surch double £1400 £850
58 20*e* 2 c. on 8 c. orange £180 £150
59 20*a* 2 c. on 32 c. pale red £325 £100
60 20*f* 2 c. on 32 c. pale red £375 £110
a. Surch double .. .. ..

The 8 c. was surcharged using one of two triplet settings, either 54 + 55 + 56 or 57 + 57 + 57, applied to rows 2 to 10. A single handstamp, either No. 57 or No. 58, was then used to complete row 1. The 32 c. was surcharged in the same way with a triplet of 59 + 60 + 59 and a single handstamp as No. 60.

2 Cents. (21) 4 Cents (22) 8 Cents (23)

1883 (June–July). *Nos.* 51 *and* 15 *surch with T* **21**.
61 2 c. on 4 c. rose .. .. .. 45·00 50·00
a. "s" of "Cents" inverted £850 £1000
62 2 c. on 12 c. blue (July) .. .. .. £110 60·00
a. "s" of "Cents" inverted £1700 £1400

The inverted "S" error occurred once in the setting of 60.

1883 (July)–**91**. *Wmk Crown CA. P* 14.
63 5 2 c. pale rose .. .. .. 16·00 1·75
a. Bright rose (1889) .. .. 1·50 15
64 4 c. pale brown .. .. .. 15·00 1·25
a. Deep brown .. .. .. 20·00 2·75
b. Olive-bistre £350 £275
65 18 5 c. blue (8.83) .. .. .. 4·50 30
66 5 6 c. lilac (11.84) .. .. .. 15·00 7·50
a. Violet .. .. .. 1·60 1·50
67 6 12 c. brown-purple .. .. .. 35·00 6·00
68 7 24 c. yellow-green (2.84) .. .. 50·00 3·75
a. Blue-green .. .. .. 2·75 2·75
69 8 30 c. claret (9.91) .. .. .. 7·00 4·50
70 9 32 c. orange-vermilion (1.87) .. .. 5·50 1·50
71 96 c. olive-grey (8.88) .. .. .. 70·00 32·00
63*a*/71 .. .. *Set of* 9 £130 45·00
63/65, 67 Optd "Specimen" .. .. *Set of* 4 £450

For the 12 c. in claret see No. 102.

1884 (Feb–Aug). *Nos.* 65, 15 *and* 67 *surch with T* **22** *or* **23**.
72 18 4 c. on 5 c. blue (Aug) £2000 £2500
73 4 c. on 5 c. blue (R.) (Aug) .. .. 75·00 65·00
74 6 8 c. on 12 c. blue .. .. .. £140 75·00
75 8 c. on 12 c. brown-purple (Aug) .. .. £120 85·00
a. Inverted "8" .. .. .. † —
b. "s" of "Cents" low (R. 5/1) .. ..

1884 (Aug). *No.* 65 *surch with T* **20***d*/*f*.
76 20*d* 2 c. on 5 c. blue .. .. .. 65·00 80·00
77 20*e* 2 c. on 5 c. blue .. .. .. 65·00 80·00
a. Pair, with and without surch ..
b. Surch double .. .. ..
78 20*f* 2 c. on 5 c. blue .. .. .. 65·00 80·00

Surcharged as a triplet, 77 + 76 + 78. On No. 76 "TS" are dropped below the line.

8 (24) 3 CENTS (25) THREE CENTS (26)

1884 (Sept). *No.* 75 *additionally surch with large numeral as T* **24** *in red.*
80 6 8 on 8 c. on 12 c. dull purple £130 £140
a. Surch T **24** double £2250
b. Surch T **23** in blue £3500
c. "s" of "Cents" low £9000

Examples as No. 75, but with Type **23** in blue, were further surcharged in error.

A similar "4" surcharge in red on No. 73 exists from a trial printing from which seven examples are known, all used on an official's correspondence (*Price* £7000 *used*).

1885. *No.* 65 *and T* **9** *in new colour, wmk Crown CA, surch with T* **25** *or* **26**.
82 25 3 c. on 5 c. blue (Sept) .. .. .. 75·00 £180
a. Surch double £1400
83 26 3 c. on 32 c. pl mag (Dec) (Optd S. £100) 1·40 2·50
a. Deep magenta 90 90

The surcharge on No. 82 was applied locally by a triplet setting. No. 83 was surcharged by De La Rue in complete panes.

3 cents (27) 2 Cents (28)

1886 (Apr). *No.* 48 *surch with T* **27**.
84 18 3 c. on 5 c. purple-brown £100 £110

The surcharge on No. 84 was applied by a triplet setting.

1887 (July). *No.* 65 *surch with T* **28**.
85 18 2 c. on 5 c. blue .. .. .. 13·00 27·00
a. "C" of "Cents" omitted .. .. — £1600
b. Surch double £400 £325

The surcharge on No. 85 was applied by a triplet setting.

10 CENTS (29) THIRTY CENTS (30)

1891 (Nov). *Nos.* 68 *and* 70 *surch with T* **29** *and* **30**.
86 7 10 c. on 24 c. yellow-green .. .. 1·50 1·25
a. Narrow "0" in "10" (R. 4/6) .. .. 25·00 28·00
87 9 30 c. on 32 c. orange-vermilion .. .. 4·75 3·50

The "R" of "THIRTY" and "N" of "CENTS" are found wide or narrow and in all possible combinations.

ONE CENT (31) ONE CENT (32)

1892. *Stamps of* 1882–91 (*wmk Crown CA*) *surch with T* **31**.
88 1 c. on 2 c. rose (March) 1·25 1·50
89 1 c. on 4 c. brown (April) 3·75 4·00
a. Surch double £600
90 1 c. on 6 c. lilac (Feb) 1·00 2·50
a. Surch double, one inverted £650 £550
91 1 c. on 8 c. orange (Jan) 1·00 60
92 1 c. on 12 c. brown-purple (Mar) 4·00 9·00
88/92 *Set of* 5 10·00 16·00

The three settings used for Nos. 88/92 contained various combinations of the following varieties: "ON" of "ONE" and "N" of "CENT" wide; "O" wide, "N" of "ONE" narrow and "N" of "CENT" wide; "O" narrow and both letters "N" wide; "ON" narrow, and "N" of "CENT" wide; "O" wide and both letters "N" narrow; "ON" wide and "N" of "CENT" narrow; "ON" and "N" of "CENT" narrow; "O" narrow "N" of "ONE" wide and "N" of "CENT" narrow. Antique "N" and "E" letters also occur.

1892–94. *Colours changed. Wmk Crown CA. P* 14. *Surch with T* **32** *and* **26** *by De la Rue.*
93 **6** 1 c. on 8 c. green (3.92) 40 75
94 **9** 3 c. on 32 c. carmine-rose (6.94) 2·00 70
a. Surch omitted £2250
93/94 Optd "Specimen" *Set of* 2 85·00

No. 94a comes from a sheet found at Singapore on which all stamps in the upper left pane had the surcharge omitted. Five of the vertical inter-panneau pairs still exist with the surcharge omitted on the upper stamp (*Price* £12000 *unused*). The only used example of the error is on cover.

33

34

4
cents.
(35)

1892 (Mar)–**99.** *Wmk Crown CA. P* 14.
95 **33** 1 c. green (9.92) 40 20
96 3 c. carmine-rose (2.95) 5·50 30
97 3 c. brown (3.99) 2·50 40
a. Yellow-brown 2·50 55
98 **5** 4 c. deep carmine (7.99) 2·50 1·25
99 **18** 5 c. brown (6.94) 2·25 90
100 5 c. magenta (7.99) 1·75 2·00
101 **6** 8 c. ultramarine (6.94) 3·50 30
a. Bright blue 4·50 35
102 12 c. claret (3.94) 7·50 8·00
103 **33** 25 c. purple-brown and green 12·00 4·00
a. Dull purple and green 12·00 3·75
104 50 c. olive-green and carmine 17·00 2·50
105 **34** $5 orange and carmine (10.98) £275 £275
99/105 *Set of* 11 £300 £275
99/101, 103/5 Optd "Specimen" *Set of* 10 £250

1898 (26 Dec). *T* **18** *and* **6** *surch with T* **35** *at Singapore.*
106 4 c. on 5 c. brown (No. 99) 75 4·25
107 4 c. on 5 c. blue (No. 65) 1·25 5·50
a. Surch double — £700
108 4 c. on 8 c. ultramarine (No. 101) 80 2·50
a. Surch double £600 £500
b. Bright blue (No. 101*a*) 50 70
106/8*b* *Set of* 3 2·25 9·50

Nos. 107 and 108*b* exist with stop spaced 1½ mm from the "S" (R. 10/6).

FOUR CENTS
(36)

37

38

1899 (Mar). *T* **18** (*wmk Crown CA. P* 14), *surch with T* **36** *by De La Rue.*
109 4 c. on 5 c. carmine (Optd S. £30) 30 20
a. Surch omitted £9000

No. 109a is only known unused.

1902 (Apr)–**03.** *Wmk Crown CA. P* 14.
110 **37** 1 c. grey-green (7.02) 45 90
a. Pale green 2·50 1·50
111 3 c. dull purple and orange 75 15
112 4 c. purple/*red* (9.02) 2·00 30
113 **38** 5 c. dull purple (8.02) 1·75 55
114 8 c. purple/*blue* 3·00 20
115 10 c. purple and black/*yellow* (9.02) 11·00 70
116 **37** 25 c. dull purple and green (8.02) 7·50 3·50
117 **38** 30 c. grey and carmine (7.02) 12·00 8·00
118 **37** 50 c. deep green and carmine (9.02) 14·00 14·00
a. Dull green and carmine 17·00 15·00
119 **38** $1 dull green and black (9.02) 20·00 42·00
120 **37** $2 dull purple and black (9.02) 45·00 45·00
121 **38** $5 dull green and brown-orange (10.02) £120 90·00
122 **37** $100 pur & grn/*yell* (3.03) (Optd S. £225) £5000
110/21 *Set of* 12 £200 £180
110/21 Optd "Specimen" *Set of* 12 £200

39

40

41

42

(Des N. Trotter and W. Egerton)

1903 (Dec)–**04.** *Wmk Crown CA. P* 14.
123 **39** 1 c. grey-green 40 3·50
124 **40** 3 c. dull purple (1.04) 4·00 2·25
125 **41** 4 c. purple/*red* (4.04) 1·00 30
126 **42** 8 c. purple/*blue* (7.04) 20·00 1·25
123/6 *Set of* 4 23·00 6·50
123/6 Optd "Specimen" *Set of* 4 £100

1904 (Aug)–**10.** *Wmk Multiple Crown CA. Ordinary paper* (1 c. *to* $1 *and* $5) *or chalk-surfaced paper* ($2, $25, $100). *P* 14.
127 **39** 1 c. deep green (9.04) 1·00 10
a. Chalk-surfaced paper (12.05) 2·50 75
128 **40** 3 c. dull purple 50 30
a. Chalk-surfaced paper (8.06) 2·00 35
b. Plum (2.08) 3·50 55
129 **41** 4 c. purple/*red* (6.05) 1·75 15
a. Chalk-surfaced paper (10.05) 1·75 15
130 **38** 5 c. dull purple (12.06) 2·50 2·00
a. Chalk-surfaced paper (12.06) 3·25 2·50
131 **42** 8 c. purple/*blue* (8.05) 5·00 35
a. Chalk-surfaced paper (12.05) 5·00 60
132 **38** 10 c. purple and black/*yellow* (8.05) 2·50 30
a. Chalk-surfaced paper (11.05) 4·25 60
133 **37** 25 c. dull purple and green (1.05) 9·00 11·00
a. Chalk-surfaced paper (11.05) 10·00 9·00
134 **38** 30 c. grey and carmine (3.05) 18·00 2·50
a. Chalk-surfaced paper (3.06) 20·00 2·50
135 **37** 50 c. dull green and carmine (10.05) 16·00 7·50
a. Chalk-surfaced paper (11.06) 10·00 6·00
136 **38** $1 dull green and black (3.05) 24·00 10·00
a. Chalk-surfaced paper (3.06) 17·00 7·50
137 **37** $2 dull purple and black (10.05) 65·00 65·00
138 **38** $5 dull green and brown-orange (10.05) 90·00 90·00
a. Chalk-surfaced paper (1.08) 90·00 90·00
139 **37** $25 grey-grn & blk (7.06) (Optd S. £120) £800 £800
140 $100 purple and green/*yellow* (6.10) £6500
127/38 *Set of* 12 £200 £160

STRAITS
SETTLEMENTS.
(43)

Straits Settlements.
(44)

STRAITS
SETTLEMENTS.

FOUR CENTS.
(45)

1906 (Dec)–**07.** *T* **18** *of Labuan* (*Nos.* 116*c etc.*) *optd with T* **43** *or* **44** (10 *c.*), *or additionally surch with T* **45**, *in black* (*No.* 145), *claret* (*No.* 151) *or brown-red* (*others*) *at Singapore. P* 13½–14.
141 1 c. black and purple (*p* 14½–15) 38·00 75·00
142 2 c. black and green £130 £150
a. Perf 14½–15 £130
143 3 c. black and sepia (1.07) 14·00 65·00
144 4 c. on 12 c. black and yellow 1·50 5·50
a. No stop after "CENTS" (R. 1/8, 6/8) £100
145 4 c. on 16 c. green and brown (Blk.) 1·50 4·25
a. "STRAITS SETTLEMENTS" in both brown-red and black £450 £450
b. Ditto. In vert pair with normal £1900
146 4 c. on 18 c. black and pale brown 1·00 4·25
a. No stop after "CENTS" (R. 1/8, 6/8) 90·00
b. "FOUR CENTS" and bar double £3500
c. "FOUR CENTS" and bar 1½ mm below normal position (pair with normal) £275
147 8 c. black and vermilion 1·00 5·50
148 10 c. brown and slate 3·00 4·25
a. No stop after "SETTLEMENTS" (R. 1/4, 6/4) £120
149 25 c. green and greenish blue (1.07) 4·25 18·00
a. Perf 14½–15 60·00 75·00
b. Perf 13½–14 comp 14½–15
150 50 c. dull purple and lilac (1.07) 9·00 42·00
151 $1 claret and orange (Claret) (1.07) 38·00 70·00
a. Perf 14½–15
141/51 *Set of* 11 £200 £375

Nos. 141/51 were overprinted by a setting of 50 (10×5) applied twice to the sheets of 100. The "FOUR CENTS" surcharges were applied separately by a similar setting.

No. 145a shows impressions of Type **43** in both brown-red and black. It is known from one complete sheet and the top half of another.

No. 146b occurred on row 5 from one sheet only. No. 146c occurred on R. 4/10 and 9/10 of the first printing.

The 1 c. and 2 c. also exist perf 14 all round and are rare.

46

47

1906 (Sept)–**12.** *Wmk Mult Crown CA. Ordinary paper* (1 *c. to* 10 *c.*) *or chalk-surfaced paper* (21 *c. to* $500). *P* 14.
152 **39** 1 c. blue-green (3.10) 6·00 70
153 **40** 3 c. red (6.08) 1·25 10
154 **41** 4 c. red (7.07) 4·75 90
155 4 c. dull purple (2.08) 1·50 10
a. Chalk-surfaced paper (1.12) 2·50 30
156 4 c. claret (9.11) 75 80
157 **38** 5 c. orange (4.09) 2·75 50
158 **42** 8 c. blue 1·50 25
159 **38** 10 c. purple/*yellow* (7.08) 1·00 15
a. Chalk-surfaced paper (5.12) 3·50 75
160 **46** 21 c. dull purple and claret (11.10) 5·50 24·00
161 **37** 25 c. dull and bright purple (7.09) 5·50 2·75
162 **38** 30 c. purple and orange-yellow (11.09) 21·00 1·50
163 **46** 45 c. black/*green* (11.10) 2·50 3·50
164 **37** 50 c. black/*green* (4.10) 3·75 1·75
165 **38** $1 black and red/*blue* (10.10) 9·50 3·50
166 **37** $2 green and red/*yellow* (12.09) 16·00 16·00
167 **38** $5 green and red/*green* (11.09) 65·00 48·00
168 **47** $25 pur & blue/*bl* (5.11) (Optd S. £150) £700 £500
169 $500 purple & orge (5.10) (Optd S. £750) £48000
152/67 *Set of* 16 £130 95·00
153/67 Optd "Specimen" *Set of* 15 £200

Beware of dangerous forgeries of No. 169.

48

49

50

51

52

53

54

1912–23. $25, $100 *and* $500 *as T* **47**, *but with head of King George V. Wmk Mult Crown CA. Ordinary paper* (*Nos.* 193/6, 198/201, 203) *or chalk-surfaced paper* (*others*). *P* 14.
193 **48** 1 c. green (9.12) 2·75 40
a. Pale green (1.14) 3·00 30
b. Blue-green (1917) 4·00 75
194 1 c. black (2.19) 30 30
195 **52** 2 c. green (10.19) 35 30
196 **49** 3 c. red (2.13) 1·25 30
a. Scarlet (2.17) 30 10
197 **50** 4 c. dull purple (3.13) 70 30
a. Wmk sideways — £1100
198 4 c. rose-scarlet (2.19) 70 15
a. Carmine 1·25 20
199 **51** 5 c. orange (8.12) 1·50 45
a. Yellow-orange 2·00 45
200 **52** 6 c. dull claret (3.20) 1·75 50
a. Deep claret 4·50 2·50
201 8 c. ultramarine (3.13) 70 30
202 **51** 10 c. purple/*yellow* (8.12) 90 30
a. White back (9.13) (Optd S. £27) 75 50
b. On lemon (1916) (Optd S. £42) 9·50 90
203 10 c. deep bright blue (2.19) 5·50 25
a. Bright blue 4·00 30
204 **53** 21 c. dull and bright purple (11.13) 4·00 7·00
205 **54** 25 c. dull purple and mauve (7.14) 5·50 3·25
206 25 c. dull purple and violet (1919) 21·00 3·75
207 **51** 30 c. dull purple and orange (12.14) 3·75 1·50
208 **53** 45 c. black/*green* (*white back*) (12.14) 6·50 13·00
a. On blue-green, olive back (7.18) (Optd S. £27) 3·00 9·00
b. On emerald back (6.22) 2·75 13·00
209 **54** 50 c. black/*green* (7.14) 5·50 1·75
a. On blue-green, olive back (1918) 9·00 2·75
b. On emerald back (10.21) 9·00 2·75
c. On emerald back (Die II) (3.23) (Optd S. £27) 2·75 2·75
210 **51** $1 black and red/*blue* (10.14) 8·50 6·00
211 **54** $2 grn & red/*yell* (7.15) (Optd S. £28) 9·50 19·00
a. White back (7.14) 6·00 20·00
b. On orange-buff (1920) 40·00 50·00
c. On pale yellow (1921) 45·00 55·00
212 **51** $5 grn & red/*grn* (4.15) (Optd S. £28) 60·00 30·00
a. White back (11.13) 50·00 24·00
b. On blue-green, olive back (1918) 80·00 38·00
c. On emerald back (6.21) £100 60·00
d. Die II (1923) (Optd S. £55) 65·00 42·00
213 – $25 purple and blue/*blue* (Optd S. £100) £600 £225
a. Break in scroll £1000
b. Broken crown and scroll £1000
214 – $100 blk & carm/*bl* (8.12) (Optd S. £225) £3000
a. Break in scroll £3750
b. Broken crown and scroll £3750
215 – $500 purple and orange-brown (8.12) (Optd S. £500) £25000
a. Break in scroll £30000
b. Broken crown and scroll £30000
193/212 *Set of* 20 85·00 65·00
193/210, 211*a*, 212*a* Optd "Specimen" *Set of* 19 £375

The 6 c. is similar to T **52**, but the head is in a beaded oval as in T **53**. The 2 c., 6 c. (and 12 c. below) have figures of value on a circular ground while in the 8 c. this is of oval shape.

For illustrations of the varieties on Nos. 213/15 see above No. 58 of Leeward Islands.

RED CROSS

2c.

(55)

MALAYA-
BORNEO
EXHIBITION.

(56)

1917 (1 May). *Surch with T* **55**.

216 **49** 2 c. on 3 c. scarlet 1·25 18·00
a. No stop (R. 2/3) £140 £250
217 **50** 2 c. on 4 c. dull purple 1·25 18·00
a. No stop (R. 2/3) £140 £250

Nos. 216a and 217a occur in the first setting only.

Type I

Type II

Two types of duty plate in the 25 c. In Type II the solid shading forming the back of the figure 2 extends to the top of the curve; the upturned end of the foot of the 2 is short; two background lines above figure 5; c close to 5; STRAITS SETTLEMENTS in taller letters.

1921–33. *Wmk Mult Script CA. Ordinary paper* (1 *c. to* 6 *c.*, 10 *c.* (*No.* 230), 12 *c.*) *or chalk-surfaced paper* (*others*). *P* 14.

218 **48** 1 c. black (3.22) 30 10
219 **52** 2 c. green (5.21) 30 10
220 2 c. brown (12.25) 5·00 2·25
221 **49** 3 c. green (9.23) 1·25 60
222 **50** 4 c. carmine-red (10.21) 2·00 2·75
223 4 c. bright violet (8.24) 30 10
224 4 c. orange (8.29) 85 10
225 **51** 5 c. orange (Die II) (5.21) 90 30
a. Die I (7.22) 85 15
ab. Wmk sideways † —
226 5 c. brown (Die II) (2.32) 1·00 10
a. Die I (1933) 2·50 10
227 **52** 6 c. dull claret (10.22) 2·00 15
228 6 c. rose-pink (2.25) 8·50 4·75
229 6 c. scarlet (1.27) 2·00 10
230 **51** 10 c. bright blue (Die I) (3.21) 1·75 30
231 10 c. purple/*yellow* (Die I) (6.25) 2·25 3·50
a. Die II. *On pale yellow* (11.26) 1·50 10
b. Die I. *On pale yellow* (1933) 1·75 15
232 **52** 12 c. bright blue (1.22) 70 10
233 **53** 21 c. dull and bright purple (2.23) 4·75 26·00
234 **54** 25 c. dull purple and mauve (Die I, Type I) (5.23) 22·00 48·00
a. Die II, Type I (9.23) 14·00 2·50
b. Die II. Type II (1927) 3·25 1·40
235 **51** 30 c. dull purple & orange (Die I) (5.21) 12·00 20·00
a. Die II (1923) 2·00 40
236 **53** 35 c. dull purple & orange-yellow (8.22) 9·00 5·00
a. *Dull purple and orange* 3·50 5·50
237 35 c. scarlet and purple (4.31) 7·50 7·00
238 **54** 50 c. black/*emerald* (9.25) 1·25 40
239 **51** $1 black and red/*blue* (6.22) 4·75 45
240 **54** $2 green and red/*pale yellow* (5.25) 9·00 8·00
240*a* **51** $5 green and red/*green* (8.26) 48·00 28·00
240*b* – $25 pur & blue/*bl* (5.23) (Optd S. £100) £300 75·00
ba. Break in scroll £550
bb. Broken crown and scroll £550
240*c* – $100 black and carmine/*blue* (5.23) (Optd S. £180) £1500 £700
ca. Break in scroll £2000
cb. Broken crown and scroll £2000
240*d* – $500 purple and orange-brown (4.23) (Optd S. £325) £15000
da. Break in scroll £18000
db. Broken crown and scroll £18000
218/40*a* *Set of* 24 £100 80·00
218/40*a* Optd/Perf "Specimen" *Set of* 24 £350

Nos. 240*b*/*d* are as Type **47**, but with portrait of George V.

An 8 c. in carmine was prepared but not issued (Optd "Specimen" £130).

The paper of No. 231b is the normal *pale yellow* at the back, but with a bright yellow surface. No. 231 is on paper of a *pale lemon* tint and the impression is smudgy.

For illustrations of the varieties on Nos. 240*b*/*d* see above No. 58 of Leeward Islands.

1922 (31 Mar). *T* **48** *and* **50** *to* **54**, *overprinted with T* **56**.

(*a*) *Wmk Mult Crown CA*

241 2 c. green 17·00 55·00
242 4 c. scarlet 3·50 15·00
243 5 c. orange 3·50 12·00
244 8 c. ultramarine 1·75 6·00
245 25 c. dull purple and mauve (No. 202) 3·00 18·00
246 45 c. black/*blue-green* (*olive back*) 3·00 15·00
a. On green (*white back*) 45·00 £110
247 $1 black and red/*blue* £100 £325
248 $2 green and red/*orange-buff* 22·00 80·00
a. On pale yellow 48·00 £130
249 $5 green and red/*blue-green* (*olive back*) £190 £275

(*b*) *Wmk Mult Script CA*

250 1 c. black 60 6·50
251 2 c. green 1·40 11·00
252 4 c. carmine-red 1·75 15·00
253 5 c. orange (Die II) 2·50 27·00
254 10 c. bright blue (Die I) 2·25 17·00
255 $1 black and red/*blue* (Die II) 15·00 70·00
241/55 *Set of* 11 £225 £475

Nos. 241/55 were overprinted by stereo which repeated a setting of 12 (6×2). The following varieties therefore occur ten times on each sheet of 120: (a) Small second "A" in "MALAYA." (b) No stop. (c) No hyphen. (d) Oval last "O" in "BORNEO," (e) "EXH.BITION".

1935 (6 May). *Silver Jubilee. As Nos.* 114/17 *of Jamaica, but ptd by Waterlow & Sons. P* 11×12.

256 5 c. ultramarine and grey 45 20
257 8 c. green and indigo 1·25 1·25
258 12 c. brown and deep blue 2·75 1·50
259 25 c. slate and purple 2·75 3·25
256/9 *Set of* 4 6·50 5·75
256/9 Perf "Specimen" *Set of* 4 85·00

57

58

1936 (1 Jan)–**37.** *Chalk-surfaced paper. Wmk Mult Script CA. P* 14.

260 **57** 1 c. black (1.1.37) 30 20
261 2 c. green (1.2.36) 30 15
262 4 c. orange (15.6.36) 50 30
263 5 c. brown (1.8.36) 30 10
264 6 c. scarlet (1.2.36) 70 40
265 8 c. grey 40 20
266 10 c. dull purple (1.7.36) 1·00 20
267 12 c. bright ultramarine (1.9.36) 2·00 2·00
268 25 c. dull purple and scarlet (1.2.36) 1·00 30
269 30 c. dull purple and orange 1·25 2·00
270 40 c. scarlet and dull purple 1·25 2·00
271 50 c. black/*emerald* (1.9.36) 1·50 70
272 $1 black and red/*blue* (1.7.36) 8·00 70
273 $2 green and scarlet (1.4.36) 14·00 10·00
274 $5 green and red/*emerald* (1.1.37) 30·00 10·00
260/74 *Set of* 15 55·00 26·00
260/74 Perf "Specimen" *Set of* 15 £150

1937 (12 May). *Coronation. As Nos.* 118/20 *of Jamaica.*

275 4 c. orange 30 10
276 8 c. grey-black 55 10
277 12 c. bright blue 65 50
275/7 *Set of* 3 1·40 55
275/7 Perf "Specimen" *Set of* 3 55·00

1937–41. *Chalk-surfaced paper. Wmk Mult Script CA. P* 14 *or* 15×14 (15 *c.*). (*a*) *Die I* (*printed at two operations*).

278 **58** 1 c. black (1.1.38) 2·00 10
279 2 c. green (6.12.37) 9·00 10
280 4 c. orange (1.1.38) 8·00 10
281 5 c. brown (19.11.37) 13·00 10
282 6 c. scarlet (10.1.38) 5·50 10
283 8 c. grey (26.1.38) 35·00 10
284 10 c. dull purple (8.11.37) 4·50 10
285 12 c. ultramarine (10.1.38) 4·50 10
286 25 c. dull purple and scarlet (11.12.37) 35·00 75
287 30 c. dull purple and orange (1.12.37) 35·00 1·25
288 40 c. scarlet and dull purple (20.12.37) 9·00 2·00
289 50 c. black/*emerald* (26.1.38) 6·00 10
290 $1 black and red/*blue* (26.1.38) 7·00 15
291 $2 green and scarlet (26.1.38) 19·00 3·00
292 $5 green and red/*emerald* (26.1.38) 23·00 3·00

(*b*) *Die II* (*printed at one operation*)

293 **58** 2 c. green (28.12.38) 20·00 10
294 2 c. orange (6.10.41) 1·00 3·75
295 3 c. green (*ordinary paper*) (5.9.41) 2·75 2·00
296 4 c. orange (29.10.38) 45·00 10
297 5 c. brown (18.2.39) 18·00 10
298 15 c. ultram (*ordinary paper*) (6.10.41) 3·50 6·00
278/98 *Set of* 18 £200 21·00
278/92, 294/5, 298 Perf "Specimen" *Set of* 18 £275

Die I. Lines of background outside central oval touch the oval and the foliage of the palm tree is usually joined to the oval frame. The downward-pointing palm frond, opposite the King's eye, has two points.

Die II. Lines of background are separated from the oval by a white line and the foliage of the palm trees does not touch the outer frame. The palm frond has only one point.

The 6 c. grey, 8 c. scarlet and $5 purple and orange were issued only with the BMA overprint, but the 8 c. without opt is known although in this state it was never issued (*Price* £11).

POSTAGE DUE STAMPS

D 1

1924 (1 Jan)–**26.** *Wmk Mult Script CA. P* 14.

D1 D 1 1 c. violet 3·75 4·75
D2 2 c. black 3·00 1·25
D3 4 c. green (5.26) 2·00 4·75
D4 8 c. scarlet 4·50 55
D5 10 c. orange 5·00 85
D6 12 c. bright blue 7·00 65
D1/6 *Set of* 6 23·00 11·50
D1/6 Optd "Specimen" *Set of* 6 £200

For later issues of Postage Due stamps, see MALAYAN POSTAL UNION.

The Straits Settlements were occupied by the Japanese in 1942. After the Second World War the stamps of MALAYA (BRITISH MILITARY ADMINISTRATION) were used. In 1946 Singapore became a separate Crown Colony and Labuan was transferred to North Borneo. Separate stamps were issued for Malacca and Penang, which both joined the Malayan Federation on 1 February 1948.

II. FEDERATED MALAY STATES

On 1 July 1896, the States of Negri Sembilan, Pahang, Perak and Selangor were organised on a federal basis to be known as the Federated Malay States. For the time being each State continued with individual issues, but stamps for the use of the Federation replaced these in 1900.

PRICES FOR STAMPS ON COVER

Nos. 1/13	*from* × 12
No. 14	—
Nos. 15/22	*from* × 10
Nos. 23/5	*from* × 3
No. 26	—
Nos. 27/50	*from* × 6
No. 51	—
Nos. 52/81	*from* × 5
No. 82	—
Nos. D1/6	*from* × 10

PRINTERS. All issues of the Federated Malay States were printed in typography by De La Rue & Co, Ltd, London, *unless otherwise stated.*

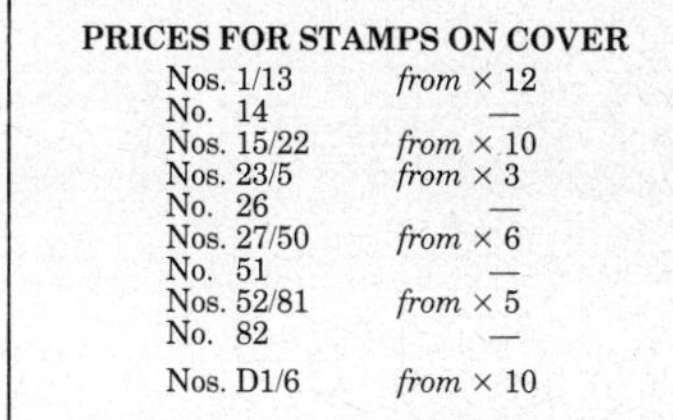

(1) (2)

1900. *Optd with T* **1** (*cent values*) *or* **2** (*dollar values*).

(*a*) *Stamps of Negri Sembilan* (*T* 3)

1 1 c. dull purple and green 1·40 3·00
2 2 c. dull purple and brown 22·00 45·00
3 3 c. dull purple and black 1·90 3·25
4 5 c. dull purple and olive-yellow 65·00 £110
5 10 c. dull purple and orange 2·00 12·00
6 20 c. green and olive 50·00 65·00
7 25 c. green and carmine £140 £170
8 50 c. green and black 60·00 80·00
1/8 *Set of* 8 £300 £425
1/8 Optd "Specimen" *Set of* 8 £160

(*b*) *Stamps of Perak* (*T* **44** *and* **45**)

9 5 c. dull purple and olive-yellow 10·00 45·00
10 10 c. dull purple and orange 55·00 60·00
11 $1 green and pale green £110 £130
12 $2 green and carmine 90·00 £120
13 $5 green and ultramarine £200 £275
14 $25 green and orange (Optd S. £250) £3750
11/13 Optd "Specimen" *Set of* 3 £110

The stamps of STRAITS SETTLEMENTS were used in Federated Malay States from 16 July 1900 until replaced by the 1900–1 issue.

3

4

1900–1. *P* 14. (*a*) *T* **3**. *Wmk Crown CA, sideways* (1901).

15 1 c. black and green 1·00 1·60
a. Grey and green 30 30
b. Grey-brown and green 3·00 25
16 3 c. black and brown 2·75 80
a. Grey and brown 1·25 35
b. Grey-brown and brown 1·25 20
17 4 c. black and carmine 8·00 1·40
a. Grey and carmine 4·00 1·40
b. Grey-brown and carmine 8·00 30
18 5 c. green and carmine/*yellow* 1·50 2·00
19 8 c. black and ultramarine 26·00 6·50
a. Grey and ultramarine 20·00 3·50
b. Grey-brown and ultramarine 22·00 2·75
20 10 c. black and claret 50·00 6·00
a. Grey and claret 35·00 3·25
b. Black and purple 55·00 5·50
c. Grey and purple 40·00 4·25
d. Grey-brown and purple 55·00 2·25
21 20 c. mauve and black 17·00 6·00
22 50 c. black and orange-brown 80·00 48·00
a. Grey and orange-brown 60·00 28·00
b. Grey-brown and orange-brown 60·00 25·00
15/22 *Set of* 8 £130 35·00
15/22 Optd "Specimen" *Set of* 8 £160

Later printings in 1903–4 show the two upper lines of shading in the background at the corner nearest to the "S" of "STATE" blurred and running into one another, whereas in earlier printings these lines are distinct. Two plates were used for printing the central design of T **3**. In Plate 1 the lines of background are regular throughout, but in Plate 2 they are lighter around the head and back of the tiger. The 5 c. was the only value with single wmk to be printed from Plate 2. Stamps with multiple wmk were printed for a short time from Plate 1, and show the two blurred lines of background near "S" of "STATE," but the majority of these stamps were printed from Plate 2 and later plates.

(*b*) *T* **4**. *Wmk Crown CC* (1900)

23 $1 green and pale green 65·00 70·00
24 $2 green and carmine 70·00 75·00
25 $5 green and bright ultramarine £120 £130
a. Green and pale ultramarine £120 £130
26 $25 green and orange (Optd S. £180) £950 £650
23/5 Optd "Specimen" *Set of* 3 £110

Two dies for 1 c. green and 4 c. scarlet

Die I. "Head" and duty plates. Thick frame line below "MALAY" and in the 1 c. the "c" is thin whilst in the 4 c. it is thick.

Die II. Single working plate. Thin frame line below "MALAY" and in the 1 c. the "c" is thicker whilst in the 4 c. it is thinner.

1904 (10 Oct)–**22**. *T* **3** *and T* **4** *(dollar values). Wmk Mult Crown CA (sideways on T* **3***). Ordinary paper (1 c. to 50 c.) or chalk-surfaced paper ($1 to $25).*

27 1 c. grey and green .. .. .. 38·00 5·00
a. Grey-brown and green .. .. .. 13·00 70
28 1 c. green (Die I) (8.7.06) .. .. .. 5·50 30
29 1 c. green (Die II) .. .. .. 1·25 20
a. Yellow-green .. .. .. 7·00 40
b. Blue-green .. .. .. 12·00 45
30 1 c. deep brown (21.1.19) .. .. 2·25 90
31 2 c. green (18.2.19) 50 30
32 3 c. grey and brown (10.04) .. .. 17·00 1·00
a. Grey-brown and brown (12.05) .. 10·00 30
ab. Chalk-surfaced paper .. .. 10·00 30
33 3 c. brown (11.7.06) .. .. .. 5·00 15
34 3 c. carmine (2.2.09) .. .. .. 2·00 10
a. Scarlet (1.17) .. .. .. 6·50 25
35 3 c. grey (29.10.18) .. .. .. 1·00 20
36 4 c. grey and scarlet .. .. .. 18·00 1·25
a. Chalk-surfaced paper. *Grey and rose* .. 8·00 85
b. Grey-brown and scarlet .. .. 16·00 1·00
c. Black and scarlet .. .. .. 17·00 1·25
d. Black and rose .. .. .. 3·50 25
e. Black and deep rose (aniline) (1909) .. 35·00 4·00
f. Jet-black and rose (1914) .. .. 10·00 55
37 4 c. scarlet (Die I) (11.2.19) .. .. 2·00 2·25
38 4 c. scarlet (Die II) (15.4.19) 80 15
a. Wmk upright (2.22) .. .. † £400
39 5 c. green and carmine/*yellow* (5.06) .. 4·00 1·50
a. Chalk-surfaced paper .. .. .. 7·00 2·25
b. Deep green and carmine/yellow .. 3·25 1·50
c. On orange-buff (1921) .. .. 7·50 3·50
d. On pale yellow (4.22) .. .. 3·00 1·75
40 6 c. orange (11.2.19) .. .. .. 2·00 1·50
41 8 c. grey and ultramarine (2.05) .. .. 27·00 9·50
a. Grey-brown and ultramarine (12.05) .. 14·00 3·50
ab. Chalk-surfaced paper .. .. 18·00 6·50
b. Wmk upright (3.07) .. .. .. 5·00 3·50
42 8 c. ultramarine (8.3.10) .. .. .. 13·00 90
a. Deep blue (1918) .. .. .. 13·00 1·25
43 10 c. grey-brown and claret .. .. .. 22·00 1·00
a. Chalk-surfaced paper (1905) .. .. 25·00 1·40
b. Black and claret .. .. .. 7·00 25
c. Grey-brown and purple (1905) .. 27·00 1·50
d. Black and purple .. .. .. 12·00 95
e. Jet-black and bright purple (1914) .. 35·00 2·00
44 10 c. deep blue (3.6.19) .. .. .. 6·00 80
a. Bright blue .. .. .. 6·50 85
b. Wmk upright (inverted) .. ..
45 20 c. mauve and black (3.05) .. .. 1·50 35
a. Chalk-surfaced paper .. .. .. 3·25 65
46 35 c. scarlet/*pale yellow* (25.8.22) .. .. 7·50 12·00
47 50 c. grey and orange (3.05) .. .. 38·00 3·25
a. Grey-brown and orange-brown (1906) 18·00 3·25
b. Chalk-surfaced paper. *Grey-brown and orange-brown* .. .. .. 20·00 3·25
ba. Grey and orange-brown .. .. 35·00 3·25
bb. Black and orange-brown .. .. 45·00 5·50
bc. Jet-black and orange-brown (1914) .. 60·00 6·00
e. Wmk upright (inverted) .. .. † —
48 $1 grey-green and green (11.07) .. .. 38·00 28·00
a. Green and pale green .. .. 38·00 28·00
49 $2 green and carmine (4.12.07) .. .. 65·00 90·00
50 $5 green and blue (1.08) .. .. .. 90·00 95·00
51 $25 green and orange (8.10) £750 £400
27/50 .. .. *Set of* 22 £275 £200
28, 30/1, 33/5, 37, 40, 42, 44, 46 Optd "Specimen" *Set of* 11 £350

Nos. 29/*b*, 30, 31, 33, 34/*a* and 35 were printed from single working plates and all the rest from double plates.

Most examples of No. 47e have fiscal cancellations, but at least one is known postally used.

1922–34. *Wmk Mult Script CA (sideways in T* **3**). *Ordinary paper (1 c. to 10 c. (No. 66), 12 c., 35 c. (No. 72)) or chalk-surfaced paper (others).*

52 **3** 1 c. deep brown (1.8.22) .. .. .. 2·50 2·25
53 1 c. black (12.6.23) 50 20
54 2 c. brown (5.8.25) .. .. .. 4·00 2·25
55 2 c. green (15.6.26) 45 10
56 3 c. grey (27.12.22) .. .. .. 1·75 4·25
57 3 c. green (22.1.24) .. .. .. 1·50 1·75
58 3 c. brown (31.5.27) 60 40
59 4 c. carmine-red (Die II) (27.11.23) .. 2·75 45
60 4 c. orange (9.11.26) 55 10
a. No watermark £200 £100
61 5 c. mauve/*pale yellow* (17.3.22) 75 20
62 5 c. brown (1.3.32) .. .. .. 1·60 10
63 6 c. orange (2.5.22) 55 45
64 6 c. scarlet (9.11.26) 80 10
65 10 c. bright blue (23.10.23) .. .. .. 1·25 6·00
66 10 c. black and blue (18.1.24*) .. .. 2·00 75
67 10 c. purple/*pale yellow* (14.7.31) .. .. 3·50 40
68 12 c. ultramarine (12.9.22) .. .. .. 1·25 10
69 20 c. dull purple and black (*chalk-surfaced paper*) (3.4.23) .. .. .. 4·00 35
a. Ordinary paper (29.12.26) .. .. 7·50 40
70 25 c. purple and bright magenta (3.9.29) .. 2·50 75
71 30 c. purple and orange-yellow (3.9.29) .. 3·25 1·25
72 35 c. scarlet/*pale yellow* (6.11.28) .. .. 3·75 12·00
73 35 c. scarlet and purple (29.9.31) .. .. 12·00 12·00
74 50 c. black and orange (24.4.24) .. .. 13·00 4·50
a. Black and orange-brown .. .. 13·00 4·50
75 50 c. black/*green* (16.6.31) .. .. 4·00 2·00
76 **4** $1 pale green and green (2.2.26) .. 17·00 48·00
a. Grey-green and emerald (5.10.26) .. 10·00 22·00
77 **3** $1 black and red/*blue* (10.3.31) .. .. 10·00 2·50
78 **4** $2 green and carmine (17.8.26) .. .. 10·00 48·00
79 **3** $2 green and red/*yellow* (6.2.34) .. .. 27·00 26·00
80 **4** $5 green and blue (24.2.25) .. .. 60·00 85·00
81 **3** $5 green and red/*green* (7.34) £120 £130
82 **4** $25 green & orange (14.2.28) (Optd S. £90) £650 £300
52/81 .. .. *Set of* 30 £275 £325
52/81 Optd/Perf "Specimen" .. *Set of* 30 £550

Nos. 52, 56 and 59 were printed from single working plates and the rest from double plates.

*No. 66 was released in London by the Crown Agents some months earlier but this is the official date of issue in the States.

The 5 c. in mauve on white Script paper is the result of soaking early printings of No. 61 in water.

POSTAGE DUE STAMPS

D 1

(Typo Waterlow)

1924 (1 Dec)–**26**. *Wmk Mult Script CA (sideways). P* 15 × 14.

D1 **D 1** 1 c. violet .. .. 3·50 7·00
D2 2 c. black .. .. 1·75 2·00
D3 4 c. green (27.4.26) .. .. .. 2·25 4·25
D4 8 c. red .. .. 4·25 14·00
D5 10 c. orange .. .. 7·50 11·00
D6 12 c. blue .. .. 8·50 18·00
D1/6 .. .. *Set of* 6 25·00 50·00
D1/6 Optd "Specimen" .. .. *Set of* 6 £140

The issues of the Federated Malay States were replaced by stamps for the individual States from 1935 onwards.

III. MALAYAN POSTAL UNION

The Malayan Postal Union was organised in 1934 and, initially, covered the Straits Settlements and the Federated Malay States. Stamps of the Straits Settlements together with issues for the individual States continued to be used, but Malayan Postal Union postage due stamps were introduced in 1936.

Following the end of the Second World War the use of these postage dues spread throughout Malaya and to Singapore.

PRICES FOR STAMPS ON COVER TO 1945	
Nos. D1/6	*from* × 10
Nos. D7/13	*from* × 4

POSTAGE DUE STAMPS

D 1

10

cents

(D 2)

(Typo Waterlow until 1961, then D.L.R.)

1936 (June)–**38**. *Wmk Mult Script CA. P* 15 × 14.

D1 **D 1** 1 c. slate-purple (4.38) .. .. .. 3·50 70
D2 4 c. green (9.36) .. .. .. 6·00 1·00
D3 8 c. scarlet .. .. 2·50 3·50
D4 10 c. yellow-orange .. .. .. 2·00 25
D5 12 c. pale ultramarine (9.36) .. .. 4·25 6·00
D6 50 c. black (1.38) .. .. .. 16·00 5·00
D1/6 .. .. *Set of* 6 30·00 15·00
D1/6 Perf "Specimen" .. .. *Set of* 6 £100

For use in Negri Sembilan, Pahang, Perak, Selangor and Straits Settlements including Singapore.

1945–49. *New values and colours. Wmk Mult Script CA. P* 15 × 14.

D 7 **D 1** 1 c. purple .. .. 2·75 1·75
D 8 3 c. green .. .. 9·00 11·00
D 9 5 c. scarlet .. .. 12·00 7·50
D10 8 c. yell-orange (1949) (Perf S. £75) .. 24·00 16·00
D11 9 c. yellow-orange .. .. .. 60·00 45·00
D12 15 c. pale ultramarine .. .. .. 80·00 35·00
D13 20 c. blue (1948) (Perf S. £75) .. .. 14·00 7·00
D7/13 .. .. *Set of* 7 £180 £110

1951 (8 Aug)–**63**. *Wmk Mult Script CA. P* 14.

D14 **D 1** 1 c. violet (21.8.52) 30 60
D15 2 c. deep slate-blue (16.11.53) 30 75
a. Perf 12½ (15.11.60) .. .. .. 40 7·00
b. Perf 12½. Chalk-surfaced paper (10.7.62) .. .. 35 5·00
ba. Ditto. Imperf between (vert pair)
D16 3 c. deep green (21.8.52) .. .. .. 12·00 10·00
D17 4 c. sepia (16.11.53) .. .. .. 45 3·00
a. Perf 12½ (15.11.60) .. .. .. 60 10·00
ab. Chalk-surfaced paper. *Bistre-brown* (10.7.62) .. .. .. 70 9·00
D18 5 c. vermilion .. .. 32·00 12·00
D19 8 c. yellow-orange .. .. .. 1·75 3·25
D20 12 c. bright purple (1.2.54) .. .. 1·00 3·75
a. Perf 12½. Chalk-surfaced paper (10.7.62) .. .. 1·50 16·00
D21 20 c. blue .. .. 4·00 6·00
a. Perf 12½. *Deep blue* (10.12.57) .. 3·25 24·00
ab. Chalk-surfaced paper (15.10.63) .. 3·00 26·00
D14/21 .. .. *Set of* 8 45·00 35·00

Nos. D7 to D21b were for use in the Federation and Singapore, and from 1963 throughout Malaysia.

1964 (14 Apr)–**65**. *Chalk-surfaced paper. Wmk w* **12** *(sideways on 1 c.). P* 12½.

D22 **D 1** 1 c. maroon .. .. 30 8·50
a. Perf 12. Wmk upright (4.5.65) .. 30 8·50
D23 2 c. deep slate-blue .. .. .. 45 10·00
a. Perf 12 (9.3.65) .. .. .. 35 16·00
D24 4 c. bistre-brown .. .. .. 75 9·50
a. Perf 12 (9.3.65) .. .. .. 40 11·00
D25 8 c. yellow-orange (p 12) (4.5.65) .. 2·00 12·00
D27 12 c. bright purple .. .. .. 1·50 16·00
a. Perf 12 (4.5.65) .. .. .. 2·25 26·00
D28 20 c. deep blue .. .. 2·50 35·00
a. Perf 12 (4.5.65) .. .. .. 3·50 45·00
D22/8 .. .. *Set of* 6 6·25 80·00

1964 (Dec). *As No.* D19 *surch locally with Type* D **2**.

D29 **D 1** 10 c. on 8 c. yellow-orange .. .. 30 1·75

First supplies of this stamp differed from No. D19 in that they had been climatically affected but later a fresh printing of No. D19 was surcharged.

1967? *Unsurfaced paper. Wmk w* **12**. *P* 15 × 14.

D30 **D 1** 50 c. black £450 £400

Nos. D22/9 were for use throughout Malaysia and Singapore. They were superseded on 15 August 1966 by the postage dues inscribed "MALAYSIA", but continued in use, together with No. D30, for Singapore until 31 January 1968 when they were replaced by Singapore Postage Dues.

IV. MALAYA (BRITISH MILITARY ADMINISTRATION)

For use throughout all Malay States and in Singapore. From 1948 this general issue was gradually replaced by individual issues for each state. The last usage was in Kelantan where B M A overprints were not withdrawn until 10 July 1951.

B M A
MALAYA

(1)

1945 (19 Oct)–**48**. *T* **58** *of Straits Settlements from Die I (double-plate printing) or Die II (single-plate printing) optd with T* **1**. *Wmk Mult Script CA. Chalk-surfaced paper. P* 14 *or* 15 × 14 *(No. 11).*

1 1 c. black (I) (R.) 20 10
a. Ordinary paper 10 10
2 2 c. orange (II) (8.7.47) .. .. .. 1·00 30
a. Ordinary paper (19.10.45) 10 10
3 2 c. orange (I) (*ordinary paper*) (9.46) .. 5·00 2·50
4 3 c. yellow-green (II) (*ordinary paper*) .. 10 10
a. Blue-green (27.1.47) .. .. .. 1·25 20
b. Chalk-surfaced paper. *Blue-grn* (8.7.47) 2·25 30
5 5 c. brown (II) (11.45) 30 10
6 6 c. grey (II) (22.3.48) .. .. .. 1·25 30
a. Ordinary paper (19.10.45) 10 10
7 8 c. scarlet (II) (*ordinary paper*) 10 10
8 10 c. purple (I) (12.45) 60 10
a. Ordinary paper (19.10.45) 30 10
b. Slate-purple (12.45) 40 10
c. Magenta (22.3.48) .. .. .. 1·00 30
9 10 c. purple (II) (28.7.48) .. .. .. 9·50 75
10 12 c. bright ultramarine (I) (11.45) .. .. 1·75 2·75
11 15 c. brt ultram (II) (*ordinary paper*) (11.45) 2·25 4·75
12 15 c. bright ultramarine (II) (R.) (22.3.48) 4·50 30
a. Ordinary paper (12.45) 30 10
b. Blue (27.11.47) .. .. .. 15·00 75
ba. Ordinary paper (8.7.47) .. .. 45·00 9·00
13 25 c. dull purple and scarlet (I) (22.3.48) .. 1·50 15
a. Ordinary paper (12.45) 70 15
ab. Opt double £1600
14 50 c. black/*emerald* (I) (R.) (12.45) .. .. 2·00 10
a. Ordinary paper 40 10
15 $1 black and red (I) (*ordinary paper*) (12.45) 1·50 10
16 $2 green & scar (I) (*ordinary paper*) (12.45) 1·75 40
17 $5 green and red/*emerald* (I) (11.45) .. 48·00 48·00
18 $5 pur & orge (I) (*ordinary paper*) (12.45) 3·00 1·50
1/18 .. .. *Set of* 15 50·00 48·00
1/11, 13/16, 18 Perf "Specimen" .. *Set of* 14 £350

The 8 c. grey with "B.M.A." opt was prepared but not officially issued (*Price* £110 *unused*).

Nos. 3 and 9 do not exist without the overprint.

Nos. 1, 2, 6, 7, 8 and 13 exist also on thin, rough ordinary paper.

No. 8 with reddish purple medallion and dull purple frame is from a 1947 printing with the head in fugitive ink which discolours with moisture.

Stamps in the Crown Colony Victory design were prepared for the Malayan Union in 1946, but not issued. Examples of the 8 c. carmine from this issue were stolen from stock awaiting destruction.

V. MALAYAN FEDERATION

The Malayan Federation, formed on 1 February 1948 by Malacca, Penang, the four Federated Malay States and the five Unfederated States, became an independent member of the British Commonwealth on 31 August 1957.

Commemoratives and a limited series of definitives were issued by the Federation and were used concurrently with the stamps from the individual States.

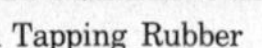

1 Tapping Rubber

4 Map of the Federation

(Centre recess, frame litho (6 c., 25 c.); centre litho, frame recess (12 c.); recess (30 c.), D.L.R.)

1957 (5 May)–**63**. *T* 1, 4 *and similar designs. W* w **12**. *P* 13×12½ *(No. 4) or* 13 *(others).*

1	6 c. deep blue, red, yellow and grey-blue	..	30	10
	a. Indigo, red, yellow and grey-blue (20.6.61)		55	20
	b. Indigo, red, yellow & slate-blue (12.2.63)		40	10
	c. Yellow (star and crescent) omitted	..	42·00	
2	12 c. red, yellow, blue, black and scarlet	..	40	10
3	25 c. maroon, red, yellow & dull greenish blue		45	10
4	30 c. orange-red and lake	..	40	20
	a. Perf 13. *Orange-red & deep lake* (20.6.61)		40	30
	ab. Orange-red and lake (10.7.62)	..	40	10
1/4	.. ..	*Set of* 4	1·40	15

Designs: *Horiz*—12 c. Federation coat of arms; 25 c. Tin dredger.

5 Prime Minister Tunku Abdul Rahman and Populace greeting Independence

(Des A. B. Saman. Recess Waterlow)

1957 (31 Aug). *Independence Day. Wmk Mult Script CA. P* 12½.

5	**5**	10 c. bistre-brown	10	10

6 United Nations Emblem **7** United Nations Emblem

(Recess D.L.R.)

1958 (5 Mar). *U.N. Economic Commission for Asia and Far East Conference, Kuala Lumpur. W* w **12**. *P* 13½ (12 c.) *or* 12½ (30 c.).

6	**6**	12 c. carmine-red	30	40
7	**7**	30 c. maroon	40	20

8 Merdeka Stadium, Kuala Lumpur **9** The Yang di-Pertuan Agong (Tuanku Abdul Rahman)

(Photo Harrison)

1958 (31 Aug). *First Anniv of Independence. W* w **12**. *P* 13½ × 14½ (10 c.) *or* 14½ × 13½ (30 c.).

8	**8**	10 c. green, yellow, red and blue ..	15	10
9	**9**	30 c. red, yellow, violet-blue and green ..	40	10

10 "Human Rights" **11** Malayan with Torch of Freedom

(Des J. P. Hendroff. Litho (10 c.), photo (30 c.) D.L.R.)

1958 (10 Dec). *Tenth Anniv of Declaration of Human Rights.*

(a) *W* w **12**. *P* 12½ × 13

10	**10**	10 c. blue, black, carmine and orange ..	10	10

(b) *Wmk Mult Script CA. P* 13 × 12½

11	**11**	30 c. deep green	30	20

12 Mace and Malayan Peoples

(Photo Enschedé)

1959 (12 Sept). *Inauguration of Parliament. No wmk. P* 13 × 14.

12	**12**	4 c. rose-red	10	10
13		10 c. violet	10	10
14		25 c. yellow-green	35	20
12/14		.. .. *Set of* 3	50	30

13 **14**

(Recess D.L.R.)

1960 (7 Apr). *World Refugee Year. W* w **12**. *P* 13½ (12 c.) *or* 12½ × 13 (30 c.).

15	**13**	12 c. purple	10	30
16	**14**	30 c. deep green	10	10

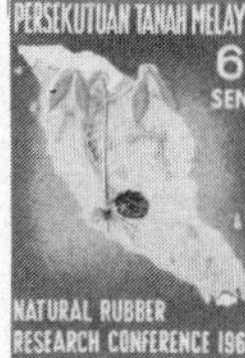

15 Seedling Rubber Tree and Map **16** The Yang di-Pertuan Agong (Tuanku Syed Putra)

(Photo Japanese Govt Ptg Wks)

1960 (19 Sept). *Natural Rubber Research Conference and 15th International Rubber Study Group Meeting, Kuala Lumpur. T* **15** *and similar vert design. No wmk. P* 13.

17		6 c. yellow-green, black, orange & red-brown	20	30
18		30 c. yellow-green, black, orange & bright blue	50	15

No. 18 is inscribed "INTERNATIONAL RUBBER STUDY GROUP 15th MEETING KUALA LUMPUR" at foot.

(Photo Harrison)

1961 (4 Jan). *Installation of Yang di-Pertuan Agong, Tuanku Syed Putra. W* w **12**. *P* 14 × 14½.

19	**16**	10 c. black and blue	10	10

17 Colombo Plan Emblem **18** Malaria Eradication Emblem

(Photo Japanese Govt Ptg Works)

1961 (30 Oct). *Colombo Plan Conference, Kuala Lumpur. P* 13.

20	**17**	12 c. black and magenta	35	1·50
21		25 c. black and apple-green	80	1·25
22		30 c. black and turquoise-blue	70	30
20/2		.. .. *Set of* 3	1·75	2·75

(Photo Harrison)

1962 (7 Apr). *Malaria Eradication. W* w **13**. *P* 14 × 14½.

23	**18**	25 c. orange-brown	20	30
24		30 c. deep lilac	20	10
25		50 c. ultramarine	40	15
23/5		.. .. *Set of* 3	70	50

19 Palmyra Palm Leaf **20** "Shadows of the Future"

(Photo Harrison)

1962 (21 July). *National Language Month. W* w **13** *(upright or inverted). P* 13½.

26	**19**	10 c. light brown and deep reddish violet	15	10
27		20 c. light brown and deep bluish green	25	25
28		50 c. light brown and magenta ..	45	60
26/8		.. .. *Set of* 3	75	80

(Photo Enschedé)

1962 (1 Oct). *Introduction of Free Primary Education. W* w **13**. *P* 13½.

29	**20**	10 c. bright purple	10	10
30		25 c. ochre	30	30
31		30 c. emerald	80	10
29/31		.. .. *Set of* 3	1·10	40

21 Harvester and Fisherman **22** Dam and Pylon

(Photo Courvoisier)

1963 (21 Mar). *Freedom from Hunger. P* 11½.

32	**21**	25 c. carmine and apple-green	85	80
33		30 c. carmine and crimson	1·50	30
34		50 c. carmine and bright blue	1·50	1·10
32/4		.. .. *Set of* 3	3·50	2·00

(Photo Harrison)

1963 (26 June). *Cameron Highlands Hydro-Electric Scheme. W* w **13**. *P* 14.

35	**22**	20 c. green and reddish violet	35	10
36		30 c. blue-green and ultramarine ..	45	40

The definitive general issue for Malaysia and the low value sets for the individual states superseded the stamps of the Malayan Federation by 15 November 1965.

VI. MALAYSIA

On 16 September 1963, the Malayan Federation, Sabah (North Borneo), Sarawak and Singapore formed the Federation of Malaysia. Singapore left the Federation on 9 August 1965, and became an independent republic.

Individual issues for the component States continued, but were restricted to low value definitives and the occasional "State" commemorative. The higher value definitives and the vast majority of commemoratives were issued on a "National" basis.

A. NATIONAL ISSUES

General issues for use throughout the Malaysian Federation.

1 Federation Map **2** Bouquet of Orchids

(Photo Harrison)

1963 (16 Sept). *Inauguration of Federation. W* w **13**. *P* 14½.

1	**1**	10 c. yellow and bluish violet	15	10
		a. Yellow omitted	85·00	
2		12 c. yellow and deep green	60	60
3		50 c. yellow and chocolate	75	10
1/3		.. .. *Set of* 3	1·40	65

(Photo Enschedé)

1963 (3 Oct). *Fourth World Orchid Conference, Singapore. No wmk. P* 13 × 14.

4	**2**	6 c. multicoloured	1·00	1·00
5		25 c. multicoloured	1·25	25

4 Parliament House, Kuala Lumpur

(Des V. Whiteley. Photo Harrison)

1963 (4 Nov). *Ninth Commonwealth Parliamentary Conference, Kuala Lumpur. W* w **13** *(inverted). P* 13½.

7	**4**	20 c. deep magenta and gold	25	40
8		30 c. deep green and gold	25	15

5 "Flame of Freedom" and Emblems of Goodwill, Health and Charity **6** Microwave Tower and I.T.U. Emblem

(Photo Harrison)

1964 (10 Oct). *Eleanor Roosevelt Commemoration. W* w **13**. *P* 14½ × 13½.

9	**5**	25 c. black, red and greenish blue ..	15	10
10		30 c. black, red and deep lilac	15	10
11		50 c. black, red and ochre-yellow ..	15	10
9/11		.. .. *Set of* 3	40	15

(Photo Courvoisier)

1965 (17 May). *I.T.U. Centenary. P* 11½.
12 **6** 2 c. multicoloured 15 80
13 25 c. multicoloured 60 40
14 50 c. multicoloured .. .. 1·25 10
12/14 .. .. *Set of* 3 1·75 1·10

7 National Mosque 8 Air Terminal

(Photo Harrison)

1965 (27 Aug). *Opening of National Mosque, Kuala Lumpur. W* w **13.** *P* 14 × 14½.
15 **7** 6 c. carmine 10 10
16 15 c. red-brown 10 10
17 20 c. deep bluish green 10 10
15/17 .. .. *Set of* 3 25 20

(Photo Harrison)

1965 (30 Aug). *Opening of International Airport, Kuala Lumpur. W* w **13.** *P* 14½ × 14.
18 **8** 15 c. black, yellow-green and new blue .. 15 10
a. Yellow-green omitted .. .. 20·00
19 30 c. black, yellow-green and magenta .. 25 20

9 Crested Wood Partridge 17 Sepak Raga (ball game) and Football

(Des A. Fraser-Brunner. Photo Harrison)

1965 (9 Sept). *T* **9** *and similar vert designs. Multicoloured. W* w **13.** *P* 14½.
20 25 c. Type **9** 50 10
21 30 c. Blue-backed Fairy Bluebird 60 10
a. Blue omitted .. .. 95·00
22 50 c. Black-eyed Oriole 70 10
a. Yellow omitted .. .. 55·00
b. Imperf (pair) £200
c. Scarlet (inscr and berries) omitted .. 30·00
23 75 c. Rhinoceros Hornbill .. .. .. 1·25 10
a. Scarlet omitted* .. .. 45·00
24 $1 Zebra Dove .. .. 1·75 10
25 $2 Great Argus Pheasant .. .. .. 4·00 30
a. Imperf (pair) £200
26 $5 Asiatic Paradise Flycatcher .. .. 13·00 1·50
27 $10 Blue-tailed Pitta .. .. 35·00 6·50
a. Imperf (pair) £275
20/7 .. .. *Set of* 8 50·00 8·00

*The inscription at foot is omitted and the background appears paler.

All values except the 75 c. and $10 exist with PVA gum as well as gum arabic.

(Des E. A. F. Anthony. Litho Japanese Govt Ptg Wks)

1965 (14 Dec). *Third South East Asian Peninsular Games. T* **17** *and similar vert designs. P* 13 × 13½.
28 25 c. black and olive-green 40 90
29 30 c. black and bright purple 40 20
30 50 c. black and light blue 70 30
28/30 .. .. *Set of* 3 1·40 1·25

Designs:—30 c. Running; 50 c. Diving.

20 National Monument 21 The Yang di-Pertuan Agong (Tuanku Ismail Nasiruddin Shah)

(Photo Harrison)

1966 (8 Feb). *National Monument, Kuala Lumpur. W* w **13.** *P* 13½.
31 **20** 10 c. multicoloured 15 10
a. Blue omitted .. .. 35·00
32 20 c. multicoloured 25 15

(Photo Japanese Govt Ptg Wks)

1966 (11 Apr). *Installation of Yang di-Pertuan Agong, Tuanku Ismail Nasiruddin Shah. P* 13½.
33 **21** 15 c. black and light yellow 10 10
34 50 c. black and greenish blue 20 15

22 School Building 23 "Agriculture"

(Photo D.L.R.)

1966 (21 Oct). *150th Anniv of Penang Free School. W* w **13** *(sideways). P* 13.
35 **22** 20 c. multicoloured 25 10
36 50 c. multicoloured 60 10

The 50 c. is also inscr "ULANG TAHUN KE-150" at foot and bears a shield at bottom left corner.

(Des Enche Ng Peng Nam. Photo Japanese Govt Ptg Wks)

1966 (1 Dec). *First Malaysia Plan. T* **23** *and similar horiz designs. Multicoloured. P* 13½.
37 15 c. Type **23** 20 10
38 15 c. "Rural Health" 20 10
39 15 c. "Communications" 75 15
40 15 c. "Education" 20 10
41 15 c. "Irrigation" 20 10
37/41 .. .. *Set of* 5 1·40 50

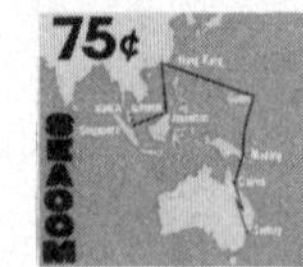

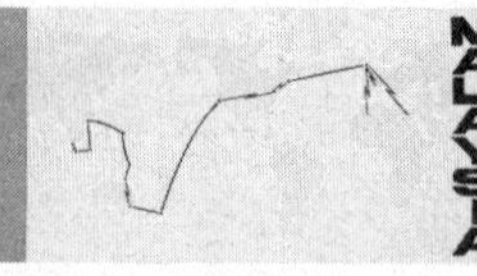

28 Cable Route Maps

(Des Enche Ng Peng Nam. Photo Japanese Govt Ptg Wks)

1967 (30 Mar). *Completion of Malaysia–Hong Kong Link of SEACOM Telephone Cable. P* 13½.
42 **28** 30 c. multicoloured 80 25
43 75 c. multicoloured .. .. 2·50 2·50

29 Hibiscus and Paramount Rulers

(Photo Harrison)

1967 (31 Aug). *Tenth Anniv of Independence. W* w **13.** *P* 14½.
44 **29** 15 c. multicoloured 20 10
45 50 c. multicoloured 50 35

30 Mace and Shield 31 Straits Settlements 1867 8 c. and Malaysia 1965 25 c. Definitive

(Des Enche Ng Peng Nam. Photo Harrison)

1967 (8 Sept). *Centenary of Sarawak Council. W* w **13.** *P* 14½.
46 **30** 15 c. multicoloured 10 10
47 50 c. multicoloured 20 20

(Des Enche Ng Peng Nam. Photo Japanese Govt Ptg Works)

1967 (2 Dec). *Stamp Centenary. T* **31** *and similar shaped designs. Multicoloured. P* 11½.
48 25 c. Type **31** .. .. 1·00 1·50
a. *Tête-bêche* (horiz pair) .. .. .. 2·00 3·00
49 30 c. Straits Settlements 1867 24 c. and Malaysia 1965 30 c. definitive .. .. 1·00 85
a. *Tête-bêche* (horiz pair) .. .. .. 2·00 1·60
50 50 c. Straits Settlements 1867 32 c. and Malaysia 1965 50 c. definitive .. .. 1·40 1·25
a. *Tête-bêche* (horiz pair) .. .. .. 2·75 2·50
48/50 .. .. *Set of* 3 3·00 3·25

Nos. 48/50 were each printed in sheets with the stamps arranged horizontally *tête-bêche*.

34 Tapping Rubber, and Molecular Unit 37 Mexican Sombrero and Blanket with Olympic Rings

(Litho B.W.)

1968 (29 Aug). *Natural Rubber Conference, Kuala Lumpur. T* **34** *and similar horiz designs. Multicoloured. W* w **13.** *P* 12.
51 25 c. Type **34** 25 10
52 30 c. Tapping rubber, and export consignment 40 20
53 50 c. Tapping rubber, and aircraft tyres .. 40 10
51/3 .. .. *Set of* 3 95 35

(Litho B.W.)

1968 (12 Oct). *Olympic Games, Mexico. T* **37** *and similar vert design. Multicoloured. W* w **13.** *P* 12 × 11½.
54 30 c. Type **37** 20 10
55 75 c. Olympic rings and Mexican embroidery 40 20

39 Tunku Abdul Rahman against background of Pandanus Weave 40

(Photo Japanese Govt Ptg Wks)

1969 (8 Feb). *Solidarity Week. T* **39**/**40** *and similar multicoloured design. P* 13½.
56 15 c. Type **39** 15 10
57 20 c. Type **40** 20 40
58 50 c. Tunku Abdul Rahman with pandanus pattern *(horiz)* 20 20
56/8 .. .. *Set of* 3 50 55

42 Peasant Girl with Sheaves of Paddy

(Des Enche Hoessein Anas. Photo Harrison)

1969 (8 Dec). *National Rice Year. W* w **13.** *P* 13½.
59 **42** 15 c. multicoloured 15 10
60 75 c. multicoloured 45 55

43 Satellite tracking Aerial

44 "Intelsat III" in Orbit

(Photo Enschedé)

1970 (6 Apr). *Satellite Earth Station. W* w **13.** *P* 14 × 13 (15 c.) *or* 13½ × 13 (30 c.).
61 **43** 15 c. multicoloured 75 15
a. *Tête-bêche* (horiz pair) .. .. .. 1·50 1·75
62 **44** 30 c. multicoloured* .. .. 75 1·40
63 30 c. multicoloured* .. .. 75 1·40
61/3 .. .. *Set of* 3 2·00 2·75

No. 61 was issued horizontally *tête-bêche* in the sheets.

*Nos. 62/3 are of the same design, differing only in the lettering colours (No. 62 white; No. 63 gold).

45 *Euploea leucostictus* 46 Emblem

(Des V. Whiteley. Litho B.W. (to 1976) or Harrison)

1970 (31 Aug–16 Nov). *Butterflies. T* **45** *and similar vert designs. Multicoloured. P* 13 × 13½.
64 25 c. Type **45** 80 10
65 30 c. *Zeuxidia amethystus* .. .. .. 1·25 10
66 50 c. *Polyura athamas* .. .. 1·50 10
67 75 c. *Papilio memnon* .. .. 1·75 10
68 $1 *Appias nero* (16.11) .. .. .. 1·75 10
69 $2 *Trogonoptera brookiana* (16.11) .. 3·00 10
70 $5 *Narathura centaurus* (16.11) .. .. 4·50 1·25
71 $10 *Terinos terpander* (16.11) .. .. 9·00 5·00
64/71 .. .. *Set of* 8 21·00 6·00

See also Nos. 144/5.

(Litho Harrison)

1970 (7 Sept). *50th Anniv of International Labour Organization. P* 14 × 13½.
72 **46** 30 c. grey and new blue 10 20
73 75 c. pink and new blue 20 30

47 U.N. Emblem encircled by Doves

50 The Yang di-Pertuan Agong (Tuanku Abdul Halim Shah)

(Des Enche Ng Peng Nam. Litho D.L.R.)

1970 (24 Oct). *25th Anniv of United Nations. T* **47** *and similar horiz designs. P* 13 × 12½.
74 25 c. gold, black and brown 35 40
75 30 c. multicoloured 45 35
76 50 c. black and dull yellow-green 75 75
74/6 .. .. *Set of* 3 1·40 1·40
Designs:—30 c. Line of doves and U.N. emblem; 50 c. Doves looping U.N. emblem.

(Des Union Art Corp. Photo Harrison)

1971 (20 Feb). *Installation of Yang di-Pertuan Agong (Paramount Ruler of Malaysia). P* 14½ × 14.
77 **50** 10 c. black, gold and lemon 20 30
a. Gold (value and inscr) omitted .. £160
78 15 c. black, gold and bright mauve .. 20 30
79 50 c. black, gold and new blue .. .. 60 1·60
77/9 .. .. *Set of* 3 90 2·00

51 Bank Negara Complex

(Photo Harrison)

1971 (15 May). *Opening of Bank Negara Building. P* 13½ *(and around design).*
80 **51** 25 c. black and silver 70 90
81 50 c. black and gold .. .. .. 70 1·10

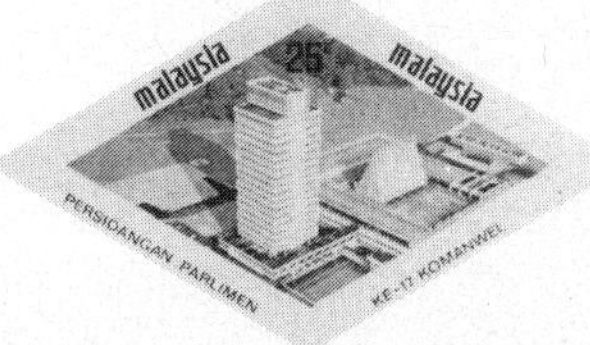

52 Aerial view of Parliament Buildings

(Des Union Art Corp. Litho Harrison)

1971 (13 Sept). *17th Commonwealth Parliamentary Association Conference, Kuala Lumpur. T* **52** *and similar multicoloured design. P* 13½ (25 c.) *or* 12½ × 13 (75c.).
82 25 c. Type **52** 90 50
83 75 c. Ground view of Parliament Buildings (73 × 23½ *mm*) .. .. 1·60 1·75

53 54 55

Malaysian Carnival

(Des locally. Litho Harrison)

1971 (18 Sept). *Visit A.S.E.A.N.* Year. P* 14½.
84 **53** 30 c. multicoloured .. .. .. 1·25 35
a. Horiz strip of 3. Nos. 84/6 .. .. 3·25
85 **54** 30 c. multicoloured .. .. .. 1·25 35
86 **55** 30 c. multicoloured .. .. .. 1·25 35
84/6 .. .. *Set of* 3 3·25 95
*A.S.E.A.N. = Association of South East Asian Nations.
Nos. 84/6 were printed together, *se-tenant*, in horizontal strips of 3 throughout the sheet, forming a composite design.

56 Trees, Elephant and Tiger

57 Athletics

(Des from children's drawings. Litho Harrison)

1971 (2 Oct). *25th Anniv of U.N.I.C.E.F. T* **56** *and similar multicoloured designs. P* 12½.
87 15 c. Type **56** .. .. 1·25 25
a. Horiz strip of 5. Nos. 87/91 .. .. 5·75
88 15 c. Cat and kittens .. .. 1·25 25
89 15 c. Sun, flower and bird (22 × 29 *mm*) .. 1·25 25
90 15 c. Monkey, elephant and lion in jungle .. 1·25 25
91 15 c. Spider and butterflies .. .. .. 1·25 25
87/91 .. .. *Set of* 5 5·75 1·10
Nos. 87/91 were issued in horizontal *se-tenant* strips of 5 throughout the sheet.

(Des Union Art Corp. Litho B.W.)

1971 (11 Dec). *Sixth S.E.A.P.* Games, Kuala Lumpur. T* **57** *and similar horiz designs. Multicoloured. P* 14½ × 14.
92 25 c. Type **57** 35 40
93 30 c. Sepak Raga players 50 50
94 50 c. Hockey 80 95
92/4 .. .. *Set of* 3 1·50 1·75
*S.E.A.P. = South East Asian Peninsula.

58 59 60

Map and Tourist Attractions

(Des locally. Litho Harrison)

1972 (31 Jan). *Pacific Area Tourist Association Conference. P* 14 × 14½.
95 **58** 30 c. multicoloured .. .. .. 1·25 35
a. Horiz strip of 3. Nos. 95/7 .. .. 3·25
96 **59** 30 c. multicoloured .. .. .. 1·25 35
97 **60** 30 c. multicoloured .. .. .. 1·25 35
95/7 .. .. *Set of* 3 3·25 95
Nos. 95/7 were printed together, *se-tenant*, in horizontal strips of 3 throughout the sheet forming a composite design.

61 Kuala Lumpur City Hall

(Des from colour transparencies. Litho Harrison)

1972 (1 Feb). *City Status for Kuala Lumpur. T* **61** *and similar horiz design. Multicoloured. P* 14½ × 14.
98 25 c. Type **61** .. .. 1·00 1·25
99 50 c. City Hall in floodlights .. .. .. 1·50 1·25

62 SOCSO Emblem

63 W.H.O. Emblem

(Des B.W. Litho Harrison)

1973 (2 July). *Social Security Organisation. P* 13½.
100 **62** 10 c. multicoloured 15 15
101 15 c. multicoloured 25 10
102 50 c. multicoloured .. .. 60 1·40
100/2 .. .. *Set of* 3 90 1·50

(Des Union Advertising. Litho B.W.)

1973 (1 Aug). *25th Anniv of W.H.O. T* **63** *and similar vert design. P* 13.
103 30 c. multicoloured 45 25
104 75 c. multicoloured .. .. 1·25 1·75

64 Fireworks, National Flag and Flower

65 Emblems of Interpol and Royal Malaysian Police

(Des Clover Associates. Litho Harrison)

1973 (31 Aug). *Tenth Anniv of Malaysia. P* 13½.
105 **64** 10 c. multicoloured 25 25
106 15 c. multicoloured 30 15
107 50 c. multicoloured .. .. 1·25 1·60
105/7 .. .. *Set of* 3 1·60 1·75

(Des Union Advertising. Litho Harrison)

1973 (15 Sept). *50th Anniv of Interpol. T* **65** *and similar vert design. Multicoloured. P* 13½.
108 25 c. Type **65** .. .. 1·00 50
109 75 c. Emblems within "50" .. .. .. 1·75 2·00

66 Aeroplane and M.A.S. Emblem

(Des Art Dept, Malaysia Airline System. Litho Harrison)

1973 (1 Oct). *Foundation of Malaysia Airline System. P* 14½.
110 **66** 15 c. multicoloured 25 10
111 30 c. multicoloured 45 60
112 50 c. multicoloured .. .. 75 1·60
110/12 .. .. *Set of* 3 1·25 2·10

67 Kuala Lumpur

(Des Malaysian Advertising Services. Litho B.W.)

1974 (1 Feb). *Establishment of Kuala Lumpur as Federal Territory. P* 12½ × 13.
113 **67** 25 c. multicoloured 50 85
114 50 c. multicoloured .. .. 1·00 1·75

68 Development Projects

69 Scout Badge and Map

(Des Malaysian Advertising Services. Litho Rosenbaum Bros, Vienna)

1974 (25 Apr). *Seventh Annual Meeting of Asian Development Bank's Board of Governors, Kuala Lumpur. P* 13½.
115 **68** 30 c. multicoloured 25 50
116 75 c. multicoloured .. .. 80 1·75

(Des Malaysian Advertising Services. Litho Harrison)

1974 (1 Aug). *Malaysian Scout Jamboree. T* **69** *and similar multicoloured designs. P* 13 × 13½ (15 c.) *or* 14 × 13½ *(others).*
117 10 c. Type **69** 30 30
118 15 c. Scouts saluting and flags (46 × 24 *mm*) 35 30
119 50 c. Scout badge .. .. 1·25 2·25
117/19 .. .. *Set of* 3 1·75 2·50

70 Coat of Arms and Power Installations

(Des Malaysian Advertising Services. Litho Harrison)

1974 (1 Sept). *25th Anniv of National Electricity Board. T* **70** *and similar multicoloured design. P* 14 (30 c.) *or* 14 × 14½ (75 c.).
120 30 c. Type **70** 30 50
121 75 c. National Electricity Board Building (37 × 27 *mm*) .. .. 1·00 2·00

71 U.P.U. and Post Office Emblems within "100"

(Des Clover Associates. Litho Harrison)

1974 (9 Oct). *Centenary of Universal Postal Union. P* 14½ × 14.
122 **71** 25 c. dull yell-grn, brt yell & lt rose-carm 20 35
123 30 c. lt new blue, brt yell & lt rose-carm 25 35
124 75 c. brownish orange, bright yellow and light rose-carmine .. .. .. 65 1·75
122/4 .. .. *Set of* 3 1·00 2·25

72 Gravel Pump in Tin Mine **73** Hockey-players, World Cup and Federation Emblem

(Des Malaysian Advertising Service. Litho D.L.R.)

1974 (31 Oct). *Fourth World Tin Conference, Kuala Lumpur. T* **72** *and similar horiz designs. Multicoloured. P* 13½.

125 15 c. Type **72** 75 15
126 20 c. Open-cast mine .. .. 1·00 70
127 50 c. Dredger within "ingot" .. .. .. 2·50 2·50
125/7 .. .. *Set of* 3 3·75 3·00

(Des Malaysian Advertising Services. Litho Harrison)

1975 (1 Mar). *Third World Cup Hockey Championships. P* 13½ × 13.

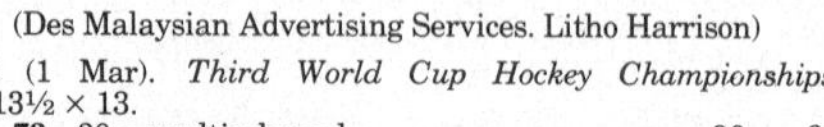

128 **73** 30 c. multicoloured 90 60
129 75 c. multicoloured .. .. 2·10 2·25

74 Congress Emblem **75** Emblem of M.K.P.W. (Malayan Women's Organisation)

(Des Malaysian Advertising Services. Litho Harrison)

1975 (1 May). *25th Anniv of Malaysian Trade Union Congress. P* 14 × 14½.

130 **74** 20 c. multicoloured 20 25
131 25 c. multicoloured 30 30
132 30 c. multicoloured 45 60
130/2 .. .. *Set of* 3 85 1·00

(Des Malaysian Advertising Services. Litho Harrison)

1975 (25 Aug). *International Women's Year. P* 14.

133 **75** 10 c. multicoloured 15 25
134 15 c. multicoloured 30 25
135 50 c. multicoloured .. .. 1·25 2·25
133/5 .. .. *Set of* 3 1·50 2·50

76 Ubudiah Mosque, Kuala Kangsar **77** Plantation and Emblem

(Des Malaysian Advertising Services. Litho Harrison)

1975 (22 Sept). *Koran Reading Competition. T* **76** *and similar horiz designs. Multicoloured. P* 14.

136 15 c. Type **76** .. .. 1·25 30
a. Horiz strip of 5. Nos. 136/40 .. .. 5·75
137 15 c. Zahir Mosque, Alor Star .. .. .. 1·25 30
138 15 c. National Mosque, Kuala Lumpur .. 1·25 30
139 15 c. Sultan Abu Bakar Mosque, Johore Bahru 1·25 30
140 15 c. Kuching State Mosque, Sarawak .. 1·25 30
136/40 .. .. *Set of* 5 5·75 1·40

The above were printed together, horizontally *se-tenant* throughout the sheet.

(Des E. Sulaiman bin Haji Hassan and E. Hoh Lian Yong. Litho Harrison)

1975 (22 Oct). *50th Anniv of Malaysian Rubber Research Institute. T* **77** *and similar horiz designs. Multicoloured. P* 14 × 14½.

141 10 c. Type **77** 35 15
142 30 c. Latex cup and emblem .. .. .. 1·00 70
143 75 c. Natural rubber in test-tubes .. .. 1·60 2·25
141/3 .. .. *Set of* 3 2·75 2·75

77a *Hebomoia glaucippe* **78** Scrub Typhus

(Photo Harrison)

1976 (19 Jan). *Coil Stamps. T* **77a** *and similar horiz design. Multicoloured. P* 13½.

144 10 c. Type **77a** .. .. 60 3·00
145 15 c. *Precis orithya* .. .. 65 3·00

(Des Lap Loy Fong (25 c.), Lee Eng Kee (others). Litho Harrison)

1976 (6 Feb). *75th Anniv of the Institute of Medical Research. T* **78** *and similar vert designs. Multicoloured. P* 14.

146 20 c. Type **78** 25 15
147 25 c. Malaria diagnosis 40 20
148 $1 Beri-beri .. .. 1·60 2·50
146/8 .. .. *Set of* 3 2·00 2·50

79 The Yang di-Pertuan Agong (Tuanku Yahya Petra) **80** State Council Complex

(Des Union Advertising. Photo Harrison)

1976 (28 Feb). *Installation of Yang di-Pertuan Agong. P* 14½ × 13½.

149 **79** 10 c. black, bistre and yellow 25 10
150 15 c. black, bistre and bright mauve .. 40 10
151 50 c. black, bistre and ultramarine .. 2·25 2·50
149/51 .. .. *Set of* 3 2·75 2·50

(Des Aini bin Abdul Rahman. Litho Harrison)

1976 (17 Aug). *Opening of the State Council Complex and Administrative Building, Sarawak. P* 12½.

152 **80** 15 c. grey-green and light yellow .. 35 10
153 20 c. grey-green and light bright mauve 45 40
154 50 c. grey-green and pale blue .. .. 1·00 1·40
152/4 .. .. *Set of* 3 1·60 1·75

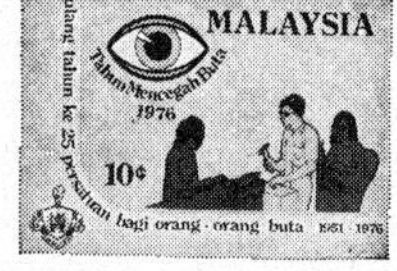

81 E.P.F. Building **82** Blind People at Work

(Litho Harrison)

1976 (18 Oct). *25th Anniv of Employees' Provident Fund. T* **81** *and similar multicoloured designs. P* 14½ (25 *c.*) *or* 13½ × 14½ (*others*).

155 10 c. Type **81** 15 10
156 25 c. E.P.F. emblems (27 × 27 *mm*) 25 35
157 50 c. E.P.F. Building at night .. .. .. 60 1·00
155/7 .. .. *Set of* 3 90 1·40

(Des Malayan Association for the Blind, Messrs Advertising Sales Promotion and Hexxon Grafic. Litho Harrison)

1976 (20 Nov). *25th Anniv of Malayan Association for the Blind. T* **82** *and similar horiz design. Multicoloured. P* 13½ × 14½.

158 10 c. Type **82** 15 15
159 75 c. Blind man and shadow .. .. .. 1·25 2·10

83 Independence Celebrations, 1957 **84** F.E.L.D.A. Village Scheme

(Des Hexxon Grafic. Photo Harrison)

1977 (14 Jan). *First Death Anniversary of Tun Abdul Razak (Prime Minister). T* **83** *and similar horiz designs, each sepia and gold. P* 14.

160 15 c. Type **83** .. .. 1·00 30
a. Horiz strip of 5. Nos. 160/4 .. .. 4·50
161 15 c. "Education" .. .. 1·00 30
162 15 c. Tun Razak and map ("Development") .. 1·00 30
163 15 c. "Rukunegara" (National Philosophy) .. 1·00 30
164 15 c. A.S.E.A.N. meeting .. .. 1·00 30
160/4 .. .. *Set of* 5 4·50 1·40

The above were printed together, horizontally *se-tenant* throughout the sheet.

(Des Halim Teh and Basyuni Sumrah. Litho Harrison)

1977 (7 July). *21st Anniv of Federal Land Development Authority (F.E.L.D.A.). T* **84** *and similar horiz design. Multicoloured. P* 13½ × 14.

165 15 c. Type **84** 25 10
166 30 c. Oil Palm settlement 60 80

85 Figure "10" **86** Games Logos

(Des Hexxon Grafic. Litho Harrison)

1977 (8 Aug). *Tenth Anniv of A.S.E.A.N. (Association of South East Asian Nations). T* **85** *and similar horiz design. Multicoloured. P* 13½ × 14½.

167 10 c. Type **85** 10 10
168 75 c. Flags of members 60 65

(Des PTM Communications & Co. Litho Harrison)

1977 (19 Nov). *9th South East Asia Games, Kuala Lumpur. T* **8** *and similar horiz designs. Multicoloured. P* 13½ × 14½.

169 10 c. Type **86** 15 1
170 20 c. "Ball" 20 1
171 75 c. Symbolic athletes .. .. 75 1·2
169/71 .. .. *Set of* 3 1·00 1·4

87 Islamic Development Bank Emblem **88** Mobile Post Office

(Des Queen's Advertising. Litho J.W.)

1978 (15 Mar). *Islamic Development Bank Board of Governors Meeting, Kuala Lumpur. P* 14.

172 **87** 30 c. multicoloured 15 15
173 75 c. multicoloured 50 55

(Des Hexxon Grafic. Litho J.W.)

1978 (10 July). *4th Commonwealth Postal Administrations Conference, Kuala Lumpur. T* **88** *and similar horiz designs. Multicoloured. P* 13½ × 13.

174 10 c. Type **88** 20 10
175 25 c. G.P.O., Kuala Lumpur 65 75
176 50 c. Postal delivery by motor-cycle .. .. 95 1·10
174/6 .. .. *Set of* 3 1·60 1·75

89 Boy Scout Emblem **90** Dome of the Rock, Jerusalem

(Des Aini bin Abdul Rahman. Litho J.W.)

1978 (26 July). *4th Malaysian Boy Scout Jamboree, Sarawak. T* **89** *and similar horiz design. Multicoloured. P* 13½ × 13.

177 15 c. Type **89** 40 10
178 $1 Bees and honeycomb .. .. 2·00 1·25

(Des Union Advertising. Litho Harrison)

1978 (21 Aug). *"Freedom for Palestine". P* 12½.

179 **90** 15 c. multicoloured 35 10
180 30 c. multicoloured 60 40

91 Globe and Emblems **92** "Seratus Tahun Getah Asli" and Tapping Knives Symbol

(Litho Harrison)

1978 (30 Sept). *Global Eradication of Smallpox. P* 13½ × 14½.

181 **91** 15 c. black, rosine and new blue 15 20
182 30 c. black, rosine and yellowish green .. 20 10
183 50 c. black, rosine and rose-pink 35 45
181/3 .. .. *Set of* 3 60 65

(Des Azmi bin Anuar. Litho J.W.)

1978 (28 Nov). *Centenary of Rubber Industry. T* **92** *and similar horiz designs. P* 13½ × 13.

184 10 c. gold and blue-green 10 10
185 20 c. ultramarine, brown & brt yellow-green .. 10 10
186 75 c. gold and blue-green 45 65
184/6 .. .. *Set of* 3 55 75

Designs:—20 c. Rubber tree seedling and part of "maxi stump"; 75 c. Graphic design of rubber tree, latex cup and globe arranged to form "100".

93 Sultan of Selangor's New Palace

(Des Queen's Advertising. Litho Harrison)

1978 (7 Dec). *Inauguration of Shah Alam New Town as State Capital of Selangor. T* **93** *and similar horiz designs. Multicoloured. P* 13½ × 14½.

187 10 c. Type **93** 10 10
188 30 c. Shah Alam (aerial view) 15 10
189 75 c. Shah Alam 45 60
187/9 .. .. *Set of* 3 65 70

94 Tiger

95 Multiple "POS" in Octagon

(Des Ong Soo Keat; adapted Malaysian Advertising Services. Litho Asher and Co, Melbourne)

1979 (4 Jan). *Wildlife. Multicoloured designs as T* **94**. *W* **95** *(inverted on $10 or sideways on others). P* 14½.
190 30 c. Type **94** 70 10
191 40 c. Malayan Flying Lemur 70 10
192 50 c. Lesser Malay Chevrotain 80 10
193 75 c. Leathery Pangolin 90 10
194 $1 Malayan Turtle .. .. 1·50 10
195 $2 Malayan Tapir .. .. 1·50 10
196 $5 Gaur .. .. 4·25 80
197 $10 Orang-Utan *(vert)* .. .. .. 7·00 3·25
190/7 .. .. *Set of* 8 16·00 4·00
For these stamps without watermark, see Nos. 272/9.

96 View of Central Bank of Malaysia

97 I.Y.C. Emblem

(Des Union Advertising. Litho J.W.)

1979 (26 Jan). *20th Anniv of Central Bank of Malaysia. T* **96** *and similar vert design showing view of bank building. P* 13.
198 10 c. multicoloured 10 10
199 75 c. multicoloured 40 45

(Des Queen's Advertising. Litho Harrison)

1979 (24 Feb). *International Year of the Child. T* **97** *and similar vert designs. P* 14½ × 14.
200 10 c. gold, blue and salmon 30 10
201 15 c. multicoloured 40 10
202 $1 multicoloured .. .. 1·75 2·00
200/2 .. .. *Set of* 3 2·25 2·00
Designs:—15 c. Children of different races holding hands in front of globe; $1 Children taking part in various activities.

98 Dam and Power Station

99 Exhibition Emblem

(Des National Electricity Board. Litho Harrison)

1979 (19 Sept). *Opening of Hydro-Electric Power Station, Temengor. T* **98** *and similar horiz designs showing views of power station and dam. P* 13½ × 14½.
203 15 c. multicoloured 15 15
204 25 c. multicoloured 25 45
205 50 c. multicoloured 45 75
203/5 .. .. *Set of* 3 75 1·25

(Des Malaysian Advertising Services. Litho J.W.)

1979 (20 Sept). *World Telecommunications Exhibition, Geneva. T* **99** *and similar designs. P* 14 (50 c.) *or* 13 *(others).*
206 10 c. orange, ultramarine and silver 10 15
207 15 c. multicoloured 15 10
208 50 c. multicoloured .. .. 40 1·25
206/8 .. .. *Set of* 3 60 1·40
Designs: (34 × 24 *mm*)—15 c. Telephone receiver joining one half of World to the other. (39 × 28 *mm*)—50 c. Communications equipment.

ALTERED CATALOGUE NUMBERS

Any Catalogue numbers altered from the last edition are shown as a list in the introductory pages.

100 Tuanku Haji Ahmad Shah

101 Pahang and Sarawak Maps within Telephone Dials

(Des Malaysian Advertising Services. Litho Harrison)

1980 (10 July). *Installation of Yang di-Pertuan Agong (Tuanku Haji Ahmad Shah). P* 14.
209 **100** 10 c. black, gold and yellow 10 10
210 15 c. black, gold and bright purple .. 15 10
211 50 c. black, gold and new blue 40 90
209/11 .. .. *Set of* 3 60 1·00

(Des Malaysian Advertising Services. Litho J.W.)

1980 (31 Aug). *Kuantan-Kuching Submarine Cable Project. T* **101** *and similar horiz designs. Multicoloured. P* 13.
212 10 c. Type **101** 10 10
213 15 c. Kuantan and Kuching views within telephone dials 15 10
214 50 c. Pahang and Sarawak Maps within telephone receiver 35 60
212/14 .. .. *Set of* 3 50 70

102 Bangi Campus

103 Mecca

(Des Malaysian Advertising Services. Litho J.W.)

1980 (2 Sept). *10th Anniv of National University of Malaysia. T* **102** *and similar horiz designs. Multicoloured. P* 13.
215 10 c. Type **102** 15 15
216 15 c. Jalan Pantai Baru campus 20 10
217 75 c. Great Hall .. .. 65 1·50
215/17 .. .. *Set of* 3 90 1·60

(Des Malaysian Advertising Services. Litho J.W.)

1980 (9 Nov). *Moslem Year* 1400 *A.H. Commemoration. P* 13.
218 **103** 15 c. multicoloured 10 10
219 50 c. multicoloured 30 75
The 50 c. value is as T **103** but the inscriptions are in Roman lettering and the country name is to the left of the design.

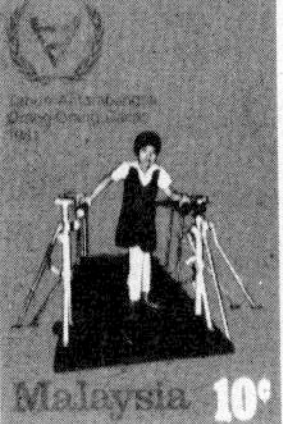

104 Disabled Child learning to Walk

105 Industrial Scene

(Des Malaysian Advertising Services. Litho J.W.)

1981 (14 Feb). *International Year for Disabled Persons. T* **104** *and similar vert designs. Multicoloured. P* 13½ × 13.
220 10 c. Type **104** 30 20
221 15 c. Disabled woman sewing 55 10
222 75 c. Disabled athlete throwing javelin .. 1·50 1·75
220/2 .. .. *Set of* 3 2·10 1·75

(Des Malaysian Advertising Services. Litho J.W.)

1981 (2 May). *"Expo '81" Industrial Training Exposition, Kuala Lumpur and Seminar, Genting Highlands. T* **105** *and similar horiz designs. Multicoloured. P* 13½ × 13.
223 10 c. Type **105** 10 10
224 15 c. Worker and bulldozer 15 10
225 30 c. Workers at ship-building yard 25 30
226 75 c. Agriculture and fishing produce, workers and machinery .. .. 65 1·25
223/6 .. .. *Set of* 4 1·00 1·60

106 "25"

(Des A. Yusof and Malaysian Advertising Services. Litho J.W.)

1981 (17 June). *25th Anniv of Malaysian National Committee for World Energy Conferences. T* **106** *and similar horiz designs. Multicoloured. P* 13½ × 13.
227 10 c. Type **106** 15 15
228 15 c. Drawings showing importance of energy sources in industry 20 10
229 75 c. Symbols of various energy sources .. 85 1·75
227/9 .. .. *Set of* 3 1·10 1·75

107 Drawing showing development of Sabah from Village to Urbanised Area

(Des Creative Concepts. Litho J.W.)

1981 (31 Aug). *Centenary of Sabah. T* **107** *and similar horiz design. Multicoloured. P* 12.
230 15 c. Type **107** 50 15
231 80 c. Drawing showing traditional and modern methods of agriculture .. .. .. 2·00 3·00

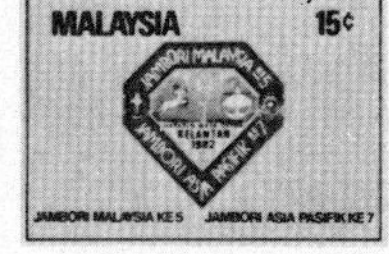

108 *Samanea saman*

109 Jamboree Emblem

(Des Yusof bin Hadji Saman. Litho J.W.)

1981 (16 Dec). *Trees. T* **108** *and similar multicoloured designs. P* 14.
232 15 c. Type **108** 55 10
233 50 c. *Dyera costulata (vert)* .. .. .. 1·50 1·00
234 80 c. *Dryobalanops aromatica (vert)* .. .. 1·75 2·50
232/4 .. .. *Set of* 3 3·50 3·25

(Des P. Lim (15 c.), Datuk Syed Hashim bin Abdullah (others). Litho J.W.)

1982 (10 Apr). *5th Malaysian/7th Asia–Pacific Boy Scout Jamboree. T* **109** *and similar horiz designs. Multicoloured. P* 13½ × 13.
235 15 c. Type **109** 30 10
236 50 c. Malaysian flag and scout emblem .. 70 80
237 80 c. Malaysian and Asia–Pacific scout emblems .. .. 1·10 2·50
235/7 .. .. *Set of* 3 1·90 3·00

110 A.S.E.A.N. Building and Emblem

111 Dome of the Rock, Jerusalem

(Litho J.W.)

1982 (8 Aug). *15th Anniv Ministerial Meeting of A.S.E.A.N. (Association of South East Asian Nations). T* **110** *and similar horiz design. Multicoloured. P* 14.
238 15 c. Type **110** 15 10
239 $1 Flags of member nations .. .. 60 1·25

(Litho J.W.)

1982 (21 Aug). *"Freedom for Palestine". P* 13½.
240 **111** 15 c. gold, blue-green and black 75 15
241 $1 silver, pale turquoise-green & blk .. 2·75 2·25

112 Views of Kuala Lumpur in 1957 and 1982

(Des Ministry of Information. Litho Rosenbaum Bros, Vienna)

1982 (31 Aug). *25th Anniv of Independence. T* **112** *and similar horiz designs. Multicoloured. P* 14 × 13½.
242 10 c. Type **112** 10 10
243 15 c. Malaysian industries 15 15
244 50 c. Soldiers on parade 40 55
245 80 c. Independence ceremony .. .. .. 70 1·50
242/5 .. .. *Set of* 4 1·25 2·00
MS246 120 × 190 mm. Nos. 242/5 .. .. 3·00 3·75

113 Shadow Play

(Des N. Ajib. Litho J.W.)

1982 (30 Oct). *Traditional Games. T* **113** *and similar horiz designs. Multicoloured. P* 13.

247	10 c. Type **113**	30	20
248	15 c. Cross Top	40	15
249	75 c. Kite flying	1·50	2·25
247/9	*Set of* 3	2·00	2·40

114 Sabah Hats

(Litho Harrison)

1982 (26 Nov). *Malaysian Handicrafts. T* **114** *and similar horiz designs. Multicoloured. P* 13 × 13½.

250	10 c. Type **114**	15	25
251	15 c. Gold-threaded cloth	15	20
252	75 c. Sarawak pottery	65	1·75
250/2	*Set of* 3	85	2·00

115 Gas Exploitation Logo

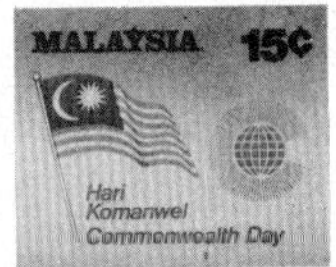

116 Flag of Malaysia

(Litho Security Printers (M), Malaysia)

1983 (22 Jan). *Export of Liquefied Natural Gas from Bintulu Field, Sarawak. T* **115** *and similar horiz designs. Multicoloured. P* 12.

253	15 c. Type **115**	45	10
	a. Perf 13½		
254	20 c. *Tenaga Satu* (liquid gas tanker)	70	40
	a. Perf 13½		
255	$1 Gas drilling equipment	2·50	3·00
	a. Perf 13½		
253/5	*Set of* 3	3·25	3·25

(Litho J.W.)

1983 (14 Mar). *Commonwealth Day. T* **116** *and similar horiz designs. Multicoloured. P* 13½ × 14.

256	15 c. Type **116**	10	10
257	20 c. The King of Malaysia	15	15
258	40 c. Oil palm tree and refinery	25	30
259	$1 Satellite view of Earth	60	1·50
256/9	*Set of* 4	1·00	1·90

117 *Tilapia nilotica*

(Des and litho Security Printers (M), Malaysia)

1983 (15 June). *Freshwater Fishes. T* **117** *and similar horiz designs. Multicoloured. P* 12.

260	20 c. Type **117**	30	30
	a. Horiz pair. Nos. 260/1	60	60
	b. Perf 13½ × 14	1·75	1·00
	ba. Horiz pair. Nos. 260b/1b	3·50	2·50
261	20 c. *Cyprinus carpio*	30	30
	b. Perf 13½ × 14	1·75	1·00
262	40 c. *Puntius gonionotus*	60	60
	a. Horiz pair. Nos. 262/3	1·10	1·10
	b. Perf 13½ × 14	3·00	2·50
	ba. Horiz pair. Nos. 262b/3b	6·00	6·00
263	40 c. *Ctenopharyngodon idellus*	60	60
	b. Perf 13½ × 14	3·00	2·50
260/3	*Set of* 4	1·60	1·60

Nos. 260/1 and 262/3 were each printed together, *se-tenant*, in horizontal pairs throughout the sheet.

118 Lower Pergau River Bridge

(Des Malaysian Public Works Dept. Litho Security Printers (M), Malaysia)

1983 (11 July). *Opening of East–West Highway. T* **118** *and similar horiz designs. Multicoloured. P* 13½.

264	15 c. Type **118**	60	15
265	20 c. Perak river reservoir bridge	70	35
266	$1 Map showing East–West highway	2·25	3·00
264/6	*Set of* 3	3·25	3·25

119 Northrop "RF-5E" Fighter

120 Helmeted Hornbill

(Des and litho J.W.)

1983 (16 Sept). *50th Anniv of Malaysian Armed Forces. T* **119** *and similar horiz designs. Multicoloured. P* 13.

267	15 c. Type **119**	40	15
268	20 c. Missile boat	65	30
269	40 c. Battle of Pasir Panjang	1·00	90
270	80 c. Trooping the Colour	1·50	2·25
267/70	*Set of* 4	3·25	3·25
MS271	130 × 85 mm. Nos. 267/70. P 13½	3·75	4·25

1983 (3 Oct)–**85**.* *As Nos.* 190/7 *but without wmk.*

272	30 c. Type **94** (1984)	90	20
273	40 c. Malayan Flying Lemur (6.10.83)	1·00	20
274	50 c. Lesser Malay Chevrotain (10.4.84)	1·25	20
275	75 c. Leathery Pangolin (19.10.85)	5·50	6·00
276	$1 Malayan Turtle (5.10.83)	2·00	20
277	$2 Malayan Tapir	3·25	70
278	$5 Gaur (1985)	10·00	9·00
279	$10 Orang-Utan (*vert*) (3.84)	13·00	11·00
272/9	*Set of* 8	32·00	25·00

*There was no official release date for these stamps. Dates shown are the earliest recorded from postmarks and may be revised should earlier examples be reported.

(Des P. Ket. Litho Security Printers (M), Malaysia)

1983 (26 Oct). *Hornbills of Malaysia. T* **120** *and similar vert designs. Multicoloured. P* 13½.

280	15 c. Type **120**	40	10
281	20 c. Wrinkled Hornbill	55	30
282	50 c. Long-crested Hornbill	85	90
283	$1 Rhinoceros Hornbill	1·60	2·50
280/3	*Set of* 4	3·00	3·50

121 Bank Building, Ipoh

122 Sky-scraper and Mosque, Kuala Lumpur

(Des P. Hoong. Litho Security Printers (M), Malaysia)

1984 (26 Jan). *25th Anniv of Bank Negara. T* **121** *and similar horiz design. Multicoloured. P* 13½ × 14.

284	20 c. Type **121**	40	30
285	$1 Bank building, Alor Setar	1·40	2·25

(Des Mara Institute of Technology. Litho Security Printers (M), Malaysia)

1984 (1 Feb). *10th Anniv of Federal Territory of Kuala Lumpur. T* **122** *and similar multicoloured designs. P* 13½ × 14 (80 c.) *or* 14 × 13½ (*others*).

286	20 c. Type **122**	50	20
287	40 c. Aerial view	1·00	1·00
288	80 c. Gardens and clock-tower (*horiz*)	1·75	2·25
286/8	*Set of* 3	3·00	3·00

123 Map showing Industries

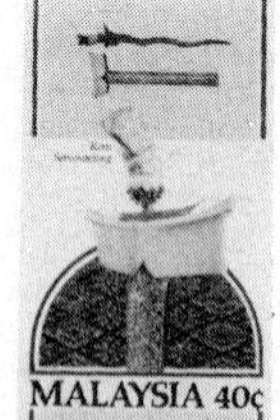

124 Semenanjung Keris

(Litho Security Printers (M), Malaysia)

1984 (16 Apr). *Formation of Labuan Federal Territory. T* **123** *and similar vert design. Multicoloured. P* 13½ × 14.

289	20 c. Type **123**	50	25
290	$1 Flag and map of Labuan	2·00	2·25

(Des P. Ket. Litho Harrison)

1984 (30 May). *Traditional Malay Weapons. T* **124** *and similar vert designs. Multicoloured. P* 13½ × 14.

291	40 c. Type **124**	70	70
	a. Block of 4. Nos. 291/4	2·50	
292	40 c. Pekakak keris	70	70
293	40 c. Jawa keris	70	70
294	40 c. Lada tumbuk	70	70
291/4	*Set of* 4	2·50	2·50

Nos. 291/4 were printed in *se-tenant* blocks of four throughout the sheet.

125 Map of World and Transmitter

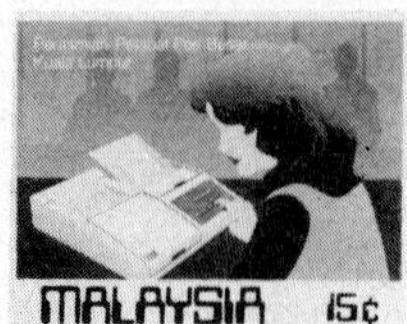

126 Facsimile Service

(Des Dept of Broadcasting. Litho Harrison)

1984 (23 June). *20th Anniv of Asia–Pacific Broadcasting Union. T* **125** *and similar horiz design. Multicoloured. P* 13½ × 14½.

295	20 c. Type **125**	40	25
296	$1 Clasped hands within "20"	2·00	2·75

(Des Mark Johan and Associates. Litho Security Printers (M), Malaysia)

1984 (29 Oct). *Opening of New General Post Office, Kuala Lumpur. T* **126** *and similar horiz designs. Multicoloured. P* 12.

297	15 c. Type **126**	30	20
298	20 c. New G.P.O. building	40	30
299	$1 Mailbag conveyor	1·75	2·50
297/9	*Set of* 3	2·25	2·75

127 Yang di Pertuan Agong (Tuanku Mahmood)

128 White Hibiscus

(Des P. Ket. Litho Security Printers (M), Malaysia)

1984 (15 Nov). *Installation of Yang di Pertuan Agong (Tuanku Mahmood). T* **127** *and similar design. P* 12.

300	**127**	15 c. multicoloured	40	20
301		20 c. multicoloured	40	20
302	–	40 c. multicoloured	75	85
303	–	80 c. multicoloured	1·40	2·00
300/3		*Set of* 4	2·75	3·00

Design: *Horiz* — 40 c., 80 c. Yang di Pertuan Agong and Federal Crest.

(Litho Security Printers (M), Malaysia)

1984 (12 Dec). *Hibiscus. T* **128** *and similar vert designs. Multicoloured. P* 13½.

304	10 c. Type **128**	35	15
305	20 c. Red Hibiscus	70	20
306	40 c. Pink Hibiscus	1·25	1·00
307	$1 Orange Hibiscus	2·25	2·75
304/7	*Set of* 4	4·00	3·75

129 Parliament Building

130 Banded Linsang

(Des P. Ket. Litho Security Printers (M), Malaysia)

1985 (30 Mar). *25th Anniv of Federal Parliament. T* **129** *and similar multicoloured design. P* 13½ × 14 (20 c.) *or* 14 × 13½ ($1).

308	20 c. Type **129**	30	15
309	$1 Parliament Building (*different*) (*horiz*)	1·75	1·50

(Des P. Ket. Litho J.W.)

1985 (25 Apr). *Protected Animals of Malaysia* (1st *series*). *T* **130** *and similar multicoloured designs. P* 14.

310	10 c. Type **130**	30	10
311	40 c. Slow Loris (*vert*)	80	80
312	$1 Spotted Giant Flying Squirrel (*vert*)	1·75	2·50
310/12	*Set of* 3	2·50	3·00

See also Nos. 383/6.

131 Stylised Figures

132 F.M.S.R. "No. 1" Steam Locomotive, 1885

(Des Amir bin Osman. Litho Security Printers (M), Malaysia)

1985 (15 May). *International Youth Year. T* **131** *and similar horiz design. Multicoloured. P* 13.

313	20 c. Type **131**	25	15
314	$1 Young workers	1·50	2·25

(Des AMW Communications Management. Litho Security Printers (M), Malaysia).

1985 (1 June). *Centenary of Malayan Railways. T* **132** *and similar horiz designs. P* 13.
315 15 c. black, carmine-verm & pale orange .. 50 15
316 20 c. multicoloured 60 20
317 $1 multicoloured .. .. 1·50 2·25
315/17 .. .. *Set of* 3 2·40 2·40
MS318 119 × 59 mm. 80 c. multicoloured. P 13½ × 13 .. .. 1·75 2·75
Designs: *Horiz* (*as T* **132**)—20 c. Class "20" diesel locomotive, 1957; $1 Class "23" diesel locomotive, 1983. (48 × 31 *mm*)—80 c. Class "56" steam locomotive, 1938.

133 Blue Proton "Saga 1.3s"

134 Penang Bridge

(Des and litho J.W.)

1985 (9 July). *Production of Proton "Saga" (Malaysian national car). T* **133** *and similar horiz designs. Multicoloured. P* 14.
319 20 c. Type **133** 30 15
320 40 c. White Proton "Saga 1.3s" 45 40
321 $1 Red Proton "Saga 1.5s" .. .. .. 80 1·75
319/21 .. .. *Set of* 3 1·40 2·10

(Des Kathy's Design. Litho Security Printers (M), Malaysia)

1985 (14 Sept). *Opening of Penang Bridge. T* **134** *and similar horiz designs. Multicoloured. P* 12 ($1) *or* 13 (*others*).
322 20 c. Type **134** 30 15
323 40 c. Penang Bridge and location map .. 55 35
324 $1 Symbolic bridge linking Penang to mainland (40 × 24 *mm*) .. .. .. 1·25 1·25
322/4 .. .. *Set of* 3 1·75 1·60

135 Offshore Oil Rig

136 Sultan Azlan Shah and Perak Royal Crest

(Des Andamaz Enterprise. Litho Security Printers (M), Malaysia)

1985 (4 Nov). *Malaysian Petroleum Production. T* **135** *and similar multicoloured designs. P* 12.
325 15 c. Type **135** 15 10
326 20 c. Malaysia's first oil refinery (*horiz*) .. 20 20
327 $1 Map of Malaysian offshore oil and gas fields (*horiz*) .. .. 90 1·25
325/7 .. .. *Set of* 3 1·10 1·40

(Des Kathy's Design. Litho J.W.)

1985 (9 Dec). *Installation of the Sultan of Perak. P* 14.
328 **136** 15 c. multicoloured 15 10
329 20 c. multicoloured 20 20
330 $1 multicoloured .. .. 1·00 2·00
328/30 .. .. *Set of* 3 1·25 2·00

137 Crested Fireback Pheasant

139 Two Indonesian Dancers

138

(Des P. Ket. Litho Security Printers (M), Malaysia)

1986 (11 Mar). *Protected Birds of Malaysia* (*1st series*). *T* **137** *and similar multicoloured designs. W* **138** (*sideways on* 40 *c.*). *Phosphorised paper. P* 13½.
331 20 c. Type **137** 70 70
a. Horiz pair. Nos. 331/2 .. .. .. 1·40 1·40
332 20 c. Malaya Peacock-pheasant 70 70
333 40 c. Bulwer's Pheasant (*horiz*) .. .. 1·00 1·00
a. Horiz pair. Nos. 333/4 .. .. .. 2·00 2·00
b. Perf 12 .. .. 1·75 2·25
ba. Horiz pair. Nos. 333b/4b .. .. 3·50 4·50
334 40 c. Great Argus Pheasant (*horiz*) .. .. 1·00 1·00
b. Perf 12 .. .. 1·75 2·25
331/4 .. .. *Set of* 4 3·00 3·00
Nos. 331/2 and 333/4 were each printed together, *se-tenant*, in horizontal pairs throughout the sheets.
See also Nos. 394/7.

(Des AMC Advertising Agencies. Litho Questa)

1986 (14 Apr). *Pacific Area Travel Association Conference, Malaysia. T* **139** *and similar vert designs. Multicoloured. P* 15 × 14.
335 20 c. Type **139** 15 20
a. Horiz strip of 3. Nos. 335/7 40
336 20 c. Dyak dancer and longhouse, Malaysia .. 15 20
337 20 c. Dancers and church, Philippines .. 15 20
338 40 c. Thai dancer and temple 30 40
a. Horiz strip of 3. Nos. 338/40 80
339 40 c. Chinese dancer, Singapore 30 40
340 40 c. Indian dancer and Hindu temple stairway 30 40
335/40 .. .. *Set of* 6 1·10 1·60
Nos. 335/7 and 338/40 were each printed together, *se-tenant*, in horizontal strips of 3 throughout the sheets.

140 Stylized Competitors

141 Rambutan

141a

(Des Design Excelsior. Litho Security Printers (M), Malaysia)

1986 (19 Apr). *Malaysia Games. T* **140** *and similar multicoloured designs. W* **138** (*sideways on* 20 *c.*). *Phosphorised paper. P* 12.
341 20 c. Type **140** 55 20
342 40 c. Games emblems (*vert*) .. .. .. 1·00 1·00
343 $1 National and state flags (*vert*) .. .. 2·50 2·75
341/3 .. .. *Set of* 3 3·50 3·75

(Des P. Ket)

1986 (5 June). *Fruits of Malaysia. T* **141** *and similar vert designs. Multicoloured.*

(*a*) *Litho Security Printers (M), Malaysia. W* **138**. *Phosphorised paper. P* 12.
344 40 c. Type **141** 15 20
345 50 c. Pineapple 20 25
346 80 c. Durian 35 40
347 $1 Mangostene 40 45

(*b*) *Photo Harrison. W* **141a**. *P* 13½.
348 $2 Star Fruit 85 90
349 $5 Banana .. .. 2·10 2·25
350 $10 Mango .. .. 4·25 4·50
351 $20 Papaya .. .. 8·50 8·75
344/51 .. .. *Set of* 8 15·00 16·00

PHOSPHORISED PAPER. From No. 352 onwards all stamps were on phosphorised paper, *unless otherwise stated.*

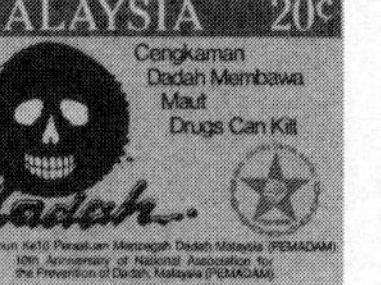

142 Skull and Slogan "Drugs Can Kill"

143 MAS Logo and Map showing Routes

(Des Kathy's Design. Litho Security Printers (M), Malaysia)

1986 (26 June). *10th Anniv of National Association for Prevention of Drug Addiction. T* **142** *and similar multicoloured designs. W* **138** (*sideways on* $1). *P* 13.
352 20 c. Type **142** 25 20
353 40 c. Bird and slogan "Stay Free From Drugs" 40 40
354 $1 Addict and slogan "Drugs Can Destroy" (*vert*) .. .. 1·00 1·60
352/4 .. .. *Set of* 3 1·50 2·00

(Des PTM Thompson Advertising. Litho Security Printers (M), Malaysia)

1986 (31 July). *Inaugural Flight of Malaysian Airlines Kuala Lumpur–Los Angeles Service. T* **143** *and similar horiz designs. Multicoloured. W* **138** (*sideways*). *P* 14 × 13½.
355 20 c. Type **143** 20 15
356 40 c. Logo, stylized aircraft and route diagram 35 35
357 $1 Logo and stylized aircraft .. .. 80 1·10
355/7 .. .. *Set of* 3 1·25 1·40

144 Building Construction

145 Old Seri Menanti Palace, Negri Sembilan

(Des M. Chin. Litho Security Printers (M), Malaysia)

1986 (3 Nov). *20th Anniv of National Productivity Council and 25th Anniv of Asian Productivity Organization* (40 *c.*, $1). *T* **144** *and similar multicoloured designs. W* **138** (*sideways on* 40 *c.*, $1). *P* 13½ × 14 (20 *c.*) *or* 14 × 13½ (*others*).
358 20 c. Type **144** 45 20
359 40 c. Planning and design (*horiz*) 80 50
360 $1 Computer-controlled car assembly line (*horiz*) .. .. 1·40 1·25
358/60 .. .. *Set of* 3 2·40 1·75

(Des P. Ket. Litho Security Printers (M), Malaysia)

1986 (20 Dec). *Historic Buildings of Malaysia* (*1st series*). *T* **145** *and similar horiz designs. Multicoloured. W* **138** (*sideways*). *P* 13.
361 15 c. Type **145** 15 15
362 20 c. Old Kenangan Palace, Perak 20 15
363 40 c. Old Town Hall, Malacca 35 35
364 $1 Astana, Kuching, Sarawak .. .. 75 1·10
361/4 .. .. *Set of* 4 1·25 1·60
See also Nos. 465/8.

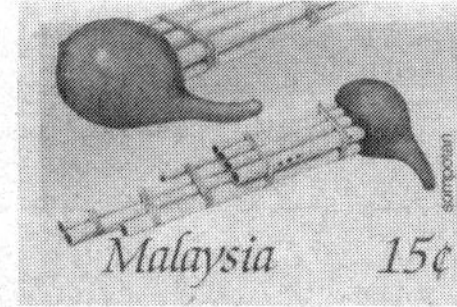

146 Sompotan (bamboo pipes)

(Des Kathy Wong. Litho Security Printers (M), Malaysia)

1987 (7 Mar). *Malaysian Musical Instruments. T* **146** *and similar multicoloured designs. W* **138** (*sideways on* 50, 80 *c.*). *P* 12.
365 15 c. Type **146** 10 10
366 20 c. Sapih (four-stringed chordophone) .. 15 15
367 50 c. Serunai (pipes) (*vert*) 30 30
368 80 c. Rebab (three-stringed fiddle) (*vert*) .. 45 45
365/8 .. .. *Set of* 4 90 90

147 Modern Housing Estate

(Litho Security Printers (M), Malaysia)

1987 (6 Apr). *International Year of Shelter for the Homeless. T* **147** *and similar horiz design. Multicoloured. W* **138**. *P* 12.
369 20 c. Type **147** 15 15
370 $1 Stylised families and houses 60 65

148 Drug Addict and Family

(Des Kathy's Design. Litho Security Printers (M), Malaysia)

1987 (8 June). *International Conference on Drug Abuse, Vienna. T* **148** *and similar horiz designs. Multicoloured. W* **138** (*sideways*). *P* 13.
371 20 c. Type **148** 20 15
a. Vert pair. Nos. 371/2 .. .. .. 40 30
372 20 c. Hands holding drugs and damaged internal organs 20 15
373 40 c. Healthy boy and broken drug capsule .. 45 30
a. Vert pair. Nos. 373/4 .. .. .. 90 60
374 40 c. Drugs and healthy internal organs .. 45 30
371/4 .. .. *Set of* 4 1·10 80
Nos. 371/2 and 373/4 were printed together, *se-tenant*, in vertical pairs throughout the sheet, each pair forming a composite design.

149 Spillway and Power Station

(Des Kathy's Design. Litho Security Printers (M), Malaysia)

1987 (13 July). *Opening of Sultan Mahmud Hydro-electric Scheme, Kenyir, Trengganu. T* **149** *and similar horiz design. Multicoloured. W* **138**. *P* 12.

375 20 c. Type **149** — 20 — 10
376 $1 Dam, spillway and reservoir — 80 — 50

150 Crossed Maces and Parliament Building, Kuala Lumpur

151 Dish Aerial, Satellite and Globe

(Des R. Zahabuddin. Litho Security Printers (M), Malaysia)

1987 (1 Sept). *33rd Commonwealth Parliamentary Conference. T* **150** *and similar horiz design. Multicoloured. W* **138**. *P* 12.

377 20 c. Type **150** — 10 — 10
378 $1 Parliament building and crossed maces emblem — 45 — 50

(Des Mark Design. Litho Security Printers (M), Malaysia)

1987 (26 Oct). *Asia/Pacific Transport and Communications Decade. T* **151** *and similar horiz designs. Multicoloured. W* **138** *(sideways). P* 13.

379 15 c. Type **151** — 15 — 10
380 20 c. Diesel train and car — 20 — 10
381 40 c. Container ships and lorry — 30 — 30
382 $1 Malaysian Airlines jumbo jet, Kuala Lumpur Airport — 65 — 90
379/82 *Set of* 4 — 1·10 — 1·25

152 Temminck's Golden Cat

153 Flags of Member Nations and "20"

(Des Ong Soo Keat. Litho Security Printers (M), Malaysia)

1987 (14 Nov). *Protected Animals of Malaysia (2nd series). T* **152** *and similar horiz designs. Multicoloured. W* **138** *(sideways on* 15, 20, 40 *c.). P* 13.

383 15 c. Type **152** — 20 — 15
384 20 c. Flatheaded Cat — 20 — 15
385 40 c. Marbled Cat — 50 — 50
386 $1 Clouded Leopard — 1·00 — 1·40
383/6 *Set of* 4 — 1·75 — 2·00

(Des P. Ket. Litho Security Printers (M), Malaysia)

1987 (14 Dec). *20th Anniv of Association of South East Asian Nations. T* **153** *and similar horiz design. Multicoloured. W* **138**. *P* 13.

387 20 c. Type **153** — 10 — 10
388 $1 Flags of member nations and globe — 45 — 70

154 Mosque and Portico

155 Aerial View

(Des R. Zahabuddin. Litho Security Printers (M), Malaysia)

1988 (11 Mar). *Opening of Sultan Salahuddin Abdul Aziz Shah Mosque. T* **154** *and similar multicoloured designs. W* **138** *(sideways on* 15, 20 *c.). P* 12.

389 15 c. Type **154** — 10 — 10
390 20 c. Dome, minarets and Sultan of Selangor — 10 — 10
391 $1 Interior and dome (*vert*) — 45 — 70
389/91 *Set of* 3 — 55 — 80

(Des Azmi bin Kassim. Litho Security Printers (M), Malaysia)

1988 (4 Apr). *Sultan Ismail Hydro-electric Power Station, Paka, Trengganu. T* **155** *and similar horiz design. Multicoloured. W* **138** *(sideways). P* 13.

392 20 c. Type **155** — 10 — 10
393 $1 Power station and pylons — 45 — 50

156 Black-naped Blue Monarch

157 Outline Map and Products of Sabah

(Des Ong Soo Keat. Litho Security Printers (M), Malaysia)

1988 (30 June). *Protected Birds of Malaysia (2nd series). T* **156** *and similar vert designs. Multicoloured. W* **138**. *P* 13.

394 20 c. Type **156** — 10 — 10
a. Horiz pair. Nos. 394/5 — 15 — 20
395 20 c. Scarlet-backed Flowerpecker — 10 — 10
396 50 c. Yellow-backed Sunbird — 20 — 25
a. Horiz pair. Nos. 396/7 — 40 — 50
397 50 c. Black and Red Broadbill — 20 — 25
394/7 *Set of* 4 — 50 — 65

The two designs of each value were printed together, *se-tenant*, in horizontal pairs throughout the sheets.

(Des P. Ket. Litho Security Printers (M), Malaysia)

1988 (31 Aug). *25th Anniv of Sabah and Sarawak as States of Malaysia. T* **157** *and similar vert designs. Multicoloured. W* **138**. *P* 13.

398 20 c. Type **157** — 10 — 10
a. Horiz pair. Nos. 398/9 — 15 — 20
399 20 c. Outline map and products of Sarawak — 10 — 10
400 $1 Flags of Malaysia, Sabah and Sarawak (30×40 *mm*) — 40 — 45
398/400 *Set of* 3 — 50 — 60

Nos. 398/9 were printed together, *se-tenant*, in horizontal pairs throughout the sheet.

158 *Glossodoris atromarginata*

159 Sultan's Palace, Malacca

(Litho Security Printers (M), Malaysia)

1988 (17 Dec). *Marine Life (1st series). T* **158** *and similar vert designs. Multicoloured. W* **138**. *P* 12.

401 20 c. Type **158** — 15 — 15
a. Horiz strip of 5. Nos. 401/5 — 70
402 20 c. *Phyllidia ocellata* — 15 — 15
403 20 c. *Chromodoris annae* — 15 — 15
404 20 c. *Flabellina macassarana* — 15 — 15
405 20 c. *Fryeria ruppelli* — 15 — 15
401/5 *Set of* 5 — 70 — 70
MS406 100×75 mm. $1 *Pomacanthus annularis* (50×40 *mm*). P 14 — 70 — 80

Nos. 401/5 were printed together, *se-tenant*, in horizontal strips of 5 throughout the sheet, forming a composite background design.

See also Nos. 410/13 and 450/3.

(Des P. Ket. Litho Security Printers (M), Malaysia)

1989 (15 Apr). *Declaration of Malacca as Historic City. T* **159** *and similar multicoloured designs. W* **138** *(sideways on* 20 *c.). P* 13.

407 20 c. Type **159** — 15 — 15
408 20 c. Independence Memorial Building — 15 — 15
409 $1 Porta De Santiago Fortress (*vert*) — 65 — 90
407/9 *Set of* 3 — 85 — 1·10

160 *Tetralia nigrolineata*

161 Map of Malaysia and Scout Badge

(Des P. Ket. Litho Security Printers (M), Malaysia)

1989 (29 June). *Marine Life (2nd series). Crustaceans. T* **160** *and similar horiz designs. Multicoloured. W* **138** *(sideways). P* 12.

410 20 c. Type **160** — 15 — 15
a. Horiz pair. Nos. 410/11 — 30 — 30
b. Wmk upright
ba. Horiz pair. Nos. 410b/11b
411 20 c. *Neopetrolisthes maculatus* (crab) — 15 — 15
b. Wmk upright
412 40 c. *Periclimenes holthuisi* (shrimp) — 20 — 25
a. Horiz pair. Nos. 412/13 — 40 — 50
413 40 c. *Synalpheus neomeris* (shrimp) — 20 — 25
410/13 *Set of* 4 — 70 — 80

Nos. 410/11 and 412/13 were each printed together, *se-tenant*, in horizontal pairs throughout the sheets.

(Des T. Teh. Litho Security Printers (M), Malaysia)

1989 (26 July). *7th National Scout Jamboree. T* **161** *and similar multicoloured designs. W* **138** *(sideways on* 10, 20 *c.). P* 13.

414 10 c. Type **161** — 10 — 10
415 20 c. Saluting national flag — 15 — 15
416 80 c. Scouts around camp fire (*horiz*) — 50 — 65
414/16 *Set of* 3 — 65 — 80

162 Cycling

163 Sultan Azlan Shah

(Litho Security Printers (M), Malaysia)

1989 (20 Aug). *15th South East Asian Games, Kuala Lumpur. T* **162** *and similar multicoloured designs. W* **138** *(sideways on* 50 *c.,* $1). *P* 13.

417 10 c. Type **162** — 15 — 15
418 20 c. Athletics — 25 — 15
419 50 c. Swimming (*vert*) — 50 — 50
420 $1 Torch bearer (*vert*) — 85 — 1·00
417/20 *Set of* 4 — 1·60 — 1·60

(Des R. Zahabuddin. Litho Security Printers (M), Malaysia)

1989 (18 Sept). *Installation of Sultan Azlan Shah as Yang di Pertuan Agong. W* **138** *(sideways). P* 13.

421 **163** 20 c. multicoloured — 15 — 15
422 40 c. multicoloured — 25 — 30
423 $1 multicoloured — 60 — 75
421/3 *Set of* 3 — 90 — 1·10

164 Putra World Trade Centre and Pan-Pacific Hotel

165 Clock Tower, Kuala Lumpur City Hall and Big Ben

(Litho Security Printers (M), Malaysia)

1989 (18 Oct). *Commonwealth Heads of Government Meeting, Kuala Lumpur. T* **164** *and similar multicoloured designs. W* **138** *(sideways on* 50 *c.). P* 13.

424 20 c. Type **164** — 15 — 10
a. Wmk sideways
425 50 c. Traditional dancers (*vert*) — 35 — 45
426 $1 National flag and map showing Commonwealth countries — 60 — 1·00
424/6 *Set of* 3 — 1·00 — 1·40

(Des AMC-Melewar Zecha Communications. Litho Security Printers (M), Malaysia)

1989 (2 Dec). *Inaugural Malaysia Airlines "747" Non-stop Flight to London. T* **165** *and similar horiz designs, each showing Malaysia Airlines Boeing "747-400". Multicoloured. W* **138**. *P* 13.

427 20 c. Type **165** — 15 — 15
a. Horiz pair. Nos. 427/9 — 30 — 30
428 20 c. Parliament Buildings, Kuala Lumpur, and Palace of Westminster — 15 — 15
429 $1 World map showing route — 70 — 80
427/9 *Set of* 3 — 90 — 1·00

Nos. 427/8 were printed together, *se-tenant*, in horizontal pairs throughout the sheet.

166 Sloth and Map of Park

167 Outline Map of South-east Asia and Logo

(Des Jermaine. Litho Security Printers (M), Malaysia)

1989 (28 Dec). *50th Anniv of National Park. T* **166** *and similar vert design. Multicoloured. W* **138**. *P* 12 (20 *c.*) *or* 13 ($1).

430 20 c. Type **166** — 15 — 1C
a. Perf $14^{1/2}$
431 $1 Pair of Crested Argus Pheasants — 75 — 1·25
a. Perf $14^{1/2}$

(Des A. Kassim. Litho Security Printers (M), Malaysia)

1990 (1 Jan). *"Visit Malaysia Year". T* **167** *and similar horiz designs. Multicoloured. W* **138** *(sideways). P* 12.

432 20 c. Type **167** — 15 — 15
433 50 c. Traditional drums — 35 — 5C
434 $1 Scuba diving, windsurfing and yachting — 65 — 1·0C
432/4 *Set of* 3 — 1·10 — 1·5C

168 *Dillenia suffruticosa*

169 Monument and Rainbow

(Litho Security Printers (M), Malaysia)

1990 (12 Mar). *Wildflowers. T* **168** *and similar vert designs. Multicoloured. W* **138**. *P* 12.

435	15 c. Type **168**	15	15
436	20 c. *Mimosa pudica*	15	15
437	50 c. *Ipmoea carnea*	35	50
438	$1 *Nymphaea pubescens*	60	1·00
435/8	*Set of* 4	1·10	1·60

(Des CD Advertising. Litho Security Printers (M), Malaysia)

1990 (14 May). *Kuala Lumpur, Garden City of Lights. T* **169** *and similar multicoloured designs. W* **138** (*sideways on* 40 *c.,* $1). *P* 12.

439	20 c. Type **169**	15	20
440	40 c. Mosque and skyscrapers at night (*horiz*)	25	30
441	$1 Kuala Lumpur skyline (*horiz*)	60	1·00
439/41	*Set of* 3	90	1·40

170 Seri Negara Building

171 Alor Setar

(Des T. Teh Chin Seng. Litho Security Printers (M), Malaysia)

1990 (1 June). *1st Summit Meeting of South–South Consultation and Co-operation Group, Kuala Lumpur. T* **170** *and similar horiz design. Multicoloured. W* **138** (*sideways*). *P* 13.

442	20 c. Type **170**	15	15
443	80 c. Summit logo	45	75

(Des Penerbit Hidayah. Litho Security Printers (M), Malaysia)

1990 (2 June). *250th Anniv of Alor Setar. T* **171** *and similar multicoloured designs. W* **138** (*sideways on* 40 *c.,* $1). *P* 12.

444	20 c. Type **171**	15	20
445	40 c. Musicians and monument (*vert*)	25	30
446	$1 Zahir Mosque (*vert*)	70	1·00
444/6	*Set of* 3	1·00	1·40

172 Sign Language Letters

173 Leatherback Turtle

(Des S. Senika. Litho Security Printers (M), Malaysia)

1990 (8 Sept). *International Literacy Year. T* **172** *and similar multicoloured designs. W* **138** (*sideways on* 20, 40 *c.*). *P* 13 (40 *c.*) *or* 12 (*others*).

447	20 c. Type **172**	10	10
	a. Perf 13		
448	40 c. People reading	25	30
449	$1 Symbolic person reading (*vert*)	65	80
447/9	*Set of* 3	90	1·10

(Des Ong Soo Keat. Litho Security Printers (M), Malaysia)

1990 (17 Nov). *Marine Life* (3rd *series*). *Sea Turtles. T* **173** *and similar horiz designs. Multicoloured. W* **138** (*sideways*). *P* 12.

450	15 c. Type **173**	15	10
451	20 c. Common Green Turtle	15	10
452	40 c. Olive Ridley Turtle	30	30
453	$1 Hawksbill Turtle	60	70
450/3	*Set of* 4	1·10	1·10

174 Safety Helmet, Dividers and Industrial Skyline

175 *Eustenogaster calyptodoma*

(Litho Security Printers (M), Malaysia)

1991 (25 Apr). *25th Anniv of MARA (Council of the Indigenous People). T* **174** *and similar horiz designs. Multicoloured. W* **138** (*sideways*). *P* 12.

454	20 c. Type **174**	15	10
455	40 c. Documents and graph	25	25
456	$1 25th Anniversary logo	65	70
454/6	*Set of* 3	95	95

(Des Loh Wen Kong. Litho Security Printers (M), Malaysia)

1991 (29 July). *Insects. Wasps. T* **175** *and similar vert designs. Multicoloured. W* **138** (*sideways*). *P* 12.

457	15 c. Type **175**	10	10
458	20 c. *Vespa affinis indonensis*	10	10
459	50 c. *Sceliphorn javanum*	20	25
460	$1 *Ampulex compressa*	40	45
457/60	*Set of* 4	75	80
MS461	130×85 mm. Nos. 457/60. P $14^1/_2$×14	80	90

176 Tunku Abdul Rahman Putra and Independence Rally

(Des Design Dimension. Litho Security Printers (M), Malaysia)

1991 (30 Aug). *Former Prime Ministers of Malaysia. T* **176** *and similar horiz designs. Multicoloured. W* **138**. *P* 12.

462	$1 Type **176**	40	45
463	$1 Tun Abdul Razak Hussein and jungle village	40	45
464	$1 Tun Hussein Onn and standard-bearers	40	45
462/4	*Set of* 3	1·10	1·25

177 Maziah Palace, Terengganu

178 Museum Building, Brass Lamp and Fabric

(Des A. Kassim. Litho Security Printers (M), Malaysia)

1991 (7 Nov). *Historic Buildings of Malaysia* (2nd *issue*). *T* **177** *and similar horiz designs. Multicoloured. W* **138**. *P* 12.

465	15 c. Type **177**	10	10
466	20 c. Grand Palace, Johore	10	10
467	40 c. Town Palace, Kuala Langat, Selangor	15	20
468	$1 Jahar Palace, Kelantan	40	45
465/8	*Set of* 4	70	75

(Des T. Seng. Litho Security Printers (M), Malaysia)

1991 (21 Dec). *Centenary of Sarawak Museum. T* **178** *and similar horiz design. Multicoloured. W* **138**. *P* 12.

469	30 c. Type **178**	10	10
470	$1 Museum building, vase and fabric	40	45

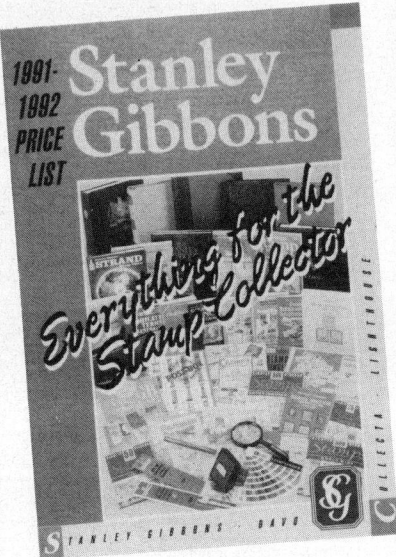

POSTAGE DUE STAMPS

Until 15 August 1966 the postage due stamps of MALAYAN POSTAL UNION were in use throughout MALAYSIA.

D 1

D 2

(Litho Harrison)

1966 (15 Aug)–**71**. *Ordinary paper.* W w **13** *(upright). P* 14½ × 14.

D1	D 1	1 c. rose	15	1·00
D2		2 c. indigo	20	1·75
D3		4 c. apple-green	60	1·75
D4		8 c. blue-green	1·00	5·50
		a. Chalk-surfaced paper. *Bright blue-green* (1.6.71)	2·50	5·50
D5		10 c. bright blue	45	2·00
		a. Chalk-surfaced paper (1.6.71)	2·50	6·00
D6		12 c. reddish violet	45	2·00
D7		20 c. red-brown	45	3·75
		a. Chalk-surfaced paper. *Brown-purple* (22.4.69)	2·50	8·00
D8		50 c. brownish bistre	1·25	6·50
		a. Chalk-surfaced paper. *Olive-bistre* (1.6.71)	3·00	9·00
D1/8		*Set of* 8	4·00	22·00

1972 (23 May). *Glazed paper.* W w **13** *(sideways). P* 14½ × 14.

D12	D 1	8 c. turquoise-green	3·75	9·00
D13		10 c. dull ultramarine	3·75	9·00
D15		20 c. pale chocolate	4·75	10·00
D16		50 c. pale olive-bistre	5·50	12·00
D12/16		*Set of* 4	16·00	35·00

1980–86. *No wmk. P* 14½×14.

D17	D 1	2 c. indigo	20	1·00
D18		8 c. blue-green	30	1·25
D19		10 c. dull ultramarine	40	1·40
D19*a*		12 c. reddish lilac (1986)	11·00	
D20		20 c. pale chocolate	50	1·75
D21		50 c. pale olive-bistre	90	2·50

(Des Kathy Wong. Litho Security Printers (M), Malaysia)

1986 (15 Sept). *P* 12 × 11½.

D22	D 2	5 c. cerise and rose-lilac	10	10
D23		10 c. brownish black & pale olive-grey	10	10
D24		20 c. dull vermilion and cinnamon	10	10
D25		50 c. dp turquoise-green & turq-bl	20	25
D26		$1 ultramarine and cobalt	40	45
D22/6		*Set of* 5	70	80

B. FEDERAL TERRITORY ISSUES

Kuala Lumpur, previously part of Selangor state, was established as a Federal Territory on 1 February 1974.

The following stamps were produced for use there, corresponding to the low value definitives provided for the states of the federation.

The island of Labuan, formerly part of Sabah, became the second Federal Territory on 16 April 1984, when Nos. K1/14 replaced the low value definitives of Sabah previously used there.

K 1 *Rafflesia hasseltii*

K 2 Coffee

(Des M. Yusof bin Mohammed; adapted Malaysian Advertising Services. Litho Asher and Co., Melbourne)

1979 (30 Apr). *Flowers. Horiz designs as Type* K **1**. *Multicoloured.* W **95** *(sideways). P* 15 × 14½.

K1	1 c. Type K 1	10	10
K2	2 c. *Pterocarpus indicus*	10	10
K3	5 c. *Lagerstroemia speciosa* (Type I)	10	10
K4	10 c. *Durio zibethinus*	10	10
K5	15 c. *Hibiscus rosa-sinensis*	15	10
K6	20 c. *Rhododendron scortechinii*	15	10
K7	25 c. *Etlingera elatior* (inscr "*Phaeomeria speciosa*")	15	10
K1/7	*Set of* 7	65	30

For higher values used in conjunction with this series see Nos. 190/7.

PRICES OF SETS

Set prices are given for many issues, generally those containing three stamps or more. Definitive sets include one of each value or major colour change, but do not cover different perforations, die types or minor shades. Where a choice is possible the set prices are based on the cheapest versions of the stamps included in the listings.

I

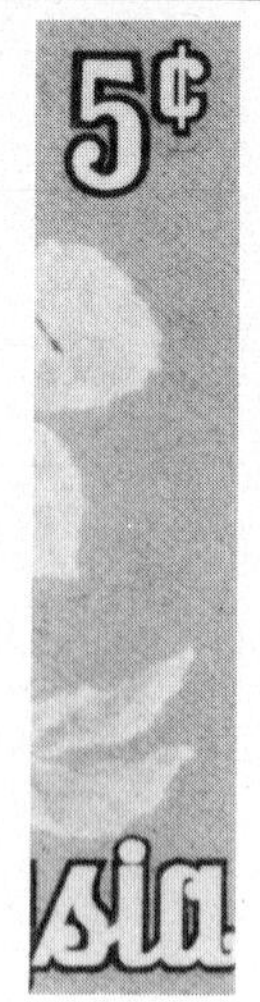

II

Two types of 5 c.:

Type I. "5" over "i" and "c" to right of "a" in "Malaysia" (Nos. K3 and K10).

Type II. "5" over "s" and "c" aligns on "a" of "Malaysia" (No. K10*a*).

1983–85.* *As Nos.* K3/7 *but without wmk.*

K10	5 c. *Lagerstroemia speciosa* (I) (turquoise-green background) (12.12.84)	6·00	3·50
K10*a*	5 c. *Lagerstroemia speciosa* (II) (turquoise-blue background) (1.85)	1·50	90
K11	10 c. *Durio zibethinus* (9.84)	35	15
K12	15 c. *Hibiscus rosa-sinensis* (5.11.83)	45	15
K13	20 c. *Rhododendron scortechinii* (blackish brown background) (1983)	8·50	1·00
K13*a*	20 c. *Rhododendron scortechinii* (bronze-green background) (13.11.83)	55	35
K14	25 c. *Etlingera elatior* (inscr "*Phaeomeria speciosa*") (1.85)	5·00	2·50

*There was no official release date for these stamps. Dates shown are the earliest recorded from postmarks and may be revised if earlier examples are reported.

The 10 c., 15 c. and 20 c. (No. K13*a*) are also from redrawn plates and show the inscriptions or the face value in slightly different positions.

(Des Kathy Wong. Litho Security Printers (M), Malaysia)

1986 (25 Oct). *Agricultural Products of Malaysia. Vert designs as Type* K **2**. *Multicoloured.* W **138**. *P* 12.

K15	1 c. Type K **2**	10	10
K16	2 c. Coconuts	10	10
K17	5 c. Cocoa	10	10
K18	10 c. Black pepper	10	10
K19	15 c. Rubber	10	10
K20	20 c. Oil palm	10	10
K21	30 c. Rice	10	15
K15/21	*Set of* 7	40	45

VII. MALAYSIAN STATES

PRINTERS. All Malaysian States stamps were printed in typography by De La Rue and Co, Ltd, London, *unless otherwise stated.*

JOHORE

A British adviser was appointed to Johore in 1914. The state joined the Federation of Malaya on 1 February 1948.

Until 1 January 1899 mail for addresses outside Malaya had the external postage paid by stamps of the STRAITS SETTLEMENTS.

PRICES FOR STAMPS ON COVER TO 1945	
Nos. 1/2	—
Nos. 3/5	*from* × 15
No. 6	*from* × 20
Nos. 7/8	—
Nos. 9/15	*from* × 25
No. 16	—
Nos. 17/20	*from* × 15
Nos. 21/31	*from* × 10
Nos. 32/8	*from* × 15
Nos. 39/53	*from* × 8
Nos. 54/60	*from* × 6
Nos. 61/74	*from* × 8
Nos. 75/7	—
Nos. 78/87	*from* × 8
No. 88	*from* × 10
Nos. 89/102	*from* × 6
Nos. 103/25	*from* × 5
Nos. 126/8	—
Nos. 129/30	*from* × 6
Nos. D1/5	*from* × 10

(1)

1876 (July). *No.* 11 *of Straits Settlements handstamped with T* **1**.

1	2 c. brown	£6500	£3000

No. 1 is known with the handstamp double.

From September 1878 to August 1884 no overprinted stamps were supplied by Singapore to Johore.

JOHORE
(2)

JOHORE
(3) ("H" and "E" wide. "J" raised. Opt 16 mm long)

JOHORE
(4) ("H" wide, "E" narrow. Opt 16 mm long)

JOHORE
(5) ("H" and "E" wide. Opt 16¾mm long)

JOHORE.
(6)

JOHORE
(7)

JOHORE
(8)

1884 (June)–**86**. *No.* 63 *of Straits Settlements optd with T* **2/8**.

2	**2**	2 c. pale rose	£1600	
3	**3**	2 c. pale rose (8.84)	£325	£140
		a. Opt double	£1000	
4	**4**	2 c. pale rose (8.84)	£400	£160
		a. Opt double		
5	**5**	2 c. pale rose (8.84)	£325	£140
		a. Opt double	—	£650
6	**6**	2 c. pale rose (3.85)	70·00	80·00
7	**7**	2 c. pale rose (1885)	£850	
8	**8**	2 c. pale rose (4.86)	35·00	48·00

Nos. 3 to 7 were from triplet settings, either 3+4+5 or three examples of the same overprint. Nos. 2 and 8 are probably single unit handstamps.

JOHOR
(9) (All letters narrow)

JOHOR
(10)

JOHOR
(11) ("H" wide)

JOHOR
(12)

JOHOR
(13)

JOHOR.
(14)

JOHOR
(15)

JOHOR
(16)

1884 (Aug)–**91**. *Nos.* 63/*a of Straits Settlements optd with T* **9/16**.

9	**9**	2 c. pale rose	6·50	9·00
10	**10**	2 c. pale rose (10.84)	4·25	4·25
		a. Thin, narrow "J" (R. 6/6)	55·00	55·00
		b. Bright rose (1890)	17·00	23·00
		ba. Thin, narrow "J" (R. 6/6)	£100	£110
11	**11**	2 c. pale rose (2.85)	35·00	35·00

12 12 2 c. pale rose (1886) .. .. 25·00 25·00
a. Opt double £650
13 13 2 c. pale rose (1886) .. .. 24·00 24·00
14 14 2 c. pale rose (1888) .. .. 42·00 30·00
a. Thin, narrow "J" £200 £200
b. Opt double £475
15 15 2 c. bright rose (9.90) .. .. 6·00 4·50
16 16 2 c. bright rose (1891) £4500

Settings:
No. 9 — various triplets with the length of the overprint varying from 12 to 15 mm
No. 10 — triplet or 60 (6×10)
No. 11 — triplet 11 + 9 + 9
No. 12 — triplet
No. 13 — triplet
No. 14 — 30 (3×10)
No. 15 — 60 (6×10)
No. 16 — not known. As no used examples are known it is possible that this stamp was not issued.

JOHOR Two CENTS
(17)

JOHOR Two CENTS
(18)

JOHOR Two CENTS
(19)

JOHOR Two CENTS
(20)

1891 (May). *No. 68 of Straits Settlements surch as T* **17/20**.
17 17 2 c. on 24 c. green .. .. 22·00 35·00
a. "CENST" (R. 5/4) £375 £250
18 18 2 c. on 24 c. green .. .. 70·00 70·00
a. Thin, narrow "J" (R. 6/6) £160 £160
19 19 2 c. on 24 c. green .. .. 28·00 45·00
20 20 2 c. on 24 c. green .. .. 65·00 65·00

Nos. 17/20 come from the same setting of 60. Type **17** occurs on horizontal rows 1 to 5, Type **18** on row 6, Type **19** on rows 7, 8 and 9 and Type **20** on row 10.

21 Sultan Aboubakar

3 cents.
(22)

KEMAHKOTAAN
(23)

1891 (16 Nov)–**94**. *No wmk. P* 14.
21 21 1 c. dull purple and mauve (7.94) .. 30 50
22 2 c. dull purple and yellow .. .. 30 1·50
23 3 c. dull purple and carmine (7.94) .. 55 50
24 4 c. dull purple and black .. .. 2·75 5·00
25 5 c. dull purple and green .. .. 8·00 20·00
26 6 c. dull purple and blue .. .. 10·00 20·00
27 $1 green and carmine .. .. .. 40·00 85·00
21/7 .. .. *Set of* 7 55·00 £120

1894 (Mar). *Surch with T* **22**.
28 21 3 c. on 4 c. dull purple and black .. 75 50
a. No stop (R. 5/11) .. .. .. 32·00 32·00
29 3 c. on 5 c. dull purple and green .. 80 2·00
a. No stop (R. 5/11) .. .. .. 40·00 45·00
30 3 c. on 6 c. dull purple and blue .. 1·00 2·00
a. No stop (R. 5/11) .. .. .. 45·00 48·00
31 3 c. on $1 green and carmine .. .. 9·50 32·00
a. No stop (R. 5/11) £140 £225
28/31 .. .. *Set of* 4 11·00 32·00

1896 (Mar). *Coronation of Sultan Ibrahim. Optd with T* **23**.
32 21 1 c. dull purple and mauve 45 85
a. "KETAHKOTAAN" .. .. .. 3·00 5·00
33 2 c. dull purple and yellow .. .. 45 1·00
a. "KETAHKOTAAN" .. .. .. 2·75 5·50
34 3 c. dull purple and carmine .. .. 55 1·00
a. "KETAHKOTAAN" .. .. .. 3·25 7·50
35 4 c. dull purple and black .. .. 80 2·25
a. "KETAHKOTAAN" .. .. .. 2·75 6·50
36 5 c. dull purple and green .. .. 5·50 7·50
a. "KETAHKOTAAN" .. .. .. 3·00 7·50
37 6 c. dull purple and blue .. .. 3·00 6·00
a. "KETAHKOTAAN" .. .. .. 3·00 6·00
38 $1 green and carmine .. .. .. 29·00 60·00
a. "KETAHKOTAAN" .. .. .. 27·00 80·00
32/8 .. .. *Set of* 7 35·00 70·00
32a/8a .. .. *Set of* 7 40·00 £110

The two spellings of the overprint occur in separate sheets.

24 Sultan Ibrahim 25

26 27

1896 (26 Aug)–**99**. *W* **27**. *P* 14.
39 24 1 c. green 70 45
40 2 c. green and blue 40 20
41 3 c. green and purple .. .. .. 1·25 40
a. Green and dull claret .. ..
42 4 c. green and carmine 50 35
43 4 c. yellow and red (1899) 75 50
44 5 c. green and brown .. .. .. 75 1·25
45 6 c. green and yellow .. .. .. 80 1·60
46 25 10 c. green and black (1898) .. .. 7·00 35·00
47 25 c. green and mauve (1898) .. .. 9·00 30·00
48 50 c. green and carmine (1898) .. .. 12·00 32·00
49 24 $1 dull purple and green (1898) .. .. 20·00 50·00
50 26 $2 dull purple and carmine (1898) .. 20·00 48·00
51 $3 dull purple and blue (1898) .. .. 28·00 75·00
52 $4 dull purple and brown (1898) .. .. 28·00 65·00
53 $5 dull purple and yellow (1898) .. .. 60·00 90·00
39/53 .. .. *Set of* 15 £170 £375

3 cents.
(28)

10 cents.
(29)

1903 (Apr). *Surch with T* **28** *or* **29**.
54 24 3 c. on 4 c. yellow and red .. .. 50 1·10
a. Original value uncancelled .. .. 3·00 12·00
55 10 c. on 4 c. green and carmine .. .. 2·50 4·50
a. Tall "1" in "10" (R. 9/12) .. .. 50·00 70·00
b. Original value uncancelled .. .. 20·00 50·00
ba. As b, with tall "1" in "10" (R. 9/12) .. £550 £650

The bars on these stamps were ruled by hand with pen and ink.

50 Cents.
(30)

One Dollar
(31)

1903 (Oct). *Surch with T* **30** *or* **31**.
56 26 50 c. on $3 dull purple and blue .. .. 18·00 55·00
57 $1 on $2 dull purple and carmine .. .. 48·00 80·00
a. "e" of "One" inverted (R. 7/9) £1100

10 CENTS.
(32)

1904. *Surch as T* **32**.
58 24 10 c. on 4 c. yellow and red (Apr) .. .. 22·00 35·00
a. Surcharge double £5500
59 10 c. on 4 c. green and carmine (Aug) .. 9·00 28·00
60 26 50 c. on $5 dull purple and yellow (May) .. 50·00 £110
58/60 .. .. *Set of* 3 75·00 £150

33 34 35 Sultan Sir Ibrahim

1904 (Sept)–**10**. *W* **27**. *Ordinary paper. P* 14.
61 33 1 c. dull purple and green 30 30
a. Chalk-surfaced paper (10.10) 80 80
62 2 c. dull purple and orange .. .. 85 1·75
a. Chalk-surfaced paper (10.10) .. .. 2·00 2·75
63 3 c. dull purple and olive-black 70 40
64 4 c. dull purple and carmine .. .. 5·00 1·60
65 5 c. dull purple and sage-green .. .. 60 2·50
66 35 8 c. dull purple and blue .. .. 2·50 4·00
67 34 10 c. dull purple and black .. .. 21·00 7·50
a. Chalk-surfaced paper (1910) .. .. 27·00 13·00
68 25 c. dull purple and green .. .. 3·50 17·00
69 50 c. dull purple and red .. .. 26·00 14·00
70 33 $1 green and mauve .. .. .. 12·00 45·00
71 35 $2 green and carmine .. .. .. 17·00 42·00
72 $3 green and blue .. .. .. 22·00 65·00
73 $4 green and brown .. .. .. 24·00 80·00
74 $5 green and orange .. .. .. 32·00 70·00
75 34 $10 green and black .. .. .. 48·00 £110
76 $50 green and ultramarine £130 £190
77 $100 green and scarlet £250 £400
61/75 .. .. *Set of* 15 £190 £425

1910–19. *Wmk Mult Rosettes (vertical). Chalk-surfaced paper. P* 14.
78 33 1 c. dull purple and green (1912) .. 15 15
79 2 c. dull purple and orange (1912) .. 2·50 65
80 3 c. dull purple and olive-black (1912) .. 2·50 65
a. Wmk horizontal (1910) .. .. 10·00 10·00
81 4 c. dull purple and carmine (1912) .. 1·50 55
a. Wmk horizontal (1910) .. .. 20·00 20·00
82 5 c. dull purple and sage-green (1912) .. 1·25 50
83 35 8 c. dull purple and blue (1912) .. .. 3·75 4·25
84 34 10 c. dull purple and black (1912) .. .. 15·00 2·50
a. Wmk horizontal (1911) .. .. 20·00 32·00
85 25 c. dull purple and green (1912) .. 3·25 15·00
86 50 c. dull purple and red (1919) .. .. 40·00 70·00
87 33 $1 green and mauve (1918) .. .. 50·00 60·00
78/87 .. .. *Set of* 10 £110 £140

3 CENTS.
(36)

37 Sultan Sin Ibrahim and Sultana

1912 (Mar). *No. 66 surch with T* **36**.
88 3 c. on 8 c. dull purple and blue .. .. 1·75 3·00
a. "T" of "CENTS" omitted £600
b. Bars double .. .. ..

No. 88b shows the bars printed twice with the upper pair partly erased.

1918–21. *Wmk Mult Crown CA. Chalk-surfaced paper. P* 14.
89 33 2 c. dull purple and green (1919) .. 40 80
90 2 c. purple and orange (1921) .. .. 50 1·00
91 4 c. dull purple and red 55 20
92 5 c. dull purple and sage-green (1920) .. 2·00 3·00
93 34 10 c. dull purple and blue .. .. 1·50 1·40
94 21 c. dull purple and orange (1919) .. 2·75 3·50
95 25 c. dull purple and green (1920) .. 8·00 13·00
96 50 c. dull purple and red (1920) .. .. 13·00 22·00
97 33 $1 green and mauve .. .. .. 9·00 35·00
98 35 $2 green and carmine .. .. .. 18·00 38·00
99 $3 green and blue .. .. .. 28·00 65·00
100 $4 green and brown .. .. .. 35·00 75·00
101 $5 green and orange .. .. .. 48·00 90·00
102 34 $10 green and black .. .. .. 95·00 £160
89/102 .. .. *Set of* 14 £225 £450
89/102 Optd "Specimen" .. .. *Set of* 14 £300

1922–40. *Wmk Mult Script CA. Chalk-surfaced paper. P* 14.
103 33 1 c. dull purple and black 30 20
104 2 c. purple and sepia (1924) .. .. 75 1·40
105 2 c. green (1928) 30 30
106 3 c. green (1925) .. .. .. 1·50 3·00
107 3 c. purple and sepia (1928) .. .. 95 1·50
108 4 c. purple and carmine (1924) .. .. 2·25 15
109 5 c. dull purple and sage-green 30 30
110 6 c. dull purple and claret 40 40
111 34 10 c. dull purple and blue .. .. 15·00 22·00
112 10 c. dull purple and yellow 25 25
113 33 12 c. dull purple and blue .. .. 1·00 1·25
114 12 c. ultramarine (1940) .. .. 20·00 10·00
115 34 21 c. dull purple and orange (1928) .. 2·50 3·00
116 25 c. dull purple and myrtle .. .. 1·40 1·00
117 35 30 c. dull purple and orange (1936) .. 2·25 2·75
118 40 c. dull purple and brown (1936) .. 2·75 3·25
119 34 50 c. dull purple and red .. .. 2·25 1·25
120 33 $1 green and mauve .. .. .. 2·00 85
121 35 $2 green and carmine (1923) .. .. 4·75 3·50
122 $3 green and blue (1925) .. .. 27·00 60·00
123 $4 green and brown (1926) .. .. 48·00 85·00
124 $5 green and orange .. .. .. 35·00 48·00
125 34 $10 green and black (1924) £110 £170
126 $50 green and ultram (Optd S. £150) £450
127 $100 green and scarlet (Optd S. £275) £1100
128 35 $500 blue and red (1926) (Optd S. £750) £16000
103/25 .. .. *Set of* 23 £250 £375
103/25 Optd/Perf "Specimen" .. *Set of* 23 £400

(Recess Waterlow)

1935 (15 May). *Wmk Mult Script CA (sideways). P* 12½.
129 37 8 c. bright violet and slate .. .. 1·00 40
129 Perf "Specimen" .. .. .. 35·00

38 Sultan Sir Ibrahim 39

(Recess D.L.R.)

1940 (Feb). *Wmk Mult Script CA. P* 13½.
130 38 8 c. black and pale blue .. .. .. 5·50 15
130 Perf "Specimen" .. .. .. 35·00

1948 (1 Dec). *Royal Silver Wedding. As Nos. 143/4 of Jamaica.*
131 10 c. violet 20 15
132 $5 green .. .. 24·00 30·00

1949 (2 May)–**55**. *Wmk Mult Script CA. Chalk-surfaced paper. P* 17½ × 18.
133 39 1 c. black 10 10
134 2 c. orange 10 10
a. Orange-yellow (22.1.52) 10 40
135 3 c. green 35 30
a. Yellow-green (22.1.52) .. .. 1·75 80
136 4 c. brown 10 10
136*a* 5 c. bright purple (1.9.52) 30 20
137 6 c. grey 20 10
a. Pale grey (22.1.52) 30 20
ac. Error. St. Edward's Crown W **9b** .. £600
138 8 c. scarlet 55 90
138*a* 8 c. green (1.9.52) .. .. .. 75 1·25
139 10 c. magenta 20 10
aa. Imperf (pair) £900
139*a* 12 c. scarlet (1.9.52) .. .. .. 1·25 2·25
140 15 c. ultramarine .. .. .. 1·00 10
141 20 c. black and green .. .. .. 45 1·00
141*a* 20 c. bright blue (1.9.52) 80 10
142 25 c. purple and orange 30 10
142*a* 30 c. scarlet and purple (5.9.55) .. 1·25 2·00
142*b* 35 c. scarlet and purple (1.9.52) .. 1·25 1·00
143 40 c. red and purple .. .. .. 1·75 4·75
144 50 c. black and blue 50 10
145 $1 blue and purple .. .. .. 2·00 75
146 $2 green and scarlet .. .. .. 10·00 3·50
147 $5 green and brown .. .. .. 26·00 9·00
133/47 .. .. *Set of* 21 45·00 24·00

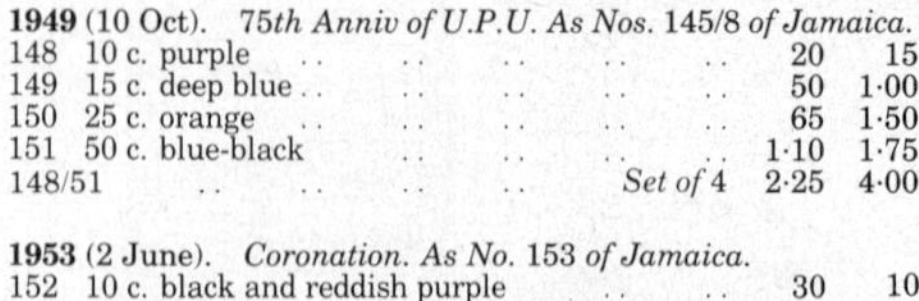

1949 (10 Oct). *75th Anniv of U.P.U. As Nos.* 145/8 *of Jamaica.*

No.	Description	Unused	Used
148	10 c. purple	20	15
149	15 c. deep blue	50	1·00
150	25 c. orange	65	1·50
151	50 c. blue-black	1·10	1·75
148/51	*Set of* 4	2·25	4·00

1953 (2 June). *Coronation. As No.* 153 *of Jamaica.*

No.	Description	Unused	Used
152	10 c. black and reddish purple	30	10

40 Sultan Sir Ibrahim

41 Sultan Sir Ismail and Johore Coat of Arms

(Recess D.L.R.)

1955 (1 Nov). *Diamond Jubilee of Sultan. Wmk Mult Script CA. P* 14.

No.	Description	Unused	Used
153 **40**	10 c. carmine-red	10	10

(Photo Courvoisier)

1960 (10 Feb). *Coronation of Sultan. No wmk. P* 11½.

No.	Description	Unused	Used
154 **41**	10 c. multicoloured	15	15

1960. *As T* **9/19** *of Kedah, but with portrait of Sultan Ismail. P* 13½ ($1); *others* 12½ × 13 (*vert*) *or* 13 × 12½ (*horiz*).

No.	Description	Unused	Used
155	1 c. black (7.10.60)	10	20
156	2 c. orange-red (7.10.60)	10	15
157	4 c. sepia (19.8.60)	10	10
158	5 c. carmine-lake (7.10.60)	10	10
159	8 c. myrtle-green (9.12.60)	1·25	1·50
160	10 c. deep maroon (10.6.60)	15	10
161	20 c. blue (9.12.60)	15	10
162	50 c. black and bright blue (19.8.60)	20	10
163	$1 ultramarine and reddish purple (9.12.60)	1·25	1·25
164	$2 bronze-green and scarlet (9.12.60)	3·75	6·00
165	$5 brown and bronze-green (7.10.60)	15·00	16·00
155/65	*Set of* 11	20·00	23·00

In No. 161 there are only two figures in the boat, the steersman being missing. In the 20 c. value for all the other States there are three figures.

The 6, 12, 25 and 30 c. values used with this issue were Nos. 1/4 of Malayan Federation.

42 *Vanda hookeriana* (Inset portrait of Sultan Ismail)

(Des A. Fraser-Brunner. Photo Harrison)

1965 (15 Nov). *T* **42** *and similar horiz designs. W* w **13** (*upright*). *P* 14½.

No.	Description	Unused	Used
166	1 c. Type **42**	10	30
	a. Black (orchid's name and part of flower) omitted	55·00	
167	2 c. *Arundina graminifolia*	10	35
168	5 c. *Paphiopedilum niveum*	10	10
	b. Yellow (flower) omitted	18·00	
169	6 c. *Spathoglottis plicata*	20	10
170	10 c. *Arachnis flos-aeris*	20	10
171	15 c. *Rhyncostylis retusa*	70	10
	b. Green (face value and leaves) omitted	85·00	
172	20 c. *Phalaenopsis violacea*	1·00	30
	a. Bright purple (blooms) omitted	35·00	
166/72	*Set of* 7	2·00	1·10

The 2 c. to 15 c. exist with both PVA gum and gum arabic.

The 2 c. with black (name of state, arms and head) omitted is listed under Sarawak No. 213*a* as there is some evidence that a sheet was issued there; if it also exists from any of the other states it would, of course, be identical.

The higher values used with this issue were Nos. 20/27 of Malaysia (National Issues).

1970. *As No.* 166 *and* 170 *but W* w **13** (*sideways*).

No.	Description	Unused	Used
173	1 c. multicoloured (20.11)	40	2·00
174	10 c. multicoloured (27.5)	40	1·50

44 *Delias ninus* (Inset portrait of Sultan Ismail)

45 *Rafflesia hasseltii* (Inset portrait of Sultan Ismail)

(Des V. Whiteley)

1971 (1 Feb)–**78**. *Butterflies. T* **44** *and similar horiz designs. Multicoloured. No wmk. P* 13½ × 13.

(*a*) *Litho by Bradbury, Wilkinson*

No.	Description	Unused	Used
175	1 c. Type **44**	15	40
176	2 c. *Danaus melanippus*	40	40
177	5 c. *Parthenos sylvia*	55	10
178	6 c. *Papilio demoleus*	55	40
179	10 c. *Hebomoia glaucippe*	55	10
180	15 c. *Precis orithya*	55	10
181	20 c. *Valeria valeria*	80	15
175/81	*Set of* 7	3·25	1·40

(*b*) *Photo Harrison* (1977–78)

No.	Description	Unused	Used
182	1 c. Type **44**	70	1·00
183	2 c. *Danaus melanippus*	55	1·40
184	5 c. *Parthenos sylvia*	2·00	30
185	10 c. *Hebomoia glaucippe*	1·00	15
186	15 c. *Precis orithya*	2·00	25
187	20 c. *Valeria valeria*	2·50	1·00
182/7	*Set of* 6	8·00	3·75

The higher values used with this issue were Nos. 64/71 of Malaysia (National Issues).

DIFFERENCES BETWEEN LITHO AND PHOTO PRINTINGS. Stamps from the photogravure printings can be easily identified by the appearance of certain features. The differences are most easily observed on the face values and inscriptions. Stamps printed by lithography show straight edges to letters and figures, but when those produced by photogravure are examined under a magnifying glass it will be seen that these edges are broken by the photogravure screen.

In addition the backgrounds and portraits of those stamps of this series printed by lithography show a regular screen of dots, a feature not visible on those printed by the photogravure process.

A number of instances have come to light of photogravure stamps which have had the top colour "removed" by means of an eraser.

(Des M. Yusof bin Mohammed; adapted Malaysian Advertising Services. Litho Asher and Co., Melbourne)

1979 (30 Apr). *Flowers. Horiz designs as T* **45**. *Multicoloured. W* **95** *of Malaysia* (*sideways*). *P* 15 × 14½.

No.	Description	Unused	Used
188	1 c. Type **45**	10	10
189	2 c. *Pterocarpus indicus*	10	10
190	5 c. *Lagerstroemia speciosa*	10	10
191	10 c. *Durio zibethinus*	10	10
192	15 c. *Hibiscus rosa-sinensis*	15	10
193	20 c. *Rhododendron scortechinii*	15	10
194	25 c. *Etlingera elatior* (inscr "*Phaeomeria speciosa*")	15	10
188/94	*Set of* 7	65	30

For higher values used in conjunction with this series see Nos. 190/7 of Malaysia.

1983 (July)–**85**.* *As Nos.* 190/3 *but without wmk.*

No.	Description	Unused	Used
197	5 c. *Lagerstroemia speciosa* (20.11.83)	45	35
198	10 c. *Durio zibethinus* (11.7.85)	50	50
199	15 c. *Hibiscus rosa-sinensis* (12.83)	55	20
200	20 c. *Rhododendron scortechinii* (blackish brown background)	5·00	75
200*a*	20 c. *Rhododendron scortechinii* (bronze-green background) (13.11.83)	65	40

*There was no official release date for these stamps. Dates shown are the earliest recorded from postmarks and may be revised if earlier examples are reported.

On Nos. 197/9 and 200*a* the "Johor" inscription is in rounded instead of square-ended letters.

WATERMARKED AND UNWATERMARKED PRINTINGS. The first printing of the 20 c, value on unwatermarked paper was from the same plates and in the same shades as the original watermarked issue.

Subsequent no watermark printings of the 20 c. and all no watermark printings of the other values were in changed shades and can be readily identified as follows:

5 c. No watermark printing has the frame in turquoise-blue instead of the dull blue of the watermarked version.

10 c. No watermark printing shows a purple-brown background instead of the sepia of the watermarked.

15 c. No watermark printing shows stronger highlights in the design and more detail on the flowers and leaves.

20 c. Later no watermark printings have a bronze-green background instead of the blackish brown shown on the watermarked and first no watermark stamps.

25 c. No watermark printing has a deep background with more detail on the flower. The latin inscription has also been moved downwards to a more central position up the side of the vignette.

Differences also occur in the plates used to apply the state names, rulers' portraits or crests. Notes on these are provided under the individual issues.

46 Coconuts (Inset portrait of Sultan Mahmood)

(Des Kathy Wong. Litho Security Printers (M), Malaysia)

1986 (25 Oct). *Agricultural Products of Malaysia. Vert designs as T* **46**. *Multicoloured. W* **138**. *Phosphorised paper. P* 12.

No.	Description	Unused	Used
202	1 c. Coffee	10	10
203	2 c. Type **46**	10	10
204	5 c. Cocoa	10	10
205	10 c. Black pepper	10	10
206	15 c. Rubber	10	10
207	20 c. Oil palm	10	10
208	30 c. Rice	10	15
202/8	*Set of* 7	40	45

ALTERED CATALOGUE NUMBERS

Any Catalogue numbers altered from the last edition are shown as a list in the introductory pages.

POSTAGE DUE STAMPS

D 1

(Typo Waterlow)

1938 (1 Jan). *Wmk Mult Script CA. P* 12½.

No.	Description	Unused	Used
D1 D 1	1 c. carmine	7·50	26·00
D2	4 c. green	25·00	38·00
D3	8 c. orange	30·00	£100
D4	10 c. brown	30·00	42·00
D5	12 c. purple	38·00	£100
D1/5	*Set of* 5	£120	£275
D1/5 Perf "Specimen"	*Set of* 5	£100	

KEDAH

Suzerainty over Kedah was transferred by Thailand to Great Britain on 15 July 1909. A British adviser was appointed in 1923.

The state joined the Federation of Malaya on 1 February 1948.

Stamps of THAILAND were used in Kedah at Alor Star (from 1883), Kuala Muda (from 1907), Kulim (from 1907) and Langkawi (from 1908) until 1909. Issues of the FEDERATED MALAY STATES were used in Kedah from 16 July 1909 until 1912.

PRICES FOR STAMPS ON COVER TO 1945	
Nos. 1/14	*from* × 15
Nos. 15/23	*from* × 10
Nos. 24/40	*from* × 8
Nos. 41/8	*from* × 12
Nos. 49/51	—
Nos. 52/9	*from* × 4
Nos. 60/8	*from* × 3
Nos. 68*a*/9*a*	*from* × 4

1 Sheaf of Rice

2 Malay ploughing

3 Council Chamber, Alor Star

1912 (16 June). *Wmk Mult Crown CA* (*sideways on* 10 *c. to* $5). *P* 14.

No.	Type	Description	Unused	Used
1	1	1 c. black and green	25	25
2		3 c. black and red	2·25	30
3		4 c. rose and grey	8·50	25
4		5 c. green and chestnut	2·00	3·00
5		8 c. black and ultramarine	1·00	2·00
6	2	10 c. blue and sepia	1·75	90
7		20 c. black and green	2·75	4·00
8		30 c. black and rose	2·25	9·00
9		40 c. black and purple	3·50	14·00
10		50 c. brown and blue	7·50	13·00
11	3	$1 black and red/*yellow*	11·00	18·00
12		$2 green and brown	11·00	50·00
13		$3 black and blue/*blue*	48·00	£100
14		$5 black and red	48·00	90·00
1/14		*Set of* 14	£130	£275
1/14 Optd "Specimen"		*Set of* 14	£275	

Due to an increase in postal rates 1 c. and 4 c. stamps of STRAITS SETTLEMENTS were used in Kedah for some months from March 1919.

(i)

(ii)

DOUBLE AND SINGLE PLATES. (i) Printed from separate plates for frame and centre, with dotted shading extending close to the central sheaf. Soft impression of centre with little clear detail.

(ii) Printed from single plate, with white space around sheaf. Centre more deeply etched with sharp image.

1919 (June)–**21**. *New colours and values. Wmk Mult Crown CA* (*sideways on* 21 *c.*, 25 *c.*). *P* 14.

No.	Type	Description	Unused	Used
15	1	1 c. brown (i) (8.19)	55	45
18		2 c. green (ii)	50	20
19		3 c. deep purple (i) (1920)	65	70
20		4 c. rose (i)	1·50	20
21		4 c. red (ii) (1920)	2·00	20
22	2	21 c. purple (8.19)	5·50	35·00
23		25 c. blue and purple (1921)	1·75	20·00
15/23		*Set of* 6	9·50	50·00
15/23 Optd "Specimen"		*Set of* 6	£130	

ONE

DOLLAR

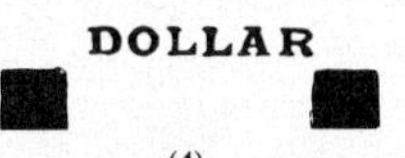

(4)

MALAYA-
BORNEO
EXHIBITION.

(5)

(Surch by Ribeiro & Co, Penang)

1919 (Mar). *Surch as T* **4**.

No.	Type	Description	Unused	Used
24	3	50 c. on $2 green and brown	40·00	48·00
		a. "C" of "CENTS" inserted by hand-stamp (R. 6/4)	£950	£1000
25		$1 on $3 black and blue/*blue*	20·00	65·00

Two types of centre plate for Type **2** wmkd Mult Script CA:

Type I (Plate 1)

Type II (Plate 2)

A new common centre plate, 2, was prepared from the orginal die in 1926. Stamps from plate 2 show considerably more detail of the ground and have the oxen, ploughman's hat and his clothing much more deeply cut as illustrated in Type II above.

1921–27. *Wmk Mult Script CA* (*sideways on* 10 *c. to* $5). *P* 14.

No.	Type	Description	Unused	Used
26	1	1 c. brown (ii)	40	20
27		2 c. dull green (ii) (Die I)*	25	20
28		3 c. deep purple (ii)	80	70
29		4 c. deep carmine (ii)	5·00	20
30	2	10 c. blue and sepia (I)	90	75
		a. Type II (1927)	8·00	2·50
31		20 c. black and yellow-green (I)	1·50	2·00
32		21 c. mauve and purple (I)	2·00	10·00
33		25 c. blue and purple (I)	2·25	5·50
		a. Type II (1927)	18·00	3·50
34		30 c. black and rose (I) (1922)	2·50	3·75
		a. Type II (1927)	18·00	2·75
35		40 c. black and purple (I)	2·50	18·00
		a. Type II (1927)	28·00	16·00
36		50 c. brown and grey-blue (I)	1·75	6·00
		a. Type II (1927)	22·00	3·50
37	3	$1 black and red/*yellow* (1924)	6·50	7·50
38		$2 myrtle and brown	13·00	55·00
39		$3 black and blue/*blue*	30·00	50·00
40		$5 black and deep carmine	45·00	90·00
26/40		*Set of* 15	95·00	£225
26/40 Optd "Specimen"		*Set of* 15	£250	

* For 2 c. Die II, see No. 69.

1922 (31 Mar). *Optd as T* **5** *at Singapore.*

I. "BORNEO" 14 *mm. long.*

(*a*) *Wmk Mult Crown CA*

No.	Type	Description	Unused	Used
41	1	2 c. green (ii)	3·50	16·00
42	2	21 c. mauve and purple (I)	17·00	70·00
43		25 c. blue and purple (I)	19·00	70·00
		a. Overprint inverted	£750	
44		50 c. brown and grey-blue (I)	19·00	85·00

(*b*) *Wmk Mult Script CA*

No.	Type	Description	Unused	Used
45	1	1 c. brown (ii)	2·25	13·00
46		3 c. purple (ii)	3·00	27·00
47		4 c. deep carmine (ii)	3·00	25·00
48	2	10 c. blue and sepia (I)	4·50	32·00
41/8		*Set of* 8	60·00	£300

There are setting variations in the size and shape of the letters, stop raised, stop omitted, etc., etc.

II. "BORNEO" 15–15½ *mm long. Wmk Mult Crown CA*

No.	Type	Description	Unused	Used
49	2	21 c. mauve and purple (I)	17·00	80·00
50		25 c. blue and purple (I)	22·00	90·00
51		50 c. brown and grey-blue (I)	45·00	£140
49/51		*Set of* 3	75·00	£275

1922–36. *New colours, etc. Wmk Mult Script CA* (*sideways on* 12, 35 *c.*). *P* 14.

No.	Type	Description	Unused	Used
52	1	1 c. black (ii) (Die I)*	15	10
53		3 c. green (ii) (1924)	1·50	65
54		4 c. violet (ii) (1926)	90	10
55		5 c. yellow (ii)	1·50	10
56		6 c. carmine (ii) (Die I) (1926)*	70	65
57		8 c. grey-black (10.36)	8·00	10
58	2	12 c. black and indigo (II) (1926)	2·00	4·00
59		35 c. purple (II) (1926)	4·50	24·00
52/9		*Set of* 8	17·00	26·00
52/9 Optd/Perf "Specimen"		*Set of* 8	£130	

*For 1 c. and 6 c. Die II, see Nos. 68*a* and 69*a*.

MINIMUM PRICE

The minimum price quote is 10p which represents a handling charge rather than a basis for valuing common stamps. For further notes about prices see introductory pages.

6 Sultan Abdul Hamid Halimshah

(Recess Waterlow)

1937 (30 June). *Wmk Mult Script CA. P* 12½.

No.	Type	Description	Unused	Used
60	6	10 c. ultramarine and sepia	1·60	30
61		12 c. black and violet	15·00	12·00
62		25 c. ultramarine and purple	4·75	4·50
63		30 c. green and scarlet	7·00	9·50
64		40 c. black and purple	1·75	11·00
65		50 c. brown and blue	2·75	4·50
66		$1 black and green	2·50	9·00
67		$2 green and brown	80·00	70·00
68		$5 black and scarlet	29·00	55·00
60/8		*Set of* 9	£130	£160
60/8 Perf "Specimen"		*Set of* 9	£170	

I II I II

1938–40. *As Nos.* 52, 27 *and* 56, *but redrawn as Dies* II.

No.	Type	Description	Unused	Used
68*a*	1	1 c. black	50·00	4·00
69		2 c. bright green (1940)	£100	10·00
69*a*		6 c. carmine-red (1940)	28·00	45·00
68*a*/9*a*		*Set of* 3	£160	55·00

1 c. Die II. Figures "1" have square-cut corners instead of rounded, and larger top serif. Larger "C". Line perf.

2 c. Die II. Figures "2" have circular instead of oval drops and the letters "c" are thin and tall instead of thick and rounded. Size of design: 19½ × 23 mm instead of about 18½ × 22½ mm. Line perf.

6 c. Die II. Design measures 19¼ × 22¼ mm instead of 18¾ × 22½ mm (No. 56). Note also shade of Die II. Line perf.

1948 (1 Dec). *Royal Silver Wedding. As Nos.* 143/4 *of Jamaica.*

No.	Description	Unused	Used
70	10 c. violet	20	20
71	$5 carmine	22·00	32·00

1949 (10 Oct). 75*th Anniv of U.P.U. As Nos.* 145/8 *of Jamaica.*

No.	Description	Unused	Used
72	10 c. purple	25	20
73	15 c. deep blue	50	1·25
74	25 c. orange	65	1·25
75	50 c. blue-black	1·25	2·25
72/5	*Set of* 4	2·40	4·50

7 Sheaf of Rice

8 Sultan Badlishah

1950 (1 June)–**55.** *Wmk Mult Script CA. Chalk-surfaced paper. P* 17½ × 18.

No.	Type	Description	Unused	Used
76	7	1 c. black	10	30
77		2 c. orange	10	15
78		3 c. green	30	1·00
79		4 c. brown	15	10
79*a*		5 c. bright purple (1.9.52)	35	40
		ab. Bright mauve (24.9.53)	35	30
80		6 c. grey	15	15
81		8 c. scarlet	30	1·75
81*a*		8 c. green (1.9.52)	75	1·75
		ab. Deep green (24.9.53)	2·25	3·75
82		10 c. magenta	15	10
82*a*		12 c. scarlet (1.9.52)	85	2·50
83		15 c. ultramarine	40	35
84		20 c. black and green	40	2·50
84*a*		20 c. bright blue (1.9.52)	85	10
85	8	25 c. purple and orange	30	30
85*a*		30 c. scarlet and purple (5.9.55)	1·25	1·25
85*b*		35 c. scarlet and purple (1.9.52)	85	1·50
86		40 c. red and purple	1·00	6·00
87		50 c. black and blue	50	10
88		$1 blue and purple	2·25	1·75
89		$2 green and scarlet	17·00	22·00
90		$5 green and brown	28·00	32·00
76/90		*Set of* 21	50·00	65·00

1953 (2 June). *Coronation. As No.* 153 *of Jamaica.*

No.	Description	Unused	Used
91	10 c. black and reddish purple	30	10

9 Copra

10 Pineapples

11 Ricefield

12 Masjid Alwi Mosque, Kangar

13 East Coast Railway

14 Tiger

15 Fishing Prau

16 Aborigines with Blowpipes

17 Government Offices

18 Bersilat

19 Weaving

(Recess D.L.R.)

1957. *Inset portrait of Sultan Badlishah.* W w **12.** *P* 13 × 12½ (1 *c. to* 8 *c.*), 12½ × 13 (10 *c.*, 20 *c.*), 12½ (50 *c.*, $2, $5) *or* 13½ ($1).

92 **9** 1 c. black (21.8) 10 35
93 **10** 2 c. orange-red (25.7) 10 40
94 **11** 4 c. sepia (21.8) 10 10
95 **12** 5 c. carmine-lake (21.8) 10 20
96 **13** 8 c. myrtle-green (21.8) .. .. .. 2·00 3·75
97 **14** 10 c. deep brown (4.8) 15 10
98 **15** 20 c. blue (26.6) 30 45
99 **16** 50 c. black and blue (25.7) .. .. 40 1·00
100 **17** $1 ultramarine & reddish purple (25.7) 2·75 5·00
101 **18** $2 bronze-green and scarlet (21.8) .. 11·00 12·00
102 **19** $5 brown and bronze-green (26.6) .. 16·00 22·00
92/102 .. .. *Set of* 11 30·00 40·00

The 6, 12, 25 and 30 c. values used with this issue were Nos. 1/4 of Malayan Federation.

20 Sultan Abdul Halim Mu'Adzam Shah

21 Sultan Abdul Halim Shah

(Photo Harrison)

1959 (20 Feb). *Installation of the Sultan.* W w **12.** *P* 14 × 14½.
103 **20** 10 c. multicoloured 10 10

1959 (1 July)–**62.** *As Nos.* 92/102 *but with inset portrait of Sultan Abdul Halim Shah as in T* **21.**

104 **21** 1 c. black 10 30
105 **10** 2 c. orange-red 10 30
106 **11** 4 c. sepia 10 10
107 **12** 5 c. carmine-lake 10 10
108 **13** 8 c. myrtle-green .. .. 2·75 1·25
109 **14** 10 c. deep brown 30 10
109*a* 10 c. deep maroon (19.12.61) .. .. 1·50 15
110 **15** 20 c. blue 20 10
111 **16** 50 c. black and blue (*p* 12½) 30 35
a. Perf 12½ × 13 (14.6.60) 30 10
112 **17** $1 ultramarine and reddish purple .. 1·50 2·25
113 **18** $2 bronze-green and scarlet .. .. 5·00 8·50
114 **19** $5 brown and bronze-green (*p* 12½) .. 11·00 17·00
a. Perf 13 × 12½ (26.11.62) .. .. 9·00 11·00
104/14 .. .. *Set of* 12 18·00 21·00

22 *Vanda hookeriana*

23 *Danaus melanippus*

1965 (15 Nov). *As Nos.* 166/72 *of Johore but with inset portrait of Sultan Abdul Halim Shah as in T* **22.** *W w* **13** *(upright).*

115 1 c. multicoloured 10 30
a. Black omitted (orchid's name and part of flower) .. .. 45·00
116 2 c. multicoloured 10 30
b. Yellow (flower) omitted .. .. 40·00
117 5 c. multicoloured 10 10
a. Black (country name and head) omitted .. .. 60·00
118 6 c. multicoloured 15 15
119 10 c. multicoloured 20 10
a. Red omitted £130
b. Green (leaves) omitted £130
120 15 c. multicoloured 70 10
121 20 c. multicoloured .. .. 1·00 40
a. Bright purple (blooms) omitted .. 85·00
b. Yellow (leaves) omitted .. .. 15·00
115/21 .. .. *Set of* 7 2·00 1·10

The 1 c. to 15 c. exist with PVA gum as well as gum arabic.

The 6 c. value exists with black (country name, arms and head) omitted and is listed under Sarawak where it was issued.

The higher values used with this issue were Nos. 20/27 of Malaysia (National Issues).

1970 (27 May). *As Nos.* 115 *and* 119 *but W w* **13** *(sideways).*
122 **22** 1 c. multicoloured .. .. .. 1·00 3·00
123 – 10 c. multicoloured .. .. .. 65 2·50

1971 (1 Feb)–**78.** *As Nos.* 175/87 *of Johore but with portrait of Sultan Abdul Halim Shah as in T* **23.** *(a) Litho by Bradbury, Wilkinson.*

124 1 c. multicoloured 15 40
125 2 c. multicoloured 35 40
126 5 c. multicoloured 45 10
127 6 c. multicoloured 45 40
128 10 c. multicoloured 45 10
129 15 c. multicoloured 60 10
130 20 c. multicoloured 95 35
124/30 .. .. *Set of* 7 3·00 1·60

(b) Photo by Harrison (1977–78)

130*a* 2 c. multicoloured .. .. 8·50 10·00
131 5 c. multicoloured .. .. 1·25 40
132 10 c. multicoloured .. .. 2·75 15
133 15 c. multicoloured .. .. 1·25 30
134 20 c. multicoloured .. .. 2·00 1·25
130*a*/4 .. .. *Set of* 5 14·00 11·00

The higher values used with this issue were Nos. 64/71 of Malaysia (National Issues).

For differences between litho and photo printings, see after Johore No. 187.

24 *Pterocarpus indicus*

25 Sultan Abdul Halim Shah

1979 (30 Apr). *As Nos.* 188/94 *of Johore but with portrait of Sultan Abdul Halim Shah as in T* **24.**

135 1 c. *Rafflesia hasseltii* 10 10
136 2 c. Type **24** 10 10
137 5 c. *Lagerstroemia speciosa* 10 10
138 10 c. *Durio zibethinus* 10 10
139 15 c. *Hibiscus rosa-sinensis* 15 10
140 20 c. *Rhododendron scortechinii* 15 10
141 25 c. *Etlingera elatior* (inscr "*Phaeomeria speciosa*") 15 10
135/41 .. .. *Set of* 7 65 30

For higher values used in conjunction with this series see Nos. 190/7 of Malaysia (National Issues).

(Des and litho Security Printers (M), Malaysia)

1983 (15 July). *Silver Jubilee of Sultan. T* **25** *and similar multicoloured designs. P* 13 × 13½ (20 *c.*) *or* 13½ × 13 (*others*).

142 20 c. Type **25** 45 25
143 40 c. Paddy fields (*horiz*) 65 40
144 60 c. Paddy fields and Mount Jerai (*horiz*) .. 90 1·10
142/4 .. .. *Set of* 3 1·75 1·60

1983 (22 Feb)–**85.*** *As Nos.* 138/40 *but without wmk.*

148 10 c. *Durio zibethinus* (27.6.85) .. .. 8·50 90
149 15 c. *Hibiscus rosa-sinensis* (12.84) .. .. 1·25 50
150 20 c. *Rhododendron scortechinii* (blackish brown background) .. .. .. 5·50 70
150*a* 20 c. *Rhododendron scortechinii* (bronze-green background) (16.12.83) 30 15

*There was no official release date for these stamps. Dates shown are the earliest recorded from postmarks and may be revised if earlier examples are reported.

For details of the shade differences between watermarked and unwatermarked printings see after Johore No. 200*a*.

Nos. 148/9 and 150*a* show "kedah" nearer to "malaysia" than on Nos. 135/41 and 150.

OMNIBUS ISSUES

Details, together with prices for complete sets, of the various Omnibus issues from the 1935 Silver Jubilee series to date are included in a special section following Zululand at the end of the catalogue.

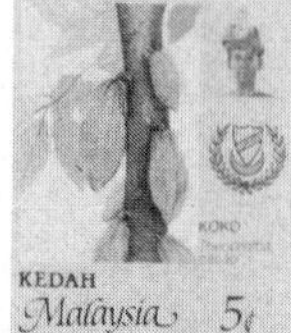

26 Cocoa

1986 (25 Oct). *As Nos.* 202/8 *of Johore but with portrait of Sultan Abdul Halim Shah as in T* **26.**

152 1 c. Coffee 10 10
153 2 c. Coconuts 10 10
154 5 c. Type **26** 10 10
155 10 c. Black pepper 10 10
156 15 c. Rubber 10 10
157 20 c. Oil palm 10 10
158 30 c. Rice 10 15
152/8 .. .. *Set of* 7 40 45

KELANTAN

Suzerainty over Kelantan was transferred by Thailand to Great Britain on 15 July 1909. A British adviser was appointed in 1923.

The state joined the Federation of Malaya on 1 February 1948.

Until 1909 the stamps of THAILAND were used by the post offices at Kota Bharu and Batu Mengkebang. From 1909 until the introduction of Kelantan stamps in 1911 the issues of the FEDERATED MALAY STATES were in use.

PRICES FOR STAMPS ON COVER TO 1945	
Nos. 1/11	*from* × 20
No. 12	—
Nos. 13/23	*from* × 20
Nos. 30/8	*from* × 15
Nos. 39/*a*	*from* × 6
Nos. 40/54	*from* × 10

1

MALAYA
BORNEO
EXHIBITION
(2)

1911 (Jan). *Wmk Mult Crown CA. Ordinary paper* (1 c. *to* 10 c.) *or chalk-surfaced paper* (30 c. *to* $25). *P* 14.

No.	Type	Description	Unused	Used
1	1	1 c. yellow-green	1·00	80
		a. Blue-green	1·00	30
2		3 c. red	1·50	15
3		4 c. black and red	80	15
4		5 c. green and red/*yellow*	4·00	20
5		8 c. ultramarine	5·00	1·00
6		10 c. black and mauve	14·00	30
7		30 c. dull purple and red	10·00	2·50
		a. Purple and carmine	26·00	13·00
8		50 c. black and orange	5·50	2·50
9		$1 green and emerald	40·00	48·00
10		$2 green and carmine	1·00	4·00
11		$5 green and blue	4·00	7·50
12		$25 green and orange	38·00	75·00
1/12		*Set of* 12	£110	£130
1/12 Optd "Specimen"		*Set of* 12	£200	

1915. *Colours changed. Wmk Mult Crown CA. Chalk-surfaced paper. P* 14.

No.	Type	Description	Unused	Used
13	1	$1 green and brown (Optd S. £45)	27·00	2·00

1921–28. *Wmk Mult Script CA. Ordinary paper* (1 c. *to* 10 c.) *or chalk-surfaced paper* (30 c. *to* $1). *P* 14.

No.	Type	Description	Unused	Used
14	1	1 c. dull green	3·75	60
15		1 c. black (1923)	40	50
16		2 c. brown (1922)	2·75	3·50
16*a*		2 c. green (1926)	90	40
16*b*		3 c. brown (1927)	2·50	1·50
17		4 c. black and red (1922)	50	10
18		5 c. green and red/*pale yellow* (1922)	50	10
19		6 c. claret (1922)	2·50	2·50
19*a*		6 c. scarlet (1928)	4·00	5·50
20		10 c. black and mauve	2·00	10
21		30 c. purple and carmine (1926)	4·00	5·50
22		50 c. black and orange (1925)	5·00	26·00
23		$1 green and brown (1924)	26·00	48·00
14/23		*Set of* 13	48·00	85·00
14/23 Optd "Specimen"		*Set of* 13	£225	

For the 4 c., 5 c. and 6 c. surcharged, see issues under "Japanese Occupation".

1922 (31 Mar). *Optd with T* 2 *by Govt Survey Office, Khota Bharu.*

No.	Type	Description	Unused	Used
		(*a*) *Wmk Mult Crown CA*		
30	1	4 c. black and red	2·75	32·00
		a. Opt double	£1500	
31		5 c. green and red/*pale yellow*	4·50	32·00
32		30 c. dull purple and red	4·50	55·00
33		50 c. black and orange	7·50	60·00
34		$1 green and brown	20·00	80·00
35		$2 green and carmine	45·00	£150
36		$5 green and blue	£130	£300
		(*b*) *Wmk Mult Script CA*		
37	1	1 c. green	2·50	26·00
		a. Opt double	£1800	
38		10 c. black and mauve	4·75	48·00
30/8		*Set of* 9	£200	£700

3 Sultan Ismail 4

(Recess D.L.R.)

1928–33. *Wmk Mult Script CA. P* 12.

No.	Type	Description	Unused	Used
39	3	$1 blue (Perf S. £40)	7·50	55·00
		a. Perf 14 (1933)	30·00	40·00

(Recess B.W.)

1937 (July)–**40.** *Wmk Mult Script CA. P* 12.

No.	Type	Description	Unused	Used
40	4	1 c. grey-olive and yellow	30	40
41		2 c. green	1·00	10
42		4 c. scarlet	3·50	45
43		5 c. red-brown	3·75	10
44		6 c. lake (10.37)	6·00	1·25
45		8 c. grey-olive	3·75	10
46		10 c. purple (10.37)	13·00	2·75
47	4	12 c. blue	1·75	3·00
48		25 c. vermilion and violet	3·75	3·50
49		30 c. violet and scarlet (10.37)	25·00	16·00
50		40 c. orange and blue-green	6·00	17·00
51		50 c. grey-olive and orange (10.37)	38·00	9·00
52		$1 violet and blue-green (10.37)	22·00	12·00
53		$2 red-brown and scarlet (3.40)	£150	£200
54		$5 vermilion and lake (3.40)	£250	£400
40/54		*Set of* 15	£450	£600
40/54 Perf "Specimen"		*Set of* 15	£375	

For above issue surcharged see issues under "Japanese Occupation".

1948 (1 Dec). *Royal Silver Wedding. As Nos.* 143/4 *of Jamaica.*

No.	Description	Unused	Used
55	10 c. violet	40	90
56	$5 carmine	23·00	48·00

1949 (10 Oct). *75th Anniv of U.P.U. As Nos.* 145/8 *of Jamaica.*

No.	Description	Unused	Used
57	10 c. purple	25	30
58	15 c. deep blue	50	90
59	25 c. orange	60	2·25
60	50 c. blue-black	1·25	2·25
57/60	*Set of* 4	2·40	5·00

5 Sultan Ibrahim 6 Sultan Yahya Petra and Crest of Kelantan

Normal No. 62a

Tiny stop (R. 1/2)

1951 (11 July)–**55.** *Chalk-surfaced paper. Wmk Mult Script CA. P* 17½ × 18.

No.	Type	Description	Unused	Used
61	5	1 c. black	10	30
62		2 c. orange	15	35
		a. Tiny stop	10·00	
		b. Orange-yellow (11.5.55)	15	30
63		3 c. green	1·25	90
64		4 c. brown	10	15
65		5 c. bright purple (1.9.52)	35	40
		a. Bright mauve (9.12.53)	30	40
66		6 c. grey	10	20
67		8 c. scarlet	30	3·00
68		8 c. green (1.9.52)	75	1·75
69		10 c. magenta	15	10
70		12 c. scarlet (1.9.52)	75	2·25
71		15 c. ultramarine	1·25	60
72		20 c. black and green	45	4·50
73		20 c. bright blue (1.9.52)	80	25
74		25 c. purple and orange	40	55
75		30 c. scarlet and purple (5.9.55)	1·25	1·75
76		35 c. scarlet and purple (1.9.52)	90	1·50
77		40 c. red and purple	1·50	7·00
78		50 c. black and blue	50	40
79		$1 blue and purple	2·75	2·50
80		$2 green and scarlet	12·00	20·00
81		$5 green and brown	38·00	38·00
		a. Green and sepia (8.12.53)	55·00	60·00
61/81		*Set of* 21	55·00	75·00

1953 (2 June). *Coronation. As No.* 153 *of Jamaica.*

No.	Description	Unused	Used
82	10 c. black and reddish purple	30	15

1957 (26 June)–**63.** *As Nos.* 92/102 *of Kedah but with inset portrait of Sultan Ibrahim.*

No.	Type	Description	Unused	Used
83	9	1 c. black (21.8.57)	10	30
84	10	2 c. orange-red (25.7.57)	30	40
		a. Red-orange (17.11.59)	1·40	4·00
85	11	4 c. sepia (21.8.57)	10	10
86	12	5 c. carmine-lake (21.8.57)	10	10
87	13	8 c. myrtle-green (21.8.57)	80	1·75
88	14	10 c. deep brown (4.8.57)	15	10
89		10 c. deep maroon (19.4.61)	3·25	3·25
90	15	20 c. blue	30	30
91	16	50 c. black and blue (*p* 12½) (25.7.57)	30	35
		a. Perf 12½ × 13 (28.6.60)	50	30
92	17	$1 ultramarine & reddish pur (25.7.57)	2·00	1·50
93	18	$2 bronze-grn & scar (*p* 12½) (21.8.57)	5·00	6·00
		a. Perf 13 × 12½ (9.4.63)	5·50	12·00
94	19	$5 brown and bronze-green (*p* 12½)	10·00	12·00
		a. Perf 13 × 12½ (13.8.63)	14·00	18·00
83/94		*Set of* 12	20·00	23·00

The 6, 12, 25 and 30 c. values used with this issue were Nos. 1/4 of Malayan Federation.

(Photo Harrison)

1961 (17 July). *Coronation of the Sultan.* W w **12**. *P* 15 × 14.

No.	Type	Description	Unused	Used
95	6	10 c. multicoloured	30	30

7 Sultan Yahya Petra 8 *Vanda hookeriana*

(Recess D.L.R.)

1961–63. *As Nos.* 92/8 *of Kedah but with inset portrait of Sultan Yahya Petra as in T* **7**. *W* w **13**. *P* 12½×13 (*vert*) *or* 13×12½ (*horiz*).

No.	Description	Unused	Used
96	1 c. black (1.3.62)	10	45
97	2 c. orange-red (1.3.62)	10	55
98	4 c. sepia (1.3.62)	10	10
99	5 c. carmine-lake (1.3.62)	10	10
100	8 c. myrtle-green (1.3.62)	2·75	3·00
	a. Deep green (15.1.63)	3·75	4·50
101	10 c. deep maroon (2.12.61)	20	10
102	20 c. blue (1.3.62)	40	30
96/102	*Set of* 7	3·25	4·00

1965 (15 Nov). *As Nos.* 166/72 *of Johore but with inset portrait of Sultan Yahya Petra as in T* **8**. *W* w **13** (*upright*).

No.	Description	Unused	Used
103	1 c. multicoloured	10	20
	b. Magenta omitted	55·00	
104	2 c. multicoloured	10	30
105	5 c. multicoloured	15	10
106	6 c. multicoloured	45	40
107	10 c. multicoloured	20	10
	a. Red omitted	28·00	
108	15 c. multicoloured	1·00	20
109	20 c. multicoloured	1·50	85
	a. Bright purple (blooms) omitted	38·00	
	b. Yellow (leaves) omitted	22·00	
103/9	*Set of* 7	3·00	1·90

The 5 c. and 10 c. exist with PVA gum as well as gum arabic.

The higher values used with this issue were Nos. 20/27 of Malaysia (National Issues).

1970 (20 Nov). *As Nos.* 103 *and* 107 *but W* w **13** (*sideways*).

No.	Type	Description	Unused	Used
110	8	1 c. multicoloured	40	2·50
111	–	10 c. multicoloured	1·40	2·25

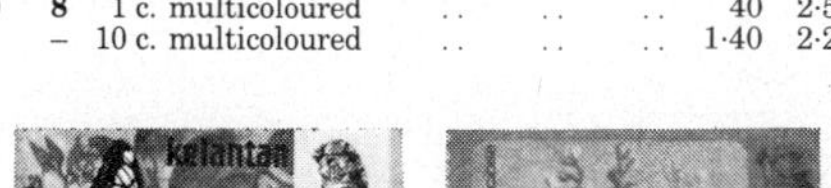

9 *Parthenos sylvia* 10 *Lagerstroemia speciosa*

1971 (1 Feb)–**78.** *As Nos.* 175/87 *of Johore but with portrait of Sultan Yahya Petra and arms, as in T* **9**. (*a*) *Litho by Bradbury, Wilkinson.*

No.	Description	Unused	Used
112	1 c. multicoloured	15	65
113	2 c. multicoloured	35	65
114	5 c. multicoloured	60	15
115	6 c. multicoloured	60	50
116	10 c. multicoloured	60	10
117	15 c. multicoloured	85	10
	a. Black (state inscription, portrait and arms) omitted	70·00	
118	20 c. multicoloured	1·00	50
112/18	*Set of* 7	3·75	2·40
	(*b*) *Photo by Harrison* (1977–78)		
119	1 c. multicoloured	40	1·50
120	5 c. multicoloured	2·50	60
121	10 c. multicoloured	2·75	60
122	15 c. multicoloured	5·00	75
119/22	*Set of* 4	9·50	3·00

The higher values used with this issue were Nos. 64/71 of Malaysia (National Issues).

For differences between litho and photo printings, see after Johore No. 187.

On No. 117a only the country inscription, portrait and arms are omitted, the remainder of the black printing being as normal. The design was produced using two black plates, one for the main design, value and inscription and the other to apply the state name, head and arms. It is this plate which is omitted from No. 117a.

1979 (30 Apr). *As Nos.* 188/94 *of Johore but with portrait of Sultan Yahya Petra as in T* **10**.

No.	Description	Unused	Used
123	1 c. *Rafflesia hasseltii*	10	30
124	2 c. *Pterocarpus indicus*	10	30
125	5 c. Type **10**	10	10
126	10 c. *Durio zibethinus*	10	10
127	15 c. *Hibiscus rosa-sinensis*	15	10
128	20 c. *Rhododendron scortechinii*	15	10
129	25 c. *Etlingera elatior* (inscr "*Phaeomeria speciosa*")	15	20
123/9	*Set of* 7	65	90

For higher values used in conjunction with this series see Nos. 190/7 of Malaysia (National Issues).

11 Sultan Tengku Ismail Petra 12 Black Pepper

(Des M. A. B. bin Saman. Litho Harrison)

1980 (30 Mar). *Coronation of Sultan Tengku Ismail Petra. P* 14.
130 **11** 10 c. multicoloured 20 20
131 15 c. multicoloured 20 15
132 50 c. multicoloured .. .. 70 1·25
130/2 .. .. *Set of* 3 1·00 1·40

1983–86.* *As Nos.* 125/6 *and* 128 *but without wmk.*
135 5 c. Type **10** (1986) .. .. 1·75 90
136 10 c. *Durio zibethinus* (18.9.84) 25 15
138 20 c. *Rhododendron scortechinii* (blackish brown background) (1983) .. .. 5·00 1·00
138*a* 20 c. *Rhododendron scortechinii* (bronze-green background) (5.10.83) 50 15

*There was no official release date for these stamps. Dates shown are the earliest recorded from postmarks and may be revised if earlier examples are reported.

For details of the shade differences between watermarked and unwatermarked printings see after Johore No. 200*a*.

On Nos. 135/6 and 138*a* the portrait and state arms have been redrawn smaller.

1986 (25 Oct). *As Nos.* 202/8 *of Johore but with portrait of Sultan Ismail Petra as in T* **12**.
140 1 c. Coffee 10 10
141 2 c. Coconuts 10 10
142 5 c. Cocoa 10 10
143 10 c. Type **12** 10 10
144 15 c. Rubber 10 10
145 20 c. Oil palm 10 10
146 30 c. Rice 10 15
140/6 .. .. *Set of* 7 40 45

MALACCA

One of the Straits Settlements.
Issues from 1965 are inscribed "MELAKA".

1948 (1 Dec). *Royal Silver Wedding. As Nos.* 143/4 *of Jamaica.*
1 10 c. violet 25 30
2 $5 brown .. .. 24·00 35·00

1949 (1 Mar)–**52.** *As T* **58** *of Straits Settlements, but inscr "MALACCA" at foot. Wmk Mult Script CA. Chalk-surfaced paper. P* 17½ × 18.
3 1 c. black 10 60
4 2 c. orange 20 45
5 3 c. green .. .. 20 1·50
6 4 c. brown 15 10
6*a* 5 c. bright purple (1.9.52) 45 85
7 6 c. grey 20 50
8 8 c. scarlet .. .. 30 2·50
8*a* 8 c. green (1.9.52) .. .. .. 85 3·25
9 10 c. purple 15 10
9*a* 12 c. scarlet (1.9.52) .. .. .. 95 1·75
10 15 c. ultramarine 30 60
11 20 c. black and green .. .. .. 30 3·25
11*a* 20 c. bright blue (1.9.52) .. .. 1·25 1·40
12 25 c. purple and orange 30 50
12*a* 35 c. scarlet and purple (1.9.52) .. 1·00 1·50
13 40 c. red and purple .. .. .. 1·25 8·50
14 50 c. black and blue 50 75
15 $1 blue and purple .. .. .. 4·00 8·50
16 $2 green and scarlet .. .. .. 11·00 16·00
17 $5 green and brown .. .. .. 28·00 32·00
3/17 .. .. *Set of* 20 45·00 75·00

1949 (10 Oct). *75th Anniv of U.P.U. As Nos.* 145/8 *of Jamaica.*
18 10 c. purple 15 45
19 15 c. deep blue .. .. 45 1·75
20 25 c. orange .. .. 45 2·50
21 50 c. blue-black .. .. 1·00 3·75
18/21 .. .. *Set of* 4 1·90 7·50

1953 (2 June). *Coronation. As No.* 153 *of Jamaica.*
22 10 c. black and reddish purple 20 10

1 Queen Elizabeth II **2** Copra

1954 (9 June)–**57.** *Chalk-surfaced paper. Wmk Mult Script CA. P* 17½×18.
23 **1** 1 c. black (27.4.55) 10 30
24 2 c. yellow-orange (27.4.55) 30 35
25 4 c. brown 30 10
a. Pale brown (24.4.57) .. .. 1·50 90
26 5 c. bright purple (12.7.54) 30 60
27 6 c. grey 10 15
28 8 c. green (5.1.55) 30 50
29 10 c. brown-purple (1.7.54) 20 10
a. Reddish purple (27.3.57) 40 15
30 12 c. rose-red (5.1.55) 20 85
31 20 c. bright blue (5.1.55) 20 15
32 25 c. brown-purple & yellow-orge (27.4.55) 20 20
33 30 c. rose-red and brown-purple (5.9.55) .. 20 15
34 35 c. rose-red and brown-purple (8.9.54) .. 20 35
35 50 c. black and bright blue (5.1.55) .. 30 40
36 $1 bright blue and brown-purple (8.9.54) 2·25 4·25
37 $2 emerald and scarlet (27.4.55) .. 13·00 18·00
38 $5 emerald and brown (27.4.55) .. 14·00 19·00
23/38 .. .. *Set of* 16 28·00 42·00

1957. *As Nos.* 92/102 *of Kedah but with inset portrait of Queen Elizabeth II.*
39 **9** 1 c. black (21.8) 10 40
40 **10** 2 c. orange-red (25.7) 10 40
41 **11** 4 c. sepia (21.8) 10 10
42 **12** 5 c. carmine-lake (21.8) 10 10
43 **13** 8 c. myrtle-green (21.8) .. .. 1·25 2·25
44 **14** 10 c. deep brown (4.8) 15 10
45 **15** 20 c. blue (26.6) 30 40
46 **16** 50 c. black and blue (25.7) 30 50
47 **17** $1 ultramarine and reddish purple (25.7) .. .. 2·00 2·50
48 **18** $2 bronze-green and scarlet (21.8) .. 6·50 12·00
49 **19** $5 brown and bronze-green (26.6) .. 8·50 13·00
39/49 .. .. *Set of* 11 17·00 29·00

The 6, 12, 25 and 30 c. values used with this issue were Nos. 1/4 of Malayan Federation.

(Recess D.L.R.)

1960 (15 Mar)–**62.** *As Nos.* 39/49, *but with inset picture of Melaka tree and Pelandok (mouse deer) as in T* **2**. *W w* **12**. *P* 13 × 12½ (1 *c. to* 8 *c.*, $2, $5), 12½ × 13 (10 *c. to* 50 *c.*) *or* 13½ ($1).
50 1 c. black 10 30
51 2 c. orange-red 10 30
52 4 c. sepia 10 10
53 5 c. carmine-lake 10 10
54 8 c. myrtle-green .. .. 1·25 80
55 10 c. deep maroon 15 10
56 20 c. blue 20 20
57 50 c. black and blue 30 30
a. Black and ultramarine (9.1.62) 45 30
58 $1 ultramarine and reddish purple .. .. 1·50 2·00
59 $2 bronze-green and scarlet .. .. 3·50 4·50
60 $5 brown and bronze-green .. .. 7·50 5·50
50/60 .. .. *Set of* 11 13·00 12·50

3 *Vanda hookeriana* **4** *Papilio demoleus*

1965 (15 Nov)–**68.** *As Nos.* 166/72 *of Johore but with Arms of Malacca inset and inscr "MELAKA" as in T* **3**. *W w* **13** *(upright).*
61 1 c. multicoloured 10 50
62 2 c. multicoloured 10 50
63 5 c. multicoloured 10 10
b. Yellow (flower) omitted .. .. 20·00
c. Red omitted .. .. 28·00
64 6 c. multicoloured 20 30
65 10 c. multicoloured 15 10
66 15 c. multicoloured .. .. 1·25 40
67 20 c. multicoloured (purple-brn background) 1·75 65
a. Red-brown background (2.4.68) .. 2·00 85
61/7 .. .. *Set of* 7 3·25 2·25

The 5 c., 6 c., 10 c. and 20 c. exist with PVA gum as well as gum arabic.

The higher values used with this issue were Nos. 20/27 of Malaysia (National Issues).

1970. *As Nos.* 61 *and* 65 *but W w* **13** *(sideways).*
68 **3** 1 c. multicoloured (27.5.70) .. .. 75 3·50
69 – 10 c. multicoloured (20.11.70) .. .. 3·00 3·50

1971 (1 Feb)–**78.** *As Nos.* 175/87 *of Johore but with arms of Malacca and inscr "melaka", as in T* **4**. *(a) Litho by Bradbury, Wilkinson.*
70 1 c. multicoloured 15 50
71 2 c. multicoloured 40 50
72 5 c. multicoloured 55 10
73 6 c. multicoloured 55 40
74 10 c. multicoloured 55 10
75 15 c. multicoloured 80 10
76 20 c. multicoloured 90 80
70/6 .. .. *Set of* 7 3·50 2·25

(b) Photo by Harrison (1977–78)
77 1 c. multicoloured .. .. 2·00 3·25
78 5 c. multicoloured .. .. 1·25 40
79 10 c. multicoloured .. .. 2·50 40
80 15 c. multicoloured .. .. 3·75 40
81 20 c. multicoloured .. .. 3·75 2·25
77/81 .. .. *Set of* 5 12·00 6·00

The higher values used with this issue were Nos. 64/71 of Malaysia (National Issues).

For differences between litho and photo printings, see after Johore No. 187.

5 *Durio zibethinus* **6** Rubber

1979 (30 Apr). *As Nos.* 188/94 *of Johore but with Arms of Malacca and inscr "melaka" as in T* **5**.
82 1 c. *Rafflesia hasseltii* 10 30
83 2 c. *Pterocarpus indicus* 10 30
84 5 c. *Lagerstroemia speciosa* 10 10
85 10 c. Type **5** 10 10
86 15 c. *Hibiscus rosa-sinensis* 15 10
87 20 c. *Rhododendron scortechinii* 15 10
88 25 c. *Etlingera elatior* (inscr "*Phaeomeria speciosa*") 15 30
82/8 .. .. *Set of* 7 65 1·00

For higher values used in conjunction with this series see Nos. 190/7 of Malaysia (National Issues).

1983 (26 Oct)–**86.*** *As Nos.* 85/7 *but without wmk.*
92 10 c. Type **5** (19.4.85) .. .. .. 3·00 2·25
93 15 c. *Hibiscus rosa-sinensis* (9.86) .. 1·25 55
94 20 c. *Rhododendron scortechinii* (blackish brown background) .. .. .. 5·50 1·25
94*a* 20 c. *Rhododendron scortechinii* (bronze-green background) (13.6.84) .. .. 1·25 60

*There was no official release date for these stamps. Dates shown are the earliest recorded from postmarks and may be revised if earlier examples are reported.

For details of the shade differences between watermarked and unwatermarked printings see after Johore No. 200*a*.

On Nos. 92/3 and 94*a* the distance between the coat of arms and the value is greater than on Nos. 85, 87 and 94.

1986 (25 Oct). *As Nos.* 202/8 *of Johore but with Arms of Malacca and inscr "MELAKA" as in T* **6**.
96 1 c. Coffee 10 10
97 2 c. Coconuts 10 10
98 5 c. Cocoa 10 10
99 10 c. Black pepper 10 10
100 15 c. Type **6** 10 10
101 20 c. Oil palm 10 10
102 30 c. Rice 10 15
96/102 .. .. *Set of* 7 40 45

NEGRI SEMBILAN

A federation of smaller states reconstituted in 1886. Sungei Ujong, taken under British protection in 1874, was absorbed into Negri Sembilan by Treaty of 8 August 1895. The Negri Sembilan federation joined the Federated Malay States in 1896.

A. SUNGEI UJONG

Until 1 January 1899, when the Federated Malay States joined the U.P.U., mail for addresses outside Malaya was franked with the stamps of the STRAITS SETTLEMENTS.

PRICES FOR STAMPS ON COVER

Nos. 1/14	—
Nos. 15/27	*from* × 25
Nos. 28/36	*from* × 8
Nos. 37/49	*from* × 10
Nos. 50/5	*from* × 25

(1)

1878. *No. 11 of Straits Settlements handstamped with T* **1**.
1 2 c. brown £1600 £1400
This overprint on India No. 54 is bogus.

SUNGEI — (**2**) (Narrow letters)
SUNGEI — (**3**) ("N" wide)
SUNGEI — (**4**) ("S" wide)

UJONG — (**5**) ("N" wide)
UJONG — (**6**) (Narrow letters, "UJ" close together)
UJONG — (**7**) Narrow letters, evenly spaced)

1881. *No. 11 of Straits Settlements optd with T* **2/7**.
2 **2+5** 2 c. brown £2000 £2000
3 **3+5** 2 c. brown £1500 £1500
4 **2+6** 2 c. brown £110
a. Opt Type **6** double £1000
5 **4+6** 2 c. brown £375
6 **2+7** 2 c. brown £190

The two lines of this surcharge were applied as separate operations. On Nos. 2/3 "SUNGEI" was printed as a triplet, probably 2+3+3, "UJONG" being added by a single unit handstamp. Nos. 4 and 5 come from a similar triplet, 4+4+5, completed by another single unit handstamp. No. 6 comes from a single type triplet with the second line added as a triplet instead of by a single unit handstamp.

The 10 c. slate overprinted Types 2 + 7 is bogus.

SUNGEI — (**8**) ("N" and "E" wide)
SUNGEI — (**9**) ("SUN" and "E" wide)
SUNGEI — (**10**) ("SUN" wide)

SUNGEI — (**11**) ("S" wide)
SUNGEI — (**12**) (Narrow letters)

UJONG — (**13**) ("U" and "NG" wide)
UJONG — (**14**) (Narrow letters)

1881. *No. 11 of Straits Settlements optd with T* **8/14**.
7 **8+13** 2 c. brown .. .. 95·00
8 **9+13** 2 c. brown .. .. 95·00
9 **10+13** 2 c. brown .. .. 95·00
10 **11+14** 2 c. brown £150
a. "S" inverted £1800
11 **12+14** 2 c. brown .. .. 95·00

Nos. 7/11 also had the two lines of the overprint applied at separate operations. "SUNGEI" as a triplet, either 7+8+9 or 10+11+11, and "UJONG" as a single unit.

S.U.

(**15**)

1882. *Nos. 50/1 of Straits Settlements optd as T* **15**.
12 2 c. brown (with stops).. .. .. .. £140
13 2 c. brown (without stops) £160 £200
14 4 c. rose (with stops) £1500 £1500

Each of the above was applied by a triplet setting.

Examples of Straits Settlements No. 11 with a similar overprint, including stops, are trials which were not issued.

SUNGEI — (**16**) ("S" and "E" wide)
SUNGEI — (**17**) ("E" wide)
UJONG — (**18**) ("N" wide)

1882 (Dec)–**84**. *Nos. 12 and 50/3 of Straits Settlements optd with T* **11/12**, **14** *and* **16/18**.
15 **12+14** 2 c. brown £225 £150
16 **11+14** 2 c. brown £325 £225
17 **12+14** 2 c. rose (1884) .. .. .. 90·00 £110
18 **11+14** 2 c. rose (1884) .. .. .. 90·00 £110
19 **16+14** 2 c. rose (1884) .. .. .. 65·00 75·00
20 **17+14** 2 c. rose (1884) .. .. .. 75·00 85·00
21 **12+18** 2 c. rose (1884) .. .. .. 75·00 85·00
a. Opt Type **18** double .. ..
22 **12+14** 4 c. rose £700 £750
23 **11+14** 4 c. rose £1100 £1200
24 **12+14** 8 c. orange £800 £700
25 **11+14** 8 c. orange £1300 £1100
26 **12+14** 10 c. slate £300 £300
27 **11+14** 10 c. slate £450 £450

Nos. 15/27 had the two lines of the overprint applied by separate triplets. Settings so far identified are Nos. 15+16+15, 17+18+19, 19+20+21, 22+23+22, 24+25+24 and 26+27+26.

The 4 c. rose overprinted Types **16**+**14** is now believed to be a trial.

UJONG. — (**19**) (With stop. Narrow letters)
UJONG. — (**20**) (With stop "N" wide)
UJONG — (**21**) (Without stop. Narrow letters)

1883–84. *Nos. 50 and 63/4 of Straits Settlements optd with T* **12**, **16/17** *and* **19/21**.
28 **12+19** 2 c. brown .. .. 28·00 70·00
29 **16+19** 2 c. brown .. .. 28·00 70·00
30 **12+20** 2 c. brown .. .. 28·00 70·00
31 **16+21** 2 c. rose (1884) .. .. .. 48·00 60·00
32 **17+21** 2 c. rose (1884) .. .. .. 48·00 60·00
33 **12+21** 2 c. rose (1884) .. .. .. 48·00 60·00
34 **16+21** 4 c. brown (1884) £110 £140
35 **17+21** 4 c. brown (1884) £110 £140
36 **12+21** 4 c. brown (1884) £110 £140
a. Opt Type **21** double £1600

Nos. 28/36 had the two lines of the overprint applied by separate triplets. Settings were Nos. 28+29+30, 31+32+33 and 34+35+36.

The 8 c. orange overprinted Types **12**+**19** is now believed to be a trial (*Price £500 unused*).

Sungei Ujong — (**22**)
SUNGEI UJONG — (**23**)
SUNGEI UJONG — (**24**)

SUNGEI UJONG — (**25**)
SUNGEI UJONG — (**26**)
SUNGEI UJONG — (**27**)

SUNGEI UJONG — (**28**)
SUNGEI UJONG. — (**29**)
SUNGEI UJONG — (**30**)

1885–90. *No. 63 of Straits Settlements optd with T* **22/30**.
37 **22** 2 c. rose .. .. 32·00 42·00
a. Opt double £300 £300
38 **23** 2 c. rose .. .. 15·00 35·00
a. Opt double £450
39 **24** 2 c. rose (1886) .. .. 85·00 95·00
40 **25** 2 c. rose (1886) .. .. 90·00 £110
a. Opt double ..
41 **26** 2 c. rose (1886) .. .. 70·00 80·00
a. Opt double ..
42 **27** 2 c. rose (1887) .. .. 7·50 23·00
43 **28** 2 c. rose (1889) .. .. 4·50 6·50
a. Narrow "E" (2 mm wide) (R. 3/4 and 4/3) .. .. 38·00
b. Antique "N" in "UJONG" (R. 10/6) .. 70·00
c. Opt double £1200
44 **29** 2 c. rose (1889) .. .. 45·00 45·00
a. "UNJOG" (R. 7/3) £2000 £1700
45 **30** 2 c. rose (1890) .. .. 13·00 13·00
a. Antique "G" in "SUNGEI" (R. 6/1) .. 90·00
b. Antique "G" in "UJONG" (R. 8/3) .. 90·00

All the above overprints had both lines applied at the same operation. Nos. 37/42 were from different triplet settings. The first printing of No. 43 was from a triplet, but this was followed by further settings of 60 (6 × 10), the first containing No. 43a and the second Nos. 43a/b. Nos. 44/5 were both from settings of 60.

SUNGEI UJONG Two CENTS — (**31**)
SUNGEI UJONG Two CENTS — (**32**)
SUNGEI UJONG Two CENTS — (**33**)

SUNGEI UJONG Two CENTS — (**34**)

1891. *No. 68 of Straits Settlements surch with T* **31/4**.
46 **31** 2 c. on 24 c. green £275 £300
47 **32** 2 c. on 24 c. green £110 £140
48 **33** 2 c. on 24 c. green £275 £300
49 **34** 2 c. on 24 c. green .. .. .. 70·00 95·00
a. Antique "G" in "SUNGEI" (R. 6/1) .. £350
b. Antique "G" in "UJONG" (R. 8/3) .. £350

Nos. 46/9 come from the same setting of 60 on which "SUNGEI UJONG" was from the same type as No. 45. No. 46 occurs in row 1. No. 47 from rows 2 to 4, No. 48 from row 5 and No. 49 from rows 6 to 10.

35

3 CENTS

(36)

37

1891–94. *Wmk Crown CA. P* 14.
50 **35** 2 c. rose .. .. 20·00 26·00
51 2 c. orange (1894).. .. .. .. 1·40 4·25
52 5 c. blue (1893) .. .. 4·50 5·50
50/2 .. .. *Set of* 3 23·00 32·00
50/2 Optd "Specimen" .. .. *Set of* 3 60·00

1894. *Surch as T* **36** *by De La Rue*.
53 **35** 1 c. on 5 c. green 65 70
54 3 c. on 5 c. rose .. .. 1·75 4·25

1895. *Wmk Crown CA. P* 14.
55 **37** 3 c. dull purple and carmine .. .. 5·00 75
53/5 Optd "Specimen" .. .. *Set of* 3 60·00

B. NEGRI SEMBILAN

Stamps of the STRAITS SETTLEMENTS were used in Negri Sembilan during 1891, until replaced by the stamps listed below. Until the Federated Malay States joined the U.P.U. On 1 January 1899 Straits Settlements stamps continued to be used for mail to addresses outside Malaya.

PRICES FOR STAMPS ON COVER TO 1945

No. 1	*from* × 200
Nos. 2/4	*from* × 8
Nos. 5/14	*from* × 5
Nos. 15/20	*from* × 6
Nos. 21/49	*from* × 4

Negri Sembilan

(1)

2

3

1891 (Aug?). *No. 63 of Straits Settlements optd with T* **1**.
1 2 c. rose .. .. 2·25 4·00

1891–94. *Wmk Crown CA. P* 14.
2 **2** 1 c. green (1893) .. .. 2·50 1·00
3 2 c. rose .. .. 3·25 3·75
4 5 c. blue (1894) .. .. 22·00 26·00
2/4 .. .. *Set of* 3 25·00 28·00
2/4 Optd "Specimen" .. .. *Set of* 3 70·00

1895–99. *Wmk Crown CA. P* 14.
5 **3** 1 c. dull purple and green (1899) .. 4·00 2·50
6 2 c. dull purple and brown (1898) .. 22·00 65·00
7 3 c. dull purple and carmine .. .. 2·50 60
8 5 c. dull purple and orange-yellow (1897) 4·50 5·50
9 8 c. dull purple and ultramarine (1898) .. 22·00 13·00
10 10 c. dull purple and orange (1897) .. 24·00 12·00
11 15 c. green and violet (1896) .. .. 27·00 48·00
12 20 c. green and olive (1897) .. .. 30·00 35·00
13 25 c. green and carmine (1896) .. .. 55·00 70·00
14 50 c. green and black (1896) .. .. 48·00 55·00
5/14 .. .. *Set of* 10 £225 £275
5/14 Optd "Specimen" .. .. *Set of* 10 £160

Four cents.

(4)

Four cents.

(5)

1898 (Dec)–**1900**. (*a*) *Surch as T* **4**.
15 **3** 1 c. on 15 c. green and violet (1900) .. 75·00 £150
a. Raised stop (R. 5/1 and R. 10/1 of each pane) £190 £350
16 **2** 4 c. on 1 c. green .. .. 1·00 9·00
17 **3** 4 c. on 3 c. dull purple and carmine .. 3·00 11·00
a. Pair, one without surch £1500 £1700
b. Surch double £475 £425
ba. Ditto. "Four cents" albino .. ..
c. Surch inverted £350 £350
d. "cents" repeated at left £300 £350
e. "Four" repeated at right £300 £350
f. Without bar £475 £375
g. Bar double .. .. † £500
18 **2** 4 c. on 5 c. blue .. .. 1·00 8·50

On Nos. 15 and 17 the bar is at the top of the stamp.

The surcharges were applied as a setting of 30 (6 × 5).

(*b*) *Surch as T* **5**
19 **3** 4 c. on 8 c. dull pur & ultram (G.) (12.98) 2·00 3·25
a. Pair, one without surch £1800 £1500
b. Surch double £900
c. Surch double (G.+R.) £700 £700
20 4 c. on 8 c. dull purple & ultramarine (Bk.) £500 £550

Pending the arrival of the permanent Federated Malay States issue the stamps of SELANGOR, FEDERATED MALAY STATES provisional overprints, STRAITS SETTLEMENTS and PERAK were used at various times between October 1899 and April 1901.

The general issues for FEDERATED MALAY STATES were used in Negri Sembilan from 29 April 1901 until 1935.

6 Arms of Negri Sembilan 7

1935 (2 Dec)–**41**. *Wmk Mult Script CA. Ordinary paper (6 c. grey, 15 c.) or chalk-surfaced paper (others). P 14.*

No.	Type			
21	6	1 c. black (1.1.36)	40	10
22		2 c. green (1.1.36)	70	20
23		2 c. orange (11.12.41)	60	24·00
24		3 c. green (21.8.41)	1·25	5·00
		a. Ordinary paper	10·00	5·00
25		4 c. orange	30	10
26		5 c. brown (5.12.35)	50	10
27		6 c. scarlet (1.1.37)	4·50	1·75
		a. Stop omitted at right (R. 10/9)	£110	80·00
28		6 c. grey (18.12.41)	2·25	45·00
		a. Stop omitted at right (R. 10/9)	55·00	£160
29		8 c. grey	1·75	10
30		10 c. dull purple (1.1.36)	30	10
31		12 c. bright ultramarine (1.1.36)	1·00	25
32		15 c. ultramarine (1.10.41)	3·25	30·00
33		25 c. dull purple and scarlet (1.4.36)	75	70
34		30 c. dull purple and orange (1.1.36)	4·00	2·00
35		40 c. scarlet and dull purple	85	2·00
36		50 c. black/*emerald* (1.2.36)	3·50	1·25
37		$1 black and red/*blue* (1.4.36)	1·60	2·00
38		$2 green and scarlet (16.5.36)	17·00	15·00
39		$5 green and red/*emerald* (16.5.36)	13·00	35·00
21/39		*Set of* 19	50·00	£150
21/39 Perf "Specimen"		*Set of* 19	£200	

An 8 c. scarlet was issued but only with opt during Japanese Occupation of Malaya. Unoverprinted specimens result from leakages.

During shortages in 1941 stamps of STRAITS SETTLEMENTS (2 c.), SELANGOR (2 c., 8 c.), PERAK (2 c., 25 c., 50 c.) and PAHANG (8 c.) were issued in Negri Sembilan.

1948 (1 Dec). *Royal Silver Wedding. As Nos. 143/4 of Jamaica.*

No.			
40	10 c. violet	15	20
41	$5 green	17·00	28·00

1949 (1 Apr)–**55**. *Chalk-surfaced paper. Wmk Mult Script CA. P* 17½ × 18.

No.	Type			
42	7	1 c. black	10	10
43		2 c. orange	10	10
44		3 c. green	10	30
45		4 c. brown	10	10
46		5 c. bright purple (1.9.52)	30	50
		a. Bright mauve (25.8.53)	30	30
47		6 c. grey	15	10
		a. Pale grey (25.8.53)	30	10
48		8 c. scarlet	20	75
49		8 c. green (1.9.52)	1·50	1·25
50		10 c. purple	15	10
51		12 c. scarlet (1.9.52)	1·50	1·50
52		15 c. ultramarine	1·00	10
53		20 c. black and green	25	75
54		20 c. bright blue (1.9.52)	80	10
55		25 c. purple and orange	25	10
56		30 c. scarlet and purple (5.9.55)	1·25	1·50
57		35 c. scarlet and purple (1.9.52)	70	1·00
58		40 c. red and purple	65	2·50
59		50 c. black and blue	40	10
60		$1 blue and purple	2·00	65
61		$2 green and scarlet	9·00	6·00
62		$5 green and brown	35·00	30·00
42/62		*Set of* 21	50·00	42·00

1949 (10 Oct). *75th Anniv of U.P.U. As Nos. 145/8 of Jamaica.*

No.			
63	10 c. purple	20	10
64	15 c. deep blue	45	70
65	25 c. orange	50	1·50
66	50 c. blue-black	80	2·50
63/6	*Set of* 4	1·75	4·25

1953 (2 June). *Coronation. As No. 153 of Jamaica.*

No.			
67	10 c. black and reddish purple	20	15

1957 (26 June)–**63**. *As Nos. 92/102 of Kedah but with inset Arms of Negri Sembilan.*

No.	Type			
68	9	1 c. black (21.8.57)	10	10
69	10	2 c. orange-red (25.7.57)	10	10
70	11	4 c. sepia (21.8.57)	10	10
71	12	5 c. carmine-lake (21.8.57)	10	10
72	13	8 c. myrtle-green (21.8.57)	85	80
73	14	10 c. deep brown (4.8.57)	15	10
74		10 c. deep maroon (10.1.61)	75	10
75	15	20 c. blue	20	10
76	16	50 c. black and blue (*p* 12½) (25.7.57)	20	20
		a. Perf 12½ × 13 (19.7.60)	20	10
77	17	$1 ultramarine & reddish pur (25.7.57)	1·25	55
78	18	$2 bronze-green & scarlet (*p* 12½) (21.8.57)	3·75	7·00
		a. Perf 13 × 12½ (15.1.63)	6·00	10·00
79	19	$5 brown and bronze-green (*p* 12½)	8·50	13·00
		a. Perf 13 × 12½ (6.3.62)	10·00	11·00
		ab. Perf 13 × 12½. *Brown and yellow-olive* (13.11.62)	£110	55·00
68/79		*Set of* 12	14·00	18·00

The 6, 12, 25 and 30 c. values used with this issue were Nos. 1/4 of Malayan Federation.

8 Tuanku Munawir 9 *Vanda hookeriana*

(Photo Enschedé)

1961 (17 Apr). *Installation of Tuanku Munawir as Yang di-Pertuan Besar of Negri Sembilan. No wmk. P* 14 × 13.

No.	Type			
80	8	10 c. multicoloured	15	15

1965 (15 Nov)–**69**. *As Nos. 166/72 of Johore but with Arms of Negri Sembilan inset and inscr* "NEGERI SEMBILAN" *as in T* **9**. *W w* **13** *(upright).*

No.			
81	1 c. multicoloured	10	30
82	2 c. multicoloured	10	30
83	5 c. multicoloured	15	10
	b. Yellow omitted	20·00	
84	6 c. multicoloured	15	30
85	10 c. multicoloured	15	10
86	15 c. multicoloured	80	10
87	20 c. jet-black and multicoloured	1·25	75
	a. Blackish brown & mult (19.12.69)	2·00	20
81/7	*Set of* 7	2·25	1·10

The 2 c., 6 c., 15 c. and 20 c. exist with PVA gum as well as gum arabic.

The higher values used with this issue were Nos. 20/27 of Malaysia (National Issues).

See also No. 90.

10 Negri Sembilan Crest and Tuanku Ja'afar 11 *Hebomoia glaucippe*

(Des Z. Noor. Photo Japanese Govt Ptg Wks)

1968 (8 Apr). *Installation of Tuanku Ja'afar as Yang di-Pertuan Besar of Negri Sembilan. P* 13.

No.	Type			
88	10	15 c. multicoloured	15	30
89		50 c. multicoloured	30	1·10

1970 (27 May). *As No.* 81 *but with W w* **13** *(sideways).*

No.	Type			
90	9	1 c. multicoloured	1·00	3·00

1971 (1 Feb)–**78**. *As Nos. 175/87 of Johore but with Arms of Negri Sembilan and inscr* "negeri sembilan", *as in T* **11**.

(a) Litho by Bradbury, Wilkinson

No.			
91	1 c. multicoloured	15	40
92	2 c. multicoloured	40	40
93	5 c. multicoloured	50	10
94	6 c. multicoloured	50	30
95	10 c. multicoloured	50	10
96	15 c. multicoloured	70	10
97	20 c. multicoloured	80	20
91/7	*Set of* 7	3·25	1·40

(b) Photo by Harrison (1977–78)

98	2 c. multicoloured	75	1·50
99	5 c. multicoloured	60	40
100	10 c. multicoloured	4·00	30
101	15 c. multicoloured	5·50	30
102	20 c. multicoloured	2·25	1·25
98/102	*Set of* 5	12·00	3·25

The higher values used with this issue were Nos. 64/71 of Malaysia (National Issues).

For differences between litho and photo printings, see after Johore No. 187.

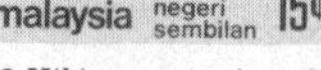

12 *Hibiscus rosa-sinensis* 13 Oil Palm

1979 (30 Apr). *As Nos. 188/94 of Johore but with Arms of Negri Sembilan and inscr* "negeri sembilan" *as in T* **12**.

No.			
103	1 c. *Rafflesia hasseltii*	10	20
104	2 c. *Pterocarpus indicus*	10	20
105	5 c. *Lagerstroemia speciosa*	10	10
106	10 c. *Durio zibethinus*	10	10
107	15 c. Type **12**	15	10
108	20 c. *Rhododendron scortechinii*	15	10
109	25 c. *Etlingera elatior* (inscr "*Phaeomeria speciosa*")	15	10
103/9	*Set of* 7	65	60

For higher values used in conjunction with this series see Nos. 190/7 of Malaysia (National Issues).

1983 (Oct)–**84**.* *As Nos. 105/8 but without wmk.*

No.			
112	5 c. *Lagerstroemia speciosa* (25.5.84)	2·25	1·10
113	10 c. *Durio zibethinus* (24.10.84)	30	20
114	15 c. Type **12** (11.8.84)	1·50	45
115	20 c. *Rhododendron scortechinii* (blackish brown background)	5·00	85
115*a*	20 c. *Rhododendron scortechinii* (bronze-green background) (1983)	30	15

*There was no official release date for these stamps. Dates shown are the earliest recorded from postmarks and may be revised if earlier examples are reported.

For details of the shade differences between watermarked and unwatermarked printings see after Johore No. 200*a*.

Nos. 112/14 and 115*a* show a larger crest, further from the face value than on Nos. 105/8 and 115.

1986 (25 Oct). *As Nos. 202/8 of Johore but with Arms of Negri Sembilan and inscr* "NEGERI SEMBILAN" *as in T* **13**.

No.			
117	1 c. Coffee	10	10
118	2 c. Coconuts	10	10
119	5 c. Cocoa	10	10
120	10 c. Black pepper	10	10
121	15 c. Rubber	10	10
122	20 c. Type **13**	10	10
123	30 c. Rice	10	15
117/23	*Set of* 7	40	45

PAHANG

The first British Resident was appointed in 1888. Pahang joined the Federated Malay States in 1896.

Until 1 January 1899, when the Federated Malay States joined the U.P.U., mail for addresses outside Malaya was franked with stamps of the STRAITS SETTLEMENTS.

PRICES FOR STAMPS ON COVER TO 1945

Nos. 1/3	*from* × 12
Nos. 4/6	*from* × 20
Nos. 7/10	*from* × 8
Nos. 11/13	*from* × 20
Nos. 14/16	*from* × 10
Nos. 17/18	*from* × 5
Nos. 19/24	*from* × 4
No. 25	*from* × 12
Nos. 26/7	—
No. 28	*from* × 10
Nos. 29/46	*from* × 6

PAHANG (1) PAHANG (2) PAHANG (2*a*) (Antique letters)

1889 (Jan). *Nos. 52/3 and 63 of Straits Settlements optd with T* 1.
1 2 c. rose . . 60·00 35·00
2 8 c. orange . . £1600 £1300
3 10 c. slate . . £250 £250

All three values were overprinted from a triplet setting, but the 2 c. also exists from a similar setting of 30 or 60.

1889. *No. 63 of Straits Settlements optd with T* **2**.
4 2 c. rose . . 3·75 6·50
a. Opt Type **2*a***. Antique letters . . £375

No. 4 was overprinted from a setting of 60. No. 4a usually occurs on R. 10/1, but has also been found on R. 8/1 as the result of revision to the setting.

PAHANG (3) PAHANG (4)

1890. *No. 63 of Straits Settlements optd.*
5 **3** 2 c. rose . . £1800 £800
6 **4** 2 c. rose . . 55·00 14·00

No. 5 may have been overprinted from a triplet setting. No. 6 was from a setting of 60.

PAHANG Two CENTS (5) PAHANG Two CENTS (6)

PAHANG Two CENTS (7) PAHANG Two CENTS (8)

1891. *No. 68 of Straits Settlements surch with T* **5/8**.
7 **5** 2 c. on 24 c. green . . 55·00 75·00
8 **6** 2 c. on 24 c. green . . £250
9 **7** 2 c. on 24 c. green . . 75·00 £100
10 **8** 2 c. on 24 c. green . . £250

Nos. 7/10 come from one setting used to surcharge the panes of sixty. No. 7 occurs in rows 1 to 5, No. 8 on row 6, No. 9 on rows 7 to 9 and No. 10 on row 10.

9

10

1891–95. *Wmk Crown CA. P* 14.
11 **9** 1 c. green (1895) . . 3·50 2·50
12 2 c. rose . . 1·75 90
13 5 c. blue (1893) . . 7·00 19·00
11/13 . . *Set of* 3 11·00 20·00
11/13 Optd "Specimen" . . *Set of* 3 60·00

OMNIBUS ISSUES

Details, together with prices for complete sets, of the various Omnibus issues from the 1935 Silver Jubilee series to date are included in a special section following Zululand at the end of the catalogue.

Following an increase of postage rates on 1 March 1894 1 cent stamps of STRAITS SETTLEMENTS were used in Pahang until the autumn of the following year.

1895–99. *Wmk Crown CA. P* 14.
14 **10** 3 c. dull purple and carmine . . 2·25 1·00
15 4 c. dull purple and carmine (1899) . . 9·00 4·00
16 5 c. dull purple and olive-yellow (1897) . . 16·00 12·00
14/16 . . *Set of* 3 24·00 15·00
14/16 Optd "Specimen" . . *Set of* 3 60·00

1897 (2 Aug). *No. 13 bisected, surch in red manuscript at Kuala Lipis and initialled "JFO". (a) Bisected horizontally.*
17 2 c. on half 5 c. blue (surch "2" and bar across "5") . . — £700
17*a* 3 c. on half of 5 c. blue (surch "3") . . — £700

(b) Bisected diagonally
18 2 c. on half of 5 c. blue (surch "2" and bar across "5") . . £750 £250
a. Unsevered pair. Nos. 18 and 18d . . £4500 £1600
b. *Se-tenant* pair. Nos. 18 and 18d . . £2250 £650
c. Surch in black manuscript . . £4500 £2000
18*d* 3 c. on half of 5 c. blue (surch "3") . . £750 £250
dc. Surch in black manuscript . . £4500 £2000

The initials are those of John Fortescue Owen, the District Treasurer at Kuala Lipis.

Nos. 17 and 18 only occur on the bottom half of the 5 c. and Nos. 17*a* and 18*d* on the top half. No. 18a is a complete example of No. 13 showing the two surcharges. No. 18b is a *se-tenant* pair of bisects from adjoining stamps.

Pahang. (11) Pahang. (12)

1898–99. *(a) Nos. 72/5 of Perak optd with T* **11**.
19 10 c. dull purple and orange . . 14·00 23·00
20 25 c. green and carmine . . 60·00 85·00
21 50 c. dull purple and greenish black . . £130 £140
22 50 c. green and black (1899) . . 95·00 £100

(b) Nos. 76 and 79 of Perak optd with T **12**
23 $1 green and pale green . . £140 £150
24 $5 green and ultramarine . . £450 £550

Pahang Four cents (13) Four cents. (14)

1898. *(a) T 44 of Perak surch with T* **13**.
25 4 c. on 8 c. dull purple and ultramarine . . 2·50 5·50
a. Surch inverted . . £1500 £750
b. Surch double . . £475

(b) T **13** *on plain paper (no stamp), but issued for postage. Imperf.*
26 4 c. black . . — £900
27 5 c. black . . £650

No. 26 also exists pin-perforated.

1899. *No. 16 surch with T* **14**.
28 **10** 4 c. on 5 c. dull purple and olive-yellow . . 6·50 29·00

Pending the arrival of the permanent Federated Malay States issue the stamps of SELANGOR, FEDERATED MALAY STATES provisional overprints and PERAK were used at various times between November 1899 and July 1902.

The general issues for the FEDERATED MALAY STATES were used in Pahang from July 1902 until 1935.

15 Sultan Sir Abu Bakar

16 Sultan Sir Abu Bakar

1935 (2 Dec)–**41**. *Chalk-surfaced paper. Wmk Mult Script CA. P* 14.
29 **15** 1 c. black (1.1.36) . . 10 20
30 2 c. green (1.1.36) . . 50 15
31 3 c. green (21.8.41) . . 1·25 5·50
a. Ordinary paper . . 3·00 4·25
32 4 c. orange . . 30 10
33 5 c. brown (5.12.35) . . 50 10
34 6 c. scarlet (1.1.37) . . 4·50 2·25
35 8 c. grey . . 50 10
36 8 c. scarlet (11.12.41) . . 70 27·00
37 10 c. dull purple (1.1.36) . . 30 10
38 12 c. bright ultramarine (1.1.36) . . 1·50 1·75
39 15 c. ultram (*ordinary paper*) (1.10.41) . . 2·50 32·00
40 25 c. dull purple and scarlet (1.4.36) . . 80 1·00
41 30 c. dull purple and orange (1.1.36) . . 55 80
42 40 c. scarlet and dull purple . . 75 1·40
43 50 c. black/*emerald* (1.2.36) . . 3·25 1·75
44 $1 black and red/*blue* (1.4.36) . . 2·25 4·75
45 $2 green and scarlet (16.5.36) . . 18·00 26·00
46 $5 green and red/*emerald* (16.5.36) . . 8·00 48·00
29/46 . . *Set of* 18 40·00 £140
29/46 Perf "Specimen" . . *Set of* 18 £180

A 2 c. orange and a 6 c. grey were prepared but not officially issued. (*Price mint £4 each*).

During shortages in 1941 stamps of STRAITS SETTLEMENTS (2 c.), SELANGOR (2 c., 8 c.) and PERAK (2 c.) were issued in Pahang.

1948 (1 Dec). *Royal Silver Wedding. As Nos. 143/4 of Jamaica.*
47 10 c. violet . . 15 40
48 $5 green . . 20·00 40·00

1949 (10 Oct). *75th Anniv of U.P.U. As Nos. 145/8 of Jamaica.*
49 10 c. purple . . 20 20
50 15 c. deep blue . . 35 70
51 25 c. orange . . 35 1·10
52 50 c. blue-black . . 70 2·00
49/52 . . *Set of* 4 1·40 3·50

1950 (1 June)–**56**. *Wmk Mult Script CA. Chalk-surfaced paper. P* 17½×18.
53 **16** 1 c. black . . 10 10
54 2 c. orange . . 10 10
55 3 c. green . . 20 25
56 4 c. brown . . 15 10
a. Chocolate (24.3.54) . . 1·50 85
57 5 c. bright purple (1.9.52) . . 25 30
a. Bright mauve (10.9.53) . . 25 15
58 6 c. grey . . 15 10
59 8 c. scarlet . . 20 1·00
60 8 c. green (1.9.52) . . 85 75
61 10 c. magenta . . 15 10
62 12 c. scarlet (1.9.52) . . 85 1·25
63 15 c. ultramarine . . 30 10
64 20 c. black and green . . 25 1·75
65 20 c. bright blue (1.9.52) . . 75 10
a. Ultramarine (8.3.56) . . 1·75 1·25
66 25 c. purple and orange . . 20 10
67 30 c. scarlet and brown-purple (5.9.55) . . 1·25 35
a. Scarlet and purple (8.3.56) . . 4·25 1·40
68 35 c. scarlet and purple (1.9.52) . . 60 25
69 40 c. red and purple . . 90 6·00
70 50 c. black and blue . . 40 10
71 $1 blue and purple . . 2·00 90
72 $2 green and scarlet . . 9·50 16·00
73 $5 green and brown . . 38·00 35·00
a. Green and sepia (24.3.54) . . 45·00 55·00
53/73 . . *Set of* 21 50·00 60·00

1953 (2 June). *Coronation. As No. 153 of Jamaica.*
74 10 c. black and reddish purple . . 20 10

1957 (26 June)–**62**. *As Nos. 92/102 of Kedah but with inset portrait of Sultan Sir Abu Bakar.*
75 **9** 1 c. black (21.8.57) . . 10 10
76 **10** 2 c. orange-red (25.7.57) . . 10 10
77 **11** 4 c. sepia (21.8.57) . . 10 10
78 **12** 5 c. carmine-lake (21.8.57) . . 10 10
79 **13** 8 c. myrtle-green (21.8.57) . . 80 80
80 **14** 10 c. deep brown (4.8.57) . . 15 10
81 10 c. deep maroon (21.2.61) . . 65 10
82 **15** 20 c. blue . . 20 10
83 **16** 50 c. black and blue (*p* 12½) (25.7.57) . . 20 10
a. Perf 12½ × 13 (17.5.60) . . 30 10
84 **17** $1 ultramarine & reddish pur (25.7.57) 1·50 1·00
85 **18** $2 bronze-grn & scar (*p* 12½) (21.8.57) 3·00 5·50
a. Perf 13 × 12½ (13.11.62) . . 4·50 8·50
86 **19** $5 brown and bronze-green (*p* 12½) . . 6·00 8·50
a. Perf 13 × 12½ (17.5.60) . . 9·00 9·00
b. Perf 13 × 12½. Brown and yellow-olive (23.10.62) . . 18·00 23·00
75/86 . . *Set of* 12 11·50 14·00

The 6, 12, 25 and 30 c. values used with this issue were Nos. 1/4 of Malayan Federation.

17 *Vanda hookeriana*

18 *Precis orithya*

1965 (15 Nov). *As Nos. 166/72 of Johore but with inset portrait of Sultan Sir Abu Bakar as in T* **17**. *W w* **13** *(upright).*
87 1 c. multicoloured . . 10 20
c. Grey (flower name, etc) omitted . . 20·00
88 2 c. multicoloured . . 10 15
89 5 c. multicoloured . . 10 10
c. Red (leaves, etc) omitted . . 22·00
90 6 c. multicoloured . . 15 10
91 10 c. multicoloured . . 15 10
a. Red omitted . . 22·00
92 15 c. multicoloured . . 80 10
93 20 c. multicoloured . . 1·40 25
87/93 . . *Set of* 7 2·50 80

The 2 c., 5 c. and 6 c. exist with PVA gum as well as gum arabic.

The higher values used with this issue were Nos. 20/27 of Malaysia (National Issues).

1970 (27 May). *As Nos.* 87 *and* 91 *but W w* **13** *(sideways).*
94 **17** 1 c. multicoloured . . 30 3·00
95 – 10 c. multicoloured . . 70 2·50

(Litho B.W.)

1971 (1 Feb). *As Nos. 175/81 of Johore but with portrait of Sultan Sir Abu Bakar and arms, as in T* **18**.
96 1 c. multicoloured . . 15 30
97 2 c. multicoloured . . 40 30
98 5 c. multicoloured . . 50 10
99 6 c. multicoloured . . 50 20
100 10 c. multicoloured . . 50 10
101 15 c. multicoloured . . 70 10
102 20 c. multicoloured . . 85 20
96/102 . . *Set of* 7 3·25 1·10

The higher values used with this issue were Nos. 64/71 of Malaysia (National Issues).

19 Sultan Haji Ahmad Shah
20 *Rhododendron scortechinii*

(Des Union Advertising. Litho Harrison)

1975 (8 May). *Installation of the Sultan. P* 14 × 14½.
103 **19** 10 c. slate-green, light lilac and gold .. 50 30
104 15 c. greenish black, yellow & dp green .. 60 10
105 50 c. black, light violet-bl & greenish blk 1·75 2·25
103/5 .. .. *Set of* 3 2·50 2·40

(Photo Harrison)

1977 (5 Sept)–**78**. *As Nos.* 97/8, 100/2 *but with portraits of Sultan Haji Ahmad Shah.*
106 2 c. multicoloured (1978) .. .. .. 25·00 25·00
107 5 c. multicoloured 60 20
108 10 c. multicoloured (10.2.78) 80 10
109 15 c. multicoloured (13.1.78) 80 20
a. Black (face value, etc.)* omitted.. .. 60·00
110 20 c. multicoloured (1978) .. .. .. 2·50 1·25
106/10 .. .. *Set of* 5 27·00 25·00
*There were two black cylinders used for No. 109, one to apply the portrait and state details, the other the face value and parts of the main design.
The higher values used with this issue were Nos. 64/71 of Malaysia (National Issues).

1979 (30 Apr). *As Nos.* 188/94 *of Johore but with portrait of Sultan Haji Ahmad Shah as in T* **20**.
111 1 c. *Rafflesia hasseltii* 10 10
112 2 c. *Pterocarpus indicus* 10 10
113 5 c. *Lagerstroemia speciosa* 10 10
114 10 c. *Durio zibethinus* 10 10
115 15 c. *Hibiscus rosa-sinensis* 15 10
116 20 c. Type **20** 15 10
117 25 c. *Etlingera elatior* (inscr "*Phaeomeria speciosa*") 15 10
111/17 .. .. *Set of* 7 65 40
For higher values used in conjunction with this series see Nos. 190/7 of Malaysia (National Issues).

1983 (5 Oct)–**85**.* *As Nos.* 113/16 *but without wmk.*
120 5 c. *Lagerstroemia speciosa* (17.11.83) .. 30 15
121 10 c. *Durio zibethinus* (8.1.85) .. .. 2·75 1·25
123 20 c. Type **20** (blackish brown background).. 5·50 1·00
123*a* 20 c. Type **20** (bronze-green background) (20.8.84).. .. .. 30 15
*There was no official release date for these stamps. Dates shown are the earliest recorded from postmarks and may be revised if earlier examples are reported.
For details of the shade differences between watermarked and unwatermarked printings see after Johore No. 200*a*.
On Nos. 120/1 and 123*a* "pahang" is one millimetre nearer "malaysia" than on Nos. 113/16 and 123.

21 Rice

1986 (25 Oct). *As Nos.* 202/8 *of Johore but with portrait of Sultan Ahmad Shah as in T* **21**.
125 1 c. Coffee 10 10
126 2 c. Coconuts.. .. .. 10 10
127 5 c. Cocoa 10 10
128 10 c. Black pepper 10 10
129 15 c. Rubber 10 10
130 20 c. Oil Palm.. .. .. 10 10
131 30 c. Type **21** 10 15
125/31 .. .. *Set of* 7 40 45

PENANG

One of the Straits Settlements.
Issues from 1965 are inscribed "PULAU PINANG".

1948 (1 Dec). *Royal Silver Wedding. As Nos.* 143/4 *of Jamaica.*
1 10 c. violet 25 15
2 $5 brown .. .. 24·00 24·00

1949 (21 Feb)–**52**. *As T* **58** *of Straits Settlements, but inscr* "PENANG" *at foot. Wmk Mult Script CA. Chalk-surfaced paper. P* 17½ × 18.
3 1 c. black 10 10
4 2 c. orange 10 10
5 3 c. green 10 15
6 4 c. brown 10 10
7 5 c. bright purple (1.9.52) 40 80
8 6 c. grey 15 10
9 8 c. scarlet .. .. 30 2·25
10 8 c. green (1.9.52) .. .. 65 1·00
11 10 c. purple 15 10
12 12 c. scarlet (1.9.52) .. .. 65 2·25
13 15 c. ultramarine 20 30
14 20 c. black and green .. .. 20 1·00
15 20 c. bright blue (1.9.52) 55 15
16 25 c. purple and orange 30 10
17 35 c. scarlet and purple (1.9.52) 60 70
18 40 c. red and purple .. .. 55 4·75
19 50 c. black and blue 40 15
20 $1 blue and purple .. .. 3·50 30
21 $2 green and scarlet.. .. .. .. 6·00 60
22 $5 green and brown .. .. 27·00 80
3/22 .. .. *Set of* 20 38·00 13·50

1949 (10 Oct). *75th Anniv of U.P.U. As Nos.* 145/8 *of Jamaica.*
23 10 c. purple 15 10
24 15 c. deep blue 35 40
25 25 c. orange 35 50
26 50 c. blue-black .. .. 1·00 1·40
23/6 .. .. *Set of* 4 1·75 2·10

1953 (2 June). *Coronation. As No.* 153 *of Jamaica.*
27 10 c. black and reddish purple 30 10

1954 (9 June)–**57**. *As T* **1** *of Malacca (Queen Elizabeth II) but inscr* "PENANG" *at foot. Chalk-surfaced paper. Wmk Mult Script CA. P* 17½×18.
28 1 c. black (5.1.55) 10 30
29 2 c. yellow-orange (8.9.54) 30 30
30 4 c. brown (1.9.54) 15 10
a. Yellow-brown (17.7.57) .. .. .. 1·00 80
31 5 c. bright purple (1.10.54) 85 60
a. Bright mauve (17.7.57) .. .. .. 75 1·25
32 6 c. grey 15 10
33 8 c. green (5.1.55) .. .. 20 1·75
34 10 c. brown-purple (1.9.54) 15 10
35 12 c. rose-red (5.1.55) .. .. 30 1·75
36 20 c. bright blue (1.9.54) 30 10
37 25 c. brown-purple & yellow-orange (1.12.54) 20 10
38 30 c. rose-red and brown-purple (5.9.55) .. 20 10
39 35 c. rose-red and brown-purple (8.9.54) .. 30 15
40 50 c. black and bright blue (1.12.54) 30 10
41 $1 bright blue and brown-purple (1.10.54) 2·00 10
42 $2 emerald and scarlet (1.10.54) .. .. 4·50 2·50
43 $5 emerald and brown (5.1.55) .. .. 19·00 3·00
28/43 .. .. *Set of* 16 26·00 9·50

1957. *As Nos.* 92/102 *of Kedah, but with inset portrait of Queen Elizabeth II.*
44 **9** 1 c. black (21.8) 10 20
45 **10** 2 c. orange-red (25.7) 10 30
46 **11** 4 c. sepia (21.8) 10 10
47 **12** 5 c. carmine-lake (21.8).. .. .. 10 10
48 **13** 8 c. myrtle-green (21.8).. .. .. 80 50
49 **14** 10 c. deep brown (4.8) 15 10
50 **15** 20 c. blue (26.6) 20 30
51 **16** 50 c. black and blue (25.7) 25 10
52 **17** $1 ultramarine and reddish purple (25.7) .. .. 2·25 25
53 **18** $2 bronze-green and scarlet (21.8) .. 3·50 4·00
54 **19** $5 brown and bronze-green (26.6) .. 7·50 4·00
44/54 .. .. *Set of* 11 13·50 8·75
The note after No. 86 of Pahang also applies here.

1 Copra
2 *Vanda hookeriana*

(Recess D.L.R.)

1960 (15 Mar). *As Nos.* 44/54, *but with inset Arms of Penang as in T* **1**. *W w* **12**. *P* 13 × 12½ (1 *c. to* 8 *c.,* $2, $5), 12½ × 13 (10 *c. to* 50 *c.*) *or* 13½ ($1).
55 1 c. black 10 15
56 2 c. orange-red 10 20
57 4 c. sepia 10 10
58 5 c. carmine-lake 10 10
59 8 c. myrtle-green .. .. 1·00 1·25
60 10 c. deep maroon 15 10
61 20 c. blue 20 10
62 50 c. black and blue 20 10
a. Imperf (pair) £250
63 $1 ultramarine and reddish purple.. .. 1·25 10
64 $2 bronze-green and scarlet.. .. .. 2·25 1·25
65 $5 brown and bronze-green.. .. .. 6·50 2·50
55/65 .. .. *Set of* 11 10·50 5·00
No. 62a comes from a sheet purchased at the Penang Post Office which had the upper five horizontal rows imperforate.

1965 (15 Nov)–**68**. *As Nos.* 166/72 *of Johore but with Arms of Penang inset and inscr* "PULAU PINANG" *as in T* **2**. *W w* **13** *(upright).*
66 1 c. multicoloured 10 30
67 2 c. multicoloured 10 30
68 5 c. multicoloured 20 10
b. Yellow (flower) omitted .. .. 15·00
c. Red omitted .. .. 25·00
d. Blue (background and inscr) omitted .. 30·00
da. Blue and yellow omitted .. .. 40·00
69 6 c. multicoloured 20 20
b. Yellow omitted .. .. 18·00
70 10 c. grey and multicoloured 15 10
a. Jet-black and multicoloured (12.11.68) 15 10
71 15 c. multicoloured 90 10
b. Green (value and leaves) omitted .. 75·00
72 20 c. multicoloured .. .. 1·40 20
a. Bright purple (blooms) omitted .. £100
b. Yellow (leaves) omitted £100
66/72 .. .. *Set of* 7 2·75 1·00
The 2 c., 5 c., 6 c., 10 c. and 20 c. exist with PVA gum as well as gum arabic.
The higher values used with this issue were Nos. 20/27 of Malaysia (National Issues).

1970. *As Nos.* 66 *and* 70 *but W w* **13** *(sideways).*
73 **2** 1 c. multicoloured (27.5.70) .. .. 30 2·50
74 – 10 c. multicoloured (20.11.70) .. .. 3·50 3·50

3 *Valeria valeria*
4 *Etlingera elatior* (inscr "*Phaeomeria speciosa*")

1971 (1 Feb)–**78**. *As Nos.* 175/87 *of Johore, but with Arms of Penang and inscr* "pulau pinang", *as in T* **3**.

(*a*) *Litho by Bradbury Wilkinson*
75 1 c. multicoloured 15 30
76 2 c. multicoloured 40 30
77 5 c. multicoloured 55 10
78 6 c. multicoloured 55 20
79 10 c. multicoloured 55 10
80 15 c. multicoloured 55 10
81 20 c. multicoloured 65 30
75/81 .. .. *Set of* 7 3·00 1·10

(*b*) *Photo by Harrison* (1977–78)
81*a* 1 c. multicoloured .. .. 5·00 3·25
82 5 c. multicoloured .. .. 1·00 40
83 10 c. multicoloured .. .. 2·00 40
84 15 c. multicoloured .. .. 3·25 30
85 20 c. multicoloured .. .. 3·50 85
81*a*/5 .. .. *Set of* 5 13·50 4·75
The higher values used with this issue were Nos. 64/71 of Malaysia (National Issues).
For differences between litho and photo printings, see after Johore No. 187.

1979 (30 Apr). *As Nos.* 188/94 *of Johore but with Arms of Penang and inscr* "pulau pinang" *as in T* **4**.
86 1 c. *Rafflesia hasseltii* 10 10
87 2 c. *Pterocarpus indicus* 10 10
88 5 c. *Lagerstroemia speciosa* 10 10
89 10 c. *Durio zibethinus* 10 10
90 15 c. *Hibiscus rosa-sinensis* 15 10
91 20 c. *Rhododendron scortechinii* 15 10
92 25 c. Type **4** 15 10
86/92 .. .. *Set of* 7 65 30
For higher values used in conjunction with this series see Nos. 190/7 of Malaysia (National Issues).

1983–85.* *As Nos.* 88/91 *but without wmk.*
95 5 c. *Lagerstroemia speciosa* (1.84) 30 30
96 10 c. *Durio zibethinus* (2.7.85) .. .. 5·50 1·50
97 15 c. *Hibiscus rosa-sinensis* (27.12.83) .. 1·75 60
98 20 c. *Rhododendron scortechinii* (blackish brown background) (21.10.85) .. .. 15·00 60
98*a* 20 c. *Rhododendron scortechinii* (bronze-green background) (3.84) 30 30
*There was no official release date for these stamps. Dates shown are the earliest recorded from postmarks and may be revised if earlier examples are reported.
For details of the shade differences between watermarked and unwatermarked printings see after Johore No. 200*a*.
On Nos. 95/7 and 98*a* the state arms are larger than on the watermarked printing and No. 98.

5 Cocoa

1986 (25 Oct). *As Nos.* 202/8 *of Johore but with Arms of Penang and inscr* "PULAU PINANG" *as in T* **5**.
100 1 c. Coffee 10 10
101 2 c. Coconuts.. .. .. 10 10
102 5 c. Type **5** 10 10
103 10 c. Black pepper 10 10
104 15 c. Rubber 10 10
105 20 c. Oil palm.. .. .. 10 10
106 30 c. Rice 10 15
100/6 .. .. *Set of* 7 40 45

NEW INFORMATION

The editor is always interested to correspond with people who have new information that will improve or correct the Catalogue.

PERAK

Perak accepted a British Resident in 1874, although he was later murdered.
The state joined the Federated Malay States in 1896.

The stamps of the STRAITS SETTLEMENTS were used in Perak during 1877/8.
Until 1 January 1899, when the Federated Malay States joined the U.P.U., mail for addresses outside Malaya was franked with stamps of the STRAITS SETTLEMENTS.

PRICES FOR STAMPS ON COVER TO 1945

No. 1	—
Nos. 2/9	*from* × 60
Nos. 10/13	*from* × 30
Nos. 14/16	*from* × 8
Nos. 17/22	*from* × 20
No. 23	—
Nos. 24/5	—
Nos. 26/8	*from* × 15
No. 29	*from* × 75
No. 30	*from* × 20
Nos. 31/2	—
Nos. 33/40	*from* × 15
Nos. 43/60	*from* × 6
Nos. 61/5	*from* × 20
Nos. 66/79	*from* × 12
No. 80	—
Nos. 81/7	*from* × 8
Nos. 88/102	*from* × 4
Nos. 103/21	*from* × 3

The Official stamps of Perak are rare used on cover.

(1)

1878. *No. 11 of Straits Settlements handstamped with T* **1**.
1 2 c. brown £950 £850

PERAK (2) (14½ mm long) — PERAK (3) (11 mm long) — PERAK (4) (10¼ mm long)

PERAK (5) (17 mm long) — PERAK (6) ("RA" narrow) — PERAK (7) ("R" narrow)

PERAK (8) ("P" and "K" wide) — PERAK (9) (12 to 13½ mm long)

1880–81. *No. 11 (wmk Crown CC) of Straits Settlements optd with T* **2/9**.

2 **2**	2 c. brown	£450	£250
3 **3**	2 c. brown	£425	£225
4 **4**	2 c. brown	£225	£180
5 **5**	2 c. brown (1881)	25·00	35·00
6 **6**	2 c. brown (1881)	80·00	95·00
7 **7**	2 c. brown (1881)	70·00	85·00
8 **8**	2 c. brown (1881)	£160	£150
9 **9**	2 c. brown (1881)	70·00	80·00

Of the above No. 2 is from a single unit overprint, No. 5 from a setting of sixty and the remainder from settings applied as horizontal strips of three. Nos. 6/8 come from mixed triplets, either 6 + 7 + 7 or 7 + 7 + 8. No. 4 is believed to come from a single unit overprint in addition to a triplet.

PERAK (10) ("A" wide) — PERAK (11) ("E" wide)

1882–83. *Nos. 50 (wmk Crown CA) and 63 of Straits Settlements optd with T* **9/11**.

10 **9**	2 c. brown	13·00	19·00
	a. Opt double	£400	
11	2 c. rose (1883)	8·00	16·00
12 **10**	2 c. rose (1883)	10·00	20·00
13 **11**	2 c. rose (1883)	10·00	20·00
	a. Opt double	£450	

The above were all overprinted as triplet settings. Those for the 2 c. rose were 11 + 12 + 13, 13 + 11 + 11 and 13 + 11 + 12.

2 CENTS PERAK (12) — 2 CENTS (13)

1883 (July). *No. 51 (wmk Crown CA) of Straits Settlements surch.*

(a) Surch with T **12**

14	2 c. on 4 c. rose	£1400	
	a. On Straits Settlements No. 12 (wmk Crown CC)	£7000	

(b) Optd as T **9** *or* **11** *and surch with T* **13**

15 **11**	2 c. on 4 c. rose	£500	£350
16 **9**	2 c. on 4 c. rose	£350	£225

It is believed that No. 14 occurred on the top row of the sheet with the remaining nine rows surcharged with a triplet containing 15 + 16 + 16.

PERAK (14) ("E" wide) — PERAK (15) ("E" narrow) — PERAK (16) (12½–13 mm long)

PERAK (17) (12–12½ mm long) — PERAK (18) (10½ mm long) — PERAK (19) (10 mm long)

PERAK (20) (13 mm long)

1884–91. *No. 63 of Straits Settlements optd with T* **14/20**.

17 **14**	2 c. rose	70	70
	a. Opt double	—	£500
	b. Opt inverted	£275	£400
18 **15**	2 c. rose	26·00	27·00
	b. Opt inverted	£550	£650
19 **16**	2 c. rose (1886)	1·00	4·25
	a. Optd "FERAK"	£160	£200
20 **17**	2 c. rose (1886)	2·75	8·50
	a. Opt double	£1100	
21 **18**	2 c. rose (1886)	50·00	65·00
22 **19**	2 c. rose (1890)	7·00	19·00
23 **20**	2 c. rose (1891)	£1400	

Settings:
Nos. 17/18 – triplets (either 17 + 17 + 17 or 18 + 17 + 17)
– 30 (3 × 10) (containing twenty-eight as No. 17 and two as No. 18)
– 60 (6 × 10) (containing either fifty-seven as No. 17 and three as No. 18 or all as No. 17)
No. 19 – 60 (6 × 10) (No. 19a occurs on one position of the setting, it is often found amended in manuscript)
No. 20 – triplet
No. 21 – triplet
No. 22 – 60 (6 × 10)
No. 23 – not known

1 CENT (21)

1886. *No. 17 surch with T* **21**.
24 **14** 1 c. on 2 c. rose £1300 £1300

ONE CENT PERAK (22) — ONE CENT PERAK. (23) — ONE CENT PERAK. (24) ("N" wide in "ONE" and "CENT")

1886. *No. 63 of Straits Settlements surch with T* **22/4**.

25 **22**	1 c. on 2 c. rose	£275	
26 **23**	1 c. on 2 c. rose	27·00	40·00
	a. Surch double	£500	
27 **24**	1 c. on 2 c. rose	45·00	60·00

Nos. 26/7 are from a triplet setting, 26 + 27 + 26, used on the top nine rows of the sheet. No. 25 may have been used on the bottom row.

1 CENT PERAK (25) — One CENT PERAK (26) — ONE CENT PERAK (27)

1886. *No. 63 of Straits Settlements surch with T* **25**.

28	1 c. on 2 c. rose	50·00	60·00
	a. Surch double	£1500	

No. 28 comes from a triplet setting.

1886. *No. 63 of Straits Settlements surch with T* **26**.

29	1 c. on 2 c. rose	85	4·00
	a. "One" inverted	£1300	
	b. Surch double	£750	

No. 29 comes from a triplet setting. It is believed that No. 29a occurred when the type was dropped and "One" replaced upside down.

1887. *No. 63 of Straits Settlements surch with T* **27** *in blue.*

30	1 c. on 2 c. rose	17·00	23·00
	a. Optd in black	£1000	£750

No. 30 was printed from a setting of 60.

1 CENT PERAK (28) — 1 CENT PERAK (29)

1887. *No. 63 of Straits Settlements surch with T* **28**.
31 1 c. on 2 c. rose £250 £275
No. 31 comes from a triplet setting.

1887. *No. 63 of Straits Settlements surch with T* **29**.
32 1 c. on 2 c. rose £800 £1000
The size of setting used for No. 32 is not known.

One CENT PERAK (30) — One CENT PERAK (31) — One CENT PERAK (32) — One CENT PERAK (33)

One CENT PERAK (34) — One CENT PERAK (35) — One CENT PERAK (36) — One CENT PERAK (37)

1887–89. *No. 63 of Straits Settlements surch with T* **30/7**.

33 **30**	1 c. on 2 c. rose	45	1·25
	a. Surch double		
34 **31**	1 c. on 2 c. rose (1889)	70·00	80·00
35 **32**	1 c. on 2 c. rose (1889)	6·50	13·00
	a. "PREAK" (R. 6/1)	£225	£275
36 **33**	1 c. on 2 c. rose (1889)	3·50	4·75
37 **34**	1 c. on 2 c. rose (1889)	3·50	6·50
38 **35**	1 c. on 2 c. rose (1889)	£275	£300
39 **36**	1 c. on 2 c. rose (1889)	£120	£130
40 **37**	1 c. on 2 c. rose (1889)	8·50	16·00

Settings. No. 33 originally appeared as a triplet, then as a block of 30 (3 × 10) and, finally, as part of a series of composite settings of 60. Specialists recognise four such composite settings:
Setting I contained No. 33 in Rows 1 to 4, R. 5/1 to 5/5 and Row 7; No. 34 on R. 5/6, 6/1 and 6/2; No. 35 on R. 6/3–6; No. 36 on Row 8; No. 37 on Rows 9 and 10.
Setting II was similar, but had the example of No. 33 on R. 3/5 replaced by No. 38 and those on R. 7/4 and R. 7/6 by No. 39.
Setting III contained No. 33 in Rows 1 to 5; No. 35 in Row 6; No. 36 in Row 7; No. 37 in Rows 8 and 9; No. 40 in Row 10.
Setting IV was similar, but showed the "PREAK" error on R. 6/1 corrected.

ONE CENT. (38) — ONE CENT (39)

1889–90. *No. 17 surch with T* **38/9**.

41 **38**	1 c. on 2 c. rose	90·00	90·00
42 **39**	1 c. on 2 c. rose (1890)	—	£140

PERAK Two CENTS (40) — PERAK One CENT (41)

1891. *Nos. 63, 66 and 68 of Straits Settlements surch.*

(a) As T **30, 32/4** *and* **37**, *but with "PERAK" at top and a bar through the original value*

43 **30**	1 c. on 6 c. lilac	30·00	24·00
44 **32**	1 c. on 6 c. lilac	75·00	80·00
45 **33**	1 c. on 6 c. lilac	75·00	80·00
46 **34**	1 c. on 6 c. lilac	50·00	55·00
47 **37**	1 c. on 6 c. lilac	75·00	80·00

(b) With T **40** *and as T* **32/4** *and* **37** *but with "PERAK" at top, all with a bar through the original value*

48 **40**	2 c. on 24 c. green	8·50	8·50
49 **32**	2 c. on 24 c. green	55·00	60·00
50 **33**	2 c. on 24 c. green	55·00	50·00
51 **34**	2 c. on 24 c. green	26·00	22·00
52 **37**	2 c. on 24 c. green	55·00	50·00

(c) With T **41** *and as T* **30, 34** *and* **37**, *but with "PERAK" at top.*
(i) Without bar over original value

53 **30**	1 c. on 2 c. rose	£130	
	a. Narrow "O" in "One" (R. 3/3)	£1200	
54 **41**	1 c. on 2 c. rose	£500	
55 **34**	1 c. on 2 c. rose	£200	
56 **37**	1 c. on 2 c. rose	£500	

(ii) With bar through original value

57 **30**	1 c. on 2 c. rose	55	1·75
	a. Narrow "O" in "One" (R. 3/3)	13·00	28·00
58 **41**	1 c. on 2 c. rose	3·75	8·00
59 **34**	1 c. on 2 c. rose	75	2·25
60 **37**	1 c. on 2 c. rose	3·75	8·00

Settings. Nos. 43/7 were arranged as Setting IV described under Nos. 33/40.
Nos. 48/52 were similar except that Type **40** replaced Type **30** on the first five rows.
The first printing of the 1 c. on 2 c. was without a bar through the original face value. Both printings, Nos. 53/60, were from the same setting with Type **30** on Rows 1 to 5, **41** on Row 6, **34** on Rows 7 to 9 and **37** on Row 10.

42

3 CENTS

(43)

1892 (1 Jan)–**95.** *Wmk Crown CA. P* 14.
61 **42** 1 c. green .. 2·25 15
62 2 c. rose .. 1·25 30
63 2 c. orange (9.9.95) .. 35 3·25
64 5 c. blue .. 2·75 6·00
61/4 .. *Set of* 4 6·00 8·75
61/4 Optd "Specimen" .. *Set of* 4 75·00

1895 (18 Apr). *Surch with T* **43.**
65 **42** 3 c. on 5 c. rose (Optd S. £25) .. 50 1·40

44

45

1895 (2 Sept)–**99.** *P* 14. (*a*) *Wmk Crown CA.*
66 **44** 1 c. dull purple and green .. 70 40
67 2 c. dull purple and brown .. 75 40
68 3 c. dull purple and carmine .. 1·50 20
69 4 c. dull purple and carmine (1899) .. 5·50 4·25
70 5 c. dull purple and olive-yellow .. 2·50 55
71 8 c. dull purple and ultramarine .. 26·00 65
72 10 c. dull purple and orange .. 6·00 45
73 25 c. green and carmine (1897) .. 90·00 11·00
74 50 c. dull purple and greenish black .. 25·00 25·00
75 50 c. green and black (2.99) .. £110 £110

(*b*) *Wmk Crown CC*
76 **45** $1 green and pale green (1896) .. 65·00 75·00
77 $2 green and carmine (1896) .. £130 £130
78 $3 green and ochre (1898) .. £100 £120
79 $5 green and ultramarine (1896) .. £300 £275
80 $25 green and orange (1899?) (S. £130) .. £4000 £1100
66/76 .. *Set of* 11 £300 £200
66/79 Optd "Specimen" .. *Set of* 14 £225

Pending the arrival of the permanent Federated Malay States issue the stamps of FEDERATED MALAY STATES provisional overprints, SELANGOR and STRAITS SETTLEMENTS were used at various times between June 1900 and February 1901.
The general issues for the FEDERATED MALAY STATES were used in Perak from 1901 until 1935.

One Cent. (46)

ONE CENT. (47)

Three Cent. (48)

Three Cent. (49)

1900. *Stamps of* 1895–99 *surch.*
81 **46** 1 c. on 2 c. dull purple and brown (13 July*) 40 1·25
a. Antique "e" in "One" (R. 5/2) .. 40·00 55·00
b. Antique "e" in "Cent" (R. 9/4) .. 40·00 55·00
82 **47** 1 c. on 4 c. dull purple and carmine .. 55 3·50
a. Surch double .. £600
83 **46** 1 c. on 5 c. dull purple & ol-yell (30 June*) 70 5·50
a. Antique "e" in "One" (R. 5/2) .. 42·00 75·00
b. Antique "e" in "Cent" (R. 9/4) .. 42·00 75·00
84 **48** 3 c. on 8 c. dull purple & ultram (26 Sept*) 2·50 3·25
a. Antique "e" in "Cent" (R. 9/4) .. 65·00 75·00
b. No stop after "Cent" (R. 9/5) .. 65·00 75·00
c. Surch double .. £180 £180
85 3 c. on 50 c. green and black (31 Aug*) .. 1·00 3·75
a. Antique "e" in "Cent" (R. 9/4) .. 55·00 80·00
b. No stop after "Cent" (R. 9/5) .. 55·00 80·00
86 **49** 3 c. on $1 green and pale green (21 Oct*) .. 50·00 95·00
a. Small "t" in "Cent" .. £225 £300
b. Surch double ..
87 3 c. on $2 green and carmine (24 Oct*) .. 26·00 65·00
81/7 .. *Set of* 7 65·00 £160
*Earliest known postmark date.
With the exception of No. 86a, whose sheet position is not known, the remaining surcharge varieties all occur in the left-hand pane.

50 Sultan Iskandar **51**

1935 (2 Dec)–**37.** *Chalk-surfaced paper. Wmk Mult Script CA. P* 14.
88 **50** 1 c. black (1.1.36) .. 15 10
89 2 c. green (1.1.36) .. 30 10
90 4 c. orange .. 30 10
91 5 c. brown (5.12.35) .. 30 10
92 6 c. scarlet (1.1.37) .. 5·00 2·50
93 8 c. grey .. 40 10
94 10 c. dull purple (1.1.36) .. 30 15
95 12 c. bright ultramarine (1.1.36) .. 60 90
96 25 c. dull purple and scarlet (1.4.36) .. 75 85
97 30 c. dull purple and orange (1.1.36) .. 80 1·50
98 40 c. scarlet and dull purple .. 2·00 4·25
99 50 c. black/*emerald* (1.2.36) .. 3·25 80
100 $1 black and red/*blue* (1.4.36) .. 2·00 80
101 $2 green and scarlet (16.5.36) .. 8·00 8·50
102 $5 green and red/*emerald* (16.5.36) .. 35·00 22·00
88/102 .. *Set of* 15 55·00 38·00
88/102 Perf "Specimen" .. *Set of* 15 £150
No. 91 exists in coils constructed from normal sheets in 1936.

1938 (2 May)–**41.** *Wmk Mult Script CA. Chalk-surfaced paper. P* 14.
103 **51** 1 c. black (4.39) .. 2·50 10
104 2 c. green (13.1.39) .. 2·00 10
105 2 c. orange (30.10.41) .. 50 4·75
a. Ordinary paper .. 80 7·50
106 3 c. green (21.8.41) .. 75 55
107 4 c. orange (5.39) .. 23·00 10
108 5 c. brown (1.2.39) .. 1·50 10
109 6 c. scarlet (12.39) .. 16·00 10
110 8 c. grey (1.12.38) .. 16·00 10
111 8 c. scarlet (18.12.41) .. 1·00 30·00
112 10 c. dull purple (17.10.38) .. 17·00 10
113 12 c. bright ultramarine (17.10.38) .. 11·00 2·00
114 15 c. brt ultram (*ordinary paper*) (8.41) 1·75 13·00
115 25 c. dull purple and scarlet (12.39) .. 65·00 4·25
116 30 c. dull purple and orange (17.10.38) 8·00 3·00
117 40 c. scarlet and dull purple .. 35·00 2·00
118 50 c. black/*emerald* (17.10.38) .. 18·00 75
119 $1 black and red/*blue* (7.40) .. 80·00 14·00
120 $2 green and scarlet (9.40) .. 90·00 50·00
121 $5 green and red/*emerald* (1.41) .. £170 £190
103/21 .. *Set of* 19 £500 £275
103/21 Perf "Specimen" .. *Set of* 19 £250
No. 108 exists in coils constructed from normal sheets.

During shortages in 1941 stamps of STRAITS SETTLEMENTS (2 c.), SELANGOR (2 c., 3 c.) and PAHANG (8 c.) were issued in Perak.

1948 (1 Dec). *Royal Silver Wedding. As Nos.* 143/4 *of Jamaica.*
122 10 c. violet .. 15 10
123 $5 green .. 20·00 20·00

1949 (10 Oct). *75th Anniv of U.P.U. As Nos.* 145/8 *of Jamaica.*
124 10 c. purple .. 15 10
125 15 c. deep blue .. 45 35
126 25 c. orange .. 45 45
127 50 c. blue-black .. 1·25 1·50
124/7 .. *Set of* 4 2·10 2·10

52 Sultan Yussuf 'Izzuddin Shah

53 Sultan Idris Shah

1950 (17 Aug)–**56.** *Chalk-surfaced paper. Wmk Mult Script CA. P* $17\frac{1}{2}$×18.
128 **52** 1 c. black .. 10 10
129 2 c. orange .. 10 10
130 3 c. green .. 85 10
a. Yellowish green (15.11.51) .. 1·00 1·50
131 4 c. brown .. 10 10
a. Yellow-brown (20.6.56) .. 35 10
132 5 c. bright purple (1.9.52) .. 35 40
a. Bright mauve (10.11.54) .. 35 30
133 6 c. grey .. 10 10
134 8 c. scarlet .. 30 75
135 8 c. green (1.9.52) .. 1·00 60
136 10 c. purple .. 10 10
a. Brown-purple (20.6.56) .. 30 10
137 12 c. scarlet (1.9.52) .. 1·00 80
138 15 c. ultramarine .. 30 10
139 20 c. black and green .. 30 20
140 20 c. bright blue (1.9.52) .. 75 10
141 25 c. purple and orange .. 30 10
142 30 c. scarlet and purple (5.9.55) .. 1·25 20
143 35 c. scarlet and purple (1.9.52) .. 70 25
144 40 c. red and purple .. 85 3·00
145 50 c. black and blue .. 40 10
146 $1 blue and purple .. 3·75 15
147 $2 green and scarlet .. 7·50 70
148 $5 green and brown .. 27·00 7·50
128/48 .. *Set of* 21 42·00 13·50

1953 (2 June). *Coronation. As No.* 153 *of Jamaica.*
149 10 c. black and reddish purple .. 20 10

1957 (26 June)–**61.** *As Nos.* 92/102 *of Kedah but with inset portrait of Sultan Yussuf 'Izzuddin Shah.*
150 1 c. black (21.8.57) .. 10 15
151 2 c. orange-red (25.7.57) .. 10 10
a. Red-orange (15.12.59) .. 10 30
152 4 c. sepia (21.8.57) .. 10 10
153 5 c. carmine-lake (21.8.57) .. 10 10
154 8 c. myrtle-green (21.8.57) .. 1·40 30
155 10 c. deep brown (4.8.57) .. 15 10
156 10 c. deep maroon (21.2.61) .. 30 10
157 20 c. blue .. 20 10
158 50 c. black and blue (*p* $12\frac{1}{2}$) (25.7.57) .. 30 10
a. Perf $12\frac{1}{2}$ × 13 (24.5.60) .. 20 10
159 $1 ultramarine and reddish purple (25.7.57) 1·75 10
160 $2 bronze-green & scar (*p* $12\frac{1}{2}$) (21.8.57) .. 2·50 1·50
a. Perf 13 × $12\frac{1}{2}$ (21.2.61) .. 2·50 1·25
161 $5 brown and bronze-green (*p* $12\frac{1}{2}$) .. 6·50 4·50
a. Perf 13 × $12\frac{1}{2}$ (24.5.60) .. 6·50 3·00
150/61 .. *Set of* 12 11·50 4·25
The 6, 12, 25 and 30 c. values used with this issue were Nos. 1/4 of Malayan Federation.

(Photo Harrison)

1963 (26 Oct). *Installation of the Sultan of Perak. W w* **13.** *P* $14\frac{1}{2}$.
162 **53** 10 c. red, black, blue and yellow .. 10 10

54 *Vanda hookeriana*

55 *Delias ninus*

1965 (15 Nov)–**68.** *As Nos.* 166/72 *of Johore but with inset portrait of Sultan Idris as in T* **54.** *W w* **13** (*upright*).
163 1 c. multicoloured .. 10 20
164 2 c. multicoloured .. 10 25
165 5 c. pale black and multicoloured .. 10 10
a. Grey-black and multicoloured (2.4.68) 10 10
b. Yellow (flower) omitted .. 18·00
166 6 c. multicoloured .. 15 10
167 10 c. multicoloured .. 15 10
168 15 c. multicoloured .. 65 10
a. Black (country name and head) omitted £110
c. Magenta (background) omitted .. 90·00
169 20 c. multicoloured .. 1·00 10
a. Bright purple (blooms) omitted .. 25·00
163/9 .. *Set of* 7 2·00 65
No. 168a comes from a horizontal strip of three, the centre stamp having the black completely omitted. The two outer stamps show the colour partly omitted.
The 2 c. to 15 c. exist with PVA gum as well as gum arabic.
The higher values used with this issue were Nos. 20/27 of Malaysia (National Issues).

1970. *As Nos.* 163 *and* 167, *but W w* **13** (*sideways*).
170 **54** 1 c. multicoloured (27.5.70) .. 75 2·75
171 – 10 c. multicoloured (20.11.70) .. 2·75 2·25

1971 (1 Feb)–**78.** *As Nos.* 175/87 *of Johore, but with portrait of Sultan Idris and arms, as in T* **55.**

(*a*) *Litho by Bradbury, Wilkinson*
172 1 c. multicoloured .. 15 30
173 2 c. multicoloured .. 40 40
174 5 c. multicoloured .. 50 10
175 6 c. multicoloured .. 50 15
176 10 c. multicoloured .. 50 10
177 15 c. multicoloured .. 70 10
178 20 c. multicoloured .. 85 15
172/8 .. *Set of* 7 3·25 1·10

(*b*) *Photo by Harrison* (1977–78)
179 1 c. multicoloured .. 45 1·50
180 5 c. multicoloured .. 2·25 35
181 10 c. multicoloured .. 1·75 40
182 15 c. multicoloured .. 3·75 30
183 20 c. multicoloured .. 2·00 65
179/83 .. *Set of* 5 9·00 3·00
The higher values used with this issue were Nos. 64/71 of Malaysia (National Issues).
For differences between litho and photo printings, see after Johore, No. 187.

56 *Rafflesia hasseltii*

57 Coffee

1979 (30 Apr). *As Nos.* 188/94 *of Johore but with portrait of Sultan Idris as in T* **56.**
184 1 c. Type **56** .. 10 10
185 2 c. *Pterocarpus indicus* .. 10 10
186 5 c. *Lagerstroemia speciosa* .. 10 10
187 10 c. *Durio zibethinus* .. 10 10
188 15 c. *Hibiscus rosa-sinensis* .. 15 10
189 20 c. *Rhododendron scortechinii* .. 15 10
190 25 c. *Etlingera elatior* (inscr "*Phaeomeria speciosa*") .. 15 10
184/90 .. *Set of* 7 65 30
For higher values used in conjunction with this series see Nos. 190/7 of Malaysia (National Issues).

1983 (15 Oct)–**84.*** *As Nos.* 186/9 *but without wmk.*
193 5 c. *Lagerstroemia speciosa* (9.9.83) .. 30 20
194 10 c. *Durio zibenthinus* (1984) .. 30 20
195 15 c. *Hibiscus rosa-sinensis* (9.9.83) .. 2·50 65
196 20 c. *Rhododendron scortechinii* (blackish brown background) .. 5·00 55
196*a* 20 c. *Rhododendron scortechinii* (bronze-green background) (20.3.84) .. 30 10
*There was no official release date for these stamps. Dates shown are the earliest recorded from postmarks and may be revised if earlier examples are reported.
For details of the shade differences between watermarked and unwatermarked printings see after Johore No. 200*a*.
On Nos. 193/5 and 196*a* the portrait and arms are redrawn smaller.

1986 (25 Oct). *As Nos. 202/8 of Johore but with portrait of Sultan Azlan Shah as in T* **57**.

198	1 c. Type **57**	10	10
199	2 c. Coconuts	10	10
200	5 c. Cocoa	10	10
201	10 c. Black pepper	10	10
202	15 c. Rubber	10	10
203	20 c. Oil palm	10	10
204	30 c. Rice	10	15
198/204	*Set of* 7	40	45

OFFICIAL STAMPS

P.G.S. (O 1) **Service.** (O 2)

1889 (1 Nov). *Stamps of Straits Settlements optd with Type* O **1**. *Wmk Crown CC (Nos. O6 and O8) or Crown CA (others).*

O1	2 c. rose	2·00	2·50
	a. Overprint double	£850	£850
	b. Wide space between "G" and "S"	35·00	45·00
	c. No stop after "S"	35·00	45·00
O2	4 c. brown	6·50	12·00
	a. Wide space between "G" and "S"	55·00	75·00
	b. No stop after "S"	80·00	£100
O3	6 c. lilac	18·00	28·00
	a. Wide space between "G" and "S"	85·00	£110
O4	8 c. orange	22·00	55·00
	a. Wide space between "G" and "S"	£100	£150
O5	10 c. slate	65·00	65·00
	a. Wide space between "G" and "S"	£180	£190
O6	12 c. blue (CC)	£110	£120
	a. Wide space between "G" and "S"	£400	
O7	12 c. brown-purple (CA)	£160	£190
	a. Wide space between "G" and "S"	£550	
O8	24 c. green (CC)	£425	£475
	a. Wide space between "G" and "S"	£1400	
O9	24 c. green (CA)	£100	£120
	a. Wide space between "G" and "S"	£400	

Nos. O1/9 were overprinted from a setting of 30 (3 × 10). The variety "wide space between G and S" occurs on R. 10/3 and R. 10/6 of the original printing. A later printing of the 2 c. and 4 c. values had this variety corrected, but was without a stop after "S" on R. 10/1 and R. 10/4.

1894 (1 June). *No. 64 optd with Type* O **2**.

O10	5 c. blue	24·00	80
	a. Overprint inverted	£450	£350

1897. *No. 70 optd with Type* O **2**.

O11	5 c. dull purple and olive-yellow	1·40	35
	a. Overprint double	£350	£375

PERLIS

Suzerainty over Perlis was transferred by Thailand to Great Britain in 1909. A British adviser was appointed in 1930.

The State joined the Federation of Malaya on 1 February 1948.

The stamps of THAILAND were used in Perlis at Kangar (Muang Perlis) until 1909. Issues of the FEDERATED MALAY STATES were in use from 10 July 1909 until 1912 and these were replaced by the stamps of KEDAH between 1912 and 1951.

1948 (1 Dec). *Royal Silver Wedding. As Nos. 143/4 of Jamaica.*

1	10 c. violet	30	1·25
2	$5 brown	25·00	42·00

1949 (10 Oct). *75th Anniv of U.P.U. As Nos. 145/8 of Jamaica.*

3	10 c. purple	25	60
4	15 c. deep blue	50	2·00
5	25 c. orange	55	1·75
6	50 c. blue-black	90	3·50
3/6	*Set of* 4	2·00	7·00

1 Raja Syed Putra

2 *Vanda hookeriana*

1951 (26 Mar)–**55**. *Chalk-surfaced paper. Wmk Mult Script CA. P* 17½ × 18.

7	**1**	1 c. black	10	40
8		2 c. orange	10	40
9		3 c. green	40	1·25
10		4 c. brown	20	20
11		5 c. bright purple (1.9.52)	30	65
12		6 c. grey	20	25
13		8 c. scarlet	30	2·00
14		8 c. green (1.9.52)	75	1·50
15		10 c. purple	15	20
16		12 c. scarlet (1.9.52)	75	1·75
17		15 c. ultramarine	70	1·50
18		20 c. black and green	70	2·25
19		20 c. bright blue (1.9.52)	85	65
20		25 c. purple and orange	50	90
21		30 c. scarlet and purple (5.9.55)	1·75	4·25
22		35 c. scarlet and purple (1.9.52)	75	2·50
23		40 c. red and purple	1·25	9·00
24		50 c. black and blue	1·00	1·75
25		$1 blue and purple	3·00	7·00
26		$2 green and scarlet	9·50	17·00
27		$5 green and brown	42·00	48·00
7/27		*Set of* 21	60·00	90·00

1953 (2 June). *Coronation. As No. 153 of Jamaica.*

28	10 c. black and reddish purple	30	1·50

1957 (26 June)–**62**. *As Nos. 92/102 of Kedah but with inset portrait of Raja Syed Putra.*

29	**9**	1 c. black (21.8.57)	10	20
30	**10**	2 c. orange-red (25.7.57)	10	20
31	**11**	4 c. sepia (21.8.57)	10	10
32	**12**	5 c. carmine-lake (21.8.57)	10	10
33	**13**	8 c. myrtle-green (21.8.57)	1·25	80
34	**14**	10 c. deep brown (4.8.57)	15	30
35		10 c. deep maroon (14.3.61)	80	35
36	**15**	20 c. blue	20	50
37	**16**	50 c. black and blue (*p* 12½) (25.7.57)	20	60
		a. Perf 12½ × 13 (8.5.62)	70	80
38	**17**	$1 ultram & reddish purple (25.7.57)	2·50	3·50
39	**18**	$2 bronze-green and scarlet (25.7.57)	3·75	5·00
40	**19**	$5 brown and bronze-green (21.8.57)	6·50	7·50
29/40		*Set of* 12	14·00	17·00

The 6, 12, 25 and 30 c. values used with this issue were Nos. 1/4 of Malayan Federation.

1965 (15 Nov). *As Nos. 166/72 of Johore but with inset portrait of Tunku Bendahara Abu Bakar as in T* **2**.

41	1 c. multicoloured	10	60
42	2 c. multicoloured	10	70
43	5 c. multicoloured	15	15
44	6 c. multicoloured	40	30
45	10 c. multicoloured	45	15
46	15 c. multicoloured	75	35
47	20 c. multicoloured	1·00	85
41/7	*Set of* 7	2·75	2·75

The 6 c. exists with PVA gum as well as gum arabic.

The higher values used with this issue were Nos. 20/27 of Malaysia (National Issues).

3 *Danaus melanippus*

4 Raja Syed Putra

1971 (1 Feb)–**78**. *As Nos. 175/87 of Johore but with portrait of Raja Syed Putra and Arms, as in T* **3**.

(*a*) *Litho by Bradbury, Wilkinson*

48	1 c. multicoloured	15	60
49	2 c. multicoloured	20	70
50	5 c. multicoloured	55	20
51	6 c. multicoloured	55	40
52	10 c. multicoloured	55	20
53	15 c. multicoloured	55	25
54	20 c. multicoloured	65	80
48/54	*Set of* 7	3·00	2·75

(*b*) *Photo by Harrison* (1977–78)

54*a*	10 c. multicoloured		
55	15 c. multicoloured	3·50	1·25
55*a*	20 c. multicoloured	11·00	13·00

The higher values used with this issue were Nos. 64/71 of Malaysia (National Issues).

For differences between litho and photo printings, see after Johore No. 187.

(Des Citizen Studio and Engravers. Litho Enschedé)

1971 (28 Mar). *25th Anniv of Installation of Raja Syed Putra. P* 13½ × 13.

56	**4**	10 c. multicoloured	20	50
57		15 c. multicoloured	20	30
58		50 c. multicoloured	70	1·75
56/8		*Set of* 3	1·00	2·25

5 *Pterocarpus indicus*

6 Coconuts

1979 (30 Apr). *As Nos. 188/94 of Johore but with portrait of Raja Syed Putra as in T* **5**.

59	1 c. *Rafflesia hasseltii*	10	30
60	2 c. Type **5**	10	30
61	5 c. *Lagerstroemia speciosa*	10	10
62	10 c. *Durio zibethinus*	10	10
63	15 c. *Hibiscus rosa-sinensis*	15	10
64	20 c. *Rhododendron scortechinii*	15	10
65	25 c. *Etlingera elatior* (inscr "*Phaeomeria speciosa*")	15	30
59/65	*Set of* 7	65	1·10

For higher values used in conjunction with this series see Nos. 190/7 of Malaysia (National Issues).

1983–84*. *As No. 64 but without wmk.*

71	20 c. *Rhododendron scortechinii* (blackish brown background)	7·00	3·50
71*a*	20 c. *Rhododendron scortechinii* (bronze-green background) (4.12.84)	1·50	1·50

*There was no official release date for these stamps. Dates shown are the earliest recorded from postmarks and may be revised if earlier examples are reported.

For details of the shade differences between watermarked and unwatermarked printings see after Johore No. 200*a*.

No. 71*a* shows the Sultan's head larger than on Nos. 64 and 71 and has "perlis" in rounded, instead of square-ended, letters.

1986 (25 Oct). *As Nos. 202/8 of Johore but with portrait of Raja Syed Putra as in T* **6**.

73	1 c. Coffee	10	10
74	2 c. Type **6**	10	10
75	5 c. Cocoa	10	10
76	10 c. Black pepper	10	10
77	15 c. Rubber	10	10
78	20 c. Oil palm	10	10
79	30 c. Rice	10	15
73/9	*Set of* 7	40	45

SELANGOR

The first British Resident was appointed in 1874. Selangor joined the Federated Malay States in 1896.

> The stamps of the STRAITS SETTLEMENTS were used in Selangor from 1879 until 1881.
> Until 1 January 1899, when the Federated Malay States joined the U.P.U., mail for addresses outside Malaya was franked with stamps of the STRAITS SETTLEMENTS.

PRICES FOR STAMPS ON COVER TO 1945

Nos. 1/8	—
Nos. 9/19	*from* × 10
Nos. 20/30	*from* × 12
Nos. 31/3	*from* × 25
Nos. 34/6	*from* × 20
Nos. 37/8	*from* × 15
Nos. 38*a*/40	—
Nos. 41/2	*from* × 8
No. 43	—
Nos. 44/8	*from* × 8
Nos. 49/53	*from* × 30
Nos. 54/66	*from* × 10
Nos. 66*a*/7	*from* × 4
Nos. 68/85	*from* × 3
Nos. 86/7	*from* × 4

The Straits Settlements 1867 2 c. brown with Crown CC watermark (No. 11) has been known since 1881 overprinted in black with a crescent and star over a capital S, all within an oval, similar in style to the overprints listed for Perak and Sungei Ujong.

The status of this item remains unclear, but it may well represent the first issue of distinctive stamps for Selangor. This overprint should not be confused with a somewhat similar cancellation used on Selangor stamps of the same period. This cancellation differs in having a circular frame with the capital S shown above the crescent and star. It is usually struck in red.

A similar overprint in red on the Straits Settlements 2 c. brown with Crown CA watermark is known to be bogus.

SELANGOR (1) ("S" inverted and narrow letters) — SELANGOR (2) ("S" wide) — SELANGOR (3) (narrow letters)

SELANGOR (4) ("N" wide) — SELANGOR (5) ("SE" and "AN" wide) — SELANGOR (6) ("SEL" and "N" wide)

SELANGOR (7) ("SELAN" wide)

1881–82. *No. 11 (wmk Crown CC) of Straits Settlements optd with T* **1/7**.

No.	Type	Description	Unused	Used
1	**1**	2 c. brown	£180	£200
2	**2**	2 c. brown	75·00	85·00
3	**3**	2 c. brown	55·00	60·00
4	**4**	2 c. brown	—	£1800
5	**5**	2 c. brown (1882)	90·00	£100
6	**6**	2 c. brown (1882)	90·00	£100
7	**7**	2 c. brown (1882)	90·00	£100

Nos. 1/3 and 5/7 have been identified as coming from triplet settings, either Nos. 1 + 2 + 3, 2 + 3 + 3 or 5 + 6 + 7. The setting for No. 4 is unknown.

S. (8)

1882. *No. 50 (wmk Crown CA) of Straits Settlements optd with T* **8**.

No.	Type	Description	Unused	Used
8	**8**	2 c. brown	—	£1300

SELANGOR (9) ("SEL" and "NG" wide) — SELANGOR (10) ("E" and "ANG" wide) — SELANGOR (11) ("ELANG" wide)

SELANGOR (12) ("S" and "L" wide) — SELANGOR (13) ("S" and "A" wide) — SELANGOR (14) ("E" wide)

SELANGOR (15) ("EL" wide) — SELANGOR (16) ("SE" and "N" wide) — SELANGOR (17) ("S" and "N" wide)

1882–83. *No. 50 (wmk Crown CA) of Straits Settlements optd with T* **2/3** *and* **9/17**.

No.	Type	Description	Unused	Used
9	**9**	2 c. brown	85·00	85·00
10	**10**	2 c. brown	85·00	85·00
11	**11**	2 c. brown	85·00	85·00
12	**2**	2 c. brown (1883)	65·00	60·00
13	**3**	2 c. brown (1883)	£100	60·00
14	**12**	2 c. brown (1883)	—	£1400
15	**13**	2 c. brown (1883)	£200	£170
16	**14**	2 c. brown (1883)	£100	90·00
17	**15**	2 c. brown (1883)	£100	90·00
18	**16**	2 c. brown (1883)	65·00	65·00
19	**17**	2 c. brown (1883)	65·00	65·00

The above were all printed from triplet settings. Those so far identified are Nos. 9 + 10 + 11, 12 (with defective "G") + 13 + 13, 15 + 16 + 17 and 18 + 12 + 19. No. 14 occurs as the first position of a triplet, but the second and third units are not yet known.

SELANGOR (18) ("E" and "A" wide) — SELANGOR (19) ("A" wide) — SELANGOR (20) ("L" wide)

SELANGOR (21) ("L" narrow) — SELANGOR (22) ("A" narrow) — SELANGOR (23) (wide letters)

1883–85. *No. 63 of Straits Settlements optd with T* **2**, **4**, **12**, **14/15** *and* **18/23**.

No.	Type	Description	Unused	Used
20	**12**	2 c. rose	80·00	80·00
21	**14**	2 c. rose	60·00	60·00
		a. Opt double		
22	**4**	2 c. rose (1884)	90·00	90·00
23	**15**	2 c. rose (1884)	60·00	60·00
24	**2**	2 c. rose (1884)	65·00	65·00
25	**18**	2 c. rose (1884)	65·00	65·00
26	**19**	2 c. rose (1884)	£120	90·00
27	**20**	2 c. rose (1884)	£160	£120
28	**21**	2 c. rose (1885)	55·00	65·00
29	**22**	2 c. rose (1885)	75·00	85·00
30	**23**	2 c. rose (1885)	£120	£100

The above come from triplet settings with Nos. 20 + 21 + 21, 22 + 22 + 23, 24 + 25 + 23 and 28 + 29 + 28 so far identified. The triplets for Nos. 26, 27 and 30 are not known, although the first two may come from the same setting.

SELANGOR (24) — Selangor (25) — SELANGOR (26)

SELANGOR (27) — SELANGOR (28) — SELANGOR (29) — SELANGOR (30)

SELANGOR (31) — SELANGOR (32) — SELANGOR (33) — *SELANGOR* (34)

1885–91. *No. 63 of Straits Settlements optd with T* **24/34**.

No.	Type	Description	Unused	Used
31	**24**	2 c. rose	3·25	7·50
		a. Opt double	—	£650
32	**25**	2 c. rose	£650	£700
33	**26**	2 c. rose	11·00	16·00
34	**27**	2 c. rose (1886)	30·00	30·00
		a. Opt double	†	£600
35	**28**	2 c. rose (horiz opt without stop) (1887)	3·00	2·25
36		2 c. rose (horiz opt with stop) (1887)	22·00	22·00
37	**29**	2 c. rose (1889)	£120	70·00
38	**30**	2 c. rose (vert opt) (1889)	35·00	6·00
38*a*		2 c. rose (horiz opt) (1889)	£3000	
39	**31**	2 c. rose (diagonal opt) (1889)	£1000	
40	**32**	2 c. rose (1889)	£200	20·00
41	**28**	2 c. rose (vert opt without stop) (1890)	9·00	14·00
42	**33**	2 c. rose (1890)	75·00	2·25
43	**34**	2 c. rose (1891)	£225	£160

Settings:
- Nos. 31/4 – each in triplet containing three examples of the same stamp
- No. 35 – triplet or 60 (6 × 10)
- No. 36 – 60 (6 × 10)
- Nos. 37/8 – 60 (6 × 10) containing both overprints in an unknown combination, but with No. 38 predominating
- No. 38*a*/9 – not known
- Nos. 40/3 – each in 60 (6 × 10)

SELANGOR Two CENTS (35) — SELANGOR Two CENTS (36) — SELANGOR Two CENTS (37)

SELANGOR Two CENTS (38) — SELANGOR Two CENTS (39)

1891. *No. 68 of Straits Settlements, surch with T* **35/9**, *each with bar obliterating old value.*

No.	Type	Description	Unused	Used
44	**35**	2 c. on 24 c. green	12·00	30·00
45	**36**	2 c. on 24 c. green	90·00	£140
46	**37**	2 c. on 24 c. green	90·00	£140
47	**38**	2 c. on 24 c. green	55·00	90·00
		a. "SELANGCR"		
48	**39**	2 c. on 24 c. green	90·00	£140

Nos. 44/8 come from the one setting used to surcharge the panes of sixty. No. 44 occurs in rows 1 to 5, No. 45 on row 6, No. 46 on row 7, No. 47 on rows 8 and 9, and No. 48 on row 10.

The error, No. 47a, occurs in the first printing only and is No. 45 (R.8/3) on the pane.

40

3 CENTS

(41)

1891 (Nov)–**95.** *Wmk Crown CA. P* 14.

No.	Type	Description	Unused	Used
49	**40**	1 c. green (1893)	70	25
50		2 c. rose	2·50	45
51		2 c. orange (1895)	75	40
52		5 c. blue (1892)	9·00	3·75
49/52		*Set of* 4	11·50	4·25
49/52 Optd "Specimen"		*Set of* 4	70·00	

1894. *Surch with T* **41**.

No.	Type	Description	Unused	Used
53	**40**	3 c. on 5 c. rose (Optd S. £30)	1·00	30

42

43

1895–99. *Wmk Crown CA or Crown CC (dollar values). P* 14.

No.	Type	Description	Unused	Used
54	**42**	3 c. dull purple and carmine	4·25	20
55		5 c. dull purple and olive-yellow	80	30
56		8 c. dull purple and ultramarine (1898)	50·00	7·00
57		10 c. dull purple and orange	5·50	35
58		25 c. green and carmine (1896)	60·00	35·00
59		50 c. dull purple and greenish black (1896)	21·00	15·00
60		50 c. green and black (1898)	£150	85·00
61	**43**	$1 green and yellow-green	32·00	50·00
62		$2 green and carmine (1897)	£100	£100
63		$3 green and ochre (1897)	£200	£150
64		$5 green and blue	95·00	£130
65		$10 green and purple (1899) (S. £90)	£275	£275
66		$25 green and orange (1899?) (S. £170)	£1200	
54/62		*Set of* 9	£375	£250
54/64 Optd "Specimen"		*Set of* 11	£190	

> Pending the arrival of the permanent Federated Malay States issue the stamps of STRAITS SETTLEMENTS and PERAK were used at various times between July 1900 and March 1901.
> The general issues for the FEDERATED MALAY STATES were used in Selangor from 1901 until 1935.

One cent. (44) — Three cents. (45)

1900 (Oct). *Nos. 55 and 59 surch with T* **44** *or* **45**.

No.	Type	Description	Unused	Used
66*a*	**42**	1 c. on 5 c. dull purple & ol-yell (31 Oct*)	50·00	65·00
66*b*		1 c. on 50 c. green and black (22 Oct*)	90	14·00
		bc. "cent" repeated at left	£1100	
67		3 c. on 50 c. green and black (30 Oct*)	6·00	15·00
		a. Antique "t" in "cents"	£100	£150

*Earliest known postmark date.

It is believed that these stamps were surcharged from settings of 30, repeated four times to complete the sheet of 120.

No. 66bc occurred on two separate vertical strips of five stamps where two impressions of the setting overlapped.

The position in the setting of No. 67a is not known.

46 Mosque at Palace, Klang

47 Sultan Suleiman

(Des E. J. McNaughton)

1935 (2 Dec)–**41.** *Wmk Mult Script CA (sideways on T* **46**). *Chalk-surfaced paper. P* 14 *or* 14×14½ *(No. 70).*

No.	Type	Description	Unused	Used
68	**46**	1 c. black (1.1.36)	20	10
69		2 c. green (1.1.36)	30	10
70		2 c. orange (*ordinary paper*) (*p* 14×14½) (21.8.41)	30	1·10
		a. Perf 14. Ordinary paper (9.41)	11·00	2·50
		ab. Chalk-surfaced paper	11·00	2·50
71		3 c. green (21.8.41)	3·00	2·50
		a. Ordinary paper	50	4·00
72		4 c. orange	30	10
73		5 c. brown (5.12.35)	30	10
74		6 c. scarlet (1.1.37)	3·25	10
75		8 c. grey	40	10
76		10 c. dull purple (1.1.36)	40	10
77		12 c. bright ultramarine (1.1.36)	1·50	10
78		15 c. brt ultram (*ordinary paper*) (1.10.41)	4·25	23·00
79		25 c. dull purple and scarlet (1.4.36)	1·50	60
80		30 c. dull purple and orange (1.1.36)	1·25	85
81		40 c. scarlet and dull purple	1·75	1·25
82		50 c. black/*emerald* (1.2.36)	1·50	15
83	**47**	$1 black and rose/*blue* (1.4.36)	4·00	40
84		$2 green and scarlet (16.5.36)	15·00	7·00
85		$5 green and red/*emerald* (16.5.36)	45·00	23·00
68/85		*Set of* 18	75·00	55·00
68/85 Perf "Specimen"		*Set of* 18	£250	

Supplies of an unissued 8 c. scarlet were diverted to Australia in 1941. Examples circulating result from leakages of this supply.

48 Sultan Hisamud-din Alam Shah **49**

1941. *Wmk Mult Script CA. Chalk-surfaced paper. P* 14.

No.	Type	Description	Unused	Used
86	**48**	$1 black and red/*blue* (15.4.41)	7·00	5·00
87		$2 green and scarlet (7.7.41) (Perf S. £70)	40·00	27·00

A $5 green and red on emerald, T **48**, was issued overprinted during the Japanese occupation of Malaya. Unoverprinted examples are known, but were not issued (*Price* £70).

During shortages in 1941 stamps of STRAITS SETTLEMENTS (2 c.) and PERAK (25 c.) were issued in Selangor.

1948 (1 Dec). *Royal Silver Wedding. As Nos.* 143/4 *of Jamaica.*

No.	Description	Unused	Used
88	10 c. violet	20	10
89	$5 green	23·00	14·00

1949 (12 Sept)–**55.** *Wmk Mult Script CA. Chalk-surfaced paper. P* 17½×18.

No.	Type	Description	Unused	Used
90	**49**	1 c. black	10	10
91		2 c. orange	10	10
92		3 c. green	20	65
93		4 c. brown	10	10
94		5 c. bright purple (1.9.52)	30	40
		a. Bright mauve (17.9.53)	30	10
95		6 c. grey	10	10
96		8 c. scarlet	25	65
97		8 c. green (1.9.52)	65	50
98		10 c. purple	10	10
99		12 c. scarlet (1.9.52)	80	1·25
100		15 c. ultramarine	35	10
101		20 c. black and green	30	10
102		20 c. bright blue (1.9.52)	80	10
103		25 c. purple and orange	30	10
104		30 c. scarlet and purple (5.9.55)	1·25	50
105		35 c. scarlet and purple (1.9.52)	70	80
106		40 c. scarlet and purple	1·25	2·00
107		50 c. black and blue	40	10
108		$1 blue and purple	2·00	10
109		$2 green and scarlet	5·00	15
110		$5 green and brown	30·00	80
90/110		*Set of* 21	40·00	7·00

1949 (10 Oct). *75th Anniv of U.P.U. As Nos.* 145/8 *of Jamaica.*

No.	Description	Unused	Used
111	10 c. purple	15	10
112	15 c. deep blue	45	45
113	25 c. orange	50	90
114	50 c. blue-black	1·10	80
111/14	*Set of* 4	2·00	2·00

1953 (2 June). *Coronation. As No.* 153 *of Jamaica.*

No.	Description	Unused	Used
115	10 c. black and reddish purple	30	10

1957 (26 June)–**61.** *As Nos.* 92/102 *of Kedah but with inset portrait of Sultan Hisamud-din Alam Shah.*

No.	Description	Unused	Used
116	1 c. black (21.8.57)	10	30
117	2 c. orange-red (25.7.57)	10	20
	a. Red-orange (10.11.59)	75	1·50
118	4 c. sepia (21.8.57)	10	10
119	5 c. carmine-lake (21.8.57)	10	10
120	8 c. myrtle-green (21.8.57)	1·10	25
121	10 c. deep brown (4.8.57)	15	10
122	10 c. deep maroon (9.5.61)	1·25	10
123	20 c. blue	25	10
124	50 c. black and blue (*p* 12½) (25.7.57)	25	10
	a. Perf 12½ × 13 (10.5.60)	25	10
125	$1 ultramarine and reddish purple (25.7.57)	1·25	10
126	$2 bronze-green & scarlet (*p* 12½) (21.8.57)	2·25	85
	a. Perf 13 × 12½ (6.12.60)	2·00	1·40
127	$5 brown and bronze-green (*p* 12½)	6·50	1·50
	a. Perf 13 × 12½ (10.5.60)	4·25	1·00
116/27a	*Set of* 12	9·00	2·50

The 6, 12, 25 and 30 c. values used with this issue were Nos. 1/4 of Malayan Federation.

50 Sultan Salahuddin Abdul Aziz Shah **51**

(Photo Harrison)

1961 (28 June). *Coronation of the Sultan. W w* **12**. *P* 15×14.

No.	Type	Description	Unused	Used
128	**50**	10 c. multicoloured	10	10
		a. Black ptg misplaced	£130	

No. 128*a* is "The Double-headed Sultan" error, from one sheet where the majority of the stamps showed considerable black printing misplacement.

1961–62. *As Nos.* 92/8 *of Kedah but with inset portrait of Sultan Salahuddin Abdul Aziz as in T* **51**. *W w* **13**. *P* 12½×13 (*vert*) *or* 13×12½ (*horiz*).

No.	Description	Unused	Used
129	1 c. black (1.3.62)	10	30
130	2 c. orange-red (1.3.62)	10	30
131	4 c. sepia (1.3.62)	10	10
132	5 c. carmine-lake (1.3.62)	10	10
133	8 c. myrtle-green (1.3.62)	70	80
134	10 c. deep maroon (1.11.61)	10	10
135	20 c. blue (1.3.62)	40	10
129/35	*Set of* 7	1·25	1·40

52 *Vanda hookeriana* **53** *Parthenos sylvia*

1965 (15 Nov). *As Nos.* 166/72 *of Johore but with inset portrait of Sultan Salahuddin Abdul Aziz Shah as in T* **52**.

No.	Description	Unused	Used
136	1 c. multicoloured	10	10
	b. Magenta omitted	30·00	
137	2 c. multicoloured	10	30
	b. Yellow (flower) omitted	18·00	
138	5 c. multicoloured	15	10
	b. Yellow (flower) omitted	16·00	
	c. Red (leaves, etc) omitted	25·00	
139	6 c. multicoloured	15	10
140	10 c. multicoloured	15	10
	a. Red omitted	28·00	
141	15 c. multicoloured	85	10
	b. Green (value and leaves) omitted	£100	
142	20 c. multicoloured	1·25	15
	a. Bright purple (blooms) omitted	30·00	
	b. Yellow (leaves) omitted	18·00	
136/42	*Set of* 7	2·40	60

The 2 c. to 20 c. values exist with PVA gum as well as gum arabic.

The higher values used with this issue were Nos. 20/27 of Malaysia (National Issues).

1970 (20 Nov). *As Nos.* 136 *etc. but W w* **13** (*sideways*).

No.	Type	Description	Unused	Used
143	**52**	1 c. multicoloured	50	2·25
144		10 c. multicoloured	2·00	30
145	–	20 c. multicoloured	3·50	2·75
143/5		*Set of* 3	5·50	4·75

1971 (1 Feb)–**78.** *As Nos.* 175/87 *of Johore but with portrait of Sultan Salahuddin Abdul Aziz Shah and Arms, as in T* **53**.

(*a*) *Litho by Bradbury, Wilkinson*

No.	Description	Unused	Used
146	1 c. multicoloured	15	30
147	2 c. multicoloured	40	40
148	5 c. multicoloured	50	10
149	6 c. multicoloured	50	15
150	10 c. multicoloured	50	10
	a. Black (state inscr, portrait and arms) omitted	60·00	
151	15 c. multicoloured	55	10
152	20 c. multicoloured	90	15
146/52	*Set of* 7	3·25	1·00

(*b*) *Photo by Harrison* (1977–78)

No.	Description	Unused	Used
153	1 c. multicoloured	50	2·00
154	5 c. multicoloured	2·50	30
155	10 c. multicoloured	3·25	50
156	15 c. multicoloured	3·25	30
157	20 c. multicoloured	3·25	85
153/7	*Set of* 5	11·50	3·50

The higher values used with this issue were Nos. 64/71 of Malaysia (National Issues).

For differences between litho and photo printings see after Johore No. 187.

A used example of No. 150 has been seen with the magenta apparently missing.

For explanation of No. 150a, see note below No. 122 of Kelantan.

54 *Lagerstroemia speciosa* **55** Sultan Salahuddin Abdul Aziz Shah and Royal Crest

1979 (30 Apr). *As Nos.* 188/94 *of Johore but with portrait of Sultan Salahuddin Abdul Aziz Shah as in T* **54**.

No.	Description	Unused	Used
158	1 c. *Rafflesia hasseltii*	10	10
159	2 c. *Pterocarpus indicus*	10	10
160	5 c. Type **54**	10	10
161	10 c. *Durio zibethinus*	10	10
162	15 c. *Hibiscus rosa-sinensis*	15	10
163	20 c. *Rhododendron scortechinii*	15	10
164	25 c. *Etlingera elatior* (inscr "*Phaeomeria speciosa*")	15	10
158/64	*Set of* 7	65	30

For higher values used in conjunction with this series see Nos. 190/7 of Malaysia (National Issues).

1983 (6 Oct)–**85.*** *As Nos.* 160/3 *but without wmk.*

No.	Description	Unused	Used
166	5 c. Type **54** (20.11.83)	30	20
167	10 c. *Durio zibethinus* (3.85)	2·00	95
168	15 c. *Hibiscus rosa-sinensis* (20.11.83)	2·00	60
169	20 c. *Rhododendron scortechinii* (blackish brown background)	5·00	75
169*a*	20 c. *Rhododendron scortechinii* (bronze-green background) (12.12.83)	60	40

*There was no official release date for these stamps. Dates shown are the earliest recorded from postmarks and may be revised if earlier examples are reported.

For details of the shade differences between watermarked and unwatermarked printings see after Johore No. 200*a*.

On Nos. 166/8 and 169*a* the ruler's headdress is bolder than on Nos. 160/3 and 169.

(Des P. Ket. Litho Security Printers (M), Malaysia)

1985 (5 Sept). *Silver Jubilee of Sultan. P* 13.

No.	Type	Description	Unused	Used
173	**55**	15 c. multicoloured	55	10
174		20 c. multicoloured	70	15
175		$1 multicoloured	1·90	2·00
173/5		*Set of* 3	2·75	2·00

56 Black Pepper

1986 (25 Oct). *As Nos.* 202/8 *of Johore but with portrait of Sultan Salahuddin Abdul Aziz Shah as in T* **56**.

No.	Description	Unused	Used
176	1 c. Coffee	10	10
177	2 c. Coconuts	10	10
178	5 c. Cocoa	10	10
179	10 c. Type **56**	10	10
180	15 c. Rubber	10	10
181	20 c. Oil palm	10	10
182	30 c. Rice	10	15
176/82	*Set of* 7	40	45

TRENGGANU

Suzerainty over Trengganu was transferred by Thailand to Great Britain in 1909. A British adviser was appointed in 1919.
The state joined the Federation of Malaya on 1 February 1948.

PRICES FOR STAMPS ON COVER TO 1945

Nos. 1/17	*from* × 12
No. 18	—
Nos. 19/22	*from* × 10
Nos. 23/33	*from* × 12
Nos. 34/6	—
Nos. 37/47	*from* × 15
Nos. 48/60	*from* × 6
Nos. D1/4	*from* × 10

RED CROSS

2c.

1 Sultan Zain ul ab din **2** **(3)**

1910 (14 Dec)–**19**. *Wmk Mult Crown CA. Ordinary paper* (1 *c. to* 10 *c.*) *or chalk-surfaced paper* (20 *c. to* $25). *P* 14.

1 **1** 1 c. blue-green .. 50 1·00
a. Green .. 95 1·00
2 2 c. brown and purple (1915) .. 40 90
3 3 c. carmine-red .. 1·75 1·50
4 4 c. orange .. 3·00 5·00
5 4 c. red-brown and green (1915) .. 2·00 3·75
5*a* 4 c. carmine-red (1919) .. 60 1·75
6 5 c. grey .. 1·25 2·00
7 5 c. grey and brown (1915) .. 2·25 2·00
8 8 c. ultramarine .. 1·25 5·50
9 10 c. purple/*yellow* .. 5·00 8·00
a. On pale yellow .. 3·00 1·75
10 10 c. green and red/*yellow* (1915) .. 1·00 2·25
11 20 c. dull and bright purple .. 2·50 3·25
12 25 c. green and dull purple (1915) .. 5·00 20·00
13 30 c. dull purple and black (1915) .. 6·50 27·00
14 50 c. black/*green* .. 4·50 5·50
15 $1 black and carmine/*blue* .. 9·50 16·00
16 $3 green and red/*green* (1915) .. 70·00 £140
17 **2** $5 green and dull purple (1912) .. 90·00 £275
18 $25 rose-carmine and green (1912) (Optd S. £150) .. £700
1/17 .. *Set of* 18 £180 £450
1/17 Optd "Specimen" .. *Set of* 18 £375

1917 (June)–**18**. *Surch with T* **3**.

19 **1** 2 c. on 3 c. carmine-red .. 30 2·25
a. Comma after "2 c." .. 4·00 15·00
b. "SS" in "CROSS" inverted .. £200 £225
c. "CSOSS for "CROSS" .. 60·00 90·00
d. "2" in thick block type .. 15·00 38·00
e. Surch inverted .. £500 £550
f. Pair, one without surch .. £1400 £1300
g. "RED CROSS" omitted .. £120
h. "RED CROSS" twice .. £200
i. "2 c." omitted .. £120
j. "2 c." twice .. £180
20 2 c. on 4 c. orange .. 70 9·50
a. Comma after "2 c." .. 13·00 45·00
b. "SS" in "CROSS" inverted .. £900 £650
c. "CSOSS" for "CROSS" .. £130 £190
d. Surch double .. £500
e. "RED CROSS" omitted .. £190
f. "RED CROSS" twice .. £325
g. "2 c." omitted .. £190
h. "2 c." twice .. £275
21 2 c. on 4 c. red-brown and green (1918) .. 1·10 20·00
a. Pair, one without surch .. £1200
22 2 c. on 8 c. ultramarine (1917) .. 50 20·00
a. Comma after "2 c." .. 11·00 65·00
b. "SS" in "CROSS" inverted .. £600
c. "CSOSS"" for "CROSS" .. £100 £150
d. "RED CROSS" omitted .. £180
e. "RED CROSS" twice .. £300
f. "2 c." omitted .. £180
g. "2 c." twice .. £250

The surcharges on Nos. 19/22 were arranged in settings of 18 (6×3) applied three times to cover the top nine rows of the sheet with the tenth row completed by a further impression so that "RED CROSS" from the centre row of the setting appears on the bottom sheet margin. Specialists recognise six different settings:

Setting I — Shows comma after "2" on both R.1/3 and 1/5, "SS" inverted on R.1/6 and "CSOSS" for "CROSS" on R.2/1. Used for 4 c. orange and 8 c.
Setting Ia — Inverted "SS" on R.1/6 corrected. Other varieties as Setting I. Used for 3 c., 4 c. orange and 8 c.
Setting II — "CSOSS" on R.2/1 corrected. Comma varieties as Setting I. Used for 3 c., 4 c. orange and 8 c.
Setting III — Both comma varieties now corrected. Used for 3 c., both 4 c. and 8 c.
Setting IIIa — "SS" inverted on R.2/5. Used for 3 c. only
Setting IV — Thick block "2" on R. 2/2. Inverted "SS" on R. 2/5 corrected. Used for 3 c. only.

Nos. 19g/j, 20e/h and 22d/g result from the misplacement of the surcharge.

MINIMUM PRICE

The minimum price quote is 10p which represents a handling charge rather than a basis for valuing common stamps. For further notes about prices see introductory pages.

During a temporary shortage between March and August 1921 2 c., 4 c. and 6 c. stamps of the STRAITS SETTLEMENTS were authorised for use in Trengganu.

2 CENTS

4 Sultan Suleiman **5** **(6)**

1921. *Chalk-surfaced paper. P* 14. (*a*) *Wmk Mult Crown CA.*

23 **4** $1 purple and blue/*blue* .. 11·00 15·00
24 $3 green and red/*emerald* .. 60·00 £120
25 **5** $5 green and red/*pale yellow* .. 65·00 £150

(*b*) *Wmk Mult Script CA*

26 **4** 2 c. green .. 75 30
27 4 c. carmine-red .. 75 10
28 5 c. grey and deep brown .. 2·00 2·50
29 10 c. bright blue .. 2·00 15
30 20 c. dull purple and orange .. 2·00 1·50
31 25 c. green and deep purple .. 2·25 2·00
32 30 c. dull purple and black .. 3·25 1·00
33 50 c. green and bright carmine .. 4·50 1·00
34 **5** $25 purple and blue (S. £70) .. £450 £600
35 $50 green and yellow (S. £150) .. £1000 £1400
36 $100 green and scarlet (S. £300) .. £3500
23/33 .. *Set of* 11 £130 £250
23/33 Optd "Specimen" .. *Set of* 11 £250

1922 (31 Mar). *Optd* "MALAYA–BORNEO EXHIBITION" *as T* **56** *of Straits Settlements at Singapore.*

37 **4** 2 c. green .. 75 24·00
38 4 c. carmine-red .. 3·50 24·00
39 **1** 5 c. grey and brown .. 2·50 25·00
40 10 c. green and red/*yellow* .. 2·50 30·00
41 20 c. dull and bright purple .. 2·00 35·00
42 25 c. green and dull purple .. 2·00 35·00
43 30 c. dull purple and black .. 2·25 35·00
44 50 c. black/*green* .. 2·50 35·00
45 $1 black and carmine/*blue* .. 10·00 65·00
46 $3 green and red/*green* .. £110 £350
47 **2** $5 green and dull purple .. £190 £600
37/47 .. *Set of* 11 £300 £1100

Minor varieties of this overprint exist as in Straits Settlements.

1924–38. *New values, etc. Wmk Mult Script CA. Chalk-surfaced paper. P* 14.

48 **4** 1 c. black (1926) .. 50 45
49 3 c. green (1926) .. 65 75
50 3 c. brown (1938) .. 10·00 4·75
51 5 c. purple/*yellow* (1926) .. 1·25 55
52 6 c. orange .. 2·25 30
53 8 c. grey (1938) .. 10·00 90
54 12 c. bright ultramarine (1926) .. 3·50 3·25
55 35 c. carmine/*yellow* (1926) .. 3·50 8·00
56 $1 purple and blue/*blue* (1929) .. 9·00 3·50
57 $3 green and red/*green* (1926) .. 30·00 65·00
58 **5** $5 green and red/*yellow* (1938) .. £200 £750
48/58 .. *Set of* 11 £225 £750
48/58 Optd/Perf "Specimen" .. *Set of* 11 £300

The 2 c. yellow, 6 c. grey, 8 c. red and 15 c. blue were prepared, but not officially issued.

1941 (1 May). *Nos.* 51 *and* 29 *surch as T* **6**.

59 **4** 2 c. on 5 c. purple/*yellow* .. 6·00 4·50
60 8 c. on 10 c. bright blue .. 7·00 4·50

1948 (2 Dec). *Royal Silver Wedding. As Nos.* 143/4 *of Jamaica.*

61 10 c. violet .. 15 25
62 $5 carmine .. 20·00 30·00

1949 (10 Oct). *75th Anniv of U.P.U. As Nos.* 145/8 *of Jamaica.*

63 10 c. purple .. 20 35
64 15 c. deep blue .. 55 1·60
65 25 c. orange .. 55 2·25
66 50 c. blue-black .. 90 2·50
63/6 .. *Set of* 4 2·00 6·00

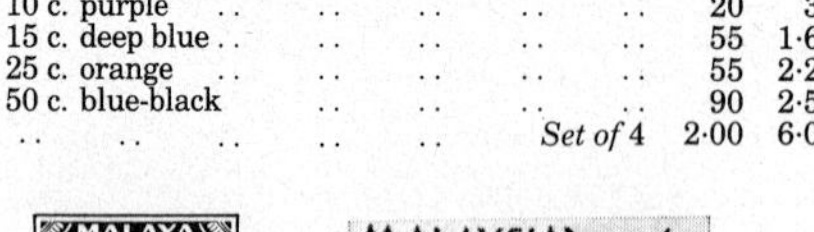

7 Sultan Ismail **8** *Vanda hookeriana*

1949 (27 Dec)–**55**. *Wmk Mult Script CA. Chalk-surfaced paper. P* 17½×18.

67 **7** 1 c. black .. 10 20
68 2 c. orange .. 10 20
69 3 c. green .. 20 80
70 4 c. brown .. 10 15
71 5 c. bright purple (1.9.52) .. 30 50
72 6 c. grey .. 15 15
73 8 c. scarlet .. 20 1·25
74 8 c. green (1.9.52) .. 65 1·00
a. Deep green (11.8.53) .. 1·25 2·50
75 10 c. purple .. 15 10
76 12 c. scarlet (1.9.52) .. 65 1·75
77 15 c. ultramarine .. 30 25
78 20 c. black and green .. 30 1·25
79 20 c. bright blue (1.9.52) .. 80 25
80 25 c. purple and orange .. 30 55
81 30 c. scarlet and purple (5.9.55) .. 1·25 1·25
82 35 c. scarlet and purple (1.9.52) .. 70 1·00
83 **7** 40 c. red and purple .. 1·00 7·00
84 50 c. black and blue .. 40 60
85 $1 blue and purple .. 2·00 2·75
86 $2 green and scarlet .. 9·50 13·00
87 $5 green and brown .. 38·00 38·00
67/87 .. *Set of* 21 50·00 65·00

1953 (2 June). *Coronation. As No.* 153 *of Jamaica.*

88 10 c. black and reddish purple .. 30 30

1957 (26 June)–**63.** *As Nos.* 92/102 *of Kedah, but with inset portrait of Sultan Ismail.*

89 1 c. black (21.8.57) .. 10 20
90 2 c. orange-red (25.7.57) .. 40 30
a. Red-orange (21.2.61) .. 5·50 7·00
91 4 c. sepia (21.8.57) .. 10 10
92 5 c. carmine-lake (21.8.57) .. 10 10
93 8 c. myrtle-green (21.8.57) .. 3·25 60
94 10 c. deep brown (4.8.57) .. 15 10
94*a* 10 c. deep maroon (21.2.61) .. 1·50 10
95 20 c. blue .. 20 30
96 50 c. black and blue (*p* 12½) (25.7.57) .. 30 70
a. Perf 12½ × 13 (17.5.60) .. 30 60
ab. Black and ultramarine (20.3.62) .. 60 60
97 $1 ultramarine and reddish purple (25.7.57) 3·00 3·00
98 $2 bronze-green and scarlet (21.8.57) .. 5·00 6·00
99 $5 brown and bronze-green .. 7·00 8·00
a. Perf 13 × 12½ (13.8.63) .. 10·00 9·00
89/99 .. *Set of* 12 19·00 17·00

The 6, 12, 25 and 30 c. values used with this issue were Nos. 1/4 of Malayan Federation.

1965 (15 Nov). *As Nos.* 166/72 *of Johore but with inset portrait of Sultan Ismail Nasiruddin Shah as in T* **8**.

100 1 c. multicoloured .. 10 30
101 2 c. multicoloured .. 10 30
102 5 c. multicoloured .. 10 10
103 6 c. multicoloured .. 15 30
104 10 c. multicoloured .. 20 10
105 15 c. multicoloured .. 85 10
106 20 c. multicoloured .. 1·25 30
a. Bright purple (blooms) omitted .. 30·00
100/6 .. *Set of* 7 2·40 1·25

The 5 c. value exists with PVA gum as well as gum arabic.
No. 101a, formerly listed here, is now listed as Sarawak No. 213a.
The higher values used with this issue were Nos. 20/27 of Malaysia (National Issues).

9 Sultan of Trengganu **10** *Papilio demoleus*

(Des Enche Nik Zainal Abidin. Photo Harrison)

1970 (16 Dec). *25th Anniv of Installation of H.R.H. Tuanku Ismail Nasiruddin Shah as Sultan of Trengganu. P* 14½ × 13½.

107 **9** 10 c. multicoloured .. 25 50
108 15 c. multicoloured .. 30 60
109 50 c. multicoloured .. 65 1·60
107/9 .. *Set of* 3 1·10 2·40

1971 (1 Feb)–**78.** *As Nos.* 175/87 *of Johore but with portrait of Sultan Ismail Nasiruddin Shah and Arms, as in T* **10**.

(*a*) *Litho by Bradbury, Wilkinson*

110 1 c. multicoloured .. 15 60
111 2 c. multicoloured .. 30 60
112 5 c. multicoloured .. 40 10
113 6 c. multicoloured .. 40 30
114 10 c. multicoloured .. 40 10
115 15 c. multicoloured .. 55 10
116 20 c. multicoloured .. 75 40
110/16 .. *Set of* 7 2·75 1·90

(*b*) *Photo by Harrison* (1977–78)

116*a* 5 c. multicoloured .. 11·00 3·50
117 10 c. multicoloured .. 2·50 1·00
117*a* 15 c. multicoloured .. 3·50 1·00

The higher values used with this issue were Nos. 64/71 of Malaysia (National Issues).
For differences between litho and photo printings, see after Johore No. 187.

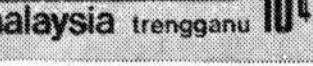

11 *Durio zibethinus* **12** Sultan Mahmud

1979 (30 Apr). *As Nos.* 188/94 *of Johore but with portrait of Sultan Ismail Nasiruddin Shah as in T* **11**.

118 1 c. *Rafflesia hasseltii* .. 10 30
119 2 c. *Pterocarpus indicus* .. 10 30
120 5 c. *Lagerstroemia speciosa* .. 10 10
121 10 c. Type **11** .. 10 10
122 15 c. *Hibiscus rosa-sinensis* .. 15 10
123 20 c. *Rhododendron scortechinii* .. 15 10
124 25 c. *Etlingera elatior* (inscr "*Phaeomeria speciosa*") .. 15 10
118/24 .. *Set of* 7 65 80

For higher values used in conjunction with this series see Nos. 190/7 of Malaysia (National Issues).

(Des Malaysian Advertising Services. Litho Harrison)

1981 (21 Mar). *Installation of Sultan Mahmud. P* 14.

125	**12**	10 c. black, gold and new blue	15	40
126		15 c. black, gold and yellow	20	30
127		50 c. black, gold and bright purple	50	1·50
125/7		*Set of* 3	75	2·00

1983 (Oct)–**86**.* *As Nos.* 121/4 *but without wmk.*

131	10 c. Type **11** (5.2.86)	11·00	3·00
132	15 c. *Hibiscus rosa-sinensis* (24.1.85)	2·25	1·00
133	20 c. *Rhododendron scortechinii* (blackish brown background)	13·00	4·50
133*a*	20 c. *Rhododendron scortechinii* (bronze-green background) (2.3.84)	4·25	3·00
134	25 c. *Etlingera elatior* (inscr "*Phaeomeria speciosa*") (13.11.83)	30	15

*There was no official release date for these stamps. Dates shown are the earliest recorded from postmarks and may be revised if earlier examples are reported.

For details of the shade differences between watermarked and unwatermarked printings see after Johore No. 200*a*.

On Nos. 131/2, 133*a* and 134 the portrait and state arms have been redrawn smaller.

13 Rubber

1986 (25 Oct). *As Nos.* 202/8 *of Johore but with portrait of Sultan Mahmud and inscr* "TERENGGANU" *as in T* **13**.

135	1 c. Coffee	10	10
136	2 c. Coconuts	10	10
137	5 c. Cocoa	10	10
138	10 c. Black pepper	10	10
139	15 c. Type **13**	10	10
140	20 c. Oil palm	10	10
141	30 c. Rice	10	15
135/41	*Set of* 7	40	45

POSTAGE DUE STAMPS

D 1

1937 (10 Aug). *Wmk Mult Script CA. P* 14.

D1	D 1	1 c. scarlet	6·50	50·00
D2		4 c. green	6·50	50·00
D3		8 c. yellow	48·00	£250
D4		10 c. brown	80·00	90·00
D1/4		*Set of* 4	£130	£400
D1/4 Perf "Specimen"		*Set of* 4	£130	

VIII. JAPANESE OCCUPATION OF MALAYA

PRICES FOR STAMPS ON COVER

Nos. J1/55	*from* × 10
Nos. J56/76	*from* × 12
Nos. J77/89	*from* × 20
Nos. J90/1	*from* × 15
Nos. J92/115	*from* × 6
Nos. J116/18	—
Nos. J119/32	*from* × 12
Nos. J133/45	*from* × 10
Nos. J146/223	*from* × 6
Nos. J224/58	*from* × 12
No. J259	*from* × 15
Nos. J260/96	*from* × 12
Nos. J297/310	*from* × 20
Nos. J311/17	—
Nos. JD1/10	*from* × 30
Nos. JD11/16	*from* × 12
Nos. JD17/20	*from* × 30
Nos. JD21/7	*from* × 20
Nos. JD28/33	*from* × 12
Nos. JD34/41	*from* × 30

Japanese forces invaded Malaya on 8 December 1941 with the initial landings taking place at Kota Bharu on the east coast. Penang fell, to a force which crossed the border from Thailand, on 20 December, Kuala Lumpur on 11 January 1942 and the conquest of the Malay penisula was completed by the capture of Singapore on 15 February.

The Japanese authorities issued instructions to their State Governors to recommence postal services on 1 April 1942, if they had not already done so. A number of the States produced their own provisional issues before the use of the stamps intended to be used throughout Malaya became general.

In addition to those listed some other stamps can be found overprinted with Types **2** or **4**. These additional values were overprinted by favour and, although valid for postal purposes, were never available to the public from post offices.

Collectors are warned against forgeries, particularly of the scarcer overprints.

JOHORE

The postal service in Johore was reconstituted at the end of April 1942 using Nos. J146/60 and subsequently other general issues. Stamps of Johore overprinted "DAI NIPPON 2602" were, however, only used for fiscal purposes. Overprinted Johore postage due stamps were not issued for use elsewhere in Malaya.

POSTAGE DUE STAMPS

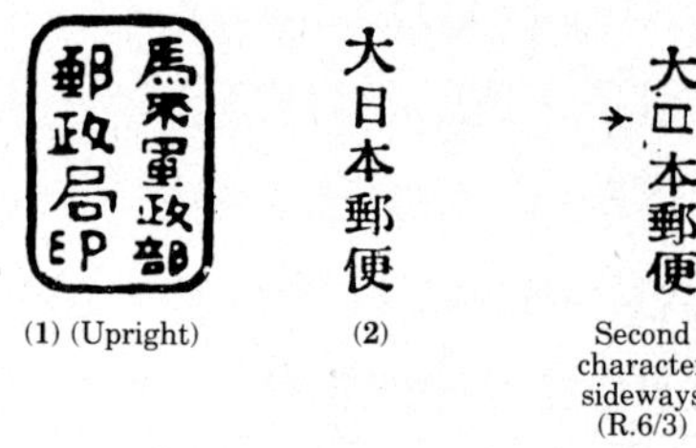

(**1**) (Upright) (**2**) Second character sideways (R.6/3)

1942 (Apr). *Nos.* D1/5 *of Johore optd as T* **1**. A. *In red*. B. *In black*.

			A		B	
JD1	D 1	1 c. carmine	60·00	—	45·00	—
JD2		4 c. green	60·00	—	55·00	—
JD3		8 c. orange	75·00	—	48·00	—
JD4		10 c. brown	26·00	—	15·00	—
JD5		12 c. purple	32·00	—	24·00	—

1943. *Nos.* D1/5 *of Johore optd with T* **2**.

JD 6	D 1	1 c. carmine	1·75	8·00
		a. Second character sideways	65·00	£110
JD 7		4 c. green	1·75	8·00
		a. Second character sideways	65·00	£110
JD 8		8 c. orange	3·50	10·00
		a. Second character sideways	90·00	£160
JD 9		10 c. brown	3·00	14·00
		a. Second character sideways	90·00	£160
JD10		12 c. purple	4·00	18·00
		a. Second character sideways	90·00	£160

KEDAH

Postal services resumed in February 1942 using unoverprinted Kedah values from 1 c. to 8 c.

During the Japanese occupation Perlis was administered as part of Kedah.

DAI NIPPON

2602

(**3**)

DAI NIPPON

2602

(**4**)

1942 (13 May)–**43**. *Stamps of Kedah (Script wmk) optd with T* **3** (1 *c. to* 8 *c.*) *or* **4** (10 *c. to* $5), *both in red*.

J 1	1	1 c. black	1·75	3·50
J 2		2 c. bright green	23·00	30·00
J 3		4 c. violet	2·75	4·00
J 4		5 c. yellow	1·50	3·25
		a. Black opt (1943)	£200	£200
J 5	1	6 c. carmine-red (Blk.)	1·50	4·75
J 6		8 c. grey-black	2·25	1·75
J 7	6	10 c. ultramarine and sepia	5·50	6·50
J 8		12 c. black and violet	10·00	17·00
J 9		25 c. ultramarine and purple	4·00	8·00
		a. Black opt (1943)	£180	£200
J10		30 c. green and scarlet	55·00	65·00
J11		40 c. black and purple	14·00	24·00
J12		50 c. brown and blue	16·00	27·00
J13		$1 black and green	£130	£150
		a. Opt inverted	£425	£450
J14		$2 green and brown	£120	£140
J15		$5 black and scarlet	45·00	55·00
		a. Black opt (1943)	£425	£450

Nos. J1/15 were gradually replaced by issues intended for use throughout Malaya. Kedah and Perlis were ceded to Thailand by the Japanese on 19 October 1943.

KELANTAN

Postal services resumed in mid-June 1942. Stamps used in Kelantan were overprinted with the personal seals of Sunagawa, the Japanese Governor, and of Handa, the Assistant Governor.

(**5**) Sunagawa Seal

(**6**) Handa Seal

(**7**) (**8**)

1 Cents

(**9**)

1942 (June). *Stamps of Kelantan surch*

(*a*) *As T* **7** *or* **8** (*dollar values*). *Optd with T* **5** *in red*

J16	4	1 c. on 50 c. grey-olive and orange	£120	£130
J17		2 c. on 40 c. orange and blue-green	£150	£160
J18		4 c. on 30 c. violet and scarlet	£750	£800
J19		5 c. on 12 c. blue (R.)	£120	£130
J20		6 c. on 25 c. vermilion and violet	£110	£130
J21		8 c. on 5 c. red-brown (R.)	£130	£130
J22		10 c. on 6 c. lake	70·00	80·00
J23		12 c. on 8 c. grey-olive (R.)	45·00	65·00
J24		25 c. on 10 c. purple (R.)	£800	£850
J25		30 c. on 4 c. scarlet	£1200	£1300
J26		40 c. on 2 c. green (R.)	48·00	60·00
J27		50 c. on 1 c. grey-olive and yellow	£750	£800
J28	1	$1 on 4 c. black & red (R., bars Blk.)	45·00	60·00
J29		$2 on 5 c. green and red/*yellow*	45·00	60·00
J30		$5 on 6 c. scarlet	45·00	60·00

(*b*) *As T* **7**. *Optd with T* **6** *in red*.

J31	4	12 c. on 8 c. grey-olive	95·00	£110

(*c*) *As T* **9**. *Optd with T* **5** *in red*.

J32	4	1 c. on 50 c. grey-olive and orange	65·00	65·00
		a. "Cente" for "Cents" (R. 5/1)	£450	
J33		2 c. on 40 c. orange and blue-green	65·00	70·00
		a. "Cente" for "Cents" (R. 5/1)	£450	
J34		5 c. on 12 c. blue (R.)	50·00	55·00
		a. "Cente" for "Cents" (R. 5/1)	£375	
J35		8 c. on 5 c. red-brown (R.)	50·00	55·00
		a. "Cente" for "Cents" (R. 5/1)	£375	
J36		10 c. on 6 c. lake	50·00	60·00
		a. "Cente" for "Cents" (R. 5/1)	£375	
J37		12 c. on 8 c. grey-olive (R.)	70·00	80·00
		a. "Cente" for "Cents" (R. 5/1)	£475	
J38		30 c. on 4 c. scarlet	£800	£850
		a. "Cente" for "Cents" (R. 5/1)		
J39		40 c. on 2 c. green (R.)	80·00	90·00
		a. "Cente" for "Cents" (R. 5/1)	£550	
J40		50 c. on 1 c. grey-olive and yellow	£375	£400
		a. "Cente" for "Cents" (R. 5/1)		

(*d*) *As T* **9**. *Optd with T* **6** *in red*.

J41	4	1 c. on 50 c. grey-olive and orange	75·00	85·00
		a. "Cente" for "Cents" (R. 5/1)	£500	
J42		2 c. on 40 c. orange and blue-green	70·00	90·00
		a. "Cente" for "Cents" (R. 5/1)	£475	
J43		8 c. on 5 c. red-brown (R.)	60·00	80·00
		a. "Cente" for "Cents" (R. 5/1)	£450	
J44		10 c. on 6 c. lake	75·00	90·00
		a. "Cente" for "Cents" (R. 5/1)	£500	

As stamps of the above series became exhausted the equivalent values from the series intended for use throughout Malaya were introduced. Stamps as Nos. J28/30, J32/3 and J36/40, but without Type **5** or **6**, are from remainders sent to Singapore or Kuala Lumpur after the state had been ceded to Thailand (*Price from £12 each unused*).

Kelantan was ceded to Thailand by the Japanese on 19 October 1943.

MALACCA

Postal services from Malacca resumed on 21 April 1942, but there were no stamps available for two days.

PRICES. Those quoted are for single stamps. Blocks of four showing the complete handstamp are worth from six times the price of a single stamp.

(**10**) Seal of the Government Office of the Malacca Military Dept

1942 (23 Apr). *Stamps of Straits Settlememts handstamped as T* **10**, *in red, each impression covering four stamps.*

			Single Un.	Used
J45	58	1 c. black	60·00	55·00
J46		2 c. orange	55·00	55·00
J47		3 c. green	55·00	55·00
J48		5 c. brown	85·00	90·00
J49		8 c. grey	£100	90·00
J50		10 c. dull purple	65·00	60·00
J51		12 c. ultramarine	80·00	80·00
J52		15 c. ultramarine	60·00	60·00
J53		40 c. scarlet and dull purple	£450	£450
J54		50 c. black/*emerald*	£650	£650
J55		$1 black and red/*blue*	£700	£700

The 30c., $2 and $5 also exist with this overprint, but these values were not available to the public.

POSTAGE DUE STAMPS

1942 (23 Apr). *Postage Due stamps of Malayan Postal Union handstamped as T* **10**, *in red, each impression covering four stamps.*

JD11	D 1	1 c. slate-purple	£130	£130
JD12		4 c. green	£190	£190
JD13		8 c. scarlet	£1000	£1000
JD14		10 c. yellow-orange	£200	£200
JD15		12 c. ultramarine	£250	£275
JD16		50 c. black	£1000	£1000

Nos. J45/55 and JD11/16 were replaced during May 1942 by the overprinted issues intended for use throughout Malaya.

PENANG

Postal services on Penang Island resumed on 30 March 1942 using Straits Settlements stamps overprinted by Japanese seals.

(**11**) Okugawa Seal

(**12**) Ochiburi Seal

DAI NIPPON

2602

PENANG

(**13**)

1942 (30 Mar). *Straits Settlements stamps optd.*

(*a*) *As T* **11** (*three forms of the seal*)

J56	58	1 c. black	6·50	8·00
J57		2 c. orange	18·00	16·00
J58		3 c. green	14·00	16·00
J59		5 c. brown	18·00	18·00
J60		8 c. grey	20·00	20·00
J61		10 c. dull purple	30·00	30·00
J62		12 c. ultramarine	18·00	22·00
J63		15 c. ultramarine	19·00	24·00
J64		40 c. scarlet and dull purple	65·00	70·00
J65		50 c. black/*emerald*	95·00	£100
J66		$1 black and red/*blue*	£160	£170
J67		$2 green and scarlet	£300	£325
J68		$5 green and red/*emerald*	£800	£900

(*b*) *With T* **12**

J69	58	1 c. black	32·00	42·00
J70		2 c. orange	32·00	42·00
J71		3 c. green	32·00	42·00
J72		5 c. brown	£425	£425
J73		8 c. grey	28·00	32·00
J74		10 c. dull purple	28·00	32·00
J75		12 c. ultramarine	28·00	32·00
J76		15 c. ultramarine	28·00	32·00

Straits Settlements stamps overprinted with a similar seal impression, but circular and containing four characters, are believed to be fiscal issues.

1942 (15 Apr). *Straits Settlements stamps optd with T* **13**.

J77	58	1 c. black (R.)	1·00	1·00
		a. Opt inverted	£110	£110
J78		2 c. orange	3·50	2·75
		a. "PE" for "PENANG"	55·00	60·00
		b. Opt inverted	£120	
		c. Opt double		
J79		3 c. green (R.)	1·40	1·75
J80		5 c. brown (R.)	1·00	2·00
		a. "N PPON"	90·00	
		b. Opt double	£130	
J81		8 c. grey (R.)	2·25	1·40
		a. "N PPON"	38·00	45·00
		b. Opt double, one inverted	£140	
J82		10 c. dull purple (R.)	1·50	2·00
		a. Opt double	£180	
		b. Opt double, one inverted	£325	
J83		12 c. ultramarine (R.)	2·00	4·50
		a. "N PPON"	£200	
		b. Opt double	£200	
		c. Opt double, one inverted	£300	£325

J84 58 15 c. ultramarine (R.) 1·75 2·00
a. "N PPON" 90·00 95·00
b. Opt inverted £275 £275
c. Opt double £275
J85 40 c. scarlet and dull purple 2·50 5·50
J86 50 c. black/*emerald* (R.) 3·50 10·00
J87 $1 black and red/*blue* 6·00 15·00
J88 $2 green and scarlet 22·00 45·00
J89 $5 green and red/*emerald* £300 £400

Nos. J77/89 were replaced by the overprinted issues intended for use throughout Malaya.

SELANGOR

Postal services resumed in the Kuala Lumpur area on 3 April 1942 and gradually extended to the remainder of the state. Stamps of the general overprinted issue were used, but the following commemorative set was only available in Selangor.

SELANGOR
EXHIBITION
DAI NIPPON
2602
MALAYA

(14)

1942 (3 Nov). *Agri-horticultural Exhibition. Nos.* 294 *and* 283 *of Straits Settlements optd with T* **14**.

J90 58 2 c. orange 12·00 18·00
a. "C" for "G" in "SELANGOR" (R.1/2) £180 £225
b. Opt inverted £300 £375
J91 8 c. grey 11·00 17·00
a. "C" for "G" in "SELANGOR" (R.1/2) £180 £225
b. Opt inverted £300 £375

SINGAPORE

The first post offices re-opened in Singapore on 16 March 1942.

(**15**) Seal of Post Office of Malayan Military Dept

(Handstamped at Singapore)

1942 (16 Mar). *Stamps of Straits Settlements optd with T* **15** *in red*.

J92 58 1 c. black 8·50 13·00
J93 2 c. orange 9·50 13·00
J94 3 c. green 42·00 60·00
J95 8 c. grey 15·00 17·00
J96 15 c. ultramarine 13·00 15·00

The overprint Type **15** has a double-lined frame, although the two lines are not always apparent, as in the illustration. Three chops were used, differing slightly in the shape of the characters, but forgeries also exist. It is distinguishable from Type **1**, used for the general issues, by its extra width, measuring approximately 14 mm against 12½ mm.

The 6, 10, 30, 40, 50 c., $2 and $5 also exist with this overprint, but were not sold to the public.

Nos. J92/6 were replaced on the 3 May 1942 by the stamps overprinted with Type **1** which were intended for use throughout Malaya.

TRENGGANU

Postal services resumed in Trengganu during April 1942 using unoverprinted stamps up to the 20 c. value.

1942 (Sept). *Stamps of Trengganu (Script wmk) optd as T* **1** *at Kuala Lumpur*.

J 97 4 1 c. black 90·00 85·00
a. Red opt £130 £140
b. Brown opt £200 £180
J 98 2 c. green £130 £140
a. Red opt £150 £160
b. Brown opt £200 £200
J 99 2 c. on 5 c. purple/*yellow* (No. 59) 70·00 70·00
a. Red opt 45·00 55·00
J100 3 c. brown 80·00 80·00
a. Brown opt £250 £250
J101 4 c. carmine-red £140 £130
J102 5 c. purple/*yellow* 7·50 12·00
a. Red opt 15·00
J103 6 c. orange 6·50 16·00
a. Red opt 22·00
b. Brown opt £110 £110
J104 8 c. grey 8·00 12·00
a. Brown to red opt 30·00
J105 8 c. on 10 c. bright blue (No. 60) 12·00 20·00
a. Red opt 21·00
J106 10 c. bright blue 8·00 16·00
a. Red opt 30·00
b. Brown opt £120 £120
J107 12 c. bright ultramarine 7·00 15·00
a. Red opt 26·00
J108 20 c. dull purple and orange 8·00 16·00
a. Red opt 16·00
J109 4 25 c. green and deep purple 7·00 16·00
a. Red opt 20·00
b. Brown opt £100 £100
J110 30 c. dull purple and black 7·00 16·00
a. Red opt 17·00
J111 35 c. carmine/*yellow* 11·00 17·00
a. Red opt 17·00
J112 50 c. green and bright carmine 50·00 60·00
J113 $1 purple and blue/*blue* £1100 £1100
J114 $3 green and red/*green* 42·00 65·00
a. Red opt 50·00
J115 5 $5 green and red/*yellow* £110 £160
J116 $25 purple and blue £650
a. Red opt £1500
J117 $50 green and yellow £3500
J118 $100 green and scarlet £750

DAI NIPPON
2602
MALAYA

(16)

1942 (Sept). *Stamps of Trengganu (Script wmk) optd with T* **16**.

J119 4 1 c. black 6·00 8·00
J120 2 c. green £130 £180
J121 2 c. on 5 c. purple/*yellow* (No. 59) 5·50 7·00
J122 3 c. brown 8·50 13·00
J123 4 c. carmine-red 6·50 9·50
J124 5 c. purple/*yellow* 4·75 7·50
J125 6 c. orange 4·25 9·50
J126 8 c. grey 55·00 16·00
J127 8 c. on 10 c. bright blue (No. 60) 5·00 9·00
J128 12 c. bright ultramarine 4·25 10·00
J129 20 c. dull purple and orange 6·50 12·00
J130 25 c. green and deep purple 7·00 15·00
J131 30 c. dull purple and black 7·00 15·00
J132 $3 green and red/*green* 48·00 90·00

1943. *Stamps of Trengganu (Script wmk) optd with T* **2**.

J133 4 1 c. black 5·50 14·00
J134 2 c. green 6·00 17·00
J135 2 c. on 5 c. purple/*yellow* (No. 59) 4·75 17·00
J136 5 c. purple/*yellow* 4·75 17·00
J137 6 c. orange 6·50 20·00
J138 8 c. grey 40·00 45·00
J139 8 c. on 10 c. bright blue (No. 60) 13·00 32·00
J140 10 c. bright blue 70·00 £110
J141 12 c. bright ultramarine 8·50 26·00
J142 20 c. dull purple and orange 9·00 26·00
J143 25 c. green and deep purple 8·50 30·00
J144 30 c. dull purple and black 8·50 30·00
J145 35 c. carmine/*yellow* 8·50 30·00

POSTAGE DUE STAMPS

1942 (Sept). *Nos.* D1/4 *of Trengganu optd with T* **1** *sideways*.

JD17 D 1 1 c. scarlet 45·00 70·00
JD18 4 c. green 50·00 65·00
a. Red opt 45·00 65·00
JD19 8 c. yellow 14·00 38·00
JD20 10 c. brown 14·00 38·00

The Trengganu 8 c. postage due also exists overprinted with Type **16**, but this was not issued (*Price £225 unused*).

Trengganu was ceded to Thailand by the Japanese on 19 October 1943.

GENERAL ISSUES

The following stamps were produced for use throughout Malaya, except for Trengganu.

1942 (3 Apr). *Stamps optd as T* **1**. (*a*) *On Straits Settlements*.

J146 58 1 c. black (R.) 3·00 3·25
a. Black opt £130 £150
b. Violet opt £160 £160
J147 2 c. green (V.) £900 £900
J148 2 c. orange (R.) 2·50 2·25
a. Black opt 55·00 60·00
b. Violet opt 60·00 55·00
c. Brown opt £180 £200
J149 3 c. green (R.) 2·50 2·25
a. Black opt £140 £150
b. Violet opt £160 £170
J150 5 c. brown (R.) 16·00 18·00
a. Black opt £170 £170
J151 8 c. grey (R.) 2·75 2·25
a. Black opt £150 £170
J152 10 c. dull purple (R.) 28·00 30·00
a. Brown opt £300 £300
J153 12 c. ultramarine (R.) 65·00 80·00
J154 15 c. ultramarine (R.) 3·50 2·75
a. Violet opt £200 £225
J155 30 c. dull purple and orange (R.) £750 £800
J156 40 c. scarlet and dull purple (R.) 65·00 80·00
a. Brown opt £180 £180
J157 50 c. black/*emerald* (R.) 40·00 40·00
J158 $1 black and red/*blue* (R.) 70·00 75·00
J159 $2 green and scarlet (R.) £120 £130
J160 $5 green and red/*emerald* (R.) £150 £160

(*b*) *On Negri Sembilan*

J161 6 1 c. black (R.) 16·00 13·00
a. Violet opt 18·00 18·00
b. Brown opt 14·00 14·00
c. Black opt 23·00 28·00
J162 2 c. orange (R.) 10·00 12·00
a. Violet opt 30·00 26·00
b. Black opt 28·00 28·00
c. Brown opt 30·00 35·00
J163 3 c. green (R.) 14·00 18·00
a. Violet opt 23·00 29·00
b. Violet opt (sideways) £140 £140
c. Brown opt 35·00 38·00
J164 6 5 c. brown 17·00 20·00
a. Brown opt 15·00 14·00
b. Red opt 12·00 11·00
c. Violet opt 30·00 30·00
J165 6 c. grey £120 £120
a. Brown opt £325 £325
J166 8 c. scarlet 25·00 35·00
J167 10 c. dull purple 48·00 55·00
a. Red opt 40·00 45·00
b. Brown opt £110 £110
J168 12 c. bright ultramarine (Br.) £550 £550
J169 15 c. ultramarine (R.) 14·00 8·00
a. Violet opt 28·00 28·00
J170 25 c. dull purple and scarlet 25·00 30·00
a. Red opt 60·00 70·00
b. Brown opt £140 £150
J171 30 c. dull purple and orange £110 £120
a. Brown opt £375 £375
J172 40 c. scarlet and dull purple £475 £475
a. Brown opt £650 £650
J173 50 c. black/*emerald* £140 £150
J174 $1 black and red/*blue* 85·00 95·00
a. Red opt £110 £120
b. Brown opt £325 £325
J175 $5 green and red/*emerald* £325 £350
a. Red opt £375 £400

(*c*) *On Pahang*

J176 15 1 c. black 24·00 28·00
a. Red opt 24·00 28·00
b. Violet opt £120 £130
c. Brown opt 95·00 95·00
J177 3 c. green 65·00 70·00
a. Red opt £225 £275
b. Violet opt £375 £375
J178 5 c. brown 8·50 6·00
a. Red opt 70·00 75·00
b. Brown opt £100 95·00
c. Violet opt £200 £200
J179 8 c. grey £110 £110
J180 8 c. scarlet 16·00 10·00
a. Red opt 55·00 55·00
b. Violet opt 55·00 60·00
c. Brown opt 65·00 70·00
J181 10 c. dull purple 32·00 38·00
a. Red opt 50·00 55·00
b. Brown opt £140 £150
J182 12 c. bright ultramarine £950 £1000
a. Red opt £1100 £1100
J183 15 c. ultramarine 48·00 48·00
a. Red opt 70·00 70·00
b. Violet opt £325 £325
c. Brown opt £160 £180
J184 25 c. dull purple and scarlet 17·00 27·00
J185 30 c. dull purple and orange 12·00 23·00
a. Red opt £140 £170
J186 40 c. scarlet and dull purple 15·00 25·00
a. Brown opt £120 £130
b. Red opt 30·00 32·00
J187 50 c. black/*emerald* £160 £180
a. Red opt £275 £300
J188 $1 black and red/*blue* (R.) 75·00 85·00
a. Black opt £140 £140
b. Brown opt £425 £425
J189 $5 green and red/*emerald* £550 £600
a. Red opt £700 £750

(*d*) *On Perak*

J190 51 1 c. black 26·00 26·00
a. Violet opt 55·00 60·00
b. Brown opt 70·00 70·00
J191 2 c. orange 17·00 17·00
a. Violet opt 55·00 60·00
b. Red opt 24·00 23·00
c. Brown opt 48·00 48·00
J192 3 c. green 22·00 25·00
a. Violet opt £130 £140
b. Brown opt £110 £120
c. Red opt £110 £120
J193 5 c. brown 5·50 5·50
a. Brown opt 19·00 19·00
b. Violet opt 80·00 90·00
c. Red opt 80·00 90·00
J194 8 c. grey 26·00 26·00
a. Red opt £150 £160
b. Brown opt £140 £150
J195 8 c. scarlet 13·00 32·00
a. Violet opt £150
J196 10 c. dull purple 12·00 20·00
a. Red opt 80·00 85·00
J197 12 c. bright ultramarine 85·00 95·00
J198 15 c. ultramarine 14·00 21·00
a. Red opt 48·00 48·00
b. Violet opt £100 £100
c. Brown opt 95·00 £100
J199 25 c. dull purple and scarlet 13·00 20·00
J200 30 c. dull purple and orange 17·00 32·00
a. Brown opt £100 £110
b. Red opt 32·00 45·00
J201 40 c. scarlet and dull purple £150 £160
a. Brown opt £300 £300
J202 50 c. black/*emerald* 26·00 38·00
a. Red opt 32·00 45·00
b. Brown opt £100 £100
J203 $1 black and red/*blue* £200 £225
a. Brown opt £700
J204 $2 green and scarlet £1200 £1200
J205 $5 green and red/*emerald* £425
a. Brown opt £850

(*e*) *On Selangor*

J206 46 1 c. black, S 9·00 12·00
a. Red opt, SU 13·00 18·00
b. Violet opt, SU 25·00 32·00
J207 2 c. green, U £400 £450
a. Violet opt, U £550 £600
J208 2 c. orange (*p* 14 × 15), S 35·00 40·00
a. Red opt, U 75·00 80·00
b. Violet opt, U £110 90·00
c. Brown opt, S 35·00 40·00
J209 2 c. orange (*p* 14), S 40·00 45·00
a. Red opt, U 85·00 85·00
b. Violet opt, U £180 £180

J210 46 3 c. green, SU 13·00 14·00
a. Red opt, SU 14·00 15·00
b. Violet opt, SU 48·00 48·00
c. Brown opt, SU 15·00 15·00
J211 5 c. brown, S 4·50 4·50
a. Red opt, S 10·00 13·00
b. Violet opt, SU 21·00 23·00
c. Brown opt, SU 42·00 42·00
J212 6 c. scarlet, S £150 £150
a. Red opt, S £180 £180
b. Brown opt, S £275
J213 8 c. grey, S 14·00 15·00
a. Red opt, SU 23·00 23·00
b. Violet opt, U 28·00 30·00
c. Brown opt, S 42·00 29·00
J214 10 c. dull purple, S 9·50 18·00
a. Red opt, S 32·00 32·00
b. Brown opt, S 32·00 25·00
J215 12 c. bright ultramarine, S 28·00 26·00
a. Red opt, S 65·00 65·00
b. Brown opt, S 70·00 70·00
J216 15 c. ultramarine, S 13·00 16·00
a. Red opt, SU 32·00 32·00
b. Violet opt, U 95·00 85·00
c. Brown opt, S 30·00 30·00
J217 25 c. dull purple and scarlet, S 65·00 75·00
a. Red opt, S 55·00 65·00
J218 30 c. dull purple and orange, S 11·00 22·00
a. Brown opt, S £100 £100
J219 40 c. scarlet and dull purple, S 48·00 55·00
a. Brown opt, S £120 £110
J220 50 c. black/*emerald*, S 32·00 35·00
a. Red opt, S 45·00 55·00
b. Brown opt, S 80·00 85·00
J221 47 $1 black and red/*blue* 30·00 40·00
a. Red opt 90·00 95·00
J222 $2 green and scarlet 35·00 50·00
a. Red opt £160 £180
J223 $5 green and red/*emerald* 55·00 65·00

On T 46 the overprint is normally sideways (with "top" to either right or left), but on T 47 it is always upright.
S=Sideways
U=Upright
SU=Sideways or upright (our prices being for the cheaper).

Specialists recognise nine slightly different chops as Type 1. Initial supplies with the overprint in red were produced at Singapore. Later overprintings took place at Kuala Lumpur in violet, red or brown and, finally, black. No. J155 was from the Kuala Lumpur printing only. Except where noted these overprints were used widely in Malaya and, in some instances, Sumatra.

The following stamps also exist with this overprint, but were not available to the public:
Straits Settlements (in red) 6, 25 c.
Kelantan (in black) 10 c.
Negri Sembilan 2 c. green (Blk. or Brn.), 4 c. (Blk.), 6 c. scarlet (Blk.), 8 c. grey (Blk.), 12 c. (Blk.), $2 (Blk. or Brn.)
Pahang (in black, 2 c. also in brown) 2, 4, 6 c., $2
Perak 2 c. green (R.), 6 c. (Blk.)
Selangor 4 c. (Blk.)

1942 (May). *Optd with T* **16**. (*a*) *On Straits Settlements.*
J224 58 2 c. orange 50 50
a. Opt inverted 7·00 12·00
b. Opt double, one inverted 38·00 48·00
J225 3 c. green 42·00 50·00
J226 8 c. grey 2·25 1·75
a. Opt inverted 13·00 24·00
J227 15 c. blue 6·00 5·00

(*b*) *On Negri Sembilan*
J228 6 1 c. black 80 60
a. Opt inverted 9·00 18·00
b. Opt double, one inverted 32·00 42·00
J229 2 c. orange 1·40 50
J230 3 c. green 90 45
J231 5 c. brown 45 55
J232 6 c. grey 1·25 1·00
a. Opt inverted — £600
b. Stop omitted at right (R.10/9) 40·00 42·00
J233 8 c. scarlet 1·75 1·25
J234 10 c. dull purple 3·00 3·00
J235 15 c. ultramarine 5·00 3·00
J236 25 c. dull purple and scarlet 2·00 4·75
J237 30 c. dull purple and orange 3·25 3·00
J238 $1 black and red/*blue* £100 £110

(*c*) *On Pahang*
J239 15 1 c. black 80 50
J240 5 c. brown 55 70
J241 8 c. scarlet 22·00 2·50
J242 10 c. dull purple 8·50 5·00
J243 12 c. bright ultramarine 1·00 2·75
J244 25 c. dull purple and scarlet 3·75 6·50
J245 30 c. dull purple and orange 80 3·00

(*d*) *On Perak*
J246 51 2 c. orange 75 70
a. Opt inverted 14·00 20·00
J247 3 c. green 50 60
a. Opt inverted 10·00 19·00
J248 8 c. scarlet 60 40
a. Opt inverted 4·50 7·00
b. Opt double, one inverted £140 £160
c. Opt omitted (in pair with normal) £300
J249 10 c. dull purple 4·25 5·00
J250 15 c. ultramarine 3·00 2·00
J251 50 c. black/*emerald* 1·75 2·75
J252 $1 black and red/*blue* £275 £325
J253 $5 green and red/*emerald* 28·00 45·00
a. Opt inverted £275 £325

(*e*) *On Selangor*
J254 46 3 c. green 40 60
J255 12 c. bright ultramarine 1·10 4·00
J256 15 c. ultramarine 2·75 2·00
J257 40 c. scarlet and dull purple 2·00 2·50
J258 48 $2 green and scarlet 10·00 18·00

On T 46 the overprint is sideways, with "top" to left or right.

The following stamps also exist with this overprint, but were not available to the public.
Perak 1, 5, 30 c. (*Price for set of* 3 £180 *unused*)
Selangor 1, 5, 10, 30 c., $1, $5 (*Price for set of* 6 £350 *unused*)

DAI NIPPON
2602
MALAYA
2 Cents
(17)

DAI NIPPON
YUBIN
2 Cents
(18)
"Japanese Postal Service"

1942. *No.* 108 *of Perak surch with T* **17**.
J259 51 2 c. on 5 c. brown 1·25 1·00

1942 (7 Dec). *Perak stamps surch or optd only, as in T* **18**.
J260 51 1 c. black 2·00 3·50
a. Opt inverted 19·00 28·00
J261 2 c. on 5 c. brown 2·00 5·00
a. "DAI NIPPON YUBIN" inverted 17·00 26·00
b. Ditto and "2 Cents" omitted 35·00 50·00
J262 8 c. scarlet 2·75 1·25
a. Opt inverted 11·00 18·00

A similar overprint exists on the Selangor 3 c., but this was not available to the public (*Price* £225 *unused*).

On 8 December 1942 contemporary Japanese 3, 5, 8 and 25 s. stamps were issued without overprint in Malaya and the 1, 2, 4, 6, 7, 10, 30 and 50 s. and 1 y. values followed on 15 February 1943.

大日本郵便
(19)

6cts. (20) **6 cts.** (21) **2 Cents** (22)

6 cts. (23) **$1.00** (24)

1943 (Feb)–**45**. *Stamps of various Malayan territories optd "Japanese Postal Service" in Kanji characters as T* **2** *or* **19**, *some additionally surch as T* **20** *to* **24**.

(*a*) *Stamps of Straits Settlements optd with T* **2**
J263 58 8 c. grey (Blk.) 1·00 50
a. Opt inverted 18·00 35·00
b. Red opt 90 90
J264 12 c. ultramarine 55 2·75
J265 40 c. scarlet and dull purple 65 1·75

(*b*) *Stamps of Negri Sembilan optd with T* **2** *or surch also*
J266 6 1 c. black 30 40
a. Opt inverted 8·00 14·00
b. Sideways second character 16·00 18·00
ba. Opt inverted with sideways second character £375
J267 2 c. on 5 c. brown (surch as T **20**) 40 45
J268 6 c. on 5 c. brown (surch T **21**) 40 60
J269 25 c. dull purple and scarlet 1·10 5·00

(*c*) *Stamp of Pahang optd with T* **2** *and surch also*
J270 15 6 c. on 5 c. brown (surch T **20**) 50 75
J271 6 c. on 5 c. brown (surch T **21**) 1·00 1·50

(*d*) *Stamps of Perak optd with T* **2** *or surch also*
J272 51 1 c. black 80 60
a. Sideways second character £100 £110
J273 2 c. on 5 c. brown (surch as T **20**) 50 50
a. Opt Type **2** and surch Type **20** both inverted 18·00 29·00
b. Opt Type **2** inverted 18·00 29·00
c. Sideways second character 35·00 38·00
J274 2 c. on 5 c. brown (surch T **22**) 45 45
a. Opt Type **2** and surch Type **22** both inverted 18·00 29·00
b. Surch Type **22** inverted 18·00 29·00
c. Sideways second character 25·00 27·00
ca. Opt Type **2** with sideways second character and surch T **22** both inverted £650
cb. Surch Type **22** inverted £600
J275 5 c. brown 45 40
a. Opt inverted 26·00 30·00
b. Sideways second character £190 £300
J276 8 c. scarlet 55 50
a. Opt inverted 15·00 24·00
b. Sideways second character 48·00 55·00
ba. Opt inverted with sideways second character £600
J277 10 c. dull purple 60 50
J278 30 c. dull purple and orange 1·25 2·50
J279 50 c. black/*emerald* 3·00 8·00
J280 $5 green and red/*emerald* 40·00 60·00

(*e*) *Stamps of Selangor optd with T* **2** (*sideways on T* **46**)
J281 46 1 c. black 90 90
J282 3 c. green 40 45
a. Sideways second character 15·00 21·00
J283 12 c. bright ultramarine 45 1·25
a. Sideways second character 20·00 30·00
J284 15 c. ultramarine 2·75 3·00
a. Sideways second character 35·00 40·00
J285 48 $1 black and red/*blue* 3·00 8·50
a. Opt inverted £225 £225
b. Sideways second character £200 £225
J286 $2 green and scarlet 10·00 22·00
J287 $5 green and red/*emerald* 22·00 50·00
a. Opt inverted £225 £225

(*f*) *Stamps of Selangor optd with T* **19** *or surch also*
J288 46 1 c. black (R.) 35 50
J289 2 c. on 5 c. brown (surch as T **21**) (R.) 30 50
J290 3 c. on 5 c. brown (surch as T **21**) 30 1·25
a. "s" in "cts." inverted (R.4/3) 25·00 40·00
b. Comma after "cts" (R.9/3) 25·00 40·00
J291 5 c. brown (R.) 30 1·25
J292 46 6 c. on 5 c. brown (surch T **21**) 30 80
J293 6 c. on 5 c. brown (surch T **23**) 20 70
a. "6" inverted (R.7/8) £400
J294 15 c. ultramarine 4·00 4·00
J295 $1 on 10 c. dull purple (surch T **24**) 30 1·00
J296 $1.50 on 30 c. dull purple and orange (surch T **24**) 30 1·00

The error showing the second character in Type **2** sideways occurred on R.6/3 in the first of four settings only.

The 2 c. orange, 3 c. and 5 c. grey of Perak also exist overprinted with Type **2**, but these stamps were not available to the public (*Price for set of* 3 £90 *unused*).

25 Tapping Rubber

26 Fruit

27 Japanese Shrine, Singapore

(Litho Kolff & Co, Batavia)

1943 (29 Apr–1 Oct). *T* **25/7** *and similar designs. P* 12½.
J297 25 1 c. grey-green (1 Oct) 15 35
J298 26 2 c. pale emerald (1 June) 15 15
J299 25 3 c. drab (1 Oct) 15 15
J300 – 4 c. carmine-rose 15 15
J301 – 8 c. dull blue 15 15
J302 – 10 c. brown-purple (1 Oct) 15 15
J303 27 15 c. violet (1 Oct) 35 65
J304 – 30 c. olive-green (1 Oct) 35 35
J305 – 50 c. blue (1 Oct) 75 75
J306 – 70 c. blue (1 Oct) 11·00 10·00
J297/306 *Set of* 10 12·00 11·50

Designs: *Vert*—4 c. Tin dredger; 8 c. War memorial; 10 c. Huts; 30 c. Sago palms; 50 c. Straits of Johore. *Horiz*—70 c. Malay Mosque, Kuala Lumpur.

28 Ploughman

29 Rice-planting

1943 (1 Sept). *Savings Campaign. Litho. P* 12½.
J307 28 8 c. violet 7·00 2·75
J308 15 c. scarlet 6·00 2·75

(Des Hon Chin. Litho)

1944 (15 Feb). *"Re-birth" of Malaya. P* 12½.
J309 29 8 c. rose-red 8·00 2·75
J310 15 c. magenta 4·00 3·00

大日本
マライ郵便
50 セント
(30)

大日本
マライ郵便
1ドル
(31)

大日本
マライ郵便
1½ドル
(32)

1944 (16 Dec). *Stamps intended for use on Red Cross letters. Surch with T* **30/2** *in red.* (*a*) *On Straits Settlements.*
J311 58 50 c. on 50 c. black/*emerald* 8·50 18·00
J312 $1 on $1 black and red/*blue* 13·00 24·00
J313 $1.50 on $2 green and scarlet 21·00 55·00

(*b*) *On Johore*
J314 29 50 c. on 50 c. dull purple and red 7·00 15·00
J315 $1.50 on $2 green and carmine 5·50 11·00

(*c*) *On Selangor*
J316 48 $1 on $1 black and red/*blue* 4·00 11·00
J317 $1.50 on $2 green and scarlet 6·00 14·00

Nos. J311/17 were issued in Singapore but were withdrawn after one day, probably because supplies of Nos. J295/6 were received and issued on the 18 December.

POSTAGE DUE STAMPS

Postage Due stamps of the Malayan Postal Union overprinted.

1942 (3 Apr). *Handstamped as T* **1** *in black.*
JD21 D 1 1 c. slate-purple 10·00 12·00
a. Red opt 22·00 25·00
b. Brown opt 42·00 50·00
JD22 3 c. green 18·00 20·00
a. Red opt 40·00 55·00
JD23 4 c. green 12·00 12·00
a. Red opt 20·00 30·00
b. Brown opt 50·00 60·00
JD24 8 c. scarlet 18·00 22·00
a. Red opt 42·00 42·00
b. Brown opt 60·00 60·00
JD25 10 c. yellow-orange 14·00 17·00
a. Red opt 24·00 27·00
b. Brown opt 26·00 32·00
JD26 12 c. ultramarine 16·00 20·00
a. Red opt 48·00 55·00
JD27 50 c. black 38·00 45·00
a. Red opt £100 £110

1942. *Optd with T* **16**.
JD28 D 1 1 c. slate-purple .. .. .. 1·00 3·25
JD29 3 c. green .. .. 4·50 7·50
JD30 4 c. green .. .. 4·50 7·50
JD31 8 c. scarlet .. .. 5·50 8·50
JD32 10 c. yellow-orange .. .. .. 1·60 5·50
JD33 12 c. ultramarine .. .. .. 1·60 8·50

The 9 c. and 15 c. also exist with this overprint, but these were not issued (*Price £200 each unused*).

1943–45. *Optd with T* **2**.
JD34 D 1 1 c. slate-purple .. .. .. 30 1·50
JD35 3 c. green .. .. 30 1·75
JD36 4 c. green .. .. 23·00 28·00
JD37 5 c. scarlet .. .. 50 2·25
JD38 9 c. yellow-orange .. .. .. 60 3·00
a. Opt inverted .. .. .. 24·00 32·00
JD39 10 c. yellow-orange .. .. .. 60 3·00
a. Opt inverted .. .. .. 38·00 42·00
JD40 12 c. ultramarine .. .. .. 60 4·00
JD41 15 c. ultramarine .. .. .. 60 4·00

IX. THAI OCCUPATION OF MALAYA

Stamps issued for use in the four Malay States of Kedah, Kelantan, Perlis and Trengganu, ceded by Japan to Thailand on 19 October 1943 and restored to British rule on the defeat of the Japanese.

Before the appearance of Nos. TM1/6 Japanese Occupation issues continued in use.

PRICES FOR STAMPS ON COVER	
Nos. TK1/5	*from* × 30
Nos. TM1/6	*from* × 40
Nos. TT1/29	*from* × 12

KELANTAN

TK 1

(Ptd at Khota Baru)

1943 (15 Nov). *Surch with value and inscr in black. No gum. P* 11.
TK1 TK 1 1 c. violet .. .. 55·00 70·00
TK2 2 c. violet .. .. 60·00 75·00
a. Violet omitted £300
TK3 4 c. violet .. .. 60·00 75·00
a. Violet omitted .. .. ..
TK4 8 c. violet .. .. 60·00 75·00
a. Violet omitted £300
TK5 10 c. violet .. .. 65·00 90·00

The above bear sheet watermarks in the form of "STANDARD" in block capitals with curved "CROWN" above and "AGENTS" below in double-lined capitals. This watermark occurs four times in the sheet.

These stamps but with centres printed in red were for fiscal use.

GENERAL ISSUE

TM 1 War Memorial

(Litho Defence Ministry, Bangkok)

1943 (Dec). *Thick opaque, or thin semi-transparent paper. Gummed or ungummed. P* 12½.
TM1 TM 1 1 c. yellow .. .. 9·00 10·00
TM2 2 c. red-brown .. .. 3·25 6·00
a. Imperf (pair) £250
b. Perf 11½×11 .. .. ..
TM3 3 c. green .. .. 5·50 11·00
a. Perf 11½×11 .. .. ..
TM4 4 c. purple .. .. 3·75 6·00
a. Perf 11½×11 .. .. ..
TM5 8 c. carmine .. .. 2·50 7·50
a. Perf 11½×11 .. .. ..
TM6 15 c. blue .. .. 6·50 12·00
a. Perf 11½×11 .. .. ..

5 c. and 10 c. stamps in this design were prepared, but never issued.

TRENGGANU

TRENGGANU

(TT 1)

(Overprinted at Trengganu Survey Office)

1944 (1 Oct). *Various stamps optd with Type* TT **1**.

(i) *On Trengganu stamp optd as T* **1**
TT 1 4 8 c. grey (J104) .. .. .. £130 75·00

(ii) *On stamps optd with T* **16**. (a) *Pahang*
TT 2 15 12 c. bright ultramarine (J243) .. £130 75·00

(b) *Trengganu*
TT 3 4 2 c. on 5 c. purple/*yellow* (J121)* .. £130 £130
TT 4 8 c. on 10 c. brt blue (J127) (inverted) 75·00 75·00
TT 5 12 c. brt ultramarine (J128) (inverted) 75·00 75·00

*This is spelt "TRENGANU" with one "G".

(iii) *On stamps optd with T* **2**. (a) *Straits Settlements*
TT 6 58 12 c. ultramarine (J264) £130 £130
TT 7 40 c. scarlet and dull purple (J265) .. £130 £130

(b) *Perak*
TT 8 51 30 c. dull purple and orange (J278) .. £250 £130

(c) *Selangor*
TT 9 46 3 c. green (J282) .. .. .. 75·00 70·00
TT10 12 c. brt ultramarine (J283) (L. to R.) 70·00 65·00
TT11 12 c. brt ultramarine (J283) (R. to L.) 60·00 60·00
a. Sideways second character .. £800 £800

(iv) *On Selangor stamps optd with T* **19**
TT12 46 2 c. on 5 c. brown (J289) £130 £130
TT13 3 c. on 5 c. brown (J290) £130 £130

(v) *On pictorials of* 1943 (*Nos.* J297/306)
TT14 25 1 c. grey-green £130 £150
TT15 26 2 c. pale emerald .. .. .. £130 85·00
TT16 25 3 c. drab £140 £140
TT17 – 4 c. carmine-rose £140 £140
TT18 – 8 c. dull blue £250 £250
TT19 – 10 c. brown-purple £500 £500
TT20 27 15 c. violet £160 £130
TT21 – 30 c. olive-green £160 £100
TT22 – 50 c. blue £250 £250
TT23 – 70 c. blue £400 £400

(vi) *On Savings Campaign stamps* (*Nos.* J307/8)
TT24 28 8 c. violet £225 £225
TT25 15 c. scarlet £225 £225

(vii) *On stamps of Japan*
TT26 – 5 s. claret (No. 396) £170 £190
TT27 – 25 s. brown and chocolate (No. 329) .. 95·00 70·00
TT28 – 30 s. blue-green (No. 330) £170 £130

(viii) *On Trengganu Postage Due stamp optd with T* **1**
TT29 D 1 1 c. scarlet (JD17) £700 £700

X. LABUAN

CROWN COLONY

The island of Labuan, off the northern coast of Borneo, was ceded to Great Britain by the Sultan of Brunei in December 1846.

Stamps of STRAITS SETTLEMENTS were used from 1867 until 1879. Covers of 1864 and 1865 are known from Labuan franked with stamps of INDIA or HONG KONG.

PRICES FOR STAMPS ON COVER	
Nos. 1/4	—
Nos. 5/10	*from* × 15
Nos. 11/13	—
Nos. 14/21	*from* × 10
Nos. 22/5	—
Nos. 26/38	*from* × 10
Nos. 39/47	*from* × 100
Nos. 49/50	*from* × 10
Nos. 51/7	*from* × 60
Nos. 62/74	*from* × 15
Nos. 75/9	*from* × 30
Nos. 80/8	*from* × 20
Nos. 89/97	*from* × 15
Nos. 98/110	*from* × 10
Nos. 111/35	*from* × 30
Nos. 136/40	—
Nos. D1/9	*from* × 15

1

8 (2) 8 (3)

(Recess D.L.R.)

1879 (May). *Wmk CA over Crown, sideways. P* 14.
1 1 2 c. blue-green £550 £450
2 6 c. orange-brown £140 £120
3 12 c. carmine £800 £400
a. No right foot to second Chinese character (R. 2/3) £1100 £550
4 16 c. blue .. .. 40·00 55·00

This watermark is always found sideways, and extends over two stamps, a single specimen showing only a portion of the Crown or the letters CA, these being tall and far apart. This paper was chiefly used for long fiscal stamps.

1880 (Jan)–**82**. *Wmk Crown CC. P* 14.
5 1 2 c. yellow-green .. .. .. 9·50 13·00
6 6 c. orange-brown .. .. .. 60·00 70·00
7 8 c. carmine (4.82) .. .. .. 65·00 75·00
8 10 c. brown .. .. 55·00 70·00
9 12 c. carmine £160 £180
a. No right foot to second Chinese character £275 £300
10 16 c. blue (1881) .. .. .. 55·00 45·00
5/10 .. .. *Set of* 6 £350 £400

1880 (Aug). (a) *No.* 9 *surch with T* **2** *in black and with the original value obliterated by manuscript bar in red or black.*
11 8 c. on 12 c. carmine £550 £450
a. Type **2** inverted £550 £450
b. "12" not obliterated £700 £600
c. As b. with Type **2** inverted .. ..
d. No right foot to second Chinese character £750 £650

(b) *No.* 4 *surch with two upright figures and No.* 9 *surch with two at right angles as T* **3**.
12 6 c. on 16 c. blue (R.) £950 £550
a. With one "6" only .. .. ..
13 8 c. on 12 c. carmine £650 £500
a. Both "8's" upright .. .. ..
b. Upright "8" inverted £700 £550
c. No right foot to second Chinese character £850 £700

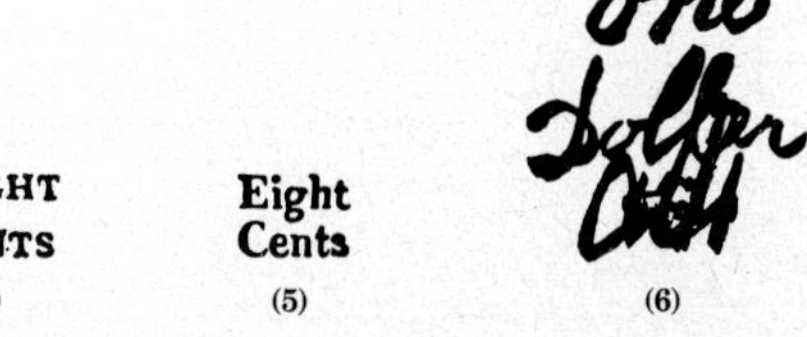

(4) (5) (6)

1881 (Mar). *No.* 9 *handstamped with T* **4**.
14 8 c. on 12 c. carmine £150 £180
a. No right foot to second Chinese character £275 £325

1881 (June). *No.* 9 *surch with T* **5**.
15 8 c. on 12 c. carmine .. .. .. 65·00 75·00
a. Surch double £500 £500
b. Surch inverted £4500
c. "Eighr" £6500
d. No right foot to second Chinese character £120 £140

The error "Eighr" occurred on R. 2/1 of the first printing, but was soon corrected.

1883. *Wmk Crown CA. P* 14.
17 1 2 c. yellow-green .. .. .. 10·00 13·00
a. Imperf between (horiz pair) £3750
18 8 c. carmine .. .. £110 65·00
19 10 c. yellow-brown .. .. .. 19·00 28·00
20 16 c. blue .. .. 65·00 75·00
21 40 c. amber .. .. 8·50 22·00
17/21 .. .. *Set of* 5 £190 £180

1883 (May). *No.* 10 *surch "One Dollar A.S.H." by hand, as T* **6**.
22 1 $1 on 16 c. blue (R.) £1900

The initials are those of the postmaster, Mr. A. S. Hamilton.

2 CENTS (7) 2 Cents (8) 2 Cents (9)

1885 (June). *Nos.* 18 *and* 10 *handstamped as T* **7**.
23 1 2 c. on 8 c. carmine .. .. .. 65·00
24 2 c. on 16 c. blue £650 £650

1885 (July). *No.* 20 *surch as T* **8**.
25 1 2 c. on 16 c. blue .. .. .. 85·00 £100
a. Surch double .. .. .. — £1300

1885 (Sept). *No.* 18 *handstamped diag as T* **9**.
26 1 2 c. on 8 c. carmine .. .. .. 38·00 50·00

1885–86. *Wmk Crown CA. P* 14.
30 1 2 c. rose-red .. .. 1·50 4·75
a. Pale rose-red (1886) .. .. 1·50 4·75
31 8 c. deep violet .. .. .. 12·00 7·00
a. Mauve (1886) .. .. .. 14·00 8·00
32 10 c. sepia (1886) .. .. .. 4·50 13·00
33 16 c. grey (1886) .. .. .. 65·00 50·00
30/3 .. .. *Set of* 4 75·00 65·00
30/3 Optd "Specimen" .. .. *Set of* 4 £350

ISSUES OF BRITISH NORTH BORNEO COMPANY

From 1 January 1890 while remaining a Crown Colony, the administration of Labuan was transferred to the British North Borneo Co, which issued the following stamps.

6 Cents (10) Two CENTS (11) Six CENTS (12)

1891 (July)–**92**. *Handstamped with T* **10**.
34 1 6 c. on 8 c. deep violet (No. 31) .. .. 30·00 26·00
a. Surch inverted .. .. .. 55·00 50·00
b. Surch double £160
c. Surch double, one inverted £300
d. "Cents" omitted £225 £225
e. Imperf between (horiz pair) .. ..
f. Pair, one without surch, one surch inverted £550

35 1 6 c. on 8 c. mauve (No. 31*a*) .. .. 4·50 4·50
a. Surch inverted .. .. 26·00 26·00
b. Surch double, one inverted .. £325
c. Surch double, both inverted .. £325
d. "6" omitted £300
e. Pair, one without surcharge .. £450 £450
f. Inverted. "Cents" omitted £300
g. Pair, one without surch, one surch inverted £550
36 6 c. on 8 c. mauve (R.) (No. 31*a*) (2.92) .. £375 £200
a. Surch inverted £475 £250
37 6 c. on 16 c. blue (No. 4) (3.92) .. £1300 £1200
a. Surch inverted £2500 £2000
38 6 c. on 40 c. amber (No. 21) £4000 £2500
a. Surch inverted £3000 £3000

There are two different versions of Type **10** with the lines of the surcharge either 1 mm or 2 mm apart.

(Recess D.L.R.)

1892–93. *No wmk. P* 14.
39 1 2 c. rose-lake .. .. 1·00 3·50
40 6 c. bright green .. .. 5·00 4·50
41 8 c. violet .. .. 2·25 4·50
a. Pale violet (1893) .. .. .. 3·25 4·50
43 10 c. brown .. .. 3·75 7·00
a. Sepia-brown (1893).. .. .. 3·75 7·50
45 12 c. bright blue .. .. 3·25 6·00
46 16 c. grey .. .. 3·25 6·00
47 40 c. ochre .. .. 16·00 24·00
a. Brown-buff (1893) .. .. .. 17·00 30·00
39/47 .. .. *Set of* 7 30·00 50·00

The 6 c., 12 c., 16 c. and 40 c. are in sheets of 10, as are all the earlier issues. The other values are in sheets of 30.

1892 (Dec). *Nos.* 47 *and* 46 *surch locally as T* **11** *or* **12**.
49 1 2 c. on 40 c. ochre (13 December) .. £100 75·00
a. Surch inverted £250 £325
50 6 c. on 16 c. grey (20 December) .. £180 £110
a. Surch inverted £200 £190

There are 10 slightly different versions of each of these surcharges.

CANCELLED-TO-ORDER. Prices are separately indicated, in a third price column, for stamps showing the recognisable black bars remainder cancellation. Earlier issues of the Company administration were also so treated, but, as postal cancellations were used, these cannot be identified.

(Litho D.L.R.)

1894 (April). *No wmk. P* 14.
51 1 2 c. carmine-pink .. .. .. 1·10 4·75 20
52 6 c. bright green .. .. .. 5·50 9·00 20
a. Imperf between (horiz pair) .. £3000
53 8 c. bright mauve .. .. .. 5·00 7·50 20
54 10 c. brown .. .. 11·00 11·00 20
55 12 c. pale blue .. .. 13·00 18·00 25
56 16 c. grey .. .. 15·00 25·00 25
57 40 c. orange-buff .. .. .. 20·00 32·00 30
51/57 .. .. .. *Set of* 7 65·00 95·00 1·25
51/57 H/S "Specimen" .. *Set of* 7 £100

Collectors are warned against forgeries of this issue.

PERFORATION. There are a number of small variations in the perforation of the Waterlow issues of 1894 to 1905 which we believe to be due to irregularity of the pins rather than different perforators.

In the following lists, stamps perf 12, 12½, 13 or compound are described as perf 12–13, stamps perf 13½, 14 or compound are described as perf 13½–14 and those perf 14½, 15 or compound are listed as perf 14½–15. In addition the 13½–14 perforation exists compound with 14½–15 and with 12–13, whilst perf 16 comes from a separate perforator.

13

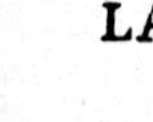
LABUAN

40

CENTS

(14)

1894 (May)–**96.** *T* 24/32 *of North Borneo (colours changed), with "LABUAN" engraved on vignette plate as T* **13** *(8, 12, 24 c.) or horizontally (others). P* 14½–15.

(*a*) *Name and central part of design in black*

62 24 1 c. grey-mauve .. .. .. 1·50 3·50 20
a. Imperf between (vert pair) .. £375 — £250
b. Perf 13½–14 .. .. .. 4·00 6·00 —
c. Perf 13½–14, comp 14½–15 ..
d. Perf 13½–14, comp 12–13 .. 9·00 8·00 —
e. Perf 12–13 .. .. ..
63 25 2 c. blue .. .. 2·50 4·00 20
a. Imperf (pair) £375
b. Perf 13½–14 .. .. .. 2·75 4·50 —
c. Perf 13½–14, comp 14½–15 ..
d. Perf 13½–14, comp 12–13 ..
e. Perf 12–13
64 26 3 c. ochre .. .. 2·75 6·00 20
a. Perf 13½–14 .. .. .. 3·50 6·00 —
b. Perf 13½–14, comp 14½–15 ..
c. Perf 13½–14, comp 12–13 ..
d. Perf 12–13
65 27 5 c. green .. .. 15·00 13·00 20
a. Perf 13½–14 .. .. .. 15·00 7·00 —
ab. Imperf between (horiz pair) ..
b. Perf 13½–14, comp 12–13 .. 15·00
67 28 6 c. brown-lake .. .. .. 2·50 5·50 20
a. Imperf (pair) .. .. .. £375 — £225
b. Perf 13½–14 .. .. .. — — 1·25
c. Perf 13½–14, comp 14½–15 .. — — 70
d. Perf 13½–14, comp 12–13
e. Perf 12–13 .. .. ..

68 29 8 c. rose-red .. .. 9·00 15·00 30
a. Perf 13½–14 .. .. .. 12·00 17·00 —
69 8 c. pink (1896) .. .. .. 7·00 18·00 30
a. Perf 13½–14 .. .. .. 12·00
70 30 12 c. orange-vermilion .. .. 16·00 30·00 30
a. Perf 13½–14 .. .. .. 28·00 32·00 2·00
b. Perf 12–13 .. .. ..
c. Perf 13½–14, comp 12–13 ..
71 31 18 c. olive-brown .. .. .. 22·00 32·00 30
a. Perf 13½–14 .. .. .. 26·00
72 18 c. olive-bistre (1896) .. .. 26·00 32·00 30
a. Perf 13½–14 .. .. .. 26·00 32·00 —
b. Perf 13½–14, comp 12–13 ..
c. Imperf between (vert pair) .. — — £375

(*b*) *Name and central part in blue*

73 32 24 c. pale mauve .. .. .. 13·00 28·00 30
a. Perf 13½–14 .. .. .. 13·00 28·00 —
74 24 c. dull lilac (1896) .. .. 13·00 28·00 30
a. Perf 13½–14 .. .. .. 13·00 28·00 —
62/74 .. .. *Set of* 9 75·00 £120 2·00
62/74 Optd "Specimen" .. *Set of* 9 £120

1895 (June). *No.* 83 *of North Borneo* ($1 *inscr* "STATE OF NORTH BORNEO") *surch as T* **14**.
75 32*c* 4 c. on $1 scarlet .. .. .. 1·00 1·25 30
76 10 c. on $1 scarlet .. .. .. 1·25 1·40 30
77 20 c. on $1 scarlet .. .. .. 11·00 6·00 30
78 30 c. on $1 scarlet .. .. .. 15·00 16·00 30
79 40 c. on $1 scarlet .. .. .. 10·00 10·00 30
75/9 .. .. *Set of* 5 35·00 32·00 1·40
75/9 Optd "Specimen" .. *Set of* 5 80·00

No. 76 exists with the figures of the surcharge 2½ mm away from "CENTS". The normal setting has a space of 4 mm. Examples of the narrow setting have, so far, only been seen on cancelled-to-order stamps.

LABUAN
(15)

1846
JUBILEE
1896
(16)

4
CENTS
(17)

1896. *T* **32***a to* **32***c of North Borneo (as Nos.* 81 *to* 83, *but colours changed) optd with T* **15**.
80 25 c. green .. .. 15·00 15·00 50
a. Opt omitted .. .. .. 11·00 — 1·25
b. Imperf (pair) .. .. ..
ba. Opt omitted .. .. .. 26·00
bb. Stamps ptd double, one inverted
81 50 c. maroon .. .. 15·00 16·00 50
a. Opt omitted .. .. .. 12·00 — 1·25
b. Imperf (pair) .. .. ..
ba. Opt omitted .. .. .. 27·00
bb. Stamps ptd double .. ..
82 $1 blue .. .. 30·00 22·00 50
a. Opt omitted .. .. .. 15·00 — 1·25
b. Imperf (pair) .. .. ..
ba. Opt omitted .. .. .. 30·00
80/82 Optd "Specimen" .. *Set of* 3 60·00

Nos. 80bb and 81bb are from waste sheets subsequently sold by the British North Borneo Company to collectors.

1896 (24 Sept). *Jubilee of Cession of Labuan to Gt Britain. Nos.* 62 *to* 68 *optd with T* **16**. *P* 14½–15.
83 1 c. black and grey-mauve .. .. 13·00 16·00 50
b. Opt in orange .. .. .. £150 £150 —
c. "JEBILEE" .. .. .. — £350 £250
d. "JUBILE" (R. 3/10) .. ..
e. Perf 13½–14 .. .. .. 13·00 20·00 —
ea. Opt double .. .. .. £150 £150 —
eb. Opt in orange .. .. .. £150 £150 —
f. Perf 13½–14, comp 12–13 .. 15·00 11·00 —
g. Perf 12–13 .. .. ..
84 2 c. black and blue .. .. .. 16·00 12·00 50
a. Imperf horiz (vert pair) .. £300 £350 —
b. "JEBILEE" .. .. .. £450 £450 —
c. "JUBILE" (R. 3/10) .. ..
d. Perf 13½–14 .. .. .. 16·00 12·00 —
e. Perf 13½–14, comp 14½–15 ..
f. Perf 13½–14, comp 12–13 .. 25·00
85 3 c. black and ochre .. .. .. 18·00 20·00 50
c. "JEBILEE" .. .. .. — £850 £600
d. Perf 13½–14 .. .. .. 25·00 25·00 —
db. Opt treble £650
e. Perf 13½–14, comp 14½–15 ..
f. Perf 13½–14, comp 12–13
fa. Opt double £150 £150 £120
86 5 c. black and green .. .. .. 30·00 16·00 50
a. Opt double .. .. .. £180 £180 —
b. Perf 13½–14 .. .. .. 30·00 16·00 —
c. Perf 13½–14, comp 12–13
87 6 c. black and brown-lake .. .. 14·00 17·00 50
a. Opt double .. .. .. £225 £225 —
b. "JUBILE" (R. 3/10) £850
c. Perf 13½–14, comp 14½–15 ..
88 8 c. black and pink .. .. .. 21·00 11·00 50
a. Perf 13½–14 .. .. .. 19·00 11·00 —
b. Perf 13½–14, comp 14½–15 .. 30·00
83/8 .. .. *Set of* 6 £100 80·00 2·75
83/8 Optd "Specimen" .. *Set of* 6 £140

No. 84b is known in a vertical strip of 3 imperf horizontally except at the base of the bottom stamp.

1897 (Apr)–**1901.** *T* 34/45 *of North Borneo (colours changed), with "LABUAN" engraved on vignette plate as T* **13** *(8, 10, 12, 24 c.) or horizontally (others). Name and central part in black (24 c. in blue). P* 13½–14.
89 34 1 c. greyish purple (*p* 14½–15) .. 2·25 3·25 20
a. Perf 13½–14, comp 14½–15
b. Brown (1901) .. .. .. 2·50 5·00 —
ba. Perf 14½–15 .. .. .. 3·75
bb. Perf 16 .. .. 9·00 12·00 —
90 35 2 c. blue .. .. 5·50 3·00 20
a. Imperf between (vert pair) .. † † £250
b. Imperf between (horiz pair) .. † † £275
c. Perf 14½–15 .. .. ..
d. Perf 13½–14, comp 12–13 .. 18·00
e. Perf 16 .. .. — — 5·00

91 36 3 c. ochre .. .. 8·00 9·00 20
a. Imperf between (vert pair) .. † † —
b. Perf 14½–15 .. .. .. 6·50 5·00 —
c. Perf 13½–14, comp 12–13 ..
92 38 5 c. green .. .. 22·00 24·00 25
a. Perf 14½–15 .. .. .. 20·00 24·00 —
b. Perf 13½–14, comp 12–13 ..
93 39 6 c. brown-lake .. .. .. 6·00 14·00 25
b. Perf 14½–15 .. .. .. 3·50 14·00 —
ba. Imperf between (vert pair) .. † † £225
c. Perf 13½–14, comp 12–13 .. — — 3·00
94 40 8 c. rose-red .. .. — — 30
a. Perf 14½–15 .. .. .. 13·00 9·00 —
b. Perf 13½–14, comp 12–13 .. 17·00 — 2·75
c. Vermilion .. .. .. 5·50 — 30
ca. Perf 16 .. .. — — 3·00
95 42 12 c. vermilion .. .. .. 30·00 40·00 40
a. Perf 14½–15 .. .. .. 18·00 30·00 —
96 44 18 c. olive-bistre .. .. .. 22·00 26·00 40
a. Imperf between (vert pair) .. † † —
b. Perf 16 .. .. 15·00 25·00 —
97 45 24 c. grey-lilac .. .. .. 12·00 28·00 40
a. Perf 14½–15 .. .. .. 10·00
89/97 .. .. *Set of* 9 75·00 £120 2·25
89/97 Optd "Specimen" .. *Set of* 9 £120

The 12, 18 and 24 c. above were errors; in the 12 c., "LABUAN" is over the value at the top; the 18 c. has "POSTAL REVENUE" instead of "POSTAGE AND REVENUE", and the 24 c. is without "POSTAGE AND REVENUE".

1897 (Nov)–**98.** (*a*) *Types of North Borneo (colours changed), with "LABUAN" engraved on the vignette plate as in T* **13**. *P* 13½–14.
98 42 12 c. black and vermilion (3.98) .. † — 1·50
a. Perf 14½–15 .. .. .. 26·00 30·00 —
b. Perf 13½–14, comp 14½–15 ..
c. Perf 16 .. .. 28·00 32·00 —
99 46 18 c. black and olive-bistre ..
a. Perf 14½–15 .. .. .. 60·00 60·00 —
b. Perf 16 .. .. † — 6·50
100 47 24 c. blue and lilac-brown .. 15·00 38·00 —
a. Perf 14½–15 .. .. .. 15·00 38·00 —
b. Perf 13½–14, comp 12–13 ..
c. Perf 16 .. .. ..
d. Blue and ochre (*p* 14½–15) ..
98/100 Optd "Specimen" .. *Set of* 2 38·00

In the 12 c. "LABUAN" is now correctly placed at foot of stamp. The 18 c. and 24 c. have the inscriptions on the stamps corrected, but the 18 c. still has "LABUAN" *over* the value at foot, and was further corrected as follows.

(*b*) *As No.* 99, *but "LABUAN" at top*

101 46 18 c. black and olive-bistre (Optd S. £25) 28·00 35·00
a. Perf 14½–15 .. .. .. 23·00 38·00
b. Perf 13½–14, comp 12–13 .. .. 22·00 32·00
c. Perf 12–13 .. .. ..

1899. *Surch with T* **17**. (*a*) *P* 14½–15.
102 38 4 c. on 5 c. (No. 92a) .. .. .. 18·00 26·00
103 39 4 c. on 6 c. (No. 93b) .. .. .. 15·00 19·00
a. Perf 13½–14 .. .. .. 20·00
b. Perf 13½–14, comp 12–13 ..
104 40 4 c. on 8 c. (No. 94a) .. .. .. 30·00 32·00
a. Perf 13½–14 .. .. .. 14·00 25·00
b. Perf 13½–14, comp 12–13 .. 22·00
c. Perf 12–13 .. .. ..
105 42 4 c. on 12 c. (No. 98a) .. .. .. 20·00 27·00
a. Perf 13½–14 .. .. .. 22·00
b. Perf 16 .. .. 22·00 32·00
c. Perf 13½–14, comp 12–13 ..
106 46 4 c. on 18 c (No. 101a) .. .. .. 15·00 17·00
a. Surch double £225 £275
107 47 4 c. on 24 c. (No. 100a) .. .. 15·00 20·00
a. Perf 13½–14 .. .. .. 14·00 25·00
b. Perf 13½–14, comp 12–13 .. 18·00 22·00
c. Perf 16 .. .. 25·00

(*b*) *P* 14

108 32*a* 4 c. on 25 c. (No. 80) .. .. .. 5·50 7·50
109 32*b* 4 c. on 50 c. (No. 81) .. .. .. 5·50 7·50
110 32*c* 4 c. on $1 (No. 82) .. .. .. 5·50 7·50
102/110 Optd "Specimen" .. *Set of* 9 £120

The 1 c., 2 c. and 3 c. values of this set were also surcharged "4 CENTS" but were not issued. They exist overprinted "Specimen" (*Price* £80 *the set of three*).

1900–02. *Types of North Borneo with "LABUAN" engraved on the vignette plate as in T* **13**, *in green on* 16 *c. P* 13½–14.
111 35 2 c. black and green .. .. 3·50 2·50 20
a. Perf 13½–14, comp 12–13 ..
112 37 4 c. black and yellow-brown .. 4·25 13·00 25
a. Imperf between (vert pair) .. £350
b. Perf 13½–14, comp 12–13
113 4 c. black and carmine (8.1900) .. 7·00 2·75 20
a. Perf 14½–15 .. .. .. 6·00 4·25 —
b. Perf 13½–14, comp 12–13 .. 14·00 4·75 —
c. Perf 16 .. .. ..
114 38 5 c. black and pale blue .. .. 17·00 18·00 50
a. Perf 13½–14, comp 12–13 ..
115 41 10 c. brown & slate-lilac (*p* 14½–15) 28·00 42·00 40
(1902) .. ..
116 43 16 c. green and chestnut (1902) .. 38·00 45·00 1·50
a. Perf 13½–14, comp 12–13 .. 38·00 45·00 —
b. Perf 12–13 .. ..
c. Perf 14½–15 .. .. ..
111/16 Optd "Specimen" .. *Set of* 6 £100

18

4
cents
(19)

(Recess Waterlow)

1902 (Sept)–**03**. *P* 13½–14.
116*d* **18** 1 c. black and purple (10.03) .. 2·00 3·25 20
da. Perf 14½–15 .. .. .. — 4·50 —
117 2 c. black and green .. .. 2·00 2·50 20
a. Perf 14½–15 .. .. .. — 3·75 —
117*b* 3 c. black and sepia (10.03) .. 2·00 3·00 20
118 4 c. black and carmine .. .. 2·00 2·50 20
a. Perf 14½–15 .. .. .. 2·25 2·75 —
119 8 c. black and vermilion .. .. 1·50 3·75 20
a. Perf 14½–15 .. .. .. 8·50
120 10 c. brown and slate-blue .. 2·00 4·50 20
b. Perf 14½–15 .. .. 2·25
ba. Imperf between (vert pair) † † £350
121 12 c. black and yellow .. .. 2·50 5·00 20
a. Imperf between (vert strip of 3) .. .. † † £2000
b. Perf 16 .. .. .. 2·75
122 16 c. green and brown .. .. 2·00 6·50 20
a. Imperf between (vert pair) † — —
123 18 c. black and pale brown .. 2·00 6·00 20
124 25 c. green and greenish blue .. 2·00 7·50 20
a. Perf 14½–15 .. .. .. 10·00
b. Error. Black and greenish blue .. .. — † £225
125 50 c. dull purple and lilac .. 8·50 17·00 30
a. Perf 13½–14, comp 12–13 .. 13·00
126 $1 claret and orange .. 3·00 19·00 40
a. Perf 14½–15 .. .. 11·00
116*d*/26 .. .. .. *Set of* 12 28·00 70·00 2·40
116*d*/26 Optd "Specimen" .. *Set of* 12 £150

1904 (Dec). *Issues of 1895 and 1897–8 surch with T* **19**.

(*a*) *P* 14½–15.
127 **38** 4 c. on 5 c. (No. 92a) .. .. 18·00 26·00 1·00
128 **39** 4 c. on 6 c. (No. 93b) .. .. 12·00 25·00 1·00
129 **40** 4 c. on 8 c. (No. 94a) .. .. 16·00 27·00 1·00
130 **42** 4 c. on 12 c. (No. 98a) .. .. 19·00 27·00 1·00
a. Perf 16 .. .. .. 20·00 28·00
131 **46** 4 c. on 18 c. (No. 101) (*p* 13½–14) .. 15·00 25·00 1·00
a. Perf 13½–14, comp 12–13 .. 20·00
b. Perf 12–13 .. ..
132 **47** 4 c. on 24 c. (No. 100a) .. .. 13·00 25·00 1·00
a. Perf 13½–14 .. .. 13·00
b. Perf 13½–14, comp 12–13 .. 20·00
c. Perf 16 .. .. .. 26·00

(*b*) *P* 14
133 **32*a*** 4 c. on 25 c. (No. 80) .. .. 8·50 18·00 1·00
134 **32*b*** 4 c. on 50 c. (No. 81) .. .. 8·50 18·00 1·00
a. Surch double £225
b. Surch triple .. ..
135 **32*c*** 4 c. on $1 (No. 82) .. .. 8·50 18·00 1·00

LABUAN (20) **LABUAN** (21)

1905 (Feb-Nov). *Nos.* 81, 83 (*in Labuan colour*), *and* 84/6 *of North Borneo optd locally with T* **20** (25 c., $2) *or* **21** *others*).
136 **32*a*** 25 c. indigo .. .. £700 † £400
137 **32*c*** $1 blue .. .. † † £425
138 **32*d*** $2 dull green £2250 £2250 £750
139 **14** $5 bright purple .. £3000 † £750
140 **15** $10 brown (11.05) .. £10000 † £4000
Dangerous forgeries exist.
The overprint on No. 138 is 12 mm long.
No. 137 is said to have been issued in 1899.

POSTAGE DUE STAMPS

POSTAGE DUE

(D 1)

1901. *Optd with Type* D 1, *reading vertically upwards*. *P* 13½–14.
D1 **35** 2 c. black and green (111) .. .. 8·50 12·00 30
a. Opt double £190
b. Perf 13½–14, comp 12–13
D2 **36** 3 c. black and ochre (91) .. .. 13·00 50·00 40
a. Perf 13½–14, comp 12–13
D3 **37** 4 c. black and carmine (113) .. 15·00 50·00 40
a. Opt double .. .. † † £190
b. Perf 14½–15 .. .. 17·00
D4 **38** 5 c. black and pale blue (114) .. 20·00 50·00 50
a. Perf 14½–15 .. .. 24·00
b. Perf 13½–14, comp 12–13
D5 **39** 6 c. black and brown-lake (93) .. 11·00 50·00 50
a. Perf 14½–15 .. .. 16·00
b. Perf 16 .. .. .. 22·00
D6 **40** 8 c. black and vermilion (94c) .. 25·00 50·00 60
a. Frame inverted (*p* 14½–15) † † £3500
b. Perf 14½–15 .. .. 18·00 — 75
c. Perf 16 .. .. .. 26·00
d. Black and rose-red (94) .. 30·00
da. Perf 14½–15 .. .. — — 6·50
db. Perf 13½–14, comp 12–13
D7 **42** 12 c. black and vermilion (98) .. 42·00 50·00 2·00
a. Opt reading downwards .. † † £200
b. Perf 14½–15 .. .. 45·00
D8 **46** 18 c. blk & ol-bistre (101) (*p* 14½–15) 13·00 50·00 1·00
D9 **47** 24 c. blue and lilac-brown (100) .. 22·00 50·00 1·00
a. Perf 13½–14, comp 12–13
b. Perf 14½–15 .. .. 22·00
ba. Blue and ochre .. .. 30·00
c. Perf 16 .. .. .. 22·00 50·00 —
D1/9 .. .. .. *Set of* 9 £140 £375 6·00

By Letters Patent dated 30 October 1906, Labuan was incorporated with Straits Settlements and ceased issuing its own stamps. In 1946 it became part of the Colony of North Borneo.

NEW INFORMATION

The editor is always interested to correspond with people who have new information that will improve or correct the Catalogue.

XI. SABAH

(*formerly* North Borneo)

NORTH BORNEO

PRICES FOR STAMPS ON COVER TO 1945	
No. 1	*from* × 100
Nos. 2/3	*from* × 10
Nos. 4/5	—
Nos. 6/19	*from* × 10
Nos. 19*b*/21*b*	—
Nos. 22/8	*from* × 50
Nos. 29/35	—
Nos. 36/44	*from* × 100
Nos. 45/50	—
Nos. 51/2	*from* × 10
No. 54	—
Nos. 55/65	*from* × 10
Nos. 66/79	*from* × 4
Nos. 81/6	—
Nos. 87/91	*from* × 12
Nos. 92/111	*from* × 4
Nos. 112/26	*from* × 10
Nos. 127/40	*from* × 6
Nos. 141/5	—
Nos. 146/57	*from* × 5
Nos. 158/79	*from* × 8
Nos. 181/5	—
Nos. 186/8	*from* × 10
Nos. 189/230	*from* × 4
Nos. 231/4	—
Nos. 235/49	*from* × 3
Nos. 250/2	—
Nos. 253/75	*from* × 12
Nos. 276/92	*from* × 7
Nos. 293/4	—
Nos. 295/300	*from* × 6
Nos. 301/2	—
Nos. 303/17	*from* × 3
Nos. 318/19	*from* × 20
Nos. 320/34	*from* × 3
Nos. D1/26	*from* × 20
Nos. D27/8	—
Nos. D29/35	*from* × 7
No. D35*a*	—
Nos. D36/65	*from* × 20
Nos. D66/70	*from* × 5

BRITISH NORTH BORNEO COMPANY ADMINISTRATION

PRINTERS. The stamps of this country up to 1894 were designed by T. Macdonald and printed in lithography by Blades, East and Blades, London.

1   **8 Cents.** (2)   **EIGHT CENTS** (3)

1883. *P* 12.
1 1 2 c. red-brown .. .. 15·00 30·00
a. Imperf between (horiz pair) ..
The figure "2" varies in size.

1883. *No.* 1 *surch as T* **2** *or* **3**.
2 **2** 8 c. on 2 c. red-brown £800 £550
3 **3** 8 c. on 2 c. red-brown £350 £150
a. Surch double .. .. .. — £3250
Type **2** was handstamped and stamps without stop are generally forgeries. Type **3** was a setting of 50 (10 × 5) providing ten varieties; it normally has a stop which sometimes failed to print.

CANCELLED-TO-ORDER—Prices are separately indicated in a third price column, for stamps showing the recognisable black bars remainder cancellation. The issues since 1916 have not been thus cancelled.

It should be noted, however, that a postmark of this form was in use for postal purposes up to this period, and was used at one or two of the smaller post-offices until 1949. A small oval with five bars was used to mark railway mail during 1945/55 and also as a paquebot mark at Jesselton *c.* 1950.

4

5

and Revenue (6)

1883. *P* 14.
4 4 50 c. violet .. .. .. 70·00 — 12·00
a. Inverted "L" for first "F" in "FIFTY" (R.5/2) .. .. £425 — £100
5 5 $1 scarlet .. .. .. 50·00 — 8·00

1883. *P* 12.
6 1 4 c. pink .. .. 20·00 35·00
a. Imperf (horiz pair) .. .. † —
7 8 c. green .. .. 40·00 45·00

1886. *P* 14.
8 1 ½ c. magenta .. .. .. 45·00 £100
9 1 c. orange £140 £200
a. Imperf (pair) £225
b. Imperf horiz (vert pair) ..
10 2 c. brown .. .. .. 12·00 14·00
a. Imperf between (horiz pair) .. £450
11 4 c. pink .. .. .. 12·00 35·00
12 8 c. green .. .. .. 14·00 35·00
a. Imperf between (horiz pair) .. £700
13 10 c. blue .. .. .. 14·00 32·00
a. Imperf (pair) £250
8/13 .. .. .. *Set of* 6 £200 £375
Imperforate examples of the 4 c. pink are listed under No. 6a.

1886. *Nos.* 8 *and* 13 *optd with T* **6**.
14 ½ c. magenta .. .. .. 50·00 £110
15 10 c. blue .. .. .. 90·00 £140

3 CENTS (7)   **5 CENTS** (8)   **3 CENTS** Small "3" variety (R.3/1, 3/4, 3/7)

(Surchd by *North Borneo Herald*, Sandakan)

1886. *T* 1 *surch as T* **7/8**. (*a*) *P* 12.
16 **7** 3 c. on 4 c. pink .. .. 75·00 £150
a. Small "3" .. .. — £3500
17 **8** 5 c. on 8 c. green £110 £160

(*b*) *P* 14
18 **7** 3 c. on 4 c. pink .. .. 48·00 85·00
a. Small "3" £950
19 **8** 5 c. on 8 c. green .. .. 60·00 85·00
a. Surch inverted £1400

9

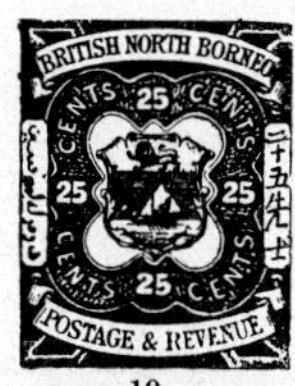

10

11

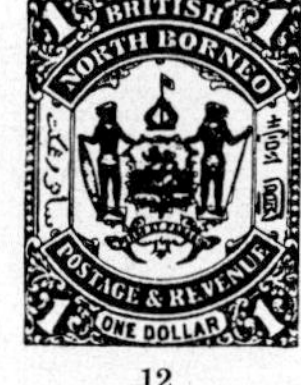

12

13

1886–87. (*a*) *P* 14.
21*b* **9** ½ c. magenta .. .. .. 11·00 26·00
22 ½ c. rose .. .. .. 1·75 8·50
a. Imperf (pair) .. .. 10·00
23 1 c. orange-yellow .. .. 4·00 13·00
a. Imperf between (vert pair) .. £300
b. Imperf (pair) .. .. 9·00
24 1 c. orange .. .. .. 1·25 5·50
a. Imperf (pair) .. .. 6·00
25 2 c. brown .. .. .. 1·50 6·00
a. Imperf (pair) .. .. 6·00
26 4 c. pink .. .. .. 1·25 6·00
a. Imperf (pair) .. .. 6·00
b. Imperf between (horiz or vert pair) £190
c. Imperf vert (horiz pair) .. £225
d. Error. 1 c. pink (R. 2/3) (centre stamp of strip of 3) £120 £250
da. Imperf between (pair) ..
db. Imperf (pair) £2000
27 8 c. green .. .. .. 2·25 11·00
a. Imperf (pair) .. .. 8·50
28 10 c. blue .. .. .. 4·50 18·00
a. Imperf between (vert pair) .. £300
b. Imperf (pair) .. .. 8·50
29 **10** 25 c. indigo .. .. .. 85·00 7·00
a. Imperf between (vert pair) ..
b. Imperf (pair) .. .. 70·00 10·00
30 **11** 50 c. violet .. .. .. 90·00 9·00
a. Imperf (pair) .. .. 60·00 6·00
31 **12** $1 scarlet .. .. .. £140 7·00
a. Imperf (pair) .. .. 75·00 6·00
32 **13** $2 sage-green .. .. .. £170 15·00
a. Imperf (pair) .. .. 90·00 13·00
21*b*/32 .. .. .. *Set of* 10 £450 85·00

(*b*) *P* 12
34 **9** ½ c. magenta .. .. .. 90·00 £180
35 1 c. orange .. .. .. 70·00 £100

Nos. 21*b*/32 are known to have been sold as cancelled remainders, but these are difficult to distinguish from postally used. Values above 10 c. are infrequently found postally used so that the used prices quoted are for the remainders.

14

15

16

17

18

1887–92. *T* **14** (*as T* **9** *but inscr* "POSTAGE & REVENUE") *and T* **15/18** (*T* **10/13** *redrawn*). *P* 14.

36	**14**	½ c. magenta (1889)	2·50	11·00	—
		a. Imperf vert (horiz pair)	†	†	£200
		b. Rose	30	2·25	30
		ba. Imperf between (horiz pair)	£350		
37		1 c. orange (1892)	50	2·25	30
		a. Imperf vert (horiz pair)	£300		
38		2 c. brown (1889)	4·50	6·00	30
		a. Imperf between (horiz pair)			
		b. Lake-brown	1·00	6·00	30
39		3 c. violet	1·50	8·50	30
		a. Printed triple, one inverted			
40		4 c. rose-pink (1889)	2·25	13·00	30
		a. Imperf between (pair)	—	£120	—
41		5 c. slate	2·00	9·00	30
		a. Imperf between (pair)			
42		6 c. lake (1892)	4·50	11·00	45
43		8 c. blue-green (1891)	7·00	12·00	45
		a. Yellow-green	7·00	12·00	45
		b. Printed triple, one inverted			
44		10 c. blue (1891)	4·25	12·00	50
		a. Imperf between (vert pair)	†	†	£200
		b. Dull blue	4·25	12·00	50
		ba. Imperf between (horiz pair)			
		c. Printed double			
45	**15**	25 c. indigo (1888)	19·00	65·00	50
		a. Imperf (pair)	80·00	—	3·00
		b. Imperf vert (horiz pair)	†	†	£250
46	**16**	50 c. violet (1888)	35·00	95·00	50
		a. Imperf (pair)	85·00	—	3·00
		b. Chalky blue	†	90·00	†
47	**17**	$1 scarlet (1888)	20·00	90·00	50
		a. Imperf (pair)	80·00	—	3·00
48	**18**	$2 dull green (1888)	65·00	£130	1·10
		a. Imperf (pair)	£100	—	3·50
36*b*/48		*Set of* 13	£150	£400	4·75

Nos. 36/44 also exist imperf (*Price* £6 *per pair unused*; £4 *cancelled*).

Nos. 39a, 43b and 44c are from waste sheets subsequently sold by the British North Borneo Company to collectors.

These stamps to the 10 c. value were forged on several occasions. Most forgeries of the ½ c. value can be identified by the presence of a diagonal line joining the top two horizontal strokes of the uppermost Chinese character.

The new 25 c. has the inscription "BRITISH NORTH BORNEO" in taller capitals. In the 50 c. the "0" of the numerals "50" in the two upper corners is square-shaped at the top and bottom instead of being oval. The 1 dollar has 14 pearls instead of 13 at each side, and on the 2 dollars the word "BRITISH" measures 10½ to 11 mm in length in place of 12 mm.

19

20

1889. *P* 14.

49	**19**	$5 bright purple	80·00	90·00	6·00
		a. Imperf (pair)	£150	—	16·00
50	**20**	$10 brown	£120	£160	9·00
		a. Imperf (pair)	£250	—	20·00
		b. "DOLLAPS" for "DOLLARS" (R.2/1)	£900	£1100	£325
		ba. Ditto. Imperf (pair)	£1500	—	£800

Two Cents. (21) **6 cents.** (22) **1 cent.** (23)

1890. *Surch as T* **21**, *in red.*

51	**15**	2 c. on 25 c. indigo	40·00	65·00
		a. Surch inverted	£275	£275
52		8 c. on 25 c. indigo	60·00	80·00

The first printing of Nos. 51/2 had the two lines of the surcharge 3.5 mm apart. On a second printing of both values this gap widened to 5 mm.

1891–92. *Surch with T* **22**.

54	**9**	6 c. on 8 c. green (1892)	£5000	£3500
		a. Large "s" in "cents"	£10000	
55	**14**	6 c. on 8 c. yellow-green	7·00	8·50
		a. Surch inverted	£180	£250
		b. Inverted "c" in "cents" (R.5/4)	£250	£300
		c. "cetns." for "cents" (R.3/7)	£275	£325
		d. Large "s" in "cents" (R.2/9 or 3/7)	95·00	95·00
56	**9**	6 c. on 10 c. blue	32·00	17·00
		a. Surch inverted	£130	£130
		b. Surch double		
		c. Surch treble	£275	
		d. Large "s" in "cents"	£120	£110
57	**14**	6 c. on 10 c. blue	70·00	24·00
		a. Large "s" in "cents"	£225	£140

Unused examples of Nos. 55 and 57 are normally without gum.

There were three settings of the surcharge for No. 55. On the first two the large "s" in "cents" occurred on R.2/9 with the other two listed varieties also included. Nos. 55b/c were corrected on the third setting and the large "s" in cents occurred on R.3/7.

1892. *Surch as T* **23** ("Cents." *with capital* "C" *as in T* **21** *on No.* 65), *in red.*

63	**14**	1 c. on 4 c. rose-pink	12·00	14·00
		a. Surch double	£650	
		b. Surch on back and on front	—	£500
		ba. As b, but with surch double on front		
64		1 c. on 5 c. slate	6·00	6·00
65	**15**	8 c. on 25 c. indigo	£110	£130

Unused examples of Nos. 63/5 are normally without gum.

24 Dyak Chief

25 Sambar Stag (*Cervus unicolor*)

26 Sago Palm

27 Great Argus Pheasant

28 Arms of the Company

29 Malay Dhow

30 Estuarine Crocodile

31 Mount Kinabalu

32 Arms of the Company with Supporters

PERFORATION. There are a number of small variations in the perforation of the Waterlow issues of 1894 to 1922 which we believe were due to irregularity of the pins rather than different perforators.

In the following lists, stamps perf 12, 12½, 13 or compound are described as perf 12–13, stamps perf 13½, 14 or compound are described as perf 13½–14 and those perf 14½, 15 or compound are listed as perf 14½–15. In addition the 13½–14 perforation exists compound with 14½–15 and with 12–13, whilst perf 15½–16 comes from a separate perforator.

(Recess Waterlow)

1894. *P* 14½–15.

66	**24**	1 c. black and olive-bistre	1·25	6·00	20
		a. Imperf between (horiz or vert pair)	£475		
		b. Perf 13½–14	1·25	6·00	20
		c. Perf 13½–14, comp 14½–15	22·00	32·00	—
		d. Perf 13½–14, comp 12–13	11·00	26·00	—
		e. Perf 12–13			
67	**24**	1 c. black and bistre-brown	1·00	6·00	20
		a. Perf 13½–14	1·25	6·00	20
		b. Perf 13½–14, comp 12–13	14·00	30·00	—
		c. Perf 12–13			
68	**25**	2 c. black and rose-lake	3·50	4·50	30
		a. Imperf between (horiz or vert pair)	£400	£450	†
		b. Perf 13½–14	22·00	26·00	—
69		2 c. black and lake	3·25	4·00	30
		a. Perf 13½–14	25·00	30·00	—
		b. Perf 13½–14, comp 12–13	18·00	20·00	—
		c. Imperf between (horiz pair)			
70	**26**	3 c. olive-green and mauve	2·25	7·00	30
		a. Imperf between (horiz pair)	—	£350	†
		b. Bronze-green and mauve			
		c. Perf 13½–14			
71		3 c. olive-green & violet (*p* 13½–14)	9·50	27·00	—
		a. Imperf between (horiz pair)			
72	**27**	5 c. black and vermilion	6·00	10·00	40
		a. Imperf between (horiz or vert pair)	£300		
		b. Perf 13½–14	30·00	50·00	—
		c. Perf 13½–14, comp 12–13	—	55·00	—
		d. Perf 13½–14, comp 14½–15			
		e. Perf 12–13			
73	**28**	6 c. black and bistre-brown	38·00	60·00	—
		a. Perf 13½–14	3·50	13·00	40
		b. Perf 13½–14, comp 12–13	—	50·00	—
		c. Perf 13½–14, comp 14½–15	42·00		
		d. Imperf between (horiz pair)			
74	**29**	8 c. black and dull purple	2·50	8·00	50
		a. Imperf between (vert pair)	£350		
		b. Perf 13½–14	7·00	20·00	50
		ba. Imperf between (vert pair)	£350	†	£300
		d. Perf 13½–14, comp 12–13			
75	**30**	12 c. black and blue	24·00	60·00	2·00
		a. Perf 13½–14	24·00	60·00	2·00
		b. Imperf between (horiz pair)	†	†	£400
76		12 c. black and ultramarine	32·00	65·00	2·00
		a. Perf 13½–14	30·00	65·00	2·00
		b. Imperf between (pair)			
78	**31**	18 c. black and deep green	15·00	40·00	2·00
		a. Perf 13½–14	20·00	40·00	2·00
79	**32**	24 c. blue and rose-lake	16·00	48·00	2·00
		a. Imperf between (vert pair)	—	—	£250
		b. Imperf between (vert strip of 3)	†	†	£350
		c. Perf 13½–14	16·00	48·00	2·00
		d. Perf 13½–14, comp 14½–15			
66/79		*Set of* 9	65·00	£180	7·50

32*a*

32*b*

32*c*

32*d*

(Litho Blades, East & Blades, London)

1894. *T* **32***a to* **32***d*, *and T* **19** *and* **20**, *but inscribed* "THE STATE OF NORTH BORNEO". *P* 14.

81	25 c. indigo	8·00	26·00	70
	a. Imperf (pair)	16·00	—	2·75
	b. Imperf between (horiz or vert pair)	£550	—	75·00
	c. Printed double, one inverted	†	†	55·00
82	50 c. deep slate-purple	9·00	40·00	70
	a. Imperf (pair)	—	—	2·50
	b. Imperf between (horiz pair)			
	c. Printed double			
	d. Chalky blue	—	50·00	—
83	$1 scarlet	10·00	22·00	90
	a. Perf 14 × 11	£150		
	b. Imperf (pair)	14·00	—	5·00
	c. Printed both sides	25·00		
84	$2 dull green	13·00	55·00	90
	a. Imperf (pair)	—	—	4·50
	b. Printed double			
85	$5 bright purple	£130	£180	9·50
	a. Imperf (pair)	85·00	—	14·00
	b. Dull purple	65·00	£100	3·50
86	$10 brown	£130	£190	5·00
	a. Imperf (pair)	85·00	—	11·00
81/6	*Set of* 6	£200	£350	10·50
81/6 Optd "Specimen"	*Set of* 6	£120		

For Nos. 81 to 83 in other colours, see Labuan 80*a*, 81*a* and 82*a*.

Nos. 81c, 82c, 83c and 84b are from waste sheets subsequently sold by the British North Borneo Company to collectors.

4

CENTS

(33 (3½ mm between lines of surcharge))

(Surcharged by Waterlow)

1895 (June). *No.* 83 *surch as T* **33**.

87	4 cents on $1 scarlet	2·50	1·50	30
	a. Surch double	£550		
88	10 cents on $1 scarlet	4·75	1·75	30
89	20 cents on $1 scarlet	15·00	9·50	30

90	30 cents on $1 scarlet	10·00	13·00	30
91	40 cents on $1 scarlet	15·00	23·00	30
87/91	*Set of* 5	42·00	45·00	1·40
87/91	Optd "Specimen" *Set of* 5	85·00		

For 4 c. on $1 with wider spacing see No. 121.

No. 88 exists with the figures of the surcharge 2½ mm away from "CENTS". The normal setting has a space of 4 mm. Examples of the narrow setting have, so far, only been seen on cancelled-to-order stamps.

34 35 36

37 Orang-Utan 38 39

40 41 Sun Bear

42 43 Borneo Railway Train

44 45

(Recess Waterlow)

1897 (Mar)–**1902.** *T* **34** *to* **45.** *New frames. P* 13½–14.

92	1 c. black and bistre-brown	4·00	2·50	20
	aa. Perf 16			
	a. Perf 14½–15	3·75	2·00	20
	b. Perf 13½–14, comp 12–13	35·00	35·00	—
	c. Imperf between (horiz pair)	†	†	£325
93	1 c. black and ochre	23·00	12·00	—
	a. Perf 14½–15	15·00	9·00	20
	ab. Imperf between (horiz pair)	†	†	£325
	b. Perf 13½–14, comp 12–13			
94	2 c. black and lake	10·00	2·75	20
	a. Perf 14½–15	6·00	2·75	20
	ab. Imperf between (horiz pair)	†	†	£325
	b. Perf 13½–14, comp 12-13	—	13·00	—
	c. Perf 12–13			
	d. Imperf between (vert pair)	†	†	£325
95	2 c. black and green (1900)	21·00	1·50	20
	a. Perf 14½–15	38·00	10·00	—
	b. Perf 13½–14, comp 12–13	65·00	19·00	—
	c. Perf 12–13			
	d. Imperf between (pair)	—	£425	†
96	3 c. green and rosy mauve	17·00	7·00	30
	a. Perf 14½–15	35·00	38·00	—
	b. Perf 13½–14, comp 12–13	60·00	60·00	—
97	3 c. green & dull mauve (*p* 14½–15)	4·50	3·00	30
98	4 c. black and green (1900)	6·00	—	40
	a. Perf 13½–14, comp 12–13			
99	4 c. black and carmine (1900)	13·00	4·75	30
	a. Perf 16	40·00	28·00	—
	b. Perf 14½–15	23·00	2·00	30
	c. Perf 13½–14, comp 12–13	19·00	20·00	—
	d. Perf 12–13			
100	5 c. black and orange-vermilion	40·00	3·50	30
	a. Perf 14½–15	45·00	2·75	30
	b. Perf 13½–14, comp 12–13	48·00	12·00	—
	c. Perf 12–13			
101	6 c. black and bistre-brown	15·00	9·50	30
	a. Perf 14½–15	8·00	3·00	30
102	8 c. black and brown-purple	35·00	35·00	—
	a. Perf 16	70·00	13·00	40
	ab. Imperf between (vert pair)	£350	£350	—
	b. Perf 14½–15	14·00	2·75	40
103	8 c. black and brown	7·00	16·00	40
	a. Perf 14½–15	30·00	35·00	—
	b. Perf 16			
104	10 c. brown and slate-lilac (1902)	45·00	27·00	1·00
	a. Imperf between (vert pair)			
105	10 c. brown and slate-blue (1902)	80·00	55·00	1·00
106	12 c. black and dull blue	80·00	40·00	1·00
	a. Imperf between (vert pair)	†	†	£325
	b. Perf 14½–15	48·00	28·00	1·00
	c. Perf 13½–14, comp 12–13	95·00	55·00	—
	d. Perf 12–13			
107	16 c. green and chestnut (1902)	75·00	70·00	2·50
	a. Perf 14½–15	75·00	£100	—
108	18 c. black and green (*p* 16)	12·00	27·00	50
	a. Imperf vert (horiz pair)	†	†	60·00
	b. Imperf between (vert pair)	†	†	£200
	c. Imperf (pair)	†	†	—
109	24 c. blue and lake	8·50	48·00	1·00
	a. Perf 13½–14, comp 12–13	24·00	65·00	—
	b. Perf 12–13	70·00		
92/109	(*one of each value*) *Set of* 12	£250	£200	6·75
92/109	(*excl* 93, 97, 103) Optd "Specimen" *Set of* 14	£170		

In the above the 18 c. has "POSTAL REVENUE" instead of "POSTAGE AND REVENUE" and the 24 c. has those words omitted. These stamps were replaced by others with corrected inscriptions; see Nos. 110 and 111.

46 47

1897. *Corrected inscriptions. P* 13½–14.

110	**46**	18 c. black and green	42·00	12·00	75
		a. Imperf between (horiz pair)	†	†	£325
		b. Perf 14½–15	45·00	12·00	75
		c. Perf 13½–14, comp 12–13			
111	**47**	24 c. blue and lake	35·00	30·00	1·00
		a. Perf 16	70·00	70·00	—
		b. Perf 14½–15	28·00	42·00	1·00
		c. Perf 13½–14, comp 12–13			
		d. Perf 12–13			
110/11		Optd "Specimen" *Set of* 2	45·00		

4 CENTS — **(48)** (4½ mm between lines of surcharge)

BRITISH PROTECTORATE. — **(49)**

4 cents — **(50)**

1899. *Surch with T* **48.** (*a*) *P* 14½–15.

112	4 c. on 5 c. (No. 100a)	27·00	
	a. Perf 13½–14	10·00	10·00
	b. Perf 13½–14, comp 12–13	28·00	38·00
113	4 c. on 6 c. (No. 101a)	16·00	20·00
	a. Perf 13½–14	10·00	26·00
114	4 c. on 8 c. (No. 102b)	12·00	10·00
115	4 c. on 12 c. (No. 106b)	11·00	13·00
	a. Imperf between (horiz pair)	£400	
	b. Imperf between (vert pair)	—	£400
	c. Perf 13½–14		
	d. Perf 12–13		
	e. Perf 13½–14, comp 12–13	22·00	
116	4 c. on 18 c. (No. 110a)	9·50	13·00
	a. Perf 13½–14		
117	4 c. on 24 c. (No. 111b)	11·00	12·00
	a. Perf 16	35·00	45·00
	b. Perf 13½–14	12·00	32·00
	c. Perf 13½–14, comp 12–13	26·00	35·00
	d. Perf 12–13	25·00	32·00
	(*b*) *P* 14		
118	4 c. on 25 c. indigo (No. 81)	5·00	8·50
	a. Imperf between (horiz strip of 3)	£800	
119	4 c. on 50 c. deep slate-purple (No. 82)	6·00	12·00
	a. Chalky blue	24·00	30·00
121	4 c. on $1 scarlet (No. 83)	5·00	8·50
122	4 c. on $2 dull green (No. 84)	5·00	12·00
123	4 c. on $5 bright purple (No. 85)	£100	£160
	a. Dull purple	60·00	£120
124	4 c. on $10 brown (No. 86)	60·00	£120
112/24	*Set of* 12	£180	£325
112/24	Optd "Specimen" *Set of* 12	£150	

No. 121 differs only from No. 87 in having the "4" and "cents" wider apart.

Examples of the Kudat postmark dated "AU 15 1899" struck on Nos. 112/24 are generally considered to be faked.

A new setting of the surcharge, with 5 mm between "4" and "CENTS", was used for the Specimen overprints, including unissued surcharges on the 1 c., 2 c. and 3 c. values (*price* £90 *the set of three*).

1899. *Surch as T* **48** *but* 8½ *mm between lines of surcharge. P* 14.

125	4 c. on $5 (No. 85)	5·50	11·00
126	4 c. on $10 (No. 86)	5·50	11·00

(Surcharged by Waterlow)

1901 (8 Oct)–**05.** *Optd as T* **49.** (*a*) *P* 13½–14.

127	1 c. (No. 92) (R.)	2·25	1·50	10
	a. Perf 14½–15	1·50	1·60	10
128	2 c. (No. 95) (R.)	2·25	1·75	10
	a. Perf 16	3·50	4·75	15
	b. Perf 14½–15	5·00	6·00	15
129	3 c. (No. 96)	1·10	2·50	10
	a. Imperf between (vert pair)			
	b. Perf 14½–15	5·50	2·00	10
	c. Perf 13½–14, comp 14½–15	35·00		
130	4 c. (No. 99) (G.)	4·50	1·50	10
	a. Perf 14½–15	10·00	1·50	10
131	5 c. (No. 100) (G.)	17·00	3·00	15
	a. Perf 14½–15	4·75	2·25	15
132	6 c. (No. 101) (R.)	25·00	40·00	—
	a. No stop after "Protectorate"	65·00	65·00	—
	b. Perf 16	2·50	6·00	20
133	8 c. (No. 103) (B.)	2·75	3·00	20
	a. No stop after "Protectorate"	3·00	17·00	—
	b. Perf 13½–14, comp 12–13	35·00	12·00	—
	c. Imperf between (vert pair)	†	†	£300
134	10 c. (No. 104) (R.) (7.02)	11·00	4·50	30
	a. Perf 14½–15	45·00	20·00	—
	c. Perf 13½–14. No stop after "Protectorate"	95·00		
	d. Opt double	£350	†	£225
	e. On 10 c. (No. 105)	90·00		
	f. Imperf vert (horiz pair)	†	†	£300
135	12 c. (No. 106) (R.)	23·00	12·00	1·00
136	16 c. (No. 107) (7.02)	50·00	20·00	1·50
	a. Perf 14½–15	55·00	28·00	1·50
	b. Perf 13½–14, comp 12–13	85·00	48·00	—
137	18 c. (No. 110) (R.)	8·00	19·00	60
	a. No stop after "Protectorate"			
	b. Perf 13½–14, comp 12–13			
138	24 c. (No. 111)	14·00	26·00	1·00
	a. Perf 14½–15	45·00	55·00	1·25
	b. Imperf between (horiz pair)			
	(*b*) *P* 14			
139	25 c. (No. 81) (R.)	2·00	10·00	30
	a. No stop after "Protectorate"	90·00	£110	—
	b. Overprints *tête-bêche* (horiz pair)			
	c. Overprint inverted	£350		

140 50 c. (No. 82) (R.) .. .. .. 2·75 11·00 40
a. No stop after "Protectorate" .. 45·00 75·00 —
b. Chalky blue .. .. ..
141 $1 (No. 83) (R.) (1.04) .. .. 10·00 50·00 —
142 $1 (No. 83) .. .. .. 6·50 28·00 2·50
a. Imperf horiz (vert pair) .. £400
b. Opt double .. .. .. † † £275
c. Opt treble .. .. ..
143 $2 (No. 84) (R.) (1903) .. .. 25·00 75·00 3·50
a. Opt double .. .. .. £950 — £325
144 $5 (No. 85*b*) (R.) (2.05) .. .. £130 £300 4·00
145 $10 (No. 86) (R.) (2.05) .. .. £190 £375 7·00
a. Opt inverted .. .. .. £1100 † £350
127/45 .. .. .. *Set of* 18 £425 £800 23·00
127/40 Optd "Specimen" .. *Set of* 14 £250

There was more than one setting of the overprint for some of the values. Full sheets of the 6 c. and 8 c. are known, without stop throughout.

1904–5. *Surch locally with T* **50.** *(a) P* 14½–15.
146 4 c. on 5 c. (No. 100a) .. .. 15·00 26·00 3·00
a. Surch omitted (in pair with normal) .. .. ..
147 4 c. on 6 c. (No. 101a) .. .. 5·00 15·00 2·00
a. Surch inverted £160
148 4 c. on 8 c. (No. 102b) .. .. 11·00 23·00 2·25
a. Surch inverted £180
149 4 c. on 12 c. (No. 106b) .. .. 17·00 30·00 2·50
a. Perf 13½–14 .. .. .. 35·00 48·00 2·50
b. Perf 13½–14, comp 12–13 .. 24·00 48·00 —
c. Surch omitted (in pair with normal) .. .. ..
150 4 c. on 18 c. (No. 110a) .. .. 14·00 28·00 3·00
a. Perf 13½–14 .. .. ..
151 4 c. on 24 c. (No. 111b) .. .. 17·00 38·00 3·00
a. Perf 16 .. .. .. 15·00 38·00 3·00
b. Perf 13½–14 .. .. .. 18·00 38·00 3·00
c. Perf 12–13 .. .. ..

(b) P 14
152 4 c. on 25 c. (No. 81) .. .. .. 3·50 22·00 2·50
153 4 c. on 50 c. (No. 82) .. .. .. 3·50 28·00 2·50
154 4 c. on $1 (No. 83) .. .. .. 4·25 40·00 3·00
155 4 c. on $2 (No. 84) .. .. .. 5·50 42·00 3·25
156 4 c. on $5 (No. 85) .. .. .. 11·00 45·00 3·50
a. Surch on No. 85*b* .. .. 30·00 45·00
157 4 c. on $10 (No. 86) .. .. .. 11·00 45·00 3·50
a. Surch inverted £1200
b. Surch omitted (in pair with normal) .. .. ..
146/57 .. .. *Set of* 12 £100 £350 30·00

51 Malayan Tapir

52 Travellers' Tree

53 Railway at Jesselton

54 The Sultan of Sulu, his staff and W. C. Cowie, Managing Director of the Company

55 Indian Elephant

56 Sumatran Rhinoceros

57 Ploughing with Buffalo

58 Wild Boar

59 Palm Cockatoo

60 Rhinoceros Hornbill

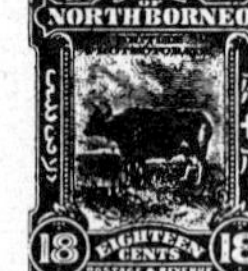
61 Banteng

62 Dwarf Cassowary

(Recess Waterlow)

1909 (1 July)–**24.** *Centres in black. P* 13½–14.
158 **51** 1 c. chocolate-brown .. .. 3·00 70 10
a. Perf 14½–15 .. .. 14·00 7·50 —
159 1 c. brown .. .. .. 6·50 90 —
a. Perf 14½–15 .. .. 12·00 2·00 20
b. Imperf between (vert pair) .. £750
160 **52** 2 c. green 75 30 10
a. Imperf between (pair) ..
b. Perf 14½–15 .. .. 2·00 60 10
161 **53** 3 c. lake .. .. .. 2·00 90 10
162 3 c. rose-lake .. .. .. 2·50 70 10
a. Perf 14½–15 .. .. 25·00 — 40
163 3 c. green (1924) .. .. 5·50 80 —
164 **54** 4 c. scarlet .. .. .. 1·25 15 10
a. Imperf between (vert pair) ..
b. Perf 14½–15 .. .. 6·50 1·60 30
165 **55** 5 c. yellow-brown .. .. 6·50 3·00 10
a. Perf 14½–15 .. ..
166 5 c. dark brown .. .. 7·00 2·00 —
167 **56** 6 c. olive-green .. .. 5·00 90 10
a. Perf 14½–15 .. .. 42·00 5·50 60
168 6 c. apple-green .. .. 15·00 2·00 —
169 **57** 8 c. lake .. .. .. 2·00 1·25 10
a. Perf 14½–15 .. ..
170 **58** 10 c. greyish blue .. .. 23·00 6·00 20
a. Perf 14½–15 .. .. 42·00 14·00 —
171 10 c. blue .. .. .. 29·00 2·00 —
172 10 c. turquoise-blue .. .. 13·00 1·75 —
a. Perf 14½–15 .. .. 30·00 5·00 —
173 **59** 12 c. deep blue .. .. 17·00 1·60 20
a. Perf 14½–15 .. ..
b. Imperf between (horiz pair) † † £350
173*c* 12 c. deep bright blue .. ..
174 **60** 16 c. brown-lake .. .. 14·00 5·00 40
175 **61** 18 c. blue-green .. .. 55·00 27·00 50
176 **62** 24 c. deep rose-lilac .. .. 16·00 2·25 30
a. Deep lilac .. ..
158/76 .. .. *Set of* 13 £130 40·00 —
158/76 Optd "Specimen" .. *Set of* 13 £275

For this issue perf 12½ see Nos. 277, etc.

(63)

64

65

1909 (7 Sept). *No.* 175 *surch with T* **63** *by Waterlow. P* 13½–14.
177 20 c. on 18 c. blue-green (R.) (Optd S. £35) .. .. .. 4·00 35 10
a. Perf 14½–15 .. .. .. £140 60·00 —

(Recess Waterlow)

1911 (7 Mar). *P* 13½–14.
178 **64** 25 c. black and yellow-green .. 4·00 3·25 1·00
a. Perf 14½–15 .. .. 8·50 24·00 —
b. Imperf (pair) .. .. 38·00
178*c* 25 c. black and blue-green .. 30·00
179 50 c. black and steel-blue .. 5·50 3·25 1·25
a. Perf 14½–15 .. .. 15·00 18·00 —
ab. Imperf between (horiz pair) £1000
c. Imperf (pair) .. .. 55·00
180 $1 black and chestnut .. .. 11·00 3·25 1·25
a. Perf 14½–15 .. .. 28·00 14·00 —
b. Imperf (pair) .. .. 70·00
181 $2 black and lilac .. .. 27·00 11·00 3·00
182 **65** $5 black and lake .. .. 55·00 60·00 20·00
a. Imperf (pair) £130
183 $10 black and brick-red .. £140 £170 40·00
a. Imperf (pair) £180
178/83 .. .. .. *Set of* 6 £225 £225 60·00
178/83 Optd "Specimen" .. *Set of* 6 £225

BRITISH

PROTECTORATE
(66)

2
cents
(67)

(68)

1912 (July). *Nos.* 85 *and* 86 *optd with T* **66.**
184 $5 dull purple (R.) .. .. .. £750 — 6·00
185 $10 brown (R.) .. .. .. £900 — 6·00
a. Opt inverted .. .. .. † † —

1916 (Feb). *Stamps of* 1909–22 *surch as T* **67** *by Govt Printing Office, Sandakan. P* 13½–14.
186 2 c. on 3 c. black and rose-lake .. .. 9·50 7·50
a. "s" inverted (R. 2/5) .. .. 85·00 85·00
b. Surch double .. .. ..
187 4 c. on 6 c. black and olive-green (R.) .. 9·50 9·50
a. "s" inverted (R. 2/5) .. .. 85·00 85·00
b. "s" inserted by hand .. .. — £550
c. Perf 14½–15 .. .. ..
ca. "s" inverted .. .. ..
188 10 c. on 12 c. black and deep blue (R.) .. 25·00 35·00
a. "s" inverted (R. 2/5) .. .. 90·00 90·00
186/8 .. .. .. *Set of* 3 40·00 48·00
186/8 Optd "Specimen" .. *Set of* 3 £100

Nos. 186/8 were surcharged from a setting of 25 (5×5) on which the required face values were inserted.

1916 (May). *Stamps of* 1909–11 *optd with T* **68** *by Waterlow. P* 13½–14. *Centres in black. (a) Cross in vermilion.*
189 **51** 1 c. brown .. .. .. 6·50 26·00
190 **52** 2 c. green .. .. .. 27·00 65·00
a. Perf 14½–15 .. .. 32·00 70·00
191 **53** 3 c. rose-lake .. .. .. 20·00 35·00
a. Nos. 191 and 204 *se-tenant* (vert pair) £750
192 **54** 4 c. scarlet .. .. .. 5·50 23·00
a. Perf 14½–15 .. .. £130 £110
193 **55** 5 c. yellow-brown .. .. 18·00 50·00
a. Perf 14½–15 .. ..
194 **56** 6 c. apple-green .. .. 38·00 60·00
a. Perf 14½–15 .. .. £130
195 **57** 8 c. lake .. .. .. 17·00 50·00
196 **58** 10 c. blue .. .. .. 35·00 65·00
197 **59** 12 c. deep blue .. .. 60·00 70·00
198 **60** 16 c. brown-lake .. .. 60·00 70·00
199 **61** 20 c. on 18 c. blue-green .. 25·00 70·00
200 **62** 24 c. dull mauve .. .. 60·00 70·00
a. Imperf between (vert pair) ..
201 **64** 25 c. green (*p* 14½–15) £250 £350
189/201 .. .. .. *Set of* 13 £500 £900

(b) Cross in carmine
202 **51** 1 c. brown .. .. .. 20·00 50·00
a. Perf 14½–15 .. .. £130
203 **52** 2 c. green .. .. .. 26·00 38·00
b. Perf 14½–15 .. .. £130
ba. Opt double .. .. .. † —
204 **53** 3 c. rose-lake .. .. .. 24·00 55·00
204*a* **54** 4 c. scarlet £350
205 **55** 5 c. yellow-brown .. .. 30·00 65·00
206 **56** 6 c. apple-green .. .. 26·00 65·00
a. Perf 14½–15 .. .. £130
207 **57** 8 c. lake .. .. .. 18·00 55·00
208 **58** 10 c. blue .. .. .. 30·00 60·00
209 **59** 12 c. deep blue .. .. 55·00 90·00
210 **60** 16 c. brown-lake .. .. 55·00 90·00
211 **61** 20 c. on 18 c. blue-green .. 55·00 90·00
212 **62** 24 c. dull mauve .. .. 65·00 £120
213 **64** 25 c. green £600
a. Perf 14½–15 .. .. £400 £475
202/13 (*ex* 4 c.) .. .. *Set of* 12 £650 £1100

The British North Borneo Company donated a proportion of the above issue to be sold by the National Philatelic War Fund for the benefit of the Red Cross and St. John's Ambulance Brigade.

RED CROSS ✚

TWO CENTS
(69)

FOUR CENTS
(70)

1918 (Aug). *Stamps of* 1909–11 *surch as T* **69.** *P* 13½–14.
(a) Lines of surcharge 9 *mm apart*
214 **51** 1 c. + 2 c. brown .. .. 2·25 7·00
a. Imperf between (horiz pair) .. £1000
215 **52** 2 c. + 2 c. green .. .. 70 7·00
a. Imperf between (horiz or vert pair) £1000
b. Imperf (pair) .. ..
c. Perf 14½–15 .. ..
216 **53** 3 c. + 2 c. rose-red .. .. 4·50 12·00
a. Imperf between (horiz pair) .. £1000
b. Perf 14½–15 .. .. 24·00 60·00
217 3 c. + 2 c. dull rose-carmine .. £130
a. Perf 14½–15 .. .. £160
218 **54** 4 c. + 2 c. scarlet .. .. 55 3·75
a. Surch inverted £275
219 **55** 5 c. + 2 c. deep brown .. .. 4·50 14·00
220 5 c. + 2 c. pale brown .. .. 5·50 20·00
221 **56** 6 c. + 2 c. olive-green .. .. 3·50 17·00
a. Perf 14½–15 .. .. £130
221*b* 6 c. + 2 c. apple-green .. ..
c. Perf 14½–15 .. .. £225
222 **57** 8 c. + 2 c. lake .. .. 4·00 7·00
a. Inverted figure "3" for "C" in "CENTS" .. ..
223 **58** 10 c. + 2 c. blue .. .. 6·50 22·00
224 **59** 12 c. + 2 c. deep bright blue .. 10·00 30·00
a. Surch inverted £500
225 **60** 16 c. + 2 c. brown-lake .. .. 11·00 30·00
226 **62** 24 c. + 2 c. mauve .. .. 12·00 30·00

(b) Lines of surch 13–14 *mm apart*
227 **52** 2 c. + 2 c. green .. .. 55·00 £100
228 **56** 6 c. + 2 c. olive-green £225 £500
229 **64** 25 c. + 2 c. green .. .. 10·00 38·00
230 50 c. + 2 c. steel-blue .. .. 12·00 38·00
231 $1 + 2 c. chestnut .. .. 38·00 48·00
232 $2 + 2 c. lilac .. .. 55·00 90·00
233 **65** $5 + 2 c. lake £250 £400
234 $10 + 2 c. brick-red £250 £400
214/34 .. .. .. *Set of* 17 £600 £1000

The above stamps were dispatched from London in three consignments, of which two were lost through enemy action at sea.

Only one sheet was found of No. 228.

These stamps were sold at a premium of 2 c. per stamp, which went to the Red Cross Society.

1918 (Oct). *Stamps of* 1909–11 *surch with T* **70**, *in red. P* 13½–14.
235 **51** 1 c. + 4 c. chocolate .. .. 50 3·50
a. Imperf between (horiz pair) .. £1000
236 **52** 2 c. + 4 c. green .. .. 65 6·50
237 **53** 3 c. + 4 c. rose-lake .. .. 80 3·25
238 **54** 4 c. + 4 c. scarlet .. .. 40 4·50
239 **55** 5 c. + 4 c. brown .. .. 1·75 16·00

No.	Type	Description	Unused	Used
240	56	6 c. + 4 c. apple-green	1·75	11·00
		a. Imperf between (vert pair)	£1000	
241	57	8 c. + 4 c. lake	1·10	9·00
242	58	10 c. + 4 c. turquoise-blue	2·00	12·00
242*a*		10 c. + 4 c. greenish blue	5·50	30·00
243	59	12 c. + 4 c. deep blue	6·00	12·00
		a. Surch double	£600	
244	60	16 c. + 4 c. brown-lake	5·00	16·00
245	62	24 c. + 4 c. mauve	5·00	20·00
246	64	25 c. + 4 c. yellow-green	3·25	38·00
247		25 c. + 4 c. blue-green	23·00	70·00
248		50 c. + 4 c. steel-blue	14·00	38·00
		a. Perf 14½–15	55·00	
249		$1 + 4 c. chestnut	14·00	50·00
		a. Perf 14½–15	60·00	
250		$2 + 4 c. lilac	40·00	75·00
251	65	$5 + 4 c. lake	£200	£400
252		$10 + 4 c. brick-red	£200	£400
235/52		*Set of* 17	£450	£1000

Nos. 235/52 were sold at face, plus 4 c. on each stamp for Red Cross Funds.

MALAYA-BORNEO
EXHIBITION
1922.
(71)

THREE
CENTS
(72)

1922 (31 Mar). *Malaya-Borneo Exhibition, Singapore. Stamps of* 1909–22 *optd as T* **71** *by Govt Printing Office, Sandakan. P* 13½–14.

No.	Type	Description	Unused	Used
253	51	1 c. brown (R.)	5·50	40·00
		a. "BORHEO"	£275	£325
		b. "BORNEQ"	£400	£450
		c. Stop after "EXHIBITION."	42·00	
		d. Raised stop after "1922"	£275	
		e. "EXHIBITICN." with stop	£400	
		f. Perf 14½–15	14·00	50·00
		fa. "BORHEO"	£375	
		fb. "BORNEQ"	£550	
		fc. Raised stop after "1922"	£375	
		fd. "EXHIBITICN." with stop	£550	
		fe. "MHLAYA" and stop after "EXHIBITION"		
		ff. Stop after "EXHIBITION."	50·00	
253*g*		1 c. brown (B.)(*p* 14½–15)	£700	
		ga. Vert pair, with and without opt	£2000	
		gb. Raised stop after "1922."	£1300	
		gc. "BORHEO"	£1300	
		gd. "BORNEQ"	£1700	
		gf. "EXHIBITICN." with stop	£1700	
		gg. "MHLAYA" and stop after EXHIBITION"		
254		1 c. orange-brown (R.)	13·00	45·00
255	52	2 c. green (R.)	1·40	14·00
		a. Stop after "EXHIBITION."	20·00	
256	53	3 c. rose-lake (B.)	5·00	30·00
		a. Stop after "EXHIBITION."	38·00	
		b. "EXHIBITICN." with stop	£1100	
		c. Raised stop after "1922"	£750	
257	54	4 c. scarlet (B.)	1·40	24·00
		a. Stop after "EXHIBITION."	19·00	
		b. Perf 14½–15		
		ba. Stop after "EXHIBITION."		
258	55	5 c. orange-brown (B.)	6·00	42·00
		a. Imperf between (vert pair)	£900	£900
		b. Stop after "EXHIBITION."	38·00	
		c. Opt double	£1600	
		d. Opt double (with stop)	£2750	
259		5 c. chestnut (B.)	15·00	48·00
		a. Stop after "EXHIBITION."	55·00	
260	56	6 c. apple-green (R.)	2·75	38·00
		a. Stop after "EXHIBITION."	30·00	
		b. Opt double	£1600	
		c. Opt double (with stop)	£2750	
261	57	8 c. dull rose (B.)	4·00	38·00
		a. Stop after "EXHIBITION."	38·00	
262		8 c. deep rose-lake (B.)	4·00	38·00
		a. Stop after "EXHIBITION."	38·00	
263	58	10 c. turquoise-blue (R.)	4·50	38·00
		a. Stop after "EXHIBITION."	38·00	
		b. Perf 14½–15	23·00	
		ba. Stop after "EXHIBITION."		
264		10 c. greenish blue (R.)	5·50	45·00
		a. Stop after "EXHIBITION."	38·00	
265	59	12 c. deep blue (R.)	3·75	20·00
		a. Stop after "EXHIBITION."	42·00	
266		12 c. deep bright blue (R.)	26·00	
		a. Stop after "EXHIBITION."	£130	
267	60	16 c. brown-lake (B.)	6·50	45·00
		a. Stop after "EXHIBITION."	42·00	
		b. Opt in red	£2500	
268	61	20 c. on 18 c. blue-green (B.)	7·00	45·00
		a. Stop after "EXHIBITION."	80·00	
269		20 c. on 18 c. blue-green (R.)	25·00	£130
		a. Stop after "EXHIBITION."	£200	£275
270	62	24 c. mauve (R.)	16·00	48·00
		a. Stop after "EXHIBITION."	50·00	
271		24 c. lilac (R.)	16·00	48·00
		a. Stop after "EXHIBITION."	50·00	
272		24 c. reddish lilac (R.)	26·00	60·00
		a. Stop after "EXHIBITION."	75·00	
273	64	25 c. blue-green (R.)	9·50	50·00
		a. Stop after "EXHIBITION."	45·00	
274		25 c. yellow-green (R.)	3·75	45·00
		a. Stop after "EXHIBITION."	40·00	
		b. Opt double	£1300	
		c. Perf 14½–15	13·00	55·00
		ca. Stop after "EXHIBITION."	£200	
		cb. Opt double	£1100	
275		50 c. steel-blue (R.)	6·00	35·00
		a. Stop after "EXHIBITION."	55·00	
		b. Perf 14½–15	20·00	
		ba. Stop after "EXHIBITION."	£100	
253/75		*Set of* 14	65·00	£450
253/75 Optd "Specimen"		*Set of* 14	£400	

These overprints were applied from a number of settings covering 10, 20, 25 or 30 stamps at a time.

Of the ten settings known for the horizontal stamps the earliest were only used for the 1 c. on which most of the varieties occur. Of the others the vast majority come from settings of 20 (10 × 2) with the stop after "EXHIBITION" variety on R. 2/7, or 25 (5 × 5) on which the same variety can be found on R. 5/4. In addition the 3 c. comes from a different setting of 20 (10 × 2) on which there is a raised stop after "1922" on R. 2/8 and "EXHIBITICN." on R. 2/9.

The 1 c. sequence is complicated, but additionally includes a setting of 10 with "BORHEO" on stamps 3 and 10, "BORNEQ" on stamp 4, raised stop on stamp 8 and "EXHIBITICN." on stamp 9. A setting of 20 repeats this sequence on its bottom line as does one of 30, although in this instance "MHLAYA" replaces "EXHIBITICN" as the variety on stamp 9.

For the vertical stamps (2, 6, 10, 12, 16 and 20 c. on 18 c.) the settings were of 20 (10 × 2) or 25 (5 × 5). The stop after "EXHIBITION" occurs on R. 2/7 of the former and R. 5/4 of the latter.

The 25 c. and 50 c. high values were overprinted from a setting of 20 (10 × 2), with the stop after "EXHIBITION" on R. 2/7, or 25 (5 × 5).

1923 (Oct). *T* **54** *surch with T* **72**.

No.	Description	Unused	Used
276	3 c. on 4 c. black and scarlet (Optd S. £50)	1·00	4·00
	a. Surch double	£550	

1925–28. *As* 1909–22. *Centres in black, and some frame colours changed. P* 12½.

No.	Type	Description	Unused	Used
277	51	1 c. chocolate-brown	75	70
		a. Imperf between (horiz pair)	£550	
278	52	2 c. claret	35	50
		a. Imperf between (horiz or vert pair)	—	£450
279	53	3 c. green (1925)	2·00	1·25
		a. Imperf between (horiz pair)		
280	54	4 c. scarlet	45	10
		a. Imperf between (vert pair)	£275	
		b. Imperf between (horiz pair)	£600	
281	55	5 c. yellow-brown	3·00	2·00
		a. Imperf between (vert pair)	£400	
282	56	6 c. olive-green	2·50	40
283	57	8 c. carmine	1·50	10
		a. Imperf between (horiz or vert pair)	£350	
284	58	10 c. turquoise-blue	1·75	40
		a. Imperf between (horiz or vert pair)	£500	
285	59	12 c. deep blue	5·50	40
286	60	16 c. red-brown	18·00	60·00
287	61	20 c. on 18 c. blue-green (R.)	3·25	3·00
288	62	24 c. violet	42·00	55·00
289	64	25 c. green	4·25	4·25
290		50 c. steel-blue	6·50	11·00
291		$1 chestnut	15·00	80·00
292		$2 mauve	45·00	£110
293	65	$5 lake (1928)	£110	£275
294		$10 orange-red (1928)	£200	£325
277/94		*Set of* 18	£400	£800

Examples of No. 278 were supplied for U.P.U. distribution punched with a 3½ mm diameter hole.

73 Head of a Murut

76 Mount Kinabalu

(Eng J. A. C. Harrison. Recess Waterlow)

1931 (1 Jan). *50th Anniv of British North Borneo Company. T* **73**, **76** *and similar designs. P* 12½.

No.	Description	Unused	Used
295	3 c. black and blue-green	80	50
296	6 c. black and orange	12·00	3·00
297	10 c. black and scarlet	2·75	9·00
298	12 c. black and ultramarine	3·75	7·00
299	25 c. black and violet	28·00	27·00
300	$1 black and yellow-green	15·00	55·00
301	$2 black and chestnut	35·00	75·00
302	$5 black and purple	£110	£200
295/302	*Set of* 8	£180	£325
295/302 Optd "Specimen"	*Set of* 8	£275	

Designs: *Vert*—6 c. Orang-Utan; 10 c. Dyak warrior; $1 Badge of the Company; $5 Arms of the Company. *Horiz*—25 c. Clouded Leopard; $2 Arms of the Company.

81 Buffalo Transport

82 Palm Cockatoo

(Eng J. A. C. Harrison. Recess Waterlow)

1939 (1 Jan). *T* **81/2** *and similar designs. P* 12½.

No.	Description	Unused	Used
303	1 c. green and red-brown	30	20
304	2 c. purple and greenish blue	1·50	25
305	3 c. slate-blue and green	45	80
306	4 c. bronze-green and violet	65	25
307	6 c. deep blue and claret	45	1·25
308	8 c. scarlet	4·00	65
309	10 c. violet and bronze-green	24·00	4·25
310	12 c. green and royal blue	6·00	2·50
	a. Green and blue	8·00	3·75
311	15 c. blue-green and brown	10·00	4·00
312	20 c. violet and slate-blue	5·50	3·00
313	25 c. green and chocolate	6·50	4·50
314	50 c. chocolate and violet	8·00	4·00
315	$1 brown and carmine	38·00	15·00
316	$2 violet and olive-green	70·00	60·00
317	$5 indigo and pale blue	£225	£160
303/17	*Set of* 15	£350	£225
303/17 Perf "Specimen"	*Set of* 15	£250	

Designs: *Vert*—3 c. Native; 4 c. Proboscis Monkey; 6 c. Mounted Bajaus; 10 c. Orang-Utan; 15 c. Dyak; $1, $2 Badge of the Company. *Horiz*—8 c. Eastern Archipelago; 12 c. Murut with blow-pipe; 20 c. River scene; 25 c. Native boat; 50 c. Mt Kinabalu; $5 Arms of the Company.

WAR TAX
(96)

WAR
TAX
(97)

1941 (24 Feb). *Nos.* 303/4 *optd with T* **96/7**.

No.	Description	Unused	Used
318	1 c. green and red-brown	10	30
319	2 c. purple and greenish blue	45	1·75

BRITISH MILITARY ADMINISTRATION

North Borneo, including Labuan, was occupied by the Japanese in January 1942. Following the defeat of Japan Allied troops landed in September 1945 and the territory was placed under British Military Administration on 5 January 1946.

BMA
(98)

(99)

1945 (17 Dec). *Nos.* 303/17 *optd with T* **98**.

No.	Description	Unused	Used
320	1 c. green and red-brown	2·00	40
321	2 c. purple and greenish blue	4·50	75
	a. Opt double	£2750	
322	3 c. slate-blue and green	1·00	80
323	4 c. bronze-green and violet	14·00	9·00
324	6 c. deep blue and claret	1·00	30
325	8 c. scarlet	1·25	45
326	10 c. violet and bronze-green	1·75	30
327	12 c. green and blue	2·25	80
	a. Green and royal blue		
328	15 c. blue-green and brown	1·00	1·00
329	20 c. violet and slate-blue	1·00	1·00
330	25 c. green and chocolate	2·25	75
331	50 c. chocolate and violet	2·00	1·00
332	$1 brown and carmine	18·00	15·00
333	$2 violet and olive-green	18·00	15·00
	a. Opt double	£1700	
334	$5 indigo and pale blue	8·00	8·00
320/34	*Set of* 15	70·00	48·00

These stamps and the similarly overprinted stamps of Sarawak were obtainable at all post offices throughout British Borneo (Brunei, Labuan, North Borneo and Sarawak), for use on local and overseas mail.

CROWN COLONY

North Borneo became a Crown Colony on 15 July 1946.

Lower bar broken at right (R. 8/3)

Lower bar broken at left (R. 8/4)

1947 (1 Sept–22 Dec). *Nos.* 303 *to* 317 *optd with T* **99** *and bars obliterating words* "THE STATE OF" *and* "BRITISH PROTECTORATE".

No.	Description	Unused	Used
335	1 c. green and red-brown (15.12)	15	40
	b. Lower bar broken at right	8·00	
	c. Lower bar broken at left	8·00	
336	2 c. purple and greenish blue (22.12)	45	50
337	3 c. slate-blue and green (R.) (22.12)	15	15
338	4 c. bronze-green and violet	20	10
339	6 c. deep blue and claret (R.) (22.12)	15	20
340	8 c. scarlet	20	15
	b. Lower bar broken at right	10·00	
341	10 c. violet and bronze-green (15.12)	40	15
342	12 c. green and royal blue (22.12)	70	85
	a. Green and blue		
343	15 c. blue-green and brown (22.12)	1·00	30
344	20 c. violet and slate-blue (22.12)	35	30
	b. Lower bar broken at right	15·00	
345	25 c. green and chocolate (22.12)	40	30
	b. Lower bar broken at right	15·00	
346	50 c. chocolate and violet (22.12)	75	55
	b. Lower bar broken at right	25·00	
	c. Lower bar broken at left	25·00	
347	$1 brown and carmine (22.12)	60	85
348	$2 violet and olive-green (22.12)	2·25	4·25
349	$5 indigo and pale blue (R.) (22.12)	8·50	7·00
	b. Lower bar broken at right	55·00	
335/49	*Set of* 15	14·50	14·50
335/49 Perf "Specimen"	*Set of* 15	£250	

1948 (1 Nov). *Royal Silver Wedding. As Nos.* 143/4 *of Jamaica.*

No.	Description	Unused	Used
350	8 c. scarlet	30	40
351	$10 mauve	11·00	24·00

1949 (10 Oct). *75th Anniv of U.P.U. As Nos.* 145/8 *of Jamaica.*

No.	Description	Unused	Used
352	8 c. carmine	30	30
353	10 c. brown	60	30
354	30 c. orange-brown	70	80
355	55 c. blue	75	90
352/5	*Set of* 4	2·10	2·10

100 Mount Kinabalu **102** Coconut Grove

(Photo Harrison)

1950 (1 July)–**52.** *T* **100, 102** *and similar designs. Wmk Mult Script CA. Chalk-surfaced paper. P* 13½ × 14½ (*horiz*), 14½ × 13½ (*vert*).

356 1 c. red-brown 15 30
357 2 c. blue 15 15
358 3 c. green 15 10
359 4 c. bright purple 15 10
360 5 c. violet 15 10
361 8 c. scarlet 30 45
362 10 c. maroon 30 10
363 15 c. ultramarine 30 30
364 20 c. brown 40 10
365 30 c. olive-brown 45 10
366 50 c. rose-carmine ("JESSLETON") .. .. 45 1·75
366*a* 50 c. rose-carmine ("JESSELTON") (1.5.52) .. 2·00 50
367 $1 red-orange .. .. 1·25 55
368 $2 grey-green .. .. 2·00 6·00
369 $5 emerald-green .. .. 9·50 11·00
370 $10 dull blue .. .. 24·00 32·00
356/70 .. .. *Set of* 16 38·00 48·00

Designs: *Horiz*—2 c. Native musical instrument; 8 c. Map; 10 c. Log pond; 15 c. Malay prau, Sandakan; 20 c. Bajau Chief; $2 Murut with blowpipe; $5 Net-fishing; $10 Arms of North Borneo. *Vert*—4 c. Hemp drying; 5 c. Cattle at Kota Belud; 30 c. Suluk river canoe, Lahad Datu; 50 c. Clock tower, Jesselton; $1 Bajau horsemen.

1953 (3 June). *Coronation. As No.* 153 *of Jamaica.*
371 10 c. black and bright scarlet 30 20

115 Log Pond

(Photo Harrison)

1954 (1 Mar)–**59.** *Designs previously used for King George VI issue, but with portrait of Queen Elizabeth II as in T* **115.** *Chalk-surfaced paper. Wmk Mult Script CA. P* 14½×13½ (*vert*) *or* 13½×14½ (*horiz*).

372 1 c. red-brown (1.10.54) 10 30
373 2 c. blue (1.6.56) 30 15
374 3 c. green (1.2.57) .. .. 30 1·50
a. Deep green (14.1.59) .. .. .. 80 1·50
375 4 c. bright purple (16.5.55) 30 20
376 5 c. reddish violet (1.7.54) 40 10
377 8 c. scarlet (1.10.54) 30 15
378 10 c. maroon 15 10
379 15 c. bright blue (16.5.55) 25 10
380 20 c. brown (3.8.54) 15 15
381 30 c. olive-brown (3.8.54) 40 15
382 50 c. rose-carm ("JESSELTON") (10.2.56) 2·50 10
a. Rose (9.12.59) .. .. .. 3·75 45
383 $1 red-orange (1.4.55) .. .. .. 3·00 20
384 $2 deep green (1.10.55) .. .. .. 7·00 40
a. Grey-green (22.1.58) .. .. .. 8·50 3·50
385 $5 emerald-green (1.2.57) .. .. 8·00 17·00
386 $10 deep blue (1.2.57) .. .. .. 20·00 28·00
372/86 .. .. *Set of* 15 38·00 42·00

Designs: *Horiz*—1 c. Mount Kinabalu; 2 c. Native musical instrument; 8 c. Map; 15 c. Native prahu, Sandakan; 20 c. Bajau chief; $2 Murut with blowpipe; $5 Net-fishing; $10 Arms of North Borneo. *Vert*—3 c. Coconut grove; 4 c. Hemp drying; 5 c. Cattle at Kota Belud; 30 c. Suluk boat, Lahad Datu; 50 c. Clock Tower, Jesselton; $1 Bajau horseman.

Plate 2 of the 30 c., released 10 August 1960, had a finer, 250 screen, instead of the previous 200 (*price* £1.75 *mint*).

116 Borneo Railway, 1902 **119** Arms of Chartered Company

(Recess Waterlow)

1956 (1 Nov). *75th Anniv of British North Borneo Co. T* **116, 119** *and similar designs. Wmk Mult Script CA. P* 13 × 13½ (*horiz*) *or* 13½ × 13 (*vert*).

387 10 c. black and rose-carmine .. .. .. 1·00 30
388 15 c. black and red-brown 25 30
389 35 c. black and bluish green 30 75
390 $1 black and slate .. .. 65 1·25
387/90 .. .. *Set of* 4 2·00 2·40

Designs: *Horiz*—15 c. Malay prau; 35 c. Mount Kinabalu.

NEW INFORMATION

The editor is always interested to correspond with people who have new information that will improve or correct the Catalogue.

120 Sambar Stag **121** Orang-Utan

(Des Chong Yun Fatt. Recess Waterlow (until 1962), then D.L.R.)

1961 (1 Feb). *Horiz designs as T* **120** *or vert designs as T* **121.** *W w* **12.** *P* 13.

391 1 c. emerald and brown-red 10 10
392 4 c. bronze-green and orange 15 40
393 5 c. sepia and violet 15 10
394 6 c. black and blue-green 10 30
395 10 c. green and red 15 10
396 12 c. brown and grey-green 15 10
397 20 c. blue-green and ultramarine .. .. 2·25 10
398 25 c. grey-black and scarlet 45 40
399 30 c. sepia and olive 20 10
400 35 c. slate-blue and red-brown 45 10
401 50 c. emerald and yellow-brown 45 10
402 75 c. grey-blue and bright purple .. .. 3·00 75
403 $1 brown and yellow-green .. .. .. 6·50 55
404 $2 brown and slate .. .. 9·50 2·25
405 $5 emerald and maroon .. .. .. 22·00 11·00
406 $10 carmine and blue .. .. .. 20·00 16·00
391/406 .. .. *Set of* 16 55·00 28·00

Designs: *Horiz*—4 c. Sun Bear; 5 c. Clouded Leopard; 6 c. Dusun woman with gong; 10 c. Map of Borneo; 12 c. Banteng; 20 c. Butterfly orchid; 25 c. Sumatran Rhinoceros; 30 c. Murut with blow-pipe; 35 c. Mount Kinabalu; 50 c. Dusun and buffalo transport; 75 c. Bajau horsemen. *Vert*—$2 Rhinoceros Hornbill; $5 Crested Wood Partridge; $10 Arms of North Borneo.

1963 (4 June). *Freedom from Hunger. As No.* 80 *of Lesotho.*
407 12 c. ultramarine 70 15

North Borneo joined the Federation of Malaysia on 16 September 1963 and was renamed Sabah.

SABAH

STATE OF MALAYSIA

SABAH (136) **SABAH** (137)

1964 (1 July)–**65.** *Nos.* 391/406 *of North Borneo* (*D.L.R. printings*), *optd with T* **136** (*Nos.* 408/19) *or T* **137** (*Nos.* 420/3).

408 1 c. emerald and brown-red 10 10
409 4 c. bronze-green and orange 15 50
410 5 c. sepia and violet 15 10
a. Light sepia and deep violet (17.8.65) 40 30
411 6 c. black and blue-green 10 10
412 10 c. green and red 15 10
413 12 c. brown and grey-green 15 10
414 20 c. blue-green and ultramarine .. .. 1·25 10
415 25 c. grey-black and scarlet 45 80
416 30 c. sepia and olive 25 10
417 35 c. slate-blue and red-brown 30 20
418 50 c. emerald and yellow-brown 30 10
419 75 c. grey-blue and bright purple .. .. 2·25 65
420 $1 brown and yellow-green .. .. .. 3·50 50
421 $2 brown and slate .. .. 6·00 2·75
422 $5 emerald and maroon .. .. .. 8·00 10·00
423 $10 carmine and blue .. .. .. 13·00 15·00
408/23 .. .. *Set of* 16 32·00 27·00

Old stocks bearing Waterlow imprints of the 4 c., 5 c., 20 c. and 35 c. to $10 were used for overprinting, but in addition new printings of all values by De La Rue using the original plates with the De La Rue imprint replacing the Waterlow imprint were specially made for overprinting.

138 *Vanda hookeriana* **139** *Hebomoia glaucippe*

1965 (15 Nov)–**68.** *As Nos.* 166/72 *of Johore, but with Arms of Sabah inset as in T* **138.** *W w* **13** (*upright*).

424 1 c. multicoloured 10 30
425 2 c. multicoloured 10 40
426 5 c. multicoloured 10 10
427 6 c. multicoloured 20 40
428 10 c. multicoloured 20 10
429 15 c. multicoloured (pale black panel) .. 1·00 10
a. Brown-black panel (20.2.68) .. .. 1·25 10
430 20 c. multicoloured .. .. 1·40 30
424/30 .. .. *Set of* 7 2·75 1·40

The 5 c. to 15 c. exist with PVA gum as well as gum arabic.

The higher values used with this issue were Nos. 20/27 of Malaysia (National Issues).

1970 (20 Nov). *As No.* 428, *but W w* **13** (*sideways*).
431 10 c. multicoloured .. .. 2·50 2·75

1971 (1 Feb)–**78.** *As Nos.* 175/87 *of Johore but with Arms of Sabah, as in T* **139.** (*a*) *Litho by Bradbury, Wilkinson.*

432 1 c. multicoloured 10 50
433 2 c. multicoloured 30 50
434 5 c. multicoloured 45 10
435 6 c. multicoloured 45 40
436 10 c. multicoloured 45 10
437 15 c. multicoloured 60 10
438 20 c. multicoloured 70 40
432/8 .. .. *Set of* 7 2·75 1·90

(*b*) *Photo by Harrison* (1977–78)

439 1 c. multicoloured .. .. 1·25 2·50
440 2 c. multicoloured .. .. 1·25 3·25
441 5 c. multicoloured .. .. 6·50 2·75
442 10 c. multicoloured .. .. 1·75 35
443 15 c. multicoloured .. .. 2·25 45
444 20 c. multicoloured .. .. 5·50 1·75
439/44 .. .. *Set of* 6 17·00 10·00

For differences between litho and photo printings, see after Johore No. 187.

The higher values used with this issue were Nos. 64/71 of Malaysia (National Issues).

140 *Hibiscus rosa-sinensis* **141** Coffee

1979 (30 Apr). *As Nos.* 188/94 *of Johore but with Arms of Sabah as in T* **140.**

445 1 c. *Rafflesia hasseltii* 10 20
446 2 c. *Pterocarpus indicus* 10 20
447 5 c. *Lagerstroemia speciosa* 10 10
448 10 c. *Durio zibethinus* 10 10
449 15 c. Type **140** 20 10
450 20 c. *Rhododendron scortechinii* 25 10
451 25 c. *Etlingera elatior* (inscr "*Phaeomeria speciosa*") 25 10
445/51 .. .. *Set of* 7 90 55

For higher values used in conjunction with this series see Nos. 190/7 of Malaysia (National Issues).

1983–85.* *As Nos.* 447/8 *and* 450 *but without wmk.*

454 5 c. *Lagerstroemia speciosa* (1.85) .. .. 3·50 2·75
455 10 c. *Durio zibethinus* (1.85) .. .. .. 7·00 6·00
456 15 c. Type **140** (5.85) .. .. 5·50 3·50
457 20 c. *Rhododendron scortechinii* (blackish brown background) (1983) .. .. 11·00 1·75
457*a* 20 c. *Rhododendron scortechinii* (bronze-green background) (29.11.83) .. .. 8·50 80
454/7*a* .. .. *Set of* 5 32·00 13·50

*There was no official release date for these stamps. Dates shown are the earliest recorded from postmarks and may be revised if earlier examples are reported.

For details of the shade differences between watermarked and unwatermarked printings see after Malaysia–Johore, No. 200*a*.

On Nos. 454/6 and 457*a* the state crest is redrawn larger.

1986 (25 Oct). *As Nos.* 202/8 *of Johore but with Arms of Sabah as in T* **141.**

459 1 c. Type **141** 10 10
460 2 c. Coconuts 10 10
461 5 c. Cocoa 10 10
462 10 c. Black pepper 10 10
463 15 c. Rubber 10 10
464 20 c. Oil palm 10 10
465 30 c. Rice 10 15
459/65 .. .. *Set of* 7 40 45

POSTAL FISCALS

Three Cents. Revenue (F 1) (Raised stop) **Ten Cents. Revenue** (F 2)

1886. *Regular issues surch as Type* F **1** *or* F **2.**

F1 1 3 c. on 4 c. pink (No. 6) .. .. .. 65·00 85·00
a. Raised stop after "Cents" .. .. 60·00 80·00
F2 5 c. on 8 c. green (No. 7) .. .. .. 65·00 85·00
a. Raised stop after "Cents" .. .. 60·00 80·00
F3 4 10 c. on 50 c. violet (No. 4) .. .. 75·00 £100
a. Surch double .. .. — £650
b. No stop after "Cents" and stop after "Revenue." £225 £300
c. Inverted "L" for first "F" in "FIFTY" (R.5/2) .. .. — £400

It is believed that Nos. F1/2 were each surcharged from a horizontal setting of five so that the raised stop variety occurs on every stamp in the first, second, third, sixth, seventh and eighth vertical columns in the sheets of 50 (10×5).

POSTAGE DUE STAMPS

POSTAGE DUE (D 1)

1895 (1 Aug). *Stamps of* 1894 *optd with Type* D **1.** *P* 14½–15.

A. *Vertically* (*reading upwards*)

D 1 **25** 2 c. black and rose-lake .. .. 13·00 23·00 1·50
a. Opt double .. .. .. † † £225
b. Opt reading downwards .. .. † † £275

D 2 25 2 c. black and lake .. .. 9·00 15·00 60
a. Perf 13½–14 ..
b. Opt omitted (in vert pair with normal) † † £1000
D 3 26 3 c. olive-green and mauve .. 3·75 9·00 75
a. Bronze-green and mauve
b. Opt reading downwards
D 3c 3 c. olive-green and violet
ca. Opt double † † £350
cb. Perf 13½–14 ..
D 4 27 5 c. black and vermilion .. 20·00 20·00 1·50
a. Printed double † — —
b. Stop after "DUE" 50·00
c. Perf 13½–14 .. — 50·00 —
ca. Opt double
d. Perf 13½–14, comp 12–13 — 55·00 —
D 5 28 6 c. black and bistre-brown 18·00 40·00 1·50
a. Perf 13½–14 .. 7·00 28·00 1·50
b. Perf 12–13
c. Perf 13½–14, comp 12–13
d. Opt reading downwards
D 6 31 18 c. black and deep green 38·00 60·00 3·00
a. Opt reading downwards £300 £200 †
D3/4 & D6 Optd "Specimen" *Set of* 3 90·00

B. Horizontally

D 7 29 8 c. black and dull purple 18·00 32·00 1·50
a. Opt double — † £300
b. Perf 13½–14 ..
ba. Opt inverted † † £120
c. Perf 13½–14, comp 12–13 30·00
D 8 30 12 c. black and blue — 35·00 1·50
a. Opt double † † £300
b. Perf 13½–14 .. 26·00 29·00 1·50
D 9 12 c. black & ultram (*p* 13½–14) 50·00 50·00 —
D10 31 18 c. black and deep green 32·00 45·00 3·00
a. Opt inverted £170 £350 †
b. Perf 13½–14 .. 45·00 55·00 3·00
ba. Opt double † † £200
D11 32 24 c. blue and rose-lake 35·00 55·00 3·00
a. Opt double † † £250
b. Perf 13½–14 .. 16·00 45·00 —
c. Perf 13½–14, comp 14½–15
D8 & D11 Optd "Specimen" *Set of* 2 50·00

1897. *Stamps of* 1897 *optd with Type* D 1. *P* 14½–15.

A. *Vertically*

D12 2 c. black and lake 3·50 6·50 50
a. Perf 13½–14 17·00

B. *Horizontally*

D13 2 c. black and lake 25·00 50·00
D14 8 c. black and brown-purple 25·00 35·00
a. Stop after "DUE." 18·00 50·00
D12 & D14 Optd "Specimen" *Set of* 2 45·00

1901. *Issue of* 1897–1902 *optd with Type* D 1. *P* 13½–14.

A. *Vertically* (*reading upwards*)

D15 2 c. black and green 15·00 22·00 60
a. Perf 13½–14, comp 12–13 — 50·00 —
b. Perf 16
c. Perf 12–13
d. Opt reading downwards
D16 3 c. green and rosy mauve 11·00 13·00 60
a. Stop after "DUE" 35·00 55·00 —
b. Perf 14½–15 4·25 12·00 40
c. Perf 13½–14, comp 14½–15
d. Opt double
e. Opt double. Stop after "DUE" £150
D17 3 c. green & dull mauve (*p* 14½–15) 8·50 17·00 75
a. Stop after "DUE" 35·00 55·00 —
b. Opt double. Stop after "DUE" £200 £225 —
D18 4 c. black and carmine 14·00 15·00 50
a. Perf 14½–15
D19 5 c. black and orange-vermilion 13·00 19·00 75
a. Perf 14½–15 25·00 26·00 —
b. Stop after "DUE" 32·00
D20 6 c. black and bistre-brown (Optd "Specimen" £25) — 17·00 40
a. Perf 14½–15 3·00 13·00 40
b. Perf 13½–14, comp 12–13
D20c 8 c. black and brown-purple (*p* 16)
D21 8 c. black and brown
a. Perf 14½–15 3·00 13·00 40
ab. Opt reading downwards † † —
D22 12 c. black and dull blue 35·00 85·00 2·00
a. Perf 14½–15
D23 18 c. black and green (No. 108)
a. Perf 16
D24 18 c. black and green (No. 110) 24·00 85·00 2·00
a. Perf 13½–14, comp 12–13 35·00 85·00 2·00
D25 24 c. blue and lake (No. 109) — 32·00 60
D26 24 c. blue and lake (No. 111)
a. Perf 14½–15 12·00 70·00 1·00

B. *Horizontally*

D27 2 c. black and green 50·00 65·00 3·00
D28 8 c. black and brown (*p* 14½–15) 60·00 70·00 4·00
a. Stop after "DUE" 75·00 90·00 —

An example of the 5 c. value, No. D19a, has been seen clearly postmarked 1899.

1902–5. *Stamps of* 1901–5 *optd* "British Protectorate," *further optd with Type* D 1. *P* 13½–14. A. *Vertically* (1902).

D29 2 c. black and green (*p* 16) £160 £140
D30 3 c. green and rosy mauve 70·00 85·00
D31 5 c. black and orange-vermilion (*p* 14½–15) £100 85·00
D32 8 c. black and brown 90·00 75·00
D33 24 c. blue and lake £110 70·00

B. *Horizontally, at top of stamp* (1904–5)

D34 2 c. black and green (*p* 14½–15) 80·00 50·00
a. Perf 16 60·00 70·00
D35 4 c. black and carmine 60·00 19·00

C. *Horizontally, at centre of stamp* (1904–5)

D35*a* 1 c. black and bistre-brown — — 23·00
b. Perf 14½–15 £200 — 23·00
D36 2 c. black and green 3·75 1·50 10
a. Perf 14½–15 45·00 45·00 —
D37 3 c. green and rosy mauve 1·75 1·50 10
a. Perf 14½–15 45·00 30·00 —
ab. "POSTAGE DUE" double
D38 4 c. black and carmine 4·50 4·25 20
a. "POSTAGE DUE" double — † £120
b. Perf 14½–15 3·00 6·50 20
D39 5 c. black and orange-vermilion 5·00 3·00 20
a. Perf 14½–15 25·00 20·00 —
D40 6 c. black and bistre-brown 6·50 6·00 25
a. "POSTAGE DUE" inverted £350 † 90·00
b. "POSTAGE DUE" double † — —
c. No stop after "PROTECTORATE"
d. Perf 16 24·00 24·00 —
D41 8 c. black and brown 13·00 4·00 40
a. No stop after "PROTECTORATE" 38·00 35·00 —
D42 10 c. brown and slate-lilac 65·00 28·00 1·00
a. No stop after "PROTECTORATE"
D42*b* 10 c. brown and slate-blue 29·00 12·00 1·00
D43 12 c. black and blue 6·50 11·00 1·00
D44 16 c. green and chestnut 14·00 14·00 1·00
D45 18 c. black and green 4·00 11·00 1·00
a. "POSTAGE DUE" double £400 † 45·00
b. Imperf between (vert pair) — — £350
D46 24 c. blue and lake 6·50 17·00 1·00
a. Perf 14½–15
b. "POSTAGE DUE" double £200 † 75·00

D. *Horizontally. Optd locally, with stop after* "DUE." (1904–5)

D47 1 c. black and bistre-brown 3·25 45·00 —
a. With raised stop after "DUE." 4·75 45·00 —

No. D35*a*/b are usually found cancelled-to-order suggesting that they came from remainder stocks which were not issued, but we have also seen one unused example of No. D35a and several of No. D35b.

1919–24. *Stamps of* 1909–22, *optd with Type* D 1. *P* 13½–14.

A. *Horizontally at top of stamp*

D48 4 c. black and scarlet (1919) 55·00 12·00

B. *Horizontally towards foot of stamp*

D49 2 c. black and green (2.24) 5·50 45·00
a. Perf 14½–15 8·00 45·00
D50 3 c. black and green 3·50 18·00
D51 4 c. black and scarlet 70 1·00
D52 5 c. black and yellow-brown 4·00 10·00
D53 6 c. black and olive-green 3·75 7·50
D53*a* 6 c. black and apple-green
D54 8 c. black and rose-lake 1·25 1·25
D55 10 c. black and turquoise-blue (7.24) 7·00 12·00
a. Perf 14½–15 42·00 75·00
D56 12 c. black and deep blue (7.24) 19·00 25·00
a. Horiz pair, one with opt omitted £5000
D56*b* 16 c. black and red-brown 16·00 60·00
ba. Black and brown-lake 6·00 40·00
D49/56*b* *Set of* 9 45·00 £140
D49 & D56*b* Optd "Specimen" *Set of* 2 45·00

Nos. D51/3 also exist with the overprint towards the centre of the stamp.

1926–31. *As* 1920–31, *but perf* 12½.

D57 2 c. black and claret 40 1·75
D58 3 c. black and green 2·25 11·00
D59 4 c. black and scarlet 50 1·25
D60 5 c. black and yellow-brown 3·75 38·00
D61 6 c. black and olive-green 2·75 2·00
D62 8 c. black and carmine 2·00 8·00
D63 10 c. black and turquoise-blue 4·50 42·00
D64 12 c. black and deep blue 11·00 70·00
D65 16 c. black and red-brown (1931) 26·00 95·00
D57/65 *Set of* 9 48·00 £250

Nos. D49/65 exist with two types of opt; A. Thick letters; pointed beard to "G". B. Thinner letters; "G" with square end to beard and "D" more open. No. D56*a* is Type B. and D56*b*, Type A.

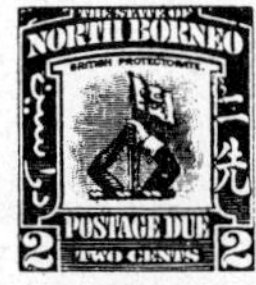

D 2 Crest of the Company

(Recess Waterlow)

1939 (1 Jan). *P* 12½.

D66 D 2 2 c. brown 4·50 55·00
D67 4 c. scarlet 5·50 60·00
D68 6 c. violet 12·00 75·00
D69 8 c. green 12·00 £120
D70 10 c. blue 25·00 £160
D66/70 *Set of* 5 55·00 £425
D66/70 Perf "Specimen" *Set of* 5 £140

XII. JAPANESE OCCUPATION OF NORTH BORNEO

Japanese forces landed in Northern Borneo on 16 December 1941 and the whole of North Borneo had been occupied by 19 January 1942.

Brunei, North Borneo, Sarawak and, after a short period, Labuan, were administered as a single territory by the Japanese. Until September–October 1942, previous stamp issues, without overprint, continued to be used in conjunction with existing postmarks. From the Autumn of 1942 onwards unoverprinted stamps of Japan were made available and examples can be found used from the area for much of the remainder of the War. Japanese Occupation issues for Brunei, North Borneo and Sarawak were equally valid throughout the combined territory but not, in practice, equally available.

PRICES FOR STAMPS ON COVER
Nos. J1/17 *from* × 4
Nos. J18/19 *from* × 5
Nos. J20/32 *from* × 25
Nos. J33/4 *from* × 2
Nos. J35/48 *from* × 6

(1)

2 Mt Kinabalu

3 Borneo Scene

1942 (Sept). *Stamps of North Borneo handstamped with T* **1**.

(*a*) *In violet or black on Nos.* 303/17

J 1 1 c. green and red-brown 85·00 £120
J 2 2 c. purple and greenish blue 80·00 £110
J 3 3 c. slate-blue and green 75·00 £110
J 4 4 c. bronze-green and violet 38·00 75·00
J 5 6 c. deep blue and claret 75·00 £110
J 6 8 c. scarlet 75·00 £110
a. Pair, one without opt £600
J 7 10 c. violet and bronze-green 75·00 £110
J 8 12 c. green and bright blue 95·00 £170
J 9 15 c. blue-green and brown 95·00 £170
J10 20 c. violet and slate-blue £130 £190
J11 25 c. green and chocolate £130 £190
J12 50 c. chocolate and violet £180 £250
J13 $1 brown and carmine £160 £300
J14 $2 violet and olive-green £275 £400
a. Pair, one without opt £1100
J15 $5 indigo and pale blue £325 £500

(*b*) *In black on Nos.* 318/19 ("WAR TAX")

J16 1 c. green and red-brown £250 £160
J17 2 c. purple and greenish blue £550 £225

(Litho G. Kolff, Batavia)

1943 (29 Apr). *P* 12½.

J18 2 4 c. red 10·00 18·00
J19 3 8 c. blue 10·00 18·00

本 日 大
便 郵 國 帝
オネルボ北

(4)

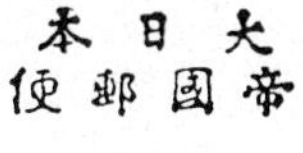

(5)

("Imperial Japanese Postal Service North Borneo")

1944 (30 Sept). *Nos.* 303/15 *of North Borneo optd as T* **4**.

J20 1 c. green and red-brown 2·25 5·00
J21 2 c. purple and greenish blue 3·25 5·00
J22 3 c. slate-blue and green 2·00 3·50
J23 4 c. bronze-green and violet 2·50 4·75
J24 6 c. deep blue and claret 2·25 3·50
J25 8 c. scarlet 3·75 8·50
J26 10 c. violet and bronze-green 2·50 6·50
J27 12 c. green and bright blue 2·75 6·50
J28 15 c. blue-green and brown 3·25 8·50
J29 20 c. violet and slate-blue 9·50 20·00
J30 25 c. green and chocolate 9·50 20·00
J31 50 c. chocolate and violet 32·00 48·00
J32 $1 brown and carmine 48·00 75·00
J20/32 *Set of* 13 £110 £190

The spacing between the second and third lines of the overprint is 12 mm on the horizontal stamps, and 15 mm on the upright.

1944. *No.* J7 *with T* **4** *opt in addition.*

J32*a* 10 c. violet and bronze-green £160 £325

The 2 c., 3 c., 8 c., 12 c. and 15 c. stamps of the 1942 issue are also known with Type **4** opt.

1945. *No.* J1 *surch with T* **5**.

J33 81 $2 on 1 c. green and red-brown £3250 £2500

本 日 大

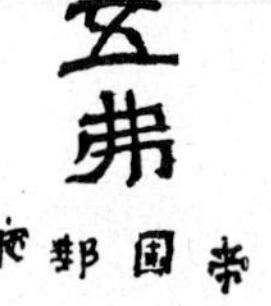

(6)

7 Girl War-worker

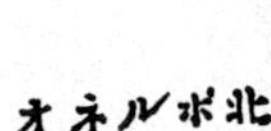

(8) ("North Borneo")

1945 (?). *North Borneo No.* 315 *surch with T* **6**.

J34 $5 on $1 brown and carmine £2750 £2250

1945. *Contemporary stamps of Japan as T 7 (various subjects) optd with T 8 at Chinese Press, Kuching.*

J35	1 s. red-brown (No. 391)	2·00	5·50
J36	2 s. scarlet (No. 318)	2·25	5·50
J37	3 s. emerald-green (No. 319)	1·50	5·50
J38	4 s. yellow-green (No. 395)	2·00	5·50
J39	5 s. claret (No. 396)	2·25	6·00
J40	6 s. orange (No. 322)	2·25	7·00
J41	8 s. violet (No. 324)	1·75	7·00
J42	10 s. carmine and pink (No. 399)	2·25	7·00
J43	15 s. blue (No. 401)	2·25	7·00
J44	20 s. blue-slate (No. 328)	65·00	80·00
J45	25 s. brown and chocolate (No. 329)	55·00	65·00
J46	30 s. turquoise-blue (No. 330)	£150	95·00
J47	50 s. olive and bistre (No. 331)	50·00	60·00
J48	1 y. red-brown and chocolate (No. 332) ..	48·00	65·00
J35/48	.. .. *Set of* 14	£350	£375

Designs:—2 s. General Nogi; 3 s. Hydro-electric Works; 4 s. Hyuga Monument and Mt Fuji; 5 s. Admiral Togo; 6 s. Garambi Lighthouse, Formosa; 8 s. Meiji Shrine; 10 s. Palms and map of S.E. Asia; 15 s. Airman; 20 s. Mt Fuji and cherry blossoms; 25 s. Horyu Temple; 30 s. Torii, Itsukushima Shrine at Miyajima; 50 s. Kinkaku Temple; 1 y. Great Buddha, Kamakura.

Examples of some values have been found with hand-painted forged overprints.

XIII. SARAWAK

Sarawak was placed under British protection in 1888. It was ceded to Great Britain on 1 July 1946 and was administered as a Crown Colony until 16 September 1963 when it became a state of the Federation of Malaysia.

Stamps of INDIA were used in Sarawak from *circa* 1859. They were replaced by Sarawak issues from 1869, although these were only valid for "local" postage as far as Singapore. Mail for further afield needed a combination of Sarawak and STRAITS SETTLEMENTS stamps, a stock of the latter being kept by the Sarawak Post Office. This arrangement continued until 1 July 1897 when Sarawak joined the U.P.U.

PRICES FOR STAMPS ON COVER TO 1945

No. 1	—
Nos. 2/7	*from* × 50
Nos. 8/21	*from* × 8
Nos. 22/6	*from* × 6
No. 27	*from* × 40
Nos. 28/35	*from* × 6
Nos. 36/47	*from* × 8
No. 48	†
No. 49	*from* × 10
Nos. 50/61	*from* × 6
No. 62	†
Nos. 63/71	*from* × 4
Nos. 72/3	*from* × 8
Nos. 74/5	—
Nos. 76/90	*from* × 7
Nos. 91/105	*from* × 5
Nos. 106/25	*from* × 3
Nos. 126/45	*from* × 2

BROOKE FAMILY ADMINISTRATION

Sir James Brooke. 1842–11 June 1868
Sir Charles Brooke. 11 June 1868–17 May 1917

UNUSED PRICES. Nos. 1/7, 27 and 32/5 in unused condition are normally found to be without gum. Prices in the unused column are for stamps in this state. Examples of these issues with original gum are worth considerably more.

1 Sir James Brooke

2 Sir Charles Brooke

The initials in the corners of T 1 and 2 stand for "James (Charles) Brooke, Rajah (of) Sarawak".

(T 1 and 2. Die eng Wm. Ridgway. Litho Maclure, Macdonald & Co, Glasgow)

1869 (1 Mar). *P* 11.

1	1	3 c. brown/*yellow*	40·00	£200

Specimens are known printed from the engraved die in orange-brown on orange surface-coloured paper, and perf 12. These were submitted to the Sarawak authorities as examples of the stamps and exist both with and without obliterations.

1871 (1 Jan). *P* 11 (*irregular*).

2	2	3 c. brown/*yellow*	1·25	3·00
		a. Stop after "THREE"	35·00	48·00
		b. Imperf between (vert pair)	£350	
		c. Imperf between (horiz pair)	£475	

The "stop" variety, No. 2a, which occurs on R. 10/7 is of no more philatelic importance than any of the numerous other variations, such as narrow first "A" in "SARAWAK" (R. 2/7) and "R" with long tail in left lower corner (R. 9/10), but it has been accepted by collectors for many years, and we therefore retain it. The papermaker's wmk "L N L" appears once or twice in sheets of No. 2.

Specimens are known, recess-printed, similar to those mentioned in the note after No. 1.

TWO CENTS

Copies of No. 2 surcharged as above were first reported in 1876 but following the discovery of dies for forgeries and faked postmarks in 1891 it was concluded that the issue was bogus, especially as the availability of the 2 c. of 1875 made it unnecessary to issue a provisional. It has now been established that a 2 c. postal rate was introduced from 1 August 1874 for the carriage of newspapers. Moreover four examples are known with a stop after "CENTS." and showing other minor differences from the forgery illustrated. This version could be genuine and if others come to light we will reconsider listing it.

1875 (1 Jan). *P* 11½–12.

3	2	2 c. mauve/*lilac* (*shades*)	2·50	11·00
4		4 c. red-brown/*yellow*	2·75	3·00
		a. Imperf between (vert pair)	£475	
5		6 c. green/*green*	2·75	3·50
6		8 c. bright blue/*blue*	2·50	3·50
7		12 c. red/*pale rose*	6·50	6·50
3/7		.. .. *Set of* 5	15·00	25·00

Nos. 3, 4, 6 and 7 have the watermark "L N L" in the sheet, as No. 2. No. 5 is watermarked "L N T".

All values exist imperf and can be distinguished from the proofs by shade and impression. Stamps rouletted, pin-perf, or roughly perf 6½ to 7 are proofs clandestinely perforated.

The 12 c. "laid" paper, formerly listed, is not on a true laid paper, the "laid" effect being accidental and not consistent.

The lithographic stones for Nos. 3 to 7 were made up from strips of five distinct impressions hence there are five types of each value differing mainly in the lettering of the tablets of value. There are flaws on nearly every individual stamp, from which they can be plated.

4 Sir Charles Brooke

(Typo D.L.R.)

1888 (10 Nov)–**1897.** *No wmk. P* 14.

8	4	1 c. purple and black (6.6.92)	80	45
9		2 c. purple and carmine (11.11.88) ..	85	65
		a. *Purple and rosine* (1897)	4·00	1·50
10		3 c. purple and blue (11.11.88)	1·25	1·00
11		4 c. purple and yellow	9·50	24·00
12		5 c. purple and green (12.6.91)	8·00	1·50
13		6 c. purple and brown (11.11.88) ..	7·00	28·00
14		8 c. green and carmine (11.11.88) ..	4·50	2·50
		a. *Green and rosine* (1897)	12·00	8·50
15		10 c. green and purple (12.6.91)	22·00	13·00
16		12 c. green and blue (11.11.88)	4·00	6·50
17		16 c. green and orange (28.12.97) ..	28·00	42·00
18		25 c. green and brown (19.11.88)	28·00	32·00
19		32 c. green and black (28.12.97)	24·00	35·00
20		50 c. green (26.7.97)	25·00	55·00
21		$1 green and black (2.11.97)	35·00	50·00
8/21		.. .. *Set of* 14	£170	£250

Prepared for use but not issued

21*a*	$2 green and blue	£350
21*b*	$5 green and violet	£350
21*c*	$10 green and carmine	£350

On No. 21 the value is in black on an uncoloured ground.

The tablet of value in this and later similar issues is in the second colour given.

One Cent. (5) one cent. (6)

2c. (7) 5c (8) 5c. (9)

1889 (3 Aug)–**92.** *T* 4 *surch. P* 14.

22	5	1 c. on 3 c. (12.1.92)	20·00	22·00
		a. Surch double	£400	£300
23	6	1 c. on 3 c. (2.92)	2·75	2·75
		a. No stop after "cent" (R. 2/6) ..	80·00	
24	7	2 c. on 8 c. (3.8.89)	2·25	5·00
		a. Surch double	£275	
		b. Surch inverted	£1800	
		c. Surch omitted (in pair with normal) ..	£2250	
25	8	5 c. on 12 c. (with stop after "C") (17.2.91) ..	17·00	27·00
		a. No stop after "C"	17·00	26·00
		b. "C" omitted	£250	£250
		c. Surch double	£900	
		d. Surch double, one vertical	£1700	
		e. Surch omitted (in pair with normal) ..	£5500	
26	9	5 c. on 12 c. (17.2.91)	70·00	90·00
		a. No stop after "C"	60·00	75·00
		b. "C" omitted	£325	£275
		c. Surch double	£800	

ONE
CENT

(10)

1892 (23 May). *No.* 2 *surch with T* 10.

27	2	1 c. on 3 c. brown/*yellow*	50	90
		a. Stop after "THREE."	16·00	24·00
		b. Imperf between (vert pair)	£400	
		c. Imperf horiz (vert pair)	£400	
		d. Bar omitted (1st ptg)	£130	
		e. Bar at top and bottom (1st ptg) ..	£180	
		f. Surch double (2nd ptg)	£300	£325

No. 27 was surcharged with a setting of 100 (10 × 10). It was originally intended that there should be no bar at foot, but this was then added at a second operation before the stamps were issued. Subsequent supplies were surcharged with "ONE CENT" and bar at one operation.

Varieties with part of the surcharge missing are due to gum on the face of the unsurcharged stamps receiving part of the surcharge, which was afterwards washed off.

11

12

13 Sir Charles Brooke 14

(Die eng Wm. Ridgway. Recess P.B.)

1895 (1 Jan–Sept). *No wmk. P* 11½–12.
28 11 2 c. brown-red 3·75 5·50
 a. Imperf between (vert pair) £250
 b. Imperf between (horiz pair) £225
 c. Second ptg. Perf 12½ (Sept). 3·75 4·50
 ca. Perf 12½. Imperf between (horiz pair) £250
29 12 4 c. black 3·75 2·50
 a. Imperf between (horiz pair) £275
30 13 6 c. violet 3·25 7·00
31 14 8 c. green 12·00 6·00
28/31 *Set of* 4 20·00 18·00

Stamps of these types, printed in wrong colours, are trials and these, when surcharged with values in "pence", are from waste sheets that were used by Perkins, Bacon & Co as trial paper when preparing an issue of stamps for British South Africa.

4
CENTS.

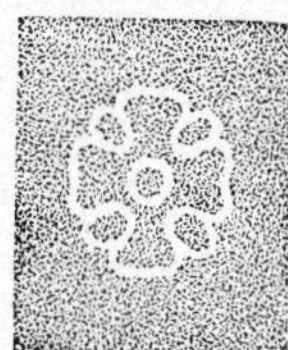

(15) 16

1899. *Surch as T* **15**.
32 2 2 c. on 3 c. brown/*yellow* (19.9.99) 80 90
 a. Stop after "THREE" 35·00
 b. Imperf between (vert pair) £650
33 2 c. on 12 c. red/*pale rose* (29.6.99) 2·50 3·00
 a. Surch inverted £700 £900
34 4 c. on 6 c. green/*green* (R.) (16.11.99) 15·00 38·00
35 4 c. on 8 c. bright blue/*blue* (R.) (29.6.99) 2·50 4·50
32/5 *Set of* 4 19·00 42·00

A variety of surcharge with small "S" in "CENTS" may be found in the 2 c. on 12 c. and 4 c. on 8 c. and a raised stop after "CENTS" on the 4 c. on 6 c.

The omission of parts of the surcharge is due to gum on the surface of the stamps (see note after No. 27).

A block of 50 of No. 35 from the right of the pane is known line perforated 12.7 between the stamps and the margins at top and right.

(Typo D.L.R.)

1899 (10 Nov)–**1908.** *Inscribed* "POSTAGE POSTAGE." *No wmk. P* 14.
36 4 1 c. grey-blue and rosine (1.1.01) 30 50
 a. Grey-blue and red 1·00 40
 b. Ultramarine and rosine 2·75 1·00
 c. Dull blue and carmine 7·00 3·75
37 2 c. green (16.12.99) 40 30
38 3 c. dull purple (1.2.08) 2·50 15
39 4 c. rose-carmine (10.11.99) 3·50 1·60
 a. Aniline carmine 1·75 15
40 8 c. yellow and black (6.12.99) 1·75 70
41 10 c. ultramarine (10.11.99) 1·75 50
42 12 c. mauve (16.12.99) 2·00 1·50
 a. Bright mauve (1905) 11·00 6·00
43 16 c. chestnut and green (16.12.99) 1·75 1·50
44 20 c. bistre and bright mauve (4.00) 4·00 2·25
45 25 c. brown and blue (16.12.99) 2·75 3·50
46 50 c. sage-green and carmine (16.12.99) 11·00 18·00
47 $1 rose-carmine and green (16.12.99) 27·00 45·00
 a. Rosine and pale green 42·00 55·00
36/47 *Set of* 12 50·00 65·00

Prepared for use but not issued
48 4 5 c. olive-grey and green 12·00

The figures of value in the $1 are in colour on an uncoloured ground.

1902. *Inscribed* "POSTAGE POSTAGE". *W* **16**. *P* 14.
49 4 2 c. green 12·00 11·00

Sir Charles Vyner Brooke. 17 May 1917–1 June 1946

17 Sir Charles Vyner Brooke

ONE
cent

(18)

(Typo D.L.R.)

1918 (26 Mar). *No wmk. Chalk-surfaced paper. P* 14.
50 17 1 c. slate-blue and red 30 40
 a. Dull blue and carmine 35 70
51 2 c. green 75 65
52 3 c. brown-purple 1·75 1·40
53 4 c. rose-carmine 1·75 1·60
 a. Rose-red 1·40 1·40
54 8 c. yellow and black 4·50 23·00
55 10 c. blue (*shades*) 2·00 2·25
56 12 c. purple 6·00 8·00
57 16 c. chestnut and green 5·00 4·25
58 20 c. olive and violet (*shades*) 3·50 4·75
59 25 c. brown and bright blue 4·00 7·50
60 50 c. olive-green and carmine 5·50 10·00
61 $1 bright rose and green 11·00 17·00
50/61 *Set of* 12 40·00 70·00
50/61 Optd "Specimen" *Set of* 12 £190

Prepared for use but not issued
62 17 1 c. slate-blue and slate 20·00

On the $1 the figures of value are in colour on an uncoloured ground.

1922–23. *New colours and values. No wmk. Chalk-surfaced paper. P* 14.
63 17 2 c. purple (5.3.23) 60 1·00
64 3 c. dull green (23.3.22) 45 65
65 4 c. brown-purple (10.4.23) 60 15
66 5 c. yellow-orange 40 90
67 6 c. claret (1.22) 85 1·00
68 8 c. bright rose-red 1·75 15·00
69 10 c. black (1923) 1·75 2·25
70 12 c. bright blue (12.22) 7·00 16·00
 a. Pale dull blue 7·00 13·00
71 30 c. ochre-brown and slate 3·50 3·75
63/71 *Set of* 9 15·00 35·00

1923 (Jan). *Surch as T* **18.** (*a*) *First printing. Bars* 1¼ *mm apart.*
72 17 1 c. on 10 c. dull blue 12·00 40·00
 a. "cnet" for "cent" (R. 9/5) £300 £600
73 2 c. on 12 c. purple 5·00 23·00
 a. Thick, narrower "W" in "TWO" 17·00 50·00

(*b*) *Second printing. Bars* ¾ *mm apart*
74 17 1 c. on 10 c. dull blue 80·00 £140
 b. "cnet" for "cent" (R.9/5) £8000
 c. "en" of "cent" scratched out and "ne" overprinted (R.9/5) £3000
75 2 c. on 12 c. purple 45·00 80·00
 a. Thick, narrower "W" in "TWO" £100

In the 2 c. on 12 c. the words of the surcharge are about 7½ mm from the bars.

The "cnet" error occurred on R.9/5 of all sheets from the first printing of the 1 c. on 10 c. A single example of the error, No. 74b, is known from the second printing, but the error was then corrected, as shown by the evidence of a surviving plate block, only to have the correct spelling scratched out, by a local employee, and "ne" substituted (No. 74c).

The thick "W" variety occurs on all stamps of the last two horizontal rows of the first printing (12 stamps per sheet), and in the last two vertical rows of the second (20 stamps per sheet).

1928 (Apr)–**29.** *W* **16** (*Multiple*). *Chalk-surfaced paper. P* 14.
76 17 1 c. slate-blue and carmine 45 35
77 2 c. bright purple 50 40
78 3 c. green 50 2·50
79 4 c. brown-purple 1·25 10
80 5 c. yellow-orange (5.8.29) 3·25 3·00
81 6 c. claret 70 30
82 8 c. bright rose-red 1·75 5·50
83 10 c. black 1·25 1·75
84 12 c. bright blue 1·75 6·50
85 16 c. chestnut and green 1·75 2·50
86 20 c. olive-bistre and violet 1·75 2·75
87 25 c. brown and bright blue 2·50 6·00
88 30 c. bistre-brown and slate 3·00 8·00
89 50 c. olive-green and carmine 3·50 5·50
90 $1 bright rose and green 8·50 18·00
76/90 *Set of* 15 29·00 60·00
76/90 Optd/Perf "Specimen" *Set of* 15 £200

In the $1 the value is as before.

19 Sir Charles Vyner Brooke

20

(Recess Waterlow)

1932 (1 Jan). *W* **20.** *P* 12½.
91 19 1 c. indigo 70 35
92 2 c. green 70 30
93 3 c. violet 2·25 60
94 4 c. red-orange 80 15
95 5 c. deep lake 2·25 60
96 6 c. scarlet 3·00 5·00
97 8 c. orange-yellow 3·00 4·50
98 10 c. black 2·25 2·50
99 12 c. deep ultramarine 2·75 5·00
100 15 c. chestnut 3·50 6·00
101 20 c. red-orange and violet 3·00 6·00
102 25 c. orange-yellow and chestnut 4·50 7·00
103 30 c. sepia and vermilion 4·50 12·00
104 50 c. carmine-red and olive-green 4·50 6·00
105 $1 green and carmine 7·00 18·00
91/105 *Set of* 15 40·00 65·00
91/105 Perf "Specimen" *Set of* 15 £200

21 Sir Charles Vyner Brooke

B M A

(22)

(Recess B.W.)

1934 (1 May)–**41.** *No wmk. P* 12.
106 21 1 c. purple 15 10
107 2 c. green 15 10
107*a* 2 c. black (1.3.41) 80 1·40
108 3 c. black 15 10
108*a* 3 c. green (1.3.41) 70 1·25
109 4 c. bright purple 15 15
110 5 c. violet 20 10
111 6 c. carmine 15 40
111*a* 21 6 c. lake-brown (1.3.41) 1·40 4·50
112 8 c. red-brown 15 10
112*a* 8 c. carmine (1.3.41) 1·00 10
113 10 c. scarlet 75 40
114 12 c. blue 30 25
114*a* 12 c. orange (1.3.41) 80 3·75
115 15 c. orange 40 2·75
115*a* 15 c. blue (1.3.41) 1·25 4·25
116 20 c. olive-green and carmine 90 40
117 25 c. violet and orange 50 1·00
118 30 c. red-brown and violet 60 1·25
119 50 c. violet and scarlet 60 60
120 $1 scarlet and sepia 60 50
121 $2 bright purple and violet 4·00 6·00
122 $3 carmine and green 15·00 12·00
123 $4 blue and scarlet 15·00 15·00
124 $5 scarlet and red-brown 16·00 23·00
125 $10 black and yellow 16·00 27·00
106/25 *Set of* 26 70·00 95·00
106/25 Perf "Specimen" *Set of* 26 £450

For the 3 c. green, wmkd Mult Script CA, see No. 152a.

BRITISH MILITARY ADMINISTRATION

Following the Japanese surrender elements of the British Military Administration reached Kuching on 11 September 1945. From 6 November 1945 Australian stamps, initially the 3d. value and later the 1d., 6d. and 1s., were made available for civilian use until replaced by Nos. 126/45.

1945 (17 Dec). *Optd with T* **22**.
126 21 1 c. purple 20 40
127 2 c. black (R.) 20 40
 a. Opt double † £2500
128 3 c. green 20 30
129 4 c. bright purple 20 30
130 5 c. violet (R.) 30 50
131 6 c. lake-brown 50 75
132 8 c. carmine 9·00 9·00
133 10 c. scarlet 50 60
134 12 c. orange 60 3·75
135 15 c. blue 85 40
136 20 c. olive-green and carmine 1·25 1·40
137 25 c. violet and orange (R.) 1·25 1·75
138 30 c. red-brown and violet 1·25 2·75
139 50 c. violet and scarlet 1·25 35
140 $1 scarlet and sepia 2·50 1·25
141 $2 bright purple and violet 9·00 4·50
142 $3 carmine and green 17·00 22·00
143 $4 blue and scarlet 25·00 25·00
144 $5 scarlet and red-brown 75·00 90·00
145 $10 black and yellow (R.) 90·00 £110
126/45 *Set of* 20 £200 £250

These stamps, and the similarly overprinted stamps of North Borneo, were obtainable at all post offices throughout British Borneo (Brunei, Labuan, North Borneo and Sarawak), for use on local and overseas mail.

The administration of Sarawak was returned to the Brooke family on 15 April 1946, but the Rajah, after consulting the inhabitants ceded the territory to Great Britain on 1 June 1946.

23 Sir James Brooke, Sir Charles Vyner Brooke and Sir Charles Brooke

(24)

(Recess B.W.)

1946 (18 May). *Centenary Issue. P* 12.
146 23 8 c. lake 20 15
147 15 c. blue 20 90
148 50 c. black and scarlet 35 80
149 $1 black and sepia 50 7·00
146/9 *Set of* 4 1·10 8·00
146/9 Perf "Specimen" *Set of* 4 90·00

CROWN COLONY

1947 (16 Apr). *Optd with T* **24**, *typo by B.W. in blue-black or red. Wmk Mult Script CA. P* 12.
150 21 1 c. purple 15 20
151 2 c. black (R.) 15 10
152 3 c. green (R.) 15 15
 a. Albino opt £2750
153 4 c. bright purple 15 15
154 6 c. lake-brown 20 50
155 8 c. carmine 20 10
156 10 c. scarlet 20 20
157 12 c. orange 15 70
158 15 c. blue (R.) 15 40
159 20 c. olive-green and carmine (R.) 30 50
160 25 c. violet and orange (R.) 30 30
161 50 c. violet and scarlet (R.) 30 30
162 $1 scarlet and sepia 60 80
163 $2 bright purple and violet 90 3·00
164 $5 scarlet and red-brown 1·75 3·00
150/64 *Set of* 15 5·00 9·25
150/64 Perf "Specimen" *Set of* 15 £250

No. 152a shows an uninked impression of T **24**.

1948 (25 Oct). *Royal Silver Wedding. As Nos.* 143/4 *of Jamaica.*
165 8 c. scarlet 30 20
166 $5 brown 23·00 24·00

1949 (10 Oct). *75th Anniv of U.P.U. As Nos.* 145/8 *of Jamaica.*
167 8 c. carmine 60 50
168 15 c. deep blue 1·40 2·25
169 25 c. deep blue-green 1·40 1·50
170 50 c. violet 2·00 3·00
167/70 *Set of* 4 4·75 6·50

25 *Trogonoptera brookiana* **26** Western Tarsier

(Recess; Arms typo B.W.)

1950 (3 Jan). *T* **25/6** *and similar designs. Wmk Mult Script CA. P* 11½ × 11 (*horiz*) *or* 11 × 11½ (*vert*).

171		1 c. black	30	30
172		2 c. red-orange	20	40
173		3 c. green	10	50
174		4 c. chocolate	10	20
175		6 c. turquoise-blue	10	15
176		8 c. scarlet	10	30
177		10 c. orange	50	2·50
178		12 c. violet	1·50	1·25
179		15 c. blue	70	10
180		20 c. purple-brown and red-orange	60	20
181		25 c. green and scarlet	70	30
182		50 c. brown and violet	70	15
183		$1 green and chocolate	4·50	1·25
184		$2 blue and carmine	12·00	4·50
185		$5 black, yellow, red and purple	16·00	7·00
171/85		*Set of* 15	35·00	17·00

Designs: *Horiz*—8 c. Dayak dancer; 10 c. Malayan Pangolin; 12 c. Kenyah boys; 15 c. Fire-making; 20 c. Kelemantan rice barn; 25 c. Pepper vines; $1 Kelabit smithy; $2 Map of Sarawak; $5 Arms of Sarawak. *Vert*—3 c. Kayan tomb; 4 c. Kayan girl and boy; 6 c. Bead work; 50 c. Iban woman.

40 Map of Sarawak

(Recess B.W.)

1952 (1 Feb). *Wmk Mult Script CA. P* 11½ × 11.

186	**40**	10 c. orange	20	30

1953 (3 June). *Coronation. As No.* 153 *of Jamaica.*

187		10 c. black and deep violet-blue	85	55

41 Logging **44** Malabar Pied Hornbill

51 Queen Elizabeth II **52** Queen Elizabeth II (after Annigoni)

(Des M. Thoma (1, 2 c.), R. Turrell (4 c.), J. D. Hughes (6, 12 c.), A. Hakim bin Moliti (8 c.), J. Woodcock (10 c.), J. Browning (15 c.), G. Gundersen (20 c.), K. Munich (25 c.). Recess, Arms typo ($5). B.W.)

1955 (1 June)–**59**. *T* **41, 44, 51/2** *and similar designs. Wmk Mult Script CA. P* 11×11½ (1 *c.,* 2 *c.,* 4 *c.*), 12×13 (30 *c.,* 50 *c.,* $1, $2) *or* 11½×11 (*others*).

188	**41**	1 c. green (1.10.57)	10	30
189	–	2 c. red-orange (1.10.57)	20	55
190	–	4 c. lake-brown (1.10.57)	30	30
		a. Brown-purple (18.3.59)	1·75	1·50
191	**44**	6 c. greenish blue (1.10.57)	2·75	35
192	–	8 c. rose-red (1.10.57)	20	30
193	–	10 c. deep green (1.10.57)	15	10
194	–	12 c. plum (1.10.57)	2·75	55
195	–	15 c. ultramarine (1.10.57)	80	15
196	–	20 c. olive and brown (1.10.57)	80	10
197	–	25 c. sepia and green (1.10.57)	4·25	15
198	**51**	30 c. red-brown and deep lilac	1·75	15
199		50 c. black and carmine (1.10.57)	1·75	15
200	**52**	$1 myrtle-green & orange-brn (1.10.57)	2·00	40
201		$2 violet and bronze-green (1.10.57)	4·50	1·75
202	–	$5 multicoloured (1.10.57)	13·00	5·50
188/202		*Set of* 15	32·00	9·75

Designs: *Horiz*—8 c. Shield with spears; 10 c. Kenyah ceremonial carving; 12 c. Barong panau (sailing prau); 15 c. Turtles; 20 c. Melanan basket-making; 25 c. Astana, Kuching; $5 Arms of Sarawak. *Vert* (*as T* **41**)—2 c. Young Orang-Utan; 4 c. Kayan dancing; 50 c. Queen Elizabeth II; $2 Queen Elizabeth II (after Annigoni).

1963 (4 June). *Freedom from Hunger. As No.* 80 *of Lesotho.*

203		12 c. sepia	1·50	35

STATE OF MALAYSIA

1964–65. *As* 1955–57 *but wmk* w **12.** *Perfs as before.*

204	**41**	1 c. green (8.9.64)	10	30
205	–	2 c. red-orange (17.8.65)	50	2·25
206	**44**	6 c. greenish blue (8.9.64)	3·50	2·25
207	–	10 c. deep green (8.9.64)	50	50
208	–	12 c. plum (8.9.64)	1·25	4·00
209	–	15 c. ultramarine (17.8.65)	1·25	7·00
210	–	20 c. olive and brown (9.6.64)	50	50
211	–	25 c. deep sepia and bluish green (8.9.64)	1·50	3·00
204/11		*Set of* 8	8·00	18·00

53 *Vanda hookeriana* **54** *Precis orithya*

1965 (15 Nov). *As Nos.* 166/72 *of Johore but with Arms of Sarawak inset as in T* **53.**

212		1 c. multicoloured	10	50
		c. Grey omitted	35·00	
213		2 c. multicoloured	15	50
		a. Black (country name and shield) omitted	65·00	
		c. Yellow-olive (stems) omitted	30·00	
214		5 c. multicoloured	35	10
215		6 c. multicoloured	50	40
		a. Black (country name and shield) omitted	65·00	
216		10 c. multicoloured	55	10
		a. Red omitted	35·00	
217		15 c. multicoloured	1·25	10
218		20 c. multicoloured	1·75	40
212/18		*Set of* 7	4·25	1·90

The 1 c., 6 c., 10 c. and 15 c. exist with PVA gum as well as gum arabic.

No. 213a was formerly listed with Trengganu No. 101 but there is evidence that it was issued in Sarawak.

A used example of No. 218 is known with the bright purple (blooms) omitted.

The higher values used with this issue were Nos. 20/7 of Malaysia (National Issues).

(Litho B.W.)

1971 (1 Feb). *As Nos.* 175/81 *of Johore but with Arms of Sarawak inset as in T* **54.**

219		1 c. multicoloured	15	55
220		2 c. multicoloured	35	60
221		5 c. multicoloured	55	10
222		6 c. multicoloured	70	40
223		10 c. multicoloured	70	10
224		15 c. multicoloured	1·00	10
225		20 c. multicoloured	1·25	45
219/25		*Set of* 7	4·25	2·00

The higher values used with this issue were Nos. 64/71 of Malaysia (National Issues).

55 *Precis orithya* (different crest at right) **56** *Rhododendron scortechinii*

(Photo Harrison)

1977 (12 Feb)–**78.** *As Nos.* 219/21 *and* 223/5 *but ptd in photogravure showing new State Crest as T* **55.**

226		1 c. multicoloured (1978)	4·25	5·50
227		2 c. multicoloured (1978)	3·50	4·50
228		5 c. multicoloured	80	55
230		10 c. multicoloured (4.4.77)	65	20
231		15 c. multicoloured (19.4.77)	1·00	20
232		20 c. multicoloured (1978)	5·50	3·50
226/32		*Set of* 6	14·00	13·00

1979 (30 Apr). *As Nos.* 188/94 *of Johore but with Arms of Sarawak as in T* **56.**

233		1 c. *Rafflesia hasseltii*	10	20
234		2 c. *Pterocarpus indicus*	10	20
235		5 c. *Lagerstroemia speciosa*	10	10
236		10 c. *Durio zibethinus*	10	10
237		15 c. *Hibiscus rosa-sinensis*	20	10
238		20 c. Type **56**	25	10
239		25 c. *Etlingera elatior* (inscr "*Phaeomeria speciosa*")	25	10
233/9		*Set of* 7	95	55

For higher values used in conjunction with this series see Nos. 190/7 of Malaysia (National Issues).

1983 (11 Oct)–**86.*** *As Nos.* 235/6 *and* 238 *but without wmk.*

242		5 c. *Lagerstroemia speciosa* (4.4.86)	4·25	3·25
243		10 c. *Durio zibethinus* (9.9.85)	3·25	2·50
245		20 c. Type **56** (blackish brown background)	5·50	2·50
245*a*		20 c. Type **56** (bronze-green background) (2.8.84)	1·50	1·00
242/5*a*		*Set of* 4	13·00	8·50

* There was no official release date for these stamps. Dates shown are the earliest recorded from postmarks and may be revised if earlier examples are reported.

For details of the shade differences between watermarked and unwatermarked printings see after Malaysia–Johore No. 200*a*.

On Nos. 242/3 and 245*a* the crest is closer to the face value than on Nos. 235/6, 238 and 245.

57 Coffee

1986 (25 Oct). *As Nos.* 202/8 *of Johore but with Arms of Sarawak as in T* **57.**

247		1 c. Type **57**	10	10
248		2 c. Coconuts	10	10
249		5 c. Cocoa	10	10
250		10 c. Black pepper	10	10
251		15 c. Rubber	10	10
252		20 c. Oil palm	10	10
253		30 c. Rice	10	15
247/53		*Set of* 7	40	45

XIV. JAPANESE OCCUPATION OF SARAWAK

Japanese forces landed in North Borneo in 16 December 1941 and Sarawak was attacked on 23 December 1941.

Brunei, North Borneo, Sarawak and, after a short period, Labuan, were administered as a single territory by the Japanese. Until September–October 1942, previous stamp issues, without overprint, continued to be used in conjunction with existing postmarks. From the Autumn of 1942 onwards unoverprinted stamps of Japan were made available and examples can be found used from the area for much of the remainder of the War. Japanese Occupation issues for Brunei, North Borneo and Sarawak were equally valid throughout the combined territory but not, in practice, equally available.

PRICES FOR STAMPS ON COVER	
Nos. J1/21	*from* × 8
Nos. J22/6	—

府政国帝本日大

(1)

("Imperial Japanese Government")

1942 (Oct). *Stamps of Sarawak handstamped with T* **1** *in violet.*

J 1	**21**	1 c. purple	22·00	27·00
J 2		2 c. green	60·00	75·00
J 3		2 c. black	38·00	50·00
J 4		3 c. black	£110	£130
J 5		3 c. green	32·00	38·00
J 6		4 c. bright purple	24·00	30·00
J 7		5 c. violet	26·00	30·00
J 8		6 c. carmine	45·00	55·00
J 9		6 c. lake-brown	30·00	38·00
J10		8 c. red-brown	£100	£130
J11		8 c. carmine	90·00	£110
J12		10 c. scarlet	30·00	38·00
J13		12 c. blue	70·00	75·00
J14		12 c. orange	80·00	£100
J15		15 c. orange	£120	£130
J16		15 c. blue	40·00	50·00
J17		20 c. olive-green and carmine	28·00	38·00
J18		25 c. violet and orange	32·00	38·00
J19		30 c. red-brown and violet	32·00	42·00
J20		50 c. violet and scarlet	32·00	42·00
J21		$1 scarlet and sepia	38·00	55·00
J22		$2 bright purple and violet	90·00	£110
J23		$3 carmine and green	£550	£650
J24		$4 blue and scarlet	£100	£130
J25		$5 scarlet and red-brown	£100	£130
J26		$10 black and yellow	£110	£150

The overprint, being handstamped, exists inverted on all values.

Stamps of T **21** optd with Japanese symbols within an oval frame are revenue stamps, while the same stamps overprinted with three Japanese characters between two vertical double rules, were used as seals.

Maldive Islands

PRICES FOR STAMPS ON COVER TO 1945

Nos. 1/6	*from* × 10
Nos. 7/10	*from* × 50
Nos. 11/20	*from* × 20

BRITISH PROTECTORATE

MALDIVES

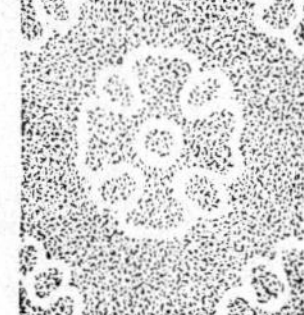

(1) 2 Minaret, Juma Mosque, Malé 3

1906. *Nos. 277/9, 280a and 283/4 of Ceylon optd with T* **1**. *Wmk Mult Crown CA. P* 14.

No.	Type	Description	Unused	Used
1	**44**	2 c. red-brown	11·00	23·00
2	**45**	3 c. green	15·00	23·00
3		4 c. orange and ultramarine	32·00	65·00
4	**46**	5 c. dull purple	4·50	6·50
5	**48**	15 c. blue	50·00	90·00
6		25 c. bistre	60·00	90·00
1/6		*Set of* 6	£150	£250

(Recess D.L.R.)

1909 (May). *T* **2** (18½ × 22½ *mm*). *W* **3**. *P* 14.

No.	Type	Description	Unused	Used
7	**2**	2 c. orange-brown	2·25	70
8		3 c. deep myrtle	40	70
9		5 c. purple	40	35
10		10 c. carmine	2·75	80
7/10		*Set of* 4	5·25	2·25

4

(Photo Harrison)

1933. *T* **2** *redrawn (reduced to* 18 × 21½ *mm). W* **4**. *P* 15 × 14.

No.	Type	Description	Unused	Used
11	**2**	2 c. grey	1·50	1·50
12		3 c. red-brown	70	1·60
13		5 c. claret (*sideways wmk*)	12·00	15·00
14		5 c. mauve (*upright wmk*)	5·50	8·50
15		6 c. scarlet	1·25	2·25
16		10 c. green	55	55
17		15 c. black	3·75	5·50
18		25 c. brown	4·25	5·50
19		50 c. purple	3·75	3·75
20		1 r. deep blue	5·50	2·75
11/20		*Set of* 10	35·00	42·00

The 2, 3, 6, 10, 15, 25, 50 c. and 1 r. values exist with both upright and sideways watermarks.

(New Currency. 100 larees=1 rupee)

5 Palm Tree and Dhow

(Recess B.W.)

1950 (24 Dec). *P* 13.

No.	Type	Description	Unused	Used
21	**5**	2 l. olive-green	65	40
22		3 l. blue	3·00	40
23		5 l. emerald-green	3·25	50
24		6 l. red-brown	35	20
25		10 l. scarlet	50	20
26		15 l. orange	50	30
27		25 l. purple	35	30
28		50 l. violet	40	30
29		1 r. chocolate	6·50	19·00
21/9		*Set of* 9	14·00	19·00

7 Fish 8 Native Products

(Recess B.W.)

1952. *P* 13.

No.	Type	Description	Unused	Used
30	**7**	3 l. blue	40	20
31	**8**	5 l. emerald	30	30

The Maldive Islands became a republic on 1 January 1953, but reverted to a sultanate in 1954.

9 Malé Harbour 10 Fort and Building

(Recess B.W.)

1956 (Feb). *P* 13½ (*T* **9**) *or* 11½ × 11 (*T* **10**).

No.	Type	Description	Unused	Used
32	**9**	2 l. purple	10	10
33		3 l. slate	10	10
34		5 l. red-brown	10	10
35		6 l. blackish violet	10	10
36		10 l. emerald	10	10
37		15 l. chocolate	10	10
38		25 l. rose-red	10	10
39		50 l. orange	10	10
40	**10**	1 r. bluish green	15	10
41		5 r. blue	60	20
42		10 r. magenta	85	40
32/42		*Set of* 11	1·75	80

11 Cycling 12 Basketball

(Des C. Bottiau. Recess and typo B.W.)

1960 (20 Aug). *Olympic Games. P* 11½ × 11 (*T* **11**) *or* 11 × 11½ (*T* **12**).

No.	Type	Description	Unused	Used
43	**11**	2 l. purple and green	10	10
44		3 l. greenish slate and purple	10	10
45		5 l. red-brown and ultramarine	10	10
46		10 l. emerald-green and brown	10	10
47		15 l. sepia and blue	10	10
48	**12**	25 l. rose-red and olive	10	10
49		50 l. orange and violet	10	10
50		1 r. emerald and purple	20	45
43/50		*Set of* 8	60	75

13 Tomb of Sultan 14 Custom House

(Recess B.W.)

1960 (15 Oct). *T* **13, 14** *and similar horiz designs. P* 11½ × 11.

No.	Description	Unused	Used
51	2 l. purple	10	10
52	3 l. emerald-green	10	10
53	5 l. orange-brown	50	30
54	6 l. bright blue	10	10
55	10 l. carmine	10	10
56	15 l. sepia	10	10
57	25 l. deep violet	10	10
58	50 l. slate-grey	10	10
59	1 r. orange	15	10
60	5 r. deep ultramarine	1·75	60
61	10 r. grey-green	4·50	1·25
51/61	*Set of* 11	7·00	2·40

Designs:—5 l. Cowrie shells; 6 l. Old Royal Palace; 10 l. Road to Juma Mosque, Malé; 15 l. Council house; 25 l. New Government Secretariat; 50 l. Prime Minister's office; 1 r. Old Ruler's tomb; 5 r. Old Ruler's tomb (distant view); 10 r. Maldivian Port.

Higher values were also issued, intended mainly for fiscal use.

24 "Care of Refugees"

(Recess B.W.)

1960 (15 Oct). *World Refugee Year. P* 11½ × 11.

No.	Type	Description	Unused	Used
62	**24**	2 l. deep violet, orange and green	10	10
63		3 l. brown, green and red	10	10
64		5 l. deep green, sepia and red	10	10
65		10 l. bluish green, reddish violet and red	10	10
66		15 l. reddish violet, grey-green and red	10	10
67		25 l. blue, red-brown and bronze-green	10	10
68		50 l. yellow-olive, rose-red and blue	10	10
69		1 r. carmine, slate and violet	15	35
62/9		*Set of* 8	30	45

MINIMUM PRICE

The minimum price quote is 10p which represents a handling charge rather than a basis for valuing common stamps. For further notes about prices see introductory pages.

25 Coconuts 26 Map of Malé

(Photo Harrison)

1961 (20 Apr). *P* 14 × 14½ (*Nos. 70/74*) *or* 14½ × 14 (*others*).

No.	Type	Description	Unused	Used
70	**25**	2 l. yellow-brown and deep green	10	10
71		3 l. yellow-brown and bright blue	10	10
72		5 l. yellow-brown and magenta	10	10
73		10 l. yellow-brown and red-orange	10	10
74		15 l. yellow-brown and black	10	10
75	**26**	25 l. multicoloured	10	10
76		50 l. multicoloured	10	10
77		1 r. multicoloured	20	30
70/7		*Set of* 8	45	55

27 5 c. Stamp of 1906 30 Malaria Eradication Emblem

(Des M. Shamir. Photo Harrison)

1961 (9 Sept). *55th Anniv of First Maldivian Stamp. T* **27** *and similar horiz designs. P* 14½ × 14.

No.	Description	Unused	Used
78	2 l. brown-purple, ultramarine & lt green	10	10
79	3 l. brown-purple, ultramarine & lt green	10	10
80	5 l. brown-purple, ultramarine & lt green	10	10
81	6 l. brown-purple, ultramarine & lt green	10	10
82	10 l. green, claret and maroon	10	10
83	15 l. green, claret and maroon	10	10
84	20 l. green, claret and maroon	10	10
85	25 l. claret, green and black	10	10
86	50 l. claret, green and black	20	40
87	1 r. claret, green and black	35	75
78/87	*Set of* 10	75	1·40
MS87*a*	114 × 88 mm. No. 87 (block of four). Imperf	1·50	2·75

Designs:—2 to 6 l. Type **27**; 10 to 20 l. 1906 3 c. and posthorn; 25 l. to 1 r. 1906 2 c. and olive sprig.

(Recess B.W.)

1962 (7 Apr). *Malaria Eradication. P* 13½ × 13.

No.	Type	Description	Unused	Used
88	**30**	2 l. chestnut	10	10
89		3 l. emerald	10	10
90		5 l. turquoise-blue	10	10
91		10 l. red	10	10
92	–	15 l. deep purple-brown	10	10
93	–	25 l. deep blue	10	10
94	–	50 l. deep green	15	10
95	–	1 r. purple	35	25
88/95		*Set of* 8	65	45

Nos. 92/5 are as T **30**, but have English inscriptions at the side.

31 Children of Europe and America 33 Sultan Mohamed Farid Didi

(Des C. Bottiau. Photo Harrison)

1962 (9 Sept). *15th Anniv of U.N.I.C.E.F. T* **31** *and similar horiz design. Multicoloured. P* 14½ × 14.

No.	Description	Unused	Used
96	2 l. Type **31**	10	10
97	6 l. Type **31**	10	10
98	10 l. Type **31**	10	10
99	15 l. Type **31**	10	10
100	25 l. Children of Middle East and Far East	10	10
101	50 l. As 25 l.	10	10
102	1 r. As 25 l.	10	20
103	5 r. As 25 l.	45	1·75
96/103	*Set of* 8	70	2·00

(Photo Harrison)

1962 (29 Nov). *Ninth Anniv of Enthronement of Sultan. P* 14 × 14½.

No.	Type	Description	Unused	Used
104	**33**	3 l. orange-brown and bluish green	10	10
105		5 l. orange-brown and indigo	10	10
106		10 l. orange-brown and blue	10	10
107		20 l. orange-brown and olive-green	10	10
108		50 l. orange-brown and deep magenta	10	10
109		1 r. orange-brown and slate-lilac	15	25
104/9		*Set of* 6	35	45

34 Angel Fish

(Des R. Hegeman. Photo Enschedé)

1963 (2 Feb). *Tropical Fish. T* **34** *and similar triangular designs. Multicoloured. P* 13½.

110 2 l. Type **34** 10 10
111 3 l. Type **34** 10 10
112 5 l. Type **34** 10 10
113 10 l. Moorish Idol 10 10
114 25 l. As 10 l. 10 10
115 50 l. Soldier Fish 10 10
116 1 r. Surgeon Fish 30 30
117 5 r. Butterfly Fish .. .. 2·75 4·25
110/17 .. .. *Set of* 8 3·00 4·50

39 Fishes in Net **40** Handful of Grain

(Photo State Ptg Wks, Vienna)

1963 (21 Mar). *Freedom from Hunger. P* 12.

118 **39** 2 l. brown and deep bluish green .. 30 60
119 **40** 5 l. brown and orange-red 50 50
120 **39** 7 l. brown and turquoise 70 50
121 **40** 10 l. brown and blue 85 50
122 **39** 25 l. brown and brown-red .. .. 3·00 2·75
123 **40** 50 l. brown and violet .. .. .. 4·75 5·50
124 **39** 1 r. brown and deep magenta .. .. 7·50 9·50
118/24 .. .. *Set of* 7 16·00 18·00

41 Centenary Emblem **42** Maldivian Scout Badge

(Photo Harrison)

1963 (Oct). *Centenary of Red Cross. P* 14 × 14½.

125 **41** 2 l. red and deep purple 30 70
126 15 l. red and deep bluish green 50 65
127 50 l. red and deep brown.. .. .. 1·25 1·50
128 1 r. red and indigo .. .. .. 2·00 1·75
129 4 r. red and deep brown-olive .. .. 6·50 17·00
125/9 .. .. *Set of* 5 9·50 19·00

(Photo Enschedé)

1964. *World Scout Jamboree, Marathon* (1963). *P* 13½.

130 **42** 2 l. green and violet 10 10
131 3 l. green and bistre-brown 10 10
132 25 l. green and blue 10 10
133 1 r. green and crimson 45 85
130/3 .. .. *Set of* 4 60 95

43 Mosque, Malé **44** Putting the Shot

(Recess B.W.)

1964 (10 Aug). *"Maldives Embrace Islam". W* w **12.** *P* 11½.

134 **43** 2 l. purple 10 10
135 3 l. emerald-green 10 10
136 10 l. carmine 10 10
137 40 l. deep dull purple 15 10
138 60 l. blue 20 10
139 85 l. orange-brown 20 15
134/9 .. .. *Set of* 6 65 40

(Litho Enschedé)

1964 (Oct). *Olympic Games, Tokyo. T* **44** *and similar horiz design. W* w **12.** *P* 14 × 13½.

140 2 l. deep maroon and turquoise-blue .. 10 10
141 3 l. crimson and chestnut 10 10
142 5 l. bronze-green and deep green 10 10
143 10 l. slate-violet and reddish purple .. 15 10
144 15 l. sepia and yellow-brown 15 10
145 25 l. indigo and deep blue 25 10
146 50 l. deep olive-green and yellow-olive .. 45 20
147 1 r. deep maroon and olive-grey 85 40
140/7 .. .. *Set of* 8 1·75 70
MS147*a* 126 × 140 mm. Nos. 145/7. Imperf .. 2·00 2·25

Designs:—2 to 10 l. Type **44**; 15 l. to 1 r. Running.

46 Telecommunications Satellite

(Des M. Shamir. Photo Harrison)

1965 (1 July). *International Quiet Sun Years. P* 14½.

148 **46** 5 l. blue 10 10
149 10 l. brown 15 10
150 25 l. green 25 10
151 1 r. deep magenta 50 35
148/51 .. .. *Set of* 4 90 50

On 26 July 1965, Maldive Islands became independent and left the British Commonwealth.

INDEPENDENT SULTANATE

Sultan Mohamed Farid Didi
29 November 1953–10 November 1968

47 Isis (wall carving, Abu Simbel) **48** President Kennedy and Doves

(Des M. and G. Shamir. Litho Harrison)

1965 (1 Sept). *Nubian Monuments Preservation. T* **47** *and similar vert design. W* w **12.** *P* 14½.

152 **47** 2 l. bluish green and brown-purple .. 10 10
153 – 3 l. lake and deep green 10 10
154 **47** 5 l. dull green and brown-purple .. 10 10
155 – 10 l. steel-blue and orange 10 10
156 **47** 15 l. red-brown and deep violet 10 10
157 – 25 l. reddish purple and deep blue .. 15 10
158 **47** 50 l. yellow-green and sepia 25 15
159 – 1 r. ochre and myrtle-green 50 30
152/9 .. .. *Set of* 8 1·00 70

Design:—3, 10, 25 l., 1 r. Rameses II on throne (wall carving, Abu Simbel).

(Photo State Ptg Wks, Vienna)

1965 (10 Oct). *Second Death Anniv of President Kennedy. T* **48** *and similar horiz design. P* 12.

160 **48** 2 l. black and mauve 10 10
161 5 l. bistre-brown and mauve 10 10
162 25 l. indigo and mauve 10 10
163 – 1 r. brt reddish purple, yellow & bl-grn 25 25
164 – 2 r. bronze-green, yellow & blue-green 40 40
160/4 .. .. *Set of* 5 75 75
MS164*a* 150 × 130 mm. No. 164 in block of four. Imperf .. .. 2·75 3·00

Design:—1 r., 2 r. Pres. Kennedy and hands holding olive-branch.

49 "XX" and U.N. Flag **50** I.C.Y. Emblem

(Des O. Adler. Photo State Ptg Wks, Vienna)

1965 (24 Nov). *20th Anniv of U.N. P* 12.

165 **49** 3 l. turquoise-blue and red-brown .. 10 10
166 10 l. turquoise-blue and violet 10 10
167 1 r. turquoise-blue and bronze-green .. 35 35
165/7 .. .. *Set of* 3 40 40

(Des M. and G. Shamir. Photo State Ptg Wks, Vienna)

1965 (20 Dec). *International Co-operation Year. P* 12.

168 **50** 5 l. brown and yellow-bistre 15 10
169 15 l. brown and slate-lilac 20 10
170 50 l. brown and yellow-olive 45 30
171 1 r. brown and orange-red .. .. 1·25 1·50
172 2 r. brown and new blue .. .. 1·75 3·00
168/72 .. .. *Set of* 5 3·50 4·50
MS173 101 × 126 mm. Nos. 170/2. Imperf .. 6·00 6·50

51 Seashells

(Des M. and G. Shamir. Photo State Ptg Wks, Vienna)

1966 (1 June). *T* **51** *and similar multicoloured designs. P* 12.

174 2 l. Type **51** 20 30
175 3 l. Yellow flowers 20 30
176 5 l. Seashells (*different*) 30 15
177 7 l. Camellias 30 15
178 10 l. Type **51** 40 15
179 15 l. Crab Plover and Seagull.. .. .. 1·50 30
180 20 l. Yellow flowers 70 30
181 30 l. Type **51** .. .. 1·25 35
182 50 l. Crab Plover and Seagull.. .. .. 2·50 55
183 1 r. Type **51** .. .. 2·00 55
184 1 r. Camellias .. .. 2·00 55
185 1 r. 50, Yellow flowers .. .. .. 2·75 1·25
186 2 r. Camellias .. .. 3·75 1·75
187 5 r. Crab Plover and Seagull.. .. .. 11·00 7·00
188 10 r. Seashells (*different*) .. .. .. 14·00 11·00
174/88 .. .. *Set of* 15 38·00 22·00

The 3 l., 7 l., 20 l., 1 r. (No. 184), 1 r. 50 and 2 r. are diamond-shaped (43½ × 43½ mm); the others are horizontal designs as T **51**.

52 Maldivian Flag

(Des M. and G. Shamir. Litho Harrison)

1966 (26 July). *First Anniv of Independence. P* 14 × 14½.

189 **52** 10 l. green, red and turquoise 10 10
190 1 r. green, red, brown & orange-yellow 40 30

53 "Luna 9" on Moon

(Des M. and G. Shamir. Litho Harrison)

1966 (1 Nov). *Space Rendezvous and Moon Landing. T* **53** *and similar horiz designs. W* w **12.** *P* 15 × 14.

191 10 l. light brown, grey-blue and bright blue .. 10 10
192 25 l. green and carmine 15 10
193 50 l. orange-brown and green.. .. .. 20 15
194 1 r. turquoise-blue and chestnut 45 35
195 2 r. green and violet 75 65
196 5 r. rose-pink and deep turquoise-blue .. 1·75 1·60
191/6 .. .. *Set of* 6 2·75 2·50
MS197 108 × 126 mm. Nos. 194/6. Imperf .. 3·25 3·75

Designs:—25 l., 1 r., 5 r. "Gemini 6" and "7" rendezvous in space; 2 r. "Gemini" spaceship as seen from the other spaceship; 50 l. Type **53**.

54 U.N.E.S.C.O. Emblem, and Owl on Book **55** Sir Winston Churchill and Cortège

(Litho Harrison)

1966 (15 Nov). *20th Anniv of U.N.E.S.C.O. T* **54** *and similar vert designs. W* w **12.** *Multicoloured. P* 15 × 14.

198 1 l. Type **54** 10 30
199 3 l. U.N.E.S.C.O. emblem, and globe and microscope 10 30
200 5 l. U.N.E.S.C.O. emblem, and mask, violin and palette 15 15
201 50 l. Type **54** 70 45
202 1 r. Design as 3 l. .. .. 1·25 75
203 5 r. Design as 5 l. .. .. 5·50 7·50
198/203 .. .. *Set of* 6 7·00 8·50

(Des M. and G. Shamir. Litho Harrison)

1967 (1 Jan). *Churchill Commemoration. T* **55** *and similar horiz design. Flag in red and blue. P* 14½ × 13½.

No.	Type	Description	Unused	Used
204	**55**	2 l. olive-brown	15	30
205	–	10 l. turquoise-blue	40	10
206	**55**	15 l. green	55	10
207	–	25 l. violet	95	10
208	–	1 r. brown	3·25	75
209	**55**	2 r. 50, crimson	7·00	8·00
204/9		*Set of* 6	11·00	8·50

Design:—10 l., 25 l., 1 r. Churchill and catafalque.

IMPERFORATE STAMPS. From No. 210 onwards some sets and perforated miniature sheets exist imperforate from limited printings.

56 Footballers and Jules Rimet Cup

(Des M. and G. Shamir. Photo Govt Printer, Israel)

1967 (22 Mar). *England's Victory in World Cup Football Championship. T* **56** *and similar horiz designs. Multicoloured. P* 14×13½.

No.	Description	Unused	Used
210	2 l. Type **56**	10	30
211	3 l. Player in red shirt kicking ball	10	30
212	5 l. Scoring goal	10	10
213	25 l. As 3 l.	20	10
	a. Emerald (face value and inscr) omitted	£130	
214	50 l. Making a tackle	45	20
215	1 r. Type **56**	1·25	45
216	2 r. Emblem on Union Jack	2·00	2·50
210/16	*Set of* 7	3·75	3·50
MS217	100×121 mm. Nos. 214/16. Imperf	4·50	4·50

57 Clown Butterfly Fish

(Des M. and G. Shamir. Photo Govt Printer, Israel)

1967 (1 May). *Tropical Fishes. T* **57** *and similar horiz designs. Multicoloured. P* 14.

No.	Description	Unused	Used
218	2 l. Type **57**	10	30
219	3 l. Striped Puffer	10	30
220	5 l. Blue Spotted Boxfish	15	10
221	6 l. Picasso Fish	15	20
222	50 l. Blue Angelfish	1·50	30
223	1 r. Blue Spotted Boxfish	3·00	75
224	2 r. Blue Angelfish	5·00	5·00
218/24	*Set of* 7	9·00	6·00

58 Hawker Siddeley "HS748" over Airport Building

(Des M. and G. Shamir. Photo Govt Printer, Israel)

1967 (26 July). *Inauguration of Hulule Airport. T* **58** *and similar horiz design. P* 14 × 13½.

No.	Description	Unused	Used
225	2 l. reddish violet and yellow-olive	10	30
226	5 l. deep green and lavender	10	10
227	10 l. reddish violet and light turquoise-green	10	10
228	15 l. deep green and yellow-ochre	15	10
229	30 l. deep ultramarine and light blue	40	10
230	50 l. deep brown and magenta	60	20
231	5 r. deep ultramarine and yellow-orange	2·75	3·50
232	10 r. deep brown and blue	4·75	5·75
225/32	*Set of* 8	8·00	9·00

Designs:—2 l., 10 l., 30 l., 5 r. T **58**; 5 l., 15 l., 50 l., 10 r. Airport building and aircraft. Higher values were also issued, intended mainly for fiscal use.

International Tourist Year 1967

59 "Man and Music" Pavilion (**60**)

(Des M. and G. Shamir. Photo Govt Printer, Israel)

1967 (Sept). *World Fair, Montreal. T* **59** *and similar horiz design. Multicoloured. P* 14 × 13½.

No.	Description	Unused	Used
233	2 l. Type **59**	10	10
234	5 l. "Man and His Community" Pavilion	10	10
235	10 l. Type **59**	10	10
236	50 l. As 5 l.	25	20
237	1 r. Type **59**	50	40
238	2 r. As 5 l.	80	90
233/8	*Set of* 6	1·50	1·50
MS239	102 × 137 mm. Nos. 237/8. Imperf	2·50	2·25

1967 (1 Dec). *International Tourist Year. Nos. 225/32 optd as T* **60** *(in one or three lines), in gold.*

No.	Description	Unused	Used
240	2 l. reddish violet and yellow-olive	10	30
241	5 l. deep green and lavender	10	15
242	10 l. reddish violet and light turquoise-green	10	15
243	15 l. deep green and yellow-ochre	10	15
244	30 l. deep ultramarine and light blue	20	20
245	50 l. deep brown and magenta	25	30
246	5 r. deep ultramarine and yellow-orange	2·25	3·00
247	10 r. deep brown and blue	3·75	5·00
240/7	*Set of* 8	6·00	8·25

61 Cub signalling and Lord Baden-Powell **62** French Satellite "A 1"

(Litho Harrison)

1968 (1 Jan). *Maldivian Scouts and Cubs. T* **61** *and similar vert design. P* 14 × 14½.

No.	Type	Description	Unused	Used
248	**61**	2 l. brown, green and yellow	10	30
249	–	3 l. carmine, bright blue and light blue	10	30
250	**61**	25 l. bluish violet, lake and orange-red	1·25	30
251	–	1 r. blackish green, chest & apple-green	3·25	1·60
248/51		*Set of* 4	4·00	2·25

Design:—3 l., 1 r. Scouts and Lord Baden-Powell.

(Des M. and G. Shamir. Photo Govt Printer, Israel)

1968 (27 Jan). *Space Martyrs. Triangular designs as T* **62**. *P* 14.

No.	Description	Unused	Used
252	2 l. magenta and ultramarine	10	30
253	3 l. violet and yellow-brown	10	30
254	7 l. olive-brown and lake	10	30
255	10 l. deep blue, pale drab and black	10	15
256	25 l. bright emerald and reddish violet	35	15
257	50 l. blue and orange-brown	65	30
258	1 r. purple-brown and deep bluish green	85	50
259	2 r. deep brown, pale blue and black	1·50	1·75
260	5 r. magenta, light drab and black	2·75	3·00
252/60	*Set of* 9	5·75	6·00
MS261	110 × 155 mm. Nos. 258/9. Imperf	3·25	3·25

Designs:—2 l., 50 l. Type **62**; 3 l., 25 l. "Luna 10"; 7 l., 1 r. "Orbiter" and "Mariner"; 10 l., 2 r. Astronauts White, Grissom and Chaffee; 5 r. Cosmonaut V. M. Komarov.

63 Putting the Shot **64** "Adriatic Seascape" (Bonington)

(Des M. Shamir. Litho Harrison)

1968 (Feb). *Olympic Games, Mexico (1967) (1st issue). T* **63** *and similar vert design. Multicoloured. P* 14½.

No.	Description	Unused	Used
262	2 l. Type **63**	10	15
263	6 l. Throwing the discus	10	15
264	10 l. Type **63**	10	10
265	15 l. As 6 l.	10	10
266	1 r. Type **63**	35	35
267	2 r. 50, As 6 l.	65	85
262/7	*Set of* 6	1·10	1·40

See also Nos. 294/7.

(Des M. Shamir. Litho Govt Printer, Israel)

1968 (1 Apr). *Paintings. T* **64** *and similar horiz designs. Multicoloured. P* 14.

No.	Description	Unused	Used
268	50 l. Type **64**	40	20
269	1 r. "Ulysses deriding Polyphemus" (Turner)	70	35
270	2 r. "Sailing Boat at Argenteuil" (Monet)	1·25	1·25
271	5 r. "Fishing Boats at Les Saintes-Maries" (Van Gogh)	3·00	3·50
268/71	*Set of* 4	4·75	4·75

65 *Graf Zeppelin* and Montgolfier's Balloon

(Des M. Shamir. Photo Govt Printer, Israel)

1968 (1 June). *Development of Civil Aviation. T* **65** *and similar horiz designs. P* 14 × 13½.

No.	Description	Unused	Used
272	2 l. orange-brown, yellow-green & ultram	15	40
273	3 l. turquoise-blue, violet & orange-brown	15	40
274	5 l. slate-green, crimson and turquoise-blue	15	15
275	7 l. bright blue, purple and red-orange	60	35
276	10 l. brown, turquoise-blue and bright purple	30	15
277	50 l. crimson, slate-green and yellow-olive	1·25	20
278	1 r. emerald, blue and vermilion	2·00	50
279	2 r. maroon, bistre and bright blue	12·00	9·00
272/9	*Set of* 8	15·00	10·00

Designs:—3 l., 1 r. Boeing "707" and Douglas "DC-3"; 5 l., 50 l. Wright Brothers aircraft and Lilienthal's glider; 7 l., 2 r. Projected Boeing Supersonic "733" and "Concorde"; 10 l. Type **65**.

International Boy Scout Jamboree, Farragut Park, Idaho, U.S.A. August 1-9, 1967

66 W.H.O. Building, Geneva (**67**)

(Litho Harrison)

1968 (15 July). *20th Anniv of World Health Organisation. P* 14½ × 13½.

No.	Type	Description	Unused	Used
280	**66**	10 l. violet, turquoise-bl & lt greenish bl	40	10
281		25 l. bronze-green, yell-brn & orge-yell	80	10
282		1 r. deep brown, emerald & brt green	2·25	75
283		2 r. bluish violet, magenta and mauve	3·75	4·25
280/3		*Set of* 4	6·50	4·75

1968 (1 Aug). *First Anniv of Scout Jamboree, Idaho. Nos.* 248/51 *optd with T* **67**.

No.	Description	Unused	Used
284	2 l. brown, green and yellow	10	30
285	3 l. carmine, bright blue and light blue	10	30
286	25 l. bluish violet, lake and orange-red	1·00	30
287	1 r. blackish green, chestnut & apple-green	3·50	1·60
284/7	*Set of* 4	4·25	2·25

68 Curlew and Redshank

1968 (24 Sept). *T* **68** *and similar horiz designs. Photo. Multicoloured. P* 14 × 13½.

No.	Description	Unused	Used
288	2 l. Type **68**	30	50
289	10 l. Conches	80	20
290	25 l. Shells	1·25	25
291	50 l. Type **68**	3·75	90
292	1 r. Conches	3·75	95
293	2 r. Shells	4·25	4·00
288/93	*Set of* 6	13·00	6·25

69 Throwing the Discus

(Des M. Shamir. Photo Govt Printer, Israel)

1968 (12 Oct). *Olympic Games, Mexico (2nd issue). T* **69** *and similar multicoloured designs. P* 14.

No.	Description	Unused	Used
294	10 l. Type **69**	10	10
295	50 l. Running	10	10
296	1 r. Cycling	35	35
297	2 r. Basketball	75	1·00
294/7	*Set of* 4	1·10	1·40

INDEPENDENT REPUBLIC

11 November 1968

70 Fishing Dhow **71** "The Thinker" (Rodin)

(Photo Harrison)

1968 (11 Nov). *Republic Day. T* **70** *and similar horiz design. P* 14 × 14½.
298 10 l. brown, ultramarine and lt yellow-green 50 15
299 1 r. green, red and bright blue .. .. 1·75 60
Design:—1 r. National flag, crest and map.

(Des M. Shamir. Litho Rosenbaum Brothers, Vienna)

1969 (10 Apr). *U.N.E.S.C.O. "Human Rights". T* **71** *and similar vert designs, showing sculptures by Rodin. Multicoloured. P* 13½.
300 6 l. Type **71** 30 15
301 10 l. "Hands" 30 15
302 1 r. 50, "Eve" .. .. 1·75 1·75
303 2 r. 50, "Adam" .. .. 2·25 2·50
300/3 .. .. *Set of* 4 4·25 4·00
MS304 112 × 130 mm. Nos. 302/3. Imperf .. 3·25 3·75

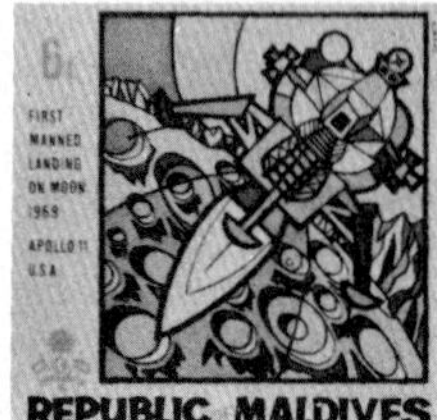

72 Module nearing Moon's Surface

(Des M. Shamir. Litho Govt Printer, Israel)

1969 (25 Sept). *First Man on the Moon. T* **72** *and similar square designs. Multicoloured. P* 14.
305 6 l. Type **72** 15 15
306 10 l. Astronaut with hatchet 15 15
307 1 r. 50, Astronaut and module .. .. 90 1·00
308 2 r. 50, Astronaut using camera .. .. 1·50 1·75
305/8 .. .. *Set of* 4 2·40 2·75
MS309 101 × 130 mm. Nos. 305/8. Imperf .. 1·75 2·75

Gold Medal Winner
Mohamed Gammoudi
5000 m. run
Tunisia
REPUBLIC OF MALDIVES

(**73**)

1969 (1 Dec). *Gold-medal Winners, Olympic Games, Mexico (1968). Nos. 295/6 optd with T* **73**, *or similar inscr honouring P. Trentin (cycling) of France.*
310 50 l. multicoloured 40 40
311 1 r. multicoloured 60 60

74 Red-striped Butterfly Fish

(Des M. Shamir. Litho)

1970 (Jan). *Tropical Fish. T* **74** *and similar diamond-shaped designs. Multicoloured. P* 10½.
312 2 l. Type **74** 30 50
313 5 l. Spotted Triggerfish 45 20
314 25 l. Scorpion Fish .. .. 1·25 30
315 50 l. Forceps Fish .. .. 1·75 75
316 1 r. Imperial Angelfish .. .. .. 2·50 90
317 2 r. Regal Angelfish .. .. 3·75 4·00
312/17 .. .. *Set of* 6 9·00 6·00

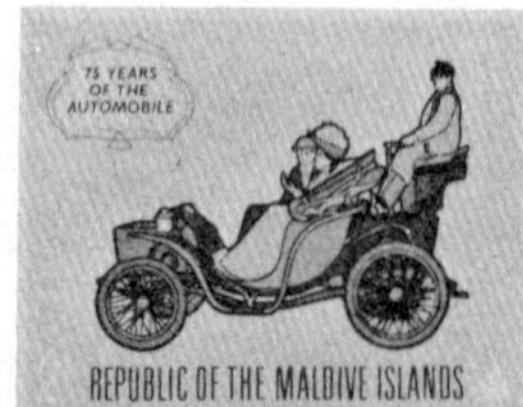

75 Columbia Dauman Victoria, 1899

(Des M. Shamir. Litho)

1970 (1 Feb). *"75 Years of the Automobile". T* **75** *and similar horiz designs. Multicoloured. P* 12.
318 2 l. Type **75** 10 20
319 5 l. Duryea phaeton, 1902 .. .. .. 15 20
320 7 l. Packard S-24, 1906 .. .. .. 20 20
321 10 l. Autocar Runabout, 1907 .. .. .. 25 20
322 25 l. Type **75** 60 20
323 50 l. As 5 l. .. .. 1·50 40
324 1 r. As 7 l. .. .. 2·25 70
325 2 r. As 10 l. .. .. 3·50 3·75
318/25 .. .. *Set of* 8 7·75 5·25
MS326 95 × 143 mm. Nos. 324/5. P 11½ .. 3·25 3·75

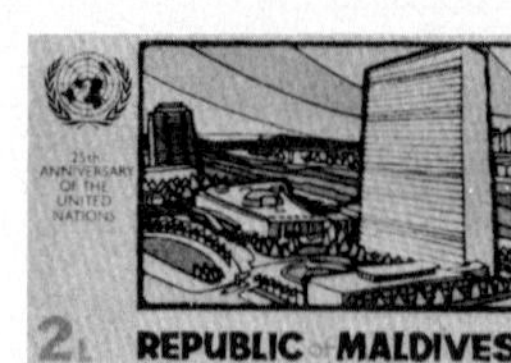

76 U.N. Headquarters, New York **77** Ship and Light Buoy

(Des M. Shamir. Litho Rosenbaum Brothers, Vienna)

1970 (26 June). *25th Anniv of United Nations. T* **76** *and similar horiz designs. Multicoloured. P* 13½.
327 2 l. Type **76** 10 40
328 10 l. Surgical operation (W.H.O.) 45 10
329 25 l. Student, actress and musician (U.N.E.S.C.O.) .. .. .. 1·00 25
330 50 l. Children at work and play (U.N.I.C.E.F.) 1·25 50
331 1 r. Fish, corn and farm animals (F.A.O.) .. 1·50 80
332 2 r. Miner hewing coal (I.L.O.) .. .. 3·00 3·25
327/32 .. .. *Set of* 6 6·50 4·75

(Des M. Shamir. Litho)

1970 (26 July). *10th Anniv of Inter-governmental Maritime Consultative Organization. T* **77** *and similar vert design. Multicoloured. P* 13½.
333 50 l. Type **77** 45 40
334 1 r. Ship and lighthouse .. .. .. 1·00 85

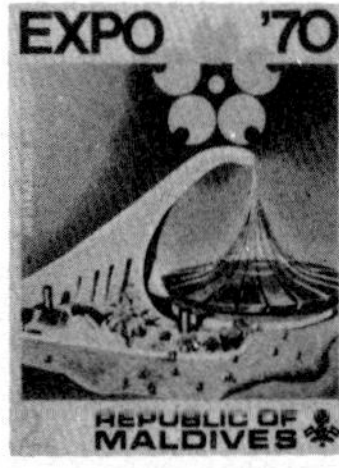

78 "Guitar-player and Masqueraders" (A. Watteau) **79** Australian Pavilion

(Des M. Shamir. Litho Govt Printer, Israel)

1970 (1 Aug). *Famous Paintings showing the Guitar. T* **78** *and similar vert designs. Multicoloured. P* 14.
335 3 l. Type **78** 10 30
336 7 l. "Spanish Guitarist" (E. Manet) 10 30
337 50 l. "Costumed Player" (Watteau) 50 35
338 1 r. "Mandoline-player" (Roberti) 85 55
339 2 r. 50, "Guitar-player and Lady" (Watteau) 2·25 2·50
340 5 r. "Mandoline-player" (Frans Hals) .. 4·00 4·25
335/40 .. .. *Set of* 6 7·00 7·50
MS341 132 × 80 mm. Nos. 339/40. Roul .. .. 4·25 4·75

(Des M. Shamir. Litho Rosenbaum Brothers, Vienna)

1970 (1 Aug). *"EXPO 70" World Fair, Osaka, Japan. T* **79** *and similar vert designs. Multicoloured. P* 13½.
342 2 l. Type **79** 10 40
343 3 l. West German Pavilion 10 40
344 10 l. U.S.A. Pavilion 15 10
345 25 l. British Pavilion 20 15
346 50 l. Soviet Pavilion 35 35
347 1 r. Japanese Pavilion 65 65
342/7 .. .. *Set of* 6 1·25 1·75

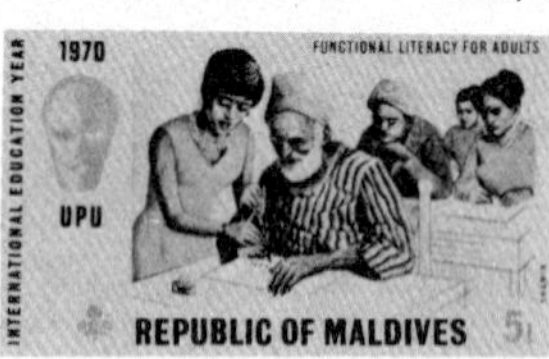

80 Learning the Alphabet

(Des M. Shamir. Litho Govt Printer, Israel)

1970 (7 Sept). *International Education Year. T* **80** *and similar horiz designs. Multicoloured. P* 14.
348 5 l. Type **80** 10 15
349 10 l. Training teachers 15 10
350 25 l. Geography lesson 30 15
351 50 l. School inspector 45 45
352 1 r. Education by television 75 75
348/52 .. .. *Set of* 5 1·60 1·40

MINIMUM PRICE

The minimum price quote is 10p which represents a handling charge rather than a basis for valuing common stamps. For further notes about prices see introductory pages.

Philympia
London 1970

(**81**)

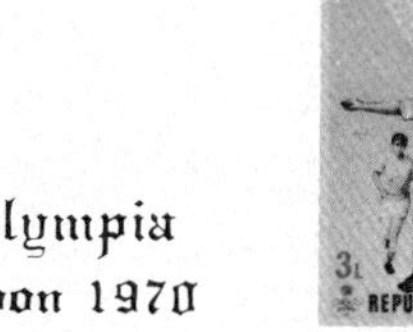

82 Footballers

1970 (18 Sept). *"Philympia 1970" Stamp Exhibition, London. Nos. 306/***MS***309 optd with T* **81**, *in silver.*
353 10 l. multicoloured 10 10
354 1 r. 50, multicoloured 65 65
355 2 r. 50, multicoloured .. .. .. 1·00 1·25
353/5 .. .. *Set of* 3 1·50 1·75
MS356 101 × 130 mm. Nos. 305/8 optd. Imperf .. 5·50 6·50

(Des M. Shamir. Litho Rosenbaum Brothers, Vienna)

1970 (Dec). *World Cup Football Championships, Mexico. T* **82** *and similar vert designs, each showing football scenes and outline of the Jules Rimet Trophy. P* 13½.
357 3 l. multicoloured 10 30
358 6 l. multicoloured 10 30
359 7 l. multicoloured 10 20
360 25 l. multicoloured 50 15
361 1 r. multicoloured .. .. 1·75 80
357/61 .. .. *Set of* 5 2·25 1·60

83 Little Boy and U.N.I.C.E.F. Flag **84** Astronauts Lovell, Haise and Swigert

(Des M. Shamir. Litho State Printing Works, Budapest)

1971 (1 Apr). *25th Anniv of U.N.I.C.E.F. T* **83** *and similar vert design. Multicoloured. P* 12.
362 5 l. Type **83** 10 15
363 10 l. Little girl with U.N.I.C.E.F. balloon .. 10 15
364 1 r. Type **83** 80 55
365 2 r. As 10 l. .. .. 1·75 1·90
362/5 .. .. *Set of* 4 2·50 2·50

(Des M. Shamir. Litho Govt Printer, Israel)

1971 (27 Apr). *Safe Return of "Apollo 13". T* **84** *and similar vert designs. Multicoloured. P* 14.
366 5 l. Type **84** 15 15
367 20 l. Explosion in Space 15 15
368 1 r. Splashdown 50 50
366/8 .. .. *Set of* 3 70 70

85 "Multiracial Flower" **86** "Mme. Charpentier and her Children" (Renoir)

(Des M. Shamir. Litho)

1971 (3 May). *Racial Equality Year. P* 14.
369 **85** 10 l. multicoloured 10 10
370   25 l. multicoloured 20 10

1971 (Aug). *Famous Paintings showing "Mother and Child". T* **86** *and similar vert designs. Multicoloured. Litho. P* 12.
371 5 l. Type **86** 10 10
372 7 l. "Susanna van Collen and her Daughter" (Rembrandt) 15 10
373 10 l. "Madonna nursing the Child" (Titian) .. 20 10
374 20 l. "Baroness Belleli and her Children" (Degas) 40 15
375 25 l. "The Cradle" (Morisot) 45 15
376 1 r. "Helena Fourment and her Children" (Rubens) .. .. 1·50 75
377 3 r. "On the Terrace" (Renoir) .. .. 3·50 3·75
371/7 .. .. *Set of* 7 5·75 4·50

87 Alan Shepard

88 "Ballerina" (Degas)

(Photo State Ptg Works, Vienna)

1971 (11 Nov). *Moon Flight of "Apollo 14". T* **87** *and similar vert designs. Multicoloured. P* 12½.

378 6 l. Type **87** 30 10
379 10 l. Stuart Roosa 35 10
380 1 r. 50, Edgar Mitchell .. .. .. 2·50 2·00
381 5 r. Mission insignia .. .. 5·75 5·50
378/81 .. .. *Set of* 4 8·00 7·00

(Litho Rosenbaum Brothers, Vienna)

1971 (19 Nov). *Famous Paintings showing "Dancers". T* **88** *and similar vert designs. Multicoloured. P* 14.

382 5 l. Type **88** 15 10
383 10 l. "Dancing Couple" (Renoir) 20 10
384 2 r. "Spanish Dancer" (Manet) .. .. 2·50 2·25
385 5 r. "Ballerinas" (Degas) .. .. .. 4·50 4·00
386 10 r. "La Goulue at the Moulin Rouge" (Toulouse-Lautrec) .. .. .. 6·50 5·75
382/6 .. .. *Set of* 5 12·50 11·00

ROYAL VISIT 1972

(89)

90 Book Year Emblem

1972 (13 Mar). *Visit of Queen Elizabeth II and Prince Philip. Nos. 382/6 optd with T* **89**.

387 5 l. multicoloured 15 10
388 10 l. multicoloured 20 10
389 2 r. multicoloured .. .. 4·00 3·50
390 5 r. multicoloured .. .. 7·00 6·00
391 10 r. multicoloured .. .. 8·50 8·00
387/91 .. .. *Set of* 5 18·00 16·00

(Des M. Shamir. Litho Bradbury, Wilkinson)

1972 (1 May). *International Book Year. P* 13 × 13½.

392 **90** 25 l. multicoloured 15 10
393 5 r. multicoloured .. .. 1·60 2·00

91 Scottish Costume

93 Cross-country Skiing

92 Stegosaurus

(Des M. Shamir. Litho State Printing Works, Budapest)

1972 (15 May). *National Costumes of the World. T* **91** *and similar vert designs. Multicoloured. P* 12.

394 10 l. Type **91** 20 10
395 15 l. Netherlands 20 15
396 25 l. Norway 40 15
397 50 l. Hungary 70 45
398 1 r. Austria .. .. 1·25 70
399 2 r. Spain .. .. 2·50 2·25
394/9 .. .. *Set of* 6 4·75 3·50

(Des M. Shamir. Litho Rosenbaum Brothers, Vienna)

1972 (31 May). *Prehistoric Animals. T* **92** *and similar horiz designs. Multicoloured. P* 14.

400 2 l. Type **92** 20 30
401 7 l. Edaphosaurus 40 20
402 25 l. Diplodocus 75 40
403 50 l. Triceratops .. .. 1·00 60
404 2 r. Pteranodon .. .. 3·50 4·00
405 5 r. Tyrannosaurus .. .. 7·00 7·50
400/5 .. .. *Set of* 6 11·50 11·50

An imperforate miniature sheet containing Nos. 404/5 also exists, but was never freely available.

(Des M. Shamir. Litho Rosenbaum Brothers, Vienna)

1972 (June). *Winter Olympic Games, Sapporo, Japan. T* **93** *and similar vert designs. Multicoloured. P* 14.

406 3 l. Type **93** 10 30
407 6 l. Bob-sleighing 10 30
408 15 l. Speed-skating 20 20
409 50 l. Ski-jumping 85 45
410 1 r. Figure-skating (pair) .. .. 1·40 70
411 2 r. 50, Ice-hockey .. .. 4·00 3·25
406/11 .. .. *Set of* 6 6·00 4·75

94 Scout Saluting

95 Cycling

(Des M. Shamir. Litho Govt Printer, Israel)

1972 (1 Aug). *13th World Scout Jamboree, Asagiri, Japan* (1971). *T* **94** *and similar vert designs. Multicoloured. P* 14.

412 10 l. Type **92** 55 20
413 15 l. Scout signalling 70 20
414 50 l. Scout blowing bugle .. .. 2·50 1·00
415 1 r. Scout beating drum .. .. 3·25 2·00
412/15 .. .. *Set of* 4 6·25 3·00

PRINTERS AND PROCESS. *Unless otherwise stated*, all the following issues to No. 1277 were lithographed by Format International Security Printers Ltd, London.

1972 (30 Oct). *Olympic Games, Munich. T* **95** *and similar vert designs. Multicoloured. P* 14½ × 14.

416 5 l. Type **95** 10 10
417 10 l. Running 10 10
418 25 l. Wrestling 15 10
419 50 l. Hurdling 30 25
420 2 r. Boxing .. .. 1·00 1·25
421 5 r. Volleyball .. .. 2·10 2·50
416/21 .. .. *Set of* 6 3·25 3·75
MS422 92 × 120 mm. 3 r. As 50 l.; 4 r. As 10 l. P 15 5·25 6·00

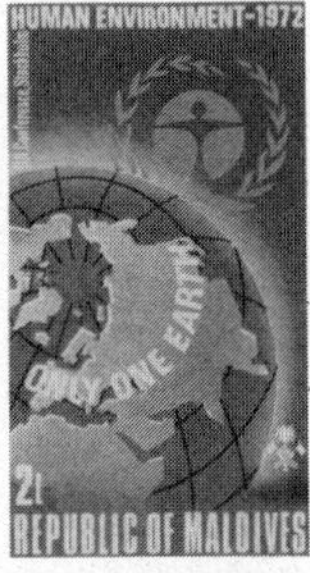

96 Globe and Conference Emblem

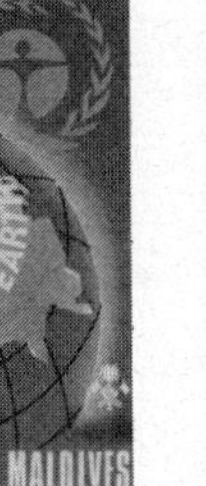

97 "Flowers" (Van Gogh)

(Litho Harrison)

1972 (15 Nov). *U.N. Environmental Conservation Conference, Stockholm. P* 14½.

423 **96** 2 l. multicoloured 10 30
424 3 l. multicoloured 10 30
425 15 l. multicoloured 30 15
426 50 l. multicoloured 75 40
427 2 r. 50, multicoloured .. .. 3·25 3·75
423/7 .. .. *Set of* 5 4·00 4·50

(Des M. Shamir)

1973 (Mar). *Floral Paintings. T* **97** *and similar vert designs. Multicoloured. P* 13½.

428 1 l. Type **97** 10 20
429 2 l. "Flowers in Jug" (Renoir) 10 20
430 3 l. "Chrysanthemums" (Renoir) 10 20
431 50 l. "Mixed Bouquet" (Bosschaert) 30 15
432 1 r. As 3 l. 55 40
433 5 r. As 2 l. .. .. 2·75 3·00
428/33 .. .. *Set of* 6 3·50 3·75
MS434 120 × 94 mm. 2 r. as 50 l.; 3 r. Type **97**. P 15 4·50 5·50

LEMECHEV
MIDDLE-WEIGHT
GOLD MEDALLIST

(98)

99 Animal Care

1973 (Apr). *Gold-medal Winners, Munich Olympic Games. Nos.* 420/**MS**422 *optd with T* **98** *or similar commemorative inscr, in blue.*

435 2 r. multicoloured .. .. 2·25 1·75
436 5 r. multicoloured .. .. 3·25 2·75
MS437 92 × 120 mm. 3 r. multicoloured; 4 r. multicoloured .. .. 5·50 6·50

Overprints:—2 r. Type **98**; 5 r. "JAPAN GOLD MEDAL WINNERS" (volleyball). Miniature sheet:—3 r. "EHRHARDT 100 METER HURDLES GOLD MEDALLIST"; 4 r. "SHORTER MARATHON GOLD MEDALLIST".

(Des M. Shamir)

1973 (Aug). *International Scouting Congress, Nairobi and Addis Ababa. T* **99** *and similar horiz designs. Multicoloured. P* 14½.

438 1 l. Type **99** 10 20
439 2 l. Lifesaving 10 20
440 3 l. Agricultural training 10 20
441 4 l. Carpentry 10 20
442 5 l. Playing leapfrog 10 20
443 1 r. As 2 l. .. .. 2·25 75
444 2 r. As 4 l. .. .. 4·25 3·25
445 3 r. Type **99** .. .. 5·50 4·50
438/45 .. .. *Set of* 8 11·00 8·50
MS446 101 × 79 mm. 5 r. As 3 l. .. .. 8·00 10·00

100 *Makaira herscheli*

1973 (Aug). *Fishes. T* **100** *and similar horiz designs. Multicoloured. P* 14½.

447 1 l. Type **100** 10 20
448 2 l. *Katsuwonus pelamys* 10 20
449 3 l. *Thunnus thynnus* 10 20
450 5 l. *Coryphaena hippurus* 10 20
451 60 l. *Lutjanus gibbus* 40 30
452 75 l. As 60 l. 50 30
453 1 r. 50, *Variola louti* .. .. 1·10 1·10
454 2 r. 50, As 5 l. .. .. 1·60 1·40
455 3 r. *Plectropoma maculatum* .. .. 1·75 2·00
456 10 r. *Scomberomorus commerson* .. .. .. 4·75 6·00
447/56 .. .. *Set of* 10 9·00 10·50
MS457 119 × 123 mm. 4 r. As 2 l.; 5 r. Type **100** .. 10·00 12·00

Nos. 451/2 are smaller, size 29 × 22 mm.

101 Golden-fronted Leafbird

102 *Lantana camara*

(Des M. Shamir)

1973 (Oct). *Fauna. T* **101** *and similar diamond-shaped designs. Multicoloured. P* 14½.

458 1 l. Type **101** 10 15
459 2 l. Indian Flying Fox 10 15
460 3 l. Land tortoise 10 15
461 4 l. *Kallima inachus* (butterfly) 15 15
462 50 l. As 3 l. 40 25
463 2 r. Type **101** .. .. 3·00 2·75
464 3 r. As 2 l. .. .. 3·00 2·75
458/64 .. .. *Set of* 7 6·25 5·75
MS465 66 × 74 mm. 5 r. As 4 l. .. .. .. 14·00 13·00

(Litho Questa)

1973 (19 Dec). *Flowers of the Maldive Islands. T* **102** *and similar vert designs. Multicoloured. P* 14.

466 1 l. Type **102** 10 10
467 2 l. *Nerium oleander* 10 10
468 3 l. *Rosa polyantha* 10 10
469 4 l. *Hibiscus manihot* 10 10
470 5 l. *Bougainvillea glabra* 10 10
471 10 l. *Plumera alba* 10 10
472 50 l. *Poinsettia pulcherrima* 55 20
473 5 r. *Ononis natrix* .. .. 3·75 3·50
466/73 .. .. *Set of* 8 4·00 3·75
MS474 110 × 100 mm. 2 r. As 3 l.; 3 r. As 10 l. .. 3·25 4·25

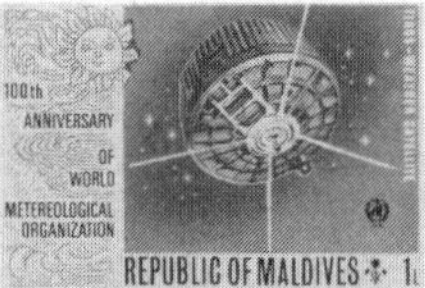

103 "Tiros" Weather Satellite

(Des M. Shamir)

1974 (10 Jan). *Centenary of World Meteorological Organization. T* **103** *and similar horiz designs. Multicoloured. P* 14½.

No.	Description	Unused	Used
475	1 l. Type **103**	10	10
476	2 l. "Nimbus" satellite	10	10
477	3 l. *Nomad* (weather ship)	10	10
478	4 l. Scanner, A.P.T. Instant Weather Picture equipment	10	10
479	5 l. Richard's wind-speed recorder	10	10
480	2 r. Type **103**	2·00	1·50
481	3 r. As 3 l.	2·25	1·75
475/81	*Set of* 7	4·00	3·25
MS482	110 × 79 mm. 10 r. As 2 l.	8·50	11·00

104 "Apollo" Spacecraft and Pres. Kennedy

(Des M. Shamir)

1974 (1 Feb). *American and Russian Space Exploration Projects. T* **104** *and similar horiz designs. Multicoloured. P* 14½.

No.	Description	Unused	Used
483	1 l. Type **104**	10	15
484	2 l. "Mercury" capsule and John Glenn	10	15
485	3 l. "Vostok 1" and Yuri Gagarin	10	15
486	4 l. "Vostok 6" and Valentina Tereshkova	10	15
487	5 l. "Soyuz 11" and "Salyut" space-station	10	15
488	2 r. "Skylab" space laboratory	2·50	2·25
489	3 r. As 2 l.	3·00	2·75
483/9	*Set of* 7	5·50	5·25
MS490	103 × 80 mm. 10 r. Type **104**	8·00	10·00

105 Copernicus and "Skylab" Space Laboratory

106 "Maternity" (Picasso)

(Des G. Vasarhelyi)

1974 (10 Apr). *500th Birth Anniv of Nicholas Copernicus (astronomer). T* **105** *and similar horiz designs. Multicoloured. P* 14½.

No.	Description	Unused	Used
491	1 l. Type **105**	10	15
492	2 l. Orbital space-station of the future	10	15
493	3 l. Proposed "Space-shuttle" craft	10	15
494	4 l. "Mariner 2" Venus probe	10	15
495	5 l. "Mariner 4" Mars probe	10	15
496	25 l. Type **105**	55	15
497	1 r. 50, As 2 l.	2·50	2·25
498	5 r. As 3 l.	6·00	6·00
491/8	*Set of* 8	8·50	8·00
MS499	106 × 80 mm. 10 r. "Copernicus" orbital observatory	10·00	13·00

(Des M. Shamir. Litho Questa)

1974 (May). *Paintings by Picasso. T* **106** *and similar vert designs. Multicoloured. P* 14.

No.	Description	Unused	Used
500	1 l. Type **106**	10	10
501	2 l. "Harlequin and Friend"	10	10
502	3 l. "Pierrot Sitting"	10	10
503	20 l. "Three Musicians"	15	15
504	75 l. "L'Aficionado"	30	30
505	5 r. "Still Life"	2·50	2·50
500/5	*Set of* 6	2·75	2·75
MS506	100 × 101 mm. 2 r. As 20 l.; 3 r. As 5 r.	3·00	3·50

107 U.P.U. Emblem, Steam and Diesel Locomotives

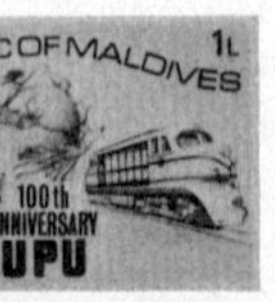

108 Footballers

(Des M. Shamir)

1974 (May). *Centenary of Universal Postal Union. T* **107** *and similar horiz designs. Multicoloured. P* 14½.

No.	Description	Unused	Used
507	1 l. Type **107**	10	10
508	2 l. Paddle-steamer and modern mailboat	10	10
509	3 l. Airship and Boeing "747" airliner	10	10
510	1 r. 50, Mailcoach and motor van	85	85
511	2 r. 50, As 2 l.	1·60	1·60
512	5 r. Type **107**	3·50	3·50
507/12	*Set of* 6	5·50	5·50
MS513	126 × 105 mm. 4 r. Type **107**	4·50	6·00

Nos. 507/12 were first issued in sheets of 50, but were later released in small sheets of five stamps and one label. These small sheets were perforated 13½.

(Des M. Shamir)

1974 (June). *World Cup Football Championships, West Germany. T* **108** *and similar vert designs, showing football scenes. P* 14½.

No.	Description	Unused	Used
514	1 l. multicoloured	10	15
515	2 l. multicoloured	10	15
516	3 l. multicoloured	10	15
517	4 l. multicoloured	10	15
518	75 l. multicoloured	90	50
519	4 r. multicoloured	3·00	2·25
520	5 r. multicoloured	3·25	2·50
514/20	*Set of* 7	6·50	5·25
MS521	88 × 95 mm. 10 r. multicoloured	7·50	7·50

109 "Capricorn"

110 Churchill and Bomber Aircraft

(Des G. Vasarhelyi)

1974 (3 July). *Signs of the Zodiac. T* **109** *and similar horiz designs. Multicoloured. P* 14½.

No.	Description	Unused	Used
522	1 l. Type **109**	10	15
523	2 l. "Aquarius"	10	15
524	3 l. "Pisces"	10	15
525	4 l. "Aries"	10	15
526	5 l. "Taurus"	10	15
527	6 l. "Gemini"	10	15
528	7 l. "Cancer"	10	15
529	10 l. "Leo"	10	15
530	15 l. "Virgo"	15	15
531	20 l. "Libra"	15	15
532	25 l. "Scorpio"	15	15
533	5 r. "Sagittarius"	8·00	6·00
522/33	*Set of* 12	8·00	7·00
MS534	119 × 99 mm. 10 r. "The Sun" (49 × 37 *mm*). P 13½	14·00	15·00

(Des M. Shamir)

1974 (30 Nov). *Birth Centenary of Sir Winston Churchill. T* **110** *and similar horiz designs. Multicoloured. P* 14½.

No.	Description	Unused	Used
535	1 l. Type **110**	10	20
536	2 l. Churchill as pilot	10	20
537	3 l. Churchill as First Lord of the Admiralty	10	20
538	4 l. Churchill and H.M.S. *Indomitable* (aircraft carrier)	10	20
539	5 l. Churchill and fighter aircraft	10	20
540	60 l. Churchill and anti-aircraft battery	2·00	1·25
541	75 l. Churchill and tank in desert	2·25	1·25
542	5 r. Churchill and flying-boat	9·50	8·50
535/42	*Set of* 8	13·00	11·00
MS543	113 × 83 mm. 10 r. As 4 l.	15·00	15·00

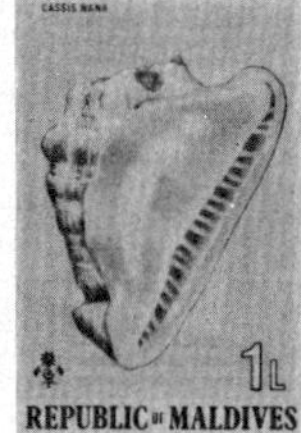

111 *Cassia nana*

112 Royal Throne

(Des M. Shamir)

1975 (25 Jan). *Seashells and Cowries. T* **111** *and similar multicoloured designs. P* 14 × 13½ (60 *l.*, 75 *l.*) *or* 14½ (*others*).

No.	Description	Unused	Used
544	1 l. Type **111**	10	15
545	2 l. *Murex triremus*	10	15
546	3 l. *Harpa major*	10	15
547	4 l. *Lambis chiragra*	10	15
548	5 l. *Conus pennaceus*	10	15
549	60 l. *Cypraea diliculum* (22 × 30 *mm*)	1·75	1·00
550	75 l. *Clanculus pharaonis* (22 × 30 *mm*)	2·25	1·10
551	5 r. *Chicoreus ramosus*	7·00	6·50
544/51	*Set of* 8	10·00	8·50
MS552	152 × 126 mm. 2 r. As 3 l.; 3 r. as 2 l.	9·00	10·00

(Des M. Shamir. Litho Questa)

1975 (22 Feb). *Historical Relics and Monuments. T* **112** *and similar multicoloured designs. P* 14.

No.	Description	Unused	Used
553	1 l. Type **112**	10	10
554	10 l. Candlesticks	10	10
555	25 l. Lamp-tree	15	10
556	60 l. Royal umbrellas	30	20
557	75 l. Eid-Miskith Mosque (*horiz*)	35	25
558	3 r. Tomb of Al-Hafiz Abu-al Barakath-al Barubari (*horiz*)	1·60	2·00
553/8	*Set of* 6	2·25	2·50

113 Guavas

114 *Phyllangia*

(Des M. Shamir)

1975 (Mar). *Fruits. T* **113** *and similar vert designs. Multicoloured. P* 14½.

No.	Description	Unused	Used
559	2 l. Type **113**	10	15
560	4 l. Maldive mulberry	10	15
561	5 l. Mountain apples	10	15
562	10 l. Bananas	15	15
563	20 l. Mangoes	30	15
564	50 l. Papaya	65	30
565	1 r. Pomegranates	1·50	45
566	5 r. Coconut	7·00	7·00
559/66	*Set of* 8	9·00	7·50
MS567	136 × 102 mm. 2 r. As 10 l.; 3 r. As 2 l.	7·50	8·50

(Des M. Shamir)

1975 (6 June). *Marine Life. T* **114** *and similar triangular designs. Multicoloured. P* 14½.

No.	Description	Unused	Used
568	1 l. Type **114**	10	10
569	2 l. *Madrepora oculata*	10	10
570	3 l. *Acropora gravida*	10	10
571	4 l. *Stylotella*	10	10
572	5 l. *Acrophora cervicornis*	10	10
573	60 l. *Strongylocentrotus purpuratus*	55	55
574	75 l. *Pisaster ochraceüs*	65	65
575	5 r. *Marthasterias glacialis*	3·75	4·25
568/75	*Set of* 8	4·75	5·25
MS576	155 × 98 mm. 4 r. As 1 l. Imperf	9·00	11·00

115 Clock Tower and Customs Building within "10"

14th Boy Scout Jamboree
July 29 – August 7, 1975

(116)

(Des M. Shamir)

1975 (26 July). *10th Anniv of Independence. T* **115** *and similar horiz designs. Multicoloured. P* 14½.

No.	Description	Unused	Used
577	4 l. Type **115**	10	10
578	5 l. Government Offices	10	10
579	7 l. Waterfront	10	10
580	15 l. Mosque and minaret	10	10
581	10 r. Sultan Park and museum	4·00	6·00
577/81	*Set of* 5	4·00	6·00

1975 (26 July). *"Nordjamb 75" World Scout Jamboree, Norway. Nos.* 443/5 *and* **MS**446 *optd with T* **116**.

No.	Description	Unused	Used
582	1 r. multicoloured	30	30
583	2 r. multicoloured	50	50
584	3 r. multicoloured	1·00	1·00
582/4	*Set of* 3	1·60	1·60
MS585	101 × 79 mm. 5 r. multicoloured	4·75	5·50

117 Madura Prau

118 *Brahmophthalma wallichi* (moth)

(Des M. Shamir)

1975 (Aug). *Ships. T* **117** *and similar multicoloured designs. P* 14½.

No.	Description	Unused	Used
586	1 l. Type **117**	10	10
587	2 l. Ganges patela	10	10
588	3 l. Indian palla (*vert*)	10	10
589	4 l. Odhi (dhow) (*vert*)	10	10
590	5 l. Maldivian schooner	10	10
591	25 l. *Cutty Sark*	35	20
592	1 r. Maldivian baggala (*vert*)	85	70
593	5 r. Freighter *Maldive Courage*	3·75	4·25
586/93	*Set of* 8	4·75	5·00
MS594	99 × 85 mm. 10 r. As 1 l.	7·00	9·00

(Des M. Shamir)

1975 (7 Sept). *Butterflies and Moth. T* **118** *and similar horiz designs. Multicoloured. P* 14½.

No.	Description	Unused	Used
595	1 l. Type **118**	10	10
596	2 l. *Teinopalpus imperialis*	10	10
597	3 l. *Cethosia biblis*	10	10
598	4 l. *Idea jasonia*	10	10
599	5 l. *Apatura ilia*	10	10
600	25 l. *Kallima horsfieldi*	55	35
601	1 r. 50, *Hebomoia leucippe*	2·50	2·50
602	5 r. *Papilio memnon*	7·00	6·00
595/602	*Set of* 8	9·00	8·00
MS603	134×97 mm. 10 r. As 25 l.	17·00	17·00

119 "The Dying Captive"

120 Beaker and Vase

1975 (9 Oct). *500th Birth Anniv of Michelangelo. T* **119** *and similar vert designs. Multicoloured. P* 14½.

604 1 l. Type **119** 10 10
605 2 l. Detail of "The Last Judgement" 10 10
606 3 l. "Apollo" 10 10
607 4 l. Detail of Sistine Chapel ceiling 10 10
608 5 l. "Bacchus" 10 10
609 1 r. Detail of "The Last Judgement" (*different*) 80 30
610 2 r. "David" 1·50 1·25
611 5 r. "Cumaean Sibyl" 3·50 3·50
604/11 *Set of* 8 5·50 4·75
MS612 123 × 113 mm. 10 r. As 2 r. 6·50 8·50

The 1, 3, 5 l. and 2, 10 r. are sculptures; the other values show details of the frescoes in the Sistine Chapel.

(Des M. Shamir. Litho Questa)

1975 (Dec). *Maldivian Lacquerware. T* **120** *and similar vert designs. Multicoloured. P* 14.

613 2 l. Type **120** 10 10
614 4 l. Boxes 10 10
615 50 l. Jar with lid 40 20
616 75 l. Bowls with covers 50 30
617 1 r. Craftsman at work 65 40
613/17 *Set of* 5 1·50 90

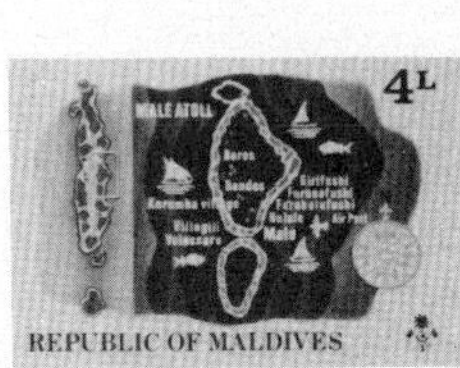

121 Map of Maldives

122 Cross-country Skiing

(Des M. Shamir. Litho Questa)

1975 (25 Dec). *Tourism. T* **121** *and similar horiz designs. Multicoloured. P* 14.

618 4 l. Type **121** 10 10
619 5 l. Motor launch and small craft 10 10
620 7 l. Sailing boats 10 10
621 15 l. Underwater fishing 10 10
622 3 r. Hulule Airport 1·40 1·60
623 10 r. Motor cruisers 4·00 5·00
618/23 *Set of* 6 5·00 6·00

(Des M. Shamir)

1976 (10 Jan). *Winter Olympic Games, Innsbruck, Austria. T* **122** *and similar vert designs. Multicoloured. P* 15.

624 1 l. Type **122** 10 10
625 2 l. Speed ice-skating 10 10
626 3 l. Pairs figure-skating 10 10
627 4 l. Four-man bobsleigh 10 10
628 5 l. Ski-jumping 10 10
629 25 l. Women's figure-skating 15 10
630 1 r. 15, Slalom skiing 65 75
631 4 r. Ice-hockey 2·25 2·50
624/31 *Set of* 8 3·00 3·25
MS632 93 × 117 mm. 10 r. Downhill skiing 7·00 8·50

123 "General Burgoyne" (Reynolds)

124 Thomas Edison

1976 (15 Feb). *Bicentenary of American Revolution. T* **123** *and similar multicoloured designs. P* 15.

633 1 l. Type **123** 10 10
634 2 l. "John Hancock" (Copley) 10 10
635 3 l. "Death of General Montgomery" (Trumbull) (*horiz*) 10 10
636 4 l. "Paul Revere" (Copley) 10 10
637 5 l. "Battle of Bunker Hill" (Trumbull) (*horiz*) 10 10
638 2 r. "The Crossing of the Delaware" (Sully) (*horiz*) 1·75 1·50
639 3 r. "Samuel Adams" (Copley) 2·25 2·00
640 5 r. "Surrender of Cornwallis" (Trumbull) (*horiz*) 2·75 2·50
633/40 *Set of* 8 6·25 5·75
MS641 147 × 95 mm. 10 r. "Washington at Dorchester Heights" (Stuart) 9·50 12·00

1976 (10 Mar). *Telephone Centenary. T* **124** *and similar horiz designs. Multicoloured. P* 15.

642 1 l. Type **124** 10 10
643 2 l. Alexander Graham Bell 10 10
644 3 l. Telephones of 1919, 1937 and 1972 10 10
645 10 l. Cable entrance into station 10 10
646 20 l. Equaliser circuit assembly 15 10
647 1 r. *Salernum* (cable ship) 70 55
648 10 r. "Intelsat IV-A" and Earth Station 4·25 5·50
642/8 *Set of* 7 4·75 5·75
MS649 156 × 105 mm. 4 r. Early telephones 5·50 6·00

MAY 29TH–JUNE 6TH "INTERPHIL" 1976

(125)

126 Wrestling

1976 (29 May). *"Interphil 76" International Stamp Exhibition, Philadelphia. Nos. 638/MS641 optd with T* **125**, *in blue* (5 *r.*) *or silver* (*others*).

650 2 r. multicoloured 1·25 1·50
651 3 r. multicoloured 1·75 2·00
652 5 r. multicoloured 2·25 2·50
650/2 *Set of* 3 4·75 5·50
MS653 147 × 95 mm. 10 r. multicoloured 8·00 10·00

(Des M. Shamir)

1976 (June). *Olympic Games, Montreal. T* **126** *and similar vert designs. Multicoloured. P* 15.

654 1 l. Type **126** 10 10
655 2 l. Putting the shot 10 10
656 3 l. Hurdling 10 10
657 4 l. Hockey 10 10
658 5 l. Running 10 10
659 6 l. Javelin-throwing 10 10
660 1 r. 50, Discus-throwing 1·25 1·50
661 5 r. Volleyball 3·50 4·00
654/61 *Set of* 8 4·75 5·50
MS662 135 × 106 mm. 10 r. Throwing the hammer 6·50 9·00

127 *Dolichos lablab*

128 "Viking" approaching Mars

(Des M. Shamir. Litho Questa)

1976 (26 July)–**77**. *Vegetables. T* **127** *and similar vert designs. Multicoloured. P* 14.

663 2 l. Type **127** 10 10
664 4 l. *Moringa pterygosperma* 10 10
665 10 l. *Solanum melongena* 10 10
666 20 l. *Moringa pterygosperma* (1977) 75 75
667 50 l. *Cucumis sativus* 80 65
668 75 l. *Trichosanthes anguina* 85 75
669 1 r. *Momordica charantia* 95 85
670 2 r. *Trichosanthes anguina* (1977) 3·00 3·50
663/70 *Set of* 8 6·00 6·00

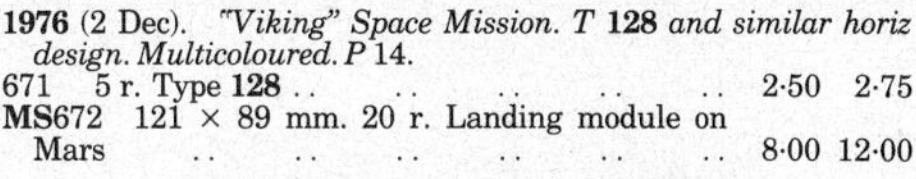

1976 (2 Dec). *"Viking" Space Mission. T* **128** *and similar horiz design. Multicoloured. P* 14.

671 5 r. Type **128** 2·50 2·75
MS672 121 × 89 mm. 20 r. Landing module on Mars 8·00 12·00

129 Coronation Ceremony

1977 (6 Feb). *Silver Jubilee of Queen Elizabeth II. T* **129** *and similar horiz designs. Multicoloured. P* 14 × 13½.

673 1 l. Type **129** 10 10
674 2 l. Queen and Prince Philip 10 10
675 3 l. Royal couple with Princes Andrew and Edward 10 10
676 1 r. 15, Queen with Archbishops 35 25
677 3 r. State coach in procession 85 55
678 4 r. Royal couple with Prince Charles and Princess Anne 1·10 90
673/8 *Set of* 6 2·25 1·60
MS679 120 × 77 mm. 10 r. Queen and Prince Charles 3·00 3·25

Nos. 673/8 also exist perf 12 (*Price per set of* 6 £1·75 *mint or used*) from additional sheetlets of five stamps and one label in changed colours.

130 Beethoven and Organ

(Des M. Shamir)

1977 (26 Mar). *150th Death Anniv of Ludwig van Beethoven (composer). T* **130** *and similar horiz designs. Multicoloured. P* 14.

680 1 l. Type **130** 10 10
681 2 l. Portrait and manuscript of *Moonlight Sonata* 10 10
682 3 l. With Goethe at Teplitz 10 10
683 4 l. Portrait and string instruments 10 10
684 5 l. Beethoven's home, Heiligenstadt 10 10
685 25 l. Hands and gold medals 40 15
686 2 r. Portrait and part of *Missa solemnis* 2·00 1·60
687 5 r. Portrait and hearing-aids 3·75 3·00
680/7 *Set of* 8 5·75 4·50
MS688 121 × 92 mm. 4 r. Death mask and room where composer died 3·75 5·00

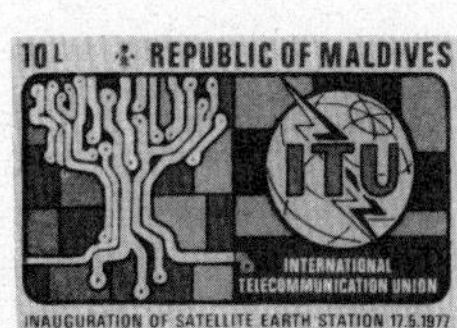

131 Printed Circuit and I.T.U. Emblem

132 "Miss Anne Ford" (Gainsborough)

(Des M. Shamir. Litho Questa)

1977 (17 May). *Inauguration of Satellite Earth Station. T* **131** *and similar horiz designs. Multicoloured. P* 14.

689 10 l. Type **131** 10 10
690 90 l. Central telegraph office 45 45
691 10 r. Satellite Earth station 5·00 6·00
689/91 *Set of* 3 5·00 6·00
MS692 100 × 85 mm. 5 r. "Intelsat IV-A" satellite over Maldives 2·75 3·50

(Des M. Shamir. Litho Questa)

1977 (20 May). *Artists' Birth Anniversaries. T* **132** *and similar vert designs. Multicoloured. P* 14.

693 1 l. Type **132** (250th anniv) 10 10
694 2 l. Group painting by Rubens (400th anniv) 10 10
695 3 l. "Girl with Dog" (Titian) (500th anniv) 10 10
696 4 l. "Mrs. Thomas Graham" (Gainsborough) 10 10
697 5 l. "Artist with Isabella Brant" (Rubens) 10 10
698 95 l. Portrait by Titian 40 40
699 1 r. Portrait by Gainsborough 40 40
700 10 r. "Isabella Brant" (Rubens) 3·50 4·50
693/700 *Set of* 8 4·00 5·00
MS701 152 × 116 mm. 5 r. "Self-portrait" (Titian) 2·25 3·00

133 Lesser Frigate Birds

134 Charles Lindbergh

(Des M. Shamir)

1977 (26 July). *Birds. T* **133** *and similar vert designs. Multicoloured. P* 14½.

702 1 l. Type **133** 10 10
703 2 l. Crab Plover 10 10
704 3 l. White-tailed Tropic Bird 10 10
705 4 l. Wedge-tailed Shearwater 10 10
706 5 l. Grey Heron 10 10
707 20 l. White Tern 30 20
708 95 l. Cattle Egret 1·25 95
709 1 r. 25, Black-naped Tern 1·75 1·40
710 5 r. Pheasant Coucal 6·50 6·50
702/10 *Set of* 9 9·00 8·25
MS711 124 × 117 mm. 10 r. Green Heron 19·00 20·00

(Des M. Shamir)

1977 (31 Oct). *50th Anniv of Lindbergh's Transatlantic Flight and 75th Anniv of First Navigable Airships. T* **134** *and similar multicoloured designs. P* 14½.

712 1 l. Type **134** 10 10
713 2 l. Lindbergh and *Spirit of St. Louis* 10 10
714 3 l. "Mohawk" aircraft (*horiz*) 10 10
715 4 l. Julliot's airship *Lebaudy I* (*horiz*) 10 10
716 5 l. Airship *Graf Zeppelin* and portrait of Zeppelin 10 10
717 1 r. Airship *Los Angeles* (*horiz*) 60 30
718 3 r. Lindbergh and Henry Ford 1·40 1·50
719 10 r. Vickers rigid airship 3·50 4·00
712/19 *Set of* 8 5·00 5·50
MS720 148 × 114 mm. 5 r. *Spirit of St. Louis*, Statue of Liberty and Eiffel Tower; 7 r. 50, Airship *L* 31 over German battleship 10·00 11·00

ALTERED CATALOGUE NUMBERS

Any Catalogue numbers altered from the last edition are shown as a list in the introductory pages.

135 Boat Building

136 Rheumatic Heart

(Des M. Shamir. Litho J.W.)

1977 (11 Nov). *Occupations. T* **135** *and similar multicoloured designs. P* 13½ × 13 (2 *r.*) *or* 13 × 13½ (*others*).

721	6 l. Type **135**	30	15
722	15 l. Fishing	35	15
723	20 l. Cadjan weaving	40	15
724	90 l. Mat weaving	1·00	70
725	2 r. Lace making (*vert*)	2·00	2·00
721/5	*Set of* 5	3·50	2·75

(Des M. Shamir. Litho Questa)

1977 (Dec). *World Rheumatism Year. T* **136** *and similar vert designs. Multicoloured. P* 14.

726	1 l. Type **136**	10	10
727	50 l. Rheumatic shoulder	20	10
728	2 r. Rheumatic fingers	85	1·00
729	3 r. Rheumatic knee	1·10	1·25
726/9	*Set of* 4	2·00	2·25

137 Lilienthal's Glider

138 Newgate Prison

(Des M. Shamir. Litho Questa)

1978 (27 Feb). *75th Anniv of First Powered Aircraft. T* **137** *and similar horiz designs. Multicoloured. P* 13 × 13½.

730	1 l. Type **137**	10	15
731	2 l. Chanute's glider	10	15
732	3 l. Wright testing glider, 1900	10	15
733	4 l. Roe's aircraft	10	15
734	5 l. Wright demonstrating aircraft to King Alfonso of Spain	10	15
735	10 l. Roe's second biplane	15	15
736	20 l. Wright Brothers and A. G. Bell	30	15
737	95 l. Hadley's triplane	1·25	1·00
738	5 r. "BE 2"s at Upavon, 1914	4·75	5·00
730/8	*Set of* 9	6·00	6·50
MS739	98 × 82 mm. 10 r. Wright Brothers' *Flyer*	9·00	10·00

1978 (15 Mar). *World Eradication of Smallpox. T* **138** *and similar multicoloured designs. P* 14.

740	15 l. Foundling Hospital, London (*horiz*)	45	25
741	50 l. Type **138**	1·00	45
742	2 r. Edward Jenner	3·00	2·25
740/2	*Set of* 3	4·00	2·75

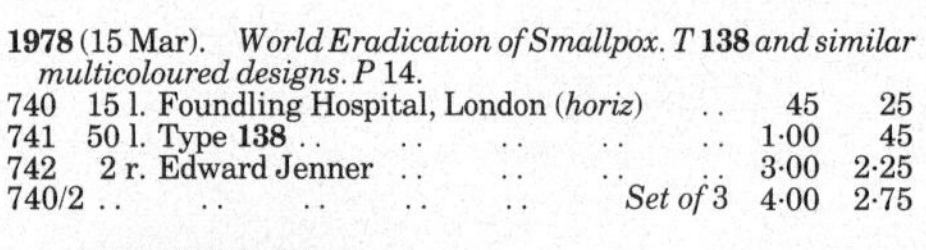

139 Television Set

140 Mas Odi

(Des M. Shamir. Litho J.W.)

1978 (29 Mar). *Inauguration of Television in Maldives. T* **139** *and similar multicoloured designs. P* 13 × 13½ (1 *r.* 50) *or* 13½ × 13 (*others*).

743	15 l. Type **139**	30	20
744	25 l. Television aerials	40	25
745	1 r. 50, Control desk (*horiz*)	1·60	1·60
743/5	*Set of* 3	2·10	1·90

(Des M. Shamir)

1978 (27 Apr). *Ships. T* **140** *and similar multicoloured designs. P* 14½.

746	1 l. Type **140**	10	10
747	2 l. Battela	10	10
748	3 l. Bandu odi (*vert*)	10	10
749	5 l. *Maldive Trader* (freighter)	10	10
750	1 r. *Fath-hul Baaree* (brigantine) (*vert*)	35	30
751	1 r. 25, Mas dhoni	55	55
752	3 r. Baggala (*vert*)	1·25	1·25
753	4 r. As No. 751	1·60	1·60
746/53	*Set of* 8	3·50	3·50
MS754	152 × 138 mm. 1 r. As No. 747; 4 r. As No. 751	3·25	3·50

Nos. 746/8, 750 and 752/4 exist imperforate from stock dispersed by the liquidator of Format International Security Printers Ltd.

141 Ampulla

142 Capt. Cook

(Des M. Shamir. Litho Questa)

1978 (15 May). *25th Anniv of Coronation of Queen Elizabeth II. T* **141** *and similar vert designs. Multicoloured. P* 14.

755	1 l. Type **141**	10	10
756	2 l. Sceptre with dove	10	10
757	3 l. Golden orb	10	10
758	1 r. 15, St. Edward's Crown	15	15
759	2 r. Sceptre with cross	30	25
760	5 r. Queen Elizabeth II	80	70
755/60	*Set of* 6	1·10	1·00
MS761	108 × 106 mm. 10 r. Anointing spoon	2·00	2·00

Nos. 755/60 were also each issued in small sheets of three stamps and one label, perf 12, in changed colours.

(Des M. Shamir)

1978 (15 July). *250th Birth Anniv of Capt. James Cook and Bicentenary of Discovery of Hawaii. T* **142** *and similar multicoloured designs. P* 14½.

762	1 l. Type **142**	10	15
763	2 l. Statue of Kamehameha I of Hawaii	10	15
764	3 l. H.M.S. *Endeavour*	10	15
765	25 l. Route of Cook's third voyage	45	45
766	75 l. H.M.S. *Resolution*, H.M.S. *Discovery* and map of Hawaiian Islands (*horiz*)	1·25	1·25
767	1 r. 50, Cook meeting Hawaiian islanders on ship (*horiz*)	2·00	2·00
768	10 r. Death of Cook (*horiz*)	7·50	8·00
762/8	*Set of* 7	10·50	11·00
MS769	100 × 92 mm. 5 r. H.M.S. *Endeavour* (*different*)	16·00	16·00

Nos. 763/4 exist imperforate from stock dispersed by the liquidator of Format International Security Printers Ltd.

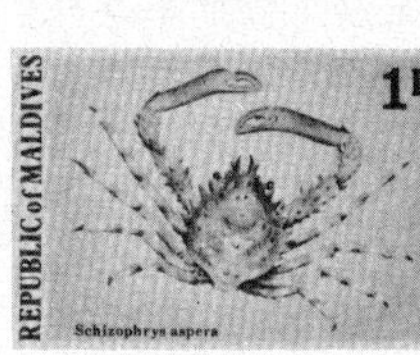

143 *Schizophrys aspera*

144 "Four Apostles"

1978 (30 Aug). *Crustaceans. T* **143** *and similar multicoloured designs. P* 14.

770	1 l. Type **143**	10	10
771	2 l. *Atergatis floridus*	10	10
772	3 l. *Perenon planissimum*	10	10
773	90 l. *Portunus granulatus*	50	40
774	1 r. *Carpilius maculatus*	50	40
775	2 r. *Huenia proteus*	1·00	1·25
776	25 r. *Etisus laevimanus*	9·00	12·00
770/6	*Set of* 7	10·00	13·00
MS777	147 × 146 mm. 2 r. *Panulirus longipes* (*vert*)	1·75	2·50

(Des BG Studio. Litho Questa)

1978 (28 Oct). *450th Death Anniv of Albrecht Dürer (artist). T* **144** *and similar designs. P* 14.

778	10 l. multicoloured	10	10
779	20 l. multicoloured	10	10
780	55 l. multicoloured	20	20
781	1 r. black, cinnamon and brown	30	30
782	1 r. 80, multicoloured	50	60
783	3 r. multicoloured	1·00	1·25
778/83	*Set of* 6	1·90	2·25
MS784	141 × 122 mm. 10 r. multicoloured	5·00	6·00

Designs: *Vert*—20 l. "Self-portrait at 27", 55 l. "Madonna and Child with a Pear"; 1 r. 80, "Hare"; 3 r. "Great Piece of Turf"; 10 r. "Columbine". *Horiz*— 1 r. "Rhinoceros".

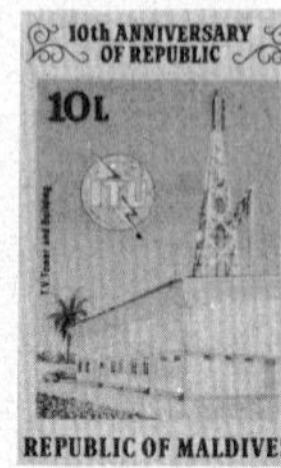

145 T.V. Tower and Building

146 Human Rights Emblem

(Des M. Shamir)

1978 (11 Nov). *Tenth Anniv of Republic. T* **145** *and similar horiz designs. Multicoloured. P* 14½.

785	1 l. Fishing boat	10	10
786	5 l. Montessori School	10	10
787	10 l. Type **145**	10	10
788	25 l. Islet	15	15
789	50 l. Boeing "737"	20	15
790	95 l. Beach scene	30	30
791	1 r. 25, Dhow at night	50	45
792	2 r. President's official residence	75	90
793	5 r. Masjidh Afeefuddin (mosque)	1·75	2·00
785/93	*Set of* 9	3·50	3·50
MS794	119 × 88 mm. 3 r. Fisherman casting net	2·75	3·25

1978 (10 Dec). *30th Anniv of Declaration of Human Rights. P* 14.

795 **146**	30 l. pale magenta, dp mauve and green	15	15
796	90 l. yellow-ochre, red-brown and green	40	50
797	1 r. 80, lt greenish blue, dp blue & grn	70	85
795/7	*Set of* 3	1·10	1·40

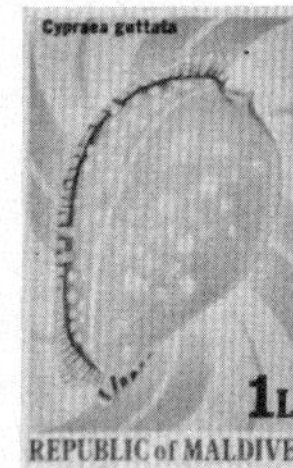

147 *Cypraea guttata*

148 Delivery by Bellman

(Des M. Shamir. Litho Questa)

1979 (Jan). *Shells. T* **147** *and similar vert designs. Multicoloured. P* 14.

798	1 l. Type **147**	10	10
799	2 l. *Conus imperialis*	10	10
800	3 l. *Turbo marmoratus*	10	10
801	10 l. *Lambis truncata*	15	10
802	1 r. *Cypraea leucodon*	70	40
803	1 r. 80, *Conus figulinus*	1·25	1·25
804	3 r. *Conus gloria-maris*	1·90	2·00
798/804	*Set of* 7	3·75	3·50
MS805	141 × 110 mm. 5 r. *Vasum turbinellus*	4·50	4·75

(Des M. Shamir. Litho Questa)

1979 (28 Feb). *Death Centenary of Sir Rowland Hill. T* **148** *and similar multicoloured designs. P* 14.

806	1 l. Type **148**	10	10
807	2 l. Mail coach, 1840 (*horiz*)	10	10
808	3 l. First London letter box, 1855	10	10
809	1 r. 55, Penny Black stamps and posthorn	65	75
810	5 r. Maldives 15 c. stamp, 1906, and carrier pigeon	2·00	2·25
806/10	*Set of* 5	2·50	3·00
MS811	132 × 107 mm. 10 r. Sir Rowland Hill	4·00	4·50

Nos. 806/10 were also each issued in small sheets of five stamps and one label, perf 12, in changed colours.

149 Girl with Teddy Bear

150 "White Feathers"

(Des M. Sharmir. Litho Questa)

1979 (10 May). *International Year of the Child* (1st issue). *T* **149** *and similar vert designs. Multicoloured. P* 14.

812	5 l. Type **149**	10	10
813	1 r. 25, Boy with model sailing boat	40	50
814	2 r. Boy with toy rocket	45	55
815	3 r. Boy with toy airship	60	75
812/15	*Set of* 4	1·40	1·60
MS816	108 × 109 mm. 5 r. Boy with toy train	1·60	2·00

See also Nos. 838/**MS**847.

(Des M. Shamir)

1979 (25 June). *25th Death Anniv of Henri Matisse (artist). T* **150** *and similar horiz designs. Multicoloured. P* 14.

817	20 l. Type **150**	15	15
818	25 l. "Joy of Life"	15	15
819	30 l. "Eggplants"	15	15
820	1 r. 50, "Harmony in Red"	55	55
821	5 r. "Still-life"	1·50	1·75
817/21	*Set of* 5	2·25	2·50
MS822	135 × 95 mm. 4 r. "Water Pitcher"	2·00	2·25

151 Sari with Overdress

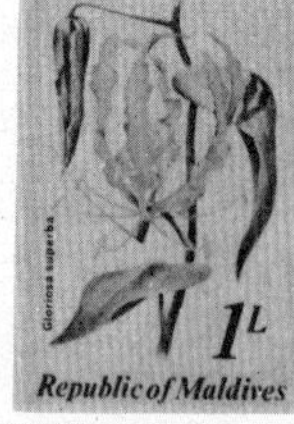

152 *Gloriosa superba*

(Des M. Shamir. Litho Questa)

1979 (22 Aug). *National Costumes. T* **151** *and similar vert designs. Multicoloured. P* 14.
823 50 l. Type **151** 25 25
824 75 l. Sashed apron dress 40 40
825 90 l. Serape 45 45
826 95 l. Ankle-length printed dress 55 55
823/6 .. .. *Set of* 4 1·50 1·50

(Des M. Shamir. Litho Questa)

1979 (29 Oct). *Flowers. T* **152** *and similar vert designs. Multicoloured. P* 14.
827 1 l. Type **152** 10 10
828 3 l. *Hibiscus tiliaceus* 10 10
829 50 l. *Barringtonia asiatica* 20 20
830 1 r. *Abutilon indicum* 40 40
831 5 r. *Guettarda speciosa* .. .. .. 1·75 2·00
827/31 .. .. *Set of* 5 2·10 2·40
MS832 94 × 85 mm. 4 r. *Pandanus odoratissimus* 1·75 2·25

153 Weaving

(Litho Questa)

1979 (11 Nov). *Handicraft Exhibition. T* **153** *and similar horiz designs. Multicoloured. P* 14.
833 5 l. Type **153** 10 10
834 10 l. Lacquerwork 10 10
835 1 r. 30, Tortoiseshell jewellery 45 50
836 2 r. Carved woodwork 70 80
833/6 .. .. *Set of* 4 1·10 1·25
MS837 125 × 85 mm. 5 r. Gold and silver jewellery 1·50 2·25

154 Mickey Mouse attacked by Bird

(Des Walt Disney Productions)

1979 (10 Dec). *International Year of the Child (2nd issue). T* **154** *and similar multicoloured designs. P* 11.
838 1 l. Goofy delivering parcel on motor-scooter (*vert*) 10 10
839 2 l. Type **154** 10 10
840 3 l. Goofy half-covered with letters 10 10
841 4 l. Pluto licking Minnie Mouse's envelopes 10 10
842 5 l. Mickey Mouse delivering letters on roller-skates (*vert*) 10 10
843 10 l. Donald Duck placing letter in mail-box 10 10
844 15 l. Chip and Dale carrying letter 10 10
845 1 r. 50, Donald Duck on monocycle (*vert*) .. 75 75
846 5 r. Donald Duck with ostrich in crate (*vert*) 2·25 2·50
838/46 .. .. *Set of* 9 3·00 3·25
MS847 127 × 102 mm. 4 r. Pluto putting parcel in mail-box. P 13½ .. .. 4·75 4·25

155 Post-Ramadan Dancing

(Litho Questa)

1980 (19 Jan). *National Day. T* **155** *and similar horiz designs. Multicoloured. P* 14.
848 5 l. Type **155** 10 10
849 15 l. Musicians and dancer, Eeduu Festival .. 10 10
850 95 l. Sultan's ceremonial band 30 30
851 2 r. Dancer and drummers, Circumcision Festival 55 70
848/51 .. .. *Set of* 4 90 1·10
MS852 131 × 99 mm. 5 r. Swordsmen .. .. 1·40 1·75

156 Leatherback Turtle (*Dermochelys coriacea*)

157 Paul Harris (founder)

(Des M. Shamir. Litho Questa)

1980 (17 Feb). *Turtle Conservation Campaign. T* **156** *and similar horiz designs. Multicoloured. P* 14.
853 1 l. Type **156** 10 10
854 2 l. Flatback turtle (*Chelonia depressa*) .. 10 10
855 5 l. Hawksbill turtle (*Eretmochelys imbricata*) 10 10
856 10 l. Loggerhead turtle (*Caretta caretta*) .. 10 10
857 75 l. Olive Ridley turtle (*Lepidochelys olivacea*) 30 30
858 10 r. Atlantic Ridley turtle (*Lepidochelys kempii*) .. .. 3·25 3·50
853/8 .. .. *Set of* 6 3·25 3·50
MS859 85 × 107 mm. 4 r. Green turtle (*Chelonia mydas*) .. .. 1·50 2·25

(Des J.W. Litho Questa)

1980 (7 Apr). *75th Anniv of Rotary International. T* **157** *and similar vert designs. Multicoloured. P* 14.
860 75 l. Type **157** 25 10
861 90 l. Family (Humanity) 30 20
862 1 r. Wheat (Hunger) 30 25
863 10 r. Caduceus of Hermes (Health) .. 3·00 3·75
860/3 .. .. *Set of* 4 3·50 3·75
MS864 109 × 85 mm. 5 r. Globe .. .. .. 1·50 2·25

LONDON 1980

(158)

159 Swimming

1980 (6 May). *"London 1980" International Stamp Exhibition. Nos.* 809/**MS**811 *optd with T* **158**.
865 1 r. 55, multicoloured .. .. .. 1·00 75
866 5 r. multicoloured .. .. 2·25 2·00
MS867 132 × 107 mm. 10 r. multicoloured .. 5·50 6·00
On No. **MS**867 the overprint is horizontal.

(Des J.W. Litho Questa)

1980 (4 June). *Olympic Games, Moscow. T* **159** *and similar horiz designs. Multicoloured. P* 14.
868 10 l. Type **159** 10 10
869 50 l. Running 20 15
870 3 r. Putting the shot .. .. 90 1·00
871 4 r. High jump .. .. 1·10 1·25
868/71 .. .. *Set of* 4 2·00 2·25
MS872 105 × 85 mm. 5 r. Weightlifting .. .. 1·25 2·00

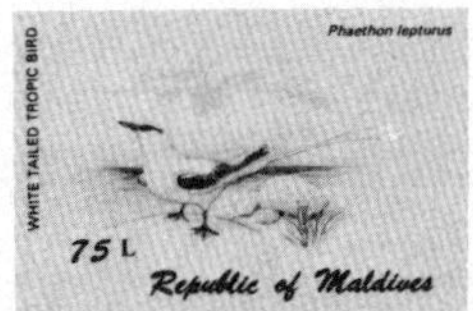

160 White-tailed Tropic Bird

(Des A. Abbas. Litho Questa)

1980 (10 July). *Birds. T* **160** *and similar horiz designs. Multicoloured. P* 14.
873 75 l. Type **160** 25 15
874 95 l. Sooty Tern 35 30
875 1 r. Common Noddy 35 30
876 1 r. 55, Curlew 50 40
877 2 r. Wilson's Petrel 60 50
878 4 r. Caspian Tern .. .. 1·10 1·00
873/8 .. .. *Set of* 6 2·75 2·40
MS879 124 × 85 mm. 5 r. Red-footed Booby and Brown Booby .. .. 4·75 5·00

161 Seal of Ibrahim II

(Litho Questa)

1980 (26 July). *Seals of the Sultans. T* **161** *and similar horiz designs. Each purple-brown and black. P* 14.
880 1 l. Type **161** 10 10
881 2 l. Mohammed Imadudeen II 10 10
882 5 l. Bin Haji Ali 10 10
883 1 r. Kuda Mohammed Rasgefaanu 30 30
884 2 r. Ibrahim Iskander I 50 60
880/4 .. .. *Set of* 5 80 90
MS885 131 × 95 mm. 3 r. Ibrahim Iskander I (*different*) .. .. 85 1·25

162 Queen Elizabeth the Queen Mother

(Des and litho Questa)

1980 (29 Sept). *Queen Mother's 80th Birthday. P* 14.
886 **162** 4 r. multicoloured .. .. .. 2·00 1·25
MS887 85 × 110 mm. **162** 5 r. multicoloured .. 2·75 2·75

163 Munnaru

(Des A. Abbas and M. Hassan)

1980 (9 Nov). *1400th Anniv of Hegira. T* **163** *and similar horiz designs. Multicoloured. P* 15.
888 5 l. Type **163** 10 10
889 10 l. Hukuru Miskiiy mosque.. .. .. 10 10
890 30 l. Medhuziyaaraiy (shrine of saint) .. 25 15
891 55 l. Writing tablets with verses of Koran .. 30 25
892 90 l. Mother teaching child Koran 50 45
888/92 .. .. *Set of* 5 1·10 85
MS893 124 × 101 mm. 2 r. Map of Maldives and coat of arms .. .. 80 1·25

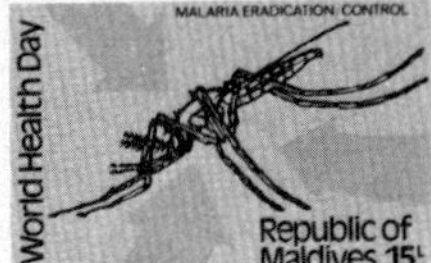

164 Malaria Eradication

(Des J.W. Litho Questa)

1980 (30 Nov). *World Health Day. T* **164** *and similar horiz designs. P* 14.
894 15 l. black, yellow and vermilion 10 10
895 25 l. multicoloured 15 10
896 1 r. 50, orange-brown, yellow-ochre & black 80 70
897 5 r. multicoloured .. .. 1·75 2·00
894/7 .. .. *Set of* 4 2·50 2·50
MS898 68 × 85 mm. 4 r. black, greenish blue and azure .. .. 1·25 1·75
Designs:—25 l. Food (Nutrition); 1 r. 50, Molar and toothbrush (Dental health); 4, 5 r. People and medical equipment (Clinics).

165 White Rabbit

(Des Walt Disney Productions)

1980 (22 Dec). *Scenes from Film "Alice in Wonderland". T* **165** *and similar horiz designs. Multicoloured. P* 11.
899 1 l. Type **165** 10 10
900 2 l. Alice falling into Wonderland 10 10
901 3 l. Alice too big to go through door.. .. 10 10
902 4 l. Alice and Tweedledum and Tweedledee 10 10
903 5 l. Alice and the caterpillar.. .. .. 10 10
904 10 l. Cheshire cat 10 10
905 15 l. Alice painting the roses 10 10
906 2 r. 50, Alice and the Queen of Hearts .. 1·25 1·25
907 4 r. Alice on trial .. .. 1·75 1·75
899/907 .. .. *Set of* 9 3·00 3·00
MS908 126 × 101 mm. 5 r. Alice at the Mad Hatter's tea-party. P 13½.. .. .. .. 4·25 4·25

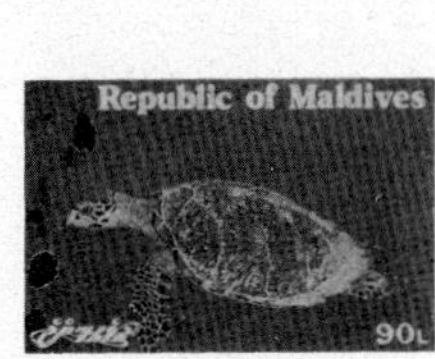

166 Indian Ocean Ridley Turtle

167 Pendant Lamp

(Des A. Abbas and Maniku. Litho Questa)

1980 (29 Dec). *Marine Life. T* **166** *and similar horiz designs. Multicoloured. P* 14.
909 90 l. Type **166** .. .. 1·00 50
910 1 r. 25, Angel fishes .. .. 1·25 85
911 2 r. Spiny lobster .. .. 1·75 1·40
909/11 .. .. *Set of* 3 3·50 2·50
MS912 140 × 94 mm. 4 r. Fishes .. .. .. 1·50 2·00

1981 (7 Jan). *National Day. T* **167** *and similar multicoloured designs. P* 14½.
913 10 l. Tomb of Ghaazee Muhammad Thakurufaan (*horiz*) 10 10
914 20 l. Type **167** 10 10
915 30 l. Chair used by Muhammad Thakurufaan 15 10
916 95 l. Muhammad Thakurufaan's palace (*horiz*) 35 30
917 10 r. Cushioned divan .. .. 2·75 3·25
913/17 .. .. *Set of* 5 3·00 3·50

168 Prince Charles and Lady Diana Spencer

169 First Majlis Chamber

(Des and litho J.W.)

1981 (22 June). *Royal Wedding. T* **168** *and similar vert designs. Multicoloured. P* 14.

918 1 r. Type **168** 25 25
919 2 r. Buckingham Palace 40 40
920 5 r. Prince Charles, polo player 75 75
918/20 .. .. *Set of* 3 1·25 1·25
MS921 95 × 83 mm. 10 r. State coach .. .. 2·25 2·50

Nos. 918/20 also exist perforated 12 (*Price for set of* 3 £1.25 *mint or used*) from additional sheets of five stamps and one label. These stamps have changed background colours.

(Des I. Azeez)

1981 (27 June). *50th Anniv of Citizens' Majlis (grievance rights). T* **169** *and similar multicoloured designs. P* 14½.

922 95 l. Type **169** 30 30
923 1 r. Sultan Muhammed Shamsuddin III .. 35 35
MS924 137 × 94 mm. 4 r. First written constitution (*horiz*) .. .. 2·75 3·25

170 "Self-portrait with a Palette"

171 Airmail Envelope

(Des J.W. Litho Questa)

1981 (July). *Birth Centenary of Pablo Picasso. T* **170** *and similar vert designs. Multicoloured. P* 13½ × 14.

925 5 l. Type **170** 10 10
926 10 l. "Woman in Blue" 10 10
927 25 l. "Boy with Pipe" 20 10
928 30 l. "Card Player" 20 10
929 90 l. "Sailor" 45 30
930 3 r. "Self-portrait" .. .. 1·00 75
931 5 r. "Harlequin" .. .. 1·50 1·25
925/31 .. .. *Set of* 7 3·00 2·40
MS932 106 × 130 mm. 10 r. "Child holding a Dove". Imperf .. .. 4·00 4·50

(Des and litho Questa)

1981 (9 Sept). *75th Anniv of Postal Service. P* 14.

933 **171** 25 l. multicoloured 15 10
934 75 l. multicoloured 35 30
935 5 r. multicoloured .. .. 1·25 1·40
933/5 .. .. *Set of* 3 1·60 1·60

172 Aircraft taking off

173 Homer

(Des A. Abbas. Litho Questa)

1981 (11 Nov). *Male International Airport. T* **172** *and similar horiz designs. Multicoloured. P* 14.

936 5 l. Type **172** 10 10
937 20 l. Passengers leaving aircraft 20 15
938 1 r. 80, Refuelling 75 75
939 4 r. Plan of airport .. .. 1·40 1·40
936/9 .. .. *Set of* 4 2·25 2·10
MS940 106 × 79 mm. 5 r. Aerial view of airport .. 1·50 2·25

(Des J.W.)

1981 (18 Nov). *International Year of Disabled People. T* **173** *and similar vert designs. Multicoloured. P* 14½.

941 2 l. Type **173** 10 10
942 5 l. Miguel Cervantes 10 10
943 1 r. Beethoven .. .. 1·75 75
944 5 r. Van Gogh .. .. 3·00 2·75
941/4 .. .. *Set of* 4 4·75 3·25
MS945 116 × 91 mm. 4 r. Helen Keller and Anne Sullivan .. .. 3·25 3·50

174 Preparation of Maldive Fish

175 Collecting Bait

(Des Central Art Palace. Litho Questa)

1981 (25 Nov). *Decade for Women. T* **174** *and similar vert designs. Multicoloured. P* 14.

946 20 l. Type **174** 10 10
947 90 l. 16th century Maldive women 25 25
948 1 r. Farming 30 30
949 2 r. Coir rope making 55 55
946/9 .. .. *Set of* 4 1·10 1·10

(Des I. Azeez. Litho Questa)

1981 (10 Dec). *Fishermen's Day. T* **175** *and similar horiz designs. Multicoloured. P* 14.

950 5 l. Type **175** 30 15
951 15 l. Fishing boats 45 25
952 90 l. Fisherman with catch 90 50
953 1 r. 30, Sorting fish .. .. 1·25 65
950/3 .. .. *Set of* 4 2·50 1·40
MS954 147 × 101 mm. 3 r. Loading fish for export 1·00 1·50

176 Bread Fruit

(Des Design Images. Litho Questa)

1981 (30 Dec). *World Food Day. T* **176** *and similar horiz designs. Multicoloured. P* 14.

955 10 l. Type **176** 15 10
956 25 l. Hen with chicks 40 15
957 30 l. Maize 40 20
958 75 l. Skipjack Tuna 85 40
959 1 r. Pumpkin .. .. 1·00 50
960 2 r. Coconuts .. .. 1·50 1·75
955/60 .. .. *Set of* 6 4·00 2·75
MS961 110 × 85 mm. 5 r. Eggplant .. .. 1·75 2·25

177 Pluto and Cat

178 Balmoral

(Des Walt Disney Productions)

1982 (29 Mar). *50th Anniv of Pluto (Walt Disney cartoon character). T* **177** *and similar multicoloured design. P* 13½.

962 4 r. Type **177** .. .. 2·50 2·00
MS963 127 × 101 mm. 6 r. Pluto (scene from *The Pointer*) .. .. 3·00 3·00

(Des PAD Studio. Litho Questa)

1982 (1 July). *21st Birthday of Princess of Wales. T* **178** *and similar vert designs. Multicoloured. P* 14½ × 14.

964 95 l. Type **178** 20 20
965 3 r. Prince and Princess of Wales 55 55
966 5 r. Princess on aircraft steps 85 85
964/6 .. .. *Set of* 3 1·40 1·40
MS967 103 × 75 mm. 8 r. Princess of Wales .. 1·50 1·60

Nos. 964/6 also exist in sheetlets of 5 stamps and 1 label.

Nos. 964/7 and the sheetlets exist imperforate from a restricted printing.

COMMONWEALTH MEMBER
9 July 1982

179 Scout saluting and Camp-site

180 Footballer

(Des D. Miller. Litho Questa)

1982 (9 Aug). *75th Anniv of Boy Scout Movement. T* **179** *and similar horiz designs. Multicoloured. P* 14.

968 1 r. 30, Type **179** 40 40
969 1 r. 80, Lighting a fire 50 50
970 4 r. Life-saving .. .. 1·10 1·10
971 5 r. Map-reading .. .. 1·40 1·40
968/71 .. .. *Set of* 4 3·00 3·00
MS972 128 × 66 mm. 10 r. Scout emblem and flag of the Maldives .. .. 2·00 2·50

(Des M. and S. Gerber Studio. Litho Questa)

1982 (4 Oct). *World Cup Football Championship, Spain. T* **180** *and similar square designs. P* 13½.

973 90 l. multicoloured 70 50
974 1 r. 50, multicoloured .. .. 1·10 70
975 3 r. multicoloured .. .. 1·75 1·25
976 5 r. multicoloured .. .. 2·25 2·00
973/6 .. .. *Set of* 4 5·25 4·00
MS977 94 × 63 mm. 10 r. multicoloured .. .. 3·00 3·50

1982 (18 Oct). *Birth of Prince William of Wales. Nos. 964/7 optd with T* 212*a of Jamaica.*

978 95 l. Type **178** 20 20
979 3 r. Prince and Princess of Wales 55 55
980 5 r. Princess on aircraft steps 85 85
978/80 .. .. *Set of* 3 1·40 1·40
MS981 103 × 75 mm. 8 r. Princess of Wales .. 2·25 2·50

Nos. 978/80 also exist in sheetlets of 5 stamps and 1 label.

Nos. 978/81 and the sheetlets exist imperforate from a restricted printing.

181 Basic Education Scheme

182 Koch isolates the Bacillus

(Des and litho Harrison)

1982 (15 Nov). *National Education. T* **181** *and similar horiz designs. Multicoloured. P* 14.

982 90 l. Type **181** 15 20
983 95 l. Primary education 15 20
984 1 r. 30, Teacher training 20 25
985 2 r. 50, Printing educational material .. 40 45
982/5 .. .. *Set of* 4 80 1·00
MS986 100 × 70 mm. 6 r. Thaana typewriter keyboard .. .. 1·00 1·60

(Des Artists International)

1982 (22 Nov). *Centenary of Robert Koch's Discovery of Tubercle Bacillus. T* **182** *and similar multicoloured designs. P* 14.

987 5 l. Type **182** 10 10
988 15 l. Micro-organism and microscope 10 10
989 95 l. Dr. Robert Koch in 1905 .. .. .. 25 25
990 3 r. Dr. Koch and plates from publication .. 65 65
987/90 .. .. *Set of* 4 95 95
MS991 77 × 61 mm. 5 r. Koch in his laboratory (*horiz*) .. .. 80 1·25

183 Blohm and Voss "Ha 139" Seaplane

(Des W. Wright. Litho Questa)

1983 (28 July). *Bicentenary of Manned Flight. T* **183** *and similar horiz designs. Multicoloured. P* 14.

992 90 l. Type **183** .. .. 1·25 50
993 1 r. 45, Macchi-Castoldi "MC.72" .. .. 1·75 1·25
994 4 r. Boeing "F4B-3" .. .. 3·25 2·50
995 5 r. *La France* airship .. .. .. 3·50 2·75
992/5 .. .. *Set of* 4 8·75 6·25
MS996 110 × 85 mm. 10 r. Nadar's *Le Geant* .. 3·00 4·00

184 "Curved Dash" Oldsmobile, 1902

(Des Publishers Graphics Inc)

1983 (Aug). *Classic Motor Cars. T* **184** *and similar horiz designs. Multicoloured. P* 14½.

997 5 l. Type **184** 10 15
998 30 l. Aston Martin "Tourer", 1932 .. .. 35 15
999 40 l. Lamborghini "Muira", 1966 .. .. 40 20
1000 1 r. Mercedes-Benz "300SL", 1945 .. .. 80 40
1001 1 r. 45, Stutz "Bearcat", 1913 .. .. 1·25 90
1002 5 r. Lotus "Elite", 1958 .. .. .. 3·00 3·00
997/1002 .. .. *Set of* 6 5·50 4·25
MS1003 132 × 103 mm. 10 r. Grand Prix "Sunbeam", 1924. P 14½ .. .. 7·50 7·50

Nos. 997/1002 were each issued in sheets of 9, including one *se-tenant* label.

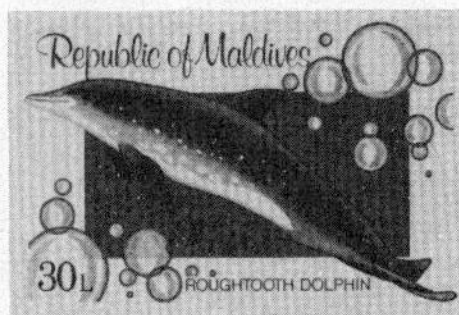

185 Rough-toothed Dolphin

(Des D. Miller. Litho Questa)

1983 (6 Sept). *Marine Mammals. T* **185** *and similar horiz designs. Multicoloured. P* 14.

1004	30 l. Type **185**	1·00	40
1005	40 l. Indo-Pacific Hump-backed Dolphin	1·10	45
1006	4 r. Finless Porpoise	4·00	2·50
1007	6 r. Pygmy Sperm Whale	5·50	4·00
1004/7	*Set of* 4	10·50	6·50
MS1008	82 × 90 mm. 5 r. Striped Dolphin	2·50	3·25

186 Dish Aerial

(Des PAD Studio. Litho Questa)

1983 (9 Oct). *World Communications Year. T* **186** *and similar horiz designs. Multicoloured. P* 14.

1009	50 l. Type **186**	15	10
1010	1 r. Land, sea and air communications	45	45
1011	2 r. Ship-to-shore communication	55	55
1012	10 r. Air traffic controller	1·90	2·50
1009/12	*Set of* 4	2·75	3·25
MS1013	91 × 76 mm. 20 r. Telecommunications	3·75	4·50

187 "La Donna Gravida"

(Des M. Diamond)

1983 (25 Oct). *500th Birth Anniv of Raphael. T* **187** *and similar vert designs showing paintings. Multicoloured. P* 13½.

1014	90 l. Type **187**	20	25
1015	3 r. "Giovanna d'Aragona" (detail)	60	65
1016	4 r. "Woman with Unicorn"	80	85
1017	6 r. "La Muta"	1·25	1·40
1014/17	*Set of* 4	2·50	2·75
MS1018	121 × 97 mm. 10 r. "The Knight's Dream" (detail)	1·90	2·75

Nos. 1014/17 exist imperforate from stock dispersed by the liquidator of Format International Security Printers Ltd.

188 Refugee Camp

(Litho Questa)

1983 (29 Nov). *Solidarity with the Palestinians. T* **188** *and similar horiz designs each showing the Dome of the Rock, Jerusalem. Multicoloured. P* 13½ × 14.

1019	4 r. Type **188**	1·50	1·50
1020	5 r. Refugee holding dead child	1·60	1·60
1021	6 r. Child carrying food	1·90	1·90
1019/21	*Set of* 3	4·50	4·50

189 Education Facilities

190 Baseball

(Des I. Azeez. Litho Questa)

1983 (10 Dec). *National Development Programme. T* **189** *and similar horiz designs. Multicoloured. P* 13½.

1022	7 l. Type **189**	10	10
1023	10 l. Health service and education	10	10
1024	5 r. Growing more food	1·25	1·25
1025	6 r. Fisheries development	1·50	1·50
1022/5	*Set of* 4	2·50	2·50
MS1026	134 × 93 mm. 10 r. Air transport	2·25	2·75

(Des PAD Studio. Litho Questa)

1984 (10 Mar). *Olympic Games, Los Angeles. T* **190** *and similar vert designs. Multicoloured. P* 14.

1027	50 l. Type **190**	15	15
1028	1 r. 55, Backstroke swimming	40	40
1029	3 r. Judo	80	90
1030	4 r. Shot-putting	1·25	1·40
1027/30	*Set of* 4	2·40	2·50
MS1031	85 × 105 mm. 10 r. Team Handball	2·40	2·75

Rf1.45

19th UPU
CONGRESS HAMBURG

(191) (192)

1984 (19 June). *Universal Postal Union Congress, Hamburg. Nos.* 994/6 *optd as T* **191**.

1032	4 r. Boeing "F4B-3"	1·40	1·40
1033	5 r. *La France* airship	1·60	1·60
MS1034	110 × 85 mm. 10 r. Nadar's *Le Geant*	2·75	3·75

1984 (20 Aug). *Surch as T* **192**. A. *In black.* B. *In gold.*

(*a*) *On Nos.* 964/7

		A		B	
1035	1 r. 45 on 95 l. Type **178**	5·00	3·00	5·00	3·00
1036	1 r. 45 on 3 r. Prince and Princess of Wales	5·00	3·00	5·00	3·00
1037	1 r. 45 on 5 r. Princess on aircraft steps	5·00	3·00	5·00	3·00
1035/7	*Set of* 3	13·50	8·00	13·50	8·00
MS1038	103 × 75 mm. 1 r. 45 on 8 r. Princess of Wales	4·00	7·00	4·00	7·00

(*b*) *On Nos.* 978/81

1039	1 r. 45 on 95 l. Type **178**	5·00	3·00	5·00	3·00
1040	1 r. 45 on 3 r. Prince and Princess of Wales	5·00	3·00	5·00	3·00
1041	1 r. 45 on 5 r. Princess on aircraft steps	5·00	3·00	5·00	3·00
1039/41	*Set of* 3	13·50	8·00	13·50	8·00
MS1042	103 × 75 mm. 1 r. 45 on 8 r. Princess of Wales	4·00	7·00	4·00	7·00

Stamps from the sheetlets of five plus one label were also surcharged, either in black or gold, using a slightly different type.

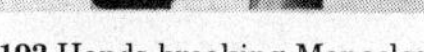

193 Hands breaking Manacles

194 Island Resort and Sea Birds

1984 (26 Aug). *Namibia Day. T* **193** *and similar horiz designs. Multicoloured. P* 15.

1043	6 r. Type **193**	1·50	1·60
1044	8 r. Namibia family	2·00	2·10
MS1045	129 × 104 mm. 10 r. Map of Namibia	2·40	2·75

(Litho Questa)

1984 (12 Sept). *Tourism. T* **194** *and similar vert designs. Multicoloured. P* 14.

1046	7 l. Type **194**	10	10
1047	15 l. Dhow	10	10
1048	20 l. Snorkelling	10	10
1049	2 r. Wind-surfing	35	40
1050	4 r. Aqualung diving	70	75
1051	6 r. Night fishing	1·00	1·25
1052	8 r. Game fishing	1·40	1·50
1053	10 r. Turtle on beach	1·60	1·75
1046/53	*Set of* 8	4·75	5·25

195 Frangipani

1984 (21 Sept). *"Ausipex" International Stamp Exhibition, Melbourne. T* **195** *and similar horiz designs showing flowers. Multicoloured. P* 15.

1054	5 r. Type **195**	1·75	1·75
1055	10 r. Cooktown Orchid	3·75	3·75
MS1056	105 × 77 mm. 15 r. Sun Orchid	7·50	5·50

196 Facade of the Malé Mosque

1984 (11 Nov). *Opening of Islamic Centre. T* **196** *and similar multicoloured design. P* 15.

1057	2 r. Type **196**	45	50
1058	5 r. Malé Mosque and minaret (*vert*)	1·10	1·25

197 Air Maldives Boeing "737"

(Des G. Drummond. Litho Questa)

1984 (19 Nov). *40th Anniv of International Civil Aviation Authority. T* **197** *and similar horiz designs. Multicoloured. P* 14.

1059	7 l. Type **197**	15	15
1060	4 r. Airlanka Lockheed "L–1011 TriStar"	1·10	1·25
1061	6 r. Air Alitalia McDonnell Douglas "DC10–30"	1·50	1·60
1062	8 r. L.T.U. Lockheed "L–1011 TriStar"	2·00	2·25
1059/62	*Set of* 4	4·25	4·75
MS1063	110 × 92 mm. 15 r. Air Maldives Shorts "SC7 Skyvan"	3·25	4·00

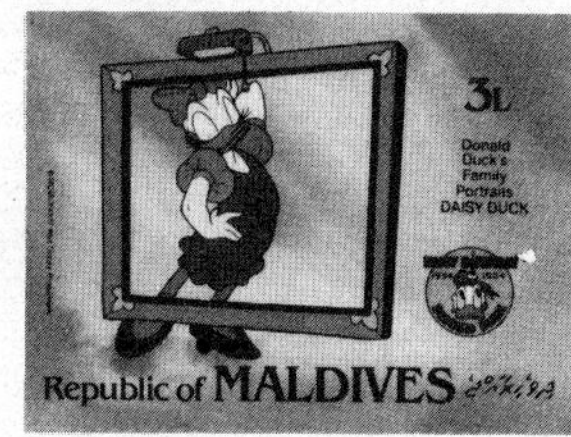

198 Daisy Duck

(Litho Questa)

1984 (26 Nov–1 Dec). *50th Anniv of Donald Duck (Walt Disney cartoon character). T* **198** *and similar horiz designs. Multicoloured. P* 12 (5 *r.*) *or* 14 × 13½ (*others*).

1064	3 l. Type **198**	10	10
1065	4 l. Huey, Dewey and Louie	10	10
1066	5 l. Ludwig von Drake	10	10
1067	10 l. Gyro Gearloose	10	10
1068	15 l. Uncle Scrooge painting self portrait	10	10
1069	25 l. Donald Duck with camera	10	10
1070	5 r. Donald Duck and Gus Goose (1.12)	1·00	1·00
1071	8 r. Gladstone Gander	1·60	1·60
1072	10 r. Grandma Duck	2·00	2·00
1064/72	*Set of* 9	4·25	4·25
MS1073	102 × 126 mm. 15 r. Uncle Scrooge and Donald Duck in front of camera	2·75	3·25
MS1074	126 × 102 mm. 15 r. Uncle Scrooge (1.12)	2·75	3·25

No. 1070 was printed in sheetlets of 8 stamps.

199 "The Day" (detail)

200 "Edmond Iduranty" (Degas)

(Litho Questa)

1984 (10 Dec). *450th Death Anniv of Correggio (artist). T* **199** *and similar vert designs. Multicoloured. P* 14.

1075	5 r. Type **199**	95	1·25
1076	10 r. "The Night" (*detail*)	1·60	2·00
MS1077	60 × 80 mm. 15 r. "Portrait of a Man"	2·75	3·25

(Litho Questa)

1984 (15 Dec). *150th Birth Anniv of Edgar Degas (artist). T* **200** *and similar vert designs. P* 14.

1078	75 l. Type **200**	15	20
1079	2 r. "James Tissot"	45	50
1080	5 r. "Achille de Gas in Uniform"	1·10	1·25
1081	10 r. "Lady with Chrysanthemums"	2·25	2·75
1078/81	*Set of* 4	3·40	4·25
MS1082	100 × 70 mm. 15 r. "Self-portrait"	3·25	3·75

201 Pale-footed Shearwater

202 Squad Drilling

(Des I. MacLaury. Litho Questa)

1985 (9 Mar). *Birth Bicentenary of John J. Audubon (ornithologist) (1st issue). T* **201** *and similar multicoloured designs showing original paintings. P* 14.

1083 3 r. Type **201** .. .. 1·00 80
1084 3 r. 50, Little Grebe (*horiz*) .. .. 1·10 90
1085 4 r. Common Cormorant .. .. 1·25 1·00
1086 4 r. 50, White-faced Storm Petrel (*horiz*) .. 1·50 1·10
1083/6 .. .. *Set of* 4 4·25 3·50
MS1087 108×80 mm. 15 r. Red-necked Phalarope (*horiz*) .. .. 2·75 3·25
See also Nos. 1192/200.

(Des and litho Questa)

1985 (6 June). *National Security Service. T* **202** *and similar multicoloured designs. P* 13½×14 *(No.* 1092) *or* 14×13½ *(others).*

1088 15 l. Type **202** 15 10
1089 20 l. Combat patrol 15 10
1090 1 r. Fire fighting 35 25
1091 2 r. Coastguard cutter 65 55
1092 10 r. Independence Day Parade (*vert*) .. 2·00 2·50
1088/92 .. .. *Set of* 5 3·00 3·00
MS1093 128×85 mm. 10 r. Cannon on saluting base and National Security Service badge .. 1·90 2·25

GOLD MEDALIST
THERESA ANDREWS
USA

(203)

204 Queen Elizabeth the Queen Mother, 1981

1985 (17 July). *Olympic Games Gold Medal Winners, Los Angeles. Nos.* 1027/31 *optd as T* **203** *or in larger capitals* (50 *l.*, 10 *r.*).

1094 50 l. Type **190** (optd "JAPAN") 10 10
1095 1 r. 55, Backstroke swimming (opt T **203**) 30 35
1096 3 r. Judo (Optd "GOLD MEDALIST FRANK WIENEKE USA") 55 60
1097 4 r. Shot-putting (optd "GOLD MEDALIST CLAUDIA LOCH WEST GERMANY") 80 85
1094/7 .. .. *Set of* 4 1·60 1·75
MS1098 85×105 mm. 10 r. Team Handball (opt "U.S.A.") .. .. 1·90 2·00

(Des J.W. Litho Questa)

1985 (20 Aug). *Life and Times of Queen Elizabeth the Queen Mother. T* **204** *and similar multicoloured designs. P* 14.

1099 3 r. Type **204** 55 60
1100 5 r. Visiting the Middlesex Hospital (*horiz*) .. .. 95 1·00
1101 7 r. The Queen Mother .. .. 1·40 1·50
1099/101 .. .. *Set of* 3 2·50 2·75
MS1102 56×85 mm. 15 r. With Prince Charles at Garter Ceremony .. .. 3·25 3·25

Stamps as Nos. 1099/101, but with face values of 1 r., 4 r. and 10 r., exist from additional sheetlets of 5 plus a label issued 4 January 1986. These also have changed background colours and are perforated 12½×12 (4 r.) or 12×12½ (others) (*Price for set of 3 stamps £2.50 mint*).

204*a* Liro da Braccio

205 Mas Odi (fishing boat)

(Des Susan David. Litho Questa)

1985 (3 Sept). *300th Birth Anniv of Johann Sebastian Bach (composer). T* **204*a*** *and similar vert designs. P* 14.

1103 15 l. multicoloured 10 10
1104 2 r. multicoloured 50 45
1105 4 r. multicoloured 90 85
1106 10 r. multicoloured .. .. 1·90 2·25
1103/6 .. .. *Set of* 4 3·00 3·25
MS1107 104×75 mm. 15 r. black and reddish orange .. .. 3·00 3·50

Designs:—2 r. Tenor oboe; 4 r. Serpent; 10 r. Table organ; 15 r. Johann Sebastian Bach.

(Des H. Afeef. Litho Questa)

1985 (23 Sept). *Maldives Ships and Boats. T* **205** *and similar horiz designs. Multicoloured. P* 14.

1108 3 l. Type **205** 10 10
1109 5 l. Battela (dhow) 10 10
1110 10 l. Addu odi (dhow) 10 10
1111 2 r. 60, Modern dhoni (fishing boat) .. 30 35
1112 2 r. 70, Mas dhoni (fishing boat) 30 35
1113 3 r. Baththeli dhoni 35 40
1114 5 r. *Inter* 1 (inter-island vessel) 55 60
1115 10 r. Dhoni-style yacht .. .. 1·10 1·25
1108/15 .. .. *Set of* 8 2·50 2·75

206 Windsurfing

207 United Nations Building, New York

(Des H. Afeef. Litho Questa)

1985 (2 Oct). *10th Anniv of World Tourism Organization. T* **206** *and similar horiz designs. Multicoloured. P* 14.

1116 6 r. Type **206** .. .. 1·10 1·40
1117 8 r. Scuba diving .. .. 1·50 1·75
MS1118 171×114 mm. 15 r. Kuda Hithi Resort 2·75 3·00

(Litho Questa)

1985 (24 Oct). *40th Anniv of United Nations Organization and International Year of Peace. T* **207** *and similar multicoloured designs. P* 14.

1119 15 l. Type **207** 10 10
1120 2 r. Hands releasing peace dove 40 45
1121 4 r. U.N. Security Council meeting (*horiz*) 80 85
1122 10 r. Lion and lamb .. .. 1·90 2·25
1119/22 .. .. *Set of* 4 2·75 3·25
MS1123 76×92 mm. 15 r. U.N. Building and peace dove .. .. 2·75 3·00

208 Maldivian Delegate voting in U.N. General Assembly

(Des BG Studio. Litho Questa)

1985 (24 Oct). *20th Anniv of United Nations Membership. T* **208** *and similar horiz design. Multicoloured. P* 14.

1124 20 l. Type **208** 10 10
1125 15 r. U.N. and Maldivian flags, and U.N. Building, New York .. .. .. 2·75 3·25

209 Youths playing Drums

(Des BG Studio)

1985 (20 Nov). *International Youth Year. T* **209** *and similar multicoloured designs. P* 15.

1126 90 l. Type **209** 15 20
1127 6 r. Tug-of-war .. .. 1·10 1·40
1128 10 r. Community service (*vert*) .. .. 1·90 2·25
1126/8 .. .. *Set of* 3 2·75 3·50
MS1129 85×84 mm. 15 r. Raising the flag at youth camp (*vert*) .. .. 2·75 3·00

210 Quotation and Flags of Member Nations

(Litho Questa)

1985 (8 Dec) *1st Summit Meeting of South Asian Association for Regional Co-operation, Dhaka, Bangladesh. P* 14.

1130 **210** 3 r. multicoloured .. .. 90 1·00

211 Frigate Tuna

212 Player running with Ball

(Litho Questa)

1985 (10 Dec). *Fishermen's Day. Species of Tuna. T* **211** *and similar horiz designs. Multicoloured. P* 14.

1131 25 l. Type **211** 10 10
1132 75 l. Little Tuna 15 15
1133 3 r. Dogtooth Tuna 55 60
1134 5 r. Yellowfin Tuna .. .. 95 1·00
1131/4 .. .. *Set of* 4 1·50 1·60
MS1135 130×90 mm. 15 r. Skipjack Tuna .. 2·75 3·00

(Des Walt Disney Productions. Litho Questa)

1985 (21 Dec). *150th Birth Anniv of Mark Twain. Vert designs as T* **160*a*** *of Lesotho showing Walt Disney cartoon characters illustrating various Mark Twain quotations. Multicoloured. P* 12 (4 *r.*) *or* 13½×14 *(others).*

1136 2 l. Winnie the Pooh 10 10
1137 3 l. Gepetto and Figaro the cat 10 10
1138 4 l. Goofy and basket of broken eggs .. 10 10
1139 20 l. Goofy as doctor scolding Donald Duck 10 10
1140 4 r. Mowgli and King Louis 75 80
1141 13 r. The wicked Queen and mirror .. 2·50 3·00
1136/41 .. .. *Set of* 6 3·00 3·75
MS1142 126×101 mm. 15 r. Mickey Mouse as Tom Sawyer on comet's tail .. .. .. 2·75 3·00
No. 1140 was issued in sheetlets of 8 stamps.

(Des Walt Disney Productions. Litho Questa)

1985 (21 Dec). *Birth Bicentenaries of Grimm Brothers (folklorists). Multicoloured designs as T* **160*b*** *of Lesotho, but horiz, showing Walt Disney cartoon characters in scenes from "Dr. Knowall". P* 12 (3 *r.*) *or* 14×13½ *(others).*

1143 1 l. Donald Duck as Crabb driving oxcart .. 10 10
1144 5 l. Donald Duck as Dr. Knowall 10 10
1145 10 l. Dr. Knowall in surgery 10 10
1146 15 l. Dr. Knowall with Uncle Scrooge as a lord 10 10
1147 3 r. Dr. and Mrs. Knowall in pony trap .. 55 65
1148 14 r. Dr. Knowall and thief .. .. .. 2·75 3·25
1143/8 .. .. *Set of* 6 3·00 3·75
MS1149 126×101 mm. 15 r. Donald and Daisy Duck as Dr. and Mrs. Knowall .. .. .. 2·75 3·00
No. 1147 was printed in sheetlets of 8 stamps.

(Des W. Hanson. Litho Questa)

1986 (29 Apr). *Appearance of Halley's Comet (1st issue). Horiz designs as T* **162*a*** *of Lesotho. Multicoloured. P* 14.

1150 20 l. N.A.S.A. space telescope and Comet .. 40 15
1151 1 r. 50, E.S.A. *Giotto* spacecraft and Comet 1·00 85
1152 2 r. Japanese *Planet A* spacecraft and Comet .. .. 1·25 1·10
1153 4 r. Edmond Halley and Stonehenge .. 2·50 2·25
1154 5 r. Russian *Vega* spacecraft and Comet .. 2·75 2·50
1150/4 .. .. *Set of* 5 7·25 6·25
MS1155 101×70 mm. 15 r. Halley's Comet .. 6·00 6·50
See also Nos. 1206/11.

(Des J. Iskowitz. Litho Questa)

1986 (5 May). *Centenary of Statue of Liberty. Multicoloured designs as T* **163*b*** *of Lesotho showing the Statue of Liberty and immigrants to the U.S.A. P* 14.

1156 50 l. Walter Gropius (architect) 30 15
1157 70 l. John Lennon (musician) .. .. 1·25 60
1158 1 r. George Balanchine (choreographer) .. 1·25 60
1159 10 r. Franz Werfel (writer) .. .. .. 3·25 3·50
1156/9 .. .. *Set of* 4 5·50 4·50
MS1160 100×72 mm. 15 r. Statue of Liberty (*vert*) .. .. 4·50 5·50

(Des Walt Disney Productions)

1986 (22 May). *"Ameripex" International Stamp Exhibition, Chicago. Horiz designs as T* **163*c*** *of Lesotho showing Walt Disney cartoon characters and U.S.A. stamps. Multicoloured. P* 11.

1161 3 l. Johnny Appleseed and 1966 Johnny Appleseed stamp 10 10
1162 4 l. Paul Bunyan and 1958 Forest Conservation stamp 10 10
1163 5 l. Casey and 1969 Professional Baseball Centenary stamp 10 10
1164 10 l. Ichabod Crane and 1974 "Legend of Sleepy Hollow" stamp 10 10
1165 15 l. John Henry and 1944 75th anniv of completion of First Transcontinental Railroad stamp 10 10
1166 20 l. Windwagon Smith and 1954 Kansas Territory Centenary stamp 10 10
1167 13 r. Mike Fink and 1970 Great Northwest stamp .. .. 2·75 3·00
1168 14 r. Casey Jones and 1950 Railroad Engineers stamp .. .. 3·00 3·25
1161/8 .. .. *Set of* 8 5·75 6·25
MS1169 Two sheets, each 127×101 mm. (a) 15 r. Davy Crockett and 1967 Davy Crockett stamp. (b) 15 r. Daisy Duck as Pocahontas saving Captain John Smith (Donald Duck). P 14×13½. .. .. *Set of* 2 *sheets* 5·50 7·00

(Litho Questa)

1986 (29 May). *60th Birthday of Queen Elizabeth II. Vert designs as T* **163***a of Lesotho. P* 14.
1170 1 r. black and chrome-yellow 35 25
1171 2 r. multicoloured 55 55
1172 12 r. multicoloured .. .. 2·75 2·75
1170/2 .. .. *Set of* 3 3·25 3·25
MS1173 120×85 mm. 15 r. black and grey-brown 3·75 4·25
Designs:—1 r. Royal Family at Girl Guides Rally, 1938; 2 r. Queen in Canada; 12 r. At Sandringham, 1970; 15 r. Princesses Elizabeth and Margaret at Royal Lodge, Windsor, 1940.
Nos. 1170/2 were each issued in sheetlets of five stamps and one stamp-size label.

(Des BG Studio. Litho Questa)

1986 (8 June). *World Cup Football Championship, Mexico. T* **212** *and similar vert designs. Multicoloured. P* 14.
1174 15 l. Type **212** 20 15
1175 2 r. Player gaining control of ball .. 1·00 80
1176 4 r. Two players competing for ball .. 1·90 1·40
1177 10 r. Player bouncing ball on knee .. .. 4·00 4·00
1174/7 .. .. *Set of* 4 6·50 5·75
MS1178 95×114 mm. 15 r. Player kicking ball .. 3·00 4·00

(Litho Questa)

1986 (1 July). *Royal Wedding. Vert designs as T* **170***a of Lesotho. Multicoloured. P* 14.
1179 10 l. Prince Andrew and Miss Sarah Ferguson 10 10
1180 2 r. Prince Andrew 60 60
1181 12 r. Prince Andrew in naval uniform .. 2·75 3·00
1179/81 .. .. *Set of* 3 3·00 3·25
MS1182 88×88 mm. 15 r. Prince Andrew and Miss Sarah Ferguson (*different*) .. .. .. 4·00 4·25

WINNERS
Argentina 3
W.Germany 2

213 Moorish Idol and Sea Fan (**213***a*)

(Des Mary Walters)

1986 (22 Sept). *Marine Wildlife. T* **213** *and similar horiz designs. Multicoloured. P* 15.
1183 50 l. Type **213** 50 30
1184 90 l. Regal Angelfish 70 45
1185 1 r. Anemone Fish 75 45
1186 2 r. Tiger Cowrie and Stinging Coral .. 1·25 1·00
1187 3 r. Emperor Angelfish and Staghorn Coral .. .. 1·50 1·25
1188 4 r. Black-naped Tern .. .. 2·25 2·00
1189 5 r. Fiddler Crab and Staghorn Coral .. 2·25 2·00
1190 10 r. Hawksbill Turtle .. .. 3·25 3·25
1183/90 .. .. *Set of* 8 11·00 9·50
MS1191 Two sheets, each 107×76 mm. (a) 15 r. Long Nosed Butterfly Fish. (b) 15 r. Trumpet Fish .. .. .. *Set of* 2 *sheets* 7·00 8·50

(Litho Questa)

1986 (9 Oct). *Birth Bicentenary of John J. Audubon* (*ornithologist*) (1985) (2*nd issue*). *Multicoloured designs as T* **201** *showing original paintings. P* 14.
1192 3 l. Little Blue Heron (*horiz*) 10 10
1193 4 l. White-tailed Kite 10 10
1194 5 l. Greater Shearwater (*horiz*) 10 10
1195 10 l. Magnificent Frigate Bird 15 10
1196 15 l. Black-necked Grebe 25 20
1197 20 l. Goosander 30 20
1198 13 r. Peregrine Falcon (*horiz*) .. .. 4·50 4·50
1199 14 r. Prairie Chicken (*horiz*) .. .. 4·50 4·50
1192/9 .. .. *Set of* 8 9·00 8·50
MS1200 Two sheets, each 74×104 mm. (a) 15 r. Fulmar. (b) 15 r. White-fronted Goose (*horiz*) *Set of* 2 *sheets* 13·00 14·00
Nos. 1192/9 were each issued in sheetlets of five stamps and one stamp-size label, which appears in the centre of the bottom row.

1986 (25 Oct). *World Cup Football Championship Winners, Mexico. Nos.* 1174/8 *optd with T* **213***a in gold.*
1201 15 l. Type **212** 10 10
1202 2 r. Player gaining control of ball .. 40 45
1203 4 r. Two players competing for ball .. 75 80
1204 10 r. Player bouncing ball on knee .. .. 1·90 2·25
1201/4 .. .. *Set of* 4 2·75 3·25
MS1205 95×114 mm. 15 r. Player kicking ball .. 2·75 3·50

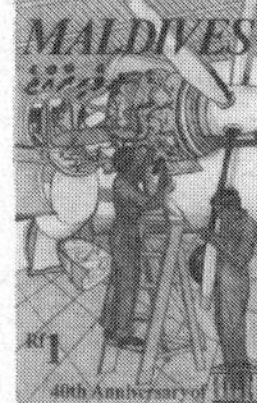

(**213***b*) **214** Servicing Aircraft

1986 (30 Oct). *Appearance of Halley's Comet* (2*nd issue*). *Nos.* 1150/5 *optd with T* **213***b in silver.*
1206 20 l. N.A.S.A. space telescope and Comet .. 10 10
1207 1 r. 50, E.S.A. *Giotto* spacecraft and Comet 30 35
1208 2 r. Japanese *Planet A* spacecraft and Comet 40 45
1209 4 r. Edmond Halley and Stonehenge .. 75 80
1210 5 r. Russian *Vega* spacecraft and Comet .. 95 1·00
1206/10 .. .. *Set of* 5 2·25 2·40
MS1211 101×70 mm. 15 r. Halley's Comet .. 3·00 3·50

(Des BG Studio)

1986 (4 Nov). *40th Anniv of U.N.E.S.C.O. T* **214** *and similar vert designs. Multicoloured. P* 15.
1212 1 r. Type **214** 20 25
1213 2 r. Boat building 40 45
1214 3 r. Children in classroom 55 60
1215 5 r. Student in laboratory .. .. .. 95 1·00
1212/15 .. .. *Set of* 4 1·90 2·10
MS1216 77×100 mm. 15 r. Diving bell on sea bed .. .. 2·75 3·50

215 *Hypholoma fasciculare* **216** Ixora

(Des Mary Walters)

1986 (31 Dec). *Fungi of the Maldives. T* **215** *and similar multicoloured designs. P* 15.
1217 15 l. Type **215** 40 15
1218 50 l. *Kuehneromyces mutabilis* (*vert*) .. 65 30
1219 1 r. *Amanita muscaria* (*vert*) 85 40
1220 2 r. *Agaricus campestris* .. .. .. 1·25 85
1221 3 r. *Amanita pantherina* (*vert*) .. .. 1·40 1·10
1222 4 r. *Coprinus comatus* (*vert*) .. .. 1·60 1·50
1223 5 r. *Pholiota spectabilis* .. .. .. 1·75 2·00
1224 10 r. *Pluteus cervinus* .. .. .. 3·00 3·25
1217/24 .. .. *Set of* 8 9·75 8·50
MS1225 Two sheets, each 100×70 mm. (a) 15 r. *Armillaria mellea*. (b) 15 r. *Stropharia aeruginosa* (*vert*) .. .. *Set of* 2 *sheets* 7·00 8·50

(Des Mary Walters)

1987 (29 Jan). *Flowers. T* **216** *and similar vert designs. Multicoloured. P* 15.
1226 10 l. Type **216** 10 10
1227 20 l. Frangipani 10 10
1228 50 l. Crinum 25 15
1229 2 r. Pink Rose 50 50
1230 4 r. Flamboyant Flower 80 80
1231 10 r. Ground Orchid .. .. 2·75 3·00
1226/31 .. .. *Set of* 6 4·00 4·25
MS1232 Two sheets, each 100×70 mm. (a) 15 r. Gardenia. (b) 15 r. Oleander *Set of* 2 *sheets* 4·75 6·50
Similar 1, 7 and 12 r. stamps were prepared but not issued. They exist from stock dispersed by the liquidator of Format International Security Printers Ltd.

217 Guides studying Wild Flowers **218** *Thespesia populnea*

(Des R. Vigurs)

1987 (4 Apr). *75th Anniv of Girl Guide Movement* (1985). *T* **217** *and similar horiz designs. Multicoloured. P* 15.
1233 15 l. Type **217** 10 10
1234 2 r. Guides with pet rabbits 40 40
1235 4 r. Guide observing spoonbill 80 90
1236 12 r. Lady Baden-Powell and Guide flag .. 2·50 3·00
1233/6 .. .. *Set of* 4 3·50 4·00
MS1237 104×78 mm. 15 r. Guides in sailing dinghy .. .. 2·75 3·00

(Litho Questa)

1987 (22 Apr). *Trees and Plants. T* **218** *and similar multicoloured designs. P* 14.
1238 50 l. Type **218** 10 10
1239 1 r. *Cocos nucifera* 15 20
1240 2 r. *Calophyllum mophyllum* 30 35
1241 3 r. *Xyanthosoma indica* (*horiz*) 45 50
1242 5 r. *Ipomoea batatas* (*horiz*) 80 85
1243 7 r. *Artocarpus altilis* .. .. .. 1·10 1·25
1238/43 .. .. *Set of* 6 2·50 3·00
MS1244 75×109 mm. 15 r. *Cocos nucifera* (*different*) .. .. 2·25 2·75

218*a Intrepid*, 1970 **219** *Precis octavia*

(Des J. Iskowitz)

1987 (4 May). *America's Cup Yachting Championship. T* **218***a and similar multicoloured designs. P* 15.
1245 15 l. Type **218***a* 10 10
1246 1 r. *France II*, 1974 .. .. 20 20
1247 2 r. *Gretel*, 1962 .. .. 40 50
1248 12 r. *Volunteer*, 1887 .. .. 2·00 2·50
1245/8 .. .. *Set of* 4 2·40 3·00
MS1249 113×83 mm. 15 r. Helmsman and crew on deck of *Defender*, 1895 (*horiz*) .. .. 2·25 2·75

1987 (16 Dec). *Butterflies. T* **219** *and similar vert designs. Multicoloured. P* 15.
1250 15 l. Type **219** 35 30
1251 20 l. *Atrophaneura hector* 35 30
1252 50 l. *Teinopalpus imperialis* 60 40
1253 1 r. *Kallima horsfieldi* 80 45
1254 2 r. *Cethosia biblis* .. .. 1·25 1·00
1255 4 r. *Idea jasonia* .. .. 2·00 1·60
1256 7 r. *Papilio memnon* .. .. 2·75 2·75
1257 10 r. *Aeropetes tulbaghia* .. .. .. 3·50 3·75
1250/7 .. .. *Set of* 8 10·50 9·50
MS1258 Two sheets, each 135×102 mm. (a) 15 r. *Acraea violae*. (b) 15 r. *Hebomoia leucippe* *Set of* 2 *sheets* 7·00 9·00

220 Isaac Newton experimenting with Spectrum

(Des J. Martin. Litho Questa)

1988 (10 Jan). *Great Scientific Discoveries. T* **220** *and similar multicoloured designs. P* 14.
1259 1 r. 50, Type **220** 60 60
1260 3 r. Euclid composing *Principles of Geometry* (*vert*) .. .. 1·00 1·00
1261 4 r. Mendel formulating theory of Genetic Evolution (*vert*) .. .. 1·25 1·25
1262 5 r. Galileo and moons of Jupiter .. .. 1·50 1·50
1259/62 .. .. *Set of* 4 4·00 4·00
MS1263 102×72 mm. 15 r. "Apollo" lunar module (*vert*) .. .. 3·50 4·00

221 Donald Duck and Weather Satellite

(Des Walt Disney Co. Litho Questa)

1988 (15 Feb). *Space Exploration. T* **221** *and similar multicoloured designs showing Walt Disney cartoon characters. P* $14\times13\frac{1}{2}$ (*horiz*) *or* $13\frac{1}{2}\times14$ (*vert*).
1264 3 l. Type **221** 10 10
1265 4 l. Minnie Mouse and navigation satellite 10 10
1266 5 l. Mickey Mouse's nephews talking via communication satellite 10 10
1267 10 l. Goofy in lunar rover (*vert*) 10 10
1268 20 l. Minnie Mouse delivering pizza to flying saucer (*vert*) 10 10
1269 13 r. Mickey Mouse directing spacecraft docking (*vert*) .. .. 1·60 1·75
1270 14 r. Mickey Mouse and "Voyager 2" .. 1·75 1·90
1264/70 .. .. *Set of* 7 3·25 3·50
MS1271 Two sheets, each 127×102 mm. (a) 15 r. Mickey Mouse at first Moon landing, 1969. (b) 15 r. Mickey Mouse and nephews in space station swimming pool (*vert*) .. *Set of* 2 *sheets* 3·50 4·00

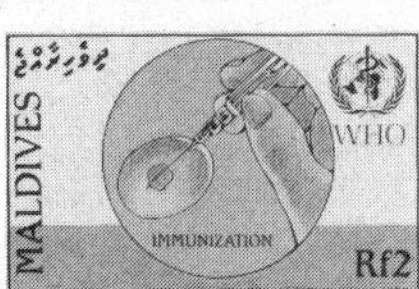

222 Syringe and Bacterium ("Immunization")

(Des Mary Walters. Litho Questa)

1988 (7 Apr). *40th Anniv of World Health Organization. T* **222** *and similar horiz design. Multicoloured. P* 14.
1272 2 r. Type **222** 25 30
1273 4 r. Tap ("Clean Water") 50 55

223 Water Droplet and Atoll **224** Globe, Carrier Pigeon and Letter

(Des I. Rasheed)

1988 (9 May). *World Environment Day* (1987). *T* **223** *and similar multicoloured designs. P* 15.

1274 15 l. Type **223** 10 10
1275 75 l. Coral reef 20 20
1276 2 r. Audubon's Shearwaters in flight .. 60 60
1274/6 .. .. *Set of* 3 80 80
MS1277 105×76 mm. 15 r. Banyan Tree (*vert*) 1·75 2·25

(Litho Questa)

1988 (31 May). *Transport and Telecommunications Decade. T* **224** *and similar horiz designs, each showing central globe. Multicoloured. P* 14.

1278 2 r. Type **224** 40 40
1279 3 r. Dish aerial and girl using telephone 50 50
1280 5 r. Satellite, television, telephone and antenna tower 90 90
1281 10 r. Car, ship and airliner .. .. .. 1·75 2·00
1278/81 .. .. *Set of* 4 3·25 3·50

40TH WEDDING ANNIVERSARY
H.M.QUEEN ELIZABETH II
H.R.H. THE DUKE OF EDINBURGH

(**225**)

226 Discus-throwing

1988 (7 July). *Royal Ruby Wedding. Nos.* 1170/3 *optd with T* **225** *in gold.*

1282 1 r. black and chrome-yellow 20 20
1283 2 r. multicoloured 35 35
1284 12 r. multicoloured .. .. 1·90 2·40
1282/4 .. .. *Set of* 3 2·25 2·75
MS1285 120×85 mm. 15 r. black and grey-brown 2·25 2·50

(Des B. Bundock. Litho Questa)

1988 (16 July). *Olympic Games, Seoul. T* **226** *and similar multicoloured designs. P* 14.

1286 15 l. Type **226** 10 10
1287 2 r. 100 metres race 35 35
1288 4 r. Gymnastics (*horiz*) 65 65
1289 12 r. Three-day equestrian event (*horiz*) 1·90 2·25
1286/9 .. .. *Set of* 4 2·75 3·00
MS1290 106×76 mm. 20 r. Tennis (*horiz*) .. 2·40 2·75

227 Immunization at Clinic

228 Breadfruit

(Des A. DiLorenzo. Litho Questa)

1988 (20 July). *International Year of Shelter for the Homeless. T* **227** *and similar vert designs. Multicoloured. P* 14.

1291 50 l. Type **227** 20 20
1292 3 r. Prefab housing estate 80 80
MS1293 63×105 mm. 15 r. Building site .. 1·75 2·25

(Des G. Watkins. Litho Questa)

1988 (30 July). 10*th Anniv of International Fund for Agricultural Development. T* **228** *and similar multicoloured designs. P* 14.

1294 7 r. Type **228** 85 90
1295 10 r. Mangos (*vert*) .. .. 1·25 1·40
MS1296 103×74 mm. 15 r. Coconut palm, fishing boat and Yellowtail Tuna .. .. 1·75 2·25

(**229**)

230 Pres. Kennedy and Launch of "Apollo" Spacecraft

1988 (1 Dec). *World Aids Day. Nos.* 1272/3 *optd with T* **229**.

1297 2 r. Type **222** 20 25
1298 4 r. Tap ("Clean Water") 45 50

(Des A. Nahigian. Litho Questa)

1989 (13 Feb). 25*th Death Anniv of John F. Kennedy (American statesman). U.S. Space Achievements. T* **230** *and similar vert designs. Multicoloured. P* 14.

1299 5 r. Type **230** 60 65
a. Horiz strip of 4. Nos. 1299/1302 .. 2·10
1300 5 r. Lunar module and astronaut on Moon 60 65
1301 5 r. Astronaut and buggy on Moon .. 60 65
1302 5 r. President Kennedy and spacecraft .. 60 65
1299/1302 .. .. *Set of* 4 2·10 2·40
MS1303 108 × 77 mm. 15 r. President Kennedy making speech .. .. 1·75 2·25

Nos. 1299/1302 were printed together, *se-tenant*, in horizontal strips of 4 throughout the sheet.

J. SCHULT
DDR

(**231**)

ASIA-PACIFIC
TELECOMMUNITY
10 YEARS

(**232**)

1989 (29 Apr). *Olympic Medal Winners, Seoul. Nos.* 1286/90 *optd as T* **231**.

1304 15 l. Type **226** (optd with T **231**) 10 10
1305 2 r. 100 metres race (optd "C. LEWIS USA") 20 25
1306 4 r. Gymnastics (*horiz*) (optd "MEN'S ALL AROUND V. ARTEMOV USSR") .. 45 50
1307 12 r. Three-day equestrian event (*horiz*) (optd "TEAM SHOW JUMPING W. GERMANY") .. .. .. 1·25 1·40
1304/7 .. .. *Set of* 4 1·75 2·00
MS1308 106×76 mm. 20 r. Tennis (*horiz*) (optd "OLYMPIC WINNERS MEN'S SINGLES GOLD M. MECIR CZECH. SILVER T. MAYOTTE USA BRONZE B. GILBERT USA") 2·25 2·40

On No. **MS**1308 the overprint appears on the sheet margin and not the 20 r. stamp.

(Litho Questa)

1989 (20 May). 500*th Birth Anniv of Titian (artist). Vert designs as T* **186a** *of Lesotho showing paintings. Multicoloured. P* 13½×14.

1309 15 l. "Benedetto Varchi" 10 10
1310 1 r. "Portrait of a Young Man" 10 15
1311 2 r. "King Francis I of France" 20 25
1312 5 r. "Pietro Aretino" 55 60
1313 15 r. "The Bravo" .. .. 1·60 1·75
1314 20 r. "The Concert" (detail) .. .. .. 2·25 2·40
1309/14 .. .. *Set of* 6 4·25 4·75
MS1315 Two sheets. (a) 112×96 mm. 20 r. "An Allegory of Prudence" (detail). (b) 96×110 mm. 20 r. "Francesco Maria della Rovere" *Set of* 2 *sheets* 4·50 4·75

1989 (10 July). 10*th Anniv of Asia-Pacific Telecommunity. Nos.* 1279/80 *optd with T* **232** *in silver.*

1316 3 r. Dish aerial and girl using telephone 35 40
1317 5 r. Satellite, television, telephone and antenna tower 55 60

(Litho Questa)

1989 (2 Sept–16 Oct). *Japanese Art. Paintings by Hokusai. Horiz designs as T* **187a** *of Lesotho. Multicoloured. P* 14×13½.

1318 15 l. "Fuji from Hodogaya" 10 10
1319 50 l. "Fuji from Lake Kawaguchi" .. 10 10
1320 1 r. "Fuji from Owari" 10 15
1321 2 r. "Fuji from Tsukudajima in Edo" .. 20 25
1322 4 r. "Fuji from a Teahouse at Yoshida" .. 45 50
1323 6 r. "Fuji from Tagonoura" 65 70
1324 10 r. "Fuji from Mishima-goe" .. .. 1·10 1·25
1325 12 r. "Fuji from the Sumida River in Edo" 1·25 1·40
1318/25 .. .. *Set of* 8 3·50 4·00
MS1326 Two sheets, each 101×77 mm. (a) 18 r. "Fuji from Inume Pass" (2 Sept). (b) 18 r. "Fuji from Fukagawa in Edo" (16 Oct) *Set of* 2 *sheets* 4·00 4·25

Nos. 1318/25 were each printed in sheetlets of 10 containing two horizontal strips of 5 stamps separated by printed labels commemorating Emperor Hirohito.

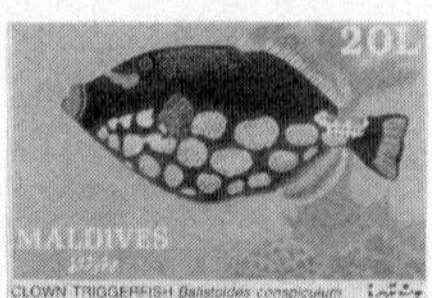

233 Clown Triggerfish

(Des L. Birmingham. Litho Questa)

1989 (16 Oct). *Tropical Fishes. T* **233** *and similar horiz designs. Multicoloured. P* 14.

1327 20 l. Type **233** 10 10
1328 50 l. Bluestripe Snapper 10 10
1329 1 r. Blue Surgeonfish 10 15
1330 2 r. Oriental Sweetlips 20 25
1331 3 r. Wrasse 35 40
1332 8 r. Threadfin Butterflyfish 90 95
1333 10 r. Bicolour Parrotfish .. .. .. 1·10 1·25
1334 12 r. Sabre Squirrelfish .. .. .. 1·25 1·40
1327/34 .. .. *Set of* 8 3·50 4·00
MS1335 Two sheets, each 101×73 mm. (a) 15 r. Butterfly Perch. (b) 15 r. Semicircle Angelfish *Set of* 2 *sheets* 3·25 3·50

234 Goofy, Mickey and Minnie Mouse with Takuri "Type 3", 1907

(Des Walt Disney Co. Litho Questa)

1989 (17 Nov). *"World Stamp Expo '89" International Stamp Exhibition, Washington* (1*st issue*). *T* **234** *and similar horiz designs showing Walt Disney cartoon characters with Japanese cars. Multicoloured. P* 14×13½.

1336 15 l. Type **234** 10 10
1337 50 l. Donald and Daisy Duck in Mitsubishi "Model A", 1917 .. .. .. 10 10
1338 1 r. Goofy in Datsun "Roadstar", 1935 .. 10 15
1339 2 r. Donald and Daisy Duck with Mazda, 1940 .. .. 20 25
1340 4 r. Donald Duck with Nissan "Bluebird 310", 1959 .. .. 45 50
1341 6 r. Donald and Daisy Duck with Subaru "360", 1958 .. .. 65 70
1342 10 r. Mickey Mouse and Pluto in Honda "5800", 1966 .. .. 1·10 1·25
1343 12 r. Mickey Mouse and Goofy in Daihatsu "Fellow", 1966 .. .. .. 1·25 1·40
1336/43 .. .. *Set of* 8 3·50 4·00
MS1344 Two sheets, each 127×102 mm. (a) 20 r. Daisy Duck with Chip n'Dale and Isuzu "Trooper II", 1981 (b) 20 r. Mickey Mouse with tortoise and Toyota "Supra", 1985 .. *Set of* 2 *sheets* 4·50 4·75

(Des Design Element. Litho Questa)

1989 (17 Nov). *"World Stamp Expo '89" International Stamp Exhibition, Washington* (2*nd issue*). *Landmarks of Washington. Sheet* 62×78 *mm containing multicoloured designs as T* **193a** *of Lesotho, but vert. P* 14.

MS1345 8 r. Marine Corps Memorial, Arlington National Cemetery 90 95

235 Lunar Module *Eagle*

(Des W. Hanson Studio. Litho Questa).

1989 (24 Nov). 20*th Anniv of First Manned Landing on Moon. T* **235** *and similar multicoloured designs. P* 14.

1346 1 r. Type **235** 10 15
1347 2 r. Astronaut Aldrin collecting dust samples 20 25
1348 6 r. Aldrin setting up seismometer .. 65 70
1349 10 r. Pres. Nixon congratulating "Apollo 11" astronauts .. .. .. 1·10 1·25
1346/9 .. .. *Set of* 4 1·90 2·10
MS1350 107×75 mm. 18 r. Television picture of Armstrong about to step onto Moon (34×47 *mm*). P 13½×14 .. .. .. 2·00 2·10

236 Jawaharlal Nehru with Mahatma Gandhi

237 Sir William van Horne, Locomotive and Map of Canadian Pacific Railway, 1894

(Des Design Element. Litho B.D.T.)

1989 (20 Dec)–**90**. *Anniversaries and Events. T* **236** *and similar multicoloured designs. P* 14.

1351 20 l. Type **236** (birth centenary) 10 10
1352 50 l. Opium poppies and logo (anti-drugs campaign) (*vert*) 10 10
1353 1 r. William Shakespeare (425th birth anniv) (15.2.90) 10 15
1354 2 r. Storming the Bastille (bicent of French Revolution) (*vert*) (15.2.90) .. 20 25
1355 3 r. "Concorde" (20th anniv of first flight) (15.2.90) 35 40
1356 8 r. George Washington (bicent of inauguration) 90 95
1357 10 r. William Bligh (bicent of mutiny on the *Bounty*) .. .. 1·10 1·25

1358 12 r. Hamburg Harbour (800th anniv) (*vert*) (15.2.90) . . . . 1·25 1·40
1351/8 . . . . *Set of* 8 3·50 4·00
MS1359 Two sheets. (a) 115×85 mm. 18 r. Baseball players (50th anniv of first televised game) (*vert*). (b) 110×80 mm. 18 r. Franz von Taxis (500th anniv of regular European postal services) (*vert*) (15.2.90) . . . . *Set of 2 sheets* 4·00 4·25

(Des A. Fagbohun. Litho Questa)

1989 (26 Dec). *Railway Pioneers. T* **237** *and similar vert designs. Multicoloured. P* 14.
1360 10 l. Type **237** 10 10
1361 25 l. Matthew Murray and Middleton Colliery rack locomotive, 1811 . . 10 10
1362 50 l. Louis Favre and locomotive entering tunnel, 1856 . . . . 10 10
1363 2 r. George Stephenson and *Locomotion*, 1825 . . . . 20 25
1364 6 r. Richard Trevithick and Pen-y-darran locomotive, 1804 . . . . . . 65 70
1365 8 r. George Nagelmackers and "Orient Express" dining car, 1869 . . . . 90 95
1366 10 r. William Jessop and horse-drawn line, 1770 . . . . 1·10 1·25
1367 12 r. Isambard Brunel and G.W.R. train, 1833 . . . . 1·25 1·40
1360/7 . . . . *Set of* 8 3·75 4·25
MS1368 Two sheets, each 71×103 mm. (a) 18 r. George Pullman (inventor of sleeping cars), 1864. (b) 18 r. Rudolf Diesel (inventor of diesel engine), 1892 . . . . . . *Set of 2 sheets* 4·00 4·25

238 Bodu Thakurufaanu Memorial Centre, Utheemu

239 "Louis XVI in Coronation Robes" (Duplesis)

(Litho B.D.T.)

1990 (1 Jan). *25th Anniv of Independence. T* **238** *and similar horiz designs. Multicoloured. P* 14.
1369 20 l. Type **238** 10 10
1370 25 l. Islamic Centre, Malé 10 10
1371 50 l. National flag and logos of international organizations 10 10
1372 2 r. Presidential Palace, Malé 20 25
1373 5 r. National Security Service 55 60
1369/73 . . . . *Set of* 5 80 90
MS1374 128×90 mm. 10 r. National emblem . . 1·10 1·25

(Litho Questa)

1990 (11 Jan). *Bicentenary of French Revolution and "Philexfrance 89" International Stamp Exhibition, Paris. French Paintings. T* **239** *and similar multicoloured designs. P* 13½×14.
1375 15 l. Type **239** 10 10
1376 50 l. "Monsieur Lavoisier and his Wife" (David) 10 10
1377 1 r. "Madame Pastoret" (David) 10 15
1378 2 r. "Oath of Lafayette, 14 July 1790" (anon) 20 25
1379 4 r. "Madame Trudaine" (David) 45 50
1380 6 r. "Chenard celebrating the Liberation of Savoy" (Boilly) 65 70
1381 10 r. "An Officer swears Allegiance to the Constitution" (anon) . . . . . . 1·10 1·25
1382 12 r. "Self Portrait" (David) . . . . . . 1·25 1·40
1375/82 . . . . *Set of* 8 3·50 4·00
MS1383 Two sheets. (a) 104×79 mm. 20 r. "The Oath of the Tennis Court, 20 June 1789" (David) (*horiz*). P 14×13½. (b) 79×104 mm. 20 r. "Rousseau and Symbols of the Revolution" (Jeaurat). P 13½×14 . . . . *Set of 2 sheets* 4·50 4·75

239*a* Donald Duck, Mickey Mouse and Goofy playing Rugby

(Des Walt Disney Co. Litho Questa)

1990 (3 May). *"Stamp World London 90" International Stamp Exhibition. T* **239*a*** *and similar horiz designs showing Walt Disney cartoon characters playing British sports. Multicoloured. P* 14×13½.
1384 15 l. Type **239*a*** 10 10
1385 50 l. Donald Duck and Chip-n-Dale curling 10 10
1386 1 r. Goofy playing polo 10 15
1387 2 r. Mickey Mouse and nephews playing soccer 20 25
1388 4 r. Mickey Mouse playing cricket 45 50
1389 6 r. Minnie and Mickey Mouse at Ascot races 65 70
1390 10 r. Mickey Mouse and Goofy playing tennis . . . . 1·10 1·25
1391 12 r. Donald Duck and Mickey Mouse playing bowls . . . . 1·25 1·40
1384/91 . . . . *Set of* 8 3·50 4·00
MS1392 Two sheets, each 126×101 mm. (a) 20 r. Minnie Mouse fox-hunting. (b) 20 r. Mickey Mouse playing golf . . . . *Set of 2 sheets* 4·50 4·75

240 Silhouettes of Queen Elizabeth II and Queen Victoria

241 Sultan's Tomb

(Des S. Pollard. Litho B.D.T.)

1990 (6 May). *150th Anniv of the Penny Black. T* **240** *and similar horiz designs. P* 15×14.
1393 8 r. black and olive-green 90 95
1394 12 r. black and deep dull blue . . . . . . 1·25 1·40
MS1395 109×84 mm. 18 r. black & yellow-brown 2·00 2·10
Designs:—12 r. As Type **240**, but with position of silhouettes reversed; 18 r. Penny Black.

(Des Young Phillips Studio. Litho Questa)

1990 (8 July). *90th Birthday of Queen Elizabeth the Queen Mother. Vert designs as T* **198*a*** *of Lesotho showing portraits, 1920–29. P* 14.
1396 6 r. brownish blk, brt mag & turquoise-bl 65 70
a. Strip of 3. Nos. 1396/8 . . . . . . 1·75
1397 6 r. brownish blk, brt mag & turquoise-bl 65 70
1398 6 r. brownish blk, brt mag & turquoise-bl 65 70
1396/8 . . . . *Set of* 3 1·75 1·90
MS1399 90×75 mm. 18 r. multicoloured . . 2·00 2·10
Designs:—No. 1396, Lady Elizabeth Bowes-Lyon; No. 1397, Lady Elizabeth Bowes-Lyon wearing headband; No. 1398, Lady Elizabeth Bowes-Lyon leaving for her wedding; No. **MS**1399, Lady Elizabeth Bowes-Lyon wearing wedding dress.
Nos. 1396/8 were printed together, horizontally and vertically *se-tenant*, in sheetlets of 9 (3×3).

(Litho Questa)

1990 (21 July). *Islamic Heritage Year. T* **241** *and similar horiz designs, each black and light cobalt. P* 14.
1400 1 r. Type **241** 10 15
a. Block of 6. Nos. 1400/5 80
1401 1 r. Thakurufaan's Palace 10 15
1402 1 r. Malé Mosque 10 15
1403 2 r. Veranda of Friday Mosque 20 25
1404 2 r. Interior of Friday Mosque 20 25
1405 2 r. Friday Mosque and Monument 20 25
1400/5 . . . . *Set of* 6 80 1·10
Nos. 1400/5 were printed together, *se-tenant*, in blocks of 6 (3×2) within the sheet of 36.

242 Defence of Wake Island, 1941

(Des W. Wright. Litho Questa)

1990 (9 Aug). *50th Anniv of Second World War. T* **242** *and similar horiz designs. Multicoloured. P* 14.
1406 15 l. Type **242** 10 10
1407 25 l. Stilwell's army in Burma, 1944 . . 10 10
1408 50 l. Normandy offensive, 1944 . . . . 10 10
1409 1 r. Capture of Saipan, 1944 . . . . 10 15
1410 2 r. 50, D-Day landings, 1944 . . . . 25 30
1411 3 r. 50, Allied landings in Norway, 1940 40 45
1412 4 r. Lord Mountbatten, Head of Combined Operations, 1943 . . . . 45 50
1413 6 r. Japanese surrender, Tokyo Bay, 1945 65 70
1414 10 r. Potsdam Conference, 1945 . . . . 1·10 1·25
1415 12 r. Allied invasion of Sicily, 1943 . . 1·25 1·40
1406/15 . . . . *Set of* 10 3·75 4·25
MS1416 115×87 mm. 18 r. Atlantic convoy . . 2·00 2·10

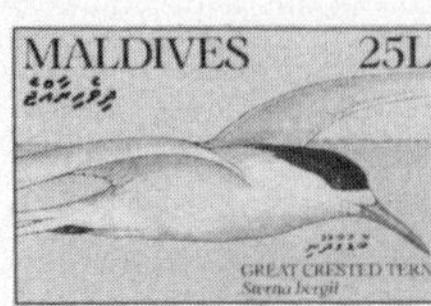

243 Great Crested Tern

(Des Mary Walters. Litho Questa)

1990 (9 Aug). *Birds. T* **243** *and similar horiz designs. Multicoloured. P* 14.
1417 25 l. Type **243** 10 10
1418 50 l. Koel 10 10
1419 1 r. White Tern 10 15
1420 3 r. 50, Cinnamon Bittern 40 45
1421 6 r. Sooty Tern 65 70
1422 8 r. Audubon's Shearwater 90 95
1423 12 r. Common Noddy . . . . 1·25 1·40
1424 15 r. Lesser Frigate Bird . . . . . . 1·60 1·75
1417/24 . . . . *Set of* 8 4·25 4·75
MS1425 Two sheets, each 100×69 mm. (a) 18 r. Grey Heron. (b) 18 r. White-tailed Tropic Bird *Set of 2 sheets* 4·00 4·25

244 Emblem, Dish Aerial and Sailboards

245 *Spathoglottis plicata*

(Litho Questa)

1990 (21 Nov). *Fifth South Asian Association for Regional Co-operation Summit. T* **244** *and similar horiz designs. P* 14.
1426 75 l. black and brown-orange 10 10
1427 3 r. 50, multicoloured 40 45
MS1428 112×82 mm. 20 r. multicoloured . . 2·25 2·50
Designs:—3 r. 50, Flags of member nations; 20 r. Global warming diagram.

(Des Dot Barlowe. Litho Questa)

1990 (9 Dec). *"EXPO '90" International Garden and Greenery Exhibition, Osaka. Flowers. T* **245** *and similar multicoloured designs. P* 14.
1429 20 l. Type **245** 10 10
1430 75 l. *Hippeastrum puniceum* 10 10
1431 2 r. *Tecoma stans* (*horiz*) 20 25
1432 3 r. 50 *Catharanthus roseus* (*horiz*) . . 40 45
1433 10 r. *Ixora coccinea* (*horiz*) . . . . . . 1·10 1·25
1434 12 r. *Clitorea ternatea* (*horiz*) . . . . 1·25 1·40
1435 15 r. *Caesalpinia pulcherrima* . . . . 1·60 1·75
1429/35 . . . . *Set of* 7 4·25 4·75
MS1436 Four sheets, each 111×79 mm. (a) 20 r. *Plumeria obtusa* (*horiz*). (b) 20 r. *Jasminum grandiflorum* (*horiz*). (c) 20 r. *Rosa* sp (*horiz*). (d) 20 r. *Hibiscus tiliaceous* (*horiz*) . . *Set of 4 sheets* 9·00 9·25

246 The Hare and the Tortoise

1990 (11 Dec). *International Literacy Year. T* **246** *and similar multicoloured designs showing Walt Disney cartoon characters illustrating fables by Aesop. P* 14×13½.
1437 15 l. Type **246** 10 10
1438 50 l. The Town Mouse and the Country Mouse 10 10
1439 1 r. The Fox and the Crow 10 15
1440 3 r. 50, The Travellers and the Bear . . 40 45
1441 4 r. The Fox and the Lion 45 50
1442 6 r. The Mice Meeting 65 70
1443 10 r. The Fox and the Goat . . . . . . 1·10 1·25
1444 12 r. The Dog in the Manger . . . . . . 1·25 1·40
1437/44 . . . . *Set of* 8 3·50 4·00
MS1445 Two sheets, each 127×102 mm. (a) 20 r. The Miller, his Son and the Ass (*vert*). (b) 20 r. The Miser's Gold (*vert*). P 13½×14 *Set of 2 sheets* 4·50 4·75

247 East African Class "31" Locomotive

248 Rudd Gullit of Holland

(Des T. Agans. Litho Questa)

1990 (15 Dec). *Steam Railway Locomotives. T* **247** *and similar vert designs. Multicoloured. P* 14.
1446 20 l. Type **247** 10 10
1447 50 l. Sudan Railways Class "Mikado" . . 10 10
1448 1 r. South African Beyer-Garratt Class "GM" 10 15
1449 3 r. Rhodesia Railways Class "7" 35 40
1450 5 r. U.S.A. Central Pacific Class "229" . . 55 60
1451 8 r. U.S.A. Reading Class "415" 90 95
1452 10 r. Canada Porter narrow gauge . . . . 1·10 1·25
1453 12 r. U.S.A. Great Northern Class "515" . . 1·25 1·40
1446/53 . . . . *Set of* 8 4·00 4·25
MS1454 Two sheets, each 90×65 mm. (a) 20 r. 19th-century standard American locomotive. (b) 20 r. East African Railways locomotive No. 5950 *Set of 2 sheets* 4·50 4·75

(Des Young Phillips Studio. Litho Questa)

1990 (27 Dec). *World Cup Football Championship, Italy. T* **248** *and similar multicoloured designs. P* 14.

1455 1 r. Type **248** 10 15
1456 2 r. 50, Paul Gascoigne of England .. 25 30
1457 3 r. 50, Brazilian challenging Argentine player 40 45
1458 5 r. Brazilian taking control of ball .. 55 60
1459 7 r. Italian and Austrian jumping for header 75 80
1460 10 r. Russian being chased by Turkish player .. .. 1·10 1·25
1461 15 r. Andres Brehme of West Germany .. 1·60 1·75
1455/61 .. .. *Set of* 7 4·25 4·75
MS1462 Four sheets, each 77×92 mm. (a) 18 r. Head of an Austrian player (*horiz*). (b) 18 r. Head of a South Korean player (*horiz*). (c) 20 r. Diego Maradonna of Argentina (*horiz*). (d) 20 r. Schilacci of Italy (*horiz*) .. .. *Set of* 4 *sheets* 8·25 8·50

249 Winged Euonymus

250 "Summer" (Rubens)

(Des N. Waldman. Litho Questa)

1991 (29 Jan). *Bonsai Trees and Shrubs. T* **249** *and similar vert designs. Multicoloured. P* 14.

1463 20 l. Type **249** 10 10
1464 50 l. Japanese Black Pine 10 10
1465 1 r. Japanese Five Needle Pine 10 15
1466 3 r. 50, Flowering Quince 40 45
1467 5 r. Chinese Elm 55 60
1468 8 r. Japanese Persimmon 90 95
1469 10 r. Japanese Wisteria .. .. .. 1·10 1·25
1470 12 r. Satsuki Azalea .. .. .. 1·25 1·40
1463/70 .. .. *Set of* 8 4·00 4·50
MS1471 Two sheets, each 89×88 mm. (a) 20 r. Trident Maple. (b) 20 r. Sargent Juniper *Set of* 2 *sheets* 4·50 4·75

(Litho Questa)

1991 (7 Feb). *350th Death Anniv of Rubens. T* **250** *and similar horiz designs. Multicoloured. P* 14×13½.

1472 20 l. Type **250** 10 10
1473 50 l. "Landscape with Rainbow" (detail) .. 10 10
1474 1 r. "Wreck of Aeneas" 10 15
1475 2 r. 50, "Château de Steen" (detail) .. 25 30
1476 3 r. 50, "Landscape with Herd of Cows" .. 40 45
1477 7 r. "Ruins on the Palantine" 75 80
1478 10 r. "Landscape with Peasants and Cows" 1·10 1·25
1479 12 r. "Wagon fording Stream" .. .. 1·25 1·40
1472/9 .. .. *Set of* 8 3·50 4·00
MS1480 Four sheets, each 100×71 mm. (a) 20 r. "Landscape at Sunset". (b) 20 r. "Peasants with Cattle by a Stream". (c) 20 r. "Shepherd with Flock". (d) 20 r. "Wagon in Stream" *Set of* 4 *sheets* 9·00 9·50

251 Greek Messenger from Marathon, 490 BC (2480th anniv)

252 Arctic Iceberg and Maldives Dhoni

(Des W. Wright. Litho Questa)

1991 (11 Mar). *Anniversaries and Events* (1990). *T* **251** *and similar multicoloured designs. P* 14.

1481 50 l. Type **251** 10 10
1482 1 r. Anthony Fokker in early aircraft (birth cent) 10 15
1483 3 r. 50, "Early Bird" satellite (25th anniv) 40 45
1484 7 r. Signing Reunification of Germany agreement (*horiz*) 75 80
1485 8 r. King John signing Magna Carta (775th anniv) 90 95
1486 10 r. Dwight D. Eisenhower (birth cent) .. 1·10 1·25
1487 12 r. Sir Winston Churchill (25th death anniv) .. .. 1·25 1·40
1488 15 r. Pres. Reagan at Berlin Wall (German reunification) (*horiz*) .. .. 1·60 1·75
1481/8 .. .. *Set of* 8 5·50 6·00
MS1489 Two sheets. (a) 180×81 mm. 20 r. German "Ju 88" bomber (50th anniv of Battle of Britain) (*horiz*). (b) 160×73 mm. 20 r. Brandenburg Gate (German reunification) (*horiz*) .. .. .. *Set of* 2 *sheets* 4·50 4·75

(Litho Questa)

1991 (10 Apr). *Global Warming. T* **252** *and similar horiz design. Multicoloured. P* 14.

1490 3 r. 50, Type **252** 40 45
1491 7 r. Antarctic iceberg and *Maldive Trader* (freighter) 75 80

253 S.A.A.R.C. Emblem and Medal

254 Children on Beach

(Litho Questa)

1991 (10 Apr). *Year of the Girl Child. P* 14.

1492 **253** 7 r. multicoloured 75 80

(Litho Questa)

1991 (14 Apr). *Year of the Maldivian Child. Children's Paintings. T* **254** *and similar horiz designs. Multicoloured. P* 14.

1493 3 r. 50, Type **254** 40 45
1494 5 r. Children in a park 55 60
1495 10 r. Hungry child dreaming of food .. 1·10 1·25
1496 25 r. Scuba diver .. .. 2·75 3·00
1493/6 .. .. *Set of* 4 4·25 4·75

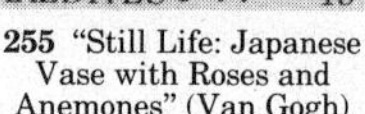

255 "Still Life: Japanese Vase with Roses and Anemones" (Van Gogh)

256 Boy painting

(Litho Walsall)

1991 (6 June). *Death Centenary of Vincent van Gogh* (*artist*) (1990). *T* **255** *and similar multicoloured designs. P* 13½.

1497 15 l. Type **255** 10 10
1498 20 l. "Still Life: Red Poppies and Daisies" 10 10
1499 2 r. "Vincent's Bedroom in Arles" (*horiz*) 20 25
1500 3 r. 50, "The Mulberry Tree" (*horiz*) 40 45
1501 7 r. "Blossoming Chestnut Branches" (*horiz*) 75 80
1502 10 r. "Peasant Couple going to Work" (*horiz*) .. .. 1·10 1·25
1503 12 r. "Still Life: Pink Roses" (*horiz*) .. 1·25 1·50
1504 15 r. "Child with Orange" .. .. 1·60 1·75
1497/1504 .. .. .. *Set of* 8 4·75 5·50
MS1505 Two sheets. (a) 77×101 mm. 25 r. "House in Auvers" (70×94 *mm*). (b) 101×77 mm. 25 r. "The Courtyard of the Hospital at Arles" (94×70 *mm*). Imperf .. .. *Set of* 2 *sheets* 5·50 5·75

(Des D. Miller. Litho Walsall)

1991 (4 July). *65th Birthday of Queen Elizabeth II. Horiz designs as T* **210** *of Lesotho. Multicoloured. P* 14.

1506 2 r. Queen at Trooping the Colour, 1990 20 25
1507 5 r. Queen with Queen Mother and Princess Margaret, 1973 .. .. 55 60
1508 8 r. Queen and Prince Philip in open carriage, 1986 .. .. .. 90 95
1509 12 r. Queen at Royal Estates Ball .. .. 1·25 1·50
1506/9 .. .. *Set of* 4 2·50 3·00
MS1510 68×90 mm. 25 r. Separate photographs of Queen and Prince Philip .. .. .. 2·75 3·00

(Des D. Miller. Litho Walsall)

1991 (4 July). *10th Wedding Anniv of Prince and Princess of Wales. Horiz designs as T* **210** *of Lesotho. Multicoloured. P* 14.

1511 1 r. Prince and Princess skiing, 1986 .. 10 10
1512 3 r. 50, Separate photographs of Prince, Princess and sons 40 45
1513 7 r. Prince Henry in Christmas play and Prince William watching polo .. 75 80
1514 15 r. Princess Diana at Ipswich, 1990, and Prince Charles playing polo .. 1·60 1·75
1511/14 .. .. *Set of* 4 2·50 2·75
MS1515 68×90 mm. 25 r. Prince and Princess of Wales in Hungary, and Princes William and Henry going to school .. .. 2·75 3·00

(Litho Questa)

1991 (25 July). *Hummel Figurines. T* **256** *and similar vert designs. Multicoloured. P* 14.

1516 10 l. Type **256** 10 10
1517 25 l. Boy reading at table 10 10
1518 50 l. Boy with school satchel 10 10
1519 2 r. Girl with basket 20 25
1520 3 r. 50, Boy reading 40 45
1521 8 r. Girl and young child reading .. 90 95
1522 10 r. School girls .. .. 1·10 1·25
1523 25 r. School boys .. .. 2·75 3·00
1516/23 .. .. *Set of* 8 5·00 5·50
MS1524 Two sheets, each 97×197 mm. (a) 5 r. As No. 1519; 5 r. As No. 1520; 5 r. As No. 1521; 5 r. As No. 1522; (b) 8 r. As Type **256**; 8 r. As No. 1517; 8 r. As No. 1518; 8 r. As No. 1523 *Set of* 2 *sheets* 5·75 6·00

257 Class "C 57" Steam Locomotive

(Litho B.D.T.)

1991 (25 Aug). *"Philanippon '91" International Stamp Exhibition, Tokyo. Japanese Steam Locomotives. T* **257** *and similar multicoloured designs. P* 14.

1525 15 l. Type **257** 10 10
1526 25 l. Class "6250" locomotive (*horiz*) .. 10 10
1527 1 r. Class "D 51" locomotive 10 10
1528 3 r. 50, Class "8620" locomotive (*horiz*) .. 40 45
1529 5 r. Class "10" locomotive (*horiz*) .. 55 60
1530 7 r. Class "C 61" locomotive 75 80
1531 10 r. Class "9600" locomotive (*horiz*) .. 1·10 1·25
1532 12 r. Class "D 52" locomotive (*horiz*) .. 1·25 1·50
1525/32 .. .. *Set of* 8 3·75 4·25
MS1533 Two sheets, each 118×80 mm. (a) 20 r. Class "C 56" locomotive (*horiz*). (b) 20 r. Class "1080" locomotive (*horiz*) .. *Set of* 2 *sheets* 4·50 4·75

Malta

Early records of the postal services under the British Occupation are fragmentary, but it is known that an Island Postmaster was appointed in 1802. A British Packet Agency was established in 1806 and it later became customary for the same individual to hold the two appointments together. The inland posts continued to be the responsibility of the local administration, but the overseas mails formed part of the British G.P.O. system.

The stamps of Great Britain were used on overseas mails from September 1857. Previously during the period of the Crimean War letters franked with Great Britain stamps from the Crimea were cancelled at Malta with a wavy line obliterator. Such postmarks are known between April 1855 and September 1856.

The British G.P.O. relinquished control of the overseas posts on 31 December 1884 when Great Britain stamps were replaced by those of Malta.

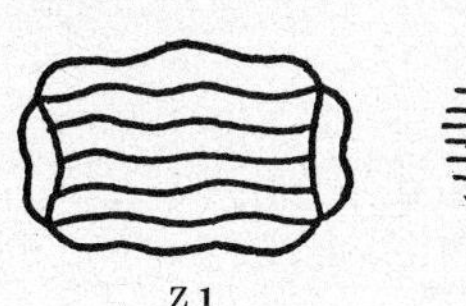

Z 1

Z 2

1855–56. *Stamps of* GREAT BRITAIN *cancelled with wavy lines obliteration, Type* Z **1.**

Z1 1d. red-brown (1854), Die I, *wmk* Small Crown, *perf* 16 .. £800
Z2 1d. red-brown (1855), Die II, *wmk* Small Crown, *perf* 14 .. £800
a. Very blued paper ..
Z3 1d. red-brown (1855), Die II, *wmk* Large Crown, *perf* 16 .. £800
Z3*a* 1d. red-brown (1855), Die II, *wmk* Large Crown, *perf* 14 .. £800
Z4 2d. blue (1855), *wmk* Large Crown, *perf* 14
Plate No. 5 ..
Z5 6d. (1854) embossed .. £4000
Z6 1s. (1847) embossed .. £4500

It is now established that this obliterator was sent to Malta and used on mail in transit emanating from the Crimea.

1857 (18 Aug)**–59.** *Stamps of* GREAT BRITAIN *cancelled* "M", *Type* Z **2.**

Z 7 1d. red-brown (1841) .. £1000
Z 8 1d. red-brown, Die I, *wmk* Small Crown, *perf* 16 .. 75·00
Z 9 1d. red-brown, Die II, *wmk* Small Crown, *perf* 16 £800
Z10 1d. red-brown, Die II (1855), *wmk* Small Crown, *perf* 14 .. £170
Z11 1d. red-brown, Die II (1855), *wmk* Large Crown, *perf* 14 .. 65·00
Z12 1d. rose-red (1857), *wmk* Large Crown, *perf* 14 .. 17·00
Z13 2d. blue (1841), *imperf* .. £2500
Z14 2d. blue (1854) *wmk* Small Crown, *perf* 16 .. £600
Plate No. 4.
Z15 2d. blue (1855), *wmk* Large Crown, *perf* 14 *From* 45·00
Plate Nos. 5, 6.
Z16 2d. blue (1858), *wmk* Large Crown, *perf* 16 .. £225
Plate No. 6.
Z17 2d. blue (1858) (Plate Nos. 7, 8, 9) .. *From* 35·00
Z18 4d. rose (1857) .. 35·00
a. Thick glazed paper .. £170
Z19 6d. violet (1854), embossed .. £1600
Z20 6d. lilac (1856) .. 40·00
a. Thick paper .. £190
Z21 6d. lilac (1856) (blued *paper*) .. £850
Z22 1s. green (1856) .. £110
a. Thick paper .. £160

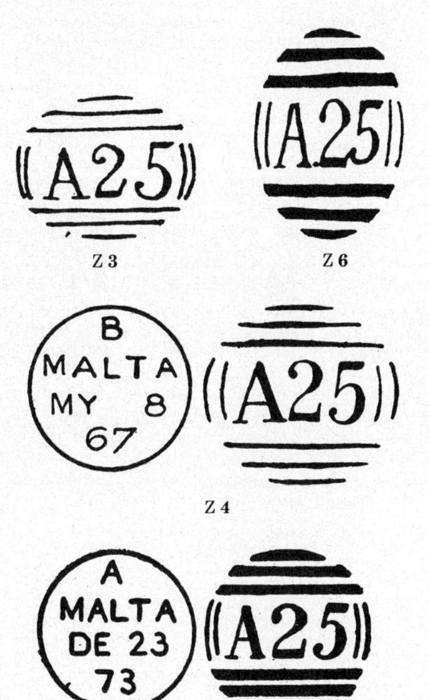

Z 3 Z 6

Z 4

Z 5

Z 7

1859–84. *Stamps of* GREAT BRITAIN *cancelled* "A 25" *as in Types* Z **3/7.**

Z23 ½d. rose-red (1870–79) .. *From* 18·00
Plate Nos. 4, 5, 6, 8, 9, 10, 11, 12, 13, 14, 15, 19, 20.
Z24 1d. red-brown (1841), *imperf* .. £2000
Z25 1d. red-brown (1854), *wmk* Small Crown, *perf* 16 £225
Z26 1d. red-brown (1855), *wmk* Large Crown, *perf* 14 55·00
Z27 1d. rose-red (1857), *wmk* Large Crown, *perf* 14 .. 7·50
Z28 1d. rose-red (1861), Alphabet IV .. £450
Z30 1d. rose-red (1864–79) .. *From* 12·00
Plate Nos. 71, 72, 73, 74, 76, 78, 79, 80, 81, 82, 83, 84, 85, 86, 87, 88, 89, 90, 91, 92, 93, 94, 95, 96, 97, 98, 99, 100, 101, 102, 103, 104, 105, 106, 107, 108, 109, 110, 111, 112, 113, 114, 115, 116, 117, 118, 119, 120, 121, 122, 123, 124, 125, 127, 129, 130, 131, 132, 133, 134, 135, 136, 137, 138, 139, 140, 141, 142, 143, 144, 145, 146, 147, 148, 149, 150, 151, 152, 153, 154, 155, 156, 157, 158, 159, 160, 161, 162, 163, 164, 165, 166, 167, 168, 169, 170, 171, 172, 173, 174, 175, 176, 177, 178, 179, 180, 181, 182, 183, 184, 185, 186, 187, 188, 189, 190, 191, 192, 193, 194, 195, 196, 197, 198, 199, 200, 201, 202, 203, 204, 205, 206, 207, 208, 209, 210, 211, 212, 213, 214, 215, 216, 217, 218, 219, 220, 221, 222, 223, 224.
Z31 1½d. lake-red (1870–79) (Plate Nos. 1, 3) .. *From* £275
Z32 2d. blue (1841), *imperf* .. £3500
Z33 2d. blue (1855) *wmk* Large Crown *perf* 14 .. 55·00
Z34 2d. blue (1858–69) .. *From* 15·00
Plate Nos. 7, 8, 9, 12, 13, 14, 15.
Z35 2½d. rosy mauve (1875) (blued *paper*) .. *From* 50·00
Plate Nos. 1, 2.
Z36 2½d. rosy mauve (1875–76) (Plate Nos. 1, 2, 3) *From* 27·00
Z37 2½d. rosy mauve (*Error of Lettering*) .. £2250
Z38 2½d. rosy mauve (1876–79) .. *From* 15·00
Plate Nos. 3, 4, 5, 6, 7, 8, 9, 10, 11, 12, 13, 14, 15, 16, 17.
Z39 2½d. blue (1880–81) (Plate Nos. 17, 18, 19, 20) *From* 9·00
Z40 2½d. blue (1881) (Plate Nos. 21, 22, 23) .. *From* 6·00
Z41 3d. carmine-rose (1862) .. £100
Z42 3d. rose (1865) (Plate No. 4) .. 50·00
Z43 3d. rose (1867–73) .. *From* 18·00
Plate Nos. 4, 5, 6, 7, 8, 9, 10.
Z44 3d. rose (1873–76) .. *From* 22·00
Plate Nos. 11, 12, 14, 15, 16, 17, 18, 19, 20.
Z45 3d. rose (1881) (Plate Nos. 20, 21) .. *From* £750
Z46 3d. on 3d. lilac (1883) .. £450
Z47 4d. rose (or rose-carmine) (1857) .. 27·00
a. Thick glazed paper .. £110
Z48 4d. red (1862) (Plate Nos. 3, 4) .. *From* 30·00
Z49 4d. vermilion (1865–73) .. *From* 15·00
Plate Nos. 7, 8, 9, 10, 11, 12, 13, 14.
Z50 4d. vermilion (1876) (Plate No. 15) .. £160
Z51 4d. sage-green (1877) (Plate Nos. 15, 16) .. *From* 85·00
Z52 4d. grey-brown (1880) *wmk* Large Garter .. £120
Plate No. 17.
Z53 4d. grey-brown (1880) *wmk* Crown .. *From* 25·00
Plate Nos. 17, 18.
Z54 6d. violet (1854), embossed .. £1500
Z55 6d. lilac (1856) .. 35·00
a. Thick paper ..
Z56 6d. lilac (1862) (Plate Nos. 3, 4) .. *From* 30·00
Z57 6d. lilac (1865–67) (Plate Nos. 5, 6) .. *From* 28·00
Z58 6d. lilac (1865–67) (*Wmk error*) .. £1200
Z59 6d. lilac (1867) (Plate No. 6) .. 32·00
Z60 6d. violet (1867–70) (Plate Nos. 6, 8, 9) .. *From* 25·00
Z61 6d. buff (1872–73) (Plate Nos. 11, 12) .. *From* £100
Z62 6d. chestnut (1872) (Plate No. 11) .. 30·00
Z63 6d. grey (1873) (Plate No. 12) .. 70·00
Z64 6d. grey (1873–80) .. *From* 20·00
Plate Nos. 13, 14, 15, 16, 17.
Z65 6d. grey (1881–82) (Plate Nos. 17, 18) .. *From* 26·00
Z66 6d. on 6d. lilac (1883) .. £110
Z67 8d. orange (1876) .. £250
Z68 9d. straw (1862) .. £475
Z69 9d. bistre (1862) .. £475
Z70 9d. straw (1865) .. £475
Z71 9d. straw (1867) .. £600
Z72 10d. red-brown (1867) .. £130
Z73 1s. (1847), embossed .. £1500
Z74 1s. green (1856) .. 70·00
Z75 1s. green (1856) (thick *paper*) .. £250
Z76 1s. green (1862) .. 60·00
Z77 1s. green ("K" *variety*) .. £2250
Z78 1s. green (1865) (Plate No. 4) .. 35·00
Z79 1s. green (1867–73) (Plate Nos. 4, 5, 6, 7) .. *From* 10·00
Z80 1s. green (1873–77) .. *From* 30·00
Plate Nos. 8, 9, 10, 11, 12, 13.
Z81 1s. orange-brown (1880) (Plate No. 13) .. £225
Z82 1s. orange-brown (1881) (Plate Nos. 13, 14) *From* 45·00
Z83 2s. blue (*shades*) (1867) .. *From* 90·00
Z84 2s. brown (1880) .. £1700
Z85 5s. rose (1867–74) (Plate Nos. 1, 2) .. *From* £300
Z86 5s. rose (1882) (Plate No. 4), blue *paper* .. £1100
Z87 5s. rose (1882) (Plate No. 4), white *paper* .. £1000
Z88 10s. grey-green (1878) .. £1600

1880.

Z89 ½d. deep green .. 8·50
Z90 ½d. pale green .. 8·50
Z91 1d. Venetian red .. 7·50
Z92 1½d. Venetian red .. £250
Z93 2d. pale rose .. 30·00
Z94 2d. deep rose .. 30·00
Z95 5d. indigo .. 50·00

1881.

Z96 1d. lilac (14 *dots*) .. 15·00
Z97 1d. lilac (16 *dots*) .. 6·00

1883–4.

Z 98–Z102 ½d. slate-blue; 1½d., 2d, 2½d., 3d. *From* 8·50
Z103–Z107 4d. 5d., 6d., 9d., 1s. .. *From* 60·00
Z108 5s. rose (blued *paper*) .. £1000
Z109 5s. rose (white *paper*) .. £750

POSTAL FISCALS

Z110 1d. purple (1871) *wmk* Anchor .. £750
Z111 1d. purple (1881) *wmk* Orb .. £600

PRICES FOR STAMPS ON COVER TO 1945

Nos. 1/3	*from* × 4
Nos. 4/19	*from* × 5
Nos. 20/9	*from* × 6
No. 30	—
Nos. 31/3	*from* × 4
Nos. 34/7	*from* × 10
Nos. 38/88	*from* × 4
Nos. 92/3	*from* × 5
Nos. 97/103	*from* × 3
Nos. 104/5	—
Nos. 106/20	*from* × 3
No. 121	—
Nos. 122/38	*from* × 3
Nos. 139/40	—
Nos. 141/72	*from* × 4
Nos. 173/209	*from* × 3
Nos. 210/31	*from* × 2
Nos. D1/10	*from* × 30
Nos. D11/20	*from* × 15

CROWN COLONY

PRINTERS. Nos. 1/156. Printed by De La Rue; typographed *except where otherwise stated.*

1

Type 1

The first Government local post was established on 10 June 1853 and, as an experiment, mail was carried free of charge. During 1859 the Council of Government decided that a rate of ½d. per ½ ounce should be charged for this service and stamps in Type I were ordered for this purpose. Both the new rate and the stamps were introduced on 1 December 1860. Until 1 January 1885 the ½d. stamps were intended for the local service only; mail for abroad being handled by the British Post Office on Malta, using G.B. stamps.

Specialists now recognise 29 printings in shades of yellow and one in green during the period to 1884. These printings can be linked to the changes in watermark and perforation as follows:

Ptg 1—Blued paper without wmk. P 14.
Ptgs 2 and 3—White paper without wmk. P 14.
Ptgs 4 to 9, 11, 13 to 19, 22 to 24—Crown CC wmk. P 14.
Ptg 10—Crown CC wmk. P 12½ (rough).
Ptg 12—Crown CC wmk. P 12½ (clean-cut).
Ptgs 20 and 21—Crown CC wmk. P 14 × 12½.
Ptgs 25 to 28, 30—Crown CA wmk. P 14.
Ptg 29—In green (No. 20).

1860 (1 Dec)**–63.** *No wmk. P* 14. (*a*) *Blued paper.*

1 ½d. buff (1.12.60) .. £850 £425

(*b*) *Thin, hard white paper*

2 ½d. brown-orange (11.61) .. £750 £325
3 ½d. buff (1.63) .. £550 £275
a. Pale buff .. £550 £275

No. 1 is printed in fugitive ink. It is known imperforate but was not issued in that state (*Price* £9000 *unused*).

The printing on No. 2 gives a very blurred and muddy impression; on Nos. 3/3*a* the impression is clear.

Specks of carmine can often be detected with a magnifying glass on Nos. 2/3*a*, and also exist on No. 4. Examples also exist on which parts of the design are in pure rose, due to defective mixing of the ink.

(Des E. Fuchs)

1863–81. *Wmk Crown CC.* (*a*) *P* 14.

4 ½d. buff (6.63) .. 75·00 45·00
5 ½d. bright orange (11.64) .. £225 95·00
6 ½d. orange-brown (4.67) .. £275 70·00
7 ½d. dull orange (4.70) .. £140 55·00
8 ½d. orange-buff (5.72) .. £130 55·00
9 ½d. golden yellow (aniline) (10.74) .. £250 £300
10 ½d. yellow-buff (9.75) .. 60·00 55·00
11 ½d. pale buff (3.77) .. £110 55·00
12 ½d. bright orange-yellow (4.80) .. 90·00 60·00
13 ½d. yellow (4.81) .. 70·00 45·00

(*b*) *P* 12½ *rough* (*No.* 14) *or clean-cut* (*No.* 15)

14 ½d. buff-brown (11.68) .. 80·00 65·00
a. Imperf between (vert pair) ..
15 ½d. yellow-orange (5.71) .. £225 £150

(*c*) *P* 14 × 12½

16 ½d. yellow-buff (7.78) .. £150 85·00
a. Perf 12½ × 14 ..
17 ½d. yellow (2.79) .. £150 85·00

Examples of No. 4 from the 1863 printing are on thin, surfaced paper; later printings in the same shade were on unsurfaced paper.

The ink used for No. 5 is mineral and, unlike that on No. 9, does not stain the paper.

Some variations of shade on No. 6 may be described as chestnut. The ink of No. 6 is clear and never muddy, although some examples are over-inked. Deeper shades of No. 4, with which examples of No. 6 might be confused, have muddy ink.

1882 (Mar)–**84**. *Wmk Crown CA. P* 14.
18 ½d. orange-yellow .. .. 19·00 35·00
19 ½d. red-orange (9.84).. .. .. .. 17·00 35·00

MALTA ONE PENNY
2

MALTA TWO PENCE
3

MALTA TWO PENCE HALFPENNY
4

MALTA FIVE SHILLINGS
5

1885 (1 Jan)–**90**. *Wmk Crown CA. P* 14.
20 **1** ½d. green .. .. 1·25 35
21 **2** 1d. rose .. .. 65·00 25·00
22 1d. carmine (*shades*) (1890) .. .. 1·75 35
23 **3** 2d. grey .. .. 3·75 1·25
24 **4** 2½d. dull blue .. .. 26·00 90
25 2½d. bright blue .. .. 26·00 90
26 2½d. ultramarine .. .. 26·00 90
27 **3** 4d. brown .. .. 8·50 3·00
a. Imperf (pair) £3750 £4000
28 1s. violet .. .. 28·00 9·00
29 1s. pale violet (1890) .. .. .. 45·00 15·00
20/29 .. .. *Set of* 6 60·00 14·00
20/28 Optd "Specimen" .. .. *Set of* 6 £2000

Although not valid for postage until 1 January 1885 these stamps were available at the G.P.O., Valletta from 27 December 1884.

Three unused examples of the ½d. green, No. 20, are known line perforated 12. It is believed that these originated from proof books, the stamp not being issued for use with this perforation.

1886 (1 Jan). *Wmk Crown CC. P* 14.
30 **5** 5s. rose (Optd S. £450) .. .. .. £110 80·00

6 Harbour of Valletta

7 Gozo Fishing Boat

8 Galley of Knights of St. John

9 Emblematic figure of Malta

10 Shipwreck of St. Paul

(T **6/10** recess)

1899 (4 Feb)–**1901**. *P* 14. (*a*) *Wmk Crown CA* (*sideways on* ¼*d*).
31 **6** ¼d. brown (4.1.01) .. .. 1·75 1·50
a. Red-brown 90 40
32 **7** 4½d. sepia .. .. 11·00 8·50
33 **8** 5d. vermilion .. .. 25·00 13·00

(*b*) *Wmk Crown CC*
34 **9** 2s. 6d. olive-grey .. .. .. 32·00 12·00
35 **10** 10s. blue-black .. .. 75·00 60·00
31/5 .. .. *Set of* 5 £130 85·00
31/5 Optd "Specimen" .. .. *Set of* 5 £250

One Penny
(11)

MALTA HALFPENNY
12

1902 (4 July). *Nos. 24 and 25 surch locally at Govt Ptg Office with T* **11**.
36 1d. on 2½d. dull blue (Optd S. £70).. .. 40 65
a. Surch double .. .. — £3250
b. "One Pnney" (R. 9/2) .. .. 27·00 50·00
ba. Surch double, with "One Pnney" ..
37 1d. on 2½d. bright blue 40 65
a. "One Pnney" (R. 9/2) .. .. 27·00 50·00

(Des E. Fuchs)

1903 (12 Mar)–**4**. *Wmk Crown CA. P* 14.
38 **12** ½d. green .. .. 3·00 10
39 1d. black and red (7.5.03) .. .. 7·50 10
40 2d. purple and grey .. .. .. 13·00 6·00
41 2½d. maroon and blue (9.03) .. .. 13·00 2·00
42 **12** 3d. grey and purple (26.3.03) 80 50
43 4d. black and brown (19.5.04) .. .. 24·00 11·00
44 1s. grey and violet (6.4.03) .. .. 13·00 6·00
38/44 .. .. *Set of* 7 65·00 23·00
38/44 Optd "Specimen" .. .. *Set of* 7 £130

1904–**14**. *Wmk Mult Crown CA* (*sideways on* ¼*d.*). *P* 14.
45 **6** ¼d. red-brown (10.10.05) 75 15
a. Deep brown (2.4.10*) 75 10
47 **12** ½d. green (6.11.04) .. .. .. 2·75 25
a. Deep green (1909) .. .. .. 1·50 10
48 1d. black and red (24.4.05) .. .. 4·50 10
49 1d. red (2.4.07) 80 10
50 2d. purple and grey (22.2.05) .. .. 4·50 45
51 2d. grey (4.10.11) .. .. .. 1·25 3·25
52 2½d. maroon and blue (10.04) .. .. 9·00 40
53 2½d. bright blue (15.1.11) .. .. 4·00 1·25
54 4d. black and brown (1.4.06) .. .. 8·00 5·00
55 4d. black and red/*yellow* (21.11.11) .. 3·50 3·00
57 **7** 4½d. brown (27.2.05) .. .. .. 17·00 5·50
58 4½d. orange (2.8.12*) .. .. .. 3·00 3·25
59 **8** 5d. vermilion (20.2.05) .. .. .. 20·00 3·75
60 5d. pale sage-green (1909) .. .. 3·00 3·25
a. Deep sage-green (1914) .. .. 9·50 14·00
61 **12** 1s. grey and violet (14.12.04) .. .. 42·00 1·75
62 1s. black/*green* (15.3.11) .. .. 6·00 2·00
63 5s. green and red/*yellow* (22.3.11) .. 60·00 65·00
45/63 .. .. *Set of* 17 £160 90·00
45*a*, 47*a*, 49, 51, 53, 55, 58, 60, 62,
63 Optd "Specimen" .. .. *Set of* 10 £350

*These are the earliest known dates of use.

13

14

15

1914–**21**. *Wmk Mult Crown CA. Ordinary paper* (¼*d. to* 2½*d.*, 2*s.* 6*d.*) *or chalk-surfaced paper* (*others*). *P* 14.
69 **13** ¼d. brown (2.1.14) 30 10
a. Deep brown (1919) 30 30
71 ½d. green (20.1.14) .. .. .. 1·25 10
aa. Wmk sideways .. .. .. † £3250
a. Deep green (1919) 60 15
73 1d. carmine-red (15.4.14) 60 10
a. Scarlet (1915) .. .. .. 1·25 30
75 2d. grey (12.8.14) .. .. .. 4·50 2·50
a. Deep slate (1919) .. .. .. 8·00 9·00
77 2½d. bright blue (11.3.14) 70 20
78 **14** 3d. purple/*yellow* (1.5.20) .. .. 2·50 5·00
a. On orange-buff .. .. .. 15·00 28·00
79 **6** 4d. black (21.8.15) .. .. .. 10·00 2·50
a. Grey-black (28.10.16) .. .. 18·00 7·50
80 **13** 6d. dull and bright purple (10.3.14) .. 7·00 11·00
a. Dull purple and magenta (1918) .. 8·00 10·00
81 **14** 1s. black/*green* (*white back*) (2.1.14) .. 8·00 17·00
a. On green, green back (Optd S. £45) (1915) .. .. 10·00 13·00
ab. Wmk sideways .. .. .. † £1800
b. On blue-green, olive back (1918) .. 11·00 16·00
c. On emerald surface (1920) .. .. 8·50 17·00
d. On emerald back (1921) .. .. 21·00 29·00
86 **15** 2s. purple and bright blue/*blue* (15.4.14) 50·00 28·00
a. Break in scroll £180
b. Broken crown and scroll £180
c. Dull purple and blue/blue (1921) .. 50·00 40·00
ca. Break in scroll £170
cb. Broken crown and scroll £170
87 **9** 2s. 6d. olive-green (1919) .. .. 45·00 65·00
a. Olive-grey (1920) .. .. .. 45·00 70·00
88 **15** 5s. green and red/*yellow* (21.3.17) .. 70·00 85·00
a. Break in scroll £250
b. Broken crown and scroll £250
69/88 .. .. *Set of* 12 £170 £190
69/88 (*excl* 87) Optd "Specimen" .. *Set of* 11 £450

The design of Nos. 79/*a* differs in various details from that of Type **6**.

We have only seen one copy of No. 71aa; it is in used condition.

A 3d. purple on yellow on white back, Type **14**, was prepared for use but not issued. It exists overprinted "Specimen" (*Price* £275).

For illustrations of the varieties on Nos. 86 and 88 see above No. 58 of Leeward Islands.

WAR TAX
(16)

17

18

1917–**18**. *Optd with T* **16**, *by De La Rue*.
92 **13** ½d. deep green (14.12.17*) 20 15
93 **12** 3d. grey and purple (15.2.18*) .. .. 1·75 6·50
92/3 Optd "Specimen" .. .. *Set of* 2 £130

*These are the earliest known dates of use.

(T **17** recess)

1919 (6 Mar). *Wmk Mult Crown CA. P* 14.
96 **17** 10s. black (Optd S. £750) £3000 £3500

Dark flaw on scroll (R. 2/4 1st state)

Lines omitted from scroll (R. 2/4 2nd state)

1921 (16 Feb)–**22**. *Wmk Mult Script CA. Chalk-surfaced paper* (*6d., 2s.*) *or ordinary paper* (*others*). *P* 14.
97 **13** ¼d. brown (12.1.22) .. .. .. 40 20·00
98 ½d. green (19.1.22) .. .. .. 90 15·00
99 1d. scarlet (24.12.21) 40 65
100 **18** 2d. grey .. .. 2·50 80
101 **13** 2½d. bright blue (15.1.22) .. .. 2·75 16·00
102 6d. dull purple and brt purple (19.1.22) 24·00 45·00
103 **15** 2s. purple and blue/*blue* (19.1.22) .. 60·00 £160
a. Break in scroll £190
b. Broken crown and scroll £190
c. Dark flaw on scroll £1500
d. Lines omitted from scroll £250
104 **17** 10s. black (19.1.22) £300 £475
97/104 .. .. *Set of* 8 £350 £650
97/104 Optd "Specimen" .. .. *Set of* 8 £450

For illustrations of other varieties on No. 103 see above No. 58 of Leeward Islands.

SELF-GOVERNMENT
(19)

SELF-GOVERNMENT
(20)

1922 (12 Jan–Apr). *Optd with T* **19** *or T* **20** (*large stamps*), *at Govt Printing Office, Valletta.* (*a*) *On No.* 35. *Wmk Crown CC.*
105 **10** 10s. blue-black (R.) £170 £275

(*b*) *On Nos.* 71, 77, 78*a*, 80, 81*d*, 86*c*, 87*a and* 88. *Wmk Mult Crown CA*
106 **13** ½d. green 20 40
107 2½d. bright blue .. .. .. 4·50 15·00
108 **14** 3d. purple/*orange-buff* .. .. 1·25 9·50
109 **13** 6d. dull and bright purple .. .. 1·25 9·50
110 **14** 1s. black/*emerald* .. .. .. 2·50 8·00
111 **15** 2s. dull purple and blue/*blue* (R.) .. £200 £325
a. Break in scroll £550
b. Broken crown and scroll £550
112 **9** 2s. 6d. olive-grey .. .. .. 17·00 27·00
113 **15** 5s. green and red/*yellow* .. .. 50·00 75·00
a. Break in scroll £180
b. Broken crown and scroll £180
c. Lines omitted from scroll £180
106/13 .. .. *Set of* 8 £250 £425

(*c*) *On Nos.* 97/104. *Wmk Mult Script CA*
114 **13** ¼d. brown 10 20
115 ½d. green (29.4) .. .. .. 60 3·00
116 1d. scarlet 20 15
117 **18** 2d. grey 80 45
118 **13** 2½d. bright blue (15.1) 30 45
119 6d. dull and bright purple (19.4) .. 6·00 16·00
120 **15** 2s. purple and blue/*blue* (R.) (25.1) .. 35·00 70·00
a. Break in scroll £130
b. Broken crown and scroll £130
c. Lines omitted from scroll £150
121 **17** 10s. black (R.) (9.3) £100 £150
114/21 .. .. *Set of* 8 £130 £200

One Farthing
(21)

22

23

1922 (15 Apr). *No.* 100 *surch with T* **21**, *at Govt Printing Office, Valletta.*
122 **18** ¼d. on 2d. grey.. .. .. .. 15 25

(Des C. Dingli (T **22**) and G. Vella (**23**))

1922 (1 Aug)–**26**. *Wmk Mult Script CA* (*sideways on T* **22**, *except No.* 140). *P* 14. (*a*) *Typo. Chalk-surfaced paper.*
123 **22** ¼d. brown (22.8.22) 40 45
a. Chocolate-brown 30 15
124 ½d. green 55 10
125 1d. orange and purple .. .. .. 1·25 15
126 1d. bright violet (25.4.24) 90 35
127 1½d. brown-red (1.10.23) .. .. 1·00 10
128 2d. bistre-brown and turquoise (28.8.22) 55 20
129 2½d. ultramarine (16.2.26) .. .. 1·00 4·50
130 3d. cobalt (28.8.22) .. .. .. 1·75 50
a. Bright ultramarine .. .. .. 1·75 50
131 3d. black/*yellow* (16.2.26) .. .. 1·00 6·50

132	22	4d. yellow and bright blue (28.8.22)	1·25	1·60
133		6d. olive-green and reddish violet	1·75	1·25
134	23	1s. indigo and sepia	3·75	2·50
135		2s. brown and blue	5·50	8·50
136		2s. 6d. brt magenta & black (28.8.22)	7·00	8·50
137		5s. orange-yell & brt ultram (28.8.22)	15·00	25·00
138		10s. slate-grey and brown (28.8.22)	45·00	80·00
		(b) Recess		
139	22	£1 black and carmine-red (28.8.22)	£100	£190
140		£1 black and bright carmine (14.5.25)	£100	£190
123/39		*Set of* 17	£160	£300
123/39 Optd "Specimen"		*Set of* 17	£500	

No. 139 has the watermark sideways and No. 140 has it upright.

Two pence halfpenny (24)

POSTAGE (25)

1925. *Surch with T* **24**, *at Govt Printing Office, Valletta.*

141	22	2½d. on 3d. cobalt (3 Dec)	30	1·00
142		2½d. on 3d. bright ultramarine (9 Dec)	40	1·00

1926 (1 April). *Optd with T* **25**, *at Govt Printing Office, Valletta.*

143	22	¼d. brown	15	80
144		½d. green	15	15
145		1d. bright violet	40	25
146		1½d. brown-red	45	25
147		2d. bistre-brown and turquoise	30	20
148		2½d. ultramarine	55	40
149		3d. black/*yellow*	30	50
		a. Opt inverted	£190	£450
150		4d. yellow and bright blue	3·00	6·50
151		6d. olive-green and violet	1·50	1·40
152	23	1s. indigo and sepia	4·50	7·00
153		2s. brown and blue	35·00	80·00
154		2s. 6d. bright magenta and black	9·00	22·00
155		5s. orange-yellow & brt ultramarine	8·00	25·00
156		10s. slate-grey and brown	6·00	14·00
143/156		*Set of* 14	60·00	£140

26

27 Valletta Harbour

28 St. Publius

33 St. Paul

(T 26 typo, others recess Waterlow)

1926 (6 Apr)–**27.** *T* **26/8, 33** *and similar designs. Inscr* "POSTAGE". *Wmk Mult Script CA. P* 15 × 14 (*T* **26**) *or* 12½ (*others*).

157	26	¼d. brown	20	15
158		½d. yellow-green (5.8.26)	30	15
159		1d. rose-red (1.4.27)	40	40
160		1½d. chestnut (7.10.26)	60	10
161		2d. greenish grey (1.4.27)	2·25	5·50
162		2½d. blue (1.4.27)	2·50	20
162*a*		3d. violet (1.4.27)	2·50	1·50
163		4d. black and red	2·75	7·00
164		4½d. lavender and ochre	2·50	2·50
165		6d. violet and scarlet (5.5.26)	2·50	2·00
166	27	1s. black	3·00	2·25
167	28	1s. 6d. black and green	5·00	9·00
168	–	2s. black and purple	5·50	13·00
169	–	2s. 6d. black and vermilion	10·00	27·00
170	–	3s. black and blue	13·00	25·00
171	–	5s. black and green (5.5.26)	18·00	38·00
172	33	10s. black and carmine (9.2.27)	55·00	85·00
157/72		*Set of* 17	£110	£190
157/72 Optd "Specimen"		*Set of* 17	£325	

Designs: *Vert*—2s. 6d. Gozo fishing boat; 3s. Neptune; *Horiz*—2s. Mdina (Notabile); 5s. Neolithic temple, Mnajdra.

AIR MAIL (34)

POSTAGE AND REVENUE (35)

POSTAGE AND REVENUE. (36)

1928 (1 Apr). *Air. Optd with T* **34**.

173	26	6d. violet and scarlet	1·75	1·25

1928 (1 Oct–5 Dec). *As Nos.* 157/72, *optd.*

174	35	¼d. brown	30	10
175		½d. yellow-green	30	10
176		1d. rose-red	1·50	1·25
177		1d. chestnut (5.12.28)	2·50	10
178		1½d. chestnut	1·00	30
179		1½d. rose-red (5.12.28)	2·75	10
180		2d. greenish grey	3·25	8·00
181		2½d. blue	1·25	10
182		3d. violet	1·25	30
183		4d. black and red	1·25	1·00
184	35	4½d. lavender and ochre	2·25	1·50
185		6d. violet and scarlet	2·25	1·00
186	36	1s. black (R.)	2·25	2·00
187		1s. 6d. black and green (R.)	5·00	9·00
188		2s. black and purple (R.)	17·00	30·00
189		2s. 6d. black and vermilion (R.)	13·00	23·00
190		3s. black and blue (R.)	17·00	30·00
191		5s. black and green (R.)	26·00	60·00
192		10s. black and carmine (R.)	50·00	85·00
174/92		*Set of* 19	£120	£225
174/92 Optd "Specimen"		*Set of* 19	£325	

1930 (20 Oct). *As Nos.* 157/172, *but inscr* "POSTAGE (&) REVENUE".

193	¼d. brown	30	10
194	½d. yellow-green	30	10
195	1d. chestnut	30	10
196	1½d. rose-red	50	10
197	2d. greenish grey	75	20
198	2½d. blue	1·50	10
199	3d. violet	1·50	20
200	4d. black and red	1·25	2·25
201	4½d. lavender and ochre	1·75	1·50
202	6d. violet and scarlet	1·25	75
203	1s. black	4·00	8·00
204	1s. 6d. black and green	5·00	12·00
205	2s. black and purple	6·50	15·00
206	2s. 6d. black and vermilion	13·00	35·00
207	3s. black and blue	20·00	45·00
208	5s. black and green	25·00	55·00
209	10s. black and carmine	60·00	95·00
193/209	*Set of* 17	£130	£250
193/209 Perf "Specimen"	*Set of* 17	£325	

1935 (6 May). *Silver Jubilee. As Nos.* 114/17 *of Jamaica.*

210	½d. black and green	30	35
	a. Extra flagstaff	25·00	
	b. Short extra flagstaff	28·00	
	c. Lightning conductor	25·00	
211	2½d. brown and deep blue	2·00	2·50
	a. Extra flagstaff	£130	
	b. Short extra flagstaff	£130	
	c. Lightning conductor	£100	
212	6d. light blue and olive-green	4·50	2·75
	a. Extra flagstaff	£180	
	b. Short extra flagstaff	£160	
	c. Lightning conductor	£130	
213	1s. slate and purple	8·50	11·00
	a. Extra flagstaff	£425	
	b. Short extra flagstaff	£350	
	c. Lightning conductor	£250	
210/13	*Set of* 4	14·00	15·00
210/13 Perf "Specimen"	*Set of* 4	£130	

For illustrations of plate varieties see Omnibus section following Zimbabwe.

Sheets from the second printing of the ½d., 6d. and 1s. in November 1935 had the extra flagstaff partially erased from the stamp with a sharp point.

1937 (12 May). *Coronation. As Nos.* 118/20 *of Jamaica.*

214	½d. green	10	10
215	1½d. scarlet	35	15
	a. Brown-lake	£425	£450
216	2½d. bright blue	50	35
214/16	*Set of* 3	85	50
214/16 Perf "Specimen"	*Set of* 3	60·00	

37 Grand Harbour, Valletta

38 H.M.S. *St. Angelo*

39 Verdala Palace

40 Hypogeum, Hal Saflieni

Broken cross (Right pane R. 5/7)

Damaged value tablet (R. 4/9)

Semaphore flaw (R. 2/7)

(Recess Waterlow)

1938 (17 Feb*)–**43.** *T* **37/40** *and similar designs. Wmk Mult Script CA (sideways on No.* 217). *P* 12½.

217	37	¼d. brown	10	10
218	38	½d. green	30	10
218*a*		½d. red-brown (8.3.43)	15	10
219	39	1d. red-brown	3·50	20
219*a*		1d. green (8.3.43)	20	10
220	40	1½d. scarlet	15	15
		a. Broken cross	16·00	
220*b*		1½d. slate-black (8.3.43)	20	15
		ba. Broken cross	16·00	
221	–	2d. slate-black	30	70
221*a*	–	2d. scarlet (8.3.43)	15	10
222	–	2½d. greyish blue	15	30
222*a*	–	2½d. dull violet (8.3.43)	60	10
223	–	3d. dull violet	20	60
223*a*	–	3d. blue (8.3.43)	30	10
224	–	4½d. olive-green and yellow-brown	50	10
225	–	6d. olive-green and scarlet	30	15
226	–	1s. black	50	30
227	–	1s. 6d. black and olive-green	4·50	3·50
228	–	2s. green and deep blue	3·25	2·75
229	–	2s. 6d. black and scarlet	6·00	4·50
		a. Damaged value tablet	75·00	
230	–	5s. black and green	6·00	5·50
		a. Semaphore flaw	50·00	
231	–	10s. black and carmine	13·00	14·00
217/231		*Set of* 21	35·00	30·00
217/31 Perf "Specimen"		*Set of* 21	£350	

Designs: *Horiz* (*as T* **39**)—2d. Victoria and citadel, Gozo; 2½d. De l'Isle Adam entering Mdina; 4½d. Ruins at Mnajdra; 1s. 6d. St. Publius; 2s. Mdina Cathedral; 2s. 6d. Statue of Neptune, *Vert* (*as T* **40**)—3d. St. John's Co-Cathedral; 6d. Statue of Manoel de Vilhena; 1s. Maltese girl wearing faldetta; 5s. Palace Square, Valletta; 10s. St. Paul.

*This is the local date of issue but the stamps were released in London on 15 February.

1946 (3 Dec). *Victory. As Nos.* 141/2 *of Jamaica, but inscr* "MALTA" *between Maltese Cross and George Cross.*

232	1d. green	10	10
233	3d. blue	10	10
232/3 Perf "Specimen"	*Set of* 2	50·00	

SELF-GOVERNMENT

(52)

"NT" joined (R. 4/10)

Halation flaw (Pl 2 R. 2/5) (ptg of 8 Jan 1953)

Cracked plate (Pl 2 R. 5/1) (ptg of 8 Jan 1953)

(Optd by Waterlow)

1948 (25 Nov)–**53.** *New Constitution. As Nos.* 217/31 *but optd as T* **52**; *reading up on* ½d. *and* 5s., *down on other values, and smaller on* ¼d. *value.*

234	37	¼d. brown	10	20
235	38	½d. red-brown	15	10
		a. "NT" joined	7·00	
236	39	1d. green	15	10
236*a*		1d. grey (R.) (8.1.53)	10	10
237	40	1½d. blue-black (R.)	30	10
		a. Broken cross	18·00	
237*b*		1½d. green (8.1.53)	10	10
		ba. Albino opt	†	£10000
238	–	2d. scarlet	30	10
238*a*	–	2d. yellow-ochre (8.1.53)	10	10
		ab. Halation flaw	60·00	
		ac. Cracked plate	70·00	
239	–	2½d. dull violet (R.)	40	10
239*a*	–	2½d. scarlet-vermilion (8.1.53)	25	65
240	–	3d. blue (R.)	20	15
240*a*	–	3d. dull violet (R.) (8.1.53)	35	15
241	–	4½d. olive-green and yellow-brown	1·25	1·50
241*a*	–	4½d. olive-green & dp ultram (R.) (8.1.53)	50	90

242 – 6d. olive-green and scarlet 25 15
243 – 1s. black 90 40
244 – 1s. 6d. black and olive-green .. 2·50 45
245 – 2s. green and deep blue (R.).. .. 4·00 1·50
246 – 2s. 6d. black and scarlet .. .. 8·00 2·50
247 – 5s. black and green (R.) .. .. 13·00 5·50
a. "NT" joined £100
248 – 10s. black and carmine .. .. 17·00 16·00
234/248 .. .. *Set of* 21 45·00 27·00

1949 (4 Jan). *Royal Silver Wedding. As Nos. 143/4 of Jamaica, but inscr* "MALTA" *between Maltese Cross and George Cross and with* £1 *ptd in recess.*
249 1d. green 30 10
250 £1 indigo .. .. 40·00 35·00

1949 (10 Oct). *75th Anniv of U.P.U. As Nos. 145/8 of Jamaica, but inscr* "MALTA" *in recess.*
251 2½d. violet 30 10
252 3d. deep blue .. .. 1·60 40
253 6d. carmine-red .. .. 1·60 40
254 1s. blue-black .. .. 1·60 1·50
251/4 .. .. *Set of* 4 4·50 2·25

53 Queen Elizabeth II when Princess

54 "Our Lady of Mount Carmel" (attrib Palladino)

(T **53**/4. Recess B.W.)

1950 (1 Dec). *Visit of Princess Elizabeth to Malta. Wmk Mult Script CA. P* 12 × 11½.
255 **53** 1d. green 10 10
256 3d. blue 20 10
257 1s. black 40 45
255/7 .. .. *Set of* 3 60 55

1951 (12 July). *Seventh Centenary of the Scapular. Wmk Mult Script CA. P* 12 × 11½.
258 **54** 1d. green 10 10
259 3d. violet 15 10
260 1s. black 30 40
258/60 .. .. *Set of* 3 50 50

1953 (3 June). *Coronation. As No. 153 of Jamaica.*
261 1½d. black and deep yellow-green 30 10

55 St. John's Co-Cathedral

56 "Immaculate Conception" (Caruana) (altar-piece, Cospicua)

(Recess Waterlow)

1954 (3 May). *Royal Visit. Wmk Mult Script CA. P* 12½.
262 **55** 3d. violet 15 10

(Photo Harrison)

1954 (8 Sept). *Centenary of Dogma of the Immaculate Conception. Wmk Mult Script CA. Chalk-surfaced paper. P* 14½ × 14.
263 **56** 1½d. emerald 10 10
264 3d. bright blue 10 10
265 1s. grey-black 10 10
263/5 .. .. *Set of* 3 15 15

57 Monument of the Great Siege, 1565

62 Auberge de Castile

(Recess Waterlow (2s. 6d. to £1). B.W. (others))

1956 (23 Jan)–**58**. *T* **57**, **62** *and similar designs. Wmk Mult Script CA. P* 14×13½ (2s. 6d. *to* £1) *or* 11½ (*others*).
266 ¼d. violet 10 10
267 ½d. orange 30 10
268 1d. black (9.2.56) 40 10
269 1½d. bluish green (9.2.56) 30 10
270 2d. brown (9.2.56) 40 10
a. Deep brown (26.2.58) 30 10
271 2½d. orange-brown 30 30
272 3d. rose-red (22.3.56) 40 10
273 4½d. deep blue 50 20
274 6d. indigo (9.2.56) 30 10
275 8d. bistre-brown .. .. 1·00 1·00
276 1s. deep reddish violet 35 10
277 1s. 6d. deep turquoise-green .. .. .. 4·25 20
278 2s. olive-green .. .. 5·00 80
279 2s. 6d. chestnut (22.3.56) .. .. .. 5·50 2·25
280 5s. green (11.10.56) .. .. 9·00 2·75
281 10s. carmine-red (19.11.56) .. .. .. 40·00 10·00
282 £1 yellow-brown (5.1.57) .. .. .. 40·00 25·00
266/82 .. .. *Set of* 17 95·00 38·00

Designs:—*Vert*—½d. Wignacourt aqueduct horsetrough; 1d. Victory church; 1½d. War memorial; 2d. Mosta dome; 3d. The King's scroll; 4½d. Roosevelt's scroll; 8d. Vedette; 1s. Mdina gate; 1s. 6d. "Les Gavroches" (statue); 2s. Monument of Christ the King; 2s. 6d. Grand Master Cottoner's monument; 5s. Grand Master Perellos's monument; 10s. St. Paul; £1 Baptism of Christ. *Horiz*—6d. Neolithic Temples at Tarxien.

See also Nos. 314/15.

74 "Defence of Malta"

75 Searchlights over Malta

(Des E. Cremona. Photo Harrison)

1957 (15 Apr). *George Cross Commemoration. Cross in silver. T* **74/5** *and similar design. Wmk Mult Script CA. P* 14½ × 14 (3*d.*) *or* 14 × 14½ (*others*).
283 1½d. deep dull green.. .. .. 15 10
284 3d. vermilion 15 10
285 1s. reddish brown 15 10
283/5 .. .. *Set of* 3 40 20

Design: *Vert*—1s. Bombed buildings.

77 "Design"

(Des E. Cremona. Photo Harrison)

1958 (15 Feb). *Technical Education in Malta. T* **77** *and similar designs. W w* **12**. *P* 14 × 14½ (3*d.*) *or* 14½ × 14 (*others*).
286 1½d. black and deep green 10 10
287 3d. black, scarlet and grey.. .. .. 10 10
288 1s. grey, bright purple and black 15 10
286/8 .. .. *Set of* 3 30 15

Designs: *Vert*—3d. "Construction". *Horiz*—1s. Technical School, Paola.

80 Bombed-out Family

81 Sea Raid on Grand Harbour, Valletta

(Des E. Cremona. Photo Harrison)

1958 (15 Apr). *George Cross Commemoration. Cross in first colour, outlined in silver. T* **80/1** *and similar design. W w* **12**. *P* 14 × 14½ (3*d.*) *or* 14½ × 14 (*others*).
289 1½d. blue-green and black 10 10
290 3d. red and black 10 10
291 1s. reddish violet and black 15 10
a. Silver (outline) omitted £225
289/91 .. .. *Set of* 3 30 15

Design: *Horiz*—1s. Searchlight crew.

83 Air Raid Casualties

84 "For Gallantry"

(Des E. Cremona. Photo Harrison)

1959 (15 Apr). *George Cross Commemoration. T* **83/4** *and similar design. W w* **12**. *P* 14½ × 14 (3*d.*) *or* 14 × 14½ (*others*).
292 1½d. grey-green, black and gold 15 10
293 3d. reddish violet, black and gold 15 10
294 1s. blue-grey, black and gold 55 55
292/4 .. .. *Set of* 3 75 55

Design: *Vert*—1s. Maltese under bombardment.

86 Shipwreck of St. Paul (after Palombi)

87 Statue of St. Paul, Rabat, Malta

(Des E. Cremona. Photo Harrison)

1960 (9 Feb). *19th Centenary of the Shipwreck of St. Paul. T* **86/7** *and similar designs. W w* **12**. *P* 13 (1½*d.*, 3*d.*, 6*d.*) *or* 14 × 14½ (*others*).
295 1½d. blue, gold and yellow-brown 15 10
a. Gold (dates and crosses) omitted .. 55·00
296 3d. bright purple, gold and blue 15 10
297 6d. carmine, gold and pale grey 25 10
298 8d. black and gold 30 40
299 1s. maroon and gold 25 10
300 2s. 6d. blue, deep bluish green and gold .. 1·00 1·50
a. Gold omitted £300
295/300 .. .. *Set of* 6 1·90 1·90

Designs: *Vert as T* **86**—3d. Consecration of St. Publius (first Bishop of Malta) (after Palombi); 6d. Departure of St. Paul (after Palombi). *Diamond shaped as T* **87**—1s. Angel with *Acts of the Apostles*; 2s. 6d. St. Paul with *Second Epistle to the Corinthians*.

92 Stamp of 1860

(Centre litho; frame recess. Waterlow)

1960 (1 Dec). *Stamp Centenary. W w* **12**. *P* 13½.
301 **92** 1½d. buff, pale blue and green 20 10
a. Buff, pale bl & myrtle (white paper) 3·00 1·50
302 3d. buff pale blue and deep carmine .. 25 10
a. Blank corner £100
303 6d. buff, pale blue and ultramarine .. 35 25
301/3 .. .. *Set of* 3 70 30

No. 302a shows the right-hand bottom corner of the 1860 stamp blank. It occurs on R. 4/7 from early trial plates and sheets containing the error should have been destroyed, but some were sorted into good stock and issued at a post office.

93 George Cross

(Photo Harrison)

1961 (15 Apr). *George Cross Commemoration. T* **93** *and similar designs showing medal. W w* **12**, *P* 15 × 14.
304 1½d. black, cream and bistre 15 10
305 3d. olive-brown and greenish blue.. .. 30 10
306 1s. olive-green, lilac & dp reddish violet .. 60 70
304/6 .. .. *Set of* 3 95 75

96 "Madonna Damascena"

(Photo Harrison)

1962 (7 Sept). *Great Siege Commemoration. T* **96** *and similar vert designs. W w* **12**. *P* 13 × 12.
307 2d. bright blue 10 10
308 3d. red 10 10
309 6d. bronze-green 10 10
310 1s. brown-purple 15 20
307/10 .. .. *Set of* 4 30 30

Designs:—3d. Great Siege Monument; 6d. Grand Master La Valette; 1s. Assault on Fort St. Elmo.

1963 (4 June). *Freedom from Hunger. As No. 80 of Lesotho.*
311 1s. 6d. sepia .. .. 4·50 2·75

1963 (2 Sept). *Red Cross Centenary. As Nos. 203/4 of Jamaica.*
312 2d. red and black 25 15
313 1s. 6d. red and blue .. .. 3·75 3·75

1963 (15 Oct)–**64.** *As Nos.* 268 *and* 270, *but wmk* w **12**.

No.	Type	Description	Unused	Used
314	**59**	1d. black	40	30
315	**61**	2d. deep brown (11.7.64*)	1·50	2·25

*This is the earliest known date recorded in Malta.

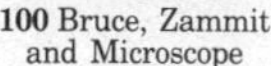

100 Bruce, Zammit and Microscope — **101** Goat and Laboratory Equipment

(Des E. Cremona. Photo Harrison)

1964 (14 April). *Anti-Brucellosis Congress. W* w **12**. *P* 14.

No.	Type	Description	Unused	Used
316	**100**	2d. light brown, black and bluish green	10	10
		a. Black (microscope, etc) omitted	£225	
317	**101**	1s. 6d. black and maroon	55	20

102 "Nicola Cotoner tending Sick Man" (M. Preti)

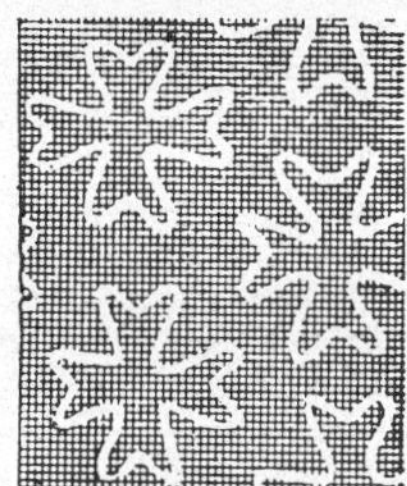

105 Maltese Cross (*Upright*)

In this illustration the points of the crosses meet in a vertical line. When the watermark is sideways they meet in a horizontal line.

(Des E. Cremona. Photo Harrison)

1964 (5 Sept). *First European Catholic Doctors' Congress, Vienna. T* **102** *and similar horiz designs. W* **105** (*sideways*). *P* 13½ × 11½.

No.	Type	Description	Unused	Used
318		2d. red, black, gold and grey-blue	20	10
319		6d. red, black, gold and bistre	45	15
320		1s. 6d. red, black, gold and reddish violet	85	85
318/20		*Set of* 3	1·40	1·00

Designs:—6d. St. Luke and Hospital; 1s. 6d. Sacra Infermeria, Valletta.

INDEPENDENT

106 Dove and British Crown — **109** "The Nativity"

(Des E. Cremona. Photo Harrison)

1964 (21 Sept). *Independence. T* **106** *and similar vert designs. W* **105**. *P* 14½ × 13½.

No.	Type	Description	Unused	Used
321		2d. olive-brown, red and gold	30	10
		a. Gold omitted	70·00	
322		3d. brown-purple, red and gold	30	10
		a. Gold omitted	70·00	
323		6d. slate, red and gold	90	15
324		1s. blue, red and gold	90	15
325		1s. 6d. indigo, red and gold	2·50	1·50
326		2s. 6d. deep violet-blue, red and gold	2·50	2·75
321/6		*Set of* 6	6·50	4·00

Designs:—2d., 1s. Type **106**; 3d., 1s. 6d. Dove and Pope's Tiara; 6d., 2s. 6d. Dove and U.N. emblem.

(Des E. Cremona. Photo D.L.R.)

1964 (3 Nov). *Christmas. W* **105** (*sideways*). *P* 13 × 13½.

No.	Type	Description	Unused	Used
327	**109**	2d. bright purple and gold	10	10
328		4d. bright blue and gold	20	15
329		8d. deep bluish green and gold	45	45
327/9		*Set of* 3	65	60

110 Neolithic Era — **117** Galleys of Knights of St. John

119 British Rule

(Des E. Cremona. Photo Harrison)

1965 (7 Jan)–**70.** *Chalk-surfaced paper. T* **110**, **117**, **119** *and similar designs. W* **105**. *P* 14 × 14½ (*vert*) *or* 14½ (*horiz*).

No.	Description	Unused	Used
330	½d. multicoloured	10	10
	a. "½d" (white) printed twice†	10·00	
	b. White (face value) omitted	38·00	
331	1d. multicoloured	10	10
	a. Gold (ancient lettering) omitted	48·00	
	b. White (Greek lettering and "PUNIC") omitted	48·00	
	d. "PUNIC" omitted	80·00	
332	1½d. multicoloured	10	10
333	2d. multicoloured	10	10
	a. Gold omitted	28·00	
	b. Imperf (pair)	£275	
334	2½d. multicoloured	30	10
	a. Orange omitted*	55·00	
	b. Gold ("SARACENIC") omitted	50·00	
	c. Salmon printed twice †	50·00	
335	3d. multicoloured	10	10
	a. Gold (windows) omitted	60·00	
	b. "MALTA" (silver) omitted	32·00	
	c. Imperf (pair)	£300	
336	4d. multicoloured	30	10
	a. "KNIGHTS OF MALTA" (silver) omitted	45·00	
	b. "MALTA" (silver) omitted	40·00	
	c. Black (shield surround) omitted	45·00	
	d. Imperf (pair)	£300	
337	4½d. multicoloured	40	30
	a. Silver ("MALTA", etc) omitted	£250	
337*b*	5d. multicoloured (1.8.70)	30	20
	ba. "FORTIFICATIONS" (gold) omitted	60·00	
338	6d. multicoloured	20	10
	a. "MALTA" (silver) omitted	42·00	
	b. Black omitted	55·00	
339	8d. multicoloured	20	10
	a. Gold (centre) omitted	32·00	
	b. Gold (frame) omitted	55·00	
339*c*	10d. multicoloured (1.8.70)	45	1·00
	ca. "NAVAL ARSENAL" (gold) omitted	70·00	
340	1s. multicoloured	30	10
	a. Gold (centre) omitted	75·00	
	b. Gold (framework) omitted	38·00	
341	1s. 3d. multicoloured	1·50	1·40
	a. Gold (centre) omitted	50·00	
	b. Gold (framework) omitted	75·00	
	c. Imperf (pair)	£350	
342	1s. 6d. multicoloured	60	10
	a. Head (black) omitted	£225	
	b. Gold (centre) omitted	38·00	
	c. Gold (frame) omitted	55·00	
343	2s. multicoloured	70	10
	a. Gold (centre) omitted	65·00	
	b. Gold (framework) omitted	42·00	
344	2s. 6d. multicoloured	70	50
345	3s. multicoloured	1·25	75
	a. Gold (framework) omitted	30·00	
346	5s. multicoloured	4·50	1·00
	a. Gold (framework) omitted	60·00	
347	10s. multicoloured	3·50	3·00
	a. Gold (centre) omitted	75·00	
348	£1 multicoloured	3·50	5·00
	a. Pink omitted	25·00	
330/48	*Set of* 21	17·00	12·00

Designs: *Vert*—1d. Punic era; 1½d. Roman era; 2d. Proto Christian era; 2½d. Saracenic era; 3d. Siculo Norman era; 4d. Knights of Malta; 5d. Fortifications; 6d. French occupation. *Horiz*—10d. Naval arsenal; 1s. Maltese corps of the British army; 1s. 3d. International Eucharistic congress, 1913; 1s. 6d. Self-government, 1921; 2s. Gozo civic council; 2s. 6d. State of Malta; 3s. Independence, 1964; 5s. HAFMED (Allied forces, Mediterranean); 10s. The Maltese Islands (map); £1 Patron saints.

*The effect of this is to leave the Saracenic pattern as a pink colour.

†On the ½d. the second impression is 6½ mm lower or 3 mm to the left, and on the 2½d. 1 mm lower so that it falls partly across "MALTA" and "2½d". Stamps with almost coincidental double impression are common.

The ½d. and 1d. had white printing plates. Two silver plates were used on the 4d., one for "KNIGHTS OF MALTA" and the other for "MALTA". Two gold plates were used for the 8d. to 10s., one for the framework and the other for the gold in the central part of the designs.

No. 337a comes from a sheet on which the silver printing was so misplaced that it missed the top horizontal row entirely.

The ½d. to 4d., 1s. and 1s. 6d. to 5s. values exist with PVA gum as well as gum arabic and the 5d. and 10d. have PVA gum only.

129 "Dante" (Raphael)

(Des E. Cremona. Photo Govt Ptg Works, Rome)

1965 (7 July). 700*th Birth Anniv of Dante. P* 14.

No.	Type	Description	Unused	Used
349	**129**	2d. indigo	10	10
350		6d. bronze-green	15	10
351		2s. chocolate	50	70
349/51		*Set of* 3	65	70

130 Turkish Camp — **131** Turkish Fleet

(Des E. Cremona. Photo Harrison)

1965 (1 Sept). 400*th Anniv of Great Siege. T* **130/1** *and similar designs. W* **105** (*sideways*). *P* 13 (6*d*., 1*s*.) *or* 14½ × 14 (*others*).

No.	Description	Unused	Used
352	2d. olive-green, red and black	25	10
353	3d. olive-green, red, black and light drab	25	10
354	6d. multicoloured	50	10
	a. Gold (framework and dates) omitted	£180	
	b. Black (on hulls) omitted	£180	
355	8d. red, gold, indigo and blue	75	75
356	1s. red, gold and deep grey-blue	55	10
357	1s. 6d. ochre, red and black	1·00	30
358	2s. 6d. sepia, black, red and yellow-olive	1·50	2·00
352/8	*Set of* 7	4·25	2·75

Designs: *Square* (*as T* **130**)—3d. Battle scene; 8d. Arrival of relief force; 1s. 6d. "Allegory of Victory" (from mural by M. Preti); 2s. 6d. Victory medal. *Vert* (*as T* **131**)—1s. Grand Master J. de La Valette's arms.

137 "The Three Kings" — **138** Sir Winston Churchill

(Des E. Cremona. Photo Enschedé)

1965 (7 Oct). *Christmas. W* **105** (*sideways*). *P* 11 × 11½.

No.	Type	Description	Unused	Used
359	**137**	1d. slate-purple and red	10	10
360		4d. slate-purple and blue	30	25
361		1s. 3d. slate-purple and bright purple	30	30
359/61		*Set of* 3	60	50

(Des E. Cremona. Photo Harrison)

1966 (24 Jan). *Churchill Commemoration. T* **138** *and similar square design. W* **105** (*sideways*). *P* 14½ × 14.

No.	Type	Description	Unused	Used
362	**138**	2d. black, red and gold	15	10
363	–	3d. bronze-green, yellow-olive and gold	15	10
364	**138**	1s. maroon, red and gold	20	10
		a. Gold (shading) omitted	£250	
365	–	1s. 6d. chalky blue, violet-blue and gold	35	40
362/5		*Set of* 4	75	55

Design:—3d., 1s. 6d. Sir Winston Churchill and George Cross.

140 Grand Master La Valette — **145** President Kennedy and Memorial

(Des E. Cremona. Photo State Ptg Works, Vienna)

1966 (28 Mar). 400*th Anniv of Valletta. T* **140** *and similar square designs. Multicoloured. W* **105** (*sideways*). *P* 12.

No.	Description	Unused	Used
366	2d. Type **140**	10	10
367	3d. Pope Pius V	10	10
	a. Gold omitted	£275	
368	6d. Map of Valletta	10	10
369	1s. Francesco Laparelli (architect)	10	10
370	2s. 6d. Girolamo Cassar (architect)	20	30
366/70	*Set of* 5	40	45

(Des E. Cremona. Photo Harrison)

1966 (28 May). *President Kennedy Commemoration. W* **105** *(sideways). P* 15 × 14.

371	**145**	3d. olive, gold and black	10	10
		a. Gold inscr omitted	£225	
372		1s. 6d. Prussian blue, gold and black	10	10

146 "Trade"

(Des E. Cremona. Photo D.L.R.)

1966 (16 June). *Tenth Malta Trade Fair. W* **105** *(sideways). P* 13½.

373	**146**	2d. multicoloured	10	10
374		8d. multicoloured	20	25
375		2s. 6d. multicoloured	20	25
373/5		*Set of* 3	45	50

147 "The Child in the Manger" **148** George Cross

(Des E. Cremona. Photo D.L.R.)

1966 (7 Oct). *Christmas. W* **105**. *P* 13½.

376	**147**	1d. black, gold, turquoise-bl & slate-pur	10	10
377		4d. black, gold, ultramarine & slate-pur	10	10
378		1s. 3d. black, gold, brt pur & slate-pur	10	10
		a. Gold omitted	70·00	
376/8		*Set of* 3	15	10

(Des E. Cremona. Photo Harrison)

1967 (1 Mar). *25th Anniv of George Cross Award to Malta. W* **105** *(sideways). P* 14½ × 14.

379	**148**	2d. multicoloured	10	10
380		4d. multicoloured	10	10
381		3s. multicoloured	15	15
379/81		*Set of* 3	15	15

149 Crucifixion of St. Peter

150 Open Bible and Episcopal Emblems

(Des E. Cremona. Photo Harrison)

1967 (28 June). *1900th Anniv of Martyrdom of Saints Peter and Paul. T* **149/50** *and similar design. W* **105** *(sideways). P* 13½ × 14½ *(8d.) or* 14½ *(others).*

382	2d. chestnut, orange and black	10	10
383	8d. yellow-olive, gold and black	10	10
384	3s. blue, light blue and black	15	10
382/4	*Set of* 3	20	15

Design:—*Square as T* **149**—3s. Beheading of St. Paul.

152 "St. Catherine of Siena" **156** Temple Ruins, Tarxien

(Des E. Cremona. Photo Enschedé)

1967 (1 Aug). *300th Death Anniv of Melchior Gafa (sculptor). T* **152** *and similar horiz designs. Multicoloured. W* **105** *(sideways). P* 13½ × 13.

385	2d. Type **152**	10	10
386	4d. "St. Thomas of Villanova"	10	10
387	1s. 6d. "Baptism of Christ" (detail)	10	10
388	2s. 6d. "St. John the Baptist" (from "Baptism of Christ")	10	10
385/8	*Set of* 4	20	15

(Des E. Cremona. Photo Harrison)

1967 (12 Sept). *15th International Historical Architecture Congress, Valletta. T* **156** *and similar square designs. Multicoloured. W* **105**. *P* 15 × 14½.

389	2d. Type **156**	10	10
390	6d. Facade of Palazzo Falzon, Notabile	10	10
391	1s. Parish Church, Birkirkara	10	10
392	3s. Portal, Auberge de Castille	15	15
389/92	*Set of* 4	20	20

160 "Angels" **161** "Crib" **162** "Angels"

(Des E. Cremona. Photo D.L.R.)

1967 (20 Oct). *Christmas. W* **105** *(sideways). P* 14.

393	**160**	1d. multicoloured	10	10
		a. In triptych with Nos. 394/5	10	10
		b. White stars (red omitted)	70·00	
394	**161**	8d. multicoloured	10	10
395	**162**	1s. 4d. multicoloured	10	10
393/5		*Set of* 3	10	10

Nos. 393/5 were issued in sheets of 60 of each value (arranged *tête-bêche*), and also in sheets containing the three values *se-tenant*, thus forming a triptych of the Nativity.

163 Queen Elizabeth II and Arms of Malta

(Des E. Cremona. Photo Harrison)

1967 (13 Nov). *Royal Visit. T* **163** *and similar designs. W* **105** *(sideways on 2d., 3s.). P* 14 × 15 *(4d.) or* 15 × 14 *(others).*

396	2d. multicoloured	10	10
	a. Cream omitted*		
397	4d. black, brown-purple and gold	10	10
398	3s. multicoloured	15	15
396/8	*Set of* 3	20	20

Designs: *Vert*—4d. Queen in Robes of Order of St. Michael and St. George. *Horiz*—3s. Queen and outline of Malta.

*This affects the Queen's face.

166 Human Rights Emblem and People **167**

(Des E. Cremona. Photo Harrison)

1968 (2 May). *Human Rights Year. W* **105**. *P* 12½ *(6d.) or* 14½ *(others).*

399	**166**	2d. multicoloured	10	10
400	**167**	6d. multicoloured	10	10
401	–	2s. multicoloured	10	10
399/401		*Set of* 3	15	10

The design of the 2s. value is a reverse of Type **166**.

169 Fair "Products"

(Des E. Cremona. Photo Harrison)

1968 (1 June). *Malta International Trade Fair. W* **105** *(sideways). P* 14½ × 14.

402	**169**	4d. multicoloured	10	10
403		8d. multicoloured	10	10
404		3s. multicoloured	15	10
402/4		*Set of* 3	20	15

170 Arms of the Order of St. John and La Valette **171** "La Valette" (A. de Favray)

172 La Valette's Tomb **173** Angels and Scroll bearing Date of Death

(Des E. Cremona. Photo Govt Printer, Israel)

1968 (1 Aug). *Fourth Death Centenary of Grand Master La Valette. W* **105** *(upright, 1s. 6d.; sideways, others). P* 13 × 14 *(1d., 1s. 6d.) or* 14 × 13 *(others).*

405	**170**	1d. multicoloured	10	10
406	**171**	8d. multicoloured	10	10
407	**172**	1s. 6d. multicoloured	10	10
408	**173**	2s. 6d. multicoloured	15	20
405/8		*Set of* 4	30	30

174 Star of Bethlehem and Angel waking Shepherds **177** "Agriculture"

(Des E. Cremona. Photo Harrison)

1968 (3 Oct). *Christmas. T* **174** *and similar shaped designs. Multicoloured. W* **105** *(sideways). P* 14½ × 14.

409	1d. Type **174**	10	10
410	8d. Mary and Joseph with shepherd watching over cradle	10	10
411	1s. 4d. Three Wise Men and Star of Bethlehem	10	10
409/11	*Set of* 3	15	15

The shortest side at top and the long side at the bottom both gauge 14½, the other three sides are 14. Nos. 409/11 were issued in sheets of 60 arranged in ten strips of six, alternately upright and inverted.

(Des E. Cremona. Photo Enschedé)

1968 (21 Oct). *Sixth Food and Agricultural Organization Regional Conference for Europe. T* **177** *and similar vert designs. Multicoloured. W* **105** *(sideways). P* 12½ × 12.

412	4d. Type **177**	10	10
413	1s. F.A.O. emblem and coin	10	10
414	2s. 6d. "Agriculture" sowing seeds	10	15
412/14	*Set of* 3	15	20

180 Mahatma Gandhi **181** I.L.O. Emblem

(Des E. Cremona. Photo Enschedé)

1969 (24 Mar). *Birth Centenary of Mahatma Gandhi. W* **105**. *P* 12 × 12½.

415	**180**	1s. 6d. blackish brown, black and gold	15	10

(Des E. Cremona. Photo Harrison)

1969 (26 May). *50th Anniv of International Labour Organization. W* **105** *(sideways). P* 13½ × 14½.

416	**181**	2d. indigo, gold and turquoise	10	10
417		6d. sepia, gold and chestnut	10	10

182 Robert Samut

(Des E. Cremona. Photo D.L.R.)

1969 (26 July). *Birth Centenary of Robert Samut (composer of Maltese National Anthem). W* **105** *(sideways). P* 13.
418 **182** 2d. multicoloured 10 10

183 Dove of Peace, U.N. Emblem and Sea-Bed

(Des E. Cremona. Photo D.L.R.)

1969 (26 July). *United Nations Resolution on Oceanic Resources. W* **105** *(sideways). P* 13.
419 **183** 5d. multicoloured 10 10

184 "Swallows" returning to Malta

(Des E. Cremona. Photo D.L.R.)

1969 (26 July). *Maltese Migrants' Convention. W* **105** *(sideways). P* 13.
420 **184** 10d. black, gold and yellow-olive .. 10 10

185 University Arms and Grand Master de Fonseca (founder)

(Des E. Cremona. Photo D.L.R.)

1969 (26 July). *Bicentenary of University of Malta. W* **105** *(sideways). P* 13.
421 **185** 2s. multicoloured 10 20

186 1919 Monument **187** Flag of Malta and Birds

(Des E. Cremona. Photo Enschedé)

1969 (20 Sept). *Fifth Anniv of Independence. T* **186/7** *and similar designs. W* **105** *(upright on 5d., sideways others). P* 13½ × 12½ *(2d.)*, 12 × 12½ *(5d.)*, *or* 12½ × 12 *(others)*.
422 2d. multicoloured 10 10
423 5d. black, red and gold 10 10
424 10d. black, turquoise-blue and gold 10 10
425 1s. 6d. multicoloured 10 20
426 2s. 6d. black, olive-brown and gold 15 25
422/6 .. .. *Set of* 5 30 55

Designs:—*Vert as T* **187**—10d. "Tourism"; 1s. 6d. U.N. and Council of Europe emblems; 2s. 6d. "Trade and Industry".

191 Peasants playing Tambourine and Bagpipes

(Des E. Cremona. Litho D.L.R.)

1969 (8 Nov). *Christmas. Children's Welfare Fund. T* **191** *and similar horiz designs. Multicoloured. W* **105** *(sideways). P* 12½.
427 1d. + 1d. Type **191** 10 10
a. Gold omitted .. .. 90·00
b. In triptych with Nos. 428/9 .. .. 15 20
428 5d. + 1d. Angels playing trumpet and harp 10 10
429 1s. 6d. + 3d. Choir boys singing 10 15
427/9 .. .. *Set of* 3 15 20

Nos. 427/9 were issued in sheets of 60 of each value, and also in sheets containing the three values *se-tenant*, thus forming the triptych No. 427b.

194 "The Beheading of St. John" (Caravaggio)

(Des E. Cremona. Photo Enschedé)

1970 (21 Mar). *13th Council of Europe Art Exhibition. T* **194** *and similar multicoloured designs. W* **105** *(upright, 10d., 2s.; sideways, others). P* 14 × 13 *(1d., 8d.)*, 12 *(10d., 2s.) or* 13 × 13½ *(others)*.
430 1d. Type **194** 10 10
431 2d. "St. John the Baptist" (M. Preti) (45 × 32 *mm*) 10 10
432 5d. Interior of St. John's Co-Cathedral, Valletta (39 × 39 *mm*) 10 10
433 6d. "Allegory of the Order" (Neapolitan School) (45 × 32 *mm*) 10 10
434 8d. "St. Jerome" (Caravaggio) 10 20
435 10d. Articles from the Order of St. John in Malta (63 × 21 *mm*) 10 10
436 1s. 6d. "The Blessed Gerard receiving Godfrey de Bouillon" (A. de Favray) (45 × 35 *mm*) 15 25
437 2s. Cape and Stolone (16th-century) (63 × 21 *mm*) 20 35
430/37 .. .. *Set of* 8 60 85

202 Artist's Impression of Fujiyama

(Des E. Cremona. Photo D.L.R.)

1970 (29 May). *World Fair, Osaka. W* **105** *(sideways). P* 15.
438 **202** 2d. multicoloured 10 10
439 5d. multicoloured 10 10
440 3s. multicoloured 15 15
438/40 .. .. *Set of* 3 15 15

203 "Peace and Justice" **204** Carol-Singers, Church and Star

(Des J. Casha. Litho Harrison)

1970 (30 Sept). *25th Anniv of United Nations. W* **105**. *P* 14 × 14½.
441 **203** 2d. multicoloured 10 10
442 5d. multicoloured 10 10
443 2s. 6d. multicoloured 15 15
441/3 .. .. *Set of* 3 15 15

(Des E. Cremona. Photo Govt Printer, Israel)

1970 (7 Nov). *Christmas. T* **204** *and similar vert designs. Multicoloured. W* **105** *(sideways). P* 14 × 13.
444 1d. + ½d. Type **204** 10 10
445 10d. + 2d. Church, star and angels with Infant 10 15
446 1s. 6d. + 3d. Church, star and nativity scene 15 25
444/6 .. .. *Set of* 3 20 40

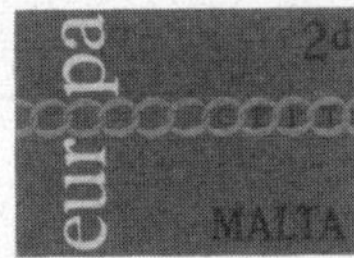

207 Books and Quill **208** Dun Karm, Books, Pens and Lamp

(Des H. Alden (1s. 6d.), A. Agius (2s.). Litho D.L.R.)

1971 (20 Mar). *Literary Anniversaries. Death Bicentenary* (1970) *of De Soldanis (historian)* (1s. 6d.) *and Birth Centenary of Dun Karm (poet)* (2s.). *W* **105** *(sideways). P* 13 × 13½.
447 **207** 1s. 6d. multicoloured 10 10
448 **208** 2s. multicoloured 10 15

209 Europa "Chain"

(Des H. Haflidason; adapted E. Cremona. Litho Harrison)

1971 (3 May). *Europa. W* **105** *(sideways). P* 13½ × 14½.
449 **209** 2d. orange, black and yellow-olive .. 10 10
450 5d. orange, black and vermilion .. 10 10
451 1s. 6d. orange, black and slate .. 20 55
449/51 .. .. *Set of* 3 30 55

210 "St. Joseph, Patron of the Universal Church" (G. Cali) **211** *Centaurea spathulata*

(Des E. Cremona. Litho D.L.R.)

1971 (24 July). *Centenary of Proclamation of St. Joseph as Patron Saint of Catholic Church, and 50th Anniv of the Coronation of the Statue of "Our Lady of Victories". T* **210** *and similar horiz design. Multicoloured. W* **105** *(sideways). P* 13 × 13½.
452 2d. Type **210** 10 10
453 5d. Statue of "Our Lady of Victories" and galley 10 10
454 10d. Type **210** 10 10
455 1s. 6d. As 5d. 20 40
452/5 .. .. *Set of* 4 30 50

(Des Reno Psaila. Litho Harrison)

1971 (18 Sept). *National Plant and Bird of Malta. T* **211** *and similar horiz design. Multicoloured. W* **105** *(sideways on 5d. and 10d.). P* 14½ × 14.
456 2d. Type **211** 10 10
457 5d. Blue Rock Thrush 10 10
458 10d. As 5d. 20 15
459 1s. 6d. Type **211** 20 80
456/9 .. .. *Set of* 4 50 1·00

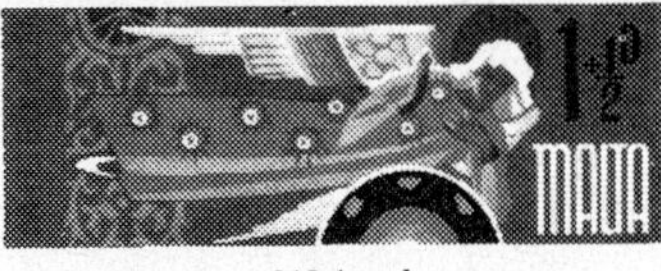

212 Angel

(Des E. Cremona. Litho Format)

1971 (8 Nov). *Christmas. T* **212** *and similar horiz designs. Multicoloured. W* **105** *(sideways). P* 13½ × 14.
460 1d. + ½d. Type **212** 10 10
461 10d. + 2d. Mary and the Child Jesus 15 20
462 1s. 6d. + 3d. Joseph lying awake 20 30
460/2 .. .. *Set of* 3 35 55
MS463 131 × 113 mm. Nos. 460/2. P 15 .. .. 75 1·75

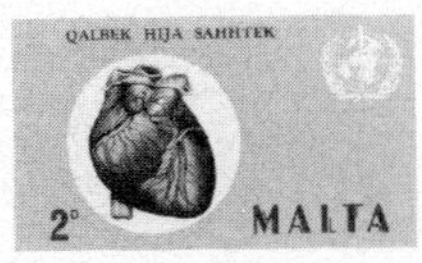

213 Heart and W.H.O. Emblem **214** Maltese Cross

(Des A. Agius. Litho Format)

1972 (20 Mar). *World Health Day. W* **105**. *P* 13½ × 14.
464 **213** 2d. multicoloured 10 10
465 10d. multicoloured 15 10
466 2s. 6d. multicoloured 40 80
464/6 .. .. *Set of* 3 55 85

(New Currency. 10 mils = 1 cent; 100 cents = 1 Maltese pound)

(Des G. Pace. Litho Format)

1972 (16 May). *Decimal Currency. T* **214** *and similar vert designs showing decimal coins. Multicoloured. W* **105**. *P* 14 *(2 m., 3 m., 2 c.)*, 14½ × 14 *(5 m., 1 c., 5 c.) or* 13½ *(10 c., 50 c.)*.
467 2 m. Type **214** 10 10
468 3 m. Bee on honeycomb 10 10
469 5 m. Earthen lampstand 10 10
470 1 c. George Cross 10 10
471 2 c. Classical head 10 10
472 5 c. Ritual altar 10 10
473 10 c. Grandmaster's galley 20 10
474 50 c. Great Siege Monument .. .. .. 80 1·25
467/74 .. .. *Set of* 8 1·25 1·25

Sizes:—2 m., 3 m. and 2 c. as T **214**; 5 m., 1 c. and 5 c. 22 × 27 mm; 10 c. and 50 c. 27 × 35 mm.

No. 467 exists imperforate from stock dispersed by the liquidator of Format International Security Printers Ltd.

= 1c3

(215)

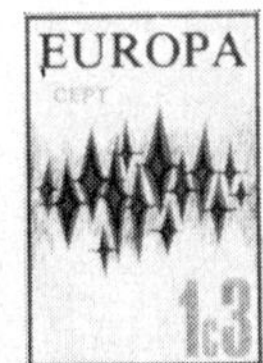

216 "Communications"

1972 (30 Sept). *Nos. 337a, 339 and 341 surch as T* **215**, *by Govt. Printing Works, Valletta.*

475 1 c. 3 on 5d. multicoloured 10 10
476 3 c. on 8d. multicoloured 15 10
a. Surch inverted .. .. 50·00
b. Gold (frame) omitted .. .. 60·00
477 5 c. on 1s. 3d. multicoloured 15 20
a. Surch double .. .. 55·00
b. Surch inverted .. .. 30·00
c. Gold (centre) omitted .. .. 45·00
475/7 .. .. *Set of* 3 30 35

PRINTERS. All stamps from No. 478 onwards were printed in lithography by Printex Ltd, Malta.

(Des P. Huovinen; adapted G. Pace)

1972 (11 Nov). *Europa. W* **105** *(sideways). P* 13.

478 **216** 1 c. 3, multicoloured 10 10
479 3 c. multicoloured 10 10
480 5 c. multicoloured 15 35
481 7 c. 5, multicoloured 20 75
478/81 .. .. *Set of* 4 50 1·10

Nos. 478/81 were each printed in sheets including two *se-tenant* stamp-size labels.

217 Angel

(Des E. Cremona)

1972 (9 Dec). *Christmas. T* **217** *and similar horiz designs. W* **105** *(sideways). P* 13½.

482 8 m. + 2 m. dull sepia, brownish grey and gold 10 10
483 3 c. + 1 c. plum, lavender and gold 15 35
484 7 c. 5 + 1 c. 5, indigo, azure and gold .. 20 45
482/4 .. .. *Set of* 3 35 75
MS485 137 × 113 mm. Nos. 482/4 .. .. .. 1·75 3·00

Designs:—No. 483, Angel with tambourine; No. 484, Singing angel.

See also Nos. 507/10.

218 Archaeology

219 Europa "Posthorn"

(Des E. Cremona)

1973 (31 Mar)–**76**. *T* **218** *and similar designs. Multicoloured. W* **105** *(sideways). P* 13½ × 14 *(Nos. 500/a) or* 13½ *(others).*

486 2 m. Type **218** 10 10
487 4 m. History 10 10
a. Gold (inscr and decoration) omitted .. 75·00
b. Imperf (pair) £325
488 5 m. Folklore 10 10
489 8 m. Industry 10 10
490 1 c. Fishing industry 10 10
491 1 c. 3, Pottery 10 10
492 2 c. Agriculture 10 10
493 3 c. Sport 10 10
494 4 c. Yacht marina 15 10
495 5 c. Fiesta 15 10
496 7 c. 5, Regatta 25 10
497 10 c. Voluntary service 25 10
498 50 c. Education .. .. 75 1·00
499 £1 Religion .. .. 2·00 2·75
500 £2 Coat of arms *(horiz)* .. .. .. 14·00 16·00
a. Gold omitted
500*b* £2 National Emblem *(horiz)* (28.1.76) .. 9·00 10·00
486/500*b* .. .. *Set of* 16 24·00 27·00

Nos. 500/*b* are larger, 32 × 27 mm.

(Des L. Anisdahl; adapted G. Pace)

1973 (2 June). *Europa. W* **105**. *P* 14.

501 **219** 3 c. multicoloured 15 10
502 5 c. multicoloured 15 35
503 7 c. 5, multicoloured 25 60
501/3 .. .. *Set of* 3 50 95

Nos. 501/3 were each printed in sheets containing two *se-tenant* stamp-size labels.

220 Emblem, and Woman holding Corn

221 Girolamo Cassar (architect)

(Des H. Alden)

1973 (6 Oct). *Anniversaries. T* **220** *and similar vert designs showing emblem and allegorical figures. W* **105** *(sideways). P* 13½.

504 1 c. 3, multicoloured 10 10
505 7 c. 5, multicoloured 25 40
506 10 c. multicoloured 30 50
504/6 .. .. *Set of* 3 55 85

Anniversaries:—1 c. 3, Tenth Anniv of World Food Programme; 7 c. 5, 25th Anniv of W.H.O.; 10 c. 25th Anniv of Universal Declaration of Human Rights.

(Des E. Cremona)

1973 (10 Nov). *Christmas. Horiz designs as T* **217**. *Multicoloured. W* **105** *(sideways). P* 13½.

507 8 m. + 2 m. Angels and organ pipes 15 10
508 3 c. + 1 c. Madonna and Child 25 40
509 7 c. 5 + 1 c. 5, Buildings and Star 45 65
507/9 .. .. *Set of* 3 75 1·00
MS510 137 × 112 mm. Nos. 507/9 .. .. 4·25 6·00

(Des E. Cremona)

1974 (12 Jan). *Prominent Maltese. T* **221** *and similar vert designs. W* **105**. *P* 14.

511 1 c. 3, dull myrtle-grn, dull grey-grn & gold .. 10 10
512 3 c. deep turquoise, grey-blue and gold .. 10 10
513 5 c. dull sepia, deep slate-green and gold .. 15 15
514 7 c. 5, slate-blue, light slate-blue and gold .. 20 30
515 10 c. purple, dull purple and gold 20 40
511/15 .. .. *Set of* 5 60 85

Designs:—3 c. Giuseppe Barth (ophthalmologist); 5 c. Nicolo' Isouard (composer); 7 c. 5, John Borg (botanist); 10 c. Antonio Sciortino (sculptor).

222 "Air Malta" Emblem

(Des E. Cremona)

1974 (30 Mar). *Air. T* **222** *and similar horiz design. Multicoloured. W* **105** *(sideways). P* 13½.

516 3 c. Type **222** 10 10
517 4 c. Boeing "707" 15 10
518 5 c. Type **222** 15 10
519 7 c. 5, As 4 c. 20 10
520 20 c. Type **222** 55 60
521 25 c. As 4 c. 55 60
522 35 c. Type **222** .. .. 1·00 1·40
516/22 .. .. *Set of* 7 2·40 2·50

223 Prehistoric Sculpture

(Des E. Cremona)

1974 (13 July). *Europa. T* **223** *and similar designs. W* **105** *(sideways on Nos. 523 and 525). P* 13½.

523 1 c. 3, slate-blue, grey-black and gold .. 15 10
524 3 c. light bistre-brown, grey-black and gold 20 15
525 5 c. purple, grey-black and gold 25 45
526 7 c. 5, dull green, grey-black and gold .. 35 80
523/6 .. .. *Set of* 4 85 1·40

Designs: *Vert*—3 c. Old Cathedral Door, Mdina; 7 c. 5, "Vetlina" (sculpture by A. Sciortino). *Horiz*—5 c. Silver Monstrance.

Nos. 523/6 were each printed in sheets including two *se-tenant* stamp-size labels.

224 Heinrich von Stephan (founder) and Land Transport

225 Decorative Star and Nativity Scene

(Des S. and G. Sullivan)

1974 (20 Sept). *Centenary of Universal Postal Union. T* **224** *and similar horiz designs. W* **105**. *P* 13½ × 14.

527 1 c. 3, blue-green, lt violet-blue & yell-orge .. 30 10
528 5 c. brown, dull vermilion and yellow-green 30 10
529 7 c. 5, dp dull blue, lt violet-blue & yell-grn .. 35 20
530 50 c. purple, dull vermilion and yellow-orange 1·00 1·25
527/30 .. .. *Set of* 4 1·75 1·50
MS531 126 × 91 mm. Nos. 527/30 .. .. 3·50 4·50

Designs (each containing portrait as T **224**):—5 c. *Washington* (paddle-steamer) and *Royal Viking Star* (liner); 7 c. 5, Balloon and Boeing "747"; 50 c. U.P.U. Buildings, 1874 and 1974.

(Des E. Cremona)

1974 (22 Nov). *Christmas. T* **225** *and similar vert designs, each with decorative star. Multicoloured. W* **105** *(sideways). P* 14.

532 8 m. + 2 m. Type **225** 10 10
533 3 c. + 1 c. "Shepherds" 15 20
534 5 c. + 1 c. "Shepherds with gifts" 20 35
535 7 c. 5 + 1 c. 5, "The Magi" 30 40
532/5 .. .. *Set of* 4 65 95

REPUBLIC

226 Swearing-in of Prime Minister

(Des E. Cremona)

1975 (31 Mar). *Inauguration of Republic. T* **226** *and similar horiz designs. W* **105** *(sideways). P* 14.

536 1 c. 3, multicoloured 10 10
537 5 c. rose-red and grey-black 20 10
538 25 c. multicoloured .. .. 60 1·00
536/8 .. .. *Set of* 3 75 1·10

Designs:—5 c. National flag; 25 c. Minister of Justice, President and Prime Minister.

227 Mother and Child ("Family Life")

(Des D. Friggieri)

1975 (30 May). *International Women's Year. T* **227** *and similar horiz design. W* **105**. *P* 13½ × 14.

539 **227** 1 c. 3, light violet and gold 15 10
540 – 3 c. light blue and gold 20 10
541 **227** 5 c. dull olive-sepia and gold 50 20
542 – 20 c. chestnut and gold .. .. .. 2·25 3·00
539/42 .. .. *Set of* 4 2·75 3·00

Design:—3 c., 20 c. Office secretary ("Public Life").

228 "Allegory of Malta" (Francesco de Mura)

(Des E. Cremona)

1975 (15 July). *Europa. T* **228** *and similar horiz design. Multicoloured. W* **105**. *P* 14 × 13½.

543 5 c. Type **228** 30 10
544 15 c. "Judith and Holofernes" (Valentin de Boulogne) 50 65

The 15 c. is a smaller design than the 5 c. (47 × 23 mm), though the perforated area is the same.

Nos. 543/4 were each printed in sheets including two *se-tenant* stamp-size labels.

229 Plan of Ggantija Temple

(Des R. England)

1975 (16 Sept). *European Architectural Heritage Year. T* **229** *and similar horiz designs. W* **105** *(sideways). P* 13½.

545 1 c. 3, brownish black and light orange-red .. 10 10
546 3 c. dull purple, lt orange-red & blackish brn 20 10
547 5 c. blackish brown and light orange-red .. 40 35
548 25 c. dull grey-olive, light orange-red and brownish black .. .. 1·75 3·25
545/8 .. .. *Set of* 4 2·25 3·50

Designs:—3 c. Mdina skyline; 5 c. View of Victoria, Gozo; 25 c. Silhouette of Fort St. Angelo.

230 Farm Animals

231 "The Right to Work"

(Des E. Cremona)

1975 (4 Nov). *Christmas. T* **230** *and similar multicoloured designs. W* **105** *(sideways). P* 13½.

549 8 m. + 2 m. Type **230** 30 25
a. In triptych with Nos. 550/1 .. .. 2·25 5·00
550 3 c. + 1 c. Nativity scene (50 × 23 *mm*) .. 60 75
551 7 c. 5 + 1 c. 5, Approach of the Magi .. 1·50 1·75
549/51 .. .. *Set of* 3 2·25 2·50

Nos. 549/51 were issued in sheets of 50 of each value, and also in sheets containing the three values horizontally *se-tenant*, thus forming the triptych No. 549a which is a composite design of "The Nativity" by Master Alberto.

(Des A. de Giovanni)

1975 (12 Dec). *First Anniv of Republic. T* **231** *and similar vert designs. W* **105**. *P* 14.

552 1 c. 3, multicoloured 10 10
553 5 c. multicoloured 20 10
554 25 c. deep rose, light steel-blue and black .. 70 1·10
552/4 .. .. *Set of* 3 80 1·10

Designs:—5 c. "Safeguarding the Environment"; 25 c. National Flag.

232 "Festa Tar-Rahal"

233 Waterpolo

(Des M. Camilleri)

1976 (26 Feb). *Maltese Folklore. T* **232** *and similar multicoloured designs. W* **105** *(sideways on 5 c. and 7 c. 5). P* 14.

555 1 c. 3, Type **232** 10 10
556 5 c. "L-Imnarja" *(horiz)* 15 10
557 7 c. 5, "Il-Karnival" *(horiz)* 45 70
558 10 c. "Il-Gimgha L-Kbira" .. .. 70 1·40
555/8 .. .. *Set of* 4 1·25 2·00

(Des H. Alden)

1976 (28 Apr). *Olympic Games, Montreal. T* **233** *and similar horiz designs. Multicoloured. W* **105**. *P* 13½ × 14.

559 1 c. 7, Type **233** 10 10
560 5 c. Sailing 20 10
561 30 c. Athletics .. .. 65 1·50
559/61 .. .. *Set of* 3 85 1·50

234 Lace-making

(Des F. Portelli)

1976 (8 July). *Europa. T* **234** *and similar horiz design. Multicoloured. W* **105** *(sideways). P* 13½ × 14.

562 7 c. Type **234** 20 30
563 15 c. Stone carving 25 40

Nos. 562/3 were each printed in sheets including two *se-tenant* stamp-size labels.

235 Nicola Cotoner

(Des E. Cremona)

1976 (14 Sept). *300th Anniv of School of Anatomy and Surgery. T* **235** *and similar horiz designs. Multicoloured. W* **105** *(sideways). P* 13½.

564 2 c. Type **235** 10 10
565 5 c. Arm 10 10
566 7 c. Giuseppe Zammit 15 10
567 11 c. Sacra Infermeria 25 65
564/7 .. .. *Set of* 4 50 75

1c7

236 St. John the Baptist and St. Michael

237 Jean de la Valette's Armour

(238)

(Des E. Cremona)

1976 (23 Nov). *Christmas. Designs showing portions of "Madonna and Saints" by Domenico di Michelino. Multicoloured. W* **105** *(sideways on No. 571). P* 13½ × 14 *(No. 571) or* 13½ *(others).*

568 1 c. + 5 m. Type **236** 15 20
569 5 c. + 1 c. Madonna and Child 50 70
570 7 c. + 1 c. 5, St. Christopher and St. Nicholas 65 1·00
571 10 c. + 2 c. Complete painting (32 × 27 *mm*) .. 75 1·40
568/71 .. .. *Set of* 4 1·90 3·00

(Des J. Briffa)

1977 (20 Jan). *Suits of Armour. T* **237** *and similar vert designs. Multicoloured. W* **105**. *P* 13½.

572 2 c. Type **237** 10 10
573 7 c. Aloph de Wignacourt's armour 20 10
574 11 c. Jean Jacques de Verdelin's armour .. 25 50
572/4 .. .. *Set of* 3 45 60

1977 (24 Mar). *No. 336 surch with T* **238** *by Govt Printing Press, Malta.*

575 **116** 1 c. 7 on 4d. multicoloured 25 25
a. "KNIGHTS OF MALTA" (silver) omitted .. .. 65·00

239 "Annunciation"

240 Map and Radio Aerial

(Des E. Cremona)

1977 (30 Mar). *400th Birth Anniversary of Rubens. Flemish tapestries (1st series) showing his paintings as T* **239**. *Multicoloured. W* **105** *(sideways). P* 14.

576 2 c. Type **239** 10 10
577 7 c. "Four Evangelists" 20 10
578 11 c. "Nativity" 40 45
579 20 c. "Adoration of the Magi" .. .. .. 65 1·00
576/9 .. .. *Set of* 4 1·25 1·50

See also Nos. 592/5, 615/18 and 638/40.

(Des H. Borg)

1977 (17 May). *World Telecommunication Day. T* **240** *and similar design. W* **105** *(sideways on 1 and 6 c.). P* 14 × 13½ *(1 and 6 c.) or* 13½ × 14 *(others).*

580 **240** 1 c. black, green and vermilion 10 10
581 6 c. black, grey-blue and vermilion .. 15 10
582 – 8 c. black, chestnut and vermilion .. 15 10
583 – 17 c. black, dull mauve and vermilion .. 30 40
580/3 .. .. *Set of* 4 55 55

Design: *Horiz*—8 and 17 c. Map, aerial and aeroplane tail-fin.

241 Ta' L-Isperanza

242 "Aid to Handicapped Workers" (detail from Workers' Monument)

(Des G. French)

1977 (5 July). *Europa. T* **241** *and similar horiz design. Multicoloured. W* **105** *(sideways). P* 13½.

584 7 c. Type **241** 30 15
585 20 c. Is-Salini 35 80

Nos. 584/5 were each printed in sheets including two *se-tenant* stamp-size labels.

(Des A. Agius)

1977 (12 Oct). *Maltese Worker Commemoration. T* **242** *and similar designs. W* **105** *(sideways on 20 c.). P* 13½.

586 2 c. orange-brown and light brown 10 10
587 7 c. chestnut and brown 15 10
588 20 c. multicoloured 40 60
586/8 .. .. *Set of* 3 55 60

Designs: *Vert*—7 c. "Stoneworker, modern industry and shipbuilding" (monument detail). *Horiz*—20 c. "Mother with Dead Son" and Service Medal.

243 The Shepherds

244 "Young Lady on Horseback and Trooper"

(Des E. Cremona)

1977 (16 Nov). *Christmas. T* **243** *and similar horiz designs. Multicoloured. W* **105** *(sideways). P* 13½ × 14.

589 1 c. + 5 m. Type **243** 10 20
a. In triptych with Nos. 590/1 40
590 7 c. + 1 c. The Nativity 15 30
591 11 c. + 1 c. 5, Flight into Egypt 20 45
589/91 .. .. *Set of* 3 40 85

Nos. 589/91 were issued in sheets of 50 of each value, and also in sheets containing the three values *se-tenant*, thus forming the triptych No. 589a.

(Des E. Cremona)

1978 (26 Jan). *Flemish Tapestries (2nd series). Horiz designs similar to T* **239**. *Multicoloured. W* **105** *(sideways). P* 14.

592 2 c. "The Entry into Jerusalem" (artist unknown) 10 10
593 7 c. "The Last Supper" (after Poussin) .. 20 10
594 11 c. "The Raising of the Cross" (after Rubens) 25 25
595 25 c. "The Resurrection" (after Rubens) .. 60 80
592/5 .. .. *Set of* 4 1·00 1·10

(Des A. Camilleri)

1978 (7 Mar). *450th Death Anniv of Albrecht Dürer. T* **244** *and similar vert designs. W* **105**. *P* 14.

596 1 c. 7, black, vermilion and deep blue .. 10 10
597 8 c. black, vermilion and slate 15 10
598 17 c. black, vermilion and deep slate 40 45
a. Vermilion (monogram) omitted .. 75·00
596/8 .. .. *Set of* 3 55 55

Designs:—8 c. "The Bag-piper"; 17 c. "The Virgin and Child with a Monkey".

245 Monument to Grand Master Nicola Cotoner (Foggini)

246 Goalkeeper

(Des E. Cremona)

1978 (26 Apr). *Europa. Monuments. T* **245** *and similar vert design. Multicoloured. W* **105**. *P* 14 × 13½.

599 7 c. Type **245** 15 10
600 25 c. Monument to Grand Master Ramon Perellos (Mazzuoli) 35 55

Nos. 599/600 were each printed in sheets including two *se-tenant* stamp-size labels.

(Des A. de Giovanni)

1978 (6 June). *World Cup Football Championship, Argentina. T* **246** *and similar vert designs. Multicoloured. W* **105** *(sideways). P* 14 × 13½.

601 2 c. Type **246** 10 10
602 11 c. Players heading ball 15 10
603 15 c. Tackling 25 35
601/3 .. .. *Set of* 3 45 45
MS604 125 × 90 mm. Nos. 601/3 .. .. .. 1·50 2·25

247 Airliner over Megalithic Temple

(Des R. Caruana)

1978 (3 Oct). *Air. Horiz designs as T* **247**. *Multicoloured. W* **105** *(sideways). P* 13½.

605 5 c. Type **247** 15 10
606 7 c. Air Malta Boeing "720B" 15 10
607 11 c. Boeing "747" taking off from Luqa Airport 25 10
608 17 c. Type **247** 35 30
609 20 c. As 7 c. 50 40
610 75 c. As 11 c. .. .. 1·50 2·25
605/10 .. .. *Set of* 6 2·75 2·75

248 Folk Musicians and Village Church

249 Luzzu and Aircraft Carrier

(Des E. Cremona)

1978 (9 Nov). *Christmas. T* **248** *and similar multicoloured designs. W* **105** *(sideways). P* 13½ *(11 c.) or* 14 *(others).*

611 1 c. + 5 m. Type **248** 10 10
612 5 c. + 1 c. Choir of Angels 10 15
613 7 c. + 1 c. 5, Carol singers 15 20
614 11 c. + 3 c. Folk musicians, church, angels and carol singers (58 × 23 *mm*) 20 30
611/14 .. .. *Set of* 4 50 65

The 1, 5 and 7 c. values depict details of the complete design shown on the 11 c. value.

(Des E. Cremona)

1979 (24 Jan). *Flemish Tapestries (3rd series). Horiz designs as T* **239** *showing paintings by Rubens. Multicoloured. W* **105** *(sideways). P* 14.

615 2 c. "The Triumph of the Catholic Church" .. 10 10
616 7 c. "The Triumph of Charity" 15 10
617 11 c. "The Triumph of Faith" 25 20
618 25 c. "The Triumph of Truth" 70 55
615/18 .. .. *Set of* 4 1·10 80

(Des E. Cremona)

1979 (31 Mar). *End of Military Facilities Agreement. T* **249** *and similar vert designs. Multicoloured. W* **105** *(sideways). P* 13½.

619 2 c. Type **249** 10 10
620 5 c. Raising the flag ceremony 10 10
621 7 c. Departing soldier and olive sprig .. 15 10
622 8 c. Type **249** 30 40
623 17 c. As 5 c. 50 60
624 20 c. As 7 c. 50 60
619/24 .. .. *Set of* 6 1·40 1·60

250 Speronara (fishing boat) and Tail of Air Malta Airliner

251 Children on Globe

(Des E. Cremona)

1979 (9 May). *Europa. Communications. T* **250** *and similar vert design. Multicoloured.* W **105** (*sideways*). *P* 14.

625 7 c. Type **250** 15 10
626 25 c. Coastal watch tower and radio link towers 35 50

Nos. 625/6 were each printed in sheets including two *se-tenant* stamp-size labels.

(Des A. Bonnici (2 c.), A. Pisani (7 c.), M. French (11 c.))

1979 (13 June). *International Year of the Child. T* **251** *and similar multicoloured designs.* W **105** (*sideways*). *P* 14 × 13½ (2 c.) *or* 14 (*others*).

627 2 c. Type **251** 10 10
628 7 c. Children flying kites (27 × 33 *mm*) .. 15 10
629 11 c. Children in circle (27 × 33 *mm*) 20 35
627/9 .. .. *Set of* 3 35 45

252 Shells (*Gibbula nivosa*)

(Des R. Pitré)

1979 (10 Oct). *Marine Life. T* **252** *and similar horiz designs. Multicoloured.* W **105**. *P* 13½.

630 2 c. Type **252** 10 10
631 5 c. Loggerhead Turtle (*Garetta garetta*) .. 20 10
632 7 c. Dolphin Fish (*Coryphaena hippurus*) .. 25 10
633 25 c. Noble Pen Shell (*Pinna nobilis*) .. .. 90 1·25
630/3 .. .. *Set of* 4 1·25 1·25

253 "The Nativity" (detail)

(Des E. Cremona)

1979 (14 Nov). *Christmas. Paintings by G. Calì. T* **253** *and similar horiz designs. Multicoloured.* W **105**. *P* 14 × 13½.

634 1 c. + 5 m. Type **253** 10 10
635 5 c. + 1 c. "The Flight into Egypt" (detail) .. 10 15
636 7 c. + 1 c. 5, "The Nativity" 15 20
637 11 c. + 3 c. "The Flight into Egypt" 25 50
634/7 .. .. *Set of* 4 50 85

(Des E. Cremona)

1980 (30 Jan). *Flemish Tapestries (4th series). Horiz designs as T* **239** *taken from paintings. Multicoloured.* W **105** (*sideways*). *P* 14.

638 2 c. "The Institution of Corpus Domini" (Rubens) 10 10
639 8 c. "The Destruction of Idolatry" (Rubens) .. 20 20
MS640 114 × 86 mm. 50 c. "Grand Master Perellos with St. Jude and St. Simon" (unknown Maltese artist) (*vert*) .. .. 80 1·40

254 Hal Saflieni Hypogeum, Paola

255 Dun Gorg Preca

1980 (15 Feb). *International Restoration of Maltese Monuments Campaign. T* **254** *and similar multicoloured designs.* W **105** (*sideways on* 8 *and* 12 *c.*). *P* 14.

641 2 c. 5, Type **254** 10 15
642 6 c. Vilhena Palace, Mdina 25 20
643 8 c. Victoria Citadel, Gozo (*horiz*) 30 35
644 12 c. Fort St. Elmo, Valletta (*horiz*) 40 55
641/4 .. .. *Set of* 4 95 1·10

(Des R. Pitré)

1980 (12 Apr). *Birth Centenary of Dun Gorg Preca (founder of Society of Christian Doctrine).* W **105** (*sideways*). *P* 14 × 13½.

645 **255** 2 c. 5, black and grey 10 10

256 Ruzar Briffa (poet)

257 "Annunciation"

(Des V. Apap)

1980 (29 Apr). *Europa. Personalities. T* **256** *and similar horiz design.* W **105** (*sideways*). *P* 13½ × 14.

646 8 c. black, brown-ochre and bronze-green .. 20 10
647 30 c. brown, brown-olive and brown-lake .. 55 70

Design:—30 c. Nikiol Anton Vassalli (scholar and patriot).

Nos. 646/7 were each printed in sheets including two *se-tenant* stamp-size labels.

(Des R. Pitré)

1980 (7 Oct). *Christmas. Paintings by A. Inglott. T* **257** *and similar multicoloured designs.* W **105** (*sideways on* 12 *c.*). *P* 14 (12 *c.*) *or* 13½ (*others*).

648 2 c. + 5 m. Type **257** 10 10
649 6 c. + 1 c. "Conception" 15 10
650 8 c. + 1 c. 5, "Nativity" 20 25
651 12 c. + 3 c. "Annunciation", "Conception" and "Nativity" (47 × 38 *mm*) 25 30
648/51 .. .. *Set of* 4 60 60

The paintings from the 2, 6 and 8 c. values are united to form the triptych on the 12 c. value.

258 Chess Pieces

259 Barn Owl (*Tyto alba*)

(Des H. Borg)

1980 (20 Nov). *Chess Olympiad and F.I.D.E. (International Chess Federation) Congress. T* **258** *and similar multicoloured designs.* W **105** (*sideways on* 30 *c.*). *P* 14 × 13½ (30 *c.*) *or* 13½ × 14 (*others*).

652 2 c. 5, Type **258** 20 10
653 8 c. Chess pieces (*different*) 50 15
654 30 c. Chess pieces (*vert*) .. .. .. 1·00 80
652/4 .. .. *Set of* 3 1·50 95

(Des M. Burlò)

1981 (20 Jan). *Birds. T* **259** *and similar vert designs. Multicoloured.* W **105** (*sideways*). *P* 13½.

655 3 c. Type **259** 30 15
656 8 c. Sardinian Warbler (*Sylvia melanocephala*) 50 20
657 12 c. Woodchat Shrike (*Lanius senator*) 60 60
658 23 c. British Storm Petrel (*Hydrobates pelagicus*) .. .. 1·10 1·25
655/8 .. .. *Set of* 4 2·25 2·00

260 Traditional Horse Race

261 Stylised "25"

(Des H. Borg)

1981 (28 Apr). *Europa. Folklore. T* **260** *and similar vert design. Multicoloured.* W **105** (*sideways*). *P* 14.

659 8 c. Type **260** 20 10
660 30 c. Attempting to retrieve flag from end of "gostra" (greasy pole) 40 65

The two values were each printed in sheets including two *se-tenant* stamp-size labels.

(Des A. de Giovanni)

1981 (12 June). *25th Maltese International Trade Fair.* W **105** (*sideways*). *P* 13½.

661 **261** 4 c. multicoloured 15 15
662 25 c. multicoloured 50 60

OMNIBUS ISSUES

Details, together with prices for complete sets, of the various Omnibus issues from the 1935 Silver Jubilee series to date are included in a special section following Zimbabwe at the end of Volume 2.

262 Disabled Artist at Work

263 Wheat Ear in Conical Flask

(Des A. Camilleri)

1981 (17 July). *International Year for Disabled Persons. T* **262** *and similar vert design. Multicoloured.* W **105** (*sideways*). *P* 13½.

663 3 c. Type **262** 15 10
664 35 c. Disabled child playing football 55 75

(Des R. Caruana)

1981 (16 Oct). *World Food Day.* W **105** (*sideways*). *P* 14.

665 **263** 8 c. multicoloured 15 15
666 23 c. multicoloured 60 50

264 Megalithic Building

265 Children and Nativity Scene

(Des F. Portelli)

1981 (31 Oct). *History of Maltese Industry. Horiz designs as T* **264**. *Multicoloured.* W **105**. *P* 14.

667 5 m. Type **264** 10 10
668 1 c. Cotton production 10 10
669 2 c. Early ship-building 10 10
670 3 c. Currency minting 10 10
671 5 c. "Art" 20 25
672 6 c. Fishing 20 25
673 7 c. Agriculture 25 30
674 8 c. Stone quarrying 30 35
675 10 c. Grape pressing 35 40
676 12 c. Modern ship-building 40 45
677 15 c. Energy 50 55
678 20 c. Telecommunications 70 75
679 25 c. "Industry" 90 95
680 50 c. Drilling for water .. .. 1·75 1·90
681 £1 Sea transport .. .. 3·50 3·75
682 £3 Air transport .. .. 10·50 11·00
667/82 .. .. *Set of* 16 17·00 18·00

(Des A. Bugeja)

1981 (18 Nov). *Christmas. T* **265** *and similar multicoloured designs.* W **105** (*sideways*). *P* 14.

683 2 c. + 1 c. Type **265** 15 10
684 8 c. + 2 c. Christmas Eve procession (*horiz*) .. 25 20
685 20 c. + 3 c. Preaching midnight sermon .. 50 60
683/5 .. .. *Set of* 3 80 80

266 Shipbuilding

267 Elderly Man and Has-Serh (home for elderly)

(Des N. Attard)

1982 (29 Jan). *Shipbuilding Industry. T* **266** *and similar vert designs showing different scenes.* W **105** (*sideways*). *P* 13½.

686 3 c. multicoloured 15 10
687 8 c. multicoloured 30 30
688 13 c. multicoloured 55 55
689 27 c. multicoloured .. .. 1·25 1·25
686/9 .. .. *Set of* 4 2·00 2·00

(Des R. Pitré)

1982 (16 Mar). *Care of Elderly. T* **267** *and similar horiz design. Multicoloured.* W **105**. *P* 14 × 13½.

690 8 c. Type **267** 40 20
691 30 c. Elderly woman and Has-Zmien (hospital for elderly) .. .. 1·40 1·40

268 Redemption of Islands by Maltese, 1428

(Des F. Portelli)

1982 (29 Apr). *Europa. Historical Events. T* **268** *and similar horiz design. Multicoloured. W* **105**. *P* 14 × 13½.
692 8 c. Type **268** 40 20
693 30 c. Declaration of rights by Maltese, 1802 .. 1·00 1·40
Nos. 692/3 were each printed in sheets containing 2 *se-tenant* stamp-size labels.

269 Stylised Footballer

(Des R. Caruana)

1982 (11 June). *World Cup Football Championship, Spain. T* **269** *and similar horiz designs showing stylised footballers. W* **105**. *P* 14.
694 3 c. multicoloured 20 10
695 12 c. multicoloured 60 55
696 15 c. multicoloured 70 65
694/6 .. .. *Set of* 3 1·40 1·25
MS697 125 × 90 mm. Nos. 694/6 .. .. .. 2·25 2·50

270 Angel appearing to Shepherds

(Des J. Mallia)

1982 (8 Oct). *Christmas. T* **270** *and similar multicoloured designs. W* **105** (*sideways*). *P* 14 (*No.* 700) *or* 13½ (*others*).
698 2 c. + 1 c. Type **270** 15 10
699 8 c. + 2 c. Nativity and Three Wise Men bearing gifts 40 40
700 20 c. + 3 c. Nativity scene (*larger* 45 × 37 *mm*) 85 85
698/700 .. .. *Set of* 3 1·25 1·25
The designs from the 2 and 8 c. values are united to form the design of the 20 c. stamp.

271 *Ta' Salvo Serafino* (bared brigantine), 1531

(Des N. Attard)

1982 (13 Nov). *Maltese Ships* (*1st series*). *T* **271** *and similar horiz designs. Multicoloured. W* **105**. *P* 14 × 13½.
701 3 c. Type **271** 40 10
702 8 c. *La Madonna del Rosaria* (tartane), 1740 .. .. 80 30
703 12 c. *San Paulo* (xebec), 1743 .. .. .. 1·25 55
704 20 c. *Ta' Pietro Saliba* (xprunara), 1798 .. 1·60 90
701/4 .. .. *Set of* 4 3·50 1·60
See also Nos. 725/8, 772/5, 792/5 and 809/12.

272 *Manning Wardle*, 1883

(Des R. Caruana)

1983 (21 Jan). *Centenary of Malta Railway. T* **272** *and similar horiz designs. Multicoloured. W* **105**. *P* 14 × 13½.
705 3 c. Type **272** 45 10
706 13 c. *Black Hawthorn*, 1884 .. .. .. 1·00 55
707 27 c. *Beyer Peacock*, 1895 .. .. .. 2·00 1·25
705/7 .. .. *Set of* 3 3·00 1·75

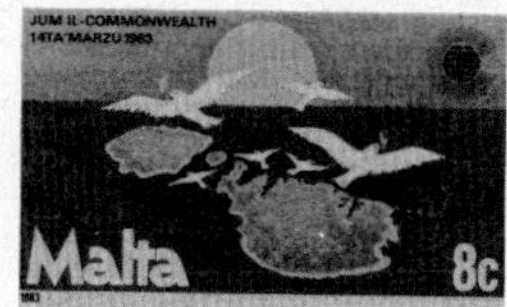

273 Peace Doves leaving Malta

(Des C. Cassar)

1983 (14 Mar). *Commonwealth Day. T* **273** *and similar multicoloured designs. W* **105** (*sideways on vert designs*). *P* 14 × 13½ (8, 12 c.) *or* 13½ × 14 (*others*).
708 8 c. Type **273** 30 30
709 12 c. Tourist landmarks 40 40
710 15 c. Holiday beach (*vert*) 50 50
711 23 c. Ship-building (*vert*) 70 75
708/11 .. .. *Set of* 4 1·75 1·75

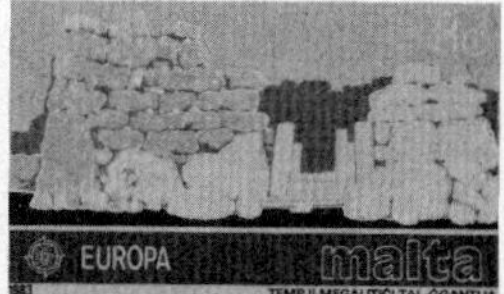

274 Ggantija Megalithic Temples, Gozo

(Des T. Bugeja (8 c.), R. Caruana (30 c.))

1983 (5 May). *Europa. T* **274** *and similar horiz design. Multicoloured. W* **105**. *P* 14 × 13½.
712 8 c. Type **274** 65 30
713 30 c. Fort St. Angelo .. .. 1·75 1·40
Nos. 712/13 were each printed in sheets including two *se-tenant* stamp-size labels.

275 Dish Aerials (World Communications Year)

(Des D. Friggieri)

1983 (14 July). *Anniversaries and Events. T* **275** *and similar horiz designs. Multicoloured. W* **105** (*sideways*). *P* 13½ × 14.
714 3 c. Type **275** 35 15
715 7 c. Ships' prows and badge (25th anniv of I.M.O. Convention) 60 40
716 13 c. Container lorries and badge (30th anniv of Customs Co-operation Council) .. 80 60
717 20 c. Stadium and emblem (9th Mediterranean Games) .. .. 1·00 1·00
714/17 .. .. *Set of* 4 2·50 2·00

276 Monsignor Giuseppe de Piro

MALTA 2c+1c

277 Annunciation

(Des E. Barthet)

1983 (1 Sept). *50th Death Anniv of Monsignor Giuseppe de Piro. W* **105** (*sideways*). *P* 14.
718 **276** 3 c. multicoloured 10 10

(Des N. Attard)

1983 (6 Sept). *Christmas. T* **277** *and similar vert designs. Multicoloured. W* **105** (*sideways*). *P* 13½ × 14.
719 2 c. + 1 c. Type **277** 30 15
720 8 c. + 2 c. The Nativity 75 40
721 20 c. + 3 c. Adoration of the Magi .. .. 1·40 85
719/21 .. .. *Set of* 3 2·25 1·25

278 Workers at Meeting

(Des F. Portelli)

1983 (5 Oct). *40th Anniv of General Workers' Union. T* **278** *and similar horiz designs. Multicoloured. W* **105**. *P* 14 × 13½.
722 3 c. Type **278** 25 10
723 8 c. Worker with family 50 30
724 27 c. Union H.Q. Building .. .. 1·50 1·40
722/4 .. .. *Set of* 3 2·00 1·75

(Des N. Attard)

1983 (17 Nov). *Maltese Ships* (*2nd series*). *Horiz designs as T* **271**. *Multicoloured. W* **105**. *P* 14 × 13½.
725 2 c. *Strangier* (full-rigged ship), 1813 .. 20 15
726 12 c. *Tigre* (topsail schooner), 1839 .. .. 90 60
727 13 c. *La Speranza* (brig), 1844 .. .. .. 1·00 70
728 20 c. *Wignacourt* (barque), 1844 .. .. 1·50 1·00
725/8 .. .. *Set of* 4 3·25 2·25

279 Boeing "737"

(Des R. Caruana)

1984 (26 Jan). *Air. T* **279** *and similar horiz designs. Multicoloured. W* **105**. *P* 14 × 13½.
729 7 c. Type **279** 25 30
730 8 c. Boeing "720B" 30 35
731 16 c. Vickers "Vanguard" 55 60
732 23 c. Vickers "Viscount" 80 85
733 27 c. Douglas "DC.3 Dakota" .. .. .. 95 1·00
734 38 c. A.W. "Atlanta" .. .. 1·40 1·50
735 75 c. Dornier "Wal" .. .. 2·75 3·00
729/35 .. .. *Set of* 7 6·25 6·75

280 C.E.P.T. 25th Anniversary Logo

Malta 3c

281 Early Policeman

(Des J. Larrivière and L. Borg)

1984 (27 Apr). *Europa. W* **105**. *P* 13½.
736 **280** 8 c. green, black and gold 35 35
737 30 c. carmine-lake, black and gold .. 1·25 1·25
Nos. 736/7 were each printed in sheets including two *se-tenant* stamp-size labels.

(Des T. Bugeja)

1984 (14 June). *170th Anniv of Malta Police Force. T* **281** *and similar vert designs. Multicoloured. W* **105**. *P* 14 × 13½.
738 3 c. Type **281** 55 15
739 8 c. Mounted police .. .. 1·25 55
a. Pale Venetian red (background) omitted .. .. 95·00
740 11 c. Motorcycle policeman .. .. 1·50 1·25
741 25 c. Policeman and fireman .. .. .. 2·50 2·50
738/41 .. .. *Set of* 4 5·25 4·00

282 Running

283 "The Visitation" (Pietro Caruana)

(Des L. Micallef)

1984 (26 July). *Olympic Games, Los Angeles. T* **282** *and similar vert designs. Multicoloured. W* **105** (*sideways*). *P* 14.
742 7 c. Type **282** 25 30
743 12 c. Gymnastics 50 60
744 23 c. Swimming .. .. 85 1·10
742/4 .. .. *Set of* 3 1·50 1·75

(Des L. Micallef)

1984 (5 Oct). *Christmas. Paintings from Church of Our Lady of Porto Salvo, Valletta. T* **283** *and similar multicoloured designs. W* **105** (*sideways on horiz designs*). *P* 14.
745 2 c. + 1 c. Type **283** 45 45
746 8 c. + 2 c. "The Epiphany" (Rafel Caruana) (*horiz*) 85 85
747 20 c. + 3 c. "Jesus among the Doctors" (Rafel Caruana) (*horiz*) .. .. 1·75 2·50
745/7 .. .. *Set of* 3 2·75 3·50

284 Dove on Map

285 1885 ½d. Green Stamp

(Des L. Micallef)

1984 (12 Dec). *10th Anniv of Republic. T* **284** *and similar vert designs. Multicoloured. W* **105** (*sideways*). *P* 14.
748 3 c. Type **284** 40 20
749 8 c. Fort St. Angelo 75 50
750 30 c. Hands .. .. 2·50 3·50
748/50 .. .. *Set of* 3 3·25 3·75

(Des N. Attard)

1985 (2 Jan). *Centenary of Malta Post Office. T* **285** *and similar vert designs showing stamps of* 1885. *Multicoloured. W* **105**. *P* 14.
751 3 c. Type **285** 35 15
752 8 c. 1885 1d. rose 55 40
753 12 c. 1885 2½d. dull blue 75 95
754 20 c. 1885 4d. brown .. .. 1·25 1·90
751/4 .. .. *Set of* 4 2·50 3·00
MS755 165 × 90 mm. Nos. 751/4. Wmk sideways 2·50 3·25

286 Boy, and Hands planting Vine

(Des T. Bugeja)

1985 (7 Mar). *International Youth Year. T* **286** *and similar multicoloured designs. W* **105** *(sideways on* 13 *c.). P* 14.
756 2 c. Type **286** 10 15
757 13 c. Young people and flowers (*vert*) .. 55 60
758 27 c. Girl holding flame in hand .. .. 1·25 1·40
756/8 .. .. *Set of* 3 1·75 1·90

287 Nicolo Baldacchino (tenor) **288** Guzeppi Bajada and Manwel Attard (victims)

(Des L. Micallef)

1985 (25 Apr). *Europa. European Music Year. T* **287** *and similar vert design. Multicoloured. W* **105**. *P* 14.
759 8 c. Type **287** .. .. 1·50 30
760 30 c. Francesco Azopardi (composer) .. 2·50 1·50
Nos. 759/60 were each printed in sheets including two *se-tenant* stamp-size labels.

(Des L. Micallef)

1985 (7 June). 66*th Anniv of* 7 *June* 1919 *Demonstrations. T* **288** *and similar multicoloured designs. W* **105** *(sideways on* 3 *c.,* 7 *c.). P* 14.
761 3 c. Type **288** 35 15
762 7 c. Karmnu Abela and Wenzu Dyer (victims) 75 35
763 35 c. Model of projected Demonstration monument by Anton Agius (*vert*) .. 2·25 1·75
761/3 .. .. *Set of* 3 3·00 2·00

289 Stylized Birds

290 Giorgio Mitrovich (nationalist) (Death Centenary)

(Des D. Friggieri)

1985 (26 July). 40*th Anniv of United Nations Organization. T* **289** *and similar horiz designs. Multicoloured. W* **105** *(sideways). P* 13½ × 14.
764 4 c. Type **289** 20 15
765 11 c. Arrow-headed ribbons 75 80
766 31 c. Stylized figures .. .. 1·75 2·75
764/6 .. .. *Set of* 3 2·40 3·25

(Des R. Pitre)

1985 (3 Oct). *Celebrities' Anniversaries. T* **290** *and similar vert design. Multicoloured. W* **105** *(sideways). P* 14.
767 8 c. Type **290** 70 35
768 12 c. Pietru Caxaru (poet and administrator) (400th death anniv) .. .. .. 1·40 90

COVER PRICES

Cover factors are quoted at the beginning of each country for most issues to 1945. An explanation of the system can be found on page x. The factors quoted do not, however, apply to philatelic covers.

291 The Three Wise Men **292** John XXIII Peace Laboratory and Statue of St. Francis of Assisi

(Des G. Bonnici)

1985 (10 Oct). *Christmas. T* **291** *and similar vert designs showing details of terracotta relief by Ganni Bonnici. Multicoloured. W* **105** *(sideways). P* 14.
769 2 c. + 1 c. Type **291** 55 60
770 8 c. + 2 c. Virgin and Child .. .. 1·25 1·50
771 20 c. + 3 c. Angels .. .. 2·25 2·75
769/71 .. .. *Set of* 3 3·50 4·25

(Des N. Attard)

1985 (27 Nov). *Maltese Ships (3rd series). Steamships. Horiz designs as T* **271**. *Multicoloured. W* **105**. *P* 14.
772 3 c. *Scotia* (paddle-steamer), 1844 .. .. 55 20
773 7 c. *Tagliaferro* (screw steamer), 1882 .. 1·00 70
774 15 c. *Gleneagles* (screw steamer), 1885 .. 1·50 1·75
775 23 c. *L'Isle Adam* (screw steamer), 1886 .. 2·25 2·50
772/5 .. .. *Set of* 4 4·75 4·75

(Des A. Agius (8 c.), T. Bugeja (11, 27 c.))

1986 (28 Jan). *International Peace Year. T* **292** *and similar horiz designs. Multicoloured. W* **105** *(sideways). P* 14 *(8, 27 c.) or* 13½ × 14 *(11 c.).*
776 8 c. Type **292** .. .. 1·00 50
777 11 c. Dove and hands holding olive branch (40 × 19 *mm*) .. .. 1·50 1·50
778 27 c. Map of Africa, dove and two heads .. 3·00 3·50
776/8 .. .. *Set of* 3 5·00 5·00

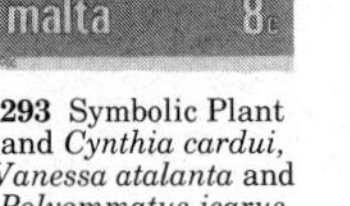

293 Symbolic Plant and *Cynthia cardui, Vanessa atalanta* and *Polyommatus icarus* (butterflies) **294** Heading the Ball

(Des M. Burló)

1986 (3 Apr). *Europa. Environmental Conservation. T* **293** *and similar vert design. Multicoloured. W* **105**. *P* 14.
779 8 c. Type **293** .. .. 1·75 50
780 35 c. Island, Neolithic frieze, sea and sun .. 3·25 4·00
Nos. 779/80 were each printed in sheets including two *se-tenant* stamp-size labels.

(Des T. Bugeja)

1986 (30 May). *World Cup Football Championship, Mexico. T* **294** *and similar horiz designs. Multicoloured. W* **105**. *P* 14.
781 3 c. Type **294** 60 20
782 7 c. Saving a goal .. .. 1·25 65
783 23 c. Controlling the ball .. .. 4·00 4·50
781/3 .. .. *Set of* 3 5·25 4·75
MS784 125 × 90 mm. Nos. 781/3. Wmk sideways 5·25 5·50

295 Father Diegu **296** "Nativity"

(Des L. Micallef)

1986 (28 Aug). *Maltese Philanthropists. T* **295** *and similar vert designs. Multicoloured. W* **105**. *P* 14.
785 2 c. Type **295** 40 30
786 3 c. Adelaide Cini 50 30
787 8 c. Alfonso Maria Galea .. .. 1·25 60
788 27 c. Vincenzo Bugeja .. .. 3·25 4·00
785/8 .. .. *Set of* 4 5·00 4·75

(Des L. Micallef)

1986 (10 Oct). *Christmas. T* **296** *and similar multicoloured designs showing paintings by Giuseppe D'Arena. W* **105** *(sideways on horiz designs). P* 14.
789 2 c. + 1 c. Type **296** 50 60
790 8 c. + 2 c. "Nativity" (detail) (*vert*) .. .. 1·50 1·75
791 20 c. + 3 c. "Epiphany" .. .. 2·75 3·50
789/91 .. .. *Set of* 3 4·25 5·25

(Des N. Attard)

1986 (19 Nov). *Maltese Ships (4th series). Horiz designs as T* **271**. *Multicoloured. W* **105**. *P* 14.
792 7 c. *San Paul* (freighter), 1921 .. .. 1·25 50
793 10 c. *Knight of Malta* (cargo liner), 1930 .. 1·50 1·10
794 12 c. *Valetta City* (freighter), 1948 .. .. 1·75 1·75
795 20 c. *Saver* (freighter), 1959 .. .. .. 3·00 3·50
792/5 .. .. *Set of* 4 6·75 6·25

297 European Robin

(Des R. Caruana)

1987 (26 Jan). 25*th Anniv of Malta Ornithological Society. T* **297** *and similar multicoloured designs. W* **105** *(sideways on* 3, 23 *c.). P* 14.
796 3 c. Type **297** 60 40
797 8 c. Peregrine Falcon (*vert*) .. .. .. 1·50 75
798 13 c. Hoopoe (*vert*) .. .. 2·00 2·00
799 23 c. Cory's Shearwater .. .. 2·75 3·25
796/9 .. .. *Set of* 4 6·25 5·75

298 Aquasun Lido **299** 16th-century Pikeman

(Des R. England)

1987 (15 Apr). *Europa. Modern Architecture. T* **298** *and similar vert design. Multicoloured. W* **105**. *P* 14.
800 8 c. Type **298** .. .. 1·25 65
801 35 c. Church of St. Joseph, Manikata .. 3·50 4·25
Nos. 800/1 were each printed in sheets including two *se-tenant* stamp-size labels.

(Des L. Micallef)

1987 (10 June). *Maltese Uniforms (1st series). T* **299** *and similar vert designs. Multicoloured. W* **105** *(sideways). P* 14.
802 3 c. Type **299** 55 40
803 7 c. 16th-century officer .. .. .. 1·00 70
804 10 c. 18th-century standard bearer .. .. 1·50 1·40
805 27 c. 18th-century General of the Galleys .. 3·25 3·75
802/5 .. .. *Set of* 4 5·75 5·50
See also Nos. 832/5, 851/4, 880/3 and 893/6.

300 Maltese Scenes, Wheat Ears and Sun (European Environment Year)

(Des A. Camilleri)

1987 (18 Aug). *Anniversaries and Events. T* **300** *and similar horiz designs. Multicoloured. W* **105** *(sideways). P* 14.
806 5 c. Type **300** 75 50
807 8 c. Esperanto star as comet (Centenary of Esperanto) .. .. 1·00 60
808 23 c. Family at house door (International Year of Shelter for the Homeless) .. 2·75 2·25
806/8 .. .. *Set of* 3 4·00 3·00

(Des N. Attard)

1987 (16 Oct). *Maltese Ships (5th series). Horiz designs as T* **271**. *Multicoloured. W* **105**. *P* 14.
809 2 c. *Medina* (freighter), 1969 .. .. 40 40
810 11 c. *Rabat* (container ship), 1974 .. .. 1·40 1·40
811 13 c. *Ghawdex* (passenger ferry), 1979 .. 1·60 1·60
812 20 c. *Pinto* (car ferry), 1987 .. .. .. 2·25 2·50
809/12 .. .. *Set of* 4 5·00 5·50

301 "The Visitation"

(Des R. Caruana)

1987 (6 Nov). *Christmas. T* **301** *and similar horiz designs, each showing illuminated illustration, score and text from 16th-century choral manuscript. Multicoloured. W* **105** *(sideways). P* 14.
813 2 c. + 1 c. Type **301** 40 40
814 8 c. + 2 c. "The Nativity" .. .. 1·25 1·50
815 20 c. + 3 c. "The Adoration of the Magi" .. 2·50 2·75
813/15 .. .. *Set of* 3 3·75 4·25

302 Dr. Arvid Pardo (U.N. representative)
303 Ven. Nazju Falzon (Catholic catechist)

(Des S. Mallia)

1987 (18 Dec). *20th Anniv of United Nations Resolution on Peaceful Use of the Seabed. T* **302** *and similar vert design. Multicoloured. W* **105**. *P* 14.
816 8 c. Type **302**.. .. .. 1·00 65
817 12 c. U.N. emblem and sea .. .. .. 1·75 2·00
MS818 125×90 mm. Nos. 816/17. Wmk sideways. P 13×13½ .. .. 2·75 2·75

(Des E. Barthet)

1988 (23 Jan). *Maltese Personalities. T* **303** *and similar vert designs. Multicoloured. W* **105**. *P* 14.
819 2 c. Type **303** 25 30
820 3 c. Mgr. Sidor Formosa (philanthropist) .. 25 30
821 4 c. Sir Luigi Preziosi (ophthalmologist) .. 30 30
822 10 c. Fr. Anastasju Cuschieri (poet) .. 70 75
823 25 c. Mgr. Pietru Pawl Saydon (Bible translator) .. .. 2·00 2·50
819/23 .. .. *Set of* 5 3·25 3·75

304 "St. John Bosco with Youth" (statue) (Death Centenary)
305 Bus, Ferry and Airplane

(Des F. Portelli)

1988 (5 Mar). *Religious Anniversaries. T* **304** *and similar vert designs. Multicoloured. W* **105** *(sideways). P* 14.
824 10 c. Type **304** 80 80
825 12 c. "Assumption of Our Lady" (altarpiece by Perugino, Ta' Pinu, Gozo) (Marian Year) .. .. 1·00 1·00
826 14 c. "Christ the King" (statue by Sciortino) (75th anniv of International Eucharistic Congress, Valletta) .. 1·50 1·75
824/6 .. .. *Set of* 3 3·00 3·25

(Des F. Fenech)

1988 (9 Apr). *Europa. Transport and Communications. T* **305** *and similar vert design. Multicoloured. W* **105** *(sideways). P* 13½.
827 10 c. Type **305** .. .. 1·00 75
828 35 c. Control panel, dish aerial and pylons 2·75 3·00
Nos. 827/8 were each printed in sheets including two *se-tenant* stamp-size labels.

NEW INFORMATION

The editor is always interested to correspond with people who have new information that will improve or correct the Catalogue.

306 Globe and Red Cross Emblems (125th anniv of International Red Cross)
307 Athletics

(Des M. Cremona)

1988 (28 May). *Anniversaries and Events. T* **306** *and similar horiz designs. Multicoloured. W* **105**. *P* 13½.
829 4 c. Type **306** 40 30
830 18 c. Divided globe (Campaign for North-South Interdependence and Solidarity) 1·75 1·75
831 19 c. Globe and symbol (40th anniv of World Health Organization) .. .. .. 1·75 1·75
829/31 .. .. *Set of* 3 3·50 3·50

(Des L. Micallef)

1988 (23 July). *Maltese Uniforms (2nd issue). Vert designs as T* **299**. *Multicoloured. W* **105** *(sideways). P* 14.
832 3 c. Private, Maltese Light Infantry, 1800 30 30
833 4 c. Gunner, Malta Coast Artillery, 1802 .. 35 35
834 10 c. Field Officer, 1st Maltese Provincial Battalion, 1805 .. .. 85 85
835 25 c. Subaltern, Royal Malta Regiment, 1809 .. .. 2·25 2·50
832/5 .. .. *Set of* 4 3·25 3·50

(Des R. Gauci)

1988 (17 Sept). *Olympic Games, Seoul. T* **307** *and similar vert designs. Multicoloured. W* **105** *(sideways). P* 14×13½.
836 4 c. Type **307** 30 30
837 10 c. Diving 70 70
838 35 c. Basketball .. .. 2·00 2·50
836/8 .. .. *Set of* 3 2·75 3·25

308 Shepherd with Flock
309 Commonwealth Emblem

(Des R. Gauci)

1988 (5 Nov). *Christmas. T* **308** *and similar vert designs. Multicoloured. W* **105**. *P* 14.
839 3 c. + 1 c. Type **308** 25 30
840 10 c. + 2 c. The Nativity 60 70
841 25 c. + 3 c. Three Wise Men .. .. 1·50 1·75
839/41 .. .. *Set of* 3 2·10 2·50

(Des F. Portelli)

1989 (28 Jan). *25th Anniv of Independence. T* **309** *and similar multicoloured designs. W* **105** *(sideways). P* 14 *(25 c.) or* 13½ *(others).*
842 2 c. Type **309** 25 25
843 3 c. Council of Europe flag 25 25
844 4 c. U. N. flag 30 30
845 10 c. Workers hands gripping ring and national flag 75 75
846 12 c. Scales and allegorical figure of Justice 90 90
847 25 c. Prime Minister Borg Olivier with Independence constitution (42 × 28 *mm*) .. 1·90 2·40
842/7 .. .. *Set of* 6 4·00 4·25

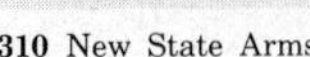

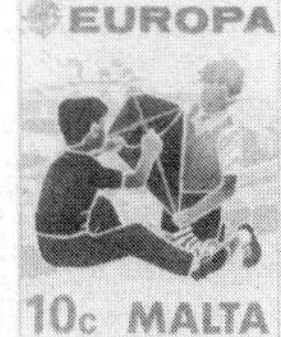

310 New State Arms
311 Two Boys flying Kite

(Des F. Portelli)

1989 (25 Mar). *W* **105**. *P* 14.
848 **310** £1 multicoloured .. .. .. 3·50 3·75

(Des R. Gauci)

1989 (6 May). *Europa. Children's Games. T* **311** *and similar vert design. Multicoloured. W* **105** *(sideways). P* 13½.
849 10 c. Type **311** .. .. 1·25 75
850 35 c. Two girls with dolls .. .. .. 3·25 3·50
Nos. 849/50 were each printed in sheets including two *se-tenant* stamp-size labels.

(Des L. Micallef)

1989 (24 June). *Maltese Uniforms (3rd series). Vert designs as T* **299**. *Multicoloured. W* **105** *(sideways). P* 14.
851 3 c. Officer, Maltese Veterans, 1815 .. 35 35
852 4 c. Subaltern, Royal Malta Fencibles, 1839 40 40
853 10 c. Private, Malta Militia, 1856 .. .. 1·00 1·00
854 25 c. Colonel, Royal Malta Fencible Artillery, 1875 .. .. 2·25 2·75
851/4 .. .. *Set of* 4 3·50 4·00

312 Human Figures and Buildings
313 Angel and Cherub

(Des L. Casha)

1989 (17 Oct). *Anniversaries and Commemorations. T* **312** *and similar horiz designs showing logo and stylized human figures. Multicoloured. W* **105** *(sideways). P* 14.
855 3 c. Type **312** (20th anniv of U.N. Declaration on Social Progress and Development) 30 30
856 4 c. Workers and figure in wheelchair (Malta's Ratification of European Social Charter) 35 35
857 10 c. Family (40th anniv of Council of Europe) 80 80
858 14 c. Teacher and children (70th anniv of Malta Union of Teachers) .. .. 1·00 1·25
859 25 c. Symbolic knights (Knights of the Sovereign Military Order of Malta Assembly) .. .. 2·25 2·50
855/9 .. .. *Set of* 5 4·25 4·75

(Des J. Mallia)

1989 (11 Nov). *Christmas. T* **313** *and similar horiz designs showing vault paintings by Mattia Preti from St. John's Co-Cathedral, Valletta. Multicoloured. W* **105**. *P* 13½.
860 3 c. + 1 c. Type **313** 40 40
861 10 c. + 2 c. Two angels 90 90
862 20 c. + 3 c. Angel blowing trumpet .. 1·60 1·75
860/2 .. .. *Set of* 3 2·50 2·75

314 Presidents Bush and Gorbachev
315 General Post Office, Auberge d'Italie, Valletta

1989 (2 Dec). *U.S.A.–U.S.S.R. Summit Meeting, Malta. W* **105**. *P* 14.
863 **314** 10 c. multicoloured .. .. .. 85 1·00

(Des R. Caruana)

1990 (9 Feb). *Europa. Post Office Buildings. T* **315** *and similar multicoloured design. W* **105** *(sideways on 10 c.). P* 14.
864 10 c. Type **315** 75 50
865 35 c. Branch Post Office, Zebbug (*horiz*) 2·25 2·75
Nos. 864/5 were each printed in sheets including two *se-tenant* stamp-size labels.

316 Open Book and Letters from Different Alphabets (International Literacy Year)
317 Samuel Taylor Coleridge (poet) and Government House

(Des T. Bugeja)

1990 (7 Apr). *Anniversaries and Events. T* **316** *and similar multicoloured designs. W* **105** *(sideways on 4, 19 c.). P* 14.
866 3 c. Type **316** 25 25
867 4 c. Count Roger of Sicily and Norman soldiers (900th anniv of Sicilian rule) (*horiz*) 30 30
868 19 c. Communications satellite (25th anniv of International Telecommunication Union membership) (*horiz*) .. .. 1·50 1·75
869 20 c. Football and map of Malta (Union of European Football Associations 20th Ordinary Congress, Malta) .. .. 1·50 1·75
866/9 .. .. *Set of* 4 3·25 3·50

(Des A. Grech)

1990 (3 May). *British Authors. T* **317** *and similar horiz designs. Multicoloured. W* **105** *(sideways). P* 13½.
870 4 c. Type **317** 25 30
871 10 c. Lord Byron (poet) and map of Valletta 50 60
872 12 c. Sir Walter Scott (novelist) and Great Siege 60 75
873 25 c. William Makepeace Thackeray (novelist) and Naval Arsenal .. .. 1·25 1·75
870/3 .. .. *Set of* 4 2·40 3·00

318 St. Paul

319 Flags and Football

(Des N. Bason)

1990 (25 May). *Visit of Pope John Paul II. T* **318** *and similar vert design showing bronze bas-reliefs. W* **105** *(sideways). P* 14.
874 4 c. brownish black, flesh and carmine .. 50 60
a. Pair. Nos. 874/5 .. .. .. 2·00 2·25
875 25 c. brownish black, flesh and carmine .. 1·50 1·75
Design:—25 c. Pope John Paul II.
Nos. 874/5 were printed together in a sheet of 12 (4×3) containing 10 stamps, *se-tenant* horizontally or vertically, and two stamp-size labels on R. 2/1 and 2/4.

(Des T. Bugeja)

1990 (8 June). *World Cup Football Championship, Italy. T* **319** *and similar horiz designs. Multicoloured. W* **105**. *P* 14.
876 5 c. Type **319** 35 30
877 10 c. Football in net 65 75
878 14 c. Scoreboard and football .. .. 1·00 1·10
876/8 .. .. *Set of* 3 1·75 2·00
MS879 123×90 mm. Nos. 876/8. Wmk sideways 1·75 2·00

(Des L. Micallef)

1990 (25 Aug). *Maltese Uniforms* (4*th series*). *Vert designs as T* **299**. *Multicoloured. W* **105** *(sideways). P* 14.
880 3 c. Captain, Royal Malta Militia, 1889 .. 30 30
881 4 c. Field officer, Royal Malta Artillery, 1905 .. .. 35 35
882 10 c. Labourer, Malta Labour Corps, 1915 65 65
883 25 c. Lieutenant, King's Own Malta Regiment of Militia, 1918 .. .. 1·50 1·50
880/3 .. .. *Set of* 4 2·50 2·50

320 Innkeeper

321 1899 10s. Stamp under Magnifying Glass

(Des J. Smith)

1990 (10 Nov). *Christmas. Figures from Crib by Austin Galea, Marco Bartolo and Rosario Zammit. T* **320** *and similar multicoloured designs. W* **105** *(sideways). P* 14×14½ (10 *c.*) *or* 13½×14 (*others*).
884 3 c. + 1 c. Type **320** 30 30
885 10 c. + 2 c. Nativity (41×28 *mm*) 70 80
886 25 c. + 3 c. Shepherd with sheep .. .. 1·60 1·75
884/6 .. .. *Set of* 3 2·40 2·50

(Des J. Mallia)

1991 (6 Mar). 25*th Anniv of Philatelic Society of Malta. W* **105** *(sideways). P* 14.
887 **321** 10 c. multicoloured 50 55

322 "Eurostar" Satellite and V.D.U. Screen

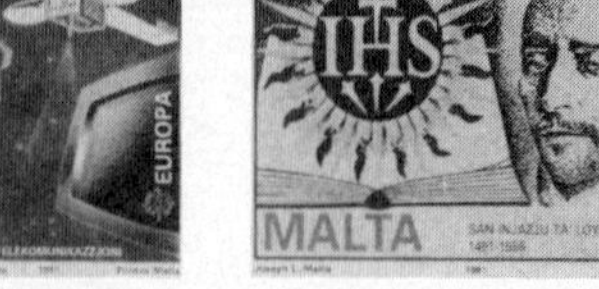

323 St. Ignatius Loyola (founder of Jesuits) (500th birth anniv)

(Des R. Caruana)

1991 (16 Mar). *Europa. Europe in Space. T* **322** *and similar vert design. Multicoloured. W* **105** *(sideways). P* 14.
888 10 c. Type **322** 60 70
889 35 c. "Ariane 4" rocket and projected HOTOL aerospaceplane .. .. 2·00 2·10
Nos. 888/9 were each printed in sheets including two *se-tenant* stamp-size labels.

(Des J. Mallia)

1991 (29 Apr). *Religious Commemorations. T* **323** *and similar multicoloured designs. W* **105** *(sideways on* 3, 30 *c.*). *P* 14.
890 3 c. Type **323** 20 20
891 4 c. Abbess Venerable Maria Adeodata Pisani (185th birth anniv) (*vert*) .. 25 25
892 30 c. St. John of the Cross (400th death anniv) .. .. 1·75 1·75
890/2 .. .. *Set of* 3 2·00 2·00

(Des L. Micallef)

1991 (13 Aug). *Maltese Uniforms* (5*th series*). *Vert designs as T* **299**. *Multicoloured. W* **105** *(sideways). P* 14.
893 3 c. Officer with colour, Royal Malta Fencibles, 1860 .. .. .. 25 25
894 10 c. Officer with colour, Royal Malta Regiment of Militia, 1903 .. .. 60 60
895 19 c. Officer with Queen's colour, King's Own Malta Regiment, 1968 .. .. 1·10 1·10
896 25 c. Officer with colour, Malta Armed Forces, 1991 .. .. 1·60 1·60
893/6 .. .. *Set of* 4 3·25 3·25

324 Interlocking Arrows

325 Honey Buzzard

(Des N. Attard)

1991 (23 Sept). 25*th Anniv of Union Haddiema Maghqudin (public services union). W* **105** *(sideways). P* 13½.
897 **324** 4 c. multicoloured 25 30

(Des H. Borg)

1991 (3 Oct). *Endangered Species. Birds. T* **325** *and similar vert designs. Multicoloured. W* **105**. *P* 14.
898 4 c. Type **325** 30 35
a. Horiz strip of 4. Nos. 898/901 .. 1·75
899 4 c. Marsh Harrier 30 35
900 10 c. Eleonora's Falcon 70 80
901 10 c. Lesser Kestrel 70 80
898/901 .. .. *Set of* 4 1·75 2·10
Nos. 898/901 were printed together, *se-tenant*, in horizontal strips of 4 throughout the sheet.

326 Three Wise Men

327 Ta' Hagrat Neolithic Temple

(Des H. Borg)

1991 (6 Nov). *Christmas. T* **326** *and similar vert designs. Multicoloured. W* **105**. *P* 14.
902 3 c. + 1 c. Type **326** 25 25
903 10 c. + 2 c. Holy Family 65 65
904 25 c. + 3 c. Two shepherds .. .. .. 1·25 1·25
902/4 .. .. *Set of* 3 2·00 2·00

(Des F. Portelli)

1991 (9 Dec). *National Heritage of the Maltese Islands. T* **327** *and similar multicoloured designs. W* **105** *(sideways on* £2). *P* 13½.
905 1 c. Type **327** 10 10
906 2 c. Cottoner Gate 10 10
907 3 c. St. Michael's Bastion, Valletta .. 10 15
908 4 c. Spinola Palace, St. Julian's 15 20
909 5 c. Birkirkara Church 20 25
910 10 c. Mellieha Bay 35 40
911 12 c. Wied iz-Zurrieq 40 45
912 14 c. Mgarr harbour, Gozo 50 55
913 20 c. Yacht marina 70 75
914 50 c. Gozo Channel .. .. .. 1·75 1·90
915 £1 "Arab Horses" (sculpture by Antonio Sciortino) .. .. 3·50 3·75
916 £2 Independence Monument (Ganni Bonnici) (*vert*) .. .. 7·00 7·25
905/16 .. .. *Set of* 12 13·50 14·50

MINIMUM PRICE

The minimum price quote is 10p which represents a handling charge rather than a basis for valuing common stamps. For further notes about prices see introductory pages.

328 Aircraft Tailfins and Terminal

(Des. H. Borg)

1992 (8 Feb). *Opening of International Air Terminal. T* **328** *and similar horiz design. W* **105** *(sideways). P* 14.
917 4 c. Type **328** 15 20
918 10 c. National flags and terminal 35 40

329 Ships of Columbus

(Des H. Borg)

1992 (20 Feb). *Europa. 500th Anniv of Discovery of America by Columbus. T* **329** *and similar horiz design. W* **105** *(sideways). P* 14.
919 10 c. Type **329** 35 40
920 35 c. Columbus and map of Americas .. 1·25 1·50
Nos. 919/20 were each printed in sheets including two *se-tenant* stamp-size labels.

POSTAGE DUE STAMPS

POSTAGE DUE ½d. MALTA.

D 1

D 2

D 3 Maltese Lace

1925 (16 Apr). *Type-set by Govt. Printing Office, Valletta. Imperf.*
D 1 D 1 ½d. black .. .. 1·25 3·75
D 2 1d. black .. .. 2·00 2·50
D 3 1½d. black .. .. 2·25 3·50
D 4 2d. black .. .. 3·25 6·00
D 5 2½d. black .. .. 2·75 2·75
a. "2" of "½" omitted £900 £1200
D 6 3d. black/*grey* .. .. 8·00 11·00
D 7 4d. black/*buff* .. .. 4·50 9·00
D 8 6d. black/*buff* .. .. 4·50 11·00
D 9 1s. black/*buff* .. .. 7·50 15·00
D10 1s. 6d. black/*buff* .. .. .. 13·00 35·00
D1/10 .. .. *Set of* 10 45·00 90·00
Nos. D1/10 were each issued in sheets containing 4 panes (6×7) printed separately. Examples exist in *tête-bêche* pairs from the junction of the panes, price about four times that of a single stamp.
No. D5a occurred on R. 4/4 of the last 2½d. pane position to be printed. Forgeries exist, but can be detected by comparison with a normal example under ultra-violet light. They are often found in pair with normal, showing forged cancellations of "VALLETTA AP20 25" or "G.P.O" MY 7 25".

(Typo B.W.)

1925 (20 July). *Wmk Mult Script CA (sideways). P* 12.
D11 D **2** ½d. green .. .. 1·25 60
D12 1d. violet .. .. 1·25 45
D13 1½d. brown .. .. 1·50 1·25
D14 2d. grey .. .. 11·00 1·50
D15 2½d. orange .. .. 2·00 1·25
D16 3d. blue .. .. 3·25 1·25
D17 4d. olive-green .. .. .. 12·00 11·00
D18 6d. purple .. .. 2·50 3·25
D19 1s. black .. .. 5·50 10·00
D20 1s. 6d. carmine .. .. .. 7·00 16·00
D11/20 .. .. *Set of* 10 42·00 42·00
D11/20 Optd "Specimen" .. .. *Set of* 10 £200

1953 (5 Nov)–**63**. *Wmk Mult Script CA (sideways). Chalk-surfaced paper. P* 12.
D21 D **2** ½d. emerald .. .. 70 1·00
D22 1d. purple .. .. 70 1·00
a. Deep purple (17.9.63) .. .. 75 2·00
D23 1½d. yellow-brown .. .. .. 4·00 6·00
D24 2d. grey-brown (20.3.57) .. .. 7·00 7·00
a. Blackish brown (3.4.62) .. 11·00 12·00
D25 3d. deep slate-blue .. .. .. 1·50 2·00
D26 4d. yellow-olive .. .. .. 6·00 8·00
D21/6 .. .. *Set of* 6 18·00 23·00

1966 (Oct). *As No.* D24, *but wmk* w **12** *(sideways).*
D27 D **2** 2d. grey-brown .. .. .. 25·00 25·00

1967–70. *Ordinary paper. W* **105** *(sideways).*

(a) P 12, line (9.11.67)
D28 D **2** ½d. emerald .. .. 4·00 9·00
D29 1d. purple .. .. 4·00 9·00
D30 2d. blackish brown .. .. .. 4·00 9·00
D31 4d. yellow-olive .. .. .. 60·00 £100
D28/31 .. .. *Set of* 4 65·00 £120

(b) P 12½, *comb* (30.5.68–70)

D32	D 2	½d. emerald	35	1·00
D33		1d. purple	30	65
D34		1½d. yellow-brown	35	1·50
		a. Orange-brown (23.10.70)	90	2·00
D35		2d. blackish brown	85	70
		a. Brownish black (23.10.70)	1·25	2·00
D36		2½d. yellow-orange	60	70
D37		3d. deep slate-blue	60	60
D38		4d. yellow-olive	1·00	80
D39		6d. purple	75	1·00
D40		1s. black	90	1·50
D41		1s. 6d. carmine	2·25	4·25
D32/41		*Set of* 10	7·00	11·50

The above are the local release dates. In the 12½ perforation the London release dates were 21 May for the ½d. to 4d. and 4 June for the 6d. to 1s. 6d.

Nos. D34*a* and D35*a* are on glazed paper.

(Des G. Pace. Litho Printex Ltd, Malta)

1973 (28 Apr). *W* **105**. *P* 13 × 13½.

D42	D 3	2 m. grey-brown and reddish brown	10	10
D43		3 m. dull orange and Indian red	10	10
D44		5 m. rose and bright scarlet	10	10
D45		1 c. turquoise and bottle green	10	10
D46		2 c. slate and black	10	10
D47		3 c. light yellow-brown and red-brown	10	10
D48		5 c. dull blue and royal blue	15	20
D49		10 c. reddish lilac and plum	30	35
D42/9		*Set of* 8	70	80

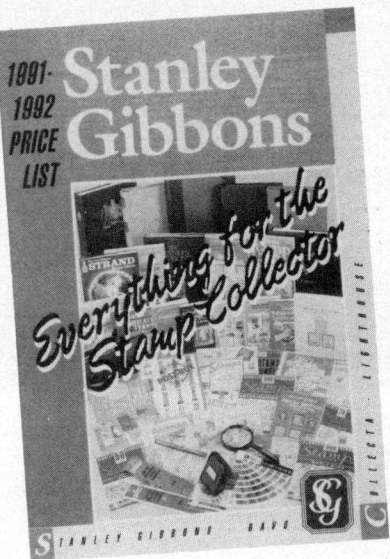

Mauritius

GREAT BRITAIN STAMPS USED IN MAURITIUS. We no longer list the Great Britain stamps with obliteration "B 53" as there is no evidence that British stamps were available from the Mauritius Post Office.

See under SEYCHELLES for stamps of Mauritius used at Victoria with "B 64" cancellations between 1861 and 1890.

A similar "B 65" cancellation was used on the island of Rodrigues, a dependency of Mauritius, from 11 December 1861 onwards.

PRICES FOR STAMPS ON COVER TO 1945
The classic issues, Nos. 1/25 and 36/44, are rare used on cover

Nos. 26/9	*from* × 2
Nos. 32/5	*from* × 3
Nos. 48/72	*from* × 3
Nos. 76/82	*from* × 5
Nos. 83/91	*from* × 6
Nos. 92/100	*from* × 4
Nos. 101/11	*from* × 3
Nos. 117/24	*from* × 8
Nos. 127/32	*from* × 7
No. 133	*from* × 4
Nos. 134/5	*from* × 10
No. 136	*from* × 8
Nos. 137/56	*from* × 6
Nos. 157/63	*from* × 5
Nos. 164/221	*from* × 3
No. 222	—
Nos. 223/41	*from* × 3
Nos. 242/4	*from* × 10
Nos. 245/8	*from* × 3
Nos. 249/63	*from* × 2
Nos. E1/6	*from* × 10
Nos. D1/7	*from* × 40
Nos. R1/4	*from* × 15

CROWN COLONY

Nos. 1/25*b* and 36/44 were printed in Mauritius.

1
("POST OFFICE")

2
("POST PAID")

(Engraved on copper by J. O. Barnard)

1847 (21 Sept). *Head of Queen on groundwork of diagonal and perpendicular lines. Imperf.*
1 **1** 1d. orange-red .. £400000 £150000
2 2d. deep blue .. £250000 £150000

A single plate contained one example of each value.

It is generally agreed that fifteen examples of No. 1 have survived (including two unused) and twelve of No. 2 (including four unused).

NOTE. Our prices for early Mauritius are for stamps in very fine condition. Exceptional copies are worth more, poorer copies considerably less.

(Engraved on copper by J. O. Barnard)

1848 (June)–**59**. *Imperf.*

A. *Earliest impressions. Design deep, sharp and clear. Diagonal lines predominate. Thick paper (Period of use: 1d. 1853–54, 2d. 1848–49)*
3 **2** 1d. orange-vermilion/*yellowish* .. £19000 £13000
4 2d. indigo-blue/*grey to bluish* .. £23000 £13000
a. "PENOE" for "PENCE" (R. 3/1) .. £34000 £23000
5 2d. deep blue/*grey to bluish* .. £25000 £13000
a. "PENOE" for "PENCE" (R. 3/1) .. — £26000

B. *Early impressions. Design sharp and clear but some lines slightly weakened. Paper not so thick, grey to yellowish white or bluish (Period of use: 1d. 1853–55, 2d. 1849–54).*
6 **2** 1d. vermilion .. £11000 £5000
7 1d. orange-vermilion .. £12000 £5000
8 2d. blue .. £15000 £5500
a. "PENOE" for "PENCE" (R. 3/1) .. £18000 £9000
9 2d. deep blue .. £19000 £6000

C. *Intermediate impressions. White patches appear where design has worn. Paper yellowish white, grey or bluish, of poorish quality (Period of use: 1d and 2d. 1854–57)*
10 **2** 1d. bright vermilion .. £7500 £2000
11 1d. dull vermilion .. £7500 £2000
12 1d. red .. £7500 £1900
13 2d. deep blue .. £7000 £2000
14 2d. blue .. £5000 £2000
a. "PENOE" for "PENCE" (R. 3/1) *from* £10000 £4000
15 2d. light blue .. £5000 £2000

D. *Worn impressions. Much of design worn away but some diagonal lines distinct. Paper yellowish, grey or bluish, of poorish quality (Period of use: 1d. 1857–59, 2d. 1855–58)*
16 **2** 1d. red/*yellowish or grey* .. £1500 £325
17 1d. red-brown/*yellowish or grey* .. £1500 £325
18 1d. red/*bluish* .. £900 £325
19 1d. red-brown/*bluish* .. £850 £325
20 2d. blue (*shades*)/*yellowish or grey* .. £1500 £650
a. "PENOE" for "PENCE" (R. 3/1) *from* — £900
21 2d. grey-blue/*yellowish or grey* .. £1700 £650
22 2d. blue (*shades*)/*bluish* .. £1500 £600
a. Doubly printed

E. *Latest impressions. Almost none of design showing except part of Queen's head and frame. Paper yellowish, grey or bluish, of poorish quality (Period of use: 1d. 1859, 2d. 1856–58)*
23 **2** 1d. red .. £850 £325
24 1d. red-brown .. £900 £325
25 2d. grey-blue/*bluish* .. £950 £375
a. "PENOE" for "PENCE" (R. 3/1) .. £1600 £700

F. *Retouched impression. Retouching to Queen's head and frame. Paper bluish of poor quality (Period of use 2d. 1857–58)*
25*b* **2** 2d. greyish blue/*bluish*

Earliest known use of the 2d. value is on 19 June 1848, but the 1d. value is not known used before 27 September 1853.

There were separate plates for the 1d. and 2d. values, each of 12 (3×4).

3

(4)

5

(Recess P.B.)

1858*. *Surch with T* **4**. *Imperf.*
26 **3** 4d. green .. £650 £350

*Although originally gazetted for use from 8 April 1854, research into the archives indicates that No. 26 was not actually issued until 1858, when the stamps were mentioned in an ordinance of 30 April. The earliest dated postmark known is 27 March 1858.

1858–62. *No value expressed. Imperf.*
27 **3** (4d.) green .. £400 £200
28 (6d.) vermilion .. 17·00 25·00
29 (9d.) dull magenta (1859) .. £475 £200
a. Reissued as (1d.) value (11.62) .. † £160

Use of the dull magenta as a 1d. value can be confirmed by the presence of the "B 53" cancellation which was first introduced in 1861.

Prepared for use, but not issued
30 **3** (No value), red-brown .. 5·00
31 (No value), blue .. 2·75

Remainders of these were overprinted "L.P.E. 1890" in red, perforated at the London Philatelic Exhibition and sold as souvenirs.

(Recess P.B.)

1859–61. *Imperf.*
32 **5** 6d. blue .. £425 28·00
33 6d. dull purple-slate (1861) .. 15·00 20·00
34 1s. vermilion .. £1800 45·00
35 1s. yellow-green (1861) .. £180 70·00

The 1859 printings had the colours transposed by mistake.

6

7

8

(Engraved on copper by J. Lapirot)

1859 (Mar–Oct). *Imperf. (a) Early impressions.*
36 **6** 2d. deep blue .. £3500 £1700
37 2d. blue .. £2500 £1500

(*b*) *Intermediate prints. Lines of background, etc, partly worn away* (July)
38 **6** 2d. blue .. £1800 £600

(*c*) *Worn impressions, bluish-paper* (Oct)
39 **6** 2d. blue .. £800 £375

Nos. 36/9 were printed from a plate of 12 (4×3).

(1848 plate re-engraved by R. Sherwin)

1859 (Oct). *Bluish paper. Imperf.*
40 **7** 2d. deep blue .. £22000 £3000

The 1d. plate was also re-engraved, but was not put into use. Reprints in black were made in 1877 from both 1d. and 2d. re-engraved plates. Coloured autotype illustrations were prepared from these reprints and 600 were included in the R.P.S.L. handbook on *British Africa* in 1900. Further reprints in black were made in 1911 after the plates had been presented to the R.P.S.L. and defaced.

(Lithographed by L. A. Dardenne)

1859 (Dec). *White laid paper. Imperf.*
41 **8** 1d. deep red .. £2000 £900
41*a* 1d. red .. £1600 £600
42 1d. dull vermilion .. £1100 £550
43 2d. slate-blue .. £2000 £600
43*a* 2d. blue .. £950 £400
44 2d. pale blue .. £850 £300
a. Heavy retouch on neck .. — £1000
b. Slight retouches (several varieties) .. — £550

9

10

(Typo D.L.R.)

1860 (Apr)–**63.** *No wmk. P* 14.
46 **9** 1d. purple-brown .. 80·00 15·00
47 2d. blue .. £100 22·00
48 4d. rose .. 95·00 17·00
49 6d. green (1862) .. £450 95·00
50 6d. slate (1863) .. £120 70·00
51 9d. dull purple .. 65·00 30·00
52 1s. buff (1862) .. £170 55·00
53 1s. green (1863) .. £425 £120

1862. *Intermediate perf* 14 *to* 16.
54 **5** 6d. slate .. 14·00 24·00
a. Imperf between (pair) .. £2500
55 1s. deep green .. £1400 £300

1863–72. *Wmk Crown CC. P* 14.
56 **9** 1d. purple-brown .. 30·00 6·50
57 1d. brown .. 45·00 5·00
58 1d. bistre (1872) .. 65·00 5·00
59 2d. pale blue .. 48·00 4·50
60 2d. bright blue .. 48·00 4·50
a. Imperf (pair) .. £1000 £1100
61 3d. deep red .. 80·00 19·00
61*a* 3d. dull red .. 30·00 8·00
62 4d. rose .. 55·00 1·75
63 6d. dull violet .. 90·00 23·00
64 6d. yellow-green (1865) .. 85·00 9·00
65 6d. blue-green .. 75·00 3·75
66 9d. yellow-green (1872) .. £100 £100
67 **10** 10d. maroon (1872) .. £100 20·00
68 **9** 1s. yellow .. £100 12·00
69 1s. blue (1866) .. £120 18·00
70 1s. orange (1872) .. 95·00 12·00
71 5s. rosy mauve .. £110 32·00
72 5s. bright mauve (1865) .. £130 30·00

HALF PENNY
(11)

½ d
HALF PENNY
(12)

1876. (*a*) *Nos.* 51 *and* 67 *surch with T* **11** *locally.*
76 **9** ½d. on 9d. dull purple .. 2·75 6·50
a. Surch inverted .. £250
b. Surch double
77 **10** ½d. on 10d. maroon .. 80 9·00

(*b*) *Prepared for use, but not issued. No.* 51 *surch with T* **12**.
78 **9** ½d. on 9d. dull purple (R.) .. £550
a. "PRNNY"
b. Black surch .. £650

HALF PENNY
(13)

One Penny
(14)

One Shilling
(15)

1877 (Apr–Dec). *Nos.* 62, 67 (*colour changed*) *and* 71/2 *surch with T* **13**/**15** *locally.*
79 **10** ½d. on 10d. rose .. 2·00 20·00
80 **9** 1d. on 4d. rose-carmine (6 Dec) .. 7·50 12·00
81 1s. on 5s. rosy mauve (6 Dec) .. £170 85·00
82 1s. on 5s. bright mauve (6 Dec) .. £200 £100

(New Currency. 100 cents = 1 rupee)

"CANCELLED" OVERPRINTS. Following the change of currency in 1878 various issues with face values in sterling were overprinted "CANCELLED" in serifed type and sold as remainders. The stamps involved were Nos. 51, 56/62, 65, 67/8, 71/2, 76, 78/b, 79 and 81/2.

Examples of such overprints on stamps between Nos. 51 and 72 are worth about the same as the prices quoted for used, on Nos. 78/b they are worth 12% of the unused price, on No. 79 65% and on Nos. 81/2 20%.

2 CENTS
(16)

2 Rs.50 C.
(17)

1878 (3 Jan). *Surch as T* **16** *or* **17** (*No.* 91). *Wmk Crown CC. P* 14.
83 **10** 2 c. dull rose (lower label blank) .. 5·00 4·25
84 **9** 4 c. on 1d. bistre .. 7·00 3·75
85 8 c. on 2d. blue .. 55·00 75
86 13 c. on 3d. orange-red .. 7·00 17·00
87 17 c. on 4d. rose .. 75·00 1·50
88 25 c. on 6d. slate-blue .. £110 4·75
89 38 c. on 9d. pale violet .. 18·00 32·00
90 50 c. on 1s. green .. 65·00 2·50
91 2 r. 50 on 5s. bright mauve .. 12·00 9·00
83/91 .. *Set of* 9 £325 65·00

NEW INFORMATION

The editor is always interested to correspond with people who have new information that will improve or correct the Catalogue.

18

19

20

21

22

23

24 25 26

(Typo D.L.R.)

1879 (Mar)–**80**. *Wmk Crown CC. P* 14.

92 **18** 2 c. Venetian red (1.80) .. .. 28·00 11·00
93 **19** 4 c. orange .. .. .. 45·00 3·25
94 **20** 8 c. blue (1.80) .. .. .. 11·00 75
95 **21** 13 c. slate (1.80) £110 £110
96 **22** 17 c. rose (1.80) .. .. .. 32·00 3·50
97 **23** 25 c. olive-yellow .. .. .. £150 8·00
98 **24** 38 c. bright purple (1.80) £130 £140
99 **25** 50 c. green (1.80) .. .. .. 2·50 1·75
100 **26** 2 r. 50, brown-purple (1.80) .. .. 23·00 40·00
92/100 .. .. *Set of* 9 £475 £275

27

(Typo D.L.R.)

1883–94. *Wmk Crown CA. P* 14.

101 **18** 1 c. pale violet (1893) 30 45
102 2 c. Venetian red .. .. .. 17·00 4·75
103 2 c. green (1885) 90 30
104 **19** 4 c. orange .. .. .. 45·00 2·50
105 4 c. carmine (1885) .. .. .. 1·00 20
106 **20** 8 c. blue (1891) 65 65
107 **27** 15 c. chestnut (1893) .. .. .. 1·00 35
108 15 c. blue (1894) .. .. .. 5·00 40
109 16 c. chestnut (1885) .. .. .. 2·00 45
110 **23** 25 c. olive-yellow .. .. .. 3·00 1·50
111 **25** 50 c. orange (1887) .. .. .. 26·00 7·50
101/11 .. .. .. *Set of* 11 90·00 17·00
101, 103, 105, 107/9, 111 Optd "Specimen" *Set of* 7 £300

16 CENTS (28) SIXTEEN CENTS (29)

(*a*) Surcharge 14 mm long and 3 high.
(*b*) Surcharge 15 mm long and 3½ high.
(*c*) Surcharge 15 mm long and 2½ high.

1883 (26 Feb). *No.* 96 *surch as T* **28** *locally.*

112 **22** 16 c. on 17 c. rose (*a*) .. .. .. 70·00 38·00
a. Surch double .. .. ..
113 16 c. on 17 c. rose (*b*) .. .. .. 75·00 38·00
114 16 c. on 17 c. rose (*c*) .. .. .. £150 85·00

1883 (14 July). *Surch with T* **29** *by D.L.R. Wmk Crown CA. P* 14.

115 **22** 16 c. on 17 c. rose .. .. .. 32·00 80

2 CENTS (30) 2 CENTS (31)

1885 (11 May). *No.* 98 *surch with T* **30** *locally.*

116 **24** 2 c. on 38 c. bright purple .. .. .. 65·00 32·00
a. Without bar .. .. .. — 80·00
b. Surch inverted £250 £250
c. Surch double £325

1887 (6 July). *No.* 95 *surch with T* **31** *locally.*

117 **21** 2 c. on 13 c. slate (R.) .. .. .. 25·00 42·00
a. Surch inverted .. .. .. 80·00 95·00
b. Surch double .. .. .. — £275
c. Surch double, one on back of stamp £325

TWO CENTS (32) TWO CENTS (33)

1891 (10–16 Sept). *Nos.* 88, 96, 98 *and* 105 *surch locally as T* **32** (*Nos.* 118/19, 121) *or T* **33** (*No.* 120).

118 **19** 2 c. on 4 c. carmine (No. 105) (12 Sept) 35 20
a. Surch inverted .. .. .. 55·00
b. Surch double .. .. .. 65·00 60·00
c. Surch double, one inverted .. .. 65·00 60·00
119 **22** 2 c. on 17 c. rose (No. 96) (16 Sept) .. 55·00 55·00
a. Surch inverted £150
b. Surch double £250 £250
120 **9** 2 c. on 38 c. on 9d. pale violet (No. 89) (16 Sept) .. .. .. 1·00 3·50
a. Surch inverted £110
b. Surch double £275 £275
c. Surch double, one inverted .. .. 55·00
121 **24** 2 c. on 38 c. bright purple (No. 98) .. 2·00 2·50
a. Surch inverted £250
b. Surch double .. .. .. 65·00
c. Surch double, one inverted .. .. 65·00

Minor varieties are also known with portions of the surcharge missing, due to defective printing.

ONE CENT (34) ONE CENT (35)

1893 (1–7 Jan). *Surch with T* **34** *by D.L.R. or T* **35** *locally. Wmk Crown CA. P* 14.

123 **18** 1 c. on 2 c. pale violet (Optd S. £27) .. 30 35
124 **27** 1 c. on 16 c. chestnut (7 Jan) 30 80

36

37

(Typo D.L.R.)

1895–9. *Wmk Crown CA. P* 14.

127 **36** 1 c. dull purple and ultramarine (8.7.97) 35 40
128 2 c. dull purple and orange (8.7.97) .. 2·00 10
129 3 c. dull purple and deep purple .. 50 30
130 4 c. dull purple and emerald (8.7.97) .. 3·25 30
131 6 c. green and rose-red (1899) .. .. 3·00 2·00
132 18 c. green and ultramarine (8.7.97) .. 6·50 5·00
128/32 .. .. *Set of* 6 14·00 7·25
128/32 Optd "Specimen" .. .. *Set of* 6 70·00

(Des L. Duvergé. Typo D.L.R.)

1898 (15 Apr). *Diamond Jubilee. Wmk CA over Crown* (*sideways*). *P* 14.

133 **37** 36 c. orange & ultramarine (Optd S. £40) 9·00 12·00

6 CENTS (38) 15 CENTS (39)

1899 (23–28 May). *Nos.* 132/3 *surcharged with T* **38/9** *locally.*

134 **36** 6 c. on 18 c. green and ultramarine (R.) 40 50
a. Surch inverted £200 £160
135 **37** 15 c. on 36 c. orge & ultram (R.) (28 May) 1·00 80
a. Bar of surch omitted £160

The space between "6" and "CENTS" varies from 2½ to 4 mm.

40 Admiral Mahé de Labourdonnais, Governor of Mauritius, 1735–46

4 Cents (41)

(Recess D.L.R.)

1899 (13 Dec). *Birth Bicentenary of Labourdonnais. Wmk Crown CC. P* 14.

136 **40** 15 c. ultramarine (Optd S. £60) .. .. 9·50 1·75

1900. *No.* 109 *surch with T* **41** *locally.*

137 **27** 4 c. on 16 c. chestnut .. .. .. 70 3·25

ALTERED CATALOGUE NUMBERS

Any Catalogue numbers altered from the last edition are shown as a list in the introductory pages.

42

12 CENTS (43)

(Typo D.L.R.)

1900–05. *Wmk Crown CC* (1 *r.*) *or Crown CA* (*others*) (*sideways on* 2 *r.* 50, 5 *r.*). *Ordinary paper. P* 14.

138 **36** 1 c. grey and black (1901) 50 10
139 2 c. dull purple and bright purple (4.01) 30 10
140 3 c. green and carmine/*yellow* (1902) .. 1·00 30
141 4 c. purple and carmine/*yellow* .. 1·10 10
142 4 c. grey-green and violet (1903) .. 60 85
143 4 c. black and carmine/*blue* (14.10.04) 2·75 10
144 5 c. dull purple & brt pur/*buff* (8.10.02) 3·00 35·00
145 5 c. dull purple and black/*buff* (2.03) .. 1·60 1·75
146 6 c. purple and carmine/*red* (1902) .. 1·25 15
147 8 c. green and black/*buff* (16.7.02) .. 80 3·00
148 12 c. grey-black and carmine (16.7.02) .. 1·50 70
149 15 c. green and orange .. .. .. 5·25 6·00
150 15 c. black and blue/*blue* (1905) .. 28·00 1·25
151 25 c. green and carmine/*green* (1902) .. 3·25 7·50
a. Chalk-surfaced paper .. .. 2·00 6·50
152 50 c. dull green & dp green/*yellow* (1902) 7·50 15·00
153 **42** 1 r. grey-black and carmine (1902) .. 38·00 23·00
154 2 r. 50, green and black/*blue* (1902) .. 11·00 40·00
155 5 r. purple and carmine/*red* (1902) .. 45·00 75·00
138/55 .. .. .. *Set of* 18 £130 £190
138/55 Optd "Specimen" .. .. *Set of* 18 £170

1902. *No.* 132 *surch with T* **43**.

156 **36** 12 c. on 18 c. green and ultramarine .. 80 5·00

The bar cancelling the original value seems in some cases to be one thick bar and in others two thin ones.

Postage & Revenue. (44)

1902 (7 July). *Various stamps optd with T* **44** *locally.*

157 **36** 4 c. purple and carmine/*yellow* (No. 141) 20 20
158 6 c. green and rose-red (No. 131) .. 35 2·25
159 15 c. green and orange (No. 149) .. 45 30
160 **23** 25 c. olive-yellow (No. 110) .. .. 50 2·25
161 **25** 50 c. green (No. 99) .. .. .. 3·75 1·00
162 **26** 2 r. 50, brown-purple (No. 100) .. 45·00 60·00
157/62 .. .. .. *Set of* 6 45·00 60·00

Nos. 157/62 were overprinted to make surplus stocks of postage stamps available for revenue (fiscal) purposes also.

1902 (22 Sept). *No.* 133 *surch as T* **43**, *but with longer bar.*

163 **37** 12 c. on 36 c. orange and ultramarine .. 1·00 1·00
a. Surch inverted £300 £250

The note below No. 156 also applies to No. 163.

Forged double surcharge errors show a straight, instead of a curved, serif to the "1" of "12".

1904–7. *Wmk Mult Crown CA. Ordinary paper* (2 c., 4 c., 6 c.) *or chalk-surfaced paper* (*others*). *P* 14.

164 **36** 1 c. grey and black (1907) .. .. 7·00 90
165 2 c. dull and bright purple (1905) .. 5·50 30
a. Chalk-surfaced paper .. .. 5·50 20
166 3 c. green and carmine/*yellow* .. .. 17·00 2·75
167 4 c. black and carmine/*blue* .. .. 3·50 30
a. Chalk-surfaced paper .. .. 1·00 10
168 6 c. purple and carmine/*red* .. .. 1·75 10
a. Chalk-surfaced paper .. .. 1·00 10
171 15 c. black and blue/*blue* (1907) .. 4·00 35
174 50 c. green and deep green/*yellow* .. 1·00 2·25
175 1 r. grey-black and carmine (1907) .. 19·00 28·00
164/75 .. .. *Set of* 8 50·00 30·00

46

47

(Typo D.L.R.)

1910 (17 Jan). *Wmk Mult Crown CA. Ordinary paper* (1 c. *to* 15 c.) *or chalk-surfaced paper* (25 c. *to* 10 *r.*). *P* 14.

181 **46** 1 c. black 55 10
182 2 c. brown .. .. 1·25 10
183 3 c. green 60 10
184 4 c. pale yellow-green and carmine .. 80 10
185 **47** 5 c. grey and carmine .. .. .. 50 1·50
186 **46** 6 c. carmine-red 40 10
a. Pale red .. .. .. 2·50 35
187 8 c. orange .. .. 1·10 1·25
188 **47** 12 c. greyish slate 30 50
189 **46** 15 c. blue .. .. 5·50 10
190 **47** 25 c. black and red/*yellow* .. .. 1·75 8·50
191 50 c. dull purple and black .. .. 1·75 9·50
192 1 r. black/*green* .. .. .. 3·75 6·00

193 **47** 2 r. 50, black and red/*blue* .. .. 7·50 35·00
194 5 r. green and red/*yellow* .. .. 24·00 55·00
195 10 r. green and red/*green* .. .. 80·00 £140
181/95 .. .. *Set of* 15 £110 £225
181/95 Optd "Specimen" .. .. *Set of* 15 £200
On Nos. 188, 190 and 195 the value labels are as in T **49**.

48

49

(Typo D.L.R.)

1913–21. *Wmk Mult Crown CA. Ordinary paper* (5 *c.*, 12 *c.*) *or chalk-surfaced paper* (*others*). *P* 14.
196 **48** 5 c. grey and carmine (5.8.15) .. .. 90 1·00
a. *Slate-grey and carmine* .. .. 7·50 6·00
198 **49** 12 c. greyish slate (1915) .. .. 1·50 30
199 25 c. black and red/*yellow* (1913) .. 40 1·40
a. *White back* (1916) .. .. .. 50 10·00
b. *On orange-buff* .. .. .. 30·00 60·00
c. *On pale yellow* (Die I) (Optd S. £25) 27·00 35·00
d. *On pale yellow* (Die II) (Optd S. £25) 50 13·00
200 **48** 50 c. dull purple and black (Die I) (1921) 17·00 35·00
201 1 r. black/*blue-green* (*olive back*) (1917) 1·50 9·00
a. *On emerald surface* .. .. 7·00 32·00
b. *On emerald back* (Die II) (Optd S. £25) .. .. 1·25 6·00
202 2 r. 50, black and red/*blue* (1916) .. 14·00 27·00
203 5 r. green and red/*orange-buff* (1921) .. 35·00 60·00
a. *On pale yellow* (Die I) .. .. 35·00 60·00
b. *On pale yellow* (Die II) .. .. 30·00 70·00
204 **49** 10 r. green and red/*green* (1913) .. 40·00 75·00
a. *On blue-green, olive back* £700
b. *On emerald surface* .. .. 40·00 75·00
c. *On emerald back* (Die I) .. .. 35·00 70·00
d. *On emerald back* (Die II) (Optd S. £28) .. .. 23·00 60·00
196/204 .. .. *Set of* 8 80·00 £170
196/204 Optd "Specimen" (Die I) .. *Set of* 8 £150

1921–26. *Wmk Mult Script CA. Chalk-surfaced paper* (50 *r.*). *P* 14.
205 **46** 1 c. black 35 90
206 2 c. brown 50 10
207 2 c. purple/*yellow* (1926) 30 20
208 3 c. green (1926) .. .. .. 1·50 1·00
209 4 c. pale olive-green and carmine .. 1·50 1·75
210 4 c. green (1922) 90 10
211 4 c. brown (1926) 60 60
212 6 c. carmine .. .. 10·00 6·00
213 6 c. bright mauve (1922) 90 10
214 8 c. orange (1925) .. .. .. 2·25 8·00
215 10 c. grey (1922) .. .. .. 2·00 3·25
216 10 c. carmine-red (1926) .. .. 2·00 80
217 12 c. carmine-red (1922) 80 40
218 12 c. grey (1926) .. .. .. 35 1·50
219 15 c. blue .. .. 4·75 2·00
a. *Cobalt* (1926) 45 25
220 20 c. blue (1922) .. .. .. 2·00 50
221 20 c. purple (1926) .. .. .. 4·50 8·50
222 – 50 r. dull pur & grn (1924) (Optd S. £170) £700 £1300
205/21 .. .. *Set of* 17 28·00 30·00
205/21 Optd "Specimen" .. .. *Set of* 17 £225
No. 222 is as Type **46**, but measures 25×35 mm.

A

B

Two types of duty plate in the 12 c. In Type B the letters of "MAURITIUS" are larger; the extremities of the downstroke and the tail of the "2" are pointed, instead of square, and the "c" is larger.

1921–34. *Wmk Mult Script CA. Chalk-surfaced paper* (25 *c. to* 10 *r.*). *P* 14.
223 **49** 1 c. black (1926) 30 35
224 2 c. brown (1926) 30 10
225 3 c. green (1926) 35 30
226 4 c. sage-green & carm (Die II) (1926) 35 30
a. Die I (1932) .. .. .. 4·75 20·00
226*b* 4 c. green (Die I) (1932) .. .. 1·25 45
227 **48** 5 c. grey and carmine (Die II) (1922) 40 10
a. Die I (1932) .. .. .. 1·50 60
228 **49** 6 c. sepia (1927) 30 60
229 8 c. orange (1926) .. .. .. 30 5·50
230 10 c. carmine-red (Die II) (1926) .. 40 10
a. Die I (1932) .. .. .. 2·50 4·00
231 12 c. grey (Type A) .. .. .. 30 6·50
232 12 c. carmine-red (Type A) (1922) .. 15 2·50
232*a* 12 c. pale grey (Type A) (1926) (Optd S. £24) .. .. 30 4·00
232*b* 12 c. grey (Type B) (1934) 60 10
233 15 c. Prussian blue (1926) 45 20
234 20 c. purple (1927) 30 40
235 20 c. Prussian blue (Die I) (1932) .. 7·00 80
a. Die II (1934) .. .. .. 9·00 30
236 25 c. black & red/*pale yell* (Die II) (1922) 20 15
a. Die I (1932) .. .. .. 1·50 17·00
237 **48** 50 c. dull purple and black (Die II) (1922) 6·50 4·00
238 1 r. black/*emerald* (Die II) (1922) .. 55 40
a. Die I (1932) .. .. .. 7·50 15·00
239 2 r. 50, black and red/*blue* (1922) .. 13·00 6·00
240 5 r. green and red/*yellow* (1924) .. 17·00 45·00
241 **49** 10 r. green and red/*emerald* (1924) .. 45·00 80·00
223/41 .. .. *Set of* 20 85·00 £130
223/41 Optd/Perf "Specimen" .. *Set of* 20 £300

3
Cents

(50)

51

1925 (25 Nov). *Nos.* 210, 217 *and* 220 *surch locally as T* **50.**
242 **46** 3 c. on 4 c. green .. .. .. 2·50 3·25
243 10 c. on 12 c. carmine-red 15 10
244 15 c. on 20 c. blue 40 15
242/4 .. .. *Set of* 3 2·75 3·25
242/4 Optd "Specimen" .. .. *Set of* 3 60·00

1935 (6 May). *Silver Jubilee. As Nos.* 114/17 *of Jamaica but ptd by D.L.R. P* 13½×14.
245 5 c. ultramarine and grey 20 10
f. Diagonal line by turret .. .. 25·00
g. Dot to left of chapel .. .. 25·00
h. Dot by flagstaff .. .. .. 25·00
246 12 c. green and indigo .. .. .. 1·75 10
g. Dot to left of chapel .. .. .. 45·00
247 20 c. brown and deep blue .. .. 2·75 20
g. Dot to left of chapel .. .. .. 55·00
248 1 r. slate and purple .. .. .. 24·00 26·00
h. Dot by flagstaff £140
245/8 .. .. *Set of* 4 26·00 26·00
245/8 Perf "Specimen" .. .. *Set of* 4 75·00
For illustrations of plate varieties see Omnibus section following Zimbabwe.

Line by sceptre (R. 5/3)

1937 (12 May). *Coronation. As Nos.* 118/20 *of Jamaica.*
249 5 c. violet 30 10
250 12 c. scarlet 30 40
251 20 c. bright blue 30 10
a. Line by sceptre .. .. 24·00
249/51 .. .. *Set of* 3 80 55
249/251 Perf "Specimen" .. .. *Set of* 3 45·00

"IJ" flaw (R. 3/6 of right pane)

Battered "A" (R. 6/1 of right pane)

(Typo D.L.R.)

1938–49. *T* **51** *and similar types. Wmk Mult Script CA. Chalk-surfaced paper* (25 *c. to* 10 *r.*). *P* 14.
252 2 c. olive-grey (9.3.38) 15 10
a. Perf 15×14 (1942) .. .. .. 1·00 10
253 3 c. reddish purple and scarlet (27.10.38) 1·00 40
a. Reddish lilac and red (4.43) 60 70
254 4 c. dull green (26.2.38) .. .. .. 1·25 50
a. Deep dull green (4.43) 50 50
255 5 c. slate-lilac (23.2.38) .. .. .. 2·00 20
a. Pale lilac (*shades*) (4.43) 70 10
b. Perf 15×14 (1942) .. .. .. 22·00 10
256 10 c. rose-red (9.3.38) .. .. .. 1·00 15
a. Deep reddish rose (*shades*) (4.43) .. 1·00 10
b. Perf 15×14. *Pale reddish rose* (1942) 22·00 30
257 12 c. salmon (*shades*) (26.2.38) 60 10
a. Perf 15×14 (1942) .. .. .. 50·00 75
258 20 c. blue (26.2.38) .. .. .. 1·00 10
259 25 c. brown-purple (2.3.38) .. .. 2·00 10
a. "IJ" flaw .. .. 60·00
b. Ordinary paper (8.4.43) .. .. 1·50 10
ba. "IJ" flaw .. .. 45·00
260 1 r. grey-brown (2.3.38) .. .. .. 5·50 70
a. Battered "A" .. .. 80·00
b. Ordinary paper (8.4.43) .. .. 3·25 60
ba. Battered "A" .. .. 60·00
c. Drab (4.49) .. .. 6·00 1·50
261 2 r. 50, pale violet (2.3.38) .. .. 16·00 6·00
a. Ordinary paper (8.4.43) .. .. 12·00 6·00
b. Slate-violet (4.48) .. .. .. 30·00 14·00
262 5 r. olive-green (2.3.38) .. .. .. 26·00 18·00
a. Ordinary paper. *Sage-green* (8.4.43) 24·00 17·00
263 10 r. reddish purple (*shades*) (2.3.38) .. 20·00 17·00
a. Ordinary paper (8.4.43) .. .. 8·00 13·00
252/63 .. .. *Set of* 12 48·00 35·00
252/63 Perf "Specimen" .. .. *Set of* 12 £140
The stamps perf 15 × 14 were printed by Bradbury, Wilkinson from De La Rue plates and issued only in the colony in 1942. De La Rue printings of the 2 c. to 20 c. in 1943–45 were on thin, whiter paper. 1943–45 printings of the 25 c. to 10 r. were on unsurfaced paper.

1946 (20 Nov). *Victory. As Nos.* 141/2 *of Jamaica.*
264 5 c. lilac 10 10
265 20 c. blue 10 10
264/5 Perf "Specimen" .. .. *Set of* 2 45·00

52 1d. "Post Office" Mauritius and King George VI

(Recess B.W.)

1948 (22 Mar). *Centenary of First British Colonial Postage Stamp. Wmk Mult Script CA. P* 11½×11.
266 **52** 5 c. orange and magenta 10 20
267 12 c. orange and green 10 10
268 – 20 c. blue and light blue 10 10
269 – 1 r. blue and red-brown.. .. .. 15 20
266/9 .. .. *Set of* 4 40 45
266/9 Perf "Specimen" .. .. *Set of* 4 90·00
Design:–20 c., 1 r. As T **52** but showing 2d. "Post Office" Mauritius.

1948 (25 Oct). *Royal Silver Wedding. As Nos.* 143/4 *of Jamaica.*
270 5 c. violet 10 10
271 10 r. magenta .. .. 8·00 12·00

1949 (10 Oct). *75th Anniv of U.P.U. As Nos.* 145/8 *of Jamaica.*
272 12 c. carmine 60 60
273 20 c. deep blue 60 60
274 35 c. purple 60 40
275 1 r. sepia 60 20
272/5 .. .. *Set of* 4 2·25 1·60

53 Labourdonnais Sugar Factory

55 Aloe Plant

(Photo Harrison)

1950 (1 July). *T* **53, 55** *and similar designs. Wmk Mult Script CA. Chalk surfaced paper. P* 13½ × 14½ (*horiz*), 14½ × 13½ (*vert*).
276 1 c. bright purple 10 40
277 2 c. rose-carmine 15 10
278 3 c. yellow-green .. .. 60 1·25
279 4 c. green 20 30
280 5 c. blue 15 10
281 10 c. scarlet 30 75
282 12 c. olive-green .. .. 1·25 30
283 20 c. ultramarine 40 15
284 25 c. brown-purple 65 40
285 35 c. violet 30 10
286 50 c. emerald-green .. .. 1·25 50
287 1 r. sepia .. .. 2·00 10
288 2 r. 50, orange .. .. 7·50 5·50
289 5 r. red-brown .. .. 8·50 10·00
290 10 r. dull blue .. .. 12·00 14·00
276/290 .. .. *Set of* 15 32·00 30·00
Designs: *Horiz*—2 c. Grand Port; 5 c. Rempart Mountain; 10 c. Transporting cane; 12 c. Mauritius Dodo and map; 35 c. Government House, Reduit; 1 r. Timor Deer; 2 r. 50, Port Louis; 5 r. Beach scene; 10 r. Arms of Mauritius. *Vert*—4 c. Tamarind Falls; 20 c. Legend of Paul and Virginie (inscr "VIRGINIA"); 25 c. Labourdonnais statue; 50 c. Pieter Both Mountain.
The latitude is incorrectly shown on No. 282. This was corrected before the same design was used for No. 302*a*.

1953 (2 June). *Coronation. As No.* 153 *of Jamaica.*
291 10 c. black and emerald 35 10

68 Tamarind Falls

69 Historical Museum, Mahebourg

(Photo Harrison)

1953 (3 Nov)–**58**. *Designs previously used for King George VI issue, but with portrait of Queen Elizabeth II as in T* **68/9**. *Wmk Mult Script CA. Chalk-surfaced paper. P* 13½×14½ *(horiz) or* 14½×13½ *(vert).*

293 2 c. bright carmine (1.6.54) 10 10
294 3 c. yellow-green (1.6.54) 30 40
295 4 c. bright purple 10 40
296 5 c. Prussian blue (1.6.54) 10 10
297 10 c. bluish green 10 10
a. *Yellowish green* (9.2.55) 20 10
298 15 c. scarlet 10 10
299 20 c. brown-purple 15 20
300 25 c. bright ultramarine 35 10
a. *Bright blue* (19.6.57) 30 10
301 35 c. reddish violet (1.6.54) 20 10
302 50 c. bright green 45 35
302*a* 60 c. deep green (2.8.54) .. .. 6·50 10
ab. Bronze-green (27.8.58) .. .. 8·00 10
303 1 r. sepia 30 10
a. *Deep grey-brown* (19.6.57) 90 65
304 2 r. 50, orange (1.6.54) .. .. 8·00 4·50
305 5 r. red-brown (1.6.54) .. .. 7·50 4·00
a. *Orange-brown* (19.6.57) .. .. 13·00 4·50
306 10 r. deep grey-blue (1.6.54) .. .. 10·00 60
293/306 .. .. *Set of* 15 30·00 9·50

Designs: *Horiz*—2 c. Grand Port; 4 c. Sugar factory; 5 c. Rempart Mountain; 35 c. Government House; 60 c. Mauritius Dodo and map; 1 r. Timor Deer; 2 r. 50, Port Louis; 5 r. Beach scene; 10 r. Arms of Mauritius. *Vert*—3 c. Aloe plant; 20 c. Labourdonnais statue; 25 c. Legend of Paul and Virginie; 50 c. Pieter Both Mountain.

Nos. 296 and 300 exist in coils, constructed from normal sheets.

See also Nos. 314/16.

70 Queen Elizabeth II and King George III (after Lawrence)

(Litho Enschedé)

1961 (11 Jan). *150th Anniv of British Post Office in Mauritius. W* w **12**. *P* 13½ × 14.

307 **70** 10 c. black and brown-red 10 10
308 20 c. ultramarine and light blue 15 25
309 35 c. black and yellow 20 25
310 1 r. deep maroon and green 20 25
307/10 .. .. *Set of* 4 60 70

1963 (4 June). *Freedom from Hunger. As No. 80 of Lesotho.*

311 60 c. reddish violet 40 10

1963 (2 Sept). *Red Cross Centenary. As Nos. 203/4 of Jamaica.*

312 10 c. red and black 15 10
313 60 c. red and blue 60 20

1963 (12 Nov)–**65**. *As Nos.* 297, 302*a and* 304 *but wmk* w **12**.

314 **68** 10 c. bluish green (1964) 15 10
a. *Yellowish green* (21.1.65) 25 10
315 – 60 c. bronze-green (28.5.64) .. .. 1·50 10
316 – 2 r. 50, orange .. .. .. 2·75 5·00
314/16 .. .. *Set of* 3 4·00 5·00

71 Bourbon White Eye

(Des D. M. Reid-Henry. Photo Harrison)

1965 (16 Mar). *Horiz designs as T* **71**. *W* w **12** *(upright). Multicoloured; background colours given. P* 14½ × 14.

317 2 c. lemon 10 15
a. Grey (leg) omitted .. .. .. 45·00
318 3 c. brown 10 15
a. Black (eye and beak) omitted .. .. 40·00
319 4 c. light reddish purple 10 15
a. Mauve-pink omitted* .. .. .. 35·00
b. Pale grey omitted .. .. .. 55·00
c. Orange omitted .. .. 95·00
320 5 c. grey-brown .. .. 1·00 10
321 10 c. light grey-green 25 10
322 15 c. pale grey 70 20
a. Red (beak) omitted .. .. .. 40·00
323 20 c. light yellow-bistre 70 10
324 25 c. bluish grey 80 10
325 35 c. greyish blue .. .. 1·00 10
326 50 c. light yellow-buff 35 35
327 60 c. light greenish yellow 40 10
328 1 r. light yellow-olive 75 10
a. Pale orange omitted .. .. .. 70·00
b. Light grey (ground) omitted .. .. 70·00
329 2 r. 50, pale stone .. .. .. 4·50 5·00
330 5 r. pale grey-blue .. .. .. 13·00 5·50
a. Brown-red omitted .. .. .. 70·00
331 10 r. pale bluish green .. .. .. 18·00 8·00
317/31 .. .. *Set of* 15 38·00 18·00

Designs:—3 c. Rodriguez Fody; 4 c. Olive White-eye; 5 c. Mascarene Paradise Flycatcher; 10 c. Mauritius Fody; 15 c. Mauritius Parakeet; 20 c. Mauritius Greybird; 25 c. Mauritius Kestrel; 35 c. Pink Pigeon; 50 c. Reunion Bulbul; 60 c. Mauritius Blue Pigeon (extinct); 1 r. Mauritius Dodo (extinct); 2 r. 50, Rodriguez Solitaire (extinct); 5 r. Mauritius Red Rail (extinct); 10 r. Broad-billed Parrot (extinct).

*On the 4 c. the background is printed in two colours so that in No. 319a the background colour is similar to that of the 5 c.

On No. 317a it is the deep grey which is missing, affecting the leg, beak and part of the branch. On No. 319c the missing orange affects the under breast of the bird, which appears much paler. On No. 328a the omission affects the legs and part of the body and on No. 330a the whole of the bird appears in the same colour as the legs.

The 50 c. and 2 r. 50 exist with PVA gum as well as gum arabic.

Nos. 320 and 324 exist in coils, constructed from normal sheets.

See also Nos. 340/1 and 370/5.

1965 (17 May). *I.T.U. Centenary. As Nos. 98/9 of Lesotho.*

332 10 c. red-orange and apple-green 15 10
333 60 c. yellow and bluish violet 40 20

1965 (25 Oct). *International Co-operation Year. As Nos. 100/1 of Lesotho.*

334 10 c. reddish purple and turquoise-green .. 15 10
335 60 c. deep bluish green and lavender 30 20

1966 (24 Jan). *Churchill Commemoration. As Nos. 102/5 of Lesotho.*

336 2 c. new blue 10 50
337 10 c. deep green 25 10
338 60 c. brown .. .. 1·10 15
339 1 r. bluish violet .. .. 1·25 15
336/9 .. .. *Set of* 4 2·40 80

1966–67. *As Nos.* 320, 325 *but wmk* w **12** *sideways.*

340 5 c. grey-brown (1966) 10 15
341 35 c. greyish blue (27.6.67) 20 15

No. 340 exists in coils, constructed from normal sheets.

72 "Education"

73 "Science"

74 "Culture"

(Des Jennifer Toombs. Litho Harrison)

1966 (1 Dec). *20th Anniv of U.N.E.S.C.O. W* w **12** *(sideways). P* 14.

342 **72** 5 c. slate-violet, red, yellow and orange 15 20
343 **73** 10 c. orange-yellow, violet and deep olive 25 10
344 **74** 60 c. black, bright purple and orange .. 50 15
342/4 .. .. *Set of* 3 80 35

SELF-GOVERNMENT

86 Red-tailed Tropic Bird

(Des D. M. Reid-Henry. Photo Harrison)

1967 (1 Sept). *Self-Government. T* **86** *and similar horiz designs. Multicoloured. W* w **12**. *P* 14½.

345 2 c. Type **86** 10 25
346 10 c. Rodriguez Brush Warbler 10 10
347 60 c. Rose-ringed Parakeet (extinct) 15 10
348 1 r. Grey-rumped Swiftlet 25 10
345/8 .. .. *Set of* 4 55 30

NEW INFORMATION

The editor is always interested to correspond with people who have new information that will improve or correct the Catalogue.

SELF GOVERNMENT 1967

(90)

1967 (1 Dec). *Self-Government. As Nos. 317/31 but wmk sideways on Nos. 352/3 and 357. Optd with T* **90**. *P* 14 × 14½.

349 2 c. lemon 10 50
350 3 c. brown 10 50
351 4 c. light reddish purple 10 50
a. Orange omitted .. .. 32·00
352 5 c. grey-brown 10 10
353 10 c. light grey-green 10 10
354 15 c. pale grey 10 20
355 20 c. light yellow-bistre 15 10
356 25 c. bluish grey 15 10
357 35 c. greyish blue 20 10
358 50 c. light yellow-buff 25 15
359 60 c. light greenish yellow 25 10
360 1 r. light yellow-olive 35 10
361 2 r. 50, pale stone .. .. 1·00 2·00
362 5 r. pale grey-blue .. .. 2·50 3·25
363 10 r. pale bluish green .. .. .. 4·75 7·00
349/63 .. .. *Set of* 15 9·00 12·00

INDEPENDENT

91 Flag of Mauritius

(Litho D.L.R.)

1968 (12 Mar). *Independence. T* **91** *and similar horiz design. P* 13½ × 13.

364 **91** 2 c. multicoloured 10 35
365 – 3 c. multicoloured 10 35
366 **91** 15 c. multicoloured 10 10
367 – 20 c. multicoloured 10 10
368 **91** 60 c. multicoloured 10 10
369 – 1 r. multicoloured 20 10
364/9 .. .. *Set of* 6 45 85

Design:—3 c., 20 c. and 1 r. Arms and Mauritius Dodo emblem.

1968 (12 July). *As Nos. 317/18, 322/3 and 327/8 but background colours changed as below.*

370 2 c. olive-yellow .. .. 20 1·00
371 3 c. cobalt .. .. 1·25 1·75
372 15 c. cinnamon 55 20
a. Greenish blue omitted .. .. ..
373 20 c. buff .. .. 2·25 60
374 60 c. rose 90 15
375 1 r. reddish purple .. .. 1·75 1·00
370/5 .. .. *Set of* 6 6·25 4·25

93 Dominique rescues Paul and Virginie

(Des V. Whiteley, from prints. Litho Format)

1968 (2 Dec). *Bicentenary of Bernardin de St. Pierre's Visit to Mauritius. Multicoloured designs as T* **93**. *P* 13½.

376 2 c. Type **93** 10 40
377 15 c. Paul and Virginie crossing the river .. 15 10
378 50 c. Visit of Labourdonnais to Madame de la Tour *(horiz)* 25 10
379 60 c. Meeting of Paul and Virginie in Confidence *(vert)* 25 10
380 1 r. Departure of Virginie for Europe *(horiz)* 35 20
381 2 r. 50, Bernardin de St. Pierre *(vert)* .. 95 2·25
376/81 .. .. *Set of* 6 1·90 2·75

99 Batardé

(Des J. Vinson (3 c., 20 c., 1 r.), R. Granger Barrett (others). Photo Harrison)

1969 (12 Mar)–**73**. *W* w **12** *(sideways on* 2, 3, 4, 5, 10, 15, 60 *and* 75 *c.). Chalk-surfaced paper. P* 14.

382 2 c. multicoloured 10 35
a. Pale green printed double* .. .. 23·00
383 3 c. multicoloured 10 50
384 4 c. multicoloured .. .. 90 1·25
385 5 c. multicoloured 30 10
386 10 c. scarlet, black and flesh .. .. .. 1·00 10
387 15 c. ochre, black and cobalt 30 10
388 20 c. multicoloured 65 30
a. Glazed ordinary paper (20.2.73) .. .. 30 1·75

389 25 c. red, black and pale apple-green 30 55
a. Glazed ordinary paper (22.1.71) 3·50 1·50
390 30 c. multicoloured 1·50 75
a. Glazed, ordinary paper (20.2.73) 3·50 3·75
391 35 c. multicoloured 65 40
a. Glazed ordinary paper (3.2.71) 90 40
392 40 c. multicoloured 35 1·25
a. Glazed ordinary paper (20.2.73) 2·50 3·25
393 50 c. multicoloured 1·00 10
a. Red omitted 50·00
b. Glazed ordinary paper (22.1.71) 1·25 10
ba. Red printed double
394 60 c. black, rose and ultramarine 1·50 10
395 75 c. multicoloured 1·50 1·25
396 1 r. multicoloured 60 10
a. Glazed ordinary paper (22.1.71) 1·75 15
397 2 r. 50, multicoloured 2·75 4·25
a. Glazed ordinary paper (20.2.73) 2·00 6·50
398 5 r. multicoloured 6·50 6·00
a. Glazed ordinary paper (22.1.71) 8·50 5·50
399 10 r. multicoloured 2·50 4·00
382/99 *Set of* 18 20·00 19·00
388a/98a *Set of* 9 22·00 20·00

Designs:—3 c. Red Reef Crab; 4 c. Episcopal Mitre; 5 c. Bourse; 10 c. Starfish; 15 c. Sea Urchin; 20 c. Fiddler Crab; 25 c. Spiny Shrimp; 30 c. Single Harp Shells, and Double Harp Shell; 35 c. Argonaute; 40 c. Nudibranch; 50 c. Violet and Orange Spider Shells; 60 c. Blue Marlin; 75 c. *Conus clytospira*; 1 r. Dolphin; 2 r. 50, Spiny Lobster, 5 r. Sacré Chien Rouge; 10 r. Croissant Queue Jaune.

*No. 382a. occurs from a sheet on which a second printing of the pale green appears above the normal.

Nos. 385/6 and 389 exist in coils constructed from normal sheets.

See also Nos. 437/54 and 475/91.

117 Gandhi as Law Student

124 Frangourinier Cane-crusher (18th cent)

(Des J. W. Litho Format)

1969 (1 July). *Birth Centenary of Mahatma Gandhi. T* **117** *and similar vert designs. Multicoloured. W w* **12**. *P* 13½.

400 2 c. Type **117** 10 10
401 15 c. Gandhi as stretcher-bearer during Zulu Revolt 20 10
402 50 c. Gandhi as Satyagrahi in South Africa 25 20
403 60 c. Gandhi at No. 10 Downing Street, London 25 10
404 1 r. Gandhi in Mauritius, 1901 30 10
405 2 r. 50, Gandhi, the "Apostle of Truth and Non-Violence" 80 1·00
400/5 *Set of* 6 1·75 1·25
MS406 153 × 153 mm. Nos. 400/5 3·75 6·00

(Des V. Whiteley. Photo Enschedé)

1969 (22 Dec).* *150th Anniv of Telfair's Improvements to the Sugar Industry. T* **124** *and similar multicoloured designs. W w* **12** *(sideways on* 2 *c. to* 1 *r.), P* 11½ × 11 *(2 r.* 50) *or* 11 × 11½ *(others).*

407 2 c. Three-roller Vertical Mill 10 20
408 15 c. Type **124** 10 10
409 60 c. Beau Rivage Factory, 1867 10 10
410 1 r. Mon Désert-Alma Factory, 1969 10 10
411 2 r. 50, Dr. Charles Telfair (*vert*) 25 50
407/11 *Set of* 5 45 60
MS412 159 × 88 mm. Nos. 407/11†. Wmk sideways. P 11 × 11½ 1·25 2·00

*This was the local release date but the Crown Agents issued the stamps on 15 December.

† In the miniature sheet the 2 r. 50 is perf 11 at the top and imperf on the other three sides.

(128)

129 Morne Plage, Mountain and Lufthansa Airliner

1970 (7 Apr). *World Fair, Osaka. Nos.* 394 *and* 396 *optd with T* **128** *by Harrison & Sons.*

413 60 c. black, rose and ultramarine 10 10
414 1 r. multicoloured 10 10

(Des H. Rose. Litho G. Gehringer, Kaiserslautern, Germany)

1970 (2 May). *Inauguration of Lufthansa Flight, Mauritius-Frankfurt. T* **129** *and similar multicoloured design. P* 14.

415 25 c. Type **129** 10 10
416 50 c. Airliner and Map (*vert*) 10 10

131 Lenin as a Student

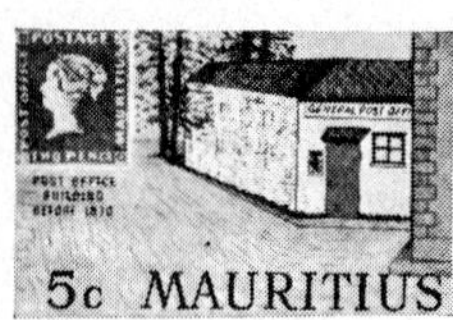
133 2d. "Post Office" Mauritius and original Post Office

(Photo State Ptg Works, Moscow)

1970 (15 May). *Birth Centenary of Lenin. T* **131** *and similar vert design. P* 12 × 11½.

417 15 c. blackish green and silver 10 10
418 75 c. blackish brown and gold 20 20

Design:—75 c. Lenin as Founder of U.S.S.R.

(Des and litho D.L.R.)

1970 (15 Oct). *Port Louis, Old and New. T* **133** *and similar horiz designs. Multicoloured. W w* **12** *(sideways). P* 14.

419 5 c. Type **133** 10 10
420 15 c. G.P.O. Building (built 1870) 10 10
421 50 c. Mail Coach (c. 1870) 15 10
422 75 c. Port Louis Harbour (1970) 20 10
423 2 r. 50, Arrival of Pierre A. de Suffren (1783) 35 60
419/23 *Set of* 5 70 70
MS424 165 × 95 mm. Nos. 419/23 2·75 6·00

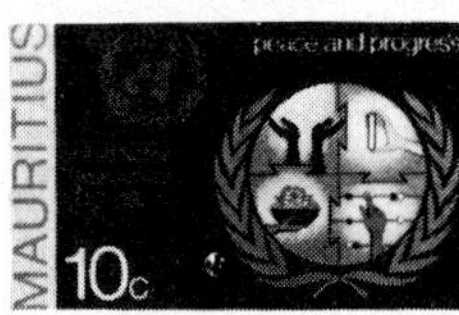
138 U.N. Emblem and Symbols

(Des Jennifer Toombs. Litho Format)

1970 (24 Oct). *25th Anniv of United Nations. W w* **12** *(sideways). P* 14½.

425 **138** 10 c. multicoloured 10 10
426 60 c. multicoloured 20 10

139 Rainbow over Waterfall

(Des R. Granger Barrett from local ideas (60 c.), R. Granger Barrett from local ideas and adapted by N. Mossae (others). Litho Format)

1971 (12 Apr). *Tourism. T* **139** *and similar horiz designs. Multicoloured. W w* **12** *(sideways). P* 14.

427 10 c. Type **139** 20 10
428 15 c. Trois Mamelles Mountains 20 10
429 60 c. Beach scene 35 10
430 2 r. 50, Marine life 1·25 1·50
427/30 *Set of* 4 1·75 1·50

Nos. 427/30 are inscribed on the reverse with details of tourist attractions in Mauritius.

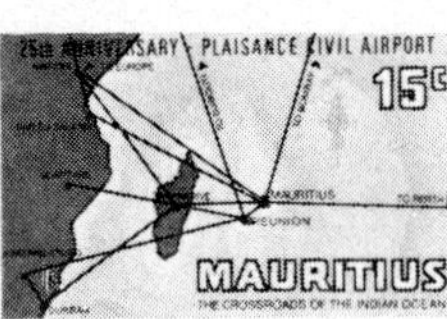
140 "Crossroads" of Indian Ocean

(Des R. Granger Barrett (60 c.) or V. Whiteley (others). Litho Harrison)

1971 (23 Oct). *25th Anniv of Plaisance Airport. T* **140** *and similar horiz designs. Multicoloured. W w* **12** *(sideways on* 15 *c.). P* 14.

431 15 c. Type **140** 10 10
432 60 c. "Boeing 707" and Terminal Buildings 25 10
433 1 r. Air Hostesses on gangway 30 10
434 2 r. 50, *Roland Garros* (aeroplane), Choisy Airfield. 1937 1·50 2·75
431/4 *Set of* 4 1·90 2·75

141 Princess Margaret Orthopaedic Centre

(Des and litho Harrison)

1971 (2 Nov). *Third Commonwealth Medical Conference. T* **141** *and similar horiz design. Multicoloured. W w* **12**. *P* 14 × 13½.

435 10 c. Type **141** 10 10
436 75 c. Operation Theatre in National Hospital 20 20

1972–74. *As Nos.* 382/99 *but W w* **12** *upright* (2, 3, 4, 5, 10, 15, 60, 75 c.) *or sideways (others).*

A. *Glazed, ordinary paper.* B. *Chalk-surfaced paper*

No.	Description	A		B	
437	2 c. multicoloured	10	30	40	1·25
438	3 c. multicoloured	1·00	2·50	30	1·00
439	4 c. multicoloured	†		3·00	3·50
440	5 c. multicoloured	2·50	30	30	10
441	10 c. scarlet, black and flesh	3·00	30	3·25	45
442	15 c. ochre, black and cobalt	50	70	35	10
443	20 c. multicoloured	†		35	75
444	25 c. red, black & apple-green	†		35	80
445	30 c. multicoloured	†		2·25	2·75
446	35 c. multicoloured	†		4·00	50
	a. Orange-brown omitted	†		55·00	—
447	40 c. multicoloured	†		3·50	4·00
448	50 c. multicoloured	†		45	10
	a. Red omitted	†		—	—
449	60 c. black, rose & ultramarine	60	60	65	10
	a. Rose omitted	†		50·00	—
450	75 c. multicoloured	1·75	5·50	2·75	1·10
451	1 r. multicoloured	†		1·00	20
452	2 r. 50, multicoloured	†		2·00	3·50
453	5 r. multicoloured	†		3·00	2·00
	a. Greenish blue printed double	†		32·00	—
454	10 r. multicoloured	†		5·00	8·00
437/450A	*Set of* 7	8·50	9·00		
437/454B	*Set of* 18			29·00	27·00

Nos. 440B and 444B exist in coils, constructed from normal sheets.

Dates of issue:

Glazed paper—10.1.72, 5 c., 10 c.; 20.2.73, 2 c., 3 c., 15 c., 60 c., 75 c.

Chalk-surfaced paper—8.11.73, 10 c., 20 c., 30 c., 35 c., 40 c., 75 c., 1 r., 10 r.; 12.12.73, 25 c., 50 c., 2 r. 50, 5 r.; 25.2.74, 5 c., 15 c., 60 c.; 13.6.74, 2 c., 3 c., 4 c.

142 Queen Elizabeth and Prince Philip

(Des and photo Harrison)

1972 (24 Mar). *Royal Visit. T* **142** *and similar multicoloured design. W w* **12**. *P* 14.

455 15 c. Type **142** 15 10
456 2 r. 50, Queen Elizabeth II (*vert*) 2·00 2·00

143 Theatre Façade

(Des and litho Harrison)

1972 (26 June). *150th Anniversary of Port Louis Theatre. T* **143** *and similar horiz design. Multicoloured. W w* **12**. *P* 14.

457 10 c. Type **143** 10 10
458 1 r. Theatre Auditorium 30 10

144 Pirate Dhow

(Des and litho Harrison)

1972 (17 Nov). *Pirates and Privateers. T* **144** *and similar multicoloured designs. W w* **12** *(sideways on* 60 *c. and* 1 *r.). P* 14½ × 14 *(60 c.,* 1 *r.) or* 14 × 14½ *(others).*

459 15 c. Type **144** 45 10
460 60 c. Treasure chest (*vert*) 75 15
461 1 r. Lemene and *L'Hirondelle* (*vert*) 90 15
462 2 r. 50, Robert Surcouf 3·50 5·50
459/62 *Set of* 4 5·00 5·50

145 Mauritius University   146 Map and Hands

(Des and litho Harrison)

1973 (10 Apr). *Fifth Anniv of Independence. T* **145** *and similar horiz designs. Multicoloured.* W w **12** (*sideways*). *P* 14.

463		15 c. Type **145**	10	10
464		60 c. Tea Development	10	10
465		1 r. Bank of Mauritius	10	10
463/5		*Set of* 3	20	15

(Des and litho Harrison)

1973 (25 Apr). *O.C.A.M.* Conference. T* **146** *and similar multi-coloured design.* W w **12** (*sideways on* 10 *c.*). *P* 14½ × 14 (10 *c.*) *or* 14 × 14½ (2 *r.* 50).

466		10 c. O.C.A.M. emblem (*horiz*)	10	10
467		2 r. 50, Type **146**	40	45

*O.C.A.M. = Organisation Commune Africaine Malgache et Mauricienne.

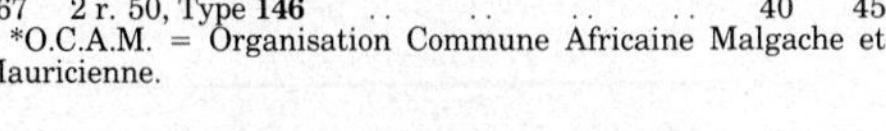

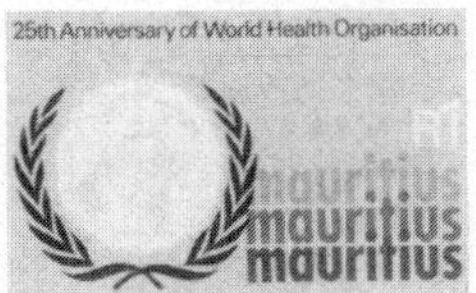

147 W.H.O. Emblem

(Des and litho Harrison)

1973 (20 Nov). *25th Anniv of W.H.O.* W w **12**. *P* 14.

468	**147**	1 r. multicoloured	10	10
		a. Wmk sideways	20	10

148 Meteorological Station, Vacoas.

(Des and litho Harrison)

1973 (27 Nov). *I.M.O./W.M.O. Centenary.* W w **12** (*sideways*). *P* 14.

469	**148**	75 c. multicoloured	20	30

149 Capture of the *Kent*, 1800   150 P. Commerson (naturalist)

(Des and litho Harrison)

1974 (21 Mar). *Birth Bicent of Robert Surcouf (privateer).* W w **12** (*sideways*). *P* 14.

470	**149**	60 c. multicoloured	40	50

(Des and litho Harrison)

1974 (18 Apr). *Death Bicent of Philibert Commerson* (1973). W w **12**. *P* 14½.

471	**150**	2 r. 50, multicoloured	30	40

PRICES OF SETS

Set prices are given for many issues, generally those containing three stamps or more. Definitive sets include one of each value or major colour change, but do not cover different perforations, die types or minor shades. Where a choice is possible the set prices are based on the cheapest versions of the stamps included in the listings.

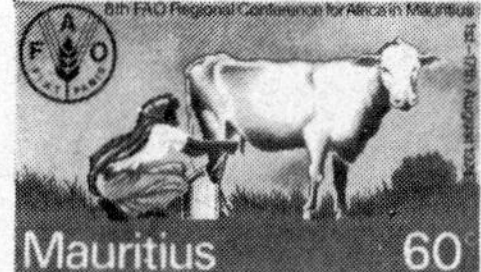

151 Cow being Milked

(Des and litho Harrison)

1974 (23 Oct). *Eighth F.A.O. Regional Conference for Africa, Mauritius.* W w **12** (*sideways*). *P* 14.

472	**151**	60 c. multicoloured	10	10

152 Mail Train

(Des and litho Harrison)

1974 (4 Dec). *Centenary of Universal Postal Union. T* **152** *and similar horiz design. Multicoloured.* W w **12**. *P* 14.

473		15 c. Type **152**	40	15
474		1 r. New G.P.O., Port Louis	40	20

1975–77. *As Nos.* 382/99 *but* W w **14** (*sideways on* 2 *to* 15 *c.*, 60 *c. and* 75 *c.*). *Chalk-surfaced paper.*

475		2 c. multicoloured (16.8.77)	2·00	50
476		3 c. multicoloured (16.8.77)	2·00	50
477		4 c. multicoloured (16.8.77)	2·25	50
478		5 c. multicoloured (19.3.75)	55	40
479		15 c. ochre, black and cobalt (21.1.75)	1·40	65
480		20 c. multicoloured (19.3.76)	30	30
		a. Grey (background) omitted	£120	
481		25 c. red, black and apple-green (19.3.75)	60	1·75
482		30 c. multicoloured (21.1.75)	35	2·25
		a. Yellow omitted		
483		35 c. multicoloured (19.3.76)	60	15
		a. Orange-brown omitted	45·00	
484		40 c. multicoloured (19.3.76)	75	60
485		50 c. multicoloured (19.3.76)	75	10
486		60 c. black, rose and ultramarine (16.8.77)	3·75	25
487		75 c. multicoloured (19.4.77)	1·25	40
488		1 r. multicoloured (19.3.76)	75	20
		a. Deep bluish green (fin and tail markings) omitted		
489		2 r. 50, multicoloured (16.8.77)	13·00	4·00
490		5 r. multicoloured (21.1.75)	5·00	13·00
491		10 r. multicoloured (21.1.75)	7·50	12·00
475/91		*Set of* 17	38·00	35·00

No. 492 is vacant.

153 "Cottage Life" (F. Leroy)

(Des and litho Harrison)

1975 (6 Mar). *Aspects of Mauritian Life. T* **153** *and similar multi-coloured designs showing paintings.* W w **14** (*sideways on* 15 *c.*, 60 *c. and* 2 *r.* 50). *P* 14.

493		15 c. Type **153**	10	10
494		60 c. "Milk Seller" (A. Richard) (*vert*)	30	10
		a. Brown and stone (ornaments and frame) double		
495		1 r. "Entrance of Port Louis Market" (Thuillier)	30	10
496		2 r. 50, "Washerwoman" (Max Boulleé) (*vert*)	85	60
493/6		*Set of* 4	1·40	65

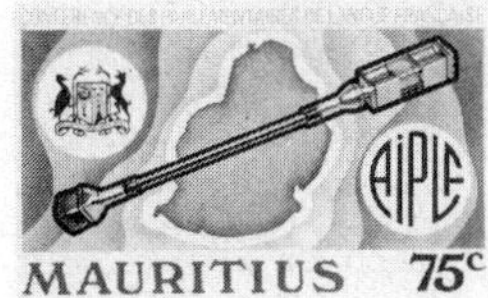

154 Mace across Map

(Des Harrison. Litho Questa)

1975 (21 Nov). *French-speaking Parliamentary Assemblies Conference. Port Louis.* W w **14** (*sideways*). *P* 14.

497	**154**	75 c. multicoloured	30	45

155 Woman with Lamp ("The Light of the World")

(Des A. H. Abdoolah; adapted Harrison. Litho Questa)

1975 (5 Dec). *International Women's Year.* W w **14** (*sideways*). *P* 14½.

498	**155**	2 r. 50, multicoloured	35	1·00

156 Parched Landscape

(Des Harrison (50 c.), J.W. Ltd (60 c.) Litho Questa)

1976 (26 Feb). *Drought in Africa. T* **156** *and similar design. Multicoloured.* W w **14** (*sideways on* 50 *c.*). *P* 14.

499		50 c. Type **156**	15	15
500		60 c. Map of Africa and carcass (*vert*)	15	15

157 *Pierre Loti*, 1953–70

(Des J. W. Litho Questa)

1976 (2 July). *Mail Carriers to Mauritius. T* **157** *and similar horiz designs. Multicoloured.* W w **14** (*sideways*). *P* 14½ × 14.

501		10 c. Type **157**	15	10
502		15 c. *Secunder*, 1907	20	10
503		50 c. *Hindoostan*, 1842	45	15
504		60 c. *St. Geran*, 1740	50	15
505		2 r. 50, *Maën*, 1638	2·00	4·00
501/5		*Set of* 5	3·00	4·00
MS506		115 × 138 mm. Nos. 501/5	4·25	5·50

158 "The Flame of Hindi carried across the Seas"   159 Conference Logo and Map of Mauritius

(Des N. Nagalingum (Type **158**), C. R. Prakashi and R. B. Kailash (1 r. 20); adapted J. W. Litho Questa)

1976 (28 Aug). *Second World Hindi Convention. T* **158** *and similar horiz design. Multicoloured.* W w **14** (*sideways*). *P* 14.

507		10 c. Type **158**	10	10
508		75 c. Type **158**	10	15
509		1 r. 20, Hindi script	20	40
507/9		*Set of* 3	30	50

(Des J. W. Litho Questa)

1976 (22 Sept). *22nd Commonwealth Parliamentary Association Conference. T* **159** *and similar vert design. Multicoloured.* W w **14**. *P* 14.

510		1 r. Type **159**	25	10
511		2 r. 50, Conference logo	70	80

160 King Priest and Breastplate   161 Sega Scene

(Des J. W. Litho Walsall)

1976 (15 Dec). *Moenjodaro Excavations, Pakistan. T* **160** *and similar vert designs. Multicoloured.* W w **14**. *P* 14.

512		60 c. Type **160**	15	10
513		1 r. House with well and goblet	30	10
514		2 r. 50, Terracotta figurine and necklace	90	45
512/14		*Set of* 3	1·25	50

(Des BG Studio. Litho J.W.)

1977 (20 Jan). *Second World Black and African Festival of Arts and Culture, Nigeria.* W w **14** (*sideways*). *P* 13.

515	**161**	1 r. multicoloured	30	15

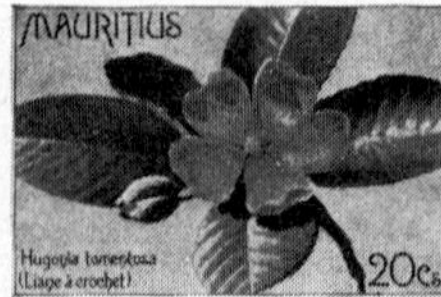

162 The Queen with Sceptre and Rod
163 *Hugonia tomentosa*

(Des L. Curtis. Litho Harrison)

1977 (7 Feb). *Silver Jubilee. T* **162** *and similar vert designs. Multicoloured. W* w **14** (*sideways*). *P* 14½ × 14.

516	50 c. The Queen at Mauritius Legislative Assembly, 1972	20	10
517	75 c. Type **162**	25	10
518	5 r. Presentation of Sceptre and Rod	75	75
516/18	*Set of* 3	1·10	75

(Des Jennifer Toombs. Litho Questa)

1977 (22 Sept). *Indigenous Flowers. T* **163** *and similar multi-coloured designs. W* w **14** (*sideways on* 20 *c. and* 1 *r.* 50). *P* 14.

519	20 c. Type **163**	10	10
520	1 r. *Ochna mauritiana* (*vert*)	20	10
521	1 r. 50, *Dombeya acutangula*	30	20
522	5 r. *Trochetia blackburniana* (*vert*)	1·00	1·25
519/22	*Set of* 4	1·40	1·40
MS523	130 × 130 mm. Nos. 519/22. Wmk sideways	3·00	5·50

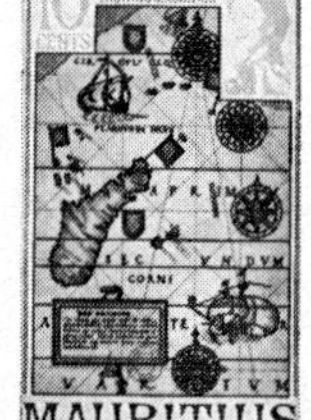

164 "Twin Otter"
165 Portuguese Map of Mauritius, 1519

(Des A. Theobald. Litho Questa)

1977 (31 Oct). *Inaugural International Flight of Air Mauritius. T* **164** *and similar horiz designs. Multicoloured. W* w **14** (*sideways*). *P* 14½ × 14.

524	25 c. Type **164**	15	10
525	50 c. "Twin Otter" and Air Mauritius emblem	20	10
526	75 c. Piper "Navajo" and Boeing "747"	30	10
527	5 r. Boeing "707"	1·60	1·50
524/7	*Set of* 4	2·00	1·50
MS528	110 × 152 mm. Nos. 524/7	2·50	2·75

(Des Harrison. Litho J.W.)

1978 (12 Mar)–**84**. *Designs as T* **165** *in light brown, chestnut and black* (25 *r.*) *or multicoloured* (*others*). *W* w **14** (*sideways on horiz designs*). *P* 13½. A. *Without imprint.* B. *With imprint date at foot.*

		A		B	
529	10 c. Type **165**	20	20	20	20
530	15 c. Dutch Occupation, 1638–1710 (*horiz*)	30	30	†	
531	20 c. Van Keulen's map, *c.* 1700 (*horiz*)	40	30	†	
532	25 c. Settlement on Rodriguez, 1691	30	30	50	30
533	35 c. French charter, 1715	20	20	50	10
534	50 c. Construction of Port Louis, *c.* 1736 (*horiz*)	20	20	40	10
535	60 c. Pierre Poivre, *c.* 1767	30	30	†	
536	70 c. Bellin's map, 1763 (*horiz*)	30	30	†	
537	75 c. First coinage, 1794	50	30	30	10
538	90 c. Battle of Grand Port, 1810 (*horiz*)	30	30	†	
539	1 r. British landing, 1810 (*horiz*)	30	10	30	10
540	1 r. 20, Government House, *c.* 1840 (*horiz*)	35	35	†	
541	1 r. 25, Lady Gomm's ball, 1847	50	15	40	10
542	1 r. 50, Indian immigration, 1835 (*horiz*)	35	15	†	
543	2 r. Race course, *c.* 1870 (*horiz*)	50	30	1·00	20
544	3 r. Place d'Armes, *c.* 1880 (*horiz*)	50	30	†	
545	5 r. Royal Visit postcard, 1901 (*horiz*)	60	50	1·25	1·25
546	10 r. Royal College, 1914 (*horiz*)	90	90	†	
547	15 r. Unfurling Mauritian flag, 1968	1·00	1·10	†	
548	25 r. First Mauritian Governor-General and Prime Minister (*horiz*)	2·00	2·25	†	
529A/48A	*Set of* 20	9·00	8·00		
529B/45B	*Set of* 9			4·25	2·25

Dates of issue:—12.3.78, Nos. 529A/48A; 15.6.83, Nos. 537B, 541B, 543B; 1.84, No. 533B; 11.84, Nos. 529B, 532B, 534B; 4.85, No. 539B; 8.5.85, No. 545B.

Nos. 533B, 537B, 541B and 543B exist with different imprint dates.

For 35 c. as Nos. 533B, but perforated 14½ see No. 737 and for values watermarked w **16** see Nos. 740/57.

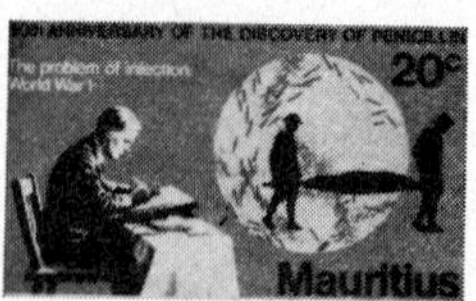

166 Mauritius Dodo
167 Problem of Infection, World War I

(Des Jennifer Toombs. Litho Questa)

1978 (21 Apr). *25th Anniv of Coronation. T* **166** *and similar vert designs. P* 15.

549	3 r. grey-blue, black and new blue	25	45
	a. Sheetlet, Nos. 549/51, each × 2	1·75	
550	3 r. multicoloured	25	45
551	3 r. grey-blue, black and new blue	25	45
549/51	*Set of* 3	65	1·25

Designs:—No. 549, Antelope of Bohun; 550, Queen Elizabeth II.

Nos. 549/51 were printed together in small sheets of 6, containing two *se-tenant* strips of 3 with horizontal gutter margin between.

(Des Jennifer Toombs. Litho Enschedé)

1978 (3 Aug). *50th Anniv of Discovery of Penicillin. T* **167** *and similar horiz designs. W* w **14** (*sideways*). *P* 13½ × 14.

552	20 c. multicoloured	20	10
553	1 r. multicoloured	50	10
554	1 r. 50, black, olive-bistre & dp bluish grn	75	20
555	5 r. multicoloured	1·60	2·00
552/5	*Set of* 4	2·75	2·00
MS556	150 × 90 mm. Nos. 552/5	2·75	3·75

Designs:—1 r. First mould-growth, 1928; 1 r. 50, *Penicillium notatum*; 5 r. Sir Alexander Fleming.

168 *Papilio manlius* (butterfly)
169 Ornate Table

(Des G. Drummond. Litho Walsall)

1978 (21 Sept). *World Wildlife. T* **168** *and similar horiz designs. Multicoloured. W* w **14** (*sideways*). *P* 13½ × 14.

557	20 c. Type **168**	20	10
558	1 r. Geckos	20	10
559	1 r. 50 Greater Mascarene Flying Fox	30	30
560	5 r. Mauritius Kestrel	2·25	2·75
557/60	*Set of* 4	2·75	2·75
MS561	154 × 148 mm. Nos. 557/60	4·50	5·50

(Des C. Abbott. Litho Questa)

1978 (21 Dec). *Bicentenary of Reconstruction of Chateau Le Réduit. T* **169** *and similar vert designs. Multicoloured. W* w **14**. *P* 14½ × 14.

562	15 c. Type **169**	10	10
563	75 c. Chateau Le Réduit	10	10
564	3 r. Le Réduit gardens	30	45
562/4	*Set of* 3	40	50

20c
MAURITIUS

170 Whitcomb Diesel Locomotive "65H.P.", 1949
171 Father Laval and Crucifix

(Des G. Hutchins. Litho Questa)

1979 (1 Feb). *Railway Locomotives. T* **170** *and similar horiz designs. Multicoloured. W* w **14** (*sideways*). *P* 14½.

565	20 c. Type **170**	10	10
566	1 r. *Sir William*, 1922	25	10
567	1 r. 50, Kitson type, 1930	35	45
568	2 r. Garratt type, 1927	50	85
565/8	*Set of* 4	1·10	1·25
MS569	128 × 128 mm. Nos. 565/8	1·75	2·25

(Des J. W. Litho Questa)

1979 (30 Apr). *Beatification of Father Laval* (*missionary*). *T* **171** *and similar multicoloured designs. W* w **14** (*sideways on* 5 *r*). *P* 14.

570	20 c. Type **171**	10	10
571	1 r. 50, Father Laval	10	10
572	5 r. Father Laval's tomb (*horiz*)	35	50
570/2	*Set of* 3	40	55
MS573	150 × 96 mm. Nos. 570/2 (wmk upright)	90	1·40

172 Astronaut descending from Lunar Module
173 Great Britain 1855 4d. Stamp and Sir Rowland Hill

(Manufactured by Walsall)

1979 (20 July). *10th Anniv of Moon Landing. T* **172** *and similar vert designs. Multicoloured. Imperf × roul 5*. Self-adhesive* (*from booklets*).

574	20 c. Type **172**	15	15
	a. Booklet pane. Nos. 574/6	2·25	
	b. Booklet pane. Nos. 574/5, each × 3	2·25	
575	3 r. Astronaut performing experiment on Moon	70	90
576	5 r. Astronaut on Moon	2·00	3·25
574/6	*Set of* 3	2·50	4·00

*Nos. 574/6 are separated by various combinations of rotary-knife (giving a straight edge) and roulette.

(Des J. W. Litho Questa)

1979 (27 Aug). *Death Centenary of Sir Rowland Hill. T* **173** *and similar vert designs showing stamps and Sir Rowland Hill. Multicoloured. W* w **14**. *P* 14.

577	25 c. Type **173**	10	10
578	2 r. 1954 60 c. definitive	45	40
579	5 r. 1847 1d. "POST OFFICE"	90	1·00
577/9	*Set of* 3	1·25	1·25
MS580	120 × 89 mm. 3 r. 1847 2d. "POST OFFICE"	80	1·10

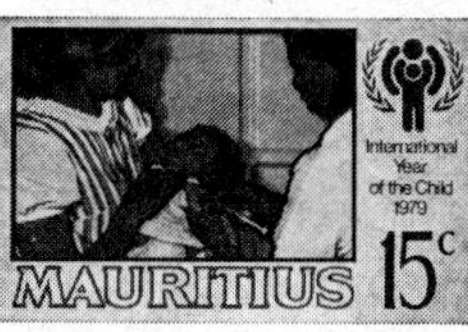

174 Young Child being Vaccinated

(Des V. Whiteley Studio. Litho Questa)

1979 (11 Oct). *International Year of the Child. T* **174** *and similar designs in black, ultramarine and bright blue* (1 *r.*) *or multi-coloured* (*others*). *W* w **14** (*sideways on* 15, 25 *c.*, 1 *r.* 50, *and* 3 *r.*). *P* 14½ × 14.

581	15 c. Type **174**	10	10
582	25 c. Children playing	10	10
583	1 r. I.Y.C. emblem (*vert*)	10	10
584	1 r. 50, Girls in chemistry laboratory	20	20
585	3 r. Boy operating lathe	35	50
581/5	*Set of* 5	70	75

175 The Liénard Obelisk
176 *Emirne*

(Des L. Curtis. Litho Questa)

1980 (24 Jan). *Pamplemousses Botanical Gardens. T* **175** *and similar horiz designs. Multicoloured. W* w **14** (*sideways*). *P* 14 × 14½.

586	20 c. Type **175**	10	10
587	25 c. Poivre Avenue	10	10
588	1 r. Varieties of Vacoas	20	10
589	2 r. Giant Water Lilies	35	35
590	5 r. Mon Plaisir (mansion)	60	1·00
586/90	*Set of* 5	1·25	1·50
MS591	152 × 105 mm. Nos. 586/90	1·75	1·90

(Des J. W. Litho Walsall)

1980 (6 May). *"London 1980" International Stamp Exhibition. Mail-carrying Ships. T* **176** *and similar horiz designs. Multi-coloured. W* w **14** (*sideways*). *P* 14½ × 14.

592	25 c. Type **176**	10	10
593	1 r. *Boissevain*	20	10
594	2 r. *La Boudeuse*	35	10
595	5 r. *Sea Breeze*	55	55
592/5	*Set of* 4	1·00	75

PRICES OF SETS

Set prices are given for many issues, generally those containing three stamps or more. Definitive sets include one of each value or major colour change, but do not cover different perforations, die types or minor shades. Where a choice is possible the set prices are based on the cheapest versions of the stamps included in the listings.

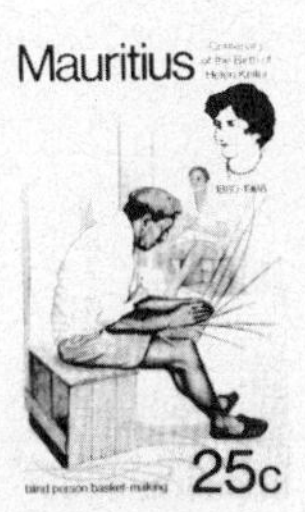

177 Blind Person Basket-making

178 Prime Minister Sir Seewoosagur Ramgoolam

(Des J. W. Litho Harrison)

1980 (27 June). *Birth Centenary of Helen Keller (campaigner for the handicapped). T* **177** *and similar vert designs. Multicoloured.* W w **14**. *P* 14.

596 25 c. Type **177** 10 10
597 1 r. Deaf child under instruction 30 10
598 2 r. 50, Helen reading braille 50 25
599 5 r. Helen at graduation, 1904 .. .. 90 70
596/9 .. .. *Set of* 4 1·60 90

(Des Walsall. Litho and gold foil embossed Questa)

1980 (18 Sept). *80th Birthday and 40th Year in Parliament of Prime Minister Sir Seewoosagur Ramgoolam.* W w **14**. *P* 13½.

600 **178** 15 r. multicoloured .. .. .. 1·25 1·40

No. 600 was printed in sheets of 4 stamps.

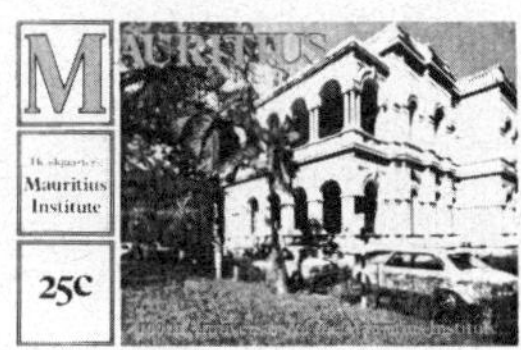

179 Headquarters, Mauritius Institute

(Des BG Studio. Litho J.W.)

1980 (1 Oct). *Centenary of Mauritius Institute. T* **179** *and similar horiz designs. Multicoloured.* W w **14** (*sideways*). *P* 13.

601 25 c. Type **179** 10 10
602 2 r. Rare copy of Veda 25 10
603 2 r. 50, Rare cone 30 15
604 5 r. "Le Torrent" (painting by Harpignies) .. 45 50
601/4 .. .. *Set of* 4 1·00 70

180 *Hibiscus liliiflorus*

181 Beau-Bassin/Rose Hill

(Des Jennifer Toombs. Litho Questa)

1981 (15 Jan). *Flowers. T* **180** *and similar vert designs. Multicoloured.* W w **14**. *P* 14.

605 25 c. Type **180** 10 10
606 2 r. *Erythrospermum monticolum* 35 40
607 2 r. 50, *Chasalia boryana* 45 50
608 5 r. *Hibiscus columnaris* .. .. .. 85 1·25
605/8 .. .. *Set of* 4 1·60 2·00

(Des. L. Curtis. Litho J.W.)

1981 (10 Apr). *Coats of Arms of Mauritius Towns. T* **181** *and similar vert designs. Multicoloured.* W w **14**. *P* 13½ × 13.

609 25 c. Type **181** 10 10
610 1 r. 50, Curepipe 25 20
611 2 r. Quatre-Bornes 30 25
612 2 r. 50, Vacoas/Phoenix 35 30
613 5 r. Port Louis 65 55
609/13 .. .. *Set of* 5 1·50 1·25
MS614 130 × 130 mm. Nos. 609/13. *P* 14.. .. 2·00 3·00

182 Prince Charles as Colonel-in-Chief, Royal Regiment of Wales

183 Emmanuel Anquetil and Guy Rozemont

(Des J. W. Litho Questa)

1981 (22 July). *Royal Wedding. T* **182** *and similar vert designs. Multicoloured.* W w **14**. *P* 14.

615 25 c. Wedding bouquet from Mauritius .. 10 10
616 2 r. 50, Type **182** 55 15
617 10 r. Prince Charles and Lady Diana Spencer 1·40 90
615/17 .. .. *Set of* 3 1·75 1·00

(Des G. Vasarhelyi. Litho Questa)

1981 (27 Aug). *Famous Politicians and Physician* (5 *r*). *T* **183** *and similar horiz designs.* W w **14** (*sideways*). *P* 14½.

618 20 c. black and carmine 10 10
619 25 c. black and lemon 10 10
620 1 r. 25, black and emerald 25 15
621 1 r. 50, black and rose-red 30 15
622 2 r. black and ultramarine 40 20
623 2 r. 50, black and orange-brown 45 25
624 5 r. black and turquoise-blue 80 70
618/24 .. .. *Set of* 7 2·00 1·40

Designs:—25 c. Remy Ollier and Sookdeo Bissoondoyal; 1 r. 25, Maurice Curé and Barthélemy Ohsan; 1 r. 50, Sir Guy Forget and Renganaden Seeneevassen; 2 r. Sir Abdul Razak Mohamed and Jules Koenig; 2 r. 50, Abdoollatiff Mahomed Osman and Dazzi Rama (Pandit Sahadeo); 5 r. Sir Thomas Lewis and electrocardiogram.

184 Drummer and Piper

185 "Skills"

(Des Jennifer Toombs. Litho Format)

1981 (16 Sept). *Religion and Culture. T* **184** *and similar multicoloured designs.* W w **14** (*sideways on* 20 *c. and* 5 *r.*). *P* 14 × 13½ (20 *c.*), 13½ × 14 (2 *r.*) *or* 13½ (5 *r.*).

625 20 c. Type **184** 10 10
626 2 r. Swami Sivananda (*vert*) 45 50
627 5 r. Chinese Pagoda .. .. 75 1·75
625/7 .. .. *Set of* 3 1·10 2·10

The 20 c. value commemorates the World Tamil Culture Conference (1980).

(Des BG Studio. Litho Questa)

1981 (15 Oct). *25th Anniv of Duke of Edinburgh Award Scheme. T* **185** *and similar vert designs. Multicoloured.* W w **14**. *P* 14.

628 25 c. Type **185** 10 10
629 1 r. 25, "Service" 10 10
630 5 r. "Expeditions" 25 30
631 10 r. Duke of Edinburgh 50 70
628/31 .. .. *Set of* 4 75 1·00

186 Ka'aba (sacred shrine, Great Mosque of Mecca)

187 Scout Emblem

(Des Jennifer Toombs. Litho Questa)

1981 (26 Nov). *Moslem Year 1400A.H. Commemoration. T* **186** *and similar vert designs. Multicoloured.* W w **14**. *P* 14½ × 14.

632 25 c. Type **186** 10 10
633 2 r. Mecca 40 50
634 5 r. Mecca and Ka'aba .. .. .. 85 1·60
632/4 .. .. *Set of* 3 1·25 2·00

(Des C. Abbott. Litho Walsall)

1982 (22 Feb). *75th Anniv of Boy Scout Movement and 70th Anniv of Scouting in Mauritius. T* **187** *and similar horiz designs.* W w **14** (*sideways*). *P* 14 × 14½.

635 25 c. deep lilac and light green 10 10
636 2 r. deep brown and brown-ochre 30 30
637 5 r. deep green and yellow-olive .. .. 70 1·00
638 10 r. deep green and new blue .. .. 1·25 2·00
635/8 .. .. *Set of* 4 2·00 3·00

Designs:—2 r. Lord Baden-Powell and Baden-Powell House; 5 r. Grand Howl; 10 r. Ascent of Pieter Both.

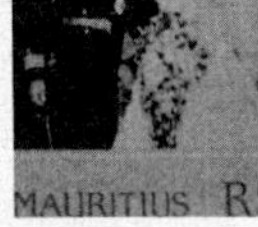

188 Charles Darwin

189 Bride and Groom at Buckingham Palace

(Des L. Curtis. Litho Questa)

1982 (19 Apr). *150th Anniv of Charles Darwin's Voyage. T* **188** *and similar horiz designs. Multicoloured.* W w **14** (*sideways*). *P* 14.

639 25 c. Type **188** 10 10
a. Yellow (background to side panels) omitted .. ..
640 2 r. Darwin's telescope 30 45
641 2 r. 50, Darwin's elephant ride 35 55
642 10 r. H.M.S. *Beagle* beached for repairs .. 1·40 2·50
639/42 .. .. *Set of* 4 1·90 3·25

(Des Jennifer Toombs. Litho J. W.)

1982 (1 July). *21st Birthday of Princess of Wales. T* **189** *and similar vert designs. Multicoloured.* W w **14**. *P* 13.

643 25 c. Mauritius coat of arms 10 10
644 2 r. 50, Princess Diana in Chesterfield, November 1981 .. .. 45 35
645 5 r. Type **189** 75 80
646 10 r. Formal portrait .. .. 1·25 1·75
643/6 .. .. *Set of* 4 2·25 2·75

190 Prince and Princess of Wales with Prince William

191 Bois Fandamane Plant

(Des Harrison. Litho Walsall)

1982 (22 Sept). *Birth of Prince William of Wales.* W w **14** (*sideways*). *P* 14 × 14½.

647 **190** 2 r. 50, multicoloured 55 30

(Des Harrison. Litho Format)

1982 (15 Dec). *Centenary of Robert Koch's Discovery of Tubercle Bacillus. T* **191** *and similar vert designs. Multicoloured.* W w **14**. *P* 14.

648 25 c. Type **191** 10 10
649 1 r. 25, Central market, Port Louis 30 30
650 2 r. Bois Banane plant 45 45
651 5 r. Platte de Lézard plant .. .. .. 95 1·40
652 10 r. Dr. Robert Koch .. .. 1·75 2·50
648/52 .. .. *Set of* 5 3·00 4·25

192 Arms and Flag of Mauritius

193 Early Wall-mounted Telephone

(Des and litho J.W.)

1983 (14 Mar). *Commonwealth Day. T* **192** *and similar horiz designs. Multicoloured.* W w **14** (*sideways*). *P* 13.

653 25 c. Type **192** 10 10
654 2 r. 50, Satellite view of Mauritius 15 30
655 5 r. Harvesting sugar cane 30 75
656 10 r. Port Louis harbour .. .. .. 70 1·50
653/6 .. .. *Set of* 4 1·10 2·40

(Des G. Vasarhelyi. Litho Format)

1983 (24 June). *World Communications Year. T* **193** *and similar multicoloured designs.* W w **14** (*sideways on* 1 *r.* 25 *and* 10 *r.*). *P* 14.

657 25 c. Type **193** 10 10
658 1 r. 25, Early telegraph apparatus (*horiz*) .. 40 15
659 2 r. Earth satellite station 70 40
660 10 r. First hot air balloon in Mauritius, 1784 (*horiz*) .. .. 2·00 2·50
657/60 .. .. *Set of* 4 2·75 2·75

194 Map of Namibia

195 Fish Trap

(Des J. W. Litho Questa)

1983 (26 Aug). *Namibia Day. T* **194** *and similar vert designs. Multicoloured.* W w **14**. *P* 14.

661 25 c. Type **194** 20 10
662 2 r. 50, Hands breaking chains 70 45
663 5 r. Family and settlement .. .. .. 1·25 1·25
664 10 r. Diamond mining .. .. 2·00 2·50
661/4 .. .. *Set of* 4 3·75 3·75

(Des Walsall. Litho Format)

1983 (25 Sept). *Fishery Resources. T* **195** *and similar multi-coloured designs.* W w**14** *(sideways on* 1 *r. and* 10 *r.). P* 14.

665 25 c. Type **195** 15 10
666 1 r. Fishing boat *(horiz)* 45 15
667 5 r. Game fishing .. .. 1·25 1·25
668 10 r. Octopus drying *(horiz)* .. .. .. 1·75 2·50
665/8 .. .. *Set of* 4 3·25 3·75

196 Swami Dayananda

197 Adolf von Plevitz

(Des A. Theobald. Litho Questa)

1983 (3 Nov). *Death Centenary of Swami Dayananda. T* **196** *and similar vert designs. Multicoloured.* W w **14**. *P* 14.

669 25 c. Type **196** 10 10
670 35 c. Last meeting with father 10 10
671 2 r. Receiving religious instruction 30 35
672 5 r. Swami demonstrating strength .. .. 70 1·25
673 10 r. At a religious gathering .. .. .. 1·10 2·50
669/73 .. .. *Set of* 5 2·00 3·75

(Des L. Curtis. Litho Harrison)

1983 (8 Dec). *125th Anniv of the Arrival in Mauritius of Adolf von Plevitz (social reformer). T* **197** *and similar horiz designs. Multicoloured.* W w **14** *(sideways). P* 14 × 14½.

674 25 c. Type **197** 10 10
675 1 r. 25, La Laura Government school .. 30 30
676 5 r. Von Plevitz addressing 1872 Commission of Enquiry .. .. 90 1·25
677 10 r. Von Plevitz with Indian farm workers .. 1·50 2·25
674/7 .. .. *Set of* 4 2·50 3·50

198 Courtship Chase

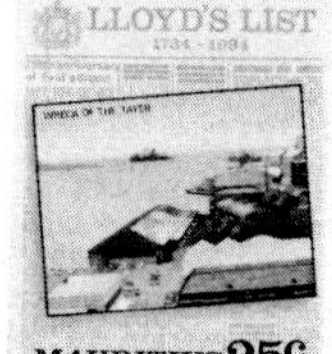

199 Wreck of S.S. *Tayeb*

(Des N. Arlott. Litho Format)

1984 (26 Mar). *Mauritius Kestrel. T* **198** *and similar multi-coloured designs.* W w **14** *(sideways on* 25 *c. and* 2 *r.* 50*). P* 14.

678 25 c. Type **198** 45 10
679 2 r. Kestrel in tree *(vert)* .. .. .. 1·00 65
680 2 r. 50, Young Kestrel .. .. .. 1·25 90
681 10 r. Head *(vert)* .. .. 2·75 4·00
678/81 .. .. *Set of* 4 5·00 5·00

(Des M. Joyce. Litho Questa)

1984 (23 May). *250th Anniv of "Lloyd's List" (newspaper). T* **199** *and similar vert designs. Multicoloured.* W w **14**. *P* 14½ × 14.

682 25 c. Type **199** 15 10
683 1 r. S.S. *Taher* 55 15
684 5 r. East Indiaman *Triton* .. .. .. 1·50 2·00
685 10 r. M.S. *Astor* .. .. 2·00 3·00
682/5 .. .. *Set of* 4 3·75 4·75

200 Blue Latan Palm

201 Slave Girl

(Des Jennifer Toombs. Litho Format)

1984 (23 July). *Palm Trees. T* **200** *and similar vert designs. Multicoloured.* W w **14**. *P* 14½.

686 25 c. Type **200** 10 10
687 50 c. *Hyophorbe vaughanii* 20 15
688 2 r. 50, *Tectiphiala ferox* .. .. .. 1·25 65
689 5 r. Round Island Bottle-palm .. .. 2·00 2·25
690 10 r. *Hyophorbe amaricaulis* .. .. .. 3·25 3·75
686/90 .. .. *Set of* 5 6·25 6·25

(Des C. Abbott. Litho Walsall)

1984 (20 Aug). *150th Anniv of the Abolition of Slavery and of the Introduction of Indian Immigrants. T* **201** *and similar designs.* W w **14** *(sideways on* 2 *r.,* 10 *r.). P* 14½.

691 25 c. deep rose-lilac, rose-lilac and bistre .. 10 10
692 1 r. deep rose-lilac, rose-lilac and bistre .. 40 10
693 2 r. deep rose-lilac and rose-lilac 75 50
694 10 r. deep rose-lilac and rose-lilac .. .. 2·50 3·00
691/4 .. .. *Set of* 4 3·25 3·25

Designs: *Vert*—1 r. Slave market. *Horiz*—2 r. Indian immigrant family; 10 r. Arrival of Indian immigrants.

202 75th Anniversary Production of *Faust* and Leoville L'Homme

203 The Queen Mother on Clarence House Balcony, 1980

(Des Walsall. Litho Questa)

1984 (10 Sept). *Centenary of Alliance Francaise (cultural organization). T* **202** *and similar horiz designs. Multicoloured.* W w **14** *(sideways). P* 14½ × 14.

695 25 c. Type **202** 15 10
696 1 r. 25, Prize-giving ceremony and Aunauth Beejadbur 40 40
697 5 r. First headquarters and Hector Clarenc .. 1·25 1·60
698 10 r. Lion Mountain and Labourdonnais .. 1·75 2·50
695/8 .. .. *Set of* 4 3·25 4·25

(Des A. Theobald (15 r.), C. Abbott (others). Litho Questa)

1985 (7 June). *Life and Times of Queen Elizabeth the Queen Mother. T* **203** *and similar vert designs. Multicoloured.* W w **16**. *P* 14½ × 14.

699 25 c. The Queen Mother in 1926 .. .. 10 10
700 2 r. With Princess Margaret at Trooping the Colour 30 30
701 5 r. Type **203** .. .. 60 1·00
702 10 r. With Prince Henry at his christening (from photo by Lord Snowdon) .. .. 1·10 1·75
699/702 .. .. *Set of* 4 1·90 2·75
MS703 91 × 73 mm. 15 r. Reopening the Stratford Canal, 1964. Wmk sideways .. .. .. 2·50 2·00

204 High Jumping

205 Adult and Fledgling Pink Pigeons

(Des Joan Thompson. Litho Walsall)

1985 (24 Aug). *2nd Indian Ocean Islands Games. T* **204** *and similar vert designs. Multicoloured.* W w **14**. *P* 14½.

704 25 c. Type **204** 15 10
705 50 c. Javelin-throwing 25 15
706 1 r. 25, Cycling 55 45
707 10 r. Wind surfing .. .. 2·50 3·00
704/7 .. .. *Set of* 4 3·00 3·25

(Des N. Arlott. Litho Walsall)

1985 (2 Sept). *Pink Pigeon. T* **205** *and similar vert designs. Multicoloured.* W w **16**. *P* 14.

708 25 c. Type **205** 50 15
709 2 r. Pink Pigeon displaying at nest .. .. 1·25 75
710 2 r. 50, On nest .. .. 1·50 1·10
711 5 r. Pair preening .. .. 2·25 2·75
708/11 .. .. *Set of* 4 5·00 4·25

206 Caverne Patates, Rodrigues

(Des D. Miller. Litho Walsall)

1985 (27 Sept). *10th Anniv of World Tourism Organization T* **206** *and similar horiz designs. Multicoloured.* W w **16** *(sideways). P* 14½.

712 25 c. Type **206** 20 10
713 35 c. Coloured soils, Chamarel 20 10
714 5 r. Serpent Island .. .. 1·75 2·00
715 10 r. Coin de Mire Island .. .. .. 2·75 3·25
712/15 .. .. *Set of* 4 4·50 5·00

207 Old Town Hall, Port Louis

(Des Jennifer Toombs. Litho J.W.)

1985 (22 Nov). *250th Anniv of Port Louis. T* **207** *and similar horiz designs. Multicoloured.* W w **16** *(sideways). P* 13 × 13½.

716 25 c. Type **207** 10 10
717 1 r. Al-Aqsa Mosque (180th anniv) 25 10
718 2 r. 50, Vase and trees (250th anniv of settlement of Tamil-speaking Indians) .. 55 40
719 10 r. Port Louis Harbour .. .. .. 1·50 2·50
716/19 .. .. *Set of* 4 2·25 2·75

208 Edmond Halley and Diagram

209 Maize (World Food Day)

(Des D. Hartley. Litho Walsall)

1986 (21 Feb). *Appearance of Halley's Comet. T* **208** *and similar horiz designs. Multicoloured.* W w **16** *(sideways). P* 14.

720 25 c. Type **208** 10 10
721 1 r. 25, Halley's Comet (1682) and Newton's Reflector 30 20
722 3 r. Halley's Comet passing Earth 65 50
723 10 r. *Giotto* spacecraft .. .. .. 1·50 2·00
720/3 .. .. *Set of* 4 2·25 2·50

(Des A. Theobald. Litho Harrison)

1986 (21 Apr). *60th Birthday of Queen Elizabeth II. Vert designs as T* **230***a of Jamaica. Multicoloured.* W w **16**. *P* 14½×14.

724 25 c. Princess Elizabeth wearing badge of Grenadier Guards, 1942 .. .. .. 10 10
725 75 c. Investiture of Prince of Wales, 1969 .. 10 10
726 2 r. With Prime Minister of Mauritius, 1972 20 25
727 3 r. In Germany, 1978 .. .. .. 30 35
728 15 r. At Crown Agents Head Office, London, 1983 .. .. 1·50 1·75
724/8 .. .. *Set of* 5 1·90 2·25

(Des O. Bell. Litho Walsall)

1986 (25 July). *International Events. T* **209** *and similar vert designs. Multicoloured.* W w **16**. *P* 14.

729 25 c. Type **209** 10 10
730 1 r. African Regional Industrial Property Organization emblem (10th anniv) .. 30 10
731 1 r. 25, International Peace Year emblem .. 45 20
732 10 r. Footballer and Mauritius Football Association emblem (World Cup Football Championship, Mexico) .. .. 2·25 2·25
729/32 .. .. *Set of* 4 2·75 2·40

210 *Cryptopus elatus*

211 Hesketh Bell Bridge

(Des Harrison. Litho Walsall)

1986 (3 Oct). *Orchids. T* **210** *and similar vert designs. Multicoloured.* W w **16**. *P* 14½ × 14.

733 25 c. Type **210** 30 10
734 2 r. *Jumellea recta* 90 40
735 2 r. 50, *Angraecum mauritianum* .. .. 1·10 50
736 10 r. *Bulbophyllum longiflorum* .. .. 2·25 2·50
733/6 .. .. *Set of* 4 4·00 3·25

1986 (Nov). *As No.* 533B, *but printed litho by Questa. P* 14½.

737 35 c. French charter, 1715 .. .. .. 30 30

(Litho Questa)

1987 (11 Jan)–**89**. *As Nos.* 531/2, 534, 543/5 *and* 548 *but* W w **16** *(sideways on horiz designs). P* 14½.

740 20 c. Van Keulen's map, c. 1700 *(horiz)* .. 20 20
741 25 c. Settlement on Rodriguez, 1691 .. 20 20
743 50 c. Construction of Port Louis, *c.* 1736 *(horiz)* (16.1.89) 30 20
752 2 r. Race course, *c.* 1870 *(horiz)* 35 20
753 3 r. Place d'Armes, *c.* 1880 *(horiz)* (16.1.89) 60 50
754 5 r. Royal Visit postcard, 1901 *(horiz)* (16.1.89) 70 70
757 25 r. First Mauritian Governor-General and Prime Minister *(horiz)* (16.1.89) .. 2·50 3·00
740/57 .. .. *Set of* 7 4·25 4·50

No. 752 exists with different imprint dates below the design.

(Des D. Hartley. Litho Format)

1987 (22 May). *Mauritius Bridges. T* **211** *and similar horiz designs. Multicoloured.* W w **16** *(sideways). P* 14½.

758 25 c. Type **211** 15 10
759 50 c. Sir Colville Deverell Bridge 20 10
760 2 r. 50, Cavendish Bridge 70 45
761 5 r. Tamarin Bridge .. .. 1·25 1·25
762 10 r. Grand River North West Bridge .. 2·00 2·25
758/62 .. .. *Set of* 5 4·00 3·75

212 Supreme Court, Port Louis **213** Dodo Mascot

(Des N. Shewring. Litho Walsall)

1987 (2 June). *Bicentenary of the Mauritius Bar. T* **212** *and similar horiz designs. Multicoloured. W w* **16** *(sideways). P* 14×14½.
763 25 c. Type **212** 10 10
764 1 r. District Court, Flacq 20 10
765 1 r. 25, Statue of Justice 30 20
766 10 r. Barristers of 1787 and 1987 .. .. 1·25 1·50
763/6 .. .. *Set of* 4 1·60 1·75

(Des O. Bell. Litho Format)

1987 (5 Sept). *International Festival of the Sea. T* **213** *and similar multicoloured designs. W w* **16** *(sideways on 25 c., 5 r.). P* 14×14½ *(vert) or* 14½×14 *(horiz)*.
767 25 c. Type **213** 10 10
768 1 r. 50, Yacht regatta *(horiz)* 50 30
769 3 r. Water skiing *(horiz)* 90 65
770 5 r. *Svanen* (barquentine) .. .. 1·40 1·40
767/70 .. .. *Set of* 4 2·50 2·25

214 Toys **215** Maison Ouvriere (Int Year of Shelter for the Homeless)

(Des G. Vasarhelyi. Litho Walsall)

1987 (30 Oct). *Industrialisation. T* **214** *and similar horiz designs. Multicoloured. W w* **14** *(sideways). P* 14.
771 20 c. Type **214** 10 10
772 35 c. Spinning factory 10 10
773 50 c. Rattan furniture 10 10
774 2 r. 50, Spectacle factory 55 45
775 10 r. Stone carving .. .. 1·60 1·75
771/5 .. .. *Set of* 5 2·10 2·10

(Des D. Miller. Litho Walsall)

1987 (30 Dec). *Art and Architecture. T* **215** *and similar horiz designs. W w* **16** *(sideways). P* 14×14½.
776 25 c. multicoloured 10 10
777 1 r. black and brownish grey 10 10
778 1 r. 25, multicoloured 15 15
779 2 r. multicoloured 30 30
780 5 r. multicoloured 75 80
776/80 .. .. *Set of* 5 1·25 1·25
Designs:—1 r. "Paul et Virginie" (lithograph); 1 r. 25, Chateau de Rosnay; 2 r. "Vielle Ferme" (Boulle); 5 r. "Trois Mamelles".

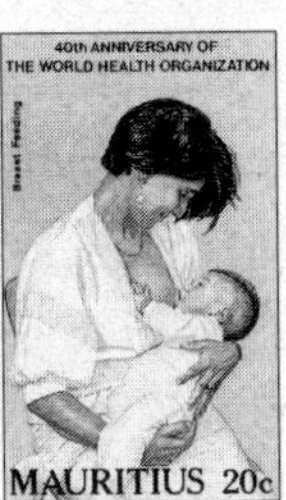

216 University of Mauritius **217** Breast Feeding

(Des A. Theobald. Litho B.D.T.)

1988 (11 Mar). *20th Anniv of Independence. T* **216** *and similar horiz designs. Multicoloured. W w* **14** *(sideways). P* 13½.
781 25 c. Type **216** 10 10
782 75 c. Anniversary gymnastic display .. 15 10
783 2 r. 50, Hurdlers and aerial view of Sir Maurice Rault Stadium 45 35
784 5 r. Air Mauritius aircraft at Sir Seewoosagur Ramgoolam International Airport 90 90
785 10 r. Governor-General Sir Veerasamy Ringadoo and Prime Minister Anerood Jugnauth .. .. 1·60 1·75
781/5 .. .. *Set of* 5 2·75 2·75

(Des D. Ashby. Litho B.D.T.)

1988 (1 July). *40th Anniv of World Health Organization. T* **217** *and similar vert designs. Multicoloured. W w* **14**. *P* 13½.
786 20 c. Type **217** 10 10
787 2 r. Baby under vaccination umbrella and germ droplets 60 40
788 3 r. Nutritious food 70 60
789 10 r. W.H.O. logo .. .. 1·75 2·00
786/9 .. .. *Set of* 4 2·75 2·75

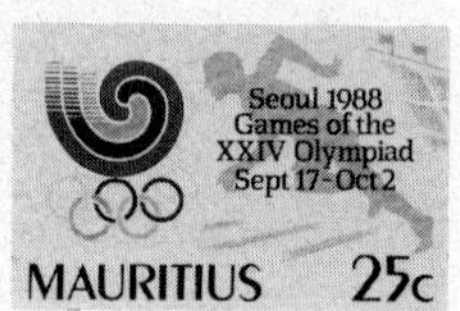

218 Modern Bank Building **219** Olympic Rings and Athlete

(Des N. Shewring (25 r.). Litho B.D.T.)

1988 (1 Sept). *150th Anniv of Mauritius Commercial Bank Ltd. T* **218** *and similar multicoloured designs. W w* **14** *(sideways on* 1, 25 *r.). P* 13½.
790 25 c. black, blue-green and new blue .. 10 10
791 1 r. black and brown-lake 15 10
792 1 r. 25, multicoloured 20 20
793 25 r. multicoloured .. .. 3·75 4·00
790/3 .. .. *Set of* 4 3·75 4·00
Designs: *Horiz*—1 r. Mauritius Commercial Bank, 1897; 25 r. Fifteen dollar bank note of 1838. *Vert*—1 r. 25, Bank arms.

(Des P. Broadbent. Litho B.D.T.)

1988 (1 Oct). *Olympic Games, Seoul. T* **219** *and similar horiz designs. Multicoloured. W w* **14** *(sideways). P* 14.
794 25 c. Type **219** 10 10
795 35 c. Wrestling 10 10
796 1 r. 50, Long distance running 40 30
797 10 r. Swimming .. .. 1·75 2·25
794/7 .. .. *Set of* 4 2·00 2·25

220 Nature Park **221** La Tour Sumeire, Port Louis

(Des D. Miller. Litho Harrison (40 c. (No. 807), 3 r., 4 r., 6 r., 10 r.) or B.D.T. (others))

1989 (11 Mar)–**91**. *Protection of the Environment. T* **220** *and similar multicoloured designs. P* 14. *(a) W w* **14** *(sideways on horiz designs)*
799 15 c. Underwater view (29.11.90) 10 10
800 40 c. Type **220** (19.2.91) 10 10
801 1 r. 50, Whimbrel (29.11.90) 10 15
802 3 r. Marine life 20 25
803 4 r. Fern Tree *(vert)* 30 35
804 6 r. Ecological scenery *(vert)* 40 45
805 25 r. Migratory birds and map *(vert)* (29.11.90) .. .. 1·75 1·90

(b) W w **16** *(sideways on horiz designs)*
806 30 c. Greenshank (29.11.90) 10 10
807 40 c. Type **220** 10 10
808 50 c. Round Island *(vert)* (4.10.91) .. 10 10
809 75 c. Bassin Blanc (4.10.91) 10 10
810 1 r. Mangrove *(vert)* (29.11.90) 10 10
811 2 r. Le Morne (4.10.91) 15 20
812 5 r. Rivière du Poste estuary (4.10.91) .. 35 40
813 10 r. *Phelsuma ornata* (gecko) on plant *(vert)* 70 75
814 15 r. Benarès waves (4.10.91) .. .. 1·10 1·25
799/814 .. .. *Set of* 16 5·00 5·50
No. 800, unlike No. 807, shows an imprint date.

(Des A. Theobald. Litho B.D.T.)

1989 (14 July). *Bicentenary of the French Revolution. T* **221** *and similar vert designs. W w* **14**. *P* 14.
818 30 c. black, emerald & pale greenish yellow 10 10
819 1 r. black, orange-brown and cinnamon .. 20 10
820 8 r. multicoloured .. .. 1·25 1·25
821 15 r. multicoloured .. .. 2·00 2·00
818/21 .. .. *Set of* 4 3·25 3·00
Designs:—1 r. Salle de Spectacle du Jardin; 8 r. Portrait of Comte de Malartic; 15 r. Bicentenary logo.

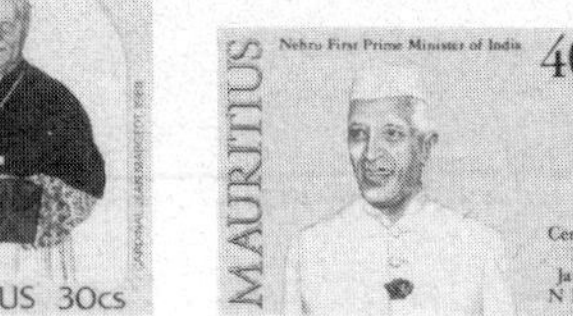

222 Cardinal Jean Margeot **223** Nehru

(Des L. Curtis. Litho B.D.T.)

1989 (13 Oct). *Visit of Pope John Paul II. T* **222** *and similar vert designs. Multicoloured. W w* **14**. *P* 14×13½.
822 30 c. Type **222** 15 10
823 40 c. Pope John Paul II and Prime Minister Jugnauth, Vatican, 1988 .. .. 20 15
824 3 r. Mère Marie Magdeleine de la Croix and Chapelle des Filles de Marie, Port Louis, 1864 .. .. 55 45
825 6 r. St. Francois d'Assise Church, Pamplemousses, 1756 .. .. 1·00 1·00
826 10 r. Pope John Paul II .. .. 1·75 1·75
822/6 .. .. *Set of* 5 3·25 3·00

(Des K. Clarkson. Litho B.D.T.)

1989 (14 Nov). *Birth Centenary of Jawaharlal Nehru (Indian statesman). T* **223** *and similar horiz designs. Multicoloured. W w* **16** *(sideways). P* 14.
827 40 c. Type **223** 15 10
828 1 r. 50, Nehru with daughter, Indira, and grandsons 30 30
829 3 r. Nehru and Gandhi 75 75
830 4 r. Nehru with Presidents Nasser and Tito 1·00 1·00
831 10 r. Nehru with children .. .. 2·25 2·50
827/31 .. .. *Set of* 5 4·00 4·25

224 Cane cutting **225** Industrial Estate

(Des D. Miller. Litho B.D.T.)

1990 (10 Jan). *350th Anniv of Introduction of Sugar Cane to Mauritius. T* **224** *and similar horiz designs. Multicoloured. W w* **16** *(sideways). P* 13½.
832 30 c. Type **224** 10 10
833 40 c. Sugar factory, 1867 .. .. 10 10
834 1 r. Mechanical loading of cane 15 10
835 25 r. Modern sugar factory .. .. 3·25 3·75
832/5 .. .. *Set of* 4 3·25 3·75

(Des L. Curtis. Litho B.D.T.)

1990 (29 Mar). *60th Birthday of Prime Minister Sir Anerood Jugnauth. T* **225** *and similar horiz designs. Multicoloured. W w* **14** *(sideways). P* 13½.
836 35 c. Type **225** 10 10
837 40 c. Sir Anerood Jugnauth at desk .. 10 10
838 1 r. 50, Mauritius Stock Exchange symbol 15 15
839 4 r. Jugnauth with Governor-General Sir Seewoosagur Ramgoolam 55 55
840 10 r. Jugnauth greeting Pope John Paul II 1·25 1·50
836/40 .. .. *Set of* 5 1·90 2·00

226 Desjardins (naturalist) (150th death anniv) **227** Letters from Alphabets

(Des D. Miller. Litho B.D.T.)

1990 (5 July). *Anniversaries. T* **226** *and similar multicoloured designs. W w* **14** *(sideways on* 35 *c.,* 8 *r.). P* 14.
841 30 c. Type **226** 10 10
842 35 c. Logo on TV screen (25th anniv of Mauritius Broadcasting Corporation) *(horiz)* 10 10
843 6 r. Line Barracks (now Police Headquarters) (250th anniv) 70 70
844 8 r. Town Hall, Curepipe (centenary of municipality) *(horiz)* 90 90
841/4 .. .. *Set of* 4 1·60 1·60

(Des G. Vasarhelyi. Litho B.D.T.)

1990 (28 Sept). *International Literacy Year. T* **227** *and similar horiz designs. Multicoloured. W w* **14** *(sideways). P* 14.
845 30 c. Type **227** 10 10
846 1 r. Blind child reading Braille 15 10
847 3 r. Open book and globe 40 40
848 10 r. Book showing world map with quill pen 1·25 1·40
845/8 .. .. *Set of* 4 1·60 1·75

(Des D. Miller. Litho Questa)

1991 (17 June). *65th Birthday of Queen Elizabeth II and 70th Birthday of Prince Philip. Vert designs as T* **58** *of Kiribati. Multicoloured. W w* **16** *(sideways). P* 14½×14.
849 8 r. Queen Elizabeth II 90 90
a. Horiz pair. Nos. 849/50 separated by label .. .. 1·75 1·75
850 8 r. Prince Philip in Grenadier Guards ceremonial uniform 90 90
Nos. 849/50 were printed together in a similar sheet format to Nos. 366/7 of Kiribati.

NEW INFORMATION

The editor is always interested to correspond with people who have new information that will improve or correct the Catalogue.

228 City Hall, Port Louis (25th anniv of City status)

229 *Euploea euphon*

(Des G. Vasarhelyi. Litho Questa)

1991 (18 Aug). *Anniversaries and Events. T* **228** *and similar multicoloured designs. W* w **14** *(sideways on 40 c., 10 r.). P* 14.

851 40 c. Type **228** 10 10
852 4 r. Colonel Draper (race course founder) (150th death anniv) (*vert*) 50 50
853 6 r. Joseph Barnard (engraver) and "POST PAID" 2d. stamp (175th birth anniv) (*vert*) 65 65
854 10 r. Spitfire *Mauritius II* (50th anniv of Second World War) .. .. .. 1·10 1·25
851/4 .. .. *Set of* 4 2·00 2·25

(Des I. Loe. Litho Walsall)

1991 (15 Nov). *"Philanippon '91" International Stamp Exhibition, Tokyo. Butterflies. T* **229** *and similar horiz designs. W* w **14** *(sideways). P* 14×14½.

855 40 c. Type **229** 10 10
856 3 r. *Hypolimnas misippus* (female) .. 20 25
857 8 r. *Papilio manlius* 60 65
858 10 r. *Hypolimnas misippus* (male) .. 70 75
855/8 .. .. *Set of* 4 1·40 1·50

230 Green Turtle, Tromelin

(Des G. Vasarhelyi. Litho Walsall)

1991 (13 Dec). *Indian Ocean Islands. T* **230** *and similar horiz designs. Multicoloured. W* w **14** *(sideways). P* 14.

859 40 c. Type **230** 10 10
860 1 r. Ibis, Agalega 10 10
861 2 r. Takamaka flowers, Chagos Archipelago 15 20
862 15 r. *Lambis violacea* sea shell, St. Brandon 1·10 1·25
859/62 .. .. *Set of* 4 1·25 1·50

231 Pres. Veerasamy Ringadoo and President's Residence

(Des G. Vasarhelyi. Litho Walsall)

1992 (12 Mar). *Proclamation of Republic. T* **231** *and similar horiz designs. W* w **14** *(sideways). P* 13½×14.

862 40 c. Type **231** 10 10
863 4 r. Prime Minister Anerood Jugnauth and Government House 30 35
864 8 r. Children and rainbow 60 65
865 10 r. Presidential flag 70 75
863/6 .. .. *Set of* 4 1·50 1·60

EXPRESS DELIVERY STAMPS

EXPRESS DELIVERY 15c.
(E 1)

EXPRESS DELIVERY (INLAND) 15c.
(E 2)

EXPRESS DELIVERY (INLAND) 15 c.
(E 3)

EXPRESS DELIVERY (INLAND) 15 c
(E 4)

Type E 2. "(INLAND)" was inserted at a second printing on stamps already surcharged with Type E 1 (No. E1).
Type E 3. New setting made at one printing. More space above and below "(INLAND)".
Type E 4. New setting with smaller "15 c" and no stop.

1903 (10 Aug)–**04**. *No.* 136 *surch locally in red.*

E1 E 1 15 c. on 15 c. ultramarine .. .. 4·00 14·00
E2 E 2 15 c. on 15 c. ultramarine (28.3.04) .. 13·00 20·00
a. "A" inverted £275 £275
E3 E 3 15 c. on 15 c. ultramarine (4.04) .. 4·00 85
a. Surch inverted .. .. .. — £200
b. Surch double, both inverted ..
c. Imperf between (vert pair) .. £1800
E4 E 4 15 c. on 15 c. ultramarine (1904) .. £160 £170
a. Surch inverted .. .. ..
b. Surch double .. .. ..
c. Surch double, both inverted ..
d. "c" omitted .. .. .. — £1000

(FOREIGN) EXPRESS DELIVERY 18 CENTS
(E 5)

1904. *T* 42 *(without value in label), surch with Type* E **5** *locally. Wmk Crown CC. P* 14.

E5 18 c. green .. .. 1·50 10·00
a. Exclamation mark for "I" in "FOREIGN" £225

1904. *T* 42 *(without value in label) surch with Type* E **3** *locally.*

E6 15 c. grey-green (R.) .. .. 1·00 1·25
a. Surch inverted £225 £225
b. Surch double £190
c. Surch double, one "LNIAND" £190 £190

POSTAGE DUE STAMPS

D 1

POSTAGE DUE 10c
(D 2)

(Typo Waterlow)

1933–54. *Wmk Mult Script CA. P* 15 × 14.

D1 D 1 2 c. black 35 50
D2 4 c. violet 40 65
D3 6 c. scarlet 40 80
D4 10 c. green 40 70
D5 20 c. bright blue 50 90
D6 50 c. deep magenta (1.3.54) .. .. 40 6·50
D7 1 r. orange (1.3.54) .. .. .. 65 9·00
D1/7 .. .. *Set of* 7 2·75 17·00
D1/5 Perf "Specimen" .. .. *Set of* 5 60·00

(Typo D.L.R.)

1966–72. *Wmk* w **12**. *Chalk-surfaced paper. P* 13½×14 *(2 c.) or* 15×14 *(others).*

D 8 D 1 2 c. black (11.7.67) .. .. .. 1·25 2·25
D 9 4 c. slate-lilac (7.1.69) .. .. 1·50 4·00
D10 6 c. red-orange (7.1.69) .. .. 2·50 8·00
a. Perf 13½×14 .. .. .. 18·00
D11 10 c. yellow-green (16.2.67) .. .. 30 1·00
D12 20 c. blue (3.1.66) .. .. .. 1·25 3·75
a. Deep blue (7.1.69) .. .. 1·00 4·25
D13 50 c. deep magenta (7.1.69) .. .. 75 6·50
a. Magenta (10.1.72) .. .. 75 8·00
D8/13 .. .. *Set of* 6 6·50 23·00

1982 (25 Oct). *Nos.* 530A/1A, 535A, 540A, 542A *and* 547A *optd as Type* D **2**, *by J. W. Dunn Printers Ltd.*

D14 10 c. on 15 c. Dutch Occupation, 1638–1710 .. 10 10
D15 20 c. on 20 c. Van Keulen's map, *circa* 1700 .. 10 10
D16 50 c. on 60 c. Pierre Poivre, *circa* 1767 .. 10 10
D17 1 r. on 1 r. 20, Government House, *circa* 1840 10 10
D18 1 r. 50 on 1 r. 50, Indian immigration, 1835 10 10
D19 5 r. on 15 r. Unfurling Mauritian flag, 1968 30 35
D14/19 .. .. *Set of* 6 55 60

FISCALS USED FOR POSTAGE

INLAND REVENUE
(F 1)

INLAND REVENUE
(F 2)

MAURITIUS INLAND REVENUE 4c
F 3

1889. *T* 19, *wmk Crown CA, optd. P* 14.

R1 F 1 4 c. carmine .. .. 4·00 5·00
R2 F 2 4 c. lilac .. .. 2·50 10·00

(Typo D.L.R.)

1896. *Wmk Crown CA. P* 14.

R3 F 3 4 c. dull purple .. .. 15·00

Montserrat

A local post office operated on Montserrat from some time early in the 18th century, although the first recorded postal marking does not occur until 1791. A branch of the British G.P.O. was established at Plymouth, the island capital, in 1852.

The stamps of Great Britain were used from 1858 until the overseas postal service reverted to local control on 1 April 1860.

In the interim period between 1860 and the introduction of Montserrat stamps in 1876 No. CC1 and a similar "uncrowned" handstamp were again used.

PLYMOUTH

CROWNED-CIRCLE HANDSTAMPS

C 1

CC1 **C 1** MONTSERRAT (R.) (15.7.1852) *Price on cover* £2500

No. CC1 was used as an emergency measure, struck in black, during 1886.

Stamps of GREAT BRITAIN *cancelled* "A 08" *as Type* Z **1** *of Jamaica.*

1858 (8 May) *to* **1860.**
Z1 1d. rose-red (1857), *perf* 14 .. .. £1100
Z2 4d. rose (1857) .. ..
Z3 6d. lilac (1856) £450
Z4 1s. green (1856) .. ..

PRICES FOR STAMPS ON COVER TO 1945	
Nos. 1/2	*from* × 40
No. 3	†
Nos. 4/5	*from* × 8
Nos. 6/13	*from* × 12
Nos. 14/22	*from* × 4
No. 23	—
Nos. 24/33	*from* × 4
Nos. 35/47	*from* × 3
No. 48	—
Nos. 49/59	*from* × 3
Nos. 60/2	*from* × 15
Nos. 63/83	*from* × 3
Nos. 84/93	*from* × 4
Nos. 94/7	*from* × 3
Nos. 98/100	*from* × 8
Nos. 101/12	*from* × 5

1

MONTSERRAT

(2)

3 (Die I)

(T **1** recess D.L.R.)

1876 (Sept). *Stamps of Antigua optd with T* **2**. *Wmk Crown CC. P* 14.
1 **1** 1d. red .. .. 18·00 15·00
a. Bisected (½d.) (on cover) .. .. † £1400
b. Inverted "S" £1600 £1600
2 6d. green .. .. 55·00 40·00
a. Bisect (used as 2½d.) (on cover) .. † £5000
b. Inverted "S" £2000 £2000
3 6d. blue-green £1100
a. Inverted "S" £5500

Nos. 1/3 were overprinted either from a setting of 120 (12×10) or from a setting of 60 (6×10) applied twice to each sheet. This setting of 60 had an inverted "S" on R. 3/3. The same setting was subsequently used for some sheets of Nos. 7 and 13.

No. 1 was bisected and used for a ½d. in 1883. This bisected stamp is found surcharged with a small "½" in *black* and also in *red*; both were unofficial and they did not emanate from the Montserrat P.O.

The 6d. in blue-green is only known unused.

(T **3** typo D.L.R.)

1880 (Jan). *Wmk Crown CC. P* 14.
4 **3** 2½d. red-brown £250 £180
5 4d. blue .. .. £140 40·00

1884–85. *Wmk Crown CA. P* 14.
6 **3** ½d. dull green .. .. 1·00 5·50
7 **1** 1d. red .. .. 8·00 17·00
a. Inverted "S" £1300 £1300
b. Rose-red (1885) .. .. 13·00 14·00
ba. Bisected vert (½d.) (on cover) .. † £1300
bb. Inverted "S" £1500 £1500
9 **3** 2½d. red-brown .. .. £225 65·00
10 2½d. ultramarine (1885) .. .. .. 14·00 16·00
11 4d. blue £2750 £250
12 4d. mauve (1885) .. .. 3·00 3·00
10, 12 Optd "Specimen" .. .. *Set of* 2 £275

1884 (May). *Wmk Crown CA. P* 12.
13 **1** 1d. red .. .. 70·00 45·00
a. Inverted "S" £2750 £1900
b. Bisected (½d.) (on cover) .. .. † £1600

The stamps for Montserrat were superseded by the general issue for Leeward Islands in November 1890, but the following issues were in concurrent use with the stamps inscribed "LEEWARD ISLANDS" until 1 July 1956, when Leeward Islands stamps were withdrawn and invalidated.

4 Device of the Colony

5

(Typo D.L.R.)

1903 (Aug). (*a*) *Wmk Crown CA. P* 14.
14 **4** ½d. grey-green and green .. .. .. 65 5·50
15 1d. grey-black and red 60 40
16 2d. grey and brown .. .. 5·00 11·00
17 2½d. grey and blue .. .. 1·50 1·75
18 3d. dull orange and deep purple .. .. 4·00 15·00
19 6d. dull purple and olive .. .. .. 4·00 24·00
20 1s. green and bright purple .. .. .. 10·00 16·00
21 2s. green and brown-orange .. .. .. 22·00 16·00
22 2s. 6d. green and black .. .. 15·00 30·00

(*b*) *Wmk Crown CC. P* 14
23 **5** 5s. black and scarlet .. .. 80·00 £140
14/23 .. .. *Set of* 10 £120 £225
14/23 Optd "Specimen" .. .. *Set of* 10 £160

1904–08. *Wmk Mult Crown CA. Ordinary paper* (½d., 2d., 3d., 6d.) *or chalk-surfaced paper* (*others*). *P* 14.
24 **4** ½d. grey-green and green 65 65
a. Chalk-surfaced paper (3.06) 40 75
25 1d. grey-black and red (1905) .. .. 12·00 20·00
26 2d. grey and brown .. .. 65 2·00
a. Chalk-surfaced paper (5.06) .. .. 80 1·00
27 2½d. grey and blue (1905) .. .. .. 2·50 6·50
28 3d. dull orange and deep purple .. .. 3·00 3·25
a. Chalk-surfaced paper (1908) .. .. 3·00 2·50
29 6d. dull purple and olive .. .. .. 2·50 7·00
a. Chalk-surfaced paper (1908) .. .. 3·00 5·00
30 1s. green and bright purple (1908) .. 8·50 4·75
31 2s. green and orange (1908) .. .. 23·00 35·00
32 2s. 6d. green and black (1908) .. .. 35·00 35·00
33 **5** 5s. black and red (1907) .. .. .. 65·00 £100
24/33 .. .. *Set of* 10 £120 £180

1908 (June)–**14.** *Wmk Mult Crown CA. Ordinary paper* (½d. *to* 2½d.) *or chalk-surfaced paper* (3d. *to* 5s.). *P* 14.
35 **4** ½d. deep green (4.10) .. .. 1·50 80
36 1d. rose-red .. .. 1·40 30
38 2d. greyish slate (9.09) .. .. 1·75 8·00
39 2½d. blue .. .. 2·25 3·50
40 3d. purple/*yellow* (9.09) .. .. .. 1·00 10·00
a. White back (1.14) (Optd S. £25) .. 2·25 20·00
43 6d. dull and deep purple (9.09) .. .. 6·50 28·00
a. Dull and bright purple (1914) .. 7·50 28·00
44 1s. black/*green* (9.09) .. .. 3·50 16·00
45 2s. purple and bright blue/*blue* (9.09) 24·00 35·00
46 2s. 6d. black and red/*blue* (9.09) .. 30·00 48·00
47 **5** 5s. red and green/*yellow* (9.09) .. .. 48·00 60·00
35/47 .. .. *Set of* 10 £100 £180
35/47 Optd "Specimen" .. .. *Set of* 10 £190

7

8

WAR STAMP

(9)

(T **7/8** typo D.L.R.)

1914. *Wmk Mult Crown CA. Chalk-surfaced paper. P* 14.
48 **7** 5s. red and green/*yellow* .. .. .. 48·00 75·00
48 Optd "Specimen" .. .. 75·00

1916 (10 Oct)–**23.** *Wmk Mult Crown CA. Ordinary paper* (½d. *to* 2½d.) *or chalk-surfaced paper* (3d. *to* 5s.). *P* 14.
49 **8** ½d. green .. .. 30 1·50
50 1d. scarlet 35 75
a. Carmine-red .. .. 6·50 4·50
51 2d. grey .. .. 1·00 4·00
52 2½d. bright blue .. .. 1·50 8·00
53 3d. purple/*yellow* .. .. 75 5·00
a. On pale yellow (1922) (Optd S. £20) 75 6·00
54 4d. grey-black and red/*pale yellow* (1923) 4·75 16·00
55 6d. dull and deep purple .. .. .. 2·75 14·00
56 1s. black/*blue-green* (*olive back*) .. 2·75 13·00
57 2s. purple and blue/*blue* .. .. .. 9·00 15·00
58 2s. 6d. black and red/*blue* .. .. .. 20·00 30·00
59 5s. green and red/*yellow* .. .. .. 35·00 48·00
49/59 .. .. *Set of* 11 65·00 £140
49/59 Optd "Specimen" .. .. *Set of* 11 £160

1917 (Oct)–**18.** *No.* 49 *optd with T* **9**.
60 **8** ½d. green (R.) 10 80
61 ½d. green (Blk.) (6.18) .. .. 15 1·00
a. Deep green (10.18) 15 90
ab. "C" and "A" missing from wmk

No. 61ab shows the "C" omitted from one impression and the "A" missing from the next.

1919 (Mar). *T* **8**. *Special printing in orange. Value and* "WAR STAMP" *as T* **9** *inserted in black at one printing.*
62 1½d. black and orange 10 30
60/2 Optd "Specimen" .. .. *Set of* 3 80·00

1922 (13 July)–**29.** *Wmk Mult Script CA. Ordinary paper* (¼d. *to* 3d. (*No.* 73) *or chalk-surfaced paper* (*others*). *P* 14.
63 **8** ¼d. brown .. .. 15 2·50
64 ½d. green (5.4.23) 20 30
65 1d. bright violet (5.4.23) 25 30
66 1d. carmine (1929) 75 70
67 1½d. orange-yellow .. .. 1·75 9·50
68 1½d. carmine (5.4.23) .. .. 20 1·50
69 1½d. red-brown (1929) 70 50
70 2d. grey .. .. 45 1·00
71 2½d. deep bright blue .. .. 6·00 12·00
a. Pale brt blue (17.8.26) (Optd S. £30) 60 90
72 2½d. orange-yellow (5.4.23) .. .. .. 1·25 17·00
73 3d. dull blue (5.4.23) .. .. 50 10·00
74 3d. purple/*yellow* (2.1.27) .. .. .. 1·10 4·75
75 4d. black and red/*pale yellow* .. .. 60 4·50
76 5d. dull purple and olive .. .. .. 2·50 10·00
77 6d. pale and bright purple (5.4.23) .. 1·00 5·50
78 1s. black/*emerald* (5.4.23) .. .. .. 3·00 7·00
79 2s. purple and blue/*blue* .. .. .. 3·50 10·00
80 2s. 6d. black and red/*blue* (5.4.23) .. 11·00 28·00
81 3s. green and violet .. .. 12·00 17·00
82 4s. black and scarlet .. .. 13·00 20·00
83 5s. green and red/*pale yellow* (6.23) .. 18·00 26·00
63/83 .. .. *Set of* 21 55·00 £150
63/83 Optd/Perf "Specimen" .. *Set of* 21 £275

10 Plymouth

(Recess D.L.R.)

1932 (18 April). *Tercentenary. Wmk Mult Script CA. P* 14.
84 **10** ½d. green .. .. 75 3·00
85 1d. scarlet .. .. 75 2·50
86 1½d. red-brown .. .. 1·25 1·75
87 2d. grey .. .. 1·25 10·00
88 2½d. ultramarine .. .. 1·25 9·00
89 3d. orange .. .. 1·50 9·00
90 6d. violet .. .. 2·25 17·00
91 1s. olive-brown .. .. 8·00 25·00
92 2s. 6d. purple .. .. 48·00 60·00
93 5s. chocolate £100 £130
84/93 .. .. *Set of* 10 £150 £225
84/93 Perf "Specimen" .. .. *Set of* 10 £225

1935 (6 May). *Silver Jubilee. As Nos.* 114/17 *of Jamaica, but ptd by Waterlow & Sons. P* 11×12.
94 1d. deep blue and scarlet .. .. .. 85 1·50
95 1½d. ultramarine and grey .. .. .. 75 2·25
96 2½d. brown and deep blue .. .. .. 2·25 1·25
97 1s. slate and purple .. .. 3·00 7·50
94/7 .. .. *Set of* 4 6·25 11·00
94/7 Perf "Specimen" .. .. *Set of* 4 75·00

1937 (12 May). *Coronation. As Nos.* 118/20 *of Jamaica.*
98 1d. scarlet 20 40
99 1½d. yellow-brown 30 25
100 2½d. bright blue 30 60
98/100 .. .. *Set of* 3 70 1·10
98/100 Perf "Specimen" .. .. *Set of* 3 50·00

11 Carr's Bay

12 Sea Island Cotton

13 Botanic Station

(Recess D.L.R.)

1938 (2 Aug)–**48.** *Wmk Mult Script CA. P* 12 (10s., £1) *or* 13 (*others*).
101 **11** ½d. blue-green 55 75
a. Perf 14 (1942) 10 10
102 **12** 1d. carmine 40 40
a. Perf 14 (1943) 20 10
103 1½d. purple .. .. 9·00 50
a. Perf 14 (1942) 20 30
104 **13** 2d. orange .. .. 5·00 60
a. Perf 14 (1942) 20 30
105 **12** 2½d. ultramarine 45 30
a. Perf 14 (1943) 30 15
106 **11** 3d. brown 70 30
a. Perf 14, *Red-brown* (1942) 30 20
ab. Deep brown (1943) .. .. 6·00 4·25
107 **13** 6d. violet .. .. 2·50 60
a. Perf 14 (1943) 60 20
108 **11** 1s. lake .. .. 4·25 70
a. Perf 14 (1942) 40 20

109 **13** 2s. 6d. slate-blue 7·50 70
a. Perf 14 (1943) 8·50 2·25
110 **11** 5s. rose-carmine 17·00 7·00
a. Perf 14 (1942) 9·00 2·50
111 **13** 10s. pale blue (1948) 12·00 16·00
112 **11** £1 black (1948) 12·00 22·00
101a/12 *Set of* 12 38·00 38·00
101/12 Perf "Specimen" *Set of* 12 £250

1946 (1 Nov). *Victory. As Nos.* 141/2 *of Jamaica.*
113 1½d. purple 10 10
114 3d. chocolate 10 10
113/14 Perf "Specimen" *Set of* 2 55·00

1949 (3 Jan). *Royal Silver Wedding. As Nos.* 143/4 *of Jamaica.*
115 2½d. ultramarine 10 10
116 5s. carmine 4·50 2·50

1949 (10 Oct). *75th Anniv of U.P.U. As Nos.* 145/8 *of Jamaica.*
117 2½d. ultramarine 15 20
118 3d. brown 30 20
119 6d. purple 30 20
120 1s. purple 35 25
117/20 *Set of* 4 1·00 75

(New Currency. 100 cents = 1 dollar)

1951 (16 Feb). *Inauguration of B.W.I. University College. As Nos.* 149/50 *of Jamaica.*
121 3 c. black and purple 20 15
122 12 c. black and violet 20 20

14 Government House **18** Badge of Presidency

(Recess B.W.)

1951 (17 Sept). *T* **14**, **18** *and similar horiz designs. Wmk Mult Script CA. P* 11½ × 11.
123 **14** 1 c. black 10 45
124 – 2 c. green 15 40
125 – 3 c. orange-brown 30 45
126 – 4 c. carmine 30 20
127 – 5 c. reddish violet 30 40
128 **18** 6 c. olive-brown 30 20
129 – 8 c. deep blue 35 20
130 – 12 c. blue and chocolate 35 30
131 – 24 c. carmine and yellow-green 45 30
132 – 60 c. black and carmine 2·50 1·75
133 – $1.20, yellow-green and blue 5·50 2·75
134 – $2.40, black and green 4·50 11·00
135 **18** $4.80, black and purple 14·00 15·00
123/135 *Set of* 13 26·00 30·00
Designs:—2 c., $1.20, Sea Island cotton: cultivation; 3 c. Map of colony; 4, 24 c. Picking tomatoes; 5, 12 c. St. Anthony's Church; 8, 60 c. Sea Island cotton: ginning; $2.40, Government House.

1953 (2 June). *Coronation. As No.* 153 *of Jamaica.*
136 2 c. black and deep green 10 10

19 Government House **20** Shakespeare and Memorial Theatre, Stratford-upon-Avon

Types **16** and **18**: I. inscr "PRESIDENCY". II. inscr "COLONY".

(Recess B.W.)

1953 (15 Oct)–**62**. *As King George VI issue, but with portrait of Queen Elizabeth II as in T* **19**. *Wmk Mult Script CA. P* 11½×11.
136*a* – ½ c. deep violet (I) (3.7.56) 15 10
136*b* – ½c. deep violet (II) (1.9.58) 30 10
137 **19** 1 c. black 10 10
138 – 2 c. green 10 10
139 – 3 c. orange-brown (I) 30 10
139*a* – 3 c. orange-brown (II) (1.9.58) 35 15
140 – 4 c. carmine-red (1.6.55) 30 15
141 – 5 c. reddish lilac (1.6.55) 30 30
142 **18** 6 c. deep bistre-brown (I) (1.6.55) 15 10
142*a* 6 c. deep bistre-brown (II) (1.9.58) 40 15
ab. Deep sepia-brown (30.7.62) 1·75 80
143 – 8 c. deep bright blue (1.6.55) 30 10
144 – 12 c. blue and red-brown (1.6.55) 75 10
145 – 24 c. carmine-red and green (1.6.55) 80 10
145*a* – 48 c. yellow-olive and purple (15.10.57) 8·50 2·00
146 – 60 c. black and carmine (1.6.55) 4·50 80
147 – $1.20, green and greenish blue (1.6.55) 7·50 3·75
148 – $2.40, black and bluish green (1.6.55) 5·00 8·00
149 **18** $4.80, black & deep purple (I) (1.6.55) 6·00 10·00
149*a* $4.80, black & deep purple (II) (1.9.58) 6·00 7·00
136*a*/149*a* *Set of* 15 30·00 20·00
Extra designs:—½, 3 c. Map of colony; 48 c. Sea Island cotton: cultivation.
See also No. 157.

1958 (22 Apr). *Inauguration of British Caribbean Federation. As Nos.* 175/7 *of Jamaica.*
150 3 c. deep green 25 15
151 6 c. blue 30 20
152 12 c. scarlet 40 10
150/2 *Set of* 3 85 40

1963 (8 July). *Freedom from Hunger. As No.* 80 *of Lesotho.*
153 12 c. reddish violet 30 15

1963 (2 Sept). *Red Cross Centenary. As Nos.* 203/4 *of Jamaica.*
154 4 c. red and black 10 10
155 12 c. red and blue 25 25

(Des R. Granger Barrett. Photo Harrison)

1964 (23 Apr). *400th Birth Anniv of William Shakespeare.* W w **12**. *P* 14×14½.
156 **20** 12 c. indigo 10 10

1964 (29 Oct). *As No.* 138 *but wmk* w **12**.
157 2 c. green 15 15

1965 (17 May). *I.T.U. Centenary. As Nos.* 98/9 *of Lesotho.*
158 4 c. vermilion and violet 15 10
159 48 c. light emerald and carmine 30 20

21 Pineapple **22** Avocado

(Des Sylvia Goaman. Photo Harrison)

1965 (16 Aug). *T* **21/2** *and similar vert designs showing vegetables, fruit or plants. Multicoloured.* W w **12** (*upright*). *P* 15×14.
160 1 c. Type **21** 10 10
161 2 c. Type **22** 10 10
162 3 c. Soursop 10 10
163 4 c. Pepper 10 10
164 5 c. Mango 10 10
165 6 c. Tomato 10 10
166 8 c. Guava 10 10
167 10 c. Ochro 10 10
168 12 c. Lime 15 10
169 20 c. Orange 20 10
170 24 c. Banana 20 10
171 42 c. Onion 75 60
172 48 c. Cabbage 1·00 75
173 60 c. Pawpaw 1·75 90
174 $1.20, Pumpkin 2·00 1·75
175 $2.40, Sweet potato 5·00 2·50
176 $4.80, Egg plant 5·00 6·00
160/76 *Set of* 17 15·00 12·00
See also Nos. 213/22.

1965 (25 Oct). *International Co-operation Year. As Nos.* 100/1 *of Lesotho.*
177 2 c. reddish purple and turquoise-green 10 10
178 12 c. deep bluish green and lavender 25 10

1966 (26 Jan). *Churchill Commemoration. As Nos.* 102/5 *of Lesotho.*
179 1 c. new blue 10 10
a. Cerise (sky) omitted £180
180 2 c. deep green 10 10
181 24 c. brown 15 10
182 42 c. bluish violet 20 15
179/82 *Set of* 4 40 30

23 Queen Elizabeth II and Duke of Edinburgh

(Des H. Baxter. Litho B.W.)

1966 (4 Feb). *Royal Visit.* W w **12**. *P* 11×12.
183 **23** 14 c. black and ultramarine 30 15
184 24 c. black and magenta 50 15

24 W.H.O. Building

(Des M. Goaman. Litho Harrison)

1966 (20 Sept). *Inauguration of W.H.O. Headquarters, Geneva.* W w **12** (*sideways*). *P* 14.
185 **24** 12 c. black, yellow-green and light blue 10 10
186 60 c. black, light purple and yellow-brown 25 20

1966 (1 Dec). *20th Anniv of U.N.E.S.C.O. As Nos.* 342/4 *of Mauritius.*
187 4 c. slate-violet, red, yellow and orange 10 10
a. Orange omitted 50·00
188 60 c. orange-yellow, violet and deep olive 20 10
189 $1.80, black, bright purple and orange 70 70
187/9 *Set of* 3 80 75
On No. 187a the omission of the orange only affects the squares of the lower case letters so that they appear yellow, the same as the capital squares.

25 Yachting **(26)**

(Des and photo Harrison)

1967 (29 Dec). *International Tourist Year. T* **25** *and similar multicoloured designs.* W w **12** (*sideways on* 15 c.). *P* 14.
190 5 c. Type **25** 10 10
191 15 c. Waterfall near Chance Mountain (*vert*) 15 10
192 16 c. Fishing, skin-diving and swimming 15 10
193 24 c. Playing golf 30 10
190/3 *Set of* 4 55 30

1968 (6 May). *Nos.* 168, 170, 172 *and* 174/6 *surch as T* **26**. W w **12** (*upright*).
194 15 c. on 12 c. Lime 20 15
195 25 c. on 24 c. Banana 25 15
196 50 c. on 48 c. Cabbage 45 15
197 $1 on $1.20, Pumpkin 1·50 40
198 $2.50 on $2.40, Sweet potato 2·00 3·00
199 $5 on $4.80, Egg plant 2·50 3·75
194/9 *Set of* 6 6·00 7·00
See also Nos. 219 etc.

27 Sprinting **28** Sprinting, and Aztec Pillars

(Des G. Vasarhelyi. Photo Harrison)

1968 (31 July). *Olympic Games, Mexico. T* **27/8** *and similar designs.* W w **12** (*sideways on* $1). *P* 14.
200 15 c. deep claret, emerald and gold 10 10
201 25 c. blue, orange and gold 10 10
202 50 c. green, red and gold 10 10
203 $1 multicoloured 20 20
200/3 *Set of* 4 35 30
Designs: *Horiz as T* **27**—25 c. Weightlifting; 50 c. Gymnastics.

31 Alexander Hamilton

(Des and photo Harrison)

1968 (6 Dec*). *Human Rights Year. T* **31** *and similar horiz designs. Multicoloured.* W w **12**. *P* 14 × 14½.
204 5 c. Type **31** 10 10
205 15 c. Albert T. Marryshow 10 10
206 25 c. William Wilberforce 10 10
207 50 c. Dag Hammarskjöld 10 10
208 $1 Dr. Martin Luther King 25 30
204/8 *Set of* 5 40 45
*Although first day covers were postmarked 2 December, these stamps were not put on sale in Montserrat until 6 December.

32 "The Two Trinities" (Murillo) **33** "The Adoration of the Kings" (detail, Botticelli)

(Des and photo Harrison)

1968 (16 Dec). *Christmas. W* w **12** *(sideways). P* 14½ × 14.

No.	Type	Description	Unused	Used
209	**32**	5 c. multicoloured	10	10
210	**33**	15 c. multicoloured	10	10
211	**32**	25 c. multicoloured	10	10
212	**33**	50 c. multicoloured	15	20
209/12		*Set of* 4	30	30

1969–70. *As Nos.* 160/4, 167, 169 *and* 194/6 *but wmk* w **12** *sideways.*

No.	Description	Unused	Used
213	1 c. Type **21** (24.6.69)	10	10
214	2 c. Type **22** (23.4.70)	60	75
215	3 c. Soursop (24.6.69)	20	15
216	4 c. Pepper (24.6.69)	35	15
217	5 c. Mango (23.4.70)	80	85
218	10 c. Ochro (24.6.69)	50	25
219	15 c. on 12 c. Lime (24.6.69)	60	40
220	20 c. Orange (17.3.69)	65	45
221	25 c. on 24 c. Banana (24.6.69)	90	85
222	50 c. on 48 c. Cabbage (24.6.69)	3·00	5·50
213/22	*Set of* 10	7·00	8·50

The 1 c., 3 c., 4 c., 10 c., 15 c. and 20 c. exist with PVA gum as well as gum arabic, but the 2 c. and 5 c. exist with PVA gum only.

34 Map showing "CARIFTA" Countries

35 "Strength in Unity"

(Des J. Cooter. Photo Harrison)

1969 (27 May). *First Anniv of CARIFTA (Caribbean Free Trade Area). W* w **12** *(sideways on T* **34**). *P* 14.

No.	Type	Description	Unused	Used
223	**34**	15 c. multicoloured	10	10
224		20 c. multicoloured	10	10
225	**35**	35 c. multicoloured	10	10
226		50 c. multicoloured	15	15
223/6		*Set of* 4	30	30

36 Telephone Receiver and Map of Montserrat

40 Dolphin

(Des R. Reid, adapted by V. Whiteley. Litho P.B.)

1969 (29 July). *Development Projects. T* **36** *and similar vert designs. Multicoloured. W* w **12**. *P* 13½.

No.	Description	Unused	Used
227	15 c. Type **36**	10	10
228	25 c. School symbols and map	10	10
229	50 c. "HS 748" aircraft and map	15	10
230	$1 Electricity pylon and map	25	20
227/30	*Set of* 4	35	30

(Des Harrison. Photo Enschedé)

1969 (1 Nov). *Game Fish. T* **40** *and similar horiz designs. Multicoloured. P* 13 × 13½.

No.	Description	Unused	Used
231	5 c. Type **40**	15	10
232	15 c. Atlantic sailfish	30	10
233	25 c. Blackfin tuna	35	10
234	40 c. Spanish mackerel	55	20
231/4	*Set of* 4	1·25	40

41 King Caspar before the Virgin and Child (detail) (Norman 16th-cent stained glass window)

42 "Nativity" (Leonard Limosin)

(Des J. Cooter. Litho D.L.R.)

1969 (10 Dec). *Christmas. Paintings multicoloured; frame colours given. W* w **12** *(sideways on* 50 c.). *P* 13.

No.	Type	Description	Unused	Used
235	**41**	15 c. black, gold and violet	10	10
236		25 c. black and vermilion	10	10
237	**42**	50 c. black, ultramarine & yellow-orange	15	15
235/7		*Set of* 3	30	20

43 "Red Cross Sale"

(Des and litho J.W.)

1970 (13 Apr). *Centenary of British Red Cross. T* **43** *and similar horiz designs. Multicoloured. W* w **12** *(sideways). P* 14½ × 14.

No.	Description	Unused	Used
238	3 c. Type **43**	10	10
239	4 c. School for deaf children	10	10
240	15 c. Transport services for disabled	10	10
241	20 c. Workshop	10	20
238/41	*Set of* 4	30	30

44 Red-footed Booby

45 "Madonna and Child with Animals" (Brueghel the Elder, after Dürer)

(Des V. Whiteley. Photo Harrison)

1970 (2 July)–**74**. *Birds. T* **44** *and similar multicoloured designs. W* w **12** *(sideways on vert designs and upright on horiz designs). P* 14 × 14½ *(horiz) or* 14½ × 14 *(vert).*

A. *Chalk-surfaced paper* (2.7.70).
B. *Glazed, ordinary paper* (30.10.74, $10; 22.1.71, *others*).

No.	Description	A Unused	A Used	B Unused	B Used
242	1 c. Type **44**	10	10	†	
243	2 c. American Kestrel	15	15	65	1·50
244	3 c. Magnificent Frigate Bird	15	15	†	
245	4 c. Great Egret	30	15	†	
246	5 c. Brown Pelican	50	10	65	1·00
247	10 c. Bananaquit	30	10	1·00	1·50
248	15 c. Smooth-billed Ani	30	15	3·75	3·75
249	20 c. Red-billed Tropic Bird	35	15	1·50	1·75
250	25 c. Montserrat Oriole	50	50	4·00	4·50
251	50 c. Green-throated Carib	3·00	1·00	4·00	4·00
252	$1 Antillean Crested Humming-bird	3·00	1·00	4·25	4·50
253	$2.50, Little Blue Heron	3·00	4·00	8·00	9·50
254	$5 Purple-throated Carib	7·50	9·00	13·00	16·00
254*a*	$10 Forest Thrush	†		15·00	15·00
242A/54A	*Set of* 13	17·00	15·00		
243B/54*a*B	*Set of* 11			50·00	55·00

The 1 c. 15 c., 20 c., 25 c., $1, $5 and $10 are horizontal, and the remainder are vertical designs.

See also Nos. 295/302.

(Des G. Drummond. Litho D.L.R.)

1970 (1 Oct).* *Christmas. T* **45** *and similar multicoloured design. W* w **12**. *P* 13½ × 14.

No.	Description	Unused	Used
255	5 c. Type **45**	10	10
256	15 c. "The Adoration of the Shepherds" (Domenichino)	10	10
257	20 c. Type **45**	10	10
258	$1 As 15 c.	35	60
255/8	*Set of* 4	55	70

*This was the local date of issue but the stamps were released by the Crown Agents on 21 September.

46 War Memorial

47 Girl Guide and Badge

(Des V. Whiteley. Litho J.W.)

1970 (30 Nov). *Tourism. T* **46** *and similar horiz designs. Multicoloured. W* w **12** *(sideways). P* 14½ × 14.

No.	Description	Unused	Used
259	5 c. Type **46**	10	10
260	15 c. Plymouth from Fort St. George	10	10
261	25 c. Carr's Bay	15	10
262	50 c. Golf Fairway	55	30
259/62	*Set of* 4	75	45
MS263	135 × 109 mm. Nos. 259/62	1·50	2·00

(Des V. Whiteley. Litho Questa)

1970 (31 Dec). *Diamond Jubilee of Montserrat Girl Guides. T* **47** *and similar vert design. Multicoloured. W* w **12**. *P* 14.

No.	Description	Unused	Used
264	10 c. Type **47**	10	10
265	15 c. Brownie and Badge	10	10
266	25 c. As 15 c.	15	10
267	40 c. Type **47**	20	20
264/7	*Set of* 4	50	30

48 "Descent from the Cross" (Van Hemessen)

49 D.F.C. and D.F.M. in Searchlights

(Des J.W. Photo Enschedé)

1971 (22 Mar). *Easter. T* **48** *and similar vert design. Multicoloured. W* w **12**. *P* 13½.

No.	Description	Unused	Used
268	5 c. Type **48**	10	10
269	15 c. "Noli me tangere" (Orcagna)	10	10
270	20 c. Type **48**	10	10
271	40 c. As 15 c.	15	15
268/71	*Set of* 4	30	30

(Des Col. A. Maynard. Litho Questa)

1971 (8 July). *Golden Jubilee of Commonwealth Ex-Services League. T* **49** *and similar vert designs. Multicoloured. W* w **12**. *P* 14.

No.	Description	Unused	Used
272	10 c. Type **49**	10	10
273	20 c. M.C., M.M. and jungle patrol	15	10
274	40 c. D.S.C., D.S.M. and submarine action	20	15
275	$1 V.C. and soldier attacking bunker	50	70
272/5	*Set of* 4	85	85

50 "The Nativity with Saints" (Romanino)

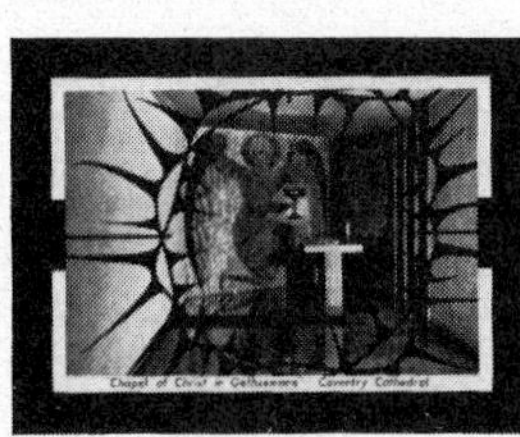

51 Piper "Apache"

(Des G. Drummond. Litho Questa)

1971 (16 Sept). *Christmas. T* **50** *and similar vert design. Multicoloured. W* w **12**. *P* 14 × 13½.

No.	Description	Unused	Used
276	5 c. Type **50**	10	10
277	15 c. "Choir of Angels" (Simon Marmion)	10	10
278	20 c. Type **50**	10	10
279	$1 As 15 c.	35	40
276/9	*Set of* 4	50	50

(Des and litho J.W.)

1971 (16 Dec). *14th Anniv of Inauguration of L.I.A.T. (Leeward Islands Air Transport). T* **51** *and similar horiz designs. Multicoloured. W* w **12** *(sideways). P* 13½.

No.	Description	Unused	Used
280	5 c. Type **51**	10	10
281	10 c. Beech "Twin Bonanza"	15	15
282	15 c. De Havilland "Heron"	30	15
283	20 c. Britten Norman "Islander"	35	15
284	40 c. De Havilland "Twin Otter"	65	45
285	75 c. Hawker Siddeley "748"	2·00	2·25
280/5	*Set of* 6	3·25	3·00
MS286	203 × 102 mm. Nos. 280/5	10·00	11·00

52 "Chapel of Christ in Gethsemane", Coventry Cathedral

53 Lizard

(Des G. Drummond. Litho A. & M.)

1972 (9 Mar). *Easter. T* **52** *and similar horiz design. Multicoloured. W* w **12**. *P* 13.

No.	Description	Unused	Used
287	5 c. Type **52**	10	10
288	10 c. "The Agony in the Garden" (Bellini)	10	10
289	20 c. Type **52**	10	10
290	75 c. As 10 c.	35	50
287/90	*Set of* 4	45	60

(Des G. Drummond. Litho Questa)

1972 (20 July). *Reptiles. T* **53** *and similar multicoloured designs. W* w **12** *(sideways on* 40 c. *and* $1). *P* 14½.

No.	Description	Unused	Used
291	15 c. Type **53**	15	10
292	20 c. Mountain Chicken (frog)	20	10
293	40 c. Iguana (*horiz*)	35	20
294	$1 Tortoise (*horiz*)	2·00	2·00
291/4	*Set of* 4	2·40	2·00

1972 (21 July)–**74**. *As No.* 242 *etc., but W* w **12**, *sideways on horiz designs* (1, 15, 20, 25 c.) *and upright on vert designs* (*others*). *Glazed, ordinary paper.*
295 1 c. Type **44** 30 45
a. Chalk-surfaced paper (4.2.74) .. 45 45
296 2 c. American Kestrel .. 50 45
a. Chalk-surfaced paper (4.2.74) .. 1·75 45
297 3 c. Magnificent Frigate Bird .. 7·00 4·25
298 4 c. Great Egret (*chalk-surfaced paper*) (4.2.74) .. 75 2·50
299 5 c. Brown Pelican (8.3.73) .. 40 30
a. Chalk-surfaced paper (4.2.74) .. 40 55
300 15 c. Smooth-billed Ani (8.3.73) .. 50 45
a. Chalk-surfaced paper (2.10.73) .. 85 1·00
301 20 c. Red-billed Tropic Bird (*chalk-surfaced paper*) (2.10.73) .. 1·40 1·50
302 25 c. Montserrat Oriole (*chalk-surfaced paper*) (17.5.74) .. 3·25 3·50
295/302 .. *Set of* 8 13·00 12·00

In 1973–74, during shortages of the 5 c. value, letters can be found posted unstamped and franked with a "postage paid" mark. Other covers exist with the word "paid" in manuscript.

54 "Madonna of the Chair" (Raphael)

(Des J. Cooter. Litho Format)

1972 (18 Oct). *Christmas. T* **54** *and similar horiz designs. Multicoloured. W* w **12**. *P* 13½.
303 10 c. Type **54** .. 10 10
304 35 c. "Virgin and Child with Cherub" (Fungai) 15 10
305 50 c. "Madonna of the Magnificat" (Botticelli) 25 30
306 $1 "Virgin and Child with St. John and an Angel" (Botticelli) .. 40 65
303/6 .. *Set of* 4 70 90

55 Lime, Tomatoes and Pawpaw **56** *Passiflora herbertiana*

(Des (from photographs by D. Groves) and photo Harrison)

1972 (20 Nov). *Royal Silver Wedding. Multicoloured; background colour given. W* w **12**. *P* 14 × 14½.
307 **55** 35 c. rose .. 10 10
308 $1 bright blue .. 20 20

(Des J. Cooter. Litho Walsall)

1973 (9 Apr). *Easter. T* **56** *and similar vert designs showing passion-flowers. Multicoloured. W* w **12**. *P* 13½.
309 20 c. Type **56** .. 25 10
310 35 c. *P. vitifolia* .. 35 10
311 75 c. *P. amabilis* .. 1·40 1·40
312 $1 *P. alata-caerulea* .. 1·75 1·75
309/12 .. *Set of* 4 3·50 3·00

Nos. 309/12 are inscribed on the reverse with information about the passion-flower.

57 Montserrat Monastery, Spain **58** "Virgin and Child" (School of Gerard David)

(Des J. Cooter. Litho Format)

1973 (9 July). 480*th Anniv of Columbus's Discovery of Montserrat. T* **57** *and similar horiz designs. Multicoloured. W* w **12**. *P* 13½.
313 10 c. Type **57** .. 15 10
314 35 c. Columbus sighting Montserrat .. 30 15
315 60 c. Columbus's ship off Montserrat .. 1·50 1·50
316 $1 Colony badge and map of voyage .. 1·75 1·75
313/16 .. *Set of* 4 3·50 3·00
MS317 126 × 134 mm. Nos. 313/16 .. 16·00 16·00

(Des J. Cooter. Litho Questa)

1973 (22 Oct). *Christmas. T* **58** *and similar vert designs. Multicoloured. W* w **12** (*sideways*). *P* 13½.
318 20 c. Type **58** .. 20 10
319 35 c. "The Holy Family with St. John" (Jordaens) .. 25 10
320 50 c. "Virgin and Child" (Bellini) .. 50 50
321 90 c. "Virgin and Child with Flowers" (Dolci) 80 1·00
318/21 .. *Set of* 4 1·60 1·40

58*a* Princess Anne and Captain Mark Phillips **59** Steel Band

(Des PAD Studio. Litho Questa)

1973 (14 Nov). *Royal Wedding. Centre multicoloured. W* w **12** (*sideways*). *P* 13½.
322 **58***a* 35 c. sage-green .. 10 10
323 $1 violet-blue .. 20 20

(Des J. W. Litho Questa)

1974 (8 Apr). 25*th Anniv of University of West Indies. T* **59** *and similar designs. Multicoloured. W* w **12** (*sideways on* 20 *c.*, $1 *and* **MS**328).
324 20 c. Type **59** .. 15 10
325 35 c. Masqueraders (*vert*) .. 20 10
326 60 c. Student weaving (*vert*) .. 1·00 1·00
327 $1 University Centre, Montserrat .. 1·10 1·25
324/7 .. *Set of* 4 2·25 2·25
MS328 130 × 89 mm. Nos. 324/7 .. 4·00 7·50

60 Hands with Letters

02¢

(61)

(Des P. Powell. Litho Walsall)

1974 (3 July). *Centenary of Universal Postal Union. T* **60** *and similar horiz design. W* w **12**. *P* 14½ × 14.
329 **60** 1 c. multicoloured .. 10 10
330 – 2 c. lt rose-red, orange-verm & blk .. 10 10
331 **60** 3 c. multicoloured .. 10 10
332 – 5 c. lt yellow-orange, reddish orge & blk 10 10
333 **60** 50 c. multicoloured .. 20 20
334 – $1 pale blue, turquoise-blue and black 40 65
329/34 .. *Set of* 6 75 90

Designs:—2 c., 5 c., $1 Figures from U.P.U. Monument.

1974 (2 Oct). *Various stamps surch as T* **61**.
335 2 c. on $1 (No. 252B) .. 30 50
336 5 c. on 50 c. (No. 333) .. 40 60
337 10 c. on 60 c. (No. 326) .. 1·75 2·25
338 20 c. on $1 (No. 252B) .. 30 40
a. "2" with seriffs (Pl 1B R. 3/1) .. 10·00
b. Bottom bar of surch omitted (Pl 1B R. 5/1-5) .. 5·00
339 35 c. on $1 (No. 334) .. 75 1·25
335/9 .. *Set of* 5 3·25 4·50

62 Churchill and Houses of Parliament **63** Carib "Carbet"

(Des R. Granger Barrett. Litho D.L.R.)

1974 (30 Nov). *Birth Centenary of Sir Winston Churchill. T* **62** *and similar vert design. Multicoloured. No wmk. P* 13 × 13½.
340 35 c. Type **62** .. 15 10
341 70 c. Churchill and Blenheim Palace .. 20 20
MS342 81 × 85 mm. Nos. 340/1 .. 50 70

(Des C. Abbott. Litho Walsall)

1975 (3 Mar). *Carib Artefacts. T* **63** *and similar horiz designs.*

(*a*) *W* w **12** (*sideways*). *From sheets. P* 14
343 5 c. lake-brown, yellow and black .. 10 10
344 20 c. black, lake-brown and yellow .. 10 10
345 35 c. black, yellow and lake-brown .. 15 10
346 70 c. yellow, lake-brown and black .. 25 40
343/6 .. *Set of* 4 50 60

(*b*) *No wmk. Self-adhesive with advertisements on the reverse. From booklets. Rouletted*
347 5 c. lake-brown, yellow and black .. 15 25
a. Booklet pane. Nos. 347/50 *se-tenant* .. 90
348 20 c. black, lake-brown and yellow .. 15 25
a. Booklet pane. Nos. 348 × 3 and No. 349 × 3 .. 90
349 35 c. black, yellow and lake-brown .. 15 25
350 70 c. yellow, lake-brown and black .. 55 70
347/50 .. *Set of* 4 90 1·25

Designs:—20 c. "Caracoli"; 35 c. Club or mace; 70 c. Canoe.

64 One-Bitt Coin

(Des J. Cooter. Litho Questa)

1975 (1 Sept). *Local Coinage*, 1785–1801. *T* **64** *and similar diamond-shaped designs. W* w **14** (*sideways*). *P* 13½.
351 5 c. black, light violet-blue and silver .. 10 10
352 10 c. black, salmon and silver .. 15 10
353 35 c. black, light blue-green and silver .. 20 15
354 $2 black, bright rose and silver .. 1·25 1·50
351/4 .. *Set of* 4 1·50 1·60
MS355 142 × 142 mm. Nos. 351/4 .. 1·75 2·75

Designs:—10 c. Eighth dollar; 35 c. Quarter dollar; $2 One dollar.

No. **MS**355 has details of the coins depicted printed on the reverse side, beneath the gum.

65 1d. and 6d. Stamps of 1876 **66** "The Trinity"

(Des J. Cooter. Litho J. W.)

1976 (5 Jan). *Centenary of First Montserrat Postage Stamp. T* **65** *and similar horiz designs. W* w **12** (*sideways*). *P* 13.
356 5 c. deep carmine, yellowish green and black 10 10
357 10 c. light yellow-ochre, scarlet and black .. 15 10
358 40 c. multicoloured .. 40 40
359 55 c. deep mauve, yellowish green and black 50 50
360 70 c. multicoloured .. 70 70
361 $1.10, yellowish green, brt blue & grey-blk .. 1·00 1·00
356/61 .. *Set of* 6 2·50 2·50
MS362 170 × 159 mm. Nos. 356/61. P 13½ .. 3·50 4·50

Designs:—10 c. G.P.O. and bisected 1d. stamp; 40 c. Bisects on cover; 55 c. G.B. 6d. used in Montserrat and local 6d. of 1876; 70 c. Stamps for 2½d. rate, 1876; $1.10, Packet boat *Antelope* and 6d. stamp.

(Des J. Cooter. Litho Questa)

1976 (5 Apr). *Easter. Unissued stamps prepared for Easter* 1975 *with values and date obliterated by black bars. T* **66** *and similar vert designs showing paintings by Orcagna. Multicoloured. W* w **14**. *P* 13½.
363 15 c. on 5 c. Type **66** .. 10 10
a. Surch omitted .. 50·00
364 40 c. on 35 c. "The Resurrection" .. 15 15
a. Surch omitted .. 50·00
365 55 c. on 70 c. "The Ascension" .. 15 15
a. Surch omitted .. 50·00
366 $1.10 on $1 "Pentecost" .. 30 40
a. Surch omitted .. 50·00
363/6 .. *Set of* 4 55 65
MS367 160 × 142 mm. Nos. 363/6 .. 1·25 2·00
a. Surch omitted .. £200

For No. 363 the "1" was added to the original 5 c. to make 15 c.

2¢

(67)

68 White Frangipani

1976 (12 Apr). *Nos.* 244A, 246A *and* 247A *surch as T* **67**.

368	2 c. on 5 c. Brown Pelican	10	15
369	30 c. on 10 c. Bananaquit	30	20
370	45 c. on 3 c. Magnificent Frigate Bird	40	25
	a. Surch triple		
	b. Surch double	40·00	
368/70	*Set of* 3	70	55

(Des J. Cooter. Litho Questa)

1976 (5 July)–**80**. *Various horiz designs showing Flowering Trees as T* **68**. *Multicoloured. Ordinary paper.* W w **14** (*sideways*). *P* 13½.

371	1 c. Type **68**	10	10
372	2 c. Cannon-ball Tree	10	10
373	3 c. Lignum vitae	10	10
374	5 c. Malay apple	15	10
375	10 c. Jacaranda	20	10
376	15 c. Orchid Tree	25	10
	a. Chalk-surfaced paper (8.80)	75	1·25
377	20 c. Manjak	25	10
	a. Chalk-surfaced paper (8.80)	75	1·25
378	25 c. Tamarind	25	10
379	40 c. Flame of the Forest	35	20
380	55 c. Pink Cassia	40	25
381	70 c. Long John	50	30
382	$1 Saman	65	40
383	$2.50, Immortelle	1·25	1·50
384	$5 Yellow Poui	2·00	2·25
385	$10 Flamboyant	3·00	4·25
371/85	*Set of* 15	8·00	8·50

69 Mary and Joseph **70** Hudson River Review, 1976

(Des L. Curtis. Litho Format)

1976 (4 Oct). *Christmas. T* **69** *and similar vert designs. Multicoloured.* W w **14**. *P* 14.

386	15 c. Type **69**	10	10
387	20 c. The Shepherds	10	10
388	55 c. Mary and Jesus	15	15
389	$1.10, The Magi	30	50
386/9	*Set of* 4	50	65
MS390	95 × 135 mm. Nos. 386/9	60	1·75

(Des and litho J.W.)

1976 (13 Dec). *Bicentenary of American Revolution. T* **70** *and similar vert designs. Multicoloured.* W w **14**. *P* 13.

391	15 c. Type **70**	30	15
392	40 c. } The *Raleigh* attacking	60	40
393	75 c. } H.M.S. *Druid*, 1777*	60	40
394	$1.25, Hudson River Review	1·10	60
391/4	*Set of* 4	2·40	1·40
MS395	95 × 145 mm. Nos. 391/4. P 13½	2·50	2·75

*The date is wrongly given on the stamps as "1776".

Nos. 392/3 and 391 and 394 were printed in horizontal *se-tenant* pairs throughout the sheet, each pair forming a composite design.

71 The Crowning **72** *Ipomoea alba*

(Des G. Vasarhelyi. Litho J.W.)

1977 (7 Feb). *Silver Jubilee. T* **71** *and similar horiz designs. Multicoloured.* W w **14** (*sideways*). *P* 13.

396	30 c. Royal Visit, 1966	15	15
397	45 c. Cannons firing salute	20	20
398	$1 Type **71**	35	60
396/8	*Set of* 3	60	85

(Des J. Cooter. Litho Questa)

1977 (1 June). *Flowers of the Night. T* **72** *and similar multicoloured designs.* W w **14** (*sideways on* 40 *and* 55 c.). *P* 14.

399	15 c. Type **72**	15	10
400	40 c. *Epiphyllum hookeri* (*horiz*)	40	30
401	55 c. *Cereus hexagonus* (*horiz*)	55	45
402	$1.50, *Cestrum nocturnum*	1·50	1·25
399/402	*Set of* 4	2·40	1·90
MS403	126 × 130 mm. Nos. 399/402. Wmk sideways	2·25	3·00

MINIMUM PRICE

The minimum price quote is 10p which represents a handling charge rather than a basis for valuing common stamps. For further notes about prices see introductory pages.

73 Princess Anne laying Foundation Stone of Glendon Hospital

(Des BG Studio. Litho Questa)

1977 (3 Oct). *Development. T* **73** *and similar horiz designs. Multicoloured.* W w **14** (*sideways*). *P* 14½ × 14.

404	20 c. Type **73**	15	10
405	40 c. *Statesman* (freighter) at Plymouth	25	15
406	55 c. Glendon Hospital	30	20
407	$1.50, Jetty at Plymouth Port	80	1·00
404/7	*Set of* 4	1·40	1·25
MS408	146 × 105 mm. Nos. 404/7	2·00	2·50

$1.00

SILVER JUBILEE 1977

ROYAL VISIT

TO THE CARIBBEAN

(74)

1977 (28 Oct). *Royal Visit. Nos.* 380/1 *and* 383 *surch locally with T* **74**.

409	$1 on 55 c. Pink Cassia	30	45
410	$1 on 70 c. Long John	30	45
411	$1 on $2.50, Immortelle	30	45
409/11	*Set of* 3	80	1·25

75 The Stable at Bethlehem **76** Four-eye Butterflyfish

(Des L. Curtis. Litho Walsall)

1977 (14 Nov). *Christmas. T* **75** *and similar vert designs. Multicoloured.* W w **14**. *P* 14 × 14½.

412	5 c. Type **75**	10	10
413	40 c. The Three Kings	15	10
414	55 c. Three Ships	20	10
415	$2 Three Angels	55	75
412/15	*Set of* 4	80	85
MS416	119 × 115 mm. Nos. 412/15	1·00	1·75

(Des J.W. Litho Walsall)

1978 (15 Mar). *Fish. T* **76** *and similar horiz designs. Multicoloured.* W w **14** (*sideways*). *P* 14.

417	30 c. Type **76**	20	10
418	40 c. French Angelfish	25	15
419	55 c. Blue Tang	35	15
420	$1.50, Queen Triggerfish	80	90
417/20	*Set of* 4	1·40	1·10
MS421	152 × 102 mm. Nos. 417/20	2·00	2·75

77 St. Paul's Cathedral **78** *Alpinia speciosa*

(Des G. Drummond. Litho J.W.)

1978 (2 June). *25th Anniv of Coronation. T* **77** *and similar horiz designs. Multicoloured.* W w **14** (*sideways*). *P* 13.

422	40 c. Type **77**	10	10
423	55 c. Chichester Cathedral	10	10
424	$1 Lincoln Cathedral	20	25
425	$2.50, Llandaff Cathedral	30	50
422/5	*Set of* 4	55	75
MS426	130 × 102 mm. Nos. 422/5. P 13½ × 14	70	1·25

Nos. 422/5 were each printed in sheets including two *se-tenant* stamp-size labels.

(Des J. Cooter. Litho J.W.)

1978 (18 Sept). *Flowers. T* **78** *and similar vert designs. Multicoloured.* W w **14**. *P* 13½ × 13.

427	40 c. Type **78**	20	10
428	55 c. *Allamanda cathartica*	25	15
429	$1 *Petrea volubilis*	45	45
430	$2 *Hippeastrum puniceum*	70	80
427/30	*Set of* 4	1·40	1·40

79 Private, 21st (Royal North British Fusiliers), 1796 **80** Cub Scouts

(Des J.W. Litho Questa)

1978 (20 Nov). *Military Uniforms* (1*st series*). *T* **79** *and similar vert designs showing soldiers from British infantry regiments. Multicoloured.* W w **14**. *P* 14 × 14½.

431	30 c. Type **79**	15	15
432	40 c. Corporal, 86th (Royal County Down), 1831	20	15
433	55 c. Sergeant, 14th (Buckinghamshire) 1837	30	20
434	$1.50, Officer, 55th (Westmorland), 1784	75	80
431/4	*Set of* 4	2·00	1·75
MS435	140 × 89 mm. Nos. 431/4	2·00	2·75

See also Nos. 441/5.

(Des J. W. Litho Walsall)

1979 (2 Apr). *50th Anniv of Boy Scout Movement on Montserrat. T* **80** *and similar multicoloured designs.* W w **14** (*sideways on* 40 *and* 55 c). *P* 14.

436	40 c. Type **80**	25	10
437	55 c. Scouts with signalling equipment	35	20
438	$1.25, Camp fire (*vert*)	60	55
439	$2 Oath ceremony (*vert*)	1·00	1·00
436/9	*Set of* 4	2·00	1·75
MS440	120 × 110 mm. Nos. 436/9	2·25	2·25

(Des J.W. Litho Questa)

1979 (4 June). *Military Uniforms* (2*nd series*). *Vert designs as T* **79** *showing soldiers from infantry regiments. Multicoloured.* W w **14**. *P* 14 × 14½.

441	30 c. Private, 60th (Royal American), 1783	15	15
442	40 c. Private, 1st West India, 1819	20	15
443	55 c. Officer, 5th (Northumberland), 1819	30	25
444	$2.50, Officer, 93rd (Sutherland Highlanders), 1830	1·00	1·10
441/4	*Set of* 4	1·50	1·50
MS445	139 × 89 mm. Nos. 441/4	2·00	2·50

81 Child reaching out to Adult

(Des G. Vasarhelyi. Litho Questa)

1979 (17 Sept). *International Year of the Child.* W w **14** (*sideways*). *P* 13½ × 14.

446	**81**	$2 black, orange-brown and flesh	50	55
MS447		85 × 99 mm. No. 446	50	2·00

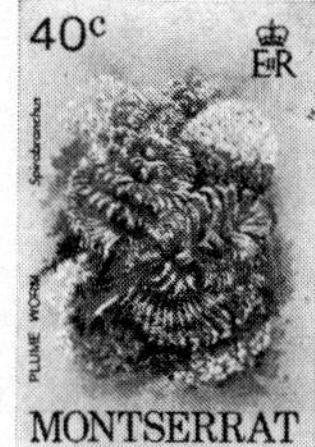

82 Sir Rowland Hill with Penny Black and Montserrat 1876 1d. Stamp **83** Plume Worm

(Des G. Vasarhelyi. Litho Questa)

1979 (1 Oct). *Death Centenary of Sir Rowland Hill and Centenary of U.P.U. Membership. T* **82** *and similar horiz designs. Multicoloured.* W w **14** (*sideways*). *P* 14.

448	40 c. Type **82**	20	10
449	55 c. U.P.U. emblem and notice announcing Leeward Islands entry into Union	25	15
450	$1 1883 Letter following U.P.U. membership	35	50
451	$2 Great Britain Post Office Regulations notice and Sir Rowland Hill	60	80
448/51	*Set of* 4	1·25	1·40
MS452	135 × 154 mm. Nos. 448/51	3·25	5·00

(Des G. Drummond. Litho Walsall)

1979 (26 Nov). *Marine Life. T* **83** *and similar vert designs. Multicoloured.* W w **14**. *P* 14.

453	40 c. Type **83**	20	15
454	55 c. Sea Fans	30	20
455	$2 Coral and Sponge	80	1·00
453/5	*Set of* 3	1·10	1·25

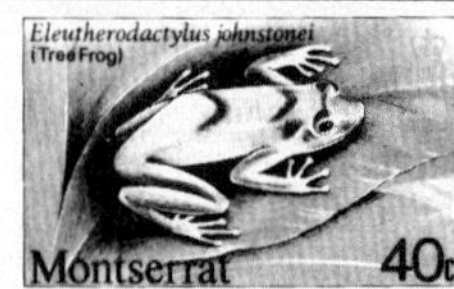

84 Tree Frog

(Des J. Cooter. Litho Rosenbaum Bros, Vienna)

1980 (4 Feb). *Reptiles and Amphibians. T* **84** *and similar horiz designs. Multicoloured.* W w **14** (*sideways*). *P* 13½.

456	40 c. Type **84**	20	15
457	55 c. Tree Lizard	25	25
458	$1 Crapaud	45	50
459	$2 Wood Slave	80	90
456/9	*Set of* 4	1·50	1·60

75th Anniversary of
Rotary International

85 *Marquess of Salisbury* and 1838 Handstamps

(86)

(Des BG Studio. Litho Questa)

1980 (14 Apr). *"London 1980" International Stamp Exhibition. T* **85** *and similar horiz designs. Multicoloured.* W w **14** (*sideways*). *P* 14.

460	40 c. Type **85**	20	15
461	55 c. "H.S. 748" aircraft and 1976 55 c. definitive	25	25
462	$1.20, *La Plata* (liner) and 1903 5s. stamp	45	45
463	$1.20, *Lady Hawkins* (packet steamer) and 1932 Tercentenary 5s. commemorative	45	45
464	$1.20, *Avon* (paddle-steamer) and Penny Red stamp with "A 08" postmark	45	45
465	$1.20, "Aeronca" aeroplane and 1953 $1.20 definitive	45	45
460/5	*Set of* 6	2·00	2·00
MS466	115 × 110 mm. Nos. 460/5. P 12	1·60	2·50

Nos. 460/5 were each printed in sheets of 4 stamps and two *se-tenant* stamp-size labels.

Some sheets of No. 462 showed the red colour omitted from the map in the right-hand label.

1980 (7 July). *75th Anniv of Rotary International. No.* 383 *optd with T* **86**.

467	$2.50, Immortelle	70	85

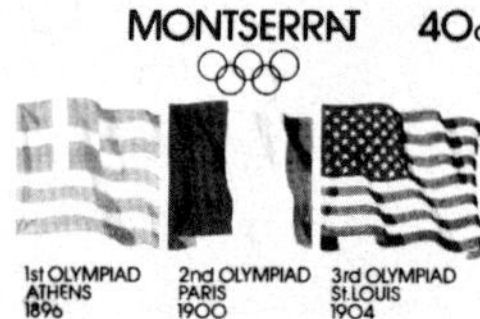

87 Greek, French and U.S.A. Flags

(Des A. Theobald. Litho Questa)

1980 (7 July). *Olympic Games, Moscow. T* **87** *and similar horiz designs. Multicoloured.* W w **14** (*sideways*). *P* 13½ × 14.

468	40 c. Type **87**	15	15
469	55 c. Union, Swedish and Belgian flags	15	15
470	70 c. French, Dutch and U.S.A. flags	20	20
471	$1 German, Union and Finnish flags	25	25
472	$1.50, Australian, Italian and Japanese flags	30	30
473	$2 Mexican, West German and Canadian flags	35	50
474	$2.50, "The Discus Thrower" (sculpture by Miron)	40	65
468/74	*Set of* 7	1·60	2·00
MS475	150 × 100 mm. Nos. 468/74	1·60	3·00
	a. Bottom row of stamps in miniature sheet imperf on 3 sides	£475	

Nos. 468/74 were each printed in small sheets of 4 including one *se-tenant* stamp-size label.

No. **MS**475a shows the three stamps in the bottom row of the miniature sheet imperforate vertically and with no perforations between the stamps and the bottom margin.

XX 5¢

(88)

89 S.S. *Lady Nelson*, 1928

1980 (30 Sept). *Nos.* 371, 373, 376 *and* 379 *surch as T* **88**.

476	5 c. on 3 c. Lignum vitae	10	10
	a. Surch double, one inverted	45·00	
477	35 c. on 1 c. Type **68**	20	15
	a. Surch omitted (in vert pair with normal)	60·00	
478	35 c. on 3 c. Lignum vitae	20	15
479	35 c. on 15 c. Orchid Tree	20	15
480	55 c. on 40 c. Flame of the Forest	25	15
	a. Surch inverted	60·00	
481	$5 on 40 c. Flame of the Forest	1·25	2·00
476/81	*Set of* 6	2·00	2·25

The surcharge omitted error, No. 477a, occurs on the lower stamp of a vertical pair. On the upper stamp the surcharge is at the foot of the design.

(Des J.W. Litho Walsall)

1980 (3 Nov). *Mail Packet Boats* (1*st series*). *T* **89** *and similar horiz designs. Multicoloured.* W w **14** (*sideways*). *P* 14.

482	40 c. Type **89**	20	15
483	55 c. R.M.S.P. *Chignecto*, 1913	30	25
484	$1 R.M.S.P. *Solent*, 1878	50	50
485	$2 R.M.S.P. *Dee*, 1841	75	85
482/5	*Set of* 4	1·60	1·60

See also Nos. 615/19.

90 *Heliconius charitonia*

91 Spadefish

(Des J.W. Litho Questa)

1981 (2 Feb). *Butterflies. T* **90** *and similar square designs. Multicoloured.* W w **14** (*inverted*). *P* 14.

486	50 c. Type **90**	60	40
487	65 c. *Pyrgus oileus*	70	45
488	$1.50, *Phoebis agarithe*	90	85
489	$2.50, *Danaus plexippus*	1·25	1·10
486/9	*Set of* 4	3·00	2·50

Nos. 486/9 were each printed in sheets including two *se-tenant* stamp-size labels.

(Des G. Drummond. Litho J.W.)

1981 (20 Mar). *Fishes. Vert designs as T* **91**. *Multicoloured.* W w **14**. *P* 13½ × 13.

490	5 c. Type **91**	40	10
491	10 c. Hogfish	40	10
492	15 c. Creole Wrasse	50	10
493	20 c. Yellow Damselfish	60	10
494	25 c. Sergeant Major	60	10
495	35 c. Clown Wrasse	50	20
496	45 c. Schoolmaster	50	25
497	55 c. Striped Parrotfish	95	30
498	65 c. Bigeye	50	30
499	75 c. French Grunt	60	40
500	$1 Rock Beauty	75	55
501	$2 Blue Chromis	1·75	1·10
502	$3 Fairy Basslet and Blueheads	1·90	1·75
503	$5 Cherubfish	2·75	2·75
504	$7.50, Longspine Squirrelfish	5·50	4·75
505	$10 Longsnout Butterflyfish	6·50	6·50
490/505	*Set of* 16	22·00	17·00

For stamps watermarked with W w **15** see Nos. 555/70.

92 Fort St. George

(Des J. Cooter. Litho Format)

1981 (18 May). *Montserrat National Trust. T* **92** *and similar horiz designs. Multicoloured.* W w **14** (*sideways*). *P* 13½ × 14.

506	50 c. Type **92**	30	20
507	65 c. Bird sanctuary, Fox's Bay	45	35
508	$1.50, Museum	85	75
509	$2.50, Bransby Point Battery, *circa* 1780	1·40	1·40
506/9	*Set of* 4	2·75	2·40

(Des D. Shults. Litho Questa)

1981 (17 July–19 Nov). *Royal Wedding. Horiz designs as T* **26/27** *of Kiribati. Multicoloured.* (a) W w **15**. *P* 14.

510	90 c. *Charlotte*	25	25
	a. Sheetlet. No. 510 × 6 and No. 511	2·25	
511	90 c. Prince Charles and Lady Diana Spencer	1·00	1·00
512	$3 *Portsmouth*	60	60
	a. Sheetlet. No. 512 × 6 and No. 513	4·75	
513	$3 As No. 511	1·75	1·75
514	$4 *Britannia*	75	75
	a. Sheetlet. No. 514 × 6 and No. 515	6·00	
515	$4 As No. 511	2·25	2·25
510/15	*Set of* 6	6·00	6·00
MS516	120 × 109 mm. $5 As No. 511. Wmk sideways. P 12 (19 Nov)	1·50	1·50

(*b*) *Booklet stamps. No wmk. P* 12 (19 Nov)

517	90 c. As No. 510	45	45
	a. Booklet pane. No. 517 × 4	1·75	
518	$3 As No. 513	1·60	1·75
	a. Booklet pane No. 518 × 2	3·25	

Nos. 510/15 were printed in sheetlets of seven stamps of the same face value, each containing six of the "Royal Yacht" design and one of the larger design showing Prince Charles and Lady Diana.

Nos. 517/18 come from $13.20 stamp booklets.

93 H.M.S. *Dorsetshire* and Seaplane

94 Methodist Church, Bethel

(Des Court House Advertising Ltd. Litho Questa)

1981 (31 Aug). *50th Anniv of Montserrat Airmail Service. T* **93** *and similar horiz designs. Multicoloured.* W w **14** (*sideways*). *P* 14.

519	50 c. Type **93**	30	30
520	65 c. Beechcraft "Twin Bonanza" aeroplane	45	50
521	$1.50, De Havilland "Dragon Rapide" R.M. *Lord Shaftesbury* aeroplane	85	1·00
522	$2.50, Hawker Siddeley Avro "748" aeroplane and maps of Montserrat and Antigua	1·25	1·50
519/22	*Set of* 4	2·50	3·00

(Des J. Cooter. Litho Walsall)

1981 (16 Nov). *Christmas. Churches. T* **94** *and similar vert designs. Multicoloured.* W w **14**. *P* 14 × 13½.

523	50 c. Type **94**	20	15
524	65 c. St George's Anglican Church, Harris	25	15
525	$1.50, St Peter's Anglican Church, St Peters	60	60
526	$2.50, St Patrick's R.C. Church, Plymouth	75	1·00
523/6	*Set of* 4	1·75	1·75
MS527	176 × 120 mm. Nos. 523/6	3·00	3·50

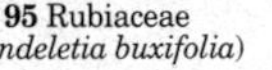

95 Rubiaceae (*Rondeletia buxifolia*)

96 Plymouth

(Des local artist. Litho Questa)

1982 (18 Jan). *Plant Life. T* **95** *and similar multicoloured designs.* W w **14** (*sideways on* 65 c. *and* $2.50). *P* 14½.

528	50 c. Type **95**	30	30
529	65 c. Boraginaceae (*Heliotropium ternatum*) (*horiz*)	40	40
530	$1.50, Simarubaceae (*Picramnia pentandra*)	85	85
531	$2.50, Ebenaceae (*Diospyrus revoluta*) (*horiz*)	1·25	1·25
528/31	*Set of* 4	2·50	2·50

(Litho Format)

1982 (17 Apr). *350th Anniv of Settlement of Montserrat by Sir Thomas Warner.* W w **14** (*sideways*). *P* 14½.

532	**96**	40 c. green	30	30
533		55 c. red	35	35
534		65 c. chestnut	40	40
535		75 c. olive-grey	45	50
536		85 c. bright blue	50	60
537		95 c. bright orange	55	65
538		$1 bright reddish violet	60	70
539		$1.50, brown-olive	80	1·00
540		$2 deep claret	1·10	1·25
541		$2.50, bistre-brown	1·40	1·60
532/41		*Set of* 10	5·75	6·50

Nos. 532/41 are based on the 1932 Tercentenary set.

97 Catherine of Aragon, Princess of Wales, 1501

98 Local Scout

(Des D. Shults and J. Cooter. Litho Format)

1982 (16 June). *21st Birthday of Princess of Wales. T* **97** *and similar vert designs. Multicoloured.* W w **15**. *P* 13½ × 14.

542	75 c. Type **97**	20	15
543	$1 Coat of Arms of Catherine of Aragon	30	20
544	$5 Diana, Princess of Wales	1·50	1·75
542/4	*Set of* 3	1·75	1·90

(Des D. Shults. Litho Format)

1982 (13 Sept). *75th Anniv of Boy Scout Movement. T* **98** *and similar vert design. Multicoloured. W* w **15**. *P* 14.
545 $1.50, Type **98** 85 70
546 $2.50, Lord Baden-Powell .. .. .. 1·25 1·10

99 Annunciation

(Des Jennifer Toombs. Litho Walsall)

1982 (18 Nov). *Christmas. T* **99** *and similar horiz designs. Multicoloured. W* w **14** *(sideways). P* 14.
547 35 c. Type **99** 20 15
548 75 c. Shepherd's Vision 40 35
549 $1.50, The Stable 85 85
550 $2.50, Flight into Egypt .. .. .. 1·00 1·10
547/50 .. .. *Set of* 4 2·25 2·25

100 *Lepthemis vesiculosa* **101** Blue-headed Hummingbird

(Des J. Cooter. Litho Walsall)

1983 (19 Jan). *Dragonflies. T* **100** *and similar horiz designs. Multicoloured. W* w **14** *(sideways). P* 13½ × 14.
551 50 c. Type **100** 25 20
552 65 c. *Orthemis ferruginea* 30 25
553 $1.50, *Triacanthagyna trifida* 70 75
554 $2.50, *Erythrodiplax umbrata* .. .. 1·25 1·25
551/4 .. .. *Set of* 4 2·25 2·25

1983 (12 Apr). *As Nos.* 490/505, *but W* w **15** *and imprint date "1983" added. P* 13½ × 13.
555 5 c. Type **91** 15 10
556 10 c. Hogfish 15 10
559 25 c. Sergeant Major 25 20
560 35 c. Clown Wrasse 35 30
564 75 c. French Grunt 60 55
565 $1 Rock Beauty 70 65
568 $5 Cherubfish .. .. 2·75 3·00
570 $10 Longsnout Butterflyfish .. .. 5·50 6·00
555/70 .. .. *Set of* 8 9·50 10·00

(Des G. Drummond. Litho Format)

1983 (24 May). *Hummingbirds. T* **101** *and similar vert designs. Multicoloured. W* w **14**. *P* 14.
571 35 c. Type **101** .. .. 1·25 35
572 75 c. Green-throated Carib .. .. .. 1·50 55
573 $2 Antillean Crested Hummingbird .. 2·50 1·40
574 $3 Purple-throated Carib .. .. .. 3·00 1·75
571/4 .. .. *Set of* 4 7·50 3·50

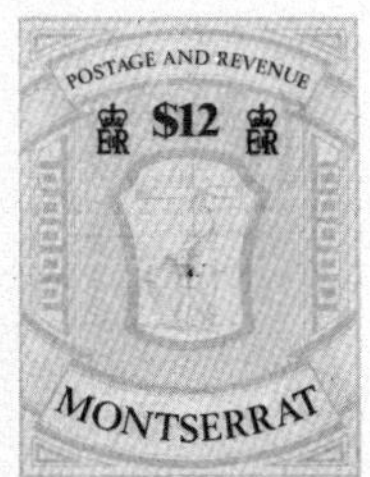

40¢

102 Montserrat Emblem (**103**)

(Litho Harrison)

1983 (25 July). *W* w **14**. *P* 14½.
575 **102** $12 royal blue and rose .. .. .. 4·25 5·00
576 $30 rose and royal blue .. .. .. 11·00 12·00

1983 (15 Aug). *Various stamps surch as T* **103**. *(a) Nos.* 491, 498, 501 *(all W* w **14**), 559, 564 *(both W* w **15**).
577 40 c. on 25 c. Sergeant Major (No. 559) .. 20 20
a. Surch inverted .. .. 38·00
b. Surch on No. 494 .. .. 12·00 12·00
c. Error. Surch on 10 c. (No. 491) .. .. 26·00
d. Surch double .. .. 45·00
578 70 c. on 10 c. Hogfish (No. 491) 35 35
a. Surch inverted .. .. 38·00
b. Surch on No. 556 .. .. 27·00 27·00
c. Surch omitted (in pair with normal) .. £130
d. Surch double .. .. 45·00
579 90 c. on 65 c. Bigeye (No. 498) 50 55
a. Error. Surch on 10 c. (No. 491) .. ..
b. Error. Surch on 75 c. (No. 499) .. .. 80·00
c. Surch double .. .. 45·00
580 $1.15 on 75 c. French Grunt (No. 564) .. 60 65
a. Surch on No. 499 .. .. 14·00 14·00
b. Error. Surch on 25 c. (No. 559) .. .. 40·00
c. Surch inverted .. .. 50·00
581 $1.50 on $2 Blue Chromis (No. 501) .. 80 85
a. Surch inverted .. .. 60·00
b. Error. Surch on 75 c. (No. 499) .. .. 80·00
c. Error. Surch on 75 c. (No. 564) .. ..

(*b*) *Nos.* 512/15
582 70 c. on $3 *Portsmouth* 60 70
a. Sheetlet. No. 582 × 6 and No. 583 .. 4·00
b. Surch double .. .. 5·00
c. Surch inverted .. .. 20·00
d. Surch inverted (horiz pair) .. .. 40·00
583 70 c. on $3 Prince Charles and Lady Diana Spencer 60 70
b. Surch double .. .. 45·00
c. Surch inverted .. .. 90·00
584 $1.15 on $4 *Britannia* .. .. .. 1·00 1·10
a. Sheetlet. No. 584 × 6 and No. 585 .. 7·00
b. Surch double .. .. 23·00
c. Surch inverted .. .. 15·00
d. Surch inverted (horiz pair) .. .. 30·00
e. Error. Surch on $3 (No. 512) .. .. 6·50
585 $1.15 on $4 As No. 583 .. .. .. 1·00 1·10
b. Surch double .. .. 40·00
c. Surch inverted .. .. 65·00
e. Error. Surch on $3 (No. 513) .. .. 70·00
577/85 .. .. *Set of* 9 4·75 5·25

Nos. 582d and 584d show the long surcharge intended for Nos. 583 or 585 inverted across horizontal pairs of the smaller design. Nos. 583c and 585c show two examples of the smaller surcharge inverted.

104 Montgolfier Balloon, 1783 **105** Boys dressed as Clowns

(Des A. Theobald. Litho Format)

1983 (19 Sept). *Bicentenary of Manned Flight. T* **104** *and similar multicoloured designs. W* w **14** *(sideways on* 75 c. *to* $2). *P* 14.
586 35 c. Type **104** 15 15
587 75 c. De Havilland "Twin Otter" (*horiz*) .. 35 30
588 $1.50, Lockheed "Vega" (*horiz*) 70 75
589 $2 *R 34* airship (*horiz*) .. .. .. 1·00 1·25
586/9 .. .. *Set of* 4 2·00 2·25
MS590 109 × 145 mm. Nos. 586/9. Wmk sideways 2·10 2·50

Nos. 586/9 were re-issued on 15 December 1983 overprinted "INAUGURAL FLIGHT Montserrat-Nevis-St. Kitts". It is understood nearly all of these overprints were used on Flown First Flight/Day Covers (*Price for set of* 4 *on First Flight Cover* £30).

(Des Jennifer Toombs. Litho Format)

1983 (18 Nov). *Christmas. Carnival. T* **105** *and similar horiz designs. Multicoloured. W* w **15** *(sideways). P* 14.
591 55 c. Type **105** 25 20
592 90 c. Girls dressed as silver star bursts .. 40 35
593 $1.15, Flower girls 50 60
594 $2 Masqueraders .. .. 95 1·00
591/4 .. .. *Set of* 4 1·90 1·90

106 Statue of Discus-thrower **107** Cattle Egret

(Des Court House Studio. Litho Questa)

1984 (26 Mar). *Olympic Games, Los Angeles. T* **106** *and similar vert designs. Multicoloured. W* w **15** *(sideways). P* 14.
595 90 c. Type **106** 35 35
596 $1 Olympic torch 40 45
597 $1.15, Olympic stadium, Los Angeles .. 45 50
598 $2.50, Olympic and American flags .. 80 1·00
595/8 .. .. *Set of* 4 1·75 2·10
MS599 110 × 110 mm. Nos. 595/8. Wmk upright 1·75 2·25

(Des G. Drummond. Litho Walsall)

1984 (28 May). *Birds of Montserrat. T* **107** *and similar multicoloured designs. W* w **15** *(sideways on* 5 c. *to* 90 c.). *P* 14.
600 5 c. Type **107** 15 20
601 10 c. Carib Grackle 15 20
602 15 c. Moorhen ("Common Gallinule") .. 15 20
603 20 c. Brown Booby 20 20
604 25 c. Black-whiskered Vireo 20 20
605 40 c. Scaly-breasted Thrasher 35 25
606 55 c. Laughing Gull 50 30
607 70 c. Glossy Ibis 60 45
608 90 c. Green Heron 75 50
609 $1 Belted Kingfisher (*vert*) 90 65
610 $1.15, Bananaquit (*vert*) .. .. .. 1·10 1·25
611 $3 American Kestrel ("Sparrow Hawk") (*vert*) .. .. 2·25 3·25
612 $5 Forest Thrush (*vert*) .. .. .. 3·50 5·50
613 $7.50, Black-crowned Night Heron (*vert*) .. 5·50 8·50
614 $10 Bridled Quail Dove (*vert*) .. .. 7·00 11·00
600/14 .. .. *Set of* 15 21·00 29·00

(Des J.W. Litho Format)

1984 (9 July). *Mail Packet Boats (2nd series). Multicoloured designs as T* **89**. *W* w **15** *(sideways). P* 14.
615 55 c. R.M.S.P. *Tagus*, 1907 .. .. .. 50 40
616 90 c. R.M.S.P. *Cobequid*, 1913 .. .. 75 65
617 $1.15, S.S. *Lady Drake*, 1942 .. .. 1·00 1·00
618 $2 M.V. *Factor*, 1948 .. .. .. 1·75 2·00
615/18 .. .. *Set of* 4 3·50 3·50
MS619 152 × 100 mm. Nos. 615/18 .. .. 3·25 4·25

No. **MS**619 also commemorates the 250th anniversary of *Lloyd's List* (newspaper).

108 Hermit Crab and Top Shell

(Des G. Drummond. Litho Questa)

1984 (24 Sept). *Marine Life. T* **108** *and similar horiz designs. Multicoloured. W* w **15** *(sideways). P* 14.
620 90 c. Type **108** 85 50
621 $1.15, Rough File Shell .. .. .. 1·10 70
622 $1.50, True Tulip Snail .. .. .. 1·50 90
623 $2.50, West Indian Fighting Conch .. 2·25 1·75
620/3 .. .. *Set of* 4 5·00 3·50

109 "Bull Man" **110** Mango

(Des Jennifer Toombs. Litho Questa)

1984 (12 Nov). *Christmas. Carnival Costumes. T* **109** *and similar horiz designs. Multicoloured. W* w **15** *(sideways). P* 14.
624 55 c. Type **109** 30 25
625 $1.15, Masquerader Captain 90 70
626 $1.50, "Fantasy" Carnival Queen .. .. 1·00 85
627 $2.30, "Ebony and Ivory" Carnival Queen .. 1·60 1·40
624/7 .. .. *Set of* 4 3·50 2·75

(Des G. Drummond. Litho Format)

1985 (8 Feb). *National Emblems. T* **110** *and similar vert designs. Multicoloured. W* w **15**. *P* 14.
628 $1.15, Type **110** .. .. 1·00 75
629 $1.50, Lobster Claw .. .. 1·50 95
630 $3 Montserrat Oriole .. .. 2·75 1·90
628/30 .. .. *Set of* 3 4·75 3·75

IMPERFORATES AND MISSING COLOURS. Various issues between Nos. 631 and 695 exist either imperforate or with colours omitted. Such items are not listed as there is no evidence that they fulfil the criteria outlined on page xi of this catalogue.

111 *Oncidium urophyllum* **112** Queen Elizabeth the Queen Mother

(Des J. Cooter. Litho Format)

1985 (9 May). *Orchids of Montserrat. T* **111** *and similar vert designs. Multicoloured. W* w **15**. *P* 14.
631 90 c. Type **111** 80 55
632 $1.15, *Epidendrum difforme* 90 70
633 $1.50, *Epidendrum ciliare* .. .. .. 1·00 85
634 $2.50, *Brassavola cucullata* .. .. 1·40 1·40
631/4 .. .. *Set of* 4 3·75 3·25
MS635 120 × 140 mm. Nos. 631/4 .. .. 4·25 5·00

(Des D. Ewart ($2), Maxine Marsh (others). Litho Format)

1985 (7 Aug). *Life and Times of Queen Elizabeth the Queen Mother. Various vertical portraits as T* **112**. *P* 12½.

636 55 c. multicoloured 30 35
a. Horiz pair. Nos. 636/7 .. .. 60 70
637 55 c. multicoloured 30 35
638 90 c. multicoloured 40 55
a. Horiz pair. Nos. 638/9 .. .. 80 1·10
639 90 c. multicoloured 40 55
640 $1.15, multicoloured 50 65
a. Horiz pair. Nos. 640/1 .. .. 1·00 1·25
641 $1.15, multicoloured 50 65
642 $1.50, multicoloured 65 70
a. Horiz pair. Nos. 642/3 .. .. 1·25 1·40
643 $1.50, multicoloured 65 70
636/43 .. .. *Set of* 8 3·25 4·00
MS644 85×113 mm. $2 multicoloured; $2 multicoloured .. .. 1·40 1·90

The two designs of each value were issued, *se-tenant*, in horizontal pairs within the sheets. Each *se-tenant* pair shows a floral pattern across the bottom of the portraits which stops short of the left-hand edge on the left-hand stamp and of the right-hand edge on the right-hand stamp.

Designs as Nos. 636/7 and 642/3 but with face values of $3.50×2 and $6×2, also exist in additional miniature sheets from a restricted printing issued 10 January 1986.

Nos. 636/43 and an unissued 15 c. also exist in separate miniature sheets, combining the two designs for each value, from stock dispersed by the liquidator of Format International Security Printers Ltd.

113 Cotton Plants

(Des G. Drummond. Litho Format)

1985 (18 Oct). *Montserrat Sea Island Cotton Industry. T* **113** *and similar horiz designs. Multicoloured.* W w **15**. *P* 15.

645 90 c. Type **113**.. .. .. 65 60
646 $1 Operator at carding machine 70 65
647 $1.15, Threading loom 85 85
648 $2.50, Weaving with hand loom .. .. 1·75 2·00
645/8 .. .. *Set of* 4 3·50 3·75
MS649 148×103 mm. Nos. 645/8. Wmk sideways .. .. 3·50 3·75

CARIBBEAN ROYAL VISIT 1985
(114)

115 Black-throated Blue Warbler

1985 (25 Oct). *Royal Visit. Nos.* 514/15, 543, 587/8 *and* 640/1 *optd as T* **114** *or surch also.*

650 75 c. multicoloured (No. 587) .. .. 2·50 2·50
651 $1 multicoloured (No. 543) .. .. 4·00 3·00
652 $1.15, multicoloured (No. 640) .. .. 4·00 3·00
a. Horiz pair. Nos. 652/3 .. .. 8·00 7·00
653 $1.15, multicoloured (No. 641) .. .. 4·00 3·50
654 $1.50, multicoloured (No. 588) .. .. 5·50 5·00
655 $1.60 on $4 multicoloured (No. 514) .. 3·50 3·50
a. Sheetlet. No. 655×6 and No. 656 .. 28·00
ab. Sheetlet No. 655×6 and No. 656a .. 28·00
656 $1.60 on $4 multicoloured (No. 515) (surch $1.60 only) .. .. 10·00 10·00
a. Additionally optd "CARIBBEAN ROYAL VISIT—1985" .. .. .. 10·00 10·00
650/6 .. .. *Set of* 7 30·00 28·00

No. 656 shows a new face value only; "CARIBBEAN ROYAL VISIT" being omitted from the surcharge. No. 656a is the corrected version issued subsequently.

(Des R. Vigurs. Litho Format)

1985 (29 Nov). *Leaders of the World. Birth Bicentenary of John J. Audubon (ornithologist). T* **115** *and similar vert designs showing original paintings. Multicoloured. P* 12½.

657 15 c. Type **115**.. .. .. 15 15
a. Horiz pair. Nos. 657/8 .. .. .. 30 30
658 15 c. Palm Warbler 15 15
659 30 c. Bobolink.. .. .. 20 20
a. Horiz pair. Nos. 659/60 .. .. .. 40 40
660 30 c. Lark Sparrow 20 20
661 55 c. Chipping Sparrow 30 30
a. Horiz pair. Nos. 661/2 .. .. .. 60 60
662 55 c. Northern Oriole.. .. .. .. 30 30
663 $2.50, American Goldfinch .. .. .. 1·00 1·00
a. Horiz pair. Nos. 663/4 .. .. .. 2·00 2·00
664 $2.50, Blue Grosbeak .. .. 1·00 1·00
657/64 .. .. *Set of* 8 3·00 3·00

Nos. 657/8, 659/60, 661/2 and 663/4 were printed together, *se-tenant*, in horizontal pairs throughout the sheets.

NEW INFORMATION

The editor is always interested to correspond with people who have new information that will improve or correct the Catalogue.

116 Herald Angel appearing to Goatherds

117 Lord Baden-Powell

(Des Jennifer Toombs. Litho Format)

1985 (2 Dec). *Christmas. T* **116** *and similar horiz designs showing a Caribbean Nativity. Multicoloured. P* 15.

665 70 c. Type **116**.. .. .. 40 45
666 $1.15, Three Wise Men following the Star 65 70
667 $1.50, Carol singing around War Memorial, Plymouth 80 85
668 $2.30, Praying to "Our Lady of Montserrat" Church of Our Lady, St. Patrick's Village .. .. 1·25 1·40
665/8 .. .. *Set of* 4 2·75 3·00

(Des G. Vasarhelyi. Litho Format)

1986 (11 Apr). *50th Anniv of Montserrat Girl Guide Movement. T* **117** *and similar vert designs. Multicoloured.* W w **15** *(sideways). P* 15.

669 20 c. Type **117**.. .. .. 25 25
a. Horiz pair. Nos. 669/70.. .. .. 50 50
670 20 c. Girl Guide saluting 25 25
671 75 c. Lady Baden-Powell 65 65
a. Horiz pair. Nos. 671/2 .. .. .. 1·25 1·25
672 75 c. Guide assisting in old people's home .. 65 65
673 90 c. Lord and Lady Baden-Powell 80 80
a. Horiz pair. Nos. 673/4 .. .. .. 1·60 1·60
674 90 c. Guides serving meal in old people's home 80 80
675 $1.15, Girl Guides of 1936.. .. .. 1·00 1·00
a. Horiz pair. Nos. 675/6 .. .. .. 2·00 2·00
676 $1.15, Two Guides saluting .. .. 1·00 1·00
669/76 .. .. *Set of* 8 4·75 4·75

Nos. 669/70, 671/2, 673/4 and 675/6 were each printed together, *se-tenant*, in horizontal pairs throughout the sheets.

117*a* Queen Elizabeth II

(Des Court House Studio. Litho Format)

1986 (21 Apr). *60th Birthday of Queen Elizabeth II. T* **117*a*** *and similar multicoloured designs. P* 12½.

677 10 c. Type **117*a*** 10 10
678 $1.50, Princess Elizabeth in 1928 .. 70 70
679 $3 In Antigua, 1977 .. .. .. 1·25 1·25
680 $6 In Canberra, 1982 (*vert*) .. .. 2·25 2·25
677/80 .. .. *Set of* 4 4·25 4·25
MS681 85×115 mm. $8 Queen with bouquet .. 4·50 5·00

The 10 c., $1.50 and $3 also exist watermarked w **16** (sideways), but no examples of these used from Montserrat have been seen.

Nos. 677/80 also exist in individual miniature sheets from stock dispersed by the liquidator of Format International Security Printers Ltd.

118 King Harold and Halley's Comet, 1066 (from Bayeux Tapestry)

(Des Court House Studio. Litho Format)

1986 (9 May). *Appearance of Halley's Comet. T* **118** *and similar horiz designs. Multicoloured. P* 14×13½.

682 35 c. Type **118**.. .. .. 30 30
683 50 c. Comet of 1301 (from Giotto's "Adoration of the Magi") 40 40
684 70 c. Edmond Halley and Comet of 1531 .. 55 55
685 $1 Comets of 1066 and 1910 .. .. 70 70
686 $1.15, Comet of 1910 .. .. .. 80 80
687 $1.50, E.S.A. *Giotto* spacecraft and Comet 95 95
688 $2.30, U.S. Space Telescope and Comet .. 1·40 1·40
689 $4 Computer reconstruction of 1910 Comet 2·50 2·50
682/9 .. .. *Set of* 8 7·00 7·00
MS690 Two sheets, each 140×115 mm. (a) 40 c. Type **118**; $1.75, As No. 683; $2 As No. 684; $3 As No. 685. (b) 55 c. As No. 686; 60 c. As No. 687; 80 c. As No. 688; $5 As No. 689 *Set of* 2 *sheets* 7·00 8·00

118*a* Prince Andrew

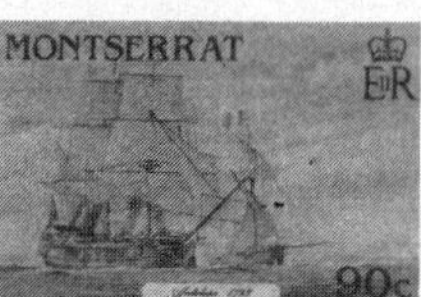

119 *Antelope* (1793)

(Des Court House Studio. Litho Format)

1986 (23 July–15 Oct). *Royal Wedding (1st issue). T* **118*a*** *and similar multicoloured designs. P* 12½.

691 70 c. Type **118*a*** 30 35
a. Pair. Nos. 691/2 .. .. 60 70
692 70 c. Miss Sarah Ferguson.. .. .. .. 30 35
693 $2 Prince Andrew wearing stetson (*horiz*) 75 90
a. Pair. Nos. 693/4 .. .. 1·50 1·75
694 $2 Miss Sarah Ferguson on skiing holiday (*horiz*) 75 90
691/4 .. .. *Set of* 4 2·00 2·25
MS695 115×85 mm. $10 Duke and Duchess of York on Palace balcony after wedding (*horiz*) (15.10) .. .. 3·50 3·75

Nos. 691/2 and 693/4 were printed together, *se-tenant*, in horizontal and vertical pairs throughout the sheets.

Nos. 691/4 imperforate come from souvenir stamp booklets.

See also Nos. 705/8.

A set of eight was prepared for the 1986 World Cup Football Championships, but was not issued. Examples exist from stock dispersed by the liquidator of Format International Security Printers Ltd.

(Des T. Hadler. Litho Questa)

1986 (29 Aug). *Mail Packet Sailing Ships. T* **119** *and similar horiz designs. Multicoloured.* W w **15**. *P* 14.

696 90 c. Type **119**.. .. .. 1·50 1·25
697 $1.15, *Montagu* (1810) .. .. .. 1·75 1·50
698 $1.50, *Little Catherine* (1813) .. .. 2·25 2·25
699 $2.30, *Hinchingbrook* (1813) .. .. 2·75 3·00
696/9 .. .. *Set of* 4 7·50 7·25
MS700 165×123 mm. Nos. 696/9. Wmk sideways 8·00 8·50

120 Radio Montserrat Building, Dagenham

(Des G. Vasarhelyi. Litho Questa)

1986 (29 Sept). *Communications. T* **120** *and similar horiz designs. Multicoloured.* W w **15**. *P* 14.

701 70 c. Type **120**.. .. .. 1·00 70
702 $1.15, Radio Gem dish aerial, Plymouth .. 1·50 1·25
703 $1.50, Radio Antilles studio, O'Garro's .. 1·75 1·75
704 $2.30, Cable and Wireless building, Plymouth .. .. 2·25 3·00
701/4 .. .. *Set of* 4 6·00 6·00

Congratulations to
T.R.H. The Duke & Duchess of York
(121)

121*a* Statue of Liberty

1986 (14 Nov). *Royal Wedding (2nd issue). Nos.* 691/4 *optd as T* **121** *in silver.*

705 70 c. Type **118*a*** 50 50
a. Pair. Nos. 705/6 .. .. 1·00 1·00
706 70 c. Miss Sarah Ferguson 50 50
707 $2 Prince Andrew wearing stetson (*horiz*) 1·25 1·25
a. Pair. Nos. 707/8.. .. .. .. 2·50 2·50
708 $2 Miss Sarah Ferguson on skiing holiday (*horiz*) .. .. 1·25 1·25
705/8 .. .. *Set of* 4 3·25 3·25

(Des Court House Studio. Litho Format)

1986 (18 Nov). *Centenary of Statue of Liberty. Vert views of Statue as T* **121*a*** *in separate miniature sheets. Multicoloured. P* 14×13½.

MS709 Three sheets, each 85×115 mm. $3; $4.50; $5 .. .. .. *Set of* 3 *sheets* 7·00 8·00

122 Sailing and Windsurfing

123 Christmas Rose

(Des J. Cooter. Litho Format)

1986 (10 Dec). *Tourism. T* **122** *and similar horiz designs. Multicoloured. P* 15.
710 70 c. Type **122** .. 1·00 70
711 $1.15, Golf .. 2·50 1·50
712 $1.50, Plymouth market .. 2·50 2·25
713 $2.30, Air Recording Studios .. 2·75 3·25
710/13 .. *Set of* 4 8·00 7·00

(Des Jennifer Toombs. Litho Questa)

1986 (12 Dec). *Christmas. Flowering Shrubs. T* **123** *and similar vert designs. Multicoloured. P* 14.
714 70 c. Type **123** .. 60 40
715 $1.15, Candle Flower .. 85 70
716 $1.50, Christmas Tree Kalanchoe .. 1·25 1·00
717 $2.30, Snow on the Mountain .. 1·75 2·00
714/17 .. *Set of* 4 4·00 3·75
MS718 150×110 mm. Nos. 714/17. P 12 .. 4·50 5·50

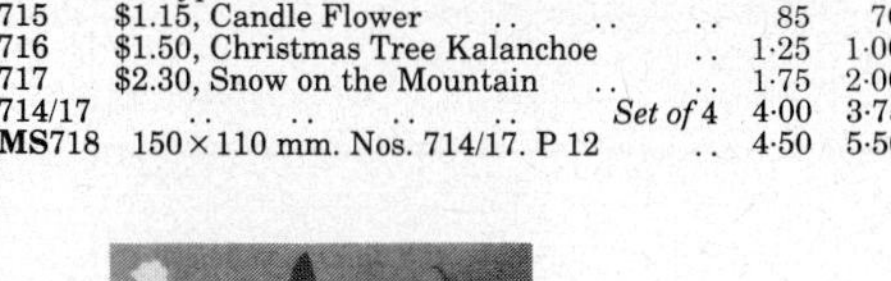

124 Tiger Shark

5c ▬

(**125**)

(Des M. Hillier. Litho Questa)

1987 (2 Feb). *Sharks. T* **124** *and similar horiz designs. Multicoloured. W w* **15**. *P* 14.
719 40 c. Type **124** .. 75 55
720 90 c. Lemon Shark .. 1·50 90
721 $1.15, White Shark .. 1·75 1·50
722 $3.50, Whale Shark .. 3·50 3·75
719/22 .. *Set of* 4 6·75 6·00
MS723 150×102 mm. Nos. 719/22. Wmk sideways. P 12 .. 7·50 8·00

1987 (6 Apr). *Nos.* 601, 603, 607/8 *and* 611 *surch as T* **125**.
724 5 c. on 70 c. Glossy Ibis .. 15 15
725 $1 on 20 c. Brown Booby .. 80 80
726 $1.15 on 10 c. Carib Grackle .. 90 90
727 $1.50 on 90 c. Green Heron .. 1·10 1·10
728 $2.30 on $3 American Kestrel (*vert*) .. 1·75 2·00
724/8 .. *Set of* 5 4·25 4·50

(**126**)

127 *Phoebis trite*

1987 (13 June). *"Capex '87" International Stamp Exhibition, Toronto. No.* **MS**690 *optd with T* **126** *in black and red.*
MS729 Two sheets. As No. **MS**690 *Set of* 2 *sheets* 6·50 7·00
No. **MS**729 also carries an overprint commemorating the exhibition on the lower sheet margins.

(Des M. Hillier. Litho Questa)

1987 (10 Aug). *Butterflies. T* **127** *and similar square designs. Multicoloured. W w* **15**. *P* 14.
730 90 c. Type **127** .. 1·00 65
731 $1.15, *Biblis hyperia* .. 1·50 1·00
732 $1.50, *Polygonus leo* .. 1·75 1·50
733 $2.50, *Hypolimnas misippus* .. 2·25 2·75
730/3 .. *Set of* 4 6·00 5·50

128 *Oncidium variegatum*

(Des R. Vigurs. Litho Questa)

1987 (13 Nov). *Christmas. Orchids. T* **128** *and similar multicoloured designs. P* 14×13½ (90 c., $1.50) *or* 13½×14 (*others*).
734 90 c. Type **128** .. 60 45
735 $1.15, *Vanilla planifolia* (*horiz*) .. 85 55
736 $1.50, *Gongora quinquenervis* .. 1·10 75
737 $3.50, *Brassavola nodosa* (*horiz*) .. 2·00 1·75
734/7 .. *Set of* 4 4·00 3·25
MS738 100×75 mm. $5 *Oncidium lanceanum* (*horiz*) .. 5·00 5·50

40th Wedding Anniversary
HM Queen Elizabeth II
HRH Duke of Edingburgh.
November 1987.
$2.30 ==

(**129**)

130 Free-tailed Bat

1987 (29 Nov). *Royal Ruby Wedding. Nos* 601, 604/5 *and* 608 *surch as T* **129**. A. *Surch* "Edingburgh". B. *Surch* "Edinburgh".

		A		B	
739	5 c. on 90 c. Green Heron	1·50	1·50	15	15
740	$1.15 on 10 c. Carib Grackle	3·25	3·25	65	65
741	$2.30 on 25 c. Black-whiskered Vireo	6·00	6·00	1·40	1·40
742	$5 on 40 c. Scaly-breasted Thrasher	9·00	9·00	2·75	3·00
739/42	*Set of* 4	18·00	18·00	4·50	4·75

Nos. 739A/42A were from the first printing using Type **129**. After the spelling mistake was noticed it was corrected on sheets subsequently surcharged.

(Des M. Pollard. Litho Questa)

1988 (8 Feb). *Bats. T* **130** *and similar vert designs. Multicoloured. W w* **15** (*sideways*). *P* 14.
743 55 c. Type **130** .. 35 35
744 90 c. *Chiroderma improvisum* (fruit bat) .. 55 55
745 $1.15, Fisherman Bat .. 75 75
746 $2.30, *Brachyphylla cavernarum* (fruit bat) 1·40 1·40
743/6 .. *Set of* 4 2·75 2·75
MS747 133×110 mm. $2.50, Funnel-eared Bat. Wmk upright .. 2·00 2·50

131 Magnificent Frigate Bird

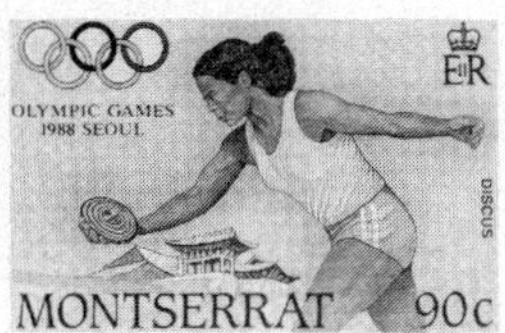

132 Discus throwing

(Des R. Vigurs. Litho Questa)

1988 (2 Apr). *Easter. Birds. T* **131** *and similar vert designs. Multicoloured. P* 14×13½.
748 90 c. Type **131** .. 60 45
749 $1.15, Caribbean Elaenia .. 80 65
750 $1.50, Glossy Ibis .. 1·00 1·00
751 $3.50, Purple-throated Carib .. 2·00 2·25
748/51 .. *Set of* 4 4·00 4·00
MS752 100 × 75 mm. $5 Brown Pelican .. 2·50 3·25

(Des R. Vigurs. Litho Questa)

1988 (29 July). *Olympic Games, Seoul. T* **132** *and similar horiz designs. Multicoloured. P* 13½×14.
753 90 c. Type **132** .. 40 45
754 $1.15, High jumping .. 50 55
755 $3.50, Athletics .. 1·60 1·75
753/5 .. *Set of* 3 2·25 2·50
MS756 103×77 mm. $5 Rowing .. 2·25 2·75

133 Golden Tulip

134 University Crest

(Des R. Vigurs. Litho Questa)

1988 (30 Aug). *Sea Shells. T* **133** *and similar horiz designs. Multicoloured. P* 14.
757 5 c. Type **133** .. 10 10
758 10 c. Little Knobby Scallop .. 10 10
759 15 c. Sozoni's Cone .. 10 10
760 20 c. Globular Coral Shell .. 10 10
761 25 c. Sundial .. 10 15
762 40 c. King Helmet .. 15 20
763 55 c. Channelled Turban .. 25 30
764 70 c. True Tulip Shell .. 30 35
765 90 c. Music Volute .. 40 45
766 $1 Flame Auger .. 40 45
767 $1.15, Rooster Tail Conch .. 50 55
768 $1.50, Queen Conch .. 65 70
769 $3 Teramachi's Slit Shell .. 1·25 1·40
770 $5 Florida Crown Conch .. 2·10 2·25
771 $7.50, Beau's Murex .. 3·25 3·50
772 $10 Triton's Trumpet .. 4·25 4·50
757/72 .. *Set of* 16 12·50 13·50

(Des R. Vigurs. Litho Questa)

1988 (14 Oct). *40th Anniv of University of West Indies. P* 14×13½.
773 **134** $5 multicoloured .. 2·40 2·50

=
HRH PRINCESS
ALEXANDRA'S VISIT
NOVEMBER 1988
40¢

(**135**)

1988 (4 Nov). *Princess Alexandra's Visit. Nos.* 763, 766 *and* 769/70 *surch as T* **135**.
774 40 c. on 55 c. Channelled Turban .. 35 35
775 90 c. on $1 Flame Auger .. 55 55
776 $1.15 on $3 Teramachi's Slit Shell .. 70 70
a. Surch double .. 55·00
777 $1.50 on $5 Florida Crown Conch .. 85 85
774/7 .. *Set of* 4 2·25 2·25

136 Spotted Sandpiper

(Des R. Vigurs. Litho Questa)

1988 (4 Dec). *Christmas. Sea Birds. T* **136** *and similar horiz designs. Multicoloured. P* 13½×14.
778 90 c. Type **136** .. 60 45
779 $1.15, Turnstone .. 70 55
780 $3.50, Red-footed Booby .. 1·75 2·00
778/80 .. *Set of* 3 2·75 2·75
MS781 105×79 mm. $5 Audubon's Shearwater 2·75 3·25

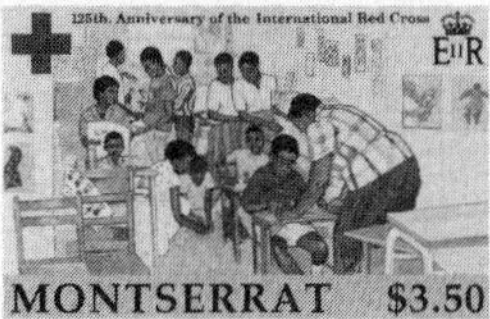

137 Handicapped Children in Classroom

(Des R. Vigurs. Litho Questa)

1988 (16 Dec). *125th Anniv of International Red Cross. P* 13½ × 14.
782 **137** $3.50, multicoloured .. 1·50 1·60

138 Drum Major in Ceremonial Uniform

139 Amazon Lily

(Des R. Vigurs. Litho Questa)

1989 (24 Feb). *75th Anniv of Montserrat Defence Force* (1988). *Uniforms. T* **138** *and similar vert designs. Multicoloured. P* 14×13½.
783 90 c. Type **138** .. 70 55
784 $1.15, Field training uniform .. 85 75
785 $1.50, Cadet in ceremonial uniform .. 1·25 1·25
786 $3.50, Gazetted Police Officer in ceremonial uniform .. 2·50 2·75
783/6 .. *Set of* 4 4·75 4·75
MS787 102×76 mm. $5 Island Girl Guide Commissioner and Brownie .. 3·25 4·00

(Litho Questa)

1989 (21 Mar). *Easter. Lilies. T* **139** *and similar multicoloured designs. P* 13½×14 (90 *c.*) *or* 14×13½ (*others*).
788 90 c. Type **139** 50 50
789 $1.15, Salmon Blood Lily (*vert*) 70 70
790 $1.50, Amaryllis (*Hippeastrum vittatum*) (*vert*) 85 85
791 $3.50, Amaryllis (*Hippeastrum* hybrid) (*vert*) .. .. 1·90 1·90
788/91 .. .. *Set of* 4 3·50 3·50
MS792 103×77 mm. $5 Resurrection Lily (*vert*) 3·50 4·00

140 *Morning Prince* (schooner), 1942

141 The Scarecrow

(Des R. Vigurs. Litho Questa)

1989 (30 June). *Shipbuilding in Montserrat. T* **140** *and similar horiz designs. Multicoloured. P* 13½×14.
793 90 c. Type **140** 40 45
794 $1.15, *Western Sun* (inter-island freighter) 55 60
795 $1.50, *Kim G* (inter-island freighter) under construction 70 75
796 $3.50, *Romaris* (island ferry), *c.* 1942 1·60 1·75
793/6 .. .. *Set of* 4 3·00 3·25

(Litho Questa)

1989 (22 Sept). 50*th Anniv of* The Wizard of Oz (*film*). *T* **141** *and similar multicoloured designs. P* 14.
797 90 c. Type **141** 40 45
798 $1.15, The Lion 55 60
799 $1.50, The Tin Man 70 75
800 $3.50, Dorothy .. .. 1·60 1·75
797/800 .. .. *Set of* 4 3·00 3·25
MS801 113×84 mm. $5 Characters from film (*horiz*) .. .. 2·40 2·50

Hurricane Hugo
Relief Surcharge $2.50

(142)

1989 (20 Oct). *Hurricane Hugo Relief Fund. Nos.* 795/6 *surch with T* **142**.
802 $1.50 + $2.50, *Kim G* (inter-island freighter) under construction .. 1·90 2·00
803 $3.50 + $2.50, *Romaris* (island ferry), *c.* 1942 .. .. 2·75 3·00

143 "Apollo 11" above Lunar Surface

(Litho Questa)

1989 (19 Dec). 20*th Anniv of First Manned Landing on Moon. T* **143** *and similar multicoloured designs. P* 13½×14.
804 90 c. Type **143** 35 40
805 $1.15, Astronaut alighting from lunar module *Eagle* 45 50
806 $1.50, *Eagle* and astronaut conducting experiment 60 65
807 $3.50, Opening "Apollo 11" hatch after splashdown .. .. 1·40 1·50
804/7 .. .. *Set of* 4 2·50 2·75
MS808 101×76 mm. $5 Astronaut on Moon. P 14×13½ .. .. 2·25 2·50

144 *Yamato* (Japanese battleship)

145 The Empty Tomb

(Litho Questa)

1990 (12 Feb). *World War II Capital Ships. T* **144** *and similar horiz designs. Multicoloured. P* 14.
809 70 c. Type **144** 40 40
810 $1.15, U.S.S. *Arizona* at Pearl Harbour .. 60 60
811 $1.50, *Bismarck* (German battleship) in action 90 90
812 $3.50, H.M.S. *Hood* (battle cruiser) .. 1·75 1·75
809/12 .. .. *Set of* 4 3·25 3·25
MS813 118×90 mm. $5 *Bismarck* and map of North Atlantic .. .. 3·50 3·75

(Des R. Vigurs. Litho Questa)

1990 (12 Apr). *Easter. T* **145** *and similar vert designs showing stained glass windows from St. Michael's Parish Church, Bray, Berkshire. Multicoloured. P* 14×15.
814 $1.15, Type **145** 45 50
a. Horiz strip of 3. Nos. 814/16 .. .. 2·25
815 $1.50, The Ascension 60 65
816 $3.50, The Risen Christ with Disciples .. 1·40 1·50
814/16 .. .. *Set of* 3 2·25 2·40
MS817 65×103 mm. $5 The Crucifixion .. 2·25 2·50
Nos. 814/16 were printed together, *se-tenant*, in sheets of 6 (3×2).

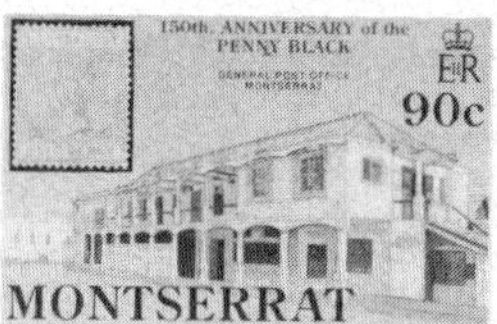

(146)

1990 (3 May). *"Stamp World London 90" International Stamp Exhibition. Nos.* 460/4 *surch as T* **146** *in bright purple.*
818 70 c. on 40 c. Type **85** 25 30
819 90 c. on 55 c. "H.S. 748" aircraft and 1976 55 c. definitive 35 40
820 $1 on $1.20, *La Plata* (liner) and 1903 5s. stamp 40 45
821 $1.15 on $1.20, *Lady Hawkins* (packet steamer) and 1932 Tercentenary 5s. commemorative 45 50
822 $1.50 on $1.20, *Avon* (paddle-steamer) and Penny Red stamp with "A 08" postmark 60 65
818/22 .. .. *Set of* 5 1·90 2·10
Nos. 818/22 also show the "Stamp World London 90" emblem overprinted on one of the *se-tenant* labels.

147 General Office, Montserrat, and 1884 ½d. Stamp

(Litho Questa)

1990 (1 June). 150*th Anniv of the Penny Black. T* **147** *and similar multicoloured designs. P* 13½×14 (*horiz*) *or* 14×13½ (*vert*).
823 90 c. Type **147** 35 40
824 $1.15, Sorting letters and Montserrat 1d. stamp of 1876 (*vert*) 45 50
825 $1.50, Posting letters and Penny Black (*vert*) 60 65
826 $3.50, Postman delivering letters and 1840 Twopence Blue .. .. 1·40 1·50
823/6 .. .. *Set of* 4 2·50 2·75
MS827 102×75 mm. $5 Montserrat soldier's letter of 1836 and Penny Black .. .. .. 2·25 2·50

149 Spinner Dolphin

(Des Jennifer Toombs. Litho Questa)

1990 (25 Sept). *Dolphins. T* **149** *and similar horiz designs. Multicoloured. P* 14.
833 90 c. Type **149** 35 40
834 $1.15, Common Dolphin 45 50
835 $1.50, Striped Dolphin 60 65
836 $3.50, Atlantic Spotted Dolphin .. .. 1·40 1·50
833/6 .. .. *Set of* 4 2·50 2·75
MS837 103×76 mm. $5 Atlantic White-sided Dolphin .. .. 2·00 2·10

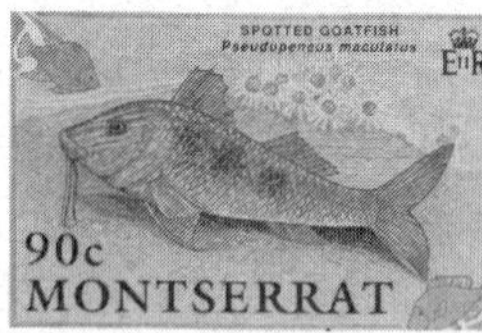

150 Spotted Goatfish

148 Montserrat v. Antigua Match

(Litho Questa)

1990 (8 July). *World Cup Football Championship, Italy. T* **148** *and similar multicoloured designs. P* 14.
828 90 c. Type **148** 35 40
829 $1.15, U.S.A v. Trinidad match 45 50
830 $1.50, Montserrat team 60 65
831 $3.50, West Germany v. Wales match .. 1·40 1·50
828/31 .. .. *Set of* 4 2·50 2·75
MS832 77×101 mm. $5 World Cup trophy (*vert*) 2·25 2·50

COVER PRICES

Cover factors are quoted at the beginning of each country for most issues to 1945. An explanation of the system can be found on page x. The factors quoted do not, however, apply to philatelic covers.

(151)

(Litho Questa)

1991 (7 Feb). *Tropical Fishes. T* **150** *and similar horiz designs. Multicoloured. P* 13½×14.
838 90 c. Type **150** 40 45
839 $1.15, Cushion Star 50 55
840 $1.50, Rock Beauty 65 70
841 $3.50, French Grunt .. .. 1·50 1·60
838/41 .. .. *Set of* 4 2·75 3·00
MS842 103×76 mm. $5 Trunkfish .. .. 2·10 2·25

1991 (27 Feb). *Nos.* 760/1, 768 *and* 771 *surch as T* **151.**
843 5 c. on 20 c. Globular Coral Shell 10 10
844 5 c. on 25 c. Sundial 10 10
845 $1.15 on $1.50, Queen Conch 50 55
846 $1.15 on $7.50, Beau's Murex 50 55
843/6 .. .. *Set of* 4 1·00 1·10

152 Duck

153 *Panaeolus antillarum*

(Des K. West. Litho Questa)

1991 (29 May). *Domestic Birds. T* **152** *and similar horiz designs. Multicoloured. P* 14.
847 90 c. Type **152** 40 45
848 $1.15, Hen and chicks 50 55
849 $1.50, Rooster 65 70
850 $3.50, Helmeted Guinea Fowl .. .. 1·50 1·60
847/50 .. .. *Set of* 4 2·75 3·00

(Des M. Pollard. Litho Questa)

1991 (13 June). *Fungi. T* **153** *and similar square designs. P* 14.
851 90 c. olive-grey 40 45
852 $1.15, rosine 50 55
853 $1.50, yellow-brown 65 70
854 $2 maroon 85 90
855 $3.50, dull ultramarine .. .. .. 1·50 1·60
851/5 .. .. *Set of* 5 3·50 3·75
Designs:—$1.15, *Cantharellus cinnabarinus*; $1.50, *Gymnopilus chrysopellus*; $2.00, *Psilocybe cubensis*; $3.50, *Leptonia caeruleocapitata*.

154 Red Water Lily

155 Tree Frog

(Des M. Pollard. Litho Questa)

1991 (8 Aug). *Lilies. T* **154** *and similar vert designs. Multicoloured. P* 14.
856 90 c. Type **154** 40 45
857 $1.15, Shell Ginger 50 55
858 $1.50, Early Day Lily 65 70
859 $3.50, Anthurium .. .. 1·50 1·60
856/9 .. .. *Set of* 4 2·75 3·00

(Des M. Pollard. Litho B.D.T.)

1991 (9 Oct). *Frogs and Toad. T* **155** *and similar multi-coloured designs. P* 14.

860 $1.15, Type **155** 50 55
861 $2 Crapaud Toad 85 90
862 $3.50, Mountain Chicken (frog) 1·50 1·60
860/2 *Set of* 3 2·50 2·75
MS863 110×110 mm. $5 Tree Frog, Crapaud Toad and Mountain Chicken (76½×44 *mm*). P 15×14 2·10 2·25

156 Black British Shorthair Cat

(Des M. Pollard. Litho B.D.T.)

1991 (5 Dec). *Cats. T* **156** *and similar horiz designs. Multicoloured. P* 14.

864 90 c. Type **156** 40 45
865 $1.15, Seal Point Siamese 50 55
866 $1.50, Silver Tabby Persian 60 65
867 $2.50, Birman Temple Cat 1·00 1·10
868 $3.50, Egyptian Mau 1·40 1·50
864/8 *Set of* 5 3·50 3·75

157 Navigational Instruments

(Des M. Pollard. Litho Questa)

1992 (16 Jan). *500th Anniv of Discovery of America by Columbus. T* **157** *and similar horiz designs. Multicoloured. P* 14.

869 $1.50, Type **157** 65 70
 a. Sheetlet. Nos. 869/75 5·25
870 $1.50, Columbus and coat of arms 65 70
871 $1.50, Landfall on the Bahamas 65 70
872 $1.50, Petitioning Queen Isabella 65 70
873 $1.50, Tropical birds 65 70
874 $1.50, Tropical fruits 65 70
875 $3 Ships of Columbus (81×26 *mm*) 1·25 1·50
869/75 *Set of* 7 5·25 5·75

Nos. 869/75 were printed together, *se-tenant*, in sheetlets of 7 with decorative margins.

OFFICIAL STAMPS

O.H.M.S. **O.H.M.S.**
(O 1) (O 2)

1976 (12 Apr). *Various stamps, some already surcharged, optd locally with Type* O 1.

O1 5 c. multicoloured (No. 246A) † 65
O2 10 c. multicoloured (No. 247A) † 75
 a. Opt double † 25·00
 b. Horiz pair, one stamp without opt † £250
O3 30 c. on 10 c. multicoloured (No. 369) † 1·50
 a. Opt double † 40·00
O4 45 c. on 3 c. multicoloured (No. 370) † 2·00
O5 $5 multicoloured (No. 254A) † £100
O6 $10 multicoloured (No. 254*a*B) † £550
O1/6 *Set of* 6 † £600

These stamps were issued for use on mail from the Montserrat Philatelic Bureau. They were not available for sale in either unused or used condition.

1976 (1 Oct)–**80**. *Nos.* 374/8, 380/2 *and* 384/5 *optd with Type* O **2** locally.

O 7 5 c. Malay Apple † 15
 a. Opt inverted † —
 b. Missing stop after "S" † 1·50
O 8 10 c. Jacaranda † 20
 a. Missing stop after "S" † 1·50
O 9 15 c. Orchid Tree † 25
 a. Opt inverted † 70·00
 b. Missing stop after "S" † 1·50
O10 20 c. Manjak † 30
 a. Opt inverted † 70·00
 b. Chalk-surfaced paper (1980) † —
 c. Missing stop after "S" † 1·50
O11 25 c. Tamarind † 35
 a. Missing stop after "S" † 1·50
O12 55 c. Pink Cassia † 55
 a. Opt inverted † —
 b. Opt double † —
 c. Missing stop after "S" † 2·50
O13 70 c. Long John † 60
 a. Missing stop after "S" † 3·50
O14 $1 Saman † 95
 a. Opt inverted † —
 b. Missing stop after "S" † 5·00
O15 $5 Yellow Poui † 4·50
 a. Missing stop after "S" † 13·00
O16 $10 Flamboyant (14.4.80) † 7·50
 a. Missing stop after "S" † 20·00
O7/16 *Set of* 10 † 14·00

Nos. O7/16 were not available in an unused condition, but were sold to the public cancelled-to-order.

The missing stop after "S" variety occurs on R. 1/3 and 3/5.

O.H.M.S. O.H.M.S. O.H.M.S. 45¢
(O 3) (O 4) (O 5)

1980 (7 July). *Nos.* 374/8, 380/2 *and* 384/5 *optd with Type* O 3 *in Great Britain.*

O17 5 c. Malay Apple † 10
 a. Opt double † —
O18 10 c. Jacaranda † 10
O19 15 c. Orchid Tree † 10
O20 20 c. Manjak † 10
 a. Opt double † 70·00
O21 25 c. Tamarind † 15
O22 55 c. Pink Cassia † 35
 a. Opt double † 25·00
O23 70 c. Long John † 45
O24 $1 Saman † 60
O25 $5 Yellow Poui † 2·75
O26 $10 Flamboyant † 5·50
O17/26 *Set of* 10 † 9·00

Nos. O17/26 were not available in an unused condition, but were sold to the public cancelled-to-order. At least two values, the 20 c. and $1 are, however, known uncancelled.

These stamps were originally intended for issue on 3 November 1980, but certain values were placed on sale from 7 July onwards to meet shortages. Bulk supplies did not arrive on the island until early December 1980.

O.H. M.S.

Spaced "H" and "M" (R. 3/4)

1980 (30 Sept). *Nos.* 374/82, 384/5 *and* 476, *together with surcharges on Nos.* 372, 376 *and* 379, *optd as Type* O **4** *locally.*

O27 5 c. Malay Apple † 10
O28 5 c. on 3 c. Lignum vitae † 10
O29 10 c. Jacaranda † 10
O30 15 c. Orchid Tree † 10
 a. Opt double † —
O31 20 c. Manjak † 15
 a. Opt double † 20·00
O32 25 c. Tamarind † 15
O33 30 c. on 15 c. Orchid Tree † 20
O34 35 c. on 2 c. Cannon-ball Tree † 20
 a. Spaced "H" and "M" † 3·50
O35 40 c. Flame of the Forest † 25
O36 55 c. Pink Cassia † 35
O37 70 c. Long John † 50
O38 $1 Saman † 60
O39 $2.50 on 40 c. Flame of the Forest † 1·75
 a. "O.H.M.S." opt omitted £160
O40 $5 Yellow Poui † 3·50
O41 $10 Flamboyant † 6·50
 a. Opt double † 75·00
O27/41 *Set of* 15 † 13·00

Nos. O27/41 were not available in an unused condition, but were sold to the public cancelled-to-order. No. O39a was, however, found amongst supplies of the postage series.

1981 (20 Mar). *Nos.* 490/4, 496, 498, 500, 502/3 *and* 505 *optd with Type* O **4**.

O42 5 c. Type **91** 10 10
 a. Opt inverted 26·00
O43 10 c. Hogfish 10 10
O44 15 c. Creole Wrasse 10 10
 a. Opt double † —
O45 20 c. Yellow Damselfish 15 15
O46 25 c. Sergeant Major 15 15
O47 45 c. Schoolmaster 25 20
 a. Opt double 38·00
 ab. Opt double, one on reverse 22·00
 b. Opt inverted 38·00
O48 65 c. Bigeye 35 30
 a. Opt inverted 65·00
O49 $1 Rock Beauty 65 65
O50 $3 Fairy Basslet and Blueheads 1·75 1·75
O51 $5 Cherubfish 3·00 3·00
O52 $10 Longsnout Butterflyfish 5·50 3·50
O42/52 *Set of* 11 11·00 9·00

1982 (17 Nov). *Nos.* 510/15 *surch as Type* O **5** *(in one line on Nos.* O54, O56 *and* O58).

O53 45 c. on 90 c. *Charlotte* 25 30
 a. Sheetlet. No. O53 × 6 and No. O54 1·75
 b. Surch double 25·00
 c. Surch inverted 16·00
 d. Surch inverted (horiz pair) 32·00
 e. Horiz pair, one without surch 70·00
O54 45 c. on 90 c. Prince Charles and Lady Diana Spencer 30 30
 b. Surch double 70·00
 c. Surch inverted 50·00
O55 75 c. on $3 *Portsmouth* 35 35
 a. Sheetlet. No. O55 × 6 and No. O56 2·25
 b. Surch double 30·00
 c. Surch inverted 22·00
 d. Surch inverted (horiz pair) 27·00
 e. Horiz pair, one without surch 70·00
 f. Error. Surch on $4 (No. 514) 15·00
 fa. Sheetlet. No. O55f × 6 and No. O56f £150
O56 75 c. on $3 Prince Charles and Lady Diana Spencer 45 45
 b. Surch double 75·00
 c. Surch inverted 30·00
 f. Error. Surch on $4 (No. 515) 70·00
O57 $1 on $4 *Britannia* 50 50
 a. Sheetlet. No. O57 × 6 and No. O58 3·50
 b. Surch double 32·00
 c. Surch inverted 10·00
 d. Surch inverted (horiz pair) 30·00
 e. Horiz pair, one without surch
O58 $1 on $4 Prince Charles and Lady Diana Spencer 60 60
 b. Surch double 80·00
 c. Surch inverted 35·00
O53/8 *Set of* 6 2·00 2·10

Nos. O53d, O55d and O57d show the long surcharge, intended for Nos. O54, O56 or O58, inverted across horizontal pairs of the smaller design. Nos. O54c, O56c and O58c show two examples as Type O **5** inverted on the same stamp.

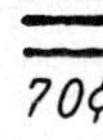

O.H.M.S. O H M S O H M S
(O 6) (O 7) (O 8)

1983 (19 Oct). *Nos.* 542/4 *surch as Type* O **6** *or optd only* ($1).

O59 70 c. on 75 c. Type **97** 60 40
O60 $1 Coat of Arms of Catherine of Aragon 70 50
 a. Opt inverted 40·00
O61 $1.50 on $5 Diana, Princess of Wales 1·00 80
O59/61 *Set of* 3 2·10 1·60

1985 (12 Apr). *Nos.* 600/12 *and* 614 *opt with Type* O **7** *(horizontally on Nos.* O71/5).

O62 5 c. Type **107** 15 15
O63 10 c. Carib Grackle 15 15
O64 15 c. Moorhen 15 15
O65 20 c. Brown Booby 15 15
O66 25 c. Black-whiskered Vireo 20 15
O67 40 c. Scaly-breasted Thrasher 25 20
 a. Opt double † —
O68 55 c. Laughing Gull 35 25
O69 70 c. Glossy Ibis 45 35
O70 90 c. Green Heron 55 40
O71 $1 Belted Kingfisher 70 45
O72 $1.15, Bananaquit 80 60
O73 $3 American Kestrel 1·75 2·00
O74 $5 Forest Thrush 2·50 2·75
O75 $10 Bridled Quail Dove 4·75 3·50
O62/75 *Set of* 14 11·50 10·00

1989 (9 May). *Nos.* 757/70 *and* 772 *optd with Type* O **8**.

O76 5 c. Type **133** 10 10
O77 10 c. Little Knobby Scallop 10 10
O78 15 c. Sozoni's Cone 10 10
O79 20 c. Globular Coral Shell 10 10
O80 25 c. Sundial 10 15
O81 40 c. King Helmet 15 20
O82 55 c. Channelled Turban 25 30
O83 70 c. True Tulip Shell 30 35
O84 90 c. Music Volute 40 45
O85 $1 Flame Auger 40 45
O86 $1.15, Rooster Tail Conch 50 55
O87 $1.50, Queen Conch 65 70
O88 $3 Teramachi's Slit Shell 1·25 1·40
O89 $5 Florida Crown Conch 2·10 2·25
O90 $10 Triton's Trumpet 4·25 4·50
O76/90 *Set of* 15 9·50 10·50

70¢

OHMS

(O 9)

1989 (26 May). *Nos.* 578 *and* 580/1 *optd with Type* O **9**.

O91	70 c. on 10 c. Hogfish	30	35
O92	$1.15 on 75 c. French Grunt	50	55
O93	$1.50 on $2 Blue Chromis	65	70
O91/3	.. .. *Set of* 3	1·25	1·40

Morocco Agencies
(British Post Offices)

With the growth of trade and commerce during the 19th century European powers opened post offices or postal agencies in various ports along the Moroccan coast from the early 1850's onwards. French and, in the north, Spanish influence eventually became predominant, leading to the protectorates of 1912. The British, who had inaugurated a regular postal service between Gibraltar and Tangier or Tetuan in May 1778, established their first postal agency in 1857. German offices followed around the turn of the century.

Before 1892 there was no indigenous postal service and those towns where there was no foreign agency were served by a number of private local posts which continued to flourish until 1900. In November 1892 the Sultan of Morocco established the Cherifian postal service, but this was little used until after its reorganization at the end of 1911. The Sultan's post was absorbed by the French postal service on 1 October 1913. Issues of the local posts and of the Sultan's post can occasionally be found used on cover in combination with stamps of Gibraltar or the Morocco Agencies.

In 1857 the first British postal agency was established at Tangier within the precincts of the Legation and was run by the official interpreter. From 1 March 1858 all letters for Great Britain sent via the British mail packets from Gibraltar required franking with Great Britain stamps.

In 1872 the Tangier office was relocated away from the Legation and the interpreter was appointed British Postal Agent. At the same time the agency was placed under the control of the Gibraltar postmaster. When the colonial posts became independent of the British G.P.O. on 1 January 1886 Gibraltar retained responsibility for the Morocco Agencies. Further offices, each under the control of the local Vice-Consul, were opened from 1886 onwards.

I. GIBRALTAR USED IN MOROCCO

Details of the various agencies are given below. Type C, the "A26" killer, is very similar to postmarks used at Gibraltar during this period. In addition to the town name postmarks as Types A, B and D from Fez, Mazagan, Saffi and Tetuan were also inscribed "MOROCCO".

Postmark Types used on Gibraltar issues.

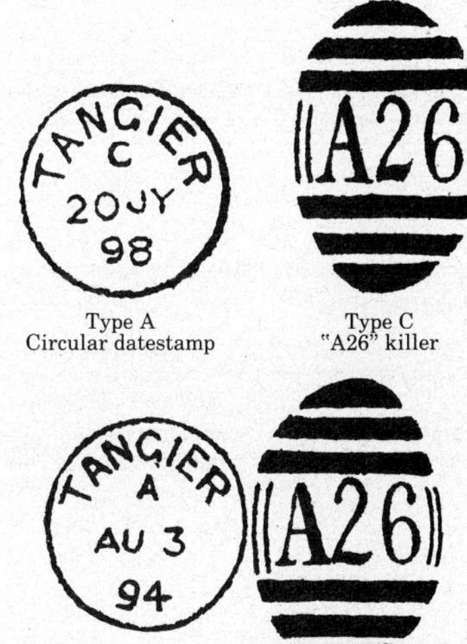

Type A Circular datestamp

Type C "A26" killer

Type B Duplex cancellation

Type D Registered oval

BISECTS. The 10 c., 40 c. and 50 c. values of the 1889 surcharges and of the 1889–96 issue are known bisected and used for half their value from various of the Morocco Agencies. These bisects were never authorised by the Gibraltar Post Office.

CASABLANCA

The British postal agency opened on 1 January 1887 and was initially supplied with ½d., 4d. and 6d. stamps from the Gibraltar 1886 overprinted on Bermuda issue and 1d., 2d. and 2½d. values from the 1886–87 set.

Stamps of GIBRALTAR *cancelled with Types* A (*without code or code* "C"), B (*without code or code* "A") *or* D.

1886 (*Nos.* 1/7).
Z1 ½d. dull green .. 45·00
Z2 4d. orange-brown .. £250
Z3 6d. deep lilac .. £250

1886–87 (*Nos.* 8/14).
Z 4 ½d. dull green .. 20·00
Z 5 1d. rose .. 22·00
Z 6 2d. brown-purple .. 45·00
Z 7 2½d. blue .. 30·00
Z 8 4d. orange-brown .. 70·00
Z10 1s. bistre .. £250

1889 (*Nos.* 15/21).
Z11 5 c. on ½d. green .. 35·00
Z12 10 c. on 1d. rose .. 30·00
Z13 25 c. on 2d. brown-purple .. 40·00
Z14 25 c. on 2½d. bright blue .. 25·00
Z15 40 c. on 4d. orange-brown .. 75·00
Z16 50 c. on 6d. bright lilac .. 65·00
Z17 75 c. on 1s. bistre .. £100

1889–96 (*Nos.* 22/33).
Z18 5 c. green .. 10·00
Z19 10 c. carmine .. 10·00
Z20 20 c. olive-green and brown .. 20·00
Z22 25 c. ultramarine .. 10·00
Z23 40 c. orange-brown .. 25·00
Z24 50 c. bright lilac .. 20·00
Z25 75 c. olive-green .. 55·00
Z26 1 p. bistre .. 50·00
Z28 1 p. bistre and ultramarine .. 25·00
Z29 2 p. black and carmine .. 35·00

FEZ

The British postal agency in this inland town opened on 24 February 1892 and was initially supplied with stamps up to the 50 c. value from the Gibraltar 1889–96 issue.

Stamps of GIBRALTAR *cancelled with Types* A (*without code*) *or* D.

1889–96 (*Nos.* 22/33).
Z31 5 c. green .. 20·00
Z32 10 c. carmine .. 22·00
Z33 20 c. olive-green and brown .. 40·00
Z35 25 c. ultramarine .. 35·00
Z36 40 c. orange-brown .. 60·00
Z37 50 c. bright lilac .. 45·00

LARAICHE

The British postal agency at Laraiche opened in March 1886, although the first postmark, an "A26" killer, was not supplied until May.

Stamps of GIBRALTAR *cancelled with Types* B (*without code*) *or* D.

1886 (*Nos.* 1/7).
Z39 ½d. dull green ..
Z40 1d. rose-red ..
Z41 2½d. ultramarine ..

1886–87 (*Nos.* 8/14).
Z42 ½d. dull green .. 75·00
Z43 1d. rose .. 75·00
Z45 2½d. blue .. 80·00

1889 (*Nos.* 15/21).
Z47 5 c. on ½d. green .. 50·00
Z48 10 c. on 1d. rose ..
Z49 25 c. on 2½d. bright blue ..

It is believed that the other surcharges in this series were not supplied to Laraiche.

1889–96 (*Nos.* 22/23).
Z50 5 c. green .. 20·00
Z51 10 c. carmine .. 30·00
Z52 20 c. olive-green and brown ..
Z54 25 c. ultramarine .. 30·00
Z55 40 c. orange-brown ..
Z56 50 c. bright-lilac .. 65·00
Z57 1 p. bistre and ultramarine ..

MAZAGAN

This was the main port for the inland city of Marrakesh. The British postal agency opened on 1 March 1888 and was initially supplied with stamps from the Gibraltar 1886–87 series.

Stamps of GIBRALTAR *cancelled with Types* A (*codes* "A" *or* "C") *or* D (*without code, code* "A" *or code* "C").

1886–87 (*Nos.* 8/14).
Z58 ½d. dull green .. 18·00
Z59 1d. rose .. 18·00
Z60 2d. brown-purple ..
Z61 2½d. blue .. 25·00
Z62 4d. orange-brown .. 75·00
Z63 6d. lilac .. 90·00

1889 (*Nos.* 15/21).
Z64 5 c. on ½d. green ..
Z65 10 c. on 1d. rose ..
Z66 25 c. on 2½d. bright blue ..

It is believed that the other surcharges in this series were not supplied to Mazagan.

1889–96 (*Nos.* 22/33).
Z67 5 c. green .. 14·00
Z68 10 c. carmine .. 12·00
Z69 20 c. olive-green and brown .. 38·00
Z70 25 c. ultramarine .. 35·00
Z71 40 c. orange-brown ..
Z72 50 c. bright lilac ..
Z74 1 p. bistre and ultramarine ..
Z75 2 p. black and carmine ..

MOGADOR

The British postal agency at this port opened in May 1887 and was initially supplied with stamps from the Gibraltar 1886–87 series.

Stamps of GIBRALTAR *cancelled with Types* A (*code* "C"), B (*code* "C") *or* D.

1886–87 (*Nos.* 8/14).
Z76 ½d. dull green .. 22·00
Z77 1d. rose .. 30·00
Z78 2d. brown-purple .. 45·00
Z79 2½d. blue .. 30·00

1889 (*Nos.* 15/21).
Z80 5 c. on ½d. green .. 35·00
Z81 10 c. on 1d. rose .. 35·00
Z82 25 c. on 2½d. bright blue .. 35·00

It is believed that the other surcharges in this series were not supplied to Mogador.

1889–96 (*Nos.* 22/33).
Z83 5 c. green .. 10·00
Z84 10 c. carmine .. 12·00
Z85 20 c. olive-green and brown ..
Z87 25 c. ultramarine .. 16·00
Z88 40 c. orange-brown .. 25·00
Z89 50 c. bright lilac .. 25·00

RABAT

The British postal agency at this port on the north-west coast of Morocco opened in March 1886, although the first cancellation, an "A26" killer, was not supplied until May. The initial stock of stamps was from the Gibraltar 1886 overprinted on Bermuda issue.

Stamps of GIBRALTAR *cancelled with Types* B (*code* "O") *or* D.

1886 (*Nos.* 1/7).
Z92 ½d. dull green ..
Z93 1d. rose-red ..
Z94 2½d. ultramarine .. £100

1886–87 (*Nos.* 8/14).
Z 95 ½d. dull green .. 20·00
Z 96 1d. rose .. 20·00
Z 97 2d. brown-purple .. 50·00
Z 98 2½d. blue .. 30·00
Z101 1s. bistre .. £300

1889 (*Nos.* 15/21).
Z102 5 c. on ½d. green .. 38·00
Z103 10 c. on 1d. rose .. 35·00
Z104 25 c. on 2½d. bright blue .. 38·00

It is believed that the other surcharges in this series were not supplied to Rabat.

1889–96 (*Nos.* 22/33).
Z105 5 c. green .. 14·00
Z106 10 c. carmine .. 14·00
Z107 20 c. olive-green and brown .. 28·00
Z108 25 c. ultramarine .. 15·00
Z109 40 c. orange-brown .. 35·00
Z110 50 c. bright lilac .. 32·00

SAFFI

The British postal agency at this port opened on 1 July 1891 and was supplied with stamps from the Gibraltar 1889–96 series.

Stamps of GIBRALTAR *cancelled with Types* B (*code* "C") *or* D (*code* "C").

1889–96 (*Nos.* 22/33).
Z111 5 c. green .. 14·00
Z112 10 c. carmine .. 14·00
Z113 20 c. olive-green and brown .. 30·00
Z115 25 c. ultramarine .. 16·00
Z116 40 c. orange-brown ..
Z117 50 c. bright lilac .. 40·00
Z118 1 p. bistre and ultramarine .. 45·00
Z119 2 p. black and carmine .. 50·00

TANGIER

The British postal agency in Tangier opened on 1 April 1857 and from 1 March of the following year letters from it sent via the packet service to Great Britain required franking with Great Britain stamps.

No identifiable postmark was supplied to Tangier until 1872 and all earlier mail was cancelled with one of the Gibraltar marks. In April 1872 a postmark as Type A was supplied on which the "N" of "TANGIER" was reversed. A corrected version, with code letter "A", followed in 1878, but both were used as origin or arrival marks and the Great Britain stamps continued to be cancelled with Gibraltar obliterators. The Type A postmarks generally fell into disuse after 1880 and very few identifiable marks occur on mail from Tangier until the introduction of Gibraltar stamps in 1886.

Stamps of GIBRALTAR *cancelled with Types* A (*codes* "A" *or* "C"), B (*code* "A") *or* D.

1886 (*Nos.* 1/7).
Z120 ½d. dull green .. 40·00
Z121 1d. rose-red .. 50·00
Z122 2d. purple-brown .. £130
Z123 2½d. ultramarine .. 40·00
Z124 4d. orange-brown .. £160
Z125 6d. deep lilac .. £200
Z126 1s. yellow-brown .. £500

1886–87 (*Nos.* 8/14).
Z127 ½d. dull green .. 15·00
Z128 1d. rose .. 15·00
Z129 2d. brown-purple .. 40·00
Z130 2½d. blue .. 25·00
Z131 4d. orange-brown .. 65·00
Z132 6d. lilac .. £100
Z133 1s. bistre .. £225

1889 (*Nos.* 15/21).

Z134 5 c. on ½d. green .. .. 24·00
Z135 10 c. on 1d. rose .. .. 17·00
Z136 25 c. on 2d. brown-purple .. .. 30·00
Z137 25 c. on 2½d. bright blue .. .. 25·00
Z138 40 c. on 4d. orange-brown .. .. 75·00
Z139 50 c. on 6d. bright lilac .. .. 60·00
Z140 75 c. on 1s. bistre £100

1889–96 (*Nos.* 22/33).

Z141 5 c. green .. .. 5·00
Z142 10 c. carmine .. .. 5·00
Z143 20 c. olive-green and brown .. .. 16·00
Z144 20 c. olive-green .. .. 18·00
Z145 25 c. ultramarine .. .. 8·00
Z146 40 c. orange-brown .. .. 10·00
Z147 50 c. bright lilac .. .. 9·00
Z148 75 c. olive-green .. .. 40·00
Z149 1 p. bistre .. .. 50·00
Z150 1 p. bistre and ultramarine .. .. 15·00
Z151 2 p. black and carmine .. .. 35·00
Z152 5 p. slate-grey .. .. 80·00

TETUAN

The British postal agency in this northern town was opened in 1890 and was supplied with stamps from the Gibraltar 1889–96 series.

Stamps of GIBRALTAR *cancelled with Types* A (*code* "C"), B (*code* "C" *often inverted*) *or* D (*code* "C").

1889–96 (*Nos.* 22/33).

Z153 5 c. green .. .. 15·00
Z154 10 c. carmine .. .. 22·00
Z155 20 c. olive-green and brown .. .. 35·00
Z157 25 c. ultramarine .. .. 25·00
Z158 40 c. orange-brown .. .. 40·00
Z159 50 c. bright lilac .. .. 45·00
Z161 1 p. bistre and ultramarine .. ..

PRICES FOR STAMPS ON COVER TO 1945

Nos. 1/16	*from* × 7
Nos. 17/30	*from* × 3
Nos. 31/74	*from* × 3
Nos. 75/6	*from* × 4
Nos. 112/24	*from* × 4
No. 125	—
Nos. 126/35	*from* × 5
Nos. 136/42	*from* × 2
Nos. 143/59	*from* × 3
Nos. 160/75	*from* × 8
Nos. 191/9	*from* × 5
Nos. 200/1	*from* × 3
Nos. 202/11	*from* × 4
Nos. 212/15	*from* × 5
Nos. 216/24	*from* × 8
Nos. 225/6	*from* × 2
Nos. 227/30	*from* × 8
Nos. 231/52	*from* × 6

The above prices apply to stamps used on cover from Morocco. Examples of Nos. 31/76 and 231/52 used on cover in Great Britain after 1950 have little additional value.

II. GIBRALTAR ISSUES OVERPRINTED

With the reversion of Gibraltar to sterling in 1898 it became necessary to provide separate issues for the Morocco Agencies which continued to use Spanish currency.

The following were used in all the British postal agencies.

Morocco Agencies (1)   Morocco Agencies (2)

Agencies — "Λ" for "A" (Right-hand pane R.6/6)   Agencies — Long tail to "S" (Right-hand pane R.8/2)

1898 (1 June)–**1900**. *Stamps of Gibraltar optd with T* **1** (*wide* "M" *and ear of* "g" *projecting upwards*), *in black at* Gibraltar Chronicle *office*.

1 **7** 5 c. green 30 35
a. "Λ" for "A" .. .. 20·00 24·00
b. Long tail to "S" .. .. 20·00 24·00
2 10 c. carmine 30 20
b. Bisected (5 c.) (on cover) .. .. † £1100
c. "Λ" for "A" £225 £275
d. Long tail to "S" £225
e. Lines of opt 5 mm apart (6.00) .. 2·00 1·00
ea. Opt double £550
3 20 c. olive-green .. .. 2·75 2·75
a. Opt double £450
b. "Λ" for "A" .. .. 27·00 32·00
c. Long tail to "S" .. .. 27·00 32·00
d. *Olive-green and brown* .. .. .. 1·50 1·25
db. "Λ" for "A" .. .. 24·00 26·00
dc. Long tail to "S" .. .. 24·00 26·00
4 25 c. ultramarine .. .. 1·50 60
a. "Λ" for "A" £100 £120
b. Long tail to "S" £100 £120
5 40 c. orange-brown (2.6.98) .. .. 2·50 3·25
a. "Λ" for "A" £150 £180
b. Long tail to "S" £150 £180
c. Blue opt (7.98) .. .. 26·00 32·00
6 50 c. bright lilac (2.6.98) .. .. .. 14·00 23·00
a. "Λ" for "A" £250 £275
b. Long tail to "S" £250 £275
c. Blue opt (7.98) .. .. 8·00 12·00
7 1 p. bistre and ultramarine (2.6.98) .. 8·00 20·00
a. "Λ" for "A" £180 £250
b. Long tail to "S" £180 £250
c. Blue opt (7.98) £140 £150
8 **7** 2 p. black and carmine (4.6.98) .. .. 5·00 20·00
a. "Λ" for "A" £225 £275
b. Long tail to "S" £225 £275
1/8 .. .. *Set of* 8 24·00 60·00

The blue overprint can be easily distinguished by looking through the stamp in front of a strong light.

The listed varieties of overprint occur from the first setting. They were corrected on the second setting of July 1898, which produced Nos. 5c, 6c, 7c and further supplies of No. 8. The corrected type was subsequently used to produce additional stocks of Nos. 1/2. Numerous more minor varieties exist from these settings.

No. 2e comes from two further printings in 1900 using a third setting on which the two lines of the overprint were 5 mm apart instead of the 4 mm space used previously.

Agencies — "CD" sideways flaw (Left-hand pane R.1/5)   Morocco — Broad top to "M" (Left-hand pane R.7/3)   Agencies — Hyphen between "nc" (Right-hand pane R.3/5)

1899 (Feb)–**1902**. *Stamps of Gibraltar optd with T* **2** (*narrow* "M" *and ear of* "g" *horizontal*), *in black by D.L.R., London*.

9 **7** 5 c. green (4.99) 25 15
a. "CD" sideways .. .. 8·00 8·00
b. Broad top to "M" .. .. 7·00 7·00
c. Hyphen between "nc" .. .. .. 7·00 7·00
10 10 c. carmine 35 15
a. "CD" sideways .. .. 8·00 8·00
b. Broad top to "M" .. .. 7·00 7·00
c. Hyphen between "nc" .. .. .. 7·00 7·00
d. Opt double £700 £700
11 20 c. olive-green (5.02) .. .. .. 1·50 70
b. Broad top to "M" .. .. 19·00 19·00
c. Hyphen between "nc" .. .. .. 19·00 19·00
12 25 c. ultramarine (10.99) .. .. .. 3·00 90
a. "CD" sideways .. .. 24·00 24·00
b. Broad top to "M" .. .. 20·00 20·00
c. Hyphen between "nc" .. .. .. 20·00 20·00
13 40 c. orange-brown (3.02) .. .. .. 19·00 16·00
b. Broad top to "M" £100 £110
c. Hyphen between "nc" £100 £110
14 50 c. bright lilac (4.99) .. .. .. 5·50 3·50
b. Broad top to "M" .. .. 90·00 £100
c. Hyphen between "nc" .. .. .. 90·00 £100
15 1 p. bistre and ultramarine (4.99) .. 13·00 20·00
b. Broad top to "M" £110 £140
c. Hyphen between "nc" £110 £140
16 2 p. black and carmine (3.01) .. .. 19·00 38·00
b. Broad top to "M" £250 £325
c. Hyphen between "nc" £250 £325
9/16 .. .. *Set of* 8 55·00 70·00
9/16 Optd "Specimen" .. .. *Set of* 8 £180

1903–5. *As T* **8** *of Gibraltar, but with value in Spanish currency, optd with T* **2**. *Wmk Crown CA. P* 14.

17 5 c. grey-green and green (1.03) .. .. 2·50 70
a. "CD" sideways .. .. 22·00 22·00
b. Broad top to "M" .. .. 22·00 22·00
c. Hyphen between "nc" .. .. .. 22·00 22·00
18 10 c. dull purple/*red* (8.03) .. .. .. 2·00 30
a. "CD" sideways .. .. 22·00 22·00
b. Broad top to "M" .. .. 22·00 22·00
c. Hyphen between "nc" .. .. .. 22·00 22·00
19 20 c. grey-green and carmine (9.04) .. 7·00 30·00
a. "CD" sideways .. .. 55·00 £100
b. Broad top to "M" .. .. 55·00 £100
c. Hyphen between "nc" .. .. .. 55·00 £100
20 25 c. purple and black/*blue* (1.7.03) .. 90 15
a. "CD" sideways .. .. 32·00 32·00
b. Broad top to "M" .. .. 32·00 32·00
c. Hyphen between "nc" .. .. .. 35·00 35·00
21 50 c. purple and violet (3.7.05) .. .. 55·00 £110
a. "CD" sideways £250 £400
b. Broad top to "M" £250 £400
c. Hyphen between "nc" £250 £400
22 1 p. black and carmine (19.11.05) .. 45·00 £120
a. "CD" sideways £225 £425
b. Broad top to "M" £225 £425
c. Hyphen between "nc" £225 £425
23 2 p. black and blue (19.11.05) .. .. 48·00 95·00
a. "CD" sideways £250 £400
b. Broad top to "M" £250 £400
c. Hyphen between "nc" £250 £400
17/23 .. .. *Set of* 7 £140 £325
17/23 Optd "Specimen" .. .. *Set of* 7 £180

1905 (Jan)–**06**. *As Nos.* 17/23 *but wmk Mult Crown CA. Ordinary paper* (5, 10, 20 *c.*) *or chalk-surfaced paper* (*others*).

24 5 c. grey-green and green (4.05) 70 75
a. "CD" sideways .. .. 20·00 22·00
b. Broad top to "M" .. .. 20·00 22·00
c. Hyphen between "nc" £600 £650
d. Chalk-surfaced paper (1.06) 70 75
da. "CD" sideways .. .. 20·00 22·00
db. Broad top to "M" .. .. 20·00 22·00
25 10 c. dull purple/*red* .. .. 1·25 30
a. "CD" sideways .. .. 22·00 20·00
b. Broad top to "M" .. .. 22·00 20·00
d. Chalk-surfaced paper (12.05) 65 30
da. "CD" sideways .. .. 20·00 20·00
db. Broad top to "M" .. .. 20·00 20·00
26 20 c. grey-green and carmine (1.06) .. .. 1·50 18·00
a. "CD" sideways .. .. 27·00 70·00
b. Broad top to "M" .. .. 27·00 70·00
27 25 c. purple and black/*blue* (6.06) .. .. 22·00 5·00
a. "CD" sideways £140 £110
b. Broad top to "M" £140 £110
28 50 c. purple and violet (7.06) .. .. 6·00 18·00
a. "CD" sideways £130 £180
b. Broad top to "M" £130 £180
29 1 p. black and carmine (11.05) .. .. 22·00 60·00
a. "CD" sideways £180 £275
b. Broad top to "M" £180 £275
30 2 p. black and blue (11.05) .. .. .. 15·00 32·00
a. "CD" sideways £160 £225
b. Broad top to "M" £160 £225
24/30 .. .. *Set of* 7 60·00 £120

Control of the British postal agencies in Morocco returned to the G.P.O., London, from 1 January 1907.

All the following issues are overprinted on Great Britain

III. BRITISH CURRENCY

Stamps overprinted "MOROCCO AGENCIES" only were primarily intended for use on parcels (and later, air-mail correspondence), and were on sale at British P.Os throughout Morocco including Tangier, until 1937.

PRICES. Our prices for used stamps with these overprints are for specimens used in Morocco. These stamps could be used in the United Kingdom, with official sanction, from the summer of 1950 onwards with U.K. postmarks are worth about 50 per cent less.

MOROCCO AGENCIES (4)   MOROCCO AGENCIES (5)   MOROCCO AGENCIES (6)

1907–13. *King Edward VII optd as T* **4** *or* **5** (*2s. 6d.*)

(*a*) *De La Rue printings. Ordinary paper* (*½d., 1d., 4d.*) *or chalk-surfaced paper* (*others*)

31 ½d. pale yellowish green .. .. .. 75 5·50
32 1d. scarlet .. .. 2·25 2·75
33 2d. grey-green and carmine .. .. .. 2·50 4·50
34 4d. green and chocolate-brown .. .. 15·00 3·25
35 4d. orange (1912) .. .. 3·75 3·50
36 6d. dull purple .. .. 4·75 7·50
37 1s. dull green and carmine .. .. .. 12·00 16·00
38 2s. 6d. pale dull purple .. .. .. 48·00 75·00
39 2s. 6d. dull purple .. .. 48·00 80·00
31/9 .. .. *Set of* 8 80·00 £110
37/8 Optd "Specimen" .. .. *Set of* 2 £140

(*b*) *Later printings* (1913)

40 4d. bright orange (No. 286) .. .. .. 8·00 18·00
41 2s. 6d. dull purple (No. 315) .. .. .. 65·00 £110

1914–31. *King George V.* (*a*) *Optd with T* **4**. *W* **100**.

42 **105** ½d. green 20 45
43 **104** 1d. scarlet 50 10
44 **105** 1½d. red-brown (1921) .. .. .. 1·00 11·00
45 **106** 2d. orange (Die I) .. .. 1·00 35
46 3d. bluish violet (1921) .. .. .. 1·00 35
47 4d. grey-green (1921) .. .. 1·00 70
48 **107** 6d. reddish pur (*chalk-surfaced paper*) (1921) .. .. 3·00 13·00
49 **108** 1s. bistre-brown (1917) .. .. .. 5·00 75
a. Opt triple, two albino .. .. .. 90·00

(*b*) *Optd with T* **6**. (i) *Waterlow printing*

50 **109** 2s. 6d. sepia-brown (1914) .. .. .. 28·00 40·00
a. Re-entry £450 £450
b. Opt double, one albino £150

(ii) *De La Rue printings*

51 **109** 2s. 6d. yellow-brown (1917) .. .. .. 28·00 28·00
a. Opt double (1917) £1500 £1000
52 2s. 6d. grey-brown .. .. 25·00 42·00

(iii) *Bradbury Wilkinson printings*

53 **109** 2s. 6d. chocolate-brown .. .. .. 28·00 25·00
a. Opt double, one albino* £150
54 5s. rose-red (1931) .. .. 48·00 70·00
a. Opt triple, two albino .. .. ..
42/54 .. .. *Set of* 10 80·00 £110
49/50, 54 Optd "Specimen" .. .. *Set of* 3 £200

*The albino overprint is quite clear, with the "MOROCCO" appearing just below "AGENCIES" of the normal overprint and a little to the right as seen from the back. There is also a second faint albino impression just below the normal overprint.

MOROCCO AGENCIES (7)   S (A)   MOROCCO AGENCIES (8)   S (B)

(A) Opt 14 mm long; ends of "s" cut off diagonally.
(B) Opt 15½ mm long; ends of "s" cut off horizontally

1925–36. *King George V, optd with T* **7** (A) *or T* **8** (B). *W* **111**.

				A		B	
55	**105**	½d. green	..	60	30	1·25	20·00
56		1½d. chestnut (1931)	..	9·00	13·00	†	
57	**106**	2d. orange	..	2·00	1·00	†	
58	**104**	2½d. blue ..	..	2·00	5·00	10·00	30·00
59	**106**	4d. grey-green (1.36)		†		3·50	30·00
60	**107**	6d. purple (1931)	..	2·00	8·50	40	60
61	**108**	1s. bistre-brown	..	15·00	5·00	48·00	55·00
55/61 (*cheapest*)		.. *Set of* 7		29·00	50·00		
61A Optd "Specimen"		..	..	60·00			

1935 (8 May). *Silver Jubilee stamps. Optd* "MOROCCO AGENCIES" *only, as in T* **17**.

62 **123** ½d. green (B.) .. .. 1·25 1·75
63 1d. scarlet (B.) .. .. 1·25 3·25
64 1½d. red-brown (B.) .. .. 1·50 7·00
65 2½d. blue (R.) .. .. 1·50 2·50
62/5 .. .. *Set of* 4 5·00 13·00

1935–37. *King George V.* (*a*) *Harrison photo ptgs optd with T* **8**.

66 **119** 1d. scarlet (4.35) .. .. .. 3·00 2·00
67 **118** 1½d. red-brown (28.4.36) .. .. .. 2·00 10·00
68 **120** 2d. orange (1.5.36) 35 60
69 **119** 2½d. ultramarine (11.2.36) .. .. .. 1·75 4·25
70 **120** 3d. violet (2.3.36) 40 15
71 4d. deep grey-green (14.5.36) 40 15
72 **122** 1s. bistre-brown (31.8.36) 80 90

(*b*) *Waterlow re-engraved ptg optd with T* **6**

73 **109** 2s. 6d. chocolate-brown (No. 450) .. 30·00 30·00
74 5s. bright rose-red (No. 451) (2.3.37) .. 22·00 55·00
66/74 .. .. *Set of* 9 55·00 95·00
72/3 Optd "Specimen" .. .. *Set of* 2 £130

1936 (26 Oct)–**37**. *King Edward VIII, optd* "MOROCCO AGENCIES" *only, as in T* **18**.
A. MOROCCO 14½ mm long.
B. MOROCCO 15¼ mm long (5.1.37)

				A		B	
75	**124**	1d. scarlet	.. ..	10	30	2·00	6·50
76		2½d. bright blue	..	10	15	80	4·00

The first two printings of both values showed all the stamps with the short overprint, Nos. 75A/6A.

On 5 January 1937 a further printing of both values was placed on sale in London which had all stamps, 24 in all, from the bottom two horizontal rows (Rows 19 and 20) with the long overprint, Nos. 75B/6B. Subsequent printings increased the number of long overprints in the sheet to 25 by the addition of R. 8/9, and, finally, to 31 (R. 1/7, R. 7/1, R. 8/1, R. 13/3, 4 and 10, R 14/6, but without R. 8/9).

For the 1d. value all sheets from cylinder 2 show the first setting. Sheets from cylinder 6 were also used for the first, and for all subsequent settings. The 2½d. value was overprinted on sheets from cylinder 2 throughout.

From 3 June 1937 unoverprinted stamps of Great Britain were supplied to the post offices at Tangier and Tetuan (Spanish Zone) as local stocks of issues overprinted "MOROCCO AGENCIES" were exhausted.

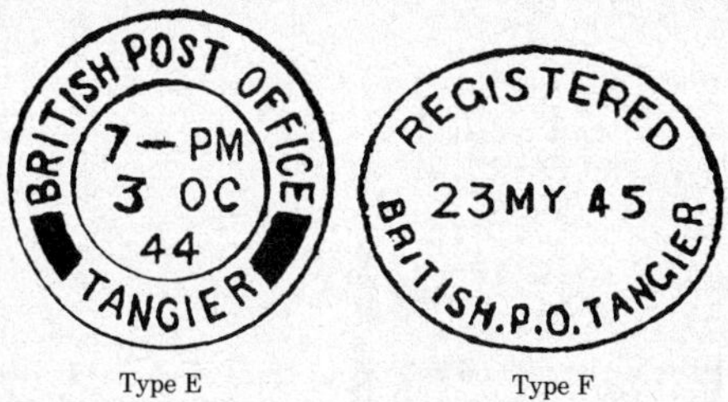

Type E Type F

Stamps of GREAT BRITAIN *cancelled as Types* E *or* F *at Tangier.*

1937. *King George V issues.*
Z170 **118** 1½d. red-brown (No. 441) .. .. ..
Z171 **120** 2d. orange (No. 442) .. .. ..
Z172 3d. violet (No. 444) .. .. ..
Z173 4d. deep grey-green (No. 445) .. ..
Z174 **107** 6d. purple (No. 426*a*) .. .. ..
Z175 **122** 1s. bistre-brown (No. 449) .. ..
Z176 **109** 2s. 6d. chocolate-brown (No. 450) ..
Z177 5s. bright rose-red (No. 451) .. ..

1937–39. (*Nos.* 462/75).
Z178 **128** ½d. green .. ..
Z179 1d. scarlet .. ..
Z180 1½d. red-brown .. ..
Z181 2d. orange .. ..
Z182 2½d. ultramarine .. ..
Z183 3d. violet .. ..
Z184 **129** 4d. grey-green .. ..
Z185 5d. brown .. ..
Z186 6d. purple .. ..
Z187 **130** 7d. emerald-green .. ..
Z188 8d. bright carmine .. ..
Z189 9d. deep olive-green .. ..
Z190 10d. turquoise-blue .. ..
Z191 1s. bistre-brown .. ..

1939–42. (*Nos.* 476/8*a*).
Z192 **131** 2s. 6d. brown .. ..
Z193 2s. 6d. yellow-green .. .. ..
Z194 5s. red .. ..
Z195 **132** 10s. dark blue .. ..
Z196 10s. ultramarine .. ..

1941–42. (*Nos.* 485/90).
Z197 **128** ½d. pale green .. ..
Z198 1d. pale scarlet .. ..
Z199 1½d. pale red-brown .. ..
Z200 2d. pale orange .. ..
Z201 2½d. light ultramarine .. .. ..
Z202 3d. pale violet .. ..

1946. *Victory* (*Nos.* 491/2).
Z203 **135** 2½d. ultramarine .. ..
Z204 **136** 3d. violet .. ..

Type G

Stamps of GREAT BRITAIN *cancelled as Type* G *at Tetuan.*

1937. *King George V issue.*
Z210 **107** 6d. purple (No. 426*a*) .. .. ..

1937–39. (*Nos.* 465/75)
Z211 **128** 2d. orange .. ..
Z212 2½d. ultramarine .. ..
Z213 3d. violet .. ..
Z214 **129** 4d. grey-green .. ..
Z215 6d. purple .. ..
Z216 **130** 9d. deep olive-green .. ..
Z217 1s. bistre-brown .. ..

1939–42. (*Nos.* 476/7).
Z218 **131** 2s. 6d. brown .. ..
Z219 2s. 6d. yellow-green .. .. ..
Z220 5s. red .. ..

1941. (*Nos.* 485/90).
Z221 **128** ½d. pale green .. ..
Z222 2d. pale orange .. ..
Z223 2½d. light ultramarine .. ..
Z224 3d. pale violet .. ..

Other unoverprinted stamps of Great Britain are known with Morocco Agencies postmarks during this period, but it is believed that only Nos. Z170/224 were sold by the local post offices.

The use of unoverprinted stamps in Tangier ceased with the issue of Nos. 261/75 on 1 January 1949. Stamps overprinted "MOROCCO AGENCIES" replaced the unoverprinted values at Tetuan on 16 August 1949.

MOROCCO AGENCIES (9) MOROCCO AGENCIES (10)

1949 (16 Aug). *King George VI, optd with T* **9** *or* **10** (2*s.* 6*d.*, 5*s.*).
77 **128** ½d. pale green .. .. 1·25 1·25
78 1d. pale scarlet .. .. 1·75 3·50
79 1½d. pale red-brown .. .. 2·00 2·75
80 2d. pale orange .. .. 2·00 3·50
81 2½d. light ultramarine .. .. .. 2·25 3·50
82 3d. pale violet 80 45
83 **129** 4d. grey-green 35 50
84 5d. brown .. .. 2·00 5·50
85 6d. purple .. .. 70 1·00
86 **130** 7d. emerald-green .. .. 40 7·50
87 8d. bright carmine .. .. 1·75 4·25
88 9d. deep olive-green .. .. 40 6·00
89 10d. turquoise-blue .. .. 40 4·00
90 11d. plum .. .. 70 3·75
91 1s. bistre-brown .. .. 2·00 3·25
92 **131** 2s. 6d. yellow-green .. .. 8·50 18·00
93 5s. red .. .. 26·00 35·00
77/93 .. .. *Set of* 17 48·00 90·00

1951 (3 May). *King George VI* (Nos. 503/7, 509/10), *optd with T* **9** *or* **10** (2*s.* 6*d.*, 5*s.*).
94 **128** ½d. pale orange 70 30
95 1d. light ultramarine 70 30
96 1½d. pale green 70 50
97 2d. pale red-brown 70 75
98 2½d. pale scarlet 70 40
99 **147** 2s. 6d. yellow-green .. .. 8·50 13·00
100 **148** 5s. red .. .. 10·00 16·00
94/100 .. .. *Set of* 7 20·00 28·00

1952–55. *Queen Elizabeth II* (*Tudor Crown wmk*), *optd with T* **9**.
101 **154** ½d. orange-red (31.8.53) 10 10
102 1d. ultramarine (31.8.53) 15 40
103 1½d. green (5.12.52) 15 10
104 2d. red-brown (31.8.53) 20 50
105 **155** 2½d. carmine-red (5.12.52) 25 10
106 **156** 4d. ultramarine (1.3.55) .. .. 60 1·50
107 **157** 5d. brown (6.7.53) 65 60
108 6d. reddish purple (1.3.55) .. .. 50 1·50
109 **158** 8d. magenta (6.7.53) .. .. .. 1·25 1·00
110 **159** 1s. bistre-brown (6.7.53) 70 60
101/110 .. .. *Set of* 10 4·00 5·50

1956 (10 Sept). *Queen Elizabeth II* (*St. Edward's Crown wmk*), *optd with T* **9**.
111 **155** 2½d. carmine-red (No. 544) .. .. 55 2·25

Stamps overprinted "MOROCCO AGENCIES" were withdrawn from sale on 31 December 1956.

IV. SPANISH CURRENCY

Stamps surcharged in Spanish currency were sold at British P.Os. throughout Morocco until the establishment of the French Zone and the Tangier International Zone, when their use was confined to the Spanish Zone.

During this period further British postal agencies were opened at Alcazar (1907–1916), Fez-Mellah (Jewish quarter) (1909), Marrakesh (1909), Marrakesh–Mellah (Jewish quarter) (1912–14), and Mequinez (1907–1916).

MOROCCO AGENCIES 5 CENTIMOS (11) MOROCCO AGENCIES 6 PESETAS (12)

1907–13. *King Edward VII, surch as T* **11** (5 *c. to* 1 *p.*) *or* **12** (3 *p. to* 12 *p.*). (*a*) *De La Rue printings. Ordinary paper* (*Nos.* 112/13, 116, 118, 122/3) *or chalk-surfaced paper* (*others*).
112 5 c. on ½d. pale yellowish green 45 15
113 10 c. on 1d. scarlet 85 10
114 15 c. on 1½d. purple and green 70 15
a. "1" of "15" omitted £2750
115 20 c. on 2d. grey-green and carmine .. 60 15
116 25 c. on 2½d. ultramarine 85 15
117 40 c. on 4d. green and chocolate-brown .. 90 1·75
118 40 c. on 4d. orange (1910) 35 60
119 50 c. on 5d. purple and ultramarine .. 1·10 80
120 1 p. on 10d. purple and carmine .. .. 6·00 5·50
a. No cross on crown
121 3 p. on 2s. 6d. pale dull purple .. .. 17·00 23·00
122 6 p. on 5s. carmine .. .. .. 35·00 45·00
123 12 p. on 10s. ultramarine .. .. .. 75·00 75·00
112/123 .. .. *Set of* 12 £120 £130
117, 123 Optd "Specimen" .. .. *Set of* 2 £140

(*b*) *Harrison printing*
124 25 c. on 2½d. bright blue (No. 283) (1912) .. 16·00 14·00

(*c*) *Somerset House printing*
125 12 p. on 10s. bright blue (No. 319) (1913) .. £140 £200

1912. *King George V, surch as T* **11**.
126 5 c. on ½d. green (No. 339) 90 10
127 10 c. on 1d. scarlet (No. 342) 50 10
a. No cross on crown .. .. .. £110 55·00

MOROCCO AGENCIES 3 CENTIMOS (13) MOROCCO AGENCIES 10 CENTIMOS (14)

MOROCCO AGENCIES 15 CENTIMOS (15) MOROCCO AGENCIES 6 PESETAS (16)

1914–26. *King George V.* (*a*) *Surch as T* **11** (5 *c.*), **13** (3 *c. and* 40 *c*)*, **15** (15 *c.*) *and* **14** (*remainder*). *W* **100**.
128 **105** 3 c. on ½d. green (1917) .. .. 20 2·50
129 5 c. on ½d. green 30 10
130 **104** 10 c. on 1d. scarlet 30 10
131 **105** 15 c. on 1½d. red-brown (1915) 30 10
a. Surch double, one albino .. .. 75·00
132 **106** 20 c. on 2d. orange (Die I) 25 25
a. Surch double, one albino .. .. 75·00
133 **104** 25 c. on 2½d. blue (*shades*) 50 25
134 **106** 40 c. on 4d. grey-green (1917) .. .. 1·50 4·00
a. Surch double, one albino .. ..
135 **108** 1p. on 10d. turquoise-blue .. .. 1·25 3·00

*The surcharge on Nos. 134, 148 and 158 is as T **13** for the value and T **15** for "MOROCCO AGENCIES".

(*b*) *Surch as T* **16**. (i) *Waterlow printings*
136 **109** 6 p. on 5s. rose-carmine .. .. .. 27·00 48·00
a. Surch double, one albino £110
b. Surch triple, two albino .. ..
137 6 p. on 5s. pale rose-carmine £130 £180
a. Surch double, one albino £150
138 12 p. on 10s. indigo-blue (R.) £100 £150
a. Surch double, one albino £250
b. Surch triple, two albino .. ..
136, 138 Optd "Specimen" .. .. *Set of* 2 £180

(ii) *De La Rue printings*
139 **109** 3 p. on 2s. 6d. grey-brown (1918) .. 25·00 70·00
a. Surch double, one albino ..
140 3 p. on 2s. 6d. yellow-brown .. .. 25·00 85·00
a. Surch double, one albino ..
141 12 p. on 10s. blue (R.) £110 £160
a. Surch double, one albino £300

(iii) *Bradbury Wilkinson printings*
142 **109** 3 p. on 2s. 6d. chocolate-brown (1926) 23·00 50·00
128/142 .. .. *Set of* 11 £140 £225

1925–31. *King George V, surch as T* **11**, **13**, **14** *or* **15**. *W* **111**.
143 **105** 5 c. on ½d. green (1931) .. .. 40 6·50
144 **104** 10 c. on 1d. scarlet (1929) .. .. 9·00 14·00
145 **105** 15 c. on 1½d. red-brown .. .. 7·00 14·00
146 **106** 20 c. on 2d. orange (1931) .. .. 3·00 5·50
a. Surch double, one albino .. .. 85·00
147 **104** 25 c. on 2½d. blue 65 30
148 **106** 40 c. on 4d. grey-green (1930) 65 30
a. Surch double, one albino .. ..
143/148 .. .. *Set of* 6 18·00 35·00

MOROCCO AGENCIES 10 CENTIMOS (17) MOROCCO AGENCIES 10 CENTIMOS (18)

1935 (8 May). *Silver Jubilee, surch as T* **17**.
149 **123** 5 c. on ½d. green (B.) .. .. .. 1·00 45
150 10 c. on 1d. scarlet (B) .. .. .. 2·75 2·25
a. Pair, one with "CENTIMES" .. £1100
151 15 c. on 1½d. red-brown (B.) .. .. 1·40 7·50
152 25 c. on 2½d. blue (R.) .. .. .. 5·50 2·25
149/52 .. .. *Set of* 4 9·50 11·00

No. 150a occurred on R. 5/4 of a small second printing made in June 1935. The error can only be identified when *se-tenant* with a normal No. 150. Beware of forgeries.

1935–37. *King George V, surch as T* **11**, **13**, **14** *or* **15**.
153 **118** 5 c. on ½d. green (9.6.36) .. .. 65 5·50
154 **119** 10 c. on 1d. scarlet (11.36) .. .. 2·25 2·75
155 **118** 15 c. on 1½d. red-brown (4.35) .. .. 2·50 3·25
156 **120** 20 c. on 2d. orange (26.10.36) 30 25
157 **119** 25 c. on 2½d. ultramarine (8.9.36) .. 1·25 3·75
158 **120** 40 c. on 4d. deep grey-green (18.5.37) .. 35 3·00
159 **122** 1 p. on 10d. turquoise-blue (14.4.37) .. 50 30
153/159 .. .. *Set of* 7 7·00 17·00

1936 (26 Oct)–**37**. *King Edward VIII, surch as T* **18**.
A. "MOROCCO" 14¼ mm long.
B. "MOROCCO" 15¼ mm long (5.1.37)

			A		B	
160 **124**	5 c. on ½d. green ..		10	10	†	
161	10 c. on 1d scarlet ..		50	50	1·50	3·25
162	15 c. on 1½d. red-brown		10	10	†	
163	25 c. on 2½d. bright blue		10	10	†	
160/3 ..	.. *Set of* 4		65	65		

The first three printings of the 10 c. on 1d. (from cyls 4, 5 and 6) showed all stamps with the short surcharge (No. 161A).

On 5 January 1937 a further printing was placed on sale in

London which had 49 stamps in the sheet (R. 1/2 to 11, R. 2/1, 5 and 6, 8 and 9, R. 3/5, R. 4/5, R. 5/4 and 5, 10, R. 6/6 and 7, R. 7/8, R. 8/8, R. 9/8, R. 11/7, 9, R.13/2 to 5, 7 and 8, R. 14/1, 7, R. 15/7, 11, R. 16/5, 10, R. 17/4, 10 and 11, R. 18/1, R. 19/2, R. 20/1 and 2, 3, 7, 9) with the long surcharge (No. 161B). The next printing increased the number of long surcharges in the sheet to 50 (R. 10/2), but the final version, although retaining 50 long surcharges, showed them on R. 1/2 to 11, R. 17/5 to 8 and the entire rows 18, 19 and 20. The first two printings with long surcharges were from cylinder 6 and the last from cylinder 13.

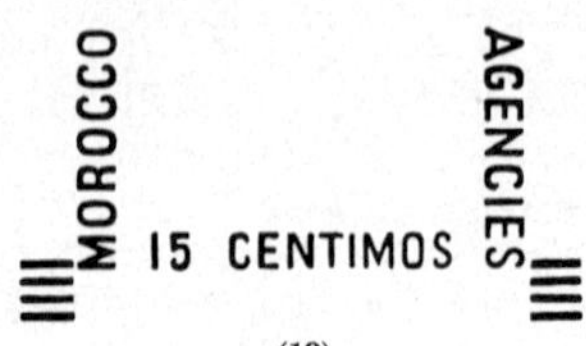

(19)

1937 (13 May). *Coronation, surch as T* **19**.
164 **126** 15 c. on 1½d. maroon (B.) 30 20

MOROCCO AGENCIES (20) — MOROCCO AGENCIES (21)

10 CENTIMOS (20) — 10 CENTIMOS (21)

1937 (June)–**52**. *King George VI, surch as T* **20**.
165 **128** 5 c. on ½d. green (B.) 45 15
166 10 c. on 1d. scarlet 40 10
167 15 c. on 1½d. red-brown (B.) (4.8.37) 45 25
168 25 c. on 2½d. ultramarine 50 50
169 **129** 40 c. on 4d. grey-green (9.40) 6·50 6·00
170 **130** 70 c. on 7d. emerald-green (9.40) 50 5·00
171 1 p. on 10d. turquoise-blue (16.6.52) 30 3·50
165/171 *Set of* 7 8·00 14·00

1940 (6 May). *Centenary of First Adhesive Postage Stamps, surch as T* **21**.
172 **134** 5 c. on ½d. green (B.) 25 1·00
173 10 c. on 1d. scarlet 1·00 1·50
174 15 c. on 1½d. red-brown (B.) 25 1·25
175 25 c. on 2½d. ultramarine 25 50
172/5 *Set of* 4 1·60 3·75

25 CENTIMOS

45 PESETAS MOROCCO AGENCIES

MOROCCO AGENCIES (22) — (23)

1948 (26 Apr). *Silver Wedding, surch with T* **22** *or* **23**.
176 **137** 25 c. on 2½d. ultramarine 30 15
177 **138** 45 p. on £1 blue 15·00 22·00

1948 (29 July). *Olympic Games, variously surch as T* **22**.
178 **139** 25 c. on 2½d. ultramarine 30 40
179 **140** 30 c. on 3d. violet 30 40
180 **141** 60 c. on 6d. bright purple 30 40
181 **142** 1 p. 20 c. on 1s. brown 45 40
a. Surch double £550
178/81 *Set of* 4 1·25 1·40

1951 (3 May)–**52**. *King George VI, surch as T* **20**.
182 **128** 5 c. on ½d. pale orange 1·25 1·25
183 10 c. on 1d. light ultramarine 2·00 1·00
184 15 c. on 1½d. pale green 1·25 3·00
185 25 c. on 2½d. pale scarlet 1·25 1·50
186 **129** 40 c. on 4d. light ultramarine (26.5.52) 50 8·00
182/6 *Set of* 5 5·75 13·50

1954–55. *Queen Elizabeth II (Tudor Crown wmk), surch as T* **20**.
187 **154** 5 c. on ½d. orange-red (1.9.54) 10 50
188 10 c. on 1d. ultramarine (1.3.55) 30 40

1956. *Queen Elizabeth II (St. Edward's Crown wmk), surch as T* **20**.
189 **154** 5 c. on ½d. orange-red (June) 15 30
190 **156** 40 c. on 4d. ultramarine (15 Aug) 70 1·50

The British postal agency at Laraiche closed on 30 June 1938. Stamps surcharged in Spanish currency were withdrawn from sale when the Tetuan agency closed on 31 December 1956.

V. FRENCH CURRENCY

For use in the British postal agencies at Casablanca (closed 14.8.37), Fez (closed 8.1.38), Fez–Mellah (closed after 1930), Marrakesh (closed 14.8.37), Mazagan (closed 14.8.37), Mogador (closed 31.10.33), Rabat (closed 8.1.38) and Saffi (closed 14.8.37).

MOROCCO AGENCIES 25 CENTIMES (24) — MOROCCO AGENCIES 1 FRANC (25)

1917–24. *King George V, surch as T* **24** *or* **25** (1 *f*.). W **100**.
191 **105** 3 c. on ½d. green (R.) 15 2·50
192 5 c. on ½d. green 10 10
193 **104** 10 c. on 1d. scarlet 75 15
194 **105** 15 c. on 1½d. red-brown 80 15
195 **104** 25 c. on 2½d. blue 30 15
196 **106** 40 c. on 4d. slate-green 70 25
197 **107** 50 c. on 5d. yellow-brown (1923) 70 2·50
198 **108** 75 c. on 9d. olive-green (1924) 50 75
199 1 f. on 10d. turquoise-blue 1·50 70
a. Opt double, one albino 85·00
191/9 *Set of* 9 4·75 6·50

1924–32. *King George V, surch as T* **25**, *but closer vertical spacing*.
200 **109** 3 f. on 2s 6d. chocolate brown 7·50 2·00
a. Major re-entry £275 £275
b. *Reddish brown* 20·00 10·00
201 6 f. on 5s. rose-red (1932) 38·00 40·00
200/1 Optd "Specimen" *Set of* 2 £120

1925–34. *King George V, surch as T* **24** *or* **25** (1 *f*.). W **111**.
202 **105** 5 c. on ½d. green 25 5·00
203 **104** 10 c. on 1d. scarlet 30 25
204 **105** 15 c. on 1½d. red-brown 85 1·75
205 **104** 25 c. on 2½d. blue 30 25
206 **106** 40 c. on 4d. grey-green 50 70
207 **107** 50 c. on 5d. yellow-brown 50 10
208 **108** 75 c. on 9d. olive-green 1·50 15
209 90 c. on 9d. olive-green 2·25 3·00
210 1 f. on 10d. turquoise-blue 70 10
211 1 f. 50 on 1s. bistre-brown (Optd S. £50) 3·00 2·25
202/211 *Set of* 10 9·00 12·00

1935 (8 May). *Silver Jubilee, surch as T* **17**, *but in French currency*.
212 **123** 5 c. on ½d. green (B.) 15 15
213 10 c. on 1d. scarlet (B.) 35 50
214 15 c. on 1½d. red-brown (B.) 15 50
215 25 c. on 2½d. blue (R.) 20 15
212/15 *Set of* 4 75 1·10

1935–37. *King George V, surch as T* **24** *or* **25** (1 *f*.).
216 **118** 5 c. on ½d. green (10.35) 45 1·25
217 **119** 10 c. on 1d. scarlet (2.3.36) 35 30
218 **118** 15 c. on 1½d. red brown 1·25 1·50
219 **119** 25 c. on 2½d. ultramarine (25.9.36) 30 15
220 **120** 40 c. on 4d. deep grey-green (2.12.36) 30 15
221 **121** 50 c. on 5d. yellow-brown (15.9.36) 30 15
222 **122** 90 c. on 9d. deep olive-green (15.2.37) 35 55
223 1 f. on 10d. turquoise-blue (10.2.37) 30 30
224 1 f. 50 on 1s. bistre-brown (20.7.37) (Optd S. £50) 30 55

1935–36. *King George V (Waterlow re-engraved ptgs), surch as T* **25**, *but closer vertical spacing*.
225 **109** 3 f. on 2s. 6d. chocolate-brown (No. 450) 4·75 12·00
226 6 f. on 5s. bright rose-red (No. 451) (17.6.36) 6·00 20·00
216/226 *Set of* 11 13·00 32·00
225/6 Optd "Specimen" *Set of* 2 £120

1936 (26 Oct). *King Edward VIII, surch as T* **18**, *but in French currency*.
227 **124** 5 c. on ½d. green 10 15
a. Bar through "POSTAGE" £400
228 15 c. on 1½d. red-brown 10 15

No. 227a was probably caused by a piece of printer's rule. It can be found on various stamps from Row 18, righthand pane.

1937 (13 May). *Coronation, surch as T* **19**, *but in French currency*.
229 **126** 15 c. on 1½d. maroon (B.) 30 20

1937 (June). *King George VI, surch as T* **20**, *but in French currency*.
230 **128** 5 c. on ½d. green (B.) 30 70

Stamps surcharged in French currency were withdrawn from sale on 8 January 1938.

VI. TANGIER INTERNATIONAL ZONE

By an agreement between Great Britain, France and Spain Tangier was declared an international zone in 1924. Stamps overprinted "Morocco Agencies" or surcharged in Spanish currency were used there until replaced by Nos. 231/4.

PRICES. Our note *re* U.K. usage (at beginning of Section III) also applies to "TANGIER" optd stamps.

TANGIER TANGIER (26) — TANGIER (27)

1927. *King George V, optd with T* **26**. W **111**.
231 **105** ½d. green 50 10
a. Opt double, one albino
232 **104** 1d. scarlet 40 10
a. Inverted "Q" for "O" (R. 20/3) £800
233 **105** 1½d. chestnut 2·00 2·00
234 **106** 2d. orange 3·25 10
a. Opt double, one albino 75·00
231/4 *Set of* 4 5·50 2·00

1934 (Dec)–**35**. *King George V, optd with T* **26**.
235 **118** ½d. green (2.35) 1·00 1·40
236 **119** 1d. scarlet 65 70
237 **118** 1½d. red-brown 15 10
235/7 *Set of* 3 1·60 2·00

1935 (8 May). *Silver Jubilee, optd with T* **27**.
238 **123** ½d. green (B.) 1·00 85
239 1d. scarlet 4·25 3·25
240 1½d. red-brown (B.) 1·25 15
238/40 *Set of* 3 6·00 3·50

1936 (26 Oct). *King Edward VIII, optd with T* **26**.
241 **124** ½d. green 10 10
242 1d. scarlet 10 10
243 1½d. red-brown 10 10
241/3 *Set of* 3 25 20

TANGIER TANGIER (28) — TANGIER (29)

1937 (13 May). *Coronation, optd with T* **28**.
244 **126** 1½d. maroon (B.) 40 15

1937. *King George VI, optd with T* **29**.
245 **128** ½d. green (B.) (June) 40 15
246 1d. scarlet (June) 65 20
247 1½d. red-brown (B.) (4 Aug) 60 10
245/7 *Set of* 3 1·50 40

TANGIER (30) — TANGIER (31)

1940 (6 May). *Centenary of First Adhesive Postage Stamps, optd with T* **30**.
248 **134** ½d. green (B.) 20 1·50
249 1d. scarlet 35 30
250 1½d. red-brown (B.) 80 30
248/50 *Set of* 3 1·25 1·90

1944. *King George VI, optd with T* **29**.
251 **128** ½d. pale green (B.) 1·75 60
252 1d. pale scarlet 2·50 1·00

1946 (11 June). *Victory, optd as T* **31**.
253 **135** 2½d. ultramarine 30 20
254 **136** 3d. violet 30 20

The opt on No. 254 is smaller (23 × 2½ mm).

1948 (26 Apr). *Royal Silver Wedding, optd with T* **30**.
255 **137** 2½d. ultramarine 30 15
a. Opt omitted (in vert pair with stamp optd at top) £2250
256 **138** £1 blue 24·00 27·00

No. 255a comes from a sheet in which the overprint is misplaced downwards resulting in the complete absence of the opt from the six stamps of the top row. On the rest of the sheet the opt falls at the top of each stamp instead of at the foot.

1948 (29 July). *Olympic Games, optd with T* **30**.
257 **139** 2½d. ultramarine 55 40
258 **140** 3d. violet 55 30
259 **141** 6d. bright purple 55 40
260 **142** 1s. brown 55 15
257/60 *Set of* 4 2·00 1·10

1949 (1 Jan). *King George VI, optd with T* **29**.
261 **128** 2d. pale orange 2·00 2·00
262 2½d. light ultramarine 35 70
263 3d. pale violet 35 20
264 **129** 4d. grey-green 2·00 4·25
265 5d. brown 75 4·50
266 6d. purple 35 30
267 **130** 7d. emerald-green 55 5·00
268 8d. bright carmine 1·00 4·50
269 9d. deep olive-green 50 5·00
270 10d. turquoise-blue 50 5·50
271 11d. plum 50 6·00
272 1s. bistre-brown 50 75
273 **131** 2s. 6d. yellow-green 4·00 7·50
274 5s. red 9·00 26·00
275 **132** 10s. ultramarine 35·00 65·00
261/275 *Set of* 15 48·00 £120

1949 (10 Oct). *75th Anniv of U.P.U., optd with T* **30**.
276 **143** 2½d. ultramarine 40 50
277 **144** 3d. violet 40 50
278 **145** 6d. bright purple 40 40
279 **146** 1s. brown 40 1·00
276/9 *Set of* 4 1·40 2·25

1950 (2 Oct)–**51**. *King George VI, optd with T* **29** *or* **30** (*shilling values*).
280 **128** ½d. pale orange (3.5.51) 30 30
281 1d. light ultramarine (3.5.51) 50 60
282 1½d. pale green (3.5.51) 50 3·50
283 2d. pale red-brown (3.5.51) 50 90
284 2½d. pale scarlet (3.5.51) 55 45
285 **129** 4d. light ultramarine 45 2·25
286 **147** 2s. 6d. yellow-green (3.5.51) 3·25 2·25
287 **148** 5s. red (3.5.51) 8·50 8·50
288 **149** 10s. ultramarine (3.5.51) 13·00 13·00
280/288 *Set of* 9 25·00 28·00

1952–54. *Queen Elizabeth II (Tudor Crown wmk), optd with T* **29**.
289 **154** ½d. orange-red (31.8.53) 10 20
290 1d. ultramarine (31.8.53) 15 20
291 1½d. green (5.12.52) 10 20
292 2d. red-brown (31.8.53) 20 20
293 **155** 2½d. carmine-red (5.12.52) 10 20
294 3d. deep lilac (B.) (18.1.54) 20 20
295 **156** 4d. ultramarine (2.11.53) 45 85
296 **157** 5d. brown (6.7.53) 60 90
297 6d. reddish purple (18.1.54) 45 15
298 7d. bright green (18.1.54) 80 1·60
299 **158** 8d. magenta (6.7.53) 80 1·50
300 9d. bronze-green (8.2.54) 1·25 75
301 10d. Prussian blue (8.2.54) 1·40 2·75
302 11d. brown-purple (8.2.54) 1·40 3·25
303 **159** 1s. bistre-brown (6.7.53) 50 30
304 **160** 1s. 3d. green (2.11.53) 65 55
305 **159** 1s. 6d. grey-blue (2.11.53) 80 1·75
289/305 *Set of* 17 9·00 14·00

1953 (3 June). *Coronation, optd with T* **30**.

306	**161**	2½d. carmine-red	50	30
307	**162**	4d. ultramarine	1·00	30
308	**163**	1s. 3d. deep yellow-green	1·25	1·25
309	**164**	1s. 6d. deep grey-blue	1·25	60
306/9		*Set of* 4	3·50	2·25

1955 (23 Sept). *Queen Elizabeth II, optd with T* **30**.

310	**166**	2s. 6d. black-brown	3·25	4·50
311	**167**	5s. rose-red	5·00	8·50
312	**168**	10s. ultramarine	18·00	20·00
310/12		*Set of* 3	24·00	30·00

1956. *Queen Elizabeth II (St. Edward's Crown wmk), optd with T* **29**.

313	**154**	½d. orange-red (21 March)	10	10
314		1d. ultramarine (13 April)	20	20
315		1½d. green (22 Oct)	40	75
316		2d. red-brown (25 July)	80	1·50
317		2d. light red-brown (10 Dec)	50	30
318	**155**	2½d. carmine-red (19 Dec)	40	30
319		3d. deep lilac (B.) (22 Oct)	40	50
320	**156**	4d. ultramarine (25 June)	65	2·00
321	**157**	6d. reddish purple (22 Oct)	50	55
322	**160**	1s. 3d. green (26 Nov)	1·75	12·00
313/22		*Set of* 10	5·00	16·00

1857-1957　　**1857-1957**
TANGIER

TANGIER

(32)　　(33)

1957 (1 Apr). *Centenary of British Post Office in Tangier.*

(*a*) *Nos. 540/2 and 543b/56 optd as T* **32** *or* **33** *(7d)*

323	**154**	½d. orange-red	10	10
324		1d. ultramarine	10	10
325		1½d. green	10	10
326		2d. light red-brown	10	10
327	**155**	2½d. carmine-red	15	15
328		3d. deep lilac (B.)	15	10
329	**156**	4d. ultramarine	30	20
330	**157**	5d. brown	30	35
331		6d. reddish purple	30	15
332		7d. bright green	30	30
333	**158**	8d. magenta	30	40
334		9d. bronze-green	30	30
		a. "TANGIER" omitted	£3500	
335		10d. Prussian blue	30	30
336		11d. brown-purple	30	30
337	**159**	1s. bistre-brown	30	30
338	**160**	1s. 3d. green	45	50
339	**159**	1s. 6d. grey-blue	50	55

(*b*) *Nos. 536/8 optd as T* **32**

340	**166**	2s. 6d. black-brown	2·00	2·25
		a. Hyphen omitted	60·00	
		b. Hyphen inserted	20·00	
341	**167**	5s. rose-red	2·75	2·25
		a. Hyphen omitted	60·00	
		b. Hyphen inserted	10·00	
342	**168**	10s. ultramarine	3·50	3·00
		a. Hyphen omitted	70·00	
		b. Hyphen inserted	15·00	
323/42		*Set of* 20	10·50	10·00

Nos. 340a/b, 341a/b and 342a/b occur on R.9/2 in the sheet of 40 (4×10). They are best collected in marginal blocks of four from the bottom left corner of the sheet. Specialists recognise two forms of No. 340b; one where the hyphen on R.9/2 was inserted separately to correct the error, No. 340a; the other from a later printing where a new and corrected overprinting plate was used. (*Price £10 un.*)

All stamps overprinted "TANGIER" were withdrawn from sale on 30 April 1957.

Mosul
see Iraq

Muscat

An independent Arab Sultanate in Eastern Arabia with an Indian postal administration.

The Indian post office at Muscat town is officially recorded as having opened on 1 May 1864. Stamps of India were provided for its use, most surviving examples being of the ½ a. value, although others to the 8 a. are known.

The office was initially included in the Bombay Postal Circle and the first postmark, so far only recorded on stampless covers, was a single circle, 21½ mm in diameter, broken at the top by "MUSCAT" and with the date in two lines across the centre. This was followed by a cancellation showing the post office number, "309", within a diamond of 13, later 16, bars. It is believed that this was used in conjunction with a single ring date stamp inscribed "MUSCAT".

1864 Diamond

In 1869 the office was transferred to the Sind Circle, assigned a new number, "23", and issued with a duplex cancellation. Major reorganisation of the postal service in 1873 resulted in Muscat becoming office "K-4". For ten years from 1873 the cancellations do not, very confusingly, carry any indication of the year of use.

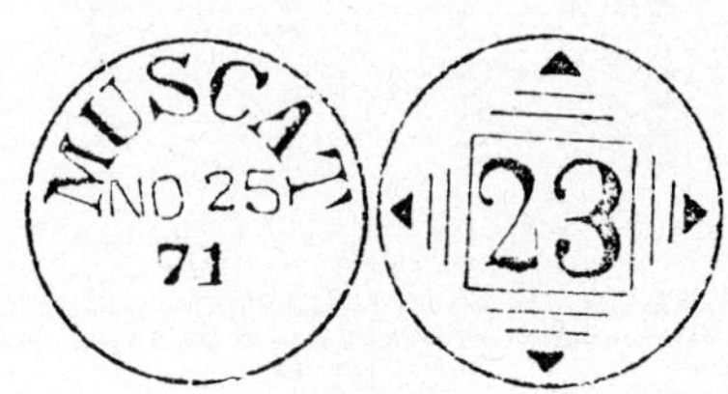

1869 Duplex

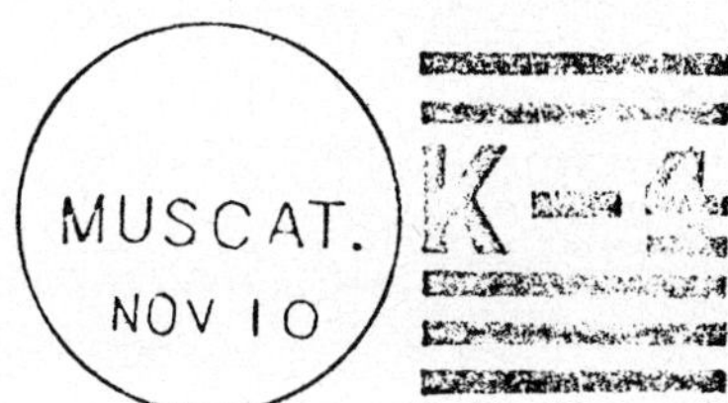

1873 Duplex

Muscat rejoined the Bombay Circle in 1879 and was issued with a cancellation showing a "B" within a square of horizontal bars. The date stamp used at this time was unique in that it carried the inscription "MASKAT", although the spelling reverted to the more usual form by 1882. The square cancellation had been replaced by a similar circular mark by 1884.

Subsequent postmarks were of various circular types, all inscribed "MUSCAT".

There was only one Indian post office in Muscat, but a further office did exist, from 12 April 1868, at the Muscat dependency of Guadur, a port on the Mekran coast of Baluchistan.

No cancellations have been reported from Guadur before its transfer to the Sind Circle in 1869. Cancellations are all similar in style to those for Muscat, Guadur being initially assigned number "24", although an office in Southern India is also known to have used this numeral. The 1869 duplex is interesting in that it is inscribed "GWADUR". Under the 1873 reorganisation the office became "4/K-1", this postmark using the "GUADUR" spelling.

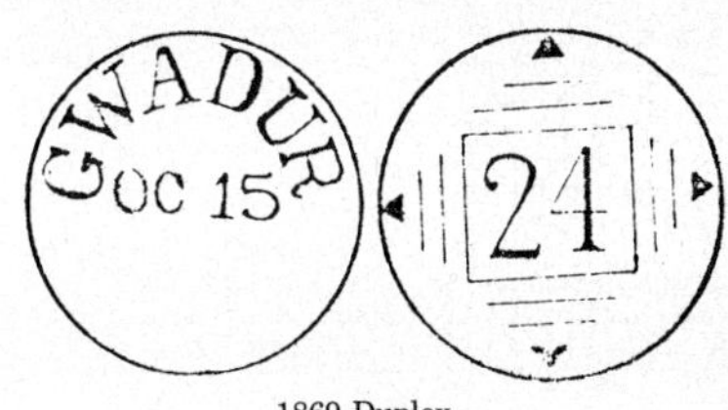

1869 Duplex

PRICES FOR STAMPS ON COVER	
Nos. 1/15	*from* × 100
Nos. O1/10	*from* × 100

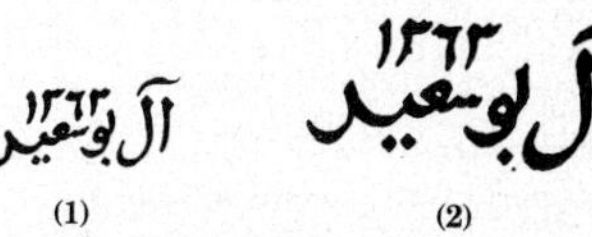

(1)　　(2)

1944 (20 Nov). *Bicentenary of Al-Busaid Dynasty. Stamps of India optd ("AL BUSAID 1363" in Arabic script) as T* **1** *or* **2** *(rupee values).*

1	**100a**	3 p. slate	30	2·50
2		½ a. purple	30	2·50
3		9 p. green	30	2·50
4		1 a. carmine	30	2·50
5	**101**	1½ a. dull violet	30	2·50
6		2 a. vermilion	30	2·50
7		3 a. bright violet	30	2·50
8		3½ a. bright blue	30	2·50
9	**102**	4 a. brown	30	2·50
10		6 a. turquoise-green	45	2·50
11		8 a. slate-violet	40	3·00
12		12 a. lake	70	3·75
13	**103**	14 a. purple	40	5·00
14	**93**	1 r. grey and red-brown	45	7·00
15		2 r. purple and brown	50	12·00
1/15		*Set of* 15	5·00	50·00

OFFICIAL STAMPS

1944 (20 Nov). *Bicentenary of Al-Busaid Dynasty. Official stamps of India optd as T* **1** *or* **2** *(1 r).*

O 1	**O 20**	3 p. slate	50	4·50
O 2		½ a. purple	50	4·50
O 3		9 p. green	50	4·50
O 4		1 a. carmine	50	4·50
O 5		1½ a. dull violet	50	4·50
O 6		2 a. vermilion	50	4·50
O 7		2½ a. bright violet	50	4·50
O 8		4 a. brown	50	5·00
O 9		8 a. slate-violet	50	5·50
O10	**93**	1 r. grey and red-brown (No. O138)	2·00	13·00
O1/O10		*Set of* 10	6·00	50·00

From December 1947 there was a Pakistani postal administration and stamps of Pakistan were used until 31 March 1948. The subsequent British administration operated from 1 April 1948 to 29 April 1966 when the stamps of the BRITISH POSTAL AGENCIES IN EASTERN ARABIA were used.

Later issues for this area will be found listed under OMAN in Part 19 (*Middle East*) of this catalogue.

Nagaland

Labels inscribed "NAGALAND" with currency in cents and chaplees are considered to be propaganda labels.

Namibia

(*formerly* South West Africa)

SOUTH WEST AFRICA

The stamps of Germany were used in the colony from July 1886 until the introduction of issues for GERMAN SOUTH-WEST AFRICA in May 1897. Following occupation by South African forces in 1914–15 the issues of SOUTH AFRICA were used, being replaced by the overprinted issues in 1923.

Walvis (or Walfish) Bay, the major anchorage on the South West Africa coast, was claimed by Great Britain as early as 1796. In 1878 the 430 sq mile area around the port, together with a number of offshore islands, was annexed to Cape Province, passing to the Union of South Africa in 1910.

Stamps of the Cape of Good Hope and South Africa were used at Walfish Bay, often cancelled with numeral obliterator 300, until the enclave was transferred to the South West Africa administration on 1 October 1922.

The Walfish Bay territory reverted to South Africa on 30 August 1977 and from that date the stamps of South Africa were, once again, in use.

PRICES FOR STAMPS ON COVER TO 1945	
Nos. 1/40*a*	*from* × 6
Nos. 41/133	*from* × 2
Nos. D1/5	*from* × 10
Nos. D6/51	*from* × 20
Nos. O1/4	*from* × 3
Nos. O5/20	*from* × 15
No. O21	—
No. O22	*from* × 15

INSCRIPTIONS. Most of the postage stamps up to No. 140 are inscribed alternately in English and Afrikaans throughout the sheets and the same applies to all the Official stamps and to Nos. D30/33.

PRICES for Nos. 1/140 are for unused horizontal pairs, used horizontal pairs or used singles (either inscr), *unless otherwise indicated.*

OVERPRINT SETTINGS. Between 1923 and 1928 the King George V definitives of South Africa, Types **2** and **3**, and the various postage due stamps were issued overprinted for use in South West Africa. A number of overprint settings were used:

- Setting I – Overprint Types 1 and 2 ("Zuid-West Afrika"). 14 mm between lines of overprint. See Nos. 1/12 and D1/9
- Setting II – As Setting I, but 10 mm between lines of overprint. See Nos. 13/15 and D10/13
- Setting III – Overprint Types 3 ("Zuidwest Afrika") and 4. "South West" 14 mm long. "Zuidwest" 11 mm long. 14 mm between lines of overprint. See Nos. 16/27 and D14/17
- Setting IV – As Setting III, but "South West" 16 mm long, "Zuidwest" 12 mm long and 14 mm between lines of overprint. See Nos. 28 and D17*a*/20
- Setting V – As Setting IV, but 12 mm between lines of overprint. See Nos. D21/4
- Setting VI – As Setting IV, but 9½ mm between lines of overprint. See Nos. 29/40 and D25/32.

South West Zuid-West

Africa. Afrika.

(1) (2)

1923 (1 Jan–17 June). *Nos.* 3/4, 6 *and* 9/17 *of South Africa optd alternately with T* **1** *and* **2** *by typography.*

Un pair / *Us pair* / *Us single*

(*a*) *Setting* I (14 *mm between lines of opt*)

1 ½d. green .. .. 1·25 4·50 1·00
 a. "Wes" for "West" (R. 20/8) .. 80·00 £110
 b. "Afr ica" (R. 20/2) £120
 c. Litho opt in shiny ink (17 June) 8·50 32·00 4·00
2 1d. rose-red .. .. .. 1·50 4·50 1·00
 a. Opt inverted £450
 b. "Wes" for "West" (R. 12/2) .. £150
 c. "Af.rica" for "Africa" (R. 20/6) £140 £160
 d. Opt double £750
 e. "Afr ica" (R. 20/2) £120
 f. "Afrika" without stop (R. 17/8) £225
3 2d. dull purple .. .. .. 2·25 7·00 1·50
 a. Opt inverted £550 £600
 b. "Wes" for "West" (R. 20/8) .. £225
 c. Litho opt in shiny ink (30 Mar) 20·00 50·00 8·00
4 3d. ultramarine .. .. .. 7·50 16·00 2·75
5 4d. orange-yellow and sage-green .. 13·00 35·00 4·00
 a. Litho opt in shiny ink (19 Apr) 35·00 60·00 8·00
6 6d. black and violet .. .. 8·00 35·00 4·00
 a. Litho opt in shiny ink (19 Apr) 35·00 65·00 7·50
7 1s. orange-yellow .. .. .. 23·00 48·00 5·00
 a. Litho opt in shiny ink (19 Apr) 60·00 95·00 11·00
8 1s. 3d. pale violet .. .. .. 30·00 55·00 5·50
 a. Opt inverted £250
 b. Litho opt in shiny ink (19 Apr) 75·00 £120 14·00
9 2s. 6d. purple and green .. .. 70·00 £130 18·00
 a. Litho opt in shiny ink (19 Apr) £150 £250 35·00
10 5s. purple and blue .. .. £160 £325 50·00
11 10s. blue and olive-green £1800 £2750 £400
12 £1 green and red £1000 £1800 £250
1/12 .. .. .. *Set of* 12 £2750 £4500 £650
1/12 Optd "Specimen" .. *Set of* 12 *singles* £1500

Nos. 1/12 were overprinted in complete sheets of 240 (4 panes 6×10).

No. 3b shows traces of a type spacer to the right of where the "t" should have been. This spacer is not visible on Nos. 1a and 2b.

Minor varieties, such as broken "t" in "West", were caused by worn type. Stamps showing one line of overprint only or with the lower line above the upper line due to overprint misplacement may also be found. All values exist showing a faint stop after "Afrika" on R.17/8, but only the 1d. has been confirmed as existing with it omitted.

(*b*) *Setting* II (10 *mm between lines of opt*) (31 Mar)

13 5s. purple and blue .. .. £180 £300 60·00
 a. "Afrika" without stop (R.6/1) .. £1700
14 10s. blue and olive-green £650 £1100 £180
 a. "Afrika" without stop (R.6/1) .. £3000 £3500
15 £1 green and red £1300 £1800 £250
 a. "Afrika" without stop (R.6/1) .. £6000
13/15 .. .. .. *Set of* 3 £1900 £3000 £450

Nos. 13/15 were overprinted in separate panes of 60 (6×10).

Zuidwest South West

Afrika. Africa.

(3) (4)

1923 (15 July)–**26**. *Nos.* 3/4, 6 *and* 9/17 *of South Africa optd as T* **3** (*"Zuidwest" in one word, without hyphen*) *and* **4** *alternately.*

(*a*) *Setting* III ("South West" 14 *mm long*, "Zuidwest" 11 *mm long*, 14 *mm between lines of opt*)

16 ½d. green (5.9.24) .. .. 3·25 15·00 2·50
 a. "outh" for "South" (R.1/1) .. £1300
17 1d. rose-red (28.9.23) .. .. 3·25 7·50 1·40
 a. "outh" for "South" (R.1/1) .. £1300
18 2d. dull purple (28.9.23) .. .. 3·25 4·50 1·00
 a. Opt double £850
19 3d. ultramarine .. .. .. 3·50 6·00 1·25
20 4d. orange-yellow and sage-green .. 4·75 14·00 2·50
21 6d. black and violet (28.9.23) .. 11·00 30·00 4·00
22 1s. orange-yellow .. .. .. 14·00 42·00 5·00
23 1s. 3d. pale violet .. .. .. 28·00 45·00 5·50
24 2s. 6d. purple and green .. .. 45·00 80·00 10·00
25 5s. purple and blue .. .. 70·00 £130 18·00
26 10s. blue and olive-green .. .. £200 £300 50·00
27 £1 green and red (28.9.23) .. .. £350 £475 70·00
16/27 .. .. .. *Set of* 12 £650 £1000 £150

Nos. 16/27 were overprinted in complete sheets of 240 (4 panes 6×10).

Two sets may be made with this overprint, one with bold lettering, and the other from September 1924, with thinner lettering and smaller stops.

(*b*) *Setting* IV ("South West" 16 *mm long*, "Zuidwest" 12 *mm long*, 14 *mm between lines of opt*)

28 2s. 6d purple and green (29.6.24) .. 80·00 £150 28·00

No. 28 was overprinted on two panes of 60 horizontally side by side.

(*c*) *Setting* VI ("South West" 16 *mm long*, "Zuidwest" 12 *mm long*, 9½ *mm between lines of opt*)

29 ½d. green (16.12.25) .. .. 4·50 26·00 4·00
30 1d. rose-red (9.12.24) .. .. 1·75 7·00 1·25
31 2d. dull purple (9.12.24) .. .. 3·50 12·00 1·50
32 3d. ultramarine (31.1.26) .. .. 3·50 18·00 2·50
 a. Deep bright blue (20.4.26) .. 50·00 80·00 12·00
33 4d. orge-yellow & sage-grn (9.12.24) 5·00 24·00 3·00
34 6d. black and violet (9.12.24) .. 6·50 30·00 3·75
35 1s. orange-yellow (9.12.24) .. .. 11·00 38·00 4·25
36 1s. 3d. pale violet (9.12.24) .. 14·00 42·00 5·00
37 2s. 6d. purple and green (9.12.24) 35·00 70·00 10·00
38 5s. purple and blue (31.1.26) .. 55·00 £100 14·00
39 10s. blue and olive-green (9.12.24) .. 85·00 £130 20·00
40 £1 green and red (9.1.26) .. .. £350 £450 70·00
 a. Pale olive-green and red (8.11.26) £300 £450 90·00
29/40*a* .. .. .. *Set of* 12 £450 £850 £140
35, 39/40 H/S "Specimen" .. *Set of* 3 £500

Nos. 29/40 were overprinted in complete sheets of 240 (4 panes of 6×10) with, initially, "South West Africa" 16½ mm long on the upper two panes and 16 mm long on the lower two. This order was subsequently reversed. For printings from 8 November 1926 all four panes showed the 16½ mm measurement. No. 40*a* only comes from this printing.

Suidwes Afrika. South West Africa.

(5) (6)

1926 (1 Jan–1 May). *Nos.* 30/2 *of South Africa optd with T* **5** (*on stamps inscr in Afrikaans*) *and* **6** (*on stamps inscr in English*) *sideways, alternately in black.*

41 ½d. black and green .. .. 2·25 8·50 1·00
42 1d. black and carmine .. .. 2·00 7·00 75
43 6d. green and orange (1 May) .. 25·00 48·00 7·00
41/3 .. .. .. *Set of* 3 26·00 55·00 8·00

SOUTH WEST AFRICA SUIDWES-AFRIKA

(7) (8)

1926. *No.* 33 *of South Africa, imperf, optd with T* **7** (E.) *or T* **8** (A.).

Single stamps E A

44 4d. grey-blue .. .. .. 65 2·00 65 2·00

1927. *As Nos.* 41/3, *but Afrikaans opt on stamp inscr in English and vice versa.*

45 ½d. black and green .. .. 1·40 4·50 75
 a. "Africa" without stop (R.13/8) .. £150
46 1d. black and carmine .. .. 1·40 2·50 50
 a. "Africa" without stop (R.13/8) .. £225
47 6d. green and orange .. .. 13·00 25·00 3·00
 a. "Africa" without stop (R.13/8) .. £170
45/7 .. .. .. *Set of* 3 14·50 29·00 3·75

SOUTH WEST AFRICA S.W.A. S.W.A.

(9) (10) (11)

1927. *As No.* 44E, *but overprint T* **9**.

Single stamps

48 4d. grey-blue (H/S S. £70) .. .. .. 7·50 19·00

1927 (Apr). *Nos.* 34/9 *of South Africa optd alternately as T* **5** *and* **6**, *in blue, but with lines of overprint spaced* 16 *mm.*

49 2d. grey and purple .. .. .. 3·75 15·00 1·75
50 3d. black and red .. .. .. 3·75 22·00 2·25
51 1s. brown and blue .. .. .. 14·00 32·00 4·00
52 2s. 6d. green and brown .. .. 45·00 65·00 12·00
53 5s. black and green .. .. .. 75·00 £120 20·00
54 10s. blue and bistre-brown .. .. 85·00 £130 20·00
49/54 .. .. .. *Set of* 6 £200 £350 50·00
49/51, 54 H/S "Specimen" .. *Set of* 4 £350

A variety of Nos. 49, 50, 51 and 54, with spacing 16½ mm between lines of overprint, occurs in the third vertical row of each sheet.

1927. *As No.* 44, *but perf* 11½ *by John Meinert, Ltd, Windhoek.*

Single stamps E A

55 4d. grey-blue .. .. .. 70 3·50 70 3·50
 a. Imperf between (pair) .. 30·00 60·00 30·00 60·00
55 H/S "Specimen" .. .. .. 70·00 70·00

1927 (Aug)–**30**. *Optd with T* **10**. (*a*) *On Nos.* 13 *and* 17*a of South Africa.*

Single stamps

56 1s. 3d. pale violet (H/S S. £70) .. .. 1·25 6·00
 a. Without stop after "A" (R.3/4) .. 90·00
57 £1 pale olive-green and red £140 £180
 a. Without stop after "A" (R.3/4) .. £2250 £3000

(*b*) *On Nos.* 30/2 *and* 34/9 *of South Africa*

Un pair / *Us pair* / *Us single*

58 ½d. black and green .. .. 1·50 4·25 70
 a. Without stop after "A" .. .. 50·00 75·00
 b. "S.W.A." opt above value .. 2·75 13·00 2·25
 c. As b, in vert pair, top stamp without opt £450
59 1d. black and carmine .. .. 1·25 3·25 55
 a. Without stop after "A" .. .. 50·00 75·00
 b. "S.W.A." opt at top (30.4.30) .. 1·75 10·00 1·60
 c. As b, vert pair, top stamp without opt £375
60 2d. grey and maroon .. .. 4·50 8·00 1·10
 a. Without stop after "A" .. .. 75·00 £110
 b. Opt double, one inverted .. £650 £850
61 3d. black and red .. .. .. 6·00 23·00 3·25
 a. Without stop after "A" .. .. 75·00 £120
62 4d. brown (4.28) .. .. .. 18·00 48·00 7·00
 a. Without stop after "A" .. .. 85·00 £130
63 6d. green and orange .. .. 13·00 22·00 2·75
 a. Without stop after "A" £110
64 1s. brown and deep blue .. .. 24·00 42·00 5·00
 a. Without stop after "A" £1700
65 2s. 6d. green and brown .. .. 45·00 75·00 10·00
 a. Without stop after "A" £160 £250
66 5s. black and green .. .. .. 65·00 £100 18·00
 a. Without stop after "A" £225 £350
67 10s. bright blue and brown .. .. £120 £180 28·00
 a. Without stop after "A" £325 £500
58/67 .. .. .. *Set of* 10 £250 £425 70·00
58/61, 63/7 H/S "Specimen" *Set of* 9 £550

On the ½d., 1d. and 6d. the missing stop variety occurs three times on each sheet, R.1/7, 13/4 and one position not yet identified. For the other values it comes on R.2/3 of the right pane and, for the 2s. 6d., 5s. and 10s., on R.8/1 of the left pane.

The overprint is normally found at the base of the ½d., 1d., 6d., 1s. 3d. and £1 values and at the top on the remainder.

1930–31. *Nos.* 42 *and* 43 *of South Africa* (*rotogravure printing*) *optd with T* **10**.

68 ½d. black and green (1931) .. .. 7·00 17·00 2·50
69 1d. black and carmine .. .. 6·00 17·00 2·50

1930 (27 Nov–Dec). *Air. Nos.* 40/1 *of South Africa optd.*

(*a*) *As T* **10**.

Un single / *Us single*

70 4d. green (*first printing*) .. .. .. 12·00 24·00
 a. No stop after "A" of "S.W.A." .. .. 80·00 £110
 b. Later printings .. .. 7·00 24·00
71 1s. orange (*first printing*) .. .. .. 70·00 £110
 a. No stop after "A" of "S.W.A." £400 £500
 b. Later printings .. .. 15·00 48·00

First printing: Thick letters, blurred impression. Stops with rounded corners.

Later printings: Thinner letters, clear impression. Clean cut, square stops.

(*b*) *As T* **11** (12.30)

72 4d. green .. .. 1·25 5·00
 a. Opt double £140
 b. Opt inverted £130
73 1s. orange .. .. 1·50 13·00
 a. Opt double .. ..

12 Kori Bustard

13 Cape Cross

14 Bogenfels

15 Windhoek

16 Waterberg

17 Luderitz Bay

18 Bush Scene

19 Elands

20 Mountain Zebra and Blue Wildebeests

21 Herero Huts

22 Welwitschia Plant

23 Okuwahaken Falls

24 Monoplane over Windhoek

25 Biplane over Windhoek

(Recess B.W.)

1931 (5 Mar). *T* **12** *to* **25** *(inscr alternately in English and Afrikaans).* W **9** *of South Africa. P* 14 × 13½. *(a) Postage.*

74	½d. black and emerald	1·40	1·00	10
75	1d. indigo and scarlet	1·00	2·00	10
76	2d. blue and brown	50	2·00	15
77	3d. grey-blue and blue	50	2·50	15
78	4d. green and purple	80	5·00	20
79	6d. blue and brown	60	6·50	20
80	1s. chocolate and blue	1·00	6·50	25
81	1s. 3d. violet and yellow	8·50	11·00	50
82	2s. 6d. carmine and grey	19·00	22·00	1·75
83	5s. sage-green and red-brown	20·00	40·00	2·75
84	10s. red-brown and emerald	55·00	60·00	7·00
85	20s. lake and blue-green	£110	£110	12·00
	(b) Air			
86	3d. brown and blue	32·00	40·00	3·00
87	10d. black and purple-brown	55·00	80·00	8·50
74/87	*Set of* 14	£275	£350	32·00

26

(Recess B.W.)

1935 (1 May). *Silver Jubilee. Inscr bilingually.* W **9** *of South Africa. P* 14 × 13½.

			Un single	*Us single*
88	**26**	1d. black and scarlet	40	25
89		2d. black and sepia	90	25
90		3d. black and blue	9·00	13·00
91		6d. black and purple	4·50	3·50
88/91		*Set of* 4	13·50	15·00

1935–36. *Voortrekker Memorial Fund. Nos.* 50/3 *of South Africa optd with T* **10**.

92	½d. + ½d. black and green	1·00	4·50	65
	a. Opt inverted	£225		
93	1d. + ½d. grey-black and pink	1·50	3·25	40
94	2d. + 1d. grey-green and purple	5·00	6·00	80
	a. Without stop after "A"	£190		
	b. Opt double	£180		
95	3d. + 1½d. grey-green and blue	15·00	24·00	3·25
	a. Without stop after "A"	£200	£225	
92/5	*Set of* 4	20·00	35·00	4·75

27 Mail Train

28

(Recess B.W.)

1937 (1 Mar). W **9** *of South Africa. P* 14 × 13½.

96	**27**	1½d. purple-brown	8·00	1·50	15

(Recess B.W.)

1937 (12 May). *Coronation.* W **9** *of South Africa (sideways). P* 13½ × 14.

97	**28**	½d. black and emerald	45	15	10
98		1d. black and scarlet	45	15	10
99		1½d. black and orange	55	15	10
100		2d. black and brown	60	15	10
101		3d. black and blue	65	15	10
102		4d. black and purple	70	20	10
103		6d. black and yellow	80	1·50	20
104		1s. black and grey-black	1·25	1·25	20
97/104		*Set of* 8	5·00	3·25	60

1938 (14 Dec). *Voortrekker Centenary Memorial. Nos.* 76/9 *of South Africa optd as T* **11**.

105	½d. + ½d. blue and green	5·50	8·00	1·00
106	1d. + 1d. blue and carmine	12·00	4·50	60
107	1½d. + 1½d. chocolate & blue-green	14·00	15·00	2·00
108	3d. + 3d. bright blue	35·00	25·00	3·75
105/8	*Set of* 4	60·00	48·00	6·50

1938 (14 Dec). *Voortrekker Commemoration. Nos.* 80/1 *of South Africa optd as T* **11**.

109	1d. blue and carmine	5·50	5·50	75
110	1½d. greenish blue and brown	7·50	8·00	1·00

1939 (17 July). *250th Anniv of Landing of Huguenots in South Africa and Huguenot Commemoration Fund. Nos.* 82/4 *of South Africa optd as T* **11**.

111	½d. + ½d. brown and green	4·75	5·00	70
112	1d. + 1d. green and carmine	7·00	6·50	85
113	1½d. + 1½d. blue-green and purple	10·00	9·50	1·25
111/13	*Set of* 3	20·00	19·00	2·50

SWA (29) SWA (30) SWA (31) S W A (32)

1941 (1 Oct)–**43**. *War Effort. Nos.* 88/96 *of South Africa optd with T* **29** *or* **30** *(3d. and 1s.). (a) Inscr alternately.*

114	½d. green (1.12.41)	75	1·25	15
	a. Blue-green (1942)	65	90	15
115	1d. carmine (1.11.41)	55	1·00	15
116	1½d. myrtle-green (21.1.42)	55	1·00	15
117	3d. blue	9·50	5·50	75
118	4d. orange-brown	6·50	4·50	60
	a. Red-brown	10·00	15·00	2·50
119	6d. red-orange	2·50	3·00	50
120	1s. 3d. olive-brown (15.1.43)	7·00	5·50	75

(b) Inscr bilingually

		Un single	*Us single*
121	2d. violet	40	30
122	1s. brown (17.11.41)	60	40
114/22	*Set of 7 pairs and 2 singles*	26·00	20·00

1943–44. *War Effort (reduced sizes). Nos.* 97/104 *of South Africa, optd with T* **29** *(1½d. and 1s., No. 130), or T* **31** *(others).*

(a) Inscr alternately

		Un unit	*Us unit*	*Us single*
123	½d. blue-green (T)	40	1·25	10
	a. Green	2·25	2·50	15
	b. Greenish blue	1·50	1·50	10
124	1d. carmine-red (T)	70	1·00	10
	a. Bright carmine	1·40	1·40	10
125	1½. red-brown (P)	45	50	10
126	2d. violet (P)	2·00	1·50	10
	a. Reddish violet	2·50	1·50	10
127	3d. blue (T)	2·50	5·50	35
128	6d. red-orange (P)	2·00	2·25	30
	a. Opt inverted	£375		
	(b) Inscr bilingually			
129	4d. slate-green (T)	2·00	6·00	40
	a. Opt inverted	£350	£275	50·00
130	1s. brown (opt T **29**) (P)	10·00	12·00	1·40
	a. Opt inverted	£375		
	b. Opt T **31** (1944)	3·25	2·75	30
	c. Opt T **31** inverted	£350	£275	40·00
123/30b	*Set of* 8	12·00	19·00	2·75

The "units" referred to above consist of pairs (P) or triplets (T).

No. 128 exists with another type of opt as Type **31**, but with broader "s", narrower "w" and more space between the letters.

1945. *Victory. Nos.* 108/10 *of South Africa optd with T* **30**.

131	1d. brown and carmine	25	30	10
	a. Opt inverted	£200	£225	
132	2d. slate-blue and violet	30	35	10
133	3d. deep blue and blue	65	55	10
131/3	*Set of* 3	1·10	1·10	20

1947 (17 Feb). *Royal Visit. Nos.* 111/13 *of South Africa optd as T* **31**, *but* 8½ × 2 *mm.*

134	1d. black and carmine	10	10	10
135	2d. violet	10	15	10
136	3d. blue	15	15	10
134/6	*Set of* 3	30	35	15

1948 (26 Apr). *Royal Silver Wedding. No.* 125 *of South Africa, optd as T* **31**, *but* 4 × 2 *mm.*

137	3d. blue and silver	1·25	35	10

1949 (1 Oct). *75th Anniv of U.P.U. Nos.* 128/30 *of South Africa optd as T* **30**, *but* 13 × 4 *mm.*

138	½d. blue-green	1·25	1·50	20
139	1½d. brown-red	1·25	80	15
140	3d. bright blue	1·75	1·00	20
	a. "Lake" in East Africa	20·00		
138/40	*Set of* 3	3·75	3·00	50

1949 (1 Dec). *Inauguration of Voortrekker Monument, Pretoria. Nos.* 131/3 *of South Africa optd with T* **32**.

		Un single	*Us single*
141	1d. magenta	10	10
142	1½d. blue-green	10	10
143	3d. blue	10	20
141/3	*Set of* 3	20	25

1952 (14 Mar). *Tercentenary of Landing of Van Riebeeck. Nos.* 136/40 *of South Africa optd as T* **30**, *but* 8 × 3½ *mm (1d., 4½d.) or* 11 × 4 *mm (others).*

144	½d. brown-purple and olive-grey	10	30	
145	1d. deep blue-green	10	10	
146	2d. deep violet	50	10	
147	4½d. blue	30	90	
148	1s. brown	1·00	10	
144/8	*Set of* 5	1·75	1·40	

PRINTERS. The following stamps were printed by the Government Printer, Pretoria, in photogravure (Nos. 149/234) or lithography (subsequent issues), *unless stated otherwise.*

33 Queen Elizabeth II and *Catophracties Alexandri*

1953 (2 June). *Coronation. T* **33** *and similar horiz designs.* W **9** *of South Africa. P* 14.

149	1d. bright carmine	75	10
150	2d. deep bluish green	75	10
151	4d. magenta	1·60	55
152	6d. dull ultramarine	1·75	1·25
153	1s. deep orange-brown	1·75	40
149/53	*Set of* 5	6·00	2·25

Designs:—2d. *Bauhinia macrantha*, 4d. *Caralluma nebrownii*, 6d. *Gloriosa virescens*, 1s. *Rhigozum tricholotum*.

34 "Two Bucks" (rock painting)

36 "Rhinoceros Hunt" (rock painting)

38 Karakul Lamb

39 Ovambo Woman blowing Horn

(Des O. Schroeder (1d, to 4d.), M. Vandenschen (4½d. to 10s.))

1954 (15 Nov). *T* **34, 36, 38/9** *and similar designs.* W **9** *of South Africa (sideways on vert designs). P* 14.

154	1d. brown-red	30	10
155	2d. deep brown	35	10
156	3d. dull purple	2·00	10
157	4d. blackish olive	1·75	10
158	4½d. deep blue	1·25	15
159	6d. myrtle-green	1·25	10
160	1s. deep mauve	1·25	30
161	1s. 3d. cerise	5·00	30
162	1s. 6d. purple	5·00	35
163	2s. 6d. bistre-brown	9·00	60
164	5s. deep bright blue	14·00	2·75
165	10s. deep myrtle-green	42·00	15·00
154/65	*Set of* 12	75·00	18·00

Designs: *Vert (as T* **34**)—2d. "White Lady" (rock painting). *(As T* **38**)—2s. 6d. Lioness; 5s. Gemsbok; 10s. African Elephant. *(As T* **39**)—1s. Ovambo woman; 1s. 3d. Herero woman; 1s. 6d. Ovambo girl. *Horiz (as T* **36**)—4d. "White Elephant and Giraffe" (rock painting).

1960 *As Nos.* 154/7, 162, *but* W **102** *of South Africa (sideways on vert designs). P* 14.

166	1d. brown-red	55	55
167	2d. deep brown	70	55
168	3d. dull purple	1·40	1·50
169	4d. blackish olive	4·25	4·50
170	1s. 6d. purple	18·00	15·00
166/70	*Set of* 5	22·00	20·00

(New Currency. 100 cents=1 rand)

46 G.P.O. Windhoek

47 Finger Rock

48 Mounted Soldier Monument

49 Quivertree

50 S.W.A. House, Windhoek

50*a* Greater Flamingoes and Swakopmund Lighthouse

51 Fishing Industry

52 Greater Flamingo

53 German Lutheran Church, Windhoek

54 Diamond

55 Fort Namutoni

55*a* Hardap Dam

56 Topaz

57 Tourmaline

58 Heliodor

1961 (14 Feb)–**63**. *Unsurfaced paper.* W **102** *of South Africa (sideways on vert designs). P* 14.

171	**46**	½ c. brown and pale blue	60	10
172	**47**	1 c. sepia and reddish lilac	15	10
173	**48**	1½ c. slate-violet and salmon	20	10
174	**49**	2 c. deep green and yellow	75	10
175	**50**	2½ c. red-brown and light blue ..	35	10
176	**50*a***	3 c. ultramarine and rose-red (1.10.62)	3·75	15
177	**51**	3½ c. indigo and blue-green	70	15
178	**52**	5 c. scarlet and grey-blue	3·75	10
179	**53**	7½ c. sepia and pale lemon	70	15
180	**54**	10 c. blue and greenish yellow ..	1·75	15
181	**55**	12½ c. indigo and lemon	85	30
182	**55*a***	15 c. chocolate and light blue (16.3.63)	14·00	3·25
183	**56**	20 c. brown and red-orange	6·00	30
184	**57**	50 c. deep bluish green & yellow-orge	10·00	1·50
185	**58**	1 r. yellow, maroon and blue ..	16·00	12·00
171/185		.. .. *Set of* 15	55·00	16·00

See also Nos. 186/91, 202/16, 224/6 and 240.

1962–66. *As No.* 171, *etc., but without watermark.*

186	**46**	½ c. brown and pale blue (8.62) ..	50	1·25
187	**48**	1½ c. slate-violet and salmon (9.62) ..	4·00	35
188	**49**	2 c. deep green and yellow (5.62) ..	2·25	1·25
189	**50**	2½ c. red-brown and light blue (1964) ..	4·00	1·75
190	**51**	3½ c. indigo and blue-green (1966) ..	8·50	4·00
191	**52**	5 c. scarlet and grey-blue (9.62) ..	6·00	35
186/91		.. .. *Set of* 6	23·00	8·00

59 "Agricultural Development"

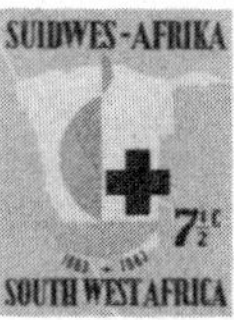

60 Centenary Emblem and Map

61 Centenary Emblem and part of Globe

1963 (16 Mar). *Opening of Hardap Dam.* W **102** *of South Africa (sideways). P* 14.

192	**59**	3 c. chocolate and light green	30	15

1963 (30 Aug). *Centenary of Red Cross. P* 14.

193	**60**	7½ c. red, black and light blue	7·00	3·00
194	**61**	15 c. red, black and orange-brown ..	10·00	5·00

62 Interior of Assembly Hall

63 Calvin

1964 (14 May). *Opening of Legislative Assembly Hall, Windhoek.* W **102** *of South Africa. P* 14.

195	**62**	3 c. ultramarine and salmon	50	30

1964 (1 Oct). *400th Death Anniv of Calvin (Protestant reformer). P* 14.

196	**63**	2½ c. brown-purple and gold	50	15
197		15 c. deep bluish green and gold	2·50	1·25

ALTERED CATALOGUE NUMBERS

Any Catalogue numbers altered from the last edition are shown as a list in the introductory pages.

64 Mail Runner of 1890

65 Kurt von François (founder)

66 Dr. H. Vedder

(Des D. Aschenborn)

1965 (18 Oct). *75th Anniv of Windhoek. Chalk-surfaced paper.* W **127** *of South Africa (sideways). P* 14.

198	**64**	3 c. sepia and scarlet	50	15
199	**65**	15 c. red-brown and blue-green	1·25	85

1966 (4 July). *90th Birth Anniv of Dr. H. Vedder (philosopher and writer). Chalk-surfaced paper.* W **127** *of South Africa (sideways). P* 14.

200	**66**	3 c. blackish green and salmon ..	50	15
201		15 c. deep sepia and light blue	1·25	65

Nos. 200/1 exist on Swiss-made paper with *tête-bêche* watermark from a special printing made for use in presentation albums for delegates to the U.P.U. Congress in Tokyo in 1969, as supplies of the original Harrison paper were by then exhausted (*Set of* 2 *price* £17 *mint*).

1966–72. *As* 1961–66 *but chalk-surfaced paper and* W **127** *of South Africa* (sideways on vert designs).*

202	**46**	½ c. brown and pale blue (1967) ..	1·25	10
203	**47**	1 c. sepia and light reddish lilac (1967)	1·00	10
		a. Grey-brown and lilac (9.72) ..	1·25	10
204	**48**	1½ c. slate-violet and salmon (1968) ..	5·50	30
205	**49**	2 c. deep bluish green and yellow ..	2·25	10
206	**50**	2½ c. dp red-brown & lt turquoise-blue	2·00	10
		a. Dp red-brown & pale blue (1967)	70	10
207	**50*a***	3 c. ultramarine and rose-red (1970)	6·50	50
208	**51**	3½ c. indigo and blue-green (1967) ..	4·00	1·75
209	**50**	4 c. dp red-brown & lt turq-bl (1.4.71)	1·50	1·25
210	**52**	5 c. scarlet and grey-blue (1968) ..	3·50	10
211	**53**	6 c. sepia & greenish yellow (31.8.71)	8·00	7·50
212		7½ c. sepia and pale lemon (1967) ..	2·50	30
213	**55**	9 c. indigo & greenish yellow (1.7.71)	8·00	7·50
214	**54**	10 c. brt blue & greenish yellow (6.70)	15·00	1·50
		a. Whiter background† (9.72) ..	15·00	2·00
215	**55*a***	15 c. chocolate and light blue (1.72) ..	16·00	5·50
216	**56**	20 c. brown and red-orange (1968) ..	12·00	1·25
202/16		.. .. *Set of* 15	75·00	24·00

*The watermark in this issue is indistinct but the stamps can be distinguished from the stamps without watermark by their shades and the chalk-surfaced paper which is appreciably thicker and whiter. The 1, 1½, 3, 4, 5, 6, 9, 10, 15 and 20 c. are known only with the watermark *tête-bêche* but the ½ c. and 2½ c. exist with both forms, the remainder being as illustrated.

† No. 214a, printed from sheets, has a much whiter background around the value and behind "SOUTH WEST AFRICA" compared with No. 214, which was issued in coils only.

See also Nos. 224/6 and 240.

67 Camelthorn Tree

(Des D. Aschenborn (2½ c., 3 c.), Govt Printer, Pretoria (15 c.))

1967 (6 Jan). *Verwoerd Commemoration. Chalk-surfaced paper. T* **67** *and similar designs.* W **127** *of South Africa (sideways on vert designs). P* 14.

217		2½ c. black and emerald-green	20	10
218		3 c. brown and new blue	30	10
219		15 c. blackish brown and reddish purple ..	1·10	45
217/19		.. .. *Set of* 3	1·40	60

Designs: *Vert.*—3 c. Waves breaking against rock; 15 c. Dr. H. F. Verwoerd.

70 President Swart

71 President and Mrs. Swart

1968 (2 Jan). *Swart Commemoration. Chalk-surfaced paper.* W **127** *of South Africa (tête-bêche, sideways). P* 14 × 15.

220	**70**	3 c. orange-red, black & turquoise-blue		
		G. Inscribed in German	45	15
		A. Inscribed in Afrikaans	45	15
		E. Inscribed in English	45	15
221	**71**	15 c. red, blackish olive and dull green		
		G. Inscribed in German	1·50	1·75
		A. Inscribed in Afrikaans	1·50	1·75
		E. Inscribed in English	1·50	1·75
		a. Red, brownish olive & bronze-green		
		G. Inscribed in German	3·00	2·25
		A. Inscribed in Afrikaans	3·00	2·25
		E. Inscribed in English	3·00	2·25
220/1		.. .. *Set of 2 values in strips of three*	12·00	
		Set of 6 *singles*	5·00	5·00

The three languages appear, *se-tenant*, both horizontally and vertically, throughout the sheet.

1970 (14 Feb). *Water 70 Campaign. As Nos.* 299/300 *of South Africa, but without phosphor band and inscr* "SWA".

222		2½ c. green, bright blue and chocolate ..	75	30
223		3 c. Prussian blue, royal blue and buff ..	75	30

72 G.P.O., Windhoek

73 "Red Sand-dunes, Eastern South West Africa"

1970–71. *As Nos.* 202 *and* 204/5 *but* "POSGELD INKOMSTE" *omitted and larger figure of value as in T* **72**. W **127** *of South Africa (tête-bêche, sideways on* 1½ *and* 2 *c.).*

224	**72**	½ c. brown and pale blue (6.70)	1·25	30
225	–	1½ c. slate-violet and salmon (1.6.71) ..	13·00	13·00
226	–	2 c. deep bluish green and lemon (11.70)	5·00	40
224/6		.. .. *Set of* 3	17·00	13·00

1970 (24 Aug). *150th Anniv of Bible Society of South Africa. As Nos.* 301/2 *of South Africa, but inscr* "SWA".

228		2½ c. multicoloured	1·50	10
229		12½ c. gold, black and blue	8·00	6·50

No. 228 has a phosphor frame, probably added in error.

A mint example of No. 229 exists with a second, blind, impression of the die-stamped features.

1971 (31 May). *"Interstex" Stamp Exhibition, Cape Town. As No.* 303A *of South Africa, but without phosphor frame and inscr* "SWA".

230		5 c. light greenish blue, black and pale yellow	4·75	1·50

1971 (31 May). *Tenth Anniv of Antarctic Treaty. As No.* 304 *of South Africa, but without phosphor frame, and inscr* "SWA".

231		12½ c. blue-black, greenish blue & orge-red	45·00	25·00

1971 (31 May). *Tenth Anniv of the South African Republic. As Nos.* 305/6 *of South Africa, but without phosphor frame, and inscr* "SWA".

232		2 c. pale flesh and brown-red	3·25	75
233		4 c. green and black	3·25	75

1972 (19 Sept). *Centenary of S.P.C.A. As No.* 312 *of South Africa, but inscr* "SWA".

234		5 c. multicoloured	3·50	55

WATERMARK. All issues from this date are on unwatermarked paper.

(Lettering by E. de Jong)

1973 (1 May). *Scenery. T* **73** *and similar multicoloured designs showing paintings by Adolph Jentsch. P* 11½ × 12½ (10 *and* 15 *c.*) *or* 12½ × 11½ (*others*).

235		2 c. Type **73**	75	75
236		4 c. "After the Rain"	1·25	1·25
237		5 c. "Barren Country"	1·50	1·50
238		10 c. "Schaap River" (*vert*)	2·75	2·75
239		15 c. "Namib Desert" (*vert*)	4·00	4·00
235/9		.. .. *Set of* 5	9·00	9·00

1973 (28 May). *As Nos.* 207 *but without wmk. Phosphorised paper.*

240	**50*a***	3 c. ultramarine and rose-red	2·50	1·25

No. 240 is also distinguishable in that the lettering of "SOUTH WEST AFRICA" is whiter.

74 *Sarcocaulon rigidum*

75 *Euphorbia virosa*

(Des D. Findlay)

1973 (1 Sept)–**79**. *Succulents. Various multicoloured designs as T* **74/5**. *Phosphorised glossy paper (original printing of all values) or ordinary paper* (1, 2, 3, 4, 5, 9, 10, 15, 20, 30, 50 *c.*).

(*a*) *As T* **74**. *P* 12½.

241	1 c. Type **74**	15	10
	a. Black (face value, etc.) omitted	£120	
242	2 c. *Lapidaria margaretae*	80	40
	a. Perf 14 × 13½ (4.8.79)	20	10
243	3 c. *Titanopsis schwantesii*	20	10
	a. Black (face value, etc.) omitted ..	£120	
	b. Perf 14 × 13½ (8.8.79)	30	15
244	4 c. *Lithops karasmontana*	25	10
245	5 c. *Caralluma lugardii*	40	30
	a. Black (face value, etc.) omitted ..	£120	
	b. Perf 14 × 13½ (12.12.79)	40	20
246	6 c. *Dinteranthus microspermus* ..	70	40
247	7 c. *Conophytum gratum*	55	45
248	9 c. *Huernia oculata*	65	40
249	10 c. *Gasteria pillansii*	60	35
	a. Black (face value, etc.) omitted ..	£200	
	b. Perf 14 × 13½ (13.8.79)	40	30
250	14 c. *Stapelia pedunculata*	1·25	90
251	15 c. *Fenestraria aurantiaca*	65	30
252	20 c. *Decabelone grandiflora*	3·75	80
253	25 c. *Hoodia bainii*	2·25	1·25

(*b*) *As T* **75**. *P* 11½ × 12½ (30 *c*., 1 *r*.) *or* 12½ × 11½ (50 *c*.)
254 30 c. Type **75** 1·00 50
a. Perf 13½ × 14 (27.12.79) 90 90
255 50 c. *Pachypodium namaquanum* (*vert*) 1·25 2·00
a. Perf 14 × 13½ (18.12.79) 1·50 1·50
256 1 r. *Welwitschia bainesii* 2·00 4·00
241/56 *Set of* 16 14·00 10·00

1973 (1 Sept)–**80**. *Coil stamps. As Nos.* 241/2 *and* 245 *but photo, colours changed. P* 14.
257 1 c. black and light mauve 60 45
a. Chalk-surfaced paper (7.76?) 60 30
b. Imperf × perf 14. Chalk-surfaced paper (1980) 2·50 3·00
258 2 c. black and yellow 40 40
a. Chalk-surfaced paper (7.76?) 75 40
b. Imperf × perf 14. Chalk-surfaced paper (1.79) 70 40
259 5 c. black and light rose-red 1·25 45
a. Imperf × perf 14. Chalk-surfaced paper (8.2.78) 90 45
257/9 *Set of* 3 1·75 1·10
Coils of Nos. 257b, 258b and 259a come with every fifth stamp numbered on the reverse.

76 Chat-shrike

77 Giraffe, Antelope and Spoor

(Des D. Findlay)

1974 (13 Feb). *Rare Birds. T* **76** *and similar vert designs. Multicoloured. P* 12½ × 11½.
260 4 c. Type **76** 2·75 75
261 5 c. Peach-faced Lovebirds 3·50 1·25
262 10 c. Damaraland Rock Jumper 9·00 3·50
263 15 c. Rüppell's Parrots 13·00 8·50
260/3 *Set of* 4 25·00 12·50

(Des O. Schröder)

1974 (10 Apr). *Twyfelfontein Rock-engravings. T* **77** *and similar multicoloured designs. P* 11½ × 12½ (15 *c*.) *or* 12½ (*others*).
264 4 c. Type **77** 1·50 50
265 5 c. Elephant, hyena, antelope and spoor 1·50 80
a. Black (value and "SWA") omitted £550
266 15 c. Kudu Cow (38 × 21 *mm*) 7·00 6·00
264/6 *Set of* 3 9·00 6·50

78 Cut Diamond

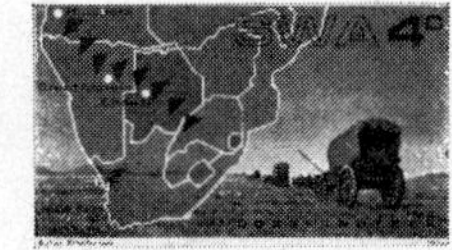

79 Wagons and Map of the Trek

(Des M. Barnett)

1974 (30 Sept). *Diamond Mining. T* **78** *and similar vert design. Multicoloured. P* 12½ × 11½.
267 10 c. Type **78** 4·00 3·00
268 15 c. Diagram of shore workings 4·50 4·00

(Des K. Esterhuysen)

1974 (13 Nov). *Centenary of Thirstland Trek. P* 11½ × 12½.
269 **79** 4 c. multicoloured 1·00 75

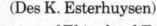

80 Peregrine Falcon

81 Kolmannskop (ghost town)

(Des D. Findlay)

1975 (19 Mar). *Protected Birds of Prey. T* **80** *and similar vert designs. Multicoloured. P* 12½ × 11½.
270 4 c. Type **80** 2·00 70
271 5 c. Verreaux's Eagle 2·25 1·25
272 10 c. Martial Eagle 6·00 4·00
273 15 c. Egyptian Vulture 7·50 7·00
270/3 *Set of* 4 16·00 11·50

(Des A. H. Barrett)

1975 (23 July). *Historic Monuments. T* **81** *and similar horiz designs. Multicoloured. P* 11½ × 12½.
274 5 c. Type **81** 30 15
275 9 c. "Martin Luther" (steam tractor) 50 50
276 15 c. Kurt von Francois and Old Fort, Windhoek 1·00 80
274/6 *Set of* 3 1·60 1·25

82 "View of Lüderitz"

(Des J. Hoekstra)

1975 (15 Oct). *Otto Schröder. T* **82** *and similar horiz designs showing his paintings. Multicoloured. P* 11½ × 12½.
277 15 c. Type **82** 55 45
a. Block of 4. Nos. 277/80 2·00
278 15 c. "View of Swakopmund" 55 45
279 15 c. "Harbour Scene" 55 45
280 15 c. "Quayside, Walvis Bay" 55 45
277/80 *Set of* 4 2·00 1·60
MS281 122 × 96 mm. Nos. 277/80 2·25 4·50
Nos. 277/80 were printed together, in *se-tenant* blocks of four within the sheet.

83 Elephants

(Des H. Pager)

1976 (31 Mar). *Prehistoric Rock Paintings. T* **83** *and similar horiz designs. Multicoloured. P* 11½ × 12½.
282 4 c. Type **83** 40 10
283 10 c. Rhinoceros 65 30
284 15 c. Antelope 80 60
285 20 c. Man with bow and arrow 1·10 85
282/5 *Set of* 4 2·75 1·60
MS286 121 × 95 mm. Nos. 282/5 2·75 4·00

84 Schwerinsburg

(Des H. Pager)

1976 (14 May). *Castles. T* **84** *and similar horiz designs. Multicoloured. P* 11½ × 12½.
287 10 c. Type **84** 50 30
288 15 c. Schloss Duwisib 70 50
289 20 c. Heynitzburg 1·00 80
287/9 *Set of* 3 2·00 1·40

85 Large-toothed Rock Hyrax

(Des D. Findlay)

1976 (16 July). *Fauna Conservation. T* **85** *and similar horiz designs. Multicoloured. P* 11½ × 12½.
290 4 c. Type **85** 50 20
291 10 c. Kirk's Dik-Dik 1·50 75
292 15 c. Kuhl's Tree Squirrel 2·25 1·40
290/2 *Set of* 3 3·75 2·10

86 The Augustineum, Windhoek

(Des H. Pager)

1976 (17 Sept). *Modern Buildings. T* **86** *and similar horiz design. P* 11½ × 12½.
293 15 c. black and yellow 40 40
294 20 c. black and light yellow 50 50
Design:—20 c. Katutura Hospital, Windhoek.

87 Ovambo Water Canal System

(Des A. H. Barrett)

1976 (19 Nov). *Water and Electricity Supply. T* **87** *and similar horiz design. Multicoloured. P* 11½ × 12½.
295 15 c. Type **87** 30 30
296 20 c. Ruacana Falls Power Station 40 40

88 Coastline near Pomona

(Des A. H. Barrett)

1977 (29 Mar). *Namib Desert. T* **88** *and similar horiz designs. Multicoloured. P* 12½.
297 4 c. Type **88** 20 15
298 10 c. Bush and dunes, Sossusvlei 30 30
299 15 c. Plain near Brandberg 50 50
300 20 c. Dunes, Sperr Gebiet 60 60
297/300 *Set of* 4 1·40 1·40

89 Kraal

(Des A. H. Barrett)

1977 (15 July). *The Ovambo People. T* **89** *and similar horiz designs. P* 11½ × 12½.
301 4 c. multicoloured 10 10
302 10 c. black, dull orange and cinnamon 30 20
303 15 c. multicoloured 30 25
304 20 c. multicoloured 35 45
301/4 *Set of* 4 95 90
Designs—10 c. Grain baskets; 15 c. Pounding grain; 20 c. Women in tribal dress.

90 Terminal Buildings

(Des H. Pager and A. H. Barrett)

1977 (22 Aug). *J. G. Strijdom Airport, Windhoek. P* 12½.
305 **90** 20 c. multicoloured 30 30

91 Drostdy, Lüderitz

92 Side-winding Adder

(Des A. H. Barrett)

1977 (4 Nov). *Historic Houses. T* **91** *and similar horiz designs. Multicoloured. P* 12 × 12½.
306 5 c. Type **91** 15 10
307 10 c. Woermannhaus, Swakopmund 40 30
308 15 c. Neu-Heusis, Windhoek 45 35
309 20 c. Schmelenhaus, Bethanie 65 40
306/9 *Set of* 4 1·50 1·10
MS310 122 × 96 mm. Nos. 306/9 1·50 2·25

(Des D. Findlay)

1978 (6 Feb). *Small Animals. T* **92** *and similar horiz designs. Multicoloured. P* 12½.
311 4 c. Type **92** 15 10
312 10 c. Grant's Desert Golden Mole 30 30
313 15 c. Palmato Gecko 50 30
314 20 c. Namaqua Chameleon 65 40
311/14 *Set of* 4 1·40 1·00

93 Ostrich Hunting

(Des A. H. Barrett)

1978 (14 Apr). *The Bushmen. T* **93** *and similar horiz designs in light grey-brown, stone and black. P* 12 × 12½.
315 4 c. Type **93** 15 10
316 10 c. Woman carrying fruit 25 20
317 15 c. Hunters kindling fire 35 30
318 20 c. Woman with musical instrument 40 40
315/18 *Set of* 4 1·00 90

MINIMUM PRICE

The minimum price quote is 10p which represents a handling charge rather than a basis for valuing common stamps. For further notes about prices see introductory pages.

ALGEMENE
STEMREG

94 Lutheran Church, Windhoek   **(95)**

(Des A. H. Barrett)

1978 (16 June). *Historic Churches. T* **94** *and similar horiz designs. P* 12½.

319 4 c. grey-black and cinnamon 10 10
320 10 c. grey-black and ochre 15 20
321 15 c. grey-black and light brown-rose 20 25
322 20 c. grey-black and light grey-blue 30 35
319/22 *Set of* 4 65 80
MS323 125 × 90 mm. Nos. 319/22 1·00 1·75

Designs:—10 c. Lutheran Church, Swakopmund; 15 c. Rhenish Mission Church, Otjimbingwe; 20 c. Rhenish Missionary Church, Keetmanshoop.

1978 (1 Nov). *Universal Suffrage. Designs as Nos.* 244/5, 249 *and* 251/3 *optd with T* **95** *(or similar inscr in English or German).*

324 4 c. *Lithops karasmontana*
A. Opt in Afrikaans 10 10
E. Opt in English 10 10
G. Opt in German 10 10
325 5 c. *Caralluma lugardii*
A. Opt in Afrikaans 10 10
E. Opt in English 10 10
G. Opt in German 10 10
326 10 c. *Gasteria pillansii*
A. Opt in Afrikaans 10 10
E. Opt in English 10 10
G. Opt in German 10 10
327 15 c. *Fenestraria aurantiaca*
A. Opt in Afrikaans 15 15
E. Opt in English 15 15
G. Opt in German 15 15
328 20 c. *Decabelone grandiflora*
A. Opt in Afrikaans 20 20
E. Opt in English 20 20
G. Opt in German 20 20
329 25 c. *Hoodia bainni*
A. Opt in Afrikaans 25 25
E. Opt in English 25 25
G. Opt in German 25 25
324/9 *Set of* 18 *(6 strips of* 3) 2·40 2·40

Nos. 324A/G, 325A/G, 326A/G, 327A/G, 328A/G and 329A/G were each printed together, *se-tenant*, in horizontal and vertical strips of 3 throughout the sheets.

96 Greater Flamingo

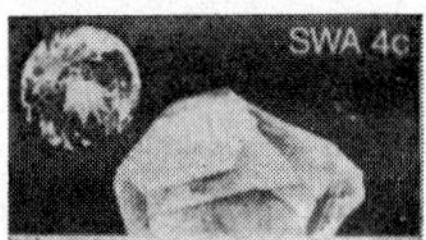

97 Silver Topaz

(Des D. Findlay)

1979 (5 Apr). *Water Birds. T* **96** *and similar vert designs. Multicoloured. P* 14.

330 4 c. Type **96** 20 10
331 15 c. White-breasted Cormorant 45 25
332 20 c. Chestnut-banded Sand Plover 50 35
333 25 c. Eastern White Pelican 55 40
330/3 *Set of* 4 1·50 1·00

(Des H. Botha)

1979 (26 Nov). *Gemstones. T* **97** *and similar horiz designs. Multicoloured. P* 14.

334 4 c. Type **97** 25 10
335 15 c. Aquamarine 55 20
336 20 c. Malachite 60 25
337 25 c. Amethyst 60 30
334/7 *Set of* 4 1·75 75

98 Killer Whale

99 Impala

(Des A. H. Barrett)

1980 (25 Mar). *Whales. T* **98** *and similar multicoloured designs. P* 14.

338 4 c. Type **98** 35 10
339 5 c. Humpback Whale (38 × 22 *mm*) 40 10
340 10 c. Black Right Whale (38 × 22 *mm*) 55 30
341 15 c. Sperm Whale (58 × 22 *mm*) 1·00 60
342 20 c. Fin Whale (58 × 22 *mm*) 1·25 80
343 25 c. Blue Whale (88 × 22 *mm*) 1·60 1·10
338/43 *Set of* 6 4·50 2·75
MS344 202 × 95 mm. Nos. 338/43 5·50 6·00

(Des P. Bosman)

1980 (25 June). *25th Anniv of Division of Nature Conservation and Tourism. Antelopes. T* **99** *and similar horiz designs. Multicoloured. P* 14.

345 5 c. Type **99** 15 10
346 10 c. Topi 20 10
347 15 c. Roan Antelope 40 15
348 20 c. Sable Antelope 50 20
345/8 *Set of* 4 1·10 45

100 Black-backed Jackal

101 Meerkat

(Des Sheila Nowers (11, 12, 14, 16 c.), P. Bosman (others))

1980 (1 Oct)–**89**. *Wildlife. Multicoloured designs as T* **100**. *Ordinary paper. P* 14.

349 1 c. Type **100** 15 10
a. Chalk-surfaced paper (11.6.85) 50 50
350 2 c. Hunting Dog 30 10
a. Chalk-surfaced paper (4.6.86) 55 55
351 3 c. Brown Hyena 20 10
a. Chalk-surfaced paper (10.2.88) 50 60
352 4 c. Springbok 20 10
a. Chalk-surfaced paper (29.7.87) 50 60
353 5 c. Gemsbok 20 10
a. Chalk-surfaced paper (11.6.85) 60 60
354 6 c. Greater Kudu 20 10
a. Chalk-surfaced paper (8.8.88) 70 70
355 7 c. Mouuntain Zebra (*horiz*) 40 20
a. Chalk-surfaced paper (19.3.86) 50 60
356 8 c. Cape Porcupine (*horiz*) 30 10
a. Chalk-surfaced paper (11.6.85) 60 60
357 9 c. Ratel (*horiz*) 30 10
a. Chalk-surfaced paper (10.2.88) 60 60
358 10 c. Cheetah (*horiz*) 30 10
358*a* 11 c. Blue Wildebeest (2.4.84) 40 30
358*b* 12 c. African Buffalo (*horiz*) (1.4.85) 60 45
ba. Booklet pane of 10 with margins all round (1.8.85) 6·00
358*c* 14 c. Caracal (*horiz*) (*chalk-surfaced paper*) (1.4.86) 1·50 70
359 15 c. Hippopotamus (*horiz*) 30 10
a. Chalk-surfaced paper (10.2.88) 50 60
359*b* 16 c. Warthog (*horiz*) (*chalk-surfaced paper*) (1.4.87) 1·00 80
ba. Ordinary paper (15.2.89) 60 40
360 20 c. Eland (*horiz*) 30 10
a. Chalk-surfaced paper (11.6.85) 50 60
361 25 c. Black Rhinoceros (*horiz*) 40 20
a. Chalk-surfaced paper (11.6.85) 55 65
362 30 c. Lion (*horiz*) 60 20
a. Chalk-surfaced paper (4.6.86) 60 60
363 50 c. Giraffe 50 30
a. Chalk-surfaced paper (21.4.88) 80 1·00
364 1 r. Leopard 90 55
a. Chalk-surfaced paper (4.6.86) 1·50 1·75
365 2 r. African Elephant 1·00 90
a. Chalk-surfaced paper (10.2.88) 1·75 2·00
349/65 *Set of* 21 9·00 5·00

Some printings of the 4, 15 and 25 c. from 1983/4 were on phosphorescent paper. The same paper was used for printings of the 1, 2, 3, 8, 9, 10, 16 c. (No. 359ba), 20, 30 c. and 1 r. during 1989.

(Des P. Bosman. Photo)

1980 (1 Oct). *Coil stamps. Wildlife. Vert designs as T* **101**. *Imperf × perf* 14.

366 1 c. yellow-brown 10 10
367 2 c. deep dull blue 10 10
368 5 c. yellow-olive 15 15
366/8 *Set of* 3 30 30

Designs:—2 c. Savanna Monkey; 5 c. Chacma Baboon.

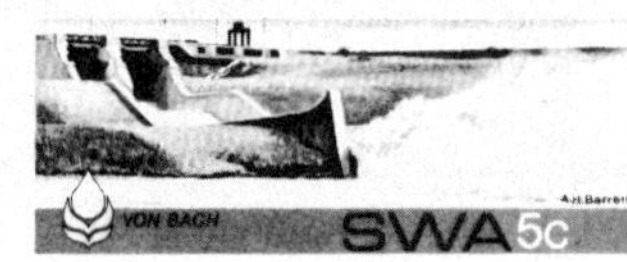

102 Von Bach

(Des A. H. Barrett)

1980 (25 Nov). *Water Conservation. Dams. T* **102** *and similar horiz designs. Multicoloured. P* 14.

369 5 c. Type **102** 10 10
370 10 c. Swakoppoort 15 10
371 15 c. Naute 20 20
372 20 c. Hardap 25 25
369/72 *Set of* 4 60 60

103 View of Fish River Canyon

104 *Aloe erinacea*

(Des A. H. Barrett)

1981 (20 Mar). *Fish River Canyon. T* **103** *and similar horiz designs showing various views of canyon. P* 14.

373 5 c. multicoloured 10 10
374 15 c. multicoloured 20 20
375 20 c. multicoloured 25 25
376 25 c. multicoloured 30 30
373/6 *Set of* 4 75 70

(Des D. Findlay)

1981 (14 Aug). *Aloes. T* **104** *and similar vert designs. Multicoloured. P* 14 × 13½.

377 5 c. Type **104** 10 10
378 15 c. *Aloe viridiflora* 30 25
379 20 c. *Aloe pearsonii* 35 25
380 25 c. *Aloe littoralis* 40 30
377/80 *Set of* 4 1·00 75

105 Paul Weiss-Haus

(Des A. H. Barrett)

1981 (16 Oct). *Historic Buildings of Lüderitz. T* **105** *and similar horiz designs. Multicoloured. P* 14.

381 5 c. Type **105** 10 10
382 15 c. Deutsche Afrika Bank 20 20
383 20 c. Schroederhaus 30 30
384 25 c. Altes Postamt 30 35
381/4 *Set of* 4 75 80
MS385 125 × 90 mm. Nos. 381/4 85 90

106 Salt Pan

107 Kalahari Starred Tortoise (*Psammobates oculifer*)

(Des A. H. Barrett)

1981 (4 Dec). *Salt Industry. T* **106** *and similar horiz designs. Multicoloured. P* 14.

386 5 c. Type **106** 10 10
387 15 c. Dumping and washing 20 20
388 20 c. Loading by conveyor 25 30
389 25 c. Dispatch to refinery 30 35
386/9 *Set of* 4 70 80

(Des A. H. Barrett)

1982 (12 Mar). *Tortoises. T* **107** *and similar horiz designs. Multicoloured. P* 14.

390 5 c. Type **107** 10 10
391 15 c. Leopard Tortoise (*Geochelone pardalis*) 20 20
392 20 c. Angulate Tortoise (*Chersina angulata*) 25 30
393 25 c. Speckled Padloper (*Homopus signatus*) 30 35
390/3 *Set of* 4 70 80

108 Mythical Sea-monster

(Des Sheila Nowers)

1982 (28 May). *Discoverers of South West Africa. (1st series). Bartolomeu Dias. T* **108** *and similar horiz designs. Multicoloured. P* 14.

394 15 c. Type **108** 20 20
395 20 c. Bartolomeu Dias and map of Africa showing voyage 30 30
396 25 c. Dias' caravel 45 40
397 30 c. Dias erecting commemorative cross, Angra das Voltas, 25 July 1488 45 45
394/7 *Set of* 4 1·25 1·25

See also Nos. 455/8.

109 Brandberg **110** Otjikaeva Head-dress of Herero Woman

(Des A. H. Barrett)

1982 (3 Aug). *Mountains of South West Africa. T* **109** *and similar horiz designs. Multicoloured. P* 13½ × 14.
398 6 c. Type **109** 10 10
399 15 c. Omatako 20 20
400 20 c. Die Nadel 25 30
401 25 c. Spitzkuppe 30 35
398/401 .. .. *Set of* 4 75 85

(Des A. H. Barrett)

1982 (15 Oct). *Traditional Head-dresses of South West Africa.* (*1st series*). *T* **110** *and similar vert designs. Multicoloured. P* 14.
402 6 c. Type **110** 10 10
403 15 c. Ekori head-dress of Himba 25 35
404 20 c. Oshikoma hair-piece and iipando plaits of Ngandjera 35 45
405 25 c. Omhatela head-dress of Kwanyama .. 35 60
402/5 .. .. *Set of* 4 95 1·40
See also Nos. 427/30.

111 Fort Vogelsang **112** Searching for Diamonds, Kolmanskop, 1908

(Des J. van Ellinckhuijzen)

1983 (16 Mar). *Centenary of Lüderitz. T* **111** *and similar designs. P* 14.
406 6 c. brownish black and deep carmine-red .. 10 10
407 20 c. brownish black and yellow-brown .. 25 30
408 25 c. brownish black and chestnut 30 35
409 30 c. brownish black and brown-purple .. 35 40
410 40 c. brownish black and bright green .. 50 55
406/10 .. .. *Set of* 5 1·40 1·50
Designs: *Vert* (23 × 29 *mm*)—20 c. Chief Joseph Fredericks; 30 c. Heinrich Vogelsang (founder); 40 c. Adolf Lüderitz (colonial promoter). *Horiz* (*As T* **111**)—25 c. Angra Pequena.

(Des J. van Ellinckhuijzen)

1983 (8 June). *75th Anniv of Discovery of Diamonds. T* **112** *and similar designs. P* 13½ × 14 (10, 20 *c.*) *or* 14 × 13½ (*others*).
411 10 c. deep brown and pale stone 15 15
412 20 c. maroon and pale stone 30 30
413 25 c. Prussian blue and pale stone 35 35
414 40 c. brownish black and pale stone 55 55
411/14 .. .. *Set of* 4 1·25 1·25
Designs: *Horiz* (34 × 19 *mm*)—20 c. Digging for diamonds, Kolmanskop, 1908. *Vert* (19 × 26 *mm*)—25 c. Sir Ernest Oppenheimer (industrialist); 40 c. August Stauch (prospector).

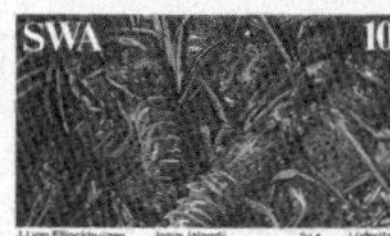

113 "Common Zebras drinking" (J. van Ellinckhuijzen) **114** The Rock Lobster

1983 (1 Sept). *Painters of South West Africa. T* **113** *and similar horiz designs. Multicoloured. P* 13½ × 14.
415 10 c. Type **113** 15 15
416 20 c. "Rossing Mountain" (H. Henckert) .. 25 30
417 25 c. "Stampeding African Buffalo" (F. Krampe) 30 35
418 40 c. "Erongo Mountains" (J. Blatt) 50 55
415/18 .. .. *Set of* 4 1·10 1·25

(Des J. van Ellinckhuijzen)

1983 (23 Nov). *Lobster Industry. T* **114** *and similar horiz designs. Multicoloured. P* 13½ × 14.
419 10 c. Type **114** 15 15
420 20 c. Mother ship and fishing dinghies .. 25 30
421 25 c. Netting lobsters from dinghy 30 35
422 40 c. Packing lobsters 50 55
419/22 .. .. *Set of* 4 1·10 1·25

115 Hohenzollern House

(Des A. H. Barrett)

1984 (8 Mar). *Historic Buildings of Swakopmund. T* **115** *and similar horiz designs. P* 14.
423 10 c. grey-black and orange-brown 15 15
424 20 c. grey-black and new blue 30 25
425 25 c. grey-black and yellow-green 30 30
426 30 c. grey-black and ochre 35 30
423/6 .. .. *Set of* 4 1·00 90
Designs:—20 c. Railway Station; 25 c. Imperial District Bureau; 30 c. Ritterburg.

(Des A. H. Barrett)

1984 (25 May). *Traditional Head-dresses of South West Africa* (*2nd series*). *Multicoloured designs as T* **110**. *P* 14.
427 11 c. Eendjushi head-dress of Kwambi .. 25 15
428 20 c. Bushman woman 40 25
429 25 c. Omulenda head-dress of Kwaluudhi .. 45 30
430 30 c. Mbukushu women 45 30
427/30 .. .. *Set of* 4 1·40 90

116 Map and German Flag **117** Sweet Thorn

(Des J. van Ellinckhuijzen)

1984 (7 Aug). *Centenary of German Colonisation. T* **116** *and similar horiz designs. Multicoloured. P* 14 × 14½.
431 11 c. Type **116** 25 15
432 25 c. Raising the German flag, 1884 .. 50 50
433 30 c. German Protectorate boundary marker 50 50
434 45 c. *Elizabeth* and *Leipzig* (German corvettes) .. .. 1·25 1·40
431/4 .. .. *Set of* 4 2·25 2·25

(Des Eva-Maria Linsmayer)

1984 (22 Nov). *Spring in South West Africa. T* **117** *and similar vert designs. Multicoloured. P* 14.
435 11 c. Type **117** 20 15
436 25 c. Camel Thorn 40 35
437 30 c. Hook Thorn 45 35
438 45 c. Candle-pod Acacia 60 50
435/8 .. .. *Set of* 4 1·50 1·25

118 Head of Ostrich

(Des J. van Ellinckhuijzen)

1985 (15 Mar). *Ostriches. T* **118** *and similar horiz designs. Multicoloured. P* 14.
439 11 c. Type **118** 35 10
440 25 c. Ostrich on eggs 60 30
441 30 c. Newly-hatched chick and eggs 70 50
442 50 c. Mating dance .. .. 1·00 75
439/42 .. .. *Set of* 4 2·40 1·50

119 Kaiserstrasse

(Des A. H. Barrett)

1985 (6 June). *Historic Buildings of Windhoek. T* **119** *and similar horiz designs. P* 14.
443 12 c. black and brown-ochre 20 10
444 25 c. black and grey-olive 35 25
445 30 c. black and brown 35 30
446 50 c. black and yellow-brown 80 70
443/6 .. .. *Set of* 4 1·50 1·25
Designs:—25 c. Turnhalle; 30 c. Old Supreme Court Building; 50 c. Railway Station.

120 Zwilling Locomotive **121** Lidumu-dumu (keyboard instrument)

(Des J. van Ellinckhuijzen)

1985 (2 Aug). *Narrow-gauge Railway Locomotives. T* **120** *and similar horiz designs. Multicoloured. P* 14.
447 12 c. Type **120** 30 10
448 25 c. Feldspur side-tank locomotive 60 25
449 30 c. Jung and Henschel side-tank locomotive 70 35
450 50 c. Henschel Hd locomotive 90 60
447/50 .. .. *Set of* 4 2·25 1·10

(Des J. van Ellinckhuijzen)

1985 (17 Oct). *Traditional Musical Instruments. T* **121** *and similar horiz designs. Multicoloured. P* 14.
451 12 c. Type **121** 10 10
452 25 c. Ngoma (drum) 20 20
453 30 c. Okambulumbumbwa (stringed instrument) 25 25
454 50 c. // Gwashi (stringed instrument) 35 35
451/4 .. .. *Set of* 4 80 80

122 Erecting Commemorative Pillar at Cape Cross, 1486 **123** Ameib, Erongo Mountains

(Des J. van Ellinckhuijzen)

1986 (24 Jan). *Discoverers of South West Africa* (*2nd series*). *Diogo Cao. T* **122** *and similar horiz designs. P* 14.
455 12 c. black, brownish grey & deep dull green 25 10
456 20 c. black, brownish grey & pale red-brown 40 20
457 25 c. black, brownish grey and dull blue .. 50 30
458 30 c. black, brownish grey & dull reddish pur 60 40
455/8 .. .. *Set of* 4 1·60 90
Designs:—20 c. Diogo Cao's coat of arms; 25 c. Caravel; 30 c. Diogo Cao.

(Des J. van Niekerk)

1986 (24 Apr). *Rock Formations. T* **123** *and similar horiz designs. Multicoloured. P* 14.
459 14 c. Type **123** 50 15
460 20 c. Vingerklip, near Outjo 60 25
461 25 c. Petrified sand dunes, Kuiseb River .. 70 40
462 30 c. Orgelpfeifen, Twyfelfontein 85 55
459/62 .. .. *Set of* 4 2·40 1·25

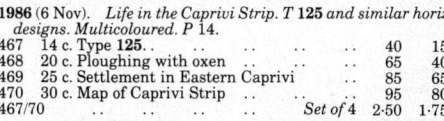

124 Model wearing Swakara Coat **125** Pirogue, Lake Liambezi

(Des J. van Ellinckhuijzen)

1986 (10 July). *Karakul Industry. T* **124** *and similar vert designs. Multicoloured. P* 14.
463 14 c. Type **124** 30 15
464 20 c. Weaving karakul wool carpet 45 20
465 25 c. Flock of karakul ewes on veld 45 30
466 30 c. Karakul rams 65 40
463/6 .. .. *Set of* 4 1·75 95

1986 (6 Nov). *Life in the Caprivi Strip. T* **125** *and similar horiz designs. Multicoloured. P* 14.
467 14 c. Type **125** 40 15
468 20 c. Ploughing with oxen 65 40
469 25 c. Settlement in Eastern Caprivi 85 65
470 30 c. Map of Caprivi Strip 95 80
467/70 .. .. *Set of* 4 2·50 1·75

126 "Gobabis Mission Station", 1863 **127** *Garreta nitens* (beetle)

1987 (19 Feb). *Paintings by Thomas Baines. T* **126** *and similar horiz designs. Multicoloured. P* 14.
471 14 c. Type **126** 40 15
472 20 c. "Outspan at Koobie", 1861 .. .. .. 65 50
473 25 c. "Outspan under Oomahaama Tree", 1862 .. .. 85 70
474 30 c. "Swakop River", 1861 .. .. 95 85
471/4 .. .. *Set of* 4 2·50 2·00

(Des E. Holm)

1987 (7 May). *Useful Insects. T* **127** *and similar horiz designs. Multicoloured. P* 14.
475 16 c. Type **127** 40 15
476 20 c. *Alcimus stenurus* (fly) 60 50
477 25 c. *Anthophora caerulea* (bee) 80 70
478 30 c. *Hemiempusa capensis* (mantid) 90 85
475/8 .. .. *Set of* 4 2·50 2·00

128 Okaukuejo

(Des J. van Niekerk)

1987 (23 July). *Tourist Camps. T* **128** *and similar horiz designs. Multicoloured. P* 14½×14.

479	16 c. Type **128**	40	15
480	20 c. Daan Viljoen	50	35
481	25 c. Ai-Ais	60	50
482	30 c. Hardap	65	55
479/82	*Set of* 4	2·00	1·40

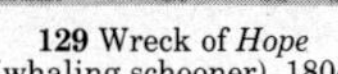

129 Wreck of *Hope* (whaling schooner), 1804 — **130** Bartolomeu Dias

(Des Sheila Nowers)

1987 (15 Oct). *Shipwrecks. T* **129** *and similar horiz designs. Multicoloured. P* 14.

483	16 c. Type **129**	50	15
484	30 c. *Tilly*, 1885	80	65
485	40 c. *Eduard Bohlen*, 1909	1·00	90
486	50 c. *Dunedin Star*, 1942	1·25	1·00
483/6	*Set of* 4	3·25	2·40

(Des Sheila Nowers)

1988 (7 Jan). *500th Anniv of Discovery of Cape of Good Hope by Bartolomeu Dias. T* **130** *and similar vert designs. Multicoloured. P* 14.

487	16 c. Type **130**	25	15
488	30 c. Caravel	50	35
489	40 c. Map of South West Africa, *c.* 1502	60	50
490	50 c. King João II of Portugal	75	60
487/90	*Set of* 4	1·90	1·40

131 Sossusvlei

(Des J. van Niekerk)

1988 (3 Mar). *Landmarks of South West Africa. T* **131** *and similar horiz designs. Multicoloured. P* 14.

491	16 c. Type **131**	30	15
492	30 c. Sesriem Canyon	55	40
493	40 c. Hoaruseb "clay castles"	70	50
494	50 c. Hoba meteorite	85	65
491/4	*Set of* 4	2·25	1·50

MACHINE LABELS. From 30 March 1988 gummed labels in the above design numbered "PT01", ranging in value from 1 c. to 99 r. 99, were available from a machine located at the Windhoek Post Office. During March 1989 three further machines at Ausspanplatz (PT02), Swakopmund (PT03) and Keetmanshoop (PT04) were added.

132 First Postal Agency, Otyimbingue, 1888 — **133** Herero Chat

(Des H. Pulon)

1988 (7 July). *Centenary of Postal Service in South West Africa. T* **132** *and similar horiz designs. Multicoloured. P* 14.

495	16 c. Type **132**	30	15
496	30 c. Post Office, Windhoek, 1904	50	30
497	40 c. Mail-runner and map	65	40
498	50 c. Camel mail, 1904	75	55
495/8	*Set of* 4	2·00	1·25

(Des G. Arnott)

1988 (3 Nov). *Birds of South West Africa. T* **133** *and similar vert designs. Multicoloured. P* 14.

499	16 c. Type **133**	30	15
500	30 c. Gray's Lark	50	30
501	40 c. Rüppell's Bustard	60	40
502	50 c. Monteiro's Hornbill	75	55
499/502	*Set of* 4	2·00	1·25

134 Dr. C. H. Hahn and Gross-Barmen Mission — **135** Beechcraft "1900"

(Des H. Pulon)

1989 (16 Feb). *Missionaries. T* **134** *and similar horiz designs. Multicoloured. P* 14.

503	16 c. Type **134**	30	10
504	30 c. Revd. J. G. Krönlein and Berseba Mission	50	30
505	40 c. Revd. F. H. Kleinschmidt and Rehoboth Mission	60	40
506	50 c. Revd. J. H. Schmelen and Bethanien Mission	70	55
503/6	*Set of* 4	1·90	1·25

(Des M. Botha)

1989 (18 May). *75th Anniv of Aviation in South West Africa. T* **135** *and similar horiz designs. Multicoloured. P* 14.

507	18 c. Type **135**	20	15
508	30 c. Ryan "Navion"	30	30
509	40 c. Junkers "F13"	40	40
510	50 c. Pfalz "Otto" biplane	50	50
507/10	*Set of* 4	1·25	1·25

136 Barchan Dunes

(Des A. H. Barrett)

1989 (14 Aug). *Namib Desert Sand Dunes. T* **136** *and similar horiz designs. Multicoloured. P* 14.

511	18 c. Barchan dunes	20	15
512	30 c. Star dunes (36×20 *mm*)	40	40
513	40 c. Transverse dunes	50	50
514	50 c. Crescentic dunes (36×20 *mm*)	70	70
511/14	*Set of* 4	1·60	1·60

137 Ballot Box and Outline Map of South West Africa

1989 (24 Aug). *South West Africa Constitutional Election. P* 14.

515	**137**	18 c. purple-brown and salmon	20	15
516		35 c. deep grey-blue and pale emerald	40	40
517		45 c. plum and lemon	55	55
518		60 c. dull green and deep yellow-ochre	70	70
515/18		*Set of* 4	1·75	1·60

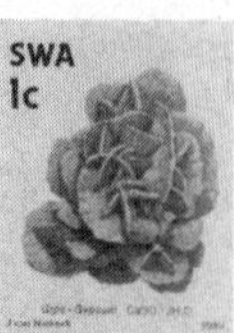

138 Gypsum — **139** Oranjemund Alluvial Diamond Field

(Des J. van Niekerk)

1989 (16 Nov)–**90.** *Minerals. T* **138/9** *and similar multicoloured designs. Phosphorised paper* (25 *c.*) *or chalk-surfaced paper* (30, 35, 50 *c.*, 1 *r.*). *P* 14.

519	1 c. Type **138**	10	10
520	2 c. Fluorite	10	10
521	5 c. Mimetite	10	10
522	7 c. Cuprite	10	10
523	10 c. Azurite	10	10
524	18 c. Boltwoodite (inscr "K (H3O) (UO2) (SiO4)")	20	10
	a. Formula corrected to "K2 (UO2) 2 (SiO3) 2 (OH) 2 5 H2O" (25.10.90)	2·00	1·50
525	20 c. Dioptase	20	15
526	25 c. Type **139**	25	15
527	30 c. Tsumeb lead and copper complex	35	20
528	35 c. Rosh Pinah zinc mine	35	20
529	40 c. Diamonds	50	30
530	45 c. Wulfenite	50	30
531	50 c. Uis tin mine	60	30
532	1 r. Rössing uranium mine	1·10	80
533	2 r. Gold	1·50	1·50
519/33	*Set of* 15	5·50	4·00

The 1, 2, 5, 7, 10, 18, 20, 40, 45 c. and 2 r. are vertical as T **138**, and the 25, 30, 35, 50 c. and 1 r. horizontal as T **139**.

140 Arrow Poison

(Des Eva-Maria Linsmayer)

1990 (1 Feb). *Flora. T* **140** *and similar vert designs. Multicoloured. P* 14.

534	18 c. Type **140**	30	10
535	35 c. Baobab flower	55	35
536	45 c. Sausage Tree flowers	60	40
537	60 c. Devil's Claw	75	75
534/7	*Set of* 4	2·00	1·40

South West Africa became independent on 21 March 1990 and was renamed Namibia.

NAMIBIA

PRINTERS. The following stamps were printed in lithography by the Government Printer, Pretoria, South Africa.

141 Pres. Sam Nujoma, Map of Namibia and National Flag — **142** Fish River Canyon

(Des T. Marais)

1990 (21 Mar). *Independence. T* **141** *and similar multicoloured designs. P* 14.

538	18 c. Type **141**	20	15
539	45 c. Hands releasing dove and map of Namibia (*vert*)	45	35
540	60 c. National flag and map of Africa	70	55
538/40	*Set of* 3	1·25	95

(Des J. van Ellinckhuijzen)

1990 (26 Apr). *Namibia Landscapes. T* **142** *and similar horiz designs. Multicoloured. P* 14.

541	18 c. Type **142**	20	20
542	35 c. Quiver-tree forest, Keetmanshoop	35	35
543	45 c. Tsaris Mountains	40	40
544	60 c. Dolerite boulders, Keetmanshoop	50	50
541/4	*Set of* 4	1·25	1·25

143 Stores on Kaiser Street, *c.* 1899 — **144** Maizefields

(Des J. van Ellinckhuijzen)

1990 (26 July). *Centenary of Windhoek. T* **143** *and similar horiz designs. Multicoloured. P* 14.

545	18 c. Type **143**	15	15
546	35 c. Kaiser Street, 1990	25	25
547	45 c. City Hall, 1914	30	30
548	60 c. City Hall, 1990	40	40
545/8	*Set of* 4	1·00	1·00

1990 (11 Oct). *Farming. T* **144** *and similar horiz designs. Multicoloured. P* 14.

549 20 c. Type **144** 15 15
550 35 c. Sanga bull 25 25
551 50 c. Damara ram 35 35
552 65 c. Irrigation in Okavango 45 45
549/52 .. .. *Set of* 4 1·10 1·10

145 Gypsum **146** Radiosonde Weather Balloon

(Des J. van Niekerk)

1991 (2 Jan–14 June). *Minerals. Designs as Nos.* 519/21 *and* 523/33, *some with values changed, and new design* (5 *r.*), *inscr* "Namibia" *as T* **145**. *Multicoloured. Chalk-surfaced paper* (25, 30, 35, 50 *c.*, 1 *r.*). *P* 14.

553 1 c. Type **145** 10 10
554 2 c. Fluorite 10 10
555 5 c. Mimetite 10 10
556 10 c. Azurite 10 10
557 20 c. Dioptase 10 10
558 25 c. Type **139** 10 15
a. Ordinary paper (14 June) 10 15
559 30 c. Tsumeb lead and copper complex .. 10 15
560 35 c. Rosh Pinah zinc mine 15 20
561 40 c. Diamonds 15 20
562 50 c. Uis tin mine 20 25
563 65 c. Boltwoodite 25 30
564 1 r. Rössing uranium mine 40 45
565 1 r. 50, Wulfenite 60 65
566 2 r. Gold 80 85
567 5 r. Willemite (vert as T **145**) .. .. 2·00 2·10
553/67 .. .. *Set of* 15 4·50 5·00

Printings of the 5 c. and 10 c. in 1992 were on phosphorescent paper.

(Des L. Kriedemann)

1991 (1 Feb). *Centenary of Weather Service. T* **146** *and similar horiz designs. Multicoloured. P* 14.

568 20 c. Type **146** 20 20
569 35 c. Sunshine recorder 30 30
570 50 c. Measuring equipment 40 40
571 65 c. Meteorological station, Gobabeb .. 50 50
568/71 .. .. *Set of* 4 1·25 1·25

147 Herd of Zebras **148** Karas Mountains

1991 (18 Apr). *Endangered Species. Mountain Zebra. T* **147** *and similar horiz designs. Multicoloured. P* 14.

572 20 c. Type **147** 25 25
573 25 c. Mare and foal 30 30
574 45 c. Zebras and foal 50 50
575 60 c. Two zebras 65 65
572/5 .. .. *Set of* 4 1·50 1·50

(Des A. H. Barrett)

1991 (18 July). *Mountains of Namibia. T* **148** *and similar horiz designs. Multicoloured. P* 14.

576 20 c. Type **148** 20 20
577 25 c. Gamsberg Mountains 25 25
578 45 c. Mount Brukkaros 45 45
579 60 c. Erongo Mountains 50 50
576/9 .. .. *Set of* 4 1·25 1·25

149 Bernabe de la Bat Camp **150** Artist's Pallet

(Des J. van Niekerk)

1991 (24 Oct). *Tourist Camps. T* **149** *and similar horiz designs. Multicoloured. P* 14.

580 20 c. Type **149** 20 20
581 25 c. Von Bach Dam Recreation Resort .. 25 25
582 45 c. Gross Barmen Hot Springs 40 40
583 60 c. Namutoni Rest Camp 50 50
580/3 .. .. *Set of* 4 1·25 1·25

(Des H. Pulon)

1992 (30 Jan). *21st Anniv of Windhoek Conservatoire. T* **150** *and similar horiz designs. Multicoloured. P* 14.

584 20 c. Type **150** 10 10
585 25 c. French horn and cello 10 10
586 45 c. Theatrical masks 20 25
587 60 c. Ballet dancers 25 30
584/7 .. .. *Set of* 4 60 70

151 Blue Kurper

(Des B. Jackson)

1992 (16 Apr). *Freshwater Angling. T* **151** *and similar horiz designs. Multicoloured. P* 14.

588 20 c. Type **151** 10 10
589 25 c. Largemouthed Yellow Fish 10 10
590 45 c. Carp 20 25
591 60 c. Sharptoothed Catfish 25 30
588/91 .. .. *Set of* 4 60 70

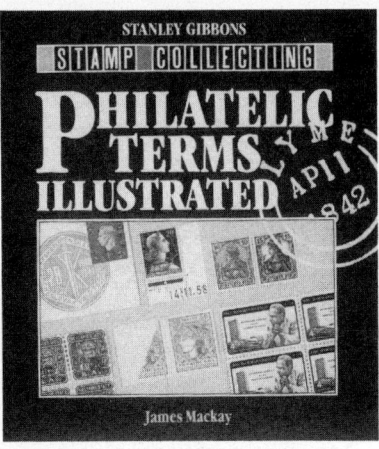

POSTAGE DUE STAMPS

PRICES for Nos. D1/39 are for unused horizontal pairs, used horizontal pairs and used singles.

1923 (1 Jan–July). *Optd with T* **1** *and* **2** *alternately.*

(*a*) *Setting* I (14 *mm between lines of overprint*) (i) *On Nos.* D5/6 *of Transvaal*

D1 5d. black and violet .. .. 4·00 30·00 8·50
a. "Wes" for "West" (R. 8/6, 10/2 left pane) £120
b. "Afrika" without stop (R. 6/1) 80·00
D2 6d. black and red-brown .. .. 17·00 32·00 9·00
a. "Wes" for "West" (R. 10/2) .. £225
b. "Afrika" without stop (R. 6/1, 7/2) £130

(ii) *On Nos.* D3/4 *and* D6 *of South Africa* (*De La Rue printing*)

D3 2d. black and violet .. .. 14·00 30·00 8·50
a. "Wes" for "West" (R. 10/2) .. £130 £160
b. "Afrika" without stop (R. 6/1, 7/2) £130
D4 3d. black and blue .. .. 8·00 30·00 8·50
a. "Wes" for "West" (R. 10/2) .. £100
D5 6d. black and slate (20 Apr) .. 22·00 38·00 10·00
a. "Wes" for "West" (R. 8/6) .. £130

(iii) *On Nos.* D9/10, D11 *and* D14 *of South Africa* (*Pretoria printings*)

D6 ½d. black and green (*p* 14) .. 3·50 17·00 4·50
a. Opt inverted £300
b. Opt double £550 £600
c. "Wes" for "West" (R. 10/2) .. 65·00
d. "Afrika" without stop (R. 6/1, 7/2) .. .. 65·00
D7 1d. black and rose (*roul*) .. 6·00 17·00 4·50
a. "Wes" for "West" (R. 10/2) .. 75·00
b. "Afrika" without stop (R. 6/1) 75·00
c. Imperf between (horiz pair) .. £900
D8 1½d. black and yellow-brown (*roul*) 75 8·50 2·25
a. "Wes" for "West" (R. 8/6, 10/2) 60·00
b. "Afrika" without stop (R. 6/1) 60·00
D9 2d. black and violet (*p* 14) (21 June) 1·75 16·00 4·25
a. "Wes" for "West" (R. 8/6) .. 75·00
b. "Afrika" without stop (R. 6/1) 75·00

Nos. D1/9 were initially overprinted as separate panes of 60, but some values were later done as double panes of 120.

A variety of Nos. D1, D4/5 and D9 with 15 mm between the lines of overprint occurs on four positions in each pane from some printings.

(*b*) *Setting* II (10 *mm between lines of overprint*). (i) *On No.* D5 *of Transvaal*

D10 5d. black and violet (20 Apr) .. 55·00 £110

(ii) *On Nos.* D3/4 *of South Africa* (*De La Rue printing*)

D11 2d. black and violet (20 Apr) .. 12·00 26·00 7·50
a. "Afrika" without stop (R.6/1) £110
D12 3d. black and blue (20 Apr) .. 7·00 20·00 5·50
a. "Afrika" without stop (R.6/1) 75·00

(iii) *On No.* D9 *of South Africa* (*Pretoria printing*). *Roul*

D13 1d. black and rose (July) .. £7000 — £1500

1923 (30 July)–**26**. *Optd as T* **3** ("Zuidwest" *in one word without hyphen*) *and* **4**.

(*a*) *Setting* III ("South West" 14 *mm long*, "Zuidwest" 11 *mm long and* 14 *mm between lines of overprint*).

(i) *On No.* D6 *of Transvaal*

D14 6d. black and red-brown .. .. 18·00 55·00 18·00

(ii) *On Nos.* D9 *and* D11/12 *of South Africa* (*Pretoria printing*)

D15 ½d. black and green (*p* 14) .. 6·00 16·00 3·75
D16 1d. black and rose (*roul*) .. 1·75 14·00 3·50
D17 1d. black and rose (*p* 14) (2.8.23) 6·00 16·00 3·75

(*b*) *Setting* IV ("South West" 16 *mm long*, "Zuidwest" 12 *mm long and* 14 *mm between lines of overprint*).

(i) *On No.* D5 *of Transvaal*

D17*a* 5d. black and violet (1.7.24) .. £400 £650

(ii) *On Nos.* D11/12 *and* D16 *of South Africa* (*Pretoria printing*). *P* 14

D18 ½d. black and green (1.7.24) .. 3·25 16·00 3·75
D19 1d. black and rose (1.7.24) .. 4·50 17·00 4·00
D20 6d. black and slate (1.7.24) .. 2·25 26·00 8·00
a. "Africa" without stop (R.9/5) £100

(*c*) *Setting* V (12 *mm between lines of overprint*).

(i) *On No.* D5 *of Transvaal*

D21 5d. black and violet (6.8.24) .. 2·50 23·00 7·00

(ii) *On No.* D4 *of South Africa* (*De La Rue printing*)

D22 3d. black and blue (6.8.24) .. 10·00 30·00 9·00

(iii) *On Nos.* D11 *and* D13 *of South Africa* (*Pretoria printing*). *P* 14

D23 ½d. black and green (6.8.24) .. 2·00 18·00 4·75
D24 1½d. black & yellow-brown (6.8.24) 4·00 18·00 4·75

(*d*) *Setting* VI (9½ *mm between lines of overprint*).

(i) *On No.* D5 *of Transvaal*

D25 5d. black and violet (7.9.24) .. 2·00 11·00 3·00
a. "Africa" without stop (R. 9/5) 55·00

(ii) *On No.* D4 *of South Africa* (*De La Rue printing*)

D26 3d. black and blue (3.2.26) .. 5·00 28·00 8·50

(iii) *On Nos.* D11/16 *of South Africa* (*Pretoria printing*). *P* 14

D27 ½d. black and green (1.3.26) .. 3·75 18·00 4·75
D28 1d. black and rose (16.3.25) .. 1·10 6·50 1·50
a. "Africa" without stop (R. 9/5 right pane) .. .. .. 60·00
D29 1½d. black & yellow-brown (1.10.26) 2·00 17·00 4·50
a. "Africa" without stop (R. 9/5 right pane) .. .. .. 60·00
D30 2d. black and violet (7.9.24) .. 2·50 10·00 2·75
a. "Africa" without stop (R. 9/5 right pane) .. .. .. 50·00
D31 3d. black and blue (6.5.26) .. 2·50 11·00 3·00
a. "Africa" without stop (R. 9/5 right pane) .. .. .. 55·00
D32 6d. black and slate (1.10.26) .. 8·50 38·00 11·00
a. "Africa" without stop (R. 9/5 right pane) £110
D27/32 .. .. .. *Set of* 6 18·00 90·00 25·00

For Setting VI the overprint was applied to sheets of 120 (2 panes of 60) of the 1d., 3d. and 6d., and to individual panes of 60 for the other values. The two measurements of "South West", as detailed under No. 40, also occur on the postage dues. Nos. D25 and D31/2 show it 16 mm long, No. 27 16½ mm long and the other stamps can be found with either measurement. In addition to the complete panes the 16½ mm long "South West" also occurs on R.2/4 in the 16 mm left pane for Nos. D28 and D30/2.

Suidwes **South West**

Afrika. **Africa.**

(D 1) (D 2)

1927 (14 May–27 Sept). *Optd as Types* D **1** *and* D **2**, *alternately,* 12 *mm between lines of overprint.* (*a*) *On No.* D5 *of Transvaal.*

D33 5d. black and violet (27 Sept) .. 16·00 55·00 18·00

(*b*) *On Nos.* D13/16 *of South Africa* (*Pretoria printing*). *P* 14

D34 1½d. black and yellow-brown .. 55 10·00 3·00
D35 2d. black and pale violet (27 Sept) 2·50 10·00 2·50
a. Black and deep violet .. 2·75 11·00 2·75
D37 3d. black and blue (27 Sept) .. 8·50 30·00 9·00
D38 6d. black and slate (27 Sept) .. 5·50 23·00 6·50

(*c*) *On No.* D18 *of South Africa* (*Pretoria printing*). *P* 14

D39 1d. black and carmine .. 1·00 8·00 2·25
D33/9 .. .. .. *Set of* 6 30·00 £120 38·00

No. D33 was overprinted in panes of 60 and the remainder as complete sheets of 120.

Examples of all values can be found with very small or very faint stops from various positions in the sheet.

1928–29. *Optd with T* **10**. (*a*) *On Nos.* D15/16 *of South Africa*

		Un Single	*Us Single*
D40	3d. black and blue	50	10·00
	a. Without stop after "A" (R.3/6) ..	25·00	
D41	6d. black and slate	7·50	20·00
	a. Without stop after "A" (R.3/6) ..	£110	
	(*b*) *On Nos.* D17/21 *of South Africa*		
D42	½d. black and green	40	7·00
D43	1d. black and carmine	40	3·25
	a. Without stop after "A" (R.3/6) ..	38·00	
D44	2d. black and mauve	40	3·50
	a. Without stop after "A" (R.3/6) ..	50·00	
D45	3d. black and blue	1·75	17·00
D46	6d. black and slate	1·00	17·00
	a. Without stop after "A" (R.3/6) ..	38·00	
D42/6	.. .. .. *Set of* 6	3·50	42·00

D 3

D 4

D 5

(Litho B.W.)

1931 (23 Feb). *Inscribed bilingually.* W **9** *of South Africa. P* 12.

D47 D **3** ½d. black and green .. .. .. 60 5·00
D48 1d. black and scarlet .. .. .. 60 1·25
D49 2d. black and violet .. .. .. 70 2·50
D50 3d. black and blue .. .. .. 1·50 14·00
D51 6d. black and slate .. .. .. 7·00 20·00
D47/51 .. .. .. *Set of* 5 9·50 38·00

PRINTER. The following issues have been printed by the South African Government Printer, Pretoria.

1959 (18 May). *Centre typo; frame roto.* W **9** *of South Africa. P* 15 × 14.

D52 D **4** 1d. black and scarlet .. .. 1·00 10·00
D53 2d. black and reddish violet .. 1·00 11·00
D54 3d. black and blue .. .. 1·00 12·00
D52/4 .. .. .. *Set of* 3 2·75 30·00

1960 (Dec). *As Nos.* D52 *and* D54 *but* W **102** *of South Africa.*

D55 1d. black and scarlet .. .. .. 2·50 4·50
D56 3d. black and blue .. .. .. 2·50 6·50

1961 (14 Feb). *As Nos.* D52 *etc, but whole stamp roto, and value in cents.* W **102** *of South Africa.*

D57 1 c. black and blue-green .. .. 30 2·50
D58 2 c. black and scarlet .. .. .. 30 2·50
D59 4 c. black and reddish violet .. .. 40 2·50
D60 5 c. black and light blue .. .. 65 3·25
D61 6 c. black and green .. .. .. 65 4·50
D62 10 c. black and yellow .. .. .. 1·25 6·00
D57/62 .. .. .. *Set of* 6 3·25 19·00

1972 (22 Mar). W **127** (*sideways tête-bêche*). *Phosphorised chalk-surfaced paper. P* 14 × 13½.

D63 D **5** 1 c. emerald .. .. .. 75 3·50
D64 8 c. ultramarine .. .. .. 3·00 6·50

The use of Postage Due stamps ceased in April 1975.

OFFICIAL STAMPS

OFFICIAL / **South West Africa.** (O 1) **OFFISIEEL** / **Suidwes Afrika.** (O 2)

1926 (Dec). *Nos.* 30, 31, 6 *and* 32 *of South Africa optd with Type* O 1 *on English stamp and* O 2 *on Afrikaans stamp alternately.*

		Un pair	*Us pair*	*Us single*
O1	½d. black and green	65·00	£140	30·00
O2	1d. black and carmine	65·00	£140	30·00
O3	2d. dull purple	£140	£200	45·00
O4	6d. green and orange	85·00	£140	30·00
O1/4	.. .. .. *Set of* 4	£325	£550	£120

OFFICIAL / **S.W.A.** (O 3) **OFFISIEEL** / **S.W.A.** (O 4)

1929 (May). *Nos.* 30, 31, 32 *and* 34 *of South Africa optd with Type* O **3** *on English stamp and* O **4** *on Afrikaans stamp.*

O5 ½d. black and green .. .. 1·00 10·00 2·50
O6 1d. black and carmine .. .. 1·00 10·00 2·50
O7 2d. grey and purple .. .. 1·50 12·00 3·00
a. Pair, stamp without stop after "OFFICIAL" .. .. 5·00 35·00
b. Pair, stamp without stop after "OFFISIEEL" .. .. 5·00 35·00
c. Pair, comprising a and b .. 16·00 75·00
O8 6d. green and orange .. .. 3·00 13·00 3·25
O5/8 .. .. *Set of* 4 6·00 40·00 10·00

Types O **3** and O **4** are normally spaced 17 mm between lines on all except the 2d. value, which is spaced 13 mm.

Except on No. O7, the words "OFFICIAL" or "OFFISIEEL" normally have no stops after them.

OFFICIAL **S.W.A.** (O 5) **OFFISIEEL** **S.W.A.** (O 6)

OFFICIAL. S.W.A. (O 7) **OFFISIEEL. S.W.A.** (O 8)

1929 (Aug). *Nos.* 30, 31 *and* 32 *of South Africa optd with Types* O **5** *and* O **6**, *and No.* 34 *with Types* O **7** *and* O **8**, *languages to correspond.*

O 9 ½d. black and green .. .. 65 10·00 2·50
O10 1d. black and carmine .. .. 75 10·00 2·50
O11 2d. grey and purple .. .. 90 12·00 3·00
a. Pair, one stamp without stop after "OFFICIAL" .. .. 3·75 35·00
b. Pair, one stamp without stop after "OFFISIEEL" .. .. 3·75 35·00
c. Pair, comprising a and b .. 18·00 75·00
O12 6d. green and orange .. .. 3·00 26·00 6·50
O9/12 .. .. *Set of* 4 4·75 50·00 13·00

OFFICIAL (O 9) **OFFISIEEL** (O 10)

1931. *English stamp optd with Type* O **9** *and Afrikaans stamp with Type* O **10** *in red.*

O13 **12** ½d. black and emerald .. .. 6·00 14·00 3·25
O14 **13** 1d. indigo and scarlet .. .. 75 14·00 3·25
O15 **14** 2d. blue and brown .. .. 70 10·00 2·25
O16 **17** 6d. blue and brown .. .. 2·25 13·00 3·00
O13/16 .. .. *Set of* 4 8·75 45·00 10·50

OFFICIAL (O 11) OFFISIEEL (O 12)

1938 (1 July). *English stamp optd with Type* O **11** *and Afrikaans with Type* O **12** *in red.*

O17 **27** 1½d. purple-brown .. .. 18·00 28·00 4·75

OFFICIAL (O 13) **OFFISIEEL** (O 14)

1945–50. *English stamp optd with Type* O **13**, *and Afrikaans stamp with Type* O **14** *in red.*

O18 **12** ½d. black and emerald .. .. 6·00 18·00 3·75
O19 **13** 1d. indigo and scarlet (1950) .. 2·25 12·00 3·00
a. Opt double £400
O20 **27** 1½d. purple-brown .. .. 25·00 22·00 4·25
O21 **14** 2d. blue and brown (1947?) .. £425 £600 £100
O22 **17** 6d. blue and brown .. .. 6·50 23·00 4·50
O18/20, O22 .. .. *Set of* 4 35·00 65·00 14·00

OFFICIAL (O 15) **OFFISIEEL** (O 16)

1951 (16 Nov)–**52**. *English stamp optd with Type* O **15** *and Afrikaans stamp with Type* O **16**, *in red.*

O23	**12**	½d. black and emerald (1952)	8·00	12·00	3·50
O24	**13**	1d. indigo and scarlet	1·00	9·00	1·60
		a. Opts transposed	40·00	70·00	
O25	**27**	1½d. purple-brown	20·00	16·00	4·00
		a. Opts transposed	55·00	80·00	
O26	**14**	2d. blue and brown	1·00	12·00	3·00
		a. Opts transposed	27·00	75·00	
O27	**17**	6d. blue and brown	2·75	28·00	6·50
		a. Opts transposed	20·00	75·00	
O23/7		*Set of* 5	29·00	70·00	17·00

The above errors refer to stamps with the English overprint on Afrikaans stamp and *vice versa*.

The use of official stamps ceased in January 1955.

Natal
see South Africa

Nauru

Stamps of MARSHALL ISLANDS were used in Nauru from the opening of the German Colonial Post Office on 14 July 1908 until 8 September 1914.

Following the occupation by Australian forces the "N.W. PACIFIC ISLANDS" overprints on Australia (see NEW GUINEA) were used during the early months of 1916.

PRICES FOR STAMPS ON COVER TO 1945	
Nos. 1/12	*from* × 10
Nos. 13/16	*from* × 3
Nos. 17/25	—
Nos. 26/39	*from* × 6
Nos. 40/3	*from* × 10
Nos. 44/7	*from* × 15

BRITISH MANDATE

NAURU (1) **NAURU** (2) **NAURU** (3)

1916 (2 Sept)–**23**. *Stamps of Great Britain* (1912–22) *overprinted at Somerset House.*

(a) With T **1** *(12½ mm long) at foot*

No.	Type	Description	Unused	Used
1	**105**	½d. green	30	3·00
		a. "NAUP.U"	£275	
		b. Double opt, one albino	60·00	
2	**104**	1d. bright scarlet	60	2·50
		a. "NAUP.U"	£450	
2*b*		1d. carmine-red	10·00	
		bb. Double opt, one albino	£200	
3	**105**	1½d. red-brown (1923)	55·00	80·00
4	**106**	2d. orange (Die I)	1·75	8·00
		a. "NAUP.U"	£300	
		b. Double opt, one albino	£100	
5		2d. orange (Die II) (1923)	70·00	£100
6	**104**	2½d. blue	2·75	5·00
		a. "NAUP.U"	£375	
		b. Double opt, one albino	£200	
7	**106**	3d. bluish violet	2·00	3·50
		a. "NAUP.U"	£375	
		b. Double opt, one albino	£200	
8		4d. slate-green	2·00	8·00
		a. "NAUP.U"	£500	
		b. Double opt, one albino	£200	
9	**107**	5d. yellow-brown	2·25	8·50
		a. "NAUP.U"	£600	
		b. Double opt, one albino	£140	
10		6d. purple, C	3·25	10·00
		a. "NAUP.U"	£500	
		b. Double opt, one albino	£225	
11	**108**	9d. agate	8·00	19·00
		a. Double opt, one albino	£225	
12		1s. bistre-brown (Optd S. £130)	7·00	19·00
		a. Double opt, one albino	£250	
1/12		*Set of* 11	75·00	£140

(b) With T **2** *(13½ mm long) at centre* (1923)

No.	Type	Description	Unused	Used
13	**105**	½d. green	4·50	55·00
14	**104**	1d. scarlet	24·00	45·00
15	**105**	1½d. red-brown	28·00	55·00
		a. Double opt, one albino	£140	
16	**106**	2d. orange (Die II)	45·00	80·00
13/16		*Set of* 4	90·00	£200

The "NAUP.U" errors occur on R.6/2 from Control I 16 only. The ink used on this batch of overprints was shiny jet-black.

There is a constant variety consisting of short left stroke to "N" which occurs on Nos. 1, 2, 2*b*, 4 (£30 *each*); 3 (£175); 5 (£200); 6,7 (£40 *each*); 8, 9, 10 (£60 *each*); 11, 12 (£75 *each*). All unused prices.

(c) T **109** *optd with T* **3**. (i) *Waterlow printing*

No.	Description	Unused	Used
17	5s. rose-carmine	£2500	£2000
18	10s. indigo-blue (R.) (Optd S. £1400)	£6000	£5000
	a. Double opt, one albino	£8000	£8000

(ii) *De La Rue printing*

No.	Description	Unused	Used
19	2s. 6d. deep brown (Optd S. £250)	£550	£650
	a. Double opt, one albino	£1200	
	b. Treble opt, two albino	£1300	
20	2s. 6d. yellow-brown	65·00	90·00
21	2s. 6d. pale brown (worn plate) (Optd S. £250)	70·00	85·00
	a. Re-entry		
22	5s. bright carmine (*shades*) (Optd S. £250)	£110	£150
	a. Treble opt, two albino	£550	
23	10s. pale blue (R.)	£300	£400
	a. Treble opt. (Blk. + R. + albino)		
23*b*	10s. deep bright blue (R.)	£600	£650

(iii) *Bradbury, Wilkinson printing* (1919)

No.	Description	Unused	Used
24	2s. 6d. chocolate-brown	75·00	£100
	a. Major re-entry		
	b. Double opt, one albino	£325	
25	2s. 6d. pale brown	60·00	85·00
	a. Double opt, one albino	£300	

AUSTRALIAN MANDATE

4 *Century* (freighter)

(Des R. A. Harrison. Eng T. S. Harrison. Recess Note Printing Branch of the Treasury, Melbourne and from 1926 by the Commonwealth Bank of Australia)

1924–48. *T* **4**. *No wmk. P* 11.
I. Rough surfaced, greyish paper (1924–34).
II. Shiny surfaced, white paper (1937–48).

No.	Description	I		II	
26	½d. chestnut	60	2·75	7·50	13·00
	a. Perf 14 (1947)	†		1·25	6·00
27	1d. green	1·50	2·75	2·50	3·00
28	1½d. scarlet	2·25	3·50	90	1·50
29	2d. orange	2·25	6·00	1·50	7·50
30	2½d. slate-blue	4·00	12·00	†	
30*a*	2½d. greenish blue (1934)	4·00	11·00	†	
30*b*	2½d. dull blue (1948)	†		1·25	3·50
	ba. Imperf between (vert pair)	†		£4000	£4000
	bb. Imperf between (horiz pair)	†		£4000	£4000
31	3d. pale blue	2·50	7·00	†	
31*a*	3d. greenish grey (1947)	†		1·50	5·50
32	4d. olive-green	3·75	9·00	3·50	6·00
33	5d. brown	2·50	6·00	3·25	3·75
34	6d. dull violet	3·00	11·00	3·00	3·50
35	9d. olive-brown	5·50	17·00	7·50	16·00
36	1s. brown-lake	6·00	13·00	5·00	2·75
37	2s. 6d. grey-green	25·00	35·00	24·00	28·00
38	5s. claret	50·00	75·00	35·00	48·00
39	10s. yellow	90·00	£110	85·00	85·00
26I/39I	*Set of* 14	£180	£275	†	
26II/39II	*Set of* 15	†		£160	£190

(5) 6

1935 (12 July). *Silver Jubilee. T* **4** (*shiny surfaced, white paper*) *optd with T* **5**.

No.	Description	Unused	Used
40	1½d. scarlet	60	80
41	2d. orange	1·00	4·00
42	2½d. dull blue	1·50	1·50
43	1s. brown-lake	4·00	3·50
40/3	*Set of* 4	6·50	9·00

(Recess John Ash, Melbourne)

1937 (10 May). *Coronation. P* 11.

No.	Type	Description	Unused	Used
44	**6**	1½d. scarlet	45	40
45		2d. orange	45	75
46		2½d. blue	45	30
47		1s. purple	85	75
44/7		*Set of* 4	2·00	2·00

7 Nauruan Netting Fish

8 Anibare Bay

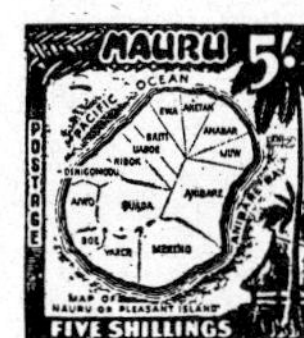

15 Map of Nauru

(Recess Note Printing Branch, Commonwealth Bank, Melbourne, and from 1960 by Note Ptg Branch, Reserve Bank of Australia, Melbourne)

1954 (6 Feb)–**65**. *T* **7/8**, **15** *and similar designs. Toned paper. P* 13½×14½ (*horiz*) *or* 14½×13½ (*vert*).

No.	Description	Unused	Used
48	½d. deep violet	20	10
	a. Violet (8.5.61)	20	20
49	1d. bluish green	30	20
	a. Emerald-green (8.5.61)	20	15
	b. Deep green (1965)	35	25
50	3½d. scarlet	1·50	15
	a. Vermilion (1958)	2·25	60
51	4d. grey-blue	1·50	60
	a. Deep blue (1958)	3·00	1·25
52	6d. orange	70	15
53	9d. claret	60	15
54	1s. deep purple	30	15
55	2s. 6d. deep green	2·50	60
56	5s. magenta	8·00	2·00
48/56	*Set of* 9	14·00	3·50

Designs: *Horiz*—3½d. Loading phosphate from cantilever; 4d. Great Frigate Bird; 6d. Nauruan canoe; 9d. Domaneab (meeting-house); 2s. 6d. Buada lagoon. *Vert*—1s. Palm trees.

Nos. 48*a*, 49*a*/*b*, 50*a* and 51*a* are on white paper.

16 Micronesian Pigeon

17 Poison Nut

20 Capparis

21 White Tern

(Recess (10d., 2s. 3d.) or photo (others) Note Ptg Branch, Reserve Bank of Australia, Melbourne)

1963–65. *T* **16/17**, **20/1** *and similar designs. P* 13½ × 13 (5*d.*), 13 × 13½ (8*d.*), 14 × 13½ (10*d.*), 15 × 14½ (1*s.* 3*d.*) *or* 13½ (*others*).

No.	Description	Unused	Used
57	2d. black, blue, red-brn & orge-yell (3.5.65)	1·00	1·50
58	3d. multicoloured (16.4.64)	75	35
59	5d. multicoloured (22.4.63)	75	75
60	8d. black and green (1.7.63)	2·00	80
61	10d. black (16.4.64)	50	30
62	1s. 3d. blue, black & yellow-green (3.5.65)	3·50	1·75
63	2s. 3d. ultramarine (16.4.64)	3·00	55
64	3s. 3d. multicoloured (3.5.65)	4·50	2·50
57/64	*Set of* 8	14·50	7·75

Designs: *Vert*—5d. "Iyo" (*calophyllum*). *Horiz*—8d. Black Lizard; 2s. 3d. Coral pinnacles; 3s. 3d. Finsch's Reed Warbler.

22 "Simpson and his Donkey"

(Des C. Andrew (after statue, Shrine of Remembrance, Melbourne. Photo Note Ptg Branch, Reserve Bank of Australia, Melbourne)

1965 (14 Apr). 50*th Anniv of Gallipoli Landing. P* 13½.

No.	Type	Description	Unused	Used
65	**22**	5d. sepia, black and emerald	15	10

(New Currency. 100 cents = $1 Australian)

24 Anibare Bay

25 "Iyo" (*calophyllum*)

(Recess (1, 2, 3, 5, 8, 19, 25 c. and $1) or photo (others))

1966 (14 Feb–25 May). *Decimal Currency. Various stamps with values in cents and dollars as T* **24/5** *and some colours changed. Recess printed stamps on helecon paper.*

No.	Type	Description	Unused	Used
66	**24**	1 c. deep blue	15	10
67	**7**	2 c. brown-purple (25 May)	15	20
68	–	3 c. bluish green (as 3½d.) (25 May)	30	30
69	**25**	4 c. multicoloured	25	10
70	–	5 c. deep ultramarine (as 1s.) (25 May)	25	30
71	–	7 c. black and chestnut (as 8d.)	25	10
72	**20**	8 c. olive-green	30	10
73	–	10 c. red (as 4d.)	40	10

74	21	15 c. blue, black & yellow-green (25 May)	80	1·00
75	–	25 c. deep brown (as 2s. 3d.) (25 May) ..	45	40
76	17	30 c. multicoloured	70	30
77	–	35 c. multicoloured (as 3s. 3d.) (25 May) ..	1·25	35
78	16	50 c. multicoloured	2·50	80
79	–	$1 magenta (as 5s.)	2·00	1·00
66/79		.. .. *Set of* 14	8·50	4·50

The 25 c. is as No. 63, but larger, 27½ × 24½ mm.

REPUBLIC

Nauru became independent on 31 January 1968 and was later admitted into special membership of the Commonwealth.

REPUBLIC OF NAURU

(26)

1968 (31 Jan–15 May). *Nos. 66/79 optd with T* **26**.

80	24	1 c. deep blue (R.)	10	20
81	7	2 c. brown-purple	10	10
82	–	3 c. bluish green	15	10
83	25	4 c. multicoloured (15.5.68)	15	10
84	–	5 c. deep ultramarine (R.)	15	10
85	–	7 c. black and chestnut (R.) (15.5.68) ..	25	10
86	20	8 c. olive-green (R.)	25	10
87	–	10 c. red	30	15
88	21	15 c. blue, black and yellow-green ..	2·75	2·50
89	–	25 c. deep brown (R.)	30	15
90	17	30 c. multicoloured (15.5.68)	55	15
91	–	35 c. multicoloured (15.5.68)	1·25	30
92	16	50 c. multicoloured	2·00	50
93		$1 magenta	1·25	75
80/93		.. .. *Set of* 14	8·00	4·50

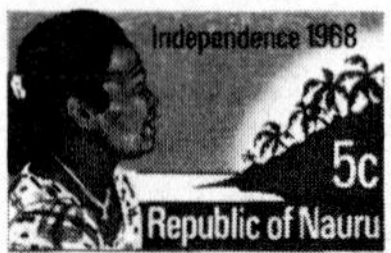

27 "Towards the Sunrise"

28 Planting Seedling, and Map

(Des H. Fallu (5 c.), Note Ptg Branch (10 c.). Photo Note Ptg Branch, Reserve Bank of Australia, Melbourne)

1968 (11 Sept). *Independence. P* 13½.

94	27	5 c. black, slate-lilac, orange-yellow and yellow-green	10	10
95	28	10 c. black, yellow-green and new blue ..	10	10

29 Flag of Independent Nauru

30 Island, "C" and Stars

(Des J. Mason. Photo Note Ptg Branch, Reserve Bank of Australia, Melbourne)

1969 (31 Jan). *P* 13½.

96	29	15 c. yellow, orange and royal blue ..	15	15

This is a definitive issue which was put on sale on the first anniversary of Independence.

(Des R. Brooks, Litho Format)

1972 (7 Feb). *25th Anniv of South Pacific Commission. P* 14½ × 14.

97	30	25 c. multicoloured	30	25

Independence 1968-1973

(31)

1973 (31 Jan). *Fifth Anniv of Independence. No. 96 optd with T* **31** *in gold.*

98	29	15 c. yellow, orange and royal blue ..	20	30

32 Denea

33 Artefacts and Map

(Des locally; adapted G. Vasarhelyi. Litho Format)

1973 (28 Mar*–25 July). *Various multicoloured designs as T* **32** *(1 to 5 c.) or T* **33** *(others). P* 14 *(1 to 5 c.),* 14½ × 14 *(7, 8, 10, 30, 50 c.) or* 14 × 14½ *(others).*

99	1 c. Ekwenababae	40	20
100	2 c. Kauwe Iud	55	20
101	3 c. Rimone	55	20
102	4 c. Type **32**	55	30
103	5 c. Erekogo	55	30
104	7 c. Ikimago (fish) (25.7)	30	20
105	8 c. Catching flying-fish (23.5)	30	20
106	10 c. Itsibweb (ball game) (23.5)	30	20
107	15 c. Nauruan wrestling (23.5)	35	20
108	20 c. Snaring Frigate Birds (23.5)	50	30
109	25 c. Nauruan girl (25.7)	50	30
110	30 c. Catching Noddy Birds (25.7)	85	40
111	50 c. Great Frigate Birds (25.7)	1·75	75
112	$1 Type **33**	2·00	75
99/112	.. .. .. *Set of* 14	8·25	4·00

The 1 to 5 c. show flowers, and the 7, 8, 10, 30, 50 c. are horiz designs.

*This is the local release date but the Crown Agents issued the stamps on 21 March.

34 Co-op Store

35 Phosphate Mining

(Des G. Vasarhelyi. Litho Format)

1973 (20 Dec). *50th Anniv of Nauru Co-operative Society. T* **34** *and similar multicoloured designs. P* 14 × 14½ *(50 c.) or* 14½ × 14 *(others).*

113	5 c. Type **34**	20	30
114	25 c. Timothy Detudamo (founder)	20	15
115	50 c. N.C.S. trademark (*vert*)	45	55
113/15	.. .. .. *Set of* 3	75	90

(Des G. Vasarhelyi (7 c. from original by J. Mason; 10 c. from original by K. Depaune). Litho Format)

1974 (21 May). *175th Anniv of First Contact with the Outside World. T* **35** *and similar horiz designs. Multicoloured. P* 13 × 13½ *(7, 35, 50 c.) or* 13½ × 13 *(others).*

116	7 c. M.V. *Eigamoiya* (bulk carrier) ..	1·25	90
117	10 c. Type **29**	1·00	25
118	15 c. Fokker Friendship *Nauru Chief* ..	1·00	30
119	25 c. Nauruan chief in early times ..	1·25	35
120	35 c. Capt. Fearn and H.M.S. *Hunter* ..	5·50	2·50
121	50 c. H.M.S. *Hunter* off Nauru ..	2·50	1·40
116/121	.. .. .. *Set of* 6	11·00	5·25

The 7, 35 and 50 c. are larger, 70 × 22 mm.

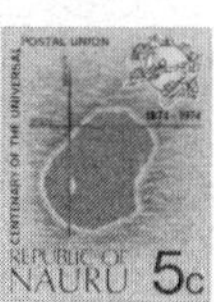

36 Map of Nauru

37 Rev. P. A. Delaporte

(Des G. Vasarhelyi. Litho Format)

1974 (23 July). *Centenary of Universal Postal Union. T* **36** *and similar multicoloured designs. P* 13½ × 14 *(5 c.),* 13 × 13½ *($1) or* 13½ × 13 *(others).*

122	5 c. Type **36**	20	20
123	8 c. Nauru Post Office	20	20
124	20 c. Nauruan postman	20	10
125	$1 U.P.U. Building and Nauruan flag ..	50	60
122/5	.. .. .. *Set of* 4	1·00	1·00
MS126	157 × 105 mm. Nos. 122/5. Imperf ..	3·50	5·50

The 8 and 20 c. are horiz (33 × 21 mm), and the $1 is vert (21 × 33 mm).

(Des J.W. Litho Format)

1974 (10 Dec). *Christmas and 75th Anniv of Rev. Delaporte's Arrival. P* 14½.

127	37	15 c. multicoloured	20	20
128		20 c. multicoloured	30	30

38 Map of Nauru, Lump of Phosphate Rock and Albert Ellis

39 Micronesian Outrigger

(Des M. and Sylvia Goaman. Litho Format)

1975 (23 July). *Phosphate Mining Anniversaries. T* **38** *and similar horiz designs. Multicoloured. P* 14½ × 14.

129	5 c. Type **38**	30	30
130	7 c. Coolies and mine	40	30
131	15 c. Electric railway, barges and ship ..	1·00	90
132	25 c. Modern ore extraction	1·25	1·00
129/32	.. .. .. *Set of* 4	2·75	2·25

Anniversaries:—5 c. 75th Anniv of discovery; 7 c. 70th Anniv of Mining Agreement; 15 c. 55th Anniv of British Phosphate Commissioners; 25 c. 5th Anniv of Nauru Phosphate Corporation.

(Des M. and Sylvia Goaman. Litho Format)

1975 (1 Sept). *South Pacific Commission Conference, Nauru (1st issue). T* **39** *and similar horiz designs. Multicoloured. P* 13½ × 14.

133	20 c. Type **39**	75	40
	a. Block of 4. Nos. 133/6	2·75	
134	20 c. Polynesian double-hull	75	40
135	20 c. Melanesian outrigger	75	40
136	20 c. Polynesian outrigger	75	40
133/6	.. .. .. *Set of* 4	2·75	1·40

Nos. 133/6 were printed in *se-tenant* blocks of four throughout the sheet.

40 New Civic Centre

41 "Our Lady" (Yaren Church)

(Des M. and Sylvia Goaman. Litho Format)

1975 (29 Sept). *South Pacific Commission Conference, Nauru (2nd issue). T* **40** *and similar horiz design. Multicoloured. P* 14.

137	30 c. Type **40**	15	15
138	50 c. Domaneab (meeting-house)	30	30

(Des M. and Sylvia Goaman. Litho Format)

1975 (7 Nov). *Christmas. T* **41** *and similar vert design showing stained-glass window. Multicoloured. P* 14½ × 14.

139	5 c. Type **41**	15	10
140	7 c. "Suffer little children. . ." (Orro Church)	15	10
141	15 c. As 7 c.	30	20
142	25 c. Type **41**	45	35
139/42	.. .. .. *Set of* 4	95	65

42 Flowers floating towards Nauru

(Des M. and Sylvia Goaman. Litho Format)

1976 (31 Jan*). *30th Anniv of the Return from Truk. T* **42** *and similar horiz designs. Multicoloured. P* 14½.

143	10 c. Type **42**	10	10
144	14 c. Nauru encircled by garland ..	15	10
145	25 c. Finsch's Reed Warbler and maps ..	35	25
146	40 c. Return of the islanders	45	35
143/6	.. .. .. *Set of* 4	95	65

*This is the local date of issue; the Crown Agents released the stamps one day earlier.

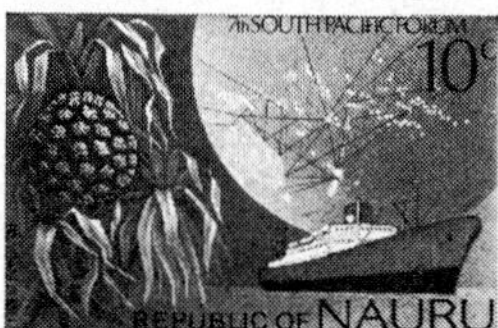

43 3d. and 9d. Stamps of 1916

(Des M. and Sylvia Goaman. Litho Format)

1976 (6 May). *60th Anniv of Nauruan Stamps. T* **43** *and similar horiz designs. Multicoloured. P* 13½.

147	10 c. Type **43**	15	15
148	15 c. 6d. and 1s. stamps	20	15
149	25 c. 2s. 6d. stamp	30	25
150	50 c. 5s. "Specimen" stamp	40	35
147/50	.. .. .. *Set of* 4	95	80

Nos. 147/8 show stamps with errors: the 3d. "Short N" and the 6d. "P" for "R".

44 *Pandanus mei* and *Enna G* (cargo liner)

(Des M. and Sylvia Goaman. Litho Format)

1976 (26 July). *South Pacific Forum, Nauru. T* **44** *and similar horiz designs. Multicoloured. P* 13½.

151	10 c. Type **44**	15	10
152	20 c. *Tournefortia argentea* and Nauruan aircraft	20	15
153	30 c. *Thespesia populnea* and Nauru Tracking Station	25	15
154	40 c. *Cordia subcordata* and produce ..	35	25
151/4	.. .. .. *Set of* 4	85	60

45 Nauruan Choir

46 Nauru House and Coral Pinnacles

(Des G. Vasarhelyi. Litho Format)

1976 (17 Nov). *Christmas. T* **45** *and similar vert designs. Multicoloured. P* 13½.

155 15 c. Type **45** 10 10
 a. Horiz pair. Nos. 155/6 . . 20 20
156 15 c. Nauruan choir . . 10 10
157 20 c. Angel in white dress . . 15 15
 a. Horiz pair. Nos. 157/8 . . 30 30
158 20 c. Angel in red dress . . 15 15
155/8 . . *Set of* 4 50 50

Nos. 155/6 and 157/8 were printed horizontally *se-tenant* throughout the sheet, both forming composite designs.

(Des D. Gentleman. Photo Harrison)

1977 (25 Apr*). *Opening of Nauru House, Melbourne. T* **46** *and similar vert design. Multicoloured. P* 14.

159 15 c. Type **46** 15 15
160 30 c. Nauru House and Melbourne skyline . . 25 25

*This is the local release date. The London agency released the stamps on 14 April.

47 Cable Ship *Anglia*

48 Father Kayser and First Catholic Church

(Des D. Gentleman. Photo Harrison)

1977 (7 Sept). *75th Anniv of First Trans-Pacific Cable and 20th Anniv of First Artificial Earth Satellite. T* **47** *and similar vert designs. P* 14 × 14½.

161 7 c. multicoloured . . 25 10
162 15 c. light blue, grey and black . . 35 15
163 20 c. light blue, grey and black . . 35 20
164 25 c. multicoloured . . 35 20
161/4 . . *Set of* 4 1·10 60

Designs:—15 c. Tracking station, Nauru; 20 c. Stern of *Anglia*; 25 c. Dish aerial.

(Des D. Gentleman. Photo Harrison)

1977 (28 Nov). *Christmas. T* **48** *and similar vert designs. Multicoloured. P* 14½.

165 15 c. Type **48** . . 10 10
166 25 c. Congregational Church, Orro . . 15 15
167 30 c. Catholic Church, Arubo . . 15 15
165/7 . . *Set of* 3 30 30

No. 165 also commemorates the 75th anniversary of the Catholic Church on Nauru.

49 Arms of Nauru

=
4c
(50)

(Des G. Vasarhelyi. Litho Format)

1978 (31 Jan). *Tenth Anniv of Independence. P* 14½.

168 **49** 15 c. multicoloured . . 20 15
169 60 c. multicoloured . . 35 30

1978 (29 Mar). *Nos. 159/60 surch as T* **50** *by Format.*

170 4 c. on 15 c. Type **46** . . 2·50 4·50
171 5 c. on 15 c. Type **46** . . 2·50 4·50
172 8 c. on 30 c. No. 160 . . 2·50 4·50
173 10 c. on 30 c. No. 160 . . 2·50 4·50
170/3 . . *Set of* 4 9·00 16·00

COVER PRICES

Cover factors are quoted at the beginning of each country for most issues to 1945. An explanation of the system can be found on page x. The factors quoted do not, however, apply to philatelic covers.

51 Collecting Shellfish

52 A.P.U. Emblem

(Des D. Gentleman. Photo Harrison)

1978 (17 May)–**79**. *Horiz designs as T* **51** *in brown, blue and black (4 c.), grey, black and light blue (20 c., $5) or multicoloured (others). P* 14½.

174 1 c. Type **51** . . 20 20
175 2 c. Coral outcrop (6.6.79) . . 20 20
176 3 c. Reef scene (6.6.79) . . 20 20
177 4 c. Girl with fish (6.6.79) . . 25 20
178 5 c. Eastern Reef Heron (6.6.79) . . 60 30
179 7 c. Catching fish, Buada Lagoon . . 20 10
180 10 c. Ijuw Lagoon . . 20 15
181 15 c. Girl framed by coral . . 20 30
182 20 c. Pinnacles, Anibare Bay reef . . 30 25
183 25 c. Pinnacle at Meneng . . 20 30
184 30 c. Head of Great Frigate Bird . . 1·00 45
185 32 c. White-capped Noddy in coconut palm . . 85 35
186 40 c. Wandering Tattler . . 1·25 55
187 50 c. Great Frigate Birds on perch . . 85 45
188 $1 Old coral pinnacles at Topside . . 70 55
189 $2 New pinnacles at Topside . . 95 1·00
190 $5 Blackened pinnacles at Topside . . 1·75 2·25
174/90 . . *Set of* 17 9·00 7·00

(Litho Toppan Ptg Co, Ltd)

1978 (28 Aug). *14th General Assembly of Asian Parliamentarians' Union. T* **52** *and similar vert design. P* 13.

191 15 c. multicoloured . . 20 25
192 20 c. black, deep ultramarine and gold . . 20 25

Design:—20 c. As T **52** but different background.

53 Virgin and Child

54 Baden-Powell and Cub Scout

(Des R. Vigurs. Litho Format)

1978 (1 Nov). *Christmas. T* **53** *and similar multicoloured design. P* 14.

193 7 c. Type **53** . . 10 10
194 15 c. Angel in sun-rise scene (*horiz*) . . 10 10
195 20 c. As 15 c. . . 15 15
196 30 c. Type **53** . . 20 20
193/6 . . *Set of* 4 40 40

(Des J. Charles. Litho Format)

1978 (1 Dec). *70th Anniv of Boy Scout Movement. T* **54** *and similar horiz designs. Multicoloured. P* 13½.

197 20 c. Type **54** . . 20 15
198 30 c. Baden-Powell and Boy Scout . . 25 20
199 50 c. Baden-Powell and Rover Scout . . 35 30
197/9 . . *Set of* 3 70 60

55 Wright *Flyer* over Nauru

(Des D. Gentleman. Litho Format)

1979 (24 Jan). *Flight Anniversaries. T* **55** *and similar horiz designs. Multicoloured. P* 14.

200 10 c. Type **55** . . 15 10
201 15 c. *Southern Cross* superimposed on nose of Boeing "727" . . 25 15
 a. Pair. Nos. 201/2 . . 50 30
202 15 c. *Southern Cross* and Boeing "727" (front view) . . 25 15
203 30 c. Wright *Flyer* over Nauru airfield . . 35 20
200/3 . . *Set of* 4 90 55

Commemorations:—10, 30 c. 75th anniversary of powered flight; 15 c. 50th anniversary of Kingsford-Smith's Pacific flight.

Nos. 201/2 were printed together, *se-tenant*, in horizontal and vertical pairs throughout the sheet.

56 Sir Rowland Hill and Marshall Islands 10 pf. Stamp of 1901

(Des R. Granger Barrett. Litho Format)

1979 (27 Feb). *Death Centenary of Sir Rowland Hill. T* **56** *and similar horiz designs showing stamps and Sir Rowland Hill. Multicoloured. P* 14½.

204 5 c. Type **56** . . 15 10
 a. Imperf (pair) . . £375
205 15 c. "NAURU" opt on Great Britain 10s. "Seahorse" of 1916–23 . . 25 20
 a. Imperf (pair) . . £375
206 60 c. 1978 10th Anniversary of Independence 60 c. commemorative . . 55 40
 a. Imperf (pair)
204/6 . . *Set of* 3 85 60
MS207 159 × 101 mm. Nos. 204/6 . . 85 1·10
 a. Error. Imperf . . £650

57 Dish Antenna, Transmitting Station and Radio Mast

58 Smiling Child

(Des G. Vasarhelyi. Litho Format)

1979 (22 Aug). *50th Anniv of International Consultative Radio Committee. T* **57** *and similar horiz designs. Multicoloured. P* 14½.

208 7 c. Type **57** . . 15 10
209 32 c. Telex operator . . 35 25
210 40 c. Radio operator . . 40 25
208/10 . . *Set of* 3 80 55

(Des G. Vasarhelyi. Litho Format)

1979 (3 Oct). *International Year of the Child. T* **58** *and similar vert designs showing smiling children. P* 14½.

211 8 c. multicoloured . . 10 10
 a. Horiz strip of 5. Nos. 211/15 . . 70
212 15 c. multicoloured . . 15 15
213 25 c. multicoloured . . 20 20
214 32 c. multicoloured . . 20 20
215 50 c. multicoloured . . 25 25
211/15 . . *Set of* 5 70 70

Nos. 211/15 were printed together, *se-tenant*, in horizontal strips of 5 throughout the sheet, forming a composite design.

59 Ekwenababae (flower), Scroll inscribed "Peace on Earth" and Star

(Des G. Vasarhelyi. Litho Format)

1979 (14 Nov). *Christmas. T* **59** *and similar horiz designs. Multicoloured. P* 14½.

216 7 c. Type **59** . . 10 10
217 15 c. *Thespia populnea* (flower), scroll inscribed "Goodwill toward Men" and star . . 10 10
218 20 c. Denea (flower), scroll inscribed "Peace on Earth" and star . . 10 10
219 30 c. Erekogo (flower), scroll inscribed "Goodwill toward Men" and star . . 20 20
216/19 . . *Set of* 4 40 40

60 Dassult "Falcon" over Melbourne

(Des G. Vasarhelyi. Litho Format)

1980 (28 Feb). *10th Anniv of Air Nauru. T* **60** *and similar horiz designs. Multicoloured. P* 14½.

220 15 c. Type **60** . . 30 15
221 20 c. Fokker "F28 (Fellowship)" over Tarawa . . 35 15
222 25 c. Boeing "727" over Hong Kong . . 35 15
223 30 c. Boeing "737" over Auckland . . 35 15
220/3 . . *Set of* 4 1·25 55

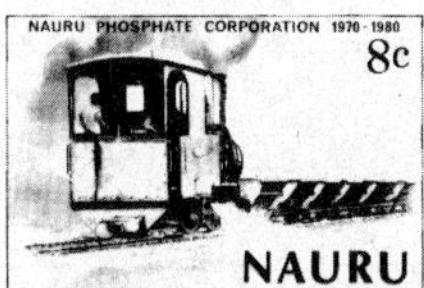

61 Steam Locomotive

(Des G. Vasarhelyi. Litho Format)

1980 (6 May). *10th Anniv of Nauru Phosphate Corporation. Railway Locomotives.* *T* **61** *and similar horiz designs. Multicoloured. P* 14½.

224 8 c. Type **61** 10 10
225 32 c. Electric locomotives 20 20
226 60 c. Diesel locomotive 35 35
224/6 . . . . *Set of* 3 60 60
MS227 168 × 118 mm. Nos. 224/6. P 13 . . . . 1·75 1·75

No. **MS**227 also commemorates the "London 1980" International Stamp Exhibition.

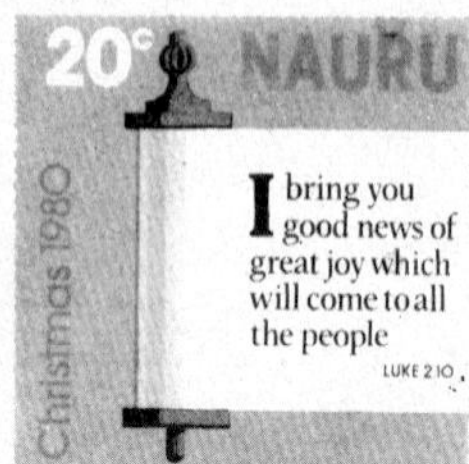

62 Verse 10 from Luke, Chapter 2 in English

(Des C. Abbott. Litho Format)

1980 (24 Sept). *Christmas.* *T* **62** *and similar square designs showing verses from Luke, chapter 2. Multicoloured. P* 14½.

228 20 c. Type **62** 10 10
a. Horiz pair. Nos. 228/9 . . . . . . 20 20
229 20 c. Verse 10 in Nauruan 10 10
230 30 c. Verse 14 in English 15 15
a. Horiz pair. Nos. 230/1 . . . . . . 30 30
231 30 c. Verse 14 in Nauruan 15 15
228/31 . . . . *Set of* 4 50 50

Nos. 228/9 and 230/1 were each printed together, *se-tenant*, in horizontal pairs throughout the sheet.

See also Nos. 248/51.

63 Nauruan, Australian, Union and New Zealand Flags on Aerial View of Nauru

(Des H. Woods. Litho Format)

1980 (3 Dec)–**81**. *20th Anniv of U.N. Declaration on the Granting of Independence to Colonial Countries and Peoples.* *T* **63** *and similar multicoloured designs. P* 14½ (25 *c.*) *or* 13½ (*others*).

232 25 c. Type **63** 15 15
233 30 c. U.N. Trusteeship Council (72 × 23 *mm*) (11.2.81) 15 15
234 50 c. Nauru independence ceremony, 1968 (72 × 23 *mm*) 25 25
232/4 . . . . *Set of* 3 50 50

The 25 c. value was printed in sheets including 5 *se-tenant* stamp-size labels; the other two values were each printed in sheets including 5 *se-tenant* half stamp-size labels.

Nos. 233/4 exist imperforate from stock dispersed by the liquidator of Format International Security Printers Ltd.

64 Timothy Detudamo

(Des R. Granger Barrett. Litho Format)

1981 (11 Feb). *30th Anniv of Nauru Local Government Council. Head Chiefs.* *T* **64** *and similar horiz designs. Multicoloured. P* 14½.

235 20 c. Type **64** 15 15
236 30 c. Raymond Gadabu 15 15
237 50 c. Hammer DeRoburt 25 25
235/7 . . . . *Set of* 3 50 50

65 Casting Net by Hand

(Litho Questa)

1981 (22 May). *Fishing.* *T* **65** *and similar horiz designs. Multicoloured. P* 12 × 11½.

238 8 c. Type **65** 10 10
239 20 c. Outrigger canoe 20 15
240 32 c. Outboard motor boat 25 20
241 40 c. Trawler 30 25
238/41 . . . . *Set of* 4 75 60
MS242 167 × 116 mm. No. 241 × 4. P 14 . . 1·90 2·00

No. **MS**242 was issued to commemorate the "WIPA 1981" International Stamp Exhibition, Vienna.

66 Bank of Nauru Emblem and Building **67** Inaugural Speech

(Des H. Woods. Litho Harrison)

1981 (21 July). *Fifth Anniv of Bank of Nauru. P* 14 × 14½.

243 **66** $1 multicoloured 60 60

(Des G. Vasarhelyi. Litho Questa)

1981 (24 Oct). *U.N. Day. E.S.C.A.P. (United Nations Economic and Social Commission for Asia and the Pacific) Events.* *T* **67** *and similar square designs. Multicoloured. P* 14 × 14½.

244 15 c. Type **67** 15 15
245 20 c. Presenting credentials 15 15
246 25 c. Unveiling plaque 20 20
247 30 c. Raising U.N. flag 25 25
244/7 . . . . *Set of* 4 65 65

(Des C. Abbott. Litho Format)

1981 (14 Nov). *Christmas. Bible Verses. Square designs as T* **62**. *Multicoloured. P* 14½.

248 20 c. Matthew 1, 23 in English 15 15
a. Horiz pair. Nos. 248/9 . . . . . . 30 30
249 20 c. Matthew 1, 23 in Nauruan 15 15
250 30 c. Luke 2, 11 in English 20 20
a. Horiz pair. Nos. 250/1 . . . . . . 40 40
251 30 c. Luke 2, 11 in Nauruan 20 20
248/51 . . . . *Set of* 4 70 70

Nos. 248/9 and 250/1 were each printed together, *se-tenant*, in horizontal pairs throughout the sheet.

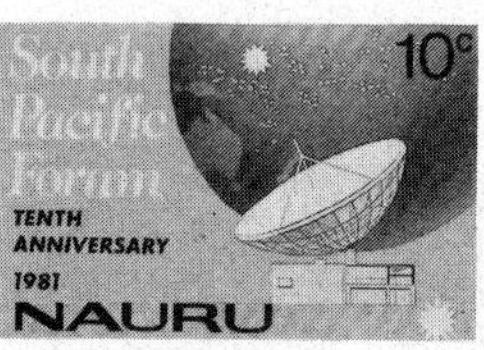

68 Earth Satellite Station

(Des M. Rickards. Litho Format)

1981 (9 Dec). *Tenth Anniv of South Pacific Forum.* *T* **68** *and similar horiz designs. Multicoloured. P* 13½ × 14.

252 10 c. Type **68** 30 20
253 20 c. *Enna G* (cargo liner) 35 25
254 30 c. Airliner 35 30
255 40 c. Local produce 45 40
252/5 . . . . *Set of* 4 1·25 1·00

69 Nauru Scouts leaving for 1935 Frankston Scout Jamboree

(Des C. Abbott. Litho Format)

1982 (23 Feb). *75th Anniv of Boy Scout Movement.* *T* **69** *and similar multicoloured designs. P* 14.

256 7 c. Type **69** 15 15
257 8 c. Two Nauru scouts on *Nauru Chief*, 1935 (*vert*) 15 15
258 15 c. Nauru scouts making pottery, 1935 (*vert*) 20 20
259 20 c. Lord Huntingfield addressing Nauru scouts, Frankston Jamboree, 1935 . . 25 25
260 25 c. Nauru cub and scout, 1982 . . . . 30 30
261 40 c. Nauru cubs, scouts and scouters, 1982 . . 45 45
256/61 . . . . *Set of* 6 1·40 1·40
MS262 152 × 114 mm. Nos. 256/61. Imperf . . 1·75 2·00

No. **MS**262 also commemorates Nauru's participation in the "Stampex" National Stamp Exhibition, London.

Nos. 256/61 were each printed in sheets including four *se-tenant* stamp-size labels.

70 100kw Electricity Generating Plant under Construction (left side)

(Litho Irish Security Stamp Printing Ltd)

1982 (10 June). *Ocean Thermal Energy Conversion.* *T* **70** *and similar horiz designs. Multicoloured. P* 13½.

263 25 c. Type **70** 50 30
a. Horiz pair. Nos. 263/4 . . . . . . 1·00 60
264 25 c. 100kw Electricity Generating Plant under construction (right side) . . 50 30
265 40 c. Completed plant (left) 70 40
a. Horiz pair. Nos. 265/6 . . . . . . 1·40 80
266 40 c. Completed plant (right) 70 40
263/6 . . . . *Set of* 4 2·25 1·25

Nos. 263/4 and 265/6 were printed together, *se-tenant*, in horizontal pairs forming composite designs throughout sheets which also included two stamp-size and twelve half stamp-size labels.

71 S.S. *Fido*

72 Queen Elizabeth II on Horseback

(Des R. Littleford (5 c.), Debbie Ryder (10, 30 c.), Cecilia Eales (60 c.), Jane Evans ($1). Litho Format)

1982 (11 Oct). *75th Anniv of Phosphate Shipments.* *T* **71** *and similar horiz designs. Multicoloured. P* 14.

267 5 c. Type **71** 40 10
268 10 c. Steam locomotive *Nellie* 75 20
269 30 c. Modern "Clyde" class diesel loco . . 1·00 50
270 60 c. M.V. *Eigamoiya* (bulk carrier) . . 1·40 80
267/70 . . . . *Set of* 4 3·25 1·40
MS271 165 × 107 mm. $1 *Eigamoiya*, *Rosie-D* and *Kolle-D* (bulk carriers) (67 × 27 *mm*) . . 1·75 1·75

No. **MS**271 was issued to commemorate "ANPEX 82" National Stamp Exhibition, Brisbane.

(Des G. Vasarhelyi. Litho Format)

1982 (21 Oct). *Royal Visit.* *T* **72** *and similar multicoloured designs. P* 14½.

272 20 c. Type **72** 40 30
273 50 c. Prince Philip, Duke of Edinburgh . . 75 60
274 $1 Queen Elizabeth II and Prince Philip (*horiz*) . . . . 1·40 1·25
272/4 . . . . *Set of* 3 2·25 1·90

73 Father Bernard Lahn **74** Speaker of the Nauruan Parliament

(Des G. Vasarhelyi. Litho Format)

1982 (17 Nov). *Christmas.* *T* **73** *and similar horiz designs. Multicoloured. P* 14½.

275 20 c. Type **73** 35 30
276 30 c. Reverend Itubwa Amram 40 45
277 40 c. Pastor James Aingimen 45 60
278 50 c. Bishop Paul Mea 50 90
275/8 . . . . *Set of* 4 1·50 2·00

Nos. 275/8 were printed in sheets of 25 including 5 *se-tenant*, stamp-size, labels.

(Des G. Vasarhelyi. Litho Walsall)

1983 (23 Mar). *15th Anniv of Independence.* *T* **74** *and similar multicoloured designs. W w* **14** (*sideways on* 30, 50 *c.*). *P* 14.

279 15 c. Type **74** 15 15
280 20 c. Family Court in session 20 20
281 30 c. Law Courts building (*horiz*) 25 25
282 50 c. Parliamentary chamber (*horiz*) . . 40 40
279/82 . . . . *Set of* 4 90 90

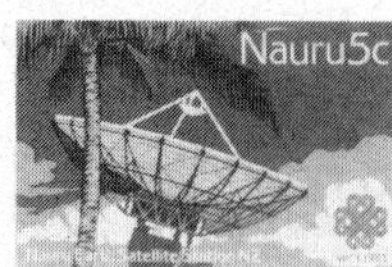

75 Nauru Satellite Earth Station

(Des C. Abbott. Litho Questa)

1983 (11 May). *World Communications Year.* *T* **75** *and similar horiz designs. Multicoloured. W w* **14** (*sideways*). *P* 14.

283 5 c. Type **75** 10 10
284 10 c. Omni-directional range installation . . 15 15
285 20 c. Emergency short-wave radio 20 25
286 25 c. Radio Nauru control room 30 30
287 40 c. Unloading air mail 45 45
283/7 . . . . *Set of* 5 1·00 1·10

76 Return of Exiles from Truk on M.V. *Trienza*, 1946

77 "The Holy Virgin, the Holy Child and St. John" (School of Raphael)

(Des D. Slater. Litho Format)

1983 (14 Sept). *Angam Day. T* **76** *and similar multicoloured designs. W* w **14** (*sideways on* 15 *c.*). *P* 13½ (15 *c.*) *or* 14 (*others*).

288	15 c. Type **76**	20	25
289	20 c. Mrs. Elsie Agio (exile community leader)	20	25
290	30 c. Child on scales	35	40
291	40 c. Nauruan children	45	50
288/91	*Set of* 4	1·10	1·25

Nos. 289/91 are vertical designs, each 25 × 41 mm.

(Des L. Curtis. Litho Questa)

1983 (16 Nov). *Christmas. T* **77** *and similar multicoloured designs. W* w **14** (*sideways on* 50 *c.*). *P* 14 × 14½ (50 *c.*) *or* 14½ × 14 (*others*).

292	5 c. Type **77**	10	10
293	15 c. "Madonna on the Throne surrounded by Angels" (School of Seville)	15	15
294	50 c. "The Mystical Betrothal of St. Catherine with Jesus" (School of Veronese) (*horiz*)	40	40
292/4	*Set of* 3	55	55

78 S.S. *Ocean Queen*

79 1974 U.P.U. $1 Stamp

(Des Beverley Barnard and L. Curtis. Litho Questa)

1984 (23 May). *250th Anniv of "Lloyd's List" (newspaper). T* **78** *and similar vert designs. Multicoloured. W* w **14**. *P* 14½ × 14.

295	20 c. Type **78**	45	30
296	25 c. M.V. *Enna G*	50	35
297	30 c. M.V. *Baron Minto*	55	40
298	40 c. Sinking of M.V. *Triadic*, 1940	75	55
295/8	*Set of* 4	2·00	1·40

(Des L. Curtis. Litho Format)

1984 (4 June). *Universal Postal Union Congress, Hamburg. W* w **14**. *P* 14.

299	**79**	$1 multicoloured	1·10	1·25

80 *Hypolimnas bolina* (female)

(Des I. Loe. Litho B.D.T.)

1984 (24 July). *Butterflies. T* **80** *and similar horiz designs. Multicoloured. W* w **14** (*sideways*). *P* 14.

300	25 c. Type **80**	50	40
301	30 c. *Hypolimnas bolina* (male)	55	55
302	50 c. *Danaus plexippus*	70	85
300/2	*Set of* 3	1·60	1·60

81 Coastal Scene

82 Buada Chapel

(Des A. Theobald. Litho Enschedé)

1984 (21 Sept). *Life in Nauru. T* **81** *and similar multicoloured designs. W* w **14** (*sideways on horiz designs*). *P* 13½ × 14 (1, 5, 10, 25, 40 *c.*, $2) *or* 14 × 13½ (*others*).

303	1 c. Type **81**	10	15
304	3 c. Nauruan woman (*vert*)	10	15
305	5 c. Modern trawler	15	15
306	10 c. Golfer on the links	30	20
307	15 c. Excavating phosphate (*vert*)	35	30
308	20 c. Surveyor (*vert*)	30	30
309	25 c. Air Nauru airliner	35	35
310	30 c. Elderly Nauruan (*vert*)	35	35
311	40 c. Loading hospital patient on to aircraft	40	40
312	50 c. Skin-diver with fish (*vert*)	55	55
313	$1 Tennis player (*vert*)	1·25	1·25
314	$2 Anabar Lagoon	1·75	1·75
303/14	*Set of* 12	5·50	5·50

Nos. 303/14 were each issued in sheets of 9 with decorative margins.

(Des L. Curtis. Litho Format)

1984 (14 Nov). *Christmas. T* **82** *and similar multicoloured designs. W* w **14** (*sideways on* 50 *c.*). *P* 14.

315	30 c. Type **82**	60	50
316	40 c. Detudamo Memorial Church	80	65
317	50 c. Candle-light service, Kayser College (*horiz*)	90	70
315/17	*Set of* 3	2·10	1·75

83 Air Nauru Jet on Tarmac

(Des L. Curtis. Litho Walsall)

1985 (26 Feb). *15th Anniv of Air Nauru. T* **83** *and similar multicoloured designs. W* w **14** (*sideways on* 20 *c.*, 40 *c.*). *P* 14.

318	20 c. Type **83**	55	35
319	30 c. Stewardess on aircraft steps (*vert*)	70	60
320	40 c. Fokker "F28" over Nauru	85	75
321	50 c. Freight being loaded onto Boeing "727" (*vert*)	1·00	85
318/21	*Set of* 4	2·75	2·25

84 Open Cut Mining

85 Mother and Baby on Beach

(Des L. Curtis. Litho B.D.T.)

1985 (31 July). *15th Anniv of Nauru Phosphate Corporation. T* **84** *and similar horiz designs. Multicoloured. W* w **14** (*sideways*). *P* 14.

322	20 c. Type **84**	70	60
323	25 c. Locomotive hauling crushed ore	1·25	1·00
324	30 c. Phosphate drying plant	1·25	1·00
325	50 c. Early steam locomotive	2·00	1·75
322/5	*Set of* 4	4·75	4·00

(Des A. Theobald. Litho Questa)

1985 (15 Nov). *Christmas. T* **85** *and similar vert design. Multicoloured. W* w **16** (*sideways*). *P* 14.

326	50 c. Beach scene	1·25	1·25
	a. Horiz pair. Nos. 326/7	2·50	2·50
327	50 c. Type **85**	1·25	1·25

Nos. 326/7 were printed in sheets of 16 made up of two strips of four *se-tenant* pairs, each pair forming a composite design. The two strips were divided by a horizontal gutter.

86 Adult Common Noddy with Juvenile

(Des N. Arlott. Litho Questa)

1985 (31 Dec). *Birth Bicentenary of John J. Audubon (ornithologist). Common "Brown" Noddy. T* **86** *and similar horiz designs. Multicoloured. W* w **16**. *P* 14.

328	10 c. Type **86**	35	35
329	20 c. Adult and immature birds in flight	50	70
330	30 c. Adults in flight	65	85
331	50 c. "Brown Noddy" (John J. Audubon)	80	1·10
328/31	*Set of* 4	2·10	2·75

87 Douglas Motor Cycle

(Des M. Joyce. Litho Questa)

1986 (5 Mar). *Early Transport on Nauru. T* **87** *and similar horiz designs. Multicoloured. W* w **16**. *P* 14.

332	15 c. Type **87**	60	60
333	20 c. Primitive lorry	75	75
334	30 c. German 2 ft gauge locomotive (1910)	1·00	1·00
335	40 c. "Baby" Austin car	1·25	1·25
332/5	*Set of* 4	3·25	3·25

88 Island and Bank of Nauru

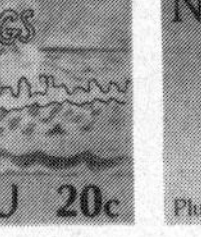

89 *Plumeria rubra*

(Des G. Vasarhelyi. Litho Format)

1986 (21 July). *10th Anniv of Bank of Nauru. Children's Paintings. T* **88** *and similar horiz designs. Multicoloured. W* w **16** (*sideways*). *P* 14.

336	20 c. Type **88**	30	30
337	25 c. Borrower with notes and coins	35	35
338	30 c. Savers	40	40
339	40 c. Customers at bank counter	55	55
336/9	*Set of* 4	1·40	1·40

(Des Doreen McGuinness. Litho Questa)

1986 (30 Sept). *Flowers. T* **89** *and similar horiz designs. Multicoloured. W* w **16**. *P* 14.

340	20 c. Type **89**	55	70
341	25 c. *Tristellateia australis*	65	85
342	30 c. *Bougainvillea cultivar*	75	1·00
343	40 c. *Delonix regia*	1·00	1·25
340/3	*Set of* 4	2·75	3·50

90 Carol Singers

91 Young Girls Dancing

(Des M. Joyce. Litho Questa)

1986 (8 Dec). *Christmas. T* **90** *and similar horiz design. Multicoloured. W* w **16** (*sideways*). *P* 14.

344	20 c. Type **90**	45	30
345	$1 Carol singers and hospital patient	2·00	1·75

(Des Joan Thompson. Litho Questa)

1987 (31 Jan). *Nauruan Dancers. T* **91** *and similar multicoloured designs. W* w **16** (*sideways on* 20, 30 *c.*). *P* 14.

346	20 c. Type **91**	55	55
347	30 c. Stick dance	75	85
348	50 c. Boy doing war dance (*vert*)	1·25	1·50
346/8	*Set of* 3	2·25	2·75

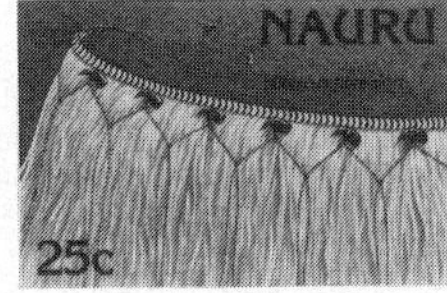

92 Hibiscus Fibre Skirt

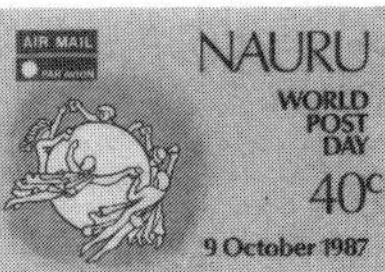

93 U.P.U. Emblem and Air Mail Label

(Des L. Curtis. Litho B.D.T.)

1987 (30 July). *Personal Artifacts. T* **92** *and similar horiz designs. Multicoloured. W* w **16** (*sideways*). *P* 14.

349	25 c. Type **92**	75	75
350	30 c. Headband and necklets	85	85
351	45 c. Decorative necklets	1·10	1·10
352	60 c. Pandanus leaf fan	1·60	1·60
349/52	*Set of* 4	3·75	3·75

(Des D. Miller. Litho Format)

1987 (20 Oct). *World Post Day. T* **93** *and similar multicoloured design. W* w **16**. *P* 14½ × 14.

353	40 c. Type **93**	65	65
MS354	122 × 82 mm. $1 U.P.U. emblem and map of Pacific showing mail routes (114 × 74 *mm*). Wmk sideways. Imperf	1·75	2·00

94 Open Bible

95 Nauruan Children's Party

(Des Janet Boschen. Litho Walsall)

1987 (5 Nov). *Centenary of Nauru Congregational Church. W* w **14**. *P* 13 × 13½.

355	**94**	40 c. multicoloured	65	80

(Des M. Joyce. Litho Format)

1987 (27 Nov). *Christmas. T* **95** *and similar horiz design. Multicoloured. W* w **16** (*sideways*). *P* 14.

356	20 c. Type **95**	75	35
357	$1 Nauruan Christmas dinner	2·75	2·75

96 Loading Phosphate on Ship

97 Map of German Marshall Is. and 1901 5 m. Yacht Definitive

(Des B. Clinton. Litho CPE Australia Ltd, Melbourne)

1988 (31 Jan). *20th Anniv of Independence. T* **96** *and similar multicoloured designs. P* 13½ × 14 (25 c.), 14 × 13½ (40, 55 c.) *or* 13 ($1).

358 25 c. Type **96** 70 70
359 40 c. Tomano flower (*vert*) .. .. 1·25 1·25
360 55 c. Frigate Bird (*vert*) .. .. 1·75 1·75
361 $1 Arms of Republic (35 × 35 *mm*) .. 2·00 2·25
358/61 .. .. *Set of* 4 5·25 5·50

(Des O. Bell. Litho Format)

1988 (29 July). *80th Anniv of Nauru Post Office. T* **97** *and similar horiz designs. Multicoloured. W w* **16** *(sideways). P* 14.

362 30 c. Type **97** 30 35
363 50 c. Letter and post office of 1908 .. .. 50 55
364 70 c. Nauru Post Office and airmail letter .. 65 70
362/4 .. .. *Set of* 3 1·25 1·40

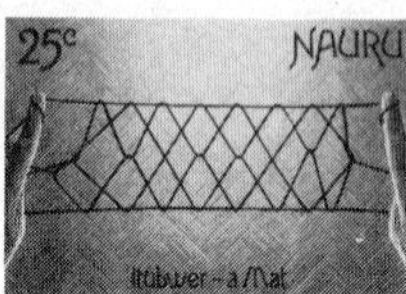

98 "Itubwer" (mat)

99 U.P.U. Emblem and National Flag

(Des Jennifer Toombs. Litho CPE Australia Ltd, Melbourne)

1988 (1 Aug). *String Figures. T* **98** *and similar horiz designs. Multicoloured. P* 13½ × 14.

365 25 c. Type **98** 25 30
366 40 c. "Etegerer–the Pursuer" 40 45
367 55 c. "Holding up the Sky" 50 55
368 80 c. "Manujie's Sword" 75 80
365/8 .. .. *Set of* 4 1·75 1·90

(Des Elisabeth Innes. Litho CPE Australia Ltd, Melbourne)

1988 (1 Oct). *Centenary of Nauru's Membership of Universal Postal Union. P* 13½ × 14.

369 **99** $1 multicoloured .. .. 95 1·00

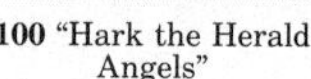

100 "Hark the Herald Angels"

101 Logo (15th anniv of Nauru Insurance Corporation)

(Des Elisabeth Innes. Litho CPE Australia Ltd, Melbourne)

1988 (28 Nov). *Christmas. T* **100** *and similar square designs showing words and music from "Hark the Herald Angels Sing". P* 13.

370 20 c. black, orange-vermilion and lemon .. 20 25
371 60 c. black, orange-vermilion and mauve .. 55 60
372 $1 black, orange-vermilion & bright green 95 1·00
370/2 .. .. *Set of* 3 1·50 1·60

(Litho Note Ptg Branch, Reserve Bank of Australia)

1989 (19 Nov). *Anniversaries and Events. T* **101** *and similar vert designs. Multicoloured. P* 14×15.

373 15 c. Type **101** 15 30
374 50 c. Logos (World Telecommunications Day and 10th anniv of Asian Pacific Telecommunity) 50 75
375 $1 Photograph of island scene (150 years of photography) .. .. 95 1·40
376 $2 Capitol and U.P.U. emblem (20th U.P.U. Congress, Washington) .. 1·90 2·50
373/6 .. .. *Set of* 4 3·25 4·50

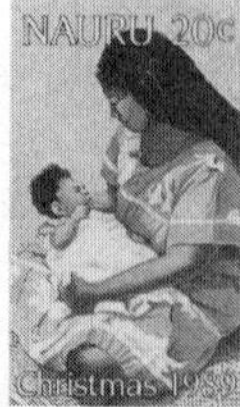

102 Mother and Baby

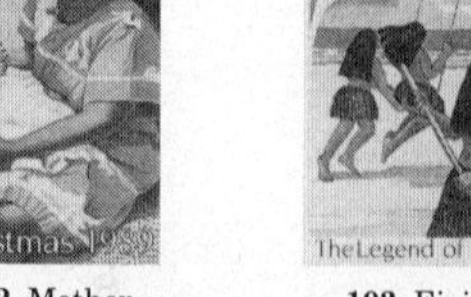

103 Eigigu working while Sisters play

(Des Robin White. Litho Note Ptg Branch, Reserve Bank of Australia)

1989 (15 Dec). *Christmas. T* **102** *and similar vert design. Multicoloured. P* 14×15.

377 20 c. Type **102** 30 30
378 $1 Children opening presents .. .. 1·50 1·75

(Des Anita Cecil. Litho Note Ptg Branch, Reserve Bank of Australia)

1989 (22 Dec). *20th Anniv of First Manned Landing on Moon. Legend of Eigigu, the Girl in the Moon. T* **103** *and similar vert designs. Multicoloured. P* 14×15.

379 25 c. Type **103** 70 70
380 30 c. Eigigu climbing tree 80 80
381 50 c. Eigigu stealing toddy from blind woman .. .. 1·50 1·50
382 $1 Eigigu on Moon .. .. 2·75 2·75
379/82 .. .. *Set of* 4 5·25 5·25

104 Early Mining by Hand

105 Sunday School Class

(Des Robin White. Litho Note Ptg Branch. Reserve Bank of Australia)

1990 (3 July). *20th Anniv of Nauru Phosphate Corporation. T* **104** *and similar vert design. Multicoloured. P* 14×15.

383 50 c. Type **104** 65 65
384 $1 Modern mining by excavator .. .. 1·25 1·25

(Litho Note Ptg Branch, Reserve Bank of Australia)

1990 (26 Nov). *Christmas. T* **105** *and similar vert design. Multicoloured. P* 14×15.

385 25 c. Type **105** 40 40
a. Horiz pair. Nos. 385/6 .. .. .. 80 80
386 25 c. Teacher telling Christmas story .. 40 40

Nos. 385/6 were printed together, *se-tenant*, in horizontal pairs throughout the sheet, each pair forming a composite design.

106 Eoiyepiang laying Baby on Mat

107 Oleander

(Des Robin White. Litho Note Ptg Branch, Reserve Bank of Australia)

1990 (24 Dec). *Legend of "Eoiyepiang, the Daughter of Thunder and Lightning". T* **106** *and similar vert designs. Multicoloured. P* 14×15.

387 25 c. Type **106** 20 25
388 30 c. Eoiyepiang making floral decoration .. 25 30
389 50 c. Eoiyepiang left on snow-covered mountain 45 50
390 $1 Eoiyepiang and warrior 85 90
387/90 .. .. *Set of* 4 1·60 1·75

(Litho Leigh-Mardon Ltd, Melbourne)

1991 (22 July). *Flowers. T* **107** *and similar multicoloured designs. P* 14½.

391 15 c. Type **107** 15 20
392 20 c. Lily 20 25
393 25 c. Passion Flower 20 25
394 30 c. Lily (*different*) 30 35
395 35 c. Caesalpinia 30 35
396 40 c. Clerodendron 35 40
397 45 c. *Baubina pinnata* 40 45
398 50 c. Hibiscus (*vert*) 45 50
399 75 c. Apocymaceae 70 75
400 $1 Bindweed (*vert*) 90 95
401 $2 Tristellateia (*vert*) .. .. 1·90 2·00
402 $3 Impala Lily (*vert*) .. .. 2·75 3·00
391/402 .. .. *Set of* 12 7·75 8·50

108 Jesus Christ and Children (stained glass window)

(Des R. Varma. Litho Leigh-Mardon Ltd, Melbourne)

1991 (12 Dec). *Christmas. Sheet* 124×82 *mm. P* 14.

MS403 **108** $2 multicoloured .. .. 2·50 2·50

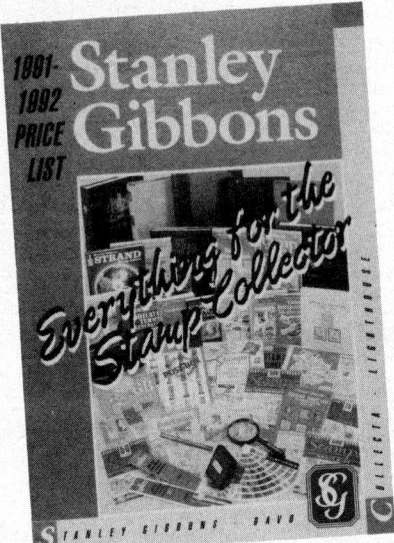

Nevis
see St. Kitts-Nevis

New Brunswick
see Canada

Newfoundland
see Canada

New Guinea
see Papua New Guinea

New Hebrides
see Vanuatu

New Republic
see South Africa

New South Wales
see Australia

New Zealand

From 1831 mail from New Zealand was sent to Sydney, New South Wales, routed through an unofficial postmaster at Kororareka.

The first official post office opened at Kororareka in January 1840 to be followed by others at Auckland, Britannia, Coromandel Harbour, Hokianga, Port Nicholson, Russell and Waimate during the same year. New South Wales relinquished control of the postal service when New Zealand became a separate colony on 3 May 1841.

The British G.P.O. was responsible for the operation of the overseas mails from 11 October 1841 until the postal service once again passed under colonial control on 18 November 1848.

CC 1

CC 2

AUCKLAND

CROWNED-CIRCLE HANDSTAMPS

CC1	CC 1	AUCKLAND NEW ZEALAND (R.) (31.10.1846) .. .. *Price on cover*	£250

NELSON

CROWNED-CIRCLE HANDSTAMPS

CC2	CC 1	NELSON NEW ZEALAND (R.) (31.10.1846) *Price on cover*	£900

NEW PLYMOUTH

CROWNED-CIRCLE HANDSTAMPS

CC3	CC 1	NEW PLYMOUTH NEW ZEALAND (R. *or* Black) (31.10.1846) .. *Price on cover*	£1500
CC3*a*	CC **2**	NEW PLYMOUTH NEW ZEALAND (R. *or* Black) (1854) .. *Price on cover*	£2000

OTAGO

CROWNED-CIRCLE HANDSTAMPS

CC4	CC **2**	OTAGO NEW ZEALAND (R.) (1851) *Price on cover*	£1500

PETRE

CROWNED-CIRCLE HANDSTAMPS

CC5	CC 1	PETRE NEW ZEALAND (R.) (31.10.1846) *Price on cover*	£1200

PORT VICTORIA

CROWNED-CIRCLE HANDSTAMPS

CC6	CC **2**	PORT VICTORIA NEW ZEALAND (R.) (1851) .. .. .. *Price on cover*	£1000

RUSSELL

CROWNED-CIRCLE HANDSTAMPS

CC7	CC 1	RUSSELL NEW ZEALAND (R.) (31.10.1846) *Price on cover*	£3000

WELLINGTON

CROWNED-CIRCLE HANDSTAMPS

CC8	CC 1	WELLINGTON NEW ZEALAND (R.) (31.10.1846) .. .. *Price on cover*	£300

A similar mark for Christchurch as Type CC **2** is only known struck, in black, as a cancellation after the introduction of adhesive stamps.

No. CC3*a* is a locally-cut replacement with the office name around the circumference, but a straight "PAID AT" in the centre.

PRICES FOR STAMPS ON COVER TO 1945

Nos. 1/125	*from* × 2
Nos. 126/36	*from* × 3
Nos. 137/9	*from* × 2
No. 140	—
No. 141	*from* × 2
No. 142	—
Nos. 143/8	*from* × 2
Nos. 149/51	*from* × 10
Nos. 152/84	*from* × 2
Nos. 185/6	—
Nos. 187/203	*from* × 3
Nos. 205/7*e*	—
Nos. 208/13	*from* × 2
Nos. 214/16*j*	—
Nos. 217/58	*from* × 3
No. 259	—
Nos. 260/9	*from* × 3
No. 270	—
Nos. 271/6	*from* × 3
Nos. 277/307	*from* × 2
Nos. 308/16	*from* × 3
No. 317	—
Nos. 318/28	*from* × 3
Nos. 329/48	—
No. 349	*from* × 5
Nos. 350/1	—
No. 352	*from* × 5
Nos. 353/69	—
Nos. 370/86	*from* × 2
No. 387	*from* × 4
Nos. 388/99	*from* × 3
Nos. 400/666	*from* × 2
Nos. E1/5	*from* × 5
No. E6	*from* × 10
Nos. D1/8	*from* × 3
Nos. D9/16	*from* × 5
Nos. D17/20	*from* × 3
Nos. D21/47	*from* × 6
Nos. O1/24	*from* × 12
Nos. O59/66	*from* × 4
Nos. O67/8	—
Nos. O69/81	*from* × 5
Nos. O82/7	—
Nos. O88/93	*from* × 20
Nos. O94/9	*from* × 12
Nos. O100/11	*from* × 5
Nos. O112/13	—
Nos. O115/19	*from* × 15
Nos. O120/33	*from* × 10
Nos. O134/51	*from* × 4
Nos. P1/7	*from* × 8
Nos. L1/9	*from* × 10
Nos. L9*a*/12	—
Nos. L13/20	*from* × 15
Nos. L21/3	—
Nos. L24/41	*from* × 12
No. F1	—
No. F2	*from* × 5
Nos. F3/144	—
Nos. F145/58	*from* × 3
Nos. F159/68	—
Nos. F169/79	*from* × 3
Nos. F180/6	—
Nos. F187/90	*from* × 2
Nos. F191/203	*from* × 3
Nos. F204/11	—
Nos. F212/18	*from* × 2
Nos. A1/3	*from* × 2

CROWN COLONY

1

2

(Eng by Humphreys. Recess P.B.)

1855 (18 July). *Wmk Large Star, W* w **1**. *Imperf.*

1	1	1d. dull carmine (*white paper*) ..	£27000	£8000
2		2d. dull blue (*blued paper*) ..	£14000	£550
3		1s. pale yellow-green (*blued paper*) ..	£25000	£5000
		a. Bisected (6d.) (on cover) ..	†	£20000

The 2d. and 1s. on white paper formerly listed are now known to be stamps printed on blued paper which have had the bluing washed out.

Nos. 3a and 6a. were used at Dunedin from March 1857 when the rate for ½ oz letters to Great Britain was reduced to 6d. All known examples are bisected vertically.

(Printed by J. Richardson, Auckland, N.Z.)

1855 (Dec). *First printing. Wmk Large Star. White paper. Imperf.*

3*b*	1	1d. orange	£15000	

1855 (Dec)–**57.** *No wmk. Blue paper. Imperf.*

4	1	1d. red	£6500	£1400
5		2d. blue (3.56)	£2250	£300
		a. Without value		
6		1s. green (9.57)	£12000	£3500
		a. Bisected (6d.) (on cover)	†	£15000

These stamps on blue paper may occasionally be found watermarked double-lined letters, being portions of the paper-maker's name.

No. 6a was used at Otago during November 1858 on letters to Great Britian.

1857 (Jan). *Wmk Large Star. White paper similar to the issue of July* 1855.

7	1	1d. dull orange	—	£12000

This stamp is in the precise shade of the 1d. of the 1858 printing by Richardson on *no wmk* white paper. An unsevered pair is known with Dunedin cancellation on a cover front showing an Auckland arrival postmark of 19.1.1857.

1858–63. *Hard or soft white paper. No wmk.* (*a*) *Imperf.*

8	1	1d. dull orange (1858)	£1500	£350
8*a*		2d. deep ultramarine (1858)	£1500	£750
9		2d. pale blue	£750	£180
10		2d. blue	£750	£180
11		2d. dull deep blue	—	£250
12		6d. bistre-brown (Aug 1859)	£2250	£500
13		6d. brown	£1100	£300
14		6d. pale brown	£1100	£300
15		6d. chestnut	£2250	£550
16		1s. dull emerald-green	£7000	£1000
17		1s. blue-green	£7000	£1200
		(*b*) *Pin-roulette, about* 10 *at Nelson* (1862)		
18	1	1d. dull orange	—	£4500
19		2d. blue	—	£4500
20		6d. brown	—	£4500
21		1s. blue-green	—	£6500
		(*c*) *Serrated perf about* 16 *or* 18 *at Nelson* (1862)		
22	1	1d. dull orange	—	£3250
23		2d. blue	—	£2750
24		6d. brown	—	£2750
25		6d. chestnut	—	£5500
26		1s. blue-green	—	£4750
		(*d*) *Rouletted* 7 *at Auckland* (April 1859)		
27	1	1d. dull orange	£4250	£3000
28		2d. blue	£5500	£2750
29		6d. brown	£3750	£2750
		a. Imperf between (pair)	£10000	£9000
30		1s. dull emerald-green	£5500	£3500
31		1s. blue-green	£6500	£3500
		(*e*) *P* 13 *at Dunedin* (1863)		
31*a*	1	1d. dull orange	—	£2500
31*b*		2d. pale blue	£2750	£1800
32		6d. pale brown	—	£5000

Other forms of separation, in addition to those shown above, are known, both on the stamps of this issue and on those of 1862. Some of the varieties are extremely rare, only single copies being known.

The 2d. in a distinctive deep bright blue on white paper wmkd. Large Star is believed by experts to have been printed by Richardson in 1861 or 1862. This also exists doubly printed and with serrated perf.

(Printed by John Davies at the G.P.O., Auckland, N.Z.)

1862 (Feb–Dec). *Wmk Large Star.* (*a*) *Imperf.*

33	1	1d. orange-vermilion	£400	£120
34		1d. vermilion	£400	£120
35		1d. carmine-vermilion	£350	£150
36		2d. deep blue (Plate I)	£300	60·00
		a. Double print	—	£2500
37		2d. slate-blue (Plate I)	£1500	£180
37*a*		2d. milky blue (Plate I, worn)	—	£225
38		2d. pale blue (Plate I, worn)	£225	70·00
39		2d. blue (*to* deep) (Plate I, very worn) ..	£225	70·00
40		3d. brown-lilac (Dec 1862)	£300	£100

NEW ZEALAND

SG L21

and the *British Empire 1840-1936*

— Bought & Sold —

WANT LISTS filled from our comprehensive, 30 volume stock of stamps, varieties and postal history (**references please**).

We hold several British Empire **public auctions** annually. Subscription: £25

George W. Holschauer

Colonial Stamp Co.

5410 Wilshire Blvd., Suite 202
Los Angeles, CA 90036, U.S.A.
(213)933-9435• FAX(213)939-9930

Members: IFSDA,PTS,ASDA,Int'l Soc. of Appraisers

NEW ZEALAND

1855 – date

Major specialists in this fascinating country, with regular specialised and general lists.

WRITE FOR DETAILS OF OUR SERVICES

J. M. A. GREGSON Ltd.

P.O. Box 11, Patchway, Bristol, BS12 4BH
Tel: 0454–617600 Fax: 0454–617600

MIGHT IT BE THE 'GOOD PERF'?

Jamaica 132a, The King George VI 5s. line perf 14 is currently catalogued at £2000 mint, £130 used. The original, comb perf 14 stamp is £6.00 mint, £2.00 used. In a footnote below the set it states that the gauges are 14–14.5 and 13.8 × 13.7 respectively. To identify these stamps correctly we recommend the

Stanley Gibbons Instanta Perforation Gauge

Accurate to one decimal point for the specialist yet practical and simple to use for the beginner, the Instanta can measure stamps wherever they are – loose, on cover, in your album – or even in the middle of a sheet or block.

The World's best perforation gauge.

For further details write to:

Stanley Gibbons Publications Ltd.,
5 Parkside, Christchurch Road,
Ringwood, Hampshire BH24 3SH
Telephone 0425 472363

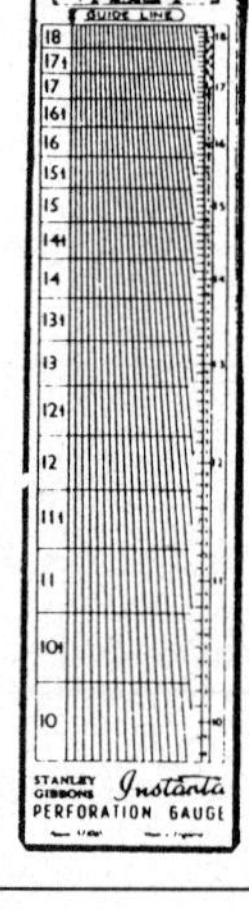

A Choice of Albums for the New Zealand Collector

The Stanley Gibbons New Zealand One Country Album (Item 5262)
This elegant 4-ring album provides the perfect home for any straightforward NZ collection. Housed in a rich burgundy leather effect binder with gold tooling on the spine, the high quality cartridge leaves are laid out and written up to ensure that your collection is attractively displayed whatever its stage of development. Every stamp illustrated and identified by its SG catalogue number.

The Stanley Gibbons New Zealand Luxury Hingeless Album (Item 5288/9)
This impressive two-volume album represents the very ultimate in luxury, convenience and style, its padded binders are covered in navy blue leatherette rexine and decorated with the country's crest in traditional heraldic colours. The leaves are of the highest quality, tastefully laid out to give a superbly attractive display with a crystal clear mount already affixed in each space for the immediate insertion of your stamps. Each album is presented in its own matching slip case for added protection.

Item 5288 New Zealand Luxury Hingeless Album Volume 1 1855–1967
Item 5289 New Zealand Luxury Hingeless Album Volume 2 1967–date

For further details visit your favourite stamp shop or write to:
Stanley Gibbons Publications Ltd.,
5 Parkside, Christchurch Road, Ringwood, Hampshire BH24 3SH. Telephone 0425 472363

41 1 6d. black-brown .. .. £650 80·00
42 6d. brown .. .. £650 80·00
43 6d. red-brown .. .. £500 65·00
44 1s. green £750 £160
45 1s. yellow-green £700 £150
46 1s. deep green £850 £190

Nos. 37*a*/38 show some signs of wear on right of Queen's head and shades of No. 39 show moderate to advanced states of wear.

(*b*) *Rouletted* 7 *at Auckland* (5.62)

47 1 1d. orange-vermilion £3000 £650
48 1d. vermilion £1800 £600
48*a* 1d. carmine-vermilion £2500 £750
49 2d. deep blue £1700 £400
50 2d. slate-blue £2750 £700
51 2d. pale blue £1500 £500
52 3d. brown-lilac £1700 £650
53 6d. black-brown £2000 £400
54 6d. brown £1700 £500
55 6d. red-brown £1700 £400
56 1s. green £2000 £550
57 1s. yellow-green £3000 £550
58 1s. deep green £3000 £650

(*c*) *Serrated perf* 16 *or* 18 *at Nelson* (8.62)

59 1 1d. orange-vermilion .. .. — £1200
60 2d. deep blue .. .. — £750
a. Imperf between (pair) £5500 £2750
61 2d. slate-blue .. ..
62 3d. brown-lilac £2750 £1400
63 6d. black-brown .. .. — £1500
64 6d. brown .. .. — £1500
65 1s. yellow-green .. .. — £2500

(*d*) *Pin-perf* 10 *at Nelson* (8.62)

66 1 2d. deep blue .. .. — £1800
67 6d. black-brown .. .. — £3000

The dates put to above varieties are the earliest that have been met with.

1862. *Wmk Large Star. P* 13 (*at Dunedin*).

68 1 1d. orange-vermilion £600 £150
69 1d. carmine-vermilion £600 £150
70 2d. deep blue (Plate II) .. .. .. £300 40·00
71 2d. slate-blue (Plate I) .. .. .. — £700
72 2d. blue (Plate I) .. .. .. £225 30·00
72*a* 2d. milky blue (Plate I) .. .. .. — £500
73 2d. pale blue (Plate I) .. .. .. £225 30·00
74 3d. brown-lilac £550 £130
75 6d. black-brown £550 £110
a. Imperf between (horiz pair) .. ..
76 6d. brown .. .. .. £500 50·00
77 6d. red-brown .. .. .. £375 30·00
78 1s. dull green £500 £200
79 1s. deep green £550 £180
80 1s. yellow-green £550 £160

See also Nos. 110/125 and the note that follows these.

1862. *Pelure paper. No wmk.* (*a*) *Imperf.*

81 1 1d. orange-vermilion £5500 £1700
82 2d. ultramarine £3250 £750
83 2d. pale ultramarine £3250 £750
84 3d. lilac .. .. £25000 †
85 6d. black-brown £1400 £225
86 1s. deep green £6000 £800

The 3d. is known only unused.

(*b*) *Rouletted* 7 *at Auckland*

87 1 1d. orange-vermilion .. .. .. — £4000
88 6d. black-brown £2000 £450
89 1s. deep green £3500 £1100

(*c*) *P* 13 *at Dunedin*

90 1 1d. orange-vermilion £9500 £3000
91 2d. ultramarine £4500 £550
92 2d. pale ultramarine £4500 £550
93 6d. black-brown £3500 £325
94 1s. deep green £7000 £1100

(*d*) *Serrated perf* 15 *at Nelson*

95 1 6d. black-brown .. .. — £4000

1863 (early). *Hard or soft white paper. No wmk.* (*a*) *Imperf.*

96 1 2d. dull deep blue (*shades*) £2250 £800

(*b*) *P* 13

96*a* 1 2d. dull deep blue (*shades*) £1600 £475

These stamps show slight beginnings of wear of the printing plate in the background to right of the Queen's ear, as one looks at the stamps. By the early part of 1864, the wear of the plate had spread, more or less, all over the background of the circle containing the head. The major portion of the stamps of this printing appears to have been consigned to Dunedin and to have been there perforated 13.

1864. *Wmk* "N Z", *W* **2.** (*a*) *Imperf.*

97 1 1d. carmine-vermilion £700 £200
98 2d. pale blue (Plate I worn) £750 £200
99 6d. red-brown £2000 £475
100 1s. green £900 £250

(*b*) *Rouletted* 7 *at Auckland*

101 1 1d. carmine-vermilion £4500 £2750
102 2d. pale blue (Plate I worn) £1400 £700
103 6d. red-brown £4250 £2750
104 1s. green £2750 £1000

(*c*) *P* 13 *at Dunedin*

104*a* 1 1d. carmine-vermilion £5000 £3500
105 2d. pale blue (Plate I worn) £550 £160
106 1s. green £1100 £450
a. Imperf between (horiz pair) .. £7500

(*d*) *P* 12½ *at Auckland*

106*b* 1 1d. carmine-vermilion £3750 £2000
107 2d. pale blue (Plate I worn) .. .. £225 50·00
108 6d. red-brown .. .. £225 30·00
109 1s. yellow-green £4000 £2000

1864–67. *Wmk Large Star. P* 12½ (*at Auckland*)

110 1 1d. carmine-vermilion (1864) .. .. 80·00 18·00
111 1d. pale orange-vermilion .. .. £100 18·00
a. Imperf (pair) £1700 £1100
112 1d. orange .. .. .. £250 42·00
113 2d. pale blue (Plate I worn) (1864) .. 85·00 14·00
114 2d. deep blue (Plate II) (1866) .. .. 90·00 14·00
a. Imperf between (pair) .. .. — £2250

115 1 2d. blue (Plate II) .. .. .. 90·00 17·00
a. Retouched (Plate II) (1867) .. .. £130 19·00
c. Imperf (pair) (Plate II) £1200 £1200
d. Retouched. Imperf (pair) £1700 £1900
116 3d. brown-lilac (1864) £700 £500
117 3d. lilac .. .. 65·00 17·00
a. Imperf (pair) £1800 £1200
118 3d. deep mauve .. .. .. £325 45·00
a. Imperf (pair) £1800 £1200
119 4d. deep rose (1865) £1800 £250
120 4d. yellow (1865) .. .. .. 85·00 45·00
121 4d. orange £1100 £800
122 6d. red-brown (1864) .. .. .. 85·00 17·00
122*a* 6d. brown .. .. 90·00 18·00
b. Imperf (pair) £1100 £1000
123 1s. deep green (1864) £500 £160
124 1s. green .. .. £275 48·00
125 1s. yellow-green .. .. .. £100 45·00

The above issue is sometimes difficult to distinguish from Nos. 68/80 because the vertical perforations usually gauge 12¾ and sometimes a full 13. However stamps of this issue invariably gauge 12½ horizontally, whereas the 1862 stamps measure a full 13.

Nos. 111a, 115c/d, 117a, 118a and 122b were issued during problems with the perforation machine which occurred in 1866–67, 1869–70 and 1871–73. Imperforate sheets of the 1s. were also released, but these stamps are very similar to Nos. 44/6.

The 1d., 2d. and 6d. were officially reprinted imperforate, without gum, in 1884 for presentation purposes. They can be distinguished from the errors listed by their shades which are pale orange, dull blue and dull chocolate-brown respectively, and by the worn state of the plates from which they were printed.

1871. *Wmk Large Star.* (*a*) *P* 10.

126 1 1d. brown .. .. £375 50·00

(*b*) *P* 12½ × 10

127 1 1d. deep brown .. .. — £750

(*c*) *P* 10 × 12½

128 1 1d. brown .. .. £110 20·00
a. Perf 12½ comp 10 (1 side) .. .. £225 60·00
129 2d. deep blue (Plate II) .. .. .. — £5000
a. Perf 10* .. .. † £9000
130 2d. vermilion .. .. £120 16·00
a. Retouched .. .. £160 20·00
b. Perf 12½ comp 10 (1 side) £650 £275
c. Perf 10* .. .. † £9000
131 6d. deep blue £1000 £500
a. Blue £750 £275
b. Imperf between (vert pair) .. .. — £4250
c. Perf 12½ comp 10 (1 side) £700 £200
ca. Imperf vert (horiz pair) .. ..

(*d*) *P* 12½

132 1 1d. red-brown .. .. 90·00 18·00
a. Brown (shades, worn plate) .. .. 90·00 18·00
b. Imperf horiz (vert pair) .. .. — £2750
133 2d. orange .. .. 50·00 15·00
a. Retouched .. .. £110 40·00
134 2d. vermilion .. .. 85·00 15·00
a. Retouched .. .. £150 50·00
135 6d. blue .. .. 85·00 25·00
136 6d. pale blue .. .. 50·00 25·00

*Only one used copy each of Nos. 129a and 130c have been reported.

1872. *No wmk. P* 12½.

137 1 1d. brown .. .. £275 40·00
138 2d. vermilion .. .. 48·00 18·00
a. Retouched .. .. £150 25·00
139 4d. orange-yellow £120 £400

In or about 1872 1d., 2d. and 4d. stamps were printed on paper showing sheet watermarks of either "W. T. & Co." (Wiggins Teape & Co.) in script letters or "T. H. Saunders" in double-lined capitals; portions of these letters are occasionally found on stamps.

1872. *Wmk* "N Z", *W* **2.** *P* 12½.

140 1 1d. brown .. .. — £2500
141 2d. vermilion .. .. £300 65·00
a. Retouched £600 £150

1872. *Wmk Lozenges, with* "INVICTA" *in double-lined capitals four times in the sheet. P* 12½.

142 1 2d. vermilion £2750 £550
a. Retouched £3750 £800

3 4

(Des John Davies. Die eng on wood in Melbourne. Printed from electrotypes at Govt Ptg Office, Wellington)

1873 (1 Jan). (*a*) *Wmk* "NZ", *W* **2.**

143 3 ½d. pale dull rose (*p* 10) .. .. .. 60·00 14·00
144 ½d. pale dull rose (*p* 12½) .. .. £180 55·00
145 ½d. pale dull rose (*p* 12½ × 10) .. £110 45·00

(*b*) *No wmk*

146 3 ½d. pale dull rose (*p* 10) .. .. .. 70·00 23·00
147 ½d. pale dull rose (*p* 12½) .. .. £190 60·00
148 ½d. pale dull rose (*p* 12½ × 10) .. £150 55·00

As the paper used for Nos. 143/5 was originally intended for fiscal stamps which were more than twice as large, about one-third of the impressions fall on portions of the sheet showing no watermark, giving rise to varieties Nos. 146/8. In later printings of No. 151 a few stamps in each sheet are without watermark. These can be distinguished from No. 147 by the shade.

1875 (Jan). *Wmk Star, W* **4.**

149 3 ½d. pale dull rose (*p* 12½) .. .. 11·00 90
a. Imperf horiz (vert pair) £600 £325
b. Imperf between (horiz pair) .. .. † £500
150 ½d. dull pale rose (*p nearly* 12) .. .. 60·00 5·50

1892 (May). *Wmk "NZ and Star". W* **12***b*. *P* 12½.

151 3 ½d. bright rose (*shades*) .. .. 5·00 30
a. No wmk .. .. 7·50 2·25

5 6 7

8 9 10

11 12 12*a* 6 mm

12*b* 7 mm 12*c* 4 mm

(T **5/10** eng De La Rue. T **11** and **12** des, eng & plates by W. R. Bock. Typo Govt Ptg Office, Wellington)

1874 (2 Jan)–**78.** *W* **12***a*. A. *White paper.* (*a*) *P* 12½.

152 5 1d. lilac .. .. 45·00 3·50
a. Imperf £400
153 6 2d. rose .. .. 45·00 1·75
154 7 3d. brown .. .. 95·00 55·00
155 8 4d. maroon .. .. £250 50·00
156 9 6d. blue .. .. £180 10·00
157 10 1s. green .. .. £650 25·00

(*b*) *Perf nearly* 12

158 6 2d. rose (1878) £600 £180

(*c*) *Perf compound of* 12½ *and* 10

159 5 1d. lilac .. .. £150 40·00
160 6 2d. rose .. .. £350 65·00
161 7 3d. brown .. .. £160 60·00
162 8 4d. maroon £350 £100
163 9 6d. blue .. .. £225 45·00
164 10 1s. green £650 £100
aa. Imperf between (vert pair) .. .. † —

(*d*) *Perf nearly* 12 × 12½

164*a* 5 1d. lilac (1875) £650 £250
165 6 2d. rose (1878) £650 £190

B. *Blued paper.* (*a*) *P* 12½

166 5 1d. lilac .. .. 70·00 29·00
167 6 2d. rose .. .. 95·00 29·00
168 7 3d. brown .. .. £225 75·00
169 8 4d. maroon £425 £100
170 9 6d. blue .. .. £325 48·00
171 10 1s. green £1000 £190

(*b*) *Perf compound of* 12½ *and* 10

172 5 1d. lilac .. .. £180 50·00
173 6 2d. rose .. .. £500 80·00
174 7 3d. brown .. .. £190 65·00
175 8 4d. maroon £450 £110
176 9 6d. blue .. .. £300 90·00
177 10 1s. green £1000 £200

1875. *Wmk Large Star, W w* **1.** *P* 12½.

178 5 1d. deep lilac £500 £100
179 6 2d. rose .. .. £300 15·00

1878. *W* **12***a*. *P* 12 × 11½ (*comb*).

180 5 1d. mauve-lilac .. .. 35·00 2·50
181 6 2d. rose .. .. 35·00 1·40
182 8 4d. maroon .. .. £130 38·00
183 9 6d. blue .. .. 80·00 10·00
184 10 1s. green .. .. £110 27·00
185 11 2s. deep rose (1 July) £300 £275
186 12 5s. grey (1 July) £325 £275

This perforation is made by a horizontal "comb" machine, giving a gauge of 12 horizontally and about 11¾ vertically. Single specimens can be found apparently gauging 11½ all round or 12 all round, but these are all from the same machine. The perforation described above as "nearly 12" was from a single-line machine.

ALTERED CATALOGUE NUMBERS

Any Catalogue numbers altered from the last edition are shown as a list in the introductory pages.

Description of Watermarks

W12*a*. 6 mm between "N Z" and star; broad irregular star; comparatively wide "N"; "N Z" 11½ mm wide.

W12*b*. 7 mm between "N Z" and star; narrower star; narrow "N"; "N Z" 10 mm wide.

W12*c*. 4 mm between "N Z" and star; narrow star; wide "N"; "N Z" 11½ mm wide.

Description of Papers

1882–88. Smooth paper with horizontal mesh. W **12***a*.

1888–98. Smooth paper with vertical mesh. *W* **12***b*.

1890–91. Smooth paper with vertical mesh. *W* **12***c*.

1898. Thin yellowish toned, coarse paper with clear vertical mesh. *W* **12***b*. Perf 11 only.

In 1899–1900 stamps appeared on medium to thick white coarse paper but we do not differentiate these (except where identifiable by shade) as they are more difficult to distinguish.

PAPER MESH. This shows on the back of the stamp as a series of parallel grooves, either vertical or horizontal. It is caused by the use of a wire gauze conveyor-belt during paper-making.

Description of Dies

1d.

Die 1

Die 2

Die 3

1882. Die 1. Background shading complete and heavy.

1886. Die 2. Background lines thinner. Two lines of shading weak or missing left of Queen's forehead.

1889. Die 3. Shading on head reduced; ornament in crown left of chignon clearer, with unshaded "arrow" more prominent.

PRICES OF SETS

Set prices are given for many issues, generally those containing three stamps or more. Definitive sets include one of each value or major colour change, but do not cover different perforations, die types or minor shades. Where a choice is possible the set prices are based on the cheapest versions of the stamps included in the listings.

2d.

Die 1

Die 2

Die 3

1882. Die 1. Background shading complete and heavy.

1886. Die 2. Weak line of shading left of forehead and missing shading lines below "TA".

1889. Die 3. As Die 2 but with comma-like white notch in hair below "&".

6d.

Die 1

Die 2

1882. Die 1. Shading heavy. Top of head merges into shading.

1892. Die 2. Background lines thinner. Shading on head more regular with clear line of demarcation between head and background shading.

STAMPS WITH ADVERTISEMENTS. During November 1891 the New Zealand Post Office invited tenders for the printing of advertisements on the reverse of the current 1d. to 1s. stamps. The contract was awarded to Messrs Miller, Truebridge & Reich and the first sheets with advertisements on the reverse appeared in February 1893.

Different advertisements were applied to the backs of the individual stamps within the sheets of 240 (four panes of 60).

On the first setting those in a vertical format were inverted in relation to the stamps and each of the horizontal advertisements had its base at the left-hand side of the stamp when seen from the back. For the second and third settings the vertical advertisements were the same way up as the stamps and the bases of those in the horizontal format were at the right as seen from the back. The third setting only differs from the second in the order of the individual advertisements.

The experiment was not, however, a success and the contract was cancelled at the end of 1893.

(Des F. W. Sears (½d.), A. E. Cousins (2½d.), A. W. Jones (5d.); others adapted from 1874 issue by W. H. Norris. Dies eng A. E. Cousins (½d., 2½d., 5d.), W. R. Bock (others). Typo Govt Ptg Office)

1882–1900. *Inscr* "POSTAGE & REVENUE".

A. *W* **12***a*. *Paper with horiz mesh* (1.4.82–86). (*a*) *P* 12 × 11½

No.	Type	Description	Unused	Used
187	**14**	1d. rose *to* rose-red (Die 1)	35·00	4·25
		a. Imperf (pair)	£275	
		b. Imperf between (vert pair)		
		c. Die 2. *Pale rose to carmine-rose* (1886)	30·00	4·25
188	**15**	2d. lilac *to* lilac-purple (Die 1)	40·00	4·00
		a. Imperf (pair)	£300	
		b. Imperf between (vert pair)	£300	
		c. Die 2. *Lilac* (1886)	55·00	5·00
189	**17**	3d. yellow (1884)	48·00	4·75
190	**18**	4d. blue-green	65·00	4·50
191	**20**	6d. brown (Die 1)	70·00	3·75
192	**21**	8d. blue (1885)	65·00	45·00
193	**22**	1s. red-brown	75·00	12·00

(*b*) *P* 12½ (1884?)

No.	Type	Description	Unused	Used
193*a*	**14**	1d. rose *to* rose-red (Die 1)	£170	70·00

B. *W* **12***b*. *Paper with vert mesh* (1888–95)

(*a*) *P* 12×11½ (1888–95)

No.	Type	Description	Unused	Used
194	**13**	½d. black (1.4.95)	25·00	55·00
195	**14**	1d. rose *to* rosine (Die 2)	38·00	3·50
		a. Die 3. *Rose to carmine* (1889)	38·00	3·50
		ab. Red-brn advert (1st setting) (2.93)		
		ac. Red advert (1st setting) (3.93)	50·00	10·00
		ad. Blue advert (2nd setting) (4.93)	60·00	25·00
		ae. Mauve advert (2nd setting) (5.93)	38·00	6·00
		af. Green advert (2nd setting) (6.93)		
		ag. Brn-red advert (3rd setting) (9.93)	38·00	6·00
196	**15**	2d. lilac (Die 2)	40·00	3·75
		a. Die 3. *Lilac to purple* (1889)	40·00	3·75
		ab. Red advert (1st setting) (3.93)	60·00	15·00
		ac. Mauve advert (2nd setting) (5.93)	50·00	
		ad. Sepia advert (2nd setting) (5.93)	50·00	20·00
		ae. Green advert (2nd setting) (6.93)	—	75·00
		af. Brn-red advert (3rd setting) (9.93)		
197	**16**	2½d. pale blue (1891)	45·00	5·50
		a. Brn-red advert (2nd setting) (4.93)	45·00	10·00
		b. *Ultramarine* (green advert. 2nd setting) (6.93)	55·00	12·00
198	**17**	3d. yellow	40·00	6·00
		a. Brn-red advert (2nd setting) (4.93)	60·00	10·00
		b. Sepia advert (2nd setting) (5.93)		
199	**18**	4d. green *to* bluish green	48·00	2·75
		a. Sepia advert (2nd setting) (5.93)	60·00	10·00
200	**19**	5d. olive-black (1.2.91)	40·00	9·00
		a. Imperf (pair)	£300	
		b. Brn-pur advert (3rd setting) (9.93)	60·00	25·00
201	**20**	6d. brown (Die 1)	60·00	2·25
		a. Die 2 (1892)	£110	50·00
		ab. Sepia advert (2nd setting) (5.93)		
		ac. Brn-red advert (3rd setting) (9.93)	£140	60·00
202	**21**	8d. blue	65·00	38·00
203	**22**	1s. red-brown	75·00	6·00
		a. Black advert (2nd setting) (5.93)	£300	£150
		b. Brn-pur advert (3rd setting) (9.93)	£100	15·00

(*b*) *Perf compound of* 12 *and* 12½ (1888–91)

No.	Type	Description	Unused	Used
204	**14**	1d. rose (Die 2)	£190	75·00
		a. Die 3 (1889)		

(*c*) *P* 12½ (1888–89)

No.	Type	Description	Unused	Used
205	**14**	1d. rose (Die 3) (1889)	£160	90·00
		a. Mauve advert (2nd setting) (5.93)		
206	**15**	2d. lilac (Die 2)	£160	80·00
		a. Die 3. *Deep lilac* (1889)	£120	65·00
		ab. Brn-red advert (3rd setting) (9.93)	£120	75·00
207	**16**	2½d. blue (1891)	£170	90·00

(*d*) *Mixed perfs* 12×11½ *and* 12½ (1891–93)

No.	Type	Description	Unused	Used
207*a*	**14**	1d. rose (Die 3)		
207*b*	**15**	2d. lilac (Die 3)		
		ba. Brn-red advert (3rd setting) (9.93)		
207*c*	**18**	4d. green	—	50·00
207*d*	**19**	5d. olive-black	—	95·00
207*e*	**20**	6d. brown (Die 1)	—	£100
		ea. Die 2	—	£150

C. *W* **12***c*. *Paper with vert mesh* (1890). (*a*) *P* 12 × 11½

No.	Type	Description	Unused	Used
208	**14**	1d. rose (Die 3)	65·00	5·50
209	**15**	2d. purple (Die 3)	65·00	5·50
210	**16**	2½d. ultramarine (27.12)	60·00	9·50
211	**17**	3d. yellow	65·00	11·00
		a. Lemon-yellow	65·00	12·00
212	**20**	6d. brown (Die 1)	£110	20·00
213	**22**	1s. deep red-brown	£130	38·00

(*b*) *P* 12½

No.	Type	Description	Unused	Used
214	**14**	1d. rose (Die 3)	£170	£100
215	**15**	2d. purple (Die 3)	£180	90·00
216	**16**	2½d. ultramarine	£200	95·00

(*c*) *Perf compound of* 12 *and* 12½

No.	Type	Description	Unused	Used
216*a*	**20**	6d. brown (Die 1)	£180	£130

D. *Continuation of W* **12***b*. *Paper with vert mesh* (1891–1900)

(*a*) *Perf compound of* 10 *and* 12½ (1891–94)

No.	Type	Description	Unused	Used
216*b*	**14**	1d. rose (Die 3)	£180	85·00
		ba. Red-brn advert (1st setting) (2.93)	£180	£100
		bb. Brn-red advert (2nd setting) (4.93)	£150	70·00
		bc. Mauve advert (2nd setting) (5.93)	£150	70·00
		bd. Green advert (2nd setting) (6.93)	£200	£120
216*c*	**15**	2d. lilac (Die 3)	£150	55·00
216*d*	**16**	2½d. blue (1893)	£130	60·00
216*e*	**17**	3d. yellow	£150	70·00
216*f*	**18**	4d. green	£170	£140
216*g*	**19**	5d. olive-black (1894)	£180	£170
216*h*	**20**	6d. brown (Die 1)	£190	£190
		i. Die 2 (1892)	£150	£150
		ia. Brn-pur advert (3rd setting) (9.93)	£180	£180
216*j*	**22**	1s. red-brown	£170	£160

(*b*) *P* 10 (1891–95)

No.	Type	Description	Unused	Used
217	**13**	½d. black (1895)	2·75	20
218	**14**	1d. rose (Die 3)	3·00	10
		a. Carmine	6·00	1·25
		b. Imperf (pair)	£250	£250
		c. Imperf between (pair)	£275	
		d. Imperf horiz (vert pair)	£200	
		e. Mixed perfs 10 and 12½	£250	£120
		f. Red-brown advert (1st setting) (2.93)	14·00	4·00
		g. Red advert (1st setting) (3.93)	14·00	5·00
		h. Brown-red advert (2nd and 3rd settings) (4.93)	7·00	2·50
		i. Blue advert (2nd setting) (4.93)	50·00	20·00
		j. Mauve advert (2nd setting) (5.93)	7·00	2·50
		k. Green advert (2nd setting) (6.93)	50·00	16·00
		l. Brown-purple advert (3rd setting) (9.93)	7·00	2·50
219	**15**	2d. lilac (Die 3)	7·00	20
		a. Purple	8·50	25
		b. Imperf between (pair)	£180	
		c. Mixed perfs 10 and 12½	£200	90·00
		d. Red-brown advert (1st setting) (2.93)	22·00	5·00
		e. Red advert (1st setting) (3.93)	22·00	5·00
		f. Brown-red advert (2nd and 3rd settings) (4.93)	11·00	2·50
		g. Sepia advert (2nd setting) (5.93)	15·00	3·00
		h. Green advert (2nd setting) (6.93)	32·00	8·00
		i. Brown-purple advert (3rd setting) (9.93)	11·00	2·50

220 16 2½d. blue (1892) 42·00 3·50
a. *Ultramarine* 42·00 4·00
b. Mixed perfs 10 and 12½ £170 80·00
c. Mauve advert (2nd setting) (5.93) 42·00 6·00
d. Green advert (2nd setting) (6.93) 70·00 9·00
e. Brown-purple advert (3rd setting) (9.93) 42·00 6·00
221 17 3d. pale orange-yellow 35·00 7·00
a. *Orange* 35·00 7·50
b. *Lemon-yellow* 42·00 8·50
c. Mixed perfs 10 and 12½ £160 £120
d. Brown-red advert (2nd and 3rd settings) (4.93) 38·00 11·00
e. Sepia advert (2nd setting) (5.93) 75·00 24·00
f. Brown-purple advert (3rd setting) (9.93) 35·00 8·00
222 18 4d. green (1892) 45·00 2·50
a. *Blue-green* 50·00 3·50
b. Mixed perfs 10 and 12½ £190 80·00
c. Brown-red advert (2nd setting) (4.93) 60·00 4·00
d. Brown-purple advert (3rd setting) (9.93) 55·00 4·00
223 19 5d. olive-black (1893) 42·00 10·00
a. Brown-purple advert (3rd setting) (9.93) 65·00 14·00
224 20 6d. brown (Die 1) 80·00 15·00
a. Mixed perfs 10 and 12½
b. Die 2 (1892) 45·00 4·50
ba. *Black-brown* 48·00 4·50
bb. Imperf (pair) £225
bc. Mixed perfs 10 and 12½ 90·00 50·00
bd. Sepia advert (2nd setting) (4.93) 60·00 9·50
be. Brown-red advert (3rd setting) (9.93) 60·00 9·50
bf. Brown-purple advert (3rd setting) (9.93) 60·00 9·50
225 21 8d. blue (brown-purple advert. 3rd setting) (9.93) 65·00 45·00
226 22 1s. red-brown 75·00 5·00
a. Imperf between (pair) £350
b. Mixed perfs 10 and 12½ £150 £110
c. Sepia advert (2nd setting) (5.93) £100 12·00
d. Black advert (2nd setting) (5.93) £180 £110
e. Brown-red advert (3rd setting) (9.93) £100 12·00
f. Brown-purple advert (3rd setting) (9.93) £100 12·00

(c) *Perf compound of* 11 *and* 10 (1895)

226c 13 ½d. black 24·00 9·50
226d 14 1d. rose (Die 3) 50·00 5·50
226e 20 6d. brown (Die 2) £160 70·00

(d) *Perf compound of* 10 *and* 11 (1895–97)

227 13 ½d. black (1896) 3·25 30
a. Mixed perfs 10 and 11 80·00 26·00
228 14 1d. rose (Die 3) 4·25 15
a. Mixed perfs 10 and 11 85·00 50·00
229 15 2d. purple (Die 3) 7·50 15
a. Mixed perfs 10 and 11 60·00 50·00
230 16 2½d. blue (1896) 38·00 3·50
a. *Ultramarine* 38·00 4·25
b. Mixed perfs 10 and 11 — 65·00
231 17 3d. lemon-yellow (1896) 60·00 6·50
232 18 4d. pale green (1896) 70·00 6·00
a. Mixed perfs 10 and 11 — 80·00
233 19 5d. olive-black (1897) 48·00 10·00
234 20 6d. deep brown (Die 2) (1896) 55·00 4·00
a. Mixed perfs 10 and 11
235 22 1s. red-brown (1896) 75·00 8·00
a. Mixed perfs 10 and 11 £140 70·00

(e) *P* 11 (1895–1900)

236 13 ½d. black (1897) 2·50 15
a. Thin coarse toned paper (1898) 22·00 1·25
b. Ditto. Wmk sideways — £150
237 14 1d. rose (Die 3) 3·50 10
a. *Deep carmine* 5·50 1·00
b. Imperf between (pair) £300
c. *Deep carmine/thin coarse toned* (1898) 8·00 1·00
d. Ditto. Wmk sideways — £200
238 15 2d. mauve (Die 3) 7·00 20
a. *Purple* 7·00 20
b. *Deep purple/thin coarse toned* (1898) 8·00 90
c. Ditto. Wmk sideways — £180
239 16 2½d. blue (1897) 38·00 3·50
a. Thin coarse toned paper (1898) 50·00 12·00
240 17 3d. pale yellow (1897) 48·00 4·50
a. *Pale dull yellow/thin coarse toned* (1898) 55·00 7·00
b. *Orange* (1899) 40·00 5·50
c. *Dull orange-yellow* (1900) 48·00 6·50
241 18 4d. yellowish green 48·00 3·00
a. *Bluish green* (1897) 48·00 2·75
242 19 5d. olive-black/*thin coarse toned* (1899) 50·00 16·00
243 20 6d. brown (Die 2) (1897) 55·00 3·00
a. *Black-brown* 55·00 3·00
b. *Brown/thin coarse toned* (1898) 60·00 4·50
244 21 8d. blue (1898) 65·00 45·00
245 22 1s. red-brown (1897) 70·00 5·50

Only the more prominent shades have been included.

Stamps perf compound of 11 and 12½ exist but we do not list them as there is some doubt as to whether they are genuine.

For the ½d. and 2d. with double-lined watermark, see Nos. 271/2.

23 Mount Cook or Aorangi

24 Lake Taupo and Mount Ruapehu

25 Pembroke Peak, Milford Sound

26 Lake Wakatipu and Mount Earnslaw, inscribed "WAKITIPU"

27 Lake Wakatipu and Mount Earnslaw, inscribed "WAKATIPU"

28 Sacred Huia Birds

29 White Terrace, Rotomahana

30 Otira Gorge and Mount Ruapehu

31 Brown Kiwi

32 Maori War Canoe

33 Pink Terrace, Rotomahana

34 Kea and Kaka

35 Milford Sound

36 Mount Cook

(Des H. Young (½d.), J. Gaut (1d.), W. Bock (2d., 3d., 9d., 1s.), E. Howard (4d., 6d., 8d.), E. Luke (others). Eng A. Hill (2½d., 1s.), J. A. C. Harrison (5d.), Rapkin (others). Recess Waterlow)

1898 (5 Apr). *No wmk. P* 12 *to* 16.

246 23 ½d. purple-brown 3·75 35
a. Imperf between (pair) £650 £650
b. *Purple-slate* 4·00 45
c. *Purple-black* 6·50 1·75
247 24 1d. blue and yellow-brown 2·50 20
a. Imperf between (pair) £600
b. Imperf vert (horiz pair) £450
c. Imperf horiz (vert pair) £450 £500
d. *Blue and brown* 3·00 65
da. Imperf between (pair) £600
248 25 2d. lake 20·00 20
a. Imperf vert (horiz pair) £400
b. *Rosy lake* 20·00 20
ba. Imperf between (pair) £550
bb. Imperf vert (horiz pair) £400
249 26 2½d. sky-blue (inscr "WAKITIPU") 6·00 18·00
a. *Blue* 6·00 18·00
250 27 2½d. blue (inscr "WAKATIPU") 13·00 1·25
a. *Deep blue* 13·00 1·50
251 28 3d. yellow-brown 20·00 5·50
252 29 4d. bright rose 12·00 14·00
a. *Lake-rose* 14·00 15·00
b. *Dull rose* 12·00 14·00
253 30 5d. sepia 55·00 £110
a. *Purple-brown* 30·00 12·00
254 31 6d. green 48·00 22·00
a. *Grass-green* 55·00 32·00
255 32 8d. indigo 35·00 24·00
a. *Prussian blue* 35·00 20·00
256 33 9d. purple 35·00 20·00
257 34 1s. vermilion 55·00 15·00
a. *Dull red* 55·00 15·00
ab. Imperf between (pair) £1200
258 35 2s. grey-green 90·00 55·00
a. Imperf between (vert pair) £1200 £1200
259 36 5s. vermilion £200 £170
246/59 *Set of* 13 £450 £275

37 Lake Taupo and Mount Ruapehu

(Recess Govt Printer, Wellington)

1899 (May)–**03.** *Thick, soft ("Pirie") paper. No wmk. P* 11.

260 27 2½d. blue (6.99) 11·00 1·75
a. Imperf between (pair) £500
b. Imperf horiz (vert pair) £300
c. *Deep blue* 11·00 1·75
261 28 3d. yellow-brown (5.00) 22·00 1·00
a. Imperf between (pair) £650
b. Imperf vert (horiz pair) £350
c. *Deep brown* 22·00 1·00
ca. Imperf between (pair) £650
262 37 4d. indigo and brown (8.99) 7·00 1·25
a. *Bright blue and chestnut* 7·00 1·25
b. *Deep blue and bistre-brown* 7·00 1·25
263 30 5d. purple-brown (6.99) 18·00 2·25
a. *Deep purple-brown* 18·00 2·25
ab. Imperf between (pair) £700
264 31 6d. deep green 48·00 48·00
a. *Yellow-green* 65·00 75·00
265 6d. pale rose (5.5.00) 35·00 2·50
a. Imperf vert (horiz pair) £350
b. *Rose-red* 35·00 2·50
ba. Printed double £350
bb. Imperf between (pair) £500
bc. Imperf vert (horiz pair) £200
bd. Showing part of sheet wmk (7.02)* 60·00 25·00
c. *Scarlet* 45·00 8·00
ca. Imperf vert (horiz pair) £375
266 32 8d. indigo 26·00 9·00
a. *Prussian blue* 26·00 9·00
267 33 9d. deep purple (8.99) 40·00 22·00
a. *Rosy purple* 27·00 8·50
268 34 1s. red (5.00) 48·00 6·50
a. *Dull orange-red* 48·00 3·00
b. *Dull brown-red* 48·00 6·50
c. *Bright red* 60·00 20·00
269 35 2s. blue-green (7.99) 75·00 30·00
a. Laid paper (1.03) £170 £190
b. *Grey-green* 75·00 35·00
270 36 5s. vermilion (7.99) £200 £140
a. *Carmine-red* £300 £225
260/70 *Set of* 11 £425 £200

*No. 265bd is on paper without general watermark, but showing the words "LISBON SUPERFINE" wmkd once in the sheet; the paper was obtained from Parsons Bros, an American firm with a branch at Auckland.

38

1900. *Thick, soft ("Pirie") paper. Wmk double-lined "NZ" and Star, W* 38 *(sideways). P* 11.

271 13 ½d. black 4·50 3·00
272 15 2d. bright purple 10·50 3·00

39 White Terrace, Rotomahana

41

40 Commemorative of the New Zealand Contingent in the South African War

(Des J. Nairn (1½d.). Recess Govt Printer, Wellington)

1900 (Mar–Dec). *Thick, soft ("Pirie") paper.* W 38. *P* 11.

273 23 ½d. pale yellow-green (7.3.00) 7·50 2·50
a. *Yellow-green* 5·00 20
b. *Green* 4·25 10
ba. Imperf between (pair) £275
c. *Deep green* 4·25 10
274 39 1d. crimson (7.3.00) 9·50 10
a. *Rose-red* 9·50 10
ab. Imperf between (pair) £550 £550
ac. Imperf vert (horiz pair) £275
b. *Lake* 18·00 2·75
275 40 1½d. khaki (7.12.00) £650 £475
a. *Brown* 50·00 50·00
ab. Imperf vert (horiz pair) £450
ac. Imperf (pair) £550
b. *Chestnut* 7·50 4·00
ba. Imperf vert (horiz pair) £450
bb. Imperf horiz (vert pair) £550
c. *Pale chestnut* 7·50 4·00
ca. Imperf (pair) £550

276 **41** 2d. dull violet (3.00) 6·00 35
a. Imperf between (pair) £650
b. Mauve 8·00 1·50
c. Purple 6·50 35
ca. Imperf between (pair) £450

The above ½d. stamps are slightly smaller than those of the previous printing. A new plate was made to print 240 stamps instead of 120 as previously, and to make these fit the watermarked paper the border design was redrawn and contracted, the centre vignette remaining as before. The 2d. stamp is also from a new plate providing smaller designs.

42

(Des G. Bach. Eng J. A. C. Harrison. Recess Waterlow)

1901 (1 Jan). *Universal Penny Postage. No wmk. P* 12 *to* 16.
277 **42** 1d. carmine 5·00 2·50

All examples of No. 277 show a small dot above the upper left corner of the value tablet which is not present on later printings.

(Recess Govt Printer, Wellington)

1901 (Feb–Dec). *Thick, soft ("Pirie") paper.* **W 38**. *(a) P* 11.
278 **42** 1d. carmine 6·00 15
a. Imperf vert (horiz pair) £225
b. Deep carmine 6·00 15
ba. Imperf vert (horiz pair) £225
c. Carmine-lake 20·00 7·50

(b) P 14
279 **23** ½d. green (11.01) 9·00 2·75
280 **42** 1d. carmine 38·00 8·00
a. Imperf vert (horiz pair) £225

(c) Perf compound of 11 *and* 14
281 **23** ½d. green 10·00 4·00
a. Deep green 10·00 4·00
282 **42** 1d. carmine £250 75·00

(d) P 11 *and* 14 *mixed**
283 **23** ½d. green 55·00 35·00
284 **42** 1d. carmine £250 75·00

*The term "mixed" is applied to stamps from sheets which were at first perforated 14, or 14 and 11 compound, and either incompletely or defectively perforated. These sheets were patched on the back with strips of paper, and re-perforated 11 in those parts where the original perforation was defective.

Nos. 278/84 were printed from new plates supplied by Waterlow. These were subsequently used for Nos. 285/307 with later printings on Cowan paper showing considerable plate wear.

(Recess Govt Printer, Wellington)

1901 (Dec.) *Thin, hard ("Basted Mills") paper.* **W 38**. *(a) P* 11.
285 **23** ½d. green 50·00 50·00
286 **42** 1d. carmine 60·00 50·00

(b) P 14
287 **23** ½d. green 30·00 11·00
a. Imperf vert (horiz pair) £325
288 **42** 1d. carmine 14·00 2·25
a. Imperf between (pair) £275

(c) Perf compound of 11 *and* 14
289 **23** ½d. green 26·00 30·00
a. Deep green 26·00 30·00
290 **42** 1d. carmine 14·00 2·75

(d) Mixed perfs
291 **23** ½d. green 75·00 75·00
292 **42** 1d. carmine 75·00 50·00

(Recess Govt Printer, Wellington)

1902 (Jan). *Thin, hard ("Cowan") paper. No wmk. (a) P* 11.
293 **23** ½d. green 90·00 90·00

(b) P 14
294 **23** ½d. green 9·00 3·50
295 **42** 1d. carmine 15·00 1·25

(c) Perf compound of 11 *and* 14
296 **23** ½d. green 90·00 90·00
297 **42** 1d. carmine £110 £110

(d) Mixed perfs
298 **23** ½d. green 90·00 90·00
299 **42** 1d. carmine £120 £120

43 "Single" Wmk

(Recess Govt Printer, Wellington)

1902 (Apr). *Thin, hard ("Cowan") paper.* **W 43**. *(a) P* 11.
300 **23** ½d. green 60·00 70·00
301 **42** 1d. carmine £550 £400

(b) P 14
302 **23** ½d. green 2·75 15
a. Imperf vert (horiz pair) £170
b. Deep green 3·25 30
ba. Imperf vert (horiz pair) £170
c. Yellow-green 2·75 30
d. Pale yellow-green 12·00 2·25
303 **42** 1d. carmine 3·00 10
a. Imperf between (pair) £170
b. Booklet pane of 6 (21.8.02) £190
c. Pale carmine 3·00 10
ca. Imperf between (pair) £170
cb. Booklet pane of 6 £190
*d. Deep carmine** 32·00 4·00

(c) Perf compound of 11 *and* 14
304 **23** ½d. green 14·00 30·00
a. Deep green 20·00 35·00
305 **42** 1d. carmine £100 80·00
*a. Deep carmine** £400 £300

(d) Mixed perfs
306 **23** ½d. green 30·00 35·00
a. Deep green 35·00 40·00
307 **42** 1d. carmine 35·00 40·00
a. Pale carmine 35·00 40·00
*b. Deep carmine** £250 £250

*Nos. 303*d*, 305*a* and 307*b* were printed from a plate made by Waterlow & Sons, known as the "Reserve" plate. The stamps do not show evidence of wearing and the area surrounding the upper part of the figure is more deeply shaded. This plate was subsequently used to produce Nos. 362, 364, and 366/9.

A special plate, made by W. R. Royle & Sons, showing a minute dot between the horizontal rows, was introduced in 1902 to print the booklet pane, No. 303b. A special characteristic of the booklet pane was that the pearl in the top left-handed corner was large. Some panes exist with the outer edges imperforate.

(Recess Govt Printer, Wellington)

1902 (28 Aug)–**09**. *Thin, hard ("Cowan") paper.* **W 43** *(sideways on 3d., 5d., 6d., 8d., 1s. and 5s.). (a) P* 11
308 **27** 2½d. blue (5.03) 11·00 11·00
a. Deep blue 13·00 11·00
309 **28** 3d. yellow-brown 16·00 35
a. Bistre-brown 16·00 35
b. Pale bistre 25·00 2·75
310 **37** 4d. deep blue and deep brown/*bluish* (27.11.02) 8·50 40·00
a. Imperf vert (horiz pair) £450
311 **30** 5d. red-brown (4.03) 16·00 5·50
a. Deep brown 16·00 2·50
b. Sepia 32·00 12·00
312 **31** 6d. rose (9.02) 35·00 3·50
a. Rose-red 35·00 4·00
ab. Wmk upright £475 £300
b. Rose-carmine 40·00 4·00
ba. Imperf vert (horiz pair) £400
bb. Imperf horiz (vert pair)
c. Bright carmine-pink 50·00 5·50
d. Scarlet 50·00 15·00
313 **32** 8d. blue (2.03) 26·00 6·00
a. Steel-blue 26·00 6·00
ab. Imperf vert (horiz pair) £500
ac. Imperf horiz (vert pair) £500
314 **33** 9d. purple (5.03) 27·00 9·50
315 **34** 1s. brown-red (11.02) 48·00 5·00
a. Bright red 48·00 5·50
b. Orange-red 48·00 3·25
ba. Error. Wmk W **12b** (inverted) † £1200
c. Orange-brown 60·00 7·50
316 **35** 2s. green (4.03) 70·00 35·00
a. Blue-green 70·00 35·00
317 **36** 5s. deep red (6.03) £190 £150
a. Wmk upright £200 £160
b. Vermilion £190 £150
ba. Wmk upright £200 £160

(b) P 14
318 **40** 1½d. chestnut (2.07) 11·00 30·00
319 **41** 2d. grey-purple (12.02) 5·50 50
a. Purple 5·50 50
ab. Imperf vert (horiz pair) £350
ac. Imperf horiz (vert pair) £350
b. Bright reddish purple 6·50 1·10
320 **27** 2½d. blue (1906) 7·00 1·25
a. Deep blue 7·00 1·50
321 **28** 3d. bistre-brown (1906) 23·00 1·00
a. Imperf vert (horiz pair) £450
b. Bistre 23·00 1·00
c. Pale yellow-bistre 48·00 8·00
322 **37** 4d. deep blue and deep brown/*bluish* (1903) 6·00 2·00
a. Imperf vert (horiz pair) £400
b. Imperf horiz (vert pair) £400
c. Centre inverted † £25000
d. Blue and chestnut/bluish 6·00 60
e. Blue and ochre-brown/bluish 6·00 60
323 **30** 5d. black-brown (1906) 50·00 15·00
a. Red-brown 23·00 5·50
324 **31** 6d. bright carmine-pink (1906) 60·00 6·00
a. Imperf vert (horiz pair) £400
b. Rose-carmine 60·00 6·50
325 **32** 8d. steel-blue (1907) 25·00 4·50
326 **33** 9d. purple (1906) 25·00 6·00
327 **34** 1s. orange-brown (1906) 60·00 4·50
a. Orange-red 55·00 4·50
b. Pale red 75·00 24·00
328 **35** 2s. green (1.06) 65·00 20·00
a. Blue-green 65·00 20·00
329 **36** 5s. deep red (1906) £190 £150
a. Wmk upright £200 £160
b. Dull red £190 £150
ba. Wmk upright £200 £160

(c) Perf compound of 11 *and* 14
330 **40** 1½d. chestnut (1907) £600
331 **41** 2d. purple (1903) £275
332 **28** 3d. bistre-brown (1906) £500 £450
333 **37** 4d. blue and yellow-brown (1903) £300 £300
334 **30** 5d. red-brown (1906) £400 £400
335 **31** 6d. rose-carmine (1907) £300 £200
336 **32** 8d. steel-blue (1907) £600 £600
337 **33** 9d. purple (1906) £800 £800
338 **36** 5s. deep red (1906) £1200 £1200

(d) Mixed perfs
339 **40** 1½d. chestnut (1907) £600
340 **41** 2d. purple (1903) £140
341 **28** 3d. bistre-brown (1906) £500 £450
342 **37** 4d. blue and chestnut/*bluish* (1904) £250 £250
a. Blue and yellow-brown/bluish £250 £250
343 **30** 5d. red-brown (1906) £400 £400
344 **31** 6d. rose-carmine (1907) £250 £200
a. Bright carmine-pink £250 £200
345 **32** 8d. steel-blue (1907) £550 £550
346 **33** 9d. purple (1906) £700 £700
347 **35** 2s. blue-green (1906) £800 £800
348 **36** 5s. vermilion (1906) £1200 £1200

Two sizes of paper were used for the above stamps:—

(1) A sheet containing 240 wmks, with a space of 9 mm between each.

(2) A sheet containing 120 wmks, with a space of 24 mm between each vertical row.

Size (1) was used for the ½d., 1d., 2d., and 4d., and size (2) for 2½d., 5d., 9d., and 2s. The paper in each case exactly fitted the plates, and had the watermark in register, though in the case of the 4d., the plate of which contained only 80 stamps, the paper was cut up to print it. The 3d., 6d., 8d., and 1s. were printed on variety (1), but with watermark sideways: by reason of this, specimens from the margins of the sheets show parts of the words "NEW ZEALAND POSTAGE" in large letters, and some copies have no watermark at all. For the 1½d. and 5s. stamps variety (1) was also used, but two watermarks appear on each stamp.

(Recess Govt Printer, Wellington)

1904 (Feb). *Printed from new "dot" plates made by W.R. Royle & Sons. Thin, hard ("Cowan") paper.* **W 43** *(a) P* 14.
349 **42** 1d. rose-carmine 7·50 40
a. Pale carmine 7·50 40

(b) Perf compound of 11 *and* 14
350 **42** 1d. rose-carmine £120 £110

(c) Mixed perfs
351 **42** 1d. rose-carmine 20·00 20·00
a. Pale carmine 20·00 20·00

These plates have a minute dot in the horizontal margins between the rows, centred under each stamp, but it is frequently cut out by the perforations. However, they can be further distinguished by the notes below.

In 1906 fresh printings were made from four new plates, two of which, marked in the margin "W1" and "W2", were supplied by Waterlow Bros and Layton, and the other two, marked "R1" and "R2", by W. R. Royle & Son. The intention was to note which pair of plates wore the best and produced the best results. They can be distinguished as follows:—

(a) *(b)* *(c)*

(d) *(e)* *(f)*

(a) Four o'clock flaw in rosette at top right corner. Occurs in all these plates but not in the original Waterlow plates.
(b) Pearl at right strong.
(c) Pearl at right weak.
(d) Dot at left and S-shaped ornament unshaded.
(e) S-shaped ornament with one line of shading within.
(f) As *(e)* but with line from left pearl to edge of stamp.

"Dot" plates comprise *(a)* and *(d)*.
Waterlow plates comprise *(a)*, *(b)* and *(e)*.
Royle plates comprise *(a)*, *(c)* and *(e)* and the line in *(f)* on many stamps but not all.

(Recess Govt Printer, Wellington)

1906. *Thin, hard ("Cowan") paper.* **W 43**.
(a) Printed from new Waterlow plates. (i) P 14
352 **42** 1d. deep rose-carmine 17·00 1·00
a. Imperf between (pair) £200
b. Aniline carmine 16·00 1·00
ba. Imperf between (pair) £200
c. Rose-carmine 16·00 1·00

(ii) P 11
353 **42** 1d. aniline carmine £325 £325

(iii) Perf compound of 11 *and* 14
354 **42** 1d. rose-carmine £300 £300

(iv) Mixed perfs
355 **42** 1d. deep rose-carmine £225 £225

(b) Printed from new Royle plates. (i) P 14
356 **42** 1d. rose-carmine 10·00 1·25
a. Imperf horiz (vert pair) £225 £225
b. Bright rose-carmine 12·00 1·40

(ii) P 11
357 **42** 1d. bright rose-carmine £150 £150

(iii) Perf compound of 11 *and* 14
358 **42** 1d. rose-carmine 85·00 85·00

(iv) Mixed perfs
359 **42** 1d. rose-carmine £100 85·00

(v) P 14 × 14½ *(comb)*
360 **42** 1d. bright rose-carmine 60·00 40·00
a. Rose-carmine 60·00 40·00

Nos. 360/*a* are known both with and without the small dot. See also No. 386.

1905 (15 June)–**06**. *Stamps supplied to penny-in-the-slot machines.*

(i) *"Dot" plates of* 1904. (ii) Waterlow *"reserve" plate of* 1902

(a) Imperf top and bottom; zigzag roulette 9½ on one or both sides, two large holes at sides

361 **42** 1d. rose-carmine (i) £120
362 1d. deep carmine (ii) £140

(b) As last but rouletted 14½ (8.7.05)

363 **42** 1d. rose-carmine (i) £140
364 1d. deep carmine (ii) .. ..

(c) Imperf all round, two large holes each side (6.3.06)

365 **42** 1d. rose-carmine (i) £120
366 1d. deep carmine (ii) £140

(d) Imperf all round (21.6.06)

367 **42** 1d. deep carmine (ii) £130

(e) Imperf all round. Two small indentations on back of stamp (1.06)

368 **42** 1d. deep carmine (ii) £160 £130

(f) Imperf all round; two small pin-holes in stamp (21.6.06)

369 **42** 1d. deep carmine (ii) £140 £130

No. 365 *only* exists from strips of Nos. 361 or 363 (resulting from the use of successive coins) which have been separated by scissors. Similarly strips of Nos. 362 and 364 can produce single copies of No. 366 but this also exists in singles from a different machine.

Most used copies of Nos. 361/7 are forgeries and they should only be collected on cover.

44 Maori Canoe, *Te Arawa*

(Des L. J. Steele. Eng W. R. Bock. Typo Govt Printer, Wellington)

1906 (1–17 Nov). *New Zealand Exhibition, Christchurch. T* **44** *and similar horiz designs. W* **43** *(sideways). P* 14.

370 ½d. emerald-green .. .. 16·00 23·00
371 1d. vermilion .. .. 13·00 15·00
a. Claret £7000 £8000
372 3d. brown and blue .. .. 45·00 55·00
373 6d. pink and olive-green (17.11) £140 £225
370/3 .. .. *Set of* 4 £200 £275

Designs:—1d. Maori art; 3d. Landing of Cook; 6d. Annexation of New Zealand.

The 1d. in claret was the original printing, which was considered unsatisfactory.

47 (T **28** reduced) **48** (T **31** reduced) **49** (T **34** reduced)

(New plates (except 4d.), supplied by Perkins Bacon. Recess Govt Printer, Wellington).

1907–8. *Thin, hard ("Cowan") paper. W* **43**. *(a) P* 14 *(line).*

374 **23** ½d. green (1907) .. .. 32·00 7·00
a. Imperf (pair) £120
b. Yellow-green .. .. 22·00 2·50
c. Deep yellow-green .. .. 18·00 1·75
375 **47** 3d. brown (6.07) .. .. 55·00 18·00
376 **48** 6d. carmine-pink (3.07) .. .. 48·00 6·00
a. Red .. .. 80·00 28·00

(b) P 14 × 13, 13½ *(comb)*

377 **23** ½d. green (1907) .. .. 20·00 5·00
a. Yellow-green .. .. 8·00 85
378 **47** 3d. brown (2.08) .. .. 48·00 22·00
a. Yellow-brown .. .. 48·00 25·00
379 **37** 4d. blue and yellow-brown/*bluish* (6.08) 27·00 20·00
380 **48** 6d. pink (2.08) .. .. £250 80·00
381 **49** 1s. orange-red (12.07) .. .. £130 48·00

(c) P 14 × 15 *(comb)*

382 **23** ½d. yellow-green (1907) .. .. 14·00 60
383 **47** 3d. brown (8.08) .. .. 48·00 7·00
a. Yellow-brown .. .. 48·00 7·00
384 **48** 6d. carmine-pink (8.08) .. .. 48·00 9·50
385 **49** 1s. orange-red (8.08) .. .. £120 24·00
a. Deep orange-brown £300

The ½d. stamps of this 1907–8 issue have a minute dot in the margin between the stamps, where not removed by the perforation. (See note after No. 351*a*). Those perforated 14 can be distinguished from the earlier stamps, Nos. 302/*d*, by the absence of plate wear. This is most noticeable on the 1902 printings as a white patch at far left, level with the bottom of the "P" in "POSTAGE". Such damage is not present on the new plates used for Nos. 374/*c*.

Stamps of T **47**, **48** and **49** also have a small dot as described in note after No. 351*a*.

TYPOGRAPHY PAPERS. 1908–30. De La Rue paper is chalk-surfaced and has a smooth finish. The watermark is as illustrated. The gum is toned and strongly resistant to soaking. **Jones paper** is chalk-surfaced and has a coarser texture, is poorly surfaced and the ink tends to peel. The outline of the watermark commonly shows on the surface of the stamp. The gum is colourless or only slightly toned and washes off readily. **Cowan paper** is chalk-surfaced and is white and opaque. The watermark is usually smaller than in the "Jones" paper and is often barely visible.

Wiggins Teape paper is chalk-surfaced and is thin and hard. It has a vertical mesh with a narrow watermark, whereas the other papers have a horizontal mesh and a wider watermark.

50

(Typo Govt Printer, Wellington, from Perkins Bacon plate).

1908 (1 Dec). *De La Rue chalk-surfaced paper. W* **43**. *P* 14×15 *(comb).*

386 **50** 1d. carmine .. .. 30·00 50

The design of Type **50** differs from Type **42** by alterations in the corner rosettes and by the lines on the globe which are diagonal instead of vertical.

51 **52** **53**

(Eng. P.B. Typo Govt Printer, Wellington)

1909 (8 Nov)–**12**. *De La Rue chalk-surfaced paper with toned gum. W* **43**. *P* 14 × 15 *(comb).*

387 **51** ½d. yellow-green .. .. 3·00 10
aa. Deep green .. .. 3·00 20
a. Imperf (pair) £140
b. Booklet pane. Five stamps plus label in position 1 (4.10) £400
c. Ditto, but label in position 6 (4.10) .. £400
d. Booklet pane of 6 (4.10) £140
e. Ditto, but with coloured bars on selvedge (5.12) £140

Stamps with blurred and heavy appearance are from booklets.

(Eng W. R. Royle & Son, London. Recess Govt Printer, Wellington)

1909 (8 Nov)–**16**. *T* **52** *and similar portraits.*

(a) W **43**. *P* 14×14½ *(comb)*

388 2d. mauve .. .. 14·00 5·00
a. Deep mauve .. .. 18·00 5·00
389 3d. chestnut .. .. 18·00 30
390 4d. orange-red .. .. 22·00 22·00
a. Orange-yellow (1912) .. .. 7·00 2·00
391 5d. brown (1910) .. .. 13·00 80
a. Red-brown .. .. 11·00 80
392 6d. carmine (1910) .. .. 26·00 40
a. Deep carmine (29.10.13) .. .. 26·00 70
393 8d. indigo-blue .. .. 9·00 65
a. Deep bright blue .. .. 11·00 65
394 1s. vermilion (1910) .. .. 48·00 1·75
388/94 .. .. *Set of* 8 £140 28·00

(b) W **43**. *P* 14 *(line)**

395 3d. chestnut (1910) .. .. 38·00 4·00
396 4d. orange (1910) .. .. 15·00 5·00
397 5d. brown .. .. 22·00 3·00
a. Red-brown (15.9.11) .. .. 24·00 3·50
398 6d. carmine .. .. 38·00 6·50
399 1s. vermilion .. .. 48·00 6·50
395/9 .. .. *Set of* 5 £140 22·00

(c) W **43** *(sideways) (paper with widely spaced watermark as used for Nos.* 308 *and* 320 *– see note below No.* 348). *P* 14 *(line)**

400 8d. indigo-blue (8.16) .. .. 13·00 35·00
a. No wmk .. .. 55·00 90·00

(d) W **43**. *P* 14 × 13½ *(comb)*†

401 3d. chestnut (1915) .. .. 60·00 65·00
a. Vert pair. P 14 × 13½ and 14 × 14½ .. £225 £275
402 5d. red-brown (1916) .. .. 17·00 1·75
a. Vert pair. P 14 × 13½ and 14 × 14½ .. 50·00 70·00
403 6d. carmine (1915) .. .. 70·00 70·00
a. Vert pair. P 14 × 13½ and 14 × 14½ .. £225 £275
404 8d. indigo-blue (3.16) .. .. 22·00 1·75
a. Vert pair. P 14 × 13½ and 14 × 14½ .. 50·00 70·00
b. Deep bright blue .. .. 22·00 1·75
ba. Vert pair. P 14 × 13½ and 14 × 14½ .. 50·00 70·00
401/4 .. .. *Set of* 4 £150 £120

*In addition to showing the usual characteristics of a line perforation, these stamps may be distinguished by their vertical perforation which measures 13.8. Nos. 388/94 generally measure vertically 14 to 14.3. An exception is 13.8 one vertical side but 14 the other.

†The 3d. and 6d. come in full sheets perf 14 × 13½. The 3d., 5d. and 6d. values also exist in two combinations: *(a)* five top rows perf 14 × 13½ with five bottom rows perf 14 × 14½ and *(b)* four top rows perf 14 × 13½ with six bottom rows perf 14 × 14½. The 8d. perf 14 × 13½ only exists from combination *(b)*.

(Eng P.B. Typo Govt Printer, Wellington)

1909 (8 Nov)–**26**. *P* 14 × 15 *(comb).*

(a) W **43**. *De La Rue chalk-surfaced paper with toned gum*

405 **53** 1d. carmine .. .. 1·25 10
a. Imperf (pair) £200
b. Booklet pane of 6 (4.10) £110
c. Ditto, but with coloured bars on selvedge (5.12) £110

(b) W **43**. *Jones chalk-surfaced paper with white gum*

406 **53** 1d. deep carmine (1924) .. .. .. 11·00 4·00
a. On unsurfaced paper. *Pale carmine* £275
b. Booklet pane of 6 with bars on selvedge (1.12.24) .. .. 95·00

(c) W **43**. *De La Rue unsurfaced medium paper with toned gum*

407 **53** 1d. rose-carmine (4.25) .. .. .. 24·00 55·00

(d) W **43** *(sideways). De La Rue chalk-surfaced paper with toned gum*

408 **53** 1d. bright carmine (4.25) .. .. .. 6·50 18·00
a. No wmk .. .. 20·00 40·00
b. Imperf (pair) .. .. 50·00

(e) No wmk, but bluish "NZ" and Star lithographed on back. Art paper

409 **53** 1d. rose-carmine (1925) .. .. .. 2·25 1·00
a. "NZ" and Star in black .. .. .. 10·00
b. "NZ" and Star colourless .. .. .. 24·00

(f) W **43**. *Cowan thick, opaque, chalk-surfaced paper with white gum*

410 **53** 1d. deep carmine (8.25) .. .. .. 4·25 1·00
a. Imperf (pair) .. .. 65·00 70·00
b. Booklet pane of 6 with bars and adverts on selvedge .. .. 45·00

(g) W **43**. *Wiggins Teape thin, hard, chalk-surfaced paper with white gum*

411 **53** 1d. rose-carmine (6.26) .. .. .. 22·00 8·50

Examples of No. 405 with a blurred and heavy appearance are from booklets.

No. 406a comes from a sheet on which the paper coating was missing from the right-hand half.

Many stamps from the sheets of No. 408 were without watermark or showed portions of "NEW ZEALAND POSTAGE" in double-lined capitals.

AUCKLAND
EXHIBITION,
1913.

(59)

60

1913 (1 Dec). *Auckland Industrial Exhibition. Nos.* 387*aa*, 389, 392 *and* 405 *optd with T* **59** *by Govt Printer, Wellington.*

412 **51** ½d. deep green .. .. 10·00 23·00
413 **53** 1d. carmine .. .. 15·00 26·00
414 **52** 3d. chestnut £100 £160
415 6d. carmine £100 £180
412/15 .. .. *Set of* 4 £200 £350

These overprinted stamps were only available for letters in New Zealand and to Australia.

(Des H. L. Richardson. Recess Govt Printer, Wellington, from plates made in London by P.B.)

1915 (30 July)–**29**. *P* 14×14½, *comb (See notes below).*

(a) W **43**. *Cowan unsurfaced paper*

416 **60** 1½d. grey-slate .. .. 2·75 40
a. Perf 14×13½ .. .. 1·75 50
b. Vert pair, 416/a .. .. 35·00 50·00
417 2d. bright violet .. .. 6·50 17·00
a. Perf 14×13½ .. .. 6·50 17·00
b. Vert pair, 417/a .. .. 24·00 50·00
418 2d. yellow (15.1.16) .. .. 4·50 13·00
a. Perf 14×13½ .. .. 4·50 13·00
b. Vert pair, 418/a .. .. 18·00 48·00
419 2½d. blue .. .. 8·50 4·50
a. Perf 14×13½ (1916) .. .. 3·25 1·50
b. Vert pair, 419/a .. .. 35·00 65·00
420 3d. chocolate .. .. 7·50 60
a. Perf 14×13½ .. .. 7·50 50
b. Vert pair, 420/a .. .. 35·00 55·00
421 4d. yellow .. .. 4·25 30·00
a. Perf 14×13½ .. .. 4·25 30·00
b. Vert pair, 421/a .. .. 26·00 £120
c. Re-entry (Pl 20 R. 1/6) .. .. 30·00
d. Re-entry (Pl 20 R. 4/10) .. .. 35·00
422 4d. bright violet (7.4.16) .. .. 7·00 20
a. Perf 14×13½ .. .. 5·00 20
b. Imperf (pair) £750
c. Vert pair, 422/a .. .. 35·00 65·00
d. Re-entry (Pl 20 R. 1/6) .. .. 35·00
e. Re-entry (Pl 20 R. 4/10) .. .. 40·00
423 4½d. deep green .. .. 18·00 14·00
a. Perf 14×13½ .. .. 12·00 2·50
b. Vert pair, 423/a .. .. 48·00 65·00
424 5d. light blue (4.22) .. .. 16·00 14·00
a. Perf 14×13½ .. .. 6·00 50
b. Imperf (pair) £110 £120
c. Pale ultramarine (5.29) .. .. 12·00 6·50
ca. Perf 14×13½ .. .. 8·00 3·75
cb. Vert pair, 424c/ca .. .. 55·00 75·00
425 6d. carmine .. .. 6·50 30
a. Perf 14×13½ .. .. 5·50 20
b. Vert pair, 425/a (1916) .. .. 65·00 95·00
c. Imperf three sides (pair) £1200
d. Carmine-lake. Perf 14×13½ (11.27) £500 £325
426 7½d. red-brown .. .. 30·00 32·00
a. Perf 14×13½ (10.20) .. .. 12·00 17·00
b. Vert pair, 426/a .. .. 50·00 80·00
427 8d. indigo-blue (19.4.21) .. .. 17·00 32·00
a. Perf 14×13½ .. .. 15·00 30·00
b. Vert pair, 427/a .. .. 38·00 80·00
428 8d. red-brown (*p* 14×13½) (2.22) .. .. 15·00 55
429 9d. sage-green .. .. 17·00 4·25
a. Perf 14×13½ .. .. 13·00 60
b. Vert pair, 429/a .. .. 70·00 £100
c. Imperf three sides (pair) £1300
d. Imperf (pair) £1000
e. Yellowish ol. Perf 14×13½ (12.25) 28·00 7·00
430 1s. vermilion .. .. 13·00 30
a. Perf 14×13½ .. .. 13·00 95
b. Imperf (pair) £2250
c. Vert pair, 430/a .. .. 75·00 £100
d. Pale orange-red (1925) .. .. 30·00 6·50
da. Imperf (pair) £325
db. Orange-brown (1.2.28) £850 £425
416/30 .. .. *Set of* 15 £100 £100

(b) W **43** *(sideways on 2d., 3d. and 6d.). Thin paper with widely spaced watermark as used for Nos.* 308 *and* 320 *– see note below No.* 348)

431 **60** 1½d. grey-slate (3.16) .. .. 1·50 3·50
a. No wmk .. .. 2·00 7·00
b. Perf 14 × 13½ .. .. 1·50 3·50
ba. No wmk .. .. 2·00 7·00
c. Vert pair, 431/b .. .. 20·00 35·00
ca. Vert pair, 431a/ba .. .. 28·00 50·00
432 2d. yellow (*p* 14, *line*) (6.16) .. .. 4·50 32·00
a. No wmk .. .. 30·00 65·00
433 3d. chocolate (*p* 14, *line*) (6.16) .. .. 6·00 10·00
a. No wmk .. .. 26·00 55·00

434 **60** 6d. carmine (*p* 14, *line*) (8.16) .. 6·00 40·00
a. No wmk .. .. 35·00 80·00
431/4 .. .. *Set of* 4 16·00 75·00

The 1½d., 2½d., 4½d. and 7½d. have value tablets as shown in T **60**. In the other values, the tablets are shortened, and the ornamental border at each side of the crown correspondingly extended.

During the laying-down of plate 20 for the 4d., from the roller-die which also contained dies of other values, an impression of the 4½d. value was placed on R.1/6 and of the 2½d. on R.4/10. These errors were subsequently corrected by re-entries of the 4d. impression, but on R.1/6 traces of the original impression can be found in the right-hand value tablet and above the top frame line, while on R.4/10 the foot of the "2" is visible in the left-hand value tablet with traces of "½" to its right.

Of this issue the 1½d., 2½d., 4d. (both), 4½d., 5d., 6d., 7½d., 9d. and 1s are known from sheets perforated 14 × 13½ throughout and the 4d. violet, 5d., 6d. and 1s. from sheets perforated 14 × 14½ throughout.

All values from 1½d. to 1s. were also produced showing the use of the two different perforations within the same sheet as described beneath No. 404ba. In most instances the top four rows were perforated 14 × 13½ and the bottom six 14 × 14½. For one printing of the 4d. violet and for all printings of the 5d. pale ultramarine with two perforations on the same sheet the arrangement differed in that the top five rows were perforated 14 × 14½ and the bottom five 14 × 13½.

With the exception of Nos. 432/4 any with perforations measuring 14 × 14 or nearly must be classed as 14 × 14½, this being an irregularity of the comb machine, and not a product of the 14-line machine.

61

62

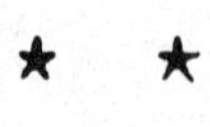

(**63**)

Type **62** (from local plates) can be identified from Type **61** (prepared by Perkins Bacon) by the shading on the portrait. This is diagonal on Type **62** and horizontal on Type **61**.

(Die eng W. R. Bock. Typo Govt Printer, Wellington, from plates made by P.B. (T **61**) or locally (T **62**))

1915 (30 July)–**34**. *P* 14×15.

(*a*) *W* **43**. *De La Rue chalk-surfaced paper with toned gum.*
435 **61** ½d. green 70 10
a. Booklet pane of 6 with bars on selvedge .. .. 95·00
b. Yellow-green .. .. .. 3·25 60
ba. Booklet pane of 6 with bars on selvedge .. .. 80·00
c. Very thick, hard, highly surfaced paper with white gum (12.15) .. 12·00 18·00
436 **62** 1½d. grey-black (4.16) .. .. .. 3·00 30
a. Black .. .. 4·50 35
437 **61** 1½d. slate (5.9.16) .. .. .. 5·50 10
438 1½d. orange-brown (9.18) .. .. 1·50 10
439 2d. yellow (9.16) 80 10
a. Pale yellow .. .. .. 3·75 60
440 3d. chocolate (5.19) .. .. .. 6·00 30
435/40 .. .. *Set of* 6 16·00 70

(*b*) *W* **43**. *Jones chalk-surfaced paper with white gum*
441 **61** ½d. green (10.24) .. .. .. 6·50 3·75
a. Booklet pane of 6 with bars on selvedge (1.12.24) .. .. .. 85·00
442 2d. dull yellow (7.24) .. .. .. 4·00 16·00
443 3d. deep chocolate (3.25) .. .. 18·00 5·50
441/3 .. .. *Set of* 3 26·00 23·00

(*c*) *No wmk, but bluish* "NZ" *and Star lithographed on back. Art paper*
444 **61** ½d. apple-green (4.25) .. .. 1·50 90
a. "NZ" and Star almost colourless .. 4·25
445 2d. yellow (7.25) .. .. .. 6·00 32·00

(*d*) *W* **43**. *Cowan thick, opaque, chalk-surfaced paper with white gum*
446 **61** ½d. green (8.25) 40 10
a. Booklet pane of 6 with bars and adverts on selvedge .. .. 85·00
ab. Booklet pane of 6 with bars on selvedge (1934) .. .. ..
b. Perf 14 (1927) 50 20
ba. Booklet pane of 6 with bars on selvedge (1928) .. .. 45·00
bb. Booklet pane of 6 with bars and adverts on selvedge (1928) .. 45·00
447 1½d. orange-brown (*p* 14) (8.29) .. 8·50 11·00
a. Perf 14×15 (7.33) .. .. .. 45·00 50·00
448 2d. yellow (8.25) .. .. .. 3·50 20
a. Perf 14 (1929) .. .. .. 2·75 10
449 3d. chocolate (8.25) .. .. .. 6·50 20
a. Perf 14 (1929) .. .. .. 7·50 1·25
446/9 .. .. *Set of* 4 17·00 11·00

(*e*) *W* **43**. *Wiggins Teape thin, hard, chalk-surfaced paper*
450 **61** 1½d. orange-brown (*p* 14) (1930) .. 30·00 60·00
451 2d. yellow (5.26) .. .. .. 7·50 15·00
a. Perf 14 (10.27) .. .. .. 6·50 15·00

The designs of these stamps also differ as described beneath No. 434.

Stamps from booklet panes often have blurred, heavy impressions. Different advertisements can be found on the listed booklet panes.

1915 (24 Sept). *No.* 435 *optd with T* **63**.
452 **61** ½d. green .. .. 1·60 20

64 "Peace" and Lion

65 "Peace" and Lion

(Des and typo D.L.R. from plates by P.B., Waterlow and D.L.R.)

1920 (27 Jan). *Victory. T* **64**/**5** *and similar designs. W* **43** (*sideways on* ½*d.,* 1½*d.,* 3*d. and* 1*s.*). *De La Rue chalk-surfaced paper. P* 14.
453 ½d. green .. .. 2·00 1·40
a. Pale yellow-green .. .. .. 24·00 14·00
454 1d. carmine-red .. .. .. 4·00 30
a. Bright carmine .. .. .. 6·00 40
455 1½d. brown-orange .. .. .. 3·50 20
456 3d. chocolate .. .. 13·00 11·00
457 6d. violet .. .. 13·00 13·00
458 1s. orange-red .. .. .. 24·00 42·00
453/8 .. .. *Set of* 6 55·00 60·00

Designs: *Horiz* (*as T* **65**)—1½d. Maori chief. (*As T* **64**)—3d. Lion; 1s. King George V. *Vert* (*as T* **64**)—6d. "Peace" and "Progress".

The above stamps were placed on sale in London in November, 1919.

2d. 2d.

TWOPENCE

(**68**)

69

1922 (Mar). *Surch with T* **68**.
459 **64** 2d. on ½d. green (R.) .. .. .. 2·00 60

(Des and eng W. R. Bock. Typo Govt Printer, Wellington)

1923 (1 Oct)–**25**. *Restoration of Penny Postage. W* **43**. *P* 14 × 15.

(*a*) *De La Rue chalk-surfaced paper with toned gum.*
460 **69** 1d. carmine .. .. 1·50 30

(*b*) *Jones chalk-surfaced paper with white gum*
461 **69** 1d. carmine (3.24) .. .. .. 3·75 2·50

(*c*) *Cowan unsurfaced paper with very shiny gum*
462 **69** 1d. carmine-pink (4.25) .. .. .. 27·00 23·00

The paper used for No. 462 is similar to that of Nos. 416/30.

70 Exhibition Buildings

(Des H. L. Richardson. Eng and typo Govt Printer, Wellington)

1925 (17 Nov). *Dunedin Exhibition. W* **43**. *Cowan chalk-surfaced paper. P* 14 × 15.
463 **70** ½d. yellow-green/*green* .. .. .. 2·00 11·00
464 1d. carmine/*rose* .. .. .. 2·50 5·00
465 4d. mauve/*pale mauve* .. .. .. 38·00 60·00
a. "POSTAGF" at right (R.1/2, R.10/1) £120 £170
463/5 .. .. *Set of* 3 38·00 70·00

71

72

(Des H. L. Richardson; plates by B.W. (1d. from sheets), P.B. (1d. from booklets), Royal Mint, London (others). Typo Govt Printer, Wellington)

1926 (12 July)–**34**. *W* **43**. *P* 14. (*a*) *Jones chalk-surfaced paper with white gum.*
466 **72** 2s. deep blue .. .. 42·00 48·00
467 3s. mauve .. .. 70·00 90·00

(*b*) *Cowan thick, opaque, chalk-surfaced paper with white gum*
468 **71** 1d. rose-carmine (15.11.26) 40 10
a. Imperf (pair) .. .. 45·00
b. Booklet pane of 6 with bars on selvedge (1928) .. .. .. 45·00
c. Booklet pane of 6 with bars and adverts on selvedge (1928) .. .. 45·00
d. Perf 14 × 15 (3.27) 45 10
da. Booklet pane of 6 with bars and adverts on selvedge (1934) .. .. 60·00
469 **72** 2s. light blue (5.27) .. .. .. 42·00 15·00
470 3s. pale mauve (9.27) .. .. .. 70·00 85·00
468/70 .. .. *Set of* 3 £100 90·00

(*c*) *Wiggins Teape thin, hard, chalk-surfaced paper with white gum*
471 **71** 1d. rose-carmine (6.30) .. .. .. 14·00 6·00

No. 468 exists in a range of colours including scarlet and deep carmine to magenta but we have insufficient evidence to show that these were issued.

73 Nurse

74 Smiling Boy

(Typo Govt Printing Office, Wellington)

1929–30. *Anti-Tuberculosis Fund. T* **73** *and similar type. W* **43**. *P* 14. (*a*) *Inscribed* "HELP STAMP OUT TUBERCULOSIS".
544 1d. + 1d. scarlet (11.12.29) .. .. .. 11·00 14·00

(*b*) *Inscribed* "HELP PROMOTE HEALTH"
545 1d. + 1d. scarlet (29.10.30) .. .. .. 17·00 22·00

(Des L. C. Mitchell. Dies eng and plates made Royal Mint, London (1d.), Govt Ptg Office, Wellington from W. R. Bock die (2d.). Typo Govt Ptg Office, Wellington)

1931 (31 Oct). *Health Stamps. W* **43** (*sideways*). *P* 14½ × 14.
546 **74** 1d. + 1d. scarlet .. .. .. 75·00 75·00
547 2d. + 1d. blue .. .. 75·00 65·00

75 New Zealand Lake Scenery

FIVE PENCE

(**76**)

(Des L. C. Mitchell. Plates, Royal Mint, London. Typo Govt Ptg Office)

1931 (10 Nov)–**35**. *Air. W* **43**. *P* 14×14½.
548 **75** 3d. chocolate .. .. 18·00 11·00
a. Perf 14×15 (4.35) £190 £425
549 4d. blackish purple .. .. .. 20·00 11·00
550 7d. brown-orange .. .. .. 22·00 7·50
548/50 .. .. *Set of* 3 55·00 27·00

1931 (18 Dec). *Air. Surch with T* **76**.
551 **75** 5d. on 3d. green (R.) .. .. .. 9·00 6·50

77 Hygeia, Goddess of Health

78 The Path to Health

(Des R. E. Tripe and W. J. Cooch. Eng H. T. Peat. Recess Govt Printing Office, Wellington)

1932 (18 Nov). *Health Stamp. W* **43**. *P* 14.
552 **77** 1d. + 1d. carmine .. .. .. 20·00 22·00

(Des J. Berry. Eng H. T. Peat. Recess Govt Printing Office, Wellington)

1933 (8 Nov). *Health Stamp. W* **43**. *P* 14.
553 **78** 1d. + 1d. carmine .. .. .. 7·50 13·00

TRANS-TASMAN
AIR MAIL
"FAITH IN AUSTRALIA."

(**79**)

80 Crusader

1934 (17 Jan). *Air. T* **75** *in new colour optd with T* **79**. *W* **43**. *P* 14×14½.
554 **75** 7d. light blue (B.) .. .. .. 35·00 38·00

(Des J. Berry. Recess D.L.R.)

1934 (25 Oct). *Health Stamp. W* **43**. *P* 14×13½.
555 **80** 1d. + 1d. carmine .. .. .. 5·50 7·00

81 Collared Grey Fantail

82 Brown Kiwi

83 Maori Woman

84 Maori Carved House

85 Mt Cook

86 Maori Girl

87 Mitre Peak

88 Swordfish

89 Harvesting

90 Tuatara Lizard

91 Maori Panel

92 Tui

93 Capt. Cook at Poverty Bay

94 Mt Egmont

Die I Die II

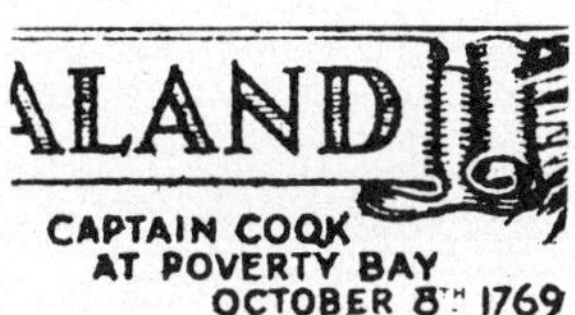

"Captain Coqk"
(R. 1/4)

(Des J. Fitzgerald (½d., 4d.), C. H. and R. J. G. Collins (1d.), M. Matthews (1½d.), H. W. Young (2d.), L. C. Mitchell (2½d., 3d., 8d., 1s., 3s.), W. J. Cooch and R. E. Tripe (5d.), T. I. Archer (6d.), I. F. Calder (9d.) and I. H. Jenkins (2s.). Litho Waterlow (9d.). Recess D.L.R. (remainder))

1935 (1 May). W **43**.
556 **81** ½d. bright green, *p* 14 × 13½ .. .. 1·50 30
557 **82** 1d. scarlet (Die I), *p* 14 × 13½ .. 1·50 20
a. Perf 13½ × 14 .. .. .. 50·00 19·00
b. Die II. Perf 14 × 13½ .. .. 4·50 1·25
ba. Booklet pane of 6 with adverts on selvedge .. .. 27·00
558 **83** 1½d. red-brown, *p* 14 × 13½ .. .. 4·00 4·50
a. Perf 13½ × 14 .. .. .. 4·00 3·50
559 **84** 2d. orange, *p* 14 × 13½ .. .. 1·50 30
560 **85** 2½d. chocolate and slate, *p* 13–14 × 13½ 4·00 12·00
a. Perf 13½ × 14 .. .. .. 3·50 11·00
561 **86** 3d. brown, *p* 14 × 13½ .. .. 8·00 80
562 **87** 4d. black and sepia, *p* 14 .. .. 2·25 55
563 **88** 5d. ultramarine, *p* 13–14 × 13½ .. 9·00 13·00
a. Perf 13½ × 14 .. .. .. 14·00 14·00
564 **89** 6d. scarlet, *p* 13½ × 14 .. .. 4·00 3·00
565 **90** 8d. chocolate, *p* 14 × 13½ .. .. 4·00 3·00
566 **91** 9d. scarlet and black, *p* 14 × 14½ .. 9·00 2·50
567 **92** 1s. deep green, *p* 14 × 13½ .. .. 14·00 3·75
568 **93** 2s. olive-green, *p* 13–14 × 13½ .. 24·00 16·00
a. "CAPTAIN COQK" .. .. 40·00
b. Perf 13½ × 14 .. .. .. 32·00 19·00
ba. "CAPTAIN COQK" .. .. 50·00
569 **94** 3s. chocolate & yell-brn, *p* 13–14 × 13½ .. .. 15·00 30·00
a. Perf 13½ × 14 .. .. .. 14·00 28·00
556/69a .. .. *Set of* 14 90·00 75·00

In the 2½d., 5d., 2s. and 3s. perf 13–14 × 13½ the horizontal perforations of each stamp are in two sizes, one half of each horizontal side measuring 13 and the other 14.

See also Nos. 577/90 and 630/1.

95 Bell Block Aerodrome

96 King George V and Queen Mary

(Des J. Berry. Eng Stamp Printing Office, Melbourne. Recess Govt Printing Office, Wellington)

1935 (4 May). *Air*. W **43**. *P* 14.
570 **95** 1d. carmine 30 30
571 3d. violet .. .. 2·75 2·50
572 6d. blue .. .. 6·00 1·75
570/2 .. .. *Set of* 3 8·00 4·00

(Frame by J. Berry. Recess B.W.)

1935 (7 May). *Silver Jubilee*. W **43**. *P* 11 × 11½.
573 **96** ½d. green .. .. 1·00 60
574 1d. carmine .. .. 1·40 40
575 6d. red-orange .. .. 12·00 16·00
573/5 .. .. *Set of* 3 13·00 16·00

97 "The Key to Health"

98 "Multiple Wmk"

(Des S. Hall. Recess John Ash, Melbourne)

1935 (30 Sept). *Health Stamp*. W **43**. *P* 11.
576 **97** 1d. + 1d. scarlet .. .. .. 1·50 2·25

WATERMARKS. In W **43** the wmk units are in vertical columns widely spaced and the sheet margins are unwatermarked or wmkd "NEW ZEALAND POSTAGE" in large letters.

In W **98** the wmk units are arranged alternately in horizontal rows closely spaced and are continued into the sheet margins.

(Litho Govt Ptg Office, Wellington (9d.). Recess Waterlow or D.L.R. (others))

1936–43. W **98**.
577 **81** ½d. bright green, *p* 14×13½ 80 10
578 **82** 1d. scarlet (Die II), *p* 14×13½ .. 40 10
579 **83** 1½d. red-brown, *p* 14×13½ .. .. 5·00 1·75
580 **84** 2d. orange, *p* 14×13½ 15 10
b. Perf 12½† (6.41) .. .. 2·50 10
c. Perf 14 (6.41) .. .. 11·00 70
d. Perf 14×15 (6.41) .. .. 20·00 4·00
581 **85** 2½d. chocolate and slate, *p* 13–14×13½ 75 2·75
a. Perf 14 .. .. .. 1·75 1·25
b. Perf 14×13½ (1942) .. .. 50 1·75
582 **86** 3d. brown, *p* 14×13½ .. .. 27·00 15
583 **87** 4d. black and sepia, *p* 14×13½ .. 3·00 10
a. Perf 12½* (1941) .. .. 14·00 80
b. Perf 14, line (1941) .. .. 50·00 40·00
c. Perf 14×14½ comb (7.42) .. 80 10
584 **88** 5d. ultramarine, *p* 13–14×13½ .. 4·25 1·10
b. Perf 12½*† (7.41, 1942) .. 16·00 95
c. Perf 14×13½ (1942) .. .. 2·25 65
585 **89** 6d. scarlet, *p* 13½×14 .. .. 4·50 30
a. Perf 12½* (1941) .. .. 2·50 50
b. Perf 14½×14 (1942) 75 10
586 **90** 8d. choc, *p* 14×13½ (*wmk sideways*) .. 3·00 90
aa. Wmk upright (1939) .. .. 2·50 75
a. Perf 12½* (*wmk sideways*) (1941) 2·00 60
b. Perf 14×14½ (*wmk sideways*) (1943) .. .. 1·00 20
587 **91** 9d. red & grey, *p* 14×15 (*wmk sideways*) 32·00 1·75
a. Red and grey-black. Perf 13½×14 (1.3.38) .. .. 38·00 1·50
588 **92** 1s. deep green, *p* 14×13½ .. .. 1·75 20
b. Perf 12½* (11.41) .. .. 50·00 8·50
589 **93** 2s. olive-green, *p* 13–14×13½ .. 16·00 1·75
a. "CAPTAIN COQK" .. .. 40·00
b. Perf 13½×14 (1938) .. .. £160 2·00
ba. "CAPTAIN COQK" £170
c. Perf 12½*† (1941, 1942) .. 23·00 2·25
ca. "CAPTAIN COQK" .. .. 40·00
d. Perf 14×13½ (1942) .. .. 12·00 1·25
da. "CAPTAIN COQK" .. .. 50·00
590 **94** 3s. chocolate & yell-brn, *p* 13–14×13½ 25·00 4·00
a. Perf 12½* (1941) .. .. 50·00 23·00
b. Perf 14×13½ (1942) .. .. 6·00 1·50
577/90b .. .. *Set of* 14 80·00 8·00

*†Stamps indicated with an asterisk were printed and perforated by Waterlow; those having a dagger were printed by D.L.R. and perforated by Waterlow. No. 580d was printed by D.L.R. and perforated by Harrison and No. 583b was printed by Waterlow and perforated by D.L.R. These are all known as "Blitz perfs" because De La Rue were unable to maintain supplies after their works were damaged by enemy action. All the rest, except the 9d., were printed and perforated by D.L.R.

On stamps printed and perforated by De La Rue the perf 14 × 13½ varies in the sheet and is sometimes nearer 13½. 2d. perf 14 × 15 is sometimes nearer 14 × 14½.

2½d., 5d., 2s. and 3s. In perf 13–14 × 13½ one half the length of each horizontal perforation measures 13 and the other 14. In perf 14 × 13½ the horizontal perforation is regular.

4d. No. 583b is line-perf measuring 14 exactly and has a blackish sepia frame. No. 583c is a comb-perf measuring 14 × 14.3 or 14 × 14.2 and the frame is a warmer shade.

2s. No. 589b is comb-perf and measures 13.5 × 13.75.

For 9d. typographed, see Nos. 630/1.

99 N.Z. Soldier at Anzac Cove

100 Wool

(Des L. C. Mitchell. Recess John Ash, Melbourne)

1936 (27 Apr). *Charity. 21st Anniv of "Anzac" Landing at Gallipoli*. W **43**. *P* 11.
591 **99** ½d. + ½d. green .. .. .. 30 1·10
592 1d. + 1d. scarlet 30 90

(Des L. C. Mitchell. Recess John Ash, Melbourne)

1936 (1 Oct). *Congress of British Empire Chambers of Commerce, Wellington. Industries Issue. T* **100** *and similar horiz designs*. W **43** (*sideways*). *P* 11½.
593 ½d. emerald-green 20 30
594 1d. scarlet 20 20
595 2½d blue .. .. 1·00 5·00
596 4d. violet .. .. 80 4·50
597 6d. red-brown .. .. 1·25 3·50
593/7 .. .. *Set of* 5 3·00 12·00

Designs:—1d. Butter; 2½d. Sheep; 4d. Apples; 6d. Exports.

105 Health Camp

106 King George VI and Queen Elizabeth

(Des J. Berry. Recess John Ash, Melbourne)

1936 (2 Nov). *Health Stamp*. W **43**. *P* 11.
598 **105** 1d. + 1d. scarlet .. .. .. 1·00 3·25

(Recess B.W.)

1937 (13 May). *Coronation*. W **98**. *P* 14 × 13½.
599 **106** 1d. carmine 30 10
600 2½d. Prussian blue .. .. .. 1·50 1·60
601 6d. red-orange .. .. 1·90 1·25
599/601 .. .. *Set of* 3 3·25 2·50

107 Rock climbing

108 King George VI

108*a*

(Des G. Bull and J. Berry. Recess John Ash, Melbourne)

1937 (1 Oct). *Health Stamp*. W **43**. *P* 11.
602 **107** 1d. + 1d. scarlet .. .. .. 1·50 2·50

Broken ribbon flaw (R. 6/6 of Pl 8)

(Des W. J. Cooch. Recess B.W.)

1938–44. W **98**. *P* 14 × 13½.
603 **108** ½d. green (1.3.38) .. .. .. 5·50 10
604 ½d. brown-orange (10.7.41) 10 10
605 1d. scarlet (1.7.38) .. .. .. 5·00 10
a. Broken ribbon .. .. ..
606 1d. green (21.7.41) 10 10
607 **108a** 1½d. purple-brown (26.7.38) .. .. 21·00 1·00
608 1½d. scarlet (1.2.44) 10 10
609 3d. blue (26.9.41) 10 10
603/9 .. .. *Set of* 7 28·00 1·00

For other values see Nos. 680/9.

109 Children playing

110 Beach Ball

(Des J. Berry. Recess B.W.)

1938 (1 Oct). *Health Stamp*. W **98**. *P* 14 × 13½.
610 **109** 1d. + 1d. scarlet .. .. .. 2·50 1·60

(Des S. Hall. Recess Note Printing Branch, Commonwealth Bank of Australia, Melbourne)

1939 (16 Oct). *Health Stamps. Surcharged with new value*. W **43**. *P* 11.
611 **110** 1d. on ½d. + ½d. green .. .. 1·50 3·25
612 2d. on 1d. + 1d. scarlet .. .. .. 2·25 3·25

111 Arrival of the Maoris, 1350

115 Signing Treaty of Waitangi, 1840

(Des L. C. Mitchell (½d., 3d., 4d.); J. Berry (others). Recess B.W.)

1940 (2 Jan–8 Mar). *Centenary of Proclamation of British Sovereignty. T* **111, 115** *and similar designs. W* **98.** *P* 14 × 13½ (2½*d.*), 13½ × 14 (5*d.*) *or* 13½ (*others*).

613 ½d. blue-green 30 10
614 1d. chocolate and scarlet .. .. .. 2·50 10
615 1½d. light blue and mauve 30 20
616 2d. blue-green and chocolate .. .. 1·50 10
617 2½d. blue-green and blue 70 20
618 3d. purple and carmine .. .. .. 2·50 25
619 4d. chocolate and lake .. .. .. 11·00 50
620 5d. pale blue and brown .. .. .. 4·50 2·25
621 6d. emerald-green and violet .. .. 11·00 35
622 7d. black and red .. .. 1·25 3·50
623 8d. black and red (8.3) .. .. .. 11·00 1·50
624 9d. olive-green and orange .. .. .. 6·50 75
625 1s. sage-green and deep green .. .. 12·00 2·50
613/25 .. .. *Set of* 13 55·00 11·00

Designs: *Horiz* (*as T* **111**)—1d. H.M.S. *Endeavour*, chart of N.Z., and Capt. Cook; 1½d. British Monarchs; 2d. Tasman with *Heemskerk* and chart; 3d. Landing of immigrants, 1840; 4d. Road, Rail, Sea and Air transport; 6d. *Dunedin* and "Frozen Mutton Route" to London; 7d., 8d. Maori council; 9d. Gold mining in 1861 and 1940. (*As T* **115**)—5d. H.M.S. *Britomart* at Akaroa, 1840. *Vert* (*as T* **111**)—1s. Giant Kauri tree.

1940 (1 Oct). *Health Stamps. As T* **110**, *but without extra surcharge. W* **43.** *P* 11.

626 **110** 1d. + ½d. blue-green .. .. .. 4·00 7·50
627 2d. + 1d. brown-orange .. .. .. 4·00 7·50

1ᴰ 1ᴰ

(123)

2ᴰ

Inserted "2"

1941

(124)

1941. *Surch as T* **123.**

628 **108** 1d. on ½d. green (1.5.41) 30 10
629 **108*a*** 2d. on 1½d. purple-brown (4.41) .. 30 10
a. Inserted "2" £475 £300

The surcharge on No. 629 has only one figure, at top left, and there is only one square to obliterate the original value at bottom right.

The variety "Inserted 2" occurs on the 10th stamp, 10th row. It is identified by the presence of remnants of the damaged "2", and by the spacing of "2" and "D" which is variable and different from the normal.

(Typo Govt Printing Office, Wellington)

1941. *As T* **91**, *but smaller* (17½ × 20½ *mm*). *P* 14 × 15. (*a*) *W* **43.**

630 **91** 9d. scarlet and black (5.41) .. .. 70·00 12·00

(*b*) *W* **98**

631 **91** 9d. scarlet and black (29.9.41) .. .. 2·00 1·00

1941 (4 Oct). *Health Stamps. Nos.* 626/7 *optd with T* **124.**

632 **110** 1d. + ½d. blue-green .. .. .. 25 1·40
633 2d. + 1d. brown-orange .. .. .. 25 1·40

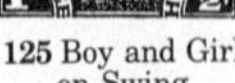

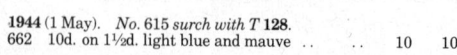

125 Boy and Girl on Swing

126 Princess Margaret

(Des S. Hall. Recess Note Printing Branch, Commonwealth Bank of Australia, Melbourne)

1942 (1 Oct). *Health Stamps. W* **43.** *P* 11.

634 **125** 1d. + ½d. blue-green 15 35
635 2d. + 1d. orange-red 15 30

(Des J. Berry. Recess B.W.)

1943 (1 Oct). *Health Stamps. T* **126** *and similar triangular design. W* **98.** *P* 12.

636 1d. + ½d. green 10 40
a. Imperf between (vert pair) £4000
637 2d. + 1d. red-brown 10 10
a. Imperf between (vert pair) £4000 £4000

Design:—2d. Queen Elizabeth II as Princess.

(128)

1944 (1 May). *No.* 615 *surch with T* **128.**

662 10d. on 1½d. light blue and mauve 10 10

129 Queen Elizabeth II as Princess and Princess Margaret

130 Statue of Peter Pan, Kensington Gardens

(Recess B.W.)

1944 (9 Oct). *Health Stamps. W* **98.** *P* 13½.

663 **129** 1d. + ½d. green 10 15
664 2d. + 1d. blue 10 15

(Des J. Berry. Recess B.W.)

1945 (1 Oct). *Health Stamps. W* **98.** *P* 13½.

665 **130** 1d. + ½d. green and buff 10 10
666 2d. + 1d. carmine and buff 10 10

131 Lake Matheson

132 King George VI and Parliament House, Wellington

133 St. Paul's Cathedral

139 "St. George" (Wellington College War Memorial Window)

Printer's guide mark (R. 12/3)

Completed rudder (R. 2/4 of Pl 42883 and R. 3/2 of Pl 42796)

(Des J. Berry. Photo Harrison (1½d. and 1s.). Recess B.W. (1d. and 2d.) and Waterlow (others))

1946 (1 Apr). *Peace issue. T* **131/3, 139** *and similar designs. W* **98** (*sideways on* 1½*d.*). *P* 13 (1*d.*, 2*d.*), 14 × 14½ (1½*d.*, 1*s.*), 13½ (*others*).

667 ½d. green and brown 15 20
a. Printer's guide mark .. .. .. 2·50
668 1d. green 10 10
669 1½d. scarlet 10 10
670 2d. purple 15 10
671 3d. ultramarine and grey 20 15
a. Completed rudder .. .. .. 3·25
672 4d. bronze-green and orange 20 20
673 5d. green and ultramarine 20 15
674 6d. chocolate and vermilion 15 10
675 8d. black and carmine 15 10
676 9d. blue and black 15 10
677 1s. grey-black 15 15
667/77 .. .. *Set of* 11 1·50 1·25

Designs: *Horiz* (*as T* **132**)—2d. The Royal Family. (*As T* **131**)—3d. R.N.Z.A.F. badge and aeroplanes; 4d. Army badge, tank and plough; 5d. Navy badge, H.M.N.Z.S. *Achilles* (cruiser) and *Dominion Monarch* (liner); 6d. N.Z. coat of arms, foundry and farm; 9d. Southern Alps and Franz Josef Glacier. *Vert* (*as T* **139**)—1s. National Memorial Campanile.

142 Soldier helping Child over Stile

(Des J. Berry. Recess Waterlow)

1946 (24 Oct). *Health Stamps. W* **98.** *P* 13½.

678 **142** 1d. + ½d. green and orange-brown .. 10 10
a. Yellow-green and orange-brown .. 3·75 3·75
679 2d. + 1d. chocolate and orange-brown 10 10

144 King George VI

145 Statue of Eros

Plate 1

Plate 2

(Des W. J. Cooch. Recess T **108*a***, B.W.; T **144**, D.L.R.)

1947–52. *W* **98** (*sideways on "shilling" values*). (*a*) *P* 14 × 13½.

680 **108*a*** 2d. orange 15 10
681 4d. bright purple 35 20
682 5d. slate 50 40
683 6d. carmine 40 10
684 8d. violet 65 20
685 9d. purple-brown 70 20

(*b*) *P* 14

686 **144** 1s. red-brown and carmine (Plate 1) .. 1·40 30
a. Wmk upright (Plate 1) 50 30
b. Wmk upright (Plate 2) .. .. 1·75 30
687 1s. 3d. red-brown and blue (Plate 2) .. 70 40
a. Wmk upright (14.1.52) .. .. 2·00 3·00
688 2s. brown-orange and green (Plate 1) .. 1·25 80
a. Wmk upright (Plate 1) .. .. 2·00 2·00
689 3s. red-brown and grey (Plate 2) .. 1·75 1·50
680/9 .. .. *Set of* 10 6·00 3·75

In head-plate 2 the diagonal lines of the background have been strengthened and result in the upper corners and sides appearing more deeply shaded.

(Des J. Berry. Recess Waterlow)

1947 (1 Oct). *Health Stamps. W* **98** (*sideways*). *P* 13½.

690 **145** 1d. + ½d. green 10 10
691 2d. + 1d. carmine 10 10

146 Port Chalmers, 1848

148 First Church, Dunedin

(Des J. Berry. Recess B.W.)

1948 (23 Feb). *Centennial of Otago. T* **146, 148** *and similar designs. W* **98** (*sideways on* 3*d.*). *P* 13½.

692 1d. blue and green 10 10
693 2d. green and brown 10 10
694 3d. purple 10 15
695 6d. black and rose 10 15
692/5 .. .. *Set of* 4 30 45

Designs: *Horiz*—2d. Cromwell, Otago; 6d. University of Otago.

150 Boy Sunbathing and Children Playing

151 Nurse and Child

(Des E. Linzell. Recess B.W.)

1948 (1 Oct). *Health Stamps. W* **98.** *P* 13½.

696 **150** 1d. + ½d. blue and green 10 10
697 2d. + 1d. purple and scarlet 10 10

1949 ROYAL VISIT ISSUE. Four stamps were prepared to commemorate this event: 2d. Treaty House, Waitangi; 3d. H.M.S. *Vanguard*; 5d. Royal portraits; 6d. Crown and sceptre. The visit did not take place and the stamps were destroyed, although a few examples of the 3d. later appeared on the market. A similar set was prepared in 1952, but was, likewise, not issued.

(Des J. Berry. Photo Harrison)

1949 (3 Oct). *Health Stamps. W* **98.** *P* 14 × 14½.

698	**151**	1d. + ½d. green	10	10
699		2d. + 1d. ultramarine	10	10
		a. No stop below "D" of "1D." (R.1/2)	6·50	13·00

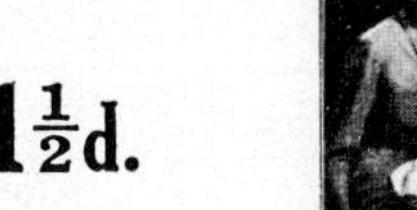

(152)

153 Queen Elizabeth II and Prince Charles

1950 (28 July). *As Type* F **6**, *but without value, surch with T* **152.** *W* **98** *(inverted). Chalk-surfaced paper. P* 14.

700	**F 6**	1½d. carmine	10	10

Originally issued with the watermark inverted, this later appeared with it upright.

(Des J. Berry and R. S. Phillips. Photo Harrison)

1950 (2 Oct). *Health Stamps. W* **98.** *P* 14 × 14½.

701	**153**	1d. + ½d. green	10	10
702		2d. + 1d. plum	10	10

154 Christchurch Cathedral

155 Cairn on Lyttleton Hills

(Des L. C. Mitchell (2d.), J. A. Johnstone (3d.) and J. Berry (others). Recess B.W.)

1950 (20 Nov). *Centennial of Canterbury, N.Z. T* **154/5** *and similar designs. W* **98** *(sideways on 1d. and 3d.). P* 13½.

703	1d. green and blue		15	10
704	2d. carmine and orange		15	10
705	3d. dark blue and blue		20	10
706	6d. brown and blue		20	25
707	1s. reddish purple and blue		20	30
703/7		*Set of* 5	80	80

Designs: *Vert (as T* **154**)—3d. John Robert Godley. *Horiz (as T* **155**)—6d. Canterbury University College; 1s. Aerial view of Timaru.

159 "Takapuna" class Yachts

(Des J. Berry and R. S. Phillips. Recess B.W.)

1951 (1 Nov). *Health Stamps. W* **98.** *P* 13½.

708	**159**	1½d. + ½d. scarlet and yellow	10	20
709		2d. + 1d. deep green and yellow	10	10

160 Princess Anne

161 Prince Charles

3D

(162)

(From photographs by Marcus Adams. Photo Harrison)

1952 (1 Oct). *Health Stamps. W* **98.** *P* 14 × 14½.

710	**160**	1½d. + ½d. carmine-red	10	10
711	**161**	2d. + 1d. brown	10	10

1952–53. *Nos.* 604 *and* 606 *surch as T* **162.**

712	**108**	1d. on ½d. brown-orange (11.9.53)	10	20
		a. "D" omitted	†	—
713		3d. on 1d. green (12.12.52*)	10	10

*Earliest known date used.

163 Buckingham Palace

164 Queen Elizabeth II

(Des L. C. Mitchell (1s. 6d.), J. Berry (others). Recess D.L.R. (2d., 4d.), Waterlow (1s. 6d.) Photo Harrison (3d., 8d.))

1953 (25 May). *Coronation. T* **163/4** *and similar designs. W* **98.** *P* 13 *(2d., 4d.),* 13½ *(1s. 6d.) or* 14 × 14½ *(3d., 8d.).*

714	2d. deep bright blue		20	15
715	3d. brown		20	10
716	4d. carmine		75	1·50
717	8d. slate-grey		70	70
718	1s. 6d. purple and ultramarine		1·25	80
714/18		*Set of* 5	2·75	2·75

Designs: *Horiz (as T* **163**)—4d. Coronation State Coach; 1s. 6d. St. Edward's Crown and Royal Sceptre. *Vert (as T* **164**)—8d. Westminster Abbey.

168 Girl Guides

169 Boy Scouts

(Des J. Berry. Photo Harrison)

1953 (7 Oct). *Health Stamps. W* **98.** *P* 14 × 14½.

719	**168**	1½d. + ½d. blue	10	10
720	**169**	2d. + 1d. deep yellow-green	10	20
		a. Imperf 3 sides (block of 4)		

No. 720a shows the left-hand vertical pair imperforate at right and the right-hand pair imperforate at left, top and bottom.

170 Queen Elizabeth II

171 Queen Elizabeth II and Duke of Edinburgh

(Des L. C. Mitchell. Recess Waterlow)

1953 (9 Dec). *Royal Visit. W* **98.** *P* 13 × 14 *(3d.) or* 13½ *(4d.).*

721	**170**	3d. dull purple	10	10
722	**171**	4d. deep ultramarine	10	25

172

173 Queen Elizabeth II

174

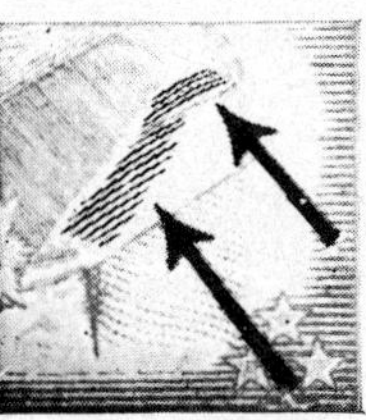

Die I

Die II

(Des L. C. Mitchell (T **172/3**), J. Berry (T **174**). Recess D.L.R. (T **173**), B.W. (others))

1953 (15 Dec)–**58.** *W* **98.** *P* 14 × 13½ *(T* **172**), 14 *(T* **173**) *or* 13½ *(T* **174**).

723	**172**	½d. slate-black (1.3.54)	15	30
724		1d. orange (1.3.54)	15	10
725		1½d. brown-lake	20	10
726		2d. bluish green (1.3.54)	20	10
727		3d. vermilion (1.3.54)	20	10
728		4d. blue (1.3.54)	40	30
729		6d. purple (1.3.54)	70	90
730		8d. carmine (1.3.54)	60	30
731	**173**	9d. brown and bright green (1.3.54)	60	20
732		1s. black & carm-red (Die I) (1.3.54)	65	10
		a. Die II (1958)	55·00	10·00
733		1s. 6d. black and bright blue (1.3.54)	1·75	30
733*a*		1s. 9d. black and red-orange (1.7.57)	5·50	75
733*b*	**174**	2s. 6d. brown (1.7.57)	23·00	5·00
734		3s. bluish green (1.3.54)	11·00	30
735		5s. carmine (1.3.54)	17·00	2·50
736		10s. deep ultramarine (1.3.54)	45·00	15·00
723/36		*Set of* 16	95·00	23·00

1s. Dies I and II. The two dies of the Queen's portrait differ in the shading on the sleeve at right. The long lines running upwards from left to right are strong in Die I and weaker in Die II. In the upper part of the shading the fine cross-hatching is visible in Die I only between the middle two of the four long lines, but in Die II it extends clearly across all four lines.

In the lower part of the shading the strength of the long lines in Die I makes the cross-hatching appear subdued, whereas in Die II the weaker long lines make the cross-hatching more prominent.

Centre plates 1A, 1B and 2B are Die I; 3A and 3B are Die II.

For stamps as T **172** but with larger figures of value see Nos. 745/51.

1958 NEW PAPER. A new white opaque paper first came into use in August 1958 and was used for later printings of Nos. 733*a*, 745, 747/9, O159, O161, O163/4, O166 and L54. It is slightly thicker than the paper previously used, but obviously different in colour (white, against cream) and opacity (the previous paper being *relatively* transparent).

175 Young Climber and Mts Aspiring and Everest

(Des J. Berry. Recess; vignette litho B.W.)

1954 (4 Oct). *Health Stamps. W* **98.** *P* 13½.

737	**175**	1½d. + ½d. sepia and deep violet	10	10
738		2d. + 1d. sepia and blue-black	10	10

176 Maori Mail-carrier

177 Queen Elizabeth II

178 Douglas "DC 3" Airliner

(Des R. M. Conly (2d.), J. Berry (3d.), A. G. Mitchell (4d.). Recess D.L.R.)

1955 (18 July). *Centenary of First New Zealand Postage Stamps. W* **98.** *P* 14 *(2d.),* 14 × 14½ *(3d.) or* 13 *(4d.).*

739	**176**	2d. sepia and deep green	10	10
740	**177**	3d. brown-red	10	10
741	**178**	4d. black and bright blue	15	25
739/41		*Set of* 3	30	35

179 Children's Health Camps Federation Emblem

180

(Des E. M. Taylor. Recess B.W.)

1955 (3 Oct). *Health Stamps. W* **98** *(sideways). P* 13½ × 13.

742	**179**	1½d. + ½d. sepia and orange-brown	10	25
743		2d. + 1d. red-brown and green	10	15
744		3d. + 1d. sepia and deep rose-red	15	10
		a. Centre omitted		
742/4		*Set of* 3	30	45

1955–59. *As Nos.* 724/30 *but larger figures of value and stars omitted from lower right corner.*

745	**180**	1d. orange (12.7.56)	50	10
746		1½d. brown-lake (1.12.55)	60	60
747		2d. bluish green (19.3.56)	40	10
748		3d. vermilion (1.5.56)	1·10	10
749		4d. blue (3.2.58)	1·75	35
750		6d. purple (20.10.55)	7·50	10
751		8d. chestnut (1.12.59)	5·50	5·00
745/51		*Set of* 7	15·00	5·50

See note *re* white opaque paper after No. 736. No. 751 exists only on white paper.

181 "The Whalers of Foveaux Strait"

183 Takahe

(Des E. R. Leeming (2d.), L. C. Mitchell (3d.), M. R. Smith (8d.). Recess D.L.R.)

1956 (16 Jan). *Southland Centennial. T* **181, 183** *and similar design.* *W* **98.** *P* 13½ × 13 (8d.) *or* 13 × 12½ (*others*).

752	2d. deep blue-green		10	10
753	3d. sepia		10	10
754	8d. slate-violet and rose-red		40	60
752/4		*Set of* 3	50	70

Design: *Horiz*—3d. "Farming".

184 Children picking Apples

(Des L. C. Mitchell, after photo by J. F. Louden. Recess B.W.)

1956 (24 Sept). *Health Stamps.* *W* **98.** *P* 13 × 13½.

755	**184**	1½d. + ½d. purple-brown		10	20
		a. Blackish brown		60	4·25
756		2d. + 1d. blue-green		10	15
757		3d. + 1d. claret		15	10
755/7 ..		.. ..	*Set of* 3	30	40

185 New Zealand Lamb and Map

186 Lamb, *Dunedin* and *Port Brisbane* (refrigerated freighter)

(Des M. Goaman. Photo Harrison)

1957 (15 Feb). *75th Anniv of First Export of N.Z. Lamb.* *W* **98** (*sideways on* 4d.). *P* 14 × 14½ (4d.) *or* 14½ × 14 (8d.).

758	**185**	4d. blue	40	45
759	**186**	8d. deep orange-red	60	65

187 Sir Truby King

(Des M. R. Smith. Recess B.W.)

1957 (14 May). *50th Anniv of Plunket Society.* *W* **98.** *P* 13.

760	**187**	3d. bright carmine-red	10	10

188 Life-savers in Action

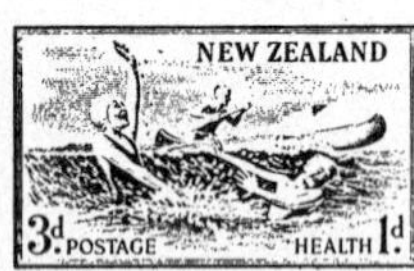

189 Children on Seashore

(Des L. Cutten (2d.), L. C. Mitchell (3d.). Recess Waterlow)

1957 (25 Sept). *Health Stamps.* *W* **98** (*sideways*). *P* 13½.

761	**188**	2d. + 1d. black and emerald	15	20
762	**189**	3d. + 1d. ultramarine and rose-red ..	15	10
MS762*b*		Two sheets each 112 × 96 mm with Nos. 761 and 762 in blocks of 6 (2 × 3) .. *Per pair*	12·00	18·00
MS762*c*		As last but with wmk upright *Per pair*	16·00	32·00

2d
●

(190)

191 Girls' Life Brigade Cadet

192 Boys' Brigade Bugler

1958 (6 Jan–Mar). *No.* 746 *surch as T* **190.**

763	**180**	2d. on 1½d. brown-lake	40	10
		a. Smaller dot in surch	15	10
		b. Error. Surch on No. 725 (3.58) ..	£110	£150

Diameter of dot on No. 763 is 4¼ mm; on No. 763a 3¾ mm.
Forgeries of No. 763b are known.

(Des J. Berry. Photo Harrison)

1958 (20 Aug). *Health Stamps.* *W* **98.** *P* 14 × 14½.

764	**191**	2d. + 1d. green	15	10
765	**192**	3d. + 1d. blue	15	10
MS765*a*		Two sheets each 104 × 124 mm with Nos. 764/5 in blocks of 6 (3 × 2) .. *Per pair*	14·00	12·00

193 Sir Charles Kingsford Smith and *Southern Cross*

194 Seal of Nelson

(Des J. E. Lyle. Eng F. D. Manley. Recess Commonwealth Bank of Australia Note Ptg Branch)

1958 (27 Aug). *30th Anniv of First Air Crossing of the Tasman Sea.* *W* **98** (*sideways*). *P* 14 × 14½.

766	**193**	6d. deep ultramarine	30	30

(Des M. J. Macdonald. Recess B.W.)

1958 (29 Sept). *Centenary of City of Nelson.* *W* **98.** *P* 13½×13.

767	**194**	3d. carmine	10	10

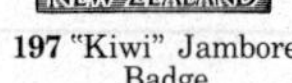

195 "Pania" Statue, Napier

196 Australian Gannets on Cape Kidnappers

(Des M. R. Smith (2d.), J. Berry (3d.), L. C. Mitchell (8d.). Photo Harrison)

1958 (3 Nov). *Centenary of Hawke's Bay Province. T* **195/6** *and similar design.* *W* **98** (*sideways on* 3d.). *P* 14½×14 (3d.) *or* 13½×14½ (*others*).

768	2d. yellow-green		10	10
769	3d. blue		15	10
770	8d. red-brown		45	75
768/70		*Set of* 3	60	80

Design:—*Vert* 8d. Maori sheep-shearer.

197 "Kiwi" Jamboree Badge

198 Careening H.M.S. *Endeavour* at Ship Cove

(Des Mrs. S. M. Collins. Recess B.W.)

1959 (5 Jan). *Pan-Pacific Scout Jamboree, Auckland.* *W* **98.** *P* 13½×13.

771	**197**	3d. sepia and carmine	10	10

(Des G. R. Bull and G. R. Smith. Photo Harrison)

1959 (2 Mar). *Centenary of Marlborough Province. T* **198** *and similar horiz designs.* *W* **98** (*sideways*). *P* 14½ × 14.

772	2d. green		15	10
773	3d. deep blue		15	10
774	8d. light brown		60	60
772/4		*Set of* 3	80	70

Designs:—3d. Shipping wool, Wairau Bar, 1857; 8d. Salt industry, Grassmere.

201 Red Cross Flag

(Photo Harrison)

1959 (3 June). *Red Cross Commemoration.* *W* **98** (*sideways*). *P* 14½×14.

775	**201**	3d. + 1d. red and ultramarine	10	10
		a. Red Cross omitted	£1000	

202 Grey Teal

203 New Zealand Stilt

(Des Display Section, G.P.O. Photo Harrison)

1959 (16 Sept). *Health Stamps.* *W* **98** (*sideways*). *P* 14 × 14½.

776	**202**	2d. + 1d. greenish yellow, ol & rose-red	15	15
777	**203**	3d. + 1d. black, pink and light blue ..	15	15
		a. Pink ptg omitted	£100	
MS777*c*.		Two sheets each 95 × 109 mm. with Nos. 776/7 in blocks of 6 (3 × 2). .. *Per pair*	6·50	14·00

204 "The Explorer"

205 "The Gold Digger"

(Des G. R. Bull and G. R. Smith. Photo Harrison)

1960 (16 May). *Centenary of Westland Province. T* **204/5** *and similar vert design.* *W* **98.** *P* 14 × 14½.

778	2d. deep dull green		15	10
779	3d. orange-red		15	10
780	8d. grey-black		40	1·50
778/80		*Set of* 3	60	1·50

Design:—8d. "The Pioneer Woman".

207 Manuka (Tea Tree)

214 National Flag

216 Trout

219 Taniwha (Maori Rock Drawing)

220 Butter Making

221 Tongariro National Park and Château

221*a* Tongariro National Park and Château

(Des Harrison (½d.), G. F. Fuller (1d., 3d., 6d.), A. G. Mitchell (2d., 4d., 5d., 8d., 3s., 10s., £1), P.O. Public Relations Division (7d.), P.O. Publicity Section (9d.), J. Berry (1s., 1s. 6d.), R. E. Barwick (1s. 3d.), J. C. Boyd (1s. 9d.), D. F. Kee (2s.), L. C. Mitchell (2s. 6d., 5s.). Photo D.L.R. (½d., 1d., 2d., 3d., 4d., 6d., 8d.) or Harrison (others))

1960 (11 July)–**66**. *T* **207, 214, 216, 219/21a** *and similar designs. Chalk-surfaced paper* (2½d., 5d., 7d., 1s. 9d. (No. 795), 3s. (No. 799). *W* **98** (*sideways on* 2½d., 5d., 1s. 3d., 1s. 6d., 2s. 6d., 3s. *and* 10s.)). *P* 14×14½ (1s. 3d., 1s. 6d., 2s., 5s., £1) *or* 14½×14 (*others*).

781	**207**	½d. grey, green and cerise (1.9.60)	10	10
		a. Grey omitted	35·00	
		b. Green omitted	60·00	
782	–	1d. orge, green, lake & brn (1.9.60)	10	10
		a. Orange omitted	£150	
		b. Coil. Perf 14½×13. Wmk sideways (11.63)	1·00	1·75
		c. Chalk-surfaced paper (1965?) ..	10	30
783	–	2d. carmine, black, yellow & green	10	10
		a. Black omitted	£130	
		b. Yellow omitted	£150	
784	–	2½d. red, yellow, blk & grn (1.11.61)	60	10
		a. Red omitted	£180	
		b. Yellow omitted	70·00	
		c. Green omitted	80·00	
		d. Red and green omitted	£300	

785 – 3d. yellow, green, yellow-brown and deep greenish blue (1.9.60) .. 30 10
a. Yellow omitted .. .. 70·00
b. Green omitted .. .. 70·00
c. Yellow-brown omitted .. 70·00
e. Coil. Perf 14½×13. Wmk sideways (3.10.63) .. .. 1·00 1·50
f. Chalk-surfaced paper (1965?) .. 30 40
786 – 4d. purple, buff, yellow-green & lt bl 40 10
a. Purple omitted £100
b. Buff omitted £130
d. Chalk-surfaced paper (1965?) .. £160 7·00
787 – 5d. yell, dp grn, blk & vio (14.5.62) 60 10
a. Yellow omitted £110
788 – 6d. lilac, green and deep bluish green (1.9.60) 50 10
a. No wmk .. .. .. 20·00 13·00
ab. Lilac omitted .. .. .. 70·00
ac. Green omitted .. .. .. 60·00
c. Chalk-surfaced paper (1966?) .. 55 1·00
788*d* – 7d. red, green, yellow and pale red (16.3.66) 35 80
789 – 8d. rose-red, yellow, green and grey (1.9.60) 40 10
790 **214** 9d. red and ultramarine (1.9.60) .. 30 10
a. Red omitted £140
791 – 1s. brown and deep green 25 10
792 **216** 1s. 3d. carmine, sepia & bright blue 4·00 50
a. Carmine omitted £150
b. Carmine, sepia and greyish blue 80 10
793 – 1s. 6d. olive-green & orange-brown 50 10
794 – 1s. 9d. bistre-brown .. .. 15·00 15
795 – 1s. 9d. orange-red, blue, green and yellow (4.11.63) .. .. 6·50 50
796 **219** 2s. black and orange-buff .. 3·00 10
a. Chalk-surfaced paper (1966) .. 2·25 1·50
797 **220** 2s. 6d. yellow and light brown .. 1·75 65
a. Yellow omitted £225
798 **221** 3s. blackish brown .. .. 48·00 65
799 **221*a*** 3s. bistre, blue and green (1.4.64) 7·50 1·50
800 – 5s. blackish green .. .. 5·50 80
a. Chalk-surfaced paper (1966) .. 2·25 4·50
801 – 10s. steel-blue .. .. .. 9·00 1·25
a. Chalk-surfaced paper (1966) .. 4·00 10·00
802 – £1 deep magenta .. .. .. 8·50 6·00
781/802 .. .. *Set of* 23 80·00 11·00

Designs: *Vert* (*as T* **207**)—1d. Karaka; 2d. Kowhai Ngutu-kaka (Kaka Beak); 2½d. Titoki; 3d. Kowhai; 4d. Puarangi (Hibiscus); 5d. Matua Tikumu (Mountain Daisy); 6d. Pikiarero (Clematis); 7d. Koromiko; 8d. Rata. (*As T* **216**)—1s. 6d. Tiki. (*As T* **219**)—5s. Sutherland Falls; £1 Pohutu Geyser. *Horiz* (*as T* **214**)—1s. Timber industry—1s. 9d. Aerial top dressing. (*As T* **221**)—10s. Tasman Glacier.

Nos. 782b and 785e were replaced by coils with upright watermark perf 14½×14 in 1966.

CHALKY PAPER. The chalk-surfaced paper is not only whiter but also thicker, making the watermark difficult to see. Examples of the 4d. value can be found on a thick surfaced paper. These should not be confused with the rare chalk-surfaced printing, No. 786d, which can be identified by its positive reaction to the silver test.

225 Sacred Kingfisher

226 New Zealand Pigeon

(Des Display Section, G.P.O. Recess B.W.)

1960 (10 Aug). *Health Stamps. W* **98**. *P* 13½.
803 **225** 2d. + 1d. sepia and turquoise-blue .. 30 30
804 **226** 3d. + 1d. deep purple-brown and orange 30 35
MS804*b* Two sheets each 95 × 107 mm with Nos. 803 and 804 in blocks of 6. *P* 11½ × 11 *Per pair* 30·00 32·00

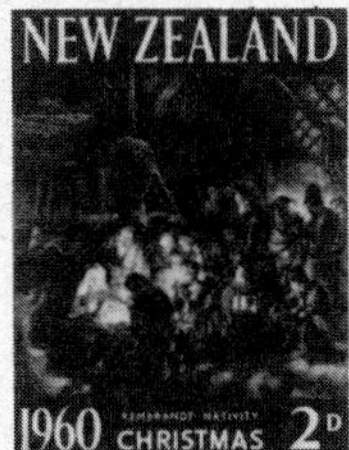

227 "The Adoration of the Shepherds" (Rembrandt)

(Photo Harrison)

1960 (1 Nov). *Christmas. W* **98**. *P* 12.
805 **227** 2d. red and deep brown/*cream* 15 10
a. Red omitted £250

MINIMUM PRICE

The minimum price quote is 10p which represents a handling charge rather than a basis for valuing common stamps. For further notes about prices see introductory pages.

228 Great Egret

229 New Zealand Falcon

(Des Display Section, G.P.O. Recess B.W.)

1961 (2 Aug). *Health Stamps. W* **98**. *P* 13½.
806 **228** 2d. + 1d. black and purple 20 20
807 **229** 3d. + 1d. deep sepia and yellow-green 20 20
MS807*a* Two sheets each 97 × 121 mm with Nos. 806/7 in blocks of 6 (3 × 2) .. *Per pair* 25·00 25·00

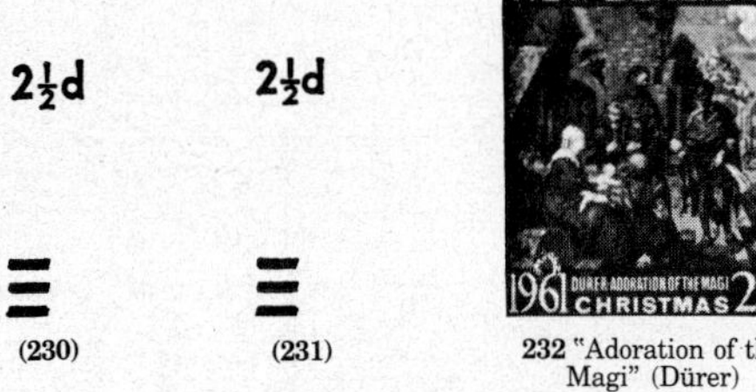

(230) **(231)**

232 "Adoration of the Magi" (Dürer)

1961 (1 Sept). *No. 748 surch with T* **230** (*wide setting*).
808 **180** 2½d. on 3d. vermilion 15 15
a. Narrow setting (T **231**) 15 15
b. Pair, wide and narrow .. .. 16·00 24·00

The difference in the settings is in the overall width of the new value, caused by two different spacings between the "2", "½" and "d".

(Photo Harrison)

1961 (16 Oct). *Christmas. W* **98** (*sideways*). *P* 14½ × 14.
809 **232** 2½d. multicoloured 10 10

233 Morse Key and Port Hills, Lyttelton

(Des A. G. Mitchell (3d.) and L. C. Mitchell (8d.). Photo Harrison)

1962 (1 June). *Telegraph Centenary. T* **233** *and similar horiz design. W* **98** (*sideways*). *P* 14½ × 14.
810 3d. sepia and bluish green 10 10
a. Green omitted £350
811 8d. black and brown-red 35 55
a. Imperf (pair) £800
b. Black omitted £325

Design:—8d. Modern teleprinter.

No. 811a comes from a sheet with the two top rows imperforate and the third row imperforate on three sides.

235 Red-fronted Parakeet

236 Tieke Saddleback

(Des Display Section, G.P.O. Photo D.L.R.)

1962 (3 Oct). *Health Stamps. W* **98**. *P* 15 × 14.
812 **235** 2½d. + 1d. multicoloured 20 30
a. Orange omitted .. .. ..
813 **236** 3d. + 1d. multicoloured 20 30
a. Orange omitted £900
MS813*b* Two sheets each 96 × 101 mm with Nos. 812/3 in blocks of 6 (3 × 2) . .. *Per pair* 45·00 32·00

237 "Madonna in Prayer" (Sassoferrato)

(Photo Harrison)

1962 (15 Oct). *Christmas. W* **98**. *P* 14½ × 14.
814 **237** 2½d. multicoloured 10 10

238 Prince Andrew **239**

(Design after photographs by Studio Lisa, London. Recess D.L.R.)

1963 (7 Aug). *Health Stamps. W* **98**. *P* 14.
815 **238** 2½d. + 1d. dull ultramarine .. 10 20
a. Ultramarine 20 20
b. Deep blue 30 35
816 **239** 3d. + 1d. carmine 10 10
MS816*a* Two sheets each 93×100 mm with Nos. 815/16 in blocks of 6 (3 × 2) .. *Per pair* 21·00 24·00

240 "The Holy Family" (Titian)

(Photo Harrison)

1963 (14 Oct). *Christmas. W* **98** (*sideways*). *P* 12½.
817 **240** 2½d. multicoloured 10 10
a. Imperf (pair) £150
b. Yellow omitted £250

241 Steam Locomotive *Pilgrim* and "DG" Diesel Electric Loco

242 Diesel Express and Mt Ruapehu

(Des Commercial Art Section, N.Z. Railways. Photo D.L.R.)

1963 (25 Nov). *Railway Centenary. W* **98** (*sideways*). *P* 14.
818 **241** 3d. multicoloured 30 10
a. Blue (sky) omitted £250
819 **242** 1s. 9d. multicoloured .. .. .. 1·60 80
a. Red (value) omitted £650

243 "Commonwealth Cable"

(Des P. Morriss. Photo Note Printing Branch, Reserve Bank of Australia)

1963 (3 Dec). *Opening of COMPAC* (*Trans-Pacific Telephone Cable*). *No wmk. P* 13½.
820 **243** 8d. red, blue and yellow 50 90

244 Road Map and Car Steering-wheel

245 Silver Gulls

(Des L. C. Mitchell. Photo Harrison)

1964 (1 May). *Road Safety Campaign. W* **98**. *P* 15 × 14.
821 **244** 3d. black, ochre-yellow and blue .. 10 10

(Des Display Section G.P.O., after Miss T. Kelly. Photo Harrison)

1964 (5 Aug). *Health Stamps. T* **245** *and similar horiz design. Multicoloured. W* **98**. *P* 14½.
822 2½d. + 1d. Type **245** 20 15
a. Red (beak and legs) omitted £100
823 3d. + 1d. Little Penguin 20 15
MS823*a* Two sheets each 171 × 84 mm with Nos. 822/3 in blocks of 8 (4 × 2) . .. *Per pair* 45·00 48·00

246 Rev. S. Marsden taking first Christian service at Rangihoua Bay, 1814

7D
POSTAGE
(247)

(Des L. C. Mitchell. Photo Harrison)

1964 (12 Oct). *Christmas. W* **98** *(sideways). P* 14 × 13½.
824 **246** 2½d. multicoloured 10 10

1964 (14 Dec). *As Type* F **6**, *but without value, surch with T* **247**. *W* **98**. *Unsurfaced paper. P* 14 × 13½.
825 F **6** 7d. carmine-red 30 80

248 Anzac Cove

(Des R. M. Conly. Photo Harrison)

1965 (14 Apr). *50th Anniv of Gallipoli Landing. T* **248** *and similar horiz design. W* **98**. *P* 12½.
826 4d. yellow-brown 10 10
827 5d. green and red 10 30
Design:—5d. Anzac Cove and poppy.

249 I.T.U. Emblem and Symbols

250 Sir Winston Churchill

(Photo Harrison)

1965 (17 May). *I.T.U. Centenary. W* **98**. *P* 14½×14.
828 **249** 9d. blue and pale chocolate 30 35

(Des P. Morriss from photograph by Karsh. Photo Note Ptg Branch, Reserve Bank of Australia)

1965 (24 May). *Churchill Commemoration. P* 13½.
829 **250** 7d. black, pale grey and light blue .. 15 50

251 Wellington Provincial Council Building

(Des from painting by L. B. Temple (1867). Photo Harrison)

1965 (26 July). *Centenary of Government in Wellington. W* **98** *(sideways). P* 14½ × 14.
830 **251** 4d. multicoloured 10 10

252 Kaka

253 Collared Grey Fantail (after Miss T. Kelly)

(Des Display Section, G.P.O. Photo Harrison)

1965 (4 Aug). *Health Stamps. W* **98**. *P* 14 × 14½.
831 **252** 3d. + 1d. multicoloured 25 15
832 **253** 4d. + 1d. multicoloured 25 15
a. Green ("POSTAGE HEALTH" and on leaves) omitted £140
MS832*b* Two sheets each 100 × 109 mm with Nos. 831/2 in blocks of 6 (3 × 2) .. *Per pair* 32·00 35·00

NEW INFORMATION

The editor is always interested to correspond with people who have new information that will improve or correct the Catalogue.

254 I.C.Y. Emblem

255 "The Two Trinities" (Murillo)

(Litho D.L.R.)

1965 (28 Sept). *International Co-operation Year. W* **98** *(sideways). P* 14.
833 **254** 4d. carmine-red and light yellow-olive 15 10

(Photo Harrison)

1965 (11 Oct). *Christmas. W* **98**. *P* 13½ × 14.
834 **255** 3d. multicoloured 10 10
a. Gold (frame) omitted £600

256 Arms of New Zealand

259 "Progress" Arrowhead

(Des Display Section, G.P.O. Photo D.L.R.)

1965 (30 Nov). *11th Commonwealth Parliamentary Conference. T* **256** *and similar horiz designs. Multicoloured. P* 14.
835 4d. Type **256** 25 20
a. Blue (incl value) omitted £325
836 9d. Parliament House, Wellington and Badge 45 75
837 2s. Wellington from Mt Victoria .. .. 80 2·25
a. Carmine omitted £275
835/7 .. .. *Set of* 3 1·40 3·00

(Des Display Section, G.P.O. Photo Harrison)

1966 (5 Jan). *Fourth National Scout Jamboree, Trentham. W* **98**. *P* 14 × 15.
838 **259** 4d. gold and myrtle-green 10 10
a. Gold (arrowhead) omitted £475

260 New Zealand Bell Bird

262 "The Virgin with Child" (Maratta)

(Des Display Section, G.P.O. Photo Harrison)

1966 (3 Aug). *Health Stamps. T* **260** *and similar vert design. Multicoloured. W* **98** *(sideways). P* 14 × 14½.
839 3d. + 1d. Type **260** 15 20
840 4d. + 1d. Weka Rail 15 20
a. Deep brown (values and date) omitted .. £650
MS841 Two sheets each 107 × 91 mm. Nos. 839/40 in blocks of 6 (3 × 2) .. .. *Per pair* 18·00 32·00
In No. 840a besides the value, "1966" and "Weka" are also omitted and the bird, etc. appears as light brown.

(Photo Harrison)

1966 (3 Oct). *Christmas. W* **98** *(sideways). P* 14½.
842 **262** 3d. multicoloured 10 10
a. Red omitted £100

263 Queen Victoria and Queen Elizabeth II

264 Half-sovereign of 1867 and Commemorative Dollar Coin

(Des Display Section, G.P.O. Photo Harrison)

1967 (3 Feb). *Centenary of New Zealand Post Office Savings Bank. W* **98** *(sideways on 4d.). P* 14 × 14½.
843 **263** 4d. black, gold and maroon 10 10
844 **264** 9d. gold, silver, black, lt blue & dp grn 10 15

(New Currency. 100 cents = 1 dollar)

265 Manuka (Tea Tree)

266 Pohutu Geyser

1967 (10 July)–**70**. *Decimal Currency. Designs as* 1960–66 *issue, but with values inscr in decimal currency as T* **265/6**. *Chalky paper. W* **98** *(sideways on* 8 *c.,* 10 *c.,* 20 *c.,* 50 *c. and* $2). *P* 13½ × 14 (½ *c. to* 3 *c.,* 5 *c. and* 7 *c.*), 14½ × 14 (4 *c.,* 6 *c.,* 8 *c.,* 10 *c.,* 25 *c.,* 30 *c. and* $1) *or* 14 × 14½ (15 *c.,* 20 *c.,* 50 *c. and* $2).
845 **265** ½ c. pale blue, yellow-green and cerise 10 10
846 – 1 c. yellow, carmine, green & lt brown (as 1d.) 10 10
a. Booklet pane. Five stamps plus one printed label .. .. .. 1·50
847 – 2 c. carmine, black, yellow and green (as 2d.) 10 10
848 – 2½ c. yellow, green, yellow-brown and deep bluish green (as 3d.) .. 10 10
a. Deep bluish green omitted* .. £425
b. Imperf (pair)† £100
849 – 3 c. purple, buff, yellow-green and light greenish blue (as 4d.) .. 10 10
850 – 4 c. yellow, deep green, black and violet (as 5d.) 30 10
851 – 5 c. lilac, yellow-olive and bluish green (as 6d.) 65 10
852 – 6 c. red, green, yellow and light pink (as 7d.) 70 10
853 – 7 c. rose-red, yellow, green and grey (as 8d.) 85 15
854 **214** 8 c. red and ultramarine 85 10
a. Red omitted £190
855 – 10 c. brown and deep green (as 1s.) .. 60 10
856 – 15 c. olive-green and orange-brown (as 1s. 6d.) 60 60
857 **219** 20 c. black and buff .. .. .. 2·00 10
858 **220** 25 c. yellow and light brown .. .. 6·00 90
859 **221***a* 30 c. olive-yellow, green & greenish blue .. .. 4·25 25
a. No wmk (1970) .. .. .. 3·50 3·75
860 – 50 c. blackish green (as 5s.) .. .. 4·00 75
861 – $1 Prussian blue (as 10s.) .. .. 16·00 1·25
862 **266** $2 deep magenta .. .. .. 10·00 11·00
845/62 .. .. *Set of* 18 40·00 14·00
*This occurred on one horizontal row of ten, affecting the background colour so that the value is also missing. In the row above and the row below, the colour was partially omitted. The price is for a vertical strip.
The 2½ c. value has been seen with the yellow omitted, but only on a used example.
†This comes from a sheet of which the six right-hand vertical rows were completely imperforate and the top, bottom and left-hand margins had been removed.
The 4 c., 30 c. and 50 c. exist with PVA gum as well as gum arabic. No. 859a exists with PVA gum only.
For $4 to $10 in the "Arms" type, see under Postal Fiscal stamps. See also Nos. 870, etc.

268 Running with Ball

(Des L. C. Mitchell. Photo Harrison)

1967 (2 Aug). *Health Stamps. Rugby Football. T* **268** *and similar multicoloured design. W* **98** *(sideways on* 2½ *c.). P* 14½ × 14 (2½ *c.*) *or* 14 × 14½ (3 *c.*).
867 2½ c. + 1 c. Type **268** 10 10
868 3 c. + 1 c. Positioning for a place-kick (*horiz*) 10 10
MS869 Two sheets; (*a*) 76 × 130 mm (867); (*b*) 130 × 76 mm (868). Containing blocks of six .. .. *Per pair* 23·00 24·00

270 *Kaita* (trawler) and Catch

271 Brown Trout

276 Dairy Farm, Mt Egmont and Butter Consignment

277 Fox Glacier, Westland National Park

(Des Display Section, G.P.O. (7, 8, 10, 18, 20, 25 c. and 28 c. from photo), R. M. Conly (7½ c.). Litho B.W. (7, 8, 18, 20 c.) or photo D.L.R. (7½ c.) and Harrison (10, 25, 28 c.). Others (15 c., $2) as before)

1967–69. *T* **270/1**, **276/7** *and similar designs. Chalky paper (except 7, 8, 18, 20 c.). No wmk (7, 8, 20 c.) or W* **98** *(sideways on 7½, 10, 15, 25 c., upright on 18, 28 c., $2). P 13½ (7, 7½ c.), 13 × 13½ (8, 18, 20 c.), 14½ × 14 (10, 25 c.) or 14 × 14½ (15, 28 c., $2).*

870 7 c. multicoloured (3.12.69) .. .. .. 1·25 75
871 7½ c. multicoloured* (29.8.67) 30 70
a. Wmk upright (10.68) 50 60
872 8 c. multicoloured (8.7.69) 75 70
873 10 c. multicoloured (2.4.68) 50 10
a. Green (background) omitted £275
874 15 c. apple-green, myrtle-green and carmine (as No. 856†) (19.3.68) .. .. .. 1·00 50
875 18 c. multicoloured (8.7.69) .. .. .. 1·40 55
876 20 c. multicoloured (8.7.69) .. .. .. 1·40 20
877 25 c. multicoloured (10.12.68) .. .. 6·00 2·00
878 28 c. multicoloured (30.7.68) 60 10
879 $2 black, ochre & pale blue (as No. 862) (10.12.68) .. .. 35·00 19·00
870/79 .. .. *Set of* 10 42·00 22·00

Designs: *Horiz*—8 c. Apples and orchard; 10 c. Forest and timber; 18 c. Sheep and the "Woolmark"; 20 c. Consignments of beef and herd of cattle.

*No. 871 was originally issued to commemorate the introduction of the brown trout into New Zealand.

† No. 874 is slightly larger than No. 856, measuring 21 × 25 mm and the inscriptions and numerals differ in size.

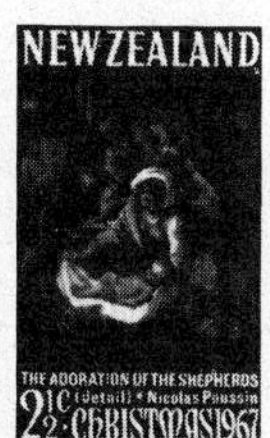

278 "The Adoration of the Shepherds" (Poussin)

279 Mount Aspiring, Aurora Australis and Southern Cross

280 Sir James Hector (founder)

(Photo Harrison)

1967 (3 Oct). *Christmas. W* **98** *(sideways). P 13½ × 14.*

880 **278** 2½ c. multicoloured 10 10

(Des J. Berry. Litho D.L.R.)

1967 (10 Oct). *Centenary of the Royal Society of New Zealand. W* **98** *(sideways on 4 c.). P 14 (4 c) or 13 × 14 (8 c.).*

881 **279** 4 c. multicoloured 15 20
882 **280** 8 c. multicoloured 15 30

281 Open Bible

282 Soldiers and Tank

(Des Display Section, G.P.O. Litho D.L.R.)

1968 (23 Apr). *Centenary of Maori Bible. W* **98**. *P 13½.*

883 **281** 3 c. multicoloured 10 10
a. Gold (inscr etc.) omitted £110

(Des L. C. Mitchell. Litho D.L.R.)

1968 (7 May). *New Zealand Armed Forces. T* **282** *and similar horiz designs. Multicoloured. W* **98** *(sideways). P 14 × 13½.*

884 4 c. Type **282** 30 15
885 10 c. Airmen, "Canberra" and "Kittyhawk" aircraft 50 25
886 28 c. Sailors and H.M.N.Z.S. *Achilles*, 1939, and H.M.N.Z.S. *Waikato*, 1968 .. 70 1·40
884/6 .. .. *Set of* 3 1·40 1·60

285 Boy breasting Tape, and Olympic Rings

287 Placing Votes in Ballot Box

(Des L. C. Mitchell. Photo Harrison)

1968 (7 Aug). *Health Stamps. T* **285** *and similar horiz design. Multicoloured. P 14½ × 14.*

887 2½ c. + 1 c. Type **285** 10 10
888 3 c. + 1 c. Girl swimming and Olympic rings 10 10
a. Red (ring) omitted £750
b. Blue (ring) omitted £350
MS889 Two sheets each 145×95 mm. Nos. 887/8 in blocks of six .. .. .. *Per pair* 15·00 24·00

No. 888a occurred in one miniature sheet. Six examples are known, one being used. No. 888b occurred from a second miniature sheet.

(Des J. Berry. Photo Japanese Govt Ptg Bureau, Tokyo)

1968 (19 Sept). *75th Anniv of Universal Suffrage in New Zealand. P 13.*

890 **287** 3 c. ochre, olive-green and light blue .. 10 10

288 Human Rights Emblem

289 "Adoration of the Holy Child" (G. van Honthorst)

(Photo Japanese Govt Ptg Bureau, Tokyo)

1968 (19 Sept). *Human Rights Year. P 13.*

891 **288** 10 c. scarlet, yellow and deep green .. 10 30

(Photo Harrison)

1968 (1 Oct). *Christmas. W* **98** *(sideways). P 14 × 14½.*

892 **289** 2½ c. multicoloured 10 10

290 I.L.O. Emblem

(Photo Harrison)

1969 (11 Feb). *50th Anniv of International Labour Organization. W* **98** *(sideways). P 14½ × 14.*

893 **290** 7 c. black and carmine-red 15 30

291 Supreme Court Building, Auckland

292 Law Society's Coat of Arms

(Des R. M. Conly. Litho B.W.)

1969 (8 Apr). *Centenary of New Zealand Law Society. T* **291/2** *and similar design. P 13½ × 13 (3 c.) or 13 × 13½ (others).*

894 3 c. multicoloured (*shades*) 10 10
895 10 c. multicoloured 35 45
896 18 c. multicoloured (*shades*) 45 70
894/6 .. .. *Set of* 3 80 1·10

Design:—*Vert*—18 c. "Justice" (from Memorial Window in University of Canterbury, Christchurch).

295 Student being conferred with Degree

(Des R. M. Conly. Litho B.W.)

1969 (3 June). *Centenary of Otago University T* **295** *and similar multicoloured design. P 13 × 13½ (3 c.) or 13½ × 13 (10 c.).*

897 3 c. Otago University (*vert*) 10 10
898 10 c. Type **295** 20 25

OMNIBUS ISSUES

Details, together with prices for complete sets, of the various Omnibus issues from the 1935 Silver Jubilee series to date are included in a special section following Zimbabwe at the end of Volume 2.

296 Boys playing Cricket

298 Dr. Elizabeth Gunn (founder of First Children's Health Camp)

(Des R. M. Conly (4 c.); L. C. Mitchell (others). Litho B.W.)

1969 (6 Aug). *Health Stamps. T* **296** *and similar horiz design and T* **298**. *P 12½ × 13 (No. 901) or 13 × 12½ (others).*

899 2½ c. + 1 c. multicoloured 40 40
900 3 c. + 1 c. multicoloured 40 40
901 4 c. + 1 c. brown and ultramarine .. .. 40 1·25
899/901 .. .. *Set of* 3 1·10 1·75
MS902 Two sheets each 144 × 84 mm. Nos. 899/900 in blocks of six .. .. *Per pair* 20·00 38·00

Design:—3 c. Girls playing cricket.

299 Oldest existing House in New Zealand, and Old Stone Mission Store, Kerikeri

(Litho D.L.R.)

1969 (18 Aug). *Early European Settlement in New Zealand, and 150th Anniv of Kerikeri. T* **299** *and similar horiz design. Multicoloured. W* **98** *(sideways). P 13 × 13½.*

903 4 c. Type **299** 20 25
904 6 c. View of Bay of Islands .. .. .. 30 1·00

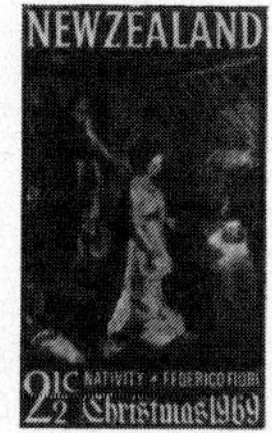

301 "The Nativity" (Federico Fiori (Barocci))

302 Captain Cook, Transit of Venus and "Octant"

(Photo Harrison)

1969 (1 Oct). *Christmas. P 13 × 14. A. W* **98**. *B. No wmk.*

				A		B	
905	**301**	2½ c. multicoloured	..	10	10	10	10

(Des Eileen Mayo. Photo; portraits embossed Harrison)

1969 (9 Oct). *Bicentenary of Captain Cook's Landing in New Zealand. T* **302** *and similar horiz designs. P 14½ × 14.*

906 4 c. black, cerise and blue 75 35
907 6 c. slate-green, purple-brown & black .. 1·00 2·75
908 18 c. purple-brown, slate-green & black .. 2·50 2·75
909 28 c. cerise, black and blue .. .. .. 4·00 4·75
906/9 .. .. *Set of* 4 7·50 9·50
MS910 109 × 90 mm. Nos. 906/9 .. .. .. 18·00 30·00

Designs:—6 c. Sir Joseph Banks (naturalist) and outline of H.M.S. *Endeavour*; 18 c. Dr. Daniel Solander (botanist) and his plant; 28 c. Queen Elizabeth II and Cook's chart, 1769.

The miniature sheet exists additionally inscribed on the selvedge at bottom. "A SOUVENIR FROM NEW ZEALAND STAMP EXHIBITION, NEW PLYMOUTH 6TH–11TH OCTOBER. 1969". These were not sold from Post Offices.

306 Girl, Wheat Field and C.O.R.S.O. Emblem

307 Mother feeding her Child, Dairy Herd and C.O.R.S.O. Emblem

(Des L. C. Mitchell. Photo Japanese Govt Printing Bureau, Tokyo)

1969 (18 Nov). *25th Anniv of C.O.R.S.O. (Council of Organizations for Relief Services Overseas). P 13.*

911 **306** 7 c. multicoloured 20 90
912 **307** 8 c. multicoloured 20 90

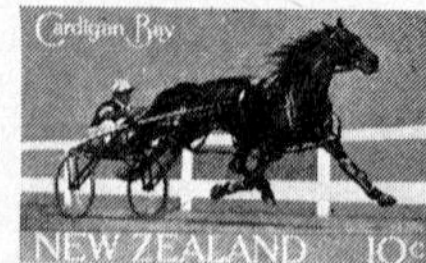

308 "Cardigan Bay" (champion trotter)

(Des L. C. Mitchell. Photo Courvoisier)

1970 (28 Jan). *Return of "Cardigan Bay" to New Zealand. P* 11½.
913 **308** 10 c. multicoloured 20 25

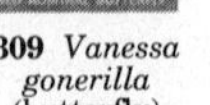

309 *Vanessa gonerilla* (butterfly) **310** Queen Elizabeth II and New Zealand Coat of Arms

(Des Enid Hunter (½ c., 1 c., 2 c., 18 c., 20 c.), Eileen Mayo (2½ c. to 7 c.), D. B. Stevenson (7½ c., 8 c.), M. Cleverley (10 c., 15 c., 25 c., 30 c., $1, $2), M. V. Askew (23 c., 50 c.). Photo Harrison (½ c. to 20 c.), Enschedé (23 c., 50 c.), Courvoisier ($1, $2) or Litho B.W. (25 c., 30 c.))

1970 (12 Mar)–**76**. *Various designs at T* **309/10**. *W* **98** (*sideways on* 10, 15 *and* 20 *c.*) *or No wmk* (23 *c.*, *to* $2).

(*a*) *Size as T* **309**. *P* 13½ × 13
914 ½ c. multicoloured (2.9.70) 10 20
915 1 c. multicoloured (2.9.70) 10 10
a. Wmk sideways (booklets) (6.7.71) .. 70 1·00
b. Booklet pane. No. 915a × 3 with three *se-tenant* printed labels (6.7.71) .. .. 2·00
916 2 c. multicoloured (2.9.70) 10 10
a. Black (inscr, etc.) omitted £110
917 2½ c. multicoloured (2.9.70) 40 10
918 3 c. black, brown and orange (2.9.70) .. 15 10
a. Wmk sideways (booklets) (6.7.71) .. 55 75
919 4 c. multicoloured (2.9.70) 15 10
a. Wmk sideways (booklets) (6.7.71) .. 55 75
920 5 c. multicoloured (4.11.70) 45 10
921 6 c. blackish grn, yell-grn & carm (4.11.70) 45 20
922 7 c. multicoloured (4.11.70) 55 40
923 7½ c. multicoloured (4.11.70) .. .. .. 1·00 1·50
924 8 c. multicoloured (4.11.70) 65 40

(*b*) *Size as T* **310**. *Various Perfs*
925 10 c. multicoloured (*p* 14½×14) 40 15
926 15 c. black, flesh and pale brown (*p* 13½×13) (20.1.71) .. .. 1·50 50
927 18 c. chestnut, black and apple-green (*p* 13×13½) (20.1.71) .. .. 1·50 40
928 20 c. black & yell-brn (*p* 13½×13) (20.1.71) 1·50 15
929 23 c. multicoloured (*p* 13½×12½) (1.12.71) 80 20
930 25 c. multicoloured (*p* 13×13½) (1.9.71) .. 1·75 35
b. Perf 14 (11.76?) 70 40
931 30 c. multicoloured (*p* 13×13½) (1.9.71) .. 2·75 15
a. Perf 14 (9.76?) .. .. .. 2·75 2·25
932 50 c. multicoloured (*p* 13½×12½) (1.9.71) 80 20
a. Apple green (hill) omitted .. .. 25·00
b. Buff (shore) omitted .. .. 55·00
933 $1 multicoloured (*p* 11½) (14.4.71) .. 2·00 85
934 $2 multicoloured (*p* 11½) (14.4.71) .. 5·00 1·25
914/34 .. .. *Set of* 21 18·00 6·50

Designs: *Vert*—½ c. *Lycaena salustius* (butterfly); 2 c. *Argyrophenga antipodum* (butterfly); 2½ c. *Nyctemera annulata* (moth); 3 c. *Detunda egregia* (moth); 4 c. *Charagia virescens* (moth); 5 c. Scarlet Parrot Fish; 6 c. Sea Horses; 7 c. Leather Jacket (fish); 7½ c. Garfish; 8 c. John Dory (fish); 18 c. Maori club; 25 c. Hauraki Gulf Maritime Park; 30 c. Mt Cook National Park. *Horiz*—10 c. Type **310**: 15 c. Maori fish hook; 20 c. Maori tattoo pattern; 23 c. Egmont National Park; 50 c. Abel Tasman National Park; $1 Geothermal Power; $2 Agricultural Technology.

Although issued as a definitive No. 925 was put on sale on the occasion of the Royal Visit to New Zealand.

See also Nos. 1008, etc.

311 Geyser Restaurant **312** U.N. H.Q. Building

(Des M. Cleverley. Photo Japanese Govt Printing Bureau, Tokyo)

1970 (8 Apr). *World Fair, Osaka. T* **311** *and similar horiz designs. Multicoloured. P* 13.
935 7 c. Type **311** 40 65
936 8 c. New Zealand Pavilion 40 65
937 18 c. Bush Walk 60 65
935/7 .. .. *Set of* 3 1·25 1·75

(Des R. M. Conly (3 c.), L. C. Mitchell (10 c.). Litho D.L.R.)

1970 (24 June). *25th Anniv of United Nations. T* **312** *and similar vert design. P* 13½.
938 3 c. multicoloured 10 10
939 10 c. scarlet and yellow 20 20

Design:—10 c. Tractor on horizon.

313 Soccer

(Des L. C. Mitchell. Litho D.L.R.)

1970 (5 Aug). *Health Stamps. T* **313** *and similar multicoloured design. P* 13½.
940 2½ c. + 1 c. Netball (*vert*) 10 15
941 3 c. + 1 c. Type **313** 10 15
MS942 Two sheets: (*a*) 102 × 125 mm (940); (*b*) 125 × 102 mm (941), containing blocks of six *Per pair* 17·00 25·00

314 "The Virgin adoring the Child" (Correggio) **315** "The Holy Family" (stained glass window, Invercargill Presbyterian Church)

(Litho D.L.R.)

1970 (1 Oct). *Christmas. T* **314/15** *and similar design. P* 12½.
943 2½ c. multicoloured 10 10
944 3 c. multicoloured 10 10
a. Green (inscr and value) omitted .. £150
945 10 c. black, orange and silver 30 75
943/5 .. .. *Set of* 3 35 75

Design: *Horiz*—10 c. Tower of Roman Catholic Church, Sockburn.

316 Chatham Islands Lily

(Des Eileen Mayo. Photo Japanese Govt Printing Bureau, Tokyo)

1970 (2 Dec). *Chatham Islands. T* **316** *and similar horiz design. Multicoloured. P* 13.
946 1 c. Type **316** 10 15
947 2 c. Shy Albatross 20 25

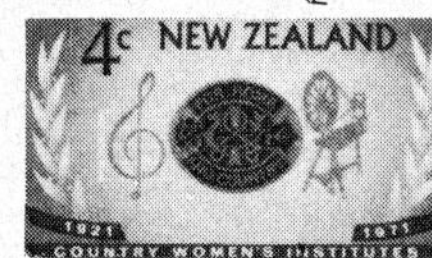

317 Country Women's Institute Emblem

(Des L. C. Mitchell. Photo Japanese Govt Ptg Bureau, Tokyo)

1971 (10 Feb). *50th Anniversaries of Country Women's Institutes and Rotary International in New Zealand. T* **317** *and similar horiz design. Multicoloured. P* 13.
948 4 c. Type **317** 10 10
949 10 c. Rotary emblem and map of New Zealand 10 20

318 *Rainbow II* (yacht)

(Des J. Berry (5 c.), G. F. Fuller (8 c.). Litho B.W.)

1971 (3 Mar). *One Ton Cup Racing Trophy. T* **318** *and similar horiz design. Multicoloured. P* 13½ × 13.
950 5 c. Type **318** 15 20
951 8 c. One Ton Cup 25 65

319 Civic Arms of Palmerston North

(Des R. M. Conly. Photo Japanese Govt Ptg Bureau, Tokyo)

1971 (12 May). *City Centenaries. T* **319** *and similar horiz designs. Multicoloured. P* 13.
952 3 c. Type **319** 10 10
953 4 c. Arms of Auckland 10 10
954 5 c. Arms of Invercargill 15 40
952/4 .. .. *Set of* 3 30 50

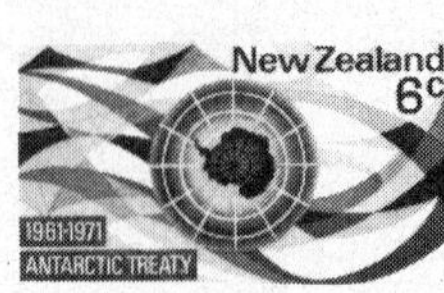

320 Antarctica on Globe **321** Child on Swing

(Des Eileen Mayo. Photo Japanese Govt Ptg Bureau, Tokyo)

1971 (9 June). *Tenth Anniv of Antarctic Treaty. P* 13.
955 **320** 6 c. multicoloured .. .. .. 1·50 1·50

(Des Eileen Mayo. Photo Japanese Govt Ptg Bureau, Tokyo)

1971 (9 June). *25th Anniv of U.N.I.C.E.F. P* 13.
956 **321** 7 c. multicoloured 50 70

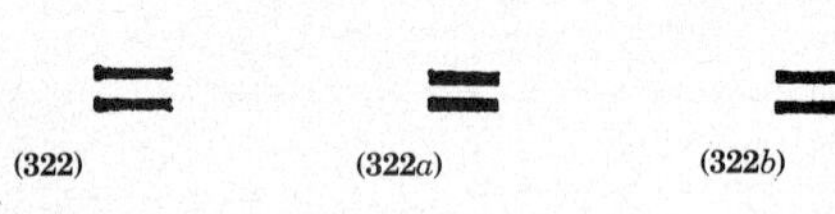

(**322**) (**322***a*) (**322***b*)

T **322**. Photo, showing screening dots; thin bars, wide apart.
T **322***a*. Typo, without screening dots; thick bars, closer together.
T **322***b*. Typo; bars similar to T **322**.

1971–73. *No.* 917 *surcharged.*

(*a*) *In photogravure, by Harrison* (23.6.71*)
957 **322** 4 c. on 2½ c. multicoloured 15 10

(*b*) *Typographically, by Harrison* (13.7.72*)
957*a* **322***a* 4 c. on 2½ c. multicoloured 45 10
ab. Albino surch £110
ac. Surch double, one albino .. .. 15·00

(*c*) *Typographically, locally* (18.6.73*)
957*b* **322***b* 4 c. on 2½ c. multicoloured 15 10

*Earliest known postmarks.

323 Satellite-tracking Aerial

(Des M. Cleverley. Photo Courvoisier)

1971 (14 July). *Opening of Satellite Earth Station. T* **323** *and similar horiz design. P* 11½.
958 8 c. black, drab-grey and vermilion .. .. 60 1·00
959 10 c. black, turquoise-grn & pale bluish vio .. 65 1·00

Design:—10 c. Satellite.

324 Girls playing Hockey

(Des L. C. Mitchell. Litho Harrison)

1971 (4 Aug). *Health Stamps. T* **324** *and similar horiz designs. Multicoloured. W* **98** (*sideways on* 5 *c.*). *P* 13½ × 13.
960 3 c. + 1 c. Type **324** 35 40
961 4 c. + 1 c. Boys playing hockey 35 40
962 5 c. + 1 c. Dental Health .. .. .. 90 1·60
960/2 .. .. *Set of* 3 1·40 2·25
MS963 Two sheets each 122 × 96 mm. Nos. 960/1 in blocks of six .. .. .. *Per pair* 20·00 30·00

325 "Madonna bending over the Crib" (Maratta) **326** "Tiffany" Rose

(Des Enid Hunter (10 c.), D. A. Hatcher (others). Photo Harrison)

1971 (6 Oct). *Christmas. T* **325** *and similar vert designs. Multicoloured. P* 13 × 13½.
964 3 c. Type **325** 10 10
965 4 c. "The Annunciation" (stained-glass window) (21½ × 38 *mm*) 10 10
966 10 c. "The Three Kings" (21½ × 38 *mm*) .. 70 1·25
964/6 .. .. *Set of* 3 80 1·25

(Des A. G. Mitchell. Photo Courvoisier)

1971 (3 Nov). *First World Rose Convention, Hamilton. T* **326** *and similar vert designs showing roses. Multicoloured. P* 11½.

967 2 c. Type **326** .. 15 30
968 5 c. "Peace" .. 35 35
969 8 c. "Chrysler Imperial" .. 60 1·10
967/9 .. *Set of* 3 1·00 1·60

327 Lord Rutherford and Alpha Particles

328 Benz (1895)

(Des M. Cleverley. Litho B.W.)

1971 (1 Dec). *Birth Centenary of Lord Rutherford (scientist). T* **327** *and similar horiz design. Multicoloured. P* 13½ × 13.

970 1 c. Type **327** .. 25 40
971 7 c. Lord Rutherford and formula .. 85 1·40

(Des A. G. Mitchell. Litho B.W.)

1972 (2 Feb). *International Vintage Car Rally. T* **328** *and similar horiz designs. Multicoloured. P* 14.

972 3 c. Type **328** .. 20 10
973 4 c. Oldsmobile (1904) .. 25 10
974 5 c. Ford "Model T" (1914) .. 35 10
975 6 c. Cadillac Service car (1915) .. 55 45
976 8 c. Chrysler (1924) .. 1·25 1·00
977 10 c. Austin "7" (1923) .. 1·25 1·00
972/7 .. *Set of* 6 3·50 2·50

329 Coat of Arms of Wanganui

330 Black Scree Cotula

(Des M. Cleverley. Litho Harrison)

1972 (5 Apr). *Anniversaries. T* **329** *and similar designs. P* 13 × 13½ (3, 5 *and* 8 c.) *or* 13½ × 13 (*others*).

978 3 c. multicoloured .. 15 10
979 4 c. red-orange, brown-bistre and black .. 15 10
980 5 c. multicoloured .. 25 10
981 8 c. multicoloured .. 1·50 1·50
982 10 c. multicoloured .. 1·50 1·50
978/82 .. *Set of* 5 3·25 3·00

Designs and Events: *Vert*—3 c. Type **329** (Centenary of Wanganui Council govt); 5 c. De Havilland DH89 "Rapide" *Dominie* and Boeing "737" (25th Anniv National Airways Corp); 8 c. French frigate and Maori palisade (Bicent of landing by Marion du Fresne). *Horiz*—4 c. Postal Union symbol (Tenth Anniv of Asian-Oceanic Postal Union); 10 c. Stone cairn (150th Anniv of New Zealand Methodist Church).

(Des Eileen Mayo. Litho Harrison)

1972 (7 June). *Alpine Plants. T* **330** *and similar vert designs. Multicoloured. P* 13½.

983 4 c. Type **330** .. 30 10
984 6 c. North Island Eidelweiss .. 75 60
985 8 c. Haast's Buttercup .. 1·25 1·25
986 10 c. Brown Mountain Daisy .. 1·75 1·75
983/6 .. *Set of* 4 3·50 3·25

331 Boy playing Tennis

332 "Madonna with Child" (Murillo)

(Des L. C. Mitchell. Litho Harrison)

1972 (2 Aug). *Health Stamps. T* **331** *and similar vert design. P* 13 × 13½.

987 3 c. + 1 c. light grey and chestnut .. 25 35
988 4 c. + 1 c. light red-brown, grey and lemon 25 35
MS989 Two sheets each 107 × 123 mm. Nos. 987/8 in blocks of six .. *Per pair* 20·00 30·00

Design:—No. 988, Girl playing tennis.

(Des D. A. Hatcher. Photo Courvoisier)

1972 (4 Oct). *Christmas. T* **332** *and similar vert designs. Multicoloured. P* 11½.

990 3 c. Type **332** .. 10 10
991 5 c. "The Last Supper" (stained-glass window, St. John's Church, Levin) .. 15 10
992 10 c. Pohutukawa flower .. 55 1·00
990/2 .. *Set of* 3 70 1·00

333 Lake Waikaremoana

334 Old Pollen Street

(Des D. A. Hatcher. Photo Courvoisier)

1972 (6 Dec). *Lake Scenes. T* **333** *and similar vert designs. Multicoloured. P* 11½.

993 6 c. Type **333** .. 1·00 1·25
994 8 c. Lake Hayes .. 1·10 1·25
995 18 c. Lake Wakatipu .. 2·00 2·25
996 23 c. Lake Rotomahana .. 2·25 2·75
993/6 .. *Set of* 4 5·75 6·75

(Des Miss V. Jepsen (3 c.), B. Langford (others). Litho Harrison)

1973 (7 Feb). *Commemorations. T* **334** *and similar horiz designs. Multicoloured* (*except* 8 c.). *P* 13½ × 13.

997 3 c. Type **334** .. 15 10
998 4 c. Coal-mining and pasture .. 15 10
999 5 c. Cloister .. 15 15
1000 6 c. Forest, birds and lake .. 50 80
1001 8 c. Rowers (light grey, indigo and gold) .. 45 1·00
1002 10 c. Graph and people .. 50 1·60
997/1002 .. *Set of* 6 1·75 3·25

Events:—3 c. Centennial of Thames Borough; 4 c. Centennial of Westport Borough; 5 c. Centennial of Canterbury University; 6 c. 50th Anniv of Royal Forest and Bird Protection Society; 8 c. Success of N.Z. Rowers in 1972 Olympics; 10 c. 25th Anniv of E.C.A.F.E.

335 Class "W" Locomotive

336 "Maori Woman and Child"

(Des R. M. Conly. Litho Harrison)

1973 (4 Apr). *New Zealand Steam Locomotives. T* **335** *and similar horiz designs. Multicoloured. P* 14 × 14½.

1003 3 c. Type **335** .. 45 10
1004 4 c. Class "X" .. 55 10
1005 5 c. Class "Ab" .. 60 10
1006 10 c. Class "Ja" .. 2·50 1·75
1003/6 .. *Set of* 4 3·50 1·75

1973–76. *As Nos.* 914 *etc., but no wmk.*

1008 1 c. multicoloured (7.9.73) .. 90 50
a. Booklet pane. No. 1008 × 3 with three *se-tenant* printed labels (8.74) .. 2·40
b. Red (wing markings) omitted .. £130
c. Blue (spots on wings) omitted .. 60·00
1009 2 c. multicoloured (6.73?) .. 30 10
1010 3 c. black, light brown and orange (1974) 2·25 70
1011 4 c. multicoloured (7.9.73) .. 70 10
a. Bright green (wing veins) inverted .. £275
b. Purple-brown omitted .. £170
c. Orange-yellow omitted .. £200
d. Greenish blue (background) omitted £150
e. Bright green (wing veins) omitted .. 6·00
f. Apple green (wings) omitted .. £130
1012 5 c. multicoloured (1973) .. 1·75 90
1013 6 c. blackish green, yellow-green and rose-carmine (7.9.73) .. 40 30
a. Yellow-grn (part of sea horse) omitted £170
1014 7 c. multicoloured (1974) .. 3·50 2·50
1015 8 c. multicoloured (1974) .. 4·25 1·50
a. Blue-green (background) omitted .. £200
1017 10 c. multicoloured, *p* 13½×13 (6.73?) .. 80 10
a. Silver (Arms) omitted .. £110
b. Imperf (vert pair) .. £180
c. Deep blue (Queen's head, face value etc.) omitted .. £180
d. Red (hair ribbon) omitted .. 20·00
1018 15 c. black, flesh & pale brown, *p* 13½×13 (2.8.76) .. 2·00 10
1019 18 c. chestnut, black & apple-green (1974) 1·00 90
a. Black (inscr, etc.) omitted .. £160
1020 20 c. black and yellow-brown (1974) .. 80 10
1008/20 .. *Set of* 12 17·00 7·00

(Des and photo Courvoisier)

1973 (6 June). *Paintings by Frances Hodgkins. T* **336** *and similar vert designs. Multicoloured. P* 11½.

1027 5 c. Type **336** .. 40 15
1028 8 c. "Hilltop" .. 75 75
1029 10 c. "Barn in Picardy" .. 1·00 1·25
1030 18 c. "Self Portrait Still Life" .. 1·50 2·50
1027/30 .. *Set of* 4 3·25 2·50

COVER PRICES

Cover factors are quoted at the beginning of each country for most issues to 1945. An explanation of the system can be found on page x. The factors quoted do not, however, apply to philatelic covers.

337 Prince Edward

338 "Tempi Madonna" (Raphael)

(Des and litho Harrison)

1973 (1 Aug). *Health Stamps. P* 13 × 13½.

1031 **337** 3 c. + 1 c. dull yellowish green and reddish brown .. 30 30
1032 4 c. + 1 c. rose-red and blackish brown 30 30
MS1033 Two sheets each 96 × 121 mm with Nos. 1031/2 in blocks of 6 (3 × 2) .. *Per pair* 18·00 27·00

(Des A. G. Mitchell. Photo Enschedé)

1973 (3 Oct). *Christmas. T* **338** *and similar vert designs. Multicoloured. P* 12½ × 13½.

1034 3 c. Type **338** .. 10 10
1035 5 c. "Three Kings" (stained-glass window, St. Theresa's Church, Auckland) .. 10 10
1036 10 c. Family entering church .. 25 50
1034/6 .. *Set of* 3 40 50

339 Mitre Peak

340 Hurdling

(Des D. A. Hatcher. Photo Enschedé)

1973 (5 Dec). *Mountain Scenery. T* **339** *and similar multicoloured designs. P* 13 × 13½ (6, 8 c.) *or* 13½ × 13 (*others*).

1037 6 c. Type **339** .. 80 90
1038 8 c. Mt Ngauruhoe .. 1·00 1·50
1039 18 c. Mt Sefton (*horiz*) .. 1·75 3·00
1040 23 c. Burnett Range (*horiz*) .. 2·00 3·00
1037/40 .. *Set of* 4 5·00 7·50

(Des M. Cleverley. Litho Harrison)

1974 (9 Jan). *Tenth British Commonwealth Games, Christchurch. T* **340** *and similar vert designs.* 5 c. *black and violet-blue, others multicoloured. P* 13 × 14.

1041 4 c. Type **340** .. 10 10
1042 5 c. Ball-player .. 15 10
1043 10 c. Cycling .. 20 15
1044 18 c. Rifle-shooting .. 35 65
1045 23 c. Bowls .. 50 85
1041/5 .. *Set of* 5 1·10 1·60

No. 1042 does not show the Games emblem, and commemorates the Fourth Paraplegic Games, held at Dunedin.

341 Queen Elizabeth II

342 "Spirit of Napier" Fountain

(Des D. A. Hatcher and A. G. Mitchell. Litho Harrison)

1974 (5 Feb). *New Zealand Day. Sheet* 131 × 74 mm. *containing T* **341** *and similar horiz designs, size* 37 × 20 mm. *Multicoloured. P* 13.

MS1046 4 c. × 5 Treaty House, Waitangi; Signing Waitangi Treaty; Type **341**; Parliament Buildings Extensions; Children in Class .. 60 2·00

(Des Miss V. Jepsen. Photo Courvoisier)

1974 (3 Apr). *Centenaries of Napier and U.P.U. T* **342** *and similar vert designs. Multicoloured. P* 11½.

1047 4 c. Type **342** .. 10 10
1048 5 c. Clock Tower, Berne .. 10 15
1049 8 c. U.P.U. Monument, Berne .. 35 90
1047/9 .. *Set of* 3 50 1·00

343 Boeing Seaplane, 1919

344 Children, Cat and Dog

(Des R. M. Conly. Litho Harrison)

1974 (5 June). *History of New Zealand Airmail Transport. T* **343** *and similar horiz designs. Multicoloured. P* 14 × 13.
1050 3 c. Type **343** 25 10
1051 4 c. Lockheed "Electra", 1937 .. .. 30 10
1052 5 c. Bristol Freighter, 1958 .. .. .. 35 10
1053 23 c. Empire "S 30" flying-boat, 1940.. .. 1·50 1·50
1050/3 .. .. *Set of* 4 2·25 1·60

(Des B. Langford. Litho Harrison)

1974 (7 Aug). *Health Stamps. P* 13 × 13½.
1054 **344** 3 c. + 1 c. multicoloured 20 30
1055 – 4 c. + 1 c. multicoloured 25 30
1056 – 5 c. + 1 c. multicoloured .. .. 1·00 1·25
1054/6 .. .. *Set of* 3 1·25 1·75
MS1057 145 × 123 mm. No. 1055 in block of ten 21·00 30·00
Nos. 1055/6 are as T **344**, showing children and pets.

345 "The Adoration of the Magi" (Konrad Witz)

346 Great Barrier Island

(Des Eileen Mayo. Photo Courvoisier)

1974 (2 Oct). *Christmas. T* **345** *and similar horiz designs. Multicoloured. P* 11½.
1058 3 c. Type **345** 10 10
1059 5 c. "The Angel Window" (stained-glass window, Old St. Pauls Church, Wellington) 10 10
1060 10 c. Madonna Lily 30 50
1058/60 .. .. *Set of* 3 40 55

(Des D. A. Hatcher. Photo Enschedé)

1974 (4 Dec). *Off-shore Islands. T* **346** *and similar horiz designs. Multicoloured. P* 13½ × 13.
1061 6 c. Type **346** 30 40
1062 8 c. Stewart Island 40 80
1063 18 c. White Island .. .. 70 1·50
1064 23 c. The Brothers .. .. 1·00 2·00
1061/4 .. .. *Set of* 4 2·25 4·25

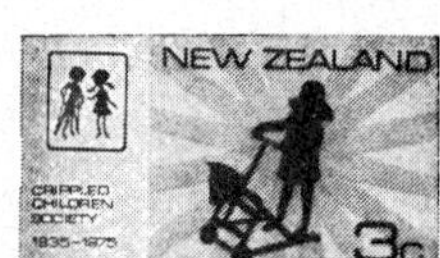

347 Crippled Child

(Des Miss V. Jepsen (3 c., 5 c.), A. G. Mitchell (10 c., 18 c.). Litho Harrison)

1975 (5 Feb). *Anniversaries and Events. T* **347** *and similar horiz designs. Multicoloured. P* 13½.
1065 3 c. Type **347** 10 10
1066 5 c. Farming family 15 10
1067 10 c. I.W.Y. symbols 20 55
1068 18 c. Medical School Building, Otago University 35 80
1065/8 .. .. *Set of* 4 70 1·40
Commemorations:—3 c. 40th Anniv of N.Z. Crippled Children Society; 5 c. 50th Anniv of Women's Division, Federated Farmers of N.Z.; 10 c. International Women's Year; 18 c. Centenary of Otago Medical School.

348 Scow *Lake Erie*

(Des R. M. Conly. Litho Harrison)

1975 (2 Apr). *Historic Sailing Ships. T* **348** *and similar horiz designs. P* 13½ × 13.
1069 4 c. black and red 30 10
1070 5 c. black and turquoise-blue 30 10
1071 8 c. black and yellow 45 35
1072 10 c. black and olive-yellow 45 40
1073 18 c. black and light brown 70 90
1074 23 c. black and slate-lilac .. .. .. 80 1·25
1069/74 .. .. *Set of* 6 2·75 2·75
Ships:—5 c. Schooner *Herald*; 8 c. Brigantine *New Zealander*; 10 c. Topsail schooner *Jessie Kelly*; 18 c. Barque *Tory*; 23 c. Full-rigged clipper *Rangitiki*.

349 Lake Summer Forest Park

(Des and photo Enschedé)

1975 (4 June). *Forest Park Scenes. T* **349** *and similar horiz designs. Multicoloured. P* 13.
1075 6 c. Type **349** 50 70
1076 8 c. North-west Nelson .. .. .. 60 1·00
1077 18 c. Kaweka .. .. 1·25 1·75
1078 23 c. Coromandel .. .. 1·50 2·00
1075/8 .. .. *Set of* 4 3·50 5·00

350 Girl feeding Lamb

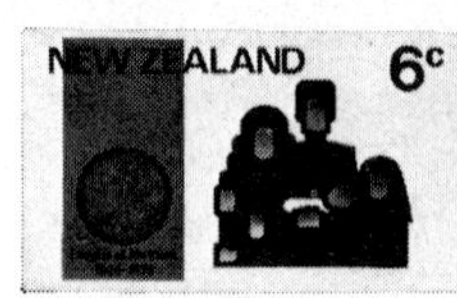

351 "Virgin and Child" (Zanobi Machiavelli)

(Des Margaret Chapman. Litho Harrison)

1975 (6 Aug). *Health Stamps. T* **350** *and similar horiz designs. Multicoloured. P* 13½ × 13.
1079 3 c. + 1 c. Type **350** 20 25
1080 4 c. + 1 c. Boy with hen and chicks 20 25
1081 5 c. + 1 c. Boy with duck and duckling .. 60 1·10
1079/81 .. .. *Set of* 3 90 1·40
MS1082 123 × 146 mm. No. 1080 × 10 .. .. 14·00 25·00

(Des Enid Hunter. Photo Harrison)

1975 (1 Oct). *Christmas. T* **351** *and similar horiz designs. Multicoloured. P* 13 × 13½ (3 c.) *or* 13½ × 13 (*others*).
1083 3 c. Type **351** 10 10
a. Red omitted* £150
1084 5 c. "Cross in Landscape" (stained-glass window, Greendale Church) 10 10
a. Brown (face value) omitted £160
1085 10 c. "I saw three ships . . ." (carol) 35 65
1083/5 .. .. *Set of* 3 60 65
*This occurred in the last two vertical rows of the sheet with the red partially omitted on the previous row.
Used copies of No. 1083 have been seen with the orange ("Christmas 1975") omitted.

352 "Sterling Silver"

353 Queen Elizabeth II (photograph by W. Harrison)

353*a* Maripi (knife)

353*b* Paua

353*c* "Beehive" (section of Parliamentary Buildings, Wellington)

(Des A. G. Mitchell (1 to 14 c.), I. Hulse (20 c. to $2), R. Conly ($5). Photo Harrison (1 to 10 c.), Courvoisier (11 to 14 c.), Heraclio Fournier (20 c. to $5))

1975 (26 Nov)–**81**. (*a*) *Vert designs as T* **352** *showing garden roses. Multicoloured. P* 14½ (6 *to* 8 c.) *or* 14½ × 14 (*others*).
1086 1 c. Type **352** 10 10
1087 2 c. "Lilli Marlene" 10 10
1088 3 c. "Queen Elizabeth" 60 10
a. Perf 14½ (6.79) 60 10
1089 4 c. "Super Star" 10 10
1090 5 c. "Diamond Jubilee" 10 10
1091 6 c. "Cresset" 90 85
a. Perf 14½ × 14 (8.76?) 40 30
1092 7 c. "Michele Meilland" .. .. .. 2·00 50
a. Perf 14½ × 14 (6.76?) 40 10
1093 8 c. "Josephine Bruce" .. .. .. 2·00 90
a. Perf 14½ × 14 (8.76?) 65 10
1094 9 c. "Iceberg" 15 15

(*b*) *Type* **353**. *P* 14½ × 14 (7.12.77)
1094*a* 10 c. multicoloured 85 20
ab. Perf 14½ (2.79) 30 10

(*c*) *Vert designs as T* **353*a*** *showing Maori artefacts. P* 11½ (24.11.76)
1095 11 c. reddish brown, lemon & blackish brown 45 30
1096 12 c. reddish brown, lemon & blackish brown 30 10
1097 13 c. reddish brown, greenish blue and blackish brown 60 30
1098 14 c. reddish brown, lemon & blackish brown 30 20
Designs:—12 c. Putorino (flute); 13 c. Wahaika (club); 14 c. Kotiate (club).

(*d*) *Horiz designs as T* **353*b*** *showing seashells. Multicoloured. P* 13
1099 20 c. Type **353*b*** (29.11.78) 15 20
1100 30 c. Toheroa (29.11.78) 25 30
1101 40 c. Coarse Dosinia (29.11.78) 30 35
1102 50 c. Spiny Murex (29.11.78).. .. .. 40 45
1103 $1 Scallop (26.11.79) 70 85
a. Imperf between (vert pair) £400
1104 $2 Circular Saw (26.11.79) .. .. 1·00 1·75

(*e*) *Type* **353*c***. *P* 13 (2.12.81)
1105 $5 multicoloured .. .. .. 3·00 2·00
a. Imperf (vert pair) .. ..
1086/105 .. .. .. *Set of* 21 9·00 6·75
Faked "missing colour errors" exist of No. 1094*a*, involving parts of the portrait.
A used example of No. 1099 exists with the black colour omitted so that the body of the shell appears in blue instead of green.
No. 1103a occurs on the top two rows of the sheet; the lower stamp being imperforate on three edges except for two perforation holes at the foot of each vertical side.

354 Family and League of Mothers Badge

(Des A. P. Derrick. Litho J.W.)

1976 (4 Feb). *Anniversaries and Metrication. T* **354** *and similar horiz designs. Multicoloured. P* 13½ × 14.
1110 6 c. Type **354** 10 10
1111 7 c. Weight, temperature, linear measure and capacity 10 10
1112 8 c. *William Bryan* (immigrant ship), mountain and New Plymouth .. 15 10
1113 10 c. Two women shaking hands and Y.W.C.A. badge 15 40
1114 25 c. Map of the world showing cable links.. 30 1·25
1110/14 .. .. *Set of* 5 70 1·60
Anniversaries:—6 c. League of Mothers, 50th Anniv; 7 c. Metrication; 8 c. Centenary of New Plymouth; 10 c. 50th Anniv of New Zealand Y.W.C.A.; 25 c. Centenary of link with International Telecommunications Network.

355 Gig

356 Purakaunui Falls

(Des G. F. Fuller. Litho Harrison)

1976 (7 Apr). *Vintage Farm Transport. T* **355** *and similar horiz designs. Multicoloured. P* 13½ × 13.
1115 6 c. Type **355** 15 20
1116 7 c. Thorneycroft lorry 20 10
1117 8 c. Scandi wagon 50 20
1118 9 c. Traction engine 30 40
1119 10 c. Wool wagon 30 75
1120 25 c. Cart .. .. 80 1·75
1115/20 .. .. *Set of* 6 2·00 2·75

(Des and photo Courvoisier)

1976 (2 June). *Waterfalls. T* **356** *and similar vert designs. Multicoloured. P* 11½.
1121 10 c. Type **356** 40 10
1122 14 c. Marakopa Falls 75 55
1123 15 c. Bridal Veil Falls 80 60
1124 16 c. Papakorito Falls 90 70
1121/4 .. .. *Set of* 4 2·50 1·75

357 Boy and Pony

358 "Nativity" (Spanish carving)

(Des Margaret Chapman. Litho Harrison)

1976 (4 Aug). *Health Stamps. T* **357** *and similar vert designs. Multicoloured. P* 13 × 13½.
1125 7 c. + 1 c. Type **357** 25 30
1126 8 c. + 1 c. Girl and calf 25 30
1127 10 c. + 1 c. Girls and bird 50 65
1125/7 .. .. *Set of* 3 90 1·10
MS1128 96 × 121 mm. Nos. 1125/7 × 2 .. .. 7·00 9·00

(Des Margaret Chapman (18 c.), D. A. Hatcher (others). Photo Harrison)

1976 (6 Oct). *Christmas. T* **358** *and similar horiz designs. Multicoloured. P* 14 × 14½ (7 *c.*) *or* 14½ × 14 (*others*).

1129 7 c. Type **358** 15 10
1130 11 c. "Resurrection" (stained-glass window, St. Joseph's Catholic Church, Grey Lynn) 25 30
1131 18 c. Angels 40 60
1129/31 .. .. *Set of* 3 70 85

359 Arms of Hamilton **360** Queen Elizabeth II

(Des P. L. Blackie. Litho Harrison)

1977 (19 Jan). *Anniversaries. T* **359** *and similar vert designs. Multicoloured. P* 13 × 13½.

1132 8 c. Type **359** 15 10
a. Horiz strip of 3, Nos. 1132/4 45
1133 8 c. Arms of Gisborne 15 10
1134 8 c. Arms of Masterton 15 10
1135 10 c. A.A. emblem 15 30
a. Horiz pair. Nos. 1135/6 .. .. .. 30 90
1136 10 c. Arms of the College of Surgeons .. 15 30
1132/6 .. .. *Set of* 5 75 80

Events:—Nos. 1132/4, City Centenaries; No. 1135, 75th Anniv of the Automobile Association in New Zealand; No. 1136, 50th Anniv of Royal Australasian College of Surgeons.

Designs of each value were printed in the same sheet horizontally *se-tenant*.

(Des and photo Harrison from photographs by Warren Harrison)

1977 (23 Feb). *Silver Jubilee. Sheet* 178 × 82 *mm containing T* **360** *and similar vert designs showing different portraits. P* 14 × 14½.

MS1137 8 c. × 5 multicoloured .. .. .. 80 1·50
a. Imperf £1400
ab. Ditto, and silver omitted £2000
b. Silver omitted £550
c. Indian red omitted £250

361 Physical Education and Maori Culture **(362)**

(Des A. G. Mitchell. Litho Harrison)

1977 (6 Apr). *Education. T* **361** *and similar vert designs. Multicoloured. P* 13 × 13½.

1138 8 c. Type **361** 30 60
a. Horiz strip of 5, Nos. 1138/42 .. .. 1·40
1139 8 c. Geography, science and woodwork .. 30 60
1140 8 c. Teaching the deaf, kindergarten and woodwork 30 60
1141 8 c. Tertiary and language classes 30 60
1142 8 c. Home science, correspondence school and teacher training 30 60
1138/42 .. .. *Set of* 5 1·40 2·75

Nos. 1138/42 were printed horizontally *se-tenant* throughout the sheet.

1977 (Apr). *Coil Stamps. Nos.* 1010/11 *surch as T* **362** *by Govt Printer, Wellington.*

1143 7 c. on 3 c. *Detunda egregia* (moth) (19.4) 40 65
1144 8 c. on 4 c. *Charagia virescens* (moth) (21.4) 40 65
a. Bright green (wing veins) omitted .. 85·00

Forged "7 c." surcharges, similar to No. 1143, but in smaller type, are known applied to Nos. 918 and 1010.

363 Karitane Beach **364** Girl with Pigeon

(Des D. A. Hatcher. Photo Heraclio Fournier)

1977 (1 June). *Seascapes. T* **363** *and similar horiz designs. Multicoloured. P* 14½.

1145 10 c. Type **363** 20 10
1146 16 c. Ocean Beach, Mount Maunganui .. 35 35
1147 18 c. Piha Beach 40 40
1148 30 c. Kaikoura Coast 50 50
1145/8 .. .. *Set of* 4 1·25 1·25

(Des A. P. Derrick. Litho Harrison)

1977 (3 Aug). *Health Stamps. T* **364** *and similar vert designs. Multicoloured. P* 13 × 13½.

1149 7 c. + 2 c. Type **364** 20 30
1150 8 c. + 2 c. Boy with frog 25 35
1151 10 c. + 2 c. Girl with butterfly 45 70
1149/51 .. .. *Set of* 3 80 1·25
MS1152 97 × 120 mm. Nos. 1149/51 × 2 .. .. 5·50 10·00

Stamps from the miniature sheet are without white border and together form a composite design.

365 "The Holy Family" (Correggio)

(Des Margaret Chapman (23 c.), graphics for all values produced by printer. Photo Courvoisier)

1977 (5 Oct). *Christmas. T* **365** *and similar vert designs. Multicoloured. P* 11½.

1153 7 c. Type **365** 15 10
1154 16 c. "Madonna and Child" (stained-glass window, St. Michael's and All Angels, Dunedin) 25 20
1155 23 c. "Partridge in a Pear Tree" 40 45
1153/5 .. .. *Set of* 3 70 65

366 Merryweather Manual Pump, 1860 **367** Town Clock and Coat of Arms, Ashburton

(Des R. M. Conly. Litho Harrison)

1977 (7 Dec). *Fire Fighting Appliances. T* **366** *and similar horiz designs. Multicoloured. P* 14 × 13.

1156 10 c. Type **366** 15 10
1157 11 c. 2-wheel hose, reel and ladder, 1880 .. 15 10
1158 12 c. Shand Mason steam fire engine, 1873 .. 20 15
1159 23 c. Chemical fire engine, 1888 .. .. 30 30
1156/9 .. .. *Set of* 4 70 60

(Des P. L. Blackie (No. 1162), Harrison (No. 1163), P. J. Durrant (others), Litho Harrison)

1978 (8 Mar). *Centenaries. T* **367** *and similar multicoloured designs. P* 14.

1160 10 c. Type **367** 15 10
a. Horiz pair. Nos. 1160/1 .. .. 30 50
1161 10 c. Stratford and Mt Egmont 15 10
1162 12 c. Early telephone 15 15
1163 20 c. Bay of Islands (*horiz*) 20 30
1160/3 .. .. *Set of* 4 60 85

Centenaries commemorated are those of the towns of Ashburton and Stratford, of the telephone in New Zealand, and of the Bay of Islands County.

The 10 c. values were printed together, *se-tenant*, in horizontal pairs throughout the sheet.

368 Students and Ivey Hall, Lincoln College **369** **370** Maui Gas Drilling Platform

(Des A. P. Derrick. Litho Harrison)

1978 (26 Apr). *Land Resources and Centenary of Lincoln College of Agriculture. T* **368** *and similar vert designs. Multicoloured. P* 14½.

1164 10 c. Type **368** 15 10
1165 12 c. Sheep grazing 20 25
1166 15 c. Fertiliser ground spreading 20 30
1167 16 c. Agricultural Field Days 20 30
1168 20 c. Harvesting grain 25 40
1169 30 c. Dairy farming 40 70
1164/9 .. .. *Set of* 6 1·25 1·90

(Photo Harrison)

1978 (3 May–9 June). *Coil Stamps. P* 14½ × 14 (10 *c.*) *or* 14 × 13 (*others*).

1170 **369** 1 c. bright purple (9.6) 10 30
1171 2 c. bright orange (9.6) 10 30
1172 5 c. red-brown (9.6) 10 30
1173 10 c. bright blue 30 45
1170/3 .. .. *Set of* 4 45 1·25

(Des R. M. Conly. Litho Harrison)

1978 (7 June). *Resources of the Sea. T* **370** *and similar vert designs. Multicoloured. P* 13 × 14.

1174 12 c. Type **370** 20 15
1175 15 c. Trawler 30 25
1176 20 c. Map of 200 mile fishing limit 40 35
1177 23 c. Humpback Whale and Bottle-nosed Dolphins 50 40
1178 35 c. Kingfish, snapper, grouper and squid .. 75 75
1174/8 .. .. *Set of* 5 1·90 1·75

371 First Health Charity Stamp **372** "The Holy Family" (El Greco) **373** Sir Julius Vogel

(Des A. G. Mitchell. Litho Harrison)

1978 (2 Aug). *Health Stamps. Health Services Commemorations. T* **371** *and similar vert design. P* 13 × 14.

1179 10 c. + 2 c. black, red and gold 25 35
1180 12 c. + 2 c. multicoloured 25 40
MS1181 97 × 124 mm. Nos. 1179/80 × 3 .. .. 3·50 4·75

Designs and commemorations:—10 c. Type **371** (50th anniversary of health charity stamps); 12 c. Heart operation (National Heart Foundation).

(Des R. M. Conly. Photo Courvoisier)

1978 (4 Oct). *Christmas. T* **372** *and similar multicoloured designs. P* 11½.

1182 7 c. Type **372** 10 10
1183 16 c. All Saints' Church, Howick 25 30
1184 23 c. Beach scene 30 45
1182/4 .. .. *Set of* 3 60 70

(Des A. G. Mitchell. Litho J.W.)

1979 (7 Feb). *Statesmen. T* **373** *and similar vert designs in sepia and drab. P* 13 × 13½.

1185 10 c. Type **373** 30 55
a. Horiz strip of 3, Nos. 1185/7 90
1186 10 c. Sir George Grey 30 55
1187 10 c. Richard John Seddon 30 55
1185/7 .. .. *Set of* 3 90 1·50

Nos. 1185/7 were printed together, *se-tenant*, in horizontal strips of 3 throughout the sheet.

Nos. 1185/7 have matt, almost invisible gum.

374 Riverlands Cottage, Blenheim **375** Whangaroa Harbour

(Des P. Leitch. Litho Enschedé)

1979 (4 Apr). *Architecture* (1*st series*). *T* **374** *and similar horiz designs. P* 13½ × 13.

1188 10 c. black, new blue and deep blue 10 10
1189 12 c. black, pale green and bottle green .. 15 20
1190 15 c. black and grey 20 25
1191 20 c. black, yellow-brown and sepia 25 30
1188/91 .. .. *Set of* 4 65 80

Designs:—12 c. The Mission House, Waimate North; 15 c. "The Elms", Tauranga; 20 c. Provincial Council Buildings, Christchurch.

See also Nos. 1217/20 and 1262/5.

(Photo Heraclio Fournier)

1979 (6 June). *Small Harbours. T* **375** *and similar multicoloured designs. P* 13.

1192 15 c. Type **375** 20 10
1193 20 c. Kawau Island 25 30
1194 23 c. Akaroa Harbour (*vert*) 30 35
1195 35 c. Picton Harbour (*vert*) 45 50
1192/5 .. .. *Set of* 4 1·10 1·10

376 Children with Building Bricks

(Des W. Kelsall. Litho J.W.)

1979 (6 June). *International Year of the Child. P* 14.

1196 **376** 10 c. multicoloured 15 10

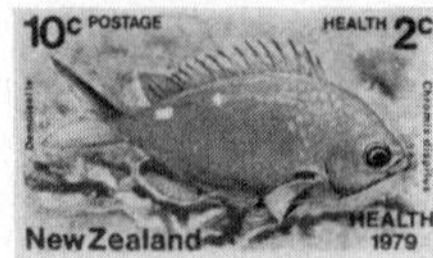

4c

377 Demoiselle (**378**)

(Des P. Blackie (12 c.), G. Fuller (others). Litho Harrison)

1979 (25 July). *Health Stamps. Marine Life. T* **377** *and similar multicoloured designs. P* 13 × 13½ (12 c.) *or* 13½ × 13 (*others*).
1197 10 c. + 2 c. Type **377** 40 50
a. Horiz pair. Nos. 1197/8 . . . . 80 1·00
1198 10 c. + 2 c. Sea Urchin 40 50
1199 12 c. + 2 c. Fish and underwater cameraman (*vert*) 40 50
1197/9 . . . . *Set of* 3 1·10 1·40
MS1200 144 × 72 mm. Nos. 1197/9, each × 2. P 14 × 14½ (12 c.) or 14½ × 14 (others) . . . . 4·00 5·50
Nos. 1197/8 were printed together, *se-tenant*, in horizontal pairs throughout the sheet.

1979 (31 Aug)–**80**. *Nos.* 1091a, 1092a, 1093a *and* 1094ab *surch as T* **378** *by Govt Printer, Wellington.*
1201 4 c. on 8 c. "Josephine Bruce" (24.9.79) . . 10 15
1202 14 c. on 10 c. Type **353** . . 40 20
a. Surch double, one albino . .
1203 17 c. on 6 c. "Cresset" (9.10.79) . . 40 60
1203*a* 20 c. on 7 c. "Michele Meilland" (29.9.80) . . 35 10
1201/3*a* . . *Set of* 4 1·10 85

379 "Madonna and Child" (sculpture by Ghiberti)

380 Chamber, House of Representatives

(Des D. Hatcher. Photo Courvoisier)

1979 (3 Oct). *Christmas. T* **379** *and similar vert designs. Multicoloured. P* 11½.
1204 10 c. Type **379** . . 15 10
1205 25 c. Christ Church, Russell . . 30 40
1206 35 c. Pohutukawa (tree) . . 40 55
1204/6 . . *Set of* 3 75 90

(Des D. Hatcher. Litho J.W.)

1979 (26 Nov). *25th Commonwealth Parliamentary Conference, Wellington. T* **380** *and similar vert designs. Multicoloured. P* 13½.
1207 14 c. Type **380** . . 15 10
1208 20 c. Mace and Black Rod . . 20 20
1209 30 c. Wall hanging from the "Beehive" . . 30 45
1207/9 . . *Set of* 3 60 60

381 1855 1d. Stamp

(Des D. Hatcher (14 c. (all designs)), R. Conly (others). Litho Harrison)

1980 (7 Feb). *Anniversaries and Events. T* **381** *and similar designs. P* 13½×13 (14 c. (*all designs*)) *or* 14 (*others*).
1210 14 c. black, brown-red and yellow . . 20 20
a. Horiz strip of 3. Nos. 1210/12 . . 60
ab. Black (inscription) omitted (*strip of* 3) . . £120
1211 14 c. black, deep turquoise-blue and yellow . . 20 20
1212 14 c. black, dull yellowish green and yellow . . 20 20
1213 17 c. multicoloured . . 20 25
1214 25 c. multicoloured . . 25 30
1215 30 c. multicoloured . . 25 35
1210/15 . . *Set of* 6 1·10 1·40
MS1216 146×96 mm. Nos. 1210/12 (as horiz strip). P 14½×14 (*sold at* 52 *c.*) . . 2·75 4·50
Designs and commemorations; (38 × 22 *mm*)—No. 1210, Type **381**; No. 1211, 1855 2d. stamp; No. 1212, 1855 1s. stamp (125th anniversary of New Zealand stamps). (40 × 23 *mm*)—No. 1213, Geyser, wood-carving and building (centenary of Rotorua (town)); No. 1214, *Earina autumnalis* and *thelymitra venosa* (International Orchid Conference, Auckland); No. 1215; Ploughing and Golden Plough Trophy (World Ploughing Championships, Christchurch).
The premium on No. **MS**1216 was used to help finance the "Zeapex 80" International Stamp Exhibition, Auckland.
Nos. 1210/12 were printed together, *se-tenant*, in horizontal strips of 3 throughout the sheet.

382 Ewelme Cottage, Parnell

383 Auckland Harbour

(Des P. Leitch. Litho Enschedé)

1980 (2 Apr). *Architecture (2nd series). T* **382** *and similar horiz designs. Multicoloured. P* 13½ × 12½.
1217 14 c. Type **382** . . 15 10
1218 17 c. Broadgreen, Nelson . . 25 30
1219 25 c. Courthouse, Oamaru . . 30 40
1220 30 c. Government Buildings, Wellington . . 35 45
1217/20 . . *Set of* 4 95 1·10

(Des D. Hatcher. Photo Heraclio Fournier)

1980 (4 June). *Large Harbours. T* **383** *and similar horiz designs. Multicoloured. P* 13.
1221 25 c. Type **383** . . 30 25
1222 30 c. Wellington Harbour . . 35 30
1223 35 c. Lyttelton Harbour . . 40 40
1224 50 c. Port Chalmers . . 65 65
1221/4 . . *Set of* 4 1·50 1·40

384 Surf-fishing

385 "Madonna and Child with Cherubim" (sculpture by Andrea della Robbia)

(Des Margaret Chapman. Litho Enschedé)

1980 (6 Aug). *Health Stamps. Fishing. T* **384** *and similar horiz designs. Multicoloured. P* 13 × 12½.
1225 14 c. + 2 c. Type **384** . . 45 55
a. Horiz pair. Nos. 1225/6 . . 90 1·10
1226 14 c. + 2 c. Wharf-fishing . . 45 55
1227 17 c. + 2 c. Spear-fishing . . 45 55
1225/7 . . *Set of* 3 1·25 1·50
MS1228 148 × 75 mm. Nos. 1225/7 each × 2. P 13½ × 13 . . 2·50 3·50
Nos. 1225/6 were printed together, *se-tenant*, in horizontal pairs throughout the sheet.

(Des P. Durrant. Photo Courvoisier)

1980 (1 Oct). *Christmas. T* **385** *and similar vert designs. Multicoloured. P* 11½.
1229 10 c. Type **385** . . 15 10
1230 25 c. St. Mary's Church, New Plymouth . . 25 25
1231 35 c. Picnic scene . . 40 45
1229/31 . . *Set of* 3 70 70

386 Te Heu Heu (chief)

387 Lt.-Col. the Hon W. H. A. Feilding and Borough of Feilding Crest

(Des R. Conly. Litho Heraclio Fournier)

1980 (26 Nov). *Maori Personalities. Vert designs as T* **386**. *Multicoloured. P* 12½ × 13.
1232 15 c. Type **386** . . 10 10
1233 25 c. Te Hau (chief) . . 15 10
1234 35 c. Te Puea (princess) . . 20 10
1235 45 c. Ngata (politician) . . 30 15
1236 60 c. Te Ata-O-Tu (warrior) . . 35 20
1232/6 . . *Set of* 5 1·00 50

(Des R. Conly. Litho Harrison)

1981 (4 Feb). *Commemorations. T* **387** *and similar horiz design. P* 14½.
1237 20 c. multicoloured . . 20 20
1238 25 c. black and brown-ochre . . 25 25
Designs and Commemorations:—20 c. Type **387** (Centenary of Feilding (town)); 25 c. I.Y.D. emblem and cupped hands (International Year of the Disabled).

388 The Family at Play

389 Kaiauai River

(Des A. Derrick. Litho J.W.)

1981 (1 Apr). *"Family Life." T* **388** *and similar vert designs. Multicoloured. P* 13½ × 13.
1239 20 c. Type **388** . . 20 10
1240 25 c. The family, young and old . . 25 25
1241 30 c. The family at home . . 30 30
1242 35 c. The family at church . . 35 40
1239/42 . . *Set of* 4 1·00 95

(Des D. Hatcher. Photo Heraclio Fournier)

1981 (3 June). *River Scenes. T* **389** *and similar multicoloured designs. P* 13½ × 13 (30, 35 c.) *or* 13 × 13½ (*others*).
1243 30 c. Type **389** . . 30 30
1244 35 c. Mangahao . . 40 40
1245 40 c. Shotover (*horiz*) . . 45 45
1246 60 c. Cleddau (*horiz*) . . 75 75
1243/6 . . *Set of* 4 1·75 1·75

390 St. Paul's Cathedral

391 Girl with Starfish

(Des and litho Harrison)

1981 (29 July). *Royal Wedding. T* **390** *and similar horiz design. Multicoloured. P* 14½.
1247 20 c. Type **390** . . 20 30
a. Pair. Nos. 1247/8 . . 40 60
ab. Deep grey (inscriptions and date) omitted £800
1248 20 c. Prince Charles and Lady Diana Spencer 20 30
Nos. 1247/8 were printed together, *se-tenant*, in horizontal and vertical pairs throughout the sheet.

(Des P.O. Litho Harrison)

1981 (5 Aug). *Health Stamps. Children playing by the Sea. T* **391** *and similar vert designs. Multicoloured. P* 14½.
1249 20 c. + 2 c. Type **391** . . 25 40
a. Horiz pair. Nos. 1249/50 . . 50 80
1250 20 c. + 2 c. Boy fishing . . 25 40
1251 25 c. + 2 c. Children exploring rock pool . . 25 30
1249/51 . . *Set of* 3 70 1·00
MS1252 100 × 125 mm. Nos. 1249/51, each × 2 . . 2·00 2·50
The 20 c. values were printed together, *se-tenant*, in horizontal pairs throughout the sheet, forming a composite design.
The stamps from No. **MS**1252 were printed together, *se-tenant*, in two horizontal strips of 3, each forming a composite design.

392 "Madonna Suckling the Child" (painting, d'Oggiono)

393 Tauranga Mission House

(Des Margaret Chapman. Photo Courvoisier)

1981 (7 Oct). *Christmas. T* **392** *and similar vert designs. Multicoloured. P* 11½.
1253 14 c. Type **392** . . 15 10
1254 30 c. St. John's Church, Wakefield . . 35 25
1255 40 c. Golden Tainui (flower) . . 45 35
1253/5 . . *Set of* 3 85 60

(Des A. Derrick. Litho Walsall)

1982 (3 Feb). *Commemorations. T* **393** *and similar vert designs. Multicoloured. P* 14½.
1256 20 c. Type **393** . . 25 10
a. Horiz pair. Nos. 1256/7 . . 50 60
1257 20 c. Water tower, Hawera . . 25 10
1258 25 c. Cat . . 35 35
1259 30 c. *Dunedin* (refrigerated sailing ship) . . 35 40
1260 35 c. Scientific research equipment . . 40 45
1256/60 . . *Set of* 5 1·40 1·60
Commemorations:—No. 1256, Centenary of Tauranga (town); No. 1257, Centenary of Hawera (town); No. 1258, Centenary of S.P.C.A. (Society for the Prevention of Cruelty to Animals in New Zealand); No. 1259, Centenary of Frozen Meat Exports; No. 1260, International Year of Science.
The 20 c. values were printed together, *se-tenant*, in horizontal pairs throughout the sheet.

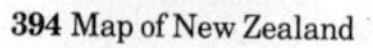

394 Map of New Zealand **395** Alberton, Auckland

(Des A. G. Mitchell. Litho Leigh-Mardon Ltd, Melbourne)

1982 (1 Apr–13 Dec). *P* 12½.
1261 **394** 24 c. pale yellowish green and ultram .. 20 10
a. Perf 14½ × 14 (13.12.82) .. 20 10

(Des P. Leitch. Litho Walsall)

1982 (7 Apr). *Architecture (3rd series). T* **395** *and similar horiz designs. Multicoloured. P* 14 × 14½.
1262 20 c. Type **395** 20 15
1263 25 c. Caccia Birch, Palmerston North .. 25 25
1264 30 c. Railway station, Dunedin 30 30
1265 35 c. Post Office, Ophir 35 40
1262/5 .. .. *Set of* 4 1·00 1·00

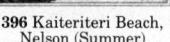

396 Kaiteriteri Beach, Nelson (Summer) **397** Labrador

(Des D. Hatcher. Photo Heraclio Fournier)

1982 (2 June). *"The Four Seasons". New Zealand Scenes. T* **396** *and similar horiz designs. Multicoloured. P* 13 × 13½.
1266 35 c. Type **396** 40 40
1267 40 c. St. Omer Park, Queenstown (Autumn) 45 45
1268 45 c. Mt Ngauruhoe, Tongariro National Park (Winter) 50 50
1269 70 c. Wairarapa farm (Spring) 75 75
1266/9 .. .. *Set of* 4 1·90 1·90

(Des R. Conly. Litho Enschedé)

1982 (4 Aug). *Health Stamps. Dogs. T* **397** *and similar vert designs. Multicoloured. P* 13 × 13½.
1270 24 c. + 2 c. Type **397** 65 70
a. Horiz pair. Nos. 1270/1 .. .. .. 1·25 1·40
1271 24 c. + 2 c. Border Collie 65 70
1272 30 c. + 2 c. Cocker Spaniel 65 70
1270/2 .. .. *Set of* 3 1·75 1·90
MS1273 98 × 125 mm. Nos. 1270/2, each × 2. P 14 × 13½ .. .. 3·50 3·75

The 24 c. values were printed together, *se-tenant*, in horizontal pairs throughout the sheet.

398 "Madonna with Child and Two Angels" (paintings by Piero di Cosimo)

(Des Margaret Chapman. Photo Heraclio Fournier)

1982 (6 Oct). *Christmas. T* **398** *and similar vert designs. Multicoloured. P* 14 × 13½.
1274 18 c. Type **398** 20 10
1275 35 c. Rangiatea Maori Church, Otaki .. 35 30
1276 45 c. Surf life-saving 50 40
1274/6 .. .. *Set of* 3 95 65

399 Nephrite **399a** Grapes

399b Kokako

(Des P. Durrant (Nos. 1277/82), D. Little (Nos. 1283/7), Janet Marshall (Nos. 1288/97). Litho Leigh-Mardon Ltd. Melbourne)

1982 (1 Dec)–**89**. *Multicoloured. P* 14½×14 (*Nos.* 1277/87) *or* 14½ (*Nos.* 1288/97).

(*a*) *Minerals. T* **399** *and similar vert designs*
1277 1 c. Type **399** 10 10
a. Perf 12½ 40 10
1278 2 c. Agate 10 10
a. Perf 12½ .. .. 1·00 75
1279 3 c. Iron Pyrites 10 10
1280 4 c. Amethyst 10 10
1281 5 c. Carnelian 10 10
1282 9 c. Native Sulphur 20 10

(*b*) *Fruits. T* **399a** *and similar vert designs*
1283 10 c. Type **399a** (7.12.83) 55 10
1284 20 c. Citrus Fruit (7.12.83) 35 10
1285 30 c. Nectarines (7.12.83) 30 10
1286 40 c. Apples (7.12.83) 35 10
1287 50 c. Kiwifruit (7.12.83) 40 10

(*c*) *Native Birds. T* **399b** *and similar vert designs*
1288 30 c. Kakapo (1.5.86) 50 25
1289 40 c. Mountain ("Blue") Duck (2.2.87) .. 60 35
1290 45 c. New Zealand Falcon (1.5.86) .. 1·00 35
1291 60 c. New Zealand Teal (2.2.87) .. .. 1·00 40
1292 $1 Type **399b** (24.4.85) .. .. .. 1·00 30
1293 $2 Chatham Island Robin (24.4.85) .. 1·40 50
1294 $3 Stitchbird (23.4.86) .. .. .. 1·75 1·40
1295 $4 Saddleback (23.4.86) .. .. .. 2·50 2·00
1296 $5 Takahe (20.4.88) .. .. 3·25 3·50
1297 $10 Little Spotted Kiwi (19.4.89) .. 5·75 6·00
1277/97 .. .. *Set of* 21 19·00 14·00
1292/7 Optd "Specimen" .. .. *Set of* 6 7·50

Nos. 1292/7 overprinted "Specimen" come from a special "NEW ZEALAND 1990" Presentation Pack issued on 19 April 1989.

A miniature sheet containing No. 1293 was only available from the New Zealand stand at "PHILEXFRANCE '89" International Stamp Exhibition or the Philatelic Bureau at Wanganui.

400 Old Arts Building, Auckland University **401** Queen Elizabeth II

(Des G. Emery (35 c.), P. Durrant (others). Litho Cambec Press, Melbourne (35 c.), J.W. (others))

1983 (2 Feb). *Commemorations. T* **400** *and similar vert designs. Multicoloured. P* 13 × 13½ (35 *c.*) *or* 14 × 13½ (*others*).
1303 24 c. Salvation Army Centenary logo .. 30 10
1304 30 c. Type **400** 40 35
1305 35 c. Stylised Kangaroo and Kiwi 45 35
1306 40 c. Rainbow Trout 50 45
1307 45 c. Satellite over Earth 55 50
1303/7 .. .. *Set of* 5 2·00 1·50

Commemorations:—24 c. Centenary of Salvation Army; 30 c. Centenary of Auckland University; 35 c. Closer Economic Relationship agreement with Australia; 40 c. Centenary of introduction of Rainbow Trout into New Zealand; 45 c. World Communications Year.

(Des P. Durrant. Litho Harrison)

1983 (14 Mar). *Commonwealth Day. T* **401** *and similar horiz designs. Multicoloured. P* 13½.
1308 24 c. Type **401** 20 10
1309 35 c. Maori rock drawing 30 40
1310 40 c. Woolmark and wool-scouring symbols .. 35 45
1311 45 c. Coat of arms 40 55
1308/11 .. .. *Set of* 4 1·10 1·40

402 "Boats, Island Bay" (Rita Angus) **403** Mt Egmont

(Des D. Hatcher. Litho Leigh-Mardon Ltd, Melbourne)

1983 (6 Apr). *Paintings by Rita Angus. T* **402** *and similar vert designs. Multicoloured. P* 14½.
1312 24 c. Type **402** 25 10
1313 30 c. "Central Otago Landscape" 30 45
1314 35 c. "Wanaka Landscape" 35 50
1315 45 c. "Tree" 45 70
1312/15 .. .. *Set of* 4 1·25 1·60

(Des P. Durrant. Photo Heraclio Fournier)

1983 (1 June). *Beautiful New Zealand. T* **403** *and similar multicoloured designs. P* 13.
1316 35 c. Type **403** 30 35
1317 40 c. Cooks Bay 35 40
1318 45 c. Lake Matheson (*horiz*) 40 45
1319 70 c. Lake Alexandrina (*horiz*) 65 70
1316/19 .. .. *Set of* 4 1·50 1·75

404 Tabby **405** "The Family of the Holy Oak Tree" (Raphael)

(Des R. Conly. Litho Harrison)

1983 (3 Aug). *Health Stamps. Cats. T* **404** *and similar vert designs. Multicoloured. P* 14.
1320 24 c. + 2 c. Type **404** 30 25
a. Horiz pair. Nos. 1320/1 .. .. .. 60 50
1321 24 c. + 2 c. Siamese 30 25
1322 30 c. + 2 c. Persian 50 30
1320/2 .. .. *Set of* 3 1·00 80
MS1323 100 × 126 mm. Nos. 1320/2, each × 2 .. 2·00 1·75

The 24 c. values were printed together, *se-tenant*, in horizontal pairs throughout the sheet.

(Des R. Conly (45 c.), M. Wyatt (others). Photo Courvoisier)

1983 (5 Oct). *Christmas. T* **405** *and similar vert designs. Multicoloured. P* 12 × 11½.
1324 18 c. Type **405** 10 10
1325 35 c. St. Patrick's Church, Greymouth .. 30 35
1326 45 c. "The Glory of Christmas" (star and flowers) 40 45
1324/6 .. .. *Set of* 3 75 75

406 Geology

(Des R. Conly. Litho Cambec Press, Melbourne)

1984 (1 Feb). *Antarctic Research. T* **406** *and similar horiz designs. Multicoloured. P* 13½ × 13.
1327 24 c. Type **406** 25 10
1328 40 c. Biology 35 40
1329 58 c. Glaciology 50 55
1330 70 c. Meteorology 60 70
1327/30 .. .. *Set of* 4 1·60 1·60
MS1331 126 × 110 mm. Nos. 1327/30 .. .. 1·75 3·00

407 *Mountaineer*, Lake Wakatipu **408** Mount Hutt

(Des M. Wyatt. Litho Cambec Press, Melbourne)

1984 (4 Apr). *New Zealand Ferry Boats. T* **407** *and similar horiz designs. Multicoloured. P* 13½ × 13.
1332 24 c. Type **407** 30 10
1333 40 c. *Waikana*, Otago 40 40
1334 58 c. *Britannia*, Waitemata 55 55
1335 70 c. *Wakatere*, Firth of Thames 65 65
1332/5 .. .. *Set of* 4 1·75 1·60

(Des D. Little. Litho Cambec Press, Melbourne)

1984 (6 June). *Ski-slope Scenery. T* **408** *and similar horiz designs. Multicoloured. P* 13½ × 13.
1336 35 c. Type **408** 40 40
1337 40 c. Coronet Park 45 45
1338 45 c. Turoa 50 50
1339 70 c. Whakapapa 75 75
1336/9 .. .. *Set of* 4 1·90 1·90

409 Hamilton's Frog

(Des A. G. Mitchell. Litho Cambec Press, Melbourne)

1984 (11 July). *Amphibians and Reptiles. T* **409** *and similar horiz designs. Multicoloured. P* 13½.
1340 24 c. Type **409** 30 30
a. Horiz pair. Nos. 1340/1 .. .. .. 60 60
1341 24 c. Great Barrier Skink 30 30
1342 30 c. Harlequin Gecko 35 35
1343 58 c. Otago Skink 70 70
1344 70 c. Gold-striped Gecko 75 75
1340/4 .. .. *Set of* 5 2·25 2·25

Nos. 1340/1 were printed together, *se-tenant*, in horizontal pairs throughout the sheet.

410 Clydesdales ploughing Field

(Des Margaret Chapman. Litho Harrison)

1984 (1 Aug). *Health Stamps. Horses. T* **410** *and similar horiz designs. Multicoloured. P* 14½.

1345	24 c. + 2 c. Type **410**	30	30
	a. Horiz pair. Nos. 1345/6	60	60
1346	24 c. + 2 c. Shetland ponies	30	30
1347	30 c. + 2 c. Thoroughbreds	45	35
1345/7	*Set of* 3	1·00	85
MS 1348	148 × 75 mm. Nos. 1345/7, each × 2	1·60	1·75

Nos. 1345/6 were printed together, *se-tenant*, in horizontal pairs throughout the sheet.

MACHINE LABELS. An automatic machine dispensing labels, ranging in value from 1 c. to $99.99, was installed at the Queen Street Post Office, Auckland, on 3 September 1984 for a trial period. The oblong designs, framed by simulated perforations at top and bottom and vertical rules at the sides, showed the "Southern Cross", face value and vertical column of six horizontal lines between the "NEW ZEALAND" and "POSTAGE" inscriptions. The trial period ended abruptly on 16 October 1984.

Similar labels, with the face value and inscriptions within a plain oblong, were introduced on 12 February 1986 and from 22 August 1988 they were printed on paper showing New Zealand flags. On 12 September 1990 the design printed on the paper was changed to show seaplanes.

411 "Adoration of the Shepherds" (Lorenzo di Credi)

(Des R. Conly (45 c.), P. Durrant (others). Photo Heraclio Fournier)

1984 (26 Sept). *Christmas. T* **411** *and similar multicoloured designs. P* 13½ × 14 *(18 c.) or* 14 × 13½ *(others).*

1349	18 c. Type **411**	20	10
1350	35 c. Old St. Paul's, Wellington (*vert*)	40	35
1351	45 c. "The Joy of Christmas" (*vert*)	50	45
1349/51	*Set of* 3	1·00	80

412 Mounted Riflemen, South Africa, 1901

(Des R. Conly. Litho Harrison)

1984 (7 Nov). *New Zealand Military History. T* **412** *and similar horiz designs. Multicoloured. P* 15 × 14.

1352	24 c. Type **412**	30	10
1353	40 c. Engineers, France, 1917	45	45
1354	58 c. Tanks of 2nd N.Z. Divisional Cavalry, North Africa, 1942	60	60
1355	70 c. Infantryman in jungle kit, and 25-pounder gun, Korea and South-East Asia, 1950–72	70	75
1352/5	*Set of* 4	1·90	1·75
MS1356	122 × 106 mm. Nos. 1352/5	1·75	1·90

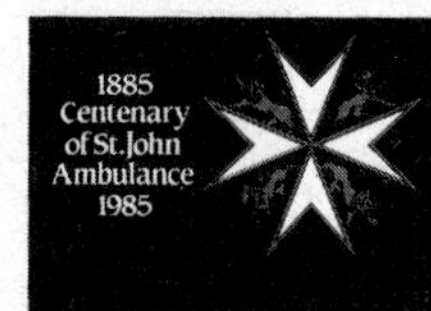

413 St. John Ambulance Badge

(Des Lindy Fisher. Litho J.W.)

1985 (16 Jan). *Centenary of St. John Ambulance in New Zealand. P* 14.

1357	**413**	24 c. black, gold and bright rosine	25	10
1358		30 c. black, sil & bright ultram	35	30
1359		40 c. black and grey	40	45
1357/9		*Set of* 3	90	75

The colours of the badge depicted are those for Bailiffs and Dames Grand Cross (24 c.), Knights and Dames of Grace (30 c.) and Serving Brothers and Sisters (40 c.).

MINIMUM PRICE

The minimum price quote is 10p which represents a handling charge rather than a basis for valuing common stamps. For further notes about prices see introductory pages.

414 Nelson Horse-drawn Tram, 1862 **415** Shotover Bridge

(Des. R. Conly. Litho Cambec Press, Melbourne)

1985 (6 Mar). *Vintage Trams. T* **414** *and similar horiz designs. Multicoloured. P* 13½.

1360	24 c. Type **414**	25	10
1361	30 c. Graham's Town steam tram, 1871	35	50
1362	35 c. Dunedin cable car, 1881	35	60
1363	40 c. Auckland electric tram, 1902	35	60
1364	45 c. Wellington electric tram, 1904	40	70
1365	58 c. Christchurch electric tram, 1905	50	1·10
1360/5	*Set of* 6	2·00	3·25

TARAPEX '86. To support this National Philatelic Exhibition the New Zealand Post Office co-operated with the organisers in the production of a set of "postage imprint labels". Five of the designs showed drawings of Maoris, taken from originals by Arthur Herbert Messenger and the sixth the Exhibition logo.

The sheetlets of 6 gummed and perforated labels were released by the Exhibition organisers on 3 April 1985. Although such labels were valid for postage, and could be so used by the general public, the sheetlets were not available from any New Zealand post office or from the Philatelic Bureau.

(Des R. Freeman. Photo Courvoisier)

1985 (12 June). *Bridges of New Zealand. T* **415** *and similar multicoloured designs. Granite paper. P* 11½.

1366	35 c. Type **415**	40	50
1367	40 c. Alexandra Bridge	45	55
1368	45 c. South Rangitikei Railway Bridge (*vert*)	50	65
1369	70 c. Twin Bridges (*vert*)	70	95
1366/9	*Set of* 4	1·90	2·40

416 Queen Elizabeth II (from photo by Camera Press) **417** Princess of Wales and Prince William

(Des B. Clinton. Litho Leigh-Mardon Ltd, Melbourne)

1985 (1 July). *Multicoloured, background colours given. P* 14½ × 14.

1370	**416**	25 c. rosine	50	10
1371		35 c. new blue	90	10

Examples of the 25 c. value exist with the orders on the sash omitted. These are believed to originate from unissued sheets sent for destruction in March 1986.

(Des D. Little. Litho Cambec Press, Melbourne)

1985 (31 July). *Health Stamps. T* **417** *and similar vert designs showing photographs by Lord Snowdon. Multicoloured. P* 13½.

1372	25 c. + 2 c. Type **417**	35	55
	a. Horiz pair. Nos. 1372/3	70	1·10
1373	25 c. + 2 c. Princess of Wales and Prince Henry	35	55
1374	35 c. + 2 c. Prince and Princess of Wales with Princes William and Henry	35	55
1372/4	*Set of* 3	95	1·50
MS1375	118 × 84 mm. Nos. 1372/4, each × 2	1·75	3·00

Nos. 1372/3 were printed together, *se-tenant*, in horizontal pairs throughout the sheet.

418 The Holy Family in the Stable **419** H.M.N.Z.S. *Philomel* (1914–47)

(Des Eileen Mayo. Photo Enschedé)

1985 (18 Sept). *Christmas. T* **418** *and similar vert designs. Multicoloured. P* 13½ × 12½.

1376	18 c. Type **418**	20	10
1377	40 c. The shepherds	40	75
1378	50 c. The angels	45	90
1376/8	*Set of* 3	95	1·60

Examples of the 18 c. and 50 c. stamps exist showing the spelling error "CRISTMAS". These are believed to originate from unissued sheets sent for destruction in March 1986. The New Zealand Post Office has stated that no such stamps were issued and that existing examples "were removed unlawfully during the destruction process".

(Des P. Durrant. Litho Cambec Press, Melbourne)

1985 (6 Nov). *New Zealand Naval History. T* **419** *and similar horiz designs. Multicoloured. P* 13½.

1379	25 c. Type **419**	60	15
1380	45 c. H.M.N.Z.S. *Achilles* (1936–46)	95	1·25
1381	60 c. H.M.N.Z.S. *Rotoiti* (1949–65)	1·25	1·50
1382	75 c. H.M.N.Z.S. *Canterbury* (from 1971)	1·50	1·75
1379/82	*Set of* 4	4·00	4·25
MS1383	124 × 108 mm. Nos. 1379/82	4·00	4·25

420 Police Computer Operator **421** Indian "Power Plus" 1000cc Motor Cycle (1920)

(Des A. Mitchell. Litho Leigh-Mardon Ltd, Melbourne)

1986 (15 Jan). *Centenary of New Zealand Police. T* **420** *and similar vert designs, each showing historical aspects above modern police activities. Multicoloured. P* 14½ × 14.

1384	25 c. Type **420**	35	50
	a. Horiz strip of 5. Nos. 1384/8	1·60	
1385	25 c. Detective and mobile control room	35	50
1386	25 c. Policewoman and badge	35	50
1387	25 c. Forensic scientist, patrol car and policeman with child	35	50
1388	25 c. Police College, Porirua, Patrol boat *Lady Elizabeth II* and dog handler	35	50
1384/8	*Set of* 5	1·60	2·25

Nos. 1384/8 were printed together, *se-tenant*, in horizontal strips of 5 throughout the sheet.

(Des M. Wyatt. Litho J.W.)

1986 (5 Mar). *Vintage Motor Cycles. T* **421** *and similar horiz designs. Multicoloured. P* 13 × 12½.

1389	35 c. Type **421**	40	30
1390	45 c. Norton "CS1" 500cc (1927)	50	45
1391	60 c. B.S.A. "Sloper" 500cc (1930)	65	65
1392	75 c. Triumph "Model H" 550cc (1915)	75	85
1389/92	*Set of* 4	2·10	2·00

422 Tree of Life **423** Knights Point

(Des Margaret Clarkson. Litho J.W.)

1986 (5 Mar). *International Peace Year. T* **422** *and similar horiz design. Multicoloured. P* 13 × 12½.

1393	25 c. Type **422**	30	30
	a. Horiz pair. Nos. 1393/4	60	60
1394	25 c. Peace dove	30	30

Nos. 1393/4 were printed together, *se-tenant*, in horizontal pairs throughout the sheet.

(Des P. Durrant. Photo Heraclio Fournier)

1986 (11 June). *Coastal Scenery. T* **423** *and similar horiz designs. Multicoloured. P* 14.

1395	55 c. Type **423**	55	45
1396	60 c. Becks Bay	55	45
1397	65 c. Doubtless Bay	60	50
1398	80 c. Wainui Bay	75	65
1395/8	*Set of* 4	2·25	1·90
MS1399	124 × 99 mm. No. 1398 (*sold at* $1.20)	85	90

The 40 c. premium on No. **MS**1399 was to support "New Zealand 1990" International Stamp Exhibition, Auckland.

No. **MS**1399 exists overprinted for "Stockholmia". Such miniature sheets were only available at this International Stamp Exhibition in Stockholm and were not placed on sale in New Zealand.

424 "Football" (Kylie Epapara) **425** "A Partridge in a Pear Tree"

(Litho Leigh-Mardon Ltd, Melbourne)

1986 (30 July). *Health Stamps. Children's Paintings (1st series). T* **424** *and similar multicoloured designs. P* 14½×14 (30 c.) *or* 14×14½ (45 c.).
1400 30 c. + 3 c. Type **424** 30 40
a. Horiz pair. Nos. 1400/1 .. .. 60 80
1401 30 c. + 3 c. "Children at Play" (Phillip Kata) 30 40
1402 45 c. + 3 c. "Children Skipping" (Mia Flannery) (*horiz*) 40 50
1400/2 .. .. *Set of* 3 90 1·10
MS1403 144×81 mm. Nos. 1400/2, each×2 .. 2·00 2·25
Nos. 1400/1 were printed together, *se-tenant*, in horizontal pairs throughout the sheet.
No. **MS**1403 exists overprinted for "Stockholmia". Such miniature sheets were only available at this International Stamp Exhibition in Stockholm and were not placed on sale in New Zealand.
See also Nos. 1433/6.

(Des Margaret Halcrow-Cross. Photo Heraclio Fournier)

1986 (17 Sept). *Christmas. "The Twelve Days of Christmas" (carol). T* **425** *and similar vert designs. Multicoloured. P* 14½.
1404 25 c. Type **425** 20 10
1405 55 c. "Two turtle doves" 45 45
1406 65 c. "Three French hens" 50 50
1404/6 .. .. *Set of* 3 1·00 95

426 Conductor and Orchestra

427 Jetboating

(Des R. Freeman. Litho Leigh-Mardon Ltd, Melbourne)

1986 (5 Nov). *Music in New Zealand. T* **426** *and similar vert designs. P* 14½×14.
1407 30 c. multicoloured 25 10
1408 60 c. black, new blue and yellow-orange .. 45 50
1409 80 c. multicoloured 70 75
1410 $1 multicoloured 80 85
1407/10 .. .. *Set of* 4 2·00 2·00
Designs:—60 c. Cornet and brass band; 80 c. Piper and Highland pipe band; $1 Guitar and country music group.

(Des M. Wyatt. Litho Leigh-Mardon Ltd, Melbourne)

1987 (14 Jan). *Tourism. T* **427** *and similar vert designs. Multicoloured. P* 14½×14.
1411 60 c. Type **427** 50 50
1412 70 c. Sightseeing flights 60 60
1413 80 c. Camping 70 75
1414 85 c. Windsurfing 70 75
1415 $1.05, Mountaineering .. .. 90 1·00
1416 $1.30, River rafting .. .. 1·10 1·25
1411/16 .. .. *Set of* 6 4·00 4·25

428 Southern Cross Cup

(Des R. Proud. Litho Leigh-Mardon Ltd, Melbourne)

1987 (2 Feb). *Yachting Events. T* **428** *and similar horiz designs showing yachts. Multicoloured. P* 14×14½.
1417 40 c. Type **428** 35 15
1418 80 c. Admiral's Cup 70 80
1419 $1.05, Kenwood Cup .. .. 85 1·25
1420 $1.30, America's Cup .. .. 1·10 1·40
1417/20 .. .. *Set of* 4 2·75 3·25

429 Hand writing Letter and Postal Transport

(Des Communication Arts Ltd. Litho C.P.E. Australia Ltd, Melbourne)

1987 (1 Apr). *New Zealand Post Ltd Vesting Day. T* **429** *and similar horiz design. Multicoloured. P* 13½.
1421 40 c. Type **429** 75 80
a. Horiz pair. Nos. 1421/2 .. .. .. 1·50 1·60
1422 40 c. Posting letter, train and mailbox .. 75 80
Nos. 1421/2 were printed together, *se-tenant*, in horizontal pairs throughout the sheet.

430 Avro "626" and Wigram Airfield, 1937

431 Urewera National Park and Fern Leaf

(Des P. Leitch. Litho Leigh-Mardon Ltd, Melbourne)

1987 (15 Apr). *50th Anniv of Royal New Zealand Air Force. T* **430** *and similar horiz designs. Multicoloured. P* 14×14½.
1423 40 c. Type **430** 35 15
1424 70 c. "P-40 Kittyhawk" over World War II Pacific airstrip 55 60
1425 80 c. Short "Sunderland" flying boat and Pacific lagoon 60 70
1426 85 c. A-4 "Skyhawk" and Mt Ruapehu .. 65 75
1423/6 .. .. *Set of* 4 2·00 2·00
MS1427 115×105 mm. Nos. 1423/6 .. .. 3·00 2·50
No. **MS**1427 overprinted on the selvedge with the "CAPEX" logo was only available from the New Zealand stand at this International Philatelic Exhibition in Toronto.

(Des Tracey Purkis. Litho Leigh-Mardon Ltd, Melbourne)

1987 (17 June). *Centenary of National Parks Movement. T* **431** *and similar vert designs. Multicoloured. P* 14½.
1428 70 c. Type **431** 70 55
1429 80 c. Mt Cook and buttercup 75 60
1430 85 c. Fiordland and pineapple shrub 80 65
1431 $1.30, Tongariro and tussock .. .. .. 1·40 95
1428/31 .. .. *Set of* 4 3·25 2·50
MS1432 123×99 mm. No. 1431 (*sold at* $1.70) .. 1·75 1·75
The 40 c. premium on No. **MS**1432 was to support "New Zealand 1990" International Stamp Exhibition, Auckland.
No. **MS**1432 overprinted on the selvedge with the "CAPEX" logo was only available from the New Zealand stand at this International Philatelic Exhibition in Toronto.

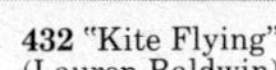

432 "Kite Flying" (Lauren Baldwin)

433 "Hark the Herald Angels Sing"

(Adapted D. Little. Litho Leigh-Mardon Ltd, Melbourne)

1987 (29 July). *Health Stamps. Children's Paintings (2nd series). T* **432** *and similar multicoloured designs. P* 14½.
1433 40 c. + 3 c. Type **432** 65 75
a. Horiz pair. Nos. 1433/4 .. .. 1·25 1·50
1434 40 c. + 3 c. "Swimming" (Ineke Schoneveld) 65 75
1435 60 c. + 3 c. "Horse Riding" (Aaron Tylee) (*vert*) .. .. 85 1·00
1433/5 .. .. *Set of* 3 2·00 2·25
MS1436 100×117 mm. Nos. 1433/5, each×2 .. 3·75 4·00
Nos. 1433/4 were printed together, *se-tenant*, in horizontal pairs throughout the sheet.

(Des Ellen Giggenbach. Litho Leigh-Mardon Ltd, Melbourne)

1987 (16 Sept). *Christmas. T* **433** *and similar vert designs. Multicoloured. P* 14½.
1437 35 c. Type **433** 40 10
1438 70 c. "Away in a Manger" 80 55
1439 85 c. "We Three Kings of Orient Are" .. 1·00 65
1437/9 .. .. *Set of* 3 2·00 1·25

434 Knot ("Pona")

435 "Geothermal"

(Des Nga Puna Waihanga. Litho Security Printers (M), Malaysia)

1987 (4 Nov). *Maori Fibre-work. T* **434** *and similar vert designs. Multicoloured. W* **138** *of Malaysia. P* 12.
1440 40 c. Type **434** 35 10
1441 60 c. Binding ("Herehere") 45 45
1442 80 c. Plait ("Whiri") 60 65
1443 85 c. Cloak weaving ("Korowai") with flax fibre ("Whitau") 65 70
1440/3 .. .. *Set of* 4 1·90 1·75

(Des Fay McAlpine. Litho Leigh-Mardon Ltd, Melbourne)

1988 (13 Jan). *Centenary of Electricity. T* **435** *and similar horiz designs, each showing radiating concentric circles representing energy generation. P* 14×14½.
1444 40 c. multicoloured 30 35
1445 60 c. black, rosine and brownish black .. 40 45
1446 70 c. multicoloured 50 55
1447 80 c. multicoloured 55 60
1444/7 .. .. *Set of* 4 1·60 1·75
Designs:—60 c. "Thermal"; 70 c. "Gas"; 80 c. "Hydro".

436 Queen Elizabeth II and 1882 Queen Victoria 1d. Stamp

437 "Mangopare"

(Des A. G. Mitchell (40 c.), M. Conly and M. Stanley ($1). Litho Leigh-Mardon Ltd, Melbourne)

1988 (13 Jan). *Centenary of Royal Philatelic Society of New Zealand. T* **436** *and similar multicoloured designs. P* 14×14½.
1448 40 c. Type **436** 35 40
a. Horiz pair. Nos. 1448/9 .. .. .. 70 80
1449 40 c. As Type **436**, but 1882 Queen Victoria 2d. 35 40
MS1450 107×160 mm. $1 "Queen Victoria" (Chalon) (*vert*). P 14½×14 .. .. .. 70 75
Nos. 1448/9 were printed together, *se-tenant*, in horizontal pairs throughout the sheet.
No. **MS**1450 overprinted on the selvedge with the "SYDPEX" logo was only available from the New Zealand stand at this International Philatelic Exhibition in Sydney and from the Philatelic Bureau at Wanganui.

(Des S. Adsett. Litho Leigh-Mardon Ltd, Melbourne)

1988 (2 Mar). *Maori Rafter Paintings. T* **437** *and similar vert designs. Multicoloured. P* 14½.
1451 40 c. Type **437** 40 40
1452 40 c. "Koru" 40 40
1453 40 c. "Raupunga" 40 40
1454 60 c. "Koiri" 55 65
1451/4 .. .. *Set of* 4 1·60 1·75

438 "Good Luck"

439 Paradise Shelduck

(Des Communication Arts Ltd. Litho CPE Australia Ltd, Melbourne)

1988 (18 May). *Greetings Booklet Stamps. T* **438** *and similar multicoloured designs. P* 13½.
1455 40 c. Type **438** 25 30
a. Booklet pane. Nos. 1455/9 .. .. 1·10
1456 40 c. "Keeping in touch" 25 30
1457 40 c. "Happy birthday" 25 30
1458 40 c. "Congratulations" (41×27 *mm*) .. 25 30
1459 40 c. "Get well soon" (41×27 *mm*) 25 30
1455/9 .. .. *Set of* 5 1·10 1·40
Nos. 1455/9 only exist from $2 stamp booklets.

(Des Pauline Morse. Litho Leigh-Mardon Ltd, Melbourne)

1988 (7 June)–**91**. *Native Birds. Multicoloured. P* 14½×14.
1459*a* 5 c. Spotless Crake (1.7.91) 10 10
1460 10 c. Banded Dotterel (2.11.88) 10 10
1461 20 c. Yellowhead (2.11.88) 10 15
1462 30 c. Silvereye (2.11.88) 20 25
1463 40 c. Brown Kiwi (2.11.88) 25 30
a. Perf 13½×13 (8.11.89) 80 80
ab. Pack pane. No. 1463a×10 with margins all round .. .. 8·00
1463*b* 45 c. Rock Wren (1.7.91) 30 35
ba Booklet pane. No. 1463*b*×10 with horiz sides of pane imperf (1.10.91) 3·00
1464 50 c. Kingfisher (2.11.88) 35 40
1465 60 c. Spotted Shag (2.11.88) 40 45
1466 70 c. Type **439** 45 50
1467 80 c. Fiordland Crested Penguin (2.11.88) 55 60
1468 90 c. South Island Robin (2.11.88) 60 65
1460/8 .. .. *Set of* 11 3·00 3·50
No. 1463a was only issued in panes of ten with margins on all four sides. These panes were initially included in "Stamp Pads" of 50 such panes, but subsequently appeared in $4 stamp packs.
No. 1463ba comes from the $4.50 "hanging" booklet.
A miniature sheet containing No. 1466 was only available from the New Zealand stand at "WORLD STAMP EXPO '89" International Stamp Exhibition or the Philatelic Bureau, Wanganui. It was subsequently overprinted with the "New Zealand 1990" emblem.

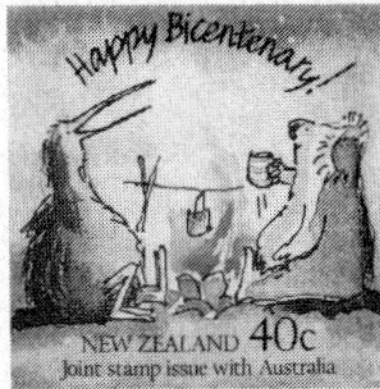

440 Milford Track

441 Kiwi and Koala at Campfire

(Des H. Thompson. Litho Leigh-Mardon Ltd, Melbourne)

1988 (8 June). *Scenic Walking Trails. T* **440** *and similar vert designs. Multicoloured. P* 14½.

1469 70 c. Type **440** 50 60
1470 80 c. Heaphy Track 55 70
1471 85 c. Copland Track 60 75
1472 $1.30, Routeburn Track .. .. .. 90 1·10
1469/72 .. .. *Set of* 4 2·25 2·75
MS1473 124 × 99 mm. No. 1472 (*sold at* $1.70) 1·50 1·50

The 40 c. premium on No. **MS**1473 was to support "New Zealand 1990" International Stamp Exhibition, Auckland.

(Des R. Harvey. Litho Leigh-Mardon Ltd, Melbourne)

1988 (21 June). *Bicentenary of Australian Settlement. P* 14½.

1474 **441** 40 c. multicoloured 45 35

A stamp in a similar design was also issued by Australia.

442 Swimming

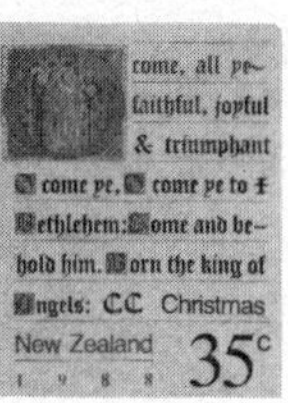

443 "O Come All Ye Faithful"

(Des R. Proud. Litho Leigh-Mardon Ltd, Melbourne)

1988 (27 July). *Health Stamps. Olympic Games, Seoul. T* **442** *and similar horiz designs. Multicoloured. P* 14½.

1475 40 c. + 3 c. Type **442** 35 45
1476 60 c. + 3 c. Athletics 50 65
1477 70 c. + 3 c. Canoeing 60 75
1478 80 c. + 3 c. Show-jumping 70 85
1475/8 .. .. *Set of* 4 1·90 2·40
MS1479 120 × 90 mm. Nos. 1475/8 .. .. 1·90 2·40

(Des Fay McAlpine. Litho Leigh-Mardon Ltd, Melbourne)

1988 (14 Sept). *Christmas. Carols. T* **443** *and similar vert designs, each showing illuminated verses. Multicoloured. P* 14½.

1480 35 c. Type **443** 30 30
1481 70 c. "Hark the Herald Angels Sing" .. 55 65
1482 80 c. "Ding Dong Merrily on High" .. 60 70
1483 85 c. "The First Nowell" 65 80
1480/3 .. .. *Set of* 4 1·90 2·25

444 "Lake Pukaki" (John Gully)

445 Brown Kiwi

(Litho Leigh-Mardon Ltd, Melbourne)

1988 (5 Oct). *New Zealand Heritage (1st issue). The Land. T* **444** *and similar horiz designs showing 19th-century paintings. Multicoloured. P* 14 × 14½.

1484 40 c. Type **444** 35 35
1485 60 c. "On the Grass Plain below Lake Arthur" (William Fox) 45 45
1486 70 c. "View of Auckland" (John Hoyte) .. 55 55
1487 80 c. "Mt. Egmont from the Southward" (Charles Heaphy) 60 60
1488 $1.05, "Anakiwa, Queen Charlotte Sound" (John Kinder) 80 80
1489 $1.30, "White Terraces, Lake Rotomahana" (Charles Barraud) 95 95
1484/9 .. .. *Set of* 6 3·25 3·25

See also Nos. 1505/10, 1524/9, 1541/6, 1548/53 and 1562/7.

(Des A. Mitchell. Eng. G. Prosser of B.A.B.N. Recess Leigh-Mardon Ltd, Melbourne)

1988 (19 Oct)–**91.** *P* 14½ (*and around design*).

1490 **445** $1 bronze-green .. .. .. 1·25 1·60
a. Booklet pane. No. 1490×6 .. 6·75
1490*b* $1 bright scarlet (17.4.91) 65 70

No. 1490 was only issued in $6 stamp booklets with the horizontal edges of the booklet pane imperforate. Each circular stamp was also separated by vertical perforations.

No. 1490*b* was printed in sheets of 24 (6×4).

446 Humpback Whale and Calf

447 Clover

(Des Lindy Fisher. Litho Govt Ptg Office, Wellington)

1988 (2 Nov). *Whales. T* **446** *and similar horiz designs. Multicoloured. P* 13½.

1491 60 c. Type **446** 70 55
1492 70 c. Killer Whales 85 65
1493 80 c. Southern Right Whale 90 70
1494 85 c. Blue Whale 95 75
1495 $1.05, Southern Bottlenose Whale and calf .. .. 1·25 90
1496 $1.30, Sperm Whale .. .. .. 1·40 1·10
1491/6 .. .. *Set of* 6 5·50 4·25

Although inscribed "ROSS DEPENDENCY" Nos. 1491/6 were available from post offices throughout New Zealand.

(Des Heather Arnold. Litho Leigh-Mardon Ltd, Melbourne)

1989 (18 Jan). *Wild Flowers. T* **447** *and similar horiz designs. Multicoloured. P* 14½.

1497 40 c. Type **447** 40 35
1498 60 c. Lotus 50 55
1499 70 c. Montbretia 60 65
1500 80 c. Wild Ginger 70 75
1497/1500 .. .. .. *Set of* 4 2·00 2·10

448 Katherine Mansfield

449 Moriori Man and Map of Chatham Islands

(Des A. G. Mitchell. Litho Harrison)

1989 (1 Mar). *New Zealand Authors. T* **448** *and similar vert designs. Multicoloured. P* 12½.

1501 40 c. Type **448** 30 35
1502 60 c. James K. Baxter 40 50
1503 70 c. Bruce Mason 50 60
1504 80 c. Ngaio Marsh 55 70
1501/4 .. .. *Set of* 4 1·60 1·90

(Des D. Gunson. Litho Leigh-Mardon Ltd, Melbourne)

1989 (17 May). *New Zealand Heritage (2nd issue). The People. T* **449** *and similar horiz designs. P* 14×14½.

1505 40 c. multicoloured 45 35
1506 60 c. orge-brn, brownish grey & reddish brn 60 70
1507 70 c. yellow-grn, brownish grey & dp olive 65 75
1508 80 c. bright greenish blue, brownish grey and deep dull blue 75 85
1509 $1.05, grey, brownish grey & grey-black 1·00 1·10
1510 $1.30, bright rose-red, brownish grey, and lake-brown .. .. .. 1·25 1·40
1505/10 .. .. *Set of* 6 4·25 4·50

Designs:—60 c. Gold prospector; 70 c. Settler ploughing; 80 c. Whaling; $1.05, Missionary preaching to Maoris; $1.30, Maori village.

450 White Pine (Kahikatea)

451 Duke and Duchess of York with Princess Beatrice

(Des D. Gunson. Litho Questa)

1989 (7 June). *Native Trees. T* **450** *and similar vert designs. Multicoloured. P* 14×14½.

1511 80 c. Type **450** 75 80
1512 85 c. Red Pine (Rimu) 80 85
1513 $1.05, Totara .. .. 1·00 1·10
1514 $1.30, Kauri .. .. 1·25 1·40
1511/14 .. .. *Set of* 4 3·50 3·75
MS1515 102×125 mm. No. 1514 (*sold at* $1.80) 1·75 1·75

The 50 c. premium on No. **MS**1515 was to support "New Zealand 1990" International Stamp Exhibition, Auckland.

(Des and litho Leigh-Mardon Ltd, Melbourne)

1989 (26 July). *Health Stamps. T* **451** *and similar vert designs. Multicoloured. P* 14½.

1516 40 c. + 3 c. Type **451** 50 55
a. Horiz pair. Nos. 1516/17 .. .. 1·00 1·10
1517 40 c. + 3 c. Duchess of York with Princess Beatrice 50 55
1518 80 c. + 3 c. Princess Beatrice .. .. 1·25 90
1516/18 .. .. *Set of* 3 1·40 1·10
MS1519 120×89 mm. Nos. 1516/18, each ×2 .. 5·50 4·25

Nos. 1516/17 were printed together, *se-tenant*, in horizontal pairs throughout the sheet.

No. **MS**1519 overprinted on the selvedge with the "WORLD STAMP EXPO '89" logo was only available from the New Zealand stand at this International Stamp Exhibition and from the Philatelic Bureau at Wanganui.

MINIMUM PRICE

The minimum price quote is 10p which represents a handling charge rather than a basis for valuing common stamps. For further notes about prices see introductory pages.

452 One Tree Hill, Auckland, through Bedroom Window

453 Windsurfing

(Des H. Chapman. Litho Leigh-Mardon Ltd, Melbourne)

1989 (13 Sept). *Christmas. T* **452** *and similar vert designs showing Star of Bethlehem. Multicoloured. P* 14½.

1520 35 c. Type **452** 35 30
1521 65 c. Shepherd and dog in mountain valley 65 70
1522 80 c. Star over harbour 85 90
1523 $1 Star over globe .. .. .. 1·25 1·40
1520/3 .. .. *Set of* 4 2·75 3·00

(Des M. Bailey. Litho Leigh-Mardon Ltd, Melbourne)

1989 (11 Oct). *New Zealand Heritage (3rd issue). The Sea. T* **453** *and similar horiz designs. Multicoloured. P* 14×14½.

1524 40 c. Type **453** 40 35
1525 60 c. Fishes of many species 60 70
1526 65 c. Marlin and game fishing launch .. 65 75
1527 80 c. Rowing boat and yachts in harbour .. 80 85
1528 $1 Coastal scene .. .. .. 1·00 1·10
1529 $1.50, Container ship and tug .. .. 1·50 1·60
1524/9 .. .. *Set of* 6 4·50 4·75

454 Games Logo

(Des Heather Arnold. Litho Leigh-Mardon Ltd, Melbourne)

1989 (8 Nov)–**90.** *14th Commonwealth Games. Auckland. T* **454** *and similar horiz designs. Multicoloured. P* 14½.

1530 40 c. Type **454** 40 35
1531 40 c. Goldie (games kiwi mascot) 40 35
1532 40 c. Gymnastics 40 35
1533 50 c. Weightlifting 50 55
1534 65 c. Swimming 65 70
1535 80 c. Cycling 80 90
1536 $1 Lawn bowling .. .. .. 1·00 1·25
1537 $1.80, Hurdling .. .. .. 1·75 1·90
1530/7 .. .. *Set of* 8 5·50 5·75
MS1538 Two sheets, each 105×92 mm. with different margin designs. (a) Nos. 1530/1 (horiz pair). (b) Nos. 1530/1 (vert pair) (24.1.90) *Set of 2 sheets* 1·10 1·25

455 Short "S.30" Empire Flying Boat and Boeing "747"

456 Chief Kawiti signing Treaty

(Des R. Proud. Litho Enschedé)

1990 (17 Jan). *50th Anniv of Air New Zealand. P* 13×14½.

1539 **455** 80 c. multicoloured .. .. .. 1·00 80

(Des A. G. Mitchell from painting by L. C. Mitchell. Litho Enschedé)

1990 (17 Jan). *150th Anniv of Treaty of Waitangi. Sheet 80×118 mm, containing T* **456** *and similar multicoloured design. P* 13½.

MS1540 40 c. Type **456**; 40 c. Chief Hone Heke (first signatory) and Lieut-Governor Hobson (*horiz*) 60 65

457 Maori Voyaging Canoe

458 *Thelymitra pulchella*

(Des G. Fuller. Litho Leigh-Mardon Ltd, Melbourne)

1990 (7 Mar). *New Zealand Heritage (4th issue). The Ships. T* **457** *and similar horiz designs. Multicoloured. P* 14×14½.

1541	40 c. Type **457**	55	35
1542	50 c. H.M.S. *Endeavour* (Cook), 1769	70	50
1543	60 c. *Tory* (barque), 1839	80	60
1544	80 c. *Crusader* (full-rigged immigrant ship), 1871	1·10	85
1545	$1 *Edwin Fox* (full-rigged immigrant ship), 1873	1·25	1·10
1546	$1.50, *Arawa* (steamer), 1884	2·00	1·75
1541/6	*Set of* 6	5·75	4·50

A miniature sheet containing No. 1542 was only available from the New Zealand stand at "Stamp World London '90" International Stamp Exhibition or from the Philatelic Bureau, Wanganui.

(Des Lindy Fisher. Litho Leigh-Mardon Ltd, Melbourne)

1990 (18 Apr). *"New Zealand 1990" International Stamp Exhibition, Auckland. Native Orchids. Sheet* 179×80 *mm. containing T* **458** *and similar vert designs. Multicoloured. P* 14½.

MS1547 40 c. Type **458**; 40 c. *Corybas macranthus*; 40 c. *Dendrobium cunninghamii*; 40 c. *Pterostylis banksii*; 80 c. *Aporostylis bifolia* (*sold at* $4.90) . . 4·25 4·25

The stamps in No. **MS**1547 form a composite design.

The $2.50 premium on No. **MS**1547 was used to support the Exhibition.

Miniature sheets as No. **MS**1547, but imperforate are from a limited printing distributed to those purchasing season tickets for the exhibition.

459 Grace Neill (social reformer) and Maternity Hospital, Wellington

460 Akaroa

(Des Elspeth Williamson. Litho Leigh-Mardon Ltd, Melbourne)

1990 (16 May). *New Zealand Heritage (5th issue). Famous New Zealanders. T* **459** *and similar horiz designs. Multicoloured. P* 14×14½.

1548	40 c. Type **459**	40	30
1549	50 c. Jean Batten (pilot) and Percival "Gull" aircraft	45	45
1550	60 c. Katherine Sheppard (suffragette) and 19th-century women	60	60
1551	80 c. Richard Pearse (inventor) and early flying machine	75	75
1552	$1 Lt.-Gen. Sir Bernard Freyberg and tank	95	95
1553	$1.50, Peter Buck (politician) and Maori pattern	1·25	1·40
1548/53	*Set of* 6	4·00	4·00

(Des Lindy Fisher. Litho Leigh-Mardon Ltd, Melbourne)

1990 (13 June). *150th Anniversary of European Settlements. T* **460** *and similar vert designs. Multicoloured. P* 14½.

1554	80 c. Type **460**	75	75
1555	$1 Wanganui	95	95
1556	$1.50, Wellington	1·40	1·40
1557	$1.80, Takapuna Beach, Auckland	1·60	1·60
1554/7	*Set of* 4	4·25	4·25
MS1558	125×100 mm. No. 1557 (*sold at* $2.30)	3·25	3·50

The 50 c. premium on No. **MS**1558 was to support "New Zealand 1990" International Stamp Exhibition, Auckland.

461 Jack Lovelock (athlete) and Race

462 Creation Legend of Rangi and Papa

(Des T. Crilley. Litho Questa)

1990 (25 July). *Health Stamps. Sportsmen. T* **461** *and similar horiz design. Multicoloured. P* 14½×13½.

1559	40 c. + 5 c. Type **461**	50	50
1560	80 c. + 5 c. George Nepia (rugby player) and match	75	75
MS1561	115×96 mm. Nos. 1559/60, each × 2	2·25	2·25

(Des K. Hall. Litho Leigh-Mardon Ltd, Melbourne)

1990 (24 Aug). *New Zealand Heritage (6th issue). The Maori. T* **462** *and similar horiz designs. Multicoloured. P* 14×14½.

1562	40 c. Type **462**	40	30
	a. Violet-blue (face value) omitted		
1563	50 c. Pattern from Maori feather cloak	55	50
1564	60 c. Maori women's choir	60	60
1565	80 c. Maori facial tattoos	75	75
1566	$1 War canoe prow (detail)	90	95
1567	$1.50, Maori haka	1·40	1·50
1562/7	*Set of* 6	4·25	4·25

463 Queen Victoria

464 Angel

(Des A. G. Mitchell. Recess Leigh-Mardon Ltd, Melbourne)

1990 (29 Aug). *150th Anniv of the Penny Black. Sheet* 169×70 *mm containing T* **463** *and similar vert designs. P* 14½×14.

MS1568 40 c.×6 indigo (Type **463**, King Edward VII, King George V, King Edward VIII, King George VI, Queen Elizabeth II) . . 1·90 1·90

(Des Sally Simons. Litho Leigh-Mardon Ltd, Melbourne)

1990 (12 Sept). *Christmas. T* **464** *and similar vert designs showing angels. P* 14½.

1569	40 c. purple, dp greenish bl & dp yellow-brn	40	30
1570	$1 purple, blue-green & dp yellow-brown	80	80
1571	$1.50, pur, brt crimson & dp yellow-brn	1·40	1·60
1572	$1.80, purple, red and deep yellow-brown	1·60	1·75
1569/72	*Set of* 4	3·75	4·00

465 Antarctic Petrel

466 Coopworth Ewe and Lambs

(Des Janet Luxton. Litho Heraclio Fournier)

1990 (7 Nov). *Antarctic Birds. T* **465** *and similar vert designs. Multicoloured. P* 13½×13.

1573	40 c. Type **465**	40	30
1574	50 c. Wilson's Petrel	50	50
1575	60 c. Snow Petrel	60	60
1576	80 c. Fulmar	75	75
1577	$1 Chinstrap Penguin	85	85
1578	$1.50, Emperor Penguin	1·40	1·50
1573/8	*Set of* 6	4·00	4·00

Although inscribed "Ross Dependency" Nos. 1573/8 were available from post offices throughout New Zealand.

(Des Lindy Fisher. Litho Leigh-Mardon Ltd, Melbourne)

1991 (23 Jan). *New Zealand Farming and Agriculture. Sheep Breeds. T* **466** *and similar vert designs. Multicoloured. P* 14½×14.

1579	40 c. Type **466**	40	30
1580	60 c. Perendale	55	55
1581	80 c. Corriedale	70	70
1582	$1 Drysdale	85	85
1583	$1.50, South Suffolk	1·25	1·25
1584	$1.80, Romney	1·50	1·60
1579/84	*Set of* 6	4·75	4·75

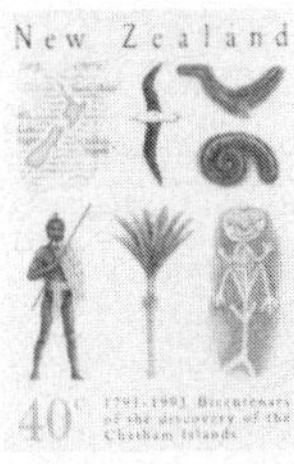

467 Moriori, Royal Albatross, Nikau Palm and Artefacts

468 Goal and Footballers

(Des K. Hall. Litho Southern Colour Print Ltd, Dunedin)

1991 (6 Mar). *Bicentenary of Discovery of Chatham Islands. T* **467** *and similar vert design. Multicoloured. P* 13½.

1585	40 c. Type **467**	40	40
1586	80 c. Carvings, H.M.S. *Chatham*, Moriori house of 1870, and Tommy Solomon	70	70

(Des T. Crilley. Litho Southern Colour Print Ltd, Dunedin)

1991 (6 Mar). *Centenary of New Zealand Football Association. T* **468** *and similar horiz design. Multicoloured. P* 13½.

1587	80 c. Type **468**	75	75
	a. Horiz pair. Nos. 1587/8	1·50	1·50
1588	80 c. Five footballers and referee	75	75

Nos. 1587/8 were printed together, *se-tenant*, in horizontal pairs throughout the sheet, each pair forming a composite design.

(Des Pauline Morse. Litho Printset, Australia)

1991 (17 Apr–1 July). *As Nos.* 1463/*b*, *but self-adhesive. P* 11½.

1589	40 c. Brown Kiwi	25	30
1589*a*	45 c. Rock Wren (1.7.91)	30	35

Nos. 1589/*a* were only available in coils of 100, each stamp, with die-cut perforations, being separate on the imperforate backing paper. The 45 c. shows the surplus surface paper removed.

A limited quantity of the 45 c. in sheets of 200 (8×25) was produced for use on official first day covers. It is reported that a small number of such sheets were subsequently sold by the Philatelic Bureau.

469 Tuatara on Rocks

470 Clown

(Des Pauline Morse. Litho Leigh-Mardon Ltd, Melbourne)

1991 (17 Apr). *Endangered Species. The Tuatara. T* **469** *and similar horiz designs. Multicoloured. P* 14½.

1590	40 c. Type **469**	40	45
1591	40 c. Tuatara in crevice	40	45
1592	40 c. Tuatara with foliage	40	45
1593	40 c. Tuatara in dead leaves	40	45
1590/3	*Set of* 4	1·40	1·60

(Des Helen Crawford. Litho Leigh-Mardon Ltd, Melbourne)

1991 (15 May–1 July). *Booklet Stamps. "Happy Birthday". T* **470** *and similar multicoloured designs. P* 13½.

1594	40 c. Type **470**	25	30
	a. Booklet pane. Nos. 1594/8	1·25	
1595	40 c. Balloons	25	30
1596	40 c. Party hat	25	30
1597	40 c. Birthday present (41×27 *mm*)	25	30
1598	40 c. Birthday cake (41×27 *mm*)	25	30
1599	45 c. Type **470**	30	35
	a. Booklet pane. Nos. 1599/1603	1·50	
1600	45 c. As No. 1595 (1 July)	30	35
1601	45 c. As No. 1596 (1 July)	30	35
1602	45 c. As No. 1597 (1 July)	30	35
1603	45 c. As No. 1598 (1 July)	30	35
1594/1603	*Set of* 10	2·50	3·00

The above were only issued in $2 (Nos. 1594/8) or $2.25 (Nos. 1599/603) stamp booklets.

471 Cat at Window

472 Punakaiki Rocks

(Des Jennifer Lautusi. Litho Leigh-Mardon Ltd, Melbourne)

1991 (15 May–1 July). *Booklet Stamps. "Thinking of You". T* **471** *and similar multicoloured designs. P* 13½.

1604	40 c. Type **471**	25	30
	a. Booklet pane. Nos. 1604/8	1·25	
1605	40 c. Cat playing with slippers	25	30
1606	40 c. Cat with alarm clock	25	30
1607	40 c. Cat in window (41×27 *mm*)	25	30
1608	40 c. Cat at door (41×27 *mm*)	25	30
1609	45 c. Type **471** (1 July)	30	35
	a. Booklet pane. Nos. 1609/13	1·50	
1610	45 c. As No. 1605 (1 July)	30	35
1611	45 c. As No. 1606 (1 July)	30	35
1612	45 c. As No. 1607 (1 July)	30	35
1613	45 c. As No. 1608 (1 July)	30	35
1604/13	*Set of* 10	2·50	3·00

The above were only issued in $2 (Nos. 1604/8) or $2.25 (Nos. 1609/13) stamp booklets.

(Des H. Thompson. Litho Leigh-Mardon Ltd, Melbourne)

1991 (12 June). *Scenic Landmarks. T* **472** *and similar horiz designs. Multicoloured. P* 14½.

1614	40 c. Type **472**	35	30
1615	50 c. Moeraki Boulders	50	45
1616	80 c. Organ Pipes	75	75
1617	$1 Castle Hill	85	85
1618	$1.50, Te Kaukau Point	1·40	1·50
1619	$1.80, Ahuriri River Clay Cliffs	1·60	1·75
1614/19	*Set of* 6	5·00	5·00

473 Dolphins Underwater

474 Children's Rugby

(Des Heather Arnold. Litho Leigh-Mardon Ltd, Melbourne)

1991 (24 July). *Health Stamps. Hector's Dolphin. T* **473** *and similar horiz design. Multicoloured. P* 14½.

1620 45 c. + 5 c. Type **473** 45 50
1621 80 c. + 5 c. Dolphins leaping 80 90
MS1622 115×100 mm. Nos. 1620/1, each × 2 2·50 2·75

(Des A.G. Mitchell. Litho Leigh-Mardon Ltd, Melbourne)

1991 (21 Aug). *World Cup Rugby Championship. T* **474** *and similar vert designs. Multicoloured. P* 14½×14.

1623 80 c. Type **474** 75 75
1624 $1 Women's rugby 85 85
1625 $1.50, Senior rugby .. .. .. 1·40 1·40
1626 $1.80, "All Blacks" (national team) .. 1·60 1·60
1623/6 .. .. *Set of* 4 4·25 4·25
MS1627 113×90 mm. No. 1626 (*sold at* $2.40) 2·00 2·25

No. **MS**1627 additionaly inscribed "PHILANIPPON '91" was available, at $1.80, from the New Zealand stand at this International Stamp Exhibition in Tokyo and from the Philatelic Bureau at Wanganui.

475 Three Shepherds

476 *Dodonidia helmsii*

(Des Designworks Communications. Litho Southern Colour Print, Dunedin)

1991 (18 Sept). *Christmas. T* **475** *and similar vert designs. Multicoloured. P* 13½.

1628 45 c. Type **475** 45 45
a. Block of four. Nos 1628/31 .. .. 1·60
1629 45 c. Two Kings on camels 45 45
1630 45 c. Mary and Baby Jesus 45 45
1631 45 c. King with gift 45 45
1632 65 c. Star of Bethlehem 60 60
1633 $1 Crown 85 85
1634 $1.50, Angel .. .. 1·40 1·40
1628/34 .. .. *Set of* 7 4·00 4·00

Nos. 1628/31 were printed together, *se-tenant,* in blocks of four throughout the sheet.

(Des Pauline Morse. Litho Leigh-Mardon Ltd, Melbourne)

1991 (6 Nov). *Butterflies. T* **476** *and similar vert designs. Multicoloured. P* 14½.

1635 $1 Type **476** 65 70
1636 $2 *Zizina otis oxleyi* .. .. .. 1·25 1·40
1637 $3 *Vanessa itea* .. .. .. 2·00 2·10
1635/7 .. .. *Set of* 3 3·50 3·75

A miniature sheet containing No. 1637 was only available from the New Zealand stand at "PHILANIPPON '91" International Stamp Exhibition, Tokyo, or the Philatelic Bureau, Wanganui.

479 Yacht *Kiwi Magic,* 1987

480 *Heemskerk*

(Des R. Proud. Litho Leigh-Mardon Ltd, Melbourne)

1992 (22 Jan). *New Zealand Challenge for America's Cup. T* **479** *and similar horiz designs. Multicoloured. P* 14.

1655 45 c. Type **479** 30 35
1656 80 c. Yacht *New Zealand,* 1988 .. .. 55 60
1657 $1 Yacht *America,* 1851 .. .. 65 70
1658 $1.50, Yacht *New Zealand,* 1992 .. 1·00 1·25
1655/8 .. .. *Set of* 4 2·25 2·50

(Des G. Fuller. Litho Enschedé)

1992 (12 Mar). *Great Voyages of Discovery. T* **480** *and similar horiz designs. Multicoloured. P* 13×14½.

1659 45 c. Type **480** 30 35
1660 80 c. *Zeehan* 55 60
1661 $1 *Santa Maria* 65 70
1662 $1.50, *Pinta* and *Nina* .. .. .. 1·00 1·10
1659/62 .. .. *Set of* 4 2·25 2·50

Nos. 1659/60 commemorate the 350th anniversary of Tasman's discovery of New Zealand and Nos. 1661/2 the 500th anniversary of discovery of America by Columbus.

481 Sprinters

482 Weddell Seal and Pup

(Des Sheryl McCammon. Litho Southern Colour Print, Dunedin)

1992 (3 Apr). *Olympic Games, Barcelona. P* 13½.

1663 **481** 45 c. multicoloured 30 35

(Des Lindy Fisher. Litho Southern Colour Print, Dunedin)

1992 (8 Apr). *Antarctic Seals. T* **482** *and similar horiz designs. Multicoloured. P* 13½.

1664 45 c. Type **482** 30 35
1665 50 c. Crabeater Seals swimming 35 40
1666 65 c. Leopard Seal and penguins 45 50
1667 80 c. Ross Seal 55 60
1668 $1 Southern Elephant Seal and harem 65 70
1669 $1.80, Hooker's Sea Lion and pup .. 1·25 1·50
1664/9 .. .. *Set of* 6 3·25 3·75

Although inscribed "Ross Dependency" Nos. 1664/9 were available from post offices throughout New Zealand.

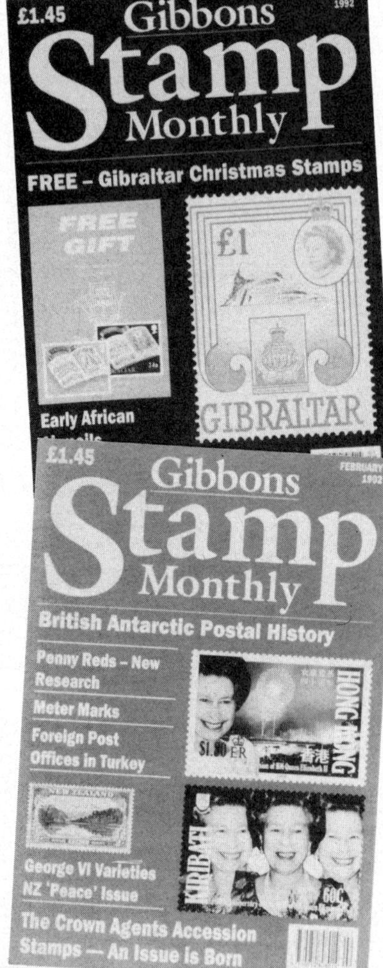

Index to New Zealand Stamp Designs from 1946

The following index is intended to facilitate the identification of all New Zealand stamps from 1946 onwards. Portrait stamps are usually listed under surnames only, views under the name of the town or city and other issues under the main subject or a prominent word and date chosen from the inscription. Simple abbreviations have occasionally been resorted to and when the same design or subject appears on more than one stamp, only the first of each series is indicated.

EXPRESS DELIVERY STAMPS

E 1

(Typo Govt Printing Office, Wellington)

1903 (9 Feb). *Value in first colour. W 43 (sideways). P 11.*
E1 E 1 6d. red and violet .. .. .. 32·00 20·00

1926–36. *Thick, white, opaque chalk-surfaced "Cowan" paper.* **W 43.**
(*a*) *P 14 × 14½*
E2 E 1 6d. vermilion and bright violet .. 35·00 18·00
(*b*) *P 14 × 15* (1936)
E3 E 1 6d. carmine and bright violet .. .. 32·00 45·00

1937–39. *Thin, hard, chalk-surfaced "Wiggins Teape" paper.*
(*a*) *P 14 × 14½*
E4 E 1 6d. carmine and bright violet .. .. 60·00 35·00
(*b*) *P 14 × 15* (1939)
E5 E 1 6d. vermilion and bright violet .. 85·00 85·00

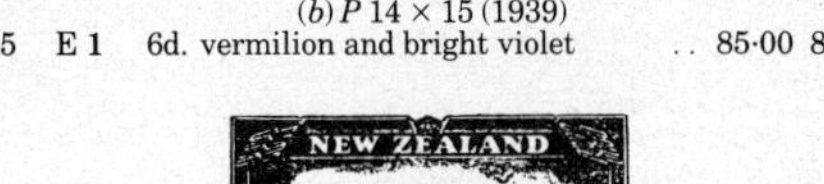

E 2 Express Mail Delivery Van

(Des J. Berry. Eng Stamp Ptg Office, Melbourne Recess Govt Ptg Office, Wellington)

1939 (16 Aug). **W 43.** *P 14.*
E6 E 2 6d. violet .. .. 1·50 1·75

POSTAGE DUE STAMPS

D 1

(I)

(II)

3D. (*a*) Large "D"

5D. (*b*) Small "D"

(Typo Govt Printing Office, Wellington)

1899 (1 Dec). **W 12*b*.** *Coarse paper. P 11.*

I. Type I. *Circle of 14 ornaments, 17 dots over "N.Z.", "N.Z." large.*
(*a*) *Large "D"*
D1 D 1 ½d. carmine and green .. .. 12·00 24·00
a. No stop after "D" (Right pane R. 2/3) 80·00 £130
D2 8d. carmine and green .. .. 60·00 75·00
D3 1s. carmine and green .. .. 65·00 60·00
D4 2s. carmine and green £110 £130
D1/4 .. .. *Set of* 4 £225 £250

To avoid further subdivision the 1s. and 2s. are placed with the pence values, although the two types of "D" do not apply to the higher values.

(*b*) *Small "D"*
D6 D 1 5d. carmine and green .. .. .. 19·00 18·00
D7 6d. carmine and green .. .. .. 22·00 18·00
D8 10d. carmine and green .. .. .. 70·00 80·00
D6/8 .. .. *Set of* 3 £100 £100

II. Type II. *Circle of 13 ornaments, 15 dots over "N.Z.", "N.Z." small.*
(*a*) *Large "D"*
D 9 D 1 ½d. vermilion and green .. .. 2·50 14·00
a. No stop after "D" (Right pane R. 2/3) .. .. .. 50·00 85·00
D10 1d. vermilion and green .. .. 8·50 1·00
D11 2d. vermilion and green .. .. 48·00 9·00
D12 3d. vermilion and green .. .. 12·00 3·50
D9/12 .. .. *Set of* 4 65·00 23·00

(*b*) *Small "D"*
D14 D 1 1d. vermilion and green .. .. 13·00 1·50
D15 2d. vermilion and green .. .. 28·00 4·75
D16 4d. vermilion and green .. .. 26·00 9·00
D14/16 .. .. *Set of* 3 60·00 14·00

Nos. D9/16 were printed from a common frame plate of 240 (4 panes of 60) used in conjunction with centre plates of 120 (2 panes of 60) for the ½d. and 4d. or 240 for the other values. Sheets of the 1d. and 2d. each contained two panes with large "D" and two panes with small "D".

D 2

D 3

(Des W. R. Bock. Typo Govt Printing Office)

1902 (28 Feb). *No wmk. P 11.*
D17 D 2 ½d. red and deep green .. .. 1·00 6·00

1904–08. *"Cowan" unsurfaced paper.* **W 43** *(sideways).* (*a*) *P 11.*
D18 D 2 ½d. red and green (4.04) .. .. 1·50 1·50
a. Imperf between (horiz pair) .. £600
D19 1d. red and green (5.12.05) .. .. 8·50 3·25
D20 2d. red and green (5.4.06) .. .. 90·00 90·00
D18/20 .. .. *Set of* 3 90·00 90·00

(*b*) *P 14*
D21 D 2 1d. carmine and green (12.06) .. 11·00 1·00
a. Rose-pink and green (9.07) .. 10·00 1·00
D22 2d. carmine and green (10.06) .. 8·50 4·50
a. Rose-pink and green (6.08) .. 4·75 1·00

1919 (Jan)–**20.** *"De La Rue" chalky paper. Toned gum.* **W 43.** *P 14 × 15.*
D23 D 2 ½d. carmine and green (6.19).. .. 3·25 2·50
D24 1d. carmine and green .. .. 4·50 30
D25 2d. carmine and green (8.20).. .. 8·00 2·50
D23/5 .. .. *Set of* 3 14·00 4·75

1925 (May). *"Jones" chalky paper. White gum.* **W 43.** *P 14 × 15.*
D26 D 2 ½d. carmine and green .. .. 35·00 35·00

1925 (July). *No wmk, but bluish "N Z" and Star lithographed on back. P 14 × 15.*
D27 D 2 ½d. carmine and green .. .. 1·75 18·00
D28 2d. carmine and green .. .. 2·75 14·00

1925 (Nov)–**35.** *"Cowan" thick, opaque chalky paper.* **W 43.**
(*a*) *P 14 × 15*
D29 D 2 ½d. carmine and green (12.26) .. 1·75 7·50
D30 1d. carmine and green .. .. 3·25 80
D31 2d. carmine and green (6.26).. .. 16·00 3·75
D32 3d. carmine and green (6.35).. .. 45·00 50·00
D29/32 .. .. *Set of* 4 60·00 55·00
(*b*) *P 14*
D33 D 2 ½d. carmine and green (10.28) .. .. 24·00 27·00
D34 1d. rose and pale yellow-green (6.28) .. 3·50 1·00
D35 2d. carmine and green (10.29) .. .. 7·00 2·50
D36 3d. carmine and green (5.28) .. .. 15·00 38·00
D33/6 .. .. *Set of* 4 45·00 60·00

1937–38. *"Wiggins Teape" thin, hard chalky paper.* **W 43.** *P 14 × 15.*
D37 D 2 ½d. carmine and yellow-green (2.38) .. 15·00 27·00
D38 1d. carmine and yellow-green (1.37) .. 10·00 3·75
D39 2d. carmine and yellow-green (6.37) .. 18·00 8·00
D40 3d. carmine and yellow-green (11.37) 65·00 50·00
D37/40 .. .. *Set of* 4 95·00 80·00

(Des J. Berry. Typo Govt Printing Office, Wellington)

1939–49. *P 15 × 14.* (*a*) **W 43** *(sideways)* (16.8.39).
D41 D 3 ½d. turquoise-green .. .. .. 3·25 4·00
D42 1d. carmine .. .. .. 1·25 30
D43 2d. bright blue .. .. .. 4·50 2·75
D44 3d. orange-brown .. .. .. 13·00 20·00
D41/4 .. .. *Set of* 4 20·00 24·00
(*b*) **W 98** *sideways*
D45 D 3 1d. carmine (4.49) .. .. .. 4·50 4·50*
D46 2d. bright blue (12.46) .. .. 1·00 80
D47 3d. orange-brown (6.45) .. .. 4·00 5·00
a. Wmk upright (1943) .. .. 35·00 30·00
D45/6 .. .. *Set of* 3 8·50 9·25*

*The use of Postage Due stamps ceased in 1951, our used price for No. D45 being for stamps postmarked after this date (*price for examples clearly cancelled* 1949–51, £25).

OFFICIAL STAMPS

1891 (Dec)–**1906.** *Contemporary issues handstamped "O.P.S.O." diagonally.* (*a*) *Stamps of* 1873 *type.* **W 12*b*.** *P 12½.*
O 1 3 ½d. rose (V.) .. .. — £450
(*b*) *Stamps of 1882–97 optd in rose or magenta.* **W 12*b*.**
O 2 13 ½d. black (*p* 10).. .. .. .. — £170
a. Violet opt .. .. .. — £200
O 3 ½d. black (*p* 10 × 11) .. .. .. — £170
O 4 14 1d. rose (*p* 12 × 11½) .. .. .. — £180
O 5 1d. rose (*p* 11) .. .. — £180
O 6 15 2d. purple (*p* 11) .. .. .. — £325
O 7 2d. mauve-lilac (*p* 10) .. .. .. — £325
a. Violet opt
O 8 16 2½d. blue (*p* 11) .. .. — £225
O 9 2½d. ultramarine (*p* 10) .. .. .. — £225
O10 2½d. ultramarine (*p* 10 × 11) .. .. — £225
O11 19 5d. olive-black (*p* 12 × 11½) .. .. — £375
O12 20 6d. brown (*p* 12 × 11½) .. .. .. — £475
(*c*) *Stamps of 1898–1903 optd in violet. P 11.* (i) *No wmk*
O13 23 ½d. green (*p* 14) (No. 294) .. .. — £160
O14 26 2½d. blue (*p* 12–16) (No. 249*a*).. .. — £400
O15 27 2½d. blue (No. 260) .. .. .. — £325
O16 37 4d. indigo and brown (No. 262) .. .. — £375
O17 30 5d. purple-brown (No. 263) .. .. — £400
a. Green opt .. .. .. — £375
O18 32 8d. indigo (No. 266) .. .. .. — £450
(ii) **W 38**
O19 42 1d. carmine (No. 278) .. .. .. — £180
(iii) **W 43** *(sideways on 3d., 1s.)*
O20 42 1d. carmine (*p* 14) (No. 303) .. .. — £180
a. Green opt .. .. .. — £180
O21 27 2½d. blue (No. 308) .. .. .. — £275
O22 28 3d. yellow-brown (No. 309) .. .. — £400
O23 34 1s. orange-red (No. 315*b*) .. .. — £750
O24 35 2s. green (No. 316) .. .. .. — £1100

The letters signify "On Public Service Only", and stamps so overprinted were used by the Post Office Department on official correspondence between the department and foreign countries.

MINIMUM PRICE

The minimum price quote is 10p which represents a handling charge rather than a basis for valuing common stamps. For further notes about prices see introductory pages.

OFFICIAL.

(O 3)

1907–08. *Stamps of 1902–6 optd with Type O 3 (vertically upwards).* **W 43** *(sideways on 3d., 6d., 1s. and 5s.). P 14.*
O59 23 ½d. yellow-green .. .. .. 7·00 50
a. Perf compound of 11 and 14 .. 65·00
b. Mixed perfs .. .. 65·00
O60 42 1d. carmine (No. 303) (1908)* .. 7·00 7·00
a. Booklet pane of 6 .. .. 30·00
O60*b* 1d. rose-carmine (Waterlow) (No. 352) 7·00 30
ba. Perf compound of 11 and 14 .. £275 £225
bb. Mixed perfs £275 £225
O60*c* 1d. carmine (Royle) .. .. 7·00 30
ca. Perf compound of 11 and 14 .. £200 £160
cb. Mixed perfs £200 £160
O61 41 2d. purple .. .. .. 7·50 1·25
a. Bright reddish purple .. 7·00 1·00
ab. Mixed perfs £180 £180
O63 28 3d. bistre-brown .. .. 35·00 1·75
O64 31 6d. bright carmine-pink .. .. £110 15·00
a. Imperf vert (horiz pair) .. £750
b. Mixed perfs £400 £350
O65 34 1s. orange-red .. .. .. 85·00 15·00
O66 35 2s. blue-green .. .. .. 70·00 48·00
a. Imperf between (pair) £1100
b. Imperf vert (horiz pair) £900
O67 36 5s. deep red £150 £160
a. Wmk upright £700 £650

*Though issued in 1908, a large quantity of booklets was mislaid and not utilized until they were found in 1930.

1908–09. *Optd as Type O 3.* **W 43.**
O69 23 ½d. green (*p* 14 × 15) .. .. 6·00 1·50
O70 50 1d. carmine (*p* 14 × 15) .. .. 60·00 1·25
O71 48 6d. pink (*p* 14 × 13, 13½) .. .. £140 38·00
O72 6d. pink (*p* 14 × 15) (1909) .. .. £110 35·00
O72*a* F 4 £1 rose-pink (*p* 14) (No. F89) .. £500 £400

1910. *No. 387 optd with Type O 3.*
O73 51 ½d. yellow-green .. .. .. 3·75 30
a. Opt inverted (reading downwards) † £1200

1910–16. *Nos. 389 and 392/4 optd with Type O 3. P 14 × 14½.*
O74 52 3d. chestnut .. .. .. 14·00 80
a. Perf 14 × 13½ (1915) .. .. 60·00 70·00
ab. Vert pair, O74/a £300 £350
O75 – 6d. carmine .. .. .. 18·00 3·75
a. Deep carmine (1913) .. .. 24·00 4·25
O76 – 8d. indigo-blue (R.) (5.16) .. 14·00 18·00
a. Perf 14 × 13½ .. .. 14·00 18·00
ab. Vert pair, O76/a .. .. 45·00 60·00
O77 – 1s. vermilion .. .. .. 45·00 12·00
O74/7 .. .. .. *Set of* 4 80·00 30·00

1910–25. *Optd with Type O 3.* (*a*) **W 43.** *De La Rue chalk-surfaced paper with toned gum.*
O78 53 1d. carmine (No. 405) .. .. .. 3·00 10
(*b*) **W 43.** *Jones chalk-surfaced paper with white gum*
O79 53 1d. deep carmine (No. 406) (1925) .. 9·50 4·00
(*c*) *No wmk, but bluish "NZ" and Star lithographed on back. Art paper*
O80 53 1d. rose-carmine (No. 409) (1925) .. 6·00 8·00
(*d*) **W 43.** *Cowan thick, opaque, chalk-surfaced paper with white gum*
O81 53 1d. deep carmine (No. 410) (1925) .. 7·50 1·25

1913–25. *Postal Fiscal stamps optd with Type O 3.*
(i) *Chalk-surfaced De La Rue paper.* (*a*) *P 14* (1913–14)
O82 F 4 2s. blue (30.9.14) .. .. .. 40·00 27·00
O83 5s. yellow-green (13.6.13) .. .. 70·00 75·00
O84 £1 rose-carmine (1913) £550 £450
O82/4 .. .. .. *Set of* 3 £600 £500
(*b*) *P 14½ × 14, comb* (1915)
O85 F 4 2s. deep blue (Aug) .. .. 42·00 24·00
a. No stop after "OFFICIAL" .. £120 80·00
O86 5s. yellow-green (Jan).. .. 65·00 65·00
a. No stop after "OFFICIAL" .. £200 £200
(ii) *Thick, white, opaque chalk-surfaced Cowan paper. P 14½ × 14* (1925)
O87 F 4 2s. blue .. .. .. 55·00 60·00
a. No stop after "OFFICIAL" .. £160 £160

The overprint on these last, and on Nos. O69 and O72*a*, is from a new set of type, giving a rather sharper impression than Type O 3, but otherwise resembling it closely.

1915 (12 Oct)–**34.** *Optd with Type O 3. P 14 × 15.* (*a*) *On Nos. 435/40 (De La Rue chalk-surfaced paper with toned gum).*
O88 61 ½d. green .. .. .. 1·25 10
O89 62 1½d. grey-black (6.16) .. .. 4·75 2·50
O90 61 1½d. slate (12.16) .. .. 3·25 40
O91 1½d. orange-brown (4.19) .. .. 3·25 30
O92 2d. yellow (4.17) .. .. 3·25 10
O93 3d. chocolate (11.19) .. .. 8·50 35
O88/93 .. .. .. *Set of* 6 22·00 3·50
(*b*) *On Nos. 441 and 443 (Jones chalk-surfaced paper with white gum)*
O94 61 ½d. green (1924) .. .. 4·00 2·25
O95 3d. deep chocolate (1924) .. 32·00 4·00
(*c*) *On Nos. 446/7 and 448a/9 (Cowan thick, opaque, chalk-surfaced paper with white gum)*
O96 61 ½d. green (1925) 50 10
a. Perf 14 (1929) .. .. 1·75 35
ab. No stop after "OFFICIAL" .. 22·00 24·00
O97 1½d. orange-brown (*p* 14) (1929) .. 9·50 11·00
a. No stop after "OFFICIAL" .. 40·00 50·00
b. Perf 14 × 15 (1934) .. .. 20·00 24·00
O98 2d. yellow (*p* 14) (1931) .. .. 1·50 20
a. No stop after "OFFICIAL" .. 32·00 20·00

O99 **61** 3d. chocolate (1925) . . . . 3·50 40
a. No stop after "OFFICIAL" . . 45·00 30·00
b. Perf 14 (1930) . . . . 24·00 1·75
ba. No stop after "OFFICIAL" . . 85·00 40·00
O96/9 . . . . *Set of* 4 13·50 11·00

1915 (Dec)–**27**. *Optd with Type* O **3**. *P* 14 × 14½. (*a*) *Nos.* 420, 422, 425, 428 *and* 429a/30 (*Cowan unsurfaced paper*).
O100 **60** 3d. chocolate . . . . . . 3·00 70
a. Perf 14×13½ . . . . . . 3·00 70
ab. Vert pair, O100/a . . . . 35·00 50·00
O101 4d. bright violet (*p* 14×13½) (4.25) . . 12·00 2·00
a. Re-entry (Pl 20 R. 1/6) . . 40·00
b. Re-entry (Pl 20 R. 4/10) . . 45·00
c. Perf 14×14½ (4.27) . . . . 22·00 1·00
O102 6d. carmine (6.16) . . . . 4·50 75
a. Perf 14×13½ . . . . 3·75 60
ab. Vert pair, O102/a . . . . 50·00 60·00
O103 8d. red-brown (*p* 14×13½) (8.22) . . 70·00 85·00
O104 9d. sage-green (*p* 14×13½) (4.25) . . 35·00 30·00
O105 1s. vermilion (9.16) . . . . 5·50 2·00
a. Perf 14×13½ . . . . 16·00 9·00
ab. Vert pair, O105/a . . . . 65·00 90·00
c. *Pale orange-red* . . . . 28·00 9·00
O100/5 . . . . . . *Set of* 6 £120 £110
(*b*) *No.* 433 (*Thin paper with widely spaced sideways wmk*)
O106 **60** 3d. chocolate (*p* 14) (7.16) . . 3·00 4·25
a. No wmk . . . . . . 30·00 50·00

1927–33. *Optd with Type* O **3**. **W 43**. *P* 14.
O111 **71** 1d. rose-carmine (No. 468) . . 1·00 10
a. No stop after "OFFICIAL" . . 20·00 13·00
b. Perf 14 × 15 . . . . 1·25 10
O112 **72** 2s. light blue (No. 469) (2.28) . . 70·00 70·00
O113 **F 6** 5s. green (1933) £250 £250
O111/13 . . . . . . *Set of* 3 £300 £275

Official (O 4)   *Official* (O 5)

1936–61. *Pictorial issue optd horiz or vert* (2s.) *with Type* O **4**.
(*a*) **W 43** (*Single* "N Z" *and Star*)
O115 **82** 1d. scarlet (Die I) (*p* 14 × 13½) . . 1·00 30
a. Perf 13½ × 14 . . . . 75·00 35·00
O116 **83** 1½d. red-brown (*p* 13½ × 14) . . 17·00 18·00
a. Perf 14 × 13½ £4500
O118 **92** 1s. deep green (*p* 14 × 13½) . . 19·00 23·00
O119 **F 6** 5s. green (*p* 14) (12.38) . . 75·00 22·00
O115/19 . . . . . . *Set of* 4 £100 55·00
The watermark of No. O119 is almost invisible.
Only four examples of No. O116a exist. The error occurred when a sheet of No. 558a was found to have a block of four missing. This was replaced by a block of No. 558 and the sheet was then sent for overprinting.
(*b*) **W 98** (*Mult* "N Z" *and Star*)
O120 **81** ½d. bright green, *p* 14 × 13½ (7.37) . . 4·25 3·75
O121 **82** 1d. scarlet (Die II), *p* 14 × 13½ (11.36) 2·75 20
O122 **83** 1½d. red-brown, *p* 14 × 13½ (7.36) . . 8·00 4·00
O123 **84** 2d. orange, *p* 14 × 13½ (1.38) . . 1·25 10
a. Perf 12½ (1942) . . . . £150 42·00
c. Perf 14 (1942) . . . . 28·00 7·50
O124 **85** 2½d. chocolate and slate, *p* 13–14 × 13½ (26.7.38) . . . . 32·00 40·00
a. Perf 14 (1938) . . . . 10·00 9·00
O125 **86** 3d. brown, *p* 14 × 13½ (1.3.38) . . 40·00 2·00
O126 **87** 4d. black and sepia, *p* 14 × 13½ (8.36) 6·50 75
a. Perf 14 (8.41) . . . . 3·50 1·00
b. Perf 12½ (1941) . . . . 2·75 1·75
c. Perf 14 × 14½ (10.42) . . 3·00 40
O127 **89** 6d. scarlet, *p* 13½ × 14 (12.37) . . 7·00 40
a. Perf 12½ (1941) . . . . 6·50 3·00
b. Perf 14½ × 14 (7.42) . . 3·50 30
O128 **90** 8d. chocolate, *p* 12½ (*wmk sideways*) (1942) . . . . 10·00 10·00
a. Perf 14 × 14½ (*wmk sideways*) (1945) . . . . 5·50 9·00
b. Perf 14 × 13½ . . . . † £1600
O129 **91** 9d. red and grey-black (G.) (No. 587*a*), *p* 13½ × 14 (1.3.38) . . 48·00 35·00
O130 9d. scarlet and black (Blk.)(No.631), *p* 14 × 15 (1943) . . 13·00 18·00
O131 **92** 1s. deep green, *p* 14 × 13½ (2.37) . . 25·00 85
a. Perf 12½ (1942) . . . . 14·00 85
O132 **93** 2s. olive-green, *p* 13–14 × 13½ (5.37) 55·00 20·00
a. "CAPTAIN COQK" . . . . 65·00
b. Perf 13½ × 14 (1939) . . 90·00 5·50
ba. "CAPTAIN COQK" £110
c. Perf 12½ (1942) . . . . 70·00 22·00
ca. "CAPTAIN COQK" . . . . 95·00
d. Perf 14 × 13½ (1944) . . 30·00 7·00
da. "CAPTAIN COQK" . . . .
O133 **F 6** 5s. green, C, *p* 14 (3.43) . . 27·00 5·00
a. Perf 14 × 13½. *Yellow-green*, **O** (10.61) . . . . 15·00 22·00
O120/33 . . . . . . *Set of* 14 £180 85·00
The opt on No. O127a was sometimes applied at the top of the stamp, instead of always at the bottom, as on No. O127.
All examples of No. O128b were used by a government office in Whangerei.
See notes on perforations after No. 590b.

1938–51. *Nos.* 603 *etc., optd with Type* O **4**.
O134 **108** ½d. green (1.3.38) . . . . 8·50 1·00
O135 ½d. brown-orange (1946) . . 1·25 1·00
O136 1d. scarlet (1.7.38) . . . . 8·00 15
O137 1d. green (10.7.41) . . . . 1·25 10
O138 **108a** 1½d. purple-brown (26.7.38) . . 60·00 18·00
O139 1½d. scarlet (2.4.51) . . . . 7·50 2·50
O140 3d. blue (16.10.41) . . . . 1·75 10
O134/40 . . . . . . *Set of* 7 80·00 20·00

1940 (2 Jan–8 Mar). *Centennial. Nos.* 613, *etc., optd with Type* O **5**.
O141 ½d. blue-green (R.) 60 35
a. "ff" joined, as Type O 4 . . 35·00 40·00
O142 1d. chocolate and scarlet . . 3·00 10
a. "ff" joined, as Type O 4 . . 45·00 40·00
O143 1½d. light blue and mauve . . 1·50 2·00
O144 2d. blue-green and chocolate . . 2·75 10
a. "ff" joined, as Type O 4 . . 45·00 40·00
O145 2½d. blue-green and ultramarine . . 2·25 2·75
a. "ff" joined, as Type O 4 . . 40·00 45·00
O146 3d. purple and carmine (R.) . . 6·50 80
a. "ff" joined, as Type O 4 . . 30·00 40·00
O147 4d. chocolate and lake . . 35·00 2·00
a. "ff" joined, as Type O 4 . . 90·00 50·00
O148 6d. emerald-green and violet . . 19·00 2·00
a. "ff" joined, as Type O 4 . . 60·00 50·00
O149 8d. black and red (8.3) . . 20·00 14·00
a. "ff" joined, as Type O 4 . . 60·00 70·00
O150 9d. olive-green and vermilion . . 7·50 7·00
O151 1s. sage-green and deep green . . 38·00 4·00
O141/51 . . . . . . *Set of* 11 £120 32·00

1947–49. *Nos.* 680, *etc., optd with Type* O **4**.
O152 **108a** 2d. orange 75 10
O153 4d. bright purple . . . . 2·00 50
O154 6d. carmine . . . . 6·50 40
O155 8d. violet . . . . 8·00 6·00
O156 9d. purple-brown . . . . 9·00 6·50
O157 **144** 1s. red-brown and carmine (*wmk upright*) (Plate 1) . . 10·00 85
a. Wmk sideways (Plate 1) (1949) . . 8·00 3·50
b. Wmk upright (Plate 2) . . 14·00 5·00
O158 2s. brown-orange and green (*wmk sideways*) (Plate 1) . . 17·00 12·00
a. Wmk upright (Plate 1) . . 26·00 23·00
O152/8 . . . . . . *Set of* 7 45·00 24·00

O **6** Queen Elizabeth II   (O **7**)

(Des J. Berry. Recess B.W.)

1954 (1 Mar)–**63**. **W 98**. *P* 14 × 13½.
O159 **O 6** 1d. orange 45 20
O160 1½d. brown-lake . . . . 55 2·50
O161 2d. bluish green 30 15
O162 2½d. olive (1.3.63) . . . . 3·75 1·50
O163 3d. vermilion 40 10
O164 4d. blue 70 15
O165 9d. carmine . . . . 2·50 60
O166 1s. purple 50 10
O167 3s. slate (1.3.63) . . . . 35·00 45·00
O159/67 . . . . . . *Set of* 9 40·00 45·00
See note *re* white opaque paper after No. 736. Nos. O162 and O167 exist only on white paper.

1959 (1 Oct). *No.* O160 *surch with Type* O **7**.
O168 **O 6** 6d. on 1½d. brown-lake . . 20 85

1961 (1 Sept). *No.* O161 *surch as Type* O **7**.
O169 **O 6** 2½d. on 2d. bluish green . . 35 1·00
Owing to the greater use of franking machines by Government Departments, the use of official stamps was discontinued on 31 March 1965, but they remained on sale at the G.P.O. until 31 December 1965.

PROVISIONALS ISSUED AT REEFTON AND USED BY THE POLICE DEPARTMENT

1907 (Jan). *Current stamps of* 1906, *overwritten* "Official," *in red ink, and marked* "Greymouth—PAID—3" *inside a circular postmark stamp. P* 14.
P1 **23** ½d. green £450 £650
P2 **40** 1d. carmine £450 £700
P3 **38a** 2d. purple £700 £850
P4 **28** 3d. bistre £650 £800
P5 **31** 6d. pink £850 £950
P6 **34** 1s. orange-red £1100 £1300
P7 **35** 2s. green . . . . — £5000

LIFE INSURANCE DEPARTMENT

L **1**   Lighthouse   L **2**

(Des W. B. Hudson and J. F. Rogers; eng A. E. Cousins. Typo Govt Printing Office, Wellington)

1891 (2 Jan)–**98**. A. **W 12c**. *P* 12×11½.
L 1 **L 1** ½d. bright purple . . . . 55·00 7·00
L 2 1d. blue . . . . 55·00 9·00
a. Wmk **12b** . . . . 90·00 20·00
L 3 2d. brown-red . . . . 85·00 4·00
a. Wmk **12b** . . . . 95·00 12·00
L 4 3d. deep brown . . . . £190 20·00
L 5 6d. green . . . . £275 60·00
L 6 1s. rose £650 £120
L1/6 . . . . . . *Set of* 6 £1100 £200
B. **W 12b** (1893–98). (*a*) *P* 10 (1893)
L 7 **L 1** ½d. bright purple . . . . 55·00 7·00
L 8 1d. blue . . . . 55·00 1·25
L 9 2d. brown-red . . . . 75·00 3·75
L7/9 . . . . . . *Set of* 3 £160 11·00
(*b*) *Perf compound of* 11 *and* 10 (1896)
L 9*a* **L 1** ½d. bright purple . . . . 90·00 26·00
L 9*b* 1d. blue . . . . 55·00 11·00
(*c*) *Perf compound of* 10 *and* 11 (1897)
L10 **L 1** ½d. bright purple . . . . — 60·00
L11 1d. blue
(*d*) *Mixed perfs* 10 *and* 11 (1897)
L12 **L 1** 2d. brown-red £550 £550
(*e*) *P* 11 (1897–98)
L13 **L 1** ½d. bright purple . . . . 55·00 2·75
a. Thin coarse toned paper (1898) . . 65·00 5·50
L14 1d. blue . . . . 55·00 75
a. Thin coarse toned paper (1898) . . 65·00 1·25
L15 2d. brown-red . . . . 70·00 3·25
a. Chocolate . . . . £110 24·00
b. Thin coarse toned paper (1898) . . 70·00 3·50
L13/15 . . . . . . *Set of* 3 £160 6·00

1902–04. **W 43** (*sideways*). (*a*) *P* 11.
L16 **L 1** ½d. bright purple (1903) . . 55·00 4·00
L17 1d. blue (1902) . . . . 55·00 90
L18 2d. brown-red (1904) . . 80·00 4·25
L16/18 . . . . . . *Set of* 3 £170 8·00
(*b*) *Perf compound of* 11 *and* 14
L19 **L 1** ½d. bright purple (1903) . . £1100
L20 1d. blue (1904) . . . . 90·00 10·00
Nos. L16/17 and L20 are known without watermark from the margins of the sheet.

1905–6. *Redrawn, with* "V.R." *omitted*. **W 43** (*sideways*). (*a*) *P* 11.
L21 **L 2** 2d. brown-red (12.05) . . £1200 80·00
(*b*) *P* 14
L22 **L 2** 1d. blue (1906) . . . . £150 30·00
(*c*) *Perf compound of* 11 *and* 14
L23 **L 2** 1d. blue (1906) £475 £150
a. Mixed perfs . . . . — £375
Between January 1907 and the end of 1912 the Life Insurance Department used ordinary Official stamps.

1913 (2 Jan)–**37**. *New values and colours*. **W 43**.
(*a*) "*De La Rue paper*". *P* 14 × 15
L24 **L 2** ½d. green . . . . 7·00 80
a. Yellow-green . . . . 7·00 80
L25 1d. carmine . . . . 7·00 80
a. Carmine-pink . . . . 13·00 90
L26 1½d. black (1917) . . . . 35·00 6·00
L27 1½d. chestnut-brown (1919) . . 1·25 2·25
L28 2d. bright purple . . . . 40·00 19·00
L29 2d. yellow (1920) . . . . 3·50 2·00
L30 3d. yellow-brown . . . . 40·00 23·00
L31 6d. carmine-pink . . . . 28·00 17·00
L24/31 . . . . . . *Set of* 8 £150 60·00
(*b*) "*Cowan*" *paper*. (i) *P* 14 × 15
L31*a* **L 2** ½d. yellow-green (1925) . . 20·00 4·00
L31*b* 1d. carmine-pink (1925) . . 21·00 3·25
(ii) *P* 14
L32 **L 2** ½d. yellow-green (1926) . . 8·50 1·50
L33 1d. scarlet (1931) . . . . 7·00 1·50
L34 2d. yellow (1937) . . . . 5·00 3·50
L35 3d. brown-lake (1931) . . 17·00 21·00
L36 6d. pink (1925) . . . . 21·00 24·00
L32/6 . . . . . . *Set of* 5 55·00 45·00
(*c*) "*Wiggins Teape*" *paper*. *P* 14 × 15
L36*a* **L 2** ½d. yellow-green (3.37) . . 4·50 6·00
L36*b* 1d. scarlet (3.37) . . . . 9·00 2·25
L36*c* 6d. pink (7.37) . . . . 22·00 32·00
L36*a/c* . . . . . . *Set of* 3 32·00 35·00
For descriptions of the various types of paper, see after No. 518.
In the 1½d. the word "POSTAGE" is in both the side-labels instead of at left only.

1944–47. **W 98**. *P* 14 × 15.
L37 **L 2** ½d. yellow-green (7.47) . . 2·50 4·25
L38 1d. scarlet (6.44) . . . . 1·50 1·50
L39 2d. yellow (1946) . . . . 6·00 7·00
L40 3d. brown-lake (10.46) . . 11·00 14·00
L41 6d. pink (7.47) . . . . 7·50 20·00
L37/41 . . . . . . *Set of* 5 26·00 42·00

L **3** Castlepoint Lighthouse   L **6** Cape Campbell Lighthouse

(Des J. Berry. Recess B.W.).

1947 (1 Aug)–**65**. *Type* L **3**, L **6** *and similar designs*. **W 98** (*sideways on* 1d., 2d., 2½d.). *P* 13½.
L42 ½d. grey-green and orange-red . . 80 60
L43 1d. olive-green and pale blue . . 50 30
L44 2d. deep blue and grey-black . . 70 25
L45 2½d. black and bright blue (*white opaque paper*) (4.11.63) . . . . 9·00 12·00
L46 3d. mauve and pale blue . . 2·25 35
L47 4d. brown and yellow-orange . . 1·75 40
a. Wmk sideways (*white opaque paper*) (13.10.65) . . . . 5·00 13·00
L48 6d. chocolate and blue . . 1·75 1·25
L49 1s. red-brown and blue . . 2·25 75
L42/49 . . . . . . *Set of* 8 17·00 14·50
Designs: *Horiz* (*as Type* L **3**)—1d Taiaroa lighthouse; 2d. Cape Palliser lighthouse; 6d. The Brothers lighthouse. *Vert* (*as Type* L **6**)—3d. Eddystone lighthouse; 4d. Stephens Island lighthouse; 1s. Cape Brett lighthouse.

(L **11**)   (L **12**)

1967 (10 July)–**68**. *Decimal currency. Stamps of* 1947–65, *surch as Type* L **12** *or* L **11** (2 c.).
L50 1 c. on 1d. (No. L43) .. 2·25 4·00
a. Wmk upright (*white opaque paper*) (10.5.68) .. 2·25 3·25
L51 2 c. on 2½d. (No. L45) .. 5·50 8·00
L52 2½ c. on 3d. (No. L46) .. 1·75 4·50
a. Horiz pair, one without surcharge .. £1700
b. Wmk sideways (*white opaque paper*) (4.68?) .. 2·50 4·50
L53 3 c. on 4d. (No. L47a) .. 4·50 4·75
L54 5 c. on 6d. (No. L48) .. 2·00 6·50
L55 10 c. on 1s. (No. L49) .. 3·00 11·00
a. Wmk sideways (*white opaque paper*) 1·25 4·00
L50/55a .. *Set of* 6 16·00 28·00

See note *re* white opaque paper below No. 736.
No. L54 exists on both ordinary and whiter paper.

L **13** Moeraki Point Lighthouse   L **14** Puyesegur Point Lighthouse

(Des J. Berry. Litho B.W.)

1969 (27 Mar)–**77**. *Types* L **13/14** *and similar designs. No wmk. Chalk-surfaced paper* (8, 10 c.), *ordinary paper* (*others*). *P* 14 (8, 10 c.) *or* 13½ (*others*).
L56 ½ c. greenish yellow, red and deep blue .. 2·00 2·00
L57 2½ c. ultramarine, green and pale buff .. 1·00 1·25
L58 3 c. reddish brown and yellow .. 75 75
a. Chalk-surfaced paper (16.6.77) 80 2·00
L59 4 c. lt new blue, yellowish grn & apple-grn 1·00 1·00
a. Chalk-surfaced paper (16.6.77) 65 2·00
L60 8 c. multicoloured (17.11.76) .. 45 2·25
L61 10 c. multicoloured (17.11.76) .. 45 2·25
L62 15 c. black, light yellow and ultramarine .. 60 1·75
a. Perf 14. Chalk-surfaced paper (24.12.76) 1·50 2·00
L56/62 .. *Set of* 7 5·00 10·00

Designs: *Horiz*—4 c. Cape Egmont Lighthouse; *Vert*—3c. Baring Head Lighthouse; 8 c. East Cape; 10 c. Farewell Spit; 15 c. Dog Island Lighthouse.

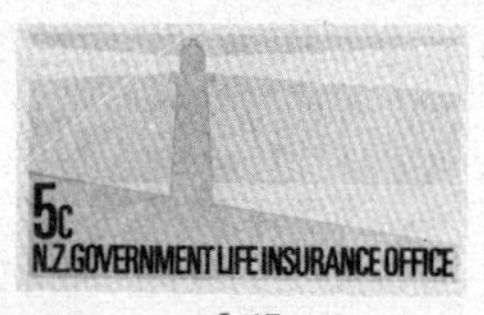

(L **16**)   L **17**

1978 (8 Mar). *No.* L 57 *surch with Type* L **16**. *Chalky paper.*
L63 L **14** 25 c. on 2½ c. ultramarine, grn & buff 75 1·75

(Des A. G. Mitchell. Litho Harrison)

1981 (3 June). *P* 14½.
L64 L **17** 5 c. multicoloured .. 10 10
L65 10 c. multicoloured .. 10 10
L66 20 c. multicoloured .. 15 15
L67 30 c. multicoloured .. 25 25
L68 40 c. multicoloured .. 35 30
L69 50 c. multicoloured .. 45 35
L64/9 .. *Set of* 6 1·25 1·00

Issues for the Government Life Insurance Department were withdrawn on 1 December 1989 when it became the privatised Tower Corporation.

POSTAL FISCAL STAMPS

As from 1 April 1882 fiscal stamps were authorised for postal use and conversely postage stamps became valid for fiscal use. Stamps in the designs of 1867 with "STAMP DUTY" above the Queen's head were withdrawn and although some passed through the mail quite legitimately they were mainly "philatelic" and we no longer list them. The issue which was specifically authorised in 1882 was the one which had originally been put on sale for fiscal use in 1880.

Although all fiscal stamps were legally valid for postage only values between 2s. and £1 were stocked at ordinary post offices. Other values could only be obtained by request from the G.P.O., Wellington or from offices of the Stamp Duties Department. Later the Arms types above £1 could also be obtained from the head post offices in Auckland, Christchurch, Dunedin and also a branch post office at Christchurch North where there was a local demand for them.

It seems sensible to list under Postal Fiscals the Queen Victoria stamps up to the £1 value and the Arms types up to the £5 because by 1931 the higher values were genuinely needed for postal purposes. Even the £10 was occasionally used on insured airmail parcels.

Although 2s. and 5s. values were included in the 1898 pictorial issue, it was the general practice for the Postal Department to limit the postage issues to 1s. until 1926 when the 2s. and 3s. appeared. These were then dropped from the fiscal issues and when in turn the 5s. and 10s. were introduced in 1953 and the £1 in 1960 no further printings of these values occurred in the fiscal series.

FORGED POSTMARKS. Our prices are for stamps with genuine postal cancellations. Beware of forged postmarks on stamps from which fiscal cancellations have been cleaned off.

Many small post offices acted as agents for government departments and it was the practice to use ordinary postal date-stamps on stamps used fiscally, so that when they are removed from documents they are indistinguishable from postally used specimens unless impressed with the embossed seal of the Stamp Duties Department.

Date-stamps very similar to postal date-stamps were sometimes supplied to offices of the Stamp Duties Department and it is not clear when this practice ceased. Prior to the Arms types the only sure proof of the postal use of off-cover fiscal stamps is when they bear a distinctive duplex, registered or parcel post cancellation, but beware of forgeries of the first two.

F **1**   F **2**   F **3**

(Die eng W. R. Bock. Typo Govt Ptg Office)

1882 (Feb). *W* **12***a*. *P* 12 × 11½.
F1 F **1** 1d. lilac .. £160 £300
F2 1d. blue .. 75·00 25·00

The 1d. fiscal was specifically authorised for postal use in February 1882 owing to a shortage of the 1d. Type **5** and pending the introduction of the 1d. Type **14** on 1 April.

The 1d. lilac fiscal had been replaced by the 1d. blue in 1878 but postally used copies with 1882 duplex postmarks are known although most postally used examples are dated from 1890 and these must have been philatelic.

(Des and dies eng W. R. Bock. Typo Govt Ptg Office)

1882 (early). *W* **12***a*. *P* 12 × 11½.
F3 F **2** 1s. grey green ..
F4 F **3** 1s. grey-green and red ..

Copies of these are known postally used in 1882 and although not specifically authorised for postal use it is believed that their use was permitted where there was a shortage of the 1s. postage stamp.

The 2s. value Type F **3** formerly listed is not known with 1882–83 postal date-stamps.

WMK TYPE F 5. The balance of the paper employed for the 1867 issue was used for early printings of Type F **4** introduced in 1880 before changing over to the "N Z" and Star watermark. The values we list with this watermark are known with 1882–83 postal date stamps. Others have later dates and are considered to be philatelic but should they be found with 1882–83 postal dates we would be prepared to add them to the list.

In the following list the 4d., 6d., 8d. and 1s. are known with early 1882 postal date-stamps and, like Nos. F3/4, it is assumed that they were used to meet a temporary shortage of postage stamps.

F **4**   F **5**

The 12s. 6d. value has the head in an oval (as Type **10**), and the 15s. and £1 values have it in a broken circle (as Type **7**).

(Dies eng W. R. Bock. Typo Govt Ptg Office)

1882 (1 Apr). *Type* F **4** *and similar types. "De La Rue" paper.*

A. *W* **12***a* (6 *mm*). (*a*) *P* 12 (1882)
F 5 4d. orange-red (*Wmk* F **5**) .. — £130
F 6 6d. lake-brown .. — £130
F 7 8d. green (*Wmk* F **5**)
F 8 1s. pink
F 9 2s. blue .. 50·00 4·50
F10 2s. 6d. grey-brown .. 85·00 4·50
a. Wmk F **5**
F11 3s. mauve .. £110 5·50
F12 4s. brown-rose .. £110 11·00
F13 5s. green .. £140 11·00
a. Yellow-green .. £140 11·00
F14 6s. rose .. £150 27·00
F15 7s. ultramarine .. £160 40·00
F16 7s. 6d. bronze-grey .. £160 45·00
F17 8s. deep blue .. £160 40·00
F18 9s. orange .. £150 45·00
F19 10s. brown-red .. £140 14·00
a. Wmk F **5**
F20 15s. green .. £190 45·00
F21 £1 rose-pink .. £190 45·00

(*b*) *P* 12½ (1886)
F22 2s. blue .. 50·00 4·50
F23 2s. 6d. grey-brown .. 85·00 4·50
F24 3s. mauve .. £110 5·50
F25 4s. purple-claret .. £110 11·00
a. Brown-rose .. £110 11·00
F26 5s. green .. £140 11·00
a. Yellow-green .. £140 11·00
F27 6s. rose .. £150 27·00
F28 7s. ultramarine .. £160 40·00
F29 8s. deep blue .. £160 40·00
F30 9s. orange .. £150 45·00
F31 10s. brown-red .. £140 14·00
F32 15s. green .. £190 45·00
F33 £1 rose-pink .. £190 45·00

B. *W* **12***b* (7 *mm*). *P* 12½ (1888)
F34 2s. blue .. 45·00 4·50
F35 2s. 6d. grey-brown .. 80·00 4·50
F36 3s. mauve .. £100 5·50
F37 4s. brown-rose .. £100 11·00
a. Brown-red .. £100 11·00
F38 5s. green .. £130 11·00
a. Yellow-green .. £130 11·00
F39 6s. rose .. £150 27·00
F40 7s. ultramarine .. £160 40·00
F41 7s. 6d. bronze-grey .. £160 45·00
F42 8s. deep blue .. £160 40·00
F43 9s. orange .. £150 45·00
F44 10s. brown-red .. £140 12·00
a. Maroon .. £140 12·00
F45 £1 pink .. £190 45·00

C. *W* **12***c* (4 *mm*). *P* 12½ (1890)
F46 2s. blue .. 75·00 11·00
F47 3s. mauve .. £150 27·00
F48 4s. brown-red .. £120 15·00
F49 5s. green .. £140 12·00
F50 6s. rose .. £160 27·00
F51 7s. ultramarine .. £170 40·00
F52 8s. deep blue .. £170 40·00
F53 9s. orange .. £150 45·00
F54 10s. brown-red .. £140 13·00
F55 15s. green .. £250 60·00

D. *Continuation of W* **12***b*. *P* 11 (1895–1901)
F56 2s. blue .. 27·00 5·50
F57 2s. 6d. grey-brown .. 80·00 4·50
a. Inscr "COUNTERPART" (1901)* .. £150 £110
F58 3s. mauve .. £100 5·50
F59 4s. brown-red .. £100 10·00
F60 5s. yellow-green .. £130 12·00
F61 6s. rose .. £140 27·00
F62 7s. pale blue .. £160 40·00
F63 7s. 6d. bronze-grey .. £160 45·00
F64 8s. deep blue .. £160 40·00
F65 9s. orange .. £150 45·00
a. Imperf between (horiz pair) .. £700
F66 10s. brown-red .. £140 12·00
a. Maroon .. £140 12·00
F67 15s. green .. £190 45·00
F68 £1 rose-pink .. £190 45·00

*The plate normally printed in yellow and inscribed "COUNTERPART" just above the bottom value panel, was for use on the counterparts of documents but was issued in error in the colour of the normal fiscal stamp and accepted for use.

E. *W* **43** (*sideways*)
(i) *Unsurfaced "Cowan" paper.* (*a*) *P* 11 (1903)
F69 2s. 6d. grey-brown .. 80·00 4·50
F70 3s. mauve .. £100 5·50
F71 4s. orange-red .. £100 10·00
F72 6s. rose .. £140 27·00
F73 7s. pale blue .. £160 40·00
F74 8s. deep blue .. £150 40·00
F75 10s. brown-red .. £130 14·00
a. Maroon .. £130 14·00
F76 15s. green .. £190 45·00
F77 £1 rose-pink .. £170 45·00

(*b*) *P* 14 (1906)
F78 2s. 6d. grey-brown .. 80·00 4·50
F79 3s. mauve .. £100 5·50
F80 4s. orange-red .. £100 7·50
F81 5s. yellow-green .. 70·00 7·50
F82 6s. rose .. £140 27·00
F83 7s. pale blue .. £150 40·00
F84 7s. 6d. bronze-grey .. £150 45·00
F85 8s. deep blue .. £150 40·00
F86 9s. orange .. £140 45·00
F87 10s. maroon .. £130 12·00
F88 15s. green .. £190 45·00
F89 £1 rose-pink .. £170 45·00

(*c*) *P* 14½ × 14, *comb* (*clean-cut*) (1907)
F90 2s. blue .. 25·00 4·00
F91 2s. 6d. grey-brown .. 80·00 4·50
F92 3s. mauve .. £100 5·50
F93 4s. orange-red .. 90·00 7·50
F94 6s. rose .. £140 27·00
F95 10s. maroon .. £130 12·00
F96 15s. green .. £170 45·00
F97 £1 rose-pink .. £170 45·00

(ii) *Chalk-surfaced "De La Rue" paper.* (*a*) *P* 14 (1913)
F 98 2s. blue .. 25·00 4·00
F 99 2s. 6d. grey-brown .. 27·00 4·50
F100 3s. purple .. 70·00 5·50
F101 4s. orange-red .. 70·00 7·00
F102 5s. yellow-green .. 70·00 7·50
F103 6s. rose .. £100 14·00
F104 7s. pale blue .. £100 15·00
F105 7s. 6d. bronze-grey .. £150 45·00
F106 8s. deep blue .. £130 24·00
F107 9s. orange .. £140 45·00
F108 10s. maroon .. £130 12·00
F109 15s. green .. £170 40·00
F110 £1 rose-carmine .. £170 45·00

(*b*) *P* 14½ × 14, *comb* (1913–21)
F111 2s. deep blue .. 25·00 4·00
F112 2s. 6d. grey-brown .. 27·00 4·50
F113 3s. purple .. 70·00 5·50
F114 4s. orange-red .. 70·00 7·00
F115 5s. yellow-green .. 70·00 7·50
F116 6s. rose .. £100 14·00
F117 7s. pale blue .. £100 15·00
F118 8s. deep blue .. £130 24·00
F119 9s. orange .. £130 45·00
F120 10s. maroon .. £130 12·00
F121 12s. 6d. deep plum (1921) .. £2250 £600
F122 15s. green .. £170 40·00
F123 £1 rose-carmine .. £170 45·00

The "De La Rue" paper has a smooth finish and has toned gum which is strongly resistant to soaking.

(iii) *Chalk-surfaced "Jones" paper. P* 14½ × 14, *comb* (1924)
F124 2s. deep blue .. 30·00 4·00
F125 2s. 6d. deep grey-brown .. 32·00 4·50
F126 3s. purple .. 80·00 5·50
F127 5s. yellow-green .. 80·00 7·50
F128 10s. brown-red .. £140 12·00
F129 12s. 6d deep purple .. £2250 £600
F130 15s. green .. £190 40·00

The "Jones" paper has a coarser texture, is poorly surfaced and the ink tends to peel. The outline of the watermark commonly shows on the surface of the stamp. The gum is colourless or only slightly toned and washes off readily.

(iv) *Thick, opaque, chalk-surfaced "Cowan" paper. P* 14½ × 14, *comb* (1925–30)
F131 2s. blue .. 25·00 4·00
F132 2s. 6d. deep grey-brown .. 27·00 4·50
F133 3s. mauve .. £100 10·00

F134 4s. orange-red .. 70·00 7·00
F135 5s. yellow-green .. 70·00 7·50
F136 6s. rose .. £100 14·00
F137 7s. pale blue .. £100 15·00
F138 8s. deep blue .. £130 24·00
a. Error. Blue (as 2s.) (1930) .. £500
F139 10s. brown-red .. £130 12·00
F140 12s. 6d. blackish purple .. £2250 £600
F141 15s. green .. £170 40·00
F142 £1 rose-pink .. £170 45·00

The "Cowan" paper is white and opaque and the watermark, which is usually smaller than in the "Jones" paper, is often barely visible.

(v) *Thin, hard, chalk-surfaced "Wiggins Teape" paper. P* 14½ × 14, *comb* (1926)

F143 4s. orange-red .. 75·00 7·00
F144 £1 rose-pink .. £180 80·00

The "Wiggins Teape" paper has a vertical mesh with narrow watermark, whereas other chalk-surfaced papers with this perforation have a horizontal mesh and wider watermark.

35/-

F 6 (F 7)

(Des H. L. Richardson. Typo Govt Ptg Office)

1931–40. *As Type* F **6** (*various frames*). *W* **43**. *P* 14.

(i) *Thick, opaque, chalk-surfaced "Cowan" paper, with horizontal mesh* (1931–35)

F145 1s. 3d. lemon (4.31) .. 10·00 35·00
F146 1s. 3d. orange-yellow .. 4·00 3·00
F147 2s. 6d. deep brown .. 12·00 2·50
F148 4s. red .. 14·00 3·00
F149 5s. green .. 15·00 4·50
F150 6s. carmine-rose .. 23·00 8·00
F151 7s. blue .. 26·00 11·00
F152 7s. 6d. olive-grey .. 55·00 60·00
F153 8s. slate-violet .. 28·00 22·00
F154 9s. brown-orange .. 30·00 23·00
F155 10s. carmine-lake .. 24·00 6·50
F156 12s. 6d. deep plum (9.35) .. £140 £140
F157 15s. sage-green .. 60·00 18·00
F158 £1 pink .. 60·00 15·00
F159 25s. greenish blue .. £225 £300
F160 30s. brown (1935) .. £250 £120
F161 35s. orange-yellow .. £2000 £2000
F162 £2 bright purple .. £300 50·00
F163 £2 10s. red .. £180 £225
F164 £3 green .. £300 £150
F165 £3 10s. rose (1935) .. £1200 £950
F166 £4 light blue (1935) .. £300 £120
F167 £4 10s. deep olive-grey (1935) .. £1300 £1000
F168 £5 indigo-blue .. £325 90·00

(ii) *Thin, hard "Wiggins Teape" paper with vertical mesh* (1936–40)

(*a*) *Chalk-surfaced* (1936–39)

F169 1s. 3d. pale orange-yellow .. 4·25 1·25
F170 2s. 6d. dull brown .. 18·00 1·40
F171 4s. pale red-brown .. 27·00 3·25
F172 5s. green .. 27·00 4·25
F173 6s. carmine-rose .. 29·00 12·00
F174 7s. pale blue .. 32·00 16·00
F175 8s. slate-violet .. 50·00 32·00
F176 9s. brown-orange .. 55·00 35·00
F177 10s. pale carmine-lake .. 48·00 6·00
F178 15s. sage-green .. 80·00 28·00
F179 £1 pink .. 65·00 20·00
F180 30s. brown (1.39) .. £250 95·00
F181 35s. orange-yellow .. £2500 £2000
F182 £2 bright purple (1937) .. £300 60·00
F183 £3 green (1937) .. £300 £150
F184 £5 indigo-blue (1937) .. £375 £110

(*b*) *Unsurfaced* (1940)

F185 7s. 6d. olive-grey .. £120 90·00

Not all values listed above were stocked at ordinary post offices as some of them were primarily required for fiscal purposes but all were valid for postage.

1939. *No.* F161 *surch with Type* F **7**.

F186 35/- on 35s. orange-yellow .. £325 £200

Because the 35s. orange-yellow could so easily be confused with the 1s. 3d. in the same colour it was surcharged.

1940 (June). *New values surch as Type* F **7**. *W* **43**. *"Wiggins Teape" chalk-surfaced paper. P* 14.

F187 3/6 on 3s. 6d. grey-green .. 35·00 11·00
F188 5/6 on 5s. 6d. lilac .. 50·00 32·00
F189 11/- on 11s. yellow .. £110 75·00
F190 22/- on 22s. scarlet .. £250 £180
F187/90 .. *Set of* 4 £400 £250

These values were primarily needed for fiscal use.

1940–58. *As Type* F **6** (*various frames*). *W* **98**.

(i) *P* 14. *"Wiggins Teape" chalk-surfaced paper with vertical mesh* (1940–56)

F191 1s. 3d. orange-yellow .. 3·50 70
F192 1s. 3d. yell & blk (*wmk inverted*) (14.6.55) 1·00 30
b. Error. Yellow & bl (wmk inverted) (7.56) 3·00 5·50
F193 2s. 6d. deep brown .. 5·00 30
F194 4s. red-brown .. 9·00 50
F195 5s. green .. 12·00 60
F196 6s. carmine-rose .. 24·00 2·50
F197 7s. pale blue .. 25·00 4·25
F198 7s. 6d. olive-grey (*wmk inverted*) (21.12.50) 55·00 48·00
F199 8s. slate-violet .. 32·00 16·00
F200 9s. brown-orange (1.46) .. 20·00 27·00
F201 10s. carmine-lake .. 20·00 2·25
F202 15s. sage-green .. 38·00 17·00
F203 £1 pink .. 24·00 3·50
F204 25s. greenish blue (1946) .. £300 £300
F205 30s. brown (1946) .. £190 95·00
F206 £2 bright purple (1946) .. 65·00 18·00
F207 £2 10s. red (*wmk inverted*) (9.8.51) .. £225 £190
F208 £3 green (1946) .. 80·00 45·00
F209 £3 10s. rose (11.48) .. £1200 £1000
F210 £4 light blue (*wmk inverted*) (12.2.52) .. £100 55·00
F211 £5 indigo-blue .. £130 45·00
F191/211 .. *Set of* 21 £2250 £1600

THREE SHILLINGS I.

THREE SHILLINGS II.

3s. 6d.

Type I. Broad serifed capitals

Type II. Taller capitals, without serifs

Surcharged as Type F **7**

F212 3/6 on 3s. 6d. grey-green (I) (1942) .. 20·00 5·00
F213 3/6 on 3s. 6d. grey-green (II) (6.53) .. 12·00 26·00
F214 5/6 on 5s. 6d. lilac (1944) .. 22·00 11·00
F215 11/- on 11s. yellow (1942) .. 60·00 40·00
F216 22/- on 22s. scarlet (1945) .. £180 £120
F212/16 .. *Set of* 5 £250 £180

(ii) *P* 14 × 13½. *"Wiggins Teape" unsurfaced paper with horizontal mesh* (1956–58)

F217 1s. 3d. yellow and black (11.56) .. 1·50 1·00
F218 £1 pink (20.10.58) .. 32·00 20·00

No. F192b had the inscription printed in blue in error but as many as 378,000 were printed.

From about 1949–53 inferior paper had to be used and for technical reasons it was necessary to feed the paper into the machine in a certain way which resulted in whole printings with the watermark inverted for most values. These are fully listed in the *New Zealand Concise Catalogue*. In the above list the prices are for the cheapest form.

F 8

1967 (10 July). *Decimal currency. W* **98** (*sideways*). *Unsurfaced paper. P* 14.

F219 F **8** $4 deep reddish violet .. 2·00 55
F220 $6 emerald .. 3·00 1·50
F221 $8 light greenish blue .. 4·00 3·50
F222 $10 deep ultramarine .. 5·00 3·50
F219/22 .. *Set of* 4 12·50 8·00

The original printings were line perf on paper with the sideways watermark inverted ("N Z" to right of star when viewed from the front). From 1968 the stamps were comb perforated with the sideways watermark normal. The prices quoted are for the cheaper printings. Both are listed in the *New Zealand Concise Catalogue*.

1986 (Apr). *As Nos.* F220/2 *but without wmk. Chalk-surfaced paper.*

F223 F **8** $6 bright green .. 5·50 5·50
F224 $8 light greenish blue .. 7·00 8·00
F225 $10 deep ultramarine .. 8·00 9·00
F223/5 .. *Set of* 3 18·00 20·00

No further printings were made of the $4 after the introduction of a $5 postage stamp in 1981.

ANTARCTIC EXPEDITIONS

VICTORIA LAND

These issues were made under authority of the New Zealand Postal Department and, while not strictly necessary, they actually franked correspondence to New Zealand. They were sold to the public at a premium.

1908 (15 Jan). *Shackleton Expedition. T* **42** *of New Zealand* (*p* 14), *optd* "King Edward VII Land", *in two lines, reading up, by Coulls, Culling and Co., Wellington.*

A1 1d. rose-carmine (No. 356 Royle) (G.) .. £400 35·00
a. Opt double .. — £1500
A1*b* 1d. rose-carmine (No. 352c Waterlow) (G.) .. £1300 £800

Nos. A1/1*b* were used on board the expedition ship, *Nimrod*, and at the Cape Royds base in McMurdo Sound. Due to adverse conditions Shackleton landed in Victoria Land rather than King Edward VII Land the intended destination.

1911 (9 Feb)–**13**. *Scott Expedition. Stamps of New Zealand optd* "VICTORIA LAND.", *in two lines by Govt Printer, Wellington.*

A2 **50** ½d. deep green (No. 387*aa*) (18.1.13) .. £500 £500
A3 **52** 1d. carmine (No. 405) .. 45·00 70·00
a. No stop after "LAND" .. £375 £550

Nos. A2/3 were used at the Cape Evans base on McMurdo Sound or on the *Terra Nova*.

ROSS DEPENDENCY

This comprises a sector of the Antarctic continent and a number of islands. It was claimed by Great Britain on 30 July 1923 and soon afterward put under the jurisdiction of New Zealand.

1 H.M.S. *Erebus*

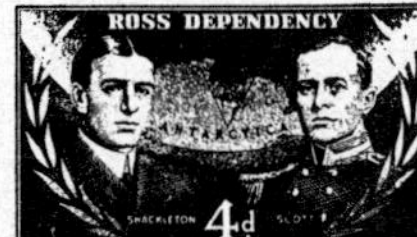

2 Shackleton and Scott

3 Map of Ross Dependency and New Zealand

4 Queen Elizabeth II

(Des E. M. Taylor (3d.), L. C. Mitchell (4d.), R. Smith (8d.), J.Berry (1s. 6d.). Recess D.L.R.)

1957 (11 Jan). *W* **98** *of New Zealand* (*Mult* N Z *and Star*). *P* 13 (1*s*. 6*d*.) *or* 14 (*others*).

1 **1** 3d. indigo .. 2·50 75
2 **2** 4d. carmine-red .. 2·50 75
3 **3** 8d. bright carmine-red and ultramarine .. 2·50 1·00
a. Bright carmine-red and blue .. 7·50 6·00
4 **4** 1s. 6d. slate-purple .. 2·50 1·25
1/4 .. *Set of* 4 9·00 3·25

(New Currency. 100 cents = 1 dollar)

5 H.M.S. *Erebus*

1967 (10 July). *Decimal currency. As Nos.* 1/4 *but with values inscr in decimal currency as T* **5**. *Chalky paper* (*except* 15 *c*.). *W* **98** *of New Zealand* (*sideways on* 7 *c*.). *P* 13 (15 *c*.) *or* 14 (*others*).

5 **5** 2 c. indigo .. 8·00 4·75
a. Deep blue .. 11·00 7·00
6 **2** 3 c. carmine-red .. 7·00 4·75
7 **3** 7 c. bright carmine-red and ultramarine .. 11·00 7·50
8 **4** 15 c. slate-purple .. 12·00 12·00
5/8 .. *Set of* 4 35·00 26·00

6 Great Skua

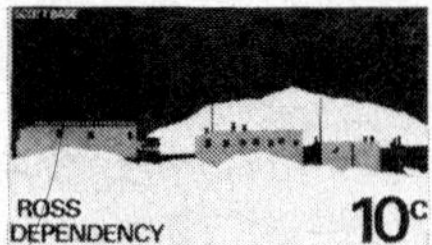

7 Scott Base

(Des M. Cleverley. Litho B.W.)

1972 (18 Jan)–**79**. *Horiz design as T* **6** (3 *to* 8 *c*.) *or* **7** (10, 18 *c*.). *Ordinary paper. P* 14½ × 14 (10, 18 *c*.) *or* 13 (*others*).

9 3 c. black, brownish grey and pale blue .. 1·25 1·25
a. Chalk-surfaced paper (2.79) .. 65 85
10 4 c. black, royal blue and violet .. 80 1·00
a. Chalk-surfaced paper (2.79) .. 40 80
11 5 c. black, brownish grey and rose-lilac .. 70 1·00
a. Chalk-surfaced paper (2.79) .. 30 80
12 8 c. black, yellow-brown and brownish grey 70 1·10
a. Chalk-surfaced paper (2.79) .. 40 85
13 10 c. black, turquoise-green and slate-green .. 1·00 1·50
a. Perf 13½ × 13. Chalk-surfaced paper (2.79) .. 40 90
14 18 c. black, violet and bright violet .. 2·25 2·50
a. Perf 13½ × 13. Chalk-surfaced paper (2.79) .. 50 1·25
9/14 .. *Set of* 6 6·00 7·50
9a/14a .. *Set of* 6 2·40 5·00

Designs:—4 c. "Hercules" aeroplane at Williams Field; 5 c. Shackleton's Hut; 8 c. Supply ship H.M.N.Z.S. *Endeavour*; 18 c. Tabular ice floe.

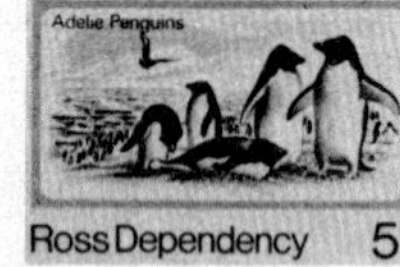

8 Adelie Penguins

(Des R. Conly. Litho Asher and Co, Melbourne)

1982 (20 Jan). *Horiz designs as T* **8**. *Multicoloured. P* 15½.

15 5 c. Type **8** .. 65 40
16 10 c. Tracked vehicles .. 30 30
17 20 c. Scott Base .. 40 30
18 30 c. Field party .. 40 30
19 40 c. Vanda Station .. 40 30
20 50 c. Scott's hut, Cape Evans .. 50 35
15/20 .. *Set of* 6 2·25 1·75

The post office at Scott Base closed on 30 September 1987 and Nos. 15/20 were withdrawn from sale at philatelic counters in New Zealand on 31 December 1987. Local stamps were subsequently issued by the Armed Forces Canteen Council to cover the cost of mail carriage from Scott Base to New Zealand. These are not listed as they had no national or international validity.

TOKELAU

Formerly known as the Union Islands, and administered as part of the Gilbert & Ellice Islands Colony, they were transferred to New Zealand on 4 November 1925 and then administered by Western Samoa. The islands were finally incorporated in New Zealand on 1 January 1949 and became a dependency. The name Tokelau was adopted on 7 May 1946.

> Stamps of GILBERT AND ELLICE ISLANDS were used in Tokelau from February 1911 until June 1926 when they were replaced by those of SAMOA. These were current until 1948.
> The post office on Atafu opened in 1911, but the cancellations for the other two islands, Fakaofo and Nukunono, did not appear until 1926.

1 Atafu Village and Map

(Des J. Berry from photographs by T. T. C. Humphrey. Recess B.W.)

1948 (22 June). *T* **1** *and similar horiz designs. Wmk T* **98** *of New Zealand (Mult* N Z *and Star). P* 13½.

1	½d. red-brown and purple		15	20
2	1d. chestnut and green		15	20
3	2d. green and ultramarine		15	20
1/3		*Set of* 3	40	55

Designs:—1d. Nukunono hut and map; 2d. Fakaofo village and map.

Covers are known postmarked 16 June 1948, but this was in error for 16 July.

1953 (15 June*). *Coronation. As No.* 715 *of New Zealand, but inscr* "TOKELAU ISLANDS".

4	**164**	3d. brown	3·50	3·75

*This is the date of issue in Tokelau. The stamps were released in New Zealand on 25 May.

ONE SHILLING

(4)

6D
TOKELAU
ISLANDS

(5)

1956 (27 Mar). *No.* 1 *surch with T* **4** *by Govt Printer, Wellington.*

5	**1**	1s. on ½d. red-brown and purple	4·00	3·50

1966 (8 Nov). *Postal fiscal stamps of New Zealand (Type* **F 6**), *but without value, surch as T* **5** *by Govt Printer, Wellington. W* **98** *of New Zealand. P* 14.

6	6d. light blue		65	1·25
7	8d. light emerald		75	1·00
8	2s. light pink		85	1·40
6/8		*Set of* 3	2·00	3·25

(New Currency. 100 cents = 1 dollar (New Zealand))

1c

(6)

5c
TOKELAU
ISLANDS

(7)

1967 (4 Sept*). *Decimal currency.*

(*a*) *Nos.* 1/3 *surch in decimal currency as T* **6** *by Govt Printer, Wellington*

9	1c. on 1d.		60	60
10	2 c. on 2d.		1·00	1·00
11	10 c. on ½d.		2·00	2·00

(*b*) *Postal Fiscal stamps of New Zealand (Type* **F 6**), *but without value, surch as T* **7** *by Govt Printer, Wellington. W* **98** *of New Zealand (sideways). P* 14 *(line or comb)*

12	**F 6**	3 c. reddish lilac		50	30
13		5 c. light blue		50	30
14		7 c. light emerald		50	30
15		20 c. light pink		65	40
9/15			*Set of* 7	5·25	4·50

*This is the date of issue in Tokelau. The stamps were released in New Zealand on 10 July.

8 British Protectorate (1877)

12 H.M.S. *Dolphin*, 1765

(Des New Zealand P.O. artists from suggestions by Tokelau Administration. Litho B.W.)

1969 (8 Aug). *History of Tokelau. T* **8** *and similar horiz designs. W* **98** *of New Zealand. P* 13 × 12½.

16	5 c. ultramarine, yellow and black		25	10
17	10 c. vermilion, yellow and black		30	10
18	15 c. green, yellow and black		35	15
19	20 c. yellow-brown, yellow and black		40	15
16/19		*Set of* 4	1·10	45

Designs:—10 c. Annexed to Gilbert and Ellice Islands, 1916: 15 c. New Zealand Administration, 1925; 20 c. New Zealand Territory, 1948.

1969 (1 Oct). *Christmas. As T* **301** *of New Zealand, but inscr* "TOKELAU ISLANDS". *W* **98** *of New Zealand. P* 13½ × 14½.

20	**301**	2 c. multicoloured	10	15

1970 (1 Oct). *Christmas. As T* **314** *of New Zealand but inscr* "TOKELAU ISLANDS". *P* 12½.

21	**341**	2 c. multicoloured	10	20

(Des D. B. Stevenson. Litho B.W.)

1970 (9 Dec). *Discovery of Tokelau. T* **12** *and similar multicoloured designs. P* 13½.

22	5 c. Type **12**		1·50	35
23	10 c. H.M.S. *Pandora*, 1791		1·50	35
24	25 c. *General Jackson*, 1835 *(horiz)*		3·25	70
22/4		*Set of* 3	5·75	1·25

13 Fan

14 Windmill Pump

(Des Enid Hunter. Litho Harrison)

1971 (20 Oct). *Various horiz designs as T* **13** *showing handicrafts. Multicoloured. P* 14.

25	1 c. Type **13**		20	20
26	2 c. Hand-bag		30	30
27	3 c. Basket		40	40
28	5 c. Hand-bag		50	65
29	10 c. Shopping-bag		60	80
30	15 c. Fishing box		1·00	1·50
31	20 c. Canoe		1·25	2·00
32	25 c. Fishing hooks		1·25	2·00
25/32		*Set of* 8	5·00	7·00

(Des A. G. Mitchell. Litho Questa)

1972 (6 Sept). *25th Anniversary of South Pacific Commission. T* **14** *and similar vert designs. Multicoloured. P* 14 × 13½.

33	5 c. Type **14**		35	60
34	10 c. Community well		45	75
35	15 c. Pest eradication		55	1·00
36	20 c. Flags of member nations		60	1·25
33/6		*Set of* 4	1·75	3·25

On No. 35 "PACIFIC" is spelt "PACFIC".

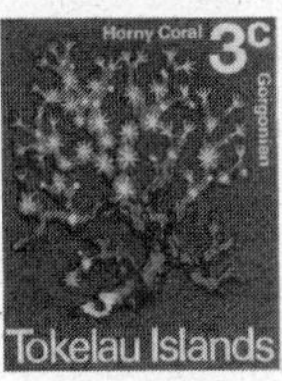

15 Horny Coral

16 Hump-back Cowrie

(Des Eileen Mayo. Litho B.W.)

1973 (12 Sept). *Coral. T* **15** *and similar vert designs. Multicoloured P.* 13.

37	3 c. Type **15**		1·00	80
38	5 c. Soft Coral		1·00	90
39	15 c. Mushroom Coral		1·75	1·50
40	25 c. Staghorn Coral		2·00	1·75
37/40		*Set of* 4	5·25	4·50

(Des G. F. Fuller. Litho Questa)

1974 (13 Nov). *"Shells of the Coral Reef". T* **16** *and similar horiz designs. Multicoloured. P* 14.

41	3 c. Type **16**		1·50	1·25
42	5 c. Tiger Cowrie		1·75	1·50
43	15 c. Mole Cowrie		3·00	3·00
44	25 c. Eyed Cowrie		4·00	3·50
41/4		*Set of* 4	9·00	8·25

17 Moorish Idol

18 Canoe Building

(Des Eileen Mayo. Litho Questa)

1975 (19 Nov). *Fishes. T* **17** *and similar vert designs. Multicoloured. P* 14.

45	5 c. Type **17**		50	1·00
46	10 c. Long-nosed Butterfly-fish		70	1·25
47	15 c. Lined Butterfly-fish		85	1·75
48	25 c. Red Fire-fish		1·10	2·00
45/8		*Set of* 4	2·75	5·50

(Des F. Paulo. Litho Questa)

1976 (27 Oct)–**81**. *T* **18** *and similar multicoloured designs showing local life. P* 14 × 13½ *(9 c. to $1) or* 13½ × 14 *(others).*

49	1 c. Type **18**		20	50
	a. Perf 14½ × 15 (15.7.81)		10	15
50	2 c. Reef fishing		20	1·00
51	3 c. Weaving preparation		25	50
	a. Perf 14½ × 15 (15.7.81)		10	15
52	5 c. Umu (kitchen)		30	50
	a. Perf 14½ × 15 (15.7.81)		10	15
53	9 c. Carving *(vert)*		10	55
	a. Perf 15 × 14½ (15.7.81)		10	15
54	20 c. Husking coconuts *(vert)*		15	45
	a. Perf 15 × 14½ (15.7.81)		15	20
55	50 c. Wash day *(vert)*		20	70
	a. Perf 15 × 14½ (15.7.81)		20	20
56	$1 Meal time *(vert)*		35	1·50
	a. Perf 15 × 14½ (15.7.81)		30	30
49a/56a		*Set of* 8	1·10	2·00

19 White Tern

20 Westminster Abbey

(Des F. Paulo. Litho Questa)

1977 (16 Nov). *Birds of Tokelau. T* **19** *and similar horiz designs. Multicoloured. P* 14½.

57	8 c. Type **19**		30	40
58	10 c. Turnstone		35	45
59	15 c. White-capped Noddy		60	70
60	30 c. Common Noddy		90	1·25
57/60		*Set of* 4	2·00	2·50

(Des Eileen Mayo. Litho Questa)

1978 (28 June). *25th Anniv of Coronation. T* **20** *and similar vert designs. Multicoloured. P* 14.

61	8 c. Type **20**		20	20
62	10 c. King Edward's Chair		20	20
63	15 c. Coronation regalia		30	35
64	30 c. Queen Elizabeth II		50	60
61/4		*Set of* 4	1·10	1·25

21 Canoe Race

22 Rugby

(Des F. Paulo. Photo Heraclio Fournier)

1978 (8 Nov). *Canoe Racing. T* **21** *and similar horiz designs showing races. P* 13½ × 14.

65	8 c. multicoloured		20	20
66	12 c. multicoloured		25	25
67	15 c. multicoloured		30	30
68	30 c. multicoloured		50	50
65/8		*Set of* 4	1·10	1·10

(Des F. Paulo. Photo Heraclio Fournier)

1979 (7 Nov). *Sports. T* **22** *and similar horiz designs. Multicoloured. P* 13½.

69	10 c. Type **22**		15	15
70	15 c. Cricket		40	60
71	20 c. Rugby *(different)*		40	65
72	30 c. Cricket *(different)*		60	80
69/72		*Set of* 4	1·40	2·00

23 Surfing

24 Pole Vaulting

(Des F. Paulo. Litho J.W.)

1980 (5 Nov). *Water Sports. T* **23** *and similar horiz designs. Multicoloured. P* 13.

73	10 c. Type **23**		10	10
74	20 c. Surfing *(different)*		15	15
75	30 c. Swimming		20	25
76	50 c. Swimming *(different)*		25	35
73/6		*Set of* 4	60	75

(Des F. Paulo. Photo Heraclio Fournier)

1981 (4 Nov). *Sports. T* **24** *and similar vert designs. Multicoloured. P* 14 × 13½.

77 10 c. Type **24** 10 10
78 20 c. Volleyball 20 20
79 30 c. Running 25 30
80 50 c. Volleyball (*different*) 30 35
77/80 .. .. *Set of* 4 75 85

25 Wood Carving **26** Octopus Lure

(Des R. Conly. Litho Enschedé)

1982 (5 May). *Handicrafts. T* **25** *and similar vert designs. Multicoloured. P* 14 × 13½.

81 10 s. Type **25** 10 10
82 22 s. Bow-drilling sea shell 15 25
83 34 s. Bowl finishing 20 35
84 60 s. Basket weaving 35 50
81/4 .. .. *Set of* 4 70 1·10

(Des R. Conly. Litho Questa)

1982 (3 Nov). *Fishing Methods. T* **26** *and similar vert designs. Multicoloured. P* 14.

85 5 s. Type **26** 10 10
86 18 s. Multiple-hook fishing 30 20
87 23 s. Ruvettus fishing 35 25
88 34 s. Netting flying fish 40 30
89 63 s. Noose fishing 50 40
90 75 s. Bonito fishing 60 45
85/90 .. .. *Set of* 6 2·00 1·50

27 Outrigger Canoe **28** Javelin Throwing

(Des R. Conly. Litho Cambec Press, Melbourne)

1983 (4 May). *Transport. T* **27** *and similar horiz designs. Multicoloured. P* 13 × 13½.

91 5 s. Type **27** 10 10
92 18 s. Wooden whaleboat 15 15
93 23 s. Aluminium whaleboat 15 20
94 34 s. *Alia* (fishing catamaran) 25 25
95 63 s. M.V. *Frysna* (freighter) 35 40
96 75 s. McKinnon "Goose" flying boat .. 45 50
91/6 .. .. *Set of* 6 1·25 1·40

(Des R. Conly. Litho Questa)

1983 (2 Nov). *Traditional Pastimes. T* **28** *and similar horiz designs. Multicoloured. P* 14.

97 5 s. Type **28** 10 10
98 18 s. String game 15 15
99 23 s. Fire making 15 20
100 34 s. Shell throwing 25 25
101 63 s. Hand-ball game 35 40
102 75 s. Mass wrestling 45 50
97/102 .. .. *Set of* 6 1·25 1·40

29 Planting and Harvesting **30** Convict Tang ("Manini")

(Des R. Conly. Litho J.W.)

1984 (2 May). *Copra Industry. T* **29** *and similar vert designs. Multicoloured. P* 13½ × 13.

103 48 s. Type **29** 40 45
a. Horiz strip of 5. Nos. 103/7 .. 1·90
104 48 s. Husking and splitting 40 45
105 48 s. Drying 40 45
106 48 s. Bagging 40 45
107 48 s. Shipping 40 45
103/7 .. .. *Set of* 5 1·90 2·00

Nos. 103/7 were printed together, *se-tenant*, in horizontal strips of 5 throughout the sheet.

(Des R. Conly. Litho B.D.T.)

1984 (5 Dec). *Fishes. T* **30** *and similar horiz designs. Multicoloured. P* 15 × 14.

108 1 s. Type **30** 10 10
109 2 s. Flying Fish ("Hahave") 10 10
110 5 s. Fire Wrasse ("Uloulo") 10 10
111 9 s. Unicorn Fish ("Ume ihu") 10 10
112 23 s. Napoleon Fish ("Lafilafi") 15 20
113 34 s. Red Snapper ("Fagamea") 20 25
114 50 s. Yellow Fin Tuna ("Kakahi") 35 40
115 75 s. Castor-oil Fish ("Palu po") 50 55
116 $1 Grey Shark ("Mokoha") 65 70
117 $2 Black Marlin ("Hakula") .. .. 1·25 1·40
108/17 .. .. *Set of* 10 3·00 3·25

Examples of Nos. 108/17 are known postmarked at Nukunonu on 23 November 1984.

The 50 s., No. 114 was sold at the "STAMPEX 86" Stamp Exhibition, Adelaide, overprinted "STAMPEX 86 4–10 AUGUST 1986" in three lines. These overprinted stamps were not available from post offices in Tokelau. Used examples come from dealers' stocks subsequently sent to the islands for cancellation.

31 *Ficus tinctoria* ("Mati") **32** Administration Centre, Atafu

(Des R. Conly. Litho Wyatt and Wilson Ltd, Christchurch, N.Z.)

1985 (26 June). *Native Trees. T* **31** *and similar vert designs. Multicoloured. P* 13.

118 5 c. Type **31** 10 10
119 18 c. *Morinda citrifolia* ("Nonu") 15 15
120 32 c. Breadfruit Tree ("Ulu") 20 25
121 48 c. *Pandanus tectorius* ("Fala") 35 40
122 60 c. *Cordia subcordata* ("Kanava") 40 45
123 75 c. Coconut Palm ("Niu") 50 55
118/23 .. .. *Set of* 6 1·50 1·60

Nos. 118/23 were issued with matt, almost invisible PVA gum.

(Des R. Conly. Litho Questa)

1985 (4 Dec). *Tokelau Architecture* (1*st series*). *Public Buildings. T* **32** *and similar horiz designs. Multicoloured. P* 14.

124 5 c. Type **32** 10 10
125 18 c. Administration Centre, Nukunonu .. 15 15
126 32 c. Administration Centre, Fakaofo .. 20 25
127 48 c. Congregational Church, Atafu .. 35 40
128 60 c. Catholic Church, Nukunonu .. 40 45
129 75 c. Congregational Church, Fakaofo .. 50 55
124/9 .. .. *Set of* 6 1·50 1·60

33 Atafu Hospital

(Des R. Conly. Litho Cambec Press, Melbourne)

1986 (7 May). *Tokelau Architecture* (2*nd series*). *Hospitals and Schools. T* **33** *and similar horiz designs. Multicoloured. P* 13½.

130 5 c. Type **33** 10 10
131 18 c. St. Joseph's Hospital, Nukunonu .. 10 10
132 32 c. Fenuafala Hospital, Fakaofo .. 20 25
133 48 c. Matauala School, Atafu .. 35 40
134 60 c. Matiti School, Nukunonu .. 40 45
135 75 c. Fenuafala School, Fakaofo .. 55 60
130/5 .. .. *Set of* 6 1·50 1·60

34 Coconut Crab

(Des R. Conly. Litho Questa)

1986 (3 Dec). *Agricultural Livestock. T* **34** *and similar horiz designs. Multicoloured. P* 14.

136 5 c. Type **34** 10 10
137 18 c. Pigs 15 15
138 32 c. Chickens 25 25
139 48 c. Reef Hawksbill Turtle 40 40
140 60 c. Goats 45 45
141 75 c. Ducks 60 60
136/41 .. .. *Set of* 6 1·75 1·75

35 *Scaevola taccada* ("Gahu")

(Des R. Conly. Litho Questa)

1987 (6 May). *Tokelau Flora. T* **35** *and similar horiz designs. Multicoloured. P* 14.

142 5 c. Type **35** 25 20
143 18 c. *Hernandia nymphaeifolia* ("Puka") .. 40 30
144 32 c. *Pandanus tectorius* ("Higano") .. 60 50
145 48 c. *Gardenia taitensis* ("Tialetiale") .. 80 70
146 60 c. *Pemphis acidula* ("Gagie") .. 1·00 90
147 75 c. *Guettarda speciosa* ("Puapua") .. 1·25 1·00
142/7 .. .. *Set of* 6 4·00 3·25

36 Javelin-throwing

(Des F. Paulo. Litho Leigh-Mardon Ltd, Melbourne)

1987 (2 Dec). *Tokelau Olympic Sports. T* **36** *and similar horiz designs. Multicoloured. P* 14 × 14½.

148 5 c. Type **36** 15 15
149 18 c. Shot-putting 30 30
150 32 c. Long jumping 45 45
151 48 c. Hurdling 60 60
152 60 c. Sprinting 80 80
153 75 c. Wrestling 95 95
148/53 .. .. *Set of* 6 3·00 3·00

37 Small Boat Flotilla in Sydney Harbour **38** Island Maps and Ministerial Representatives

(Des and litho CPE Australia Ltd, Melbourne)

1988 (30 July). *Bicentenary of Australian Settlement and "Sydpex '88" National Stamp Exhibition, Sydney. T* **37** *and similar square designs. Multicoloured. P* 13.

154 50 c. Type **37** 70 70
a. Horiz strip of 5. Nos. 154/8 .. 3·25
155 50 c. Sailing ships and liners 70 70
156 50 c. Sydney skyline and Opera House .. 70 70
157 50 c. Sydney Harbour Bridge 70 70
158 50 c. Sydney waterfront 70 70
154/8 .. .. *Set of* 5 3·25 3·25

Nos. 154/8 were printed together, *se-tenant*, in horizontal strips of five throughout the sheet, forming a composite aerial view of the re-enactment of First Fleet's arrival.

(Des F. Paulo. Litho Leigh-Mardon Ltd, Melbourne)

1988 (10 Aug). *Political Development. T* **38** *and similar horiz designs. Multicoloured. P* 14½.

159 5 c. Type **38** (administration transferred to N.Z. Foreign Affairs Ministry, 1975) .. 10 10
160 18 c. General Fono (island assembly) meeting, 1977 .. .. 15 15
161 32 c. Arms of New Zealand (first visit by New Zealand Prime Minister, 1985) .. 20 25
162 48 c. U.N. logo (first visit by U.N. representative, 1976) 35 40
163 60 c. Canoe and U.N. logo (first Tokelau delegation to U.N., 1987) 40 45
164 75 c. Secretary and N.Z. flag (first islander appointed as Official Secretary, 1987) 50 55
159/64 .. .. *Set of* 6 1·50 1·60

39 Three Wise Men in Canoe and Star

(Des F. Paulo. Litho Govt Ptg Office, Wellington)

1988 (7 Dec). *Christmas. T* **39** *and similar horiz designs showing Christmas in Tokelau. Multicoloured. P* 13½.

165 5 c. Type **39** 10 10
166 20 c. Tokelau Nativity 20 20
167 40 c. Flight to Egypt by canoe 35 35
168 60 c. Children's presents 45 45
169 70 c. Christ child in Tokelauan basket .. 55 55
170 $1 Christmas parade 75 75
165/70 .. .. *Set of* 6 2·10 2·10

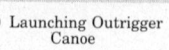

40 Launching Outrigger Canoe **41** Basketwork

(Des F. Paulo. Litho Leigh-Mardon Ltd, Melbourne)

1989 (28 June). *Food Gathering. T* **40** *and similar horiz designs. Multicoloured. P* 14×14½.

171	50 c. Type **40**		60	60
	a. Horiz strip of 3. Nos. 171/3		1·60	
172	50 c. Paddling canoe away from shore		60	60
173	50 c. Fishing punt and sailing canoe		60	60
174	50 c. Canoe on beach		60	60
	a. Horiz strip of 3. Nos. 174/6		1·60	
175	50 c. Loading coconuts into canoe		60	60
176	50 c. Tokelauans with produce		60	60
171/6		*Set of* 6	3·00	3·00

Nos. 171/3 and 174/6 were each printed together, *se-tenant*, in horizontal strips of three throughout the sheets, forming composite designs.

A $3 miniature sheet commemorating the 150th anniversary of the Penny Black and "Stamp World London 90" International Stamp Exhibition exists, but was not issued or used by the New Zealand Post offices on the islands.

(Litho Leigh-Mardon Ltd, Melbourne)

1990 (2 May). *Women's Handicrafts. T* **41** *and similar horiz designs. Multicoloured. P* 14½.

177	5 c. Type **41**		25	25
178	20 c. Preparing cloth		55	55
179	40 c. Tokelau fabrics		75	75
180	60 c. Mat weaving		1·25	1·25
181	80 c. Weaving palm fronds		1·50	1·50
182	$1 Basket making		1·60	1·60
177/82		*Set of* 6	5·50	5·50

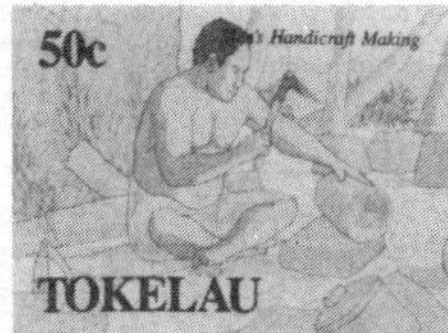

42 Man with Adze and Wood Blocks

(Des F. Paulo. Litho Wyatt & Wilson, Christchurch)

1990 (1 Aug). *Men's Handicrafts. T* **42** *and similar horiz designs. Multicoloured. P* 13½.

183	50 c. Type **42**		75	75
	a. Horiz strip of 3. Nos. 183/5		2·00	
184	50 c. Making fishing boxes		75	75
185	50 c. Fixing handles to fishing boxes		75	75
186	50 c. Two men decorating fishing boxes		75	75
	a. Horiz strip of 3. Nos. 186/8		2·00	
187	50 c. Canoe building (two men)		75	75
188	50 c. Canoe building (three men)		75	75
183/8		*Set of* 6	4·00	4·00

Nos. 183/5 and 186/8 were each printed together, *se-tenant*, in horizontal strips of 3 throughout the sheets, and have matt, almost invisible, gum.

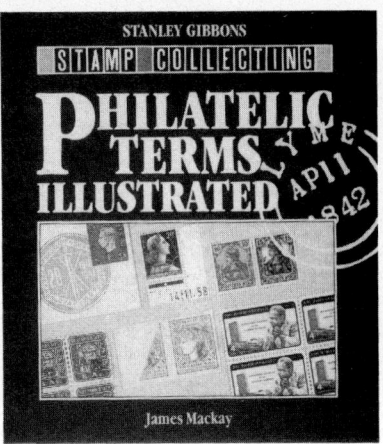

Nigeria

LAGOS

A British Consul was established at Lagos during 1853 as part of the anti-slavery policy, but the territory was not placed under British administration until the treaty of August 1861. From 1866 Lagos was administered with Sierra Leone and from July 1874 as part of Gold Coast. It became a separate colony in January 1886.

Although a postal service had been established by the British G.P.O. in 1851 no postal markings were supplied to Lagos until 1859. The British G.P.O. retained control of the postal service until 1874, when it became the responsibility of the colonial authorities.

CROWNED-CIRCLE HANDSTAMPS

CC 1

CC1 CC 1 LAGOS (19.2.1859) .. .. *Price on cover* £1500

PRICES FOR STAMPS ON COVER	
Nos. 1/9	*from* × 6
Nos. 10/41	*from* × 5
No. 42	*from* × 15
Nos. 44/53	*from* × 5
Nos. 54/63	*from* × 4

PRINTERS. All the stamps of Lagos were typographed by D.L.R.

1

1874 (10 June)–**75**. *Wmk Crown CC. P* 12½.

1	1	1d. lilac-mauve	48·00	28·00
2		2d. blue	48·00	26·00
3		3d. red-brown (3.75)	90·00	40·00
4		3d. red-brown and chestnut	75·00	48·00
5		4d. carmine	60·00	40·00
6		6d. blue-green	75·00	10·00
8		1s. orange (value 15½ mm) (3.75)	£300	£130
9		1s. orange (value 16½ mm)	£225	60·00
1/9		*Set of* 6	£475	£180

1876. *Wmk Crown CC. P* 14.

10	1	1d. lilac-mauve	32·00	14·00
11		2d. blue	35·00	11·00
12		3d. red-brown	90·00	18·00
13		3d. chestnut	£110	30·00
14		4d. carmine	£160	11·00
		a. Wmk sideways	£850	£130
15		6d. green	75·00	6·00
16		1s. orange (value 16½ mm long)	£450	65·00
10/16		*Set of* 6	£750	£110

1882 (June). *Wmk Crown CA. P* 14.

17	1	1d. lilac-mauve	15·00	10·00
18		2d. blue	£110	4·75
19		3d. chestnut	10·00	5·00
20		4d. carmine	£100	11·00
17/20		*Set of* 4	£200	28·00

1884 (Dec)–**86**. *New values and colours. Wmk Crown CA. P* 14.

21	1	½d. dull green (2.86)	50	20
22		1d. rose-carmine	60	25
23		2d. grey	35·00	5·00
24		4d. pale violet	65·00	8·50
25		6d. olive-green	5·00	20·00
26		1s. orange (3.85)	5·00	13·00
27		2s. 6d. olive-black (10.86)	£275	£250
28		5s. blue (10.86)	£550	£400
29		10s. purple-brown (10.86)	£1200	£800
21/9		*Set of* 9	£1800	£1300
27/9 Optd "Specimen"		*Set of* 3	£450	

We would warn collectors against clever forgeries of Nos. 27 to 29 on genuinely watermarked paper.

2½ PENNY A

2½ PENNY B

1887 (Mar)–**1902**. *Wmk Crown CA. P* 14.

30	1	2d. dull mauve and blue	1·25	1·00
31		2½d. ultramarine (A) (12.90)	1·25	1·75
		a. Larger letters of value (B)	18·00	17·00
		b. Blue (A)	80·00	50·00
32	1	3d. dull mauve and chestnut (4.91)	2·50	3·25
33		4d. dull mauve and black	2·00	1·75
34		5d. dull mauve and green (2.94)	2·00	11·00
35		6d. dull mauve and mauve	4·50	3·00
		a. Dull mauve and carmine (10.02)	4·50	12·00
36		7½d. dull mauve and carmine (2.94)	2·00	22·00
37		10d. dull mauve and yellow (2.94)	2·75	13·00
38		1s. yellow-green and black	3·00	14·00
		a. Blue-green and black	4·00	16·00
39		2s. 6d. green and carmine	22·00	50·00
40		5s. green and blue	32·00	90·00
41		10s. green and brown	60·00	£130
30/41		*Set of* 12	£120	£300
30/41 Optd "Specimen"		*Set of* 12	£250	

HALF PENNY

(2)

3

1893 (Aug). *No.* 33 *surch with T* **2**.

42	1	½d. on 4d. dull mauve and black	2·25	2·50
		a. Surch double	55·00	55·00
		b. Surch treble	80·00	
		c. Error. ½d. on 2d. (No. 30)	—	£11000

There were four settings of this surcharge, a scarce setting in which "HALF PENNY" is 16½ mm and three others in which the length is 16 mm. Of No. 42c, one copy is known unused and one used.

1904 (22 Jan–Nov). *Wmk Crown CA. P* 14.

44	3	½d. dull green and green	1·50	5·50
45		1d. purple and black/*red*	60	15
46		2d. dull purple and blue	6·00	12·00
47		2½d. dull purple and blue/*blue* (B)	1·00	1·50
		a. Smaller letters of value as A	3·00	8·00
48		3d. dull purple and brown	1·00	2·75
49		6d. dull purple and mauve	35·00	10·00
50		1s. green and black	35·00	30·00
51		2s. 6d. green and carmine	80·00	£150
52		5s. green and blue	£150	£275
53		10s. green and brown (Nov)	£300	£750
44/53		*Set of* 10	£550	£1100
44/53 Optd "Specimen"		*Set of* 10	£225	

1904–06. *Wmk Mult Crown CA. Ordinary paper. P* 14.

54	3	½d. dull green and green (30.10.04)	3·75	1·75
		a. Chalk-surfaced paper (12.3.06)	3·25	1·75
55		1d. purple and black/*red* (22.10.04)	1·25	10
		a. Chalk-surfaced paper (21.9.05)	50	10
56		2d. dull purple and blue (2.05)	1·75	75
		a. Chalk-surfaced paper (25.9.06)	4·25	1·50
57		2½d. dull purple and blue/*blue* (B) (*chalk-surfaced paper*) (13.10.05)	1·50	15·00
		a. Smaller letters of values as A	55·00	£100
58		3d. dull purple and brown (27.4.05)	2·75	90
		a. Chalk-surfaced paper (2.8.06)	6·00	1·75
59		6d. dull purple and mauve (31.10.05)	3·25	1·25
		a. Chalk-surfaced paper (1.3.06)	3·25	1·25
60		1s. green and black (15.10.04)	3·25	4·50
		a. Chalk-surfaced paper (4.06)	8·00	2·00
61		2s. 6d. green and carmine (3.12.04)	10·00	23·00
		a. Chalk-surfaced paper (21.10.06)	16·00	23·00
62		5s. green and blue (1.05)	16·00	60·00
		a. Chalk-surfaced paper (21.10.06)	24·00	75·00
63		10s. green and brown (3.12.04)	48·00	£110
		a. Chalk-surfaced paper (12.3.06)	55·00	£110
54/63		*Set of* 10	80·00	£190

Lagos was incorporated into the Colony and Protectorate of Southern Nigeria, previously formed from Niger Coast Protectorate and part of the Niger Company territories, on 16 February 1906. Stamps of Lagos were then authorised for use throughout Southern Nigeria.

NIGER COAST PROTECTORATE

OIL RIVERS PROTECTORATE

A British consulate for the Bights of Benin and Biafra was established in 1849 on the off-shore Spanish island of Fernando Poo. In 1853 the appointment was divided with a consul for the Bight of Benin at Lagos. The consulate for the Bight of Biafra was transferred to Old Calabar in 1882.

A British protectorate was proclaimed over the coastal area, with the exceptions of the colony of Lagos and the centre of the Niger delta, in June 1885. It was not, however, until 1891 that steps were taken to set up an admininistration with a consul-general at Old Calabar and vice-consuls at some of the river ports.

The consulate-general at Old Calabar and the vice-consulates at Benin, Bonny, Brass, Forcados and Opobo acted as collection and distribution centres for mail from November 1891, but were not recognised as post offices until 20 July 1892.

For a few months from July 1892 local administrative handstamps, as Type Z 1, were in use either as obliterators or in conjunction with the c.d.s.

Z 1

These oval handstamps are usually found on the 1892 overprinted issue, but the following are known on unoverprinted stamps of Great Britain:

1892

BENIN

Stamps of GREAT BRITAIN *cancelled with oval postmark, Type* Z **1**, *inscribed* "BENIN".

Z1 2½d. purple/*blue* (V.) £1000

BONNY

Stamps of GREAT BRITAIN *cancelled with oval postmark, Type* Z **1**, *inscribed* "BONNY".

Z2 2½d. purple/*blue* (V.) .. ..

BRASS RIVER

Stamps of GREAT BRITAIN *cancelled with oval postmark, Type* Z **1**, *inscribed* "BRASS".

Z3 2½d. purple/*blue* (Blk.) £750

OLD CALABAR RIVER

Stamps of GREAT BRITAIN *cancelled with oval postmark, Type* Z **1**, *inscribed* "OLD CALABAR".

Z4 2½d. purple/*blue* (Blk.) .. .. ..

Stamps of GREAT BRITAIN *cancelled* "BRITISH VICE-CONSULATE OLD CALABAR" *within double-lined circle.*

Z5 2½d. purple/*blue* (V.) £400

Z6 5d. dull purple and blue (V.) .. ..

For later use of Type Z 1 and the circular Vice-Consulate marks see note beneath No. 6.

Z 2.

Unoverprinted stamps of Great Britain remained officially valid for postage in the Protectorate until 30 September 1892, but were available from post offices in the Niger Company Territories up to the end of 1899. The two areas were so closely linked geographically that offices in the Protectorate continued to accept letters franked with Great Britain stamps until the reorganisation of 1900. The listing below covers confirmed examples, known on cover or piece, the prices quoted being for the latter.

1892 *to* **1899**

Stamps of GREAT BRITAIN *cancelled with circular postmarks as Type* Z **2**.

BENIN RIVER

Z 7	2d. green and carmine	
Z 8	2½d. purple/*blue*	
Z 9	3d. purple/*yellow*	
Z10	5d. dull purple and blue	
Z11	1s. green	

BONNY RIVER

Z12	½d. vermilion	
Z13	2½d. purple/*blue*	£250
Z14	5d. dull purple and blue	£350
Z15	6d. deep purple/*red*	£350

BRASS RIVER

Z16	1½d. dull purple and green	
Z17	2½d. purple/*blue*	£850
Z17*a*	2½d. purple/*blue* (squared-circle cancellation)	
Z18	6d. purple/*red*	£700

FORCADOS RIVER

Z19	1d. lilac	£550
Z20	2½d. purple/*blue*	
Z21	5d. dull purple and blue (m/s cancellation)	
Z22	10d. dull purple and carmine	

OLD CALABAR RIVER

Z23	½d. vermilion	£300
Z24	1d. lilac	£250
Z25	1½d. dull purple and green	
Z26	2d. green and vermilion	
Z27	2½d. purple/*blue*	£250
Z28	5d. dull purple and blue	
Z29	6d. purple/*red*	
Z30	1s. green	

OPOBO RIVER

Z31	2½d. purple/*blue*	
Z32	10d. dull purple and carmine	

Some later covers are known franked with G.B. stamps, but the origin of the stamps involved is uncertain.

PRICES FOR STAMPS ON COVER	
Nos. 1/6	*from* × 10
Nos. 7/36	*from* × 3
Nos. 37/44	—
Nos. 45/50	*from* × 10
Nos. 51/6	*from* × 12
Nos. 57/65	*from* × 3
Nos. 66/73	*from* × 12

BRITISH
PROTECTORATE

OIL RIVERS

(1)

(2)

1892 (20 July)–**94.** *Stamps of Great Britain optd by D.L.R. with T* **1**.

1 **71** ½d. vermilion .. .. 5·50 4·50
2 **57** 1d. lilac .. .. 5·50 4·50
a. Opt reversed "OIL RIVERS" at top £4000
b. Bisected (½d.) (on cover) .. .. † £2500
3 **73** 2d. green and carmine .. .. .. 13·00 8·00
a. Bisected (1d.) (on cover) .. .. † £4000
4 **74** 2½d. purple/*blue* .. .. 6·50 2·00
5 **78** 5d. dull purple & blue (No. 207*a* Die II) 7·50 7·50
a. On No. 207 (Die I) .. ..
6 **82** 1s. green .. .. 45·00 55·00
1/6 .. .. *Set of* 6 75·00 70·00
1/6 H/S "Specimen" .. .. .. *Set of* 6 £300

Nos. 2b and 3a were used at Bonny River during August and September 1894.

OVAL HANDSTAMPS. In addition to Nos. Z1/4 postmarks as Type Z 1 are also known used on the 1892–94 overprinted issue from the following offices:

Bakana (Nos. 2, 4/6)
Benin (Nos. 1/6)
Bonny (No. 2)
Brass (Nos. 3/5)
Buguma (Nos. 4 and 6)
Old Calabar (No. 4)
Opobo (Nos. 1/3)
Sombreiro River (Nos. 1/6)

The Vice-Consulate marks, as Nos. Z5/6, are also known struck on examples of No. 4 from Bonny, Forcados or Old Calabar.

Nos. 2 to 6 surcharged locally

1893 (3 Sept). *Issued at Old Calabar. Surch with T* **2** *and then bisected.*

7 ½d. on half of 1d. (R.) £150 £140
a. Unsevered pair £450 £425
ab. Surch inverted and dividing line reversed (unsevered pair) .. .. — £6500
b. Surch reversed (dividing line running from left to right) (unsevered pair) .. — £6500
c. Straight top to "1" in "½" £350 £350
d. "½" omitted .. ..
e. Surch double (unsevered pair with normal) .. .. — £1500
f. *Se-tenant* pair. Nos. 7a/8a .. .. — £8500
8 ½d. on half of 1d. (V.) £3000 £2750
a. Unsevered pair £7000 £6500
b. Surch double (pair) £10000

The surcharge was applied in a setting covering one horizontal row at a time. Violet ink was used for the top row in the first sheet, but was then replaced with red.

HALF PENNY.

(3)

HALF PENNY.

(4)

1893 (Dec). *Issued at Old Calabar. Nos. 3/6 handstamped.*

(*a*) *With T* **3**

9 ½d. on 2d. (V.) £500 £300
a. Surch inverted £3000
b. Surch diagonal (up or down) £2250
c. Surch vertical (up or down) £2250
10 ½d. on 2½d. (Verm.) £6500
a. Surch in carmine £10000

(*b*) *With T* **4**

11 ½d. on 2½d. (G.) £250 £250
a. Surch double £2000 £2000
b. Surch diagonally inverted £2000
12 ½d. on 2½d. (Verm) £375 £275
13 ½d. on 2½d. (C.) £325 £325
a. Surch omitted (in pair) .. .. ..
14 ½d. on 2½d. (B.) £325 £325
15 ½d. on 2½d. (Blk.) £2750
a. Surch inverted £4000
b. Surch diagonal inverted (up or down) .. £3000
16 ½d. on 2½d. (B.-Blk.) £3000

In T 3 "HALF" measures 9½ mm and "PENNY" 12½ mm with space 1½ mm between the words. Bar 14½ mm ending below the stop. The "F" is nearly always defective.

In T 4 "HALF" is 8½ mm, "PENNY" 12½ mm, spacing 2½ mm, and bar 16 mm, extending beyond the stop.

HALF PENN.Y

5 (Stop after "N")

HALF PENNY

6 (No stop after "N")

(*c*) *With T* **5**

17 ½d. on 2½d. (Verm.) £350 £200
a. Surch double .. .. — £1300
b. Surch vertical (up) .. .. .. — £2000

(*d*) *With T* **6**

18 ½d. on 2d. (V.) £550 £400
19 ½d. on 2½d. (Verm.) £225 £225
a. Surch inverted £1400
b. Surch double .. .. — £1600
c. Surch diagonal (up or down) £1200
d. Surch omitted (in strip of 3) £6500
e. Surch vertical (up or down) £1400
f. Surch diagonal, inverted (up or down) £1600

In T **5** the "P" and "Y" are raised, and the space between the words is about 4 mm. Bar is short, approx 13½ mm. T **6** is similar but without the stop after "N".

Half Penny

(7)

Half Penny

(8)

(*e*) *With T* **7**

20 ½d. on 2d. (V.) £250 £225
a. Surch double .. .. — £5500
b. Surch vertical (up or down) £1600
c. Surch diagonal (up or down) £1500
d. Surch diagonal (inverted) £3000
21 ½d. on 2½d. (Verm.) £225 £200
a. Surch double £4000
b. Surch vertical (up or down) £1400
c. Surch inverted £1600
d. Surch diagonal (up or down) £1200
e. Surch diagonal, inverted (up) £3000
22 ½d. on 2½d. (B.) £6500 £6500
23 ½d. on 2½d. (C.) £5500
24 ½d. on 2½d. (V.) £3500

(*f*) *With T* **8**

25 ½d. on 2½d. (Verm.) £300 £325
a. Surch diagonal (up) £1800
26 ½d. on 2½d. (B.) £7500
27 ½d. on 2½d. (G.) £275 £350
a. Surch double £5000
28 ½d. on 2½d. (C.) £10000 £10000

In T 7 the "a" and "e" are narrow and have a short upward terminal hook. The "l" has a very small hook. The letters "nny" have curved serifs, and the distance between the words is 5½ mm.

In T 8 the "a" and "e" are wider. The "l" has a wider hook. The letters "nny" have straight serifs, and the distance between the words is 4¼ mm.

HALF PENNY.

(9)

HALF PENNY

(10)

(*g*) *With T* **9**

29 ½d. on 2d. (V.) £300 £300
30 ½d. on 2d. (B.) £900 £550
a. Surch double .. ..
31 ½d. on 2½d. (Verm.) £400 £500
a. Surch double .. ..
32 ½d. on 2½d. (B.) £300 £300
33 ½d. on 2½d. (G.) £300 £300
a. Surch double (G.) £1600
b. Surch double (G. + Verm.) .. ..
34 ½d. on 2½d. (V.) £3250

(*h*) *With T* **10**

35 ½d. on 2½d. (G.) £400 £500
36 ½d. on 2½d. (Verm.) £4250

One Shilling

(11)

5/-

(12)

(*i*) *With T* **11**

37 1s. on 2d. (V.) £450 £400
a. Surch inverted £2750
b. Surch vertical (up or down) £2500
c. Surch diagonal (up or down) £2250
d. Surch diagonal, inverted (up or down) £2750
38 1s. on 2d. (Verm.) £550 £650
a. Surch inverted £3750
b. Surch diagonal (up or down) £3250
c. Surch vertical (up or down) £3750
39 1s. on 2d. (Blk.) £5000
a. Surch inverted £8000
b. Surch vertical (up or down) £6500

There are two main types of the "One Shilling" surcharge:—

Type A. The "O" is over the "hi" of "Shilling" and the downstrokes of the "n" in "One", if extended, would meet the "ll" of "Shilling". The "g" is always raised. Type A is known in all three colours.

Type B. The "O" is over the first "i" of "Shilling" and the downstrokes of the "n" would meet the "li" of "Shilling". Type B is known in violet and vermilion.

There is a third, minor type of the black surcharge, but the differences are very slight.

Various types of the surcharges on Nos. 9 to 39 were printed on the same sheet, and different types in different colours may be found *se-tenant*. These are of great rarity.

(*j*) *As T* **12**

40 5s. on 2d. (V.) £7000 £8000
a. Surch inverted £10000
b. Surch vertical (up or down) £10000 £10000
c. Surch diagonal (down) £10000
41 10s. on 5d. (Verm.) £6000 £8000
a. Surch inverted £10000
b. Surch vertical (up or down) £10000
c. Surch diagonal (down) .. ..
42 20s. on 1s (V.) £65000
a. Surch inverted £80000
43 20s. on 1s. (Verm.) £65000
44 20s. on 1s. (Blk.) £65000

NIGER COAST PROTECTORATE

The name of the protectorate was changed on 12 May 1893.

PERFORATION. There are a number of small variations in the perforation of the Waterlow issues of 1893 to 1898 which were due to irregularity of the pins rather than different perforators.

In the following lists, stamps perf 12, 12½, 13 or compound are described as perf 12–13, stamps perf 13½, 14 or compound are described as perf 13½–14 and those perf 14½, 15 or compound are listed as perf 14½–15. In addition the 13½–14 perforation exists compound with 14½–15 and with 12–13, whilst perf 15½–16 comes from a separate perforator.

13

14

(Des G. D. Drummond. Recess Waterlow)

1894 (1 Jan). *T* **13** (*with* "OIL RIVERS" *obliterated and* "NIGER COAST" *in top margin*). *Various frames. No wmk. Thick and thin papers. P* 14½–15.

45 ½d. vermilion .. .. 4·00 3·75
a. Perf 13½–14 .. ..
46 1d. pale blue .. .. 3·75 3·25
a. Bisected (½d.) (on cover) .. .. † £550
b. Dull blue .. .. 3·75 3·25
ba. Bisected (½d.) (on cover) .. .. † £450
c. Perf 13½–14 .. ..
d. Perf 13½–14, comp 12–13 .. ..
47 2d. green .. .. 14·00 13·00
a. Imperf between (horiz pair) .. .. — £3000
b. Bisected (1d.) (on cover) .. .. † £700
c. Perf 14½–15, comp 12–13 .. ..
d. Perf 13½–14 .. .. 14·00 13·00
e. Perf 13½–14, comp 12–13 .. .. — 18·00
d. Perf 12–13 .. ..
48 2½d. carmine-lake .. .. 3·50 3·50
a. Perf 13½–14 .. ..
b. Perf 13½–14, comp 12–13 .. ..
c. Perf 12–13 .. ..
49 5d. grey-lilac .. .. 9·50 9·00
a. Lilac (1894) .. .. 9·00 12·00
b. Perf 13½–14 .. ..
50 1s. black .. .. 14·00 12·00
a. Perf 14½–15, comp 12–13 .. ..
b. Perf 13½–14 .. ..
c. Perf 13½–14, comp 12–13 .. ..
45/50 .. .. *Set of* 6 42·00 42·00

There were three printings of each value, in November 1893, Jan 1894 and March 1894.

Nos. 46a, 46ba and 47b were used at Bonny River during August and September 1894.

(Recess Waterlow)

1894 (June). *T* **14** (*various frames*). *No wmk. P* 14½–15.

51 ½d. yellow-green .. .. 1·40 2·50
a. Deep green .. .. 1·75 3·50
b. Perf 14½–15, comp 13½–14 .. ..
c. Perf 13½–14 .. ..
d. Perf 13½–14, comp 12–13 .. ..
52 1d. orange-vermilion .. .. .. 7·50 6·50
a. Vermilion .. .. 6·00 3·25
b. Bisected diagonally (½d.) (on cover) .. † £500
c. Perf 15½–16 .. ..
d. Perf 13½–14 .. ..
e. Perf 13½–14, comp 12–13 .. ..
53 2d. lake .. .. 7·00 3·75
a. Bisected diagonally (1d.) (on cover) ..
b. Perf 13½–14 .. .. 7·50 3·25
54 2½d. blue .. .. 7·50 3·25
a. Pale blue .. .. 6·00 5·00
55 5d. purple .. .. 4·50 5·50
a. Deep violet .. .. 4·50 5·50
56 1s.black
a. Perf 13½–14 .. .. 10·00 7·00
b. Perf 13½–14, comp 12–13 .. ..
51/6 .. .. *Set of* 6 32·00 22·00

Nos. 52b and 53a were used at Bonny River during August and September 1894.

1/2

(15)

1

(16)

ONE = = HALF PENNY

(17)

1894. *Provisionals. Issued at Opobo.*

(*a*) *Nos.* 46*b and* 46 *bisected vertically and surch with T* **15** (May–June)

57 "½" on half of 1d dull blue (R.) (May) .. £750 £250
a. Surch inverted (in strip of 3 with normals) £6500
58 "½" on half of 1d. pale blue (R.) (June) .. £550 £225
a. Surch *tête-bêche* (pair) .. .. ..
b. Surcharge inverted £2500

(*b*) *No.* 3 *bisected vertically and surch*

(i) *With T* **16** (12 *mm high*) (June-Oct)

59 "1" on half of 2d. (Verm.) £500 £300
a. Surch double £1100 £950
b. Surch inverted .. .. — £1100

(ii) *Smaller* "1" (4¾ *mm high*)

60 "1" on half of 2d. (C.).. .. .. .. — £2500

(iii) *Smaller* "1" (3¾ mm high)

61 "1" on half on 2d. (C.)

Nos. 60 and 61 exist *se-tenant*. (*Price* £18000 *used*.)

(c) *No.* 52a *bisected, surch with T* 15 (Aug–Sept)

62 ½ on half of 1d. vermilion (Blk.) £1600 £450
63 ½ on half of 1d. vermilion (V.) £1400 £325
64 ½ on half of 1d. vermilion (B.) £1200 £250
a. "½" double .. .. — £2000

The stamp is found divided down the middle and also diagonally.

1894 (10 Aug). *Issued at Old Calabar. No.* 54 *surch with T* 17 *and two bars through value at foot.*

65 ½d. on 2½d. blue £275 £200
a. Surch double £1600 £1300
b. "OIE" for "ONE" £1400 £1000
c. Ditto. Surch double .. .. .. — £2250

There are eight types in the setting of T 17.

(Recess Waterlow)

1897 (Mar)–**98**. *As T* 14 (*various frames*). *Wmk Crown CA. P* 14½–15.

66 ½d. green (7.97) .. .. 1·50 1·00
a. Sage-green .. .. 2·00 1·75
b. Perf 13½–14 .. .. — 2·25
67 1d. orange-vermilion .. .. 2·00 1·00
a. Vermilion .. .. 2·25 1·00
b. Imperf between (pair) £2000
c. Perf 15½–16
d. Perf 13½–14 .. .. — 1·75
68 2d. lake (7.97) .. .. 1·50 1·00
a. Perf 15½–16 .. .. — 2·00
69 2½d. slate-blue (8.97) .. .. 2·75 2·00
a. Deep bright blue .. .. 2·75 1·00
b. Perf 13½–14
70 5d. red-violet (1898) .. .. 7·50 45·00
a. Purple .. .. 7·50 45·00
b. Perf 13½–14
71 6d. yellow-brown (6.98) .. .. 7·00 6·50
a. Perf 13½–14
72 1s. black (1898) .. .. 14·00 13·00
a. Perf 13½–14 .. .. 14·00 14·00
73 2s. 6d. olive-bistre (6.98)
a. Perf 15½–16 .. .. 30·00
b. Perf 13½–14 .. .. 20·00 55·00
74 10s. deep violet (6.98) .. .. 75·00 £140
a. Bright violet .. .. 80·00 £140
b. Perf 13½–14 .. .. 80·00 £140
66/74 .. .. *Set of* 9 £120 £225
71, 73/4 Optd "Specimen" .. .. *Set of* 3 £225

Owing to temporary shortages in Southern Nigeria, the above issue was again in use at various times from 1902 until 1907.

On 1 January 1900 the Niger Coast Protectorate together with the southern portion of the Niger Company Territories became the protectorate of Southern Nigeria.

NIGER COMPANY TERRITORIES

Following the development of trade along the Niger, British commercial interests formed the United African Company in 1879 which became, in 1886, the Royal Niger Company. A charter was granted to the Company in the same year to administer territory along the Rivers Niger and Benue over which a British protectorate had been proclaimed. The Company's territories extended to the Niger delta to provide access to the interior.

Post Offices were opened at Akassa (1887), Burutu (1896), Lokoja (1898) and Abutshi (1899). The stamps of Great Britain were used from 1888.

On the establishment of postal services in 1887 the Company arranged with the British G.P.O. that unstamped mail marked with their handstamps would be delivered in Great Britain, the recipients only being charged the normal rate of postage from West Africa. This system was difficult to administer, however, so the British authorities agreed to the supply of G.B. stamps for use at the Company post offices.

Initially the stamps on such covers were left uncancelled until the mail arrived in the United Kingdom, the Company handstamp being struck elsewhere on the address side. This method continued to be used until early 1896, although a number of covers from the twelve months prior to that date do show the Company handstamp cancelling the stamps. Some of these covers were later recancelled on arrival in Great Britain. From May 1896 the postage stamps were cancelled in the Niger Territories.

In the following listings no attempt has been made to cover the use of the Company marks on the reverse of envelopes.

Dates given are those of earliest known postmarks. Colour of postmarks in brackets. Where two or more colours are given, price is for cheapest. Illustrations are reduced to two-thirds linear of the actual size.

Stamps of GREAT BRITAIN *cancelled as indicated below.*

ABUTSHI

1899 (4 Oct *to* 31 Dec). *Cancelled as T* 8, *but inscribed* "THE ROYAL NIGER CO. C. & L. ABUTSHI" *with* "CUSTOMS (date) OFFICE" *in central oval.*

Z1 ½d. vermilion (V.) £250
Z2 1d. lilac (V.) £180
Z3 2½d. purple/*blue* (V.) £275
Z4 5d. dull purple and blue (V.) £300
Z5 10d. dull purple and carmine (V.) £350
Z6 2s. 6d. deep lilac (V.) £400

AKASSA

The listings for Nos. Z7/15 are for *covers* on which the Akassa handstamp appears on the front, but is *not* used as a cancellation for the G.B. stamps. Examples of Nos. Z16/26 occur, from 1895–96, with the handstamp struck on the front of the cover away from the stamps, or, from 1896, used as a cancellation. The prices quoted are for *single stamps* showing the cancellation; covers from either period being worth considerably more. On Nos. Z27/42 the handstamp was used as a cancellation and the prices quoted are for *single stamps.*

1

2

1888. *Cancelled as T* 3 *but with Maltese cross each side of* "AKASSA". *Size* 36 × 22 *mm.*

Z 7 6d. deep purple/*red*

1890 (24 June). *Size* 39 × 24 *mm.*

Z 8 1 2½d. purple/*blue* (V.)
Z 9 3d. purple/*yellow* (V.)
Z10 5d. dull purple and blue (V.)
Z11 6d. deep purple/*red* (V.)
Z12 10d. dull purple and carmine (V.)
Z12*a* 1s. green (V.)
Z13 2s. 6d. lilac (V.)

1894.

Z14 2 1d. lilac (V.) (July) .. .. .. 75·00
Z15 2½d. purple/*lilac* (V.) (3 Oct)

3

THE ROYAL NIGER COMPANY
CHARTERED & LIMITED.
7- AUG. 98
POST OFFICE
AKASSA.

4

1895 (7 March). *Size* 39 × 25 *mm.*

Z16 3 2½d. purple/*blue* (V.)

1895 (1 June)–**99**.

Z17 4 ½d. vermilion (V.) .. .. .. 27·00
Z18 1d. lilac (V.) .. .. .. 25·00
Z19 2d. green and vermilion (V.) £180
Z20 2½d. purple/*blue* (V.) .. .. .. 24·00
Z21 3d. purple/*yellow* (V.) £130
Z22 5d. dull purple and blue (V.) .. .. 28·00
Z23 6d. deep purple/*red* (V.) .. .. 60·00
Z24 9d. dull purple and blue (V.) £130
Z25 10d. dull purple and carmine (V.) .. .. 65·00
Z26 2s. 6d. deep lilac (V.) £120

1899 (20 May). *Cancelled as T* 4, *but* "CUSTOMS DEPT" *in place of* "POST OFFICE".

Z27 1d. lilac (V.) £170
Z28 2½d. purple/*blue* (V.) £170

THE ROYAL NIGER COMPANY,
CHARTERED & LIMITED.
4 NOV.1889
POST OFFICE,
AKASSA.

5

1897 (Jan) *to* **1899** (Dec).

Z29 5 ½d. vermilion (V.) .. .. .. 27·00
Z30 1d. lilac (V.) .. .. .. 26·00
a. "RECD" for year in postmark
Z31 2d. green and vermilion (V.) .. .. 65·00
Z32 2½d. purple/*blue* (V.) .. .. .. 35·00
a. "RECD" for year in postmark (1898)
Z33 3d. purple/*yellow* (V.) .. .. .. 95·00
Z34 4d. green and brown (V.) .. .. 70·00
Z35 4½d. green and carmine (V.) £450
Z36 5d. dull purple and blue (V.) .. .. 45·00
Z37 6d. deep purple/*red* (V.) £100
Z38 9d. dull purple and blue (V.) £150
Z39 10d. dull purple and carmine (V.) .. .. 65·00
Z40 1s. green (V.) £225
Z41 2s. 6d. deep lilac (V.) £120

1899 (9 Jan). *Cancelled as T* 7, *but inscribed* "AKASSA".

Z42 5d. dull purple and blue (V.)

BURUTU

THE ROYAL NIGER COMPANY
CHARTERED & LIMITED.
31 MAR 1898
POST OFFICE.
BURUTU.

6

1897 (20 Jan) *to* **1898** (30 Oct). *Cancelled as T* 6, "BURUTU" *in sans-serif caps. Size* 44 × 24 *mm.*

Z43 6 ½d. vermilion (V.) .. .. .. 42·00
Z44 1d. lilac (V.) .. .. .. 42·00
Z45 1½d. dull purple and green (V.) £120
Z46 2d. green and carmine (V.) .. .. 70·00
Z47 2½d. purple/*blue* (V.) .. .. .. 26·00
Z48 3d. purple/*yellow* (V.) .. .. .. 80·00
Z49 4d. green and brown (V.) .. .. 60·00
Z50 5d. dull purple and blue (V.) .. .. 45·00
Z51 6d. deep purple/*red* (V.) .. .. 85·00
Z52 9d. dull purple and blue (V.) £120
Z53 6 10d. dull purple and carmine (V.) .. .. 65·00
Z54 1s. green (V.) £250
Z55 2s. 6d. lilac (V.) £110

The 2½d. is also known with this postmark in blue (6.9.97) and violet-black (Apr 1898) and the ½d., 2½d., 3d., 5d. and 10d. with it in black.

1898 *to* **1899**. *Cancelled as T* 4, *but inscribed* "BURUTU" *in serifed caps. Size* 44 × 27 *mm.*

Z56 ½d. vermilion (V., Blk.) .. .. .. 45·00
Z57 1d. lilac (V., Blk.) .. .. .. 45·00
Z58 2d. green and vermilion (V.) £120
Z59 2½d. purple/*blue* (V., Blk.) .. .. 38·00
Z60 3d. purple/*yellow* (V.) .. .. .. 95·00
Z61 4d. green and brown (V.) .. .. 80·00
Z62 4½d. green and carmine (V.) £475
Z63 5d. dull purple and blue (V.) .. .. 48·00
Z64 6d. deep purple/*red* (V.) £120
Z65 9d. dull purple and blue (V.) £150
Z66 10d. dull purple and carmine (V., Blk.) .. 65·00
Z67 2s. 6d. lilac (V., Blk.) £150

7

1898 (9 July) *to* **1899** (Feb).

Z68 7 1d. lilac (V.)
Z69 2½d. purple/*blue* (V.) £190

1899 (20 May). *Cancelled as T* 4, *but inscribed* "CUSTOM DEPT. BURUTU".

Z70 1d. lilac (V.)

There is some doubt as to the use of this cancellation for postal purposes.

LOKOJA

8

1899 (30 June *to* 31 Dec).

Z71 8 ½d. vermilion (V.) .. .. .. 60·00
Z72 1d. lilac (V.) .. .. .. 50·00
Z73 2½d. purple/*blue* (V.) £160
Z74 5d. dull purple and blue (V.) £170
Z75 10d. dull purple and carmine (V.) £160
Z76 2s. 6d. deep lilac (V.) £350

AGENT GENERAL NIGER TERRITORIES

The listings for Nos. Z78/9 are for covers showing a handstamp struck on the address side, but *not* used as a cancellation for the G.B. stamp.

1894. *Cancelled as T* 8 *but inscribed* "AGENT GENERAL NIGER TERRITORIES".

Z78 2½d. purple/*blue* (V.) (3.10.94) £1000

1895 (4 Aug). *Cancelled as T* 7 *but inscribed as last.*

Z79 2½d. purple/*blue* (V.) £1000

It is now believed that these cancellations may have been used at Asaba.

The British Government purchased the Royal Niger Company territories and from 1 January 1900 they were incorporated into the protectorates of Northern and Southern Nigeria. Of the post offices listed above only Lokoja was then situated in Northern Nigeria, the remainder joining Niger Coast in forming Southern Nigeria.

Issues for Northern Nigeria did not reach Lokoja until sometime in March 1900 and the post office there continued to use unoverprinted stamps of Great Britain until these supplies arrived.

NORTHERN NIGERIA

The Protectorate of Northern Nigeria was formed on 1 January 1900 from the northern part of the Niger Company Territories. Only one post office existed in this area, at Lokoja, and this continued to use unoverprinted stamps of GREAT BRITAIN until the arrival of Nos. 1/9 during March 1900.

PRICES FOR STAMPS ON COVER	
Nos. 1/7	*from* × 6
Nos. 8/9	—
Nos. 10/16	*from* × 5
Nos. 17/19	—
Nos. 20/6	*from* × 5
No. 27	—
Nos. 28/37	*from* × 5
Nos. 38/9	—
Nos. 40/9	*from* × 5
Nos. 50/2	—

PRINTERS. All issues were typographed by De La Rue & Co.

1

2

1900 (Mar). *Wmk Crown CA. P* 14.
1 1 ½d. dull mauve and green .. .. 1·00 5·50
2 1d. dull mauve and carmine .. .. 1·60 2·25
3 2d. dull mauve and yellow .. .. 3·00 17·00
4 2½d. dull mauve and ultramarine .. 6·00 17·00
5 2 5d. dull mauve and chestnut .. .. 10·00 24·00
6 6d. dull mauve and violet .. .. 13·00 17·00
7 1 1s. green and black .. .. .. 13·00 35·00
8 2s. 6d. green and ultramarine .. .. 60·00 £150
9 10s. green and brown £160 £375
1/9 .. .. *Set of* 9 £225 £550
1/9 Optd "Specimen" .. .. .. *Set of* 9 £200

3

4

1902 (1 July). *Wmk Crown CA. P* 14.
10 3 ½d. dull purple and green 65 60
11 1d. dull purple and carmine 80 20
12 2d. dull purple and yellow .. .. 60 1·40
13 2½d. dull purple and ultramarine .. .. 55 2·75
14 4 5d. dull purple and chestnut .. .. 1·50 4·50
15 6d. dull purple and violet .. .. 3·00 4·50
16 3 1s. green and black .. .. .. 2·50 3·50
17 2s. 6d. green and ultramarine .. .. 8·00 20·00
18 10s. green and brown .. .. .. 45·00 48·00
10/18 .. .. *Set of* 9 55·00 75·00
10/18 Optd "Specimen" .. .. *Set of* 9 £150

1904 (April). *Wmk Mult Crown CA. P* 14.
19 4 £25 green and carmine £25000

1905 (Aug)–**06**. *Wmk Mult Crown CA. Ordinary paper. P* 14.
20 3 ½d. dull purple and green (10.05) .. 4·00 2·50
a. Chalk-surfaced paper (1906) .. 2·25 2·25
21 1d. dull purple and carmine .. .. 2·75 30
a. Chalk-surfaced paper (1906) .. 1·50 40
22 2d. dull purple and yellow (10.05) .. 6·00 12·00
a. Chalk-surfaced paper (1906) .. 4·75 7·50
23 2½d. dull purple and ultramarine (10.05) 4·25 3·75
24 4 5d. dull purple and chestnut (10.05) .. 9·00 18·00
a. Chalk-surfaced paper (1906) .. 12·00 18·00
25 6d. dull purple and violet (10.05) .. 12·00 17·00
a. Chalk-surfaced paper (1906) .. 13·00 13·00
26 3 1s. green and black (10.05) .. .. 25·00 38·00
a. Chalk-surfaced paper (1906) .. 15·00 23·00
27 2s. 6d. green and ultramarine (10.05) .. 32·00 38·00
a. Chalk-surfaced paper (1906) .. 23·00 27·00
20/7 .. .. *Set of* 8 65·00 85·00

1910 (Jan)–**11**. *Wmk Mult Crown CA. Ordinary paper* (½*d. to* 2½*d.*) *or chalk-surfaced paper* (*others*). *P* 14.
28 3 ½d. green (4.10) 60 30
29 1d. carmine (1.10) 50 15
30 2d. grey (10.11) .. .. 1·00 2·00
31 2½d. blue (10.10) .. .. 60 2·75
32 4 3d. purple/*yellow* (9.11) .. .. .. 1·00 30
34 5d. dull purple and olive-green (2.11) 2·00 3·75
35 6d. dull purple and purple (11.10) .. 4·50 8·50
a. Dull and bright purple (1911) .. 1·25 3·50
36 3 1s. black/*green* (11.10) 90 55
37 2s. 6d. black and red/*blue* (3.11) .. 7·50 15·00
38 4 5s. green and red/*yellow* (9.11) .. 17·00 48·00
39 3 10s. green and red/*green* (3.11) .. .. 42·00 45·00
28/39 .. .. *Set of* 11 65·00 £110
28/39 Optd "Specimen" .. .. *Set of* 11 £180

5

6

1912. *Wmk Mult Crown CA. Ordinary paper* (½*d.*, 1*d.*, 2*d.*) *or chalk-surfaced paper* (*others*). *P* 14.
40 5 ½d. deep green 30 20
41 1d. red 30 15
42 2d. grey .. .. 1·25 2·25
43 6 3d. purple/*yellow* 60 65
44 4d. black and red/*yellow* 40 50
45 5d. dull purple and olive-green .. .. 1·25 4·00
46 6d. dull and bright purple .. .. 1·25 2·75
47 9d. dull purple and carmine .. .. 1·00 5·50
48 5 1s. black/*green* .. .. 1·50 50
49 2s. 6d. black and red/*blue* .. .. 7·00 22·00
50 6 5s. green and red/*yellow* .. .. 16·00 50·00
51 5 10s. green and red/*green* .. .. 30·00 45·00
52 6 £1 purple and black/*red* £170 £140
40/52 .. .. *Set of* 13 £200 £225
40/52 Optd "Specimen" .. .. *Set of* 13 £225

On 1 January 1914 Northern Nigeria became part of Nigeria.

SOUTHERN NIGERIA

The Colony and Protectorate of Southern Nigeria was formed on 1 January 1900 by the amalgamation of Niger Coast Protectorate with the southern part of the Niger Territories. Lagos was incorporated into the territory on 16 February 1906.

The stamps of NIGER COAST PROTECTORATE were used in Southern Nigeria until the introduction of Nos. 1/9, and also during a shortage of these values in mid-1902. The issues of LAGOS were utilized throughout Southern Nigeria after 16 February 1906 until supplies were exhausted.

PRICES FOR STAMPS ON COVER

Nos. 1/7	*from* × 8
Nos. 8/9	—
Nos. 10/18	*from* × 4
Nos. 19/20	—
Nos. 21/30	*from* × 4
Nos. 31/2	—
Nos. 33/42	*from* × 4
Nos. 43/4	—
Nos. 45/53	*from* × 4
Nos. 55/6	—

PRINTERS. All issues of Southern Nigeria were typographed by De La Rue & Co, Ltd, London.

1

2

3

1901 (Mar)–**02**. *Wmk Crown CA. P* 14.
1 1 ½d. black and pale green 60 75
a. Black and green (1902) 45 50
2 1d. black and carmine 50 50
3 2d. black and red-brown .. .. 1·75 3·50
4 4d. black and sage-green .. .. 1·75 6·00
5 6d. black and purple .. .. .. 1·75 3·50
6 1s. green and black .. .. .. 7·00 13·00
7 2s. 6d. black and brown .. .. 28·00 50·00
8 5s. black and orange-yellow .. .. 38·00 70·00
9 10s. black and purple/*yellow* .. .. 65·00 £130
1/9 .. .. *Set of* 9 £120 £250
1/9 Optd "Specimen" .. .. *Set of* 9 £120

1903 (Mar)–**04**. *Wmk Crown CA. P* 14.
10 2 ½d. grey-black and pale green 50 15
11 1d. grey-black and carmine .. .. 1·25 15
12 2d. grey-black and chestnut .. .. 2·25 90
13 2½d. grey-black and blue (1904) .. .. 2·00 75
14 4d. grey-black and olive-green .. .. 1·75 3·25
15 6d. grey-black and purple .. .. 3·25 8·00
16 1s. green and black .. .. .. 15·00 9·50
17 2s. 6d. grey-black and brown .. .. 10·00 29·00
a. Grey and yellow-brown .. .. 55·00 75·00
18 5s. grey-black and yellow .. .. 35·00 75·00
19 10s. grey-black and purple/*yellow* .. 25·00 60·00
20 £1 green and violet £225 £350
10/20 .. .. *Set of* 11 £275 £475
10/20 Optd "Specimen" .. .. *Set of* 11 £160

1904 (June)–**08**. *Wmk Mult Crown CA. Ordinary paper. P* 14.
21 2 ½d. grey-black and pale green 40 10
a. Chalk-surfaced paper (1905) .. 50 20
22 1d. grey-black and carmine .. .. 3·50 20
a. Chalk-surfaced paper (1905) .. 4·00 10
23 2d. grey-black and chestnut .. .. 2·00 45
a. Pale grey and chestnut (1907) .. 3·25 40
24 2½d. grey-black and bright blue (1905) .. 80 95
25 3d. orange-brown & bright purple (*chalk-surfaced paper*) (1907) (Optd S. £20) 8·50 1·25
26 4d. grey-black and olive-green (1905) .. 14·00 14·00
a. Chalk-surfaced paper (1906) .. 15·00 15·00
ab. Grey-black & pale olive-green (1907) 14·00 15·00
27 6d. grey-black and bright purple (1905) 5·00 1·00
a. Chalk-surfaced paper (1905) .. 6·50 70
28 1s. grey-green and black .. .. 2·25 1·25
a. Chalk-surfaced paper (1907) .. 5·50 1·00
29 2s. 6d. grey-black and brown (1905) .. 15·00 9·00
a. Chalk-surfaced paper (1905) .. 17·00 8·50
30 5s. grey-black and yellow (1905) .. 30·00 45·00
a. Chalk-surfaced paper (1907) .. 38·00 45·00
31 10s. grey-black and purple/*yellow* (*chalk-surfaced paper*) (1908) .. .. 70·00 £110
32 £1 green and violet (1905) £130 £160
a. Chalk-surfaced paper (1905) .. £100 £140
21/32 .. .. *Set of* 12 £225 £275

I

II

Die I. Thick "1"; small "d".
Die II. Thinner "1"; larger "d".

1907–11. *Colours changed. Ordinary paper* (½*d. to* 2½*d.*) *or chalk-surfaced paper* (*others*). *Wmk Mult Crown CA. P* 14.
33 2 ½d. pale green 45 20
a. Blue-green (1910) 30 20
34 1d. carmine (I) 80 15
a. Die II. *Carmine-red* (1910) 30 10
35 2d. greyish slate (1909) 70 70
36 2½d. blue (1909) .. .. 1·00 3·50
37 3d. purple/*yellow* (1909) 90 30
38 2 4d. black and red/*yellow* (1909) 60 80
39 6d. dull purple and purple (1909) .. 10·00 3·00
a. Dull purple and bright purple (1911) 13·00 2·50
40 1s. black/*green* (1909) .. .. .. 6·00 40
41 2s. 6d. black and red/*blue* (1909) .. 4·00 90
42 5s. green and red/*yellow* (1909) .. 24·00 42·00
43 10s. green and red/*green* (1909) .. .. 55·00 80·00
44 £1 purple and black/*red* (1909) .. £140 £150
33/44 .. .. *Set of* 12 £200 £225
33/44 Optd "Specimen" .. .. *Set of* 12 £225

It was formerly believed that the plate used for printing the head was retouched in 1907 but the fact that the 1d. Die II, which did not appear until 1910, only exists in the first state of the head threw some doubts on this theory. Specialists now recognise that two dies of the head existed and that plates from both were used in Southern Nigeria.

The differences are very small and we refrain from listing them until more research is done, both in this country and in others where they may have been used. The differences are illustrated below:

A

B

In Head A the fifth line of shading on the king's cheek shows as a line of dots and the lines of shading up to the king's hair are broken in places. In Head B the lines of shading are more regular, especially the fifth line.

The following stamps are known:

Ordinary colours: 21 ordinary and chalky, A; 22 ordinary and chalky, A; 23, A; 23*a*, B; 24, A; 25, B; 26 ordinary and chalky, A; 27 ordinary, A; 27 chalky, B; 28 ordinary, A; 28 chalky, B; 29 ordinary, A; 29 chalky, A and B; 30 ordinary, A; 30 chalky, B; 31, B; 32 ordinary, A; 32 chalky, B.

New colours: 33, A and B; 33*a*, B; 34, A and B; 34*a*, A; 35/44, B.

1912. *Wmk Mult Crown CA. P* 14.
45 3 ½d. green 40 10
46 1d. red 50 10
47 2d. grey 50 85
48 2½d. bright blue .. .. 2·00 2·75
49 3d. purple/*yellow* 75 30
50 4d. black and red/*yellow* .. .. .. 70 2·00
51 6d. dull and bright purple 75 90
52 1s. black/*green* .. .. 2·00 60
53 2s. 6d. black and red/*blue* .. .. 4·50 11·00
54 5s. green and red/*yellow* .. .. 8·00 40·00
55 10s. green and red/*green* .. .. 32·00 70·00
56 £1 purple and black/*red* £140 £150
45/56 .. .. *Set of* 12 £170 £225
45/56 Optd "Specimen" .. .. *Set of* 12 £225

On 1 January 1914 Southern Nigeria became part of Nigeria.

NIGERIA

Nigeria was formed on 1 January 1914 from the former protectorates of Northern and Southern Nigeria.

PRICES FOR STAMPS ON COVER TO 1945

Nos. 1/10	*from* × 3
Nos. 11/13	—
Nos. 15/24	*from* × 3
No. 25	—
Nos. 25*a*/9*d*	*from* × 3
No. 29*e*	—
Nos. 30/3	*from* × 3
Nos. 34/59	*from* × 2

CROWN COLONY

1

2

(Typo D.L.R.)

1914–27. *Wmk Mult Crown CA. Ordinary paper* (½*d. to* 2½*d.*) *or chalk-surfaced paper* (*others*). *P* 14.

A. *Die I.* (1.6.14–21)
1 1 ½d. green 40 30
2 1d. carmine-red .. .. 1·00 10
a. Scarlet (6.17) .. .. .. 1·50 10
3 2d. grey .. .. 2·00 70
a. Slate-grey (1918) .. .. .. 2·50 65
4 2½d. bright blue .. .. 1·00 80
a. Dull blue (1915) .. .. ..
5 2 3d. purple/*yellow* (*white back*) .. .. 1·50 4·50
a. On yellow (*lemon back*) (8.15) .. 1·25 90
b. On deep yellow (*yellow back, thick paper*) (1915) (Optd S. £30) .. 14·00 7·50
c. On pale yellow (*orange-buff back*) (12.20) .. .. 4·00 14·00
d. On pale yellow (*pale yellow back*) (1921) .. .. 4·00 13·00

6 2 4d. black and red/*yellow* (*white back*) .. 1·00 4·25
a. On yellow (*lemon back*) (8.15) .. 80 2·75
b. On deep yellow (*yellow back, thick paper*) (1915) (Optd S. £30) .. 13·00 6·00
c. On pale yellow (*orange-buff back*) (1921) .. 5·00 5·50
d. On pale yellow (*pale yellow back*) (1921) .. 6·50 15·00
7 6d. dull and bright purple (*shades*) .. 1·75 2·50
8 1 1s. black /*pale blue-green* (*white back*) .. 80 4·00
a. On yellow-green (*white back*) ..
b. On pale blue-green (*yellow-green back*) (1915) .. 8·00 12·00
c. On pale blue-green (*blue-green back*) (1915) (Optd S. £30) .. 1·00 3·50
d. On pale blue-green (*pale olive back*) (1918) .. 9·50 13·00
e. On emerald-green (*pale olive back*) (12.20) .. 4·50 13·00
f. On emerald-green (*emerald-green back*) (1921) .. 1·00 8·00
9 2s. 6d. black and red/*blue* .. 5·00 3·00
10 2 5s. green and red/*yellow* (*white back*) .. 6·00 17·00
a. On yellow (*lemon back*) (8.15) .. 16·00 32·00
b. On deep yellow (*yellow back, thick paper*) (1915) (Optd S. £30) .. 22·00 45·00
c. On yellow (*orange-buff back*) (1921) 24·00 55·00
d. On pale yellow (*pale yellow back*) (1921) .. 40·00 75·00
11 1 10s. green and red/*blue-green* (*white back*) 38·00 75·00
a. On blue-green (*blue-green back*) (8.15) (Optd S. £35) .. 35·00 60·00
b. On blue-green (*pale olive back*) (1918) £650 £1100
c. On emerald green (*pale olive back*) (12.20) .. 70·00 90·00
d. On emerald-green (*emerald back*) (1921) .. 27·00 65·00
12 2 £1 deep purple and black/*red* .. £150 £180

B. *Change to Die II* (19.1.27)
13 2 £1 purple and black/*red* .. £160 £200
1/12 .. *Set of* 12 £170 £225
1/12 Optd "Specimen" .. *Set of* 12 £350

1921–32. *Wmk Mult Script CA. Ordinary paper* (½d. *to* 3d.) *or chalk-surfaced paper* (*others*). *P* 14.

A. *The basic issue. Die I for the* ½d., 1d., 2d., 2½d., 3d *and* 6d., *Die II remainder* (1921–26)
15 1 ½d. green (1921) .. 60 30
16 1d. rose-carmine (1921) .. 40 15
17 2d. grey (5.21) .. 1·50 1·50
18 2½d. bright blue (5.21) .. 50 1·60
19 2 3d. bright violet (1.24) .. 3·75 3·25
20 4d. black and red/*pale yellow* (10.23) .. 50 55
21 6d. dull and bright purple (5.21) .. 4·00 4·75
22 1 1s. black/*emerald* (7.24) .. 65 70
23 2s. 6d. black and red/*blue* (8.25) .. 6·00 14·00
24 2 5s. green and red/*yellow* (10.26) .. 10·00 42·00
25 1 10s. green and red/*green* (4.26) .. 45·00 90·00
15/25 .. *Set of* 11 65·00 £140
15/25 Optd "Specimen" .. *Set of* 11 £250

B. *Change to Die II* (1924–25)
25*a* 1 ½d. green (5.25) .. 1·00 65
25*b* 1d. rose-carmine (5.25) .. 50 45
25*c* 2d. grey (1924) .. 2·50 30
25*d* 2 3d. bright violet (5.25) .. 5·50 1·50
25*e* 6d. dull and bright purple (7.24) .. 4·00 4·00
25*a*/*e* .. *Set of* 5 12·00 6·25

C. *New value and colours changed. Die II* (1927–31)
26 2 1½d. orange (1.4.31) .. 1·50 15
27 1 2d. chestnut (1.10.27) .. 1·50 1·00
28 2d. chocolate (1.7.28) .. 45 15
29 2 3d. bright blue (1.4.31) .. 2·25 2·00
26/7, 29 .. *Set of* 3 5·00 3·00
26/7, 29 Optd/Perf "Specimen" .. *Set of* 3 75·00

D. *Reappearance of Die I* (*Key Plate* 23) (Mar to Aug 1932)
29*a* 1 2d. chocolate (Mar) .. 4·50 75
29*b* 2 4d. black and red/*pale yellow* .. 5·50 7·00
29*c* 1 2s. 6d. black and red/*blue* .. 27·00 32·00
29*d* 2 5s. green and red/*yellow* .. 45·00 80·00
29*e* 1 10s. green and red/*green* .. 75·00 £170
29*a*/*e* .. *Set of* 5 £140 £250

1935 (6 May). *Silver Jubilee. As Nos.* 114/17 *of Jamaica, but ptd by Waterlow. P* 11×12.
30 1½d. ultramarine and grey .. 60 30
31 2d. green and indigo .. 1·50 30
j. Kite and vertical log .. 40·00
32 3d. brown and deep blue .. 2·25 4·00
33 1s. slate and purple .. 2·75 11·00
30/3 .. *Set of* 4 6·50 14·00
30/3 Perf "Specimen" .. *Set of* 4 75·00

For illustration of plate variety see Omnibus section following Zimbabwe.

3 Apapa Wharf

4 Fishing Village

5 Victoria-Buea Road

(Recess D.L.R.)

1936 (1 Feb). *Designs as T* **3**/**5**. *Wmk Mult Script CA.*

(*a*) *P* 11½ × 13
34 ½d. green .. 65 65
35 1d. carmine .. 30 35
36 1½d. brown .. 30 30
a. Perf 12½ × 13½ .. 26·00 2·00
37 2d. black .. 30 55
38 3d. blue .. 50 75
a. Perf 12½ × 13½ .. 70·00 24·00
39 4d. red-brown .. 1·25 2·00
40 6d. dull violet .. 40 60
41 1s. sage-green .. 1·10 1·40

(*b*) *P* 14
42 2s. 6d. black and ultramarine .. 3·50 12·00
43 5s. black and olive-green .. 6·00 17·00
44 10s. black and grey .. 42·00 60·00
45 £1 black and orange .. 75·00 £120
34/45 .. *Set of* 12 £120 £190
34/45 Perf "Specimen" .. *Set of* 12 £225

Designs: *Vert as T* **3**/**4**—1d. Cocoa; 1½d. Tin dredger; 2d. Timber industry; 4d. Cotton ginnery; 6d. Habe minaret; 1s. Fulani Cattle. *Horiz as T* **5**—5s. Oil Palms; 10s. River Niger at Jebba; £1, Canoe pulling.

1937 (12 May). *Coronation. As Nos.* 118/20 *of Jamaica, but ptd by B.W. & Co. P* 11×11½.
46 1d. carmine .. 30 65
47 1½d. brown .. 75 55
48 3d. blue .. 1·25 1·75
46/8 .. *Set of* 3 2·10 2·75
46/8 Perf "Specimen" .. *Set of* 3 55·00

15 King George VI

16 Victoria-Buea Road

(Recess B.W. (T **15**), D.L.R. (others))

1938 (1 May)–**51.** *Designs as T* **15**/**16**. *Wmk Mult Script CA. P* 12 (*T* **15**) *or* 13 × 11½ (*others*).
49 **15** ½d. green .. 10 10
a. Perf 11½ (15.2.50) .. 20 10
50 1d. carmine .. 18·00 2·25
a. Rose-red (1941) .. 20 10
50*b* 1d. bright purple (1.12.44) .. 10 10
ba. Perf 11½ (15.2.50) .. 10 20
51 1½d. brown .. 10 10
a. Perf 11½ (15.11.50) .. 10 10
52 2d. black .. 10 40
52*aa* 2d. rose-red (1.12.44) .. 10 40
ab. Perf 11½ (15.2.50) .. 10 40
52*a* 2½d. orange (4.41) .. 10 35
53 3d. blue .. 10 10
a. Wmk sideways .. † —
53*b* 3d. black (1.12.44) .. 10 10
54 4d. orange .. 45·00 2·50
54*a* 4d. blue (1.12.44) .. 10 80
55 6d. blackish purple .. 10 10
a. Perf 11½ (17.4.51) .. 20 30
56 1s. sage-green .. 40 10
a. Perf 11½ (15.2.50) .. 10 10
57 1s. 3d. light blue (1940) .. 30 10
a. Perf 11½ (14.6.50) .. 30 50
b. Wmk sideways (Perf 11½) .. — £1400
58 **16** 2s. 6d. black and blue .. 40·00 8·50
a. Perf 13½ (6.42) .. 1·50 2·00
ab. Perf 13½. *Black and deep blue* (1946) 26·00 21·00
b. Perf 14 (1942) .. 1·25 90
c. Perf 12 (15.8.51) .. 1·25 90
59 – 5s. black and orange .. 75·00 9·00
a. Perf 13½ (8.42) .. 3·50 2·50
b. Perf 14 (1948) .. 3·25 2·50
c. Perf 12 (19.5.49) .. 3·25 1·00
49/59c .. *Set of* 16 45·00 6·25
49/52*aa*, 53/9 Perf "Specimen" .. *Set of* 15 £200

Design: *Horiz as T* **16**—5s. R. Niger at Jebba.

1946 (21 Oct). *Victory. As Nos.* 141/2 *of Jamaica.*
60 1½d. chocolate .. 15 10
61 4d. blue .. 15 35
60/1 Perf "Specimen" .. *Set of* 2 55·00

1948 (20 Dec). *Royal Silver Wedding. As Nos.* 143/4 *of Jamaica.*
62 1d. bright purple .. 35 10
63 5s. brown-orange .. 5·00 7·00

1949 (10 Oct). 75*th Anniv of U.P.U. As Nos.* 145/8 *of Jamaica.*
64 1d. bright reddish purple .. 15 10
65 3d. deep blue .. 35 55
66 6d. purple .. 50 1·00
67 1s. olive .. 70 1·40
64/7 .. *Set of* 4 1·50 2·75

1953 (2 June). *Coronation. As No.* 153 *of Jamaica, but ptd by B.W.*
68 1½d. black and emerald .. 30 10

18 Old Manilla Currency

21 "Tin"

Die I Flat-bed Die Ia Rotary

Two types of 1d.:

The Belgian rotary printings have thicker lines of shading giving blotches of black colour instead of fine lines, particularly in the stirrups.

Major re-entry showing duplication of steps of the terraces (Pl 3, R. 1/5)

Type A
Gap in row of dots

Type B
Unbroken row of dots

Two types of 2d. slate-violet:

Nos. 72c/cc. The original cylinder used was Type A (July 1956); later Type B (Sept 1957). The above illustrations will help classification, but two stamps per sheet of 60 of Type A show faint dots. However, one of these has the "2d." re-entry which does not exist in Type B sheets, and shades are distinctive.

Die I Flat-bed

Die 1a Rotary

Two types of 3d.:

As in the 1d. the Belgian rotary printings have thicker lines of shading and this is particularly noticeable in the dark hills in the background.

24 Ife Bronze

26 Victoria Harbour

29 New and Old Lagos

(Des M. Fievet. Recess Waterlow)

1953 (1 Sept)–**58**. *T* **18**, **21**, **24**, **26**, **29** *and similar designs. Wmk Mult Script CA. P* 14.

69 **18** ½d. black and orange 15 20
70 – 1d. black and bronze-green (Die I) .. 20 10
a. Die Ia (1.9.58) 20 10
71 – 1½d. blue-green 35 30
72 **21** 2d. black and yellow-ochre .. .. 2·75 15
a. Black and ochre (18.8.54) .. .. 3·00 15
b. Re-entry .. .. 65·00
72c 2d. slate-violet (Type A) (23.7.56) .. 2·50 60
ca. Slate-blue (*shades*) (Type A) .. 3·75 20
cb. Bluish grey (Type B) (25.9.57) .. 2·50 20
cc. Grey (*shades*) (Type B) .. .. 2·50 10
73 – 3d. black and purple (Die I) 55 10
a. Die Ia. *Black & reddish pur* (1.9.58) 55 10
b. Imperf (pair) £200
74 – 4d. black and blue .. .. .. 1·50 10
75 **24** 6d. orange-brown and black 20 10
a. Chestnut and black (18.8.54) .. 25 10
76 – 1s. black and maroon 40 10
77 **26** 2s. 6d. black and green .. .. 3·50 20
a. Black and deep green (18.8.54) .. 4·50 20
78 – 5s. black and red-orange .. .. 3·25 60
79 – 10s. black and red-brown .. .. 5·00 1·25
80 **29** £1 black and violet .. .. .. 10·00 4·50
69/80 .. .. *Set of* 13 27·00 7·00

Designs: *Horiz* (*as T* **18**)—1d. Bornu horsemen; 1½d. "Groundnuts"; 3d. Jebba bridge and R. Niger; 4d. "Cocoa"; 1s. "Timber". (*As T* **26**)—5s. "Palm-oil"; 10s. "Hides and skins".

Nos. 70a, 72c/cc and 73a were printed on rotary machines by a subsidiary company, Imprimerie Belge de Securité, in Belgium.

Nos. 72ca and 72cc were only available in Nigeria.

ROYAL VISIT
1956

(30) **31** Victoria Harbour

1956 (28 Jan). *Royal Visit. No.* 72 *optd with T* **30**.
81 **21** 2d. black and ochre 30 10
a. Opt inverted £160

(Recess Waterlow)

1958 (1 Dec). *Centenary of Victoria. W* w **12**. *P* 13½ × 14.
82 **31** 3d. black and purple 10 10

32 Lugard Hall

(Recess Waterlow)

1959 (14 Mar). *Attainment of Self-Government, Northern Region of Nigeria. T* **32** *and similar horiz design. W* w **12**. *P* 13½ (3*d*.) *or* 13½ × 14 (1*s*.).
83 3d. black and purple 10 10
84 1s. black and green 35 35
Design:—1s. Kano Mosque.

INDEPENDENT FEDERATION

34

35 Legislative Building **38** Dove, Torch and Map

(Des L. J. Wittington (1d.), R. Crawford (3d.), R. D. Baxter (6d.), J. White (1s. 3d.), Photo Waterlow)

1960 (1 Oct). *Independence. T* **35**, **38** *and similar horiz designs. W* **34**. *P* 13½ (1*s*. 3*d*.) *or* 14 (*others*).
85 1d. black and scarlet 10 10
86 3d. black and greenish blue 10 10
87 6d. green and red-brown 15 10
88 1s. 3d. bright blue and yellow 20 10
85/8 .. .. *Set of* 4 45 30
Designs: (As *T* **35**)—3d. African paddling canoe; 6d. Federal Supreme Court.

39 Groundnuts **48** Central Bank

1961 (1 Jan). *T* **39**, **48**, *and similar designs. W* **34**. *P* 15 × 14 (½*d. to* 1*s* 3*d*.) *or* 14½ (*others*).
89 ½d. emerald 10 40
90 1d. reddish violet 40 10
91 1½d. carmine-red .. .. 40 1·25
92 2d. deep blue 20 10
93 3d. deep green 30 10
94 4d. blue 30 35
95 6d. yellow and black 40 10
a. Yellow omitted .. .. — £275
96 1s. yellow-green .. .. 1·75 10
97 1s. 3d. orange 30 10
98 2s. 6d. black and yellow 75 15
99 5s. black and emerald 50 25
100 10s. black and ultramarine 75 90
101 £1 black and carmine-red .. .. .. 5·00 3·75
89/101 .. .. *Set of* 13 10·00 6·50

Designs: *Vert* (*as T* **39**)—1d. Coal mining; 1½d. Adult education; 2d. Pottery; 3d. Oyo carver; 4d. Weaving; 6d. Benin mask; 1s. Yellow-casqued Hornbill; 1s. 3d. Camel train. *Horiz* (*as T* **48**)—5s. Nigeria Museum; 10s. Kano airport; £1 Lagos railway station.

PRINTERS. The above and all following issues to No. 206 were printed in photogravure by Harrison & Sons, *except where otherwise stated.*

52 Globe and Railway Locomotive **56** Coat of Arms

(Des M. Goaman)

1961 (25 July). *Admission of Nigeria into U.P.U. T* **52** *and similar horiz designs. W* **34**. *P* 14½.
102 1d. red-orange and blue 10 10
103 3d. olive-yellow and black 10 10
104 1s. 3d. blue and carmine-red 15 10
105 2s. 6d. deep green and blue 25 35
102/5 .. .. *Set of* 4 45 40
Designs:—3d. Globe and mail-van; 1s. 3d. Globe and aircraft; 2s. 6d. Globe and liner.

(Des S. Bodo (3d.), R. Hopeman (4d.), C. Adesina (6d.), M. Shamir (1s. 6d.), B. Enweonwu (2s. 6d.))

1961 (1 Oct). *First Anniv of Independence. T* **56** *and similar designs. W* **34**. *P* 14½.
106 3d. multicoloured 10 10
107 4d. yellow-green and yellow-orange 10 10
108 6d. emerald-green 15 10
109 1s. 3d. grey, emerald and blue 20 10
110 2s. 6d. green and grey-blue 25 20
106/10 .. .. *Set of* 5 65 35
Designs: *Horiz*—4d. Natural resources and map; 6d. Nigerian Eagle; 1s. 3d. Eagles in flight; 2s. 6d. Nigerians and flag.

A used copy of No. 106 has been seen with both the silver (large "Y" appearing grey) and the yellow (appearing white) omitted.

61 "Health" **66** Malaria Eradication Emblem and Parasites

(Des M. Shamir)

1962 (25 Jan). *Lagos Conference of African and Malagasy States. T* **61** *and similar vert designs. W* **34**. *P* 14 × 14½.
111 1d. yellow-bistre 10 10
112 3d. deep reddish purple 10 10
113 6d. deep green 10 10
114 1s. brown 15 10
115 1s. 3d. blue 20 15
111/15 .. .. *Set of* 5 50 30
Designs:—3d. "Culture"; 6d. "Commerce"; 1s. "Communications"; 1s. 3d. "Co-operation".

1962 (7 Apr). *Malaria Eradication. T* **66** *and similar horiz designs. W* **34**. *P* 14½.
116 3d. green and orange-red 10 10
117 6d. blue and bright purple 10 10
118 1s. 3d. magenta and violet-blue 15 10
119 2s. 6d. blue and yellow-brown 25 20
116/19 .. .. *Set of* 4 50 30
Designs:—6d. Insecticide spraying; 1s. 3d. Aerial spraying; 2s. 6d. Mother, child and microscope.

70 National Monument **71** Benin Bronze

(Des S. Bodo (3d.), B. Enweonwu (5s.))

1962 (1 Oct). *Second Anniv of Independence. W* **34**. *P* 14½ × 14 (3*d*.) *or* 14 × 14½ (5*s*.).
120 **70** 3d. emerald and blue 10 10
a. Emerald omitted .. .. ..
121 **71** 5s. red, emerald and violet 80 30

72 Fair Emblem **73** "Cogwheels of Industry"

(Des M. Goaman (1d., 2s. 6d.), J. O. Gbagbeolu and M. Goaman (6d.), R. Hegeman (1s.))

1962 (27 Oct). *International Trade Fair, Lagos. W* **34**. *T* **72/3** *and similar designs. P* 14½.
122 1d. olive-brown and orange-red 10 10
123 6d. carmine-red and black 10 10
124 1s. orange-brown and black 10 10
125 2s. 6d. ultramarine and yellow 20 20
122/5 .. .. *Set of* 4 40 30
Designs: *Horiz as T* **73**—1s. "Cornucopia of Industry; 2s. 6d. Oilwells and tanker.

76 "Arrival of Delegates" **77** Mace as Palm Tree

(Des S. Akosile (2½d.), M. Goaman (others))

1962 (5 Nov). *Eighth Commonwealth Parliamentary Conference, Lagos. T* **76/77** *and similar design. W* **34**. *P* 14½.
126 2½d. greenish blue 10 15
127 4d. indigo and rose-red 10 10
128 1s. 3d. sepia and lemon 15 20
126/8 .. .. *Set of* 3 30 35
Design: *Horiz*—4d. National Hall.

80 Tractor and Maize **81** Mercury Capsule and Kano Tracking Station

(Des M. Goaman)

1963 (21 Mar). *Freedom from Hunger. T* **80** *and similar design. W* **34**. *P* 14.
129 3d. olive-green 30 15
130 6d. magenta 70 15
Design: *Vert*—3d. Herdsman.

(Des R. Hegeman)

1963 (21 June). *"Peaceful Use of Outer Space". T* **81** *and similar vert design. W* **34**. *P* 14½ × 14.
131 6d. blue and yellow-green 20 10
132 1s. 3d. black and blue-green 30 10
Design:—1s. 3d. Satellite and Lagos Harbour.

83 Scouts shaking Hands

(Des S. Apostolou (3d.), G. Okiki (1s.))

1963 (1 Aug). *11th World Scout Jamboree, Marathon. T* **83** *and similar triangular-shaped design.* W **34**. *P* 14.
133 3d. red and bronze-green 15 15
134 1s. black and red 35 35
MS134*a* 93 × 95 mm. Nos. 133/4 .. .. .. 1·50 1·50
ab. Red omitted (on 3d. value) £225
Design:—1s. Campfire.

85 Emblem and First Aid Team **88** President Azikiwe and State House

(Des M. Goaman)

1963 (1 Sept). *Red Cross Centenary. T* **85** *and similar horiz designs.* W **34**. *P* 14½.
135 3d. red and deep ultramarine 45 10
136 6d. red and deep green 70 10
137 1s. 3d. red and deep sepia .. .. .. 1·25 45
135/7 .. .. *Set of* 3 2·25 55
MS137*a* 102 × 102 mm. No. 137 (block of four) .. 6·00 6·00
Designs:—6d. Emblem and "Hospital Services"; 1s. 3d. Patient and emblem.

(Des M. Shamir. Photo Govt Printer, Israel)

1963 (1 Oct). *Republic Day. T* **88** *and similar vert designs showing administrative buildings and President Azikiwe. P* 14 × 13.
138 3d. yellow-olive and grey-green 10 10
139 1s. 3d. yellow-brown and sepia 10 10
a. Yellow-brown (portrait) omitted ..
140 2s. 6d. turquoise-blue and deep violet-blue .. 15 15
138/40 .. .. *Set of* 3 30 30
Designs:—1s. 3d. Federal Supreme Court Building; 2s. 6d. Parliament Building.

89 Charter and Broken Whip **90** "Freedom of Worship"

(Des S. Apostolou (3d.), Mrs. F. P. Effiong (others). Photo D.L.R.)

1963 (10 Dec). *15th Anniv of Declaration of Human Rights. T* **89/90** *and similar designs.* W **34**. *P* 13.
141 3d. vermilion 10 10
142 6d. blue-green 10 10
143 1s. 3d. ultramarine 15 10
144 2s. 6d. bright purple 30 30
141/4 .. .. *Set of* 4 50 35
Designs: *Vert as T* **90**—1s. 3d. "Freedom from want"; 2s. 6d. "Freedom of speech".

93 Queen Nefertari **94** Rameses II

(Des M. Shamir)

1964 (8 Mar). *Nubian Monuments Preservation.* W **34**. *P* 14½.
145 **93** 6d. yellow-olive and emerald 30 10
146 **94** 2s. 6d. brown, deep olive and emerald 1·25 1·40

NEW INFORMATION

The editor is always interested to correspond with people who have new information that will improve or correct the Catalogue.

95 President Kennedy

(Des M. Shamir (1s. 3d.), M. Goaman (2s. 6d.), Mr. Bottiau (5s.). Photo Govt Printer, Israel (1s. 3d.); litho Lewin-Epstein, Bat Yam, Israel (others))

1964 (27 Aug). *President Kennedy Memorial Issue. T* **95** *and similar horiz designs. P* 13 × 14 (1*s*. 3*d*.) *or* 14 (*others*).
147 1s. 3d. light violet and black 30 15
148 2s. 6d. black, red, blue and green 45 50
149 5s. black, deep blue, red and green .. .. 70 1·25
147/9 .. .. *Set of* 3 1·25 1·75
MS149*a* 154 × 135 mm. No. 149 (block of four). Imperf .. .. 8·00 9·00
Designs:—2s. 6d. President Kennedy and flags; 5s. President Kennedy (U.S. coin head) and flags.

98 President Azikiwe **99** Herbert Macaulay

(Des S. Apostolou (3d.), W. H. Irvine (others). Photo Govt Printer, Israel (3d.); Harrison (others))

1964 (1 Oct). *First Anniv of Republic. T* **98** *or* **99** *and similar vert design. P* 14 × 13 (3*d*.) *or* 14½ (*others*).
150 3d. red-brown 10 10
151 1s. 3d. green 20 10
152 2s. 6d. deep grey-green 30 20
150/2 .. .. *Set of* 3 50 30
Design:—2s. 6d. King Jaja of Opobo.

101 Boxing Gloves

102 Hurdling

(Des A. Adalade (3d.), S. Medahunsi (6d.), M. Shamir (1s. 3d.), M. Goaman (2s. 6d.))

1964 (10 Oct). *Olympic Games, Tokyo. T* **101** *and similar designs, and T* **102**. W **34**. *P* 14 (2*s*. 6*d*.) *or* 14½ (*others*).
153 3d. sepia and olive-green 10 10
154 6d. emerald and indigo 15 10
155 1s. 3d. sepia and yellow-olive 35 10
156 2s. 6d. sepia and chestnut 75 90
153/6 .. .. *Set of* 4 1·25 1·00
MS156*a* 102 × 102 mm. No. 156 (block of four). Imperf .. .. 2·75 4·00
Designs: *Horiz*—6d. High-jumping. *Vert*—1s. 3d. Running.

105 Scouts on Hill-top

(Des S. Apostolou (1d., 1s. 3d.), H. N. G. Cowham and Eagle Scout N. A. Lasisi (3d.), W. H. Irvine (6d.))

1965 (1 Jan). *50th Anniv of Nigerian Scout Movement. T* **105** *and similar vert designs. P* 14 × 14½.
157 1d. brown 10 10
158 3d. red, black and emerald 15 10
159 6d. red, sepia and yellow-green 25 15
160 1s. 3d. bistre-brown, greenish yellow and black-green 40 55
157/60 .. .. *Set of* 4 75 75
MS160*a* 76 × 104 mm. No. 160 (block of four). Imperf .. .. 5·50 7·00
Designs:—3d. Scout badge on shield; 6d. Scout badges; 1s. 3d. Chief Scout and Nigerian scout.

109 "Telstar" **110** Solar Satellite

(Des M. Shamir. Photo Govt Printer, Israel)

1965 (1 Apr). *International Quiet Sun Years. P* 14 × 13.
161 **109** 6d. reddish violet and turquoise-blue .. 10 10
162 **110** 1s. 3d. green and reddish lilac 10 10

111 Native Tom-tom and Modern Telephone

(Des C. Botham (5s.), H. N. G. Cowham (others). Photo Enschedé)

1965 (2 Aug). *I.T.U. Centenary. T* **111** *and similar designs. P* 11½ × 11 (1*s*. 3*d*.) *or* 11 × 11½ (*others*).
163 3d. black, carmine and yellow-brown .. 15 10
164 1s. 3d. black, blue-green and chalky blue .. 1·25 1·00
165 5s. black, carmine, blue & brt greenish blue 3·75 4·50
163/5 .. .. *Set of* 3 4·50 5·00
Designs: *Vert*—1s. 3d. Microwave aerial. *Horiz*—5s. Telecommunications satellite and part of globe.

114 I.C.Y. Emblem and Diesel Locomotive **117** Carved Frieze

(Des W. H. Irvine. Photo D.L.R.)

1965 (1 Sept). *International Co-operation Year. T* **114** *and similar horiz designs.* W **34**. *P* 14 × 15.
166 3d. green, red and orange .. .. .. 1·50 10
167 1s. black, bright blue and lemon .. .. 1·75 40
168 2s. 6d. green, bright blue and yellow .. 5·50 4·00
166/8 .. .. *Set of* 3 8·00 4·00
Designs:—1s. Students and Lagos Teaching Hospital; 2s. 6d. Kainji (Niger) Dam.

(Des S. Apostolou (3d.), W. H. Irvine (others). Photo D.L.R.)

1965 (1 Oct). *2nd Anniv of Republic. T* **117** *and similar designs. P* 14 × 15 (3*d*.) *or* 15 × 14 (*others*).
169 3d. black, red and orange-yellow 10 10
170 1s. 3d. red-brown, dp green & lt ultramarine 55 20
171 5s. brown, blackish brown and light green .. 1·60 2·00
169/71 .. .. *Set of* 3 2·00 2·00
Designs: *Vert*—1s. 3d. Stone images at Ikom; 5s. Tada bronze.

120 Lion and Cubs **121** African Elephants

132 Hippopotamus **133** African Buffalo

(Des M. Fievet. Photo Harrison (1d., 2d., 3d., 4d. (No. 177a), 9d.) or Delrieu (others))

1965 (1 Nov)–**66**. *T* **120/1**, **132/3** *and similar designs. Without printer's imprint. Chalk-surfaced paper* (1*d*., 2*d*., 3*d*., 4*d*., 9*d*.). *P* 12 × 12½ (½*d*., 6*d*.), 12½ × 12 (1½*d*., 4*d*.), 14 × 13½ (1*d*., 2*d*., 3*d*., 9*d*.) *or* 12½ (*others*).
172 ½d. multicoloured (1.11.65) 40 60
173 1d. multicoloured (1.11.65) 20 15
174 1½d. multicoloured (2.5.66) .. .. .. 3·75 4·00
175 2d. multicoloured (1.4.66) .. .. .. 2·00 15

176 3d. multicoloured (17.10.66) 80 15
177 4d. multicoloured (2.5.66) 50 1·50
a. Perf 14 × 13½ (1966) 20 30
178 6d. multicoloured (2.5.66) 1·00 30
179 9d. Prussian blue and orange-red (17.10.66) 2·25 40
180 1s. multicoloured (2.5.66) 1·50 40
181 1s. 3d. multicoloured (2.5.66) 6·50 45
182 2s. 6d. orange-brown, buff and brown (2.5.66) 75 30
183 5s. chestnut, light yellow and brown (2.5.66) 1·50 1·25
a. Pale chestnut, yellow and brown-purple (1966) 1·50 1·25
184 10s. multicoloured (2.5.66) 5·50 3·00
185 £1 multicoloured (2.5.66) 13·00 8·50
172/85 *Set of* 14 32·00 18·00

Designs: *Horiz* (*as T* **121**)—1½d. Splendid Sunbird; 2d. Village Weaver and Red-headed Malimbe; 3d. Cheetah; 4d. Leopards; 9d. Grey Parrots. (*As T* **133**)—1s. Blue-breasted Kingfishers; 1s. 3d. Crowned Cranes; 2s. 6d. Kobs; 5s. Giraffes. *Vert* (*as T* **120**)—6d. Saddle-bill Stork.

The 2d. and 3d. exist with PVA gum as well as gum arabic.

See also Nos. 220, etc.

The 1d., 3d., 4d. (No. 177a), 1s., 1s. 3d., 2s. 6d., 5s. and £1 values exist overprinted "F.G.N." (Federal Government of Nigeria) twice in black. They were prepared in November 1968 at the request of one of the State Governments for use as official stamps but the scheme was abandoned and meter machines were used instead. Some stamps held at Lagos Post Office were sold over the counter in error and passed through the post. The Director of Posts made limited stocks of all values, except the 1s., available from the Philatelic Bureau from 11 April 1969 "in order not to create an artificial scarcity", but they had no postal validity. Covers do, however, exist showing the 4d. value used by Lagos Federal Income Tax Office in April 1969 and others from the Office of the Secretary to the Military Government in 1973 carry the 3d., 4d. and 2s. 6d. values.

(134)

135 Y.M.C.A. Emblem and H.Q., Lagos

1966 (11 Jan). *Commonwealth Prime Ministers' Meeting, Lagos. No 98 optd with T* **134** *by the Nigerian Security Printing and Minting Co, Lagos, in red.*
186 **48** 2s. 6d. black and yellow 30 30

(Des S. B. Ajayi. Litho Nigerian Security Printing & Minting Co Ltd)

1966 (1 Sept). *Nigerian Y.W.C.A.'s Diamond Jubilee. P* 14.
187 **135** 4d. yellow-orange, ultramarine, orange-brown and yellow-green 10 10
188 9d. yellow-orange, ultramarine, brown and turquoise-green 10 30

137 Telephone Handset and Linesman

139 "Education, Science and Culture"

(Des S. B. Ajayi (4d.), N. Lasisi (1s. 6d.), B. Enweonwu (2s. 6d))

1966 (1 Oct). *Third Anniv of Republic. T* **137** *and similar designs. W* **34**. *P* 14½ × 14.
189 4d. green 10 10
190 1s. 6d. black, brown and reddish violet 45 50
191 2s. 6d. indigo, blue, yellow and green 1·25 2·00
189/91 *Set of* 3 1·60 2·25

Designs: *Vert*—4d. Dove and flag. *Horiz*—2s. 6d. Niger Bridge, Jebba.

(Des V. Whiteley from sketch by B. Salisu)

1966 (4 Nov). *20th Anniv of U.N.E.S.C.O. W* **34** (*sideways*). *P* 14½ × 14.
192 **139** 4d. black, lake and orange-yellow 40 10
193 1s. 6d. black, lake and turquoise-green 1·50 2·00
194 2s. 6d. black, lake and rose-pink 2·50 4·00
192/4 *Set of* 3 4·00 5·50

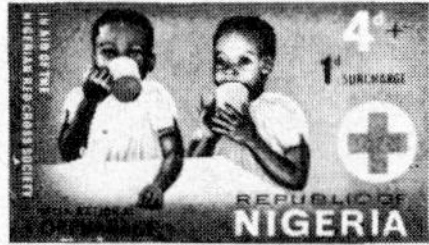

140 Children drinking

(Des V. Whiteley, after M. O. Afamefuna (4d.), I. U. Anawanti (1s. 6d.) and S. Adeyemi (2s. 6d.))

1966 (1 Dec). *Nigerian Red Cross. T* **140** *and similar designs. W* **34**. *P* 14 × 14½ (1*s.* 6*d.*) *or* 14½ × 14 (*others*).
195 4d. + 1d. black, reddish violet and red 30 25
196 1s. 6d. + 3d. multicoloured 1·00 3·50
197 2s. 6d. + 3d. multicoloured 1·25 4·00
195/7 *Set of* 3 2·25 7·00

Designs: *Vert*—1s. 6d. Tending patient. *Horiz*—2s. 6d. Tending casualties, and badge.

143 Surveying

(Des M. Goaman)

1967 (1 Feb). *International Hydrological Decade. T* **143** *and similar multicoloured design. W* **34**. *P* 14½ × 14 (4*d.*) *or* 14 × 14½ (2*s.* 6*d.*).
198 4d. Type **143** 10 10
199 2s. 6d. Water gauge on dam (*vert*) 25 60

145 Globe and Weather Satellite **147** Eyo Masqueraders

(Des M. Shamir (4d.), S. Bodo (1s. 6d.))

1967 (23 Mar). *World Meteorological Day. T* **145** *and similar horiz design. W* **34**. *P* 14½ × 14.
200 4d. magenta and blue 10 10
201 1s. 6d. black, yellow and blue 40 50

Design:—1s. 6d. Passing storm and sun.

(Des G. A. Okiki (4d.), A. B. Saka Lawal (1s. 6d.), S. Bodo (2s. 6d.). Photo Enschedé)

1967 (1 Oct). *4th Anniv of Republic. T* **147** *and similar multicoloured designs. P* 11½ × 11 (2*s.* 6*d.*) *or* 11 × 11½ (*others*).
202 4d. Type **147** 20 10
203 1s. 6d. Crowd watching acrobat 1·25 1·25
204 2s. 6d. Stilt dancer (*vert*) 1·50 2·25
202/4 *Set of* 3 2·75 3·25

150 Tending Sick Animal **151** Smallpox Vaccination

(Des G. Drummond)

1967 (1 Dec). *Rinderpest Eradication Campaign. P* 14½ × 14.
205 **150** 4d. multicoloured 10 10
206 1s. 6d. multicoloured 45 65

PRINTERS AND PROCESS. Nos. 207/89 were printed in photogravure by the Nigerian Security Printing and Minting Co Ltd, *unless otherwise stated.*

(Des J. Owei. Litho)

1968 (7 Apr). *20th Anniv of World Health Organization. T* **151** *and similar horiz design. P* 14.
207 4d. magenta and black 10 10
208 1s. 6d. orange, lemon and black 45 40

Design:—1s. 6d. African and mosquito.

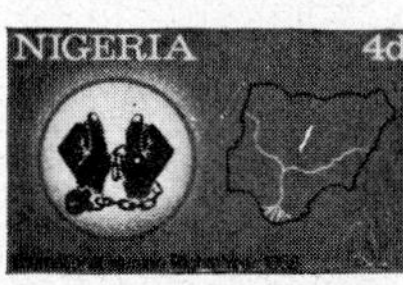

153 Chained Hands and Outline of Nigeria **155** Hand grasping at Doves of Freedom

(Des Jennifer Toombs)

1968 (1 July). *Human Rights Year. T* **153** *and similar design. P* 14.
209 4d. greenish blue, black and yellow 10 10
210 1s. 6d. myrtle-green, orange-red and black 20 30

Design: *Vert*—1s. 6d. Nigerian flag and Human Rights emblem.

(Des G. Vasarhelyi)

1968 (1 Oct). *5th Anniv of Federal Republic. P* 13½ × 14.
211 **155** 4d. multicoloured 10 10
212 1s. 6d. multicoloured 20 20

156 Map of Nigeria and Olympic Rings **158** G.P.O., Lagos

(Des J. Owei)

1968 (14 Oct). *Olympic Games, Mexico. T* **156** *and similar horiz design. P* 14.
213 4d. black, green and scarlet 10 10
214 1s. 6d. multicoloured 20 20

Design:—1s. 6d. Nigerian athletes, flag and Olympic rings.

(Des D.L.R.)

1969 (11 Apr). *Inauguration of Philatelic Service. P* 14.
215 **158** 4d. black and green 10 10
216 1s. 6d. black and blue 20 20

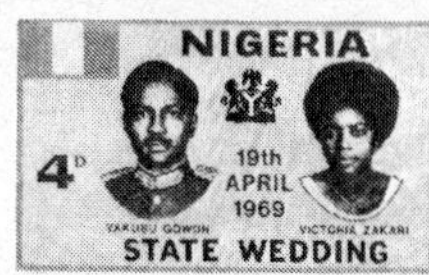

159 Yakubu Gowon and Victoria Zakari

(Des adapted from photo by Jackie Phillips. Litho)

1969 (20 Sept). *Wedding of General Gowon. P* 13 × 13½.
217 **159** 4d. chocolate and emerald 10 10
218 1s. 6d. black and emerald 20 20

1969–72. (*a*) *As No.* 173 *etc, but printed by Nigerian Security Printing and Minting Co Ltd. With printer's imprint* "N.S.P. & M. CO. LTD." *P* 13½ (6*d.*) *or P* 13 × 13½ (*others*).
220 1d. multicoloured 1·75 40
222 2d. multicoloured 1·25 50
a. Smaller imprint* (13.1.71) 1·25 90
223 3d. multicoloured (7.71) 65 40
a. Larger imprint* (22.10.71) 1·00 90
224 4d. multicoloured 5·00 60
a. Smaller imprint* †
225 6d. multicoloured (1971) 1·00 70
226 9d. Prussian blue and orange-red (1970) 5·00 3·00
a. "TD" of "LTD" omitted from imprint (Pl. 1B, R. 10/2) 23·00
227 1s. multicoloured (8.71) 2·00 40
228 1s. 3d. multicoloured (1971) 8·00 3·25
229 2s. 6d. multicoloured (1972) 4·00 6·00
230 5s. multicoloured (1972) 3·00 7·00
220/30 *Set of* 10 28·00 20·00

*On No. 222a the designer's name measures 4¾ mm. On No. 223a the imprints measure 9 and 8½ mm respectively. The normal imprints on Nos. 222/3 both measure 5½ mm.

The date given for Nos. 222a and 223a are for the earliest known used copies.

†No. 224 has the left-hand imprint 6 mm long and the right-hand 5½ mm. On No. 224a the imprints are 5½ mm and 4½ mm respectively. The width of the design is also ½ mm smaller.

Imperforate proofs of similar 10s. and £1 values are known.

(*b*) *As Nos.* 222 *and* 224, *but redrawn, and printed by Enschedé. No printer's imprint; designer's name at right. P* 14½ × 13.
231 2d. multicoloured (9.70) 23·00 5·00
232 4d. multicoloured (3.71) 1·50 1·75

In the 2d. the face value is white instead of yellow, and in the 4d. the white lettering and value are larger.

160 Bank Emblem and "5th Anniversary" **161** Bank Emblem and Rays

(Des J. Owei (4d.), B. Salisu (1s. 6d.). Litho)

1969 (18 Oct). *Fifth Anniv of African Development Bank. P* 14.
233 **160** 4d. orange, black and blue 10 10
234 **161** 1s. 6d. lemon, black and plum 20 20

162 I.L.O. Emblem **164** Olumo Rock

(Des D. West)

1969 (15 Nov). *50th Anniv of International Labour Organisation. T* **162** *and similar horiz design. P* 14.
235 4d. black and bright reddish violet 10 10
236 1s. 6d. emerald and black 20 25

Design:—1s. 6d. World map and I.L.O. emblem.

(Des A. Onwudimegwu)

1969 (30 Dec). *International Year of African Tourism. T* **164** *and similar designs. P* 14.
237 4d. multicoloured 10 10
238 1s. black and bright emerald 15 10
239 1s. 6d. multicoloured 30 20
237/9 *Set of* 3 50 30

Designs: *Vert*—1s. Traditional musicians; 1s. 6d. Assob Falls.

167 Symbolic Tree **168** U.P.U. H.Q. Building

(Des E. Emokpae (4d., 1s., 2s.), B. Onobrakpeya (1s. 6d.). Photo Enschedé)

1970 (28 May). *"Stamp of Destiny"; End of Civil War. T* **167** *and similar designs. P* 11 × 11½ (2*s*.) *or* 11½ × 11 (*others*).

240	4d. gold, new blue and black	10	10
241	1s. multicoloured	10	10
242	1s. 6d. yellow-green and black	10	10
243	2s. multicoloured	15	20
240/3	*Set of* 4	30	30

Designs: *Vert*—1s. Symbolic Wheel; 1s. 6d. United Nigerians supporting Map. *Horiz*—2s. Symbolic Torch.

(Des A. Onwudimegwu)

1970 (29 June). *New U.P.U. Headquarters Building. P* 14.

244 **168**	4d. reddish violet and greenish yellow	10	10
245	1s. 6d. light greenish blue and deep blue	20	20

169 Scroll **170** Oil Rig

(Des A. Onwudimegwu)

1970 (1 Sept). *25th Anniv of United Nations. T* **169** *and similar vert design. P* 14.

246	4d. orange-brown, buff and black	10	10
247	1s. 6d. steel-blue, cinnamon and gold	20	20

Design:—1s. 6d. U.N. Building.

(Des E. Emokpae. Litho Enschedé)

1970 (30 Sept). *Tenth Anniv of Independence. T* **170** *and similar vert designs. Multicoloured. P* 13½ × 13.

248	2d. Type **170**	10	10
249	4d. University Graduate	15	10
250	6d. Durbar Horsemen	15	10
251	9d. Servicemen raising Flag	20	10
252	1s. Footballer	20	10
253	1s. 6d. Parliament Building	20	25
254	2s. Kainji Dam	50	70
255	2s. 6d. Agricultural Produce	50	75
248/55	*Set of* 8	1·75	1·75

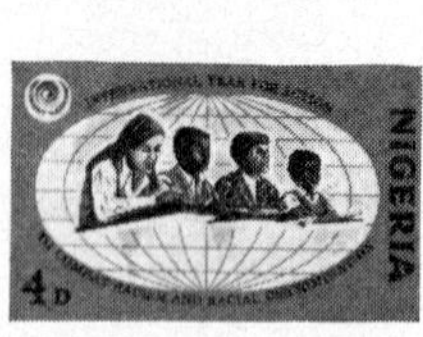

171 Children and Globe **172** Ibibio Face Mask

(Des E. Emokpae and A. Onwudimegwu. Photo Enschedé)

1971 (21 Mar). *Racial Equality Year. T* **171** *and similar multicoloured designs. P* 13 × 13½ (4*d*., 2*s*.) *or* 13½ × 13 (*others*).

256	4d. Type **171**	10	10
257	1s. Black and white men uprooting "Racism" (*vert*)	10	10
258	1s. 6d. The world in black and white (*vert*)	15	50
259	2s. Black and white men united	15	75
256/9	*Set of* 4	35	1·25

(Des A. Onwudimegwu)

1971 (30 Sept). *Antiquities of Nigeria. T* **172** *and similar vert designs. P* 13½ × 14.

260	4d. black and pale blue	10	10
261	1s. 3d. blackish brown and ochre	15	30
262	1s. 9d. emerald, sepia and olive-yellow	20	80
260/2	*Set of* 3	35	1·00

Designs:—1s. 3d. Benin bronze; 1s. 9d. Ife bronze.

MINIMUM PRICE

The minimum price quote is 10p which represents a handling charge rather than a basis for valuing common stamps. For further notes about prices see introductory pages.

173 Children and Symbol **174** Mast and Dish Aerial

(Des E. Emokpae)

1971 (11 Dec). *25th Anniv of U.N.I.C.E.F. T* **173** *and similar vert designs, each incorporating the U.N.I.C.E.F. symbol. P* 13½ × 14.

263	4d. multicoloured	10	10
264	1s. 3d. yellow-orange, orge-red & carm-lake	15	40
265	1s. 9d. pale greenish blue & dp greenish blue	15	85
263/5	*Set of* 3	30	1·25

Designs:—1s. 3d. Mother and child; 1s. 9d. Mother carrying child.

(Des A. Onwudimegwu)

1971 (30 Dec). *Opening of Nigerian Earth Satellite Station. T* **174** *and similar horiz designs. P* 14.

266 **174**	4d. multicoloured	15	10
267 –	1s. 3d. green, blue and black	30	50
268 –	1s. 9d. brown, orange and black	40	1·00
269 –	3s. mauve, black and magenta	85	2·00
266/9	*Set of* 4	1·50	3·25

Designs:—Nos. 267/9, as T **174**, but showing different views of the Satellite Station.

The 4d. has been seen on a cover from Ilorin, postmarked 23.12.71.

175 Trade Fair Emblem **176** Traffic

(Des E. Emokpae (4d.), A. Onwudimegwu (others). Litho D.L.R.)

1972 (23 Feb). *All-Africa Trade Fair. T* **175** *and similar designs. P* 13.

270	4d. multicoloured	10	10
271	1s. 3d. deep lilac, lemon and gold	15	35
272	1s. 9d. yellow-orange, orange-yellow & black	15	90
270/2	*Set of* 3	30	1·25

Designs: *Horiz*—1s. 3d. Map of Africa with pointers to Nairobi. *Vert*—1s. 9d. Africa on globe.

(Des A. Onwudimegwu (4d., 3s.), E. Emokpae (1s. 3d.), J. Owei (1s. 9d.). Litho D.L.R.)

1972 (23 June). *Change to Driving on the Right. T* **176** *and similar horiz designs. Multicoloured (except 4d.). P* 13.

273	4d. Type **176** (yellow-orge, dp chest & black)	15	10
274	1s. 3d. Roundabout	70	70
275	1s. 9d. Highway	80	1·25
276	3s. Road junction	2·00	3·00
273/6	*Set of* 4	3·25	4·50

177 Nok Style Terracotta Head **178** Hides and Skins

(Des G. Okiki (1s. 3d.), A. Aiyegbusi (others). Litho D.L.R.)

1972 (1 Sept). *All-Nigeria Arts Festival. T* **177** *and similar multicoloured designs. P* 13.

277	4d. Type **177**	10	10
278	1s. 3d. Bronze pot from Igbo-Ukwu	25	60
279	1s. 9d. Bone harpoon (*horiz*)	30	1·00
277/9	*Set of* 3	60	1·50

(New Currency. 100 kobo = 1 naira)

(Des E. Emokpae (8, 25, 30, 50 k., 1 n.), A. Onwudimegwu (others))

1973–74. *T* **178** *and similar designs. P* 14.

(*a*) *Photo. Left-hand imprint* 5¼ *mm long* (2 Jan–2 Apr)

280	1 k. multicoloured (deep green foliage)	40	40
	*a. Light emerald foliage** (2.4.73)	20	10
281	2 k. black, pale turquoise-blue and bright purple	35	10
282	5 k. multicoloured (emerald hills)	60	30
	*a. Bright yellow-green hills** (2.4.73)	50	10
283	10 k. black, orange-yellow and lilac	70	30
284	12 k. black, pale emerald and deep cobalt	7·00	6·00
285	18 k. multicoloured	6·00	2·00
286	20 k. multicoloured	9·00	3·00
287	30 k. black, chrome-yellow and new blue	9·00	5·00
288	50 k. multicoloured (black background and figure)	5·00	2·75
	*a. Deep chocolate background and figure** (2.4.73)	1·50	90
289	1 n. multicoloured	12·00	12·00
280/9	*Set of* 10	42·00	26·00

(*b*) *Litho. Left-hand imprint* 6 *mm long* (2 Apr 1973†–74)

290	1 k. multicoloured (8.73)	10	10
291	2 k. black, pale turquoise-blue and bright purple (27.6.74)**	1·75	50
292	3 k. multicoloured	15	10
293	5 k. multicoloured (*shades*) (2.74)	2·50	60
294	7 k. multicoloured	30	50
295	8 k. multicoloured	40	10
296	10 k. black, orange-yellow and lilac (8.73)	3·50	15
297	12 k. black, green and cobalt (*shades*)	20	60
298	15 k. multicoloured	20	40
299	18 k. multicoloured	50	30
300	20 k. multicoloured	65	30
301	25 k. multicoloured	85	45
302	30 k. black, chrome-yellow and new blue	40	70
303	35 k. multicoloured	3·50	2·00
305	1 n. multicoloured (*shades*)	1·25	1·10
306	2 n. multicoloured (*shades*)	3·50	3·75
290/306	*Set of* 16	18·00	10·50

Designs: *Horiz*—2 k. Natural gas tanks; 3 k. Cement works; 5 k. Cattle-ranching; 7 k. Timber mill; 8 k. Oil refinery; 10 k. Cheetahs, Yankari Game Reserve; 12 k. New Civic Building; 15 k. Sugar-cane harvesting; 20 k. Vaccine production; 25 k. Modern wharf; 35 k. Textile machinery; 1 n. Eko Bridge; 2 n. Teaching Hospital, Lagos. *Vert*— 18 k. Palm oil production; 30 k. Argungu Fishing Festival; 50 k. Pottery.

*On Nos. 280*a*, 282*a* and 288*a* other colours also differ, but the shades can best be identified by the distinctive features noted.

Used copies of No. 282*a* have been seen with orange omitted.

†Although First Day Covers of Nos. 290/306 were dated 1 April the stamps were not placed on sale until 2 April. Later, post-dated, covers included No. 291.

**This is the earliest known postmark date. No. 291 was not released by the Crown Agents in London until 11 September 1975.

Differences between printings:

1 k. In photogravure printings the stretched hide at left is in brownish black; on the litho stamps this hide is brown and yellow.

2 k. On the litho stamp the line of division between the black and pale blue colours of the gas tanks is a regular curve; on the photogravure printing it is horizontal and irregular. The litho stamp also has a wider mauve border at top.

5 k. The litho printing differs from the photogravure (Nos. 282/*a*) in having brown on the herdsman, instead of black.

10 k. The litho version has much less black on the cheetahs and tree trunk. It also shows black details at the left-hand end of the trunk, which do not appear on the photogravure version.

12 k. No. 284 is much darker than the litho version, especially within the building and amongst the trees at right.

18 k. The lithographed printing shows two oildrums in the foreground which are not present on the photogravure stamp.

20 k. The lithographed printing includes a brown plate not present on the photogravure version and this shows on the chemist. The liquid in the flasks is grey-blue instead of black. On the watermarked version, No. 348, the liquid is turquoise-blue.

30 k. No. 287 is much darker, with greater use of black in the design.

50 k. The litho version (No. 352) has solid shading on the potter's upper arm and lacks a black inner frame-line beneath the potter's wheel. No. 352 has a green printer's imprint at foot (instead of black) and its background is similar to that of No. 288*a*.

1 n. On the photogravure stamp the traffic is shown driving on the left. For the litho version the traffic is corrected to show it driving on the right.

See also Nos. 338/54.

PROCESS. From No. 307 onwards all stamps were lithographed by the Nigerian Security Printing and Minting Co Ltd.

179 Athlete

1973 (8 Jan). *Second All-African Games. Lagos. T* **179** *and similar multicoloured designs (except 5 k.). P* 13.

307	5 k. Type **179** (lt lilac, lt greenish bl & blk)	15	10
308	12 k. Football	25	50
309	18 k. Table-tennis	60	1·00
310	25 k. National Stadium (*vert*)	70	1·50
307/10	*Set of* 4	1·50	2·75

180 All-Africa House, Addis Ababa **181** Dr. Hansen

1973 (25 May). *Tenth Anniv of O.A.U. T* **180** *and similar vert designs. Multicoloured. P* 14.
311 5 k. Type **180** 10 10
312 18 k. O.A.U. flag 30 40
313 30 k. O.A.U. emblem and symbolic flight of ten stairs 50 80
311/13 .. .. *Set of* 3 70 1·10

(Des A. Onwudimegwu)

1973 (30 July). *Centenary of Discovery of Leprosy Bacillus. P* 14.
314 **181** 5 k. + 2 k. lt red-brown, flesh & black .. 20 50

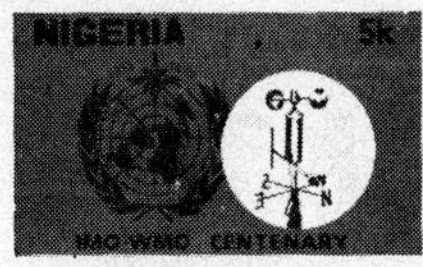

182 W.M.O. Emblem and Weather-vane

183 University Complex

(Des O. I. Oshiga)

1973 (4 Sept). *I.M.O./W.M.O. Centenary. P* 14.
315 **182** 5 k. multicoloured 15 10
316 30 k. multicoloured .. .. .. 85 1·75

(Des A. Onwudimegwu (5, 18 k.), C. Okechukwu (12 k.), O. I. Oshiga (30 k.))

1973 (17 Nov). *25th Anniv of Ibadan University. T* **183** *and similar multicoloured designs. P* 13½ × 14 (12 *k.*) *or* 14 × 13½ (*others*).
317 5 k. Type **183** 10 10
318 12 k. Students' population growth (*vert*) .. 25 30
319 18 k. Tower and students 35 55
320 30 k. Teaching Hospital 50 85
317/20 .. .. *Set of* 4 1·10 1·50

184 Lagos 1d. Stamp of 1874

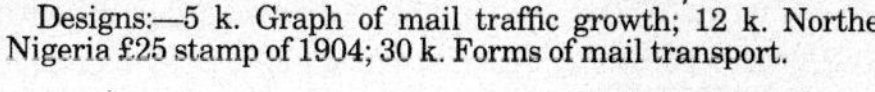

(Des A. Onwudimegwu (30 k.), S. Eluare (others))

1974 (10 June). *Stamp Centenary. T* **184** *and similar horiz designs. P* 14 × 13½.
321 5 k. light emerald, yellow-orange and black 15 10
322 12 k. multicoloured 40 60
323 18 k. light yellowish green, mauve and black 70 1·00
324 30 k. multicoloured .. .. 1·60 2·50
321/4 .. .. *Set of* 4 2·50 3·75
Designs:—5 k. Graph of mail traffic growth; 12 k. Northern Nigeria £25 stamp of 1904; 30 k. Forms of mail transport.

185 U.P.U. Emblem on Globe

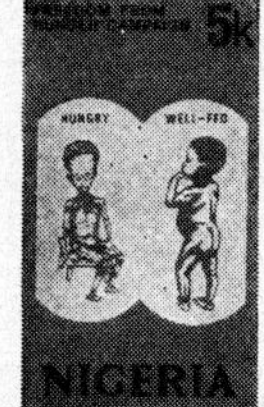

186 Starving and Well-fed Children

(Des S. Eluare (5 k.). A. Onwudimegwu (18 k.), O. I. Oshiga (30 k.))

1974 (9 Oct). *Centenary of Universal Postal Union. T* **185** *and similar horiz designs. P* 14.
325 5 k. lt greenish blue, yellow-orange & black 15 10
326 18 k. multicoloured .. .. 1·00 60
327 30 k. bistre-brown, lt greenish blue & black .. 1·50 1·75
325/7 .. .. *Set of* 3 2·40 2·25
Designs:—18 k. World transport map; 30 k. U.P.U. emblem and letters.

(Des A. Onwudimegwu (12 k.), S. Eluare (others))

1974 (25 Nov). *Freedom from Hunger Campaign. T* **186** *and similar designs. P* 14.
328 5 k. apple-green, buff and grey-black .. 10 10
329 12 k. multicoloured 40 50
330 30 k. multicoloured .. .. 1·10 1·75
328/30 .. .. *Set of* 3 1·40 2·00
Designs: *Horiz*—12 k. Poultry battery. *Vert*—30 k. Water-hoist.

187 Telex Network and Teleprinter

188 Queen Amina of Zaria

(Des S. Eluare)

1975 (3 July). *Inauguration of Telex Network. T* **187** *and similar vert designs. P* 13½ × 14.
331 5 k. black, yellow-orange & light olive-green 10 10
332 12 k. black, lemon and orange-brown 20 20
333 18 k. multicoloured 30 30
334 30 k. multicoloured 50 50
331/4 .. .. *Set of* 4 1·00 1·00
Nos. 332/4 are as T **187** but have the motifs arranged differently.

(Des A. Onwudimegwu)

1975 (18 Aug). *International Women's Year. P* 14.
335 **188** 5 k. deep olive, light yellow and azure .. 15 10
336 18 k. purple, pale blue and light mauve .. 50 65
337 30 k. multicoloured .. .. .. 60 1·10
335/7 .. .. *Set of* 3 1·10 1·75

189

1975–82*. *As Nos.* 290 *etc., but W* **189** (*sideways on* 18, 50 *k.*).
338 1 k. multicoloured (6.4.77) 40 55
339 2 k. black, pale turq-bl & bright purple (9.75) 75 10
340 3 k. multicoloured (10.75) 15 10
341 5 k. multicoloured (1.76) 80 10
342 7 k. multicoloured (16.5.80) .. .. .. 1·50 60
343 8 k. multicoloured (12.76) .. .. .. 1·00 60
344 10 k. blk, orange-yell & lilac (*shades*) (7.4.76) 1·00 20
346 15 k. multicoloured (5.82) .. .. .. — 1·25
347 18 k. multicoloured (12.78) .. .. .. 2·25 1·50
348 20 k. multicoloured (9.79) .. .. .. 2·25 1·50
349 25 k. multicoloured (21.3.77) .. .. .. 2·25 25
352 50 k. multicoloured (2.9.77) .. .. .. 3·25 3·25
354 2 n. multicoloured (11.77) .. .. .. 6·00 6·00
*Earliest known dates of use.

190 Alexander Graham Bell

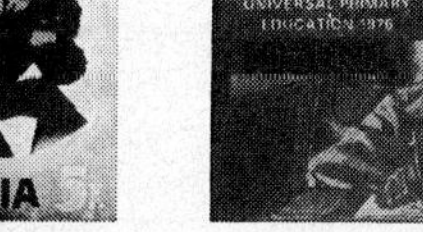

191 Child Writing

(Des A. Onwudimegwu)

1976 (10 Mar). *Telephone Centenary. T* **190** *and similar designs. W* **189** (*sideways on* 5 *and* 25 *k.*). *P* 13½.
355 5 k. multicoloured 10 10
356 18 k. multicoloured 40 55
357 25 k. royal blue, pale blue and blackish brown 70 1·00
a. No wmk .. .. 10·00
355/7 .. .. *Set of* 3 1·10 1·50
Designs: *Horiz*—18 k. Gong and modern telephone system. *Vert*—25 k. Telephones, 1876 and 1976.

(Des A. Onwudimegwu (5 k.), S. Eluare (18 k.), N. Lasisi (25 k.))

1976 (20 Sept). *Launching of Universal Primary Education. T* **191** *and similar designs. W* **189** (*sideways on* 18 *and* 25 *k.*). *P* 14.
358 5 k. lemon, light violet and bright mauve .. 10 10
359 18 k. multicoloured 45 60
360 25 k. multicoloured 70 85
358/60 .. .. *Set of* 3 1·10 1·40
Designs: *Vert*—18 k. Children entering school; 25 k. Children in class.

192 Festival Emblem

(Des O. I. Oshiga (5 k., 30 k.), A. Onwudimegwu (10 k., 12 k.), N. Lasisi (18 k.))

1976–77. *Second World Black and African Festival of Arts and Culture, Nigeria. T* **192** *and similar horiz designs. W* **189**. *P* 14.
361 5 k. gold and blackish brown (1.11.76) .. 15 10
362 10 k. lt red-brown, lt yellow & black (15.1.77) 35 40
363 12 k. multicoloured (15.1.77) 40 55
364 18 k. chrome-yellow, lt brown & blk (1.11.76) 60 80
365 30 k. magenta and black (15.1.77) .. .. 1·00 1·50
361/5 .. .. *Set of* 5 2·25 3·00
Designs:—10 k. National Arts Theatre; 12 k. African hair styles; 18 k. Musical instruments; 30 k. "Nigerian arts and crafts".

193 General Murtala Muhammed and Map of Nigeria

194 Scouts Saluting

(Des A. Onwudimegwu (5, 18 k.), O. I. Oshiga (30 k.))

1977 (12 Feb). *First Death Anniv of General Muhammed (Head of State). T* **193** *and similar vert designs. Multicoloured. W* **189** (*sideways on* 18 *and* 30 *k.*). *P* 14.
366 5 k. Type **193** 10 10
367 18 k. General in dress uniform 20 35
368 30 k. General in battle dress 30 70
366/8 .. .. *Set of* 3 50 1·00

(Des N. Lasisi (18 k.), A. Onwudimegwu (others))

1977 (2 Apr). *First All-Africa Scout Jamboree, Jos, Nigeria. T* **194** *and similar horiz designs. Multicoloured. W* **189** (*sideways on* 5 *k.*). *P* 14.
369 5 k. Type **194** 15 10
370 18 k. Scouts cleaning street 70 70
371 25 k. Scouts working on farm 85 95
372 30 k. Jamboree emblem and map of Africa .. 1·10 1·40
369/72 .. .. *Set of* 4 2·50 2·75

195 Trade Fair Complex

(Des S. Eluare (5 k.), A. Onwudimegwu (others))

1977 (27 Nov). *1st Lagos International Trade Fair. T* **195** *and similar horiz designs. W* **189**. *P* 14.
373 5 k. black, new blue and yellow-green .. 10 10
374 18 k. black, new blue and magenta 20 25
375 30 k. multicoloured 30 45
373/5 .. .. *Set of* 3 50 70
Designs:—18 k. Globe and Trade Fair emblem; 30 k. Weaving and basketry.

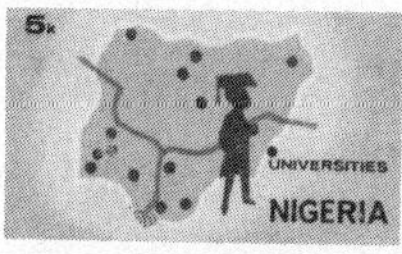

196 Map showing Nigerian Universities

(Des M. O. Shadare (5 k.), C. Okechukwu (12 k.), A. Onwudimegwu (18 k.), N. Lasisi (30 k.))

1978 (28 Apr). *Global Conference on Technical Co-operation between Developing Countries, Buenos Aires. T* **196** *and similar horiz designs. W* **189**. *P* 14.
376 5 k. multicoloured 10 10
377 12 k. multicoloured 15 15
378 18 k. multicoloured 25 25
379 30 k. yellow, bluish violet and black 45 60
376/9 .. .. *Set of* 4 80 1·00
Designs:—12 k. Map of West African highways and telecommunications; 18 k. Technologists undergoing training; 30 k. World map.

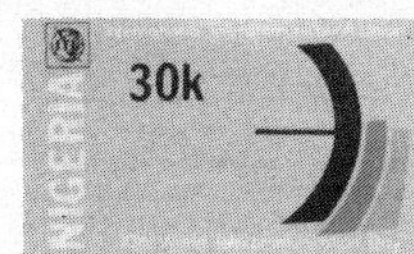

197 Microwave Antenna

1978 (17 May). *10th World Telecommunications Day. W* **189**. *P* 14.
380 **197** 30 k. multicoloured 50 60

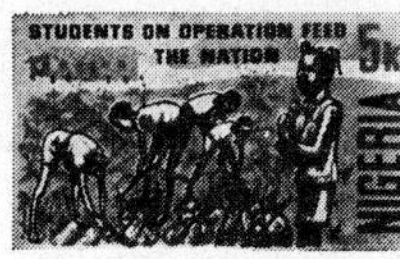

198 Students on "Operation Feed the Nation"

199 Mother with Infected Child

(Des J. Salisu (5 k.), N. Lasisi (18 k.), A. Onwudimegwu (30 k.))

1978 (7 July). *"Operation Feed the Nation" Campaign. T* **198** *and similar multicoloured designs. W* **189** (*sideways on* 30 *k.*). *P* 14.
381 5 k. Type **198** 10 10
382 18 k. Family backyard farm 20 20
383 30 k. Plantain farm (*vert*) 35 60
381/3 .. .. *Set of* 3 55 75

(Des G. Osuji (30 k.), N. Lasisi (others))

1978 (31 Aug). *Global Eradication of Smallpox. T* **199** *and similar designs. W* **189** *(sideways on* 30 *k.). P* 14.
384 5 k. black, orange-brown and rose-lilac .. 10 10
385 12 k. multicoloured 25 20
386 18 k. black, lake-brown and greenish yellow .. 40 30
387 30 k. black, silver and rose-pink 60 50
384/7 .. .. *Set of* 4 1·25 1·00
Designs: *Horiz*—12 k. Doctor and infected child; 18 k. Group of children being vaccinated. *Vert*—30 k. Syringe.

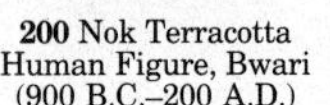

200 Nok Terracotta Human Figure, Bwari (900 B.C.–200 A.D.)

201 Anti-Apartheid Emblem

(Des local artists)

1978 (27 Oct). *Antiquities. T* **200** *and similar designs. W* **189** *(sideways on* 5, 18 *and* 30 *k.). P* 14.
388 5 k. black, new blue and carmine-red .. 10 10
389 12 k. multicoloured 10 10
390 18 k. black, greenish blue and carmine-red .. 15 15
391 30 k. multicoloured 20 20
388/91 .. .. *Set of* 4 45 45
Designs: *Horiz*—12 k. Igbo-Ukwu bronze snail shell, Igbo Isaiah (9th-century A.D.). *Vert*—18 k. Ife bronze statue of king (12th–15th century A.D.); 30 k. Benin bronze equestrian figure (about 1700 A.D.).

(Des A. Onwudimegwu)

1978 (10 Dec). *International Anti-Apartheid Year. W* **189** *(sideways). P* 14.
392 **201** 18 k. black, greenish yellow & vermilion 15 15

202 Wright Brothers and *Flyer*

203 Murtala Muhammed Airport

(Des A. Onwudimegwu)

1978 (28 Dec). *75th Anniv of Powered Flight. T* **202** *and similar horiz design. W* **189**. *P* 14.
393 5 k. multicoloured 15 10
394 18 k. black, ultramarine and light blue .. 50 20
Design:—18 k. Nigerian Air Force formation.

(Des A. Onwudimegwu)

1979 (15 Mar). *Opening of Murtala Muhammed Airport. W* **189**. *P* 14.
395 **203** 5 k. black, grey-blk & brt greenish blue 20 20

204 Child with Stamp Album

205 Mother and Child

1979 (11 Apr). *10th Anniv of National Philatelic Service. W* **189**. *P* 14.
396 **204** 5 k. multicoloured 10 10

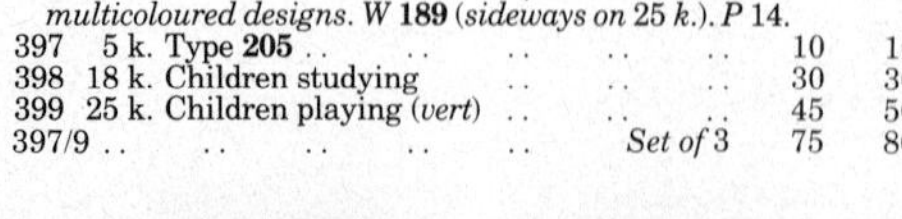

1979 (28 June). *International Year of the Child. T* **205** *and similar multicoloured designs. W* **189** *(sideways on* 25 *k.). P* 14.
397 5 k. Type **205** 10 10
398 18 k. Children studying 30 30
399 25 k. Children playing (*vert*) 45 50
397/9 .. .. *Set of* 3 75 80

206 Trainee Teacher making Audio Visual Aid Materials

207 Necom House

(Des M. Shadare and O. Oshiga)

1979 (25 July). *50th Anniv of International Bureau of Education. T* **206** *and similar vert design. Multicoloured. W* **189** *(sideways). P* 14.
400 10 k. Type **206** 10 10
401 30 k. Adult education class 25 30

(Des A. Onwudimegwu)

1979 (20 Sept). *50th Anniv of Consultative Committee of International Radio. W* **189** *(sideways). P* 14.
402 **207** 10 k. multicoloured 15 20

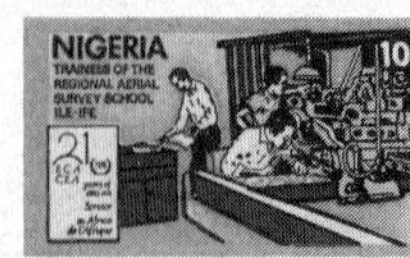

208 Trainees of the Regional Aerial Survey School, Ile-Ife

(Des A. Onwudimegwu)

1979 (12 Dec). *21st Anniv of the Economic Commission for Africa. W* **189**. *P* 14.
403 **208** 10 k. multicoloured 20 20

209 Football, Cup and Map of Nigeria

210 Wrestling

(Des G. Akinola (10 k.), Mrs. O. Adeyeye (30 k.)

1980 (8 Mar). *African Cup of Nations Football Competition, Nigeria. T* **209** *and similar multicoloured design. W* **189** *(sideways on* 30 *k.). P* 14.
404 10 k. Type **209** 15 10
405 30 k. Footballer (*vert*) 50 50

(Des M. Shadare (10 k.), Mrs. O. Adeyeye (others))

1980 (19 July). *Olympic Games, Moscow. T* **210** *and similar designs. W* **189** *(sideways on* 10, 20 *and* 45 *k.). P* 14.
406 10 k. multicoloured 10 10
407 20 k. black and bright yellow-green 10 10
408 30 k. black, reddish orange and blue 15 15
409 45 k. multicoloured 20 20
406/9 .. .. *Set of* 4 45 45
Designs: *Vert*—20 k. Long jump; 45 k. Netball. *Horiz*—30 k. Swimming.

211 Figures supporting O.P.E.C. Emblem

212 Steam Locomotive

(Des G. Oluwasegun)

1980 (15 Sept). *20th Anniv of O.P.E.C. (Organization of Petroleum Exporting Countries). T* **211** *and similar design. W* **189** *(sideways on* 45 *k.). P* 14.
410 10 k. black, ultramarine and greenish yellow 15 10
411 45 k. black, deep turquoise-blue and magenta 55 60
Design: *Vert*—45 k. O.P.E.C. emblem on globe.

1980 (2 Oct). *25th Anniv of Nigerian Railway Corporation. T* **212** *and similar horiz designs. Multicoloured. W* **189**. *P* 14.
412 10 k. Type **212** 45 10
413 20 k. Loading goods train 85 60
414 30 k. Freight train 95 70
412/14 .. .. *Set of* 3 2·00 1·25

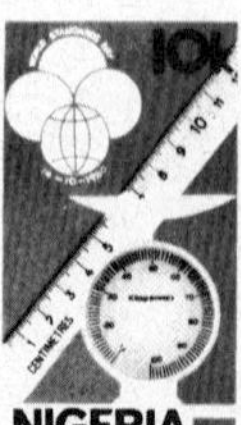

213 Metric Scales

214 "Communications" Symbols and Map of West Africa

(Des G. Akinola (10 k.), M. Shadare (30 k.))

1980 (14 Oct). *World Standards Day. T* **213** *and similar design. W* **189** *(sideways on* 10 *k.). P* 14.
415 10 k. red and black 10 10
416 30 k. multicoloured 35 40
Design: *Horiz*—30 k. Quality control.

1980 (5 Nov). *5th Anniv of E.C.O.W.A.S. (Economic Community of West African States). T* **214** *and similar horiz designs showing symbols of economic structure and map of West Africa. W* **189**. *P* 14.
417 10 k. black, yellow-orange and grey-olive .. 10 10
418 25 k. black, emerald and bright rose 10 10
419 30 k. black, greenish yellow and yellow-brown 15 15
420 45 k. black, turquoise-blue and bright blue .. 20 25
417/20 .. .. *Set of* 4 45 50
Designs:—25 k. "Transport"; 30 k. "Agriculture"; 45 k. "Industry".

215 Disabled Woman Sweeping

216 President launching "Green Revolution" (food production campaign)

(Des N. Lasisi (10 k.), G. Akinola (30 k.))

1981 (25 June). *International Year for Disabled Persons. T* **215** *and similar vert design. W* **189** *(sideways). P* 14.
421 10 k. multicoloured 20 10
422 30 k. black, chestnut and new blue 65 65
Design:—30 k. Disabled man filming.

(Des Mrs. A. Adeyeye (10 k.), G. Akinola (30 k.), S. Eluare (others))

1981 (16 Oct). *World Food Day. T* **216** *and similar designs. W* **189** *(sideways on* 25 *and* 30 *k.). P* 14.
423 10 k. multicoloured 10 10
424 25 k. black, greenish yellow and emerald .. 20 50
425 30 k. multicoloured 25 55
426 45 k. black, yellow-brown and orange-yellow 45 85
423/6 .. .. *Set of* 4 85 1·75
Designs: *Vert*—25 k. Food crops; 30 k. Harvesting tomatoes. *Horiz*—45 k. Pig farming.

217 Rioting in Soweto

218 "Preservation of Wildlife"

(Des G. Osuji)

1981 (10 Dec). *Anti-Apartheid Movement. T* **217** *and similar design. W* **189** *(sideways on* 45 *k.). P* 14.
427 30 k. multicoloured 35 45
428 45 k. black, vermilion and light green .. 50 80
Design: *Vert*—45 k. "Police brutality".

(Des G. Akinola)

1982 (22 Feb). *75th Anniv of Boy Scout Movement. T* **218** *and similar horiz design. Multicoloured. W* **189**. *P* 14.
429 30 k. Type **218** 75 55
430 45 k. Lord Baden-Powell taking salute .. 1·00 95

219 Early Inoculation

220 "Keep Your Environment Clean"

(Des G. Osuji (10 k.), C. Ogbebor (30 k.), N. Lasisi (45 k.))

1982 (24 Mar). *Centenary of Robert Koch's Discovery of Tubercle Bacillus. T* **219** *and similar designs. W* **189** *(sideways on* 45 *k.). P* 14.
431 10 k. multicoloured 25 15
432 30 k. grey-black, brown and turquoise-green .. 65 55
433 45 k. grey-black, light brown and bright green 1·10 85
431/3 .. .. *Set of* 3 1·75 1·40
Designs: *Horiz*—30 k. Technician and microscope. *Vert*—45 k. Patient being X-rayed.

(Des C. Ogbebor (10 k.), N. Lasisi (others))

1982 (10 June). *10th Anniv of U.N. Conference on Human Environment. T* **220** *and similar horiz designs. W* **189**. *P* 14.
434 10 k. multicoloured 15 10
435 20 k. yellow-orange, greenish grey and black .. 40 40
436 30 k. multicoloured 55 60
437 45 k. multicoloured 80 85
434/7 .. .. *Set of* 4 1·75 1·75
Designs:—20 k. "Check air pollution"; 30 k. "Preserve natural environment"; 45 k. "Reafforestation concerns all".

COVER PRICES

Cover factors are quoted at the beginning of each country for most issues to 1945. An explanation of the system can be found on page x. The factors quoted do not, however, apply to philatelic covers.

221 *Salamis parhassus* **222** Carving of "Male and Female Twins"

(Des G. Akinola)

1982 (15 Sept). *Nigerian Butterflies. T* **221** *and similar horiz designs. Multicoloured. W* **189**. *P* 14.

438	10 k. Type **221**	15	10
439	20 k. *Iterus zalmoxis*	40	40
440	30 k. *Cymothoe beckeri*	55	60
441	45 k. *Papilio hesperus*	80	85
438/41	*Set of* 4	1·75	1·75

(Des C. Ogbebor (10 k.), G. Akinola (20 k.), S. Eluare (30 k.), N. Lasisi (45 k.))

1982 (18 Nov). *25th Anniv of National Museum. T* **222** *and similar multicoloured designs. W* **189** (*sideways on* 10, 30, 45 *k.*). *P* 14.

442	10 k. Type **222**	25	10
443	20 k. Royal bronze leopard (*horiz*)	50	55
444	30 k. Soapstone seated figure	80	1·25
445	45 k. Wooden helmet mask	1·25	1·75
442/5	*Set of* 4	2·50	3·25

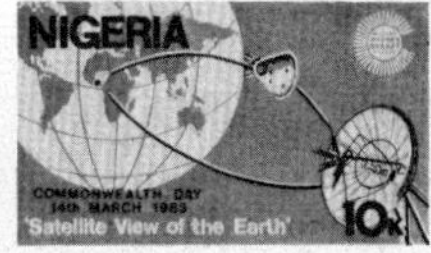

223 Three Generations **224** Satellite View of Globe

(Des G. Akinola)

1983 (8 Mar). *Family Day. T* **223** *and similar multicoloured design. W* **189** (*sideways on* 30 *k.*). *P* 14.

446	10 k. Type **223**	15	10
447	30 k. Parents with three children (*vert*)	50	65

(Des N. Lasisi (30 k.), C. Ogbebor (others))

1983 (14 Mar). *Commonwealth Day. T* **224** *and similar designs. W* **189** (*sideways on* 30, 45 *k.*). *P* 14.

448	10 k. yellow-brown and black	15	10
449	25 k. multicoloured	45	50
450	30 k. black, magenta and pale grey	50	55
451	45 k. multicoloured	80	85
448/51	*Set of* 4	1·75	1·75

Designs: *Horiz*—25 k. National Assembly Buildings. *Vert*—30 k. Drilling for oil; 45 k. Athletics.

225 Corps Members on Building Project **226** Postman on Bicycle

(Des Mrs. A. Adeyeye (25 k.), G. Akinola (others))

1983 (25 May). *10th Anniv of National Youth Service Corps. T* **225** *and similar multicoloured designs. W* **189** (*sideways on* 25, 30 *k.*). *P* 14.

452	10 k. Type **225**	15	10
453	25 k. On the assault-course (*vert*)	45	50
454	30 k. Corps members on parade (*vert*)	50	60
452/4	*Set of* 3	1·00	1·10

(Des N. Lasisi (25 k.), O. Ogunfowora (30 k.), Mrs. A. Adeyeye (others))

1983 (20 July). *World Communications Year. T* **226** *and similar multicoloured designs. W* **189** (*sideways on* 10 *k.*). *P* 14.

455	10 k. Type **226**	15	10
456	25 k. Newspaper kiosk (*horiz*)	45	50
457	30 k. Town crier blowing elephant tusk (*horiz*)	50	55
458	45 k. T.V. newsreader (*horiz*)	80	85
455/8	*Set of* 4	1·75	1·75

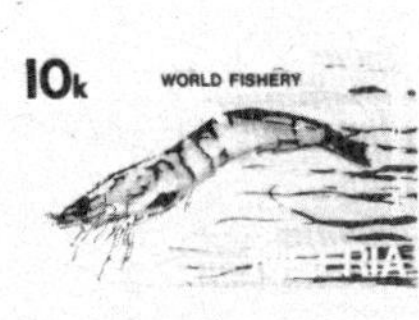

227 Pink Shrimp **228** On Parade

(Des Hilda Woods (10 k.), G. Osuji (25 k.), Mrs. A. Adeyeye (30 k.), O. Ogunfowora (45 k.))

1983 (22 Sept). *World Fishery Resources. T* **227** *and similar horiz designs. W* **189**. *P* 14.

459	10 k. rose, new blue and black	15	10
460	25 k. multicoloured	35	50
461	30 k. multicoloured	40	55
462	45 k. multicoloured	65	85
459/62	*Set of* 4	1·40	1·75

Designs:—25 k. Long Neck Croaker; 30 k. Barracuda; 45 k. Fishing techniques.

(Des F. Nwaije (10 k.), Mrs A. Adeyeye (30 k.), G. Osuji (45 k.))

1983 (14 Oct). *Boys' Brigade Centenary and 75th Anniv of Movement in Nigeria. T* **228** *and similar multicoloured designs. W* **189** (*sideways on* 10 *k.*). *P* 14.

463	10 k. Type **228**	40	10
464	30 k. Members working on cassava plantation (*horiz*)	1·25	1·25
465	45 k. Skill training (*horiz*)	2·00	2·25
463/5	*Set of* 3	3·25	3·25

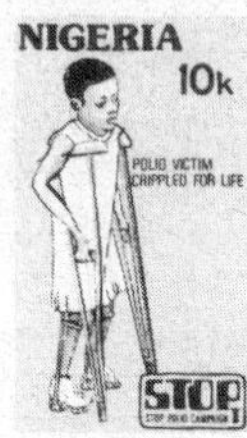

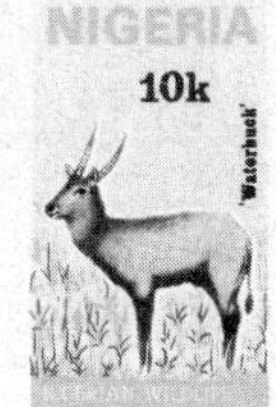

229 Crippled Child **230** Waterbuck

(Des S. Eluare (10 k.), G. Osuji (others))

1984 (29 Feb). *Stop Polio Campaign. T* **229** *and similar designs. W* **189** (*sideways on* 10 *k. and* 30 *k.*). *P* 14.

466	10 k. light blue, black and light brown	20	15
467	25 k. pale orange, black and greenish yellow	45	60
468	30 k. carmine-rose, black and orange-brown	55	75
466/8	*Set of* 3	1·10	1·40

Designs: *Horiz*—25 k. Child receiving vaccine. *Vert*—30 k. Healthy child.

(Des O. Ogunfowora (30 k.), Mrs. A. Adeyeye (45 k.), N. Lasisi (others))

1984 (25 May). *Nigerian Wildlife. T* **230** *and similar designs. W* **189** (*inverted on* 30 *k.*, *sideways on* 10 *k.*, 45 *k.*). *P* 14.

469	10 k. light green, light brown and black	20	10
470	25 k. multicoloured	50	50
471	30 k. yellow-brown, black and light green	60	70
472	45 k. new blue, pale orange and black	80	95
469/72	*Set of* 4	1·90	2·00

Designs: *Horiz*—25 k. Hartebeest; 30 k. African Buffalo. *Vert*—45 k. Diademed Monkey ("African Golden Monkey").

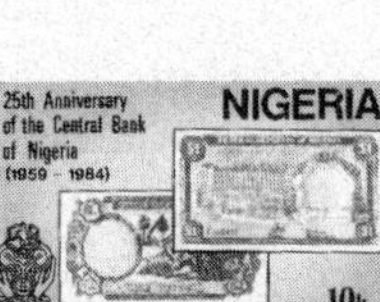

231 Obverse and Reverse of 1969 £1 Note **232** Boxing

1984 (2 July). *25th Anniv of Nigerian Central Bank. T* **231** *and similar horiz designs. W* **189** (*inverted on* 30 *k.*). *P* 14.

473	10 k. multicoloured	20	10
474	25 k. deep cinnamon, black and light green	45	50
475	30 k. light rose, black and grey-olive	55	60
473/5	*Set of* 3	1·10	1·10

Designs:—25 k. Central Bank; 30 k. Obverse and reverse of 1959 £5 note.

1984 (20 July). *Olympic Games, Los Angeles. T* **232** *and similar vert designs. Multicoloured. W* **189** (*sideways*). *P* 14.

476	10 k. Type **232**	15	10
477	25 k. Discus-throwing	35	50
478	30 k. Weightlifting	40	60
479	45 k. Cycling	60	90
476/9	*Set of* 4	1·40	1·90

233 Irrigation Project, Lesotho **234** Pin-tailed Whydah

(Des Mrs. A. Adeyeye (10 k.), S. Eluare (25 k.), Hilda Woods (30 k.), O. Ogunfowora (45 k.))

1984 (10 Sept). *20th Anniv of African Development Bank. T* **233** *and similar designs. W* **189** (*sideways on* 10 *k.*). *P* 14.

480	10 k. multicoloured	20	10
481	25 k. multicoloured	50	50
482	30 k. black, chrome yell & bright greenish bl	60	60
483	45 k. black, orange-brn & bright greenish bl	1·75	90
480/3	*Set of* 4	2·75	1·90

Designs: *Horiz*—25 k. Bomi Hills Road, Liberia; 30 k. School building project, Seychelles; 45 k. Coal mining, Niger.

(Des S. Eluare (25 k.), O. Ogunfowora (45 k.), F. Isibor (others))

1984 (24 Oct). *Rare Birds. T* **234** *and similar vert designs. Multicoloured. W* **189** (*sideways*). *P* 14.

484	10 k. Type **234**	65	10
485	25 k. Spur-winged Plover	1·50	60
486	30 k. Red Bishop	1·50	1·25
487	45 k. Double-spurred Francolin	1·75	1·75
484/7	*Set of* 4	4·75	3·25

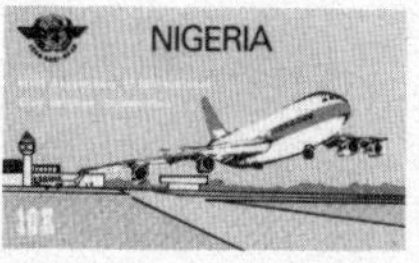

235 Aircraft taking-off **236** Office Workers and Clocks ("Punctuality")

(Des. F. Isibor (10 k.), O. Ogunfowora (45 k.))

1984 (7 Dec). *40th Anniv of International Civil Aviation Organization. T* **235** *and similar horiz design. Multicoloured. W* **189** (*inverted on* 45 *k.*). *P* 14.

488	10 k. Type **235**	50	10
489	45 k. Aircraft circling globe	1·75	1·50

(Des O. Ogunfowora)

1985 (27 Feb). *"War against Indiscipline". T* **236** *and similar horiz design. Multicoloured. W* **189** (*inverted on* 20 *k.*). *P* 14.

490	20 k. Type **236**	30	35
491	50 k. Cross over hands passing banknotes ("Discourage Bribery")	70	75

237 Footballers receiving Flag from Major-General Buhari **238** Globe and O.P.E.C. Emblem

(Des F. Isibor (50 k.), G. Akinola (others))

1985 (5 June). *International Youth Year. T* **237** *and similar multicoloured designs. W* **189** (*sideways on* 50, 55 *k.*). *P* 14.

492	20 k. Type **237**	30	35
493	50 k. Girls of different tribes with flag (*vert*)	70	75
494	55 k. Members of youth organizations with flags (*vert*)	75	80
492/4	*Set of* 3	1·60	1·75

1985 (15 Sept). *25th Anniv of Organization of Petroleum Exporting Countries. T* **238** *and similar design. W* **189** (*sideways on* 20 *k.*). *P* 14.

495	20 k. greenish blue and orange-vermilion	1·00	35
496	50 k. black and ultramarine	1·75	75

Design: *Horiz*—50 k. World map and O.P.E.C. emblem.

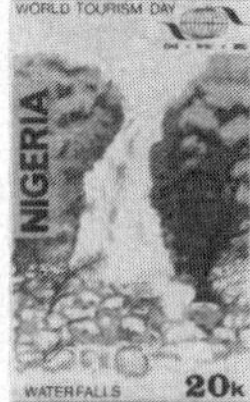

239 Rolling Mill **240** Waterfall

1985 (25 Sept). *25th Anniv of Independence. T* **239** *and similar horiz designs. Multicoloured. W* **189**. *P* 14.

497	20 k. Type **239**	40	10
498	50 k. Map of Nigeria	60	35
499	55 k. Remembrance Arcade	60	40
500	60 k. Eleme, first Nigerian oil refinery	85	50
497/500	*Set of* 4	2·25	1·25
MS501	101 × 101 mm. Nos. 497/500. Wmk sideways	4·00	4·75

(Des S. Eluare (55 k.), F. Isibor (60 k.), Mrs. A. Adeyeye (others))

1985 (27 Sept). *World Tourism Day. T* **240** *and similar multicoloured designs. W* **189** (*sideways on* 20, 55, 60 *k.*, *inverted on* 50 *k.*). *P* 14.

502	20 k. Type **240**	45	10
503	50 k. Pottery, carved heads and map of Nigeria (*horiz*)	55	40
504	55 k. Calabash carvings and Nigerian flag	55	40
505	60 k. Leather work	55	45
502/5	*Set of* 4	1·90	1·25

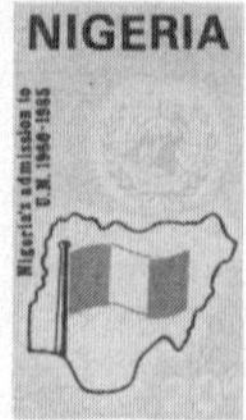
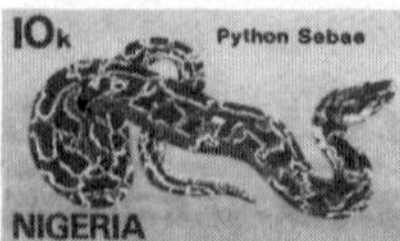

241 Map of Nigeria and National Flag 242 Rock Python

(Des N. Lasisi (20 k.), Mrs. A. Adeyeye (50 k.), O. Ogunfowora (55 k.))

1985 (7 Oct). *40th Anniv of United Nations Organization and 25th Anniv of Nigerian Membership. T* **241** *and similar designs. W* **189** *(sideways on 20 k., inverted on 50 k.). P* 14.

506 20 k. black, light green and pale blue .. 15 10
507 50 k. black, dull ultramarine and cerise .. 30 30
508 55 k. black, new blue and carmine 30 30
506/8 .. *Set of* 3 65 65

Designs: *Horiz*—50 k. United Nations Building, New York; 55 k. United Nations logo.

IMPERFORATE STAMPS. Nos. 509/12, 528/38, 543/6, 555/7, 560/7, 572/9, 582/5 and 607/9 exist imperforate from restricted printings. Such printings may also exist for other issues.

(Des Hilda Woods (10, 30 k.), G. Akinola (20 k.), F. Isibor (25 k.))

1986 (15 Apr). *African Reptiles. T* **242** *and similar horiz designs. W* **189** *(inverted on 10 k.). P* 14.

509 10 k. multicoloured .. 35 10
510 20 k. black, orange-brown and pale new blue 65 50
511 25 k. multicoloured .. 70 65
512 30 k. multicoloured .. 70 85
509/12 .. *Set of* 4 2·25 1·90

Designs:—20 k. Long Snouted Crocodile; 25 k. Gopher Tortoise; 30 k. Chameleon.

243 Social Worker with Children 244 Emblem and Globe

(Des G. Akinola (1, 35 k.), S. Eluare (5 k.), O. Ogunfowora (10, 15 k.), Mrs. A. Adeyeye (40, 45 k.), G. Osuji (50 k.), C. Ogbebor (others))

1986 (16 June). *Nigerian Life. T* **243** *and similar multicoloured designs. W* **189** *(sideways on* 1, 10, 20, 40 *k. and inverted on* 2, 5, 25, 50 *k.,* 1, 2 *n.). P* 14.

513 1 k. Type **243** .. 10 10
514 2 k. Volkswagen motor assembly line (*horiz*) .. 10 10
515 5 k. Modern housing estate (*horiz*) .. 10 10
516 10 k. Harvesting oil palm fruit .. 10 10
517 15 k. Unloading freighter (*horiz*) .. 10 10
518 20 k. *Tecoma stans* (flower) .. 10 10
519 25 k. Hospital ward (*horiz*) .. 10 10
519*a* 30 k. Birom dancers .. 10 10
520 35 k. Telephonists operating switchboard (*horiz*) .. 10 10
521 40 k. Nkpokiti dancers .. 10 10
522 45 k. Hibiscus (*horiz*) .. 10 10
523 50 k. Post Office counter (*horiz*) .. 10 10
524 1 n. Stone quarry (*horiz*) .. 10 15
525 2 n. Students in laboratory (*horiz*) .. 25 30
513/25 .. *Set of* 14 85 95

Nos. 513/25 were originally scheduled for issue during 1984, but were delayed. The 5 k. and 20 k. appear to have been released for postal purposes during 1984 and are known postmarked from 2 November (5 k.) or 3 July (20 k.). The 30 k. value, No. 519*a*, was not included in the 1986 philatelic release.

(Des Mrs. A. Adeyeye)

1986 (20 June). *International Peace Year. T* **244** *and similar horiz design. Multicoloured. W* **189**. *P* 14.

526 10 k. Type **244** .. 10 10
527 20 k. Hands of five races holding globe .. 10 10

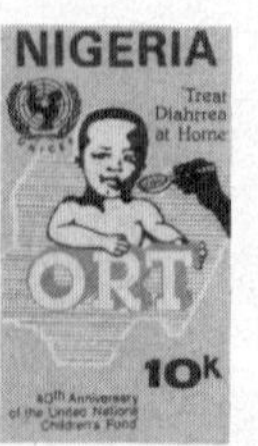

245 *Goliathus goliathus* (beetle) 246 Oral Rehydration Therapy

(Des Hilda Woods (25 k.), S. Eluare (others))

1986 (14 July). *Nigerian Insects. T* **245** *and similar horiz designs. Multicoloured. W* **189** *(inverted on 20 k.). P* 14.

528 10 k. Type **245** .. 35 10
529 20 k. *Vespa vulgaris* (wasp) .. 45 40
530 25 k. *Acheta domestica* (cricket) .. 55 55
531 30 k. *Anthrenus verbaxi* (beetle) .. 75 85
528/31 .. *Set of* 4 1·90 1·75
MS532 119×101 mm. Nos. 528/31. Wmk sideways .. 4·00 4·75

(Des N. Lasisi (10 k.), F. Isibor (30 k.), Mrs. A. Adeyeye (others))

1986 (11 Nov). *40th Anniv of United Nations Children's Fund. T* **246** *and similar vert designs. W* **189** *(sideways). P* 14.

533 10 k. multicoloured .. 30 10
534 20 k. black, reddish brown & greenish yellow 50 30
535 25 k. multicoloured .. 55 40
536 30 k. multicoloured .. 70 55
533/6 .. *Set of* 4 1·75 1·25

Designs:—20 k. Immunisation; 25 k. Breast feeding; 30 k. Mother and child.

247 Stylized Figures on Wall ("International Understanding") 248 Freshwater Clam

(Des S. Eluare (20 k.), Hilda Woods (30 k.))

1986 (12 Dec). *25th Anniv of Nigerian Institute of International Affairs. T* **247** *and similar design. W* **189** *(sideways on 30 k.). P* 14.

537 20 k. black, greenish blue and light green .. 50 40
538 30 k. multicoloured .. 75 1·00

Design: *Vert*—30 k. "Knowledge" (bronze sculpture).

(Des G. Osuji (20 k.), F. Isibor (others))

1987 (31 Mar). *Shells. T* **248** *and similar horiz designs. W* **189** *(inverted on* 10, 25 *k.). P* 14.

539 10 k. multicoloured .. 35 10
540 20 k. black, reddish brown & pale rose-pink 60 60
541 25 k. multicoloured .. 60 60
542 30 k. multicoloured .. 75 90
539/42 .. *Set of* 4 2·10 2·00

Design:—20 k. Periwinkle; 25 k. Bloody Cockle (inscr "BLODDY COCKLE"); 30 k. Mangrove Oyster.

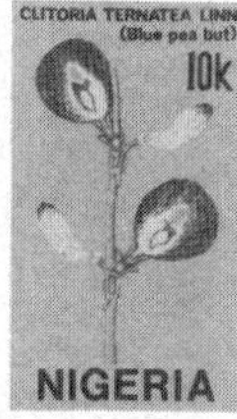
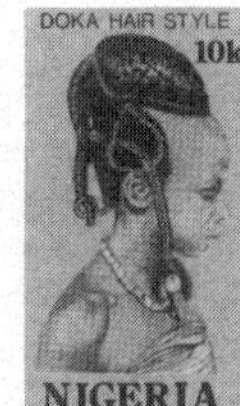

249 *Clitoria ternatea* 250 Doka Hairstyle

(Des S. Eluare (10 k.), Hilda Woods (20 k.), Mrs. A. Adeyeye (others))

1987 (28 May). *Nigerian Flowers. T* **249** *and similar vert designs. W* **189** *(sideways). P* 14.

543 10 k. multicoloured .. 10 10
544 20 k. lake-brown, greenish yellow & emerald 15 10
545 25 k. multicoloured .. 15 15
546 30 k. multicoloured .. 20 20
543/6 .. *Set of* 4 55 45

Designs:—20 k. *Hibiscus tiliaceus*; 25 k. *Acanthus montanus*; 30 k. *Combretum racemosum*.

(Des G. Akinola (25 k.), S. Eluare (30 k.), Mrs. A. Adeyeye (others))

1987 (15 Sept). *Women's Hairstyles. T* **250** *and similar vert designs. W* **189** *(sideways). P* 14.

547 10 k. black, orange-brown and olive-grey .. 10 10
548 20 k. multicoloured .. 10 10
549 25 k. black, brown and vermilion .. 10 10
550 30 k. multicoloured .. 10 10
547/50 .. *Set of* 4 30 30

Designs:—20 k. Eting; 25 k. Agogo; 30 k. Goto.

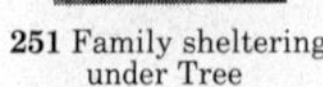

251 Family sheltering under Tree 252 Red Cross Worker distributing Food

(Des S. Nwasike (20 k.), Mrs. A. Adeyeye (30 k.))

1987 (10 Dec). *International Year of Shelter for the Homeless. T* **251** *and similar vert design. Multicoloured. W* **189** *(sideways). P* 14.

551 20 k. Type **251** .. 15 10
552 30 k. Family and modern house .. 15 20

(Des G. Osuji)

1988 (17 Feb). *125th Anniv of International Red Cross. T* **252** *and similar vert design. Multicoloured. W* **189** *(sideways). P* 14.

553 20 k. Type **252** .. 15 10
554 30 k. Carrying patient to ambulance .. 15 40

253 Doctor vaccinating Baby 254 O.A.U. Logo

(Des C. Ogbebor (10 k.), G. Osuji (others))

1988 (7 Apr). *40th Anniv of World Health Organization. T* **253** *and similar horiz designs. Multicoloured. W* **189** *(inverted). P* 14.

555 10 k. Type **253** .. 10 10
556 20 k. W.H.O. logo and outline map of Nigeria 15 15
557 30 k. Doctor and patients at mobile clinic .. 15 15
555/7 .. *Set of* 3 30 30

(Des O. Ojo (10 k.), Mrs. A. Adeyeye (20 k.))

1988 (25 May). *25th Anniv of Organization of African Unity. T* **254** *and similar vert design. W* **189** *(sideways). P* 14.

558 10 k. olive-bistre, emerald and bright orange 15 15
559 20 k. multicoloured .. 15 15

Design:—20 k. Four Africans supporting map of Africa.

255 Pink Shrimp 256 Weightlifting

(Des S. Eluare)

1988 (2 June). *Shrimps. T* **255** *and similar horiz designs. W* **189**. *P* 14.

560 10 k. multicoloured .. 15 10
561 20 k. black and pale yellow-olive .. 20 10
562 25 k. black, orange-vermilion & yell-brown 20 10
563 30 k. reddish orange, olive-bistre and black 25 10
560/3 .. *Set of* 4 70 30
MS564 120 × 101 mm. Nos. 560/3. Wmk sideways .. 40 50

Designs:—20 k. Tiger Shrimp; 25 k. Deepwater Roseshrimp; 30 k. Estuarine Prawn.

(Des G. Osuji (30 k.), Mrs. A. Adeyeye (others))

1988 (6 Sept). *Olympic Games, Seoul. T* **256** *and similar multicoloured designs. W* **189** *(sideways on 30 k.). P* 14.

565 10 k. Type **256** .. 15 10
566 20 k. Boxing .. 20 10
567 30 k. Athletics (*vert*) .. 30 15
565/7 .. *Set of* 3 60 30

257 Banknote Production Line

(Des Mrs. A. Adeyeye (25 k.), G. Akinola (30 k.), O. Ojo (others))

1988 (28 Oct). *25th Anniv of Nigerian Security Printing and Minting Co Ltd. T* **257** *and similar designs. W* **189** *(inverted on 10 k.). P* 14.

568 10 k. multicoloured .. 10 10
569 20 k. black, silver and emerald .. 10 10
570 25 k. multicoloured .. 10 10
571 30 k. multicoloured .. 15 15
568/71 .. *Set of* 4 30 30

Designs: *Horiz (as T* **257***)*—20 k. Coin production line. *Vert* (37 × 44 *mm*)—25 k. Montage of products; 30 k. Anniversary logos.

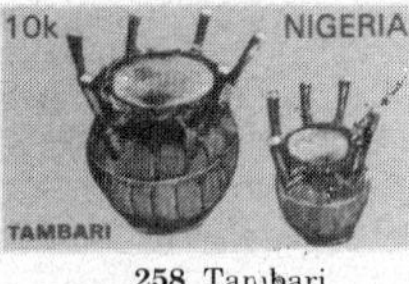

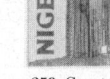

258 Tambari 259 Construction of Water Towers, Mali

(Des S. Nwasike (10 k.), N. Lasisi (20 k.), S. Eluare (others))

1989 (29 June). *Nigerian Musical Instruments. T* **258** *and similar horiz designs. W* **189** *(inverted). P* 14.

572 10 k. multicoloured .. 10 10
573 20 k. multicoloured .. 10 10
574 25 k. chestnut, bronze-green and black .. 10 10
575 30 k. red-brown and black .. 15 15
572/5 .. *Set of* 4 30 30

Designs:—20 k. Kundung, 25 k. Ibid; 30 k. Dundun.

(Des Hilda Woods (10 k.), F. Abdul (20, 25 k.), S. Eluare (30 k.))

1989 (10 Sept). *25th Anniv of African Development Bank. T* **259** *and similar multicoloured designs. W* **189** *(inverted on 10, 25 k. and sideways on 30 k.). P* 14.

576 10 k. Type **259** 10 10
577 20 k. Paddy field, Gambia 10 10
578 25 k. Bank Headquarters, Abidjan, Ivory Coast 10 10
579 30 k. Anniversary logo *(vert)* 15 15
576/9 .. .. *Set of* 4 30 30

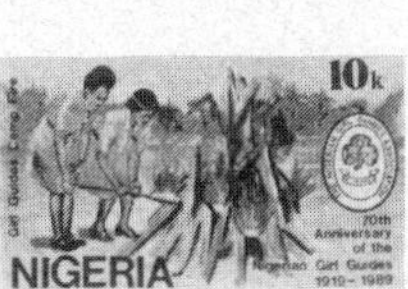

260 Lighting Camp Fire

261 Etubom Costume

(Des F. Abdul (10 k.), Mrs. A. Adeyeye (20 k.))

1989 (16 Sept). *70th Anniv of Nigerian Girl Guides Association. T* **260** *and similar multicoloured design. W* **189** *(inverted on 10 k. and sideways on 20 k.). P* 14.

580 10 k. Type **260** 15 10
581 20 k. Guide on rope bridge *(vert)* 15 20

(Des S. Eluare (10 k.), Mrs. A. Adeyeye (20 k.), F. Abdul (others))

1989 (26 Oct). *Traditional Costumes. T* **261** *and similar vert designs. Multicoloured. W* **189** *(sideways). P* 14.

582 10 k. Type **261** 15 10
583 20 k. Fulfulde 20 10
584 25 k. Aso-Ofi 25 10
585 30 k. Fuska Kura 30 15
582/5 .. .. *Set of* 4 80 30

262 Dove with Letter and Map of Africa

263 Oil Lamps

1990 (18 Jan). *10th Anniv of Pan African Postal Union. T* **262** *and similar vert design. Multicoloured. W* **189** *(sideways). P* 14.

586 10 k. Type **262** 15 10
587 20 k. Parcel and map of Africa 15 20

1990 (24 May). *Nigerian Pottery. T* **263** *and similar horiz designs. W* **189** *(inverted on 10 k.). P* 14.

588 10 k. brownish black, orange-brn & slate-vio 10 10
589 20 k. brownish black, red-brown & slate-vio 10 10
590 25 k. reddish brown and slate-violet .. 10 10
591 30 k. multicoloured 15 15
588/91 .. .. *Set of* 4 30 30
MS592 120×100 mm. Nos. 588/91. Wmk sideways 30 35

Designs:—20 k. Water pots; 25 k. Musical pots; 30 k. Water jugs.

264 Teacher and Class

(Des Mrs. A. Adeyeye (20 k.), G. Osuji (30 k.))

1990 (8 Aug). *International Literacy Year. T* **264** *and similar horiz design. W* **189** *(inverted). P* 14.

593 20 k. multicoloured 10 10
594 30 k. blackish brn, greenish bl & orange-yell 15 15

Design:—30 k. Globe and book.

265 Globe and OPEC Logo

266 Grey Parrot

1990 (14 Sept). *30th Anniv of the Organisation of Petroleum Exporting Countries. T* **265** *and similar multicoloured designs. W* **189** *(inverted on 10, 25 k. and sideways on others). P* 14.

595 10 k. Type **265** 10 10
596 20 k. Logo and flags of member countries *(vert)* 10 10
597 25 k. World map and logo 15 15
598 30 k. Logo within inscription "Co-operation for Global Energy Security" *(vert)* .. 15 15
595/8 .. .. *Set of* 4 35 35

(Des C. Ogbebor (20 k.), G. Osuji (30 k, 2 n. 50), S. Eluare (1 n. 50))

1990 (8 Nov). *Wildlife. T* **266** *and similar vert designs. Multicoloured. W* **189** *(sideways). P* 14.

599 20 k. Type **266** 10 10
600 30 k. Roan Antelope 10 10
601 1 n. 50, Grey-necked Bald Crow ("Rock-fowl") 20 25
602 2 n. 50, Mountain Gorilla 35 40
599/602 .. .. *Set of* 4 55 60
MS603 118×119 mm. Nos. 599/602. Wmk inverted 65 75

267 Eradication Treatment

268 Hand holding Torch (Progress)

(Des C. Ogbebor (20 k.), G. Osuji (others))

1991 (20 Mar). *National Guineaworm Eradication Day. T* **267** *and similar multicoloured designs. W* **189** *(sideways on 10, 30 k.). P* 14.

604 10 k. Type **267** 10 10
605 20 k. Women collecting water from river *(horiz)* 10 10
606 30 k. Boiling pot of water 10 10
604/6 .. .. *Set of* 3 15 15

1991 (26 May). *Organization of African Unity Heads of State and Governments Meeting, Abuja. T* **268** *and similar vert designs each showing outline map of Africa. Multicoloured. W* **189** *(sideways). P* 14.

607 20 k. Type **268** 10 10
608 30 k. Cog wheel (Unity) 10 10
609 50 k. O.A.U flag (Freedom) 10 10
607/9 .. .. *Set of* 3 15 15

269 National Flags

270 Electric Catfish

(Des G. Osuji)

1991 (4 July). *Economic Community of West African States Summit Meeting, Abuja. T* **269** *and similar horiz design. Multicoloured. W* **189** *(inverted). P* 14.

610 20 k. Type **269** 10 10
611 50 k. Map showing member states 10 10

(Des R. Adeyemi (10 k.), C. Ogbebor (20 k.), N. Lasisi (others))

1991 (30 July). *Nigerian Fishes. T* **270** *and similar horiz designs. Multicoloured. W* **189** *(inverted on 20 k.). P* 14.

612 10 k. Type **270** 10 10
613 20 k. Niger Perch 10 10
614 30 k. Talapia 10 10
615 50 k. African Catfish 10 10
612/15 .. .. *Set of* 4 20 20

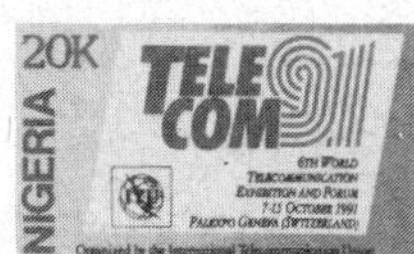

271 Telecom '91 Emblem

(Des S. Eluare)

1991 (7 Oct). *"Telecom '91" 6th World Telecommunication Exhibition, Geneva. T* **271** *and similar design. W* **189** *(sideways on 50 k.). P* 14.

617 20 k. black, deep green and deep violet .. 10 10
618 50 k. multicoloured 10 10

Design: *Vert*—50 k. Emblem and patchwork.

POSTAGE DUE STAMPS

D 1

(Litho B.W.)

1959 (4 Jan). *Wmk Mult Script CA. P* 14½ × 14.

D1 D 1 1d. red-orange 10 55
D2 2d. red-orange 15 70
D3 3d. red-orange .. .. 20 1·00
D4 6d. red-orange .. .. 20 3·00
D5 1s. grey-black .. .. 45 4·25
D1/5 .. .. *Set of* 5 1·00 8·50

1961 (1 Aug). *W* **34**. *P* 14½ × 14.

D 6 D 1 1d. red 10 25
D 7 2d. light blue 10 30
D 8 3d. emerald 15 50
D 9 6d. yellow 30 70
D10 1s. blue *(shades)* .. .. 45 1·75
D6/10 .. .. *Set of* 5 1·00 3·25

(Typo Nigerian Security Printing & Minting Co)

1973 (3 May)–**90**. *New Currency. No wmk. P* 12½×13½.

D11 D 1 2 k. red 10 10
a. Roul 9 (1990) .. .. 1·50
D12 3 k. blue 10 10
D13 5 k. orange-yellow *(shades)* 10 10
D14 10 k. light apple-green *(shades)* 10 10
a. Roul 9. *Emerald* (1987) .. .. 4·00
D11/14 .. .. *Set of* 4 20 20

Nos. D11a and D14a are known postally used at Ibadan in January 1990 and August 1987.

BIAFRA

The following stamps were issued by Biafra (the Eastern Region of Nigeria) during the civil war with the Federal Government, 1967–70.

They were in regular use within Biafra from the time when supplies of Nigerian stamps were exhausted; and towards the end of the conflict they began to be used on external mail carried by air via Libreville.

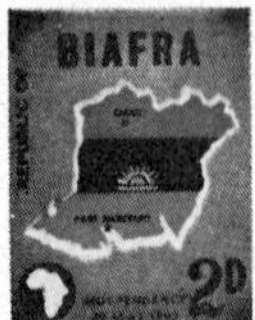

1 Map of Republic

2 Arms, Flag and Date of Independence

3 Mother and Child

(Typo and litho Mint, Lisbon)

1968 (5 Feb). *Independence. P* 12½.
1 **1** 2d. multicoloured 10 30
2 **2** 4d. multicoloured 10 40
3 **3** 1s. multicoloured 15 90
1/3 .. .. *Set of* 3 30 1·40

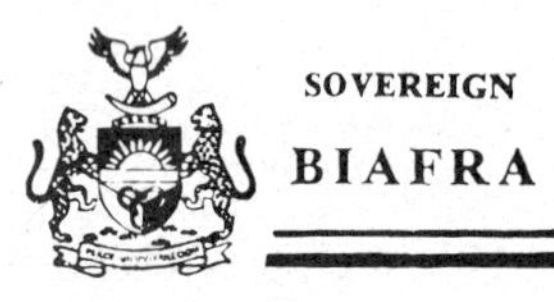

(4)

1968 (Apr). *Nos.* 172/5 *and* 177/85 *of Nigeria optd as T* **4** (*without* "SOVEREIGN" *on* 10s.).
4 ½d. multicoloured (No. 172) .. .. 75 2·00
5 1d. multicoloured (No. 173) .. .. 1·25 3·25
a. Opt double £150
b. Opt omitted (in pair with normal) .. £325
6 1½d. multicoloured (No. 174) .. .. 3·75 6·50
7 2d. multicoloured (No. 175) .. .. 17·00 42·00
8 4d. multicoloured (No. 177a) .. .. 17·00 42·00
9 6d. multicoloured (No. 178) .. .. 3·50 5·50
10 9d. Prussian blue and orange-red (No. 179) 1·00 2·00
11 1s. multicoloured (Blk. + R.) (No. 180) .. 50·00 85·00
12 1s. 3d. multicoloured (Blk. + R.) (No. 181) 32·00 50·00
13 2s. 6d. orange-brown, buff and brown (Blk. + R.) (No. 182) .. .. 1·75 5·50
a. Red opt omitted £160
14 5s. chestnut, lt yell & brn (Blk. + R.) (No. 183) .. .. 1·75 5·50
a. Red opt omitted £160
b. Black opt omitted £150
c. *Pale chestnut, yellow & brn-pur* (No. 183*a*) .. .. 2·25 5·50
15 10s. multicoloured (No. 184) .. .. 9·00 24·00
16 £1 multicoloured (Blk. + R.) (No. 185) .. 10·00 24·00
a. Black ("SOVEREIGN BIAFRA") omitted £170
b. Red (coat of arms) omitted £170
4/16 .. .. *Set of* 13 £120 £275

Nos. 172/3 of Nigeria also exist surcharged "BIAFRA – FRANCE FRIENDSHIP 1968 SOVEREIGN BIAFRA", clasped hands and "+5/-" (½d.) or "+£1" (1d.). There is no evidence that these two surcharges were used for postage within Biafra (*Price for set of* 2 £20 *mint*).

5 Weapon Maintenance

8 Biafran Arms and Banknote

9 Orphaned Child

(Litho Mint, Lisbon)

1968 (30 May). *First Anniv of Independence. T* **5**, **8/9** *and similar vert designs. P* 12½.
17 4d. multicoloured 15 10
18 1s. multicoloured 20 20
19 2s. 6d. multicoloured .. .. 45 1·00
20 5s. multicoloured .. .. 60 1·75
a. Indigo (banknote) omitted .. .. 40·00
b. Red (from flag) omitted .. .. .. 40·00
21 10s. multicoloured .. .. 1·00 2·75
a. Bright green (from flag) omitted .. 30·00
17/21 .. .. *Set of* 5 2·10 5·25

Designs:—1s. Victim of atrocity; 2s. 6d. Nurse and refugees.

Nos. 17/21 also exist surcharged "HELP BIAFRAN CHILDREN" and different charity premium ranging from 2d. on the 4d. to 2s. 6d. on the 10s. There is no evidence that these surcharges were used for postage within Biafra (*Price for set of* 5 £1.50 *mint*).

In late 1968 a set of four values, showing butterflies and plants, was offered for sale outside Biafra. The same stamps also exist overprinted "MEXICO OLYMPICS 1968" and Olympic symbol. There is no evidence that either of these issues were used for postage within Biafra (*Price for set of* 4 £4 (*Butterflies and Plants*) *or* £3.50 (*Olympic overprints*), *both mint*).

CANCELLED-TO-ORDER. Many issues of Biafra, including the three unissued sets mentioned above, were available cancelled-to-order with a special "UMUAHIA" handstamp. This was the same diameter as postal cancellations, but differed from them by having larger letters, 3 mm. high, and the year date in full. Where such cancellations exist on issued stamps the used prices quoted are for c-t-o examples. Postally used stamps are worth considerably more.

16 Child in Chains and Globe

17 Pope Paul VI, Map of Africa and Papal Arms

1969 (30 May). *Second Anniv of Independence. Multicoloured; frame colours given. Litho. P* 13 × 13½.
35 **16** 2d. yellow-orange .. .. 60 2·00
36 4d. red-orange .. .. 60 2·00
a. Green (wreath) and orange (Sun) omitted .. ..
37 1s. new blue .. .. 85 3·50
38 2s. 6d. emerald .. .. 1·50 7·50
35/8 .. .. *Set of* 4 3·25 13·50

A miniature sheet with a face value of 10s. was also released.

1969 (1 Aug). *Visit of Pope Paul to Africa. T* **17** *and similar vert designs. Multicoloured. Litho. P* 13×13½.
39 4d. Type **17** .. .. 40 1·75
40 6d. Pope Paul VI, Map of Africa and arms of the Vatican .. .. 55 3·50
41 9d. Pope Paul VI, map of Africa and St. Peter's Basilica, Vatican .. .. .. 75 4·75
42 3s. Pope Paul VI, map of Africa and Statue of St. Peter .. .. 2·25 10·00
39/42 .. .. *Set of* 4 3·50 18·00

A miniature sheet with a face value of 10s. was also released.

No. 42 has a magenta background. This value is also known with the background in brown-red or brown.

Biafra was overrun by Federal troops on 10 January 1970 and surrender took place on 15 January.

On 17 December the French Agency released a Christmas issue consisting of Nos. 39/42 overprinted "CHRISTMAS 1969 PEACE ON EARTH AND GOODWILL TO ALL MEN" together with the miniature sheet overprinted "CHRISTMAS 1969" and surcharged £1. Later Nos. 35/38 were released overprinted in red "SAVE BIAFRA 9TH JAN 1970" with a premium of 8d., 1s. 4d., 4s., and 10s. respectively together with the miniature sheet with a premium of £1. We have no evidence that these issues were actually put on sale in Biafra before the collapse, but it has been reported that the 4d. Christmas issue and 2d. + 8d. Save Biafra exist genuinely used before capitulation.

Nos. 40/41 have been seen surcharged "+ 10/–HUMAN RIGHTS" and the United Nations emblem but it is doubtful if they were issued.

No. 81 of Nigeria has also been reported with the original "ROYAL VISIT 1956" overprint, together with "NIGERIA" from the basic stamp, obliterated and a "SERVICE" overprint added. Such stamps were not used for official mail in Biafra, although an example is known with the "UMUAHIA" c-t-o mark.

Niue

PRICES FOR STAMPS ON COVER TO 1945	
No. 1	*from* × 2
Nos. 2/5	*from* × 8
Nos. 6/7	—
Nos. 8/9	*from* × 30
Nos. 10/12	—
Nos. 13/31	*from* × 3
Nos. 32/7c	—
Nos. 38/47	*from* × 5
Nos. 48/9	—
No. 50	*from* × 15
Nos. 51/4	—
Nos. 55/61	*from* × 8
Nos. 62/8	*from* × 12
Nos. 69/71	*from* × 3
Nos. 72/4	*from* × 10
Nos. 75/8	*from* × 8
Nos. 79/88	—
Nos. 89/97	*from* × 2

NEW ZEALAND DEPENDENCY

Stamps of New Zealand overprinted

NIUE

(1)

1902 (4 Jan). *Handstamped with T* **1**, *in green or bluish green. Pirie paper. Wmk double-lined "N Z" and Star, W* **38** *of New Zealand. P* 11.
1 **42** 1d. carmine £375 £375

A few overprints were made with a *greenish violet* ink. These occurred only in the first vertical row and part of the second row of the first sheet overprinted owing to violet ink having been applied to the pad (*Price* £1400 *un*).

NIUE. **½ PENI.** (2)   **NIUE.** **TAHA PENI.** (3) 1d.   **NIUE.** **2½ PENI.** (4)

1902 (4 Apr). *Type-set surcharges. T* **2**, **3**, *and* **4**.
(*i*) *Pirie paper. No wmk. P* 11.
2 **27** 2½d. blue (R.) .. .. 1·25 2·75
a. No stop after "PENI" .. .. 25·00 40·00
b. Surch double £2000

(ii) *Basted Mills paper. Wmk double-lined "N Z" and Star, W* **38** *of New Zealand.*
(*a*) *Perf* 14
3 **23** ½d. green (R.) .. .. 75 2·50
a. Spaced "U" and "E" (R. 3/3, 3/6, 8/3, 8/6) .. .. 5·50 10·00
b. Surch inverted £250 £400
c. Surch double .. ..
4 **42** 1d. carmine (B.) .. .. 6·50 8·50
a. Spaced "U" and "E" (R. 3/3, 3/6, 8/6) .. 50·00 65·00
b. No stop after "PENI" (R. 9/3) £130 £140
c. Varieties a. and b. on same stamp (R. 8/3) £130 £140
(*b*) *P* 11 *and* 14 *compound*
5 **42** 1d. carmine (B.) .. .. 85 1·40
a. Spaced "U" and "E" (R. 3/3, 3/6, 8/6) 6·50 8·00
b. No stop after "PENI" (R. 9/3) .. .. 28·00 35·00
c. Varieties a. and b. on same stamp (R. 8/3) .. .. 28·00 35·00
(*c*) *Mixed perfs*
6 **23** ½d. green (R.) £425
7 **42** 1d. carmine (B.) £400

1902 (2 May). *Type-set surcharges, T* **2**, **3**. *Cowan paper. Wmk single-lined "N Z" and Star, W* **43** *of New Zealand.* (*a*) *P* 14.
8 **23** ½d. green (R.) 65 80
a. Spaced "U" and "E" (R. 3/3, 3/6, 8/3, 8/6) .. .. 5·50 6·00
9 **42** 1d. carmine (B.) 50 65
a. Surch double £750
b. Spaced "U" and "E" (R. 3/3, 3/6, 8/6) 9·00 11·00
c. No stop after "PENI" (R. 5/3, 7/3, 9/3, 10/3, 10/6) .. .. 9·00 11·00
d. Varieties b. and c. on same stamp (R. 8/3) .. .. 28·00 35·00
e. "I" of "NIUE" omitted (R. 6/5 from end of last ptg) .. ..
(*b*) *Perf* 11 *and* 14 *compound*
10 **23** ½d. green (R.) .. ..
(*c*) *Mixed perfs*
11 **23** ½d. green (R.) £400
12 **42** 1d. carmine (B.) £170
a. Spaced "U" and "E" (R. 3/3, 3/6, 8/3, 8/6) £325
b. No stop after "PENI" (R. 5/3, 7/3, 9/3, 10/3, 10/6) £300

NIUE. (5)   **Tolu e Pene.** (6) 3d.

Ono e Pene. (7) 6d.   **Taha e Sileni.** (8) 1s.

1903 (2 July). *Optd with name at top, T* **5**, *and values at foot, T* **6/8**, *in blue. W* **43** *of New Zealand. P* 11.
13 **28** 3d. yellow-brown .. .. .. 5·00 5·00
14 **31** 6d. rose-red .. .. 5·00 10·00
15 **34** 1s. brown-red ("Tahae" joined) £650
16 1s. bright red .. .. 24·00 25·00
a. Orange-red .. .. 30·00 35·00
13/16 .. .. *Set of* 3 30·00 35·00

NIUE. **½ PENI.** (9)   **NIUE.** (10)

1911 (30 Nov). *½d. surch with T* **9**, *others optd at top as T* **5** *and values at foot as T* **7**, **8**. *W* **43** *of New Zealand. P* 14×14½.
17 **51** ½d. green (C.) 45 40
18 **52** 6d. carmine (B.) .. .. 2·00 7·00
19 1s. vermilion (B.) .. .. 6·50 35·00
17/19 .. .. *Set of* 3 8·00 38·00

1915 (Sept). *Surch as T* **4**. *W* **43** *of New Zealand. P* 14.
20 **27** 2½d. deep blue (C.) .. .. .. 9·00 17·00

1917 (Aug). *1d. surch as T* **3**, *3d. optd as T* **5** *with value as T* **6**. *W* **43** *of New Zealand.*
21 **53** 1d. carmine (*p* 14×15) (Br.) .. .. 5·00 5·50
a. No stop after "PENI" (R.10/16) .. £140
22 **60** 3d. chocolate (*p* 14×14½) (B.) .. .. 48·00 75·00
a. No stop after "PENE" (R.10/4) .. £475
b. Perf 14×13½ .. .. .. 60·00 85·00
c. Vert pair, Nos. 22/b £180

1917–21. *Optd with T* **10**. *W* **43** *of New Zealand.* (*a*) *P* 14×15.
23 **61** ½d. green (R.) (2.20) 50 85
24 **53** 1d. carmine (B.) (10.17) .. .. 2·00 3·25
25 **61** 1½d. slate (R.) (11.17) .. .. .. 80 1·75
26 1½d. orange-brown (R.) (2.19) .. .. 70 2·25
27 3d. chocolate (B.) (6.19) .. .. .. 1·40 13·00
(*b*) *P* 14×14½
28 **60** 2½d. deep blue (R.) (10.20) .. .. 90 2·75
a. Perf 14×13½ .. .. .. 1·75 4·00
b. Vert pair, Nos. 28/a .. .. 18·00 32·00

29 **60** 3d. chocolate (B.) (10.17) .. .. 1·25 1·50
a. Perf 14 × 13½ .. .. .. 1·60 2·50
b. Vert pair, Nos. 29/a .. .. 27·00 38·00
30 6d. carmine (B.) (8.21) .. .. 4·25 15·00
a. Perf 14 × 13½ .. .. .. 4·75 15·00
b. Vert pair, Nos. 30/a .. .. 38·00 60·00
31 1s. vermilion (B.) (10.18) .. .. 4·75 15·00
a. Perf 14 × 13½ .. .. .. 7·50 15·00
b. Vert pair, Nos. 31/a .. .. 42·00 65·00
23/31 .. .. *Set of* 9 15·00 50·00

1918–29. *Postal Fiscal stamps as Type* F 4 *of New Zealand optd with T* **10**. *W* **43** *of New Zealand (sideways).*

(i) *Chalk-surfaced "De La Rue" paper.* (a) *P* 14
32 5s. yellow-green (R.) (7.18) .. .. .. 75·00 90·00
(b) *P* 14½ × 14, *comb*
33 2s. deep blue (R.) (9.18) .. .. .. 15·00 32·00
34 2s. 6d. grey-brown (B.) (2.23) .. .. 17·00 38·00
35 5s. yellow-green (R.) (10.18).. .. .. 20·00 48·00
36 10s. maroon (B.) (2.23) .. .. .. 70·00 90·00
37 £1 rose-carmine (B.) (2.23) £130 £150
33/7 .. .. *Set of* 5 £225 £300

(ii) *Thick, opaque, white chalk-surfaced "Cowan" paper.* *P* 14½ × 14
37*a* 5s. yellow-green (R.) (10.29) .. .. 22·00 48·00
37*b* 10s. brown-red (B.) (2.27) .. .. .. 70·00 90·00
37*c* £1 rose-pink (B.) (2.28) £130 £150
37*a*/*c* .. .. *Set of* 3 £200 £250

11 Landing of Captain Cook

12 Landing of Captain Cook

(Des, eng and recess P.B.)

1920 (23 Aug). *T* **11** *and similar designs. No wmk. P* 14.
38 ½d. black and green .. .. .. 2·25 3·25
39 1d. black and dull carmine .. .. 1·75 1·25
40 1½d. black and red .. .. 2·50 3·50
41 3d. black and blue .. .. 60 4·75
42 6d. red-brown and green .. .. .. 80 11·00
43 1s. black and sepia.. .. .. .. 1·50 11·00
38/43 .. .. *Set of* 6 8·50 32·00

Designs: *Vert*—1d. Wharf at Avarua; 1½d. "Capt Cook (Dance)"; 3d. Palm tree. *Horiz*—6d. Huts at Arorangi; 1s. Avarua Harbour.

Examples of the 6d. with inverted centre were not supplied to the Post Office.

1925–27. *As Nos. 38/9 and new values. W* **43** *of New Zealand. P* 14.
44 ½d. black and green (1927).. .. .. 1·25 4·50
45 1d. black and deep carmine (1925) .. 75 75
46 2½d. black and blue (10.27) .. .. .. 1·50 6·00
47 4d. black and violet (10.27) .. .. 2·00 8·00
44/7 .. .. *Set of* 4 5·00 17·00

Designs: *Vert*—2½d. Te Po, Rarotongan chief. *Horiz*—4d. Harbour, Rarotonga, and Mount Ikurangi.

1927–28. *Admiral type of New Zealand optd as T* **10**. *W* **43** *of New Zealand. P* 14.

(*a*) *"Jones" paper*
48 **72** 2s. deep blue (2.27) (R.) .. .. .. 15·00 42·00
(*b*) *"Cowan" paper*
49 **72** 2s. light blue (R.) (2.28) .. .. .. 15·00 30·00

1931 (Apr). *No. 40 surch as T* **18** *of Cook Is.*
50 2d. on 1½d. black and red .. .. .. 1·25 90

1931 (12 Nov). *Postal Fiscal stamps as Type* F **6** *of New Zealand optd as T* **10**. *W* **43** *of New Zealand. Thick, opaque, chalk-surfaced "Cowan" paper. P* 14.
51 2s. 6d. deep brown (B.) .. .. .. 5·50 11·00
52 5s. green (R.) .. .. 26·00 55·00
53 10s. carmine-lake (B.) .. .. .. 35·00 70·00
54 £1 pink (B.).. .. .. 55·00 95·00
51/4 .. .. *Set of* 4 £110 £200

See also Nos. 79/82 for different type of overprint.

(Des L. C. Mitchell. Recess P.B.)

1932 (16 Mar). *T* **12** *and similar designs inscr* "NIUE" *and* "COOK ISLANDS". *No wmk. P* 13.
55 ½d. black and emerald .. .. .. 4·50 9·50
a. Perf 13×14×13×13 .. .. .. £250
56 1d. black and deep lake .. .. .. 1·00 30
57 2d. black and red-brown .. .. .. 75 2·75
a. Perf 14×13×13×13 .. .. .. 90·00 £150
58 2½d. black and slate-blue .. .. .. 5·00 26·00
59 4d. black and greenish blue .. .. 7·00 24·00
a. Perf 14 .. .. 8·00 21·00
60 6d. black and orange-vermilion .. .. 2·00 2·00
61 1s. black and purple (*p* 14) .. .. 2·00 5·00
55/61 .. .. *Set of* 7 20·00 60·00

Designs: *Vert*—1d. Capt. Cook; 1s. King George V. *Horiz*—2d. Double Maori canoe; 2½d. Islanders working cargo; 4d. Port of Avarua; 6d. R.M.S. *Monowai*.

Examples of the 2½d. with inverted centre were not supplied to the Post Office.

Nos. 55a and 57a are mixed perforations, each having one side perforated 14 where the original perforation, 13, was inadequate.

(Recess from Perkins, Bacon's plates at Govt Ptg Office, Wellington, N.Z.)

1932–36. *As Nos. 55/61, but W* **43** *of New Zealand. P* 14.
62 ½d. black and emerald 50 75
63 1d. black and deep lake 50 30
64 2d. black and yellow-brown (1.4.36) .. 40 70
65 2½d. black and slate-blue .. .. .. 40 2·75
66 4d. black and greenish blue .. .. 1·00 1·25
67 6d. black and red-orange (1.4.36) 70 65
68 1s. black and purple (1.4.36) .. .. 4·25 13·00
62/68 .. .. *Set of* 7 7·00 17·00

Imperforate proofs of No. 65 are known used on registered mail from Niue postmarked 30 August 1945 or 29 October 1945.

See also Nos. 89/97.

SILVER JUBILEE
OF
KING GEORGE V.
1910-1935.

(12)

Normal letters
B K E N
B K E N
Narrow letters

1935 (7 May). *Silver Jubilee. Designs as Nos.* 63, 65 *and* 67 *(colours changed) optd with T* **12** *(wider vertical spacing on 6d.). W* **43** *of New Zealand. P* 14.
69 1d. red-brown and lake .. .. .. 60 1·50
a. Narrow "K" in "KING".. .. .. 2·75 8·00
b. Narrow "B" in JUBILEE .. .. 2·75 8·00
70 2½d. dull and deep blue (R.) .. .. .. 3·25 2·50
a. Narrow first "E" in "GEORGE" .. 4·00 12·00
71 6d. green and orange .. .. .. 3·25 5·00
a. Narrow "N" in "KING".. .. .. 12·00 32·00
69/71 .. .. *Set of* 3 6·50 8·00

Examples of No. 70 imperforate horizontally are from proof sheets not issued through the Post and Telegraph Department (*Price* £350 *for vert pair*).

NIUE

(13)

14 King George VI

15 Tropical Landscape

1937 (13 May). *Coronation Issue. Nos. 599/601 of New Zealand optd with T* **13**.
72 1d. carmine 30 10
73 2½d. Prussian blue 40 20
74 6d. red-orange 40 10
72/4 .. .. *Set of* 3 1·00 35

1938 (2 May). *T* **14** *and similar designs inscr* "NIUE COOK ISLANDS". *W* **43** *of New Zealand. P* 14.
75 1s. black and violet .. .. 3·25 4·00
76 2s. black and red-brown .. .. .. 8·50 7·50
77 3s. light blue and emerald-green .. .. 15·00 7·00
75/7 .. .. *Set of* 3 27·00 19·00

Designs: *Vert*—2s. Island village. *Horiz*—3s. Cook Islands canoe.

1940 (2 Sept). *Surch as in T* **15**. *W* **98** *of New Zealand. P* 13½×14.
78 3d. on 1½d. black and purple 10 10

NIUE.

(16)

1941–67. *Postal Fiscal stamps as Type* F **6** *of New Zealand with thin opt, T* **16**. *P* 14.

(i) *Thin, hard, chalk-surfaced "Wiggins Teape" paper with vertical mesh* (1941–43). (*a*) *W* **43** *of New Zealand*
79 2s. 6d. deep brown (B.) (4.41) .. .. 35·00 30·00
80 5s. green (R.) (4.41) £170 £140
81 10s. pale carmine-lake (B.) (6.42) £100 £140
82 £1 pink (B.) (2.43?) £170 £200
79/82 .. .. *Set of* 4 £425 £450
(*b*) *W* **98** *of New Zealand* (1944–45)
83 2s. 6d. deep brown (B.) (3.45) .. .. 3·00 6·50
84 5s. green (R.) (11.44).. .. .. .. 5·50 9·00
85 10s. carmine-lake (B.) (11.45) .. .. 45·00 60·00
86 £1 pink (B.) (6.42) .. .. 38·00 45·00
83/6 .. .. *Set of* 4 80·00 £110

(ii) *Unsurfaced "Wiggins Teape" paper with horizontal mesh. W* **98** *of New Zealand* (1957–67)
87 2s. 6d. deep brown (*p* 14 × 13½) (1.11.57) .. 3·75 4·50
88 5s. pale yellowish green (*wmk sideways*) (6.67) .. .. 50·00 75·00

Nos. 83/5 were later printed with the watermark inverted for technical reasons and the prices quoted are for the cheapest form. They are fully listed in the *Two Reigns Catalogue*.

No. 88 came from a late printing made to fill demands from Wellington, but no supplies were sent to Niue. It exists in both line and comb perf.

1944–46. *As Nos. 62/7 and 75/7, but W* **98** *of New Zealand (sideways on ½d., 1d., 1s. and 2s.).*
89 **12** ½d. black and emerald 50 60
90 – 1d. black and deep lake 50 60
91 – 2d. black and red-brown .. .. .. 2·50 2·25
92 – 2½d. black and slate-blue (1946) 60 85
93 – 4d. black and greenish blue 60 90
94 – 6d. black and red-orange .. .. .. 70 1·40
95 **14** 1s. black and violet .. .. .. 1·25 85
96 – 2s. black and red-brown (1945) .. .. 4·00 2·75
97 – 3s. light blue and emerald-green (1945) 8·50 6·00
89/97 .. .. *Set of* 9 17·00 14·50

1946 (4 June). *Peace. Nos.* 668, 670, 674/5 *of New Zealand optd as T* **16** *without stop (twice, reading up and down on 2d.).*
98 1d. green (Blk.) 10 10
99 2d. purple (B.) 10 10
100 6d. chocolate and vermilion (Blk.) .. 10 10
a. Opt double, one albino £200
101 8d. black and carmine (B.) 10 10
98/101 .. .. *Set of* 4 35 30

Nos. 102/112 are no longer used.

17 Map of Niue

18 H.M.S. *Resolution*

23 Bananas

24 Matapa Chasm

(Des J. Berry. Recess B.W.)

1950 (3 July). *T* **17/18**, **23/24** *and similar designs. W* **98** *of New Zealand (sideways inverted on 1d., 2d., 3d., 4d., 6d. and 1s.). P* 13½×14 *(horiz) or* 14×13½ *(vert).*
113 ½d. orange and blue 10 10
114 1d. brown and blue-green .. .. .. 2·00 55
115 2d. black and carmine 10 10
116 3d. blue and violet-blue 10 10
117 4d. olive-green and purple-brown 10 10
118 6d. green and brown-orange.. .. .. 45 15
119 9d. orange and brown 10 15
120 1s. purple and black 10 10
121 2s. brown-orange and dull green .. .. 75 2·00
122 3s. blue and black .. .. 3·50 3·75
113/22 .. .. *Set of* 10 6·50 6·25

Designs: *Horiz (as T* **18**)—2d. Alofi landing; 3d. Native hut; 4d. Arch at Hikutavake; 6d. Alofi bay; 1s. Cave, Makefu. *Vert (as T* **17**)–9d. Spearing fish.

1953 (25 May). *Coronation. As Nos. 715 and 717 of New Zealand, but inscr* "NIUE".
123 3d. brown 65 30
124 6d. slate-grey 95 30

(New Currency. 100 cents = 1 dollar)

1c

(25)

26

1967 (10 July–7 Aug). *Decimal currency.* (*a*) *Nos.* 113/22 *surch as T* **25**.
125 ½ c. on ½d. 10 10
126 1 c. on 1d. 80 15
127 2 c. on 2d. 10 10
128 2½ c. on 3d. 10 10
129 3 c. on 4d. 10 10
130 5 c. on 6d. 10 10
131 8 c. on 9d. 10 10
132 10 c. on 1s. 10 10
133 20 c. on 2s. .. .. 60 1·25
134 30 c. on 3s. .. .. 1·50 1·75
125/34 .. .. *Set of* 10 2·75 3·00

(*b*) *Arms type of New Zealand without value, surch as in T* **26**. *W* **98** *of New Zealand (sideways). P* 14.
135 **26** 25 c. deep yellow-brown 65 65
a. Rough perf 11 .. .. .. 8·00 14·00
136 50 c. pale yellowish green .. .. .. 1·00 1·00
a. Rough perf 11 .. .. .. 9·00 16·00
137 $1 magenta .. .. 80 1·50
a. Rough perf 11 .. .. .. 13·00 15·00
138 $2 light pink .. .. 1·40 2·50
a. Rough perf 11 .. .. .. 15·00 20·00
135/8 .. .. *Set of* 4 3·50 5·00
135a/8a .. .. *Set of* 4 40·00 60·00

The 25 c., $1 and $2 perf 14 exist both line and comb perforated. The 50 c. is comb perforated only. The perf 11 stamps resulted from an emergency measure in the course of printing.

1967 (3 Oct). *Christmas. As T* **278** *of New Zealand, but inscr* "NIUE".
139 2½ c. multicoloured 10 10

1969 (1 Oct). *Christmas. As T* **301** *of New Zealand, but inscr* "NIUE". *W* **98** *of New Zealand. P* 13½ × 14½.
140 2½ c. multicoloured 10 10

27 "Pua"   37 Kalahimu

(Des Mrs. K. W. Billings. Litho Enschedé)

1969 (27 Nov). *T* **27** *and similar vert designs. Multicoloured. P* 12½ × 13½.

141 ½ c. Type **27** 10 10
142 1 c. "Golden Shower" 10 10
143 2 c. Flamboyant 10 10
144 2½ c. Frangipani 10 10
145 3 c. Niue Crocus 10 10
146 5 c. Hibiscus 10 10
147 8 c. "Passion Fruit" 10 10
148 10 c. "Kampui" 10 10
149 20 c. Queen Elizabeth II (after Anthony Buckley) .. .. 1·00 1·25
150 30 c. Tapeu Orchid .. .. 1·75 1·75
141/150 .. .. *Set of* 10 3·00 3·00

(Des G. F. Fuller. Photo Enschedé)

1970 (19 Aug). *Indigenous Edible Crabs. T* **37** *and similar horiz designs. Multicoloured. P* 13½ × 12½.

151 3 c. Type **37** 10 10
152 5 c. Kalavi 10 10
153 30 c. Unga 30 25
151/3 .. .. *Set of* 3 45 40

1970 (1 Oct). *Christmas. As T* **314** *of New Zealand, but inscr* "NIUE".

154 2½ c. multicoloured 10 10

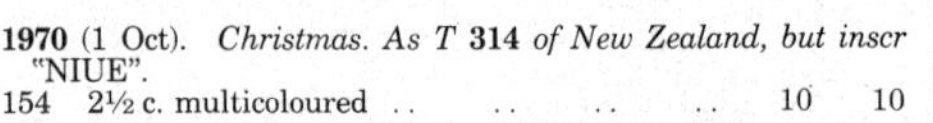

38 Outrigger Canoe and Aircraft over Jungle   39 Spotted Triller

(Des L. C. Mitchell. Litho B.W.)

1970 (9 Dec). *Opening of Niue Airport. T* **38** *and similar horiz designs. Multicoloured. P* 13½.

155 3 c. Type **38** 10 10
156 5 c. Cargo liner, and aircraft over harbour .. 15 10
157 8 c. Aircraft over Airport 15 20
155/7 .. .. *Set of* 3 35 35

(Des A. G. Mitchell. Litho B.W.)

1971 (23 June). *Birds. T* **39** *and similar horiz designs. Multicoloured. P* 13½.

158 5 c. Type **39** 15 10
159 10 c. Purple-capped Fruit Dove 70 15
160 20 c. Blue-crowned Lory 80 20
158/60 .. .. *Set of* 3 1·50 40

1971 (6 Oct). *Christmas. As T* **325** *of New Zealand, but inscr* "NIUE".

161 3 c. multicoloured 10 10

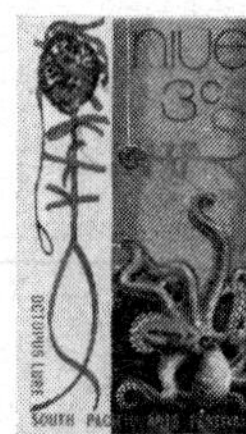

40 Niuean Boy   41 Octopus Lure

(Des L. C. Mitchell. Litho Harrison)

1971 (17 Nov). *Niuean Portraits. T* **40** *and similar vert designs. Multicoloured. P* 13 × 14.

162 4 c. Type **40** 10 10
163 6 c. Girl with garland 10 10
164 9 c. Man 10 10
165 14 c. Woman with garland 15 20
162/5 .. .. *Set of* 4 35 35

(Des A. G. Mitchell. Litho B.W.)

1972 (3 May). *South Pacific Arts Festival, Fiji. T* **41** *and similar multicoloured designs. P* 13½.

166 3 c. Type **41** 10 10
167 5 c. War weapons 15 10
168 10 c. Sika throwing (*horiz*) 20 10
169 25 c. Vivi dance (*horiz*) 30 20
166/9 .. .. *Set of* 4 65 40

42 Alofi Wharf

(Des A. G. Mitchell. Litho Questa)

1972 (6 Sept). *25th Anniversary of South Pacific Commission. T* **42** *and similar horiz designs. Multicoloured. P* 14.

170 4 c. Type **42** 10 10
171 5 c. Medical Services 15 10
172 6 c. Schoolchildren 15 10
173 18 c. Dairy cattle 25 20
170/3 .. .. *Set of* 4 60 40

1972 (4 Oct). *Christmas. As T* **332** *of New Zealand but inscr* "NIUE".

174 3 c. multicoloured 10 10

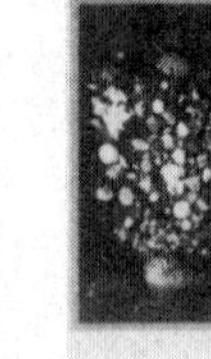

43 Kokio   44 "Large Flower Piece" (Jan Brueghel)

(Des G. F. Fuller. Litho Harrison)

1973 (27 June). *Fishes. T* **43** *and similar horiz designs. Multicoloured. P* 14 × 13½.

175 8 c. Type **43** 25 25
176 10 c. Loi 30 30
177 15 c. Malau 40 40
178 20 c. Palu 45 45
175/8 .. .. *Set of* 4 1·25 1·25

(Des and litho Enschedé)

1973 (21 Nov). *Christmas. T* **44** *and similar vert designs showing flower studies by the artists listed. Multicoloured. P* 14 × 13½.

179 4 c. Type **44** 10 10
180 5 c. Bollongier 10 10
181 10 c. Ruysch 20 20
179/81 .. .. *Set of* 3 30 30

45 Capt. Cook and Bowsprit   46 King Fataaiki

(Des A. G. Mitchell. Litho Questa)

1974 (20 June). *Bicentenary of Capt. Cook's Visit. T* **45** *and similar horiz designs each showing Cook's portrait. Multicoloured. P* 13½ × 14.

182 2 c. Type **45** 30 20
183 3 c. Niue landing place 30 25
184 8 c. Map of Niue 50 40
185 20 c. Ensign of 1774 and Administration Building 70 80
182/5 .. .. *Set of* 4 1·60 1·50

SELF-GOVERNMENT

(Des A. G. Mitchell. Litho Questa)

1974 (19 Oct). *Self-Government. T* **46** *and similar multicoloured designs. P* 14 × 13½ (4 *and* 8 *c.*) *or* 13½ × 14 (*others*).

186 4 c. Type **46** 10 10
187 8 c. Annexation Ceremony, 1900 .. .. 10 10
188 10 c. Legislative Assembly Chambers (*horiz*) 10 10
189 20 c. Village meeting (*horiz*) 15 15
186/9 .. .. *Set of* 4 35 30

47 Decorated Bicycles   48 Children going to Church

(Des B. C. Strong. Litho D.L.R.)

1974 (13 Nov). *Christmas. T* **47** *and similar vert designs. P* 12½.

190 3 c. multicoloured 10 10
191 10 c. multicoloured 10 10
192 20 c. dull red-brown, slate and black 20 20
190/2 .. .. *Set of* 3 30 30

Designs:—10 c. Decorated motorcycles; 20 c. Motor transport to church.

(Des Enid Hunter. Litho Questa)

1975 (29 Oct). *Christmas. T* **48** *and similar horiz designs. Multicoloured. P* 14.

193 4 c. Type **48** 10 10
194 5 c. Child with balloons on bicycle 10 10
195 10 c. Balloons and gifts on tree 20 20
193/5 .. .. *Set of* 3 30 30

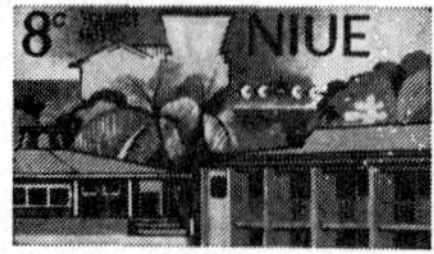

49 Hotel Buildings   50 Preparing Ground for Taro

(Des B. C. Strong. Litho Harrison)

1975 (19 Nov). *Opening of Tourist Hotel. T* **49** *and similar horiz design. Multicoloured. P* 13½ × 13.

196 8 c. Type **49** 10 10
197 20 c. Ground-plan and buildings 20 20

(Des A. G. Mitchell. Litho Questa)

1976 (3 Mar). *T* **50** *and similar horiz designs showing food gathering. Multicoloured. P* 13½ × 14.

198 1 c. Type **50** 10 10
199 2 c. Planting taro 10 10
200 3 c. Banana gathering 10 10
201 4 c. Harvesting taro 10 10
202 5 c. Gathering shell fish 15 10
203 10 c. Reef fishing 15 10
204 20 c. Luku gathering 20 15
205 50 c. Canoe fishing 40 60
206 $1 Coconut husking 60 80
207 $2 Uga gathering .. .. 1·00 1·40
198/207 .. .. *Set of* 10 2·50 2·75

See also Nos. 249/58 and 264/73.

51 Water   52 Christmas Tree, Alofi

(Des A. G. Mitchell. Litho Questa)

1976 (7 July). *Utilities. T* **51** *and similar vert designs. Multicoloured. P* 14.

208 10 c. Type **51** 10 10
209 15 c. Telecommunications 15 15
210 20 c. Power 15 15
208/10 .. .. *Set of* 3 30 30

(Des A. G. Mitchell. Litho Questa)

1976 (15 Sept). *Christmas. T* **52** *and similar horiz design. Multicoloured. P* 14.

211 9 c. Type **52** 15 15
212 15 c. Church Service, Avatele 15 15

53 Queen Elizabeth II and Westminster Abbey

(Des and photo Heraclio Fournier)

1977 (7 June). *Silver Jubilee. T* **53** *and similar horiz design. Multicoloured. P* 13½.

213 $1 Type **53** .. .. 1·50 75
214 $2 Coronation regalia .. .. 2·00 1·00
MS215 72 × 104 mm. Nos. 213/14 .. .. .. 3·50 2·50

Stamps from the miniature sheet have a blue border.

54 Child Care   55 "The Annunciation"

(Des R. M. Conly. Litho Questa)

1977 (29 June). *Personal Services. T* **54** *and similar horiz designs. Multicoloured. P* 14½.

216	10 c. Type **54**	15	10
217	15 c. School dental clinic	20	20
218	20 c. Care of the aged	20	20
216/18	*Set of* 3	50	45

(Des and photo Heraclio Fournier)

1977 (15 Nov). *Christmas. T* **55** *and similar vert designs showing paintings by Rubens. Multicoloured. P* 13.

219	10 c. Type **55**	20	10
220	12 c. "Adoration of the Magi"	20	10
221	20 c. "Virgin in a Garland"	35	20
222	35 c. "The Holy Family"	55	35
219/22	*Set of* 4	1·10	65
MS223	82 × 129 mm. Nos. 219/22	1·50	2·25

(56)

1977 (15 Nov). *Nos.* 198 *etc.,* 214, 216 *and* 218 *surch as T* **56** *by New Zealand Govt Printer.*

224	12 c. on 1 c. Type **50**	25	25
225	16 c. on 2 c. Planting taro	30	30
226	30 c. on 3 c. Banana gathering	40	40
227	35 c. on 4 c. Harvesting taro	45	45
228	40 c. on 5 c. Gathering shell fish	50	50
229	60 c. on 20 c. Luku gathering	70	65
230	70 c. on $1 Coconut husking	75	70
231	85 c. on $2 Uga gathering	80	70
232	$1.10 on 10 c. Type **54**	90	75
233	$2.60 on 20 c. Care of the aged	1·50	1·25
234	$3.20 on $2 Coronation regalia (Gold)	1·75	1·50
224/34	*Set of* 11	7·50	6·50

57 "An Island View in Atooi"

(Photo Heraclio Fournier)

1978 (18 Jan). *Bicentenary of Discovery of Hawaii. T* **57** *and similar horiz designs showing paintings by John Webber. Multicoloured. P* 13.

235	12 c. Type **57**	75	30
236	16 c. "View of Karakaooa, in Owhyhee"	85	40
237	20 c. "Offering before Capt. Cook in the Sandwich Islands"	1·00	45
238	30 c. "Tereoboo, King of Owhyhee bringing presents to Capt. Cook"	1·25	50
239	35 c. "Canoe in the Sandwich Islands, the rowers masked"	1·25	55
235/9	*Set of* 5	4·50	2·00
MS240	121 × 121 mm. Nos. 235/9	4·50	4·25

Nos. 235/9 were each printed in small sheets of 6, including 1 *se-tenant* stamp-size label.

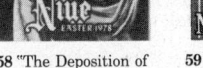

58 "The Deposition of Christ" (Caravaggio)

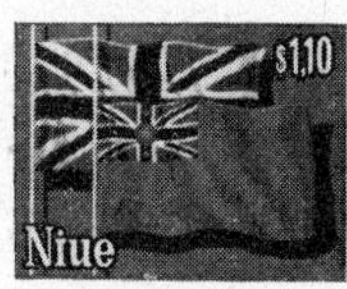

59 Flags of Niue and U.K.

(Photo Heraclio Fournier)

1978 (15 Mar). *Easter. Paintings from the Vatican Galleries. T* **58** *and similar vert design. Multicoloured. P* 13.

241	10 c. Type **58**	15	10
242	20 c. "The Burial of Christ" (Bellini)	35	25
MS243	102 × 68 mm. Nos. 241/2	60	75

1978 (15 Mar). *Easter. Children's Charity. Designs as Nos.* 241/2 *in separate miniature sheets* 64 × 78 *mm, each with a face value of* 70 *c.* + 5 *c. P* 13.

MS244	As Nos. 241/2 .. *Set of* 2 *sheets*	1·75	2·00

(Photo Heraclio Fournier)

1978 (26 June). 25*th Anniv of Coronation. T* **59** *and similar horiz designs. Multicoloured.* A. *White border.* B. *Turquoise-green border. P* 13.

		A		B	
245	$1.10 Type **59**	1·25	1·00	1·25	1·00
246	$1.10 Coronation portrait by Cecil Beaton	1·25	1·00	1·25	1·00
247	$1.10 Queen's personal flag for New Zealand	1·25	1·00	1·25	1·00
245/7	*Set of* 3	3·25	2·75	3·25	2·75
MS248	87 × 98 mm. Nos. 245/7	4·25	3·50		†

Nos. 245/7 were printed together in small sheets of 6, containing two *se-tenant* strips of 3, with horizontal gutter margin between. The upper strip has white borders, the lower turquoise-green.

(Litho Questa)

1978 (27 Oct). *Designs as Nos.* 198/207 *but margin colours changed and silver frame. P* 13½ × 14.

249	12 c. Type **50**	20	20
250	16 c. Planting taro	20	20
251	30 c. Banana gathering	30	25
252	35 c. Harvesting taro	30	30
253	40 c. Gathering shell fish	40	30
254	60 c. Reef fishing	45	35
255	75 c. Luku gathering	50	40
256	$1.10, Canoe fishing	1·10	80
257	$3.20, Coconut husking	1·25	1·25
258	$4.20, Uga gathering	1·40	1·40
249/58	*Set of* 10	5·50	5·00

See also Nos. 264/73.

60 "Festival of the Rosary"

(Des and photo Heraclio Fournier)

1978 (30 Nov). *Christmas.* 450*th Death Anniv of Dürer. T* **60** *and similar horiz designs. Multicoloured. P* 13.

259	20 c. Type **60**	40	20
260	30 c. "The Nativity"	50	30
261	35 c. "Adoration of the Magi"	60	35
259/61	*Set of* 3	1·40	75
MS262	143 × 82 mm. Nos. 259/61	1·50	1·75

Nos. 259/61 were each printed in small sheets of 6.

1978 (30 Nov). *Christmas. Children's Charity. Designs as Nos.* 259/61 *in separate miniature sheets* 74 × 66 *mm., each with a face value of* 60 *c.* + 5 *c. P* 13.

MS263	As Nos. 259/61 .. *Set of* 3 *sheets*	2·00	2·00

(Litho Questa)

1979 (26 Feb–28 May). *Air. Designs as Nos.* 249/58 *but gold frames and additionally inscr* "AIRMAIL". *P* 13½ × 14.

264	15 c. Planting taro	20	15
265	20 c. Banana gathering	25	15
266	23 c. Harvesting taro	30	15
267	50 c. Canoe fishing	70	20
268	90 c. Reef fishing	85	35
269	$1.35, Type **50** (30.3)	1·25	1·50
270	$2.10, Gathering shell fish (30.3)	2·00	2·25
271	$2.60, Luku gathering (30.3)	2·00	2·50
272	$5.10, Coconut husking (28.5)	2·25	3·50
273	$6.35, Uga gathering (28.5)	2·50	4·50
264/73	*Set of* 10	11·00	14·00

PRINTERS. The following stamps were printed in photogravure by Heraclio Fournier, Spain, *except where otherwise stated.*

61 "Pietà" (Gregorio Fernandez)

62 "The Nurse and Child" (Franz Hals)

1979 (2 Apr). *Easter. Paintings. T* **61** *and similar horiz design. Multicoloured. P* 13.

274	30 c. Type **61**	30	25
275	35 c. "Burial of Christ" (Pedro Roldan)	35	25
MS276	82 × 82 mm. Nos. 274/5	1·50	1·50

1979 (2 Apr). *Easter. Children's Charity. Designs as Nos.* 274/5 *in separate miniature sheets* 86 × 69 *mm., each with a face value of* 70 *c.* + 5 *c. P* 13.

MS277	As Nos. 274/5 .. *Set of* 2 *sheets*	1·75	1·75

1979 (31 May). *International Year of the Child. Details of Paintings. T* **62** *and similar vert designs. Multicoloured. P* 14 × 13½.

278	16 c. Type **62**	30	15
279	20 c. "Child of the Duke of Osuna" (Goya)	35	20
280	30 c. "Daughter of Robert Strozzi" (Titian)	55	35
281	35 c. "Children eating Fruit" (Murillo)	60	40
278/81	*Set of* 4	1·60	1·00
MS282	80 × 115 mm. Nos. 278/81. P 13	1·60	2·25

1979 (31 May). *International Year of the Child. Children's Charity. Designs as Nos.* 278/81 *in separate miniature sheets* 99 × 119 *mm, each with a face value of* 70 *c.* + 5 *c. P* 13.

MS283	As Nos. 278/81 .. *Set of* 4 *sheets*	3·00	2·50

63 Penny Black Stamp

64 Cook's Landing at Botany Bay

1979 (3 July). *Death Centenary of Sir Rowland Hill. T* **63** *and similar vert designs. Multicoloured. P* 14 × 13½.

284	20 c. Type **63**	20	15
285	20 c. Sir Rowland Hill and original Bath mail coach	20	15
286	30 c. Basel 1845 2½ r. stamp	30	20
287	30 c. Sir Rowland Hill and Alpine village coach	30	20
288	35 c. U.S.A. 1847 5 c. stamp	35	25
289	35 c. Sir Rowland Hill and first Transatlantic U.S.A. mail vessel	35	25
290	50 c. France 1849 20 c. stamp	50	35
291	50 c. Sir Rowland Hill and French Post Office railway van, 1849	50	35
292	60 c. Bavaria 1849 1 k. stamp	55	40
293	60 c. Sir Rowland Hill and Bavarian coach with mail	55	40
284/93	*Set of* 10	3·50	2·50
MS294	143 × 149 mm. Nos. 284/93	3·50	3·75

Nos. 284/5, 286/7, 288/9, 290/1 and 292/3 were each printed together, *se-tenant,* in horizontal pairs throughout the sheet forming composite designs.

1979 (30 July). *Death Bicentenary of Captain Cook. T* **64** *and similar horiz designs. Multicoloured. P* 14.

295	20 c. Type **64**	55	30
296	30 c. Cook's men during a landing on Erromanga	75	40
297	35 c. H.M.S. *Resolution* and H.M.S. *Discovery* in Queen Charlotte's Sound	85	45
298	75 c. Death of Captain Cook, Hawaii	1·50	70
295/8	*Set of* 4	3·25	1·75
MS299	104 × 80 mm. Nos. 295/8. P 13½	3·25	3·00

65 Launch of "Apollo 11"

66 "Virgin of Tortosa" (P. Serra)

1979 (27 Sept). 10*th Anniv of Moon Landing. T* **65** *and similar vert designs. Multicoloured. P* 13½.

300	30 c. Type **65**	25	20
301	35 c. Lunar module on Moon	30	25
302	60 c. Helicopter, recovery ship and command module after splashdown	40	40
300/2	*Set of* 3	85	75
MS303	120 × 82 mm. Nos. 300/2	1·00	1·40

Stamps from No. **MS**303 have the inscription in gold on a blue panel.

1979 (29 Nov). *Christmas. Paintings. T* **66** *and similar vert designs. Multicoloured. P* 13.

304	20 c. Type **66**	10	10
305	25 c. "Virgin with Milk" (R. di Mur)	15	15
306	30 c. "Virgin and Child" (S. di G. Sassetta)	20	20
307	50 c. "Virgin and Child" (J. Huguet)	25	25
304/7	*Set of* 4	60	60
MS308	95 × 113 mm. Nos. 304/7	75	1·25

1979 (29 Nov). *Christmas. Children's Charity. Designs as Nos.* 304/7 *in separate miniature sheets,* 49 × 84 *mm, each with a face value of* 85 *c.* + 5 *c. P* 13.

MS309	As Nos. 304/7 .. *Set of* 4 *sheets*	1·50	2·00

HURRICANE
RELIEF
Plus 2c

(67)

68 "Pietà" (Bellini)

1980 (25 Jan). *Hurricane Relief. Various stamps surch as T* **67** *in black (Nos.* 310/19) *or silver* (320/30).

(*a*) *Nos.* 284/93 (*Death Centenary of Sir Rowland Hill*)

310	20 c. + 2 c. Type **63**	20	25
311	20 c. + 2 c. Sir Rowland Hill and original Bath mail coach	20	25
312	30 c. + 2 c. Basel 1845 2½ r. stamp	30	35
313	30 c. + 2 c. Sir Rowland Hill and Alpine village coach	30	35
314	35 c. + 2 c. U.S.A. 1847 5 c. stamp	35	40

315 35 c. + 2 c. Sir Rowland Hill and first Transatlantic U.S.A. mail vessel 35 40
316 50 c. + 2 c. France 1849 20 c. stamp 50 55
317 50 c. + 2 c. Sir Rowland Hill and French Post Office railway van, 1849.. .. .. 50 55
318 60 c. + 2 c. Bavaria 1849 1 k. stamp 60 65
319 60 c. + 2 c. Sir Rowland Hill and Bavarian coach with mail 60 65

(b) *Nos. 295/8 (Death Bicentenary of Captain Cook)*

320 20 c. + 2 c. Type **64** 20 25
321 30 c. + 2 c. Cook's men during a landing on Erromanga 30 35
322 35 c. + 2 c. H.M.S. *Resolution* and H.M.S. *Discovery* in Queen Charlotte's Sound .. 35 40
323 75 c. + 2 c. Death of Captain Cook, Hawaii .. 75 80

(c) *Nos. 300/2 (10th Anniv of Moon Landing)*

324 30 c. + 2 c. Type **65** 30 35
325 35 c. + 2 c. Lunar module on Moon 35 40
326 60 c. + 2 c. Helicopter, recovery ship and command module after splashdown .. 60 65

(d) *Nos. 304/7 (Christmas)*

327 20 c. + 2 c. Type **66** 20 25
328 25 c. + 2 c. "Virgin with Milk" (R. de Mur) .. 25 30
329 30 c. + 2 c. "Virgin and Child" (S. di G. Sassetta) 30 35
330 50 c. + 2c. "Virgin and Child" (J. Huguet) .. 50 55
310/30 .. .. *Set of* 21 7·50 8·00

On Nos. 310/19 "HURRICANE RELIEF" covers the two designs of each value.

1980 (2 Apr). *Easter. Paintings. T* **68** *and similar horiz designs showing "Pietà" paintings by various artists. Multicoloured. P* 13½ × 13.

331 25 c. Type **68** 30 15
332 30 c. Botticelli 35 20
333 35 c. Antony van Dyck 35 20
331/3 .. .. *Set of* 3 90 50
MS334 75 × 104 mm. As Nos. 331/3, but each with additional premium of "+ 2 c." 55 90

The premiums on No. **MS**334 were used to support Hurricane Relief.

1980 (2 Apr). *Easter. Hurricane Relief. Designs as Nos. 331/3 in separate miniature sheets, 75 × 52 mm, each with a face value of* 85 c. + 5 c. *P* 13 × 14.

MS335 As Nos. 331/3 .. .. *Set of 3 sheets* 1·25 1·75

69 Ceremonial Stool, New Guinea

1980 (30 July). *South Pacific Festival of Arts, New Guinea. T* **69** *and similar vert designs. Multicoloured. P* 13.

336 20 c. Type **69** 20 20
337 20 c. Ku-Tagwa plaque, New Guinea 20 20
338 20 c. Suspension hook, New Guinea 20 20
339 20 c. Ancestral board, New Guinea 20 20
340 25 c. Platform post, New Hebrides 25 25
341 25 c. Canoe ornament, New Ireland 25 25
342 25 c. Carved figure, Admiralty Islands .. 25 25
343 25 c. Female with child, Admiralty Islands .. 25 25
344 30 c. The God A'a, Rurutu (Austral Islands) .. 25 30
345 30 c. Statue of Tangaroa, Cook Islands .. 25 30
346 30 c. Ivory pendant, Tonga 25 30
347 30 c. Tapa (Hiapo) cloth, Niue.. .. .. 25 30
348 35 c. Feather box (Waka), New Zealand .. 30 35
349 35 c. Hei-Tiki amulet, New Zealand 30 35
350 35 c. House post, New Zealand 30 35
351 35 c. Feather image of god Ku, Hawaii .. 30 35
336/51 .. .. *Set of* 16 3·75 4·00
MS352 Four sheets, each 86 × 124 mm. (a) Nos. 336, 340, 344, 348; (b) Nos. 337, 341, 345, 349; (c) Nos. 338, 342, 346, 350; (d) Nos. 339, 343, 347, 351. Each stamp with an additional premium of 2 c... .. .. *Set of 4 sheets* 4·00 4·25

Nos. 336/9, 340/3, 344/7 and 348/51 were each printed together, *se-tenant*, in horizontal strips of 4 throughout the sheet.

NEW ZEALAND STAMP EXHIBITION

ZEAPEX '80 AUCKLAND

(70) (71)

1980 (22 Aug). *"Zeapex '80" International Stamp Exhibition, Auckland. Nos. 284, 286, 288, 290 and 292 optd with T* **70** *and Nos. 285, 287, 289, 291 and 293 optd with T* **71**, *both in black on silver background.*

353 20 c. Type **63** 20 20
354 20 c. Sir Rowland Hill and original Bath mail coach 20 20
355 30 c. Basel 1845 2½ r. stamp 30 25
356 30 c. Sir Rowland Hill and Alpine village coach 30 25
357 35 c. U.S.A. 1847 5 c. stamp 35 25
358 35 c. Sir Rowland Hill and first Transatlantic U.S.A. mail vessel 35 25
359 50 c. France 1849 20 c. stamp.. .. .. 45 30
360 50 c. Sir Rowland Hill and French Post Office railway van, 1849 .. .. .. 45 30
361 60 c. Bavaria 1849 1 k. stamp.. .. .. 55 35
362 60 c. Sir Rowland Hill and Bavarian coach with mail 55 35
353/62 .. .. *Set of* 10 3·50 2·50
MS363 143 × 149 mm. Nos. 353/62, each additionally surcharged "+ 2 c." .. .. 4·00 3·25

72 Queen Elizabeth the Queen Mother

73 100 Metre Dash

1980 (15 Sept). *80th Birthday of Queen Elizabeth the Queen Mother. P* 13.

364 **72** $1.10 multicoloured .. .. .. 1·25 1·50
MS365 55 × 80 mm. **72** $3 multicoloured .. 3·00 3·00

No. 364 was printed in small sheets of 6 including one *se-tenant* stamp-size label.

1980 (30 Oct). *Olympic Games, Moscow. T* **73** *and similar horiz designs. Multicoloured. P* 14 × 13½.

366 20 c. Type **73** 15 15
367 20 c. Allen Wells, Great Britain (winner of 100 metre dash).. .. .. .. 15 15
368 25 c. } 400 metre freestyle (winner, Ines Diers, 15 20
369 25 c. } D.D.R.) 15 20
370 30 c. } "Soling" Class Yachting (winner, 20 20
371 30 c. } Denmark) 20 20
372 35 c. } Football (winner, Czechoslovakia) .. 20 25
373 35 c. } .. 20 25
366/73 .. .. *Set of* 8 1·25 1·40
MS374 119 × 128 mm. Nos. 366/73, each stamp including premium of 2 c... .. .. .. 1·60 2·00

Nos. 366/7, 368/9, 370/1 and 372/3 were each printed together, *se-tenant*, in horizontal pairs throughout the sheet, forming composite designs. On the 25 c. and 35 c. stamps the face value is at right on the first design and at left on the second in each pair. For the 30 c. No. 370 has a yacht with a green sail at left and No. 371 a yacht with a red sail.

74 "The Virgin and Child"

75 *Phalaenopsis sp.*

1980 (28 Nov). *Christmas and 450th Death Anniv of Andrea del Sarto (painter). T* **74** *and similar vert designs showing different "The Virgin and Child" works. P* 13.

375 20 c. multicoloured 15 15
376 25 c. multicoloured 15 15
377 30 c. multicoloured 20 20
378 35 c. multicoloured 20 20
375/8 .. .. *Set of* 4 60 60
MS379 87 × 112 mm. Nos. 375/8 .. .. .. 85 95

1980 (28 Nov). *Christmas. Children's Charity. Designs as Nos. 375/8 in separate miniature sheets 62 × 84 mm, each with a face value of* 80 c. + 5 c. *P* 13.

MS380 As Nos. 375/8 .. .. *Set of 4 sheets* 2·75 3·00

1981 (2 Apr)–**82**. *Flowers (1st series). Horiz designs as T* **75**. *Multicoloured. P* 13.

381 2 c. Type **75** 10 10
382 2 c. Moth Orchid 10 10
383 5 c. *Euphorbia pulcherrima* 10 10
384 5 c. Poinsettia 10 10
385 10 c. *Thunbergia alata* 10 10
386 10 c. Black-eyed Susan 10 10
387 15 c. *Cochlospermum hibiscoides* 15 15
388 15 c. Buttercup Tree 15 15
389 20 c. *Begonia sp.* 20 20
390 20 c. Begonia 20 20
391 25 c. *Plumeria sp.* 25 25
392 25 c. Frangipani 25 25
393 30 c. *Strelitzia reginae* (26 May) 30 30
394 30 c. Bird of Paradise (26 May) 30 30
395 35 c. *Hibiscus syriacus* (26 May) 30 30
396 35 c. Rose of Sharon (26 May).. .. .. 30 30
397 40 c. *Nymphaea sp.* (26 May) 35 35
398 40 c. Water Lily (26 May) 35 35
399 50 c. *Tibouchina sp.* (26 May).. .. .. 45 45
400 50 c. Princess Flower (26 May) 45 45
401 60 c. *Nelumbo sp.* (26 May) 55 55
402 60 c. Lotus (26 May) 55 55
403 80 c. *Hybrid hibiscus* (26 May) 75 75
404 80 c. Yellow Hibiscus (26 May) 75 75
405 $1 Golden Shower Tree (*Cassia fistula*) (9.12.81) .. .. 1·00 1·00
406 $2 *Orchid var.* (9.12.81) .. .. .. 2·50 2·50
407 $3 *Orchid sp.* (9.12.81) .. .. .. 3·50 3·50
408 $4 *Euphorbia pulcherrima poinsettia* (15.1.82) .. .. 3·00 3·25
409 $6 *Hybrid hibiscus* (15.1.82) .. .. 4·50 4·75
410 $10 Scarlet Hibiscus (*Hibiscus rosasinensis*) (12.3.82) .. .. 7·50 7·75
381/410 .. .. *Set of* 30 26·00 26·00

The two designs of the 2 c. to 80 c. show different drawings of the same flower, one inscribed with its name in Latin, the other giving the common name. These were printed together, *se-tenant*, in horizontal and vertical pairs throughout the sheet.

Nos. 405/10 are larger, 47 × 33 mm.

See also Nos. 527/36.

76 "Jesus Defiled" (El Greco)

77 Prince Charles

1981 (10 Apr). *Easter. Details of Paintings. T* **76** *and similar horiz designs. Multicoloured. P* 14.

425 35 c. Type **76** 30 30
426 50 c. "Pietà" (Fernando Gallego) 50 50
427 60 c. "The Supper of Emmaus" (Jacopo da Pontormo) 55 55
425/7 .. .. *Set of* 3 1·25 1·25
MS428 69 × 111 mm. As Nos. 425/7, but each with charity premium of 2 c. P 13½ .. .. .. 1·40 1·60

1981 (10 Apr). *Easter. Children's Charity. Designs as Nos. 425/7 in separate miniature sheets 78 × 86 mm, each with a face value of* 80 c. + 5 c. *P* 13½ × 14.

MS429 As Nos. 425/7 .. .. *Set of 3 sheets* 2·50 2·75

1981 (26 June). *Royal Wedding. T* **77** *and similar vert designs. Multicoloured. P* 14.

430 75 c. Type **77** 90 80
431 95 c. Lady Diana Spencer .. .. .. 1·00 90
432 $1.20, Prince Charles and Lady Diana .. 1·25 1·00
430/2 .. .. *Set of* 3 2·75 2·50
MS433 78 × 85 mm. Nos. 430/2 .. .. .. 3·00 3·25

Nos. 430/2 were each printed in small sheets of 6, including one *se-tenant* stamp-size label.

+5c

78 Footballer Silhouettes **(79)**

1981 (16 Oct). *World Cup Football Championship, Spain* (1982). *T* **78** *and similar horiz designs showing footballer silhouettes. P* 13.

434 30 c. blue-green, gold & new blue (Type **78**) .. 20 20
435 30 c. blue-green, gold and new blue (gold figure 3rd from left of stamp) 20 20
436 30 c. blue-green, gold and new blue (gold figure 4th from left) 20 20
437 35 c. new blue, gold and reddish orange (gold figure 3rd from left) 25 25
438 35 c. new blue, gold and reddish orange (gold figure 4th from left) 25 25
439 35 c. new blue, gold and reddish orange (gold figure 2nd from left) 25 25
440 40 c. reddish orange, gold and blue-green (gold figure 3rd from left, displaying close control) 25 25
441 40 c. reddish orange, gold and blue-green (gold figure 2nd from left) 25 25
442 40 c. reddish orange, gold and blue-green (gold figure 3rd from left, heading) 25 25
434/42 .. .. *Set of* 9 1·90 1·90
MS443 162 × 122 mm. 30 c. + 3 c., 35 c. + 3 c., 40 c. + 3 c. (each × 3). As Nos. 434/42 .. .. 2·00 2·50

The three designs of each value were printed together, *se-tenant*, in horizontal strips of 3 throughout the sheets.

1981 (3 Nov). *International Year for Disabled Persons. Nos. 430/3 surch as T* **79**.

444 75 c. + 5 c. Type **77** .. .. 2·25 1·50
445 95 c. + 5 c. Lady Diana Spencer .. .. 2·75 1·75
446 $1.20 + 5 c. Prince Charles and Lady Diana 3·75 2·00
444/6 .. .. *Set of* 3 8·00 4·75
MS447 78×85 mm. As Nos. 444/6, with each surcharged "+ 10 c." .. .. 6·50 5·25

Nos. 444/6 have a commemorative inscription overprinted on the sheet margins.

OMNIBUS ISSUES

Details, together with prices for complete sets, of the various Omnibus issues from the 1935 Silver Jubilee series to date are included in a special section following Zimbabwe at the end of Volume 2.

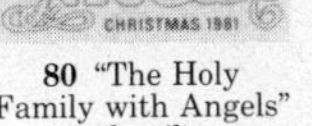

80 "The Holy Family with Angels" (detail)

81 Prince of Wales

1981 (11 Dec). *Christmas and 375th Birth Anniv of Rembrandt. T* **80** *and similar vert designs. Multicoloured. P* 14 × 13.
448 20 c. Type **80** 35 20
449 35 c. "Presentation in the Temple" 50 30
450 50 c. "Virgin and Child in Temple" 60 40
451 60 c. "The Holy Family" 70 45
448/51 .. .. *Set of* 4 1·90 1·25
MS452 79 × 112 mm. Nos. 448/51 .. .. .. 1·90 1·75

1982 (22 Jan). *Christmas. Children's Charity. Designs as Nos. 448/51 in separate miniature sheets 66 × 80 mm, each with a face value of* 80 c. + 5 c. *P* 14 × 13.
MS453 As Nos. 448/51 .. .. *Set of 4 sheets* 2·50 2·75

1982 (1 July). *21st Birthday of Princess of Wales. T* **81** *and similar horiz designs. Multicoloured. P* 14.
454 50 c. Type **81** 55 55
455 $1.25, Prince and Princess of Wales .. 1·25 1·25
456 $2.50, Princess of Wales .. .. .. 2·00 2·00
454/6 .. .. *Set of* 3 3·50 3·50
MS457 81 × 101 mm. Nos. 454/6 .. .. .. 3·75 4·00
Nos. 454/6 were each printed in small sheets of 6 including one *se-tenant* stamp-size label.
The stamps from No. **MS**457 are without white borders.

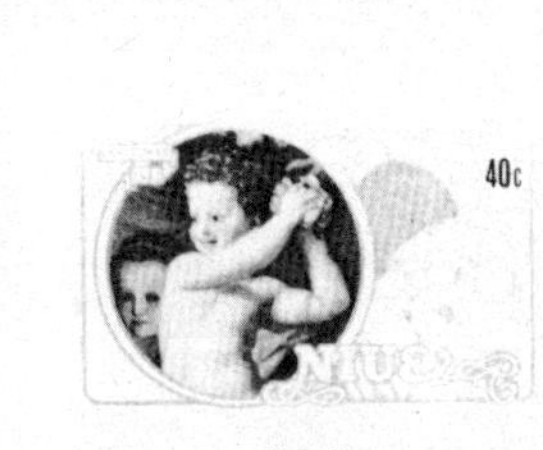

(82) 83 Infant

1982 (23 July). *Birth of Prince William of Wales* (1*st issue*). *Nos. 430/3 optd as T* **82**.
458 75 c. Type **77** (optd with T **82**) .. .. .. 2·25 1·75
a. Pair. Nos. 458/9 .. .. 4·50 3·50
459 75 c. Type **77** (optd "BIRTH OF PRINCE WILLIAM OF WALES 21 JUNE 1982") 2·25 1·75
460 95 c. Lady Diana Spencer (optd with T **82**) .. 3·25 2·25
a. Pair. Nos. 460/1 .. .. 6·50 4·50
461 95 c. Lady Diana Spencer (optd "BIRTH OF PRINCE WILLIAM OF WALES 21 JUNE 1982") .. .. 3·25 2·25
462 $1.20, Prince Charles and Lady Diana Spencer (optd with T **82**) .. .. .. 4·25 2·75
a. Pair. Nos. 462/3 .. .. 8·50 5·50
463 $1.20, Prince Charles and Lady Diana Spencer (optd "BIRTH OF PRINCE WILLIAM OF WALES 21 JUNE 1982") 4·25 2·75
458/63 .. .. *Set of* 6 18·00 12·00
MS464 78 × 85 mm. Nos. 430/2 each optd "PRINCE WILLIAM OF WALES 21 JUNE 1982" .. .. 8·50 6·00
Nos. 458/9, 460/1 and 462/3 were each printed *se-tenant* in small sheets of 6, containing three stamps overprinted with Type **82**, two with "BIRTH OF PRINCE WILLIAM OF WALES 21 JUNE 1982" and one stamp-size label.

1982 (10 Sept). *Birth of Prince William of Wales* (2*nd issue*). *Designs as Nos. 454/7 but with changed inscriptions. Multicoloured. P* 14.
465 50 c. Type **81** 55 55
466 $1.25, Prince and Princess of Wales .. 1·25 1·25
467 $2.50, Princess of Wales .. .. .. 2·00 2·00
465/7 .. .. *Set of* 3 3·50 3·50
MS468 81 × 101 mm. As Nos. 465/7 .. .. 3·75 4·00
Nos. 465/7 were each printed in small sheets of 6 including one *se-tenant*, stamp-size, label.

1982 (3 Dec). *Christmas. Paintings of Infants by Bronzino, Murillo and Boucher. T* **83** *and similar horiz designs. P* 13 × 14½.
469 40 c. multicoloured 55 35
470 52 c. multicoloured 65 45
471 83 c. multicoloured .. .. 1·10 80
472 $1.05, multicoloured .. .. 1·25 95
469/72 .. .. *Set of* 4 3·25 2·25
MS473 110 × 76 mm. Designs as Nos. 469/72 (*each* 31 × 27 *mm*), but without portrait of Princess and Prince William. P 13½ .. .. 2·50 2·75

MINIMUM PRICE

The minimum price quote is 10p which represents a handling charge rather than a basis for valuing common stamps. For further notes about prices see introductory pages.

84 Prince and Princess of Wales with Prince William

85 Prime Minister Robert Rex

1982 (3 Dec). *Christmas. Children's Charity. Sheet* 72 × 58 *mm. P* 13 × 13½.
MS474 **84** 80 c. + 5 c. multicoloured .. .. 1·00 1·00
No. **MS**474 occurs with four different designs in the sheet margin.

1983 (14 Mar). *Commonwealth Day. T* **85** *and similar horiz designs. Multicoloured. P* 13.
475 70 c. Type **85** 65 70
476 70 c. H.M.S. *Resolution* and H.M.S. *Adventure* off Niue, 1774 .. .. .. 65 70
477 70 c. Passion flower 65 70
478 70 c. Limes 65 70
475/8 .. .. *Set of* 4 2·40 2·50
Nos. 475/8 were issued together, *se-tenant*, in blocks of four throughout the sheet.

86 Scouts signalling (87)

1983 (28 Apr). *75th Anniv of Boy Scout Movement and 125th Birth Anniv of Lord Baden-Powell. T* **86** *and similar vert designs. Multicoloured. P* 13.
479 40 c. Type **86** 35 40
480 50 c. Planting sapling 45 50
481 83 c. Map-reading 85 90
479/81 .. .. *Set of* 3 1·50 1·60
MS482 137 × 90 mm. As Nos. 479/81, but each with premium of 3 c. .. .. 1·60 1·75

1983 (14 July). *15th World Scout Jamboree, Alberta, Canada. Nos. 479/82 optd with T* **87**, *in black on silver background.*
483 40 c. Type **86** 35 40
484 50 c. Planting sapling 45 50
485 83 c. Map-reading 85 90
483/5 .. .. *Set of* 3 1·50 1·60
MS486 137 × 90 mm. As Nos. 483/5, but each with premium of 3 c. .. .. 1·60 1·75

88 Black Right Whale

1983 (15 Aug). *Protect the Whales. T* **88** *and similar horiz designs. Multicoloured. P* 13 × 14.
487 12 c. Type **88** 55 45
488 25 c. Fin Whale 75 60
489 35 c. Sei Whale .. .. 1·00 90
490 40 c. Blue Whale .. .. 1·25 1·00
491 58 c. Bowhead Whale .. .. 1·40 1·10
492 70 c. Sperm Whale .. .. 1·75 1·50
493 83 c. Humpback Whale .. .. .. 2·00 1·75
494 $1.05, Minke Whale ("Lesser Rorqual") .. 2·50 2·00
495 $2.50, Grey Whale .. .. 3·75 3·50
487/95 .. .. *Set of* 9 13·50 11·50

89 Montgolfier Balloon, 1783 90 "The Garvagh Madonna"

1983 (14 Oct). *Bicentenary of Manned Flight. T* **89** *and similar horiz designs. Multicoloured.* (a) *Postage. P* 13½.
496 25 c. Type **89** 20 20
497 40 c. Wright Brothers' *Flyer*, 1903 .. .. 35 35
498 58 c. *Graf Zeppelin*, 1928 .. .. .. 50 50
499 70 c. Boeing "247", 1933 .. .. .. 65 65
500 83 c. "Apollo 8", 1968 .. .. 80 80
501 $1.05, Space shuttle *Columbia*, 1982 .. 95 95
496/501 .. .. *Set of* 6 3·00 3·00
(b) *Air. Inscr* "AIRMAIL"
MS502 118 × 130 mm. Nos. 496/501. P 13 .. 3·00 3·25

1983 (25 Nov). *Christmas. 500th Birth Anniv of Raphael. T* **90** *and similar vert designs. Multicoloured. P* 14 × 13½.
503 30 c. Type **90** 25 30
504 40 c. "Madonna of the Granduca" 30 35
505 58 c. "Madonna of the Goldfinch" 45 50
506 70 c. "The Holy Family of Francis I" 55 60
507 83 c. "The Holy Family with Saints" 65 70
503/7 .. .. *Set of* 5 2·00 2·25
MS508 120 × 114 mm. As Nos. 503/7 but each with a premium of 3 c. .. .. 2·25 2·50

1983 (30 Nov). *Various stamps surch as T* **56**.
(a) *Nos.* 393/4, 399/404 *and* 407
509 52 c. on 30 c. *Strelitzia reginae* 40 45
510 52 c. on 30 c. Bird of Paradise 40 45
511 58 c. on 50 c. *Tibouchina sp.* 50 55
512 58 c. on 50 c. Princess Flower 50 55
513 70 c. on 60 c. *Nelumbo sp.* 55 60
514 70 c. on 60 c. Lotus 55 60
515 83 c. on 80 c. *Hybrid hibiscus* 70 75
516 83 c. on 80 c. Yellow Hibiscus 70 75
517 $3.70 on $3 *Orchid sp.* .. .. .. 3·00 3·25
(b) *Nos.* 431/2 *and* 455/6
518 $1.10 on 95 c. Lady Diana Spencer .. .. 3·00 2·25
a. Error. Surch on No. 458 .. .. .. 6·00 6·00
ab. Pair. Nos. 518a/b .. .. 15·00 15·00
b. Error. Surch on No. 459 .. .. .. 9·00 9·00
519 $1.10 on $1.25, Prince and Princess of Wales 2·25 2·00
520 $2.60 on $1.20, Prince Charles and Lady Diana .. .. 5·50 3·50
a. Error. Surch on No. 462 .. .. .. 6·00 6·00
ab. Pair. Nos. 520a/b .. .. 15·00 15·00
b. Error. Surch on No. 463 .. .. .. 9·00 9·00
521 $2.60 on $2.50, Princess of Wales .. .. 3·50 3·25
509/21 .. .. *Set of* 13 19·00 17·00

1983 (29 Dec). *Christmas. 500th Birth Anniv of Raphael. Children's Charity. Designs as Nos. 503/7 in separate miniature sheets, 65 × 80 mm, each with face value of* 85 c. + 5 c. *P* 13½.
MS522 As Nos. 503/7 .. .. *Set of 5 sheets* 3·25 3·50

91 Morse Key Transmitter 92 *Phalaenopsis sp.*

1984 (23 Jan). *World Communications Year. T* **91** *and similar vert designs. Multicoloured. P* 13 × 13½.
523 40 c. Type **91** 30 35
524 52 c. Wall-mounted phone 40 45
525 83 c. Communications satellite 60 65
523/5 .. .. *Set of* 3 1·10 1·25
MS526 114 × 90 mm. Nos. 523/5 .. .. .. 1·10 1·50

1984 (20 Feb–23 July). *Flowers* (2*nd series*). *Designs as Nos. 381 etc., but with gold frames and redrawn inscr as in T* **92**. *Multicoloured. P* 13 (*Nos.* 537/42) *or* 13 × 13½ (*others*).
527 12 c. Type **92** 10 10
528 25 c. *Euphorbia pulcherrima* 15 20
529 30 c. *Cochlospermum hibiscoides* 20 25
530 35 c. *Begonia sp.* 25 30
531 40 c. *Plumeria sp.* 25 30
532 52 c. *Strelitzia reginae* 35 40
533 58 c. *Hibiscus syriacus* 40 45
534 70 c. *Tibouchina sp.* 45 50
535 83 c. *Nelumbo sp.* 55 60
536 $1.05, *Hybrid hibiscus* 70 75
537 $1.75, *Cassia fistula* (10.5) .. .. .. 1·10 1·25
538 $2.30, *Orchid var.* (10.5) .. .. .. 1·50 1·60
539 $3.90, *Orchid sp.* (10.5) .. .. .. 2·50 2·75
540 $5 *Euphorbia pulcherrima poinsettia* (18.6) 3·25 3·50
541 $6.60, *Hybrid hibiscus* (18.6) .. .. .. 4·25 4·50
542 $8.30, *Hibiscus rosasinensis* (23.7) .. .. 5·50 5·75
527/42 .. .. *Set of* 16 18·00 20·00
Nos. 537/42 are larger, 39 × 31 mm.

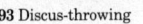

93 Discus-throwing 94 Koala

1984 (15 Mar). *Olympic Games, Los Angeles. T* **93** *and similar multicoloured designs showing ancient Greek sports. P* 14.

547 30 c. Type **93** 25 30
548 35 c. Sprinting (*horiz*) 30 35
549 40 c. Horse racing (*horiz*) 35 40
550 58 c. Boxing (*horiz*) 50 55
551 70 c. Javelin-throwing 60 65
547/51 .. .. *Set of* 5 1·75 2·00

1984 (24 Aug). *"Ausipex" International Stamp Exhibition, Melbourne* (*1st issue*). *P* 14. (*a*) *Postage. Vert designs as T* **94** *showing Koala Bears.*

552 25 c. multicoloured 40 30
553 35 c. multicoloured 45 35
554 40 c. multicoloured 50 40
555 58 c. multicoloured 70 55
556 70 c. multicoloured 85 65

(*b*) *Air. Vert designs showing Red Kangaroos*

557 83 c. multicoloured .. .. 1·00 75
558 $1.05, multicoloured .. .. .. 1·25 95
559 $2.50, multicoloured .. .. .. 2·75 2·25
552/9 .. .. *Set of* 8 7·00 5·50
MS560 110 × 64 mm. $1.75, Wallaby; $1.75, Koala Bear. P 13½ .. .. 3·25 3·75
See also Nos. **MS**566/7.

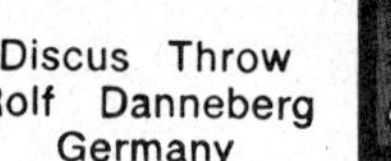

(**95**)

96 Niue National Flag and Premier Sir Robert Rex

1984 (7 Sept). *Olympic Gold Medal Winners, Los Angeles. Nos.* 547/51 *optd as T* **95** *in red* (35 c.) *or gold* (*others*).

561 30 c. Type **93** (opt T **95**) 25 30
562 35 c. Sprinting (optd "1,500 Metres Sebastian Coe Great Britain") 30 35
563 40 c. Horse racing (optd "Equestrian Mark Todd New Zealand") 30 35
564 58 c. Boxing (optd "Boxing Tyrell Biggs United States") 45 50
565 70 c. Javelin-throwing (optd "Javelin Throw Arto Haerkoenen Finland") 55 60
561/5 .. .. *Set of* 5 1·75 1·90

1984 (20 Sept). *"Ausipex" International Stamp Exhibition, Melbourne* (*2nd issue*). *Designs as Nos.* 552/60 *in miniature sheets of six or four. Multicoloured. P* 13½.

MS566 109 × 105 mm. Nos. 552/6 and $1.75, Koala Bear (as No. **MS**560) .. .. .. 3·00 3·50
MS567 80 × 105 mm. Nos. 557/9 and $1.75, Wallaby (as No. **MS**560) .. .. 4·50 4·75

1984 (19 Oct). *10th Anniv of Self-Government. T* **96** *and similar horiz designs. Multicoloured. P* 13.

568 40 c. Type **96** 30 35
569 58 c. Map of Niue and Premier Rex 45 50
570 70 c. Premier Rex receiving proclamation of self-government 55 60
568/70 .. .. *Set of* 3 1·10 1·25
MS571 110 × 83 mm. Nos. 568/70 .. .. 1·25 1·40
MS572 100 × 74 mm. $2.50, As 70 c. (50 × 30 *mm*) .. .. 1·75 1·90

(**97**)

98 "The Nativity" (A. Vaccaro)

1984 (22 Oct). *Birth of Prince Henry. Nos.* 430 *and* 454 *optd as T* **97**.

573 $2 on 50 c. Type **81** (Sil.) .. .. .. 2·50 1·75
574 $2 on 75 c. Type **77** (R.) .. .. .. 2·50 1·75

1984 (23 Nov). *Christmas. T* **98** *and similar vert designs. Multicoloured. P* 13 × 13½.

575 40 c. Type **98** 30 35
576 58 c. "Virgin with Fly" (anon, 16th-century) 45 50
577 70 c. "The Adoration of the Shepherds" (B. Murillo) 55 60
578 83 c. "Flight into Egypt" (B. Murillo) .. 65 70
575/8 .. .. *Set of* 4 1·75 1·90
MS579 115 × 111 mm. As Nos. 575/8 but each stamp with a 5 c. premium .. .. .. 2·00 2·25
MS580 Four sheets, each 66 × 98 mm. As Nos. 575/8, but each stamp 30 × 42 mm. with a face value of 95 c. + 10 c. P 13½ *Set of* 4 *sheets* 3·00 3·25

99 House Wren

1985 (15 Apr). *Birth Bicentenary of John J. Audubon* (*ornithologist*). *T* **99** *and similar horiz designs showing original paintings. Multicoloured. P* 14.

581 40 c. Type **99** .. .. 1·00 35
582 70 c. Veery .. .. 1·40 60
583 83 c. Grasshopper Sparrow .. .. .. 1·50 70
584 $1.05, Henslow's Sparrow .. .. .. 2·00 85
585 $2.50, Vesper Sparrow .. .. .. 2·75 2·00
581/5 .. .. *Set of* 5 7·75 4·00
MS586 Five sheets, each 54 × 60 mm. As Nos. 581/5 but each stamp 34 × 26 mm with a face value of $1.75 and without the commemorative inscription .. .. .. *Set of* 5 *sheets* 7·50 8·50

100 The Queen Mother in Garter Robes

1985 (14 June). *Life and Times of Queen Elizabeth the Queen Mother. T* **100** *and similar horiz designs. Multicoloured. P* 13.

587 70 c. Type **100** 55 60
588 $1.15, In open carriage with the Queen .. 90 95
589 $1.50, With Prince Charles during 80th birthday celebrations .. .. .. 1·10 1·25
587/9 .. .. *Set of* 3 2·25 2·50
MS590 70 × 70 mm. $3 At her desk in Clarence House (38 × 35 *mm*) .. .. 2·25 2·50
Nos. 587/9 were each issued in sheetlets of five stamps and one stamp-size label at top left, showing the Queen Mother's arms.
For Nos. 587/9 in miniature sheet see No. **MS**627.

MINI SOUTH PACIFIC GAMES, RAROTONGA

52
c

(**101**)

1985 (26 July). *South Pacific Mini Games, Rarotonga. Nos.* 547/8 *and* 550/1 *surch as T* **101** *in black and gold.*

591 52 c. on 70 c. Javelin-throwing 40 45
592 83 c. on 58 c. Boxing 65 70
593 95 c. on 35 c. Sprinting 75 80
594 $2 on 30 c. Type **93** .. .. 1·50 1·60
591/4 .. .. *Set of* 4 3·00 3·25
On Nos. 591/4 the new face values and inscriptions are surcharged in black on gold panels. The Games emblem is in gold only.

PACIFIC ISLANDS CONFERENCE, RAROTONGA

(**102**)

103 "R. Strozzi's Daughter" (Titian)

1985 (26 July). *Pacific Islands Conference, Rarotonga. Nos.* 475/8 *optd with T* **102** *in black on silver.*

595 70 c. Type **85** 55 60
596 70 c. *Resolution* and *Adventure* off Niue, 1774 .. .. 55 60
597 70 c. Passion flower 55 60
598 70 c. Limes 55 60
595/8 .. .. *Set of* 4 2·00 2·25
No. 595 also shows an overprinted amendment to the caption which now reads "Premier Sir Robert Rex K.B.E.".

1985 (11 Oct). *International Youth Year. T* **103** *and similar vert designs. Multicoloured. P* 13.

599 58 c. Type **103** 75 50
600 70 c. "The Fifer" (E. Manet) 90 60
601 $1.15, "Portrait of a Young Girl" (Renoir) .. .. 1·40 1·25
602 $1.50, "Portrait of M. Berard" (Renoir) .. 1·75 1·50
599/602 .. .. *Set of* 4 4·25 3·50
MS603 Four sheets, each 63 × 79 mm. As Nos. 599/602 but each with a face value of $1.75 + 10 c. .. .. *Set of* 4 *sheets* 7·00 6·50

104 "Virgin and Child"

1985 (29 Nov). *Christmas. Details of Paintings by Correggio. T* **104** *and similar vert designs. Multicoloured. P* 13 × 13½.

604 58 c. Type **104** 60 50
605 85 c. "Adoration of the Magi" 80 70
606 $1.05, "Virgin with Child and St. John" .. 1·00 85
607 $1.45, "Virgin and Child with St. Catherine" .. .. 1·50 1·25
604/7 .. .. *Set of* 4 3·50 3·00
MS608 83 × 123 mm. As Nos. 604/7, but each stamp with a face value of 60 c. + 10 c. .. .. 2·10 2·25
MS609 Four sheets, each 80 × 90 mm. 65 c. Type **104**; 95 c. As No. 605; $1.20, As No. 606; $1.75, As No. 607 (each stamp 49 × 59 mm). Imperf .. *Set of* 4 *sheets* 3·50 4·00

105 "The Constellations" (detail)

106 Queen Elizabeth II and Prince Philip

1986 (24 Jan). *Appearance of Halley's Comet. T* **105** *and similar horiz designs showing details from ceiling painting "The Constellations" by Giovanni de Vecchi. Nos.* 611/13 *show different spacecraft at top left. P* 13½.

610 60 c. multicoloured 50 50
611 75 c. multicoloured (*Vega* spacecraft) .. 65 65
612 $1.10, multicoloured (*Planet A* spacecraft) 90 90
613 $1.50, multicoloured (*Giotto* spacecraft) .. 1·25 1·25
610/13 .. .. *Set of* 4 3·00 3·00
MS614 125 × 91 mm. As Nos. 610/13 but each stamp with a face value of 95 c. .. .. .. 3·00 3·25
Stamps from No. **MS**614 are without borders.

1986 (28 Apr). *60th Birthday of Queen Elizabeth II. T* **106** *and similar vert designs. Multicoloured. P* 14½ × 13.

615 $1.10, Type **106** .. .. 1·00 1·00
616 $1.50, Queen and Prince Philip at Balmoral 1·25 1·25
617 $2 Queen at Buckingham Palace .. .. 1·75 1·75
615/17 .. .. *Set of* 3 3·50 3·50
MS618 110 × 70 mm. As Nos. 615/17, but each stamp with a face value of 75 c. .. .. .. 2·50 2·75
MS619 58 × 89 mm. $3 Queen and Prince Philip at Windsor Castle .. .. 3·50 3·75

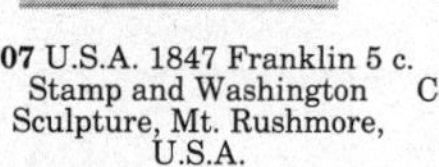
107 U.S.A. 1847 Franklin 5 c. Stamp and Washington Sculpture, Mt. Rushmore, U.S.A.

108 "Statue under Construction, Paris, 1883" (Victor Dargaud)

1986 (22 May). *"Ameripex '86" International Stamp Exhibition, Chicago. T* **107** *and similar vert design. Multicoloured. P* 14.

620 $1 Type **107** .. .. 1·40 1·40
a. Horiz pair. Nos. 620/1 .. .. .. 2·75 2·75
621 $1 Flags of Niue and U.S.A. and Mt. Rushmore sculptures .. .. 1·40 1·40
Nos. 620/1 were printed together, *se-tenant*, in horizontal pairs, within sheetlets of 8 stamps, each pair forming a composite design.

1986 (4 July). *Centenary of Statue of Liberty* (1*st issue*). *T* **108** *and similar vert design. Multicoloured. P* 13 × 13½.
622 $1 Type **108** .. .. 1·50 1·50
623 $2.50, "Unveiling of the Statue of Liberty" (Edmund Morand).. .. .. .. 2·25 2·25
MS624 107 × 73 mm. As Nos. 622/3, but each stamp with a face value of $1.25 .. .. 2·50 3·00
See also No. **MS**648.

109 Prince Andrew, Miss Sarah Ferguson and Westminster Abbey

1986 (23 July). *Royal Wedding. T* **109** *and similar horiz design. Multicoloured. P* 13½ × 13.
625 $2.50, Type **109** .. .. 2·75 2·75
MS626 106 × 68 mm. $5 Prince Andrew and Miss Sarah Ferguson (43 × 30 *mm*) .. .. .. 5·50 6·00

1986 (4 Aug). 86*th Birthday of Queen Elizabeth the Queen Mother. Nos.* 587/9 *in miniature sheet,* 109 × 83 *mm. P* 13.
MS627 Nos. 587/9 .. .. 4·50 4·75

110 Great Egret

111 "Virgin and Child" (Perugino)

1986 (4 Aug). *"Stampex '86" Stamp Exhibition, Adelaide. Australian Birds. T* **110** *and similar multicoloured designs. P* 13 × 13½ (40, 75 *c.,* $1, $2.20) *or* 13½ × 13 (*others*).
628 40 c. Type **110**.. .. .. 1·25 75
629 60 c. Painted Finch (*horiz*) .. .. .. 1·50 85
630 75 c. Australian King Parrot .. .. 1·75 1·10
631 80 c. Variegated Wren (*horiz*) .. .. 2·00 1·40
632 $1 Peregrine Falcon .. .. .. 2·25 1·75
633 $1.65, Azure Kingfisher (*horiz*) .. .. 3·00 2·25
634 $2.20, Budgerigars.. .. .. 3·75 3·25
635 $4.25, Emu (*horiz*) .. .. 5·50 5·00
628/35 .. .. *Set of* 8 19·00 15·00

1986 (14 Nov). *Christmas. Paintings from the Vatican Museum. T* **111** *and similar vert designs. Multicoloured. P* 14.
636 80 c. Type **111**.. .. .. 1·00 1·00
637 $1.15, "Virgin of St. N. dei Frari" (Titian) 1·25 1·25
638 $1.80, "Virgin with Milk" (Lorenzo di Credi) .. .. 1·90 1·90
639 $2.60, "Madonna of Foligno" (Raphael) .. 2·75 2·75
636/9 .. .. *Set of* 4 6·25 6·25
MS640 87 × 110 mm. As Nos. 636/9, but each stamp with a face value of $1.50. P 13½ .. 4·00 4·50
MS641 70 × 100 mm. $7.50, As No. 639, but 27 × 43 mm. P 14½ × 13 .. .. 6·50 7·50

+10c

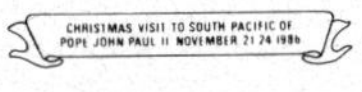

(**112**)

1986 (21 Nov). *Visit of Pope John Paul II to South Pacific. Nos.* 636/41 *surch as T* **112** *in black on silver.*
642 80 c. + 10 c. Type **111** .. .. .. 1·40 1·40
643 $1.15 + 10 c. "Virgin of St. N. dei Frari" (Titian) .. .. 1·75 1·75
644 $1.80 + 10 c. "Virgin with Milk" (Lorenzo di Credi).. .. .. 2·75 2·75
645 $2.60 + 10 c. "Madonna of Foligno" (Raphael) .. .. 3·25 3·25
642/5 .. .. *Set of* 4 8·25 8·25
MS646 87 × 110 mm. As Nos. 642/5, but each stamp with a face value of $1.50 + 10 c.. .. 7·00 7·50
MS647 70 × 100 mm. $7.50 + 50 c. As No. 645, but 27 × 43 mm .. .. 8·50 9·00

1987 (20 May). *Centenary of Statue of Liberty* (1986) (2*nd issue*). *Two sheets, each* 122 × 122 *mm, containing multi-coloured designs as T* **63** *of Cook Islands* (*Penrhyn*). *Litho. P* 13½ × 14 (*horiz*) *or* 14 × 13½ (*vert*).
MS648 Two sheets (a) 75 c. Sailing ship under Brooklyn Bridge; 75 c. Restoring Statue's flame; 75 c. Steam-cleaning Statue's torch; 75 c. *Esmerelda* (Chilean cadet ship) off Manhattan; 75 c. Cadet barque at dusk. (b) 75 c. Statue of Liberty at night (*vert*); 75 c. Statue at night (side view) (*vert*); 75 c. Cleaning Statue's crown (*vert*); 75 c. Statue at night (rear view) (*vert*); 75 c. Cleaning a finial (*vert*) .. ..*Set of* 2 *sheets* 4·25 4·75

113 Boris Becker, Olympic Rings and Commemorative Coin

(Des G. Vasarhelyi. Litho Questa)

1987 (25 Sept). *Olympic Games, Seoul* (1988). *Tennis* (1*st issue*). *T* **113** *and similar horiz designs showing Boris Becker in play. P* 13½ × 14.
649 80 c. multicoloured .. .. 1·00 1·00
650 $1.15, multicoloured .. .. .. 1·25 1·25
651 $1.40, multicoloured .. .. .. 1·50 1·50
652 $1.80, multicoloured .. .. .. 1·75 1·75
649/52 .. .. *Set of* 4 5·00 5·00

(Des G. Vasarhelyi. Litho Questa)

1987 (20 Oct). *Olympic Games, Seoul* (1988). *Tennis* (2*nd issue*). *Horiz designs as T* **113**, *but showing Steffi Graf. P* 13½ × 14.
653 85 c. multicoloured .. .. 1·00 1·00
654 $1.05, multicoloured .. .. .. 1·25 1·25
655 $1.30, multicoloured .. .. .. 1·50 1·50
656 $1.75, multicoloured .. .. .. 1·75 1·75
653/6 .. .. *Set of* 4 5·00 5·00

40TH
WEDDING
ANNIV.

(**114**)

115 "The Nativity"

1987 (20 Nov). *Royal Ruby Wedding. Nos.* 616/17 *optd with T* **114**.
657 $4.85 on $1.50, Queen and Prince Philip at Balmoral .. .. 3·50 3·75
658 $4.85 on $2 Queen at Buckingham Palace .. 3·50 3·75
On Nos. 657/8 the original values are obliterated in gold.

1987 (4 Dec). *Christmas. Religious Paintings by Dürer. T* **115** *and similar horiz designs. Multicoloured. P* 13½.
659 80 c. Type **115**.. .. .. 55 60
660 $1.05, "Adoration of the Magi" 75 80
661 $2.80, "Celebration of the Rosary" .. 2·00 2·10
659/61 .. .. *Set of* 3 3·00 3·25
MS662 100 × 140 mm. As Nos. 659/61, but each size 48 × 37 mm with a face value of $1.30 .. 2·75 3·25
MS663 90 × 80 mm. $7.50, As No. 661, but size 51 × 33 mm .. .. 5·50 6·00
Nos. 659/61 each include a detail of an angel with lute as in T **115**. Stamps from the miniature sheets are without this feature.

116 Franz Beckenbauer in Action

(Des G. Vasarhelyi. Litho Questa)

1988 (20 June). *European Cup Football Championship, West Germany. T* **116** *and similar horiz designs. Multicoloured. P* 13½ × 14.
664 20 c. Type **116** 30 30
665 40 c. German "All Star" team in action .. 45 45
666 60 c. Bayern Munich team with European Cup, 1974 .. .. 55 55
667 80 c. World Cup match, England, 1966 .. 75 75
668 $1.05, World Cup match, Mexico, 1970 .. 1·00 1·00
669 $1.30, Beckenbauer with pennant, 1974 1·40 1·40
670 $1.80, Beckenbauer and European Cup, 1974 .. .. 1·75 1·75
664/70 .. .. *Set of* 7 5·50 5·50

NEW INFORMATION

The editor is always interested to correspond with people who have new information that will improve or correct the Catalogue.

Australia 24 Jan 88
French Open 4 June 88

(**117**)

118 Angels

1988 (14 Oct). *Steffi Graf's Tennis Victories. Nos.* 653/6 *optd as T* **117**.
671 85 c. multicoloured (optd with T **117**) .. 60 65
672 $1.05, mult (optd "Wimbledon 2 July 88 U S Open 10 Sept. 88") 75 80
673 $1.30, mult (optd "Women's Tennis Grand Slam: 10 September 88") 90 95
674 $1.75, multicoloured (optd "Seoul Olympic Games Gold Medal Winner") .. .. 1·25 1·40
671/4 .. .. *Set of* 4 3·25 3·50

1988 (28 Oct). *Christmas. T* **118** *and similar vert designs showing details from "The Adoration of the Shepherds" by Rubens. Multicoloured. P* 13½.
675 60 c. Type **118** 60 60
676 80 c. Shepherds 80 80
677 $1.05, Virgin Mary .. .. 1·25 1·25
678 $1.30, Holy Child .. .. 1·50 1·50
675/8 .. .. *Set of* 4 3·75 3·75
MS679 83 × 103 mm. $7.20, The Nativity (38 × 49 *mm*) .. .. 5·00 6·00

119 Astronaut and "Apollo 11" Emblem

(Des G. Vasarhelyi)

1989 (20 July). 20*th Anniv of First Manned Landing on Moon. T* **119** *and similar horiz designs. Multicoloured. P* 14.
680 $1.50, Type **119** .. .. 2·00 2·00
a. Horiz strip of 3. Nos. 680/2 .. .. 5·50
681 $1.50, Earth and Moon .. .. .. 2·00 2·00
682 $1.50, Astronaut and "Apollo 1" emblem 2·00 2·00
680/2 .. .. *Set of* 3 5·50 5·50
MS683 160 × 64 mm. As Nos. 680/2, but each stamp with a face value of $1.15. P 13 .. .. 3·00 3·50
Nos. 680/2 were printed together, *se-tenant*, in horizontal strips of 3 throughout the sheet.

120 Priests

1989 (22 Nov). *Christmas. T* **120** *and similar multicoloured designs showing details from "Presentation in the Temple" by Rembrandt. P* 13.
684 70 c. Type **120** 75 75
685 80 c. Virgin and Christ Child in Simeon's arms 85 85
686 $1.05, Joseph .. .. 1·25 1·25
687 $1.30, Simeon and Christ Child .. .. 1·50 1·50
684/7 .. .. *Set of* 4 4·00 4·00
MS688 84 × 110 mm. $7.20, "Presentation in the Temple" (39 × 49 *mm*). P 13½ .. .. .. 8·00 8·50

121 Fritz Walter

1990 (5 Feb). *World Cup Football Championship, Italy. German Footballers. T* **121** *and similar horiz designs. Multicoloured. P* 13½ × 13.
689 80 c. Type **121** .. .. 1·40 1·40
690 $1.15, Franz Beckenbauer .. .. .. 1·75 1·75
691 $1.40, Uwe Seeler .. .. 2·00 2·00
692 $1.80, German team emblem and signatures of former captains .. .. .. 2·50 2·50
689/92 .. .. *Set of* 4 7·00 7·00

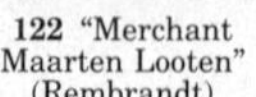

122 "Merchant Maarten Looten" (Rembrandt)

123 Queen Elizabeth the Queen Mother

1990 (2 May). *150th Anniv of the Penny Black. T* **122** *and similar vert designs showing Rembrandt paintings. Multicoloured. P* 13½.

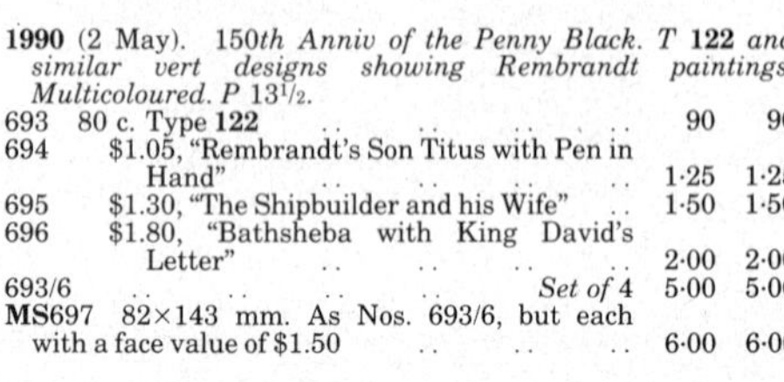

693 80 c. Type **122** 90 90
694 $1.05, "Rembrandt's Son Titus with Pen in Hand" .. .. 1·25 1·25
695 $1.30, "The Shipbuilder and his Wife" .. 1·50 1·50
696 $1.80, "Bathsheba with King David's Letter" .. .. 2·00 2·00
693/6 .. .. *Set of* 4 5·00 5·00
MS697 82×143 mm. As Nos. 693/6, but each with a face value of $1.50 .. .. .. 6·00 6·00

1990 (23 July). *90th Birthday of Queen Elizabeth the Queen Mother. P* 13×13½.
698 **123** $1.25, multicoloured .. .. .. 2·00 2·00
MS699 84×64 mm. **123** $7 multicoloured .. 8·50 8·50

124 "Adoration of the Magi" (Dirk Bouts)

(125)

(Litho Questa)

1990 (27 Nov). *Christmas. Religious Paintings. T* **124** *and similar vert designs. Multicoloured. P* 14.
700 70 c. Type **124** 75 75
701 80 c. "Holy Family" (Fra Bartolommeo) .. 90 90
702 $1.05, "Nativity" (Memling) .. .. 1·10 1·10
703 $1.30, "Adoration of the Kings" (Bruegel the Elder) .. .. 1·40 1·40
700/3 .. .. *Set of* 4 3·75 3·75
MS704 100×135 mm. $7.20, "Virgin and Child Enthoned" (detail, Cosimo Tura) .. .. 6·50 7·00

1990 (5 Dec). *"Birdpex '90" Stamp Exhibition, Christchurch, New Zealand. No.* 410 *optd with T* **125** *in silver.*
705 $10 Scarlet Hibiscus .. .. .. 8·00 8·50

SIXTY FIFTH BIRTHDAY
QUEEN ELIZABETH II

(126)

1991 (22 Apr). *65th Birthday of Queen Elizabeth II. No.* 409 *optd with T* **126.**
706 $6 *Hybrid hibiscus* .. .. .. 5·50 6·00

T E N T H ANNIVERSARY (127)

T E N T H ANNIVERSARY (128)

1991 (26 June). *10th Wedding Anniv of Prince and Princess of Wales. Nos.* 430/2 *optd. A. With T* **127** *in typography* (75 c. *in silver*). *B. With T* **128** *in lithography* (75 c. *in black*).

		A		B	
707	75 c. Type **77** ..	70	70	70	70
708	95 c. Lady Diana Spencer ..	85	85	85	85
709	$1.20, Prince Charles and Lady Diana ..	1·25	1·25	1·25	1·25
707/9	.. .. *Set of* 3	2·50	2·50	2·50	2·50

Nos. 707A/9A come from small sheets of 6, including one *se-tenant* stamp-size label, and Nos. 707B/9B from uncut sheets containing four such small sheets.

MINIMUM PRICE

The minimum price quote is 10p which represents a handling charge rather than a basis for valuing common stamps. For further notes about prices see introductory pages.

129 "The Virgin and Child with Sts Jerome and Dominic" (Lippi)

130 Banded Rail

(Des G. Vasarhelyi. Litho Questa)

1991 (11 Nov). *Christmas. Religious Paintings. T* **129** *and similar vert designs. Multicoloured. P* 14.
710 20 c. Type **129** 10 15
711 50 c. "The Isenheim Altarpiece" (M. Grunewald) 35 40
712 $1 "The Nativity" (G. Pittoni) 60 70
713 $2 "Adoration of the Kings" (J. Brueghel the Elder) .. .. 1·25 1·40
710/13 .. .. *Set of* 4 2·10 2·40
MS714 79×104 mm. $7 "Adoration of the Shepherds" (G. Reni) .. .. 4·50 4·75

(Litho B.D.T.)

1992 (19 Feb–20 Mar). *Birds. T* **130** *and similar vert designs. Multicoloured. P* 14.
718 20 c. Type **130** 10 10
719 50 c. Red-tailed Tropic Bird 35 40
720 70 c. Purple Swamphen 45 50
721 $1 Pacific Pigeon 65 70
722 $1.50, White-collared Kingfisher (20.3.92) 1·00 1·10
723 $2 Blue-crowned Lory (20.3.92) .. .. 1·25 1·40
718/23 .. .. *Set of* 6 3·50 3·75

OFFICIAL STAMPS

O.H.M.S. (O 1) **O.H.M.S.** (O 2)

1985 (1 July)–**87.** *Nos.* 408/10 *optd with Type* O **2** *in gold and Nos.* 527/42 *optd with Type* O **1** *in blue, all by foil embossing.*
O 1 12 c. Type **92** 10 10
O 2 25 c. *Euphorbia pulcherrima* 15 20
O 3 30 c. *Cochlospermum hibiscoides* 20 25
O 4 35 c. *Begonia sp.* 25 30
O 5 40 c. *Plumeria sp.* 25 30
O 6 52 c. *Strelitzia reginae* 35 40
O 7 58 c. *Hibiscus syriacus* 40 45
O 8 70 c. *Tibouchina sp.* 45 50
O 9 83 c. *Nelumbo sp.* 55 60
O10 $1.05, *Hybrid hibiscus* 70 75
O11 $1.75, *Cassia fistula* .. .. .. 1·10 1·25
O12 $2.30, *Orchid var.* (29.11.85) .. .. 1·50 1·60
O13 $3.90, *Orchid sp.* (29.11.85) .. .. 2·50 2·75
O14 $4 *Euphorbia pulcherrima poinsettia* (1.4.86) .. .. 2·75 3·00
O15 $5 *Euphorbia pulcherrima poinsettia* (1.4.86) .. .. 3·25 3·50
O16 $6 *Hybrid hibiscus* (29.4.87) .. .. 4·00 4·25
O17 $6.60, *Hybrid hibiscus* (15.9.86) .. .. 4·25 4·50
O18 $8.30, *Hibiscus rosasinensis* (15.9.86) .. 5·50 5·75
O19 $10 Scarlet Hibiscus (29.4.87) .. .. 6·50 6·75
O1/19 .. .. *Set of* 19 29·00 32·00

Norfolk Island

The stamps of TASMANIA were used on Norfolk Island from mid-1854 until May 1855, such use being identified by the "72" numeral cancellation. From 1877 the stamps of NEW SOUTH WALES were in regular use, being replaced by issues for AUSTRALIA from 1913 to 1947.

AUSTRALIAN ADMINISTRATION

PRINTERS. Nos. 1 to 42 were printed at the Note Printing Branch Reserve Bank of Australia (until 14 Jan 1960, known as the Note Printing Branch, Commonwealth Bank) by recess. See note at the beginning of Australia *re* imprints.

1 Ball Bay

1947 (10 June)–**59**. *Toned paper. P* 14.

No.	Type	Description	Unused	Used
1	1	½d. orange	35	40
		a. White paper (11.56)	1·50	3·50
2		1d. bright violet	50	40
		a. White paper (11.56)	7·50	14·00
3		1½d. emerald-green	50	40
		a. White paper (11.56)	13·00	22·00
4		2d. reddish violet	55	30
		a. White paper (11.56)	£130	£130
5		2½d. scarlet	80	30
6		3d. chestnut	70	45
6a		3d. emerald-green (*white paper*) (6.7.59)	14·00	3·75
7		4d. claret	70	40
8		5½d. indigo	70	30
9		6d. purple-brown	70	30
10		9d. magenta	1·25	40
11		1s. grey-green	70	40
12		2s. yellow-bistre	4·00	1·25
12a		2s. deep blue (*white paper*) (6.7.59)	24·00	5·00
1/12a		*Set of* 14	45·00	12·50

Stamps of T 1, perf 11, or in different colours, perf 11, are printer's waste which leaked from the Note Ptg Branch. They were never distributed to post offices for sale to the public.

2 Warder's Tower

3 Airfield

1953 (10 June). *T* **2/3** *and similar designs. P* 14½ × 15 (*vert*) *or* 15 × 14½ (*horiz*).

No.	Description	Unused	Used
13	3½d. brown-lake	3·00	90
14	6½d. deep green	3·00	1·00
15	7½d. deep blue	4·00	3·00
16	8½d. chocolate	7·00	3·50
17	10d. reddish violet	5·00	75
18	5s. sepia	38·00	8·00
13/18	*Set of* 6	55·00	15·00

Designs: *Horiz* (*as T* 3)—7½d. Old Stores (Crankmill); 5s. Bloody Bridge. *Vert* (*as T* 2)—8½d. Barracks entrance; 10d. Salt House.

8 Norfolk Island Seal and Pitcairners Landing

Two types of 2s.:

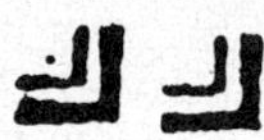

Type I   Type II

Alternate stamps on each horizontal row are with or without a dot in bottom right corner.

1956 (8 June). *Centenary of Landing of Pitcairn Islanders on Norfolk Island. P* 15 × 14½.

No.	Type	Description	Unused	Used
19	8	3d. deep bluish green	1·25	30
20		2s. violet (I)	1·75	50
		a. Type II	1·75	50
		b. Deep violet (I)	2·75	1·75
		ba. Type II	2·75	1·75

7d

NORFOLK ISLAND

8d 5D

(9) (10) (11)

1958 (1 July). *Nos.* 15/16 *surch with T* **9/10**.

No.	Description	Unused	Used
21	7d. on 7½d. deep blue	1·00	45
22	8d. on 8½d. chocolate	1·00	45

1959 (7 Dec). *150th Anniv of Australian Post Office. No.* 331 *of Australia surch with T* **11**.

No.	Description	Unused	Used
23	5d. on 4d. slate (R.)	35	15

12 *Hibiscus insularis*

14 White Tern

16 Red Hibiscus

17 Queen Elizabeth II and Cereus

21 Rose Apple

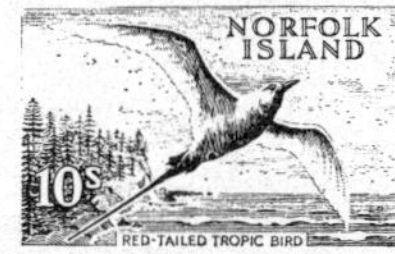

22 Red-tailed Tropic Bird

(Design recess; centre typo (T **21**))

1960–62. *T* **12, 14, 16/17, 21/2** *and similar designs. P* 14½ *or* 14½ × 14 (10*s*.).

No.	Description	Unused	Used
24	1d. bluish green (23.5.60)	15	10
25	2d. rose and myrtle-green (23.5.60)	20	10
26	3d. green (1.5.61)	70	15
27	5d. bright purple (20.6.60)	55	20
28	8d. red (20.6.60)	80	50
29	9d. ultramarine (23.5.60)	80	45
30	10d. brown and reddish violet (as No. 17) (27.2.61)	2·50	1·25
31	1s. 1d. carmine-red (16.10.61)	80	35
32	2s. sepia (1.5.61)	6·00	90
33	2s. 5d. deep violet (5.2.62)	1·00	40
34	2s. 8d. cinnamon and deep green (9.4.62)	2·00	55
35	5s. sepia and deep green (as No. 18) (27.2.61)	6·00	75
36	10s. emerald-green (14.8.61) (Optd S. £48)	60·00	26·00
24/36	*Set of* 13	70·00	28·00

Designs: *Vert* (*as T* **12**)—2d. *Lagunaria patersonii*; 5d. Lantana. (*As T* **21**); 1s. 1d. Fringed Hibiscus; 2s. 5d. Passion-flower. (*As T* **14**)—2s. Solander's Petrel.

Nos. 30 and 35 are redrawn.

The Specimen overprint on No. 36 is from sets sold by the Australian Post Office.

2/8

1/1   2/5

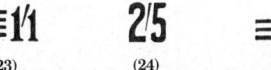

(23) (24) (25)

1960. *As Nos.* 13/15 *but colours changed, surch with T* **23/5**.

No.	Description	Unused	Used
37	1s. 1d. on 3½d. deep ultramarine (26.9.60)	3·50	1·25
38	2s. 5d. on 6½d. bluish green (26.9.60)	3·50	1·25
39	2s. 8d. on 7½d. sepia (29.8.60)	8·00	2·25
37/9	*Set of* 3	13·50	4·25

26 Queen Elizabeth II and Map

27 Open Bible and Candle

1960 (24 Oct). *Introduction of Local Government. P* 14.

No.	Type	Description	Unused	Used
40	26	2s. 8d. reddish purple	15·00	6·00

(Des K. McKay. Adapted and eng B. Stewart. Recess)

1960 (21 Nov). *Christmas. P* 15×14½.

No.	Type	Description	Unused	Used
41	27	5d. bright purple	80	30

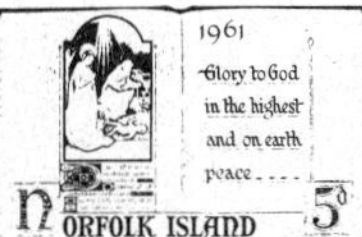

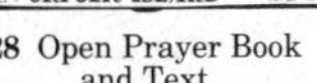

28 Open Prayer Book and Text

29 "Tweed Trousers" (*Atypichthys latus*)

(Des G. Lissenden. Eng P. Morriss. Recess)

1961 (20 Nov). *Christmas. P* 14½×14.

No.	Type	Description	Unused	Used
42	28	5d. slate-blue	30	30

PRINTERS. All the following issues to No. 233 were printed in photogravure by Harrison and Sons, Ltd, London, *except where otherwise stated*.

1962–63. *Fishes. Horiz designs as T* **29**. *P* 14½×14.

No.	Description	Unused	Used
43	6d. sepia, yellow & dp bluish green (16.7.62)	1·00	25
44	11d. red-orange, brown and blue (25.2.63)	2·50	80
45	1s. blue, pink and yellow-olive (17.9.62)	1·00	25
46	1s. 3d. blue, red-brown and green (15.7.63)	2·50	1·75
47	1s. 6d. sepia, violet and light blue (6.5.63)	3·00	80
48	2s. 3d. dp blue, red & greenish yell (23.9.63)	4·50	80
43/8	*Set of* 6	13·00	4·25

Designs:—11d. "Trumpeter"; 1s. "Po'ov"; 1s. 3d. "Dreamfish"; 1s. 6d. "Hapoéka"; 2s. 3d. "Ophie" (*carangidae*).

30 "Madonna and Child"

31 "Peace on Earth..."

(Des and eng G. Lissenden. Recess Note Ptg Branch, Reserve Bank of Australia)

1962 (19 Nov). *Christmas. P* 14½.

No.	Type	Description	Unused	Used
49	30	5d. ultramarine	35	15

(Des R. Warner. Eng B. Stewart. Recess Note Ptg Branch, Reserve Bank of Australia)

1963 (11 Nov). *Christmas. P* 14½.

No.	Type	Description	Unused	Used
50	31	5d. red	30	15

32 Overlooking Kingston

33 Norfolk Pine

1964 (24 Feb–28 Sept). *Views. Horiz designs as T* **32**. *Multicoloured. P* 14½×14.

No.	Description	Unused	Used
51	5d. Type **32**	50	15
52	8d. Kingston	1·00	20
53	9d. The Arches (Bumboras) (11.5)	2·00	15
54	10d. Slaughter Bay (28.9)	3·00	25
51/4	*Set of* 4	6·00	65

(Photo Note Ptg Branch, Reserve Bank of Australia, Melbourne)

1964 (1 July). *50th Anniv of Norfolk Island as Australian Territory. P* 13½.

No.	Type	Description	Unused	Used
55	33	5d. black, red and orange	20	10
56		8d. black, red and grey-green	30	10

34 Child looking at Nativity Scene

35 Nativity Scene

(Des P. Morriss and J. Mason. Photo Note Ptg Branch, Reserve Bank of Australia)

1964 (9 Nov). *Christmas. P* 13½.

No.	Type	Description	Unused	Used
57	34	5d. green, blue, buff and violet	30	10

1965 (14 Apr). *50th Anniv of Gallipoli Landing. As T* **22** *of Nauru. P* 13½.

No.	Description	Unused	Used
58	5d. sepia, black and emerald	10	10

(Des J. Mason. Photo Note Ptg Branch, Reserve Bank of Australia)

1965 (25 Oct). *Christmas. Helecon paper. P* 13½.

No.	Type	Description	Unused	Used
59	35	5d. multicoloured	10	10

ALTERED CATALOGUE NUMBERS

Any Catalogue numbers altered from the last edition are shown as a list in the introductory pages.

(New Currency. 100 cents = $1 Australian)

38 *Hibiscus insularis*

39 Headstone Bridge

1966 (14 Feb). *Decimal currency. Various stamps surch in black on silver tablets, which vary slightly in size, obliterating old value as in T* **38**. *Surch typo.*

60 **38** 1 c. on 1d. bluish green (*value tablet* 4×5 *mm*) 20 10
a. Value tablet larger, 5½×5½ mm .. 40 30
61 – 2 c. on 2d. rose & myrtle-green (No. 25) 20 10
62 **14** 3 c. on 3d. green 50 10
a. Silver tablet omitted £250
63 – 4 c. on 5d. bright purple (No. 27) .. 25 10
64 **16** 5 c. on 8d. red 30 10
65 – 10 c. on 10d. brown & reddish vio (No. 30) 40 15
66 – 15 c. on 1s. 1d. carmine-red (No. 31) .. 45 15
67 – 20 c. on 2s. sepia (No. 32).. .. .. 3·50 1·75
68 – 25 c. on 2s. 5d. deep violet (No. 33) .. 1·50 40
69 **21** 30 c. on 2s. 8d. cinnamon and deep green 1·00 50
70 – 50 c. on 5s. sepia and deep green (No. 35) 4·50 75
71 **22** $1 on 10s. emerald-green (*value tablet* 7×6½ *mm*) .. .. 3·50 1·75
a. Value tablet smaller, 6½×4 mm .. 3·50 1·75
60/71 .. .. *Set of* 12 14·50 5·25

1966 (27 June). *Horiz designs as T* **39**. *Multicoloured. P* 14½ × 14.
72 7 c. Type **39** 40 15
73 9 c. Cemetery Road 40 15

41 St. Barnabas' Chapel (interior)

42 St. Barnabas' Chapel (exterior)

1966 (23 Aug). *Centenary of Melanesian Mission. P* 14 × 14½.
74 **41** 4 c. multicoloured 10 10
75 **42** 25 c. multicoloured 20 10

43 Star over Philip Island

44 H.M.S. *Resolution*, 1774

(Des B. G. W. McCoy)

1966 (24 Oct). *Christmas. P* 14½.
76 **43** 4 c. multicoloured 10 10

(Des Harrison)

1967 (17 Apr)–**68**. *T* **44** *and similar horiz designs showing ships. Multicoloured. P* 14 × 14½.
77 1 c. Type **44** 10 10
78 2 c. *La Boussole* and *L'Astrolabe*, 1788 .. 15 10
79 3 c. H.M.S. *Supply*, 1788 .. .. .. 15 10
80 4 c. H.M.S. *Sirius*, 1790 .. .. .. 15 10
81 5 c. *Norfolk* (cutter), 1798 (14.8.67) 20 10
82 7 c. H.M.S. *Mermaid* (survey cutter), 1825 (14.8.67) 20 10
83 9 c. *Lady Franklin*, 1853 (14.8.67) 20 10
84 10 c. *Morayshire*, 1856 (14.8.67) 20 20
85 15 c. *Southern Cross*, 1866 (18.3.68) 45 30
86 20 c. *Pitcairn*, 1891 (18.3.68) 60 40
87 25 c. Norfolk Island whaleboat, 1895 (18.3.68) 1·00 75
88 30 c. *Iris* (cable ship), 1907 (18.6.68) .. .. 2·00 1·50
89 50 c. *Resolution*, 1926 (18.6.68) .. .. 3·00 2·00
90 $1 *Morinda*, 1931 (18.6.68) .. .. .. 5·50 2·50
77/90 .. .. *Set of* 14 12·50 7·50

45 Lions Badge and 50 Stars

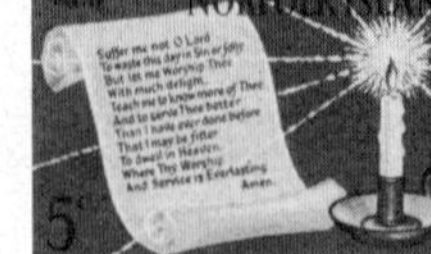

46 Prayer of John Adams and Candle

(Des M. Ripper. Photo Note Ptg Branch, Reserve Bank of Australia)

1967 (7 June). *50th Anniv of Lions International. P* 13½.
91 **45** 4 c. black, bluish green and olive-yellow .. 10 10

(Des B. G. W. McCoy)

1967 (16 Oct). *Christmas. P* 14.
92 **46** 5 c. black, light yellow-olive and red .. 10 10

47 Queen Elizabeth II

(Photo Note Ptg Branch, Reserve Bank of Australia)

1968 (5 Aug)–**71**. *Coil stamps. P* 15×*imperf.*
93 **47** 3 c. black, light brown and vermilion .. 10 10
94 4 c. black, light brown and blue-green .. 10 10
95 5 c. black, light brown and deep violet .. 10 10
95*a* 6 c. black, lt brown & lake-brn (25.8.71) 30 35
93/5*a* .. .. *Set of* 4 45 45

59 "Skymaster" and "Lancastrian" Aircraft

60 Bethlehem Star and Flowers

(Des Harrison)

1968 (25 Sept). *21st Anniv of QANTAS Air Service, Sydney–Norfolk Island. P* 14.
96 **59** 5 c. bluish black, carmine-red & lt blue 10 10
97 7 c. blackish brown, carmine-red & turq 10 10

(Des Mrs. B. L. Laing)

1968 (24 Oct). *Christmas. P* 14 × 14½.
98 **60** 5 c. multicoloured 10 10

61 Captain Cook, Quadrant and Chart of Pacific Ocean

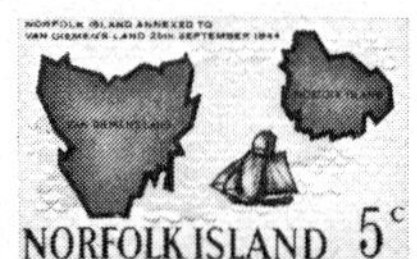

62 Van Diemen's Land, Norfolk Island and Sailing Cutter

(Des V. Whiteley from sketch by J. G. Cowan)

1969 (3 June). *Captain Cook Bicentenary* (*1st issue*). *Observation of the transit of Venus across the Sun, from Tahiti. P* 14.
99 **61** 10 c. multicoloured 10 10
See also Nos. 118/19, 129, 152/5, 200/2 and 213/14.

(Des Mrs. A. Bathie and Mrs. M. J. McCoy)

1969 (29 Sept). *125th Anniv of the Annexation of Norfolk Island to Van Diemen's Land. P* 14 × 14½.
100 **62** 5 c. multicoloured 10 10
101 30 c. multicoloured 20 10

63 "The Nativity" (carved mother-of-pearl plaque)

64 New Zealand Grey Flyeater

(Des J. G. Cowan)

1969 (27 Oct). *Christmas. P* 14½ × 14.
102 **63** 5 c. multicoloured 10 10

(Des G. Mathews)

1970–71. *Birds. T* **64** *and similar multicoloured designs. Chalk-surfaced paper. P* 14.
103 1 c. Scarlet Robins (22.7.70) 30 10
104 2 c. Golden Whistler (24.2.71) 30 20
105 3 c. Type **64** (25.2.70).. .. .. .. 30 10
106 4 c. Long-tailed Koels (25.2.70) 60 10
107 5 c. Red-fronted Parakeet (24.2.71) .. .. 1·50 45
108 7 c. Long-tailed Triller (22.7.70) 45 10
109 9 c. Island Thrush (25.2.70) 70 10
110 10 c. Boobook Owl (22.7.70) .. .. .. 1·75 40
111 15 c. Norfolk Island Pigeon (24.2.71) .. .. 1·50 65
112 20 c. White-chested White Eye (16.6.71) .. 4·50 2·50
113 25 c. Norfolk Island Parrots (22.7.70) .. 2·50 40
a. Error. Glazed, ordinary paper .. ..
114 30 c. Collared Grey Fantail (16.6.71) .. .. 4·50 1·75
115 45 c. Norfolk Island Starlings (25.2.70) .. 3·50 80
116 50 c. Crimson Rosella (24.2.71) .. .. 4·00 1·75
117 $1 Sacred Kingfisher (16.6.71) .. .. 9·00 8·00
103/17 .. .. *Set of* 15 32·00 15·00
Nos. 105, 106, 109, 112, 114, 115 and 117 are horizontal, and the remainder vertical designs.

65 Capt. Cook and Map of Australia

66 First Christmas Service, 1788

(Des R. Bates)

1970 (29 Apr). *Captain Cook Bicentenary* (*2nd issue*). *Discovery of Australia's East Coast. T* **65** *and similar horiz design. Multi-coloured. P* 14.
118 5 c. Type **65** 10 10
119 10 c. H.M.S. *Endeavour* and aborigine .. 20 10

(Des R. Bates)

1970 (15 Oct). *Christmas. P* 14.
120 **66** 5 c. multicoloured 10 10

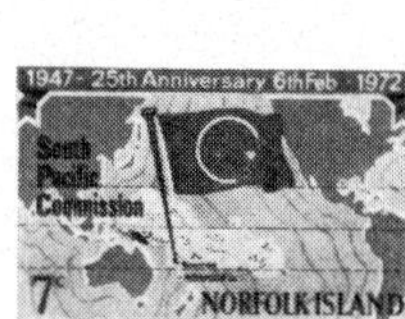

67 Bishop Patteson and Martyrdom of St. Stephen

68 Rose Window, St. Barnabas Chapel, Kingston

(Des R. Bates)

1971 (20 Sept). *Death Centenary of Bishop Patteson. T* **67** *and similar horiz designs. Multicoloured. P* 14 × 14½.
121 6 c. Type **67** 10 10
a. Pair. Nos. 121/2 .. .. 10 10
122 6 c. Bible, Martyrdom of St. Stephen and knotted palm-frond 10 10
123 10 c. Bishop Patteson and stained-glass .. 10 10
a. Pair. Nos. 123/4 .. .. 20 20
124 10 c. Cross and Bishop's Arms 10 10
121/4 .. .. *Set of* 4 30 30
Nos. 121/2 and 123/4 were printed in *se-tenant* pairs throughout the sheet.

(Des G. Hitch. Photo Heraclio Fournier, Spain)

1971 (25 Oct). *Christmas. P* 14 × 13½.
125 **68** 6 c. multicoloured 10 10

69 Map and Flag

70 "St. Mark" (stained-glass window, All Saints, Norfolk Is)

(Des G. Hitch)

1972 (7 Feb). *25th Anniv of South Pacific Commission. P* 14 × 14½.
126 **69** 7 c. multicoloured 15 10

(Des Mrs. M. J. McCoy)

1972 (16 Oct). *Christmas. P* 14.
127 **70** 7 c. multicoloured 10 10

71 Cross and Pines. (stained-glass window, All Saints Church)

72 H.M.S. *Resolution* in the Antarctic

(Des Harrison)

1972 (20 Nov). *Centenary of First Pitcairner-built Church. P* 14.
128 **71** 12 c. multicoloured 10 10
a. Purple (background to dates) omitted .. ..

(Des G. Hitch)

1973 (17 Jan). *Captain Cook Bicentenary* (3rd *issue*). *Crossing of the Antarctic Circle. P* 14.
129 **72** 35 c. multicoloured .. .. .. 3·00 2·25

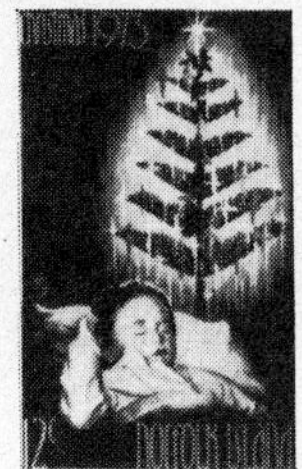

73 Child and Christmas Tree

74 Protestant Clergyman's Quarters

(Des B. W. McCoy (T **73**), R. Westwood (35 c.))

1973 (22 Oct). *Christmas. T* **73** *and similar vert design. Multicoloured. P* 14.
130 7 c. Type **73** 20 10
131 12 c. Type **73** 25 10
132 35 c. Fir trees and star 70 80
130/2 .. .. *Set of* 3 1·00 90

(Des G. Hitch)

1973 (19 Nov)–**75.** *Historic Buildings. T* **74** *and similar horiz designs. Multicoloured. P* 14 × 14½.
133 1 c. Type **74** 10 10
134 2 c. Royal Engineers' Office (1.5.74) 10 10
135 3 c. Double Quarters for Free Overseers (19.2.75) 25 15
136 4 c. Guard House (12.7.74) 20 20
137 5 c. Entrance to Pentagonal Gaol 25 15
138 7 c. Pentagonal Gaol (1.5.74) 35 35
139 8 c. Prisoners' Barracks (19.2.75) .. .. 1·00 35
140 10 c. Officers' Quarters, New Military Barracks 50 45
141 12 c. New Military Barracks (1.5.74) 50 30
142 14 c. Beach Stores (12.7.74) 60 60
143 15 c. The Magazine (19.2.75) .. .. .. 1·50 50
144 20 c. Entrance, Old Military Barracks (12.7.74) 80 80
145 25 c. Old Military Barracks (19.2.75) .. .. 1·50 90
146 30 c. Old Stores (Crankmill) (1.5.74) .. .. 1·00 60
147 50 c. Commissariat Stores .. .. .. 1·25 1·75
148 $1 Government House (12.7.74) .. .. 2·25 3·75
133/48 .. .. *Set of* 16 11·00 10·00

75 Royal Couple and Map

(Des Harrison)

1974 (8 Feb). *Royal Visit. P* 14 × 14½.
149 **75** 7 c. multicoloured 40 15
150 25 c. multicoloured .. .. 1·25 75

76 Chichester's *Madame Elijah*

(Des B. McCoy. Litho State Bank Note Printing Works, Helsinki)

1974 (28 Mar). *First Aircraft Landing on Norfolk Island. P* 14.
151 **76** 14 c. multicoloured .. .. 1·00 70

77 "Captain Cook" (engraving by J. Basire)

78 Nativity Scene (pearl-shell pew carving)

(Des C. I. Buffett. Litho Questa)

1974 (8 Oct). *Captain Cook Bicentenary* (4*th issue*). *Discovery of Norfolk Is. T* **77** *and similar vert designs. Multicoloured. P* 14.
152 7 c. Type **77** .. .. 1·50 75
153 10 c. "H.M.S. *Resolution*" (H. Roberts) .. 2·50 1·75
154 14 c. Norfolk Island Pine .. .. 2·75 2·00
155 25 c. "Norfolk Island flax" (G. Raper) .. .. 3·25 2·75
152/5 .. .. *Set of* 4 9·00 6·50

(Des G. Hitch)

1974 (18 Oct). *Christmas. P* 14½.
156 **78** 7 c. multicoloured 15 10
157 30 c. multicoloured 60 75

79 Norfolk Pine

(Manufactured by Walsall)

1974 (16 Dec). *Centenary of Universal Postal Union. T* **79** *and similar "island"-shaped designs. Multicoloured. Imperf* (*backing-paper roul* 20). *Self-adhesive.*
158 10 c. Type **79** 35 40
159 15 c. Offshore islands 40 45
160 35 c. Crimson Rosella and Sacred Kingfisher 70 75
161 40 c. Pacific map 75 90
158/61 .. .. *Set of* 4 2·00 2·25
MS162 106 × 101 mm. Map of Norfolk Is. cut-to-shape with reduced-size replicas of Nos. 158/61 23·00 27·00

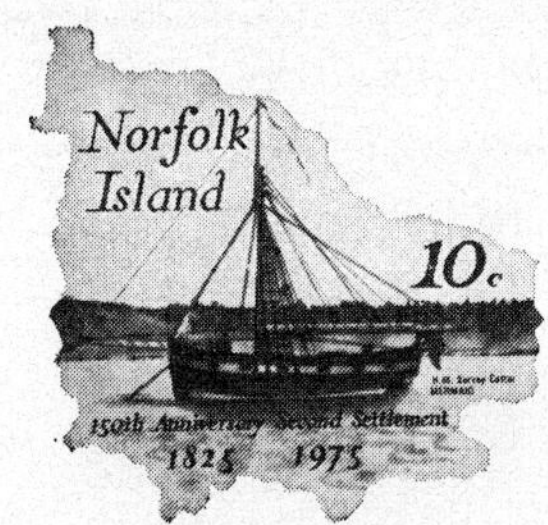

80 H.M.S. *Mermaid* (survey cutter)

(Manufactured by Walsall)

1975 (18 Aug). *150th Anniv of Second Settlement. T* **80** *and similar "island"-shaped design. Multicoloured. Imperf* (*backing-paper roul* 20). *Self-adhesive.*
163 10 c. Type **80** 45 45
164 35 c. Kingston, 1835 (from painting by T. Seller) 80 80

81 Star on Norfolk Island Pine

82 Memorial Cross

(Des Harrison)

1975 (6 Oct). *Christmas. P* 14.
165 **81** 10 c. multicoloured 15 10
166 15 c. multicoloured 20 10
167 35 c. multicoloured 30 35
165/7 .. .. *Set of* 3 60 45

(Des Harrison)

1975 (24 Nov). *Centenary of St. Barnabas Chapel. T* **82** *and similar horiz design. Multicoloured. P* 14.
168 30 c. Type **82** 20 15
169 60 c. Laying foundation stone and Chapel in 1975 .. .. 40 40

83 Launching of *Resolution*

84 Whaleship *Charles W. Morgan*

(Des Harrison)

1975 (1 Dec). *50th Anniv of Launching of Schooner "Resolution". T* **83** *and similar horiz design. Multicoloured. P* 14.
170 25 c. Type **83** 25 30
171 45 c. *Resolution* at sea 40 55

(Des Harrison)

1976 (5 July). *Bicentenary of American Revolution. T* **84** *and similar horiz designs. Multicoloured. P* 14.
172 18 c. Type **84** 30 15
173 25 c. Thanksgiving Service 40 20
174 40 c. "Flying Fortress" over Norfolk Is .. 75 45
175 45 c. California Quail .. .. 1·00 55
172/5 .. .. *Set of* 4 2·25 1·25

85 Swallow-tailed Tern and Sun

86 *Vanessa ita*

(Des Harrison)

1976 (4 Oct). *Christmas. P* 14.
176 **85** 18 c. multicoloured 25 15
177 25 c. multicoloured 40 20
178 45 c. multicoloured 85 50
176/8 .. .. *Set of* 3 1·40 75

(Des B. Hargreaves)

1976 (17 Nov)–**77.** *Butterflies and Moths. T* **86** *and similar horiz designs. Multicoloured. P* 14.
179 1 c. Type **86** 10 40
180 2 c. *Utetheisa pulchelloides* (moth) (22.2.77) 10 40
181 3 c. *Agathia asterias* (moth) (5.7.77) 10 20
182 4 c. *Cynthia kershawi* (5.7.77) 10 25
183 5 c. *Leucania loreyimima* (moth) 15 30
184 10 c. *Hypolimnas bolina* 30 35
185 15 c. *Pyrrhorachis pyrrhogona* (moth) (22.2.77) 30 30
186 16 c. *Austrocarea iocephala* (moth) 30 30
187 17 c. *Pseudocoremia christiani* (moth) (10.5.77) 35 30
188 18 c. *Cleora idiocrossa* (moth) 35 30
189 19 c. *Simplicia caeneusalis* (moth) (10.5.77) 35 30
190 20 c. *Austrocidaria ralstonae* (moth) (10.5.77) 40 30
191 30 c. *Hippotion scrofa* (moth) (22.2.77) .. 50 40
192 40 c. *Papilio amynthor* (*ilioneus*) (10.5.77) 55 40
193 50 c. *Tiracola plagiata* (moth) (22.2.77) .. 70 60
194 $1 *Precis villida* .. .. 1·00 75
195 $2 *Cepora perimale* (5.7.77) .. .. .. 1·75 1·40
179/95 .. .. *Set of* 17 6·50 6·50

87 Queen's View, Kingston

(Des Harrison)

1977 (10 June). *Silver Jubilee. P* 14.
196 **87** 25 c. multicoloured 35 30

88 Hibiscus Flowers and Oil Lamp

89 Captain Cook (from a portrait by Nathaniel Dance)

(Des Mrs. M. J. McCoy)

1977 (4 Oct). *Christmas. P* 14 × 14½.
197 **88** 18 c. multicoloured 15 10
198 25 c. multicoloured 15 10
199 45 c. multicoloured 30 35
197/9 .. .. *Set of* 3 55 50

(Des Harrison)

1978 (18 Jan). *Captain Cook Bicentenary* (5*th issue*). *Discovery of Hawaii. T* **89** *and similar horiz designs. Multicoloured. P* 14½.
200 18 c. Type **89** 30 20
201 25 c. Discovery of Northern Hawaiian islands 40 30
202 80 c. British flag against island background .. 90 70
200/2 .. .. *Set of* 3 1·40 1·10

90 Guide Flag and Globe

(Manufactured by Walsall)

1978 (22 Feb). *50th Anniv of Girl Guides. T* **90** *and similar "island"-shaped designs. Multicoloured. Imperf (backing paper roul 20). Self-adhesive.*

203 18 c. Type **90** .. 30 15
204 25 c. Emblem and scarf badge .. 45 25
a. Horiz roul omitted (vert pair)
205 35 c. Emblem and Queen Elizabeth .. 60 35
a. Horiz roul omitted (vert pair)
206 45 c. Emblem and Lady Baden-Powell .. 75 45
203/6 .. *Set of* 4 1·90 1·10

Nos. 204a and 205a each come from sheets of 20 on which all the horizontal roulettes were omitted.

91 St. Edward's Crown

(Des Harrison)

1978 (29 June). *25th Anniv of Coronation. T* **91** *and similar horiz design. Multicoloured. P* 14½.

207 25 c. Type **91** .. 15 15
208 70 c. Coronation regalia .. 40 45

92 View of Duncombe Bay with Scout at Camp Fire

(Des S. Jensen. Manufactured by Walsall)

1978 (22 Aug). *50th Anniv of Boy Scouts. T* **92** *and similar "island"-shaped designs. Multicoloured. Imperf (backing paper roul 20). Self-adhesive.*

209 20 c. Type **92** .. 35 30
210 25 c. View from Kingston and emblem .. 55 40
211 35 c. View of Anson Bay and Link Badge .. 85 75
212 45 c. Sunset scene and Lord Baden-Powell .. 1·00 85
209/12 .. *Set of* 4 2·50 2·10

93 Chart showing Route of Arctic Voyage

94 Poinsettia and Bible

(Des G. Hitch)

1978 (29 Aug). *Captain Cook Bicentenary (6th issue). Northernmost Voyages. T* **93** *and similar horiz design. Multicoloured. P* 14½.

213 25 c. Type **93** .. 60 30
214 90 c. "H.M.S. *Resolution* and H.M.S. *Discovery* in Pack Ice" (painting by Webber) .. 1·50 80

(Des Mrs. M. J. McCoy)

1978 (3 Oct). *Christmas. T* **94** *and similar vert designs. Multicoloured. P* 14½ × 14.

215 20 c. Type **94** .. 15 10
216 30 c. Native Oak and Bible .. 20 15
217 55 c. Hibiscus and Bible .. 30 30
215/17 .. *Set of* 3 60 50

95 Cook and Village of Staithes near Marton

(Des Harrison)

1978 (27 Oct). *250th Birth Anniv of Captain Cook. T* **95** *and similar horiz design. Multicoloured. P* 14½.

218 20 c. Type **95** .. 35 25
219 80 c. Cook and Whitby Harbour .. 1·40 1·25

MINIMUM PRICE

The minimum price quote is 10p which represents a handling charge rather than a basis for valuing common stamps. For further notes about prices see introductory pages.

96 H.M.S. *Resolution*

97 Assembly Building

(Des G. Hitch)

1979 (14 Feb). *Death Bicentenary of Captain Cook. T* **96** *and similar horiz designs. Multicoloured. P* 14.

220 20 c. Type **96** .. 80 30
a. Pair. Nos. 220/1 .. 1·60 60
221 20 c. Cook (statue) .. 80 30
222 40 c. Cook's death .. 90 50
a. Pair. Nos. 222/3 .. 1·75 1·00
223 40 c. Cook's death (*different*) .. 90 50
220/23 .. *Set of* 4 3·00 1·60

The 20 c. designs depict the *Resolution* and Cook's statue on a map showing the last voyage. The 40 c. designs show Cook's death from an aquatint by John Clevely.

Nos. 220/1 and 222/3 were each printed together, *se-tenant*, in horizontal pairs throughout the sheets, forming composite designs.

1979 (10 Aug). *First Norfolk Island Legislative Assembly. P* 14½ × 14.

224 **97** $1 multicoloured .. 50 50

98 Tasmania 1853 1d. Stamp and Sir Rowland Hill

1979 (27 Aug). *Death Centenary of Sir Rowland Hill. T* **98** *and similar horiz designs showing stamps and Sir Rowland Hill. P* 14 × 14½.

225 20 c. new blue and sepia .. 20 10
226 30 c. brown-red and olive-grey .. 25 15
227 55 c. violet and indigo .. 40 30
225/7 .. *Set of* 3 75 50
MS228 142 × 91 mm. No. 227. P 14 .. 55 1·00

Designs:—30 c. Penny Red; 55 c. 1d. "Ball Bay".

99 I.Y.C. Emblem and Map of Pacific showing Norfolk Island as Pine Tree

(Des Claire Walters. Litho Asher and Co, Melbourne)

1979 (25 Sept). *International Year of the Child. P* 15.

229 **99** 80 c. multicoloured .. 40 45

100 Emily Bay

101 Lions International Emblem

1979 (5 Nov).* *Christmas. T* **100** *and similar horiz designs showing different aspects of Emily Bay. P* 12½ × 13.

230 15 c. multicoloured .. 15 15
a. Horiz strip of 3. Nos. 230/2 .. 40
231 20 c. multicoloured .. 15 15
232 30 c. multicoloured .. 15 15
230/2 .. *Set of* 3 40 40
MS233 152 × 83 mm. Nos. 230/2. P 14 × 14½ .. 1·00 1·25

Nos. 230/2 were printed together, *se-tenant*, in horizontal strips of 3 throughout the sheet, forming a composite design.

*Although released by the Crown Agents in London on 2 October the stamps were not released locally until 5 November.

(Des Norfolk Island Lions Club. Litho Asher and Co, Melbourne)

1980 (25 Jan). *Lions Convention. P* 15.

234 **101** 50 c. multicoloured .. 35 30

102 Rotary International Emblem

(Des E. Lenthall. Litho Asher and Co, Melbourne)

1980 (21 Feb). *75th Anniv of Rotary International. P* 15.

235 **102** 50 c. multicoloured .. 35 30
a. Black (face value and "NORFOLK ISLAND") omitted ..

103 "D.H. 60 (Gypsy Moth)" *Mme Elijah*

(Des G. Hitch. Litho Harrison)

1980 (25 Mar)–**81.** *Aeroplanes. Horiz designs as T* **103.** *Multicoloured. P* 14½ × 14.

236 1 c. Hawker Siddeley "H.S. 748" (3.3.81) .. 15 20
237 2 c. Type **103** .. 15 20
238 3 c. Curtis "P-40 Kittyhawk" .. 15 20
239 4 c. Chance Vought "F4U-1 Corsair" (19.8.80) .. 15 20
240 5 c. Grumman "TBF-1c Avenger" (19.8.80) .. 15 20
241 15 c. Douglas "SBD-5 Dauntless" (19.8.80) .. 30 30
242 20 c. Cessna "172" .. 30 30
243 25 c. Lockheed "Hudson" (3.3.81) .. 30 35
244 30 c. Lockheed "PV-1 Ventura" (13.1.81) .. 40 35
245 40 c. Avro "York" (3.3.81) .. 50 45
246 50 c. Douglas "DC-3" (13.1.81) .. 65 55
247 60 c. Avro "691 Lancastrian" (13.1.81) .. 75 65
248 80 c. Douglas "DC-4" (13.1.81) .. 95 85
249 $1 Beechcraft "Super King Air" (3.3.81) .. 1·25 90
250 $2 Fokker "F-27 Friendship" (19.8.80) .. 2·50 90
251 $5 Lockheed "C-130 Hercules" .. 6·00 2·00
236/51 .. *Set of* 16 13·00 7·75

104 Queen Elizabeth the Queen Mother

(Des K. Williams. Litho Harrison)

1980 (4 Aug). *80th Birthday of Queen Elizabeth the Queen Mother. P* 14.

252 **104** 22 c. multicoloured .. 30 20
253 60 c. multicoloured .. 65 40

105 Red-tailed Tropic Birds

(Des K. Williams. Litho Harrison)

1980 (28 Oct). *Christmas. Birds. T* **105** *and similar horiz designs. Multicoloured. P* 14 × 14½.

254 15 c. Type **105** .. 35 25
a. Horiz strip of 3. Nos. 254/6 .. 95
255 22 c. White Terns .. 35 25
256 35 c. White-capped Noddys .. 35 25
257 60 c. White Terns (*different*) .. 60 45
254/7 .. *Set of* 4 1·50 1·10

Nos. 254/6 were printed together, *se-tenant*, in horizontal strips of 3 throughout the sheet.

106 *Morayshire* and View of Norfolk Island

107 Wedding Bouquet from Norfolk Island

(Des Jennifer Toombs. Litho Harrison)

1981 (5 June). *125th Anniv of Pitcairn Islanders' Migration to Norfolk Island. T* **106** *and similar horiz designs. Multicoloured. P* 14½.

258 5 c. Type **106** .. 15 15
259 35 c. Islanders arriving ashore .. 55 30
260 60 c. View of new settlement .. 85 45
258/60 .. *Set of* 3 1·40 80
MS261 183 × 127 mm. Nos. 258/60 .. 2·00 1·75

(Des J.W. Litho Harrison)

1981 (22 July). *Royal Wedding. T* **107** *and similar vert designs. Multicoloured. P* 14.

262 35 c. Type **107** .. 20 15
263 55 c. Prince Charles at horse trials .. 35 25
264 60 c. Prince Charles and Lady Diana Spencer 35 35
262/4 .. *Set of* 3 80 65

108 Uniting Church of Australia

109 Pair of White-chested White Eyes

(Des K. Williams. Litho Harrison)

1981 (15 Sept). *Christmas. Churches. T* **108** *and similar horiz designs. Multicoloured. P* 14½ × 14.
265 18 c. Type **108** 20 10
266 24 c. Seventh Day Adventist Church 25 15
267 30 c. Church of the Sacred Heart 30 20
268 $1 St. Barnabas Chapel 70 70
265/8 .. .. *Set of* 4 1·25 1·00

(Des P. Slater. Litho Questa)

1981 (10 Nov). *White-chested White Eye ("Silvereye"). T* **109** *and similar horiz designs. Multicoloured. P* 14 × 14½.
269 35 c. Type **109** 45 40
a. Horiz strip of 5. Nos. 269/73 .. .. 2·25
270 35 c. Bird on nest 45 40
271 35 c. Bird with egg 45 40
272 35 c. Parents with chicks 45 40
273 35 c. Fledgelings 45 40
269/73 .. .. *Set of* 5 2·25 2·00
Nos. 269/73 were printed together, *se-tenant*, in horizontal strips of 5 throughout the sheet.

110 Aerial View of Philip Island

(Des local artist. Litho Harrison)

1982 (12 Jan). *Philip and Nepean Islands. T* **110** *and similar horiz designs. Multicoloured. P* 14 × 13½.
274 24 c. Type **110** 30 25
a. Horiz strip of 5. Nos. 274/8 .. .. 1·40
275 24 c. Close-up view of Philip Island landscape 30 25
276 24 c. Gecko (*Phyllodactylus guentheri*), Philip Island 30 25
277 24 c. Sooty Tern (*Sterna fuscata*), Philip Island 30 25
278 24 c. Philip Island Hibiscus (*Hibiscus insularis*) 30 25
279 35 c. Aerial view of Nepean Island 40 35
a. Horiz strip of 5. Nos. 279/83 .. .. 1·75
280 35 c. Close-up view of Nepean Island landscape 40 35
281 35 c. Gecko (*Phyllodactylus guentheri*), Nepean Island 40 35
282 35 c. Blue-faced Boobies (*Sula dactylatra*), Nepean Island 40 35
283 35 c. *Carpobrotus glaucescens* (flower), Nepean Island 40 35
274/83 .. .. *Set of* 10 3·00 2·50
The five designs of each value were printed together, *se-tenant*, in horizontal strips of 5 throughout the sheet.

111 Sperm Whale

(Des Jennifer Toombs. Litho Harrison)

1982 (23 Feb). *Whales. T* **111** *and similar horiz designs. P* 14½.
284 24 c. multicoloured 45 35
285 55 c. multicoloured 85 75
286 80 c. black, mauve and stone .. .. .. 1·10 1·00
284/6 .. .. *Set of* 3 2·25 1·90
Designs:—55 c. Black Right Whale; 80 c. Humpback Whale.

112 *Diocet*, Wrecked 20 April 1873

(Litho Harrison)

1982 (18 May–27 July). *Shipwrecks. T* **112** *and similar horiz designs. Multicoloured. P* 14½ × 14.
287 24 c. H.M.S. *Sirius*, wrecked 19 March 1790 (27 July) 50 50
288 27 c. Type **112** 50 50
289 35 c. *Friendship*, wrecked 17 May 1835 (27 July) 70 70
290 40 c. *Mary Hamilton*, wrecked 6 May 1873 .. 80 80
291 55 c. *Fairlie*, wrecked 14 February 1840 (27 July) 95 95
292 65 c. *Warrigal*, wrecked 18 March 1918 .. 1·25 1·25
287/92 .. .. *Set of* 6 4·25 4·25

C-KURITY PAPER. The following issues up to No. 342 were all printed on this type of security paper, *unless otherwise stated.* It shows a pattern of blue fluorescent markings, resembling rosettes, on the reverse beneath the gum.

113 R.N.Z.A.F. "Hudson" dropping Christmas Supplies, 1942

114 50th (Queen's Own) Regiment

(Des A. Theobald. Litho Walsall)

1982 (7 Sept). *Christmas. 40th Anniv of first Supply-plane Landings on Norfolk Island (Christmas Day 1942). T* **113** *and similar horiz designs. Multicoloured. P* 14.
293 27 c. Type **113** 30 35
294 40 c. "Hudson" landing Christmas supplies, 1942 .. .. 45 65
295 75 c. Christmas, 1942 .. .. 90 1·40
293/5 .. .. *Set of* 3 1·50 2·25

(Des W. Fenton. Litho Questa)

1982 (9 Nov). *Military Uniforms. T* **114** *and similar vert designs. Multicoloured. P* 14½ × 14.
296 27 c. Type **114** 30 35
297 40 c. 58th (Rutlandshire) Regiment 45 75
298 55 c. 80th (Staffordshire Volunteers) Battalion Company 65 95
299 65 c. 11th (North Devonshire) Regiment .. 80 1·25
296/9 .. .. *Set of* 4 2·00 3·00

115 *Panaeolus papilionaceus*

116 Beechcraft "18" Aircraft

(Des Jane Thatcher. Litho Enschedé)

1983 (29 Mar). *Fungi. T* **115** *and similar vert designs. Multicoloured. P* 13½ × 13.
300 27 c. Type **115** 45 35
301 40 c. *Coprinus domesticus* 70 50
302 55 c. *Marasmius niveus* 95 70
303 65 c. *Cymatoderma elegans* var *lamellatum* 1·25 85
300/3 .. .. *Set of* 4 3·00 2·25

(Des Walsall. Litho Format)

1983 (12 July). *Bicentenary of Manned Flight. T* **116** *and similar horiz designs. Multicoloured. P* 14½ × 14.
304 10 c. Type **116** 15 15
305 27 c. Fokker "F28 Fellowship" 30 35
306 45 c. French military "DC 4" 50 60
307 75 c. Sikorsky helicopter 90 95
304/7 .. .. *Set of* 4 1·60 1·90
MS308 105 × 100 mm. Nos. 304/7 .. .. 2·00 2·50

117 St. Matthew

118 Cable Ship *Chantik*

(Des McCombie-Skinner Studio. Litho Format)

1983 (13 Sept). *Christmas. 150th Birth Anniv of Sir Edward Burne-Jones. T* **117** *and similar vert designs showing stained-glass windows from St. Barnabas Chapel, Norfolk Island. Multicoloured. P* 14.
309 5 c. Type **117** 10 10
310 24 c. St. Mark 30 30
311 30 c. Jesus Christ 40 40
312 45 c. St. Luke 55 55
313 85 c. St. John .. .. 1·10 1·10
309/13 .. .. *Set of* 5 2·25 2·25

(Des G. Drummond. Litho Format)

1983 (15 Nov). *World Communications Year. ANZCAN Cable. T* **118** *and similar horiz designs. Multicoloured. Ordinary paper. P* 14½ × 14.
314 30 c. Type **118** 40 40
315 45 c. *Chantik* during in-shore operations .. 55 55
316 75 c. Cable ship *Mercury* 95 95
317 85 c. Diagram of cable route .. .. .. 1·10 1·10
314/17 .. .. *Set of* 4 2·75 2·75

119 Popwood

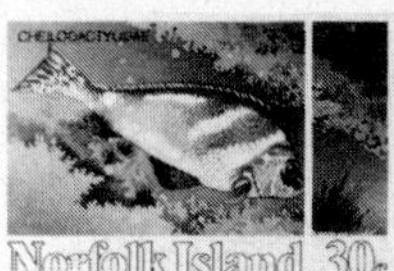

120 *Cheilodactylidae*

(Des I. Loe. Litho B.D.T.)

1984 (10 Jan–27 Mar). *Flowers. T* **119** *and similar vert designs. Multicoloured. P* 14.
318 1 c. Type **119** (27.3) 20 20
319 2 c. Strand Morning Glory 30 20
320 3 c. Native Phreatia 35 20
321 4 c. Philip Island Wisteria (27.3) 35 20
322 5 c. Norfolk Island Palm (27.3) 35 20
323 10 c. Evergreen 40 20
324 15 c. Bastard Oak (27.3) 50 30
325 20 c. Devil's Guts 50 30
326 25 c. White Oak 60 35
327 30 c. Ti (27.3) 70 40
328 35 c. Philip Island Hibiscus (27.3) 70 40
329 40 c. Native Wisteria 80 45
330 50 c. Native Jasmine .. .. 1·25 50
331 $1 Norfolk Island Hibiscus (27.3) .. .. 1·25 1·00
332 $3 Native Oberonia (27.3) .. .. .. 3·00 2·75
333 $5 Norfolk Island Pine .. .. 4·50 4·00
318/33 .. .. *Set of* 16 14·00 10·50

(Des Marg Towt. Litho Cambec Press, Melbourne)

1984 (17 Apr). *Reef Fishes. T* **120** *and similar horiz designs. Multicoloured. Ordinary paper. P* 13½ × 14.
334 30 c. Type **120** 40 45
335 45 c. *Pseudopeneus signatus* 60 65
336 75 c. *Acanthuridae* .. .. 1·00 1·10
337 85 c. *Chaeton ancinetus* .. .. 1·25 1·40
334/7 .. .. *Set of* 4 2·75 3·25

121 Owl with Eggs

122 1953 7½d. and 1974 Cook Bicent 10 c. Stamps

(Des P. Slater. Litho Questa)

1984 (17 July). *Boobook Owl. T* **121** *and similar vert designs. Multicoloured. P* 14.
338 30 c. Type **121** 65 50
a. Horiz strip of 5. Nos. 338/42 .. .. 3·00
339 30 c. Fledgeling 65 50
340 30 c. Young owl on stump 65 50
341 30 c. Adult on branch 65 50
342 30 c. Owl in flight 65 50
338/42 .. .. *Set of* 5 3·00 2·25
Nos. 338/42 were printed together, *se-tenant*, in horizontal strips of 5 throughout the sheet.

(Des D. Miller. Litho Harrison)

1984 (18 Sept). *"Ausipex" International Stamp Exhibition, Melbourne. T* **122** *and similar horiz designs. Multicoloured. W w* 14 (*sideways*). *P* 14.
343 30 c. Type **122** 30 35
344 45 c. John Buffett commemorative postal stationery envelope 45 75
345 75 c. Design from Presentation Pack for 1982 Military Uniforms issue .. .. .. 90 1·75
343/5 .. .. *Set of* 3 1·50 2·50
MS346 151 × 93 mm. Nos. 343/5. P 14½ .. .. 3·50 3·75

123 Font, Kingston Methodist Church

124 The Revd. Nobbs teaching Pitcairn Islanders

(Des R. Murphy. Litho Questa)

1984 (9 Oct). *Christmas. Centenary of Methodist Church on Norfolk Island. T* **123** *and similar vert designs. Multicoloured. W w* **14**. *P* 14.
347 5 c. Type **123** 10 10
348 24 c. Church service in Old Barracks, Kingston, late 1800's 35 40
349 30 c. The Revd. & Mrs. A. H. Phelps and sailing ship 40 45
350 45 c. The Revd. A. H. Phelps and First Congregational Church, Chester, U.S.A. 60 65
351 85 c. Interior of Kingston Methodist Church .. 1·25 1·40
347/51 .. .. *Set of* 5 2·40 2·50

(Des D. Hopkins. Litho B.D.T.)

1984 (6 Nov). *Death Centenary of the Revd. George Hunn Nobbs (leader of Pitcairn community). T* **124** *and similar vert designs. Multicoloured. W w* **14.** *P* 14 × 15.

352 30 c. Type **124** 40 45
353 45 c. The Revd. Nobbs with sick islander .. 60 65
354 75 c. Baptising baby .. .. 1·00 1·10
355 85 c. Presented to Queen Victoria, 1852 .. 1·25 1·40
352/5 .. .. *Set of* 4 3·00 3·25

125 *Fanny Fisher*

126 The Queen Mother (from photo by Norman Parkinson)

(Des D. Hopkins. Litho Cambec Press, Melbourne)

1985 (19 Feb). *19th-Century Whaling Ships* (*1st series*). *T* **125** *and similar horiz designs. Multicoloured. P* 13½ × 14.

356 5 c. Type **125** 30 15
357 33 c. *Costa Rica Packet* 85 55
358 50 c. *Splendid* .. .. 1·25 1·00
359 90 c. *Onward* .. .. 1·75 1·75
356/9 .. .. *Set of* 4 3·75 3·00
See also Nos. 360/3.

(Des D. Hopkins. Litho Cambec Press, Melbourne)

1985 (30 Apr). *19th-Century Whaling Ships* (*2nd series*). *Horiz designs as T* **125**. *Multicoloured. P* 13½ × 14.

360 15 c. *Waterwitch* 50 50
361 20 c. *Canton* 60 60
362 60 c. *Aladdin* .. .. 1·25 1·25
363 80 c. *California* .. .. 1·60 1·75
360/3 .. .. *Set of* 4 3·50 3·75

(Des A. Theobald ($1), C. Abbott (others). Litho Questa)

1985 (6 June). *Life and Times of Queen Elizabeth the Queen Mother. T* **126** *and similar vert designs. Multicoloured. W w* **16.** *P* 14½ × 14.

364 5 c. The Queen Mother (from photo by Dorothy Wilding) 10 10
365 33 c. With Princess Anne at Trooping the Colour 35 40
366 50 c. Type **126**.. .. .. 50 55
367 90 c. With Prince Henry at his christening (from photo by Lord Snowdon).. .. 95 1·00
364/7 .. .. *Set of* 4 1·75 1·90
MS368 91 × 73 mm. $1 With Princess Anne at Ascot Races. Wmk sideways .. .. .. 1·10 1·25

127 "Swimming"

128 Prize-winning Cow and Owner

(Des from children's paintings. Litho Cambec Press, Melbourne)

1985 (9 July). *International Youth Year. T* **127** *and similar horiz design. Multicoloured. P* 13½ × 14.

369 33 c. Type **127**.. .. .. 75 40
370 50 c. "A Walk in the Country" .. .. .. 1·50 85

(Des Flett Henderson & Arnold. Litho Cambec Press, Melbourne)

1985 (10 Sept). *125th Anniv of Royal Norfolk Island Agricultural and Horticultural Show. T* **128** *and similar horiz design. Multicoloured. P* 13½ × 14.

371 80 c. Type **128**.. .. .. 75 80
372 90 c. Show exhibits 85 90
MS373 132 × 85 mm. Nos. 371/2 .. .. .. 1·75 2·50

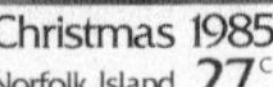

129 Shepherds with Flock

130 Long-spined Sea Urchin

(Des R. Murphy. Litho Cambec Press, Melbourne)

1985 (3 Oct). *Christmas. T* **129** *and similar vert designs. Multicoloured. P* 13½.

374 27 c. Type **129**.. .. .. 60 30
375 33 c. Mary and Joseph with donkey.. .. 75 40
376 50 c. The Three Wise Men .. .. .. 1·40 65
377 90 c. The Nativity .. .. 1·75 1·25
374/7 .. .. *Set of* 4 4·00 2·25

(Des L. Curtis. Litho Cambec Press, Melbourne)

1986 (14 Jan). *Marine Life. T* **130** *and similar horiz designs. Multicoloured. P* 13½ × 14.

378 5 c. Type **130**.. .. .. 10 10
379 33 c. Blue Starfish 40 35
380 55 c. Eagle Ray 60 75
381 75 c. Moray Eel .. .. 85 1·00
378/81 .. .. *Set of* 4 1·75 2·00
MS382 100 × 95 mm. Nos. 378/81 .. .. .. 2·75 3·00

131 *Giotto* Spacecraft

132 Isaac Robinson (U.S. Consul 1887–1908)

(Des G. Revell. Litho Leigh-Mardon Ltd, Melbourne)

1986 (11 Mar). *Appearance of Halley's Comet. T* **131** *and similar vert design. Multicoloured. P* 14½ × 15.

383 $1 Type **131** .. .. 1·50 1·75
a. Horiz pair. Nos. 383/4 .. .. .. 3·00 3·50
384 $1 Halley's Comet .. .. 1·50 1·75
Nos. 383/4 were printed together, *se-tenant*, in horizontal pairs throughout the sheet, each pair forming a composite design.

(Des G. Revell. Litho Cambec Press, Melbourne)

1986 (22 May). *"Ameripex'86" International Stamp Exhibition, Chicago. T* **132** *and similar multicoloured designs. P* 13½.

385 33 c. Type **132**.. .. .. 60 35
386 50 c. Ford "Model T" (first vehicle on island) (*horiz*) 80 50
387 80 c. Statue of Liberty .. .. 1·10 80
385/7 .. .. *Set of* 3 2·25 1·50
MS388 125 × 100 mm. Nos. 385/7 .. .. 2·50 2·50
No. 387 also commemorates the Centenary of the Statue of Liberty.

133 Princess Elizabeth and Dog

134 Stylized Dove and Norfolk Island

(Des Allison Ryves. Litho Cambec Press, Melbourne)

1986 (12 June). *60th Birthday of Queen Elizabeth II. T* **133** *and similar vert designs. Multicoloured. P* 13½.

389 5 c. Type **133**.. .. .. 10 10
390 33 c. Queen Elizabeth II 50 35
391 80 c. Opening Norfolk Island Golf Club .. 1·25 1·40
392 90 c. With Duke of Edinburgh in carriage .. 1·50 1·60
389/92 .. .. *Set of* 4 3·00 3·00

(Des Lyn Studham. Litho Cambec Press, Melbourne)

1986 (23 Sept). *Christmas. P* 13½ × 14.

393 **134** 30 c. multicoloured 35 30
394 40 c. multicoloured 50 45
395 $1 multicoloured .. .. 1·40 1·50
393/5 .. .. *Set of* 3 2·00 2·00

135 British Convicts, 1787

136 Stone Tools

(Des Josephine Martin. Litho Cambec Press, Melbourne)

1986 (14 Oct–16 Dec). *Bicentenary of Norfolk Island Settlement* (1988) (*1st issue*). *Governor Phillip's Commission. T* **135** *and similar vert designs. Multicoloured. P* 14 × 13½.

396 36 c. Type **135**.. .. .. 75 35
397 55 c. Judge passing sentence of transportation .. .. 1·25 65
398 90 c. Governor Phillip meeting Home Secretary (inscr "Home Society") .. .. 1·90 1·25
399 90 c. As No. 398, but correctly inscr "Home Secretary" (16.12) .. .. .. 1·90 1·25
400 $1 Captain Arthur Phillip.. .. .. 2·00 1·40
396/400 .. .. *Set of* 5 7·00 4·50
See also Nos. 401/4, 421/4, 433/5, 436/7 and 438/43.

(Des B. Clinton. Litho Cambec Press, Melbourne)

1986 (16 Dec). *Bicentenary of Norfolk Island Settlement* (1988) (*2nd issue*). *Pre-European Occupation. T* **136** *and similar horiz designs. Multicoloured. P* 13½.

401 36 c. Type **136**.. .. .. 65 45
402 36 c. Bananas and taro 65 45
403 36 c. Polynesian outrigger canoe 65 45
404 36 c. Maori chief 65 45
401/4 .. .. *Set of* 4 2·40 1·60

137 Philip Island from Point Ross

138 Male Red-fronted Parakeet

(Des C. Abbott. Litho CPE Australia Ltd, Melbourne)

1987 (17 Feb)–**88**. *Norfolk Island Scenes. T* **137** *and similar square designs. Multicoloured. P* 13½.

405 1 c. Cockpit Creek Bridge (17.5.88) 20 30
406 2 c. Cemetery Bay Beach (17.5.88) 20 30
407 3 c. Island guesthouse (17.5.88) 20 30
408 5 c. Type **137**.. .. .. 20 15
409 15 c. Cattle in pasture (27.7.87) 25 30
410 30 c. Rock fishing (7.4.87) 30 30
411 37 c. Old Pitcairner-style house (27.7.87) .. 50 50
412 40 c. Shopping centre (7.4.87) 35 35
413 50 c. Emily Bay 45 45
414 60 c. Bloody Bridge (27.7.87) 65 75
415 80 c. Pitcairner-style shop (7.4.87) 85 95
416 90 c. Government House .. .. 85 1·10
417 $1 Melanesian Memorial Chapel 90 95
418 $2 Convict Settlement, Kingston (7.4.87).. 1·75 1·75
419 $3 Ball Bay (27.7.87) .. .. 3·00 3·25
420 $5 Northern cliffs (17.5.88) .. .. 4·75 5·50
405/20 .. .. *Set of* 16 14·00 15·00

(Des Josephine Martin. Litho CPE Australia Ltd, Melbourne)

1987 (13 May). *Bicentenary of Norfolk Island Settlement* (1988) (*3rd issue*). *The First Fleet. Vert designs as T* **135**. *Multicoloured. P* 14 × 13½.

421 5 c. Loading supplies, Deptford 40 40
422 55 c. Fleet leaving Spithead .. .. .. 1·40 1·50
a. Horiz pair. Nos. 422/3 .. .. .. 2·75 3·00
423 55 c. H.M.S. *Sirius* leaving Spithead .. 1·40 1·50
424 $1 Female convicts below decks .. .. 2·25 2·25
421/4 .. .. *Set of* 4 4·75 5·00
Nos. 422/3 were printed together, *se-tenant*, in horizontal pairs throughout the sheet, forming a composite design.

(Des P. Slater. Litho CPE Australia Ltd, Melbourne)

1987 (16 Sept). *Red-fronted Parakeet* ("*Green Parrot*"). *T* **138** *and similar vert designs. Multicoloured. P* 14 × 13½.

425 5 c. Type **138**.. .. .. 60 60
a. Horiz strip of 4. Nos. 425/8 .. .. 4·75
426 15 c. Adult with fledgeling and egg.. .. 1·00 1·00
427 36 c. Young parakeets .. .. 1·75 1·75
428 55 c. Female parakeet .. .. 2·00 2·00
425/8 .. .. *Set of* 4 4·75 4·75
Nos. 425/8 were printed together, *se-tenant*, in horizontal strips of four throughout the sheet.

139 Christmas Tree and Restored Garrison Barracks

140 Airliner, Container Ship and Sydney Harbour Bridge

(Des T. Bland and Alison Ryves. Litho CPE Australia Ltd, Melbourne)

1987 (13 Oct). *Christmas. T* **139** *and similar horiz designs. Multicoloured. P* 13½ × 14.

429 30 c. Type **139**.. .. .. 30 30
430 42 c. Children opening presents 45 55
431 58 c. Father Christmas with children .. 60 65
432 63 c. Children's party 70 80
429/32 .. .. *Set of* 4 1·90 2·10

(Des Josephine Martin. Litho CPE Australia Ltd, Melbourne)

1987 (8 Dec). *Bicentenary of Norfolk Island Settlement* (1988) (*4th issue*). *Visit of La Perouse* (*navigator*). *Vert designs as T* **135**. *Multicoloured. P* 14 × 13½.

433 37 c. La Perouse with King Louis XVI .. 75 55
434 90 c. *L'Astrolabe* and *La Boussole* off Norfolk Island .. .. 1·75 2·00
435 $1 *L'Astrolabe* wrecked in Solomon Islands 2·25 2·50
433/5 .. .. *Set of* 3 4·25 4·50

(Des Josephine Martin. Litho CPE Australia Ltd, Melbourne)

1988 (25 Jan). *Bicentenary of Norfolk Island Settlement* (*5th issue*). *Arrival of First Fleet at Sydney. Vert designs as T* **135**. *Multicoloured. P* 14 × 13½.

436 37 c. Ship's cutter approaching Port Jackson 90 65
437 $1 Landing at Sydney Cove .. .. .. 2·10 2·10

(Des Josephine Martin. Litho CPE Australia Ltd, Melbourne)

1988 (4 Mar). *Bicentenary of Norfolk Island Settlement (6th issue). Foundation of First Settlement. Vert designs as T* **135**. *Multicoloured. P* 14 × 13½.

438 5 c. Lt. Philip Gidley King 20 20
439 37 c. Raising the flag, March 1788 .. .. 75 75
440 55 c. King exploring .. .. 1·25 1·25
441 70 c. Landing at Sydney Bay, Norfolk Island 1·50 1·50
442 90 c. H.M.S. *Supply* (brig) .. .. .. 1·75 1·75
443 $1 Sydney Bay settlement, 1788 .. .. 1·90 1·90
438/43 .. .. *Set of* 6 6·50 6·50

(Des Janet Boschen. Litho CPE Australia Ltd, Melbourne)

1988 (30 July). *"Sydpex '88" National Stamp Exhibition, Sydney. T* **140** *and similar multicoloured designs. P* 14 × 13½ *(vert) or* 13½ × 14 *(horiz).*

444 37 c. Type **140** 55 65
445 37 c. Exhibition label under magnifying glass *(horiz)* 55 65
446 37 c. Telephone and dish aerial 55 65
444/6 .. .. *Set of* 3 1·50 1·75
MS447 118×84 mm. Nos. 444/6 .. .. .. 2·00 2·25

In No. **MS**447 the horizontal design is perforated 14 at foot and 13½ on the other three sides.

141 Flowers and Decorations

142 Pier Store and Boat Shed

(Des Sue Pearson. Litho CPE Australia Ltd, Melbourne)

1988 (27 Sept). *Christmas. T* **141** *and similar vert designs. Multicoloured. P* 14 × 13½.

448 30 c. Type **141** 40 40
449 42 c. Flowers 60 70
450 58 c. Fishes and beach 75 85
451 63 c. Norfolk Island .. .. 85 1·00
448/51 .. .. *Set of* 4 2·40 2·75

(Des R. Murphy. Litho CPE Australia Ltd, Melbourne)

1988 (6 Dec). *Restored Buildings from the Convict Era. T* **142** *and similar horiz designs. Multicoloured. P* 13½ × 14.

452 39 c. Type **142** 35 40
453 55 c. Royal Engineers Building 50 55
454 90 c. Old Military Barracks 85 90
455 $1 Commissariat Store and New Military Barracks .. .. 95 1·00
452/5 .. .. *Set of* 4 2·40 2·50

143 *Lamprima aenea*

144 H.M.S. *Bounty* off Tasmania

(Des T. Nolan. Litho CPE Australia Ltd, Melbourne)

1989 (14 Feb). *Endemic Insects. T* **143** *and similar horiz designs. Multicoloured. P* 13½ × 14.

456 39 c. Type **143** 45 40
457 55 c. *Insulascirtus nythos* 60 70
458 90 c. *Caedicia araucariae* .. .. .. 1·00 1·10
459 $1 *Thrincophora aridela* .. .. .. 1·10 1·25
456/9 .. .. *Set of* 4 2·75 3·00

(Des C. Abbott. Litho CPE Australia Ltd, Melbourne (Nos. 460/3), B.D.T. (No. **MS**464))

1989 (28 Apr). *Bicentenary of the Mutiny on the* Bounty. *T* **144** *and similar horiz designs. Multicoloured. P* 13½.

460 5 c. Type **144** 30 30
461 39 c. Mutineers and Polynesian women, Pitcairn Island .. .. 1·25 1·25
462 55 c. Lake Windermere, Cumbria (Christian's home county) .. .. 1·75 1·75
463 $1.10, "Mutineers casting Bligh adrift" (Robert Dodd) .. .. .. 2·50 2·50
460/3 .. .. *Set of* 4 5·25 5·25
MS464 110×85 mm. 39 c. No. 461; 90 c. Isle of Man 1989 Mutiny 35p., No. 414; $1 Pitcairn Islands 1989 Settlement Bicent 90 c., No. 345. P 14 .. .. 4·00 4·00

145 Norfolk Island Flag

146 Red Cross

(Des R. Fletcher. Litho CPE Australia Ltd, Melbourne)

1989 (10 Aug). *10th Anniv of Internal Self-Government. T* **145** *and similar vert designs. Multicoloured. P* 14×13½.

465 41 c. Type **145** 60 55
466 55 c. Old ballot box 70 65
467 $1 Norfolk Island Act, 1979 .. .. 1·40 1·40
468 $1.10, Island crest .. .. 1·50 1·60
465/8 .. .. *Set of* 4 3·75 3·75

(Des E. Lenthall. Litho CPE Australia Ltd, Melbourne)

1989 (25 Sept). *75th Anniv of Red Cross on Norfolk Island. P* 13½.

469 **146** $1 bright rose-red and ultramarine .. 2·00 1·75

147 "Gethsemane"

148 John Royle (first announcer)

(Des Sue Pearson. Litho CPE Australia Ltd, Melbourne)

1989 (9 Oct). *Christmas. T* **147** *and similar horiz designs showing opening lines of hymns and local scenes. Multicoloured. P* 13½×14.

470 36 c. Type **147** 70 40
471 60 c. "In the Sweet Bye and Bye" .. .. 1·10 1·10
472 75 c. "Let the Lower Lights Be Burning" .. 1·40 1·40
473 80 c. "The Beautiful Stream" .. .. .. 1·50 1·75
470/3 .. .. *Set of* 4 4·25 4·25

(Des Philatelic Studios. Litho Leigh-Mardon Ltd, Melbourne)

1989 (21 Nov). *50th Anniv of Radio Australia. T* **148** *and similar vert designs each showing Kingston buildings. Multicoloured. P* 14×13½.

474 41 c. Type **148** 75 55
475 65 c. Radio waves linking Australia and Norfolk Island .. .. 1·25 1·25
476 $1.10, Anniversary kookaburra logo .. 2·00 2·00
474/6 .. .. *Set of* 3 3·50 3·50

149 H.M.S. *Bounty* on fire, Pitcairn Island, 1790

150 H.M.S. *Sirius* striking Reef

(Des G. Hitch. Litho Leigh-Mardon Ltd, Melbourne)

1990 (23 Jan). *History of the Norfolk Islanders (1st series). Settlement on Pitcairn Island. T* **149** *and similar vert design. Multicoloured. P* 14½.

477 70 c. Type **149** .. .. 1·50 1·50
478 $1.10, Arms of Norfolk Island .. .. 1·75 1·75

See also Nos. 503/4 and 516/17.

(Des Maree Edmiston. Litho Leigh-Mardon Ltd, Melbourne)

1990 (19 Mar). *Bicentenary of Wreck of H.M.S.* Sirius. *T* **150** *and similar horiz designs. Multicoloured. P* 13½.

479 41 c. Type **150** .. .. 1·00 1·00
a. Horiz pair. Nos. 479/80 .. .. .. 2·00 2·00
480 41 c. H.M.S. *Sirius* failing to clear bay .. 1·00 1·00
481 65 c. Divers at work on wreck .. .. 1·40 1·40
482 $1 Recovered artifacts and chart of site 2·00 2·00
479/82 .. .. *Set of* 4 5·00 5·00

Nos. 479/80 were printed together, *se-tenant*, in horizontal pairs throughout the sheet, each pair forming a composite design.

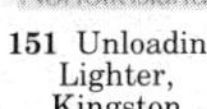

151 Unloading Lighter, Kingston

152 *Ile de Lumiere* (freighter)

(Des Philatelic Studios. Litho Leigh-Mardon Ltd, Melbourne)

1990 (17 July)–**91**. *Ships. T* **151** *and horiz designs as T* **152**. *P* 14×14½ *(5, 10 c.) or* 14½ *(others).*

483 **151** 5 c. purple-brown 10 10
484 10 c. ochre 10 10
485 – 45 c. multicoloured (19.2.91) 40 45
486 – 50 c. multicoloured (19.2.91) 45 50
487 – 65 c. multicoloured (19.2.91) 60 65
488 **152** 70 c. multicoloured 65 70
489 – 75 c. multicoloured (13.8.91) 70 75
490 – 80 c. multicoloured (13.8.91) 75 80
491 – 90 c. multicoloured (13.8.91) 85 90
492 – $1 multicoloured (13.8.91) 90 95
493 – $2 multicoloured .. .. 1·90 2·00
494 – $5 multicoloured (19.2.91) .. .. 4·50 4·75
483/94 .. .. *Set of* 12 10·50 11·50

Designs: *Horiz (as T* **152**)—45 c. *La Dunkerquoise* (French patrol vessel); 50 c. *Dmitri Mendeleev* (Soviet research vessel); 65 c. *Pacific Rover* (tanker); 75 c. *Norfolk Trader* (freighter); 80 c. *Roseville* (transport); 90 c. *Kalia* (container ship); $1 *Bounty* (replica); $2 H.M.A.S. *Success* (supply ship); $5 H.M.A.S. *Whyalla* (patrol vessel).

153 Santa on House Roof

154 William Charles Wentworth

(Des G. Hitch, adapted Philatelic Studios. Litho Leigh-Mardon Ltd, Melbourne)

1990 (25 Sept). *Christmas. T* **153** *and similar multicoloured designs. P* 14½.

499 38 c. Type **153** 50 45
500 43 c. Santa at Kingston Post Office 55 50
501 65 c. Santa over Sydney Bay, Kingston *(horiz)* 85 75
502 85 c. Santa on Officers' Quarters *(horiz)* .. 1·10 1·10
499/502 .. .. *Set of* 4 2·75 2·50

(Des G. Hitch. Litho Leigh-Mardon Ltd, Melbourne)

1990 (11 Oct). *History of the Norfolk Islanders (2nd series). The First Generation. T* **154** *and similar vert design. P* 14½.

503 70 c. reddish brown and pale cinnamon .. 85 85
504 $1.20, reddish brown and pale cinnamon 1·40 1·40

Designs:—$1.20, Thursday October Christian.

155 Adult Robin and Chicks in Nest

156 Map of Norfolk Island

(Des E. Monks. Litho Leigh-Mardon Ltd, Melbourne)

1990 (3 Dec). *"Birdpex '90" Stamp Exhibition, Christchurch, New Zealand. Scarlet Robin. T* **155** *and similar vert designs. Multicoloured. P* 14½.

505 65 c. Type **155** 75 75
506 $1 Hen on branch .. .. 1·25 1·25
507 $1.20, Cock on branch .. .. .. 1·40 1·40
505/7 .. .. *Set of* 3 3·00 3·00
MS508 70×90 mm. $1 Hen; $1 Cock and hen .. 2·40 2·50

(Des Philatelic Studios. Litho Leigh-Mardon Ltd, Melbourne)

1991 (9 Apr). *Ham Radio Network. T* **156** *and similar vert designs. Multicoloured. P* 14½.

509 43 c. Type **156** 60 50
510 $1 Globe showing Norfolk Island .. .. 1·40 1·40
511 $1.20, Map of South-west Pacific .. .. 1·60 1·75
509/11 .. .. *Set of* 3 3·25 3·25

157 Display in *Sirius* Museum

158 H.M.S. *Pandora* wrecked on Great Barrier Reef (1791)

(Des Philatelic Studios. Litho Leigh-Mardon Ltd, Melbourne)

1991 (16 May). *Norfolk Island Museums. T* **157** *and similar multicoloured designs. P* 14½

512 43 c. Type **157** 60 50
513 70 c. 19th-century sitting room, House Museum *(horiz)* 95 95
514 $1 Carronade, *Sirius* Museum *(horiz)* .. 1·40 1·40
515 $1.20, Reconstructed jug and beaker, Archaeological Museum .. .. .. 1·60 1·60
512/15 .. .. *Set of* 4 4·00 4·00

(Des Philatelic Studios. Litho Leigh-Mardon, Melbourne)

1991 (2 July). *History of the Norfolk Islanders (3rd series). Search for the* Bounty. *T* **158** *and similar horiz design. Multicoloured. P* 13½×14.

516 $1 Type **158** .. .. 1·40 1·40
517 $1.20, H.M.S. *Pandora* leaving bay .. 1·60 1·60

159 Hibiscus and Island Scene

160 Tank and Soldier in Jungle

(Des Philatelic Studios. Litho Leigh-Mardon Ltd, Melbourne)

1991 (23 Sept). *Christmas. P* 14½.

518 **159** 38 c. multicoloured 50 40
519 43 c. multicoloured 60 55
520 65 c. multicoloured 80 80
521 85 c. multicoloured .. .. .. 1·00 1·10
518/21 .. .. *Set of* 4 2·50 2·50

(Des Philatelic Studios. Litho Leigh-Mardon Ltd, Melbourne)

1991 (9 Dec). *50th Anniv of Outbreak of Pacific War. T* **160** *and similar horiz designs. Multicoloured. P* 14½.

522 43 c. Type **160** 55 45
523 70 c. B17 Flying Fortress on jungle airstrip 90 90
524 $1 Warships .. .. 1·40 1·50
522/4 .. .. *Set of* 3 2·50 2·50

161 Coat of Arms

(Des Philatelic Studios. Litho Leigh-Mardon Ltd, Melbourne)

1992 (11 Feb). *500th Anniv of Discovery of America by Columbus. T* **161** *and similar vert designs. Multicoloured. P* 14½.

525 45 c. Type **161** 40 45
526 $1.05, *Santa Maria* .. .. .. 95 1·00
527 $1.20, Columbus and globe .. .. 1·10 1·25
525/7 .. .. *Set of* 3 2·25 2·50

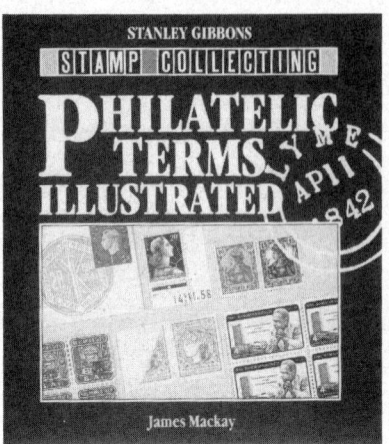

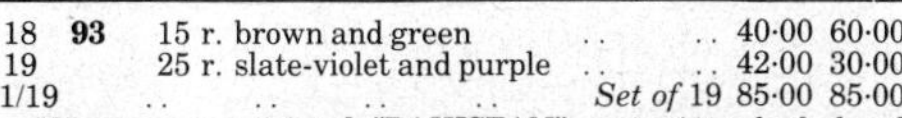

North Borneo
see Malaysia

Northern Nigeria
see Nigeria

Northern Rhodesia
see Zambia

North-West Pacific Islands
see Papua New Guinea

Nova Scotia
see Canada

Nyasaland Protectorate
see Malawi

Orange Free State
see South Africa

Pakistan

DOMINION

PAKISTAN (1) **PAKISTAN** (2)

1947 (1 Oct). *Stamps of India, optd by litho at Nasik, as T* **1** (*3 p. to 12 a.*) *or* **2** (*14 a. and rupee values*).

No.	Type	Value	Unused	Used
1	**100*a***	3 p. slate	10	10
2		½ a. purple	10	10
3		9 p. green	10	10
4		1 a. carmine	10	10
5	**101**	1½ a. dull violet	10	10
6		2 a. vermilion	10	10
7		3 a. bright violet	10	10
8		3½ a. bright blue	45	2·00
9	**102**	4 a. brown	10	10
10		6 a. turquoise-green	40	20
11		8 a. slate-violet	20	15
12		12 a. lake	1·00	15
13	**103**	14 a. purple	1·40	35
14	**93**	1 r. grey and red-brown	1·00	15
15		2 r. purple and brown	1·50	40
16		5 r. green and blue	2·75	1·25
17		10 r. purple and claret	4·00	90
18	**93**	15 r. brown and green	40·00	60·00
19		25 r. slate-violet and purple	42·00	30·00
1/19		*Set of* 19	85·00	85·00

Numerous provisional "PAKISTAN" overprints, both hand-stamped and machine-printed, in various sizes and colours, on Postage and Official stamps, also exist.

These were made under authority of Provincial Governments, District Head Postmasters or Local Postmasters and are of considerable philatelic interest.

The 1 a. 3 p. (India No. 269) exists only as a local issue (*price, Karachi opt, 70p. unused; £1.25 used*).

The 12 a., as No. 12 but overprinted at Karachi exists with overprint inverted (*Price £60 unused*).

The 1 r. value with local overprint exists with overprint inverted (*Price £150 unused*) or as a pair with one stamp without overprint (*Price £600 unused*).

3 Constituent Assembly Building, Karachi

6 Crescent and Stars

(Des A. R. Chughtai (1 r.). Recess D.L.R.)

1948 (9 July). *Independence. T* **3, 6** *and similar horiz designs. P* 13½ × 14 *or* 11½ (1 r.).

No.	Value	Unused	Used
20	1½ a. ultramarine	20	30
21	2½ a. green	20	10
22	3 a. purple-brown	20	10
23	1 r. scarlet	40	20
	a. Perf 14 × 13½	3·50	10·00
20/3	*Set of* 4	90	60

Designs:—2½ a. Karachi Airport entrance; 3 a. Gateway to Lahore Fort.

7 Scales of Justice

8 Star and Crescent

9 Lloyds Barrage

10 Karachi Airport

13 Khyber Pass

(Des M. M. A. Suharwardi (T **8**). Recess Pakistan Security Ptg Corp Ltd, Karachi (P 13 and 13½), D.L.R. (others))

1948 (14 Aug)–**56**?. *T* **7/10, 13** *and similar designs.*

No.	Type	Value	Unused	Used
24	**7**	3 p. red (*p* 12½)	10	10
		a. Perf 13½ (1954?)	10	10
25		6 p. violet (*p* 12½)	30	10
		a. Perf 13½ (1954?)	55	30
26		9 p. green (*p* 12½)	20	10
		a. Perf 13½ (1954?)	10	10
27	**8**	1 a. blue (*p* 12½)	10	10
28		1½ a. grey-green (*p* 12½)	10	10
29		2 a. red (*p* 12½)	20	10
30	**9**	2½ a. green (*p* 14×13½)	90	2·50
31	**10**	3 a. green (*p* 14)	60	20
32	**9**	3½ a. bright blue (*p* 14×13½)	55	2·00
33		4 a. reddish brown (*p* 12½)	25	10
34	–	6 a. blue (*p* 14×13½)	30	50
35	–	8 a. black (*p* 12½)	30	30
36	**10**	10 a. scarlet (*p* 14)	60	2·50
37	–	12 a. scarlet (*p* 14×13½)	1·75	30
38	–	1 r. ultramarine (*p* 14)	2·50	10
		a. Perf 13½ (1954?)	7·00	1·25
39	–	2 r. chocolate (*p* 14)	17·00	30
		a. Perf 13½ (1954?)	17·00	75
40	–	5 r. carmine (*p* 14)	11·00	30
		a. Perf 13½ (7.53)	8·50	20
41	**13**	10 r. magenta (*p* 14)	6·00	7·00
		a. Perf 12	35·00	3·00
		b. Perf 13 (1951)	11·00	30
42		15 r. blue-green (*p* 12)	13·00	8·50
		a. Perf 14	12·00	23·00
		b. Perf 13 (1956?)	15·00	12·00
43		25 r. violet (*p* 14)	35·00	38·00
		a. Perf 12	20·00	25·00
		b. Perf 13 (1954)	27·00	13·00
24/43		*Set of* 20	65·00	28·00

Designs: *Vert* (*as T* **7**)—6 a., 8 a., 12 a. Karachi Port Trust. (*As T* **10**)—1 r., 2 r., 5 r. Salimullah Hostel, Dacca.

For 25 r. with W **98**, see No. 210.

14 Star and Crescent

15 Karachi Airport

(Recess Pakistan Security Ptg Corp (P 13½), D.L.R. (others).

1949 (Feb)–**53**? *Redrawn. Crescent moon with points to left as T* **14/15**.

No.	Type	Value	Unused	Used
44	**14**	1 a. blue (*p* 12½)	1·75	10
		a. Perf 13½ (1953?)	1·75	10
45		1½ a. grey-green (*p* 12½)	1·75	10
		a. Perf 13½ (1952?)	1·75	10
46		2 a. red (*p* 12½)	1·75	10
		a. Perf 13½ (1953?)	1·75	10
47	**15**	3 a. green (*p* 14)	1·75	65
48	–	6 a. blue (as No. 34) (*p* 14×13½)	5·50	15
49	–	8 a. black (as No. 35) (*p* 12½)	2·75	35
50	**15**	10 a. scarlet (*p* 14)	5·00	60
51	–	12 a. scarlet (as No. 37) (*p* 14×13½)	8·50	15
44/51		*Set of* 8	26·00	1·90

16

(Recess D.L.R.)

1949 (11 Sept). *First Death Anniv of Mohammed Ali Jinnah. T* **16** *and similar design. P* 14.

No.	Type	Value	Unused	Used
52	**16**	1½ a. brown	1·25	55
53		3 a. green	1·25	55
54	–	10 a. black	2·75	4·25
52/4		*Set of* 3	4·75	4·75

Design:—10 a. Similar inscription reading "QUAID-I-AZAM/ MOHAMMAD ALI JINNAH" etc.

17 Pottery

18 Aeroplane and Hour-glass

Two Types of 3½ a.:

I

II

19 Saracenic Leaf Pattern

20 Archway and Lamp

(Des A. R. Chughtai. Recess D.L.R., later printings, Pakistan Security Ptg Corp)

1951 (14 Aug)–**56**. *Fourth Anniv of Independence. P* 13.

No.	Type	Value	Unused	Used
55	**17**	2½ a. carmine	70	35
56	**18**	3 a. purple	40	10
57	**17**	3½ a. blue (I)	60	1·00
57*a*		3½ a. blue (II)(12.56)	2·00	60
58	**19**	4 a. green	35	10
59		6 a. brown-orange	45	10
60	**20**	8 a. sepia	3·50	10
61		10 a. violet	80	10
62	**18**	12 a. slate	80	10
55/62		*Set of* 9	8·50	2·00

The above and the stamps issued on the 14 August 1954, 1955 and 1956, are basically definitive issues, although issued on the Anniversary date of Independence.

21 "Scinde Dawk" stamp and Ancient and Modern Transport

(Recess D.L.R.)

1952 (14 Aug). *Centenary of "Scinde Dawk" Issue of India. P* 13.

No.	Type	Value	Unused	Used
63	**21**	3 a. deep olive/*yellow-olive*	75	50
64		12 a. deep brown/*salmon*	1·00	15

PRINTERS. All issues up to No. 219 were recess-printed by the Pakistan Security Printing Corporation, *unless otherwise stated.*

22 Kaghan Valley 23 Mountains, Gilgit

24 Tea Plantation, East Pakistan

1954 (14 Aug). *Seventh Anniv of Independence. T* **22/4** *and similar designs. P* 13½ (14 *a.,* 1 *r.,* 2 *r.) or* 13 (*others*).
65 6 p. reddish violet 10 10
66 9 p. blue .. .. 1·25 70
67 1 a. carmine 10 10
68 1½ a. red 10 10
69 14 a. deep green 55 10
70 1 r. green .. .. 8·00 10
71 2 r. red-orange .. .. 2·00 10
65/71 .. .. *Set of* 7 11·00 75
Designs: *As T* **22**—1½ a. Mausoleum of Emperor Jehangir, Lahore. *As T* **23**—1 a. Badshahi Mosque, Lahore. *As T* **24**—1 r. Cotton plants, West Pakistan; 2 r. Jute fields and river, East Pakistan.

29 View of K 2

1954 (25 Dec). *Conquest of K 2 (Mount Godwin-Austen). P* 13.
72 **29** 2 a. deep violet 30 15

30 Karnaphuli Paper Mill, Type I (Arabic fraction on left) Type II (Arabic fraction on right)

1955 (14 Aug)–**56**. *Eighth Anniv of Independence. T* **30** *and similar horiz designs. P* 13.
73 2½ a. scarlet (I) 30 30
73*a* 2½ a. scarlet (II) (12.56) 30 30
74 6 a. deep ultramarine 60 10
75 8 a. deep reddish violet .. .. 2·25 10
76 12 a. carmine and orange .. .. 2·00 10
73/6 .. .. *Set of* 5 5·00 55
Designs:—6 a. Textile mill, West Pakistan; 8 a. Jute mill, East Pakistan; 12 a. Main Sui gas plant.

TENTH
ANNIVERSARY
UNITED NATIONS

24.10.55.

(34)

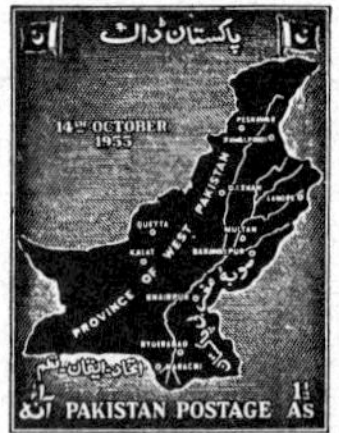

35 Map of West Pakistan

TENTH
ANNIVERSARY
UNITED NATIONS

24.10.55.

"UNITED NATIONS" shifted 1 mm to left (1½ a. R. 7/10; 12 a. R. 3/8, 5/8, 7/8, 9/8)

1955 (24 Oct). *Tenth Anniv of United Nations. Nos.* 68 *and* 76 *optd as T* **34**.
77 1½ a. red (B.) .. .. 1·75 5·00
a. "UNITED NATIONS" 1 mm to left 3·50 6·00
78 12 a. carmine and orange (B.) .. .. 75 4·50
a. "UNITED NATIONS" 1 mm to left 3·50 6·00
Forgeries exist of the overprint on No. 77. These are in very uneven thin type and measure 20×18 mm instead of the genuine 19½×19 mm.

1955 (7 Dec). *West Pakistan Unity. P* 13½.
79 **35** 1½ a. myrtle-green 15 10
80 2 a. sepia 15 10
81 12 a. deep rose-red 55 15
79/81 .. .. *Set of* 3 75 30

REPUBLIC

36 Constituent Assembly Building, Karachi

(Litho D.L.R.)

1956 (23 Mar). *Republic Day. P* 13.
82 **36** 2 a. myrtle-green 35 10

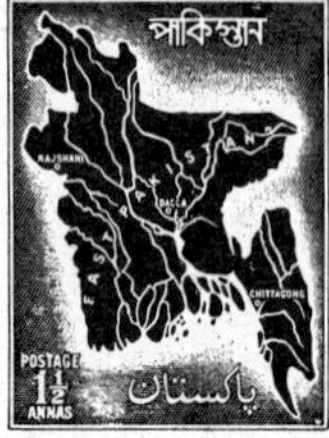

37 **38** Map of East Pakistan

1956 (14 Aug). *Ninth Anniv of Independence. P* 13½.
83 **37** 2 a. scarlet 20 10

1956 (15 Oct). *First Session of National Assembly of Pakistan at Dacca. P* 13½.
84 **38** 1½ a. myrtle-green 15 60
85 2 a. sepia 15 10
86 12 a. deep rose-red 20 30
84/6 .. .. *Set of* 3 45 90

39 Karnaphuli Paper Mill, East Bengal **40** Pottery

41 Orange Tree

1957 (23 Mar). *First Anniv of Republic. P* 13.
87 **39** 2½ a. scarlet 20 10
88 **40** 3½ a. blue 30 10
89 **41** 10 r. myrtle-green and yellow-orange .. 80 20
87/9 .. .. *Set of* 3 1·10 30
The above and No. 95 are primarily definitive issues, although issued on the Anniversary of Republic Day.
For 10 r. with W **98**, see No. 208.

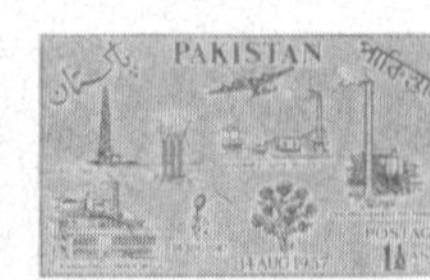

42 Pakistani Flag **43** Pakistani Industries

(Litho D.L.R.)

1957 (10 May). *Centenary of Struggle for Independence (Indian Mutiny). P* 13.
90 **42** 1½ a. bronze-green 20 10
91 12 a. light blue 45 10

(Litho D.L.R.)

1957 (14 Aug). *Tenth Anniv of Independence. P* 14.
92 **43** 1½ a. ultramarine 15 10
93 4 a. orange-red 25 30
94 12 a. mauve 30 40
92/4 .. .. *Set of* 3 65 70

44 Coconut Tree **45**

1958 (23 Mar). *Second Anniv of Republic. P* 13.
95 **44** 15 r. red and deep reddish purple .. 4·25 3·00
This is a definitive issue, see note below No. 89.
See No. 209 for this stamp with W **98**.

(Photo Harrison)

1958 (21 Apr). *20th Death Anniv of Mohammed Iqbal (poet). P* 14½ × 14.
96 **45** 1½ a. yellow-olive and black 20 10
97 2 a. orange-brown and black 20 10
98 14 a. turquoise-blue and black 45 10
96/8 .. .. *Set of* 3 75 20

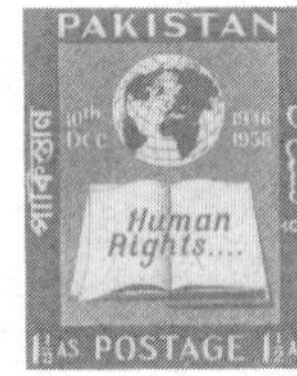

46 U.N. Charter and Globe

PAKISTAN
BOY SCOUT
2nd NATIONAL
JAMBOREE

CHITTAGONG
Dec. 58—Jan. 59

(47)

1958 (10 Dec). *Tenth Anniv of Declaration of Human Rights. P* 13.
99 **46** 1½ a. turquoise-blue 10 10
100 14 a. sepia 40 10

1958 (28 Dec). *Second Pakistan Boy Scouts National Jamboree, Chittagong. Nos.* 65 *and* 75 *optd with T* **47**.
101 6 p. reddish violet 15 10
102 8 a. deep reddish violet 30 10

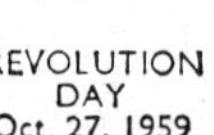

(48)

49 "Centenary of An Idea"

1959 (27 Oct). *Revolution Day. No.* 74 *optd with T* **48** *in red.*
103 6 a. deep ultramarine 30 10

1959 (19 Nov). *Red Cross Commemoration. Recess; cross typo. P* 13.
104 **49** 2 a. red and green 15 10
105 10 a. red and deep blue 55 10

50 Armed Forces Badge **51** Map of Pakistan

(Litho D.L.R.)

1960 (10 Jan). *Armed Forces Day. P* 13½ × 13.
106 **50** 2 a. red, ultramarine and blue-green .. 20 10
107 14 a. red and bright blue 65 10

1960 (23 Mar). *P* 13 × 13½.
108 **51** 6 p. deep purple 15 10
109 2 a. brown-red 30 10
110 8 a. deep green 60 10
111 1 r. blue 70 10
108/11 .. .. *Set of* 4 1·60 15

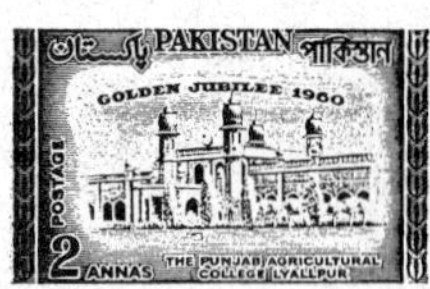

52 Uprooted Tree **53** Punjab Agricultural College

1960 (7 Apr). *World Refugee Year. P* 13.
112 **52** 2 a. rose-carmine 10 10
113 10 a. green 20 10

1960 (10 Oct). *Golden Jubilee of Punjab Agricultural College, Lyallpur. T* **53** *and similar horiz design. P* 12½ × 14.
114 2 a. slate-blue and carmine-red 10 10
115 8 a. bluish green and reddish violet 10 10
Design:—8 a. College arms.

55 "Land Reforms, Rehabilitation and Reconstruction" **56** Caduceus

(Des M. H. Hanjra. Photo D.L.R.)

1960 (27 Oct). *Revolution Day. P* 13 × 13½.
116 **55** 2 a. green, pink and brown 10 10
a. Green and pink omitted .. .. 9·00
b. Pink omitted .. .. .. 5·00
117 14 a. green, yellow and ultramarine .. 20 20

(Photo D.L.R.)

1960 (16 Nov). *Centenary of King Edward Medical College, Lahore. P* 13.
118 **56** 2 a. yellow, black and blue 30 10
119 14 a. emerald, black and carmine .. 70 10

57 "Economic Co-operation" **58** Zam-Zama Gun, Lahore ("Kim's Gun," after Rudyard Kipling)

1960 (5 Dec). *International Chamber of Commerce C.A.F.E.A. Meeting, Karachi. P* 13.
120 **57** 14 a. orange-red 15 10

(Centre typo, background recess Pakistan Security Ptg Corp)

1960 (24 Dec). *Third Pakistan Boy Scouts National Jamboree, Lahore. P* 12½ × 14.
121 **58** 2 a. carmine, yellow & dp bluish green 30 10

(New Currency. 100 paisa=1 rupee)

1 PAISA
(59)

1961 (1 Jan–14 Feb). *Nos.* 24a, 67/8, 83 *and* 108/9, *surch as T* **59**. *Nos.* 123/4 *and* 126 *surch by Pakistan Security Ptg Corp and others by the Times Press, Karachi.*
122 1 p. on 1½ a. red (10.1) 15 10
123 2 p. on 3 p. red 10 10
124 3 p. on 6 p. deep purple 10 10
a. "PASIA" for "PAISA" .. .. .. 2·50
125 7 p. on 1 a. carmine (14.2) 20 10
126 13 p. on 2 a. brown-red (14.2) 20 10
a. "PAIS" for "PAISA" .. .. .. 2·50
127 13 p. on 2 a. scarlet (14.2) 15 10
122/7 .. .. *Set of* 6 70 20
No. 122. Two settings were used, the first with figure "1" 2½ mm tall and the second 3 mm.
On the 1 p. with tall "1" and the 13 p. (No. 127), the space between the figures of value and "P" of "PAISA" varies between 1½ mm and 3 mm.
See also Nos. 262/4.

ERRORS. In the above issue and the corresponding official stamps we have listed errors in the stamps surcharged by the Pakistan Security Printing Corp but have not included the very large number of errors which occurred in the stamps surcharged by the less experienced Times Press. This was a very hurried job and there was no time to carry out the usual checks. It is also known that some errors were not issued to the public but came on the market by other means.

NOTE. Stamps in the old currency were also *handstamped* with new currency equivalents and issued in various districts but these local issues are outside the scope of this catalogue.

60 Khyber Pass **61** Shalimar Gardens, Lahore

62 Chota Sona Masjid (gateway)

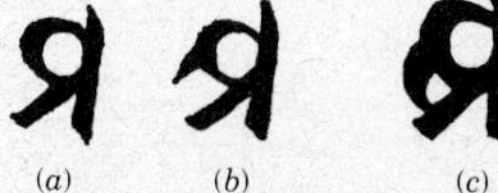

(*a*) (*b*) (*c*)

Types (*a*) and (*b*) show the first letter in the top right-hand inscription; (*a*) wrongly engraved, "SH" (*b*) corrected to "P".
On Nos. 131/2 and 134 the corrections were made individually on the plate, so that each stamp in the sheet may be slightly different.
Type (*c*) refers to No. 133a only.

1961–63. *No wmk. P* 13 (*T* **62**) *or* 14 (*others*).

(*a*) *Inscribed* "SHAKISTAN" *in Bengali*
128 **60** 1 p. violet (1.1.61) 50 10
129 2 p. rose-red (12.1.61) 50 10
130 5 p. ultramarine (23.3.61) 40 10

(*b*) *Inscribed* "PAKISTAN" *in Bengali*
131 **60** 1 p. violet 30 10
132 2 p. rose-red 10 10
133 3 p. reddish purple (27.10.61) 30 10
a. Re-engraved. First letter of Bengali inscription as Type (*c*) (1963) .. 1·25 1·50
134 5 p. ultramarine 60 10
135 7 p. emerald (23.3.61) 50 10
136 **61** 10 p. brown (14.8.61) 20 10
137 13 p. slate-violet (14.8.61) 10 10
138 25 p. deep blue (1.1.62) .. .. .. 3·50 10
139 40 p. deep purple (1.1.62) 40 10
140 50 p. deep bluish green (1.1.62) 35 10
141 75 p. carmine-red (23.3.62) 40 10
142 90 p. yellow-green (1.1.62) 40 10
143 **62** 1 r. vermilion (7.1.63) .. .. .. 1·75 10
a. Imperf (pair) .. ..
144 1 r. 25, reddish violet (27.10.61) 75 10
144*a* 2 r. orange (7.1.63) .. .. .. 4·50 15
144*b* 5 r. green (7.1.63) .. .. .. 6·00 1·00
128/44*b* .. .. *Set of* 19 19·00 1·90
See also Nos. 170/81 and 204/7.

(63) **64** Warsak Dam and Power Station

1961 (12 Feb). *Lahore Stamp Exhibition. No.* 110 *optd with T* **63**.
145 **51** 8 a. deep green (R.) 40 70

1961 (1 July). *Completion of Warsak Hydro-Electric Project. P* 12½ × 14.
146 **64** 40 p. black and blue 40 10

65 Narcissus **66** Ten Roses

1961 (2 Oct). *Child Welfare Week. P* 14.
147 **65** 13 p. turquoise-blue 15 10
148 90 p. bright purple 35 20

1961 (4 Nov). *Co-operative Day. P* 13.
149 **66** 13 p. rose-red and deep green 30 10
150 90 p. rose-red and blue 70 20

67 Police Crest and "Traffic Control" **68** Locomotive *Eagle* of 1861

(Photo D.L.R.)

1961 (30 Nov). *Police Centenary. P* 13.
151 **67** 13 p. silver, black and blue 40 10
152 40 p. silver, black and red 85 20

(Des M. Thoma. Photo D.L.R.)

1961 (31 Dec). *Railway Centenary. T* **68** *and similar horiz design. P* 14.
153 13 p. green, black and yellow 50 40
154 50 p. yellow, black and green 75 40
Design:—50 p. Diesel locomotive and tracks forming "1961".

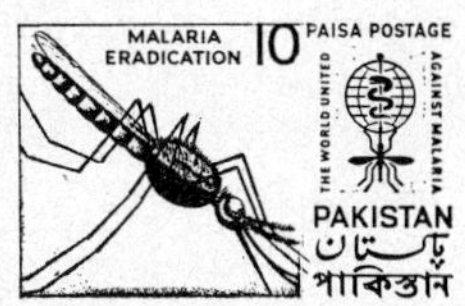

(70) **71** *Anopheles* sp (mosquito)

1962 (6 Feb). *First Karachi–Dacca Jet Flight. No.* 87 *surch with T* **70**.
155 **39** 13 p. on 2½ a. scarlet (R.) 50 30

(Photo D.L.R.)

1962 (7 Apr). *Malaria Eradication. T* **71** *and similar horiz design. P* 14.
156 10 p. black, yellow and red 20 10
157 13 p. black, greenish yellow and red 20 10
Design:—13 p. Mosquito pierced by blade.

73 Pakistan Map and Jasmine

(Photo Courvoisier)

1962 (8 June). *New Constitution. P* 12.
158 **73** 40 p. yellow-green, bluish green and grey 45 10

74 Football **78** Marble Fruit Dish and Bahawalpuri Clay Flask

1962 (14 Aug). *Sports. T* **74** *and similar horiz designs. P* 12½ × 14.
159 7 p. black and blue 10 10
160 13 p. black and green 10 10
161 25 p. black and purple 10 10
162 40 p. black and orange-brown .. .. .. 1·40 80
159/62 .. .. *Set of* 4 1·50 90
Designs:—13 p. Hockey; 25 p. Squash; 40 p. Cricket.

1962 (10 Nov). *Small Industries. T* **78** *and similar vert designs. P* 13.
163 7 p. brown-lake 10 10
164 13 p. deep green .. .. 1·75 50
165 25 p. reddish violet 10 10
166 40 p. yellow-green 10 10
167 50 p. deep red 10 10
163/7 .. .. *Set of* 5 1·75 65
Designs:—13 p. Sports equipment; 25 p. Camel-skin lamp and brassware; 40 p. Wooden powderbowl and basket-work; 50 p. Inlaid cigarette-box and brassware.

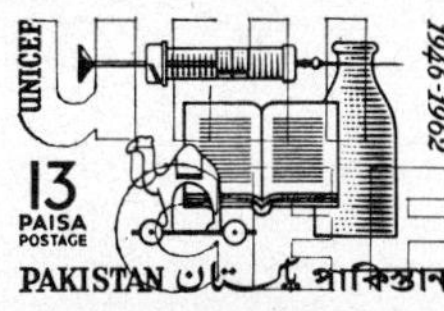

83 "Child Welfare"

(Des M. Thoma. Photo D.L.R.)

1962 (11 Dec). *16th Anniv of U.N.I.C.E.F. P* 14.
168 **83** 13 p. black, light blue and maroon .. 15 10
169 40 p. black, yellow and turquoise-blue .. 15 10

Nos. 170, etc. Nos. 131/42

1962–70. *As T* **60/1** *but with redrawn Bengali inscription at top right. No wmk.*
170 **60** 1 p. violet (1963) 10 10
171 2 p. rose-red (1964) 50 10
a. Imperf (pair) .. .. 2·75
172 3 p. reddish purple (1970) .. .. .. 2·00 90
173 5 p. ultramarine (1963) 10 10
174 7 p. emerald (1964) .. .. 3·00 85
175 **61** 10 p. brown (1963) 10 10
176 13 p. slate-violet 10 10
176*a* 15 p. bright purple (31.12.64) 15 10
ab. Imperf (pair) .. .. 3·75
176*b* 20 p. myrtle-green (26.1.70) 30 10
ba. Imperf (pair) .. .. 2·75
177 25 p. deep blue (1963) .. .. 2·50 10
a. Imperf (pair) .. .. 5·00
178 40 p. deep purple (1964) 15 10
a. Imperf (pair) .. .. 6·00
179 50 p. deep bluish green (1964) 15 10
180 75 p. carmine-red (1964) 30 30
181 90 p. yellow-green (1964) 30 45
170/81 .. .. *Set of* 14 8·50 2·75
Other values in this series and the high values (Nos. 204/10) are known imperforate but we are not satisfied as to their status.

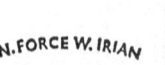

U.N.FORCE W.IRIAN

(84)

85 "Dancing" Horse, Camel and Bull

1963 (15 Feb). *Pakistan U.N. Force in West Irian. No.* 176 *optd with T* **84**.
182 **61** 13 p. slate-violet (R.) 10 10

(Des S. Jahangir. Photo Courvoisier)

1963 (13 Mar). *National Horse and Cattle Show. P* 11½.
183 **85** 13 p. blue, sepia and cerise 10 10

86 Wheat and Tractor

1963 (21 Mar). *Freedom from Hunger. T* **86** *and similar horiz design. P* 12½ × 14.
184 13 p. orange-brown 50 10
185 50 p. bistre-brown .. .. 1·50 40
Design:—50 p. Rice.

(88)

89 Centenary Emblem

1963 (23 Mar). *2nd International Stamp Exhibition, Dacca. No.* 109 *surch with T* **88**.
186 **51** 13 p. on 2 a. brown-red 30 10

1963 (25 June). *Centenary of Red Cross. Recess; cross typo. P* 13.
187 **89** 40 p. red and deep olive 85 15

90 Paharpur

100 YEARS OF P.W.D.
OCTOBER, 1963
13

(94)

1963 (16 Sept). *Archaeological Series. T* **90** *and similar designs. P* 14 × 12½ (13 *p.*) *or* 12½ × 15 (*others*).
188 7 p. ultramarine 15 10
189 13 p. sepia 20 10
190 40 p. carmine 25 10
191 50 p. deep reddish violet 30 10
188/91 .. .. *Set of* 4 80 30
Designs: *Vert*—13 p. Moenjodaro; *Horiz*—40 p. Taxila; 50 p. Mainamati.

1963 (7 Oct). *Centenary of Public Works Department. No.* 133 *surch with T* **94** *by typography*.
192 **60** 13 p. on 3 p. reddish purple 10 10
Forged surcharges applied in *lithography* exist.

95 Ataturk's Mausoleum

1963 (10 Nov). *25th Death Anniv of Kemal Atatürk. P* 13½.
193 **95** 50 p. red 35 10

96 Globe and U.N.E.S.C.O. Emblem

(Photo D.L.R.)

1963 (10 Dec). *15th Anniv of Declaration of Human Rights. P* 14.
194 **96** 50 p. brown, red and ultramarine 30 10

COVER PRICES

Cover factors are quoted at the beginning of each country for most issues to 1945. An explanation of the system can be found on page x. The factors quoted do not, however, apply to philatelic covers.

97 Thermal Power Installations

1963 (25 Dec). *Completion of Multan Thermal Power Station. P* 12½ × 14.
195 **97** 13 p. ultramarine 10 10

98 Multiple Star and Crescent

99 Temple of Thot, Queen Nefertari and Maids

1963–79. *As Nos.* 43*b*, 89, 95 *and* 143/44*b*, *but W* **98**.
204 **62** 1 r. vermilion 30 10
b. Imperf (pair) .. .. 7·00
205 1 r. 25, reddish violet (1964) .. .. .. 1·00 10
a. *Purple* (1975?) .. .. 1·00 10
ab. Imperf (pair) .. .. 6·00
206 2 r. orange (1964) 55 15
a. Imperf (pair) .. .. 8·00
207 5 r. green (1964) .. .. 3·50 40
a. Imperf (pair) .. .. 14·00
208 **41** 10 r. myrtle-green & yellow-orge (1968) 3·50 3·25
a. Imperf (pair) .. ..
b. Wmk sideways 75 75
209 **44** 15 r. red and deep reddish purple (*wmk sideways*) (20.3.79) .. .. 80 1·00
a. Imperf (pair) .. .. 18·00
210 **13** 25 r. violet (1968) .. .. 12·00 15·00
a. Wmk sideways .. .. 2·00 2·50
ab. Imperf (pair) .. .. 15·00
204/10a .. .. *Set of* 7 8·00 4·50

1964 (30 Mar). *Nubian Monuments Preservation. T* **99** *and similar horiz design. P* 13 × 13½.
211 13 p. turquoise-blue and red 20 10
212 50 p. bright purple and black 60 10
Design:—50 p. Temple of Abu Simbel.

101 "Unisphere" and Pakistan Pavilion

103 Shah Abdul Latif's Mausoleum

1964 (22 Apr). *New York World's Fair. T* **101** *and similar design. P* 12½ × 14 (13 *p.*) *or* 14 × 12½ (1 *r.* 25).
213 13 p. ultramarine 10 10
214 1 r. 25, ultramarine and red-orange 30 20
Design: *Vert*—1 r. 25, Pakistan Pavilion on "Unisphere".

1964 (25 June). *Death Bicentenary of Shah Abdul Latif of Bhit. P* 13½ × 13.
215 **103** 50 p. bright blue and carmine-lake .. 40 10

104 Mausoleum of Quaid-i-Azam

105 Mausoleum

1964 (11 Sept). *16th Death Anniv of Mohammed Ali Jinnah (Quaid-i-Azam). P* 13½ (15 *p.*) *or* 13 (50 *p.*).
216 **104** 15 p. emerald-green 15 10
217 **105** 50 p. bronze-green 50 10

106 Bengali and Urdu Alphabets

107 University Building

1964 (5 Oct). *Universal Children's Day. P* 13.
218 **106** 15 p. brown 10 10

1964 (21 Dec). *First Convocation of the West Pakistan University of Engineering and Technology, Lahore. P* 12½ × 14.
219 **107** 15 p. chestnut 10 10

PROCESS. All the following issues were lithographed by the Pakistan Security Printing Corporation, *unless otherwise stated.*

108 "Help the Blind"

109 "I.T.U. Emblem and Symbols

(Des A. Chughtai)

1965 (28 Feb). *Blind Welfare. P* 13.
220 **108** 15 p. ultramarine and yellow 10 10

1965 (17 May). *I.T.U. Centenary. Recess. P* 12½ × 14.
221 **109** 15 p. reddish purple .. .. 1·25 30

110 I.C.Y. Emblem

1965 (26 June). *International Co-operation Year. P* 13 × 13½.
222 **110** 15 p. black and light blue 40 15
223 50 p. green and yellow 85 40

111 "Co-operation"

112 Globe and Flags of Turkey, Iran and Pakistan

1965 (21 July). *First Anniv of Regional Development Co-operation Pact. P* 13½ × 13 (15 *p.*) *or* 13 (50 *p.*).
224 **111** 15 p. multicoloured 15 10
225 **112** 50 p. multicoloured 45 10

113 Soldier and Tanks

1965 (25 Dec). *Pakistan Armed Forces. T* **113** *and similar horiz designs. Multicoloured. P* 13½ × 13.
226 7 p. Type **113** 35 15
227 15 p. Naval officer and *Tughril* (destroyer) .. 60 10
228 50 p. Pilot and "F-104" Starfighters 95 15
226/8 .. .. *Set of* 3 1·75 30

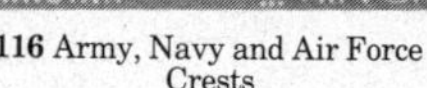

116 Army, Navy and Air Force Crests

117 Atomic Reactor, Islamabad

1966 (13 Feb). *Armed Forces Day. P* 13½ × 13.
229 **116** 15 p. royal blue, dull grn, brt blue & buff 10 10

1966 (30 Apr). *Inauguration of Pakistan's First Atomic Reactor. Recess. P* 13.
230 **117** 15 p. black 10 10

118 Bank Crest   119 Children

1966 (25 Aug). *Silver Jubilee of Habib Bank. P* 12½ × 14.
231 **118** 15 p. blue-green, yellow-orange & sepia   10   10

1966 (3 Oct). *Universal Children's Day. P* 13½.
232 **119** 15 p. black, red and pale yellow   10   10

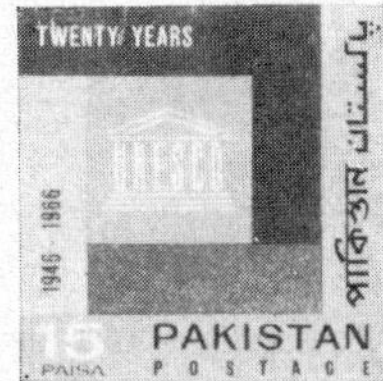

120 U.N.E.S.C.O. Emblem

1966 (24 Nov). *20th Anniv of U.N.E.S.C.O. P* 14.
233 **120** 15 p. multicoloured . . . . 1·60   30

121 Flag, Secretariat Building and President Ayub

1966 (29 Nov). *Islamabad (new capital). P* 13.
234 **121** 15 p. deep bluish green, chestnut, light blue and bistre-brown   10   10
235   50 p. deep bluish green, chestnut, light blue and black   30   10

122 Avicenna   123 Mohammed Ali Jinnah

1966 (3 Dec). *Foundation of Health and Tibbi Research Institute. P* 13 × 13½.
236 **122** 15 p. dull green and salmon   15   10
  a. Imperf (pair) . . . . . . 55·00

1966 (25 Dec). *90th Birth Anniv of Mohammed Ali Jinnah. T* **123** *and similar design bearing same portrait but in different frame. Litho and recess. P* 13.
237 **123** 15 p. black, orange and greenish blue . .   10   10
238 – 50 p. black, purple and ultramarine . .   30   10

124 Tourist Year Emblem   125 Emblem of Pakistan T.B. Association

1967 (1 Jan). *International Tourist Year. P* 13½ × 13.
239 **124** 15 p. black, light blue and yellow-brown   10   10

1967 (10 Jan). *Tuberculosis Eradication Campaign. P* 13½ × 13.
240 **125** 15 p. red, sepia and chestnut   10   10

126 Scout Salute and Badge   127 "Justice"

1967 (29 Jan). *4th National Scout Jamboree. Photo. P* 12½ × 14.
241 **126** 15 p. light orange-brown and maroon . .   15   10

1967 (17 Feb). *Centenary of West Pakistan High Court. P* 13.
242 **127** 15 p. black, slate, light red and slate-blue   10   10

128 Dr. Mohammed Iqbal (philosopher)

1967 (21 Apr). *Iqbal Commemoration. P* 13.
243 **128** 15 p. sepia and light red   10   10
244   1 r. sepia and deep green   30   10

129 Hilal-i-Isteqlal Flag

1967 (15 May). *Award of Hilal-i-Isteqlal (for Valour) to Lahore, Sialkot, and Sargodha. P* 13.
245 **129** 15 p. multicoloured   10   10

130 "20th Anniversary"

1967 (14 Aug). *20th Anniv of Independence. Photo. P* 13.
246 **130** 15 p. red and deep bluish green   10   10

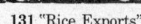

131 "Rice Exports"   132 Cotton Plant, Yarn and Textiles

1967 (26 Sept). *Pakistan Exports. T* 131/2 *and similar design. Photo. P* 13 × 13½.
247 10 p. yellow, deep bluish green and deep blue   10   15
248 15 p. multicoloured   10   10
  a. Pale orange (top panel) omitted . . . . 10·00
249 50 p. multicoloured   20   15
247/9 . . . . *Set of* 3   30   30
Design: *Vert as T* **132**—50 p. Raw jute, bale and bags.

134 Clay Toys

1967 (2 Oct). *Universal Children's Day. P* 13.
250 **134** 15 p. multicoloured   10   10

135 Shah and Empress of Iran and Gulistan Palace, Teheran

1967 (26 Oct). *Coronation of Shah Mohammed Riza Pahlavi and Empress Farah of Iran. Recess and litho. P* 13.
251 **135** 50 p. purple, blue and light yellow-ochre   30   10

136 "Each For All–All For Each"

1967 (4 Nov). *Co-operative Day. P* 13.
252 **136** 15 p. multicoloured   10   10

137 Mangla Dam

1967 (23 Nov). *Indus Basin Project. P* 13.
253 **137** 15 p. multicoloured   10   10

138 Crab pierced by Sword   139 Human Rights Emblem

1967 (26 Dec). *The Fight Against Cancer. P* 13.
254 **138** 15 p. red and black   40   10

1968 (31 Jan). *Human Rights Year. Photo. P* 14 × 13.
255 **139** 15 p. red and deep turquoise-blue . .   10   15
256   50 p. red, yellow and silver-grey   10   15

140 Agricultural University, Mymensingh   141 W.H.O. Emblem

1968 (28 Mar). *First Convocation of East Pakistan Agricultural University. Photo. P* 13½ × 13.
257 **140** 15 p. multicoloured   10   10

1968 (7 Apr). *20th Anniv of World Health Organization. Photo. P* 14 × 13.
258 **141** 15 p. green and orange-red   10   15
  a. "PAIS" for "PAISA" (R.4/5) . . 1·00
259   50 p. red-orange and indigo   10   15

142 Kazi Nazrul Islam (poet, composer and patriot)

1968 (25 June). *Nazrul Islam Commemoration. Recess and litho. P* 13.
260 **142** 15 p. sepia and pale yellow   15   15
261   50 p. sepia and pale rose-red   35   15
Nos. 260/1 with a two-line inscription giving the wrong date of birth ("1889") were prepared but not issued. Some are known to have been released in error.

4 PAISA

(143)

1968 (18 July–Aug). *Nos.* 56, 74 *and* 61 *surch as T* **143**.

262	4 p. on 3 a. purple	20	45
263	4 p. on 6 a. deep ultramarine (R.) (Aug)	40	55
264	60 p. on 10 a. violet (R.)	30	35
	a. Surch in black	30	55
	b. Surch triple	30·00	
262/4	*Set of* 3	80	1·25

144 Children running with Hoops

1968 (7 Oct). *Universal Children's Day. P* 13.

265	**144**	15 p. multicoloured	10	10

145 "National Assembly"

1968 (27 Oct). *"A Decade of Development". T* **145** *and similar horiz designs. P* 13.

266	10 p. multicoloured	10	10
267	15 p. multicoloured	15	10
268	50 p. multicoloured	40	15
269	60 p. light blue, dull purple and vermilion	40	15
266/9	*Set of* 4	95	45

Designs:—15 p. Industry and agriculture; 50 p. Army, Navy and Air Force; 60 p. Minaret and atomic reactor plant.

149 Chittagong Steel Mill

1969 (7 Jan). *Pakistan's First Steel Mill, Chittagong. P* 13.

270	**149**	15 p. grey, light blue & pale yellow-olive	10	10

150 "Family" **151** Olympic Gold Medal and Hockey Player

1969 (14 Jan). *Family Planning. P* 13½ × 13.

271	**150**	15 p. bright purple & pale greenish blue	10	10

1969 (30 Jan). *Olympic Hockey Champions. Photo. P* 13½.

272	**151**	15 p. black, gold, deep green & pale blue	55	35
273		1 r. black, gold, dp green & flesh-pink	1·50	60

152 Mirza Ghalib and Lines of Verse

1969 (15 Feb). *Death Centenary of Mirza Ghalib (poet). P* 13.

274	**152**	15 p. multicoloured	15	15
275		50 p. multicoloured	40	15

The lines of verse on No. 275 are different from those in T **152**.

153 Dacca Railway Station

1969 (27 Apr). *First Anniv of New Dacca Railway Station. P* 13.

276	**153**	15 p. multicoloured	30	10

154 I.L.O. Emblem and "1919–1969" **155** Mughal Miniature (Pakistan)

1969 (15 May). *50th Anniv of International Labour Organisation. P* 13½.

277	**154**	15 p. buff and bluish green	10	10
278		50 p. cinnamon and cerise	30	10

1969 (21 July). *Fifth Anniv of Regional Co-operation for Development. T* **155** *and similar vert designs. Multicoloured. P* 13.

279	20 p. Type **155**	15	10
280	50 p. Safav miniature (Iran)	15	10
281	1 r. Ottoman miniature (Turkey)	20	10
279/81	*Set of* 3	45	30

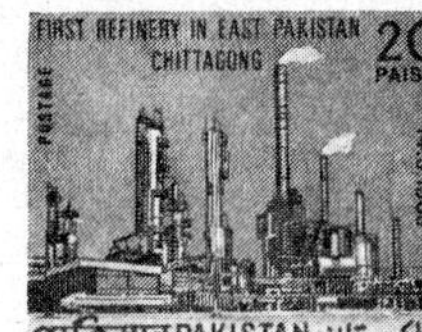

158 Eastern Refinery, Chittagong

1969 (14 Sept). *First Oil Refinery in East Pakistan. Photo. P* 13½ × 13.

282	**158**	20 p. multicoloured	10	10

159 Children playing Outside "School"

1969 (6 Oct). *Universal Children's Day. Photo. P* 13.

283	**159**	20 p. multicoloured	10	10

160 Japanese Doll and P.I.A. Air Routes

1969 (1 Nov). *Inauguration of P.I.A. Pearl Route, Dacca–Tokyo. P* 13½ × 13.

284	**160**	20 p. multicoloured	20	10
		a. Yellow and pink omitted	7·00	
285		50 p. multicoloured	35	40
		a. Yellow and pink omitted	7·00	

161 "Reflection of Light" Diagram

1969 (4 Nov). *Millenary Commemorative of Ibn-al-Haitham (physicist). Photo. P* 13.

286	**161**	20 p. black, lemon and light blue	10	10

162 Vickers "Vimy" and Karachi Airport **163** Flags, Sun Tower and Expo Site Plan

1969 (2 Dec). *50th Anniv of First England–Australia Flight. Photo. P* 13½ × 13.

287	**162**	50 p. multicoloured	40	35

1970 (15 Mar). *World Fair, Osaka. P* 13.

288	**163**	50 p. multicoloured	15	30

164 New U.P.U. H.Q. Building

1970 (20 May). *New U.P.U. Headquarters Building. P* 13½ × 13.

289	**164**	20 p. multicoloured	10	10
290		50 p. multicoloured	20	25

The above, in a miniature sheet, additionally inscr "U.P.U. Day 9th Oct, 1971", were put on sale on that date in very limited numbers.

165 U.N. H.Q. Building

1970 (26 June). *25th Anniv of United Nations. T* **165** *and similar horiz design. Multicoloured. P* 13 × 13½.

291	20 p. Type **165**	15	10
292	50 p. U.N. emblem	15	20

167 I.E.Y. Emblem, Book and Pen

1970 (6 July). *International Education Year. P* 13.

293	**167**	20 p. multicoloured	10	10
294		50 p. multicoloured	20	20

168 Saiful Malook Lake (Pakistan)

1970 (21 July). *Sixth Anniv of Regional Co-operation for Development. T* **168** *and similar square designs. Multicoloured. P* 13.

295	20 p. Type **168**	15	10
296	50 p. Seeyo-Se-Pol Bridge, Esfahan (Iran)	20	10
297	1 r. View from Fethiye (Turkey)	20	15
295/7	*Set of* 3	50	30

171 Asian Productivity Symbol **172** Dr. Maria Montessori

1970 (18 Aug). *Asian Productivity Year. Photo. P* 12½ × 14.
298 **171** 50 p. multicoloured 10 15

1970 (31 Aug). *Birth Centenary of Dr. Maria Montessori (educationist). P* 13.
299 **172** 20 p. multicoloured 10 10
300 50 p. multicoloured 10 20

173 Tractor and Fertilizer Factory

1970 (12 Sept). *Tenth Near East F.A.O. Regional Conference, Islamabad. P* 13.
301 **173** 20 p. bright green, and orange-brown 10 15

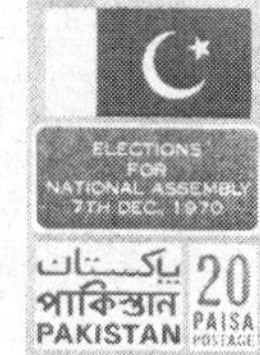

174 Children and Open Book

175 Pakistan Flag and Text

1970 (5 Oct). *Universal Children's Day. Photo. P* 13.
302 **174** 20 p. multicoloured 10 10

1970 (7 Dec). *General Elections for National Assembly. P* 13½ × 13.
303 **175** 20 p. green and bluish violet 10 10

1970 (17 Dec). *General Elections for Provincial Assemblies. As No.* 303, *but inscr* "PROVINCIAL ASSEMBLIES 17TH DEC., 1970".
304 **175** 20 p. green and pale magenta 10 10

176 Conference Crest and burning Al-Aqsa Mosque

1970 (26 Dec). *Conference of Islamic Foreign Ministers. Karachi. P* 13.
305 **176** 20 p. multicoloured 10 10

177 Coastal Embankments

1971 (25 Feb). *Coastal Embankments in East Pakistan Project. P* 13.
306 **177** 20 p. multicoloured 10 10

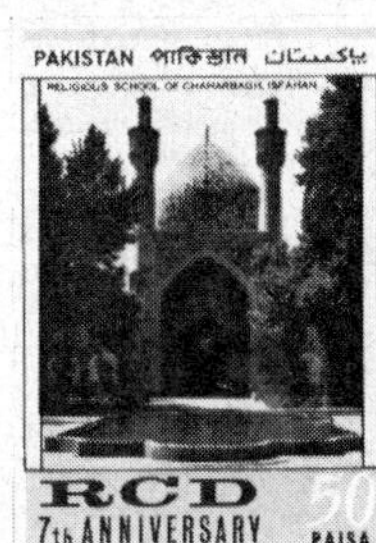

178 Emblem and United Peoples of the World

180 Chaharbagh School (Iran)

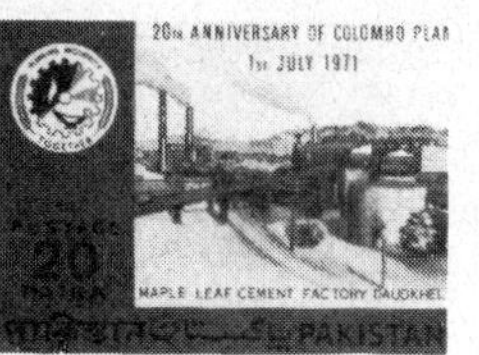

179 Maple Leaf Cement Factory, Daudkhel

1971 (21 Mar). *Racial Equality Year. P* 13.
307 **178** 20 p. multicoloured 10 10
308 50 p. multicoloured 20 20

1971 (1 July). *20th Anniv of Colombo Plan. P* 13.
309 **179** 20 p. brown, black and reddish violet .. 10 10

1971 (21 July). *Seventh Anniv of Regional Co-operation for Development. T* **180** *and similar horiz designs. Multicoloured. P* 13.
310 10 p. Selimiye Mosque (Turkey) 10 15
311 20 p. Badshahi Mosque (Lahore) 20 25
312 50 p. Type **180** 30 35
310/12 .. .. *Set of* 3 55 65

181 Electric Locomotive and Boy with Toy Train

1971 (4 Oct). *Universal Children's Day. P* 13.
313 **181** 20 p. multicoloured .. .. .. 1·00 30

182 Horseman and Symbols

1971 (15 Oct). *2500th Anniv of Persian Monarchy. P* 13.
314 **182** 10 p. multicoloured 25 30
315 20 p. multicoloured 35 40
316 50 p. multicoloured 45 50
314/16 .. .. *Set of* 3 95 1·10

The above exist in a miniature sheet, but only a very limited quantity was placed on sale.

183 Hockey-player and Trophy

1971 (24 Oct). *World Cup Hockey Tournament, Barcelona. P* 13.
317 **183** 20 p. multicoloured .. .. .. 1·00 45

184 Great Bath, Moenjodaro

1971 (4 Nov). *25th Anniv of U.N.E.S.C.O. and Campaign to save the Moenjodaro Excavations. P* 13.
318 **184** 20 p. multicoloured 15 20

185 U.N.I.C.E.F. Symbol

1971 (11 Dec). *25th Anniv of U.N.I.C.E.F. P* 13.
319 **185** 50 p. multicoloured 30 30

186 King Hussein and Jordanian Flag

1971 (25 Dec). *50th Anniv of Hashemite Kingdom of Jordan. P* 13.
320 **186** 20 p. multicoloured 15 15

187 Badge of Hockey Federation and Trophy

188 Reading Class

1971 (31 Dec). *Hockey Championships Victory. P* 13.
321 **187** 20 p. multicoloured .. .. .. 1·50 90

1972 (15 Jan). *International Book Year. P* 13½.
322 **188** 20 p. multicoloured 20 20

OUTSIDE THE COMMONWEALTH

On 30 January 1972 Pakistan left the Commonwealth.

189 View of Venice

1972 (7 Feb). *U.N.E.S.C.O. Campaign to Save Venice. P* 13.
323 **189** 20 p. multicoloured 30 30

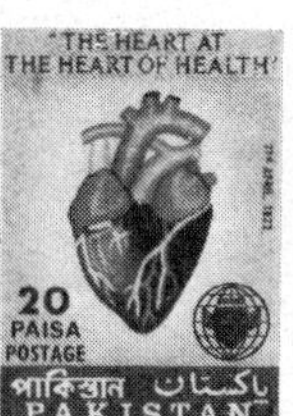

190 E.C.A.F.E. Emblem and Discs

191 Human Heart

1972 (28 Mar). *25th Anniv of E.C.A.F.E. (Economic Commission for Asia and the Far East). P* 13.
324 **190** 20 p. multicoloured 10 20

1972 (7 Apr). *World Health Day. P* 13 × 13½.
325 **191** 20 p. multicoloured 20 20

192 "Only One Earth"

193 "Fisherman" (Cevat Dereli)

1972 (5 June). *U.N. Conference on the Human Environment, Stockholm. P* 13 × 13½.
326 **192** 20 p. multicoloured 20 20

1972 (21 July). *Eighth Anniv of Regional Co-operation for Development. T* **193** *and similar vert designs. Multicoloured. P* 13.
327 10 p. Type **193** 10 20
328 20 p. "Iranian Woman" (Behzad) 15 25
329 50 p. "Will and Power" (A. R. Chughtai) .. 35 45
a. Brown-ochre (border) omitted .. .. 15·00
327/9 .. .. *Set of* 3 55 80

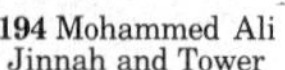

194 Mohammed Ali Jinnah and Tower

195 Donating Blood

1972 (14 Aug). *25th Anniv of Independence. T* **194** *and similar horiz designs. Multicoloured. P* 13 (10 *and* 60 *p.*) *or* 14 × 12½ (20 *p.*).
330 10 p. Type **194** 10 10
331 20 p. "Land Reform" (74 × 23½ *mm*) 15 20
a. Horiz strip of 4. Nos. 331/4 55
332 20 p. "Labour Reform" (74 × 23½ *mm*) .. 15 20
333 20 p. "Education Policy" (74 × 23½ *mm*) .. 15 20
334 20 p. "Health Policy" (74 × 23½ *mm*) .. 15 20
335 60 p. National Assembly Building (46 × 28 *mm*) 25 25
330/5 .. .. *Set of* 6 80 1·00
Nos. 331/4 were printed horizontally *se-tenant* throughout the sheet.

1972 (6 Sept). *National Blood Transfusion Service. P* 13½×12½.
336 **195** 20 p. multicoloured 15 30

196 People and Squares

1972 (16 Sept). *Centenary of Population Census. P* 13½.
337 **196** 20 p. multicoloured 15 20

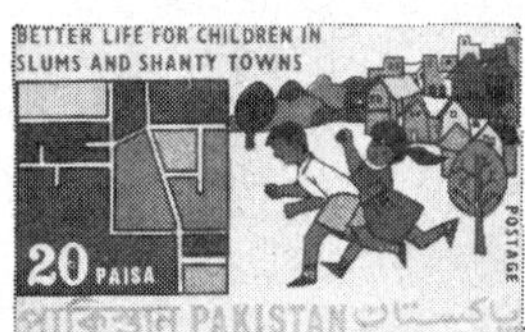

197 Children from Slums

1972 (2 Oct). *Universal Children's Day. P* 13.
338 **197** 20 p. multicoloured 15 30

198 People and Open Book

1972 (23 Oct). *Education Week. P* 13.
339 **198** 20 p. multicoloured 20 20

199 Nuclear Power Plant

1972 (28 Nov). *Inauguration of Karachi Nuclear Power Plant. P* 13.
340 **199** 20 p. multicoloured 15 30

200 Copernicus in Observatory

1973 (19 Feb). *500th Birth Anniv of Nicholas Copernicus (astronomer). P* 13.
341 **200** 20 p. multicoloured 20 30

201 Moenjodaro Excavations

202 Elements of Meteorology

1973 (23 Feb). *50th Anniv of Moenjodaro Excavations. P* 13 × 13½.
342 **201** 20 p. multicoloured 20 30

1973 (23 Mar). *I.M.O./W.M.O. Centenary. P* 13.
343 **202** 20 p. multicoloured 20 30

203 Prisoners-of-war

1973 (18 Apr). *Prisoners-of-war in India. P* 13.
344 **203** 1 r. 25, multicoloured .. .. .. 1·50 1·50

204 National Assembly Building and Constitution Book

1973 (21 Apr). *Constitution Week. P* 12½ × 13½.
345 **204** 20 p. multicoloured 40 40

205 Badge and State Bank Building

1973 (1 July). *25th Anniv of Pakistan State Bank. P* 13.
346 **205** 20 p. multicoloured 15 20
347 1 r. multicoloured 30 40

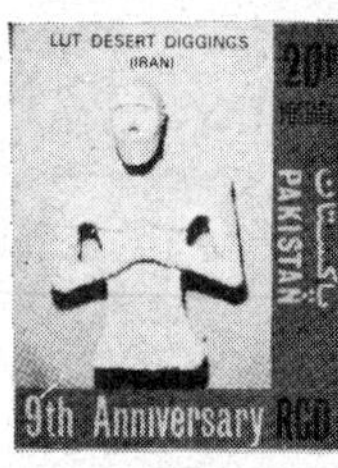

206 Lut Desert Excavations (Iran)

207 Constitution Book and Flag

1973 (21 July). *9th Anniv of Regional Co-operation for Development. T* **206** *and similar vert designs. Multicoloured. P* 13 × 13½.
348 20 p. Type **206** 30 20
349 60 p. Main Street, Moenjodaro (Pakistan) .. 55 40
350 1 r. 25, Mausoleum of Antiochus I (Turkey) 75 1·00
348/50 .. .. *Set of* 3 1·40 1·40

1973 (14 Aug). *Independence Day and Enforcement of the Constitution. P* 13.
351 **207** 20 p. multicoloured 15 20

208 Mohammed Ali Jinnah (Quaid-i-Azam)

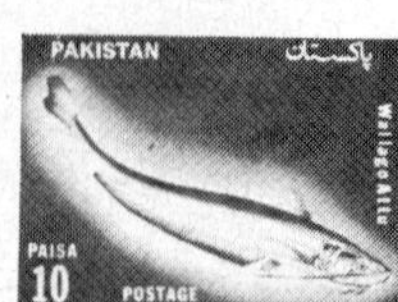

209 *Wallago attu*

1973 (11 Sept). *25th Death Anniv of Mohammed Ali Jinnah. P* 13.
352 **208** 20 p. light emerald, pale yellow and black 15 20

1973 (24 Sept). *Fishes. T* **209** *and similar horiz designs. Multicoloured. P* 13½.
353 10 p. Type **209** 80 80
a. Horiz strip of 4. Nos. 353/6 .. .. 3·50
354 20 p. *Labeo rohita* 90 90
355 60 p. *Tilapia mossambica* .. .. .. 1·00 1·00
356 1 r. *Catla catla* .. .. 1·25 1·25
353/6 .. .. *Set of* 4 3·50 3·50
Nos. 353/6 were printed within one sheet, horizontally *se-tenant*.

210 Children's Education

1973 (1 Oct). *Universal Children's Day. P* 13.
357 **210** 20 p. multicoloured 15 30

211 Harvesting

1973 (15 Oct). *Tenth Anniv of World Food Programme. P* 13.
358 **211** 20 p. multicoloured 50 30

212 Ankara and Kemal Atatürk

1973 (29 Oct). *50th Anniv of Turkish Republic. P* 13.
359 **212** 50 p. multicoloured 45 35

213 Boy Scout

214 "Basic Necessities"

1973 (11 Nov). *National Silver Jubilee Scout Jamboree. P* 13.
360 **213** 20 p. multicoloured 80 50

1973 (16 Nov). *25th Anniv of Declaration of Human Rights. P* 13.
361 **214** 20 p. multicoloured 30 30

215 Al-Biruni and Nandana Hill

216 Dr. Hansen, Microscope and Bacillus

1973 (26 Nov). *Al-Biruni Millennium Congress. P* 13.
362 **215** 20 p. multicoloured 40 20
363 1 r. 25, multicoloured 85 75

1973 (29 Dec). *Centenary of Hansen's Discovery of Leprosy Bacillus. P* 13.
364 **216** 20 p. multicoloured 75 50

217 Family and Emblem

218 Conference Emblem

1974 (1 Jan). *World Population Year. P* 13.
365 **217** 20 p. multicoloured 10 10
366 1 r. 25, multicoloured 30 40

1974 (22 Feb). *Islamic Summit Conference, Lahore. T* **218** *and similar design. P* 14 × 12½ (20 *p.*) *or* 13 (65 *p.*).
367 20 p. Type **218** 10 10
368 65 p. Emblem on "Sun" (42 × 30 *mm*) . .. 25 45
MS369 102 × 102 mm. Nos. 367/8. Imperf .. 2·50 5·00

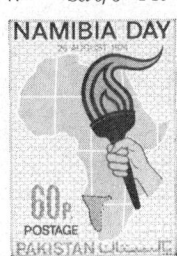

219 Units of Weight and Measurement **220** "Chand Chauthai" Carpet, Pakistan

1974 (1 July). *Adoption of International Weights and Measures System. P* 13.
370 **219** 20 p. multicoloured 15 25

1974 (21 July). *Tenth Anniv of Regional Co-operation for Development. Vert designs as T* **220** *showing carpets from member countries. Multicoloured. P* 13.
371 20 p. Type **220** 15 15
372 60 p. Persian carpet, 16th-century 45 50
373 1 r. 25, Anatolian carpet, 15th-century .. 65 1·00
371/3 .. .. *Set of* 3 1·10 1·50

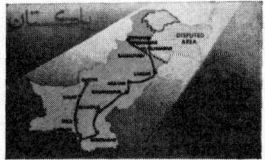

221 Hands protecting Sapling **222** Torch and Map

1974 (9 Aug). *Tree Planting Day. P* 13.
374 **221** 20 p. multicoloured 50 30

1974 (26 Aug). *Namibia Day. P* 13.
375 **222** 60 p. multicoloured 35 60

223 Highway Map

1974 (23 Sept). *Shahrah-e-Pakistan (Pakistan Highway). P* 13.
376 **223** 20 p. multicoloured 50 40

224 Boy at Desk **225** U.P.U. Emblem

1974 (7 Oct). *Universal Children's Day. P* 13.
377 **224** 20 p. multicoloured 30 30

1974 (9 Oct). *Centenary of Universal Postal Union. T* **225** *and similar vert design. Multicoloured. P* 13 × 13½ (20 *p.*) *or* 13 (2 *r.* 25).
378 20 p. Type **225** 20 20
379 2 r. 25, U.P.U. emblem, aeroplane and mail-wagon (30 × 41 *mm*) .. .. .. 55 1·40
MS380 100 × 101 mm. Nos. 378/9. Imperf .. 4·00 8·50

226 Liaquat Ali Khan **227** Dr. Mohammed Iqbal (poet and philosopher)

1974 (16 Oct). *Liaquat Ali Khan (First Prime Minister of Pakistan). P* 13 × 13½.
381 **226** 20 p. black and light vermilion 30 30

1974 (9 Nov). *Birth Centenary of Dr. Iqbal* (1977) (*1st issue*). *P* 13.
382 **227** 20 p. multicoloured 30 30
See also Nos. 399, 433 and 445/9.

228 Dr. Schweitzer and River Scene

1975 (14 Jan). *Birth Centenary of Dr. Albert Schweitzer. P* 13.
383 **228** 2 r. 25, multicoloured .. .. .. 1·75 2·00

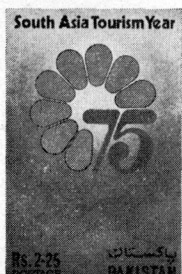

229 Tourism Year Symbol

1975 (15 Jan). *South East Asia Tourism Year. P* 13.
384 **229** 2 r. 25, multicoloured 55 80

230 Assembly Hall, Flags and Prime Minister Bhutto

(Des A. Salahuddin)

1975 (22 Feb). *First Anniv of Islamic Summit Conference, Lahore. P* 13.
385 **230** 20 p. multicoloured 35 25
386 1 r. multicoloured .. .. .. 90 1·00

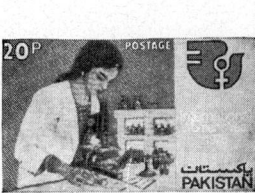

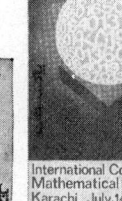

231 "Scientific Research" **232** "Globe" and Algebraic Symbol

(Des A. Salahuddin (20 p.), M. Ahmed (2 r. 25))

1975 (15 June). *International Women's Year. T* **231** *and similar horiz design. Multicoloured. P* 13.
387 20 p. Type **231** 20 25
388 2 r. 25, Girl teaching woman ("Adult Education") .. .. 1·10 1·75

1975 (14 July). *International Congress of Mathematical Sciences, Karachi. P* 13.
389 **232** 20 p. multicoloured 40 30

233 Pakistani Camel-skin Vase **234** Sapling and Dead Trees

(Des I. Gilani)

1975 (21 July). *Eleventh Anniv of Regional Co-operation for Development. T* **233** *and similar multicoloured designs. P* 13.
390 20 p. Type **233** 25 30
391 60 p. Iranian tile (*horiz*) 50 70
392 1 r. 25, Turkish porcelain vase .. .. 75 1·25
390/2 .. .. *Set of* 3 1·40 2·00

1975 (9 Aug). *Tree Planting Day. P* 13 × 13½.
393 **234** 20 p. multicoloured 35 30

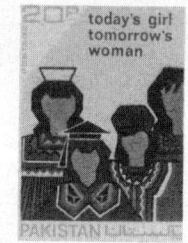

235 Black Partridge **236** "Today's Girls"

(Des A. Salahuddin)

1975 (30 Sept). *Wildlife Protection* (*1st series*). *P* 13.
394 **235** 20 p. multicoloured .. .. .. 1·00 35
395 2 r. 25, multicoloured .. .. .. 3·75 3·50
See also Nos. 400/1, 411/12, 417/18, 493/6, 560, 572/3, 581/2, 599, 600, 605, 621/2, 691, 702, 780/3 and 853.

1975 (6 Oct). *Universal Children's Day. P* 13.
396 **236** 20 p. multicoloured 30 30

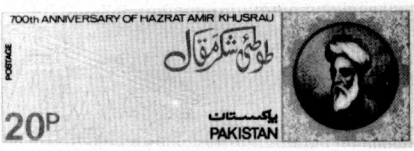

237 Hazrat Amir Khusrau, Sitar and Tabla

(Des A. Salahuddin)

1975 (24 Oct). *700th Birth Anniv of Hazrat Amir Khusrau (poet and musician). P* 13½ × 12½.
397 **237** 20 p. multicoloured 20 45
398 2 r. 25, multicoloured .. .. .. 75 1·60

238 Dr. Mohammed Iqbal **239** Urial (wild sheep)

(Des A. Salahuddin)

1975 (9 Nov). *Birth Centenary of Dr. Iqbal* (1977) (*2nd issue*). *P* 13.
399 **238** 20 p. multicoloured 30 30

(Des M. Ahmed)

1975 (31 Dec). *Wildlife Protection* (*2nd series*). *P* 13.
400 **239** 20 p. multicoloured 40 30
401 3 r. multicoloured .. .. .. 2·50 3·00

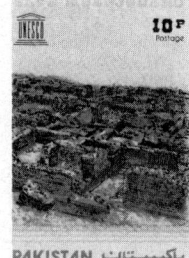

240 Moenjodaro Remains **241** Dome and Minaret of Rauza-e-Mubarak

(Des A. Salahuddin)

1976 (29 Feb). *"Save Moenjodaro" (1st series). T* **240** *and similar vert designs. Multicoloured. P* 13.
402 10 p. Type **240** 65 75
a. Horiz strip of 5. Nos. 402/6 .. .. 3·25
403 20 p. Remains (*different*) 75 85
404 65 p. The Citadel 75 85
405 3 r. Well inside a house 75 85
406 4 r. The "Great Bath" 85 95
402/6 .. .. *Set of* 5 3·25 3·75
Nos. 402/6 were printed horizontally *se-tenant* within the sheet, the five stamps forming a composite design of the excavations.
See also Nos. 414 and 430.

(Des A. Ghani. Photo)

1976 (3 Mar). *International Congress on Seerat. P* 13 × 13½.
407 **241** 20 p. multicoloured 20 20
408 3 r. multicoloured 70 90

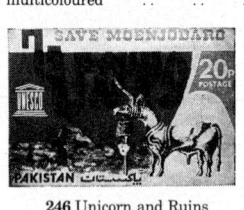

242 Alexander Graham Bell and Telephone Dial

(Des M. M. Saeed. Photo)

1976 (10 Mar). *Telephone Centenary. P* 13.
409 **242** 3 r. multicoloured .. .. .. 1·25 2·00

243 College Arms within "Sun"

(Des A. Salahuddin)

1976 (15 Mar). *Centenary of National College of Arts, Lahore. P* 13.
410 **243** 20 p. multicoloured 30 40

244 Common Peafowl

(Des A. Salahuddin)

1976 (31 Mar). *Wildlife Protection* (3*rd series*). *P* 13.
411 **244** 20 p. multicoloured 75 35
412 3 r. multicoloured .. .. .. 3·25 4·00

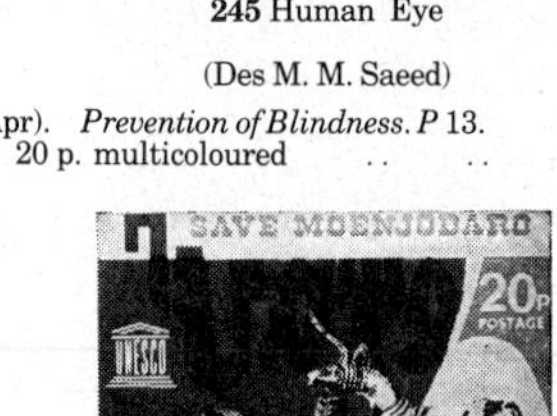

245 Human Eye

(Des M. M. Saeed)

1976 (7 Apr). *Prevention of Blindness. P* 13.
413 **245** 20 p. multicoloured 40 40

246 Unicorn and Ruins

(Des I. Gilani)

1976 (31 May). *"Save Moenjodaro"* (2*nd series*). *P* 13.
414 **246** 20 p. multicoloured 30 35

247 Jefferson Memorial

248 Ibex

(Des I. Gilani (90 p.), A. Salahuddin (4 r.))

1976 (4 July). *Bicentenary of American Revolution. T* **247** *and similar horiz design. Multicoloured. P* 13 (90 *p.*) *or* 13½ (4 *r.*).
415 90 p. Type **247** .. .. .. 1·00 60
416 4 r. "Declaration of Independence" (47 × 36 *mm*) .. .. .. 3·75 4·50

(Des M. Ahmed)

1976 (12 July). *Wildlife Protection* (4*th series*). *P* 13.
417 **248** 20 p. multicoloured 30 35
418 3 r. multicoloured .. .. .. 1·75 2·50

249 Mohammed Ali Jinnah

(Des A. Salahuddin)

1976 (21 July). *Twelfth Anniv of Regional Co-operation for Development. T* **249** *and similar diamond-shaped designs. Multicoloured. P* 14.
419 20 p. Type **249** 50 50
a. Vert strip of 3. Nos. 419/21 .. .. 1·40
420 65 p. Reza Shah the Great (Iran) 50 50
421 90 p. Kemal Atatürk (Turkey) 50 50
419/21 .. .. .. *Set of* 3 1·40 1·40
Nos. 419/21 were printed vertically *se-tenant* throughout the sheet.

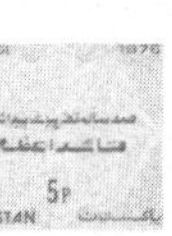

250 Urdu Text

251 Mohammed Ali Jinnah and Wazir Mansion

1976 (14 Aug). *Birth Centenary of Mohammed Ali Jinnah* (1*st issue*). *P* 13. (*a*) *Type* **250**.
422 5 p. black, new blue and yellow 20 25
a. Block of 8. Nos. 422/9 .. .. 1·75
423 10 p. black, yellow and magenta 20 25
424 15 p. black and violet-blue 20 25
425 1 r. black, yellow and new blue 30 30

(*b*) *Multicoloured designs as T* **251**, *different buildings in the background*
426 20 p. Type **251** 20 25
427 40 p. Sind Madressah 20 25
428 50 p. Minar Qarardad-e-Pakistan 20 25
429 3 r. Mausoleum 45 50
422/9 .. .. .. *Set of* 8 1·75 2·10
Nos. 422/9 were printed in *se-tenant* blocks of 8 throughout the sheet.
See also No. 436.

252 Dancing-girl, Ruins and King Priest

(Des A. Salahuddin)

1976 (31 Aug). *"Save Moenjodaro"* (3*rd series*). *P* 14.
430 **252** 65 p. multicoloured 35 35

253 U.N. Racial Discrimination Emblem

(Des A. Salahuddin)

1976 (15 Sept). *U.N. Decade to Combat Racial Discrimination. P* 12½ × 13½.
431 **253** 65 p. multicoloured 30 40

254 Child in Maze and Basic Services

(Des M. Ahmed)

1976 (4 Oct). *Universal Children's Day. P* 13.
432 **254** 20 p. multicoloured 20 30

Stamps commemorating the visit of King Khalid of Saudi Arabia and showing the Islamabad Mosque were prepared for release on 11 October 1976, but withdrawn before issue. Some are known to have been released in error.

255 Verse from "Allama Iqbal"

256 Mohammed Ali Jinnah giving Scout Salute

(Des M. A. Javed)

1976 (9 Nov). *Birth Centenary of Dr. Iqbal* (1977) (3*rd issue*). *P* 13.
433 **255** 20 p. multicoloured 15 20

(Des I. Gilani)

1976 (20 Nov). *Quaid-i-Azam Centenary Jamboree. P* 13½.
434 **256** 20 p. multicoloured 45 30

257 Children Reading

258 Mohammed Ali Jinnah

(Des M. Ahmed)

1976 (15 Dec). *Children's Literature. P* 13.
435 **257** 20 p. multicoloured 20 30

(Litho and embossed Cartor S.A., France)

1976 (25 Dec). *Birth Centenary of Mohammed Ali Jinnah* (2*nd issue*). *P* 12½.
436 **258** 10 r. emerald and gold .. .. .. 2·50 3·50

259 Rural Family

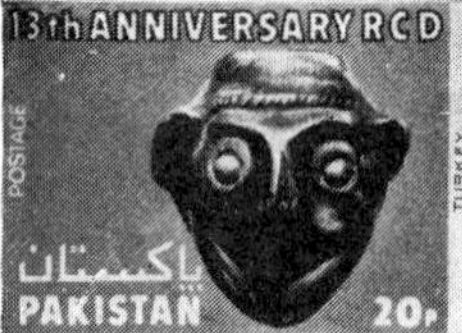

260 Turkish Vase, 1800 B.C.

(Des M. Ahmed)

1977 (14 Apr). *Social Welfare and Rural Development Year. P* 13.
437 **259** 20 p. multicoloured 15 10

(Des A. Salahuddin)

1977 (21 July). 13*th Anniv of Regional Co-operation for Development. T* **260** *and similar horiz designs. P* 13.
438 20 p. red-orange, violet-blue and black .. 25 10
439 65 p. multicoloured 35 15
440 90 p. multicoloured 45 30
438/40 .. .. .. *Set of* 3 95 45
Designs:—60 p. Pakistani toy bullock cart, Moenjodaro; 90 p. Pitcher with spout, Sialk Hill, Iran.

261 Forest

262 Desert Scene

(Des A. Ahmed)

1977 (9 Aug). *National Tree Plantation Campaign. P* 13.
441 **261** 20 p. multicoloured 10 10

(Des M. A. Javed)

1977 (5 Sept). *U.N. Conference on Desertification, Nairobi. P* 13.
442 **262** 65 p. multicoloured 30 20

263 "Water for the Children of the World"

264 Aga Khan III

(Des A. Salahuddin)

1977 (3 Oct). *Universal Children's Day. P* 13½ × 12½.
443 **263** 50 p. multicoloured 40 20

(Des A. Rauf)

1977 (2 Nov). *Birth Centenary of Aga Khan III. P* 13.
444 **264** 2 r. multicoloured 55 85

265 Iqbal and Spirit of the Poet Roomi (from painting by Behzad)

266 The Holy "Khana-Kaaba" (House of God, Mecca)

(Des A. Ahmed)

1977 (9 Nov). *Birth Centenary of Dr. Mohammed Iqbal* (*4th issue*). *T* **265** *and similar vert designs. Multicoloured. P* 13.
445 20 p. Type **265** 25 35
a. Horiz strip of 5. Nos. 445/9 .. .. 1·40
446 65 p. Iqbal looking at Jamaluddin Afghani and Saeed Haleem Pasha at prayer (Behzad) 25 35
447 1 r. 25, Urdu verse 30 40
448 2 r. 25, Persian verse.. .. .. .. 35 45
449 3 r. Iqbal 40 50
445/9 .. .. *Set of* 5 1·40 1·90
Nos. 445, 448/9, 447 and 446 (in that order) were issued in horizontal *se-tenant* strips of 5.

(Des I. Gilani)

1977 (21 Nov). *Haj* (*pilgrimage to Mecca*). *P* 14.
450 **266** 65 p. multicoloured 30 30

267 Rheumatic Patient and Healthy Man

268 Woman in Costume of Rawalpindi-Islamabad

(Des T. Hameed)

1977 (19 Dec). *World Rheumatism Year. P* 13.
451 **267** 65 p. turquoise-blue, black and yellow .. 30 20

(Des A. Salahuddin)

1978 (5 Feb). *Indonesia–Pakistan Economic and Cultural Co-operation Organization. P* 12½ × 13½.
452 **268** 75 p. multicoloured 30 20

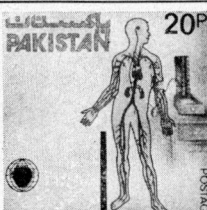

269 Human Body and Sphygmomanometer

270 Henri Dunant

(Des A. Salahuddin)

1978 (20 Apr). *World Hypertension Month. P* 13.
453 **269** 20 p. multicoloured 15 10
454 – 2 r. multicoloured 60 60
The 2 r. value is as T **269**, but has the words "Down with high blood pressure" instead of the Urdu inscription at bottom left.

(Des A. Salahuddin)

1978 (8 May). *150th Birth Anniv of Henri Dunant* (*founder of Red Cross*). *P* 14.
455 **270** 1 r. black, new blue and vermilion .. 45 20

271 Red Roses (Pakistan)

272 "Pakistan, World Cup Hockey Champions"

(Des A. Salahuddin)

1978 (21 July). *14th Anniv of Regional Co-operation for Development. T* **271** *and similar vert designs. Multicoloured. P* 13½.
456 20 p. Type **271** 35 20
a. Horiz strip of 3. Nos. 456/8 .. .. 1·40
457 90 p. Pink roses (Iran).. .. .. .. 50 20
458 2 r. Yellow rose (Turkey) 75 25
456/8 .. .. *Set of* 3 1·40 60
Nos. 456/8 were printed together, *se-tenant*, in horizontal strips of 3 throughout the sheet.

(Des M. Munawar)

1978 (26 Aug). *"Riccione '78" International Stamp Fair. T* **272** *and similar vert design. Multicoloured. P* 13.
459 1 r. Type **272** .. .. 1·00 25
460 2 r. Fountain at Plazza Turismo .. .. 1·25 35

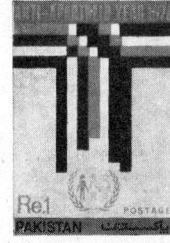

273 Cogwheels within Globe Symbol

274 St. Patrick's Cathedral

(Des A. Salahuddin)

1978 (3 Sept). *U.N. Technical Co-operation amongst Developing Countries Conference. P* 13.
461 **273** 75 p. multicoloured 15 10

(Des A. Salahuddin)

1978 (29 Sept). *Centenary of St. Patrick's Cathedral, Karachi. T* **274** *and similar vert design. Multicoloured. P* 13.
462 1 r. Type **274** 10 10
463 2 r. Stained glass window 25 25

275 Minar-i-Qarardad-e-Pakistan

276 Tractor

276*a* Mausoleum of Ibrahim Khan Makli, Thatta

Two Dies of 75 p. value:

Die I　　Die II

Die I. Size of design 26½ × 21½ mm. Figures of value large; "p" small. Plough does not touch left-hand frame.
Die II. Size of design 25½ × 21 mm. Smaller figures; larger "p". Plough touches left-hand frame.

(Des A. Salahuddin. Litho (10, 25, 40, 50, 90 p.), recess (others))

1978 (7 Nov)–**81**. *No wmk* (*2 to 90 p.*) *or W* **98** (*1 to 5 r.*). *P* 14×13½ (*2 to 5 p.*), 13½×14 (*10 to 90 p.*) *or* 13 (*1 to 5 r.*).
464 **275** 2 p. deep grey-green 10 10
465 3 p. black 10 10
a. Imperf (pair) .. .. .. 5·00
466 5 p. deep ultramarine 10 10
467 **276** 10 p. new blue & greenish bl (7.10.79) .. 10 10
468 20 p. deep yellow-green (25.3.79) .. 50 10
469 25 p. dp green & dull magenta (19.3.79) 50 10
470 40 p. new blue and magenta (16.12.78) 10 10
471 50 p. slate-lilac & turq-green (19.3.79) .. 30 10
472 60 p. black (16.12.78) 10 10
a. Imperf (pair) .. .. .. 5·00
473 75 p. dull vermilion (I) (16.12.78) .. 60 10
a. Imperf (pair) .. .. .. 16·00
b. Die II (1980) 45 10
ba. Imperf (pair) .. .. .. 7·00
474 90 p. magenta and new blue (16.12.78) 20 10
475 **276***a* 1 r. bronze-green (2.8.80) 10 10
a. Imperf (pair) .. .. .. 20·00
476 1 r. 50, red-orange (17.11.79) 10 10
a. Imperf (pair) .. .. .. 6·00
477 2 r. carmine-red (17.11.79) 15 10
a. Imperf (pair) .. .. .. 7·00
478 3 r. blue-black (4.6.80) 20 10
a. Imperf (pair) .. .. .. 9·00
479 4 r. black (1.1.81) 30 10
a. Imperf (pair) .. .. ..
480 5 r. sepia (1.1.81) 30 10
a. Imperf (pair) .. .. ..
464/80 .. .. *Set of* 17 3·00 75
The remaining values as Type **276** printed in recess, are from Die II.
Postal forgeries exist of the 2 r. and 3 r. values. These are poorly printed with perforations which do not match those of the genuine stamps.

GUM. Later printings of the 10 p., 20 p., 25 p., 4 r. and 5 r. values (Nos. 467/9 and 479/80) occur with matt, almost invisible gum of a PVA type, instead of the gum arabic used previously.

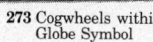

277 Emblem and "United Races" Symbol

278 Maulana Mohammad Ali Jauhar

(Des M. Munawar)

1978 (20 Nov). *International Anti-Apartheid Year. P* 13.
481 **277** 1 r. multicoloured 15 15

(Des A. Salahuddin)

1978 (10 Dec). *Birth Centenary of Maulana Mohammad Ali Jauhar* (*patriot*). *P* 13.
482 **278** 50 p. multicoloured 40 20

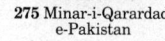

279 "Tornado", "Rapide" and Wright *Flyer*

(Des A. Salahuddin)

1978 (24 Dec). *75th Anniv of Powered Flight. T* **279** *and similar diamond-shaped designs. Multicoloured. P* 13.

483 65 p. Type **279** 75 75
a. Block of 4. Nos. 483/6 .. .. 3·50
484 1 r. "Phantom F4F", "Tri-star" and Wright *Flyer* 90 90
485 2 r. "X15", Tu. "104" and Wright *Flyer* .. 1·10 1·10
486 2 r. 25, Mig "15", "Concorde" and Wright *Flyer* .. .. 1·25 1·25
483/6 .. .. *Set of* 4 3·50 3·50

Nos. 483/6 were printed together, *se-tenant*, in blocks of 4 throughout the sheet.

280 "Holy Koran illuminating Globe" and Raudha-e-Mubarak (mausoleum)

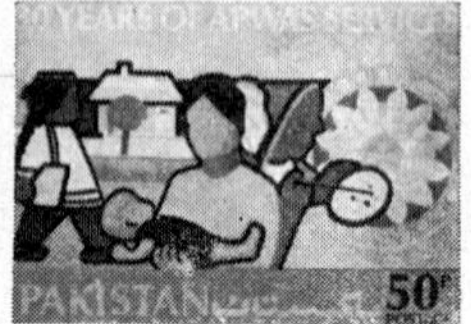

281 "Aspects of A.P.W.A."

(Des A. Salahuddin)

1979 (10 Feb). *"12th Rabi-ul-Awwal" (Prophet Mohammed's birthday). P* 13.

487 **280** 20 p. multicoloured 30 15

(Des M. Saeed)

1979 (25 Feb). *30th Anniv of A.P.W.A. (All Pakistan Women's Association). P* 13.

488 **281** 50 p. multicoloured 40 15

282 Tippu Sultan Shaheed of Mysore

(Des A. Rauf)

1979 (23 Mar). *Pioneers of Freedom (1st series). T* **282** *and similar diamond-shaped designs. Multicoloured. W* **98**. *P* 14.

490 10 r. Type **282** 50 55
a. Horiz strip of 3. Nos. 490/2 .. .. 2·25
491 15 r. Sir Syed Ahmad Khan 70 75
492 25 r. Altaf Hussain Hali .. .. .. 1·25 1·40
490/2 .. .. *Set of* 3 2·25 2·40

Nos. 490/2 were printed together *se-tenant* in the same sheet: there being ten horizontal strips of 3 values and ten additional 10 r. stamps.

See also Nos. 757, 801/27 and 838/46.

283 Himalayan Monal Pheasant

(Des M. Ahmed)

1979 (17 June). *Wildlife Protection (5th series). Pheasants. T* **283** *and similar horiz designs. Multicoloured. P* 13.

493 20 p. Type **283** 75 40
494 25 p. Kalij 75 45
495 40 p. Koklass .. .. 1·00 75
496 1 r. Cheer .. .. 2·00 1·50
493/6 .. .. *Set of* 4 4·00 2·75

284 "Pakistan Village Scene" (Ustad Bakhsh)

(Des A. Rauf)

1979 (21 July). *15th Anniv of Regional Co-operation for Development. Paintings. T* **284** *and similar horiz designs. Multicoloured. P* 14 × 12½.

497 40 p. Type **284** 20 25
a. Vert strip of 3. Nos. 497/9 60
498 75 p. "Iranian Goldsmith" (Kamal al Molk) .. 20 25
499 1 r. 60, "Turkish Harvest" (Namik Ismail) .. 25 30
497/9 .. .. *Set of* 3 60 70

Nos. 497/9 were printed together, *se-tenant*, in vertical strips of 3 throughout the sheet.

285 Guj Embroidered Shirt (detail)

1979 (23 Aug). *Handicrafts (1st series). T* **285** *and similar horiz designs. Multicoloured. P* 14 × 12½.

500 40 p. Type **285** 20 20
a. Block of 4. Nos. 500/3 .. .. .. 1·00
501 1 r. Enamel inlaid brass plate 25 25
502 1 r. 50, Baskets 30 30
503 2 r. Chain-stitch embroidered rug (detail) .. 40 40
500/3 .. .. *Set of* 4 1·00 1·00

Nos. 500/3 were printed together, *se-tenant*, in blocks of 4 throughout the sheet.

See also Nos. 578/9, 595/6 and 625/8.

286 Children playing on Climbing Frame

(Des A. Rauf)

1979 (10 Sept). *S.O.S. Children's Village, Lahore (orphanage). P* 13.

504 **286** 50 p. multicoloured 30 30

287 "Island" (Z. Maloof)

(Des A. Salahuddin)

1979 (22 Oct). *International Year of the Child. Children's Paintings. T* **287** *and similar horiz designs. Multicoloured. P* 14 × 12½.

505 40 p. Type **287** 15 15
a. Block of 4. Nos. 505/8 85
506 75 p. "Playground" (R. Akbar) 25 25
507 1 r. "Fairground" (M. Azam) 25 25
508 1 r. 50, "Hockey Match" (M. Tayyab) .. 30 30
505/8 .. .. *Set of* 4 85 85
MS509 79 × 64 mm. 2 r. "Child looking at Faces in the Sky" (M. Mumtaz) (*vert*). Imperf .. .. 3·25 3·25

Nos. 505/8 were printed together, *se-tenant*, in blocks of 4 throughout the sheet.

Examples of No. **MS**509 are known overprinted in gold for the "PHILEXFRANCE" International Stamp Exhibition in 1982. The Pakistan Post Office has declared such overprints to be bogus.

288 Warrior attacking Crab

289 Pakistan Customs Emblem

(Des A. Salahuddin)

1979 (12 Nov). *Fight Against Cancer. P* 14.

510 **288** 40 p. black, greenish yellow and magenta 40 30

(Des A. Salahuddin)

1979 (10 Dec). *Centenary of Pakistan Customs Service. P* 13 × 13½.

511 **289** 1 r. multicoloured 20 30

290 Boeing "747 (Jumbo)" and Douglas "DC-3" Airliners

291 Islamic Pattern

(Des A. Salahuddin)

1980 (10 Jan). *25th Anniv of Pakistan International Air Lines. P* 13.

512 **290** 1 r. multicoloured 50 50

(Des and litho Secura, Singapore)

1980 (15 Jan–10 Mar). *Matt, almost invisible PVA gum. P* 12.

513 **291** 10 p. slate-green and orange-yellow .. 10 10
514 15 p. slate-green and bright yellow-green 10 10
515 25 p. violet and brown-red (10.3) .. 10 10
516 35 p. carmine & brt yellow-green (10.3) .. 10 10
517 – 40 p. rosine and olive-sepia 15 10
518 – 50 p. violet and dull yellow-green (10.3) 10 10
519 – 80 p. brt yellow-green & black (10.3) .. 15 15
513/19 .. .. *Set of* 7 70 55

The 40 to 80 p. values also show different Islamic patterns, the 40 p. being horizontal and the remainder vertical.

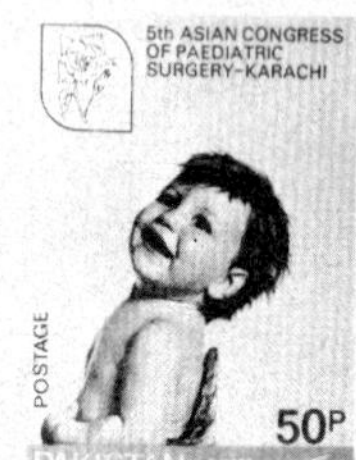

292 Young Child

293 Conference Emblem

(Des M. Saeed)

1980 (16 Feb). *5th Asian Congress of Paediatric Surgery, Karachi. P* 13.

530 **292** 50 p. multicoloured 40 40

(Des A. Salahuddin)

1980 (17 May). *11th Islamic Conference of Foreign Ministers, Islamabad. P* 13.

531 **293** 1 r. multicoloured 30 45

294 Karachi Port

(Des A. Salahuddin)

1980 (15 July). *Centenary of Karachi Port Authority. P* 13 × 13½.

532 **294** 1 r. multicoloured 60 60

RICCIONE 80

(295)

296 College Emblem with Old and New Buildings

1980 (30 Aug). *"Riccione 80" International Stamp Exhibition. Nos. 505/8 optd with T* **295** *in red.*

533 40 p. Type **287** 25 25
534 75 p. "Playground" (R. Akbar) 30 30
535 1 r. "Fairground" (M. Azam) 35 35
536 1 r. 50, "Hockey Match" (M. Tayyab) .. 45 45
533/6 .. .. *Set of* 4 1·25 1·25

(Des M. Munawar)

1980 (18 Sept). *75th Anniv of Command and Staff College, Quetta. P* 13.

537 **296** 1 r. multicoloured 10 15

WORLD TOURISM CONFERENCE
MANILA 80

(297)

1980 (27 Sept). *World Tourism Conference, Manila. No. 496 optd with T* **297**.

538 1 r. Cheer 30 15

298 Birth Centenary Emblem

(Des A. Salahuddin)

1980 (5 Oct). *Birth Centenary of Hafiz Mahmood Shairani. P* 13.
539 **298** 40 p. multicoloured 30 40

299 Shalimar Gardens, Lahore

(Des A. Salahuddin)

1980 (23 Oct). *Aga Khan Award for Architecture. P* 13.
540 **299** 2 r. multicoloured 30 60

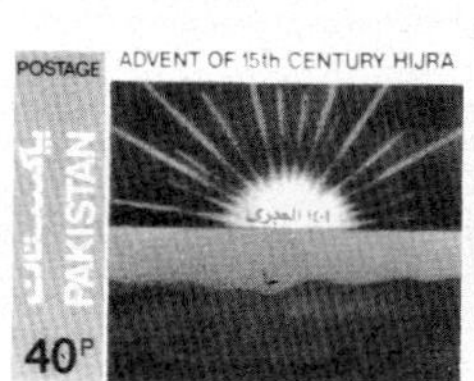

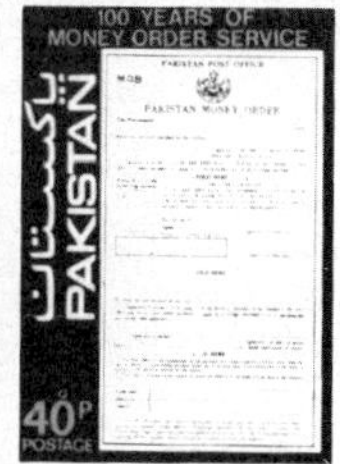

300 Rising Sun **301** Money Order Form

(Des S. Ahmed (40 p.), J. Sultana (2 r.), A. Salahuddin (others))

1980 (10 Nov). *1400th Anniv of Hegira (1st issue). T* **300** *and similar multicoloured designs. P* 14 (2 *r.*) *or* 13 (*others*).
541 40 p. Type **300** 10 10
542 2 r. Ka'aba and symbols of Moslem achievement (34 × 34 *mm*) 25 40
543 3 r. Holy Koran illuminating World (31 × 54 *mm*) 30 60
541/3 .. .. *Set of* 3 55 95
MS544 106 × 84 mm. 4 r. Candles. Imperf .. .. 45 1·00
See also No. 549.

(Des A. Ahmed)

1980 (20 Dec). *Centenary of Money Order Service. P* 13.
545 **301** 40 p. multicoloured 15 30

302 Postcards encircling Globe **303** Heinrich von Stephan and U.P.U. Emblem

(Des A. Ahmed)

1980 (27 Dec). *Centenary of Postcard Service. P* 13.
546 **302** 40 p. multicoloured 15 30

(Des J. Sultana)

1981 (7 Jan). *150th Birth Anniv of Heinrich von Stephan (founder of U.P.U.). P* 13.
547 **303** 1 r. multicoloured 20 15

304 Aircraft and Airmail Letters

(Des J. Sultana)

1981 (15 Feb). *50th Anniv of Airmail Service. P* 13.
548 **304** 1 r. multicoloured 20 15

305 Mecca **306** Conference Emblem and Afghan Refugees

1981 (7 Mar). *1400th Anniv of Hegira (2nd issue). P* 13.
549 **305** 40 p. multicoloured 15 20

(Des Z. Akhlaq (Nos. 550 and 552), A. Ahmed (Nos. 551 and 553), M. Jafree (No. 554))

1981 (29 Mar). *Islamic Summit Conference (1st issue). T* **306** *and similar multicoloured designs. P* 13.
550 40 p. Type **306** 25 10
551 40 p. Conference emblem encircled by flags and Afghan refugees (28 × 58 *mm*) 25 10
552 1 r. Type **306** 40 10
553 1 r. As No. 551 .. .. 40 10
554 2 r. Conference emblem and map showing Afghanistan (48 × 32 *mm*) 55 50
550/4 .. .. *Set of* 5 1·75 75

307 Conference Emblem **308** Kemal Atatürk

(Des A. Salahuddin (Nos. 555, 557), A. Irani (Nos. 556, 558))

1981 (20 Apr). *Islamic Summit Conference (2nd issue). T* **307** *and similar multicoloured design. P* 13.
555 40 p. Type **307** 10 10
556 40 p. Conference emblem and flags (28 × 46 *mm*) 10 10
557 85 p. Type **307** 20 15
558 85 p. As No. 556 .. .. 20 15
555/8 .. .. *Set of* 4 55 30

(Des A. Salahuddin)

1981 (19 May). *Birth Centenary of Kemal Atatürk (Turkish statesman). P* 13.
559 **308** 1 r. multicoloured 20 15

309 Green Turtle **310** Dome of the Rock

(Des Jamal. Litho Secura, Singapore)

1981 (20 June). *Wildlife Protection (6th series). Matt, almost invisible PVA gum. P* 12 × 11½.
560 **309** 40 p. multicoloured 65 20

(Des A. Salahuddin)

1981 (25 July). *Palestinian Welfare. P* 13.
561 **310** 2 r. multicoloured 35 35

311 Malubiting West

(Litho Secura, Singapore)

1981 (20 Aug). *Mountain Peaks (1st series). Karakoram Range. T* **311** *and similar multicoloured designs. Matt, almost invisible PVA gum. P* 14 × 13½.
562 40 p. Type **311** 40 35
a. Horiz pair. Nos. 562/3 .. .. 80 70
563 40 p. Malubiting West (24 × 31 *mm*) 40 35
564 1 r. Haramosh 75 55
a. Horiz pair. Nos. 564/5 .. .. 1·50 1·10
565 1 r. Haramosh (24 × 31 *mm*) 75 55
566 1 r. 50, K6 .. .. 90 70
a. Horiz pair. Nos. 566/7 .. .. 1·75 1·40
567 1 r. 50, K6 (24 × 31 *mm*) 90 70
568 2 r. K2, Broad Peak, Gasherbrum 4 and Gasherbrum 2 .. .. 1·00 1·00
a. Horiz pair. Nos. 568/9 .. .. 2·00 2·00
569 2 r. K2 (24 × 31 *mm*) .. .. 1·00 1·00
562/9 .. .. *Set of* 8 5·50 4·75
The two designs of each value were printed together, *se-tenant*, in horizontal pairs throughout the sheet.
See also Nos. 674/5.

312 Pakistan Steel "Furnace No. 1" **313** Western Tragopan

(Des A. Ahmed)

1981 (31 Aug). *First Firing of Pakistan Steel "Furnace No. 1", Karachi. P* 13.
570 **312** 40 p. multicoloured 15 10
571 2 r. multicoloured 35 30

(Litho Secura, Singapore)

1981 (15 Sept). *Wildlife Protection (7th series). Matt, almost invisible PVA gum. P* 14.
572 **313** 40 p. multicoloured .. .. 1·25 50
573 – 2 r. multicoloured .. .. 3·00 3·25
The 2 r. value is as Type **313** but the background design shows a winter view.

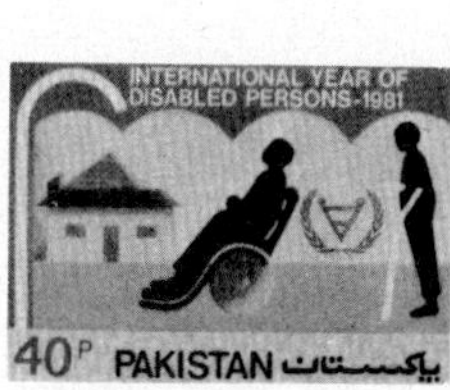
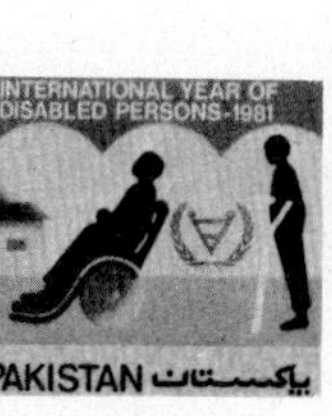

314 Disabled People and I.Y.D.P. Emblem **315** World Hockey Cup below flags of participating Countries

(Des M. Saeed)

1981 (12 Dec). *International Year for Disabled Persons. P* 13.
574 **314** 40 p. multicoloured 20 20
575 2 r. multicoloured 70 90

(Des A. Salahuddin)

1982 (31 Jan). *Pakistan—World Cup Hockey Champions. T* **315** *and similar vert design. Multicoloured. P* 13.
576 1 r. Type **315** .. .. 1·50 90
577 1 r. World Hockey Cup above flags of participating countries .. .. 1·50 90

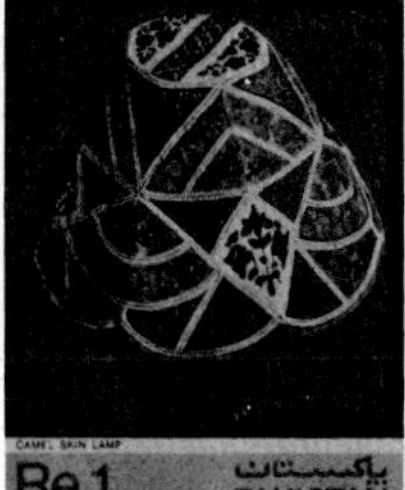

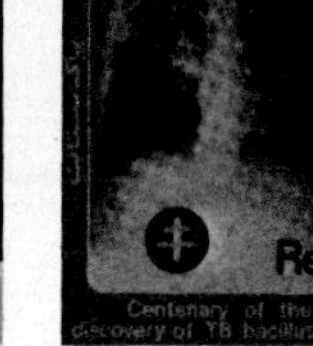

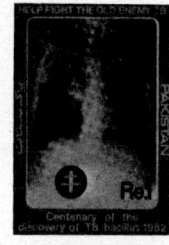

316 Camel Skin Lamp **317** Chest X-Ray of Infected Person

(Des A. Salahuddin. Litho Secura, Singapore)

1982 (20 Feb). *Handicrafts (2nd series). T* **316** *and similar vert design. Multicoloured. P* 14.
578 1 r. Type **316** 30 25
579 1 r. Hala pottery 30 25
See also Nos. 595/6.

(Des A. Ahmed)

1982 (24 Mar). *Centenary of Robert Koch's Discovery of Tubercle Bacillus. P* 13.
580 **317** 1 r. multicoloured 70 60

318 Indus Dolphin

(Des A. Salahuddin. Litho Secura, Singapore)

1982 (24 Apr). *Wildlife Protection* (8*th series*). *P* 12 × 11½.
581 **318** 40 p. multicoloured .. .. .. 1·25 90
582 – 1 r. multicoloured .. .. .. 2·25 2·10
The 1 r. value is as Type **318** but the design is reversed.

319 "Apollo–Soyuz" Link-up, 1975

(Des A. Salahuddin)

1982 (7 June). *Peaceful Uses of Outer Space. P* 13.
583 **319** 1 r. multicoloured 90 55

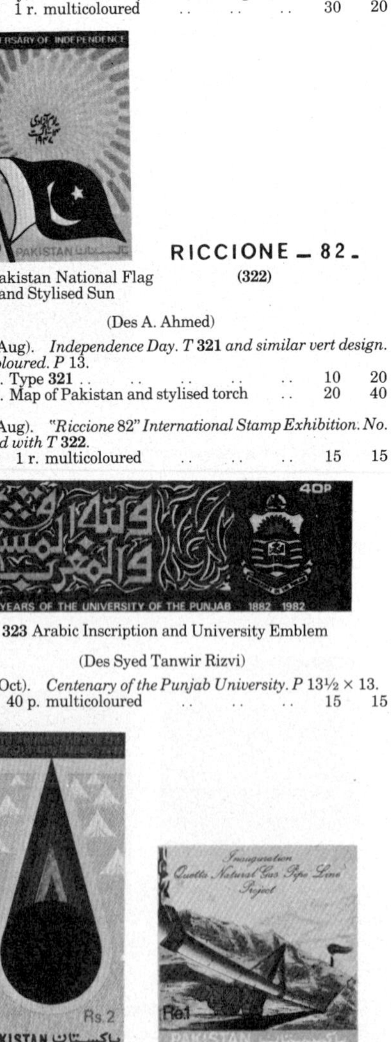

320 Sukkur Barrage

(Des A. Salahuddin)

1982 (17 July). 50*th Anniv of Sukkur Barrage. P* 13.
584 **320** 1 r. multicoloured 30 20

321 Pakistan National Flag and Stylised Sun

(322)

(Des A. Ahmed)

1982 (14 Aug). *Independence Day. T* **321** *and similar vert design. Multicoloured. P* 13.
585 40 p. Type **321** 10 20
586 85 p. Map of Pakistan and stylised torch .. 20 40

1982 (28 Aug). *"Riccione 82" International Stamp Exhibition. No.* 584 *optd with T* **322**.
587 **320** 1 r. multicoloured 15 15

323 Arabic Inscription and University Emblem

(Des Syed Tanwir Rizvi)

1982 (14 Oct). *Centenary of the Punjab University. P* 13½ × 13.
588 **323** 40 p. multicoloured 15 15

324 Scout Emblem and Tents **325** Laying Pipeline

(Des M. Saeed)

1982 (23 Dec). 75*th Anniv of Boy Scout Movement. P* 13.
589 **324** 2 r. multicoloured 30 30

(Des A. Salahuddin)

1983 (6 Jan). *Inauguration of Quetta Natural Gas Pipeline Project. P* 13.
590 **325** 1 r. multicoloured 15 20

326 *Papilio polyctor*

(Litho Secura, Singapore)

1983 (15 Feb). *Butterflies. T* **326** *and similar horiz designs. Multicoloured. Matt, almost invisible PVA gum. P* 13½.
591 40 p. Type **326** 70 20
592 50 p. *Atrophaneura aristolochiae* 70 20
593 60 p. *Danaus chrysippus* 80 30
594 1 r. 50, *Papilio demoleus* .. .. .. 1·10 70
591/4 .. .. *Set of* 4 3·00 1·25

(Litho Secura, Singapore)

1983 (9 Mar). *Handicrafts* (3*rd series*). *Vert designs as T* **316**. *Multicoloured. Matt, almost invisible PVA gum. P* 14.
595 1 r. Five flower motif needlework, Sind .. 15 15
596 1 r. Straw mats 15 15

327 School of Nursing and University Emblem

(Des A. Salahuddin)

1983 (16 Mar). *Presentation of Charter to Aga Khan University, Karachi. P* 13½ × 13.
597 **327** 2 r. multicoloured 30 30
No. 597 was issued in sheets of 8 (2 × 4), each horizontal pair being separated by a different *se-tenant* label showing views of the University.

328 Yak Caravan crossing Zindiharam-Darkot Pass, Hindu Kush

(Des A. Salahuddin)

1983 (28 Apr). *Trekking in Pakistan. P* 13.
598 **328** 1 r. multicoloured 40 30

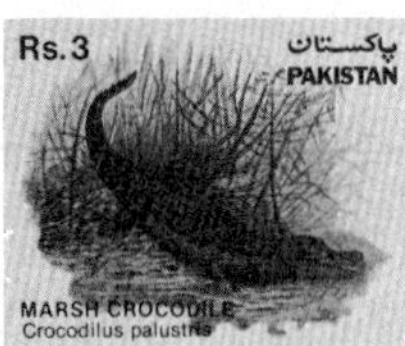

329 Marsh Crocodile

(Litho Secura, Singapore)

1983 (19 May). *Wildlife Protection* (9*th series*). *Matt, almost invisible PVA gum. P* 13½.
599 **329** 3 r. multicoloured .. .. .. 1·75 1·25

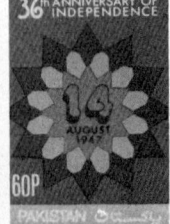

330 Goitred Gazelle **331** Floral Design

(Litho Secura, Singapore)

1983 (20 June). *Wildlife Protection* (10*th series*). *Matt, almost invisible PVA gum. P* 14 × 13½.
600 **330** 1 r. multicoloured .. .. .. 1·25 75

(Des A. Ahmed)

1983 (14 Aug). 36*th Anniv of Independence. T* **331** *and similar vert design. Multicoloured. P* 13.
601 60 p. Type **331** 10 10
602 4 r. Hand holding flaming torch 40 45

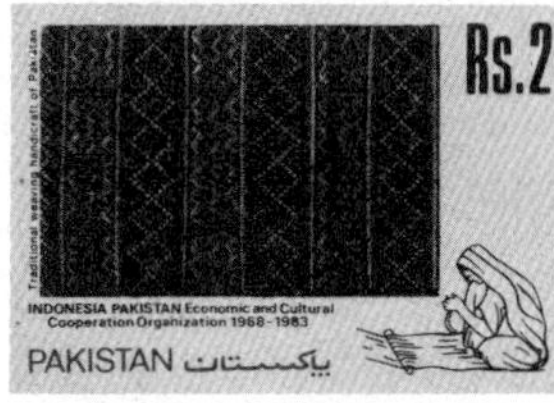

332 Traditional Weaving, Pakistan

(Des A. Salahuddin)

1983 (19 Aug). *Indonesian–Pakistan Economic and Cultural Cooperation Organization,* 1969–1983. *T* **332** *and similar horiz design. Multicoloured. P* 13.
603 2 r. Type **332** 20 25
604 2 r. Traditional weaving, Indonesia 20 25

333 "Siberian Cranes" (Great White Cranes) (Sir Peter Scott)

1983 (8 Sept). *Wildlife Protection* (11*th series*). *P* 13.
605 **333** 3 r. multicoloured .. .. .. 1·75 90

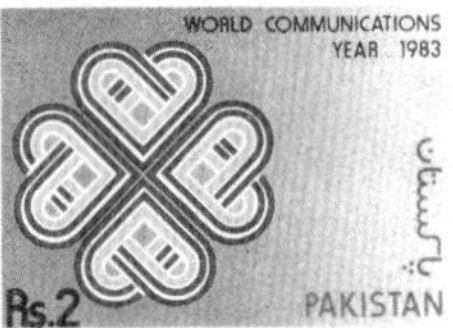

334 W.C.Y. Emblem

1983 (9 Oct). *World Communications Year. T* **334** *and similar multicoloured design. P* 13 (2 *r.*) *or* 14 (3 *r.*).
606 2 r. Type **334** 20 25
607 3 r. W.C.Y. emblem (*different*) (33 × 33 *mm*) 30 35

335 Farm Animals **336** Agricultural Produce and Fertiliser Factory

(Des A. Salahuddin)

1983 (24 Oct). *World Food Day. T* **335** *and similar horiz designs. Multicoloured. P* 13.
608 3 r. Type **335** .. .. 1·00 1·00
a. Horiz strip of 4. Nos. 608/11 .. .. 3·50
609 3 r. Fruit .. .. 1·00 1·00
610 3 r. Crops .. .. 1·00 1·00
611 3 r. Sea food .. .. 1·00 1·00
608/11 .. .. *Set of* 4 3·50 3·50
Nos. 608/11 were printed together, *se-tenant*, in horizontal strips of four throughout the sheet.

(Des J. Sultana)

1983 (24 Oct). *National Fertiliser Corporation. P* 13 × 13½.
612 **336** 60 p. multicoloured 15 20

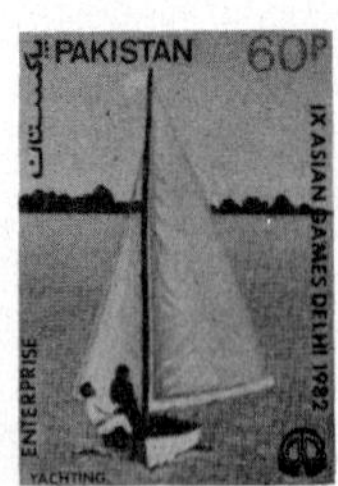

337 Lahore, 1852 **338** Winner of "Enterprise" Event

(Des A. Salahuddin)

1983 (13 Nov). *National Stamp Exhibition, Lahore. T* **337** *and similar vert designs showing panoramic view of Lahore in* 1852. *Multicoloured. P* 13 × 13½.

613	60 p. Musti Durwaza Dharmsala	15	15
	a. Horiz strip of 6. Nos. 613/18	80	
614	60 p. Khabgha	15	15
615	60 p. Type **337**	15	15
616	60 p. Summan Burj Hazuri	15	15
617	60 p. Flower Garden, Samadhi Northern Gate	15	15
618	60 p. Budda Darya, Badshahi Masjid	15	15
613/18	*Set of* 6	80	80

Nos. 613/18 were printed together, *se-tenant* in sheets of twelve, containing two horizontal strips of six.

(Des J. Sultana)

1983 (31 Dec). *Yachting Champions, Asian Games, Delhi. T* **338** *and similar vert design. Multicoloured. P* 13.

619	60 p. Type **338**	75	40
620	60 p. Winner of "OK" Dinghy event	75	40

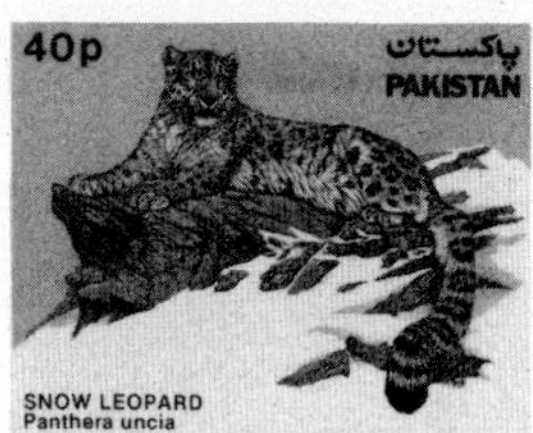

339 Snow Leopard

(Litho Secura, Singapore)

1984 (21 Jan). *Wildlife Protection* (12*th series*). *Matt, almost invisible PVA gum. P* 14.

621 **339**	40 p. multicoloured	1·25	50
622	1 r. 60, multicoloured	2·75	3·00

340 Jahangir Khan (World Squash Champion)

341 P.I.A. Airliner

1984 (17 Mar). *Squash. P* 13.

623 **340**	3 r. multicoloured	1·00	75

(Des A. Salahuddin)

1984 (29 Apr). 20*th Anniv of Pakistan International Airways' Service to China. P* 13.

624 **341**	3 r. multicoloured	3·00	3·00

342 Glass-work

343 Attock Fort

(Des A. Salahuddin. Litho Secura, Singapore)

1984 (31 May). *Handicrafts* (4*th series*). *T* **342** *and similar designs showing glass-work in Sheesh Mahal, Lahore Fort. P* 13½.

625	1 r. multicoloured (blue frame)	10	15
626	1 r. multicoloured (red frame)	10	15
627	1 r. multicoloured (green frame) (*horiz*)	10	15
628	1 r. multicoloured (violet frame) (*horiz*)	10	15
625/8	*Set of* 4	35	55

(Des J. Sultana)

1984 (16 June)–**86**. *Forts. T* **343** *and similar horiz designs. P* 11.

629	5 p. brownish black & brown-pur (1.11.84)	10	10
630	10 p. brownish black and rose-red (25.9.84)	10	10
631	15 p. reddish violet & bistre-brown (1.12.86)	10	10
632	20 p. black and bright reddish violet	10	10
633	50 p. sepia and Venetian red (10.4.86)	10	10
634	60 p. blackish brown and light brown	10	10
635	70 p. greenish blue (3.8.86)	10	10
636	80 p. bistre-brown and dull scarlet (1.7.86)	10	10
629/36	*Set of* 8	40	40

Design:—5 p. Kot Diji Fort; 10 p. Rohtas Fort; 15 p. Bala Hisar Fort; 50 p. Hyderabad Fort; 60 p. Lahore Fort; 70 p. Sibi Fort; 80 p. Ranikot Fort.

344 Shah Rukn i Alam's Tomb, Multan

1984 (26 June). *Aga Khan Award for Architecture. P* 13.

647 **344**	60 p. multicoloured	60	60

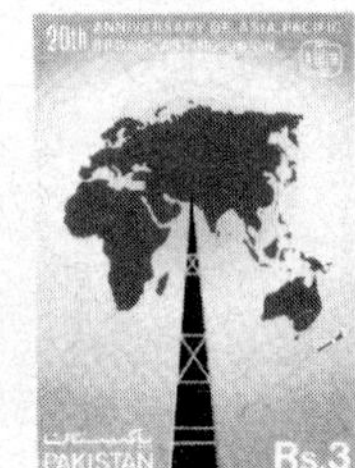

345 Radio Mast and Map of World

1984 (1 July). 20*th Anniv of Asia–Pacific Broadcasting Union. P* 13.

648 **345**	3 r. multicoloured	80	60

346 Wrestling

(Des A. Salahuddin)

1984 (31 July). *Olympic Games, Los Angeles. T* **346** *and similar horiz designs. Multicoloured. P* 13.

649	3 r. Type **346**	85	55
650	3 r. Boxing	85	55
651	3 r. Athletics	85	55
652	3 r. Hockey	85	55
653	3 r. Yachting	85	55
649/53	*Set of* 5	3·75	2·50

347 Jasmine (National flower) and Inscription

348 Gearwheel Emblem and Flags of Participating Nations

(Des M. Munawar)

1984 (14 Aug). *Independence Day. T* **347** *and similar horiz design. Multicoloured. P* 13.

654	60 p. Type **347**	10	10
655	4 r. Symbolic torch	45	50

(Des A. Zafar)

1984 (1 Sept). *Pakistan International Trade Fair. P* 13.

656 **348**	60 p. multicoloured	30	20

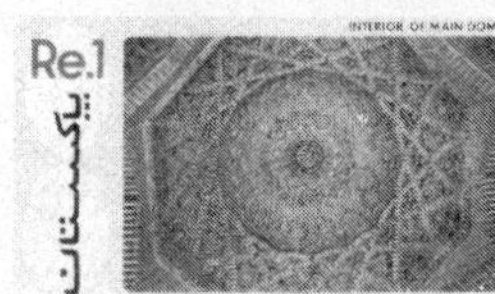

349 Interior of Main Dome

1984 (5 Nov). *Tourism Convention. Shahjahan Mosque, Thatta. T* **349** *and similar horiz designs. Multicoloured. P* 13½.

657	1 r. Type **349**	20	20
	a. Horiz strip of 5. Nos. 657/61	90	
658	1 r. Brick and glazed tile work	20	20
659	1 r. Gateway	20	20
660	1 r. Symmetrical archways	20	20
661	1 r. Interior of a dome	20	20
657/61	*Set of* 5	90	90

Nos. 657/61 were printed together, *se-tenant*, in horizontal strips of 5 throughout the sheet

350 Bank Emblem in Floral Pattern

(Des A. Zafar)

1984 (7 Nov). 25*th Anniv of United Bank Ltd. P* 13½.

662 **350**	60 p. multicoloured	40	40

351 Conference Emblem

352 Postal Life Insurance Emblem within Hands

(Des A. Salahuddin)

1984 (24 Dec). 20*th United Nations Conference on Trade and Development. P* 14.

663 **351**	60 p. multicoloured	40	20

(Des A. Zafar and J. Sultana)

1984 (29 Dec). *Centenary of Postal Life Insurance. T* **352** *and similar vert design. Multicoloured. P* 13½.

664	60 p. Type **352**	25	15
665	1 r. "100" and Postal Life Insurance emblem	35	15

353 Bull (Wall painting)

354 International Youth Year Emblem and "75"

(Des A. Salahuddin and M. Munawar)

1984 (31 Dec). *U.N.E.S.C.O. Save Moenjadoro Campaign. T* **353** *and similar vert design. Multicoloured. P* 13½.

666	2 r. Type **353**	70	70
	a. Horiz pair. Nos. 666/7	1·40	1·40
667	2 r. Bull (seal)	70	70

Nos. 666/7 were printed together, *se-tenant*, in horizontal pairs throughout the sheet.

(Des A. Salahuddin)

1985 (6 Jan). 75*th Anniv of Girl Guide Movement. P* 13½.

668 **354**	60 p. multicoloured	1·00	30

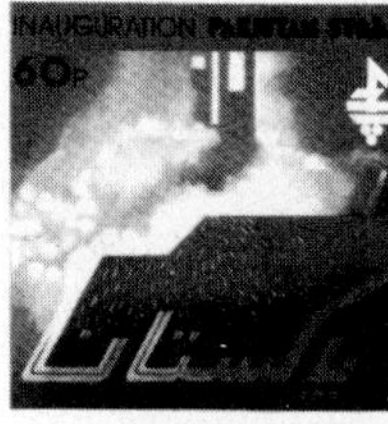

355 Smelting Ore

356 Map of Pakistan and Rays of Sun

1985 (15 Jan). *Inauguration of Pakistan Steel Corporation. T* **355** *and similar multicoloured design. P* 13.

669	60 p. Type **355**	30	10
670	1 r. Pouring molten steel from ladle (28 × 46 *mm*)	40	20

(Des A. Salahuddin)

1985 (20 Mar). *Presidential Referendum of* 19 *December* 1984. *P* 13.

671 **356**	60 p. multicoloured	40	20

357 Ballot Box and Voting Paper

(Des A. Salahuddin (No. 672), Sultana Shamim Haider (No. 673))

1985 (23 Mar). *March Elections. T* **357** *and similar multi-coloured design. P* 13.
672 1 r. Type **357** 30 15
673 1 r. Minar-e-Qarardad-e-Pakistan Tower, and word "Democracy" (31 × 43 *mm*) .. 30 15

(Des and litho Secura, Singapore)

1985 (27 May). *Mountain Peaks (2nd series). Horiz designs as T* **311**. *Multicoloured. Matt, almost invisible PVA gum.* P 14 × 13½.
674 40 p. Rakaposhi (Karakoram Range) .. 75 35
675 2 r. Nangaparbat (Western Himalayas) .. 1·75 1·75

358 Trophy and Medals from Olympic Games 1984, Asia Cup 1985 and World Cup 1982

(Des A. Salahuddin)

1985 (5 July). *Pakistan Hockey Team "Grand Slam" Success. P* 13.
676 **358** 1 r. multicoloured 90 80

359 King Edward Medical College

(Des Sultana Shamim Haider)

1985 (28 July). *125th Anniv of King Edward Medical College, Lahore. P* 13.
677 **359** 3 r. multicoloured 70 40

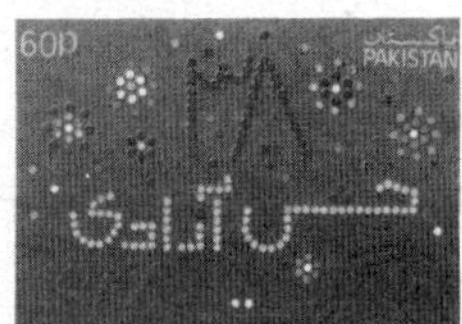

360 Illuminated Inscription in Urdu

(Des A. Salahuddin)

1985 (14 Aug). *Independence Day. T* **360** *and similar horiz design. Multicoloured. P* 13.
678 60 p. Type **360** 15 15
a. Sheetlet. Nos. 678/9 × 2 55
679 60 p. Illuminated "XXXVIII" (inscr in English) 15 15
Nos. 678/9 were issued *se-tenant*, both horizontally and vertically, in sheetlets of four stamps and four stamp-size labels inscribed in Urdu.

361 Sind Madressah-tul-Islam, Karachi

(Des A. Salahuddin)

1985 (1 Sept). *Centenary of Sind Madressah-tul-Islam (theological college), Karachi. P* 13.
680 **361** 2 r. multicoloured 80 55

362 Jamia Masjid Mosque by Day

(Des A. Salahuddin)

1985 (14 Sept). *Inauguration of New Jamia Masjid Mosque, Karachi. T* **362** *and similar horiz design. Multicoloured. P* 13.
681 1 r. Type **362** 45 30
682 1 r. Jamia Masjid illuminated at night .. 45 30

363 Lawrence College, Murree

(Des A. Salahuddin)

1985 (21 Sept). *125th Anniv of Lawrence College, Murree. P* 13.
683 **363** 3 r. multicoloured 75 45

364 United Nations Building, New York

(Des A. Salahuddin)

1985 (24 Oct). *40th Anniv of United Nations Organization. T* **364** *and similar diamond-shaped design. Multicoloured. P* 14.
684 1 r. Type **364** 15 15
685 2 r. U.N. Building and emblem 25 25

365 Tents and Jamboree Emblem

(Des A. Salahuddin)

1985 (8 Nov). *10th National Scout Jamboree. P* 13.
686 **365** 60 p. multicoloured 90 50

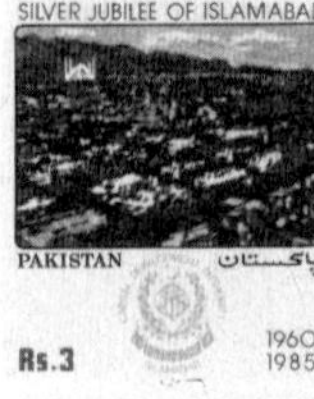

366 Islamabad

367 Map of S.A.A.R.C. Countries and National Flags

(Des H. Durrani)

1985 (30 Nov). *25th Anniv of Islamabad. P* 14½ × 14.
687 **366** 3 r. multicoloured 65 35

(Des A. Salahuddin)

1985 (8 Dec). *1st Summit Meeting of South Asian Association for Regional Cooperation, Dhaka, Bangladesh. T* **367** *and similar multicoloured design. P* 13½ × 13 *(1 r.) or* 13 *(2 r.).*
688 1 r. Type **367** .. .. 1·25 2·50
689 2 r. National flags (39 × 39 *mm*) 75 75
No. 688 is reported to have been withdrawn on 9 December 1985.

368 Globe and Peace Dove

369 Peregrine Falcon

(Des A. Salahuddin)

1985 (14 Dec). *25th Anniv of U.N. General Assembly's Declaration on Independence for Colonial Territories. P* 13.
690 **368** 60 p. multicoloured 40 30

(Des and litho Secura, Singapore)

1986 (20 Jan). *Wildlife Protection (13th series). Peregrine Falcon. Matt, almost invisible PVA gum. P* 13½.
691 **369** 1 r. 50, multicoloured .. .. .. 2·00 1·75

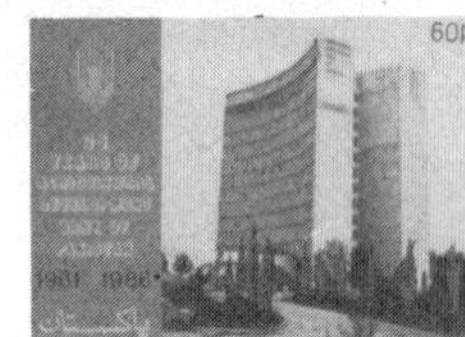

370 A.D.B.P. Building, Islamabad

(Des A. Salahuddin)

1986 (18 Feb). *25th Anniv of Agricultural Development Bank of Pakistan. P* 13.
692 **370** 60 p. multicoloured 40 30

371 Government S.E. College

372 Emblem and Bar Graph

(Des Sultana Shamim Haider)

1986 (25 Apr). *Centenary of Government Sadiq Egerton College, Bahawalpur. P* 13.
693 **371** 1 r. multicoloured 45 30

(Des Sultana Shamim Haider)

1986 (11 May). *25th Anniv of Asian Productivity Organization. P* 13½.
694 **372** 1 r. multicoloured 30 30

373 "1947 1986"

374 Open Air Class

(Des A. Salahuddin (80 p.), M. Munawar (1 r.))

1986 (14 Aug). *39th Anniv of Independence. T* **373** *and similar vert design. Multicoloured. P* 14.
695 80 p. Type **373** 15 15
696 1 r. Illuminated inscription in Urdu .. 15 15

(Des Sultana Shamim Haider)

1986 (8 Sept). *International Literacy Day. P* 13.
697 **374** 1 r. multicoloured 20 20

375 Mother and Child

376 Aitchison College

1986 (28 Oct). *U.N.I.C.E.F. Child Survival Campaign. P* 13½×13.
698 **375** 80 p. multicoloured 30 20

(Des A. Salahuddin)

1986 (3 Nov). *Centenary of Aitchison College, Lahore. P* 13½.
699 **376** 2 r. 50, multicoloured 30 30

377 Two Doves carrying Olive Branches **378** Table Tennis Players

(Des Sultana Shamim Haider)

1986 (20 Nov). *International Peace Year. P* 13.
700 **377** 4 r. multicoloured 50 50

(Des A. Salahuddin)

1986 (25 Nov). *4th Asian Cup Table Tennis Tournament, Karachi. P* 14.
701 **378** 2 r. multicoloured 50 30

379 Argali

(Des M. Jamal. Litho Secura, Singapore)

1986 (4 Dec). *Wildlife Protection* (14*th series*). *Argali. Matt, almost invisible PVA gum. P* 14.
702 **379** 2 r. multicoloured .. .. .. 1·50 65

380 Selimiye Mosque, Edirne, Turkey

(Des A. Salahuddin)

1986 (20 Dec). *"Ecophilex '86" International Stamp Exhibition, Islamabad. T* **380** *and similar vert designs. Multicoloured. P* 13.
703 3 r. Type **380** 70 70
a. Horiz strip of 3. Nos. 703/5 .. .. 1·90
704 3 r. Gawhar Shad Mosque, Mashhad, Iran .. 70 70
705 3 r. Grand Mosque, Bhong, Pakistan .. 70 70
703/5 .. .. *Set of* 3 1·90 1·90
Nos. 703/5 were printed together, *se-tenant*, in horizontal strips of three, within sheetlets of 12.

381 St. Patrick's School

(Des A. Salahuddin)

1987 (29 Jan). *125th Anniv of St. Patrick's School, Karachi. P* 13.
706 **381** 5 r. multicoloured 85 70

MINIMUM PRICE

The minimum price quote is 10p which represents a handling charge rather than a basis for valuing common stamps. For further notes about prices see introductory pages.

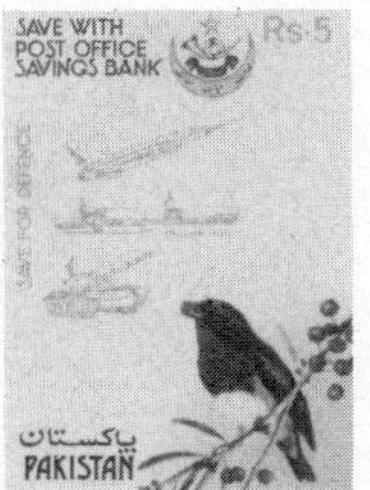

382 Mistletoe Flowerpecker and Defence Symbols

(Des A. Salahuddin)

1987 (21 Feb). *Post Office Savings Bank Week. T* **382** *and similar vert designs, each showing a different bird. Multicoloured. P* 13.
707 5 r. Type **382** 70 45
a. Block of 4. Nos. 707/10 .. .. .. 2·50
708 5 r. Spotted Pardalote and laboratory apparatus 70 45
709 5 r. Black-throated Blue Warbler and agriculture symbols 70 45
710 5 r. Red-capped Manakin and industrial skyline 70 45
707/10 .. .. *Set of* 4 2·50 1·60
Nos. 707/10 were printed together, *se-tenant*, in blocks of four throughout the sheet of 32 which contained six blocks of four and eight labels in the left and right-hand vertical columns.

383 New Parliament House, Islamabad

(Des A. Salahuddin)

1987 (23 Mar). *Inauguration of New Parliament House, Islamabad. P* 13.
711 **383** 3 r. multicoloured 30 30

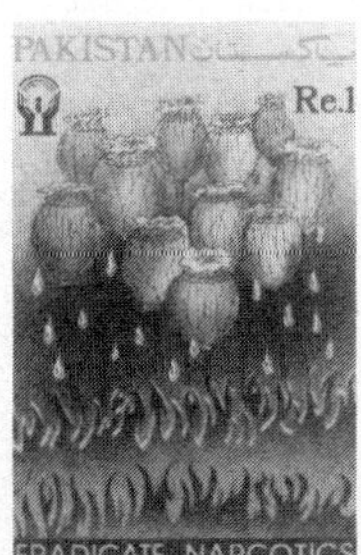

384 Opium Poppies and Flames

(Des A. Salahuddin)

1987 (30 June). *Campaign against Drug Abuse. P* 13.
712 **384** 1 r. multicoloured 30 20

385 Flag and National Anthem Score

(Des A. Salahuddin)

1987 (14 Aug). *40th Anniv of Independence. T* **385** *and similar horiz design. Multicoloured. P* 13.
713 80 p. Type **385**.. .. .. 10 10
714 3 r. Text of speech by Mohammed Ali Jinnah, Minar-e-Qardad-e-Pakistan Tower and arms 20 25

386 "Tempest II"

(Des M. Hussaini and A. Salahuddin)

1987 (7 Sept). *Air Force Day. T* **386** *and similar horiz designs showing military aircraft. Multicoloured. P* 13½.
715 3 r. Type **386** 40 40
a. Sheetlet. Nos. 715/24 .. .. .. 3·50
716 3 r. Hawker "Fury" 40 40
717 3 r. Supermarine "Attacker" 40 40
718 3 r. "F86 Sabre" 40 40
719 3 r. "F104 Star Fighter" 40 40
720 3 r. "C130 Hercules" 40 40
721 3 r. "F6" 40 40
722 3 r. "Mirage III" 40 40
723 3 r. "A5" 40 40
724 3 r. "F16 Fighting Falcon" 40 40
715/24 .. .. *Set of* 10 3·50 3·50
Nos. 715/24 were printed together, *se-tenant*, in sheetlets of 10.

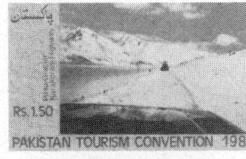

387 Pasu Glacier

(Des A. Salahuddin)

1987 (1 Oct). *Pakistan Tourism Convention. T* **387** *and similar horiz designs showing views along Karakoram Highway. Multicoloured. P* 13.
725 1 r. 50, Type **387** 20 20
a. Block of 4. Nos. 725/8 70
726 1 r. 50, Apricot trees 20 20
727 1 r. 50, Karakoram Highway 20 20
728 1 r. 50, View from Khunjerab Pass 20 20
725/8 .. .. *Set of* 4 70 70
Nos. 725/8 were printed together, *se-tenant*, in blocks of four throughout the sheet of 24.

388 Shah Abdul Latif Bhitai Mausoleum

(Des A. Salahuddin)

1987 (8 Oct). *Shah Abdul Latif Bhitai (poet) Commemoration. P* 13.
729 **388** 80 p. multicoloured 20 20

389 D. J. Sind Science College, Karachi

(Des Sultana Shamim Haider)

1987 (7 Nov). *Centenary of D. J. Sind Science College, Karachi. P* 13.
730 **389** 80 p. multicoloured 20 20

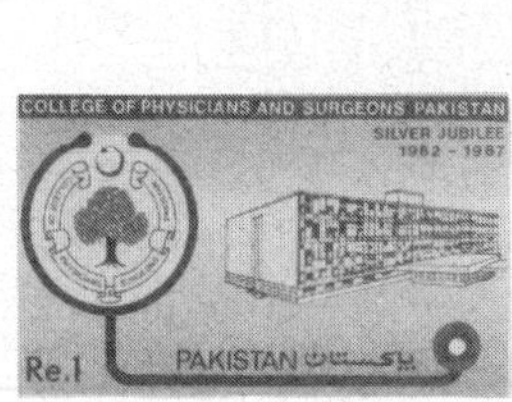

390 College Building **391** Homeless People, Houses and Rising Sun

(Des Sultana Shamim Haider)

1987 (9 Dec). *25th Anniv of College of Physicians and Surgeons. P* 13.
731 **390** 1 r. multicoloured 20 20

(Des Sultana Shamim Haider)

1987 (15 Dec). *International Year of Shelter for the Homeless. P* 13.
732 **391** 3 r. multicoloured 30 30

392 Cathedral Church of the Resurrection, Lahore

(Des A. Salahuddin)

1987 (20 Dec). *Centenary of Cathedral Church of the Resurrection, Lahore. P* 13.
733 **392** 3 r. multicoloured 30 30

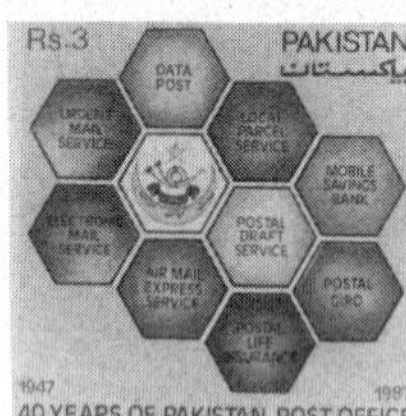

393 Honeycomb and Arms

(Des A. Salahuddin)

1987 (28 Dec). *40th Anniv of Pakistan Post Office. P* 13.
734 **393** 3 r. multicoloured 30 30

394 Corporation Emblem

(Des A. Salahuddin)

1987 (31 Dec). *Radio Pakistan's New Programme Schedules. P* 13.
735 **394** 80 p. multicoloured 15 15

395 Jamshed Nusserwanjee Mehta and Karachi Municipal Corporation Building

396 Leprosy Symbols within Flower

(Des A. Salahuddin)

1988 (7 Jan). *Birth Centenary* (1986) *of Jamshed Nusserwanjee Mehta (former President of Karachi Municipal Corporation). P* 13.
736 **395** 3 r. multicoloured 30 30

(Des Sultana Shamim Haider)

1988 (31 Jan). *World Leprosy Day. P* 13.
737 **396** 3 r. multicoloured 35 30

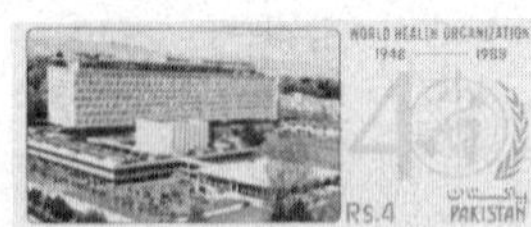

397 W.H.O. Building, Geneva

(Des A. Salahuddin)

1988 (7 Apr). *40th Anniv of World Health Organization. P* 13.
738 **397** 4 r. multicoloured 35 35

398 Globe

399 Crescent, Leaf Pattern and Archway

1988 (8 May). *125th Anniv of International Red Cross and Crescent. P* 13.
739 **398** 3 r. multicoloured 30 30

(Des A. Salahuddin)

1988 (14 Aug). *Independence Day. P* 13½.
740 **399** 80 p. multicoloured 10 10
741 4 r. multicoloured 25 30

400 Field Events

(Des A. Salahuddin)

1988 (17 Sept). *Olympic Games, Seoul. T* **400** *and similar horiz designs. Multicoloured. P* 13.
742 10 r. Type **400** 75 75
a. Sheetlet. Nos. 742/51 .. .. .. 6·75
743 10 r. Track events 75 75
744 10 r. Jumping and pole vaulting 75 75
745 10 r. Gymnastics 75 75
746 10 r. Table tennis, tennis, hockey and baseball 75 75
747 10 r. Volleyball, football, basketball and handball 75 75
748 10 r. Wrestling, judo, boxing and weightlifting 75 75
749 10 r. Shooting, fencing and archery .. 75 75
750 10 r. Water sports 75 75
751 10 r. Equestrian events and cycling .. 75 75
742/51 .. .. *Set of* 10 6·75 6·75
Nos. 742/51 were issued, *se-tenant*, in sheetlets of ten stamps and thirty-six half stamp-size labels.

401 Markhor

(Litho Secura, Singapore)

1988 (29 Oct). *Wildlife Protection (15th series). Markhor. Matt, almost invisible PVA gum. P* 14.
752 **401** 2 r. multicoloured 30 30

402 Islamia College, Peshawar

(Des A. Salahuddin)

1988 (22 Dec). *75th Anniv of Islamia College, Peshawar. P* 13½.
753 **402** 3 r. multicoloured 30 30

403 Symbols of Agriculture, Industry and Education with National Flags

(Des Sultana Shamim Haider (25 r.), G. M. Shaikh (50 r.), A. Salahuddin (75 r.))

1988 (29 Dec). *South Asian Association for Regional Co-operation, 4th Summit Meeting, Islamabad. T* **403** *and similar multicoloured designs. P* 13 (25 *r.*), 14 (50 *r.*) *or* 13½×13 (75 *r.*).
754 25 r. Type **403** .. .. 1·40 1·50
755 50 r. National flags on globe and symbols of communications (33×33 *mm*) .. 3·00 3·25
756 75 r. Stamps from member countries (52×29 *mm*) .. .. 4·25 4·50
754/6 .. .. *Set of* 3 7·75 8·25
No. 755 was printed in sheets of eight stamps and one stamp-size label, showing the S.A.A.R.C. emblem, in the central position.

(Des A. Salahuddin)

1989 (23 Jan). *Pioneers of Freedom (2nd series). Diamond-shaped design as T* **282**. *Multicoloured. W* **98**. *P* 14.
757 3 r. Maulana Hasrat Mohani 15 20

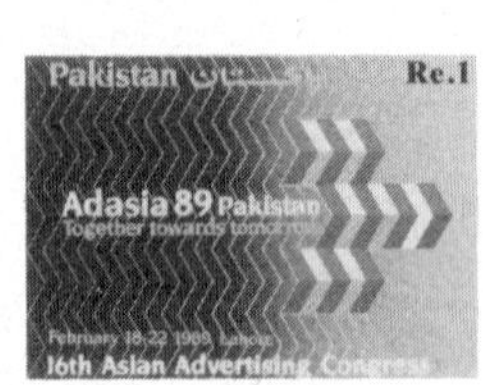

404 Logo

405 Zulfikar Ali Bhutto

(Des A. Salahuddin)

1989 (18 Feb). *"Adasia 89" 16th Asian Advertising Congress, Lahore. P* 13.
758 **404** 1 r. mult ("Pakistan" in yellow) .. 15 15
a. Sheetlet. Nos. 758/60, each × 3 1·25
759 1 r. mult ("Pakistan" in turquoise-bl) 15 15
760 1 r. mult ("Pakistan" in white) .. 15 15
758/60 .. .. *Set of* 3 40 40
Nos. 758/60 were printed together, *se-tenant*, in horizontal and vertical strips of three within the sheetlets of nine.

(Des A. Munir (1 r.), A. Salahuddin (2 r.))

1989 (4 Apr). *10th Death Anniv of Zulfikar Ali Bhutto (statesman). T* **405** *and similar vert design. Multicoloured. P* 13.
761 1 r. Type **405** 15 10
762 2 r. Zulfikar Ali Bhutto (*different*) .. 20 20

406 "Daphne" Class Submarine

(Des A. Salahuddin)

1989 (1 June). *25 Years of Pakistan Navy Submarine Operations. T* **406** *and similar horiz designs. Multicoloured. P* 13½.
763 1 r. Type **406** 20 20
a. Vert strip of 3. Nos. 763/5 55
764 1 r. "Fleet Snorkel" class submarine .. 20 20
765 1 r. "Agosta" class submarine 20 20
763/5 .. .. *Set of* 3 55 55
Nos. 763/5 were printed together, *se-tenant*, in vertical strips of three throughout the sheet.

407 "The Oath of the Tennis Court" (David)

(Des A. Salahuddin)

1989 (24 June). *Bicentenary of French Revolution. P* 13½.
766 **407** 7 r. multicoloured 60 70

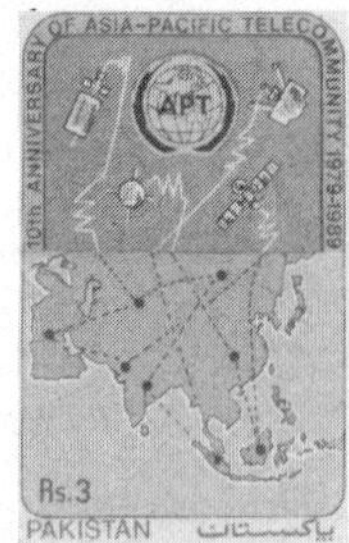

408 Pitcher, *c.* 2200 B.C.

409 Satellites and Map of Asian Telecommunications Network

(Des A. Salahuddin)

1989 (28 June). *Archaeological Artifacts. T* **408** *and similar square designs showing terracotta pottery from Baluchistan Province. Multicoloured. P* 14.

767	1 r. Type **408**	15	15
	a. Block of 4. Nos. 767/70	55	
768	1 r. Jar, *c.* 2300 B.C.	15	15
769	1 r. Vase, *c.* 3600 B.C.	15	15
770	1 r. Jar, *c.* 2600 B.C.	15	15
767/70	*Set of* 4	55	55

Nos. 767/70 were printed together, *se-tenant*, in blocks of four throughout the sheet.

(Des G. Shaikh)

1989 (1 July). 10*th Anniv of Asia-Pacific Telecommunity. P* 13½.

771	**409**	3 r. multicoloured	30	30

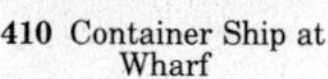

410 Container Ship at Wharf

411 Mohammad Ali Jinnah

(Des A. Salahuddin)

1989 (5 Aug). *Construction of Integrated Container Terminal, Port Qasim. P* 14.

772	**410**	6 r. multicoloured	1·00	1·25

(Des A. Salahuddin. Eng A. Munir. Recess and litho)

1989 (14 Aug). *W* **98**. *P* 13.

773	**411**	1 r. multicoloured	10	10
774		1 r. 50, multicoloured	10	10
775		2 r. multicoloured	10	15
776		3 r. multicoloured	15	20
777		4 r. multicoloured	20	25
778		5 r. multicoloured	25	30
773/8		*Set of* 6	70	90

412 Mausoleum of Shah Abdul Latif Bhitai

413 Asiatic Black Bear

(Des A. Salahuddin)

1989 (16 Sept). 300*th Birth Anniv of Shah Abdul Latif Bhitai (poet). P* 13.

779	**412**	2 r. multicoloured	20	20

COMMONWEALTH MEMBER

Pakistan rejoined the Commonwealth on 1 October 1989.

(Des A. McCoy)

1989 (7 Oct). *Wildlife Protection* (15*th series*). *Asiatic Black Bear. T* **413** *and similar horiz designs. Multicoloured. P* 13½.

780	4 r. Type **413**	45	45
	a. Block of 4. Nos. 780/3	1·60	
781	4 r. Bear among boulders	45	45
782	4 r. Standing on rock	45	45
783	4 r. Sitting by trees	45	45
780/3	*Set of* 4	1·60	1·60

Nos. 780/3 were printed together, *se-tenant*, in blocks of 4 throughout the sheet.

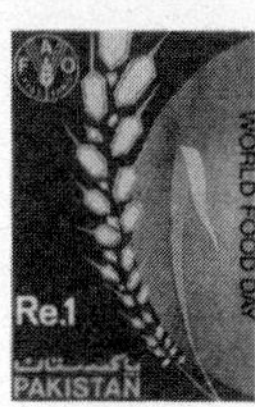

414 Ear of Wheat encircling Globe

415 Games Emblem and Flags of Member Countries

(Des A. Salahuddin)

1989 (16 Oct). *World Food Day. P* 14×12½.

784	**414**	1 r. multicoloured	35	35

(Des A. Salahuddin)

1989 (20 Oct). 4*th South Asian Sports Federation Games, Islamabad. P* 13.

785	**415**	1 r. multicoloured	35	35

416 Patchwork Kamblee (cloth) entering Gate of Heaven

(Des Farah and Fareeda Batul)

1989 (20 Oct). 800*th Birth Anniv of Baba Farid* (*Muslim spiritual leader*). *P* 13.

786	**416**	3 r. multicoloured	25	30

417 Pakistan Television Logo

418 Family of Drug Addicts in Poppy Bud

(Des A. Salahuddin)

1989 (26 Nov). 25*th Anniv of Television Broadcasting in Pakistan. P* 13½.

787	**417**	3 r. multicoloured	25	30

(Des M. Munawar)

1989 (8 Dec). *South Asian Association for Regional Co-operation Anti-Drugs Campaign. P* 13.

788	**418**	7 r. multicoloured	55	60

419 Murray College, Sialkot

(Des A. Salahuddin)

1989 (18 Dec). *Centenary of Murray College, Sialkot. P* 14.

789	**419**	6 r. multicoloured	50	50

420 Government College, Lahore

(Des N. Sheikh)

1989 (21 Dec). 125*th Anniv of Government College, Lahore. P* 13.

790	**420**	6 r. multicoloured	50	50

OMNIBUS ISSUES

Details, together with prices for complete sets, of the various Omnibus issues from the 1935 Silver Jubilee series to date are included in a special section following Zimbabwe at the end of Volume 2.

421 Fields, Electricity Pylons and Rural Buildings

(Des A. Salahuddin)

1989 (31 Dec). 10*th Anniv of Centre for Asia and Pacific Integrated Rural Development. P* 13.

791	**421**	3 r. multicoloured	30	30

422 Emblem and Islamic Patterns

(Des A. Salahuddin)

1990 (9 Feb). 20*th Anniv of Organization of the Islamic Conference. P* 13.

792	**422**	1 r. multicoloured	20	20

423 Hockey Match

(Des M. Khan)

1990 (12 Feb). 7*th World Hockey Cup, Lahore. P* 13½.

793	**423**	2 r. multicoloured	70	70

424 Mohammed Iqbal addressing Crowd and Liaquat Ali Khan taking Oath

(Des A. Zafar (1 r.), A. Salahuddin (7 r.))

1990 (23 Mar). 50*th Anniv of Passing of Pakistan Resolution. T* **424** *and similar multicoloured designs. P* 13 (1 *r.*) *or* 13½ (7 *r.*).

794	1 r. Type **424**	30	30
	a. Horiz strip of 3. Nos. 794/6	80	
795	1 r. Maulana Mohammad Ali Jauhar and Mohammed Ali Jinnah with banner	30	30
796	1 r. Women with Pakistan flag, and Mohammed Ali Jinnah taking Governor-General's oath, 1947	30	30
797	7 r. Minar-i-Qarardad-e-Pakistan Monument and Resolution in Urdu and English (86×42 *mm*)	75	75
794/7	*Set of* 4	1·50	1·50

Nos. 794/6 were printed together, *se-tenant*, in horizontal strips of 3 throughout the sheet, each strip forming a composite design.

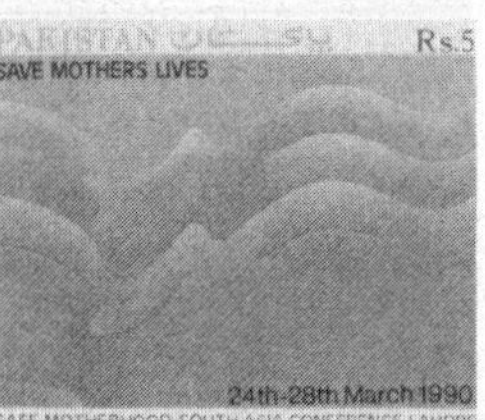

425 Pregnant Woman resting

(Des Family Planning Association of Pakistan)

1990 (24 Mar). *"Safe Motherhood" South Asia Conference, Lahore. P* $13^{1}/_{2}$.

798 **425** 5 r. multicoloured 50 50

426 "Decorated Verse by Ghalib" (Shakir Ali)

(Des A. Salahuddin)

1990 (19 Apr). *Painters of Pakistan (1st series). Shakir Ali. P* $13^{1}/_{2}\times13$.

799 **426** 1 r. multicoloured 20 20

See also Nos. 856/7.

427 Satellite in Night Sky

(Des A. Salahuddin)

1990 (26 July). *Launch of "Badr 1" Satellite. P* 13.

800 **427** 3 r. multicoloured 30 30

428 Allama Mohammed Iqbal

1990 (14 Aug). *Pioneers of Freedom (3rd series). T* **428** *and similar vert designs. Each brown and green. P* 13.

801 1 r. Type **428** 10 10
a. Sheetlet. Nos. 801/9 75
802 1 r. Mohammed Ali Jinnah 10 10
803 1 r. Sir Syed Ahmad Khan 10 10
804 1 r. Nawab Salimullah 10 10
805 1 r. Mohtarma Fatima Jinnah 10 10
806 1 r. Aga Khan III 10 10
807 1 r. Nawab Mohammad Ismail Khan . . 10 10
808 1 r. Hussain Shaheed Suhrawardy . . 10 10
809 1 r. Syed Ameer Ali 10 10
810 1 r. Nawab Bahadur Yar Jung 10 10
a. Sheetlet. Nos. 810/18 75
811 1 r. Khawaja Nazimuddin 10 10
812 1 r. Maulana Obaidullah Sindhi 10 10
813 1 r. Sahibzada Abdul Qaiyum Khan . . 10 10
814 1 r. Begum Jahanara Shah Nawaz . . 10 10
815 1 r. Sir Ghulam Hussain Hidayatullah . . 10 10
816 1 r. Qazi Mohammad Isa 10 10
817 1 r. Sir M. Shahnawaz Khan Mamdot . . 10 10
818 1 r. Pir Sahib of Manki Sharif 10 10
819 1 r. Liaquat Ali Khan 10 10
a. Sheetlet. Nos. 819/27 75
820 1 r. Maulvi A. K. Fazl-ul-Haq 10 10
821 1 r. Allama Shabbir Ahmad Usmani . . 10 10
822 1 r. Sadar Abdur Rab Nishtar 10 10
823 1 r. Bi Amma 10 10
824 1 r. Sir Abdullah Haroon 10 10
825 1 r. Chaudhry Rahmat Ali 10 10
826 1 r. Raja Sahib of Mahmudabad 10 10
827 1 r. Hassanally Effendi 10 10
801/27 . . . . *Set of* 27 2·00 2·00

Nos. 801/9, 810/18 and 819/27 were each printed together, *se-tenant*, in sheetlets of nine.

See also Nos. 838/46.

429 Cultural Aspects of Indonesia and Pakistan

(Des J. Engineer)

1990 (19 Aug). *Indonesia–Pakistan Economic and Cultural Cooperation Organization. P* 13.

828 **429** 7 r. multicoloured 50 50

430 Globe, Open Book and Pen

(Des S. Afar)

1990 (8 Sept). *International Literacy Year. P* 13

829 **430** 3 r. multicoloured 20 20

431 College Crests **432** Children and Globe

(Des I. Gilani)

1990 (22 Sept). *Joint Meeting between Royal College of Physicans, Edinburgh, and College of Physicians and Surgeons, Pakistan. P* 13.

830 **431** 2 r. multicoloured 15 20

(Des A. Salahuddin)

1990 (29 Sept). *U. N. World Summit for Children, New York. P* 13.

831 **432** 7 r. multicoloured 55 65

433 Girl within Members' Flags

(Des A. Salahuddin)

1990 (21 Nov). *South Asian Association for Regional Co-operation Year of Girl Child. P* $13^{1}/_{2}$.

832 **433** 2 r. multicoloured 15 20

434 Paper passing over Rollers **435** Civil Defence Worker protecting Islamabad

(Des I. Jillani)

1990 (8 Dec). *25th Anniv of Security Papers Limited. P* 13.

833 **434** 3 r. multicoloured 20 30

(Des I. Jillani)

1991 (1 Mar). *International Civil Defence Day. P* 13.

834 **435** 7 r. multicoloured 35 40

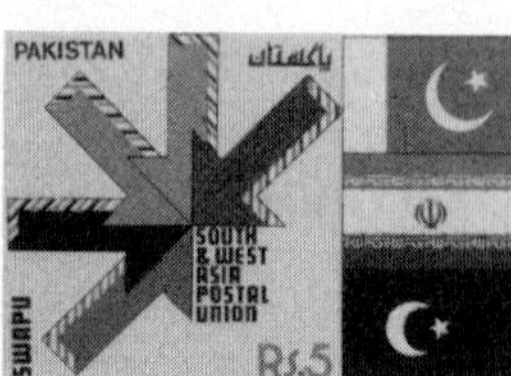

436 Logo and Flags of Member Countries

(Des A. Salahuddin)

1991 (12 Mar). *South and West Asia Postal Union Commemoration. P* 13.

835 **436** 5 r. multicoloured 25 30

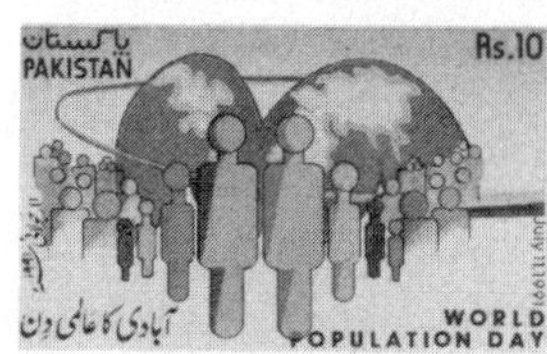

437 Globe and Figures

(Des S. Afsar)

1991 (11 July). *World Population Day. P* 13.

836 **437** 10 r. multicoloured 50 55

438 Mentally Handicapped Athlete **439** Habib Bank Headquarters and Emblem

(Des A. Salahuddin)

1991 (19 July). *Pakistan Participation in Special Olympic Games. P* 13.

837 **438** 7 r. multicoloured 35 40

1991 (14 Aug). *Pioneers of Freedom (4th series). Vert designs as T* **428**. *Each brown and green. P* 13.

838 1 r. Maulana Zafar Ali Khan 10 10
a. Sheetlet. Nos. 838/46 40
839 1 r. Maulana Mohamed Ali Jauhar . . 10 10
840 1 r. Chaudhry Khaliquzzaman 10 10
841 1 r. Hameed Nizami 10 10
842 1 r. Begum Ra'ana Liaquat Ali Khan . . 10 10
843 1 r. Mirza Abol Hassan Ispahani . . 10 10
844 1 r. Raja Ghazanfar Ali Khan 10 10
845 1 r. Malik Barkat Ali 10 10
846 1 r. Mir Jaffer Khan Jamali 10 10
838/46 . . . . *Set of* 9 40 40

Nos. 838/46 were printed together, *se-tenant*, as a sheetlet of nine.

(Des I. Jillani)

1991 (25 Aug). *50th Anniv of Habib Bank. P* 13.

847 **439** 1 r. multicoloured 10 10
848 5 r. multicoloured 25 30

440 St. Joseph's Convent School

(Des A. Salahuddin)

1991 (8 Sept). *130th Anniv (1992) of St. Joseph's Convent School, Karachi. P* 13.

849 **440** 5 r. multicoloured 25 30

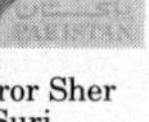

441 Emperor Sher Shah Suri **442** Jinnah Antarctic Research Station

(Des S. Akhtar)

1991 (5 Oct). *Emperor Sher Shah Suri (founder of road network) Commemoration. Multicoloured. P* 13.

850 5 r. Type **441** 25 30
MS851 92×80 mm. 7 r. Emperor on horseback and portrait as Type **441**. Imperf 35 40

(Des I. Jillani)

1991 (28 Oct). *Pakistan Scientific Expedition to Antarctica. P* 13.
852 **442** 7 r. multicoloured 35 40

443 Houbara Bustard **444** Mosque

1991 (4 Nov). *Wildlife Protection* (16*th series*). *P* 13.
853 **443** 7 r. multicoloured 35 40

1991 (22 Nov). 300*th Death Anniv of Hazrat Sultan Bahoo. P* 13.
854 **444** 7 r. multicoloured 35 40

445 Development Symbols and Map of Asia

1991 (19 Dec). 25*th Anniv of Asian Development Bank. P* 13.
855 **445** 7 r. multicoloured 35 40

1991 (24 Dec). *Painters of Pakistan* (2*nd series*). *Horiz designs as T* **426.** *Multicoloured. P* 13½×13.
856 1 r. "Procession" (Haji Muhammad Sharif) 10 10
857 1 r. "Women harvesting" (Ustad Allah Bux) 10 10

446 American Express Travellers Cheques of 1891 and 1991

1991 (26 Dec). *Centenary of American Express Travellers Cheques. P* 13½.
858 **446** 7 r. multicoloured 35 40

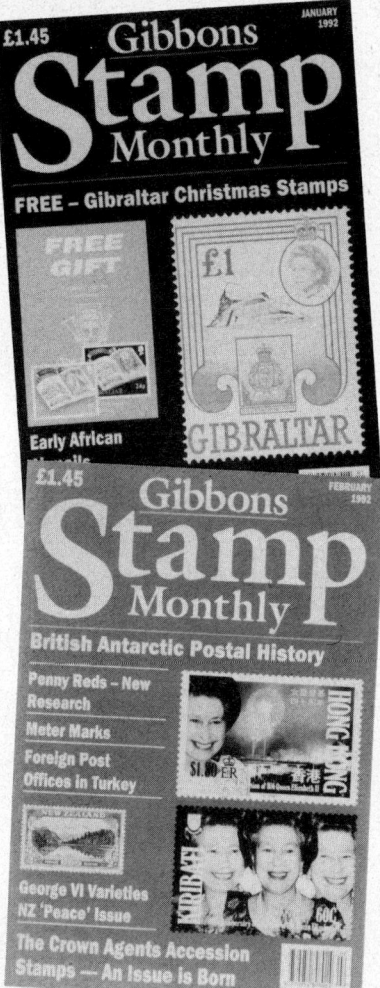

OFFICIAL STAMPS

PAKISTAN

(O 1)

1947. *Official stamps of India, Nos.* O143/50, *optd as Type* O **1** *and Nos.* O138/41 *optd as* T **2** *by litho, at Nasik.*

O 1 O **20** 3 p. slate 30 10
O 2 ½ a. purple 20 10
O 3 9 p. green .. .. 1·00 2·25
O 4 1 a. carmine 20 10
O 5 1½ a. dull violet 20 10
O 6 2 a. vermilion 20 10
O 7 2½ a. bright violet .. .. 1·75 2·50
O 8 4 a. brown 20 10
O 9 8 a. slate-violet 30 35
O10 **93** 1 r. grey and red-brown 80 50
O11 2 r. purple and brown .. .. .. 3·50 1·25
O12 5 r. green and blue .. .. 13·00 18·00
O13 10 r. purple and claret .. .. .. 24·00 50·00
O1/13 .. .. *Set of* 13 40·00 65·00

See note after No. 19. The 1 a. 3 p. (India No. O146*a*) exists only as a local issue (*Price,* Karachi opt, £2 *mint,* £5.50 *used*).

SERVICE (O 2) **SERVICE** (O 3) **SERVICE** (O 4)

NOTE. Apart from a slight difference in size, Types O **2** and O **3** can easily be distinguished by the difference in the shape of the "c". Type O **4** is taller and thinner in appearance.

PRINTERS. Type O **2** was overprinted by De La Rue and Types O **3** and O **4** by the Pakistan Security Ptg Corp.

1948 (14 Aug)–**54**? *Optd with Type* O **2**.

O14 **7** 3 p. red (No. 24) 10 10
O15 6 p. violet (No. 25) (R.) 10 10
O16 9 p. green (No. 26) (R.) 10 10
O17 **8** 1 a. blue (No. 27) (R.) .. .. .. 2·75 10
O18 1½ a. grey-green (No. 28) (R.) .. .. 2·25 10
O19 2 a. red (No. 29) .. .. 1·25 10
O20 **10** 3 a. green (No. 31) .. .. .. 7·00 1·75
O21 **9** 4 a. reddish brown (No. 33) 80 10
O22 – 8 a. black (No. 35) (R.) .. .. .. 80 2·75
O23 – 1 r. ultramarine (No. 38) .. .. 1·00 10
O24 – 2 r. chocolate (No. 39) .. .. .. 7·50 3·00
O25 – 5 r. carmine (No. 40) .. .. .. 7·50 3·75
O26 **13** 10 r. magenta (No. 41) .. .. .. 9·00 26·00
a. Perf 12 (10.10.51) .. .. 8·50 22·00
b. Perf 13 (1954?) .. .. .. 12·00 30·00
O14/26 .. .. *Set of* 13 35·00 30·00

1949. *Optd with Type* O **2**.

O27 1 a. blue (No. 44) (R.) 65 10
O28 1½ a. grey-green (No. 45) (R.) 30 10
a. Opt inverted .. .. — 35·00
O29 2 a. red (No. 46) 90 10
a. Opt omitted (in pair with normal) .. — £100
O30 3 a. green (No. 47) .. .. 5·50 2·25
O31 8 a. black (No. 49) (R.) .. .. .. 14·00 6·25
O27/31 .. .. *Set of* 5 19·00 8·00

1951 (14 Aug). *4th Anniv of Independence. As Nos.* 56, 58 *and* 60, *but inscr* "SERVICE" *instead of* "PAKISTAN POSTAGE".

O32 **18** 3 a. purple .. .. 1·25 3·00
O33 **19** 4 a. green 60 10
O34 **20** 8 a. sepia .. .. 3·00 85
O32/4 .. .. *Set of* 3 4·25 3·50

1953. *Optd with Type* O **3**.

O35 3 p. red (No. 24a) 10 10
O36 6 p. violet (No. 25a) (R.) 10 10
O37 9 p. green (No. 26a) (R.) 10 10
O38 1 a. blue (No. 44a) (R.) 10 10
O39 1½ a. grey-green (No. 45a) (R.) 10 10
O40 2 a. red (No. 46a) (1953?) 15 10
O41 1 r. ultramarine (No. 38a) .. .. .. 2·50 75
O42 2 r. chocolate (No. 39a) .. .. .. 2·25 10
O43 5 r. carmine (No. 40a) .. .. .. 7·50 3·25
O44 10 r. magenta (No. 41b) (date?) .. .. 13·00 28·00
O35/44 .. .. *Set of* 10 23·00 29·00

1954 (14 Aug). *Seventh Anniv of Independence. Nos.* 65/71 *optd with Type* O **3**.

O45 6 p. reddish violet (R.) 10 75
O46 9 p. blue (R.) .. .. 40 4·00
O47 1 a. carmine 15 60
O48 1½ a. red 15 60
O49 14 a. deep green (R.) .. .. 60 3·00
O50 1 r. green (R.) 75 10
O51 2 r. red-orange .. .. 1·25 15
O45/51 .. .. *Set of* 7 3·00 8·00

1955 (14 Aug). *Eighth Anniv of Independence. No.* 75 *optd with Type* O **3**.

O52 8 a. deep reddish violet (R.) 15 10

1957 (Jan)–**59**. *Nos.* 65/71 *optd with Type* O **4**.

O53 6 p. reddish violet (R.) 10 10
a. Opt inverted .. .. † —
O54 9 p. blue (R.) (1.59) 10 30
a. Opt inverted .. ..
O55 1 a. carmine 10 10
a. Opt inverted .. ..
O56 1½ a. red 10 10
a. Opt double .. ..
O57 14 a. deep green (R.) (2.59) .. .. .. 40 1·75
O58 1 r. green (R.) (4.58) 40 10
O59 2 r. red-orange (4.58) .. .. .. 2·25 10
O53/9 .. .. *Set of* 7 3·00 2·00

1958 (Jan)–**61**. *Optd with Type* O **4**.

O60 **7** 3 p. red (No. 24a) 10 10
O61 – 5 r. carmine (No. 40a) (7.59) .. .. 3·00 15
O62 **41** 10 r. myrtle-green and yellow-orange (No. 89) (R.) (1961) .. .. .. 6·00 6·00
a. Opt inverted .. .. 12·00
O60/2 .. .. *Set of* 3 8·00 6·00

1958 (Jan)–**61**. *Nos.* 74/5 *optd with Type* O **4**.

O63 6 a. deep ultramarine (R.) (4.61) 10 10
O64 8 a. deep reddish violet (R.) 10 10

1959 (Aug). *No.* 83 *optd with Type* O **4**.

O65 **37** 2 a. scarlet 10 10

1961 (Apr). *Nos.* 110/11 *optd with Type* O **4**.

O66 **51** 8 a. deep green 10 10
O67 1 r. blue 10 10
a. Opt inverted .. .. 6·50

NEW CURRENCY. In addition to the local *handstamped* surcharges mentioned in the note above No. 122, the following *typographed* surcharges were made at the Treasury at Mastung and issued in the Baluchi province of Kalat: 6 p. on 1 a. (No. O55), 9 p. on 1½ a. (No. O56) and 13 p. on 2 a. (No. O65). They differ in that the surcharges are smaller and "PAISA" is expressed as "Paisa". Being locals they are outside the scope of this catalogue.

1961. *Optd with Type* O **4**.

O68 1 p. on 1½ a. (No. 122) 10 10
a. Optd with Type O 3 .. .. .. 1·00 65
O69 2 p. on 3 p. (No. 123) (1.1.61) 10 10
a. Surch double .. ..
b. Optd with Type O 3 .. .. .. 2·00 2·00
O70 3 p. on 6 p. (No. 124) 10 10
O71 7 p. on 1 a. (No. 125) 10 10
a. Optd with Type O 3 .. .. .. 2·00 2·00
O72 13 p. on 2 a. (No. 126) 10 10
O73 13 p. on 2 a. (No. 127) 10 10
O68/73 .. .. *Set of* 6 30 30

No. O68 exists with small and large "1" (see note below Nos. 122/7, etc.).

ERRORS. See note after No. 127.

SERVICE (O 5) SERVICE (O 6)

1961–63. *Nos.* 128/44*b* *optd with Type* O **4** (*rupee values*) *or* O **5** (*others*). (*a*) *Inscribed* "SHAKISTAN".

O74 1 p. violet (R.) (1.1.61) 10 10
O75 2 p. rose-red (R.) (12.1.61) 10 10
O76 5 p. ultramarine (R.) (23.3.61) 15 10

(*b*) *Inscribed* "PAKISTAN"

O77 1 p. violet (R.) 40 10
O78 2 p. rose-red (R.) 10 10
O79 3 p. reddish purple (R.) (27.10.61) 10 10
O80 5 p. ultramarine (R.) .. .. .. 1·25 10
O81 7 p. emerald (R.) (23.3.61) 10 10
O82 10 p. brown (R.) 10 10
a. Opt inverted .. ..
O83 13 p. slate-violet (R.) (14.2.61) 10 10
O85 40 p. deep purple (R.) (1.1.62) 10 10
O86 50 p. deep bluish green (R.) (1.1.62) 15 10
a. Opt double .. .. † —
O87 75 p. carmine-red (R.) (23.3.62) 20 10
a. Opt double .. ..
O88 1 r. vermilion (7.1.63) 35 10
a. Opt double .. .. 8·00
b. Opt as Type O 3 .. .. .. 6·00 6·00
c. Opt inverted .. .. 6·00
O89 2 r. orange (7.1.63) .. .. 1·25 20
O90 5 r. green (R.) (7.1.63) .. .. .. 4·00 4·50
O74/90 .. .. *Set of* 16 7·50 5·00

1963–78? *Nos.* 170, *etc., optd with Type* O **5**, *in red.*

O 91 1 p. violet 10 10
O 92 2 p. rose-red (1965) 10 10
a. Opt inverted .. .. 1·25
b. Albino opt .. ..
c. Opt double, one albino .. .. ..
O 93 3 p. reddish purple (1967) .. .. .. 1·25 55
a. Opt double .. .. 3·50
b. Opt inverted .. .. 1·25
O 94 5 p. ultramarine 10 10
a. Opt inverted .. .. 1·25
ab. Vert pair, top stamp without opt, lower with opt inverted .. ..
O 95 7 p. emerald (date?) .. .. 4·00 2·25
O 96 10 p. brown (1965) 10 10
a. Opt inverted .. .. 1·50
O 97 13 p. slate-violet 10 10
O 98 15 p. bright purple (31.12.64) 10 40
O 99 20 p. myrtle-green (26.1.70) 10 30
a. Opt double .. .. 20·00
O100 25 p. deep blue (1977) .. .. 2·75 65
O101 40 p. deep purple (1972?) .. .. .. 3·75 1·75
O102 50 p. deep bluish green (1965) 10 15
O103 75 p. carmine-red (date?) .. .. .. 3·50 3·00
O104 90 p. yellow-green (5.78?) .. .. .. 2·00 2·00
O91/104 .. .. *Set of* 14 16·00 10·00

1968–(?). *Nos.* 204, 206 *and* 207 *optd with Type* O **4**.

O105 **62** 1 r. vermilion 65 30
a. Opt inverted .. .. 6·00
O107 2 r. orange (date?) .. .. 3·75 75
a. Opt inverted .. .. 6·00
O108 5 r. green (R.) (date?) .. .. .. 7·00 2·25
a. Opt inverted .. .. 9·00
O105/8 .. .. *Set of* 3 10·00 3·00

1979–85. *Nos.* 464/72, 473*b* *and* 475/80 *optd as Type* O **5** *in black* (2 *r.*) *or in red* (*reading vertically downwards on* 2, 3 *and* 5 *p.*) (*others*).

O109 **275** 2 p. deep grey-green 10 10
a. Opt reading upwards .. .. ..
ab. Horiz pair, one with opt reading upwards, the other with opt omitted .. ..
O110 3 p. black 10 10
a. Opt reading upwards .. .. ..
O111 5 p. deep ultramarine 10 10
a. Opt reading upwards .. .. .. 1·50 1·50
b. Vert pair, top stamp without opt .. .. 3·00
O112 **276** 10 p. new blue and greenish blue 10 10
O113 20 p. deep yellow-green 10 10
O114 **276** 25 p. deep green and dull magenta 10 10
O115 40 p. new blue and magenta 30 10
a. Opt inverted .. ..
b. Albino opt .. .. 10·00
O116 50 p. slate-lilac and turquoise-green .. 10 10
O117 60 p. black .. .. 1·00 10
O118 75 p. dull vermilion (Die II) (1980) 75 10
O119 **276a** 1 r. bronze-green (1980) 75 10
O120 1 r. 50, red-orange (1979) 10 10
O121 2 r. carmine-red (1979) 15 10
O122 3 r. blue-black (1980) 20 20
O123 4 r. black (1985) 30 25
O124 5 r. sepia (1985) 35 30
O109/24 .. .. *Set of* 16 3·50 1·50

(Des and litho Secura, Singapore)

1980 (15 Jan–10 Mar). *As Nos.* 513/19 *but inscr* "SERVICE". *P* 12.

O125 **291** 10 p. slate-green and orange-yellow 40 10
O126 15 p. slate-green & brt yellow-green 10 10
O127 25 p. violet and brown-red (10 Mar) 10 10
O128 35 p. carmine & brt yell-grn (10 Mar) 10 10
O129 – 40 p. rosine and olive-sepia 10 10
O130 – 50 p. violet & dull yell-green (10 Mar) .. 15 10
O131 – 80 p. brt yellow-green & blk (10 Mar) 20 20
O125/31 .. .. *Set of* 7 80 45

1984 (25 Sept)–**89**. *Nos.* 629/30 *and* 632/6 *optd with Type* O **6** *in red.*

O132 – 5 p. brownish blk & brn-pur (1989?) .. 10 10
O133 – 10 p. brownish black and rose-red 10 10
O135 **343** 20 p. black and bright reddish violet (opt at right) (20.11.84) 10 10
a. Opt at left 10 10
O136 – 50 p. sepia and Venetian red (1988?) .. 10 10
O137 – 60 p. lt brown & blackish brown (1985) .. 10 10
O138 – 70 p. greenish blue (1988?) 10 10
O139 – 80 p. bistre-brown & dull scar (1988) .. 10 10
O132/9 .. .. *Set of* 7 35 35

1989 (24 Dec). *No.* 773 *optd with Type* O **5**.

O140 **411** 1 r. multicoloured 10 10

O **7** State Bank of Pakistan Building, Islamabad

1990 (12 Apr). *W* **98** (*sideways*). *P* 13½.

O141 O **7** 1 r. carmine and dull green 10 10
O142 2 r. carmine and rose-carmine 10 15
O143 3 r. carmine and ultramarine 15 20
O144 4 r. carmine and red-brown 20 25
O145 5 r. carmine and reddish purple 25 30
O141/5 .. .. *Set of* 5 70 85

BAHAWALPUR

PRICES FOR STAMPS ON COVER TO 1945	
Nos. O1/6	*from* × 30
Nos. O7/8	*from* × 10
Nos. O11/18	*from* × 30

(1)

1947 (15 Aug). *Nos.* 265/8, 269*a*/77 *and* 259/62 *of India optd locally with T* **1**.

No.	Type	Description	Price
1	**100*a***	3 p. slate (R.)	6·00
2		½ a. purple	6·00
3		9 p. green (R.)	6·00
4		1 a. carmine	6·00
5	**101**	1½ a. dull violet (R.)	6·50
6		2 a. vermilion	6·50
7		3 a. bright violet (R.)	6·50
8		3½ a. bright blue (R.)	6·50
9	**102**	4 a. brown	7·00
10		6 a. turquoise-green (R.)	7·00
11		8 a. slate-violet (R.)	7·00
12		12 a. lake	7·00
13	**103**	14 a. purple	40·00
14	**93**	1 r. grey and red-brown	18·00
15		2 r. purple and brown (R.)	£400
16		5 r. green and blue (R.)	£425
17		10 r. purple and claret	£450
1/17		*Set of* 17	£1200

Nos. 1/17 were issued during the interim period, following the implementation of the Indian Independence Act, during which time Bahawalpur was part of neither of the two Dominions created. The Amir acceded to the Dominion of Pakistan on 3 October 1947 and these overprinted stamps of India were then withdrawn.

The stamps of Bahawalpur only had validity for use within the state. For external mail Pakistan stamps were used.

PRINTERS. All the following issues were recess-printed by De La Rue & Co, Ltd, London.

2 Amir Muhammad Bahawal Khan I Abbasi

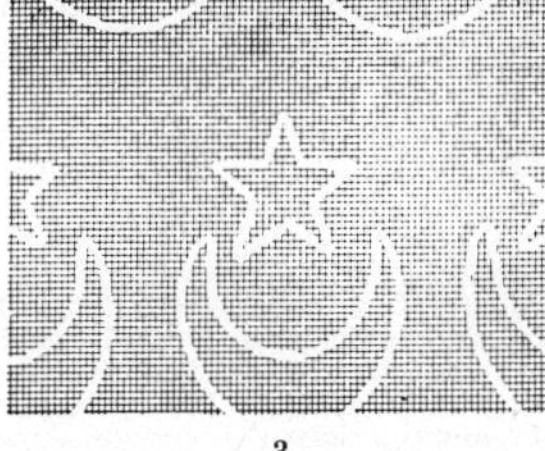

3

1947 (1 Dec). *Bicentenary Commemoration. W* **3** (*sideways*). *P* 12½ × 11½.

No.	Type	Description	Unused	Used
18	**2**	½ a. black and carmine	30	1·25

4 H.H. the Amir of Bahawalpur

5 The Tombs of the Amirs

6 Mosque in Sadiq-Garh

7 Fort Derawar from the Lake

8 Nur-Mahal Palace

9 The Palace, Sadiq-Garh

10 H.H. the Amir of Bahawalpur

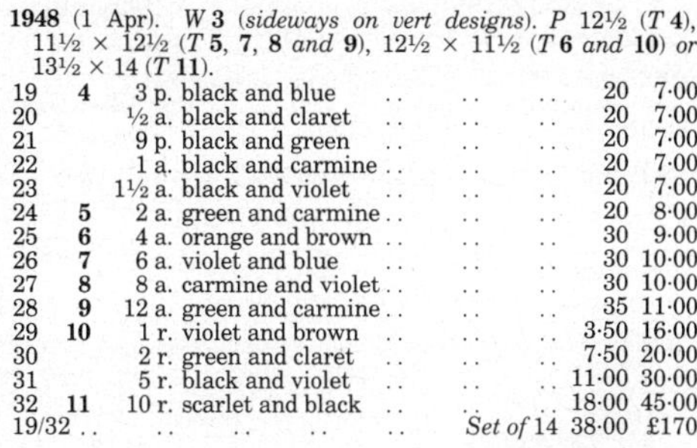

11 Three Generations of Rulers; H.H. the Amir in centre

1948 (1 Apr). *W* **3** (*sideways on vert designs*). *P* 12½ (*T* **4**), 11½ × 12½ (*T* **5**, **7**, **8** *and* **9**), 12½ × 11½ (*T* **6** *and* **10**) *or* 13½ × 14 (*T* **11**).

No.	Type	Description	Unused	Used
19	**4**	3 p. black and blue	20	7·00
20		½ a. black and claret	20	7·00
21		9 p. black and green	20	7·00
22		1 a. black and carmine	20	7·00
23		1½ a. black and violet	20	7·00
24	**5**	2 a. green and carmine	20	8·00
25	**6**	4 a. orange and brown	30	9·00
26	**7**	6 a. violet and blue	30	10·00
27	**8**	8 a. carmine and violet	30	10·00
28	**9**	12 a. green and carmine	35	11·00
29	**10**	1 r. violet and brown	3·50	16·00
30		2 r. green and claret	7·50	20·00
31		5 r. black and violet	11·00	30·00
32	**11**	10 r. scarlet and black	18·00	45·00
19/32		*Set of* 14	38·00	£170

12 H.H. The Amir of Bahawalpur and Mohammed Ali Jinnah

13 Soldiers of 1848 and 1948

1948 (3 Oct). *First Anniv of Union of Bahawalpur with Pakistan. W* **3**. *P* 13.

No.	Type	Description	Unused	Used
33	**12**	1½ a. carmine and blue-green	10	1·00

1948 (15 Oct). *Multan Campaign Centenary. W* **3**. *P* 11½.

No.	Type	Description	Unused	Used
34	**13**	1½ a. black and lake	20	4·75

1948. *As Nos.* 29/32, *but colours changed.*

No.	Type	Description	Unused	Used
35	**10**	1 r. deep green and orange	25	9·00
36		2 r. black and carmine	30	12·00
37		5 r. chocolate and ultramarine	30	20·00
38	**11**	10 r. red-brown and green	35	25·00
35/8		*Set of* 4	1·10	60·00

14 Irrigation

17 U.P.U. Monument, Berne

1949 (3 Mar). *Silver Jubilee of Accession of H.H. the Amir of Bahawalpur. T* **14** *and similar horiz designs. W* **3**. *P* 14.

No.	Description	Unused	Used
39	3 p. black and ultramarine	10	4·75
40	½ a. black and brown-orange	10	4·75
41	9 p. black and green	10	4·75
42	1 a. black and carmine	10	4·75
39/42	*Set of* 4	30	17·00

Designs:—½ a. Wheat; 9 p. Cotton; 1 a. Sahiwal bull.

1949 (10 Oct). *75th Anniv of Universal Postal Union. W* **3**. *P* 13.

No.	Type	Description	Unused	Used
43	**17**	9 p. black and green	20	2·00
		a. Perf 17½ × 17	2·25	10·00
44		1 a. black and magenta	20	2·00
		a. Perf 17½ × 17	2·25	10·00
45		1½ a. black and orange	20	2·00
		a. Perf 17½ × 17	2·25	10·00
46		2½ a. black and blue	20	2·00
		a. Perf 17½ × 17	2·25	10·00
43/6		*Set of* 4	70	7·00
43a/6a		*Set of* 4	8·00	35·00

OMNIBUS ISSUES

Details, together with prices for complete sets, of the various Omnibus issues from the 1935 Silver Jubilee series to date are included in a special section following Zimbabwe at the end of Volume 2.

OFFICIAL STAMPS

O **1** Panjnad Weir

O **2** Dromedary and Calf

O **3** Blackbuck

O **4** Eastern White Pelicans

O **5** Juma Masjid Palace, Fort Derawar

O **6** Temple at Pattan Manara

1945 (1 Jan). *Various horizontal pictorial designs, with red Arabic opt. W* **3**. *P* 14.

No.	Type	Description	Unused	Used
O1	O **1**	½ a. black and green	1·25	4·00
O2	O **2**	1 a. black and carmine	1·75	3·00
O3	O **3**	2 a. black and violet	2·75	4·50
O4	O **4**	4 a. black and olive-green	6·50	12·00
O5	O **5**	8 a. black and brown	5·50	7·00
O6	O **6**	1 r. black and orange	5·50	7·00
O1/6		*Set of* 6	21·00	35·00

O **7** Baggage Camels

(O **8**)

1945 (10 Mar). *Red Arabic opt. No wmk. P* 14.

No.	Type	Description	Unused	Used
O7	O **7**	1 a. black and brown	22·00	40·00

1945 (Mar–June). *Surch as Type* O **8** (*at Security Printing Press, Nasik*) *instead of red Arabic opt. No wmk. P* 14.

No.	Type	Description	Unused	Used
O11	O **5**	½ a. on 8 a. black and purple	4·25	2·00
O12	O **6**	1½ a. on 1 r. black and orange	14·00	3·00
O13	O **1**	1½ a. on 2 r. black and blue (1 June)	60·00	3·25
O11/13		*Set of* 3	70·00	7·50

(O **9**)

O **10** H.H. the Amir of Bahawalpur

1945. *Optd with Type* O **9** (*by D.L.R.*) *instead of red Arabic opt. No wmk. P* 14.

No.	Type	Description	Unused	Used
O14	O **1**	½ a. black and carmine	1·00	5·50
O15	O **2**	1 a. black and carmine	1·50	6·50
O16	O **3**	2 a. black and orange	2·75	17·00
O14/16		*Set of* 3	4·75	26·00

1945. *P* 14.

No.	Type	Description	Unused	Used
O17	O **10**	3 p. black and blue	60	3·25
O18		1½ a. black and violet	4·50	4·75

O **11** Allied Banners

(Des E. Meronti. Recess, background litho)

1946 (1 May). *Victory. P* 14.

No.	Type	Description	Unused	Used
O19	O **11**	1½ a. green and grey	1·75	1·75

1948. *Nos.* 19, 22, 24/5 *and* 35/8 *optd as Nos.* O1/6.

No.	Type	Description	Unused	Used
O20	**4**	3 p. black and blue (R.)	15	5·50
O21		1 a. black and carmine (Blk.)	15	4·50

No.	Type	Description	Unused	Used
O22	**5**	2 a. green and carmine (Blk.)	15	6·00
O23	**6**	4 a. orange and brown (Blk.)	15	8·00
O24	**10**	1 r. deep green and orange (R.).. ..	15	9·00
O25		2 r. black and carmine (R.)	15	11·00
O26		5 r. chocolate and ultramarine (R.) ..	20	19·00
O27	**11**	10 r. red-brown and green (R.)	30	24·00
O20/7 ..		.. .. *Set of* 8	1·25	75·00

1949 (10 Oct). *75th Anniv of Universal Postal Union. Nos.* 43/6 *optd as Nos.* O1/6.

No.	Type	Description	Unused	Used
O28	**17**	9 p. black and green	15	4·50
		a. Perf 17½ × 17	2·40	15·00
O29		1 a. black and magenta	15	4·50
		a. Perf 17½ × 17	2·40	15·00
O30		1½ a. black and orange	15	4·50
		a. Perf 17½ × 17	2·40	15·00
O31		2½ a. black and blue	15	4·50
		a. Perf 17½ × 17	2·40	15·00
O28/31		.. .. *Set of* 4	55	16·00
O28a/31a		.. .. *Set of* 4	8·50	55·00

Since 1949 only Pakistan stamps have been used in Bahawalpur for both internal and external mail.

Palestine

The stamps of TURKEY were used in Palestine from 1865.

In addition various European Powers, and Egypt, maintained post offices at Jerusalem (Austria, France, Germany, Italy, Russia), Jaffa (Austria, Egypt, France, Germany, Russia) and Haifa (Austria, France) using their own stamps or issues specially prepared for Levant post offices. All foreign post offices had closed by the time of the British Occupation.

PRICES FOR STAMPS ON COVER TO 1945

No. 1	*from* × 6
No. 2	*from* × 4
Nos. 3/4	*from* × 5
Nos. 5/15	*from* × 4
Nos. 16/29	*from* × 3
Nos. 30/42	*from* × 2
No. 43	—
Nos. 44/57	*from* × 2
Nos. 58/9	—
Nos. 60/8	*from* × 3
Nos. 69/70	—
Nos. 71/89	*from* × 3
Nos. 90/103	*from* × 4
Nos. 104/11	*from* × 8
Nos. D1/5	*from* × 30
Nos. D6/20	*from* × 10

BRITISH MILITARY OCCUPATION

Nos. 1/15 were issued by the British military authorities for use by the civilian population in territories previously part of the Ottoman Empire. In addition to Palestine they were available from E.E.F. post offices in Syria (including what subsequently became Transjordan) from 23 September 1918 to 23 February 1922, Lebanon from 21 October 1918 to September 1920 and Cilicia from 2 September 1919 to 16 July 1920. Use in the following post offices outside Palestine is recorded in *British Empire Campaigns and Occupations in the Near East, 1914–1924* by John Firebrace:

Adana, Cilicia	Hajjin ("Hadjin"), Cilicia
Akkari ("Akkar"), Syria	Hama, Syria
Aleppo ("Alep, Halep"), Syria	Hasbaya, Lebanon
Aleih ("Alie"), Lebanon	Hasine, Cilicia
Alexandretta, Syria	Hommana, Lebanon
Antakie, Syria	Homs, Syria
Ba'abda, Lebanon	Kozan, Cilicia
Baalbek, Lebanon	Lattakia ("Laskie, Lattaquie"), Syria
Bab, Syria	Massel el Chouf ("Moussalc"), Lebanon
Babitoma, Syria	Merdjajoun, Lebanon
Behamdoun, Lebanon	Mersina ("Mersine"), Cilicia
Beit ed Dine, Lebanon	Mounboudje, Syria
Bekaa, Lebanon	Nabatti, Lebanon
Beyrouth, Lebanon	Nebk ("Nebik"), Syria
Beit Mery, Beyrouth Lebanon	Payass, Syria
Bouzanti, Syria	Racheya, Lebanon
Broumana, Lebanon	Safita, Syria
Damascus ("Damas"), Syria	Savour, Tyre, Lebanon
Damour ("Damor"), Lebanon	Selimie, Syria
Der'a ("Deraa"), Syria	Sidan ("Saida (Echelle)"), Lebanon
Deurt-Yol, Syria	Suweidiya ("Suvedie"), Syria
Djey Han, Syria	Talia, Syria
Djezzin ("Djezzine"), Lebanon	Tarsous, Cilicia
Djon, Lebanon	Tartous, Turkey
Djounie, Lebanon	Tibnin, Lebanon
Djubeil, Lebanon	Tripoli, Syria
Douma, Syria	Zahle, Lebanon
Edleb, Syria	Zebdani, Syria
Feke, Turkey	
Habib Souk, Syria	

This information is reproduced here by permission of the publishers, Robson Lowe Publications.

ALTERED CATALOGUE NUMBERS

Any Catalogue numbers altered from the last edition are shown as a list in the introductory pages.

1

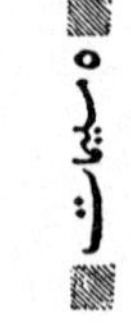

(2)

3

"E.E.F." = Egyptian Expeditionary Force

(Des G. Rowntree. Litho Typographical Dept, Survey of Egypt, Giza, Cairo)

1918 (10 Feb). *Wmk Royal Cypher in column* (*W* **100** *of Great Britain*). *Ungummed. Roul* 20.

No.	Type	Description	Unused	Used
1	**1**	1 p. indigo (Optd S. £375)	£200	£130
		a. Deep blue	£180	£120
		b. Blue	£180	£120

Control: A 18 (*Prices, corner block of* 4; No. 1 £850. No. 1*a*, £750. No. 1*b*, £850).

1918 (16 Feb). *As last* (*ungummed*), *surch with T* **2.**

No.	Type	Description	Unused	Used
2	**1**	5 m. on 1 p. cobalt-blue (Optd S. £375) ..	£120	£650
		a. "MILLILMES" (No. 10 in sheet) ..	£3250	£4000

Control: B 18 A. (*Corner block,* £1000).

1918 (5 Mar). *As No.* 1 *but colour changed. With gum.*

No.	Type	Description	Unused	Used
3	**1**	1 p. ultramarine	2·50	2·50

Control: C 18. (*Corner block,* £70).

1918 (5 Mar *and* 13 May). *No.* 3 *surch with T* **2.**

No.	Type	Description	Unused	Used
4	**1**	5 m. on 1 p. ultramarine	5·00	4·00
		a. Arabic surch wholly or partly missing (No. 11 in sheet)	£400	£400

Controls: C 18 B (Mar). (*Corner block,* £750.)
D 18 C (May). (*Corner block,* £175.)

(Typo Stamping Dept, Board of Inland Revenue, Somerset House, London)

1918 (16 July–27 Dec). *Wmk Royal Cypher in column. P* 15 × 14.

No.	Type	Description	Unused	Used
5	**3**	1 m. sepia	30	40
		a. Deep brown	40	40
6		2 m. blue-green	30	35
		a. Deep green	50	40
7		3 m. yellow-brown (17 Dec)	35	35
		a. Chestnut	9·00	6·00
8		4 m. scarlet	35	40
9		5 m. yellow-orange (25 Sept)	35	30
		a. Orange	55	45
10		1 p. deep indigo (9 Nov)	35	25
11		2 p. pale olive	60	60
		a. Olive	1·25	1·10
12		5 p. purple	1·75	2·25
13		9 p. ochre (17 Dec)	2·25	4·00
14		10 p. ultramarine (17 Dec)	2·25	3·00
15		20 p. pale grey (27 Dec)	9·00	15·00
		a. Slate-grey	12·00	20·00
5/15		.. .. *Set of* 11	16·00	24·00

There are two sizes of the design of this issue:
19 × 23 mm. 1, 2, and 4 m., and 2 and 5 p.
18 × 21½ mm. 3 and 5 m., and 1, 9, 10 and 20 p.

There are numerous minor plate varieties in this issue, such as stops omitted in "E.E.F.", malformed Arabic characters, etc.

CIVIL ADMINISTRATION UNDER BRITISH HIGH COMMISSIONER

Palestine was placed under civil administration by a British High Commissioner on 1 July 1920.

(4)	(5)	(6)
فلسطين	فلسطين	فلسطين
PALESTINE	PALESTINE	PALESTINE
פלשתינה א״י	פלשתינה א״י	פלשתינה א״י

Differences:—
T **5**. 20 mm vert and 7 mm between English and Hebrew.
T **6**. 19 mm and 6 mm respectively.

(Optd at Greek Orthodox Convent, Jerusalem)

1920 (1 Sept). *Optd with T* **4** (*Arabic* 8 *mm long*). (*a*) *P* 15 × 14.

No.	Type	Description	Unused	Used
16	**3**	1 m. sepia	1·40	1·40
17		2 m. blue-green	6·00	4·50
18		3 m. chestnut	3·50	4·50
		a. Opt inverted	£500	£550
19		4 m. scarlet	1·00	1·25
20		5 m. yellow-orange	8·00	4·00
21		1 p. deep indigo (Sil.)	1·00	80
22		2 p. deep olive	1·75	1·90
23		5 p. deep purple	7·50	13·00
24		9 p. ochre	7·50	18·00
25		10 p. ultramarine	9·00	16·00
26		20 p. pale grey	15·00	32·00
		(*b*) *P* 14		
27	**3**	2 m. blue-green	1·10	1·25
28		3 m. chestnut	35·00	35·00
29		5 m. orange	1·25	90
16/29		.. .. *Set of* 14	90·00	£110

Two settings of T 4 are known to specialists, the first, of 24, being used for all values perforated 15×14 (but only on one sheet of the 1 p.) and the second, of 12, for all values in both perforations.

Apart from minor varieties due to broken type, there are three major errors which are rare in some values. These are (*a*) two Hebrew characters at left transposed (all values of first setting only); (*b*) diamond-shaped dot over the Arabic "t" making the word read "Faleszin" for "Falestin" (2 p. to 20 p. of first setting and 1 m. and 3 m. perf 15 × 14, and 5 m. perf 14 of second setting); (*c*) "B" for final "E" of "PALESTINE" (2 p. to 20 p. of first setting and all values of second setting except 3 m. perf 14).

Faulty registration of the overprint in this issue has resulted in numerous misplaced overprints, either vertically or horizontally, which are not of great importance with the exception of Nos. 21 and 29 which exist with the overprint out of sequence, i.e. Hebrew/Arabic/English or English/Arabic/Hebrew or English/Hebrew only. Also all values are known with Arabic/English only.

1920 (22 Sept)–**21**. *Optd with T* **5*** (*Arabic* 10 *mm long*).

No.	Type	Description	Unused	Used
		(*a*) *P* 15 × 14		
30	**3**	1 m. sepia (27.12.20)	75	1·00
		a. Opt inverted	£400	†
31		2 m. blue-green (27.12.20)	3·00	4·00
32		3 m. yellow-brown (27.12.20)	85	1·00
33		4 m. scarlet (27.12.20)	1·00	1·25
34		5 m. yellow-orange	2·00	1·00
35		1 p. deep indigo (Silver) (21.6.21) ..	£600	25·00
36		2 p. olive (21.6.21)	55·00	25·00
37		5 p. deep purple (21.6.21)	20·00	8·00
		(*b*) *P* 14		
38	**3**	1 m. sepia	£600	£650
39		2 m. blue-green	2·50	4·00
40		4 m. scarlet	60·00	80·00
41		5 m. orange	£120	10·00
		a. Yellow-orange	1·25	1·10
42		1 p. deep indigo (Silver)	25·00	1·25
43		5 p. purple	£225	£500

*In this setting the Arabic and Hebrew characters are badly worn and blunted, the Arabic "S" and "T" are joined (i.e. there is no break in the position indicated by the arrow in our illustration); the letters of "PALESTINE" are often irregular or broken; and the space between the two groups of Hebrew characters varies from 1 mm to over 1¾ mm. The " character in the left-hand Hebrew word extends above the remainder of the line (*For clear, sharp overprint, see Nos.* 47/59.)

The dates of issue given are irrespective of the perforations, i.e. one or both perfs could have been issued on the dates shown.

Nos. 31 and 39 exist with any one line of the overprint partly missing.

1920 (6 Dec). *Optd with T* **6**. (*a*) *P* 15 × 14.

No.	Type	Description	Unused	Used
44	**3**	3 m. yellow-brown	30·00	35·00
44*a*		5 m. yellow-orange	£12000	£10000
		(*b*) *P* 14		
45	**3**	1 m. sepia	25·00	30·00
46		5 m. orange	£400	30·00

(6*a*)	(7)	(8)
فلسطين	فلسطين	فلسطين
PALESTINE	PALESTINE	PALESTINE
פלשתינה א״י	פלשתינה א״י	פלשתינה א״י

1921 (29 May–4 Aug). *Optd as T* **6***a*. (*a*) *P* 15×14.

No.	Type	Description	Unused	Used
47	**3**	1 m. sepia (23.6)	4·50	3·50
48		2 m. blue-green (23.6)	7·50	5·00
49		3 m. yellow-brown (23.6)	20·00	2·50
		a. "PALESTINE" omitted	£1800	
50		4 m. scarlet (23.6)	16·00	3·00
51		5 m. yellow-orange	16·00	1·00
52		1 p. deep indigo (Silver) (July)	16·00	60
53		2 p. olive (4.8)	20·00	5·00
54		5 p. purple (4.8)	18·00	8·00
55		9 p. ochre (4.8)	30·00	90·00
56		10 p. ultramarine (4.8)	30·00	14·00
57		20 p. pale grey (4.8)	75·00	50·00
47/57		.. .. *Set of* 11	£225	£160
		(*b*) *P* 14		
58	**3**	1 m. sepia	—	£2500
59		20 p. pale grey	£10000	£3000

In this setting the Arabic and Hebrew characters are sharp and pointed and there is usually a break between the Arabic "S" and "T", though this is sometimes filled with ink. The space between the two groups of Hebrew characters is always 1¾ mm. The top of the " character in the Hebrew aligns with the remainder of the word.

1921 (Sept-Oct). *Optd with T* **7** ("PALESTINE" *in sans-serif letters*) *by Stamping Dept, Board of Inland Revenue, Somerset House, London. Wmk Royal Cypher in column. P* 15 × 14.

No.	Type	Description	Unused	Used
60	**3**	1 m. sepia	35	30
61		2 m. blue-green	35	30
62		3 m. yellow-brown	35	30
63		4 m. scarlet	50	50
64		5 m. yellow-orange	40	30
65		1 p. bright turquoise-blue	60	35
66		2 p. olive	70	40
67		5 p. deep purple	4·00	5·00
68		9 p. ochre	12·00	14·00
69		10 p. ultramarine	15·00	£500
70		20 p. pale grey	45·00	£1100
60/70		.. .. *Set of* 11	70·00	

(Printed and optd by Waterlow & Sons from new plates)

1922 (Sept–Nov). *T* **3** (*redrawn*), *optd with T* **8**. *Wmk Mult Script CA*. (*a*) *P* 14.

No.	Type	Description	Unused	Used
71	**3**	1 m. sepia	30	30
		a. Deep brown	40	30
		b. Opt inverted	—	£10000
		c. Opt double	£225	£375
72		2 m. yellow	35	30
		a. Orange-yellow	1·00	50
73		3 m. greenish blue	35	15
74		4 m. carmine-pink	30	20
75		5 m. orange	35	20
76		6 m. blue-green	65	30
77		7 m. yellow-brown	65	30
78		8 m. scarlet	65	30

79 3 1 p. grey 65 30
80 13 m. ultramarine 50 15
81 2 p. olive .. .. 1·25 35
a. Opt inverted £350 £500
b. Ochre .. .. £110 5·50
82 5 p. deep purple .. .. 4·50 1·25
82*a* 9 p. ochre £1000 £250
83 10 p. light blue .. .. 22·00 7·50
a. "E.F.F." for "E.E.F." in bottom panel £550 £500
84 20 p. bright violet .. .. £120 90·00

(*b*) *P* 15 × 14

86 3 5 p. deep purple .. .. 30·00 4·00
87 9 p. ochre .. .. 9·00 9·00
88 10 p. light blue .. .. 7·50 2·50
a. "E.F.F." for "E.E.F." in bottom panel £450 £325
89 20 p. bright violet .. .. 9·00 5·50
71/89 Optd "Specimen" .. .. *Set of* 15 £400

Most values can be found on thin paper.

In this issue the design of all denominations is the same size, 18 mm × 21½ mm. Varieties may be found with one or other of the stops between "E.E.F." missing.

BRITISH MANDATE TO THE LEAGUE OF NATIONS

The League of Nations granted a mandate to Great Britain for the administration of Palestine on 29 September 1923.

9 Rachel's Tomb

10 Dome of the Rock

11 Citadel, Jerusalem

12 Sea of Galilee

(Des F. Taylor. Typo Harrison)

1927 (1 June)–**45**. *Wmk Mult Script CA. P* 13½ × 14½ (2 *m. to* 20 *m.*) *or* 14.

90 9 2 m. greenish blue (14.8.27) 30 10
91 3 m. yellow-green 30 10
92 10 4 m. rose-pink (14.8.27) .. .. .. 2·75 1·25
93 11 5 m. orange (14.8.27) 45 10
a. From coils. Perf 14½×14 (1935) 13·00 18·00
b. Yellow (12.44) 60 15
c. Yellow. From coils. Perf 14½ × 14 (1945) .. .. 23·00 23·00
94 10 6 m. pale green (14.8.27) .. .. 2·25 1·50
a. Deep green 50 20
95 11 7 m. scarlet (14.8.27) .. .. .. 4·00 1·00
96 10 8 m. yellow-brown (14.8.27) .. .. 11·00 5·00
97 9 10 m. slate (14.8.27) 40 10
a. Grey. From coils. Perf 14½ × 14 (11.38) .. .. 22·00 23·00
b. Grey (1944) 40 10
98 10 13 m. ultramarine .. .. .. 3·75 30
99 11 20 m. dull olive-green (14.8.27) .. .. 1·40 15
a. Bright olive-green (12.44) .. .. 1·40 15
100 12 50 m. deep dull purple (14.8.27) .. .. 1·00 25
a. Bright purple (12.44) .. .. 1·00 20
101 90 m. bistre (14.8.27) .. .. .. 75·00 75·00
102 100 m. turquoise-blue (14.8.27) .. .. 2·00 50
103 200 m. deep violet (14.8.27) .. .. 8·00 4·50
a. Bright violet (1928) .. .. 27·00 16·00
b. Blackish violet (12.44) .. .. 5·50 3·00
90/103*b* .. .. *Set of* 14 95·00 75·00
90/103 H/S "Specimen" .. .. *Set of* 14 £325

Three sets may be made of the above issue; one on thin paper, one on thicker paper with a ribbed appearance, and another on thick white paper without ribbing.

2 m. stamps in the grey colour of the 10 m. exist as also 50 m. stamps in blue, but it has not been established whether they were issued.

Nos. 90/1 and 93 exist in coils, constructed from normal sheets.

1932 (1 June)–**44**. *New values and colours. Wmk Mult Script CA. P* 13½ × 14½ (4 *m. to* 15 *m.*) *or* 14.

104 10 4 m. purple (1.11.32) 30 10
105 11 7 m. deep violet 45 10
106 10 8 m. scarlet 60 20
107 13 m. bistre (1.8.32) 40 10
108 15 m. ultramarine (1.8.32) 80 10
a. Grey-blue (12.44) 50 10
b. Greenish blue 65 10
109 12 250 m. brown (15.1.42) .. .. .. 2·50 2·00
110 500 m. scarlet (15.1.42) .. .. .. 4·50 2·75
111 £P1 black (15.1.42) .. .. .. 5·00 3·25
104/11 .. .. *Set of* 8 13·00 7·50
104/11 Perf "Specimen" .. .. *Set of* 8 £375

No. 108 exists in coils, constructed from normal sheets.

POSTAL FISCALS

Type-set stamps inscribed "O.P.D.A." (= Ottoman Public Debt Administration) or "H.J.Z." (Hejaz Railway); British 1d. stamps of 1912–24 and Palestine stamps overprinted with one or other of the above groups of letters, or with the word "Devair", with or without surcharge of new value, are fiscal stamps. They are known used as postage stamps, alone, or with other stamps to make up the correct rates, and were passed by the postal authorities, although they were not definitely authorised for postal use.

POSTAGE DUE STAMPS

D 1

D 2 (MILLIEME)

D 3 (MIL)

(Typo Greek Orthodox Convent Press, Jerusalem)

1923 (1 Apr). *P* 11.

D1 D 1 1 m. yellow-brown .. .. 25·00 42·00
a. Imperf (pair) £300
b. Imperf between (horiz pair) .. £1000
D2 2 m. blue-green .. .. 22·00 32·00
a. Imperf (pair) £350
D3 4 m. scarlet .. .. 22·00 38·00
D4 8 m. mauve .. .. 17·00 26·00
a. Imperf (pair) £120
b. Imperf between (horiz pair) .. — £1800
D5 13 m. steel blue .. .. 15·00 26·00
a. Imperf between (horiz pair) .. £850
D1/5 .. .. *Set of* 5 90·00 £150

Perfectly centred and perforated stamps of this issue are worth considerably more than the above prices, which are for average specimens.

(Types D **2**/**3**. Typo D.L.R.)

1924 (1 Dec). *Wmk Mult Script CA. P* 14.

D 6 D 2 1 m. deep brown .. .. .. 90 1·75
D 7 2 m. yellow .. .. 1·00 1·75
D 8 4 m. green .. .. 1·10 1·25
D 9 8 m. scarlet .. .. 2·50 90
D10 13 m. ultramarine .. .. .. 2·50 2·50
D11 5 p. violet .. .. 7·00 1·75
D6/11 .. .. *Set of* 6 13·50 9·00
D6/11 Optd "Specimen" .. .. *Set of* 6 £275

1928 (1 Feb)–**45**. *Wmk Mult Script CA. P* 14.

D12 D 3 1 m. brown 45 75
a. Perf 15 × 14 (1944) .. .. 25·00 45·00
D13 2 m. yellow 55 60
D14 4 m. green .. .. 70 1·25
a. Perf 15 × 14 (1945) .. .. 38·00 60·00
D15 6 m. orange-brown (10.33) .. .. 7·00 7·00
D16 8 m. carmine .. .. 1·50 70
D17 10 m. pale grey .. .. 1·25 60
D18 13 m. ultramarine .. .. .. 1·50 1·50
D19 20 m. pale olive-green .. .. .. 1·60 1·25
D20 50 m. violet .. .. 2·50 1·25
D12/20 .. .. *Set of* 9 15·00 13·50
D12/20 Perf (D15) or Optd (others) "Specimen" *Set of* 9 £300

The British Mandate terminated on 14 May 1948. Later issues of stamps and occupation issues will be found listed under Gaza, Israel and Jordan in Part 19 (*Middle East*) of this catalogue.

Papua New Guinea

NEW GUINEA

Stamps of Germany and later of GERMAN NEW GUINEA were used in New Guinea from 1888 until 1914.

During the interim period between the "G.R.I." surcharges and the "N.W. PACIFIC ISLANDS" overprints, stamps of AUSTRALIA perforated "OS" were utilised.

PRICES FOR STAMPS ON COVER

Nos. 1/30	*from* × 3
Nos. 31/2	—
Nos. 33/49	*from* × 3
Nos. 50/9	*from* × 2
Nos. 60/2	—
Nos. 63/4	*from* × 2
Nos. 64*c*/*q*	—
Nos. 65/81	*from* × 5
Nos. 83/5	—
Nos. 86/97	*from* × 5
No. 99	—
Nos. 100/16	*from* × 4
Nos. 117/18	—
Nos. 119/24	*from* × 4
Nos. 125/203	*from* × 2
Nos. 204/5	—
Nos. 206/11	*from* × 8
Nos. 212/25	*from* × 2
Nos. O1/33	*from* × 8

AUSTRALIAN OCCUPATION

Stamps of German New Guinea surcharged

G.R.I. 2d. (1)   G.R.I. 1s. (2)   G.R.I. 1d. (3)

SETTINGS. The "G.R.I" issues of New Guinea were surcharged on a small hand press which could only accommodate one horizontal row of stamps at a time. In addition to complete sheets the surcharges were also applied to multiples and individual stamps which were first lightly affixed to plain paper backing sheets. Such backing sheets could contain a mixture of denominations, some of which required different surcharges.

Specialists recognise twelve settings of the low value surcharges (1d. to 8d.):

Setting 1 (Nos. 1/4, 7/11) shows the bottom of the "R" 6 mm from the top of the "d"

Setting 2 (Nos. 16/19, 22/6) shows the bottom of the "R" 5 mm from the top of the "d"

Setting 3 was used for the Official stamps (Nos. O1/2)

Setting 4, which included the 2½d. value for the first time, and Setting 5 showed individual stamps with either 6 mm or 5 mm spacing.

These five settings were for rows of ten stamps, but the remaining seven, used on odd stamps handed in for surcharging, were applied as strips of five only. One has, so far, not been reconstructed, but of the remainder three show the 6 mm spacing, two the 5 mm and one both.

On the shilling values the surcharges were applied as horizontal rows of four and the various settings divide into two groups, one with 3½ to 4½ mm between the bottom of the "R" and the top of numeral, and the second with 5½ mm between the "R" and numeral. The first group includes the very rare initial setting on which the space is 4 to 4½ mm.

G.R.I, 2d. "1" for "I" (Setting 1)   G.R.I. 1d. Short "1" (Setting 1)   G.R.I. 1s. Large "S" (Setting 1)

1914 (17 Oct)–**15**. *Stamps of* 1901 *surch*.

(*a*) *As T* **1**. "G.R.I." *and value* 6 *mm apart*

1 1d. on 3 pf. brown £250 £250
a. "1" for "I" £450
b. Short "1" £450
c. "1" with straight top serif (Setting 6) .. £500
d. "I" for "1" (Setting 12) £600
2 1d. on 5 pf. green .. .. 32·00 40·00
a. "1" for "I" £160
b. Short "1" £160
c. "1" with straight top serif (Settings 6 and 9) £200
3 2d. on 10 pf. carmine .. .. .. 50·00 60·00
a. "1" for "I" £200
4 2d. on 20 pf. ultramarine .. .. .. 35·00 42·00
a. "1" for "I" £160
e. Surch double, one "G.R.I." albino £1800
f. Surch inverted £3000
5 2½d. on 10 pf. carmine (27.2.15) .. 65·00 £140
a. Fraction bar omitted (Setting 9) £1000 £1300
6 2½d. on 20 pf. ultramarine (27.2.15) .. 65·00 £140
a. Fraction bar omitted (Setting 9)
7 3d. on 25 pf. black and red/*yellow* .. £160 £190
a. "1" for "I" £425
8 3d. on 30 pf. black and orange/*buff* .. £180 £225
a. "1" for "I" £450
e. Surch double £3000 £3000
9 4d. on 40 pf. black and carmine .. £225 £275
a. "1" for "I" £550
e. Surch double £850 £1300
f. Surch inverted £3000
10 5d. on 50 pf. black and purple/*buff* .. £375 £500
a. "1" for "I" £800 £950
e. Surch double £3000
11 8d. on 80 pf. black and carmine/*rose* .. £600 £750
a. "1" for "I" £1300
d. No stop after "d" £1400
e. Error. Surch "G.R.I. 4d." £2000

(*b*) *As T* **2**. "G.R.I." *and value* 3½ *to* 4 *mm apart*

12 1s. on 1 m. carmine £1400 £1900
a. Large "s" £3500 £3500
13 2s. on 2 m. blue £1500 £2250
a. Large "s" £3500 £4500
c. Error. Surch "G.R.I. 5s." £7500
14 3s. on 3 m. violet-black £3000 £3750
a. Large "s" £5000
b. No stop after "I" (Setting 3) .. £6000 £6000
15 5s. on 5 m. carmine and black .. £5000 £6000
a. Large "s" £7500
b. No stop after "I" (Setting 3) .. £7500 £9000
c. Error. Surch "G.R.I. 1s." £14000

G.R.I. 3d. Thick "3" (Setting 2)   G.R.I. 5d. Thin "5" (Setting 2)

1914 (16 Dec)–**15**. *Stamps of* 1901 *surch*.

(*a*) *As T* **1**. "G.R.I." *and value* 5 *mm apart*

16 1d. on 3 pf. brown .. .. 40·00 50·00
a. "I" for "1" (Setting 11) £140
b. Short "1" (Setting 2) £180
c. "1" with straight top serif (Settings 2 and 6) .. .. 70·00 80·00
e. Surch double £275 £400
f. Surch double, one inverted £1300
g. Surch inverted £750 £1100
h. Error. Surch "G.R.I. 4d." £3500
17 1d. on 5 pf. green .. .. 14·00 20·00
b. Short "1" (Setting 2) £110 £130
c. "1" with straight top serif (Setting 2) 32·00 45·00
e. "d" inverted .. .. — £800
f. "1d" inverted .. .. — £2250
g. "G.R.I." without stops or spaces .. £2250
ga. "G.R.I." without stops, but with normal spaces .. .. — £2250
h. "G.I.R." instead of "G.R.I." £3000 £3500
i. Surch double £850

No.	Description	Unused	Used
18	2d. on 10 pf. carmine	18·00	25·00
	e. No stop after "d" (Setting 2)	85·00	£120
	f. Stop before, instead of after, "G" (Settings 4 and 5)	£2500	
	g. Surch double	£3500	£3500
	h. Surch double, one inverted	—	£1900
	i. In vert pair with No. 20	£8500	
	j. In horiz pair with No. 20	£8500	
	k. Error. Surch ".GR.I. 1d."	£2750	£2000
	l. Error. Surch "G.I.R. 3d."	£3500	
19	2d. on 20 pf. ultramarine	24·00	30·00
	e. No stop after "d" (Setting 2)	70·00	95·00
	f. No stop after "I" (Setting 11)	£425	
	g. "R" inverted (Settings 4 and 5)	—	£2000
	h. Surch double	£600	£1400
	i. Surch double, one inverted	£1100	£1500
	j. Surch inverted	£1800	£2750
	k. Albino surch (in horiz pair with normal)	£5000	
	l. In vert pair with No. 21	£4750	£6000
	m. Error. Surch "G.R.I. 1d."	£3500	£3500
20	2½d. on 10 pf. carmine (27.2.15)	£225	£275
21	2½d. on 20 pf. ultramarine (27.2.15)	£1200	£1500
22	3d. on 25 pf. black and red/*yellow*	75·00	95·00
	e. Thick "3"	£450	
	f. Surch double	£2000	£3000
	g. Surch inverted	£2000	£3000
	h. Surch omitted (in horiz pair with normal)	£5500	
	i. Error. Surch "G.R.I. 1d."	£5500	
23	3d. on 30 pf. black and orange/*buff*	70·00	90·00
	e. No stop after "d" (Setting 2)	£400	
	f. Thick "3"	£375	
	g. Surch double	£850	£1200
	h. Surch double, one inverted	£1000	£1500
	i. Surch double, both inverted	£2000	£3000
	j. Surch inverted	£1700	
	k. Albino surch	£5500	
	l. Surch omitted (in vert pair with normal)	£3250	
	m. Error. Surch "G.R.I. 1d."	£2500	£3500
24	4d. on 40 pf. black and carmine	85·00	£100
	e. Surch double	£800	
	f. Surch double, one inverted	£1100	
	g. Surch double, both inverted	£2750	
	h. Surch inverted	£1600	
	i. Error. Surch "G.R.I. 1d."	£1600	
	ia. Surch "G.R.I. 1d." inverted	£2500	
	j. Error. Surch "G.R.I. 3d." double	£4250	
	k. No stop after "I" (Setting 11)	£1400	
25	5d. on 50 pf. black and purple/*buff*	£120	£150
	e. Thin "5"	£650	£1100
	f. Surch double	£800	
	g. Surch double, one inverted	£1800	£3250
	h. Surch double, both inverted	£2500	£3000
	i. Surch inverted	£1400	
	j. Error. Surch "G.I.R. 3d."	£5000	
26	8d. on 80 pf. black and carmine/*rose*	£350	£450
	e. Surch double	£1600	£1800
	f. Surch double, one inverted	£1500	£1800
	g. Surch triple	£1700	£2000
	h. Surch inverted	£2750	£3250
	i. Error. Surch "G.R.I. 3d."	£5500	

(b) As T **2**. *"G.R.I." and value 5½ mm apart*

No.	Description	Unused	Used
27	1s. on 1 m. carmine	£2000	£2750
28	2s. on 2 m. blue	£2250	£3250
29	3s. on 3 m. violet-black	£3500	£4500
	a. "G.R.I." double	£10000	
30	5s. on 5 m. carmine and black	£9000	£10000

1915. *Nos.* 18 *and* 19 *further surch as in T* **3**.

No.	Description	Unused	Used
31	"1" on 2d. on 10 pf.	£9000	£9000
32	"1" on 2d. on 20 pf.	£9000	£6000

OFFICIAL STAMPS

O. S.

G.R.I.

1d.

(O 3a)

1915 (27 Feb). *Stamps of* 1901 *surch as Type* O **3a**. "G.R.I." *and value* 3½ *mm apart.*

No.	Description	Unused	Used
O1	1d. on 3 pf. brown	25·00	60·00
	a. "1" and "d" spaced	75·00	
	b. Surch double	£2000	
O2	1d. on 5 pf. green	75·00	£130
	a. "1" and "d" spaced	£150	

German New Guinea Registration Labels surcharged

4 4*a*

G.R.I.

3d.

Sans serif "G" and different "3".

1915. *Registration Labels surch* "G.R.I. 3d." *in settings of five or ten and used for postage. Each black and red on buff. Inscr* "(Deutsch Neuguinea)" *spelt in various ways as indicated.*

I. *With name of town in sans-serif letters as T* **4**

No.	Description	Unused	Used
33	Rabaul "(Deutsch Neuguinea)"	£110	£150
	a. "G.R.I. 3d." double	£1100	£1300
	b. No bracket before "Deutsch"	£425	£550
	ba. No bracket and surch double	£3000	
	d. "(Deutsch-Neuguinea)"	£170	£225
	da. "G.R.I. 3d." double	£3000	£3000
	db. No stop after "I"	£550	
	dc. "G.R.I. 3d" inverted	£2750	
	dd. No bracket before "Deutsch"	£700	
	de. No bracket after "Neuguinea"	£700	
34	Deulon "(Deutsch Neuguinea)"	£5000	
35	Friedrich-Wilhelmshafen "(Deutsch Neuguinea)"	£120	£275
	a. No stop after "d"	£275	
	b. "G" omitted	£2000	
	c. Sans-serif "G"	£3000	
	d. Sans-serif "G" and different "3"	£2500	
	e. Surch inverted	—	£2750
	f. "(Deutsch-Neuguinea)"	£140	£275
	fa. No stop after "d"	£325	
36	Herbertshöhe "(Deutsch Neuguinea)"	£170	£325
	a. No stop after "d"	£375	
	b. No stop after "I"	£650	
	c. "G" omitted	£2500	
	d. Surch omitted (in horiz pair with normal)	£4000	
	e. "(Deutsch Neu-Guinea)"	£300	
37	Käwieng "(Deutsch-Neuguinea)"	£425	
	a. No bracket after "Neuguinea"	£1700	
	b. "Deutsch Neu-Guinea"	£150	£275
	ba. No stop after "d"	£325	
	bb. "G.R.I." double	£1600	
	bc. "3d." double	£1600	
	bd. "G" omitted	£3000	
38	Kieta "(Deutsch-Neuguinea)"	£300	£475
	a. No bracket before "Deutsch"	£950	£1200
	b. No stop after "d"	£650	
	c. Surch omitted (righthand stamp of horiz pair)	£3250	
	d. No stops after "R" and "I"		
	e. No stop after "I"	£900	
	f. "G" omitted	£2750	
39	Manus "(Deutsch Neuguinea)"	£180	£325
	a. "G.R.I. 3d." double	£1600	
	b. No bracket before "Deutsch"	£700	£900
40	Stephansort "(Deutsch Neu-Guinea)"	†	£1500
	a. No stop after "d"	†	£2750

II. *With name of town in letters with serifs as T* **4a**

No.	Description	Unused	Used
41	Friedrich Wilhelmshafen "(Deutsch-Neuguinea)"	£150	£275
	b. No stop after "d"	£325	£475
	c. No stop after "I"	£600	£850
	d. No bracket before "Deutsch"	£650	£900
	e. No bracket after "Neuguinea"	£650	£900
42	Käwieng "(Deutsch Neuguinea)"	£120	£250
	a. No stop after "d"	£275	
43	Manus "(Deutsch-Neuguinea)"	£1200	£1700
	a. No stop after "I"	£2000	£2000

Stamps of Marshall Islands surcharged

SETTINGS. The initial supply of Marshall Islands stamps, obtained from Nauru, was surcharged with Setting 2 (5 mm between "R" and "d") on the penny values and with the 3½ to 4 setting on the shilling stamps.

Small quantities subsequently handed in were surcharged, often on the same backing sheet as German New Guinea values, with Settings 6, 7 or 12 (all 6 mm between "R" and "d") for the penny values and with a 5½ mm setting for the shilling stamps.

1914 (16 Dec). *Stamps of* 1901 *surch.*

(a) As T **1**. "G.R.I." *and value* 5 *mm apart*

No.	Description	Unused	Used
50	1d. on 3 pf. brown	40·00	50·00
	c. "1" with straight top serif (Setting 2)	95·00	£120
	d. ".GR.I." and "1" with straight top serif (Settings 4 and 5)	—	£3000
	e. Surch inverted	£1600	
51	1d. on 5 pf. green	42·00	50·00
	c. "1" with straight top serif (Settings 2 and 11)	£100	£120
	d. "I" for "1" (Setting 11)	£375	
	e. "1" and "d" spaced	£325	£350
	f. Surch double	£850	£1500
	g. Surch inverted	£1000	
52	2d. on 10 pf. carmine	14·00	21·00
	e. No stop after "G" (Setting 2)	£500	
	f. Surch double	£800	£1500
	g. Surch double, one inverted	£950	£1500
	h. Surch inverted	£1300	
	i. Surch sideways	£2500	
53	2d. on 20 pf. ultramarine	15·00	24·00
	e. No stop after "d" (Setting 2)	40·00	60·00
	g. Surch double	£800	£1600
	h. Surch double, one inverted	£1600	£1800
	i. Surch inverted	£1800	£1800
54	3d. on 25 pf. black and red/*yellow*	£250	£325
	e. No stop after "d" (Settings 2 and 11)	£500	£650
	f. Thick "3"	£700	
	g. Surch double	£1000	£1400
	h. Surch double, one inverted	£1000	
	i. Surch inverted	£1800	
55	3d. on 30 pf. black and orange/*buff*	£275	£350
	e. No stop after "d" (Setting 2)	£550	
	f. Thick "3"	£750	
	g. Surch inverted	£1500	£1700
56	4d. on 40 pf. black and carmine	85·00	£110
	e. No stop after "d" (Setting 2)	£250	£325
	f. "d" omitted (Setting 2)	—	£2500
	g. Surch double	£1500	£1700
	h. Surch triple	£2500	
	i. Surch inverted	£1600	
	j. Error. Surch "G.R.I. 1d."	£3750	
	k. Error. Surch "G.R.I. 3d."	£3750	
57	5d. on 50 pf. black and purple/*buff*	£120	£160
	e. Thin "5"	£2250	
	f. "d" omitted (Setting 2)	£700	
	g. Surch double	£2000	
	h. Surch inverted	£2500	
58	8d. on 80 pf. black and carmine/*rose*	£450	£550
	e. Surch double	£1700	
	f. Surch double, both inverted	£2250	£2750
	g. Surch triple	£3000	
	h. Surch inverted	£2000	£2750

(b) As T **2**. "G.R.I." *and value* 3½-4 *mm apart*

No.	Description	Unused	Used
59	1s. on 1 m. carmine	£1600	£2250
	b. No stop after "I"	£2750	
	e. Surch double	£7000	
60	2s. on 2 m. blue	£1000	£1500
	b. No stop after "I"	£2250	£3000
	e. Surch double	£6500	
	f. Surch double, one inverted	£5500	£5500
61	3s. on 3 m. violet-black	£2750	£3750
	b. No stop after "I"	£4000	
	e. Surch double	£6500	£8000
62	5s. on 5 m. carmine and black	£4750	£6000
	e. Surch double, one inverted	—	£11000

1915. *Nos.* 52 *and* 53 *further surch as in T* **3**.

No.	Description	Unused	Used
63	"1" on 2d. on 10 pf. carmine	£140	£170
	a. "1" double	£5500	
	b. "1" inverted	£5500	£5500
64	"1" on 2d. on 20 pf. ultramarine	£3000	£2000
	a. On No 53e.	£5000	£2750
	b. "1" inverted	£6500	£6500

1915. *Stamps of* 1901 *surch.*

(a) As T **1**. "G.R.I." *and value* 6 *mm apart*

No.	Description	Unused	Used
64*c*	1d. on 3 pf. brown	£550	
	cc. "1" with straight top serif (Setting 6)	—	£1500
	cd. "I" for "1" (Setting 12)	£800	
	ce. Surch inverted	£2750	
64*d*	1d. on 5 pf. green	£600	£1100
	dc. "1" with straight top serif (Setting 6)	£800	
	dd. "I" for "1" (Setting 12)	£800	
	de. Surch inverted	£2750	
	df. Surch double	£2750	
64*e*	2d. on 10 pf. carmine	£850	£1300
	ea. Surch sideways	£3000	
64*f*	2d. on 20 pf. ultramarine	£700	£1300
	fe. Surch inverted	£2750	
64*g*	2½d. on 10 pf. carmine	£4250	
64*h*	2½d. on 20 pf. ultramarine	£6500	
64*i*	3d. on 25 pf. black and red/*yellow*	£950	£1500
64*j*	3d. on 30 pf. black and orange/*buff*	£1000	£1500
	je. Error. Surch "G.R.I. 1d."	£3750	
64*k*	4d. on 40 pf. black and carmine	£950	£1500
	ke. Surch double	£3000	
	kf. Surch inverted	£3000	
64*l*	5d. on 50 pf. black and purple/*buff*	£850	£1500
	le. Surch double	£3000	
64*m*	8d. on 80 pf. black and carmine/*rose*	£1500	£2000
	me. Surch inverted	£3500	

(b) As T **2**. "G.R.I." *and value* 5½ *mm apart*

No.	Description	Unused	Used
64*n*	1s. on 1 m. carmine	£4500	
	na. Large "s" (Setting 5)	£5500	
64*o*	2s. on 2 m. blue	£3500	
	oe. Surch double, one inverted	£10000	
64*p*	3s. on 3 m. violet-black	£6000	
	pe. Surch inverted	£10000	
64*q*	5s. on 5 m. carmine and black	£8500	
	qa. Large "s" (Setting 5)	£10000	

Stamps of Australia overprinted

N. W. PACIFIC ISLANDS.	N. W. PACIFIC ISLANDS.	N. W. PACIFIC ISLANDS.
(*a*)	(*b*)	(*c*)

(**6**)

W **5** *of Australia*

W **2** *of Australia*

W **6** *of Australia*

1915–16. *Stamps of Australia optd in black as T* **6** (*a*), (*b*) *or* (*c*).

(i) *W* **5** *of Australia. P* 14 (4 Jan–15 March 1915)

No.	Type	Description	Unused	Used
65	**5a**	½d. green	1·25	5·00
66		½d. bright green	1·75	5·50
67		1d. pale rose (Die I) (4.1)	3·75	3·75
68		1d. dull red (Die I)	5·00	4·25
69		1d. carmine-red (Die I)	4·50	4·00
		a. Substituted cliché	—	£700
69*b*		1d. carmine-red (Die II)	£250	£200
		c. Substituted cliché	£1100	
70		4d. yellow-orange	3·50	9·00
		a. Line through "FOUR PENCE"	£350	£550
		b. Pale orange-yellow	15·00	24·00
71		4d. chrome-yellow	£250	£275
72		5d. brown	3·25	15·00

(ii) *W* 2 *of Australia. P* 12 (4 Jan 1915–March 1916)

73 1 2d. grey (Die I) .. 17·00 30·00
74 2½d. indigo (4.1.15) .. 2·75 15·00
76 3d. yellow-olive (Die I) .. 17·00 35·00
a. Die II .. £300 £350
ab. In pair with Die I .. £500 £550
77 3d. greenish olive (Die I) .. £190 £250
a. Die II .. £1300
ab. In pair with Die I .. £2250
78 6d. ultramarine .. 26·00 50·00
a. Retouched "E" .. £5000
79 9d. violet .. 35·00 55·00
81 1s. green .. 38·00 55·00
83 5s. grey and yellow (3.16) .. £750 £900
84 10s. grey and pink (12.15) .. £110 £160
85 £1 brown and ultramarine (12.15) .. £450 £650

(iii) *W* 5 *of Australia. P* 12 (Oct 1915–July 1916)

86 1 2d. grey (Die I) .. 6·50 12·00
87 2½d. indigo (7.16) .. £9500 £9000
88 6d. ultramarine .. 9·50 12·00
89 9d. violet (12.15) .. 13·00 15·00
90 1s. emerald (12.15) .. 9·00 23·00
91 2s. brown (12.15) .. 80·00 £100
92 5s. grey and yellow (12.15) .. 80·00 £100

(iv) *W* 6 *of Australia. P* 12 (Dec 1915–Aug 1916)

94 1 2d. grey (Die I) .. 4·50 11·00
a. In pair with Die IIA .. £180
96 3d. yellow-olive (Die I) .. 4·75 11·00
a. Die II .. 75·00 £100
ab. In pair with Die I .. £140
97 2s. brown (8.16) .. 27·00 45·00
99 £1 brown and ultramarine (8.16) .. £300 £450

Dates for Nos. 67 and 74 are issue dates. All other dates are those of despatch. Nos. 65/6, 68/73, 76/81 were despatched on 15 March 1915.

For Die IIA of 2d. see note below Australia No. 45.

SETTINGS. Type **6** exists in three slightly different versions, illustrated above as (*a*), (*b*), *and* (*c*). These differ in the letters "S" of "ISLANDS" as follows:

(*a*) Both "SS" normal.
(*b*) First "S" with small head and large tail and second "S" normal.
(*c*) Both "SS" with small head and large tail.

Type **11**, which also shows the examples of "S" as the normal version, can be identified from Type **6**(*a*) by the relative position of the second and third lines of the overprint. On Type **6***a* the "P" of "PACIFIC" is exactly over the first "S" of "ISLANDS". On Type **11** the "P" appears over the space between "I" and "S".

It has been established, by the study of minor variations, that there are actually six settings of the "N.W. PACIFIC ISLANDS" overprint, including that represented by T **11**, but the following are the different arrangements of Type **6**(*a*), (*b*), and (*c*) which occur.

A. Horizontal rows 1 and 2 all Type (*a*). Row 3 all Type (*b*). Rows 4 and 5 all Type (*c*).

B. (½d. green only). As A, except that the types in the bottom row run (*c*) (*c*) (*c*) (*b*) (*c*).

C. As A, but bottom row now shows types (*a*) (*c*) (*c*) (*c*) (*b*) (*c*).

Horizontal strips and pairs showing varieties (*a*) and (*c*), or (*b*) and (*c*) *se-tenant* are scarce.

The earliest printing of the 1d. and 2½d. values was made on sheets with margin attached on two sides, the later printings being on sheets from which the margins had been removed. In this printing the vertical distances between the overprints are less than in later printings, so that in the lower horizontal rows of the sheet the overprint is near the top of the stamp.

The settings used on King George stamps and on the Kangaroo type are similar, but the latter stamps being smaller the overprints are closer together in the vertical rows.

PURPLE OVERPRINTS. We no longer differentiate between purple and black overprints in the above series. In our opinion the two colours are nowadays insufficiently distinct to warrant separation.

PRICES. The prices quoted for Nos. 65 to 101 apply to stamps with opts Types **6** (*a*) or **6** (*c*). Stamps with opt Type **6** (*b*) are worth a 25 per cent premium. Vertical strips of three, showing (*a*), (*b*) and (*c*), are worth from four times the prices quoted for singles as Types **6** (*a*) or **6** (*c*).

One Penny
(10)

**N. W.
PACIFIC
ISLANDS.**
(11)

1918 (23 May). *Nos.* 72 *and* 81 *surch locally with T* **10**.

100 1d. on 5d. brown .. 90·00 80·00
101 1d. on 1s. green .. 90·00 80·00

Types **6** (*a*), (*b*), (*c*) occur on these stamps also.

1918–23. *Stamps of Australia optd with T* **11** ("P" *of* "PACIFIC" *over space between* "I" *and* "S" *of* "ISLANDS").

(i) *T* **5***a* (*King*). *W* **5** *of Australia. P* 14

102 ½d. green .. 50 3·25
103 1d. carmine-red (Die I) .. 1·40 1·60
a. Substituted cliché .. £800 £500
b. Rosine. Rough paper, locally gummed (perfd "OS") .. £400 £120
103*c* 1d. carmine-red (Die II) .. £120 48·00
d. Substituted cliché .. £800 £500
e. Rosine. Rough paper, locally gummed (perfd "OS") .. — £400
104 4d. yellow-orange (1919) .. 3·25 16·00
a. Line through "FOUR PENCE" .. £1000 £1200
105 5d. brown (1919) .. 1·75 12·00

(ii) *T* **1** (*Kangaroo*). *W* **6** *of Australia. P* 12

106 2d. grey (Die I) (1919) .. 2·50 16·00
a. Die II .. 9·00 35·00
107 2½d. indigo (1919) .. 3·00 15·00
a. "1" of "½" omitted .. £5500 £5500
108 2½d. blue (1920) .. 6·50 24·00
109 3d. greenish olive (Die I) (1919) .. 16·00 21·00
a. Die II .. 42·00 60·00
ab. In pair with Die I .. £300
b. Light olive (Die II) (1923) .. 11·00 18·00
110 6d. ultramarine (1919) .. 4·50 14·00
111 6d. greyish ultramarine (1922) .. 42·00 65·00
112 9d. violet (1919) .. 6·50 35·00
113 1s. emerald .. 6·50 28·00
114 1s. pale blue-green .. 13·00 28·00
115 2s. brown (1919) .. 28·00 38·00
116 5s. grey and yellow (1919) .. 60·00 60·00
117 10s. grey and bright pink (1919) .. £150 £200
118 £1 brown and ultramarine (1922) .. £2750

(iii) *T* **5***a*. *W* **6***a of Australia* (*Mult Crown* A). *P* 14

119 ½d. green (1919) .. 40 3·50

Type **11** differs from Type **6** (*a*) in the position of the "P" of "PACIFIC", which is further to the left in Type **11**.

1921–22. *T* **5***a of Australia. W* **5** *of Australia. Colour changes and new value. Optd with T* **11**.

120 1d. bright violet (1922) .. 1·00 5·50
121 2d. orange .. 2·75 4·50
122 2d. scarlet (1922) .. 4·00 8·00
123 4d. violet (1922) .. 26·00 45·00
a. "FOUR PENCE" in thinner letters .. £750
124 4d. ultramarine (1922) .. 10·00 45·00
a. "FOUR PENCE" in thinner letters .. £750
120/4 .. *Set of* 5 40·00 95·00

MANDATED TERRITORY OF NEW GUINEA

PRINTERS. See note at the beginning of Australia.

12 Native Village

(13)

(Des R. Harrison. Eng T. Harrison. Recess Note Printing Branch, Treasury, Melbourne, from 1926 Note Ptg Branch, Commonwealth Bank of Australia, Melbourne).

1925–28. *P* 11.

125 **12** ½d. orange .. 1·75 3·75
126 1d. green .. 1·75 3·75
126*a* 1½d. orange-vermilion (1926) .. 1·75 2·25
127 2d. claret .. 1·75 4·50
128 3d. blue .. 4·00 4·00
129 4d. olive-green .. 11·00 15·00
130 6d. dull yellow-brown .. 17·00 40·00
a. Olive-bistre (1927) .. 6·00 40·00
b. Pale yellow-bistre (1928) .. 4·50 40·00
131 9d. dull purple (*to violet*) .. 13·00 38·00
132 1s. dull blue-green .. 15·00 22·00
133 2s. brown-lake .. 30·00 40·00
134 5s. olive-bistre .. 48·00 65·00
135 10s. dull rose .. £110 £160
136 £1 dull olive-green .. £200 £250
125/36 .. *Set of* 13 £400 £550

1931 (8 June). *Air. Optd with T* **13**. *P* 11.

137 **12** ½d. orange .. 60 3·00
138 1d. green .. 1·40 3·25
139 1½d. orange-vermilion .. 1·00 4·50
140 2d. claret .. 1·00 7·00
141 3d. blue .. 1·50 10·00
142 4d. olive-green .. 1·25 7·50
143 6d. pale yellow-bistre .. 1·75 13·00
144 9d. violet .. 3·00 16·00
145 1s. dull blue-green .. 3·00 16·00
146 2s. brown-lake .. 7·00 29·00
147 5s. olive-bistre .. 20·00 55·00
148 10s. bright pink .. 65·00 90·00
149 £1 olive-grey .. £110 £150
137/49 .. *Set of* 13 £200 £350

14 Raggiana Bird of Paradise (Dates either side of value)

AIR
MAIL

(15)

(Recess John Ash, Melbourne)

1931 (2 Aug). *Tenth Anniv of Australian Administration. T* **14** (*with dates*). *P* 11.

150 **14** 1d. green .. 1·25 40
151 1½d. vermilion .. 4·00 8·50
152 2d. claret .. 2·50 2·00
153 3d. blue .. 3·00 4·00
154 4d. olive-green .. 5·00 11·00
155 5d. deep blue-green .. 3·50 14·00
156 6d. bistre-brown .. 3·00 14·00
157 9d. violet .. 5·50 14·00
158 1s. pale blue-green .. 5·00 14·00
159 2s. brown-lake .. 6·50 24·00
160 5s. olive-brown .. 35·00 48·00
161 10s. bright pink .. 75·00 £120
162 £1 olive-grey .. £140 £200
150/62 .. *Set of* 13 £250 £425

1931 (2 Aug). *Air. Optd with T* **15**.

163 **14** ½d. orange .. 55 1·25
164 1d. green .. 1·50 2·75
165 1½d. vermilion .. 1·40 6·50
166 2d. claret .. 1·00 2·75
167 3d. blue .. 3·00 3·25
168 4d. olive-green .. 3·00 5·00
169 5d. deep blue-green .. 3·50 6·50
170 6d. bistre-brown .. 6·00 21·00
171 9d. violet .. 7·50 15·00
172 1s. pale blue-green .. 6·50 15·00
173 2s. dull lake .. 10·00 42·00
174 **14** 5s. olive-brown .. 32·00 60·00
175 10s. bright pink .. 60·00 £100
176 £1 olive-grey .. £100 £170
163/76 .. *Set of* 14 £200 £350

1932 (30 June)–**1934.** *T* **14** (*redrawn without dates*). *P* 11.

177 1d. green .. 50 20
178 1½d. claret .. 60 7·00
179 2d. vermilion .. 55 20
179*a* 2½d. green (14.9.34) .. 4·00 9·00
180 3d. blue .. 90 80
180*a* 3½d. aniline carmine (14.9.34) .. 10·00 9·00
181 4d. olive-green .. 75 2·50
182 5d. deep blue-green .. 75 70
183 6d. bistre-brown .. 1·00 3·00
184 9d. violet .. 7·50 17·00
185 1s. blue-green .. 4·00 10·00
186 2s. dull lake .. 4·00 16·00
187 5s. olive .. 27·00 45·00
188 10s. pink .. 60·00 80·00
189 £1 olive-grey .. 90·00 £100
177/89 .. *Set of* 15 £190 £250

1932 (30 June)–**34.** *Air. T* **14** (*redrawn without dates*), *optd with T* **15**. *P* 11.

190 ½d. orange .. 40 1·50
191 1d. green .. 40 1·50
192 1½d. claret .. 60 4·50
193 2d. vermilion .. 60 30
193*a* 2½d. green (14.9.34) .. 3·50 2·25
194 3d. blue .. 1·10 1·60
194*a* 3½d. aniline carmine (14.9.34) .. 3·50 3·25
195 4d. olive-green .. 2·50 6·50
196 5d. deep blue-green .. 4·50 7·50
197 6d. bistre-brown .. 2·75 10·00
198 9d. violet .. 5·50 9·00
199 1s. pale blue-green .. 4·50 7·50
200 2s. dull lake .. 5·50 28·00
201 5s. olive-brown .. 40·00 55·00
202 10s. pink .. 65·00 70·00
203 £1 olive-grey .. 75·00 55·00
190/203 .. *Set of* 16 £180 £200

Two sheets were reported of the ½d. without overprint but it is believed they were not issued (*Price* £125 *un.*).

16 Bulolo Goldfields

(Recess John Ash, Melbourne)

1935 (1 May). *Air. P* 11.

204 **16** £2 bright violet .. £225 £150
205 £5 emerald-green .. £600 £500

**HIS MAJESTY'S
JUBILEE.
1910 — 1935**
(17)

18

1935 (27 June). *Silver Jubilee. As Nos.* 177 *and* 179, *but shiny paper. Optd with T* **17**.

206 1d. green .. 45 35
207 2d. vermilion .. 55 35

(Recess John Ash, Melbourne)

1937 (18 May). *Coronation. P* 11.

208 **18** 2d. scarlet .. 50 30
209 3d. blue .. 60 30
210 5d. green .. 50 35
a. Re-entry (design completely duplicated) .. 65·00 80·00
211 1s. purple .. 85 35
208/11 .. *Set of* 4 2·25 1·10

(Recess John Ash, Melbourne)

1939 (1 Mar). *Air. Inscr* "AIR MAIL POSTAGE" *at foot. P* 11.

212 **16** ½d. orange .. 80 3·75
213 1d. green .. 2·00 2·50
214 1½d. claret .. 80 5·50
215 2d. vermilion .. 3·75 3·00
216 3d. blue .. 4·00 9·50
217 4d. yellow-olive .. 3·00 7·50
218 5d. deep green .. 3·00 2·25
219 6d. bistre-brown .. 6·00 9·50
220 9d. violet .. 6·00 14·00
221 1s. pale blue-green .. 7·50 15·00
222 2s. dull lake .. 45·00 40·00
223 5s. olive-brown .. 85·00 85·00
224 10s. pink .. £225 £190
225 £1 olive-green .. £110 £120
212/25 .. *Set of* 14 £450 £450

OFFICIAL STAMPS

Australian stamps perforated "O S" exist with overprint Type **11** for use in New Guinea. We do not list such varieties.

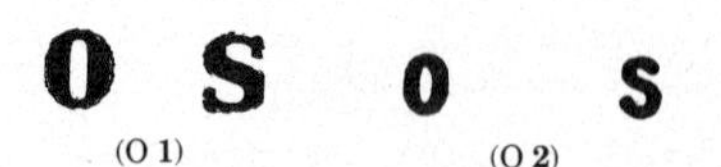

(O 1) (O 2)

1925–31. *Optd with Type* O **1.** *P* 11.

No.	Type	Description	Unused	Used
O3	**12**	1d. green	80	4·25
O4		1½d. orange-vermilion (1931)	5·50	17·00
O5		2d. claret	1·60	3·75
O6		3d. blue	2·00	5·50
O7		4d. olive-green	3·00	8·50
O8		6d. olive-bistre	16·00	40·00
		a. Pale yellow-bistre (1931)	7·00	40·00
O9		9d. violet	3·75	40·00
O10		1s. dull blue-green	5·00	40·00
O11		2s. brown-lake	27·00	75·00
O3/11		*Set of* 9	50·00	£200

1931 (2 Aug). *Optd with Type* O **2.** *P* 11.

No.	Type	Description	Unused	Used
O12	**14**	1d. green	1·50	11·00
O13		1½d. vermilion	2·25	12·00
O14		2d. claret	3·75	7·00
O15		3d. blue	2·25	6·00
O16		4d. olive-green	2·25	8·50
O17		5d. deep blue-green	5·00	12·00
O18		6d. bistre-brown	8·00	17·00
O19		9d. violet	8·50	28·00
O20		1s. pale blue-green	12·00	28·00
O21		2s. brown-lake	35·00	75·00
O22		5s. olive-brown	£120	£180
O12/22		*Set of* 11	£180	£325

1932 (30 June)–**34.** *T* **14** (*redrawn without dates*), *optd with Type* O **2.** *P* 11.

No.	Description	Unused	Used
O23	1d. green	2·00	3·50
O24	1½d. claret	2·75	12·00
O25	2d. vermilion	2·75	2·75
O26	2½d. green (14.9.34)	2·75	7·50
O27	3d. blue	5·50	14·00
O28	3½d. aniline carmine (14.9.34)	3·00	10·00
O29	4d. olive-green	4·50	14·00
O30	5d. deep blue-green	4·50	14·00
O31	6d. bistre-brown	6·00	27·00
O32	9d. violet	10·00	40·00
O33	1s. pale blue-green	15·00	28·00
O34	2s. dull lake	35·00	85·00
O35	5s. olive-brown	£120	£170
O23/35	*Set of* 13	£190	£375

Civil Administration in New Guinea was suspended in 1942, following the Japanese invasion. It is believed that the Japanese intended to issue various New Guinea stamps overprinted with Japanese characters and an anchor, but such issues were never made available for postal purposes.

On resumption, after the Japanese defeat in 1945. Australian stamps were used until the appearance of the issue for the combined territories of Papua & New Guinea.

PAPUA (BRITISH NEW GUINEA)

Stamps of QUEENSLAND were used in British New Guinea (Papua) from at least 1885 onwards. Post Offices were opened at Daru (1894), Kulumadau (Woodlarks) (1899), Nivani (1899), Port Moresby (1885), Samarai (1888), Sudest (1899) and Tamata (1899). Stamps were usually cancelled "N.G." (at Port Moresby from 1885) or "BNG" (without stops at Samarai or with stops at the other offices) from 1888. Queensland stamps were replaced in Papua by the issue of 1901.

PRICES FOR STAMPS ON COVER

Nos. 1/7	*from* × 15
No. 8	—
Nos. 9/14*a*	*from* × 20
Nos. 14*c*/21	*from* × 5
No. 22	—
Nos. 23/9*a*	*from* × 6
No. 29*b*	—
Nos. 30/2	*from* × 9
Nos. 34/8*b*	*from* × 5
No. 38*c*	—
Nos. 38*d*/71	*from* × 8
Nos. 72/4	—
Nos. 75/92*a*	*from* × 8
Nos. 93/8	*from* × 10
Nos. 99/109	*from* × 6
Nos. 110/11	—
Nos. 112/14	*from* × 6
No. 115	—
Nos. 116/28	*from* × 5
Nos. 130/53	*from* × 4
Nos. 154/7	*from* × 12
Nos. 158/67	*from* × 4
No. 168	*from* × 3
Nos. O1/54	*from* × 10
Nos. O55/66*a*	*from* × 7

1 Lakatoi (trading canoe) with Hanuabada Village in Background

2 (Horizontal)

(Recess D.L.R.)

1901 (1 July)–**05.** *Wmk Mult Rosettes, W* **2.** *P* 14.

No.	Type	Description	Unused	Used
		I. *Thick paper. Wmk horizontal*		
1	**1**	½d. black and yellow-green	6·50	10·00
2		1d. black and carmine	5·00	7·00
3		2d. black and violet	7·00	7·00
4		2½d. black and ultramarine	13·00	11·00
5		4d. black and sepia	45·00	35·00
6		6d. black and myrtle-green	42·00	35·00
7		1s. black and orange	60·00	65·00
8		2s. 6d. black and brown (1905)	£600	£550
		II. *Thick paper. Wmk vertical*		
9	**1**	½d. black and yellow-green	3·00	3·75
10		1d. black and carmine	3·00	2·00
11		2d. black and violet	4·75	4·00
12		2½d. black and ultramarine	8·00	12·00
13		4d. black and sepia	32·00	48·00
14		6d. black and myrtle-green	48·00	70·00
14*a*		1s. black and orange	55·00	75·00
14*b*		2s. 6d. black and brown	£2250	£1900
		III. *Thin paper. Wmk horizontal*		
14*c*	**1**	½d. black and yellow-green	£150	£130
14*d*		2½d. black and ultramarine	£190	£150
14*e*		2½d. black and dull blue	£325	£225
		IV. *Thin paper. Wmk vertical*		
15	**1**	½d. black and yellow-green	8·00	15·00
16		1d. black and carmine		
17		2d. black and violet	42·00	16·00
18		2½d. black and ultramarine		
18*a*		2½d. black and dull blue		
19		4d. black and sepia	£190	£450
20		6d. black and myrtle-green	£550	£900
21		1s. black and orange	£475	£900
22		2s. 6d. black and brown	£550	£1000
1/22		*Set of* 8	£650	£650

The sheets of the ½d., 2d. and 2½d. show a variety known as "white leaves" on R. 4/5 while the 2d. and 2½d. (both R. 6/2) and the ½d. and 1s. (both R. 6/3) show what is known as the "unshaded leaves" variety.

Papua. (3) **Papua.** (4)

1906–7. A. *Optd with T* **3** (*large opt*), *at Port Moresby* (8 Nov 1906).

No.	Type	Description	Unused	Used
		I. *Thick paper. Wmk horizontal*		
23	**1**	4d. black and sepia	£200	£180
24		6d. black and myrtle-green	38·00	40·00
25		1s. black and orange	20·00	38·00
26		2s. 6d. black and brown	£140	£150
		II. *Thick paper. Wmk vertical*		
27	**1**	2½d. black and ultramarine	3·75	13·00
28		4d. black and sepia	£160	£160
29		6d. black and myrtle-green	18·00	38·00
29*a*		1s. black and orange	£850	£750
29*b*		2s. 6d. black and brown	£3500	£3000
		III. *Thin paper. Wmk vertical*		
30	**1**	½d. black and yellow-green	4·50	17·00
31		1d. black and carmine	7·50	13·00
32		2d. black and violet	4·50	3·00
23/32 (*cheapest*)		*Set of* 8	£325	£350

B. *Optd with T* **4** (*small opt*), *at Brisbane* (May–June 1907)

No.	Type	Description	Unused	Used
		I. *Thick paper. Wmk horizontal*		
34	**1**	½d. black and yellow-green	75·00	95·00
35		2½d. black and ultramarine	75·00	95·00
36		1s. black and orange	95·00	£140
37		2s. 6d. black and brown	30·00	50·00
		a. Opt reading downwards	£2250	
		c. Opt double (horiz)	—	£1900
		d. Opt triple (horiz)	—	£1600
		II. *Thick paper. Wmk vertical*		
38	**1**	2½d. black and ultramarine	6·00	18·00
		a. Opt double		
38*b*		1s. black and orange	60·00	70·00
38*c*		2s. 6d. black and brown	£2750	£2750
		III. *Thin paper. Wmk horizontal*		
38*d*	**1**	½d. black and yellow-green	50·00	55·00
39		2½d. black and ultramarine	22·00	48·00
		a. Opt double		
39*b*		2½d. black and dull blue	95·00	95·00
		IV. *Thin paper. Wmk vertical*		
40	**1**	½d. black and yellow-green	3·50	5·50
		a. Opt double	£1600	
41		1d. black and carmine	3·75	6·00
		a. Opt reading upwards	£950	£700
42		2d. black and violet	4·50	2·25
42*a*		2½d. black and ultramarine		
43		4d. black and sepia	25·00	45·00
44		6d. black and myrtle-green	21·00	35·00
		a. Opt double	£1800	£3250
45		1s. black and orange	27·00	40·00
		a. Opt double, one diagonal	£2750	£2250
46		2s. 6d. black and brown	38·00	48·00
34/46 (*cheapest*)		*Set of* 8	£110	£180

In the setting of this overprint Nos. 10, 16, and 21 have the "p" of "Papua" with a defective foot or inverted "d" for "p", and in No. 17 the "pua" of "Papua" is a shade lower than the first "a".

No. 37a comes from a single sheet on which the overprints were sideways. Examples exist showing one, two or four complete or partial overprints.

PRINTERS. All the following issues were printed at Melbourne by the Stamp Ptg Branch (to 1928) or Note Ptg Branch.

5 Large "PAPUA"

B

C

Three types of the 2s. 6d.:—

A. Thin top to "2" and small ball. Thin "6" and small ball. Thick uneven stroke.

B. Thin top to "2" and large, well shaped ball. Thin "6" and large ball. Very thick uneven stroke.

C. Thick top to "2" and large, badly shaped ball. Thick "6" and uneven ball. Thin even line.

Type A is not illustrated as the stamp is distinguishable by perf and watermark.

The litho stones were prepared from the engraved plates of the 1901 issue, value for value except the 2s. 6d. for which the original plate was mislaid. No. 48 containing Type A was prepared from the original ½d. plate with the value inserted on the stone and later a fresh stone was prepared from the 1d. plate and this contained Type B. Finally, the original plate of the 2s. 6d. was found and a third stone was prepared from this, and issued in 1911. These stamps show Type C.

6 Small "PAPUA"

(Litho Stamp Ptg Branch, Melbourne, from transfers taken from original engraved plates)

1907–10. *Wmk Crown over A, W* w **11.**

No.	Type	Description	Unused	Used
		A. *Large* "PAPUA". (*a*) *Wmk upright. P* 11		
47	**5**	½d. black and yellow-green (11.07)	1·00	3·00
		(*b*) *Wmk sideways. P* 11		
48	**5**	2s. 6d. black and chocolate (A) (12.09)	48·00	60·00
		a. "POSTAGIE" at left (R. 1/5)	£375	
		B. *Small* "PAPUA"		
		I. *Wmk upright.* (*a*) *P* 11 (1907–8)		
49	**6**	1d. black and rose (6.08)	4·75	2·00
50		2d. black and purple (10.08)	6·00	4·50
51		2½d. black & bright ultramarine (7.08)	13·00	22·00
		a. Black and pale ultramarine	5·50	6·50
52		4d. black and sepia (20.1.07)	4·00	6·50
53		6d. black and myrtle-green (4.08)	11·00	15·00
54		1s. black and orange (10.08)	16·00	18·00
		(*b*) *P* 12½ (1907–9)		
55	**6**	2d. black and purple (10.08)	12·00	6·00
56		2½d. black and bright ultramarine (7.08)	55·00	70·00
		b. Black and pale ultramarine	38·00	55·00
57		4d. black and sepia (20.1.07)	7·50	8·00
58		1s. black and orange (1.09)	50·00	75·00
		II. *Wmk sideways.* (*a*) *P* 11 (1909–10)		
59	**6**	½d. black and yellow-green (12.09)	2·25	2·75
		a. Black and deep green (1910)	28·00	42·00
60		1d. black and carmine (1.10)	8·50	7·00
61		2d. black and purple (1.10)	4·50	2·75
62		2½d. black and dull blue (1.10)	4·25	17·00
63		4d. black and sepia (1.10)	3·50	6·50
64		6d. black and myrtle-green (11.09)	10·00	10·00
65		1s. black and orange (3.10)	40·00	48·00
		(*b*) *P* 12½ (1909–10)		
66	**6**	½d. black and yellow-green (12.09)	1·40	2·00
		a. Black and deep green (1910)	30·00	38·00
67		1d. black and carmine (12.09)	6·00	7·00
68		2d. black and purple (1.10)	3·00	2·50
69		2½d. black and dull blue (1.10)	7·50	26·00
70		6d. black and myrtle-green (11.09)	£2000	£2750
71		1s. black and orange (3.10)	12·00	25·00
		(*c*) *Perf compound of* 11 *and* 12½		
72	**6**	½d. black and yellow-green	£1900	£1900
73		2d. black and purple	£700	
		(*d*) *Mixed perfs* 11 *and* 12½		
74	**6**	4d. black and sepia	£3250	

(Litho Stamp Ptg Branch, Melbourne, by J. B. Cooke, from new stones made by fresh transfers)

1910 (Sept)–**11.** *Large* "PAPUA". *W* w **11** (*upright*). *P* 12½.

No.	Type	Description	Unused	Used
75	**5**	½d. black and green (12.10)	3·50	8·00
76		1d. black and carmine	9·00	3·00
77		2d. black and dull purple (*shades*) (12.10)	4·00	4·00
		a. "C" for "O" in "POSTAGE" (R.4/3)	60·00	60·00
78		2½d. black and blue-violet (10.10)	4·50	16·00
79		4d. black and sepia (10.10)	2·75	9·50
80		6d. black and myrtle-green	5·50	7·50
81		1s. black and deep orange (12.10)	5·50	15·00
82		2s. 6d. black and brown (B)	45·00	65·00
83		2s. 6d. black and brown (C) (1911)	45·00	65·00
75/83		*Set of* 8	70·00	£110

A variety showing a white line or "rift" in clouds occurs on R. 5/3 in Nos. 49/74 and the "white leaves" variety mentioned below No. 22 occurs on the 2d. and 2½d. values in both issues. They are worth about four times the normal price.

8

ONE PENNY

(9)

(Typo J. B. Cooke)

1911–15. *Printed in one colour. W* **8** (*sideways*).

No.	Type	Description	Unused	Used
		(*a*) *P* 12½ (1911–12)		
84	**6**	½d. yellow-green	70	3·25
		a. Green	30	2·00
85		1d. rose-pink	70	40
86		2d. bright mauve	70	75

87 6 2½d. bright ultramarine . . . . . . 4·75 8·50
a. Dull ultramarine . . . . . . 5·50 8·50
88 4d. pale olive-green . . . . . . 2·00 11·00
89 6d. orange-brown . . . . . . 3·75 5·00
90 1s. yellow . . . . . . 8·50 14·00
91 2s. 6d. rose-carmine . . . . . . 28·00 38·00
a. Rose-red (aniline) . . . .
84/91 . . . . . . *Set of* 8 45·00 70·00

No. 91*a* always shows the watermark Crown to right of A, *as seen from the back of the stamp.*

(*b*) *P* 14

92 6 1d. rose-pink (6.15) . . . . . . 18·00 5·00
a. Pale scarlet . . . . . . 5·50 2·00

1917. *Above issue surch with T* **9** *at Port Moresby.*

93 6 1d. on ½d. yellow-green . . . . . . 90 1·40
a. Green . . . . . . 50 1·00
94 1d. on 2d. bright mauve . . . . . . 12·00 14·00
95 1d. on 2½d. ultramarine . . . . 1·25 3·75
96 1d. on 4d. pale olive-green . . . . 1·00 4·50
97 1d. on 6d. orange-brown . . . . . . 8·00 13·00
98 1d. on 2s. 6d. rose-carmine . . . . 1·50 8·00
93/98 . . . . . . *Set of* 6 22·00 40·00

(Typo J. B. Cooke (1916–18), T. S. Harrison (1918–26), A. J. Mullett (No. 101*a* only) (1926–27), or John Ash (1927–31))

1916–31. *Printed in two colours.* W **8** (*sideways*). *P* 14.

99 6 ½d. myrtle and apple green (Harrison and Ash) (1919) 80 70
a. Myrtle and pale olive-green (1927) 55 80
100 1d. black and carmine-red (1916) . . 1·40 80
a. Grey-black and red (1918) . . . . 1·60 30
b. Intense black and red (Harrison) (1926) . . . . . . 1·90 1·90
101 1½d. pale grey-blue (*shades*) and brown (1925) . . . . . . 1·00 50
a. *Cobalt and light brown* (Mullett) (1927) . . . . . . 6·00 3·25
b. Bright blue and bright brown (1929) 1·75 1·60
c. "POSTACE" at right (R. 1/1) (all ptgs) . . . . *From* 35·00 38·00
102 2d. brown-purple and brown-lake (1919) . . . . . . 1·25 75
a. Deep brown-purple and lake (1931) 21·00 1·25
b. Brown-purple and claret (1931) . . 2·00 75
103 2½d. myrtle and ultramarine (1919) . . 4·25 9·00
104 3d. black and bright blue-green (1916) 1·25 1·75
a. Error. Black and deep greenish Prussian blue* £450 £450
b. Sepia-black and bright blue-green (Harrison) . . . . . . 20·00 17·00
c. Black and blue-green (1927) . . 3·75 6·00
105 4d. brown and orange (1919) . . . . 2·50 4·50
a. Light brown and orange (1927) . . 5·00 13·00
106 5d. bluish slate and pale brown (1931) 4·25 15·00
107 6d. dull and pale purple (1919) . . 2·75 8·50
a. Dull purple and red-purple (1927) 8·00 15·00
b. "POSTACE" at left (R.6/2) (all ptgs) . . . . . . *From* 65·00 95·00
108 1s. sepia and olive (1919) . . . . 3·50 6·00
a. Brown and yellow-olive (1927) . . 6·00 12·00
109 2s. 6d. maroon and pale pink (1919) . . 18·00 35·00
a. Maroon and bright pink (*shades*) (1927) . . . . . . 18·00 45·00
110 5s. black and deep green (1916) . . 40·00 45·00
111 10s. green and pale ultramarine (1925) £140 £180
99/111 . . . . . . *Set of* 13 £200 £250

*Beware of similar shades produced by removal of yellow pigment. No. 104*a* is a colour trial, prepared by Cooke, of which, it is believed, five sheets were sold in error.

The printers of the various shades can be determined by their dates of issue. The Ash printings are on whiter paper.

For 9d. and 1s 3d. values, see Nos. 127/8.

AIR MAIL

(10) (11)

1929 (Oct)–**30.** *Air. Optd with T* **10** *by Govt Printer, Port Moresby.*

(*a*) *Cooke printing. Yellowish paper*

112 6 3d. black and bright blue-green . . 1·10 6·50
a. Opt omitted in vert pair with normal £2250

(*b*) *Harrison printing. Yellowish paper*

113 6 3d. sepia-black and bright blue-green 50·00 60·00

(*c*) *Ash printing. White paper*

114 6 3d. black and blue-green . . . . 80 6·50
a. Opt omitted in horiz pair with normal £3250
b. Ditto, but vert pair £2750
c. Opt vertical, on back £2750
d. Opts *tête-bêche* (pair) £2000

1930 (15 Sept). *Air. Optd with T* **11**, *in carmine by Govt Printer, Port Moresby.* (*a*) *Harrison printings. Yellowish paper.*

115 6 3d. sepia-black and bright blue-green £1200 £1900
116 6d. dull and pale purple . . . . 3·00 15·00
a. "POSTACE" at left (R. 6/2) . . 65·00 £100
117 1s. sepia and olive . . . . 7·00 27·00
a. Opt inverted £2750

(*b*) *Ash printings. White paper*

118 6 3d. black and blue-green . . . . 55 5·00
119 6d. dull purple and red-purple . . 7·00 10·00
a. "POSTACE" at left (R. 6/2) . . 65·00 £100
120 1s. brown and yellow-olive . . . . 4·00 15·00
118/20 . . . . . . *Set of* 3 10·50 27·00

5d.

TWO PENCE FIVE PENCE

(12) (13)

1931 (1 Jan). *Surch with T* **12** *by Govt Printer, Port Moresby.*

(*a*) *Mullett printing*

121 6 2d. on 1½d. cobalt and light brown . . 16·00 40·00
a. "POSTACE" at right (R. 1/1) . . £150 £250

(*b*) *Ash printing*

122 6 2d. on 1½d. bright blue and bright brown . . . . . . 80 2·00
a. "POSTACE" at right (R. 1/1) . . 32·00 48·00

1931. *Surch as T* **13** *by Govt Printer, Port Moresby.*

(*a*) *Cooke printing*

123 6 1s. 3d. on 5s. black and deep green . . 4·00 9·00

(*b*) *Harrison printing. Yellowish paper*

124 6 9d. on 2s. 6d. maroon and pale pink (Dec) 5·50 16·00

(*c*) *Ash printings. White paper*

125 6 5d. on 1s. brown and yellow-olive (26.7) 60 1·75
126 9d. on 2s. 6d. maroon and bright pink 5·00 8·50

(Typo J. Ash)

1932. *W* **15** *of Australia* (*Mult* "C of A"). *P* 11.

127 5 9d. lilac and violet . . . . . . 4·00 25·00
128 1s. 3d. lilac and pale greenish blue . . 7·00 30·00
127/8 Optd "Specimen" . . . . *Set of* 2 £450

15 Motuan Girl

18 Raggiana Bird of Paradise

20 Native Mother and Child

22 Papuan Motherhood

(Des F. E. Williams (2s., £1 and frames of other values), E. Whitehouse (2d., 4d., 6d., 1s., and 10s.); remaining centres from photos by Messrs F. E. Williams and Gibson. Recess J. Ash (all values) and W. C. G. McCracken (½d., 1d., 2d., 4d.))

1932 (14 Nov). *T* **15, 18, 20, 22** *and similar designs. No wmk. P* 11.

130 ½d. black and orange . . . . . . 35 2·50
a. Black and buff (McCracken) . . . . 12·00 20·00
131 1d. black and green 50 30
132 1½d. black and lake . . . . . . 60 5·00
133 2d. red . . . . . . 5·50 30
134 3d. black and blue . . . . . . 2·00 6·50
135 4d. olive-green . . . . . . 3·00 8·50
136 5d. black and slate-green . . . . 2·00 4·00
137 6d. bistre-brown . . . . . . 4·00 7·00
138 9d. black and violet . . . . . . 7·00 17·00
139 1s. dull blue-green . . . . . . 2·50 11·00
140 1s. 3d. black and dull purple . . . . 8·50 20·00
141 2s. black and slate-green . . . . 11·00 20·00
142 2s. 6d. black and rose-mauve . . . . 24·00 38·00
143 5s. black and olive-brown . . . . 48·00 55·00
144 10s. violet . . . . . . 75·00 75·00
145 £1 black and olive-grey £170 £170
130/145 . . . . . . *Set of* 16 £325 £375

Designs: *Vert* (*as T* **15**)—1d. A Chieftain's son; 1½d. Tree-houses; 3d. Papuan dandy; 5d. Masked dancer; 9d. Papuan shooting fish; 1s. 3d. Lakatoi; 2s. Papuan art; 2s. 6d. Pottery making; 5s. Native policeman; £1 Delta house. (*As T* **18**)—1s. *Dubu*—or ceremonial platform. *Horiz* (*as T* **20**)—10s. Lighting a fire.

31 Hoisting the Union Jack

32 Scene on H.M.S. *Nelson*

(Recess J. Ash)

1934 (6 Nov). *50th Anniv of Declaration of British Protectorate. P* 11.

146 **31** 1d. green . . . . . . 80 2·25
147 **32** 2d. scarlet . . . . . . 1·75 2·25
148 **31** 3d. blue . . . . . . 1·50 3·00
149 **32** 5d. purple . . . . . . 5·50 7·00
146/9 . . . . . . *Set of* 4 8·50 13·00

HIS MAJESTY'S JUBILEE.

1910 1935

(33)

HIS MAJESTY'S
JUBILEE.
1910 — 1935

(34)

MAJESTY'S MAJESTY'S

Normal "Accent" flaw (R. 5/4)

1935 (9 July). *Silver Jubilee. Nos.* 131, 133/4 *and* 136 *optd with T* **33** *or* **34** (2*d.*).

150 1d. black and green 55 80
a. "Accent" flaw . . . . . . 22·00 35·00
151 2d. scarlet . . . . . . 1·25 60
152 3d. black and blue . . . . . . 1·25 2·50
a. "Accent" flaw . . . . . . 40·00 60·00
153 5d. black and slate-green . . . . 2·75 2·75
a. "Accent" flaw . . . . . . 55·00 70·00
150/3 . . . . . . *Set of* 4 5·25 6·00

35

36 Port Moresby

(Recess J. Ash)

1937 (14 May). *Coronation. P* 11.

154 **35** 1d. green 40 15
155 2d. scarlet 40 15
156 3d. blue 40 20
157 5d. purple 40 45
154/7 . . . . . . *Set of* 4 1·40 85

(Recess J. Ash)

1938 (6 Sept). *Air. 50th Anniv of Declaration of British Possession. P* 11.

158 **36** 2d. rose-red . . . . . . 3·75 2·25
159 3d. bright blue . . . . . . 3·75 2·25
160 5d. green . . . . . . 3·75 3·25
161 8d. brown-lake . . . . . . 9·00 9·50
162 1s. mauve . . . . . . 22·00 13·00
158/62 . . . . . . *Set of* 5 38·00 27·00

37 Natives poling Rafts

(Recess J. Ash)

1939 (6 Sept). *Air. P* 11.

163 **37** 2d. rose-red . . . . . . 5·00 2·50
164 3d. bright blue . . . . . . 5·00 4·00
165 5d. green . . . . . . 8·00 1·50
166 8d. brown-lake . . . . . . 9·00 2·50
167 1s. mauve . . . . . . 12·00 5·00

(Recess W. C. G. McCracken)

1941 (2 Jan). *Air. P* 11½.

168 **37** 1s. 6d. olive-green . . . . . . 42·00 30·00
163/168 . . . . . . *Set of* 6 75·00 40·00

OFFICIAL STAMPS

1908 (Oct). *Punctured* "OS".

O1 1 2s. 6d. black and brown (No. 37) . . . . — 40·00
O2 2s. 6d. black and brown (No. 38*c*) . . £1400 £1400
O3 2s. 6d. black and brown (No. 46) £500 £375

1909–10. *Nos.* 49/71 *punctured* "OS". I. *Wmk upright.* (*a*) *P* 11.

O 4 6 1d. black and rose . . . . 7·50 2·50
O 5 2d. black and purple . . . . 8·50 3·75
O 6 2½d. black and bright ultramarine . . 18·00 12·00
a. Black and pale ultramarine . . 8·00 4·00
O 7 4d. black and sepia . . . . 8·00 4·25
O 8 6d. black and myrtle-green . . 16·00 11·00
O 9 1s. black and orange . . . . 18·00 13·00
O4/9 . . . . . . *Set of* 6 60·00 35·00

(*b*) *P* 12½

O10 6 2d. black and purple . . . . 10·00 4·50
O11 2½d. black and bright ultramarine . . 45·00 35·00
b. Black and pale ultramarine . . 30·00 25·00
O12 4d. black and sepia . . . . 12·00 6·00
O13 1s. black and orange . . . . 55·00 38·00
O10/13 . . . . . . *Set of* 4 95·00 65·00

II. *Wmk sideways.* (*a*) *P* 11

O14 6 ½d. black and yellow-green . . . . 6·50 3·50
a. Black and deep green . . 35·00 26·00
O15 1d. black and carmine . . . . 13·00 5·50
O16 2d. black and purple . . . . 7·50 2·00
O17 2½d. black and dull blue . . . . 8·50 5·00
O18 4d. black and sepia . . . . 7·50 4·00
O19 6d. black and myrtle-green . . 18·00 5·00
O20 1s. black and orange . . . . 50·00 28·00
O14/20 . . . . . . *Set of* 7 £100 48·00

(b) P 12½

O21	6	½d. black and yellow-green	3·50	1·50
		a. *Black and deep green*	35·00	26·00
O22		1d. black and carmine	9·00	4·00
O23		2d. black and purple	6·00	1·50
O24		2½d. black and dull blue	15·00	10·00
O25		6d. black and myrtle-green	—	£650
O26		1s. black and orange	22·00	13·00

1910. *Nos.* 47/8 *punctured* "OS".

O27	5	½d. black & yellow-green (*wmk upright*)	4·50	4·50
O28		2s. 6d. black & chocolate (*wmk sideways*)	95·00	75·00

1910–11. *Nos.* 75/83 *punctured* "OS".

O29	5	½d. black and green	5·50	2·50
O30		1d. black and carmine	8·00	2·50
O31		2d. black and dull purple	6·50	2·50
		a. "C" for "O" in "POSTAGE"	75·00	50·00
O32		2½d. black and blue-violet	8·50	6·00
O33		4d. black and sepia	8·50	5·00
O34		6d. black and myrtle-green	8·50	6·00
O35		1s. black and deep orange	15·00	9·00
O36		2s. 6d. black and brown (B)	55·00	35·00
O37		2s. 6d. black and brown (C)	60·00	40·00
O29/37		*Set of* 8	£100	60·00

1911–12. *Nos.* 84/91 *punctured* "OS".

O38	6	½d. yellow-green	2·25	2·00
O39		1d. rose-pink	2·75	1·25
O40		2d. bright mauve	2·75	1·25
O41		2½d. bright ultramarine	7·00	6·00
O42		4d. pale olive-green	7·50	10·00
O43		6d. orange-brown	6·50	6·00
O44		1s. yellow	11·00	11·00
O45		2s. 6d. rose-carmine	35·00	40·00
O38/45		*Set of* 8	65·00	70·00

1930. *Nos.* 99/102*a and* 104*c*/9 *punctured* "OS".

O46	6	½d. myrtle and apple green	1·40	2·25
O47		1d. intense black and red	2·00	2·25
O48		1½d. bright blue and bright brown	1·75	2·25
		a. "POSTACE" at right	40·00	50·00
O49		2d. deep brown-purple and lake	10·00	10·00
O50		3d. black and blue-green	16·00	20·00
O51		4d. light brown and orange	7·50	11·00
O52		6d. dull purple and pale purple	6·00	7·50
		a. "POSTACE" at left	80·00	£100
O53		1s. brown and yellow-olive	8·00	12·00
O54		2s. 6d. maroon and pale pink	32·00	42·00
O46/54		*Set of* 9	75·00	95·00

(O 1)

(Typo T. S. Harrison (1d. and 2s. 6d.) and J. Ash)

1931 (29 July)–**32.** *Optd with Type* O 1. *W* 8 *or W* 15 *of Australia* (9*d.*, 1*s.* 3*d.*). *P* 14 *or* 11 (9*d.*, 1*s.* 3*d.*).

O55	6	½d. myrtle and apple-green	1·00	4·00
O56		1d. grey-black and red		
		a. *Intense black and red*	3·00	4·00
O57		1½d. bright blue and bright brown	1·40	8·50
		a. "POSTACE" at right	45·00	80·00
O58		2d. brown-purple and claret	2·25	8·00
O59		3d. black and blue-green	2·25	14·00
O60		4d. light brown and orange	2·25	13·00
O61		5d. bluish slate and pale brown	6·00	30·00
O62		6d. dull purple and red-purple	4·00	8·50
		a. "POSTACE" at left	80·00	£140
O63		9d. lilac and violet (1932)	35·00	50·00
O64		1s. brown and yellow-olive	8·00	24·00
O65		1s. 3d. lilac & pale greenish blue (1932)	35·00	55·00
O66		2s. 6d. maroon and pale pink (Harrison)	38·00	80·00
		a. *Maroon and bright pink* (Ash)	38·00	80·00
O55/66		*Set of* 12	£120	£275

Civil Administration, in Papua, was suspended in 1942; on resumption, after the Japanese defeat in 1945, Australian stamps were used until the appearance of the issue of the combined territories of Papua & New Guinea.

PAPUA NEW GUINEA

AUSTRALIAN TRUST TERRITORY

The name of the combined territory was changed from "Papua and New Guinea" to "Papua New Guinea" at the beginning of 1972.

SPECIMEN OVERPRINTS. These come from specimen sets in which the lower values were cancelled-to-order, but stamps above the value of 10s. were overprinted "Specimen". These overprints are listed as they could be purchased from the Post Office.

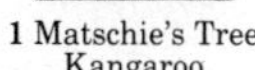

1 Matschie's Tree Kangaroo

2 Buka Head-dresses

3 Native Youth

14 Map of Papua and New Guinea

15 Papuan shooting Fish

(Recess Note Printing Branch, Commonwealth Bank, Melbourne)

1952 (30 Oct)–**58.** *T* 1/3, 14/15 *and similar designs. P* 14.

1	½d. emerald	30	10
2	1d. deep brown	20	10
3	2d. blue	35	10
4	2½d. orange	1·75	40
5	3d. deep green	1·25	10
6	3½d. carmine-red	60	10
6*a*	3½d. black (2.6.58)	9·50	4·25
7	6½d. dull purple	2·25	10
	a. *Maroon* (1956)	4·50	15
8	7½d. blue	10·00	4·50
9	9d. brown	6·00	60
10	1s. yellow-green	2·75	10
11	1s. 6d. deep green	12·00	80
12	2s. indigo	8·00	10
13	2s. 6d. brown-purple	7·50	40
14	10s. blue-black	60·00	11·00
15	£1 deep brown	75·00	11·00
1/15	*Set of* 16	£170	30·00
14/15	Optd "Specimen" *Set of* 2	£120	

Designs: *Vert* (*as T* 1/3)—2½d. Greater Bird of Paradise; 3d. Native policeman; 3½d. Papuan head-dress. (*As T* 15)—6½d. Kiriwina Chief House; 7½d. Kiriwina yam house; 1s. 6d. Rubber tapping; 2s. Sepik dancing masks. *Horiz* (*as T* 14)—9d. Copra making; 1s. Lakatoi; 2s. 6d. Native shepherd and flock.

(16) (17)

1957 (29 Jan). *Nos.* 4 *and* 10 *surch with T* 16 *or T* 17.

16	4d. on 2½d. orange	30	10
17	7d. on 1s. yellow-green	20	10

18 Cacao Plant

19 Klinki Plymill

20 Cattle

21 Coffee Beans

(Recess Note Ptg Branch, Commonwealth Bank, Melbourne)

1958 (2 June)–**60.** *New values. P* 14.

18	18	4d. vermilion	1·00	10
19		5d. green (10.11.60)	1·75	10
20	19	7d. bronze-green	10·00	10
21		8d. deep ultramarine (10.11.60)	1·50	2·00
22	20	1s. 7d. red-brown	30·00	20·00
23		2s. 5d. vermilion (10.11.60)	4·25	3·25
24	21	5s. crimson and olive-green	11·00	1·50
18/24		*Set of* 7	55·00	24·00

(22)

23 Council Chamber, Port Moresby

1959 (1 Dec). *No.* 1 *surch with T* 22.

25	1	5d. on ½d. emerald	50	10

(Photo Harrison)

1961 (10 Apr). *Reconstitution of Legislative Council. P* 15 × 14.

26	23	5d. deep green and yellow	1·50	25
27		2s. 3d. deep green and light salmon	5·50	1·50

24 Female, Goroka, New Guinea

26 Female Dancer

28 Traffic Policeman

(Des Pamela M. Prescott, Recess Note Ptg Branch, Reserve Bank of Australia, Melbourne)

1961 (26 July)–**62.** *T* 24, 26, 28 *and similar designs. P* 14½ × 14 (1*d.*, 3*d.*, 3*s.*) *or* 14 × 14½ (*others*).

28	1d. lake	1·00	10
29	3d. indigo	30	10
30	1s. bronze-green	3·25	15
31	2s. maroon	45	15
32	3s. deep bluish green (5.9.62)	1·75	1·00
28/32	*Set of* 5	6·00	1·25

Designs:—*Vert* (*as T* 24)—3d. Tribal Elder, Tari, Papua. (*As T* 26)—2s. Male dancer.

29 Campaign Emblem

30 Map of South Pacific

(Recess Note Ptg Branch, Reserve Bank of Australia, Melbourne)

1962 (7 Apr). *Malaria Eradication. P* 14.

33	29	5d. carmine-red and light blue	45	15
34		1s. red and sepia	1·00	25
35		2s. black and yellow-green	1·40	70
33/5		*Set of* 3	2·50	1·00

(Des Pamela M. Prescott. Recess Note Ptg Branch, Reserve Bank of Australia, Melbourne)

1962 (9 July). *Fifth South Pacific Conference, Pago Pago. P* 14½ × 14.

36	30	5d. scarlet and light green	70	15
37		1s. 6d. deep violet and light yellow	2·00	60
38		2s. 6d. deep green and light blue	2·00	1·00
36/8		*Set of* 3	4·25	1·60

31 Throwing the Javelin

33 Runners

(Des G. Hamori. Photo Courvoisier)

1962 (24 Oct). *Seventh British Empire and Commonwealth Games, Perth. T* 31, 33 *and similar design. P* 11½.

39	5d. brown and light blue	30	10
	a. Pair. Nos. 39/40	60	50
40	5d. brown and orange	30	10
41	2s. 3d. brown and light green	1·75	75
39/41	*Set of* 3	2·10	1·25

Design: (*As T* 31)—5d. High jump.

Nos. 39/40 are arranged together *se-tenant* in sheets of 100.

34 Raggiana Bird of Paradise

35 Common Phalanger

36 Rabaul

37 Queen Elizabeth II

(Des S. T. Cham (10s.), A. Buckley (photo) (£1). Photo Harrison (£1), Courvoisier (others)).

1963. *P* 14½ (£1) *or* 11½ (*others*).
42 **34** 5d. yellow, chestnut and sepia (27 Mar) .. 1·75 10
43 **35** 6d. red, yellow-brown and grey (27 Mar) .. 1·00 90
44 **36** 10s. multicoloured (13 Feb) .. .. 17·00 7·00
45 **37** £1 sepia, gold and blue-green (3 July) .. 12·00 2·50
42/5 .. .. *Set of* 4 29·00 9·50
44/5 Optd "Specimen" .. .. *Set of* 2 90·00

38 Centenary Emblem

39 Waterfront, Port Moresby

(Des G. Hamori. Photo Note Ptg Branch, Reserve Bank of Australia, Melbourne)

1963 (1 May). *Red Cross Centenary. P* 13½×13.
46 **38** 5d. red, grey-brown and bluish green .. 60 10

(Des J. McMahon (8d.), Pamela M. Prescott (2s. 3d.). Recess Note Ptg Branch, Reserve Bank of Australia, Melbourne)

1963 (8 May). *T* **39** *and similar horiz design. P* 14×13½.
47 **39** 8d. green 40 15
48 – 2s. 3d. ultramarine 30 15
Design:—2s. 3d. Piaggio "P-166" aircraft landing at Tapini.

40 Games Emblem

41 Watam Head

(Des Pamela M. Prescott. Recess Note Ptg Branch, Reserve Bank of Australia, Melbourne)

1963 (14 Aug). *First South Pacific Games, Suva. P* 13½ × 14½.
49 **40** 5d. bistre 10 10
50 1s. deep green 20 20

(Des Pamela M. Prescott. Photo Courvoisier)

1964 (5 Feb). *Native Artefacts. T* **41** *and similar vert designs. Multicoloured. P* 11½.
51 11d. Type **41** .. .. 1·00 10
52 2s. 5d. Watam Head (*different*) .. .. 1·00 75
53 2s. 6d. Bosmun Head .. .. .. 1·00 10
54 5s. Medina Head .. .. 1·25 15
51/4 .. .. *Set of* 4 3·75 90

45 Casting Vote

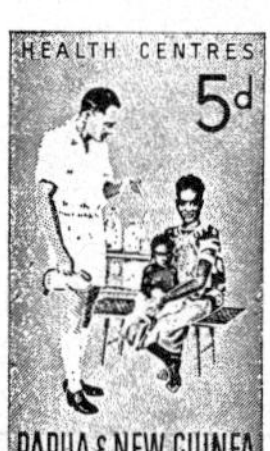

46 "Health Centres"

(Photo Courvoisier)

1964 (4 Mar). *Common Roll Elections. P* 11½.
55 **45** 5d. brown and drab 10 10
56 2s. 3d. brown and pale blue 20 25

(Recess Note Ptg Branch, Reserve Bank of Australia, Melbourne)

1964 (5 Aug). *Health Services. T* **46** *and similar vert designs. P* 14.
57 5d. violet 10 10
58 8d. bronze-green 10 10
59 1s. blue 10 10
60 1s. 2d. brown-red 15 30
57/60 .. .. *Set of* 4 40 40
Designs:—8d. "School health"; 1s. "Infant, child and maternal health"; 1s. 2d. "Medical training".

50 Striped Gardener Bowerbird

51 Emperor of Germany Bird of Paradise

(Photo Courvoisier)

1964 (28 Oct)–**65**. *Vert designs as T* **50** (*1d. to 8d.*) *or* **51** (*others*). *Multicoloured; background colours given. P* 11½ (*1d. to 8d.*) *or* 12 × 11½ (*1s. to 10s.*).
61 1d. pale olive-yellow (20.1.65) 40 10
62 3d. light grey (20.1.65) 50 10
63 5d. pale red (20.1.65) 55 10
64 6d. pale green 75 10
65 8d. lilac .. .. 1·25 20
66 1s. salmon .. .. 1·25 10
67 2s. light blue (20.1.65) .. .. .. 1·00 30
68 2s. 3d. light green (20.1.65) .. .. .. 1·00 85
69 3s. pale yellow (20.1.65) .. .. .. 1·25 1·25
70 5s. cobalt (20.1.65) .. .. .. 16·00 2·00
71 10s. pale drab (Optd S. £120) .. .. 11·00 4·00
61/71 .. .. *Set of* 11 32·00 8·00
Designs:—3d. Adelbert Bowerbird; 5d. Blue Bird of Paradise; 6d. Lawes's Parotia; 8d. Black-billed Sicklebill; 2s. Brown Sicklebill; 2s. 3d. Lesser Bird of Paradise; 3s. Magnificent Bird of Paradise; 5s. Twelve-wired Bird of Paradise; 10s. Magnificent Riflebird.

61 Canoe Prow

(Des Pamela M. Prescott. Photo Courvoisier)

1965 (24 Mar). *Sepik Canoe Prows in Port Moresby Museum. T* **61** *and similar horiz designs showing carved prows. P* 11½.
72 4d. multicoloured 40 10
73 1s. 2d. multicoloured .. .. .. 1·75 85
74 1s. 6d. multicoloured 50 10
75 4s. multicoloured .. .. 1·50 25
72/5 .. .. *Set of* 4 3·50 1·10

1965 (14 Apr). *50th Anniv of Gallipoli Landing. As T* **22** *of Nauru. P* 13½.
76 2s. 3d. sepia, black and emerald 20 10

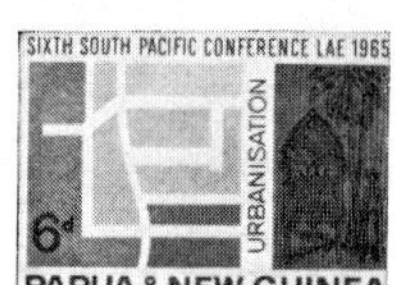

65 Urban Plan and Native House

(Des G. Hamori. Photo Courvoisier)

1965 (7 July). *Sixth South Pacific Conference, Lae. T* **65** *and similar horiz design. P* 11½.
77 6d. multicoloured 10 10
78 1s. multicoloured 10 10
No. 78 is similar to T **65** but with the plan on the right and the house on the left. Also "URBANISATION" reads downwards.

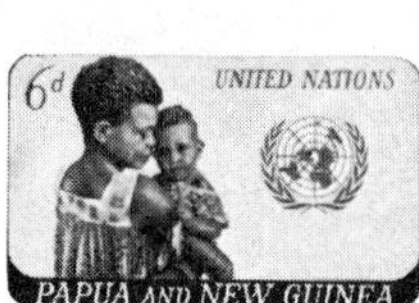

66 Mother and Child

67 Globe and U.N. Emblem

(Photo Courvoisier)

1965 (13 Oct). *20th Anniv of U.N.O. T* **66/7** *and similar vert design. P* 11½.
79 6d. sepia, blue and pale turquoise-blue .. 10 10
80 1s. orange-brown, blue & dp reddish violet .. 10 10
81 2s. blue, blue-green and light yellow-olive .. 10 10
79/81 .. .. *Set of* 3 15 15
Design:—2s. U.N. Emblem and globes.

69 *Papilio ulysses*

71 *Ornithoptera priamus*

(Photo Courvoisier)

1966 (14 Feb–12 Oct). *Decimal Currency. Butterflies. Vert designs as T* **69** (*1 to 5 c.*), *or horiz as T* **71** (*others*). *Multicoloured. P* 11½.
82 1 c. Type **69** 30 30
83 3 c. *Cyrestis acilia* 40 40
84 4 c. *Graphium weiskei* 40 20
85 5 c. *Terinos alurgis* 40 10
86 10 c. Type **71** 50 30
86*a* 12 c. *Euploea callithoe* (12.10) .. .. 2·25 2·25
87 15 c. *Papilio euchenor* .. .. .. 4·25 80
88 20 c. *Parthenos sylvia* .. .. .. 2·50 25
89 25 c. *Delias aruna* .. .. 4·50 70
90 50 c. *Apaturina erminea* .. .. .. 12·00 1·25
91 $1 *Doleschallia dascylus* .. .. .. 3·50 1·25
92 $2 *Ornithoptera paradisea* .. .. 6·50 5·00
82/92 .. .. *Set of* 12 35·00 11·50

80 "Molala Harai"

84 Throwing the Discus

(Des Rev. H. A. Brown. Photo Courvoisier)

1966 (8 June). *Folklore. Elema Art (1st series). T* **80** *and similar vert designs. P* 11½.
93 2 c. black and carmine 10 10
94 7 c. black, light yellow and light blue .. 10 10
95 30 c. black, carmine and apple-green 15 10
96 60 c. black, carmine and yellow 40 20
93/6 .. .. *Set of* 4 65 35
Designs:—7 c. "Marai"; 30 c. "Meavea Kivovia"; 60 c. "Toivita Tapaivita".
Nos. 93/6 were supplementary values to the decimal currency definitive issue.
See also Nos. 152/5 and 342/5.

(Photo Courvoisier)

1966 (31 Aug). *South Pacific Games, Nouméa. T* **84** *and similar vert designs. Multicoloured. P* 11½.
97 5 c. Type **84** 10 10
98 10 c. Football 10 10
99 20 c. Tennis 15 10
97/9 .. .. *Set of* 3 30 15

87 *Mucuna novoguineensis*

91 "Fine Arts"

(Des Mrs. D. Pearce. Photo Courvoisier)

1966 (7 Dec). *Flowers. T* **87** *and similar vert designs. Multicoloured. P* 11½.
100 5 c. Type **87** 15 10
101 10 c. *Tecomanthe dentrophila* 15 10
102 20 c. *Rhododendron macgregoriae* 25 10
103 60 c. *Rhododendron konori* 55 40
100/3 .. .. *Set of* 4 1·00 55

(Des G. Hamori. Photo Courvoisier)

1967 (8 Feb). *Higher Education. T* **91** *and similar horiz designs. Multicoloured. P* 12½ × 12.
104 1 c. Type **91** 10 10
105 3 c. "Surveying" 10 10
106 4 c. "Civil Engineering" 10 10
107 5 c. "Science" 10 10
108 20 c. "Law" 10 10
104/8 .. .. *Set of* 5 20 20

96 *Sagra speciosa*

100 Laloki River

(Des Pamela M. Prescott. Photo Courvoisier)

1967 (12 Apr). *Fauna Conservation (Beetles). T* **96** *and similar vert designs. Multicoloured. P* 11½.
109 5 c. Type **96** 20 10
110 10 c. *Eupholus schoenherri* 30 10
111 20 c. *Sphingnotus albertisi* 50 10
112 25 c. *Cyphogastra albertisi* 55 10
109/12 .. .. *Set of* 4 1·40 30

(Des G. Wade. Photo Courvoisier)

1967 (28 June). *Laloki River Hydro-Electric Scheme, and "New Industries". T* **100** *and similar vert designs. Multicoloured. P* 12½.
113 5 c. Type **100** 10 10
114 10 c. Pyrethrum 10 10
115 20 c. Tea Plant 10 10
116 25 c. Type **100** 10 10
113/16 .. .. *Set of* 4 30 20

103 Air Attack at Milne Bay **107** Papuan Lory

(Des R. Hodgkinson (2 c.), F. Hodgkinson (5 c.), G. Wade (20 c., 50 c.). Photo Courvoisier)

1967 (30 Aug). *25th Anniv of the Pacific War. T* **103** *and similar multicoloured designs. P* 11½.

117 2 c. Type **103** 10 10
118 5 c. Kokoda Trail (*vert*) 10 10
119 20 c. The Coast Watchers 15 10
120 50 c. Battle of the Coral Sea 50 25
117/20 . . . . *Set of* 4 60 40

(Des T. Walcot. Photo Courvoisier)

1967 (29 Nov). *Christmas. Territory Parrots. T* **107** *and similar vert designs. Multicoloured. P* 12½.

121 5 c. Type **107** 20 10
122 7 c. Pesquet's Parrot 25 15
123 20 c. Dusky Lory 60 10
124 25 c. Edward's Fig Parrot 60 10
121/4 . . . . *Set of* 4 1·50 30

111 Chimbu Head-dresses **112**

(Des P. Jones. Photo Courvoisier)

1968 (21 Feb). *"National Heritage". T* **111/12** *and similar multicoloured designs. P* 12 × 12½ (5, 60 c.) *or* 12½ × 12 (10, 20 c.).

125 5 c. Type **111** 10 10
126 10 c. Southern Highlands Head-dress (*horiz*) 10 10
127 20 c. Western Highlands Head-dress (*horiz*) . . 15 10
128 60 c. Type **112** 40 20
125/8 . . . . *Set of* 4 60 40

115 *Hyla thesaurensis* **119** Human Rights Emblem and Papuan Head-dress (abstract)

(Des and photo Courvoisier)

1968 (24 Apr). *Fauna Conservation (Frogs). T* **115** *and similar horiz designs. Multicoloured. P* 11½.

129 5 c. Type **115** 15 15
130 10 c. *Hyla iris* 15 10
131 15 c. *Ceratobatrachas guentheri* 15 10
132 20 c. *Nyctimystes narinosa* 20 10
129/32 . . . . *Set of* 4 60 30

(Des G. Hamori. Litho Enschedé)

1968 (26 June). *Human Rights Year. T* **119** *and similar horiz design. Multicoloured. P* 13½ × 12½.

133 5 c. Type **119** 10 10
134 10 c. Human Rights in the World (abstract) . . 10 10

121 Leadership (abstract) **123** Egg Cowry

(Des G. Hamori. Litho Enschedé)

1968 (26 June). *Universal Suffrage. T* **121** *and similar horiz design. Multicoloured. P* 13½ × 12½.

135 20 c. Type **121** 15 10
136 25 c. Leadership of the Community (abstract) 15 10

(Des P. Jones. Photo Courvoisier)

1968–69. *Seashells. Multicoloured designs as T* **123**. *P* 12 × 12½ ($2), 12½ × 12 (1 *c. to* 20 *c.*) *or* 11½ (*others*).

137 1 c. Type **125** (29.1.69) 10 10
138 3 c. Laciniated Conch (30.10.68) 30 20
139 4 c. Lithograph Cone (29.1.69) 20 30
140 5 c. Marbled Cone (28.8.68) 25 10
141 7 c. Episcopal Mitre (29.1.69) 35 10
142 10 c. Red Volute (30.10.68) 45 10
143 12 c. Areola Bonnet (29.1.69) . . . . . . 1·50 90
144 15 c. Scorpion Conch (30.10.68) 80 30
145 20 c. Fluted Clam (28.8.68) 90 10
146 25 c. Chocolate Flamed Venus Shell (28.8.68) 90 30
147 30 c. Giant Murex (28.8.68) . . . . . . 1·25 45
148 40 c. Chambered Nautilus (30.10.68) . . . . 1·00 40
149 60 c. Pacific Triton (28.8.68) . . . . . . 1·25 20
150 $1 Emerald Snail (30.10.68) . . . . 3·00 50
151 $2 Glory of the Sea (*vert*) (29.1.69) . . . . 19·00 4·25
137/51 . . . . *Set of* 15 28·00 7·25

The 1, 5, 7, 15, 40, 60 c. and $1 exist with PVA gum as well as gum arabic.

138 Tito Myth **140** Luvuapo Myth

139 Iko Myth **141** Miro Myth

(Des from native motifs by Revd. H. A. Brown. Litho Enschedé)

1969 (9 Apr). *Folklore. Elema Art* (*2nd series*). *P* 12½ × 13½ × *Roul* 9 *between se-tenant pairs.*

152 **138** 5 c. black, yellow and red 10 10
a. Pair. Nos. 152/3 . . . . 20 20
153 **139** 5 c. black, yellow and red 10 10
154 **140** 10 c. black, grey and red 15 20
a. Pair. Nos. 154/5 . . . . 30 40
155 **141** 10 c. black, grey and red 15 20
152/5 . . . . *Set of* 4 50 60

Nos. 152/3 and 154/5 were issued in vertical *se-tenant* pairs, separated by a line of roulette.

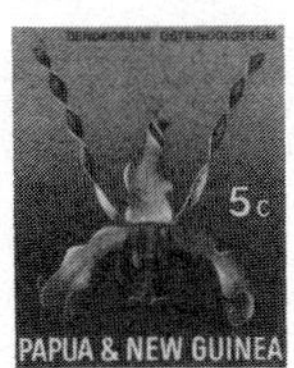

142 "Fireball" Class Yacht **145** *Dendrobium ostinoglossum*

(Des J. Fallas. Recess Note Ptg Branch, Reserve Bank of Australia)

1969 (25 June). *Third South Pacific Games, Port Moresby. T* **142** *and similar designs. P* 14 × 14½ (5 *c.*) *or* 14½ × 14 (*others*).

156 5 c. black 10 10
157 10 c. deep bluish violet 10 10
158 20 c. myrtle-green 15 15
156/8 . . . . *Set of* 3 30 30

Designs: *Horiz*—10 c. Swimming pool, Boroko; 20 c. Games arena, Konedobu.

(Des P. Jones. Photo Courvoisier)

1969 (27 Aug). *Flora Conservation (Orchids). T* **145** *and similar vert designs. Multicoloured. P* 11½.

159 5 c. Type **145** 25 10
160 10 c. *Dendrobium lawesii* 35 40
161 20 c. *Dendrobium pseudofrigidum* 55 60
162 30 c. *Dendrobium conanthum* 70 40
159/62 . . . . *Set of* 4 1·75 1·25

149 Bird of Paradise **150** Native Potter

(Des G. Hamori. Photo Note Ptg Branch, Reserve Bank of Australia)

1969 (24 Sept)–**71**. *Coil stamps. P* 15 × *imperf.*

162*a* **149** 2 c. blue, black and red (1.4.71) . . 10 15
163 5 c. bright green, brown and red-orange 10 10

(Des G. Hamori. Photo Courvoisier)

1969 (24 Sept). *50th Anniv of International Labour Organization. P* 11½.

164 **150** 5 c. multicoloured 10 10

NEW INFORMATION

The editor is always interested to correspond with people who have new information that will improve or correct the Catalogue.

151 Tareko **155** Prehistoric Ambun Stone

(Des G. Hamori. Photo Courvoisier)

1969 (29 Oct). *Musical Instruments. T* **151** *and similar horiz designs. P* 12½ × 12.

165 5 c. multicoloured 10 10
166 10 c. black, olive-green and pale yellow . . 10 10
167 25 c. black, yellow and brown 15 10
168 30 c. multicoloured 25 10
165/8 . . . . *Set of* 4 55 30

Designs:—10 c. Garamut; 25 c. Iviliko; 30 c. Kundu.

(Des R. Bates. Photo Courvoisier)

1970 (11 Feb). *"National Heritage". T* **155** *and similar horiz designs. Multicoloured. P* 12½ × 12.

169 5 c. Type **155** 15 10
170 10 c. Masawa canoe of Kula Circuit 20 15
171 25 c. Torres' Map, 1606 . . . . . . 45 15
172 30 c. H.M.S. *Basilisk* (paddle-sloop), 1873 . . 60 20
169/72 . . . . *Set of* 4 1·25 50

159 King of Saxony Bird of Paradise

(Des T. Walcot. Photo Courvoisier)

1970 (13 May). *Fauna Conservation (Birds of Paradise). T* **159** *and similar vert designs. Multicoloured. P* 12.

173 5 c. Type **159** . . . . 1·00 15
174 10 c. King Bird of Paradise . . . . . . 1·50 60
175 15 c. Raggiana Bird of Paradise . . . . 2·25 1·00
176 25 c. Sickle-crested Bird of Paradise . . . . 2·50 70
173/6 . . . . *Set of* 4 6·50 2·25

163 McDonnell Douglas "DC-6B" and Mt Wilhelm **164** Lockheed "Electra" and Mt Yule

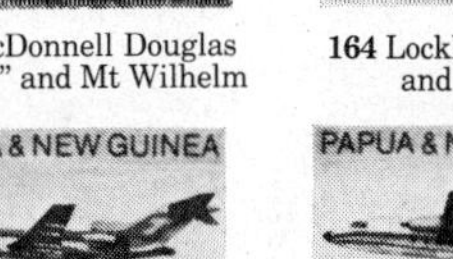

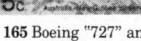

165 Boeing "727" and Mt Giluwe **166** Fokker "Friendship" and Manam Island

(Des D. Gentleman. Photo Harrison)

1970 (8 July). *Australian and New Guinea Air Services. T* **163/6** *and similar horiz designs. Multicoloured. P* 14½ × 14.

177 5 c. Type **163** 25 10
a. Block of 4. Nos. 177/80 90
178 5 c. Type **164** 25 10
179 5 c. Type **165** 25 10
180 5 c. Type **166** 25 10
181 25 c. McDonnell Douglas "DC-3" and Matupi Volcano 60 40
182 30 c. Boeing "707" and Hombrom's Bluff . . 70 60
177/82 . . . . *Set of* 6 2·00 1·25

Nos. 177/80 were issued together, *se-tenant*, in blocks of 4 throughout the sheet.

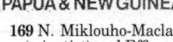

169 N. Miklouho-Maclay (scientist) and Effigy **170** Wogeo Island Food Bowl

(Des D. Gentleman. Photo Courvoisier)

1970 (19 Aug). *42nd ANZAAS (Australian-New Zealand Association for the Advancement of Science) Congress, Port Moresby. T* **169** *and similar horiz designs. P* 11½.

183 5 c. multicoloured 10 10
184 10 c. multicoloured 15 10
185 15 c. multicoloured 50 15
186 20 c. multicoloured 50 15
183/6 . . . . *Set of* 4 1·10 35

Designs:—10 c. B. Malinowski (anthropologist) and native hut; 15 c. T. Salvadori (ornithologist) and Dwarf Cassowary; 20 c. F. R. R. Schlechter (botanist) and flower.

(Des P. Jones. Photo Courvoisier)

1970 (28 Oct). *Native Artefacts. T* **170** *and similar multicoloured designs. P* 12½ × 12 (30 c.) *or* 12 × 12½ (*others*).

187	5 c. Type **170**	10	10
188	10 c. Lime Pot	20	10
189	15 c. Aibom Sago Storage Pot	20	10
190	30 c. Manus Island Bowl (*horiz*)	25	20
187/90	*Set of* 4	70	40

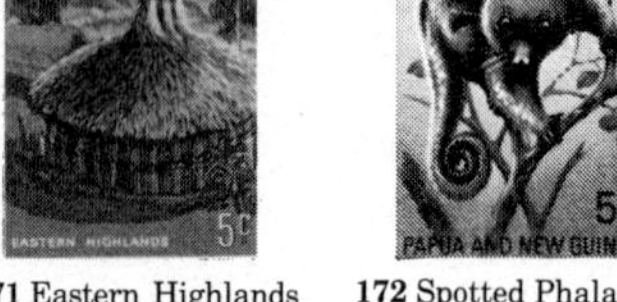

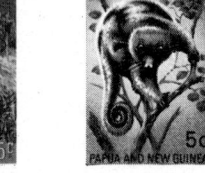

171 Eastern Highlands Dwelling　**172** Spotted Phalanger

(Des G. Wade. Photo Courvoisier)

1971 (27 Jan). *Native Dwellings. T* **171** *and similar vert designs showing dwellings from the places given. Multicoloured. P* 11½.

191	5 c. Type **171**	15	10
192	7 c. Milne Bay	15	15
193	10 c. Purari Delta	15	10
194	40 c. Sepik	35	60
191/4	*Set of* 4	70	80

(Des R. Bates. Photo Courvoisier)

1971 (31 Mar). *Fauna Conservation. T* **172** *and similar multicoloured designs. P* 11½.

195	5 c. Type **172**	30	10
196	10 c. Long-fingered Possum	60	15
197	15 c. Feather-tailed Possum	1·25	1·00
198	25 c. Long-nosed Echidna (*horiz*)	1·75	1·00
199	30 c. Ornate Tree Kangaroo (*horiz*)	1·75	70
195/9	*Set of* 5	5·00	2·50

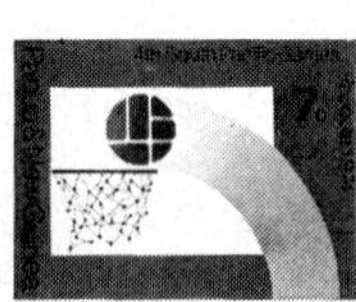

173 "Basketball"　**174** Bartering Fish for Vegetables

(Des G. Hamori, Litho D.L.R.)

1971 (9 June). *Fourth South Pacific Games, Papeete, Tahiti. T* **173** *and similar horiz designs. Multicoloured. P* 13½ × 14.

200	7 c. Type **173**	10	10
201	14 c. "Sailing"	15	20
202	21 c. "Boxing"	15	25
203	28 c. "Athletics"	15	35
200/3	*Set of* 4	50	75

(Des G. Wade. Photo Courvoisier)

1971 (18 Aug). *Primary Industries. T* **174** *and similar vert designs. Multicoloured. P* 11½.

204	7 c. Type **174**	15	10
205	9 c. Man stacking yams	20	25
206	14 c. Vegetable market	30	10
207	30 c. Highlanders cultivating garden	50	50
204/7	*Set of* 4	1·00	80

175 Sia Dancer　**176** Papuan Flag over Australian Flag

(Des Bette Hays. Photo Courvoisier)

1971 (27 Oct). *Native Dancers. T* **175** *and similar multicoloured designs. P* 11½.

208	7 c. Type **175**	20	10
209	9 c. Urasena dancer	30	20
210	20 c. Siassi Tubuan dancers (*horiz*)	80	90
211	28 c. Sia dancers (*horiz*)	1·00	1·10
208/11	*Set of* 4	2·10	2·00

(Des R. Bates. Photo Courvoisier)

1972 (26 Jan). *Constitutional Development. T* **176** *and similar horiz design. P* 12½ × 12.

212 **176**	7 c. multicoloured	30	10
	a. Pair. Nos. 212/13	60	90
213 –	7 c. multicoloured	30	10

Design:—No. 213, Crest of Papua New Guinea and Australian coat of arms.

Nos. 212/13 were printed vertically *se-tenant* within the sheet.

177 Map of Papua New Guinea and Flag of South Pacific Commission　**178** Turtle

(Des R. Bates. Photo Courvoisier)

1972 (26 Jan). *25th Anniv of South Pacific Commission. T* **177** *and similar horiz design. P* 12½ × 12.

214 **177**	15 c. multicoloured	65	55
	a. Pair. Nos. 214/15	1·25	2·00
215 –	15 c. multicoloured	65	55

Design:—No. 215, Man's face and flag of the Commission.

Nos. 214/15 were printed vertically *se-tenant* within the sheet.

(Des R. Bates. Photo Courvoisier)

1972 (17 Mar). *Fauna Conservation (Reptiles). T* **178** *and similar horiz designs. Multicoloured. P* 11½.

216	7 c. Type **178**	40	10
217	14 c. Rainforest Dragon	1·00	1·25
218	21 c. Green Python	1·25	1·50
219	30 c. Salvador's Monitor	1·75	1·25
216/19	*Set of* 4	4·00	3·50

179 Curtiss "Seagull MF6" Aircraft and *Eureka* (schooner)　**180** New National Flag

(Des Major L. G. Halls. Photo Courvoisier)

1972 (7 June). *50th Anniv of Aviation. T* **179** *and similar horiz designs. Multicoloured. P* 11½.

220	7 c. Type **179**	40	10
221	14 c. De Havilland "37" and native porters	1·00	1·25
222	20 c. Junkers "G-31" and gold dredger	1·10	1·25
223	25 c. Junkers "F-13" and mission church	1·10	1·25
220/3	*Set of* 4	3·25	3·50

(Des R. Bates. Photo Courvoisier)

1972 (16 Aug). *National Day. T* **180** *and similar vert designs. Multicoloured. P* 11½.

224	7 c. Type **180**	30	10
225	10 c. Native drum	35	25
226	30 c. Blowing conch-shell	60	50
224/6	*Set of* 3	1·10	70

181 Rev. Copland King　**182** Mt Tomavatur Station

(Des G. Wade. Photo Courvoisier)

1972 (25 Oct). *Christmas (Missionaries). T* **181** *and similar horiz designs. Multicoloured. P* 11½.

227	7 c. Type **181**	25	40
228	7 c. Rev. Dr. Flierl	25	40
229	7 c. Bishop Verjus	25	40
230	7 c. Pastor Ruatoka	25	40
227/30	*Set of* 4	90	1·40

(Des R. Bates. Photo Courvoisier)

1973 (24 Jan). *Completion of Telecommunications Project, 1968–72. T* **182** *and similar horiz designs. Multicoloured. P* 12½ (*Nos.* 231/4) *or* 11½ (*others*).

231	7 c. Type **182**	45	20
	a. Block of 4. Nos. 231/4	1·60	
232	7 c. Mt Kerigomma Station	45	20
233	7 c. Sattelburg Station	45	20
234	7 c. Wideru Station	45	20
235	9 c. Teleprinter (36 × 26 *mm*)	45	55
236	30 c. Network Map (36 × 26 *mm*)	1·25	1·50
231/6	*Set of* 6	3·00	2·50

Nos. 231/4 were printed in *se-tenant* blocks of four within the sheet.

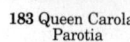

183 Queen Carola's Parotia　**184** Wood Carver

(Des W. Cooper. Photo Courvoisier)

1973 (30 Mar). *Birds of Paradise. T* **183** *and similar vert designs. Multicoloured. P* 11½.

237	7 c. Type **183**	1·50	35
238	14 c. Goldie's Bird of Paradise	2·75	1·25
239	21 c. Ribbon-tailed Bird of Paradise (18 × 49 *mm*)	3·25	2·00
240	28 c. Princess Stephanie's Bird of Paradise (18 × 49 *mm*)	4·50	2·50
237/40	*Set of* 4	11·00	5·50

(Des R. Bates. Photo Courvoisier)

1973 (13 June)–**74**. *T* **184** *and similar horiz designs. Multicoloured. P* 11½.

241	1 c. Type **184**	10	10
242	3 c. Wig-makers (23.1.74)	40	10
243	5 c. Mt Bagana (22.8.73)	55	10
244	6 c. Pig Exchange (7.8.74)	70	80
245	7 c. Coastal village	30	10
246	8 c. Arawe mother (23.1.74)	35	20
247	9 c. Fire dancers	30	20
248	10 c. Tifalmin hunter (23.1.74)	55	10
249	14 c. Crocodile hunters (22.8.73)	45	60
250	15 c. Mt Elimbari	50	30
251	20 c. Canoe-racing, Manus (23.1.74)	1·50	40
252	21 c. Making sago (22.8.73)	65	65
253	25 c. Council House	70	45
254	28 c. Menyamya bowmen (22.8.73)	80	75
255	30 c. Shark-snaring (22.8.73)	1·25	75
256	40 c. Fishing canoes, Madang	1·50	80
257	60 c. Tapa cloth-making (23.1.74)	3·50	1·00
258	$1 Asaro Mudmen (23.1.74)	5·00	3·25
259	$2 Enga "Sing Sing" (7.8.74)	10·00	8·50
241/59	*Set of* 19	26·00	18·00

185 Stamps of German New Guinea, 1897

(Des R. Bates. Photo (1 c.), litho and recess (6 c.) or litho (7 c.) State Printing Works, Berlin. Photo and recess D.L.R. (9 c.). Recess and typo Reserve Bank of Australia (25 and 30 c.))

1973 (24 Oct). *75th Anniv of Papua New Guinea Stamps. T* **185** *and similar horiz designs. Chalky paper* (25, 30 *c.*). *P* 13½ (1, 6, 7 *c.*), 14 × 13½ (9 *c.*) *or* 14 × 14½ (25, 30 *c.*).

260	1 c. multicoloured	15	15
261	6 c. indigo, new blue and silver	25	35
262	7 c. multicoloured	30	35
263	9 c. multicoloured	35	45
264	25 c. orange and gold	60	1·00
265	30 c. plum and silver	75	1·25
260/65	*Set of* 6	2·25	3·25

Designs: *As T* **185**—6 c. 2 mark stamp of German New Guinea, 1900; 7 c. Surcharged registration label of New Guinea, 1914. 46 × 35 *mm.*—9 c. Papua 1s. stamp, 1901. 45 × 38 *mm*—25 c. ½d. stamp of New Guinea, 1925; 30 c. Papua 10s. stamp, 1932.

SELF-GOVERNMENT

186 Native Carved Heads　**187** Queen Elizabeth II (from photograph by Karsh)

(Des G. Wade. Photo Courvoisier)

1973 (5 Dec). *Self-Government. P* 11½.

266 **186**	7 c. multicoloured	30	15
267	10 c. multicoloured	50	65

(Des and photo Harrison)

1974 (22 Feb). *Royal Visit. P* 14 × 14½.

268 **187**	7 c. multicoloured	25	15
269	30 c. multicoloured	1·00	1·75

188 Blyth's Hornbill　**189** *Dendrobium bracteosum*

(Des T. Nolan. Photo Courvoisier)

1974 (12 June). *Birds' Heads. T* **188** *and similar multicoloured designs. P* 11½ (10 c.) *or* 12 (*others*).
270 7 c. Type **188** .. .. 1·50 70
271 10 c. Double-wattled Cassowary (33 × 49 *mm*) 2·50 2·75
272 30 c. New Guinea Harpy Eagle .. .. 6·00 7·50
270/2 .. .. *Set of* 3 9·00 10·00

(Des T. Nolan. Photo Courvoisier)

1974 (20 Nov). *Flora Conservation. T* **189** *and similar vert designs. Multicoloured. P* 11½.
273 7 c. Type **189** 50 10
274 10 c. *D. anosmum* .. .. 1·00 50
275 20 c. *D. smillieae* .. .. 1·40 1·25
276 30 c. *D. insigne* .. .. 1·75 1·75
273/6 .. .. *Set of* 4 4·25 3·25

190 Motu Lakatoi

191 1-toea Coin

(Des G. Wade. Photo Courvoisier)

1975 (26 Feb). *National Heritage—Canoes. T* **190** *and similar horiz designs. Multicoloured. P* 11½.
277 7 c. Type **190** 30 10
278 10 c. Tami two-master morobe 45 60
279 25 c. Aramia racing canoe .. .. .. 1·10 1·75
280 30 c. Buka Island canoe .. .. .. 1·10 1·25
277/80 .. .. *Set of* 4 2·75 3·25

(New Currency. 100 toea = 1 kina)

(Des G. Wade. Photo Courvoisier)

1975 (21 Apr). *New Coinage. T* **191** *and similar multicoloured designs. P* 11½.
281 1 t. Type **191** 10 10
282 7 t. New 2 t. and 5 t. coins (45 × 26 *mm*) .. 40 10
283 10 t. New 10 t. coin 60 30
284 20 t. New 20 t. coin .. .. 1·00 80
285 1 k. New 1 k. coin (45 × 26 *mm*) .. .. 3·50 4·00
281/5 .. .. *Set of* 5 5·00 4·50

192 *Ornithoptera alexandrae*

193 Boxing

(Des R. Bates. Photo Courvoisier)

1975 (11 June). *Fauna Conservation (Birdwing Butterflies). T* **192** *and similar vert designs. Multicoloured. P* 11½.
286 7 t. Type **192** 50 10
287 10 t. *O. victoriae* 80 65
288 30 t. *O. allottei* .. .. 1·75 2·00
289 40 t. *O. chimaera* .. .. 2·25 2·75
286/9 .. .. *Set of* 4 4·75 5·00

(Des R. Bates. Photo Courvoisier)

1975 (2 Aug). *Fifth South Pacific Games, Guam. T* **193** *and similar vert designs. Multicoloured. P* 11½.
290 7 t. Type **193** 15 10
291 20 t. Running 25 30
292 25 t. Basketball 30 45
293 30 t. Swimming 35 50
290/3 .. .. *Set of* 4 95 1·10

INDEPENDENT

194 Map and National Flag

(Des and photo Courvoisier)

1975 (10 Sept). *Independence. T* **194** *and similar horiz design. Multicoloured. P* 11½.
294 7 t. Type **194** 20 10
295 30 t. Map and National emblem 40 65
MS296 116 × 58 mm. Nos. 294/5 .. .. .. 1·50 1·75

MINIMUM PRICE

The minimum price quote is 10p which represents a handling charge rather than a basis for valuing common stamps. For further notes about prices see introductory pages.

195 M.V. *Bulolo*

196 Rorovana Carvings

(Des R. Bates. Photo Courvoisier)

1976 (21 Jan). *Ships of the* 1930*s. T* **195** *and similar horiz designs. Multicoloured. P* 11½.
297 7 t. Type **195** 30 10
298 15 t. M.V. *Macdhui* 45 30
299 25 t. M.V. *Malaita* 65 65
300 60 t. S.S. *Montoro* .. .. 1·75 2·50
297/300 .. .. *Set of* 4 2·75 3·25

(Des R. Bates. Photo Courvoisier)

1976 (17 Mar). *Bougainville Art. T* **196** *and similar horiz designs. Multicoloured. P* 11½.
301 7 t. Type **196** 20 10
302 20 t. Upe hats 40 75
303 25 t. Kapkaps 50 85
304 30 t. Canoe paddles 55 90
301/4 .. .. *Set of* 4 1·50 2·25

197 Rabaul House

198 Landscouts

(Des G. Wade. Photo Courvoisier)

1976 (9 June). *Native Dwellings. T* **197** *and similar horiz designs. Multicoloured. P* 11½.
305 7 t. Type **197** 20 10
306 15 t. Aramia house 35 30
307 30 t. Telefomin house 70 75
308 40 t. Tapini house .. .. 80 1·00
305/8 .. .. *Set of* 4 1·75 1·90

(Des R. Bates. Photo Courvoisier)

1976 (18 Aug). *50th Anniversaries of Survey Flight and Scouting in Papua New Guinea. T* **198** *and similar horiz designs. Multicoloured. P* 11½.
309 7 t. Type **198** 30 10
310 10 t. D. H. floatplane 40 30
311 15 t. Seascouts 50 65
312 60 t. Floatplane on water .. .. .. 1·25 2·25
309/12 .. .. *Set of* 4 2·25 3·00

199 Father Ross and New Guinea Highlands

(Des R. Bates. Photo Courvoisier)

1976 (28 Oct). *William Ross Commemoration. P* 11½.
313 **199** 7 t. multicoloured 40 15

200 Clouded Rainbow Fish

(Des P. Jones. Photo Courvoisier)

1976 (28 Oct). *Fauna Conservation (Tropical Fish). T* **200** *and similar horiz designs. Multicoloured. P* 11½.
314 5 t. Type **200** 30 10
315 15 t. Emperor or Imperial Angel Fish 60 45
316 30 t. Freckled Rock Cod .. .. 1·10 70
317 40 t. Threadfin Butterfly Fish .. .. .. 1·40 1·00
314/17 .. .. *Set of* 4 3·00 2·00

201 Man from Kundiawa

202 Headdress, Wasara Tribe

(Des R. Bates. Litho Questa (1, 2 k.) or photo Courvoisier (others))

1977 (12 Jan)–**78**. *T* **201/2** *and similar multicoloured designs showing headdresses. P* 14 (1, 2 *k.*) *or* 11½ (*others*).
318 1 t. Type **201** (29.3.78) 10 10
319 5 t. Masked dancer, Abelam area of Maprik (29.3.78) 10 10
320 10 t. Headdress from Koiari (7.6.78) 30 15
321 15 t. Woman with face paint, Hanuabada (29.3.78) 30 20
322 20 t. Orokaiva dancer (7.6.78) 50 30
323 25 t. Haus Tambaran dancer, Abelam area of Maprik (29.3.78) 40 30
324 30 t. Asaro Valley headdress (29.3.78) .. 45 35
325 35 t. Singsing costume, Garaina (7.6.68) .. 70 45
326 40 t. Waghi Valley headdress (29.3.78) .. 60 35
327 50 t. Trobriand Island dancer (7.6.78) .. 1·25 60
328 1 k. Type **202** .. .. 1·50 1·50
329 2 k. Headdress, Mekeo tribe .. .. .. 3·00 3·00
318/29 .. .. *Set of* 12 8·00 6·50
Sizes:—1, 5, 20 t. 25 × 31 *mm*; 35, 40 t. 23 × 38 *mm*; 1 k. 28 × 35 *mm*; 2 k. 33 × 23 *mm*; others 26 × 26 *mm*.

203 National Flag and Queen Elizabeth II

204 White-breasted Ground Pigeon

(Des and photo Harrison)

1977 (16 Mar). *Silver Jubilee. Horiz designs showing Queen Elizabeth as T* **203**. *Multicoloured. P* 14½ × 14.
330 7 t. Type **203** 25 10
a. Silver (face value and inscr) omitted .. £450
331 15 t. National emblem 35 35
332 35 t. Map of P.N.G. 65 70
330/2 .. .. *Set of* 3 1·10 1·00

(Des W. Cooper. Photo Courvoisier)

1977 (8 June). *Fauna Conservation (Birds). T* **204** *and similar horiz designs. Multicoloured. P* 11½.
333 5 t. Type **204** 35 10
334 7 t. Victoria Crowned Pigeon 35 10
335 15 t. Pheasant Pigeon 65 65
336 30 t. Orange-fronted Fruit Dove .. .. 1·00 1·00
337 50 t. Banded Imperial Pigeon .. .. .. 1·60 2·00
333/7 .. .. *Set of* 5 3·50 3·50

205 Guides and Gold Badge

206 Kari Marupi Myth

(Des R. Bates. Litho Questa)

1977 (10 Aug). *50th Anniv of Guiding in Papua New Guinea. Horiz designs showing badge as T* **205**. *Multicoloured. P* 14½.
338 7 t. Type **205** 20 10
339 15 t. Guides mapping 35 20
340 30 t. Guides washing 55 50
341 35 t. Guides cooking 60 60
338/41 .. .. *Set of* 4 1·50 1·25

(Des Revd. H. A. Brown. Litho Enschedé)

1977 (19 Oct). *Folklore. Elema Art (3rd series). T* **206** *and similar vert designs. P* 13½ × 13.
342 7 t. multicoloured 20 10
343 20 t. multicoloured 45 35
344 30 t. orange-red, light blue and black 50 75
345 35 t. orange-red, yellow and black 50 75
342/5 .. .. *Set of* 4 1·50 1·75
Designs:—20 t. Savoripi clan myth; 30 t. Oa-Laea myth; 35 t. Oa-Iriarapo myth.

207 Blue-tailed Skink

208 *Roboastra arika*

(Des T. Nolan. Photo Courvoisier)

1978 (25 Jan). *Fauna Conservation (Skinks). T* **207** *and similar horiz designs. Multicoloured. P* 11½.
346 10 t. Type **207** 30 10
347 15 t. Green Tree Skink 35 20
348 35 t. Crocodile Skink 55 55
349 40 t. New Guinea Blue-tongued Skink 75 70
346/9 .. .. *Set of* 4 1·75 1·40

(Des B. Twigden. Photo Courvoisier)

1978 (29 Aug). *Sea Slugs. T* **208** *and similar horiz designs. Multicoloured. P* 11½.
350 10 t. Type **208** 30 10
351 15 t. *Chromodoris fidelis* 35 30
352 35 t. *Flabellina macassarana* 70 90
353 40 t. *Chromodoris trimarginata* .. .. .. 75 1·25
350/3 .. .. *Set of* 4 1·90 2·25

209 Present Day Royal Papua New Guinea Constabulary   **210** Ocarina

(Des R. Bates. Photo Harrison)

1978 (26 Oct). *History of Royal Papua New Guinea Constabulary. T* **209** *and similar horiz designs showing uniformed police and constabulary badges. Multicoloured. P* 14½.

354 10 t. Type **209** . . 30 10
355 15 t. Mandated New Guinea Constabulary, 1921–1941 . . 40 15
356 20 t. British New Guinea Armed Constabulary, 1890–1906 . . 45 40
357 25 t. German New Guinea Police, 1899–1914 50 45
358 30 t. Royal Papua and New Guinea Constabulary, 1906–1964 . . 60 60
354/8 . . *Set of* 5 2·00 1·50

(Des R. Bates. Litho Questa)

1979 (24 Jan). *Musical Instruments. T* **210** *and similar multicoloured designs. P* 14½ × 14 (7, 28 *t.*) *or* 14 × 14½ (*others*).

359 7 t. Type **210** . . 15 10
360 20 t. Musical bow (*horiz*) . . 25 20
361 28 t. Launut . . 30 30
362 35 t. Nose flute (*horiz*) . . 40 45
359/62 . . *Set of* 4 1·00 90

211 East New Britain Canoe   **212** Katudababila (waist belt)

(Des G. Wade. Litho Questa)

1979 (28 Mar). *Traditional Canoe Prows and Paddles. T* **211** *and similar vert designs. Multicoloured. P* 14½.

363 14 t. Type **211** . . 15 15
364 21 t. Sepik war canoe . . 25 25
365 25 t. Trobriand Island canoe . . 25 30
366 40 t. Milne Bay canoe . . 40 60
363/6 . . *Set of* 4 95 1·10

(Des R. Bates. Photo Courvoisier)

1979 (6 June). *Traditional Currency. T* **212** *and similar horiz designs. Multicoloured. P* 12½ × 12.

367 7 t. Type **212** . . 10 10
368 15 t. Doga (chest ornament) . . 20 30
369 25 t. Mwali (armshell) . . 35 55
370 35 t. Soulava (necklace) . . 45 75
367/70 . . *Set of* 4 1·00 1·50

213 *Aenetus cyanochlora*   **214** "The Right to Affection and Love"

(Des T. Nolan. Photo Courvoisier)

1979 (29 Aug). *Fauna Conservation. Moths. T* **213** *and similar multicoloured designs. P* 11½.

371 7 t. Type **213** . . 20 10
372 15 t. *Celerina vulgaris* . . 30 35
373 20 t. *Alcidis aurora* (*vert*) . . 40 60
374 25 t. *Phyllodes conspicillator* . . 45 70
375 30 t. *Lyssa patroclus* (*vert*) . . 55 75
371/5 . . *Set of* 5 1·75 2·25

(Des G. Wade. Litho Enschedé)

1979 (24 Oct). *International Year of the Child. T* **214** *and similar vert designs. Multicoloured. P* 13½ × 13.

376 7 t. Type **214** . . 10 10
377 15 t. "The right to adequate nutrition and medical care" . . 15 15
378 30 t. "The right to play" . . 20 20
379 60 t. "The right to a free education" . . 45 60
376/9 . . *Set of* 4 80 90

215 "Post Office Service"   **216** Detail from Betrothal Ceremony Mural, Minj District, Western Highlands Province

(Des G. Wade. Litho Enschedé)

1980 (23 Jan). *Admission to U.P.U.* (1979). *T* **215** *and similar horiz designs. Multicoloured. P* 13 × 13½.

380 7 t. Type **215** . . 10 10
381 25 t. "Wartime mail" . . 25 25
382 35 t. U.P.U. emblem . . 35 40
383 40 t. "Early postal services" . . 40 50
380/3 . . *Set of* 4 1·00 1·10

(Des W. Tubun. Photo Courvoisier)

1980 (26 Mar). *South Pacific Festival of Arts. T* **216** *and similar vert designs showing different details from mural of betrothal ceremony, Minj District, Western Highlands Province. P* 11½.

384 20 t. black, greenish yellow and pale orange . . 25 35
a. Strip of 5. Nos. 384/8 . . 1·10
385 20 t. multicoloured (two figures—left-hand black and yellow; right-hand black, yellow and red) . . 25 35
386 20 t. multicoloured (two figures—left-hand black and orange; right-hand black) . . 25 35
387 20 t. multicoloured (two figures, one behind the other) . . 25 35
388 20 t. multicoloured (one figure) . . 25 35
384/8 . . *Set of* 5 1·10 1·60

Nos. 384/8 were printed together, *se-tenant*, in horizontal strips of 5 throughout the sheet.

217 Family being Interviewed

(Des R. Bates. Litho Questa)

1980 (4 June). *National Census. T* **217** *and similar horiz designs. Multicoloured. P* 14 × 13½.

389 7 t. Type **217** . . 10 10
390 15 t. Population symbol . . 15 15
391 40 t. Figures and map of Papua New Guinea 30 40
392 50 t. Heads symbolising population growth . . 35 50
389/92 . . *Set of* 4 80 1·00

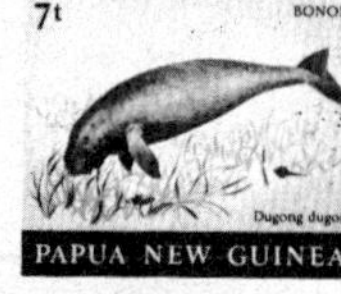

218 Donating Blood   **219** Dugong

(Des R. Bates. Litho Questa)

1980 (27 Aug). *Red Cross Blood Bank. T* **218** *and similar horiz designs. Multicoloured. P* 14½.

393 7 t. Type **218** . . 15 10
394 15 t. Receiving transfusion . . 20 20
395 30 t. Map of Papua New Guinea showing blood transfusion centres . . 25 25
396 60 t. Blood and its components . . 40 60
393/6 . . *Set of* 4 90 1·00

(Des Dr. E. Lindgren (35 t.), T. Nolan (others). Photo Courvoisier)

1980 (29 Oct). *Mammals. T* **219** *and similar multicoloured designs. P* 11½.

397 7 t. Type **219** . . 10 10
398 30 t. New Guinea Marsupial Cat (*vert*) . . 40 40
399 35 t. Tube-nosed Bat (*vert*) . . 40 40
400 45 t. Rufescent Bandicoot ("Mumut") . . 50 50
397/400 . . *Set of* 4 1·25 1·25

PRICES OF SETS

Set prices are given for many issues, generally those containing three stamps or more. Definitive sets include one of each value or major colour change, but do not cover different perforations, die types or minor shades. Where a choice is possible the set prices are based on the cheapest versions of the stamps included in the listings.

220 White-headed Kingfisher   **221** Native Mask

(Des W. Peckover. Photo Courvoisier)

1981 (21 Jan). *Kingfishers. T* **220** *and similar multicoloured designs. P* 11½.

401 3 t. Type **220** . . 15 20
402 7 t. Forest Kingfisher . . 15 10
403 20 t. Sacred Kingfisher . . 50 50
404 25 t. White-tailed Kingfisher (26 × 46 *mm*) . . 60 85
405 60 t. Blue-winged Kookaburra . . 1·40 2·00
401/5 . . *Set of* 5 2·50 3·25

(Des R. Bates. Photo Note Ptg Branch, Reserve Bank of Australia)

1981 (21 Jan). *Coil stamps. Vert designs as T* **221**. *P* 15 × *imperf.*

406 2 t. reddish violet and orange . . 10 20
407 5 t. cerise and blue-green . . 10 20

Design:—5 t. Hibiscus flower.

222 Mortar Team   **223** M.A.F. (Missionary Aviation Fellowship) Aeroplane

(Des T. Reilly (15 t.), R. Bates (others). Litho Enschedé)

1981 (25 Mar). *Defence Force. T* **222** *and similar horiz designs. Multicoloured. P* 13 × 13½.

408 7 t. Type **222** . . 15 10
409 15 t. Aeroplane and aircrew . . 30 25
410 40 t. *Aitape* (patrol boat) and seamen . . 70 65
411 50 t. Medical team examining children . . 75 75
408/11 . . *Set of* 4 1·75 1·50

(Des G. Wade. Litho Questa)

1981 (17 June). *"Mission Aviation". T* **223** *and similar vert designs. Multicoloured. P* 14.

412 10 t. Type **223** . . 20 10
413 15 t. Catholic mission aeroplane . . 25 25
414 20 t. S.I.L. (Summer Institute of Linguistics) helicopter . . 35 35
415 30 t. Lutheran mission aeroplane . . 55 55
416 35 t. S.D.A. (Seventh Day Adventist Church) aeroplane . . 65 65
412/16 . . *Set of* 5 1·75 1·75

224 Scoop Net Fishing   **225** *Forcartia buhleri*

(Des G. Wade. Litho Questa)

1981 (26 Aug). *Fishing. T* **224** *and similar horiz designs. Multicoloured. P* 14.

417 10 t. Type **224** . . 15 10
418 15 t. Kite fishing . . 30 30
419 30 t. Rod fishing . . 50 50
420 60 t. Scissor net fishing . . 95 85
417/20 . . *Set of* 4 1·75 1·60

(Des P. Jones. Photo Courvoisier)

1981 (28 Oct). *Land Snail Shells. T* **225** *and similar horiz designs. Multicoloured. P* 11½ × 12.

421 5 t. Type **225** . . 10 10
422 15 t. *Naninia citrina* . . 25 25
423 20 t. *Papuina adonis* and *papuina hermione* . . 35 35
424 30 t. *Papustyla hindei* and *papustyla novaepommeraniae* . . 50 50
425 40 t. *Rhynchotrochus strabo* . . 70 80
421/5 . . *Set of* 5 1·75 1·75

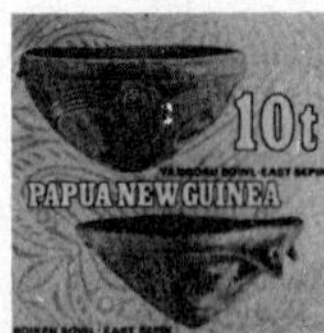

226 Lord Baden-Powell and Flag-raising Ceremony   **227** Yangoru and Boiken Bowls, East Sepik

(Des G. Wade. Photo Courvoisier)

1982 (20 Jan). *75th Anniv of Boy Scout Movement. T* **226** *and similar horiz designs. Multicoloured. P* 11½.
426 15 t. Type **226** 40 25
427 25 t. Scout leader and camp 60 50
428 35 t. Scout, and hut building 75 65
429 50 t. Percy Chaterton, and Scouts administering first aid 90 85
426/9 .. .. *Set of* 4 2·40 2·00

(Des R. Bates. Litho Questa)

1982 (24 Mar). *Native Pottery. T* **227** *and similar multicoloured designs. P* 14 (10, 20 *t.*) *or* 14½ (*others*).
430 10 t. Type **227** 15 10
431 20 t. Utu cooking pot and small Gumalu pot, Madang 30 30
432 40 t. Wanigela pots, Northern District (37 × 23 *mm*) 55 55
433 50 t. Ramu Valley pots, Madang (37 × 23 *mm*) 70 80
430/3 .. .. *Set of* 4 1·50 1·60

228 "Eat Healthy Foods"

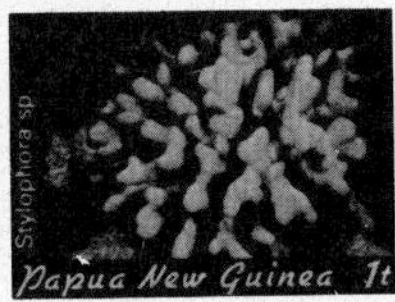

229 *Stylophora sp*

(Des G. Wade, Litho J.W.)

1982 (21 May). *Food and Nutrition. T* **228** *and similar horiz designs. Multicoloured. P* 14½ × 14.
434 10 t. Type **228** 15 10
435 15 t. Protein foods 30 30
436 30 t. Protective foods 55 55
437 40 t. Energy foods 65 70
434/7 .. .. *Set of* 4 1·50 1·50

(Des Courvoisier or W. Peckover (5 k.). Photo Courvoisier)

1982 (21 July)—**85**. *Granite paper.* (*a*) *Corals. Multicoloured designs as T* **229**. *P* 11½.
438 1 t. Type **229** 10 10
439 3 t. *Dendrophyllia sp.* (*vert*) (12.1.83) .. 50 20
440 5 t. *Acropora humilis* 15 10
441 10 t. *Dendronephthya sp.* (*vert*) (12.1.83) .. 60 10
442 12 t. As 10 t. (29.5.85) .. .. .. 2·50 1·50
443 15 t. *Distichopora sp* 30 20
444 20 t. *Isis sp.* (*vert*) (9.11.83) 60 25
445 25 t. *Acropora sp.* (*vert*) (9.11.83) 40 30
446 30 t. *Dendronephthya sp.* (*diff*) (*vert*) (12.1.83) 1·25 60
447 35 t. *Stylaster elegans* (*vert*) (9.11.83) 80 50
448 40 t. *Antipathes sp.* (*vert*) (12.1.83) .. .. 1·50 50
449 45 t. *Turbinarea sp.* (*vert*) (9.11.83) .. .. 1·50 60
450 1 k. *Xenia sp* .. .. 1·25 1·25
451 3 k. *Distichopora sp.* (*vert*) (12.1.83) .. .. 3·75 3·50
(*b*) *Bird of Paradise. Multicoloured square design,* 33 × 33 *mm*
452 5 k. Raggiana Bird of Paradise (15.8.84) .. 6·00 6·50
438/52 .. .. *Set of* 15 19·00 14·50

230 Missionaries landing on Beach

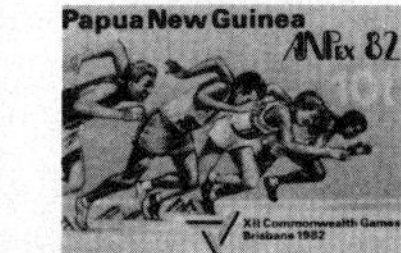

231 Athletics

(Des B. To Una. Photo Courvoisier)

1982 (15 Sept). *Centenary of Catholic Church in Papua New Guinea. Mural on wall of Nordup Catholic Church, East New Britain. T* **230** *and similar vert designs. Multicoloured. P* 11½.
457 10 t. Type **230** 25 20
a. Horiz strip of 3. Nos. 457/9 65
458 10 t. Missionaries talking to natives 25 20
459 10 t. Natives with slings and spears ready to attack 25 20
457/9 .. .. *Set of* 3 65 55
Nos. 457/9 come in *se-tenant* strips of 3 horizontally throughout the sheet, each strip forming a composite design.

(Des R. Bates. Litho Questa)

1982 (6 Oct). *Commonwealth Games and "Anpex 82" Stamp Exhibition, Brisbane. T* **231** *and similar horiz designs. Multicoloured. P* 14½.
460 10 t. Type **231** 15 10
461 15 t. Boxing 25 25
462 45 t. Rifle-shooting 55 70
463 50 t. Bowls 65 75
460/3 .. .. *Set of* 4 1·40 1·60

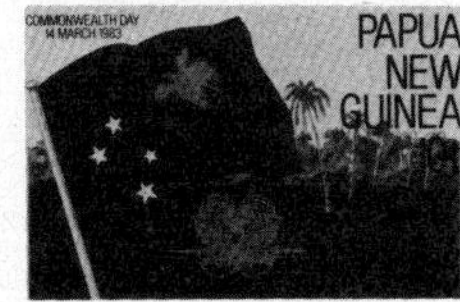

232 National Flag

(Des Walsall. Litho Harrison)

1983 (9 Mar). *Commonwealth Day. T* **232** *and similar horiz designs. Multicoloured. P* 14.
464 10 t. Type **232** 15 10
465 15 t. Basket-weaving and cabbage-picking .. 20 30
466 20 t. Crane hoisting roll of material 25 35
467 50 t. Lorries and ships.. .. .. .. 60 75
464/7 .. .. *Set of* 4 1·10 1·40

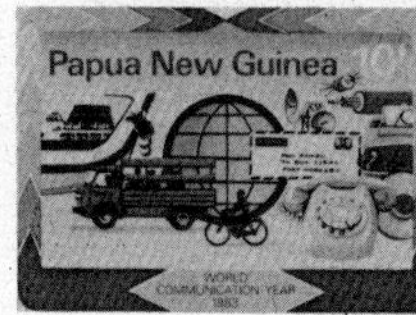

233 Transport Communications

234 *Chelonia depressa*

(Des G. Wade. Litho J.W.)

1983 (7 Sept). *World Communications Year. T* **233** *and similar horiz designs. Multicoloured. P* 14.
468 10 t. Type **233** 30 10
469 25 t. "Postal service" 70 45
470 30 t. "Telephone service" 80 50
471 60 t. "Transport service" .. .. 1·50 90
468/71 .. .. *Set of* 4 3·00 1·75

(Des R. Bates. Photo Courvoisier)

1984 (8 Feb). *Turtles. T* **234** *and similar horiz designs. Multicoloured. P* 11½.
472 5 t. Type **234** 20 10
473 10 t. *Chelonia mydas* 35 10
474 15 t. *Eretmochelys imbricata* 50 30
475 20 t. *Lepidochelys olivacea* 65 35
476 25 t. *Caretta caretta* 70 50
477 40 t. *Dermochelys coriacea* 95 75
472/7 .. .. *Set of* 6 3·00 1·75

235 Avro "X VH-UXX" *Faith in Australia*

(Des T. Reilly. Litho Format)

1984 (9 May). *50th Anniv of First Airmail Australia-Papua New Guinea. T* **235** *and similar horiz designs. Multicoloured. P* 14½ × 14.
478 20 t. Type **235** 40 30
479 25 t. "DH86B VH-UYU" *Carmania* 50 45
480 40 t. Westland "Widgeon VH-UGI" 90 80
481 60 t. Consolidated "Catalina NC777" *Guba* .. 1·40 1·25
478/81 .. .. *Set of* 4 3·00 2·50

236 Parliament House

237 Ceremonial Shield and Club, Central Province

(Des A. Brennan, adapted G. Vasarhelyi. Litho Harrison)

1984 (7 Aug). *Opening of New Parliament House. P* 13½ × 14.
482 **236** 10 t. multicoloured 30 30

(Des Revd. A. H. Brown. Photo Courvoisier)

1984 (21 Sept). *Ceremonial Shields. T* **237** *and similar vert designs. Multicoloured. Granite paper. P* 11½.
483 10 t. Type **237** 30 10
484 20 t. Ceremonial shield, West New Britain .. 50 50
485 30 t. Ceremonial shield, Madang Province .. 75 90
486 50 t. Ceremonial shield, East Sepik .. .. 1·25 1·50
483/6 .. .. *Set of* 4 2·50 2·75

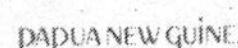

238 H.M.S. *Nelson* at Port Moresby, 1884

239 Fergusson Island

(Des R. Bates, Litho Format)

1984 (6 Nov). *Centenary of Protectorate Proclamations for British New Guinea and German New Guinea. T* **238** *and similar horiz designs. Multicoloured. P* 14½ × 14.
487 10 t. Type **238** 35 35
a. Horiz pair. Nos. 487/8 .. .. .. 70 70
488 10 t. Papua New Guinea flag and Port Moresby, 1984 .. .. 35 35
489 45 t. Papua New Guinea flag and Rabaul, 1984 1·25 1·50
a. Horiz pair. Nos. 489/90 .. .. .. 2·50 3·00
490 45 t. German warship *Elisabeth* at Rabaul, 1884 .. .. 1·25 1·50
487/90 .. .. *Set of* 4 3·00 3·25
The two designs for each value were issued together, *se-tenant*, as horizontal pairs throughout the sheets, each pair forming a composite picture.

(Des R. Bates. Photo Courvoisier)

1985 (6 Feb). *Tourist Scenes. T* **239** *and similar multicoloured designs. Granite paper. P* 11½.
491 10 t. Type **239** 30 10
492 25 t. Sepik River 65 55
493 40 t. Chimbu Gorge (*horiz*) 95 80
494 60 t. Dali Beach, Vanimo (*horiz*) .. .. 1·40 1·40
491/4 .. .. *Set of* 4 3·00 2·50

12t
(**240**)

241 Dubu Platform, Central Province

1985 (1 Apr). *No.* 408 *surch with T* **240**.
495 12 t. on 7 t. Type **222** 50 50
a. Surch omitted (in horiz pair with normal) £110
b. Surch inverted .. .. † —
At least one sheet of No. 495 exists with the surcharge completely omitted on five positions of the sheet and poorly printed on the remainder.

(Des G. Wade. Photo Heraclio Fournier)

1985 (1 May). *Ceremonial Structures. T* **241** *and similar vert designs. Multicoloured. P* 13.
496 15 t. Type **241** 45 15
497 20 t. Tamuniai house, West New Britain .. 60 50
498 30 t. Traditional yam tower, Trobriand Island 85 80
499 60 t. Huli grave, Tari .. .. 1·25 1·75
496/9 .. .. *Set of* 4 2·75 3·00

242 Head of New Britain Sparrow Hawk

243 National Flag and Parliament House

(Des P. Slater. Litho Format)

1985 (26 Aug). *Birds of Prey. T* **242** *and similar vert designs, Multicoloured. P* 14 × 14½.
500 12 t. Type **242** 55 55
a. Horiz pair. Nos. 500/1 .. .. .. 1·10 1·10
501 12 t. New Britain Sparrow Hawk in flight .. 55 55
502 30 t. Doria's Goshawk 80 80
a. Horiz pair. Nos. 502/3 .. .. .. 1·60 1·60
503 30 t. Doria's Goshawk in flight 80 80
504 60 t. Long-tailed Honey Buzzard .. .. 1·50 1·50
a. Horiz pair. Nos. 504/5 .. .. .. 3·00 3·00
505 60 t. Long-tailed Honey Buzzard in flight .. 1·50 1·50
500/5 .. .. *Set of* 6 5·25 5·25
Nos. 500/1, 502/3 and 504/5 were each printed together, *se-tenant*, in horizontal pairs throughout the sheets.

(Des R. Bates. Litho B.D.T.)

1985 (11 Sept). *10th Anniv of Independence. P* 14 × 15.
506 **243** 12 t. multicoloured 50 40

244 Early Postcard, Aerogramme, Inkwell and Spectacles

245 Figure with Eagle

(Des R. Bates. Litho Walsall)

1985 (9 Oct). *Centenary of the Papua New Guinea Post Office. T* **244** *and similar horiz designs. Multicoloured. P* 14½ × 14.

507 12 t. Type **244** 40 10
508 30 t. Queensland 1897 1d. die with proof and modern press printing stamps 85 70
509 40 t. Newspaper of 1885 announcing shipping service and loading mail into aircraft .. .. 1·10 85
510 60 t. Friedrich-Wilhelmshafen postmark of 1892 and Port Moresby F.D.C. postmark of 9 Oct 1985. .. .. .. 1·60 1·75
507/10 .. .. *Set of* 4 3·50 3·00
MS511 90 × 79 mm. Nos. 507/10 .. .. .. 3·50 4·00

(Des R. Bates. Photo Courvoisier)

1985 (13 Nov). *Nombowai Wood Carvings. T* **245** *and similar vert designs. Multicoloured. Granite paper. P* 11½.

512 12 t. Type **245** 50 10
513 30 t. Figure with clamshell .. .. .. 1·25 75
514 60 t. Figure with dolphin .. .. .. 2·00 2·00
515 80 t. Figure of woman with cockerel .. 2·50 2·75
512/15 .. .. *Set of* 4 5·75 5·00

246 *Cypraea valentia* **247** Rufous Fantail

(Des R. Bates. Photo Courvoisier)

1986 (12 Feb). *Seashells. T* **246** *and similar horiz designs. Multicoloured. Granite paper. P* 11½.

516 15 t. Type **246** 55 15
517 35 t. *Oliva buelowi* .. .. 1·25 1·00
518 45 t. *Oliva parkinsoni* .. .. .. 1·50 1·40
519 70 t. *Cypraea aurantium* .. .. .. 2·00 2·50
516/19 .. .. *Set of* 4 4·75 4·50

(Des A. Theobald. Litho Harrison)

1986 (21 Apr). *60th Birthday of Queen Elizabeth II. Vert designs as T* **110** *of Ascension. Multicoloured. P* 14½ × 14.

520 15 t. Princess Elizabeth in A.T.S. uniform, 1945 .. .. 20 15
521 35 t. Silver Wedding Anniversary photograph (by Patrick Lichfield), Balmoral, 1972 .. .. 50 55
522 50 t. Queen inspecting guard of honour, Port Moresby, 1982 .. .. 70 75
523 60 t. On board Royal Yacht *Britannia*, Papua New Guinea, 1982 .. .. .. 85 90
524 70 t. At Crown Agents' Head Office, London, 1983 .. .. 95 1·10
520/4 .. .. *Set of* 5 3·00 3·00

(Des W. Peckover. Photo Courvoisier)

1986 (22 May). *"Ameripex '86" International Stamp Exhibition, Chicago. Small Birds (1st series). T* **247** *and similar multicoloured designs. Granite paper. P* 12½.

525 15 t. Type **247** 70 15
526 35 t. Streaked Berrypecker .. .. .. 1·40 65
527 45 t. Red-breasted Pitta .. .. .. 1·50 80
528 70 t. Olive-yellow Robin (*vert*) .. .. 2·00 2·00
525/8 .. .. *Set of* 4 5·00 3·25

The scientific name on the 15 t. value refers to the 45 t. design, and vice versa.

See also Nos. 597/601.

248 Martin Luther nailing Theses to Cathedral Door, Wittenberg, and Modern Lutheran Pastor

249 *Dendrobium vexillarius*

(Des local artist. Litho Questa)

1986 (3 July). *Centenary of Lutheran Church in Papua New Guinea. T* **248** *and similar vert design. Multicoloured. P* 14 × 15.

529 15 t. Type **248** 75 15
530 70 t. Early church, Finschhafen, and modern Martin Luther Chapel, Lae Seminary .. 2·00 1·50

(Des Harrison. Litho B.D.T.)

1986 (4 Aug). *Orchids. T* **249** *and similar vert designs. Multicoloured. P* 13½.

531 15 t. Type **249** 75 15
532 35 t. *Dendrobium lineale* .. .. .. 1·40 75
533 45 t. *Dendrobium johnsoniae* .. .. 1·50 1·10
534 70 t. *Dendrobium cuthbertsonii* .. .. 2·40 1·75
531/4 .. .. *Set of* 4 5·50 3·25

COVER PRICES

Cover factors are quoted at the beginning of each country for most issues to 1945. An explanation of the system can be found on page x. The factors quoted do not, however, apply to philatelic covers.

250 Maprik Dancer **251** White Cap Anemonefish

(Des R. Bates. Litho B.D.T.)

1986 (12 Nov). *Papua New Guinea Dancers. T* **250** *and similar vert designs. Multicoloured. P* 14.

535 15 t. Type **250** 65 15
536 35 t. Kiriwina .. .. 1·40 75
537 45 t. Kundiawa .. .. 1·50 95
538 70 t. Fasu .. .. 2·40 2·25
535/8 .. .. *Set of* 4 5·50 3·75

(Des Harrison. Litho Format)

1987 (15 Apr). *Anemonefish. T* **251** *and similar horiz designs. Multicoloured. P* 15.

539 17 t. Type **251** 70 25
540 30 t. Black Anemonefish .. .. .. 1·40 80
541 35 t. Tomato Clownfish .. .. .. 1·50 90
542 70 t. Spine Cheek Anemonefish .. .. 2·50 2·50
539/42 .. .. *Set of* 4 5·50 4·00

15t =

252 *Roebuck* (Dampier), 1700 (**253**)

(Des R. Bates. Photo Courvoisier)

1987 (15 June)–**88**. *Ships. T* **252** *and similar square designs. Multicoloured. Granite paper. P* 11½.

543 1 t. *Boudeuse* (De Bougainville), 1768 (16.11.88) 10 10
544 5 t. Type **252** 10 10
545 10 t. H.M.S. *Swallow* (Philip Carteret), 1767 (16.11.88) 10 15
546 15 t. H.M.S. *Fly* (Blackwood), 1845 (17.2.88) 20 25
547 17 t. As 15 t. (16.3.88) 20 25
548 20 t. H.M.S. *Rattlesnake* (Owen Stanley), 1849 (17.2.88) 25 30
549 30 t. *Vitiaz* (Maclay), 1871 (16.11.88) .. 35 40
550 35 t. *San Pedrico* (Torres) and zabra, 1606 .. 45 50
551 40 t. *L'Astrolabe* (d'Urville), 1827 (17.2.88) .. 50 55
552 45 t. *Neva* (D'Albertis), 1876 .. .. 55 60
553 60 t. Spanish galleon (Jorge de Meneses), 1526 (17.2.88) 65 70
554 70 t. *Eendracht* (Schouten and Le Maire), 1616 .. .. 85 90
555 1 k. H.M.S. *Blanche* (Simpson), 1872 (16.3.88) .. .. 1·25 1·40
556 2 k. *Merrie England* (steamer), 1889 .. 2·50 2·75
557 3 k. *Samoa* (German colonial steamer), 1884 (16.11.88) .. .. 3·75 4·00
543/57 .. .. *Set of* 15 10·50 11·50

A printing by lithography of a 45 t. (as issued 70 t.), 70 t. (as 45 t.), 80 t. (as 35 t.) and 2 k. was originally produced, but such stamps were not issued for postal purposes. Examples in circulation are from a small quantity sold by the U.S.A. philatelic agent in error.

(Des Revd. A. H. Brown. Photo Courvoisier)

1987 (19 Aug). *War Shields. Vert designs as T* **237**. *Multicoloured. Granite paper. P* 11½.

558 15 t. Gulf Province 20 25
559 35 t. East Sepik 45 50
560 45 t. Madang Province 55 60
561 70 t. Telefomin 85 90
558/61 .. .. *Set of* 4 1·90 2·00

1987 (23 Sept). *No. 442 surch with T* **253**.

562 15 t. on 12 t. *Dendronephthya sp.* 40 40

For similar 20 t. surcharge see No. 602.

254 *Protoreaster nodosus* **255** Cessna "Stationair 6" taking off, Rabaraba

(Des Harrison. Litho B.D.T.)

1987 (30 Sept). *Starfish. T* **254** *and similar horiz designs. Multicoloured. P* 13½.

563 17 t. Type **254** 35 25
564 35 t. *Gomophia egeriae* 65 50
565 45 t. *Choriaster granulatus* 75 70
566 70 t. *Neoferdina ocellata* .. .. .. 1·25 1·00
563/6 .. .. *Set of* 4 2·75 2·25

(Des A. Theobald. Litho Questa)

1987 (11 Nov). *Aircraft in Papua New Guinea. T* **255** *and similar horiz designs. Multicoloured. P* 14.

567 15 t. Type **255** 50 25
568 35 t. Britten-Norman "Islander" over Hombrum Bluff 90 60
569 45 t. DHC "Twin Otter" over Highlands .. 1·10 80
570 70 t. Fokker "F28" over Madang .. .. 1·90 1·40
567/70 .. .. *Set of* 4 4·00 2·75

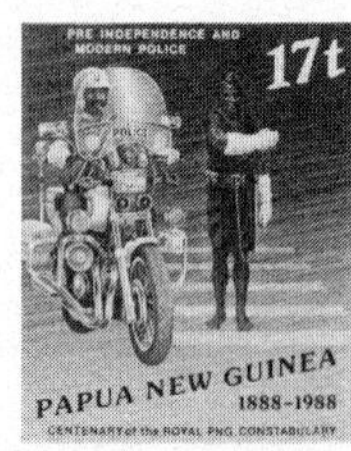

256 Pre-Independence Policeman on Traffic Duty and Present-day Motorcycle Patrol

(Des R. Bates. Litho Questa)

1988 (15 June). *Centenary of Royal Papua New Guinea Constabulary. T* **256** *and similar vert designs. Multicoloured. P* 14 × 15.

571 17 t. Type **256** 30 25
572 35 t. British New Guinea Armed Constabulary, 1890, and Governor W. MacGregor 60 50
573 45 t. Police badges 75 65
574 70 t. German New Guinea Police, 1888, and Dr. A. Hahl (founder) .. .. .. 1·25 1·50
571/4 .. .. *Set of* 4 2·50 2·50

257 Lakatoi (canoe) and Sydney Opera House

(Des R. Bates. Litho Harrison)

1988 (30 July). *"Sydpex '88" National Stamp Exhibition, Sydney. P* 14.

575 **257** 35 t. multicoloured 70 50

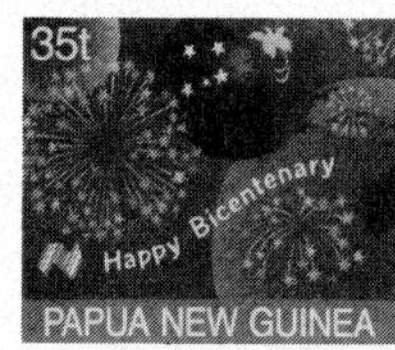

258 Papua New Guinea Flag on Globe and Fireworks

259 Male and Female Butterflies in Courtship

(Des R. Bates. Litho CPE Australia Ltd, Melbourne)

1988 (30 July). *Bicentenary of Australian Settlement. T* **258** *and similar horiz design. Multicoloured. P* 13½.

576 35 t. Type **258** 55 65
a. Horiz pair. Nos. 576/7 .. .. 1·10 1·25
577 35 t. Australian flag on globe and fireworks 55 65
MS578 90 × 50 mm. Nos. 576/7 .. .. 1·10 1·25

Nos. 576/7 were printed together, *se-tenant*, in horizontal pairs throughout the sheet, each pair forming a composite design.

(Des M. Parsons, adapted D. Miller. Litho Walsall)

1989 (19 Sept). *Endangered Species.* Ornithoptera alexandrae (*Queen Alexandra's Birdwing butterfly*). *T* **259** *and similar multicoloured designs. P* 14½.

579 5 t. Type **259** 30 10
580 17 t. Female laying eggs and mature larva (*vert*) 65 25
581 25 t. Male emerging from pupa (*vert*) .. 85 55
582 35 t. Male feeding .. .. 1·00 85
579/82 .. .. *Set of* 4 2·50 1·60

260 Athletics

(Des G. Wade. Litho CPE Australia Ltd, Melbourne)

1988 (19 Sept). *Olympic Games, Seoul. T* **260** *and similar horiz design. Multicoloured. P* 13½.

583 17 t. Type **260** 20 25
584 45 t. Weightlifting 60 65

261 *Rhododendron zoelleri*

263 Writing Letter

262

(Des N. Cruttwell and I. Loe. Litho Leigh-Mardon Ltd, Melbourne)

1989 (25 Jan). *Rhododendrons. T* **261** *and similar vert designs. Multicoloured. W* **262**. *P* 14½.
585 3 t. Type **261** 10 10
586 20 t. *Rhododendron cruttwellii* 35 30
587 60 t. *Rhododendron superbum* .. .. 1·00 1·00
588 70 t. *Rhododendron christianae* .. .. 1·10 1·10
585/8 .. .. *Set of* 4 2·25 2·25

(Des R. Bates. Litho Leigh-Mardon Ltd, Melbourne)

1989 (22 Mar). *International Letter Writing Week. T* **263** *and similar square designs. Multicoloured. W* **262**. *P* 14½.
589 20 t. Type **263** 30 30
590 35 t. Stamping letter 55 50
591 60 t. Posting letter .. .. .. 90 1·10
592 70 t. Reading letter .. .. .. 1·10 1·40
589/92 .. .. *Set of* 4 2·50 3·00

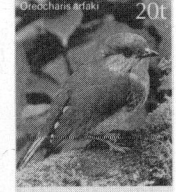

264 Village House, Buka Island, North Solomons

265 Tit Berrypecker (female)

(Des G. Wade. Litho Leigh-Mardon Ltd, Melbourne)

1989 (17 May). *Traditional Dwellings. T* **264** *and similar horiz designs. Multicoloured. W* **262**. *P* 15.
593 20 t. Type **264** 35 35
594 35 t. Koiari tree house, Central Province .. 60 60
595 60 t. Longhouse, Lauan, New Ireland .. 1·00 1·25
596 70 t. Decorated house, Basilaki, Milne Bay 1·25 1·50
593/6 .. .. *Set of* 4 3·00 3·25

(Des W. Peckover. Litho Questa)

1989 (12 July). *Small Birds (2nd issue). T* **265** *and similar vert designs. Multicoloured. P* 14½.
597 20 t. Type **265** 70 55
a. Horiz pair. Nos. 597/8 .. .. 1·40 1·10
598 20 t. Tit Berrypecker (male) 70 55
599 35 t. Blue-capped Babbler 90 75
600 45 t. Black-throated Robin .. .. 1·10 1·00
601 70 t. Large Mountain Sericornis .. .. 1·60 1·60
597/601 .. .. *Set of* 5 4·50 4·00
Nos. 597/8 were printed together, *se-tenant*, in horizontal pairs throughout the sheet.

1989 (12 July). *No.* 539 *surch as T* 253.
602 20 t. on 17 t. Type **251** 60 60

266 Motu Motu Dancer, Gulf Province

267 Hibiscus, People going to Church and Gope Board

(Des G. Wade. Litho Leigh-Mardon Ltd, Melbourne)

1989 (6 Sept). *Traditional Dancers. T* **266** *and similar vert designs. Multicoloured. W* **262**. *P* 14×14½.
603 20 t. Type **266** 50 35
604 35 t. Baining, East New Britain 85 85
605 60 t. Vailala River, Gulf Province .. .. 1·50 1·75
606 70 t. Timbunke, East Sepik Province .. 1·75 2·00
603/6 .. .. *Set of* 4 4·25 4·50

(Des R. Bates. Litho Leigh-Mardon Ltd, Melbourne)

1989 (8 Nov). *Christmas. T* **267** *and similar horiz designs showing flowers and carved panels. Multicoloured. P* 14×14½.
607 20 t. Type **267** 40 35
608 35 t. Rhododendron, Virgin and Child and mask 60 60
609 60 t. D'Albertis Creeper, Christmas candle and warshield .. .. .. 1·25 1·50
610 70 t. Pacific Frangapani, peace dove and flute mask .. .. 1·40 1·75
607/10 .. .. *Set of* 4 3·25 3·75

268 Guni Falls

269 Boys and Census Form

(Des A. Theobald. Litho Questa)

1990 (1 Feb). *Waterfalls. T* **268** *and similar vert designs. Multicoloured. P* 14.
611 20 t. Type **268** 50 35
612 35 t. Rouna Falls 75 75
613 60 t. Ambua Falls .. .. 1·25 1·50
614 70 t. Wawoi Falls .. .. 1·50 1·75
611/14 .. .. *Set of* 4 3·50 4·00

MACHINE LABELS. From 7 March 1990 gummed labels inscribed "PAPUA NEW GUINEA BOROKO" with values from 1 t. to 99 k. 99 were available from an automatic machine installed at Boroko Post Office. A second machine was operational at Rabaul Post Office from 8 February 1991.

(Des R. Bates. Litho Questa)

1990 (2 May). *National Census. T* **269** *and similar horiz design. Multicoloured. P* 14½×15.
615 20 t. Type **269** 40 30
616 70 t. Family and census form .. .. 1·50 1·60

270 Gwa Pupi Dance Mask

271 Sepik and Maori Kororu Masks

(Des G. Vasarhelyi. Litho Leigh-Mardon Ltd, Melbourne)

1990 (11 July). *Gogodala Dance Masks. T* **270** *and similar vert designs. Multicoloured. P* 13½.
617 20 t. Type **270** 50 30
618 35 t. Tauga paiyale 80 60
619 60 t. A:ga .. .. 1·40 1·50
620 70 t. Owala .. .. 1·75 2·00
617/20 .. .. *Set of* 4 4·00 4·00

(Des R. Bates. Litho Leigh-Mardon Ltd, Melbourne)

1990 (24 Aug). *"New Zealand 1990" International Stamp Exhibition, Auckland. P* 14½.
621 **271** 35 t. multicoloured 75 75

272 Dwarf Cassowary and Great Spotted Kiwi

273 Whimbrel

(Des R. Bates. Litho Leigh-Mardon Ltd, Melbourne)

1990 (24 Aug). *150th Anniv of Treaty of Waitangi. T* **272** *and similar square design. Multicoloured. P* 14½.
622 20 t. Type **272** 70 40
623 35 t. Double-wattled Cassowary and Brown Kiwi .. .. 1·10 1·25

(Des L. Curtis. Litho Questa)

1990 (26 Sept). *Migratory Birds. T* **273** *and similar horiz designs. Multicoloured. P* 14½×13½.
624 20 t. Type **273** 55 30
625 35 t. Sharp-tailed Sandpiper 85 70
626 60 t. Turnstone .. .. 1·50 1·60
627 70 t. Terek Sandpiper .. .. .. 1·75 1·90
624/7 .. .. *Set of* 4 4·25 4·00

274 Jew's Harp

275 *Rhynchotrochus weigmani*

(Des R. Bates. Litho Leigh-Mardon Ltd, Melbourne)

1990 (31 Oct). *Musical Instruments. T* **274** *and similar square designs. Multicoloured. P* 13.
628 20 t. Type **274** 35 30
629 35 t. Musical bow 60 50
630 60 t. Wantoat drum .. .. .. 1·00 1·10
631 70 t. Gogodala rattle .. .. .. 1·10 1·25
628/31 .. .. *Set of* 4 2·75 2·75

(Des P. Schouter. Litho Leigh-Mardon Ltd, Melbourne)

1991 (6 Mar). *Land Shells. T* **275** *and similar horiz designs. Multicoloured. P* 14×14½.
632 21 t. Type **275** 35 30
633 40 t. *Forcartia globula* and *Canefriula azonata* 60 50
634 50 t. *Planispira deaniana* 90 70
635 80 t. *Papuina chancel* and *Papuina xanthocheila* .. .. 1·25 1·50
632/5 .. .. *Set of* 4 2·75 2·75

276 Lesser Bird of Paradise

277 Cricket

(Des W. Peckover (10 k.), R. Bates (others). Litho Leigh-Mardon Ltd, Melbourne)

1991 (1 May)–**92**. *Birds of Paradise. T* **276** *and similar multicoloured designs. P* 13 (10 *k*.) *or* 14½ (*others*).
642 21 t. Crinkle-collared Manucode (26½×32 *mm*) (25.3.92) 25 30
643 45 t. King Bird of Paradise (26½×32 *mm*) (25.3.92) 55 60
644 60 t. Queen Carola's Parotia (26½×32 *mm*) (25.3.92) 65 70
645 90 t. Emperor of Germany Bird of Paradise (26½×32 *mm*) (25.3.92) .. .. 1·10 1·25
650 10 k. Type **276** .. .. 12·50 13·00
642/50 .. .. *Set of* 5 13·50 14·00

(Des D.D.S. Associates and T. Sipa. Litho Leigh-Mardon Ltd, Melbourne)

1991 (26 June). *9th South Pacific Games. T* **277** *and similar horiz designs. Multicoloured. P* 13.
651 21 t. Type **277** 40 30
652 40 t. Athletics 75 60
653 50 t. Baseball 85 70
654 80 t. Rugby Union .. .. 1·50 1·60
651/4 .. .. *Set of* 4 3·25 3·00

278 Cathedral of St. Peter and St. Paul, Dogura

279 Rambusto Headdress, Manus Province

(Des G. Wade. Litho Questa)

1991 (7 Aug). *Centenary of Anglican Church in Papua New Guinea. T* **278** *and similar horiz designs. Multicoloured. P* 14½.

No.	Description		Unused	Used
655	21 t. Type **278**		35	30
656	40 t. Missionaries landing, 1891, and Kaieta shrine		70	70
657	80 t. First church and Modawa tree		1·40	1·50
655/7		*Set of* 3	2·25	2·25

(Des D.D.S. Associates and T. Sipa. Litho Leigh-Mardon Ltd, Melbourne)

1991 (16 Oct). *Tribal Headdresses. T* **279** *and similar vert designs. Multicoloured. P* 13.

No.	Description		Unused	Used
658	21 t. Type **279**		35	30
659	40 t. Marawaka, Eastern Highlands		70	70
660	50 t. Tufi, Oro Province		80	80
661	80 t. Sina Sina, Simbu Province		1·40	1·50
658/61		*Set of* 4	3·00	3·00

POSTAGE DUE STAMPS

POSTAL CHARGES

6d.

● IXIXIXIXIX

(D 1)

POSTAL CHARGES

3s.

(D 2)

1960 (1 Mar). *Postage stamps surcharged.* (*a*) *No.* 8 *with Type* D 1.

No.	Description		Unused	Used
D1	6d. on 7½d. blue (R.)		£750	£400
	a. Surch double		£3250	£1800
	(*b*) *Nos.* 1, 4, 6*a*, 7/8 *as Type* D **2**			
D2	1d. on 6½d. maroon		14·00	7·00
D3	3d. on ½d. emerald (B.)		16·00	5·50
	a. Surch double		£475	
D4	6d. on 7½d. blue (R.)		32·00	13·00
	a. Surch double		£475	
D5	1s. 3d. on 3½d. black (O.)		24·00	13·00
D6	3s. on 2½d. orange		40·00	26·00
D2/6		*Set of* 5	£110	55·00

Of No. D1a, only a few copies are known from a sheet used at Goroka.

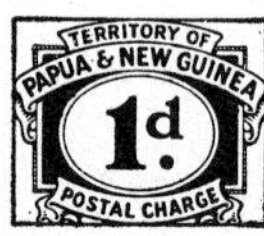

D 3

(Typo Note Ptg Branch, Reserve Bank of Australia, Melbourne)

1960 (2 June). *W* **15** *of Australia. P* 14.

No.	Type	Description		Unused	Used
D 7	D **3**	1d. orange		65	50
D 8		3d. yellow-brown		70	55
D 9		6d. blue		75	40
D10		9d. deep red		75	1·60
D11		1s. light emerald		75	50
D12		1s. 3d. violet		1·40	1·60
D13		1s. 6d. pale blue		5·50	5·00
D14		3s. yellow		6·00	1·00
D7/14			*Set of* 8	15·00	10·00

The use of Postal Charge stamps was discontinued on 12 February 1966, but they remained on sale at the Philatelic Bureau until 31 August 1966.

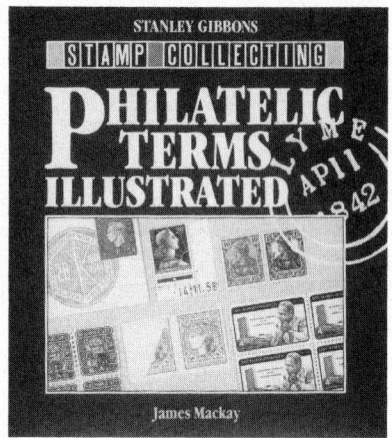

Pitcairn Islands

CROWN COLONY

Stamps of NEW ZEALAND were used by a Postal Agency operating on Pitcairn Islands from 7 June 1927 until October 1940.

PRICES FOR STAMPS ON COVER TO 1945
Nos. 1/8 *from* × 2

1 Cluster of Oranges

2 Christian on *Bounty* and Pitcairn Island

(Recess B.W. (1d., 3d., 4d., 8d. and 2s. 6d.), and Waterlow (others))

1940 (15 Oct)–**51**. *T* **1/2** *and similar horiz designs. Wmk Mult Script CA. P* 11½ × 11 (*1d., 3d., 4d., 8d. and 2s. 6d.*) *or* 12½ (*others*).
1 ½d. orange and green 40 60
2 1d. mauve and magenta 55 70
3 1½d. grey and carmine 55 50
4 2d. green and brown .. .. .. 1·75 1·40
5 3d. yellow-green and blue .. .. .. 1·25 1·40
5*a* 4d. black and emerald-green (1.9.51) .. 11·00 7·00
6 6d. brown and grey-blue .. .. .. 5·00 2·25
6*a* 8d. olive-green and magenta (1.9.51) .. 11·00 7·00
7 1s. violet and grey .. .. .. 3·00 2·00
8 2s. 6d. green and brown .. .. .. 7·00 4·25
1/8 .. .. *Set of* 10 38·00 24·00
1/8 (ex. *a* Nos.) Perf "Specimen" .. *Set of* 8 £700

Designs:—1½d. John Adams and his house; 2d. Lt. Bligh and H.M.S. *Bounty*; 3d. Pitcairn Islands and Pacific Ocean; 4d. *Bounty* Bible; 6d. H.M.S. *Bounty*; 8d. School, 1949; 1s. Fletcher Christian and Pitcairn Island; 2s. 6d. Christian on H.M.S. *Bounty* and Pitcairn Coast.

Flagstaff flaw
(R. 8/2)

1946 (2 Dec). *Victory. As Nos.* 141/2 *of Jamaica.*
9 2d. brown 30 15
10 3d. blue 30 15
a. Flagstaff flaw .. .. 18·00
9/10 Perf "Specimen" .. .. *Set of* 2 £130

1949 (1 Aug). *Royal Silver Wedding. As Nos.* 143/4 *of Jamaica.*
11 1½d. scarlet .. .. 1·50 1·00
12 10s. mauve .. .. 80·00 65·00

1949 (10 Oct). *75th Anniv of U.P.U. As Nos.* 145/8 *of Jamaica.*
13 2½d. red-brown .. .. 2·00 3·00
14 3d. deep blue .. .. 8·50 4·00
15 6d. deep blue-green .. .. 11·00 5·00
16 1s. purple .. .. 11·00 5·00
13/16 .. .. *Set of* 4 30·00 15·00

1953 (2 June). *Coronation. As No.* 153 *of Jamaica, but ptd by B.W.*
17 4d. black and deep bluish green .. .. 2·00 2·75

9 *Cordyline terminalis*

10 Pitcairn Island Map

(Recess D.L.R.)

1957 (2 July)–**63**. *T* **9/10** *and similar designs. Wmk Mult Script CA. P* 13×12½ (*horiz*) *or* 12½×13 (*vert*).
18 ½d. green and reddish lilac 80 75
a. Green and reddish purple (9.3.63) .. 1·00 2·00
19 1d. black and olive-green .. .. 1·25 80
a. Black and yellow-olive (19.2.59) .. 8·50 11·00
b. Black and light olive-green (24.2.60) 4·00 3·00
20 2d. brown and greenish blue 75 60
21 2½d. deep brown and red-orange 50 40
22 3d. emerald and deep ultramarine .. 80 40
23 4d. scarlet and deep ultramarine (I) .. 90 40
23*a* 4d. carmine-red & dp ultram (II) (5.11.58) 5·00 1·50
24 6d. pale buff and indigo .. .. .. 1·25 55
25 8d. deep olive-green and carmine-lake .. 60 40
26 1s. black and yellowish brown .. .. 1·00 40
27 2s. green and red-orange .. .. 30·00 10·00
28 2s. 6d. ultramarine and lake .. .. 12·00 6·50
a. Blue and deep lake (10.2.59) .. 18·00 10·00
18/28 .. .. *Set of* 12 48·00 20·00

Designs: *Vert*—2d. John Adams and *Bounty* Bible; 2s. Island wheelbarrow. *Horiz*—2½d. Handicrafts: Bird model; 3d. Bounty Bay; 4d. Pitcairn School; 6d. Pacific Ocean map; 8d. Inland scene; 1s. Handicrafts: Ship model; 2s. 6d. Launching new whaleboat.

Nos. 23/*a*. Type I is inscribed "PITCAIRN SCHOOL"; Type II "SCHOOLTEACHER'S HOUSE".

See also No. 33

20 Pitcairn Island and Simon Young

(Des H. E. Maud. Photo Harrison)

1961 (15 Nov). *Centenary of Return of Pitcairn Islanders from Norfolk Island. T* **20** *and similar horiz designs. W* w **12**. *P* 14½ × 13½.
29 3d. black and yellow 20 15
30 6d. red-brown and blue 50 20
31 1s. red-orange and blue-green 60 25
29/31 .. .. *Set of* 3 1·10 55

Designs:—6d. Norfolk Island and Pitcairn Islands; 1s. Migrant brigantine *Mary Ann*.

1963 (4 June). *Freedom from Hunger. As No.* 80 *of Lesotho.*
32 2s. 6d. ultramarine .. .. 22·00 3·00

1963 (4 Dec). *As No.* 18*a*, *but wmk* w **12**.
33 **9** ½d. green and reddish purple 30 60

1963 (9 Dec). *Red Cross Centenary. As Nos.* 203/4 *of Jamaica.*
34 2d. red and black .. .. 2·00 1·00
35 2s. 6d. red and blue .. .. 11·00 5·50

23 Pitcairn Is Longboat

24 Queen Elizabeth II (after Anthony Buckley)

(Des M. Farrar Bell. Photo Harrison)

1964 (5 Aug)–**65**. *T* **23/4** *and similar horiz designs. Multi-coloured. W* w **12**. *P* 14 × 14½.
36 ½d. Type **23** 10 30
37 1d. H.M.S. *Bounty* 30 30
38 2d. "Out from Bounty Bay" 30 30
39 3d. Great Frigate Bird 30 30
40 4d. White Tern 30 30
41 6d. Pitcairn Warbler 30 30
42 8d. Red-footed Booby 30 30
a. Pale blue (beak) omitted £150
43 10d. Red-tailed Tropic Birds 30 30
44 1s. Henderson Island Crake 30 30
45 1s. 6d. Stephen's Lory .. .. .. 5·50 1·25
46 2s. 6d. Murphy's Petrel .. .. .. 5·00 1·50
47 4s. Henderson Island Fruit Dove .. .. 7·00 1·75
48 8s. Type **24** (5.4.65) .. .. .. 2·50 1·75
36/48 .. .. *Set of* 13 20·00 8·00

1965 (17 May). *I.T.U. Centenary. As Nos.* 98/9 *of Lesotho.*
49 1d. mauve and orange-brown .. .. 1·00 40
50 2s. 6d. turquoise-green and bright blue .. 14·00 3·50

1965 (25 Oct). *International Co-operation Year. As Nos.* 100/1 *of Lesotho.*
51 1d. reddish purple and turquoise-green .. 1·00 40
52 1s. 6d. deep bluish green and lavender .. 14·00 4·00

1966 (24 Jan). *Churchill Commemoration. As Nos.* 102/5 *of Lesotho.*
53 2d. new blue .. .. 2·00 60
54 3d. deep green .. .. 4·50 80
55 6d. brown .. .. 7·50 1·50
56 1s. bluish violet .. .. 10·00 2·00
53/6 .. .. *Set of* 4 22·00 4·50

25 Footballer's Legs, Ball and Jules Rimet Cup

(Des V. Whiteley. Litho Harrison)

1966 (1 Aug). *World Cup Football Championships. W* w **12** (*sideways*). *P* 14.
57 **25** 4d. violet, yellow-green, lake & yellow-brn 2·00 1·00
58 2s. 6d. chocolate, blue-grn, lake & yell-brn 5·00 1·75

1966 (20 Sept). *Inauguration of W.H.O. Headquarters, Geneva. As Nos.* 185/6 *of Montserrat.*
59 8d. black, yellow-green and light blue .. 4·50 1·25
60 1s. 6d. black, light purple and yellow-brown 7·50 1·50

1966 (1 Dec). *20th Anniv of U.N.E.S.C.O. As Nos.* 342/4 *of Mauritius.*
61 ½d. slate-violet, red, yellow and orange .. 20 30
62 10d. orange-yellow, violet and deep olive .. 5·00 1·75
63 2s. black, bright purple and orange .. .. 11·00 2·25
61/3 .. .. *Set of* 3 14·50 4·00

36 Mangarevan Canoe, *circa* 1325

(Des V. Whiteley. Photo Harrison)

1967 (1 Mar). *Bicentenary of Discovery of Pitcairn Islands. T* **36** *and similar horiz designs. Multicoloured. W* w **12**. *P* 14½.
64 ½d. Type **36** 10 10
65 1d. P. F. de Quiros and *San Pedro y Pablo*, 1606 .. .. 15 10
66 8d. *San Pedro y Pablo* and *Los Tres Reyes*, 1606 .. .. 25 10
67 1s. Carteret and H.M.S. *Swallow*, 1767 .. 25 10
68 1s. 6d. *Hercules*, 1819 .. .. .. 30 10
64/8 .. .. *Set of* 5 85 35

(New Currency. 100 cents = 1 New Zealand dollar)

½c

(41 *Bounty* Anchor)

1967 (10 July). *Decimal currency. Nos.* 36/48 *surch in decimal currency by die-stamping in gold as T* **41**.
69 ½ c. on ½d. multicoloured 10 10
a. Deep brown omitted £350
b. Surch double, one albino £110
70 1 c. on 1d. multicoloured 30 30
71 2 c. on 2d. multicoloured 25 30
72 2½ c. on 3d. multicoloured 25 30
73 3 c. on 4d. multicoloured 25 15
74 5 c. on 6d. multicoloured 30 30
75 10 c. on 8d. multicoloured 30 30
a. "10 c." omitted £250
b. Pale blue (beak) omitted £150
76 15 c. on 10d. multicoloured 70 40
77 20 c. on 1s. multicoloured 80 55
78 25 c. on 1s. 6d. multicoloured .. .. 2·50 1·25
79 30 c. on 2s. 6d. multicoloured .. .. 2·75 1·25
80 40 c. on 4s. multicoloured .. .. 4·25 1·25
81 45 c. on 8s. multicoloured .. .. 4·25 1·50
69/81 .. .. *Set of* 13 15·00 7·00

On No. 75a the anchor emblem is still present. Several examples of this variety have been identified as coming from R. 9/1.

The ½ c. and 1 c. exist with PVA gum as well as gum arabic.

42 Bligh and *Bounty*'s Launch

(Des Jennifer Toombs. Litho D.L.R.)

1967 (7 Dec). *150th Death Anniv of Admiral Bligh. T* **42** *and similar horiz designs. P* 13½ × 13.
82 1 c. turq-blue, black and royal blue (*shades*) 10 10
83 8 c. black, yellow and magenta 20 10
84 20 c. black, brown and pale buff 20 15
82/4 .. .. *Set of* 3 45 30

Designs:—8 c. Bligh and followers cast adrift; 20 c. Bligh's tomb.

45 Human Rights Emblem

(Des G. Hamori. Litho D.L.R.)

1968 (4 Mar). *Human Rights Year. P* 13½ × 13.
85 **45** 1 c. multicoloured 10 10
86 2 c. multicoloured 10 10
87 25 c. multicoloured 20 20
85/7 .. .. *Set of* 3 30 30

46 Miro Wood and Flower

(Des Jennifer Toombs. Photo Harrison)

1968 (19 Aug). *Handicrafts (1st series). T* **46** *and similar designs. W* w **12** *(sideways on vert designs). P* 14 × 13½ (5, 10 c.) *or* 13½ × 14 *(others).*

88 5 c. multicoloured 15 10
89 10 c. bronze-green, brown and orange .. 20 20
90 15 c. deep bluish violet, chocolate and salmon 20 20
91 20 c. multicoloured 25 20
88/91 .. .. *Set of* 4 70 60

Designs: *Horiz*—10 c. Flying Fish model. *Vert*—15 c. "Hand" vases; 20 c. Woven baskets.

See also Nos. 207/10.

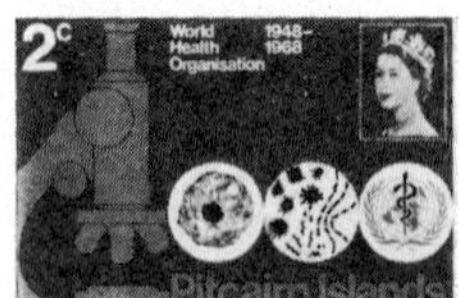

50 Microscope and Slides

(Des Jennifer Toombs. Litho D.L.R.)

1968 (25 Nov). *20th Anniv of World Health Organisation. T* **50** *and similar horiz design. W* w **12** *(sideways). P* 14.

92 2 c. black, turquoise-blue and ultramarine .. 10 10
93 20 c. black, orange and bright purple .. 25 20

Design:—20 c. Hypodermic syringe and jars of tablets.

52 Pitcairn Island **62** "Flying Fox" Cable System

(Des Jennifer Toombs. Litho Questa (50 c., $1), D.L.R. (others))

1969 (17 Sept)–**75**. *T* **52**, **62** *and similar designs. Chalk-surfaced paper. W* w **12** *(upright on 3 c., 25 c., sideways on $1 and horiz designs). P* 14½ × 14 (50 c.), 14 ($1) *or* 13 *(others).*

94 1 c. multicoloured 35 15
a. Glazed, ordinary paper (9.8.71) .. .. 1·25 65
95 2 c. multicoloured 25 15
96 3 c. multicoloured 25 15
97 4 c. multicoloured 30 15
98 5 c. multicoloured 30 15
99 6 c. multicoloured 30 20
100 8 c. multicoloured 35 20
101 10 c. multicoloured .. .. 2·00 85
a. Glazed, ordinary paper (9.8.71) .. .. 1·75 2·00
102 15 c. multicoloured 60 50
a. Queen's head omitted £450
103 20 c. multicoloured 60 40
104 25 c. multicoloured 70 40
105 30 c. multicoloured 55 45
106 40 c. multicoloured 75 60
106*a* 50 c. multicoloured *(glazed, ordinary paper)* (2.1.73) .. .. 11·00 10·00
106*b* $1 multicoloured *(glazed, ordinary paper)* (21.4.75) .. .. 16·00 15·00
94/106*b* .. .. *Set of* 15 30·00 26·00

Designs: *Horiz*—2 c. Captain Bligh and *Bounty* chronometer; 4 c. Plans and drawing of *Bounty*; 5 c. Breadfruit containers and plant; 6 c. Bounty Bay; 8 c. Pitcairn longboat; 10 c. Ship landing point; 15 c. Fletcher Christian's Cave; 20 c. Thursday October Christian's House; 30 c. Radio Station, Taro Ground; 40 c. *Bounty* Bible; 50 c. Pitcairn Coat of Arms. *Vert*—3 c. *Bounty* anchor; $1 Queen Elizabeth II.

See also No. 133.

65 Lantana **69** Auntie and Ann (grouper)

(Des Jennifer Toombs. Litho D.L.R.)

1970 (23 Mar). *Flowers. T* **65** *and similar vert designs. Multicoloured. W* w **12**. *P* 14.

107 1 c. Type **65** 20 20
108 2 c. "Indian Shot" 45 25
109 5 c. Pulau 85 40
110 25 c. Wild Gladiolus .. .. 2·00 1·10
107/10 .. .. *Set of* 4 3·25 1·75

(Des Jennifer Toombs. Photo Harrison)

1970 (12 Oct). *Fishes. T* **69** *and similar horiz designs. Multicoloured. W* w **12**. *P* 14.

111 5 c. Type **69** .. .. 2·75 70
112 10 c. Dream Fish (rudder fish) .. .. .. 2·75 85
113 15 c. Elwyn's Trousers (wrasse) .. .. 3·25 1·00
114 20 c. Whistling Daughter (wrasse) .. .. 3·50 1·25
111/14 .. .. *Set of* 4 11·00 3·50

ROYAL VISIT 1971

(70)

71 Polynesian Rock Carvings

1971 (22 Feb). *Royal Visit. No.* 101 *optd with T* **70**, *in silver.*

115 10 c. multicoloured .. .. 2·25 3·00

(Des Jennifer Toombs. Litho A & M)

1971 (3 May). *Polynesian Pitcairn. T* **71** *and similar multicoloured designs. W* w **12** *(sideways on* 10 *and* 15 *c.). P* 13½.

116 5 c. Type **71** .. .. 1·75 1·00
117 10 c. Polynesian artefacts *(horiz)* .. .. 2·25 1·25
118 15 c. Polynesian stone fish-hook *(horiz)* .. 2·50 1·25
119 20 c. Polynesian stone deity .. .. .. 2·50 1·50
116/19 .. .. *Set of* 4 8·00 4·50

72 Commission Flag **73** Red-tailed Tropic Birds and Longboat

(Des Jennifer Toombs. Litho Questa)

1972 (4 Apr). *25th Anniv of South Pacific Commission. T* **72** *and similar horiz designs. Multicoloured (except 4 c.). W* w **12** *(sideways on 4 c.). P* 14.

120 4 c. dp blue, blue-violet & brt yellow (T **72**) .. 1·00 1·00
121 8 c. Young and Elderly (Health) .. .. 1·00 1·00
122 18 c. Junior School (Education) .. .. 1·50 1·50
123 20 c. Goods store (Economy) .. .. .. 2·00 2·00
120/3 .. .. *Set of* 4 5·00 5·00

(Des (from photographs by D. Groves) and photo Harrison)

1972 (20 Nov). *Royal Silver Wedding. Multicoloured; background colour given. W* w **12**. *P* 14 × 14½.

124 **73** 4 c. slate-green 40 60
125 20 c. bright blue 60 90

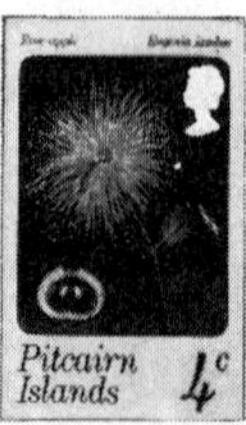

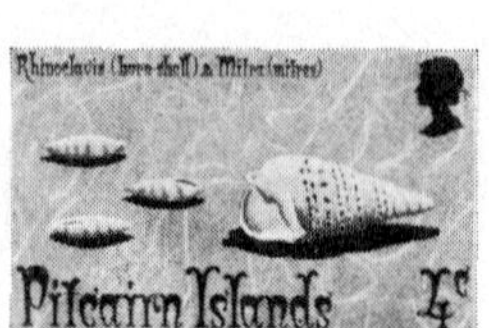

74 Rose-apple **75** Horn-shell and Mitres

(Des Jennifer Toombs. Litho J.W.)

1973 (25 June). *Flowers. T* **74** *and similar vert designs. Multicoloured. W* w **12** *(sideways). P* 14.

126 4 c. Type **74** .. .. 1·25 55
127 8 c. Mountain-apple .. .. 1·75 75
128 15 c. "Lata" .. .. 3·00 1·00
129 20 c. "Dorcas-flower" .. .. 3·25 1·25
130 35 c. Guava .. .. 4·00 1·75
126/30 .. .. *Set of* 5 12·00 4·75

1973 (14 Nov). *Royal Wedding. As Nos.* 322/3 *of Montserrat. Centre multicoloured. W* w **12** *(sideways). P* 13½.

131 10 c. bright mauve 30 15
132 25 c. emerald 35 30

1974 (4 Feb). *As No.* 94a, *but wmk upright. Glazed, ordinary paper.*

133 **52** 1 c. multicoloured .. .. 3·50 4·25

134/46 Catalogue numbers vacant.

(Des Jennifer Toombs. Litho Questa)

1974 (15 Apr). *Shells. T* **75** *and similar horiz designs. Multicoloured. W* w **12**. *P* 14.

147 4 c. Type **75** .. .. 1·50 60
148 10 c. Dove-shell .. .. 1·75 80
149 18 c. Limpet and False Limpet .. .. .. 2·00 1·00
150 50 c. Lucine shell .. .. 2·75 1·25
147/50 .. .. *Set of* 4 7·00 3·25
MS151 130 × 121 mm. Nos. 147/50 .. .. 8·00 13·00

76 Island Post Office

(Des Jennifer Toombs. Litho Questa)

1974 (22 July). *Centenary of Universal Postal Union. T* **76** *and similar horiz designs. W* w **12** *(sideways). P* 14.

152 4 c. multicoloured 25 30
153 20 c. bright purple, light cinnamon and black 40 50
154 35 c. multicoloured 50 60
152/4 .. .. *Set of* 3 1·00 1·25

Designs:—20 c. Pre-stamp letter, 1922; 35 c. Mailship and Pitcairn longboat.

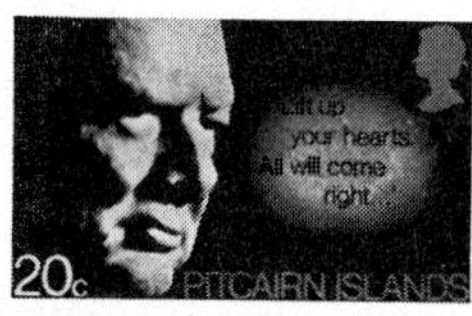

77 Churchill and Text "Lift up your Hearts . . ."

(Des Jennifer Toombs. Litho Questa)

1974 (30 Nov). *Birth Centenary of Sir Winston Churchill. T* **77** *and similar horiz design. W* w **14** *(sideways). P* 14½.

155 20 c. blackish olive, apple-green & dp slate .. 50 85
156 35 c. sepia, greenish yellow and deep slate .. 75 90

Design:—35 c. Text "Give us the tools . . .".

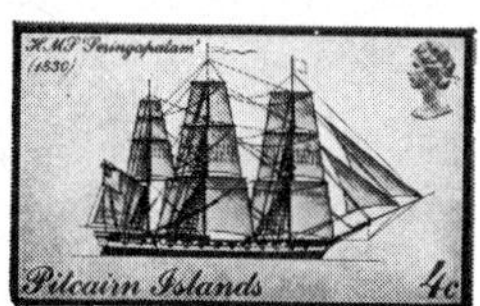

78 H.M.S. *Seringapatam*, 1830

(Des Jennifer Toombs. Litho Walsall)

1975 (22 July). *Mailboats. T* **78** *and similar horiz designs. Multicoloured. W* w **14** *(sideways). P* 14.

157 4 c. Type **78** 65 60
158 10 c. *Pitcairn* (missionary schooner), 1890 .. 70 85
159 18 c. R.M.S. *Athenic*, 1904 .. .. .. 80 1·40
160 50 c. S.S. *Gothic*, 1948 .. .. 2·00 2·75
157/60 .. .. *Set of* 4 3·50 5·00
MS161 145 × 110 mm. Nos. 157/60 .. .. 10·00 15·00

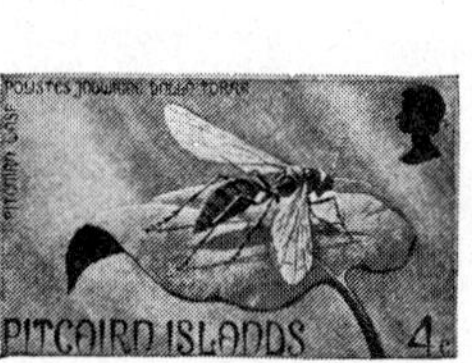

79 *Polistes jadwigae* (wasp) **80** Fletcher Christian

(Des Jennifer Toombs. Litho Questa)

1975 (9 Nov). *Pitcairn Insects. T* **79** *and similar horiz designs. Multicoloured. W* w **12** *(sideways). P* 14.

162 4 c. Type **79** 50 45
163 6 c. *Euconocephalus* sp (grasshopper) .. 70 55
164 10 c. *Anomis flavia* and *Chasmina tibialis* (moths) 80 70
165 15 c. *Pantala flavescens* (skimmer) .. .. 1·25 1·25
166 20 c. *Gnathothlibus erotus* (Banana moth) .. 1·50 1·50
162/6 .. .. *Set of* 5 4·25 4·00

(Des Jennifer Toombs. Litho J.W.)

1976 (4 July). *Bicentenary of American Revolution. T* **80** *and similar vert designs. Multicoloured. W* w **14**. *P* 13½.

167	5 c. Type **80**	40	65
	a. Horiz pair. Nos. 167 and 169	1·10	1·60
168	10 c. H.M.S. *Bounty*	50	80
	a. Horiz pair. Nos. 168 and 170	1·50	2·25
169	30 c. George Washington	75	95
170	50 c. *Mayflower*, 1620	1·00	1·50
167/70	.. .. *Set of* 4	2·50	3·50

The 5 and 30 c. and 10 and 50 c. values were each printed together, *se-tenant*, in horizontal pairs throughout the sheets.

81 Chair of Homage

82 The Island's Bell

(Des Jennifer Toombs. Litho J.W.)

1977 (6 Feb). *Silver Jubilee. T* **81** *and similar vert designs. Multicoloured. W* w **14**. *P* 13.

171	8 c. Prince Philip's visit, 1971	20	20
172	20 c. Type **81**	30	30
173	50 c. Enthronement	50	50
171/3	.. .. *Set of* 3	90	90

(Des Jennifer Toombs. Litho Walsall)

1977 (12 Sept)–**81**. *Various multicoloured designs as T* **82**. *W* w **14** (*upright on* 1 c., 9 c., 70 c. *and* $2; *sideways on others*). *P* 14.

174	1 c. Type **82**	30	40
175	2 c. Building a longboat	30	40
176	5 c. Landing cargo	35	40
177	6 c. Sorting supplies	30	40
178	9 c. Cleaning wahoo (fish)	30	40
179	10 c. Cultivation	30	40
179*a*	15 c. Sugar Mill (1.10.81)	1·25	1·00
180	20 c. Grating coconut and bananas	30	40
181	35 c. The Island church	35	70
182	50 c. Fetching miro logs, Henderson Is. ..	45	80
182*a*	70 c. Burning obsolete stamp issues (1.10.81)	1·25	1·25
183	$1 Prince Philip, Bounty Bay and Royal Yacht *Britannia*	65	1·10
184	$2 Queen Elizabeth II (photograph by Reginald Davis)	1·25	1·75
174/84	.. .. *Set of* 13	6·50	8·50

The 1 c., 9 c., 70 c. and $2 are vertical designs, the remainder horizontal.

83 Building a *Bounty* Model

84 Coronation Ceremony

(Des E. W. Roberts. Litho Questa)

1978 (9 Jan). *"Bounty Day". T* **83** *and similar horiz designs. Multicoloured. W* w **14** (*sideways*). *P* 14½.

185	6 c. Type **83**	40	35
186	20 c. The model at sea	70	60
187	35 c. Burning the model	85	70
185/7	.. .. *Set of* 3	1·75	1·50
MS188	166 × 122 mm. Nos. 185/7	7·50	9·00

(Des Jennifer Toombs. Litho Cartor S.A., France)

1978 (9 Oct). *25th Anniv of Coronation. Sheet* 94 × 78 *mm. W* w **14**. *P* 12.

MS189 **84**	$1.20, multicoloured	1·75	2·25

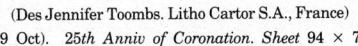

85 Harbour before Development

(Des J.W. Litho Bruder Rosenbaum, Vienna)

1978 (18 Dec). *"Operation Pallium" (Harbour Development Project). T* **85** *and similar horiz designs. Multicoloured. W* w **14** (*sideways*). *P* 13½.

190	15 c. Type **85**	30	40
191	20 c. Unloading R.F.A. *Sir Geraint*	40	50
192	30 c. Work on the jetty	45	55
193	35 c. Harbour after development	50	60
190/3	.. .. *Set of* 4	1·50	1·90

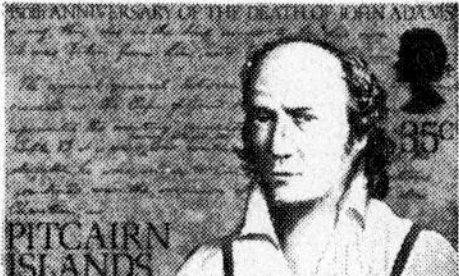

86 John Adams and Diary Extract

(Des Jennifer Toombs. Litho Questa)

1979 (5 Mar). *150th Death Anniv of John Adams (mutineer from the "Bounty"). T* **86** *and similar horiz design. Multicoloured. W* w **14** (*sideways*). *P* 14.

194	35 c. Type **86**	40	70
195	70 c. John Adams' grave and diary extract ..	60	90

87 Pitcairn's Island sketched from H.M.S. *Amphitrite*

(Des Jennifer Toombs. Litho Questa)

1979 (12 Sept). *19th-century Engravings. T* **87** *and similar horiz designs. W* w **14** (*sideways*). *P* 14.

196	6 c. black, brown-ochre and stone	15	20
197	9 c. black, violet and pale violet	15	25
198	20 c. black, brt green & pale yellowish green	15	40
199	70 c. black, scarlet and pale rose	50	1·00
196/9	.. .. *Set of* 4	85	1·75

Designs:—9 c. Bounty Bay and Village of Pitcairn; 20 c. Lookout Ridge; 70 c. Church and School House.

88 Taking Presents to the Square

(Des and litho J.W.)

1979 (28 Nov). *Christmas and International Year of the Child. T* **88** *and similar horiz designs. Multicoloured. W* w **14** (*sideways*). *P* 13.

200	6 c. Type **88**	15	20
201	9 c. Decorating trees with the presents ..	15	20
202	20 c. Chosen men distribute the gifts	25	35
203	35 c. Carrying presents home	30	40
200/3	.. .. *Set of* 4	75	1·00
MS204	198 × 73 mm. Nos. 200/3. P 13½ × 14 ..	2·00	2·00

89 Loading Mail from Supply Ship to Longboats

(Des Jennifer Toombs. Litho Format)

1980 (6 May). *"London 1980" International Stamp Exhibition. Sheet* 120 × 135 *mm containing T* **89** *and similar horiz designs. Multicoloured. W* w **14** (*sideways*). *P* 14½.

MS205	35 c. Type **89**; 35 c. Mail being conveyed by "Flying Fox" (hoisting mechanism) to the Edge; 35 c. Tractor transporting mail from the Edge to Adamstown; 35 c. Mail being off-loaded at Post Office ..	1·00	1·50

90 Queen Elizabeth the Queen Mother at Henley Regatta

(Des Harrison. Litho Questa)

1980 (4 Aug). *80th Birthday of Queen Elizabeth the Queen Mother. W* w **14** (*sideways*). *P* 14.

206 **90**	50 c. multicoloured	50	70

(Des Jennifer Toombs. Litho Questa)

1980 (29 Sept). *Handicrafts (2nd series). Multicoloured designs as T* **46**. *W* w **14** (*sideways on* 9 *and* 20 c.). *P* 14.

207	9 c. Turtles (wood carvings)	10	10
208	20 c. Pitcairn wheelbarrow (wood carving) ..	10	15
209	35 c. Gannet (wood carving) (*vert*)	15	25
210	40 c. Woven bonnet and fan (*vert*)	15	25
207/10	.. .. *Set of* 4	40	65

91 Part of Adamstown

(Des BG Studio. Litho Rosenbaum Bros, Vienna)

1981 (22 Jan). *Landscapes. T* **91** *and similar horiz designs. Multicoloured. W* w **14** (*sideways*). *P* 13½.

211	6 c. Type **91**	10	10
212	9 c. Big George	10	15
213	20 c. Christian's Cave, Gannets Ridge ..	15	20
214	35 c. Radio Station from Pawala Valley Ridge	20	30
215	70 c. Tatrimoa	30	45
211/15	.. .. *Set of* 5	75	1·10

92 Islanders preparing for Departure

93 Prince Charles as Colonel-in-Chief, Cheshire Regiment

(Des Jennifer Toombs. Litho Heraclio Fournier)

1981 (3 May). *125th Anniv of Pitcairn Islanders' Migration to Norfolk Island. T* **92** *and similar horiz designs. Multicoloured. P* 13 × 14.

216	9 c. Type **92**	15	20
217	35 c. View of Pitcairn Island from *Morayshire*	30	45
218	70 c. *Morayshire*	45	65
216/18	.. .. *Set of* 3	80	1·10

(Des J.W. Litho Format)

1981 (22 July). *Royal Wedding. T* **93** *and similar vert designs. Multicoloured. W* w **14**. *P* 14.

219	20 c. Wedding bouquet from Pitcairn Islands	25	25
220	35 c. Type **93**	40	40
221	$1.20, Prince Charles and Lady Diana Spencer	75	85
219/21	.. .. *Set of* 3	1·25	1·40

94 Lemon

95 Pitcairn Islands Coat of Arms

(Des Daphne Padden. Litho Harrison)

1982 (23 Feb). *Fruit. T* **94** *and similar horiz designs. Multicoloured. W* w **14** (*sideways*). *P* 14½.

222	9 c. Type **94**	10	10
223	20 c. Pomegranate	15	20
224	35 c. Avocado	25	30
225	70 c. Pawpaw	50	65
222/5	.. .. *Set of* 4	90	1·10

(Des Jennifer Toombs. Litho Harrison)

1982 (1 July). *21st Birthday of Princess of Wales. T* **95** *and similar vert designs. Multicoloured. W* w **14**. *P* 14½ × 14.

226	6 c. Type **95**	10	20
227	9 c. Princess at Royal Opera House, Covent Garden, December 1981	10	20
228	70 c. Balcony Kiss	50	75
229	$1.20, Formal portrait	80	1·10
226/9	.. .. *Set of* 4	1·25	2·00

96 Raphael's Angels

(Des Leslie McCombie. Litho Walsall)

1982 (19 Oct). *Christmas. T* **96** *and similar designs showing Raphael's Angels.* W w **14** (*sideways on* 15 *c. and* 20 *c.*). *P* 13½ × 14 (15 *c.*, 20 *c.*) *or* 14 × 13½ (*others*).
230 15 c. black, silver and pink 15 15
231 20 c. black, silver and pale lemon 20 20
232 50 c. yellow-brown, silver and stone 45 45
233 $1 black, silver and cobalt 85 85
230/3 .. .. *Set of* 4 1·50 1·50
The 50 c. and $1 are vertical designs.

97 Radio Operator

(Des Jennifer Toombs. Litho Harrison)

1983 (14 Mar). *Commonwealth Day. T* **97** *and similar horiz designs. Multicoloured.* W w **14** (*sideways*). *P* 13½.
234 6 c. Type **97** 10 10
235 9 c. Postal clerk 10 10
236 70 c. Fisherman 50 65
237 $1.20, Artist .. .. 80 1·10
234/7 .. .. *Set of* 4 1·25 1·60

98 *Topaz* sights Smoke on Pitcairn

(Des Jennifer Toombs. Litho B.D.T.)

1983 (14 June). *175th Anniv of Folger's Discovery of the Settlers. T* **98** *and similar horiz designs. Multicoloured.* W w **14** (*sideways*). *P* 14.
238 6 c. Type **98** 20 15
239 20 c. Three islanders approach the *Topaz* .. 30 30
240 70 c. Capt. Mayhew Folger welcomed by John Adams 75 75
241 $1.20, Folger presented with *Bounty* chronometer .. .. 1·10 1·10
238/41 .. .. *Set of* 4 2·10 2·10

99 Hattie-Tree

(Des Jennifer Toombs. Litho B.D.T.)

1983 (6 Oct). *Trees of Pitcairn Islands* (*1st series*). *T* **99** *and similar horiz designs. Multicoloured.* W w **14** (*sideways*). *P* 13½.
242 35 c. Type **99** 30 55
a. Pair. Nos. 242/3 .. .. 60 1·10
243 35 c. Leaves from Hattie-Tree 30 55
244 70 c. Pandanus 65 90
a. Pair. Nos. 244/5 .. .. 1·25 1·75
245 70 c. Pandanus and basket weaving 65 90
242/5 .. .. *Set of* 4 1·75 2·50
The two designs of each value were printed together, *se-tenant*, in horizontal and vertical pairs throughout the sheet.
See also Nos. 304/7.

100 *Pseudojuloides atavai*

(Des C. Abbott. Litho Format)

1984 (11 Jan). *Fishes* (*1st series*). *T* **100** *and similar horiz designs. Multicoloured.* W w **14** (*sideways*). *P* 14½.
246 1 c. Type **100** 20 30
247 4 c. *Halichoeres melasmapomus* 30 35
248 6 c. *Scarus longipinnis* 30 35
249 9 c. *Variola louti* 30 35
250 10 c. *Centropyge hotumatua* 30 40
251 15 c. *Stegastes emeryi* 30 40
252 20 c. *Chaetodon smithi* 40 50
253 35 c. *Xanthichthys mento* 50 60
254 50 c. *Chrysiptera galba* 50 75
255 70 c. *Genicanthus spinus* 70 95
256 $1 *Myripristis tiki* .. .. 90 1·25
257 $1.20, *Anthias ventralis* .. .. .. 1·75 2·00
258 $2 *Pseudocaranx dentex* .. .. .. 2·25 2·50
246/58 .. .. *Set of* 13 8·00 9·50
For 90 c. and $3 values see Nos. 312/13.

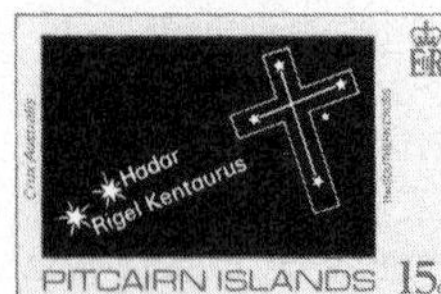

101 "Southern Cross"

(Des J. Cooter. Litho Walsall)

1984 (14 May). *Night Sky. T* **101** *and similar horiz designs.* W w **14** (*sideways*). *P* 14.
259 15 c. deep violet-blue, pale rose-lilac and gold 20 20
260 20 c. deep violet-blue, bright yell-grn & gold 30 30
261 70 c. deep violet-blue, yellow-ochre and gold .. 75 75
262 $1 deep violet-blue, pale blue and gold .. 1·00 1·00
259/62 .. .. *Set of* 4 2·00 2·00
Constellations:—20 c. "Southern Fish"; 70 c. "Lesser Dogs"; $1 "The Virgin".

102 Aluminium Longboat

103 "H.M.S. *Portland* standing off Bounty Bay" (J. Linton Palmer)

(Des C. Abbott. Litho Enschedé)

1984 (21 Sept). *"Ausipex" International Stamp Exhibition, Melbourne. Sheet* 134 × 86 *mm containing T* **102** *and similar horiz design. Multicoloured.* W w **14** (*sideways*). *P* 13½ × 14.
MS263 50 c. Type **102**; $2 Traditional-style wooden longboat .. .. 2·00 2·25

(Des Jennifer Toombs. Litho Questa)

1985 (16 Jan). *19th-Century Paintings* (*1st series*). *T* **103** *and similar horiz designs. Multicoloured.* W w **14** (*sideways*). *P* 13½ × 14 ($2) *or* 14 (*others*).
264 6 c. Type **103** 30 20
265 9 c. "Christian's Look Out" (J. Linton Palmer) 30 20
266 35 c. "The Golden Age" (J. Linton Palmer) .. 70 50
267 $2 "A View of the Village, 1825" (William Smyth) (48×31 *mm*) .. .. .. 2·00 1·60
264/7 .. .. *Set of* 4 3·00 2·25
The original printing of No. 267 was incorrectly dated "1835". The mistake was, however, spotted before issue and a replacement printing, correctly dated "1825", was provided. Those stamps dated "1835" were never issued for postal purposes, although isolated examples exist which may have been supplied by various philatelic agents in error.
See also Nos. 308/11.

104 The Queen Mother with the Queen and Princess Margaret, 1980

105 *Act* 6 (container ship)

(Des A. Theobald ($2), C. Abbott (others). Litho Questa)

1985 (7 June). *Life and Times of Queen Elizabeth the Queen Mother. T* **104** *and similar vert designs. Multicoloured.* W w **16**. *P* 14½ × 14.
268 6 c. Receiving the Freedom of Dundee, 1964 .. .. 10 20
269 35 c. Type **104** 40 55
270 70 c. The Queen Mother in 1983 .. .. .. 70 90
271 $1.20, With Prince Henry at his christening (from photo by Lord Snowdon) .. 1·10 1·40
268/71 .. .. *Set of* 4 2·10 2·75
MS272 91 × 73 mm. $2 In coach at Ascot Races. Wmk sideways .. .. 2·00 2·00

(Des E. Nisbet. Litho Format)

1985 (28 Aug). *Ships* (*1st series*). *T* **105** *and similar multicoloured designs.* W w **14** (*sideways*). *P* 14 (*Nos.* 273/4) *or* 14 × 13½ (*others*).
273 50 c. Type **105** .. .. 1·00 1·25
274 50 c. *Columbus Louisiana* (container ship) .. 1·00 1·25
275 50 c. *Essi Gina* (tanker) (48 × 35 *mm*) .. 1·00 1·25
276 50 c. *Stolt Spirit* (tanker) (48 × 35 *mm*) .. 1·00 1·25
273/6 .. .. *Set of* 4 3·50 4·50
See also Nos. 296/9.

106 "Madonna and Child" (Raphael)

107 Green Turtle

(Des Jennifer Toombs. Litho Walsall)

1985 (26 Nov). *Christmas. T* **106** *and similar vert designs showing "Madonna and Child" paintings. Multicoloured.* W w **16**. *P* 14 × 13½.
277 6 c. Type **106** 30 20
278 9 c. Krause (after Raphael) 30 20
279 35 c. Andreas Mayer 65 50
280 $2 Unknown Austrian master .. .. 2·25 2·50
277/80 .. .. *Set of* 4 3·25 3·00

(Des J. Thatcher. Litho Questa)

1986 (12 Feb). *Turtles. T* **107** *and similar horiz designs. Multicoloured.* W w **16** (*sideways*). *P* 14½.
281 9 c. Type **107** 75 75
282 20 c. Green Turtle and Pitcairn Island .. 1·25 1·25
283 70 c. Hawksbill Turtle .. .. 2·50 2·50
284 $1.20, Hawksbill Turtle and Pitcairn Island .. .. 3·25 3·25
281/4 .. .. *Set of* 4 7·00 7·00

(Des A. Theobald. Litho Questa)

1986 (21 Apr). *60th Birthday of Queen Elizabeth II. Vert designs as T* **230a** *of Jamaica. Multicoloured.* W w **16**. *P* 14½ × 14.
285 6 c. Princess Elizabeth at Royal Lodge, Windsor, 1946 .. .. 15 15
286 9 c. Wedding of Princess Anne, 1973 .. 15 15
287 20 c. At Order of St. Michael and St. George service, St. Paul's Cathedral, 1961 .. 30 30
288 $1.20, At Electrical Engineering Concert, Royal Festival Hall, 1971 .. .. 1·10 1·25
289 $2 At Crown Agents Head Office, London, 1983 .. .. 1·75 2·00
285/9 .. .. *Set of* 5 3·00 3·50

(Des D. Miller. Litho Questa)

1986 (23 July). *Royal Wedding. Square designs as T* **231a** *of Jamaica. Multicoloured.* W w **16**. *P* 14.
290 20 c. Prince Andrew and Miss Sarah Ferguson 50 50
291 $1.20, Prince Andrew aboard *Bluenose II* off Halifax, Canada, 1985 .. .. 1·75 1·75

108 John I. Tay (pioneer missionary) and First Church

109 Pitcairn Island Home

(Des A. Theobald. Litho Walsall)

1986 (18 Oct). *Centenary of Seventh-Day Adventist Church on Pitcairn. T* **108** *and similar vert designs. Multicoloured.* W w **16**. *P* 14.
292 6 c. Type **108** 40 40
293 20 c. *Pitcairn* (mission schooner) and second church (1907) .. .. 1·00 1·00
294 35 c. Baptism at Down Isaac and third church (1945) .. .. 1·50 1·50
295 $2 Islanders singing farewell hymn and present church (1954) .. .. .. 3·25 3·25
292/5 .. .. *Set of* 4 5·50 5·50

(Des E. Nisbet. Litho Format)

1987 (20 Jan). *Ships* (*2nd series*). *Multicoloured designs as T* **105**. W w **16** (*sideways on Nos.* 298/9). *P* 14 (*Nos.* 296/7) *or* 14 × 13½ (*others*).
296 50 c. *Samoan Reefer* (freighter) .. .. 1·25 1·50
297 50 c. *Brussel* (container ship) .. .. 1·25 1·50
298 50 c. *Australian Exporter* (container ship) (48 × 35 *mm*) .. .. 1·25 1·50
299 50 c. *Taupo* (cargo liner) (48 × 35 *mm*) .. 1·25 1·50
296/9 .. .. *Set of* 4 4·50 5·50

(Des E. Roberts and D. Robertson. Litho Format)

1987 (21 Apr). *Pitcairn Island Homes. T* **109** *and similar horiz designs showing different houses.* W w **14** (*sideways*). *P* 13½ × 14.
300 **109** 70 c. black, brt reddish violet & brt violet 75 60
301 – 70 c. black, pale orange-yell & brn-ochre 75 60
302 – 70 c. black, dull blue and ultramarine .. 75 60
303 – 70 c. black, blue-green & deep blue-green 75 60
300/3 .. .. *Set of* 4 2·75 2·25

(Des Jennifer Toombs. Litho Format)

1987 (10 Aug). *Trees of Pitcairn Islands (2nd series). Horiz designs as T* **99**. *Multicoloured.* W w **16** (*sideways*). *P* 14½.
304 40 c. Leaves and flowers from *Erythrina variegata* 70 70
a. Pair. Nos. 304/5 .. .. 1·40 1·40
305 40 c. *Erythrina variegata* tree 70 70
306 $1.80, Leaves from *Aleurites moluccana* and nut torch .. .. 2·00 2·00
a. Pair. Nos. 306/7 .. .. 4·00 4·00
307 $1.80, *Aleurites moluccana* tree .. .. 2·00 2·00
304/7 .. .. *Set of* 4 5·00 5·00
The two designs of each value were printed together, *se-tenant*, in horizontal and vertical pairs throughout the sheet.

(Des Jennifer Toombs. Litho Questa)

1987 (7 Dec). *19th-Century Paintings (2nd series). Horiz designs as T* **103** *showing paintings by Lt. Conway Shipley in 1848. Multicoloured.* W w **16** (*sideways*). *P* 13½ × 14 ($1.80) *or* 14 (*others*).
308 20 c. "House and Tomb of John Adams" .. 45 45
309 40 c. "Bounty Bay" 70 70
310 90 c. "School House and Chapel" .. .. 1·25 1·25
311 $1.80, "Pitcairn Island" (48 × 31 *mm*) .. 2·00 2·00
308/11 .. .. *Set of* 4 4·00 4·00

(Des C. Abbott. Litho Format)

1988 (14 Jan). *Fishes (2nd series). Horiz designs as T* **100**. *Multicoloured.* W w **16** (*sideways*). *P* 14½.
312 90 c. As No. 249 .. .. 1·75 1·75
313 $3 *Gymnothorax eurostus* .. .. .. 4·25 4·25

110 *Bounty* (replica)

111 H.M.S. *Swallow* (survey ship), 1767

(Des M. Bradbery. Litho Questa)

1988 (9 May). *Bicentenary of Australian Settlement. Sheet* 112 × 76 *mm.* W w **16**. *P* 14 × 13½.
MS314 **110** $3 multicoloured .. .. .. 2·10 2·25

(Des E. Nisbet. Litho B.D.T.)

1988 (14 Aug). *Ships. T* **111** *and similar horiz designs. Multicoloured.* W w **14** (*sideways*). *P* 13½.
315 5 c. Type **111** 10 10
316 10 c. H.M.S. *Pandora* (frigate), 1791 .. 10 10
317 15 c. H.M.S. *Briton* and H.M.S. *Tagus* (frigates), 1814 .. .. .. 10 15
318 20 c. H.M.S. *Blossom* (survey ship), 1825 .. 10 15
319 30 c. *Lucy Anne* (barque), 1831 .. .. 20 25
320 35 c. *Charles Doggett* (whaling ship), 1831 25 30
321 40 c. H.M.S. *Fly* (sloop), 1838 .. .. 25 30
322 60 c. *Camden* (missionary brig), 1840 .. 40 45
323 90 c. H.M.S. *Virago* (paddle-sloop), 1853 .. 60 65
324 $1.20, *Rakaia* (screw-steamer), 1867 .. 80 85
325 $1.80, H.M.S. *Sappho* (screw-sloop), 1882 1·25 1·40
326 $5 H.M.S. *Champion* (corvette), 1893 .. 3·25 3·50
315/26 .. .. *Set of* 12 6·50 7·25
For 20 c. and 90 c. values as above, but watermarked w **16** (sideways), see Nos. 369 and 374.

112 Raising the Union Jack, 1838

113 Angel

(Des Jennifer Toombs. Litho Walsall)

1988 (30 Nov). *150th Anniv of Pitcairn Island Constitution. T* **112** *and similar vert designs, each showing different extract from original Constitution. Multicoloured.* W w **14**. *P* 14.
327 20 c. Type **112** 15 20
328 40 c. Signing Constitution on board H.M.S. *Fly*, 1838 .. .. 30 35
329 $1.05, Voters at modern polling station .. 75 80
330 $1.80, Modern classroom .. .. .. 1·25 1·40
327/30 .. .. *Set of* 4 2·25 2·50

(Des M. Grimsdale. Litho Questa)

1988 (30 Nov). *Christmas. T* **113** *and similar vert designs. Multicoloured.* W w **16**. *P* 14 × 13½.
331 90 c. Type **113** 65 70
a. Horiz strip of 4. Nos. 331/4 .. .. 2·40
332 90 c. Holy Family 65 70
333 90 c. Two Polynesian Wise Men 65 70
334 90 c. Polynesian Wise Man and shepherd .. 65 70
331/4 .. .. *Set of* 4 2·40 2·50
Nos. 331/4 were printed together, *se-tenant*, in horizontal strips of four throughout the sheet.

114 Loading Stores, Deptford

115 R.N.Z.A.F. "Orion" making Mail Drop, 1985

(Des C. Abbott. Litho Questa)

1989 (22 Feb). *Bicentary of Pitcairn Island Settlement (1st issue). T* **114** *and similar horiz designs. Multicoloured.* W w **14** (*sideways*). *P* 14.
335 20 c. Type **114** 30 30
a. Sheetlet. Nos. 335/40 .. .. .. 1·60
336 20 c. H.M.S. *Bounty* leaving Spithead .. 30 30
337 20 c. H.M.S. *Bounty* at Cape Horn 30 30
338 20 c. Anchored in Adventure Bay, Tasmania 30 30
339 20 c. Crew collecting breadfruit 30 30
340 20 c. Breadfruit in cabin 30 30
335/40 .. .. *Set of* 6 1·60 1·60
Nos. 335/40 were printed together, *se-tenant* in sheetlets of six, as two horizontal rows of three separated by a central gutter.
See also Nos. 341/7, 356/61 and 389/94.

(Des C. Abbott. Litho Questa (Nos. 341/6), B.D.T. (No. **MS**347))

1989 (28 Apr). *Bicentenary of Pitcairn Island Settlement (2nd issue). Horiz designs as T* **114**. *Multicoloured.* W w **14** (*sideways*). *P* 14.
341 90 c. H.M.S. *Bounty* leaving Tahiti .. 1·10 1·10
a. Sheetlet. Nos. 341/6 .. .. .. 6·00
342 90 c. Bligh awoken by mutineers .. .. 1·10 1·10
343 90 c. Bligh before Fletcher Christian .. 1·10 1·10
344 90 c. Provisioning Bounty's launch .. 1·10 1·10
345 90 c. "Mutineers casting Bligh adrift" (Robert Dodd) .. .. .. 1·10 1·10
346 90 c. Mutineers discarding breadfruit plants 1·10 1·10
341/6 .. .. *Set of* 6 6·00 6·00
MS347 110 × 85 mm. 90 c. No. 345; 90 c. Isle of Man 1989 35p. Mutiny stamp; 90 c. Norfolk Island 39 c. Mutiny stamp. W w **16** (sideways) 3·50 4·00
Nos. 341/6 were printed in the same sheet format as Nos. 335/40

(Des A. Theobald. Litho Questa)

1989 (25 July). *Aircraft. T* **115** *and similar horiz designs. Multicoloured.* W w **16** (*sideways*). *P* 14×14½.
348 20 c. Type **115** 25 25
349 80 c. Beechcraft "Queen Air" on photo-mission, 1983 .. .. 80 80
350 $1.05, Helicopter landing diesel fuel from U.S.S. *Breton*, 1969 .. .. .. 1·10 1·10
351 $1.30, R.N.Z.A.F. "Hercules" dropping bulldozer, 1983 .. .. .. 1·25 1·25
348/51 .. .. *Set of* 4 3·00 3·00

116 Ducie Island

(Des A. Theobald. Litho Walsall)

1989 (23 Oct). *Islands of Pitcairn Group. T* **116** *and similar horiz designs. Multicoloured.* W w **14** (*sideways*). *P* 14.
352 15 c. Type **116** 15 15
353 90 c. Henderson Island 90 90
354 $1.05, Oeno Island .. .. .. 1·00 1·00
355 $1.30, Pitcairn Island .. .. .. 1·25 1·25
352/5 .. .. *Set of* 4 3·00 3·00

(Des C. Abbott. Litho Questa)

1990 (15 Jan). *Bicentenary of Pitcairn Island Settlement (3rd issue). Horiz designs as T* **114**. *Multicoloured.* W w **16** (*sideways*). *P* 14.
356 40 c. Mutineers sighting Pitcairn Island .. 40 40
a. Sheetlet. Nos. 356/61 .. .. .. 2·25
357 40 c. Ship's boat approaching landing .. 40 40
358 40 c. Exploring island 40 40
359 40 c. Ferrying goods ashore 40 40
360 40 c. Burning of H.M.S. *Bounty* 40 40
361 40 c. Pitcairn Island village 40 40
356/61 .. .. *Set of* 6 2·25 2·25
Nos. 356/61 were printed in the same sheet format as Nos. 335/40.

117 Ennerdale, Cumbria, and Peter Heywood

(Des D. Ashby. Litho Questa)

1990 (3 May). *"Stamp World London 90" International Stamp Exhibition, London. T* **117** *and similar horiz designs showing English landmarks and Bounty crew members. Multicoloured.* W w **14** (*sideways*). *P* 14.
362 80 c. Type **117** 75 80
363 90 c. St. Augustine's Tower, Hackney, and John Adams 85 90
364 $1.05, Citadel Gateway, Plymouth, and William Bligh .. .. .. 1·00 1·25
365 $1.30, Moorland Close, Cockermouth, and Fletcher Christian .. .. .. 1·25 1·40
362/5 .. .. *Set of* 4 3·50 4·00

(Des E. Nisbet. Litho B.D.T.)

1990 (3 May). *As Nos.* 318 *and* 323, *but* W w **16** (*sideways*). *P* 13½.
369 20 c. H.M.S. *Blossom* (survey ship), 1825 .. 10 15
a. Booklet pane. No. 369×4 with margins all round 40
374 90 c. H.M.S. *Virago* (paddle-sloop), 1853 .. 60 65
a. Booklet pane. No. 374×4 with margins all round .. .. 2·40
Nos. 369 and 374 only exist from $4.40 stamp booklets.

(Des D. Miller. Litho Questa)

1990 (4 Aug). *90th Birthday of Queen Elizabeth the Queen Mother. Vert designs as T* **107** (40 *c.*) *or* **108** ($3) *of Kenya. Multicoloured.* W w **16**. *P* 14×15 (40 *c.*) *or* 14½ ($3).
378 40 c. multicoloured 50 50
379 $3 black and dull scarlet .. .. 2·50 2·50
Designs:—40 c. Queen Elizabeth, 1937; $3 King George VI and Queen Elizabeth on way to Silver Wedding Service, 1948.

118 *Bounty* Chronometer and 1940 1d. Definitive

119 Stephen's Lory ("Redbreast")

(Des D. Miller. Litho Walsall)

1990 (15 Oct). *50th Anniv of Pitcairn Islands Stamps. T* **118** *and similar horiz designs. Multicoloured.* W w **14** (*sideways*). *P* 13½×14.
380 20 c. Type **118** 30 30
381 80 c. *Bounty* Bible and 1958 4d. definitive 80 80
382 90 c. *Bounty* Bell and 1969 30 c. definitive 90 90
383 $1.05, Mutiny on the *Bounty* and 1977 $1 definitive .. .. 1·00 1·00
384 $1.30, Penny Black and 1988 15 c. ship definitive .. .. 1·40 1·40
380/4 .. .. *Set of* 5 4·00 4·00

(Des N. Harvey from paintings by Byatt. Litho Questa)

1990 (6 Dec). *"Birdpex '90" Stamp Exhibition, Christchurch, New Zealand. T* **119** *and similar vert designs. Multicoloured.* W w **14**. *P* 14.
385 20 c. Type **119** 30 30
386 90 c. Grey-green Fruit Dove ("Wood Pigeon") 1·10 1·10
387 $1.30, Pitcairn Warbler ("Sparrow") .. 1·40 1·40
388 $1.80, Henderson Island Crake ("Chicken Bird") .. .. 1·60 1·60
385/8 .. .. *Set of* 4 4·00 4·00
Nos. 385/8 carry the "Birdpex '90" logo and inscription in the gutter between the two panes.

(Des N. Shewring. Litho Leigh-Mardon Ltd, Melbourne)

1991 (24 Mar). *Bicentenary of Pitcairn Islands Settlement (4th issue). Celebrations. Horiz designs as T* **114**. *Multicoloured.* W w **16**. *P* 14½.
389 80 c. Re-enacting landing of mutineers .. 90 1·10
a. Sheetlet. Nos. 389/94 .. .. .. 5·00
390 80 c. Commemorative plaque .. .. 90 1·10
391 80 c. Memorial church service .. .. 90 1·10
392 80 c. Cricket match .. .. .. 90 1·10
393 80 c. Burning model of *Bounty* .. .. 90 1·10
394 80 c. Firework display .. .. .. 90 1·10
389/94 .. .. *Set of* 6 5·00 6·00
Nos. 389/94 were printed in the same sheet format as Nos. 335/40.

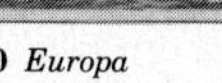
120 *Europa*

121 Bulldozer

(Des E. Nisbet. Litho Leigh-Mardon Ltd, Melbourne)

1991 (17 June). *Cruise Liners. T* **120** *and similar horiz designs. Multicoloured.* W w **16.** *P* 14½

395	15 c. Type **120**	20	20
396	80 c. *Royal Viking Star*	85	85
397	$1.30, *World Discoverer*	1·25	1·25
398	$1.80, *Sagafjord*	1·90	1·90
395/8	*Set of* 4	3·75	3·75

(Des D. Miller. Litho Questa)

1991 (12 July). *65th Birthday of Queen Elizabeth II and 70th Birthday of Prince Philip. Vert designs as T* **58** *of Kiribati. Multicoloured.* W w **16** (*sideways*). *P* 14½×14.

399	20 c. Prince Philip	40	30
	a. Horiz pair. Nos. 399/400 separated by label	2·00	1·50
400	$1.30, Queen in robes of Order of St. Michael and St. George	1·60	1·25

Nos. 399/400 were printed in a similar sheet format to Nos. 366/7 of Kiribati.

(Des O. Bell. Litho Questa)

1991 (25 Sept). *Island Transport. T* **121** *and similar diamond-shaped designs. Multicoloured.* W w **14.** *P* 14.

401	20 c. Type **121**	20	20
402	80 c. Two-wheeled motorcycle	75	75
403	$1.30, Tractor	1·25	1·25
404	$1.80, Three-wheeled motorcycle	1·90	1·90
401/4	*Set of* 4	3·75	3·75

122 The Annunciation

(Des Jennifer Toombs. Litho Questa)

1991 (18 Nov). *Christmas. T* **122** *and similar vert designs. Multicoloured.* W w **14.** *P* 14.

405	20 c. Type **122**	20	20
406	80 c. Shepherds and lamb	75	75
407	$1.30, Holy Family	1·10	1·10
408	$1.80, Three Wise Men	1·75	1·75
405/8	*Set of* 4	3·50	3·50

(Des D. Miller. Litho Questa ($1.80), Leigh-Mardon Ltd, Melbourne (others))

1992 (6 Feb). *40th Anniv of Queen Elizabeth II's Accession. Horiz designs as T* **112** *of Kenya. Multicoloured.* W w **14** (*sideways*) ($1.80) *or* w **16** (*sideways*) (*others*). *P* 14.

409	20 c. Bounty Bay	15	15
410	60 c. Sunset over Pitcairn	60	60
411	90 c. Pitcairn coastline	85	85
412	$1 Three portraits of Queen Elizabeth	90	90
413	$1.80, Queen Elizabeth II	1·60	1·60
409/13	*Set of* 5	3·75	3·75

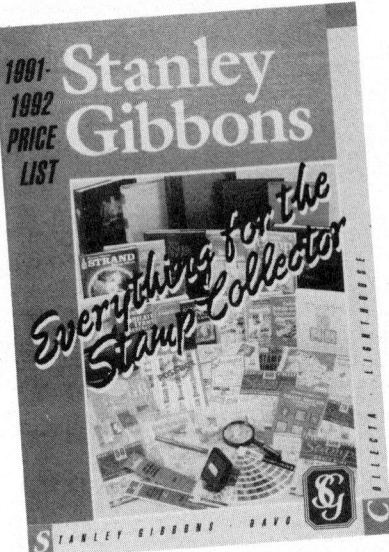

Prince Edward Island *see* Canada

Qatar

An independent Arab Shaikhdom, with a British postal administration until 23 May 1963.

There was no postal service from Qatar until 18 May 1950. Prior to this date the few foreign residents made their own arrangements for their mail to be carried to Bahrain for onward transmission through the postal services.

The first organised post from the capital, Doha, was an extension of the work in the state by the British Political Officer. From 18 May 1950 British residents were able to send mail via his office. The first three sendings had the Bahrain or British Postal Agencies in Eastern Arabia stamps cancelled by a circular office stamp, but later batches, up to the introduction of the first Doha postmark in July 1950, had the stamps cancelled on arrival at Bahrain.

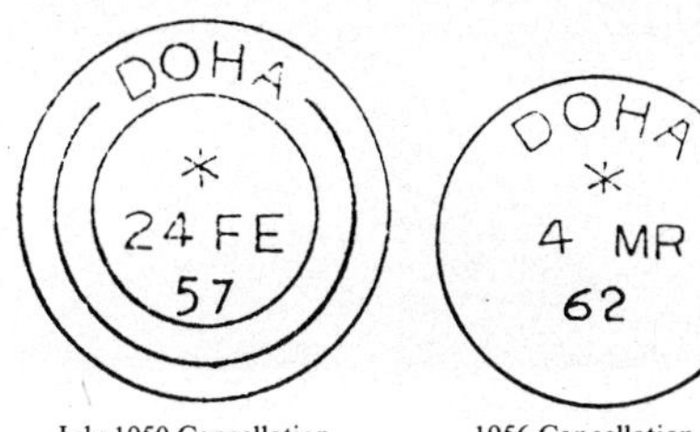

July 1950 Cancellation — 1956 Cancellation

The Post Office became a separate entity in August 1950 when its services were made available to the general public. After initially using the Bahrain surcharges on Great Britain the supply of stamps for the Qatar office was switched to the British Postal Agencies in Eastern Arabia surcharges.

The circular cancellation, dating from July 1950, continued to be used until replaced by a slightly smaller version in early 1956.

A further post office was opened on 1 February 1956 at the Umm Said oil terminal, using its own cancellation.

Both offices were issued with standard oval Registered handstamps, Doha in 1950 and Umm Said in 1956.

1956 Umm Said Cancellation

All stamps to 1960 surcharged in issues of Great Britain

QATAR NP 1 NP (1) — QATAR 3 NP NP (2) — QATAR 75 NP (3)

1957 (1 Apr)–**59**. (*a*) *T* **154/60** (*St Edward's Crown wmk, W* **165**) *surch as T* **1** *to* **3**.

No.	Type	Description	Unused	Used
1	**1**	1 n.p. on 5d. brown	10	10
2	**2**	3 n.p. on ½d. orange-red	15	15
3		6 n.p. on 1d. ultramarine	15	15
4		9 n.p. on 1½d. green	15	10
5		12 n.p. on 2d. light red-brown	20	30
6	**1**	15 n.p. on 2½d. carmine-red (I)	15	10
7	**2**	20 n.p. on 3d. deep lilac (B.)	15	10
8	**1**	25 n.p. on 4d. ultramarine	40	40
9		40 n.p. on 6d. reddish purple	15	10
		a. Deep claret (21.7.59)	30	10
10		50 n.p. on 9d. bronze-green	40	15
11	**3**	75 n.p. on 1s. 3d. green	50	50
12		1 r. on 1s. 6d. grey-blue	5·50	10
1/12		*Set of* 12	7·00	1·75

QATAR 2 RUPEES I
QATAR 2 RUPEES II
(4)

QATAR 5 RUPEES I
QATAR 5 RUPEES II
(5)

QATAR 10 RUPEES I

QATAR 10 RUPEES II
(6)

Type I (**4/6**). Type-set overprints. Bold thick letters with sharp corners and straight edges. Bars close together and usually slightly longer than in Type II.

Type II (**4/6**). Plate-printed overprints. Thinner letters, rounded corners and rough edges. Bars wider apart.

(*b*) *Nos.* 536/8 *surch with T* **4/6**

No.	Type	Description	I (1.4.57) Unused	I Used	II (18.9.57) Unused	II Used
13	**166**	2 r. on 2s. 6d. black-brown	4·00	1·00	9·00	6·00
14	**167**	5 r. on 5s. rose-red	7·00	2·75	9·00	16·00
15	**168**	10 r. on 10s. ultramarine	8·50	8·50	45·00	£100
13/15		*Set of* 3	18·00	11·00	55·00	£110

QATAR 15 NP

(7)

1957 (1 Aug). *World Scout Jubilee Jamboree. Nos.* 557/9 *surch in two lines as T* **7** (15 *n.p.*) *or in three lines* (*others*).

No.	Description	Unused	Used
16	15 n.p. on 2½d. carmine-red	25	35
17	25 n.p. on 4d. ultramarine	25	35
18	75 n.p. on 1s. 3d. green	30	35
16/18	*Set of* 3	70	95

1960 (26 Apr–28 Sept). *Q.E.II* (*Mult Crowns wmk, W* **179**) *surch as T* **1** *or* **2**.

No.	Type	Description	Unused	Used
20	**2**	3 n.p. on ½d. orange-red (28.9)	70	1·75
21		6 n.p. on 1d. ultramarine (21.6)	1·25	2·75
22		9 n.p. on 1½d. green (28.9)	75	1·50
23		12 n.p. on 2d. light red-brown (28.9)	3·75	6·50
24	**1**	15 n.p. on 2½d. carmine-red (II)	35	10
25	**2**	20 n.p. on 3d. deep lilac (B.) (28.9)	35	10
26	**1**	40 n.p. on 6d. deep claret (21.6)	60	30
20/6		*Set of* 7	7·00	11·50

8 Shaikh Ahmad bin Ali al Thani

9 Peregrine Falcon

10 Dhow

11 Oil Derrick

12 Mosque

(Des O. C. Meronti (T **8**), M. Goaman (T **9**), M. Farrar Bell (T **10**), J. Constable and O. C. Meronti (T **11/12**). Photo Harrison, (T **8/10**). Recess D.L.R. (T **11/12**))

1961 (2 Sept). *P* 14½ (5 *n.p. to* 75 *n.p.*) *or* 13 (1 *r. to* 10 *r.*).

No.	Type	Description	Unused	Used
27	**8**	5 n.p. carmine	10	10
28		15 n.p. black	10	10
29		20 n.p. reddish purple	10	10
30		30 n.p. deep green	10	10
31	**9**	40 n.p. red	85	10
32		50 n.p. sepia	1·25	10
33	**10**	75 n.p. ultramarine	60	60
34	**11**	1 r. scarlet	70	10
35		2 r. ultramarine	2·00	25
36	**12**	5 r. bronze-green	9·00	80
37		10 r. black	19·00	1·75
27/37		*Set of* 11	30·00	3·50

The Qatar Post Department took over the postal services on 23 May 1963. Later stamp issues will be found listed in Part 19 (*Middle East*) of this catalogue.

Queensland *see* Australia

Rhodesia

Stamps of BECHUANALAND (see BOTSWANA) were used in Matabeleland on the runner post between Gubulawayo and Mafeking (Bechuanaland) from 21 August 1888 until 5 May 1894. Such stamps were cancelled "GUBULAWAYO" or by the barrel oval "678" obliteration.

Between 27 June 1890 and 13 May 1892 external mail from Mashonaland sent via Bechuanaland was franked with that territory's stamps. A similar arrangement, using the stamps of MOZAMBIQUE existed for the route via Beira inaugurated on 29 August 1891. In both instances the stamps were cancelled by the post offices receiving the mail from Mashonaland. From 14 May until 31 July 1892 letters via Bechuanaland were franked with a combination of B.S.A Company and Bechuanaland issues.

Rhodesia joined the South African Postal Union on 1 August 1892 when its stamps became valid for international mail. Combination frankings with Mozambique stamps continued to be required until April 1894.

For the use of British Central Africa overprints in North-eastern Rhodesia from 1893 to 1899 see MALAWI (NYASALAND).

PRICES FOR STAMPS ON COVER TO 1945	
Nos. 1/7	*from* × 5
Nos. 8/13	—
Nos. 14/17	*from* × 2
Nos. 18/24	*from* × 10
Nos. 25/6	—
Nos. 27/8	*from* × 7
Nos. 29/35	*from* × 10
Nos. 36/7	—
Nos. 41/6	*from* × 6
Nos. 47/50	—
Nos. 51/3	*from* × 2
Nos. 58/64	*from* × 3
Nos. 66/72	*from* × 8
Nos. 73/4	—
Nos. 75/87	*from* × 6
Nos. 88/93*a*	—
Nos. 94/9	*from* × 3
Nos. 100/10	*from* × 5
Nos. 111/13*e*	—
Nos. 114/18	*from* × 7
Nos. 119/60*a*	*from* × 2
Nos. 160*b*/6*b*	—
Nos. 167/78	*from* × 2
Nos. 179/81*a*	—
Nos. 182/5*a*	*from* × 2
Nos. 186/208	*from* × 3
Nos. 209/41	*from* × 2
Nos. 242/54*a*	—
Nos. 255/77	*from* × 2
Nos. 278/9*c*	—
Nos. 280/1	*from* × 7
Nos. 282/310	*from* × 2
Nos. 311/22	—

A. ISSUES FOR THE BRITISH SOUTH AFRICA COMPANY TERRITORY

1

2

½d.

(3)

(Recess B.W.)

1892 (2 Jan)*–**93**. *Thin wove paper. P* 14, 14½.

No.	Type	Description	Unused	Used
1	**1**	1d. black	9·00	1·25
2		6d. ultramarine	48·00	20·00
3		6d. deep blue (1893)	22·00	2·50
4		1s. grey-brown	28·00	7·50
5		2s. vermilion	40·00	25·00
6		2s. 6d. grey-purple	24·00	25·00
7		2s. 6d. lilac (1893)	27·00	27·00
8		5s. orange-yellow	42·00	48·00
9		10s. deep green	60·00	90·00
10	**2**	£1 deep blue	£160	£130
11		£2 rose-red**	£375	£150
12		£5 sage-green	£1500	£450
13		£10 brown	£2750	£700
1/10		*Set of* 10	£350	£350

Great caution is needed in buying the high values in either used or unused condition, many stamps offered being revenue stamps cleaned and re-gummed or with forged postmarks.

*Printing of Nos. 1/28 commenced in 1890, although none were used for postal purposes before 2 January 1892 when the route to the East Coast was inaugurated.

**For later printings of the £2 see No. 74.

The following sheet watermarks are known on Nos. 1/26: (1) William Collins, Sons & Co's paper watermarked with the firm's monogram, and "PURE LINEN WOVE BANK" in double-lined capitals (1890 and 1891 ptgs). (2) As (1) with "EXTRA STRONG" and "139" added (1892 ptgs). (3) Paper by Wiggins, Teape & Co, watermarked "W T & Co" in script letters in double-lined wavy border (1893 ptgs). (4) The same firm's paper, watermarked "1011" in double-lined figures (1894 ptgs except ½d.). (5) "WIGGINS TEAPE & CO LONDON" in double-lined block capitals (1894 ptg of No. 18). Many values can also be found on a slightly thicker paper without wmk, but single specimens are not easily distinguishable.

1892 (2 Jan). *Nos. 2 and 4 surch as T* 3.

14 **1** ½d. on 6d. ultramarine 65·00 £110
15 2d. on 6d. ultramarine 60·00 £140
16 4d. on 6d. ultramarine 80·00 £180
17 8d. on 1s. grey-brown 90·00 £250

Caution is needed in buying these surcharges as both forged surcharges and forged postmarks exist.

4

5 (ends of scrolls behind legs of springboks)

(T 4. Centre recess; value B.W.)

1892 (2 Jan)–**94**. *Thin wove paper (wmks as note after No.* 13). *P* 14, 14½.

18 **4** ½d. dull blue and vermilion 2·50 1·00
19 ½d. deep blue and vermilion (1893) 2·50 2·75
20 2d. sea-green and vermilion 8·00 1·75
21 3d. grey-black and green (8.92) 8·00 1·75
22 4d. chestnut and black 8·00 1·75
23 8d. rose-lake and ultramarine 10·00 5·00
24 8d. red and ultramarine (1892) 10·00 5·00
25 3s. brown and green (1894) 95·00 65·00
26 4s. grey-black and vermilion (1893) 30·00 40·00
18/26 *Set of* 7 £150 £100

(Recess P.B. from the Bradbury, Wilkinson plates)

1895. *Thick soft wove paper. P* 12½.

27 **4** 2d. green and red 20·00 5·00
28 4d. yellow-brown and black 22·00 9·00
a. Imperf (pair) £1400

(Centre recess; value typo P.B.)

1896–97. *Wove paper. P* 14.

(*a*) *Die I. Plates* 1 *and* 2.

Small dot to the right of the tail of the right-hand supporter in the coat of arms. Body of lion only partly shaded.

29 **5** 1d. scarlet and emerald 10·00 3·25
a. Carmine-red and emerald
30 2d. brown and mauve 12·00 1·00
31 3d. chocolate and ultramarine 2·25 80
32 4d. ultramarine and mauve
a. Imperf between (pair)
b. Blue and mauve 9·50 8·00
33 6d. mauve and pink 60·00 7·00
34 8d. green and mauve/*buff* 4·50 45
a. Imperf between (pair
b. Imperf (pair) £1500
35 1s. green and blue 15·00 2·25
36 3s. green and mauve/*blue* 48·00 29·00
a. Imperf (pair) £2750
37 4s. orange-red and blue/*green* 40·00 2·00
29/37 *Set of* 9 £180 48·00

(*b*) *Die II. Plates* 3 *and* 4

No dot. Body of lion heavily shaded all over.

41 **5** ½d. slate and violet 1·00 1·50
42 1d. scarlet and emerald 1·50 2·25
43 2d. brown and mauve 4·00 3·50
44 4d. ultramarine and mauve 55·00 9·00
a. Blue and mauve 6·00 40
46 6d. mauve and rose 4·50 45
47 2s. indigo and green/*buff* 20·00 3·00
48 2s. 6d. brown and purple/*yellow* 55·00 38·00
49 5s. chestnut and emerald 35·00 12·00
50 10s. slate and vermilion/*rose* 80·00 60·00
41/50 *Set of* 9 £180 £110

One Penny

(6)

THREE PENCE.

(7)

(Surchd by *Bulawayo Chronicle*)

1896 (April). *Matabele Rebellion provisionals. Surch with T* 6 *and* 7.

51 **6** 1d. on 3d. (No. 21) £350 £375
a. "P" in "Penny" inverted £12000
b. "y" in "Penny" inverted
c. Surch double
52 1d. on 4s. (No. 26) £250 £225
a. "P" in "Penny" inverted £11000
b. "y" in "Penny" inverted £11000
c. Single bar through original value £800 £1000
53 **7** 3d. on 5s. (No. 8) £150 £200
a. "R" in "THREE" inverted £12000
b. "T" in "THREE" inverted £15000

Nos. 51 and 52 occur in two settings, one with 9¾ mm between value and upper bar, the other with 11 mm between value and upper bar.

BRITISH SOUTH AFRICA COMPANY.

(8)

9 (Ends of scrolls between legs of springboks)

1896 (22 May–Aug). *Cape of Good Hope stamps optd by Argus Printing Co, Cape Town, with T* 8. *Wmk Anchor (3d. wmk Crown CA). P* 14.

58 **6** ½d. grey-black (No. 48*a*) 6·00 11·00
59 **17** 1d. rose-red (No. 58) 9·50 12·00
60 **6** 2d. deep bistre (No. 50*a*) 10·00 7·00
61 3d. pale claret (No. 40) 45·00 55·00
62 4d. blue (No. 51) 12·00 12·00
a. "COMPANY," omitted £7000
63 **4** 6d. deep purple (No. 52*a*) 42·00 60·00
64 **6** 1s. yellow-ochre (No. 65) (Aug) 80·00 £110
58/64 *Set of* 7 £170 £225

(Eng J. A. C. Harrison (vignette), Bain or Rapkin (£1) (frames). Recess Waterlow)

1897. *P* 13½ *to* 16.

66 **9** ½d. grey-black and purple 1·60 3·00
67 1d. scarlet and emerald 3·00 3·75
68 2d. brown and mauve 3·25 60
69 3d. brown-red and slate-blue 2·50 30
a. Imperf between (vert pair) £1400
70 4d. ultramarine and claret 5·00 1·25
a. Imperf between (horiz pair) £4000 £4000
71 6d. dull purple and pink 5·50 3·50
72 8d. green and mauve/*buff* 8·50 40
a. Imperf between (vert pair) — £950
73 £1 black and red-brown/*green* £400 £225

(Recess Waterlow, from the Bradbury plate)

1897 (Jan). *P* 15.

74 **2** £2 rosy red £1600 £400

10

11

12

(Recess Waterlow)

1898–1908. *P* 13½ *to* 15½.

75 **10** ½d. dull bluish green 75 20
a. Yellow-green (1904) 85 30
aa. Imperf between (horiz pair) £650
ab. Imperf (pair) £600
76 ½d. deep green (*shades*) (1908) 23·00 60
77 1d. rose (*shades*) 1·00 15
a. Imperf (pair) £550 £550
b. Imperf between (vert pair) £500 £500
78 1d. red (*shades*) (1905) 2·50 30
a. Imperf between (pair) £350 £375
b. Imperf (pair) £500 £500
79 2d. brown 1·25 10
80 2½d. dull blue (*shades*) 3·75 30
a. Imperf between (horiz pair) £750 £750
b. Grey-blue (shades) (1903) 8·00 70
81 3d. claret 3·75 40
a. Imperf between (vert pair) £700
82 4d. olive 3·75 15
a. Imperf between (vert pair) £800
83 6d. reddish purple 6·50 1·75
a. Reddish mauve (1902) 12·00 5·00
84 **11** 1s. bistre 7·50 1·25
a. Imperf between (pair) £2250
b. Deep olive-bistre (1907) £275
bc. Imperf (pair) £2250
bd. Imperf between (horiz pair) £2500
c. Bistre-brown (1908) 42·00 10·00
d. Brownish yellow (1908) 14·00 4·25
85 2s. 6d. bluish grey (11.06) 28·00 55
a. Imperf between (vert pair) £900 £600
b. Imperf (vert pair) — £5000
86 3s. deep violet (1902) 9·00 50
a. Deep bluish violet (1908) 42·00 9·50
87 5s. brown-orange 24·00 8·50
88 7s. 6d. black (11.01) 45·00 14·00
89 10s. grey-green 15·00 1·50
90 **12** £1 greyish red-purple (*p* 15½) (7.01) £150 60·00
a. Perf 14. *Blackish purple* (1902) £190 60·00
91 £2 brown (5.08) 65·00 6·50
92 £5 deep blue (7.01) £3000 £2250
93 £10 lilac (7.01) £3000 £2250
93*a* £20 yellow-bistre (1901?) £8500
75/90 *Set of* 14 £250 80·00
80/1, 85/6, 88/93 Perf "Specimen" *Set of* 10 £900

A £100 cherry-red, perf 13½, was ordered in June 1901, a number of mint, together with three examples showing fiscal cancellations, being known.

13 Victoria Falls

RHODESIA.

(14)

(Recess Waterlow)

1905 (13 July). *Visit of British Association and Opening of Victoria Falls Bridge. P* 13½ *to* 15.

94 **13** 1d. red 2·75 3·00
95 2½d. deep blue 7·50 3·75
96 5d. claret (Optd S. £100) 18·00 40·00
97 1s. blue-green 18·00 23·00
a. Imperf (pair) £8000
b. Imperf between (horiz pair) £11000
c. Imperf between (vert pair) £11000
d. Imperf vert (horiz pair) £8500
98 2s. 6d. black £100 £150
99 5s. violet 85·00 40·00
94/9 *Set of* 6 £200 £225
94/9 Perf (5d.) or Optd (others) "Specimen" *Set of* 6 £250

1909 (15 Apr)–**12**. *Optd as T* 14. *P* 13½ *to* 15.

100 **10** ½d. green *to* deep green 1·25 20
a. No stop 42·00 27·00
b. Yellow-green (1911) 35·00 27·00
101 1d. carmine-rose 1·25 20
a. No stop 60·00 25·00
b. Imperf between (horiz pair) £300
c. Deep carmine-rose 1·25 20
cd. Imperf between (horiz pair) £350
102 2d. brown 1·60 2·00
a. No stop 75·00 50·00
103 2½d. pale dull blue 1·00 20
a. No stop 30·00 22·00
104 3d. claret 1·60 20
a. No stop 90·00 55·00
105 4d. olive 2·75 35
a. No stop 60·00 55·00
106 6d. reddish purple 5·00 1·25
a. No stop
b. Reddish mauve
c. Dull purple 12·00 2·50
ca. No stop 70·00 45·00
107 **11** 1s. bistre
a. No stop
b. Bistre-brown
ba. No stop
c. Deep brownish bistre 8·50 1·00
ca. No stop 75·00 32·00
108 2s. 6d. bluish grey 15·00 4·00
a. No stop 75·00 55·00
109 3s. deep violet 15·00 4·00
110 5s. orange 25·00 13·00
a. No stop 75·00 60·00
111 7s. 6d. black 55·00 11·00
112 10s. dull green 26·00 8·50
a. No stop £200 £180
113 **12** £1 grey-purple £100 60·00
a. Vert pair, one without opt £12000
b. Opt in violet £275 £225
113*c* £2 brown £3250 £325
113*d* £2 rosy brown (*bluish paper*) (*p* 14½×15) (1912) £3000 £300
113*e* £5 deep blue (*bluish paper*) £5000 £2250
100/13 *Set of* 14 £225 85·00
100/13 Perf "Specimen" *Set of* 14 £300

In some values the no stop variety occurs in every stamp in a vertical row of a sheet, in other values only once in a sheet. Other varieties, such as no serif to the right of apex of "A", no serif to top of "E", etc., exist in some values.

RHODESIA.
5d

(15)

RHODESIA.
TWO SHILLINGS.

(16)

1909 (April)–**11**. *Surch as T* 15 *and* 16 (2s.), *in black*.

114 **10** 5d. on 6d. reddish purple 6·50 7·00
a. Surcharge in violet 75·00
b. Reddish mauve
c. Dull purple 9·00 7·00
116 **11** 7½d. on 2s. 6d. bluish grey 3·50 2·25
a. Surcharge in violet 16·00 4·50
ab. Surch double † £6500
117 10d. on 3s. deep violet 13·00 14·00
a. Surcharge in violet 4·00 3·25
118 2s. on 5s. orange 12·00 7·00
114/18 Perf "Specimen" *Set of* 4 £180

In the 7½d. and 10d. surcharges the bars are spaced as in **T 16.**

17

18

(Recess Waterlow)

1910 (11 Nov)–**13**. (*a*) *P* 14.

119 **17** ½d. yellow-green 6·50 85
120 ½d. bluish green 11·00 85
a. Imperf (pair) £6500 £4000
121 ½d. olive-green 24·00 1·50
122 ½d. dull green 60·00 50·00
123 1d. bright carmine 10·00 30
a. Imperf between (pair) £15000 £10000
124 1d. carmine-lake 26·00 50
125 1d. rose-red 11·00 30
126 2d. black and grey 27·00 5·50
127 2d. black-purple and slate-grey £160
128 2d. black and slate-grey 29·00 4·00
129 2d. black and slate 29·00 5·00
130 2d. black and grey-black 32·00 7·50

131 17 2½d. ultramarine .. .. 15·00 5·00
131a 2½d. bright ultramarine .. .. .. 13·00 5·00
132 2½d. dull blue .. .. 15·00 5·00
133 2½d. chalky blue .. .. 15·00 9·00
134 3d. purple and ochre .. .. .. 20·00 20·00
135 3d. purple and yellow-ochre .. .. 22·00 6·00
136 3d. magenta and yellow-ochre .. .. 60·00 45·00
137 3d. violet and ochre .. .. .. 70·00 70·00
138 4d. greenish black and orange .. .. 75·00 70·00
139 4d. brown-purple and orange .. .. 55·00 35·00
140 4d. black and orange .. .. .. 23·00 10·00
141 5d. purple-brown and olive-green .. 20·00 32·00
141a 5d. purple-brown and olive-yellow .. 18·00 38·00
ab. Error. Purple-brown and ochre .. £550 £150
143 5d. lake-brown and olive .. .. £190 60·00
143a 5d. lake-brown and green £18000 £1500
144 6d. red-brown and mauve .. .. 18·00 19·00
145 6d. brown and purple .. .. .. 18·00 8·00
145a 6d. bright chestnut and mauve .. £650 60·00
146 8d. black and purple £3500
147 8d. dull purple and purple .. .. £100 65·00
148 8d. greenish black and purple .. £110 55·00
149 10d. scarlet and reddish mauve .. 26·00 48·00
150 10d. carmine and deep purple .. £500 70·00
151 1s. grey-black and deep blue-green 26·00 15·00
151a 1s. black and deep blue-green .. 75·00 22·00
152 1s. black and pale blue-green .. 25·00 9·00
152a 1s. purple-black and blue-green .. £200 38·00
153 2s. black and ultramarine .. .. 55·00 50·00
154 2s. black and dull blue .. .. £600 55·00
154a 2s. purple-black and ultramarine .. £2250 £200
155 2s. 6d. black and lake £300 £275
155a 2s. 6d. black and crimson £300 £275
156 2s. 6d. sepia and deep crimson .. £375 £325
156a 2s. 6d. bistre-brown and crimson .. £700 £500
157 2s. 6d. black and rose-carmine .. £275 £275
158 3s. green and violet (*shades*) .. £130 £130
158a 3s. bright green and magenta .. £950 £550
159 5s. vermilion and deep green .. £225 £200
160 5s. scarlet and pale yellow-green .. £275 £200
160a 5s. crimson and yellow-green .. £225 £200
160b 7s. 6d. carmine and pale blue .. £600 £500
161 7s. 6d. carmine and light blue .. £650 £550
162 7s. 6d. carmine and bright blue .. £1300 £700
163 10s. deep myrtle and orange £550 £250
164 10s. blue-green and orange £425 £250
165 £1 carmine-red and bluish black .. £900 £375
166 £1 rose-scarlet and bluish black .. £1000 £375
166a £1 crimson and slate-black .. £1100 £600
b. Error. Scarlet and reddish mauve £8500

(*b*) *P* 15
167 17 ½d. blue-green .. .. .. £250 13·00
168 ½d. yellow-green .. .. .. £250 11·00
169 ½d. apple-green .. .. .. £500 24·00
170 1d. carmine .. .. £250 7·00
170a 1d. carmine-lake .. .. .. £400 12·00
170b 1d. rose-carmine .. .. .. £250 9·00
171 2d. black and grey-black .. .. £600 26·00
171a 2d. black and grey .. .. .. £600 26·00
171b 2d. black and slate .. .. .. £600 26·00
172 2½d. ultramarine (*shades*) .. .. 70·00 35·00
173 3d. purple and yellow-ochre .. .. £2000 50·00
173a 3d. claret and pale yellow-ochre .. £1500 50·00
174 4d. black and orange (*shades*) .. 38·00 60·00
175 5d. lake-brown and olive-green .. £700 75·00
176 6d. brown and mauve .. .. .. £800 60·00
177 1s. black and blue-green (*shades*) .. £750 55·00
178 2s. black and dull blue £1100 £300
179 £1 red and black £11000 £3500

(*c*) *P* 15 × 14 *or* 14 × 15
179a 17 ½d. yellow-green .. .. .. † £2000
179b 1d. carmine .. .. † £3000
180 3d. purple and ochre £3000 £200
181 4d. black and orange £425
181a 1s. black and blue-green £16000 £3000

(*d*) *P* 13½
182 17 ½d. yellow-green .. .. .. £250 40·00
182a ½d. green .. .. £250 40·00
183 1d. bright carmine .. .. .. £1500 48·00
184 2½d. ultramarine (*shades*) .. .. 35·00 50·00
185 8d. black and purple (*shades*) .. 60·00 £200
185a 8d. grey-purple and dull purple £350 £350
119/185 Optd "Specimen" perf 14 except 2½d. and 8d. perf 13½ .. .. *Set of* 18 £2750

Plate varieties in T 17 are:—½d., double dot below "D" in right-hand value tablet (*from* £500 *un*. £350 *used*); 2d. to £1 excluding 2½d., straight stroke in Queen's right ear known as the "gash in ear" variety (*from* 3 *to* 8 *times normal*).

Stamps from the above and the next issue are known compound perf with 14 or 15 on one side only or on adjoining sides but we no longer list them.

(Recess Waterlow)

1913 (1 Sept)–**22**. *No wmk*. (i) *From single working plates*.

(*a*) *P* 14.
186 18 ½d. blue-green .. .. 3·75 40
187 ½d. deep green .. .. 1·50 40
a. Imperf horiz (vert pair) £500
188 ½d. yellow-green .. .. .. 4·25 40
188b ½d. dull green .. .. 2·50 40
ba. Imperf vert (horiz pair) £600 £600
189 ½d. bright green .. .. .. 5·50 50
a. Imperf between (vert pair) .. £900
190 1d. rose-carmine .. .. .. 3·00 40
a. Imperf between (pair) £425 £400
191 1d. carmine-red (*shades*) .. .. 5·00 40
a. Imperf between (pair) £800
192 1d. brown-red .. .. 2·25 30
193 1d. red .. .. 2·50 30
a. Imperf between (horiz pair) .. £600
194 1d. scarlet .. .. 8·50 55
a. Imperf between (horiz pair) .. £700
195 1d. rose-red .. .. 4·25 30
a. Imperf between (horiz pair) .. £425
b. Imperf between (vert pair) .. £1300
196 1d. rosine .. .. £500 19·00
197 1½d. brown-ochre (1919) .. .. 2·00 40
a. Imperf between (horiz pair) .. £400 £400
198 1½d. bistre-brown (1917) .. .. 2·00 40
a. Imperf between (horiz pair) .. £425 £400
199 18 1½d. drab-brown (1917) .. .. .. 2·00 40
a. Imperf between (horiz pair) .. £400
b. Imperf between (vert pair) .. £1200
200 2½d. deep blue .. .. 3·00 11·00
201 2½d. bright blue .. .. 3·00 11·00

(*b*) *P* 15
202 18 ½d. blue-green .. .. 8·50 7·00
203 ½d. green .. .. 12·00 7·00
204 1d. rose-red .. .. £500 75·00
a. Imperf between (horiz pair) .. £8000
205 1d. brown-red .. .. 2·00 3·50
206 1½d. bistre-brown (1919) .. .. 15·00 6·50
206a 1½d. brown-ochre (1917) .. .. 28·00 7·00
207 2½d. deep blue .. .. 17·00 24·00
208 2½d. bright blue .. .. 15·00 23·00

(*c*) *P* 14 × 15
208a 18 ½d. green £2250 £150

(*d*) *P* 15 × 14
208b 18 ½d. green £2250 £190

(*e*) *P* 13½
208d 18 1d. red (*shades*) .. .. — £500

Die I Die II Die III

The remaining values were printed from double, i.e. head and duty, plates. There are at least four different head plates made from three different dies, which may be distinguished as follows:—

Die I. The King's left ear is neither shaded nor outlined; no outline to top of cap. Shank of anchor in cap badge is complete.

Die II. The ear is shaded all over, but has no outline. The top of the cap has a faint outline. Anchor as Die I.

Die III. The ear is shaded and outlined; a heavy continuous outline round the cap. Shank of anchor is broken just below the lowest line which crosses it.

(ii) *Printed from double plates. Head Die* I. (*a*) *P* 14.
209 18 2d. black and grey .. .. .. 5·50 3·75
210 3d. black and yellow .. .. .. 50·00 4·00
211 4d. black and orange-red .. .. 4·00 17·00
212 5d. black and green .. .. .. 3·50 5·00
213 6d. black and mauve .. .. .. £130 23·00
213a 8d. violet and green £4000
214 2s. black and brown .. .. .. 60·00 50·00

(*b*) *P* 15
215 18 3d. black and yellow .. .. .. 4·00 9·00
216 4d. black and orange-red .. .. 90·00 11·00
217 6d. black and mauve .. .. .. 3·25 3·25
217a 8d. violet and green £13000
218 2s. black and brown .. .. .. 10·00 22·00

(iii) *Head Die* II. (*a*) *P* 14
219 18 2d. black and grey .. .. .. 7·50 1·25
220 2d. black and brownish grey .. .. 18·00 2·75
221 3d. black and deep yellow .. .. 18·00 2·75
222 3d. black and yellow .. .. .. 35·00 2·50
223 3d. black and buff .. .. .. 4·50 2·50
224 4d. black and orange-red .. .. 10·00 3·25
225 4d. black and deep orange-red .. 5·50 3·25
226 5d. black and grey-green .. .. 9·00 16·00
227 5d. black and bright green .. .. 7·50 16·00
228 6d. black and mauve .. .. .. 16·00 1·50
229 6d. black and purple .. .. .. 35·00 2·50
230 8d. violet and green .. .. .. 9·50 25·00
231 10d. blue and carmine-red .. .. 10·00 15·00
232 1s. black and greenish blue .. .. 15·00 16·00
233 1s. black and turquoise-blue .. .. 5·50 6·00
234 2s. black and brown .. .. .. 42·00 6·50
235 2s. black and yellow-brown .. .. £140 17·00
236 2s. 6d. indigo and grey-brown .. 35·00 14·00
236a 2s. 6d. pale blue and brown .. .. 75·00 22·00
236b 3s. brown and blue .. .. .. 60·00 80·00
237 3s. chestnut and bright blue .. .. 60·00 85·00
238 5s. blue and yellow-green .. .. 90·00 48·00
239 5s. blue and blue-green .. .. 42·00 48·00
240 7s. 6d. blackish purple and slate-black £170 £170
241 10s. crimson and yellow-green £150 £180
242 £1 black and purple £400 £450
243 £1 black and violet £450 £550

(*b*) *P* 15
244 18 2d. black and grey .. .. .. 3·25 3·75
245 4d. black and deep orange-vermilion .. £850 £225
246 8d. violet and green £170 £130
247 10d. blue and red .. .. .. 4·00 17·00
248 1s. black and greenish blue .. .. 20·00 5·00
249 2s. 6d. indigo and grey-brown .. 28·00 60·00
250 3s. chocolate and blue £800 £250
251 5s. blue and yellow-green .. .. 95·00 95·00
251a 5s. blue and blue-green £1300
252 7s. 6d. blackish purple and slate-black 75·00 £130
253 10s. red and green £150 £250
254 £1 black and purple £1000 £1000
254a £1 black and deep purple £2000 £2000
186/254a Optd "Specimen" (various Dies and Perfs) .. .. .. *Set of* 19 £1900

(iv) *Head Die* III. *Toned paper, yellowish gum*. (*a*) *P* 14
255 18 2d. black and brownish grey .. .. 6·50 3·00
256 2d. black and grey-black .. .. 3·50 1·40
a. Imperf between (horiz pair) .. £3750
b. Imperf between (horiz strip of 3) £5500
c. Imperf vert (horiz pair) £3250 £3250
257 2d. black and grey .. .. .. 4·00 1·90
258 2d. black and sepia .. .. .. 17·00 3·50
259 3d. black and yellow .. .. .. 3·50 1·40
260 3d. black and ochre .. .. .. 3·50 1·40
261 4d. black and orange-red .. .. 8·00 2·75
262 4d. black and dull red .. .. .. 7·00 3·25
263 5d. black and pale green .. .. 5·00 12·00
a. Imperf between (horiz strip of 3) £9000
264 18 5d. black and green .. .. .. 5·00 12·00
265 6d. black and reddish mauve .. .. 3·25 2·25
a. Imperf between (horiz pair) .. £7000
266 6d. black and dull mauve .. .. 3·25 2·25
267 8d. mauve and dull blue-green .. 15·00 32·00
268 8d. mauve and greenish blue .. .. 15·00 32·00
a. Imperf vert (horiz pair) £7000
269 10d. indigo and carmine .. .. .. 9·00 24·00
270 10d. blue and red .. .. 7·50 24·00
271 1s. black and greenish blue .. .. 5·00 2·75
272 1s. black and pale blue-green .. .. 5·00 2·75
272a 1s. black and light blue .. .. 9·00 4·50
272b 1s. black and green .. .. .. 45·00 19·00
273 2s. black and brown .. .. .. 12·00 14·00
aa. Imperf between (vert pair) .. † £14000
273a 2s. black and yellow-brown .. .. £1200 80·00
274 2s. 6d. dp ultramarine & grey-brn 23·00 27·00
274a 2s. 6d. pale blue and pale bistre-brown (*shades*) .. .. 60·00 32·00
274b 3s. chestnut and light blue .. .. £160 75·00
275 5s. deep blue and blue-green (*shades*) 60·00 48·00
276 5s. blue & pale yell-grn (*shades*) 60·00 48·00
276a 7s. 6d. maroon and slate-black .. £700 £850
277 10s. carmine-lake and yellow-green .. £300 £160
278 £1 black and bright purple £500 £500
279 £1 black and deep purple £500 £500
279a £1 black and violet-indigo £500 £500
279b £1 black and deep violet £500 £500

(*b*) *P* 15
279c 18 2d. black and brownish grey £5000 £550

Half Penny (19) Half- Penny. (20)

1917 (15 Aug). *No. 190 surch at the Northern Rhodesian Administrative Press, Livingstone, with T* **19**, *in violet or violet-black*.
280 18 ½d. on 1d. rose-carmine (*shades*) .. 2·00 4·75
a. Surch inverted £1500 £1500
b. Letters "n n" spaced wider .. 9·50 17·00
c. Letters "n y" spaced wider .. .. 6·50 11·00

The setting was in two rows of 10 repeated three times in the sheet.

The two colours of the surcharge occur on the same sheet.

1917 (22 Sept). *No. 190 surch as T* **20** (*new setting with hyphen, and full stop after* "Penny"), *in deep violet*.
281 18 ½d. on 1d. rose-carmine (*shades*) .. 1·25 3·25

1922–24. *New printings on white paper with clear white gum*.

(i) *Single working plates*. (*a*) *P* 14
282 18 ½d. dull green (1922) .. .. .. 5·50 75
a. Imperf between (vert pair) .. £1600 £1000
283 ½d. deep blue-green (1922) .. .. 4·75 1·25
284 1d. bright rose (1922) .. .. .. 4·75 2·25
285 1d. bright rose-scarlet (1923) .. .. 4·50 2·00
a. Imperf between (horiz pair) .. £1600
286 1d. aniline red (8.24) .. .. .. 20·00 3·00
287 1½d. brown-ochre (1923) .. .. .. 6·00 1·50
a. Imperf between (vert pair) .. £1600 £1000

(*b*) *P* 15
288 18 ½d. dull green (1923) .. .. .. 28·00 26·00
289 1d. bright rose-scarlet (1923) .. .. 38·00 35·00
290 1½d. brown-ochre (1923) .. .. .. 35·00 32·00

(ii) *Double plates. Head Die* III. (*a*) *P* 14
291 18 2d. black and grey-purple (1922) .. 1·75 1·00
292 2d. black and slate-purple (1923) .. 2·50 1·75
293 3d. black and yellow (1922) .. .. 10·00 12·00
294 4d. black & orange-vermilion (1922–3) 8·00 15·00
295 6d. jet-black and lilac (1922–3) .. 4·75 3·25
296 8d. mauve and pale blue-green (1922) 27·00 50·00
297 8d. violet and grey-green (1923) .. 27·00 50·00
298 10d. bright ultramarine and red (1922) 8·50 27·00
299 10d. brt ultramarine & carm-red (1923) 9·00 27·00
300 1s. black and dull blue (1922–3) .. 2·25 3·25
a. Imperf between (horiz pair) .. £6000
b. Imperf between (vert pair) .. £8000
301 2s. black and brown (1922–3) .. .. 17·00 21·00
302 2s. 6d. ultramarine and sepia (1922) .. 35·00 50·00
303 2s. 6d. violet-blue & grey-brown (1923) 35·00 50·00
304 3s. red-brown & turquoise-bl (1922) .. 50·00 75·00
305 3s. red-brown and grey-blue (1923) .. 80·00 95·00
306 5s. brt ultramarine and emerald (1922) 75·00 90·00
307 5s. deep blue and bright green (1923) 75·00 90·00
308 7s. 6d. brown-purple and slate (1922) £150 £200
309 10s. crimson and brt yellow-green (1922) £140 £170
310 10s. carmine and yellow-green (1923) .. £140 £190
311 £1 black and deep magenta (1922) .. £475 £550
311a £1 black and magenta (1923) £475 £550

(*b*) *P* 15 (1923)
312 18 2d. black and slate-purple .. .. 32·00
313 4d. black and orange-vermilion .. 35·00
314 6d. jet-black and lilac .. .. .. 40·00
315 8d. violet and grey-green .. .. 40·00
316 10d. bright ultramarine & carmine-red 50·00
317 1s. black and dull blue .. .. .. 50·00
318 2s. black and brown .. .. .. 90·00
319 2s. 6d. violet-blue and grey-brown .. £100
320 3s. red-brown and grey-blue £130
321 5s. deep blue and bright green £150
322 £1 black and magenta £600

The 1922 printing shows the mesh of the paper very clearly through the gum. In the 1923 printing the gum is very smooth and the mesh of the paper is not so clearly seen. Where date is given as "(1922–23)" two printings were made, which do not differ sufficiently in colour to be listed separately.

Nos. 312/22 were never sent out to Rhodesia but only issued in London. Any used copies could, therefore, only have been obtained by favour.

In 1924 Rhodesia was divided into NORTHERN and SOUTHERN RHODESIA (see ZAMBIA and ZIMBABWE), and between 1954 and 1964 these were merged in the Central African Federation (see RHODESIA AND NYASALAND). In 1964 there were again separate issues for Northern and Southern Rhodesia, but after the former became independent as Zambia, Southern Rhodesia was renamed Rhodesia in October 1964.

For issues inscribed "RHODESIA" between 1965 and 1978 see ZIMBABWE.

Rhodesia & Nyasaland

Stamps for the Central African Federation of Northern and Southern Rhodesia and Nyasaland Protectorate.

1

2

3 Queen Elizabeth II

(Recess Waterlow)

1954 (1 July)–**56.** *P* 13½×14 (*T* **1**), 13½×13 (*T* **2**) *or* 14½×13½ (*T* **3**).
1 **1** ½d. red-orange 15 10
a. Coil stamp. Perf 12½×14 (6.2.56) .. 25 1·50
2 1d. ultramarine 15 10
a. Coil stamp. Perf 12½×14. *Deep blue* (9.55) .. .. 40 5·00
ab. Ultramarine (1.10.55) .. .. 40 5·00
3 2d. bright green 15 10
3*a* 2½d. ochre (15.2.56) .. .. .. 2·00 10
4 3d. carmine-red 20 10
5 4d. red-brown 60 15
6 4½d. blue-green 15 25
7 6d. bright reddish purple 60 10
a. Bright purple (5.5.56) 70 10
8 9d. violet 65 70
9 1s. grey-black .. .. 1·00 10
10 **2** 1s. 3d. red-orange and ultramarine .. 2·25 10
11 2s. deep blue and yellow-brown .. 5·00 65
12 2s. 6d. black and rose-red .. .. 5·50 65
13 5s. violet and olive-green .. .. 11·00 2·00
14 **3** 10s. dull blue-green and orange .. 13·00 7·00
15 £1 olive-green and lake .. .. 22·00 20·00
1/15 .. .. *Set of* 16 55·00 29·00

Nos. 1a and 2a printed on rotary machines by subsidiary company, Imprimerie Belge de Securité, in Belgium.

4 Aeroplane over Victoria Falls

5 Livingstone and Victoria Falls

(Des J. E. Hughes (3d.), V. E. Horne (1s.). Recess Waterlow)

1955 (15 June). *Centenary of Discovery of Victoria Falls. P* 13½ (3*d.*) *or* 13 (1*s.*).
16 **4** 3d. ultramarine & dp turquoise-grn .. 20 20
17 **5** 1s. purple and deep blue 30 30

6 Tea Picking

10 Rhodes's Grave

11 Lake Bangweulu

12*a* Rhodesian Railway Trains

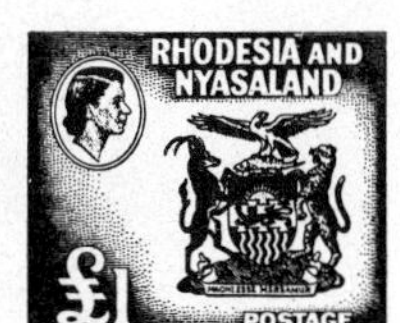

19 Federal Coat of Arms

(Des M. Kinsella (9d.). Recess Waterlow (½d., 1d., 2d., 1s.) until 1962, then D.L.R., D.L.R. (2½d., 4d., 6d., 9d., 2s., 2s. 6d.) and B.W. (others))

1959 (12 Aug)–**62.** *T* **6, 10/11, 12*a*, 19** *and similar designs. P* 13½ × 14 (½*d.*, 1*d.*, 2*d.*), 14½ (2½*d.*, 4*d.*, 6*d.*, 9*d.*, 2*s.*, 2*s.* 6*d.*), 14 × 13½ (3*d.*), 13½ × 13 (1*s.*), 14 (1*s.* 3*d.*) *or* 11 (*others*).
18 ½d. black and light emerald 40 30
a. Coil stamp. Perf 12½×14 .. .. 1·25 3·00
19 1d. carmine-red and black 15 10
a. Coil stamp. Perf 12½×14 .. .. 1·25 3·00
ab. Carmine-red and grey-black .. 1·25 3·00
ac. Carmine-red (centre) omitted .. £225
20 2d. violet and yellow-brown 40 20
21 2½d. purple and grey-blue 30 40
22 3d. black and blue 15 10
a. Centre omitted £850
23 4d. maroon and olive 70 10
24 6d. ultramarine and deep myrtle-green .. 35 10
24*a* 9d. orge-brown & reddish violet (15.5.62) 4·50 1·75
25 1s. light green and ultramarine .. 60 10
26 1s. 3d. emerald and deep chocolate .. 1·75 10
27 2s. grey-green and carmine .. .. 3·25 45
28 2s. 6d. light blue and yellow-brown .. 3·75 30
29 5s. deep chocolate and yellow-green .. 5·50 2·25
30 10s. olive-brown and rose-red .. .. 23·00 12·00
31 £1 black and deep violet .. .. 32·00 25·00
18/31 .. .. *Set of* 15 65·00 38·00

Designs: *Vert* (*as T* **6**)—1d. V.H.F. mast; 2d. Copper mining; 2½d. Fairbridge Memorial. (*As T* **11**)—6d. Eastern Cataract, Victoria Falls. *Horiz* (*as T* **12*a***)—1s. Tobacco; 1s. 3d. Lake Nyasa; 2s. Chirundu Bridge; 2s. 6d. Salisbury Airport. (*As T* **19**)—5s. Rhodes Statue; 10s. Mlanje.

20 Kariba Gorge, 1955

(Photo Harrison (3d., 6d.), D.L.R. (others))

1960 (17 May). *Opening of Kariba Hydro-Electric Scheme. T* **20** *and similar horiz designs. P* 14½ × 14 (3*d.*, 6*d.*) *or* 14 (*others*).
32 3d. blackish green and red-orange .. 35 10
a. Red-orange omitted £1000
33 6d. brown and yellow-brown 70 20
34 1s. slate-blue and green .. .. 1·75 1·50
35 1s. 3d. light blue and orange-brown .. 2·50 1·00
a. Blue and deep orange-brown .. 5·00 5·00
36 2s. 6d. deep slate-purple and orange-red .. 3·25 7·00
37 5s. reddish violet and turquoise-blue .. 6·50 11·00
32/7 .. .. *Set of* 6 13·50 19·00

Designs:—6d. 330 kV power lines; 1s. Barrage wall; 1s. 3d. Barrage and lake; 2s. 6d. Interior of power station; 5s. Barrage wall and Queen Mother (top left).

26 Miner Drilling

(Des V. Whiteley. Photo Harrison)

1961 (8 May). *Seventh Commonwealth Mining and Metallurgical Congress. T* **26** *and similar horiz design. P* 15 × 14.
38 6d. olive-green and orange-brown 30 15
39 1s. 3d. black and light blue 40 60

Design:—1s. 3d. Surface installations, Nchanga Mine.

28 D.H. "Hercules" on Rhodesian Airstrip

31 Tobacco Plant

1962 (6 Feb). *30th Anniv of First London-Rhodesia Airmail Service. T* **28** *and similar horiz designs. P* 14½ × 14.
40 6d. bronze-green and vermilion 35 25
41 1s. 3d. light blue, black and yellow .. .. 1·00 50
42 2s. 6d. rose-red and deep violet .. .. 6·00 4·25
40/2 .. .. *Set of* 3 6·50 4·50

Designs:—1s. 3d. Empire "C" class flying-boat taking off from Zambesi; 2s. 6d. "Comet" at Salisbury airport.

(Des V. Whiteley. Photo Harrison)

1963 (18 Feb). *World Tobacco Congress, Salisbury. T* **31** *and similar vert designs. P* 14 × 14½.
43 3d. green and olive-brown 15 10
44 6d. green, brown and blue 20 35
45 1s. 3d. chestnut and indigo 30 45
46 2s. 6d. yellow and brown .. .. .. 75 2·50
43/6 .. .. *Set of* 4 1·25 3·00

Designs:—6d. Tobacco field; 1s. 3d. Auction floor; 2s. 6d. Cured tobacco.

35 Red Cross Emblem

(Photo Harrison)

1963 (6 Aug). *Red Cross Centenary. P* 14½ × 14.
47 **35** 3d. red 30 10

36 African "Round Table" Emblem

(Des V. Whiteley. Photo Harrison)

1963 (11 Sept). *World Council of Young Men's Service Clubs, Salisbury. P* 14½ × 14.
48 **36** 6d. black, gold and yellow-green .. 20 50
49 1s. 3d. black, gold, yell-grn & lilac .. 30 40

POSTAGE DUE STAMPS

The 1d. and 2d. (Nos. 2/3) exist with a rubber-stamped "POSTAGE DUE" cancellation. In the absence of proper labels these values were used as postage dues at the Salisbury G.P.O. but according to the G.P.O. the handstamp was intended as a cancellation and not as an overprint (although "unused" examples of the 1d. are known). Its use was discontinued at the end of August 1959.

D 1

(Typo Federal Printing and Stationery Dept, Salisbury)

1961 (19 Apr). *P* 12½.
D1 D **1** 1d. vermilion .. .. 1·25 3·00
a. Imperf between (horiz pair) .. £275 £325
D2 2d. deep violet-blue .. .. .. 1·75 3·00
D3 4d. green .. .. 1·75 4·50
D4 6d. purple .. .. 2·50 7·00
a. Imperf between (horiz pair) .. £500
D1/4 .. .. *Set of* 4 6·50 16·00

The 2d. has a stop below the "D".

The stamps of the Federation were withdrawn on 19 February 1964 when all three constituent territories had resumed issuing their own stamps.

Sabah
see Malaysia

St. Helena

CROWN COLONY

PRICES FOR STAMPS ON COVER TO 1945	
Nos. 1/2*a*	*from* × 12
Nos. 3/5	*from* × 6
Nos. 6/45	*from* × 10
Nos. 46/52	*from* × 4
Nos. 53/67	*from* × 3
No. 71	—
Nos. 72/86	*from* × 3
Nos. 87/8	*from* × 10
Nos. 89/95	*from* × 3
No. 96	—
Nos. 97/110	*from* × 3
Nos. 111/13	—
Nos. 114/40	*from* × 2

1

ONE PENNY
(2)

FOUR PENCE
(3)

(Recess P.B.)

Wmk Large Star, W w 1

1856 (1 Jan). *Imperf.*
1 1 6d. blue .. £500 £180

1861 (April (?)). (*a*) *Clean-cut perf* 14 *to* 16.
2 1 6d. blue .. £1300 £250
(*b*) *Rough perf* 14 *to* 16
2*a* 1 6d. blue .. £400 £130

NOTE: The issues which follow consist of 6d. stamps, T 1, printed in various colours and (except in the case of the 6d. values) surcharged with a new value, as T **2** to **10**, *e.g.* stamps described as "1d." are, in fact, 1d. on 6d stamps, and so on.
The numbers in the Type column below refer to the *types of the lettering* of the surcharged value.

(Printed by D.L.R. from P.B. plate)

Two Types of Bar on 1d. value:
A. Bar 16–17 mm long.
B. Bar 18½–19 mm long.

1863 (July). *Wmk Crown CC. Surch as T* **2/3** *with thin bar approximately the same length as the words. Imperf.*
3 2 1d. lake (Type A) .. £110 £140
a. Surch double .. £4000 £2500
b. Surch omitted .. £10000
4 1d. lake (Type B) .. £110 £140
a. Vert pair. Nos. 3/4 .. £2250
5 3 4d. carmine (*bar* 15½–16½ *mm*) .. £500 £250
a. Surch double .. £7500 £7500

ONE PENNY (4 (A))
ONE PENNY (4 (B))
ONE PENNY (4 (C))
TWO PENCE (5)
THREE PENCE (6)
FOUR PENCE (7)
ONE SHILLING (8)
FIVE SHILLINGS (9)

Three Types of Bar:
A. Thin bar (16½ to 17 mm) nearly the same length as the words.
B. Thick bar (14 to 14½ mm) much shorter than the words, except on the 2d. (Nos. 9, 22, 28) where it is nearly the same length.
C. Long bar (17 to 18 mm) same length as the words.

1864–80. *Wmk Crown CC. 6d. as T* 1, *without surcharge.*

(*a*) *P* 12½ (1864–73)
6 4 1d. lake (Type A) (1864) .. 27·00 24·00
a. Surch double .. £4500
7 1d. lake (Type B) (1868) .. 80·00 50·00
a. Surch double
b. Imperf .. £2000
8 1d. lake (Type C) (1871) .. 40·00 16·00
a. Surch in blue-black .. £850 £550
9 5 2d. yellow (Type B) (1868) .. 90·00 60·00
a. Imperf .. £8000
10 2d. yellow (Type C) (1873) .. 70·00 38·00
a. Surch in blue-black .. £4500 £2750
b. Surch double, one albino
11 6 3d. deep dull purple (Type B) (1868) .. 55·00 48·00
a. Surch double .. — £6000
b. Imperf .. £750
c. Light purple .. £2750 £750
12 3d. deep dull purple (Type A) (1873) .. 75·00 48·00
13 7 4d. carmine (Type A) (1864) .. 90·00 40·00
a. Surch double .. — £5500
14 4d. carmine (Type B) (*words* 18 *mm long*) (1868) .. 70·00 45·00
a. Surch double .. — £4500
b. Surch double (18 + 19 *mm widths*) £11000 £9000
c. Imperf .. £7500
15 4d. carmine-rose (Type B) (*words* 19 *mm long*) (1868) .. £180 £120
a. Surch omitted .. † —
16 – 6d. dull blue (1871) .. £550 £100
a. Ultramarine (1873) .. £275 80·00
17 8 1s. deep yellow-green (Type A) (1864) £110 26·00
a. Surch double .. — £18000
18 1s. deep yellow-green (Type B) (1868) £325 £120
a. Surch double .. £10000
b. Imperf .. £12000
c. Surch omitted* .. £10000
19 1s. deep green (Type C) (1871) .. £190 16·00
a. Surch in blue-black
20 9 5s. orange (Type B) (1868) .. 35·00 45·00
a. Yellow .. £325 £275

(*b*) *P* 14 × 12½ (1876)
21 4 1d. lake (Type B) .. 48·00 15·00
22 5 2d. yellow (Type B) .. 60·00 50·00
23 3d. purple (Type B) .. £170 70·00
24 4d. carmine (Type B) (*words* 16½ *mm long*) .. 80·00 60·00
25 – 6d. milky blue .. £250 30·00
26 8 1s. deep green (Type C) .. £275 20·00

(*c*) *P* 14 (1880)
27 4 1d. lake (Type B) .. 55·00 16·00
28 5 2d. yellow (Type B) .. 75·00 18·00
29 – 6d. milky blue .. £250 40·00
30 8 1s. yellow-green (Type B) .. 20·00 12·00

The only known copy of No. 15a is in the Royal Collection, although a second badly damaged example may exist.
*No. 18c is from a sheet of the 1s. with surcharge misplaced, the fifth row of 12 stamps being thus doubly surcharged and the tenth row without surcharge.

2½d (10)

11

12

1884–94. *Wmk Crown CA. T* 1 *surch. Bars similar to Type* B *above (except* 2½*d., T* **10**, *and the* 1s., *in which the bar is nearly the same length as the words). The* 6d. *as before without surcharge. P* 14.
34 – ½d. green (*words* 17 *mm*) (1884) .. 2·50 5·00
a. "N" and "Y" spaced .. £350
35 – ½d. emerald (*words* 17 *mm*) (1885) .. 6·00 7·50
a. "N" and "Y" spaced .. £700
b. Surch double .. £900
ba. Ditto. "N" and "Y" spaced* .. £9000
36 – ½d. deep green (*words* 14½ *mm*) (1893) 90 1·10
37 4 1d. red (1887) .. 2·75 2·00
38 1d. pale red (1890) .. 2·75 2·00
39 5 2d. yellow (1894) .. 1·25 3·50
40 10 2½d. ultramarine (1893) .. 2·00 5·00
a. Surch double .. £10000
b. Stamp doubly printed .. £5000
41 6 3d. deep mauve (1887) .. 2·00 2·75
a. Surch double .. — £9000
42 3d. deep reddish lilac (1887) .. 4·50 7·00
a. Surch double .. £6500 £6000
43 7 4d. pale brown (*words* 16½ *mm*) (1890) 9·00 16·00
a. Additional thin bar in surch (R. 7/4) £425
43*b* 4d. sepia (*words* 17 *mm*) (1894) .. 14·00 8·00
44 – 6d. grey (1887) .. 10·00 3·50
45 8 1s. yellow-green (1894) .. 23·00 14·00
a. Surch double .. £4250
40/1, 43, 44 Optd "Specimen" .. *Set of* 4 £180

Examples of the above are sometimes found showing no watermark; these are from the bottom row of the sheet, which had escaped the watermark, the paper being intended for stamps of a different size to Type **1**.
Some are found without bar and others with bar at top of stamp, due to careless overprinting.
Of the 2½d. with double surcharge only six copies exist, and of the 2½d. double printed, one row of 12 stamps existed on one sheet only.
*No. 35ba. No. 35a occurs on stamp No. 216 in the sheet. In No. 35ba only one of the two surcharges shows the variety.

CANCELLATIONS. Nos. 36/45 and No. 20, have been sold cancelled with a violet diamond-shaped grill with four interior bars extending over two stamps. These cannot be considered as *used* stamps, and they are consequently not priced in the list.
This violet obliteration is easily removed and many of these remainders have been cleaned and offered as unused; some are repostmarked with a date and name in thin type rather larger than the original, a usual date being "Ap. 4.01."

(Typo D.L.R.)

1890–97. *Wmk Crown CA. Plate I for the* 1½*d. Plate II for the other values (for differences see Seychelles). P* 14.
46 11 ½d. green (1897) .. 2·75 4·50
47 1d. carmine (1896) .. 6·50 1·00
48 1½d. red-brown and green (1890) .. 4·25 6·00
49 2d. orange-yellow (1896) .. 4·00 8·50
50 2½d. ultramarine (1896) .. 5·00 9·00
51 5d. mauve (1896) .. 11·00 23·00
52 10d. brown (1896) .. 15·00 42·00
46/52 .. *Set of* 7 42·00 85·00
46/52 Optd "Specimen" .. *Set of* 7 £275

The note below No. 45a *re* violet diamond-shaped grill cancellation also applies to Nos. 46/52.

1902. *Wmk Crown CA. P* 14.
53 12 ½d. green (Mar) .. 1·50 90
54 1d. carmine (24 Feb) .. 3·50 70
53/4 Optd "Specimen" .. *Set of* 2 70·00

13 Government House

14 The Wharf

(Typo D.L.R.)

1903 (May). *Wmk Crown CC. P* 14.
55 13 ½d. brown and grey-green .. 2·00 2·25
56 14 1d. black and carmine .. 1·50 35
57 13 2d. black and sage-green .. 6·00 1·25
58 14 8d. black and brown .. 14·00 32·00
59 13 1s. brown and brown-orange .. 14·00 27·00
60 14 2s. black and violet .. 42·00 70·00
55/60 .. *Set of* 6 70·00 £120
55/60 Optd "Specimen" .. *Set of* 6 £200

A printing of the 1d. value in Type **14** in red only on Mult Crown CA paper was made in 1911, but not sold to the public. Examples are known overprinted "SPECIMEN" (*Price* £350).

MINIMUM PRICE

The minimum price quote is 10p which represents a handling charge rather than a basis for valuing common stamps. For further notes about prices see introductory pages.

15

(Typo D.L.R.)

1908 (May)–**11.** *P* 14. (*a*) *Wmk Mult Crown CA. Ordinary paper* (2½*d.*) *or chalk-surfaced paper* (4*d.*, 6*d.*).
64 15 2½d. blue .. 1·00 1·40
66 4d. black and red/*yellow* .. 3·00 6·50
a. Ordinary paper (1911) .. 1·25 4·25
67 6d. dull and deep purple .. 4·50 13·00
a. Ordinary paper (1911) .. 2·75 9·50
(*b*) *Wmk Crown CA. Chalk-surfaced paper.*
71 15 10s. green and red/*green* .. £180 £225
64/71 .. *Set of* 4 £180 £225
64/71 Optd "Specimen" .. *Set of* 4 £225

16

17

(Typo D.L.R.)

1912–16. *Wmk Mult Crown CA. P* 14.
72 16 ½d. black and green .. 1·25 5·00
73 17 1d. black and carmine-red .. 1·25 1·00
a. Black and scarlet (1916) .. 24·00 27·00
74 1½d. black and dull orange (1913) .. 2·00 4·25
75 16 2d. black and greyish slate .. 2·00 1·75
76 17 2½d. black and bright blue .. 1·75 5·00
77 16 3d. black and purple/*yellow* (1913) 2·00 5·00
78 17 8d. black and dull purple .. 5·50 38·00
79 16 1s. black and black/*green* .. 8·00 19·00
80 17 2s. black and blue/*blue* .. 27·00 55·00
81 3s. black and violet (1913) .. 48·00 85·00
72/81 .. *Set of* 10 90·00 £200
72/81 Optd "Specimen" .. *Set of* 10 £250
No. 73*a* is on thicker paper than 73.

18

19

TAGE
Split "A"

(Typo D.L.R.)

1912. *Wmk Mult Crown CA. Chalk-surfaced paper. P* 14.
83 18 4d. black and red/*yellow* .. 4·00 13·00
84 6d. dull and deep purple .. 2·50 5·00
83/4 Optd "Specimen" .. *Set of* 2 60·00

1913. *Wmk Mult Crown CA. P* 14.
85 19 4d. black and red/*yellow* .. 5·50 3·50
a. Split "A" .. 90·00
86 6d. dull and deep purple .. 9·50 20·00
a. Split "A" .. £150
85/6 Optd "Specimen" .. *Set of* 2 70·00

WAR TAX ONE PENNY (20)

WAR TAX 1d. (21)

1916 (Sept). *As No.* 73*a*, *on thin paper, surch with T* **20**.
87 17 1d. + 1d. black and scarlet (Optd S. £50) 85 2·25
a. Surch double .. — £6000

1919. *No.* 73 *on thicker paper, surch with T* **21**.
88 17 1d. + 1d. black and carmine-red (*shades*) (Optd S. £50) .. 40 3·00

1922 (Jan). *Printed in one colour. Wmk Mult Script CA. P* 14.
89 17 1d. green .. 50 15·00
90 1½d. rose-scarlet .. 6·00 25·00
91 16 3d. bright blue .. 12·00 35·00
89/91 .. *Set of* 3 17·00 65·00
89/91 Optd "Specimen" .. *Set of* 3 75·00

22 Badge of St. Helena

PLATE FLAWS ON THE 1922–37 ISSUE. Many constant plate varieties exist on both the vignette and duty plates of this issue.

The three major varieties are illustrated and listed below with prices for mint examples. Fine used stamps showing these flaws are worth a considerable premium over the mint prices quoted.

a. Broken mainmast. Occurs on R.2/1 of all sheets from the second printing onwards. It does not appear on Nos. 93/6 and 112/13 as these stamps only exist from the initial printing invoiced in May 1922.

b. Torn flag. Occurs on R.4/6 of all sheets from printings up to and including that invoiced in December 1922. The flaw was retouched for the printing invoiced in December 1926 and so does not occur on Nos. 99e, 103 and 107/10.

c. Cleft rock. Occurs on R.5/1 of all sheets from the second printing onwards. It does not appear on Nos. 93/6 and 112/13 as these stamps only exist from the initial printing invoiced in May 1922.

(Des T. Bruce. Typo D.L.R.)

1922 (June)–**37.** *P* 14 (*a*) *Wmk Mult Crown CA. Chalk-surfaced paper.*

No.	Type	Description	Unused	Used
92	**22**	4d. grey and black/*yellow* (2.23)	5·00	7·00
		a. Broken mainmast	90·00	
		b. Torn flag	90·00	
		c. Cleft rock	80·00	
93		1s. 6d. grey and green/*blue-green*	20·00	45·00
		b. Torn flag	£350	
94		2s. 6d. grey and red/*yellow*	22·00	48·00
		b. Torn flag	£400	
95		5s. grey and green/*yellow*	35·00	70·00
		b. Torn flag	£450	
96		£1 grey and purple/*red*	£400	£450
		b. Torn flag	£1500	
92/6 Optd "Specimen"		*Set of* 5	£500	

The paper of No. 93 is bluish on the surface with a full green back.

(*b*) *Wmk Mult Script CA. Ordinary paper* (1s. 6d., 2s. 6d., 5s.) *or chalk-surfaced paper* (others).

No.	Type	Description	Unused	Used
97	**22**	½d. grey and black (2.23)	90	1·25
		a. Broken mainmast	30·00	
		b. Torn flag	55·00	
		c. Cleft rock	27·00	
98		1d. grey and green	1·50	80
		a. Broken mainmast	35·00	
		b. Torn flag	35·00	
		c. Cleft rock	30·00	
99		1½d. rose-red (2.23)	2·50	7·00
		a. Broken mainmast	80·00	
		b. Torn flag	80·00	
		c. Cleft rock	80·00	
		d. *Carmine-rose*	19·00	21·00
		da. Broken mainmast	£200	
		db. Torn flag	£200	
		dc. Cleft rock	£200	
		e. *Deep carmine-red* (1937)	80·00	£100
		ea. Broken mainmast	£500	
		ec. Cleft rock	£500	
100		2d. grey and slate (2.23)	1·50	2·00
		a. Broken mainmast	60·00	
		b. Torn flag	60·00	
		c. Cleft rock	50·00	
101		3d. bright blue (2.23)	1·75	4·00
		a. Broken mainmast	60·00	
		b. Torn flag	60·00	
		c. Cleft rock	50·00	
103	**22**	5d. green and carmine/*green* (1927)	2·50	5·50
		a. Broken mainmast	£110	
		c. Cleft rock	£100	
104		6d. grey and bright purple	3·25	8·00
		a. Broken mainmast	£120	
		b. Torn flag	£110	
		c. Cleft rock	£100	
105		8d. grey and bright violet (2.23)	3·25	6·50
		a. Broken mainmast	£150	
		b. Torn flag	£150	
		c. Cleft rock	£130	
106		1s. grey and brown	4·75	8·50
		a. Broken mainmast	£160	
		b. Torn flag	£120	
		c. Cleft rock	£110	
107		1s. 6d. grey and green/*green* (1927)	10·00	35·00
		a. Broken mainmast	£200	
		c. Cleft rock	£200	
108		2s. purple and blue/*blue* (1927)	10·00	30·00
		a. Broken mainmast	£200	
		c. Cleft rock	£200	
109		2s. 6d. grey and red/*yellow* (1927)	12·00	40·00
		a. Broken mainmast	£200	
		c. Cleft rock	£200	
110		5s. grey and green/*yellow* (1927)	30·00	60·00
		a. Broken mainmast	£350	
		c. Cleft rock	£350	
111		7s. 6d. grey and yellow-orange	75·00	£120
		a. Broken mainmast	£650	
		b. Torn flag	£550	
		c. Cleft rock	£650	
112		10s. grey and olive-green	£110	£160
		b. Torn flag	£750	
113		15s. grey and purple/*blue*	£850	£1400
		b. Torn flag	£2750	
97/112		*Set of* 15	£250	£350
97/113 Optd "Specimen"		*Set of* 16	£1000	

23 Lot and Lot's Wife

24 The "Plantation"

30 St. Helena

32 Badge of St. Helena

(Recess B.W.)

1934 (23 April). *Centenary of British Colonisation. T* **23/4, 30, 32** *and similar horiz designs. Wmk Mult Script CA. P* 12.

No.	Description	Unused	Used
114	½d. black and purple	45	80
115	1d. black and green	50	85
116	1½d. black and scarlet	2·00	2·50
117	2d. black and orange	1·75	1·25
118	3d. black and blue	1·40	4·50
119	6d. black and light blue	3·25	3·00
120	1s. black and chocolate	6·00	18·00
121	2s. 6d. black and lake	32·00	48·00
122	5s. black and chocolate	75·00	85·00
123	10s. black and purple	£200	£250
114/123	*Set of* 10	£275	£350
114/23 Perf "Specimen"	*Set of* 10	£350	

Design:—1½d. Map of St. Helena; 2d. Quay at Jamestown; 3d. James Valley; 6d. Jamestown; 1s. Munden's Promontory; 5s. High Knoll.

1935 (6 May). *Silver Jubilee. As Nos.* 114/17 *of Jamaica, but ptd by D.L.R. P* 13½×14.

No.	Description	Unused	Used
124	1½d. deep blue and carmine	75	2·00
	f. Diagonal line by turret	45·00	
125	2d. ultramarine and grey	1·25	90
	f. Diagonal line by turret	55·00	
126	6d. green and indigo	5·50	1·75
	f. Diagonal line by turret	£100	
	h. Dot by flagstaff	£100	
127	1s. slate and purple	6·50	10·00
	h. Dot flagstaff	£120	
124/7	*Set of* 4	12·50	13·00
124/7 Perf "Specimen"	*Set of* 4	95·00	

For illustrations of plate varieties see Omnibus section following Zimbabwe.

1937 (19 May). *Coronation. As Nos.* 118/20 *of Jamaica.*

No.	Description	Unused	Used
128	1d. green	30	15
129	2d. orange	75	15
130	3d. bright blue	1·00	25
128/30	*Set of* 3	1·90	50
128/30 Perf "Specimen"	*Set of* 3	55·00	

33 Badge of St. Helena

(Recess Waterlow)

1938 (12 May)–**44.** *Wmk Mult Script CA. P* 12½.

No.	Type	Description	Unused	Used
131	**33**	½d. violet	10	30
132		1d. green	20·00	4·00
132*a*		1d. yellow-orange (8.7.40)	15	20
133		1½d. scarlet	15	30
134		2d. red-orange	15	10
135		3d. ultramarine	90·00	30·00
135*a*		3d. grey (8.7.40)	30	15
135*b*		4d. ultramarine (8.7.40)	70	20
136		6d. light blue	80	15
136*a*		8d. sage-green (8.7.40)	2·00	75
		b. Olive-green (24.5.44)	4·50	3·00
137		1s. sepia	35	25
138		2s. 6d. maroon	8·00	2·75
139		5s. chocolate	11·00	7·50
140		10s. purple	11·00	15·00
131/140		*Set of* 14	£130	55·00
131/40 Perf "Specimen"		*Set of* 14	£300	

See also Nos. 149/51.

1946 (21 Oct). *Victory. As Nos.* 141/2 *of Jamaica.*

No.	Description	Unused	Used
141	2d. red-orange	10	10
142	4d. blue	10	10
141/2 Perf "Specimen"	*Set of* 2	60·00	

1948 (20 Oct). *Royal Silver Wedding. As Nos.* 143/4 *of Jamaica.*

No.	Description	Unused	Used
143	3d. black	30	20
144	10s. violet-blue	18·00	23·00

1949 (10 Oct). *75th Anniv of U.P.U. As Nos.* 145/8 *of Jamaica.*

No.	Description	Unused	Used
145	3d. carmine	75	30
146	4d. deep blue	1·50	90
147	6d. olive	1·75	90
148	1s. blue-black	1·75	1·10
145/8	*Set of* 4	5·25	3·00

1949 (1 Nov). *Wmk Mult Script CA. P* 12½.

No.	Type	Description	Unused	Used
149	**33**	1d. black and green	40	80
150		1½d. black and carmine	40	80
151		2d. black and scarlet	40	80
149/51		*Set of* 3	1·10	2·25

1953 (2 June). *Coronation. As No.* 153 *of Jamaica.*

No.	Description	Unused	Used
152	3d. black and deep reddish violet	70	65

34 Badge of St. Helena

35 Heart-shaped Waterfall

(Recess D.L.R.)

1953 (4 Aug)–**59.** *Horiz designs as T* **34**, *and T* **35**. *Wmk Mult Script CA. P* 14.

No.	Description	Unused	Used
153	½d. black and bright green	30	30
154	1d. black and deep green	15	20
155	1½d. black and reddish purple	1·25	60
	a. Black & deep reddish purple (14.1.59)	2·75	1·75
156	2d. black and claret	50	30
157	2½d. black and red	40	30
158	3d. black and brown	2·50	30
159	4d. black and deep blue	40	40
160	6d. black and deep lilac	40	30
161	7d. black and grey-black	65	4·25
162	1s. black and carmine	40	40
163	2s. 6d. black and violet	8·50	6·50
164	5s. black and deep brown	12·00	9·00
165	10s. black and yellow-orange	40·00	20·00
153/65	*Set of* 13	60·00	35·00

Designs:—1d. Flax plantation; 2d. Lace-making; 2½d. Drying flax; 3d. St. Helena Sand Plover; 4d. Flagstaff and The Barn; 6d. Donkeys carrying flax; 7d. Island map; 1s. The Castle; 2s. 6d. Cutting flax; 5s. Jamestown; 10s. Longwood House.

45 Stamp of 1856

(Recess D.L.R.)

1956 (3 Jan). *St. Helena Stamp Centenary. Wmk Mult Script CA. P* 11½.

No.	Type	Description	Unused	Used
166	**45**	3d. Prussian blue and carmine	10	10
167		4d. Prussian blue and reddish brown	10	10
168		6d. Prussian blue & dp reddish purple	15	15
166/8		*Set of* 3	30	30

46 Arms of East India Company

(Recess Waterlow)

1959 (5 May). *Tercentenary of Settlement. T* **46** *and similar horiz designs. W* w **12**. *P* 12½ × 13.

169	3d. black and scarlet	10	10
170	6d. light emerald and slate-blue	30	25
171	1s. black and orange	30	25
169/71	*Set of* 3	65	55

Designs:—6d. East Indiaman *London* off James Bay; 1s. Commemoration Stone.

ST. HELENA
Tristan Relief
9d +

(49)

1961 (12 Oct). *Tristan Relief Fund. Nos.* 46 *and* 49/51 *of Tristan da Cunha surch as T* **49** *by Govt Printer, Jamestown.*

172	2½ c. + 3d. black and brown-red	—	£400
173	5 c. + 6d. black and blue	—	£400
174	7½ c. + 9d. black and rose-carmine	—	£475
175	10 c. + 1s. black and light brown	—	£550
172/5	*Set of* 4	£4000	£1600

The above stamps were withdrawn from sale on 19 October, 434 complete sets having been sold.

50 Cunning Fish

51 Yellow Canary

53 Queen Elizabeth II

63 Queen Elizabeth II with Prince Andrew (after Cecil Beaton)

(Des V. Whiteley. Photo Harrison)

1961 (12 Dec)–**65**. *T* **50/1**, **53**, **63** *and similar designs. W* w **12**. *P* 11½ × 12 (*horiz*), 12 × 11½ (*vert*) *or* 14½ × 14 (£1).

176	1d. brt blue, dull violet, yellow & carmine	10	10
	a. Chalk-surfaced paper (4.5.65)	1·25	20
177	1½d. yellow, green, black and light drab	30	10
178	2d. scarlet and grey	15	10
179	3d. light blue, black, pink and deep blue	50	20
	a. Chalk-surfaced paper (30.11.65)	1·00	20
180	4½d. yellow-green, green, brown and grey	60	30
181	6d. red, sepia and light yellow-olive	2·25	35
	a. Chalk-surfaced paper (30.11.65)	3·50	35
182	7d. red-brown, black and violet	35	50
183	10d. brown-purple and light blue	35	40
184	1s. greenish yellow, bluish green & brown	35	40
185	1s. 6d. grey, black and slate-blue	7·50	3·00
186	2s. 6d. red, pale yellow and turquoise (*chalk-surfaced paper*)	2·50	1·50
187	5s. yellow, brown and green	8·50	2·75
188	10s. orange-red, black and blue	17·00	8·50
189	£1 chocolate and light blue	22·00	17·00
	a. Chalk-surfaced paper (30.11.65)	30·00	32·00
176/89 (*cheapest*)	*Set of* 14	55·00	32·00

Designs: *Horiz* (*as T* **50**)—2d. Brittle Starfish; 7d. Trumpet Fish; 10d. Feather Starfish; 2s. 6d. Orange Starfish; 10s. Deep-water Bull's-eye. *Vert* (*as T* **51**)—4½d. Red-wood Flower; 6d. Madagascar Red Fody; 1s. Gum-wood Flower; 1s. 6d. White Tern; 5s. Night-blooming Cereus.

1963 (4 June). *Freedom from Hunger. As No.* 80 *of Lesotho.*

190	1s. 6d. ultramarine	2·50	40

1963 (2 Sept). *Red Cross Centenary. As Nos.* 203/4 *of Jamaica.*

191	3d. red and black	75	25
192	1s. 6d. red and blue	3·00	75

COVER PRICES

Cover factors are quoted at the beginning of each country for most issues to 1945. An explanation of the system can be found on page x. The factors quoted do not, however, apply to philatelic covers.

FIRST LOCAL POST
4th JANUARY 1965

(64)

65 Badge of St. Helena

1965 (4 Jan). *First Local Post. Nos.* 176, 179, 181 *and* 185 *optd with T* **64**.

193	1d. bright blue, dull violet, yellow & carmine	10	10
194	3d. light blue, black, pink and deep blue	10	10
195	6d. red, sepia and light yellow-olive	20	10
196	1s. 6d. grey, black and slate-blue	25	15
193/6	*Set of* 4	50	30

1965 (17 May). *I.T.U. Centenary. As Nos.* 98/9 *of Lesotho.*

197	3d. blue and grey-brown	35	15
198	6d. bright purple and bluish green	55	15

1965 (15 Oct). *International Co-operation Year. As Nos.* 100/1 *of Lesotho.*

199	1d. reddish purple and turquoise-green	20	15
200	6d. deep bluish green and lavender	55	15

1966 (24 Jan). *Churchill Commemoration. As Nos.* 102/5 *of Lesotho.*

201	1d. new blue	15	10
202	3d. deep green	35	10
203	6d. brown	50	10
204	1s. 6d. bluish violet	70	30
201/4	*Set of* 4	1·50	55

1966 (1 July). *World Cup Football Championships. As Nos.* 57/8 *of Pitcairn Islands.*

205	3d. violet, yellow-green, lake & yellow-brn	50	15
206	6d. chocolate, blue-green, lake & yellow-brn	75	15

1966 (20 Sept). *Inauguration of W.H.O. Headquarters, Geneva. As Nos.* 185/6 *of Montserrat.*

207	3d. black, yellow-green and light blue	50	15
208	1s. 6d. black, light purple and yellow-brown	2·75	40

1966 (1 Dec). *20th Anniversary of U.N.E.S.C.O. As Nos.* 342/4 *of Mauritius.*

209	3d. slate-violet, red, yellow and orange	1·50	20
210	6d. orange-yellow, violet and deep olive	2·50	30
211	1s. 6d. black, bright purple and orange	4·00	1·00
209/11	*Set of* 3	7·00	1·40

(Des W. H. Brown. Photo Harrison)

1967 (5 May). *New Constitution. W* w **12** (*sideways*). *P* 14½ × 14.

212	**65**	1s. multicoloured	10	10
213		2s. 6d. multicoloured	20	20
		a. Red (ribbon, etc.) omitted	£375	

66 Fire of London

(Des M. Goaman. Recess D.L.R.)

1967 (4 Sept). *300th Anniv of Arrival of Settlers after Great Fire of London. T* **66** *and similar horiz designs. W* w **12**. *P* 13.

214	1d. carmine-red and black	10	10
	a. Carmine and black	30	30
215	3d. ultramarine and black	10	10
216	6d. slate-violet and black	10	10
217	1s 6d. olive-green and black	10	10
214/17	*Set of* 4	35	30

Designs:—3d. East Indiaman *Charles*; 6d. Settlers landing at Jamestown; 1s. 6d. Settlers clearing scrub.

70 Interlocking Maps of Tristan and St. Helena

(Des Jennifer Toombs. Photo Harrison)

1968 (4 June). *30th Anniv of Tristan da Cunha as a Dependency of St. Helena. T* **70** *and similar horiz design. W* w **12**. *P* 14 × 14½.

218	**70**	4d. purple and chocolate	10	10
219	–	8d. olive and brown	10	10
220	**70**	1s. 9d. ultramarine and chocolate	10	15
221	–	2s. 3d. greenish blue and brown	15	15
218/21		*Set of* 4	35	35

Design:—8d., 2s. 3d. Interlocking maps of St. Helena and Tristan.

72 Queen Elizabeth and Sir Hudson Lowe

(Des M. Farrar Bell. Litho D.L.R.)

1968 (4 Sept). *150th Anniv of the Abolition of Slavery in St. Helena. T* **72** *and similar horiz design. Multicoloured. W* w **12** (*sideways*). *P* 13 × 12½.

222	3d. Type **72**	10	10
223	9d. Type **72**	10	10
224	1s. 6d. Queen Elizabeth and Sir George Bingham	15	15
225	2s. 6d. As 1s. 6d.	25	15
222/5	*Set of* 4	55	35

74 Blue Gum Eucalyptus and Road Construction

(Des Sylvia Goaman. Litho P.B.)

1968 (4 Nov). *Horiz designs as T* **74**. *Multicoloured. W* w **12** (*sideways*). *P* 13½.

226	½d. Type **74**	10	10
227	1d. Cabbage-tree and electricity development	10	10
228	1½d. St. Helena Redwood and dental unit	15	10
229	2d. Scrubweed and pest control	15	10
230	3d. Tree-fern and flats in Jamestown	30	10
231	4d. Blue gum Eucalyptus, pasture and livestock improvement	20	10
232	6d. Cabbage-tree and schools broadcasting	40	10
233	8d. St. Helena Redwood and country cottages	30	10
234	10d. Scrubweeed and new school buildings	30	10
235	1s. Tree-fern and reafforestation	20	10
236	1s. 6d. Blue gum Eucalyptus and heavy lift crane	70	1·25
237	2s. 6d. Cabbage-tree and Lady Field Children's Home	80	1·40
238	5s. St. Helena Redwood and agricultural training	90	1·75
239	10s. Scrubweed and New General Hospital	2·25	3·00
240	£1 Tree-fern and lifeboat *John Dutton*	10·00	15·00
226/40	*Set of* 15	15·00	21·00

See also No. 274 for distinct shade of £1 value.

89 Brig *Perseverance*

93 W.O. and Drummer of the 53rd Foot, 1815

(Des J.W. Litho P.B.)

1969 (19 Apr). *Mail Communications. T* **89** *and similar horiz designs. Multicoloured. W* w **12** (*sideways*). *P* 13½.

241	4d. Type **89**	20	15
242	8d. R.M.S. *Dane*	30	15
243	1s. 9d. S.S. *Llandovery Castle*	40	25
244	2s. 3d. R.M.S. *Good Hope Castle*	45	30
241/4	*Set of* 4	1·25	75

(Des R. North. Litho Format)

1969 (3 Sept). *Military Uniforms. T* **93** *and similar vert designs. Multicoloured. W* w **12**. *P* 14.

245	6d. Type **93**	30	15
246	8d. Officer and Surgeon, 20th Foot, 1816	40	15
247	1s. 8d. Drum Major, 66th Foot, 1816, and Royal Artillery Officer, 1820	50	15
248	2s. 6d. Private, 91st Foot, and 2nd Corporal, Royal Sappers and Miners, 1832	60	20
245/8	*Set of* 4	1·50	60

97 Dickens, Mr. Pickwick and Job Trotter (*Pickwick Papers*)

(Des Jennifer Toombs. Litho P.B.)

1970 (9 June). *Death Centenary of Charles Dickens. T* **97** *and similar horiz designs each incorporating a portrait of Dickens. Multicoloured. Chalk-surfaced paper. W* w **12** (*sideways*). *P* 13½ × 13.

249	4d. Type **97**	15	10
	a. Shiny unsurfaced paper	15	60
	b. Yellow omitted	£225	
250	8d. Mr. Bumble and Oliver (*Oliver Twist*)	20	10
	a. Shiny unsurfaced paper	20	85
251	1s. 6d. Sairey Gamp and Mark Tapley (*Martin Chuzzlewit*)	35	15
	a. Shiny unsurfaced paper	35	1·25

252 2s. 6d. Jo and Mr. Turveydrop (*Bleak House*) 45 30
 a. Shiny unsurfaced paper .. .. .. 45 1·75
249/52 .. .. *Set of* 4 1·00 60
249a/52a .. .. *Set of* 4 1·00 4·00

Supplies sent to St. Helena were on paper with a dull surface which reacts to the chalky test and with PVA gum. Crown Agents supplies were from a later printing on shiny paper which does not respond to the chalky test and with gum arabic.

98 "Kiss of Life" **99** Officer's Shako Plate (20th Foot)

(Des Jennifer Toombs. Litho J.W.)

1970 (15 Sept). *Centenary of British Red Cross. T* **98** *and similar horiz designs. W* w **12** (*sideways*). *P* 14.
253 6d. bistre, vermilion and black 10 10
254 9d. turquoise-green, vermilion and black .. 10 10
255 1s. 9d. pale grey, vermilion and black .. 15 10
256 2s. 3d. pale lavender, vermilion and black .. 20 20
253/6 .. .. *Set of* 4 50 45

Designs:—9d. Nurse with girl in wheelchair; 1s. 9d. Nurse bandaging child's knee; 2s. 3d. Red Cross emblem.

(Des J.W. Litho Questa)

1970 (2 Nov). *Military Equipment* (1*st issue*). *T* **99** *and similar vert designs. Multicoloured. W* w **12**. *P* 12.
257 4d. Type **99** 80 20
258 9d. Officer's Breast-plate (66th Foot) .. 1·25 30
259 1s. 3d. Officer's Full Dress Shako (91st Foot) 1·50 40
260 2s. 11d. Ensign's Shako (53rd Foot).. .. 2·00 60
257/60 .. .. *Set of* 4 5·00 1·40

See also Nos. 281/4, 285/8 and 291/4.

100 Electricity Development **101** St. Helena holding the "True Cross"

(Litho P.B.)

1971 (15 Feb). *Decimal Currency. Designs as Nos.* 227/40, *but with values inscr in decimal currency as in T* **100**. *W* w **12** (*sideways*). *P* 13½.
261 ½p. multicoloured 10 10
262 1p. multicoloured (as 1½d.) 10 10
263 1½p. multicoloured (as 2d.) 10 10
264 2p. multicoloured (as 3d.) .. .. .. 1·75 90
265 2½p. multicoloured (as 4d.) 10 10
266 3½p. multicoloured (as 6d.) 15 10
267 4½p. multicoloured (as 8d.) 10 10
268 5p. multicoloured (as 10d.).. .. .. 10 10
269 7½p. multicoloured (as 1s.) 30 35
270 10p. multicoloured (as 1s. 6d.) 30 35
271 12½p. multicoloured (as 2s. 6d.) 30 50
272 25p. multicoloured (as 5s.) .. .. .. 60 1·25
273 50p. multicoloured (as 10s.).. .. .. 1·25 2·00
274 £1 multicoloured† .. .. 21·00 18·00
261/74 .. .. *Set of* 14 23·00 22·00

†Although the design of No. 274 in no way differs from that of No. 240, it was reprinted specially for decimalisation, and differs considerably in shade from No. 240, as do others from their counterparts in the 1968 set.

The main differences in No. 274 are in the mountain which is blue rather than pinkish blue and in the sea which is light blue instead of greenish blue.

See also No. 309.

(Des R. Granger Barrett. Litho Questa)

1971 (5 Apr). *Easter. W* w **12**. *P* 14 × 14½.
275 **101** 2p. multicoloured 10 10
276 5p. multicoloured 15 15
277 7½p. multicoloured 20 20
278 12½p. multicoloured 25 25
275/8 .. .. *Set of* 4 60 60

PRICES OF SETS

Set prices are given for many issues, generally those containing three stamps or more. Definitive sets include one of each value or major colour change, but do not cover different perforations, die types or minor shades. Where a choice is possible the set prices are based on the cheapest versions of the stamps included in the listings.

102 Napoleon (after painting by J.-L. David) and Tomb on St. Helena

(Des J.W. Litho Questa)

1971 (5 May). 150*th Death Anniv of Napoleon, T* **102** *and similar vert design. Multicoloured. W* w **12**. *P* 13½.
279 2p. Type **102** 50 40
280 34p. "Napoleon at St. Helena" (H. Delaroche) 2·00 85

(Des J.W. Litho Questa)

1971 (10 Nov). *Military Equipment* (2*nd issue*). *Multicoloured designs as T* **99**. *W* w **12**. *P* 14.
281 1½p. Artillery Private's hanger .. .. 1·25 30
282 4p. Baker rifle and socket bayonet .. 2·00 60
283 6p. Infantry Officer's sword .. .. 2·00 80
284 22½p. Baker rifle and sword bayonet.. .. 2·50 1·25
281/4 .. .. *Set of* 4 7·00 2·75

(Des and litho J.W.)

1972 (19 June). *Military Equipment* (3*rd issue*). *Multicoloured designs as T* **99**. *W* w **12**. *P* 14.
285 2p. multicoloured 60 20
286 5p. reddish lilac, new blue and black .. 1·25 50
287 7½p. multicoloured .. .. 1·50 60
288 12½p. pale olive-sepia, brown and black .. 2·00 75
285/8 .. .. *Set of* 4 4·75 1·90

Designs:—2p. Royal Sappers and Miners breast-plate, *post* 1823; 5p. Infantry sergeant's spontoon, *circa* 1830; 7½p. Royal Artillery officer's breast-plate, *circa* 1830; 12½p. English military pistol, *circa* 1800.

103 St. Helena Sand Plover and White Tern

(Des (from photograph by D. Groves) and photo Harrison)

1972 (20 Nov). *Royal Silver Wedding. Multicoloured; background colour given. W* w **12**. *P* 14 × 14½.
289 **103** 2p. slate-green 25 35
290 16p. lake-brown 50 65

(Des J.W. Litho Questa)

1973 (20 Sept). *Military Equipment* (4*th issue*). *Multicoloured designs as T* **99**. *W* w **12** (*sideways*). *P* 14.
291 2p. Other Rank's shako, 53rd Foot, 1815 .. 1·00 55
292 5p. Band and Drums sword, 1830.. .. 2·00 1·00
293 7½p. Royal Sappers and Miners Officer's hat, 1830 .. .. 2·25 1·25
294 12½p. General's sword, 1831 .. .. .. 3·50 1·50
291/4 .. .. *Set of* 4 8·00 4·00

1973 (14 Nov). *Royal Wedding. As Nos.* 322/3 *of Montserrat.*
295 2p. violet-blue 15 10
296 18p. light emerald 25 20

104 *Westminster* and *Claudine* beached, 1849

(Des J.W. Litho Questa)

1973 (17 Dec). *Tercentenary of East India Company Charter. T* **104** *and similar horiz designs. Multicoloured. W* w **12**. *P* 14.
297 1½p. Type **104** 50 35
298 4p. *True Briton*, 1790 .. .. .. 60 65
299 6p. *General Goddard* in action, 1795 .. 60 65
300 22½p. *Kent* burning in the Bay of Biscay, 1825 1·50 2·00
297/300 .. .. *Set of* 4 3·00 3·25

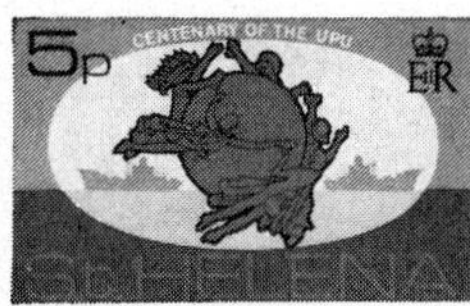

105 U.P.U. Emblem and Ships

(Des J.W. Litho Questa)

1974 (15 Oct). *Centenary of Universal Postal Union. T* **105** *and similar horiz design. Multicoloured. W* w **12** (*sideways on* **MS**303). *P* 14.
301 5p. Type **105** 25 25
302 25p. U.P.U. emblem and letters 55 55
MS303 89 × 84 mm. Nos. 301/2 .. .. .. 1·00 1·50

106 Churchill in Sailor Suit, and Blenheim Palace **107** Capt. Cook and H.M.S. *Resolution*

(Des Jennifer Toombs. Litho Questa)

1974 (30 Nov). *Birth Centenary of Sir Winston Churchill. T* **106** *and similar horiz design. W* w **14** *sideways* (*Nos.* 304/5) *or W* w **12** *sideways* (**MS**306). *P* 14.
304 5p. multicoloured 25 25
305 25p. black, flesh and reddish purple 55 75
MS306 108 × 93 mm. Nos. 304/5 .. .. .. 1·00 2·00

Design:—25p. Churchill and River Thames.

(Des J. Cooter. Litho Questa)

1975 (14 July). *Bicentenary of Capt. Cook's Return to St. Helena. T* **107** *and similar horiz design. Multicoloured. W* w **14** (*sideways on* 25p.). *P* 13½.
307 5p. Type **107** 50 50
308 25p. Capt. Cook and Jamestown .. .. 1·00 1·50

(Litho Questa)

1975 (13 Aug). *As No.* 264 *but whiter paper. P* 14.
309 2p. multicoloured .. .. 90 4·00

108 *Mellissia begonifolia* (tree) **109** £1 Note

(Des Jennifer Toombs. Litho J.W.)

1975 (20 Oct). *Centenary of Publication of "St. Helena" by J. C. Melliss. T* **108** *and similar multicoloured designs. W* w **14** (*sideways on* 12 *and* 25p.). *P* 13.
310 2p. Type **108** 25 40
311 5p. *Mellissius adumbratus* (beetle) 35 60
312 12p. St. Helena Sand Plover (*horiz*) .. .. 90 1·50
313 25p. *Scorpaenia mellissii* (fish) (*horiz*) .. 1·00 1·75
310/13 .. .. *Set of* 4 2·25 3·75

(Des V. Whiteley Studio. Litho J.W.)

1976 (15 Mar). *First Issue of Currency Notes. T* **109** *and similar horiz design. Multicoloured. W* w **12** (*sideways*). *P* 13½.
314 8p. Type **109** 40 35
315 33p. £5 Note .. .. 85 1·25

110 1d. Stamp of 1863

(Des C. Abbott. Litho J.W.)

1976 (4 May). *Festival of Stamps, London. T* **110** *and similar designs. W* w **14** (*sideways on* 5 *and* 25p.). *P* 13½.
316 5p. light red-brown, black and light flesh .. 15 15
317 8p. black, green and pale dull green .. 25 30
318 25p. multicoloured 40 45
316/18 .. .. *Set of* 3 70 80

Designs: *Vert*—8p. 1d. stamp of 1922. *Horiz*—25p. Mail carrier *Good Hope Castle*.

For miniature sheet containing No. 318 see Ascension No. **MS**218.

111 "High Knoll, 1806" (Capt. Barnett)

(Des C. Abbott. Litho Questa)

1976 (14 Sept)–**82**. *Aquatints and Lithographs of St. Helena. T* **111** *and similar horiz designs. Multicoloured. W* w **14** (*sideways*). *P* 13½ (£1, £2) *or* 14 (*others*).

A. *On white paper. Without imprint date.*

319A	1p. Type **111**	30	40
	a. Cream paper (13.6.80)	30	40
320A	3p. "The Friar Rock, 1815" (G. Bellasis)	30	40
	a. Cream paper (13.6.80)	30	40
321A	5p. "The Column Lot, 1815" (G. Bellasis)	20	40
322A	6p. "Sandy Bay Valley, 1809" (H. Salt) (23.11.76)	20	40
323A	8p. "Scene from Castle Terrace, 1815" (G. Bellasis)	30	45
324A	9p. "The Briars, 1815" (23.11.76)	30	50
325A	10p. "Plantation House, 1821" (J. Wathen)	50	60
326A	15p. "Longwood House, 1821" (J. Wathen) (23.11.76)	35	45
327A	18p. "St. Paul's Church" (V. Brooks)	35	65
328A	26p. "St. James's Valley, 1815" (Capt. Hastings)	45	65
329A	40p. "St. Matthew's Church, 1860" (V. Brooks)	70	1·25
330A	£1 "St. Helena, 1815" (G. Bellasis)	1·50	3·00
	a. Gold omitted	£750	
331A	£2 "Sugar Loaf Hill, 1821" (J. Wathen) (23.11.76)	3·50	5·50
319A/31A	*Set of* 13	8·00	13·00

B. *On cream paper with imprint date* ("1982") (10.5.82)

319B	1p. Type **111**	20	30
325B	10p. "Plantation House, 1821" (J. Wathen)	50	1·00
331B	£2 "Sugar Loaf Hill, 1821" (J. Wathen)	3·75	5·00

The £1 and £2 are larger, 47 × 34 mm.

112 Duke of Edinburgh paying Homage

(Des M. Shamir. Litho J.W.)

1977 (7 Feb). *Silver Jubilee. T* **112** *and similar horiz designs. Multicoloured. W* w **14** (*sideways*). *P* 13.

332	8p. Royal visit, 1947	20	35
333	15p. Queen's sceptre with dove	25	45
334	26p. Type **112**	35	50
332/4	*Set of* 3	70	1·10

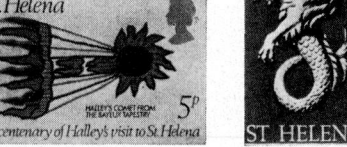

113 Halley's Comet (from Bayeux Tapestry)

114 Sea Lion

(Des C. Abbott. Litho Questa)

1977 (23 Aug). *Tercentenary of Halley's Visit. T* **113** *and similar horiz designs. Multicoloured. W* w **14** (*sideways*). *P* 14.

335	5p. Type **113**	35	20
336	8p. Late 17th-century sextant	50	20
337	27p. Halley and Halley's Mount, St. Helena	1·00	60
335/7	*Set of* 3	1·75	90

(Des Jennifer Toombs. Litho Questa)

1978 (2 June). *25th Anniv of Coronation. T* **114** *and similar vert designs. P* 15.

338	25p. agate, cerise and silver	40	50
	a. Sheetlet. Nos. 338/40 × 2	2·00	
339	25p. multicoloured	40	50
340	25p. agate, cerise and silver	40	50
338/40	*Set of* 3	1·10	1·40

Designs:—No. 338, Black Dragon of Ulster; No. 339, Queen Elizabeth II; No. 340, Type **114**.

Nos. 338/40 were printed together in small sheets of 6, containing two *se-tenant* strips of 3, with horizontal gutter margin between.

115 Period Engraving of St. Helena

(Des J.W. Litho Questa)

1978 (14 Aug). *Wreck of the "Witte Leeuw". T* **115** *and similar horiz designs. Multicoloured. W* w **14** (*sideways*). *P* 14½.

341	3p. Type **115**	15	15
342	5p. Chinese porcelain	20	20
343	8p. Bronze cannon	25	30
344	9p. Chinese porcelain (*different*)	30	35
345	15p. Pewter mug and ceramic flasks	50	55
346	20p. Dutch East Indiaman	60	70
341/6	*Set of* 6	1·75	2·00

116 H.M.S. *Discovery*

117 Sir Rowland Hill

(Des and litho (25p. also embossed) Walsall)

1979 (19 Feb). *Bicentenary of Captain Cook's Voyages*, 1768–79. *T* **116** *and similar vert designs. Multicoloured. P* 11.

347	3p. Type **116**	20	15
348	8p. Cook's portable observatory	30	25
349	12p. *Pharnaceum acidum* (based on sketch by Joseph Banks)	35	35
350	25p. Flaxman/Wedgwood medallion of Captain Cook	55	90
347/50	*Set of* 4	1·25	1·50

(Des J.W. Litho Questa)

1979 (20 Aug). *Death Centenary of Sir Rowland Hill. T* **117** *and similar designs. W* w **14** (*sideways on* 8 *to* 32*p.*). *P* 14.

351	5p. multicoloured	15	15
352	8p. multicoloured	20	20
353	20p. multicoloured	40	40
354	32p. black, magenta and deep mauve	55	55
351/4	*Set of* 4	1·10	1·10

Designs: *Horiz*—8p. 1965 1d. 1st Local Post stamp; 20p. 1863 1d. on 6d. stamp; 32p. 1902 1d. stamp.

118 R. F. Seal's Chart of 1823 showing the Elevation of the Coastline

(Des G. Vasarhelyi. Litho Questa)

1979 (10 Dec). *150th Anniv of the Inclined Plane. T* **118** *and similar designs. W* w **14** (*sideways on* 5 *and* 8*p.*). *P* 14.

355	5p. black, brownish grey and stone	20	15
356	8p. black, brownish grey and stone	20	20
357	50p. multicoloured	70	75
355/7	*Set of* 3	1·00	1·00

Designs: *Horiz*—8p. The Inclined Plane in 1829. *Vert*—50p. The Inclined Plane in 1979.

119 Napoleon's Tomb, 1848

120 East Indiaman

(Des J.W. Litho Questa)

1980 (23 Feb). *Centenary of Empress Eugenie's Visit. T* **119** *and similar horiz designs. W* w **14** (*sideways*). *P* 14.

358	5p. gold, reddish brown and pale red-brown	20	20
359	8p. gold, reddish brown and pale bistre	25	25
360	62p. gold, reddish brown & pale orange-brn	95	1·10
358/60	*Set of* 3	1·25	1·40
MS361	180 × 110 mm. Nos. 358/60	1·50	2·00

Designs:—8p. Landing at St. Helena; 62p. At the tomb of Napoleon.

(Des C. Abbott. Litho Format)

1980 (6 May). *"London 1980" International Stamp Exhibition, T* **120** *and similar vert designs. Multicoloured. W* w **14**. *P* 14½.

362	5p. Type **120**	15	15
363	8p. *Dolphin* postal stone	15	20
364	47p. Postal stone outside Castle entrance, Jamestown	60	80
362/4	*Set of* 3	80	1·00
MS365	111 × 120 mm. Nos. 362/4	85	1·50

121 Queen Elizabeth the Queen Mother in 1974

(Des and litho Harrison)

1980 (18 Aug*). *80th Birthday of Queen Elizabeth the Queen Mother. W* w **14** (*sideways*). *P* 14.

366 **121**	24p. multicoloured	50	50

*This is the local date of issue; the Crown Agents released the stamp on 4 August.

122 The Briars, 1815

(Des C. Abbott. Litho Questa)

1980 (17 Nov). *175th Anniv of Wellington's Visit. T* **122** *and similar multicoloured design. W* w **14** (*sideways on* 9*p.*). *P* 14.

367	9p. Type **122**	15	15
368	30p. "Wellington" (Goya) (*vert*)	45	45

Nos. 367/8 were each printed in small sheets of 10 stamps.

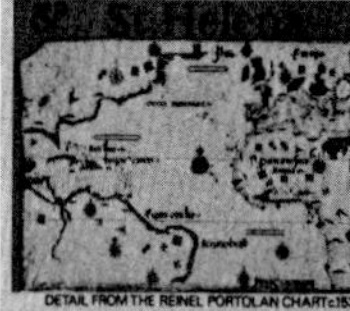

123 Redwood

124 Detail from Reinel Portolan Chart, *circa* 1530

(Des Daphne Padden. Litho Enschedé)

1981 (5 Jan). *Endemic Plants. T* **123** *and similar horiz designs. Multicoloured. W* w **14** (*sideways*). *P* 13½.

369	5p. Type **123**	15	15
370	8p. Old Father Live Forever	20	20
371	15p. Gumwood	25	25
372	27p. Black Cabbage	45	45
369/72	*Set of* 4	95	95

(Des Harrison. Litho Walsall)

1981 (22 May). *Early Maps. T* **124** *and similar horiz designs. W* w **14** (*sideways*). *P* 14 × 14½.

373	5p. multicoloured	25	15
374	8p. black, brown-lake and grey	30	20
375	20p. multicoloured	50	35
376	30p. multicoloured	55	50
373/6	*Set of* 4	1·40	1·10
MS377	114 × 83 mm. 24p. black and grey	40	65

Designs:—8p. John Thornton's Map of St. Helena, *circa* 1700; 20p. Map of St. Helena, 1815; 30p. Map of St. Helena, 1817; miniature sheet, Part of Gastaldi's map of Africa, 16th-century.

125 Prince Charles as Royal Navy Commander

126 *Charonia Variegata*

(Des J.W. Litho Questa)

1981 (22 July). *Royal Wedding. T* **125** *and similar vert designs. Multicoloured. W* w **14**. *P* 14.

378	14p. Wedding bouquet from St. Helena	25	25
379	29p. Type **125**	35	35
380	32p. Prince Charles and Lady Diana Spencer	50	50
378/80	*Set of* 3	1·00	1·00

(Des J.W. Litho Walsall)

1981 (10 Sept). *Seashells. T* **126** *and similar vert designs. Multicoloured. W* w **14**. *P* 14.

381	7p. Type **126**	35	20
382	10p. *Cypraea spurca sanctaehelenae*	40	25
383	25p. *Janthina janthina*	70	60
384	53p. *Pinna rudis*	1·25	1·25
381/4	*Set of* 4	2·40	2·10

127 Traffic Duty   **128** *Sympetrum dilatatum* (dragonfly)

(Des BG Studio. Litho Questa)

1981 (5 Nov). *25th Anniv of Duke of Edinburgh Award Scheme. T* **127** *and similar vert designs. Multicoloured.* W w **14**. *P* 14.
385 7p. Type **127** 15 15
386 11p. Signposting 15 15
387 25p. Animal care 35 35
388 50p. Duke of Edinburgh, in Guards' uniform, on horse-back 70 70
385/8 . . . . . . *Set of* 4 1·25 1·25

(Des C. Abbott. Litho Questa)

1982 (4 Jan). *Insects (1st series). T* **128** *and similar horiz designs. Multicoloured.* W w **14** (*sideways on* 7, 10 *and* 25p., *inverted on* 32p.). *P* 14½.
389 7p. Type **128** 30 25
390 10p. *Aplothorax burchelli* (beetle) . . 40 35
391 25p. *Ampulex compressa* (wasp) . . 70 60
392 32p. *Labidura herculeana* (earwig) . . 80 75
389/92 . . . . . . *Set of* 4 2·00 1·75
The 32p. is larger, 45×27 mm.
See also Nos. 411/14.

129 Charles Darwin   **130** Prince and Princess of Wales at Balmoral, Autumn 1981

(Des L. Curtis. Litho Questa)

1982 (19 Apr). *150th Anniv of Charles Darwin's Voyage. T* **129** *and similar horiz designs. Multicoloured.* W w **14** (*sideways*). *P* 14.
393 7p. Type **129** 30 30
394 14p. Flagstaff Hill and Darwin's hammer . . 45 60
395 25p. Ring-necked Pheasant and Chukar Partridge . . . . . . 75 1·00
396 29p. H.M.S. *Beagle* off St. Helena . . . . 95 1·25
393/6 . . . . . . *Set of* 4 2·25 2·75

(Des C. Abbott. Litho Format)

1982 (1 July). *21st Birthday of Princess of Wales. T* **130** *and similar vert designs. Multicoloured.* W w **14**. *P* 13½ × 14 (7, 55p.) *or* 13½ (*others*).
397 7p. St. Helena coat of arms 15 15
398 11p. Type **130** 25 25
399 29p. Bride on Palace Balcony 55 70
a. Perf 13½ × 14 . . . . . . 30·00 14·00
b. Imperf (pair) £500
400 55p. Formal portrait . . . . . . 1·00 1·40
397/400 . . . . . . *Set of* 4 1·75 2·25

1st PARTICIPATION COMMONWEALTH GAMES 1982

(**131**)   **132** Lord Baden-Powell

1982 (25 Oct). *Commonwealth Games, Brisbane. Nos.* 326 *and* 328 *optd with T* **131**.
401 15p. "Longwood House, 1821" (G. Wathen) . . 25 25
402 26p. "St. James's Valley, 1815" (Capt. Hastings) 45 45

(Des L. McCombie. Litho Walsall)

1982 (29 Nov). *75th Anniv of Boy Scout Movement. T* **132** *and similar designs.* W w **14** (*inverted on* 3p., 29p.; *sideways on* 11p., 59p.). *P* 14.
403 3p. lake-brown, grey and orange-yellow . . 15 15
404 11p. lake-brown, grey & bright yellow-green 35 25
405 29p. lake-brown, grey and reddish orange . . 70 60
406 59p. lake-brown, grey & bright yellow-green 1·25 1·25
403/6 . . . . . . *Set of* 4 2·25 2·00
Designs: *Horiz*—11p. Boy Scout (drawing by Lord Baden-Powell); 59p. Camping at Thompsons Wood. *Vert*—29p. Canon Walcott.

133 King and Queen Rocks   **134** *Coriolus versicolor*

(Des C. Abbott. Litho B.D.T.)

1983 (14 Jan). *Views of St. Helena by Roland Svensson. T* **133** *and similar multicoloured designs.* W w **14** (*sideways on* 29p., 59p.). *P* 14.
407 7p. Type **133** 20 20
408 11p. Turk's Cap 25 25
409 29p. Coastline from Jamestown (*horiz*) . . 65 65
410 59p. Mundens Point (*horiz*) . . . . 1·40 1·40
407/10 . . . . . . *Set of* 4 2·25 2·25

(Des C. Abbott. Litho Questa)

1983 (22 Apr). *Insects (2nd series). Horiz designs as T* **128**. *Multicoloured.* W w **14** (*sideways*). *P* 14½.
411 11p. *Acherontia atropos* (hawk moth) . . 35 30
412 15p. *Helenasaldula aberrans* (shore-bug) . . 40 35
413 29p. *Anchastus conpositarum* (click beetle) 65 55
414 59p. *Lamprochrus cossonoides* (weevil) . . 1·40 1·25
411/14 . . . . . . *Set of* 4 2·50 2·25

(Des Garden Studio. Litho Format)

1983 (16 June). *Fungi. T* **134** *and similar multicoloured designs.* W w **14** (*sideways on* 29p.). *P* 14.
415 11p. Type **134** 20 20
416 15p. *Pluteus brunneisucus* 30 30
417 29p. *Polyporus induratus* (*horiz*) . . 55 55
418 59p. *Coprinus angulatus* . . . . 1·25 1·25
415/18 . . . . . . *Set of* 4 2·10 2·10

135 Java Sparrow   **136** Birth of St. Helena

(Des J.W. Litho Questa)

1983 (12 Sept). *Birds. T* **135** *and similar vert designs. Multicoloured.* W w **14**. *P* 14.
419 7p. Type **135** 30 20
420 15p. Madagascar Red Fody 45 35
421 33p. Common Waxbill 80 70
422 59p. Yellow Canary . . . . . . 1·50 1·40
419/22 . . . . . . *Set of* 4 2·75 2·50

(Des Jennifer Toombs. Litho Questa)

1983 (17 Oct). *Christmas. Life of St. Helena (1st series). T* **136** *and similar vert design.* W w **14**. *P* 14 × 13½.
423 10p. Type **136** 25 35
a. Sheetlet Nos. 423/4, each ×5 . . 3·00
424 15p. St. Helena being taken to convent . . 30 35
Nos. 423/4 were printed together in small sheets of 10, containing horizontal strips of 5 for each value separated by a horizontal gutter margin.
See also Nos. 450/3 and 468/71.

137 1934 ½d. Stamp   **138** Prince Andrew and H.M.S. *Invincible* (aircraft carrier)

(Des C. Abbott. Litho Questa)

1984 (3 Jan). *150th Anniv of St. Helena as a British Colony. T* **137** *and similar square designs showing values of the* 1934 *Centenary of British Colonisation issue or Colony Arms. Multicoloured.* W w **14** (*sideways*). *P* 13½.
425 1p. Type **137** 10 20
426 3p. 1934 1d. stamp 10 20
427 6p. 1934 1½d. stamp 10 30
428 7p. 1934 2d. stamp 15 30
429 11p. 1934 3d. stamp 20 40
430 15p. 1934 6d. stamp 25 45
431 29p. 1934 1s. stamp 50 95
432 33p. 1934 5s. stamp . . . . . . 55 1·25
433 59p. 1934 10s. stamp . . . . . . 1·10 2·00
434 £1 1934 2s. 6d. stamp . . . . . . 2·75 3·25
435 £2 St. Helena Coat of Arms . . . . 3·50 5·00
425/35 . . . . . . *Set of* 11 7·50 13·00

(Des D. Bowen. Litho Format)

1984 (4 Apr). *Visit of Prince Andrew. T* **138** *and similar horiz design. Multicoloured.* W w **14** (*sideways*). *P* 14.
436 11p. Type **138** 25 25
437 60p. Prince Andrew and H.M.S. *Herald* (survey ship) . . . . . . 1·25 1·40

139 *St. Helena* (schooner)   **140** Twopenny Coin and Donkey

(Des A. Theobald. Litho Questa)

1984 (14 May). *250th Anniv of "Lloyd's List" (newspaper). T* **139** *and similar vert designs. Multicoloured.* W w **14**. *P* 14½ × 14.
438 10p. Type **139** 20 20
439 18p. Solomons Facade (local agent) . . 35 35
440 25p. Lloyd's Coffee House, London . . 50 55
441 50p. *Papanui* (freighter) . . . . 1·00 1·00
438/41 . . . . . . *Set of* 4 1·90 1·90

(Des G. Drummond. Litho Format)

1984 (23 July). *New Coinage. T* **140** *and similar horiz designs. Multicoloured.* W w **14** (*sideways*). *P* 14.
442 10p. Type **140** 35 35
443 15p. Five pence coin and St. Helena Sand Plover 45 45
444 29p. Penny coin and Yellowfin Tuna . . 75 75
445 50p. Ten pence coin and Arum Lily . . 1·25 1·25
442/5 . . . . . . *Set of* 4 2·50 2·50

141 Mrs. Rebecca Fuller (former Corps Secretary)   **142** Queen Elizabeth the Queen Mother aged Two

(Des L. Curtis. Litho Walsall)

1984 (12 Oct). *Centenary of Salvation Army on St. Helena. T* **141** *and similar multicoloured designs.* W w **14** (*sideways on* 11p., 25p.). *P* 14.
446 7p. Type **141** 35 25
447 11p. Meals-on-wheels service (*horiz*) . . 45 30
448 25p. Salvation Army Citadel, Jamestown (*horiz*) 80 60
449 60p. Salvation Army band at Jamestown Clock Tower . . . . . . 1·75 1·60
446/9 . . . . . . *Set of* 4 3·00 2·50

(Des Jennifer Toombs. Litho Questa)

1984 (9 Nov). *Christmas. Life of St. Helena (2nd series). Vert designs as T* **136**. W w **14**. *P* 14.
450 6p. St. Helena visits prisoners 20 20
451 10p. Betrothal of St. Helena 30 30
452 15p. Marriage of St. Helena to Constantius . . 40 40
453 33p. Birth of Constantine 70 70
450/3 . . . . . . *Set of* 4 1·40 1·40

(Des A. Theobald (70p.), C. Abbott (others). Litho Questa)

1985 (7 June). *Life and Times of Queen Elizabeth the Queen Mother. T* **142** *and similar vert designs. Multicoloured.* W w **16**. *P* 14½ × 14.
454 11p. Type **142** 20 25
455 15p. At Ascot with the Queen 30 35
456 29p. Attending Gala Ballet at Covent Garden 60 65
457 55p. With Prince Henry at his christening . . 1·10 1·25
454/7 . . . . . . *Set of* 4 2·00 2·25
MS458 91 × 73 mm. 70p. The Queen Mother with Ford "V8 Pilot". Wmk sideways . . . . 1·40 1·60

143 Rock Bullseye   **144** John J. Audubon

(Des L. Curtis. Litho Walsall)

1985 (12 July). *Marine Life. T* **143** *and similar horiz designs. Multicoloured.* W w **14** (*sideways*). *P* 13 × 13½.

459 7p. Type **143** 25 25
460 11p. Mackerel 30 30
461 15p. Skipjack Tuna 40 40
462 33p. Yellowfin Tuna 75 75
463 50p. Stump .. .. 1·25 1·25
459/63 .. .. *Set of* 5 2·75 2·75

(Des Josephine Martin (11p.). Litho Format)

1985 (2 Sept). *Birth Bicentenary of John J. Audubon (ornithologist). T* **144** *and similar designs.* W w **14** (*inverted on* 11p., *sideways on others*). *P* 14.

464 11p. black and blackish brown 45 25
465 15p. multicoloured 55 35
466 25p. multicoloured 75 55
467 60p. multicoloured .. .. 1·40 1·40
464/7 .. .. *Set of* 4 2·75 2·25

Designs: *Horiz* (from original Audubon paintings)—15p. Moorhen ("Common Gallinule"); 25p. White-tailed Tropic Bird; 60p. Common Noddy.

(Des Jennifer Toombs. Litho Questa)

1985 (14 Oct). *Christmas. Life of St. Helena (3rd series). Vert designs as T* **136**. *Multicoloured.* W w **14**. *P* 14 × 13½.

468 7p. St. Helena journeys to the Holy Land .. 25 25
469 10p. Zambres slays the bull 30 30
470 15p. The bull restored to life: conversion of St. Helena 40 40
471 60p. Resurrection of the corpse: the true Cross identified .. .. 1·50 1·50
468/71 .. .. *Set of* 4 2·25 2·25

145 Church Provident Society for Women Banner

146 Plaque at Site of Halley's Observatory on St. Helena

(Des A. Theobald. Litho J.W.)

1986 (7 Jan). *Friendly Societies' Banners. T* **145** *and similar horiz designs. Multicoloured.* W w **16** (*sideways*). *P* 13 × 13½.

472 10p. Type **145** 25 25
473 11p. Working Men's Christian Association .. 25 25
474 25p. Church Benefit Society for Children .. 55 55
475 29p. Mechanics and Friendly Benefit Society 65 65
476 33p. Ancient Order of Foresters 70 70
472/6 .. .. *Set of* 5 2·10 2·10

(Des A. Theobald. Litho Questa)

1986 (21 Apr). *60th Birthday of Queen Elizabeth II. Vert designs as T* **230a** *of Jamaica. Multicoloured.* W w **16**. *P* 14½×14.

477 10p. Princess Elizabeth making 21st birthday broadcast, South Africa, 1947 .. 20 25
478 15p. Silver Jubilee photograph, 1977 .. 30 35
479 20p. Princess Elizabeth on board H.M.S. *Implacable*, 1947 .. .. 40 45
480 50p. In the U.S.A., 1976 .. .. 1·00 1·10
481 65p. At Crown Agents Head Office, London, 1983 .. .. 1·25 1·40
477/81 .. .. *Set of* 5 2·75 3·25

(Des L. Curtis. Litho Walsall)

1986 (15 May). *Appearance of Halley's Comet. T* **146** *and similar vert designs. Multicoloured.* W w **14**. *P* 14½ × 14.

482 9p. Type **146** 25 25
483 12p. Edmond Halley 30 30
484 20p. Halley's planisphere of the southern stars 45 45
485 65p. *Unity* on passage to St. Helena, 1676 .. 1·40 1·40
482/5 .. .. *Set of* 4 2·10 2·10

(Des D. Miller. Litho Questa)

1986 (23 July). *Royal Wedding. Square designs as T* **231a** *of Jamaica. Multicoloured.* W w **16**. *P* 14.

486 10p. Prince Andrew and Miss Sarah Ferguson 20 25
487 40p. Prince Andrew with Governor J. Massingham on St. Helena 80 85

147 James Ross and H.M.S. *Erebus*

(Des C. Abbott. Litho Questa)

1986 (22 Sept). *Explorers. T* **147** *and similar horiz designs.* W w **16** (*sideways*). *P* 14½.

488 1p. deep brown and pink 10 10
489 3p. royal blue and grey-blue 10 10
490 5p. bronze-green and deep yellow-green .. 10 15
491 9p. purple-brown and claret 20 25
492 10p. deep brown and light brown 20 25
493 12p. myrtle-green and light green 25 30
494 15p. red-brown and brown-rose 30 35
495 20p. deep dull blue and light blue 40 45
496 25p. sepia and salmon-pink 50 55
497 40p. bottle-green and dull blue-green .. 80 85
498 60p. reddish brown and pale orange-brown .. 1·25 1·40
499 £1 deep turquoise-blue and turquoise-blue 2·00 2·10
500 £2 deep lilac and reddish lilac .. .. 4·00 4·25
488/500 .. .. *Set of* 13 9·00 10·00

Designs:—3p. Robert FitzRoy and H.M.S. *Beagle*; 5p. Adam Johann von Krusenstern and *Nadezhda*; 9p. William Bligh and H.M.S. *Resolution*; 10p. Otto von Kotzebue and *Rurik*; 12p. Philip Carteret and H.M.S. *Swallow*; 15p. Thomas Cavendish and *Desire*; 20p. Louis-Antoine de Bougainville and *La Boudeuse*; 25p. Fyedor Petrovich Lütke and *Senyavin*; 40p. Louis Isidore Duperrey and *La Coquille*; 60p. John Byron and H.M.S. *Dolphin*; £1 James Cook and H.M.S. *Endeavour*; £2 Jules Dumont d'Urville and *L'Astrolabe*.

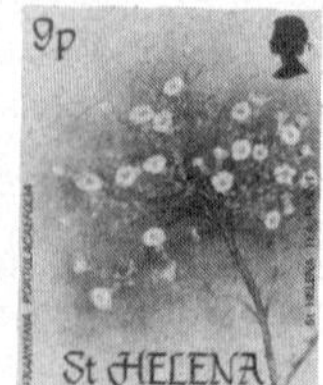

148 Prince Edward and H.M.S. *Repulse* (battle cruiser), 1925

149 St. Helena Tea Plant

(Des E. Nisbet. Litho Questa)

1987 (16 Feb). *Royal Visits to St. Helena. T* **148** *and similar horiz designs. Multicoloured.* W w **16** (*sideways*). *P* 14.

501 9p. Type **148** 50 40
502 13p. King George VI and H.M.S. *Vanguard* (battleship), 1947 .. .. 70 60
503 38p. Prince Philip and Royal Yacht *Britannia*, 1957 .. .. 1·40 1·50
504 45p. Prince Andrew and H.M.S. *Herald* (survey ship), 1984 .. .. 1·60 1·75
501/4 .. .. *Set of* 4 3·75 3·75

(Des Annette Robinson. Litho Questa)

1987 (3 Aug). *Rare Plants (1st series). T* **149** *and similar vert designs. Multicoloured.* W w **16**. *P* 14½ × 14.

505 9p. Type **149** 65 35
506 13p. Baby's Toes 80 45
507 38p. Salad Plant .. .. 1·50 1·00
508 45p. Scrubwood .. .. 1·75 1·25
505/8 .. .. *Set of* 4 4·25 2·75

See also Nos. 531/4.

150 Lesser Rorqual

151 *Defence* and Dampier's Signature, 1691

(Des A. Riley. Litho Questa)

1987 (24 Oct). *Marine Mammals. T* **150** *and similar horiz designs. Multicoloured.* W w **16** (*sideways*). *P* 14.

509 9p. Type **150** 60 35
510 13p. Risso's Dolphin 75 50
511 45p. Sperm Whale .. .. 1·75 1·40
512 60p. Euphrosyne Dolphin .. .. 2·00 1·60
509/12 .. .. *Set of* 4 4·50 3·50
MS513 102 × 72 mm. 75p. Humpback Whale (48 × 31 *mm*). P 13½ × 14 .. .. .. 2·00 2·00

1987 (9 Dec). *Royal Ruby Wedding. Nos. 477/81 optd with T* **45a** *of Kiribati in silver.*

514 10p. Princess Elizabeth making 21st birthday broadcast, South Africa, 1947 .. 20 25
515 15p. Silver Jubilee photograph, 1977 .. 30 35
a. Opt omitted (vert pair with normal) .. £150
516 20p. Princess Elizabeth on board H.M.S. *Implacable*, 1947 .. .. 40 45
517 50p. In the U.S.A., 1976 .. .. 1·00 1·10
518 65p. At Crown Agents Head Office, London, 1983 .. .. 1·25 1·40
514/18 .. .. *Set of* 5 2·75 3·25

No. 515a occurred on the top row of several sheets.

(Des A. Theobald. Litho Walsall)

1988 (1 Mar). *Bicentenary of Australian Settlement. T* **151** *and similar horiz designs showing ships and signatures. Multicoloured.* W w **16** (*sideways*). *P* 14 × 14½.

519 9p. Type **151** 75 65
520 13p. H.M.S. *Resolution* (Cook), 1775 .. .. 1·25 90
521 45p. H.M.S. *Providence* (Bligh), 1792 .. .. 2·25 2·00
522 60p. H.M.S. *Beagle* (Darwin), 1836 .. .. 2·75 2·50
519/22 .. .. *Set of* 4 6·25 5·50

ALTERED CATALOGUE NUMBERS

Any Catalogue numbers altered from the last edition are shown as a list in the introductory pages.

152 "The Holy Virgin with the Child"

153 Ebony

(Des N. Harvey. Litho Questa)

1988 (11 Oct). *Christmas. T* **152** *and similar vert designs showing religious paintings. Multicoloured.* W w **14**. *P* 14.

523 5p. Type **152** 10 15
524 20p. "Madonna" 40 45
525 38p. "The Holy Family with St. John" .. 75 80
526 60p. "The Holy Virgin with the Child" .. 1·25 1·40
523/6 .. .. *Set of* 4 2·25 2·50

(Des D. Miller (8p.), E. Nisbet and D. Miller (others). Litho Questa)

1988 (1 Nov). *300th Anniv of Lloyd's of London. Designs as T* **167a** *of Malawi.* W w **16** (*sideways on* 20, 45p.). *P* 14.

527 9p. agate and brown 20 25
528 20p. multicoloured 40 45
529 45p. multicoloured 90 95
530 60p. multicoloured .. .. 1·25 1·40
527/30 .. .. *Set of* 4 2·50 2·75

Designs: *Vert*—9p. Lloyd's Underwriting Room, 1886; 60p. *Spangereid* (full-rigged ship) on fire, St. Helena, 1920. *Horiz*—20p. *Edinburgh Castle* (liner); 45p. *Bosun Bird* (freighter).

(Des L. Ninnes. Litho Questa)

1989 (6 Jan). *Rare Plants (2nd series). T* **153** *and similar vert designs. Multicoloured.* W w **16**. *P* 14.

531 9p. Type **153** 30 30
532 20p. St. Helena Lobelia 55 55
533 45p. Large Bellflower .. .. 1·10 1·10
534 60p. She Cabbage Tree .. .. 1·40 1·40
531/4 .. .. *Set of* 4 3·00 3·00

154 Private, 53rd Foot

(**155**)

(Des C. Collins. Litho Format)

1989 (5 June). *Military Uniforms of* 1815. *T* **154** *and similar vert designs. Multicoloured.* W w **16**. *P* 14.

535 9p. Type **154** 35 35
a. Horiz strip of 5. Nos. 535/9 .. .. 3·50
536 13p. Officer, 53rd Foot 40 40
537 20p. Royal Marine 55 55
538 45p. Officer, 66th Foot .. .. 1·25 1·25
539 60p. Private, 66th Foot .. .. 1·50 1·50
535/9 .. .. *Set of* 5 3·50 3·50

Nos. 535/9 were printed together, *se-tenant*, in horizontal strips of five throughout the sheet.

1989 (7 July). *"Philexfrance 89" International Stamp Exhibition, Paris. Nos. 535/9 optd with T* **155**.

540 9p. Type **154** 35 35
a. Horiz strip of 5. Nos. 540/4 .. .. 3·50
541 13p. Officer, 53rd Foot 40 40
542 20p. Royal Marine 55 55
543 45p. Officer, 66th Foot .. .. 1·25 1·25
544 60p. Private, 66th Foot .. .. 1·50 1·50
540/4 .. .. *Set of* 5 3·50 3·50

156 Agricultural Studies

157 "The Madonna with the Pear" (Dürer)

(Des A. Edmonston. Litho Questa)

1989 (24 Aug). *New Prince Andrew Central School. T* **156** *and similar horiz designs. Multicoloured.* W w **16** (*sideways*). *P* 14 × 14½.

545 13p. Type **156** 35 35
546 20p. Geography lesson 55 55
547 25p. Walkway and classroom block 65 65
548 60p. Aerial view of School .. .. .. 1·50 1·50
545/8 .. .. *Set of* 4 2·75 2·75

(Des D. Miller. Litho Questa)

1989 (23 Oct). *Christmas. Religious Paintings. T* **157** *and similar vert designs. Multicoloured. W* w **14**. *P* 14.

549 10p. Type **157** 40 30
550 20p. "The Holy Family under the Appletree" (Rubens) 65 55
551 45p. "The Virgin in the Meadow" (Raphael) 1·40 1·25
552 60p. "The Holy Family with St. John" (Raphael) .. .. 1·75 1·60
549/52 .. .. *Set of* 4 3·75 3·25

158 Chevrolet "6" 30 cwt Lorry, 1930

159 Sheep

(Des E. Nesbit. Litho Questa)

1989 (1 Dec). *Early Vehicles. T* **158** *and similar horiz designs. Multicoloured. W* w **16** *(sideways). P* 14½.

553 9p. Type **158** 30 30
554 20p. Austin "Seven", 1929 .. .. 50 50
555 45p. Morris "Cowley" 11.9 h.p., 1929 .. 1·00 1·00
556 60p. Sunbeam 25 h.p., 1932 .. .. 1·40 1·40
553/6 .. .. *Set of* 4 3·00 3·00
MS557 93×74 mm. £1 Ford "Model A Fordor" .. 2·00 2·50

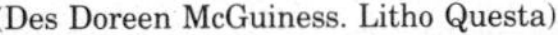

(Des Doreen McGuiness. Litho Questa)

1990 (1 Feb). *Farm Animals. T* **159** *and similar vert designs. Multicoloured. W* w **16**. *P* 14.

558 9p. Type **159** 30 30
559 13p. Pigs 35 35
560 45p. Cow and calf .. .. 1·00 1·25
561 60p. Geese .. .. 1·40 1·60
558/61 .. .. *Set of* 4 2·75 3·25

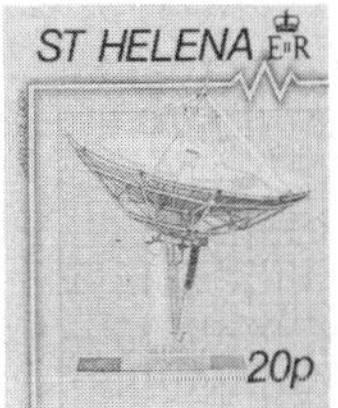

160 1840 Twopence Blue

161 Satellite Dish

(Des D. Miller. Litho Walsall)

1990 (3 May). *"Stamp World London 90" International Stamp Exhibition, London. T* **160** *and similar horiz designs. W* w **14** *(sideways). P* 14.

562 13p. black and cobalt 40 40
563 20p. multicoloured 65 65
564 38p. multicoloured .. .. 1·10 1·10
565 45p. multicoloured .. .. 1·40 1·40
562/5 .. .. *Set of* 4 3·25 3·25

Designs:—20p. 1840 Penny Black and 19th-century St. Helena postmark; 38p. Delivering mail to sub-post office; 45p. Mail van and Post Office, Jamestown.

(Des N. Shewring. Litho B.D.T.)

1990 (28 July). *Modern Telecommunications Links. T* **161** *and similar vert designs. Multicoloured. W* w **14**. *P* 13½.

566 20p. Type **161** 60 60
a. Block of 4. Nos. 566/9 .. .. 2·25
567 20p. Digital telephone exchange 60 60
568 20p. Public card phone 60 60
569 20p. Facsimile machine 60 60
566/9 .. .. *Set of* 4 2·25 2·25

Nos. 566/9 were printed together, *se-tenant*, in blocks of 4 throughout the sheet of 16.

(Des D. Miller. Litho Questa)

1990 (4 Aug). *90th Birthday of Queen Elizabeth the Queen Mother. Vert designs as T* **107** *(25p.) or* **108** *(£1) of Kenya. W* w **16**. *P* 14×15 *(25p.) or* 14½ *(£1).*

570 25p. multicoloured 75 75
571 £1 black and purple-brown .. .. .. 2·50 2·75

Designs:—25p. Lady Elizabeth Bowes-Lyon, April 1923; £1 Queen Elizabeth visiting communal kitchen, 1940.

162 *Dane* (mail ship), 1857

163 Baptist Chapel, Sandy Bay

(Des L. Curtis. Litho Walsall)

1990 (13 Sept). *Maiden Voyage of* St. Helena II. *T* **162** *and similar horiz designs. Multicoloured. W* w **14** *(sideways). P* 14×14½.

572 13p. Type **162** 40 40
573 20p. *St. Helena I* offloading at St. Helena 65 65
574 38p. Launch of *St. Helena II* .. .. 1·10 1·10
575 45p. The Duke of York launching *St. Helena II* .. .. 1·25 1·40
572/5 .. .. *Set of* 4 3·00 3·25
MS576 100×100 mm. £1 *St. Helena II* and outline map of St. Helena .. .. .. 2·75 3·25

No. **MS**576 also contains two imperforate designs of similar stamps from Ascension and Tristan da Cunha without face values.

(Des G. Vasarhelyi. Litho Questa)

1990 (18 Oct). *Christmas. Local Churches. T* **163** *and similar horiz designs. Multicoloured. W* w **14** *(sideways). P* 14.

577 10p. Type **163** 30 30
578 13p. St. Martin in the Hills Church .. 35 35
579 20p. St. Helena and the Cross Church .. 55 55
580 38p. St. James Church .. .. .. 1·00 1·00
581 45p. St. Paul's Cathedral .. .. .. 1·25 1·25
577/81 .. .. *Set of* 5 3·25 3·25

164 "Funeral Cortège, Jamestown Wharf" (detail, V. Adam)

165 Officer, Leicestershire Regiment

(Des N. Harvey. Litho Questa)

1990 (15 Dec). *150th Anniv of Removal of Napoleon's Body. T* **164** *and similar horiz designs. W* w **14** *(sideways). P* 13½×14.

582 13p. black, sepia and blue-green 40 40
583 20p. black, sepia and ultramarine .. 70 70
584 38p. black, sepia and deep magenta .. 1·25 1·25
585 45p. multicoloured .. .. .. 1·50 1·50
582/5 .. .. *Set of* 4 3·50 3·50

Designs:—20p. "Coffin being conveyed to the *Belle Poule*" (detail, V. Adam); 38p. "Transfer of the Coffin to the *Normandie*, Cherbourg" (detail, V. Adam); 45p. "Napoleon's Tomb, St. Helena" (T. Sutherland).

(Des C. Collins. Litho Questa)

1991 (2 May). *Military Uniforms of* 1897. *T* **165** *and similar vert designs. Multicoloured. W* w **14**. *P* 14.

586 13p. Type **165** 40 40
587 15p. Officer, York & Lancaster Regiment 45 45
588 20p. Colour-sergeant, Leicestershire Regt 65 65
589 38p. Bandsman, York & Lancaster Regt .. 1·25 1·25
590 45p. Lance-corporal, York & Lancaster Regt 1·50 1·50
586/90 .. .. *Set of* 5 3·75 3·75

(Des D. Miller. Litho Questa)

1991 (1 July). *65th Birthday of Queen Elizabeth II and 70th Birthday of Prince Philip. Vert designs as T* **58** *of Kiribati. Multicoloured. W* w **16** *(sideways). P* 14½×14.

591 25p. Queen Elizabeth II 75 75
a. Horiz pair. Nos. 591/2 separated by label .. .. 1·50 1·50
592 25p. Prince Philip in naval uniform .. 75 75

Nos. 591/2 were printed in similar sheet format to Nos. 366/7 of Kiribati.

166 "Madonna and Child" (T. Vecellio)

167 Matchless (346cc) Motorcycle, 1947

(Des G. Vasarhelyi. Litho Walsall)

1991 (2 Nov). *Christmas. Religious Paintings. T* **166** *and similar vert designs. Multicoloured. W* w **14**. *P* 14.

593 10p. Type **166** 35 35
594 13p. "The Holy Family" (A. Mengs) .. 45 45
595 20p. "Madonna and Child" (W. Dyce) .. 65 65
596 38p. "The Two Trinities" (B. Murillo) .. 1·10 1·10
597 45p. "The Virgin and Child" (G. Bellini) .. 1·60 1·60
593/7 .. .. *Set of* 5 3·75 3·75

(Des N. Shewring. Litho Questa)

1991 (16 Nov). *"Philanippon '91" International Stamp Exhibition, Tokyo. Motorcycles. T* **167** *and similar horiz designs. W* w **16** *(sideways). P* 14×14½.

598 13p. Type **167** 35 35
599 20p. Triumph "Tiger 100" (500cc), 1950 .. 55 55
600 38p. Honda "CD" (175cc), 1967 .. .. 95 95
601 45p. Yamaha "DTE 400", 1976 .. .. 1·40 1·40
598/601 .. .. *Set of* 4 3·00 3·00
MS602 72×49 mm. 65p. Suzuki "RM" (250cc), 1984 .. .. 1·75 2·00

168 *Eye of the Wind* (cadet ship) and Compass Rose

(Des. R. Watton. Litho Walsall)

1992 (24 Jan). *500th Anniv of Discovery of America by Columbus and Re-enactment Voyages. T* **168** *and similar horiz designs. Multicoloured. W* w **14** *(sideways). P* 13½×14.

603 15p. Type **168** 50 50
604 25p. *Soren Larsen* (cadet ship) and map of Re-enactment Voyages 80 80
605 35p. *Santa Maria, Nina* and *Pinta* .. .. 1·25 1·25
606 50p. Columbus and *Santa Maria* .. .. 1·60 1·60
603/6 .. .. *Set of* 4 3·75 3·75

(Des D. Miller. Litho Questa (50p.), Walsall (others))

1992 (6 Feb). *40th Anniv of Queen Elizabeth II's Accession. Horiz designs as T* **112** *of Kenya. Multicoloured. W* w **14** *(sideways). P* 14.

607 11p. Prince Andrew Central School .. 30 30
608 15p. Plantation House 45 45
609 25p. Jamestown 70 70
610 35p. Three portraits of Queen Elizabeth .. 95 95
611 50p. Queen Elizabeth II .. .. .. 1·25 1·25
607/11 .. .. *Set of* 5 3·25 3·25

POSTAGE DUE STAMPS

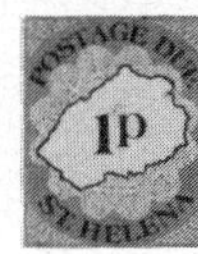

D 1 Outline Map of St. Helena

(Des L. Curtis. Litho Questa)

1986 (9 June). W w **16**. *P* 14½×14.

D1 D 1 1p. deep brown and cinnamon 10 10
D2 2p. deep brown and bright orange .. 10 10
D3 5p. deep brown and orange-vermilion .. 10 15
D4 7p. black and bright reddish violet .. 15 20
D5 10p. black and violet-blue 20 25
D6 25p. black and pale emerald 50 55
D1/6 .. .. *Set of* 6 95 1·10

St. Kitts-Nevis

ST. CHRISTOPHER

From 1760 the postal service for St. Christopher was organised by the Deputy Postmaster General on Antigua. It was not until May 1779 that the first postmaster was appointed to the island and the use of postmarks on outgoing mail commenced.

Stamps of Great Britain were used between May 1858 and the end of March 1860 when control of the postal services passed to the local authorities. In the years which followed, prior to the introduction of St. Christopher stamps in April 1870, a circular "PAID" handstamp was used on overseas mail.

BASSETERRE

Stamps of GREAT BRITAIN *cancelled* "A 12" *as Type* Z 1 *of Jamaica.*

1858 *to* **1860.**
Z1 1d. rose-red (1857), *perf* 14 .. ..
Z2 2d. blue (1858) (Plate No. 7) £900
Z3 4d. rose (1857) £300
Z4 6d. lilac (1856) £180
Z5 1s. green (1856) £900

PRICES FOR STAMPS ON COVER	
Nos. 1/5	*from* × 10
Nos. 6/8	*from* × 7
Nos. 9/10	*from* × 7
Nos. 11/21	*from* × 6
Nos. 22/3	*from* × 8
Nos. 24/8	—
Nos. R1/6	—

1

FOUR PENCE
(2)

Halfpenny
(3)

1870 (1 Apr)–**79.** *Wmk Crown CC. (a) P* 12½.
1 1 1d. dull rose .. .. 55·00 40·00
a. Wmk sideways £225 £180
2 1d. magenta (*shades*) (1871) .. .. 38·00 26·00
4 6d. yellow-green .. .. 85·00 17·00
5 6d. green (1871) .. .. 85·00 7·50

(*b*) *P* 14
6 1 1d. magenta (*shades*) (1875) .. .. 55·00 7·00
a. Bisected diag or vert (½d.) (on cover) (3.82) .. .. † £1100
7 2½d. red-brown (11.79) £170 £225
8 4d. blue (11.79) .. .. £150 15·00
a. Wmk sideways £500 £100
9 6d. green (1876) .. .. 50·00 5·00
a. Imperf between (pair) ..
b. Wmk sideways .. .. £300 90·00

The magenta used for the 1d. was a fugitive colour which reacts to both light and water.

No. 6a. was authorised for use between March and June 1882 to make up the 2½d. letter rate and for ½d. book post.

1882 (June)–**90.** *Wmk Crown CA. P* 14.
11 1 ½d. dull green 50 80
a. Wmk sideways £250
12 1d. dull magenta .. .. £475 60·00
a. Bisected diagonally (½d.) (on cover)
13 1d. carmine-rose (2.84) 60 60
a. Bisected (½d.) (on cover) .. ..
14 2½d. pale red-brown .. .. .. £170 55·00
15 2½d. deep red-brown .. .. .. £180 60·00
16 2½d. ultramarine (2.84) .. .. .. 1·50 1·50
17 4d. blue .. .. £400 20·00
18 4d. grey (10.84) .. .. 1·25 80
19 6d. olive-brown ((3.90) .. .. .. 80·00 £200
20 1s. mauve (6.86) .. .. 90·00 65·00
21 1s. bright mauve (1890) .. .. .. 80·00 £110
19/20 Optd "Specimen" .. .. *Set of* 2 £120

1884 (Dec). *No.* 9 *surch with T* 2 *by* The Advertiser Press.
22 1 4d. on 6d. green .. .. 48·00 48·00
a. Full stop after "PENCE" .. .. .. 48·00 48·00
b. Surch double £1600

No. 22a occurred on alternate stamps.

1885 (March). *No.* 13 *bisected and each half diagonally surch with T* 3.
23 1 ½d. on half of 1d. carmine-rose .. .. 24·00 32·00
a. Unsevered pair £100 £110
ab. Ditto, one surch inverted £350 £250
b. Surch inverted £250 £160
c. Surch double .. .. ..

ONE PENNY.
(4)

4d.
(5)

1886 (June). *No.* 9 *surch with T* 4 *or* 5 *each showing a manuscript line through the original value.*
24 1 1d. on 6d. green .. .. .. 16·00 28·00
a. Surch inverted £5000
b. Surch double .. .. .. — £1300
25 4d. on 6d. green .. .. .. 48·00 90·00
a. No stop after "d" £180 £200
b. Surch double £1400 £1600

No. 24b is only known penmarked with dates between 21 July and 3 August 1886, or with violet handstamp.

1887 (May). *No.* 11 *surch with T* 4 *showing a manuscript line through the original value.*
26 1 1d. on ½d. dull green .. .. .. 28·00 38·00

ONE PENNY.
(7)

1888 (May). *No.* 16 *surch.*

(*a*) *With T* 4. *Original value unobliterated*
27 1 1d. on 2½d. ultramarine £10000 £10000

(*b*) *With T* 7 *showing a manuscript line through the original value*
28 1 1d. on 2½d. ultramarine .. .. 38·00 42·00
a. Surch inverted £7000 £4750

The 1d. of Antigua was used provisionally in St. Christopher between February and March 1890 during a shortage of 1d. stamps. Such use can be distinguished by the postmark, which is "A 12" in place of "A02" (*price from* £160 *used*).

REVENUE STAMPS USED FOR POSTAGE

Saint Christopher
(R 1)

SAINT KITTS NEVIS REVENUE
(R 2)

1883. *Nos.* F6 *and* F8 *of Nevis optd with Type* R 1, *in violet. Wmk Crown CA. P* 14.
R1 1d. lilac-mauve £225
R2 6d. green .. .. 60·00 90·00

1885. *Optd with Type* R 2. *Wmk Crown CA. P* 14.
R3 1 1d. rose .. .. 1·25 7·50
R4 3d. mauve .. .. 9·00 50·00
R5 6d. orange-brown .. .. .. 4·00 35·00
R6 1s. olive .. .. 1·50 35·00

Other fiscal stamps with overprints as above also exist, but none of these was ever available for postal purposes.

The stamps for St. Christopher were superseded by the general issue for Leeward Islands on 31 October 1890.

Stamps for St. Kitts, issued from 1980 onwards will be found listed after those for the combined colony.

NEVIS

Little is known concerning the early postal affairs of Nevis, but it is recorded that the British G.P.O. was to establish a branch office on the island under an Act of Parliament, passed in 1710, although arrangements may not have been finalised for a number of years afterwards. Nevis appears as "a new office" in the P.O. Accounts of 1787.

Stamps of Great Britain were used on the island from May 1858 until the colonial authorities assumed control of the postal service on 1 May 1860. Between this date and the introduction of Nevis stamps in 1861 No. CC1 was again used on overseas mail.

CHARLESTOWN

CROWNED-CIRCLE HANDSTAMPS

CC 1

CC1 CC 1 NEVIS (R.) (9.1852) .. .. *Price on cover* £2000

No. CC1, but struck in black, was later used on several occasions up to 1886 where there were shortages of adhesive stamps.

Stamps of GREAT BRITAIN *cancelled* "A 09" *as Type* Z 1 *of Jamaica.*

1858 *to* **1860.**
Z1 1d. rose-red (1857), *perf* 14 .. .. £375
Z2 2d. blue (1858) (Plate Nos. 7, 8) .. ..
Z3 4d. rose (1857) £300
Z4 6d. lilac (1856) £275
Z5 1s. green (1856) .. ..

PRICES FOR STAMPS ON COVER	
Nos. 1/22	*from* × 8
Nos. 23/4	*from* × 4
Nos. 25/34	*from* × 6
Nos. 35/6	*from* × 7
Nos. F1/8	*from* × 12

1

2

3

4

The designs on the stamps refer to a medicinal spring on the island

(Recess Nissen & Parker, London)

1861. *Greyish paper. P* 13.
5 1 1d. dull lake .. .. 45·00 35·00
a. On blued paper .. .. £180 95·00
6 2 4d. rose .. .. 75·00 55·00
a. On blued paper £600 £140
7 3 6d. grey-lilac .. .. 70·00 40·00
a. On blued paper £500 £180
8 4 1s. green .. .. £150 50·00
a. On blued paper £750 £150

1866–76. *White paper. P* 15.
9 1 1d. pale red .. .. 30·00 24·00
10 1d. deep red .. .. 30·00 24·00
11 2 4d. orange .. .. 95·00 19·00
12 4d. deep orange .. .. 95·00 19·00
13 4 1s. blue-green .. .. £150 26·00
14 1s. yellow-green (1876) £800 £100
a. Vertically laid paper £10000 £3500
b. No. 9 on sheet with crossed lines on hill £3500 £500
c. Ditto. On laid paper .. .. .. † £6500

Examples of the 4d. exist showing part of a papermakers watermark reading "A. COWAN & SONS EXTRA SUPERFINE".

(Lithographed by transfer from the engraved plates Nissen and Parker, London)

1876–78. *P* 15.
15 1 1d. pale rose-red .. .. 15·00 12·00
a. Imperf (pair) £225
16 1d. deep rose-red .. .. 22·00 17·00
17 1d. vermilion-red (1878) .. .. .. 20·00 17·00
a. Bisected (½d.) (on cover) .. .. .. † £1100
18 2 4d. orange-yellow .. .. £140 27·00
a. Imperf between (vert pair) £3000
19 3 6d. grey (1878) £190 £170
20 4 1s. pale green (1878) .. .. .. 55·00 80·00
a. Imperf ..
b. Imperf between (horiz strip of three) £3500
c. No. 9 on sheet with crossed lines on hill £225
21 1s. deep green .. .. 60·00 90·00
c. No. 9 on sheet with crossed lines on hill

No. 21c occurs on a small part of the deep green printing only.

RETOUCHES. 1d. Lithograph.
i. No. 1 on sheet. Top of hill over kneeling figure redrawn by five thick lines and eight small slanting lines £140 £150
ii. No. 1 on sheet. Another retouch. Three series of short vertical strokes behind the kneeling figure £140 £150
iii. No. 3 on sheet. Right upper corner star and border below star retouched £140 £150
iv. No. 9 on sheet. Retouch in same position as on No. 3 but differing in detail £160 £170
v. No. 12 on sheet. Dress of standing figure retouched by a number of horizontal and vertical lines £140 £150

1878. *Litho. P* 11½.
22 1 1d. vermilion-red .. .. 38·00 48·00
a. Bisected (½d.) (on cover) .. .. .. † £1100
b. Imperf (pair) £200
c. Imperf between (horiz pair) .. ..

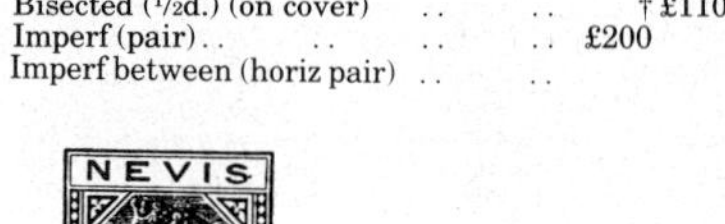

5 (Die I)

NEVIS. 1d.
(6)

(Typo D.L.R.)

1879–80. *Wmk Crown CC. P* 14.
23 5 1d. lilac-mauve (1880) .. .. .. 35·00 26·00
a. Bisected (½d.) (on cover) .. .. .. † £800
24 2½d. red-brown .. .. 85·00 75·00

1882–90. *Wmk Crown CA. P* 14.
25 5 ½d. dull green (11.83) .. .. .. 2·50 4·50
26 1d. lilac-mauve .. .. 80·00 20·00
a. Bisected (½d.) on cover (1883) .. † £700
27 1d. dull rose (11.83) .. .. .. 14·00 10·00
a. Carmine (1884) .. .. .. 3·00 3·25
28 2½d. red-brown .. .. 90·00 45·00
29 2½d. ultramarine (11.83) .. .. .. 9·00 6·00
30 4d. blue .. .. £275 45·00
31 4d. grey (1884) .. .. 3·75 2·50
32 6d. green (11.83) £350 £350
33 6d. chestnut (10.88) .. .. .. 17·00 38·00
34 1s. pale violet (3.90) .. .. .. 85·00 £150
33/4 Optd "Specimen" .. .. *Set of* 2 £110

1883. *No.* 26 *bisected vertically and surch with T* **6**, *reading upwards or downwards.*
35 ½d. on half 1d. lilac-mauve (V.) .. .. £400 27·00
a. Surch double .. .. — £275
b. Surch on half "REVENUE" stamp No. F6 — £500
36 ½d. on half 1d. lilac-mauve .. .. .. £400 25·00
a. Surch double .. .. — £275
b. Unsevered pair £1000 £200
ba. Surch on right half only .. .. ..
c. Surch on half "REVENUE" stamp No. F6 — £500

FISCALS USED FOR POSTAGE

Revenue (F 1) REVENUE (F 2)

1882. (*a*) *Stamps of* 1876 *optd with Type* F 1.
F1 1 1d. bright red .. .. 27·00
F2 2 1d. rose .. .. 27·00 13·00
F3 4d. orange .. .. 55·00
F4 3 6d. grey .. .. 90·00
F5 4 1s. green £100
a. No. 9 on sheet with crossed lines on hill

(*b*) *Nos.* 26, 30 *and* 32 *optd with Type* F **2**
F6 5 1d. lilac-mauve .. .. 24·00 26·00
a. Bisected (½d.) (on cover) .. ..
F7 4d. blue .. .. 13·00 30·00
F8 6d. green .. .. 11·00 35·00

Nos. F1/5 were produced from fresh transfers. Similar "REVENUE" handstamps, both with and without stop, were also applied to postage issues.

The stamps of Nevis were superseded by the general issue for Leeward Islands on 31 October 1890. Stamps for Nevis were again issued in 1980 and will be found listed after those for the combined colony.

ST. KITTS-NEVIS

CROWN COLONY

Stamps for the combined colony were introduced in 1903, and were used concurrently with the general issues of Leeward Islands until the latter were withdrawn on 1 July 1956.

PRICES FOR STAMPS ON COVER TO 1945	
Nos. 1/9	*from* × 3
No. 10	—
Nos. 11/20	*from* × 3
No. 21	—
Nos. 22/3	*from* × 15
Nos. 24/34	*from* × 3
Nos. 35/6	—
Nos. 37/47	*from* × 2
Nos. 47*a*/*b*	—
Nos. 48/57	*from* × 2
Nos. 58/60	—
Nos. 61/4	*from* × 2
Nos. 65/7	*from* × 5
Nos. 68/77	*from* × 2

1 Christopher Columbus

2 Medicinal Spring

(Typo D.L.R.)

1903. *Wmk Crown CA. P* 14.
1 1 ½d. dull purple and deep green .. 1·50 70
2 2 1d. grey-black and carmine .. 2·50 20
3 1 2d. dull purple and brown .. 2·25 8·00
4 2½d. grey-black and blue .. 9·00 3·50
5 2 3d. deep green and orange .. 3·00 14·00
6 1 6d. grey-black and bright purple .. 3·25 15·00
7 1s. grey-green and orange .. 6·00 11·00
8 2 2s. deep green and grey-black .. 9·00 14·00
9 1 2s. 6d. grey-black and violet .. 16·00 30·00
10 2 5s. dull purple and sage-green .. 30·00 50·00
1/10 .. .. *Set of* 10 70·00 £130
1/10 Optd "Specimen" .. .. *Set of* 10 £130

1905–18. *Wmk Mult Crown CA. Chalk-surfaced paper* (1d. (*No.* 13), 5s.) *or ordinary paper* (*others*). *P* 14.
11 1 ½d. dull purple and deep green .. .. 4·00 5·50
12 ½d. grey-green (1907) 30 35
a. Dull blue-green (1916) .. .. 30 1·25
13 2 1d. grey-black and carmine (1906) .. 1·00 25
14 1d. carmine (1907) 80 15
a. Scarlet (1916) 35 20
15 1 2d. dull purple and brown .. .. 1·25 1·75
a. Chalk-surfaced paper (1906) .. 80 1·75
16 2½d. grey-black and blue (1907) .. 14·00 2·75
17 2½d. bright blue (1907) 60 40
18 2 3d. deep green and orange .. .. 1·50 3·00
a. Chalk-surfaced paper (1906) .. 80 2·00
19 1 6d. grey-black and deep violet .. .. 8·50 25·00
a. Chalk-surfaced paper. *Grey-black and deep purple* (1908) .. .. .. 8·00 16·00
ab. Grey-black and bright purple (1916) 4·25 15·00
20 1s. grey-green and orange (1909) .. 4·00 12·00
a. Chalk-surfaced paper .. .. 1·75 16·00
21 2 5s. dull purple and sage-green (11.18) 23·00 55·00
11/21 .. .. *Set of* 11 45·00 85·00
12, 14, 17 Optd "Specimen" .. *Set of* 3 60·00

WAR TAX (3) WAR STAMP (3*a*)

1916 (Oct). *Optd with T* **3**. *Wmk Mult Crown CA. P* 14.
22 1 ½d. dull blue-green (No. 12*a*) (Optd S. £40) 15 30
a. Deep green 10 30
No. 22*a* was a special printing produced for this overprint.

1918 (Aug). *Optd with T* **3***a*. *Wmk Mult Crown CA. P* 14.
23 1 1½d. orange (Optd S. £45) 15 30
No. 23 was a special printing produced for this overprint.

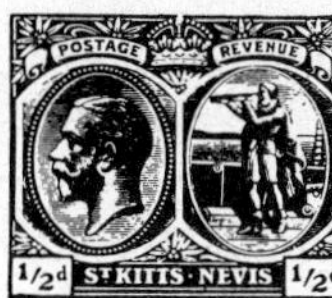

4

5

(Typo D.L.R.)

1920–22. *Wmk Mult Crown CA (sideways). Ordinary paper* (½d. *to* 2½d.) *or chalk-surfaced paper* (*others*). *P* 14.
24 4 ½d. blue-green .. .. 3·00 3·50
25 5 1d. carmine .. .. 2·00 2·00
26 4 1½d. orange-yellow .. .. .. 1·25 80
27 5 2d. slate-grey .. .. 2·25 3·00
28 4 2½d. ultramarine .. .. 1·25 4·50
29 5 3d. purple/*yellow* .. .. .. 1·00 7·00
30 4 6d. dull purple and bright mauve .. 2·50 8·50
31 5 1s. grey and black/*green* .. .. 1·25 3·00
32 4 2s. dull purple and blue/*blue* .. 6·00 15·00
33 5 2s. 6d. grey and red/*blue* .. .. 5·00 25·00
34 4 5s. green and red/*pale yellow* .. 5·00 35·00
35 5 10s. green and red/*green* .. .. 12·00 45·00
36 4 £1 purple and black/*red* (1922) .. £200 £275
24/36 .. .. *Set of* 13 £225 £375
24/36 Optd "Specimen" .. .. *Set of* 13 £275

1921–9. *Wmk Mult Script CA (sideways). Chalk-surfaced paper* (2½d.) (*No.* 44), 3d. (*No.* 45*a*) *and* 6d. *to* 5s.) *or ordinary paper* (*others*). *P* 14.
37 4 ½d. blue-green 40 65
a. Yellow-green (1922) .. .. .. 1·00 70
38 5 1d. rose-carmine 20 15
39 1d. deep violet (1922) .. .. .. 1·25 35
a. Pale violet (1929) .. .. .. 1·75 65
40 4 1½d. red (1925) .. .. 75 2·50
40*a* 1½d. red-brown (1929) 30 15
41 5 2d. slate-grey (1922) 30 60
42 4 2½d. pale bright blue (1922) .. .. 2·00 2·25
43 2½d. brown (1922) .. .. .. 75 4·50
44 2½d. ultramarine (1927) .. .. .. 1·50 3·50
45 5 3d. dull ultramarine (1922) .. .. 40 2·50
45*a* 3d. purple/*yellow* (1927) .. .. 50 2·50
46 4 6d. dull and bright purple (1924) .. 2·00 4·50
46*a* 5 1s. black/*green* (1929) .. .. .. 3·75 6·00
47 4 2s. purple and blue/*blue* (1922) .. 3·50 12·00
47*a* 5 2s. 6d. black and red/*blue* (1927) .. 12·00 24·00
47*b* 4 5s. green and red/*yellow* (1929) .. 23·00 42·00
37/47*b* .. .. *Set of* 16 45·00 95·00
37/47*b* Optd/Perf "Specimen" .. *Set of* 16 £375
In the Specimen set above No. 38 is overprinted. A later printing exists perforated "Specimen" (*Price* £70).

6 Old Road Bay and Mount Misery

(Typo D.L.R.)

1923. *Tercentenary of Colony. Chalk-surfaced paper. P* 14.
(*a*) *Wmk Mult Script CA* (*sideways*)
48 6 ½d. black and green .. .. .. 2·00 6·00
49 1d. black and bright violet .. .. 1·75 1·50
50 1½d. black and scarlet .. .. .. 3·75 7·00
51 2d. black and slate-grey .. .. 1·75 1·50
52 2½d. black and brown .. .. .. 3·00 18·00
53 3d. black and ultramarine .. .. 3·25 12·00
54 6d. black and bright purple .. .. 8·00 22·00
55 1s. black and sage-green .. .. 12·00 27·00
56 2s. black and blue/*blue* .. .. 24·00 48·00
57 2s. 6d. black and red/*blue* .. .. 38·00 65·00
58 10s. black and red/*emerald* £225 £325
(*b*) *Wmk Mult Crown CA* (*sideways*)
59 6 5s. black and red/*pale yellow* .. .. 60·00 £150
60 £1 black and purple/*red* £850 £1300
48/60 .. .. *Set of* 13 £1100 £1800
48/60 Optd "Specimen" .. .. *Set of* 13 £800

1935 (6 May). *Silver Jubilee. As Nos.* 114/17 *of Jamaica, but ptd by Waterlow. P* 11×12.
61 1d. deep blue and scarlet 75 20
j. Kite and vertical log .. .. .. 24·00
k. Kite and horizontal log .. .. .. 40·00
62 1½d. ultramarine and grey 60 75
j. Kite and vertical log .. .. .. 28·00
63 2½d. brown and deep blue .. .. .. 1·00 80
64 1s. slate and purple .. .. .. 4·75 9·50
j. Kite and vertical log .. .. .. 75·00
k. Kite and horizontal log .. .. .. 80·00
61/4 .. .. *Set of* 4 6·50 10·00
61/4 Perf "Specimen" .. .. *Set of* 4 75·00
For illustrations of plate varieties see Omnibus section following Zimbabwe.

1937 (12 May). *Coronation. As Nos.* 118/20 *of Jamaica.*
65 1d. scarlet 30 15
66 1½d. buff 35 10
67 2½d. bright blue 40 35
65/7 .. .. *Set of* 3 95 55
65/7 Perf "Specimen" .. .. *Set of* 3 50·00
Nos. 61/7 are inscribed "ST. CHRISTOPHER AND NEVIS".

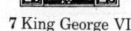

7 King George VI

8 King George VI and Medicinal Spring

9 King George VI and Christopher Columbus

10 King George VI and Anguilla Island

Break in value tablet (R. 12/5) (1947 ptg only)

Break in oval (R. 12/1) (1938 ptg only)

Break in value tablet frame (R.3/2)

Break in value tablet frame (R.12/3) (ptgs between 1941 and 1945 only)

Break in frame above ornament (R. 2/4) (ptgs between 1941 and 1944)

Break in oval (R.12/5) (ptgs between 1941 and 1945 only. Sometimes touched-in by hand painting)

(Typo; centre litho (T 10). D.L.R.)

1938 (15 Aug)–**49**. *Wmk Mult Script CA (sideways on T* **8** *and* **9**). *Chalk-surfaced paper* (10s., £1). *P* 14 (*T* **7** *and* **10**) *or* 13×12 (*T* **8/9**).

68 **7** ½d. green . . . . 1·75 10
   a. Blue-green (5.4.43) . . 10 10
69 1d. scarlet . . . . 2·50 40
   a. Carmine (5.43) . . 30 20
   b. Rose-red (1947) . . 40 20
70 1½d. orange 15 20
71 **8** 2d. scarlet and grey . . 12·00 2·25
   a. Chalk-surfaced paper. *Carmine and deep grey* (1940) . . 38·00 9·00
   b. Perf 14. *Scarlet and pale grey* (1941) 50 70
   ba. Scarlet and deep grey (5.43) . . 17·00 5·00
   bb. Chalk-surfaced paper. *Scarlet and pale grey* (8.49) . . 80 55
72 **7** 2½d. ultramarine . . 2·25 30
   a. Bright ultramarine (5.4.43) . . 15 15
73 **8** 3d. dull reddish purple and scarlet . . 7·00 90
   a. Chalk-surfaced paper. *Brown-purple & carmine-vermilion* (1940) 11·00 2·75
   b. Perf 14. Chalk-surfaced paper. *Reddish purple and scarlet* (1942) 1·00 1·50
   ba. Ordinary paper (5.43) . . 1·00 1·00
   bb. Ordinary paper. *Pur & scar* (1945) 11·00 16·00
   bc. Chalk-surfaced paper. *Reddish mauve and scarlet* (1947) . . 50·00 18·00
   bd. Break in value tablet . .
74 **9** 6d. green and bright purple . . 6·00 1·25
   a. Break in oval . .
   b. Perf 14. Chalk-surfaced paper. *Green and deep claret* (1942) . . 35·00 10·00
   ba. Ordinary paper. *Green & pur* (5.43) 2·50 90
   bb. Chalk-surfaced paper. *Green and purple* (10.48) . . 1·25 1·00
75 **8** 1s. black and green . . 10·00 1·25
   a. Break in value tablet frame . . 70·00
   b. Perf 14 (1943) . . 2·25 55
   ba. Break in value tablet frame . . 40·00
   c. Perf 14. Chalk-surfaced paper (28.7.49) . . 75 70
   ca. Break in value tablet frame . . 28·00
76 2s. 6d. black and scarlet . . 17·00 9·00
   a. Perf 14. Chalk-surfaced paper (1942) . . 6·00 3·00
   ab. Ordinary paper (5.43) . . 5·00 3·00
77 **9** 5s. green and scarlet . . 55·00 10·00
   a. Perf 14. Chalk-surfaced paper (1941) . . 17·00 7·50
   ab. Break in value tablet frame . . £120
   ac. Break in frame above ornament . . £120
   ad. Break in oval . . £120
   b. Perf 14. Ordinary paper (5.43) . . 13·00 6·00
   ba. Break in value tablet frame . . 90·00
   bb. Break in frame above ornament 90·00
   bc. Break in oval . . 90·00
77*c* **10** 10s. black and ultramarine (1.9.48) . . 12·00 18·00
77*d* £1 black and brown (1.9.48) . . 15·00 22·00
68/77*d* . . *Set of* 12 45·00 45·00
68/77 Perf "Specimen" . . *Set of* 10 £180

1946 (1 Nov). *Victory. As Nos.* 141/2 *of Jamaica.*
78 1½d. red-orange . . 10 10
79 3d. carmine . . 10 10
78/9 Perf "Specimen" . . *Set of* 2 60·00

1949 (3 Jan). *Royal Silver Wedding. As Nos.* 143/4 *of Jamaica.*
80 2½d. ultramarine . . 10 10
81 5s. carmine . . 3·50 2·50

1949 (10 Oct). *75th Anniv of U.P.U. As Nos.* 145/8 *of Jamaica.*
82 2½d. ultramarine . . 25 10
83 3d. carmine-red . . 35 25
84 6d. magenta . . 35 25
85 1s. blue-green . . 35 25
82/5 . . *Set of* 4 1·10 75

ANGUILLA   ANGUILLA

TERCENTENARY 1650-1950 (11)   TERCENTENARY 1650—1950 (12)

1950 (10 Nov). *Tercentenary of British Settlement in Anguilla. T* **7** *optd as T* **11** *and T* **8/9**, *perf* 13×12½ *optd as T* **12**. *Chalk-surfaced paper* (3d., 6d., 1s.).
86 **7** 1d. bright rose-red . . 10 10
87 1½d. orange . . 10 10
   a. Error. Crown missing, W 9*a* . . £1000
   b. Error. St. Edward's Crown, W 9*b* . . £650
88 2½d. bright ultramarine . . 10 10
89 **8** 3d. dull purple and scarlet . . 10 10
90 **9** 6d. green and bright purple . . 10 10
91 **8** 1s. black and green (R.) . . 10 10
   a. Break in value tablet frame . . 8·00
86/91 . . *Set of* 6 40 40

Nos. 87a/b occur on a row in the watermark, in which the crowns and letters "CA" alternate.

(New Currency. 100 cents = 1 West Indian dollar)

1951 (16 Feb). *Inauguration of B.W.I. University College. As Nos.* 149/50 *of Jamaica.*
92 3c. black and yellow-orange . . 15 10
93 12c. turquoise-green and magenta . . 15 20

NEW INFORMATION

The editor is always interested to correspond with people who have new information that will improve or correct the Catalogue.

ST. CHRISTOPHER, NEVIS AND ANGUILLA

LEGISLATIVE COUNCIL

13 Bath House and Spa, Nevis

14 Map of the Islands

1952 (14 June). *Vert designs as T* **14** (3, 12 *c.*) *or horiz as* **13** (*others*). *Wmk Mult Script CA. P* 12½.
94 1 c. deep green and ochre . . 15 25
95 2 c. green . . 20 30
96 3 c. carmine-red and violet . . 25 30
97 4 c. scarlet . . 20 20
98 5 c. bright blue and grey . . 20 10
99 6 c. ultramarine . . 20 15
100 12 c. deep blue and reddish brown . . 20 10
101 24 c. black and carmine-red . . 20 10
102 48 c. olive and chocolate . . 1·50 1·50
103 60 c. ochre and deep green . . 1·50 1·50
104 $1.20, deep green and ultramarine . . 4·50 1·75
105 $4.80, green and carmine . . 10·00 16·00
94/105 . . *Set of* 12 17·00 20·00

Designs:—2 c. Warner Park; 4 c. Brimstone Hill; 5 c. Nevis from the sea, North; 6 c. Pinney's Beach, Nevis; 12 c. Sir Thomas Warner's Tomb; 24 c. Old Road Bay; 48 c. Sea Island cotton, Nevis; 60 c. The Treasury; $1.20, Salt pond, Anguilla; $4.80, Sugar factory.

1953 (2 June). *Coronation. As No.* 153 *of Jamaica.*
106 2 c. black and bright green . . 10 10

25 Sombrero Lighthouse

26 Map of Anguilla and Dependencies

(Recess Waterlow (until 1961), then D.L.R.)

1954 (1 Mar)–**63**. *Designs previously used for King George VI issue, but with portrait of Queen Elizabeth II as in T* **25/6** *or new values and designs* (½ *c.*, 8 *c.*, $2.40). *Wmk Mult Script CA. P* 12½.
106*a* ½ c. deep olive (3.7.56) . . 20 10
107 1 c. deep green and ochre . . 15 10
   a. Deep green and orange-ochre (13.2.62) 60 60
   b. Imperf vert (horiz strip of three) . . † —
108 2 c. green . . 30 10
   a. Yellow-green (31.7.63) . . 2·50 2·50
109 3 c. carmine-red and violet . . 50 10
   a. Carmine and deep violet (31.7.63) . . 2·50 3·00
110 4 c. scarlet . . 15 10
111 5 c. bright blue and grey . . 15 10
112 6 c. ultramarine . . 30 10
   a. Blue (19.2.63) . . 75 20
112*b* 8 c. grey-black (1.2.57) . . 3·00 10
113 12 c. deep blue and red-brown . . 15 10
114 24 c. black and carmine-red (1.12.54) . . 15 10
115 48 c. olive-bistre and chocolate (1.12.54) . . 60 50
116 60 c. ochre and deep green (1.12.54) . . 2·00 85
117 $1.20, dp green & ultramarine (1.12.54) 7·00 90
   a. Deep green and violet-blue (19.2.63) . . 13·00 3·75
117*b* $2.40, black and red-orange (1.2.57) . . 8·00 11·00
118 $4.80, green and carmine (1.12.54) . . 12·00 11·00
106*a*/18 . . *Set of* 15 30·00 22·00

Design: *Horiz*—½ c., $1.20 Salt Pond; 1 c. Bath House and Spa; 2 c. Warner Park; 4 c. Brimstone Hill; 5 c. Nevis from the sea, North; 6 c. Pinney's Beach; 24 c. Old Road Bay; 48 c. Sea Island cotton; 60 c. The Treasury; $4.80, Sugar factory. *Vert*—3 c. Map of the islands; 12 c. Sir Thomas Warner's Tomb.

Stamps of St. Christopher, Nevis and Anguilla were in concurrent use with the stamps inscribed "LEEWARD ISLANDS" until 1 July 1956, when the general Leeward Islands stamps were withdrawn.

27 Alexander Hamilton and View of Nevis

(Des Eva Wilkin. Recess Waterlow)

1957 (11 Jan). *Birth Bicentenary of Alexander Hamilton. Wmk Mult Script CA. P* 12½.
119 **27** 24 c. green and deep blue . . 15 10

1958 (22 Apr). *Inauguration of British Caribbean Federation. As Nos.* 175/7 *of Jamaica.*
120 3 c. deep green . . 30 10
121 6 c. blue . . 55 60
122 12 c. scarlet . . 80 15
120/2 . . *Set of* 3 1·50 75

MINISTERIAL GOVERNMENT

28 One Penny Stamp of 1861

(Recess Waterlow)

1961 (15 July). *Nevis Stamp Centenary. T* **28** *and similar horiz designs. W w* **12**. *P* 14.
123 2 c. red-brown and green . . 15 15
124 8 c. red-brown and deep blue . . 15 10
125 12 c. black and carmine-red . . 20 10
126 24 c. deep bluish green and red-orange . . 25 15
123/6 . . *Set of* 4 65 40

Designs:—8 c. Fourpence stamp of 1861; 12 c. Sixpence stamp of 1861; 24 c. One shilling stamp of 1861.

1963 (2 Sept). *Red Cross Centenary. As Nos.* 203/4 *of Jamaica.*
127 3 c. red and black . . 10 10
128 12 c. red and blue . . 20 40

32 New Lighthouse, Sombrero

33 Loading Sugar Cane, St. Kitts

(Des V. Whiteley. Photo Harrison)

1963 (20 Nov)–**65**. *Vert designs as T* **32** (2, 3, 15, 25, 60 *c.*, $1, $5) *or horiz as* **33** (*others*) *in sepia and light blue* (½ *c.*), *greenish yellow and blue* ($1) *or multicoloured* (*others*). *W w* **12** (*upright*). *P* 14.
129 ½ c. Type **32** . . 10 10
130 1 c. Type **33** . . 10 10
131 2 c. Pall Mall Square, Basseterre . . 10 10
   a. White fountain and Church . . 90·00
132 3 c. Gateway, Brimstone Hill Fort, St. Kitts 10 10
133 4 c. Nelson's Spring, Nevis . . 10 10
134 5 c. Grammar School, St. Kitts . . 10 10
135 6 c. Crater, Mt Misery, St. Kitts . . 10 10
136 10 c. Hibiscus . . 15 10
137 15 c. Sea Island cotton, Nevis . . 35 10
138 20 c. Boat building, Anguilla . . 20 10
139 25 c. White-crowned Pigeon (turquoise-blue background) . . 65 10
   a. Turquoise-green background (13.4.65) 2·25 60
140 50 c. St. George's Church Tower, Basseterre 40 25
141 60 c. Alexander Hamilton . . 1·00 25
142 $1 Map of St. Kitts-Nevis . . 2·25 40
143 $2.50, Map of Anguilla . . 2·25 2·00
144 $5 Arms of St. Christopher, Nevis and Anguilla . . 3·50 3·00
129/44 . . *Set of* 16 9·50 6·00

The 1, 4, 5, 6, 10 and 20 c. values exist with PVA gum as well as gum arabic.

See also Nos. 166/71.

ARTS
FESTIVAL
ST KITTS
1964

(48)

49 Festival Emblem

1964 (14 Sept). *Arts Festival. Nos.* 132 *and* 139 *optd as T* **48**.
145 3 c. Gateway, Brimstone Hill Fort, St. Kitts 10 10
   a. Opt double . . £150
146 25 c. White-crowned Pigeon . . 20 10
   a. "FESTIVAI" (R. 1/10) . . 55·00

1965 (17 May). *I.T.U. Centenary. As Nos.* 98/9 *of Lesotho.*
147 2 c. bistre-yellow and rose-carmine . . 10 10
148 50 c. turquoise-blue and yellow-olive . . 40 35

1965 (15 Oct). *International Co-operation Year. As Nos.* 100/1 *of Lesotho.*
149 2 c. reddish purple and turquoise-green . . 10 10
150 25 c. deep bluish green and lavender . . 20 10

1966 (24 Jan). *Churchill Commemoration. As Nos.* 102/5 *of Lesotho.*
151 ½ c. new blue . . 10 10
   a. Value omitted . . £130
   b. Value at left instead of right . . 50·00
152 3 c. deep green . . 15 10
153 15 c. brown . . 30 15
154 25 c. bluish violet . . 35 15
151/4 . . *Set of* 4 75 35

1966 (4 Feb). *Royal Visit. As Nos.* 183/4 *of Montserrat.*
155 3 c. black and ultramarine 10 10
156 25 c. black and magenta 30 10

1966 (1 July). *World Cup Football Championships. As Nos.* 57/8 *of Pitcairn Islands.*
157 6 c. violet, yellow-green, lake & yellow-brn .. 10 10
158 25 c. chocolate, blue-green, lake & yell-brn .. 30 10

(Photo Harrison)

1966 (15 Aug). *Arts Festival. P* 14 × 14½.
159 **49** 3 c. black, buff, emerald-green and gold 10 10
160 25 c. black, buff, emerald-green and silver 10 10

1966 (20 Sept). *Inauguration of W.H.O. Headquarters, Geneva. As Nos.* 185/6 *of Montserrat.*
161 3 c. black, yellow-green, and light blue .. 10 10
162 40 c. black, light purple, and yellow-brown .. 20 20

1966 (1 Dec). *20th Anniv of U.N.E.S.C.O. As Nos.* 342/4 *of Mauritius.*
163 3 c. slate-violet, red, yellow and orange .. 10 10
164 6 c. orange-yellow, violet and deep olive .. 10 10
165 40 c. black, bright purple and orange .. 20 35
163/5 .. .. *Set of* 3 30 45

ASSOCIATED STATEHOOD

1967–69. *As Nos.* 129, 131/2, 137, 139 *and* 142 *but wmk sideways.*
166 **20** ½ c. sepia and light blue (9.1.69) .. 15 80
167 – 2 c. multicoloured (27.6.67) 90 10
168 – 3 c. multicoloured (16.7.68) 15 10
169 – 15 c. multicoloured (16.7.68) 70 30
170 – 25 c. multicoloured (16.7.68) .. .. 2·25 20
171 – $1 greenish yellow and blue (16.7.68) .. 5·00 4·00
a. *Greenish yellow & ultramarine-blue* (19.12.69) .. .. 8·50 5·00
166/71 .. .. *Set of* 6 8·25 5·00
The 2 c. and $1 values exist with PVA gum as well as gum arabic.
Nos. 172/81 vacant.

50 Government Headquarters, Basseterre

53 John Wesley and Cross

(Des V. Whiteley. Photo Harrison)

1967 (1 July). *Statehood. T* **50** *and similar horiz designs. Multicoloured. W w* **12**. *P* 14½ × 14.
182 3 c. Type **50** 10 10
183 10 c. National Flag 10 10
184 25 c. Coat of Arms 15 10
182/4 .. .. *Set of* 3 30 20

(Litho D.L.R.)

1967 (1 Dec). *West Indies Methodist Conference. T* **53** *and similar vert designs. P* 13 × 13½.
185 3 c. black, cerise and reddish violet 10 10
186 25 c. black, light greenish blue and blue .. 15 10
187 40 c. black, yellow and orange 15 10
185/7 .. .. *Set of* 3 30 20
Designs:—25 c. Charles Wesley and Cross; 40 c. Thomas Coke and Cross.

56 "Herald" Aircraft over *Jamaica Producer* (freighter)

57 Dr. Martin Luther King

(Des and litho D.L.R.)

1968 (30 July). *Caribbean Free Trade Area. W w* **12** *(sideways). P* 13.
188 **56** 25 c. multicoloured 15 10
189 50 c. multicoloured 15 10

(Des G. Vasarhelyi. Litho Enschedé)

1968 (30 Sept). *Martin Luther King Commemoration. W w* **12**. *P* 12 × 12½.
190 **57** 50 c. multicoloured 10 10

58 "Mystic Nativity" (Botticelli)

60 Tarpon

(Des and photo Harrison)

1968 (27 Nov). *Christmas. Paintings. T* **58** *and similar vert design. Multicoloured. W w* **12** *(sideways). P* 14½ × 14.
191 12 c. Type **58** 10 10
192 25 c. "The Adoration of the Magi" (Rubens) .. 10 10
193 40 c. Type **58** 10 10
194 50 c. As 25 c. 10 10
191/4 .. .. *Set of* 4 30 30

(Des G. Drummond. Photo Harrison)

1969 (25 Feb). *Fishes. T* **60** *and similar horiz designs. W w* **12**. *P* 14 × 14½.
195 6 c. multicoloured 10 10
196 12 c. black, turquoise-green & greenish blue 15 10
197 40 c. multicoloured 20 10
198 50 c. multicoloured 25 15
195/8 .. .. *Set of* 4 60 30
Designs:—12 c. Garfish; 40 c. Horse-eye Jack; 50 c. Redsnapper.

64 The Warner Badge and Islands

67 "The Adoration of the Kings" (Mostaert)

(Des V. Whiteley. Litho Format)

1969 (1 Sept). *Sir Thomas Warner Commemoration. T* **64** *and similar horiz designs. Multicoloured. W w* **12** *(sideways). P* 13½ × 14.
199 20 c. Type **64** 10 10
200 25 c. Sir Thomas Warner's tomb 10 10
201 40 c. Charles I's commission 15 15
199/201 .. .. *Set of* 3 30 30

(Des Enschedé. Litho B.W.)

1969 (17 Nov). *Christmas. Paintings. T* **67** *and similar vert design. Multicoloured. W w* **12** *(sideways). P* 13½.
202 10 c. Type **67** 10 10
203 25 c. Type **67** 10 10
204 40 c. "The Adoration of the Kings" (Geertgen) 10 10
205 50 c. As 40 c. 10 10
202/5 .. .. *Set of* 4 30 30

73 Portuguese Caravels (16th-cent)

(Des and litho J.W.)

1970 (2 Feb–8 Sept). *Designs as T* **73** *in black, pale orange and emerald* (½ c.) *or multicoloured (others). W w* **12** *(upright on vert designs, sideways on horiz designs). P* 14.
206 ½ c. Pirates and treasure at Frigate Bay *(vert)* 10 10
207 1 c. English two-decker warship, 1650 *(vert)* 30 10
208 2 c. Naval flags of colonizing nations *(vert)* .. 15 10
209 3 c. Rapier hilt (17th-century) *(vert)*.. .. 15 10
210 4 c. Type **73** 20 10
211 5 c. Sir Henry Morgan and fireships, 1669 .. 30 10
212 6 c. L'Ollonois and pirate carrack (16th-century) 30 10
213 10 c. 17th-century smugglers' ship 30 10
214 15 c. "Piece-of-eight" *(vert)* (I) .. .. 1·50 40
214*a* 15 c. "Piece-of-eight" *(vert)* (II) (8.9.70) .. 50 10
215 20 c. Cannon (17th-century) 35 10
216 25 c. Humphrey Cole's Astrolabe, 1574 *(vert)* 40 10
217 50 c. Flintlock pistol (17th-century) 85 80
218 60 c. Dutch flute (17th-century) *(vert)*.. .. 2·25 70
219 $1 Captain Bartholomew Roberts and his crew's death warrant *(vert)* .. .. 2·50 75
220 $2.50, Railing piece (16th-century).. .. 2·00 3·00
221 $5 Drake, Hawkins and sea battle .. .. 2·50 4·25
206/221 .. .. *Set of* 17 13·00 9·00
Nos. 214/*a*. Type I, coin inscribed "HISPANIANUM"; Type II, corrected to "HISPANIARUM". No. 214*a* also differs considerably in shade from No. 214.
See also Nos. 269/80 and 322/31.

85 Graveyard Scene (*Great Expectations*)

(Des Jennifer Toombs. Litho B.W.)

1970 (1 May). *Death Centenary of Charles Dickens. T* **85** *and similar designs. W w* **12** *(sideways on horiz designs). P* 13.
222 4 c. bistre-brown, gold and deep blue-green .. 10 10
223 20 c. bistre-brown, gold and reddish purple .. 10 10
224 25 c. bistre-brown, gold and olive-green .. 10 10
225 40 c. bistre-brown, gold and ultramarine .. 10 15
222/5 .. .. *Set of* 4 30 30
Designs: *Horiz*—20 c. Miss Havisham and Pip (*Great Expectations*). *Vert*—25 c. Dickens's Birthplace; 40 c. Charles Dickens.

86 Local Steel Band

(Des V. Whiteley. Litho Enschedé)

1970 (1 Aug). *Festival of Arts. T* **86** *and similar horiz designs. Multicoloured. W w* **12** *(sideways). P* 13½.
226 20 c. Type **86** 10 10
227 25 c. Local String Band 10 10
228 40 c. Scene from *A Midsummer Night's Dream* 15 15
226/8 .. .. *Set of* 3 30 30

87 1d. Stamp of 1870 and Post Office, 1970

88 "Adoration of the Shepherds" (detail) (Frans van Floris)

(Des J. Cooter. Litho J.W.)

1970 (14 Sept). *Stamp Centenary. T* **87** *and similar horiz designs. W w* **12** *(sideways). P* 14½.
229 ½ c. green and rose 10 10
230 20 c. deep blue, green and rose 10 10
231 25 c. brown-purple, green and rose 10 10
232 50 c. scarlet, green and black 30 45
229/32 .. .. *Set of* 4 50 50
Designs:—20 c., 25 c. 1d. and 6d. Stamps of 1870; 50 c. 6d. Stamp of 1870 and early postmark.

(Des Enschedé. Litho Format)

1970 (16 Nov). *Christmas. T* **88** *and similar vert design. Multicoloured. W w* **12**. *P* 14.
233 3 c. Type **88** 10 10
234 20 c. "The Holy Family" (Van Dyck) 10 10
235 25 c. As 20 c. 10 10
236 40 c. Type **88** 15 10
233/6 .. .. *Set of* 4 30 30

89 Monkey Fiddle

(Des Sylvia Goaman. Litho Format)

1971 (1 Mar). *Flowers. T* **89** *and similar horiz designs. Multicoloured. W w* **12** *(sideways). P* 14½.
237 ½ c. Type **89** 10 10
238 20 c. Tropical Mountain Violet 20 10
239 30 c. Trailing Morning Glory 20 10
240 50 c. Fringed Epidendrum 40 40
237/40 .. .. *Set of* 4 75 55

90 Royal Poinciana

(Des Enschedé. Litho J.W.)

1971 (1 June). *Phillipe de Poincy Commemoration. T* **90** *and similar multicoloured designs. W w* **12** (*sideways on* 20 *and* 30 *c.*). *P* 13½.
241 20 c. Type **90** 10 10
242 30 c. Château de Poincy 10 10
243 50 c. De Poincy's badge (*vert*) 20 15
241/3 .. .. *Set of* 3 35 30

91 The East Yorks **92** "Crucifixion" (Massys)

(Des V. Whiteley. Litho Walsall)

1971 (1 Sept). *Siege of Brimstone Hill,* 1782. *T* **91** *and similar horiz designs. Multicoloured. W w* **12** (*sideways*). *P* 14½.
244 ½ c. Type **91** 10 10
245 20 c. Royal Artillery 45 10
246 30 c. French infantry 55 10
247 50 c. The Royal Scots 75 20
244/7 .. .. *Set of* 4 1·60 35

(Des J. Cooter. Litho J.W.)

1972 (1 Apr). *Easter. W w* **12**. *P* 14 × 13½.
248 **92** 4 c. multicoloured 10 10
249 20 c. multicoloured 10 10
250 30 c. multicoloured 10 10
251 40 c. multicoloured 10 10
248/51 .. .. *Set of* 4 30 30

93 "Virgin and Child" (Borgognone) **94** Brown Pelicans

(Des J. Cooter. Litho J.W.)

1972 (2 Oct). *Christmas. T* **93** *and similar multicoloured designs. W w* **12** (*sideways on vert designs*). *P* 14.
252 3 c. Type **93** 10 10
253 20 c. "Adoration of the Kings" (J. Bassano) (*horiz*) 15 10
254 25 c. "Adoration of the Shepherds" (Domenichino) 15 10
255 40 c. "Virgin and Child" (Fiorenzo di Lorenzo) 20 10
252/5 .. .. *Set of* 4 45 30

(Des (from photograph by D. Groves) and photo Harrison)

1972 (20 Nov). *Royal Silver Wedding. Multicoloured; background colour given. W w* **12**. *P* 14 × 14½.
256 **94** 20 c. carmine 15 15
257 25 c. bright blue 15 15

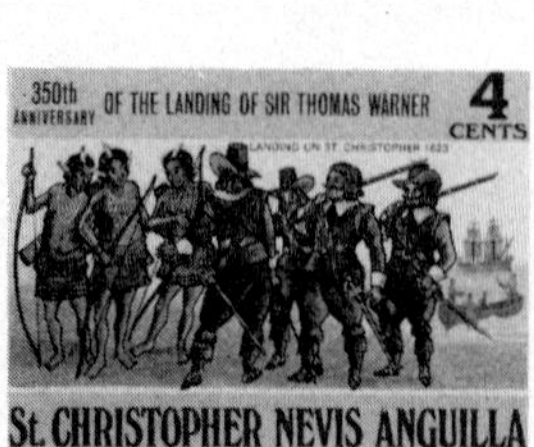

95 Landing on St. Christopher, 1623 **96** "The Last Supper" (Titian)

(Des J.W. Litho Questa)

1973 (28 Jan). 350*th Anniv of Sir Thomas Warner's landing on St. Christopher. T* **95** *and similar horiz designs. Multicoloured. W w* **12**. *P* 13½.
258 4 c. Type **95** 15 10
259 25 c. Growing tobacco 15 10
260 40 c. Building fort at Old Road 20 10
261 $2.50, *Concepcion* .. .. 80 1·10
258/61 .. .. *Set of* 4 1·10 1·25

(Des J. Cooter. Litho Walsall)

1973 (16 Apr). *Easter. T* **96** *and similar multicoloured designs showing paintings of "The Last Supper" by the artists listed. W w* **12** (*sideways on* $2.50). *P* 13½ × 14 ($2.50) *or* 14 × 13½ (*others*).
262 4 c. Type **96** 10 10
263 25 c. Ascr to Roberti 10 10
264 $2.50, Juan de Juanes (*horiz*) 70 60
262/4 .. .. *Set of* 3 75 60

VISIT OF
H. R. H. THE PRINCE OF WALES 1973
(97)

1973 (31 May). *Royal Visit. Nos.* 258/61 *optd with T* **97** *by Questa.*
265 4 c. Type **95** 10 15
266 25 c. Growing tobacco 10 15
267 40 c. Building fort at Old Road 15 15
268 $2.50 *Concepcion* 45 50
265/8 .. .. *Set of* 4 65 85

(Des J.W. Litho Harrison ($10), J.W. (others))

1973 (12 Sept)–**74**. *As Nos.* 206, 208/9, 211/13, 214*a*/17, 219 *and new horiz design* ($10), *but W w* **12** (*sideways on vert designs, upright on horiz designs*).
269 ½ c. Pirates and treasure at Frigate Bay .. 10 40
270 2 c. Naval flags of colonizing nations .. 20 45
271 3 c. Rapier hilt 20 45
272 5 c. Sir Henry Morgan and fireships, 1669 .. 35 45
273 6 c. L'Ollonois and pirate carrack (16th-century) 35 40
274 10 c. 17th-century smugglers' ship 40 60
275 15 c. "Piece-of-eight" (II) 65 85
276 20 c. Cannon (17th-century) 75 95
277 25 c. Humphrey Cole's Astrolabe, 1574 .. 80 1·75
278 50 c. Flintlock pistol (17th-century) .. .. 1·10 1·50
279 $1 Captain Bartholomew Roberts and his crew's death warrant .. .. 2·75 3·50
280 $10 "The Apprehension of Blackbeard" (Edward Teach) (16.11.74) .. .. .. 20·00 13·00
269/80 .. .. *Set of* 12 25·00 22·00
Nos. 281/4 vacant.

99 Harbour Scene and 2d. Stamp of 1903

(Des V. Whiteley Studio. Litho Enschedé)

1973 (1 Oct). 70*th Anniv of First St. Kitts-Nevis Stamps. T* **99** *and similar horiz designs. Multicoloured. W w* **12** (*sideways*). *P* 13 × 13½.
285 4 c. Type **99** 10 10
286 25 c. Sugar-mill and 1d. stamp of 1903 .. 15 10
287 40 c. Unloading boat and ½d. stamp of 1903 35 10
288 $2.50, Rock-carvings and 3d. stamp of 1903 2·00 1·00
285/8 .. .. *Set of* 4 2·25 1·10
MS289 144 × 95 mm. Nos. 285/8 .. .. .. 2·75 5·50

1973 (14 Nov). *Royal Wedding. As Nos.* 322/3 *of Montserrat.*
290 25 c. light emerald 15 10
291 40 c. brown-ochre 15 10

100 "Madonna and Child" (Murillo) **101** "Christ carrying the Cross" (S. del Piombo)

(Des J. Cooter. Litho Format)

1973 (1 Dec). *Christmas. T* **100** *and similar multicoloured designs showing "The Holy Family" by the artists listed. W w* **12** (*sideways on* $1). *P* 13½.
292 4 c. Type **100** 10 10
293 40 c. Mengs 20 10
294 60 c. Sassoferrato 25 15
295 $1 Filippino Lippi (*horiz*) 35 30
292/5 .. .. *Set of* 4 75 50

(Des J. Cooter. Litho D.L.R.)

1974 (8 Apr). *Easter. T* **101** *and similar multicoloured designs. W w* **12** (*sideways on* $2.50). *P* 13½.
296 4 c. Type **101** 10 10
297 25 c. "The Crucifixion" (Goya) 15 10
298 40 c. "The Trinity" (Ribera) 15 10
299 $2.50, "The Deposition" (Fra Bartolomeo) (*horiz*) .. .. 1·00 75
296/9 .. .. *Set of* 4 1·25 75

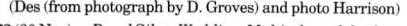

102 University Centre, St. Kitts **103** Hands reaching for Globe

(Des G. Drummond. Litho Questa)

1974 (1 June). 25*th Anniv of University of West Indies. T* **102** *and similar horiz design. Multicoloured. W w* **12** (*sideways*). *P* 13½.
300 10 c. Type **102** 10 10
301 $1 As Type **102** but showing different buildings 20 25
MS302 99 × 95 mm. Nos. 300/1 .. .. .. 35 65

(Des Jennifer Toombs. Litho Questa)

1974 (5 Aug). *Family Planning. T* **103** *and similar designs. W w* **12** (*sideways on* 25 *c. and* $2.50). *P* 14.
303 4 c. orange-brown, new blue and black .. 10 10
304 25 c. multicoloured 10 10
305 40 c. multicoloured 10 10
306 $2.50, multicoloured 35 55
303/6 .. .. *Set of* 4 50 65
Designs: *Horiz*—25 c. Instruction by nurse; $2.50, Emblem and globe on scales. *Vert*—40 c. Family group.

104 Churchill as Army Lieutenant **105** Aeroplane and Map

(Des PAD Studio. Litho Questa)

1974 (30 Nov). *Birth Centenary of Sir Winston Churchill. T* **104** *and similar vert designs. Multicoloured. W w* **12**. *P* 13½.
307 4 c. Type **104** 10 10
308 25 c. Churchill as Prime Minister 15 10
309 40 c. Churchill as Knight of the Garter .. 25 10
310 60 c. Churchill's statue, London 35 15
307/10 .. .. *Set of* 4 70 30
MS311 99 × 148 mm. Nos. 307/10 .. .. .. 1·00 1·50

(Des J.W. Litho Questa)

1974 (16 Dec). *Opening of Golden Rock Airport, St. Kitts. Sheets* 98 × 148 *mm. W w* **12**. *P* 13½.
MS312 **105** 40 c.multicoloured 20 40
MS313 45 c.multicoloured 20 40

106 "The Last Supper" (Doré) **107** E.C.C.A. H.Q. Buildings, Basseterre

(Des PAD Studio. Litho Questa)

1975 (24 Mar). *Easter. T* **106** *and similar vert designs showing paintings by Doré. Multicoloured. W w* **12**. *P* 14½.
314 4 c. Type **106** 10 10
315 25 c. "Christ Mocked" 10 10
316 40 c. "Jesus falling beneath the Cross" .. 10 10
317 $1 "The Erection of the Cross" 25 30
314/17 .. .. *Set of* 4 40 40

(Des J. Cooter. Litho Enschedé)

1975 (2 June*). *Opening of East Caribbean Currency Authority's Headquarters. T* **107** *and similar horiz designs. W w* **14** (*sideways*). *P* 13 × 13½.
318 12 c. multicoloured 10 10
319 25 c. multicoloured 10 10
320 40 c. light vermilion, silver and grey-black .. 15 10
321 45 c. multicoloured 15 15
a. Silver omitted† .. .. 85·00
318/21 .. .. *Set of* 4 30 30
Designs:—25 c. Specimen one-dollar banknote; 40 c. Half-dollar of 1801 and current 4-dollar coin; 45 c. Coins of 1801 and 1960.
*This is the local date of issue; the Crown Agents released the stamps on 28 April.
†This affects the dull silver coin on the left which on No. 321a appears in tones of the black plate.

1975–77. *As Nos.* 207, 209/13, 214*a*/15 *and* 218/19 *but* W w **14** *(sideways on* 4, 5, 6, 10, 20 *and* 60 *c.).*
A. *White, ordinary paper.*
B. *Cream, chalk-surfaced paper.*

No.	Description	A		B	
322	1 c. English two-decker war-ship, 1650	†		30	30
323	3 c. Rapier hilt (17th-century)	20	10	1·75	2·00
324	4 c. Type **73**	20	10	1·75	2·00
325	5 c. Sir Henry Morgan and fireships, 1669	30	40	3·50	3·50
326	6 c. L'Ollonois and pirate carrack (16th-century)	80	10	1·00	2·00
327	10 c. 17th-century smugglers' ship	45	15	1·00	2·00
328	15 c. "Piece-of-eight" (II)	55	15	4·50	4·50
329	20 c. Cannon (17th-century)	1·40	2·50	1·75	5·00
330	60 c. Dutch flute (17th-century)	6·00	1·75	†	
331	$1 Captain Bartholomew Roberts and his crew's death warrant	†		9·00	3·00
323A/30A	*Set of* 8	9·00	4·75		
322B/31B	*Set of* 9			22·00	22·00

Dates of issue: Ordinary paper–5, 6 and 20 c. 11.6.75; others 11.6.76. Chalk-surfaced paper–5, 15 c. and $1 16.8.77; others 17.5.77

Nos. 332/7 vacant.

108 Evangeline Booth (Salvation Army General)

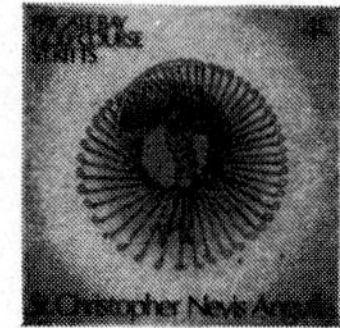

109 Golfer

(Des Jennifer Toombs. Litho Questa)

1975 (15 Sept). *International Women's Year. T* **108** *and similar vert designs. Multicoloured.* W w **12**. P 14.

No.	Description	Unused	Used
338	4 c. Type **108**	10	10
339	25 c. Sylvia Pankhurst	25	10
340	40 c. Marie Curie	50	30
341	$2.50, Lady Annie Allen (teacher and guider)	2·00	2·75
338/41	*Set of* 4	2·50	3·00

(Des Sue Lawes. Litho Questa)

1975 (1 Nov). *Opening of Frigate Bay Golf Course.* W w **14** *(sideways).* P 13½.

No.	Description	Unused	Used
342	**109** 4 c. black and rose-red	20	10
343	25 c. black and greenish yellow	35	10
344	40 c. black and light emerald	45	10
345	$1 black and new blue	1·00	70
342/5	*Set of* 4	1·75	75

110 "St. Paul" (Pier Francesco Sacchi)

111 "Crucifixion" (detail)

(Des J.W. Litho Questa)

1975 (1 Dec). *Christmas. T* **110** *and similar vert designs showing details from paintings in the National Gallery, London. Multicoloured.* W w **14**. P 13½.

No.	Description	Unused	Used
346	25 c. Type **110**	20	10
347	40 c. "St James" (Bonifazio di Pitati)	35	10
348	45 c. "St. John the Baptist" (Mola)	35	10
349	$1 "St. Mary" (Raphael)	70	60
346/9	*Set of* 4	1·40	70

(Des J. Cooter. Litho Questa)

1976 (14 Apr). *Easter. Stained-glass Windows. T* **111** *and similar vert designs. Multicoloured.* W w **14**. P 14 × 13½ (4 c.) *or* 14 *(others).*

No.	Description	Unused	Used
350	4 c. Type **111**	10	10
	a. Strip of 3. Nos. 350/2	20	
351	4 c. } "Crucifixion"	10	10
352	4 c. } "Crucifixion"	10	10
353	25 c. "Last Supper"	30	10
354	40 c. "Last Supper" *(different)*	35	10
355	$1 "Baptism of Christ"	60	55
350/5	*Set of* 6	1·25	80

Nos. 350/2 were printed horizontally *se-tenant*, together forming a composite design, No. 350 being the left-hand stamp.

Nos. 353/5 are smaller, 27 × 35 mm.

1976 (8 July). *West Indian Victory in World Cricket Cup. As Nos.* 419/20 *of Jamaica.*

No.	Description	Unused	Used
356	12 c. Map of the Caribbean	60	20
357	40 c. Prudential Cup	1·40	50
MS358	95 × 80 mm. Nos. 356/7	4·00	3·75

112 Crispus Attucks and the Boston Massacre

113 "The Nativity" (Sforza Book of Hours)

(Des J.W. Litho Questa)

1976 (26 July). *Bicentenary of American Revolution. T* **112** *and similar horiz designs. Multicoloured.* W w **14** *(sideways).* P 13½.

No.	Description	Unused	Used
359	20 c. Type **112**	15	10
360	40 c. Alexander Hamilton and Battle of Yorktown	30	10
361	45 c. Jefferson and Declaration of Independence	30	10
362	$1 Washington and the Crossing of the Delaware	60	80
359/62	*Set of* 4	1·25	95

(Des Jennifer Toombs. Litho Questa)

1976 (1 Nov). *Christmas. T* **113** *and similar vert designs. Multicoloured.* W w **14**. P 14.

No.	Description	Unused	Used
363	20 c. Type **113**	10	10
364	40 c. "Virgin and Child with St. John" (Pintoricchio)	15	10
365	45 c. "Our Lady of Good Children" (Ford Maddox-Brown)	15	10
366	$1 "Little Hands Outstretched to Bless" (Margaret Tarrant)	35	50
363/6	*Set of* 4	65	60

114 Royal Visit, 1966

115 "Christ on the Cross" (Niccolo di Liberatore)

(Des J.W. Litho Questa)

1977 (7 Feb). *Silver Jubilee. T* **114** *and similar vert designs. Multicoloured.* W w **14**. P 13½.

No.	Description	Unused	Used
367	50 c. Type **114**	15	10
368	55 c. The Sceptre	15	10
369	$1.50, Bishops paying homage	30	50
367/9	*Set of* 3	55	60

(Des G. Hutchins. Litho Questa)

1977 (14 Apr*). *Easter. T* **115** *and similar designs showing paintings from the National Gallery, London. Multicoloured.* W w **14** *(sideways on* 50 *c.).* P 14.

No.	Description	Unused	Used
370	25 c. Type **115**	10	10
371	30 c. "The Resurrection" (imitator of Mantegna)	10	10
372	50 c. "The Resurrection" (Ugolino da Siena) *(horiz)*	15	10
373	$1 "Christ Rising from the Tomb" (Gaudenzio Ferrari)	25	30
370/3	*Set of* 4	55	45

*This is the local release date; the Crown Agents released the stamps ten days earlier.

116 Estridge Mission

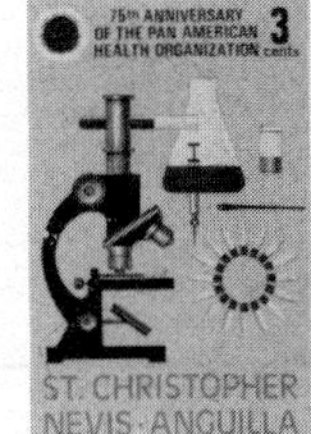

117 Laboratory Instruments

(Des Jennifer Toombs. Litho Cartor S.A., France)

1977 (27 June). *Bicentenary of Moravian Mission. T* **116** *and similar horiz designs.* W w **14** *(sideways).* P 12½.

No.	Description	Unused	Used
374	4 c. black, greenish blue and new blue	10	10
375	20 c. black, brt mauve & brt reddish violet	10	10
376	40 c. black, yellow and yellow-orange	15	15
374/6	*Set of* 3	30	30

Designs:—20 c. Mission symbol; 40 c. Basseterre Mission.

(Des G. Hutchins. Litho Questa)

1977 (11 Oct). *75th Anniv of Pan-American Health Organization. T* **117** *and similar vert designs.* W w **14**. P 14.

No.	Description	Unused	Used
377	3 c. multicoloured	10	10
378	12 c. multicoloured	15	10
379	20 c. multicoloured	20	10
380	$1 red-brown, bright orange and black	70	40
377/80	*Set of* 4	1·00	50

Designs:—12 c. Fat cells, blood cells and nerve cells; 20 c. "Community participation in health"; $1 Inoculation.

118 "Nativity" (West Window)

119 Savanna Monkey with Vervet

(Des Jennifer Toombs. Litho Rosenbaum Bros, Vienna)

1977 (15 Nov). *Christmas. Vert designs as T* **118** *showing stained-glass windows from Chartres Cathedral. Multicoloured.* W w **14** *(inverted).* P 13½.

No.	Description	Unused	Used
381	4 c. Type **118**	10	10
382	6 c. "Three Magi" (West window)	10	10
383	40 c. "La Belle Verriere"	35	10
384	$1 "Virgin and Child" (Rose window)	75	45
381/4	*Set of* 4	1·10	55

(Des BG Studio. Litho Questa)

1978 (15 Apr). *The Savanna ("Green") Monkey. T* **119** *and similar vert design.* W w **14**. P 14½.

No.	Description	Unused	Used
385	**119** 4 c. yellow-brown, rosine and black	10	10
386	– 5 c. multicoloured	10	10
387	**119** 55 c. yellow-brown, apple-green & black	30	10
388	– $1.50, multicoloured	75	60
385/8	*Set of* 4	1·10	65

Design:—5 c., $1.50 Savanna Monkeys on branch.

120 Falcon of Edward III

121 Tomatoes

(Des C. Abbott. Litho Questa)

1978 (2 June). *25th Anniv of Coronation. T* **120** *and similar vert designs.* P 15.

No.	Description	Unused	Used
389	$1 olive-brown and vermilion	20	20
	a. Sheetlet. Nos. 389/91 × 2	1·10	
390	$1 multicoloured	20	20
391	$1 olive-brown and vermilion	20	20
389/91	*Set of* 3	55	55

Designs:—No. 389, Type **120**; No. 390, Queen Elizabeth II; No. 391, Brown Pelican.

(Des BG Studio. Litho D.L.R.)

1978 (8 Sept). *Horiz designs as T* **121**. *Multicoloured.* W w **14** *(sideways).* P 14½ × 14.

No.	Description	Unused	Used
392	1 c. Type **121**	10	15
393	2 c. Defence Force band	10	15
394	5 c. Radio and T.V. station	10	10
395	10 c. Technical college	10	10
396	12 c. T.V. assembly plant	10	15
397	15 c. Sugar cane harvesting	15	10
398	25 c. Crafthouse (craft centre)	15	10
399	30 c. *Europa* (liner)	40	30
400	40 c. Lobster and sea crab	30	10
401	45 c. Royal St. Kitts Hotel and golf course	75	30
402	50 c. Pinney's Beach, Nevis	30	10
403	55 c. New runway at Golden Rock	30	10
404	$1 Cotton picking	35	30
405	$5 Brewery	1·00	1·25
406	$10 Pineapples and peanuts	2·25	2·50
392/406	*Set of* 15	5·50	4·50

122 Investiture

123 Wise Man with Gift of Gold

(Des L. Curtis. Litho Rosenbaum Bros, Vienna)

1978 (9 Oct). *50th Anniv of Boy Scout Movement on St. Christopher and Nevis. T* **122** *and similar vert designs. Multicoloured. W* w **14**. *P* 13½.

407 5 c. Type **122** 10 10
408 10 c. Map reading 10 10
409 25 c. Pitching tent 20 15
410 40 c. Cooking 35 25
411 50 c. First aid 40 35
412 55 c. Rev. W. A. Beckett (founder of scouting in St. Kitts) 45 45
407/12 .. .. *Set of* 6 1·40 1·10

(Des Jennifer Toombs. Litho Walsall)

1978 (1 Dec). *Christmas. T* **123** *and similar vert designs. Multicoloured. W* w **14**. *P* 13½.

413 5 c. Type **123** 10 10
414 15 c. Wise Man with gift of Frankincense .. 10 10
415 30 c. Wise Man with gift of Myrrh 10 10
416 $2.25, Wise Men paying homage to the infant Jesus 35 50
413/16 .. .. *Set of* 4 50 55

124 *Canna coccinea*

125 St. Christopher 1870–76 1d. Stamp and Sir Rowland Hill

(Des Daphne Padden. Litho Questa)

1979 (19 Mar). *Flowers* (*1st series*). *T* **124** *and similar vert designs. Multicoloured. W* w **14**. *P* 14.

417 5 c. Type **124** 10 10
418 30 c. *Heliconia bihai* 30 20
419 55 c. *Ruellia tuberosa* 50 30
420 $1.50, *Gesneria ventricosa* .. .. .. 1·10 1·40
417/20 .. .. *Set of* 4 1·75 1·75

See also Nos. 430/3.

(Des J.W. Litho Walsall)

1979 (2 July). *Death Centenary of Sir Rowland Hill. T* **125** *and similar horiz designs showing stamps and portrait. Multicoloured. W* w **14** (*sideways*). *P* 14½ × 14.

421 5 c. Type **125** 10 10
422 15 c. 1970 Stamp Centenary 50 c. commemorative 10 10
423 50 c. Great Britain 1841 2d. 35 35
424 $2.50, St. Kitts-Nevis 1923 300th Anniversary of Colony £1 commemorative .. 90 1·10
421/4 .. .. *Set of* 4 1·25 1·40

126 "The Woodman's Daughter"

127 Nevis Lagoon

(Des BG Studio. Litho Format)

1979 (12 Nov). *Christmas and International Year of the Child. Paintings by Sir John Millais. T* **126** *and similar vert designs. Multicoloured. W* w **14**. *P* 13½.

425 5 c. Type **126** 10 10
426 25 c. "Cherry Ripe" 25 20
427 30 c. "The Rescue" 25 20
428 55 c. "Bubbles" 30 25
425/8 .. .. *Set of* 4 75 65
MS429 100 × 68 mm. $1 "Christ in the House of His Parents" 70 55

(Des J. Cooter. Litho Questa)

1980 (4 Feb). *Flowers* (*2nd series*). *Vert designs as T* **124**. *Multicoloured. W* w **14** (*inverted*). *P* 14.

430 4 c. *Clerodendrum aculeatum* 30 10
431 55 c. *Inga laurina* 40 20
432 $1.50, *Epidendrum difforme* .. .. .. 1·00 50
433 $2 *Salvia serotina* .. .. 1·10 90
430/3 .. .. *Set of* 4 2·50 1·50

(Des and litho Secura, Singapore)

1980 (6 May). *"London 1980" International Stamp Exhibition. T* **127** *and similar multicoloured designs. W* w **14** (*sideways, on* 5 *and* 55 *c., inverted on* 30 *c.*). *P* 13.

434 5 c. Type **127** 10 10
435 30 c. Fig Tree Church (*vert*) 20 10
436 55 c. Nisbet Plantation 45 25
437 $3 "Nelson" (Fuger) (*vert*) .. .. .. 1·00 1·00
434/7 .. .. *Set of* 4 1·60 1·25
MS438 107 × 77 mm 75 c. Detail of "Nelson Falling" (D. Dighton). P 13½ × 13 .. .. 85 70
a. Wmk sideways .. .. 40·00

OFFICIAL STAMPS

OFFICIAL

(O 1)

1980 (3 Mar). *Nos.* 396, 398 *and* 400/6 *optd with Type* O **1**.

O1 12 c. T.V. assembly plant .. .. .. 1·25 1·00
O2 25 c. Crafthouse (craft centre) 15 20
O3 40 c. Lobster and sea crab 50 50
O4 45 c. Royal St. Kitts Hotel and golf course .. 45 45
O5 50 c. Pinney's Beach, Nevis 30 40
O6 55 c. New runway at Golden Rock 30 40
O7 $1 Cotton picking .. .. 1·25 2·25
O8 $5 Brewery .. .. 1·00 2·50
O9 $10 Pineapples and Peanuts .. .. .. 2·50 3·50
O1/9 .. .. *Set of* 9 7·00 10·00

From 23 June 1980 St. Kitts and Nevis had separate postal authorities, each with their own issues.

ST. KITTS

St. Kitts

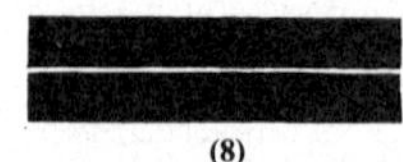

(8)

1980 (23 June). *As Nos.* 394/406 *of St. Christopher, Nevis and Anguilla optd with T* **8**. *A. W* w **14** (*sideways*). *B. No wmk*.

		A		B	
29	5 c. Radio and T.V. station ..	15	15	10	10
30	10 c. Technical college	15	15	10	10
31	12 c. T.V. assembly plant ..	80	80	†	
32	15 c. Sugar cane harvesting ..	15	15	10	10
33	25 c. Crafthouse (craft centre) ..	15	15	10	10
34	30 c. *Europa* (liner)	15	15	10	10
35	40 c. Lobster and sea crab ..	20	20	10	15
36	45 c. Royal St. Kitts Hotel and golf course	15	15	†	
37	50 c. Pinney's Beach, Nevis ..	15	15	†	
38	55 c. New runway at Golden Rock	15	15	15	15
39	$1 Cotton picking	25	25	25	25
40	$5 Brewery	1·00	1·00	1·25	1·50
41	$10 Pineapples and peanuts ..	1·75	1·75	2·00	2·50
29A/41A	.. .. *Set of* 13	4·75	4·75		
29B/41B	.. .. *Set of* 10			3·75	4·50

9 H.M.S. *Vanguard*, 1762

St.KITTS $2

80th Birthday Her Majesty Queen Elizabeth The Queen Mother

10 Queen Elizabeth the Queen Mother at Royal Variety Performance, 1978

(Litho Secura, Singapore)

1980 (8 Aug). *Ships. T* **9** *and similar horiz designs. Multicoloured. W* w **14** (*sideways*). *P* 13 × 13½.

42 4 c. Type **9** 10 10
a. Opt omitted .. .. 60·00
c. No stop after "ST" .. .. 1·00
43 10 c. H.M.S. *Boreas*, 1787 .. .. 10 10
a. Opt omitted £100
c. No stop after "ST" .. .. 1·00
44 30 c. H.M.S. *Druid*, 1827 .. .. 15 10
a. Opt omitted £100
c. No stop after "ST" .. .. 1·25
45 55 c. H.M.S. *Winchester*, 1831 .. .. .. 20 15
a. Opt inverted £120
b. Opt omitted £100
c. No stop after "ST" .. .. 1·50
46 $1.50, Harrison Line *Philosopher*, 1857 .. 40 30
a. Opt omitted £100
c. No stop after "ST" .. .. 2·00
47 $2 Harrison Line *Contractor*, 1930 .. .. 50 40
a. Opt double £100
b. Opt omitted £150
c. No stop after "ST" .. .. 2·00
42/7 .. .. *Set of* 6 1·25 90

Nos. 42/7 are overprinted "ST. KITTS" and have the previous combined inscription obliterated.

The "no stop" variety occurs on R.3/4 of the lower pane.

(Des and litho Format)

1980 (4 Sept). *80th Birthday of Queen Elizabeth the Queen Mother. W* w **14**. *P* 13½.

48 **10** $2 multicoloured 60 60

No. 48 was printed in sheets containing two *se-tenant* stamp-size labels.

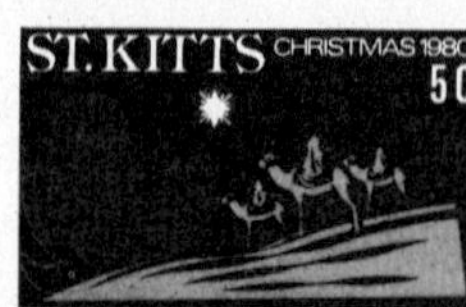

11 The Three Wise Men

(Des Walsall. Litho Questa)

1980 (10 Nov). *Christmas. T* **11** *and similar horiz designs. Multicoloured. W* w **14** (*sideways*). *P* 14½ × 14.

49 5 c. Type **11** 10 10
50 15 c. The Shepherds 10 10
51 30 c. Bethlehem 10 10
52 $4 Nativity scene 60 60
49/52 .. .. *Set of* 4 70 65

12 Purple-throated Carib

13 Bananaquit

(Des Jennifer Toombs. Litho Questa)

1981 (5 Feb)–**82**. *Birds. Vert designs as T* **12** (1 *to* 10 *c.*) *or horiz as T* **13** (15 *c. to* $10). *Multicoloured. W* w **14** (*sideways on* 1 *to* 10 *c.*). *P* 13½ × 14 (1 *to* 10 *c.*) *or* 14 (15 *c. to* $10).
A. *Without imprint date*
B. *With imprint date at foot of design*

		A		B	
53	1 c. Magnificent Frigate Bird ..	15	15	35	35
54	4 c. Wied's Crested Flycatcher	25	15	35	30
55	5 c. Type **12**	25	15	45	30
56	6 c. Burrowing Owl ..	35	25	55	40
57	8 c. Caribbean Martin	30	25	50	30
58	10 c. Yellow-crowned Night Heron	25	15	50	30
59	15 c. Type **13**	25	15	55	30
60	20 c. Scaly-breasted Thrasher ..	30	15	60	30
61	25 c. Grey Kingbird	30	15	60	30
62	30 c. Green-throated Carib ..	30	15	60	35
63	40 c. Turnstone	35	20	70	40
64	45 c. Black-faced Grassquit ..	35	25	80	45
65	50 c. Cattle Egret	40	30	90	50
66	55 c. Brown Pelican	40	30	1·00	50
67	$1 Lesser Antillean Bullfinch	60	50	1·75	80
68	$2.50, Zenaida Dove ..	1·25	1·25	2·75	2·25
69	$5 American Kestrel ..	2·25	2·50	4·50	4·50
70	$10 Antillean Crested Hummingbird ..	4·50	4·75	7·50	8·50
53/70	.. .. *Set of* 18	11·50	10·50	22·00	19·00

Dates of issue: Without imprint—5.2.81, 5 c. and 10 c. to $10; 30.5.81, 1, 4, 6, 8 c. With imprint—8.6.82, 1 c. to $10.

Nos. 59B/64B and 67B/8B exist with different imprint dates.

14 Battalion Company Sergeant, 3rd Regt of Foot ("The Buffs"), *circa* 1801

15 Miriam Pickard (first Guide Commissioner)

(Des G. Vasarhelyi. Litho Format)

1981 (5 Mar). *Military Uniforms* (*1st series*). *T* **14** *and similar vert designs. Multicoloured. W* w **14**. *P* 14½.

71 5 c. Type **14** 10 10
72 30 c. Battalion Company Officer, 45th Regt of Foot, 1796–97 .. .. 20 10
73 55 c. Battalion Company Officer, 9th Regt of Foot, 1790 .. .. 30 10
74 $2.50, Grenadier, 38th Regt of Foot, 1751 .. 90 35
71/4 .. .. *Set of* 4 1·25 45

See also Nos. 110/13 and 220/6.

(Des D. Shults. Litho Questa)

1981 (23 June–14 Dec). *Royal Wedding. Horiz designs as T* **26/27** *of Kiribati. Multicoloured.* (*a*) *W* w **14**. *P* 14.

75 55 c. *Saudadoes* 15 15
a. Sheetlet. No 75 × 6 and No. 76 .. .. 1·10
76 55 c. Prince Charles and Lady Diana Spencer 40 40
77 $2.50, *Royal George* 35 35
a. Sheetlet No. 77 × 6 and No. 78 .. .. 2·75
78 $2.50, As No. 76 .. .. 70 70
79 $4 *Britannia* 50 50
a. Sheetlet. No. 79 × 6 and No. 80 .. .. 3·50
80 $4 As No. 76 .. .. 1·00 1·00
75/80 .. .. *Set of* 6 2·75 2·75
MS81 120 × 109 mm. $5 As No. 76. Wmk sideways. P 12 (14 Dec) .. .. 3·00 1·50

(*b*) *Booklet stamps. No wmk. P* 12 (19 Nov)

82 55 c. As No. 76 .. .. 30 30
a. Booklet pane. No. 82 × 4 .. .. .. 1·00
83 $2.50, As No. 78 .. .. 1·10 1·25
a. Booklet pane. No. 83 × 2 .. .. .. 2·25

Nos. 75/80 were printed in sheetlets of seven stamps of the same face value, each containing six of the "Royal Yacht" design and one of the larger design showing Prince Charles and Lady Diana.

Nos. 82/3 come from $9.40 stamp booklets.

(Des Jennifer Toombs. Litho Walsall)

1981 (21 Sept). *50th Anniv of St. Kitts Girl Guide Movement. T* **15** *and similar vert designs. Multicoloured. W* w **14**. *P* 14.

84 5 c. Type **15** 10 10
85 30 c. Lady Baden-Powell's visit, 1964 .. .. 15 10
86 55 c. Visit of Princess Alice, 1960 .. .. 30 10
87 $2 Thinking-Day parade, 1980's 60 35
84/7 .. .. *Set of* 4 1·00 45

16 Stained-glass Windows **17** Admiral Samuel Hood

(Des Jennifer Toombs. Litho Format)

1981 (30 Nov). *Christmas. T* **16** *and similar vert designs showing stained-glass windows. W* w **14**. *P* 13 × 14.

88 5 c. multicoloured 10 10
89 30 c. multicoloured 20 10
90 55 c. multicoloured 30 10
91 $3 multicoloured 1·00 50
88/91 *Set of* 4 1·40 60

(Des D. Shults. Litho Format)

1982 (15 Mar). *Bicentenary of Brimstone Hill Siege. T* **17** *and similar horiz designs. W* w **14** (*sideways*). *P* 14.

92 15 c. multicoloured 10 10
93 55 c. multicoloured 20 10
MS94 96 × 71 mm. $5 black, red-orange & yell-brn 2·50 1·50
Designs:—55 c. Marquis De Bouillé; $5 Battle scene.

ROYAL BABY
(**19**)

18 Alexandra, Princess of Wales, 1863

(Des D. Shults and J. Cooter. Litho Format)

1982 (22 June). *21st Birthday of Princess of Wales. T* **18** *and similar vert designs. Multicoloured. W* w **14**. *P* 13½ × 14.

95 15 c. Type **18** 10 10
96 55 c. Coat of arms of Alexandra of Denmark 40 35
97 $6 Diana, Princess of Wales 1·50 1·50
95/7 *Set of* 3 1·75 1·75

1982 (12 July). *Birth of Prince William of Wales. Nos.* 95/7 *optd with T* **19**

98 15 c. Type **18** 10 10
a. Opt inverted 20·00
99 55 c. Coat of arms of Alexandra of Denmark 40 35
100 $6 Diana, Princess of Wales 1·50 1·50
98/100 *Set of* 3 1·75 1·75

20 Naturalist Badge **21** Santa with Christmas Tree and Gifts

(Des Philatelists (1980) Ltd. Litho Questa)

1982 (18 Aug). *75th Anniv of Boy Scout Movement. T* **20** *and similar vert designs. Multicoloured. W* w **14**. *P* 14 × 13½.

101 5 c. Type **20** 10 10
102 55 c. Rescuer badge 40 15
103 $2 First Aid badge 1·10 80
101/3 *Set of* 3 1·40 90

(Des Marcel Frazer (5 c.), Sinclair Herbert (55 c.), Marijka Grey ($1.10), Gary Bowrin ($3). Litho Format)

1982 (20 Oct). *Christmas. Children's Paintings. T* **21** *and similar horiz designs. Multicoloured. W* w **14** (*sideways*). *P* 14 × 13½.

104 5 c. Type **21** 10 10
105 55 c. The Inn 15 10
106 $1.10, Three Kings 30 15
107 $3 Annunciation 80 40
104/7 *Set of* 4 1·25 60

COVER PRICES

Cover factors are quoted at the beginning of each country for most issues to 1945. An explanation of the system can be found on page x. The factors quoted do not, however, apply to philatelic covers.

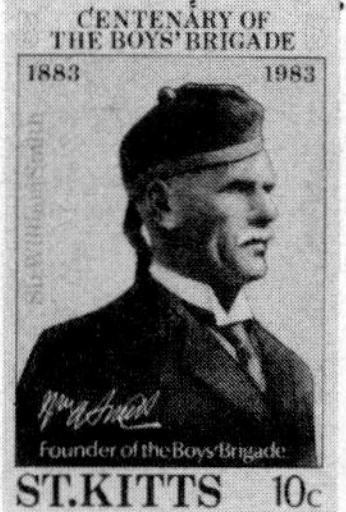

22 Cruise Ship *Stella Oceanis* at Basseterre **23** Sir William Smith (founder)

(Des G. Drummond. Litho Format)

1983 (14 Mar). *Commonwealth Day. T* **22** *and similar horiz design. Multicoloured. W* w **14** (*sideways*). *P* 14.

108 55 c. Type **22** 20 10
109 $2 *Queen Elizabeth 2* at Basseterre 50 40

(Des G. Vasarhelyi. Litho Format)

1983 (25 May). *Military Uniforms* (2nd series). *Vert designs as T* **14**. *Multicoloured. W* w **14**. *P* 14½.

110 15 c. Light Company Private, 15th Regt of Foot, *circa* 1814 20 10
111 30 c. Battalion Company Officer, 15th Regt of Foot, *circa* 1780 35 15
112 55 c. Light Company Officer, 5th Regt of Foot, *circa* 1822 55 20
113 $2.50, Battalion Company Officer, 11th Regt of Foot, *circa* 1804 1·40 1·60
110/13 *Set of* 4 2·25 1·75

(Des J. Cooter. Litho Format)

1983 (27 July). *Centenary of the Boys' Brigade. T* **23** *and similar vert designs. Multicoloured. W* w **14**. *P* 13½.

114 10 c. Type **23** 25 10
115 45 c. B.B. members on steps of Sandy Point Methodist Church 55 20
116 50 c. Brigade drummers 65 25
117 $3 Boys' Brigade badge 2·50 2·75
114/17 *Set of* 4 3·50 3·00

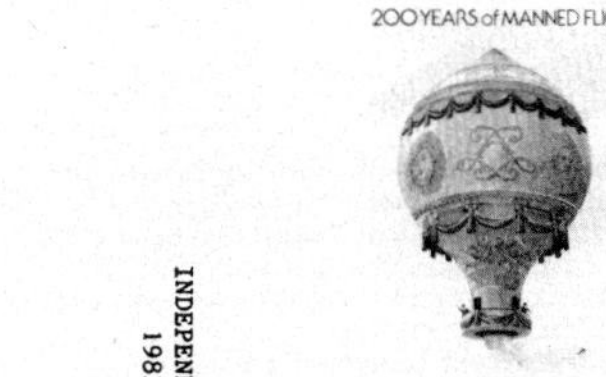

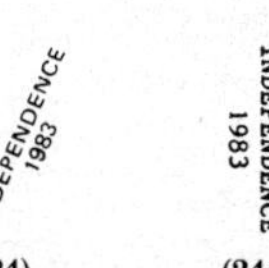

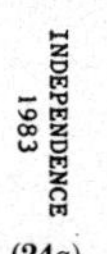

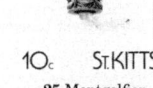

(**24**) (**24***a*) **25** Montgolfier Balloon, 1783

1983 (19 Sept). *Nos.* 55, 59/63 *and* 66/70 *optd as T* **24** (*horiz 20 mm long on Nos.* 119/28)
A. No imprint date
B. With imprint date

		A		B	
118	5 c. Type **12**	15	10	15	10
	a. Opt inverted	†		48·00	—
	b. Pair one without opt	†		80·00	—
	c. Opt with T **24***a* (local opt)	12·00	12·00	2·25	2·00
	ca. Opt inverted (reading upwards)	35·00	—	11·00	—
119	15 c. Type **13**	1·00	1·00	20	10
	a. Opt double	†		12·00	—
120	20 c. Scaly-breasted Thrasher	†		25	10
121	25 c. Grey Kingbird	†		30	10
	a. Opt inverted	†		14·00	—
122	30 c. Green-throated Carib	20·00	20·00	35	15
123	40 c. Turnstone	†		40	20
124	55 c. Brown Pelican	50	50	45	30
	a. Opt inverted	†		11·00	—
125	$1 Lesser Antillean Bullfinch	7·50	7·50	80	50
126	$2.50, Zenaida Dove	2·00	2·00	1·50	1·25
127	$5 American Kestrel	2·75	2·75	2·50	2·50
128	$10 Antillean Crested Hummingbird	6·00	6·00	5·00	5·00
118A/28A	*Set of* 8	35·00	35·00		
118B/28B	*Set of* 11			11·00	9·00

(Des A. Theobald. Litho Format)

1983 (28 Sept). *Bicentenary of Manned Flight. T* **25** *and similar multicoloured designs. W* w **15** (*sideways on Nos.* 130/3). *P* 14.

129 10 c. Type **25** 10 10
130 45 c. Sikorsky *Russian Knight* biplane (*horiz*) 15 10
131 50 c. Lockheed "Tristar" (*horiz*) 20 15
132 $2.50, Bell "XS-1" (*horiz*) 60 75
129/32 *Set of* 4 90 95
MS133 108 × 145 mm. Nos. 129/32 95 1·25

26 Star over West Indian Town **27** Parrot in Tree

(Des Jennifer Toombs. Litho Format)

1983 (7 Nov). *Christmas. T* **26** *and similar horiz designs. Multicoloured. W* w **15** (*sideways*). *P* 14.

134 15 c. Type **26** 10 10
135 30 c. Shepherds watching Star 10 10
136 55 c. Mary and Joseph 15 10
137 $2.50, The Nativity 40 40
134/7 *Set of* 4 60 55
MS138 130 × 130 mm. Nos. 134/7. Wmk upright 75 1·10

(Des Court House Studio. Litho Format)

1984 (30 Jan). *Batik Designs* (1st series). *T* **27** *and similar vert designs. W* w **15**. *P* 14 × 13½.

139 45 c. multicoloured 15 10
140 50 c. multicoloured 15 10
141 $1.50, new blue, bistre-yellow & brt mag 45 50
142 $3 multicoloured 80 1·00
139/42 *Set of* 4 1·40 1·50
Designs:—50 c. Man under coconut tree; $1.50, Women with fruit; $3 Butterflies.
See also Nos. 169/72.

28 Cushion Star

(Des G. Drummond. Litho J.W.)

1984 (4 July). *Marine Wildlife. T* **28** *and similar multicoloured designs. W* w **15** (*sideways on* 5 c. *to* 75 c.). *P* 14.

143 5 c. Type **28** 25 20
144 10 c. Rough File Shell 35 20
145 15 c. Red-lined Cleaning Shrimp 35 15
146 20 c. Bristleworm 35 15
147 25 c. Flamingo Tongue 30 15
148 30 c. Christmas Tree Worm 30 20
149 40 c. Pink-tipped Anemone 45 25
150 50 c. Smallmouth Grunt 45 30
151 60 c. Glasseye Snapper 1·00 40
152 75 c. Reef Squirrelfish 75 45
153 $1 Sea Fans and Flamefish (*vert*) 85 50
154 $2.50, Reef Butterflyfish (*vert*) 2·00 2·25
155 $5 Blackbar Soldierfish (*vert*) 4·75 5·50
156 $10 Cocoa Damselfish (*vert*) 8·50 10·00
143/56 *Set of* 14 19·00 19·00
For 10 c., 60 c., $5 and $10 with watermark w **16** see Nos. 194/206.

29 Agriculture

(Des G. Vasarhelyi. Litho Questa)

1984 (15 Aug). *25th Anniv of 4-H Organisation. T* **29** *and similar horiz designs. Multicoloured. W* w **15** (*sideways*). *P*. 14.

157 30 c. Type **29** 30 10
158 55 c. Animal husbandry 40 15
159 $1.10, The 4-H Pledge 70 60
160 $3 On parade 1·25 1·25
157/60 *Set of* 4 2·40 1·90

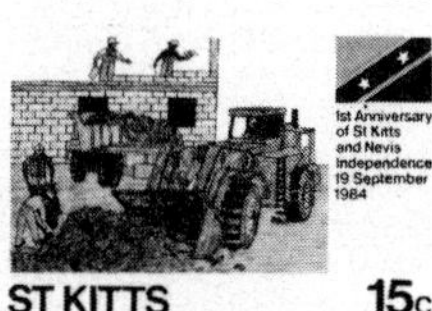

30 Construction of Royal St. Kitts Hotel

(Des K. Tatem (15 c.), Tessa Wattley (30 c.), Myrna Elcock and L. Freeman ($1.10), A. Williams ($3), adapted Jennifer Toombs. Litho Format)

1984 (18 Sept). *First Anniv of Independence of St. Kitts-Nevis. T* **30** *and similar multicoloured designs. W* w **15** (*sideways on* 15, 30 *c.*). *P* 14.

161 15 c. Type **30** 20 10
162 30 c. Independence celebrations 30 15
163 $1.10, National Anthem and aerial view (*vert*) 70 60
164 $3 "Dawn of a New Day" (*vert*) 1·60 1·40
161/4 *Set of* 4 2·50 2·00

31 Opening Presents

(Des Jennifer Toombs. Litho Questa)

1984 (1 Nov). *Christmas. T* **31** *and similar horiz designs. Multicoloured. W* w **15** (*sideways*). *P* 14.

165 15 c. Type **31** 15 10
166 60 c. Singing carols 45 35
167 $1 Nativity play 75 60
168 $2 Leaving church on Christmas Day 1·40 1·10
165/8 *Set of* 4 2·50 1·90

IMPERFORATES. Issues between Nos. 169 and 184 exist imperforate. Such items are not listed as there is no evidence that they fulfil the criteria outlined on page xi of this catalogue.

(Des Court House Studio. Litho Format)

1985 (6 Feb). *Batik Designs (2nd series). Horiz designs as T* **27**. *W w* **15** (*sideways*). *P* 13½ × 14.

169 15 c. black, bright green and light green .. 15 10
170 40 c. black, bright greenish blue and bright new blue .. 30 15
171 60 c. black, orange-vermilion and vermilion .. 45 20
172 $3 black, lake-brown and orange-brown .. 1·75 2·00
169/72 .. *Set of* 4 2·40 2·25

Designs:—15 c. Country bus; 40 c. Donkey cart; 60 c. Rum shop, and man on bicycle; $3 S.V. *Polynesia* (tourist yacht).

32 Container Ship *Tropic Jade*

33 James Derrick Cardin (leading Freemason)

(Des J. Cooter. Litho Format)

1985 (27 Mar). *Ships. T* **32** *and similar horiz designs. Multicoloured. W w* **15** (*sideways*). *P* 13½ × 14.

173 40 c. Type **32** .. 75 30
174 $1.20, *Atlantic Clipper* (schooner) .. 1·50 1·25
175 $2 *Mandalay* (schooner) .. 2·25 2·25
176 $2 *Cunard Countess* (liner) .. 2·25 2·25
173/6 .. *Set of* 4 6·00 5·50

(Des G. Vasarhelyi. Litho Format)

1985 (9 Nov). *150th Anniv of Mount Olive S.C. Masonic Lodge. T* **33** *and similar multicoloured designs. W w* **15** (*sideways on* 15, 75 *c., and* $3). *P* 15.

177 15 c. Type **33** .. 50 20
178 75 c. Banner of Mount Olive Lodge .. 1·50 1·10
179 $1.20, Masonic symbols (*horiz*) .. 2·25 2·25
180 $3 Lodge Charter (1835) .. 3·75 3·75
177/80 .. *Set of* 4 7·25 6·50

34 Map of St. Kitts

35 Queen Elizabeth and Prince Philip on St. Kitts

(Des. J. Cooter. Litho Format)

1985 (27 Nov). *Christmas. 400th Anniv of Sir Francis Drake's Visit. T* **34** *and similar vert designs. Multicoloured. P* 15.

181 10 c. Type **34** .. 30 15
182 40 c. *Golden Hind* .. 75 35
183 60 c. Sir Francis Drake .. 85 50
184 $3 Drake's heraldic shield .. 2·50 2·25
181/4 .. *Set of* 4 4·00 3·00

(Des D. Miller. Litho B.D.T.)

1986 (9 July). *60th Birthday of Queen Elizabeth II. T* **35** *and similar vert designs. Multicoloured. P* 13½.

185 10 c. Type **35** .. 15 10
186 20 c. Queen Elizabeth on St. Kitts .. 25 15
187 40 c. At Trooping the Colour .. 50 30
188 $3 In Sweden .. 2·00 2·25
185/8 .. *Set of* 4 2·50 2·50

(Des D. Miller. Litho Walsall)

1986 (23 July). *Royal Wedding. Square designs as T* **231a** *of Jamaica. Multicoloured. W w* **16**. *P* 14½×14.

189 15 c. Prince Andrew and Miss Sarah Ferguson .. 15 10
190 $2.50, Prince Andrew .. 1·50 2·00

36 Family on Smallholding

40th ANNIVERSARY
U.N. WEEK 19-26 OCT.

(**37**)

(Des K. Tatem (15 c.), A. Williams ($1.20), adapted G. Vasarhelyi. Litho Questa)

1986 (18 Sept). *Agriculture Exhibition. T* **36** *and similar horiz design. Multicoloured. W w* **16** (*sideways*). *P* 13½ × 14.

191 15 c. Type **36** .. 20 10
192 $1.20, Hands holding people, computers and crops .. 1·25 1·40

(Litho Questa)

1986 (5 Nov)–**88**. *As Nos.* 144, 151 *and* 155/6 *but W w* **16** (*sideways on* 10, 60 *c.*). *With imprint date. P* 14.

194 10 c. Rough File Shell .. 50 40
201 60 c. Glasseye Snapper (17.8.88) .. 1·40 1·10
205 $5 Blackbar Soldierfish (*vert*) (17.8.88) .. 5·00 5·50
206 $10 Cocoa Damselfish (*vert* (17.8.88) .. 9·50 11·00
194/206 .. *Set of* 4 15·00 16·00

No. 194 exists with different imprint dates below the design.

1986 (12 Nov). *40th Anniv of United Nations Week. Nos.* 185/8 *optd with T* **37** *in gold.*

207 10 c. Type **35** .. 20 15
208 20 c. Queen Elizabeth on St. Kitts .. 30 20
209 40 c. At Trooping the Colour .. 40 30
210 $3 In Sweden .. 2·25 2·75
a. Opt triple .. 75·00
207/10 .. *Set of* 4 2·75 3·00

38 Adult Green Monkey with Young

39 Frederic Bartholdi (sculptor)

(Des Doreen McGuinness. Litho Walsall)

1986 (1 Dec). *Green Monkeys on St. Kitts. T* **38** *and similar vert designs. Multicoloured. W w* **16**. *P* 14 × 13½.

211 15 c. Type **38** .. 30 15
212 20 c. Adult on ground .. 35 20
213 60 c. Young monkey in tree .. 85 65
214 $1 Adult grooming young monkey .. 1·40 1·75
211/14 .. *Set of* 4 2·50 2·50

(Des D. Miller. Litho Format)

1986 (17 Dec). *Centenary of Statue of Liberty. T* **39** *and similar multicoloured designs. W w* **16** (*sideways on* 60 *c.*, $1.50). *P* 14.

215 40 c. Type **39** .. 40 30
216 60 c. Torch (1876) and head (1878) on exhibition (*horiz*) .. 65 50
217 $1.50, French ship *Isere* carrying Statue (*horiz*) .. 1·50 1·50
218 $3 Statue of Liberty, Paris, 1884 .. 2·40 2·50
215/18 .. *Set of* 4 4·50 4·25
MS219 70 × 85 mm. $3.50, Head of Statue of Liberty .. 2·25 2·50

40 Officer, 9th Regt (East Norfolk), 1792

41 Sugar Cane Warehouse

(Des C. Collins. Litho Format)

1987 (25 Feb). *Military Uniforms (3rd series). T* **40** *and similar vert designs. Multicoloured. W w* **16**. *P* 14½.

220 15 c. Type **40** .. 40 30
221 15 c. Officer, Regt de Neustrie, 1779 .. 40 30
222 40 c. Sergeant, 3rd Regt ("The Buffs"), 1801 75 45
223 40 c. Officer, French Artillery, 1812 .. 75 45
224 $2 Light Company Private, 5th Regt, 1778 2·25 2·50
225 $2 Grenadier of the Line, 1796 .. 2·25 2·50
220/5 .. *Set of* 6 6·25 6·00
MS226 121 × 145 mm. Nos. 220/5 .. 6·25 6·50

The two designs for each value were printed in sheets of 50 containing two panes 5 × 5 with the British uniform depicted on the left-hand pane and the French on the right.

(Des G. Vasarhelyi. Litho Format)

1987 (15 Apr). *Sugar Cane Industry. T* **41** *and similar vert designs. Multicoloured (colour of panel behind* "ST. KITTS" *given). W w* **16**. *P* 14.

227 15 c. greenish yellow (Type **41**) .. 20 20
a. Horiz strip of 5. Nos. 227/31 .. 90
228 15 c. cinnamon .. 20 20
229 15 c. lilac .. 20 20
230 15 c. azure .. 20 20
231 15 c. pale greenish blue .. 20 20
232 75 c. bright green .. 75 75
a. Horiz strip of 5. Nos. 232/6 .. 3·25
233 75 c. lilac .. 75 75
234 75 c. dull green .. 75 75
235 75 c. orange-yellow .. 75 75
236 75 c. greenish blue .. 75 75
227/36 .. *Set of* 10 4·25 4·25

Designs:—Nos. 227/31, Sugar cane factory; Nos. 232/6, Loading sugar train.

Nos. 227/31 and 232/6 were each printed together, *se-tenant*, in horizontal strips of five throughout the sheets, each strip forming a composite design.

42 B.W.I.A. "L-1011-500 TriStar"

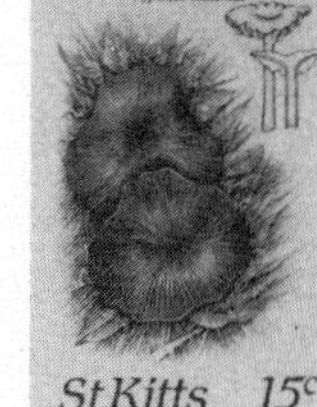

43 *Hygrocybe occidentalis*

(Des T. Hadler. Litho Format)

1987 (24 June). *Aircraft visiting St. Kitts. T* **42** *and similar horiz designs. Multicoloured. W w* **14** (*sideways*). *P* 14.

237 40 c. Type **42** .. 65 30
238 60 c. L.I.A.T. BAe "Super 748" .. 85 60
239 $1.20, W.I.A. "DHC-6 Twin Otter" .. 1·50 1·50
240 $3 American Eagle Aérospatiale "ATR-42" 2·75 3·25
237/40 .. *Set of* 4 5·25 5·00

(Des I. Loe. Litho Questa)

1987 (26 Aug). *Fungi. T* **43** *and similar vert designs. Multicoloured. W w* **16**. *P* 14.

241 15 c. Type **43** .. 45 20
242 40 c. *Marasmius haematocephalus* .. 75 40
243 $1.20, *Psilocybe cubensis* .. 1·50 1·50
244 $2 *Hygrocybe acutoconica* .. 2·25 2·25
245 $3 *Boletellus cubensis* .. 2·75 3·00
241/5 .. *Set of* 5 7·00 6·50

44 Carnival Clown

45 Ixora

(Des Rose Cameron-Smith. Litho Format)

1987 (28 Oct). *Christmas. T* **44** *and similar square designs showing different clowns. Multicoloured. W w* **16** (*sideways*). *P* 14½.

246 15 c. multicoloured .. 25 15
247 40 c. multicoloured .. 55 30
248 $1 multicoloured .. 1·25 80
249 $3 multicoloured .. 2·50 3·00
246/9 .. *Set of* 4 4·00 3·75

See also Nos. 266/9.

(Des Josephine Martin. Litho Questa)

1988 (20 Jan). *Flowers. T* **45** *and similar vert designs. Multicoloured. W w* **16**. *P* 14½ × 14.

250 15 c. Type **45** .. 30 15
251 40 c. Shrimp Plant .. 55 30
252 $1 Poinsettia .. 1·00 75
253 $3 Honolulu Rose .. 2·50 3·00
250/3 .. *Set of* 4 4·00 3·75

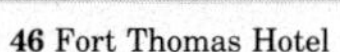

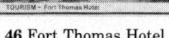

46 Fort Thomas Hotel

47 Ball, Wicket and Leeward Islands Cricket Association Emblem

(Des L. Curtis. Litho Walsall)

1988 (20 Apr). *Tourism (1st series). Hotels. T* **46** *and similar horiz designs. Multicoloured. W w* **14** (*sideways*). *P* 14 × 14½.

254 60 c. Type **46** .. 40 40
255 60 c. Fairview Inn .. 40 40
256 60 c. Frigate Bay Beach Hotel .. 40 40
257 60 c. Ocean Terrace Inn .. 40 40
258 $3 The Golden Lemon .. 1·75 2·00
259 $3 Royal St. Kitts Casino and Jack Tar Village .. 1·75 2·00
260 $3 Rawlins Plantation Hotel and Restaurant .. 1·75 2·00
254/60 .. *Set of* 7 6·25 7·00

See also Nos. 270/5.

(Des Joan Thompson. Litho Walsall)

1988 (13 July). *75th Anniv of Leeward Islands Cricket Tournament. T* **47** *and similar vert design. Multicoloured. W w* **14**. *P* 13 × 13½.

261 40 c. Type **47** .. 75 30
262 $3 Cricket match at Warner Park .. 3·25 3·75

48 Flag of St. Kitts-Nevis

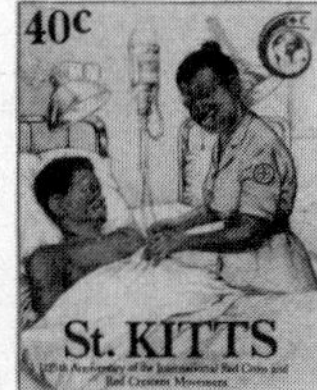

49 Red Cross Nurse with Hospital Patient

(Des L. Curtis. Litho Questa)

1988 (19 Sept). *5th Anniv of Independence. T* **48** *and similar vert designs. Multicoloured.* W w **16**. *P* 14½ × 14.
263 15 c. Type **48** 15 10
264 60 c. Arms of St. Kitts 50 50
MS265 61 × 53 mm. $5 Princess Margaret presenting Constitutional Instrument to Prime Minister Kennedy Simmonds, 1983. W w **14** 2·75 3·00

(Des Rose Cameron-Smith. Litho Format)

1988 (2 Nov). *Christmas. Square designs as T* **44** *showing carnival masqueraders.* W w **14** *(sideways). P* 14½.
266 15 c. multicoloured 10 10
267 40 c. multicoloured 20 25
268 80 c. multicoloured 40 45
269 $3 multicoloured 1·25 1·75
266/9 *Set of* 4 1·75 2·25

(Des L. Curtis. Litho Format)

1989 (25 Jan). *Tourism (2nd series). Colonial Architecture. Horiz designs as T* **46**. *Multicoloured.* W w **16** *(sideways). P* 14.
270 20 c. Georgian house 20 15
271 20 c. Colonial-style house 20 15
272 $1 Romney Manor 70 75
273 $1 Lavington Great House 70 75
274 $2 Government House 1·25 1·40
275 $2 Treasury Building 1·25 1·40
270/5 *Set of* 6 3·75 4·25

(Des C. Collins. Litho Format)

1989 (8 May). *125th Anniv of International Red Cross. T* **49** *and similar vert designs.* W w **16**. *P* 14×14½.
276 40 c. multicoloured 30 30
277 $1 multicoloured 65 65
278 $3 orange-vermilion and black 1·75 2·00
276/8 *Set of* 3 2·40 2·75
Designs:—$1 Loading patient into ambulance; $3 125th anniversary logo.

50 Battle on the Champ-de-Mars

51 Outline Map of St. Kitts

(Des D. Miller. Litho B.D.T.)

1989 (7 July). *"Philexfrance 89" International Stamp Exhibition, Paris. Sheet* 115×99 *mm.* W w **16**. *P* 14.
MS279 **50** $5 multicoloured 3·25 3·50

(Des A. Theobald ($5), D. Miller (others). Litho Questa)

1989 (20 July). *20th Anniv of First Manned Landing on Moon. Multicoloured designs as T* **51a** *of Kiribati.* W w **16** *(sideways on 20 c., $1). P* 14×13½ *(10 c., $2) or* 14 *(others).*
280 10 c. Lunar rover on Moon 10 10
281 20 c. Crew of "Apollo 13" (30×30 *mm*) 10 10
282 $1 "Apollo 13" emblem (30×30 *mm*) 45 60
283 $2 "Apollo 13" splashdown, South Pacific 95 1·25
280/3 *Set of* 4 1·40 1·75
MS284 100×83 mm. $5 Aldrin leaving "Apollo 11" lunar module. Wmk inverted. P 14×13½ 3·50 3·75

(Des D. Miller. Litho B.D.T.)

1989 (25 Oct). W w **16**. *P* 15×14.
285 **51** 10 c. deep mauve and black 10 10
286 15 c. bright carmine and black 10 10
287 20 c. yellow-orange and black 15 10
288 40 c. yellow and black 20 20
289 60 c. bright blue and black 30 30
290 $1 yellow-green and black 50 60
285/90 *Set of* 6 1·10 1·10

52 *Santa Mariagalante* passing St. Kitts, 1493

(Des L. Curtis. Litho Questa)

1989 (8 Nov). *500th Anniv of Discovery of America (1992) by Columbus. T* **52** *and similar horiz designs. Multicoloured.* W w **16** *(sideways). P* 14.
291 15 c. Type **52** 35 20
292 80 c. Arms of Columbus and map of fourth voyage, 1502-04 1·00 1·00
293 $1 Navigation instruments, c. 1500 1·25 1·25
294 $5 Columbus and map of second voyage, 1493-96 4·00 4·50
291/4 *Set of* 4 6·00 6·25

53 Poinciana Tree

54 *Junonia evarete*

(Des G. Vasarhelyi. Litho Walsall)

1989 (17 Nov). *"World Stamp Expo '89" International Stamp Exhibition, Washington. T* **53** *and similar horiz designs. Multicoloured.* W w **14** *(sideways). P* 14.
295 15 c. Type **53** 20 10
296 40 c. Fort George Citadel, Brimstone Hill 45 30
297 $1 Private, Light Company, 5th Foot, 1778 95 70
298 $3 St. George's Anglican Church 2·50 2·75
295/8 *Set of* 4 3·75 3·50

(Des I. Loe. Litho B.D.T.)

1990 (6 June). *Butterflies. T* **54** *and similar horiz designs. Multicoloured.* W w **14** *(sideways). P* 13½×14.
299 15 c. Type **54** 25 15
300 40 c. *Anartia jatrophae* 45 25
301 60 c. *Heliconius charitonia* 65 45
302 $3 *Biblis hyperia* 2·25 2·75
299/302 *Set of* 4 3·25 3·25

(55)

56 Brimstone Hill

1990 (6 June). *"EXPO 90" International Garden and Greenery Exhibition, Osaka. Nos. 299/302 optd with T* **55**.
303 15 c. Type **54** 25 15
304 40 c. *Anartia jatrophae* 45 25
305 60 c. *Heliconius charitonia* 65 45
306 $3 *Biblis hyperia* 2·25 2·75
303/6 *Set of* 4 3·25 3·25

(Des D. Miller. Litho Questa)

1990 (30 June). *300th Anniv of English Bombardment of Brimstone Hill. T* **56** *and similar horiz designs. Multicoloured.* W w **16** *(sideways). P* 14.
307 15 c. Type **56** 20 10
308 40 c. Restored Brimstone Hill fortifications 35 25
309 60 c. 17th-century English marine and Fort Charles under attack 50 50
a. Horiz pair. Nos. 309/10 2·75 2·75
310 $3 English sailors firing cannon 2·25 2·25
307/10 *Set of* 4 3·00 2·75
Nos. 307/9 were printed in complete sheets, each containing one value. No. 309 also exists *se-tenant*, as a horizontal pair, with No. 310. Each pair shows a composite design across the two stamps with no margin at the left of the 60 c. or at the right of the $3.

57 Spitfire Mk Vb *St. Kitts Nevis I*, 71 Squadron

(Des A. Theobald. Litho B.D.T.)

1990 (15 Sept). *50th Anniv of Battle of Britain. Sheet* 103×76 *mm. containing T* **57** *and similar horiz design. Multicoloured.* W w **16** *(sideways). P* 14.
MS311 $3 Type **57**; $3 Spitfire Mk Vb *St. Kitts Nevis II*, 345 Squadron 4·00 4·25

58 *Romney* (freighter)

(Des S. Williams. Litho B.D.T.)

1990 (10 Oct). *Ships. T* **58** *and similar horiz designs. Multicoloured.* W w **14** *(sideways). P* 14.
312 10 c. Type **58** 10 10
313 15 c. *Baralt* (freighter) 10 10
314 20 c. *Wear* (mail steamer) 10 10
315 25 c. *Sunmount* (freighter) 10 15
316 40 c. *Inanda* (cargo liner) 15 20
317 50 c. *Alcoa Partner* (freighter) 20 25
318 60 c. *Dominica* (freighter) 25 30
319 80 c. *C.G.M Provence* (container ship) 35 40
320 $1 *Director* (freighter) 40 45
321 $1.20, Sailing barque 50 55
322 $2 *Chignecto* (mail steamer) 85 90
323 $3 *Berbice* (mail steamer) 1·25 1·40
324 $5 *Vamos* (freighter) 2·10 2·25
325 $10 *Federal Maple* (freighter) 4·25 4·50
312/25 *Set of* 14 9·50 10·50

59 Single Fork Game

(Des G. Vasarhelyi. Litho Questa)

1990 (14 Nov). *Christmas. Traditional Games. T* **59** *and similar horiz designs. Multicoloured.* W w **16** *(sideways). P* 14.
326 10 c. Type **59** 15 10
327 15 c. Boulder breaking 15 10
328 40 c. Double fork 30 30
329 $3 The run up 1·75 1·75
326/9 *Set of* 4 2·10 2·00

60 White Periwinkle

61 Census Logo

(Des Annette Robinson. Litho Cartor, France)

1991 (8 May). *Flowers. T* **60** *and similar multicoloured designs.* W w **14** *(sideways on 10, 40 c.). P* 14×13½ *(10, 40 c.) or* 13½×14 *(others).*
330 10 c. Type **60** 15 10
331 40 c. Pink Oleander 25 25
332 60 c. Pink Periwinkle (*vert*) 40 40
333 $2 White Oleander (*vert*) 1·25 1·25
330/3 *Set of* 4 1·90 1·75

(Des G. Vasarhelyi, Litho B.D.T)

1991 (13 May). *National Census.* W w **16**. *P* 14.
333 **61** 15 c. multicoloured 15 10
334 $2.40, multicoloured 1·60 1·60
The $2.40 differs from Type **61** by showing "ST. KITTS" in a curved panel.

(Des D. Miller. Litho Questa)

1991 (17 June). *65th Birthday of Queen Elizabeth II and 70th Birthday of Prince Philip. Vert designs as T* **58** *of Kiribati.* W w **16** *(sideways). P* 14½×14.
336 $1.20, Prince Philip 75 75
a. Horiz pair. Nos. 336/7 separated by label 1·75 1·75
337 $1.80, Queen holding bouquet of flowers 1·00 1·00
Nos. 336/7 were printed together in a similar sheet format to Nos. 366/7 of Kiribati.

62 Nassau Grouper

(Des G. Drummond. Litho Questa)

1991 (28 Aug). *Fishes. T* **62** *and similar horiz designs. Multicoloured.* W w **14** *(sideways). P* 14.
338 10 c. Type **62** 15 10
339 60 c. Hogfish 40 40
340 $1 Red Hind 70 70
341 $3 Porkfish 2·00 2·00
338/41 *Set of* 4 3·00 3·00

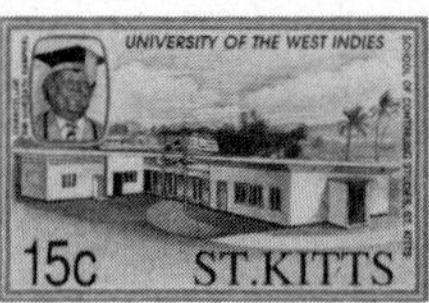

63 School of Continuing Studies, St. Kitts, and Chancellor Sir Shridath Ramphal

(Des G. Vasarhelyi. Litho Questa)

1991 (28 Sept). *40th Anniv of University of West Indies. T* **63** *and similar horiz designs. Multicoloured. W w* **16** *(sideways). P* 14.

342	15 c. Type **63**	15	10
343	50 c. Administration Building, Barbados	35	35
344	$1 Engineering Building, Trinidad and Tobago	65	65
345	$3 Mona Campus, Jamaica, and Sir Shridath Ramphal	2·00	2·00
342/5	*Set of* 4	2·75	2·75

64 Whipping The Bull

(Des Marijka Grey and G. Vasarhelyi. Litho Walsall)

1991 (6 Nov). *Christmas. "The Bull" (Carnival play). T* **64** *and similar horiz designs. Multicoloured. W w* **14** *(sideways). P* 14.

346	10 c. Type **64**	15	10
347	15 c. Death of The Bull	15	10
348	60 c. Cast of characters and musicians	45	45
349	$3 The Bull in procession	1·60	1·60
346/9	*Set of* 4	2·10	2·00

(Des D. Miller. Litho Questa ($3), Leigh-Mardon Ltd, Melbourne (others))

1992 (6 Feb). *40th Anniv of Queen Elizabeth II's Accession. Horiz designs as T* **112** *of Kenya. Multicoloured. W w* **14** *(sideways)* ($3) *or w* **16** *(sideways) (others). P* 14.

350	10 c. St. Kitts coastline	15	10
351	40 c. Warner Park Pavilion	25	25
352	60 c. Brimstone Hill	40	40
353	$1 Three portraits of Queen Elizabeth	70	70
354	$3 Queen Elizabeth II	1·90	1·90
350/4	*Set of* 5	3·00	3·00

OFFICIAL STAMPS

1980 (23 June). *Nos.* 32/41 *additionally optd with Type* O 1 *of St. Christopher, Nevis and Anguilla. A. W w* **14** *(sideways). B. No wmk.*

		A		B	
O 1	15 c. Sugar cane harvesting	10	10	†	
O 2	25 c. Crafthouse (craft centre)	10	10	10	10
O 3	30 c. *Europa* (liner)	10	10	15	15
O 4	40 c. Lobster and sea crab	10	15	15·00	27·00
O 5	45 c. Royal St. Kitts Hotel and golf course	15	15	†	
O 6	50 c. Pinney's Beach, Nevis	15	15	†	
O 7	55 c. New runway at Golden Rock	15	15	30	35
	a. Opt inverted	42·00	—	†	
O 8	$1 Cotton picking	25	25	40	50
O 9	$5 Brewery	1·00	1·50	2·25	3·50
O10	$10 Pineapples and peanuts	1·75	2·50	4·50	6·50
	a. Opt inverted	£100	—	†	
O1/10	*Set of* 10	3·50	4·50		
O2/10	*Set of* 7			20·00	35·00

OFFICIAL

(O 1)

1981 (5 Feb). *Nos.* 59A/70A *optd with Type* O **1**.

O11	15 c. Type **13**	20	10
O12	20 c. Scaly-breasted Thrasher	20	10
O13	25 c. Grey Kingbird	25	10
O14	30 c. Green-throated Carib	25	10
O15	40 c. Turnstone	35	15
O16	45 c. Black-faced Grassquit	40	20
O17	50 c. Cattle Egret	40	20
O18	55 c. Brown Pelican	50	25
O19	$1 Lesser Antillean Bullfinch	75	45
O20	$2.50, Zenaida Dove	1·60	1·00
O21	$5 American Kestrel	2·75	2·00
O22	$10 Antillean Crested Hummingbird	5·00	4·25
O11/22	*Set of* 12	11·50	8·00

1983 (2 Feb). *Nos.* 75/80 *optd with Type* O 1 (55 *c.*) *or surch also (others).*

O23	45 c. on $2.50, *Royal George* (New Blue)	25	25
	a. Sheetlet No. O23 × 6 and No. O24	1·40	
	b. Surch double	18·00	
	c. Albino surch	10·00	
	f. Deep ultramarine surch	50	
	fd. Surch inverted	7·50	
	fe. Surch inverted (horiz pair)	25·00	
	g. Black opt		
O24	45 c. on $2.50, Prince Charles and Lady Diana Spencer (New Blue)	25	25
	b. Surch double	60·00	
	c. Albino surch	30·00	
	f. Deep ultramarine surch	75	
	fd. Surch inverted	30·00	
	g. Black opt		
O25	55 c. *Saudadoes* (New Blue)	30	30
	a. Sheetlet No. O25 × 6 and No. O26	1·75	
	b. Opt double	22·00	
	c. Albino opt	12·00	
	d. Opt inverted	8·00	
	e. Opt inverted (horiz pair)	22·00	
	f. Deep ultramarine opt	60	
	fd. Opt inverted	7·00	
	fe. Opt inverted (horiz pair)	26·00	
O26	55 c. Prince Charles and Lady Diana Spencer (New Blue)	30	30
	b. Opt double	60·00	
	c. Albino opt	35·00	
	d. Opt inverted	27·00	
	f. Deep ultramarine opt	90	
	fd. Opt inverted	27·00	
O27	$1.10 on $4 *Britannia* (Blk.)	60	70
	a. Sheetlet. No. O27 × 6 and No. O28	3·50	
	b. Surch double	17·00	
	f. Deep ultramarine surch	4·00	
O28	$1.10 on $4 Prince Charles and Lady Diana Spencer (Blk.)	60	70
	b. Surch double	45·00	
	f. Deep ultramarine surch	30·00	
O23/8	*Set of* 6	2·10	2·25

Nos. O23fe, O25e and O25fe show the surcharge or overprint intended for the large design, inverted and struck across a horizontal pair of the smaller. Nos. O24fd, O26d and O26fd each show two inverted surcharges or overprints intended for a horizontal pair of the smaller design.

1984 (4 July). *Nos.* 145/56 *optd with Type* O 1.

O29	15 c. Red-lined Cleaning Shrimp	25	25
O30	20 c. Bristleworm	30	30
O31	25 c. Flamingo Tongue	35	35
O32	30 c. Christmas Tree Worm	40	40
O33	40 c. Pink-tipped Anemone	50	50
O34	50 c. Smallmouth Grunt	60	60
O35	60 c. Glasseye Snapper	70	70
O36	75 c. Reef Squirrelfish	80	80
O37	$1 Sea Fans and Flamefish (*vert*)	1·00	1·00
O38	$2.50, Reef Butterflyfish (*vert*)	2·25	2·50
O39	$5 Blackbar Soldierfish (*vert*)	4·00	4·50
O40	$10 Cocoa Damselfish (*vert*)	7·50	8·50
O29/40	*Set of* 12	17·00	18·00

NEVIS

(7)

8 Nevis Lighter

1980 (23 June). *Nos.* 394/406 *of St. Christopher, Nevis and Anguilla optd with T* **7**.

37	5 c. Radio and T.V. Station	10	10
38	10 c. Technical college	10	10
39	12 c. T.V. assembly plant	40	40
40	15 c. Sugar cane harvesting	10	10
41	25 c. Crafthouse (craft centre)	15	10
	a. No wmk	1·75	3·00
42	30 c. *Europa* (liner)	20	15
43	40 c. Lobster and sea crab	70	70
44	45 c. Royal St. Kitts Hotel and golf course	70	70
45	50 c. Pinney's Beach, Nevis	50	50
46	55 c. New runway at Golden Rock	15	15
47	$1 Picking cotton	45	45
	a. No wmk	6·00	10·00
48	$5 Brewery	75	75
49	$10 Pineapples and peanuts	1·25	1·25
37/49	*Set of* 13	4·25	4·25

1980 (4 Sept). *80th Birthday of Queen Elizabeth the Queen Mother. As T* **10** *of St. Kitts, but inscr* "NEVIS".

50	$2 multicoloured	50	50

No. 50 was printed in sheets including two *se-tenant* stamp-size labels.

(Des Jennifer Toombs. Litho Questa)

1980 (8 Oct). *Boats. T* **8** *and similar multicoloured designs. W* w **14** (*sideways on* 5, 30 *and* 55 *c.*). *P* 14.

51	5 c. Type **8**	10	10
52	30 c. Local fishing boat	15	10
53	55 c. *Caona* (catamaran)	20	10
54	$3 *Polynesia* (cruise schooner) (39 × 53 *mm*)	65	55
	a. Perf 12 (booklets)	65	1·10
	ab. Booklet pane of 3	1·90	
51/4	*Set of* 4	90	70

No. 54a comes from $12.30 stamp booklets containing No. 53 × 6 and one pane as No. 54ab. In this pane each stamp is surrounded by white margins, the pane being divided in three by vertical roulettes.

9 Virgin and Child

(Des Jennifer Toombs. Litho Format)

1980 (20 Nov). *Christmas. T* **9** *and similar vert designs. Multicoloured. W* w **14**. *P* 14.

55	5 c. Type **9**	10	10
56	30 c. Angel	10	10
57	$2.50, The Three Wise Men	30	30
55/7	*Set of* 3	35	35

10 Charlestown Pier **11** New River Mill

(Des Jennifer Toombs. Litho Questa)

1981 (5 Feb)–**82**. *Horiz designs as T* **10** (5, 10 *c.*) *or T* **11** (15 *c. to* $10). *Multicoloured. W* w **14**. *P* 14 × 13½ (5, 10 *c.*) *or* 14 (*others*).
A. *No imprint date*
B. *With imprint date at foot of design* (9.6.82.)

		A		B	
58	5 c. Type **10**	10	10	10	10
59	10 c. Court House and Library	10	10	10	10
60	15 c. Type **11**	10	10	10	10
61	20 c. Nelson Museum	10	10	10	10
62	25 c. St. James' Parish Church	15	15	15	15
63	30 c. Nevis Lane	15	15	15	15
64	40 c. Zetland Plantation	20	20	20	20
65	45 c. Nisbet Plantation	20	25	20	25
66	50 c. Pinney's Beach	25	25	25	25
67	55 c. Eva Wilkin's Studio	25	30	25	30
68	$1 Nevis at dawn	50	45	50	45
69	$2.50, Ruins of Fort Charles	90	1·10	90	1·10
70	$5 Old Bath House	1·50	1·75	1·50	1·75
71	$10 Beach at Nisbet's	2·75	3·50	2·75	3·50
58/71	*Set of* 14	6·00	7·50	6·00	7·50

Nos. 61B/7B and 69B exist with different imprint dates.

(Des D. Shults. Litho Questa)

1981 (23 June–14 Dec). *Royal Wedding. Horiz designs as T* **26/27** *of Kiribati. Multicoloured.* (*a*) *W* w **14**. *P* 14.

72	55 c. *Royal Caroline*	20	20
	a. Sheetlet. No. 72 × 6 and No. 73	1·60	
73	55 c. Prince Charles and Lady Diana Spencer	40	40
74	$2 *Royal Sovereign*	40	40
	a. Sheetlet No. 74 × 6 and No. 75	2·75	
75	$2 As No. 73	80	80
76	$5 *Britannia*	80	80
	a. Sheetlet. No. 76 × 6 and No. 77	5·75	
77	$5 As No. 73	1·50	1·50
72/7	*Set of* 6	3·75	3·75
MS78	120 × 109 mm. $4.50, As No. 73, Wmk sideways. P 12 (14 Dec)	3·00	1·50

(*b*) *Booklet stamps. No wmk. P* 12 (19 Nov).

79	55 c. As No. 72	25	30
	a. Booklet pane. No. 79 × 4	1·00	
80	$2 As No. 75	1·00	1·25
	a. Booklet pane. No. 80 × 2	2·00	

Nos. 72/7 were printed in sheetlets of seven stamps of the same face value, each containing six of the "Royal Yacht" design and one of the larger design showing Prince Charles and Lady Diana.

Nos. 79/80 come from $8.40 stamp booklets.

12 *Heliconius charithonia* **13** Caroline of Brunswick, Princess of Wales, 1793

(Des Jennifer Toombs. Litho Questa)

1982 (16 Feb). *Butterflies* (1*st series*). *T* **12** *and similar horiz designs. Multicoloured. W* w **14** (*sideways*). *P* 14.

81	5 c. Type **12**	10	10
82	30 c. *Siproeta stelenes*	15	10
83	55 c. *Marpesia petreus*	20	15
84	$2 *Phoebis agarithe*	60	70
81/4	*Set of* 4	90	90

See also Nos. 105/8.

(Des D. Shults and J. Cooter. Litho Format)

1982 (22 June). *21st Birthday of Princess of Wales. T* **13** *and similar vert designs. Multicoloured. W* w **14**. *P* 13½ × 14.

85	30 c. Type **13**	25	20
86	55 c. Coat of arms of Caroline of Brunswick	35	30
87	$5 Diana, Princess of Wales	1·25	1·40
85/7	*Set of* 3	1·75	1·75

1982 (12 July). *Birth of Prince William of Wales. Nos.* 85/7 *optd with T* **19** *of St. Kitts.*

88	30 c. Type **13**	25	20
89	55 c. Coat of arms of Caroline of Brunswick	35	30
	a. Opt triple	35·00	
90	$5 Diana, Princess of Wales	1·25	1·40
88/90	*Set of* 3	1·75	1·75

14 Cyclist

(Des Philatelists (1980) Ltd. Litho Questa)

1982 (18 Aug). *75th Anniv of Boy Scout Movement. T* **14** *and similar horiz designs. Multicoloured. W* w **14** (*sideways*). *P* 13½ × 14.

91	5 c. Type **14**	20	10
92	30 c. Athlete	50	10
93	$2.50, Camp cook	1·25	80
91/3	*Set of* 3	1·75	85

15 Santa Claus **16** Tube Sponge

(Des Eugene Seabrookes (15 c.), Kharenzabeth Glasgow (30 c.), Davia Grant (£1.50), Leonard Huggins ($2.50); adapted Jennifer Toombs. Litho Format)

1982 (20 Oct). *Christmas. Children's Paintings. T* **15** *and similar multicoloured designs. W* w **14** (*sideways on* $1.50 *and* $2.50). *P* 13½ × 14 (15 *c.*, 30 *c.*) *or* 14 × 13½ (*others*).

94	15 c. Type **15**	10	10
95	30 c. Carollers	10	10
96	$1.50, Decorated house and local band (*horiz*)	25	25
97	$2.50, Adoration of the Shepherds (*horiz*)	50	50
94/7	*Set of* 4	75	75

(Des G. Drummond. Litho Format)

1983 (12 Jan). *Corals* (1*st series*). *T* **16** *and similar vert designs. Multicoloured. W* w **14**. *P* 14.

98	15 c. Type **16**	10	10
99	30 c. Stinging coral	15	10
100	55 c. Flower coral	25	10
101	$3 Sea Rod and Red Fire Sponge	70	80
98/101	*Set of* 4	1·00	90
MS102	82 × 115 mm. Nos. 98/101	1·10	1·60

See also Nos. 423/6.

17 H.M.S. *Boreas* off Nevis

(Des G. Drummond. Litho Format)

1983 (14 Mar). *Commonwealth Day. T* **17** *and similar horiz design. Multicoloured. W* w **14** (*sideways*). *P* 14.

103	55 c. Type **17**	20	10
104	$2 Capt. Horatio Nelson and H.M.S. *Boreas* at anchor	65	75

(Des Jennifer Toombs. Litho Format)

1983 (8 June). *Butterflies* (2*nd series*). *Multicoloured designs as T* **12**. *W* w **14** (*sideways on* 30 *c. and* $2). *P* 14.

105	30 c. *Pyrgus oileus*	20	15
106	55 c. *Junonia evarete*	25	20
107	$1.10, *Urbanus proteus*	50	55
108	$2 *Hypolimnas misippus*	95	1·00
105/8	*Set of* 4	1·75	1·75

INDEPENDENCE 1983

(18)

INDEPENDENCE 1983

(18*a*)

19 Montgolfier Balloon, 1783

1983 (19 Sept). *Nos.* 58 *and* 60/71 *optd as T* **18** (20 *mm long on Nos.* 110/21).
A. *No imprint date*
B. *With imprint date.*

		A		B	
109	5 c. Type **10**	†		10	10
	a. Vert pair, lower stamp without opt.	†		65·00	—
	b. Optd with T **18***a* (local opt)	13·00	11·00	2·50	2·00
	ba. Opt T **18***a* inverted	†		45·00	—
110	15 c. Type **11**	35·00	35·00	10	10
111	20 c. Nelson Museum	5·00	5·00	10	10
112	25 c. St. James' Parish Church	5·00	5·00	10	15
113	30 c. Nevis Lane	90	90	15	15
	a. Opt inverted	†		11·00	—
114	40 c. Zetland Plantation	75	75	15	20
115	45 c. Nisbet Plantation	†		20	25
116	50 c. Pinney's Beach	†		20	25
117	55 c. Eva Wilkin's Studio	75	75	25	30
	a. Opt double	†		12·00	—
118	$1 Nevis at dawn	75	75	40	45
119	$2.50, Ruins of Fort Charles	1·10	1·10	90	1·10
120	$5 Old Bath House	1·90	2·25	1·50	1·75
121	$10 Beach at Nisbet's	3·50	4·25	2·75	3·00
	a. Opt inverted	60·00	—	†	
109bA/121A	*Set of* 11	60·00	60·00		
109B/121B	*Set of* 13			6·00	7·00

(Des A. Theobald. Litho Format)

1983 (28 Sept). *Bicentenary of Manned Flight. T* **19** *and similar multicoloured designs. W* w **15** (*sideways on* 45 *c. to* $2.50). *P* 14.

122	10 c. Type **19**	10	10
123	45 c. Sikorsky "S-38", flying boat (*horiz*)	15	10
124	50 c. Beechcraft "Twin Bonanza" (*horiz*)	15	10
125	$2.50, B. Ae. "Sea Harrier" (*horiz*)	50	60
122/5	*Set of* 4	70	70
MS126	118×145 mm. Nos. 122/5. Wmk sideways	1·00	1·00

20 Mary praying over Holy Child

(Des Jennifer Toombs. Litho Format)

1983 (7 Nov). *Christmas. T* **20** *and similar horiz designs. Multicoloured. W* w **15** (*sideways*). *P* 14.

127	5 c. Type **20**	10	10
128	30 c. Shepherds with flock	10	10
129	55 c. Three Angels	15	10
130	$3 Boy with two girls	55	60
127/30	*Set of* 4	70	70
MS131	135 × 149 mm. Nos. 127/30	1·00	1·25

21 *County of Oxford* (1945) **22** Boer War

(Des J. W. Litho Format)

1983 (10 Nov). *Leaders of the World. Railway Locomotives* (1*st series*). *T* **21** *and similar horiz designs, the first in each pair showing technical drawings and the second the locomotive at work. P* 12½.

132	55 c. multicoloured	20	25
	a. Vert pair. Nos. 132/3	40	50
133	55 c. multicoloured	20	25
134	$1 bright crimson, new blue and black	25	35
	a. Vert pair. Nos. 134/5	50	70
135	$1 multicoloured	25	35
136	$1 magenta, new blue and black	25	35
	a. Vert pair. Nos. 136/7	50	70
137	$1 multicoloured	25	35
138	$1 bright crimson, black and greenish yellow	25	35
	a. Vert pair. Nos. 138/9	50	70
139	$1 multicoloured	25	35
140	$1 multicoloured	25	35
	a. Vert pair. Nos. 140/1	50	70
141	$1 multicoloured	25	35
142	$1 greenish yellow, black and new blue	25	35
	a. Vert pair. Nos. 142/3	50	70
143	$1 multicoloured	25	35
144	$1 greenish yellow, black & brt magenta	25	35
	a. Vert pair. Nos. 144/5	50	70
145	$1 multicoloured	25	35
146	$1 multicoloured	25	35
	a. Vert pair. Nos. 146/7	50	70
147	$1 multicoloured	25	35
132/47	*Set of* 16	3·50	4·75

Designs:—Nos. 132/3, *County of Oxford*, Great Britain (1945), 134/5, *Evening Star*, Great Britain (1960); 136/7, Stanier "Class 5", Great Britain (1934); 138/9, *Pendennis Castle*, Great Britain (1924); 140/1, *Winston Churchill*, Great Britain (1946); 142/3, *Mallard*, Great Britain (1935); 144/5, *Britannia*, Great Britain (1951); 146/7, *King George V*, Great Britain (1927).

Nos. 132/3, 134/5, 136/7, 138/9, 140/1, 142/3, 144/5 and 146/7 were printed together, *se-tenant* in vertical pairs throughout the sheets.

See also Nos. 219/26, 277/84, 297/308, 352/9 and 427/42.

(Des Court House Studio. Litho Format)

1984 (11 Apr). *Leaders of the World. British Monarchs* (1*st series*). *T* **22** *and similar vert designs. Multicoloured. P* 12½.

148	5 c. Type **22**	10	10
	a. Horiz pair. Nos. 148/9	10	10
149	5 c. Queen Victoria	10	10
150	50 c. Queen Victoria at Osborne House	35	35
	a. Horiz pair. Nos. 150/1	70	70
151	50 c. Osborne House	35	35
152	60 c. Battle of Dettingen	40	40
	a. Horiz pair. Nos. 152/3	80	80
153	60 c. George II	40	40
154	75 c. George II at the Bank of England	40	40
	a. Horiz pair. Nos. 154/5	80	80
155	75 c. Bank of England	40	40
156	$1 Coat of Arms of George II	45	45
	a. Horiz pair. Nos. 156/7	90	90
157	$1 George II (*different*)	45	45
158	$3 Coat of Arms of Queen Victoria	1·00	1·10
	a. Horiz pair. Nos. 158/9	2·00	2·10
159	$3 Queen Victoria (*different*)	1·00	1·10
148/59	*Set of* 12	4·75	4·75

Nos. 148/9, 150/1, 152/3, 154/5, 156/7 and 158/9 were printed together, *se-tenant* in horizontal pairs throughout the sheet.

See also Nos. 231/6.

23 Golden Rock Inn

(Des Jennifer Toombs. Litho J.W.)

1984 (16 May). *Tourism.* (1*st series*). *T* **23** *and similar horiz designs. Multicoloured. W w* **15** (*sideways*). *P* 14.

160	55 c. Type **23**	35	20
161	55 c. Rest Haven Inn	35	20
162	55 c. Cliffdwellers Hotel	35	20
163	55 c. Pinney's Beach Hotel	35	20
160/3	*Set of* 4	1·25	70

See also Nos. 245/8.

24 Early Seal of Colony

(Des G. Drummond. Litho Format)

1984 (8 June). *W w* **15** (*sideways*). *P* 14.

164 **24**	$15 dull scarlet	4·50	5·50

IMPERFORATES AND MISSING COLOURS. Various issues between Nos. 165 and 410 exist either imperforate or with colours omitted. Such items are not listed as there is no evidence that they fulfil the criteria outlined on page xi of this catalogue.

25 Cadillac

(Des J. W. Litho Format)

1984 (25 July). *Leaders of the World. Automobiles* (1*st series*). *T* **25** *and similar horiz designs, the first in each pair showing technical drawings and the second paintings. P* 12½.

165	1 c. greenish yellow, black and magenta	10	10
	a. Vert pair. Nos. 165/6	10	10
166	1 c. multicoloured	10	10
167	5 c. new blue, magenta and black	10	10
	a. Vert pair. Nos. 167/8	10	10
168	5 c. multicoloured	10	10
169	15 c. multicoloured	15	15
	a. Vert pair. Nos. 169/70	30	30
170	15 c. multicoloured	15	15
171	35 c. magenta, greenish yellow and black	25	25
	a. Vert pair. Nos. 171/2	50	50
172	35 c. multicoloured	25	25
173	45 c. new blue, magenta and black	30	30
	a. Vert pair. Nos. 173/4	60	60
174	45 c. multicoloured	30	30
175	55 c. multicoloured	35	35
	a. Vert pair. Nos. 175/6	70	70
176	55 c. multicoloured	35	35
177	$2.50, magenta, black and greenish yellow	80	65
	a. Vert pair. Nos. 177/8	1·60	1·25
178	$2.50, multicoloured	80	65
179	$3 new blue, greenish yellow and black	85	70
	a. Vert pair. Nos. 179/80	1·60	1·40
180	$3 multicoloured	85	70
165/80	*Set of* 16	4·50	4·25

Designs:—Nos. 165/6, Cadillac "V16 Fleetwood Convertible" (1932); 167/8, Packard "Twin Six Touring Car" (1916); 169/70, Daimler, "2 Cylinder" (1886); 171/2, Porsche "911 S Targa" (1970); 173/4, Benz "Three Wheeler" (1885); 175/6, M.G. "TC" (1947); 177/8, Cobra "Roadster 289" (1966), 179/80, Aston Martin "DB6 Hardtop" (1966).

Nos. 165/6, 167/8, 169/70, 171/2, 173/4, 175/6, 177/8 and 179/80 were printed together, *se-tenant* in vertical pairs throughout the sheet.

See also Nos. 203/10, 249/64, 326/37, 360/71 and 411/22.

26 Carpentry **27** Yellow Bell

(Des Jennifer Toombs. Litho Questa)

1984 (1 Aug). *10th Anniv of Culturama Celebrations. T* **26** *and similar horiz designs. Multicoloured. W w* **15** (*sideways*). *P* 14.

181	30 c. Type **26**	10	10
182	55 c. Grass mat and basket-making	15	10
183	$1 Pottery-firing	25	25
184	$3 Culturama Queen and dancers	55	55
181/4	*Set of* 4	95	85

(Des Jennifer Toombs. Litho Format)

1984 (8 Aug)–**86**. *Flowers. T* **27** *and similar vert designs. Multicoloured. W w* **15**. *P* 14. A. *Without imprint date.* B. *With imprint date at foot of design* (23.7.86).

		A		B	
185	5 c. Type **27**	10	10	†	
186	10 c. Plumbago	10	10	†	
187	15 c. Flamboyant	10	10	†	
188	20 c. Eyelash Orchid	60	15	10	10
189	30 c. Bougainvillea	10	15	†	
190	40 c. Hibiscus *sp.*	70	25	15	20
191	50 c. Night-blooming Cereus	15	20	†	
192	55 c. Yellow Mahoe	20	25	†	
193	60 c. Spider-lily	20	25	†	
194	75 c. Scarlet Cordia	25	30	†	
195	$1 Shell-ginger	35	40	†	
196	$3 Blue Petrea	1·00	1·10	†	
197	$5 Coral Hibiscus	1·75	2·00	†	
198	$10 Passion Flower	3·25	3·50	†	
185/98	*Set of* 14	7·75	7·75	†	

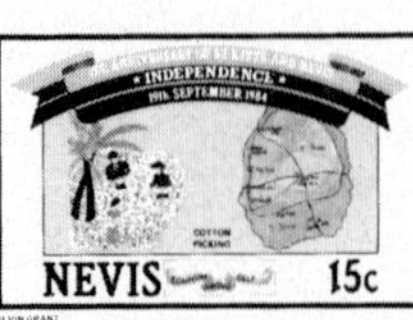

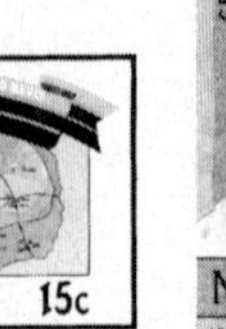

28 Cotton-picking and Map **29** C.P. Mead

(Des A. Grant (15 c.), Tracy Watkins (55 c.), C. Manners ($1.10), D. Grant ($3), adapted Court House Advertising. Litho Format)

1984 (18 Sept). *First Anniv of Independence of St. Kitts-Nevis. T* **28** *and similar horiz designs. Multicoloured. W w* **15** (*sideways*). *P* 14.

199	15 c. Type **28**	15	10
200	55 c. Alexander Hamilton's birthplace	20	10
201	$1.10, Local agricultural produce	35	40
202	$3 Nevis Peak and Pinneys Beach	75	1·00
199/202	*Set of* 4	1·25	1·40

(Des J. W. Litho Format)

1984 (23 Oct). *Leaders of the World. Automobiles* (2*nd series*). *Horiz designs as T* **25**, *the first in each pair showing technical drawings and the second paintings. P* 12½.

203	5 c. black, pale new blue and yellow-brown	10	10
	a. Vert pair. Nos. 203/4	10	10
204	5 c. multicoloured	10	10
205	30 c. black, pale turquoise-green & lake-brn	15	15
	a. Vert pair. Nos. 205/6	30	30
206	30 c. multicoloured	15	15
207	50 c. black, pale drab and red-brown	20	20
	a. Vert pair. Nos. 207/8	40	40
208	50 c. multicoloured	20	20
209	$3 black, grey-brown and dull green	60	60
	a. Vert pair. Nos. 209/10	1·10	1·10
210	$3 multicoloured	60	60
203/10	*Set of* 8	1·75	1·75

Designs:—Nos. 203/4, Lagonda "Speed Model" touring car (1929); 205/6, Jaguar "E-Type" 4.2 litre (1967); 207/8, Volkswagen "Beetle" (1947); 209/10, Pierce Arrow "V12" (1932).

Nos. 203/10 were issued in a similar sheet format to Nos. 165/80.

(Des Court House Studio. Litho Format)

1984 (23 Oct). *Leaders of the World. Cricketers* (1*st series*). *T* **29** *and similar vert designs, the first in each pair showing a head portrait and the second the cricketer in action. P* 12½.

211	5 c. multicoloured	10	10
	a. Horiz pair. Nos. 211/12	15	15
212	5 c. multicoloured	10	10
213	25 c. multicoloured	30	30
	a. Horiz pair. Nos. 213/14	60	60
214	25 c. multicoloured	30	30
215	55 c. multicoloured	40	40
	a. Horiz pair. Nos. 215/16	80	80
216	55 c. multicoloured	40	40
217	$2.50, multicoloured	1·25	1·25
	a. Horiz pair. Nos. 217/18	2·50	2·50
218	$2.50, multicoloured	1·25	1·25
211/18	*Set of* 8	3·50	3·50

Designs:—Nos. 211/12, C. P. Mead; 213/14, J. B. Statham; 215/16, Sir Learie Constantine; 217/18, Sir Leonard Hutton.

Nos. 211/12, 213/14, 215/16 and 217/18 were printed together, *se-tenant*, in horizontal pairs throughout the sheets.

See also Nos. 237/44.

(Des J. W. Litho Format)

1984 (29 Oct). *Leaders of the World. Railway Locomotives* (2*nd series*). *Horiz designs as T* **21** *the first in each pair showing technical drawings and the second the locomotive at work. P* 12½.

219	5 c. multicoloured	10	10
	a. Vert pair. Nos. 219/20	10	10
220	5 c. multicoloured	10	10
221	10 c. multicoloured	10	10
	a. Vert pair. Nos. 221/2	15	15
222	10 c. multicoloured	10	10
223	60 c. multicoloured	30	30
	a. Vert pair. Nos. 223/4	60	60
224	60 c. multicoloured	30	30
225	$2.50, multicoloured	90	90
	a. Vert pair. Nos. 225/6	1·75	1·75
226	$2.50, multicoloured	90	90
219/26	*Set of* 8	2·40	2·40

Designs:—Nos. 219/20, Class "EF81", Japan (1968); 221/2, Class "5500", France (1927); 223/4, Class "240P", France (1940); 225/6, Shinkansen train, Japan (1964).

Nos. 219/26 were issued in a similar sheet format to Nos. 132/47.

30 Fifer and Drummer from Honeybees Band

(Des Jennifer Toombs. Litho Questa)

1984 (2 Nov). *Christmas. Local Music. T* **30** *and similar horiz designs. Multicoloured. W w* **15** (*sideways*). *P* 14.

227	15 c. Type **30**	15	10
228	40 c. Guitar and "barhow" players from Canary Birds Band	25	10
229	60 c. Shell All Stars steel band	30	10
230	$3 Organ and choir, St. John's Church, Fig Tree	1·25	1·00
227/30	*Set of* 4	1·75	1·10

(Des Court House Studio. Litho Format)

1984 (20 Nov). *Leaders of the World. British Monarchs* (2*nd series*). *Vert designs as T* **22**. *Multicoloured. P* 12½.

231	5 c. King John and Magna Carta	10	10
	a. Horiz pair. Nos. 231/2	10	10
232	5 c. Barons and King John	10	10
233	55 c. King John	25	25
	a. Horiz pair Nos. 233/4	50	50
234	55 c. Newark Castle	25	25
235	$2 Coat of arms	75	75
	a. Horiz pair. Nos. 235/6	1·50	1·50
236	$2 King John (*different*)	75	75
231/6	*Set of* 6	1·75	1·75

Nos. 231/6 were issued in a similar sheet format to Nos. 148/59.

(Des Court House Studio. Litho Format)

1984 (20 Nov). *Leaders of the World. Cricketers (2nd series). Vert designs as T* **29**, *the first in each pair listed showing a head portrait and the second the cricketer in action. P* 12½.

237 5 c. multicoloured 10 10
a. Horiz pair. Nos. 237/8 .. .. 15 15
238 5 c. multicoloured 10 10
239 15 c. multicoloured 15 15
a. Horiz pair. Nos. 239/40 .. .. 30 30
240 15 c. multicoloured 15 15
241 55 c. multicoloured 30 30
a. Horiz pair. Nos. 241/2 .. .. 60 60
242 55 c. multicoloured 30 30
243 $2,50, multicoloured .. .. 1·00 1·00
a. Horiz pair. Nos. 243/4 .. .. 2·00 2·00
244 $2.50, multicoloured .. .. 1·00 1·00
237/44 .. .. *Set of* 8 2·75 2·75

Designs:—Nos. 237/8, J. D. Love; 239/40, S. J. Dennis; 241/2, B. W. Luckhurst; 243/4, B. L. D'Oliveira.

Nos. 237/44 were issued in a similar sheet format to Nos. 211/18.

(Des Jennifer Toombs. Litho Format)

1985 (12 Feb). *Tourism (2nd series). Horiz designs as T* **23**. *Multicoloured. W w* **15** *(sideways). P* 14.

245 $1.20, Croney's Old Manor Hotel 45 45
246 $1.20, Montpelier Plantation Inn 45 45
247 $1.20, Nisbet's Plantation Inn 45 45
248 $1.20, Zetland Plantation Inn 45 45
245/8 .. .. *Set of* 4 1·60 1·60

(Des G. Turner (10 c.), J.W. (others). Litho Format)

1985 (20 Feb). *Leaders of the World. Automobiles (3rd series). Horiz designs as T* **25**, *the first in each pair showing technical drawings and the second paintings. P* 12½.

249 1 c. black, light green and pale green .. 10 10
a. Vert pair. Nos. 249/50 .. .. .. 10 10
250 1 c. multicoloured 10 10
251 5 c. black, cobalt and pale violet-blue .. 10 10
a. Vert pair. Nos. 251/2 .. .. .. 10 10
252 5 c. multicoloured 10 10
253 10 c. black, grey-olive and pale green 10 10
a. Vert pair. Nos. 253/4 .. .. .. 10 10
254 10 c. multicoloured 10 10
255 50 c. black, sage-green and pale cinnamon .. 20 20
a. Vert pair. Nos. 255/6 .. .. .. 40 40
256 50 c. multicoloured 20 20
257 60 c. black, dull yellowish green and pale blue 20 20
a. Vert pair. Nos. 257/8 .. .. .. 40 40
258 60 c. multicoloured 20 20
259 75 c. black, dull vermilion and pale orange .. 25 25
a. Vert pair. Nos. 259/60 .. .. .. 50 50
260 75 c. multicoloured 25 25
261 $2.50, black, light green and azure 40 40
a. Vert pair. Nos. 261/2 .. .. .. 80 80
262 $2.50, multicoloured 40 40
263 $3 black, bright yellow-green and pale green 40 40
a. Vert pair. Nos. 263/4 .. .. .. 80 80
264 $3 multicoloured 40 40
249/64 .. .. *Set of* 16 2·75 2·75

Designs:—Nos. 249/50, Delahaye "Type 35 Cabriolet" (1935); 251/2, Ferrari "Testa Rossa" (1958); 253/4, Voisin "Aerodyne" (1934); 255/6, Buick "Riviera" (1963); 257/8, Cooper "Climax" (1960); 259/60, Ford "999" (1904); 261/2, MG "M-Type Midget" (1930); 263/4, Rolls-Royce "Corniche" (1971).

Nos. 249/64 were issued in a similar sheet format to Nos. 165/80.

31 Broad-winged Hawk **32** Eastern Bluebird

(Des Jennifer Toombs. Litho Format)

1985 (19 Mar). *Local Hawks and Herons. T* **31** *and similar horiz designs. Multicoloured. W w* **15** *(sideways). P* 14.

265 20 c. Type **31** 75 20
266 40 c. Red-tailed Hawk .. .. 1·00 30
267 60 c. Little Blue Heron .. .. 1·25 40
268 $3 Great Blue Heron (white phase) .. .. 2·50 1·90
265/8 .. .. *Set of* 4 5·00 2·50

No. 268 was re-issued on 24 May 1990 overprinted "40th Anniversary C.S.S." to mark the fortieth anniversary of Charlestown Secondary School. This oveprint was only available on First Day Covers.

(Des R. Vigurs. Litho Format)

1985 (25 Mar). *Leaders of the World. Birth Bicentenary of John J. Audubon (ornithologist) (1st issue). T* **32** *and similar vert designs. Multicoloured. P* 12½.

269 5 c. Type **32** 15 10
a. Horiz pair. Nos. 269/70 .. .. 30 20
270 5 c. Common Cardinal 15 10
271 55 c. Belted Kingfisher 65 65
a. Horiz pair. Nos. 271/2 .. .. 1·25 1·25
272 55 c. Mangrove Cuckoo 65 65
273 60 c. Yellow Warbler 65 65
a. Horiz pair. Nos. 273/4 .. .. 1·25 1·25
274 60 c. Cerulean Warbler 65 65
275 $2 Burrowing Owl .. .. 1·75 1·75
a. Horiz pair. Nos. 275/6 .. .. 3·50 3·50
276 $2 Long-eared Owl .. .. 1·75 1·75
269/76 .. .. *Set of* 8 5·75 5·75

Nos. 269/70, 271/2, 273/4 and 275/6 were printed together, *se-tenant*, in horizontal pairs throughout the sheets.

See also Nos. 285/92.

(Des J.W. Litho Format)

1985 (26 Apr). *Leaders of the World. Railway Locomotives (3rd series). Horiz designs as T* **21**, *the first in each pair showing technical drawings and the second the locomotive at work. P* 12½.

277 1 c. multicoloured 10 10
a. Vert pair. Nos. 277/8 .. .. 10 10
278 1 c. multicoloured 10 10
279 60 c. multicoloured 30 30
a. Vert pair. Nos. 279/80 .. .. 60 60
280 60 c. multicoloured 30 30
281 90 c. multicoloured 35 35
a. Vert pair. Nos. 281/2 .. .. 70 70
282 90 c. multicoloured 35 35
283 $2 multicoloured 75 75
a. Vert pair. Nos. 283/4 .. .. 1·50 1·50
284 $2 multicoloured 75 75
277/84 .. .. *Set of* 8 2·50 2·50

Designs:—Nos. 277/8, Class "Wee Bogie", Great Britain (1882); 279/80, *Comet*, Great Britain (1851); 281/2, Class "8H", Great Britain (1908); 283/4, Class "A" No. 23, Great Britain (1866).

Nos. 277/84 were issued in a similar sheet format to Nos. 132/47.

(Des R. Vigurs. Litho Format)

1985 (3 June). *Leaders of the World. Birth Bicentenary of John J. Audubon (ornithologist) (2nd issue). Vert designs as T* **32** *showing original paintings. Multicoloured. P* 12½.

285 1 c. Painted Bunting 10 10
a. Horiz pair. Nos. 285/6 .. .. 10 10
286 1 c. Golden-crowned Kinglet 10 10
287 40 c. Common Flicker 40 40
a. Horiz pair. Nos. 287/8 .. .. 80 80
288 40 c. Western Tanager 40 40
289 60 c. Varied Thrush ("Sage Thrasher") .. 45 45
a. Horiz pair. Nos. 289/90 .. .. 90 90
290 60 c. Evening Grosbeak 45 45
291 $2.50, Blackburnian Warbler .. .. .. 1·00 1·00
a. Horiz pair. Nos. 291/2 .. .. 2·00 2·00
292 $2.50, Northern Oriole .. .. 1·00 1·00
285/92 .. .. *Set of* 8 3·50 3·50

Nos. 285/92 were issued in a similar sheet format to Nos. 269/76.

Nos. 285/92 exist with yellow omitted from stock dispersed by the liquidator of Format International Security Printers Ltd.

33 Guides and Guide Headquarters **34** The Queen Mother at Garter Ceremony

(Des G. Vasarhelyi. Litho Format)

1985 (17 June). *75th Anniv of Girl Guide Movement. T* **33** *and similar multicoloured designs. W w* **15** *(inverted on 60 c., sideways on 15 c.). P* 14.

293 15 c. Type **33** 10 10
294 60 c. Girl Guide uniforms of 1910 and 1985 (*vert*) 30 30
295 $1 Lord and Lady Baden-Powell (*vert*) .. 50 50
296 $3 Princess Margaret in Guide uniform (*vert*) .. .. 1·25 1·50
293/6 .. .. *Set of* 4 1·90 2·25

(Des T. Hadler (75 c., $1, $2.50), J.W. (others). Litho Format)

1985 (26 July). *Leaders of the World. Railway Locomotives (4th series). Horiz designs as T* **21**, *the first in each pair showing technical drawings and the second the locomotive at work. P* 12½.

297 5 c. multicoloured 10 10
a. Vert pair. Nos. 297/8 .. .. 10 10
298 5 c. multicoloured 10 10
299 30 c. multicoloured 15 15
a. Vert pair. Nos. 299/300 .. .. .. 30 30
300 30 c. multicoloured 15 15
301 60 c. multicoloured 30 30
a. Vert pair. Nos. 301/2 .. .. 60 60
302 60 c. multicoloured 30 30
303 75 c. multicoloured 35 35
a. Vert pair. Nos. 303/4 .. .. 70 70
304 75 c. multicoloured 35 35
305 $1 multicoloured 35 35
a. Vert pair. Nos. 305/6 .. .. 70 70
306 $1 multicoloured 35 35
307 $2.50, multicoloured 80 80
a. Vert pair. Nos. 307/8 .. .. 1·60 1·60
308 $2.50, multicoloured 80 80
297/308 .. .. *Set of* 12 3·50 3·50

Designs:—Nos. 297/8, *Snowdon Ranger*, Great Britain (1878); 299/300, Large Belpaire passenger locomotive, Great Britain (1904); 301/2, Great Western Railway "County" Class, Great Britain (1904); 303/4, *Nord L'Outrance*, France (1877); 305/6, Q.R. "Class PB-15", Australia (1899); 307/8, D.R.G. "Class 64", Germany (1928).

Nos. 297/308 were issued in a similar sheet format to Nos. 132/47.

(Des Court House Studio. Litho Format)

1985 (31 July). *Leaders of the World. Life and Times of Queen Elizabeth the Queen Mother. Various vertical portraits as T* **34**. *P* 12½.

309 45 c. multicoloured 20 25
a. Horiz pair. Nos. 309/10 .. .. 40 50
310 45 c. multicoloured 20 25
311 75 c. multicoloured 30 35
a. Horiz pair. Nos. 311/12 .. .. 60 70
312 75 c. multicoloured 30 35
313 $1.20, multicoloured 45 55
a. Horiz pair. Nos. 313/14 .. .. 90 1·10
314 $1.20, multicoloured 45 55
315 $1.50, multicoloured 55 65
a. Horiz pair. Nos. 315/16 .. .. 1·10 1·25
316 $1.50, multicoloured 55 65
309/16 .. .. *Set of* 8 2·75 3·25
MS317 85 × 114 mm. $2 multicoloured; $2 multicoloured .. .. 1·25 1·60

The two designs of each value were issued, *se-tenant*, in horizontal pairs within the sheets.

Each *se-tenant* pair shows a floral pattern across the bottom of the portraits which stops short of the left-hand edge on the left-hand stamp and of the right-hand edge on the right-hand stamp.

Nos. 309/16 exist in unissued miniature sheets, one for each value, from stock dispersed by the liquidator of Format International Security Printers Ltd.

Designs as Nos. 309/10 and 315/16, but with face values of $3.50 × 2 and $6 × 2, also exist in additional miniature sheets from a restricted printing issued 27 December 1985.

35 Isambard Kingdom Brunel **36** St. Pauls Anglican Church, Charlestown

(Des Tudor Art Agency. Litho Format)

1985 (31 Aug). *150th Anniv of the Great Western Railway. T* **35** *and similar vert designs showing railway engineers and their achievements. Multicoloured. P* 12½.

318 25 c. Type **35** 45 45
a. Horiz pair. Nos. 318/19 .. .. 90 90
319 25 c. Royal Albert Bridge, 1859 .. .. .. 45 45
320 50 c. William Dean 55 55
a. Horiz pair. Nos. 320/1 .. .. 1·10 1·10
321 50 c. Locomotive *Lord of the Isles*, 1895 .. 55 55
322 $1 Locomotive *Lode Star*, 1907 .. .. 1·00 1·00
a. Horiz pair. Nos. 322/3 .. .. 2·00 2·00
323 $1 G. J. Churchward .. .. 1·00 1·00
324 $2.50, Locomotive *Pendennis Castle*, 1924 1·50 1·50
a. Horiz pair. Nos. 324/5 .. .. 3·00 3·00
325 $2.50, C. B. Collett .. .. 1·50 1·50
318/25 .. .. *Set of* 8 6·25 6·25

Nos. 318/19, 320/1, 322/3 and 324/5 were printed together, *se-tenant*, in horizontal pairs throughout the sheets, each pair forming a composite design.

(Des J.W. Litho Format)

1985 (4 Oct). *Leaders of the World. Automobiles (4th series). Horiz designs as T* **25**, *the first in each pair showing technical drawings and the second paintings. P* 12½.

326 10 c. black, azure and brown-red 10 10
a. Vert pair. Nos. 326/7 .. .. 10 15
327 10 c. multicoloured 10 10
328 35 c. black, pale turquoise-grn & greenish bl 20 25
a. Vert pair. Nos. 328/9 .. .. 40 50
329 35 c. multicoloured 20 25
330 75 c. black, bright green & lt purple-brown 35 40
a. Vert pair. Nos. 330/1 .. .. 70 80
331 75 c. multicoloured 35 40
332 $1.15, black, pale cinnamon & olive-green 50 60
a. Vert pair. Nos. 332/3 .. .. 1·00 1·10
333 $1.15, multicoloured 50 60
334 $1.50, black, pale blue and carmine .. 60 70
a. Vert pair. Nos. 334/5 .. .. 1·10 1·40
335 $1.50, multicoloured 60 70
336 $2 black, rose-lilac and reddish violet .. 75 1·00
a. Vert pair. Nos. 336/7 .. .. 1·50 2·00
337 $2 multicoloured .. .. 75 1·00
326/37 .. .. *Set of* 12 4·00 5·50

Designs:—Nos. 326/7, Sunbeam "Coupe de l'Auto" (1912); 328/9, Cisitalia "Pininfarina Coupe" (1948); 330/1, Porsche "928 S" (1980); 332/3, MG "K3 Magnette" (1933); 334/5, Lincoln "Zephyr" (1937); 336/7, Pontiac 2 Door (1926).

Nos. 326/37 were issued in a similar sheet format to Nos. 165/80.

1985 (23 Oct). *Royal Visit. Nos.* 76/7, 83, 86, 92/3, 98/9 *and* 309/10 *optd as T* **114** *of Montserrat or surch also.*

338 **16** 15 c. multicoloured .. .. 1·00 1·00
339 – 30 c. multicoloured (No. 92) .. .. 2·00 1·50
340 – 30 c. multicoloured (No. 99) .. .. 1·00 1·00
341 – 40 c. on 55 c. multicoloured (No. 86) .. 2·00 1·75
342 **34** 45 c. multicoloured .. .. 2·25 2·00
a. Horiz pair. Nos. 342/3 .. .. .. 4·50 4·00
343 – 45 c. multicoloured (No. 310) .. .. 2·25 2·00
344 – 55 c. multicoloured (No. 83) .. .. 1·25 1·25
345 – $1.50 on $5 multicoloured (No. 76) .. 2·25 2·25
a. Sheetlet. No. 345 × 6 and No. 346 .. 20·00
b. Error. Surch $1.60 .. .. .. 2·75 2·75
ba. Sheetlet. No. 345b × 6 and No. 346b 18·00
346 – $1.50 on $5 multicoloured (No. 77) .. 4·50 4·50
b. Error. Surch $1.60 .. .. .. 4·75 4·75
347 – $2.50, multicoloured (No. 93) .. .. 2·75 2·50
338/47 .. .. *Set of* 10 18·00 17·00

Nos. 345b/ba and 346b had the surcharge intended for similar St. Vincent sheetlets applied by mistake.

(Des G. Drummond. Litho Format)

1985 (5 Nov). *Christmas. Churches of Nevis* (1*st series*). *T* **36** *and similar horiz designs. Multicoloured. W w* **15**. *P* 15.

348 10 c. Type **36** 15 10
349 40 c. St. Theresa Catholic Church, Charlestown 30 30
350 60 c. Methodist Church, Gingerland .. 45 50
351 $3 St. Thomas Anglican Church, Lowland 2·00 2·25
348/51 .. .. *Set of* 4 2·50 2·75

See also Nos. 462/5.

(Des T. Hadler. Litho Format)

1986 (30 Jan). *Leaders of the World. Railway Locomotives* (5*th series*). *Horiz designs as T* **21**, *the first in each pair showing technical drawings and the second the locomotive at work. P* 12½.

352 30 c. multicoloured 25 25
a. Vert pair. Nos. 352/3 .. .. 50 50
353 30 c. multicoloured 25 25
354 75 c. multicoloured 50 50
a. Vert pair. Nos. 354/5 .. .. 1·00 1·00
355 75 c. multicoloured 50 50
356 $1.50, multicoloured 80 80
a. Vert pair. Nos. 356/7 .. .. 1·60 1·60
357 $1.50, multicoloured 80 80
358 $2 multicoloured .. .. 1·10 1·10
a. Vert pair. Nos. 358/9 .. .. 2·10 2·10
359 $2 multicoloured .. .. 1·10 1·10
352/9 .. .. *Set of* 8 4·75 4·75

Designs:—Nos. 342/3, *Stourbridge Lion*, U.S.A. (1829); 354/5, "EP-2 Bi-Polar", U.S.A. (1919); 356/7, U.P. "BO × 4" gas turbine, U.S.A. (1953); 358/9, N.Y., N.H. and H.R. "FL9", U.S.A (1955).

Nos. 352/9 were issued in a similar sheet format to Nos. 132/47.

(Des G. Turner (60 c.), J.W. (others). Litho Format)

1986 (30 Jan). *Leaders of the World. Automobiles* (5*th series*). *Horiz designs as T* **25**, *the first in each pair showing technical drawings and the second paintings. P* 12½.

360 10 c. black, pale cinnamon and yellow-olive.. 10 10
a. Vert pair. Nos. 360/1 .. .. 10 20
361 10 c. multicoloured 10 10
362 60 c. black, salmon and bright scarlet .. 25 30
a. Vert pair. Nos. 362/3 .. .. 50 60
363 60 c. multicoloured 25 30
364 75 c. black, pale cinnamon and cinnamon .. 30 35
a. Vert pair. Nos. 364/5 .. .. 60 70
365 75 c. multicoloured 30 35
366 $1 black, lavender-grey and violet-grey .. 30 40
a. Vert pair. Nos. 366/7 .. .. 60 80
367 $1 multicoloured 30 40
368 $1.50, black, pale olive-yellow & olive-grn 40 60
a. Vert pair. Nos. 368/9 .. .. 80 1·10
369 $1.50, multicoloured 40 60
370 $3 black, azure and cobalt.. .. .. .. 70 1·10
a. Vert pair. Nos. 370/1 .. .. 1·40 2·10
371 $3 multicoloured .. .. 70 1·10
360/71 .. .. *Set of* 12 3·50 5·00

Designs:—No. 360/1, Adler "Trumpf" (1936); 362/3, Maserati "Tipo 250F" (1957); 364/5, Oldsmobile "Limited" (1910); 366/7, Jaguar "C-Type" (1951); 368/9, ERA "1.5L B Type" (1937); 370/1 Chevrolet "Corvette" (1953).

Nos. 360/71 were issued in a similar sheet format to Nos. 165/80.

37 "Spitfire" Prototype "K.5054", 1936

(Des J. Batchelor. Litho Format)

1986 (5 Mar). 50*th Anniv of the "Spitfire"* (*fighter aircraft*). *T* **37** *and similar horiz designs. Multicoloured. P* 12½.

372 $1 Type **37** .. .. 1·00 85
373 $2.50, Mark "1A" in Battle of Britain, 1940.. 1·75 2·00
374 $3 Mark "XII" over convoy, 1944 .. .. 2·00 2·25
375 $4 Mark "XXIV", 1948 .. .. .. 2·25 2·75
372/5 .. .. *Set of* 4 6·25 7·00
MS376 114×86 mm. $6 "Seafire" Mark "III" on escort carrier H.M.S. *Hunter* .. .. .. 4·00 4·50

Nos. 372/6 exist with red omitted and No. **MS**376 with black omitted from stock dispersed by the liquidator of Format International Security Printers Ltd.

38 Head of Amerindian **39** Brazilian Player

(Litho Format)

1986 (11 Apr). 500*th Anniv of Discovery of America* (1992). *T* **38** *and similar vert designs. Multicoloured. P* 12½.

377 75 c. Type **38** 55 55
a. Horiz pair. Nos. 377/8 .. .. 1·10 1·10
378 75 c. Exchanging gifts for food from Amerindians 55 55
379 $1.75, Columbus's coat of arms .. .. 1·40 1·40
a. Horiz pair. Nos. 379/80.. .. .. 2·75 2·75
380 $1.75, Breadfruit plant .. .. .. 1·40 1·40
381 $2.50, Columbus's fleet .. .. .. 1·75 1·75
a. Horiz pair. Nos. 381/2 .. .. .. 3·50 3·50
382 $2.50, Christopher Columbus .. .. 1·75 1·75
377/82 .. .. *Set of* 6 6·50 6·50
MS383 95×84 mm. $6 Christopher Columbus (*different*) .. .. 6·50 7·00

The two designs of each value were printed together, *se-tenant*, in horizontal pairs throughout the sheets. Each pair forms a composite design showing charts of Columbus's route in the background.

Miniature sheets, each containing $2 × 2 stamps in the above designs, also exist from a restricted printing and from stock dispersed by the liquidator of Format International Security Printers Ltd.

(Des Court House Studio. Litho Format)

1986 (21 Apr). 60*th Birthday of Queen Elizabeth II. Multicoloured designs as T* **117a** *of Montserrat. P* 12½.

384 5 c. Queen Elizabeth in 1976 .. .. 10 10
385 75 c. Queen Elizabeth in 1953 .. .. 25 25
386 $2 In Australia 60 60
387 $8 In Canberra, 1982 (*vert*) .. .. 2·25 2·50
384/7 .. .. *Set of* 4 2·75 3·00
MS388 85×115 mm. $10 Queen Elizabeth II .. 6·00 6·00

The 5 c., 75 c. and $2 values exist with PVA gum as well as gum arabic.

No. 387 also exists watermarked w **15** (inverted), but no examples have been reported used from Nevis.

Nos. 384/7 exist in separate miniature sheets from unissued stock dispersed by the liquidator of Format International Security Printers Ltd.

(Des Court House Studio. Litho Format)

1986 (16 May). *World Cup Football Championship, Mexico. T* **39** *and similar multicoloured designs. P* 12½ (75 *c.*, $1, $1.75, $6) *or* 15 (*others*).

389 1 c. Official World Cup mascot (*horiz*) .. 10 10
390 2 c. Type **39** 10 10
391 5 c. Danish player 10 10
392 10 c. Brazilian player (*different*) 10 10
393 20 c. Denmark v Spain 20 20
394 30 c. Paraguay v Chile 30 30
395 60 c. Italy v West Germany 55 55
396 75 c. Danish team (56×36 *mm*) 65 65
397 $1 Paraguayan team (56×36 *mm*) .. 80 80
398 $1.75, Brazilian team (56×36 *mm*) .. 1·40 1·40
399 $3 Italy v England.. .. .. .. 2·00 2·00
400 $6 Italian team (56×36 *mm*) .. .. 3·50 3·50
389/400 .. .. *Set of* 12 8·75 8·75
MS401 Five sheets, each 85×115 mm. (a) $1.50, As No. 398. (b) $2 As No. 393. (c) $2 As No. 400. (d) $2.50, As No. 395. (e) $4 As No. 394 .. .. .. *Set of* 5 *sheets* 8·50 9·00

40 Clothing Machinist **41** Gorgonia

(Des G. Vasarhelyi. Litho Questa)

1986 (18 July). *Local Industries. T* **40** *and similar horiz designs. Multicoloured. W w* **15**. *P* 14.

402 15 c. Type **40** 20 15
403 40 c. Carpentry/joinery workshop 45 30
404 $1.20, Agricultural produce market .. 1·25 1·25
405 $3 Fishing boats landing catch .. .. 2·50 2·75
402/5 .. .. *Set of* 4 4·00 4·00

(Des Court House Studio. Litho Format)

1986 (23 July–15 Oct). *Royal Wedding* (1*st issue*). *Multicoloured designs as T* **118a** *of Montserrat. P* 12½.

406 60 c. Prince Andrew in midshipman's uniform 25 25
a. Pair. Nos. 406/7.. .. .. 50 50
407 60 c. Miss Sarah Ferguson 25 25
408 $2 Prince Andrew on safari in Africa (*horiz*) 75 85
a. Pair. Nos. 408/9.. .. .. 1·50 1·60
409 $2 Prince Andrew at the races (*horiz*) .. 75 85
406/9 .. .. *Set of* 4 2·00 2·10
MS410 115×85 mm. $10 Duke and Duchess of York on Palace balcony after wedding (*horiz*) (15.10.86) .. .. 3·50 4·50

Nos. 406/7 and 408/9 were each printed together, *se-tenant*, in horizontal and vertical pairs throughout the sheets.

Nos. 408/9 exist in *tête-bêche* pairs from unissued stock dispersed by the liquidator of Format International Security Printers Ltd.

See also Nos. 454/7.

(Litho Format)

1986 (15 Aug). *Automobiles* (6*th series*). *Horiz designs as T* **25**, *the first in each pair showing technical drawings and the second paintings. P* 12½.

411 15 c. multicoloured 10 10
a. Vert pair. Nos. 411/12 .. .. .. 20 20
412 15 c. multicoloured 10 10
413 45 c. black, light blue and grey-blue .. 25 25
a. Vert pair. Nos. 413/14 .. .. .. 50 50
414 45 c. multicoloured 25 25
415 60 c. multicoloured 30 30
a. Vert pair. Nos. 415/16 .. .. .. 60 60
416 60 c. multicoloured 30 30
417 $1 black, yellow-green and dull green .. 40 40
a. Vert pair. Nos. 417/18 .. .. .. 80 80
418 $1 multicoloured 40 40
419 $1.75, black, pale reddish lilac & deep lilac 60 60
a. Vert pair. Nos. 419/20 .. .. .. 1·10 1·10
420 $1.75, multicoloured 60 60
421 $3 multicoloured .. .. 1·10 1·10
a. Vert pair. Nos. 421/2 .. .. .. 2·10 2·10
422 $3 multicoloured .. .. 1·10 1·10
411/22 .. .. *Set of* 12 4·75 4·75

Designs:—Nos. 411/12, Riley "Brooklands Nine" (1930); 413/14, Alfa Romeo "GTA" (1966); 415/16, Pierce Arrow "Type 66" (1913); 417/18, Willys-Knight "66 A" (1928); 419/20, Studebaker "Starliner" (1953); 421/2, Cunningham "V-8" (1919).

Nos. 411/22 were issued in a similar sheet format to Nos. 165/80.

(Des G. Drummond. Litho Format)

1986 (8 Sept). *Corals* (2*nd series*). *T* **41** *and similar vert designs. Multicoloured. W w* **15** (*sideways*). *P* 15.

423 15 c. Type **41** 50 20
424 60 c. Fire Coral .. .. 1·25 65
425 $2 Elkhorn Coral .. .. 2·50 2·50
426 $3 Vase Sponge and Feather Star .. 3·50 3·50
423/6 .. .. *Set of* 4 7·00 7·00

(Des Court House Studio. Litho Format)

1986 (1 Oct). *Railway Locomotives* (6*th series*). *Horiz designs as T* **21**, *the first in each pair showing technical drawings and the second the locomotive at work. P* 12½.

427 15 c. multicoloured 10 10
a. Vert pair. Nos. 427/8 .. .. .. 20 20
428 15 c. multicoloured 10 10
429 45 c. multicoloured 25 25
a. Vert pair. Nos. 429/30 .. .. .. 50 50
430 45 c. multicoloured 25 25
431 60 c. multicoloured 30 30
a. Vert pair. Nos. 431/2 .. .. .. 60 60
432 60 c. multicoloured 30 30
433 75 c. multicoloured 40 40
a. Vert pair. Nos. 433/4 .. .. .. 80 80
434 75 c. multicoloured 40 40
435 $1 multicoloured 45 50
a. Vert pair. Nos. 435/6 .. .. .. 90 1·00
436 $1 multicoloured 45 50
437 $1.50, multicoloured 60 70
a. Vert pair. Nos. 437/8 .. .. .. 1·10 1·40
438 $1.50, multicoloured 60 70
439 $2 multicoloured 70 80
a. Vert pair. Nos. 439/40 .. .. .. 1·40 1·60
440 $2 multicoloured 70 80
441 $3 multicoloured .. .. 90 1·10
a. Vert pair. Nos. 441/2 .. .. .. 1·75 2·10
442 $3 multicoloured .. .. 90 1·10
427/42 .. .. *Set of* 16 6·50 7·50

Designs:—Nos. 427/8, Connor Single Class, Great Britain (1859); 429/30, Class "P2" *Cock o' the North*, Great Britain (1934); 431/2, Class "7000", Japan (1926); 433/4, Palatinate Railway Class "P3", Germany (1897); 435/6, *Dorchester*, Canada (1836); 437/8, "Centennial" Class diesel, U.S.A. (1969); 439/40, *Lafayette*, U.S.A. (1837); 441/2, Class "C-16", U.S.A. (1882).

Nos. 427/42 were issued in a similar sheet format to Nos. 132/47.

(Des Court House Studio. Litho Format)

1986 (28 Oct). *Centenary of Statue of Liberty. Multicoloured designs as T* **121a** *of Montserrat. P* 13½×14 ($1, $2) *or* 14×13½ (*others*).

443 15 c. Statue of Liberty and World Trade Centre, Manhattan 10 10
444 25 c. Sailing ship passing Statue 15 15
445 40 c. Statue in scaffolding 20 25
446 60 c. Statue (side view) and scaffolding .. 25 30
447 75 c. Statue and regatta 35 40
448 $1 Tall Ships parade passing Statue (*horiz*) 45 50
449 $1.50, Head and arm of Statue above scaffolding 70 75
450 $2 Ships with souvenir flags (*horiz*) .. 90 95
451 $2.50, Statue and New York waterfront .. 1·10 1·25
452 $3 Restoring Statue .. .. .. 1·40 1·50
443/52 .. .. *Set of* 10 5·00 5·50
MS453 Four sheets, each 85×115 mm. (a) $3.50, Statue at dusk. (b) $4 Head of Statue. (c) $4.50, Statue and lightning. (d) $5 Head and torch at sunset .. .. *Set of* 4 *sheets* 8·50 9·50

1986 (17 Nov). *Royal Wedding* (2*nd issue*). *Nos.* 406/9 *optd as T* **121** *of Montserrat in silver*.

454 60 c. Prince Andrew in midshipman's uniform 35 35
a. Pair. Nos. 454/5.. .. .. 70 70
455 60 c. Miss Sarah Ferguson 35 35
456 $2 Prince Andrew on safari in Africa (*horiz*) 1·10 1·10
a. Pair. Nos. 456/7.. .. .. 2·10 2·10
457 $2 Prince Andrew at the races (*horiz*) .. 1·10 1·10
454/7 .. .. *Set of* 4 2·50 2·50

42 Dinghy sailing

(Des G. Vasarhelyi. Litho Questa)

1986 (21 Nov). *Sports. T* **42** *and similar horiz designs. Multicoloured. P* 14.

458 10 c. Type **42** 10 10
459 25 c. Netball 30 15
460 $2 Cricket .. .. 1·75 1·75
461 $3 Basketball .. .. 2·00 2·00
458/61 .. .. *Set of* 4 3·75 3·75

43 St. George's Anglican Church, Gingerland

44 Constitution Document, Quill and Inkwell

(Des J. Cooter. Litho Questa)

1986 (8 Dec). *Christmas. Churches of Nevis (2nd series). T* **43** *and similar horiz designs. Multicoloured. P* 14.

462 10 c. Type **43** 10 10
463 40 c. Trinity Methodist Church, Fountain .. 20 25
464 $1 Charlestown Methodist Church .. 45 55
465 $5 Wesleyan Holiness Church, Brown Hill .. .. 2·25 2·75
462/5 .. .. *Set of* 4 2·75 3·25

(Des Maxine Marsh. Litho Questa)

1987 (11 Jan). *Bicentenary of U.S. Constitution and 230th Birth Anniv of Alexander Hamilton (U.S. statesman). T* **44** *and similar vert designs. Multicoloured. P* 14.

466 15 c. Type **44** 10 10
467 40 c. Alexander Hamilton and Hamilton House 20 25
468 60 c. Alexander Hamilton 25 35
469 $2 Washington and his Cabinet .. .. 90 1·25
466/9 .. .. *Set of* 4 1·25 1·75
MS470 70 × 82 mm. $5 Model ship *Hamilton* on float, 1788 .. .. 6·00 6·00

America's Cup
1987 Winners
'Stars & Stripes'

(45)

1987 (20 Feb). *Victory of* Stars and Stripes *in America's Cup Yachting Championship. No.* 54 *optd with T* **45**.

471 $3 Windjammer's S.V. *Polynesia* .. .. 1·40 1·75

46 Fig Tree Church

(Des Maxine Marsh. Litho Questa)

1987 (11 Mar). *Bicentenary of Marriage of Horatio Nelson and Frances Nisbet. T* **46** *and similar horiz designs. Multicoloured. W* w **15**. *P* 14.

472 15 c. Type **46** 10 10
473 60 c. Frances Nisbet 30 30
474 $1 H.M.S. *Boreas* 65 65
475 $3 Captain Horatio Nelson .. .. .. 1·90 2·00
472/5 .. .. *Set of* 4 2·75 2·75
MS476 102 × 82 mm. $3 As No. 473; $3 No. 475 .. 5·00 5·50

47 Queen Angelfish

(Des C. Abbott. Litho Format)

1987 (6 July). *Coral Reef Fishes. T* **47** *and similar triangular designs. Multicoloured. P* 14½.

477 60 c. Type **47** 70 70
a. Vert pair. Nos. 477/8 .. .. 1·40 1·40
478 60 c. Blue Angelfish 70 70
479 $1 Stoplight Parrotfish (male) 90 90
a. Vert pair. Nos. 479/80 .. .. 1·75 1·75
480 $1 Stoplight Parrotfish (female) 90 90
481 $1.50, Red Hind .. .. 1·40 1·40
a. Vert pair. Nos. 481/2 .. .. 2·75 2·75
482 $1.50, Rock Hind .. .. 1·40 1·40
483 $2.50, Coney (bicoloured phase) .. .. .. 2·25 2·25
a. Vert pair. Nos. 483/4 .. .. 4·50 4·50
484 $2.50, Coney (red-brown phase) .. .. .. 2·25 2·25
477/84 .. .. *Set of* 8 9·25 9·25

Nos. 477/8, 479/80, 481/2 and 483/4 were each printed together, *se-tenant*, in pairs throughout the sheets. The second design for each value is in the form of an inverted triangle.

Nos. 477/84 exist imperforate from stock dispersed by the liquidator of Format International Security Printers Ltd.

48 *Panaeolus antillarum*

49 Rag Doll

(Des J. Cooter. Litho Format)

1987 (16 Oct). *Fungi. T* **48** *and similar vert designs. Multicoloured. W* w **16**. *P* 14.

485 15 c. Type **48** 30 20
486 50 c. *Pycnoporus sanguineus* 75 50
487 $2 *Gymnopilus chrysopellus* .. .. .. 2·25 2·00
488 $3 *Cantharellus cinnabarinus* .. .. .. 2·75 2·75
485/8 .. .. *Set of* 4 5·50 5·00

(Des J.W. Litho Walsall)

1987 (4 Dec). *Christmas. Toys. T* **49** *and similar horiz designs. Multicoloured. W* w **16** *(sideways). P* 14½.

489 10 c. Type **49** 10 10
490 40 c. Coconut boat 20 25
491 $1.20, Sandbox cart 55 60
492 $5 Two-wheeled cart .. .. 2·25 2·75
489/92 .. .. *Set of* 4 2·75 3·25

50 Hawk-wing Conch

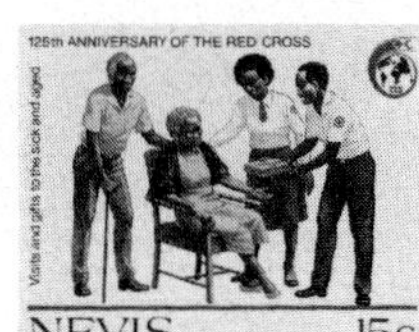

51 Visiting Pensioners at Christmas

(Des Josephine Martin. Litho Questa)

1988 (15 Feb). *Seashells and Pearls. T* **50** *and similar vert designs. Multicoloured. W* w **16**. *P* 14½ × 14.

493 15 c. Type **50** 10 10
494 40 c. Roostertail Conch 15 20
495 60 c. Emperor Helmet 25 30
496 $2 Queen Conch 85 90
497 $3 King Helmet .. .. 1·25 1·40
493/7 .. .. *Set of* 5 2·25 2·50

(Des L. Curtis. Litho Walsall)

1988 (20 June). *125th Anniv of International Red Cross. T* **51** *and similar horiz designs. Multicoloured. W* w **16** *(sideways). P* 14 × 14½.

498 15 c. Type **51** 10 10
499 40 c. Teaching children first aid 15 20
500 60 c. Providing wheelchairs for the disabled 25 30
501 $5 Helping cyclone victim .. .. .. 2·10 2·50
498/501 .. .. *Set of* 4 2·25 2·75

52 Athlete on Starting Blocks

53 Outline Map and Arms of St. Kitts–Nevis

(Des G. Vasarhelyi. Litho Format)

1988 (26 Aug). *Olympic Games, Seoul. T* **52** *and similar vert designs. Multicoloured. W* w **16**. *P* 14.

502 10 c. Type **52** 10 10
a. Horiz strip of 4. Nos. 502/5 .. .. .. 2·40
503 $1.20, At start 50 55
504 $2 During race 85 90
505 $3 At finish .. .. 1·25 1·40
502/5 .. .. *Set of* 4 2·40 2·50
MS506 137 × 80 mm. As Nos. 502/5, but each size 24 × 36 mm. Wmk sideways .. .. 2·75 3·00

Nos. 502/5 were printed together, *se-tenant*, in horizontal strips of 4 throughout the sheet, each strip forming a composite design showing an athlete from start to finish of race.

(Des L. Curtis. Litho Questa)

1988 (19 Sept). *5th Anniv of Independence. W* w **14**. *P* 14½ × 14.

507 **53** $5 multicoloured .. .. 2·10 2·25

(Des D. Miller (15 c., $2.50), E. Nisbet and D. Miller (60 c., $3). Litho Questa)

1988 (31 Oct). *300th Anniversary of Lloyd's of London. Multicoloured designs as T* **167a** *of Malawi. W* w **16** *(sideways on* 60 c., $2.50). *P* 14.

508 15 c. House of Commons passing Lloyd's Bill, 1871 .. .. 10 10
509 60 c. *Cunard Countess* (liner) (*horiz*) .. 25 30
510 $2.50, Space shuttle deploying satellite (*horiz*) .. .. 1·00 1·10
511 $3 *Viking Princess* on fire, 1966 .. .. 1·25 1·40
508/11 .. .. *Set of* 4 2·25 2·50

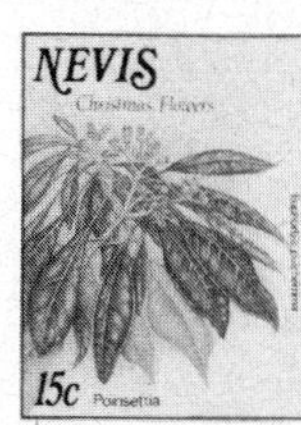

54 Poinsettia

55 British Fleet off St. Kitts

(Des I. Loe. Litho Questa)

1988 (7 Nov). *Christmas. Flowers. T* **54** *and similar vert designs. Multicoloured. W* w **16**. *P* 14½ × 14.

512 15 c. Type **54** 10 10
513 40 c. Tiger Claws 15 20
514 60 c. Sorrel Flower 25 30
515 $1 Christmas Candle 40 45
516 $5 Snow Bush .. .. 2·10 2·25
512/16 .. .. *Set of* 5 2·75 3·00

(Des Jane Hartley. Litho Format)

1989 (17 Apr). *"Philexfrance 89" International Stamp Exhibition, Paris. Battle of Frigate Bay, 1782. T* **55** *and similar vert designs. Multicoloured. W* w **16**. *P* 13½×14 ($3) *or* 14 *(others).*

517 50 c. Type **55** 20 25
a. Horiz strip of 3. Nos. 517/19 .. .. 1·50
518 $1.20, Battle off Nevis 50 55
519 $2 British and French fleets exchanging broadsides 85 90
520 $3 French map of Nevis, 1764 .. .. 1·25 1·40
517/20 .. .. *Set of* 4 2·50 2·75

Nos. 517/19 were printed together, *se-tenant*, in horizontal strips of 3 throughout the sheet, each strip forming a composite design.

56 Cicada

57 Queen Conch feeding

(Des I. Loe. Litho Questa)

1989 (15 May). *"Sounds of the Night". T* **56** *and similar vert designs. Multicoloured. W* w **16**. *P* 14.

521 10 c. Type **56** 10 10
522 40 c. Grasshopper 15 20
523 60 c. Cricket 25 30
524 $5 Tree frog .. .. 2·10 2·25
521/4 .. .. *Set of* 4 2·25 2·50
MS525 135×81 mm. Nos. 521/4 .. .. 2·50 2·75

(Des A. Theobald ($6), D. Miller (others). Litho Questa)

1989 (20 July). *20th Anniv of First Manned Landing on Moon. Multicoloured designs as T* **51a** *of Kiribati. W* w **16** *(sideways on* 40 c., $2). *P* 14×13½ (15 c., $3) *or* 14 *(others).*

526 15 c. Vehicle Assembly Building, Kennedy Space Centre 10 10
527 40 c. Crew of "Apollo 12" (30×30 *mm*) .. 15 20
528 $2 "Apollo 12" emblem (30×30 *mm*) .. 85 90
529 $3 "Apollo 12" astronaut on Moon .. 1·25 1·40
526/9 .. .. *Set of* 4 2·00 2·25
MS530 100×83 mm. $6 Aldrin undertaking lunar seismic experiment. P 14×13½ .. .. 2·50 2·75

(Des Deborah Dudley Max. Litho Questa)

1990 (31 Jan). *Queen Conch. T* **57** *and similar horiz designs. Multicoloured. P* 14.

531 10 c. Type **57** 10 10
532 40 c. Queen Conch from front 15 20
533 60 c. Side view of shell 25 30
534 $1 Back and flare 40 45
531/4 .. .. *Set of* 4 85 90
MS535 72×103 mm. $5 Underwater habitat .. 2·10 2·25

NEW INFORMATION

The editor is always interested to correspond with people who have new information that will improve or correct the Catalogue.

58 Wyon Medal Portrait   **59**

(Des M. Pollard. Litho B.D.T.)

1990 (3 May). *150th Anniv of the Penny Black. T* **58** *and similar vert designs. P* 14×15.
536 15 c. black and brown 10 10
537 40 c. black and deep blue-green 15 20
538 60 c. black 25 30
539 $4 black and ultramarine .. .. 1·75 1·90
536/9 .. .. *Set of* 4 2·00 2·25
MS540 114×84 mm. $5 blk, brn-lake & pale buff 2·10 2·25
Designs:—40 c. Engine-turned background; 60 c. Heath's engraving of portrait; $4 Essay with inscriptions; $5 Penny Black.
No. **MS**540 also commemorates "Stamp World London 90" International Stamp Exhibition.

(Des S. Pollard. Litho B.D.T.)

1990 (3 May). *500th Anniv of Regular European Postal Services. T* **59** *and similar square designs with different corner emblems. P* 13½.
541 15 c. brown 10 10
542 40 c. deep dull green 15 20
543 60 c. bright reddish violet 25 30
544 $4 ultramarine .. .. 1·75 1·90
541/4 .. .. *Set of* 4 2·00 2·25
MS545 110×82 mm. $5 brown-lake, pale buff and pale grey .. .. 2·10 2·25
Nos. 541/5 commemorate the Thurn and Taxis postal service and the designs are loosely based on those of the initial 1852–58 series.

60 Sand Fiddler Crab

(Des Mary Walters. Litho Questa)

1990 (25 June). *500th Anniv of Discovery of America by Columbus* (1992) (*3rd issue*). *New World Natural History – Crabs. T* **60** *and similar horiz designs. Multicoloured. P* 14.
546 5 c. Type **60** 10 10
547 15 c. Great Land Crab 10 10
548 20 c. Blue Crab 10 10
549 40 c. Stone Crab 15 20
550 60 c. Mountain Crab 25 30
551 $2 Sargassum Crab 85 90
552 $3 Yellow Box Crab .. .. 1·25 1·40
553 $4 Spiny Spider Crab .. .. 1·75 1·90
546/53 .. .. *Set of* 8 4·00 4·25
MS554 Two sheets, each 101×70 mm. (a) $5 Sally Lightfoot. (b) $5 Wharf Crab *Set of* 2 *sheets* 4·25 4·50

(Des Young Phillips Studio. Litho Questa)

1990 (5 July). *90th Birthday of Queen Elizabeth the Queen Mother. Vert designs as T* **198***a of Lesotho showing portraits*, 1930–39. *P* 14.
555 $2 brownish black, magenta and pale buff 85 90
a. Strip of 3. Nos. 555/7 .. .. .. 2·25
556 $2 brownish black, magenta and pale buff 85 90
557 $2 brownish black, magenta and pale buff 85 90
555/7 .. .. *Set of* 3 2·25 2·40
MS558 90×75 mm. $6 chestnut, magenta & blk 2·50 2·75
Designs:—No. 555, Duchess of York with corgi; No. 556, Queen Elizabeth in Coronation robes, 1937; No. 557, Duchess of York in garden; No. **MS**558, Queen Elizabeth in Coronation robes, 1937 (*different*).
Nos. 555/7 were printed together, horizontally and vertically *se-tenant*, in sheetlets of 9 (3×3).

61 MaKanaky, Cameroons   **62** *Cattleya deckeri*

(Des Young Phillips Studio. Litho Questa)

1990 (1 Oct). *World Cup Football Championship, Italy. Star Players. T* **61** *and similar vert designs. Multicoloured. P* 14.
559 10 c. Type **61** 10 10
560 25 c. Chovanec, Czechoslovakia 10 15
561 $2.50, Robson, England .. .. .. 1·10 1·10
562 $5 Voller, West Germany .. .. .. 2·10 2·25
559/62 .. .. *Set of* 4 3·00 3·25
MS563 Two sheets, each 90×75 mm. (a) $5 Maradona, Argentina (b) $5 Gordillo, Spain *Set of* 2 *sheets* 4·25 4·50

(Des Mary Walters. Litho B.D.T.)

1990 (19 Nov). *Christmas. Native Orchids. T* **62** *and similar vert designs. Multicoloured. P* 14.
564 10 c. Type **62** 10 10
565 15 c. *Epidendrum ciliare* 10 10
566 20 c. *Epidendrum fragrans* 10 10
567 40 c. *Epidendrum ibaguense* 15 20
568 60 c. *Epidendrum latifolium* 25 30
569 $1.20, *Maxillaria conferta* 50 55
570 $2 *Epidendrum strobiliferum* 85 90
571 $3 *Brassavola cucullata* .. .. .. 1·25 1·40
564/71 .. .. *Set of* 8 3·00 3·25
MS572 102×71 mm. $5 *Rodriguezia lanceolata* 2·10 2·25

(Des T. Agans. Litho Questa)

1991 (14 Jan). *350th Death Anniv of Rubens. Multicoloured designs as T* **250** *of Maldive Islands, showing details from "The Feast of Achelous". P* 13½×14.
573 10 c. Two jugs (*vert*) 10 10
574 40 c. Woman at table (*vert*) 15 20
575 60 c. Two servants with fruit (*vert*) 25 30
576 $4 Achelous (*vert*) .. .. 1·75 1·90
573/6 .. .. *Set of* 4 2·00 2·25
MS577 101×71 mm. $5 "The Feast of Achelous". P 14×13½ .. .. 2·10 2·25

63 *Agraulis vanillae*

(Des L. Nelson. Litho Questa)

1991 (1 Mar). *Butterflies. T* **63** *and similar horiz designs. Multicoloured. P* 14.
578 5 c. Type **63** 10 10
579 10 c. *Historis odius* 10 10
580 15 c. *Marpesia corinna* 10 10
581 20 c. *Anartia amathea* 10 10
582 25 c. *Junonia evarete* 10 15
583 40 c. *Heliconius charithonia* 15 20
584 50 c. *Marpesia petreus* 20 25
585 60 c. *Dione juno* 25 30
586 75 c. *Heliconius doris* 30 35
587 $1 *Hypolimnas misippus* 40 45
588 $3 *Danaus plexippus* .. .. 1·25 1·40
589 $5 *Heliconius sara* .. .. 2·10 2·25
590 $10 *Tithorea harmonia* .. .. 4·25 4·50
591 $20 *Dryas julia* .. .. 8·50 8·75
578/91 .. .. *Set of* 14 16·00 17·00

64 "Viking Mars Lander", 1976

(Des T. Agans. Litho Questa)

1991 (22 Apr). *500th Anniv of Discovery of America by Columbus* (1992) (*4th issue*). *History of Exploration. T* **64** *and similar multicoloured designs. P* 14.
592 15 c. Type **64** 10 10
593 40 c. "Apollo 11", 1969 .. .. 15 20
594 60 c. "Skylab", 1973 .. .. 25 30
595 75 c. "Salyut 6", 1977 .. .. 30 35
596 $1 "Voyager 1", 1977 .. .. 40 45
597 $2 "Venera 7", 1970 .. .. 85 90
598 $4 "Gemini 4", 1965 .. .. 1·75 1·90
599 $5 "Luna 3", 1959 .. .. 2·10 2·25
592/9 .. .. *Set of* 8 5·25 5·75
MS600 Two sheets each 105×76 mm. (a) $6 Bow of *Santa Maria* (*vert*). (b) $6 Christopher Columbus (*vert*) .. .. *Set of* 2 *sheets* 5·00 5·25

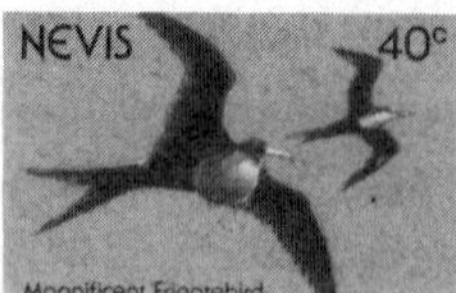

65 Magnificent Frigate Bird

(Des Jennifer Toombs. Litho Questa)

1991 (28 June). *Island Birds. T* **65** *and similar horiz designs. Multicoloured. P* 14.
601 40 c. Type **65** 15 20
a. Sheetlet. Nos. 601/20 .. .. .. 2·75
602 40 c. Roseate Tern 15 20
603 40 c. Red-tailed Hawk 15 20
604 40 c. Zenaida Dove 15 20
605 40 c. Bananaquit 15 20
606 40 c. American Kestrel 15 20
607 40 c. Grey Kingbird 15 20
608 40 c. Prothonotary Warbler 15 20
609 40 c. Blue-hooded Euphonia 15 20
610 40 c. Antillean Crested Hummingbird .. 15 20
611 40 c. White-tailed Tropic Bird 15 20
612 40 c. Yellow-bellied Sapsucker 15 20
613 40 c. Green-throated Carib 15 20
614 40 c. Purple-throated Carib 15 20
615 40 c. Black-bellied Tree-duck 15 20
616 40 c. Ringed Kingfisher 15 20
617 40 c. Burrowing Owl 15 20
618 40 c. Ruddy Turnstone 15 20
619 40 c. Great White Heron 15 20
620 40 c. Yellow-crowned Night-heron 15 20
601/20 .. .. *Set of* 20 2·75 3·50
MS621 76×59 mm. $6 Great Egret .. .. 2·50 2·75
Nos. 601/20 were printed together, *se-tenant*, in sheetlets of 20, forming a composite design.

(Des D. Miller. Litho Walsall)

1991 (5 July). *65th Birthday of Queen Elizabeth II. Horiz designs as T* **210** *of Lesotho. Multicoloured. P* 14.
622 15 c. Queen Elizabeth at polo match with Prince Charles 10 10
623 40 c. Queen and Prince Philip on Buckingham Palace balcony 15 20
624 $2 In carriage at Ascot, 1986 .. .. 85 90
625 $4 Queen Elizabeth II at Windsor polo match, 1989 .. .. 1·75 1·90
622/5 .. .. *Set of* 4 2·50 2·75
MS626 68×90 mm. $5 Queen Elizabeth and Prince Philip .. .. 2·10 2·25

(Des D. Miller. Litho Walsall)

1991 (5 July). *10th Wedding Anniv of Prince and Princess of Wales. Horiz designs as T* **210** *of Lesotho. Multicoloured. P* 14.
627 10 c. Prince Charles and Princess Diana .. 10 10
628 50 c. Prince of Wales and family 20 25
629 $1 Prince William and Prince Harry .. 40 45
630 $5 Prince and Princess of Wales .. 2·10 2·25
627/30 .. .. *Set of* 4 2·50 2·75
MS631 68×90 mm. $5 Prince and Princess of Wales in Hungary, and young princes at Christmas .. .. 2·10 2·25

(Litho Questa)

1991 (12 Aug). *"Philanippon '91" International Stamp Exhibition, Tokyo. Japanese Railway Locomotives. Multicoloured designs as T* **257** *of Maldive Islands. P* 14.
632 10 c. Class "C62" steam locomotive .. 10 10
633 15 c. Class "C56" steam locomotive (*horiz*) 10 10
634 40 c. Class "C-55" streamlined steam locomotive (*horiz*) 15 20
635 60 c. Class "1400" steam locomotive (*horiz*) 25 30
636 $1 Class "485 Bonnet" diesel rail car .. 40 45
637 $2 Class "C61" steam locomotive .. 85 90
638 $3 Class "485" express train (*horiz*) .. 1·25 1·40
639 $4 Class "7000" electric train (*horiz*) .. 1·75 1·90
632/9 .. .. *Set of* 8 4·25 4·75
MS640 Two sheets, each, 108×72 mm. (a) $5 Class "D51" steam locomotive (*horiz*). (b) $5 Hikari Bullet Train (*horiz*) .. *Set of* 2 *sheets* 4·25 4·50

(Litho B.D.T.)

1991 (20 Dec). *Christmas. Drawings by Albrecht Dürer. Vert designs as T* **211** *of Lesotho. P* 13.
641 10 c. black and apple-green 10 10
642 40 c. black and yellow-orange 15 20
643 60 c. black and new blue 25 30
644 $3 black and bright mauve .. .. 1·25 1·40
641/4 .. .. *Set of* 4 1·60 1·75
MS645 Two sheets, each 96×124 mm. (a) $6 black. (b) $6 black .. .. *Set of* 2 *sheets* 5·00 5·50
Designs:—10 c. "Mary being Crowned by an Angel"; 40 c. "Mary with the Pear"; 60 c. "Mary in a Halo"; $3 "Mary with Crown of Stars and Sceptre"; $6 (No. **MS**645a) "The Holy Family" (detail); $6 (No. **MS**645b) "Mary at the Yard Gate" (detail).

OFFICIAL STAMPS

1980 (30 July). *Nos. 40/9 additionally optd with Type* O **1** *of St. Christopher, Nevis and Anguilla.*
O 1 15 c. Sugar cane harvesting 10 10
O 2 25 c. Crafthouse (craft centre) 10 10
a. "OFFICIAL" opt double .. .. .. 55·00
b. "OFFICIAL" opt omitted (in horiz pair with normal) .. .. 85·00
c. Optd on No. 41a .. .. 5·50 8·00
O 3 30 c. *Europa* (liner) 10 10
O 4 40 c. Lobster and sea crab 15 15
O 5 45 c. Royal St. Kitts Hotel and golf course .. 20 25
a. Opt inverted .. .. 13·00
O 6 50 c. Pinney's Beach, Nevis 20 25
a. Opt inverted .. .. 75·00
O 7 55 c. New runway at Golden Rock 20 25
a. Opt double .. .. 15·00
O 8 $1 Picking cotton 30 35
O 9 $5 Brewery .. .. 1·00 1·00
a. Opt inverted .. .. 80·00
O10 $10 Pineapples and peanuts .. .. 2·25 2·25
O1/10 .. .. *Set of* 10 4·00 4·50

1981 (Mar). *Nos. 60A/71A optd with Type* O **1** *of St. Kitts.*
O11 15 c. New River Mill .. .. 10 [illegible]
O12 20 c. Nelson Museum .. .. 10 [illegible]
O13 25 c. St. James' Parish Church .. .. 10 [illegible]
O14 30 c. Nevis Lane .. .. 15 [illegible]
O15 40 c. Zetland Plantation .. .. .. 15 [illegible]
O16 45 c. Nisbet Plantation .. .. .. 20 [illegible]
O17 50 c. Pinney's Beach .. .. 20 [illegible]
O18 55 c. Eva Wilkin's Studio 25 30
O19 $1 Nevis at dawn 40 45
O20 $2.50, Ruins of Fort Charles 85 90
O21 $5 Old Bath House .. .. 1·25 1·75
O22 $10 Beach at Nisbet's .. .. .. 2·25 2·75
O11/22 .. .. *Set of* 12 5·00 6·50

Stanley Gibbons
Privilege Card
STANLEY GIBBONS
MERCURYCARD £1
STANLEY GIBBONS LTD.
399, THE STRAND, LONDON WC2R OLX

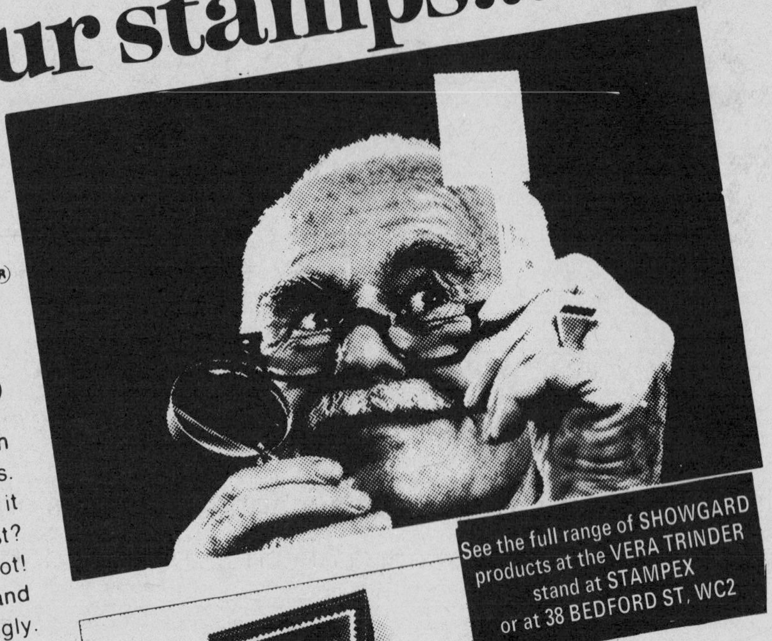

Stanley Gibbons Great Britain Luxury Hingeless Album

With a space for each stamp and crystal-clear protective mounts already affixed for the immediate insertion of your stamps, this really is the album to give your Great Britain collection a touch of class.
The leaves which are of finest quality paper, have been expertly arranged and include selected illustrations and descriptions for your guidance. Handsomely bound in navy blue leatherette, the deeply padded binders are richly embossed with the coat of arms and crest of the country on the cover and spine and each is presented in its own matching slip case to keep both binder and collection in pristine condition.

An album of this quality and craftsmanship will give real distinction to every collection and at the same time offers the security and protection which your stamps demand.
Now presented in three volumes: Volume 1, 1840–1970 (pre-decimal); Volume 2, 1970 - date and Volume 3. (binder and slip case only).
There is also a special Queen Elizabeth Volume which takes all issues from 1952 to date. Annual supplements available in the spring of each year.

Item 5484 Great Britain Luxury Hingless Album Volume 1 1840–1970

Item 5285 Great Britain Luxury Hingeless Album Volume 2 1971–date

Item 5290 Great Britain Luxury Hingeless binder and slipcase - Volume 3

Item 5546 Great Britain Luxury Hingless Album, Queen Elizabeth Volume 1952–date

For further details visit your favourite stamp shop or write to:

Stanley Gibbons Publications Ltd.,
5 Parkside, Christchurch Road,
Ringwood, Hampshire BH24 3SH
Telephone 0425 472363

The Stanley Gibbons GREAT BRITAIN SPECIALISED Stamp Catalogue

Whether you collect line-engraved or Machin cylinder blocks, the Stanley Gibbons Great Britain Specialised Catalogue provides you with the information you need for the in-depth study of your stamps.
The winner of several international awards, this detailed and authoritative handbook/catalogue is now split into five convenient volumes, each clearly laid out with thousands of illustrations and explanatory notes to cover every aspect of the postage stamps of Great Britain.
Each new edition is thoroughly revised in order not only to ensure that prices are in line with the current market, but that the most up-to-date information and research are included.
Volumes 1 and 2 available either casebound or paperback – remaining volumes paperback only.

Item 0285 Volume 1 Queen Victoria
Item 0286 Volume 2 King Edward VII to King George VI
Item 2810 Volume 3 Queen Elizabeth Pre-decimal Issues
Item 2820 Volume 4 Queen Elizabeth Decimal Definitive Issues
Item 2891 Volume 5 Queen Elizabeth Decimal Special Issues

For further details visit your favourite stamp shop or write to:

Stanley Gibbons Publications Ltd.,
5 Parkside, Christchurch Road,
Ringwood, Hampshire BH24 3SH
Telephone 0425 472363

1983 (2 Feb). *Nos. 72/7 optd with Type* O **1** *of St. Kitts* (55 c.) *or surch also* (*others*).

No.	Description	Unused	Used
O23	45 c. on $2 *Royal Sovereign* (New Blue)	20	25
	a. Sheetlet. No. O23 × 6 and No. O24	1·40	
	b. Surch inverted	10·00	
	c. Surch inverted (horiz pair)	38·00	
	d. Albino surch	9·00	
	da. Albino surch inverted		
	e. Horiz pair, one without surch		
	f. Deep ultramarine surch	40	50
	fb. Surch inverted	7·00	
	fc. Surch inverted (horiz pair)	18·00	
	g. Black surch	60·00	
O24	45 c. on $2 Prince Charles and Lady Diana Spencer (New Blue)	20	25
	b. Surch inverted	30·00	
	d. Albino surch	23·00	
	f. Deep ultramarine surch	40	50
	fb. Surch inverted	18·00	
	g. Black surch	£150	
O25	55 c. *Royal Caroline* (New Blue)	20	25
	a. Sheetlet No. O25 × 6 and No. O26	1·40	
	d. Albino opt	9·00	
	db. Albino opt inverted	11·00	
	dc. Albino opt inverted (horiz pair)	13·00	
	f. Deep ultramarine opt	75	
	fb. Opt inverted	7·00	
	fc. Opt inverted (horiz pair)	25·00	
	ff. Opt double	16·00	
	g. Black opt	60·00	
O26	55 c. Prince Charles and Lady Diana Spencer (New Blue)	25	25
	d. Albino opt	20·00	
	db. Albino opt inverted	25·00	
	f. Deep ultramarine opt	1·00	
	fb. Opt inverted	25·00	
	ff. Opt double	32·00	
	g. Black opt	£150	
O27	$1.10 on $5 *Britannia* (Blk.)	45	50
	a. Sheetlet. No. O27 × 6 and No. O28	3·00	
	d. Albino surch	9·00	
	f. Deep ultramarine surch.	6·00	
	fb. Surch inverted	8·00	
	fc. Surch inverted (horiz pair)	32·00	
O28	$1.10 on $5 Prince Charles and Lady Diana Spencer (Blk.)	55	60
	d. Albino surch	27·00	
	f. Deep ultramarine surch	40·00	
	fb. Surch inverted	50·00	
O23/28	*Set of* 6	1·75	1·75

Nos. O23c, O23fc, O25dc, O25fc and O27fc show the surcharge or overprint intended for the large design inverted and struck across a horizontal pair of the smaller. Nos. O24b, O24fb, O26db, O26fb and O28fb each show two inverted surcharges intended for a horizontal pair of the smaller design.

1985 (2 Jan). *Nos. 187/98 optd with Type* O **1** *of St. Kitts.*

No.	Description	Unused	Used
O29	15 c. Flamboyant	10	10
O30	20 c. Eyelash Orchid	10	10
O31	30 c. Bougainvillea	10	15
O32	40 c. Hibiscus sp.	15	20
O33	50 c. Night-blooming Cereus	20	25
O34	55 c. Yellow Mahoe	25	30
O35	60 c. Spider-lily	25	30
O36	75 c. Scarlet Cordia	30	35
O37	$1 Shell-ginger	40	45
O38	$3 Blue Petrea	1·25	1·40
O39	$5 Coral Hibiscus	2·10	2·25
O40	$10 Passion Flower	4·25	4·50
O29/40	*Set of* 12	8·50	9·25

St. Lucia

Although a branch office of the British G.P.O. was not opened at Castries, the island capital, until 1844 some form of postal arrangements for overseas mails existed from at least 1841 when the issue of a Ship Letter handstamp is recorded.

The stamps of Great Britain were used on the island from May 1858 until the end of April 1860 when the local authorities assumed responsibility for the postal service. No. CC1 was again used on overseas mail between 1 May and the introduction of St. Lucia stamps in December 1860.

CASTRIES

CROWN-CIRCLE HANDSTAMPS

CC1

CC1 CC1 ST. LUCIA (R.) (1.5.1844) *Price on cover* £750

No. CC1 was utilised, struck in black, during a shortage of 1d. stamps in 1904. *Price on cover* £275.

Stamps of GREAT BRITAIN *cancelled* "A 11" *as Type* Z 1 *of Jamaica.*

1858 *to* **1860**

Z1 1d. rose-red (1857), *perf* 14 £1400
Z2 2d. blue (1855)
Z3 4d. rose (1857) £325
Z4 6d. lilac (1856) £200
Z5 1s. green (1856) £750

PRICES FOR STAMPS ON COVER TO 1945

Nos. 1/8	*from* × 6
Nos. 9/10	†
Nos. 11/24	*from* × 8
Nos. 25/30	*from* × 6
Nos. 31/6	*from* × 3
Nos. 39/42	*from* × 6
Nos. 43/50	*from* × 8
Nos. 51/2	—
Nos. 53/62	*from* × 4
No. 63	*from* × 10
Nos. 64/75	*from* × 4
Nos. 76/7	—
Nos. 78/88	*from* × 3
No. 89	*from* × 4
No. 90	*from* × 20
Nos. 91/112	*from* × 3
Nos. 113/24	*from* × 2
Nos. 125/7	*from* × 10
Nos. 128/41	*from* × 2
Nos. D1/6	*from* × 20
Nos. F1/28	—

CROWN COLONY

1

Half penny

(2)

(Recess P.B.)

1860 (18 Dec). *Wmk Small Star, W w* 2. *P* 14 *to* 16.

1 1 (1d.) rose-red £100 75·00
a. Imperf vert (horiz pair)
b. Double impression £1300
2 (4d.) blue £250 £180
a. Deep blue
b. Imperf vert (horiz pair)
3 (6d.) green £300 £250
a. Imperf vert (horiz pair)
b. Deep green £300 £250

(Recess D.L.R.)

1863. *Wmk Crown CC. P* 12½.

5 1 (1d.) lake 55·00 80·00
b. Brownish lake 75·00 75·00
7 (4d.) indigo £100 £100
8 (6d.) emerald-green £200 £200

Prepared for use, but not issued. Surch as T 2

9 1 ½d. on (6d.) emerald-green 42·00
10 6d. on (4d.) indigo £1200

1864 (19 Nov)–**76.** *Wmk Crown CC.* (a) *P* 12½.

11 1 (1d.) black 16·00 12·00
a. Intense black 15·00 11·00
12 (4d.) yellow £120 30·00
b. Lemon-yellow £1500
c. Chrome-yellow £130 30·00
d. Olive-yellow £250 70·00

13 1 (6d.) violet 70·00 28·00
a. Mauve £150 28·00
b. Deep lilac 90·00 32·00
14 (1s.) brown-orange £275 25·00
b. Orange £200 25·00
c. Pale orange £150 25·00
ca. Imperf between (horiz pair)

(*b*) *P* 14

15 1 (1d.) black (6.76) 16·00 15·00
a. Imperf between (horiz pair)
16 (4d.) yellow (6.76) 60·00 18·00
a. Olive-yellow £150 80·00
17 (6d.) mauve (6.76) 60·00 30·00
a. Pale lilac 60·00 18·00
b. Violet £170 60·00
18 (1s.) orange (10.76) £225 22·00
a. Deep orange £180 16·00

HALFPENNY (3)

2½ PENCE (4)

5

1881 (Sept). *Surch with T* 3 *or* 4. *Wmk Crown CC. P* 14

23 1 ½d. green 50·00 65·00
24 2½d. brown-red 19·00 18·00

The 1d. black is known surcharged "1d." in violet ink by hand, but there is no evidence that this was done officially.

1882–84. *Surch as T* 3. *Wmk Crown CA.* (*a*) *P* 14

25 1 ½d. green (1882) 12·00 22·00
26 1d. black (C.) 18·00 8·00
a. Bisected (on cover) † —
27 4d. yellow £170 17·00
28 6d. violet 22·00 25·00
29 1s. orange £250 £160

(*b*) *P* 12

30 1 4d. yellow £250 28·00

Deep blue stamps, wmk Crown CA, perf 14 or 12, are fiscals from which the overprint "THREE PENCE—REVENUE", or "REVENUE", has been fraudulently removed.

(Typo D.L.R.)

1883 (6 July)–**86.** *Wmk Crown CA. Die* 1. *P* 14.

31 5 ½d. dull green 2·75 3·00
32 1d. carmine-rose 23·00 7·50
33 2½d. blue 15·00 1·25
34 4d. brown (1885) 16·00 70
35 6d. lilac (1886) £250 £200
36 1s. orange-brown (1885) £400 £140

We no longer list imperforate examples of stamps appearing between 1863 and 1887 as there is no evidence that these were ever issued.

1886–87. *Wmk Crown CA. Die* I. *P* 14.

39 5 1d. dull mauve 2·50 5·00
40 3d. dull mauve and green 60·00 12·00
41 6d. dull mauve and blue (1887) 3·25 7·00
42 1s. dull mauve and red (1887 60·00 15·00
39/42 *Set of* 4 £110 35·00
39/42 Optd "Specimen" *Set of* 4 £160

1891–98. *Wmk Crown CA. Die* II. *P* 14.

43 5 ½d. dull green 50 30
44 1d. dull mauve 90 15
45 2d. ultramarine and orange (1898) 70 1·00
46 2½d. ultramarine 1·75 30
47 3d. dull mauve and green 3·25 5·50
48 4d. brown 1·40 2·25
49 6d. dull mauve and blue 13·00 14·00
50 1s. dull mauve and red 2·75 5·00
51 5s. dull mauve and orange 27·00 70·00
52 10s. dull mauve and black 50·00 70·00
43/52 *Set of* 10 90·00 £150
45, 51, 52 Optd "Specimen" *Set of* 3 £120

For description and illustration of differences between Die I and Die II see Introduction.

ONE HALF PENNY (6)

½d (7)

ONE PENNY (8)

N Normal "N"

N Thick "N"

Three types of T 8

I. All letters "N" normal.
II. Thick diagonal stroke in first "N".
III. Thick diagonal stroke in second "N".

1891–92 (*a*) *Stamps of Die* I *surch.*

53 6 ½d. on 3d. dull mauve and green 60·00 65·00
a. Small "A" in "HALF" 90·00 90·00
b. Small "O" in "ONE" 90·00 90·00
54 7 ½d. on half 6d. dull mauve and blue 14·00 3·25
a. No fraction bar £150 £130
b. Surch sideways £375
c. Surch double £350 £400
d. "2" in fraction omitted £325 £450
e. Thick "1" with sloping serif £150 £130
f. Surch triple £550
g. Figure "1" used as fraction bar £375 £250

55 8 1d. on 4d. brown (I) (12.91) 3·00 3·00
a. Surch double £150
b. Surch inverted £700 £600
c. Type II 18·00 18·00
ca. Surch double £200
cb. Surch inverted — £600
d. Type III 18·00 18·00

(*b*) *Stamp of Die* II *surch*

56 6 ½d. on 3d. dull mauve and green 30·00 14·00
a. Surch double £650 £600
b. Surch inverted £1600 £650
c. Small "O" in "ONE" £130 90·00
d. Small "A" in "HALF" £130 90·00
e. "ONE" misplaced ("O" over "H") £130 90·00

9

10

(Typo D.L.R.)

1902–3. *Wmk Crown CA. P* 14.

58 9 ½d. dull purple and green 2·00 80
59 1d. dull purple and carmine 2·50 45
60 2½d. dull purple and ultramarine 9·00 5·50
61 10 3d. dull purple and yellow 4·00 8·50
62 1s. green and black 7·50 12·00
58/62 *Set of* 5 23·00 24·00
58/62 Optd "Specimen" *Set of* 5 £100

11 The Pitons

(Recess D.L.R.)

1902 (15 Dec). 400*th Anniv of Discovery by Columbus. Wmk Crown CC, sideways. P* 14

63 11 2d. green and brown 6·50 1·75
63 Optd "Specimen" 60·00

This stamp was formerly thought to have been issued on 16 December but it has been seen on a postcard clearly postmarked 15 December.

1904–10. *Wmk Mult Crown CA. Chalk-surfaced paper* (*Nos.* 71, 73/5 *and* 77) *or ordinary paper* (*others*). *P* 14.

64 9 ½d. dull purple and green 1·25 20
a. Chalk-surfaced paper 1·25 40
65 ½d. green (1907) 1·00 30
66 1d. dull purple and carmine 1·75 20
a. Chalk-surfaced paper 1·75 20
67 1d. carmine (1907) 1·00 10
68 2½d. dull purple and ultramarine 3·75 1·25
a. Chalk-surfaced paper 2·75 2·00
69 2½d. blue (1907) 3·00 1·25
70 10 3d. dull purple and yellow 3·50 3·00
71 3d. purple/*yellow* (1909) 1·75 7·50
72 6d. dull purple and violet (1905) 5·50 4·75
a. Chalk-surfaced paper 5·50 6·50
ab. Dull purple and bright purple (1907) 4·00 11·00
73 6d. dull purple (1910) 13·00 22·00
74 1s. green and black (1905) 15·00 11·00
75 1s. black/*green* (1909) 2·75 4·50
76 5s. green and carmine (1905) 30·00 70·00
77 5s. green and red/*yellow* (1907) 35·00 48·00
64/77 *Set of* 14 £100 £160
65, 67, 69, 71/2, 72*ab* and 75/7 Optd "Specimen" *Set of* 9 £170

12

13

14

15

2/6 2/6 ST. LUCIA

16

(Typo D.L.R.)

1912–20. *Wmk Mult Crown CA. Chalk-surfaced paper* (*3d. t[o] 5s.*) *P* 14.

78 12 ½d. deep green 60 4[…]
a. Yellow-green (1916) 55 3[…]
79 1d. carmine-red 1·90 1[…]
a. Scarlet (1916) 3·00 1[…]
b. Rose-red 2·50 4[…]
80 13 2d. grey 1·50 4·0[…]
a. Slate-grey (1916) 9·00 10·0[…]
81 12 2½d. ultramarine 2·25 2·7[…]
a. Bright blue (1918) 1·75 2·7[…]
b. Deep bright blue 7·00 7·5[…]

82 **15** 3d. purple/*yellow* . . . . . . 60 2·00
a. On pale yellow (Die I) . . . . 5·00 9·00
b. On pale yellow (Die II) . . . . 5·00 17·00
83 **14** 4d. black and red/*yellow* . . . . 90 1·75
a. White back (Optd S. £25) . . . . 60 1·50
84 **15** 6d. dull and bright purple . . . . 2·00 6·50
a. Grey-purple and purple (1918) . . 11·00 14·00
85 1s. black/*green* . . . . . . 2·50 4·25
a. On blue-green, olive back . . . . 3·75 6·00
86 1s. orange-brown (1920) . . . . 4·25 24·00
87 **16** 2s. 6d. black and red/*blue* . . . . 14·00 20·00
88 **15** 5s. green and red/*yellow* . . . . 18·00 55·00
78/88 . . . . . . *Set of* 11 42·00 £110
78/88 Optd "Specimen" . . . . *Set of* 11 £170

(17)

WAR TAX
(18)

1916 (June). *No. 79a optd locally with T* **17**.
89 **12** 1d. scarlet . . . . 3·25 3·25
a. Opt double £350 £375
b. Carmine . . . . . . 28·00 25·00

For the overprinting with Type **17** the top margin of the sheet was folded beneath the top row of stamps so that marginal examples from this row show an inverted albino impression of the overprint in the top margin.

1916 (Sept). *No. 79a optd in London with T* **18**.
90 **12** 1d. scarlet (Optd S. £40) 15 15

1921–26. *Wmk Mult Script CA. Chalk-surfaced paper* (3*d*. (*No.* 100) *to* 5*s*.) *P* 14.
91 **12** ½d. green 20 15
92 1d. rose-carmine . . . . . . 2·75 8·00
93 1d. deep brown (1922) 20 15
94 **14** 1½d. dull carmine (1922) 40 90
95 **13** 2d. slate-grey 20 15
96 **12** 2½d. bright blue . . . . . . 1·50 2·00
97 2½d. orange (1925) . . . . . . 5·50 26·00
98 2½d. dull blue (1926) . . . . . . 90 2·50
99 **15** 3d. bright blue (1922) . . . . 3·75 13·00
a. Dull blue (1926) . . . . . . 1·00 9·00
100 3d. purple/*yellow* (1926) . . . . 55 3·75
a. Deep purple/yellow . . . . 4·00 10·00
101 **14** 4d. black and red/*yellow* (1924) . . 80 2·50
102 **15** 6d. grey-purple and purple . . . . 1·25 4·75
103 1s. orange-brown . . . . . . 1·75 4·00
104 **16** 2s. 6d. black and red/*blue* (1924) . . 15·00 25·00
105 **15** 5s. green and red/*pale yellow* (1923) . . 27·00 50·00
91/105 . . . . . . *Set of* 15 50·00 £120
91/105 Optd "Specimen" . . . . *Set of* 15 £200

1935 (6 May). *Silver Jubilee. As Nos. 114/17 of Jamaica, but ptd by D.L.R. P* 13½×14.
109 ½d. black and green 15 25
f. Diagonal line by turret . . . . 17·00
110 2d. ultramarine and grey 45 25
111 2½d. brown and deep blue 90 65
f. Diagonal line by turret . . . . 38·00
g. Dot to left of chapel . . . . 38·00
112 1s. slate and purple . . . . . . 3·00 3·75
h. Dot by flagstaff . . . . . . 75·00
109/12 . . . . . . *Set of* 4 4·00 4·50
109/12 Perf "Specimen" . . . . *Set of* 4 75·00

For illustrations of plate varieties see Omnibus section following Zimbabwe.

19 Port Castries

20 Columbus Square, Castries

21 Ventine Falls

25 The Badge of the Colony

(Recess D.L.R.)

1936 (1 Mar-Apr). *T* **19/21**, **25** *and similar designs. Wmk Mult Script CA. P* 14 *or* 13 × 12 (1*s. and* 10*s*.).
113 **19** ½d. black and bright green 20 45
a. Perf 13 × 12 (8.4.36) . . . . 50 3·50
114 **20** 1d. black and brown 25 10
a. Perf 13 × 12 (8.4.36) . . . . 1·40 2·50
115 **21** 1½d. black and scarlet 55 30
a. Perf 12 × 13 . . . . . . 5·00 1·75
116 **19** 2d. black and grey 25 15
117 **20** 2½d. black and blue 30 15
118 **21** 3d. black and dull green . . . . 1·25 70
119 **19** 4d. black and red-brown . . . . 30 1·00
120 **20** 6d. black and orange . . . . 65 1·00
121 – 1s. black and light blue . . . . 70 2·00
122 – 2s. 6d. black and ultramarine . . 3·50 13·00
123 – 5s. black and violet . . . . 8·00 20·00
124 **25** 10s. black and carmine . . . . 40·00 50·00
113/124 . . . . . . *Set of* 12 50·00 80·00
113/24 Perf "Specimen" . . . . *Set of* 12 £180

Designs: *Vert* (*as T* **21**) 2s. 6d. Inniskilling monument. *Horiz* (*as T* **19**) 1s. Fort Rodney, Pigeon Island; 5s. Government House.

1937 (12 May). *Coronation. As Nos. 118/20 of Jamaica, but ptd by B.W. P* 11×11½.
125 1d. violet 20 15
126 1½d. carmine 30 15
127 2½d. blue 30 15
125/7 . . . . . . *Set of* 3 70 40
125/7 Perf "Specimen" . . . . *Set of* 3 55·00

26 King George VI

27 Columbus Square

28 Government House

31 Device of St. Lucia

(Des E. Crafer (T **26**), H. Fleury (5s.). Recess Waterlow (½d. to 3½d., 8d., 3s., 5s., £1), D.L.R. (6d., 1s.) and B.W. (2s., 10s.))

1938 (22 Sept)–**48**. *T* **26/8**, **31** *and similar designs. Wmk Mult Script CA* (*sideways on* 2*s*.).
128 **26** ½d. green (*p* 14½ × 14) 45 10
a. Perf 12½ (1943) 10 10
129 1d. violet (*p* 14½ × 14) 90 20
a. Perf 12½ (1938) 10 15
129*b* 1d. scarlet (*p* 12½) (1947) 10 10
c. Perf 14½ × 14 (1948) 10 10
130 1½d. scarlet (*p* 14½ × 14) 65 10
a. Perf 12½ (1943) 10 30
131 2d. grey (*p* 14½ × 14) 15 30
a. Perf 12½ (1943) 10 10
132 2½d. ultramarine (*p* 14½ × 14) . . 50 10
a. Perf 12½ (1943) 10 10
132*b* 2½d. violet (*p* 12½) (1947) 10 10
133 3d. orange (*p* 14½ × 14) 10 10
a. Perf 12½ (1943) 10 10
133*b* 3½d. ultramarine (*p* 12½) (1947) . . 30 15
134 **27** 6d. claret (*p* 13½) 35 40
a. Carmine-lake (*p* 13½) (1945) . . 1·50 35
b. Perf 12. *Claret* (1948) 40 45
134*c* **26** 8d. brown (*p* 12½) (1946) . . . . 1·25 30
135 **28** 1s. brown (*p* 13½) 15 30
a. Perf 12 (1948) 30 20
136 – 2s. blue and purple (*p* 12) . . . . 3·25 1·25
136*a* **26** 3s. bright purple (*p* 12½) (1946) . . 8·00 2·75
137 – 5s. black and mauve (*p* 12½) . . 8·00 4·00
138 **31** 10s. black/*yellow* (*p* 12) . . . . 3·50 9·00
141 **26** £1 sepia (*p* 12½) (1946) . . . . 11·00 8·00
128a/141 . . . . . . *Set of* 17 32·00 24·00
128/41 Perf "Specimen" . . . . *Set of* 17 £300

Designs: *Horiz* (*as T* **28**): 2s. The Pitons; 5s. Loading bananas.

1946 (8 Oct). *Victory. As Nos. 141/2 of Jamaica.*
142 1d. lilac 10 10
143 3½d. blue 10 10
142/3 Perf "Specimen" . . . . *Set of* 2 50·00

1948 (26 Nov). *Royal Silver Wedding. As Nos. 143/4 of Jamaica.*
144 1d. scarlet 15 10
145 £1 purple-brown . . . . . . 11·00 30·00

(New Currency. 100 cents=1 West Indian dollar)

32 King George VI

33 Device of St. Lucia

(Recess Waterlow (**32**), B.W. (**33**))

1949 (1 Oct)–**50**. *Value in cents or dollars. Wmk Mult Script CA. P* 12½ (1 *c. to* 16 *c*.), 11 × 11½ (*others*).
146 **32** 1 c. green 10 10
a. Perf 14 (1949) 75 40
147 2 c. magenta 10 10
a. Perf 14½ × 14 (1949) . . . . 1·50 1·00
148 3 c. scarlet 10 20
149 4 c. grey 10 10
a. Perf 14½ × 14 . . . . . . † £4500
150 5 c. violet 10 10
151 6 c. orange 10 20
152 7 c. ultramarine 50 30
153 12 c. claret 90 15
a. Perf 14½ × 14 (1950) £325 £190
154 16 c. brown 75 15
155 **33** 24 c. light blue 30 10
156 48 c. olive-green . . . . . . 1·50 50
157 $1.20, purple . . . . . . 2·25 4·00
158 $2.40, blue-green . . . . . . 3·00 14·00
159 $4.80, rose-carmine . . . . 7·00 18·00
146/159 . . . . . . *Set of* 14 15·00 35·00

1949 (10 Oct). *75th Anniv of U.P.U. As Nos. 145/8 of Jamaica.*
160 5 c. violet 15 15
161 6 c. orange 35 25
162 12 c. magenta 25 20
163 24 c. blue-green 50 20
160/3 . . . . . . *Set of* 4 1·10 70

1951 (16 Feb). *Inauguration of B.W.I. University College. As Nos. 149/50 of Jamaica.*
164 3 c. black and scarlet 20 10
165 12 c. black and deep carmine 20 10

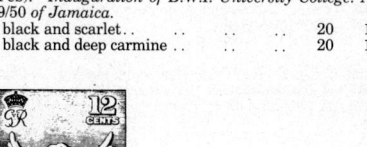

34 Phoenix rising from Burning Buildings

NEW 1951 CONSTITUTION
(35)

(Flames typo, rest recess B.W.)

1951 (19 June). *Reconstruction of Castries. Wmk Mult Script CA. P* 13½ × 13.
166 **34** 12 c. red and blue 15 30

1951 (25 Sept). *New Constitution. Optd with T* **35** *by Waterlow. P* 12½.
167 **32** 2 c. magenta 10 15
168 4 c. grey 10 15
169 5 c. violet 10 15
170 12 c. claret 10 25
167/70 . . . . . . *Set of* 4 30 60

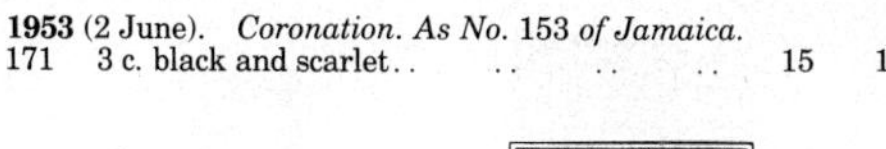

1953 (2 June). *Coronation. As No. 153 of Jamaica.*
171 3 c. black and scarlet 15 10

36 Queen Elizabeth II

37 Device of St. Lucia

(Recess Waterlow (T **36**), until 1960, then D.L.R. B.W. (T **37**))

1953 (28 Oct)–**63**. *Wmk Mult Script CA. P* 14½×14 (*T* **36**) *or* 11×11½ (*T* **37**)
172 **36** 1 c. green (1.4.54) 10 10
173 2 c. magenta 10 10
174 3 c. red (2.9.54) 10 10
175 4 c. slate (7.1.54) 10 10
176 5 c. violet (1.4.54) 10 10
a. Slate-violet (19.2.63) . . . . 1·75 60
177 6 c. orange (2.9.54) 15 10
a. Brown-orange (26.9.61) . . . . 1·25 10
178 8 c. lake (2.9.54) 10 10
179 10 c. ultramarine (2.9.54) 10 10
a. Blue (14.8.62) 20 10
180 15 c. red-brown (2.9.54) 30 10
a. Brown (30.10.57) 30 10
181 **37** 25 c. deep turquoise-blue (2.9.54) . . 20 10
182 50 c. deep olive-green (2.9.54) . . 3·50 35
183 $1 bluish green (2.9.54) . . . . 3·25 85
184 $2.50, carmine (2.9.54) . . . . 4·50 3·00
172/84 . . . . . . *Set of* 13 11·00 4·00

1958 (22 Apr). *Inauguration of British Caribbean Federation. As Nos. 175/7 of Jamaica.*
185 3 c. deep green 30 15
186 6 c. blue 55 65
187 12 c. scarlet 70 55
185/7 . . . . . . *Set of* 3 1·40 1·25

MINISTERIAL GOVERNMENT

38 Columbus's *Santa Maria* off the Pitons

39 Stamp of 1860

(Recess Waterlow)

1960 (1 Jan). *New Constitution for the Windward and Leeward Islands. W w* **12**. *P* 13.
188 **38** 8 c. carmine-red 25 15
189 10 c. red-orange 25 15
190 25 c. deep blue 35 20
188/90 . . . . . . *Set of* 3 75 45

(Eng H. Bard. Recess Waterlow)

1960 (18 Dec). *Stamp Centenary. W* w **12**. *P* 13½.

191	**39**	5 c. rose-red and ultramarine	10	10
192		16 c. deep blue and yellow-green	15	25
193		25 c. green and carmine-red	15	10
191/3		*Set of* 3	35	40

1963 (4 June). *Freedom from Hunger. As No.* 80 *of Lesotho.*

194	25 c. bluish green	30	10

1963 (2 Sept). *Red Cross Centenary. As Nos.* 203/4 *of Jamaica.*

195	4 c. red and black	15	10
196	25 c. red and blue	40	70

40 Queen Elizabeth II (after A. C. Davidson-Houston) **41**

42 Fishing Boats

43 Castries Harbour

44 Vigie Beach

45 Queen Elizabeth II

(Des V. Whiteley. Photo Harrison)

1964 (1 Mar)–**69**. *Designs as T* **40/5**, *W* w **12**. *P* 14½ (*T* **40**), *others* 14½×14 (*vert*) *or* 14×14½ (*horiz*).

197	1 c. crimson	10	10
198	2 c. bluish violet	30	10
199	4 c. turquoise-green	35	10
	a. Deep turquoise (5.8.69)	50	50
200	5 c. Prussian blue	30	10
201	6 c. yellow-brown	45	10
202	8 c. multicoloured	10	10
203	10 c. multicoloured	40	10
204	12 c. multicoloured	15	10
205	15 c. multicoloured	20	10
206	25 c. multicoloured	20	10
207	35 c. blue and buff	1·25	10
208	50 c. multicoloured	1·10	10
209	$1 multicoloured	1·25	25
210	$2.50, multicoloured	2·00	1·50
197/210	*Set of* 14	7·00	2·00

Designs:—1 to 6 c. Type **40**; 8, 10 c. Type **41**. *Horiz as T* **42/3**—15 c. Pigeon Island; 25 c. Reduit Beach; 50 c. The Pitons.

See also No. 249.

1964 (23 Apr). 400*th Birth Anniv of William Shakespeare. As No.* 156 *of Montserrat.*

211	10 c. blue-green	10	10

1965 (17 May). *I.T.U. Centenary. As Nos.* 98/9 *of Lesotho.*

212	2 c. mauve and magenta	10	10
213	50 c. lilac and light olive-green	90	35

1965 (25 Oct). *International Co-operation Year. As Nos.* 100/1 *of Lesotho.*

214	1 c. reddish purple and turquoise-green	10	10
215	25 c. deep bluish green and lavender	20	20

1966 (24 Jan). *Churchill Commemoration. As Nos.* 102/5 *of Lesotho.*

216	4 c. new blue	10	10
217	6 c. deep green	15	10
218	25 c. brown	20	15
219	35 c. bluish violet	30	20
216/19	*Set of* 4	65	45

1966 (4 Feb). *Royal Visit. As Nos.* 183/4 *of Montserrat.*

220	4 c. black and ultramarine	10	10
221	25 c. black and magenta	40	25

1966 (1 July). *World Cup Football Championship, England. As Nos.* 57/8 *of Pitcairn Islands.*

222	4 c. violet, yellow-green, lake & yellow-brn	10	10
223	25 c. chocolate, blue-green, lake & yellow-brn	30	20

1966 (20 Sept). *Inauguration of W.H.O. Headquarters, Geneva. As Nos.* 185/6 *of Montserrat.*

224	4 c. black, yellow-green and light blue	10	10
225	25 c. black, light purple and yellow-brown	25	20

1966 (1 Dec). 20*th Anniv of U.N.E.S.C.O. As Nos.* 342/4 *of Mauritius.*

226	4 c. slate-violet, red, yellow and orange	10	10
227	12 c. orange-yellow, violet and deep olive	20	15
228	25 c. black, bright purple and orange	35	30
226/8	*Set of* 3	60	45

ASSOCIATED STATEHOOD

STATEHOOD 1st MARCH 1967 (49)

STATEHOOD 1st MARCH 1967 (50)

51 Map of St. Lucia

(Optd by Art Printery, Castries from dies supplied by Harrison. Photo Harrison (No. 240))

1967 (7 Mar). *Statehood.* (*a*) *Postage. Nos.* 198 *and* 200/9 *optd with T* **49** (2, 5, 6 *c.*) *or T* **50** (*others*) *in red.*

229	2 c. bluish violet	20	15
	a. Horiz pair, one without opt		
230	5 c. Prussian blue	10	10
	a. Opt inverted	45·00	
231	6 c. yellow-brown	10	10
232	8 c. multicoloured	20	10
233	10 c. multicoloured	25	10
234	12 c. multicoloured	20	10
235	15 c. multicoloured	25	30
236	25 c. multicoloured	30	30
237	35 c. blue and buff	50	35
238	50 c. multicoloured	50	55
239	$1 multicoloured	50	55
229/39	*Set of* 11	2·75	2·25

(*b*) *Air. P* 14½ × 14.

240	**51**	15 c. new blue	10	10

Overprinted 1 c. and $2.50 stamps were prepared for issue but were not put on sale over the post office counter. Later, however, they were accepted for franking (*Price for set of* 2 £6 *mint*, £11 *used*).

52 "Madonna and Child with the Infant Baptist" (Raphael)

53 Batsman and Sir Frederick Clarke (Governor)

(Des and photo Harrison)

1967 (16 Oct). *Christmas. W* w **12** (*sideways*). *P* 14½.

241	**52**	4 c. multicoloured	10	10
242		25 c. multicoloured	20	10

(Des V. Whiteley. Photo Harrison)

1968 (8 Mar). *M.C.C.'s West Indies Tour. W* w **12** (*sideways*). *P* 14½ × 14.

243	**53**	10 c. multicoloured	20	15
244		35 c. multicoloured	45	40

54 "The Crucified Christ with the Virgin Mary, Saints and Angels" (Raphael)

55 "Noli me tangere" (detail by Titian)

(Des and photo Harrison)

1968 (25 Mar). *Easter. W* w **12** (*sideways*). *P* 14 × 14½.

245	**54**	10 c. multicoloured	10	10
246	**55**	15 c. multicoloured	10	10
247	**54**	25 c. multicoloured	15	10
248	**55**	35 c. multicoloured	15	10
		a. Yellow (sunset) omitted	£140	
245/8		*Set of* 4	40	20

1968 (14 May)*. *As No.* 205 *but W* w **12** (*sideways*).

249	15 c. multicoloured	15	15

*This is the London release date. Stamps from this printing were available some months earlier on St. Lucia.

56 Dr. Martin Luther King

57 "Virgin and Child in Glory" (Murillo)

(Des V. Whiteley. Litho D.L.R.)

1968 (4 July). *Martin Luther King Commemoration. W* w **12**. *P* 13½ × 14.

250	**56**	25 c. blue, black and flesh	10	10
251		35 c. violet-black, black and flesh	10	10

(Des and photo Harrison)

1968 (17 Oct). *Christmas. Paintings. T* **57** *and similar vert design. Multicoloured. W* w **12** (*sideways*). *P* 14½ × 14.

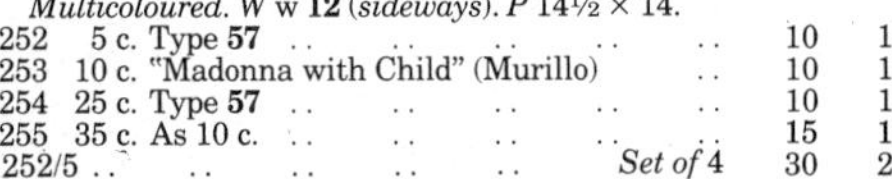

252	5 c. Type **57**	10	10
253	10 c. "Madonna with Child" (Murillo)	10	10
254	25 c. Type **57**	10	10
255	35 c. As 10 c.	15	10
252/5	*Set of* 4	30	20

59 Purple-throated Carib

(Des V. Whiteley. Litho Format)

1969 (10 Jan). *Birds. T* **59** *and similar horiz design. Multicoloured. W* w **12** (*sideways*). *P* 14.

256	10 c. Type **59**	45	20
257	15 c. St. Lucia Amazon	55	25
258	25 c. Type **59**	75	30
259	35 c. As 15 c.	90	30
256/9	*Set of* 4	2·40	95

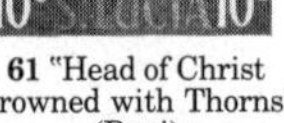

61 "Head of Christ Crowned with Thorns" (Reni)

62 "Resurrection of Christ" (Sodoma)

(Des and photo Harrison)

1969 (20 Mar). *Easter. W* w **12** (*sideways*). *P* 14½ × 14.

260	**61**	10 c. multicoloured	10	10
261	**62**	15 c. multicoloured	10	10
262	**61**	25 c. multicoloured	10	10
263	**62**	35 c. multicoloured	10	10
260/3		*Set of* 4	30	30

63 Map showing "CARIFTA" Countries

(Des J. Cooter. Photo Harrison)

1969 (29 May). *First Anniv of CARIFTA* (*Caribbean Free Trade Area*). *T* **63** *and similar horiz designs. Multicoloured. W* w **12**. *P* 14.

264	5 c. Type **63**	10	10
265	10 c. Type **63**	10	10
266	25 c. Handclasp and names of CARIFTA countries	10	10
267	35 c. As 25 c.	10	10
264/7	*Set of* 4	30	30

65 Emperor Napoleon and Empress Josephine

66 "Virgin and Child" (P. Delaroche)

(Des and litho Enschedé)

1969 (22 Sept). *Birth Bicentenary of Napoleon Bonaparte. P* 14 × 13.

268	**65**	15 c. multicoloured	10	10
269		25 c. multicoloured	10	10
270		35 c. multicoloured	10	10
271		50 c. multicoloured	15	15
268/71		*Set of* 4	30	30

(Des J. W. Photo Harrison)

1969 (27 Oct). *Christmas. Paintings. T* **66** *and similar vert design. Multicoloured. W* w **12** *(sideways). P* 14½ × 14.

272	5 c. Type **66**	10	10
273	10 c. "Holy Family" (Rubens)	10	10
274	25 c. Type **66**	10	10
275	35 c. As 10 c.	10	10
272/5	*Set of* 4	30	30

68 House of Assembly

69 "The Sealing of the Tomb" (Hogarth)

(Des J. Cooter ($10), Sylvia and M. Goaman (others). Litho Questa ($10), Format (others))

1970 (2 Feb)–**73**. *T* **68** *and similar designs. Multicoloured. W* w **12** *(sideways on* 1 *c. to* 35 *c. and* $10). *P* 14.

276	1 c. Type **68**	10	10
277	2 c. Roman Catholic Cathedral	10	10
278	4 c. The Boulevard, Castries	15	10
279	5 c. Castries Harbour	15	10
280	6 c. Sulphur springs	15	10
281	10 c. Vigie Airport	20	10
282	12 c. Reduit Beach	20	10
283	15 c. Pigeon Island	25	10
284	25 c. The Pitons and yacht	40	10
285	35 c. Marigot Bay	40	10
286	50 c. Diamond Waterfall (*vert*)	70	60
287	$1 Flag of St. Lucia (*vert*)	75	70
288	$2.50, St. Lucia Coat of Arms (*vert*)	1·50	1·75
289	$5 Queen Elizabeth II (*vert*)	3·25	4·75
289*a*	$10 Map of St. Lucia (*vert*) (3.12.73)	9·00	11·00
276/89*a*	*Set of* 15	15·00	17·00

See also Nos. 367/8 and 395/8.

(Des V. Whiteley. Litho Enschedé)

1970 (7 Mar). *Easter. Triptych by Hogarth. T* **69** *and similar multicoloured designs. W* w **12** *(sideways). Roul.* 9 × *P* 12½.

290	25 c. Type **69**	15	20
	a. Strip of 3. Nos. 290/2	55	
291	35 c. "The Three Marys at the Tomb"	15	20
292	$1 "The Ascension" (39 × 55 *mm*)	30	40
290/2	*Set of* 3	55	70

Nos. 290/2 were issued in sheets of 30 (6 × 5) containing the Hogarth Triptych spread over all three values of the set. This necessitated a peculiar arrangement with the $1 value (which depicts the centre portion of the triptych) 10 mm higher than the other values in the *se-tenant* strip.

72 Charles Dickens and Dickensian Characters

(Des V. Whiteley. Litho B.W.)

1970 (8 June). *Death Centenary of Charles Dickens. W* w **12** *(sideways). P* 14.

293	**72**	1 c. multicoloured	10	10
294		25 c. multicoloured	10	10
295		35 c. multicoloured	15	10
296		50 c. multicoloured	20	20
293/6		*Set of* 4	40	30

73 Nurse and Emblem

(Des R. Granger Barrett. Litho J.W.)

1970 (18 Aug). *Centenary of British Red Cross. T* **73** *and similar horiz design. Multicoloured. W* w **12** *(sideways). P* 14.

297	10 c. Type **73**	10	10
298	15 c. Flags of Great Britain, Red Cross and St. Lucia	15	10
299	25 c. Type **73**	25	10
300	35 c. As 15 c.	30	10
297/300	*Set of* 4	65	30

74 "Madonna with the Lilies" (Luca della Robbia)

75 "Christ on the Cross" (Rubens)

(Des P. B. Litho and embossed Walsall)

1970 (16 Nov). *Christmas. P* 11.

301	**74**	5 c. multicoloured	10	10
302		10 c. multicoloured	10	10
303		35 c. multicoloured	20	10
304		40 c. multicoloured	20	15
301/4		*Set of* 4	45	30

(Des and litho Enschedé)

1971 (29 Mar). *Easter. T* **75** *and similar vert design. Multicoloured. W* w **12**. *P* 13½ × 13.

305	10 c. Type **75**	10	10
306	15 c. "Descent from the Cross" (Rubens)	10	10
307	35 c. Type **75**	20	10
308	40 c. As 15 c.	20	15
305/8	*Set of* 4	45	30

76 Moule à Chique Lighthouse

(Des J. W. Litho Questa)

1971 (1 May). *Opening of Beane Field Airport. T* **76** *and similar horiz design. Multicoloured. W* w **12** *(sideways). P* 14½ × 14.

309	5 c. Type **76**	20	15
310	25 c. Aircraft landing at Beane Field	35	15

77 Morne Fortune

78 Morne Fortune, Modern View

(Des V. Whiteley. Litho Questa)

1971 (10 Aug.). *Old and New Views of St. Lucia. T* **77/8** *and similar horiz designs. Multicoloured. W* w **12** *(sideways). P* 13½ × 13.

311	5 c. Type **77**	10	10
312	5 c. Type **78**	10	10
313	10 c. } Castries city	10	10
314	10 c. }	10	10
315	25 c. } Pigeon Island	20	20
316	25 c. }	20	20
317	50 c. } View from grounds of Govt House	40	40
318	50 c. }	40	40
311/18	*Set of* 8	1·25	1·25

Each value of this issue was printed horizontally and vertically *se-tenant* in two designs showing respectively old and new views of St. Lucia.

The old views are taken from paintings by J. H. Caddy.

79 "Virgin and Child with Two Angels" (Verrocchio)

80 "St. Lucia" (Dolci School) and Coat of Arms

(Des J. Cooter. Litho J.W.)

1971 (15 Oct). *Christmas. T* **79** *and similar vert designs. Multicoloured. W* w **12**. *P* 14.

319	5 c. Type **79**	10	10
320	10 c. "Virgin and Child, St. John the Baptist and an Angel" (Morando)	10	10
321	35 c. "Madonna and Child" (Battista)	15	10
322	40 c. Type **79**	20	25
319/22	*Set of* 4	40	40

(Des and litho Harrison)

1971 (13 Dec). *National Day. W* w **12**. *P* 14 × 14½.

323	**80**	5 c. multicoloured	10	10
324		10 c. multicoloured	10	10
325		25 c. multicoloured	20	10
326		50 c. multicoloured	40	30
323/6		*Set of* 4	60	40

81 "The Dead Christ Mourned" (Carracci)

(Des G. Drummond. Litho Questa)

1972 (15 Feb). *Easter. T* **81** *and similar horiz design. Multicoloured. W* w **12**. *P* 14.

327	10 c. Type **81**	10	10
328	25 c. "Angels weeping over the dead Christ" (Guercino)	20	10
329	35 c. Type **81**	30	10
330	50 c. As 25 c.	40	40
327/30	*Set of* 4	85	45

82 Science Block and Teachers' College

(Des P. Powell. Litho Questa)

1972 (18 Apr). *Morne Educational Complex. T* **82** *and similar horiz designs. Multicoloured. W* w **12**. *P* 14.

331	5 c. Type **82**	10	10
332	15 c. University Centre	10	10
333	25 c. Secondary School	10	10
334	35 c. Technical College	15	10
331/4	*Set of* 4	30	30

83 Steamship Stamp and Map

Des J. Cooter. Litho Questa)

1972 (22 June). *Centenary of First Postal Service by St. Lucia Steam Conveyance Co Ltd. T* **83** *and similar horiz designs. W* w **12**. *P* 14.

335	5 c. multicoloured	15	10
336	10 c. ultramarine, mauve and black	20	10
337	35 c. light rose-carmine, pale greenish blue and black	45	10
338	50 c. multicoloured	1·00	1·00
335/8	*Set of* 4	1·60	1·00

Designs:—10 c. Steamship stamp and Castries Harbour; 35 c. Steamship stamp and Soufrière; 50 c. Steamship stamps.

84 "The Holy Family" (Sebastiano Ricci)

(Des J. Cooter. Litho J.W.)

1972 (18 Oct). *Christmas. W* w **12** *(sideways). P* 14½.
339 **84** 5 c. multicoloured 10 10
340 10 c. multicoloured 10 10
341 35 c. multicoloured 20 10
342 40 c. multicoloured 25 15
339/42 .. .. *Set of* 4 50 30

85 Arms and St. Lucia Amazon **86** Week-day Headdress

(Des (from photograph by D. Groves) and photo Harrison)

1972 (20 Nov). *Royal Silver Wedding. Multicoloured; background colour given. W* w **12**. *P* 14 × 14½.
343 **85** 15 c. carmine 20 10
344 35 c. yellow-olive 20 10

(Des Sylvia Goaman. Litho A. & M.)

1973 (1 Feb). *Local Headdresses. T* **86** *and similar vert designs. Multicoloured. W* w **12**. *P* 13.
345 5 c. Type **86** 10 10
346 10 c. Formal style 10 10
347 25 c. Unmarried girl's style 10 10
348 50 c. Ceremonial style 20 20
345/8 .. .. *Set of* 4 30 30

87 Coat of Arms **88** H.M.S. *St. Lucia*, 1803

(Des and litho Harrison)

1973–76. *Coil Stamps. P* 14½ × 14.
A. *W* w **12** *upright* (19.4.73). B. *W* w **12** *sideways* (1976).

			A		B	
349	**87**	5 c. olive-green	10	15	30	50
350		10 c. new blue	15	15	30	50
351		25 c. lake-brown	15	20	†	
349/51		.. .. *Set of* 3	35	45		

For 10 c. value watermarked w **16** see No. 953.

(Des R. Granger Barrett. Litho Questa)

1973 (24 May). *Historic Ships. T* **88** *and similar horiz designs. Multicoloured. W* w **12**. *P* 13½ × 14.
352 15 c. Type **88** 15 10
353 35 c. H.M.S. *Prince of Wales*, 1765 .. .. 20 10
354 50 c. *Oliph Blossom*, 1605 .. .. .. 30 15
355 $1 H.M.S. *Rose*, 1757 .. .. .. 45 55
352/5 .. .. *Set of* 4 1·00 70
MS356 122 × 74 mm. Nos. 352/5 .. .. .. 1·00 2·75

89 Plantation and Flower **90** "The Virgin with Child" (Maratta)

(Des PAD Studio. Litho Walsall)

1973 (26 July). *Banana Industry. T* **89** *and similar horiz designs. Multicoloured. W* w **12**. *P* 14.
357 5 c. Type **89** 10 10
358 15 c. Aerial spraying 15 10
359 35 c. Boxing plant 20 10
360 50 c. Loading a boat 40 40
357/60 .. .. *Set of* 4 75 45

(Des J. Cooter. Litho Walsall)

1973 (17 Oct). *Christmas. T* **90** *and similar vert designs. Multicoloured. W* w **12** *(sideways). P* 13½.
361 5 c. Type **90** 10 10
362 15 c. "Madonna in the Meadow" (Raphael) .. 10 10
363 35 c. "The Holy Family" (Bronzino) 15 10
364 50 c. "Madonna of the Pear" (Dürer) 20 25
361/4 .. .. *Set of* 4 45 30

1973 (14 Nov). *Royal Wedding. As Nos.* 322/3 *of Montserrat.*
365 40 c. grey-green 10 10
366 50 c. rosy lilac 10 10

1974 (15 Mar). *As Nos.* 277/8 *but wmk upright.*
367 2 c. Roman Catholic Cathedral 60 70
368 4 c. The Boulevard, Castries 80 90

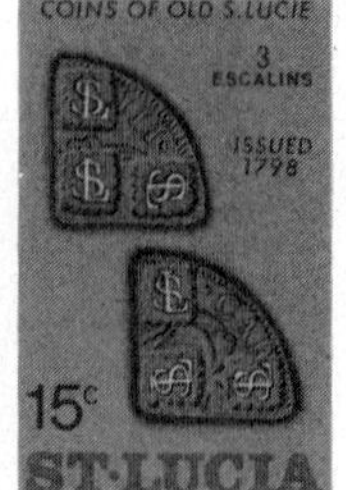

91 "The Betrayal" **92** 3-Escalins Coins, 1798

(Des J. Cooter. Litho D.L.R.)

1974 (1 Apr). *Easter. T* **91** *and similar horiz designs showing paintings by Ugolino da Siena. Multicoloured. W* w **12** *(sideways on Nos.* 369/72, *upright on* **MS**373). *P* 13.
369 5 c. Type **91** 10 10
370 35 c. "The Way to Calvary" 15 10
371 80 c. "The Deposition" 15 15
372 $1 "The Resurrection" 20 25
369/72 .. .. *Set of* 4 50 40
MS373 180 × 140 mm. Nos. 369/72 .. .. 1·25 2·00

(Des J. Cooter. Litho Format)

1974 (20 May). *Coins of Old St. Lucie. T* **92** *and similar vert designs. Multicoloured. W* w **12** *(sideways). P* 14 × 13½.
374 15 c. Type **92** 15 10
375 35 c. 6-escalins coins, 1798 .. .. .. 20 10
376 40 c. 2-livres 5-sols coins, 1813 .. .. 20 10
377 $1 6-livres 15-sols coins, 1813 .. .. 55 65
374/7 .. .. *Set of* 4 1·00 75
MS378 151 × 115 mm. Nos. 374/7 .. .. 1·60 2·50

93 Baron de Laborie **94** "Virgin and Child" (Andrea del Verrocchio)

(Des J. W. Litho Questa)

1974 (29 Aug). *Past Governors of St. Lucia. T* **93** *and similar vert designs. Multicoloured. W* w **12** *(sideways on Nos.* 379/82, *upright on* **MS**383). *P* 14.
379 5 c. Type **93** 10 10
380 35 c. Sir John Moore 10 10
381 80 c. Sir Dudley Hill 15 10
382 $1 Sir Frederick Clarke 25 35
379/82 .. .. *Set of* 4 50 50
MS383 153 × 117 mm. Nos. 379/82 .. .. 50 2·00

(Des PAD Studio. Litho D.L.R.)

1974 (18 Nov). *Christmas. T* **94** *and similar vert designs. Multicoloured. W* w **12**. *P* 13 × 13½.
384 5 c. Type **94** 10 10
385 35 c. "Virgin and Child" (Andrea della Robbia) 10 10
386 80 c. "Madonna and Child" (Luca della Robbia) 15 15
387 $1 "Virgin and Child" (Rossellino) 20 25
384/7 .. .. *Set of* 4 40 40
MS388 92 × 140 mm. Nos. 384/7 .. .. 90 1·75

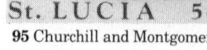

95 Churchill and Montgomery **96** "Christ on the Cross" (School of Van der Weyden)

(Des PAD Studio. Litho Format)

1974 (30 Nov). *Birth Centenary of Sir Winston Churchill. T* **95** *and similar horiz design. Multicoloured. W* w **12** *(sideways). P* 14.
389 5 c. Type **95** 10 10
390 $1 Churchill and Truman 30 35

(Des J. Cooter. Litho Questa)

1975 (27 Mar). *Easter. T* **96** *and similar vert designs. Multicoloured. W* w **12**. *P* 13½.
391 5 c. Type **96** 10 10
392 35 c. "Noli me tangere" (Romano) 10 10
393 80 c. "Calvary" (Gallego) 15 15
394 $1 "Noli me tangere" (Correggio) 20 25
391/4 .. .. *Set of* 4 40 40

1975 (28 July). *As Nos.* 278 *etc. but W* w **14** *(sideways).*
395 4 c. The Boulevard, Castries 90 90
396 5 c. Castries Harbour .. .. .. 1·00 1·00
397 10 c. Vigie Airport .. .. 1·40 1·40
398 15 c. Pigeon Island .. .. 2·00 2·00
395/8 .. .. *Set of* 4 4·75 4·75

97 "Nativity" (French Book of Hours) **98** American Schooner *Hanna*

1975 (12 Dec). *Christmas. T* **97** *and similar vert designs. Multicoloured. W* w **12**. *P* 14½.
399 5 c. Type **97** 10 10
400 10 c. } Epiphany scene 10 10
401 10 c. } (stained-glass window) .. 10 10
402 10 c. } .. 10 10
403 40 c. "Nativity" (Hastings Book of Hours) .. 30 20
404 $1 "Virgin and Child with Saints" (Borgognone) 70 50
399/404 .. .. *Set of* 6 1·25 90
MS405 105 × 109 mm. Nos. 399 and 403/4 .. 75 1·00

Nos. 400/2 were printed horizontally *se-tenant* within the sheet to form the composite design listed.

(Des J. W. Litho Format)

1976 (26 Jan). *Bicentenary of American Revolution. T* **98** *and similar horiz designs showing ships. Multicoloured. P* 14½.
406 ½ c. Type **98** 10 10
407 1 c. Mail Packet *Prince of Orange* 10 10
408 2 c. H.M.S. *Edward* 10 10
409 5 c. Merchantman *Millern* 30 10
410 15 c. American lugger *Surprise* 60 10
411 35 c. H.M.S. *Serapis* .. .. 1·10 20
412 50 c. American frigate *Randolph* .. .. 1·25 40
413 $1 American frigate *Alliance* .. .. 2·25 1·00
406/13 .. .. *Set of* 8 5·00 1·75
MS414 142 × 116 mm. Nos. 410/13. P 13 .. 3·50 4·50

99 Laughing Gull **100** H.M.S. *Ceres*

(Des J.W. Litho Questa)

1976 (17 May)–**79**. *Birds. T* **99** *and similar vert designs. Multicoloured. Ordinary paper. W* w **12** (1 c.) *or* w **14** *(others). P* 14.
415 1 c. Type **99** 20 40
416 2 c. Little Blue Heron 30 40
417 4 c. Belted Kingfisher 35 40
418 5 c. St. Lucia Amazon .. .. 1·25 40
419 6 c. St. Lucia Oriole .. .. 1·25 50
420 8 c. Brown Trembler .. .. 1·25 50
421 10 c. American Kestrel .. .. 1·25 35
422 12 c. Red-billed Tropic Bird .. .. .. 1·25 55
423 15 c. Moorhen .. .. 1·25 15
424 25 c. Common Noddy .. .. 1·25 45
a. Chalk-surfaced paper (7.79) .. .. 1·00 30
425 35 c. Sooty Tern .. .. 1·75 55
a. Chalk-surfaced paper (1979) .. .. 2·50 2·75
426 50 c. Osprey .. .. 3·25 1·00
427 $1 White-breasted Trembler .. .. .. 3·25 1·10
428 $2.50, St. Lucia Black Finch .. .. .. 3·50 3·25
429 $5 Red-necked Pigeon .. .. .. 4·25 3·50
430 $10 Caribbean Elaenia .. .. .. 6·00 7·50
a. Chalk-surfaced paper (7.79) .. .. 6·00 7·50
415/30 .. .. *Set of* 16 28·00 19·00

1976 (19 July). *West Indian Victory in World Cricket Cup. As Nos.* 419/20 *of Jamaica.*
431 50 c. Caribbean map .. .. 1·00 1·00
432 $1 Prudential Cup .. .. 1·50 2·25
MS433 92 × 79 mm. Nos. 431/2 .. .. .. 3·25 4·25

(Des J. Cooter. Litho Walsall)

1976 (4 Sept). *Royal Navy Crests. T* **100** *and similar vert designs. Multicoloured. W w* **14** *(inverted). P* 14.

434 10 c. Type **100** 30 10
435 20 c. H.M.S. *Pelican* 50 10
436 40 c. H.M.S. *Ganges* 75 10
437 $2 H.M.S. *Ariadne* .. .. 1·75 2·00
434/7 .. .. *Set of* 4 3·00 2·00

101 "Madonna and Child" (Murillo) **102** Queen Elizabeth II

(Des J. Cooter. Litho Questa)

1976 (15 Nov). *Christmas. T* **101** *and similar vert designs. Multicoloured. W w* **14**. *P* 13½.

438 10 c. Type **101** 10 10
439 20 c. "Madonna and Child with Angels" (Costa) 10 10
440 50 c. "Madonna and Child Enthroned" (Isenbrandt) 15 10
441 $2 "Madonna and Child with St. John" (Murillo) 50 65
438/41 .. .. *Set of* 4 70 75
MS442 105 × 93 mm. $2.50, As Type **101** .. .. 70 1·25

(Des Daphne Padden. Litho Questa)

1977 (7 Feb). *Silver Jubilee. W w* **14** *(sideways). P* 14.

443 **102** 10 c. multicoloured 10 10
444 20 c. multicoloured 15 15
445 40 c. multicoloured 20 25
446 $2 multicoloured 60 90
443/6 .. .. *Set of* 4 95 1·25
MS447 128 × 95 mm. **102** $2.50 multicoloured .. 60 1·00

Nos. 443/6 were each issued in sheets of five stamps and one label.

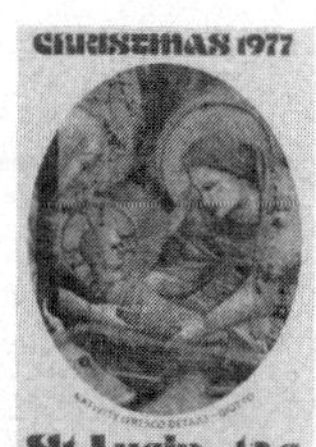

103 Scouts from Tapion School **104** "Nativity" (Giotto)

(Des J. W. Litho Format)

1977 (17 Oct). *Caribbean Boy Scout Jamboree. T* **103** *and similar vert designs. Multicoloured. P* 14½.

448 ½ c. Type **103** 10 10
449 1 c. Sea scouts 10 10
450 2 c. Scout from Micoud 10 10
451 10 c. Two scouts from Tapion School 15 10
452 20 c. Venture scouts 20 15
453 50 c. Scout from Gros Islet 45 35
454 $1 Sea scouts in motor boat 75 90
448/54 .. .. *Set of* 7 1·50 1·50
MS455 75 × 85 mm. $2.50, As $1 .. .. .. 1·50 2·50

(Des J. W. Litho Questa)

1977 (31 Oct). *Christmas. T* **104** *and similar vert designs. Multicoloured. P* 14.

456 ½ c. Type **104** 10 10
457 1 c. "Perugia triptych" (Fra Angelico) .. 10 10
458 2 c. "Virgin and Child" (El Greco) 10 10
459 20 c. "Madonna of the Rosary" (Caravaggio) .. 10 10
460 50 c. "Adoration of the Magi" (Velazquez) .. 20 10
461 $1 "Madonna of Carmel" (Tiepolo) 30 40
462 $2.50, "Adoration of the Magi" (Tiepolo) .. 55 80
456/62 .. .. *Set of* 7 1·10 1·25

105 "Susan Lunden" **106** Yeoman of the Guard and Life Guard

(Des C. Abbott. Litho Harrison)

1977 (28 Nov). *400th Birth Anniv of Rubens. T* **105** *and similar vert designs. Multicoloured. W w* **14** *(sideways). P* 14 × 15.

463 10 c. Type **105** 10 10
464 35 c. "The Rape of the Sabine Women" (detail) 15 10
465 50 c. "Ludovicus Nonnius" 25 10
466 $2.50, "Minerva protects Pax from Mars" (detail) 65 80
463/6 .. .. *Set of* 4 1·00 90
MS467 145 × 120 mm. Nos. 463/6 .. .. 1·00 1·75

(Des J. W. Litho Questa)

1978 (2 June). *25th Anniv of Coronation. T* **106** *and similar horiz designs. Multicoloured. P* 14.

468 15 c. Type **106** 10 10
469 20 c. Groom and postillion 10 10
470 50 c. Footman and coachman 15 10
471 $3 State trumpeter and herald 60 80
468/71 .. .. *Set of* 4 85 90
MS472 114 × 88 mm. $5 Master of the Horse and Gentleman-at-Arms .. .. 1·00 1·25

Nos. 468/71 also exist perf 12 (*Price for set of* 4 95p *mint or used*) from additional sheetlets of 3 stamps and one label. Stamps perforated 14 are from normal sheets of 50.

107 Queen Angelfish

(Des G. Vasarhelyi. Litho Format)

1978 (19 June). *Fishes. T* **107** *and similar horiz designs. Multicoloured. P* 15.

473 10 c. Type **107** 10 10
474 20 c. Foureye Butterflyfish 20 10
475 50 c. French Angelfish 40 20
476 $2 Yellowtail Damselfish .. .. .. 1·00 1·25
473/6 .. .. *Set of* 4 1·40 1·40
MS477 155 × 89 mm. $2.50, Rock Beauty .. 1·60 1·90

Nos. 473/6 exist imperforate from stock dispersed by the liquidator of Format International Security Printers Ltd.

108 French Grenadier and Map of the Battle **109** The Annunciation

(Des J. W. Litho Questa)

1978 (29 Nov). *Bicentenary of Battle of Cul-de-Sac. T* **108** *and similar horiz designs. Multicoloured. P* 14

478 10 c. Type **108** 15 10
479 30 c. British Grenadier officer and map of St. Lucia (Bellin), 1762 .. .. 30 10
480 50 c. Coastline from Gros Islet to Cul-de-Sac and British fleet opposing French landings 40 15
481 $2.50, General James Grant, 1798, and Light Infantrymen of 46th Regiment .. .. 1·50 1·25
478/81 .. .. *Set of* 4 2·10 1·40

(Des Jennifer Toombs. Litho Questa)

1978 (4 Dec). *Christmas. T* **109** *and similar horiz design. Multicoloured. W w* **14**. *P* 14.

482 30 c. Type **109** 10 10
483 50 c. Type **109** 15 10
484 55 c. The Nativity 15 10
485 80 c. As 55 c. 20 20
482/5 .. .. *Set of* 4 55 40

INDEPENDENT

110 Hewanorra International Air Terminal

(Des J. W. Litho Questa)

1979 (22 Feb). *Independence. T* **110** *and similar horiz designs. Multicoloured. W w* **14** *(sideways). P* 14.

486 10 c. Type **110** 10 10
487 30 c. New coat of arms 10 10
488 50 c. Government House and Sir Allen Lewis (first Governor-General) 15 10
489 $2 French, St. Lucia and Union flags on map of St. Lucia 30 45
486/9 .. .. *Set of* 4 50 55
MS490 127 × 80 mm. Nos. 486/9 .. .. .. 50 1·00

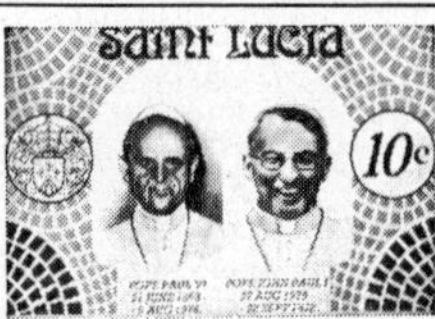

111 Popes Paul VI and John Paul I

(Des J.W. Litho Harrison)

1979 (28 May). *Pope Paul VI Commemoration. T* **111** *and similar horiz designs. Multicoloured. W w* **14** (sideways). *P* 14½ × 14.

491 10 c. Type **111** 10 10
492 30 c. President Sadat of Egypt with Pope Paul 20 10
493 50 c. Pope Paul with Secretary-General U Thant 35 20
494 55 c. Pope Paul and Prime Minister Golda Meir of Israel 40 25
495 $2 Martin Luther King received in audience by Pope Paul .. .. 1·00 80
491/5 .. .. *Set of* 5 1·75 1·25

112 Dairy Farming

(Des G. Drummond. Litho Format)

1979 (2 July). *Agriculture Diversification. T* **112** *and similar horiz designs. Multicoloured. W w* **14** *(sideways). P* 14.

496 10 c. Type **112** 10 10
497 35 c. Fruit and vegetables 10 10
498 50 c. Water conservation 10 10
499 $3 Copra industry 35 50
496/9 .. .. *Set of* 4 50 60

113 Lindbergh and Flying-boat **114** "A Prince of Saxony" (Cranach the Elder)

(Des L. Curtis. Litho Walsall)

1979 (2 Oct). *50th Anniv of Lindbergh's Inaugural Airmail Flight via St. Lucia. T* **113** *and similar horiz designs. W w* **14** *(sideways). P* 14.

500 10 c. black, Indian red and pale orange .. 10 10
501 30 c. multicoloured 10 10
502 50 c. multicoloured 10 10
503 $2 multicoloured 30 40
500/3 .. .. *Set of* 4 50 50

Designs:—30 c. Flying boat and route map; 50 c. Arrival at La Toc, September, 1929; $2 Letters on first flight.

(Litho Questa)

1979 (6 Dec). *International Year of the Child. Paintings. T* **114** *and similar vert designs. Multicoloured. P.* 14.

504 10 c. Type **114** 10 10
505 50 c. "The Infanta Margarita" (Velazquez) .. 15 10
506 $2 "Girl playing Badminton" (Chardin) .. 30 40
507 $2.50, "Mary and Francis Wilcox" (Stock) .. 35 45
504/7 .. .. *Set of* 4 70 80
MS508 113 × 94 mm. $5 "Two Children" (Picasso) 1·10 1·60

115 Notice of Introduction of Penny Post **116** "Madonna and Child" (Bernardino Fungai)

(Des J.W. Litho Questa)

1979 (10 Dec). *Death Centenary of Sir Rowland Hill. T* **115** *and similar vert designs. Multicoloured. P* 14.

509 10 c. Type **115** 10 10
510 50 c. Original stamp sketch 20 10
511 $2 1860 1d. stamp 45 50
512 $2.50, Penny Black stamp 55 60
509/12 .. .. *Set of* 4 1·10 1·10
MS513 111 × 85 mm. $5 Sir Rowland Hill .. 90 1·10

Nos. 509/12 also exist perf 12 (*Price for set of* 4 £1·10 *mint or used*) from additional sheetlets of 5 stamps and one label. Stamps perforated 14 are from normal sheets of 40.

(Des R. Vigurs. Litho Walsall)

1980 (14 Jan). *Christmas* (1979) *and International Year of the Child. T* **116** *and similar vert designs showing "Madonna and Child" paintings by various artists. Multicoloured.* W w **14**. *P* 14.

514 10 c. Type **116** 10 10
515 50 c. Carlo Dolci 25 10
516 $2 Titian 70 40
517 $2.50, Giovanni Bellini 75 50
514/17 *Set of* 4 1·60 95
MS518 94 × 120 mm. Nos. 514/17 1·60 1·60

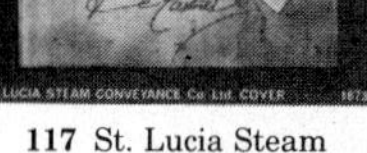

117 St. Lucia Steam Conveyance Company Cover, 1873

118 Mickey Mouse astride Rocket

(Des G. Drummond. Litho Questa)

1980 (6 May). *"London 1980" International Stamp Exhibition. T* **117** *and similar horiz designs. Multicoloured.* W w **14** (*sideways*). *P* 14.

519 10 c. Type **117** 10 10
520 30 c. S.S. *Assistance* 1d. postmark of 1879 10 10
521 50 c. Postage due handstamp of 1929 15 10
522 $2 Crowned-circle paid stamp of 1844 40 55
519/22 *Set of* 4 60 65
MS523 85 × 76 mm. Nos. 519/22 65 90

(Litho Format)

1980 (29 May). *10th Anniv of Moon Landing* (1979). *Walt Disney Cartoon Characters. T* **118** *and similar multicoloured designs showing characters in space scenes. P* 11.

524 ½ c. Type **118** 10 10
525 1 c. Donald Duck being towed by rocket (*horiz*) 10 10
526 2 c. Minnie Mouse on Moon 10 10
527 3 c. Goofy hitching lift to Mars 10 10
528 4 c. Goofy and moondog (*horiz*) 10 10
529 5 c. Pluto burying bone on Moon (*horiz*) 10 10
530 10 c. Donald Duck and love-sick martian (*horiz*) 10 10
531 $2 Donald Duck paddling spaceship (*horiz*) 1·75 1·00
532 $2.50, Mickey Mouse driving moonbuggy (*horiz*) 2·00 1·10
524/32 *Set of* 9 3·75 2·00
MS533 102 × 127 mm. $5 Goofy leaping from space-ship on to Moon. P 13½ 3·00 2·25

119 Queen Elizabeth the Queen Mother

(Litho Questa)

1980 (4 Aug). *80th Birthday of Queen Elizabeth the Queen Mother. P* 14.

534 **119** 10 c. multicoloured 20 10
535 $2.50, multicoloured 1·40 1·50
MS536 85 × 65 mm. **119** $3 multicoloured 1·50 2·10

120 Hawker Siddeley "HS 748"

(Des A. Theobald. Litho Harrison)

1980 (11 Aug). *Transport. Horiz designs as T* **120**. *Multicoloured.* W w **14** (*sideways on* 5 c. *to* $1). *P* 14½ × 14.

537 5 c. Type **120** 25 10
538 10 c. McDonnell Douglas "DC-10" airliner 35 10
539 15 c. Local bus 35 10
540 20 c. Refrigerated freighter 35 10
541 25 c. "Islander" aeroplane 50 10
542 30 c. Pilot boat 40 20
543 50 c. Boeing "727" airliner 65 40
544 75 c. *Cunard Countess* (liner) 65 75
545 $1 Lockheed "Tristar" airliner 85 85
546 $2 Cargo liner 1·25 1·50
547 $5 Boeing "707" airliner 4·50 4·50
548 $10 *Queen Elizabeth 2* (liner) 5·50 6·50
537/48 *Set of* 12 14·00 13·50

For stamps with watermark W w **15** see Nos. 690/8.

121 Shot-putting

122 Coastal Landscape within Cogwheel

(Des M. Diamond. Litho Questa)

1980 (22 Sept). *Olympic Games, Moscow. T* **121** *and similar horiz designs. Multicoloured. P* 14.

549 10 c. Type **121** 10 10
550 50 c. Swimming 15 10
551 $2 Gymnastics 60 50
552 $2.50, Weight-lifting 70 60
549/52 *Set of* 4 1·40 1·10
MS553 108 × 83 mm. $5 Athletes with Olympic Torch 1·25 1·40

(Des BG Studio. Litho Questa)

1980 (30 Sept). *75th Anniv of Rotary International. T* **122** *and similar vert designs showing different coastal landscapes within cogwheels. P* 14.

554 10 c. multicoloured 10 10
555 50 c. multicoloured 15 10
556 $2 greenish black, carmine & greenish yell 40 40
557 $2.50, multicoloured 50 55
554/7 *Set of* 4 1·00 1·00
MS558 103 × 106 mm. $5 multicoloured 1·50 1·75

123 Sir Arthur Lewis

(Des J. W. Litho Questa)

1980 (23 Oct). *Nobel Prize Winners. T* **123** *and similar vert designs. Multicoloured. P* 14.

559 10 c. Type **123** 10 10
560 50 c. Martin Luther King Jnr. 20 15
561 $2 Ralph Bunche 50 60
562 $2.50, Albert Schweitzer 70 80
559/62 *Set of* 4 1·25 1·40
MS563 115 × 91 mm. $5 Albert Einstein 1·75 2·00

1980
HURRICANE

$1.50 RELIEF

(124)

1980 (3 Nov). *Hurricane Relief. Nos.* 539/40 *and* 543 *surch with T* **124**.

564 $1.50 on 15 c. Local bus 30 40
565 $1.50 on 20 c. Refrigerated freighter 30 40
566 $1.50 on 50 c. Boeing "727" airliner 30 40
564/6 *Set of* 3 80 1·10

125 "The Nativity" (Giovanni Battista)

126 Brazilian Agouti

(Des J. Cooter. Litho Questa)

1980 (1 Dec). *Christmas. Paintings. T* **125** *and similar vert designs. Multicoloured.* W w **14**. *P* 14 × 13½.

567 10 c. Type **125** 10 10
568 30 c. "Adoration of the Kings" (Pieter the Elder) 10 10
569 $2 "Adoration of the Shepherds" (ascribed to Murillo) 40 60
567/9 *Set of* 3 50 60
MS570 102 × 88 mm. $1 × 3, Angel with people of St. Lucia (*composite design*) (*each* 30 × 75 *mm*). P 14½ × 14 65 90

(Des G. Drummond. Litho Questa)

1981 (19 Jan). *Wildlife. T* **126** *and similar vert designs. Multicoloured. P* 14.

571 10 c. Type **126** 15 10
572 50 c. St. Lucia Amazon 75 10
573 $2 Purple-throated Carib 1·00 80
574 $2.50, Fiddler Crab 1·10 1·00
571/4 *Set of* 4 2·75 1·75
MS575 103×87 mm. $5 *Danaus plexippus* (butterfly) 2·40 2·50

127 Prince Charles at Balmoral

128 Lady Diana Spencer

(Des J. W. Litho Questa)

1981 (23 June). *Royal Wedding. T* **127** *and similar vert designs. Multicoloured. P* 14.

576 25 c. Prince Charles and Lady Diana Spencer 15 10
577 50 c. Clarence House 20 10
578 $4 Type **127** 75 80
576/8 *Set of* 3 1·00 90
MS579 96 × 82 mm. $5 Glass Coach and coachman 1·25 1·00

Nos. 576/8 also exist perforated 12 (*price for set of* 3 £1 *mint or used*) from additional sheetlets of five stamps and one label. These stamps have changed background colours.

(Manufactured by Walsall)

1981 (23 June). *Royal Wedding. Booklet stamps. T* **128** *and similar vert designs. Multicoloured. Roul* 5 × *imperf** *Self-adhesive.*

580 50 c. Type **128** 15 30
a. Booklet pane. Nos. 580/1 each × 3 1·75
581 $2 Prince Charles 50 80
582 $5 Prince Charles and Lady Diana Spencer 1·75 2·50
a. Booklet pane of 1 1·75
580/2 *Set of* 3 2·25 3·25

*The 50 c. and $2 values were each separated by various combinations of rotary knife (giving a straight edge) and roulette. The $5 value exists only with straight edges.

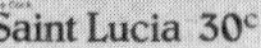

129 "The Cock"

130 "Industry"

(Des J.W. Litho Questa)

1981 (20 July). *Birth Centenary of Picasso. T* **129** *and similar vert designs. Multicoloured. P* 13½ × 14.

583 30 c. Type **129** 25 10
584 50 c. "Man with an Ice-Cream" 35 10
585 55 c. "Woman dressing her Hair" 35 10
586 $3 "Seated Woman" 95 85
583/6 *Set of* 4 1·75 1·00
MS587 128 × 102 mm. $5 "Night Fishing at Antibes" 2·00 2·50

(Des Walsall. Litho Format)

1981 (28 Sept). *25th Anniv of Duke of Edinburgh Award Scheme. T* **130** *and similar vert designs. Multicoloured.* W w **14**. *P* 14½.

588 10 c. Type **130** 10 10
589 35 c. "Community service" 15 10
590 50 c. "Physical recreation" 20 10
591 $2.50, Duke of Edinburgh speaking at Caribbean Conference, 1975 70 70
588/91 *Set of* 4 1·00 75

131 Louis Braille

132 "Portrait of Fanny Travis Cochran" (Cecilia Beaux)

(Des J.W. Litho Questa)

1981 (10 Nov). *International Year for Disabled Persons. Famous Disabled People. T* **131** *and similar horiz designs. Multicoloured. P* 14.

592 10 c. Type **131** 15 10
593 50 c. Sarah Bernhardt 30 15
594 $2 Joseph Pulitzer .. .. 1·00 90
595 $2.50, Henri de Toulouse-Lautrec .. .. 1·10 1·00
592/5 .. .. *Set of* 4 2·25 1·90
MS596 115 × 90 mm. $5 Franklin Delano Roosevelt .. .. 2·50 2·25

(Des BG Studio. Litho Questa)

1981 (1 Dec). *Decade for Women. Paintings. T* **132** *and similar vert designs. Multicoloured. P* 14.

597 10 c. Type **132** 10 10
598 50 c. "Women with Dove" (Marie Laurencin) 35 15
599 $2 "Portrait of a Young Pupil of David" (Aimee Duvivier) .. .. 1·00 90
600 $2.50, "Self-portrait" (Rosalba Carriera) .. 1·10 1·00
597/600 .. .. *Set of* 4 2·25 1·90
MS601 104 × 78 mm. $5 "Self-portrait" (Elizabeth Vigee-le-Brun) .. .. 3·00 2·50

133 "The Adoration of the Magi" (Sfoza)

134 1860 1d. Stamp

(Des BG Studio. Litho Format)

1981 (15 Dec). *Christmas Paintings. T* **133** *and similar vert designs. Multicoloured. W* w **14**. *P* 14.

602 10 c. Type **133** 15 10
603 30 c. "The Adoration of the Kings" (Orcanga) 30 10
604 $1.50, "The Adoration of the Kings" (Gerard) 1·10 60
605 $2.50, "The Adoration of the Kings" (Foppa) 1·75 1·25
602/5 .. .. *Set of* 4 3·00 1·75

(Des J.W. Litho Questa)

1981 (29 Dec). *First Anniv of U.P.U. Membership. T* **134** *and similar horiz designs. Multicoloured. P* 14.

606 10 c. Type **134** 15 10
607 30 c. 1969 First anniversary of Caribbean Free Trade Area 25 c. commemorative .. 35 10
608 50 c. 1979 Independence $2 commemorative 50 40
609 $2 U.P.U. emblem with U.P.U. and St. Lucia flags .. .. 1·60 2·25
606/9 .. .. *Set of* 4 2·40 2·50
MS610 128 × 109 mm. $5 U.P.U. Headquarters, Berne, and G.P.O. Building, Castries .. .. 3·00 2·50

135 Scene from Football Match

(Des Clover Mill. Litho Format)

1982 (15 Feb). *World Cup Football Championship, Spain. T* **135** *and similar horiz designs showing scenes from different matches. P* 15.

611 10 c. multicoloured 20 10
612 50 c. multicoloured 70 15
613 $2 multicoloured .. .. 1·75 90
614 $2.50, multicoloured .. .. 2·00 1·00
611/14 .. .. *Set of* 4 4·25 1·90
MS615 104 × 84 mm. $5 multicoloured .. .. 3·00 2·25

136 Pigeon Island National Park

137 Map-reading

(Des J. Cooter. Litho Format)

1982 (13 Apr). *Bicentenary of Battle of the Saints. T* **136** *and similar horiz designs. Multicoloured. W* w **14**. *P* 14.

616 10 c. Type **136** 25 15
617 35 c. Battle scene 80 15
618 50 c. Rodney (English admiral) and De Grasse (French admiral) .. .. 1·10 35
619 $2.50, Map of the Saints, Martinique and St. Lucia .. .. 3·25 3·50
616/19 .. .. *Set of* 4 5·00 3·75
MS620 125 × 75 mm. Nos. 616/19 .. .. .. 5·50 5·50

(Litho Questa)

1982 (4 Aug). *75th Anniv of Boy Scout Movement. T* **137** *and similar vert designs. Multicoloured. W* w **14**. *P* 14.

621 10 c. Type **137** 10 10
622 50 c. First Aid practice 30 15
623 $1.50, Camping 75 80
624 $2.50, Campfire singsong .. .. 1·25 1·50
621/4 .. .. *Set of* 4 2·25 2·25

138 Leeds Castle

139 "Adoration of the Kings" (detail, Jan Brueghel)

(Des PAD Studio. Litho Questa)

1982 (1 Sept). *21st Birthday of Princess of Wales. T* **138** *and similar vert designs. Multicoloured. P* 14½ × 14.

625 50 c. Type **138** 30 20
626 $2 Princess Diana boarding aircraft .. 90 75
627 $4 Wedding .. .. 1·60 1·40
625/7 .. .. *Set of* 3 2·50 2·10
MS628 102 × 75 mm. $5 Princess of Wales .. 2·00 2·00

(Des PAD Studio. Litho Harrison)

1982 (10 Nov). *Christmas. T* **139** *and similar vert designs depicting details from paintings. Multicoloured. W* w **14**. *P* 14.

629 10 c. Type **139** 10 10
630 30 c. "Nativity" (Lorenzo Costa) 15 10
631 50 c. "Virgin and Child" (Fra Filippo Lippi) .. 25 15
632 80 c. "Adoration of the Shepherds" (Nicolas Poussin) 40 55
629/32 .. .. *Set of* 4 75 75

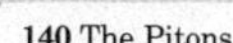

140 The Pitons

141 Crown Agents Headquarters, Millbank, London

(Des D. Bowen. Litho Questa)

1983 (14 Mar). *Commonwealth Day. T* **140** *and similar horiz designs. Multicoloured. W* w **14** (*sideways*). *P* 14.

633 10 c. Type **140** 10 10
634 30 c. Tourist beach 15 10
635 50 c. Banana harvesting 20 15
636 $2 Flag of St. Lucia .. .. 60 1·00
633/6 .. .. *Set of* 4 85 1·10

(Des L. Curtis. Litho Questa)

1983 (1 Apr). *150th Anniv of Crown Agents. T* **141** *and similar vert designs. Multicoloured. W* w **14**. *P* 14.

637 10 c. Type **141** 10 10
638 15 c. Road construction 10 10
639 50 c. Road network map 20 25
640 $2 First St. Lucia stamp .. .. 60 1·00
637/40 .. .. *Set of* 4 80 1·25

142 Communications at Sea

(Des J.W. Litho Format)

1983 (12 July). *World Communications Year. T* **142** *and similar horiz designs. Multicoloured. P* 14½.

641 10 c. Type **142** 15 10
642 50 c. Communications in the air 40 15
643 $1.50, T.V. transmission via satellite .. 90 75
644 $2.50, Computer communications .. .. 1·40 1·25
641/4 .. .. *Set of* 4 2·50 2·00
MS645 107 × 88 mm. $5 Weather satellite .. .. 2·50 2·75

143 Longspine Squirrelfish

(Des G. Drummond. Litho Format)

1983 (23 Aug). *Coral Reef Fishes. T* **143** *and similar horiz designs. Multicoloured. P* 14½.

646 10 c. Type **143** 10 10
647 50 c. Banded Butterflyfish 20 15
648 $1.50, Blackbar Soldierfish 70 75
649 $2.50, Yellowtail Snapper .. .. .. 1·10 1·25
646/9 .. .. *Set of* 4 1·90 2·00
MS650 122 × 97 mm. $5 Red Hind .. .. .. 2·50 3·00

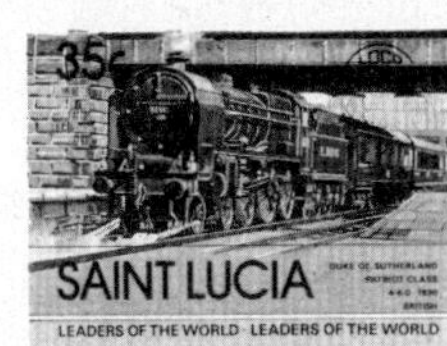

144 *Duke of Sutherland* (1930)

145 "The Niccolini-Cowper Madonna"

(Des J.W. Litho Format)

1983 (14 Oct). *Leaders of the World. Railway Locomotives (1st series). T* **144** *and similar horiz designs, the first in each pair showing technical drawings and the second the locomotive at work. P* 12½.

651 35 c. multicoloured 25 20
a. Vert pair. Nos. 651/2 .. .. 50 40
652 35 c. multicoloured 25 20
653 35 c. multicoloured 25 20
a. Vert pair. Nos. 653/4 .. .. 50 40
654 35 c. multicoloured 25 20
655 50 c. multicoloured 35 30
a. Vert pair. Nos. 655/6 .. .. 70 60
656 50 c. multicoloured 35 30
657 50 c. multicoloured 35 30
a. Vert pair. Nos. 657/8 .. .. 70 60
658 50 c. multicoloured 35 30
659 $1 multicoloured 70 50
a. Vert pair. Nos. 659/60 .. .. .. 1·40 1·00
660 $1 multicoloured 70 50
661 $1 multicoloured 70 50
a. Vert pair. Nos. 661/2 .. .. 1·40 1·00
662 $1 multicoloured 70 50
663 $2 multicoloured 90 80
a. Vert pair. Nos. 663/4 .. .. 1·75 1·60
664 $2 multicoloured 90 80
665 $2 multicoloured 90 80
a. Vert pair. Nos. 665/6 .. .. 1·75 1·60
666 $2 multicoloured 90 80
651/66 .. .. *Set of* 16 8·00 6·50

Designs:—Nos. 651/2, *Duke of Sutherland*, Great Britain (1930); 653/4, *City of Glasgow*, Great Britain (1940); 655/6, *Lord Nelson*, Great Britain (1926); 657/8, *Leeds United*, Great Britain (1928); 659/60, *Bodmin*, Great Britain (1945); 661/2, *Eton*, Great Britain (1930); 663/4, *Flying Scotsman*, Great Britain (1923); 665/6, *Rocket*, Great Britain (1829).

Nos. 651/2, 653/4, 655/6, 657/8, 659/60, 661/2, 663/4 and 665/6 were printed together, *se-tenant*, in vertical pairs throughout the sheets.

See also Nos. 715/26, 761/76, 824/31 and 858/73.

(Litho Format)

1983 (21 Nov). *Christmas. 500th Birth Anniv of Raphael. T* **145** *and similar vert designs showing details of Raphael paintings. Multicoloured. W* w **14**. *P* 14.

667 10 c. Type **145** 10 10
668 30 c. "The Holy Family with a Palm Tree" .. 20 10
669 50 c. "The Sistine Madonna" 35 20
670 $5 "The Alba Madonna" .. .. 2·50 2·25
667/70 .. .. *Set of* 4 2·75 2·25

146 George III

147 Clarke & Co's Drug Store

(Des Court House Studio. Litho Format)

1984 (13 Mar). *Leaders of the World. British Monarchs. T* **146** *and similar vert designs. Multicoloured. P* 12½.

671 5 c. Battle of Waterloo 10 10
a. Horiz pair. Nos. 671/2 .. .. 10 10
672 5 c. Type **146** 10 10
673 10 c. George III at Kew 10 10
a. Horiz pair. Nos. 673/4 .. .. 15 15
674 10 c. Kew Palace 10 10
675 35 c. Coat of Arms of Elizabeth I 20 20
a. Horiz pair. Nos. 675/6 .. .. 40 40
676 35 c. Elizabeth I 20 20
677 60 c. Coat of Arms of George III 30 30
a. Horiz pair. Nos. 677/8 .. .. 60 60
678 60 c. George III (*different*) 30 30
679 $1 Elizabeth I at Hatfield 40 40
a. Horiz pair. Nos. 679/80 .. .. 80 80

680 $1 Hatfield Palace 40 40
681 $2.50, Spanish Armada 75 75
a. Horiz pair. Nos. 681/2 .. .. .. 1·50 1·50
682 $2.50, Elizabeth I (*different*) 75 75
671/82 .. .. *Set of* 12 3·00 3·00

Nos. 671/2, 673/4, 675/6, 677/8, 679/80 and 681/2 were printed together in *se-tenant* horizontal pairs throughout the sheets.

Unissued 30, 50 c., $1, $2.50 and $5 values, showing Alfred the Great or Richard I, exist from stock dispersed by the liquidator of Format International Security Printers Ltd.

(Des J. Cooter. Litho Questa)

1984 (6 Apr). *Historic Buildings. T* **147** *and similar multi-coloured designs. W w* **15** *(sideways on* 45 *c. to* $2.50). *P* 14 × 13½ (10 *c.) or* 13½ × 14 *(others).*
683 10 c. Type **147** 10 10
684 45 c. Colonial architecture (*horiz*) 30 25
685 65 c. Colonial "chattel" house (*horiz*) 45 35
686 $2.50, Treasury after 1906 earthquake (*horiz*) 1·75 1·60
683/6 .. .. *Set of* 4 2·40 2·00

1984 (15 May). *As Nos.* 540/42, 545/6 *and* 548, *but W w* **15** *(sideways on* 20 *c. to* $1). *P* 14½ × 14.
690 20 c. Refrigerator ship 65 20
691 25 c. "Islander" aeroplane 75 25
692 30 c. Pilot boat 85 30
695 $1 Lockheed "Tristar" airliner .. .. 2·00 80
696 $2 Cargo liner .. .. 3·00 2·50
698 $10 *Queen Elizabeth 2* (liner) .. .. 8·50 11·00
690/8 .. .. *Set of* 6 14·00 13·50

148 Logwood

(Des J. Cooter. Litho Format)

1984 (12 June). *Forestry Resources. T* **148** *and similar multi-coloured designs. W w* **15** *(inverted on* 65 *c., sideways on others). P* 14 × 13½ (65 *c.) or* 13½ × 14 *(others).*
699 10 c. Type **148** 15 10
700 45 c. Calabash 60 30
701 65 c. Gommier (*vert*) 80 55
702 $2.50, Raintree .. .. 2·25 2·75
699/702 .. .. *Set of* 4 3·50 3·25

IMPERFORATES AND MISSING COLOURS. Various issues between Nos. 703 and 893 exist either imperforate or with colours omitted. Such items are not listed as there is no evidence that they fulfil the criteria outlined on page xi of this catalogue.

149 Bugatti Type "57SC Atlantic Coupe"

(Des J.W. Litho Format)

1984 (25 June). *Leaders of the World. Automobiles (1st series). T* **149** *and similar horiz designs, the first in each pair showing technical drawings and the second paintings. P* 12½.
703 5 c. black, reddish lavender and lemon .. 10 10
a. Vert pair. Nos. 703/4 .. .. .. 10 10
704 5 c. multicoloured 10 10
705 10 c. black, azure and rose-carmine 10 10
a. Vert pair. Nos. 705/6 .. .. .. 15 15
706 10 c. multicoloured 10 10
707 $1 black, pale green and orange-brown .. 35 35
a. Vert pair. Nos. 707/8 .. .. .. 70 70
708 $1 multicoloured 35 35
709 $2.50, black, pale flesh and slate-blue .. 60 60
a. Vert pair. Nos. 709/10 .. .. .. 1·10 1·10
710 $2.50, multicoloured 60 60
703/10 .. .. *Set of* 8 1·75 1·75

Designs:—Nos. 703/4, Bugatti Type "57SC Atlantic Coupe"; 705/6, Chevrolet "Bel Air Convertible"; 707/8, Alfa Romeo "1750 GS (Zagato)"; 709/10, Duesenberg "S J Roadster".

Nos. 703/4, 705/6, 707/8 and 709/10 were printed together, *se-tenant*, in vertical pairs throughout the sheets.

See also Nos. 745/60, 789/96 and 902/13.

150 Pygmy Gecko

151 Men's Volleyball

(Des Jennifer Toombs. Litho Format)

1984 (8 Aug). *Endangered Wildlife. T* **150** *and similar horiz designs. Multicoloured. W w* **15** *(sideways). P* 14.
711 10 c. Type **150** 40 10
712 45 c. Maria Island Ground Lizard .. .. 1·00 50
713 65 c. Green Iguana .. .. 1·25 85
714 $2.50, Couresse Snake .. .. .. 3·00 3·50
711/14 .. .. *Set of* 4 5·00 4·50

(Des J.W. Litho Format)

1984 (21 Sept). *Leaders of the World. Railway Locomotives (2nd series). Horiz designs as T* **144**, *the first in each pair showing technical drawings and the second the locomotive at work. P* 12½.
715 1 c. multicoloured 10 10
a. Vert pair. Nos. 715/16 .. .. .. 10 10
716 1 c. multicoloured 10 10
717 15 c. multicoloured 15 15
a. Vert pair. Nos. 717/18 .. .. .. 30 30
718 15 c. multicoloured 15 15
719 50 c. multicoloured 30 30
a. Vert pair. Nos. 719/20 .. .. .. 60 60
720 50 c. multicoloured 30 30
721 75 c. multicoloured 35 35
a. Vert pair. Nos. 721/2 .. .. .. 70 70
722 75 c. multicoloured 35 35
723 $1 multicoloured 40 40
a. Vert pair. Nos. 723/4 .. .. .. 80 80
724 $1 multicoloured 40 40
725 $2 multicoloured 70 70
a. Vert pair. Nos. 725/6 .. .. .. 1·40 1·40
726 $2 multicoloured 70 70
715/26 .. .. *Set of* 12 4·00 4·00

Designs:—Nos. 715/16, *Taw*, Great Britain (1897); 717/18, "Crocodile 1.C.C.1." type, Switzerland (1920); 719/20, *The Countess*, Great Britain (1903); 721/2, Class "GE6/6 C.C.", Switzerland (1921); 723/4, Class "P8", Germany (1906); 725/6, *Der Adler*, Germany (1835).

Nos. 715/26 were issued in a similar sheet format to Nos. 651/66.

Nos. 715/26 exist imperforate from stock dispersed by the liquidator of Format International Security Printers Ltd.

(Des Court House Studio. Litho Format)

1984 (21 Sept). *Leaders of the World. Olympic Games, Los Angeles. T* **151** *and similar vert designs. Multicoloured. P* 12½.
727 5 c. Type **151** 10 10
a. Horiz pair. Nos. 727/8 .. .. .. 10 10
728 5 c. Women's volleyball 10 10
729 10 c. Women's hurdles 10 10
a. Horiz pair. Nos. 729/30 .. .. .. 15 15
730 10 c. Men's hurdles 10 10
731 65 c. Show jumping 20 20
a. Horiz pair. Nos. 731/2 .. .. .. 40 40
732 65 c. Dressage 20 20
733 $2.50, Women's gymnastics 50 50
a. Horiz pair. Nos. 733/4 .. .. .. 1·00 1·00
734 $2.50, Men's gymnastics 50 50
727/34 .. .. *Set of* 8 1·50 1·50

Nos. 727/8, 729/30, 731/2, 733/4 were printed together, *se-tenant*, in horizontal pairs throughout the sheets.

Examples of No. 537 exist overprinted "RUMBRIDGE PACK R.F.C./1984 TOUR". This was a private souvenir, connected with a tour to St. Lucia by an English rugby club in October 1984. It was not sold by the St. Lucia Post Office or Philatelic Bureau.

152 Glass of Wine and Flowers **153** Slaves preparing Manioc

(Des G. Vasarhelyi. Litho Format)

1984 (31 Oct). *Christmas. T* **152** *and similar vert designs. Multi-coloured. W w* **15**. *P* 14.
735 10 c. Type **152** 10 10
736 35 c. Priest and decorated altar 20 15
737 65 c. Nativity scene 35 35
738 $3 Holy Family .. .. 1·50 1·60
735/8 .. .. *Set of* 4 1·90 1·90
MS739 147 × 77 mm. Nos. 735/8 .. .. 2·75 3·25

(Des J. Cooter. Litho Format)

1984 (12 Dec). *150th Anniv of Abolition of Slavery. T* **153** *and similar vert designs. Each black and yellow-ochre. W w* **15**. *P* 14 × 13½.
740 10 c. Type **153** 10 10
741 35 c. Sifting and cooking cassava flour .. 15 20
742 55 c. Cooking pot, and preparing tobacco .. 25 30
743 $5 Stripping tobacco leaves for twist tobacco 2·25 2·50
740/3 .. .. *Set of* 4 2·40 2·75
MS744 154 × 110 mm. As Nos. 740/3, but without dates and side inscription and with the face values in different positions .. .. .. 3·25 4·50

(Des Artists International (65 c.), J.W. (others). Litho Format)

1984 (19 Dec). *Leaders of the World. Automobiles (2nd series). Horiz designs as T* **149**, *the first in each pair showing technical drawings and the second paintings. P* 12½.
745 10 c. black, pale green and lake-brown .. 10 10
a. Vert pair. Nos. 745/6 .. .. .. 15 15
746 10 c. multicoloured 10 10
747 30 c. black, azure and bright yellow-green .. 15 15
a. Vert pair. Nos. 747/8 .. .. .. 30 30
748 30 c. multicoloured 15 15
749 55 c. black, greenish yellow and orange-brown 30 30
a. Vert pair. Nos. 749/50 .. .. .. 60 60
750 55 c. multicoloured 30 30
751 65 c. black, grey and brown-lilac 35 35
a. Vert pair. Nos. 751/2 .. .. .. 70 70
752 65 c. multicoloured 35 35
753 75 c. black, pale cinnamon, & orange-verm 35 35
a. Vert pair. Nos. 753/4 .. .. .. 70 70
754 75 c. multicoloured 35 35
755 $1 black, pale cinnamon and dull violet-blue 40 40
a. Vert pair. Nos. 755/6 .. .. .. 80 80
756 $1 multicoloured 40 40
757 $2 black, pale green and orange-red .. 50 50
a. Vert pair. Nos. 757/8 .. .. .. 1·00 1·00
758 $2 multicoloured 50 50
759 $3 black, pale cinnamon & orange-verm 60 60
a. Vert pair. Nos. 759/60 .. .. .. 1·10 1·10
760 $3 multicoloured 60 60
745/60 .. .. *Set of* 16 4·75 4·75

Designs:—Nos. 745/6, Panhard and Levassor; 747/8, N.S.U. "RO-80" Saloon; 749/50, Abarth "Bialbero"; 751/2, TVR "Vixen 2500M"; 753/4, Ford "Mustang" Convertible; 755/6, Ford "Model T"; 757/8, Aston Martin" DB3S"; 759/60, Chrysler "Imperial CG Dual Cowl" Phaeton.

Nos. 745/60 were issued in a similar sheet format to Nos. 703/10.

(Des T. Hadler (5, 15, 35 c.), J.W. (others). Litho Format)

1985 (4 Feb). *Leaders of the World. Railway Locomotives (3rd series). Horiz designs as T* **144**, *the first in each pair showing technical drawings and the second the locomotive at work. P* 12½.
761 5 c. multicoloured 10 10
a. Vert pair. Nos. 761/2 .. .. .. 20 20
762 5 c. multicoloured 10 10
763 15 c. multicoloured 15 10
a. Vert pair. Nos. 763/4 .. .. .. 30 20
764 15 c. multicoloured 15 10
765 35 c. multicoloured 20 20
a. Vert pair. Nos. 765/6 .. .. .. 40 40
766 35 c. multicoloured 20 20
767 60 c. multicoloured 25 25
a. Vert pair. Nos. 767/8 .. .. .. 50 50
768 60 c. multicoloured 25 25
769 75 c. multicoloured 25 25
a. Vert pair. Nos. 769/70 .. .. .. 50 50
770 75 c. multicoloured 25 25
771 $1 multicoloured 30 30
a. Vert pair. Nos. 771/2 .. .. .. 60 60
772 $1 multicoloured 30 30
773 $2 multicoloured 55 55
a. Vert pair. Nos. 773/4 .. .. .. 1·10 1·10
774 $2 multicoloured 55 55
775 $2.50, multicoloured 75 75
a. Vert pair. Nos. 775/6 .. .. .. 1·50 1·50
776 $2.50, multicoloured 75 75
761/76 .. .. *Set of* 16 4·50 4·50

Designs:—Nos. 761/2, Class "C53", Japan (1928); 763/4, Class "Heavy L", India (1885); 765/6, Class "B18¼", Australia (1926); 767/8, *Owain Glyndwr*, Great Britain (1923); 769/70, *Lion*, Great Britain (1838); 771/2, Coal type locomotive, Great Britain (1873); 773/4, No. 2238, Class "Q6", Great Britain (1921); 775/6, Class "H", Great Britain (1920).

Nos. 761/76 were issued in a similar sheet format to Nos. 651/66.

154 Girl Guide Badge in Shield and Crest of St. Lucia **155** *Clossiana selene*

(Des Court House Studio. Litho Questa)

1985 (21 Feb). *75th Anniv of Girl Guide Movement and 60th Anniv of Guiding in St. Lucia. W w* **15**. *P* 14.
777 **154** 10 c. multicoloured 20 10
778 35 c. multicoloured 60 15
779 65 c. multicoloured .. .. .. 1·00 35
780 $3 multicoloured .. .. .. 3·00 1·90
777/80 .. .. *Set of* 4 4·25 2·25

(Des Jennifer Toombs. Litho Format)

1985 (28 Feb). *Leaders of the World. Butterflies. T* **155** *and similar vert designs. Multicoloured. P* 12½.
781 15 c. Type **155** 15 10
a. Horiz pair. Nos. 781/2 .. .. .. 30 20
782 15 c. *Inachis io* 15 10
783 40 c. *Philaethria dido* (s sp *werneckei*) .. 30 30
a. Horiz pair. Nos. 783/4 .. .. .. 60 60
784 40 c. *Callicore sorana* 30 30
785 60 c. *Kallima inachus* 40 40
a. Horiz pair. Nos. 785/6 .. .. .. 80 80
786 60 c. *Hypanartia paullus* 40 40
787 $2.25, *Morpho helena* .. .. .. 1·25 1·25
a. Horiz pair. Nos. 787/8 .. .. .. 2·50 2·50
788 $2.25, *Ornithoptera meridionalis* .. 1·25 1·25
781/8 .. .. *Set of* 8 3·75 3·75

Nos. 781/2, 783/4, 785/6 and 787/8 were printed together, *se-tenant*, in horizontal pairs throughout the sheets.

(Des J.W. Litho Format)

1985 (29 Mar). *Leaders of the World. Automobiles (3rd series). Horiz designs as T* **149**, *the first in each pair showing technical drawings and the second paintings. P* 12½.
789 15 c. black, cobalt and Indian red 10 10
a. Vert pair. Nos. 789/90 .. .. .. 15 20
790 15 c. multicoloured 10 10
791 50 c. black, pale orange and deep rose-red .. 20 25
a. Vert pair. Nos. 791/2 .. .. .. 40 50
792 50 c. multicoloured 20 25
793 $1 black, pale green and reddish orange .. 30 40
a. Vert pair, Nos. 793/4 .. .. .. 60 80
794 $1 multicoloured 30 40
795 $1.50, black, pale green & pale red-brown 40 55
a. Vert pair. Nos. 795/6 .. .. .. 80 1·10
796 $1.50, multicoloured 40 55
789/96 .. .. *Set of* 8 1·75 2·40

Designs:—Nos. 789/90, Hudson "Eight" (1940); 791/2, KdF (1937); 793/4, Kissel "Goldbug" (1925); 795/6, Ferrari "246 GTS" (1973).

Nos. 789/96 were issued in a similar sheet format to Nos. 703/10.

156 Grenadier, 70th Regiment, *c* 1775 **157** Messerschmitt "109-E"

(Des J. Cooter. Litho Format)

1985 (7 May). *Military Uniforms. T* **156** *and similar vert designs. Multicoloured.* W w **15** (*sideways*). *P* 15.

797 5 c. Type **156**.. .. .. 25 15
798 10 c. Officer, Grenadier Company, 14th Regiment, 1780.. .. .. 25 15
799 20 c. Officer, Battalion Company, 46th Regiment, 1781 .. .. 40 15
800 25 c. Officer, Royal Artillery, *c*. 1782 .. 40 15
801 30 c. Officer, Royal Engineers, 1782 .. 60 15
802 35 c. Officer, Battalion Company, 54th Regiment, 1782 .. .. 50 20
803 45 c. Private, Grenadier Company, 14th Regiment, 1782.. .. .. 80 40
804 50 c. Gunner, Royal Artillery, 1796.. .. 80 40
805 65 c. Private, Battalion Company, 85th Regiment, *c*. 1796 .. .. 70 50
806 75 c. Private, Battalion Company, 76th Regiment, 1796 .. .. 75 55
807 90 c. Private, Battalion Company, 81st Regiment, *c*. 1796 .. .. 85 60
808 $1 Sergeant, 74th (Highland) Regiment, 1796 .. .. 90 60
809 $2.50, Private, Light Company, 93rd Regiment, 1803 .. .. 3·50 3·75
810 $5 Private, Battalion Company, 1st West India Regiment, 1803 .. .. .. 6·50 7·50
811 $15 Officer, Royal Artillery, 1850 .. .. .. 11·00 13·00
797/811 .. .. *Set of* 15 25·00 25·00

The 25 c. exists with different imprint dates below the design.

Examples of the 5, 10, 15, 20, 25, 40, 50 c. and $20 with "1986" imprint date, and in some cases imperforate, come from stock dispersed by the liquidator of Format International Security Printers Ltd.

For 5, 10, 30, 45, 50 c., $2.50, $5, and additional values, all without watermark see Nos. 928/46.

For 5, 10, 20, 25 c. and additional values, all watermarked w **16** (sideways) see Nos. 993/1003.

(Des J.W. Litho Format)

1985 (30 May). *Leaders of the World. Military Aircraft. T* **157** *and similar horiz designs, the first in each pair showing paintings and the second technical drawings. P* 12½.

812 5 c. multicoloured 10 10
a. Vert pair. Nos. 812/13 .. .. 10 10
813 5 c. black, pale new blue and pale yellow .. 10 10
814 55 c. multicoloured 40 35
a. Vert pair. Nos. 814/15 .. .. 80 70
815 55 c. black, pale new blue and pale yellow .. 40 35
816 60 c. multicoloured 40 40
a. Vert pair. Nos. 816/17 .. .. 80 80
817 60 c. black, pale new blue and pale yellow .. 40 40
818 $2 multicoloured 80 80
a. Vert pair. Nos. 818/19 .. .. 1·60 1·60
819 $2 black, pale new blue and pale yellow .. 80 80
812/19 .. .. *Set of* 8 3·00 3·00

Designs:—Nos. 812/13, Messerschmitt "109-E"; 814/15, Avro "683 Lancaster Mark I"; 816/17, North American "P.51-D Mustang"; 818/19, Supermarine "Spitfire Mark II".

Nos. 812/13, 814/15, 816/17 and 818/19 were printed together, *se-tenant*, in vertical pairs throughout the sheets.

158 Magnificent Frigate Birds, Frigate Island Bird Sanctuary **159** Queen Elizabeth the Queen Mother

(Des G. Drummond. Litho Format)

1985 (20 June). *Nature Reserves. T* **158** *and similar horiz designs. Multicoloured.* W w **15**. *P* 15.

820 10 c. Type **158**.. .. .. 45 20
821 35 c. Mangrove Cuckoo, Scorpion Island, Savannes Bay .. .. 1·40 45
822 65 c. Lesser Yellowlegs, Maria Island Reserve .. .. 2·00 85
823 $3 Audubon's Shearwaters, Lapins Island Reserve .. .. 4·00 5·00
820/3 .. .. *Set of* 4 7·00 6·00

(Des Tudor Art Agency ($2.50), J.W. (others). Litho Format)

1985 (26 June). *Leaders of the World. Railway Locomotives* (*4th series*). *Horiz designs as T* **144**, *the first in each pair showing technical drawings and second the locomotive at work. P* 12½.

824 10 c. multicoloured 15 10
a. Vert pair. Nos. 824/5 .. .. 30 20
825 10 c. multicoloured 15 10
826 30 c. multicoloured 20 20
a. Vert pair. Nos. 826/7 .. .. 40 40
827 30 c. multicoloured 20 20
828 75 c. multicoloured 30 30
a. Vert pair. Nos. 828/9 .. .. 60 60
829 75 c. multicoloured 30 30
830 $2.50, multicoloured 75 75
a. Vert pair. Nos. 830/1 .. .. 1·50 1·50
831 $2.50, multicoloured 75 75
824/31 .. .. *Set of* 8 2·50 2·50

Designs:—Nos. 824/5, No. 28 tank locomotive, Great Britain (1897); 826/7, No. 1621 Class "M", Great Britain (1893); 828/9, Class "Dunalastair", Great Britain (1896); 830/1, No. 2290 "Big Bertha" type, Great Britain (1919).

Nos. 824/31 were issued in a similar sheet format to Nos. 651/66.

(Des Court House Studio. Litho Format)

1985 (16 Aug). *Leaders of the World. Life and Times of Queen Elizabeth the Queen Mother. Various vertical portraits as T* **159**. *P* 12.

832 40 c. multicoloured 20 25
a. Horiz pair. Nos. 832/3 .. .. 40 50
833 40 c. multicoloured 20 25
834 75 c. multicoloured 30 40
a. Horiz pair. Nos. 834/5 .. .. 60 80
835 75 c. multicoloured 30 40
836 $1.10, multicoloured 40 55
a. Horiz pair. Nos. 836/7 .. .. 80 1·10
837 $1.10, multicoloured 40 55
838 $1.75, multicoloured 65 80
a. Horiz pair. Nos. 838/9 .. .. 1·25 1·60
839 $1.75, multicoloured 65 80
832/9 .. .. *Set of* 8 2·75 3·50
MS840 84 × 114 mm. 42 multicoloured; $2 multicoloured .. .. 1·25 1·75

The two designs of each value were issued, *se-tenant*, in horizontal pairs within the sheets.

Each *se-tenant* pair shows a floral pattern across the bottom of the portraits which stops short of the left-hand edge on the left-hand stamp and of the right-hand edge on the right-hand stamp.

Nos. 832/9, together with two unissued 25 c. designs, exist in miniature sheets, one for each value, from stock dispersed by the liquidator of Format International Security Printers Ltd.

Designs as Nos. 832/3 and 836/7, but with face values of $3 × 2 and $6 × 2, also exist in additional miniature sheets from a restricted printing issued 31 December 1985.

160 "Youth playing Banjo" (Wayne Whitfield) **161** "Papa Jab"

(Litho Format)

1985 (5 Sept). *International Youth Year. Paintings by Young St. Lucians. T* **160** *and similar designs.* W w **15** (*sideways*). *P* 15.

841 10 c. black, new blue and bright magenta .. 10 10
842 45 c. multicoloured 30 25
843 75 c. multicoloured 50 40
844 $3.50, multicoloured .. .. 2·00 1·75
841/4 .. .. *Set of* 4 2·50 2·25
MS845 123 × 86 mm. $5 multicoloured .. .. 2·25 2·75

Designs: *Vert* (*as T* **160**)—45 c. "Motorcyclist" (Mark Maragh); 75 c. "Boy and Girl at Pitons" (Bartholomew Eugene); $3.50, "Abstract" (Lyndon Samuel). *Horiz* (80 × 55 *mm*)—$5 Young people and St. Lucia landscapes.

1985 (26 Oct). *Royal Visit. Nos.* 649, 685/6, 702, 713, 778 *and* 836/7 *optd as T* **114** *of Montserrat.*

846 **154** 35 c. multicoloured .. .. .. 3·50 2·50
847 – 65 c. multicoloured (No. 685) .. .. 3·00 3·00
848 – 65 c. multicoloured (No. 713) .. .. 3·00 3·00
849 – $1.10, multicoloured (No. 836) .. 4·00 4·00
a. Horiz pair. Nos. 849/50 .. .. 8·00 8·00
850 – $1.10, multicoloured (No. 837) .. 4·00 4·00
851 – $2.50, multicoloured (No. 649) .. 4·00 4·00
852 – $2.50, multicoloured (No. 686) .. 3·50 3·50
853 – $2.50, multicoloured (No. 702) .. 3·50 3·50
846/53 .. .. *Set of* 8 26·00 25·00

(Litho Format)

1985 (24 Dec). *Christmas. Masqueraders. T* **161** *and similar vert designs. Multicoloured. P* 15.

854 10 c. Type **161**.. .. .. 10 10
855 45 c. "Paille Bananne" 20 25
856 65 c. "Cheval Bois" 30 35
854/6 .. .. *Set of* 3 50 60
MS857 70 × 83 mm. $4 "Madonna and Child" (Dunstan St. Omer) .. .. 1·75 1·90

(Des T. Hadler. Litho Format)

1986 (27 Jan). *Leaders of the World. Railway Locomotives* (*5th series*). *Horiz designs as T* **144**, *the first in each pair showing technical drawings and the second the locomotive at work. P* 12½.

858 5 c. multicoloured 15 15
a. Vert pair. Nos. 858/9 .. .. 30 30
859 5 c. multicoloured 15 15
860 15 c. multicoloured 15 15
a. Vert pair. Nos. 860/1 .. .. 30 30
861 15 c. multicoloured 15 15
862 30 c. multicoloured 30 30
a. Vert pair. Nos. 862/3 .. .. 60 60
863 30 c. multicoloured 30 30
864 60 c. multicoloured 45 45
a. Vert pair. Nos. 864/5 .. .. 90 90
865 60 c. multicoloured 45 45
866 75 c. multicoloured 50 50
a. Vert pair. Nos. 866/7 .. .. 1·00 1·00
867 75 c. multicoloured 50 50
868 $1 multicoloured 65 65
a. Vert pair. Nos. 868/9 .. .. 1·25 1·25
869 $1 multicoloured 65 65
870 $2.25, multicoloured .. .. 1·25 1·25
a. Vert pair. Nos. 870/1 .. .. 2·50 2·50
871 $2.25, multicoloured .. .. 1·25 1·25
872 $3 multicoloured .. .. 1·60 1·60
a. Vert pair. Nos. 872/3 .. .. 3·00 3·00
873 $3 multicoloured .. .. 1·60 1·60
858/73 .. .. *Set of* 16 9·00 9·00

Designs:—Nos. 858/9, Rack loco *Tip Top*, U.S.A (1983); 860/1, *Stephenson*, Great Britain (1975); 862/3, No. 737 Class "D", Great Britain (1901); 864/5, No. 13 Class "2-CO-2", Great Britain (1922); 866/7, *Electra*, Great Britain (1954); 868/9, *City of Newcastle*, Great Britain (1922); 870/1, Von Kruckenburg propeller-driven rail car, Germany (1930); 872/3, No. 860, Japan (1893).

Nos. 858/73 were issued in a similar sheet format to Nos. 651/66.

162 Campfire Cooking Utensils

(Des Court House Studio. Litho Format)

1986 (3 Mar). *75th Annivs of Girl Guide Movement and Boy Scouts of America. Two sheets, each* 85 × 113 *mm, containing vert designs as T* **162**. *Multicoloured. P* 12½.

MS874 $4 Type **162**: $4 Scout salute .. .. 3·00 3·50
MS875 $6 Wickerwork: $6 Lady Baden-Powell .. 4·00 5·00

The two stamps in each sheet were printed together, *se-tenant*, in horizontal pairs, each forming a composite design.

Nos. **MS**874/5 exist with plain or decorative margins.

Overprints on these miniature sheets commemorating "Capex '87" International Stamp Exhibition, Toronto, were not authorised by the St. Lucia administration.

(Des Court House Studio. Litho Format)

1986 (21 Apr). *60th Birthday of Queen Elizabeth II* (*1st issue*). *Multicoloured designs as T* **117***a of Montserrat. P* 12½.

876 5 c. Queen Elizabeth II 10 10
877 $1 Princess Elizabeth 40 45
878 $3.50, Queen Elizabeth II (*different*) .. 1·10 1·50
879 $6 In Canberra, 1982 (*vert*).. .. .. 1·75 2·25
876/9 .. .. *Set of* 4 3·00 3·75
MS880 85 × 115 mm. $8 Queen Elizabeth II (*different*) .. .. 5·50 6·00

Nos. 876/9 exist in separate miniature sheets from stock dispersed by the liquidator of Format International Security Printers Ltd.

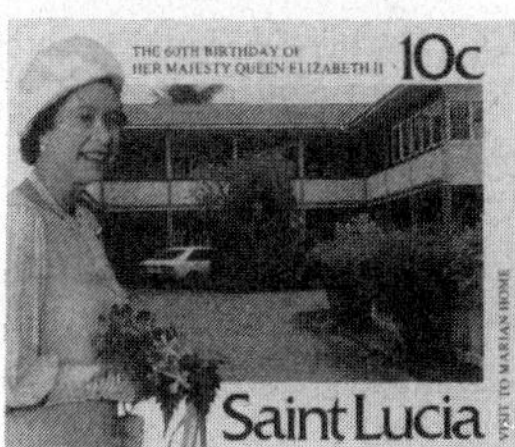

163 Queen Elizabeth and Marian Home

(Des Court House Studio. Litho Questa)

1986 (14 June). *60th Birthday of Queen Elizabeth II* (*2nd issue*). *T* **163** *and similar horiz designs. Multicoloured.* W w **15** (*sideways*). *P* 14 × 15.

881 10 c. Type **163**.. .. .. 15 15
882 45 c. Queen addressing rally, Mindoo Phillip Park, 1985 .. .. 35 35
883 50 c. Queen opening Leon Hess Comprehensive School, 1985 .. .. 40 40
884 $5 Queen Elizabeth and Government House, Castries.. .. .. 2·50 2·75
881/4 .. .. *Set of* 4 3·00 3·25
MS885 121 × 85 mm. $7 Queen Elizabeth and Royal Yacht *Britannia*, Castries.. .. .. 4·00 4·50

164 Pope John Paul II kissing Ground, Castries Airport

(Des Court House Studio. Litho Questa)

1986 (7 July). *Visit of Pope John Paul II. T* **164** *and similar multicoloured designs.* W w **15** (*sideways on* 55, 60 *c.*). *P* 14½ × 14 (80 *c.*) *or* 14 × 14½ (*others*).

886 55 c. Type **164** 70 60
887 60 c. Pope and St. Joseph's Convent . . 70 60
888 80 c. Pope and Castries Catholic Cathedral (*vert*) . . 1·10 95
886/8 . . *Set of* 3 2·25 2·00
MS889 85 × 123 mm. $6 Pope John Paul II (*vert*). P 14½ × 14 . . 5·00 5·50

(Litho Format)

1986 (12 Aug). *Royal Wedding* (1*st issue*). *Multicoloured designs as T* **118a** *of Montserrat. P* 12½.

890 80 c. Miss Sarah Ferguson . . 45 50
a. Pair. Nos. 890/1 . . 90 1·00
891 80 c. Prince Andrew . . 45 50
892 $2 Prince Andrew and Miss Sarah Ferguson (*horiz*) . . 1·25 1·40
a. Pair. Nos. 892/3 . . 2·50 2·75
893 $2 Prince Andrew with Mrs Nancy Reagan (*horiz*) . . 1·25 1·40
890/3 . . *Set of* 4 3·00 3·25

Nos. 890/1 and 892/3 were each printed together, *se-tenant*, in horizontal and vertical pairs throughout the sheets.

165 Peace Corps Teacher with Students

166 Prince Andrew in Carriage

(Des J. Cooter. Litho Questa)

1986 (25 Sept). *25th Anniv of United States Peace Corps. T* **165** *and similar multicoloured designs.* W w **15** (*sideways on* $2). *P* 14.

894 80 c. Type **165** . . 35 40
895 $2 President John Kennedy (*vert*) . . 1·10 1·25
896 $3.50, Peace Corps emblem between arms of St. Lucia and U.S.A. . . 1·60 2·00
894/6 . . *Set of* 3 2·75 3·25

(Des Court House Studio. Litho Format)

1986 (15 Oct). *Royal Wedding* (2*nd issue*). *T* **166** *and similar vert designs. Multicoloured. P* 15.

897 50 c. Type **166** . . 30 30
898 80 c. Miss Sarah Ferguson in coach . . 40 40
899 $1 Duke and Duchess of York at altar . . 45 50
900 $3 Duke and Duchess of York in carriage . . 1·25 1·75
897/900 . . *Set of* 4 2·25 2·75
MS901 115 × 85 mm. $7 Duke and Duchess of York on Palace balcony after wedding (*horiz*) . . 3·50 4·25

Examples of an unissued $10 miniature sheet exist from stock dispersed by the liquidator of Format International Security Printers Ltd.

(Des Court House Studio. Litho Format)

1986 (23 Oct). *Automobiles* (4*th series*). *Horiz designs as T* **149**, *the first in each pair showing technical drawings and the second paintings. P* 12½.

902 20 c. multicoloured . . 10 15
a. Vert pair. Nos. 902/3 . . 15 30
903 20 c. multicoloured . . 10 15
904 50 c. multicoloured . . 15 20
a. Vert pair. Nos. 904/5 . . 30 40
905 50 c. multicoloured . . 15 20
906 60 c. multicoloured . . 15 20
a. Vert pair. Nos. 906/7 . . 30 40
907 60 c. multicoloured . . 15 20
908 $1 multicoloured . . 25 30
a. Vert pair. Nos. 908/9 . . 50 60
909 $1 multicoloured . . 25 30
910 $1.50, multicoloured . . 30 35
a. Vert pair. Nos. 910/11 . . 60 70
911 $1.50, multicoloured . . 30 35
912 $3 multicoloured . . 60 75
a. Vert pair. Nos. 912/13 . . 1·10 1·50
913 $3 multicoloured . . 60 75
902/13 . . *Set of* 12 2·75 3·50

Designs:—Nos. 902/3, AMC "AMX" (1969); 904/5, Russo-Baltique (1912); 906/7, Lincoln "K.B." (1932); 908/9, Rolls Royce "Phantom II Continental" (1933); 910/11, Buick "Century" (1939); 912/13, Chrysler "300 C" (1957).

Nos. 902/13 were issued in a similar sheet format to Nos. 703/10.

167 Chak-Chak Band

(Des Jennifer Toombs. Litho Format)

1986 (7 Nov). *Tourism. T* **167** *and similar horiz designs. Multicoloured.* W w **15**. *P* 15.

914 15 c. Type **167** . . 15 10
915 45 c. Folk dancing . . 35 30
916 80 c. Steel band . . 70 60
917 $5 Limbo dancing . . 2·75 3·00
914/17 . . *Set of* 4 3·50 3·50
MS918 157 × 109 mm. $10 Fire-eating. Wmk sideways . . 6·00 7·00

168 St. Ann Catholic Church, Mon Repos

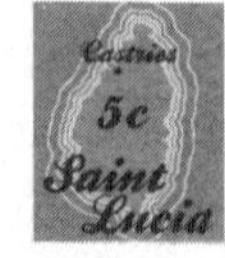

169 Outline Map of St. Lucia

(Litho Format)

1986 (3 Dec). *Christmas. T* **168** *and similar multicoloured designs. P* 15.

919 10 c. Type **168** . . 10 10
920 40 c. St. Joseph the Worker Catholic Church, Gros Islet . . 35 25
921 80 c. Holy Trinity Anglican Church, Castries 60 45
922 $4 Our Lady of the Assumption Catholic Church, Soufriere (*vert*) . . 2·25 2·75
919/22 . . *Set of* 4 3·00 3·25
MS923 120 × 101 mm $7 St. Lucy Catholic Church, Micoud . . 4·00 5·00

(Des L. Curtis. Litho Walsall)

1987 (24 Feb)–**89**. W w **14** (*sideways*). *P* 14. A. *No imprint at foot.* B. *With imprint date.*

		A		B	
924 **169** 5 c. black and cinnamon . .		15	15	20	20
925 10 c. black and pale emerald		15	15	20	20
926 45 c. black & bright orange		45	45	†	
927 50 c. black and violet-blue		45	45	50	50
927c $1 black and bright rose		65	65	†	
924/7c . . *Set of* 5		1·75	1·75	†	

Dates of issue:—24.2.87, Nos. 924A/7A; 9.88, Nos. 924B/5B; 17.3.89, Nos. 927B, 927cA.

For 5 c. and 10 c. watermarked w **16** (sideways) see Nos. 1018/19.

(Des J. Cooter. Litho Format)

1987 (16 Mar). *As Nos.* 797/8, 801, 803/4, 809/10 *and new values* (15, 60, 80 *c. and* $20), *all without wmk. P* 15.

928 5 c. Type **156** . . 20 20
929 10 c. Officer, Grenadier Company, 14th Regiment, 1780 . . 25 25
930 15 c. Private, Battalion Company, 2nd West India Regiment, 1803 . . 35 35
933 30 c. Officer, Royal Engineers, 1782 . . 45 45
935 45 c. Private, Grenadier Company, 14th Regiment, 1782 . . 50 50
936 50 c. Gunner, Royal Artillery, 1796 . . 60 60
937 60 c. Officer, Battalion Company, 5th Regiment, 1778 . . 70 70
940 80 c. Officer, Battalion Company, 27th Regiment, c. 1780 . . 90 90
943 $2.50, Private, Light Company, 93rd Regiment, 1803 . . 3·00 3·25
944 $5 Private, Battalion Company, 1st West India Regiment, 1803 . . 5·50 6·00
946 $20 Private, Grenadier Company, 46th Regiment, 1778 . . 17·00 21·00
928/46 . . *Set of* 11 26·00 30·00

For various values watermarked w **16** (sideways) see Nos. 993/1003.

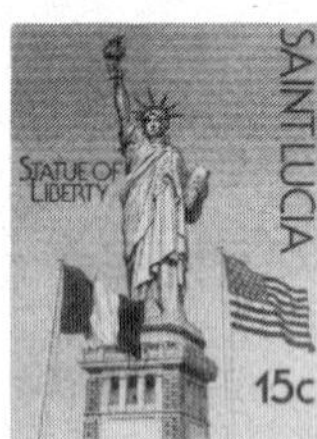

170 Statue of Liberty and Flags of France and U.S.A.

171 First Cadastral Survey Map and Surveying Instruments, 1775

(Des A. Theobald. Litho Format)

1987 (29 Apr). *Centenary of Statue of Liberty* (1986). *T* **170** *and similar vert designs. Multicoloured.* W w **16**. *P* 14½.

947 15 c. Type **170** . . 15 10
948 80 c. Statue and *Mauretania* (liner) . . 75 55
949 $1 Statue and "Concorde" . . 1·10 75
950 $5 Statue and flying boat at sunset . . 3·00 3·50
947/50 . . *Set of* 4 4·50 4·50
MS951 107 × 88 mm. $6 Statue and Manhattan at night. Wmk sideways . . 3·50 4·00

Unissued $3.50, $4 and $5 miniature sheets exist from stock dispersed by the liquidator of Format International Security Printers Ltd.

1987 (July). *Coil stamp. As No.* 350, *but* W w **16**. *P* 14½ × 14.

953 **87** 10 c. turquoise-green . . 30 30

(Des N. Shewring. Litho Walsall)

1987 (31 Aug). *New Cadastral Survey of St. Lucia. T* **171** *and similar vert designs. Multicoloured.* W w **16**. *P* 14.

955 15 c. Type **171** . . 30 15
956 60 c. Map and surveying instruments, 1814 70 55
957 $1 Map and surveying instruments, 1888 90 90
958 $2.50, Cadastral survey map and surveying instruments, 1987 . . 2·25 2·50
955/8 . . *Set of* 4 3·75 3·75

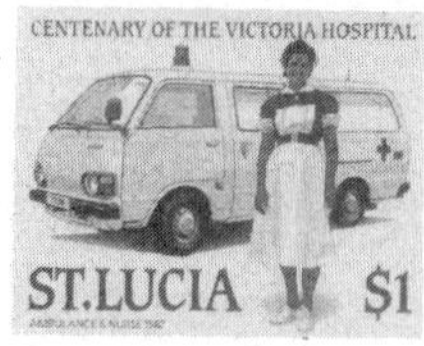

172 Ambulance and Nurse, 1987

173 "The Holy Family"

(Des C. Abbott. Litho Questa)

1987 (4 Nov). *Centenary of Victoria Hospital, Castries. T* **172** *and similar horiz designs. Multicoloured.* W w **16** (*sideways*). *P* 14 × 14½.

959 **172** $1 multicoloured . . 1·00 1·00
a. Pair. Nos. 959/60 . . 2·00 2·00
960 – $1 indigo . . 1·00 1·00
961 – $2 multicoloured . . 1·50 1·50
a. Pair. Nos. 961/2 . . 3·00 3·00
962 – $2 indigo . . 1·50 1·50
959/62 . . *Set of* 4 4·50 4·50
MS963 86 × 68 mm. $4.50, multicoloured . . 5·50 6·00

Designs:—No. 960, Nurse and carrying hammock, 1913; No. 961, $2 Victoria Hospital, 1987; No. 962, Victoria Hospital, 1887; No. **MS**963, Hospital gates, 1987.

Nos. 959/60 and 961/2 were each printed together, *se-tenant*, in horizontal and vertical pairs throughout the sheets.

(Des D. Miller. Litho Format)

1987 (30 Nov). *Christmas. T* **173** *and similar square designs showing paintings. Multicoloured.* W w **16** (*sideways*). *P* 14½.

964 15 c. Type **173** . . 30 10
965 50 c. "Adoration of the Shepherds" . . 60 30
966 60 c. "Adoration of the Magi" . . 70 55
967 90 c. "Madonna and Child" . . 1·25 1·50
964/7 . . *Set of* 4 2·50 2·25
MS968 82 × 67 mm. $6 Type **173** . . 3·50 4·00

174 St Lucia Amazon perched on Branch

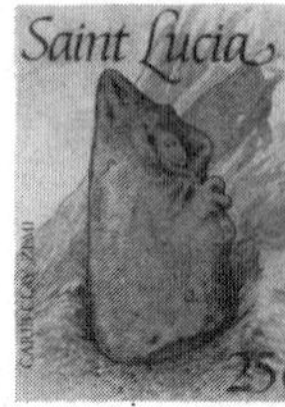

175 Carib Clay Zemi

(Des W. Oliver. Litho Walsall)

1987 (18 Dec). *St. Lucia Amazon. T* **174** *and similar vert designs. Multicoloured.* W w **16**. *P* 14.

969 15 c. Type **174** . . 35 20
970 35 c. Pair in flight . . 75 35
971 50 c. Perched on branch (rear view) . . 1·10 85
972 $1 Emerging from tree . . 2·00 2·50
969/72 . . *Set of* 4 3·75 3·50

(Des C. Collins. Litho Walsall)

1988 (24 Feb). *Amerindian Artifacts. T* **175** *and similar vert designs. Multicoloured.* W w **16**. *P* 14½ × 14.

973 25 c. Type **175** . . 15 10
974 30 c. Troumassee cylinder . . 20 15
975 80 c. Three pointer stone . . 55 45
976 $3.50, Dauphine petroglyph . . 2·25 2·50
973/6 . . *Set of* 4 2·75 2·75

176 East Caribbean Currency

177 Rural Telephone Exchange

(Des D. Miller (10 c.), S. Conlin (others). Litho B.D.T.)

1988 (29 Apr). *50th Anniv of St. Lucia Co-operative Bank. T* **176** *and similar horiz designs. Multicoloured.* W w **14** (*sideways*). *P* 15 × 14.

977 10 c. Type **176** . . 20 10
978 45 c. Castries branch . . 55 35
979 60 c. As 45 c. . . 75 80
980 80 c. Vieux Fort branch . . 1·25 1·50
977/80 . . *Set of* 4 2·50 2·50

(Des A. Theobald. Litho Walsall)

1988 (10 June). *50th Anniv of Cable and Wireless (West Indies) Ltd. T* **177** *and similar horiz designs. Multicoloured. W* w **16** *(sideways). P* 14.
981 15 c. Type **177** 10 10
982 25 c. Early and modern telephones .. 15 15
983 80 c. St. Lucia Teleport dish aerial 40 45
984 $2.50, Map showing Eastern Caribbean Microwave System .. .. .. 1·00 1·10
981/4 .. .. *Set of* 4 1·40 1·60

178 Stained Glass Window **179** Garnished Lobsters

(Des O. Bell. Litho Format)

1988 (15 Aug). *Centenary of Methodist Church in St. Lucia. T* **178** *and similar diamond-shaped designs. Multicoloured. W* w **16** *(sideways). P* 14½.
985 15 c. Type **178** 10 10
986 80 c. Church interior 40 45
987 $3.50, Methodist Church, Castries .. 1·50 1·60
985/7 .. .. *Set of* 3 1·75 1·90

(Des D. Miller. Litho Harrison)

1988 (15 Sept). *Tourism (2nd series). T* **179** *and similar vert designs showing local delicacies. Multicoloured. W* w **16**. *P* 14 × 13½.
988 10 c. Type **179** 30 30
a. Horiz strip of 4. Nos. 988/91 .. .. 3·00
989 30 c. Cocktail and tourists at buffet .. 45 45
990 80 c. Fresh fruits and roasted breadfruit .. 80 80
991 $2.50, Barbecued Red Snappers (fish) .. 1·75 1·75
988/91 .. .. *Set of* 4 3·00 3·00
MS992 88 × 104 mm. $5.50, Fruit stall, Castries market. P 14½ × 14 .. .. 2·25 2·75
Nos. 988/91 were printed together, *se-tenant*, in horizontal strips of four throughout the sheet, forming a composite design of tourists at beach barbecue.

(Des J. Cooter. Litho Format)

1988 (Sept)–**89**. *As Nos.* 797/800, 930, 937, 940 *and* 946, *but W* w **16** *(sideways). P* 15.
993 5 c. Type **156** (6.89) 25 25
994 10 c. Officer, Grenadier Company, 14th Regiment, 1780 (6.89) 30 30
995 15 c. Private, Battalion Company, 2nd West India Regiment, 1803 .. .. 40 40
996 20 c. Officer, Battalion Company, 46th Regiment, 1781 (6.89) 45 45
997 25 c. Officer, Royal Artillery, *c.* 1782 .. 45 45
999 60 c. Officer, Battalion Company, 5th Regiment, 1778 .. .. 80 80
1000 80 c. Officer, Battalion Company, 27th Regiment, *c.* 1780 .. .. .. 1·00 1·00
1003 $20 Private, Grenadier Company, 46th Regiment, 1778 (6.89) .. .. 16·00 18·00
993/1003 .. .. *Set of* 8 18·00 19·00
The 15 c. and 25 c. exist with different imprint dates below the designs.

(Des D. Miller (10 c.), L. Curtis and D. Miller (60 c.), E. Nisbet and D. Miller (80 c.), S. Noon and D. Miller ($2.50). Litho Questa)

1988 (17 Oct). *300th Anniv of Lloyd's of London. Designs as T* **167***a of Malawi. W* w **14** *(sideways on* 60, 80 *c.) P* 14.
1004 10 c. black, grey-lilac and brown 20 10
1005 60 c. multicoloured 60 45
1006 80 c. multicoloured 90 75
1007 $2.50, multicoloured .. .. 2·25 2·50
1004/7 .. .. *Set of* 4 3·50 3·50
Designs: *Vert*—10 c. San Francisco earthquake, 1906; $2.50, Castries fire, 1948. *Horiz*—60 c. Castries Harbour; 80 c. *Lady Nelson* (liner) 1942.

180 Snow on the Mountain **181** Princess Alexandra presenting Constitution

(Des R. Gorringe. Litho Format)

1988 (22 Nov). *Christmas. Flowers. T* **180** *and similar vert designs. Multicoloured. W* w **16**. *P* 14.
1008 15 c. Type **180** 30 10
1009 45 c. Christmas Candle 55 40
1010 60 c. Balisier 70 70
1011 80 c. Poinsettia .. .. 1·00 1·25
1008/11 .. .. *Set of* 4 2·25 2·25
MS1012 79 × 75 mm. $5.50, Christmas flower arrangement. Wmk sideways .. .. .. 2·50 3·25

(Des S. Noon. Litho Walsall)

1989 (22 Feb). *10th Anniv of Independence. T* **181** *and similar vert designs. Multicoloured. W* w **14**. *P* 13½ × 13.
1013 15 c. Type **181** 10 10
1014 80 c. Geothermal well 40 45
1015 $1 Sir Arthur Lewis Community College 45 50
1016 $2.50, Pointe Seraphine shopping centre 1·00 1·10
1013/16 .. .. *Set of* 4 1·75 1·90
MS1017 47 × 62 mm. $5 Man with national flag. W w **16**. .. .. 2·25 2·50

1989 (12 Apr). *As Nos.* 924B/5B, *but W* w **16** *(sideways). With imprint date. P* 14.
1018 **169** 5 c. black and cinnamon 20 20
1019 10 c. black and pale emerald 30 30

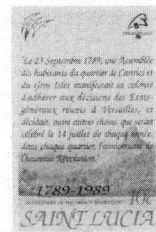

182 *Gerronema citrinum* **183** Local Revolutionary Declaration, 1789 and View of St. Lucia

(Des Josephine Martin. Litho Questa)

1989 (31 May). *Fungi. T* **182** *and similar vert designs. Multicoloured. W* w **16**. *P* 14½×14.
1022 15 c. Type **182** 35 15
1023 25 c. *Lepiota spiculata* 50 15
1024 50 c. *Calocybe cyanocephala* 90 65
1025 $5 *Russula puiggarii* .. .. 4·50 4·75
1022/5 .. .. *Set of* 4 5·50 5·00

(Litho Questa)

1989 (14 July). *Bicentenary of the French Revolution. T* **183** *and similar multicoloured designs each including the "Philexfrance" International Stamp Exhibition logo. W* w **14** *(sideways on* 60 *c.,* $3.50). *P* 14.
1026 10 c. Type **183** 20 15
1027 60 c. Hoisting Revolutionary flag, Morne Fortune, 1791 (*horiz*) 80 60
1028 $1 Declaration of Rights of Man and view of St. Lucia .. .. 1·10 85
1029 $3.50, Arrival of Capt. La Crosse, Gros Islet, 1792 (*horiz*) .. .. .. 3·50 3·75
1026/9 .. .. *Set of* 4 5·00 4·75

184 Red Cross Headquarters, St. Lucia **185** Christmas Lantern

(Des A. Theobald. Litho Questa)

1989 (10 Oct). *125th Anniv of International Red Cross. T* **184** *and similar horiz designs. Multicoloured. W* w **16** *(sideways). P* 14×14½.
1030 50 c. Type **184** 75 75
1031 80 c. Red Cross seminar, Castries, 1987 .. 1·25 1·25
1032 $1 Red Cross ambulance .. .. .. 1·40 1·40
1030/2 .. .. *Set of* 3 3·00 3·00

(Des Jennifer Toombs. Litho Questa)

1989 (17 Nov). *Christmas. T* **185** *and similar horiz designs showing decorative "building" lanterns. W* w **16** *(sideways). P* 14×14½.
1033 10 c. multicoloured 10 10
1034 50 c. multicoloured 25 30
1035 90 c. multicoloured 40 45
1036 $1 multicoloured 45 50
1033/6 .. .. *Set of* 4 1·00 1·10

MINIMUM PRICE

The minimum price quote is 10p which represents a handling charge rather than a basis for valuing common stamps. For further notes about prices see introductory pages.

186 Gwi Gwi **187** Father Tapon and Original College Building

(Des R. Gorringe. Litho B.D.T.)

1990 (21 Feb–25 June). *Endangered Trees. T* **186** *and similar vert designs. Multicoloured. W* w **16**. *P* 14.
1037 10 c. Chinna (12 Apr) 10 10
1038 15 c. Latanier (12 Apr) 10 10
1039 20 c. Type **186** 10 10
1040 25 c. L'Encens 10 15
1041 50 c. Bois Lélé 20 25
1042 80 c. Bois D'Amande (12 Apr) 35 40
1043 95 c. Mahot Piman Grand Bois (25 June) 40 45
1044 $1 Balata (25 June) 40 45
1045 $1.50, Pencil Cedar (12 Apr) 65 70
1046 $2.50, Bois Cendre (25 June) .. .. 1·00 1·10
1047 $5 Lowye Cannelle (25 June) .. .. 2·10 2·25
1048 $25 Chalantier Grand Bois .. .. 10·50 11·00
1037/48 .. .. *Set of* 12 13·50 14·50

(Des G. Vasarhelyi. Litho Questa)

1990 (6 June). *International Literacy Year. Centenary of St. Mary's College, Castries. T* **187** *and similar horiz designs. Multicoloured. W* w **14** *(sideways). P* 14.
1049 30 c. Type **187** 15 15
1050 45 c. Brother M. C. Collins and St. Mary's College 25 25
1051 75 c. Literacy class 45 45
1052 $2 Children approaching "door to knowledge" .. .. 1·50 1·50
1049/52 .. .. *Set of* 4 2·10 2·10

(Des D. Miller. Litho Questa)

1990 (3 Aug). *90th Birthday of Queen Elizabeth the Queen Mother. Vert designs as T* **107** (50 *c.*) *or* **108** ($5) *of Kenya. W* w **16**. *P* 14×15 (50 *c.*) *or* 14½ ($5).
1053 50 c. multicoloured 35 35
1054 $5 brownish black and deep violet-blue 2·75 3·00
Designs:—50 c. Crowning of Queen Consort, 1937; $5 Queen Elizabeth arriving at New Theatre, London, 1949.

(188) **189** "Adoration of the Magi" (Rubens)

1990 (13 Aug). *"EXPO 90" International Garden and Greenery Exhibition, Osaka. No.* 1047 *optd with T* **188**.
1055 $5 Lowye Cannelle .. .. 2·75 3·00

(Des D. Miller. Litho Questa)

1990 (3 Dec). *Christmas. Religious Paintings. T* **189** *and similar vert designs. Multicoloured. W* w **16**. *P* 14.
1056 10 c. Type **189** 15 10
1057 30 c. "Adoration of the Shepherds" (Murillo) 20 15
1058 80 c. "Adoration of the Magi" (Rubens) (*different*) 50 50
1059 $5 "Adoration of the Shepherds" (Philippe de Champaigne) .. .. 2·75 3·00
1056/9 .. .. *Set of* 4 3·25 3·25

190 *Vistafjord* (liner) **191** *Battus polydamas*

(Des E. Nisbet. Litho Walsall)

1991 (27 Mar). *Cruise Ships. T* **190** *and similar horiz designs. Multicoloured. W* w **14** *(sideways). P* 14½.
1060 50 c. Type **190** 35 30
1061 80 c. *Windstar* (schooner) 55 50
1062 $1 *Unicorn* (brig) 70 65
1063 $2.50, Game-fishing launch .. .. .. 2·00 2·25
1060/3 .. .. *Set of* 4 3·25 3·25
MS1064 82×65 mm. $5 Ships in Castries Harbour .. .. 3·25 3·50

(Des I. Loe. Litho Walsall)

1991 (15 Aug). *Butterflies. T* **191** *and similar vert designs. Multicoloured. W* w **16.** *P* 14.

1065	60 c. Type **191**	50	40
1066	80 c. *Strymon simaethis*	75	60
1067	$1 *Mestra cana*	85	70
1068	$2.50, *Allosmaitia piplea*	1·90	2·00
1065/8	*Set of* 4	3·50	3·25

192 Mural, Jacmel Church

193 Yacht and Map

(Des D. Miller. Litho Questa)

1991 (20 Nov). *Christmas. Paintings by Duncan St. Omer. T* **192** *and similar multicoloured designs. W* w **16** *(sideways on* 10, 80 *c.). P* 14½.

1069	10 c. Type **192**	15	10
1070	15 c. "Red Madonna" (*vert*)	15	10
1071	80 c. Mural, Monchy Church	50	45
1072	$5 "Blue Madonna" (*vert*)	2·50	2·75
1069/72	*Set of* 4	3·00	3·00

(Des P. Devarreaux. Litho Questa)

1991 (10 Dec). *Atlantic Rally for Cruising Yachts. T* **193** *and similar horiz design. Multicoloured. W* w **16** *(sideways). P* 14.

1073	60 c. Type **193**	35	35
1074	80 c. Yachts off St. Lucia	50	50

POSTAGE DUE STAMPS

No. ..4545
ST. LUCIA.
1d.
POSTAGE DUE

D 1

No. No.

Normal — Wide fount

(Type-set Government Printing Office)

1930. *Each stamp individually handstamped with different number. No wmk. No gum. Rough perf 12. (a) Horizontally laid paper.*

No.	Type	Description	Mint	Used
D1	D 1	1d. black/*blue*	2·25	7·50
		a. Wide, wrong fount "No."	8·00	19·00
		b. Missing stop after "ST"	30·00	50·00
		c. Missing stop after "LUCIA"	30·00	50·00
		d. Handstamped number double	£140	
		(b) Wove paper		
D2	D 1	2d. black/*yellow*	6·00	24·00
		a. Wide, wrong fount "No."	16·00	48·00
		b. Imperf between (vert pair)	£3500	
		c. Missing stop after "ST"	60·00	90·00
		d. Incorrect number with correction above	£225	

It is believed that there were three settings of the 1d. and two of the 2d., the same type being used for both values.

For the initial setting of the 1d. the wide "No." variety occurs on the last four stamps in the bottom row of the sheet of 60 (6 × 10). In later settings first the second and then later the first stamps in the same row were changed to show the variety. Nos. D1b and D2c occur on R.5/3 and No. D1c on R.9/2.

Some sheets from the initial printing of the 1d. show a paper-maker's watermark, "KINGSCLERE" in double-lined capitals above a crown, across a number of stamps.

The sheets had all outer edges, except that at the left, imperforate. It would appear that they were bound into books from which they could be detached, using the perforations at the left-hand edge.

The handstamped numbers were applied at the Post Office, using numbering machines. Each value had its own sequence of numbers and it is possible to recognise, by minor differences in fount, the use of two such machines. This is especially noticeable on examples of Nos. D1d and D2d where the corrections are often applied using a second machine. No. D2d shows the incorrect number partly erased and a correction struck across it.

D 2

D 3

D 4 St. Lucia Coat of Arms

(Typo D.L.R.)

1933–47. *Wmk Mult Script CA. P 14.*

No.	Type	Description	Mint	Used
D3	D 2	1d. black	4·00	4·00
D4		2d. black	9·00	6·50
D5		4d. black (28.6.47)	3·50	21·00
D6		8d. black (28.6.47)	3·50	25·00
D3/6		*Set of* 4	18·00	50·00
D3/6 Perf "Specimen"		*Set of* 4	£130	

1949 (1 Oct)**–52.** *Value in cents. Wmk Mult Script CA. Typo. P 14.*

No.	Type	Description	Mint	Used
D 7	D 3	2 c. black	1·75	14·00
		a. Chalk-surfaced paper (27.11.52)	10	3·75
		ab. Error. Crown missing, W **9***a*	65·00	
		ac. Error. St. Edward's Crown, W **9***b*	25·00	
D 8		4 c. black	3·25	11·00
		a. Chalk-surfaced paper (27.11.52)	30	4·75
		ab. Error. Crown missing, W **9***a*	80·00	
		ac. Error. St. Edward's Crown, W **9***b*	32·00	
D 9	D 3	8 c. black	2·75	14·00
		a. Chalk-surfaced paper (27.11.52)	90	15·00
		ac. Error. St. Edward's Crown, W **9***b*	£130	
D10		16 c. black	12·00	35·00
		a. Chalk-surfaced paper (27.11.52)	1·75	20·00
		ac. Error. St. Edward's Crown, W **9***b*	£160	
D7/10		*Set of* 4	18·00	65·00
D7a/10a		*Set of* 4	2·75	40·00

1965 (9 Mar). *As Nos. D7/8, but wmk w* **12**. *Ordinary paper. P* 14.

No.	Type	Description	Mint	Used
D11	D 3	2 c. black	35	5·50
D12		4 c. black	45	5·50

Nos D9a, D10a and D11/12 exist with a similar overprint to Type **49** in red (*Price for set of* 4 £150 *mint*).

(Des L. Curtis. Litho Format)

1981 (4 Aug). *W w* **14**. *P* 14.

No.	Type	Description	Mint	Used
D13	D 4	5 c. brown-purple	10	15
D14		15 c. emerald	15	20
D15		25 c. red-orange	15	20
D16		$1 deep ultramarine	50	65
D13/16		*Set of* 4	80	1·10

(Des L. Curtis. Litho Questa)

1991 (14 Feb). *W w* **16**. *P* 15×14.

No.	Type	Description	Mint	Used
D17	D 4	5 c. deep carmine	10	10
D18		15 c. emerald	10	10
D19		25 c. red-orange	10	15
D20		$1 ultramarine	40	45
D17/20		*Set of* 4	55	65

OFFICIAL STAMPS

OFFICIAL (O 1) — OFFICIAL (O 2)

1983 (13 Oct). *Nos.* 537/48 *optd with Type* O **1**.

No.	Description	Mint	Used
O 1	5 c. Type **120**	15	10
O 2	10 c. McDonnell Douglas "DC-10" airliner	15	10
O 3	15 c. Local bus	20	15
O 4	20 c. Refrigerated freighter	30	20
O 5	25 c. "Islander" aeroplane	35	20
O 6	30 c. Pilot boat	40	25
O 7	50 c. Boeing "727" airliner	55	35
O 8	75 c. *Cunard Countess* (liner)	75	50
O 9	$1 Lockheed "Tristar" airliner	95	75
O10	$2 Cargo liner	1·75	1·75
O11	$5 Boeing "707" airliner	3·50	3·50
O12	$10 *Queen Elizabeth 2* (liner)	6·50	7·50
O1/12	*Set of* 12	14·00	14·00

1985 (7 May). *Nos.* 797/811 *optd with Type* O **2**.

No.	Description	Mint	Used
O13	5 c. Type **156**	20	20
O14	10 c. Officer, Grenadier Company, 14th Regiment, 1780	20	20
O15	20 c. Officer, Battalion Company, 46th Regiment, 1781	20	20
O16	25 c. Officer, Royal Artillery, *c* 1782	20	20
O17	30 c. Officer, Royal Engineers, 1782	30	30
O18	35 c. Officer, Battalion Company, 54th Regiment, 1782	30	30
O19	45 c. Private, Grenadier Company, 14th Regiment, 1782	40	40
O20	50 c. Gunner, Royal Artillery, 1796	40	40
O21	65 c. Private, Battalion Company, 85th Regiment, *c* 1796	50	50
O22	75 c. Private, Battalion Company, 76th Regiment, 1796	60	60
O23	90 c. Private, Battalion Company, 81st Regiment, *c* 1796	65	65
O24	$1 Sergeant, 74th (Highland) Regiment, 1796	70	70
O25	$2.50, Private, Light Company, 93rd Regiment, 1803	1·75	1·75
O26	$5 Private, Battalion Company, 1st West India Regiment, 1803	3·50	4·00
O27	$15 Officer, Royal Artillery, 1850	8·00	9·00
O13/27	*Set of* 15	16·00	17·00

POSTAL FISCAL STAMPS

Nos. F1/28 were authorised for postal use from 14 April 1885.

CANCELLATIONS. Many used examples of the Postal Fiscal stamps have had previous pen cancellations removed before being used postally.

SHILLING STAMP (F 1) — One Penny Stamp (F 2) — HALFPENNY Stamp (F 3)

1881. *Wmk Crown CC. P* 14. *(a) Surch as Type* F **1**.

No.	Type	Description	Mint	Used
F1	1	ONE PENNY STAMP, black (C.)	30·00	38·00
		a. Surch inverted	£700	£700
		b. Surch double	£650	£700
F2		FOUR PENNY STAMP, yellow	50·00	60·00
		a. Bisected (2d.) (on cover)		
F3		SIX PENCE STAMP, mauve	90·00	£100
F4		SHILLING STAMP, orange	50·00	60·00
		a. "SHILEING"	£650	
		b. "SHILDING"	£650	£600
		(b) Surch as Type F **2**		
F 7	1	One Penny Stamp, black (R.)	30·00	38·00
		a. Surch double	£700	
F 8		Four Pence Stamp, yellow	50·00	50·00
F 9		Six Pence Stamp, mauve	50·00	50·00
F10		Shilling Stamp, orange	55·00	70·00
		(c) Surch as Type F **3**		
F11	1	Halfpenny Stamp, green	30·00	38·00
		a. "Stamp" double	£450	£450
F12		One Shilling Stamp, orange (*wmk Crown CA*)	55·00	55·00
		a. "Stamp" double	£450	£500

FOUR PENCE REVENUE (F 4) — Revenue (F 5) — REVENUE (F 6)

1882. *Wmk Crown CA. Surch as Type* F **4**. *(a) P* 14.

No.	Type	Description	Mint	Used
F13	1	1d. black (C.)	22·00	22·00
		a. Imperf. (pair)	£1100	
F14		2d. pale blue	11·00	9·50
		a. Imperf (pair)		
F15		3d. deep blue (C.)	38·00	38·00
F16		4d. yellow	13·00	4·00
F17		6d. mauve	24·00	23·00
		(b) P 12		
F18	1	1d. black (C.)	22·00	22·00
F19		3d. deep blue (C.)	30·00	20·00
F20		1s. orange	30·00	13·00

1883. *Nos.* 25, 26, 30 *and* 32 *optd locally as Type* F **5**.

No.	Description	Mint	Used
	(a) Word 11 mm long		
F21	1d. black (C.)	21·00	32·00
	a. Opt inverted		
	b. Opt double	£250	£350
	(b) Word 13 mm		
F22	1d. black (C.)	—	50·00
	(c) Word 15½ mm		
F23	½d. green	—	42·00
	a. "Revenue" double	—	£225
F24	1d. black (C.)	17·00	10·00
	a. "Revenue" double	£130	
	b. "Revenue" triple	£250	
	c. "Revenue" double, one inverted	£250	£300
F25	1d. rose (No. 30)	—	45·00
F26	4d. yellow	—	55·00

1884–85. *Optd with Type* F **6**. *Wmk Crown CA. P* 14.

No.	Type	Description	Mint	Used
F27	5	1d. slate (C.)	12·00	11·00
		a. Imperf (pair)		
F28		1d. dull mauve (Die I) (1885)	12·00	7·50

St. Vincent

Although postal markings for St. Vincent are recorded as early as 1793 it was not until 1852 that the British G.P.O. opened a branch office at Kingstown, the island's capital.

The stamps of Great Britain were used between May 1858 and the end of April 1860. From 1 May in that year the local authorities assumed responsibility for the postal services and fell back on the use of No. CC1 until the introduction of St. Vincent stamps in 1861.

KINGSTOWN

CROWNED-CIRCLE HANDSTAMPS

CC 1

CC1 CC 1 ST. VINCENT (R.) (30.1.1852) *Price on cover* £750

Stamps of GREAT BRITAIN *cancelled* "A 10" *as Type* Z 1 *of Jamaica*.

1858 *to* **1860**.
Z1 1d. rose-red (1857), *perf* 14 .. .. £550
Z2 2d. blue (1855) .. ..
Z3 4d. rose (1857) £350
Z4 6d. lilac (1856) £250
Z5 1s. green (1856) £950

PRICES FOR STAMPS ON COVER TO 1945	
Nos. 1/2	*from* × 5
Nos. 3/7	*from* × 8
No. 8	—
No. 9	*from* × 8
No. 10	—
Nos. 11/19	*from* × 8
Nos. 20/1	*from* × 5
Nos. 22/5	*from* × 8
Nos. 26/8	—
Nos. 29/31	*from* × 9
No. 32	—
Nos. 33/4	*from* × 8
No. 35	—
Nos. 36/8	*from* × 6
Nos. 39/41	*from* × 12
Nos. 42/5	*from* × 5
No. 46	*from* × 15
Nos. 47/54	*from* × 4
Nos. 55/8	*from* × 8
No. 59	*from* × 10
No. 60	*from* × 6
Nos. 61/3	*from* × 8
Nos. 67/75	*from* × 3
Nos. 76/84	*from* × 2
Nos. 85/92	*from* × 3
No. 93	—
Nos. 94/8	*from* × 3
Nos. 99/107	*from* × 2
Nos. 108/19	*from* × 3
No. 120	—
No. 121	*from* × 3
No. 122	*from* × 5
No. 123	—
No. 124	*from* × 5
Nos. 126/9	*from* × 10
Nos. 131/45	*from* × 3
Nos. 146/8	*from* × 6
Nos. 149/59	*from* × 2

CROWN COLONY

1

d.
1

(2)

3

(T **1**, **3** and **7** recess P.B.)

1861 (8 May). *No wmk.* (a) *Intermediate perf* 14 *to* 16.
1 1 1d. rose-red £7000 £450
a. Imperf vert (horiz pair) £450
2 6d. deep yellow-green £5500 £200

(b) *Rough perf* 14 *to* 16
3 1 1d. rose-red .. .. 35·00 14·00
a. Imperf vert (horiz pair) £350
b. Imperf (pair) £250

1862 (Sept). *No wmk. Rough perf* 14 *to* 16.
4 1 6d. deep green .. .. 50·00 18·00
a. Imperf between (horiz pair) £1400
b. Imperf (pair) £450

1863–68. *No wmk.* (a) *P* 11 *to* 12½.
5 1 1d. rose-red (3.63) .. .. .. 32·00 15·00
6 4d. deep blue (*shades*) (1866) £275 £110
a. Imperf between (horiz pair) ..
7 6d. deep green (7.68) .. .. .. £200 60·00
8 1s. slate-grey (8.66) £1800 £900

(b) *P* 14 *to* 16
9 1 1s. slate-grey (*shades*) £300 £130

(c) *P* 11 *to* 12½ × 14 *to* 16
10 1 1d. rose-red £2750 £1300
11 1s. slate-grey (*shades*) £225 £120

1869. *Colours changed. No wmk. P* 11 *to* 12½.
12 1 4d. yellow £350 £150
13 1s. indigo .. .. £325 90·00
14 1s. brown £425 £160

1871 (Apr). *Wmk Small Star, Type* w **2**. *Rough perf* 14 *to* 16.
15 1 1d. black .. .. 40·00 10·00
a. Imperf between (vert pair) £4750
16 6d. deep green .. .. £250 70·00

1872. *Colour changed.* W w **2**. *P* 11 *to* 12½.
17 1 1s. deep rose-red £750 £140

1872–75. W w **2**. (a) *Perf about* 15.
18 1 1d. black (*shades*) (1872) .. .. 38·00 7·50
19 6d. dull blue-green (*shades*) (1873) .. £600 30·00
a. *Deep blue-green* (1875) .. .. £600 38·00

(b) *P* 11 *to* 12½ × 15
20 1 1s. lilac-rose (1873) £5000 £400

No. 19*a* always has the watermark sideways and Nos. 16 and 19 normally have it upright but are known with it sideways.

1875. *Colour changed.* W w **2**. *P* 11 *to* 12½.
21 1 1s. claret £600 £250

1876–78. W w **2**. (a) *P* 11 *to* 12½ × 15.
22 1 1d. black (*shades*) (1876) .. .. 60·00 6·00
a. Imperf between (horiz pair) .. — £3750
23 6d. pale green (1877) .. .. .. £500 45·00
24 1s. vermilion (2.77) .. .. .. £750 85·00
a. Imperf vert (horiz pair) .. ..

(b) *P* 11 to 12½
25 1 4d. deep blue (7.77) .. .. .. £450 90·00

(c) *Perf about* 15
26 1 6d. pale green (3.77) £1500 £450
a. *Light yellow-green* (1878) .. .. £550 25·00
27 1s. vermilion (1878?) .. .. .. — £6500
a. Imperf .. .. — £3000

Nos. 23 and 26 always have the watermark sideways but No. 26*a* always has the watermark upright.

1880 (May). *No.* 19*a divided vertically by a line of perforation gauging* 12, *and surch locally as T* **2**.
28 1 1d. on half 6d. bright blue-green (R.) .. £375 £250
a. Unsevered pair £1300 £950

1880 (June). W w **2**. *P* 11 *to* 12½.
29 1 1d. olive-green .. .. 85·00 3·25
30 6d. bright green .. .. £300 60·00
31 1s. bright vermilion .. .. .. £650 50·00
a. Imperf between (horiz pair) £4500
32 3 5s. rose-red £1000 £1200
a. Imperf £3250

d
1
—
2

(4)

d
1
—
2

Straight serif to "1" (R. 6/20)

ONE PENNY

(5)

4d

(6)

1881. *Nos.* 30/31 *surch locally. No.* 33 *is divided vertically like No.* 28.
33 4 ½d. on half 6d. bright green (R.) (1.9) .. £160 £160
a. Unsevered pair £400 £400
b. Fraction bar omitted (pair with and without bar) £3500 £4000
c. Straight serif to "1" .. ..
34 5 1d. on 6d. bright green (30.11) £400 £275
35 6 4d. on 1s. bright vermilion (28.11) .. £1300 £700

It is believed that Type 4 was applied as a setting of 36 (6 × 6) surcharges repeated three times on each sheet across rows 1 to 9. The missing fraction bar occurs on R. 6/3 of the setting.

The tenth vertical row of stamps appears to have been surcharged from a separate setting of 12 (2 × 6) on which the "straight serif" flaw occurs on the bottom right half-stamp.

Three unused single copies of No. 33 are known with the surcharge omitted.

It is believed that Nos. 34 and 35 were surcharged in settings of 30 (10×3).

No. 34 was only on sale between the 30 November and 3 December when supplies of No. 37 became available.

7

2½ PENCE

(8)

1d
2½ PENCE

(9)

1881 (Dec). W w **2**. *P* 11 *to* 12½.
36 7 ½d. orange (*shades*) .. .. .. 7·00 2·50
37 1 1d. drab (*shades*) .. .. .. £700 4·75
38 4d. bright blue £1200 £100
a. Imperf between (horiz pair) .. ..

(Recess D.L.R. from Perkins, Bacon plates)

1882 (Nov)–**83.** *No.* 40 *is surch with T* **8**. *Wmk Crown CA. P* 14.
39 1 1d. drab .. .. 35·00 90
40 2½d. on 1d. lake (1883) .. .. .. 7·50 40
41 4d. ultramarine .. .. .. £300 28·00
a. Dull ultramarine £950 £350

1883–84. *Wmk Crown CA. P* 12.
42 7 ½d. green (1884) .. .. .. 55·00 25·00
43 1 4d. ultramarine-blue .. .. .. £275 18·00
a. Grey-blue £1000 £300
44 6d. bright green £400 £325
45 1s. orange-vermilion .. .. .. 80·00 48·00

The ½d. orange, 1d. rose-red, 1d. milky blue (without surcharge) and 5s. carmine-lake which were formerly listed are now considered to be colour trials. They are, however, of great interest. (*Prices un.* ½d. £900, 1d. red £900, 1d. blue £1200, 5s. £1500.)

1885 (Mar). *No.* 40 *surch locally as in T* **9**.
46 1 1d. on 2½d. on 1d. lake .. .. .. 10·00 11·00

Stamps with three cancelling bars instead of two are considered to be proofs.

1885–93. *No.* 49 *is surch with T* **8**. *Wmk Crown CA. P* 14.
47 7 ½d. green 60 20
a. Deep green .. .. .. 2·50 50
48 1 1d. rose-red .. .. 2·00 80
a. Rose (1886) .. .. .. 4·25 1·50
b. Red (1887) .. .. .. 1·60 35
c. Carmine-red (1889) .. .. .. 23·00 3·00
49 2½d. on 1d. milky blue (1889) .. .. 23·00 4·00
50 4d. red-brown .. .. .. £850 22·00
51 4d. purple-brown (1886) .. .. .. 38·00 75
a. Chocolate (1887) .. .. .. 38·00 1·25
52 6d. violet (1888) .. .. .. 85·00 £100
53 3 5s. lake (1888) .. .. .. 27·00 48·00
a. Printed both sides £3500
b. Brown-lake (1893) .. .. .. 29·00 48·00
49, 51, 52 Optd "Specimen" .. *Set of* 3 £160

2½d.

(10)

5
PENCE

(11)

1890 (Aug). *No.* 51*a surch with T* **10**.
54 1 2½d. on 4d. chocolate .. .. .. 48·00 65·00
a. No fraction bar (R. 1/7, 2/4) .. £225 £250

1890–93. *No.* 55 *is surch with T* **8**. *Colours changed. Wmk Crown CA. P* 14.
55 1 2½d. on 1d. grey-blue (1890) .. .. 12·00 55
a. Blue (1893) 75 35
56 4d. yellow (1893) (Optd S. £30) .. 1·60 4·75
57 6d. dull purple (1891) .. .. .. 2·00 4·75
58 1s. orange (1891) .. .. .. 5·50 9·00
a. Red-orange (1892) .. .. .. 9·00 17·00

1892 (Nov). *No.* 51*a surch with T* **11**, *in purple*.
59 1 5d. on 4d. chocolate (Optd S. £30) .. 9·00 18·00

Some letters are known double due to loose type, the best known being the first "E", but they are not constant.

FIVE PENCE

(12)

13

14

1893–94. *Surch with T* **12**. *Wmk Crown CA. P* 14.
60 1 5d. on 6d. carmine-lake (Optd S. £45) .. 12·00 24·00
a. Deep lake (1893) .. .. .. 80 1·75
b. Lake (1894) .. .. .. 1·75 4·25
c. Surch double £4000 £2750

(Recess D.L.R.)

1897 (13 July). *New values. Wmk Crown CA. P* 14.
61 1 2½d. blue .. .. 2·50 2·25
62 5d. sepia .. .. 5·50 17·00
61/2 Optd "Specimen" .. .. *Set of* 2 60·00

1897 (6 Oct). *Surch as T* **12**. *Wmk Crown CA. P* 14.
63 1 3d. on 1d. mauve (Optd S. £40) .. .. 7·50 15·00
a. Red-mauve .. .. .. 9·50 23·00

(Typo D.L.R.)

1899 (1 Jan). *Wmk Crown CA. P 14.*

No.	Type	Description	Unused	Used
67	**13**	½d. dull mauve and green	1·00	75
68		1d. dull mauve and carmine	3·25	45
69		2½d. dull mauve and blue	4·00	2·00
70		3d. dull mauve and olive	4·00	8·50
71		4d. dull mauve and orange	4·00	13·00
72		5d. dull mauve and black	7·00	13·00
73		6d. dull mauve and brown	13·00	27·00
74	**14**	1s. green and carmine	13·00	38·00
75		5s. green and blue	70·00	£120
67/75		*Set of* 9	£110	£200
67/75 Optd "Specimen"		*Set of* 9	£170	

15 16

(Typo D.L.R.)

1902. *Wmk Crown CA. P 14.*

No.	Type	Description	Unused	Used
76	**15**	½d. dull purple and green	1·00	60
77		1d. dull purple and carmine	1·25	20
78	**16**	2d. dull purple and black	1·75	2·25
79	**15**	2½d. dull purple and blue	2·00	3·25
80		3d. dull purple and olive	2·00	2·00
81		6d. dull purple and brown	9·00	22·00
82	**16**	1s. green and carmine	12·00	40·00
83	**15**	2s. green and violet	22·00	45·00
84	**16**	5s. green and blue	45·00	90·00
76/84		*Set of* 9	85·00	£180
76/84 Optd "Specimen"		*Set of* 9	£120	

1904–11. *Wmk Mult Crown CA. Ordinary paper* (½d., 1d., 1s.) *or chalk-surfaced paper* (*others*). *P 14.*

No.	Type	Description	Unused	Used
85	**15**	½d. dull purple and green (1905)	1·75	90
		a. Chalk-surfaced paper	1·00	80
86		1d. dull purple and carmine	8·00	40
		a. Chalk-surfaced paper	8·00	40
88		2½d. dull purple and blue (1906)	10·00	25·00
89		6d. dull purple and brown (1905)	11·00	25·00
90	**16**	1s. green and carmine (1906)	12·00	27·00
		a. Chalk-surfaced paper	9·00	27·00
91	**15**	2s. purple and bright blue/*blue* (3.09?)	22·00	42·00
92	**16**	5s. green and red/*yellow* (3.09?)	17·00	45·00
93		£1 purple and black/*red* (22.7.11)	£300	£350
85/93		*Set of* 8	£350	£475
91/3 Optd "Specimen"		*Set of* 3	£225	

17 18

(Recess D.L.R.)

1907–08. *Wmk Mult Crown CA. P 14.*

No.	Type	Description	Unused	Used
94	**17**	½d. green (2.7.07)	1·25	80
95		1d. carmine (26.4.07)	2·50	15
96		2d. orange (5.08)	1·00	5·50
97		2½d. blue (8.07)	11·00	8·50
98		3d. violet (1.6.07)	4·25	14·00
94/8		*Set of* 5	18·00	26·00
94/8 Optd "Specimen"		*Set of* 5	£100	

1909. *No dot below "d". Wmk Mult Crown CA. P 14.*

No.	Type	Description	Unused	Used
99	**18**	1d. carmine (3.09)	1·25	25
100		6d. dull purple (16.1.09)	5·50	24·00
101		1s. black/*green* (16.1.09)	3·75	7·00
99/101		*Set of* 3	9·50	28·00
99/101 Optd "Specimen"		*Set of* 3	60·00	

1909 (Nov)–**11.** *T* **18**, *redrawn* (*dot below* "d", *as in T* **17**). *Wmk Mult Crown CA. P 14.*

No.	Type	Description	Unused	Used
102		½d. green (31.10.10)	1·25	40
103		1d. carmine	1·50	15
104		2d. grey (3.8.11)	1·75	8·00
105		2½d. ultramarine (25.7.10)	5·00	2·00
106		3d. purple/*yellow*	2·00	3·25
107		6d. dull purple	2·00	5·00
102/7		*Set of* 6	12·00	17·00
102 and 104/6 Optd "Specimen"		*Set of* 4	80·00	

19

ONE PENNY.

(20)

(Recess D.L.R.)

1913 (1 Jan)–**17.** *Wmk Mult Crown CA. P 14.*

No.	Type	Description	Unused	Used
108	**19**	½d. green	35	20
109		1d. red	60	25
		a. Rose-red	80	45
		b. Scarlet (1.17)	7·00	3·00
110		2d. grey	5·50	20·00
		a. Slate	2·50	18·00
111		2½d. ultramarine	35	40
112		3d. purple/*yellow*	80	5·00
		a. On lemon	2·50	12·00
		b. On pale yellow	1·90	8·50
113		4d. red/*yellow*	80	2·00
114		5d. olive-green (7.11.13)	2·25	12·00
115	**19**	6d. claret	2·00	4·50
116		1s. black/*green*	1·50	3·25
117		1s. bistre (1.5.14)	3·50	12·00
118	**18**	2s. blue and purple	4·75	17·00
119		5s. carmine and myrtle	13·00	38·00
120		£1 mauve and black	70·00	£140
108/20		*Set of* 13	90·00	£225
108/20 Optd "Specimen"		*Set of* 13	£250	

Nos. 118/20 are from new centre and frame dies, the motto "PAX ET JUSTITIA" being slightly over 7 mm long, as against just over 8 mm in Nos. 99 to 107. Nos. 139/41 are also from the new dies.

1915. *Surch with T* **20.**

No.	Type	Description	Unused	Used
121	**19**	1d. on 1s. black/*green* (R.)	3·00	15·00
		a. "ONE" omitted	£850	
		b. "ONE" double	£750	
		c. "PENNY" and bar double	£700	

The spacing between the two words varies from 7¾ mm to 10 mm.

WAR STAMP. (21) WAR STAMP. (22) WAR STAMP (24)

1916 (June). *No. 109 optd locally with T* **21**. (*a*) *First and second settings; words 2 to 2½ mm apart.*

No.	Type	Description	Unused	Used
122	**19**	1d. red	1·50	2·75
		a. Opt double	£140	£140
		b. Comma for stop	7·00	11·00

In the first printing every second stamp has the comma for stop. The second printing of this setting has full stops only. These two printings can therefore only be distinguished in blocks or pairs.

(*b*) *Third setting; words only* 1½ *mm apart*

No.	Type	Description	Unused	Used
123	**19**	1d. red	55·00	
		a. Opt double	£1100	

Stamps of the first setting are offered as this rare one. Care must be taken to see that the distance between the lines is not over 1½ mm.

(*c*) *Fourth setting; optd with T* **22.** *Words* 3½ *mm apart*

No.	Type	Description	Unused	Used
124	**19**	1d. carmine-red	1·25	5·00
		a. Opt double	£200	

1916 (Aug)–**18.** *T* **19**, *new printing, optd with T* **24**.

No.	Type	Description	Unused	Used
126		1d. carmine-red (Optd S. £60)	25	50
127		1d. pale rose-red	20	50
128		1d. deep rose-red	15	50
129		1d. pale scarlet (1918)	15	50

1921–32. *Wmk Mult Script CA. P 14.*

No.	Type	Description	Unused	Used
131	**19**	½d. green (3.21)	30	20
132		1d. carmine (6.21)	30	40
		a. Red	30	15
132*b*		1½d. brown (1.12.32)	60	15
133		2d. grey (3.22)	40	30
133*a*		2½d. bright blue (12.25)	60	30
134		3d. bright blue (3.22)	90	6·00
135		3d. purple/*yellow* (1.12.26)	45	1·50
135*a*		4d. red/*yellow* (9.30)	1·75	6·00
136		5d. sage-green (8.3.24)	70	5·00
137		6d. claret (1.11.27)	80	3·50
138		1s. bistre-brown (9.21)	2·50	10·00
		a. Ochre (1927)	1·50	10·00
139	**18**	2s. blue and purple (8.3.24)	4·00	13·00
140		5s. carmine and myrtle (8.3.24)	10·00	30·00
141		£1 mauve and black (9.28)	70·00	£110
131/41		*Set of* 14	80·00	£160
131/41 Optd/Perf "Specimen"		*Set of* 14	£250	

1935 (6 May). *Silver Jubilee. As Nos. 114/17 of Jamaica, but ptd by Waterlow. P 11×12.*

No.	Type	Description	Unused	Used
142		1d. deep blue and scarlet	40	55
143		1½d. ultramarine and grey	1·00	65
144		2½d. brown and deep blue	1·50	65
145		1s. slate and purple	2·00	3·50
		k. Kite and horizontal log	£100	
142/5		*Set of* 4	4·50	4·75
142/5 Perf "Specimen"		*Set of* 4	75·00	

For illustration of plate variety see Omnibus section following Zimbabwe.

1937 (12 May). *Coronation. As Nos. 118/20 of Jamaica, but ptd by B.W. P 11×11½.*

No.	Type	Description	Unused	Used
146		1d. violet	35	15
147		1½d. carmine	55	10
148		2½d. blue	65	45
146/8		*Set of* 3	1·40	60
146/8 Perf "Specimen"		*Set of* 3	50·00	

25

26 Young's Island and Fort Duvernette

27 Kingstown and Fort Charlotte

28 Bathing Beach at Villa

29 Victoria Park, Kingstown

NEW CONSTITUTION 1951

(29*a*)

(Recess B.W.)

1938 (11 Mar)–**47.** *Wmk Mult Script CA. P 12.*

No.	Type	Description	Unused	Used
149	**25**	½d. blue and green	10	10
150	**26**	1d. blue and lake-brown	10	10
151	**27**	1½d. green and scarlet	15	10
152	**25**	2d. green and black	40	35
153	**28**	2½d. blue-black and blue-green	10	40
153*a*	**29**	2½d. green and purple-brown (1947)	15	15
154	**25**	3d. orange and purple	15	10
154*a*	**28**	3½d. blue-black and blue-green (1947)	40	75
155	**25**	6d. black and lake	50	40
156	**29**	1s. purple and green	50	40
157	**25**	2s. blue and purple	4·50	55
157*a*		2s. 6d. red-brown and blue (1947)	1·00	3·50
158		5s. scarlet and deep green	8·50	2·50
158*a*		10s. violet and brown (1947)	3·50	7·50
159		£1 purple and black	16·00	15·00
149/59		*Set of* 15	32·00	28·00
149/59 Perf "Specimen"		*Set of* 15	£250	

1946 (15 Oct). *Victory. As Nos. 141/2 of Jamaica.*

No.	Type	Description	Unused	Used
160		1½d. carmine	10	10
161		3½d. blue	10	10
160/1 Perf "Specimen"		*Set of* 2	50·00	

1948 (30 Nov). *Royal Silver Wedding. As Nos. 143/4 of Jamaica.*

No.	Type	Description	Unused	Used
162		1½d. scarlet	10	10
163		£1 bright purple	15·00	12·00

No. 163 was originally printed in black, but the supply of these was stolen in transit. A few archive examples exist, some perforated "Specimen".

(New Currency. 100 cents=1 West Indian dollar)

1949 (26 Mar)–**52.** *Value in cents and dollars. Wmk Mult Script CA. P 12.*

No.	Type	Description	Unused	Used
164	**25**	1 c. blue and green	20	15
164*a*		1 c. green and black (10.6.52)	30	40
165	**26**	2 c. blue and lake-brown	15	20
166	**27**	3 c. green and scarlet	40	15
166*a*	**25**	3 c. orange and purple (10.6.52)	30	35
167		4 c. green and black	35	20
167*a*		4 c. blue and green (10.6.52)	25	15
168	**29**	5 c. green and purple-brown	15	10
169	**25**	6 c. orange and purple	40	35
169*a*	**27**	6 c. green and scarlet (10.6.52)	25	15
170	**28**	7 c. blue-black and blue-green	2·50	30
170*a*		10 c. blue-black and blue-green (10.6.52)	50	20
171	**25**	12 c. black and lake	35	15
172	**29**	24 c. purple and green	35	30
173	**25**	48 c. blue and purple	1·50	1·50
174		60 c. red-brown and blue	1·75	1·75
175		$1.20, scarlet and deep green	4·25	4·00
176		$2.40, violet and brown	6·50	9·00
177		$4.80, purple and black	11·00	17·00
164/77		*Set of* 19	28·00	32·00

1949 (10 Oct). *75th Anniv of U.P.U. As Nos. 145/8 of Jamaica.*

No.	Type	Description	Unused	Used
178		5 c. blue	15	15
179		6 c. purple	25	25
180		12 c. magenta	30	30
181		24 c. blue-green	40	25
178/81		*Set of* 4	1·00	85

1951 (16 Feb). *Inauguration of B.W.I. University College. As Nos. 149/50 of Jamaica.*

No.	Type	Description	Unused	Used
182		3 c. deep green and scarlet	20	15
183		12 c. black and purple	25	15

1951 (21 Sept). *New Constitution. Optd with T* **29*a*** *by B.W.*

No.	Type	Description	Unused	Used
184	**27**	3 c. green and scarlet	10	15
185	**25**	4 c. green and black	10	15
186	**29**	5 c. green and purple-brown	10	15
187	**25**	12 c. black and lake	10	15
184/7		*Set of* 4	30	55

1953 (2 June). *Coronation. As No. 153 of Jamaica.*

No.	Type	Description	Unused	Used
188		4 c. black and green	30	15

30

31

(Recess Waterlow (until 1961), then D.L.R.)

1955 (16 Sept)–**63.** *Wmk Mult Script CA. P* 13½×14 (*T* **30**) *or* 14 (*T* **31**).

No.	Type	Description	Unused	Used
189	**30**	1 c. orange	10	10
		a. Deep orange (11.12.62)	1·25	1·50
190		2 c. ultramarine	10	10
		a. Blue (26.9.61)	15	10
191		3 c. slate	30	10
192		4 c. brown	15	10
193		5 c. scarlet	30	10
194		10 c. reddish violet	20	10
		a. Deep lilac (12.2.58)	20	10
195		15 c. deep blue	55	30
196		20 c. green	60	10
197		25 c. black-brown	50	10

198 31 50 c. red-brown .. .. 2·75 90
a. *Chocolate* (11.6.58) .. .. .. 2·75 75
199 $1 myrtle-green .. .. .. 4·25 1·00
a. *Deep myrtle-green* (11.6.58) .. .. 9·00 4·00
b. *Deep yellowish green* (15.1.63) .. 13·00 8·00
200 $2.50, deep blue .. .. .. 12·00 6·50
a. *Indigo-blue* (30.7.62) .. .. 25·00 12·00
189/200 .. .. *Set of* 12 19·00 8·00
See also Nos. 207/20 and **MS**633.

1958 (22 Apr). *Inauguration of British Caribbean Federation. As Nos.* 175/7 *of Jamaica.*
201 3 c. deep green 40 20
202 6 c. blue 55 35
203 12 c. scarlet 80 35
201/3 .. .. *Set of* 3 1·60 80

MINISTERIAL GOVERNMENT

1963 (4 June). *Freedom from Hunger. As No.* 80 *of Lesotho.*
204 8 c. reddish violet 60 50

1963 (2 Sept). *Red Cross Centenary. As Nos.* 203/4 *of Jamaica.*
205 4 c. red and black 15 20
206 8 c. red and blue 35 50

(Recess D.L.R.)

1964–65. *As* 1955 *but wmk* w **12.** (*a*) *P* 12½ (14 Jan–Feb 1964).
207 30 10 c. deep lilac 40 45
208 15 c. deep blue 70 50
209 20 c. green (24.2.64*) .. .. .. 5·50 2·00
210 25 c. black-brown .. .. 1·00 50
211 31 50 c. chocolate .. .. 4·50 8·00
207/11 .. .. *Set of* 5 11·00 10·00

(*b*) *P* 13 × 14 (*T* **30**) *or* 14 (*T* **31**)
212 30 1 c. orange (15.12.64) 15 10
213 2 c. blue (15.12.64) 15 10
214 3 c. slate (15.12.64) 50 10
215 5 c. scarlet (15.12.64) 15 10
216 10 c. deep lilac (15.12.64) 15 10
217 15 c. deep blue (9.11.64).. .. .. 80 30
218 20 c. green (1964) 45 10
219 25 c. black-brown (20.10.64) .. .. 1·25 25
220 31 50 c. chocolate (18.1.65).. .. .. 4·75 6·50
212/20 .. .. *Set of* 9 7·50 6·50
*This is the earliest known date recorded in St. Vincent although it may have been put on sale on 14.1.64.

32 Scout Badge and Proficiency Badges

33 Tropical Fruits

(Des V. Whiteley. Litho Harrison)

1964 (23 Nov). *50th Anniv of St. Vincent Boy Scouts Association.* W w **12.** *P* 14½.
221 32 1 c. yellow-green and chocolate .. 10 10
222 4 c. blue and brown-purple 10 10
223 20 c. yellow and black-violet 30 10
224 50 c. red and bronze-green 45 20
221/4 .. .. *Set of* 4 80 30

(Des V. Whiteley. Photo Harrison)

1965 (23 Mar). *Botanic Gardens Bicentenary. T* **33** *and similar multicoloured designs.* W w **12.** *P* 14½ × 13½ (*horiz*) *or* 13½ × 14½ (*vert*).
225 1 c. Type **33** 10 10
226 4 c. Breadfruit and H.M.S. *Providence*, 1791 10 10
227 25 c. Doric Temple and pond (*vert*) .. 15 10
228 40 c. Talipot Palm and Doric Temple (*vert*) .. 30 40
225/8 .. .. *Set of* 4 50 50

1965 (17 May). *I.T.U. Centenary. As Nos.* 98/9 *of Lesotho.*
229 4 c. light blue and light olive-green .. 25 10
230 48 c. ochre-yellow and orange.. .. 1·00 45

37 Boat-building, Bequia (inscr "BEOUIA")

(Des M. Goaman. Photo Harrison)

1965 (16 Aug)–**67.** *T* **37** *and similar multicoloured designs.* W w **12.** *P* 14½ × 13½ (*horiz designs*) *or* 13½ × 14½ (*vert*).
231 1 c. Type **37** ("BEOUIA") 10 40
231*a* 1 c. Type **37** ("BEQUIA") (27.6.67) .. 10 10
232 2 c. Friendship Beach, Bequia .. 10 10
233 3 c. Terminal Building, Arnos Vale Airport 15 10
234 4 c. Woman with bananas (*vert*) .. 1·00 30
235 5 c. Crater Lake 15 10
236 6 c. Carib Stone (*vert*) 15 30
237 8 c. Arrowroot (*vert*) 30 10
238 10 c. Owia Salt Pond 20 10
239 12 c. Deep water wharf 30 10
240 20 c. Sea Island cotton (*vert*) 30 10
241 25 c. Map of St. Vincent and islands (*vert*) .. 35 10
242 50 c. Breadfruit (*vert*).. .. .. 50 25
243 $1 Baleine Falls (*vert*) .. .. .. 4·00 30
244 $2.50, St. Vincent Amazon (*vert*) .. 16·00 4·00
245 $5 Arms of St. Vincent (*vert*) .. .. 7·00 5·50
231/45 .. .. *Set of* 16 27·00 10·00
The 1 c. (No. 231*a*), 2 c., 3 c., 5 c. and 10 c. exist with PVA gum as well as gum arabic.
See also No. 261.

1966 (24 June). *Churchill Commemoration. As Nos.* 102/5 *of Lesotho.*
246 1 c. new blue 10 10
247 4 c. deep green 35 10
248 20 c. brown 75 45
249 40 c. bluish violet .. .. 1·50 1·25
246/9 .. .. *Set of* 4 2·40 1·60

1966 (4 Feb). *Royal Visit. As Nos.* 183/4 *of Montserrat.*
250 4 c. black and ultramarine .. .. .. 1·50 25
251 25 c. black and magenta .. .. .. 4·00 1·25

1966 (20 Sept). *Inauguration of W.H.O. Headquarters, Geneva. As Nos.* 185/6 *of Montserrat.*
252 4 c. black, yellow-green and light blue .. 30 10
253 25 c. black, light purple and yellow-brown .. 95 80

1966 (1 Dec). *20th Anniv of U.N.E.S.C.O. As Nos.* 342/4 *of Mauritius.*
254 4 c. slate-violet, red, yellow and orange .. 40 10
255 8 c. orange-yellow, violet and deep olive .. 75 10
256 25 c. black, bright purple and orange.. .. 1·50 60
254/6 .. .. *Set of* 3 2·40 70

38 Coastal View of Mount Coke Area

(Des and photo Harrison)

1967 (1 Dec). *Autonomous Methodist Church. T* **38** *and similar horiz designs. Multicoloured.* W w **12.** *P* 14 × 14½.
257 2 c. Type **38** 10 10
258 8 c. Kingstown Methodist Church 10 10
259 25 c. First Licence to perform marriages .. 20 10
260 35 c. Conference Arms 20 10
257/60 .. .. *Set of* 4 45 20

1968 (20 Feb). *As No.* 234, *but* W w **12** *sideways.*
261 4 c. Woman with bananas 30 30
The above exists with PVA gum as well as gum arabic.

39 Meteorological Institute

(Des G. Vasarhelyi. Photo Harrison)

1968 (28 May). *World Meteorological Day.* W w **12.** *P* 14 × 14½.
262 39 4 c. multicoloured 10 10
263 25 c. multicoloured 10 10
264 35 c. multicoloured 15 10
262/4 .. .. *Set of* 3 30 20

40 Dr. Martin Luther King and Cotton Pickers

(Des V. Whiteley. Litho D.L.R.)

1968 (28 Aug). *Martin Luther King Commemoration.* W w **12** (*sideways*). *P* 13.
265 40 5 c. multicoloured 10 10
266 25 c. multicoloured 10 10
267 35 c. multicoloured 10 10
265/7 .. .. *Set of* 3 20 20

41 Speaker addressing Demonstrators

42 Scales of Justice and Human Rights Emblem

(Des V. Whiteley. Photo Enschedé)

1968 (1 Nov). *Human Rights Year. P* 13 × 14 (3 *c.*) *or* 14 × 13 (35 *c.*).
268 41 3 c. multicoloured 10 10
269 42 35 c. royal blue and turquoise-blue .. 20 10

43 Male Masquerader 44 Steel Bandsman

(Des V. Whiteley. Litho Format)

1969 (17 Feb). *St. Vincent Carnival. T* **43/4** *and similar designs. P* 14.
270 1 c. multicoloured 10 10
271 5 c. red and deep chocolate 10 10
272 8 c. multicoloured 10 10
273 25 c. multicoloured 15 15
270/3 .. .. *Set of* 4 30 30
Designs: *Horiz*—8 c. Carnival Revellers. *Vert*—25 c. Queen of Bands.

METHODIST
CONFERENCE
MAY
1969
(47)

1969 (14 May). *Methodist Conference. Nos.* 257/8, 241 *and* 260 *optd with T* **47**.
274 2 c. multicoloured 10 15
275 8 c. multicoloured 30 40
276 25 c. multicoloured 35 40
277 35 c. multicoloured .. .. 1·50 3·00
274/7 .. .. *Set of* 4 2·00 3·50

48 "Strength in Unity" 49 Map of "CARIFTA" Countries

(Des J. Cooter. Litho D.L.R.)

1969 (1 July). *First Anniv of CARIFTA (Caribbean Free Trade Area).* W w **12** (*sideways on T* **48**). *P* 13.
278 48 2 c. black, pale buff and red 10 10
279 49 5 c. multicoloured 10 10
280 48 8 c. black, pale buff and pale green .. 10 10
281 49 25 c. multicoloured 15 15
278/81 .. .. *Set of* 4 30 30

ASSOCIATED STATEHOOD

50 Flag of St. Vincent

(Des V. Whiteley, based on local designs. Photo Harrison)

1969 (27 Oct). *Statehood. T* **50** *and similar horiz designs.* W w **12.** *P* 14 × 14½.
282 4 c. multicoloured 10 10
283 10 c. multicoloured 10 10
284 50 c. grey, black and orange 25 10
282/4 .. .. *Set of* 3 40 20
Designs:—10 c. Battle scene with insets of Petroglyph and Carib chief Chatoyer; 50 c. Carib House with maces and scales.

51 Green Heron

(Des J.W. Photo Harrison)

1970 (12 Jan)–71. *T* **51** *and similar multicoloured designs. Chalk-surfaced paper.* W w **12** (*sideways on* 1, 2, 3, 6, 8, 20, 25 c., $1, $2.50 *and upright on others*). *P* 14.

285 ½ c. House Wren (*vert*) 10 50
286 1 c. Type **51** 35 90
a. Glazed, ordinary paper (9.8.71) 30 80
287 2 c. Lesser Antillean Bullfinches 15 30
288 3 c. St. Vincent Amazons 15 30
289 4 c. Rufous-throated Solitaire (*vert*) 20 30
290 5 c. Red-necked Pigeon (*vert*) 2·75 30
a. Glazed, ordinary paper (9.8.71) 1·25 30
291 6 c. Bananaquits 25 20
292 8 c. Purple-throated Carib 25 20
293 10 c. Mangrove Cuckoo (*vert*) 30 10
294 12 c. Common Black Hawk (*vert*) 40 10
295 20 c. Bare-eyed Thrush 60 15
296 25 c. Hooded Tanager 70 20
297 50 c. Blue Hooded Euphonia 1·50 75
298 $1 Barn Owl (*vert*) 6·50 3·50
299 $2.50, Yellow-bellied Elaenia (*vert*) 7·00 4·00
300 $5 Ruddy Quail Dove 11·00 5·50
285/300 *Set of* 16 27·00 15·00

See also Nos. 361/8 and 396/8.

52 "DHC-6" Twin Otter

(Des R. Granger Barrett. Litho Enschedé)

1970 (13 Mar). *20th Anniv of Regular Air Services. T* **52** *and similar horiz designs. Multicoloured.* W w **12** (*sideways*). *P* 14 × 13.

301 5 c. Type **52** 10 10
302 8 c. Grumman "Goose" 15 10
303 10 c. Hawker Siddeley "HS-748" 20 10
304 25 c. Douglas "DC-3" 65 30
301/4 *Set of* 4 1·00 40

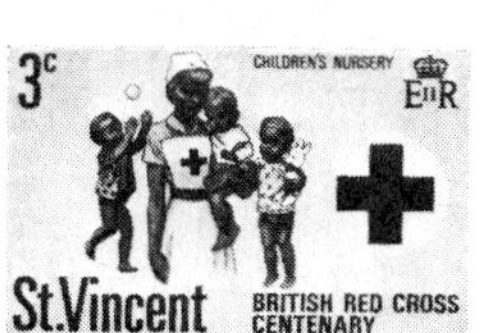

53 "Children's Nursery"

54 "Angel and the Two Marys at the Tomb" (stained-glass window)

(Des R. Granger Barrett. Photo Harrison)

1970 (1 June). *Centenary of British Red Cross. T* **53** *and similar horiz designs. Multicoloured.* W w **12**. *P* 14.

305 3 c. Type **53** 10 10
306 5 c. "First Aid" 15 10
307 12 c. "Voluntary Aid Detachment" 20 15
308 25 c. "Blood Transfusion" 30 15
305/8 *Set of* 4 65 30

(Des L. Curtis. Litho J.W.)

1970 (7 Sept). *150th Anniv of St. George's Cathedral, Kingstown. T* **54** *and similar multicoloured designs.* W w **12** (*sideways on horiz designs*). *P* 14.

309 ½ c. Type **54** 10 10
310 5 c. St. George's Cathedral (*horiz*) 10 10
311 25 c. Tower, St. George's Cathedral 10 10
312 35 c. Interior, St. George's Cathedral (*horiz*) 15 10
313 50 c. Type **54** 20 30
309/13 *Set of* 5 45 35

55 "The Adoration of the Shepherds" (Le Nain)

(Des J. Cooter. Litho Questa)

1970 (23 Nov). *Christmas. T* **55** *and similar vert design. Multicoloured.* W w **12** (*sideways on* 25 c., 50 c.). *P* 14.

314 8 c. "The Virgin and Child" (Bellini) 10 10
315 25 c. Type **55** 10 10
316 35 c. As 8 c. 10 10
317 50 c. Type **55** 15 20
314/17 *Set of* 4 35 30

56 New Post Office and 6d. Stamp of 1861

(Des J. Cooter. Litho Questa)

1971 (29 Mar). *110th Anniv of First St. Vincent Stamps. T* **56** *and similar horiz design. Multicoloured.* W w **12** (*sideways*). *P* 14.

318 2 c. Type **56** 10 10
319 4 c. 1d. Stamp of 1861 and New Post Office 10 10
320 25 c. Type **56** 10 10
321 $1 As 4 c. 35 45
318/21 *Set of* 4 45 50

57 Trust Seal and Wildlife

58 "Madonna appearing to St. Anthony" (Tiepolo)

(Des G. Drummond. Litho J.W.)

1971 (4 Aug). *St. Vincent's National Trust. T* **57** *and similar horiz design. Multicoloured.* W w **12** (*sideways*). *P* 13½ × 14.

322 12 c. Type **57** 25 10
323 30 c. Old Cannon, Fort Charlotte 40 15
324 40 c. Type **57** 55 25
325 45 c. As 30 c. 55 30
322/5 *Set of* 4 1·60 70

(Des J. Cooter. Litho Questa)

1971 (6 Oct). *Christmas. T* **58** *and similar horiz design. Multicoloured.* W w **12** (*sideways on* 10 c. *and* $1). *P* 14½ × 14 (10 *c.*, $1) *or* 14 × 14½ (5 *c.*, 25 *c.*).

326 5 c. Type **58** 10 10
327 10 c. "The Holy Family on the Flight into Egypt" (detail, Pietro da Cortona) 10 10
328 25 c. Type **58** 10 10
329 $1 As 10 c. 30 35
326/9 *Set of* 4 40 40

59 Careening

60 Private, Grenadier Company, 32nd Foot (1764)

(Des J. Cooter. Litho J.W.)

1971 (25 Nov). *The Grenadines of St. Vincent. T* **59** *and similar vert designs. Multicoloured.* W w **12**. *P* 13½.

330 1 c. Type **59** 10 10
331 5 c. Seine fishermen 10 10
332 6 c. Map of the Grenadines 10 10
333 15 c. Type **59** 10 10
334 20 c. As 5 c. 15 10
335 50 c. As 6 c. 30 60
330/5 *Set of* 6 50 80
MS336 177 × 140 mm. Nos. 330/5 7·00 11·00

(Des and litho J.W.)

1972 (14 Feb). *Military Uniforms. T* **60** *and similar vert designs. Multicoloured.* W w **12**. *P* 14 × 13½.

337 12 c. Type **60** 90 15
338 30 c. Officer, Battalion Company, 31st Foot (1772) 1·75 65
339 50 c. Private, Grenadier Company, 6th Foot (1772) 2·50 1·00
337/9 *Set of* 3 4·50 1·60

61 Breadnut Fruit

62 Candlestick Cassia

(Des P. Powell. Litho Questa)

1972 (16 May). *Fruit. T* **61** *and similar vert designs. Multicoloured.* W w **12** (*sideways*). *P* 13½.

340 3 c. Type **61** 10 10
341 5 c. Pawpaw 10 10
342 12 c. Plumrose or Roseapple 30 30
343 25 c. Mango 70 70
340/3 *Set of* 4 1·00 1·00

(Des Sylvia Goaman. Litho B.W.)

1972 (31 July). *Flowers. T* **62** *and similar vert designs. Multicoloured. P* 13 ($1) *or* 13½ × 14 (*others*).

344 1 c. Type **62** 10 10
345 30 c. Lobster Claw 20 10
346 40 c. White Trumpet 25 15
347 $1 Soufriere tree 70 80
344/7 *Set of* 4 1·10 1·00

63 Sir Charles Brisbane and Coat of Arms

(Des Jennifer Toombs. Litho J.W.)

1972 (29 Sept). *Birth Bicentenary of Sir Charles Brisbane. T* **63** *and similar horiz designs.* W w **12** (*sideways*). *P* 13½.

348 20 c. yellow-ochre, gold and red-brown 15 10
349 30 c. light yellow, light mauve and black 40 10
350 $1 multicoloured 1·40 70
348/50 *Set of* 3 1·75 75
MS351 171 × 111 mm. Nos. 348/50 (*sold at* $2) 4·50 6·50

Designs:—30 c. H.M.S. *Arethusa*, 1807; $1 H.M.S. *Blake*, 1808.

64 Arrowroot and Breadfruit

(Des (from photograph by D. Groves) and photo Harrison)

1972 (20 Nov). *Royal Silver Wedding. Multicoloured; background colour given.* W w **12**. *P* 14 × 14½.

352 **64** 30 c. red-brown 10 10
353 $1 myrtle-green 40 20

65 Sighting St. Vincent

66 "The Last Supper" (French Stained-glass Window)

(Des J. Cooter. Litho Enschedé)

1973 (31 Jan). *475th Anniv of Columbus's Third Voyage to the West Indies. T* **65** *and similar triangular designs. Multicoloured.* W w **12**. *P* 13½.

354 5 c. Type **65** 25 15
355 12 c. Caribs watching Columbus's fleet 45 20
356 30 c. Christopher Columbus 1·00 70
357 50 c. *Santa Maria* 1·50 1·10
354/7 *Set of* 4 3·00 2·00

(Des J. Cooter. Litho Questa)

1973 (19 Apr). *Easter. T* **66** *and similar vert designs. Multicoloured.* W w **12** (*sideways*). *P* 14 × 13½.

358 **66** 15 c. multicoloured 10 10
a. Horiz strip of 3. Nos. 358/60 45
359 – 60 c. multicoloured 20 20
360 – $1 multicoloured 20 20
358/60 *Set of* 3 45 45

Nos. 358, 360 and 359 were printed, in that order, horizontally *se-tenant* throughout a sheet of 45 stamps, and form a composite design of "The Last Supper".

1973 (13 June–23 Nov). *As Nos.* 285 *etc, but* W w **12** *upright on* 2, 3, 6, 20 *c. and sideways on others. Glazed paper.*

361 2 c. Lesser Antillean Bullfinches (23.11) 30 30
362 3 c. St. Vincent Amazons (23.11) 30 30
363 4 c. Rufous-throated Solitaire (*vert*) (23.11) 30 30
364 5 c. Red-necked Pigeon (*vert*) 50 20
365 6 c. Bananaquits (23.11) 40 35
366 10 c. Mangrove Cuckoo (*vert*) (23.11) 55 15
367 12 c. Common Black Hawk (*vert*) (23.11) 85 65
368 20 c. Bare-eyed Thrush (23.11) 1·25 40
361/8 *Set of* 8 4·00 2·40

For the 1 c. value with watermark upright see Grenadines of St. Vincent No. 3a.

67 William Wilberforce and Poster

68 P.P.F. Symbol

(Des Jennifer Toombs. Litho D.L.R.)

1973 (11 July). *140th Death Anniv of William Wilberforce. T* **67** *and similar horiz designs. Multicoloured. W* w **12.** *P* 14 × 13½.
369 30 c. Type **67** 15 10
370 40 c. Slaves cutting cane 20 15
371 50 c. Wilberforce and medallion 20 15
369/71 .. .. *Set of* 3 50 35

(Des PAD Studio. Litho Walsall)

1973 (3 Oct). *21st Anniv of International Planned Parenthood Federation. T* **68** *and similar vert design. Multicoloured. W* w **12** *(sideways). P* 14.
372 12 c. Type **68** 10 10
373 40 c. "IPPF" and symbol 20 20

1973 (14 Nov). *Royal Wedding. As Nos.* 322/3 *of Montserrat.*
374 50 c. deep blue 15 10
375 70 c. grey-green 20 10

69 Administrative Block, Mona

(Des PAD Studio. Litho Questa)

1973 (13 Dec). *25th Anniv of West Indies University. T* **69** *and similar multicoloured designs. W* w **12** *(sideways on* $1*). P* 14.
376 5 c. Type **69** 10 10
377 10 c. University Centre, Kingstown 10 10
378 30 c. Aerial view, Mona University 15 10
379 $1 University coat of arms (*vert*) 50 60
376/9 .. .. *Set of* 4 65 65

30c

(70)

71 "The Descent from the Cross" (Sansovino)

1973 (15 Dec). *Nos.* 297, 292 *and* 298 *surch in half sheets with T* **70**, *by the Govt Printer, St. Vincent.*
380 30 c. on 50 c. multicoloured .. .. .. 1·75 70
a. Surch double .. .. 30·00
b. Surch double (on front) and single inverted (on reverse) .. .. .. 75·00
c. Surch double, one inverted .. .. 60·00
d. Surch inverted .. ..
381 40 c. on 8 c. multicoloured .. .. .. 1·75 70
a. Surch double .. .. 35·00
b. Surch inverted .. .. 10·00
382 $10 on $1 multicoloured .. .. .. 10·00 6·50
a. Surch double .. .. 95·00
b. Surch inverted £110
c. Surch double, one inverted £110
380/2 .. .. *Set of* 3 12·00 7·00

SPECIMEN STAMPS. From No. 383 onwards the stamps of St. Vincent exist overprinted "SPECIMEN", these being produced for publicity purposes.

(Des PAD Studio. Litho Enschedé)

1974 (10 Apr). *Easter. T* **71** *and similar vert designs showing sculptures. Multicoloured. W* w **12** *(sideways). P* 14 × 13½.
383 5 c. Type **71** 10 10
384 30 c. "The Deposition" (English, 14th-century) 10 10
385 40 c. "Pieta" (Fernandez) 10 10
386 $1 "The Resurrection" (French, 16th-century) 20 25
383/6 .. .. *Set of* 4 30 30

72 *Istra*

(Des J.W. Litho Questa)

1974 (28 June). *Cruise Ships. T* **72** *and similar horiz designs. Multicoloured. W* w **12** *(sideways). P* 14.
387 15 c. Type **72** 20 10
388 20 c. *Oceanic* 25 10
389 30 c. *Aleksandr Pushkin* 25 10
390 $1 *Europa* 50 30
387/90 .. .. *Set of* 4 1·10 40
MS391 134 × 83 mm. Nos. 387/90 .. .. 1·00 2·50

73 U.P.U. Emblem

(Des J.W. Litho Questa)

1974 (25 July). *Centenary of Universal Postal Union. T* **73** *and similar horiz designs. Multicoloured. W* w **12.** *P* 14.
392 5 c. Type **73** 10 10
393 12 c. Globe within posthorn 10 10
394 60 c. Map of St. Vincent and hand-cancelling 20 10
395 90 c. Map of the World 25 30
392/5 .. .. *Set of* 4 50 40

74 Royal Tern

75 Scout Badge and Emblems

(Des J.W. Litho Questa)

1974 (29 Aug). *T* **74** *and similar vert designs. Multicoloured. Glazed paper. W* w **12** *(sideways on* 40 c. *and* $10*). P* 14.
396 30 c. Type **74** .. .. 2·00 75
397 40 c. Brown Pelican .. .. 2·00 75
398 $10 Magnificent Frigate Bird .. .. 18·00 9·00
396/8 .. .. *Set of* 3 20·00 9·50

(Des Sylvia Goaman. Litho Enschedé)

1974 (9 Oct). *Diamond Jubilee of Scout Movement in St. Vincent. W* w **12.** *P* 13 × 13½.
399 **75** 10 c. multicoloured 10 10
400 25 c. multicoloured 20 10
401 45 c. multicoloured 35 25
402 $1 multicoloured 75 50
399/402 .. .. *Set of* 4 1·25 75

76 Sir Winston Churchill

77 The Shepherds

(Des C. Abbott. Litho Questa)

1974 (28 Nov). *Birth Centenary of Sir Winston Churchill. T* **76** *and similar vert designs. Multicoloured. W* w **12.** *P* 14.
403 25 c. Type **76** 15 10
404 35 c. Churchill in military uniform 20 10
405 45 c. Churchill in naval uniform 25 10
406 $1 Churchill in air-force uniform 45 50
403/6 .. .. *Set of* 4 95 60

(Des Jennifer Toombs. Litho Enschedé)

1974 (5 Dec). *Christmas. T* **77** *and similar vert designs. W* w **12.** *P* 12 × 12½.
407 **77** 3 c. violet-blue and black 10 10
a. Horiz strip of 4. Nos. 407/10 .. 20
408 – 3 c. violet-blue and black 10 10
409 – 3 c. violet-blue and black 10 10
410 – 3 c. violet-blue and black 10 10
411 **77** 8 c. apple-green and black 10 10
412 – 35 c. rose and deep maroon 20 10
413 – 45 c. olive-bistre and brown-black .. 20 10
414 – $1 lavender and slate-black 40 50
407/14 .. .. *Set of* 8 1·00 85

Designs:—Nos. 408, 412 Mary and crib; Nos. 409, 413 Joseph, ox and ass; Nos. 410, 414 The Magi.

Nos. 407/10 were issued horizontally *se-tenant* within the sheet, together forming a composite design of the Nativity.

MINIMUM PRICE

The minimum price quote is 10p which represents a handling charge rather than a basis for valuing common stamps. For further notes about prices see introductory pages.

78 Faces

(Des G. Drummond. Litho D.L.R.)

1975 (7–27 Feb). *Kingstown Carnival. T* **78** *and similar horiz designs. Multicoloured. W* w **12.** *P* 14 × 13½.
415 1 c. Type **78** 10 10
a. Booklet pane. No. 415 × 2 plus printed label (27.2) 35
b. Booklet pane. Nos. 415, 417 and 419 (27.2) 45
416 15 c. Pineapple women 20 15
a. Booklet pane. Nos. 416, 418 and 420 (27.2) 70
417 25 c. King of the Bands 20 20
418 35 c. Carnival dancers 25 15
419 45 c. Queen of the Bands 25 20
420 $1.25, "African Splendour" 35 55
415/20 .. .. *Set of* 6 1·10 1·10
MS421 146 × 128 mm. Nos. 415/20 .. .. 1·25 3·00

79 French Angelfish

Two types of $2.50:

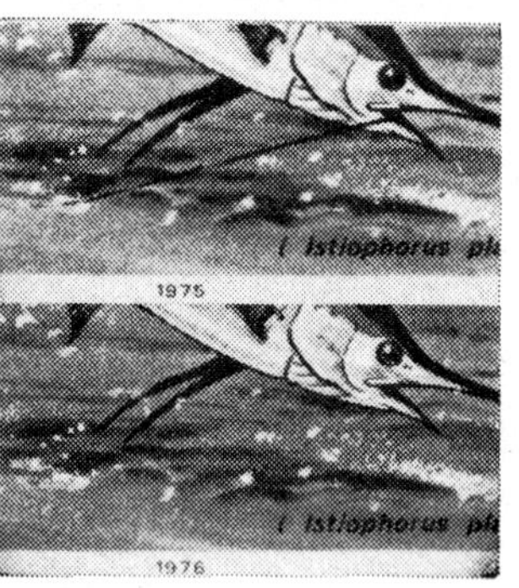

I

II

Type I. Fishing-line attached to fish's mouth. Imprint "1975".
Type II. Fishing-line omitted. Imprint "1976".

(Des G. Drummond. Litho Questa)

1975 (10 Apr)–**76.** *T* **79** *and similar horiz designs. Multicoloured. W* w **14** *(sideways). P* 14½.
422 1 c. Type **79** 15 40
423 2 c. Spotfin Butterfly-fish 15 40
424 3 c. Horse-eyed Jack 15 15
425 4 c. Mackerel 20 10
426 5 c. French Grunt 20 30
427 6 c. Spotted Goatfish 20 40
428 8 c. Ballyhoo 20 40
429 10 c. Sperm Whale 30 10
430 12 c. Humpback Whale 40 50
431 15 c. Cowfish 70 45
432 15 c. Skipjack (14.10.76) .. .. .. 3·00 35
433 20 c. Queen Angelfish 40 10
434 25 c. Princess Parrotfish 45 10
435 35 c. Red Hind 50 30
436 45 c. Atlantic Flying Fish 65 30
437 50 c. Porkfish 65 35
438 70 c. "Albacore" or Yellowfin Tuna (14.10.76) 4·25 70
439 90 c. Pompano (14.10.76) .. .. .. 4·25 70
440 $1 Queen Triggerfish 90 20
441 $2.50, Sailfish (I) .. .. 4·00 5·50
a. Type II (12.7.76) .. .. 3·50 1·50
442 $5 Dolphin Fish .. .. 5·00 2·50
443 $10 Blue Marlin .. .. 5·00 8·00
422/43 .. .. *Set of* 22 27·00 16·00

With the exception of Nos. 431, 435/6, 438/9 and 442 the above exist with different dates in the imprint at the foot of each stamp.

80 Cutting Bananas

(Des G. Drummond. Litho Questa)

1975 (26 June). *Banana Industry. T* **80** *and similar horiz designs. Multicoloured. W* w **12** *(sideways). P* 13½.
447 25 c. Type **80** 15 10
448 35 c. Packaging Station, La Croix 15 10
449 45 c. Cleaning and boxing 20 15
450 70 c. Shipping bananas aboard *Geest Tide* .. 40 30
447/50 .. .. *Set of* 4 80 50

81 Snorkel Diving

(Des G. Drummond. Litho Questa)

1975 (31 July). *Tourism. T* **81** *and similar horiz designs. Multicoloured.* W w **14** (*sideways*). *P* 13½.

451 15 c. Type **81** 15 10
452 20 c. Aquaduct Golf Course 20 10
453 35 c. Steel Band at Mariner's Inn 35 15
454 45 c. Sunbathing at Young Island 45 25
455 $1.25, Yachting marina .. .. .. 1·25 1·50
451/5 .. .. *Set of* 5 2·10 1·90

82 George Washington, John Adams, Thomas Jefferson and James Madison

(Des G. Drummond. Litho Questa)

1975 (11 Sept). *Bicentenary of American Revolution. T* **82** *and similar horiz designs. P* 14.

456 ½ c. black and lavender 10 10
457 1 c. black and light emerald 10 10
458 1½ c. black and light magenta 10 10
459 5 c. black and bright yellow-green 10 10
460 10 c. black and light violet-blue 15 10
461 25 c. black and dull orange-yellow 25 10
462 35 c. black and light greenish blue 30 15
463 45 c. black and bright rose 35 15
464 $1 black and light orange 55 40
465 $2 black and light yellow-olive 90 75
456/65 .. .. *Set of* 10 2·50 1·50
MS466 179 × 156 mm. Nos. 456/65 .. .. 5·00 4·00

Presidents:—1 c. Monroe, Quincy Adams, Jackson, van Buren; 1½ c. W. Harrison, Tyler, Polk, Taylor; 5 c. Fillmore, Pierce, Buchanan, Lincoln; 10 c. Andrew Johnson, Grant, Hayes, Garfield; 25 c. Arthur, Cleveland, B. Harrison, McKinley; 35 c. Theodore Roosevelt, Taft, Wilson, Harding; 45 c. Coolidge, Hoover, Franklin Roosevelt, Truman; $1 Eisenhower, Kennedy, Lyndon Johnson, Nixon; $2 Pres. Ford and White House.

Nos. 456/65 were each issued in sheets of ten stamps and two *se-tenant* labels.

83/4 "Shepherds"

(Des Jennifer Toombs. Litho Harrison)

1975 (4 Dec). *Christmas. T* **83/4** *and similar triangular designs. P* 13½ × 14. *A. W w* **12** (*upright*). *B. W w* **12** (*sideways*).

		A		B	
467	3 c. black and magenta ..	10	10	10	10
	a. Block of 4. Nos. 467/70	30	30	30	30
468	3 c. black and magenta ..	10	10	10	10
469	3 c. black and magenta ..	10	10	10	10
470	3 c. black and magenta ..	10	10	10	10
471	8 c. black & lt greenish blue ..	10	10	10	10
	a. Pair. Nos. 471/2 ..	15	15	15	15
472	8 c. black & lt greenish blue ..	10	10	10	10
473	35 c. black and yellow ..	20	20	20	20
	a. Pair. Nos. 473/4 ..	40	40	40	40
474	35 c. black and yellow ..	20	20	20	20
475	45 c. black and yellow-green ..	30	30	30	30
	a. Pair. Nos. 475/6 ..	60	60	60	60
476	45 c. black and yellow-green ..	30	30	30	30
477	$1 black and bright lilac ..	65	65	65	65
	a. Pair. Nos. 477/8 ..	1·25	1·25	1·25	1·25
478	$1 black and bright lilac ..	65	65	65	65
467/78	.. .. *Set of* 12	2·40	2·40	2·40	2·40

Designs:—No. 467, "Star of Bethlehem"; 468, "Holy Trinity"; 469, As T **83**; 470, "Three Kings"; 471/2, As 467; 473/4, As 468; 475/6, T **83/4**; 477/8 As 470. The two designs of each denomination (Nos. 471/8) differ in that the longest side is at the foot or at the top as shown in T **83/4**.

Each denomination was printed in sheets of 16, the designs being *se-tenant* and so arranged that the watermark comes upright, inverted, sideways right and sideways left.

85 Carnival Dancers

(Des G. Drummond. Litho Questa)

1976 (19 Feb). *Kingstown Carnival. T* **85** *and similar horiz designs. Multicoloured.* W w **14** (*sideways*). *P* 13½.

479 1 c. Type **85** 10 10
a. Booklet pane. Nos. 479 and 480 plus printed label 20
480 2 c. Humpty-Dumpty people 10 10
a. Booklet pane. Nos. 480/2 35
481 5 c. Smiling faces 10 10
482 35 c. Dragon worshippers 20 10
a. Booklet pane. Nos. 482/4 80
483 45 c. Carnival tableaux 25 15
484 $1.25, Bumble-Bee dancers 45 45
479/84 .. .. *Set of* 6 90 80

70¢

(86)

87 Blue-headed Hummingbird and Yellow Hibiscus

1976 (8 Apr). *Nos.* 424 *and* 437 *surch as T* **86**.

485 70 c. on 3 c. Horse-eyed Jack .. .. .. 1·25 1·25
a. Surch inverted .. .. 40·00
486 90 c. on 50 c. Porkfish .. .. 1·40 1·40
a. Surch inverted .. .. 45·00

(Des G. Drummond. Litho Walsall)

1976 (20 May). *Hummingbirds and Hibiscuses. T* **87** *and similar vert designs. Multicoloured.* W w **14** (*inverted*). *P* 13½.

487 5 c. Type **87** 35 10
488 10 c. Antillean Crested Hummingbird and Pink Hibiscus 60 15
489 35 c. Purple-throated Carib and White Hibiscus .. .. 1·40 55
a. No wmk .. .. 35·00
490 45 c. Blue-headed Hummingbird and Red Hibiscus .. .. 1·50 65
491 $1.25, Green-throated Carib and Peach Hibiscus .. .. 9·50 5·50
487/91 .. .. *Set of* 5 12·00 6·25

1976 (16 Sept). *West Indian Victory in World Cricket Cup. As Nos.* 419/20 *of Jamaica.*

492 15 c. Map of the Caribbean 75 25
493 45 c. Prudential Cup .. .. 1·75 1·00

88 St Mary's Church, Kingstown

(Des G. Drummond. Litho Questa)

1976 (18 Nov). *Christmas. T* **88** *and similar horiz designs. Multicoloured.* W w **14** (*sideways*). *P* 14.

494 35 c. Type **88** 15 10
495 45 c. Anglican Church, Georgetown 15 10
496 50 c. Methodist Church, Georgetown 20 10
497 $1.25, St. George's Cathedral, Kingstown .. 40 60
494/7 .. .. *Set of* 4 80 70

89 Barrancoid Pot-stand

(Des G. Vasarhelyi. Litho J.W.)

1976 (16 Dec). *National Trust. T* **89** *and similar horiz designs. Multicoloured.* W w **14** (*sideways*). *P* 13½.

498 5 c. Type **89** 10 10
499 45 c. National Museum 15 10
500 70 c. Carib sculpture 25 20
501 $1 Ciboney petroglyph 45 50
498/501 .. .. *Set of* 4 80 75

90 William I, William II, Henry I and Stephen

(Des G. Vasarhelyi. Litho J.W.)

1977 (7 Feb). *Silver Jubilee. T* **90** *and similar horiz designs. Multicoloured. P* 13½. (a) W w **14** (*sideways*). *From sheets.*

502 ½ c. Type **90** 10 10
503 1 c. Henry II, Richard I, John, Henry III .. 10 10
504 1½ c. Edward I, Edward II, Edward III, Richard II 10 10
505 2 c. Henry IV, Henry V, Henry VI, Edward IV 10 10
506 5 c. Edward V, Richard III, Henry VII, Henry VIII 10 10
507 10 c. Edward VI, Lady Jane Grey, Mary I, Elizabeth I 10 10
508 25 c. James I, Charles I, Charles II, James II 20 15
509 35 c. William III, Mary II, Anne, George I .. 30 20
510 45 c. George II, George III, George IV .. 35 25
511 75 c. William IV, Victoria, Edward VII .. 45 35
512 $1 George V, Edward VIII, George VI .. 55 45
513 $2 Elizabeth II leaving Westminster Abbey 95 70
502/13 .. .. *Set of* 12 2·75 2·40
MS514 170 × 146 mm. Nos. 502/13. P 14½ × 14 4·00 4·00

(*b*) *No wmk. From booklets*

515 ½ c. Type **90** .. .. 2·00 2·50
a. Booklet pane. Nos. 515/18 *se-tenant* .. 7·50
516 1 c. As No. 503 .. .. 2·00 2·50
517 1½ c. As No. 504 .. .. 2·00 2·50
518 2 c. As No. 505 .. .. 2·00 2·50
519 5 c. As No. 506 .. .. 2·00 2·50
a. Booklet pane. Nos. 519/22 *se-tenant* .. 7·50
520 10 c. As No. 507 .. .. 2·00 2·50
521 25 c. As No. 508 .. .. 2·00 2·50
522 35 c. As No. 509 .. .. 2·00 2·50
523 45 c. As No. 510 .. .. 2·00 2·50
a. Booklet pane. Nos. 523/6 *se-tenant* .. 7·50
524 75 c. As No. 511 .. .. 2·00 2·50
525 $1 As No. 512 .. .. 2·00 2·50
526 $2 As No. 513 .. .. 2·00 2·50
515/26 .. .. *Set of* 12 22·00 26·00

Nos. 502/13 were each issued in sheets of ten stamps and two *se-tenant* labels.

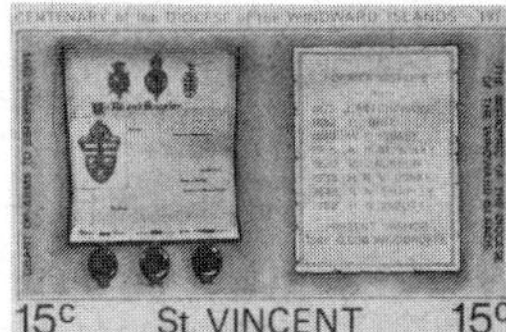

91 Grant of Arms

(Des G. Drummond. Litho Questa)

1977 (12 May). *Centenary of Windward Is Diocese. T* **91** *and similar horiz designs. Multicoloured.* W w **14** (*sideways*). *P* 13½.

527 15 c. Type **91** 10 10
528 35 c. Bishop Berkeley and mitres 10 10
529 45 c. Map and arms of diocese 10 10
530 $1.25, St. George's Cathedral and Bishop Woodroffe 30 45
527/30 .. .. *Set of* 4 45 50

(92)

1977 (2 June). *Kingstown Carnival. Nos.* 426, 429, 432/3 *and* 440 *optd with T* **92**.

531 5 c. French Grunt 10 10
a. Red opt .. .. 50·00
b. Hyphen omitted .. .. 1·40
532 10 c. Sperm Whale (R.) 10 10
a. Opt double (R. and Blk.) .. .. 60·00
b. Hyphen omitted .. .. 1·60
533 15 c. Skipjack (R.) 10 10
a. Black opt .. .. 50·00
b. Hyphen omitted .. .. 2·00
534 20 c. Queen Angel Fish (R.) 10 10
a. Opt inverted .. .. 22·00
b. Black opt .. .. 55·00
c. Hyphen omitted .. .. 2·25
535 $1 Queen Triggerfish 40 40
a. Red opt .. .. 60·00
b. Hyphen omitted .. .. 3·50
531/5 .. .. *Set of* 5 70 70

The variety showing the hyphen omitted from the second line of the overprint occurred on R.4/4 of the lower pane.

93 Guide and Emblem

CARIBBEAN VISIT 1977

(94)

(Des PAD Studio. Litho J.W.)

1977 (1 Sept). *50th Anniv of St. Vincent Girl Guides. T* **93** *and similar vert designs. The $2 value is additionally optd. "1930–1977". Multicoloured. W w* **14.** *P* 13½.

536	5 c. Type **93**	10	10
537	15 c. Early uniform, ranger, guide and brownie	15	10
538	20 c. Early uniform and guide	15	10
539	$2 Lady Baden-Powell	70	60
	a. Optd dates omitted	25·00	
	b. Optd dates double	85·00	
536/9	*Set of* 4	95	65

1977 (27 Oct). *Royal Visit. No.* 513 *optd with T* **94.**

540	$2 Queen Elizabeth leaving Westminster Abbey	40	30
	a. Opt inverted	50·00	

95 Map of St. Vincent **96** Opening Verse and Scene

(Des G. Drummond. Litho Questa)

1977–78. *Provisionals. W w* **12.** *P* 14½ × 14.

541	**95**	20 c. blk, dull violet-bl & pale bl (31.1.78)	15	15
542		40 c. black, dull orange & flesh (30.11.77)	25	20
		a. Black (value) omitted	50·00	
543		40 c. black, magenta and salmon (31.1.78)	20	15
541/3		*Set of* 3	55	45

Nos. 541/3 were printed in 1974, without value, for provisional use; they were locally surcharged before going on sale.

(Des Jennifer Toombs. Litho Enschedé)

1977 (1 Dec). *Christmas. Scenes and Verses from the carol "While Shepherds Watched their Flocks by Night". T* **96** *and similar vert designs. Multicoloured. W w* **14.** *P* 13 × 11.

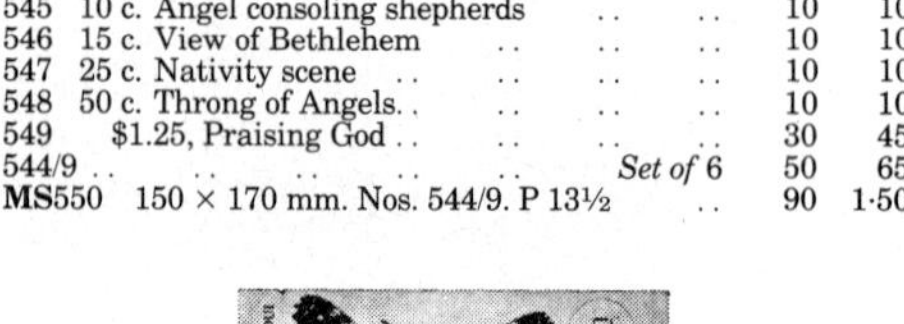

544	5 c. Type **96**	10	10
545	10 c. Angel consoling shepherds	10	10
546	15 c. View of Bethlehem	10	10
547	25 c. Nativity scene	10	10
548	50 c. Throng of Angels	10	10
549	$1.25, Praising God	30	45
544/9	*Set of* 6	50	65
MS550	150 × 170 mm. Nos. 544/9. P 13½	90	1·50

97 *Cynthia cardui* and *Bougainvillea glabra var. alba*

(Des Daphne Padden. Litho Walsall)

1978 (6 Apr). *Butterflies and Bougainvilleas. T* **97** *and similar horiz designs. Multicoloured. W w* **14** *(sideways). P* 14.

551	5 c. Type **97**	10	10
552	25 c. *Dione juno* and "Golden Glow"	15	10
553	40 c. *Anartia amathea* and "Mrs McLean"	25	10
554	50 c. *Hypolimnas misippus* and "Cyphen"	30	10
555	$1.25, *Pseudolycaena marsyas* and "Thomasii"	65	55
551/5	*Set of* 5	1·25	75

(Des G. Drummond. Litho J.W.)

1978 (2 June). *25th Anniv of Coronation. Horiz designs as Nos.* 422/5 *of Montserrat. Multicoloured. W w* **14** *(sideways). P* 13.

556	40 c. Westminster Abbey	10	10
557	50 c. Gloucester Cathedral	10	10
558	$1.25, Durham Cathedral	20	15
559	$2.50, Exeter Cathedral	30	25
556/9	*Set of* 4	55	45
MS560	130 × 102 mm. Nos. 556/9. P 13½ × 14	60	85

Nos. 556/9 were each printed in sheets of ten stamps and two *se-tenant* labels.

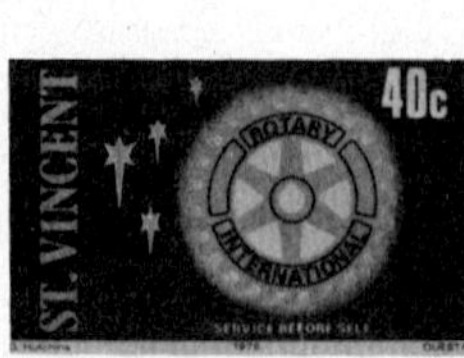

98 Rotary International Emblem and Motto **99** "Co-operation in Education Leads to Mutual Understanding and Respect"

(Des G. Hutchins. Litho Questa)

1978 (13 July). *International Service Clubs. T* **98** *and similar horiz designs showing club emblems and mottoes. Multicoloured. W w* **14** *(sideways). P* 14½.

561	40 c. Type **98**	25	10
562	50 c. Lions International	25	10
563	$1 Jaycees	50	35
561/3	*Set of* 3	90	40

(Des G. Hutchins. Litho Questa)

1978 (7 Sept). *10th Anniv of Project School to School (St. Vincent-Canada school twinning project). T* **99** *and similar multicoloured design showing flags and blackboard. W w* **14** *(sideways on $2). P* 14.

564	40 c. Type **99**	10	10
565	$2 "Co-operation in Education Leads to the Elimination of Racial Intolerance" (*horiz*)	40	50

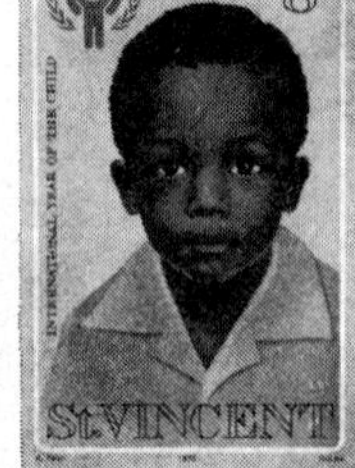

100 Arnos Vale Airport **101** Young Child

(Des G. Drummond. Litho Questa)

1978 (19 Oct). *75th Anniv of Powered Flight. T* **100** *and similar horiz designs. Multicoloured. W w* **14** *(sideways). P* 14½ × 14.

566	10 c. Type **100**	10	10
567	40 c. Wilbur Wright landing *Flyer*	15	10
568	50 c. Orville Wright in *Flyer*	15	10
569	$1.25, Orville Wright and *Flyer* airborne	45	35
566/9	*Set of* 4	70	45

(Des A. Paish. Litho Questa)

1979 (14 Feb). *International Year of the Child. T* **101** *and similar vert designs showing portraits of young children. W w* **14.** *P* 14 × 13½.

570	8 c. black, gold and pale yellow-green	10	10
571	20 c. black, gold and pale rose-lilac	15	10
572	50 c. black, gold and pale violet-blue	25	10
573	$2 black, gold and flesh	75	50
570/3	*Set of* 4	1·10	55

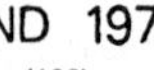

10c+5c

SOUFRIERE
RELIEF
FUND 1979

(102) **103** Sir Rowland Hill

(Des G. Drummond. Litho Questa)

1979 (17 Apr). *Soufrière Eruption Relief Fund. Designs as T* **95** *but surchd as T* **102** *by Reliance Printery, Kingstown. W w* **12.** *P* 14½ × 14.

574	10 c. + 5 c. violet-blue and pale rose-lilac	10	15
575	50 c. + 25 c. yellow-brown and buff	20	20
576	$1 + 50 c. reddish brown and brownish grey	30	30
577	$2 + $1 deep green and apple-green	50	50
574/7	*Set of* 4	1·00	1·00

(Des J.W. Litho Harrison)

1979 (31 May). *Death Centenary of Sir Rowland Hill. T* **103** *and similar horiz designs. Multicoloured. W w* **14** *(sideways). P* 14.

578	40 c. Type **103**	15	10
579	50 c. Penny Black and Twopenny Blue stamps	20	15
580	$3 1861 1d. and 6d. stamps	1·00	1·10
578/80	*Set of* 3	1·25	1·25
MS581	170 × 123 mm. Nos. 578/80, 594/5 and 599 (see footnote after No. 601)	1·75	3·00

Nos. 578/80 were each printed in sheets including two *se-tenant* stamp-size labels.

ST VINCENT AND
THE GRENADINES
AIR SERVICE 1979

104 First and Latest Buccament Postmarks and Map of St. Vincent **(105)**

(Des J.W. Litho Harrison)

1979 (31 May–1 Sept). *St. Vincent Post Offices. Horiz designs as T* **104** *showing first and latest postmarks and map of St. Vincent. Multicoloured. W w* **14** *(sideways). P* 14.

582	1 c. Type **104**	10	10
583	2 c. Sion Hill	10	10
584	3 c. Cumberland	10	10
585	4 c. Questelles	10	10
586	5 c. Layou	10	10
587	6 c. New Ground	10	10
588	8 c. Mesopotamia	10	10
589	10 c. Troumaca	10	10
590	12 c. Arnos Vale	15	10
591	15 c. Stubbs	15	10
592	20 c. Orange Hill	15	10
593	25 c. Calliaqua	15	10
594	40 c. Edinboro	25	20
595	50 c. Colonarie	30	25
596	80 c. Biabou	40	35
597	$1 Chateaubelair	50	50
598	$2 Head P.O., Kingstown	60	80
599	$3 Barrouallie	75	1·25
600	$5 Georgetown	1·25	2·00
601	$10 Kingstown	2·25	4·00
582/601	*Set of* 20	6·50	9·00

Dates of issue:—40, 50 c., $3 (from No. **MS**581 and booklets only) 31.5.79; others, and 40, 50 c., $3 from sheets, 1.9.79.

The 5, 10, 25 c. and $1 values exist with different imprint dates below the design.

See also Nos. **MS**581 and **MS**637.

1979 (6 Aug). *Opening of St. Vincent and the Grenadines Air Service. No.* 566 *optd with T* **105,** *in red, by Reliance Printery, Kingstown.*

602	10 c. Type **100**	10	10

INDEPENDENT

106 National Flag and *Ixora coccinea* (flower)

(Des J.W. Litho Enschedé)

1979 (27 Oct). *Independence. T* **106** *and similar horiz designs. Multicoloured. W w* **14** *(sideways). P* 12½ × 12.

603	20 c. Type **106**	15	10
604	50 c. House of Assembly and *Ixora stricta* (flower)	20	10
605	80 c. Prime Minister R. Milton Cato and *Ixora williamsii* (flower)	25	20
603/5	*Set of* 3	55	30

INDEPENDENCE 1979

(107)

1979 (27 Oct). *Independence. Nos.* 422, 425/30, 432, 434, 437/40, 441a *and* 443 *optd with T* **107,** *by Letchworth Press, Barbados.*

606	1 c. Type **79**	10	10
607	4 c. Mackerel	10	10
608	5 c. French Grunt	10	10
609	6 c. Spotted Goatfish	10	10
610	8 c. Ballyhoo	10	10
611	10 c. Sperm Whale	15	15
612	12 c. Humpback Whale	15	15
613	15 c. Skipjack	15	15
614	25 c. Princess Parrotfish	20	20
615	50 c. Porkfish	35	35
616	70 c. "Albacore" or Yellowfin Tuna	45	45
617	90 c. Pompano	60	50
618	$1 Queen Triggerfish	60	50
619	$2.50, Sailfish (II)	1·75	1·00
	a. Opt inverted	£100	
	b. Optd on Type I (No. 441)	9·00	9·00
620	$10 Blue Marlin	4·75	4·25
606/20	*Set of* 15	8·50	7·00

108 Virgin and Child **109** *Polistes cinctus* (wasp) and Oleander

(Des Jennifer Toombs. Litho Questa)

1979 (1 Nov). *Christmas. Scenes and Verses from the carol "Silent Night". T* **108** *and similar horiz designs. Multicoloured. W w* **14** *(sideways). P* 13½.

621	10 c. Type **108**	10	10
622	20 c. Jesus in manger	10	10
623	25 c. Shepherds	10	10
624	40 c. Angel	10	10
625	50 c. Angels with infant Jesus	10	10
626	$2 Nativity scene	40	30
621/6	*Set of* 6	55	45
MS627	151 × 170 mm. Nos. 621/6	55	1·00

(Des J.W. Litho Walsall)

1979 (13 Dec). *Flowers and Insects. T* **109** *and similar vert designs showing insects and different varieties of Oleander flower. Multicoloured. W w* **14.** *P* 14.

628	5 c. Type **109**	10	10
629	10 c. *Pyrophorus noctiluca* (click beetle)	10	10
630	25 c. *Stagmomantis limbata* (mantid)	10	10
631	50 c. *Psiloptera lampetis* (beetle)	10	10
632	$2 *Diaprepies abbreviatus* (weevil)	30	30
628/32	*Set of* 5	50	40

(Des and litho D.L.R.)

1980 (28 Feb). *Centenary of St. Vincent "Arms" Stamps. Sheet 116 × 72 mm containing designs as T* **31.** *W w* **14** *(sideways). P* 14 × 13½.
MS633 116 × 72 mm. 50 c. reddish brown; $1 deep grey-green; $2.50 deep blue .. 50 75

110 Queen Elizabeth II

(Des J.W. Litho Harrison)

1980 (24 Apr). *"London 1980" International Stamp Exhibition. T* **110** *and similar horiz designs. Multicoloured. W w* **14** *(sideways). P* 14.
634 80 c. Type **110** .. 20 20
635 $1 Great Britain 1954 3d. and St. Vincent 1954 5 c. definitive stamps .. 30 30
636 $2 Unadopted postage stamp design of 1971 60 60
634/6 .. *Set of* 3 1·00 1·00
MS637 165 × 115 mm. Nos. 596/8 and 634/6 .. 1·25 1·50
Nos. 634/6 were each printed in sheets containing 2 *se-tenant* stamp-size labels.

111 Steel Band 112 Football

(Des G. Drummond. Litho Questa)

1980 (12 June). *Kingstown Carnival. T* **111** *and similar horiz design. Multicoloured. W w* **14** *(sideways). P* 13½ × 14.
638 20 c. Type **111** 15 15
a. Pair. Nos. 638/9 .. 30 30
639 20 c. Steel band *(different)* .. 15 15
Nos. 638/9 were printed together, *se-tenant*, in horizontal and vertical pairs throughout the sheet.

(Des Polygraphic. Litho Rosenbaum Bros, Vienna)

1980 (7 Aug). *"Sport for All". T* **112** *and similar vert designs. Multicoloured. W w* **14** *(inverted). P* 13½.
640 10 c. Type **112** .. 10 10
641 60 c. Cycling .. 20 15
642 80 c. Basketball .. 30 20
643 $2.50, Boxing .. 40 70
640/3 .. *Set of* 4 90 1·00

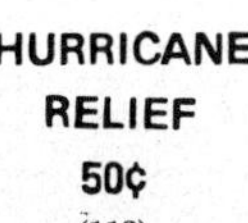

(113) 114 Brazilian Agouti

1980 (7 Aug). *Hurricane Relief. Nos. 640/3 surch with T* **113.** *W w* **14** *(upright).*
644 10 c. + 50 c. Type **112** .. 15 15
645 60 c. + 50 c. Cycling .. 25 25
646 80 c. + 50 c. Basketball .. 35 35
647 $2.50 + 50 c. Boxing .. 60 60
644/7 .. *Set of* 4 1·25 1·25

(Des L. Curtis. Litho Questa)

1980 (2 Oct). *Wildlife. T* **114** *and similar horiz designs. Multicoloured. W w* **14** *(sideways). P* 14 × 14½.
648 25 c. Type **114** .. 10 10
649 50 c. Giant Toad .. 15 10
650 $2 Small Indian Mongoose .. 40 55
648/50 .. *Set of* 3 60 60

115 Map of World showing St. Vincent 116 *Ville de Paris*, 1782

(Des G. Drummond. Litho Questa)

1980 (4 Dec). *St. Vincent "On the Map". T* **115** *and similar designs depicting maps showing St. Vincent. Multicoloured. W w* **14** *(sideways). P* 13½ × 14.
651 10 c. Type **115** .. 10 10
652 50 c. Western hemisphere .. 10 10
653 $1 Central America .. 25 15
654 $2 St. Vincent .. 40 30
651/4 .. *Set of* 4 70 50
MS655 143 × 95 mm. No. 654. P 12 .. 50 75

(Des J.W. Litho Rosenbaum Bros, Vienna)

1981 (19 Feb). *Sailing Ships. T* **116** *and similar vert designs. Multicoloured. W w* **14.** *P* 13½.
656 50 c. Type **116** .. 30 20
657 60 c. H.M.S. *Ramillies*, 1782 .. 35 30
658 $1.50, H.M.S. *Providence*, 1793 .. 80 1·25
659 $2 *Dee* (paddle-steamer packet) .. 1·10 1·50
656/9 .. *Set of* 4 2·25 2·75

117 Arrowroot Cultivation

(Des G. Drummond. Litho Format)

1981 (21 May). *Agriculture. T* **117** *and similar horiz designs. Multicoloured. W w* **14** *(sideways). P* 14.
660 25 c. Type **117** .. 10 15
a. Pair. Nos. 660/1 .. 20 30
661 25 c. Arrowroot processing .. 10 15
662 50 c. Banana cultivation .. 20 25
a. Pair. Nos. 662/3 .. 40 50
663 50 c. Banana export packaging station .. 20 25
664 60 c. Coconut plantation .. 25 30
a. Pair. Nos. 664/5 .. 50 60
665 60 c. Copra drying frames .. 25 30
666 $1 Cocoa cultivation .. 50 45
a. Pair. Nos. 666/7 .. 1·00 90
667 $1 Cocoa beans and sun drying frames .. 50 45
660/7 .. *Set of* 8 1·90 2·00
The two designs of each value were printed together, *se-tenant*, in horizontal and vertical pairs throughout the sheet.

(Des D. Shults. Litho Questa)

1981 (17 July–26 Nov). *Royal Wedding. Horiz designs as T* **26/27** *of Kiribati. Multicoloured. (a) W w* **15.** *P* 14.
668 60 c. *Isabella* .. 15 15
a. Sheetlet. No. 668 × 6 and No. 669 .. 1·10
669 60 c. Prince Charles and Lady Diana Spencer 30 30
670 $2.50, *Alberta* (tender) .. 30 30
a. Sheetlet. No. 670 × 6 and No. 671 .. 2·50
671 $2.50, As No. 669 .. 70 70
672 $4 *Britannia* .. 40 40
a. Sheetlet. No. 672 × 6 and No. 673 .. 3·25
673 $4 As No. 669 .. 1·25 1·25
668/73 .. *Set of* 6 2·75 2·75
MS674 120 × 109 mm. $5 As No. 669. Wmk sideways. P 12 (26 Nov) .. 1·25 1·00

(b) Booklet stamps. No wmk. P 12 (26 Nov)
675 60 c. As No. 668 .. 25 25
a. Booklet pane. No. 675 × 4 .. 1·00
676 $2.50, As No. 671 .. 1·25 1·25
a. Booklet pane. No. 676 × 2 .. 2·50
Nos. 668/73 were printed in sheetlets of seven stamps of the same face value, each containing six of the "Royal Yacht" design and one of the larger design showing Prince Charles and Lady Diana.
Nos. 675/6 come from $9.80 stamp booklets.

118 Kingstown General Post Office 119

(Des G. Drummond. Litho Questa)

1981 (1 Sept). *U.P.U. Membership. W w* **14** *(sideways). P* 14.
677 **118** $2 multicoloured .. 70 90
a. Horiz pair. Nos. 677/8 .. 1·40 1·75
678 **119** $2 multicoloured .. 70 90
Nos. 677/8 were printed together, *se-tenant*, in horizontal pairs throughout the sheet, forming a composite design.

120 St. Vincent Flag with Flags of other U.N. Member Nations

(Des L. Curtis. Litho Format)

1981 (11 Sept). *First Anniv of U.N. Membership. T* **120** *and similar horiz design. Multicoloured. W w* **14** *(sideways). P* 13½ × 14.
679 $1.50, Type **120** .. 55 25
680 $2.50, Prime Minister Robert Milton Cato .. 85 50
Nos. 679/80 are inscribed "ST. VINCENT and the GRENADINES" and were each printed in small sheets of 6 including one *se-tenant* stamp-size label.

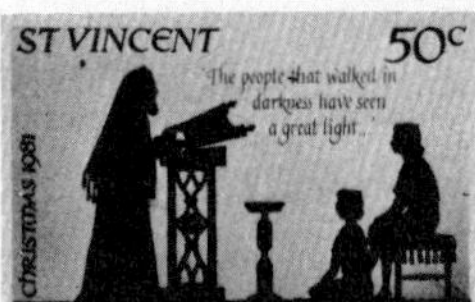

121 Silhouettes of Figures at Old Testament Reading, and Bible Extract

(Des Jennifer Toombs. Litho Security Printers (M), Malaysia)

1981 (19 Nov). *Christmas. T* **121** *and similar horiz designs showing silhouettes of figures. Multicoloured. W w* **14** *(sideways). P* 12.
681 50 c. Type **121** .. 15 10
682 60 c. Madonna, and angel .. 15 10
683 $1 Madonna, and Bible extract .. 25 25
684 $2 Joseph and Mary travelling to Bethlehem 50 50
681/4 .. *Set of* 4 95 85
MS685 129 × 127 mm. Nos. 681/4. P 13½ .. 95 1·40

122 Sugar Boilers

(Des L. Curtis. Litho Format)

1982 (5 Apr). *First Anniv of Re-introduction of Sugar Industry. T* **122** *and similar horiz designs. Multicoloured. W w* **14** *(sideways). P* 14.
686 50 c. Type **122** .. 25 15
687 60 c. Sugar drying plant .. 25 20
688 $1.50, Sugar mill machinery .. 70 75
689 $2 Crane loading sugar cane .. 95 1·00
686/9 .. *Set of* 4 1·90 1·90

123 Butterfly Float 124 Augusta of Saxe-Gotha, Princess of Wales, 1736

(Des G. Vasarhelyi. Photo Heraclio Fournier)

1982 (10 June). *Carnival 1982. T* **123** *and similar multicoloured designs. P* 13½.
690 50 c. Type **123** .. 20 15
691 60 c. Angel dancer *(vert)* .. 20 15
692 $1.50, Winged dancer *(vert)* .. 50 80
693 $2 Eagle float .. 70 1·25
690/3 .. *Set of* 4 1·50 2·10

(Des D. Shults and J. Cooter. Litho Format)

1982 (1 July). *21st Birthday of Princess of Wales. T* **124** *and similar vert designs. Multicoloured. W* **24** *of Kiribati. P* 13½ × 14.
694 50 c. Type **124** .. 25 20
695 60 c. Coat of arms of Augusta of Saxe-Gotha 25 25
696 $6 Diana, Princess of Wales .. 1·75 1·75
694/6 .. *Set of* 3 2·00 2·00

125 Scout Emblem 126 De Havilland "Moth", 1932

(Des L. Curtis. Litho Questa)

1982 (15 July). *75th Anniv of Boy Scout Movement. T* **125** *and similar vert design. Multicoloured. W w* **14.** *P* 14.
697 $1.50, Type **125** .. 70 1·00
698 $2.50, 75th anniv emblem .. 90 1·25

1982 (19 July). *Birth of Prince William of Wales. Nos. 694/6 optd with T* **19** *of St. Kitts.*
699 50 c. Type **124** .. 20 20
700 60 c. Coat of arms of Augusta of Saxe-Gotha 25 25
a. Opt inverted .. 50·00
701 $6 Diana, Princess of Wales .. 1·75 2·00
a. Opt double .. 20·00
699/701 .. *Set of* 3 2·00 2·25

(Des A. Theobald. Litho Questa)

1982 (29 July). *50th Anniv of Airmail Service. T* **126** *and similar horiz designs. Multicoloured.* W w **14** *(sideways). P* 14.

702 50 c. Type **126** 45 30
703 60 c. Grumman "Goose", 1952 .. .. 50 40
704 $1.50, Hawker-Siddeley "748", 1968 .. 95 1·00
705 $2 Britten-Norman "Trislander", 1982 .. 1·10 1·60
702/5 .. .. *Set of* 4 2·75 3·00

127 *Geestport* (freighter)

(Des G. Drummond. Litho Format)

1982 (27 Dec). *Ships. T* **127** *and similar horiz designs. Multicoloured.* W w **14** *(sideways). P* 14.

706 45 c. Type **127**.. .. .. 25 25
707 60 c. *Stella Oceanic* (liner) 30 35
708 $1.50, *Victoria* (liner) .. .. .. 70 1·00
709 $2 *Queen Elizabeth 2* (liner) .. .. 95 1·50
706/9 .. .. *Set of* 4 2·00 2·75

128 *Pseudocorynactis caribbeorum*

(Des McCombie-De Bay. Litho Security Printers (M), Malaysia)

1983 (10 Feb). *Marine Life. T* **128** *and similar multicoloured designs.* W w **14** *(sideways on* 60 c., $1.50, $2*). P* 12.

710 50 c. Type **128** 45 25
711 60 c. *Actinoporus elegans* (*vert*) 50 35
712 $1.50, *Arachnanthus nocturnus* (*vert*) .. 1·00 75
713 $2 *Hippocampus reidi* (*vert*).. .. .. 1·25 1·00
710/13 .. .. *Set of* 4 3·00 2·00

129 Satellite View of St. Vincent

45¢

(130)

(Des R. Vigurs. Litho Questa)

1983 (14 Mar). *Commonwealth Day. T* **129** *and similar horiz designs. Multicoloured.* W w **14** *(sideways). P* 14.

714 45 c. Type **129** 20 20
715 60 c. Flag of St. Vincent 25 25
716 $1.50, Prime Minister R. Milton Cato .. 50 65
717 $2 Harvesting bananas 75 90
714/17 .. .. *Set of* 4 1·50 1·75

Nos. 714/17 are inscribed "St. Vincent & The Grenadines".

1983 (26 Apr). *No.* 681 *surch with T* **130** *by Reliance Printery, Kingstown.*

718 45 c. on 50 c. Type **121**.. .. .. .. 40 30

131 Symbolic Handshake

132 Sir William Smith (founder)

(Des J.W. Litho Security Printers (M), Malaysia)

1983 (6 July). *10th Anniv of Treaty of Chaguaramas. T* **131** *and similar vert designs. Multicoloured.* W w **14** *(sideways). P* 11½ × 12.

719 45 c. Type **131** 25 20
720 60 c. Commerce emblem 30 25
721 $1.50, Caribbean map 60 65
722 $2 Flags of member countries and map of St. Vincent 85 90
719/22 .. .. *Set of* 4 1·75 1·75

(Des L. Curtis. Litho Security Printers (M), Malaysia)

1983 (6 Oct). *Centenary of Boys' Brigade. T* **132** *and similar vert designs. Multicoloured.* W w **14**. *P* 12 × 11½.

723 45 c. Type **132** 25 25
724 60 c. On parade 30 35
725 $1.50, Craftwork .. .. 70 1·10
726 $2 Community service .. .. .. 95 1·60
723/6 .. .. *Set of* 4 2·00 3·00

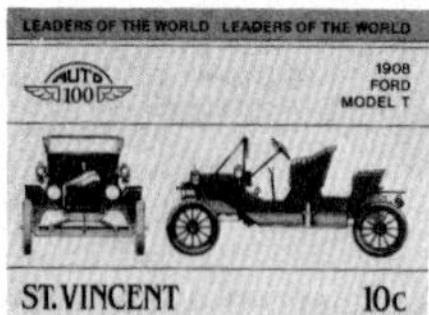

133 Ford "Model T" (1908)

(Des J.W. Litho Format)

1983 (25 Oct). *Leaders of the World. Automobiles (1st series). T* **133** *and similar horiz designs, the first in each pair showing technical drawings and the second paintings. P* 12½.

727 10 c. multicoloured 10 10
a. Vert pair. Nos. 727/8 .. .. .. 10 10
728 10 c. multicoloured 10 10
729 60 c. multicoloured 20 20
a. Vert pair. Nos. 729/30 .. .. .. 40 40
730 60 c. multicoloured 20 20
731 $1.50, multicoloured 25 25
a. Vert pair. Nos. 731/2 .. .. .. 50 50
732 $1.50, multicoloured 25 25
733 $1.50, multicoloured 25 25
a. Vert pair. Nos. 733/4 .. .. .. 50 50
734 $1.50, multicoloured 25 25
735 $2 multicoloured 40 40
a. Vert pair. Nos. 735/6 .. .. .. 80 80
736 $2 multicoloured 40 40
737 $2 multicoloured 40 40
a. Vert pair. Nos. 737/8 .. .. .. 80 80
738 $2 multicoloured 40 40
727/38 .. .. *Set of* 12 2·75 2·75

Designs:—Nos. 727/8, Ford "Model T" (1908); 729/30, Supercharged Cord "812" (1937); 731/2, Citroen "Open Tourer" (1937); 733/4, Mercedes Benz "300SL Gull-Wing" (1954); 735/6, Rolls-Royce "Phantom I" (1925); 737/8, Ferrari "Boxer 512BB" (1976).

Nos. 727/8, 729/30, 731/2, 733/4, 735/6 and 737/8 were printed together, *se-tenant*, in vertical pairs throughout the sheets.

See also Nos. 820/9, 862/7, 884/92 and 959/70.

134 Appearance of the Nativity Star

(Des Jennifer Toombs. Litho Security Printers (M), Malaysia)

1983 (15 Nov). *Christmas. T* **134** *and similar horiz designs showing the Shepherds.* W w **14**. *P* 12.

739 10 c. Type **134** 10 10
740 50 c. Message of the Angel 20 10
741 $1.50, The Heavenly Host 45 45
742 $2.40, Worshipping Jesus 65 75
739/42 .. .. *Set of* 4 1·25 1·25
MS743 130 × 130 mm. Nos. 739/42. Wmk sideways 1·25 1·75

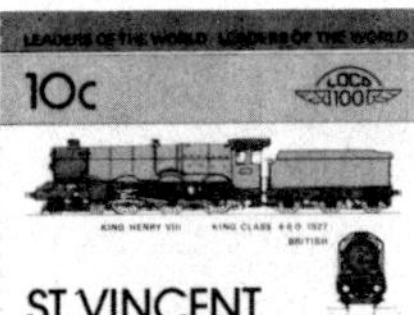

135 *King Henry VIII*

(Des J.W. Litho Format)

1983 (8 Dec). *Leaders of the World. Railway Locomotives (1st series). T* **135** *and similar horiz designs, the first in each pair showing technical drawings and the second the locomotive at work. P* 12½.

744 10 c. multicoloured 10 10
a. Vert pair. Nos. 744/5 .. .. .. 10 10
745 10 c. multicoloured 10 10
746 10 c. multicoloured 10 10
a. Vert pair. Nos. 746/7 .. .. .. 10 10
747 10 c. multicoloured 10 10
748 25 c. multicoloured 10 10
a. Vert pair. Nos. 748/9 .. .. .. 20 20
749 25 c. multicoloured 10 10
750 50 c. multicoloured 20 20
a. Vert pair. Nos. 750/1 .. .. .. 40 40
751 50 c. multicoloured 20 20
752 60 c. multicoloured 25 25
a. Vert pair Nos. 752/3 .. .. .. 50 50
753 60 c. multicoloured 25 25
754 75 c. multicoloured 35 35
a. Vert pair. Nos. 754/5 .. .. .. 70 70
755 75 c. multicoloured 35 35
756 $2.50, multicoloured 75 75
a. Vert pair. Nos. 756/7 .. .. .. 1·50 1·50
757 $2.50, multicoloured 75 75
758 $3 multicoloured 90 90
a. Vert pair. Nos. 758/9 .. .. .. 1·75 1·75
759 $3 multicoloured 90 90
744/59 .. .. *Set of* 16 4·75 4·75

Designs:—Nos. 744/5, *King Henry VIII*, Great Britain (1927); 746/7, *Royal Scots Greys*, Great Britain (1961); 748/9, *Hagley Hall*, Great Britain (1928); 750/1, *Sir Lancelot*, Great Britain (1926); 752/3 Class "B12", Great Britain (1912); 754/5, Deeley "Compound" type, Great Britain (1902); 756/7, *Cheshire*, Great Britain (1927); 758/9, Bullied "Austerity" Class Q1, Great Britain (1942).

Nos. 744/59 were issued in a similar sheet format to Nos. 727/38.

See also Nos. 792/807, 834/41, 872/83, 893/904 and 1001/8.

136 Fort Duvernette

(Des Walsall. Litho Questa)

1984 (13 Feb). *Fort Duvernette. T* **136** *and similar horiz designs. Multicoloured.* W w **15** *(sideways). P* 14 × 14½.

760 35 c. Type **136** 20 30
761 45 c. Soldiers on fortifications.. .. .. 25 30
762 $1 Cannon facing bay 40 60
763 $3 Map of St. Vincent and mortar .. .. 1·25 1·75
760/3 .. .. *Set of* 4 1·90 2·75

137 White Frangipani

(Des J. Cooter. Litho Harrison)

1984 (2 Apr). *Flowering Trees and Shrubs. T* **137** *and similar horiz designs. Multicoloured.* W w **14** *(sideways). P* 13½ × 14.

764 5 c. Type **137** 10 10
765 10 c. Genip 15 10
766 15 c. Immortelle 20 10
767 20 c. Pink Poui 25 10
768 25 c. Buttercup 30 10
769 35 c. Sandbox 40 20
770 45 c. Locust 50 25
771 60 c. Colville's Glory 65 30
772 75 c. Lignum Vitae 75 40
773 $1 Golden Shower .. .. 1·00 60
774 $5 Angelin .. .. 3·50 4·00
775 $10 Roucou .. .. 5·50 7·50
764/75 .. .. *Set of* 12 12·00 12·00

138 Trench Warfare, First World War

139 Musical Fantasy Costume

(Des Court House Studio. Litho Format)

1984 (25 Apr). *Leaders of the World. British Monarchs. T* **138** *and similar vert designs. Multicoloured. P* 12½.

776 1 c. Type **138** 10 10
a. Horiz pair. Nos. 776/7 .. .. .. 10 10
777 1 c. George V and trenches 10 10
778 5 c. Battle of Bannockburn 10 10
a. Horiz pair. Nos. 778/9 .. .. .. 10 10
779 5 c. Edward II and battle 10 10
780 60 c. George V 25 25
a. Horiz pair. Nos. 780/1 .. .. .. 50 50
781 60 c. York Cottage, Sandringham 25 25
782 75 c. Edward II 30 30
a. Horiz pair. Nos. 782/3 .. .. .. 60 60
783 75 c. Berkeley Castle 30 30
784 $1 Coat of arms of Edward II 35 35
a. Horiz pair. Nos. 784/5 .. .. .. 70 70
785 $1 Edward II (*different*) 35 35
786 $4 Coat of arms of George V .. .. 1·00 1·00
a. Horiz pair. Nos. 786/7 .. .. .. 2·00 2·00
787 $4 George V and Battle of Jutland.. .. 1·00 1·00
776/87 .. .. *Set of* 12 3·50 3·50

Nos. 776/7, 778/9, 780/1, 782/3, 784/5 and 786/7 were printed together, *se-tenant*, in horizontal pairs throughout the sheets, each pair forming a composite design.

(Des G. Vasarhelyi. Litho Questa)

1984 (25 June). *Carnival* 1984. *T* **139** *and similar horiz designs showing Carnival costumes. Multicoloured.* W w **15** *(sideways). P* 14.

788 35 c. Type **139** 15 15
789 45 c. African princess 20 20
790 $1 Market woman 40 40
791 $3 Carib hieroglyph.. .. .. .. 1·25 1·40
788/91 .. .. *Set of* 4 1·75 2·00

IMPERFORATES AND MISSING COLOURS. Various issues between Nos. 792 and 1084 exist either imperforate or with colours omitted. Such items are not listed as there is no evidence that they fulfil the criteria outlined on page xi of this catalogue.

(Des J.W. Litho Format)

1984 (27 July). *Leaders of the World. Railway Locomotives (2nd series). Horiz designs as T* **135**, *the first in each pair showing technical drawings and the second the locomotive at work. P* 12½.

792 1 c. multicoloured 10 10
a. Vert pair. Nos. 792/3 .. .. .. 10 10
793 1 c. multicoloured 10 10

794 2 c. multicoloured 10 10
a. Vert pair. Nos. 794/5 .. .. 10 10
795 2 c. multicoloured 10 10
796 3 c. multicoloured 10 10
a. Vert pair. Nos. 796/7 .. .. 10 10
797 3 c. multicoloured 10 10
798 50 c. multicoloured 30 30
a. Vert pair. Nos. 798/9 .. .. 60 60
799 50 c. multicoloured 30 30
800 75 c. multicoloured 35 35
a. Vert pair. Nos. 800/1 .. .. 70 70
801 75 c. multicoloured 35 35
802 $1 multicoloured 40 40
a. Vert pair. Nos. 802/3 .. .. 80 80
803 $1 multicoloured 40 40
804 $2 multicoloured 55 55
a. Vert pair. Nos. 804/5 .. .. 1·10 1·10
805 $2 multicoloured 55 55
806 $3 multicoloured 65 65
a. Vert pair. Nos. 806/7 .. .. 1·25 1·25
807 $3 multicoloured 65 65
792/807 .. .. *Set of* 16 4·25 4·25

Designs:—Nos. 792/3, Liberation Class, France (1945); 794/5, *Dreadnought*, Great Britain (1767); 796/7, No. 242A1, France (1946); 798/9, Class "Dean Goods", Great Britain (1883); 800/1, Hetton Colliery No. 1, Great Britain (1822); 802/3, *Penydarren*, Great Britain (1804); 804/5, *Novelty*, Great Britain (1829); 806/7, Class "44", Germany (1925).

Nos. 792/807 were issued in a similar sheet format to Nos. 727/38.

140 Slaves tilling Field

141 Weightlifting

(Des G. Vasarhelyi. Litho Questa)

1984 (1 Aug). *150th Anniv of Emancipation of Slaves on St. Vincent. T* **140** *and similar horiz designs. Multicoloured. W* w **15** *(sideways). P* 14.

808 35 c. Type **140** 20 20
809 45 c. Sugar-cane harvesting 25 25
810 $1 Cutting sugar-cane 45 45
811 $3 William Wilberforce and African slave caravan .. .. 1·25 1·40
808/11 .. .. *Set of* 4 2·00 2·10

(Des Court House Studio. Litho Format)

1984 (30 Aug). *Leaders of the World. Olympic Games, Los Angeles. T* **141** *and similar vert designs. Multicoloured. P* 12½.

812 1 c. Judo 10 10
a. Horiz pair. Nos. 812/13 .. .. .. 10 10
813 1 c. Type **141** 10 10
814 3 c. Pursuit cycling 10 10
a. Horiz pair. Nos. 814/15 .. .. .. 10 10
815 3 c. Cycle road-racing 10 10
816 60 c. Women's backstroke swimming .. 20 20
a. Horiz pair. Nos. 816/17 .. .. .. 40 40
817 60 c. Men's butterfly swimming 20 20
818 $3 Sprint start 75 75
a. Horiz pair. Nos. 818/19 .. .. .. 1·50 1·50
819 $3 Finish of long distance race 75 75
812/19 .. .. *Set of* 8 1·90 1·90

Nos. 812/13, 814/15, 816/17 and 818/19 were printed together, *se-tenant*, in horizontal pairs throughout the sheets.

(Des J.W. Litho Format)

1984 (22 Oct). *Leaders of the World. Automobiles (2nd series). Horiz designs as T* **133**, *the first in each pair showing technical drawings and the second paintings. P* 12½.

820 5 c. black, drab and bright green 10 10
a. Vert pair. Nos. 820/1 .. .. .. 10 10
821 5 c. multicoloured 10 10
822 20 c. black, pink and pale new blue 15 15
a. Vert pair. Nos. 822/3 .. .. .. 30 30
823 20 c. multicoloured 15 15
824 55 c. black, pale green and lake-brown .. 25 25
a. Vert pair. Nos. 824/5 .. .. .. 50 50
825 55 c. multicoloured 25 25
826 $1.50, black, pale turq-grn & turq-grn .. 35 35
a. Vert pair. Nos. 826/7 .. .. .. 70 70
827 $1.50, multicoloured 35 35
828 $2.50, black, turquoise-green and lilac .. 40 40
a. Vert pair. Nos. 828/9 .. .. .. 80 80
829 $2.50, multicoloured 40 40
820/9 .. .. *Set of* 10 2·10 2·10

Designs:—Nos. 820/1, Austin-Healey "Sprite" (1958); 822/3, Maserati "Ghibli Coupé" (1971); 824/5, Pontiac "GTO" (1964); 826/7, Jaguar "D-Type" (1957); 828/9, Ferrari "365 GTB4 Daytona" (1970).

Nos. 820/9 were issued in a similar sheet format to Nos. 727/38.

142 Grenadier, 70th Regt of Foot, 1773

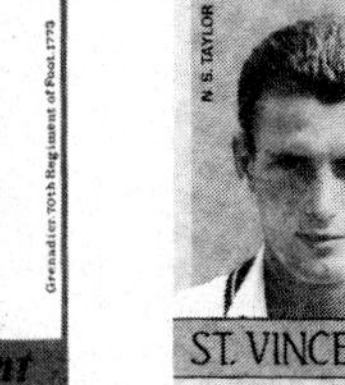

143 N. S. Taylor

(Des J. Cooter. Litho Questa)

1984 (12 Nov). *Military Uniforms. T* **142** *and similar vert designs. Multicoloured. W* w **15**. *P* 14.

830 45 c. Type **142** 25 30
831 60 c. Grenadier, 6th Regt of Foot, 1775 .. 30 35
832 $1.50, Grenadier, 3rd Regt of Foot, 1768 .. 75 80
833 $2 Battalion Company officer, 14th Regt of Foot, 1780 .. .. 1·00 1·10
830/3 .. .. *Set of* 4 2·10 2·25

(Des J.W. Litho Format)

1984 (21 Nov). *Leaders of the World. Railway Locomotives (3rd series). Horiz designs as T* **135**, *the first in each pair showing technical drawings and the second the locomotive at work. Multicoloured. P* 12½.

834 5 c. multicoloured 10 10
a. Vert pair. Nos. 834/5 .. .. .. 10 15
835 5 c. multicoloured 10 10
836 40 c. multicoloured 20 35
a. Vert pair. Nos. 836/7 .. .. .. 40 70
837 40 c. multicoloured 20 35
838 75 c. multicoloured 30 50
a. Vert pair. Nos. 838/9 .. .. .. 60 1·00
839 75 c. multicoloured 30 50
840 $2.50, multicoloured .. .. .. 1·00 1·50
a. Vert pair. Nos. 840/1 .. .. .. 2·00 3·00
841 $2.50, multicoloured .. .. .. 1·00 1·50
834/41 .. .. *Set of* 8 2·75 4·25

Designs:—Nos. 834/5 Class "20", Rhodesia (1954); 836/7, *Southern Maid*, Great Britain (1928); 838/9, *Prince of Wales*, Great Britain (1911); 840/1, Class "05", Germany (1935).

Nos. 834/41 were issued in a similar sheet format to Nos. 727/38.

(Des Court House Studio. Litho Format)

1985 (7 Jan). *Leaders of the World. Cricketers. T* **143** *and similar vert designs, the first in each pair showing a head portrait and the second the cricketer in action. P* 12½.

842 5 c. multicoloured 10 10
a. Horiz pair. Nos. 842/3 .. .. .. 10 10
843 5 c. multicoloured 10 10
844 35 c. multicoloured 25 25
a. Horiz pair. Nos. 844/5 .. .. .. 50 50
845 35 c. multicoloured 25 25
846 50 c. multicoloured 35 35
a. Horiz pair. Nos. 846/7 .. .. .. 70 70
847 50 c. multicoloured 35 35
848 $3 multicoloured .. .. 1·50 1·50
a. Horiz pair. Nos. 848/9 .. .. .. 3·00 3·00
849 $3 multicoloured .. .. 1·50 1·50
842/9 .. .. *Set of* 8 3·75 3·75

Designs:—Nos. 842/3, N. S. Taylor; 844/5. T. W. Graveney; 846/7, R. G. D. Willis; 848/9, S. D. Fletcher.

Nos. 842/3, 844/5, 846/7, and 848/9 were printed together, *se-tenant*, in vertical pairs throughout the sheets.

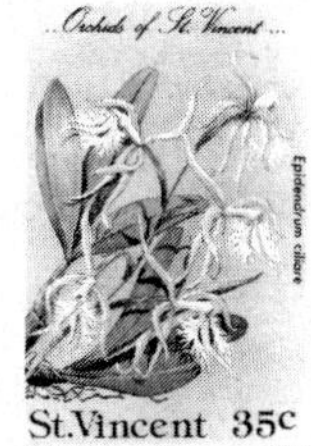

144 Eye Lash Orchid

145 Brown Pelican

(Des G. Drummond. Litho Format)

1985 (31 Jan). *Orchids. T* **144** *and similar vert designs. Multicoloured. W* w **15**. *P* 14.

850 35 c. Type **144** 40 30
851 45 c. *Ionopsis utricularioides* 50 30
852 $1 *Epidendrum secundum* 80 65
853 $3 *Oncidium altissimum* .. .. .. 1·75 2·00
850/3 .. .. *Set of* 4 3·00 3·00

(Des R. Vigurs. Litho Format)

1985 (7 Feb). *Leaders of the World. Birth Bicentenary of John J. Audubon (ornithologist). T* **145** *and similar vert designs. Multicoloured. P* 12½.

854 15 c. Type **145** 15 10
a. Horiz pair. Nos. 854/5 .. .. .. 30 20
855 15 c. Green Heron 15 10
856 40 c. Pileated Woodpecker 40 30
a. Horiz pair. Nos. 856/7 .. .. .. 80 60
857 40 c. Common Flicker 40 30
858 60 c. Painted Bunting 50 40
a. Horiz pair. Nos. 858/9 .. .. .. 1·00 80
859 60 c. White-winged Crossbill 50 40
860 $2.25, Red-shouldered Hawk .. .. 1·75 1·50
a. Horiz pair. Nos. 860/1 .. .. .. 3·50 3·00
861 $2.25, Common Caracara .. .. .. 1·75 1·50
854/61 .. .. *Set of* 8 5·00 4·25

Nos. 854/5, 856/7, 858/9 and 860/1 were printed together, *se-tenant*, in horizontal pairs throughout the sheets.

(Des Artists International. Litho Format)

1985 (11 Mar). *Leaders of the World. Automobiles (3rd series). Horiz designs as T* **133**, *the first in each pair showing technical drawings and the second paintings. P* 12½.

862 1 c. black, pale lemon and blue-green .. 10 10
a. Vert pair. Nos. 862/3 .. .. .. 10 10
863 1 c. multicoloured 10 10
864 55 c. black, pale new blue and violet-grey .. 20 20
a. Vert pair. Nos. 864/5 .. .. .. 40 40
865 55 c. multicoloured 20 20
866 $2 black, pale lemon & dull reddish purple 55 55
a. Vert pair. Nos. 866/7 .. .. .. 1·10 1·10
867 $2 multicoloured 55 55
862/7 .. .. *Set of* 6 1·40 1·40

Designs:—Nos. 862/3, Lancia "Aprilia" (1937); 864/5, Pontiac "Firebird Trans Am" (1973); 866/7, Cunningham "C-5R" (1953).

Nos. 862/7 were issued in a similar sheet format to Nos. 727/38.

146 Pepper

147 Bamboo Flute

(Des G. Drummond. Litho Format)

1985 (22 Apr). *Herbs and Spices. T* **146** *and similar vert designs. Multicoloured. W* w **15**. *P* 14.

868 25 c. Type **146** 15 15
869 35 c. Sweet Marjoram 20 25
870 $1 Nutmeg 50 60
871 $3 Ginger .. .. 1·50 2·00
868/71 .. .. *Set of* 4 2·10 2·75

(Des. T. Hadler ($2.50), J.W. (others). Litho Format)

1985 (26 Apr). *Leaders of the World. Railway Locomotives (4th series). Horiz designs as T* **135**, *the first in each pair showing technical drawings and the second the locomotive at work. P* 12½.

872 1 c. multicoloured 10 10
a. Vert pair. Nos. 872/3 .. .. .. 10 10
873 1 c. multicoloured 10 10
874 10 c. multicoloured 10 10
a. Vert pair. Nos. 874/5 .. .. .. 10 15
875 10 c. multicoloured 10 10
876 40 c. multicoloured 25 30
a. Vert pair. Nos. 876/7 .. .. .. 50 60
877 40 c. multicoloured 25 30
878 60 c. multicoloured 35 40
a. Vert pair. Nos. 878/9 .. .. .. 70 80
879 60 c. multicoloured 35 40
880 $1 multicoloured 45 50
a. Vert pair. Nos. 880/1 .. .. .. 90 1·00
881 $1 multicoloured 45 50
882 $2.50, multicoloured .. .. .. 90 1·25
a. Vert pair. Nos. 882/3 .. .. .. 1·75 2·50
883 $2.50, multicoloured .. .. .. 90 1·25
872/83 .. .. *Set of* 12 3·50 4·50

Designs:—Nos. 872/3, *Glen Douglas*, Great Britain (1913); 874/5, *Fenchurch*, Great Britain (1872); 876/7, No. 1 "Stirling Single", Great Britain (1870); 878/9, No. 158A, Great Britain (1866); 880/1, No. 103 Class "Jones Goods", Great Britain (1893); 882/3, *The Great Bear*, Great Britain (1908).

Nos. 872/83 were issued in a similar sheet format to Nos. 727/38.

(Des J.W. (25 c.), G. Turner ($1), Artists International (others). Litho Format)

1985 (7 June). *Leaders of the World. Automobiles (4th series). Horiz designs as T* **133**, *the first in each pair showing technical drawings and the second paintings. P* 12½.

884 25 c. black, greenish grey and brown-red .. 15 15
a. Vert pair. Nos. 884/5 .. .. .. 30 30
885 25 c. multicoloured 15 15
886 60 c. black, pale flesh and red-orange .. 25 25
a. Vert pair. Nos. 886/7 .. .. .. 50 50
887 60 c. multicoloured 25 25
888 $1 black, azure and dull lavender .. 30 30
a. Vert pair. Nos. 888/9 .. .. .. 60 60
889 $1 multicoloured 30 30
890 $1.50, black, pale blue and scarlet .. 40 40
a. Vert pair. Nos. 890/1 .. .. .. 80 80
891 $1.50, multicoloured 40 40
884/91 .. .. *Set of* 8 2·00 2·00
MS892 180 × 121 mm. $4 × 2 As Nos. 890/1; $5 × 2 As Nos. 888/9. P 14 .. .. .. 4·00 7·00

Designs:—Nos. 884/5, Essex "Coach" (1922); 886/7, Nash "Rambler" (1950); 888/9, Ferrari "Tipo 156" (1961); 890/1, Eagle-Weslake "Type 58" (1967).

Nos. 884/91 were issued in a similar sheet format to Nos. 727/38.

(Des J.W. (5 c., 30 c., $1), T. Hadler (others). Litho Format)

1985 (27 June). *Leaders of the World. Railway Locomotives (5th series). Horiz designs as T* **135**, *the first in each pair showing technical drawings and the second the locomotive at work. P* 12½.

893 5 c. multicoloured 10 10
a. Vert pair. Nos. 893/4 .. .. .. 10 10
894 5 c. multicoloured 10 10
895 30 c. multicoloured 15 20
a. Vert pair. Nos. 895/6 .. .. .. 30 40
896 30 c. multicoloured 15 20
897 60 c. multicoloured 30 40
a. Vert pair. Nos. 897/8 .. .. .. 60 80
898 60 c. multicoloured 30 40
899 75 c. multicoloured 30 40
a. Vert pair. Nos. 899/900 .. .. .. 60 80
900 75 c. multicoloured 30 40
901 $1 multicoloured 40 50
a. Vert pair. Nos. 901/2 .. .. .. 80 1·00
902 $1 multicoloured 40 50
903 $2.50, multicoloured .. .. .. 80 1·00
a. Vert pair. Nos. 903/4 .. .. .. 1·60 2·00
904 $2.50, multicoloured .. .. .. 80 1·00
893/904 .. .. *Set of* 12 3·50 4·50

Designs:—Nos. 893/4, Tank locomotive *Loch*, Great Britain (1874); 895/6, Class "47XX", Great Britain (1919); 897/8, Class "121", France (1876); 899/900, Class "24", Germany (1927); 901/2 Tank locomotive No. 1008, Great Britain (1889); 903/4, Class "PS-4", U.S.A. (1926).

Nos. 893/904 were issued in a similar sheet format to Nos. 727/38.

(Des Jennifer Toombs. Litho Format)

1985 (10 July). *Traditional Musical Instruments. T* **147** *and similar multicoloured designs. W w* **15** (*sideways on* $1, $2). *P* 15.

905 25 c. Type **147** 15 15
906 35 c. Quatro (four-stringed guitar) 20 25
907 $1 Ba-ha (bamboo pipe) (*vert*) 50 55
908 $2 Goat-skin drum (*vert*) . . . . . . 1·00 1·10
905/8 . . . . *Set of* 4 1·60 1·90
MS909 141 × 100 mm. Nos. 905/8 . . . . 3·50 4·00

148 Queen Elizabeth the Queen Mother

149 Elvis Presley

(Des Court House Studio. Litho Format)

1985 (9 Aug). *Leaders of the World. Life and Times of Queen Elizabeth the Queen Mother. Various vertical portraits as T* **148**. *P* 12½.

910 35 c. multicoloured 15 20
a. Horiz pair. Nos. 910/11 . . . . . . 30 40
911 35 c. multicoloured 15 20
912 85 c. multicoloured 35 45
a. Horiz pair. Nos. 912/13 . . . . . . 70 90
913 85 c. multicoloured 35 45
914 $1.20, multicoloured 40 60
a. Horiz pair. Nos. 914/15 . . . . . . 80 1·10
915 $1.20, multicoloured 40 60
916 $1.60, multicoloured 50 80
a. Horiz pair. Nos. 916/17 . . . . . . 1·00 1·60
917 $1.60, multicoloured 50 80
910/17 . . . . *Set of* 8 2·50 3·50
MS918 85 × 114 mm. $2.10, multicoloured; $2.10, multicoloured . . . . 1·00 2·00

The two designs of each value were issued, *se-tenant*, in horizontal pairs within the sheets.

Each *se-tenant* pair shows a floral pattern across the bottom of the portraits which stops short of the left-hand edge on the left-hand stamp and of the right-hand edge on the right-hand stamp.

Designs as Nos. 910/11 and 912/13, but with face values of $3.50 × 2 and $6 × 2, also exist in additional miniature sheets from a restricted printing issued 19 December 1985.

(Des Court House Studio. Litho Format)

1985 (16 Aug). *Leaders of the World. Elvis Presley* (*entertainer*). *Various vertical portraits as T* **149**. *Multicoloured, background colours given. P* 12½.

919 10 c. multicoloured (T **149**) 30 10
a. Horiz pair. Nos. 919/20 . . . . . . 60 20
920 10 c. multicoloured (bright blue) 30 10
921 60 c. multicoloured (brown) 65 35
a. Horiz pair. Nos. 921/2 . . . . . . 1·25 70
922 60 c. multicoloured (pale grey) 65 35
923 $1 multicoloured (brown) . . . . . . 1·00 55
a. Horiz pair. Nos. 923/4 . . . . . . 2·00 1·10
924 $1 multicoloured (bright blue) . . . . 1·00 55
925 $5 multicoloured (azure) . . . . . . 3·25 2·75
a. Horiz pair. Nos. 925/6 . . . . . . 6·50 5·50
926 $5 multicoloured (bright blue) . . . . 3·25 2·75
919/26 . . . . *Set of* 8 9·50 6·75
MS927 Four sheets each 145 × 107 mm. (a) 30 c. As Nos. 919/20 each × 2; (b) 50 c. As Nos. 921/2 each × 2; (c) $1.50 As Nos. 923/4 each × 2; (d) $4.50 As Nos. 925/6 each × 2 *Set of 4 sheets* 20·00 18·00

The two designs of each value were printed together, *se-tenant*, in horizontal pairs throughout the sheets.

Two similar designs, each with a face value of $4, were prepared, but not issued.

150 Silos and Conveyor Belt

151 Michael Jackson

(Des G. Vasarhelyi. Litho Format)

1985 (17 Oct). *St. Vincent Flour Milling Industry. T* **150** *and similar horiz designs. Multicoloured. W w* **15**. *P* 15.

928 20 c. Type **150** 15 15
929 30 c. Roller mills 15 20
930 75 c. Administration building 40 45
931 $3 Bran finishers . . . . 1·60 1·75
928/31 . . . . *Set of* 4 2·00 2·25

1985 (27 Oct). *Royal Visit. Nos.* 672/3, 697/8, 711, 724 *and* 912/13 *optd as T* **114** *of Montserrat or surch also.*

932 – 60 c. multicoloured (No. 711) . . . . 2·50 2·00
933 – 60 c. multicoloured (No. 724) . . . . 3·00 2·50
934 – 85 c. multicoloured (No. 912) . . . . 4·00 3·50
a. Horiz pair. Nos. 934/5 . . . . . . 8·00 7·00
935 – 85 c. multicoloured (No. 913) . . . . 4·00 3·50
936 **125** $1.50, multicoloured . . . . . . 4·00 4·00
937 – $1.60 on $4 multicoloured (No. 672) . . 2·00 2·50
a. Sheetlet. No. 937 × 6 and No. 938 . . 19·00
ab. Sheetlet. No. 937 × 6 and No. 938a . . 19·00
938 – $1.60 on $4 multicoloured (No. 673) (surch $1.60 only) . . . . . . 9·00 9·00
a. Additionally optd "CARIBBEAN ROYAL VISIT—1985" . . . . . . 9·00
939 – $2.50, multicoloured (No. 698) . . . . 5·50 4·50
932/9 . . . . *Set of* 8 30·00 29·00

No. 938 shows a new face value only. "CARIBBEAN ROYAL VISIT—1985" being omitted from the surcharge. No. 938a is the corrected version issued subsequently.

(Des Court House Studio. Litho Format)

1985 (2 Dec). *Leaders of the World. Michael Jackson* (*entertainer*). *Various vertical portraits as T* **151**. *Multicoloured. P* 12½.

940 60 c. multicoloured 25 30
a. Horiz pair. Nos. 940/1 . . . . . . 50 60
941 60 c. multicoloured 25 30
942 $1 multicoloured 40 45
a. Horiz pair. Nos. 942/3 . . . . . . 80 90
943 $1 multicoloured 40 45
944 $2 multicoloured 85 90
a. Horiz pair. Nos. 944/5 . . . . . . 1·75 1·75
945 $2 multicoloured 85 90
946 $5 multicoloured . . . . 2·10 2·25
a. Horiz pair. Nos. 946/7 . . . . . . 4·25 4·50
947 $5 multicoloured . . . . 2·10 2·25
940/7 . . . . *Set of* 8 6·50 7·00
MS948 Four sheets, each 144 × 109 mm. (a) 45 c. As Nos. 940/1 each × 2; (b) 90 c. As Nos. 942/3 each × 2; (c) $1.50 As Nos. 944/5 each × 2; (d) $4 As Nos. 946/7 each × 2. *Set of 4 sheets* 7·25 7·50

The two designs for each value were printed together, *se-tenant*, in horizontal pairs throughout the sheets. The left-hand design shows the face value at top left (as on Type **151**) and the right-hand design at top right.

152 "The Serenaders" (Kim de Freitas)

153 *Santa Maria*

(Litho Format)

1985 (9 Dec). *Christmas. Children's Paintings. T* **152** *and similar vert designs. Multicoloured. W w* **15**. *P* 13½ × 14.

949 25 c. Type **152** 15 15
950 75 c. "Poinsettia" (Jackie Douglas) 35 40
951 $2.50, "Jesus our Master" (Bernadette Payne) . . . . 1·25 1·40
949/51 . . . . *Set of* 3 1·50 1·75

(Litho Format)

1986 (23 Jan). *500th Anniv of Discovery of America* (1992) *by Columbus* (1*st issue*). *T* **153** *and similar vert designs. Multicoloured. P* 12½.

952 60 c. Type **153** 30 35
a. Horiz pair. Nos. 952/3 . . . . . . 60 70
953 60 c. Christopher Columbus 30 35
954 $1.50, Columbus at Spanish Court 75 80
a. Horiz pair. Nos. 954/5 . . . . . . 1·50 1·60
955 $1.50, King Ferdinand and Queen Isabella of Spain 75 80
956 $2.75, *Santa Maria* and fruits . . . . 1·40 1·50
a. Horiz pair. Nos. 956/7 . . . . . . 2·75 3·00
957 $2.75, Maize and fruits . . . . . . 1·40 1·50
952/7 . . . . *Set of* 6 4·50 4·75
MS958 95 × 85 mm. $6 Christopher Columbus (*different*) . . . . 3·25 3·75

The two designs of each value were printed together, *se-tenant*, in horizontal pairs within the sheets.

See also Nos. 1125/31, 1305/24, 1639/57 and 1677/85.

(Des Artists International. Litho Format)

1986 (27 Jan). *Leaders of the World. Automobiles* (5*th series*). *Horiz designs as T* **133**, *the first in each pair showing technical drawings and the second paintings. P* 12½.

959 30 c. black, cobalt and dull orange 15 15
a. Vert pair. Nos. 959/60 . . . . . . 30 30
960 30 c. multicoloured 15 15
961 45 c. black, lavender-grey and blue 20 20
a. Vert pair. Nos. 961/2 . . . . . . 40 40
962 45 c. multicoloured 20 20
963 60 c. black, bright blue and vermilion . . 25 25
a. Vert pair. Nos. 963/4 . . . . . . 50 50
964 60 c. multicoloured 25 25
965 90 c. black, greenish yellow and bright blue 30 30
a. Vert pair. Nos. 965/6 . . . . . . 60 60
966 90 c. multicoloured 30 30
967 $1.50, black, pale rose-lilac & brt magenta 40 40
a. Vert pair. Nos. 967/8 . . . . . . 80 80
968 $1.50, multicoloured 40 40
969 $2.50, black, blue and bright blue 50 50
a. Vert pair. Nos. 969/70 . . . . . . 1·00 1·00
970 $2.50, multicoloured 50 50
959/70 . . . . *Set of* 12 3·25 3·25

Designs:—Nos. 959/60, Cadillac "Type 53" (1916); 961/2, Triumph "Dolomite" (1939); 963/4, Panther "J-72" (1972); 965/6, Ferrari "275 GTB/4" (1967); 967/8, Packard "Caribbean" (1953); 969/70, Bugatti "Type 41 Royale" (1931).

Nos. 959/70 were issued in a similar sheet format to Nos. 727/38.

154 Guide Salute and Handclasp

155 Halley's Comet

(Des Court House Studio. Litho Format)

1986 (25 Feb). *75th Annivs of Girl Guide Movement and Boy Scouts of America. Two sheets, each* 85 × 113 *mm, containing vert designs as T* **154**. *Multicoloured. P* 12½.

MS971 $5 Type **154**: $5 Palette and paintbrushes 4·00 5·00
MS972 $6 Cross-tied logs: $6 Lord Baden-Powell 5·00 6·00

The two stamps in each sheet were printed together, *se-tenant*, in horizontal pairs, each forming a composite design.

Nos. **MS**971/2 exist with plain or decorative margins.

Overprints on these miniature sheets commemorating "Capex '87" International Stamp Exhibition, Toronto, were not authorised by the St. Vincent administration.

(Des G. Vasarhelyi. Litho Format)

1986 (14 Apr). *Appearance of Halley's Comet. T* **155** *and similar horiz designs. Multicoloured. W w* **15**. *P* 15.

973 45 c. Type **155** 50 30
974 60 c. Edmond Halley 60 40
975 75 c. Newton's telescope and astronomers . . 75 55
976 $3 Amateur astronomer on St. Vincent . . 2·25 2·25
973/6 . . . . *Set of* 4 3·75 3·25
MS977 155 × 104 mm. Nos. 973/6 . . . . 3·75 4·50

(Des Court House Studio. Litho Format)

1986 (21 Apr). *60th Birthday of Queen Elizabeth II* (1*st issue*). *Multicoloured designs as T* **117a** *of Montserrat. P* 12½.

978 10 c. Queen Elizabeth II 10 10
979 90 c. Princess Elizabeth 40 40
980 $2.50, Queen gathering bouquets from crowd . . . . 1·00 1·00
981 $8 In Canberra, 1982 (*vert*) . . . . . . 3·00 3·50
978/81 . . . . *Set of* 4 4·00 4·50
MS982 85 × 115 mm. $10 Queen Elizabeth II (*different*) . . . . 4·00 5·00

156 Mexican Player

157 Queen Elizabeth at Victoria Park, Kingstown

(Des Court House Studio. Litho Format)

1986 (7 May). *World Cup Football Championship, Mexico. T* **156** *and similar multicoloured designs. P* 12½ (75 c., $2, $4, $5) *or* 15 (*others*).

983 1 c. Football and world map (*horiz*) . . 10 10
984 2 c. Type **156** 10 10
985 5 c. Mexican player (*different*) 10 10
986 5 c. Hungary *v* Scotland 10 10
987 10 c. Spain *v* Scotland 10 10
988 30 c. England *v* U.S.S.R. (*horiz*) 20 20
989 45 c. Spain *v* France 30 30
990 75 c. Mexican team (56 × 36 *mm*) 45 40
991 $1 England *v* Italy 75 55
992 $2 Scottish team (56 × 36 *mm*) . . . . 1·40 1·10
993 $4 Spanish team (56 × 36 *mm*) . . . . 2·50 2·10
994 $5 English team (56 × 36 *mm*) . . . . 3·00 2·75
983/94 . . . . *Set of* 12 8·00 7·00
MS995 Four sheets, each 84 × 114 mm. (a) $1.50, As No. 993; (b) $2.25, As No. 992; (c) $2.50, As No. 990; (d) $5.50, As No. 994. P 12½ *Set of 4 sheets* 7·00 7·00

(Des Court House Studio. Litho Questa)

1986 (14 June). *60th Birthday of Queen Elizabeth II* (2*nd issue*). *T* **157** *and similar vert designs showing scenes from* 1985 *Royal Visit. Multicoloured. W w* **15**. *P* 15 × 14.

996 45 c. Type **157** 25 30
997 60 c. Queen and Prime Minister James Mitchell, Bequia 30 35
998 75 c. Queen, Prince Phillip and Mr. Mitchell, Port Elizabeth, Bequia 35 40
999 $2.50, Queen, Prince Phillip and Mr. Mitchell watching Independence Day parade, Victoria Park . . . . . . 1·25 1·40
996/9 . . . . *Set of* 4 1·90 2·25
MS1000 121 × 85 mm. $3 Queen at Victoria Park 2·00 2·40

(Des T. Hadler. Litho Format)

1986 (15 July). *Leaders of the World. Railway Locomotives* (*6th series*). *Horiz designs as T* **135**. *Multicoloured. P* 12½.
1001 30 c. multicoloured 15 15
a. Vert pair. Nos. 1001/2 .. .. 30 30
1002 30 c. multicoloured 15 15
1003 50 c. multicoloured 20 20
a. Vert pair. Nos. 1003/4 .. .. 40 40
1004 50 c. multicoloured 20 20
1005 $1 multicoloured 30 30
a. Vert pair. Nos. 1005/6 .. .. 60 60
1006 $1 multicoloured 30 30
1007 $3 multicoloured 80 80
a. Vert pair. Nos. 1007/8 .. .. 1·60 1·60
1008 $3 multicoloured 80 80
1001/8 .. .. *Set of* 8 2·50 2·50
Designs:—Nos. 1001/2, Class "ED41 BZZB" rack and adhesion locomotive, Japan (1926); 1003/4, Locomotive *The Judge*, Chicago Railroad Exposition, U.S.A. (1883); 1005/6, Class "E60C" electric locomotive, U.S.A. (1973); 1007/8, Class "SD40-2" diesel locomotive, U.S.A. (1972).
Nos. 1001/8 were issued in a similar sheet format to Nos. 727/38.
Nos. 1007/8 exist with the green omitted from stock dispersed by the liquidator of Format International Security Printers Ltd.

(Des Court House Studio. Litho Format)

1986 (18 July–15 Oct). *Royal Wedding* (*1st issue*). *Multicoloured designs as T* **118a** *of Montserrat. P* 12½.
1009 60 c. Profile of Prince Andrew 20 25
a. Pair. Nos. 1009/10 .. .. .. 40 50
1010 60 c. Miss Sarah Ferguson 20 25
1011 $2 Prince Andrew with Mrs. Nancy Reagan (*horiz*) 65 85
a. Pair. Nos. 1011/12 .. .. .. 1·25 1·60
1012 $2 Prince Andrew in naval uniform (*horiz*) 65 85
1009/12 .. .. *Set of* 4 1·60 2·10
MS1013 115 × 85 mm. $10 Duke and Duchess of York in carriage after wedding (*horiz*) (15.10) .. 3·75 4·50
Nos. 1009/10 and 1011/12 were each printed together, *se-tenant*, in horizontal and vertical pairs throughout the sheets.

158 *Acrocomia aculeata*

159 Cadet Force Emblem and Cadets of 1936 and 1986

(Des J. Cooter. Litho Questa)

1986 (30 Sept). *Timber Resources of St. Vincent. T* **158** *and similar vert designs. Multicoloured. W* w **15** (*sideways*). *P* 14.
1014 10 c. Type **158** 30 15
1015 60 c. *Pithecellobium saman* 90 60
1016 75 c. White Cedar .. .. 1·25 75
1017 $3 *Andira inermis* .. .. .. 3·25 3·50
1014/17 .. .. *Set of* 4 5·25 4·50

(Des G. Vasarhelyi. Litho Questa)

1986 (30 Sept). *50th Anniv of St. Vincent Cadet Force* (45 c., $2) *and 75th Anniv of St. Vincent Girls' High School* (*others*). *T* **159** *and similar multicoloured designs. W* w **15** (*sideways on* 45 c.). *P* 14.
1018 45 c. Type **159** 30 30
1019 60 c. Grimble Building, Girls' High School (*horiz*) 35 35
1020 $1.50, High School pupils (*horiz*) .. 80 80
1021 $2 Cadets on parade (*horiz*) .. .. 1·25 1·10
1018/21 .. .. *Set of* 4 2·40 2·25

1986 (15 Oct). *Royal Wedding* (*2nd issue*). *Nos.* 1009/12 *optd as T* **121** *of Montserrat in silver.*
1022 60 c. Profile of Prince Andrew 30 35
a. Pair. Nos. 1022/3 .. .. .. 60 70
1023 60 c. Miss Sarah Ferguson 30 35
1024 $2 Prince Andrew with Mrs. Nancy Reagan (*horiz*) .. .. 1·00 1·10
a. Pair. Nos. 1024/5 .. .. .. 2·00 2·25
1025 $2 Prince Andrew in naval uniform (*horiz*) .. .. 1·00 1·10
1022/5 .. .. *Set of* 4 2·40 2·50

160 King Arthur

(Des G. Vasarhelyi. Litho Format)

1986 (3 Nov). *The Legend of King Arthur. T* **160** *and similar horiz designs. Multicoloured. P* 14 × 13½.
1026 30 c. Type **160** 40 40
1027 45 c. Merlin taking baby Arthur 50 50
1028 60 c. Arthur pulling sword from stone .. 60 60
1029 75 c. Camelot 70 70
1030 $1 Arthur receiving Excalibur from the Lady of the Lake 80 80
1031 $1.50, Knights at the Round Table .. 1·25 1·25
1032 $2 The Holy Grail .. .. 1·50 1·50
1033 $5 Sir Lancelot jousting .. .. .. 2·75 2·75
1026/33 .. .. *Set of* 8 7·75 7·75
Nos. 1026/9 cancelled-to-order exist imperforate from stock dispersed by the liquidator of Format International Security Printers Ltd.

161 Statue of Liberty Floodlit

162 Fishing for Tri Tri

(Des Court House Studio. Litho Format)

1986 (26 Nov). *Centenary of Statue of Liberty. T* **161** *and similar vert designs showing aspects of the Statue. P* 14 × 13½.
1034 15 c. multicoloured 10 10
1035 25 c. multicoloured 15 15
1036 40 c. multicoloured 20 25
1037 55 c. multicoloured 25 30
1038 75 c. multicoloured 35 40
1039 90 c. multicoloured 45 50
1040 $1.75, multicoloured 90 95
1041 $2 multicoloured .. .. 1·00 1·10
1042 $2.50, multicoloured .. .. 1·25 1·40
1043 $3 multicoloured .. .. 1·50 1·60
1034/43 .. .. *Set of* 10 5·50 6·00
MS1044 Three sheets, each 85 × 115 mm. $3.50; $4; $5 .. .. .. *Set of* 3 *sheets* 7·00 8·50

(Des T. Hadler. Litho Format)

1986 (10 Dec). *Freshwater Fishing. T* **162** *and similar horiz designs. Multicoloured. P* 15.
1045 75 c. Type **162** 35 40
a. Pair. Nos. 1045/6 .. .. .. 70 80
1046 75 c. Tri Tri 35 40
1047 $1.50, Crayfishing 75 80
a. Pair. Nos. 1047/8 .. .. .. 1·50 1·60
1048 $1.50, Crayfish 75 80
1045/8 .. .. *Set of* 4 2·00 2·10
Nos. 1045/6 and 1047/8 were each printed together, *se-tenant*, in horizontal and vertical pairs throughout the sheets.

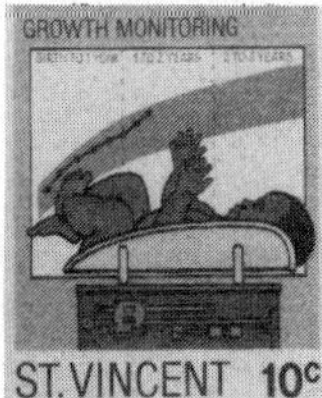

163 Baby on Scales

WORLD POPULATION
5 BILLION
11TH JULY 1987

(164)

(Litho Format)

1987 (10 June). *Child Health Campaign. T* **163** *and similar vert designs. Multicoloured. P* 14.
1049 10 c. Type **163** 10 10
1050 50 c. Oral rehydration therapy 35 40
1051 75 c. Breast feeding 50 55
1052 $1 Nurse giving injection 75 80
1049/52 .. .. *Set of* 4 1·50 1·60

1987 (10 June). *World Population Control. Nos.* 1049/52 *optd with T* **164**.
1053 10 c. Type **163** 10 10
1054 50 c. Oral rehydration therapy 40 40
1055 75 c. Breast feeding 55 55
1056 $1 Nurse giving injection 70 70
1053/6 .. .. *Set of* 4 1·60 1·60

165 Hanna Mandlikova

166 Miss Prima Donna, Queen of the Bands, 1986

(Litho Format)

1987 (22 June). *International Lawn Tennis Players. T* **165** *and similar vert designs. Multicoloured. P* 12½.
1057 40 c. Type **165** 25 25
1058 60 c. Yannick Noah 35 35
1059 80 c. Ivan Lendl 40 40
1060 $1 Chris Evert 50 50
1061 $1.25, Steffi Graf 60 60
1062 $1.50, John McEnroe 75 75
1063 $1.75, Martina Navratilova with Wimbledon trophy 85 85
1064 $2 Boris Becker with Wimbledon trophy 95 95
1057/64 .. .. *Set of* 8 4·25 4·25
MS1065 115 × 85 mm. $2.25 As No. 1063; $2.25 As No. 1064 .. .. 2·75 3·25
Designs as Nos. 1063/4, but each with a face value of $10, also exist embossed on gold foil from a restricted printing.

(Des Young Phillips. Litho Format)

1987 (29 June). *10th Anniv of Carnival. T* **166** *and similar vert designs. Multicoloured. P* 12½.
1066 20 c. Type **166** 10 15
1067 45 c. Donna Young, Miss Carnival, 1985 .. 20 25
1068 55 c. Miss St. Vincent and the Grenadines, 1986 .. .. 25 30
1069 $3.70, "Spirit of Hope" costume, 1986 .. 1·60 1·75
1066/9 .. .. *Set of* 4 1·90 2·25
The 45 c. value is inscribed "Miss Carival" in error.

(167)

168 Queen Victoria, 1841

1987 (26 Aug). *10th Death Anniv of Elvis Presley* (*entertainer*). *Nos.* 919/27 *optd with T* **167** *in silver.*
1070 10 c. multicoloured (T **149**) 10 10
a. Horiz pair. Nos. 1070/1 .. .. 10 10
1071 10 c. multicoloured (bright blue) 10 10
1072 60 c. multicoloured (brown) 25 30
a. Horiz pair. Nos. 1072/3 .. .. 50 60
1073 60 c. multicoloured (pale grey) 25 30
1074 $1 multicoloured (brown) 40 45
a. Horiz pair. Nos. 1074/5 .. .. 80 90
1075 $1 multicoloured (bright blue) 40 45
1076 $5 multicoloured (azure) .. .. .. 2·10 2·25
a. Horiz pair. Nos. 1076/7 .. .. 4·25 4·50
1077 $5 multicoloured (bright blue) .. .. 2·10 2·25
1070/7 .. .. *Set of* 8 5·00 5·50
MS1078 Four sheets, each 145 × 107 mm. (a) 30 c. As Nos. 1070/1 each × 2; (b) 50 c. As Nos. 1072/3 each × 2; (c) $1.50, As Nos. 1074/5 each × 2; (d) $4.50, As Nos. 1076/7 each × 2 .. .. 7·00 7·25

(Litho Format)

1987 (15 Oct). *Royal Ruby Wedding and 150th Anniv of Queen Victoria's Accession. T* **168** *and similar vert designs. Multicoloured. P* 12½.
1079 15 c. Type **168** 15 10
1080 75 c. Queen Elizabeth and Prince Andrew, 1960 .. .. 45 40
1081 $1 Coronation, 1953 .. .. .. 60 50
1082 $2.50, Duke of Edinburgh, 1948 .. .. 1·40 1·50
1083 $5 Queen Elizabeth II, *c.* 1980 .. .. 2·50 2·75
1079/83 .. .. *Set of* 5 4·50 4·75
MS1084 85 × 115 mm. $6 Princess Elizabeth with Prince Charles at his Christening, 1948 .. 3·75 4·00

169 Karl Benz and Benz Three-wheeler (1886)

(Litho Format)

1987 (4 Dec), *Century of Motoring. T* **169** *and similar horiz designs. Multicoloured. P* 12½.
1085 $1 Type **169** 60 60
1086 $2 Enzo Ferrari and Ferrari "Dino 206SP" (1966) .. .. 1·25 1·25
1087 $4 Charles Rolls and Sir Henry Royce and Rolls-Royce "Silver Ghost" (1907) .. 2·00 2·00
1088 $5 Henry Ford and Ford "Model T" (1908) .. 2·50 2·50
1085/8 .. .. *Set of* 4 5·75 5·75
MS1089 Four sheets, each 144 × 75 mm. (a) $3 As Type **169**. (b) $5 As No. 1086. (c) $6 As No. 1087. (d) $8 As No. 1088 .. *Set of* 4 *sheets* 17·00 18·00
Nos. 1085/8 with the gold omitted and Nos. 1088 and **MS**1089d with Henry Ford facing right all exist from stock dispersed by the liquidator of Format International Security Printers Ltd.

170 Everton Football Team

(Litho Format)

1987 (4 Dec). *English Football Teams. T* **170** *and similar horiz designs. Multicoloured. P* 12½.
1090 $2 Type **170** .. .. 1·25 1·25
1091 $2 Manchester United .. .. .. 1·25 1·25
1092 $2 Tottenham Hotspur .. .. .. 1·25 1·25
1093 $2 Arsenal .. .. 1·25 1·25
1094 $2 Liverpool .. .. 1·25 1·25
1095 $2 Derby County .. .. .. 1·25 1·25
1096 $2 Portsmouth .. .. .. 1·25 1·25
1097 $2 Leeds United .. .. .. 1·25 1·25
1090/7 .. .. *Set of* 8 9·00 9·00

171 Five Cent Coins

172 Charles Dickens

(Des Questa ($20), Young Phillips Studio (others). Litho Questa ($20) or Format (others))

1987 (11 Dec)–**89**. *East Caribbean Currency. T* **171** *and similar multicoloured designs. P* 14 ($20) *or* 15 (*others*).
1098 5 c. Type **171** 10 10
1099 6 c. Two cent coins 10 10
1100 10 c. Ten cent coins 10 10
1101 12 c. Two and ten cent coins 10 10
1102 15 c. Five cent coins 10 10
1103 20 c. Ten cent coins 10 10
1104 25 c. Twenty-five cent coins 10 15
1105 30 c. Five and twenty-five cent coins .. 10 15
1106 35 c. Twenty-five and ten cent coins .. 15 20
1107 45 c. Twenty-five and two ten cent coins .. 20 25
1108 50 c. Fifty cent coins 20 25
1109 65 c. Fifty, ten and five cent coins 25 30
1110 75 c. Fifty and twenty-five cent coins .. 30 35
1111 $1 One dollar note (*horiz*) 40 45
1112 $2 Two one dollar notes (*horiz*) 85 90
1113 $3 Three one dollar notes (*horiz*) .. 1·25 1·40
1114 $5 Five dollar note (*horiz*) .. .. 2·10 2·25
1115 $10 Ten dollar note (*horiz*) .. .. 4·25 4·50
1115*a* $20 Twenty-dollar note (*horiz*) (7.11.89) 8·50 8·75
1098/115*a* .. .. .. *Set of* 19 16·00 17·00

No. 1100 overprinted "SPECIMEN" and with the blue omitted exists from stock dispersed by the liquidator of Format International Security Printers Ltd.

(Des Jennifer Toombs. Litho Format)

1987 (17 Dec). *Christmas. 175th Birth Anniv of Charles Dickens. T* **172** *and similar vert designs. Multicoloured. P* 14 × 14½.
1116 6 c. Type **172** 10 10
a. Horiz pair. Nos. 1116/17 .. .. 15 15
1117 6 c. "Mr. Fezziwig's Ball" 10 10
1118 25 c. Type **172** 15 15
a. Horiz pair. Nos. 1118/19 .. .. 30 30
1119 25 c. "Scrooge's Third Visitor" 15 15
1120 50 c. Type **172** 30 30
a. Horiz pair. Nos. 1120/1 .. .. 60 60
1121 50 c. "The Cratchits' Christmas" 30 30
1122 75 c. Type **172** 45 45
a. Horiz pair. Nos. 1122/3 .. .. 90 90
1123 75 c. "A Christmas Carol" 45 45
1116/23 .. .. *Set of* 8 1·75 1·75
MS1124 141 × 101 mm. $5 Teacher reading to class .. .. 2·75 3·25

Nos. 1116/17, 1118/19, 1120/1 and 1122/3 were printed together, *se-tenant*, in horizontal pairs throughout the sheets, each pair forming a composite design showing an open book. The first design in each pair shows Type **172** and the second a scene from *A Christmas Carol*.

173 *Santa Maria*

174 Brown Pelican

(Des M. Pollard. Litho Format)

1988 (11 Jan). *500th Anniv of Discovery of America* (1992) *by Columbus (2nd issue). T* **173** *and similar square designs. Multicoloured. P* 14.
1125 15 c. Type **173** 15 15
1126 75 c. *Nina* and *Pinta* 50 50
1127 $1 Compass and hourglass 70 70
1128 $1.50, Claiming the New World for Spain 90 90
1129 $3 Arawak village .. .. .. 1·50 1·50
1130 $4 Parrot, hummingbird, pineapple and maize .. .. 2·00 2·00
1125/30 .. .. *Set of* 6 5·25 5·25
MS1131 114 × 86 mm. $5 Columbus, Arms and *Santa Maria*. P 13½ × 14 .. .. 4·25 4·75

Further unissued $2 and $5 miniature sheets exist from stock dispersed by the liquidator of Format International Security Printers Ltd.

(Des Maxine Marsh. Litho Format)

1988 (15 Feb). *P* 14.
1132 **174** 45 c. multicoloured 30 30

175 Windsurfing

(Litho Format)

1988 (26 Feb). *Tourism. T* **175** *and similar multicoloured designs. P* 15.
1133 10 c. Type **175** 10 10
1134 45 c. Scuba diving 20 25
1135 65 c. Aerial view of Young Island (*horiz*) .. 30 35
1136 $5 Charter yacht (*horiz*) .. .. 2·10 2·25
1133/6 .. .. *Set of* 4 2·40 2·50
MS1136*a* 115×85 mm $10 Two windsurfers off St. Vincent (60×40 *mm*). P 12½ .. .. 4·00 4·50

176 *Nuestra Sénora del Rosario* (galleon) and Spanish Knight's Cross

(Litho Format)

1988 (29 July). *400th Anniv of Spanish Armada. T* **176** *and similar horiz designs. Multicoloured. P* 12½.
1137 15 c. Type **176** 15 10
1138 75 c. *Ark Royal* and English Armada medal 30 35
1139 $1.50, English fleet and Drake's dial .. 60 65
1140 $2 Dismasted Spanish ship and 16th-century shot 80 85
1141 $3.50, Attack of English fireships at Calais and 16th-century grenade .. 1·50 1·60
1142 $5 *Revenge* and Drake's Drum .. .. 2·10 2·25
1137/42 .. .. *Set of* 6 4·75 5·25
MS1143 123 × 92 mm. $8 Sighting the Armada 3·50 3·75

177 D. K. Lillee

178 Athletics

(Litho Format)

1988 (29 July). *Cricketers of* 1988 *International Season. T* **177** *and similar square designs. Multicoloured. P* 14.
1144 15 c. Type **177** 30 30
1145 50 c. G. A. Gooch 50 50
1146 75 c. R. N. Kapil Dev 70 70
1147 $1 S. M. Gavaskar 85 85
1148 $1.50, M. W. Gatting .. .. .. 1·25 1·25
1149 $2.50, Imran Khan .. .. .. 1·75 1·75
1150 $3 I. T. Botham .. .. .. 2·00 2·00
1151 $4 I. V. A. Richards .. .. .. 2·25 2·25
1144/51 .. .. *Set of* 8 8·50 8·50
MS1152 130 × 80 mm. $2 As $4; $3.50, As $3 3·50 4·00

Examples of No. **MS**1152 imperforate or part perforate exist from stock dispersed by the liquidator of Format International Security Printers Ltd.

(Des and litho Questa)

1988 (7 Dec). *Olympic Games, Seoul. T* **178** *and similar multicoloured designs. P* 14.
1153 10 c. Type **178** 10 10
1154 50 c. Long jumping (*vert*) 20 25
1155 $1 Triple jumping 40 45
1156 $5 Boxing (*vert*) .. .. .. 2·10 2·25
1153/6 .. .. *Set of* 4 2·50 2·75
MS1157 85 × 63 mm. $10 Olympic flame .. 4·25 4·50

A different set of six values and a miniature sheet for this event was not issued, but exists from stock dispersed by the liquidator of Format International Security Printers Ltd.

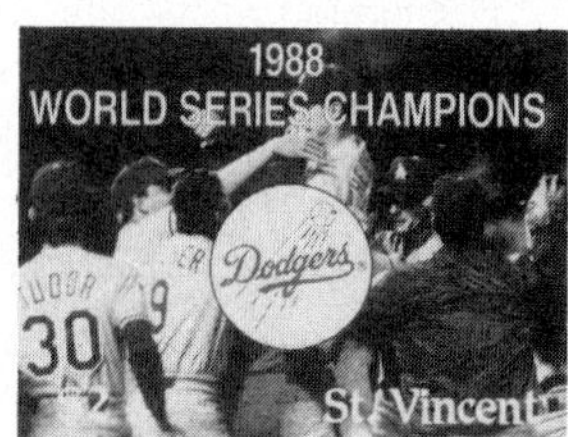

179 Babe Ruth **180** Los Angeles Dodgers (National League Champions)

(Litho Questa)

1988 (15 Dec). *Famous Baseball Players* (*1st series*). *P* 14.
1158 **179** $2 multicoloured 85 90

No. 1158 also exists embossed on gold foil from a restricted printing.

See also Nos. 1264/75, 1407 and 1408/88.

(Des W. Storozuk. Litho Questa)

1988 (15 Dec). 1988 *Baseball World Series. Sheet* 115×85 *mm containing T* **180** *and similar horiz design. Multicoloured. P* 14×13½.
MS1159 $2 Type **180**; $2 Team logos of Dodgers and Oakland Athletics .. .. .. 1·75 1·90

(Des Walt Disney Co. Litho Questa)

1988 (23 Dec). *Christmas. "Mickey's Christmas Train". Multicoloured designs as T* **171***a of Lesotho. P* 14×13½.
1160 1 c. Minnie Mouse in parcels van (*horiz*) 10 10
1161 2 c. Mordie and Ferdie on low-loader wagon (*horiz*) 10 10
1162 3 c. Chip n'Dale in wagon with Christmas trees (*horiz*) 10 10
1163 4 c. Donald Duck's nephews riding with reindeer (*horiz*) 10 10
1164 5 c. Donald and Daisy Duck in restaurant car (*horiz*) 10 10
1165 10 c. Grandma Duck, Uncle Scrooge McDuck, Goofy and Clarabelle carol singing in carriage (*horiz*) .. 10 10
1166 $5 Mickey Mouse driving locomotive (*horiz*) .. .. 2·10 2·25
1167 $6 Father Christmas in guard's van (*horiz*) .. .. 2·50 2·75
1160/7 .. .. *Set of* 8 4·50 4·75
MS1168 Two sheets, each 127 × 102 mm, (a) $5 Mickey Mouse and nephews at railway station. (b) $5 Mickey and Minnie Mouse on carousel. P 13½×14 .. .. .. *Set of* 2 *sheets* 4·25 4·50

181 Mickey Mouse as Snake Charmer

(Des Walt Disney Co. Litho Questa)

1989 (7 Feb). *"India-89" International Stamp Exhibition, New Delhi. T* **181** *and similar multicoloured designs showing Walt Disney cartoon characters in India. P* 14×13½.
1169 1 c. Type **181** 10 10
1170 2 c. Goofy with Chowsingha Antelope .. 10 10
1171 3 c. Mickey and Minnie Mouse with Blue Peacock 10 10
1172 5 c. Goofy with Briolette Diamond and Mickey Mouse pushing mine truck .. 10 10
1173 10 c. Clarabelle with Orloff Diamond .. 10 10
1174 25 c. Mickey Mouse as tourist and Regent Diamond, Louvre, Paris 10 15
1175 $4 Minnie and Mickey Mouse with Kohinoor Diamond .. .. .. 1·75 1·90
1176 $5 Mickey Mouse and Goofy with Indian Rhinoceros .. .. 2·10 2·25
1169/76 .. .. *Set of* 8 3·75 4·00
MS1177 Two sheets, each 127 × 102 mm. (a) $6 Mickey Mouse riding Indian elephant. P 14×13½. (b) $6 Mickey Mouse as postman delivering Hope Diamond to Smithsonian Museum, U.S.A. (*vert*). P 13½×14. .. .. *Set of* 2 *sheets* 5·00 5·25

182 Harry James

(Des A. Nahigian. Litho Questa)

1989 (3 Apr). *Jazz Musicians. T* **182** *and similar horiz designs. Multicoloured. P* 14.

1178 10 c. Type **182** 10 10
1179 15 c. Sidney Bechet 10 10
1180 25 c. Benny Goodman 10 15
1181 35 c. Django Reinhardt 15 20
1182 50 c. Lester Young 20 25
1183 90 c. Gene Krupa 40 45
1184 $3 Louis Armstrong .. .. .. 1·25 1·40
1185 $4 Duke Ellington .. .. .. 1·75 1·90
1178/85 .. .. *Set of* 8 3·50 4·00
MS1186 Two sheets, each 107×92 mm. (a) $5 Charlie Parker. (b) $5 Billie Holliday *Set of* 2 *sheets* 4·25 4·50

183 Head of St. Vincent Amazon

(Des L. McQueen. Litho Questa)

1989 (5 Apr). *Wildlife Conservation. St. Vincent Amazon ("St. Vincent Parrot"). T* **183** *and similar multicoloured designs. P* 14.

1187 10 c. Type **183** 10 10
1188 20 c. St. Vincent Amazon in flight .. 10 10
1189 40 c. Feeding (*vert*) 15 20
1190 70 c. At entrance to nest (*vert*) 30 35
1187/90 .. .. *Set of* 4 55 65

184 Blue-hooded Euphonia ("Mistletoe Bird")

185 Birds in Flight

(Des Tracy Pedersen. Litho Questa)

1989 (5 Apr). *Birds of St. Vincent. T* **184** *and similar multicoloured designs. P* 14.

1191 25 c. Type **184** 10 15
1192 75 c. Common Black Hawk ("Crab Hawk") 30 35
1193 $2 Mangrove Cuckoo ("Coucou") .. 85 90
1194 $3 Hooded Tanager ("Prince Bird") .. 1·25 1·40
1191/4 .. .. *Set of* 4 2·25 2·50
MS1195 (a) 75×105 mm. $5 Rufous-throated Solitaire ("Soufriere Bird") (*vert*). (b) 105×75 mm. $5 Purple-throated Carib ("Doctor Bird") *Set of* 2 *sheets* 4·25 4·50

(Des N. Waldman. Litho B.D.T.)

1989 (10 Apr). *Wildlife Conservation. Noah's Ark. T* **185** *and similar square designs. Multicoloured. P* 14.

1196 40 c. Type **185** 15 20
a. Sheetlet. Nos. 1196/220 .. .. 3·50
1197 40 c. Rainbow (left side) 15 20
1198 40 c. Noah's Ark on mountain 15 20
1199 40 c. Rainbow (right side) 15 20
1200 40 c. Birds in flight (*different*) 15 20
1201 40 c. Cow elephant 15 20
1202 40 c. Bull elephant 15 20
1203 40 c. Top of eucalyptus tree 15 20
1204 40 c. Kangaroos 15 20
1205 40 c. Hummingbird 15 20
1206 40 c. Lions 15 20
1207 40 c. White-tailed Deer 15 20
1208 40 c. Koala in fork of tree 15 20
1209 40 c. Koala on branch 15 20
1210 40 c. Hummingbird approaching flower .. 15 20
1211 40 c. Toucan and flower 15 20
1212 40 c. Toucan facing right 15 20
1213 40 c. Camels 15 20
1214 40 c. Giraffes 15 20
1215 40 c. Mountain Sheep 15 20
1216 40 c. Ladybirds on leaf 15 20
1217 40 c. Swallowtail butterfly 15 20
1218 40 c. Swallowtail butterfly behind leaves .. 15 20
1219 40 c. Pythons 15 20
1220 40 c. Dragonflies 15 20
1196/220 .. .. *Set of* 25 3·50 4·50

Nos. 1196/220 were printed together, *se-tenant*, in a sheetlet of 25, forming a composite design showing Noah's Ark and animals released after the Flood.

(Litho Questa)

1989 (17 Apr). *Easter. 500th Birth Anniv of Titian (artist). Vert designs as T* **186a** *of Lesotho. Multicoloured. P* 13½×14.

1221 5 c. "Baptism of Christ" (detail) 10 10
1222 30 c. "Temptation of Christ" 10 15
1223 45 c. "Ecce Homo" 20 25
1224 65 c. "Noli Me Tangere" (fragment) .. 25 30
1225 75 c. "Christ carrying the Cross" (detail) .. 30 35
1226 $1 "Christ crowned with Thorns" (detail) 40 45
1227 $4 "Lamentation over Christ" (detail) .. 1·75 1·90
1228 $5 "The Entombment" (detail) .. .. 2·10 2·25
1221/8 .. .. *Set of* 8 4·75 5·25
MS1229 (a) 98×111 mm. $6 "Pietà" (detail). (b) 114×95 mm. $6 "The Deposition" (detail) *Set of* 2 *sheets* 5·00 5·25

186 *Ile de France*

187 Space Shuttle deploying West German Satellite, 1983

(Des W. Wright. Litho Questa)

1989 (21 Apr). *Ocean Liners. T* **186** *and similar horiz designs. Multicoloured. P* 14.

1230 10 c. Type **186** 10 10
1231 40 c. *Liberté* 15 20
1232 50 c. *Mauretania* (launched 1906) .. 20 25
1233 75 c. *France* 30 35
1234 $1 *Aquitania* 40 45
1235 $2 *United States* 85 90
1236 $3 *Olympic* .. .. 1·25 1·40
1237 $4 *Queen Elizabeth* .. .. .. 1·75 1·90
1230/7 .. .. *Set of* 8 4·50 5·00
MS1238 Two sheets, each 141×108 mm. (a) $6 *Queen Mary* (85×28 *mm*). (b) $6 *Queen Elizabeth 2* (85×28 *mm*) .. .. .. *Set of* 2 *sheets* 5·00 5·25

(Des M. Dorfman. Litho Questa)

1989 (26 Apr). *International Co-operation in Space. T* **187** *and similar vert designs. Multicoloured. P* 14.

1239 40 c. Type **187** 15 20
1240 60 c. Vladimir Remeck (Czech cosmonaut) and "Soyuz 28", 1978 .. .. 25 30
1241 $1 Projected "Hermes" space plane and "Columbus" Space Station 40 45
1242 $4 Ulf Merbold (West German astronaut), 1983, and proposed European Spacelab .. .. .. 1·75 1·90
1239/42 .. .. *Set of* 4 2·25 2·50
MS1243 93×67 mm. $5 Meeting in space of "Apollo/Soyuz" mission crews, 1975 .. .. 2·10 2·25

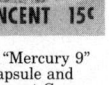

188 "Mercury 9" Capsule and Astronaut Cooper

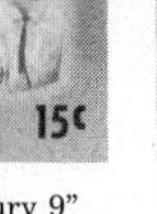

189 Schooner

(Des M. Dorfman. Litho Questa)

1989 (26 Apr). *25th Anniv of Launching of "Telstar II" Communications Satellite* (1988). *T* **188** *and similar vert designs, each showing satellite and T.V. screen. Multicoloured. P* 14.

1244 15 c. Type **188** 10 10
1245 35 c. Martin Luther King addressing crowd, 1963 .. .. .. 15 20
1246 50 c. Speedskater, Winter Olympic Games, Innsbruck, 1964 .. .. 20 25
1247 $3 Pope John XXIII blessing crowd .. 1·25 1·40
1244/7 .. .. *Set of* 4 1·50 1·75
MS1248 107×77 mm. $5 Launch of "Telstar II", 1963 .. .. 2·10 2·25

(Litho Questa)

1989 (6 July). *Japanese Art. Multicoloured designs as T* **187a** *of Lesotho. P* 14×13½.

1249 10 c. "Autumn Flowers in Front of the Full Moon" (Hiroshige) 10 10
1250 40 c. "Hibiscus" (Hiroshige) 15 20
1251 50 c. "Iris" (Hiroshige) 20 25
1252 75 c. "Morning Glories" (Hiroshige) .. 30 35
1253 $1 "Dancing Swallows" (Hiroshige) .. 40 45
1254 $2 "Sparrow and Bamboo" (Hiroshige) 85 90
1255 $3 "Yellow Bird and Cotton Rose" (Hiroshige) .. .. .. 1·25 1·40
1256 $4 "Judos Chrysanthemums in a Deep Ravine in China" (Hiroshige) .. 1·75 1·90
1249/56 .. .. *Set of* 8 4·50 5·00
MS1257 Two sheets, each 102×76 mm. (a) $6 "Rural Cottages in Spring" (Sotatsu). P 14×13½. (b) $6 "The Six Immortal Poets portrayed as Cats" (Kuniyoshi) (*vert*). P 13½×14 *Set of* 2 *sheets* 5·00 5·25

Nos. 1249/56 were each printed in sheetlets of 10 containing two horizontal strips of 5 stamps separated by printed labels commemorating Emperor Hirohito.

(Des J. Batchelor. Litho Questa)

1989 (7 July). *"Philexfrance 89" International Stamp Exhibition, Paris, and Bicentenary of French Revolution. T* **189** *and similar multicoloured designs, showing 18th-century French naval vessels. P* 13½×14.

1258 30 c. Type **189** 10 15
1259 55 c. Corvette 25 30
1260 75 c. Frigate 30 35
1261 $1 Ship of the line 40 45
1262 $3 *Ville de Paris* (ship of the line) .. 1·25 1·40
1258/62 .. .. *Set of* 5 2·10 2·40
MS1263 76×108 mm. $6 Map of St. Vincent in 18th century (*vert*). P 14×13½ .. .. 2·50 2·75

190 Johnny Bench

191 Dante Bichette, 1989

(Des Rosemary De Figlio and W. Storozuk. Litho Questa)

1989 (23 July). *Famous Baseball Players (2nd series). T* **190** *and similar vert designs. Multicoloured. P* 14.

1264 $2 Type **190** 85 90
1265 $2 Red Schoendienst 85 90
1266 $2 Carl Yastrzemski 85 90
1267 $2 Ty Cobb 85 90
1268 $2 Willie Mays 85 90
1269 $2 Stan Musial 85 90
1270 $2 Ernie Banks 85 90
1271 $2 Lou Gehrig 85 90
1272 $2 Jackie Robinson 85 90
1273 $2 Bob Feller 85 90
1274 $2 Ted Williams 85 90
1275 $2 Al Kaline 85 90
1264/75 .. .. *Set of* 12 9·25 9·75

Nos. 1264/75 also exist embossed on gold foil from a restricted printing.

(Des Rosemary De Figlio. Litho Questa)

1989 (23 July). *Major League Baseball Rookies. T* **191** *and similar vert designs. Multicoloured. P* 13½×14.

1276 60 c. Type **191** 25 30
a. Sheetlet. Nos. 1276/84 .. .. 2·25
1277 60 c. Carl Yastrzemski, 1961 .. .. 25 30
1278 60 c. Randy Johnson, 1989 .. .. 25 30
1279 60 c. Jerome Walton, 1989 .. .. 25 30
1280 60 c. Ramon Martinez, 1989 .. .. 25 30
1281 60 c. Ken Hill, 1989 .. .. .. 25 30
1282 60 c. Tom McCarthy, 1989 .. .. 25 30
1283 60 c. Gaylord Perry, 1963 .. .. 25 30
1284 60 c. John Smoltz, 1989 .. .. 25 30
1285 60 c. Bob Milacki, 1989 .. .. 25 30
a. Sheetlet. Nos. 1285/93 .. .. 2·25
1286 60 c. Babe Ruth, 1915 .. .. .. 25 30
1287 60 c. Jim Abbott, 1989 .. .. .. 25 30
1288 60 c. Gary Sheffield, 1989 .. .. 25 30
1289 60 c. Gregg Jeffries, 1989 .. .. 25 30
1290 60 c. Kevin Brown, 1989 .. .. .. 25 30
1291 60 c. Cris Carpenter, 1989 .. .. 25 30
1292 60 c. Johnny Bench, 1968 .. .. 25 30
1293 60 c. Ken Griffey Jr, 1989 .. .. 25 30
1276/93 .. .. *Set of* 18 4·00 4·75

Nos. 1276/84 and 1285/93 were each printed together, *se-tenant*, in sheetlets of 9.

192 Chris Sabo

(Des Rosemary De Figlio. Litho Questa)

1989 (23 July). *Major League Baseball Award Winners. T* **192** *and similar vert designs. Multicoloured. P* 13½×14.

1294 60 c. Type **192** 25 30
a. Sheetlet. Nos. 1294/302 .. .. 2·00
1295 60 c. Walt Weiss 25 30
1296 60 c. Willie Mays 25 30
1297 60 c. Kirk Gibson 25 30
1298 60 c. Ted Williams 25 30
1299 60 c. Jose Canseco 25 30
1300 60 c. Gaylord Perry 25 30
1301 60 c. Orel Hershiser 25 30
1302 60 c. Frank Viola 25 30
1294/1302 .. .. *Set of* 9 2·00 2·40

Nos. 1294/302 were printed together, *se-tenant*, in a sheetlet of 9.

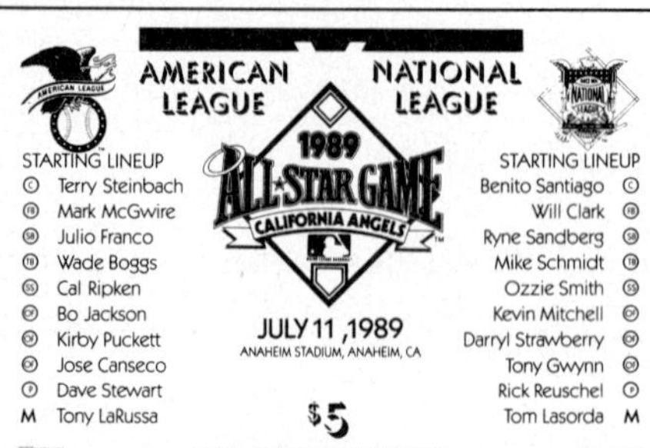

193 All-Star Game Line-up
(Illustration reduced. Actual size 115 × 80 *mm)*

(Des Rosemary De Figlio. Litho Questa)

1989 (23 July). *American League v National League All-Star Game,* 1989. *Sheet* 115×81 *mm. Imperf.*
MS1303 **193** $5 multicoloured .. .. .. 2·10 2·25

194 St. Vincent Amazon
195 Queen Conch and West Indian Purpura Shells

(Litho Questa)

1989 (31 July). *P* 15×14.
1304 **194** 55 c. multicoloured 25 30

(Des I. MacLaury. Litho B.D.T.)

1989 (31 Aug). 500*th Anniv of Discovery of America by Columbus* (1992) (3*rd issue*). *T* **195** *and similar horiz designs. P* 14.
1305 50 c. multicoloured 20 25
a. Sheetlet. Nos. 1305/24 .. .. 3·50
1306 50 c. multicoloured 20 25
1307 50 c. dull ultramarine, black & brt new blue 20 25
1308 50 c. dull ultramarine, black & brt new blue 20 25
1309 50 c. multicoloured 20 25
1310 50 c. multicoloured 20 25
1311 50 c. multicoloured 20 25
1312 50 c. black and bright new blue 20 25
1313 50 c. multicoloured 20 25
1314 50 c. multicoloured 20 25
1315 50 c. multicoloured 20 25
1316 50 c. multicoloured 20 25
1317 50 c. multicoloured 20 25
1318 50 c. multicoloured 20 25
1319 50 c. multicoloured 20 25
1320 50 c. multicoloured 20 25
1321 50 c. multicoloured 20 25
1322 50 c. multicoloured 20 25
1323 50 c. multicoloured 20 25
1324 50 c. multicoloured 20 25
1305/24 .. .. *Set of* 20 3·50 4·50

Designs:—No. 1305, Type **195**; 1306, Caribbean reef fishes; 1307, Sperm Whale; 1308, Fleet of Columbus; 1309, Remora (fish); 1310, Columbus planting flag; 1311, Navigational instruments; 1312, Sea monster; 1313, Kemp's Ridley Turtle; 1314, Magnificent Frigate Bird; 1315, Caribbean Manatee; 1316, Caribbean Monk Seal; 1317, Mayan chief, dugout canoe and caravel; 1318, Masked Boobies; 1319, Venezuelan pile village; 1320, Atlantic Wing Oyster and Lion's Paw Scallop; 1321, Great Hammerhead and Mako Sharks; 1322, Brown Pelican and Hyacinthine Macaw; 1323, Venezuelan bowmen; 1324, Capuchin and Squirrel Monkeys.

Nos. 1305/24 were printed together, *se-tenant*, in a sheetlet of 20 (4×5), forming a composite design of a Caribbean map showing the voyages of Columbus

196 Command Module *Columbia* returning to Earth

(Des W. Wright. Litho Questa)

1989 (11 Sept). 20*th Anniv of First Manned Landing on Moon. T* **196** *and similar multicoloured designs. P* 14.
1325 35 c. Type **196** 15 20
1326 75 c. Lunar module *Eagle* landing 30 35
1327 $1 "Apollo 11" launch 40 45
1328 $2 Buzz Aldrin on Moon 85 90
a. Horiz strip of 4. Nos. 1328/31 .. 3·50
1329 $2 Lunar module *Eagle* 85 90
1330 $2 Earthrise from the Moon 85 90
1331 $2 Neil Armstrong 85 90
1332 $3 *Eagle* and *Columbia* in Moon Orbit .. 1·25 1·40
1325/32 .. .. *Set of* 8 5·00 5·50
MS1333 Two sheets, each 108×79 mm. (a) $3 Command Module *Columbia*, $3 Lunar Module *Eagle*. (b) $6 Neil Armstrong stepping on to Moon (*vert*) .. .. .. *Set of* 2 *sheets* 5·00 5·25

Nos. 1328/31 were printed together, *se-tenant*, in horizontal strips of four throughout the sheet.

197 Jay Howell and Alejandro Pena

1989 (23 Sept). *Centenary of the Los Angeles Dodgers* (1*st issue*). *Baseball Players. T* **197** *and similar horiz designs. Multicoloured. Litho. P* 12½.
1334 60 c. Type **197** 25 30
a. Sheetlet. Nos. 1334/41 .. .. 2·25
1335 60 c. Mike Davis and Kirk Gibson .. 25 30
1336 60 c. Fernando Valenzuela and John Shelby 25 30
1337 60 c. Jeff Hamilton and Franklin Stubbs 25 30
1338 60 c. Aerial view of Dodger stadium .. 25 30
1339 60 c. Ray Searage and John Tudor .. 25 30
1340 60 c. Mike Sharperson and Mickey Hatcher 25 30
1341 60 c. Coaching staff 25 30
1342 60 c. John Wetteland and Ramon Martinez 25 30
1343 60 c. Tim Belcher and Tim Crews .. 25 30
a. Sheetlet. Nos. 1343/51 .. .. 2·25
1344 60 c. Orel Hershiser and Mike Morgan .. 25 30
1345 60 c. Mike Scioscia and Rick Dempsey .. 25 30
1346 60 c. Dave Anderson and Alfredo Griffin 25 30
1347 60 c. Dodgers emblem 25 30
1348 60 c. Kal Daniels and Mike Marshall .. 25 30
1349 60 c. Eddie Murray and Willie Randolph 25 30
1350 60 c. Tom Lasorda and Jose Gonzalez .. 25 30
1351 60 c. Lenny Harris, Chris Gwynn and Billy Bean 25 30
1334/51 .. .. *Set of* 18 4·00 4·75

Nos. 1334/42 and 1343/51 were each printed together, *se-tenant*, in sheetlets of 9.

For similar stamps, but rouletted 7, see Nos. 1541/58.

198 *Eurema venusta*
199 Young Footballers

(Des D. Bruckner. Litho Questa)

1989 (16 Oct). *Butterflies. T* **198** *and similar multicoloured designs. P* 14×14½.
1352 6 c. Type **198** 10 10
1353 10 c. *Historis odius* 10 10
1354 15 c. *Cynthia virginiensis* 10 10
1355 75 c. *Leptotes cassius* 30 35
1356 $1 *Battus polydamas* 40 45
1357 $2 *Astraptes talus* 85 90
1358 $3 *Danaus gilippus* .. .. .. 1·25 1·40
1359 $5 *Myscelia antholia* .. .. .. 2·10 2·25
1352/9 .. .. *Set of* 8 4·50 5·00
MS1360 Two sheets, each 76×103 mm. (a) $6 *Danaus plexippus* (*vert*). (b) $6 *Eurema daira* (*vert*). P 14½×14 .. .. *Set of* 2 *sheets* 5·00 5·25

(Des R. Vigurs. Litho B.D.T.)

1989 (16 Oct). *World Cup Football Championship, Italy* (1*st issue*) (1990). *T* **199** *and similar horiz designs. Multicoloured. P* 14.
1361 10 c. Type **199** 10 10
1362 55 c. Youth football teams 25 30
1363 $1 St. Vincent team in training .. 40 45
1364 $5 National team with trophies .. 2·10 2·25
1361/4 .. .. *Set of* 4 2·50 2·75
MS1365 Two sheets, each 103×73 mm. (a) $6 Youth team. (b) $6 National team *Set of* 2 *sheets* 5·00 5·25

See also Nos. 1559/63.

+10c

CALIF. EARTHQUAKE
RELIEF

200 St. Vincent Amazon
(**201**)

(Des Tracy Pedersen. Litho Questa)

1989 (1 Nov). *Wildlife. T* **200** *and similar multicoloured designs. P* 14.
1366 65 c. Type **200** 25 30
1367 75 c. Whistling Warbler 30 35
1368 $5 Black Snake .. .. .. 2·10 2·25
1366/8 .. .. *Set of* 3 2·40 2·50
MS1369 97×70 mm. $6 Volcano Plant (*vert*) .. 2·50 2·75

1989 (17 Nov). *California Earthquake Relief Fund. Nos.* 1276/1302 *surch as T* **201**.
1370 60 c. + 10 c. Type **191** 35 35
a. Sheetlet. Nos. 1370/8 .. .. 2·75
1371 60 c. + 10 c. Carl Yastrzemski 35 35
1372 60 c. + 10 c. Randy Johnson 35 35
1373 60 c. + 10 c. Jerome Walton 35 35
1374 60 c. + 10 c. Ramon Martinez 35 35
1375 60 c. + 10 c. Ken Hill 35 35
1376 60 c. + 10 c. Tom McCarthy 35 35
1377 60 c. + 10 c. Gaylord Perry 35 35
1378 60 c. + 10 c. John Smoltz 35 35
1379 60 c. + 10 c. Bob Milacki 35 35
a. Sheetlet. Nos. 1379/87 .. .. 2·75
1380 60 c. + 10 c. Babe Ruth 35 35
1381 60 c. + 10 c. Jim Abbott 35 35
1382 60 c. + 10 c. Gary Sheffield 35 35
1383 60 c. + 10 c. Gregg Jeffries 35 35
1384 60 c. + 10 c. Kevin Brown 35 35
1385 60 c. + 10 c. Cris Carpenter 35 35
1386 60 c. + 10 c. Johnny Bench 35 35
1387 60 c. + 10 c. Ken Griffey Jr 35 35
1388 60 c. + 10 c. Type **192** 35 35
a. Sheetlet. Nos. 1388/96 .. .. 2·75
1389 60 c. + 10 c. Walt Weiss 35 35
1390 60 c. + 10 c. Willie Mays 35 35
1391 60 c. + 10 c. Kirk Gibson 35 35
1392 60 c. + 10 c. Ted Williams 35 35
1393 60 c. + 10 c. Jose Canseco 35 35
1394 60 c. + 10 c. Gaylord Perry 35 35
1395 60 c. + 10 c. Orel Hershiser 35 35
1396 60 c. + 10 c. Frank Viola 35 35
1370/96 .. .. *Set of* 27 8·25 8·25

(Des Walt Disney Co. Litho Questa)

1989 (17 Nov). *"World Stamp Expo '89" International Stamp Exhibition, Washington* (1*st issue*). *Multicoloured designs as T* **234** *of Maldive Islands showing Walt Disney cartoon characters and U.S. monuments. P* 13½×14.
1397 1 c. Mickey and Minnie Mouse by Seagull Monument, Utah (*vert*) 10 10
1398 2 c. Mickey Mouse and Goofy at Lincoln Memorial (*vert*) 10 10
1399 3 c. Mickey and Minnie Mouse at Crazy Horse Memorial, South Dakota (*vert*) 10 10
1400 4 c. Mickey Mouse saluting "Uncle Sam" Wilson statue, New York (*vert*) .. 10 10
1401 5 c. Goofy and Mickey Mouse at Benjamin Franklin Memorial, Philadelphia (*vert*) 10 10
1402 10 c. Goofy and Mickey Mouse at George Washington statue, New York (*vert*) 10 10
1403 $3 Mickey Mouse at John F. Kennedy's birthplace, Massachusetts (*vert*) .. 1·25 1·40
1404 $6 Mickey and Minnie Mouse at Mount Vernon, Virginia (*vert*) .. .. 2·50 2·75
1397/1404 .. .. .. *Set of* 8 3·75 4·00
MS1405 Two sheets, each 127×100 mm. (a) $5 Mickey and Minnie Mouse over Mount Rushmore, South Dakota. (b) $5 Mickey Mouse and Donald Duck at Stone Mountain, Georgia. P 14×13½ .. .. .. *Set of* 2 *sheets* 4·25 4·50

(Des Design Element. Litho Questa)

1989 (17 Nov). *"World Stamp Expo '89" International Stamp Exhibition, Washington* (2*nd issue*). *Sheet* 61×78 *mm containing multicoloured designs as T* **193a** *of Lesotho. P* 14.
MS1406 $5 Washington Monument (*vert*) 2·10 2·25

202 Nolan Ryan

(Des W. Storozuk. Litho)

1989 (30 Nov). *Famous Baseball Players* (3*rd series*). *P* 12½.
1407 **202** $2 multicoloured 85 90
a. Sheetlet of 9 .. .. 7·75

No. 1407 was printed in sheetlets of 9, with each stamp showing a different commemorative inscription.

203 Early Wynn
204 Arms and 1979 Independence 50 c. Stamp

(Des Susan Gansbourg. Litho)

1989 (30 Nov). *Famous Baseball Players* (4*th series*). *T* **203** *and similar horiz designs. P* 12½.
1408/88 30 c. × 81 multicoloured .. *Set of* 81 10·00 10·50

Nos. 1408/88 were issued as nine sheetlets, each of 9 different designs. No. 1456 (Mike Greenwell) was also available in sheetlets containing nine examples of the one design.

(Des and litho Questa)

1989 (20 Dec). *10th Anniv of Independence. P* 14.

1489 **204**	65 c. multicoloured	25	30
MS1490	57×77 mm. **204** $10 multicoloured	4·25	4·50

(Litho Questa)

1989 (20 Dec). *Christmas. Paintings by Botticelli and Da Vinci. Vert designs as T* **193***b of Lesotho. Multicoloured. P* 14.

1491	10 c. Holy Family (detail, "The Adoration of the Magi") (Botticelli)	10	10
1492	25 c. Crowd (detail, "The Adoration of the Magi") (Botticelli)	10	15
1493	30 c. "The Madonna of the Magnificat" (detail) (Botticelli)	10	15
1494	40 c. "The Virgin and Child with St. Anne and St. John the Baptist" (detail) (Da Vinci)	15	20
1495	55 c. Angel (detail, "The Annunciation") (Da Vinci)	25	30
1496	75 c. Virgin Mary (detail, "The Annunciation") (Da Vinci)	30	35
1497	$5 "Madonna of the Carnation" (detail) (Da Vinci)	2·10	2·25
1498	$6 "The Annunciation" (detail) (Botticelli)	2·50	2·75
1491/8	*Set of* 8	5·00	5·50
MS1499	Two sheets, each 70×94 mm. (a) $5 "The Virgin of the Rocks" (detail) (Da Vinci). (b) $5 Holy Family (detail, "The Adoration of the Magi") (Botticelli) *Set of 2 sheets*	4·25	4·50

205 Boy Scout, 1989

206 Man and Blind Girl

(Des A. Fagbohun. Litho Questa)

1989 (20 Dec). *75th Anniv of Boy Scout and 60th Anniv of Girl Guide Movements in St. Vincent. T* **205** *and similar multicoloured designs, each showing portrait of Lord or Lady Baden-Powell. P* 14.

1500	35 c. Type **205**	15	20
1501	35 c. Guide, ranger and brownie	15	20
1502	55 c. Boy scout in original uniform	25	30
1503	55 c. Mrs. Jackson (founder of St. Vincent Girl Guides)	25	30
1504	$2 Scouts' 75th Anniv logo	85	90
1505	$2 Mrs. Russell (Girl Guide leader, 1989)	85	90
1500/5	*Set of* 6	2·25	2·50
MS1506	Two sheets, each 105×75 mm. (a) $5 Scout in canoe. (b) $5 Scout and Guide with flagpoles (*horiz*) *Set of 2 sheets*	4·25	4·50

(Des W. Hanson Studio. Litho Questa)

1990 (5 Mar). *25th Anniv of Lions Club of St. Vincent* (1989). *T* **206** *and similar multicoloured designs. P* 14.

1507	10 c. Type **206**	10	10
1508	65 c. Handing out school books (*horiz*)	25	30
1509	75 c. Teacher explaining diabetes (*horiz*)	30	35
1510	$2 Blood sugar testing machine (*horiz*)	85	90
1511	$4 Distributing book on drugs (*horiz*)	1·75	1·90
1507/11	*Set of* 5	3·00	3·25

(Des W. Wright. Litho Questa)

1990 (2 Apr). *50th Anniv of Second World War. Horiz designs as T* **242** *of Maldive Islands. Multicoloured. P* 14.

1512	5 c. Scuttling of *Admiral Graf Spee*, 1939	10	10
1513	10 c. General De Gaulle and French resistance, 1940	10	10
1514	15 c. British tank, North Africa, 1940	10	10
1515	25 c. U.S.S *Reuben James* in periscope sight, 1941	10	15
1516	30 c. General MacArthur and map of S.W. Pacific, 1942	10	15
1517	40 c. American parachute drop on Corregidor, 1945	15	20
1518	55 c. H.M.S. *King George V* engaging *Bismarck*, 1941	25	30
1519	75 c. American battleships entering Tokyo Bay, 1945	30	35
1520	$5 Hoisting the Soviet flag on the Reichstag, Berlin, 1945	2·10	2·25
1521	$6 American carriers, Battle of Philippine Sea, 1944	2·50	2·75
1512/21	*Set of* 10	5·00	5·75
MS1522	100×70 mm. $6 Japanese Zero fighter, Battle of Java Sea, 1942	2·50	2·75

207 Two Pence Blue

Sixth No-Hitter
11 June 90
Oakland Athletics

(208)

(Des M. Pollard. Litho B.D.T)

1990 (3 May). *150th Anniv of the Penny Black. T* **207** *and similar vert designs. P* 14×15.

1523	$2 black, blue-green and bright magenta	85	90
1524	$4 black and bright magenta	1·75	1·90
MS1525	130×99 mm. $6 black, scarlet & yellow	2·50	2·75

Designs:—$4, $6 Penny Black.

(Des Walt Disney Co. Litho Questa)

1990 (3 May). *"Stamp World London 90" International Stamp Exhibition. British Uniforms. Multicoloured designs as T* **239***a of Maldive Islands showing Walt Disney cartoon characters. P* 13½×14.

1526	5 c. Scrooge McDuck as 18th-century admiral (*vert*)	10	10
1527	10 c. Huey as Light Infantry bugler, 1854 (*vert*)	10	10
1528	15 c. Minnie Mouse as Irish Guards drummer, 1900 (*vert*)	10	10
1529	25 c. Goofy as Seaforth Highlanders lance-corporal, 1944 (*vert*)	10	15
1530	$1 Mickey Mouse as 58th Regiment ensign, 1879 (*vert*)	40	45
1531	$2 Donald Duck as Royal Engineers officer, 1813 (*vert*)	85	90
1532	$4 Mickey Mouse as Duke of Edinburgh's Royal Regiment drum major (*vert*)	1·75	1·90
1533	$5 Goofy as Cameronians sergeant piper, 1918 (*vert*)	2·10	2·25
1526/33	*Set of* 8	4·75	5·25
MS1534	Two sheets, each 120x100 mm. (a) $6 Goofy as officer in King's Lifeguard of Foot, 1643. P 13½×14. (b) $6 Mickey Mouse as Grenadier Guards drummer (*vert*). P 14×13½ *Set of 2 sheets*	5·00	5·25

1990 (23 June). *Nolan Ryan–Sixth No-hitter. No.* 1407 *optd with T* **208**.

1535 **202**	$2 multicoloured	85	90
	a. Sheetlet of 9	7·75	

(Des Young Phillips Studio. Litho Questa)

1990 (5 July). *90th Birthday of Queen Elizabeth the Queen Mother. Vert designs as T* **198***a of Lesotho showing portraits,* 1950–59. *P* 14.

1536	$2 black, bright sage-green and magenta	85	90
	a. Strip of 3. Nos. 1536/8	2·25	
1537	$2 black, bright sage-green and magenta	85	90
1538	$2 black, bright sage-green and magenta	85	90
1536/8	*Set of* 3	2·25	2·40
MS1539	90×75 mm. $6 multicoloured	2·50	2·75

Designs:—No. 1536, Queen Elizabeth signing visitors' book; Nos. 1537, **MS**1539, Queen Elizabeth in evening dress; No. 1538, Queen Elizabeth the Queen Mother in Coronation robes, 1953.

Nos. 1536/8 were printed together, horizontally and vertically *se-tenant*, in sheetlets of 9 (3×3).

300th Win
Milwaukee Brewers
July 31, 1990

(209)

210 Maradona, Argentina

1990 (3 Aug). *Nolan Ryan–300th Win. No.* 1407 *optd with T* **209**.

1540 **202**	$2 multicoloured	85	90
	a. Sheetlet of 9	7·75	

1990 (21 Sept). *Centenary of Los Angeles Dodgers* (2nd issue). *Baseball Players. Multicoloured designs as T* **197**. *Litho. Rouletted* 7.

1541	60 c. Mickey Hatcher and Jay Howell	25	30
	a. Sheetlet. Nos. 1541/9	2·25	
1542	60 c. Juan Samuel and Mike Scioscia	25	30
1543	60 c. Lenny Harris and Mike Hartley	25	30
1544	60 c. Ramon Martinez and Mike Morgan	25	30
1545	60 c. Aerial view of Dodger stadium	25	30
1546	60 c. Stan Javier and Don Aase	25	30
1547	60 c. Ray Searage and Mike Sharperson	25	30
1548	60 c. Tim Belcher and Pat Perry	25	30
1549	60 c. Dave Walsh, Jose Vizcaino, Jim Neidlinger, Jose Offerman and Carlos Hernandez	25	30
1550	60 c. Hubie Brooks and Orel Hershiser	25	30
	a. Sheetlet. Nos. 1550/8	2·25	
1551	60 c. Tom Lasorda and Tim Crews	25	30
1552	60 c. Fernando Valenzuela and Eddie Murray	25	30
1553	60 c. Kal Daniels and Jose Gonzalez	25	30
1554	60 c. Dodgers emblem	25	30
1555	60 c. Chris Gwynn and Jeff Hamilton	25	30
1556	60 c. Kirk Gibson and Rick Dempsey	25	30
1557	60 c. Jim Gott and Alfredo Griffin	25	30
1558	60 c. Ron Perranoski, Bill Russell, Joe Ferguson, Joe Amalfitano, Mark Cresse, Ben Hines and Manny Mota	25	30
1541/58	*Set of* 18	4·00	4·75

Nos. 1541/9 and 1550/8 were each printed together, *se-tenant*, in sheetlets of nine.

(Des Young Phillips Studio. Litho Questa)

1990 (24 Sept). *World Cup Football Championship, Italy* (2nd issue). *T* **210** *and similar vert designs. Multicoloured. P* 14.

1559	10 c. Type **210**	10	10
1560	75 c. Valderrama, Colombia	30	35
1561	$1 Francescoli, Uruguay	40	45
1562	$5 Beulemans, Belgium	2·00	2·10
1559/62	*Set of* 4	2·40	2·75
MS1563	Two sheets, each 101×85 mm. (a) $6 Klinsmann, West Germany. (b) $6 Careca, Brazil *Set of 2 sheets*	5·00	5·25

(211)

JOE DELOACH U.S.A. **STEVE LEWIS U.S.A.** **PAUL ERANG KENYA**

(212)

1990 (18 Oct). *95th Anniv of Rotary International. Nos.* 1230/8 *optd with T* **211**.

1564	10 c. Type **186**	10	10
1565	40 c. *Liberté*	15	20
1566	50 c. *Mauretania* (launched 1906)	20	25
1567	75 c. *France*	30	35
1568	$1 *Aquitania*	40	45
1569	$2 *United States*	85	90
1570	$3 *Olympic*	1·25	1·40
1571	$4 *Queen Elizabeth*	1·75	1·90
1564/71	*Set of* 8	4·50	5·00
MS1572	Two sheets, each 141×108 mm. (a) $6 *Queen Mary* (85×28 *mm*). (b) $6 *Queen Elizabeth 2* (85×28 *mm*) *Set of 2 sheets*	5·00	5·25

1990 (18 Oct). *Olympic Medal Winners, Seoul. Nos.* 1153/7 *optd as T* **212**.

1573	10 c. Type **178**	10	10
1574	50 c. Long jumping (optd "CARL LEWIS U.S.A.")	20	25
1575	$1 Triple jumping (optd "HRISTO MARKOV BULGARIA")	40	45
1576	$5 Boxing (optd "HENRY MASKE E. GERMANY")	2·00	2·10
1573/6	*Set of* 4	2·40	2·50
MS1577	85×63 mm $10 Olympic flame*	4·25	4·50

*No. **MS**1577 is overprinted "FINAL MEDAL STANDINGS" and medal totals for either South Korea and Spain or U.S.S.R. and U.S.A. on the margin (*same price for either opt*)

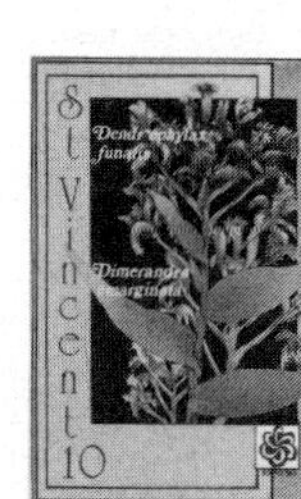

213 *Dendrophylax funalis* and *Dimerandra emarginata*

214 "Miraculous Draught of Fishes" (detail, Rubens)

(Litho B.D.T.)

1990 (23 Nov). *"EXPO 90" International Garden and Greenery Exposition, Osaka. Orchids. T* **213** *and similar vert designs. Multicoloured. P* 14.

1578	10 c. Type **213**	10	10
1579	15 c. *Epidendrum elongatum*	10	10
1580	45 c. *Comparettia falcata*	20	25
1581	60 c. *Brassia maculata*	25	30
1582	$1 *Encyclia cochleata* and *Encyclia cordigera*	40	45
1583	$2 *Cyrtopodium punctatum*	85	90
1584	$4 *Cattleya labiata*	1·75	1·90
1585	$5 *Bletia purpurea*	2·10	2·25
1578/85	*Set of* 8	5·00	5·50
MS1586	Two sheets, each 108×78 mm. (a) $6 *Vanilla planifolia Jackson*. (b) $6 *Ionopsis utricularioides* *Set of 2 sheets*	5·00	5·25

(Litho Questa)

1990 (3 Dec). *Christmas. 350th Death Anniv of Rubens. T* **214** *and similar vert designs. Multicoloured. P* 13½×14.

1587	10 c. Type **214**	10	10
1588	45 c. "Crowning of Holy Katherine" (detail)	20	25
1589	50 c. "St. Ives of Treguier" (detail)	20	25
1590	65 c. "Allegory of Eternity" (detail)	25	30
1591	$1 "St. Bavo receives Monastic Habit of Ghent" (detail)	40	45
1592	$2 "Crowning of Holy Katherine" (different detail)	85	90
1593	$4 "St. Bavo receives Monastic Habit of Ghent" (different detail)	1·75	1·90
1594	$5 "Communion of St. Francis" (detail)	2·10	2·25
1587/94	*Set of* 8	5·25	5·75
MS1595	Four sheets. (a) 70×100 mm. $6 "Allegory of Eternity" (different detail). P 13½×14. (b) 70×100 mm. $6 As 50 c. P 13½×14. (c) 100×70 mm. $6 As Type **214** (*horiz*). P 14×13½. (d) 100×70 mm. $6 "St. Bavo receives Monastic Habit of Ghent" (different detail) (*horiz*). P 14×13½ *Set of 4 sheets*	10·00	10·50

215 Geoffrey Chaucer

216 American Football Game

(Des N. Waldman. Litho Cartor)

1990 (12 Dec). *International Literacy Year. Chaucer's Canterbury Tales. T* **215** *and similar square designs. Multicoloured. P* 13½.

1596 40 c. Type **215** 15 20
a. Sheetlet. Nos. 1596/1619 .. .. 3·25
1597 40 c. "When April with his showers..." .. 15 20
1598 40 c. "When Zephyr also has..." 15 20
1599 40 c. "And many little birds..." 15 20
1600 40 c. "And palmers to go seeking out..." .. 15 20
1601 40 c. Quill in ink well and open book .. 15 20
1602 40 c. Green bird in tree 15 20
1603 40 c. Brown bird in tree and franklin's head 15 20
1604 40 c. Purple bird in tree and banner .. 15 20
1605 40 c. Canterbury 15 20
1606 40 c. Knight's head 15 20
1607 40 c. Black bird in tree and squire's head 15 20
1608 40 c. Friar 15 20
1609 40 c. Franklin 15 20
1610 40 c. Prioress and monk holding banner .. 15 20
1611 40 c. Summoner, Oxford clerk and parson 15 20
1612 40 c. Serjeant-at-Law and knight on horse-back 15 20
1613 40 c. Squire 15 20
1614 40 c. "In fellowship..." 15 20
1615 40 c. Cockerel and horse's legs 15 20
1616 40 c. Hens 15 20
1617 40 c. Hen and rabbit 15 20
1618 40 c. Horses' legs and butterfly 15 20
1619 40 c. "And briefly, when the sun..." .. 15 20
1596/1619 .. .. .. *Set of* 24 3·25 4·00

Nos. 1596/1619 were printed together, *se-tenant*, as a sheetlet of 24, forming a composite design.

(Litho Cartor)

1990 (17 Dec). *Death Centenary of Van Gogh (painter). Vert designs as T* **255** *of Maldive Islands. Multicoloured. P* 13.

1620 1 c. Self-portrait, 1889 .. .. .. 10 10
a. Vert strip of 4. Nos. 1620/3 15
1621 5 c. Self-portrait, 1886 .. .. .. 10 10
1622 10 c. Self-portrait with hat and pipe, 1888 10 10
1623 15 c. Self-portrait at easel, 1888 .. .. 10 10
1624 20 c. Self-portrait, 1887 .. .. .. 10 10
a. Vert strip of 4. Nos. 1624/7 .. .. 5·00
1625 45 c. Self-portrait, 1889 (*different*) .. 20 25
1626 $5 Self-portrait with pipe, 1889 .. 2·10 2·25
1627 $6 Self-portrait wearing straw hat, 1887 2·50 2·75
1620/7 .. .. *Set of* 8 4·50 5·00

Nos. 1620/3 and 1624/7 were each printed in sheets of 16 (4×4) with the four values vertically *se-tenant*.

(Litho Questa)

1990 (30 Dec). *Hummel Figurines. Vert designs as T* **256** *of Maldive Islands. Multicoloured. P* 14.

1628 10 c. "The Photographer" 10 10
1629 15 c. "Ladder and Rope" 10 10
1630 40 c. "Druggist" 15 20
1631 60 c. "Hello" 25 30
1632 $1 "Boots" 40 45
1633 $2 "The Artist" 85 90
1634 $4 "Waiter" .. .. 1·75 1·90
1635 $5 "The Postman" .. .. .. 2·10 2·25
1628/35 .. .. *Set of* 8 5·00 5·50
MS1636 Two sheets, each 94×121 mm. (a) Nos. 1628, 1631/2 and 1635. (b) Nos. 1629/30 and 1633/4 .. .. *Set of 2 sheets* 5·50 5·75

1991 (15 Jan). *25th Anniv of Super Bowl American Football Championship (1st issue). T* **216** *and similar vert designs. Multicoloured. Litho. P* 13½×14.

MS1637 Twenty-five sheets, each 127×101 mm, containing 50 c. × 2 as horiz pairs forming composite designs of game scenes or 50 c. × 3 (final sheet) showing Vince Lombardi Trophy and helmets of participating teams *Set of* 25 *sheets* 10·50

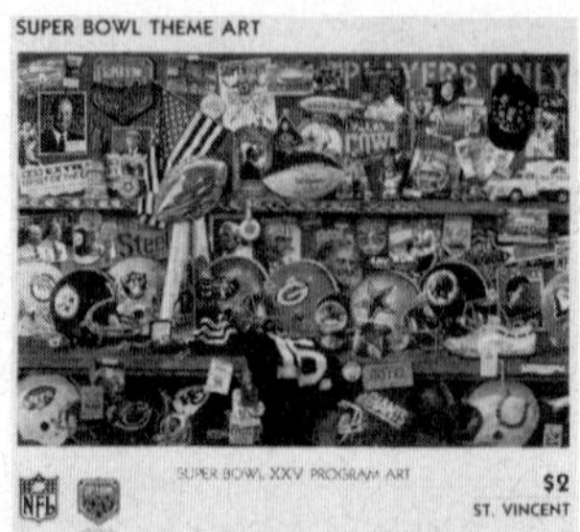

217 Programme Cover of XXV Super Bowl (*Illustration reduced. Actual size* 105×95 *mm*)

1991 (15 Jan). *25th Anniv of Super Bowl American Football Championships (2nd issue). T* **217** *and similar multicoloured designs, each showing a different programme cover illustration. Litho. Imperf.*

MS1638 Twenty-five sheets, 125×99 mm or 99×125 mm, each with a face value of $2 *Set of* 25 *sheets* 21·00

218 U.S.A. 1893 1 c. Columbus Stamp

1991 (18 Mar). *500th Anniv of Discovery of America (1992) by Columbus (4th issue). T* **218** *and similar horiz designs showing U.S.A 1893 Columbian Exposition, Chicago, stamps (Nos. 1639/54) or ships (others). Multicoloured. Litho. P* 13½×14.

1639 1 c. Type **218** 10 10
a. Sheetlet. Nos. 1639/46 and 1655 .. 4·75
1640 2 c. U.S.A. Columbus 2 c. 10 10
1641 3 c. U.S.A. Columbus 3 c. 10 10
1642 4 c. U.S.A. Columbus 4 c. 10 10
1643 5 c. U.S.A. Columbus 5 c. 10 10
1644 6 c. U.S.A. Columbus 6 c. 10 10
1645 8 c. U.S.A. Columbus 8 c. 10 10
1646 10 c. U.S.A. Columbus 10 c. 10 10
1647 15 c. U.S.A. Columbus 15 c. 10 10
a. Sheetlet. Nos. 1647/54 and 1656 .. 11·00
1648 30 c. U.S.A. Columbus 30 c. 10 10
1649 50 c. U.S.A. Columbus 50 c. 20 25
1650 $1 U.S.A. Columbus $1 .. .. 40 45
1651 $2 U.S.A. Columbus $2 .. .. 85 90
1652 $3 U.S.A. Columbus $3 .. .. 1·25 1·40
1653 $4 U.S.A. Columbus $4 .. .. 1·75 1·90
1654 $5 U.S.A. Columbus $5 .. .. 2·10 2·25
1655 $10 *Santa Maria*, parrot and tropical flower .. .. 4·25 4·50
1656 $10 Logo, *Santa Maria* and Amerindian hut .. .. 4·25 4·50
1639/56 .. .. .. *Set of* 18 14·00 15·00
MS1657 Two sheets, each 98×72 mm. (a) $6 Sailors on ship's fo'c'sle. (b) $6 Ship's figurehead *Set of 2 sheets* 5·00 5·25

Nos. 1639/46 and 1655 and Nos. 1647/54 and 1656 were each printed together, *se-tenant*, in sheetlets of 9.

219 Pebbles and Hoppy boxing

(Des Hanna-Barbera Productions. Litho Questa)

1991 (25 Mar). *Sports. T* **219** *and similar horiz designs showing characters from the Flintstones cartoons. Multicoloured. P* 14×13½.

1658 10 c. Type **219** 10 10
1659 15 c. Fred Flintstone and Dino playing football 10 10
1660 45 c. Fred losing rowing race to Barney Rubble 20 25
1661 55 c. Betty Rubble, Wilma Flintstone and Pebbles in dressage competition .. 25 30
1662 $1 Fred playing basketball 40 45
1663 $2 Bamm Bamm wrestling Barney with Fred as referee 85 90
1664 $4 Fred and Barney playing tennis .. 1·75 1·90
1665 $5 Fred, Barney and Dino cycling .. 2·10 2·25
1658/65 .. .. *Set of* 8 5·00 5·50
MS1666 Two sheets, each 117×95 mm. (a) $6 Fred at the plate in baseball game. (b) $6 Fred running to homeplate .. .. *Set of 2 sheets* 5·00 5·25

220 Board Meeting

(Des Hanna-Barbera Productions. Litho Questa)

1991 (25 March). *The Jetsons (cartoon film). T* **220** *and similar multicoloured designs. P* 14×13½ (60 c., $1, $2) *or* 13½×14 (*others*).

1667 5 c. Type **220** 10 10
1668 20 c. Jetsons with Dog 10 10
1669 45 c. Judy and Apollo Blue 20 25
1670 50 c. Cosmo Spacely and George Jetson .. 20 25
1671 60 c. George and Elroy catching cogs (*horiz*) 25 30
1672 $1 Judy, Apollo, Elroy and Teddy in cavern (*horiz*) 40 45
1673 $2 Drill destroying the cavern (*horiz*) .. 85 90
1674 $4 Jetsons celebrating with the Grungees 1·75 1·90
1675 $5 The Jetsons returning home .. 2·10 2·25
1667/75 .. .. *Set of* 9 5·25 5·75
MS1676 Two sheets, each 114×76 mm. (a) $6 The Jetsons in spacecraft (*horiz*). (b) $6 The Jetsons in control room (*horiz*). P 14×13½ *Set of 2 sheets* 5·00 5·25

(Des T. Agans. Litho Questa)

1991 (13 May). *500th Anniv of Discovery of America by Columbus, (1992) (5th issue). History of Exploration. Multicoloured designs as T* **64** *of St. Kitts-Nevis (Nevis). P* 14.

1677 5 c. "Sänger 2" (projected space shuttle) .. 10 10
1678 10 c. "Magellan" satellite, 1990 .. .. 10 10
1679 25 c. "Buran" space shuttle 10 15
1680 75 c. Projected "Freedom" space station .. 30 35
1681 $1 Projected Mars mission space craft .. 40 45
1682 $2 "Hubble" telescope, 1990 .. .. 85 90
1683 $4 Projected Mars mission "sailship" .. 1·75 1·90
1684 $5 Projected "Craf" satellite .. .. 2·10 2·25
1677/84 .. .. *Set of* 8 5·00 5·50
MS1685 Two sheets, each 105×71 mm. (a) $6 Bow of caravel (*vert*). (b) $6 Caravel under full sail .. .. *Set of 2 sheets* 5·00 5·25

(Des D. Miller. Litho Walsall)

1991 (5 July). *65th Birthday of Queen Elizabeth II. Horiz designs as T* **210** *of Lesotho. Multicoloured. P* 14.

1686 5 c. Queen and Prince Philip during visit to Spain, 1988 .. .. .. 10 10
1687 60 c. Queen and Prince Philip in landau .. 25 30
1688 $2 Queen at Caen Hill Waterway, 1990 85 90
1689 $4 Queen at Badminton, 1983 .. .. 1·75 1·90
1686/9 .. .. *Set of* 4 2·50 2·75
MS1690 68×91 mm. $5 Queen Elizabeth II in 1988 and Prince Philip in 1989 .. .. 2·10 2·25

(Des D. Miller. Litho Walsall)

1991 (5 July). *10th Wedding Anniv of the Prince and Princess of Wales. Horiz designs as T* **210** *of Lesotho. Multicoloured. P* 14.

1691 20 c. Prince and Princess in hard hats, 1987 10 10
1692 25 c. Portraits of Prince and Princess and sons 10 15
1693 $1 Prince Henry and Prince William, both in 1988 .. .. .. 40 40
1694 $5 Princess Diana in France and Prince Charles in 1987 .. .. 2·10 2·25
1691/4 .. .. *Set of* 4 2·40 2·75
MS1695 68×90 mm. $5 Princes Henry and William in Majorca, and Princess Diana presenting polo trophy to Prince Charles .. 2·10 2·25

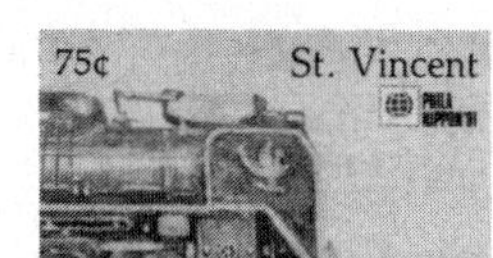

221 Class "D 51" Steam Locomotive

(Des K. Gromell. Litho Cartor)

1991 (12 Aug). *"Philanippon '91" International Stamp Exhibition, Tokyo. Japanese Trains. T* **221** *and similar multicoloured designs. P* 13½.

1696 75 c. Type **221** 30 35
a. Sheetlet. Nos. 1696/1704 .. .. 2·75
1697 75 c. Class "9600" steam locomotive .. 30 35
1698 75 c. Goods wagons and chrysanthemum emblem 30 35
1699 75 c. Passenger coach 30 35
1700 75 c. Decorated class "C 57" steam locomotive 30 35
1701 75 c. Oil tanker wagon 30 35
1702 75 c. Class "C 53" steam locomotive .. 30 35
1703 75 c. First Japanese steam locomotive .. 30 35
1704 75 c. Class "C 11" steam locomotive .. 30 35
1705 $1 Class "181" electric train 40 45
a. Sheetlet. Nos. 1705/13 .. .. 3·50
1706 $1 Class "EH-10" electric locomotive .. 40 45
1707 $1 Passenger coaches and Special Express symbol 40 45
1708 $1 Sendai City class "1" tram 40 45
1709 $1 Class "485" electric train 40 45
1710 $1 Sendai City street cleaning tram .. 40 45
1711 $1 Hakari "Bullet" train 40 45
1712 $1 Class "ED-11" electric locomotive .. 40 45
1713 $1 Class "EF-66" electric locomotive .. 40 45
1696/1713 .. .. *Set of* 18 5·75 6·50
MS1714 Four sheets, each 108×77 mm. (a) $6 Class "C 55" steam locomotive (*vert*). P 13×13½. (b) $6 Series "400" electric train. P 13½×13. (c) $6 Class "C 62" steam locomotive (*vert*). P 13×13½. (d) $6 Super Hitachi electric train. P 13×13½. .. .. .. *Set of 4 sheets* 10·00 10·50

Nos. 1696/1704 and 1705/13 were each printed together, *se-tenant*, in sheetlets of 9.

222 Marcello Mastroianni (actor)

(Des J. Iskowitz. Litho Cartor)

1991 (22 Aug). *Italian Entertainers. T* **222** *and similar multicoloured designs. P* 13.

1715 $1 Type **222** 40 45
a. Sheetlet. Nos. 1715/23 .. .. 3·25
1716 $1 Sophia Loren (actress) 40 45
1717 $1 Mario Lanza (singer) 40 45
1718 $1 Federico Fellini (director) 40 45
1719 $1 Arturo Toscanini (conductor) .. 40 45
1720 $1 Anna Magnani (actress) 40 45
1721 $1 Giancarlo Giannini (actor) 40 45
1722 $1 Gina Lollobrigida (actress) 40 45
1723 $1 Enrico Caruso (operatic tenor) .. 40 45
1715/23 .. .. *Set of* 9 3·25 3·75
MS1724 117×80 mm. $6 Luciano Pavarotti (operatic tenor) (*horiz*) .. .. .. 2·10 2·25

Nos. 1715/23 were printed together, *se-tenant*, in sheetlets of 9.

223 Madonna

(Des J. Iskowitz. Litho Cartor)

1991 (22 Aug). *Madonna (American singer). T* **223** *and similar vert portraits. Multicoloured. P* 13.

1725 $1 Type **223** 40 45
a. Sheetlet. Nos. 1725/33 .. .. 3·25
1726 $1 In strapless dress 40 45
1727 $1 Wearing necklaces, looking right .. 40 45
1728 $1 In green dress 40 45
1729 $1 Wearing necklaces, looking to front .. 40 45
1730 $1 With wrist bangles 40 45
1731 $1 With hand to face 40 45
1732 $1 In purple dress 40 45
1733 $1 With microphone 40 45
1725/33 .. .. *Set of* 9 3·25 3·75
MS1734 79×118 mm. $6 Madonna (25×40 *mm*). P 12×13 .. .. 2·10 2·25

Nos. 1725/33 were printed together, *se-tenant*, in sheetlets of 9.

224 John Lennon **225** Tales around the Camp Fire

(Des J. Iskowitz. Litho Cartor)

1991 (22 Aug). *John Lennon (British musician). T* **224** *and similar vert portraits. Multicoloured. P* 13.

1735 $1 + 2 c. Type **224** 40 45
a. Sheetlet. Nos. 1735/43 .. .. 3·25
1736 $1 + 2 c. With Beatle hair cut 40 45
1737 $1 + 2 c. In cap 40 45
1738 $1 + 2 c. In red polka-dot shirt .. 40 45
1739 $1 + 2 c. In green polo-neck jumper and jacket 40 45
1740 $1 + 2 c. In glasses and magenta jacket 40 45
1741 $1 + 2 c. With long hair and glasses .. 40 45
1742 $1 + 2 c. In black jumper 40 45
1743 $1 + 2 c. In polo-neck jumper 40 45
1735/43 .. .. *Set of* 9 3·25 3·75

Nos. 1735/43 were printed together, *se-tenant*, in sheetlets of 9.

(Litho Questa)

1991 (18 Nov). *50th Death Anniv of Lord Baden-Powell and World Scout Jamboree, Korea. T* **225** *and similar multicoloured designs. P* 14.

1744 65 c. Type **225** 25 30
1745 $1.50, British trenches and Mafeking Siege 3d. stamp (*horiz*) 60 65
1746 $3. 50, Queen Angelfish and scout diver (*horiz*) .. .. 1·50 1·75
1744/6 .. .. *Set of* 3 2·10 2·40
MS1747 117×89 mm. $5 Scout badge and Jamboree emblem (*horiz*) .. .. .. 2·10 2·25

226 Free French Resistance Fighters, 1944

(Litho Questa)

1991 (18 Nov). *Birth Centenary of Charles de Gaulle (French statesman) (1990). T* **226** *and similar multicoloured designs.*

1748 10 c. Type **226** 10 10
1749 45 c. De Gaulle with Churchill, 1944 .. 20 25
1750 75 c. Liberation of Paris, 1944 .. .. 30 35
1748/50 .. .. *Set of* 3 55 65
MS1751 76×116 mm. $5 President De Gaulle (*vert*) .. .. 2·10 2·25

227 Protester with Banner **228** Myrvyn Bennion

(Litho Questa)

1991 (18 Nov). *Bicentenary of Brandenburg Gate, Berlin. T* **227** *and similar horiz designs. Multicoloured. P* 14.

1752 50 c. Type **227** 20 25
1753 75 c. Building Berlin Wall 30 35
1754 90 c. German flag and protestors' shadows 40 45
1755 $1 Presidents Bush and Gorbachev shaking hands 40 45
1752/5 .. .. *Set of* 4 1·10 1·25
MS1756 101×72 mm. $4 Arms of Berlin .. 1·75 2·00

(Litho Questa)

1991 (18 Nov). *Death Bicentenary of Mozart. Multicoloured designs as T* **226**. *P* 14.

1757 $1 *Marriage of Figaro* 40 45
1758 $3 *The Clemency of Titus* .. .. 1·25 1·50
MS1759 77×116 mm. $4 Mozart and signature (*vert*) .. .. 1·75 2·00

(Des D. Ben-Ami. Litho Questa)

1991 (18 Nov). *50th Anniv of Japanese Attack on Pearl Harbor. T* **228** *and similar horiz designs showing recipients of Congressional Medal of Honor. Multicoloured. P* 14½×15.

1760 $1 Type **228** 40 45
a. Sheetlet. Nos. 1760/74 .. .. 5·50
1761 $1 George Cannon 40 45
1762 $1 John Finn 40 45
1763 $1 Francis Flaherty 40 45
1764 $1 Samuel Fuqua 40 45
1765 $1 Edwin Hill 40 45
1766 $1 Herbert Jones 40 45
1767 $1 Isaac Kidd 40 45
1768 $1 Jackson Pharris 40 45
1769 $1 Thomas Reeves 40 45
1770 $1 Donald Ross 40 45
1771 $1 Robert Scott 40 45
1772 $1 Franklin van Valkenburgh 40 45
1773 $1 James Ward 40 45
1774 $1 Cassin Young 40 45
1760/74 .. .. *Set of* 15 5·50 6·00

Nos. 1760/74 were printed together, *se-tenant*, in sheetlets of 15.

(Des Walt Disney Co. Litho Questa)

1991 (18 Nov). *International Literacy Year. Multicoloured designs as T* **246** *of Maldive Islands, but horiz, showing scenes from Disney cartoon film* The Prince and The Pauper. *P* 14×13½.

1775 5 c. Mickey Mouse, Goofy and Pluto as pauper pals 10 10
1776 10 c. Mickey as the bored prince 10 10
1777 15 c. Donald Duck as the valet 10 10
1778 25 c. Mickey as the prince and the pauper 10 10
1779 60 c. Exchanging clothes 25 30
1780 75 c. Prince and pauper with suit of armour 30 35
1781 80 c. Throwing food from the battlements 35 40
1782 $1 Pete as Captain of the Guard .. 40 45
1783 $2 Mickey and Donald in the dungeon .. 85 90
1784 $3 Mickey and Donald at dungeon window .. .. 1·25 1·40
1785 $4 Goofy rescuing Mickey and Donald .. 1·75 1·90
1786 $5 Crowning the real prince .. .. 2·10 2·25
1775/86 .. .. *Set of* 12 6·75 7·50
MS1787 Four sheets, each 127×101 mm. (a) $6 Crowning the wrong prince. (b) $6 Pete holding Mickey. (c) $6 The pauper on the throne. (d) $6 Mickey telling troops to seize the guard *Set of* 4 *sheets* 10·00 10·50

OFFICIAL STAMPS

OFFICIAL

(O 1)

1982 (11 Oct). *Nos. 668/73 optd with Type* O **1**.

O1 60 c. *Isabella* 25 30
a. Sheetlet. No. O1 × 6 and No. O2 .. 2·00
b. Opt double .. ..
c. Albino opt .. .. 12·00
O2 60 c. Prince Charles and Lady Diana Spencer 50 50
b. Opt double .. ..
c. Albino opt .. .. 35·00
O3 $2.50, *Alberta* (tender) 80 90
a. Sheetlet. No. O3 × 6 and No. O4 .. 5·50
b. Opt inverted .. .. 30·00
c. Opt inverted (horiz pair) .. .. 80·00
d. Albino opt .. .. 25·00
O4 $2.50, Prince Charles and Lady Diana Spencer .. .. 1·25 1·40
b. Opt inverted .. .. 80·00
c. Albino opt .. .. 65·00
O5 $4 *Britannia* .. .. 1·25 1·60
a. Sheetlet. No. O5 × 6 and No. O6 .. 9·00
b. Opt double .. ..
c. Albino opt .. .. 20·00
d. Opt inverted .. ..
e. Opt inverted (horiz pair) .. .. ..
O6 $4 Prince Charles and Lady Diana Spencer 2·00 2·25
b. Opt double .. ..
c. Albino opt .. .. 55·00
d. Opt inverted .. ..
O1/6 .. .. *Set of* 6 5·50 6·25

Nos. O3c and O5e show the long overprint, intended for Nos. O4 or O6, inverted and struck across a horizontal pair of Nos. O3 or O5. Nos. O4b and O6d show two examples of Type O **1** inverted on the same stamp.

POSTAL FISCAL STAMPS

The following were primarily intended for the payment of passport fees, but were also valid for postal purposes and are frequently found used on parcels.

$5

STAMP DUTY

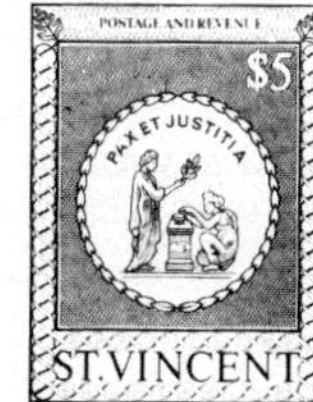

(F 1) F **2** St. Vincent Coat of Arms

1980 (Feb). *Stamps as T* **95**, *without value, surch as Type* F **1**. *W* w **12**. *P* 14½ × 14.

F1 $5 deep lavender and azure .. .. .. 3·00 2·50
F2 $10 light green and apple green .. .. 6·50 5·50
F3 $20 reddish purple and pale rose-lilac .. 12·50 12·00
F1/3 .. .. *Set of* 3 20·00 18·00

(Des Harrison. Recess D.L.R.)

1980 (19 May). *W* w **14**. *P* 14 × 13.

F4 F **2** $5 chalky blue .. .. 2·10 2·25
F5 $10 deep green .. .. 4·00 4·25
F6 $20 brown-red .. .. 9·50 9·75
F4/6 .. .. *Set of* 3 14·00 14·50

1984 (22 May). *As No.* F6, *but W* w **15**. *P* 12.

F9 F **2** $20 brown-red .. .. 8·50 8·75

GRENADINES OF ST. VINCENT

A group of islands south of St. Vincent which includes Bequia, Mustique, Canouan and Union.

For stamps inscribed "The Grenadines of St. VINCENT" issued by St. Vincent in 1971, see under St. Vincent Nos. 330/6.

Stamps of the Grenadines of St. Vincent exist overprinted "SPECIMEN", these being produced for publicity purposes.

1973 (14 Nov). *Royal Wedding. As Nos. 322/3 of Montserrat.*

1	25 c. light green	10	10
2	$1 ochre	25	15

GRENADINES
OF

(1)

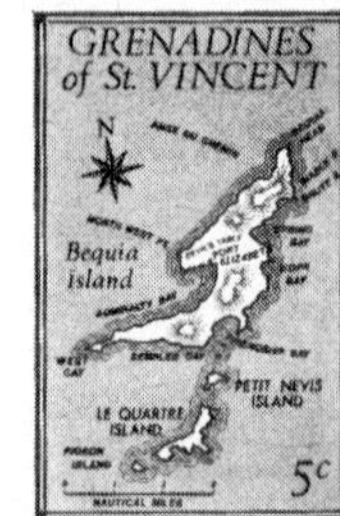

2 Map of Bequia

1974 (24 Apr). *Stamps of St. Vincent. T* **51** *etc. optd in litho with T* **1** *by Harrison & Sons. Glazed paper.* W w **12** (*sideways on* 4, 5, 10, 12, 50 *c. and* $5).

3	1 c. Green Heron	10	10
	a. Opt omitted	50·00	
	b. Albino opt	45·00	
4	2 c. Lesser Antillean Bullfinches	15	15
5	3 c. St. Vincent Amazons	75	75
6	4 c. Rufous-throated Solitaire	15	10
7	5 c. Red-necked Pigeon	15	10
8	6 c. Bananaquits	15	10
9	8 c. Purple-throated Carib	15	10
10	10 c. Mangrove Cuckoo	15	10
11	12 c. Common Black Hawk	20	15
	a. Opt double	£130	
12	20 c. Bare-eyed Thrush	35	20
13	25 c. Hooded Tanager	40	20
14	50 c. Blue-hooded Euphonia	70	40
	a. Albino opt	80·00	
15	$1 Barn Owl	1·50	75
16	$2.50, Yellow-bellied Elaenia	2·00	1·25
17	$5 Ruddy Quail Dove	3·50	2·25
3/17	*Set of* 15	9·25	6·00

(Des G. Drummond. Litho Enschedé)

1974 (9 May). *Maps* (*1st series*). *T* **2** *and similar vert designs.* W w **12** (*sideways*). *P* 13 × 12½.

18	5 c. black, light dull green and deep dull green	10	10
19	15 c. multicoloured	10	10
20	20 c. multicoloured	10	10
21	30 c. black, light rose-lilac and lake	10	10
22	40 c. black, lavender and deep ultramarine	10	10
23	$1 black, cobalt and bright ultramarine	25	20
18/23	*Set of* 6	60	35

Maps:—15 c. The Grenadines and Prune Island (inset); 20 c. Mayreau Island and Tobago Cays; 30 c. Mustique Island; 40 c. Union Island; $1 Canouan Island.

Nos. 18/23 were each issued in sheets of ten stamps and two *se-tenant* labels.

See also Nos. 85/8.

GRENADINES
OF

(3)

4 Boat-building

1974 (7 June). *Nos. 361/2 of St. Vincent optd in typo with T* **3** *by Govt Printer, St. Vincent. Glazed paper.* W w **12**.

24	2 c. Lesser Antillean Bullfinches	40	30
25	3 c. St. Vincent Amazons	40	30
	a. Opt double	45·00	
	b. Albino opt	11·00	
	c. Chalky paper. Wmk sideways (No. 288)	30·00	30·00

1974 (25 July). *Centenary of Universal Postal Union. As Nos. 392/5 of St. Vincent but colours and face-values changed and inscr* "Grenadines of St. Vincent".

26	2 c. U.P.U. emblem	10	10
	a. Red (U.P.U. emblem) omitted	£650	
27	15 c. Globe within posthorn	10	10
28	40 c. Map of St. Vincent and hand-cancelling	10	10
29	$1 Map of the world	25	15
26/9	*Set of* 4	40	25

No. 26a was caused by a paper fold.

(Des G. Drummond. Litho Questa)

1974. *Bequia Island* (*1st series*). *T* **4** *and similar horiz designs. Multicoloured. P* 14. (*a*) W w **12** (*sideways*) (26.9.74).

30	5 c. Type **4**	90	1·50
31	30 c. Careening at Port Elizabeth	10	15
32	35 c. Admiralty Bay	10	15
33	$1 Fishing boat race	20	25

(*b*) W w **14** (*sideways*) (12.74)

34	5 c. Type **4**	15	10
30/4	*Set of* 5	1·25	2·00

No. 34 differs in shade from No. 30, notably in the shirt of the man at right, which is red on No. 34 instead of purple.

Nos. 30/4 were each issued in sheets of ten stamps and two *se-tenant* labels.

See also Nos. 185/8.

5 Music Volute (imprint at foot showing designer, date and printer)

(Des R. Granger Barrett. Litho Questa)

1974 (27 Nov)–**77.** *Shells and Molluscs. Horiz designs as T* **5.** *Multicoloured.* W w **14** (*sideways*). *P* 14.

A. *No imprint.* B. *Imprint at foot*

		A		B	
35	1 c. Atlantic Thorny Oyster	10	10	†	
36	2 c. Zigzag Scallop	10	10	†	
37	3 c. Reticulated Helmet	10	10	†	
38	4 c. Type **5**	10	10	10	10
39	5 c. Amber Pen Shell	10	10	10	10
40	6 c. Angular Triton	10	10	10	10
41	8 c. Flame Helmet	10	10	10	10
42	10 c. Caribbean Olive	10	10	10	10
	a. Corrected imprint	†		70	10
43	12 c. Common Sundial	10	10	†	
44	15 c. Glory of the Atlantic Cone	25	20	80	15
45	20 c. Flame Auger	30	35	30	20
	a. Corrected imprint	†		1·25	15
46	25 c. King Venus	40	20	80	15
47	35 c. Long-spined Star-shell	35	30	35	25
	a. Corrected imprint	†		1·50	25
48	45 c. Speckled Tellin	35	30	†	
49	50 c. Rooster Tail Conch	40	25	45	30
50	$1 Green Star Shell	1·00	75	1·00	60
51	$2.50, Incomparable Cone	2·25	1·25	6·00	1·25
52	$5 Rough File Clam	4·00	2·75	8·00	3·00
52*a*	$10 Measled Cowrie	10·00	4·00	†	
35A/52aA	*Set of* 19	18·00	10·00		
38B/52B	*Set of* 13			17·00	5·50

Dates of issue: 27.11.74, Nos. 35A/52A; 12.7.76, Nos. 52aA, 38B/42B, 45B, 47B and 49B/50B; 2.6.77, Nos. 42a, 44B, 45a, 46B, 47a, 51B, 52B.

On Nos. 42a, 44B, 45a, 46B, 47a, 51B and 52B the designer's name is correctly spelt as "R. Granger Barrett". Previously the last name had been spelt "Barratt".

1974 (28 Nov). *Birth Centenary of Sir Winston Churchill. As Nos. 403/6 of St. Vincent but colours and face-values changed and inscr* "GRENADINES OF ST. VINCENT".

53	5 c. Type **75**	10	10
54	40 c. As 35 c.	10	10
55	50 c. As 45 c.	15	10
56	$1 As $1	25	20
53/6	*Set of* 4	50	40

6 Cotton House, Mustique

(Des G. Drummond. Litho Questa)

1975 (27 Feb). *Mustique Island. T* **6** *and similar horiz designs. Multicoloured.* W w **14** (*sideways*). *P* 14.

57	5 c. Type **6**	10	10
58	35 c. "Blue Waters", Endeavour Bay	10	10
59	45 c. Endeavour Bay	10	10
60	$1 "Les Jolies Eaux", Gelliceaux Bay	25	20
57/60	*Set of* 4	40	30

Nos. 57/60 were each issued in sheets of ten stamps and two *se-tenant* labels.

7 *Danaus plexippus*

(Des G. Drummond. Litho Questa)

1975 (15 May). *Butterflies. T* **7** *and similar horiz designs. Multicoloured.* W w **14** (*sideways*). *P* 14.

61	3 c. Type **7**	20	10
62	5 c. *Agraulis vanillae*	25	10
63	35 c. *Battus polydamas*	80	10
64	45 c. *Evenus dindymus* and *Junonia evarete*	1·00	10
65	$1 *Anartia jatrophae*	1·75	35
61/5	*Set of* 5	3·50	65

8 Resort Pavilion

(Des G. Drummond. Litho Harrison)

1975 (24 July). *Petit St. Vincent. T* **8** *and similar horiz designs. Multicoloured.* W w **14** (*sideways*). *P* 14.

66	5 c. Type **8**	10	10
67	35 c. The Harbour	10	10
68	45 c. The Jetty	15	10
69	$1 Sailing in coral lagoon	50	30
66/9	*Set of* 4	70	45

Nos. 66/9 were each issued in sheets of ten stamps and two *se-tenant* labels.

9 Ecumenical Church, Mustique

(Des G. Drummond. Litho Questa)

1975 (20 Nov). *Christmas. T* **9** *and similar horiz designs. Multicoloured.* W w **12** (*sideways*). *P* 14.

70	5 c. Type **9**	10	10
71	25 c. Catholic Church, Union Island	10	10
72	50 c. Catholic Church, Bequia	10	10
73	$1 Anglican Church, Bequia	25	15
70/3	*Set of* 4	40	30

10 Sunset Scene

(Des G. Drummond. Litho J.W.)

1976 (26 Feb). *Union Island* (*1st series*). *T* **10** *and similar horiz designs. Multicoloured.* W w **14** (*sideways*). *P* 13½.

74	5 c. Type **10**	10	10
75	35 c. Customs and Post Office, Clifton	10	10
76	45 c. Anglican Church, Ashton	10	10
77	$1 Mail schooner, Clifton Harbour	25	20
74/7	*Set of* 4	45	30

Nos. 74/7 were each issued in sheets of ten stamps and two *se-tenant* labels.

See also Nos. 242/5.

11 Staghorn Coral

(Des G. Drummond. Litho Questa)

1976 (13 May). *Corals. T* **11** *and similar horiz designs. Multicoloured.* W w **14** (*sideways*). *P* 14.

78	5 c. Type **11**	10	10
79	35 c. Elkhorn coral	25	10
80	45 c. Pillar coral	30	10
81	$1 Brain coral	80	20
78/81	*Set of* 4	1·25	30

12 25 c. Bicentennial Coin

(Des J. Cooter. Litho Questa)

1976 (15 July). *Bicentenary of American Revolution. T* **12** *and similar horiz designs.* W w **14** (*sideways*). *P* 13½.

82	25 c. silver, black and light violet-blue	10	10
83	50 c. silver, black and light rose-red	20	10
84	$1 silver, black and mauve	25	20
82/4	*Set of* 3	50	30

Designs:—50 c. Half-dollar coin; $1 One dollar coin.

Nos. 82/4 were each issued in sheets of ten stamps and two *se-tenant* labels.

(Des G. Drummond. Litho Questa)

1976 (23 Sept). *Maps* (*2nd series*). *Vert designs as T* **2**, *showing various islands as detailed below.* W w **14.** *P* 13½.

A. Bequia — D. Mustique — F. Prune
B. Canouan — E. Petit St. Vincent — G. Union
C. Mayreau

To indicate individual islands, use the above letters as a suffix to the following catalogue numbers.

85	5 c. black, myrtle-green and pale emerald	10	10
	a. Booklet pane. Nos. 85/6 and 88 plus printed label	45	
	b. Booklet pane. Nos. 85 × 2 and 86 plus printed label	30	

86 10 c. black, ultramarine and greenish blue .. 10 10
 a. Booklet pane. Nos. 86 × 2 and 87 plus printed label 40
87 35 c. black, red-brown and bright rose .. 20 20
 a. Booklet pane. Nos. 87 × 2 and 88 plus printed label 65
88 45 c. black, scarlet and yellow-orange .. 25 25
85/8 .. .. *Set of* 4 (*one island*) 60 60
85/8 .. .. .. *Set of* 28 (*seven islands*) 4·00 4·00
Nos. 85/8 were only issued in $2.50 stamp booklets.

13 Station Hill School and Post Office

(Des G. Drummond. Litho Questa)

1976 (2 Dec). *Mayreau Island. T* **13** *and similar horiz designs. Multicoloured. W* w **14** (*sideways*). *P* 14.
89 5 c. Type **13** 10 10
90 35 c. Church at Old Wall 10 10
91 45 c. La Sourciere Anchorage 10 10
92 $1 Saline Bay 25 15
89/92 .. .. *Set of* 4 40 30
Nos. 89/92 were each issued in sheets of ten stamps and two *se-tenant* labels.

14 Coronation Crown Coin

(Des G. Vasarhelyi. Litho Questa)

1977 (3 Mar). *Silver Jubilee. T* **14** *and similar horiz designs. Multicoloured. W* w **14** (*sideways*). *P* 14.
93 25 c. Type **14** 20 10
94 50 c. Silver Wedding Crown 25 10
95 $1 Silver Jubilee Crown 30 15
93/5 .. .. *Set of* 3 65 30
Nos. 93/5 were each issued in sheets of ten stamps and two *se-tenant* labels.

15 Fiddler Crab

(Des BG Studio. Litho Questa)

1977 (19 May). *Crustaceans. T* **15** *and similar horiz designs. Multicoloured. W* w **14** (*sideways*). *P* 14.
96 5 c. Type **15** 10 10
97 35 c. Ghost crab 20 10
98 50 c. Blue crab 25 10
99 $1.25, Spiny lobster 55 40
96/9 .. .. *Set of* 4 95 55

16 Snorkel Diving

(Des G. Drummond. Litho Questa)

1977 (25 Aug). *Prune Island. T* **16** *and similar horiz designs. Multicoloured. W* w **14** (*sideways*). *P* 14½.
100 5 c. Type **16** 10 10
101 35 c. Palm Island Resort 10 10
102 45 c. Casuarina Beach 10 10
103 $1 Palm Island Beach Club 30 30
100/3 .. .. *Set of* 4 50 40
Nos. 100/3 were each issued in sheets of ten stamps and two *se-tenant* labels.

17 Mustique Island

(Des G. Drummond. Litho Questa)

1977 (31 Oct). *Royal Visit. Previously unissued stamps without face values, locally surch with new inscription. W* w **12.** *P* 14½ × 14.
104 **17** 40 c. turquoise-green and blue-green (Blk. (value) and R.) 20 10
105 $2 yellow-ochre and yellow-brown (R. (value) and B.) 65 25

18 The Clinic, Charlestown

(Des G. Drummond. Litho Harrison)

1977 (8 Dec). *Canouan Island* (1*st series*). T **18** *and similar horiz designs. Multicoloured. W* w **14.** *P* 14½.
106 5 c. Type **18** 10 10
107 35 c. Town jetty, Charlestown 10 10
108 45 c. Mail schooner arriving at Charlestown 10 10
109 $1 Grand Bay 30 20
106/9 .. .. *Set of* 4 50 30
Nos. 106/9 were each issued in sheets of ten stamps and two *se-tenant* labels.
See also Nos. 307/10.

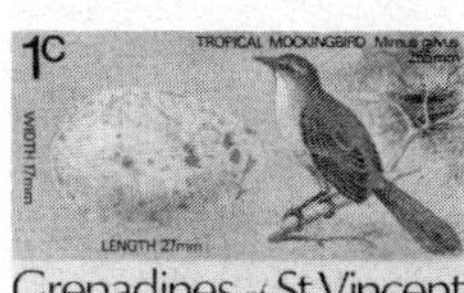

19 Tropical Mockingbird

(Des J.W. Litho Enschedé)

1978 (11 May). *Birds and their Eggs. Horiz designs as T* **19.** *Multicoloured. W* w **14** (*sideways*). *P* 12½ × 12.
110 1 c. Type **19** 10 10
111 2 c. Mangrove Cuckoo 15 10
112 3 c. Osprey 20 10
113 4 c. Smooth-billed Ani 20 10
114 5 c. House Wren 20 10
115 6 c. Bananaquit 20 10
116 8 c. Carib Grackle 20 10
117 10 c. Yellow-bellied Elaenia 20 10
118 12 c. Collared Plover 30 10
119 15 c. Cattle Egret 30 10
120 20 c. Red-footed Booby 30 10
121 25 c. Red-billed Tropic Bird 30 10
122 40 c. Royal Tern 45 15
123 50 c. Grenada Flycatcher 45 20
124 80 c. Purple Gallinule 70 30
125 $1 Broad-winged Hawk 75 50
126 $2 Scaly-breasted Ground Dove 90 75
127 $3 Laughing Gull .. .. 1·25 1·00
128 $5 Common Noddy .. .. 2·25 1·25
129 $10 Grey Kingbird .. .. 5·00 2·25
110/29 .. .. *Set of* 20 13·00 6·00
See also Nos. **MS**155 and **MS**170.

(Des G. Drummond. Litho J.W.)

1978 (2 June). *25th Anniv of Coronation. Horiz designs as Nos. 422/5 of Montserrat. Multicoloured. W* w **14** (*sideways*). *P* 13.
130 5 c. Worcester Cathedral 10 10
131 40 c. Coventry Cathedral 10 10
132 $1 Winchester Cathedral 15 10
133 $3 Chester Cathedral 25 35
130/3 .. .. *Set of* 4 45 50
MS134 130 × 102 mm. Nos. 130/3. P 13½ × 14 .. 60 80
 a. Top horiz pair imperf three sides .. £350
Nos. 130/3 were each issued in sheets of ten stamps and two *se-tenant* labels.
No. **MS**134a shows the 5 c. and 40 c. stamps in the sheet perforated along the top, but imperforate on the other three sides.

20 Green Turtle

21 Three Kings following Star

(Des R. Granger Barrett. Litho Walsall)

1978 (20 July). *Turtles. T* **20** *and similar horiz designs. Multicoloured. W* w **14** (*sideways*). *P* 14.
135 5 c. Type **20** 10 10
136 40 c. Hawksbill turtle 15 10
137 50 c. Leatherback turtle 15 10
138 $1.25, Loggerhead turtle 40 40
135/8 .. .. *Set of* 4 65 60

(Des Jennifer Toombs. Litho Questa)

1978 (2 Nov). *Christmas. Scenes and Verses from the Carol "We Three Kings of Orient Are". T* **21** *and similar vert designs. Multicoloured. W* w **14.** *P* 14 × 13½.
139 5 c. Type **21** 10 10
140 10 c. King with gift of Gold 10 10
141 25 c. King with gift of Frankincense 10 10
142 50 c. King with gift of Myrrh 10 10
143 $2 Three Kings paying homage to infant Jesus 30 20
139/43 .. .. *Set of* 5 45 30
MS144 154 × 175 mm. Nos. 139/43 .. .. 70 1·25

22 Sailing Yachts

23 False Killer Whale

(Des G. Drummond. Litho Questa)

1979 (25 Jan). *National Regatta. T* **22** *and similar vert designs showing sailing yachts. W* w **14.** *P* 14.
145 5 c. multicoloured 10 10
146 40 c. multicoloured 20 10
147 50 c. multicoloured 25 10
148 $2 multicoloured 75 60
145/8 .. .. *Set of* 4 1·10 75

(Des L. Curtis. Litho Questa)

1979 (8 Mar). *Wildlife. Horiz designs as T* **114** *of St. Vincent. Multicoloured. W* w **14** (*sideways*). *P* 14 × 14½.
149 20 c. Green Iguana 10 10
150 40 c. Common Opossum ("Manicou") .. 15 10
151 $2 Red-legged Tortoise 60 65
149/51 .. .. *Set of* 3 75 75
Nos. 149/51 were each printed in four panes of 12 throughout the sheet, each pane including two *se-tenant* labels.

(Des J.W. Litho. Enschedé)

1979 (21 May). *Death Centenary of Sir Rowland Hill. Horiz designs as T* **103** *of St. Vincent. Multicoloured. W* w **14** (*sideways*). *P* 12½ × 12.
152 80 c. Sir Rowland Hill 25 15
153 $1 Great Britain 1d. and 4d. stamps of 1858 with "A10" (Kingstown, St. Vincent) postmark 30 25
154 $2 St. Vincent ½d. and 1d. stamps of 1894 with Bequia postmark 50 40
152/4 .. .. *Set of* 3 95 70
MS155 165 × 115 mm. Nos. 124/6 and 152/4 .. 2·00 2·50
Nos. 152/4 were each printed in sheets including two *se-tenant* stamp-size labels.

1979 (24 Oct). *International Year of the Child. As Nos. 570/3 of St. Vincent.*
156 6 c. black, silver and pale blue 10 10
157 40 c. black, silver and salmon 10 10
158 $1 black, silver and buff 20 10
159 $3 black, silver and lilac 45 30
156/9 .. .. *Set of* 4 65 45

(Des J.W. Litho Enschedé)

1979 (27 Oct). *Independence. Horiz designs as T* **106** *of St. Vincent. Multicoloured. W* w **14** (*sideways*). *P* 12½ × 12.
160 5 c. National flag and *Ixora salici-folia* (flower) 10 10
161 40 c. House of Assembly and *Ixora odorata* (flower) 10 10
162 $1 Prime Minister R. Milton Cato and *Ixora javanica* (flower) 20 20
160/2 .. .. *Set of* 3 30 30

(Des R. Granger Barrett. Litho Walsall)

1980 (31 Jan). *Whales and Dolphins. T* **23** *and similar horiz designs. Multicoloured. W* w **14** (*sideways*). *P* 14.
163 10 c. Type **23** 15 10
164 50 c. Spinner Dolphin 40 20
165 90 c. Bottle-nosed Dolphin 65 40
166 $2 Short-finned Pilot Whale ("Blackfish") 1·00 65
163/6 .. .. *Set of* 4 2·00 1·10

(Des J.W. Litho Enschedé)

1980 (24 Apr). *"London 1980" International Stamp Exhibition. Horiz designs as T* **110** *of St. Vincent. Multicoloured. W* w **14** (*sideways*). *P* 12½ × 12.
167 40 c. Queen Elizabeth II 20 10
168 50 c. St. Vincent 1965 2 c. definitive 20 10
169 $3 1973 25 c. and Royal Wedding commemoratives .. .. 80 1·00
167/9 .. .. *Set of* 3 1·10 1·10
MS170 165 × 115 mm. Nos. 122/3, 127 and 167/9 2·25 2·50
Nos. 167/9 were printed in sheets including 2 *se-tenant* stamp-size labels.

(Des Polygraphic. Litho Rosenbaum Bros, Vienna)

1980 (7 Aug). *"Sport for All". Vert designs as T* **112** *of St. Vincent. Multicoloured. W* w **14.** *P* 13½.
171 25 c. Running 10 10
172 50 c. Sailing 10 10
173 $1 Long jumping 20 20
174 $2 Swimming 30 30
171/4 .. .. *Set of* 4 60 60

1980 (7 Aug). *Hurricane Relief. Nos.* 171/4 *surch with T* **113** *of St. Vincent.*
175 25 c.+50 c. Running 10 20
176 50 c.+50 c. Sailing 20 30
177 $1+50 c. Long jumping 25 40
178 $2+50 c. Swimming 40 60
175/8 .. .. *Set of* 4 85 1·40

24 Scene and Verse from the Carol "De Borning Day" **25** Post Office, Port Elizabeth

(Des Jennifer Toombs. Litho Questa)

1980 (13 Nov). *Christmas. T* **24** *and similar vert designs showing scenes and verses from the carol "De Borning Day". W w* **14**. *P* 14 × 13½.
179 5 c. multicoloured 10 10
180 50 c. multicoloured 10 10
181 60 c. multicoloured 10 10
182 $1 multicoloured 15 15
183 $2 multicoloured 25 25
179/83 .. .. *Set of* 5 50 50
MS184 159 × 178 mm. Nos. 179/83 .. .. 75 1·40

(Des G. Drummond. Litho Questa)

1981 (19 Feb). *Bequia Island (2nd series). T* **25** *and similar horiz designs. Multicoloured. W w* **14** *(sideways). P* 14½ × 14.
185 50 c. Type **25** 15 15
186 60 c. Moonhole 20 20
187 $1.50, Fishing boats, Admiralty Bay .. 40 40
188 $2 *Friendship Rose* (yacht) at jetty .. 55 55
185/8 .. .. *Set of* 4 1·10 1·10

The $2 value was originally printed with the country name in black and the face value in white. A quantity of these were stolen in transit before issue and the remainder were not placed on sale, the stamp being reprinted with the inscriptions in red.

Nos. 185/8 were each printed in sheets including two *se-tenant* stamp-size labels.

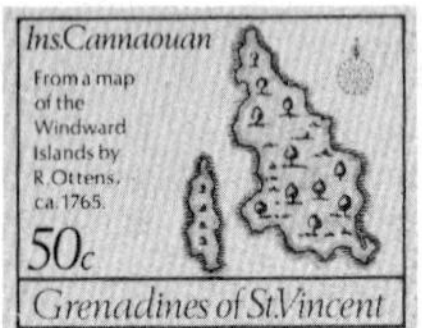

26 Ins. Cannaouan (map of Windward Islands by R. Ottens, *circa* 1765) **27** Bar Jack

(Des J. Cooter. Litho Format)

1981 (2 Apr). *Details from Early Maps. T* **26** *and similar horiz designs. Multicoloured. W w* **14** *(sideways). P* 13½.
189 50 c. Type **26** 40 30
a. Pair. Nos. 189/90 .. .. 80 60
190 50 c. Cannouan Is. (chart by J. Parsons, 1861) 40 30
191 60 c. Ins. Moustiques (map of Windward Islands by R. Ottens, *circa* 1765) .. 45 35
a. Pair. Nos. 191/2 .. .. 90 70
192 60 c. Mustique Is. (chart by J. Parsons, 1861) 45 35
193 $2 Ins. Bequia (map of Windward Islands by R. Ottens, *circa* 1765) 80 75
a. Pair. Nos. 193/4 .. .. 1·60 1·50
194 $2 Bequia Is. (map surveyed in 1763 by T. Jefferys) 80 75
189/94 .. .. *Set of* 6 3·00 2·50

The two designs of each value were printed together, *se-tenant*, in horizontal and vertical pairs throughout the sheet.

(Des D. Shults. Litho Questa)

1981 (17 July–26 Nov). *Royal Wedding. Horiz designs as T* **26/27** *of Kiribati. Multicoloured. (a) W w* **15**. *P* 14.
195 50 c. *Mary* 15 15
a. Sheetlet. No. 195 × 6 and No. 196 .. 1·10
196 50 c. Prince Charles and Lady Diana Spencer 40 40
197 $3 *Alexandra* 30 30
a. Sheetlet. No. 197 × 6 and No. 198 .. 2·50
198 $3 As No. 196 .. .. 90 90
199 $3.50, *Britannia* 35 35
a. Sheetlet. No. 199 × 6 and No. 200 .. 2·75
200 $3.50, As No. 196 .. .. 90 90
195/200 .. .. *Set of* 6 2·75 2·75
MS201 120 × 109 mm. $5 As No. 196. Wmk sideways. P 12 (26 Nov) .. .. .. 1·25 1·00

(*b*) *Booklet stamps. No wmk. P* 12 (26 Nov)
202 50 c. As No. 195 .. .. 20 30
a. Booklet pane. No. 202 × 4 80
203 $3 As No. 198 .. .. 1·50 1·60
a. Booklet pane. No. 203 × 2 .. .. 3·00

Nos. 195/200 were printed in sheetlets of seven stamps of the same face value, each containing six of the "Royal Yacht" design and one of the larger design showing Prince Charles and Lady Diana.

Nos. 202/3 come from $10 stamp booklets.

(Des N. Weaver. Litho Questa)

1981 (9 Oct). *Game Fish. T* **27** *and similar horiz designs. Multicoloured. W w* **14** *(sideways). P* 14.
204 10 c. Type **27** 15 10
205 50 c. Tarpon 25 10
206 60 c. Cobia 30 10
207 $2 Blue Marlin 90 70
204/7 .. .. *Set of* 4 1·40 85

28 H.M.S. *Experiment* **29** Prickly Pear Fruit

(Des J. Cooter. Litho Security Printers (M), Malaysia)

1982 (28 Jan). *Ships. Horiz designs as T* **28**. *Multicoloured. W* w **14**. *P* 13½ × 13.
208 1 c. Type **28** 10 10
209 3 c. *Lady Nelson* (cargo liner) 10 10
210 5 c. *Daisy* (brig) 10 10
211 6 c. Carib canoe 10 10
212 10 c. *Hairoun Star* (freighter) 10 10
213 15 c. *Jupiter* (liner) 10 10
214 20 c. *Christina* (steam yacht) 10 10
215 25 c. *Orinoco* (paddle-steamer) 10 15
216 30 c. H.M.S. *Lively* 10 15
217 50 c. *Alabama* (Confederate warship) .. 20 25
218 60 c. *Denmark* (freighter) 25 30
219 75 c. *Santa Maria* 30 35
220 $1 *Baffin* (cable ship) 40 45
221 $2 *Queen Elizabeth 2* (liner) 85 90
222 $3 R.Y. *Britannia* .. .. 1·25 1·40
223 $5 *Geeststar* (cargo liner) .. .. .. 2·10 2·25
224 $10 *Grenadines Star* (ferry) .. .. 4·25 4·50
208/24 .. .. *Set of* 17 9·25 10·00

(Des G. Drummond. Litho Harrison)

1982 (5 Apr). *Prickly Pear Cactus. T* **29** *and similar vert designs. Multicoloured. W* w **14**. *P* 14.
225 10 c. Type **29** 15 15
226 50 c. Prickly Pear flower buds 35 35
227 $1 Flower of Prickly Pear Cactus 60 60
228 $2 Prickly Pear Cactus .. .. .. 1·25 1·25
225/8 .. .. *Set of* 4 2·10 2·10

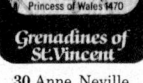

30 Anne Neville, Princess of Wales, 1470 **31** Old and New Uniforms

(Des D. Shults and J. Cooter. Litho Format)

1982 (1 July). *21st Birthday of Princess of Wales. T* **30** *and similar vert designs. Multicoloured. W* w **15**. *P* 13½ × 14.
229 50 c. Type **30** 20 20
230 60 c. Coat of arms of Anne Neville 20 20
231 $6 Diana, Princess of Wales .. .. 1·25 1·25
229/31 .. .. *Set of* 3 1·50 1·50

(Des L. Curtis. Litho W.S. Cowell Ltd)

1982 (15 July). *75th Anniv of Boy Scout Movement. T* **31** *and similar vert design. Multicoloured. W* w **14** *(inverted). P* 14½.
232 $1.50, Type **31** 60 60
233 $2.50, Lord Baden-Powell 90 90

ROYAL BABY

BEQUIA

(32)

33 Silhouette Figures of Mary and Joseph

1982 (19 July). *Birth of Prince William of Wales. Nos.* 229/31 *optd with various island names as T* **32**.
A. Bequia B. Canouan C. Mayreau
D. Mustique E. Union Island

To indicate individual islands, use the above letters as a suffix to the following catalogue numbers.
234 50 c. Type **30** 20 20
a. Opt A (Bequia) double .. .. .. 40·00
b. Opt C (Mayreau) inverted .. .. 35·00
c. Opt D (Mustique) inverted .. .. 35·00
235 60 c. Coat of arms of Anne Neville 20 20
a. Opt D (Mustique) inverted .. .. 40·00
b. Opt E (Union Island) inverted .. .. 60·00
c. Opt E (Union Island) double £110
236 $6 Diana, Princess of Wales .. .. 1·25 1·25
234/6 .. .. *Set of* 3 1·50 1·50

(Des Jennifer Toombs. Litho Security Printers (M), Malaysia)

1982 (18 Nov). *Christmas. T* **33** *and similar horiz designs showing silhouettes of figures. Multicoloured. W* w **14**. *P* 13½.
237 10 c. Type **33** 10 10
238 $1.50, Animals in stable 45 45
239 $2.50, Mary and Joseph with baby Jesus .. 60 60
237/9 .. .. *Set of* 3 1·00 1·00
MS240 168 × 99 mm. Nos. 237/9 .. .. .. 1·00 1·75

45¢

(34)

35 Power Station, Clifton

1983 (26 Apr). *No.* 123 *surch with T* **34** *by Reliance Printery, Kingstown.*
241 45 c. on 50 c. Grenada Flycatcher 20 25

(Des G. Drummond. Litho Security Printers (M), Malaysia)

1983 (12 May). *Union Island (2nd series). T* **35** *and similar horiz designs. Multicoloured. W* w **14**. *P* 13½.
242 50 c. Type **35** 15 15
243 60 c. Sunrise, Clifton harbour 15 15
244 $1.50, Junior Secondary School, Ashton .. 40 40
245 $2 Frigate Rock and Conch Shell Beach .. 55 55
242/5 .. .. *Set of* 4 1·10 1·10

Nos. 242/5 were each printed in sheets including two *se-tenant* stamp-size labels.

36 British Man-of-war **37** Montgolfier Balloon, 1783

(Des and litho J.W.)

1983 (15 Sept). *Bicentenary of Treaty of Versailles. T* **36** *and similar vert designs. Multicoloured. W* w **14**. *P* 14½.
246 45 c. Type **36** 15 15
247 60 c. American man-of-war 15 15
248 $1.50, Soldiers carrying U.S. flags 45 45
249 $2 British troops in battle 55 55
246/9 .. .. *Set of* 4 1·10 1·10

(Des A. Theobald. Litho Format)

1983 (15 Sept). *Bicentenary of Manned Flight. T* **37** *and similar multicoloured designs. W* w **14** *(sideways on Nos.* 251/53*). P* 14.
250 45 c. Type **37** 15 15
251 60 c. Ayres "Turbo-thrush Commander" (*horiz*) 15 15
252 $1.50, Lebaudy "1" dirigible (*horiz*) 45 45
253 $2 Space shuttle *Columbia* (*horiz*) 55 55
250/3 .. .. *Set of* 4 1·10 1·10
MS254 110 × 145 mm. Nos. 250/3. Wmk sideways 1·50 2·00

38 Coat of Arms of Henry VIII **39** Quarter Dollar and Half Dollar, 1797

(Des Court House Studio. Litho Format)

1983 (25 Oct). *Leaders of the World. British Monarchs. T* **38** *and similar vert designs. Multicoloured. P* 12½.
255 60 c. Type **38** 25 25
a. Horiz pair. Nos. 255/6 .. .. .. 50 50
256 60 c. Henry VIII 25 25
257 60 c. Coat of Arms of James I 25 25
a. Horiz pair. Nos. 257/8 .. .. .. 50 50
258 60 c. James I 25 25
259 75 c. Henry VIII 25 25
a. Horiz pair. Nos. 259/60 .. .. .. 50 50
260 75 c. Hampton Court 25 25
261 75 c. James I 25 25
a. Horiz pair. Nos. 261/2 .. .. .. 50 50
262 75 c. Edinburgh Castle 25 25
263 $2.50, The *Mary Rose* 35 35
a. Horiz pair. Nos. 263/4 .. .. .. 70 70
264 $2.50, Henry VIII and Portsmouth harbour 35 35
265 $2.50, Gunpowder Plot 35 35
a. Horiz pair. Nos. 265/6 .. .. .. 70 70
266 $2.50, James I and the Gunpowder Plot .. 35 35
255/66 .. .. *Set of* 12 3·00 3·00

Nos. 255/6, 257/8, 259/60, 261/2, 263/4 and 265/6 were printed together, *se-tenant*, in horizontal pairs throughout the sheets.

(Des J. Cooter. Litho Walsall)

1983 (1 Dec). *Old Coinage. T* **39** *and similar vert designs. Multicoloured.* W w **14.** *P* 14.

267 20 c. Type **39** .. 10 10
268 45 c. Nine Bitts, 1811–14 .. 15 15
269 75 c. Twelve Bitts and Six Bitts, 1811–14 .. 25 25
270 $3 Sixty-six Shillings, 1798 .. 80 80
267/70 .. *Set of* 4 1·10 1·10

40 Class "D 13"

(Des J.W. Litho Format)

1984 (15 Mar). *Leaders of the World. Railway Locomotives* (*1st series*). *T* **40** *and similar horiz designs, the first in each pair showing technical drawings and the second the locomotive at work. P* 12½.

271 5 c. multicoloured .. 10 10
a. Vert pair. Nos. 271/2 .. 10 10
272 5 c. multicoloured .. 10 10
273 10 c. multicoloured .. 10 10
a. Vert pair. Nos. 273/4 .. 15 15
274 10 c. multicoloured .. 10 10
275 15 c. multicoloured .. 15 15
a. Vert pair. Nos. 275/6 .. 30 30
276 15 c. multicoloured .. 15 15
277 35 c. multicoloured .. 20 20
a. Vert pair. Nos. 277/8 .. 40 40
278 35 c. multicoloured .. 20 20
279 45 c. multicoloured .. 20 20
a. Vert pair. Nos. 279/80 .. 40 40
280 45 c. multicoloured .. 20 20
281 60 c. multicoloured .. 25 25
a. Vert pair. Nos. 281/2 .. 50 50
282 60 c. multicoloured .. 25 25
283 $1 multicoloured .. 35 35
a. Vert pair. Nos. 283/4 .. 70 70
284 $1 multicoloured .. 35 35
285 $2.50, multicoloured .. 50 50
a. Vert pair. Nos. 285/6 .. 1·00 1·00
286 $2.50, multicoloured .. 50 50
271/86 .. *Set of* 16 3·00 3·00

Designs:—Nos. 271/2, Class "D 13", U.S.A. (1892); 273/4, High Speed Train "125", Great Britain (1980); 275/6, Class "T 9", Great Britain (1899); 277/8, *Claud Hamilton*, Great Britain (1900); 279/80, Class "J", U.S.A. (1941); 281/2, Class "D 16", U.S.A. (1895); 283/4, *Lode Star*, Great Britain (1907); 285/6, *Blue Peter*, Great Britain (1948).

Nos. 271/2, 273/4, 275/6, 277/8, 279/80, 281/2, 283/4 and 285/6 were printed together, *se-tenant* in vertical pairs throughout the sheet.

See also Nos. 311/26, 351/9, 390/7, 412/19, 443/58, 504/19 and 520/35.

41 Spotted Eagle Ray

(Des G. Drummond. Litho Format)

1984 (26 Apr). *Reef Fishes. T* **41** *and similar horiz designs. Multicoloured.* W w **15.** *P* 14.

287 45 c. Type **41** .. 25 30
288 60 c. Queen Trigger Fish .. 30 35
289 $1.50, White Spotted File Fish .. 75 80
290 $2 Schoolmaster .. 1·00 1·10
287/90 .. *Set of* 4 2·10 2·25

42 R. A. Woolmer **43** Junior Secondary School

(Des Court House Studio. Litho Format)

1984 (16 Aug). *Leaders of the World. Cricketers* (*1st series*). *T* **42** *and similar vert designs, the first in each pair showing a portrait and the second the cricketer in action. P* 12½.

291 1 c. multicoloured .. 10 10
a. Horiz pair. Nos. 291/2 .. 10 10
292 1 c. multicoloured .. 10 10
293 3 c. multicoloured .. 10 10
a. Horiz pair. Nos. 293/4 .. 10 10
294 3 c. multicoloured .. 10 10
295 5 c. multicoloured .. 10 10
a. Horiz pair. Nos. 295/6 .. 10 10
296 5 c. multicoloured .. 10 10
297 30 c. multicoloured .. 20 20
a. Horiz pair. Nos. 297/8 .. 40 40
298 30 c. multicoloured .. 20 20
299 60 c. multicoloured .. 40 40
a. Horiz pair. Nos. 299/300 .. 80 80
300 60 c. multicoloured .. 40 40
301 $1 multicoloured .. 50 50
a. Horiz pair. Nos. 301/2 .. 1·00 1·00
302 $1 multicoloured .. 50 50
303 $2 multicoloured .. 80 80
a. Horiz pair. Nos. 303/4 .. 1·60 1·60
304 $2 multicoloured .. 80 80
305 $3 multicoloured .. 1·10 1·10
a. Horiz pair. Nos. 305/6 .. 2·10 2·10
306 $3 multicoloured .. 1·10 1·10
291/306 .. *Set of* 16 5·50 5·50

Designs:—Nos. 293/4, K. S. Ranjitsinhji; 295/6, W. R. Hammond; 297/8, D. L. Underwood; 299/300, W. G. Grace; 301/2, E. A. E. Baptiste; 303/4, A. P. E. Knott; 305/6, L. E. G. Ames.

See also Nos. 331/8 and 364/9.

(Des G. Drummond. Litho Questa)

1984 (3 Sept). *Canouan Island* (*2nd series*). *T* **43** *and similar horiz designs. Multicoloured.* W w **15** (*sideways*). *P* 14.

307 35 c. Type **43** .. 20 20
308 45 c. Police Station .. 25 25
309 $1 Post Office .. 50 50
310 $3 Anglican Church .. 1·25 1·50
307/10 .. *Set of* 4 2·00 2·25

IMPERFORATES AND MISSING COLOURS. Various issues between Nos. 311 and 672 exist either imperforate or with colours omitted. Such items are not listed as there is no evidence that they fulfil the criteria outlined on page xi of this catalogue.

(Des J.W. Litho Format)

1984 (9 Oct). *Leaders of the World. Railway Locomotives* (*2nd series*). *Horiz designs as T* **40**, *the first in each pair showing technical drawings and the second the locomotive at work. P* 12½.

311 1 c. multicoloured .. 10 10
a. Vert pair. Nos. 311/12 .. 10 10
312 1 c. multicoloured .. 10 10
313 5 c. multicoloured .. 10 10
a. Vert pair. Nos. 313/14 .. 10 10
314 5 c. multicoloured .. 10 10
315 20 c. multicoloured .. 15 15
a. Vert pair. Nos. 315/16 .. 30 30
316 20 c. multicoloured .. 15 15
317 35 c. multicoloured .. 25 25
a. Vert pair. Nos. 317/18 .. 50 50
318 35 c. multicoloured .. 25 25
319 60 c. multicoloured .. 40 40
a. Vert pair. Nos. 319/20 .. 80 80
320 60 c. multicoloured .. 40 40
321 $1 multicoloured .. 50 50
a. Vert pair. Nos. 321/2 .. 1·00 1·00
322 $1 multicoloured .. 50 50
323 $1.50, multicoloured .. 55 55
a. Vert pair. Nos. 323/4 .. 1·10 1·10
324 $1.50, multicoloured .. 55 55
325 $3 multicoloured .. 80 80
a. Vert pair. Nos. 325/6 .. 1·60 1·60
326 $3 multicoloured .. 80 80
311/26 .. *Set of* 16 5·00 5·00

Designs:—Nos. 311/12, Class "C62", Japan (1948); 313/14, Class "V", Great Britain (1903); 315/16, *Catch-Me-Who-Can*, Great Britain (1808), 317/18, Class "E10", Japan (1948); 319/20, *J. B. Earle*, Great Britain (1904); 321/2, *Lyn*, Great Britain (1898); 323/4, *Talyllyn*, Great Britain (1865); 325/6, *Cardean*, Great Britain (1906).

Nos. 311/26 were issued in a similar sheet format to Nos. 271/86.

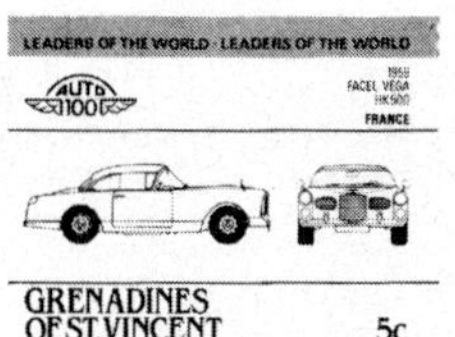

44 Lady of the Night **45** Facel "Vega HK500"

(Des Jennifer Toombs. Litho Questa)

1984 (15 Oct). *Night-blooming Flowers. T* **44** *and similar vert designs. Multicoloured.* W w **15.** *P* 14.

327 35 c. Type **44** .. 35 30
328 45 c. Four o'clock .. 45 35
329 75 c. Mother-in-Law's Tongue .. 60 50
330 $3 Queen of the Night .. 2·00 1·75
327/30 .. *Set of* 4 3·00 2·50

(Des Court House Studio. Litho Format)

1984 (28 Nov). *Leaders of the World. Cricketers* (*2nd series*). *Vert designs as T* **42**, *the first in each pair listed showing a head portrait and the second the cricketer in action. P* 12½.

331 5 c. multicoloured .. 10 10
a. Horiz pair. Nos. 331/2 .. 10 10
332 5 c. multicoloured .. 10 10
333 30 c. multicoloured .. 20 20
a. Horiz pair. Nos. 333/4 .. 40 40
334 30 c. multicoloured .. 20 20
335 $1 multicoloured .. 50 50
a. Horiz pair. Nos. 335/6 .. 1·00 1·00
336 $1 multicoloured .. 50 50
337 $2.50, multicoloured .. 1·10 1·10
a. Horiz pair. Nos. 337/8 .. 2·10 2·10
338 $2.50, multicoloured .. 1·10 1·10
331/8 .. *Set of* 8 3·25 3·25

Designs:—Nos. 331/2, S. F. Barnes; 333/4, R. Peel; 335/6, H. Larwood; 337/8, Sir John Hobbs.

Nos. 331/8 were issued in a similar sheet format to Nos. 291/306.

(Des J.W. Litho Format)

1984 (28 Nov). *Leaders of the World. Automobiles* (*1st series*). *T* **45** *and similar horiz designs, the first in each pair showing technical drawings and the second paintings. P* 12½.

339 5 c. black, azure and dull yellow-green .. 10 10
a. Vert pair. Nos. 339/40 .. 10 10
340 5 c. multicoloured .. 10 10
341 25 c. black, pale lilac and pink .. 15 15
a. Vert pair. Nos. 341/2 .. 30 30
342 25 c. multicoloured .. 15 15
343 50 c. black, pale blue and pale orange .. 20 20
a. Vert pair. Nos. 343/4 .. 40 40
344 50 c. multicoloured .. 20 20
345 $3 black, stone and brown lake .. 60 60
a. Vert pair. Nos. 345/6 .. 1·10 1·10
346 $3 multicoloured .. 60 60
339/46 .. *Set of* 8 1·60 1·60

Designs:—Nos. 339/40, Facel "Vega HK500"; 341/2, B.M.W. "328"; 343/4, Frazer-Nash "TT Replica 1.5L"; 345/6, Buick "Roadmaster Riviera".

Nos. 339/40, 341/2, 343/4 and 345/6 were printed together, *se-tenant*, in vertical pairs throughout the sheets.

See also Nos. 378/85 and 431/42.

46 The Three Wise Men and Star

(Des Jennifer Toombs. Litho Format)

1984 (3 Dec). *Christmas. T* **46** *and similar horiz designs. Multicoloured.* W w **15** (*sideways*). *P* 14½.

347 20 c. Type **46** .. 10 10
348 45 c. Journeying to Bethlehem .. 20 25
349 $3 Presenting gifts .. 1·00 1·40
347/9 .. *Set of* 3 1·10 1·60
MS350 177 × 107 mm. Nos. 347/9. Wmk inverted 1·25 2·00

(Des J.W. Litho Format)

1985 (31 Jan). *Leaders of the World. Railway Locomotives* (*3rd series*). *Horiz designs as T* **40**, *the first in each pair showing technical drawings and the second the locomotive at work. P* 12½.

351 1 c. multicoloured .. 10 10
a. Vert pair. Nos. 351/2 .. 10 10
352 1 c. multicoloured .. 10 10
353 15 c. multicoloured .. 10 10
a. Vert pair Nos. 353/4 .. 15 15
354 15 c. multicoloured .. 10 10
355 75 c. multicoloured .. 35 35
a. Vert pair. Nos. 355/6 .. 70 70
356 75 c. multicoloured .. 35 35
357 $3 multicoloured .. 1·00 1·00
a. Vert pair. Nos. 357/8 .. 2·00 2·00
358 $3 multicoloured .. 1·00 1·00
351/8 .. *Set of* 8 2·50 2·50
MS359 142 × 122 mm. Nos. 355/8. W w **15.** .. 8·00 8·00

Designs:—Nos. 351/2, P.L.M. "Grosse C", France (1898); 353/4, Class "C12", Japan (1932); 355/6, Class "D50", Japan (1923); 357/8, *Fire Fly*, Great Britain (1840).

Nos. 351/8 were issued in a similar sheet format to Nos. 271/86.

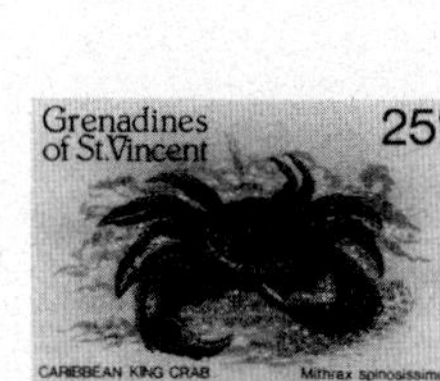

47 Caribbean King Crab **48** *Cypripedium calceolus*

(Des G. Drummond. Litho Format)

1985 (11 Feb). *Shell Fish. T* **47** *and similar horiz designs. Multicoloured.* W w **15** (*sideways*). *P* 14.

360 25 c. Type **47** .. 40 15
361 60 c. Queen Conch .. 55 35
362 $1 White Sea Urchin .. 80 60
363 $3 West Indian Top Shell .. 1·75 1·90
360/3 .. *Set of* 4 3·25 2·75

(Des Court House Studio. Litho Format)

1985 (22 Feb). *Leaders of the World. Cricketers* (*3rd series*). *Vert designs as T* **42** (*55 c., 60 c.*), *the first in each pair showing a head portrait and the second the cricketer in action, or horiz designs showing teams* (*$2*). *P* 12½.

364 55 c. multicoloured .. 30 35
a. Horiz pair. Nos. 364/5 .. 60 70
365 55 c. multicoloured .. 30 35
366 60 c. multicoloured .. 35 40
a. Horiz pair. Nos. 366/7 .. 70 80
367 60 c. multicoloured .. 35 40
368 $2 multicoloured .. 80 85
369 $2 multicoloured .. 80 85
364/9 .. *Set of* 6 2·50 2·75

Designs: *Vert* (*as T* **42**)—Nos. 364/5, M. D. Moxon; 366/7, L. Potter. *Horiz* (*59 × 42 mm*)—No. 368, Kent team; 369, Yorkshire team.

Nos. 364/5 and 366/7 were issued in a similar sheet format to Nos. 291/306.

(Des Jennifer Toombs. Litho Format)

1985 (13 Mar). *Leaders of the World. Flowers. T* **48** *and similar vert designs. Multicoloured. P* 12½.

370 5 c. Type **48** .. 10 10
a. Horiz pair. Nos. 370/1 .. 10 10
371 5 c. *Gentiana asclepiadea* .. 10 10
372 55 c. *Clianthus formosus* .. 30 35
a. Horiz pair. Nos. 372/3 .. 60 70
373 55 c. *Clemisia coriacea* .. 30 35
374 60 c. *Erythronium americanum* .. 35 40
a. Horiz pair. Nos. 374/5 .. 70 80
375 60 c. *Laelia anceps* .. 35 40
376 $2 *Leucadendron discolor* .. 75 75
a. Horiz pair. Nos. 376/7 .. 1·50 1·50
377 $2 *Meconopsis horridula* .. 75 75
370/7 .. *Set of* 8 2·50 2·75

Nos. 370/1, 372/3, 374/5 and 376/7 were printed together, *se-tenant*, in horizontal pairs throughout the sheets.

(Des J.W. (5 c.), G. Turner (others). Litho Format)

1985 (9 Apr). *Leaders of the World. Automobiles* (2nd series). *Horiz designs as T* **45**, *the first in each pair showing technical drawings and the second paintings. P* 12½.

378 5 c. black, pale lemon and turquoise-blue .. 10 10
a. Vert pair. Nos. 378/9 .. 10 10
379 5 c. multicoloured .. 10 10
380 60 c. black, pale yellow and pale orange .. 25 25
a. Vert pair. Nos. 380/1 .. 50 50
381 60 c. multicoloured .. 25 25
382 $1 black, pale green and azure .. 30 30
a. Vert pair. Nos. 382/3 .. 60 60
383 $1 multicoloured .. 30 30
384 $1.50, black, pale cobalt and light green .. 35 35
a. Vert pair. Nos. 384/5 .. 70 70
385 $1.50, multicoloured .. 35 35
378/85 .. *Set of* 8 1·60 1·60

Designs:—Nos. 378/9, Winton (1903); 380/1, Invicta 4½ litre (1931); 382/3, Daimler "SP250 Dart" (1959); 384/5, Brabham "Repco BT19" (1966).

Nos. 378/85 were issued in a similar sheet format to Nos. 339/46.

49 Windsurfing

(Des G. Vasarhelyi. Litho Format)

1985 (9 May). *Tourism. Watersports. T* **49** *and similar horiz designs. Multicoloured. W w* **15** *(sideways). P* 14.

386 35 c. Type **49** .. 20 25
387 45 c. Water-skiing .. 25 30
388 75 c. Scuba-diving .. 35 40
389 $3 Deep-sea game fishing .. 1·50 1·60
386/9 .. *Set of* 4 2·10 2·25

(Des J.W. (50 c.), T. Hadler (others). Litho Format)

1985 (17 May). *Leaders of the World. Railway Locomotives* (4*th series*). *Horiz designs as T* **40**, *the first in each pair showing technical drawings and the second the locomotive at work. P* 12½.

390 10 c. multicoloured .. 10 10
a. Vert pair. Nos. 390/1 .. 10 15
391 10 c. multicoloured .. 10 10
392 40 c. multicoloured .. 25 30
a. Vert pair. Nos. 392/3 .. 50 60
393 40 c. multicoloured .. 25 30
394 50 c. multicoloured .. 25 30
a. Vert pair. Nos. 394/5 .. 50 60
395 50 c. multicoloured .. 25 30
396 $2.50, multicoloured .. 1·00 1·10
a. Vert pair. Nos. 396/7 .. 2·00 2·10
397 $2.50, multicoloured .. 1·00 1·10
390/7 .. *Set of* 8 2·75 3·00

Designs:—Nos. 390/1, Class "581" 12-car train, Japan (1968); 392/3, Class "231-132BT", Algeria (1936); 394/5, *Slieve Gullion*, Great Britain (1913); 396/7, Class "Beattie" well tank, Great Britain (1974).

Nos. 390/7 were issued in a similar sheet format to Nos. 271/86.

50 Passion Fruits and Blossom

51 Queen Elizabeth the Queen Mother

(Des G. Drummond. Litho Format)

1985 (24 June). *Fruits and Blossoms. T* **50** *and similar horiz designs. Multicoloured. W w* **15**. *P* 15.

398 30 c. Type **50** .. 15 20
399 75 c. Guava .. 35 40
400 $1 Sapodilla .. 50 55
401 $2 Mango .. 1·00 1·10
398/401 .. *Set of* 4 1·75 2·00
MS402 145×120 mm. Nos. 398/401. Wmk sideways. P 14½×15. 2·00 2·25

(Des Court House Studio. Litho Format)

1985 (31 July). *Leaders of the World. Life and Times of Queen Elizabeth the Queen Mother. Various vertical portraits as T* **51**. *P* 12½.

403 40 c. multicoloured .. 15 20
a. Horiz pair. Nos. 403/4 .. 30 40
404 40 c. multicoloured .. 15 20
405 75 c. multicoloured .. 25 30
a. Horiz pair. Nos. 405/6 .. 50 60
406 75 c. multicoloured .. 25 30
407 $1.10, multicoloured .. 30 35
a. Horiz pair. Nos. 407/8 .. 60 70
408 $1.10, multicoloured .. 30 35
409 $1.75, multicoloured .. 45 55
a. Horiz pair. Nos. 409/10 .. 90 1·10
410 $1.75, multicoloured .. 45 55
403/10 .. *Set of* 8 2·25 2·50
MS411 85×114 mm. $2 multicoloured; $2 multicoloured .. 1·00 1·75

The two designs of each value were issued, *se-tenant*, in horizontal pairs within the sheets.

Each *se-tenant* pair shows a floral pattern across the bottom of the portraits which stops short of the left-hand edge on the left-hand stamp and of the right-hand edge on the right-hand stamp.

Designs as Nos. 403/4 and 407/8, but with face values of $4×2 and $5×2, also exist in additional miniature sheets from a restricted printing issued 19 December 1985.

(Des J.W. (35 c.), T. Hadler (others). Litho Format)

1985 (16 Sept). *Leaders of the World. Railway Locomotives* (5*th series*). *Horiz designs as T* **40**, *the first in each pair showing technical drawings and the second the locomotive at work. P* 12½.

412 35 c. multicoloured .. 20 25
a. Vert pair. Nos. 412/13 .. 40 50
413 35 c. multicoloured .. 20 25
414 70 c. multicoloured .. 35 40
a. Vert pair. Nos. 414/15 .. 70 80
415 70 c. multicoloured .. 35 40
416 $1.20, multicoloured .. 55 65
a. Vert pair. Nos. 416/17 .. 1·10 1·25
417 $1.20, multicoloured .. 55 65
418 $2 multicoloured .. 75 80
a. Vert pair. Nos. 418/19 .. 1·50 1·60
419 $2 multicoloured .. 75 80
412/19 .. *Set of* 8 3·25 3·75

Designs:—Nos. 412/13, *Coronation*, Great Britain (1937); 414/15, Class "E18", Germany (1935); 416/17, "Hayes" type, U.S.A. (1854), 418/19, Class "2120", Japan (1890).

Nos. 412/19 were issued in a similar sheet format to Nos. 271/86.

1985 (27 Oct). *Royal Visit. Nos.* 199/200, 222, 287, 398 *and* 407/8 *optd as T* **114** *of Montserrat or surch also.*

420 **50** 30 c. multicoloured .. 2·50 2·00
421 **41** 45 c. multicoloured .. 3·00 2·50
422 – $1.10, multicoloured (No. 407) .. 4·50 4·00
a. Horiz pair. Nos. 422/3 .. 9·00 8·00
423 – $1.10, multicoloured (No. 408) .. 4·50 4·00
424 – $1.50 on $3.50, mult (No. 199) 3·00 3·00
a. Sheetlet. No. 424×6 and No. 425 .. 25·00
425 – $1.50 on $3.50, mult (No. 200) 9·00 9·00
426 – $3 multicoloured (No. 222) .. 5·50 5·00
420/6 .. *Set of* 7 28·00 26·00

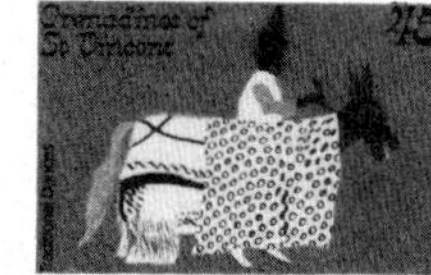

52 Donkey Man

(Des Jennifer Toombs. Litho Format)

1985 (16 Dec). *Traditional Dances. T* **52** *and similar multi-coloured designs. P* 15.

427 45 c. Type **52** .. 25 30
428 75 c. Cake Dance (*vert*) .. 35 40
429 $1 Bois-Bois Man (*vert*) .. 50 55
430 $2 Maypole Dance .. 1·00 1·10
427/30 .. *Set of* 4 1·90 2·10

(Des Artists International (15 c.), J.W. ($3), G. Turner (others). Litho Format)

1986 (20 Feb). *Leaders of the World. Automobiles* (3rd series). *Horiz designs as T* **45**, *the first in each pair showing technical drawings and the second paintings. P* 12½.

431 15 c. black, pale rose-lilac and dull mauve .. 10 10
a. Vert pair. Nos. 431/2 .. 20 20
432 15 c. multicoloured .. 10 10
433 45 c. black, pale yellow and light brown .. 25 30
a. Vert pair. Nos. 433/4 .. 50 60
434 45 c. multicoloured .. 25 30
435 60 c. black, pale green and turquoise-blue .. 25 30
a. Vert pair. Nos. 435/6 .. 50 60
436 60 c. multicoloured .. 25 30
437 $1 black, pale cinnamon and sage-green .. 35 40
a. Vert pair. Nos. 437/8 .. 70 80
438 $1 multicoloured .. 35 40
439 $1.75, black, pale yellow and pale orange .. 50 60
a. Vert pair. Nos. 439/40 .. 1·00 1·10
440 $1.75, multicoloured .. 50 60
441 $3 multicoloured .. 75 80
a. Vert pair. Nos. 441/2 .. 1·50 1·60
442 $3 multicoloured .. 75 80
431/42 .. *Set of* 12 4·00 4·50

Designs:—Nos. 431/2, Mercedes-Benz 4.5 litre (1914); 433/4, Rolls Royce "Silver Wraith" (1954); 435/6, Lamborghini "Countach" (1974); 437/8, Marmon "V-16" (1932): 439/40, Lotus-Ford "49 B" (1968); 441/2, Delage 1.5 litre (1927).

Nos. 431/42 were issued in a similar sheet format to Nos. 339/46.

(Des T. Hadler (15 c., $3), J.W. (others). Litho Format)

1986 (14 Mar). *Leaders of the World. Railway Locomotives* (6*th series*). *Horiz designs as T* **40**, *the first in each pair showing technical drawings and the second the locomotive at work. P* 12½.

443 15 c. multicoloured .. 10 10
a. Vert pair. Nos. 443/4 .. 15 20
444 15 c. multicoloured .. 10 10
445 45 c. multicoloured .. 25 30
a. Vert pair. Nos. 445/6 .. 50 60
446 45 c. multicoloured .. 25 30
447 60 c. multicoloured .. 30 35
a. Vert pair. Nos. 447/8 .. 60 70
448 60 c. multicoloured .. 30 35
449 75 c. multicoloured .. 35 40
a. Vert pair. Nos. 449/50 .. 70 80
450 75 c. multicoloured .. 35 40
451 $1 multicoloured .. 40 50
a. Vert pair. Nos. 451/2 .. 80 1·00
452 $1 multicoloured .. 40 50
453 $1.50, multicoloured .. 55 70
a. Vert pair. Nos. 453/4 .. 1·10 1·40
454 $1.50, multicoloured .. 55 70
455 $2 multicoloured .. 65 75
a. Vert pair. Nos. 455/6 .. 1·25 1·50
456 $2 multicoloured .. 65 75
457 $3 multicoloured .. 80 1·00
a. Vert pair. Nos. 457/8 .. 1·60 2·00
458 $3 multicoloured .. 80 1·00
443/58 .. *Set of* 16 6·00 7·50

Designs:—Nos. 443/4, Class "T15", Germany (1897); 445/6, Class "13", Great Britain (1900); 447/8, *Halesworth*, Great Britain (1879); 449/50, Class "Problem", Great Britain (1859); 451/2, Class "Western" diesel, Great Britain (1961); 453/4, Drummond's "Bug", Great Britain (1899); 455/6, Class "Clan", Great Britain (1951); 457/8, Class "1800", Japan (1884).

Nos. 443/58 were issued in a similar sheet format to Nos. 271/86.

(Des Court House Studio. Litho Format)

1986 (21 Apr). 60*th Birthday of Queen Elizabeth II. Multicoloured designs as T* **117a** *of Montserrat. P* 12½.

459 5 c. Queen Elizabeth II .. 10 10
460 $1 At Princess Anne's christening, 1950 .. 40 45
461 $4 Princess Elizabeth .. 1·25 1·50
462 $6 In Canberra, 1982 (*vert*) .. 2·00 2·50
459/62 .. *Set of* 4 3·25 4·25
MS463 85×115 mm. $8 Queen Elizabeth II (*different*) .. 3·25 3·75

53 Handmade Dolls

(Des G. Drummond. Litho Format)

1986 (22 Apr). *Handicrafts. T* **53** *and similar horiz designs. Multicoloured. W w* **15**. *P* 15.

464 10 c. Type **53** .. 10 10
465 60 c. Basketwork .. 35 35
466 $1 Scrimshaw work .. 55 55
467 $3 Model boat .. 1·60 1·60
464/7 .. *Set of* 4 2·40 2·40

54 Uruguayan Team

(Des Court House Studio. Litho Format)

1986 (7 May). *World Cup Football Championship, Mexico. T* **54** *and similar multicoloured designs. P* 12½ (1 c., 10 c., $4, $5) *or* 15 (*others*).

468 1 c. Type **54** .. 10 10
469 10 c. Polish team .. 10 10
470 45 c. Bulgarian player (28×42 *mm*) .. 25 30
471 75 c. Iraqi player (28×42 *mm*) .. 35 40
472 $1.50, South Korean player (28×42 *mm*) .. 75 80
473 $2 Northern Irish player (28×42 *mm*) .. 1·00 1·10
474 $4 Portuguese team .. 2·00 2·10
475 $5 Canadian team .. 2·50 2·75
468/75 .. *Set of* 8 6·25 6·75
MS476 Two sheets, 85×114 mm. (a) $1 As No. 474: (b) $3 Type **54**. P 12½ *Set of* 2 *sheets* 1·50 2·25

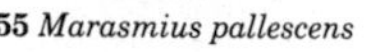

55 *Marasmius pallescens*

56 *Brachymesia furcata*

(Des G. Drummond. Litho Questa)

1986 (23 May). *Fungi. T* **55** *and similar vert designs. Multicoloured. W w* **15** *(sideways). P* 14.
477 45 c. Type **55** .. .. 1·00 55
478 60 c. *Leucocoprinus fragilissimus* .. .. 1·25 70
479 75 c. *Hygrocybe occidentalis* .. .. .. 1·50 85
480 $3 *Xerocomus hypoxanthus* .. .. 4·00 3·00
477/80 .. .. *Set of* 4 7·00 4·75

(Des Court House Studio. Litho Format)

1986 (18 July–15 Oct). *Royal Wedding (1st issue). Multicoloured designs as T* **118***a of Montserrat. P* 12½.
481 60 c. Miss Sarah Ferguson and Princess Diana applauding 30 35
a. Pair. Nos. 481/2 .. .. 60 70
482 60 c. Prince Andrew at shooting match .. 30 35
483 $2 Prince Andrew and Miss Sarah Ferguson (*horiz*) 1.00 1.10
a. Pair. Nos. 483/4 .. .. 2.00 2.25
484 $2 Prince Charles, Prince Andrew, Princess Anne and Princess Margaret on balcony (*horiz*) .. .. 1·00 1·10
481/4 .. .. *Set of* 4 2·40 2·50
MS485 115×85 mm. $8 Duke and Duchess of York in carriage after wedding (*horiz*) (15.10.86) 3·00 3·50

Nos. 481/2 and 483/4 were each printed together, *se-tenant*, in horizontal and vertical pairs throughout the sheets.

1986 (15 Oct). *Royal Wedding (2nd issue). Nos.* 481/4 *optd as T* **121** *of Montserrat in silver.*
486 60 c. Miss Sarah Ferguson and Princess Diana applauding 30 35
a. Pair. Nos. 486/7 .. .. 60 70
487 60 c. Prince Andrew at shooting match .. 30 35
488 $2 Prince Andrew and Miss Sarah Ferguson (*horiz*) .. .. 1·00 1·10
a. Pair. Nos. 488/9 .. .. 2·00 2·25
489 $2 Prince Charles, Prince Andrew, Princess Anne and Princess Margaret on balcony (*horiz*) .. .. 1·00 1·10
486/9 .. .. *Set of* 4 2·40 2·50

(Des M. Hillier. Litho Format)

1986 (19 Nov). *Dragonflies. T* **56** *and similar multicoloured designs. P* 15.
490 45 c. Type **56** 30 30
491 60 c. *Lepthemis vesiculosa* 35 35
492 75 c. *Perithemis domitta* 40 40
493 $2.50, *Tramea abdominalis* (*vert*) .. .. 1·40 1·40
490/3 .. .. *Set of* 4 2·25 2·25

(Des Court House Studio. Litho Format)

1986 (26 Nov). *Centenary of Statue of Liberty. Vert views of Statue as T* **121***a of Montserrat in separate miniature sheets. Multicoloured. P* 14×13½.
MS494 Nine sheets, each 85×115 mm. $1.50; $1.75; $2; $2.50; $3; $3.50; $5; $6; $8
Set of 9 *sheets* 15·00 18·00

57 American Kestrel

58 Santa playing Steel Band Drums

(Des Toni Lance. Litho Questa)

1986 (26 Nov). *Birds of Prey. T* **57** *and similar vert designs. Multicoloured. P* 14.
495 10 c. Type **57** 30 15
496 45 c. Common Black Hawk 75 45
497 60 c. Peregrine Falcon .. .. 1·00 55
498 $4 Osprey .. .. 3·75 4·00
495/8 .. .. *Set of* 4 5·25 4·75

(Des Court House Studio. Litho Questa)

1986 (26 Nov). *Christmas. T* **58** *and similar vert designs. Multicoloured. P* 14.
499 45 c. Type **58** 25 30
500 60 c. Santa windsurfing 30 35
501 $1.25, Santa skiing 60 65
502 $2 Santa limbo dancing .. .. 1·00 1·10
499/502 .. .. *Set of* 4 1·90 2·10
MS503 166×128 mm. Nos. 499/502 .. .. 5·50 6·00

(Litho Format)

1987 (5 May). *Railway Locomotives (7th series). Horiz designs, as T* **40**, *the first in each pair showing technical drawings and the second the locomotive at work. Multicoloured. P* 12½.
504 10 c. multicoloured 10 10
a. Vert pair. Nos. 504/5 .. .. 10 10
505 10 c. multicoloured 10 10
506 40 c. multicoloured 20 25
a. Vert pair. Nos. 506/7 .. .. 40 50
507 40 c. multicoloured 20 25
508 50 c. multicoloured 25 30
a. Vert pair. Nos. 508/9 .. .. 50 60
509 50 c. multicoloured 25 30
510 60 c. multicoloured 25 30
a. Vert pair. Nos. 510/11 .. .. 50 60
511 60 c. multicoloured 25 30
512 75 c. multicoloured 35 40
a. Vert pair. Nos. 512/13 .. .. 70 80
513 75 c. multicoloured 35 40
514 $1 multicoloured 45 50
a. Vert pair. Nos. 514/15 .. .. 90 1·00
515 $1 multicoloured 45 50
516 $1.25, multicoloured 55 60
a. Vert pair. Nos. 516/17 .. .. 1·10 1·25
517 $1.25, multicoloured 55 60
518 $1.50, multicoloured 70 75
a. Vert pair. Nos. 518/19 .. .. 1·40 1·50
519 $1.50, multicoloured 70 75
504/19 .. .. *Set of* 16 5·00 5·75

Designs:—Nos. 504/5, Class "1001", No. 1275, Great Britain (1874); 506/7, Class "4P Garratt", Great Britain (1927); 508/9, *Papyrus*, Great Britain (1929); 510/11, Class "V1", Great Britain (1930); 512/13, Class "40" diesel, No. D200, Great Britain (1958); 514/15, Class "42 Warship" diesel, Great Britain (1958); 516/17, Class "P-69", U.S.A. (1902); 518/19, Class "60-3 Shay", No. 15, U.S.A. (1913).

Nos. 504/19 were issued in a similar sheet format to Nos. 271/86.

(Litho Format)

1987 (26 Aug). *Railway Locomotives (8th series). Horiz designs as T* **40**, *the first in each pair showing technical drawings and the second the locomotive at work. P* 12½.
520 10 c. multicoloured 10 10
a. Vert pair. Nos. 520/1 .. .. 10 15
521 10 c. multicoloured 10 10
522 40 c. multicoloured 20 25
a. Vert pair. Nos. 522/3 .. .. 40 50
523 40 c. multicoloured 20 25
524 50 c. multicoloured 25 30
a. Vert pair. Nos. 524/5 .. .. 50 60
525 50 c. multicoloured 25 30
526 60 c. multicoloured 25 30
a. Vert pair. Nos. 526/7 .. .. 50 60
527 60 c. multicoloured 25 30
528 75 c. multicoloured 35 40
a. Vert pair. Nos. 528/9 .. .. 70 80
529 75 c. multicoloured 35 40
530 $1 multicoloured 45 50
a. Vert pair. Nos. 530/1 .. .. 90 1·00
531 $1 multicoloured 45 50
532 $1.50, multicoloured 70 75
a. Vert pair. Nos. 532/3 .. .. 1·40 1·50
533 $1.50, multicoloured 70 75
534 $2 multicoloured 90 95
a. Vert pair. Nos. 534/5 .. .. 1·75 1·90
535 $2 multicoloured 90 95
520/35 .. .. *Set of* 16 5·75 6·25

Designs:—Nos. 520/1, Class "142", East Germany (1977); 522/3, Class "120", West Germany (1979); 524/5, Class "X", Australia (1954); 526/7, Class "59", Great Britain (1986); 528/9, New York Elevated Railroad *Spuyten Duyvel*, U.S.A. (1875); 530/1, Camden & Amboy Railroad *Stevens* (later *John Bull*), U.S.A. (1831); 532/3, "Royal Hudson" Class "H1-d", No. 2850, Canada (1938), 534/5, "Pioneer Zephyr" 3-car set, U.S.A. (1934).

Nos. 520/35 were issued in a similar sheet format to Nos. 271/86.

59 Queen Elizabeth with Prince Andrew

60 Banded Coral Shrimp

(Litho Format)

1987 (15 Oct). *Royal Ruby Wedding and 150th Anniv of Queen Victoria's Accession. T* **59** *and similar vert designs. P* 12½.
536 15 c. multicoloured 15 15
537 45 c. deep chocolate, black & greenish yellow 30 30
538 $1.50, multicoloured 90 90
539 $3 multicoloured .. .. 1·75 1·75
540 $4 multicoloured .. .. 2·00 2·00
536/40 .. .. *Set of* 5 4·50 4·50
MS541 85×115 mm. $6 multicoloured .. .. 3·00 3·25

Designs:—45 c. Queen Victoria and Prince Albert, *c* 1855; $1.50, Queen and Prince Philip after Trooping the Colour, 1977; $3 Queen and Duke of Edinburgh, 1953; $4 Queen in her study, *c* 1980; $6 Princess Elizabeth, 1947.

(Litho Format)

1987 (17 Dec). *Marine Life. T* **60** *and similar horiz designs. Multicoloured. P* 15.
542 45 c. Type **60** 45 45
543 50 c. Arrow Crab and Flamingo Tongue .. 50 50
544 65 c. Cardinal Fish 70 70
545 $5 Moray Eel .. .. 4·00 4·00
542/5 .. .. *Set of* 4 5·00 5·00
MS546 85×115 mm. $5 Puffer Fish .. .. 3·50 4·00

MINIMUM PRICE

The minimum price quote is 10p which represents a handling charge rather than a basis for valuing common stamps. For further notes about prices see introductory pages.

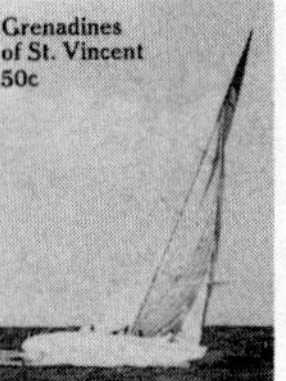

61 *Australia IV*

62 Seine-fishing Boats racing

(Litho Format)

1988 (31 Mar). *Ocean Racing Yachts. T* **61** *and similar vert designs. Multicoloured. P* 12½.
547 50 c. Type **61** 50 50
548 65 c. *Crusader II* 60 60
549 75 c. *New Zealand K27* 75 75
550 $2 *Italia* .. .. 1·50 1·50
551 $4 *White Crusader* .. .. 2·50 2·50
552 $5 *Stars and Stripes* .. .. 3·00 3·00
547/52 .. .. *Set of* 6 8·00 8·00
MS553 100 × 140 mm. $1 *Champosa V* .. 90 1·00

(Litho Format)

1988 (31 Mar). *Bequia Regatta. T* **62** *and similar horiz designs. Multicoloured. P* 15.
554 5 c. Type **62** 10 10
555 50 c. *Friendship Rose* (motor fishing boat) .. 20 25
556 75 c. Fishing boats racing 30 35
557 $3.50, Yachts racing .. .. 1·50 1·60
554/7 .. .. *Set of* 4 1·90 2·00
MS558 115 × 85 mm. $8 Port Elizabeth, Bequia (60 × 40 *mm*). P 12½ .. .. 3·75 4·50

63 "Twin-Otter" making Night Approach

(Litho Format)

1988 (26 May). *Mustique Airways. T* **63** *and similar multicoloured designs. P* 14 × 13½.
559 15 c. Type **63** 10 10
560 65 c. Beech "Baron" aircraft in flight .. 30 35
561 75 c. "Twin-Otter" over forest 30 35
562 $5 Beech "Baron" on airstrip .. .. 2·10 2·25
559/62 .. .. *Set of* 4 2·50 2·75
MS563 115 × 85 mm. $10 Baleine Falls (36 × 56 *mm*). P 12½ .. .. 4·75 5·50

64 *Sv. Petr* in Arctic (Bering)

65 Asif Iqbal Razvi

(Litho Format)

1988 (29 July). *Explorers. T* **64** *and similar square designs. Multicoloured. P* 14 × 13½.
564 15 c. Type **64** 10 10
565 75 c. Bering's ships in pack ice 30 35
566 $1 Livingstone's steam launch *Ma-Robert* on Zambesi 45 50
567 $2 Meeting of Livingstone and H. M. Stanley at Ujiji 80 85
568 $3 Speke and Burton at Tabori .. .. 1·25 1·40
569 $3.50, Speke and Burton in canoe on Lake Victoria .. .. 1·50 1·60
570 $4 Sighting the New World, 1492 .. 1·60 1·75
571 $4.50, Columbus trading with Indians .. 2·00 2·10
563/71 .. .. *Set of* 8 7·25 7·75
MS572 Two sheets, each 115 × 85 mm. (a) $5 Sextant and coastal scene. (b) $5 *Santa Maria* at anchor. P 13½ × 14 .. .. *Set of* 2 *sheets* 4·25 4·50

An unissued $6 miniature sheet, showing the *Santa Maria*, exists from stock dispersed by the liquidator of Format International Security Printers Ltd.

(Litho Format)

1988 (29 July). *Cricketers of* 1988 *International Season. T* **65** *and similar multicoloured designs. P* 15.
573 20 c. Type **65** 30 30
574 45 c. R. J. Hadlee 50 50
575 75 c. M. D. Crowe 70 70
576 $1.25, C. H. Lloyd .. .. 1·00 1·00
577 $1.50, A. R. Boarder .. .. 1·25 1·25
578 $2 M. D. Marshall .. .. 1·75 1·75
579 $2.50, G. A. Hick .. .. 2·00 2·00
580 $3.50, C. G. Greenidge (*horiz*) .. .. 2·50 2·50
573/80 .. .. *Set of* 8 9·00 9·00
MS581 115 × 85 mm. $3 As $2 .. .. .. 4·00 4·00

66 Pam Shriver

(Litho Format)

1988 (29 July). *International Tennis Players. T* **66** *and similar multicoloured designs. P* 12½.

582 15 c. Type **66** 10 10
583 50 c. Kevin Curran (*vert*) 20 25
584 75 c. Wendy Turnbull (*vert*) 30 35
585 $1 Evonne Cawley (*vert*) 45 50
586 $1.50, Ilie Nastase 60 65
587 $2 Billie Jean King (*vert*) 80 85
588 $3 Bjorn Borg (*vert*) .. .. .. 1·25 1·40
589 $3.50, Virginia Wade with Wimbledon trophy (*vert*) .. .. 1·50 1·60
582/9 .. .. *Set of* 8 4·75 5·25
MS590 115 × 85 mm. $2.25, Stefan Edberg with Wimbledon cup; $2.25, Steffi Graf with Wimbledon trophy .. .. 3·00 3·25

No. 584 is inscribed "WENDY TURNBALL" in error.

Examples of an unissued set of six values and a miniature sheet for the 1988 Olympic Games at Seoul exist from stock dispersed by the liquidator of Format International Security Printers Ltd.

67 Mickey and Minnie Mouse visiting Fatehpur Sikri

(Des Walt Disney Co. Litho Questa)

1989 (7 Feb). *"India-89" International Stamp Exhibition, New Delhi. T* **67** *and similar multicoloured designs showing Walt Disney cartoon characters in India. P* 14×13½.

591 1 c. Type **67** 10 10
592 2 c. Mickey and Minnie Mouse aboard "Palace on Wheels" train 10 10
593 3 c. Mickey and Minnie Mouse passing Old Fort, Delhi 10 10
594 5 c. Mickey and Minnie Mouse on camel, Pinjore Gardens, Haryana 10 10
595 10 c. Mickey and Minnie Mouse at Taj Mahal, Agra 10 10
596 25 c. Mickey and Minnie Mouse in Chandni Chowk, Old Delhi 10 10
597 $4 Goofy on elephant with Mickey and Minnie Mouse at Agra Fort, Jaipur .. 1·60 1·75
598 $5 Goofy, Mickey and Minnie Mouse at Gandhi Memorial, Cape Comorin .. 2·10 2·25
591/8 .. .. *Set of* 8 3·75 4·00
MS599 Two sheets, each 127 × 102 mm. (a) $6 Mickey and Minnie Mouse in vegetable cart, Jaipur. P 14 × 13½. (b) $6 Mickey and Minnie Mouse leaving carriage, Qutab Minar, New Delhi (*vert*). P 13½ × 14 .. *Set of 2 sheets* 5·00 5·50

(Litho Questa)

1989 (6 July). *Japanese Art. Horiz designs as T* **187a** *of Lesotho. Multicoloured. P* 14×13½.

600 5 c. "The View at Yotsuya" (Hokusai) .. 10 10
601 30 c. "Landscape at Ochanomizu" (Hokuju) 10 15
602 45 c. "Itabashi" (Eisen) 20 25
603 65 c. "Early Summer Rain" (Kunisada) .. 25 30
604 75 c. "High Noon at Kasumigaseki" (Kuniyoshi) 30 35
605 $1 "The Yoshiwara Embankment by Moonlight" (Kuniyoshi) 40 45
606 $4 "The Bridge of Boats at Sano" (Hokusai) .. .. 1·75 1·90
607 $5 "Lingering Snow on Mount Hira" (Kunitora) .. .. 2·10 2·25
600/7 .. .. *Set of* 8 4·75 5·25
MS608 Two sheets, each 103×76 mm. (a) $6 "Colossus of Rhodes" (Kunitora). (b) $6 "Shinobazu Pond" (Kokan) .. *Set of 2 sheets* 5·00 5·25

Nos. 600/7 were each printed in sheetlets of 10 containing two horizontal strips of 5 stamps separated by printed labels commemorating Emperor Hirohito.

68 Player with Ball and Mt Vesuvius **69** Arawak smoking Tobacco

(Des J. Genzo. Litho B.D.T.)

1989 (10 July). *World Cup Football Championship, Italy (1st issue). T* **68** *and similar vert designs each showing players and Italian landmarks. Multicoloured. P* 14.

609 $1.50, Type **68** 65 70
a. Sheetlet. Nos. 609/16 .. .. .. 4·75
610 $1.50, Fallen player, opponent kicking ball and Coliseum 65 70
611 $1.50, Player blocking ball and Venice .. 65 70
612 $1.50, Player tackling and Forum, Rome 65 70
613 $1.50, Two players competing for ball and Leaning Tower, Pisa 65 70
614 $1.50, Goalkeeper and Florence 65 70
615 $1.50, Two players competing for ball and St. Peter's, Vatican 65 70
616 $1.50, Player kicking ball and Pantheon 65 70
609/16 .. .. *Set of* 8 4·75 5·00

Nos. 609/16 were printed together, *se-tenant*, in a sheetlet of 8.

See also Nos. 680/4.

(Des D. Miller. Litho B.D.T.)

1989 (2 Oct). *500th Anniv of Discovery of America (1992) by Columbus. Pre-Columbian Arawak Society. T* **69** *and similar vert designs. Multicoloured. P* 14.

617 25 c. Type **69** 10 15
618 75 c. Arawak rolling cigar 30 35
619 $1 Applying body paint 40 45
620 $1.50, Making fire 65 70
a. Horiz strip of 4. Nos. 620/3 .. .. 2·50
621 $1.50, Cassava production 65 70
622 $1.50, Woman baking bread 65 70
623 $1.50, Using stone implement 65 70
624 $4 Arawak priest .. .. .. 1·75 1·90
617/24 .. .. *Set of* 8 4·75 5·00
MS625 Two sheets, each 70×84 mm. (a) $6 Arawak chief. (b) $6 Men returning from fishing expedition .. .. .. *Set of 2 sheets* 5·00 5·25

Nos. 620/4 were printed together, *se-tenant*, in horizontal strips of 4 throughout the sheet of 20, each strip forming a composite design.

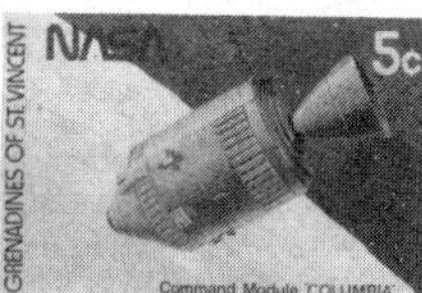
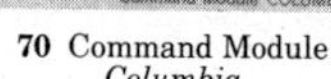

70 Command Module *Columbia* **71** *Marpesia petreus*

(Des D. Bruckner. Litho Questa)

1989 (2 Oct). *10th Anniv of First Manned Landing on Moon. T* **70** *and similar multicoloured designs. P* 14.

626 5 c. Type **70** 10 10
627 40 c. Astronaut Neil Armstrong saluting U.S. flag 15 20
628 55 c. *Columbia* above lunar surface .. 25 30
629 65 c. Lunar module *Eagle* leaving Moon .. 25 30
630 70 c. *Eagle* on Moon 30 35
631 $1 *Columbia* re-entering Earth's atmosphere 40 45
632 $3 "Apollo 11" emblem .. .. .. 1·25 1·40
633 $5 Armstrong and Aldrin on Moon .. 2·10 2·25
626/33 .. .. *Set of* 8 4·25 4·75
MS634 Two sheets, each 110×82 mm. (a) $6 Launch of "Apollo 11" (*vert*). (b) $6 "Apollo 11" splashdown .. .. .. *Set of 2 sheets* 5·00 5·25

(Des D. Bruckner. Litho Questa)

1989 (16 Oct). *Butterflies. T* **71** *and similar horiz designs. Multicoloured. P* 14½.

635 5 c. Type **71** 10 10
636 30 c. *Papilio androgeus* 10 15
637 45 c. *Strymon maesites* 20 25
638 65 c. *Junonia coenia* 25 30
639 75 c. *Eurema gratiosa* 30 35
640 $1 *Hypolimnas misippus* 40 45
641 $4 *Urbanus proteus* .. .. .. 1·75 1·90
642 $5 *Junonia evarete* .. .. .. 2·10 2·25
635/42 .. .. *Set of* 8 4·75 5·25
MS643 Two sheets. (a) 76×104 mm. $6 *Phoebis agarithe*. (b) 104×76 mm. $6 *Dryas julia* *Set of 2 sheets* 5·00 5·25

72 *Solanum urens* **73** Goofy and Mickey Mouse in Rolls-Royce "Silver Ghost", 1907

(Des Mary Walters. Litho Questa)

1989 (1 Nov). *Flowers from St. Vincent Botanical Gardens. T* **72** *and similar vert designs. Multicoloured. P* 14.

644 80 c. Type **72** 35 40
645 $1.25, *Passiflora andersonii* 50 55
646 $1.65, *Miconia andersonii* 70 75
647 $1.85, *Pitcairnia sulphurea* 80 85
644/7 .. .. *Set of* 4 2·10 2·25

(Des Walt Disney Co. Litho Questa)

1989 (20 Dec). *Christmas. T* **73** *and similar horiz designs showing Walt Disney cartoon characters and cars. Multicoloured. P* 14×13½.

648 5 c. Type **73** 10 10
649 10 c. Daisy Duck driving first Stanley Steamer, 1897 .. .. 10 10
650 15 c. Horace Horsecollar and Clarabelle Cow in Darracq "Genevieve", 1904 .. 10 10
651 45 c. Donald Duck driving Detroit electric coupe, 1914 .. .. 20 25
652 55 c. Mickey and Minnie Mouse in first Ford, 1896 .. .. 25 30
653 $2 Mickey Mouse driving Reo "Runabout", 1904 .. .. 85 90
654 $3 Goofy driving Winton mail truck, 1899 1·25 1·40
655 $5 Mickey and Minnie Mouse in Duryea car, 1893 .. .. 2·10 2·25
648/55 .. .. *Set of* 8 4·25 4·75
MS656 Two sheets, each 127×102 mm. (a) $6 Mickey and Minnie Mouse in Pope-Hartford, 1912. (b) $6 Mickey and Minnie Mouse in Buick "Model 10", 1908. P 13½×14 .. *Set of 2 sheets* 5·00 5·25

(Des W. Wright. Litho Questa)

1990 (2 Apr). *50th Anniv of Second World War. Horiz designs as T* **242** *of Maldive Islands. Multicoloured. P* 14.

657 10 c. Destroyers in action, First Battle of Narvik, 1940 .. .. 10 10
658 15 c. Allied tank at Anzio, 1944 .. .. 10 10
659 20 c. U.S. carrier under attack, Battle of Midway, 1942 .. .. 10 10
660 45 c. U.S. bombers over Gustav Line, 1944 20 25
661 55 c. Map showing Allied zones of Berlin, 1945 .. .. 25 30
662 65 c. German U-boat pursuing convoy, Battle of the Atlantic, 1943 .. .. 25 30
663 90 c. Allied tank, North Africa, 1943 .. 40 45
664 $3 U.S. forces landing on Guam, 1944 .. 1·25 1·40
665 $5 Crossing the Rhine, 1945 .. .. 2·10 2·25
666 $6 Japanese battleships under attack, Leyte Gulf, 1944 .. .. .. 2·50 2·75
657/66 .. .. *Set of* 10 6·50 7·00
MS667 100×70 mm. $6 Lancaster on "Dam-busters" raid, 1943 .. .. 2·50 2·75

(Des Walt Disney Co. Litho Questa)

1990 (3 May). *"Stamp World London 90" International Stamp Exhibition (1st issue). Mickey's Shakespeare Company. Multicoloured designs as T* **239a** *of Maldive Islands showing Walt Disney cartoon characters. P* 14×13½.

668 20 c. Goofy as Mark Anthony (*Julius Caesar*) 10 10
669 30 c. Clarabelle Cow as the Nurse (*Romeo and Juliet*) 10 15
670 45 c. Pete as Falstaff (*Henry IV*) 20 25
671 50 c. Minnie Mouse as Portia (*The Merchant of Venice*) 20 25
672 $1 Donald Duck as Hamlet (*Hamlet*) .. 40 45
673 $2 Daisy Duck as Ophelia (*Hamlet*) .. 85 90
674 $4 Donald and Daisy Duck as Benedick and Beatrice (*Much Ado About Nothing*) .. .. 1·75 1·90
675 $5 Minnie Mouse and Donald Duck as Katherine and Petruchio (*The Taming of the Shrew*) .. .. 2·10 2·25
668/75 .. .. *Set of* 8 5·25 5·75
MS676 Two sheets, each 127×101 mm. (a) $6 Clarabelle as Titania (*A Midsummer Night's Dream*) (*vert*). (b) $6 Mickey Mouse as Romeo (*Romeo and Juliet*) (*vert*). P 13½×14 *Set of 2 sheets* 5·00 5·25

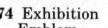

74 Exhibition Emblem **75** Scaly-breasted Ground Dove

(Des M. Pollard. Litho B.D.T.)

1990 (3 May). *"Stamp World London 90" International Stamp Exhibition (2nd issue). 150th Anniv of Penny Black. T* **74** *and similar vert designs. P* 14×15.

677 $1 black, brown-rose and magenta .. 40 45
678 $5 black, grey-lilac and ultramarine .. 2·10 2·25
MS679 130×100 mm. $6 black and pale blue .. 2·50 2·75

Designs:—$5 Negative image of Penny Black; $6 Penny Black.

(Des Young Phillips Studio. Litho Questa)

1990 (24 Sept). *World Cup Football Championship, Italy (2nd issue). Multicoloured designs as T* **210** *of St. Vincent, but horiz. P* 14.

680 25 c. McCleish, Scotland 10 15
681 50 c. Rasul, Egypt 20 25
682 $2 Lindenberger, Austria 85 90
683 $4 Murray, U.S.A. .. .. .. 1·75 1·90
680/3 .. .. *Set of* 4 2·50 3·00
MS684 Two sheets, each 102×77 mm. (a) $6 Robson, England. (b) $6 Gullit, Netherlands *Set of 2 sheets* 5·00 5·25

(Litho B.D.T.)

1990 (23 Nov). *"EXPO 90" International Garden and Greenery Exposition, Osaka. Orchids. Vert designs as T* **213** *of St. Vincent. Multicoloured. P* 14.
685 5 c. *Paphiopedilum* 10 10
686 25 c. *Dendrobium phalaenopsis* and *Cymbidium hybrid* 10 15
687 30 c. *Miltonia candida hybrid* 10 15
688 50 c. *Epidendrum ibaguense* and *Cymbidium* Elliot Rogers 20 25
689 $1 *Rossioglossum grande* 40 45
690 $2 *Phalaenopsis* Elisa Chamg Lou and *Masdevallia coccinea* 85 90
691 $4 *Cypripedium acaule* and *Cypripedium calceolus* . . . . 1·75 1·90
692 $5 *Orchis spectabilis* . . . . . . 2·10 2·25
685/92 . . . . . . *Set of* 8 5·00 5·50
MS693 Two sheets, each 108×78 mm. (a) $6 *Dendrobium anosmum.* (b) $6 *Epidendrum ibaguense* and *Phalaenopsis* . . *Set of* 2 *sheets* 5·00 5·25

(Des W. Wright. Litho B.D.T.)

1990 (26 Nov). *Birds of the Caribbean. T* **75** *and similar horiz designs. Multicoloured. P* 14.
694 5 c. Type **75** 10 10
695 25 c. Purple Martin 10 15
696 45 c. Painted Bunting 20 25
697 55 c. Blue-hooded Euphonia 25 30
698 75 c. Blue-grey Tanager 30 35
699 $1 Red-eyed Vireo 40 45
700 $2 Palm Chat 85 90
701 $3 Northern Jacana . . . . . . 1·25 1·40
702 $4 Green-throated Carib . . . . 1·75 1·90
703 $5 St. Vincent Amazon . . . . 2·10 2·25
694/703 . . . . . . *Set of* 10 6·50 7·25
MS704 Two sheets, each 117×87 mm. (a) $3 Magnificent Frigate Bird; $3 Bananaquit. (b) $6 Red-legged Honeycreeper . . *Set of* 2 *sheets* 5·00 5·25

(Des Young Phillips Studio. Litho B.D.T.)

1991 (14 Feb). *90th Birthday of Queen Elizabeth the Queen Mother. Vert designs as T* **198a** *of Lesotho. P* 14.
705 $2 multicoloured 85 90
a. Sheetlet. Nos. 705/13 . . . . 7·75
706 $2 multicoloured 85 90
707 $2 multicoloured 85 90
708 $2 multicoloured 85 90
709 $2 multicoloured 85 90
710 $2 multicoloured 85 90
711 $2 multicoloured 85 90
712 $2 multicoloured 85 90
713 $2 multicoloured 85 90
714 $2 multicoloured 85 90
a. Sheetlet. Nos. 714/22 . . . . 7·75
715 $2 multicoloured 85 90
716 $2 multicoloured 85 90
717 $2 black and rose-lilac 85 90
718 $2 black and rose-lilac 85 90
719 $2 black, pale yellow-olive and rose-lilac 85 90
720 $2 multicoloured 85 90
721 $2 black and rose-lilac 85 90
722 $2 multicoloured 85 90
723 $2 multicoloured 85 90
a. Sheetlet. Nos. 723/31 . . . . 7·75
724 $2 multicoloured 85 90
725 $2 multicoloured 85 90
726 $2 multicoloured 85 90
727 $2 multicoloured 85 90
728 $2 multicoloured 85 90
729 $2 multicoloured 85 90
730 $2 multicoloured 85 90
731 $2 multicoloured 85 90
705/31 . . . . . . *Set of* 27 21·00 22·00
MS732 Nine sheets containing details of designs indicated. (a) 120×115 mm. $5 As No. 705. (b) 115×120 mm. $5 As No. 710. (c) 115×120 mm. $5 As No. 712. (d) 115×120 mm. $5 As No. 715. (e) 120×115 mm. $5 As No. 719. (f) 120×115 mm. $5 As No. 720. (g) 120×115 mm. $5 As No. 724. (h) 120×115 mm. $5 As No. 726. (i) 120×115 mm. $5 As No. 730 . . *Set of* 9 *sheets* 19·00 20·00

Designs:—No. 705, Lady Elizabeth Bowes-Lyon with brother; No. 706, Young Lady Elizabeth in long dress; No. 707, Young Lady Elizabeth wearing a hat; No. 708, Lady Elizabeth leaning on wall; No. 709, Lady Elizabeth on pony; No. 710, Studio Portrait; No. 711, Lady Elizabeth in evening dress; No. 712, Duchess of York in fur-lined cloak; No. 713, Duchess of York holding rose; No. 714, Coronation, 1937; No. 715, King and Queen with Princess Elizabeth at Royal Lodge, Windsor; No. 716, Queen Elizabeth in blue hat; No. 717, King George VI and Queen Elizabeth; No. 718, Queen Elizabeth with Princess Elizabeth; No. 719, Queen Elizabeth watching sporting fixture; No. 720, Queen Elizabeth in white evening dress; No. 721, Princess Anne's christening, 1950; No. 722, Queen Mother with yellow bouquet; No. 723, Queen Mother and policewoman; No. 724, Queen Mother at ceremonial function; No. 725, Queen Mother in pink coat; No. 726, Queen Mother in academic robes; No. 727, Queen Mother in carriage with Princess Margaret; No. 728, Queen Mother in blue coat and hat; No. 729, Queen Mother with bouquet; No. 730, Queen Mother outside Clarence House on her birthday; No. 731, Queen Mother in turquoise coat and hat.

Nos. 705/13, 714/22 and 723/31 were printed, *se-tenant,* in sheetlets of nine.

(Litho Walsall)

1991 (11 June). *Death Centenary of Vincent van Gogh (artist)* (1990). *Multicoloured designs as T* **255** *of Maldive Islands. P* 13½.
733 5 c. "View of Arles with Irises" (*horiz*) . . 10 10
734 10 c. "Saintes-Maries" 10 10
735 15 c. "Old Woman of Arles" 10 10
736 20 c. "Orchard in Blossom, bordered by Cypresses" (*horiz*) 10 10
737 25 c. "Three White Cottages in Saintes-Maries" (*horiz*) 10 10
738 35 c. "Boats at Saintes-Maries" (*horiz*) . . 15 20
739 40 c. "Interior of a Restaurant in Arles" (*horiz*) 15 20
740 45 c. "Peasant Women" 20 25
741 55 c. "Self-portrait" 20 25
742 60 c. "Pork Butcher's Shop from a Window" 25 30
743 75 c. "The Night Cafe in Arles" (*horiz*) . . 30 35
744 $1 "2nd Lieut. Millet of the Zouaves" (*horiz*) 40 45
745 $2 "The Café Terrace, Place du Forum, Arles at Night" 85 90
746 $3 "The Zouave" . . . . . . 1·25 1·50
747 $4 "The Two Lovers" (detail) . . . . 1·75 2·00
748 $5 "Still Life" (*horiz*) . . . . . . 2·10 2·25
733/48 . . . . . . *Set of* 16 7·00 8·00
MS749 Four sheets, each 112×76 mm. (a) $5 "Street in Saintes-Maries" (*horiz*). (b) $5 "Lane near Arles" (*horiz*). (c) $6 "Harvest at La Crau, with Montmajour in the Background" (*horiz*). (d) $6 "The Sower". Imperf. . . . *Set of* 4 *sheets* 9·50 9·75

(Des D. Miller. Litho Walsall)

1991 (5 July). *65th Birthday of Queen Elizabeth II. Horiz designs as T* **210** *of Lesotho. Multicoloured. P* 14.
750 15 c. Inspecting the Yeomen of the Guard . . 10 10
751 40 c. Queen Elizabeth II with the Queen Mother at the Derby, 1988 . . . . 15 20
752 $2 The Queen and Prince Philip leaving Euston, 1986 . . . . . . 85 90
753 $4 The Queen at the Commonwealth Institute, 1987 . . . . . . 1·75 1·90
750/3 . . . . . . *Set of* 4 2·50 2·75
MS754 68×90 mm. $5 Queen Elizabeth and Prince Philip with Prince Andrew in naval uniform . . . . 2·10 2·25

(Des D. Miller. Litho Walsall)

1991 (5 July). *10th Wedding Anniv of Prince and Princess of Wales. Horiz designs as T* **210** *of Lesotho. Multicoloured. P* 14.
755 10 c. Prince and Princess at polo match, 1987 . . . . 10 10
756 50 c. Separate family portraits 20 25
757 $1 Prince William and Prince Henry at Kensington Palace, 1991 . . . . 40 45
758 $5 Portraits of Prince Charles and Princess Diana . . . . . . 2·10 2·25
755/8 . . . . . . *Set of* 4 2·50 2·75
MS759 68×90 mm. $5 Separate portraits of Prince and Princess and sons . . . . 2·10 2·25

76 First Japanese Steam Locomotive and Map

(Des K. Gromell. Litho Cartor)

1991 (12 Aug). *"Philanippon '91" International Stamp Exhibition, Tokyo. Japanese Railway Locomotives. T* **76** *and similar designs, each in black, scarlet-vermilion and dull blue-green. P* 14×13½.
760 10 c. Type **76** 10 10
761 25 c. First imported American steam locomotive 10 15
762 35 c. Class "8620" steam locomotive . . 15 20
763 50 c. Class "C53" steam locomotive . . 20 25
764 $1 Class "DD-51" diesel locomotive . . 40 45
765 $2 Class "RF22327" electric rail car . . 85 90
766 $4 Class "EF55" electric locomotive . . 1·75 1·90
767 $5 Class "EF58" electric locomotive . . 2·10 2·25
760/7 . . . . . . *Set of* 8 5·00 5·50
MS768 Four sheets, each 114×73 mm showing frontal views. (a) $6 Class "9600" steam locomotive (*vert*). (b) $6 Class "C57" steam locomotive (*vert*). (c) $6 Class "C62" steam locomotive (*vert*). (d) $6 Class "4100" steam locomotive (*vert*) . . . . *Set of* 4 *sheets* 10·00 10·50

(Litho Questa)

1991 (18 Nov). *50th Death Anniv of Lord Baden-Powell and World Scout Jamboree, Korea. Multicoloured designs as T* **225** *of St. Vincent. P* 14.
769 $2 Czechoslovakia 1918 20 h. stamp and scout delivering mail (*horiz*) 85 90
770 $4 Scouts and cog train on Snowdon . . 1·75 1·90
MS771 Two sheets, each 118×89 mm. (a). $5 Jamboree emblem (buff background). (b) $5 Jamboree emblem (bluish violet background) *Set of* 2 *sheets* 4·25 4·50

(Litho Questa)

1991 (18 Nov). *Birth Centenary of Charles de Gaulle (French statesman)* (1990). *Multicoloured designs as T* **226** *of St. Vincent. P* 14.
772 60 c. General De Gaulle in Djibouti, 1959 . . 25 30
MS773 Two sheets. (a) 77×112 mm. $5 De Gaulle in civilian dress. (b) 69×101 mm. $5 General Charles de Gaulle (*vert*) *Set of* 2 *sheets* 4·25 4·50

(Litho Questa)

1991 (18 Nov). *Bicentenary of Brandenburg Gate. Horiz designs as T* **227** *of St. Vincent. Multicoloured. P* 14.
774 45 c. President Gorbachev and photo of Gate 20 25
775 65 c. "DIE MAUER MUSS WEG!" slogan 25 30
776 80 c. East German border guard escaping to West 35 40
774/6 . . . . . . *Set of* 3 75 85
MS777 Two sheets, each 100×71 mm. (a) $5 Arms of Berlin. (b) $5 Berlin police badge *Set of* 2 *sheets* 4·25 4·50

(Litho Questa)

1991 (18 Nov). *Death Bicentenary of Mozart. Multicoloured designs as T* **226** *of St. Vincent. P* 14.
778 $1 *Abduction from the Seraglio* 40 45
779 $3 Dresden, 1749 . . . . . . 1·25 1·50
MS780 Two sheets, each 75×101 mm. (a) $5 Portrait of Mozart (*vert*). (b) $5 Bust of Mozart (*vert*) . . . . . . *Set of* 2 *sheets* 4·25 4·50

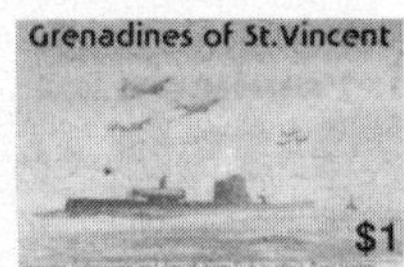

77 Japanese Aircraft and Submarines leaving Truk

(Des J. Batchelor. Litho Questa)

1991 (18 Nov). *50th Anniv of Japanese Attack on Pearl Harbor. T* **77** *and similar horiz designs. Multicoloured. P* 14½×15.
781 $1 Type **77** 40 45
a. Sheetlet. Nos. 781/90 . . . . 3·50
782 $1 *Akagi* (Japanese aircraft carrier) . . 40 45
783 $1 Nakajima B5 N2 "Kate" aircraft . . 40 45
784 $1 Torpedo bombers attacking Battleship Row 40 45
785 $1 Burning aircraft, Ford Island airfield . . 40 45
786 $1 Doris Miller winning Navy Cross . . 40 45
787 $1 U.S.S. *West Virginia* and *Tennessee* (battleships) ablaze 40 45
788 $1 U.S.S. *Arizona* (battleship) sinking . . 40 45
789 $1 U.S.S. *New Orleans* (cruiser) . . 40 45
790 $1 President Roosevelt declaring war . . 40 45
781/90 . . . . . . *Set of* 10 3·50 4·00

Nos. 781/90 were printed together, *se-tenant,* in sheetlets of 10 with the stamps arranged in two horizontal rows of 5 separated by a map of Pearl Harbor.

78 Pluto pulling Mickey Mouse in Sledge, 1974

(Des Walt Disney Co. Litho Questa)

1991 (23 Dec). *Christmas. Walt Disney Company Christmas Cards. T* **78** *and similar multicoloured designs. P* 14×13½.
791 10 c. Type **78** 10 10
792 55 c. Mickey, Pluto and Donald Duck watching toy band, 1961 . . . . 20 25
793 65 c. "The Same Old Wish", 1942 . . . . 25 30
794 75 c. Mickey, Peter Pan, Donald and Nephews with Merlin the magician, 1963 . . . . 30 35
795 $1.50, Mickey, Donald and leprechauns, 1958 . . . . 60 65
796 $2 Mickey and friends with book *Old Yeller,* 1957 . . . . . . 85 90
797 $4 Mickey controlling Pinnochio, 1953 . . 1·75 2·00
798 $5 Cinderella and Prince dancing, 1987 2·10 2·25
791/8 . . . . . . *Set of* 8 5·50 6·00
MS799 Two sheets, each 128×102 mm. (a) $6 Santa Claus and American bomber, 1942 (*vert*). (b) $6 Snow White, 1957 (*vert*). P 13½×14 *Set of* 2 *sheets* 5·00 5·25

OFFICIAL STAMPS

1982 (11 Oct). *Nos.* 195/200 *optd with Type* O 1 *of St. Vincent.*
O1 50 c. *Mary* 15 20
a. Sheetlet. No. O1 × 6 and No. O2 . . 1·10
b. Opt double . . . .
c. Albino opt . . . . . . 4·00
d. Horiz pair, one without opt . . . .
O2 50 c. Prince Charles and Lady Diana Spencer 40 45
b. Opt double . . . .
c. Albino opt . . . . . . 13·00
O3 $3 *Alexandra* 55 75
a. Sheetlet. No. O3 × 6 and No. O4 . . 4·00
b. Opt double . . . . . . 40·00
c. Albino opt . . . . . . 7·00
O4 $3 Prince Charles and Lady Diana Spencer 1·25 1·25
b. Opt double £130
c. Albino opt . . . . . . 30·00
O5 $3.50, *Britannia* . . . . . . 75 1·00
a. Sheetlet. No. O5 × 6 and No. O6 . . 5·50
c. Albino opt . . . . . . 9·00
O6 $3.50, Prince Charles and Lady Diana Spencer . . . . 1·50 1·75
c. Albino opt . . . . . . 25·00
O1/6 . . . . . . *Set of* 6 4·25 4·75

Appendix

The following issues for individual islands in the Grenadines group fall outside the criteria for full listing as detailed on page xi of the General Catalogue Information in this edition.

BEQUIA

1984

Leaders of the World. Railway Locomotives (1st series). *Two designs for each value, the first showing technical drawings and the second the locomotive at work.* 1, 5, 10, 25, 35, 45 *c.*, $1.50, $2, *each* × 2
Grenadines of St. Vincent 1982 *Ships definitives* (Nos. 208/24) *optd* "BEQUIA". 1, 3, 5, 6, 10, 15, 20, 25, 30, 50, 60, 75 *c.*, $1, $2, $3, $5, $10
Leaders of the World. Automobiles (1st series). *Two designs for each value, the first showing technical drawings and the second the car in action.* 5, 40 *c.*, $1, $1.50, *each* × 2
Leaders of the World. Olympic Games, Los Angeles. 1, 10, 60 *c.*, $3, *each* × 2
Leaders of the World. Railway Locomotives (2nd series). *Two designs for each value, the first showing technical drawings and the second the locomotive at work.* 1, 5, 10, 35, 75 *c.*, $1, $2.50, $3, *each* × 2
Leaders of the World. Automobiles (2nd series). *Two designs for each value, the first showing technical drawings and the second the car in action.* 5, 10, 20, 25, 75 *c.*, $1, $2.50, $3, *each* × 2

1985

Leaders of the World. Railway Locomotives (3rd series). *Two designs for each value, the first showing technical drawings and the second the locomotive at work.* 25, 55, 60 *c.*, $2, *each* × 2
Leaders of the World. Dogs. 25, 35, 55 *c.*, $2, *each* × 2
Leaders of the World, Warships of the Second World War. Two designs for each value, the first showing technical drawings and the second the ship at sea. 15, 50 *c.*, $1, $1.50, *each* × 2
Leaders of the World. Flowers. 10, 20, 70 *c.*, $2.50, *each* × 2
Leaders of the World. Automobiles (3rd series). *Two designs for each value, the first showing technical drawings and the second the car in action.* 5, 25, 50 *c.*, $1, $1.25, $2, *each* × 2
Leaders of the World. Railway Locomotives (4th series). *Two designs for each value, the first showing technical drawings and the second the locomotive at work.* 25, 55, 60, 75 *c.*, $1, $2.50, *each* × 2
Leaders of the World. Life and Times of Queen Elizabeth the Queen Mother. Two designs for each value, showing different portraits. 20, 65 *c.*, $1.35, $1.80, *each* × 2
Leaders of the World. Automobiles (4th series). *Two designs for each value, the first showing technical drawings and the second the car in action.* 10, 35, 75 *c.*, $1.15, $1.50, $2, *each* × 2

1986

Leaders of the World. Automobiles (5th series). *Two designs for each value, the first showing technical drawings and the second the car in action.* 25, 50, 65, 75 *c.*, $1, $3, *each* × 2
60th Birthday of Queen Elizabeth II. 5, 75 *c.*, $2, $8
World Cup Football Championship, Mexico. 1, 2, 5, 10, 45, 60, 75 *c.*, $1.50, $1.50, $2, $3.50, $6
Royal Wedding (1st issue). 60 *c.*, $2, *each* × 2
Railway Engineers and Locomotives. $1, $2.50, $3, $4
Royal Wedding (2nd issue). *Previous issue optd* "Congratulations T.R.H. The Duke & Duchess of York". 60 *c.*, $2, *each* × 2.
Automobiles (6th series). *Two designs for each value, the first showing technical drawings and the second the car in action.* 20, 60, 75, 90 *c.*, $1, $3, *each* × 2

1987

Automobiles (7th series). *Two designs for each value, the first showing technical drawings and the second the car in action.* 5, 20, 35, 60, 75, 80 *c.*, $1.25, $1.75, *each* × 2
Royal Ruby Wedding. 15, 75 *c.*, $1, $2.50, $5
Railway Locomotives (5th series). *Two designs for each value, the first showing technical drawings and the second the locomotive at work.* 15, 25, 40, 50, 60, 75 *c.*, $1, $2, *each* × 2

1988

Explorers. 15, 50 *c.*, $1.75, $2, $2.50, $3, $3.50, $4
International Lawn Tennis Players. 15, 45, 80 *c.*, $1.25, $1.75, $2, $2.50, $3

1989

"Philexfrance 89" International Stamp Exhibition, Paris. Walt Disney Cartoon Characters. 1, 2, 3, 4, 5, 10 *c.*, $5, $6

UNION ISLAND

1984

Leaders of the World. British Monarchs. Two designs for each value, forming a composite picture. 1, 5, 10, 20, 60 *c.*, $3, *each* × 2
Leaders of the World. Railway Locomotives (1st series). *Two designs for each value, the first showing technical drawings and the second the locomotive at work.* 5, 60 *c.*, $1, $2
Grenadines of St. Vincent 1982 *Ships definitives* (Nos. 208/24) *optd* "UNION ISLAND". 1, 3, 5, 6, 10, 15, 20, 25, 30, 50, 60, 75 *c.*, $1, $2, $3, $5, $10
Leaders of the World. Cricketers. Two designs for each value, the first showing a portrait and the second the cricketer in action. 1, 10, 15, 55, 60, 75 *c.*, $1.50, $3, *each* × 2
Leaders of the World. Railway Locomotives (2nd series). *Two designs for each value, the first showing technical drawings and the second the locomotive at work.* 5, 10, 20, 25, 75 *c.*, $1, $2.50, $3, *each* × 2

1985

Leaders of the World. Automobiles (1st series). *Two designs for each value, the first showing technical drawings and the second the car in action.* 1, 50, 75 *c.*, $2.50, *each* × 2
Leaders of the World. Birth Bicent of John J. Audubon (ornithologist). Birds. 15, 50 *c.*, $1, $1.50, *each* × 2
Leaders of the World. Railway Locomotives (3rd series). *Two designs for each value, the first showing technical drawings and the second the locomotive at work.* 5, 50, 60 *c.*, $2, *each* × 2
Leaders of the World. Butterflies. 15, 25, 75 *c.*, $2, *each* × 2
Leaders of the World. Automobiles (2nd series). *Two designs for each value, the first showing technical drawings and the second the car in action.* 5, 60 *c.*, $1, $1.50, *each* × 2
Leaders of the World. Automobiles (3rd series). *Two designs for each value, the first showing technical drawings and the second the car in action.* 10, 55, 60, 75, 90 *c.*, $1, $1.50, $2, *each* × 2
Leaders of the World. Life and Times of Queen Elizabeth the Queen Mother. Two designs for each value, showing different portraits. 55, 70 *c.*, $1.05, $1.70, *each* × 2

1986

Leaders of the World. Railway Locomotives (4th series). *Two designs for each value, the first showing technical drawings and the second the locomotive at work.* 15, 30, 45, 60, 75 *c.*, $1.50, $2.50, $3, *each* × 2
60th Birthday of Queen Elizabeth II. 10, 60 *c.*, $2, $8
World Cup Football Championship, Mexico. 1, 10, 30, 75 *c.*, $1, $2.50, $3, $6
Royal Wedding (1st issue). 60 *c.*, $2, *each* × 2
Automobiles (4th series). *Two designs for each value, the first showing technical drawings and the second the car in action.* 10, 60, 75 *c.*, $1, $1.50, $3, *each* × 2
Royal Wedding (2nd issue). *Previous issue optd as Bequia.* 60 *c.*, $2, *each* × 2
Railway Locomotives (5th series). *Two designs for each value, the first showing technical drawings and the second the locomotive at work.* 15, 45, 60, 75 *c.*, $1, $1.50, $2, $3, *each* × 2

1987

Railway Locomotives (6th series). *Two designs for each value, the first showing technical drawings and the second the locomotive at work.* 15, 25, 40, 50, 60, 75 *c.*, $1, $2, *each* × 2
Royal Ruby Wedding. 15, 45 *c.*, $1.50, $3, $4
Railway Locomotives (7th series). *Two designs for each value, the first showing technical drawings and the second the locomotive at work.* 15, 20, 30, 45, 50, 75 *c.*, $1, $1.50, *each* × 2

1989

"Philexfrance 89" International Stamp Exhibition, Paris. Walt Disney Cartoon Characters. 1, 2, 3, 4, 5, 10 *c.*, $5, $6

Samoa

PRICES FOR STAMPS ON COVER TO 1945

Nos. 1/20 are very rare used on cover.

Nos. 21/40	*from* × 20
Nos. 41/8	*from* × 100
Nos. 49/56	*from* × 4
Nos. 57/64	*from* × 12
Nos. 65/8	*from* × 2
Nos. 69/97	*from* × 20
Nos. 101/9	*from* × 3
Nos. 110/14	—
Nos. 115/21	*from* × 3
Nos. 122/32	—
Nos. 134/64	*from* × 3
Nos. 165/76	—
Nos. 177/214	*from* × 2

INDEPENDENT KINGDOM OF SAMOA

The first postal service in Samoa was organised by C. L. Griffiths, who had earlier run the *Fiji Times* Express post in Suva. In both instances the principal purpose of the service was the distribution of newspapers of which Griffiths was the proprietor. The first issue of the *Samoa Times* (later the *Samoa Times and South Sea Gazette*) appeared on 6 October 1877 and the newspaper continued in weekly publication until 27 August 1881.

Mail from the Samoa Express post to addresses overseas was routed via New South Wales, New Zealand or U.S.A. and received additional franking with stamps of the receiving country on landing.

Cancellations, inscribed "APIA SAMOA", did not arrive until March 1878 so that examples of Nos. 1/9 used before that date were cancelled in manuscript.

1

(Des H. H. Glover. Litho S. T. Leigh & Co, Sydney, N.S.W.)

1877 (1 Oct)–**80.**

A. 1*st state: line above "X" in* "EXPRESS" *not broken. P* 12½

1 1 1d. ultramarine .. £225 £100
2 3d. deep scarlet .. £250 £110
3 6d. bright violet .. £250 95·00
a. Pale lilac .. £275 95·00

B. 2*nd state: line above "X" broken, and dot between top of* "M" *and* "O" *of* "SAMOA". *P* 12½ (1878–79)

4 1 1d. ultramarine .. 85·00 90·00
5 3d. bright scarlet .. £250 £110
6 6d. bright violet .. £150 80·00
7 1s. dull yellow .. £130 80·00
a. Line above "X" not broken .. £150 £100
b. Perf 12 (1879) .. 70·00 85·00
c. Orange-yellow .. 85·00 90·00
8 2s. red-brown .. £250 £180
a. Chocolate .. £275 £325
9 5s. green .. £800 £1000

C. 3*rd state: line above "X" repaired, dot merged with upper right serif of* "M" (1879). (*a*) *P* 12½

10 1 1d. ultramarine .. 80·00 80·00
11 3d. vermilion .. £110 £110
12 6d. lilac .. £110 80·00
13 2s. brown .. £200 £200
a. Chocolate .. £200 £200
14 5s. green .. £500 £500
a. Line above "X" not repaired .. £600

(*b*) *P* 12

15 1 1d. blue .. 24·00 40·00
a. Deep blue .. 32·00 70·00
b. Ultramarine .. 28·00 40·00
16 3d. vermilion .. 45·00 65·00
a. Carmine-vermilion .. 45·00 75·00
17 6d. bright violet .. 40·00 48·00
a. Deep violet .. 40·00 80·00
18 2s. deep brown .. £130 £200
19 5s. yellow-green .. £400 £600
a. Deep green .. £375 £550
b. Line above "X" not repaired .. £475

D. 4*th state: spot of colour under middle stroke of* "M". *P* 12 (1880)

20 1 9d. orange-brown .. 55·00 £110

Originals exist imperf, but are not known used in this state.

On sheets of the 1d., 1st state, at least eight stamps have a stop after "PENNY". In the 2nd state, three stamps have the stop, and in the 3rd state, only one.

In the 1st state, all the stamps, 1d., 3d. and 6d., were in sheets of 20 (5 × 4) and also the 1d. in the 3rd state.

All values in the 2nd state, all values except the 1d. in the 3rd state and No. 20 were in sheets of 10 (5 × 2).

As all sheets of all printings of the originals were imperf at the outer edges, the only stamps which can have perforations on all four sides are Nos. 1 to 3*a*, 10 and 15 to 15*b*, all other originals being imperf on one or two sides.

The perf 12 stamps, which gauge 11.8, are generally very rough but later the machine was repaired and the 1d., 3d. and 6d. are known with clean-cut perforations.

Remainders of the 1d., unissued 2d. rose, 6d. (in sheets of 21 (7 × 3), 3d., 9d., 1s. (in sheets of 12 (4 × 3)) and of the 2s. and 5s. (sheet format unknown) were found in the Samoan post office when the service closed down in 1881. The remainders are rare in complete sheets, but of very little value as singles, compared with the originals.

Reprints of all values, in sheets of 40 (8 × 5), were made after the originals had been withdrawn from sale. These are practically worthless.

The majority of both reprints and remainders are in the 4th state as the 9d. with the spot of colour under the middle stroke of the "M", but a few stamps (both remainders and reprints) do not show this, while on some it is very faint.

There are three known types of forgery, one of which is rather dangerous, the others being crude.

The last mail despatch organised by the proprietors of the Samoa Express took place on 31 August 1881, although one cover is recorded postmarked 24 September 1881.

After the withdrawal of the Samoa Express service it would appear that the Apia municipality appointed a postmaster to continue the overseas post. Covers are known franked with U.S.A. or New Zealand stamps in Samoa, or routed via Fiji.

In December 1886 the municipal postmaster, John Davis, was appointed Postmaster of the Kingdom of Samoa by King Malietoa. Overseas mail sent via New Zealand was subsequently accepted without the addition of New Zealand stamps, although letters to the U.S.A. continued to require such franking until August 1891.

2 Palm Trees

3 King Malietoa Laupepa

4*a* 6 mm

4*b* 7 mm

4*c* 4 mm

Description of Watermarks

(These are the same as W **12***a*/*c* of New Zealand)

W **4***a*. 6 mm between "N Z" and star; broad irregular star; comparatively wide "N"; "N Z" 11½ mm wide.

W **4***b*. 7 mm between "N Z" and star; narrower star; narrow "N"; "N Z" 10 mm wide.

W **4***c*. 4 mm between "N Z" and star; narrow star; wide "N"; "N Z" 11 mm wide.

(Des A. E. Cousins (T **3**). Dies eng W. R. Bock and A. E. Cousins (T **2**) or A. E. Cousins (T **3**). Typo Govt Ptg Office, Wellington)

1886–1900. (i) *W* **4***a*. (*a*) *P* 12½ (Oct–Nov 1886).

21 2 ½d. purple-brown .. 16·00 28·00
22 1d. yellow-green .. 5·50 12·00
23 2d. dull orange .. 10·00 7·50
24 4d. blue .. 20·00 8·50
25 1s. rose-carmine .. 55·00 7·50
a. Bisected (2½d.) (on cover)* .. † £275
26 2s. 6d. reddish lilac .. 55·00 48·00

(*b*) *P* 12 × 11½ (July–Nov 1887)

27 2 ½d. purple-brown .. 80·00 80·00
28 1d. yellow-green .. £100 25·00
29 2d. yellow .. 85·00 £140
30 4d. blue .. £250 £200
31 6d. brown-lake .. 20·00 8·00
32 1s. rose-carmine .. — £160
33 2s. 6d. reddish lilac .. £275

(ii) *W* **4***c*. *P* 12 × 11½ (May 1890)

34 2 ½d. purple-brown .. 70·00 25·00
35 1d. green .. 50·00 27·00
36 2d. brown-orange .. 70·00 35·00
37 4d. blue .. £130 5·00
38 6d. brown-lake .. £225 11·00
39 1s. rose-carmine .. £325 13·00
40 2s. 6d. reddish lilac .. £375 8·50

(iii) *W* **4***b*. (*a*) *P* 12 × 11½ (1890–92)

41 2 ½d. pale purple-brown .. 1·75 2·50
a. Blackish purple .. 1·75 2·50
42 1d. myrtle-green (5.90) .. 11·00 1·40
a. Green .. 11·00 1·40
b. Yellow-green .. 11·00 1·40
43 2d. dull orange (5.90) .. 13·00 1·75
44 3 2½d. rose (11.92) .. 75·00 3·50
a. Pale rose .. 75·00 3·50
45 2 4d. blue .. £225 13·00
46 6d. brown-lake .. £110 8·00
47 1s. rose-carmine .. £225 4·00
48 2s. 6d. slate-lilac .. — 5·50

(*b*) *P* 12½ (Mar 1891–92)

49 2 ½d. purple-brown ..
50 1d. green ..
51 2d. orange-yellow .. — £130
52 3 2½d. rose (1.92) .. 20·00 4·50
53 2 4d. blue .. — £450
54 6d. brown-purple .. £2000 £750
55 1s. rose-carmine .. — £425
56 2s. 6d. slate-lilac ..

(*c*) *P* 11 (May 1895–1900)

57 2 ½d. purple-brown .. 75 1·75
a. Deep purple-brown .. 65 1·75
b. Blackish purple (1900) .. 65 35·00
58 2 1d. green .. 1·25 1·75
a. Bluish green (1897) .. 1·25 1·75
b. Deep green (1900) .. 1·25 22·00
59 2d. pale yellow .. 35·00 35·00
a. Orange (1896) .. 35·00 35·00
b. Bright yellow (1.97) .. 5·50 4·00
c. Pale ochre (10.97) .. 4·50 1·00
d. Dull orange (1900) .. 5·50
60 3 2½d. rose .. 70 4·50
a. Deep rose-carmine (1900) .. 1·10 42·00
61 2 4d. blue .. 5·75 2·00
a. Deep blue (1900) .. 60 50·00
62 6d. brown-lake .. 5·50 4·00
a. Brown-purple (1900) .. 1·75 60·00
63 1s. rose .. 5·50 4·50
a. Dull rose-carmine/toned (5.98) .. 2·00 35·00
b. Carmine (1900) .. 1·25
64 2s. 6d. purple .. 55·00 9·50
a. Reddish lilac (wmk inverted) (1897) 7·50 7·50
b. Deep purple/toned (wmk reversed) (5.98) .. 4·75 9·50
ba. Imperf between (vert pair) .. £350
c. Slate-violet .. £120

*Following a fire on 1 April 1895 which destroyed stocks of all stamps except the 1s. value perf 12½, this was bisected diagonally and used as a 2½d. stamp for overseas letters between 24 April and May 1895, and was cancelled in blue. Fresh supplies of the 2½d. did not arrive until July 1895, although other values were available from 23 May.

Examples of the 1s. rose perforated 11, No. 63, were subsequently bisected and supplied cancelled-to-order by the post office to collectors, often with backdated cancellations. Most of these examples were bisected vertically and all were cancelled in black (*Price* £7).

The dates given relate to the earliest dates of printing in the various watermarks and perforations and not to issue dates.

The perf 11 issues (including those later surcharged or overprinted), are very unevenly perforated owing to the large size of the pins. Evenly perforated copies are extremely hard to find.

For the 2½d. black, see Nos. 81/2 and for the ½d. green and 1d. red-brown, see Nos. 88/9.

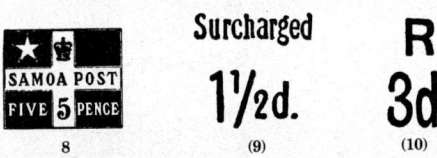

FIVE PENCE (5) FIVE PENCE (6) 5d (7)

1893 (Nov–Dec). *Handstamped singly, at Apia.*

(*a*) *In two operations*

65 5 5d. on 4d. blue (37) .. 45·00 42·00
a. Bars omitted .. — £400
66 5d. on 4d. blue (45) .. 60·00 £100
67 6 5d. on 4d. blue (37) .. 85·00 £110
68 5d. on 4d. blue (45) .. 90·00

(*b*) *In three operations* (Dec)

69 7 5d. on 4d. blue (37) (R.) .. 17·00 25·00
a. Stop after "d" .. £250 60·00
b. Bars omitted ..
70 5d. on 4d. blue (45) (R.) .. 17·00 50·00

In Types **5** and **6** the bars obliterating the original value vary in length from 13½ to 16½ mm and can occur with either the thick bar over the thin one or vice versa.

Double handstamps exist but we do not list them.

No. 69a came from a separate handstamp which applied the "5d." at one operation. Where the "d" was applied separately its position in relation to the "5" naturally varies.

SAMOA POST FIVE 5 PENCE (8) Surcharged 1½d. (9) R 3d. (10)

The "R" in Type **10** indicates use for registration fee.

(Des and die eng A. E. Cousins. Typo New Zealand Govt Ptg Office)

1894–1900. *W* **4***b* (*sideways*). (*a*) *P* 11½ × 12.

71 8 5d. dull vermilion (3.94) .. 16·00 2·75
a. Dull red .. 16·00 3·75

(*b*) *P* 11

72 8 5d. dull red (1895) .. 10·00 6·50
a. Deep red (1900) .. 1·25 13·00

1895–1900. *W* **4***b*.

(i) *Handstamped with T* **9** *or* **10**. (*a*) *P* 12 × 11½ (26.1.95)

73 2 1½d. on 2d. dull orange (B.) .. 5·50 5·00
74 3d. on 2d. dull orange .. 21·00 8·00

(*b*) *P* 11 (6.95)

75 2 1½d. on 2d. orange (B.) .. 1·50 3·00
a. Pair, one without handstamp ..
b. On 2d. yellow .. 75·00 60·00
76 3d. on 2d. orange .. 5·00 7·50
a. On 2d. yellow .. 75·00 60·00

(ii) *Surch printed**. *P* 11

77 2 1½d. on 2d. orange-yellow (B.) ..

(iii) *Handstamped as T* **9** *or* **10**.† *P* 11 (1896)

78 2 1½d. on 2d. orange-yellow (B.) .. 2·50 22·00
79 3d. on 2d. orange-yellow .. 3·00 45·00
a. Imperf between (vert pair) .. £400
b. Pair, one without handstamp

(iv) *Surch typo as T* **10**. *P* 11 (Feb 1900)

80 2 3d. on 2d. deep red-orange (G.) .. 1·50 £130

*It is believed that this was type-set from which clichés were made and set up in a forme and then printed on a hand press. This would account for the clear indentation on the back of the stamp and the variation in the position on the stamps which probably resulted from the clichés becoming loose in the forme.

†In No. 78 the "2" has a serif and the handstamp is in pale greenish blue instead of deep blue. In No. 79 the "R" is slightly narrower. In both instances the stamp is in a different shade.

A special printing in a distinctly different colour was made for No. 80 and the surcharge is in green.

Most of the handstamps exist double.

1896 (Aug). *Printed in the wrong colour. W* 4*b*. (*a*) *P* 10 × 11.

81	3	2½d. black	90	3·00
		(*b*) *P* 11		
82	3	2½d. black	60·00	65·00
		a. Mixed perfs 10 and 11	£350	

Surcharged 2½d. (11)

PROVISIONAL GOVT. (12)

1898–99. *W* 4*b*. *P* 11. (*a*) *Handstamped as T* **11** (10.98).

83	2	2½d. on 1s. dull rose-carmine/*toned*	24·00	32·00
		(*b*) *Surch as T* **11** (1899)		
84	2	2½d. on 1d. bluish green (R.)	55	2·00
		a. Surch inverted	—	£350
85		2½d. on 1s. dull rose-carmine/*toned* (R.)	3·50	8·50
		a. Surch double	£350	
86		2½d. on 1s. dull rose-carmine/*toned* (Blk.)	3·50	8·50
		a. Surch double	£450	
87		2½d. on 2s. 6d. deep purple/*toned*	4·75	11·00

The typographed surcharge was applied in a setting of nine, giving seven types differing in the angle and length of the fractional line, the type of stop, etc.

1899. *Colours changed. W* 4*b*. *P* 11.

88	2	½d. dull blue-green	65	1·40
		a. Deep green	65	1·40
89		1d. deep red-brown	55	1·25

1899–1900. *Provisional Government. New printings optd with T* **12** (*longer words and shorter letters on 5d.*). *W* 4*b*. *P* 11.

90	2	½d. dull blue-green (R.)	30	1·25
		a. Yellowish green (1900)	30	1·50
91		1d. chestnut (B.)	90	2·50
92		2d. dull orange (R.)	55	2·50
		a. Orange-yellow (1900)	40	3·00
93		4d. deep dull blue (R.)	45	2·25
94	8	5d. dull vermilion (B.)	90	4·50
		a. Red (1900)	90	4·50
95	2	6d. brown-lake (B.)	1·10	3·75
96		1s. rose-carmine (B.)	1·50	9·50
97		2s. 6d. reddish purple (R.)	4·75	17·00

The Samoan group of islands was partitioned on 1 March 1900: Western Samoa (Upolu, Savaii, Apolima and Manono) to Germany and Eastern Samoa (Tutuila, the Manu'a Is and Rose Is) to the United States. German issues of 1900–14 will be found listed in Part 7 (*Germany*) of this catalogue, there were no U.S. issues.

The Samoan Kingdom post office run by John Davis was suspended in March 1900.

WESTERN SAMOA

NEW ZEALAND OCCUPATION

The German Islands of Samoa surrendered to the New Zealand Expeditionary Force on 30 August 1914 and were administered by New Zealand until 1962.

G.R.I. 1d. (13)

G.R.I. 1 Shillings. (14)

SETTINGS. Nos. 101/9 were surcharged by a vertical setting of ten, repeated ten times across the sheet. Nos. 110/14 were from a horizontal setting of four repeated five times in the sheet.

Nos. 101b, 102a and 104a occurred on position 6. The error was corrected during the printing of No. 102.

Nos. 101c, 102c, 104d and 105b are from position 10.

Nos. 101d, 102e and 104b are from position 1.

No. 108b is from position 9.

(Surch by *Samoanische Zeitung*, Apia)

1914 (3 Sept). *German Colonial issue* (*ship*) (*no wmk*) *inscr* "SAMOA" *surch as T* **13** *or* **14** (*mark values*).

101	½d. on 3 pf. brown	16·00	8·50
	a. Surch double	£650	£500
	b. No fraction bar	50·00	30·00
	c. Comma after "I"	£600	£500
	d. "1" to left of "2" in "½"	50·00	30·00
102	½d. on 5 pf. green	35·00	10·00
	a. No fraction bar	£100	55·00
	c. Comma after "I"	£350	£170
	d. Surch double	£650	£500
	e. "1" to left of "2" in "½"	90·00	40·00
103	1d. on 10 pf. carmine	95·00	40·00
	a. Surch double	£650	£500
104	2½d. on 20 pf. ultramarine	30·00	10·00
	a. No fraction bar	60·00	38·00
	b. "1" to left of "2" in "½"	60·00	40·00
	c. Surch inverted	£800	£750
	d. Comma after "I"	£450	£325
	e. Surch double	£650	£550
105	3d. on 25 pf. black and red/*yellow*	50·00	35·00
	a. Surch double	£650	£500
	b. Comma after "I"	£3500	£800
106	4d. on 30 pf. black and orange/*buff*	£100	60·00
107	5d. on 40 pf. black and carmine	£110	70·00
108	6d. on 50 pf. black and purple/*buff*	55·00	35·00
	a. Surch double	£750	£800
	b. Inverted "9" for "6"	£160	£100
109	9d. on 80 pf. black and carmine/*rose*	£190	95·00
110	"1 shillings" on 1 m. carmine	£3000	£3250
111	"1 shilling" on 1 m. carmine	£9500	£7000
112	2s. on 2 m. blue	£3000	£2750
113	3s. on 3 m. violet-black	£1400	£1200
	a. Surch double	£8000	£9000
114	5s. on 5 m. carmine and black	£1000	£950
	a. Surch double	£11000	£11000

No. 108b is distinguishable from 108, as the "d" and the "9" are not in a line, and the upper loop of the "9" turns downwards to the left.

UNAUTHORISED SURCHARGES. Examples of the 2d. on 20 pf., 3d. on 30 pf., 3d. on 40 pf., 4d. on 40 pf., 6d. on 80 pf., 2s. on 3 m. and 2s. on Marshall Islands 2 m., together with a number of errors not listed above, were produced by the printer on stamps supplied by local collectors. These were not authorised by the New Zealand Military Administration.

SAMOA. (15)

1914 (29 Sept)–**15.** *Stamps of New Zealand. T* **50**, **51**, **52** *and* **27**, *optd as T* **15**, *but opt only* 14 *mm long on all except* 2½*d. Wmk "N Z" and Star, W* **43** *of New Zealand.*

115	½d. yellow-green (R.) (*p* 14×15)	30	30
116	1d. carmine (B.) (*p* 14×15)	30	10
117	2d. mauve (R.) (*p* 14×14½) (10.14)	60	95
118	2½d. deep blue (R.) (*p* 14) (10.14)	1·50	1·75
119	6d. carmine (B.) (*p* 14×14½) (10.14)	1·50	1·75
	a. Perf 14×13½	17·00	19·00
	b. Vert pair. Nos. 119/a (1915)	38·00	55·00
120	6d. pale carmine (B.) (*p* 14×14½) (10.14)	10·00	9·50
121	1s. vermilion (B.) (*p* 14×14½) (10.14)	3·50	9·00

1914–24. *Postal Fiscal stamps as Type* F **4** *of New Zealand optd with T* **15**. *W* **43** *of New Zealand* (*sideways*). *Chalk-surfaced "De La Rue" paper.*

	(*a*) *P* 14 (Nov 1914–17)		
122	2s. blue (R.) (9.17)	80·00	£100
123	2s. 6d. grey-brown (B.) (9.17)	4·50	8·50
124	5s. yellow-green (R.)	9·50	11·00
125	10s. maroon (B.)	20·00	28·00
126	£1 rose-carmine (B.)	60·00	50·00
	(*b*) *P* 14½ × 14, *comb* (1917–24)		
127	2s. deep blue (R.) (3.18)	4·00	5·50
128	2s. 6d. grey-brown (B.) (10.24)	£170	£130
129	3s. purple (R.) (6.23)	12·00	26·00
130	5s. yellow-green (R.) (9.17)	14·00	15·00
131	10s. maroon (B.) (3.18)	40·00	40·00
132	£1 rose-carmine (B.) (3.18)	60·00	70·00

We no longer list the £2 value as it is doubtful if this was used for postal purposes.

See also Nos. 165/6*e*.

1916–19. *King George V stamps of New Zealand optd as T* **15**, *but* 14 *mm long.* (*a*) *T* **61**. *Typo. P* 14×15.

134	½d. yellow-green (R.)	20	40
135	1½d. slate (R.) (1917)	25	25
136	1½d. orange-brown (R.) (1919)	15	40
137	2d. yellow (R.) (14.2.18)	40	15
138	3d. chocolate (B.) (1919)	75	12·00
	(*b*) *T* **60**. *Recess. P* 14 × 14½, *etc.*		
139	2½d. blue (R.)	65	60
	a. Perf 14 × 13½	35	35
	b. Vert pair. Nos. 139/9a	14·00	20·00
140	3d. chocolate (B.) (1917)	35	90
	a. Perf 14 × 13½	45	1·60
	b. Vert pair. Nos. 140/40a	14·00	23·00
141	6d. carmine (B.) (5.5.17)	1·25	90
	a. Perf 14 × 13½	1·50	3·25
	b. Vert pair. Nos. 141/1a	16·00	25·00
142	1s. vermilion (B.)	3·50	9·00
	a. Perf 14 × 13½	1·25	1·25
	b. Vert pair. Nos. 142/2a	20·00	35·00
134/42a	*Set of* 9	4·50	15·00

LEAGUE OF NATIONS MANDATE

Administered by New Zealand.

1920 (July). *Victory. Nos.* 453/8 *of New Zealand optd as T* **15**, *but* 14 *mm long.*

143	½d. green (R.)	1·25	2·25
144	1d. carmine (B.)	1·25	1·00
145	1½d. brown-orange (R.)	1·25	4·00
146	3d. chocolate (B.)	3·50	7·00
147	6d. violet (R.)	4·00	6·50
148	1s. orange-red (B.)	12·00	11·00
143/8	*Set of* 6	21·00	29·00

16 Native Hut

SILVER JUBILEE OF KING GEORGE V 1910 - 1935. (17)

(Eng B.W. Recess-printed at Wellington, N.Z.)

1921 (23 Dec). *W* **43** *of New Zealand.* (*a*) *P* 14 × 14½.

149	16	½d. green	40	3·25
150		1d. lake	40	20
151		1½d. chestnut	40	4·75
152		2d. yellow	60	1·90
149/52		*Set of* 4	1·60	9·00
		(*b*) *P* 14 × 13½		
153	16	½d. green	1·00	1·75
154		1d. lake	1·00	20
155		1½d. chestnut	6·00	7·50
156		2d. yellow	5·50	35
157	16	2½d. grey-blue	70	3·50
158		3d. sepia	75	3·00
159		4d. violet	80	3·00
160		5d. light blue	75	5·00
161		6d. bright carmine	80	3·50
162		8d. red-brown	1·25	9·00
163		9d. olive-green	1·25	10·00
164		1s. vermilion	1·25	11·00
153/64		*Set of* 12	19·00	50·00

1925–28. *Postal Fiscal stamps as Type* F **4** *of New Zealand optd with T* **15**. *W* **43** *of New Zealand* (*sideways*). *P* 14½×14.

	(*a*) *Thick, opaque, white chalk-surfaced "Cowan" paper*		
165	2s. blue (R.) (12.25)	95·00	£100
166	2s. 6d. deep grey-brown (B.) (10.28)	60·00	80·00
166*a*	3s. mauve (R.) (9.25)	45·00	55·00
166*b*	5s. yellow-green (R.) (11.26)	12·00	23·00
	ba. Opt at top of stamp	£1100	
166*c*	10s. brown-red (B.) (12.25)	60·00	50·00
166*d*	£1 rose-pink (B.) (11.26)	50·00	75·00
165/6*d*	*Set of* 6	£250	£300
	(*b*) *Thin, hard, chalk-surfaced "Wiggins Teape" paper*		
166*e*	£1 rose-pink (B.) (1928)	—	£700

1926–27. *T* **72** *of New Zealand, optd with T* **15**, *in red.*

	(*a*) *"Jones" paper*		
167	2s. deep blue (11.26)	4·50	12·00
168	3s. mauve (10.26)	7·00	22·00
	(*b*) *"Cowan" paper*		
169	2s. light blue (10.11.27)	5·00	28·00
170	3s. pale mauve (10.11.27)	42·00	65·00

1932 (Aug). *Postal Fiscal stamps as Type* F **6** *of New Zealand optd with T* **15**. *W* **43** *of New Zealand. Thick, opaque, white chalk-surfaced "Cowan" paper. P* 14.

171	2s. 6d. deep brown (B.)	15·00	27·00
172	5s. green (R.)	20·00	35·00
173	10s. carmine-lake (B.)	45·00	70·00
174	£1 pink (B.)	60·00	85·00
175	£2 bright purple (R.)	£700	
176	£5 indigo-blue (R.)	£1800	

The £2 and £5 values were primarily for fiscal use.

1935 (7 May). *Silver Jubilee. Optd with T* **17**. *P* 14 × 13½.

177	16	1d. lake	30	30
		a. Perf 14 × 14½	75·00	£110
178		2½d. grey-blue	60	65
179		6d. bright carmine	2·10	2·50
177/9		*Set of* 3	2·75	3·00

18 Samoan Girl

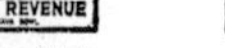

19 Apia

21 Chief and Wife

25 Lake Lanuto'o

(Recess D.L.R.)

1935 (7 Aug). *T* **18/19**, **21**, **25** *and similar designs. W* **43** *of New Zealand* ("N Z" *and Star*).

	(*a*) *P* 14 × 13½, (*b*) *P* 13½ × 14 *or* (*c*) *P* 14		
180	½d. green (*a*)	10	35
181	1d. black and carmine (*b*)	10	10
182	2d. black and orange (*c*)	2·00	1·25
	a. Perf 13½ × 14	3·75	3·50
183	2½d. black and blue (*a*)	10	10
184	4d. slate and sepia (*b*)	40	15
185	6d. bright magenta (*b*)	40	10
186	1s. violet and brown (*b*)	30	10
187	2s. green and purple-brown (*a*)	50	50
188	3s. blue and brown-orange (*a*)	1·50	3·50
180/8	*Set of* 9	4·75	5·00

Designs: *Horiz*—2d. River scene; 4d. Canoe and house; 6d. R. L. Stevenson's home "Vailima"; 1s. Stevenson's Tomb. *Vert* (*as T* **25**)—3s. Falefa Falls.

See also Nos. 200/3.

WESTERN SAMOA. (27)

1935–42. *Postal Fiscal stamps as Type* F **6** *of New Zealand optd with T* **27**. *W* **43** *of New Zealand. P* 14.

	(*a*) *Thick, opaque chalk-surfaced "Cowan" paper* (7.8.35)		
189	2s. 6d. deep brown (B.)	6·00	13·00
190	5s. green (B.)	10·00	16·00
191	10s. carmine-lake (B.)	40·00	55·00
192	£1 pink (B.)	60·00	85·00
193	£2 bright purple (R.)	£190	£275
194	£5 indigo-blue (R.)	£450	£550
	(*b*) *Thin, hard chalk-surfaced "Wiggins, Teape" paper* (1941–42)		
194*a*	5s. green (B.) (6.42)	65·00	70·00
194*b*	10s. pale carmine-lake (B.) (6.41)	£100	£110
194*c*	£2 bright purple (R.) (2.42)	£425	£500
194*d*	£5 indigo-blue (R.) (2.42)	£650	£750

The £2 and £5 values were primarily for fiscal use.

See also Nos. 207/14.

28 Coastal Scene

31 Robert Louis Stevenson

(Des J. Berry (1d. and 1½d.). L. C. Mitchell (2½d. and 7d.). Recess B.W.)

1939 (29 Aug). *25th Anniv of New Zealand Control. T* **28, 31** *and similar horiz designs. W* **98** *of New Zealand. P* 13½ × 14 *or* 14 × 13½ *(7d.).*

195 1d. olive-green and scarlet .. 30 10
196 1½d. light blue and red-brown .. 35 30
197 2½d. red-brown and blue .. 90 65
198 7d. violet and slate-green .. 4·50 1·50
195/8 .. *Set of* 4 5·50 2·25

Designs:—1½d. Western Samoa; 2½d. Samoan dancing party.

32 Samoan Chief

33 Apia Post Office

(Recess B.W.)

1940 (2 Sept). *W* **98** *of New Zealand (Mult "N Z" and Star). P* 14 × 13½.

199 **32** 3d. on 1½d. brown .. 10 10

T **32** was not issued without surcharge.

(T **33**. Des L. C. Mitchell. Recess B.W.)

1944–49. *As Nos.* 180, 182/3 *and T* **33**. *W* **98** *of New Zealand (Mult "N Z" and Star) (sideways on 2½d.). P* 14 *or* 13½ × 14 *(5d.).*

200 ½d. green .. 25 5·50
202 2d. black and orange .. 1·25 4·75
203 2½d. black and blue (1948) .. 3·00 14·00
205 5d. sepia and blue (8.6.49) .. 20 50
200/5 .. *Set of* 4 4·25 22·00

1945–48. *Postal Fiscal stamps as Type* F **6** *of New Zealand optd with T* **27**. *W* **98** *of New Zealand. Thin hard, chalk-surfaced "Wiggins Teape" paper. P* 14.

207 2s. 6d. deep brown (B.) (6.45) .. 2·25 5·50
208 5s. green (B.) (5.45) .. 5·00 7·50
209 10s. carmine-lake (B.) (4.46) .. 16·00 17·00
210 £1 pink (B.) (6.48) .. 80·00 £150
211 30s. brown (8.48) .. £140 £225
212 £2 bright purple (R.) (11.47) .. £140 £225
213 £3 green (8.48) .. £170 £300
214 £5 indigo-blue (R.) (1946) .. £250 £350
207/10 .. *Set of* 4 90·00 £160

The £2 to £5 values were mainly used for "fiscal purposes".

See also Nos. 232/5.

WESTERN
SAMOA
(34)

1946 (4 June). *Peace Issue. Nos.* 668, 670 *and* 674/5 *of New Zealand optd with T* **34** *(reading up and down at sides on 2d.).*

215 1d. green .. 10 10
216 2d. purple (B.) .. 10 10
217 6d. chocolate and vermilion .. 10 10
218 8d. black and carmine (B.) .. 10 10
215/18 .. *Set of* 4 35 20

UNITED NATIONS TRUST TERRITORY

Administered by New Zealand.

35 Making Siapo Cloth

42 Thatching a Native Hut

43 Preparing Copra

44 Samoan Chieftainess

(Recess B.W.)

1952 (10 Mar). *T* **35, 42/4** *and similar designs. W* **98** *of New Zealand (sideways on 1s. and 3s.). P* 13 *(½d., 2d., 5d. and 1s.) or* 13½ *(others).*

219 ½d. claret and orange-brown .. 10 40
220 1d. olive-green and green .. 10 10
221 2d. carmine-red .. 10 10
222 3d. pale ultramarine and indigo .. 40 10
223 5d. brown and deep green .. 3·50 70
224 6d. pale ultramarine and rose-magenta .. 40 10
225 8d. carmine .. 30 30
226 1s. sepia and blue .. 15 10
227 2s. yellow-brown .. 1·40 60
228 3s. chocolate and brown-olive .. 3·00 2·00
219/28 .. *Set of* 10 8·50 3·75

Designs: *Horiz (as T* **43**)—1d. Native houses and flags; 3d. Malifa Falls (wrongly inscribed "Aleisa Falls"); 6d. Bonito fishing canoe; 8d. Cacao harvesting. *Vert (as T* **35**)—2d. Seal of Samoa; 5d. Tooth-billed Pigeon.

1953 (25 May). *Coronation. Designs as Nos.* 715 *and* 717 *of New Zealand, but inscr* "WESTERN SAMOA".

229 2d. brown .. 75 15
230 6d. slate-grey .. 1·00 35

WESTERN

SAMOA
(45)

1955 (14 Nov). *Postal Fiscal stamps as Type* F **6** *of New Zealand optd with T* **45**. *W* **98**. *Chalk-surfaced "Wiggins, Teape" paper. P* 14.

232 5s. green (B.) .. 13·00 16·00
233 10s. carmine-lake (B.) .. 16·00 24·00
234 £1 pink (B.) .. 27·00 35·00
235 £2 bright purple (R.) .. 70·00 £130
232/5 .. *Set of* 4 £110 £170

The £2 value was mainly used for fiscal purposes.

46 Native Houses and Flags

47 Seal of Samoa

(Recess B.W.)

1958 (21 Mar). *Inauguration of Samoan Parliament. T* **46/7** *and similar horiz design. W* **98** *of New Zealand (sideways). P* 13½ × 13 *(6d.) or* 13½ *(others).*

236 4d. cerise .. 15 10
237 6d. deep reddish violet .. 15 15
238 1s. deep ultramarine .. 25 15
236/8 .. *Set of* 3 50 30

Design:—1s. Map of Samoa, and the Mace.

INDEPENDENT

Samoa became independent on 1 January 1962.

49 Samoan Fine Mat

50 Samoa College

(Litho B.W.)

1962 (2 July). *Independence. T* **49/50** *and similar designs. W* **98** *of New Zealand (sideways on horiz stamps). P* 13½.

239 1d. brown and rose-carmine .. 10 10
240 2d. brown, green, yellow and red .. 10 10
241 3d. brown, blue-green and blue .. 10 10
242 4d. magenta, yellow, blue and black .. 15 10
243 6d. yellow and blue .. 20 10
244 8d. bluish green, yellow-green and blue .. 20 10
245 1s. brown and bluish green .. 20 10
246 1s. 3d. yellow-green and blue .. 75 35
247 2s. 6d. red and ultramarine .. 1·50 1·25
248 5s. ultramarine, yellow, red and drab .. 3·25 2·50
239/48 .. *Set of* 10 5·75 4·25

Designs: *Horiz*—3d. Public library; 4d. Fono House; 6d. Map of Samoa; 8d. Airport; 1s. 3d. "Vailima"; 2s. 6d. Samoan flag; 5s. Samoan seal. *Vert*—1s. Samoan orator.

See Nos. 257/62.

59 Seal and Joint Heads of State

60 Signing the Treaty

(Des L. C. Mitchell. Photo Harrison)

1963 (1 Oct). *First Anniv of Independence. W* **98** *of New Zealand. P* 14.

249 **59** 1d. deep sepia and green .. 10 10
250 4d. deep sepia and blue .. 10 10
251 8d. deep sepia and rose-pink .. 10 10
252 2s. deep sepia and orange .. 20 10
249/52 .. *Set of* 4 35 20

(Des L. C. Mitchell. Photo Enschedé)

1964 (1 Sept). *2nd Anniv of New Zealand–Samoa Treaty of Friendship. P* 13½.

253 **60** 1d. multicoloured .. 10 10
254 8d. multicoloured .. 10 10
255 2s. multicoloured .. 20 10
256 3s. multicoloured .. 20 20
253/6 .. *Set of* 4 40 35

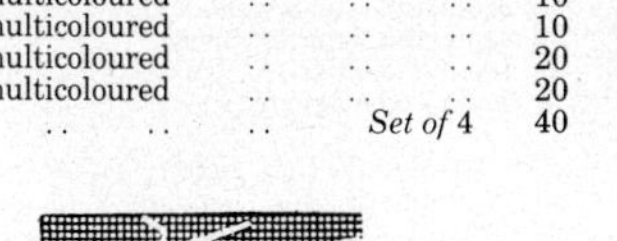

61 Kava Bowl

1965 (4 Oct)–**66?** *As Nos.* 239, 241/5, *but W* **61** *(sideways on horiz designs).*

257 1d. brown and rose-carmine .. 20 30
258 3d. brown, blue-green and blue (1966?) .. 27·00 3·75
259 4d. magenta, yellow, blue and black .. 25 30
260 6d. yellow and blue .. 35 20
261 8d. bluish green, yellow-green and blue .. 20 10
262 1s. brown and bluish green .. 25 30
257/62 .. *Set of* 6 27·00 4·50

62 Red-tailed Tropic Bird

63 Flying Fish

(Des L. C. Mitchell. Photo Harrison)

1965 (29 Dec). *Air. W* **61** *(sideways). P* 14½.

263 **62** 8d. black, red-orange and blue .. 40 10
264 **63** 2s. black and blue .. 55 20

64 Aerial View of Deep Sea Wharf

(Des Tecon Co (U.S.A.). Photo Enschedé)

1966 (3 Mar). *Opening of First Deep Sea Wharf, Apia. T* **64** *and similar horiz design. Multicoloured. W* **61** *(sideways). P* 13½.

265 1d. Type **64** .. 10 10
266 8d. Aerial view of wharf and bay .. 15 10
267 2s. As 8d. .. 25 15
268 3s. Type **64** .. 30 15
265/8 .. *Set of* 4 70 35

66 W.H.O. Building

(Des M. Goaman. Photo D.L.R.)

1966 (4 July). *Inauguration of W.H.O. Headquarters, Geneva. T* **66** *and similar horiz design. W* **61** *(sideways). P* 14.

269 3d. yellow-ochre, blue and light slate-lilac .. 30 10
270 4d. blue, yellow, green & light orange-brown 35 10
271 6d. reddish lilac, emerald and yellow-olive .. 40 15
272 1s. blue, yellow, green and turquoise-green 60 20
269/72 .. *Set of* 4 1·50 50

Designs:—3d., 6d. Type **66**; 4d., 1s. W.H.O. Building on flag.

HURRICANE RELIEF
6d
(68)

1966 (1 Sept). *Hurricane Relief Fund. No.* 261 *surch with T* **68** *by Bradbury, Wilkinson.*

273 8d. + 6d. bluish green, yellow-green and blue 10 10

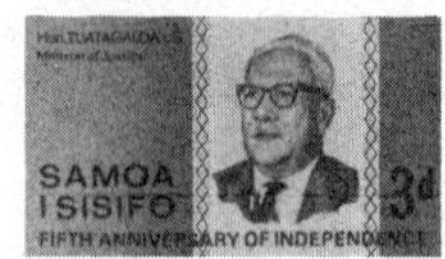

69 Hon. Tuatagaloa L. S. (Minister of Justice)

(Des and photo Harrison)

1967 (16 Jan). *Fifth Anniv of Independence. T* **69** *and similar horiz designs. W* **61** *(sideways). P* 14½ × 14.

274	3d. sepia and bluish violet	10	10
275	8d. sepia and light new blue	10	10
276	2s. sepia and olive	10	10
277	3s. sepia and magenta	15	15
274/7	*Set of* 4	30	30

Designs:—8d. Hon. F. C. F. Nelson (minister of Works, Marine and Civil Aviation); 2s. Hon. To'omata T. L. (minister of Lands); Hon. Fa'alava'au G. (minister of Post Office, Radio and Broadcasting).

73 Samoan Fales (houses), 1890

(Des V. Whiteley. Photo Harrison)

1967 (16 May). *Centenary of Mulinu'u as Seat of Government. T* **73** *and similar horiz design. Multicoloured. W* **61.** *P* 14½ × 14.

278	8d. Type **73**	15	10
279	1s. Fono (Parliament) House, 1967	15	10

(New Currency. 100 sene or cents=1 tala or dollar)

75 Carunculated Honeyeater

76 Black-breasted Honeyeater

(Des V. Whiteley. Litho Format ($2, $4). Photo Harrison (others))

1967 (10 July)–**69.** *Decimal currency. Multicoloured designs as T* **75** *(*1 *s. to* $1*) or* **76** *(*$2, $4*). W* **61** *(sideways). P* 13½ ($2, $4) *or* 14 × 14½ *(others).*

280	1 s. Type **75**	10	10
281	2 s. Pacific Pigeon	10	10
282	3 s. Samoan Starling	10	10
283	5 s. White-vented Flycatcher	15	10
284	7 s. Red-headed Parrot Finch	15	10
285	10 s. Purple Swamphen	20	10
286	20 s. Barn Owl	2·25	40
287	25 s. Tooth-billed Pigeon	1·50	15
288	50 s. Island Thrush	1·50	25
289	$1 Samoan Fantail	1·75	1·50
289*a*	$2 Type **76** (14.7.69)	5·50	7·00
289*b*	$4 Savaii White Eye (6.10.69)	40·00	45·00
280/9*b*	*Set of* 12	48·00	48·00

89 Thomas Trood

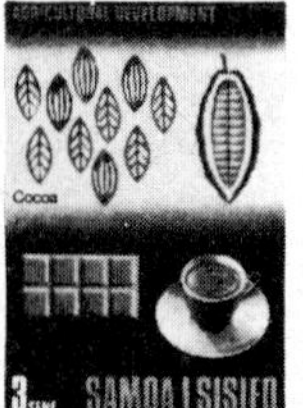

93 Cocoa

85 Nurse and Child

(Des G. Vasarhelyi. Photo D.L.R.)

1967 (1 Dec). *South Pacific Health Service. T* **85** *and similar horiz designs. Multicoloured. P* 14.

290	3 s. Type **85**	10	10
291	7 s. Leprosarium	10	10
292	20 s. Mobile X-ray Unit	20	10
293	25 s. Apia Hospital	25	15
290/3	*Set of* 4	50	30

(Des M. Farrar-Bell. Litho B.W.)

1968 (15 Jan). *6th Anniv of Independence. T* **89** *and similar horiz designs. Multicoloured. P* 13½.

294	2 s. Type **89**	10	10
295	7 s. Dr. Wilhelm Solf	10	10
296	20 s. J. C. Williams	10	10
297	25 s. Fritz Marquardt	15	10
294/7	*Set of* 4	30	30

(Des Jennifer Toombs. Photo Enschedé)

1968 (15 Feb). *Agricultural Development. T* **93** *and similar vert designs. W* **61.** *P* 13 × 12½.

298	3 s. deep red-brown, yellow-green and black	10	10
299	5 s. myrtle-green, greenish yellow & lt brn	10	10
300	10 s. scarlet, blackish brown and olive-yellow	10	10
301	20 s. yellow-bistre, yellow and blackish olive	15	15
298/301	*Set of* 4	30	30

Designs:—5 s. Breadfruit; 10 s. Copra; 20 s. Bananas.

97 Women weaving Mats

(Des G. Vasarhelyi. Photo Harrison)

1968 (22 Apr). *21st Anniv of the South Pacific Commission. T* **97** *and similar horiz designs. Multicoloured. W* **61.** *P* 14½ × 14.

302	7 s. Type **97**	10	10
303	20 s. Palm trees and bay	15	10
304	25 s. Sheltered cove	15	15
302/4	*Set of* 3	30	30

1928-1968
KINGSFORD-SMITH
TRANSPACIFIC FLIGHT
20
SENE

(100)

1968 (13 June). *40th Anniv of Kingsford Smith's Trans-Pacific Flight. No.* 285 *surch with T* **100**.

305	20 s. on 10 s. Purple Swamphen	10	10

101 Bougainville's Route

(Des Jennifer Toombs. Litho B.W.)

1968 (17 June). *Bicentenary of Bougainville's Visit to Samoa. T* **101** *and similar horiz designs. W* **61** *(sideways). P* 14.

306	3 s. new blue and black	10	10
307	7 s. light ochre and black	15	10
308	20 s. multicoloured	45	15
309	25 s. multicoloured	60	25
306/9	*Set of* 4	1·10	45

Designs:—7 s. Louis de Bougainville; 20 s. Bougainvillea flower; 25 s. Ships *La Boudeuse* and *L'Etoile*.

105 Globe and Human Rights Emblem

106 Dr. Martin Luther King

(Des G. Vasarhelyi. Photo Harrison)

1968 (26 Aug). *Human Rights Year. W* **61.** *P* 14.

310	**105**	7 s. greenish blue, brown and gold	10	10
311		20 s. orange, green and gold	10	10
312		25 s. violet, green and gold	15	10
310/12		*Set of* 3	30	20

(Des and litho D.L.R.)

1968 (23 Sept). *Martin Luther King Commemoration. W* **61.** *P* 14½ × 14.

313	**106**	7 s. black and olive-green	10	10
314		20 s. black and bright purple	10	10

107 Polynesian Version of Madonna and Child

108 Frangipani—*Plumeria acuminata*

(Des and litho D.L.R.)

1968 (14 Oct). *Christmas. W* **61.** *P* 14.

315	**107**	1 s. multicoloured	10	10
316		3 s. multicoloured	10	10
317		20 s. multicoloured	10	10
318		30 s. multicoloured	15	15
315/18		*Set of* 4	30	30

(Des J.W. Litho Format)

1969 (20 Jan). *Seventh Anniv of Independence. T* **108** *and similar multicoloured designs. P* 14½.

319	2 s. Type **108**	10	10
320	7 s. Hibiscus *(vert)*	25	10
321	20 s. Red-Ginger *(vert)*	65	10
322	30 s. "Moso'oi"	80	35
319/22	*Set of* 4	1·60	50

109 R. L. Stevenson and *Treasure Island*

110 Weightlifting

(Des Jennifer Toombs. Litho D.L.R.)

1969 (21 Apr). *75th Death Anniv of Robert Louis Stevenson. Horiz designs, each showing portrait as in T* **109.** *Multicoloured. W* **61** *(sideways). P* 14.

323	3 s. Type **109**	15	10
324	7 s. *Kidnapped*	20	10
325	20 s. *Dr. Jekyll and Mr. Hyde*	45	10
326	22 s. *Weir of Hermiston*	55	15
323/6	*Set of* 4	1·25	40

(Des J. Mason. Photo Note Ptg Branch, Reserve Bank of Australia)

1969 (21 July). *Third South Pacific Games, Port Moresby. T* **110** *and similar vert designs. P* 13½.

327	3 s. black and sage-green	10	10
328	20 s. black and light blue	10	10
329	22 s. black and dull orange	15	15
327/9	*Set of* 3	30	30

Designs:—20 s. Yachting; 22 s. Boxing.

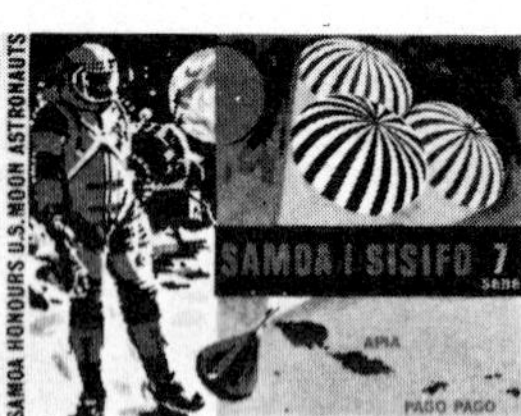

113 U.S. Astronaut on the Moon and the Splashdown near Samoan Islands

(Des J. Mason. Photo Note Ptg Branch, Reserve Bank of Australia)

1969 (24 July). *First Man on the Moon. P* 13½.

330	**113**	7 s. multicoloured	15	15
331		20 s. multicoloured	15	15

OMNIBUS ISSUES

Details, together with prices for complete sets, of the various Omnibus issues from the 1935 Silver Jubilee series to date are included in a special section following Zimbabwe at the end of Volume 2.

114 "Virgin with Child" (Murillo)

(Des and photo Heraclio Fournier)

1969 (13 Oct). *Christmas. T* **114** *and similar vert designs. Multicoloured. P* 14.

332 1 s. Type **114** 10 10
333 3 s. "The Holy Family" (El Greco) 10 10
334 20 s. "The Nativity" (El Greco) 20 10
335 30 s. "The Adoration of the Magi" (detail, Velazquez) 20 15
332/5 .. .. *Set of* 4 40 30
MS336 116 × 126 mm. Nos. 332/5 .. .. 60 1·25

115 Seventh Day Adventists' Sanatorium, Apia

(Des V. Whiteley. Litho Format)

1970 (19 Jan). *Eighth Anniv of Independence. T* **115** *and similar designs. W* **61** *(sideways on* 2, 7 *and* 22 *s.). P* 14.

337 2 s. yellow-brown, pale slate and black .. 10 10
338 7 s. violet, buff and black 10 10
339 20 s. rose, lilac and black 15 10
340 22 s. olive-green, cinnamon and black .. 15 15
337/40 .. .. *Set of* 4 30 30

Designs: *Horiz*—7 s. Rev. Father Violette and Roman Catholic Cathedral, Apia; 22 s. John Williams, 1797–1839, and London Missionary Society Church, Sapali'i. *Vert*—20 s. Mormon Church of Latter Day Saints, Tuasivi-on-Safotulafai.

119 Wreck of S.M.S. *Adler*

(Des J.W. Litho Questa)

1970 (27 Apr). *Great Apia Hurricane of* 1889. *T* **119** *and similar horiz designs. Multicoloured. W* **61** *(sideways). P* 13½.

341 5 s. Type **119** 45 10
342 7 s. U.S.S. *Nipsic* 50 10
343 10 s. H.M.S. *Calliope* 65 25
344 20 s. Apia after the hurricane .. .. .. 2·00 1·25
341/4 .. .. *Set of* 4 3·25 1·50

120 Sir Gordon Taylor's *Frigate Bird III*

(Des R. Honisett. Photo. Note Ptg Branch, Reserve Bank of Australia)

1970 (27 July). *Air. Aircraft. T* **120** *and similar horiz designs. Multicoloured. P* 13½ × 13.

345 3 s. Type **120** 35 10
346 7 s. Polynesian Airlines "DC-3" 70 10
347 20 s. Pan-American "Samoan Clipper" .. 1·75 60
348 30 s. Air Samoa Britten-Norman "Islander" 2·00 1·25
a. Pale purple omitted £250
345/8 .. .. *Set of* 4 4·25 1·75

121 Kendal's Chronometer and Cook's Sextant — **122** "Peace for the World" (F. B. Eccles)

(Des J. Berry, adapted J. Cooter. Litho Questa)

1970 (14 Sept). *Cook's Exploration of the Pacific. T* **121** *and similar designs. W* **61** *(sideways on* 30 *s.). P* 14.

349 1 s. carmine, silver and black 20 15
350 2 s. multicoloured 35 25
351 20 s. black, bright blue and gold .. .. 1·75 1·00
352 30 s. multicoloured .. .. 2·75 1·75
349/52 .. .. *Set of* 4 4·50 2·75

Designs: *Vert*—2 s. Cook's statue, Whitby; 20 s. Cook's head. *Horiz* (83 × 25 *mm*)—30 s. Cook, H.M.S. *Endeavour* and island.

(Des from paintings. Photo Heraclio Fournier)

1970 (26 Oct). *Christmas. T* **122** *and similar vert designs. Multicoloured. P* 13.

353 2 s. Type **122** 10 10
354 3 s. "The Holy Family" (W. E. Jahnke) .. 10 10
355 20 s. "Mother and Child" (F. B. Eccles) .. 15 10
356 30 s. "Prince of Peace" (Meleane Fe'ao) .. 20 15
353/6 .. .. *Set of* 4 35 30
MS357 111 × 158 mm. Nos. 353/6 .. .. 60 1·25

123 Pope Paul VI — **124** Native and Tree

(Des J. Cooter. Litho Format)

1970 (20 Nov). *Visit of Pope Paul to Samoa. W* **61**. *P* 14×14½.

358 **123** 8 s. black and grey-blue 15 15
359 20 s. black and plum 35 15

(Des G. Drummond from sketches by the American Timber Co. Litho Questa)

1971 (1 Feb). *Timber Industry. T* **124** *and similar multicoloured designs. P* 13½.

360 3 s. Type **124** 10 10
361 8 s. Bulldozer in clearing (*horiz*) 15 10
362 20 s. Log in sawmill (*horiz*) 30 10
363 22 s. Floating logs and harbour 30 15
360/3 .. .. *Set of* 4 70 30

125 Fautasi (canoe) in Apia Harbour and first stamps of Samoa and U.S.A.

(*Half-sized illustration. Actual size* 84 × 26 *mm*)

(Des E. Roberts. Photo Courvoisier)

1971 (12 Mar). *"Interpex" Stamp Exhibition, New York. Sheet* 138 × 80 *mm. P* 11½.

MS364 **125** 70 s. multicoloured .. .. .. 85 1·40

126 Siva Dance — **127** "Queen Salamasina"

(Des and litho J.W.)

1971 (9 Aug). *Tourism. T* **126** *and similar horiz designs. Multicoloured. W* **61** *(sideways). P* 14.

365 5 s. Type **126** 40 10
366 7 s. Samoan cricket .. .. 1·00 60
367 8 s. Hideaway Hotel .. .. 1·00 35
368 10 s. Aggie Grey and her hotel .. .. 1·00 60
365/8 .. .. *Set of* 4 3·00 1·40

(Des Jennifer Toombs. Litho J.W.)

1971 (20 Sept). *Myths and Legends of Old Samoa* (1st *series*). *T* **127** *and similar vert designs from carvings by S. Ortquist. Multicoloured. W* **61** *(sideways). P* 14 × 13½.

369 3 s. Type **127** 10 10
370 8 s. "Lu and his Sacred Hens" 15 10
371 10 s. "God Tagaloa fishes Samoa from the sea" 20 10
372 22 s. "Mount Vaea and the Pool of Tears" .. 35 20
369/72 .. .. *Set of* 4 70 30

See also Nos. 426/9.

128 "The Virgin and Child" (Bellini) — **129** Map and Scales of Justice

(Des J. Cooter. Litho J.W.)

1971 (4 Oct). *Christmas. T* **128** *and similar design. W* **61**. *P* 14 × 13½.

373 **128** 2 s. multicoloured 10 10
374 3 s. multicoloured 10 10
375 – 20 s. multicoloured 20 10
376 – 30 s. multicoloured 30 20
373/6 .. .. *Set of* 4 55 35

Design: *Vert*—20 s., 30 s. "The Virgin and Child with St. Anne and John the Baptist" (Leonardo da Vinci).

(Des E. Roberts. Photo Courvoisier)

1972 (10 Jan). *First South Pacific Judicial Conference. P* 11½ × 11.

377 **129** 10 s. multicoloured 15 15

Issued on matt, almost invisible gum.

130 Asau Wharf, Savaii — **131** Flags of Member Countries

(Des V. Whiteley. Litho A. & M.)

1972 (10 Jan). *Tenth Anniv of Independence. T* **130** *and similar horiz designs. Multicoloured. W* **61** *(sideways). P* 13.

378 1 s. Type **130** 10 10
379 8 s. Parliament Building 10 10
380 10 s. Mothers' Centre 10 10
381 22 s. "Vailima" Residence and rulers 20 25
378/81 .. .. *Set of* 4 40 30

(Des V. Whiteley. Litho Questa)

1972 (17 Mar). *25th Anniv of South Pacific Commission. T* **131** *and similar multicoloured designs. W* **61** *(sideways on* 8 *s. and* 10 *s.). P* 14 × 13½ (3 *and* 7 *s.*) *or* 13½ × 14 (*others*).

382 3 s. Type **131** 10 15
383 7 s. Flag and Afoafouvale Misimoa (Gen Sec) 10 15
384 8 s. H.Q. building, Nouméa (*horiz*) 15 15
385 10 s. Flags and area map (*horiz*) 15 15
382/5 .. .. *Set of* 4 40 55

132 Expedition Ships — **133** Bull Conch

(Des J. Berry; adapted J. Cooter. Litho Questa)

1972 (14 June). *250th Anniv of sighting of Western Samoa by Jacob Roggeveen. T* **132** *and similar horiz designs. Multicoloured.* **W 61** *(sideways, except 2 s.). P* 14½.

386 2 s. Type **132** 15 10
387 8 s. Ships in storm 45 10
388 10 s. Ships passing island 50 10
389 30 s. Route of Voyage (85 × 25 *mm*) .. .. 1·75 1·50
386/9 .. .. *Set of* 4 2·50 1·60

(Des Format ($5) or J.W. (others). Litho Format ($5), Questa (others))

1972 (18 Oct)–**76.** *T* **133** *and similar multicoloured designs.* **W 61** *(sideways, on 1 s. to 50 s.). White, ordinary paper. P* 13½ ($1 *to* $5) *or* 14½ *(others).*

390 1 s. Type **133** 20 10
a. Cream, chalk-surfaced paper (30.11.76) .. .. 1·50 1·50
391 2 s. *Oryctes rhinoceros* (beetle) 20 10
a. Cream, chalk-surfaced paper (30.11.76) .. .. 1·50 1·50
392 3 s. Skipjack (fish) 30 20
393 4 s. Painted Crab 30 10
a. Cream, chalk-surfaced paper (30.11.76) .. .. 1·50 1·50
394 5 s. Butterfly Fish 35 10
a. Cream, chalk-surfaced paper (30.11.76) .. .. 1·50 1·50
395 7 s. *Danaus hamata* (butterfly) .. .. 1·25 30
396 10 s. Triton Shell 80 40
397 20 s. *Chrysochroa abdominalis* (beetle) .. 1·25 30
398 50 s. Spiny Lobster .. .. .. 2·00 1·25
399 $1 *Gnathothlibus erotus* (moth) (29×45 *mm*) .. .. 7·00 2·50
399*a* $2 Green Turtle (29×45 *mm*) (18.6.73) 8·00 4·00
399*b* $4 Black Marlin (29×45 *mm*) (27.3.74) 5·00 7·00
399*c* $5 Green Tree Lizard (29×45 *mm*) (30.6.75) .. .. 5·50 7·50
390/9*c* .. .. *Set of* 13 29·00 21·00

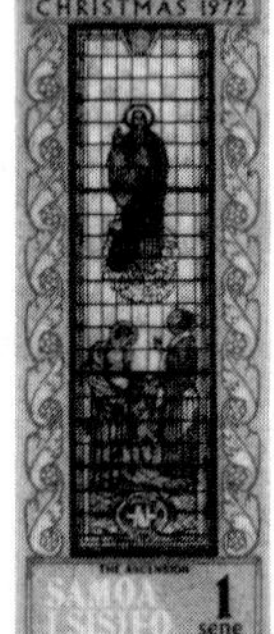

134 "The Ascension" **135** Erecting a Tent

(Des PAD Studio. Litho Harrison)

1972 (1 Nov). *Christmas. Stained-glass Windows in Apia. T* **134** *and similar vert designs. Multicoloured.* **W 61.** *P* 14 × 14½.

400 1 s. Type **134** 10 10
401 4 s. "The Blessed Virgin and Infant Christ" 10 10
402 10 s. "St. Andrew blessing Samoan canoe" .. 10 10
403 30 s. "The Good Shepherd" 40 30
400/3 .. .. *Set of* 4 50 40
MS404 70 × 159 mm. Nos. 400/3 .. .. 90 1·25

(Des G. Drummond. Litho Format)

1973 (29 Jan). *Boy Scout Movement. T* **135** *and similar horiz designs. Multicoloured.* **W 61** *(sideways). P* 14.

405 2 s. Saluting the flag 10 10
406 3 s. First-aid 10 10
407 8 s. Type **135** 25 10
408 20 s. Samoan action-song 90 85
405/8 .. .. *Set of* 4 1·10 95

136 Hawker Siddeley "748"

(Des E. Roberts. Photo Courvoisier)

1973 (9 Mar). *Air. T* **136** *and similar horiz designs showing aircraft at Faleolo Airport. Multicoloured. P* 11½.

409 8 s. Type **136** 45 15
410 10 s. H.S. "748" in flight 55 15
411 12 s. H.S. "748" on runway 65 35
412 22 s. B.A.C. 1-11 .. .. 1·00 60
409/12 .. .. *Set of* 4 2·40 1·10
Issued on matt, almost invisible gum.

ALTERED CATALOGUE NUMBERS

Any Catalogue numbers altered from the last edition are shown as a list in the introductory pages.

137 Apia General Hospital **138** Mother and Child, and Map

(Des C. Abbott. Litho Questa)

1973 (20 Aug). *25th Anniv of W.H.O. T* **137** *and similar vert designs. Multicoloured.* **W 61.** *P* 14.

413 2 s. Type **137** 10 10
414 8 s. Baby clinic 20 10
415 20 s. Filariasis research 45 20
416 22 s. Family welfare 45 30
413/16 .. .. *Set of* 4 1·10 55

(Des W. E. Jahnke (3 s.), Fiasili Keil (4 s.), E. Cooter (others); adapted Jennifer Toombs. Litho J.W.)

1973 (15 Oct). *Christmas. T* **138** *and similar vert designs. Multicoloured.* **W 61.** *P* 14.

417 3 s. Type **138** 10 10
418 4 s. Mother and child, and village 10 10
419 10 s. Mother and child, and beach 10 10
420 30 s. Samoan stable 45 50
417/20 .. .. *Set of* 4 55 55
MS421 144 × 103 mm. Nos. 417/20 .. .. 60 75

139 Boxing

(Des G. Drummond. Litho Questa)

1974 (24 Jan). *Commonwealth Games, Christchurch. T* **139** *and similar horiz designs. Multicoloured.* **W 61** *(sideways). P* 14.

422 8 s. Type **139** 10 10
423 10 s. Weightlifting 10 10
424 20 s. Bowls 20 10
425 30 s. Athletics stadium 35 45
422/5 .. .. *Set of* 4 70 60

(Des Jennifer Toombs. Litho Questa)

1974 (13 Aug). *Myths and Legends of Old Samoa (2nd series). Vert designs as T* **127** *from carvings by S. Ortquist. Multicoloured.* **W 61.** *P* 14 × 13½.

426 2 s. Tigilau and sacred dove 10 10
427 8 s. Pili, his sons and fishing net 10 10
428 20 s. Sina and the origin of the coconut .. 30 10
429 30 s. The warrior, Nafanua 45 45
426/9 .. .. *Set of* 4 80 55

140 Mail-van at Faleolo Airport

(Des E. Roberts. Photo Heraclio Fournier)

1974 (4 Sept). *Centenary of Universal Postal Union. T* **140** *and similar horiz designs. Multicoloured. P* 13 × 12½ *(50 s.) or* 13 *(others).*

430 8 s. Type **140** 15 10
431 20 s. Cargo liner at Apia Wharf 35 15
432 22 s. Early Post Office, Apia and letter .. 40 25
433 50 s. William Willis and *Age Unlimited* (sailing-raft) (87×29 *mm*) .. .. .. 80 1·00
430/3 .. .. *Set of* 4 1·50 1·40
MS434 140×82 mm. No. 433 .. .. .. 1·25 2·25

141 "Holy Family" (Sebastiano)

(Des PAD Studio. Litho Enschedé)

1974 (25 Nov). *Christmas. T* **141** *and similar horiz designs. Multicoloured.* **W 61** *(sideways). P* 13×13½.

435 3 s. Type **141** 10 10
436 4 s. "Virgin and Child with Saints" (Lotto) .. 10 10
437 10 s. "Madonna and Child with St. John" (Titian) 10 10
438 30 s. "Adoration of the Shepherds" (Rubens) .. 35 45
435/8 .. .. *Set of* 4 45 50
MS439 128 × 87 mm. Nos. 435/8 .. .. .. 70 1·40

142 Winged Passion Flower

(Des J.W. Litho Questa)

1975 (15 Jan). *Tropical Flowers. T* **142** *and similar multicoloured designs.* **W 61** *(sideways on 8 and 30 s.). P* 14.

440 8 s. Type **142** 20 10
441 20 s. Gardenia *(vert)* 50 45
442 22 s. *Barringtonia samoensis (vert)* 55 50
443 30 s. Malay apple 85 85
440/3 .. .. *Set of* 4 1·90 1·75

143 *Joyita* loading at Apia **144** "Pate" Drum

(Des E. Roberts. Photo Heraclio Fournier)

1975 (14 Mar). *"Interpex 1975" Stamp Exhibition, New York, and "Joyita Mystery". T* **143** *and similar horiz designs. Multicoloured. P* 13½.

444 1 s. Type **143** 10 10
445 8 s. *Joyita* sails for Tokelau Islands 15 10
446 20 s. Taking to rafts 35 25
447 22 s. *Joyita* abandoned 40 30
448 50 s. Discovery of *Joyita* north of Fiji .. .. 1·00 1·25
444/8 .. .. *Set of* 5 1·75 1·75
MS449 150 × 100 mm. Nos. 444/8. Imperf .. 2·50 3·50

(Des Iosua To'afa; adapted L. Curtis. Litho Harrison)

1975 (30 Sept). *Musical Instruments. T* **144** *and similar vert designs. Multicoloured.* **W 61** *(sideways). P* 14.

450 8 s. Type **144** 10 10
451 20 s. "Lali" drum 20 10
452 22 s. "Logo" drum 20 10
453 30 s. "Pu" shell horn 35 30
450/3 .. .. *Set of* 4 75 50

145 "Mother and Child" (Meleane Fe'ao) **146** "The Boston Massacre, 1770" (Paul Revere)

(Des local artists; adapted G. Vasarhelyi. Litho Walsall)

1975 (25 Nov). *Christmas. T* **145** *and similar vert designs. Multicoloured.* **W 61** *(inverted). P* 14.

454 3 s. Type **145** 10 10
455 4 s. "The Saviour" (Polataia Tuigamala) .. 10 10
456 10 s. "A Star is Born" (Iosua To'afa) 10 10
457 30 s. "Madonna and Child" (Ernesto Coter) .. 30 45
454/7 .. .. *Set of* 4 45 50
MS458 101 × 134 mm. Nos. 454/7 .. .. 60 1·25

(Des J. Cooter. Litho Walsall)

1976 (20 Jan). *Bicentenary of American Revolution. T* **146** *and similar horiz designs. Multicoloured.* **W 61** *(sideways). P* 13½.

459 7 s. Type **146** 20 15
460 8 s. "The Declaration of Independence" (Trumbull) 20 15
461 20 s. "The Ship that Sank in Victory, 1779" (Ferris) 60 35
462 22 s. "Pitt addressing the Commons, 1782" (R. A. Hickel) 60 35
463 50 s. "The Battle of Princetown" (Mercer) .. 1·50 1·75
459/63 .. .. *Set of* 5 2·75 2·50
MS464 160 × 125 mm. Nos. 459/63 .. .. 5·50 6·50

147 Mullet Fishing

(Des V. Whiteley Studio. Litho Harrison)

1976 (27 Apr). *Fishing. T* **147** *and similar horiz designs. Multicoloured.* **W 61.** *P* 14.

465 10 s. Type **147** 10 10
466 12 s. Fish traps 15 10
467 22 s. Samoan fishermen 30 10
468 50 s. Net fishing 85 70
465/8 .. .. *Set of* 4 1·25 90

148 Paul Revere's Ride

(Des J. Berry. Photo Heraclio Fournier)

1976 (29 May). *"Interphil" Stamp Exhibition. Sheet* 120 × 80 *mm. P* 13.

MS469 **148** $1 gold, black and emerald .. .. 2·75 2·50

149 Boxing   **150** Mary and Joseph going to Bethlehem

(Des C. Abbott. Litho Questa)

1976 (21 June). *Olympic Games, Montreal. T* **149** *and similar horiz designs. Multicoloured. W* **61** *(sideways). P* 14.

470 10 s. Type **149** 10 10
471 12 s. Wrestling 10 10
472 22 s. Javelin 15 10
473 50 s. Weightlifting 45 50
470/3 .. .. *Set of* 4 70 60

(Des C. Abbott. Litho Questa)

1976 (18 Oct). *Christmas. T* **150** *and similar vert designs. Multicoloured. W* **61**. *P* 13½.

474 3 s. Type **150** 10 10
475 5 s. The Shepherds 10 10
476 22 s. The Holy Family 15 10
477 50 s. The Magi 55 65
474/7 .. .. *Set of* 4 70 75
MS478 124 × 115 mm. Nos. 474/7 .. .. 80 1·75

151 Queen Elizabeth and View of Apia

(Des BG Studio. Litho Questa)

1977 (11 Feb). *Silver Jubilee and Royal Visit. T* **151** *and similar horiz designs. Multicoloured. W* **61** *(sideways). P* 13½.

479 12 s. Type **151** 20 10
480 26 s. Presentation of Spurs of Chivalry .. 35 20
481 32 s. Queen and Royal Yacht *Britannia* .. 50 25
482 50 s. Queen leaving Abbey 55 80
479/82 .. .. *Set of* 4 1·40 1·25

152 Map of Flight Route

(Des C. Abbott. Litho Walsall)

1977 (20 May). *50th Anniv of Lindbergh's Transatlantic Flight. Horiz designs showing the "Spirit of St. Louis". Multicoloured. W* **61** *(sideways). P* 14.

483 22 s. Type **152** 25 10
484 24 s. In flight 35 15
485 26 s. Landing 35 15
486 50 s. Col. Lindbergh 80 75
483/6 .. .. *Set of* 4 1·60 1·00
MS487 194 × 93 mm. Nos. 483/6 .. .. .. 2·40 2·75

153 3d. Express Stamp and First Mail Notice

(Des J. Cooter. Litho Questa)

1977 (29 Aug). *Stamp Centenary. T* **153** *and similar horiz designs. W* **61** *(sideways). P* 13½.

488 12 s. lemon, red and sepia 20 10
489 13 s. multicoloured 20 15
490 26 s. multicoloured 45 30
491 50 s. multicoloured .. .. 80 1·00
488/91 .. .. *Set of* 4 1·50 1·40

Designs:—13 s. Early cover and 6d. Express; 26 s. Apia Post Office and 1d. Express; 50 s. Schooner *Energy*, 1877, and 6d. Express.

154 Apia Automatic Telephone Exchange   **155** "Samoan Nativity" (P. Feata)

(Des J.W. Litho Questa)

1977 (28 Oct*). *Telecommunications Project. T* **154** *and similar horiz designs. Multicoloured. W* **61** *(sideways). P* 14.

492 12 s. Type **154** 15 10
493 13 s. Mulinuu Radio Terminal 15 10
494 26 s. Old and new telephones 30 20
495 50 s. "Global communication" 50 70
492/5 .. .. *Set of* 4 1·00 1·00

*The above were originally scheduled for release on 11 July and were put on sale by the Crown Agents in England on that date.

(Designs adapted by J.W. Litho Questa)

1977 (31 Oct). *Christmas. T* **155** *and similar vert designs. Multicoloured. W* **61**. *P* 14.

496 4 s. Type **155** 10 10
497 6 s. "The Offering" (E. Saofaiga) 10 10
498 26 s. "Madonna and Child" (F. Tupou) .. 20 10
499 50 s. "Emmanuel" (M. Sapa'u) 35 40
496/9 .. .. *Set of* 4 55 50
MS500 117×159 mm. Nos. 496/9 .. .. .. 55 85

156 Polynesian Airlines Boeing "737"

(Des E. Roberts. Litho Heraclio Fournier)

1978 (21 Mar). *Aviation Progress. T* **156** *and similar horiz designs. Multicoloured. P* 14.

501 12 s. Type **156** 20 10
502 24 s. Wright brothers' *Flyer* 40 20
503 26 s. Kingsford Smith's *Southern Cross* .. 40 20
504 50 s. "Concorde" .. .. 1·10 85
501/4 .. .. *Set of* 4 1·90 1·25
MS505 150 × 120 mm. Nos. 501/4 .. .. .. 2·25 2·75

157 Hatchery, Aleipata   **158** Pacific Pigeon

(Des J.W. Litho Questa)

1978 (14 Apr). *Hawksbill Turtle Conservation Project. T* **157** *and similar horiz design. Multicoloured. W* **61** *(sideways). P* 14½ × 14.

506 24 s. Type **157** 35 30
507 $1 Turtle .. .. 1·60 1·60

(Des Jennifer Toombs. Litho Questa)

1978 (21 Apr). *25th Anniv of Coronation. T* **158** *and similar vert designs. P* 15.

508 26 s. black, brown and deep magenta 25 30
a. Sheetlet. Nos. 508/10 × 2 .. .. .. 1·50
509 26 s. multicoloured 25 30
510 26 s. black, brown and deep magenta 25 30
508/10 .. .. *Set of* 3 70 80

Designs:—No. 508, King's Lion; No. 509, Queen Elizabeth II; No. 510, Type **158**.

Nos. 508/10 were printed together in small sheets of 6, containing two *se-tenant* strips of 3, with horizontal gutter margin between.

159 Flags of Western Samoa and Canada with Canadian National Tower   **160** Captain Cook

(Des BG Studio. Litho Walsall)

1978 (9 June). *"Capex '78" International Stamp Exhibition, Toronto. Sheet* 119 × 79 *mm. W* **61**. *P* 14½.

MS511 **159** $1 blue, red and black .. .. .. 1·25 1·75

(Des J. Berry. Litho Harrison)

1978 (28 Aug). *250th Birth Anniv of Captain Cook. T* **160** *and similar vert designs. Multicoloured. W* **61**. *P* 14½ × 14.

512 12 s. Type **160** 30 15
513 24 s. Cook's cottage, Gt Ayton, Yorkshire .. 60 35
514 26 s. Old drawbridge over the river Esk, Whitby 70 35
515 50 s. H.M.S. *Resolution* .. .. 1·25 1·50
512/15 .. .. *Set of* 4 2·50 2·10

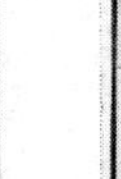

161 Thick-edged Cowry   **162** "Madonna on the Crescent"

(Photo Courvoisier)

1978 (15 Sept)–**80**. *Shells. Horiz designs as T* **161**. *Multicoloured. P* 12½.

516 1 s. Type **161** 15 10
517 2 s. Isabella cowry 15 10
518 3 s. Money cowry 25 10
519 4 s. Eroded cowry 30 10
520 6 s. Honey cowry 30 10
521 7 s. Banded cowry 35 10
522 10 s. Globe cowry 40 10
523 11 s. Mole cowry 40 10
524 12 s. Children's cowry 40 10
525 13 s. Flag cone (20.11.78) 40 10
526 14 s. Soldier cone (20.11.78) 40 10
527 24 s. Cloth-of-gold cone (20.11.78) 40 10
528 26 s. Lettered cone (20.11.78) 45 10
529 50 s. Tiled cone (20.11.78) 50 15
530 $1 Black Marble cone (20.11.78) 95 60
530*a* $2 Marlin-spike auger (18.7.79) .. .. 1·50 90
530*b* $3 Scorpion Spider Conch (18.7.79) .. .. 2·25 1·50
530*c* $5 Common Harp (26.8.80) .. .. .. 3·75 3·00
516/30*c* .. .. *Set of* 18 12·00 6·00

Nos. 530*a*/*c* are larger, size 36 × 26 mm.

Issued on matt, almost invisible gum.

(Des C. Abbott. Litho Questa)

1978 (6 Nov). *Christmas. Woodcuts by Dürer. T* **162** *and similar vert designs. W* **61**. *P* 14.

531 4 s. black and yellow-brown 10 10
532 6 s. black and turquoise-blue 10 10
533 26 s. black and bright blue 15 10
534 50 s. black and bright violet 35 50
531/4 .. .. *Set of* 4 50 55
MS535 103 × 154 mm. Nos. 531/4 .. .. .. 70 1·00

Designs:—6 s. "Nativity"; 26 s. "Adoration of the Magi"; 50 s. "Annunciation".

163 Boy with Coconuts   **164** *Charles W. Morgan*

(Des G. Drummond. Litho Questa)

1979 (10 Apr). *International Year of the Child. T* **163** *and similar horiz designs. Multicoloured. W* **61** *(sideways). P* 14.

536 12 s. Type **163** 15 10
537 24 s. White Sunday 30 15
538 26 s. Children at pump 35 15
539 50 s. Young girl with ukulele 70 80
536/9 .. .. *Set of* 4 1·40 1·10

(Des J. Cooter. Litho Format)

1979 (29 May). *Sailing Ships (1st series). Whaling Ships. T* **164** *and similar horiz designs. Multicoloured.* **W 61** *(sideways). P* 13½.

540 12 s. Type **164** 30 10
541 14 s. *Lagoda* 35 10
542 24 s. *James T. Arnold* 50 20
543 50 s. *Splendid* .. .. 1·10 85
540/3 .. .. *Set of* 4 2·00 1·10

See also Nos. 561/4 and 584/7.

165 Launch of "Apollo 11"

166 Sir Rowland Hill (statue) and Penny Black

(Des J.W. Litho Questa)

1979 (20 June). *10th Anniv of Moon Landing. T* **165** *and similar designs in chocolate and dull vermilion* (12 s.) *or multicoloured (others).* **W 61** *(sideways on* 14, 26 *s. and* $1). *P* 14½ × 14 (12, 24, 50 s.) *or* 14 × 14½ *(others).*

544 12 s. Type **165** 20 10
545 14 s. Lunar module and astronaut on Moon (*horiz*) 25 10
546 24 s. View of Earth from Moon 30 15
547 26 s. Astronaut on Moon (*horiz*) 30 15
548 50 s. Lunar and Command modules in Space 55 55
549 $1 Command module after splash-down (*horiz*) .. .. 1·25 1·50
544/9 .. .. *Set of* 6 2·50 2·25
MS550 90 × 130 mm. No. 549 .. .. .. 1·00 1·75

No. **MS**550 is inscribed "Spashdown" in error.

(Des and litho J.W.)

1979 (27 Aug). *Death Centenary of Sir Rowland Hill. T* **166** *and similar vert designs. Multicoloured.* **W 61.** *P* 14.

551 12 s. Type **166** 15 10
552 24 s. Two-penny Blue with "Maltese Cross" postmark 20 15
553 26 s. Sir Rowland Hill and Penny Black .. 20 15
554 $1 Two-penny Blue and Sir Rowland Hill (statue) 60 75
551/4 .. .. *Set of* 4 1·00 1·00
MS555 128 × 95 mm. Nos. 551/4 .. .. .. 1·00 1·60

167 Anglican Church, Apia

(Des A. Peake. Photo Courvoisier)

1979 (22 Oct). *Christmas. Churches. T* **167** *and similar horiz designs. P* 11½.

556 4 s. black and pale blue 10 10
557 6 s. black and bright yellow-green 10 10
558 26 s. black and yellow-ochre 15 10
559 50 s. black and reddish lilac 30 30
556/9 .. .. *Set of* 4 45 35
MS560 150 × 124 mm. Nos. 556/9 .. .. 50 75

Designs:—6 s. Congregational Christian, Leulumoega; 26 s. Methodist, Piula; 50 s. Protestant, Apia.

Issued on matt, almost invisible gum.

(Des J. Cooter. Litho Format)

1980 (22 Jan). *Sailing Ships (2nd series). Whaling Ships. Horiz designs as T* **164.** *Multicoloured.* **W 61** *(sideways) P* 13½.

561 12 s. *William Hamilton* 30 10
562 14 s. *California* 35 15
563 24 s. *Liverpool II* 50 25
564 50 s. *Two Brothers* .. .. 1·10 70
561/4 .. .. *Set of* 4 2·00 1·10

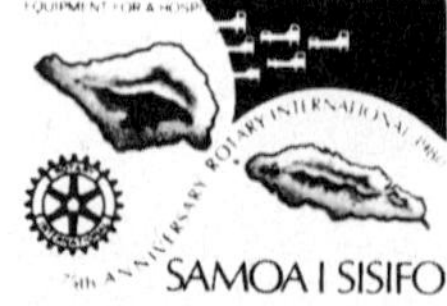

168 "Equipment for a Hospital"

(Des M. Goaman (12, 50 s.), E. Roberts (others). Photo Heraclio Fournier)

1980 (26 Mar). *Anniversaries. T* **168** *and similar horiz designs. Multicoloured. P* 13½ × 14.

565 12 s. Type **168** 30 10
566 13 s. John Williams, dove with olive twig and commemorative inscription 30 15
567 14 s. Dr. Wilhelm Solf (instigator), flag and commemorative inscription 35 15
568 24 s. Cairn Monument 45 25
569 26 s. Williams Memorial, Savai'i 45 25
570 50 s. Paul P. Harris (founder) 75 60
565/70 .. .. *Set of* 6 2·40 1·40

Commemorations:—12, 50 s. 75th anniversary of Rotary International; 13, 26 s. 150th anniversary of John Williams' (missionary) arrival in Samoa; 14, 24 s. 80th anniversary of raising of German flag.

169 Samoan Village Scene

(Des J.W. Litho Walsall)

1980 (6 May). *"London 1980" International Stamp Exhibition. Sheet* 140 × 81 *mm.* **W 61** *(sideways). P* 14.

MS571 **169** $1 multicoloured .. .. 80 1·25

170 Queen Elizabeth the Queen Mother in 1970

(Des Harrison. Litho Questa)

1980 (4 Aug). *80th Birthday of Queen Elizabeth the Queen Mother. P* 14.

572 **170** 50 s. multicoloured 50 35

171 1964 2nd Anniversary of New Zealand–Samoa Treaty of Friendship 2 s. Commemorative and "Zeapex '80" Emblem

(Des E. Roberts. Photo Heraclio Fournier)

1980 (23 Aug). *"Zeapex '80" International Stamp Exhibition, Auckland. Sheet* 130 × 80 *mm. P* 14.

MS573 **171** $1 multicoloured .. .. 1·25 1·40

172 Afiamalu Satellite Earth Station

(Des and photo Courvoisier)

1980 (20 Sept). *Afiamalu Satellite Earth Station. T* **172** *and similar horiz designs. Multicoloured. P* 11½.

574 12 s. Type **172** 15 10
575 14 s. Satellite station (*different*) 20 10
576 24 s. Satellite station and map of Savai'i and Upolu 30 15
577 50 s. Satellite and globe 60 60
574/7 .. .. *Set of* 4 1·10 85

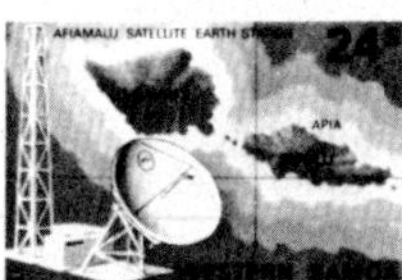

173 Afiamalu Satellite Earth Station 24 s. Commemorative Stamp and "Sydpex 80" Emblem

(Des E. Roberts. Litho Sprintpak, Mayne Nickless Ltd, Australia)

1980 (29 Sept). *"Sydpex 80" International Stamp Exhibition, Sydney. Sheet* 130 × 80 *mm. Imperf.*

MS578 **173** $2 multicoloured .. .. 2·00 2·00

174 "The Saviour" (J. Poynton)

175 President Franklin D. Roosevelt and Hyde Park (family home)

(Des G. Vasarhelyi. Litho Format)

1980 (28 Oct). *Christmas. Paintings. T* **174** *and similar vert designs. Multicoloured.* **W 61.** *P* 13½.

579 8 s. Type **174** 10 10
580 14 s. "Madonna and Child" (Lealofi F. Siaopo) 10 10
581 27 s. "Nativity" (Pasila Feata) 15 10
582 50 s. "Yuletide" (R. P. Aiono) 25 40
579/82 .. .. *Set of* 4 55 55
MS583 90 × 105 mm. Nos. 579/82 .. .. 1·00 1·50

(Des J. Cooter. Litho Format)

1981 (26 Jan). *Sailing Ships (3rd series). Horiz designs as T* **164.** *Multicoloured. P* 13½.

584 12 s. *Ocean* (whaling ship) 20 10
585 18 s. *Horatio* (whaling ship) 30 15
586 27 s. H.M.S. *Calliope* 45 25
587 32 s. H.M.S. *Calypso* 50 50
584/7 .. .. *Set of* 4 1·25 90

(Des J.W. Litho Format)

1981 (29 Apr). *International Year for Disabled Persons. President Franklin D. Roosevelt Commemoration. T* **175** *and similar horiz designs. Multicoloured. P* 14.

588 12 s. Type **175** 15 10
589 18 s. Roosevelt's inauguration, 4 March 1933 25 15
590 27 s. Franklin and Eleanor Roosevelt .. 35 20
591 32 s. Roosevelt's Lend-lease Bill (Atlantic convoy, 1941) 40 30
592 38 s. Roosevelt the philatelist 45 35
593 $1 Campobello House (summer home) .. 1·00 1·00
588/93 .. .. *Set of* 6 2·40 1·90

176 Hotel Tusitala

177 Wedding Bouquet from Samoa

(Des and litho Walsall)

1981 (29 June). *Tourism. T* **176** *and similar horiz designs. Multicoloured.* **W 61** *(sideways). P* 14½ × 14.

594 12 s. Type **176** 15 10
595 18 s. Apia Harbour 25 15
596 27 s. Aggie Grey's Hotel 25 20
597 32 s. Preparation for Ceremonial Kava .. 30 30
598 54 s. Piula water pool 55 55
594/8 .. .. *Set of* 5 1·40 1·10

(Des J.W. Litho Walsall)

1981 (22 July). *Royal Wedding. T* **177** *and similar vert designs. Multicoloured.* **W 61.** *P* 14.

599 18 s. Type **177** 25 10
600 32 s. Prince Charles as Colonel-in-Chief, Gordon Highlanders 35 20
601 $1 Prince Charles and Lady Diana Spencer 70 90
599/601 .. .. *Set of* 3 1·10 1·10

178 Tattooing Instruments

179 Black Marlin

(Des E. Roberts. Litho Cambec Press, Melbourne)

1981 (29 Sept). *Tattooing. T* **178** *and similar horiz designs. Multicoloured. P* 13½.

602 12 s. Type **178** 20 20
 a. Horiz strip of 4. Nos. 602/5 .. .. 1·25
603 18 s. First stage of tattooing 25 25
604 27 s. Progressive stage 30 30
605 $1 Completed tattoo 70 70
602/5 .. .. *Set of* 4 1·25 1·25

Nos. 602/5 were printed together, *se-tenant*, in horizontal strips of 4 throughout the sheet.

(Des E. Roberts. Litho Cambec Press, Melbourne)

1981 (9 Oct). *"Philatokyo '81" International Stamp Exhibition, Tokyo. Sheet* 130 × 80 *mm. P* 14 × 13½.

MS606 **179** $2 multicoloured .. .. 1·25 1·50

180 *Thespesia populnea*

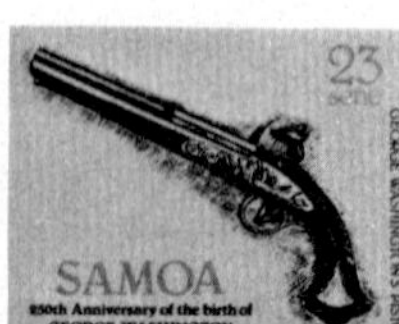

181 George Washington's Pistol

(Des and litho J.W.)

1981 (30 Nov). *Christmas. Flowers. T* **180** *and similar vert designs. Multicoloured.* **W 61.** *P* 13½.

607 11 s. Type **180** 15 10
608 15 s. Copper Leaf 20 15
609 23 s. *Allamanda cathartica* 30 25
610 $1 Mango .. .. 1·00 1·00
607/10 .. .. *Set of* 4 1·50 1·40
MS611 86 × 120 mm. Nos. 607/10 .. .. 1·60 2·25

(Des J.W. Litho Format)

1982 (26 Feb). *250th Birth Anniv of George Washington.* T **181** *and similar horiz designs, each in black, ochre and stone. P* 13½.

612 23 s. Type **181** 30 30
613 25 s. Mount Vernon (Washington's house) .. 30 30
614 34 s. George Washington 40 40
612/14 .. .. *Set of* 3 90 90
MS615 104 × 103 mm. $1 Washington taking Oath of Office as President .. .. 95 1·00

182 *Forum Samoa* (container ship)

(Des E. Roberts. Litho Cambec Press, Melbourne)

1982 (24 May). *20th Anniv of Independence.* T **182** *and similar horiz designs. Multicoloured. P* 13½ × 14.

616 18 s. Type **182** 30 20
617 23 s. "Air services" 40 30
618 25 s. N.P.F. (National Provident Fund) Building, Apia 40 30
619 $1 "Telecommunications" .. .. .. 1·10 1·00
616/19 .. .. *Set of* 4 2·00 1·60

183 Scouts map-reading and "75" **184** Boxing

(Des J.W. Litho Walsall)

1982 (20 July). *75th Anniv of Boy Scout Movement.* T **183** *and similar horiz designs. Multicoloured.* W **61** (*sideways*). *P* 14½.

620 5 s. Type **183** 10 10
621 38 s. Scout salute and "75" 40 40
622 44 s. Scout crossing river by rope, and "75" .. 50 50
623 $1 "Tower" of Scouts and "75" .. .. 1·00 1·00
620/23 .. .. *Set of* 4 1·75 1·75
MS624 93 × 81 mm. $1 As No. 623 but with portrait of Lord Baden-Powell replacing emblem (47 × 35 *mm*). *P* 11 .. .. 1·00 1·10

(Des Garden Studio. Litho Walsall)

1982 (20 Sept). *Commonwealth Games, Brisbane.* T **184** *and similar vert designs. Multicoloured.* W w **14**. *P* 14½.

625 23 s. Type **184** 25 20
626 25 s. Hurdling 25 20
627 34 s. Weightlifting 35 40
628 $1 Bowling .. .. 95 1·75
625/8 .. .. *Set of* 4 1·60 2·25

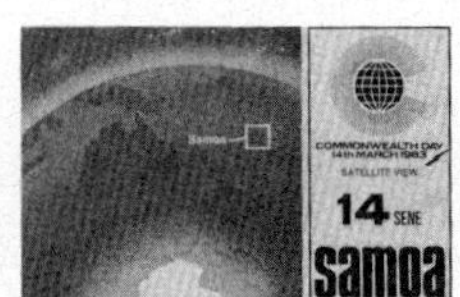

185 "Mary and Joseph" (Emma Dunlop) **186** Satellite View of Australasia

(Des J.W. Litho Questa)

1982 (15 Nov). *Christmas. Children's Pictures.* T **185** *and similar horiz designs. Multicoloured.* W **61** (*sideways*). *P* 14 × 14½.

629 11 s. Type **185** 15 10
630 15 s. "Mary, Joseph and baby Jesus" (Marie Tofaeono) 15 15
631 38 s. "Madonna and Child" (Ralph Laban and Fetalaiga Fareni) 40 30
632 $1 "Mother and Child" (Panapa Pouesi) .. 90 1·10
629/32 .. .. *Set of* 4 1·40 1·50
MS633 130 × 119 mm. Nos. 629/32 .. .. 1·60 2·25

(Des Walsall. Litho Enschedé)

1983 (23 Feb). *Commonwealth Day.* T **186** *and similar horiz designs. Multicoloured.* W w **14** (*sideways*). *P* 13 × 13½.

634 14 s. Type **186** 10 10
635 29 s. Flag of Samoa 15 20
636 43 s. Harvesting copra 25 25
637 $1 Head of State Malietoa Tanumafili II .. 50 80
634/7 .. .. *Set of* 4 90 1·25

187 Douglas "DC-1"

(Des J.W. Litho Questa)

1983 (7 June). *Bicentenary of Manned Flight and 50th Anniv of Douglas Commercial Aircraft. Sheet,* 215 × 113 *mm, containing horiz designs as* T **187**. *Multicoloured.* W w **14** (*sideways*). *P* 14.
MS638 32 s. × 10, each design showing a different Douglas aircraft from the "DC-1" to the "DC-10" .. 2·50 2·75

188 Pole-vaulting **189** Lime

(Des McCombie Skinner Studio. Litho Format)

1983 (31 Aug). *South Pacific Games.* T **188** *and similar vert designs. Multicoloured.* W w **14**. *P* 14 × 14½.

639 8 s. Type **188** 30 10
640 15 s. Netball 40 20
641 25 s. Tennis 60 40
642 32 s. Weight-lifting 60 60
643 35 s. Boxing 65 60
644 46 s. Football 80 70
645 48 s. Golf 90 85
646 56 s. Rugby .. .. 1·00 95
639/46 .. .. *Set of* 8 4·75 4·00

(Des E. Roberts. Litho Enschedé)

1983 (28 Sept)–**84**. *Fruit.* T **189** *and similar vert designs. Multicoloured.* W w **14** (*inverted on* 1 *s.*). *P* 13½ ($2 *to* $5) *or* 14 × 13½ (*others*).

647 1 s. Type **189** 10 10
648 2 s. Star fruit 10 10
649 3 s. Mangosteen 10 10
650 4 s. Lychee 10 10
651 7 s. Passion fruit 10 10
652 8 s. Mango 10 10
653 11 s. Pawpaw 10 10
654 13 s. Pineapple 15 15
655 14 s. Breadfruit 15 15
656 15 s. Banana 20 15
657 21 s. Cashew Nut (30.11.83) 60 20
658 25 s. Guava (30.11.83) 80 20
659 32 s. Water Melon (30.11.83) 65 35
660 48 s. Sasalapa (30.11.83) 80 60
661 56 s. Avocado (30.11.83) 85 60
662 $1 Coconut (30.11.83) .. .. .. 1·00 65
663 $2 Vi Apple (11.4.84) .. .. .. 1·25 1·50
664 $4 Grapefruit (11.4.84) .. .. .. 2·00 2·75
665 $5 Orange (11.4.84) .. .. 2·50 3·00
647/65 .. .. *Set of* 19 10·00 9·50

Nos. 663/5 are larger, size 25 × 35½ mm.

Samoa $1

190 On Parade **191** Togitogiga Falls, Upolu

(Des Brian Melton Studio. Litho Format)

1983 (10 Oct). *Centenary of Boys' Brigade. Sheet* 120 × 83 *mm.* W w **14**. *P* 14.
MS668 **190** $1 multicoloured .. .. .. 2·50 2·00

(Litho Format)

1984 (15 Feb). *Scenic Views.* T **191** *and similar horiz designs. Multicoloured.* W w **14** (*sideways*). *P* 14.

669 25 s. Type **191** 30 15
670 32 s. Lano Beach, Savai'i 50 50
671 48 s. Mulinu'u Point, Upolu 75 85
672 56 s. Nu'utele Island .. .. 80 1·10
669/72 .. .. *Set of* 4 2·10 2·40

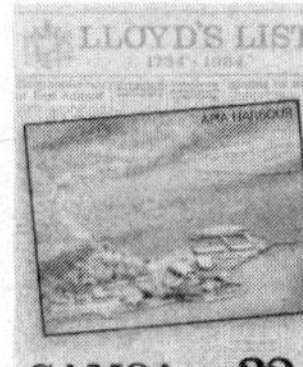

19 th U.P.U. CONGRESS
HAMBURG 1984

192 Apia Harbour **(193)**

(Des Jennifer Toombs. Litho Questa)

1984 (24 May). *250th Anniv of "Lloyd's List" (newspaper).* T **192** *and similar vert designs. Multicoloured.* W w **14**. *P* 14 × 14½.

673 32 s. Type **192** 25 20
674 48 s. Apia hurricane, 1889 .. .. .. 40 45
675 60 s. *Forum Samoa* (container ship) 45 50
676 $1 *Matua* (cargo liner) 75 80
673/6 .. .. *Set of* 4 1·75 1·75

1984 (7 June). *Universal Postal Union Congress, Hamburg. No.* 662 *optd with* T **193**.
677 $1 Coconut .. .. 1·10 80

194 Olympic Stadium

(Des Garden Studio. Litho Format)

1984 (26 June). *Olympic Games, Los Angeles.* T **194** *and similar horiz designs. Multicoloured.* W w **14** (*sideways*). *P* 14½.

678 25 s. Type **194** 20 20
679 32 s. Weightlifting 25 25
680 48 s. Boxing 40 45
681 $1 Running 75 80
678/81 .. .. *Set of* 4 1·40 1·50
MS682 170 × 120 mm. Nos. 678/81 .. .. 1·40 1·60

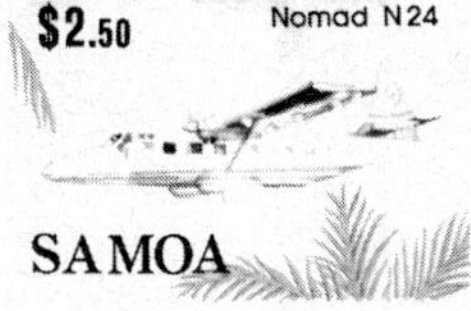

195 Nomad "N24" Aircraft

(Des E. Roberts. Litho Walsall)

1984 (21 Sept). *"Ausipex" International Stamp Exhibition, Melbourne. Sheet* 131 × 80 mm. W w **14** (*sideways*). *P* 14.
MS683 **195** $2.50, multicoloured .. .. .. 3·00 3·00

196 "Faith"

(Litho Walsall)

1984 (7 Nov). *Christmas. "The Three Virtues" (Raphael).* T **196** *and similar horiz designs. Multicoloured.* W w **14** (*sideways*). *P* 14.

684 25 s. Type **196** 20 15
685 35 s. "Hope" 25 20
686 $1 "Charity" 75 90
684/6 .. .. *Set of* 3 1·10 1·10
MS687 63 × 76 mm. Nos. 684/6 .. .. .. 1·25 1·75

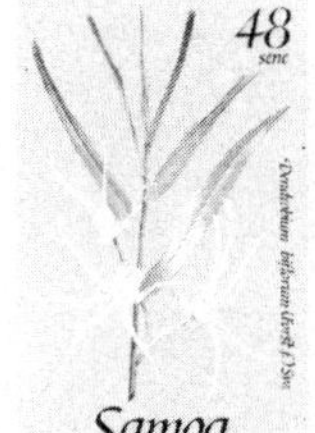

197 *Dendrobium biflorum* **198** Ford "Model A", 1903

(Des Jennifer Toombs. Litho Format)

1985 (23 Jan). *Orchids* (1*st series*). T **197** *and similar vert designs. Multicoloured. P* 14.

688 48 s. Type **197** 55 35
689 56 s. *Dendrobium vaupelianum Kraenzl* .. 65 45
690 67 s. *Glomera montana* 80 60
691 $1 *Spathoglottis plicata* .. .. .. 1·10 1·10
688/91 .. .. *Set of* 4 2·75 2·25

See also Nos. 818/21.

(Des A. Theobald. Litho Walsall)

1985 (26 Mar). *Veteran and Vintage Cars.* T **198** *and similar horiz designs. Multicoloured. P* 14.

692 48 s. Type **198** 60 35
693 56 s. Chevrolet "Tourer", 1912 .. .. 70 40
694 67 s. Morris "Oxford", 1913 .. .. .. 80 45
695 $1 Austin "Seven", 1923 .. .. .. 1·00 70
692/5 .. .. *Set of* 4 2·75 1·75

199 *Dictyophora indusiata* **200** The Queen Mother at Liverpool Street Station

(Des Doreen McGuinness. Litho Walsall)

1985 (17 Apr). *Fungi. T* **199** *and similar vert designs. Multicoloured. P* 14½.

696 48 s. Type **199**. 35 35
697 56 s. *Ganoderma tornatum* 40 40
698 67 s. *Mycena chlorophos* 45 45
699 $1 *Mycobonia flava*. 70 70
696/9 .. .. *Set of* 4 1·75 1·75

(Des A. Theobald ($2), C. Abbott (others). Litho Questa)

1985 (7 June). *Life and Times of Queen Elizabeth the Queen Mother. T* **200** *and similar vert designs. Multicoloured. W* w **16**. *P* 14½×14.

700 32 s. At Glamis Castle, aged 9 .. .. 20 25
701 48 s. At Prince Henry's Christening with other members of the Royal family .. 30 35
702 56 s. Type **200**. 35 40
703 $1 With Prince Henry at his christening (from photo by Lord Snowdon). . .. 65 70
700/3 .. .. *Set of* 4 1·40 1·50
MS704 91×73 mm. $2 Arriving at Tattenham Corner Station with the Queen. Wmk sideways. . 1·75 1·50

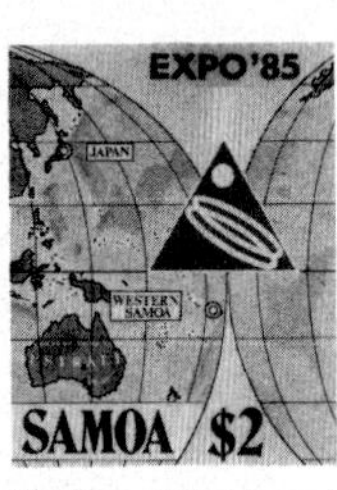

201 Map of Pacific and Exhibition Logo

202 I.Y.Y. Emblem and Map (Alaska—Arabian Gulf)

(Des D. Hartley. Litho Enschedé)

1985 (26 Aug). *"Expo '85" World Fair, Japan. Sheet* 70×45 *mm. P* 14.

MS705 **201** $2 multicoloured .. .. .. 1·25 1·40

(Des Garden Studio. Litho B.D.T.)

1985 (18 Sept) *International Youth Year. T* **202** *and similar vert designs, showing background map and emblem (Nos.* 706 *and* 710*) or raised arms (others). Multicoloured P* 14.

706 60 s. Type **202**. 40 45
a. Horiz strip of 5. Nos. 706/10 .. .. 1·75
707 60 s. Raised arms (Pakistan–Mexico) .. 40 45
708 60 s. Raised arms (Central America–China) 40 45
709 60 s. Raised arms (Japan–Greenland) .. 40 45
710 60 s. As Type **202** (Iceland–Siberia) . .. 40 45
706/10 .. .. *Set of* 5 1·75 2·00

Nos. 706/10 were printed together, *se-tenant*, in horizontal strips of 5, throughout the sheet, the background forming a composite design of three continuous world maps.

203 "System"

204 *Hypolimnas bolina*

(Des L. Curtis. Litho Format)

1985 (5 Nov). *Christmas. T* **203** *and similar vert designs showing illustrations by Millicent Sowerby for R. L. Stevenson's "A Child's Garden of Verses". Multicoloured. P* 14×14½.

711 32 s. Type **203**. 20 25
712 48 s. "Time to Rise" 30 35
713 56 s. "Auntie's Skirts" 35 40
714 $1 "Good Children" 65 70
711/14 .. .. *Set of* 4 1·40 1·50
MS715 87×109 mm. Nos. 711/14 .. .. 1·50 2·25

(Des Annette Robinson. Litho Walsall)

1986 (13 Feb). *Butterflies. T* **204** *and similar vert designs. Multicoloured. W* w **16**. *P* 14½×14.

716 25 s. Type **204** 25 15
717 32 s. *Belenois java* 30 20
718 48 s. *Deudorix epijarbas* 50 35
719 56 s. *Badamia exclamationis* 55 40
720 60 s. *Danaus hamata* 55 40
721 $1 *Catochrysops taitensis* 80 65
716/21 .. .. *Set of* 6 2·75 1·90

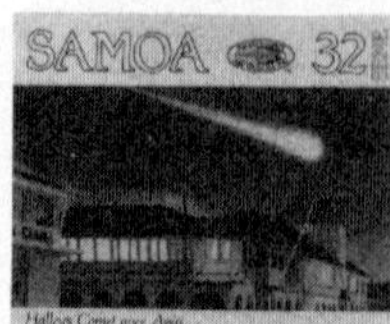

205 Halley's Comet over Apia

206 U.S.S. *Vincennes*

(Des N. Shewring. Litho Walsall)

1986 (24 Mar). *Appearance of Halley's Comet. T* **205** *and similar horiz designs. Multicoloured. W* w **16** *(sideways). P* 14×14½.

722 32 s. Type **205**. 15 20
723 48 s. Edmond Halley 30 35
724 60 s. Comet passing Earth 35 40
725 $2 Preparing *Giotto* spacecraft .. .. 1·10 1·25
722/5 .. .. *Set of* 4 1·75 2·00

(Des A. Theobald. Litho Questa)

1986 (21 Apr). *60th Birthday of Queen Elizabeth II. Vert designs as T* **230***a of Jamaica. Multicoloured. W* w **16**. *P* 14½×14.

726 32 s. Engagement photograph, 1947 .. 15 20
727 48 s. Queen with Liberty Bell, U.S.A., 1976. . 30 35
728 56 s. At Apia, 1977 .. .. 35 40
729 67 s. At Badminton Horse Trials, 1978 .. 40 45
730 $2 At Crown Agents Head Office, London, 1983 .. .. 1·10 1·25
726/30 .. .. *Set of* 5 2·10 2·40

(Des E. Nisbet. Litho Questa)

1986 (22 May). *"Ameripex '86" International Stamp Exhibition, Chicago. T* **206** *and similar horiz designs. Multicoloured. P* 14×14½.

731 48 s. Type **206**. 30 35
732 56 s. Sikorsky "S-42" flying boat 35 40
733 60 s. U.S.S. *Swan* 35 40
734 $2 "Apollo 10" descending. . .. .. 1·10 1·25
731/4 .. .. *Set of* 4 1·90 2·10

207 Vailima

(Des E. Roberts. Litho Cambec Press, Melbourne)

1986 (4 Aug). *"Stampex '86" Stamp Exhibition, Adelaide. Sheet* 158×97 *mm. P* 13½.

MS735 **207** $3 multicoloured .. .. .. 2·50 2·50

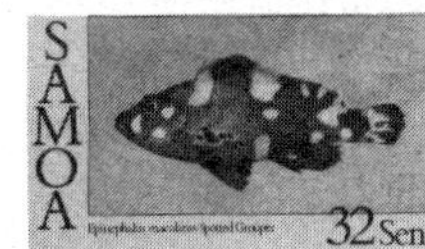

208 Spotted Grouper

(Des P. Rymers. Litho Walsall)

1986 (13 Aug). *Fishes. T* **208** *and similar horiz designs. Multicoloured. P* 14.

736 32 s. Type **208**. 25 20
737 48 s. Sabel Squirrelfish 40 35
738 60 s. Lunartail Grouper 45 40
739 67 s. Longtail Snapper 50 45
740 $1 Berndt's Soldierfish 75 65
736/40 .. .. *Set of* 5 2·10 1·90

209 Samoan Prime Ministers, American Presidents and Parliament House

210 *Hibiscus rosa-sinensis* and Map of Samoa

(Des N. Shewring. Litho Format)

1986 (1 Dec). *Christmas. 25th Anniv of United States Peace Corps. T* **209** *and similar horiz design. Multicoloured. P* 14½.

741 45 s. Type **209**. 25 30
742 60 s. French and American Presidents, Samoan Prime Minister and Statue of Liberty 35 40
MS743 131×72 mm. Nos. 741/2 . . .. .. 2·50 2·75

No. **MS**743 also commemorates the Centenary of the Statue of Liberty.

(Des local artist, adapted G. Vasarhelyi. Litho Format)

1987 (16 Feb). *25th Anniv of Independence. T* **210** *and similar multicoloured designs. P* 14½×14 *($2) or* 14×14½ *(others).*

744 15 s. Type **210**. 30 10
745 45 s. Parliament Building, Apia 50 30
746 60 s. Boat race at Independence celebration 65 40
747 70 s. Peace dove and laurel wreath 75 50
748 $2 Head of State Malietoa Tanumafili II and national flag *(horiz)* .. .. 1·60 1·75
744/8 .. .. *Set of* 5 3·50 2·75

NEW INFORMATION

The editor is always interested to correspond with people who have new information that will improve or correct the Catalogue.

211 Gulper (*Eurypharynx*)

(Des J. Walker. Litho Format)

1987 (31 Mar). *Deep Ocean Fishes. T* **211** *and similar horiz designs. Multicoloured. P* 14.

749 45 s. Type **211**. 45 30
750 60 s. Hatchet Fish 50 35
751 70 s. Angler Fish 60 45
752 $2 Gulper (*Saccopharynx*) . . .. .. 1·40 1·40
749/52 .. .. *Set of* 4 2·75 2·25

212 Workmen trimming Logs and building Fale (traditional house)

(Des Jennifer Toombs. Litho Questa)

1987 (13 June). *"Capex 87" International Stamp Exhibition, Toronto. Sheet* 122×66 *mm. P* 14½.

MS753 **212** $3 multicoloured .. .. .. 1·60 1·75

213 Lefaga Beach, Upolu

214 Abel Tasman

(Des D. Miller. Litho Questa)

1987 (29 July). *Coastal Scenery. T* **213** *and similar horiz designs. Multicoloured. P* 14.

754 45 s. Type **213**. 35 30
755 60 s. Vaisala Beach, Savaii 40 35
756 70 s. Solosolo Beach, Upolu 55 45
757 $2 Neiafu Beach, Savaii .. .. .. 1·40 1·25
754/7 .. .. *Set of* 4 2·50 2·10

(Des M. Bradbery. Litho Questa)

1987 (30 Sept). *Bicentenary of Australian Settlement* (1988) *(1st issue). Explorers of the Pacific. T* **214** *and similar horiz designs. Multicoloured. P* 14×14½.

758 40 s. Type **214**. 30 25
759 45 s. Capt. James Cook 45 30
760 80 s. Comte Louis-Antoine de Bougainville 50 50
761 $2 Comte Jean de la Perouse .. .. 1·10 1·25
758/61 .. .. *Set of* 4 2·10 2·10
MS762 90×73 mm. No. 761 .. .. .. 1·10 1·25

See also Nos. 768/72.

(**215**)

216 Christmas Tree

1987 (16 Oct). *"Hafnia" International Stamp Exhibition, Copenhagen. No.* **MS**762 *optd with T* **215** *in red.*

MS763 90×73 mm. $2 Comte Jean de la Perouse .. .. 1·10 1·25

(Des Josephine Martin. Litho Questa)

1987 (30 Nov). *Christmas. T* **216** *and similar square designs. Multicoloured. P* 14.

764 40 s. Type **216**. 20 25
765 45 s. Family going to church 25 30
766 50 s. Bamboo fire-gun 25 30
767 80 s. Inter-island transport 45 50
764/7 .. .. *Set of* 4 1·00 1·25

217 Samoa Coat of Arms and Australia Post Logo

218 Airport Terminal and Airliner taking off

(Des A. Theobald. Litho Questa)

1988 (27 Jan). *Bicentenary of Australian Settlement (2nd issue). Postal Services. T* **217** *and similar vert designs. Multicoloured. P* 14½×14.

768 45 s. Type **217** 40 40
a. Horiz strip of 5. Nos. 768/72 . . 1·75
769 45 s. Samoan mail van and aircraft . . 40 40
770 45 s. Loading mail plane . . 40 40
771 45 s. Australian mail van and aircraft . . 40 40
772 45 s. "Congratulations Australia" message on airmail letter . . 40 40
768/72 . . *Set of* 5 1·75 1·75

Nos. 768/72 were printed together, *se-tenant*, in horizontal strips of 5 throughout the sheet, Nos. 769/71 forming a composite design.

(Des E. Nisbet. Litho Walsall)

1988 (24 Mar). *Opening of Faleolo Airport. T* **218** *and similar horiz designs. Multicoloured. P* 13×13½.

773 40 s. Type **218** . . 35 25
774 45 s. Boeing "727" . . 40 30
775 60 s. DHC "Twin Otter" . . 45 35
776 70 s. Boeing "737" . . 55 50
777 80 s. Boeing "727" and control tower . . 70 60
778 $1 "DC9" over "fale" (house) . . 80 70
773/8 . . *Set of* 6 3·00 2·40

219 "Expo '88" Pacific Islands Village

220 Mormon Temple, Apia

(Des C. Abbott. Litho Walsall)

1988 (30 Apr). *"Expo '88" World Fair, Brisbane. T* **219** *and similar horiz designs. Multicoloured. P* 14 × 14½.

779 45 s. Type **219** . . 25 30
780 70 s. Expo Complex and monorail . . 35 40
781 $2 Map of Australia showing Brisbane . . 1·00 1·10
779/81 . . *Set of* 3 1·40 1·60

(Des Jennifer Toombs. Litho CPE Australia Ltd, Melbourne)

1988 (9 June). *Centenary of Arrival of the Latter-Day Saints in Samoa. Sheet* 86 × 77 *mm. P* 13½.

MS782 **220** $3 multicoloured . . 1·50 1·60

221 Athletics

222 Spotted Triller

(Des D. Miller. Litho Format)

1988 (10 Aug). *Olympic Games, Seoul. T* **221** *and similar vert designs. Multicoloured. P* 14.

783 15 s. Type **221** . . 10 10
784 60 s. Weightlifting . . 30 35
785 80 s. Boxing . . 40 45
786 $2 Olympic stadium . . 1·00 1·10
783/6 . . *Set of* 4 1·60 1·75
MS787 85 × 100 mm. Nos. 783/6 . . 1·75 2·00

(Des D. Johnston. Litho CPE Australia Ltd, Melbourne (Nos. 788/97), Questa (Nos. 798/803))

1988 (17 Aug)–**89**. *Birds. Multicoloured.*

(a) Vert designs as T **222**. *P* 13½

788 10 s. Type **222** . . 10 10
789 15 s. Samoan Wood Rail . . 10 10
790 20 s. Flat-billed Kingfisher . . 10 15
791 25 s. Samoan Fantail . . 10 15
792 35 s. Scarlet Robin . . 15 20
793 40 s. Black-breasted Honeyeater ("Mao") . . 20 25
794 50 s. Cardinal Honeyeater . . 25 30
795 65 s. Yellow-fronted Whistler . . 30 35
796 75 s. Many-coloured Fruit Dove . . 35 40
797 85 s. White-throated Pigeon . . 40 45

(b) Horiz designs, each 45 × 28 *mm. P* 13½ × 14.

798 75 s. Silver Gull (28.2.89) . . 35 40
799 85 s. Great Frigate Bird (28.2.89) . . 40 45
800 90 s. Eastern Reef Heron (28.2.89) . . 45 50
801 $3 Short-tailed Albatross (28.2.89) . . 1·50 1·60
802 $10 White Tern (31.7.89) . . 5·00 5·25
803 $20 Shy Albatross (31.7.89) . . 10·00 10·50
788/803 . . *Set of* 16 17·00 18·00

223 Forest

224 Congregational Church of Jesus, Apia

(Des G. Vasarhelyi. Litho Questa)

1988 (25 Oct). *National Conservation Campaign. T* **223** *and similar multicoloured designs. P* 14 × 13½ *(15, 40, 45 s.) or* 13½ × 14 *(others).*

807 15 s. Type **223** . . 10 10
808 40 s. Samoan handicrafts . . 20 25
809 45 s. Forest wildlife . . 25 30
810 50 s. Careful use of water (*horiz*) . . 25 30
811 60 s. Fishing (*horiz*) . . 30 35
812 $1 Coconut plantation (*horiz*) . . 55 60
807/12 . . *Set of* 6 1·50 1·75

(Des N. Shewring. Litho Format)

1988 (14 Nov). *Christmas. Samoan Churches. T* **224** *and similar vert designs. Multicoloured. P* 14.

813 15 s. Type **224** . . 10 10
814 40 s. Roman Catholic Church, Leauva'a . . 20 25
815 45 s. Congregational Christian Church, Moataa . . 25 30
816 $2 Baha'i Temple, Vailima . . 1·00 1·25
813/16 . . *Set of* 4 1·40 1·75
MS817 143 × 64 mm. Nos. 813/16 . . 1·75 1·90

225 *Phaius flavus*

226 *Eber* (German warship)

(Des H. Bevan. Litho Questa)

1989 (31 Jan). *Orchids (2nd series). T* **225** *and similar vert designs. Multicoloured. P* 14 × 13½.

818 15 s. Type **225** . . 15 10
819 45 s. *Calanthe triplicata* . . 35 30
820 60 s. *Luisia teretifolia* . . 40 35
821 $3 *Dendrobium mohlianum* . . 1·50 1·75
818/21 . . *Set of* 4 2·25 2·25

(Des E. Nisbet. Litho Walsall)

1989 (16 Mar). *Centenary of Great Apia Hurricane. T* **226** *and similar horiz designs. Multicoloured. P* 14.

822 50 s. Type **226** . . 40 40
a. Horiz strip of 4. Nos. 822/5 . . 2·75
823 65 s. *Olga* (German warship) . . 55 55
824 85 s. H.M.S. *Calliope* (screw corvette) . . 70 70
825 $2 U.S.S. *Vandalia* . . 1·50 1·75
822/5 . . *Set of* 4 2·75 3·00

Nos. 822/5 were printed together, *se-tenant*, in horizontal strips of 4 throughout the sheet.

See also No. **MS**839.

227 Samoan Red Cross Youth Group on Parade

228 Virgin Mary and Joseph

(Des L. Curtis. Litho Questa)

1989 (15 May). *125th Anniv of International Red Cross. T* **227** *and similar vert designs. Multicoloured. P* 14½×14.

826 50 s. Type **227** . . 35 30
827 65 s. Blood donors . . 45 40
828 75 s. Practising first aid . . 55 45
829 $3 Red Cross volunteers carrying patient . . 1·75 2·25
826/9 . . *Set of* 4 2·75 3·00

(Des A. Theobald ($3), D. Miller (others). Litho Questa)

1989 (20 July). *20th Anniv of First Manned Landing on Moon. Multicoloured designs as T* **126** *of Ascension. W* w **16** *(sideways on 50, 65 c.). P* 14×13½ *(18 s., $2) or* 14 *(others).*

830 18 s. Saturn rocket on mobile launcher . . 15 10
831 50 s. Crew of "Apollo 14" (30×30 *mm*) . . 30 30
832 65 s. "Apollo 14" emblem (30×30 *mm*) . . 45 45
833 $2 Tracks of lunar transporter . . 1·25 1·75
830/3 . . *Set of* 4 2·00 2·40
MS834 100×83 mm. $3 Aldrin with U.S. flag on Moon. P 14×13½ . . 1·75 2·25

(Des T. Chance. Litho Cartor, France)

1989 (1 Nov). *Christmas. T* **228** *and similar horiz designs. Multicoloured. P* 13½.

835 18 s. Type **228** . . 10 10
836 50 s. Shepherds . . 30 30
837 55 s. Donkey and ox . . 35 35
838 $2 Three Wise Men . . 1·50 1·50
835/8 . . *Set of* 4 2·00 2·00

(Litho Walsall)

1989 (17 Nov). *"World Stamp Expo '89" International Stamp Exhibition, Washington. Sheet* 91×105 *mm containing designs as Nos. 824/5. Multicoloured. W* **61**. *Imperf.*

MS839 85 s. H.M.S. *Calliope*; $2 U.S.S. *Vandalia* 3·50 3·75

229 Pao Pao Outrigger

(Des R. Roberts. Litho Note Ptg Branch, Reserve Bank of Australia)

1990 (31 Jan). *Local Transport. T* **229** *and similar horiz designs. Multicoloured. P* 14×15.

840 18 s. Type **229** . . 15 15
841 55 s. Fautasi (large canoe) . . 35 40
842 60 s. Polynesian Airlines aircraft . . 40 45
843 $3 *Lady Samoa* (ferry) . . 1·75 2·00
840/3 . . *Set of* 4 2·40 2·75

230 Bismarck and Brandenburg Gate, Berlin

(Des G. Vasarhelyi. Litho Cartor, France)

1990 (19 Apr). *Treaty of Berlin, 1889, and Opening of Berlin Wall, 1989. T* **230** *and similar horiz design. Multicoloured. P* 14×13½.

844 75 s. Type **230** . . 1·00 1·00
a. Horiz pair. Nos. 844/5 . . 3·00 3·00
845 $3 *Adler* (German steam gunboat) . . 2·00 2·00

Nos. 844/5 were printed together, *se-tenant*, in horizontal pairs throughout the sheet, each pair forming a composite design showing Berliners on the Wall near the Brandenburg Gate.

231 Penny Black and Alexandra Palace, London

(Des G. Vasarhelyi. Litho Cartor, France)

1990 (3 May). *"Stamp World London 90" International Stamp Exhibition. P* 14×13½.

846 **231** $3 multicoloured . . 2·40 2·75

232 Visitors' Bureau

(Des D. Miller. Litho B.D.T.)

1990 (30 July). *Tourism. T* **232** *and similar horiz designs. Multicoloured. P* 14.

847 18 s. Type **232** . . 20 10
848 50 s. Village resort . . 35 30
849 65 s. Aggie's Hotel . . 50 40
850 $3 Swimming pool, Tusitala Hotel . . 1·75 2·00
847/50 . . *Set of* 4 2·50 2·50

233 1964 2nd Anniv of Treaty of Friendship 3 s. Commemorative and "NZ 1990" Logo

(Des N. Eustis. Litho Leigh-Mardon Ltd, Melbourne)

1990 (24 Aug). *"New Zealand 1990" International Stamp Exhibition, Auckland. Sheet* 130×85 *mm. P* 13.

MS851	**233** $3 multicoloured	2·10	2·25

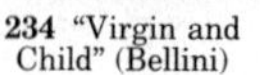

234 "Virgin and Child" (Bellini)

235 William Draper III (administrator) and 40th Anniv Logo

(Des G. Vasarhelyi. Litho Security Printers (M), Malaysia)

1990 (31 Oct). *Christmas. Paintings. T* **234** *and similar vert designs. Multicoloured. P* 12½.

852	18 s. Type **234**	20	10
853	50 s. "Virgin and Child with St. Peter and St. Paul" (Bouts)	40	25
854	55 s. "School of Love" (Correggio)	45	30
855	$3 "Virgin and Child" (Cima)	2·00	2·50
852/5	.. .. *Set of* 4	2·75	2·75

The 55 s. value should have shown "The Madonna of the Basket" by the same artist and is so inscribed.

(Des D. Miller. Litho Cartor, France)

1990 (26 Nov). *40th Anniv of U.N. Development Programme. P* 13½.

856	**235** $3 multicoloured	2·00	2·25

236 Black-capped Lory

237 Peter Fatialofa (Samoan captain)

(Des R. Roberts. Litho B.D.T.)

1991 (8 Apr). *Parrots. T* **236** *and similar vert designs. Multicoloured. P* 13½.

857	18 s. Type **236**	20	10
858	50 s. Eclectus Parrot	45	35
859	65 s. Scarlet Macaw	55	40
860	$3 Palm Cockatoo	2·50	2·50
857/60	.. .. *Set of* 4	3·25	3·00

(Des D. Miller. Litho Questa)

1991 (17 June). *65th Birthday of Queen Elizabeth II and 70th Birthday of Prince Philip. Vert designs as T* **58** *of Kiribati. Multicoloured. W w* **16** *(sideways). P* 14½×14.

861	75 s. Prince Philip in the countryside ..	60	60
	a. Horiz pair. Nos. 861/2 separated by label	2·10	2·10
862	$2 Queen wearing yellow lei	1·50	1·50

Nos. 861/2 were printed together in a similar sheet format to Nos. 366/7 of Kiribati.

(Des G. Vasarhelyi. Litho Questa)

1991 (21 Oct). *World Cup Rugby Championships. Sheet* 121×75 *mm. P* 14½×14.

MS863	**237** $5 multicoloured	2·50	2·75

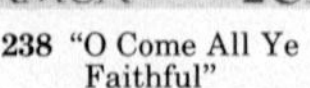

238 "O Come All Ye Faithful"

239 *Herse convolvuli*

(Des Jennifer Toombs. Litho Questa)

1991 (31 Oct). *Christmas. Carols. T* **238** *and similar horiz designs. Multicoloured. P* 14×14½.

864	20 s. Type **238**	20	15
865	60 s. "Joy to the World"	55	40
866	75 s. "Hark the Herald Angels sing" ..	65	50
867	$4 "We wish you a Merry Christmas" ..	2·75	3·00
864/7	.. .. *Set of* 4	3·75	3·50

(Des I. Loe. Litho Questa)

1991 (16 Nov). *"Philanippon '91" International Stamp Exhibition, Tokyo. Samoan Hawkmoths. T* **239** *and similar horiz designs. P* 13½×14.

868	60 s. Type **239**	50	50
869	75 s. *Gnathothlibus erotus*	55	55
870	85 s. *Deilephila celerio*	60	60
871	$3 *Cephonodes armatus*	2·00	2·00
868/71	.. .. *Set of* 4	3·25	3·25

240 Head of State inspecting Guard of Honour

241 Samoa Express 1d. Stamp, 1877

(Des G. Vasarhelyi and D. Miller. Litho Walsall)

1992 (8 Jan). *30th Anniv of Independence. T* **240** *and similar horiz designs. Multicoloured. P* 14.

872	50 s. Type **240**	35	30
873	65 s. Siva ceremony	45	40
874	$1 Commemorative float	70	70
875	$3 Raising Samoan flag	2·00	2·00
872/5	.. .. *Set of* 4	3·25	3·00

(Des D. Miller. Litho Questa ($3), Leigh-Mardon Ltd, Melbourne (others))

1992 (6 Feb). *40th Anniv of Queen Elizabeth II's Accession. Horiz designs as T* **112** *of Kenya. Multicoloured. W w* **14** *(sideways) ($3) or w* **16** *(sideways) (others). P* 14.

876	20 s. Queen and Prince Philip with umbrellas	15	10
877	60 s. Queen and Prince Philip on Royal Yacht..	40	35
878	75 s. Queen in multicoloured hat	50	40
879	85 s. Three portraits of Queen Elizabeth ..	60	50
880	$3 Queen Elizabeth II	2·00	2·00
876/80	.. .. *Set of* 5	3·25	3·00

(Des L. Curtis. Litho Questa)

1992 (17 Apr). *500th Anniv of Discovery of America by Columbus. Sheet* 91×70 *mm. P* 14½×14.

MS881	**241** $4 multicoloured	2·00	2·25

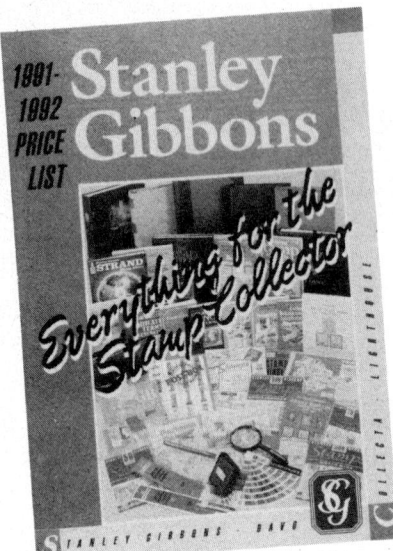

Sarawak *see* Malaysia

Seychelles

Seychelles was administered as a dependency of Mauritius from 1810 until 1903, although separate stamp issues were provided from April 1890 onwards.

The first post office was opened, at Victoria on Mahé, on 11 December 1861 and the stamps of Mauritius were used there until 1890. No further post offices were opened until 1901.

Z 1

Stamps of MAURITIUS *cancelled with Type* Z **1**.

1859–61.
Z1 6d. blue (No. 32) .. £450
Z2 6d. dull purple-slate (No. 33) .. £750
Z3 1s. vermilion (No. 34) .. £550

1860–63. (*Nos.* 45/53).
Z 4 1d. purple-brown .. £110
Z 5 2d. blue .. £140
Z 6 4d. rose .. £100
Z 7 6d. green .. £350
Z 8 6d. slate .. £275
Z 9 9d. dull purple .. 70·00
Z10 1s. buff .. £130
Z11 1s. green .. £275

1862.
Z12 6d. slate (No. 54) .. £600

1863–72. (*Nos.* 56/72).
Z13 1d. purple-brown .. 65·00
Z14 1d. brown .. 55·00
Z15 1d. bistre .. 55·00
Z16 2d. pale blue .. 75·00
Z17 2d. bright blue .. 75·00
Z18 3d. deep red .. 85·00
Z19 3d. dull red .. 65·00
Z20 4d. rose .. 45·00
Z21 6d. dull violet .. £140
Z22 6d. yellow-green .. 65·00
Z23 6d. blue-green .. 55·00
Z24 9d. yellow-green .. £450
Z25 10d. maroon .. £180
Z26 1s. yellow .. 85·00
Z27 1s. blue .. £200
Z28 1s. orange .. 85·00
Z29 5s. rosy mauve .. £400
Z30 5s. bright mauve .. £400

1876. (*Nos.* 76/7).
Z31 ½d. on 9d. dull purple .. £160
Z32 ½d. on 10d. maroon .. £160

1877. (*Nos.* 79/82).
Z33 ½d. on 10d. rose ..
Z34 1d. on 4d. rose-carmine ..
Z35 1s. on 5s. rosy mauve ..
Z36 1s. on 5s. bright mauve ..

1878. (*Nos.* 83/91).
Z37 2 c. dull rose (lower label blank) .. 50·00
Z38 4 c. on 1d. bistre .. £200
Z39 8 c. on 2d. blue .. 35·00
Z40 13 c. on 3d. orange-red .. 75·00
Z41 17 c. on 4d. rose .. 35·00
Z42 25 c. on 6d. slate-blue .. 65·00
Z43 38 c. on 9d. pale violet .. £140
Z44 50 c. on 1s. green .. 65·00
Z45 2 r. 50 on 5s. bright mauve .. £180

1879–80. (*Nos.* 92/100).
Z46 2 c. Venetian red .. £100
Z47 4 c. orange .. £110
Z48 8 c. blue .. 30·00
Z49 13 c. slate .. £500
Z50 17 c. rose .. 70·00
Z51 25 c. olive-yellow .. £120
Z52 38 c. bright purple .. £750
Z53 50 c. green .. £400
Z54 2 r. 50, brown-purple .. £500

1883–90.
Z55 2 c. Venetian red (No. 102) .. 65·00
Z56 2 c. green (No. 103) .. £110
Z57 4 c. orange (No. 104) .. 55·00
Z58 4 c. carmine (No. 105) .. 65·00
Z59 16 c. chestnut (No. 109) .. 35·00
Z60 25 c. olive-yellow (No. 110) .. 75·00
Z61 50 c. orange (No. 111) .. £350

1883.
Z62 16 c. on 17 c. rose (No. 112) ..

1883.
Z63 16 c. on 17 c. rose (No. 115) .. 30·00

1885.
Z64 2 c. on 38 c. bright purple (No. 116) ..

1887.
Z65 2 c. on 13 c. slate (No. 117) ..

POSTAL FISCAL

1889.
ZR1 4 c. lilac (No. R2) ..

We no longer list the G.B. 1862 6d. lilac with this obliteration as there is no evidence that the stamps of Great Britain were sold by the Victoria post office.

PRICES FOR STAMPS ON COVER TO 1945	
Nos. 1/8	*from* × 10
Nos. 9/21	*from* × 20
Nos. 22/5	*from* × 6
Nos. 26/7	*from* × 8
Nos. 28/36	*from* × 5
Nos. 37/40	*from* × 30
Nos. 41/5	*from* × 6
Nos. 46/81	*from* × 5
Nos. 82/131	*from* × 3
Nos. 132/4	*from* × 10
Nos. 135/49	*from* × 3

DEPENDENCY OF MAURITIUS

PRINTERS. Nos. 1 to 123 were typographed by De La Rue & Co.

1

Die I

Die II

In Die I there are lines of shading in the middle compartment of the diadem which are absent from Die II.

1890 (5 April)–**92.** *Wmk Crown CA. P* 14. (i) *Die* I.
1 1 2 c. green and carmine .. 65 7·00
2 4 c. carmine and green .. 8·50 9·00
3 8 c. brown-purple and blue .. 3·25 3·50
4 10 c. ultramarine and brown .. 3·75 9·00
5 13 c. grey and black .. 4·50 9·00
6 16 c. chestnut and blue .. 2·00 2·75
7 48 c. ochre and green .. 16·00 16·00
8 96 c. mauve and carmine .. 38·00 45·00
1/8 .. *Set of* 8 65·00 90·00
1/8 Optd "Specimen" .. *Set of* 8 £160

(ii) *Die* II (1892)
9 1 2 c. green and rosine .. 65 90
10 4 c. carmine and green .. 90 85
11 8 c. brown-purple and ultramarine .. 2·50 1·40
12 10 c. bright ultramarine and brown .. 2·75 2·00
13 13 c. grey and black .. 85 1·50
14 16 c. chestnut and ultramarine .. 27·00 7·00
9/14 .. *Set of* 6 32·00 12·50

3
cents

(2)

18 CENTS

(3)

4

1893 (1 Jan). *Surch locally as T* **2**.
15 3 c. on 4 c. (No. 10) .. 75 1·10
a. Surch inverted .. £300 £375
b. Surch double .. £450
c. Surch omitted (in pair with normal) .. £4000
16 12 c. on 16 c. (No. 6) .. 1·00 3·25
a. Surch inverted .. £450
b. Surch double .. — £4000
17 12 c. on 16 c. (No. 14) .. 2·50 1·25
a. Surch double .. £3500 £3500
b. Surch omitted (in pair with normal)
18 15 c. on 16 c. (No. 6) .. 8·00 11·00
a. Surch inverted .. £300 £350
b. Surch double .. £750 £750
19 15 c. on 16 c. (No. 14) .. 7·00 1·75
a. Surch inverted .. £650 £650
b. Surch double .. £800 £800
c. Surch treble .. £2000
20 45 c. on 48 c. (No. 7) .. 8·50 4·00
21 90 c. on 96 c. (No. 8) .. 23·00 25·00
15/21 .. *Set of* 7 45·00 42·00

Nos. 15, 16, 18, 19 and 20 exist with "cents" omitted and with "cents" above value and are due to misplacement of the surcharge.

1893 (Nov). *New values. Die* II. *Wmk Crown CA. P* 14.
22 1 3 c. dull purple and orange .. 55 30
23 12 c. sepia and green .. 55 40
24 15 c. sage-green and lilac .. 3·25 2·00
25 45 c. brown and carmine .. 22·00 25·00
22/5 .. *Set of* 4 24·00 25·00
22/5 Optd "Specimen" .. *Set of* 4 70·00

1896 (1 Aug). *No.* 25 *surch as T* **3**.
26 1 18 c. on 45 c. brown and carmine .. 6·50 2·50
a. Surch double .. £1200 £1200
b. Surch treble .. £1400
27 36 c. on 45 c. brown and carmine .. 10·00 32·00
a. Surch double .. £1100
26/27 H/S "Specimen" .. *Set of* 2 70·00

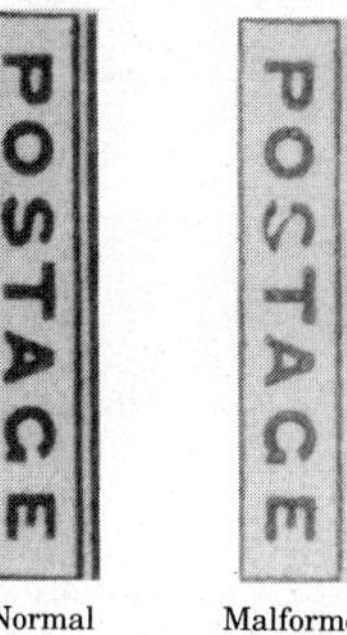

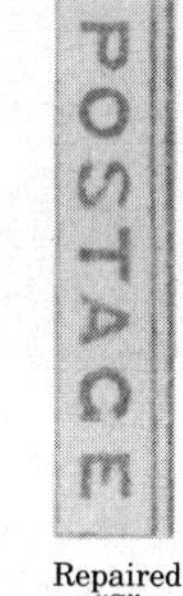

Normal Malformed "S" Repaired "S"

The malformed "S" occurs on R. 7/3 of the left pane from Key Plate 2. It is believed that the repair to it took place in mid-1898. Both states may occur on other stamps in Types **1** and **4**. Stamps subsequently printed from Key Plate 3 showed the "S" normal.

1897–1900. *Colours changed and new values. Die* II. *Wmk Crown CA. P* 14.
28 1 2 c. orange-brown and green (1900) .. 30 45
a. Repaired "S" .. 85·00
29 6 c. carmine (1900) .. 2·25 40
a. Repaired "S" .. £120
30 15 c. ultramarine (1900) .. 2·50 2·50
a. Repaired "S" .. £130
31 18 c. ultramarine .. 1·40 90
32 36 c. brown and carmine .. 15·00 4·00
33 4 75 c. yellow and violet (1900) .. 35·00 55·00
a. Repaired "S" .. £225
34 1 r. bright mauve and deep red .. 8·50 3·50
35 1 r. 50, grey and carmine (1900) .. 48·00 75·00
a. Repaired "S" .. £250
36 2 r. 25, bright mauve and green (1900) .. 55·00 75·00
a. Repaired "S" .. £250
28/36 .. *Set of* 9 £150 £190
28/36 Optd "Specimen" .. *Set of* 9 £160

3 cents
══
(5)

6 cents
(5*a*)

1901 (21 June–Oct). *Surch locally with T* **5** *or* **5a**.
37 3 c. on 10 c. bright ultramarine and brown (No. 12) (10.01) .. 30 60
a. Surch double .. £650
b. Malformed "S" .. 85·00
38 3 c. on 16 c. chestnut and ultramarine (No. 14) (8.01) .. 30 85
a. Surch inverted .. £600 £600
b. Surch double .. £500
c. "3 cents" omitted .. £550 £550
39 3 c. on 36 c. brown and carmine (No. 32) .. 30 50
a. Surch double .. £750 £900
b. "3 cents" omitted .. £600 £650
40 6 c. on 8 c. brown-purple and ultramarine (No. 11) (8.01) .. 30 1·50
a. Surch inverted .. £750 £800
37/40 .. *Set of* 4 1·00 3·00
37/40 H/S "Specimen" .. *Set of* 4 £100

1902 (June). *Surch locally as T* **5**.
41 1 2 c. on 4 c. carmine and green (No. 10) .. 90 2·75
42 4 30 c. on 75 c. yellow and violet (No. 33) .. 80 4·00
a. Narrow "0" in "30" (R. 3/6, 5/2-4) .. 10·00 40·00
b. Repaired "S" .. £120
43 30 c. on 1 r. bright mauve & dp red (No. 34) 3·25 16·00
a. Narrow "0" in "30" (R. 3/6, 5/2-4) .. 20·00 65·00
b. Surch double .. £800
44 45 c. on 1 r. bright mauve & dp red (No. 34) 3·25 16·00
45 45 c. on 2 r. 25, brt mauve & grn (No. 36) 21·00 35·00
a. Narrow "5" in "45" (R. 4/1) .. £100 £160
b. Repaired "S" .. £180
41/5 .. *Set of* 5 26·00 65·00
41/5 H/S "Specimen" .. *Set of* 5 £110

3 cents

6 7 (8)

Dented frame (R. 1/6 of left pane)

1903 (26 May). *Wmk Crown CA. P* 14.
46 **6** 2 c. chestnut and green .. 40 40
a. Dented frame .. 30·00
47 3 c. dull green .. 1·00 1·25
a. Dented frame .. 35·00
48 6 c. carmine .. 1·00 15
a. Dented frame .. 35·00
49 12 c. olive-sepia and dull green .. 1·50 1·00
a. Dented frame .. 45·00
50 15 c. ultramarine .. 2·75 1·25
a. Dented frame .. 55·00
51 18 c. sage-green and carmine .. 3·00 6·00
a. Dented frame .. 65·00
52 30 c. violet and dull green .. 5·50 8·00
a. Dented frame .. 75·00
53 45 c. brown and carmine .. 7·00 11·00
a. Dented frame .. 80·00
54 **7** 75 c. yellow and violet .. 9·00 16·00
a. Dented frame .. £110
55 1 r. 50, black and carmine .. 32·00 48·00
a. Dented frame .. £160
56 2 r. 25, purple and green .. 24·00 55·00
a. Dented frame .. £150
46/56 .. *Set of* 11 80·00 £130
46/56 Optd "Specimen" .. *Set of* 11 £180

1903. *Surch locally with T* **8**.
57 **6** 3 c. on 15 c. ultramarine (3.7) .. 55 1·00
a. Dented frame .. 50·00
58 3 c. on 18 c. sage-green and carmine (2.9) 1·75 21·00
a. Dented frame .. 90·00
59 3 c. on 45 c. brown and carmine (21.7) .. 55 1·50
a. Dented frame .. 55·00
57/9 .. *Set of* 3 2·50 21·00
57/9 H/S "Specimen" .. *Set of* 3 80·00

CROWN COLONY

The Seychelles became a Separate Crown Colony by Letters Patent dated 31 August 1903.

1906. *Wmk Mult Crown CA. P* 14.
60 **6** 2 c. chestnut and green .. 30 1·50
a. Dented frame .. 30·00
61 3 c. dull green .. 70 30
a. Dented frame .. 35·00
62 6 c. carmine .. 80 10
a. Dented frame .. 35·00
63 12 c. olive-sepia and dull green .. 3·00 1·00
a. Dented frame .. 65·00
64 15 c. ultramarine .. 1·60 2·00
a. Dented frame .. 50·00
65 18 c. sage-green and carmine .. 3·00 5·50
a. Dented frame .. 60·00
66 30 c. violet and dull green .. 6·00 7·50
a. Dented frame .. £110
67 45 c. brown and carmine .. 3·00 5·00
a. Dented frame .. £100
68 **7** 75 c. yellow and violet .. 8·50 35·00
a. Dented frame .. £120
69 1 r. 50, black and carmine .. 35·00 35·00
a. Dented frame .. £160
70 2 r. 25, purple and green .. 30·00 35·00
a. Dented frame .. £160
60/70 .. *Set of* 11 80·00 £110

9 10

1912 (Apr)–**13**. *Wmk Mult Crown CA. P* 14.
71 **9** 2 c. chestnut and green .. 20 1·10
a. Split "A" .. 20·00
72 3 c. green .. 35 30
a. Split "A" .. 30·00
73 6 c. aniline carmine (6.13) .. 8·50 4·50
a. Carmine-red .. 2·25 30
b. Split "A" .. 50·00
74 12 c. olive-sepia and dull green (1.13) .. 80 3·50
a. Split "A" .. 35·00
75 15 c. ultramarine .. 1·25 40
a. Split "A" .. 40·00
76 18 c. sage-green and carmine (1.13) .. 1·25 3·50
a. Split "A" .. 40·00
77 30 c. violet and green (1.13) .. 5·00 90
a. Split "A" .. 60·00
78 45 c. brown and carmine (1.13) .. 2·50 22·00
a. Split "A" .. 50·00
79 **10** 75 c. yellow and violet (1.13) .. 2·50 5·50
a. Split "A" .. 50·00
80 **10** 1 r. 50, black and carmine (1.13) .. 5·50 85
a. Split "A" .. 85·00
81 2 r. 25, rose-purple and green (1.13) .. 55·00 55·00
a. Bright purple and green .. 30·00 2·50
b. Split "A" .. £180
71/81*a* .. *Set of* 11 45·00 35·00
71/81 Optd "Specimen" .. *Set of* 11 £180
For illustration of "Split A" flaw see above St. Helena No. 83.

11 12 13

1917–22. *Wmk Mult Crown CA. Chalk-surfaced paper* (18 *c. to* 5 *r.*). *P* 14.
82 **11** 2 c. chestnut and green .. 15 90
83 3 c. green .. 50 30
84 **12** 5 c. deep brown (1920) .. 45 2·50
85 **11** 6 c. carmine .. 55 40
a. Rose (1919) .. 3·25 40
86 12 c. grey (1919) .. 30 1·00
87 15 c. ultramarine .. 30 85
88 18 c. purple/*yellow* (1919) .. 1·75 11·00
a. On orange-buff (1920) .. 13·00 42·00
b. On pale yellow (Die II) (1922) .. 75 13·00
89 **13** 25 c. black and red/*yellow* .. 1·50 14·00
a. On orange-buff (1920) .. 38·00 65·00
b. On pale yellow (Die II) (1922) .. 1·00 5·00
90 **11** 30 c. dull purple and olive .. 1·50 5·50
91 45 c. dull purple and orange (1919) .. 3·00 17·00
92 **13** 50 c. dull purple and black (1920) .. 3·00 11·00
93 75 c. black/*blue-green* (*olive back*) .. 1·25 7·00
a. On emerald back (Die II) (1922) .. 1·40 13·00
94 1 r. dull purple and red (1920) .. 7·00 23·00
95 1 r. 50, reddish purple and blue/*blue* .. 9·00 32·00
a. Blue-pur & blue/blue (Die II) (1922) 8·50 26·00
96 2 r. 25, yellow-green and violet .. 27·00 85·00
97 5 r. green and blue (1920) .. 40·00 £140
82/97 .. *Set of* 16 85·00 £300
82/97 Optd "Specimen" .. *Set of* 16 £250

1921–32. *Wmk Mult Script CA. Chalk-surfaced paper* (18 *c. and* 25 *c. to* 5 *r.*). *P* 14.
98 **11** 2 c. chestnut and green .. 10 15
99 3 c. green .. 20 15
100 3 c. black (1922) .. 50 30
101 4 c. green (1922) .. 60 40
102 4 c. sage-green and carmine (1928) .. 3·50 9·50
103 **12** 5 c. deep brown .. 75 3·00
104 **11** 6 c. carmine .. 1·00 4·50
105 6 c. deep mauve (1922) .. 30 10
106 **13** 9 c. red (1927) .. 1·25 2·75
107 **11** 12 c. grey (Die II) .. 50 15
108 12 c. carmine-red (1922) .. 45 15
109 12 c. grey (Die I) (1932) .. 3·75 65
110 15 c. bright blue .. 2·00 38·00
111 15 c. yellow (1922) .. 50 2·50
112 18 c. purple/*pale yellow* (1925) .. 2·00 6·50
113 **13** 20 c. bright blue (1922) .. 1·25 35
a. Dull blue (1926) .. 4·00 55
114 **11** 25 c. black and red/*pale yellow* (1925) .. 2·50 5·50
115 30 c. dull purple and olive .. 80 8·00
116 45 c. dull purple and orange .. 80 5·00
117 **13** 50 c. dull purple and black .. 90 2·25
118 75 c. black/*emerald* (1924) .. 7·50 15·00
119 1 r. dull purple and red (Die II) .. 7·00 17·00
120 1 r. dull purple and red (Die I) (1932) 12·00 27·00
121 1 r. 50, purple and blue/*blue* (1924) .. 8·00 15·00
122 2 r. 25, yellow-green and violet .. 8·00 14·00
123 5 r. yellow-green and blue .. 48·00 90·00
98/123 .. *Set of* 24 80·00 £225
98/123 Optd "Specimen" .. *Set of* 24 £350
The 3 c. green and 12 c. grey (Die II) were reissued in 1927. "Specimens" of these also exist.

1935 (6 May). *Silver Jubilee. As Nos.* 114/17 *of Jamaica. P* 11×12.
128 6 c. ultramarine and grey-black .. 70 40
a. Extra flagstaff .. £160
b. Short extra flagstaff .. £100
c. Lightning conductor .. £100
d. Flagstaff on right-hand turret .. £100
e. Double flagstaff .. £100
129 12 c. green and indigo .. 2·00 30
a. Extra flagstaff .. £2500 £2250
b. Short extra flagstaff .. £130
c. Lightning conductor .. £400
d. Flagstaff on right-hand turret .. £130
e. Double flagstaff .. £130
130 20 c. brown and deep blue .. 2·00 40
a. Extra flagstaff .. £200
b. Short extra flagstaff .. £120
c. Lightning conductor .. £120
d. Flagstaff on right-hand turret .. £120
e. Double flagstaff .. £120
131 1 r. slate and purple .. 3·00 7·75
a. Extra flagstaff .. £150
b. Short extra flagstaff .. £140
c. Lightning conductor .. £100
d. Flagstaff on right-hand turret .. £140
128/31 .. *Set of* 4 7·00 8·00
128/31 Perf "Specimen" .. *Set of* 4 80·00
For illustrations of plate varieties see Omnibus section following Zimbabwe.

1937 (12 May). *Coronation. As Nos.* 118/20 *of Jamaica, but ptd by B.W. P* 11×11½.
132 6 c. sage-green .. 35 15
133 12 c. orange .. 50 30
134 20 c. blue .. 70 40
132/4 .. *Set of* 3 1·40 75
132/4 Perf "Specimen" .. *Set of* 3 55·00

14 Coco-de-mer Palm

15 Giant Tortoise

16 Fishing Pirogue

(Photo Harrison)

1938 (1 Jan)–**49**. *Wmk Mult Script CA. Chalk-surfaced paper. P* 14½×13½ (*vert*) *or* 13½×14½ (*horiz*).
135 **14** 2 c. purple-brown (10.2.38) .. 30 30
a. Ordinary paper (18.11.42) .. 20 30
136 **15** 3 c. green .. 4·00 1·00
136*a* 3 c. orange (8.8.41) .. 35 30
ab. Ordinary paper (18.11.42) .. 40 35
137 **16** 6 c. orange .. 3·50 2·50
137*a* 6 c. greyish green (8.8.41) .. 1·75 55
ab. Ordinary paper. *Green* (18.11.42) 30 40
ac. Green (5.4.49) .. 40 55
138 **14** 9 c. scarlet (10.2.38) .. 7·00 1·75
138*a* 9 c. grey-blue (8.8.41) .. 60 30
ab. Ordinary paper (18.11.42) .. 40 40
ac. Ordinary paper. *Dull bl* (19.11.45) 1·75 60
ad. Dull blue (5.4.49) .. 1·60 60
139 **15** 12 c. reddish violet .. 24·00 70
139*a* 15 c. brown-carmine (8.8.41) .. 1·25 30
ab. Ordinary paper. *Brn-red* (18.11.42) 50 45
139*c* **14** 18 c. carmine-lake (8.8.41) .. 1·75 40
ca. Ordinary paper (18.11.42) .. 1·25 1·25
cb. Rose-carmine (5.4.49) .. 1·50 1·50
140 **16** 20 c. blue .. 32·00 5·50
140*a* 20 c. brown-ochre (8.8.41) .. 1·50 30
ab. Ordinary paper (18.11.42) .. 60 40
141 **14** 25 c. brown-ochre .. 45·00 9·50
142 **15** 30 c. carmine (10.2.38) .. 55·00 6·50
142*a* 30 c. blue (8.8.41) .. 1·25 40
ab. Ordinary paper (18.11.42) .. 40 60
143 **16** 45 c. chocolate (10.2.38) .. 1·75 40
a. Ordinary paper. *Pur-brn* (18.11.42) 75 55
b. Purple-brown (5.4.49) .. 75 55
144 **14** 50 c. deep reddish violet (10.2.38) .. 1·25 30
a. Ordinary paper (18.11.42) .. 30 70
144*b* 50 c. bright lilac (13.6.49) .. 30 75
145 **15** 75 c. slate-blue (10.2.38) .. 75·00 38·00
145*a* 75 c. deep slate-lilac (8.8.41) .. 1·25 70
ab. Ordinary paper (18.11.42) .. 40 50
146 **16** 1 r. yellow-green (10.2.38) .. 95·00 48·00
146*a* 1 r. grey-black (8.8.41) .. 50 45
ab. Ordinary paper (18.11.42) .. 80 75
147 **14** 1 r. 50, ultramarine (10.2.38) .. 2·50 90
a. Ordinary paper (18.11.42) .. 1·50 90
148 **15** 2 r. 25, olive (10.2.38) .. 4·00 3·00
a. Ordinary paper (18.11.42) .. 2·50 3·00
149 **16** 5 r. red (10.2.38) .. 3·50 2·75
a. Ordinary paper (18.11.42) .. 6·50 5·50
135/49 .. *Set of* 25 £325 £110
135/49 (*excl No.* 144*b*) Perf "Specimen" *Set of* 24 £350

Lamp on mast flaw (R. 1/5)

1946 (23 Sept). *Victory. As Nos.* 141/2 *of Jamaica.*
150 9 c. light blue .. 10 10
151 30 c. deep blue .. 10 10
a. Lamp on mast flaw .. 10·00
150/1 Perf "Specimen" .. *Set of* 2 50·00

1948 (5 Nov). *Royal Silver Wedding. As Nos.* 143/4 *of Jamaica.*
152 9 c. ultramarine .. 15 25
153 5 r. carmine .. 6·50 9·50

1949 (10 Oct). *75th Anniv of U.P.U. As Nos.* 145/8 *of Jamaica, but inscribed* "SEYCHELLES" *in recess.*
154 18 c. bright reddish purple .. 15 15
155 50 c. purple .. 35 40
156 1 r. grey .. 30 15
157 2 r. 25, olive .. 50 40
154/7 .. *Set of* 4 1·10 1·00

PRICES OF SETS

Set prices are given for many issues, generally those containing three stamps or more. Definitive sets include one of each value or major colour change, but do not cover different perforations, die types or minor shades. Where a choice is possible the set prices are based on the cheapest versions of the stamps included in the listings.

17 Sail-fish

18 Map of Indian Ocean

(Photo Harrison)

1952 (3 Mar). *Various designs as T* **14/16** *but with new portrait and crown as in T* **17/18.** *Chalk-surfaced paper. Wmk Mult Script CA. P* 14½ × 13½ *(vert) or* 13½ × 14½ *(horiz).*

158 **17** 2 c. lilac 40 40
 a. Error. Crown missing, W **9***a* .. £225
 b. Error. St. Edward's Crown, W **9***b* .. 85·00
159 **15** 3 c. orange 40 30
 a. Error. Crown missing, W **9***a* .. £200
 b. Error. St. Edward's Crown, W **9***b* .. 80·00
160 **14** 9 c. chalky blue 40 40
 a. Error. Crown missing, W **9***a* .. £300
 b. Error. St. Edward's Crown, W **9***b* .. £130
161 **16** 15 c. deep yellow-green 30 50
 a. Error. Crown missing, W **9***a* .. £300
 b. Error. St. Edward's Crown, W **9***b* .. £140
162 **18** 18 c. carmine-lake 55 20
 a. Error. Crown missing, W **9***a* .. £350
 b. Error. St. Edward's Crown, W **9***b* .. £150
163 **16** 20 c. orange-yellow 80 60
 a. Error. Crown missing, W **9***a* .. £375
 b. Error. St. Edward's Crown, W **9***b* .. £200
164 **15** 25 c. vermilion 60 70
 a. Error. Crown missing, W **9***a* .. £350
 b. Error. St. Edward's Crown, W **9***b* .. £180
165 **17** 40 c. ultramarine 60 70
 a. Error. Crown missing, W **9***a* .. £375
 b. Error. St. Edward's Crown, W **9***b* .. £200
166 **16** 45 c. purple-brown 60 30
 a. Error. Crown missing, W **9***a* .. £425
 b. Error. St. Edward's Crown, W **9***b* .. £275
167 **14** 50 c. reddish violet .. .. 1·00 60
 a. Error. Crown missing, W **9***a* .. £475
 b. Error. St. Edward's Crown, W **9***b* .. £250
168 **18** 1 r. grey-black .. .. 1·75 1·25
 b. Error. St. Edward's Crown, W **9***b* .. £475
169 **14** 1 r. 50, blue .. .. 3·25 6·00
 b. Error. St. Edward's Crown, W **9***b* .. £600
170 **15** 2 r. 25, brown-olive .. .. 3·50 7·50
 b. Error. St. Edward's Crown, W **9***b* .. £600
171 **18** 5 r. red .. .. 3·75 10·00
 b. Error. St. Edward's Crown, W **9***b* .. £500
172 **17** 10 r. green .. .. 7·00 15·00
158/72 .. .. *Set of* 15 22·00 40·00
See *Introduction* re the watermark errors.

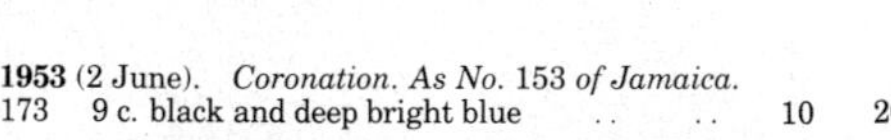

1953 (2 June). *Coronation. As No.* 153 *of Jamaica.*
173 9 c. black and deep bright blue 10 20

19 Sail-fish

20 Seychelles Flying Fox

(Photo Harrison)

1954 (1 Feb)–**61**. *Designs previously used for King George VI issue, but with portrait of Queen Elizabeth II, as in T* **19** *and T* **20.** *Chalk-surfaced paper. Wmk Mult Script CA. P* 14½ × 13½ *(vert) or* 13½ × 14½ *(horiz).*

174 **19** 2 c. lilac 10 10
175 – 3 c. orange 10 10
175*a* **20** 5 c. violet (25.10.57) 30 30
176 – 9 c. chalky blue 10 10
176*a* – 10 c. chalky blue (15.9.56) 30 30
 ab. Blue (11.7.61) .. .. 1·50 65
177 – 15 c. deep yellow-green 15 15
178 – 18 c. crimson 10 10
179 – 20 c. orange-yellow 30 20
180 – 25 c. vermilion 50 50
180*a* – 35 c. crimson (15.9.56) .. .. 1·50 90
181 **19** 40 c. ultramarine 30 25
182 – 45 c. purple-brown 20 15
183 – 50 c. reddish violet 30 20
183*a* – 70 c. purple-brown (15.9.56) .. .. .. 1·50 1·25
184 – 1 r. grey-black 50 40
185 – 1 r. 50, blue .. .. 3·25 2·50
186 – 2 r. 25, brown-olive .. .. 3·25 6·00
187 – 5 r. red .. .. 10·00 6·50
188 **19** 10 r. green .. .. 21·00 16·00
174/88 .. .. *Set of* 19 40·00 32·00

Designs: *Horiz*—15 c., 20 c., 45 c., 70 c. Fishing pirogue; 18 c., 35 c., 1 r., 5 r. Map of Indian Ocean. *Vert*—3 c., 25 c., 2 r. 25, Giant Tortoise; 9 c., 50 c., 1 r. 50, Coco de Mer Palm.

21 "La Pierre de Possession"

5
cents
(22)

(Photo Harrison)

1956 (15 Nov). *Bicentenary of "La Pierre de Possession". Wmk Mult Script CA. P* 14½ × 13½.
189 **21** 40 c. ultramarine 10 10
190 1 r. black 10 10

191 191a 191 191b 191 191c

1957 (16 Sept). *No.* 182 *surch with T* **22.**
191 5 c. on 45 c. purple-brown 10 10
 a. Italic "e" .. .. 3·00
 b. Italic "s" .. .. 3·00
 c. Italic "c" .. .. 2·50
 d. Thick bars omitted £425
 e. Surch double £225

23 Mauritius 6d. Stamp with Seychelles "B 64" Cancellation

(Recess: cancellation typo B.W.)

1961 (11 Dec). *Centenary of First Seychelles Post Office.* W w **12.** *P* 11½.
193 **23** 10 c. blue, black and purple 10 10
194 35 c. blue, black and myrtle-green 20 10
195 2 r. 25, blue, black and orange-brown .. 50 20
193/5 .. .. *Set of* 3 70 30

24 Black Parrot

29 Anse Royale Bay

40 Colony's Badge

(Des V. Whiteley. Photo Harrison)

1962 (21 Feb)–**68.** *T* **24, 29, 40** *and similar designs.* W w **12** *(upright). P* 13½ × 14½ *(horiz designs and* 10 r.*) or* 14½ × 13½ *(others).*

196 5 c. multicoloured 20 10
197 10 c. multicoloured 60 10
198 15 c. multicoloured 10 10
199 20 c. multicoloured 10 10
200 25 c. multicoloured 10 10
200*a* 30 c. multicoloured (15.7.68) .. .. .. 2·25 90
201 35 c. multicoloured .. .. 1·25 2·00
202 40 c. multicoloured 20 40
203 45 c. multicoloured (1.8.66) .. .. .. 3·50 2·75
204 50 c. multicoloured 25 25
205 70 c. ultramarine and light blue .. .. 5·50 3·00
206 75 c. multicoloured (1.8.66) .. .. .. 1·75 2·75
207 1 r. multicoloured 30 10
208 1 r. 50, multicoloured .. .. 3·00 4·50
209 2 r. 25, multicoloured .. .. 3·00 3·00
210 3 r. 50, multicoloured .. .. 2·25 4·50
211 5 r. multicoloured .. .. 3·50 2·50
212 10 r. multicoloured .. .. 11·00 4·50
196/212 .. .. *Set of* 18 35·00 27·00

Designs: *Vert (as T* **24**)—10 c. Vanilla vine; 15 c. Fisherman; 20 c. Denis Island lighthouse; 25 c. Clock Tower, Victoria; 50 c. Cascade Church; 70 c. Sail-fish; 75 c. Coco-de-Mer palm. *Horiz (as T* **29**)—30 c., 35 c. Anse Royale Bay; 40 c. Government House; 45 c. Fishing pirogue; 1 r. Cinnamon; 1r. 50, Copra; 2r. 25 Map; 3r. 50, Land settlement; 5 r. Regina Mundi convent.

The 1 r. exists with PVA gum as well as gum arabic, but the 30 c. exists with PVA gum only.

See also Nos. 233/7.

For stamps of the above issue overprinted "B.I.O.T" see under British Indian Ocean Territory.

1963 (4 June). *Freedom from Hunger. As No.* 80 *of Lesotho.*
213 70 c. reddish violet 60 25

1963 (16 Sept). *Red Cross Centenary. As Nos.* 203/4 *of Jamaica.*
214 10 c. red and black 25 10
215 75 c. red and blue 75 40

45
CENTS
(41)

42 Seychelles Flying Fox

1965 (15 Apr). *Nos.* 201 *and* 205 *surch as T* **41.**
216 45 c. on 35 c. multicoloured 10 15
217 75 c. on 70 c. ultramarine and light blue .. 20 15

1965 (1 June). *I.T.U. Centenary. As Nos.* 98/9 *of Lesotho.*
218 5 c. orange and ultramarine 15 10
219 1 r. 50, mauve and apple-green 65 25

1965 (25 Oct). *International Co-operation Year. As Nos.* 100/1 *of Lesotho.*
220 5 c. reddish purple and turquoise-green .. 10 10
221 40 c. deep bluish green and lavender 20 20

1966 (24 Jan). *Churchill Commemoration. As Nos.* 102/5 *of Lesotho.*
222 5 c. new blue 15 10
223 15 c. deep green 40 10
224 75 c. brown 80 10
225 1 r. 50, bluish violet .. .. 1·25 60
222/5 .. .. *Set of* 4 2·25 80

1966 (1 July). *World Cup Football Championships. As Nos.* 57/8 *of Pitcairn Islands.*
226 15 c. violet, yellow-green, lake & yellow-brn .. 10 10
227 1 r. chocolate, blue-green, lake & yellow-brn 20 20

1966 (20 Sept). *Inauguration of W.H.O. Headquarters, Geneva. As Nos.* 185/6 *of Montserrat.*
228 20 c. black, yellow-green and light blue .. 15 10
229 50 c. black, light purple and yellow-brown .. 25 20

1966 (1 Dec). *20th Anniv of U.N.E.S.C.O. As Nos.* 342/4 *of Mauritius.*
230 15 c. slate-violet, red, yellow and orange .. 25 10
231 1 r. orange-yellow, violet and deep olive .. 45 10
232 5 r. black, bright purple and orange .. .. 1·25 1·00
230/2 .. .. *Set of* 3 1·75 1·00

1967–69. *As Nos.* 196/7, 204 *and new values as T* **42** *but wmk* w **12** *(sideways).*
233 5 c. multicoloured (7.2.67) 35 40
234 10 c. multicoloured (4.6.68) 25 10
235 50 c. multicoloured (13.5.69) .. .. .. 1·75 2·25
236 60 c. red, blue and blackish brown (15.7.68) 1·25 45
237 85 c. ultramarine and light blue (as No. 205) (15.7.68) 90 40
233/7 .. .. *Set of* 5 4·00 3·25

The 10 c. exists with PVA gum as well as gum arabic, but the 50 c. to 85 c. exist with PVA gum only.

UNIVERSAL
ADULT
SUFFRAGE
1967
(43)

44 Cowrie Shells

1967 (18 Sept). *Universal Adult Suffrage. As Nos.* 198 *and* 206, *but W* w **12** *(sideways), and Nos.* 203 *and* 210 *(wmk upright), optd with T* **43.**
238 15 c. multicoloured 10 10
 a. Opt double .. ..
239 45 c. multicoloured 10 10
240 75 c. multicoloured 10 10
241 3 r. 50, multicoloured 20 15
238/41 .. .. *Set of* 4 30 30

(Des V. Whiteley. Photo Harrison)

1967 (4 Dec). *International Tourist Year. T* **44** *and similar horiz designs. Multicoloured.* W w **12.** *P* 14 × 13.
242 15 c. Type **44** 15 10
243 40 c. Cone Shells 20 10
244 1 r. Arthritic Spider Conch 25 10
245 2 r. 25, Subulate Auger and Triton Shells .. 55 40
242/5 .. .. *Set of* 4 1·00 45

= 30
(48)

49 Farmer with Wife and Children at Sunset

1968 (16 Apr). *Nos.* 202/3 *and as No.* 206 *surch as T* **48** *(*30 c.*) or with "CENTS" added, and three bars (others).* W w **12** *(sideways on No.* 248*).*
246 30 c. on 40 c. multicoloured 10 10
247 60 c. on 45 c. multicoloured 10 10
248 85 c. on 75 c. multicoloured 15 15
246/8 .. .. *Set of* 3 30 30

(Des Mary Hayward. Litho Harrison)

1968 (2 Sept). *Human Rights Year.* W w **12**. P 14½ × 13½.

249	**49** 20 c. multicoloured	10	10
250	50 c. multicoloured	10	10
251	85 c. multicoloured	10	10
252	2 r. 25, multicoloured	20	30
249/52	*Set of* 4	30	40

50 Expedition landing at Anse Possession

54 Apollo Launch

(Des Mary Hayward. Litho and die-stamped Harrison)

1968 (30 Dec). *Bicentenary of First Landing on Praslin. T* **50** *and similar multicoloured designs.* W w **12** (*sideways on* 50 c., 85 c.). *P* 14.

253	20 c. Type **50**	15	10
254	50 c. French warships at anchor (*vert*)	20	15
255	85 c. Coco-de-Mer and Black Parrot (*vert*)	45	20
256	2 r. 25, French warships under sail	55	50
253/6	*Set of* 4	1·25	80

(Des V. Whiteley. Litho Format)

1969 (9 Sept). *First Man on the Moon. T* **54** *and similar horiz designs. Multicoloured.* W w **12** (*sideways on horiz designs*). *P* 13½.

257	5 c. Type **54**	10	10
258	20 c. Module leaving Mother-ship for Moon	15	10
259	50 c. Astronauts and Space Module on Moon	20	15
260	85 c. Tracking station	25	15
261	2 r. 25, Moon craters with Earth on the "Horizon"	45	65
257/61	*Set of* 5	1·00	95

59 Picault's Landing, 1742

60 Badge of Seychelles

(Des Mary Hayward. Litho Enschedé)

1969 (3 Nov)–**75**. *Horiz designs as T* **59/60**. *Multicoloured.* W w **12** (*sideways*). *Slightly toned paper. P* 13 × 12½.

262	5 c. Type **59**	10	10
263	10 c. U.S. satellite-tracking station	10	10
	a. Whiter paper (8.3.73)	70	40
264	15 c. *Königsberg I* at Aldabra, 1914†	1·00	55
	a. Whiter paper (8.3.73)	3·75	1·00
265	20 c. Fleet re-fuelling off St. Anne, 1939–45	30	10
	a. Whiter paper (13.6.74)	1·25	1·50
266	25 c. Exiled Ashanti King Prempeh	20	10
	a. Whiter paper (8.3.73)	65	75
267	30 c. Laying Stone of Possession, 1756	1·00	2·75
268	40 c. As 30 c. (11.12.72)	90	1·25
	a. Whiter paper (13.6.74)	1·60	1·60
269	50 c. Pirates and treasure	30	15
	a. Whiter paper (13.6.74)	1·25	1·50
270	60 c. Corsairs attacking merchantman	1·00	1·50
271	65 c. As 60 c. (11.12.72)	2·00	3·00
	a. Whiter paper (13.8.75)	6·00	7·00
272	85 c. Impression of proposed airport	1·25	1·50
273	95 c. As 85 c. (11.12.72)	3·00	3·25
	a. Whiter paper (13.6.74)	4·00	3·25
274	1 r. French Governor capitulating to British naval officer, 1794	35	15
	a. Whiter paper (8.3.73)	1·00	70
275	1 r. 50, H.M.S. *Sybille* and *Chiffone* in battle, 1801	1·75	2·00
	a. Whiter paper (8.3.73)	3·00	5·00
276	3 r. 50, Visit of the Duke of Edinburgh, 1956	1·50	2·00
	a. Whiter paper (13.8.75)	2·50	8·00
277	5 r. Chevalier Queau de Quincy	1·50	1·75
278	10 r. Indian Ocean chart, 1574	3·00	3·50
279	15 r. Type **60**	4·00	7·50
262/79	*Set of* 18	19·00	26·00
263a/76a	*Set of* 11	23·00	28·00

†The design is incorrect in that it shows *Königsberg II* and the wrong date ("1915").

The stamps on the whiter paper are highly glazed, producing shade variations and are easily distinguishable from the original printings on toned paper.

74 White Terns, French Warship and Island

(Des A. Smith; adapted V. Whiteley. Litho D.L.R.)

1970 (27 Apr). *Bicentenary of First Settlement, St. Anne Island. T* **74** *and similar horiz designs. Multicoloured.* W w **12** (*sideways*). *P* 14.

280	20 c. Type **74**	15	10
281	50 c. Flying Fish, ship and island	15	10
282	85 c. Compass and chart	15	10
283	3 r. 50, Anchor on sea-bed	30	45
280/3	*Set of* 4	65	55

78 Girl and Optician's Chart

79 Pitcher Plant

(Des A. Smith. Litho Questa)

1970 (4 Aug). *Centenary of British Red Cross. T* **78** *and similar multicoloured designs.* W w **12** (*sideways on horiz designs*). *P* 14.

284	20 c. Type **78**	10	10
285	50 c. Baby, scales and milk bottles	15	10
286	85 c. Woman with child and umbrella (*vert*)	15	10
287	3 r. 50, Red Cross local H.Q. building	80	60
284/7	*Set of* 4	1·10	65

(Des G. Drummond. Litho J.W.)

1970 (29 Dec). *Flowers. T* **79** *and similar vert designs. Multicoloured.* W w **12**. *P* 14.

288	20 c. Type **79**	45	15
289	50 c. Wild Vanilla	55	15
290	85 c. Tropic-Bird Orchid	1·40	30
291	3 r. 50, Vare Hibiscus	2·50	1·50
288/91	*Set of* 4	4·50	1·90
MS292	81 × 133 mm. Nos. 288/91. Wmk inverted	8·00	12·00

80 Seychelles "On the Map"

81 Piper "Navajo"

(Des and litho J.W.)

1971 (18 May). *"Putting Seychelles on the Map". Sheet* 152 × 101 *mm.* W w **12** (*sideways*). *P* 13½.

MS293	**80** 5 r. multicoloured	2·25	8·50

(Des and litho J.W.)

1971 (28 June). *Airport Completion. T* **81** *and similar multi-coloured designs showing aircraft.* W w **12** (*sideways on horiz designs*). *P* 14 × 14½ (5, 20 *and* 60 c.) *or* 14½ (*others*).

294	5 c. Type **81**	10	10
295	20 c. Westland "Wessex"	20	10
296	50 c. "Catalina" flying-boat (*horiz*)	40	10
297	60 c. Grumman "Albatross"	45	10
298	85 c. Short "G" Class flying-boat (*horiz*)	65	10
299	3 r. 50, Vickers Supermarine "Walrus" (*horiz*)	3·50	3·00
294/9	*Set of* 6	4·75	3·25

82 Santa Claus delivering Gifts (Jean-Claude Waye Hive)

(**83**)

(Des Jennifer Toombs. Litho A. & M.)

1971 (12 Oct). *Christmas. Drawings by local children. T* **82** *and similar horiz designs. Multicoloured.* W w **12** (*sideways*). *P* 13½.

300	10 c. Type **82**	10	10
301	15 c. Santa Claus seated on turtle (Edison Thérésine)	10	10
302	3 r. 50, Santa Claus landing on island (Isabelle Tirant)	40	70
300/2	*Set of* 3	50	70

1971 (21 Dec). *Nos.* 267, 270 *and* 272 *surch in grey as T* **83**.

303	40 c. on 30 c. Laying Stone of Possession, 1756	30	55
304	65 c. on 60 c. Corsairs attacking merchantman	40	75
305	95 c. on 85 c. Impression of proposed airport	45	1·00
303/5	*Set of* 3	1·00	2·10

ROYAL VISIT 1972

(**84**)

85 Seychelles Brush Warbler

1972 (20 Mar). *Royal Visit. Nos.* 265 *and* 277 *optd with T* **84**.

306	20 c. Fleet re-fuelling off St. Anne, 1939–45	15	20
307	5 r. Chevalier Queau de Quincy (Gold)	1·50	2·50

(Des R. Gillmor. Litho Questa)

1972 (24 July). *Rare Seychelles Birds. T* **85** *and similar vert designs. Multicoloured.* W w **12** (*sideways*). *P* 13½.

308	5 c. Type **85**	30	10
309	20 c. Bare-legged Scops Owl	1·00	20
310	50 c. Seychelles Blue Pigeon	1·25	65
311	65 c. Seychelles Magpie Robin	1·50	75
312	95 c. Seychelles Paradise Flycatcher	2·25	2·00
313	3 r. 50, Seychelles Kestrel	6·50	8·00
308/13	*Set of* 6	11·50	10·50
MS314	144 × 162 mm. Nos. 308/13	17·00	24·00

86 Fireworks Display

87 Giant Tortoise and Sailfish

(Des V. Whiteley. Litho Questa)

1972 (18 Sept). *"Festival '72". T* **86** *and similar multicoloured designs.* W w **12** (*sideways on* 10 *and* 25 c.). *P* 14.

315	10 c. Type **86**	10	10
316	15 c. Pirogue race (*horiz*)	10	10
317	25 c. Floats and costumes	10	10
318	5 r. Water skiing (*horiz*)	60	80
315/18	*Set of* 4	65	80

(Des (from photograph by D. Groves) and photo Harrison)

1972 (20 Nov). *Royal Silver Wedding. Multicoloured; background colour given.* W w **12**. *P* 14 × 14½.

319	**87** 95 c. turquoise-blue	15	10
320	1 r. 50, red-brown	15	10

1973 (14 Nov). *Royal Wedding. As Nos.* 322/3 *of Montserrat.*

321	95 c. ochre	10	10
322	1 r. 50, dull deep blue	10	10

88 Soldier Fish

(Des G. Drummond. Litho Questa)

1974 (5 Mar). *Fishes. T* **88** *and similar horiz designs. Multicoloured.* W w **12**. *P* 14½ × 14.

323	20 c. Type **88**	15	10
324	50 c. File Fish	25	10
325	95 c. Butterfly Fish	30	20
326	1 r. 50, Gaterin	75	1·00
323/6	*Set of* 4	1·25	1·25

89 Globe and Letter

(Des Sylvia Goaman. Litho Enschedé)

1974 (9 Oct). *Centenary of Universal Postal Union. T* **89** *and similar horiz designs. Multicoloured.* W w **12** (*sideways*). *P* 12½ × 12.

327	20 c. Type **89**	10	10
328	50 c. Globe and radio beacon	20	10
329	95 c. Globe and postmark	35	40
330	1 r. 50, Emblems within "UPU"	50	70
327/30	*Set of* 4	1·00	1·10

90 Sir Winston Churchill (**91**)

(Des G. Vasarhelyi. Litho Questa)

1974 (30 Nov). *Birth Centenary of Sir Winston Churchill. T* **90** *and similar horiz design. Multicoloured. W w* **12**. *P* 14.

331 95 c. Type **90** 20 15
332 1 r. 50, Profile portrait 35 40
MS333 81 × 109 mm. Nos. 331/2 .. .. .. 60 1·75

1975 (8 Feb). *Visit of R.M.S. "Queen Elizabeth II". Nos.* 265a, 269a, 273a *and* 275a *optd with T* **91**.

334 20 c. Fleet re-fuelling off St. Anne, 1939–45 .. 15 15
335 50 c. Pirates and treasure 20 20
336 95 c. Impression of proposed airport (Sil.) .. 25 35
337 1 r. 50, H.M.S. *Sybille* and *Chiffone* in battle, 1801 .. .. 35 60
334/7 .. .. *Set of* 4 85 1·10

INTERNAL
SELF-GOVERNMENT
OCTOBER
1975

(**92**) **93** Queen Elizabeth I

1975 (1 Oct). *Internal Self-Government. Nos.* 265a, 271a, 274a *and* 276a *optd with T* **92** *in gold, by Enschedé.*

338 20 c. Fleet re-fuelling off St. Anne, 1939–45 .. 15 15
339 65 c. Corsairs attacking merchantman .. 25 30
340 1 r. French Governor capitulating to British naval officer, 1794 .. .. .. 30 35
341 3 r. 50, Visit of Duke of Edinburgh, 1956 .. 1·00 1·50
338/41 .. .. *Set of* 4 1·50 2·00

(Des C. Abbott. Litho Walsall)

1975 (15 Dec). *International Women's Year. T* **93** *and similar vert designs. Multicoloured. W w* **14** (*inverted*). *P* 13½.

342 10 c. Type **93** 10 10
343 15 c. Gladys Aylward 10 10
344 20 c. Elizabeth Fry 10 10
345 25 c. Emmeline Pankhurst 10 10
346 65 c. Florence Nightingale 25 20
347 1 r. Amy Johnson 40 35
348 1 r. 50, Joan of Arc 50 60
349 3 r. 50, Eleanor Roosevelt .. .. .. 1·50 2·25
342/9 .. .. *Set of* 8 2·50 3·25

94 Map of Praslin and Postmark

95 First Landing, 1609 (inset portrait of Premier James Mancham)

(Des J.W. Litho Questa)

1976 (30 Mar). *Rural Posts. T* **94** *and similar vert designs showing maps and postmarks. Multicoloured. W w* **14**. *P* 14.

350 20 c. Type **94** 15 10
351 65 c. La Digue 25 20
352 1 r. Mahé with Victoria postmark 30 25
353 1 r. 50, Mahé with Anse Royale postmark .. 45 70
350/3 .. .. *Set of* 4 1·00 1·10
MS354 166 × 127 mm. Nos. 350/3 .. .. .. 2·00 3·00

INDEPENDENT

(Des G. Drummond. Litho J.W.)

1976 (29 June). *Independence. T* **95** *and similar vert designs. Multicoloured. W w* **12** (*sideways*). *P* 13½.

355 20 c. Type **95** 10 10
356 25 c. The Possession Stone 10 10
357 40 c. First settlers, 1770 .. .. .. 15 15
358 75 c. Chevalier Queau de Quincy 20 20
359 1 r. Sir Bickham Sweet-Escott 25 20
360 1 r. 25, Legislative Building 40 50
361 1 r. 50, Seychelles badge 45 60
362 3 r. 50, Seychelles flag .. .. .. 90 1·40
355/62 .. .. *Set of* 8 2·25 2·75

96 Flags of Seychelles and U.S.A.

(Des and litho J.W.)

1976 (12 July). *Seychelles Independence and American Independence Bicentenary. T* **96** *and similar horiz design. Multicoloured. W w* **12** (*sideways*). *P* 13½.

363 1 r. Type **96** 25 15
364 10 r. Statehouses of Seychelles and Philadelphia .. .. 1·25 1·50

97 Swimming **98** Seychelles Paradise Flycatcher

(Des J.W. Litho Questa)

1976 (26 July). *Olympic Games, Montreal. T* **97** *and similar horiz designs. W w* **14** (*sideways*). *P* 14.

365 20 c. ultramarine, cobalt and sepia 10 10
366 65 c. bottle-green, apple-green and grey-black 20 10
367 1 r. chestnut, blue-green and grey-black .. 25 10
368 3 r. 50, crimson, rose and grey-black .. 50 80
365/8 .. .. *Set of* 4 90 95

Designs:—65 c. Hockey; 1 r. Basketball; 3 r. 50, Football.

(Des Mrs. R. Fennessy. Litho Questa)

1976–77. *Fourth Pan-African Ornithological Congress, Seychelles. T* **98** *and similar multicoloured designs. W w* **14** (*sideways on Nos.* 370/1). *P* 14. A. *Ordinary paper* (8.11.76). B. *Chalky paper* (7.3.77).

		A		B	
369	20 c. Type **98**	20	10	15	10
370	1 r. 25, Seychelles Sunbird (*horiz*)	75	65	65	65
371	1 r. 50, Seychelles Brown White Eye (*horiz*)	95	80	80	80
372	5 r. Black Parrot	2·00	2·00	2·00	2·00
369/72	.. .. .. *Set of* 4	3·50	3·25	3·25	3·25
MS373	161 × 109 mm. Nos. 369/72	4·50	5·50	†	
	a. 5 r. value in miniature sheet imperf	£850			

Independence
1976

(**99**) **100** Inauguration of George Washington

1976 (22 Nov). *Independence. Nos.* 265a, 269, 271a, 273a, 274a, 276a *and* 277/9 *optd with T* **99** (*No.* 271 *additionally surch.*). *W w* **12** (*sideways*).

374 20 c. Fleet re-fuelling off St. Anne, 1939–45 .. 25 55
375 50 c. Pirates and treasure 40 75
376 95 c. Impression of proposed airport .. .. 55 1·00
a. Opt inverted .. .. 85·00
377 1 r. French Governor capitulating to British naval officer, 1794 .. .. .. 55 1·00
378 3 r. 50, Visit of Duke of Edinburgh, 1956 .. 2·75 3·50
a. Opt inverted .. .. 75·00
b. On No. 276 .. .. 3·25 3·50
ba. Opt inverted £100
379 5 r. Chevalier Queau de Quincy .. .. 3·00 3·50
380 10 r. Indian Ocean chart, 1574 .. .. 5·50 9·00
381 15 c. Type **60** .. .. 7·50 9·00
382 25 r. on 65 c. Corsairs attacking merchantman 11·00 16·00
374/82 .. .. *Set of* 9 28·00 40·00

(Des Jennifer Toombs. Litho Questa)

1976 (21 Dec). *Bicentenary of American Revolution. T* **100** *and similar horiz designs. P* 14 × 13½.

383 1 c. crimson and light rose 10 10
384 2 c. violet and light lilac 10 10
385 3 c. bright blue and azure 10 10
386 4 c. chestnut and light yellow 10 10
387 5 c. emerald and light yellow-green 10 10
388 1 r. 50, sepia and cinnamon 60 35
389 3 r. 50, dp turquoise-blue & pale blue-green .. 80 80
390 5 r. chestnut and light yellow .. .. 1·00 1·00
391 10 r. chalky blue and azure .. .. .. 1·75 1·75
383/91 .. .. *Set of* 9 4·00 3·75
MS392 141 × 141 mm. 25 r. plum and magenta 4·00 5·50

Designs:—2 c. Jefferson and Louisiana Purchase; 3 c. William Seward and Alaska Purchase; 4 c. Pony Express, 1860; 5 c. Lincoln's Emancipation Proclamation; 1 r. 50 Transcontinental Railroad, 1869; 3 r. 50 Wright Brothers flight, 1903; 5 r. Henry Ford's assembly-line, 1913; 10 r. J. F. Kennedy and 1969 Moon-landing; 25 r. Signing Independence Declaration, 1776.

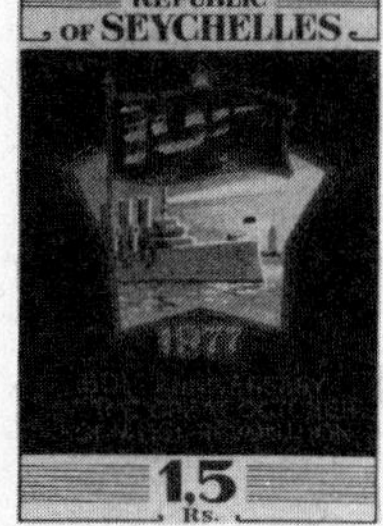

101 Silhouette of the Islands **102** Cruiser *Aurora* and Flag

(Des G. Hutchins (Nos. 395/8), J.W. (others). Litho Questa)

1977 (5 Sept). *Silver Jubilee. T* **101** *and similar multicoloured designs. W w* **14** (*sideways on* 20 *and* 40 *c.*, 5 *and* 10 *r.*). *P* 14.

393 20 c. Type **101** 10 10
394 40 c. Silhouette (*different*) 10 10
395 50 c. The Orb (*vert*) 10 10
396 1 r. St. Edward's Crown (*vert*) 15 10
397 1 r. 25, Ampulla and Spoon (*vert*) 20 15
398 1 r. 50, Sceptre with Cross (*vert*) 20 20
399 5 r. Silhouette (*different*) 50 50
400 10 r. Silhouette (*different*) 90 90
393/400 .. .. *Set of* 8 1·75 1·75
MS401 133 × 135 mm. 20 c., 50 c., 1 r., 10 r. all wmk sideways .. .. 75 1·40

(Litho State Printing Works, Moscow)

1977 (7 Nov). *60th Anniv of Russian October Revolution. P* 12 × 12½.

402 **102** 1 r. 50, multicoloured 35 30
MS403 101 × 129 mm. No. 402 .. .. .. 60 50

103 Coral Scene

(Des G. Drummond. Litho Walsall (40 c., 1 r., 1 r. 25, 1 r. 50), J.W. or Questa (25 c. (No. 408B)), J.W. (others))

1977–84. *Multicoloured designs as T* **103**. *Rupee values show* "Re" *or* "Rs". *W w* **14** (*sideways on* 10, 20, 50 *and* 75 *c.*). *P* 14½ × 14 (40 *c.*, 1 *r.*, 1 *r.* 25, 1 *r.* 50), 13 (5, 10, 15, 20 *r.*) *or* 14 (*others*).

A. *No imprint*. B. *Imprint date at foot*

		A		B	
404	5 c. Reef Fish	10	10	†	
405	10 c. Hawksbill Turtle ..	20	10	10	10
406	15 c. Coco-de-Mer	10	15	10	10
407	20 c. Wild Vanilla Orchid ..	65	10	10	10
408	25 c. *Hypolimnas misippus* (butterfly)	75	35	10	10
409	40 c. Type **103**	30	10	10	10
410	50 c. Giant Tortoise	20	10	30	10
411	75 c. Crayfish	20	10	15	20
412	1 r. Madagascar Red Fody ..	1·25	10	4·00	20
413	1 r. 25, White Tern	1·00	15	†	
414	1 r. 50, Seychelles Flying Fox	1·50	15	2·00	50
415	3 r. 50, Green Gecko	75	80	†	
416	5 r. Octopus	2·00	40	†	
417	10 r. Giant Tiger Cowrie ..	2·25	2·00	†	
418	15 r. Pitcher Plant	2·25	2·50	†	
419	20 r. Coat of arms	2·50	2·50	†	
404A/19A	.. .. *Set of* 16	14·00	8·75		
405B/14B	.. .. *Set of* 9			6·00	1·10

Dates of issue: Without imprint 10.11.77, 40 c., 1 r. to 1 r. 50; 6.2.78, 10, 20, 50, 75 c., 5 r., 20 r.; 10.4.78, others. With imprint 14.3.80, 10, 15, 25, 40, 50, 75, 1 r., 1 r. 50; 5.84, 20 c.

The 40 c., 1 r., 1 r. 25 and 1 r. 50 values are horizontal designs, 31 × 27 mm; the 5, 10, 15 and 20 r. are vertical, 28 × 36 mm; the others are horizontal, 29 × 25 mm.

The 10 c. and 25 c. (Nos. 405B and 408B) exist with different imprint dates.

For rupee values showing face value as "R" see Nos. 487/94.

For 10 c. and 50 c. with watermark w **14** (upright) and printed by Questa see Nos. 718 and 722. A printing of the 25 c. by Questa on the same date has the same perforation and watermark as J.W. printings of No. 408B.

For 50 c. and 3 r. (inscr "Rs") with watermark w **16** and printed by Questa see Nos. 732/8.

104 St. Roch Roman Catholic Church, Bel Ombre

(Des G. Drummond. Litho Walsall)

1977 (5 Dec). *Christmas. T* **104** *and similar horiz designs. Multicoloured. W w* **14** (*sideways*). *P* 13½ × 14.

420 20 c. Type **104** 10 10
421 1 r. Anglican cathedral, Victoria 10 10
422 1 r. 50, Roman Catholic cathedral, Victoria .. 15 10
423 5 r. St. Mark's Anglican church, Praslin .. 30 45
420/3 .. .. *Set of* 4 50 55

105 Liberation Day ringed on Calendar

106 Stamp Portraits of Edward VII, George V and George VI

(Des local artists; adapted L. Curtis. Litho Questa)

1978 (5 June). *Liberation Day. T* **105** *and similar vert designs. Multicoloured. W* w **14**. *P* 14 × 13½.

424 40 c. Type **105** 10 10
425 1 r. 25, Hands holding bayonet, torch and flag . . 15 10
426 1 r. 50, Fisherman and farmer . . 15 15
427 5 r. Soldiers and rejoicing people . . 35 40
424/7 . . *Set of* 4 60 60

(Des G. Drummond. Litho Questa)

1978 (21 Aug). *25th Anniv of Coronation. T* **106** *and similar vert designs. Multicoloured. W* w **14**. *P* 14.

428 40 c. Type **106** 10 10
429 1 r. 50, Victoria and Elizabeth II . . 10 10
430 3 r. Queen Victoria Monument . . 20 25
431 5 r. Queen's Building, Victoria . . 30 35
428/31 . . *Set of* 4 60 65
MS432 87 × 129 mm. Nos. 428/31 . . 60 85

107 Gardenia

(Des G. Hutchins. Litho Questa)

1978 (16 Oct). *Wildlife. T* **107** *and similar horiz designs. Multicoloured. W* w **14** (*sideways*). *P* 13½ × 14.

433 40 c. Type **107** 10 10
434 1 r. 25, Seychelles Magpie Robin . . 40 25
435 1 r. 50, Seychelles Paradise Flycatcher . . 45 35
436 5 r. Green Turtle . . 70 85
433/6 . . *Set of* 4 1·50 1·40

108 Possession Stone

109 Seychelles Fody

(Des G. Hutchins. Litho Questa)

1978 (15 Dec). *Bicentenary of Victoria. T* **108** *and similar horiz designs. Multicoloured. W* w **14** (*sideways*). *P* 13½ × 14.

437 20 c. Type **108** 10 10
438 1 r. 25, Plan of 1782 "L'Etablissement" . . 15 15
439 1 r. 50, Clock Tower . . 15 15
440 5 r. Bust of Pierre Poivre . . 40 50
437/40 . . *Set of* 4 65 75

(Des G. Drummond. Litho Questa)

1979 (27 Feb). *Birds* (*1st series*). *T* **109** *and similar vert designs. Multicoloured. W* w **14**. *P* 14.

441 2 r. Type **109** 50 50
a. Horiz strip of 5. Nos. 441/5 . . 2·25
442 2 r. Green Heron . . 50 50
443 2 r. Thick-billed Bulbul . . 50 50
444 2 r. Seychelles Cave Swiftlet . . 50 50
445 2 r. Grey-headed Lovebird . . 50 50
441/5 . . *Set of* 5 2·25 2·25

Nos. 441/5 were printed together, *se-tenant*, in horizontal strips of 5 throughout the sheet.

See also Nos. 463/7, 500/4 and 523/7.

COVER PRICES

Cover factors are quoted at the beginning of each country for most issues to 1945. An explanation of the system can be found on page x. The factors quoted do not, however, apply to philatelic covers.

110 Patrice Lumumba

111 1978 5 r. Liberation Day Commemorative and Sir Rowland Hill

(Des G. Vasarhelyi. Litho Questa)

1979 (5 June). *African Liberation Heroes. T* **110** *and similar vert designs. W* w **14**. *P* 14 × 14½.

446 40 c. black, deep violet and lilac . . 10 10
447 2 r. black, blue and pale blue . . 25 25
448 2 r. 25, black, reddish brown & orange-brn . . 30 30
449 5 r. black, bronze-green and dull green . . 65 80
446/9 . . *Set of* 4 1·10 1·25

Designs:—2 r. Kwame Nkrumah; 2 r. 25, Dr. Eduardo Mondlane; 5 r. Hamilcar Cabral.

(Des J.W. Litho Questa)

1979 (27 Aug). *Death Centenary of Sir Rowland Hill. T* **111** *and similar vert designs showing stamps and Sir Rowland Hill. Multicoloured. W* w **14**. *P* 14.

450 40 c. Type **111** 10 10
451 2 r. 25, 1972 50 c. Rare Birds commemorative 45 40
452 3 r. 1962 50 c. definitive . . 50 55
450/2 . . *Set of* 3 95 95
MS453 112 × 88 mm. 5 r. 1892 4 c. definitive. Wmk inverted . . 40 55

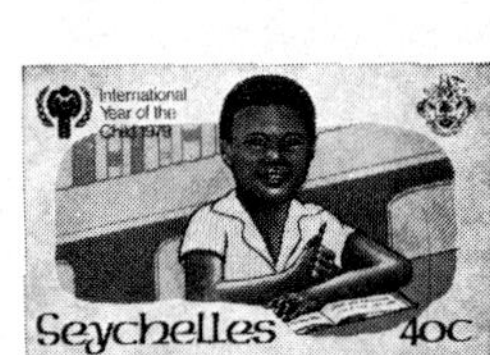

112 Child with Book

113 The Herald Angel

(Des BG Studio. Litho Questa)

1979 (26 Oct). *International Year of the Child. T* **112** *and similar multicoloured designs. W* w **14** (*sideways on* 40 *c. and* 2 *r.* 25). *P* 14½.

454 40 c. Type **112** 10 10
455 2 r. 25, Children of different races . . 20 30
456 3 r. Young child with ball (*vert*) . . 30 45
457 5 r. Girl with glove-puppet (*vert*) . . 40 65
454/7 . . *Set of* 4 85 1·25

Nos. 454/7 were each printed in sheets including two *se-tenant* stamp-size labels.

(Des J. Cooter. Litho Walsall)

1979 (3 Dec). *Christmas. T* **113** *and similar multicoloured designs. W* w **14** (*sideways on* 3 *r.*). *P* 14½ × 14 (3 *r.*) *or* 14 × 14½ (*others*).

458 20 c. Type **113** 10 10
459 2 r. 25, The Virgin and Child . . 30 30
460 3 r. The Three Kings (*horiz*) . . 40 45
458/60 . . *Set of* 3 65 70
MS461 87 × 75 mm. 5 r. The Flight into Egypt (*horiz*) (wmk sideways). P 14½ × 14 . . 50 70

R.1.10

(**114**)

115 Seychelles Kestrel

1979 (7 Dec). *As No.* 415 *but with imprint, surch with T* **114**.

462 1 r. 10 on 3 r. 50, Green Gecko . . 30 30

(Des G. Drummond. Litho Questa)

1980 (29 Feb). *Birds* (*2nd series*). *Seychelles Kestrel. T* **115** *and similar vert designs. Multicoloured. W* w **14** (*inverted*). *P* 14.

463 2 r. Type **115** 60 50
a. Horiz strip of 5. Nos. 463/7 . . 2·75
464 2 r. Pair of Seychelles Kestrels . . 60 50
465 2 r. Seychelles Kestrel with eggs . . 60 50
466 2 r. Seychelles Kestrel on nest with chick . . 60 50
467 2 r. Seychelles Kestrel chicks in nest . . 60 50
463/7 . . *Set of* 5 2·75 2·25

Nos. 463/7 were printed together, *se-tenant*, in horizontal strips of 5 throughout the sheet.

116 10 Rupees Banknote

117 Sprinting

(Des B. Grout. Litho Questa)

1980 (18 Apr). *"London 1980" International Stamp Exhibition. New Currency. T* **116** *and similar multicoloured designs showing banknotes. W* w **14** (*sideways on* 40 *c. and* 1 *r.* 50). *P* 14.

468 40 c. Type **116** 10 10
469 1 r. 50, 25 rupees . . 20 15
470 2 r. 25, 50 rupees (*vert*) . . 30 25
471 5 r. 100 rupees (*vert*) . . 60 55
468/71 . . *Set of* 4 1·00 90
MS472 119 × 102 mm. Nos. 468/71 (wmk sideways) 90 1·40

(Des J.W. Litho Questa)

1980 (13 June). *Olympic Games, Moscow. T* **117** *and similar vert designs. Multicoloured. W* w **14**. *P* 14 × 14½.

473 40 c. Type **117** 10 10
474 2 r. 25, Weightlifting . . 20 20
475 3 r. Boxing . . 30 30
476 5 r. Yachting . . 60 40
473/6 . . *Set of* 4 1·10 80
MS477 90 × 121 mm. Nos. 473/6 . . 1·10 1·90

118 "Jumbo Jet" Airliner

119 Female Palm

(Des A. Theobald. Litho Questa)

1980 (22 Aug). *International Tourism Conference, Manila. T* **118** *and similar horiz designs. Multicoloured. W* w **14** (*sideways*). *P* 14.

478 40 c. Type **118** 10 10
479 2 r. 25, Bus . . 35 35
480 3 r. Cruise liner . . 50 50
481 5 r. *La Belle Coralline* (tourist launch) . . 70 75
478/81 . . *Set of* 4 1·50 1·50

(Des L. Curtis. Litho Harrison)

1980 (14 Nov). *Coco-de-Mer* (*palms*). *T* **119** *and similar vert designs. Multicoloured. W* w **14**. *P* 14.

482 40 c. Type **119** 10 10
483 2 r. 25, Male Palm . . 25 20
484 3 r. Artefacts . . 40 35
485 5 r. Fisherman's gourd . . 55 55
482/5 . . *Set of* 4 1·10 1·00
MS486 82 × 140 mm. Nos. 482/5 . . 2·00 2·00

1981 (9 Jan)–**91**. *As Nos.* 412/14, 415 (*but new value*), *and* 416/19 *all with face values redrawn to show* "R" *instead of* "Re" *or* "Rs" *and imprint date at foot. Chalk-surfaced paper.*

487 1 r. Madagascar Red Fody . . 1·00 30
a. Ordinary paper (11.86) . . 20 25
488 1 r. 10, Green Gecko . . 25 30
489 1 r. 25, White Tern . . 1·25 40
490 1 r. 50, Seychelles Flying Fox . . 35 40
a. Ordinary paper (11.91) . . 35 40
491 5 r. Octopus . . 1·25 1·40
492 10 r. Giant Tiger Cowrie . . 2·25 2·40
493 15 r. Pitcher Plant . . 3·25 3·50
494 20 r. Coat of arms . . 4·50 4·75
487/94 . . *Set of* 8 12·00 12·00

The 1 r., 1 r. 50 and 5 r. values exist with different imprint dates below the design.

For 1 r. 25, 3 r. and 5 r. watermarked w **16** see Nos. 735/8.

120 Vasco da Gama's *Sao Gabriel*, 1497

121 Male White Tern

(Des J.W. Litho Format)

1981 (27 Feb). *Ships. T* **120** *and similar horiz designs. Multicoloured.* W w **14** (*sideways*). *P* 14½ × 14.

495 40 c. Type **120** 15 10
496 2 r. 25, Mascarenhas' caravel, 1505 . . . . 60 55
497 3 r. 50, Darwin's H.M.S. *Beagle*, 1831 . . 90 1·00
498 5 r. *Queen Elizabeth 2* (liner), 1968 . . 1·10 1·40
495/8 . . . . *Set of* 4 2·50 2·75
MS499 141 × 91 mm. Nos. 495/98 . . . . 2·50 3·25

(Des G. Drummond. Litho Questa)

1981 (10 Apr). *Birds (3rd series). White Tern. T* **121** *and similar vert designs. Multicoloured.* W w **14**. *P* 14.

500 2 r. Type **121** 85 65
a. Horiz strip of 5. Nos. 500/4 . . . . 3·75
501 2 r. Pair of White Terns 85 65
502 2 r. Female White Tern 85 65
503 2 r. Female White Tern on nest, and egg . . 85 65
504 2 r. White Tern and chick 85 65
500/4 . . . . *Set of* 5 3·75 3·00

Nos. 500/4 were printed together, *se-tenant*, in horizontal strips of 5 throughout the sheet.

(Des D. Shults. Litho Questa)

1981 (23 June–16 Nov). *Royal Wedding. Horiz designs as T* **26/27** *of Kiribati. Multicoloured.* (a) W w **15**. *P* 14.

505 1 r. 50, *Victoria and Albert I* 20 25
a. Sheetlet. No. 505 × 6 and No. 506 . . 1·60
506 1 r. 50, Prince Charles and Lady Diana Spencer 50 50
507 5 r. *Cleveland* 60 60
a. Sheetlet. No. 507 × 6 and No. 508 . . 4·50
508 5 r. As No. 506 . . . . . . 1·50 2·00
509 10 r. *Britannia* . . . . . . 1·00 1·50
a. Sheetlet. No. 509 × 6 and No. 510 . . 7·50
510 10 r. As No. 506 . . . . . . 2·25 2·25
505/10 . . . . *Set of* 6 5·50 6·50
MS511 120 × 109 mm. 7 r. 50, As No. 506. Wmk sideways. P 12 (16 Nov) . . . . 1·50 1·50

(*b*) *Booklet stamps. No wmk. P* 12 (16 Nov)

512 1 r. 50, As No. 505 . . . . . . 25 40
a. Booklet pane. No. 512 × 4 . . . . 1·00
513 5 r. As No. 508 . . . . . . 1·00 1·60
a. Booklet pane. No. 513 × 2 . . . . 2·00

Nos. 505/10 were printed in sheetlets of seven stamps of the same face value, each containing six of the "Royal Yacht" design and one of the larger design showing Prince Charles and Lady Diana.

Nos. 512/13 come from 22 r. stamp booklets.

122 Britten-Norman "Islander"

123 Seychelles Flying Foxes in Flight

(Litho Harrison)

1981 (27 July). *10th Anniv of Opening of Seychelles International Airport. Aircraft. T* **122** *and similar horiz designs. Multicoloured.* W w **14** (*sideways*). *P* 14½.

514 40 c. Type **122** 15 10
515 2 r. 25, Britten-Norman "Trislander" . . 55 45
516 3 r. 50, BAC (Vickers) "VC10" airliner . . 80 70
517 5 r. Boeing "747" airliner . . . . 1·00 1·00
514/17 . . . . *Set of* 4 2·25 2·00

(Litho Format)

1981 (9 Oct). *Seychelles Flying Fox (Roussette). T* **123** *and similar vert designs. Multicoloured.* W w **14**. *P* 14.

518 40 c. Type **123** 10 10
519 2 r. 25, Flying Fox eating 45 45
520 3 r. Flying Fox climbing across tree branch 70 70
521 5 r. Flying Fox hanging from tree branch . . 1·00 1·00
518/21 . . . . *Set of* 4 2·00 2·00
MS522 95 × 130 mm. Nos. 518/21 . . . . 3·00 3·50

124 Chinese Little Bittern (male)

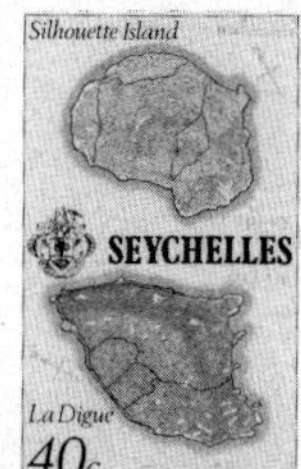

125 Silhouette Island and La Digue

(Des G. Drummond. Litho Questa)

1982 (4 Feb). *Birds (4th series). Chinese Little Bittern. T* **124** *and similar vert designs. Multicoloured.* W w **14**. *P* 14.

523 3 r. Type **124** . . . . . . 1·75 80
a. Horiz strip of 5. Nos. 523/7 . . . . 8·00
524 3 r. Chinese Little Bittern (female) . . 1·75 80
525 3 r. Hen on nest . . . . . . 1·75 80
526 3 r. Nest and eggs . . . . . . 1·75 80
527 3 r. Hen with chicks . . . . . . 1·75 80
523/7 . . . . *Set of* 5 8·00 3·50

Nos. 523/7 were printed together, *se-tenant*, in horizontal strips of 5 throughout the sheet.

(Des J. Cooter. Litho Format)

1982 (22 Apr). *Modern Maps. T* **125** *and similar vert designs. Multicoloured.* W w **14**. *P* 14½.

528 40 c. Type **125** 15 10
529 1 r. 50, Denis and Bird Islands 40 25
530 2 r. 75, Praslin 65 65
531 7 r. Mahé . . . . . . 1·60 2·00
528/31 . . . . *Set of* 4 2·50 2·75
MS532 92 × 128 mm. Nos. 528/31 . . . . 3·25 4·00

126 "Education"

(Des PAD Studio. Litho Harrison)

1982 (5 June). *5th Anniv of Liberation. T* **126** *and similar horiz designs. Multicoloured.* W w **14** (*sideways*). *P* 14.

533 40 c. Type **126** 10 10
534 1 r. 75, "Health" 25 25
535 2 r. 75, "Agriculture" 45 45
536 7 r. "Construction" . . . . . . 1·40 1·40
533/6 . . . . *Set of* 4 2·00 2·00
MS537 128 × 120 mm. Nos. 533/6. P 14½ . . 4·00 4·75

127 Tourist Board Emblem

128 Tata Bus

(Des and litho Harrison)

1982 (1 Sept). *Tourism. T* **127** *and similar horiz designs. Multicoloured.* W w **14** (*sideways*). *P* 14.

538 1 r. 75, Type **127** 40 35
539 1 r. 75, Northolme Hotel 40 35
540 1 r. 75, Reef Hotel 40 35
541 1 r. 75, Barbarous Beach Hotel 40 35
542 1 r. 75, Coral Strand Hotel 40 35
543 1 r. 75, Beau Vallon Bay Hotel 40 35
544 1 r. 75, Fisherman's Cove Hotel 40 35
545 1 r. 75, Mahé Beach Hotel 40 35
538/45 . . . . *Set of* 8 2·75 2·50

(Des C. Abbott. Litho Harrison)

1982 (18 Nov). *Land Transport. T* **128** *and similar horiz designs. Multicoloured.* W w **14** (*sideways*). *P* 14.

546 20 c. Type **128** 10 10
547 1 r. 75, Mini-moke 30 25
548 2 r. 75, Ox-cart 50 55
549 7 r. Truck . . . . . . 1·40 1·75
546/9 . . . . *Set of* 4 2·10 2·40

129 Radio Seychelles Control Room

(Des A. Theobald. Litho Questa)

1983 (25 Feb). *World Communications Year. T* **129** *and similar horiz designs. Multicoloured.* W w **14** (*sideways*). *P* 14.

550 40 c. Type **129** 10 10
551 2 r. 75, Satellite Earth Station 45 50
552 3 r. 50, Radio Seychelles Television control room 70 75
553 5 r. Postal services sorting office . . . . 1·00 1·25
550/3 . . . . *Set of* 4 2·00 2·25

130 Agricultural Experimental Station

(Des L. Curtis. Litho Questa)

1983 (14 Mar). *Commonwealth Day. T* **130** *and similar horiz designs. Multicoloured.* W w **14** (*sideways*). *P* 14.

554 40 c. Type **130** 10 10
555 2 r. 75, Food processing plant 45 50
556 3 r. 50, Unloading fish catch 70 75
557 7 r. Seychelles flag . . . . . . 1·40 1·50
554/7 . . . . *Set of* 4 2·40 2·50

131 Denis Island Lighthouse

(Des Harrison. Litho Format)

1983 (14 July). *Famous Landmarks. T* **131** *and similar horiz designs. Multicoloured.* W w **14** (*sideways*). *P* 14 × 13½.

558 40 c. Type **131** 10 10
559 2 r. 75, Victoria Hospital 40 45
560 3 r. 50, Supreme Court 60 65
561 7 r. State House . . . . . . 1·25 1·40
558/61 . . . . *Set of* 4 2·10 2·25
MS562 110 × 98 mm. Nos. 558/61 . . . . 4·50 5·50

132 *Royal Vauxhall* Balloon, 1836

(Des A. Theobald. Litho Harrison)

1983 (15 Sept). *Bicentenary of Manned Flight. T* **132** *and similar horiz designs. Multicoloured.* W w **14** (*sideways*). *P* 14.

563 40 c. Type **132** 10 10
564 1 r. 75, De Havilland "D.H.50J" 40 30
565 2 r. 75, Grumman "Albatross" flying boat . . 55 55
566 7 r. Swearingen "Merlin" . . . . 1·40 1·75
563/6 . . . . *Set of* 4 2·25 2·25

133 "DC 10" Aircraft

134 Swamp Plant and Moorhen

(Des Park Advertising. Litho Walsall)

1983 (26 Oct). *1st International Flight of Air Seychelles.* W w **14** (*sideways*). *P* 14.

567 **133** 2 r. multicoloured 60 60

(Des L. Curtis. Litho Questa)

1983 (17 Nov). *Centenary of Visit to Seychelles by Marianne North (botanic artist). T* **134** *and similar vert designs. Multicoloured.* W w **14**. *P* 14.

568 40 c. Type **134** 15 10
569 1 r. 75, *Wormia flagellaria* 50 30
570 2 r. 75, Asiatic Pancratium 65 60
571 7 r. Pitcher Plant . . . . . . 1·50 1·60
568/71 . . . . *Set of* 4 2·50 2·25
MS572 90 × 121 mm. Nos. 568/71 . . . . 3·50 4·25

50c ▬

(**135**)

1983 (28 Dec). *Nos. 505/10 surch as T* **135**.

573 50 c. on 1 r. 50, *Victoria and Albert I* . . 15 15
a. Sheetlet. No. 573 × 6 and No. 574 . . 1·10
b. Albino surch . . . . . . 32·00
c. Surch double, one albino . . . . 35·00
d. Surch double, one inverted . . . . 55·00
e. Surch double, one in 2 r. 25 value . . 45·00
574 50 c. on 1 r. 50, Prince Charles and Lady Diana Spencer 40 45
b. Albino surch . . . . . . 75·00
c. Surch double, one albino . . . . 85·00
d. Surch double, one inverted £130
e. Surch double, one in 2 r. 25 value . . £110
575 2 r. 25 on 5 r. *Cleveland* 45 50
a. Sheetlet. No. 575 × 6 and No. 576 . . 3·25
576 2 r. 25 on 5 r. As No. 574 . . . . 1·00 1·25
577 3 r. 75 on 10 r. *Britannia* 75 80
a. Sheetlet. No. 577 × 6 and No. 578 . . 5·50
b. Albino surch . . . . . . 30·00
c. Surch double . . . . . . 75·00
578 3 r. 75 on 10 r. As No. 574 . . . . 1·40 1·75
b. Albino surch . . . . . . 65·00
c. Surch double £225
573/8 . . . . *Set of* 6 3·75 4·50

MINIMUM PRICE

The minimum price quote is 10p which represents a handling charge rather than a basis for valuing common stamps. For further notes about prices see introductory pages.

136 Coconut Vessel

137 Victoria Port

(Des Jennifer Toombs. Litho Format)

1984 (29 Feb). *Traditional Handicrafts. T* **136** *and similar horiz designs. Multicoloured. W w* **14** *(sideways). P* 14.

579	50 c. Type **136**	15	10
580	2 r. Scarf and doll	50	60
581	3 r. Coconut-fibre roses	70	80
582	10 r. Carved fishing boat and doll	2·00	3·00
579/82	*Set of* 4	3·00	4·00

(Des C. Collins. Litho Questa)

1984 (21 May). *25th Anniv of "Lloyd's List" (newspaper). T* **137** *and similar vert designs. Multicoloured. W w* **14**. *P* 14½ × 14.

583	50 c. Type **137**	20	10
584	2 r. Cargo liner	55	55
585	3 r. *Sun Viking* (liner)	80	80
586	10 r. Loss of R.F.A. *Ennerdale II*	2·25	2·75
583/6	*Set of* 4	3·50	3·75

138 Old S.P.U.P. Office

(Des D. Miller. Litho B.D.T.)

1984 (2 June). *20th Anniv of Seychelles People's United Party. T* **138** *and similar multicoloured designs. W w* **14** *(sideways on 50 c., 3 r.). P* 14.

587	50 c. Type **138**	15	10
588	2 r. Liberation statue (*vert*)	40	50
589	3 r. New S.P.U.P. office	60	80
590	10 r. President René (*vert*)	2·00	3·00
587/90	*Set of* 4	2·75	4·00

139 1949 U.P.U. 2 r. 25 Stamp

(Des M. Joyce. Litho Harrison)

1984 (18 June). *Universal Postal Union Congress, Hamburg. Sheet* 70 × 85 *mm. W w* **14** *(sideways). P* 14½.

MS591	**139** 5 r. yellow-olive, flesh and black	1·40	2·25

140 Long Jumping

(Des L. Curtis. Litho Questa)

1984 (28 July). *Olympic Games, Los Angeles. T* **140** *and similar horiz designs. Multicoloured. W w* **14** *(sideways). P* 14.

592	50 c. Type **140**	10	10
593	2 r. Boxing	40	45
594	3 r. Swimming	60	75
595	10 r. Weightlifting	1·75	2·50
592/5	*Set of* 4	2·50	3·50
MS596	100 × 100 mm. Nos. 592/5	2·50	4·00

141 Sub-aqua Diving

(Des A. Theobald. Litho Questa)

1984 (24 Sept). *Water Sports. T* **141** *and similar horiz designs. Multicoloured. W w* **14** *(sideways). P* 14.

597	50 c. Type **141**	20	10
598	2 r. Paragliding	60	45
599	3 r. Sailing	80	75
600	10 r. Water-skiing	2·25	2·50
597/600	*Set of* 4	3·50	3·50

142 Humpback Whale

143 Two Bare-legged Scops Owls in Tree

(Des A. Jardine. Litho Questa)

1984 (19 Nov). *Whale Conservation. T* **142** *and similar horiz designs. Multicoloured. W w* **14** *(sideways). P* 14.

601	50 c. Type **142**	75	15
602	2 r. Sperm Whale	1·75	85
603	3 r. Black Right Whale	2·00	1·25
604	10 r. Blue Whale	4·00	4·50
601/4	*Set of* 4	7·75	6·00

(Des I. Lewington. Litho Walsall)

1985 (11 Mar). *Birth Bicentenary of John J. Audubon (ornithologist). Bare-legged Scops Owl. T* **143** *and similar vert designs. Multicoloured. W w* **14**. *P* 14.

605	50 c. Type **143**	75	15
606	2 r. Owl on branch	1·50	85
607	3 r. Owl in flight	1·75	1·25
608	10 r. Owl on ground	3·25	4·00
605/8	*Set of* 4	6·50	5·75

144 Giant Tortoises

145 The Queen Mother with Princess Anne and Prince Andrew, 1970

(Des D. Miller. Litho Format)

1985 (15 Mar). *"Expo '85" World Fair, Japan. T* **144** *and similar vert designs. Multicoloured. W w* **14**. *P* 14.

609	50 c. Type **144**	30	10
610	2 r. White Terns	1·00	60
611	3 r. Windsurfing	1·00	75
612	5 r. Coco-de-Mer	1·25	1·40
609/12	*Set of* 4	3·25	2·50
MS613	130 × 80 mm. Nos. 609/12	3·25	4·25

For these designs without "Expo '85" inscription see No. **MS**650.

(Des A. Theobald (10 r.), C. Abbott (others). Litho Questa)

1985 (7 June). *Life and Times of Queen Elizabeth the Queen Mother. T* **145** *and similar vert designs. Multicoloured. W w* **16**. *P* 14½×14.

614	50 c. The Queen Mother in 1930	10	10
615	2 r. Type **145**	45	50
616	3 r. On her 75th Birthday	65	70
617	5 r. With Prince Henry at his christening (from photo by Lord Snowdon)	1·10	1·25
614/17	*Set of* 4	2·10	2·40
MS618	91 × 73 mm. 10 r. Arriving at Blenheim Palace by helicopter. Wmk sideways	2·50	2·50

146 Boxing

147 Agriculture Students

(Des O. Bell. Litho Questa)

1985 (24 Aug). *2nd Indian Ocean Islands Games. T* **146** *and similar horiz designs. Multicoloured. W w* **14** *(sideways). P* 14.

619	50 c. Type **146**	15	10
620	2 r. Football	55	50
621	3 r. Swimming	75	70
622	10 r. Windsurfing	2·40	2·40
619/22	*Set of* 4	3·50	3·25

1985 (1 Nov). *Acquisition of 1st Air Seychelles "Airbus". As No. 735, but additionally inscribed* "AIR SEYCHELLES FIRST AIRBUS".

623	1 r. 25, White Tern	75	75

(Des Joan Thompson. Litho Questa)

1985 (28 Nov). *International Youth Year. T* **147** *and similar vert designs. Multicoloured. W w* **16**. *P* 14.

624	50 c. Type **147**	10	10
625	2 r. Construction students building wall	45	50
626	3 r. Carpentry students	65	70
627	10 r. Science students	2·25	2·40
624/7	*Set of* 4	3·00	3·25

148 Ford "Model T" (1919)

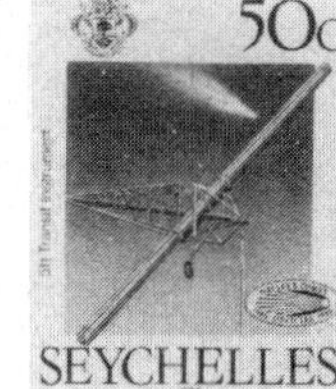

149 Five Foot Transit Instrument

(Des J.W. Litho Questa)

1985 (18 Dec). *Vintage Cars. T* **148** *and similar horiz designs. Multicoloured. W w* **16** *(sideways). P* 14.

628	50 c. Type **148**	30	10
629	2 r. Austin "Seven" (1922)	1·00	50
630	3 r. Morris "Oxford" (1924)	1·25	70
631	10 r. Humber "Coupé" (1929)	2·75	2·40
628/31	*Set of* 4	4·75	3·25

(Des Harrison. Litho Format)

1986 (28 Feb). *Appearance of Halley's Comet. T* **149** *and similar vert designs. Multicoloured. W w* **16**. *P* 14.

632	50 c. Type **149**	30	10
633	2 r. Eight foot quadrant	1·00	50
634	3 r. Comet's orbit	1·25	75
635	10 r. Edmond Halley	2·75	2·40
632/5	*Set of* 4	4·75	3·50

150 Ballerina

151 Ferry to La Digue

(Des C. Abbott. Litho Format)

1986 (4 Apr). *Visit of Ballet du Louvre Company. "Giselle". T* **150** *and similar vert designs. Multicoloured. W w* **16**. *P* 13½.

636	2 r. Type **150**	75	60
637	3 r. Male dancer	1·00	90
MS638	80 × 90 mm. 10 r. Pas de deux	2·25	2·40

(Des A. Theobald. Litho Questa)

1986 (21 Apr). *60th Birthday of Queen Elizabeth II. Vert designs as T* **230a** *of Jamaica. Multicoloured. W w* **16**. *P* 14½×14.

639	50 c. Wedding photograph, 1947	10	10
640	1 r. 25, At State Opening of Parliament, 1982	30	35
641	2 r. Queen accepting bouquet, Seychelles, 1972	45	50
642	3 r. On board Royal Yacht *Britannia*, Qatar, 1979	70	75
643	5 r. At Crown Agents Head Office, London, 1983	1·10	1·25
639/43	*Set of* 5	2·40	2·75

(Des G. Drummond. Litho Questa)

1986 (22 May). *"Ameripex '86" International Stamp Exhibition, Chicago. Inter-island Communications. T* **151** *and similar multicoloured designs. W w* **16** *(sideways on 50 c., 7 r.). P* 14.

644	50 c. Type **151**	40	10
645	2 r. Telephone kiosk (*vert*)	85	50
646	3 r. Post Office counter, Victoria (*vert*)	1·25	75
647	7 r. Air Seychelles Britten-Norman "Trislander" aircraft	2·50	1·75
644/7	*Set of* 4	4·50	2·75

152 Crests of Seychelles and Knights of Malta

LAZOURNEN ENTERNASYONAL KREOL

(153)

(Des Jennifer Toombs. Litho Format)

1986 (7 June). *Seychelles Knights of Malta Day. W w* **16** *(sideways). P* 14.

648	**152** 5 r. multicoloured	1·10	1·25
MS649	101 × 81 mm. No. 648	2·00	2·50

1986 (12 July). *Seychelles Philatelic Exhibition, Tokyo. Miniature sheet, 130×80 mm, containing stamps as Nos.* 609/12, *but without "Expo '85" inscription and emblem.* W w **16**. *P* 14.
MS650 As Nos. 609/12 . . . . 3·00 3·00

(Des D. Miller. Litho Questa)

1986 (23 July). *Royal Wedding. Vert designs as T* **231a** *of Jamaica. Multicoloured.* W w **16**. *P* 14.
651 2 r. Prince Andrew and Miss Sarah Ferguson 45 50
652 10 r. Prince Andrew boarding Wessex helicopter, 1983 . . . . 2·25 2·40

1986 (28 Oct). *International Creole Day. No.* 487a *optd with T* **153**.
653 1 r. Madagascar Red Fody . . . . 1·00 50

154 Pope John Paul at Seychelles Airport

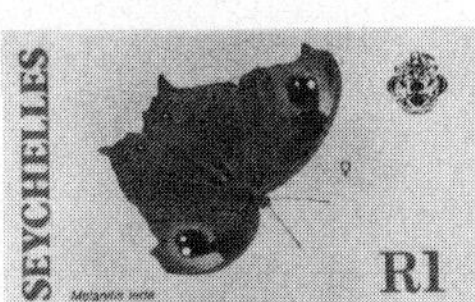

155 *Melanitis leda*

(Des L. Curtis. Litho Questa)

1986 (1 Dec). *Visit of Pope John Paul II. T* **154** *and similar vert designs, each showing Pope and Seychelles scene. Multicoloured.* W w **16**. *P* 14½×14.
654 50 c. Type **154**. 50 10
655 2 r. Catholic Cathedral, Victoria . . . . 1·50 60
656 3 r. Baie Lazare Parish Church . . . . 2·00 90
657 10 r. Aerial view of People's Stadium . . 3·25 2·75
654/7 . . . . *Set of* 4 6·50 4·00
MS658 95×106 mm. Nos. 654/7. Wmk inverted . . 8·00 8·50

(Des R. Lewington. Litho Questa)

1987 (18 Feb). *Butterflies. T* **155** *and similar horiz designs. Multicoloured.* W w **16** (*sideways*). *P* 14½.
659 1 r. Type **155**. 55 25
660 2 r. *Phalanta philiberti* 90 60
661 3 r. *Danaus chrysippus* . . . . 1·25 1·00
662 10 r. *Euploea mitra* . . . . 3·50 3·50
659/62 . . . . *Set of* 4 5·75 4·75

156 *Gloripallium pallium*

157 Statue of Liberation

(Des Josephine Martin. Litho Walsall)

1987 (7 May). *Seashells. T* **156** *and similar vert designs. Multicoloured.* W w **14**. *P* 14½×14.
663 1 r. Type **156**. 60 25
664 2 r. *Spondylus aurantius* . . . . 1·00 60
665 3 r. *Harpa ventricosa* and *Lioconcha ornata* . . . . 1·50 90
666 10 r. *Strombus lentiginosus* . . . . . . 3·25 3·00
663/6 . . . . *Set of* 4 5·75 4·25

(Des Harrison. Litho Format)

1987 (5 June). *10th Anniv of Liberation. T* **157** *and similar multicoloured designs.* W w **16** (*sideways on* 2 *r.*, 3 *r.*). *P* 14.
667 1 r. Type **157**. 20 25
668 2 r. Seychelles Hospital (*horiz*) 45 50
669 3 r. Orphanage Village (*horiz*) 70 75
670 10 r. Proposed Sail-fish Monument . . . . 2·25 2·50
667/70 . . . . *Set of* 4 3·25 3·50

158 Seychelles Savings Bank, Praslin

(Des A. Theobald. Litho Format)

1987 (25 June). *Centenary of Banking in Seychelles. T* **158** *and similar horiz designs.* W w **16** (*sideways*). *P* 14.
671 1 r. bronze-green and sage-green 20 25
672 2 r. bistre-brown and salmon 45 50
673 10 r. royal blue and cobalt . . . . . . 2·25 2·50
671/3 . . . . *Set of* 3 2·50 3·00
Designs:—2 r. Development Bank; 10 r. Central Bank.

1987 (9 Dec). *Royal Ruby Wedding. Nos.* 639/43 *optd with T* **45a** *of Kiribati in silver.*
674 50 c. Wedding photograph, 1947 . . . . 15 15
a. Opt inverted . . . . 75·00
675 1 r. 25, At State Opening of Parliament, 1982 . . . . 30 35
676 2 r. Queen accepting bouquet, Seychelles, 1972 . . . . 45 50
677 3 r. On board Royal Yacht *Britannia*, Qatar, 1979 . . . . 70 75
678 5 r. At Crown Agents Head Office, London, 1983 . . . . 1·10 1·25
674/8 . . . . *Set of* 5 2·40 2·75

159 Tuna-canning Factory

(Des O. Bell. Litho B.D.T.)

1987 (11 Dec). *Seychelles Fishing Industry. T* **159** *and similar diamond-shaped designs. Multicoloured.* W w **16**. *P* 14.
679 50 c. Type **159**. 15 15
680 2 r. Trawler 45 50
681 3 r. Weighing catch 70 75
682 10 r. Unloading net . . . . 2·25 2·40
679/82 . . . . *Set of* 4 3·25 3·50

160 Water Sports

161 Young Turtles making for Sea

(Des Jennifer Toombs. Litho Questa)

1988 (9 Feb). *Tourism. T* **160** *and similar horiz designs, each showing beach hotel. Multicoloured.* W w **16** (*sideways*). *P* 14½.
683 1 r. Type **160**. 20 25
684 2 r. Speedboat and yachts 45 50
685 3 r. Yacht at anchor. 70 75
686 10 r. Hotel at night . . . . 2·25 2·40
683/6 . . . . *Set of* 4 3·25 3·50

(Des Doreen McGuinness. Litho Questa)

1988 (22 Apr). *The Green Turtle. T* **161** *and similar vert designs. Multicoloured.* W w **14**. *P* 14½ × 14.
687 2 r. Type **161** . . . . 1·00 1·00
a. Vert pair. Nos. 687/8 . . . . . . 2·00 2·00
688 2 r. Young turtles hatching . . . . . . 1·00 1·00
689 3 r. Female turtle leaving sea . . . . 1·50 1·50
a. Vert pair. Nos. 689/90 . . . . . . 3·00 3·00
690 3 r. Female laying eggs . . . . 1·50 1·50
687/90 . . . . *Set of* 4 4·50 4·50
Nos. 687/8 and 689/90 were each printed together, *se-tenant*, in vertical pairs throughout the sheets, each pair forming a composite design.

162 Shot Put

163 Police Motorcyclists

(Des O. Bell. Litho Walsall)

1988 (29 July). *Olympic Games, Seoul. T* **162** *and similar vert designs. Multicoloured.* W w **16**. *P* 14½.
691 1 r. Type **162** 20 25
692 2 r. Type **162** 40 45
a. Horiz strip of 5. Nos. 692/6 . . . . 2·00
693 2 r. High jump 40 45
694 2 r. Gold medal winner on podium 40 45
695 2 r. Athletics 40 45
696 2 r. Javelin 40 45
697 3 r. As No. 694 . . . . 60 65
698 4 r. As No. 695 . . . . 80 85
699 5 r. As No. 696 . . . . 1·00 1·10
691/9 . . . . *Set of* 9 4·25 4·50
MS700 121 × 52 mm. 10 r. Tennis. W w **14** (sideways) . . . . 2·25 2·25
Nos. 691, 693 and 697/9 were each printed in sheets of 50 of one design. No. 693 also exists from sheets containing Nos. 692/6 printed together, *se-tenant*, in horizontal strips of five.

(Des D. Miller (1 r.), L. Curtis and D. Miller (2 r.), E. Nisbet and D. Miller (3 r.), S. Noon and D. Miller (10 r.). Litho Questa)

1988 (30 Sept). *300th Anniv of Lloyd's of London. Multicoloured designs as T* **167a** *of Malawi.* W w **16** (*sideways on* 2, 3 *r.*). *P* 14.
701 1 r. Leadenhall Street, London, 1928 . . 50 25
702 2 r. *Cinq Juin* (travelling post office) (*horiz*) 1·00 45
703 3 r. *Queen Elizabeth 2* (liner) (*horiz*) . . 1·50 65
704 10 r. Loss of *Hindenburg* (airship), 1937 . . 3·50 2·75
701/4 . . . . *Set of* 4 6·00 3·75

(Des A. Theobald. Litho Questa)

1988 (25 Nov). *1st Anniv of Defence Forces Day. T* **163** *and similar horiz designs. Multicoloured.* W w **14** (*sideways*). *P* 14.
705 1 r. Type **163** 60 25
706 2 r. Air Wing helicopter . . . . 1·00 90
707 3 r. Patrol boat . . . . 1·50 1·40
708 10 r. BRDM armoured car . . . . 3·50 4·00
705/8 . . . . *Set of* 4 6·00 6·00

164 Father Christmas with Basket of Presents

165 *Dendrobium sp.*

(Des S. Hoareau (50 c.), R. Leste (2 r.), F. Anacoura (3 r.), A. McGaw (10 r.), adapted N. Harvey. Litho B.D.T.)

1988 (1 Dec). *Christmas. T* **164** *and similar vert designs. Multicoloured.* W w **14**. *P* 13½.
709 50 c. Type **164** 10 10
710 2 r. Bird and gourd filled with presents . . 40 45
711 3 r. Father Christmas basket weaving . . 60 65
712 10 r. Christmas bauble and palm tree . . 2·00 2·10
709/12 . . . . *Set of* 4 2·75 3·00

(Des Annette Robinson. Litho Questa)

1988 (21 Dec). *Orchids (1st series). T* **165** *and similar multicoloured designs.* W w **16** (*sideways on* 2, 10 *r.*). *P* 14.
713 1 r. Type **165** 30 25
714 2 r. *Arachnis hybrid* (*horiz*) 50 45
715 3 r. *Vanda caerulea* 70 65
716 10 r. *Dendrobium phalaenopsis* (*horiz*) . . 2·00 2·50
713/16 . . . . *Set of* 4 3·25 3·50
See also Nos. 767/70 and 795/8.

(Litho Questa)

1988 (30 Dec). *As Nos.* 405B *and* 410B, *but* W w **14** (*upright*). *P* 14.
718 10 c. Hawksbill Turtle 10 10
722 50 c. Giant Tortoise 10 10
A Questa new printing of the 25 c. was issued on the same date. It has the same watermark and perforation as No. 408B.

166 India 1976 25 p. Nehru Stamp

167 Pres. Rene addressing Rally at Old Party Office

(Des O. Bell. Litho B.D.T.)

1989 (30 Mar). *Birth Centenary of Jawaharlal Nehru (Indian statesman). T* **166** *and similar horiz design, each showing flags of Seychelles and India. Multicoloured.* W w **16** (*sideways*). *P* 13½.
724 2 r. Type **166** 40 50
725 10 r. Jawaharlal Nehru . . . . 2·00 2·50

(Litho Walsall (1 r. 25), Questa (others))

1989 (May)–**91**. *As Nos.* 410, 415 (*but new value*), 489 *and* 491, *but* W w **16**. *Chalk-surfaced paper* (1 *r.* 25). *Imprint date at foot. P* 14½×14 (1 *r.* 25), 14×14½ (5 *r.*) *or* 14 (*others*).
732 50 c. Giant Tortoise (11.91) 10 10
735 1 r. 25, White Tern 25 30
736 3 r. Green Gecko (as No. 415) (11.91) . . 65 70
738 5 r. Octopus (1.91) . . . . 1·10 1·25
732/8 . . . . *Set of* 4 1·90 2·10

(Des D. Miller. Litho Walsall)

1989 (5 June). *25th Anniv of Seychelles People's United Party. T* **167** *and similar vert designs. Multicoloured.* W w **16**. *P* 14.
742 1 r. Type **167** 20 25
743 2 r. Women with Party flags and Maison du Peuple 40 45
744 3 r. President Rene making speech and Torch of Freedom 60 65
745 10 r. President Rene, Party flag and Torch of Freedom . . . . 2·00 2·25
742/5 . . . . *Set of* 4 2·75 3·25

(Des A. Theobald (10 r.), D. Miller (others). Litho Questa)

1989 (20 July). *20th Anniv of First Manned Landing on Moon. Multicoloured designs as T* **51a** *of Kiribati. W w* **16** *(sideways on 2, 3 r.). P* 14×13½ *(1, 5 r.) or* 14 *(others).*

746 1 r. Lift off of "Saturn 5" rocket 20 25
747 2 r. Crew of "Apollo 15" (30×30 *mm*) .. 40 45
748 3 r. "Apollo 15" emblem (30×30 *mm*) .. 60 65
749 5 r. James Irwin saluting U.S. flag on Moon 1·00 1·10
746/9 .. .. *Set of* 4 2·00 2·25
MS750 100×83 mm. 10 r. Aldrin alighting from "Apollo 11" on Moon. P 14×13½ .. .. 3·25 3·50

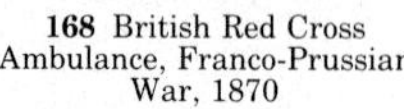

168 British Red Cross Ambulance, Franco-Prussian War, 1870

169 Black Parrot and Map of Praslin

(Des A. Theobald. Litho Questa)

1989 (12 Sept). *125th Anniv of International Red Cross. T* **168** *and similar horiz designs. W w* **16** *(sideways). P* 14½.

751 1 r. black and orange-vermilion 40 25
752 2 r. black, light green and orange-vermilion 80 70
753 3 r. black and orange-vermilion .. .. 1·25 1·00
754 10 r. black and orange-vermilion .. .. 3·50 4·00
751/4 .. .. *Set of* 4 5·50 5·50

Designs:—2 r. H.M. Hospital Ship *Liberty*, 1914-18; 3 r. Sunbeam "Standard" army ambulance, 1914-18; 10 r. "White Train", South Africa, 1899-1902.

(Des I. Loe. Litho Questa)

1989 (16 Oct). *Island Birds. T* **169** *and similar vert designs. Multicoloured. W w* **16**. *P* 14½×14.

755 50 c. Type **169** 50 15
756 2 r. Sooty Tern and Ile aux Vaches .. 1·25 1·00
757 3 r. Magpie Robin and Frégate .. .. 1·60 1·40
758 5 r. Roseate Tern and Aride .. .. 2·25 2·50
755/8 .. .. *Set of* 4 5·00 4·50
MS759 83×109 mm. Nos. 755/8 .. .. 5·50 5·50

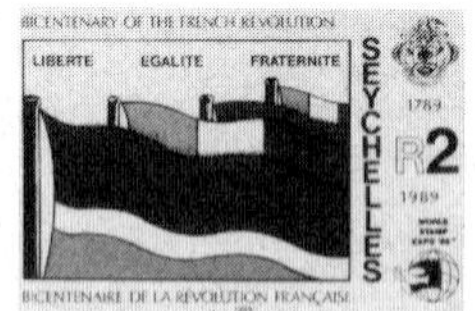

170 Flags of Seychelles and France

(Adapted D. Miller from local artwork. Litho B.D.T.)

1989 (17 Nov). *Bicentenary of French Revolution and "World Stamp Expo '89", International Stamp Exhibition, Washington. T* **170** *and similar horiz designs. W w* **16** *(sideways). P* 14.

760 2 r. multicoloured .. .. .. 1·00 1·00
761 5 r. black, new blue and scarlet .. .. 2·25 2·25
MS762 78×100 mm. 10 r. multicoloured .. 3·25 3·75

Designs:—5 r. Storming the Bastille, Paris, 1789; 10 r. Reading Revolutionary proclamation, Seychelles, 1791.

171 Beau Vallon School

172 *Disperis tripetaloides*

(Des L. Curtis. Litho B.D.T.)

1989 (29 Dec). *25th Anniv of African Development Bank. T* **171** *and similar multicoloured designs. W w* **16** *(sideways on* 1, 2 *r.). P* 14.

763 1 r. Type **171** 40 25
764 2 r. Seychelles Fishing Authority Headquarters 75 65
765 3 r. *Variola* (fishing boat) (*vert*) .. .. 1·10 1·00
766 10 r. *Deneb* (fishing boat) (*vert*) .. .. 3·25 3·75
763/6 .. .. *Set of* 4 5·00 5·00

(Des N. Shewring. Litho Questa)

1990 (26 Jan). *Orchids (2nd series). T* **172** *and similar vert designs. Multicoloured. W w* **16**. *P* 14.

767 1 r. Type **172** 40 25
768 2 r. *Vanilla phalaenopsis* 75 65
769 3 r. *Angraecum eburneum* subsp *superbum* 95 85
770 10 r. *Polystachya concreta* .. .. .. 2·50 3·00
767/70 .. .. *Set of* 4 4·25 4·25

See also Nos. 795/8.

173 Seychelles 1903 2 c. and Great Britain 1880 1½d. Stamps

174 Fumiyo Sako

(Des D. Miller. Litho Security Printers (M), Malaysia)

1990 (3 May). *"Stamp World London 90" International Stamp Exhibition. T* **173** *and similar horiz designs, each showing stamps. Multicoloured. W w* **14** *(sideways). P* 12½.

771 1 r. Type **173** 40 25
772 2 r. Seychelles 1917 25 c. and G.B. 1873 1s. 75 65
773 3 r. Seychelles 1917 2 c. and G.B. 1874 6d. 1·10 1·00
774 5 r. Seychelles 1890 2 c. and G.B. 1841 1d. red-brown .. .. 1·75 2·00
771/4 .. .. *Set of* 4 3·50 3·50
MS775 88×60 mm. 10 r. Seychelles 1961 Post Office Centenary 2 r. 25 and G.B. 1840 Penny Black. Wmk upright .. .. 3·50 4·00

(Des D. Miller. Litho B.D.T.)

1990 (8 June). *"EXPO 90" International Garden and Greenery Exhibition, Osaka. T* **174** *and similar vert designs. Multicoloured. W w* **14**. *P* 14.

776 2 r. Type **174** 75 75
777 3 r. Male and female Coco-de-Mer palms 1·00 1·00
778 5 r. Pitcher Plant and Aldabra Lily .. 1·60 1·60
779 7 r. Arms of Seychelles and Gardenia .. 2·25 2·25
776/9 .. .. *Set of* 4 5·00 5·00
MS780 130×85 mm. Nos. 776/9. Wmk inverted 5·50 6·00

175 Air Seychelles Boeing "767-200ER" over Island

176 Adult Class

(Des D. Miller. Litho Questa)

1990 (27 July). *Air Seychelles "Boeing 767-200ER" World Record-breaking Flight* (1989). *W w* **16**. *P* 14×14½.

781 **175** 3 r. multicoloured .. .. .. 1·40 1·40

No. 781 was printed in sheetlets of 10, containing two horizontal strips of 5, separated by a central gutter showing a map of the flight route from Grand Rapids, U.S.A. to the Seychelles.

(Des D. Miller. Litho Questa)

1990 (4 Aug). *90th Birthday of Queen Elizabeth the Queen Mother. Vert designs as T* **107** (2 *r.*) *or* **108** *of Kenya. W w* **16**. *P* 14×15 (2 *r.*) *or* 14½ (10 *r.*).

782 2 r. multicoloured 75 60
783 10 r. brownish black and violet .. .. 2·75 3·00

Designs:—2 r. Queen Elizabeth in Coronation robes, 1937; 10 r. Queen Elizabeth visiting Lord Roberts Workshops, 1947.

(Des G. Vasarhelyi. Litho Questa)

1990 (8 Sept). *International Literacy Year. T* **176** *and similar vert designs. Multicoloured. W w* **14**. *P* 14.

784 1 r. Type **176** 40 25
785 2 r. Reading a letter 75 65
786 3 r. Following written instructions .. 1·00 85
787 10 r. Typewriter, calculator and crossword 3·25 3·50
784/7 .. .. *Set of* 4 4·75 4·75

177 Sega Dancers

178 Beach

(Des Jennifer Toombs. Litho Cartor, France)

1990 (27 Oct). *Kreol Festival. Sega Dancing. T* **177** *and similar vert designs. Multicoloured. W w* **14**. *P* 13½×14.

788 2 r. Type **177** 65 70
a. Horiz strip of 5. Nos. 788/92 .. .. 3·00
789 2 r. Dancing couple (girl in yellow dress) 65 70
790 2 r. Female Sega dancer 65 70
791 2 r. Dancing couple (girl in floral pattern skirt) 65 70
792 2 r. Dancing couple (girl in red patterned skirt) 65 70
788/92 .. .. *Set of* 5 3·00 3·25

Nos. 788/92 were printed together, *se-tenant*, in horizontal strips of 5 throughout the sheet.

(Des D. Miller. Litho Questa)

1990 (10 Dec). *First Indian Ocean Regional Seminar on Petroleum Exploration. T* **178** *and similar horiz design. Multicoloured. W w* **16** *(sideways). P* 14½.

793 3 r. Type **178** .. .. 1·00 1·00
794 10 r. Geological map .. .. .. 3·00 3·00

(Des N. Shewring. Litho Questa)

1991 (1 Feb). *Orchids (3rd series). Vert designs as T* **172**. *Multicoloured. W w* **16**. *P* 14.

795 1 r. *Bulbophyllum intertextum* 40 25
796 2 r. *Agrostophyllum occidentale* 75 60
797 3 r. *Vanilla planifolia* .. .. .. 1·10 85
798 10 r. *Malaxis seychellarum* .. .. 3·25 3·50
795/8 .. .. *Set of* 4 5·00 4·75

(Des D. Miller. Litho Questa)

1991 (17 June). *65th Birthday of Queen Elizabeth II and 70th Birthday of Prince Philip. Vert designs as T* **58** *of Kiribati. Multicoloured. W w* **16** *(sideways). P* 14½×14.

799 4 r. Queen in evening dress .. .. 1·40 1·50
a. Horiz pair. Nos. 799/800 separated by label .. .. 2·75 3·00
800 4 r. Prince Philip in academic robes .. 1·40 1·50

Nos. 799/800 were printed in a similar sheet format to Nos. 366/7 of Kiribati.

179 *Precis rhadama*

180 "The Holy Virgin, Joseph, The Holy Child and St. John" (S. Vouillemont after Raphael)

(Des I. Loe. Litho Walsall)

1991 (15 Nov). *"Philanippon '91" International Stamp Exhibition, Tokyo. Butterflies. T* **179** *and similar horiz designs. W w* **14** *(sideways). P* 14×14½.

801 1 r. 50, Type **179** 50 40
802 3 r. *Lampides boeticus* 95 85
803 3 r. 50, *Zizeeria knysna* .. .. .. 1·10 1·00
804 10 r. *Phalanta phalantha* .. .. .. 3·00 3·00
801/4 .. .. *Set of* 4 5·00 4·75
MS805 78×81 mm. 10 r. *Eagris sabadius* .. 3·00 3·25

(Des D. Miller. Litho B.D.T.)

1991 (2 Dec). *Christmas. Woodcuts. T* **180** *and similar vert designs. W w* **16**. *P* 13½×14.

806 50 c. black, brown-ochre and bright crimson 20 15
807 1 r. black, brown-ochre and myrtle-green 35 25
808 2 r. black, brown-ochre and blue .. 60 60
809 7 r. black, brown-ochre & deep violet-blue 2·00 2·25
806/9 .. .. *Set of* 4 2·75 3·00

Designs:—1 r. "The Holy Virgin, the Child and Angel" (A. Blooting after Van Dyck); 2 r. "The Holy Family, St. John and St. Anna" (L. Vorsterman after Rubens); 7 r. "The Holy Family, Angel and St. Cathrin" (C. Bloemaert).

(Des D. Miller. Litho Questa (5 r.), Walsall (others))

1992 (6 Feb). *40th Anniv of Queen Elizabeth II's Accession. Horiz designs as T* **112** *of Kenya. Multicoloured. W w* **14** *(sideways). P* 14.

810 1 r. Seychelles coastline 35 25
811 1 r. 50, Clock Tower, Victoria 50 40
812 3 r. Victoria harbour 90 90
813 3 r. 50, Three portraits of Queen Elizabeth 1·00 1·00
814 5 r. Queen Elizabeth II .. .. .. 1·40 1·60
810/14 .. .. *Set of* 5 3·75 3·75

POSTAGE DUE STAMPS

D 1

(Frame recess, value typo B.W.)

1951 (1 Mar). *Wmk Mult Script CA. P* 11½.

D1	D 1	2 c. scarlet and carmine	80	1·50
D2		3 c. scarlet and green	1·25	1·50
D3		6 c. scarlet and bistre	1·25	1·25
D4		9 c. scarlet and orange	1·50	1·25
D5		15 c. scarlet and violet	1·75	7·50
D6		18 c. scarlet and blue	1·75	7·50
D7		20 c. scarlet and brown	1·75	7·50
D8		30 c. scarlet and claret	1·75	7·50
D1/8		.. .. *Set of* 8	10·50	32·00

1964 (7 July)–**65.** *As* 1951 *but* W w **12**.

D 9	D 1	2 c. scarlet and carmine	1·00	5·50
D10		3 c. scarlet and green (14.9.65) ..	1·00	7·50

(Litho Walsall)

1980 (29 Feb). *Design as Type* D **1** *but redrawn, size* 18 × 22 *mm.* W w **14** (*sideways*). *P* 14.

D11	5 c. rosine and magenta	10	15
D12	10 c. rosine and deep blue-green	10	15
D13	15 c. rosine and bistre	15	20
D14	20 c. rosine and orange-brown	15	25
D15	25 c. rosine and bright violet	15	25
D16	75 c. rosine and maroon	25	35
D17	80 c. rosine and deep grey-blue	25	35
D18	1 r. rosine and deep reddish purple	30	40
D11/18	.. .. *Set of* 8	1·25	1·90

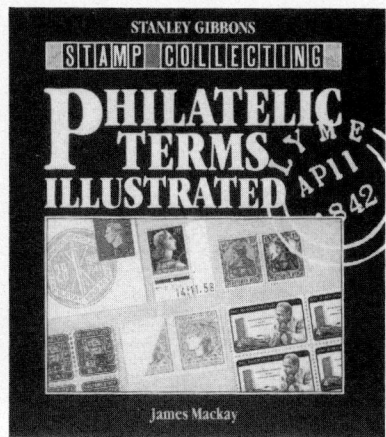

ZIL ELWANNYEN SESEL

(SEYCHELLES OUTER ISLANDS)

For use from Aldabra, Coetivy, Farquhar and the Amirante Islands, served by the M.V. *Cinq-Juin* travelling post office.

I Inscr "ZIL ELOIGNE SESEL"

1 Reef Fish

2 *Cinq Juin*

1980 (20 June)–**81.** *Designs as Nos.* 404/11 (*with imprint*) *and* 487/94 *of Seychelles but inscr.* "ZIL ELOIGNE SESEL" *as in T* **1**. *W w* **14** (*sideways on* 10, 20, 50, 75 *c.*). *P* 14½ × 14 (40 *c.*, 1 *r.*, 1 *r.* 25, 1*r.* 50), 13½ (5, 10, 15, 20 *r.*) *or* 14 (*others*).

1 5 c. Type **1** 15 20
2 10 c. Hawksbill Turtle 15 20
3 15 c. Coco-de-Mer 15 20
4 20 c. Wild Vanilla 20 20
5 25 c. *Hypolimnas misippus* (butterfly) .. 60 30
6 40 c. Coral scene 30 30
7 50 c. Giant Tortoise 30 30
8 75 c. Crayfish 35 30
9 1 r. Madagascar Red Fody 75 40
10 1 r. 10, Green Gecko 40 40
11 1 r. 25, White Tern 90 45
12 1 r. 50, Seychelles Flying Fox 45 35
13 5 r. Octopus .. .. 70 1·00
a. Perf 13 (1981) 65 90
14 10 r. Giant Tiger Cowrie .. .. 1·50 1·50
a. Perf 13 (1981) .. .. 1·00 2·00
15 15 r. Pitcher Plant .. .. 2·00 2·50
a. Perf 13 (1981) .. .. 1·75 2·50
16 20 r. Seychelles coat of arms .. .. .. 2·00 3·25
a. Perf 13 (1981) .. .. 2·00 3·75
1/16 .. .. *Set of* 16 9·00 10·50

Nos. 1/12 exist with imprint dates of either "1980" or "1981", Nos. 13/16 with "1980" only and Nos. 13a/16a "1981" only.

(Des L. Curtis. Litho Walsall)

1980 (24 Oct). *Establishment of Travelling Post Office. T* **2** *and similar horiz designs. Multicoloured. W w* **14** (*sideways*). *P* 14.

17 1 r. 50, Type **2** 30 15
18 2 r. 10, Hand-stamping covers 40 20
19 5 r. Map of Zil Eloigne Sesel 70 40
17/19 .. .. *Set of* 3 1·25 65

Nos. 17/19 were printed in sheets including two *se-tenant* stamp-size labels.

The original version of No. 19 incorrectly showed the Agalega Islands as Seychelles territory. A corrected version was prepared prior to issue and stamps in the first type were intended for destruction. Mint examples and some used on first day covers are known, originating from supplies sent to some philatelic bureau standing order customers in error. Such stamps are not listed as they were not available from Seychelles post offices or valid for postage.

3 Yellowfin Tuna

(Des G. Drummond. Litho Rosenbaum Bros, Vienna)

1980 (28 Nov). *Marine Life. T* **3** *and similar horiz designs. Multicoloured. W w* **14**. *P* 14.

20 1 r. 50, Type **3** 20 15
21 2 r. 10, Blue Marlin (fish) 35 20
22 5 r. Sperm Whale 70 50
20/2 .. .. *Set of* 3 1·10 75

Nos. 20/2 were printed in sheets including two *se-tenant* stamp-size labels.

(Des D. Shults. Litho Questa)

1981 (23 June–16 Nov). *Royal Wedding. Horiz designs as T* **26/27** *of Kiribati. Multicoloured.* (*a*) *W w* **15**. *P* 14.

23 40 c. *Royal Escape* 10 10
a. Sheetlet. No. 23 × 6 and No. 24 90
24 40 c. Prince Charles and Lady Diana Spencer 40 40
25 5 r. *Victoria and Albert II* 40 40
a. Sheetlet. No. 25 × 6 and No. 26 .. .. 3·50
26 5 r. As No. 24 .. .. 1·40 1·40
27 10 r. *Britannia* 85 85
a. Sheetlet. No. 27 × 6 and No. 28 .. .. 7·00
28 10 r. As No. 24 .. .. 2·50 2·50
23/8 .. .. *Set of* 6 5·00 5·00
MS29 120 × 109 mm. 7 r. 50, As No. 24. Wmk sideways. P 12 (16 Nov) .. .. 2·00 2·00

(*b*) *Booklet stamps. No wmk. P* 12 (16 Nov)

30 40 c. As No. 23 .. .. 35 55
a. Booklet pane. No. 30 × 4 .. .. .. 1·25
31 5 r. As No. 26 .. .. 1·00 1·50
a. Booklet pane. No. 31 × 2 .. .. .. 2·00

Nos. 23/8 were printed in sheetlets of seven stamps of the same face value, each containing six of the "Royal Yacht" design and one of the larger design showing Prince Charles and Lady Diana.

Nos. 30/1 come from 13 r. 20 stamp booklets.

4 Wright's Skink

(Des and litho Walsall)

1981 (11 Dec). *Wildlife* (1*st series*). *T* **4** *and similar horiz designs. Multicoloured. W w* **14** (*sideways*). *P* 14.

32 1 r. 40, Type **4** 15 15
33 2 r. 25, Tree Frog 20 20
34 5 r. Robber Crab 40 40
32/4 .. .. *Set of* 3 65 65

See also Nos. 45/7.

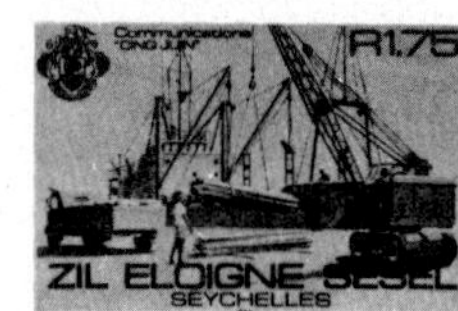

5 *Cinq Juin* ("Communications")

(Des L. Curtis. Litho Harrison)

1982 (11 Mar). *Island Development. Ships. T* **5** *and similar horiz designs. W w* **14**. *P* 14 × 14½.

35 1 r. 75, black and orange 50 20
36 2 r. 10, black and turquoise-blue 60 30
37 5 r. black and bright scarlet 70 50
35/7 .. .. *Set of* 3 1·60 90

Designs:—2 r. 10, *Junon* ("fisheries protection"); 5 r. *Diamond M. Dragon* (drilling ship).

II Inscr "ZIL ELWAGNE SESEL"

6 *Paulette*

(Des L. Curtis. Litho Harrison)

1982 (22 July). *Local Mail Vessels. T* **6** *and similar horiz designs. Multicoloured. W w* **14** (*sideways*). *P* 14.

38 40 c. Type **6** 20 10
39 1 r. 75, *Janette* 40 30
40 2 r. 75, *Lady Esme* 50 40
41 3 r. 50, *Cinq Juin* 60 50
38/41 .. .. *Set of* 4 1·50 1·10

7 Birds flying over Island

8 Red Land Crab

(Des Harrison. Litho Format)

1982 (19 Nov). *Aldabra, World Heritage Site. T* **7** *and similar horiz designs. Multicoloured. W w* **14** (*sideways*). *P* 14.

42 40 c. Type **7** 30 15
43 2 r. 75, Map of the atoll 70 35
44 7 r. Giant Tortoises .. .. 1·25 75
42/4 .. .. *Set of* 3 2·00 1·10

(Des G. Drummond. Litho Questa)

1983 (25 Feb). *Wildlife* (2*nd series*). *T* **8** *and similar horiz designs. Multicoloured. W w* **14** (*sideways*). *P* 14 × 14½.

45 1 r. 75, Type **8** 25 25
46 2 r. 75, Black Terrapin 35 35
47 7 r. Madagascar Green Gecko 80 80
45/7 .. .. *Set of* 3 1·25 1·25

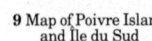

9 Map of Poivre Island and Île du Sud

10 Aldabra Warbler

(Des J. Cooter. Litho Format)

1983 (27 Apr). *Island Maps. T* **9** *and similar vert designs. Multicoloured. W w* **14**. *P* 14.

48 40 c. Type **9** 10 10
49 1 r. 50, Île des Roches 25 25
50 2 r. 75, Astove Island 40 40
51 7 r. Coëtivy Island .. .. 1·10 1·10
48/51 .. .. *Set of* 4 1·75 1·75
MS52 93 × 129 mm. Nos. 48/51 .. .. .. 2·75 3·25

(Des G. Drummond. Litho Harrison)

1983 (13 July). *Birds. T* **10** *and similar multicoloured designs. W w* **14** (*sideways on* 5 *c. to* 2 *r.* 75). *P* 14.

53 5 c. Type **10** 20 20
54 10 c. Zebra Dove 35 10
55 15 c. Madagascar Nightjar 10 10
56 20 c. Madagascar Cisticola 10 10
57 25 c. Madagascar White Eye 50 10
58 40 c. Mascarene Fody 10 10
59 50 c. White-throated Rail 50 10
60 75 c. Black Bulbul 15 20
61 2 r. Western Reef Heron .. .. 1·25 55
62 2 r. 10, Souimanga Sunbird 45 50
63 2 r. 50, Madagascar Turtle Dove 55 60
64 2 r. 75, Sacred Ibis 60 65
65 3 r. 50, Black Coucal (*vert*) 75 80
66 7 r. Seychelles Kestrel (*vert*) .. .. .. 1·50 1·60
67 15 r. Comoro Blue Pigeon (*vert*) .. .. .. 3·25 3·50
68 20 r. Greater Flamingo (*vert*) .. .. .. 4·50 4·75
53/68 .. .. *Set of* 16 13·00 12·50

For 5 c., 10 c., 25 c., 50 c. and 2 r. values in these designs, but inscribed "Zil Elwannyen Sesel", see Nos. 100/7, 165/73 and 226.

11 Windsurfing

(Des G. Wilby. Litho Questa)

1983 (27 Sept). *Tourism. T* **11** *and similar horiz designs. Multicoloured. W w* **14** (*sideways*). *P* 14.

69 50 c. Type **11** 10 10
70 2 r. Hotel 25 25
71 3 r. View of beach 35 35
72 10 r. Islands at sunset .. .. 1·40 1·75
69/72 .. .. *Set of* 4 1·75 2·10

1983 (16–28 Dec). *Nos.* 23/8 *surch as T* **135** *of Seychelles.*

73 30 c. on 40 c. *Royal Escape* 25 25
a. Sheetlet. No. 73 × 6 and No. 74 .. .. 1·50
b. Surch double .. .. 50·00
c. Error. Surch 50 c. (as Seychelles No. 573) 60·00
74 30 c. on 40 c. Prince Charles and Lady Diana Spencer 40 50
b. Surch double £130
c. Error. Surch 50 c. (as Seychelles No. 574) £140
75 2 r. on 5 r. *Victoria and Albert II* (28.12.83) .. 70 70
a. Sheetlet. No. 75 × 6 and No. 76 .. .. 4·75
b. Albino surch .. .. 40·00
c. Surch double .. .. 75·00
76 2 r. on 5 r. As No. 74 (28.12.83) .. .. .. 1·00 1·40
b. Albino surch .. .. 65·00
c. Surch double £200
77 3 r. on 10 r. *Britannia* (28.12.83) 85 85
a. Sheetlet. No. 77 × 6 and No. 78 .. .. 6·00
78 3 r. on 10 r. As No. 74 (28.12.83) .. .. 1·40 1·75
73/8 .. .. *Set of* 6 4·25 5·00

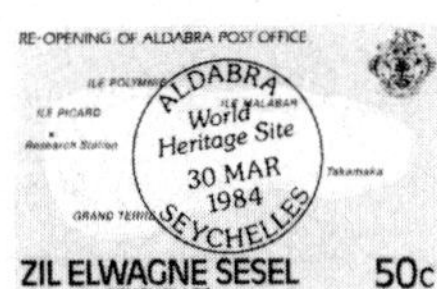

12 Map of Aldabra and Commemorative Postmark

(Des L. Curtis. Litho Questa)

1984 (30 Mar). *Re-opening of Aldabra Post Office. T* **12** *and similar horiz designs. Multicoloured. W w* **14** (*sideways*). *P* 14.

79 50 c. Type **12** 15 20
80 2 r. 75, White-throated Rail 60 85
81 3 r. Giant Tortoise 60 95
82 10 r. Red-footed Booby .. .. 2·25 2·75
79/82 .. .. *Set of* 4 3·25 4·25

13 Fishing from Launch

(Des L. Curtis. Litho Walsall)

1984 (31 May). *Game Fishing. T* **13** *and similar multicoloured designs. W w* **14** (*sideways on* 50 *c.*, 10 *r.*). *P* 14.

83 50 c. Type **13** 15 15
84 2 r. Hooked fish (*vert*) 45 55
85 3 r. Weighing catch (*vert*) 60 75
86 10 r. Fishing from boat (*different*) .. .. 2·00 2·50
83/6 .. .. *Set of* 4 2·75 3·50

14 Giant Hermit Crab   **15** Constellation of "Orion"

(Des G. Drummond. Litho Format)

1984 (24 Aug). *Crabs. T* **14** *and similar horiz designs. Multicoloured. W* w **14** *(sideways). P* 14½.

87 50 c. Type **14** 25 30
88 2 r. Fiddler Crabs 65 85
89 3 r. Sand Crab .. .. 80 1·25
90 10 r. Spotted Pebble Crab .. .. .. 2·50 3·25
87/90 .. .. *Set of* 4 3·75 5·00

(Des A. Theobald. Litho Format)

1984 (16 Oct). *The Night Sky. T* **15** *and similar vert designs. Multicoloured. W* w **14**. *P* 14.

91 50 c. Type **15** 15 15
92 2 r. "Cygnus" 50 55
93 3 r. "Virgo" 75 80
94 10 r. "Scorpio" .. .. 2·00 2·25
91/4 .. .. *Set of* 4 3·00 3·25

III Inscr "ZIL ELWANNYEN SESEL"

16 *Lenzites elegans*   **17** The Queen Mother attending Royal Opera House, Covent Garden

(Des G. Drummond. Litho Walsall)

1985 (31 Jan). *Fungi. T* **16** *and similar vert designs. Multicoloured. W* w **14**. *P* 14.

95 50 c. Type **16** 25 15
96 2 r. *Xylaria telfairei* 70 50
97 3 r. *Lentinus sajor-caju* 90 70
98 10 r. *Hexagonia tenuis* .. .. 2·75 2·50
95/8 .. .. *Set of* 4 4·25 3·50

(Litho Harrison)

1985 (May)–**87**. *As Nos.* 54, 57, 59 *and* 61 *but inscr* "Zil Elwannyen Sesel". *W* w **14** *(sideways). P* 14.

100 10 c. Zebra Dove 40 40
103 25 c. Madagascar White Eye 10 10
105 50 c. White-throated Rail (1.7.87) 40 40
107 2 r. Western Reef Heron .. .. .. 2·00 2·00
100/7 .. .. *Set of* 4 2·50 2·50

The 10 c. exists with different imprint dates below the design.

For 10 c., 50 c. and 2 r. values watermarked w **16** (sideways) see Nos. 165/73 and 226.

(Des A. Theobald (10 r.), C. Abbott (others). Litho Questa)

1985 (7 June). *Life and Times of Queen Elizabeth the Queen Mother. T* **17** *and similar vert designs. Multicoloured. W* w **16**. *P* 14½×14.

115 1 r. The Queen Mother, 1936 (from photo by Dorothy Wilding) 20 25
116 2 r. With Princess Anne at Ascot, 1974 .. 45 50
117 3 r. Type **17** 65 70
118 5 r. With Prince Henry at his christening (from photo by Lord Snowdon) .. 1·10 1·25
115/18 .. .. *Set of* 4 2·25 2·40
MS119 91×73 mm. 10 r. In a launch, Venice, 1985. Wmk sideways .. .. 2·25 2·75

18 Giant Tortoise

(Des. G. Vasarhelyi. Litho J.W.)

1985 (27 Sept). *Giant Tortoises of Aldabra* (1*st series*). *T* **18** *and similar horiz designs. Multicoloured. W* w **16** *(sideways). P* 14.

120 50 c. Type **18** 40 20
121 75 c. Giant Tortoises at stream 45 30
122 1 r. Giant Tortoises on grassland 55 35
123 2 r. Giant Tortoise (side view) 90 70
120/3 .. .. *Set of* 4 2·10 1·40
MS124 70×60 mm. 10 r. Two Giant Tortoises. P 13×13½ .. .. 2·25 2·75

For stamps as Nos. 120/3, but without circular inscription around W.W.F. emblem, see Nos. 153/6.

19 Phoenician Trading Ship (600 B.C.)   **20** *Acropora palifera* and *Tubastraea coccinea*

(Des N. Shewring. Litho Format)

1985 (25 Oct). *Famous Visitors. T* **19** *and similar horiz designs. Multicoloured. W* w **14** *(sideways). P* 14.

125 50 c. Type **19** 40 30
126 2 r. Sir Hugh Scott and H.M.S. *Sealark*, 1908 .. .. 1·25 80
127 10 r. Vasco da Gama and *Sao Gabriel*, 1502 3·50 2·75
125/7 .. .. *Set of* 3 4·75 3·50

(Des A. Theobald. Litho Questa)

1986 (21 Apr). 60*th Birthday of Queen Elizabeth II. Vert designs as T* **230a** *of Jamaica. Multicoloured. W* w **16**. *P* 14½×14.

128 75 c. Princess Elizabeth at Chester, 1951 .. 20 25
129 1 r. Queen and Duke of Edinburgh at Falklands Service, St. Paul's Cathedral, 1985 .. .. 20 25
130 1 r. 50, At Order of St. Michael and St. George service, St. Paul's Cathedral, 1968 .. .. 35 40
131 3 r. 75, In Mexico, 1975 .. .. .. 85 90
132 5 r. At Crown Agents Head Office, London, 1983 .. .. 1·10 1·25
128/32 .. .. *Set of* 5 2·40 2·75

(Des D. Miller. Litho Questa)

1986 (23 July). *Royal Wedding. Square designs as T* **231a** *of Jamaica. Multicoloured. W* w **16**. *P* 14.

133 3 r. Prince Andrew and Miss Sarah Ferguson on Buckingham Palace balcony 70 75
134 7 r. Prince Andrew in naval uniform .. 1·60 1·75

(Des I. Loe. Litho Harrison)

1986 (17 Sept). *Coral Formations. T* **20** *and similar vert designs. Multicoloured. W* w **16**. *P* 14.

135 2 r. Type **20** 60 60
a. Horiz strip of 5. Nos. 135/9 .. .. 2·75
136 2 r. *Echinopora lamellosa* and *Favia pallida* 60 60
137 2 r. *Sarcophyton sp.* and *Porites lutea* .. 60 60
138 2 r. *Goniopora sp.* and *Goniastrea retiformis* 60 60
139 2 r. *Tubipora musica* and *Fungia fungites* .. 60 60
135/9 .. .. *Set of* 5 2·75 2·75

Nos. 135/9 were printed together, *se-tenant*, in horizontal strips of 5 throughout the sheet, forming a composite design.

21 *Hibiscus tiliaceus*   **22** *Chaetodon unimaculatus*

(Des Annette Robinson. Litho Walsall)

1986 (12 Nov). *Flora. T* **21** *and similar vert designs. Multicoloured. W* w **16**. *P* 14.

140 50 c. Type **21** 35 20
141 2 r. *Crinum angustum* .. .. .. 1·40 80
142 3 r. *Phaius tetragonus* .. .. .. 1·90 1·25
143 10 r. *Rothmannia annae* .. .. .. 3·50 2·75
140/3 .. .. *Set of* 4 6·50 4·50

(Des G. Drummond. Litho Questa)

1987 (26 Mar). *Coral Reef Fishes. T* **22** *and similar vert designs. Multicoloured. W* w **16**. *P* 14.

144 2 r. Type **22** 55 55
a. Horiz strip of 5. Nos. 144/8 .. .. 2·50
145 2 r. *Ostorhincus fleurieu* 55 55
146 2 r. *Platax orbicularis* 55 55
147 2 r. *Abudefduf annulatus* 55 55
148 2 r. *Chaetodon lineolatus* 55 55
144/8 .. .. *Set of* 5 2·50 2·50

Nos. 144/8 were printed together, *se-tenant*, in horizontal strips of 5 throughout the sheet, forming a composite design.

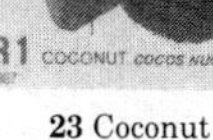

23 Coconut   **24** "Vallee de Mai" (Christine Harter)

(Des R. Gorringe. Litho Walsall)

1987 (26 Aug). *Trees. T* **23** *and similar vert designs. Multicoloured. W* w **16**. *P* 14½.

149 1 r. Type **23** 45 45
150 2 r. Mangrove 85 85
151 3 r. Pandanus Palm .. .. 1·25 1·25
152 5 r. Indian Almond .. .. 2·00 2·25
149/52 .. .. *Set of* 4 4·00 4·25

(Des G. Vasarhelyi. Litho Questa)

1987 (9 Sept). *Giant Tortoises of Aldabra* (2*nd series*). *Designs as Nos.* 120/3, *but without circular inscr around W.W.F. emblem. Multicoloured. W* w **16** *(sideways). P* 14.

153 50 c. As Type **18** 60 60
154 75 c. Giant Tortoises at stream 90 90
155 1 r. Giant Tortoises on grassland .. .. 1·10 1·10
156 2 r. Giant Tortoise (side view) .. .. 1·75 1·75
153/6 .. .. *Set of* 4 4·00 4·00

1987 (9 Dec). *Royal Ruby Wedding. Nos.* 128/32 *optd with T* **45a** *of Kiribati in silver.*

157 75 c. Princess Elizabeth at Chester, 1951 .. 20 20
158 1 r. Queen and Duke of Edinburgh at Falklands Service, St. Paul's Cathedral, 1985 .. .. 25 25
159 1 r. 50, At Order of St. Michael and St. George service, St. Paul's Cathedral, 1968 .. .. 40 40
160 3 r. 75, In Mexico, 1975 .. .. .. 90 90
161 5 r. At Crown Agents Head Office, London, 1983 .. .. 1·25 1·25
157/61 .. .. *Set of* 5 2·75 2·75

(Des D. Miller. Litho Questa)

1987 (16 Dec). *Tourism. T* **24** *and similar vert designs. Multicoloured. W* w **16**. *P* 14.

162 3 r. Type **24** .. .. 1·25 1·00
a. Horiz strip of 3. Nos. 162/4 .. .. 3·25
163 3 r. Ferns .. .. 1·25 1·00
164 3 r. Bamboo .. .. 1·25 1·00
162/4 .. .. *Set of* 3 3·25 2·75

Nos. 162/4 were printed together, *se-tenant*, in horizontal strips of 3 throughout the sheet, forming the complete picture.

(Litho Harrison)

1988 (July–24 Nov). *As No.* 53, *but inscr* "Zil Elwannyen Sesel", *and Nos.* 100, 105 *and* 107, *all W* w **16** *(sideways). P* 14.

165 5 c. Type **10** (24.11) 10 10
166 10 c. Zebra Dove (24.11) 10 10
171 50 c. White-throated Rail (24.11) 10 15
173 2 r. Western Reef Heron 75 75
165/73 .. .. *Set of* 4 85 90

For 2 r. printed by Walsall and perforated 14×14½ see No. 226.

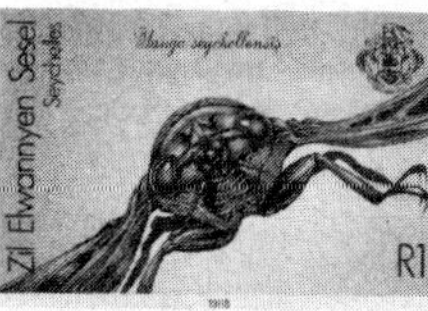

25 *Yanga seychellensis* (beetle)

(Des I. Loe. Litho Walsall)

1988 (28 July). *Insects. T* **25** *and similar horiz designs. Multicoloured. W* w **14** *(sideways). P* 14.

180 1 r. Type **25** 40 30
181 2 r. *Belenois aldabrensis* (butterfly) 65 45
182 3 r. *Polyspilota seychelliana* (mantid) .. 75 65
183 5 r. *Polposipus herculeanus* (beetle) .. .. 1·25 1·10
180/3 .. .. *Set of* 4 2·75 2·25

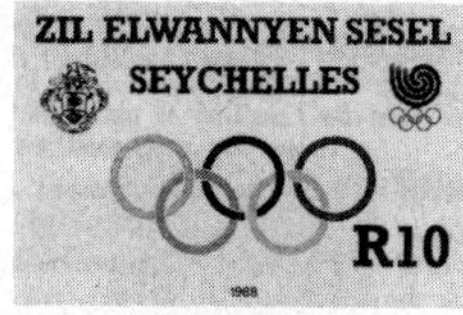

26 Olympic Rings

(Des Joan Thompson. Litho Format)

1988 (31 Aug). *Olympic Games, Seoul. Sheet* 99 × 73 *mm. W* w **16** *(sideways). P* 14.

MS184 **26** 10 r. multicoloured .. .. .. 2·00 2·10

(Des D. Miller (1 r.), E. Nisbet and D. Miller (2 r.), O. Bell and D. Miller (3 r.), A. Theobald and D. Miller (5 r.). Litho Walsall)

1988 (28 Oct). 300*th Anniv of Lloyd's of London. Multicoloured designs as T* **167a** *of Malawi. W* w **14** *(sideways on* 2, 3 *r.). P* 14.

185 1 r. Modern Lloyd's Building, London .. 50 40
186 2 r. *Retriever* (cable ship) *(horiz)* 80 60
187 3 r. *Chantel* (fishing boat) *(horiz)* .. .. 1·25 90
188 5 r. Wreck of *Torrey Canyon* (tanker), Cornwall, 1967 .. .. 1·75 1·40
185/8 .. .. *Set of* 4 4·00 3·00

COVER PRICES

Cover factors are quoted at the beginning of each country for most issues to 1945. An explanation of the system can be found on page x. The factors quoted do not, however, apply to philatelic covers.

27 "Father Christmas landing with Presents" (Jean-Claude Boniface)

(Adapted G. Vasarhelyi. Litho Questa)

1988 (18 Nov). *Christmas. Children's Paintings. T* **27** *and similar multicoloured designs. W w* **16** *(sideways on 1, 5 r.). P* 13½ × 14 *(horiz) or* 14 × 13½ *(vert).*

189 1 r. Type **27** 25 25
190 2 r. "Church" (Francois Barra) *(vert)* .. 45 45
191 3 r. "Father Christmas flying on Bird" (Wizy Ernesta) *(vert)* 65 65
192 5 r. "Father Christmas in Sleigh over Island" (Federic Lang) .. .. 1·10 1·10
189/92 .. .. *Set of* 4 2·25 2·25

(Des A. Theobald (10 r.), D. Miller (others). Litho Questa)

1989 (20 July). *20th Anniv of First Manned Landing on Moon. Multicoloured designs as T* **51a** *of Kiribati. W w* **16** *(sideways on 2, 3 r.). P* 14×13½ *(1, 5 r.) or* 14 *(others).*

193 1 r. Firing Room, Launch Control Centre .. 35 35
194 2 r. Crews of "Apollo-Soyuz" mission (30×30 *mm*) 60 60
195 3 r. "Apollo-Soyuz" emblem (30×30 *mm*) .. 80 80
196 5 r. "Apollo" and "Soyuz" docking in space 1·40 1·40
193/6 .. .. *Set of* 4 2·75 2·75
MS197 82×100 mm. 10 r. Recovery of "Apollo 11". P 14×13½ .. .. 3·50 4·00

28 Dumb Cane

29 Tec-Tec Broth

(Des Lynn Chadwick. Litho Questa)

1989 (9 Oct). *Poisonous Plants (1st series). T* **28** *and similar horiz designs. Multicoloured. W w* **16** *(sideways). P* 14.

198 1 r. Type **28** 40 40
199 2 r. Star of Bethlehem 70 70
200 3 r. Indian Liquorice 95 95
201 5 r. Black Nightshade .. .. .. 1·50 1·50
198/201 .. .. *Set of* 4 3·25 3·25

See also Nos. 214/17.

(Des O. Bell. Litho B.D.T.)

1989 (18 Dec). *Creole Cooking. T* **29** *and similar vert designs. Multicoloured. W w* **16**. *P* 14.

202 1 r. Type **29** 40 40
203 2 r. Pilaff á la Seychelloise 75 75
204 3 r. Mullet grilled in banana leaves .. 1·00 1·00
205 5 r. Daube .. .. 1·40 1·40
202/5 .. .. *Set of* 4 3·25 3·25
MS206 125×80 mm. Nos. 202/5 .. .. 4·00 4·25

Stamps from No. **MS**206 have the white margin omitted on one or both vertical sides.

30 1980 Marine Life 5 r. Stamp

(Des D. Miller. Litho Security Printers (M), Malaysia)

1990 (3 May). *"Stamp World London 90" International Stamp Exhibition. T* **30** *and similar horiz designs showing stamps. Multicoloured. W w* **14** *(sideways). P* 12½.

207 1 r. Type **30** 30 30
208 2 r. 1980 5 r. definitive 55 55
209 3 r. 1983 2 r. 75 definitive 80 80
210 5 r. 1981 Wildlife 5 r. .. .. .. 1·40 1·40
207/10 .. .. *Set of* 4 2·75 2·75
MS211 124×84 mm. Nos. 207/10. Wmk upright 3·75 4·00

(Des D. Miller. Litho Questa)

1990 (4 Aug). *90th Birthday of Queen Elizabeth the Queen Mother. Vert designs as T* **107** *(2 r.) or* **108** *(10 r.) of Kenya. W w* **16**. *P* 14×15 *(2 r.) or* 14½ *(10 r.).*

212 2 r. multicoloured 60 60
213 10 r. black and orange-brown .. .. 2·40 2·40

Designs:—2 r. Duchess of York with baby Princess Elizabeth, 1926; 10 r. King George VI and Queen Elizabeth visiting bombed district, London, 1940.

(Des Lynn Chadwick. Litho Security Printers (M), Malaysia)

1990 (5 Nov). *Poisonous Plants (2nd series). Horiz designs as T* **28**. *Multicoloured. W w* **14** *(sideways). P* 12½.

214 1 r. Ordeal Plant 40 40
215 2 r. Thorn Apple 70 70
216 3 r. Strychnine Tree 90 90
217 5 r. Bwa Zasmen .. .. 1·40 1·40
214/17 .. .. *Set of* 4 3·00 3·00

(Litho Walsall)

1991 (Jan). *As No.* 173, *but different printer. W w* **16** *(sideways). P* 14×14½.

226 2 r. Western Reef Heron 45 50

(Des D. Miller. Litho Questa)

1991 (17 June). *65th Birthday of Queen Elizabeth II and 70th Birthday of Prince Philip. Vert designs as T* **58** *of Kiribati. Multicoloured. W w* **16** *(sideways). P* 14½×14.

234 4 r. Queen Elizabeth II .. .. .. 1·40 1·50
a. Horiz pair. Nos. 234/5 separated by label .. .. 2·75 3·00
235 4 r. Prince Philip .. .. 1·40 1·50

Nos. 234/5 were printed in a similar sheet format to Nos. 366/7 of Kiribati.

31 *St. Abbs* (full-rigged ship), 1860

(Des J. Batchelor. Litho Walsall)

1991 (28 Oct). *Shipwrecks. T* **31** *and similar horiz designs. Multicoloured. W w* **14** *(sideways). P* 14.

236 1 r. 50, Type **31** 50 50
237 3 r. *Norden* (barque), 1862 .. .. 95 95
238 3 r. 50, *Clan Mackay* (freighter), 1894 .. 1·10 1·10
239 10 r. *Glenlyon* (freighter), 1905 .. .. 2·75 2·75
236/9 .. .. *Set of* 4 4·75 4·75

(Des D. Miller. Litho Questa (5 r.), Walsall (others))

1992 (6 Feb). *40th Anniv of Queen Elizabeth II's Accession. Horiz designs as T* **112** *of Kenya. Multicoloured. W w* **14** *(sideways). P* 14.

240 1 r. Beach 30 30
241 1 r. 50, Aerial view of Desroches 50 50
242 3 r. Tree-covered coastline 90 90
243 3 r. 50, Three portraits of Queen Elizabeth II 1·00 1·00
244 5 r. Queen Elizabeth II .. .. .. 1·40 1·40
240/4 .. .. *Set of* 5 3·75 3·75

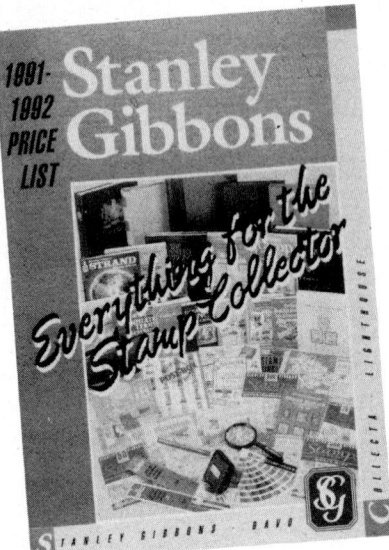

Sierra Leone

PRICES FOR STAMPS ON COVER TO 1945

Nos. 1/3	*from* × 10
Nos. 4/15	*from* × 6
Nos. 16/26	*from* × 10
Nos. 27/34	*from* × 12
Nos. 35/7	*from* × 6
No. 38	—
No. 39	*from* × 10
Nos. 41/52	*from* × 4
No. 53	—
No. 54	*from* × 25
Nos. 55/63	*from* × 3
Nos. 64/71	—
Nos. 73/84	*from* × 3
No. 85	—
Nos. 86/97	*from* × 3
No. 98	—
Nos. 99/110	*from* × 3
No. 111	—
Nos. 112/26	*from* × 2
Nos. 127/30	—
Nos. 131/45	*from* × 2
Nos. 146/8	—
Nos. 155/66	*from* × 2
No. 167	—
Nos. 168/78	*from* × 2
Nos. 179/80	—
Nos. 181/4	*from* × 6
Nos. 185/7	*from* × 5
Nos. 188/200	*from* × 2

CROWN COLONY AND PROTECTORATE

The first settlement in Sierra Leone intended as a home for repatriated Africans, and subsequently those released by the Royal Navy from slave ships, was established in 1787. The Sierra Leone Company was created by Act of Parliment in 1791, but its charter was surrendered in 1808 and the coastal settlements then became a Crown Colony. The inland region was proclaimed a British protectorate on 21 August 1896.

A post office was established in 1843 but, until the inclusion of Freetown in the British Post Office packet system in 1852, overseas mail was carried at irregular intervals by passing merchant or naval vessels.

The stamps of GREAT BRITAIN were not sold at Sierra Leone post offices, although examples from ships of the West African Squadron do exist with local cancellations.

PRINTERS. All issues of Sierra Leone until 1932 were typographed by De La Rue & Co. Ltd, London.

1

2

HALF
PENNY

(3)

1859 (21 Sept)–**74.** *No wmk. P* 14.

No.	Type	Description	Unused	Used
1	**1**	6d. dull purple	£200	45·00
2		6d. grey-lilac (1865)	£225	40·00
3		6d. reddish violet (*p* 12½) (1872)	£300	55·00
4		6d. reddish lilac (1874)	35·00	25·00

Imperforate proofs exist.

The paper used for the 6d. value often shows varying degrees of blueing, caused by a chemical reaction.

1872–73. *Wmk Crown CC. P* 12½. (*a*) *Wmk sideways* (April 1872).

No.	Type	Description	Unused	Used
7	**2**	1d. rose-red	65·00	27·00
8		3d. buff	£110	35·00
9		4d. blue	£150	38·00
10		1s. green	£250	50·00
		(*b*) *Wmk upright* (Sept 1873)		
11	**2**	1d. rose-red	55·00	28·00
12		2d. magenta	£100	48·00
13		3d. saffron-yellow	£475	85·00
14		4d. blue	£200	50·00
15		1s. green	£350	90·00

1876–77. *Wmk Crown CC. P* 14.

No.	Type	Description	Unused	Used
16	**2**	½d. brown	2·00	4·75
17		1d. rose-red	38·00	10·00
18		1½d. lilac (1877)	38·00	5·00
19		2d. magenta	42·00	3·75
20		3d. buff	40·00	4·00
21		4d. blue	90·00	6·50
22		1s. green	50·00	6·00
16/22		*Set of* 7	£250	35·00

1883 (June–26 Sept). *Wmk Crown CA. P* 14.

No.	Type	Description	Unused	Used
23	**2**	½d. brown	17·00	35·00
24		1d. rose-red (26.9.83)	£200	35·00
25		2d. magenta	35·00	6·50
26		4d. blue	£850	28·00

1884 SIERRA 5s. LEONE SURCHARGE. From 2 June 1884 the administration decided that, as a temporary measure, revenue and fiscal duties were to be paid with ordinary postage stamps. At that time there was no postage value higher than 1s., so a local surcharge, reading "SIERRA 5s. LEONE" was applied to No. 22. Until its withdrawal on 1 March 1885 this surcharge was valid for both fiscal and postal purposes, although no genuine postal cover or piece has yet been found. One mint example is known with overprint inverted.

Remainders of the surcharge were cancelled by a horizontal red brush stroke (*Price* £30).

1884 (July)–**91.** *Wmk Crown CA. P* 14.

No.	Type	Description	Unused	Used
27	**2**	½d. dull green	30	30
28		1d. carmine	1·60	35
		a. Rose-carmine (1885?)	28·00	8·50
29		1½d. pale violet (1889)	2·00	5·00
30		2d. grey	16·00	2·00
31		2½d. ultramarine (1891)	7·00	55
32		3d. yellow (1889)	1·75	3·50
33		4d. brown	1·50	1·00
34		1s. red-brown (1888)	12·00	9·00
27/34		*Set of* 8	38·00	20·00
27/8, 30/1, 33/4 (*perf* 14) Optd "Specimen"		*Set of* 6	£400	
27/8, 30, 33 (*perf* 12) Optd "Specimen"		*Set of* 4	£450	

1885–96. *Wmk Crown CC. P* 14.

No.	Type	Description	Unused	Used
35	**1**	6d. dull violet (1885)	55·00	22·00
		a. Bisected (3d.) (on cover)	†	£2250
36		6d. brown-purple (1890)	13·00	14·00
37		6d. purple-lake (1896)	2·00	6·50
36 Optd "Specimen"			60·00	

1893 (18 Jan). *Surch with T* **3**. *P* 14. (*a*) *Wmk Crown CC.*

No.	Type	Description	Unused	Used
38	**2**	½d. on 1½d. lilac	£400	£450
		a. "PFNNY" (R. 3/1)	£1800	£2250
		(*b*) *Wmk Crown CA*		
39	**2**	½d. on 1½d. pale violet	2·75	3·00
		a. Surch inverted	£100	£100
		b. "PFNNY" (R. 3/1)	70·00	70·00
		ba. Ditto. Surch inverted	£1400	

The 6d. fiscal, inscribed "STAMP DUTY" as Type **6,** surcharged "ONE-PENNY" is known used for postage between June and August 1894, but no official sanction for such usage has been found.

4

5

1896–97. *Wmk Crown CA. P* 14.

No.	Type	Description	Unused	Used
41	**4**	½d. dull mauve and green (1897)	65	85
42		1d. dull mauve and carmine	65	40
43		1½d. dull mauve and black (1897)	2·25	6·00
44		2d. dull mauve and orange	2·25	5·00
45		2½d. dull mauve and ultramarine	1·40	80
46	**5**	3d. dull mauve and slate	7·00	7·00
47		4d. dull mauve and carmine (1897)	7·00	13·00
48		5d. dull mauve and black (1897)	7·00	11·00
49		6d. dull mauve (1897)	7·00	12·00
50		1s. green and black	6·00	15·00
51		2s. green and ultramarine	20·00	26·00
52		5s. green and carmine	38·00	75·00
53		£1 purple/*red*	£140	£250
41/53		*Set of* 13	£200	£375
41/53 Optd "Specimen"		*Set of* 13	£225	

6

POSTAGE
AND
REVENUE

(7)

2½d. (8)

2½d. (9)

2½d. (10)

2½d. (11)

2½d. (12)

2½d. (13)

POSTAGE AND
REVENUE

(14)

1897 (Mar). *Fiscal stamps as T* **6**. *Wmk CA over Crown*, w **7**. *P* 14. (*a*) *Optd with T* **7**.

No.	Type	Description	Unused	Used
54		1d. dull purple and green	1·60	1·75
		a. Opt double	£1000	£1000
		(*b*) *Optd with T* **7** *and surch T* **8, 10, 11** (*with square stop*) *or* **12** *with six thin bars across the original face value.*		
55	**8**	2½d. on 3d. dull purple and green	11·00	12·00
		a. Surch double	£9000	
		b. Surch double (Types **8** + **10**)	£7000	
		c. Surch double (Types **8** + **11**)	£12000	
56	**10**	2½d. on 3d. dull purple and green	50·00	65·00
57	**11**	2½d. on 3d. dull purple and green	£140	£160
58	**12**	2½d. on 3d. dull purple and green	£300	£350
59	**8**	2½d. on 6d. dull purple and green	8·50	11·00
60	**10**	2½d. on 6d. dull purple and green	40·00	50·00
61	**11**	2½d. on 6d. dull purple and green	£100	£110
62	**12**	2½d. on 6d. dull purple and green	£225	£250

Nos. 55/8 and 59/62 were surcharged from a setting of 30 (10×3) which contained twenty-two examples of Type **8** (including three with square stops), five of Type **10,** two of Type **11** and one of Type **12.**

Two examples are known of No. 55a, five of No. 55b (of which two are in the Royal Collection) and two of No. 55c (one in the Royal Collection). A unique example of a double surcharge on No. 55 showing Types **8** + **12** is also in the Royal Collection.

(*c*) *Optd with T* **14** *and surch T* **8, 9, 10, 11** (*with round stop*) *or* **13** *with five thin bars across the original face value.*

No.	Type	Description	Unused	Used
63	**8**	2½d. on 1s. dull lilac	80·00	60·00
64	**9**	2½d. on 1s. dull lilac	£1200	£1200
65	**10**	2½d. on 1s. dull lilac	£700	£700
66	**11**	2½d. on 1s. dull lilac	£400	£400
66*a*	**13**	2½d. on 1s. dull lilac	£1200	£1200
67	**8**	2½d. on 2s. dull lilac	£1300	£1600
68	**9**	2½d. on 2s. dull lilac	£27000	
69	**10**	2½d. on 2s. dull lilac	£11000	
70	**11**	2½d. on 2s. dull lilac	£6500	
71	**13**	2½d. on 2s. dull lilac	£27000	

The setting of 30 (10×3) used for both Nos. 63/6*a* and 67/71 contained twenty-two examples of Type **8** (including one with square stop), one of Type **9,** two of Type **10,** four of Type **11** and one of Type **13.**

Most examples of Nos. 63/6*a* are water-stained. Stamps in this condition are worth about 40% of the price quoted.

15

16

1903. *Wmk Crown CA. P* 14.

No.	Type	Description	Unused	Used
73	**15**	½d. dull purple and green	2·75	2·25
74		1d. dull purple and rosine	1·00	30
75		1½d. dull purple and black	1·25	3·75
76		2d. dull purple and brown-orange	3·75	9·00
77		2½d. dull purple and ultramarine	4·50	4·50
78	**16**	3d. dull purple and grey	5·50	7·00
79		4d. dull purple and rosine	6·00	8·00
80		5d. dull purple and black	6·00	13·00
81		6d. dull purple	9·50	9·00
82		1s. green and black	11·00	23·00
83		2s. green and ultramarine	28·00	40·00
84		5s. green and carmine	45·00	65·00
85		£1 purple/*red*	£200	£225
73/85		*Set of* 13	£275	£325
73/85 Optd "Specimen"		*Set of* 13	£225	

1904–5. *Wmk Mult Crown CA. Ordinary paper* (1*d.*) *or chalk-surfaced paper* (*others*). *P* 14.

No.	Type	Description	Unused	Used
86	**15**	½d. dull purple and green (1905)	5·00	2·00
87		1d. dull purple and rosine	65	35
		a. Chalk-surfaced paper (1905)	75	70
88		1½d. dull purple and black (1905)	2·75	8·00
89		2d. dull purple and brown-orange (1905)	4·25	3·50
90		2½d. dull purple and ultramarine (1905)	4·50	2·00
91	**16**	3d. dull purple and grey (1905)	13·00	3·00
92		4d. dull purple and rosine (1905)	4·25	4·50
93		5d. dull purple and black (1905)	8·00	15·00
94		6d. dull purple (1905)	3·00	3·25
95		1s. green and black (1905)	7·50	8·50
96		2s. green and ultramarine (1905)	14·00	18·00
97		5s. green and carmine (1905)	28·00	48·00
98		£1 purple/*red* (1905)	£200	£225
86/98		*Set of* 13	£250	£300

1907–12. *Wmk Mult Crown CA. Ordinary paper* (½*d. to* 2½*d.*) *or chalk-surfaced paper* (*others*). *P* 14.

No.	Type	Description	Unused	Used
99	**15**	½d. green	35	25
100		1d. carmine	5·50	20
		a. Red	1·75	15
101		1½d. orange (1910)	30	2·00
102		2d. greyish slate (1909)	80	1·50
103		2½d. blue	1·25	1·40
104	**16**	3d. purple/*yellow* (1909)	4·25	2·75
		a. Ordinary paper (1912)	4·25	4·75
105		4d. black and red/*yellow* (1908)	2·25	1·10
106		5d. purple and olive-green (1908)	5·00	4·25
107		6d. dull and bright purple (1908)	3·25	4·50
108		1s. black/*green* (1908)	5·00	4·50
109		2s. purple and bright blue/*blue* (1908)	15·00	12·00
110		5s. green and red/*yellow* (1908)	27·00	38·00
111		£1 purple and black/*red* (1911)	£170	£170
99/111		*Set of* 13	£200	£200
99/111 Optd "Specimen"		*Set of* 13	£300	

USED HIGH VALUES. The £2 and £5 values of the King George V series were intended for fiscal use only. Before the introduction of the airmail service at the end of 1926 there was no postal rate for which they could be used. Under the airmail rates used between 1926 and 1932 it is just possible that a very heavy letter may have required a £2 value. Postmarks on the £5 and on the £2 before December 1926 can only have been applied "by favour" or, in the case of the cds type, are on stamps removed from telegraph forms. Used prices quoted for Nos. 129/30 and 147/8 are for "by favour" cancellations.

17

18

19

20

1912–21. *Wmk Mult Crown CA. Chalk-surfaced paper (3d. and 6d. to £5). P 14.*

112 **17** ½d. blue-green 75 60
a. Yellow-green 85 65
b. Deep green .. .. 2·50 1·10
113 1d. carmine-red .. .. 1·00 10
a. Scarlet (1916) .. .. 1·00 40
b. Rose-red .. .. 2·00 30
114 1½d. orange (1913) 80 85
a. Orange-yellow .. .. 2·25 95
115 2d. greyish slate (1913) .. .. .. 1·00 10
116 2½d. deep blue (1913) .. .. .. 6·50 2·25
a. Ultramarine 85 65
116*b* **20** 3d. purple/*yellow* .. .. 2·75 2·50
ba. On pale yellow .. .. 2·75 3·25
117 **18** 4d. black and red/*yellow* (Die I) (1913) 1·00 4·00
a. On lemon .. .. 3·75 5·50
b. On pale yellow (Die II) (5.21) .. 2·25 2·50
118 5d. purple and olive-green (1913) .. 70 2·75
119 6d. dull and bright purple (1913) .. 3·25 3·50
120 **19** 7d. purple and orange (1913) .. 1·75 4·00
121 9d. purple and black (1913) .. .. 5·00 5·50
122 **18** 10d. purple and red (1913) .. .. 3·00 12·00
124 **20** 1s. black/*green* .. .. 3·50 3·25
a. On blue-green, green back .. 3·25 2·50
125 2s. blue and purple/*blue* .. .. 7·50 3·25
126 5s. red and green/*yellow* .. .. 11·00 17·00
127 10s. red and green/*green* .. .. 45·00 70·00
a. Carmine and blue-green/green .. 60·00 85·00
b. Carmine and yellow-green/green 60·00 85·00
128 £1 black and purple/*red* £110 £140
129 £2 blue and dull purple (S. £100) .. £475 £600
130 £5 orange and green (S. £225) .. £1200 £1400
112/28 .. .. *Set of* 17 £180 £250
112/28 Optd "Specimen" .. .. *Set of* 17 £300

1921–28. *Wmk Mult Script CA. Chalk-surfaced paper (6d. to £5). P 14.*

131 **17** ½d. dull green 55 15
a. Bright green .. .. 1·50 60
132 1d. bright violet (Die I) (1924) .. 95 40
a. Die II (1926) .. .. 1·25 10
133 1½d. scarlet (1925) 50 30
134 2d. grey (1922) 40 10
135 2½d. ultramarine .. .. 45 1·75
136 **18** 3d. bright blue (1922) 40 25
137 4d. black and red/*pale yellow* (1925) .. 1·75 1·25
138 5d. purple and olive-green 50 55
139 6d. grey-purple and bright purple .. 1·25 2·00
140 **19** 7d. purple and orange (1928) .. 2·00 10·00
141 9d. purple and black (1922) .. .. 2·50 7·00
142 **18** 10d. purple and red (1926) .. .. 2·00 13·00
143 **20** 1s. black/*emerald* (1925) .. .. 3·25 3·75
144 2s. blue and dull purple/*blue* .. 7·00 6·50
145 5s. red and green/*yellow* (1927) .. 8·50 32·00
146 10s. red and green/*green* (1927) .. 55·00 90·00
147 £2 bl & dull pur (1923) (Optd S. £100) £425 £600
148 £5 orange & grn (1923) (Optd S. £225) £1200 £1400
131/46 .. .. *Set of* 16 75·00 £150
131/46 Optd "Specimen" .. .. *Set of* 16 £250

21 Rice Field

22 Palms and Cola Tree

(Eng J.A.C. Harrison (T **21**))

1932 (1 Mar). *Wmk Mult Script CA. (a) Recess Waterlow. P* 12½.

155 **21** ½d. green 15 20
156 1d. violet 15 10
157 1½d. carmine .. .. 20 1·25
a. Imperf between (horiz pair) ..
158 2d. brown 20 10
159 3d. blue 40 85
160 4d. orange .. .. 40 2·00
161 5d. bronze-green .. .. 50 1·40
162 6d. light blue .. .. 40 1·50
163 1s. lake .. .. 80 2·50

(*b*) *Recess B.W. P* 12.

164 **22** 2s. chocolate .. .. 2·75 3·50
165 5s. deep blue .. .. 7·00 15·00
166 10s. green .. .. 45·00 80·00
167 £1 purple .. .. 75·00 £140
155/67 .. .. *Set of* 13 £120 £225
155/67 Perf "Specimen" .. .. *Set of* 13 £180

23 Arms of Sierra Leone

24 Old Slave Market, Freetown

27 African Elephant

28 King George V

(Des Father F. Welsh. Recess B.W.)

1933 (2 Oct). *Centenary of Abolition of Slavery and of Death of William Wilberforce. T* **23/4, 27/8** *and similar designs. Wmk Mult Script CA (sideways on horiz designs). P* 12.

168 ½d. green 35 60
169 1d. black and brown 30 10
170 1½d. chestnut .. .. 3·25 4·00
171 2d. purple .. .. 2·50 20
172 3d. blue .. .. 2·00 1·50
173 4d. brown .. .. 6·00 10·00
174 5d. green and chestnut .. .. .. 6·50 16·00
175 6d. black and brown-orange .. .. 6·50 8·00
176 1s. violet .. .. 4·50 13·00
177 2s. brown and light blue .. .. 19·00 26·00
178 5s. black and purple £120 £150
179 10s. black and sage-green £130 £180
180 £1 violet and orange £375 £450
168/180 .. .. *Set of* 13 £600 £750
168/80 Perf "Specimen" .. .. *Set of* 13 £650

Designs: *Vert*—1d. "Freedom"; 1½d. Map of Sierra Leone; 4d. Government sanatorium. *Horiz*—3d. Native fruit seller; 5d. Bullom canoe; 6d. Punting near Banana; 1s. Government buildings; 2s. Bunce Island; £1 Freetown harbour.

1935 (6 May). *Silver Jubilee. As Nos.* 114/17 *of Jamaica. P* 11×12.

181 1d. ultramarine and grey-black 50 40
a. Extra flagstaff .. .. .. 40·00
b. Short extra flagstaff .. .. 45·00
c. Lightning conductor .. .. 27·00
182 3d. brown and deep blue .. .. 1·00 2·75
a. Extra flagstaff .. .. .. 60·00
b. Short extra flagstaff .. .. 70·00
c. Lightning conductor .. .. 45·00
183 5d. green and indigo .. .. .. 1·40 4·75
a. Extra flagstaff .. .. .. 90·00
b. Short extra flagstaff £100
c. Lightning conductor .. .. 70·00
184 1s. slate and purple .. .. .. 4·75 2·75
a. Extra flagstaff £180
b. Short extra flagstaff £140
c. Lightning conductor £120
181/4 .. .. *Set of* 4 7·00 9·50
181/4 Perf "Specimen" .. .. *Set of* 4 80·00

For illustrations of plate varieties see Omnibus section following Zimbabwe.

1937 (12 May). *Coronation. As Nos.* 118/20 *of Jamaica, but ptd by B.W.*

185 1d. orange 70 25
186 2d. purple 80 30
187 3d. blue .. .. 1·40 1·25
185/7 .. .. *Set of* 3 2·50 1·60
185/7 Perf "Specimen" .. .. *Set of* 3 55·00

30 Freetown from the Harbour

31 Rice Harvesting

(Recess Waterlow)

1938 (1 May)–**44**. *Wmk Mult Script CA (sideways). P* 12½.

188 **30** ½d. black and blue-green 10 15
189 1d. black and lake 20 10
a. Imperf between (vert pair) .. † —
190 **31** 1½d. scarlet .. .. 15·00 20
190*a* 1½d. mauve (1.2.41) 10 10
191 2d. mauve .. .. 35·00 1·25
191*a* 2d. scarlet (1.2.41) 10 30
192 **30** 3d. black and ultramarine 20 20
193 4d. black and red-brown (20.6.38) .. 50 60
194 **31** 5d. olive-green (20.6.38) .. .. 4·00 2·50
195 6d. grey (20.6.38) 40 20
196 **30** 1s. black and olive-green (20.6.38) .. 35 20
196*a* **31** 1s. 3d. yellow-orange (1.7.44) .. 30 20
197 **30** 2s. black and sepia (20.6.38) .. 1·50 70
198 **31** 5s. red-brown (20.6.38) .. .. 4·50 2·25
199 10s. emerald-green (20.6.38) .. 8·00 5·50
200 **30** £1 deep blue (20.6.38) .. .. 15·00 8·50
188/200 .. .. *Set of* 16 75·00 20·00
188/200 Perf "Specimen" .. .. *Set of* 16 £250

1946 (1 Oct). *Victory. As Nos.* 141/2 *of Jamaica.*

201 1½d. lilac 10 10
202 3d. ultramarine 15 10
201/2 Perf "Specimen" .. .. *Set of* 2 55·00

1948 (1 Dec). *Royal Silver Wedding. As Nos.* 143/4 *of Jamaica.*

203 1½d. bright purple 15 15
204 £1 indigo .. .. 14·00 13·00

1949 (10 Oct). *75th Anniv of U.P.U. As Nos.* 145/8 *of Jamaica.*

205 1½d. purple 15 15
206 3d. deep blue 35 70
207 6d. grey 35 70
208 1s. olive 35 80
205/8 .. .. *Set of* 4 1·10 2·10

1953 (2 June). *Coronation. As No.* 153 *of Jamaica, but ptd by B.W.*

209 1½d. black and purple 15 15

32 Cape Lighthouse

33 Cotton Tree, Freetown

(Recess Waterlow)

1956 (2 Jan)–**61**. *Designs as T* **32/3**. *Wmk Mult Script CA. P* 13½ × 13 (*horiz*) *or* 14 (*vert*).

210 ½d. black and deep lilac 40 70
211 1d. black and olive 45 20
212 1½d. black and ultramarine .. .. .. 60 1·75
213 2d. black and brown 40 10
214 3d. black and bright blue 75 10
a. Perf 13 × 13½ .. .. .. 1·25 5·50
215 4d. black and slate-blue .. .. .. 1·75 60
216 6d. black and violet 70 15
217 1s. black and scarlet 50 10
218 1s. 3d. black and sepia .. .. .. 6·00 10
219 2s. 6d. black and chestnut .. .. 6·50 2·00
220 5s. black and deep green .. .. 1·00 80
221 10s. black and bright reddish purple .. 3·00 2·50
a. Black and purple (19.4.61) .. 9·00 24·00
222 £1 black and orange .. .. .. 9·00 16·00
210/22 .. .. *Set of* 13 28·00 22·00

Designs: *Horiz*—1d. Queen Elizabeth II Quay; 1½d. Piassava workers; 4d. Iron ore production, Marampa; 6d. Whale Bay, York Village; 1s. 3d. Aeroplane and map; 10s. Law Courts, Freetown; £1, Government House. *Vert*—3d. Rice harvesting; 1s. Bullom canoe; 2s.6d. Orugu Railway Bridge; 5s. Kuranko Chief.

Nos. 210/11 and 214 exist in coils, constructed from normal sheets.

INDEPENDENT

45 Palm Fruit Gathering

46 Licensed Diamond Miner

52

(Des K. Penny (½d., 1s.), Messrs Thoma, Turrell and Larkins (1d., 3d., 6d., 2s. 6d.), W. G. Rumley (1½d., 5s.), J. H. Vandi (2d., 10s.), R. A. Sweet (4d., 1s 3d.), J. White (£1). Recess B.W.)

1961 (27 Apr). *Independence. T* **45/6** *and similar designs. W* **52**. *P* 13½.

223 ½d. chocolate and deep bluish green .. 10 10
224 1d. orange-brown and myrtle-green .. 50 10
225 1½d. black and emerald 10 10
226 2d. black and ultramarine 10 10
227 3d. orange-brown and blue 10 10
228 4d. turquoise-blue and scarlet 10 10
229 6d. black and purple 10 10
230 1s. chocolate and yellow-orange 10 10
231 1s. 3d. turquoise-blue and violet 15 10
232 2s. 6d. deep green and black .. .. 1·75 10
233 5s. black and red 90 90
234 10s. black and green .. .. .. 1·00 1·25
235 £1 carmine-red and yellow .. .. 6·00 4·00
223/235 .. .. *Set of* 13 10·00 6·50

Designs: *Vert*—1½d., 5s. Bundu mask; 2d., 10s. Bishop Crowther and Old Fourah Bay College; 1s. Palm fruit gathering; £1, Forces Bugler. *Horiz*—3d., 6d. Sir Milton Margai; 4d., 1s. 3d. Lumley Beach, Freetown; 2s. 6d. Licensed diamond miner.

53 Royal Charter, 1799

55 Old House of Representatives, Freetown, 1924

(Des C. P. Rang (3d., 4d.), F. H. Burgess (1s. 3d.). Recess B.W.)

1961 (25 Nov). *Royal Visit. T* **53**, **55** *and similar designs. W* **52**. *P* 13½.

236 3d. black and rose-red 10 10
237 4d. black and violet 10 20
238 6d. black and yellow-orange 10 10
239 1s. 3d. black and blue 1·25 20
236/9 *Set of* 4 1·40 50

Designs: *Vert*—4d. King's Yard Gate, Freetown, 1817. *Horiz*—1s. 3d. Royal Yacht *Britannia* at Freetown.

57 Campaign Emblem

(Recess B.W.)

1962 (7 Apr). *Malaria Eradication. W* **52**. *P* 11 × 11½.

240 **57** 3d. carmine-red 10 10
241 1s. 3d. deep green 10 10

58 Fireball Lily **59** Jina-gbo

(Des M. Goaman. Photo Harrison)

1963 (1 Jan). *Flowers. Vert designs as T* **58** *(½d., 1½d., 3d., 4d., 1s., 2s. 6d., 5s., 10s.) or horiz as T* **59** *(others). Multicoloured. W* **52** *(sideways on vert designs). P* 14.

242 ½d. Type **58** 10 10
243 1d. Type **59** 10 10
244 1½d. Stereospermum 10 10
245 2d. Black-eyed Susan 10 10
246 3d. Beniseed 10 10
247 4d. Blushing Hibiscus 10 10
248 6d. Climbing Lily 15 10
249 1s. Beautiful Crinum 30 10
250 1s. 3d. Blue Bells 60 20
251 2s. 6d. Broken Hearts 60 30
252 5s. Ra-ponthi 80 80
253 10s. Blue Plumbago 2·00 1·50
254 £1 African Tulip Tree 7·50 7·00
242/254 *Set of* 13 11·00 9·00

71 Threshing Machine and Corn Bins

(Des V. Whiteley. Recess B.W.)

1963 (21 Mar). *Freedom from Hunger. T* **71** *and similar horiz design. W* **52**. *P* 11½ × 11.

255 3d. black and yellow-ochre 15 10
256 1s. 3d. sepia and emerald-green 35 10

Design:—1s. 3d. Girl with onion crop.

2ND YEAR OF INDEPENDENCE 19 PROGRESS 63 DEVELOPMENT 3d. (73)

2nd Year Independence Progress Development 1963 10d. (74)

(Optd by Govt Printer, Freetown)

1963 (27 Apr). *Second Anniv of Independence. Surch or optd as T* **73/4**. *(a) Postage.*

257 3d. on ½d. black & deep lilac (No. 210) (R.) 20 10
a. Small "c" in "INDEPENDENCE" 3·00 4·50
258 4d. on 1½d. black & ultram (No. 212) (Br.) 10 10
259 6d. on ½d. black & deep lilac (No. 210) (O.) 20 10
a. Small "c" in "INDEPENDENCE" 3·50 4·75
260 10d. on 3d. black & bright blue (No. 214) (R.) 40 10
261 1s. 6d. on 3d. black & brt bl (No. 214) (V.) 20 10
262 3s. 6d. on 3d. black & brt bl (No. 214) (Ult.) 30 15

(b) *Air. Additionally optd* "AIR MAIL"

263 7d. on 1½d. black & ultram (No. 212) (C.) 10 10
264 1s. 3d. on 1½d. blk & ultram (No. 212) (R.) 10 10
265 2s. 6d. black and chestnut (No. 219) (V.) 40 15
266 3s. on 3d. black & bright blue (No. 214) (B.) 30 15
267 6s. on 3d. black & bright blue (No. 214) (R.) 80 20
268 11s. on 10s. black and bright reddish purple (No. 221) (C.) 1·25 75
269 11s. on £1 black and orange (No. 222) (C.) £500 £180
257/268 *Set of* 12 3·50 1·60

75 Centenary Emblem

(Des M. Goaman. Recess B.W.)

1963 (1 Nov). *Centenary of Red Cross. T* **75** *and similar vert designs. W* **52**. *P* 11 × 11½.

270 3d. red and violet 30 10
271 6d. red and black 30 15
272 1s. 3d. red and deep bluish green 45 20
270/2 *Set of* 3 95 40

Designs:—6d. Red Cross emblem; 1s. 3d. Centenary emblem.

1853–1859–1963 Oldest Postal Service Newest G.P.O. in West Africa 1s. (78)

1853–1859–1963 Oldest Postage Stamp Newest G.P.O. in West Africa AIRMAIL (79)

1963 (4 Nov). *Postal Commemorations. Optd or surch by Govt Printer, Freetown. (a) Postage. As T* **78**.

273 3d. black and bright blue (No. 214) 10 10
a. "1895" for "1859" (R. 3/3) 2·50
274 4d. on 1½d. black & ultram (No. 212) (C.) 10 10
a. "1895" for "1859" (R. 1/2) 3·50
275 9d. on 1½d. black & ultram (No. 212) (V.) 10 10
276 1s. on 1s. 3d. turq-blue & vio (No. 231) (C.) 10 10
277 1s. 6d. on ½d. black & deep lilac (No. 210) (Mag.) 15 10
278 2s. on 3d. black & brt blue (No. 214) (Br.) 15 10
a. "1895" for "1859" (R. 4/10) 8·00

(b) *Air. As T* **79**

279 7d. on 3d. black & rose-red (No. 236) (Br.) 10 20
a. "1895" for "1859" (R. 3/6, 4/4) 3·00
280 1s. 3d. black and blue (No. 239) (C.) 75 40
a. "1895" for "1859" (R. 7/3) 12·00
281 2s. 6d. on 4d. turquoise-bl & scar (No. 228) 40 20
a. "1895" for "1859" (R. 7/3) 35·00
282 3s. on 3d. black and rose-red (No. 236) (V.) 75 90
a. "1895" for "1859" (R. 3/3) £180
283 6s. on 6d. black & yell-orge (No. 238) (Ult.) 60 60
a. "1895" for "1859" (R. 1/1) 40·00
284 £1 black and orange (No. 222) (R.) 11·00 13·00
a. "1895" for "1859" (R. 11/4) £160
273/84 *Set of* 12 12·50 14·00

The events commemorated are: 1853, "First Post Office"; 1859, "First Postage Stamps"; and 1963, "Newest G.P.O." in West Africa. Nos. 273, 278 have the opt. in five lines; Nos. 279, 282 in six lines (incl "AIRMAIL").

80 Lion Emblem and Map **81** Globe and Map

(Recess and litho Walsall Lithographic Co, Ltd)

1964 (10 Feb). *World's Fair, New York. Imperf. Self-Adhesive.*

(a) *Postage. T* **80**

285 1d. multicoloured 10 10
286 3d. multicoloured 10 10
a. Lion omitted
287 4d. multicoloured 10 10
288 6d. multicoloured 10 10
289 1s. multicoloured 10 10
a. "POSTAGE 1/-" omitted 35·00
290 2s. multicoloured 15 10
291 5s. multicoloured 25 20
a. "POSTAGE 5/-" omitted 35·00

(b) *Air. T* **81**

292 7d. multicoloured 10 10
293 9d. multicoloured 10 10
a. "AIR MAIL 9d." omitted
294 1s. 3d. multicoloured 10 10
a. "AIR MAIL 1/3" omitted 35·00
295 2s. 6d. multicoloured 15 10
296 3s. 6d. multicoloured 15 10
a. "AIR MAIL 3/6" omitted
297 6s. multicoloured 25 25
a. "AIR MAIL 6/–" omitted 40·00
298 11s. multicoloured 35 50
a. "AIR MAIL 11/-" omitted 42·00
285/298 *Set of* 14 1·40 1·40

Nos. 285/98 were issued in sheets of 30 (6 × 5) on green (postage) or yellow (airmail) backing paper with the emblems of Samuel Jones & Co. Ltd, self-adhesive paper-makers, on the back.

WARNING. These and later self-adhesive stamps should be kept on their backing paper except commercially used, which should be retained on cover or piece.

82 Inscription and Map **83** Pres. Kennedy and Map

(Recess and litho Walsall)

1964 (11 May). *President Kennedy Memorial Issue. Imperf. Self-adhesive. (a) Postage. Green backing paper.*

299 **82** 1d. multicoloured 10 10
300 3d. multicoloured 10 10
301 4d. multicoloured 10 10
302 6d. multicoloured 10 10
303 1s. multicoloured 10 10
304 2s. multicoloured 10 10
305 5s. multicoloured 25 20

(b) *Air. Yellow backing paper*

306 **83** 7d. multicoloured 10 10
307 9d. multicoloured 10 10
308 1s. 3d. multicoloured 10 10
309 2s. 6d. multicoloured 15 20
310 3s. 6d. multicoloured 15 20
311 6s. multicoloured 30 40
312 11s. multicoloured 45 60
299/312 *Set of* 14 1·50 1·75

(New Currency. 100 cents = 1 leone)

3c (84) AIRMAIL 7c (85) LE 1·00 (86)

1964–66. *Decimal currency. Various stamps surch locally.*

(i) *First issue* (4.8.64). (a) *Postage. Surch as T* **84**

313 1 c. on 6d. multicoloured (No. 248) (R.) 10 10
314 2 c. on 3d. black and rose-red (No. 236) 10 10
315 3 c. on 3d. multicoloured (No. 246) 10 10
a. Surch inverted £140
316 5 c. on ½d. chocolate and deep bluish green (No. 223) (B.) 10 10
317 8 c. on 3d. black & yell-ochre (No. 255) (R.) 10 10
318 10 c. on 1s. 3d. multicoloured (No. 250) (R.) 10 10
319 15 c. on 1s. multicoloured (No. 249) 15 10
320 25 c. on 6d. black & yell-orge (No. 238) (V.) 25 25
321 50 c. on 2s. 6d. dp green & blk (No. 232) (O.) 50 50

(b) *Air. As T* **85** *or* **86** *(Nos. 326/7)*

322 7 c. on 1s. 3d. sepia and emerald-green (No. 256) (B.) 10 10
323 20 c. on 4d. turquoise-blue & scarlet (No. 228) 20 15
324 30 c. on 10s. black and green (No. 234) (R.) 30 30
325 40 c. on 5s. black and red (No. 233) (B.) 40 40
326 1 l. on 1s. 3d. multicoloured (No. 308) (R.) 60 80
327 2 l. on 11s. multicoloured (No. 312) 1·10 1·40
313/327 *Set of* 15 3·50 3·75

1c (87) TWO LEONES Le 2·00 (88)

(ii) *Second issue* (20.1.65). *Surch as T* **87** *or* **88** *(Nos. 332/3)*

(a) *Postage*

328 1 c. on 3d. orange-brown and blue (No. 227) 10 10
329 2 c. on 1d. multicoloured (No. 299) 10 10
330 4 c. on 3d. multicoloured (No. 300) 10 10
a. Error. 4 c. on 1d. (No. 299)
b. Stamp omitted (in pair with normal)
331 5 c. on 2d. multicoloured (No. 245) 10 10
332 1 l. on 5s. multicoloured (No. 252) (Gold) 1·25 1·25
333 2 l. on £1 carmine-red & yellow (No. 235) (B.) 2·25 2·25
a. Surch double (B. + Blk.) — 65·00

(b) *Air*

334 7 c. on 7d. multicoloured (No. 306) (R.) 10 10
335 60 c. on 9d. multicoloured (No. 307) 50 45
328/35 *Set of* 8 3·75 3·75

On No. 330b the stamp became detached before the surcharge was applied so that "4c" appears on the backing paper.

(iii) *Third issue* (4.65). *Surch in figures (various sizes). (a) Postage*

336 1 c. on 1½d. black & emerald (No. 225) (R.) 10 10
337 2 c. on 3d. multicoloured (No. 300) 10 10
338 2 c. on 4d. multicoloured (No. 287) 10 10
339 3 c. on 1d. multicoloured (No. 243) 10 10
340 3 c. on 2d. black and ultram (No. 226) (R.) 10 10
341 5 c. on 1s. 3d. turq-bl & violet (No. 231) (R.) 10 10
a. Surch inverted
342 15 c. on 6d. multicoloured (No. 302) 80 50
343 15 c. on 1s. multicoloured (No. 303) (R.) 1·25 90
344 20 c. on 6d. black and purple (No. 229) (R.) 30 15
345 25 c. on 6d. multicoloured (No. 248) (R.) 35 20
346 50 c. on 3d. orange-brn & blue (No. 227) (R.) 80 55
347 60 c. on 5s. multicoloured (No. 291) (V.) 3·00 1·75
348 1 l. on 4d. multicoloured (No. 301) (R.) 3·25 2·75
349 2 l. on £1 carmine-red & yell (No. 235) (B.) 5·00 3·75

(b) Air

350		7 c. on 9d. multicoloured (No. 293)	15	10
336/350		Set of 15	14·00	9·75

TWO
2c Leones
(89) (90)

(iv) *Fourth issue* (9.11.65). *Surch as T* **89**. (a) *Postage*

351	**80**	1 c. on 6d. multicoloured (V.)	2·75	7·00
352		1 c. on 2s. multicoloured (V.)	2·75	7·00
353	**82**	1 c. on 2s. multicoloured (V.)	2·75	7·00
354		1 c. on 5s. multicoloured (V.)	2·75	7·00

(b) *Air*

355	**81**	2 c. on 1s. 3d. multicoloured	2·75	7·00
356	**83**	2 c. on 1s. 3d. multicoloured	2·75	7·00
357		2 c. on 3s. 6d. multicoloured	2·75	7·00
358	**81**	3 c. on 7d. multicoloured	2·75	7·00
359	**83**	3 c. on 9d. multicoloured	2·75	7·00
360	**81**	5 c. on 2s. 6d. multicoloured	2·75	7·00
361	**83**	5 c. on 2s. 6d. multicoloured	2·75	7·00
362	**81**	5 c. on 3s. 6d. multicoloured	2·75	7·00
363		5 c. on 6s. multicoloured	2·75	7·00
364	**83**	5 c. on 6s. multicoloured	2·75	7·00
351/364		Set of 14	35·00	90·00

(v) *Fifth issue* (28.1.66). *Air. No.* 374 *further surch with T* **90**

365		2 l. on 30 c. on 6d. multicoloured	2·50	2·00

IN MEMORIAM 2c
TWO GREAT LEADERS

(**91** Margai and Churchill)

1965 (19 May). *Sir Milton Margai and Sir Winston Churchill Commemoration. Nos.* 242/3, 245/50 *and* 252/4 *surch as T* **91** *on horiz designs or with individual portraits on vert designs as indicated.*

(a) *Postage*

366		2 c. on 1d. Type **59**	10	10
367		3 c. on 3d. Beniseed (Margai)	10	10
368		10 c. on 1s. Beautiful Crinum (Churchill)	20	10
369		20 c. on 1s. 3d. Blue Bells	40	10
370		50 c. on 4d. Blushing Hibiscus (Margai)	90	35
371		75 c. on 5s. Ra-ponthi (Churchill)	2·25	1·25

(b) *Air. Additionally optd* "AIR MAIL"

372		7 c. on 2d. Black-eyed Susan	20	10
373		15 c. on ½d. Type **58** (Margai)	35	10
374		30 c. on 6d. Climbing Lily (O. and W.)	1·25	25
375		1 l. on £1 African Tulip Tree	4·00	1·50
376		2 l. on 10s. Blue Plumbago (Churchill)	11·00	5·00
		a. Surch value omitted	£250	
366/376		Set of 11	18·00	8·00

92 Cola Plant and Nut

93 Arms of Sierra Leone

NEW INFORMATION

The editor is always interested to correspond with people who have new information that will improve or correct the Catalogue.

94 Inscription and Necklace

(Des M. Meers. Manufactured by Walsall Lithographic Co, Ltd)

1965 (Nov). *Imperf. Self-adhesive.*

A. *Embossed on silver foil, backed with paper bearing advertisements. Emerald, olive-yellow and carmine; denominations in colours given. Postage.*

377	**92**	1 c. emerald	25	10
378		2 c. carmine	25	10
379		3 c. olive-yellow	25	10
380		4 c. silver/*emerald*	30	10
381		5 c. silver/*carmine*	30	10

B. *Typo and embossed on cream paper backed with advertisements*

(a) *Postage*

382	**93**	20 c. multicoloured	1·00	35
383		50 c. multicoloured	2·50	1·60

(b) *Air*

384	**93**	40 c. multicoloured	2·25	1·60

C. *Foil-backed and litho, with advertisements on white paper backing (see footnote). Air*

385	**94**	7 c. multicoloured	55	15
386		15 c. multicoloured	85	50
377/386		Set of 10	7·50	4·25

The above stamps were issued in single form with attached tabs to remove the backing paper, with the exception of No. 385 which was in sheets of 25 bearing a single large advertisement on the back.

For other stamps in Type **92** see Nos. 421/31 and 435/42*a*. For 10 c. stamps in Type **93** see Nos. 433/*b*.

2c 15c
AIRMAIL
FIVE YEARS INDEPENDENCE 1961-1966 (95)
FIVE YEARS INDEPENDENCE 1961-1966 (96)

1966 (27 Apr). *Fifth Anniv of Independence. Various stamps surch.*

(a) *Postage. As T* **95**

387		1 c. on 6d. multicoloured (No. 248)	10	10
388		2 c. on 4d. multicoloured (No. 247)	10	10
389		3 c. on 1½d. black & ultram (No. 212) (B.)	10	10
390		8 c. on 1s. multicoloured (No. 249) (B.)	15	10
391		10 c. on 2s. 6d. multicoloured (No. 251) (B.)	15	10
392		20 c. on 2d. black and brown (No. 213) (B.)	20	10

(b) *Air. As T* **96**

393		7 c. on 3d. red and violet (No. 270)	10	10
394		15 c. on 1s. multicoloured (No. 249)	20	10
395		25 c. on 2s. 6d. multicoloured (No. 251)	40	60
396		50 c. on 1½d. multicoloured (No. 244)	60	80
397		1 l. on 4d. multicoloured (No. 247)	1·00	1·60
387/397		Set of 11	2·50	3·00

The inscription on No. 387 is in larger type.

97 Lion's Head

98 Map of Sierra Leone

(Des and embossed Walsall)

1966 (12 Nov). *First Sierra Leone Gold Coinage Commemoration. Circular designs, embossed on gold foil, backed with paper bearing advertisements. Imperf.* (a) *Postage.*

(i) ¼ *golde coin. Diameter* 1½ *in.*

398	**97**	2 c. magenta and yellow-orange	10	10
399	**98**	3 c. emerald and bright purple	10	10

(ii) ½ *golde coin. Diameter* 2⅛ *in.*

400	**97**	5 c. vermilion and ultramarine	10	10
401	**98**	8 c. turquoise-blue and black	15	15

(iii) 1 *golde coin. Diameter* 3¼ *in.*

402	**97**	25 c. violet and emerald	35	35
403	**98**	1 l. orange and cerise	2·25	2·25

(b) *Air.* (i) ¼ *golde coin. Diameter* 1½ *in.*

404	**98**	7 c. red-orange and cerise	10	10
405	**97**	10 c. cerise and greenish blue	15	15

(ii) ½ *golde coin. Diameter* 2⅛ *in.*

406	**98**	15 c. orange and cerise	25	25
407	**97**	30 c. bright purple and black	40	45

(iii) 1 *golde coin. Diameter* 3¼ *in.*

408	**98**	50 c. bright green and purple	75	75
409	**97**	2 l. black and emerald	3·50	3·50
398/409		Set of 12	7·25	7·25

12½ 17½ =17½
(99) (100) (101)

1967 (2 Dec). *Decimal Currency Provisionals. Surch as T* **99** *(Nos. 410/13), T* **100** *(Nos. 415/17) or T* **101** *(others).* (a) *Postage.*

410		6½ c. on 75 c. on 5s. mult (No. 371) (R.)	15	15
411		7½ c. on 75 c. on 5s. mult (No. 371) (S.)	15	15
412		9½ c. on 50 c. on 4d. mult (No. 370) (G.)	20	20
413		12½ c. on 20 c. on 1s. 3d. multicoloured (No. 369) (V.)	25	25
414		17½ c. on 50 c. multicoloured (No. 383)	1·40	1·40
415		17½ c. on 1 l. on 4d. mult (No. 348) (B.)	1·40	1·40
416		18½ c. on 1 l. on 4d. multicoloured (No. 348)	1·40	1·40
417		18½ c. on 60 c. on 5s. multicoloured (No. 347)	4·00	4·00
418		25 c. on 50 c. multicoloured (No. 383)	60	60

(b) *Air*

419		11½ c. on 40 c. multicoloured (No. 384)	20	20
420		25 c. on 40 c. multicoloured (No. 384)	60	60
410/20		Set of 11	9·25	9·25

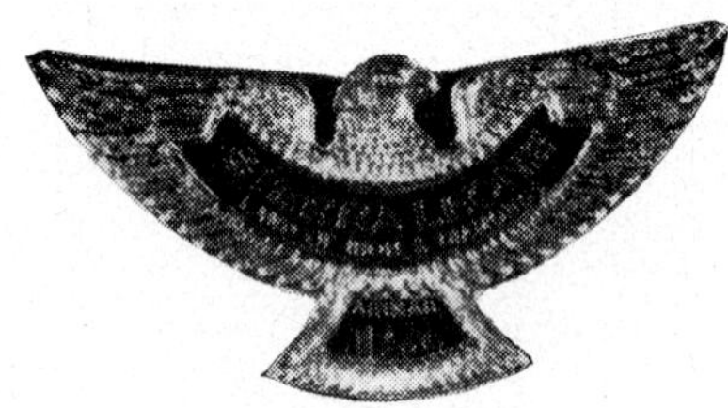

102 Eagle

(Manufactured by Walsall)

1967 (2 Dec)–**69**. *Decimal Currency. Imperf. Self-adhesive.*

(a) *Postage. As T* **92**, *but embossed on white paper, backed with paper bearing advertisements. Background colours given first, and value tablet colours in brackets*

421	**92**	½ c. carmine-red (carmine/*white*)	10	10
422		1 c. carmine (carmine/*white*)	15	10
423		1½ c. orange-yellow (green/*white*)	20	15
424		2 c. carmine-red (green/*white*)	35	10
425		2½ c. apple-green (yellow/*white*)	50	30
426		3 c. carmine-red (white/*carmine*)	30	10
427		3½ c. reddish purple (white/*green*)	50	30
428		4 c. carmine-red (white/*green*)	50	15
429		4½ c. dull green (green/*white*)	50	30
430		5 c. carmine (yellow/*white*)	50	15
431		5½ c. brown-red (green/*white*)	50	40

(b) *Air. T* **102** *embossed on black paper, backed with paper bearing advertisements; or, (No. 433), as T* **93**, *typo and embossed on cream paper, also with advertisements*

432	**102**	9½ c. red and gold/*black*	60	60
432*a*		9½ c. blue and gold/*black* (10.9.69)	3·50	3·00
433	**93**	10 c. multicoloured (red frame)	65	65
		a. Face value omitted		
433*b*		10 c. mult (black frame) (10.9.69)	3·75	3·25
434	**102**	15 c. green and gold/*black*	85	85
434*a*		15 c. red and gold/*black* (10.9.69)	4·00	4·00
421/34*a*		Set of 17	16·00	13·00

The ½, 1½, 2, 2½, 3, 3½ and 5 c. also exist without advertisements.

The footnote below Nos. 377/86 also applies here.

Although only released for collectors on 2 December, the 5 c. was known to be in use locally in February and the 3 c. in March. The 1 c. and 2 c. were also released locally some months earlier.

See also Nos. 538/44.

1968. *No advertisements on back, and colours in value tablet reversed. Background colours given first, and value tablet colours in brackets.*

435	**92**	½ c. carmine-red (white/*green*)	10	10
436		1 c. carmine (white/*carmine*)	15	10
437		2 c. carmine (white/*green*)	4·00	4·00
438		2½ c. apple-green (white/*yellow*)	4·50	4·50
439		3 c. carmine-red (carmine/*white*)	1·75	65

On Nos. 435 and 438, the figure "½" is larger than in Nos. 421 and 425.

It is believed that the ½ c. was released in February, the 2½ c. in April and the others in March.

The 1 c. also exists with advertisements on the backing paper.

The footnote below Nos. 377/86 also applies here.

1968–69. *No advertisements on back, colours changed and new value (7 c.). Background colours given first, and value tablet colours in brackets. (a) Postage.*

440	92	2 c. pink (white/*brown-lake*)	1·50	90
441		2½ c. deep bluish green (white/*orange*)	1·50	90
442		3½ c. olive-yellow (blue/*white*)	2·00	1·10
		(b) Air		
442*a*	92	7 c. yellow (carmine/*white*) (10.9.69)	6·00	3·00
435/42*a*		*Set of* 9	19·00	13·50

On Nos. 441/2 the fraction "½" is larger than in Nos. 425 and 427.

It is believed that the 3½ c. was released in March 1968 and the 2 and 2½ c. in May 1968.

The 2 c. also exists with advertisements on the backing paper.

The footnote below Nos. 377/86 also applies here.

103 Outline Map of Africa

(Litho Walsall)

1968 (25 Sept). *Human Rights Year. Each value comes in six types, showing different territories in yellow, as below. Imperf. Self-adhesive.*

A. Portuguese Guinea. D. Rhodesia.
B. South Africa. E. South West Africa.
C. Mozambique. F. Angola.

To indicate yellow territory use above letters as suffix to the following catalogue numbers.

(a) Postage

			Each Territory	
443	**103**	½ c. multicoloured	10	10
444		2 c. multicoloured	10	10
445		2½ c. multicoloured	10	10
446		3½ c. multicoloured	10	10
447		10 c. multicoloured	15	15
448		11½ c. multicoloured	20	20
449		15 c. multicoloured	25	25
		(b) Air		
450	**103**	7½ c. multicoloured	15	15
451		9½ c. multicoloured	20	20
452		14½ c. multicoloured	25	25
453		18½ c. multicoloured	30	30
454		25 c. multicoloured	40	40
455		1 l. multicoloured	6·50	5·50
456		2 l. multicoloured	14·00	12·00
443/56 Each territory		*Set of* 14	20·00	18·00
443/56 Six territories		*Set of* 84	£120	£100

Nos. 443/56 were issued in sheets of 30 (6 × 5) on backing paper depicting diamonds or the coat of arms on the reverse. The six types occur once in each horizontal row.

MEXICO 1968 OLYMPIC PARTICIPATION

POSTAGE
✱6½

(104)

1968 (30 Nov). *Mexico Olympics Participation.*

(a) Postage. No. 383 surch or optd (No. 461) as T **104**

457	**93**	6½ c. on 50 c. multicoloured	15	10
458		17½ c. on 50 c. multicoloured	20	15
459		22½ c. on 50 c. multicoloured	35	25
		a. Surch double	£170	
460		28½ c. on 50 c. multicoloured	45	35
461		50 c. multicoloured	70	50
		(b) Air. No. 384 surch or optd (No. 466) as T **104** *in red*		
462	**93**	6½ c. on 40 c. multicoloured	15	10
		a. Surch double	£190	
463		17½ c. on 40 c. multicoloured	20	15
464		22½ c. on 40 c. multicoloured	35	25
465		28½ c. on 40 c. multicoloured	45	35
466		40 c. multicoloured	70	50
457/66		*Set of* 10	3·25	2·50

105 1859 6d.

111 1965 15 c. Self-adhesive

(Litho Walsall)

1969 (1 Mar). *Fifth Anniv of World's First Self-adhesive Postage Stamps. Reproductions of earlier issues. Multicoloured. Imperf. Self-adhesive. (a) Postage. Vert designs.*

467	1 c. Type **105**	10	10
468	2 c. 1965 2 c. self-adhesive	10	10
469	3½ c. 1961 Independence 2 c. commemorative	10	10
470	5 c. 1965 20 c. self-adhesive	10	10
471	12½ c. 1948 Royal Silver Wedding £1 commemorative	30	15
472	1 l. 1923 £2	3·50	2·75
	(b) Air. Horiz designs		
473	7½ c. Type **111**	20	10
474	9½ c. 1967 9½ c. self-adhesive	20	10
475	20 c. 1964 1s. 3d. self-adhesive	40	25
476	30 c. 1964 President Kennedy Memorial 6s. commemorative self-adhesive	55	35
477	50 c. 1933 Centenary of Abolition of Slavery £1 commemorative	1·75	1·00
478	2 l. 1963 2nd Anniversary of Independence 11s. commemorative	15·00	13·00
467/478	*Set of* 12	20·00	16·00

Nos. 467 and 473 were issued with tabs as note under Nos. 377/86 and No. 474 exists with tabs and also in the normal version on backing paper.

All values are on white backing paper with advertisements printed on the reverse.

117 Ore Carrier, Globe and Flags of Sierra Leone and Japan

118 Ore Carrier, Map of Europe and Africa and Flags of Sierra Leone and Netherlands

The 3½ c., 9½ c., 2 l. and 10 c., 50 c., 1 l. are as T **118** but show respectively the flags of Great Britain and West Germany instead of the Netherlands.

(Litho Walsall)

1969 (10 July). *Pepel Port Improvements. Imperf. Self-adhesive, backed with paper bearing advertisements. (a) Postage.*

479	**117**	1 c. multicoloured	10	10
480	**118**	2 c. multicoloured	10	10
481	–	3½ c. multicoloured	10	10
482	–	10 c. multicoloured	10	10
483	**118**	18½ c. multicoloured	20	25
484	–	50 c. multicoloured	70	85
		(b) Air		
485	**117**	7½ c. multicoloured	10	10
486	–	9½ c. multicoloured	15	10
487	**117**	15 c. multicoloured	20	25
488	**118**	25 c. multicoloured	30	35
489	–	1 l. multicoloured	1·25	1·50
490	–	2 l. multicoloured	2·50	3·75
479/90		*Set of* 12	5·00	6·50

119 African Development Bank Emblem

120 Boy Scouts Emblem in "Diamond"

(Litho and embossed Walsall)

1969 (10 Sept). *Fifth Anniv of African Development Bank. Self-adhesive, backed with paper bearing advertisements. Imperf.*

		(a) Postage		
491	**119**	3½ c. deep green, gold and blue	25	20
		(b) Air		
492	**119**	9½ c. bluish violet, gold and apple-green	35	45

(Litho Walsall)

1969 (6 Dec). *Boy Scouts Diamond Jubilee. T* **120** *and similar design. Imperf. Self-adhesive, backed with paper bearing advertisements.*

		(a) Postage		
493	**120**	1 c. multicoloured	10	10
494		2 c. multicoloured	10	10
495		3½ c. multicoloured	15	10
496		4½ c. multicoloured	15	15
497		5 c. multicoloured	15	15
498		75 c. multicoloured	9·00	5·00
		(b) Air		
499	–	7½ c. multicoloured	35	30
500	–	9½ c. multicoloured	45	35
501	–	15 c. multicoloured	70	50
502	–	22 c. multicoloured	1·25	70
503	–	55 c. multicoloured	7·50	4·00
504	–	3 l. multicoloured	85·00	60·00
493/504		*Set of* 12	95·00	65·00

Design: *Octagonal Shape* (65 × 51 *mm*)—Nos. 499/504 Scout saluting, Baden-Powell and badge.

(121)

1970 (28 Mar). *Air. No. 443 surch as T* **121**.

			Each Territory	
505	**103**	7½ c. on ½ c. multicoloured (G.)	20	10
506		9½ c. on ½ c. multicoloured (P.)	20	10
507		15 c. on ½ c. multicoloured (B.)	40	25
508		28 c. on ½ c. multicoloured (G.)	70	55
509		40 c. on ½ c. multicoloured (B.)	1·25	1·40
510		2 l. on ½ c. multicoloured (Sil.)	6·00	7·50
505/10 Each Territory		*Set of* 6	8·00	9·00
505/10 Six Territories		*Set of* 36	45·00	48·00

122 Expo Symbol and Maps of Sierra Leone and Japan

(Litho Walsall)

1970 (22 June). *World Fair, Osaka. T* **122** *and similar design. Imperf. Self-adhesive, backed with paper bearing advertisements.*

		(a) Postage		
511	**122**	2 c. multicoloured	10	10
512		3½ c. multicoloured	10	10
513		10 c. multicoloured	15	10
514		12½ c. multicoloured	15	10
515		20 c. multicoloured	20	10
516		45 c. multicoloured	45	45
		(b) Air		
517	–	7½ c. multicoloured	10	10
518	–	9½ c. multicoloured	15	10
519	–	15 c. multicoloured	20	10
520	–	25 c. multicoloured	40	20
521	–	50 c. multicoloured	55	50
522	–	3 l. multicoloured	3·00	4·00
511/22		*Set of* 12	4·50	5·00

Design: *Chrysanthemum shape* (43 × 42 *mm*)—Nos. 517/22 Maps of Sierra Leone and Japan.

123 Diamond

124 Palm Nut

(Litho and embossed Walsall)

1970 (3 Oct). *Imperf. Self-adhesive, backed with paper bearing advertisements.*

523	**123**	1 c. multicoloured	10	10
524		1½ c. multicoloured	10	10
525		2 c. multicoloured	10	10
526		2½ c. multicoloured	10	10
527		3 c. multicoloured	15	10
528		3½ c. multicoloured	15	10
529		4 c. multicoloured	15	10
530		5 c. multicoloured	20	10
531	**124**	6 c. multicoloured	25	10
532		7 c. multicoloured	30	15
533		8½ c. multicoloured	40	15
534		9 c. multicoloured	40	15
535		10 c. multicoloured	45	15
536		11½ c. multicoloured	55	20
537		18½ c. multicoloured	75	45

1970 (3 Oct). *Air. As T* **102**, *but embossed on white paper. Backed with paper bearing advertisements.*

538	**102**	7½ c. gold and red	35	10
539		9½ c. rose and bright green	40	10
540		15 c. pink and greenish blue ..	55	20
541		25 c. gold and purple..	90	50
542		50 c. bright green and orange ..	2·00	1·50
543		1 l. royal blue and silver	5·00	6·50
544		2 l. ultramarine and gold	10·00	15·00
523/44		.. .. *Set of* 22	21·00	23·00

126 "Jewellery Box" and Sewa Diadem

(Litho and embossed Walsall)

1970 (30 Dec). *Diamond Industry. T* **126** *and similar design. Imperf (backing paper roul 20). Self-adhesive, backed with paper bearing advertisements. (a) Postage.*

545	**126**	2 c. multicoloured	30	10
546		3½ c. multicoloured	30	10
547		10 c. multicoloured	55	15
548		12½ c. multicoloured	75	25
549		40 c. multicoloured	1·75	1·00
550		1 l. multicoloured	9·50	8·00
		(b) Air		
551	–	7½ c. multicoloured	50	10
552	–	9½ c. multicoloured	60	10
553	–	15 c. multicoloured	95	30
554	–	25 c. multicoloured	1·40	60
555	–	75 c. multicoloured	5·00	4·00
556	–	2 l. multicoloured	22·00	17·00
545/556		.. .. .. *Set of* 12	38·00	28·00

Design: *Horiz* (63 × 61 *mm*)—Nos. 551/6, Diamond and curtain.

ALTERED CATALOGUE NUMBERS

Any Catalogue numbers altered from the last edition are shown as a list in the introductory pages.

10c
AIRMAIL

127 "Traffic Changeover" **(128)**

1971 (1 Mar). *Changeover to Driving on the Right of the Road. Imperf (backing paper roul 20). Self-adhesive, backed with paper bearing advertisements. (a) Postage.*

557	**127**	3½ c. yellow-orange, ultram & blk	1·25	40
		(b) Air		
558	**127**	9½ c. ultramarine, yell-orge & blk	1·75	1·60

1971 (1 Mar). *Air. Surch as T* **128**, *in red (No.* 559), *blue (Nos.* 560 *and* 562) *or black (others).*

559	10 c. on 2d. black and ultramarine (No. 226) ..	40	20
560	20 c. on 1s. chocolate & yell-orge (No. 230) ..	70	45
561	50 c. on 1d. multicoloured (No. 243)	1·25	1·10
562	70 c. on 30 c. multicoloured (No. 476).. ..	2·00	2·75
563	1 l. on 30 c. multicoloured (No. 476).. ..	3·00	3·75
559/63	.. .. *Set of* 5	6·50	7·50

REPUBLIC

129 Flag and Lion's Head **130** Pres. Siaka Stevens

(Manufactured by Walsall)

1971 (27 Apr). *Tenth Anniv of Independence. T* **129** *and similar design. Imperf. Self-adhesive, backed with paper bearing advertisements. (a) Postage.*

564	**129**	2 c. multicoloured	10	10
565		3½ c. multicoloured	10	10
566		10 c. multicoloured	15	10
567		12½ c. multicoloured	20	10
568		40 c. multicoloured	70	40
569		1 l. multicoloured	1·50	2·25
		(b) Air		
570	–	7½ c. multicoloured	15	10
571	–	9½ c. multicoloured	15	10
572	–	15 c. multicoloured	25	10
573	–	25 c. multicoloured	35	35
574	–	75 c. multicoloured	1·25	1·50
575	–	2 l. multicoloured	4·00	6·00
564/75		.. .. *Set of* 12	8·00	10·00

Design: *"Map" shaped as T* **129**—Nos. 570/5, Bugles and lion's head.

(Litho D.L.R.)

1972 (5 Dec)–**78.** *Multicoloured; colour of background given. P* 13.
A. *Glazed ordinary paper.*
B. *Chalk-surfaced paper* (1975–78).

			A		B	
576	**130**	1 c. light rose-lilac ..	10	10	20	30
577		2 c. lavender (*shades*) ..	10	10	20	20
578		4 c. cobalt	10	10	45	30
579		5 c. light cinnamon ..	10	10	45	20
580		7 c. light rose	15	10	60	20
581		10 c. olive-bistre	15	10	60	20
582		15 c. pale yellow-green ..	25	15	1·00	40
583		18 c. yellow-ochre	25	15	1·00	65
584		20 c. pale greenish blue ..	30	15	1·25	75
585		25 c. orange-ochre	35	15	1·25	75
586		50 c. light turquoise-green	1·00	55	3·50	2·00
587		1 l. bright reddish mauve (*shades*)	1·50	1·00	4·50	3·25
588		2 l. orange-salmon ..	3·50	3·50	10·00	14·00
589		5 l. light stone	8·00	8·50	17·00	30·00
576/89		.. .. .. *Set of* 14	14·00	13·00	38·00	48·00

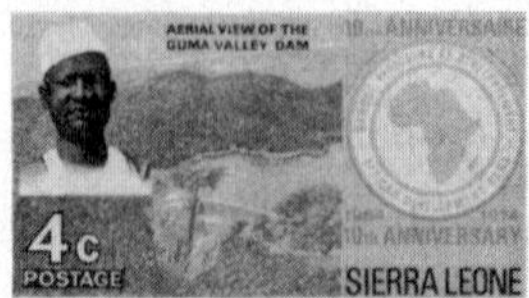

131 Guma Valley Dam and Bank Emblem

(Litho D.L.R.)

1975 (14 Jan). *Tenth Anniv of African Development Bank* (1974). *P* 13½ × 13. *(a) Postage.*

590	**131**	4 c. multicoloured	45·00	28·00
		(b) Air		
591	**131**	15 c. multicoloured	1·00	80

132 Opening Ceremony

(Litho D.L.R.)

1975 (25 Aug). *Opening of New Congo Bridge and President Stevens' 70th Birthday. P* 12½ × 13. *(a) Postage.*

592	**132**	5 c. multicoloured	5·00	1·75
		(b) Air		
593	**132**	20 c. multicoloured	70	25

133 Presidents Tolbert and Stevens, and Handclasp

(Litho D.L.R.)

1975 (3 Oct). *1st Anniv of Mano River Union. P* 12½ × 13. *(a) Postage.*

594	**133**	4 c. multicoloured	75	50
		(b) Air		
595	**133**	15 c. multicoloured	35	25

134 "Quaid-i-Azam" (Mohammed Ali Jinnah) **135** Queen Elizabeth II

(Litho Pakistan Security Printing Corporation)

1977 (28 Jan). *Birth Centenary of Mohammed Ali Jinnah (Quaid-i-Azam). P* 13.

596	**134**	30 c. multicoloured	75	30

(Des A. Larkins. Litho De La Rue, Colombia)

1977 (28 Nov). *Silver Jubilee. P* 12½ × 12.

597	**135**	5 c. multicoloured	10	10
598		1 l. multicoloured	90	80

136 College Buildings **137** St. Edward's Crown and Sceptres

(Des A. Larkins. Litho De La Rue, Colombia)

1977 (19 Dec). *150th Anniv of Fourah Bay College. T* **136** *and similar vert design. Multicoloured. P* 12 × 12½ (5 c.) *or* 12½ × 12 (20 c.).

599	5 c. Type **136**	10	10
600	20 c. The old college	35	30

(Des L. Curtis. Litho Harrison)

1978 (14 Sept). *25th Anniv of Coronation. T* **137** *and similar vert designs. Multicoloured. P* 14½ × 14.

601	5 c. Type **137**	10	10
602	50 c. Queen Elizabeth II in Coronation Coach	30	40
603	1 l. Queen Elizabeth II and Prince Philip ..	40	60
601/3	.. .. *Set of* 3	65	1·00

138 *Myrina silenus* **139** Young Child's Face

(Des J. Cooter. Litho Questa)

1979 (9 Apr). *Butterflies (1st series). T* **138** *and similar horiz designs. Multicoloured. P* 14½ × 14.

604 5 c. Type **138** .. 10 10
605 15 c. *Papilio nireus* .. 25 15
606 25 c. *Catacroptera cloanthe* .. 40 15
607 1 l. *Druryia antimachus* .. 2·00 1·50
604/7 .. *Set of* 4 2·50 1·60

See also Nos. 646/9.

(Des BG Studio. Litho Walsall)

1979 (13 Aug). *International Year of the Child and 30th Anniv of S.O.S. International (child distress organisation). T* **139** *and similar vert designs. Multicoloured. W* w **14**. *P* 14 × 13½.

608 5 c. Type **139** .. 10 10
609 27 c. Young child with baby .. 20 25
610 1 l. Mother with young child .. 50 1·10
608/10 .. *Set of* 3 65 1·25
MS611 114 × 84 mm. No. 610. Wmk sideways .. 1·00 1·75

140 Presidents Stevens (Sierra Leone) and Tolbert (Liberia), Dove with Letter and Bridge

(Des L. Curtis. Litho Questa)

1979 (3 Oct). *5th Anniv of Mano River Union and 1st Anniv of Postal Union. W* w **14** *(sideways). P* 13½ × 14.

612 **140** 5 c. sepia, orange and greenish yellow .. 10 10
613 22 c. sepia, orge-yell & brt reddish violet 10 15
614 27 c. sepia, light blue and orange .. 10 15
615 35 c. sepia, blue-green and orange-red .. 15 20
616 1 l. sepia, brt reddish violet & lt blue .. 50 1·00
612/16 .. *Set of* 5 75 1·40
MS617 144 × 73 mm. No. 616 .. 55 1·00

141 Great Britain 1848 10d. Stamp

142 Knysna Touraco

(Des J.W. Litho Walsall)

1979 (19 Dec). *Death Centenary of Sir Rowland Hill. T* **141** *and similar vert designs showing stamps. W* w **14**. *P* 14 × 14½.

618 10 c. black, orange-brown and new blue .. 15 10
619 15 c. black, brown-ochre and greenish blue .. 25 15
620 50 c. black, carmine and greenish yellow .. 60 70
618/20 .. *Set of* 3 90 85
MS621 90 × 99 mm. 1 l. black, carm-red & flesh .. 60 80

Designs:—15 c. 1872 4d.; 50 c. 1961 £1 Independence commemorative; 1 l. 1912 £1.

(Des J.W. Litho Format)

1980 (29 Jan)–**82**. *Birds. Multicoloured designs as T* **142**. *W* w **14** *(sideways on* 1, 2, 3, 5, 7 *c.,* 1, 2 *and* 5 *l.). P* 14.

A. *No imprint*. B. *Imprint date at foot*

No.			A		B	
622	1 c.	Type **142**	20	30	30	50
623	2 c.	Olive-bellied Sunbird	20	30	40	50
624	3 c.	Western Black-headed Oriole	50	30	30	50
625	5 c.	Spur-winged Goose	50	20	30	30
626	7 c.	Didric Cuckoo	40	20	4·25	2·25
627	10 c.	Grey Parrot (*vert*)	50	30	30	35
628	15 c.	Blue Quail (*vert*)	75	60	40	75
629	20 c.	African Wood Owl (*vert*)	1·00	90	40	75
630	30 c.	Great Blue Turaco (*vert*)	1·00	95	50	1·00
631	40 c.	Blue-breasted Kingfisher (*vert*)	1·25	1·00	60	1·25
632	50 c.	Black Crake (*vert*)	1·25	1·10	60	1·50
633	1 l.	Hartlaub's Duck	1·40	1·75	60	1·75
634	2 l.	Black Bee Eater	2·50	3·50	1·75	4·50
635	5 l.	Barrow's Bustard	5·50	8·50	4·25	8·50
622/35		*Set of* 14	15·00	18·00	13·50	22·00

Dates of issue: No Imprint—29.1.80. With Imprint—21.12.81 5, 10, 15, 30, 40, 50 c., 1 l., 2 l., 5 l.; 15.3.82 1, 2, 3, 20 c.; 11.10.82 7 c.

Nos. 622A/35A exist imperforate from stock dispersed by the liquidator of Format International Security Printers Ltd.

For similar stamps, but without watermark, see Nos. 760/73.

143 Paul P. Harris (founder), President Stevens of Sierra Leone and Rotary Emblem

(Des BG Studio. Litho Walsall)

1980 (23 Feb). *75th Anniv of Rotary International. W* w **14** *(sideways). P* 13½.

636 **143** 5 c. multicoloured .. 10 10
637 27 c. multicoloured .. 10 10
638 50 c. multicoloured .. 20 25
639 1 l. multicoloured .. 40 55
636/9 .. *Set of* 4 65 85

144 *Maria*, 1884

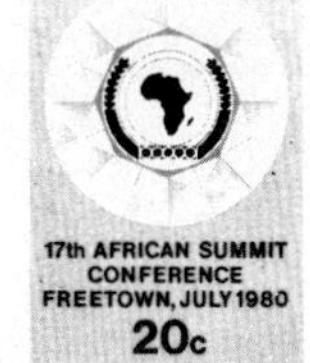

145 Organisation for African Unity Emblem

(Des L. Dunn. Litho Walsall)

1980 (6 May). *"London 1980" International Stamp Exhibition. Mail Ships. T* **144** *and similar horiz designs. Multicoloured. W* w **14** *(sideways). P* 14.

640 6 c. Type **144** .. 10 10
641 31 c. *Tarquah*, 1902 .. 25 30
642 50 c. *Aureol*, 1951 .. 40 60
643 1 l. *Africa Palm*, 1974 .. 55 95
640/3 .. *Set of* 4 1·10 1·75

(Des L. Curtis. Litho Questa)

1980 (1 July). *African Summit Conference, Freetown. W* w **14**. *P* 14 × 14½.

644 **145** 20 c. black, light blue and bright purple 10 10
645 1 l. black, bright purple and light blue 45 45

146 *Graphium policenes*

147 Arrival at Freetown Airport

(Des I. Loe. Litho Questa)

1980 (6 Oct). *Butterflies (2nd series). T* **146** *and similar vert designs. Multicoloured. W* w **14**. *P* 13½.

646 5 c. Type **146** .. 10 10
647 27 c. *Charaxes varanes* .. 30 15
648 35 c. *Charaxes brutus* .. 35 25
649 1 l. *Euphaedra zaddachi* .. 1·10 1·40
646/9 .. *Set of* 4 1·75 1·75

(Des L. Curtis. Litho Format)

1980 (5 Dec). *Tourism. T* **147** *and similar vert designs. Multicoloured. W* w **14**. *P* 13½.

650 6 c. Type **147** .. 10 10
651 26 c. Welcome to tourists .. 20 20
652 31 c. Freetown cotton tree .. 25 25
653 40 c. Beinkongo Falls .. 30 30
654 50 c. Sports facilities .. 40 40
655 1 l. African Elephant .. 95 95
650/5 .. *Set of* 6 2·00 2·00

148 Servals

149 Soldiers (Defence)

(Des P. Oxenham. Litho Questa)

1981 (28 Feb). *Wild Cats. T* **148** *and similar horiz designs. Multicoloured. W* w **14** *(sideways). P* 13½ × 14.

656 6 c. Type **148** .. 10 10
a. Horiz pair. Nos. 656/7 .. 10 10
657 6 c. Serval cubs .. 10 10
658 31 c. African Golden Cats .. 30 30
a. Horiz pair. Nos. 658/9 .. 60 60
659 31 c. African Golden Cat cubs .. 30 30
660 50 c. Leopards .. 45 45
a. Horiz pair. Nos. 660/1 .. 90 90
661 50 c. Leopard cubs .. 45 45
662 1 l. Lions .. 80 80
a. Horiz pair. Nos. 662/3 .. 1·60 1·60
663 1 l. Lion cubs .. 80 80
656/63 .. *Set of* 8 2·75 2·75

The two designs of each value were printed together, *se-tenant*, in horizontal pairs throughout the sheet, forming composite designs.

(Des G. Hutchins. Litho Walsall)

1981 (18 Apr). *20th Anniv of Independence and 10th Anniv of Republic. National Services. T* **149** *and similar multicoloured designs. W* w **14** *(sideways on* 31 *c. and* 1 *l.). P* 14½.

664 6 c. Type **149** .. 30 10
665 31 c. Nurses administering first aid, and ambulance (Health) (*horiz*) .. 75 20
666 40 c. Controlling traffic (Police Force) .. 1·25 30
667 1 l. Patrol boat (Coastguard) (*horiz*) .. 2·00 1·25
664/7 .. *Set of* 4 4·00 1·60

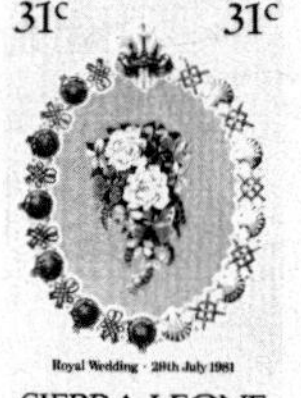

150 Wedding Bouquet from Sierra Leone

151 Sandringham

(Des J.W. Litho Harrison)

1981 (22 July). *Royal Wedding (1st issue). T* **150** *and similar vert designs. Multicoloured. W* w **14**. *P* 14.

668 31 c. Type **150** .. 20 20
669 45 c. Prince Charles as helicopter pilot .. 25 30
670 1 l. Prince Charles and Lady Diana Spencer 45 1·10
668/70 .. *Set of* 3 80 1·40

(Des J.W. Litho Format)

1981 (9 Sept–30 Nov). *Royal Wedding (2nd issue). T* **151** *and similar vert designs. Multicoloured.* (a) *Sheet stamps. P* 12.

671 35 c. Type **151** .. 30 35
672 60 c. Prince Charles in outdoor clothes .. 50 40
673 1 l. 50, Prince Charles and Lady Diana Spencer .. 1·00 1·40
671/3 .. *Set of* 3 1·60 1·90
MS674 96 × 83 mm. 3 l. Royal Landau. P 14 .. 1·75 1·75

(b) *Booklet stamps. P* 14 (30 Nov)

675 70 c. Type **151** .. 75 90
a. Booklet pane. Nos. 675/6 × 2 plus two printed labels .. 3·00
676 1 l. 30, As 60 c. .. 1·00 1·25
677 2 l. As 1 l. 50 .. 3·25 3·50
a. Booklet pane of 1 .. 3·25
675/7 .. *Set of* 3 4·50 5·00

Nos. 671/3 were each printed in small sheets of 6 including one *se-tenant* stamp-size label.

152 "Physical Recreation"

153 Pineapples

(Des BG Studio. Litho Questa)

1981 (30 Sept). *25th Anniv of Duke of Edinburgh Award Scheme and President's Award Scheme Publicity. T* **152** *and similar vert designs. Multicoloured. W* w **14**. *P* 14.

678 6 c. Type **152** .. 10 10
679 31 c. "Community service" .. 15 10
680 1 l. Duke of Edinburgh .. 40 40
681 1 l. President Siaka Stevens .. 40 40
678/81 .. *Set of* 4 90 85

(Des BG Studio. Litho Questa)

1981 (16 Oct). *World Food Day (1st issue). T* **153** *and similar vert designs. Multicoloured. W* w **14**. *P* 14.

682 6 c. Type **153** .. 10 10
683 31 c. Groundnuts .. 15 10
684 50 c. Cassava fruits .. 20 15
685 1 l. Rice plants .. 50 50
682/5 .. *Set of* 4 75 70

154 Groundnuts

(Litho Format)

1981 (2 Nov). *World Food Day (2nd issue). Agricultural Industry. T* **154** *and similar horiz designs. Multicoloured. P* 14½.

686 6 c. Type **154** .. 10 10
687 31 c. Cassava .. 25 10
688 50 c. Rice .. 45 25
689 1 l. Pineapples .. 90 70
686/9 .. *Set of* 4 1·50 1·00

Examples of Nos. 686/9 *se-tenant* come from unissued sheetlets dispersed by the liquidator of Format International Security Printers Ltd.

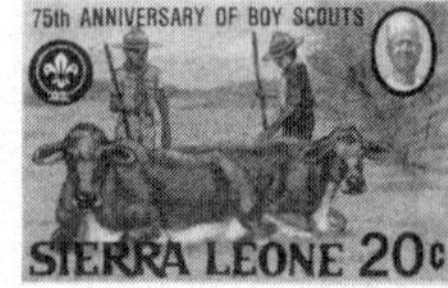

50c 50c

155 Scouts with Cattle (**156**)

(Des M. Diamond. Litho Questa)

1982 (23 Aug). *75th Anniv of Boy Scout Movement. T* **155** *and similar horiz designs. Multicoloured. P* 14.
690 20 c. Type **155** 25 10
691 50 c. Scouts picking flowers 50 40
692 1 l. Lord Baden-Powell .. .. .. 90 1·00
693 2 l. Scouts fishing .. .. 1·90 2·00
690/3 .. .. *Set of* 4 3·25 3·00
MS694 101 × 70 mm. 3 l. Scouts raising flag .. 2·75 3·25

1982 (30 Aug)–**85**. *Nos.* 668/74 *surch as T* **156**.
695 50 c. on 31 c. Type **150** 40 40
696 50 c. on 35 c. Type **151** 40 40
697 50 c. on 45 c. Prince Charles as helicopter pilot 40 40
698 50 c. on 60 c. Prince Charles in outdoor clothes 40 40
699 90 c. on 1 l. Prince Charles and Lady Diana Spencer 75 75
699*a* 1 l. 30 on 60 c. Prince Charles in outdoor clothes (1985) .. .. 1·75 1·75
699*b* 2 l. on 35 c. Type **151** (1985) .. .. 2·75 2·75
ba. Surch double .. .. 20·00
700 2 l. on 1 l. 50, Prince Charles and Lady Diana Spencer .. .. 1·50 1·50
700*a* 8 l. on 1 l. 50, Prince Charles and Lady Diana Spencer (1985) .. .. 8·75 8·75
695/700*a* .. .. *Set of* 9 15·00 15·00
MS701 95 × 83 mm. 3 l. 50 on 3 l. Royal Landau .. 1·75 1·75
Nos. 699*a/b* and 700*a* also exist surcharged in blue from a limited printing (*Price for set of* 3 £50 *mint*).

157 Heading

158 Prince and Princess of Wales

(Des PAD Studio. Litho Questa)

1982 (7 Sept). *World Cup Football Championship, Spain. T* **157** *and similar vert designs. Multicoloured. P* 14.
702 20 c. Type **157** 35 15
703 30 c. Dribbling 50 20
704 1 l. Tackling .. .. 1·60 1·40
705 2 l. Goalkeeping .. .. 2·75 3·00
702/5 .. .. *Set of* 4 4·75 4·25
MS706 92 × 75 mm. 3 l. Shooting .. .. 4·00 3·00
Nos. 702/5 were each printed in small sheets of 6 including one, *se-tenant*, stamp-sized label.

(Des PAD Studio. Litho Questa)

1982 (15 Sept). *21st Birthday of Princess of Wales. T* **158** *and similar vert designs. Multicoloured. P* 14½ × 14.
707 31 c. Caernarvon Castle 35 15
708 50 c. Type **158** 50 25
709 2 l. Princess of Wales .. .. .. 1·40 1·50
707/9 .. .. *Set of* 3 2·00 1·75
MS710 103 × 75 mm. 3 l. Princess of Wales (*different*) .. .. 2·00 2·00
Nos. 707/9 also exist in sheetlets of 5 stamps and 1 label.

1982 (15 Oct). *Birth of Prince William of Wales. Nos.* 707/10 *optd with T* **212a** *of Jamaica.*
711 31 c. Caernarvon Castle 35 15
712 50 c. Type **158** 50 25
713 2 l. Princess of Wales .. .. .. 1·40 1·50
711/13 .. .. *Set of* 3 2·00 1·75
MS714 103 × 75 mm. 3 l. Princess of Wales (*different*) .. .. 2·00 2·00
Nos. 711/13 also exist in sheetlets of 5 stamps and 1 label.

159 Washington with Troops

160 Temptation of Christ

(Des C. Mill. Litho Questa)

1982 (30 Oct). *250th Birth Anniv of George Washington. T* **159** *and similar multicoloured designs. P* 14.
715 6 c. Type **159** 10 10
716 31 c. Portrait of Washington (*vert*) 20 20
717 50 c. Washington with horse 35 35
718 1 l. Washington standing on battlefield (*vert*) 65 80
715/18 .. .. *Set of* 4 1·10 1·25
MS719 103 × 71 mm. 2 l. Washington at home .. 1·00 1·50

(Des N. Waldman Studio. Litho Questa)

1982 (18 Nov). *Christmas. Stained-glass Windows. T* **160** *and similar vert designs. Multicoloured. P* 13½ × 14.
720 6 c. Type **160** 10 10
721 31 c. Baptism of Christ 15 20
722 50 c. Annunciation 20 40
723 1 l. Nativity 55 90
720/3 .. .. *Set of* 4 85 1·40
MS724 74 × 104 mm. 2 l. Mary and Joseph .. 70 1·10

WORLD CUP
WINNERS
ITALY (3)
vs.
W. GERMANY (1)

(**161**)

162 Long Snouted Crocodile

1982 (2 Dec). *World Cup Football Championship Winners. Nos.* 702/6 *optd with T* **161**.
725 20 c. Type **157** 15 20
726 30 c. Dribbling 20 30
727 1 l. Tackling 55 55
728 2 l. Goalkeeping .. .. 1·00 1·75
725/8 .. .. *Set of* 4 1·75 2·75
MS729 91 × 75 mm. 3 l. Shooting .. .. 1·00 2·00

(Des G. Drummond. Litho Questa)

1982 (10 Dec). *Death Centenary of Charles Darwin. T* **162** *and similar horiz designs. Multicoloured. P* 14.
730 6 c. Type **162** 30 10
731 31 c. Rainbow Lizard 85 55
732 50 c. River Turtle .. .. 1·25 95
733 1 l. Chameleon .. .. 2·00 2·50
730/3 .. .. *Set of* 4 4·00 3·75
MS734 90 × 70 mm. 2 l. Royal Python (*vert*) .. 2·25 2·75

163 Diogenes

(Des Design Images. Litho Questa)

1983 (28 Jan). *500th Birth Anniv of Raphael. Details from painting "The School of Athens". T* **163** *and similar multicoloured designs. P* 13½.
735 6 c. Type **163** 10 10
736 31 c. Euclid, Ptolemy, Zoroaster, Raphael and Sodoma 20 30
737 50 c. Euclid and his pupils 35 45
738 2 l. Pythagoras, Francesco Maria della Rovere and Heraclitus .. .. .. 1·25 1·40
735/8 .. .. *Set of* 4 1·60 2·00
MS739 101 × 126 mm. 3 l. Plato and Aristotle (*vert*) 1·25 2·00

164 Agricultural Training

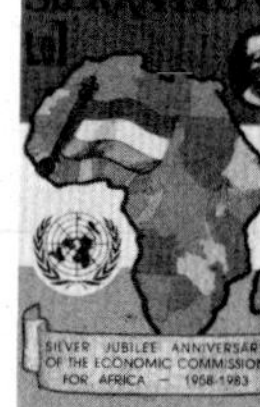

165 Map of Africa and Flag of Sierra Leone

(Litho Questa)

1983 (14 Mar). *Commonwealth Day. T* **164** *and similar horiz designs. Multicoloured. P* 14.
740 6 c. Type **164** 10 10
741 10 c. Tourism development 10 10
742 50 c. Broadcasting training 45 45
743 1 l. Airport services 90 90
740/3 .. .. *Set of* 4 1·40 1·40

(Des M. Diamond. Litho J.W.)

1983 (29 Apr). *25th Anniv of Economic Commission for Africa. P* 13.
744 **165** 1 l. multicoloured .. .. .. 80 1·10

166 Chimpanzees in Tree

(Des J. Iskowitz. Litho Questa)

1983 (19 May). *Endangered Species. T* **166** *and similar multicoloured designs. P* 14.
745 6 c. Type **166** 50 15
746 10 c. Three Chimpanzees (*vert*) 60 15
747 31 c. Chimpanzees swinging in tree (*vert*) .. 1·40 50
748 60 c. Group of Chimpanzees .. .. .. 2·50 2·75
745/8 .. .. *Set of* 4 4·50 3·25
MS749 115 × 80 mm. 3 l. African Elephant .. 1·50 2·25

167 Traditional Communications

168 Montgolfier Balloon, Paris, 1783

(Des R. Sauber. Litho Questa)

1983 (14 July). *World Communications Year. T* **167** *and similar horiz designs. Multicoloured. P* 14.
750 6 c. Type **167** 10 10
751 10 c. Mail via Mano River 10 10
752 20 c. Satellite ground station 10 10
753 1 l. British packet, *circa* 1805 .. .. 55 65
750/3 .. .. *Set of* 4 70 80
MS754 115 × 85 mm. 2 l. Telecommunications .. 80 1·25

(Des Artists International. Litho Questa)

1983 (31 Aug). *Bicentenary of Manned Flight. T* **168** *and similar multicoloured designs. P* 14.
755 6 c. Type **168** 20 10
756 20 c. *Deutschland* airship, Berlin, 1879 (*horiz*) 35 20
757 50 c. *Norge I*, North Pole, 1926 (*horiz*) .. 70 60
758 1 l. *Cape Sierra* sport balloon, Freetown, 1983 1·10 1·40
755/8 .. .. *Set of* 4 2·10 2·10
MS759 115 × 85 mm. 2 l. Airship of 21st century 1·00 1·75

1983 (Oct). *Birds. As Nos.* 622B/35B *but without wmk.*
760 1 c. Type **142** .. .. 70 1·00
761 2 c. Olive-bellied Sunbird .. .. .. 70 1·00
763 5 c. Spur-winged Goose 90 50
765 10 c. Grey Parrot (*vert*) 90 50
766 15 c. Blue Quail (*vert*) .. .. .. 1·25 60
767 20 c. African Wood Owl (*vert*) .. .. 2·25 1·00
768 30 c. Great Blue Turaco (*vert*) .. .. 1·50 1·25
769 40 c. Blue-breasted Kingfisher (*vert*) .. 2·50 2·00
770 50 c. Black Crake (*vert*) .. .. .. 2·50 2·00
772 2 l. Black Bee Eater .. .. 5·00 7·50
773 5 l. Barrow's Bustard .. .. .. 10·00 15·00
760/73 .. .. *Set of* 11 25·00 29·00
Nos. 760/73 exist imperforate from stock dispersed by the liquidator of Format International Security Printers Ltd.
The imprint date on Nos. 760/73 is 1983. Examples of the 1, 2, 3 c. and 2 l. with 1981 date come from the liquidator's stock.

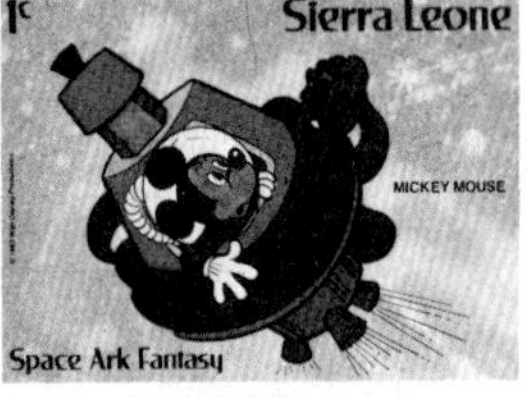

169 Mickey Mouse

(Litho Format)

1983 (18 Nov). *Space Ark Fantasy. T* **169** *and similar horiz designs featuring Disney cartoon characters. Multicoloured. P* 13½.
774 1 c. Type **169** 10 10
775 1 c. Huey, Dewey and Louie 10 10
776 3 c. Goofy in spaceship 10 10
777 3 c. Donald Duck 10 10
778 10 c. Ludwig von Drake 10 10
779 10 c. Goofy 10 10
780 2 l. Mickey Mouse and Giraffe in spaceship 1·10 1·25
781 3 l. Donald Duck floating in space .. .. 1·60 1·75
774/81 .. .. *Set of* 8 2·75 3·00
MS782 140 × 116 mm. 5 l. Mickey Mouse leaving spaceship .. .. 2·75 3·00

170 Graduates from Union Training Programme

(Des G. Vasarhelyi. Litho Format)

1984 (8 Feb). *10th Anniv of the Mano River Union. T* **170** *and similar horiz designs. Multicoloured. P* 15.
783 6 c. Type **170** 10 10
784 25 c. Intra-Union trade 10 10
785 31 c. Member Presidents on map 15 15
786 41 c. Signing ceremony marking Guinea's accession 20 20
783/6 .. .. *Set of* 4 45 45
MS787 75 × 113 mm. No. 786 .. .. .. 50 70

171 Gymnastics

172 "Apollo 11" Lift-off

(Des J. Iskowitz. Litho Questa)

1984 (27 Mar). *Olympic Games, Los Angeles. T* **171** *and similar horiz designs. Multicoloured. P* 14.

788	90 c. Type **171**	30	40
789	1 l. Hurdling	30	40
790	3 l. Javelin-throwing	75	1·25
788/90	*Set of* 3	1·25	1·90
MS791	104 × 71 mm. 7 l. Boxing	1·40	2·00

(Des J. Iskowitz. Litho Questa)

1984 (14 May). *15th Anniv of First Moonwalk. T* **172** *and similar multicoloured designs. P* 14.

792	50 c. Type **172**	20	20
793	75 c. Lunar module	30	30
794	1 l. 25, First Moonwalk	45	45
795	2 l. 50, Lunar exploration	85	85
792/5	*Set of* 4	1·60	1·60
MS796	99 × 69 mm. 5 l. Family watching Moonwalk on television (*horiz*)	1·60	2·25

173 "Concorde"

(Des Susan David. Litho Walsall)

1984 (19 June). *Universal Postal Union Congress, Hamburg. T* **173** *and similar horiz design. Multicoloured. P* 14.

797	4 l. Type **173**	2·50	1·75
MS798	100 × 70 mm. 4 l. Heinrich von Stephan (founder of U.P.U.)	2·00	2·75

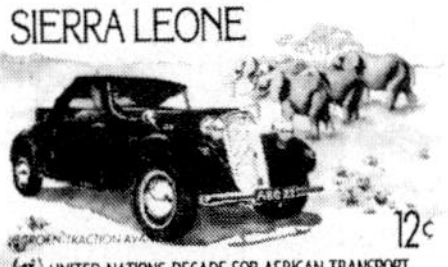

174 Citroen "Traction Avante"

25c

(175)

(Des Susan David. Litho Format)

1984 (16 July). *United Nations Decade for African Transport. T* **174** *and similar horiz designs. Multicoloured. P* 14½ × 15.

799	12 c. Type **174**	20	10
800	60 c. Locomobile	40	25
801	90 c. A.C. "Ace"	55	35
802	1 l. Vauxhall "Prince Henry"	55	35
803	1 l. 50, Delahaye "135"	70	50
804	2 l. Mazda "1105"	90	65
799/804	*Set of* 6	3·00	1·90
MS805	107 × 75 mm. 6 l. Volkswagen "Beetle". P 15	3·25	3·50

1984 (3 Aug). *Surch as T* **175**. (*a*) *On Nos.* 625, 627 *and* 634. *A. No imprint. B. Imprint date at foot.*

		A		B	
806	25 c. on 10 c. Grey Parrot (*vert*)	3·50	3·50	3·50	3·50
807	40 c. on 10 c. Grey Parrot (*vert*)	3·50	3·50	3·50	3·50
808	50 c. on 2 l. Black Bee Eater	3·50	3·50	3·50	3·50
809	70 c. on 5 c. Spur-winged Goose	3·50	3·50	3·50	3·50
810	10 l. on 5 c. Spur-winged Goose	7·00	7·00	7·00	7·00
806/10	*Set of* 5	19·00	19·00	19·00	19·00

(*b*) *On Nos.* 763, 765 *and* 772

811	25 c. on 10 c. Grey Parrot (*vert*)	75	85
812	40 c. on 10 c. Grey Parrot (*vert*)	50	70
813	50 c. on 2 l. Black Bee Eater	50	70
814	70 c. on 5 c. Spur-winged Goose	50	70
815	10 l. on 5 c. Spur-winged Goose	3·00	3·50
811/15	*Set of* 5	4·75	5·75

Nos. 806B/10B exist with either "1981" or "1982" imprint dates.

AUSIPEX 84

(176)

177 Portuguese Caravel

1984 (22 Aug). *"Ausipex" International Stamp Exhibition, Melbourne. Optd with T* **176**. (*a*) *On Nos.* 632 *and* 635. *A. No imprint. B. Imprint date at foot.*

		A		B	
816	50 c. Black Crake	5·00	5·00	5·00	5·00
817	5 l. Barrow's Bustard	15·00	15·00	15·00	15·00

(*b*) *On Nos.* 770 *and* 773

818	50 c. Black Crake	1·00	75
819	5 l. Barrow's Bustard	2·25	2·00

Nos. 816B/17B exist with either "1981" or "1982" imprint dates.

(Des G. Drummond. Litho Questa)

1984 (5 Sept)–**85**. *History of Shipping. T* **177** *and similar horiz designs. Multicoloured. A. Without imprint date below design. P* 14. *B. With imprint date below design. P* 12.

		A		B	
820	2 c. Type **177**	20	40	15	20
821	5 c. *Merlin* of Bristol	35	40	20	20
822	10 c. *Golden Hind*	45	40	30	20
823	15 c. *Mordaunt*	55	40	†	
824	20 c. *Atlantic* (transport)	60	40	30	20
825	25 c. H.M.S. *Lapwing*	60	40	30	20
826	30 c. *Traveller* (brig)	70	40	30	25
827	40 c. *Amistad* (schooner)	75	50	35	25
828	50 c. H.M.S. *Teazer*	75	45	40	25
829	70 c. *Scotia* (cable ship)	90	75	55	35
830	1 l. H.M.S. *Alecto*	1·00	75	60	35
831	2 l. H.M.S. *Blonde*	4·50	2·00	85	55
832	5 l. H.M.S. *Fox*	8·00	4·25	1·25	85
833	10 l. *Accra* (liner)	11·00	10·00	1·75	1·40
833*c*	15 l. H.M.S. *Favourite*	1·25	1·25	†	
833*d*	25 l. H.M.S. *Euryalus*	1·75	1·75	†	
820A/33dA	*Set of* 16	30·00	22·00		
820B/33B	*Set of* 13			6·50	4·75

Dates of issue:—Without imprint 5.9.84, 2 c., to 1 l.; 9.10.84, 2 l., 5 l.; 7.11.84, 10 l; 15.11.85, 15 l., 25 l. With imprint 7.85, 2 c. to 10 l.

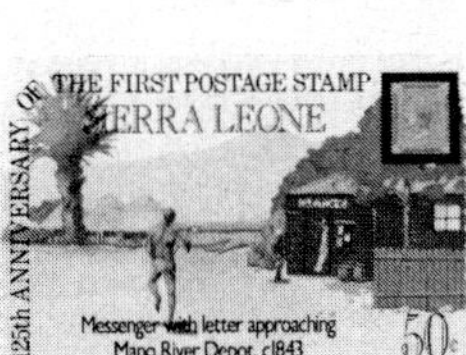

178 Mail Runner approaching Mano River Depot, *c* 1843

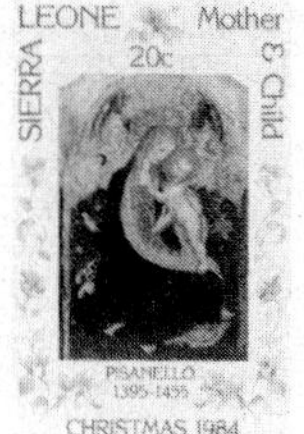

179 "Madonna and Child" (Pisanello)

(Des Susan David. Litho Walsall)

1984 (9 Oct). *125th Anniv of First Postage Stamps. T* **178** *and similar horiz designs. Multicoloured. P* 14.

834	50 c. Type **178**	30	15
835	2 l. Isaac Fitzjohn, First Postmaster, receiving letters, 1855	1·00	65
836	3 l. 1859 packet franked with four 6d. stamps	1·50	1·00
834/6	*Set of* 3	2·50	1·75
MS837	100 × 70 mm. 5 l. Sierra Leone 1859 6d. purple and Great Britain 1840 Penny Black stamps	1·50	1·60

(Litho Walsall)

1984 (15 Nov). *Christmas. Madonna and Child paintings by artists named. T* **179** *and similar vert designs. Multicoloured. P* 14.

838	20 c. Type **179**	10	10
839	1 l. Memling	40	30
840	2 l. Raphael	75	55
841	3 l. Van der Werff	1·10	80
838/41	*Set of* 4	2·00	1·60
MS842	100 × 69 mm. 6 l. Picasso	2·00	1·90

180 Donald Duck in the "The Wise Little Hen"

(Litho Questa)

1984 (26 Nov). *50th Birthday of Donald Duck. Walt Disney Cartoon Characters. T* **180** *and similar horiz designs. Multicoloured. P* 12 (2 *l.*) *or* 14 × 13½ (*others*).

843	1 c. Type **180**	10	10
844	2 c. Mickey Mouse and Donald Duck in "Boat Builders"	10	10
845	3 c. Panchito, Donald Duck and Jose Carioca in "The Three Caballeros"	10	10
846	4 c. Donald Duck meeting Pythagoras in "Mathmagic Land"	10	10
847	5 c. Donald Duck and nephew in "The Mickey Mouse Club"	10	10
848	10 c. Mickey Mouse, Goofy and Donald Duck in "Donald on Parade"	10	10
849	1 l. Donald Duck riding donkey in "Don Donald"	75	75
850	2 l. Donald Duck in "Donald Gets Drafted"	1·50	1·50
851	4 l. Donald Duck meeting children in Tokyo Disneyland	2·50	2·50
843/51	*Set of* 9	4·50	4·50
MS852	126 × 102 mm. 5 l. Style sheet for Donald Duck	2·00	1·50

No. 850 was printed in sheetlets of 8.

181 Fischer's Whydah

(Des Susan David. Litho Walsall)

1985 (31 Jan). *Birth Bicentenary of John J. Audubon (ornithologist). Songbirds of Sierra Leone. T* **181** *and similar horiz designs. Multicoloured. P* 14.

853	40 c. Type **181**	1·00	40
854	90 c. Spotted Flycatcher	2·00	1·10
855	1 l. 30, Garden Warbler	2·25	2·00
856	3 l. Speke's Weaver	3·50	4·00
853/6	*Set of* 4	8·00	6·75
MS857	100 × 70 mm. 5 l. Great Grey Shrike	2·25	3·00

182 Fishing

(Des M. Zacharow. Litho Walsall)

1985 (14 Feb). *International Youth Year. T* **182** *and similar horiz designs. Multicoloured. P* 14.

858	1 l. 15, Type **182**	30	35
859	1 l. 50, Sawing timber	40	45
860	2 l. 15, Rice farming	55	60
858/60	*Set of* 3	1·10	1·25
MS861	100 × 70 mm. 5 l. Polishing diamonds	1·25	1·50

183 Eddie Rickenbacker and Spad "XIII", 1918

(Des K. Gromol. Litho Walsall)

1985 (28 Feb). *40th Anniv of International Civil Aviation Organization. T* **183** *and similar horiz designs. Multicoloured. P* 14.

862	70 c. Type **183**	1·00	60
863	1 l. 25, Samuel P. Langley and *Aerodrome No.* 5, 1903	1·40	1·25
864	1 l. 30, Orville and Wilbur Wright with *Flyer No.* 1, 1903	1·40	1·25
865	2 l. Charles Lindbergh and *Spirit of St. Louis*, 1927	1·75	2·00
862/5	*Set of* 4	5·00	4·75
MS866	100 × 69 mm. 5 l. Sierra Leone Airlines Boeing "707-384C"	1·50	1·75

184 "Temptation of Christ" (Botticelli)

185 The Queen Mother at St. Paul's Cathedral

(Des C. Walters. Litho Questa)

1985 (29 Apr). *Easter. Religious Paintings. T* **184** *and similar multicoloured designs. P* 14.

867	45 c. Type **184**	30	15
868	70 c. "Christ at the Column" (Velasquez)	55	25
869	1 l. 55, "Pietà" (Botticelli) (*vert*)	90	45
870	10 l. "Christ on the Cross" (Velasquez) (*vert*)	4·25	3·25
867/70	*Set of* 4	5·50	3·75
MS871	106 × 76 mm. 12 l. "Man of Sorrows" (Botticelli)	3·50	3·75

(Des J.W. Litho Questa)

1985 (8 July). *Life and Times of Queen Elizabeth the Queen Mother. T* **185** *and similar multicoloured designs. P* 14.

872	1 l. Type **185**	25	30
873	1 l. 70, With her racehorse, "Double Star", at Sandown (*horiz*)	45	50
874	10 l. At Covent Garden, 1971	3·00	3·25
872/4	*Set of* 3	3·25	3·75
MS875	56 × 85 mm. 12 l. With Princess Anne at Ascot	2·50	3·50

75th ANNIVERSARY OF GIRL GUIDES

70c

(186)

1985 (25 July). *75th Anniv of Girl Guide Movement. Nos.* 690/4 *surch as T* **186**.
876 70 c. on 20 c. Type **155** 20 25
877 1 l. 30 on 50 c. Scouts picking flowers .. 35 40
878 5 l. on 1 l. Lord Baden-Powell .. .. 1·25 1·40
879 7 l. on 2 l. Scouts fishing .. .. .. 1·75 1·90
876/9 .. .. *Set of* 4 3·25 3·50
MS880 101×70 mm. 15 l. on 3 l. Scouts raising flag.. .. .. 3·75 4·00

MA YANHONJG
CHINA
GOLD MEDAL
Le2

(187)

1985 (25 July). *Olympic Gold Medal Winners, Los Angeles. Nos.* 788/91 *surch as T* **187**.
881 2 l. on 90 c. Type **171** (surch T **187**) 50 55
882 4 l. on 1 l. Hurdling (surch "E. MOSES U.S.A. GOLD MEDAL") .. .. .. 1·00 1·25
883 8 l. on 3 l. Javelin-throwing (surch "A. HAERKOENEN FINLAND GOLD MEDAL") .. .. 2·00 2·10
881/3 .. .. *Set of* 3 3·25 3·50
MS884 104×71 mm. 15 l. on 7 l. Boxing (surch "M. TAYLOR U.S.A. GOLD MEDAL") .. .. 3·25 3·75

188 Chater-Lea (1905) at Hill Station House

70c

(189)

(Des A. DiLorenzo. Litho Questa)

1985 (15 Aug). *Centenary of the Motor Cycle and Decade for African Transport. T* **188** *and similar horiz designs. Multicoloured. P* 14.
885 1 l. 40, Type **188** .. .. 1·00 1·00
886 2 l. Honda "XR 350 R" at Queen Elizabeth II Quay, Freetown .. .. 1·40 1·40
887 4 l. Kawasaki "Vulcan" at Bo Clock Tower .. 2·50 2·50
888 5 l. Harley-Davidson "Electra-Glide" in Makeni village .. .. 2·75 2·75
885/8 .. .. *Set of* 4 7·00 7·00
MS889 104×71 mm. 12 l. Millet (1893).. .. 3·00 3·50

(Des Susan David. Litho Questa)

1985 (3 Sept). *300th Birth Anniv of Johann Sebastian Bach (composer). Vert designs as T* **204a** *of Maldive Islands. P* 14.
890 70 c. multicoloured 40 25
891 3 l. multicoloured .. .. 1·10 80
892 4 l. multicoloured .. .. 1·40 1·10
893 5 l. multicoloured .. .. 1·60 1·40
890/3 .. .. *Set of* 4 4·00 3·25
MS894 103×77 mm. 12 l. black .. .. .. 3·50 3·50
Designs:—70 c. Viola pomposa; 3 l. Spinet; 4 l. Lute; 5 l. Oboe; 12 l. "Johann Sebastian Bach" (Toby E. Rosenthal).

1985 (30 Sept). *Surch as T* **189**. (*a*) *On Nos.* 707/10
895 70 c. on 31 c. Caernarvon Castle 30 30
896 4 l. on 50 c. Type **158** .. .. .. 2·50 2·50
897 5 l. on 2 l. Princess of Wales .. .. 3·00 3·00
MS898 103×75 mm. 15 l. on 3 l. Princess of Wales (*different*) .. .. 6·00 6·00

(*b*) *On Nos.* 711/14
899 1 l. 30 on 31 c. Caernarvon Castle 80 80
900 5 l. on 50 c. Type **158**.. .. .. .. 3·00 3·00
901 7 l. on 2 l. Princess of Wales .. .. .. 4·00 4·00
895/901 .. .. *Set of* 6 12·00 12·00
MS902 103×75 mm. 15 l. on 3 l. Princess of Wales (*different*) .. .. 6·00 6·00

190 "Madonna and Child" (Crivelli)

191 Player kicking Ball

(Litho Questa)

1985 (18 Oct). *Christmas. "Madonna and Child" Paintings by artists named. T* **190** *and similar vert designs. Multicoloured. P* 14.
903 70 c. Type **190**.. .. .. 20 10
904 3 l. Bouts 70 40
905 4 l. Da Messina 85 55
906 5 l. Lochner .. .. 1·00 65
903/6 .. .. *Set of* 4 2·50 1·50
MS907 113×85 mm. 12 l. Miniature from Book of Kells .. .. 1·50 1·60

(Des Walt Disney Productions. Litho Questa)

1985 (30 Oct). *150th Birth Anniv of Mark Twain (author). Vert designs as T* **160a** *of Lesotho showing Walt Disney cartoon characters illustrating Mark Twain quotations. Multicoloured. P* $13^1/_2$×14.
908 1 l. 50, Snow White and Bashful 20 25
909 3 l. Three Little Pigs 35 40
910 4 l. Donald Duck and nephew 50 55
911 5 l. Pinocchio and Figaro the cat 60 65
908/11 .. .. *Set of* 4 1·50 1·60
MS912 126×101 mm. 15 l. Winnie the Pooh .. 1·90 2·00

(Des Walt Disney Productions. Litho Questa)

1985 (3 Oct). *Birth Bicentenaries of Grimm Brothers (folklorists). Designs as T* **160b** *of Lesotho, but horiz, showing Walt Disney cartoon characters from "Rumpelstiltskin". Multicoloured. P* 14×$13^1/_2$.
913 70 c. The Miller (Donald Duck) and his daughter (Daisy Duck) meet the King (Uncle Scrooge) 20 25
914 1 l. 30, The King puts the Miller's daughter to work 35 40
915 2 l. Rumpelstiltskin demands payment .. 50 55
916 10 l. The King with gold spun from straw .. 2·75 3·00
913/16 .. .. *Set of* 4 3·50 3·75
MS917 126×100 mm. 15 l. The King and Queen with baby .. .. 4·00 4·25

(Litho Format)

1985 (28 Nov). *40th Anniv of United Nations Organization. Multicoloured designs as T* **159** *of Lesotho showing United Nations (New York) stamps. P* $14^1/_2$.
918 2 l. John Kennedy and 1954 Human Rights 8 c... .. .. 70 70
919 4 l. Albert Einstein (scientist) and 1958 Atomic Energy 3 c. .. .. 1·40 1·40
920 7 l. Maimonides (physician) and 1956 W.H.O. 8 c. .. .. 3·25 3·25
918/20 .. .. *Set of* 3 4·75 4·75
MS921 110×85 mm. 12 l. Martin Luther King (civil rights leader) (*vert*).. .. .. .. 1·50 1·75

(Des M. Lemel. Litho Questa)

1986 (3 Mar). *World Cup Football Championship, Mexico. T* **191** *and similar vert designs. Multicoloured. P* 14.
922 70 c. Type **191**.. .. .. 20 10
923 3 l. Player controlling ball 60 50
924 4 l. Player chasing ball 75 70
925 5 l. Player kicking ball (*different*) .. .. 1·00 80
922/5 .. .. *Set of* 4 2·25 1·90
MS926 105×74 mm. 12 l. Player kicking ball (*different*) .. .. 1·50 1·75

191a Times Square, 1905

192 Chicago-Milwaukee "Hiawatha Express'

(Des J. Iskowitz. Litho Questa)

1986 (11 Mar). *Centenary of Statue of Liberty (1st issue). T* **191a** *and similar multicoloured designs. P* 14.
927 40 c. Type **191a** 10 10
928 70 c. Times Square, 1986 .. .. 15 10
929 1 l. "Tally Ho" coach, *c* 1880 (*horiz*) .. 20 15
930 10 l. Express bus, 1986 (*horiz*) .. .. 1·60 1·40
927/30 .. .. *Set of* 4 1·75 1·60
MS931 105×75 mm. 12 l. Statue of Liberty .. 2·00 2·00
See also Nos. 1001/9.

(Des W. Hanson. Litho Questa)

1986 (1 Apr). *Appearance of Halley's Comet (1st issue). Horiz designs as T* **162a** *of Lesotho. Multicoloured. P* 14.
932 15 c. Johannes Kepler (astronomer) and Paris Observatory 10 10
933 50 c. N.A.S.A. Space Shuttle landing, 1985 .. 10 10
934 70 c. Halley's Comet (from Bayeux Tapestry) 10 10
935 10 l. Comet of 530 A.D. and Merlin predicting coming of King Arthur .. .. 1·25 1·40
932/5 .. .. *Set of* 4 1·40 1·50
MS936 101×70 mm. 12 l. Halley's Comet .. 1·50 1·60

(Des and litho Questa)

1986 (23 Apr). *60th Birthday of Queen Elizabeth II. Vert designs as T* **163a** *of Lesotho. P* 14.
937 10 c. black and yellow 10 10
938 1 l. 70, multicoloured 25 30
939 10 l. multicoloured .. .. 1·25 1·40
937/9 .. .. *Set of* 3 1·40 1·60
MS940 120×85 mm. 12 l. black and grey-brown 1·50 1·60
Designs:—10 c. Princess Elizabeth inspecting guard of honour, Cranwell, 1951; 1 l. 70, In Garter robes; 10 l. At Braemar Games, 1970; 12 l. Princess Elizabeth, Windsor Castle, 1943.

(Des P. Rhymer. Litho Questa)

1986 (22 May). *"Ameripex" International Stamp Exhibition, Chicago. American Trains. T* **192** *and similar horiz designs. Multicoloured. P* 14.
941 50 c. Type **192**.. .. .. 60 25
942 2 l. Rock Island Line "The Rocket" .. 1·25 80
943 4 l. Rio Grande "Prospector" .. .. 2·00 1·60
944 7 l. Southern Pacific "Daylight Express" .. 2·50 2·50
941/4 .. .. *Set of* 4 5·75 4·75
MS945 105×85 mm. 12 l. Pennsylvania "Broadway" .. .. 2·00 2·00

(Litho Questa)

1986 (1 July). *Royal Wedding. Vert designs as T* **170a** *of Lesotho. Multicoloured. P* 14.
946 10 c. Prince Andrew and Miss Sarah Ferguson 10 10
947 1 l. 70, Prince Andrew at clay pigeon shoot 30 35
948 10 l. Prince Andrew in naval uniform .. 1·40 1·75
946/8 .. .. *Set of* 3 1·60 2·00
MS949 88×88 mm. 12 l. Prince Andrew and Miss Sarah Ferguson (*different*) .. .. .. 2·00 1·60

193 *Monodora myristica*

194 Handshake and Flags of Sierra Leone and U.S.A.

(Des G. Drummond. Litho Format)

1986 (25 Aug). *Flowers of Sierra Leone. T* **193** *and similar vert designs. Multicoloured. P* 15.
950 70 c. Type **193**.. .. .. 15 10
951 1 l. 50, *Gloriosa simplex* 20 15
952 4 l. *Mussaenda erythrophylla* 35 25
953 6 l. *Crinum ornatum* 50 40
954 8 l. *Bauhinia purpurea* 60 60
955 10 l. *Bombax costatum* 70 70
956 20 l. *Hibiscus rosasinensis* .. .. .. 1·25 1·50
957 30 l. *Cassia fistula* .. .. 1·75 2·00
950/7 .. .. *Set of* 8 5·00 5·00
MS958 Two sheets, each 101×92 mm. (a) 40 l. *Clitoria ternatea*. (b) 40 l. *Plumbago auriculata* *Set of* 2 *sheets* 4·00 4·00

(Litho Questa)

1986 (26 Aug). *25th Anniv of United States Peace Corps. P* 14.
959 **194** 10 l. multicoloured 70 70

Le30

195 Transporting Goods by Canoe

(196)

70¢

(197)

(Des T. O'Toole. Litho Questa)

1986 (1 Sept). *International Peace Year. T* **195** *and similar horiz designs. Multicoloured. P* 14.
960 1 l. Type **195**.. .. .. 10 10
961 2 l. Teacher and class 15 15
962 5 l. Rural post office.. .. .. 30 30
963 10 l. Fishermen in longboat 55 55
960/3 .. .. *Set of* 4 1·00 1·00

1986 (15 Sept). *Various stamps surch.*
(*a*) *As T* **196** *on Nos.* 820A, 826/7A *and* 829A
964 30 l. on 2 c. Type **177**.. .. .. .. 1·50 1·60
965 40 l. on 30 c. *Traveller* (brig).. .. .. 2·10 2·25
966 45 l. on 40 c. *Amistad* (schooner) .. .. 2·40 2·50
967 50 l. on 70 c. *Scotia* (cable ship) .. .. 2·75 2·75
(*b*) *As T* **197** *on Nos.* 937 *and* 939/40 (*in silver on Nos.* 968/9)
968 70 c. on 10 c. black and yellow 10 10
969 45 l. on 10 l. multicoloured .. .. .. 2·40 2·50
MS970 120×85 mm. 50 l. on 12 l. black and grey-brown .. .. 3·00 3·00
(*c*) *As T* **197** *on Nos.* 946 *and* 948/9, *in silver*
971 70 c. on 10 c. Prince Andrew and Miss Sarah Ferguson.. .. .. 10 10
972 45 l. on 10 l. Prince Andrew in naval uniform 2·40 2·50
964/72 .. .. *Set of* 8 12·00 12·50
MS973 88×88 mm. 50 l. on 12 l. Prince Andrew and Miss Sarah Ferguson (*different*) .. .. 3·50 3·00

1986 (15 Sept). *World Cup Football Championship Winners, Mexico. Nos.* 922/6 *optd with T* **213a** *of Maldive Islands or surch also, all in gold.*
974 70 c.Type **191** 15 10
975 3 l. Player controlling ball 30 30
976 4 l. Player chasing ball 40 40
977 40 l. on 5 l. Player kicking ball (*different*) .. 3·00 3·50
974/7 .. .. *Set of* 4 3·50 3·75
MS978 105×74 mm. 40 l. on 12 l. Player kicking ball (*different*) .. .. 2·50 2·50

198 Mickey and Minnie Mouse as Jack and Jill

(Des Walt Disney Co. Litho Format)

1986 (22 Sept). *"Stockholmia '86" International Stamp Exhibition, Sweden. T* **198** *and similar horiz designs showing Walt Disney cartoon characters in scenes from nursery rhymes. Multicoloured. P* 11.

979 70 c. Type **198** 10 10
980 1 l. Donald Duck as Wee Willie Winkie .. 10 10
981 2 l. Minnie Mouse as Little Miss Muffet .. 15 15
982 4 l. Goofy as Old King Cole 30 30
983 5 l. Clarabelle as Mary Quite Contrary .. 40 40
984 10 l. Daisy Duck as Little Bo Peep 70 70
985 25 l. Daisy Duck and Minnie Mouse in "Polly put the Kettle on" .. .. 1·75 1·75
986 35 l. Goofy, Mickey Mouse and Donald Duck as the Three Men in a Tub .. .. 2·25 2·25
979/86 .. .. *Set of* 8 5·00 5·00
MS987 Two sheets, each 127 × 102 mm. P 14 × 13½. (a) 40 l. Aunt Matilda as the Old Woman in the Shoe. (b) 40 l. Goofy as Simple Simon .. .. .. *Set of* 2 *sheets* 4·25 4·50

1986 (15 Oct). *Appearance of Halley's Comet* (2*nd issue*). *Nos.* 932/6 *optd as T* **213***b of Maldive Islands* (*in silver on* 50 *l.*) *or surch also.*

988 50 c. N.A.S.A. Space Shuttle landing, 1985 .. 10 10
989 70 c. Halley's Comet (from Bayeux Tapestry) 10 10
990 1 l. 50 on 15 c. Johannes Kepler (astronomer) and Paris Observatory 10 10
991 45 l. on 10 l. Comet of 530 A.D. and Merlin predicting coming of King Arthur .. 3·00 3·50
988/91 .. .. *Set of* 4 3·00 3·50
MS992 101 × 70 mm. 50 l. on 12 l. Halley's Comet 3·25 3·50

199 "Virgin and Child with St. Dorothy" — **200** Nomoli (soapstone figure)

(Litho Questa)

1986 (17 Nov). *Christmas. Paintings by Titian. T* **199** *and similar multicoloured designs. P* 14.

993 70 c. Type **199** 10 10
994 1 l. 50, "The Gypsy Madonna" (*vert*) .. 15 10
995 20 l. "The Holy Family" .. .. .. 1·75 1·75
996 30 l. "Virgin and Child in an Evening Landscape" (*vert*) .. .. 2·25 2·50
993/6 .. .. *Set of* 4 3·75 4·00
MS997 76 × 102 mm. 40 l. "Madonna with the Pesaro Family" (*vert*) .. .. 4·50 4·75

(Des A. DiLorenzo. Litho Format)

1987 (2 Jan). *Bicentenary of Sierra Leone. T* **200** *and similar vert designs. Multicoloured. P* 15.

998 2 l. Type **200** 10 15
999 5 l. King's Yard Gate, Royal Hospital, 1817 .. 20 30
MS1000 100 × 70 mm. 60 l. Early 19th-century British warship at Freetown .. .. .. 2·50 2·75

201 Removing Top of Statue's Torch — **202** Emblem, Mother with Child and Syringe

(Litho Questa)

1987 (2 Jan). *Centenary of Statue of Liberty* (1986) (2*nd issue*). *T* **201** *and similar multicoloured designs. P* 14.

1001 70 c. Type **201** 10 10
1002 1 l. 50, View of Statue's torch and New York Harbour (*horiz*) 10 10
1003 2 l. Crane lifting torch 10 10
1004 3 l. Workman steadying torch 10 15
1005 4 l. Statue's crown (*horiz*) 15 20
1006 5 l. Statue of Liberty (side view) and fireworks 20 25
1007 10 l. Statue of Liberty and fireworks .. 40 45
1008 25 l. Bedloe Island, Statue and fireworks (*horiz*) .. .. 1·00 1·25
1009 30 l. Statue's face .. .. 1·25 1·60
1001/9 .. .. *Set of* 9 3·00 3·75

(Litho Questa)

1987 (18 Mar). *40th Anniv of U.N.I.C.E.F. P* 14.

1010 **202** 10 l. multicoloured 40 55

ALTERED CATALOGUE NUMBERS

Any Catalogue numbers altered from the last edition are shown as a list in the introductory pages.

203 *U.S.A.*, 1987 — **204** Mickey Mouse as Mountie and Parliament Building, Ottawa

(Des S. Heinmann. Litho Questa)

1987 (15 June). *America's Cup Yachting Championship. T* **203** *and similar multicoloured designs. P* 14.

1011 1 l. Type **203** 10 10
1012 1 l. 50, *New Zealand*, 1987 (*horiz*) .. 10 10
1013 2 l. 50, *French Kiss*, 1987 .. .. .. 10 10
1014 10 l. *Stars and Stripes*, 1987 (*horiz*) .. 40 45
1015 15 l. *Australia II*, 1983 .. .. .. 60 65
1016 25 l. *Freedom*, 1980 .. .. 1·00 1·10
1017 30 l. *Kookaburra III*, 1987 (*horiz*) .. .. 1·25 1·40
1011/17 .. .. *Set of* 7 3·00 3·50
MS1018 100 × 70 mm. 50 l. *Constellation*, 1964 .. 2·00 2·50

(Des Walt Disney Co. Litho Format)

1987 (15 June). *"Capex '87" International Stamp Exhibition, Toronto. T* **204** *and similar horiz designs showing Walt Disney cartoon characters in Canada. Multicoloured. P* 11.

1019 2 l. Type **204** 10 10
1020 5 l. Goofy dressed as Mountie and totem poles 20 25
1021 10 l. Goofy windsurfing and Donald Duck fishing off Perce Rock 40 45
1022 20 l. Goofy with mountain goat in Rocky Mountains 80 85
1023 25 l. Donald Duck and Mickey Mouse in Old Quebec .. .. 1·00 1·10
1024 45 l. Goofy emerging from igloo and *Aurora Borealis* .. .. 1·75 1·90
1025 50 l. Goofy as gold prospector and post office, Yukon .. .. 2·00 2·10
1026 75 l. Dumbo flying over Niagara Falls .. 3·25 3·25
1019/26 .. .. *Set of* 8 8·25 9·00
MS1027 Two sheets, each 127 × 101 mm. (a) 100 l. Mickey Mouse driving chuckwagon in Calgary Stampede. (b) 100 l. Mickey Mouse and Goofy as Vikings in Newfoundland. P 14 × 13½ *Set of* 2 *sheets* 8·00 8·50

205 *Salamis temora* — **206** Cycling

(Des S. Heinmann. Litho Questa)

1987 (4 Aug)–**89**. *Butterflies. T* **205** *and similar vert designs. Multicoloured. A. Without imprint date. P* 14. *B. Without imprint date. P* 12.

		A		B	
1028	10 c. Type **205** ..	30	20	20	20
1029	20 c. *Stugeta marmorea* ..	40	20	20	20
1030	40 c. *Graphium ridleyanus*	40	20	20	20
1031	1 l. *Papilio bromius* ..	40	20	30	20
1032	2 l. *Iterus zalmoxis* ..	50	40	35	30
1033	3 l. *Cymothoe sangaris* ..	50	40	35	30
1034	5 l. *Graphium tynderaeus*	75	40	10	10
1035	10 l. *Graphium policenes* ..	1·40	70	10	10
1036	20 l. *Tanuetheira timon* ..	2·25	2·00	10	10
1037	25 l. *Danaus limniace* ..	3·00	2·50	10	10
1038	30 l. *Papilio hesperus* ..	3·50	3·00	10	10
1039	45 l. *Charaxes smaragdalis*	4·50	4·00	10	15
1040	60 l. *Charaxes lucretius* ..	2·00	3·00	20	25
1041	75 l. *Antanartia delius* ..	2·50	3·25	20	25
1042	100 l. *Abisara talantus* ..	3·25	4·00	30	35
1028/42	.. .. *Set of* 15	23·00	22·00	2·25	2·40

C. *With imprint date. P* 14

1028C 10 c. Type **205** 10 10
1029C 20 c. *Stugeta marmorea* 10 10
1030C 40 c. *Graphium ridleyanus* 10 10
1031C 1 l. *Papilio bromius* 10 10
1032C 2 l. *Iterus zalmoxis* 10 10
1033C 3 l. *Cymothoe sangaris* 10 10
1028C/33C .. .. *Set of* 6 30 30

Dates of issue:—4.8.87, Nos. 1028A/42A; 6.88, Nos. 1028B/37B; 8.88, Nos. 1038B/9B; 10.88, Nos. 1040B/1B; 3.89, No. 1042B; 1989, Nos. 1028C/33C.

(Des BG Studio. Litho Questa)

1987 (10 Aug). *Olympic Games, Seoul* (1988) (1*st issue*). *T* **206** *and similar vert designs. Multicoloured. P* 14.

1043 5 l. Type **206** 20 25
1044 10 l. Three Day Eventing 40 45
1045 45 l. Athletics .. .. 1·75 1·90
1046 50 l. Tennis .. .. 2·00 2·10
1043/6 .. .. *Set of* 4 4·00 4·25
MS1047 73 × 84 mm. 100 l. Olympic gold medal .. 4·00 4·50

See also Nos. 1137/41.

206*a* "The Quarrel" (Chagall) — **206***b* "Apollo 8" Spacecraft (first manned Moon orbit), 1968

(Litho Questa)

1987 (17 Aug). *Birth Centenary of Marc Chagall* (*artist*). *T* **206***a and similar multicoloured designs. P* 13½ × 14.

1048 3 l. Type **206***a* 15 15
1049 5 l. "Rebecca giving Abraham's Servant a Drink" 20 25
1050 10 l. "The Village" 40 45
1051 20 l. "Ida at the Window" 80 85
1052 25 l. "Promenade" .. .. 1·00 1·10
1053 45 l. "Peasants" .. .. 1·75 1·90
1054 50 l. "Turquoise Plate" (ceramic) .. .. 2·00 2·10
1055 75 l. "Cemetery Gate" .. .. .. 3·00 3·25
1048/55 .. .. *Set of* 8 8·25 9·00
MS1056 Two sheets, each 110 × 95 mm. (a) 100 l. "Wedding Feast" (stage design) (104 × 78 *mm*). (b) 100 l. "The Falling Angel" (104 × 78 *mm*). Imperf .. .. .. *Set of* 2 *sheets* 8·00 8·50

(Des W. Wright. Litho Format)

1987 (28 Aug). *Milestones of Transportation. T* **206***b and similar multicoloured designs. P* 15.

1057 3 l. Type **206***b* 15 15
1058 5 l. Blanchard's balloon (first U.S. balloon flight), 1793 (*horiz*) 20 20
1059 10 l. Amelia Earhart's Lockheed "Vega" (first solo transatlantic flight by woman), 1932 (*horiz*) 40 40
1060 15 l. Vicker's "Vimy" (first non-stop transatlantic flight), 1919 (*horiz*) .. 60 60
1061 20 l. British "Mk 1" tank (first combat tank), 1916 (*horiz*) 80 80
1062 25 l. Sikorsky "VS-300" (first U.S. helicopter flight), 1939 (*horiz*) .. 90 90
1063 30 l. Wright brother's *Flyer 1* (first powered flight), 1903 (*horiz*) .. 1·10 1·10
1064 35 l. Bleriot "XI" (first cross Channel flight), 1909 (*horiz*) .. .. .. 1·25 1·25
1065 40 l. Paraplane (first flexible-wing ultra-light), 1983 .. .. 1·50 1·50
1066 50 l. Daimler's first motorcycle, 1885 .. 1·75 1·75
1057/66 .. .. *Set of* 10 7·75 7·75
MS1067 114 × 83 mm. 100 l. "Rhinegold Express" (first electric railway) (*horiz*) .. .. .. 3·75 4·00

207 Evonne Goolagong

(Des W. Storozuk. Litho Questa)

1987 (4 Sept). *Wimbledon Tennis Champions. T* **207** *and similar horiz designs. Multicoloured. P* 14.

1068 2 l. Type **207** 20 20
1069 5 l. Martina Navratilova 35 35
1070 10 l. Jimmy Connors 60 60
1071 15 l. Bjorn Borg 90 90
1072 30 l. Boris Becker .. .. 1·75 1·75
1073 40 l. John McEnroe .. .. .. 2·00 2·00
1074 50 l. Chris Evert Lloyd .. .. .. 2·25 2·25
1075 75 l. Virginia Wade .. .. .. 3·00 3·00
1068/75 .. .. *Set of* 8 10·00 10·00
MS1076 Two sheets, each 105 × 75 mm. (a) 100 l. Boris Becker (*different*). (b) 100 l. Steffi Graf *Set of* 2 *sheets* 8·50 9·00

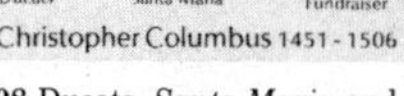

208 Ducats, *Santa Maria* and Issac Abravanel (financier) — **209** Cotton Tree

(Litho Questa)

1987 (11 Sept). *500th Anniv of Discovery of America by Columbus (1992). T* **208** *and similar horiz designs. Multicoloured. P* 14.

1077 5 l. Type **208** 15 20
1078 10 l. Astrolabe, *Pinta* and Abraham Zacuto (astronomer) 30 35
1079 45 l. Maravedis (coins), *Nina* and Luis de Santangel (financier) . . . . 1·25 1·40
1080 50 l. Carib and Spaniard with tobacco plant and Luis de Torres (translator) . . 1·50 1·60
1077/80 . . . . *Set of* 4 3·00 3·25
MS1081 101 × 70 mm. 100 l. Christopher Columbus and map . . . . 3·00 3·50

(Des Mary Walters. Litho Questa)

1987 (15 Sept). *Flora and Fauna. T* **209** *and similar horiz designs. Multicoloured. P* 14.

1082 3 l. Type **209** 10 10
1083 5 l. Dwarf Crocodile 15 20
1084 10 l. Kudu 30 35
1085 20 l. Yellowbells 60 65
1086 25 l. Hippopotamus and calf 75 80
1087 45 l. Comet Orchid . . . . 1·25 1·40
1088 50 l. Baobab Tree . . . . 1·50 1·60
1089 75 l. Elephant and calf . . . . . . 2·25 2·40
1082/9 . . . . *Set of* 8 6·25 6·75
MS1090 Two sheets, each 100 × 70 mm. (a) 100 l. Bananas, Coconut Palm, Papayas and Pineapple. (b) 100 l. Leopard . . *Set of* 2 *sheets* 5·75 6·50

210 Scouts at Ayers Rock

210a White House

(Des R. Vigurs. Litho Format)

1987 (5 Oct). *World Scout Jamboree, Australia. T* **210** *and similar horiz designs. Multicoloured. P* 15.

1091 5 l. Type **210** 15 20
1092 15 l. Scouts sailing yacht 45 50
1093 40 l. Scouts and Sydney skyline . . . . 1·25 1·40
1094 50 l. Scout, Sydney Harbour Bridge and Opera House . . . . . . 1·50 1·60
1091/4 . . . . *Set of* 4 3·00 3·25
MS1095 114 × 78 mm. 100 l. Flags of Sierra Leone, Australia and Boy Scouts . . . . 3·00 3·50

(Des and litho Questa)

1987 (9 Nov). *Bicentenary of U.S. Constitution. T* **210a** *and similar multicoloured designs. P* 14.

1096 5 l. Type **210a** 15 20
1097 10 l. George Washington (Virginia delegate) (*vert*) 30 35
1098 30 l. Patrick Henry (statesman) (*vert*) . . 90 95
1099 65 l. State Seal, New Hampshire . . . . 1·90 2·00
1096/9 . . . . *Set of* 4 3·00 3·25
MS1100 105 × 75 mm. 100 l. John Jay (jurist) (*vert*) . . . . 3·00 3·50

210b Mickey and Minnie Mouse on Space Mountain

(Des Walt Disney Company. Litho Questa)

1987 (9 Dec). *60th Anniv of Mickey Mouse (Walt Disney cartoon character). T* **210b** *and similar horiz designs showing cartoon characters at Tokyo Disneyland. Multicoloured. P* 14×13½.

1101 20 c. Type **210b** 10 10
1102 40 c. Mickey Mouse at Country Bear Jamboree 10 10
1103 80 c. Mickey Mouse as bandleader and Minnie Mouse, Goofy and Pluto as musicians 10 10
1104 1 l. Goofy, Mickey Mouse and children in canoe and Mark Twain's river boat . . 10 10
1105 2 l. Mickey Mouse, Goofy and Chip n'Dale on Western River Railroad 10 10
1106 3 l. Goofy and Mickey Mouse as Pirates of the Caribbean 10 10
1107 10 l. Mickey Mouse, Goofy and children aboard Big Thunder Mountain train 30 35
1108 20 l. Mickey Mouse, Morty and Ferdie in boat and Goofy on flying carpet . . 60 65
1109 30 l. Mickey and Minnie Mouse in kimonos at Disneyland entrance 90 95
1101/9 . . . . *Set of* 9 1·90 2·10
MS1110 127 × 102 mm. 65 l. Mickey and Minnie Mouse in kimonos at Cinderella's Castle . . 1·90 2·00

211 "The Annunciation" (detail) (Titian)

211a Wedding of Princess Elizabeth and Duke of Edinburgh, 1947

(Litho Questa)

1987 (21 Dec). *Christmas. Religious Paintings by Titian. T* **211** *and similar multicoloured designs. P* 14.

1111 2 l. Type **211** 10 10
1112 10 l. "Madonna and Child with Saints" . . 40 35
1113 20 l. "Madonna and Child with Saints Ulfus and Brigid" 75 75
1114 35 l. "The Madonna of the Cherries" . . 1·40 1·50
1111/14 . . . . *Set of* 4 2·40 2·40
MS1115 70 × 100 mm. 65 l. "The Pesaro Altarpiece" (*vert*) . . . . 2·75 3·00

(Des and litho Questa)

1988 (15 Feb). *Royal Ruby Wedding. T* **211a** *and similar vert designs. P* 14.

1116 2 l. deep brown, black and grey 10 10
1117 3 l. multicoloured 10 10
1118 10 l. deep brown, black and orange . . 30 35
1119 50 l. multicoloured . . . . 1·50 1·60
1116/19 . . . . *Set of* 4 1·75 1·90
MS1120 76 × 100 mm. 65 l. multicoloured . . 1·90 2·00

Designs:—3 l. Prince Charles' christening photograph, 1949; 10 l. Queen Elizabeth II with Prince Charles and Princess Anne, *c.* 1951; 50 l. Queen Elizabeth, *c.* 1960; 65 l. Wedding photograph, 1947.

212 *Russula cyanoxantha*

213 Golden Pheasant Fish

(Des L. Nelson. Litho Questa)

1988 (29 Feb). *Fungi. T* **212** *and similar vert designs. Multicoloured. P* 14.

1121 3 l. Type **212** 30 20
1122 10 l. *Lycoperdon perlatum* 70 50
1123 20 l. *Lactarius deliciosus* . . . . . . 1·25 1·25
1124 30 l. *Boletus edulis* . . . . 1·75 2·00
1121/4 . . . . *Set of* 4 3·50 3·50
MS1125 100 × 70 mm. 65 l. *Amanita muscaria* 2·25 2·50

(Des Mary Walters. Litho Format)

1988 (13 Apr). *Fishes of Sierra Leone. T* **213** *and similar horiz designs. Multicoloured. P* 15.

1126 3 l. Type **213** 10 10
1127 10 l. Banded Toothcarp 30 35
1128 20 l. Jewel Fish 60 65
1129 35 l. Butterfly Fish . . . . 1·00 1·10
1126/9 . . . . *Set of* 4 1·75 1·90
MS1130 99 × 69 mm. 65 l. African Longfin . . 1·90 2·25

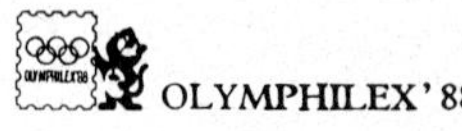

(**213a**)

1988 (19 Apr). *Stamp Exhibitions. Nos.* 1016, 1072 *and* 1079 *optd as T* **213a** *with various emblems.*

1131 25 l. *Freedom*, 1980 (optd "INDEPENDENCE 40, Israel") 75 80
1132 30 l. Boris Becker (optd Type **213a**) . . 90 95
1133 45 l. Maravedis (coins), *Nina* and Luis de Santangel (financier) (optd "PRAGA 88", Prague) . . . . 1·25 1·40
1131/3 . . . . *Set of* 3 2·50 2·75

214 Hands holding Coffee Beans and Woman with Cocoa

215 Basketball

(Des L. Lamm. Litho Questa)

1988 (3 May). *International Fund for Agricultural Development. T* **214** *and similar horiz designs. Multicoloured. P* 14.

1134 3 l. Type **214** 10 10
1135 15 l. Tropical fruits and man climbing palm tree 45 50
1136 25 l. Sheaf of rice and harvesters 75 80
1134/6 . . . . *Set of* 3 1·10 1·25

(Des L. Fried. Litho Questa)

1988 (15 June). *Olympic Games, Seoul (2nd issue). T* **215** *and similar vert designs. Multicoloured. P* 14.

1137 3 l. Type **215** 10 10
1138 10 l. Judo 30 35
1139 15 l. Gymnastics 45 50
1140 40 l. Synchronized swimming . . . . 1·25 1·40
1137/40 . . . . *Set of* 4 2·00 2·10
MS1141 73 × 101 mm. 65 l. Sierra Leone athlete 1·90 2·50

216 Swallow-tailed Bee Eater

217 *Aureol* (cargo liner)

(Des L. Nelson. Litho Questa)

1988 (25 June). *Birds. T* **216** *and similar vert designs. Multicoloured. P* 14.

1142 3 l. Type **216** 15 15
1143 5 l. Double-toothed Barbet 25 25
1144 8 l. African Golden Oriole 35 35
1145 10 l. Red Bishop 40 40
1146 12 l. Red-billed Shrike 45 45
1147 20 l. European Bee Eater 80 80
1148 35 l. Common Gonolek ("Barbary Shrike") 1·40 1·40
1149 40 l. Western Black-headed Oriole . . 1·50 1·50
1142/9 . . . . *Set of* 8 4·75 4·75
MS1150 Two sheets, each 111 × 82 mm. (a) 65 l. Purple Heron. (b) 65 l. Saddle-bill Stork *Set of* 2 *sheets* 3·75 4·50

(Des D. Miller. Litho Questa)

1988 (1 July). *Ships. T* **217** *and similar horiz designs. Multicoloured. P* 14.

1151 3 l. Type **217** 30 30
1152 10 l. *Dunkwa* (freighter) 80 80
1153 15 l. *Melampus* (container ship) . . . . 1·10 1·10
1154 30 l. *Dumbaia* (freighter) . . . . . . 1·90 1·90
1151/4 . . . . *Set of* 4 3·75 3·75
MS1155 95 × 95 mm. 65 l. Loading container ship, Freetown . . . . 1·90 2·25

(Litho Questa)

1988 (22 Aug). *500th Birth Anniv of Titian (artist). Vert designs as T* **186a** *of Lesotho showing paintings. Multicoloured. P* 13½×14.

1156 1 l. "The Concert" (detail) 10 10
1157 2 l. "Philip II of Spain" 10 10
1158 3 l. "Saint Sebastian" (detail) 10 10
1159 5 l. "Martyrdom of St. Peter Martyr" . . 15 20
1160 15 l. "St. Jerome" 45 50
1161 20 l. "St. Mark enthroned with Saints" . . 60 65
1162 25 l. "Portrait of a Young Man" 75 80
1163 30 l. "St. Jerome in Penitence" 90 95
1156/63 . . . . *Set of* 8 2·75 3·00
MS1164 Two sheets, each 110 × 95 mm. (a) 50 l. "Self Portrait". (b) 50 l. "Orpheus and Eurydice" *Set of* 2 *sheets* 3·00 3·50

218 Helicopter lowering "Mercury" Capsule to Flight Deck

219 Famine Relief Convoy crossing Desert

(Des W. Hanson. Litho B.D.T.)

1988 (26 Sept). *25th Death Anniv of John F. Kennedy (American statesman). U.S. Space Achievements. T* **218** *and similar horiz designs. Multicoloured. P* 14.

1165 3 l. Type **218** 10 10
1166 5 l. *Liberty Bell* 7 capsule descending (*vert*) 15 20
1167 15 l. Launch of first manned American capsule (*vert*) 45 50
1168 40 l. *Freedom* 7 orbiting Earth . . . . 1·25 1·40
1165/8 . . . . *Set of* 4 1·75 2·00
MS1169 98 × 69 mm. 65 l. President Kennedy and quotation . . . . 1·90 2·25

(Des J. Genzo. Litho B.D.T.)

1988 (1 Nov). *125th Anniv of International Red Cross. T* **219** *and similar multicoloured designs. P* 14.

1170 3 l. Type **219** 20 20
1171 10 l. Rifle and map of Battle of Solferino, 1859.. .. .. 50 50
1172 20 l. World War II hospital ship in Pacific 90 90
1173 40 l. Red Cross tent and World War I German biplanes .. .. .. 1·75 1·75
1170/3 .. .. *Set of* 4 3·00 3·00
MS1174 100 × 70 mm. 65 l. Henri Dunant (founder), Alfred Nobel and Peace Prize scroll (*horiz*) .. .. 1·90 2·25

(Des Walt Disney Company. Litho Questa)

1988 (1 Dec). *Christmas. "Mickey's Christmas Dance". Vert designs as T* **171a** *of Lesotho showing Walt Disney cartoon characters. Multicoloured. P* 13½×14.

1175 10 l. Donald Duck's nephews playing as band.. .. .. 35 35
a. Sheetlet. Nos. 1175/82 .. .. 2·50
1176 10 l. Clarabelle 35 35
1177 10 l. Goofy 35 35
1178 10 l. Scrooge McDuck and Grandma Duck 35 35
1179 10 l. Donald Duck 35 35
1180 10 l. Daisy Duck 35 35
1181 10 l. Minnie Mouse 35 35
1182 10 l. Mickey Mouse 35 35
1175/82 .. .. *Set of* 8 2·50 2·50
MS1183 Two sheets, each 127 × 102 mm. (a) 70 l. Mickey Mouse dancing the Charleston. (b) 70 l. Mickey Mouse jiving .. .. *Set of 2 sheets* 4·00 4·50

Nos. 1175/82 were printed together, *se-tenant* as a composite design, in sheetlets of eight.

220 "Adoration of the Magi" (detail)

GRAND SLAM WINNER

(221)

(Litho Questa)

1988 (15 Dec). *Christmas. Religious Paintings by Rubens. T* **220** *and similar vert designs. Multicoloured. P* 13½ × 14.

1184 3 l. Type **220** 10 10
1185 3 l. 60, "Adoration of the Shepherds" (detail) 10 10
1186 5 l. "Adoration of the Magi" (detail) .. 15 20
1187 10 l. "Adoration of the Shepherds" (different detail) 30 35
1188 20 l. "Virgin and Child surrounded by Flowers" 60 65
1189 40 l. "St. Gregory the Great and Other Saints" (detail) .. .. .. 1·25 1·40
1190 60 l. "Adoration of the Magi" (detail) 1·75 1·90
1191 80 l. "Madonna and Child with Saints" (detail) .. .. 2·25 2·40
1184/91 .. .. *Set of* 8 5·75 6·50
MS1192 Two sheets, each 76 × 113 mm. (a) 100 l. "Virgin and Child enthroned with Saints". (b) 100 l. "St. Gregory the Great and Other Saints" *Set of 2 sheets* 5·75 6·50

1989 (16 Jan). *Steffi Graf's "Grand Slam" Tennis Victories. No.* **MS**1076b *optd* "GOLD MEDALIST" (*No.* **MS**1193e) *or with T* **221** (*others*), *each with different inscription on sheet margin, all in gold.*

MS1193 105×75 mm. 100 l. Steffi Graf. (a) Optd "AUSTRALIAN OPEN JANUARY 11–24, 1988 GRAF v EVERET". (b) Optd "FRENCH OPEN MAY 23–JUNE 5, 1988 GRAF v ZVEREVA". (c) Optd "WIMBLEDON JUNE 20–JULY 4, 1988 GRAF v NAVRATILOVA". (d) Optd "U.S. OPEN AUGUST 29–SEPTEMBER 11, 1988 GRAF v SABATINI". (e) Optd "SEOUL OLYMPICS 1988 GRAF v SABATINI" *Set of 5 sheets* 1·50 1·60

Each marginal overprint includes score of match involved.

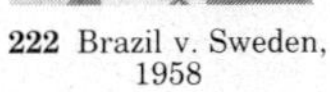

222 Brazil v. Sweden, 1958

223 Decathlon (Gold, C. Schenk, East Germany)

(Des J. McDaniel. Litho B.D.T.)

1989 (28 Apr). *World Cup Football Championship, Italy. T* **222** *and similar vert designs, each showing action from previous World Cup finals. Multicoloured. P* 14.

1194 3 l. Type **222** 10 10
1195 6 l. West Germany v. Hungary, 1954 .. 10 10
1196 8 l. England v. West Germany, 1966 .. 10 10
1197 10 l. Argentina v. Netherlands, 1978 .. 10 10
1198 12 l. Brazil v. Czechoslovakia, 1962 .. 10 10
1199 20 l. West Germany v. Netherlands, 1974 10 10
1200 30 l. Italy v. West Germany, 1982 .. 10 15
1201 40 l. Brazil v. Italy, 1970 .. .. .. 10 15
1194/201 .. .. *Set of* 8 45 55
MS1202 Two sheets, each 73×104 mm. (a) 100 l. Argentina v. West Germany, 1986. (b) 100 l. Uruguay v. Brazil, 1950 .. *Set of 2 sheets* 60 65

(Des L. Fried. Litho B.D.T.)

1989 (28 Apr). *Olympic Medal Winners, Seoul* (1988). *T* **223** *and similar horiz designs. Multicoloured. P* 14.

1203 3 l. Type **223** 10 10
1204 6 l. Men's heavyweight judo (Gold, H. Saito, Japan) 10 10
1205 10 l. Women's cycle road race (Silver, J. Niehaus, West Germany) 10 10
1206 15 l. Men's single sculls (Gold, T. Lange, East Germany) 10 10
1207 20 l. Men's 50 metres freestyle swimming (Gold, M. Biondi, U.S.A.) 10 10
1208 30 l. Men's 100 metres (Gold, C. Lewis, U.S.A.) 10 15
1209 40 l. Dressage (Gold, West Germany) .. 10 15
1210 50 l. Greco-Roman wrestling (57 kg) (Gold, A. Sike, Hungary) 15 20
1203/10 .. .. *Set of* 8 55 70
MS1211 Two sheets, each 70×100 mm. (a) 100 l. Olympic gold medal. (b) 100 l. Olympic torch and rings .. .. *Set of 2 sheets* 60 65

224 Map of Union States, Mail Lorry and Post Office

(Des J. Genzo. Litho B.D.T.)

1989 (19 May). *15th Anniv of Mano River Union. T* **224** *and similar horiz designs. Multicoloured. P* 14.

1212 1 l. Type **224** 10 10
1213 3 l. Map of West Africa and Presidents Momoh, Conte and Doe 10 10
1214 10 l. Construction of Freetown–Monrovia Highway 10 10
1212/14 .. .. *Set of* 3 10 10
MS1215 96×68 mm. 15 l. Presidents signing anniversary meeting communique .. 10 10

225 *Richard III*

SIERRA LEONE Le3

226 Centenary Logo

(Des G. Vasarhelyi. Litho B.D.T.)

1989 (30 May). *425th Birth Anniv of Shakespeare. T* **225** *and similar horiz designs. Multicoloured. P* 13.

1216 15 l. Type **225** 10 10
a. Sheetlet. Nos. 1216/23 40
1217 15 l. *Othello* (Iago) 10 10
1218 15 l. *Two Gentlemen of Verona* 10 10
1219 15 l. *Macbeth* (Lady Macbeth) 10 10
1220 15 l. *Hamlet* 10 10
1221 15 l. *The Taming of the Shrew* 10 10
1222 15 l. *The Merry Wives of Windsor* .. 10 10
1223 15 l. *Henry IV* (Sir John Falstaff) .. 10 10
1224 15 l. *Macbeth* (The Witches) 10 10
a. Sheetlet. Nos. 1224/31 40
1225 15 l. *Romeo and Juliet* 10 10
1226 15 l. *Merchant of Venice* 10 10
1227 15 l. *As You Like It* 10 10
1228 15 l. *The Taming of the Shrew* (banquet scene) 10 10
1229 15 l. *King Lear* 10 10
1230 15 l. *Othello* (Othello and Desdemona) .. 10 10
1231 15 l. *Henry IV* (Justice Shallow) 10 10
1216/31 .. .. *Set of* 16 70 70
MS1232 Two sheets, each 117×82 mm. (a) 100 l. Shakespeare and arms (49×36 *mm*). (b) 100 l. Shakespeare (49×36 *mm*) .. *Set of 2 sheets* 60 65

Nos. 1216/23 and 1224/31 were each printed together, *se-tenant*, in sheetlets of eight stamps and one central stamp-size label.

(Litho Questa)

1989 (8 June). *Centenary of Ahmadiyya Muslim Society. P* 14.

1233 **226** 3 l. brownish black and new blue .. 10 10

(Litho Questa)

1989 (3 July). *Japanese Art* (1*st series*). *Paintings by Seiho. Multicoloured designs as T* **187a** *of Lesotho. P* 14×13½ (3, 10, 12, 40 *l.*) *or* 13½×14 (*others*).

1234 3 l. "Lapping Waves" 10 10
1235 6 l. "Hazy Moon" (*vert*) 10 10
1236 8 l. "Passing Spring" (*vert*) 10 10
1237 10 l. "Mackerels" 10 10
1238 12 l. "Calico Cat" 10 10
1239 30 l. "The First Time to be a Model" (*vert*) 10 15
1240 40 l. "Kingly Lion" 10 15
1241 75 l. "After a Shower" (*vert*) 20 25
1234/41 .. .. *Set of* 8 60 70
MS1242 Two sheets, each 102×77 mm. (a) 150 l. "Dozing in the midst of all the Chirping" (detail) (*vert*). P 13½×14. (b) 150 l. "Domesticated Monkeys and Rabbits" (detail). P 14×13½ *Set of 2 sheets* 90 95

Nos. 1234/41 were each printed in sheetlets of 10 containing two horizontal or vertical strips of 5 stamps separated by printed labels commemorating Emperor Hirohito.

See also Nos. 1321/51.

227 Robespierre and Bastille

(Des Design Element. Litho B.D.T.)

1989 (13 July). *"Philexfrance 89" International Stamp Exhibition, Paris, and Bicentenary of French Revolution. T* **227** *and similar multicoloured designs. P* 14.

1243 6 l. Type **227** 10 10
1244 20 l. Danton and Louvre 10 10
1245 45 l. Queen Marie Antoinette and Notre Dame 10 15
1246 80 l. Louis XVI and Palace of Versailles .. 25 30
1243/6 .. .. *Set of* 4 40 50
MS1247 77×107 mm. 150 l. Celebrating crowd, Paris (*vert*) 45 50

228 "Sputnik" Satellite in Orbit, 1957

SIERRA LEONE Le3

229 *Bulbophyllum barbigerum*

(Des G. Vasarhelyi. Litho B.D.T.)

1989 (20 July). *History of Space Exploration. T* **228** *and similar horiz designs. P* 14.

1248/301 10 l.×27, 15 l.×27 multicoloured *Set of* 54 2·00 2·10
MS1302 Three sheets, each 112×90 mm. 100 l. ×3 multicoloured .. .. *Set of 3 sheets* 90 95

Nos. 1248/301 were issued as six sheetlets, each of nine different designs.

(Des W. Hanson Studio. Litho B.D.T.)

1989 (8 Sept). *Orchids of Sierra Leone. T* **229** *and similar vert designs. Multicoloured. P* 14.

1303 3 l. Type **229** 10 10
1304 6 l. *Bulbophyllum falcatum* 10 10
1305 12 l. *Habenaria macrara* 10 10
1306 20 l. *Eurychone rothchildiana* 10 10
1307 50 l. *Calyptrochilum christyanum* .. 15 20
1308 60 l. *Bulbophyllum distans* 20 25
1309 70 l. *Eulophia guineensis* 20 25
1310 80 l. *Diaphananthe pellucida* 25 30
1303/10 .. .. *Set of* 8 90 1·10
MS1311 Two sheets, each 112×80 mm. (a) 100 l. *Cyrtorchis arcuata* and Pagoda, Kew Gardens. (b) 100 l. *Eulophia cucullata* .. *Set of 2 sheets* 60 65

230 *Salamis temora*

(Des Mary Walters. Litho B.D.T.)

1989 (11 Sept). *Butterflies. T* **230** *and similar multicoloured designs. P* 14.

1312 6 l. Type **230** 10 10
1313 12 l. *Pseudacraea lucretia* 10 10
1314 18 l. *Charaxes boueti* (*vert*) 10 10
1315 30 l. *Graphium antheus* (*vert*) 10 15
1316 40 l. *Colotis protomedia* 10 15
1317 60 l. *Asterope pechueli* (*vert*) 20 25
1318 72 l. *Coenyra aurantiaca* 20 25
1319 80 l. *Precis octavia* (*vert*) 25 30
1312/19 .. .. *Set of* 8 90 1·10
MS1320 Two sheets, each 100×70 mm. (a) 100 l. *Charaxes cithaeron* (*vert*). (b) 100 l. *Euphaedra themis* .. .. *Set of 2 sheets* 60 65

(Litho Questa)

1989 (13 Nov). *Japanese Art (2nd series). Paintings by Hiroshige of "The Fifty-three Stations on the Tokaido Road". Horiz designs as T* **187***a of Lesotho. Multicoloured. P* 14×13½.

1321 25 l. "Ferry-boat to Kawasaki" 10 10
1322 25 l. "The Hilly Town of Hodogaya" .. 10 10
1323 25 l. "Lute Players at Fujisawa" 10 10
1324 25 l. "Mild Rainstorm at Oiso" 10 10
1325 25 l. "Lake Ashi and Mountains of Hakone" 10 10
1326 25 l. "Twilight at Numazu" 10 10
1327 25 l. "Mount Fuji from Hara" 10 10
1328 25 l. "Samurai Children riding through Yoshiwara" 10 10
1329 25 l. "Mountain Pass at Yui" 10 10
1330 25 l. "Harbour at Ejiri" 10 10
1331 25 l. "Halt at Fujieda" 10 10
1332 25 l. "Misty Kanaya on the Oi River" .. 10 10
1333 25 l. "The Bridge to Kakegawa" 10 10
1334 25 l. "Teahouse at Fukuroi" 10 10
1335 25 l. "The Ford at Mistuke" 10 10
1336 25 l. "Coolies warming themselves at Hamamatsu" 10 10
1337 25 l. "Imakiri Ford at Maisaka" 10 10
1338 25 l. "Pacific Ocean from Shirasuka" .. 10 10
1339 25 l. "Futakawa Street-singers" 10 10
1340 25 l. "Repairing Yoshida Castle" 10 10
1341 25 l. "The Inn at Akasaka" 10 10
1342 25 l. "The Bridge to Okazaki" 10 10
1343 25 l. "Samurai's Wife entering Narumi" .. 10 10
1344 25 l. "Harbour at Kuwana" 10 10
1345 25 l. "Autumn in Ishiyakushi" 10 10
1346 25 l. "Snowfall at Kameyama" 10 10
1347 25 l. "The Frontier-station of Seki" .. 10 10
1348 25 l. "Teahouse at Sakanoshita" 10 10
1349 25 l. "Kansai Houses at Minakushi" .. 10 10
1350 25 l. "Kusatsu Station" 10 10
1321/50 .. .. *Set of* 30 3·00 3·00
MS1351 Two sheets, each 102×75 mm. (a) 120 l. "Nihom Bridge, Edo". (b) 120 l. "Sanjo Bridge, Kyoto" .. .. *Set of* 2 *sheets* 70 75

The English captions of the two miniature sheets of No. **MS**1351 are transposed. The sheet showing the Nihom Bridge, Edo, has a group of fishmongers in the left foreground.

(Des Design Element. Litho Questa)

1989 (17 Nov). *"World Stamp Expo '89" International Stamp Exhibition, Washington (1st issue). Landmarks of Washington. Sheet 78×61 mm containing horiz design as T* **193***a of Lesotho. Multicoloured. P* 14.

MS1352 100 l. Jefferson Memorial 30 35

231 Formosan Sika Deer

(Des J. Genzo. Litho B.D.T.)

1989 (29 Nov). *"World Stamp Expo '89" International Stamp Exhibition, Washington (2nd issue). Endangered Fauna. T* **231** *and similar multicoloured designs. P* 14.

1353 6 l. Humpback Whale 10 10
1354 9 l. Type **231** 10 10
1355 16 l. Spanish Lynx 10 10
1356 20 l. Goitred Gazelle 10 10
1357 30 l. Japanese Sea Lion 10 15
1358 50 l. Long-eared Owl 15 20
1359 70 l. Lady Amherst's ("Chinese Copper") Pheasant 20 25
1360 100 l. Siberian Tiger 30 35
1353/60 .. .. *Set of* 8 85 1·00
MS1361 Two sheets, each 103×75 mm. (a) 150 l. Mauritius Kestrel (*vert*). (b) 150 l. Japanese Crested Ibis (*vert*) .. .. *Set of* 2 *sheets* 90 95

(Des Walt Disney Co. Litho Questa)

1989 (18 Dec). *Christmas. Horiz designs as T* **73** *of St. Vincent Grenadines showing Walt Disney cartoon characters with cars. Multicoloured. P* 14×13½.

1362 3 l. Mickey Mouse and Goofy in Rolls-Royce "Phantom II Roadstar", 1934 10 10
1363 6 l. Mickey and Minnie Mouse in Mercedes-Benz "500K", 1935 .. 10 10
1364 10 l. Mickey and Minnie Mouse with Jaguar "SS-100", 1938 .. .. 10 10
1365 12 l. Mickey Mouse and Goofy with U.S. army jeep, 1941 .. .. .. 10 10
1366 20 l. Mickey and Minnie Mouse with Buick Roadmaster Sedan "Model 91", 1937 10 10
1367 30 l. Mickey Mouse driving 1948 Tucker 10 15
1368 40 l. Mickey and Minnie Mouse in Alfa Romeo, 1933 .. .. .. 10 15
1369 50 l. Mickey and Minnie Mouse with 1937 Cord 15 20
1362/9 .. .. *Set of* 8 55 70
MS1370 Two sheets, each 127×101 mm. (a) 100 l. Mickey in Fiat Topolino, 1938. (b) 100 l. Mickey Mouse with gifts and Pontiac "Model 401", 1931 .. .. .. *Set of* 2 *sheets* 60 65

(Litho Questa)

1989 (22 Dec). *Christmas. Paintings by Rembrandt. Vert designs as T* **193***b of Lesotho. Multicoloured. P* 14.

1371 3 l. "The Adoration of the Magi" .. 10 10
1372 6 l. "The Holy Family with a Cat" .. 10 10
1373 10 l. "The Holy Family with Angels" .. 10 10
1374 15 l. "Simeon in the Temple" 10 10
1375 30 l. "The Circumcision" 10 15
1376 90 l. "The Holy Family" 25 30
1377 100 l. "The Visitation" 30 35
1378 120 l. "The Flight into Egypt" 35 40
1371/8 .. .. *Set of* 8 1·10 1·25
MS1379 Two sheets, each 70×95 mm. (a) 150 l. "The Adoration of the Shepherds" (detail). (b) 150 l. "The Presentation of Jesus in the Temple" (detail) .. .. *Set of* 2 *sheets* 90 95

232 Johann Kepler (astronomer)

(Des G. Vasarhelyi. Litho Questa)

1990 (15 Jan). *Exploration of Mars. T* **232** *and similar horiz designs showing astronomers, spacecraft and Martian landscapes. P* 14.

1380/1415 175 l. × 36 multicoloured .. *Set of* 36 19·00 20·00
MS1416 Two sheets, each 105×85 mm. (a) 150 l. The "Face" on Mars. (b) 150 l. Section of space station .. .. *Set of* 2 *sheets* 90 95

Nos. 1380/1415 were issued as four sheetlets each of nine different designs.

232*a* Dolittle's B-25 *Ruptured Duck*, 1942

(Des J. Batchelor. Litho Questa)

1990 (5 Feb). *50th Anniv of Second World War. American Aircraft. T* **232***a and similar horiz designs. Multicoloured. P* 14.

1417 1 l. Type **232***a* 10 10
1418 2 l. B-24 Liberator 10 10
1419 3 l. A-20 Boston attacking Japanese convoy, Bismark Sea, 1943 .. 10 10
1420 9 l. P-38 Lightning 10 10
1421 12 l. B-26 bomber 10 10
1422 16 l. Two B-17 F bombers 10 10
1423 50 l. B-25 D bomber 15 20
1424 80 l. B-29 Superfortress 25 30
1425 90 l. B-17 G bomber 25 30
1426 100 l. B-29 Superfortress *Enola Gay* .. 30 35
1417/26 .. .. *Set of* 10 1·10 1·25
MS1427 Two sheets, each 106×77 mm. (a) 150 l. Dolittle B-25 taking off from the U.S.S. *Hornet*, 1942. (b) 150 l. B-17 G of 447th Bomber Group *Set of* 2 *sheets* 90 95

233 Mickey Mouse at Bauxite Mine

234 Olivier as Antony in *Antony and Cleopatra*, 1951

(Des Walt Disney Co. Litho Questa)

1990 (23 Apr). *Sierra Leone Sites and Scenes. T* **233** *and similar multicoloured designs, each showing Walt Disney cartoon characters. P* 14×13½.

1428 3 l. Type **233** 10 10
1429 6 l. Scrooge McDuck panning for gold .. 10 10
1430 10 l. Minnie Mouse at Lungi Airport .. 10 10
1431 12 l. Mickey Mouse at Old Fourah Bay College 10 10
1432 16 l. Mickey Mouse mining bauxite .. 10 10
1433 20 l. Huey, Dewey and Louie harvesting rice 10 10
1434 30 l. Mickey and Minnie Mouse admire the Freetown Cotton Tree 10 15
1435 100 l. Mickey Mouse flying over Rutile Mine 30 35
1436 200 l. Mickey Mouse fishing at Goderich .. 60 65
1437 225 l. Mickey and Minnie Mouse at Bintumani Hotel 65 70
1428/37 .. .. *Set of* 10 1·75 2·00
MS1438 Two sheets, each 130×100 mm. (a) 250 l. Dwarfs with diamonds. P 14×13½. (b) 250 l. Mickey and Minnie Mouse at King Jimmy Market (*vert*). P 13½×14 .. *Set of* 2 *sheets* 1·50 1·60

(Des J. Iskowitz. Litho Questa)

1990 (27 Apr). *Sir Laurence Olivier (actor) Commemoration. T* **234** *and similar vert designs. Multicoloured. P* 14.

1439 3 l. Type **234** 10 10
1440 9 l. As King Henry V in *Henry V*, 1943 10 10
1441 16 l. As Oedipus in *Oedipus*, 1945 .. 10 10
1442 20 l. As Heathcliffe in *Wuthering Heights*, 1939 .. .. 10 10
1443 30 l. As Szell in *Marathon Man*, 1976 .. 10 15
1444 70 l. As Othello in *Othello*, 1964 .. 20 25
1445 175 l. As Michael in *Beau Geste*, 1929 .. 50 55
1446 200 l. As King Richard III in *Richard III*, 1956 .. .. 60 65
1439/46 .. .. *Set of* 8 1·40 1·60
MS1447 Two sheets, each 98×68 mm. (a) 250 l. As Hamlet in *Hamlet*, 1947. (b) 250 l. As Sir Hugh Dowding in *The Battle of Britain*, 1969 *Set of* 2 *sheets* 1·50 1·60

235 Penny Black

236 Cameroons World Cup Team

(Des M. Pollard. Litho Questa)

1990 (3 May). *150th Anniv of the Penny Black. P* 14×13½.

1448 **235** 50 l. deep ultramarine 15 20
1449 100 l. purple-brown 30 35
MS1450 145×106 mm. **235** 250 l. black .. 75 80

(Des Young Phillips Studio. Litho Questa)

1990 (11 May). *World Cup Football Championship, Italy. Finalists. T* **236** *and similar horiz designs. Multicoloured. P* 14×13½.

1451/74 15 l. × 8 (Type **236**, Colombia, Costa Rica, Egypt, Rumania, South Korea, U.A.E., Yugoslavia), 30 l. × 8 (Austria, Belgium, Czechoslovakia, Netherlands, Scotland, Sweden, Uruguay, U.S.S.R.), 45 l. × 8 (Argentina, Brazil, England, Ireland, Italy, Spain, U.S.A., West Germany) .. .. .. *Set of* 24 2·10 2·25

Each design of Nos. 1451/74 was issued in separate sheetlets of 8 stamps with a central label showing the World Cup and Championship logo.

237 Great Crested Grebe

(Des Mary Walters. Litho Questa)

1990 (4 June). *Birds. T* **237** *and similar horiz designs. Multicoloured. P* 14.

1475 3 l. Type **237** 10 10
1476 6 l. Green Woodhoopoe 10 10
1477 10 l. African Jacana 10 10
1478 12 l. Avocet 10 10
1479 20 l. Peters's Finfoot 10 15
1480 80 l. Glossy Ibis 25 30
1481 150 l. Hamerkop 45 50
1482 200 l. Black-throated Honeyguide .. 60 65
1475/82 .. .. *Set of* 8 1·40 1·50
MS1483 Two sheets, each 100×70 (a) 250 l. African Palm Swift. (b) 250 l. Painted Snipe *Set of* 2 *sheets* 1·50 1·60

(Des Walt Disney Co. Litho Questa)

1990 (6 June). *"Stamp World London 90" International Stamp Exhibition. British Costumes. Multicoloured designs as T* **239***a of Maldive Islands showing Walt Disney cartoon characters. P* 13½×14.

1484 3 l. Mickey Mouse as a Yeoman Warder (*vert*) 10 10
1485 6 l. Scrooge McDuck as a lamplighter (*vert*) 10 10
1486 12 l. Goofy as a medieval knight (*vert*) .. 10 10
1487 15 l. Clarabelle as Anne Boleyn (*vert*) .. 10 10
1488 75 l. Minnie Mouse as Queen Elizabeth I (*vert*) 20 25
1489 100 l. Donald Duck as a chimney sweep (*vert*) 30 35
1490 125 l. Pete as King Henry VIII (*vert*) .. 35 40
1491 150 l. Clarabelle, Minnie Mouse and Daisy Duck as May dancers (*vert*) .. 45 50
1484/91 .. .. *Set of* 8 1·40 1·50
MS1492 Two sheets, each 127×102 mm. (a) 250 l. Donald Duck as a lawyer (*vert*). P 13½×14. (b) 250 l. Minnie Mouse as Queen Boadicea. P 14×13½. .. .. *Set of* 2 *sheets* 1·50 1·60

(Des Young Phillips Studio. Litho Questa)

1990 (5 July). *90th Birthday of Queen Elizabeth the Queen Mother. Vert designs as T* **198a** *of Lesotho showing portraits, 1980–89. Multicoloured. P* 14.

1493	75 l. Queen Mother on Remembrance Sunday	20	25
	a. Strip of 3. Nos. 1493/5	55	
1494	75 l. Queen Mother in yellow hat	20	25
1495	75 l. Waving to crowds on 85th birthday	20	25
1493/5	*Set of* 3	55	70
MS1496	90×75 mm. 250 l. As No. 1495	75	80

Nos. 1493/5 were printed together, horizontally and vertically *se-tenant*, in sheetlets of 9 (3×3).

238 Golden Cat

239 Rabbit

(Des S. Barlowe. Litho Questa)

1990 (24 Sept). *Wildlife. T* **238** *and similar multicoloured designs. P* 14.

1497	25 l. Type **238**	10	10
	a. Sheetlet. Nos. 1497/1514	80	
1498	25 l. White-backed Night Heron	10	10
1499	25 l. Bateleur Eagle	10	10
1500	25 l. Marabou Stork	10	10
1501	25 l. White-faced Whistling Duck	10	10
1502	25 l. Aardvark	10	10
1503	25 l. Royal Antelope	10	10
1504	25 l. Pygmy Hippopotamus	10	10
1505	25 l. Leopard	10	10
1506	25 l. Sacred Ibis	10	10
1507	25 l. Mona Monkey	10	10
1508	25 l. Darter	10	10
1509	25 l. Chimpanzee	10	10
1510	25 l. African Elephant	10	10
1511	25 l. Potto	10	10
1512	25 l. African Manatee	10	10
1513	25 l. African Fish Eagle	10	10
1514	25 l. African Spoonbill	10	10
1497/1514	*Set of* 18	80	80
MS1515	106×76 mm. 150 l. Crowned Eagle (*vert*)	45	50

Nos. 1497/1514 were printed together, *se-tenant*, in sheetlets of 18 with the background forming a map of Sierra Leone.

(Litho Questa)

1990 (22 Oct). *Fairground Carousel Animals. T* **239** *and similar vert designs. Multicoloured. P* 14.

1516	5 l. Type **239**	10	10
1517	10 l. Horse with panther saddle	10	10
1518	20 l. Ostrich	10	10
1519	30 l. Zebra	10	15
1520	50 l. Horse	15	20
1521	80 l. Sea monster	25	30
1522	100 l. Giraffe	30	35
1523	150 l. Armoured horse	45	50
1524	200 l. Camel	60	65
1516/24	*Set of* 9	1·75	2·10
MS1525	Two sheets (a) 98×68 mm. 300 l. Masked horse. (b) 68×98 mm. 300 l. Baden-Powell as Centaur *Set of* 2 *sheets*	1·75	1·90

(Des B. Grout. Litho B.D.T.)

1990 (12 Nov). *Olympic Games, Barcelona* (1992). *Multicoloured designs as T* **202** *of Lesotho. P* 14.

1526	5 l. Start of Men's 100 metres	10	10
1527	10 l. Men's 4×400 metres relay	10	10
1528	20 l. Men's 100 metres in progress	10	10
1529	30 l. Weightlifting	10	15
1530	40 l. Freestyle wrestling	10	15
1531	80 l. Water polo	25	30
1532	150 l. Women's gymnastics	45	50
1533	200 l. Cycling	60	65
1526/33	*Set of* 8	1·50	1·75
MS1534	Two sheets, each 103×75 mm. (a) 400 l. Boxing (*horiz*). (b) 400 l. Olympic flag (*horiz*) *Set of* 2 *sheets*	2·40	2·50

240 Morty assembling Bicycle by Christmas Tree

241 "Holy Family with St. Elizabeth" (Mantegna)

(Des Walt Disney Co. Litho B.D.T.)

1990 (17 Dec). *Christmas. "The Night before Christmas". T* **240** *and similar designs showing Walt Disney cartoon characters in scenes from Clement Moore's poem. P* 13.

1535/58	50 l. × 8, 75 l. × 8, 100 l. × 8 *Set of* 24	5·50	5·75
MS1559	Six sheets, each 129×107 mm. 400 l. × 6 multicoloured *Set of* 6 *sheets*	7·25	7·50

Nos. 1535/58 were issued as three sheetlets of eight, each containing stamps of the same face value *se-tenant*.

Of the stamps in No. **MS**1559 four horizontal and two vertical.

(Litho Cartor, France)

1990 (17 Dec). *Christmas. Paintings. T* **241** *and similar vert designs. Multicoloured. P* 13.

1560	10 l. "Holy Family resting" (Rembrandt)	10	10
1561	20 l. Type **241**	10	10
1562	30 l. "Virgin and Child with an Angel" (Correggio)	10	15
1563	50 l. "Annunciation" (Bernardo Strozzi)	15	20
1564	100 l. "Madonna and Child appearing to St. Anthony" (Lippi)	30	35
1565	175 l. "Virgin and Child" (Giovanni Boltraffio)	50	55
1566	200 l. "Esterhazy Madonna" (Raphael)	60	65
1567	300 l. "Coronation of Mary" (Andrea Orcagna)	90	95
1560/7	*Set of* 8	2·40	2·75
MS1568	Two sheets, each 75×114 mm. (a) 400 l. "Adoration of the Shepherds" (Bronzino). (b) 400 l. "Adoration of the Shepherds" (Gerard David) *Set of* 2 *sheets*	2·40	2·50

242 "Helena Fourment as Hagar in the Wilderness" (detail, Rubens)

(Litho Questa)

1990 (24 Dec). *350th Death Anniv of Rubens. T* **242** *and similar vert designs. Multicoloured. P* $13^1/_2$×14.

1569	5 l. Type **242**	10	10
1570	10 l. "Isabella Brant"	10	10
1571	20 l. "Countess of Arundel and her Party" (detail)	10	10
1572	60 l. "Countess of Arundel and her Party" (different detail)	20	25
1573	80 l. "Nicolaas Rockox"	25	30
1574	100 l. "Adriana Perez"	30	35
1575	150 l. "George Villiers, Duke of Buckingham" (detail)	45	50
1576	300 l. "Countess of Buckingham"	90	95
1569/76	*Set of* 8	2·00	2·25
MS1577	Two sheets, each 71×100 mm. (a) 350 l. "Giovanni Carlo Dorio" (detail). (b) 350 l. "Veronica Spinola Dorio" (detail) *Set of* 2 *sheets*	2·10	2·25

Singapore

A Crown Colony until the end of 1957. From 1 August 1958, an internally self-governing territory designated the State of Singapore. From 16 September 1963, part of the Malaysian Federation until 9 August 1965, when it became an independent republic within the Commonwealth.

Stamps in the Crown Colony Victory design were prepared for Singapore in 1946, but not issued. Examples of the 8 c. carmine are known to exist.

CROWN COLONY

(Typo D.L.R.)

1948 (1 Sept)–**52.** *As T* **58** *of Malaysia (Straits Settlements), but inscribed "SINGAPORE" at foot. Wmk Mult Script CA. Chalk-surfaced paper. (a) P* 14.

No.	Description	Unused	Used
1	1 c. black	15	10
2	2 c. orange	15	10
3	3 c. green	20	10
4	4 c. brown	20	40
5	6 c. grey	25	15
6	8 c. scarlet (1.10.48)	25	15
7	10 c. purple	20	10
8	15 c. ultramarine (1.10.48)	2·75	10
9	20 c. black and green (1.10.48)	2·75	20
10	25 c. purple and orange (1.10.48)	1·50	15
11	40 c. red and purple (1.10.48)	4·75	5·00
12	50 c. black and blue (1.10.48)	3·25	10
13	$1 blue and purple (1.10.48)	10·00	60
14	$2 green and scarlet (25.10.48)	48·00	2·50
15	$5 green and brown (1.10.48)	£100	2·50
1/15	*Set of* 15	£150	11·00

(*b*) *P* 17½ × 18

No.	Description	Unused	Used
16	1 c. black (21.5.52)	50	1·75
17	2 c. orange (31.10.49)	70	80
19	4 c. brown (1.7.49)	70	10
19*a*	5 c. bright purple (1.9.52)	2·50	55
21	6 c. grey (10.12.52)	70	10
21*a*	8 c. green (1.9.52)	4·00	2·25
22	10 c. purple (9.2.50)	50	10
22*a*	12 c. scarlet (1.9.52)	4·00	3·75
23	15 c. ultramarine (9.2.50)	4·00	10
24	20 c. black and green (31.10.49)	2·75	1·10
24*a*	20 c. bright blue (1.9.52)	4·00	10
25	25 c. purple and orange (9.2.50)	80	10
25*a*	35 c. scarlet and purple (1.9.52)	4·00	90
26	40 c. red and purple (24.5.51)	16·00	8·50
27	50 c. black and blue (9.2.50)	5·50	10
28	$1 blue and purple (31.10.49)	11·00	20
	a. Error. St. Edward's Crown, W 9*b*	£3250	
29	$2 green and scarlet (24.5.51)	£100	1·75
	a. Error. St. Edward's Crown, W 9*b*	£3250	
30	$5 green and brown (19.12.51)	£140	1·75
16/30	*Set of* 18	£275	21·00

Nos. 28a and 29a occur on rows in the watermark in which the crowns and letters "CA" alternate.

1948 (25 Oct). *Royal Silver Wedding. As Nos.* 143/4 *of Jamaica.*

No.	Description	Unused	Used
31	10 c. violet	75	10
32	$5 brown	95·00	27·00

1949 (10 Oct). *75th Anniv of U.P.U. As Nos.* 145/8 *of Jamaica.*

No.	Description	Unused	Used
33	10 c. purple	75	10
34	15 c. deep blue	3·25	1·40
35	25 c. orange	3·75	1·25
36	50 c. blue-black	5·50	2·50
33/6	*Set of* 4	12·00	4·75

1953 (2 June). *Coronation. As No.* 153 *of Jamaica.*

No.	Description	Unused	Used
37	10 c. black and reddish purple	1·00	10

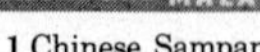

1 Chinese Sampan

2 Raffles Statue

3 Singapore River

4 Arms of Singapore

(Des Dr. C. A. Gibson-Hill, except 25 c., 30 c., 50 c. and $5 (from photographs, etc.). Photo Harrison (1 c. to 50 c.). Recess (centre typo on $5) B.W. (others))

1955 (4 Sept)–**59.** *Designs as T* **1/4**. *Wmk Mult Script CA. P* 13½×14½ (1 *c. to* 50 *c.*) *or* 14 (*others*).

No.	Description	Unused	Used
38	1 c. black	10	40
39	2 c. yellow-orange	60	1·00
40	4 c. brown	35	15
41	5 c. bright purple	35	15
42	6 c. deep grey-blue	35	30
43	8 c. turquoise-blue	55	70
44	10 c. deep lilac	2·00	10
45	12 c. rose-carmine	2·25	2·50
46	20 c. ultramarine	90	10
	a. Blue (13.3.58)	1·10	10
47	25 c. orange-red and bluish violet	75	10
	a. Orange-red and purple (21.1.59)	3·50	40
48	30 c. violet and brown-purple	2·00	10
49	50 c. blue and black	1·25	10
50	$1 blue and deep purple	22·00	10
51	$2 blue-green and scarlet	26·00	65
52	$5 yellow, red, brown and slate-black	35·00	3·00
38/52	*Set of* 15	80·00	8·00

Designs: *Horiz as T* 1—2 c. Malay kolek; 4 c. Twa-kow lighter; 5 c. Lombok sloop; 6 c. Trengganu pinas; 8 c. Palari schooner; 10 c. Timber tongkong; 12 c. Hainan junk; 20 c. Cocos-Keeling schooner; 25 c. "Argonaut" aircraft; 30 c. Oil tanker; 50 c. *Chusan III* (liner).

Plate 2A and 2B of the 10 c. (12 April 1960) and the blue "3A" and "3B" plates of the 50 c. "3A–2A", "3B–2B" (part of the 24 January 1961 issue and later printings) were printed with a finer screen (250 dots per inch, instead of the normal 200) (*Price* 10 *c.,* £2.75 *un,* 20*p us.* 50 *c.* £2 *un,* 10*p us*).

INTERNAL SELF-GOVERNMENT

16 The Singapore Lion

17 State Flag

(Photo Harrison)

1959 (1 June). *New Constitution. W w* **12**. *P* 11½ × 12.

No.	Type	Description	Unused	Used
53	**16**	4 c. yellow, sepia and rose-red	30	30
54		10 c. yellow, sepia and reddish purple	40	20
55		20 c. yellow, sepia and bright blue	1·10	2·00
56		25 c. yellow, sepia and green	1·10	1·25
57		30 c. yellow, sepia and violet	1·25	2·00
58		50 c. yellow, sepia and deep slate	1·50	2·00
53/8		*Set of* 6	5·00	7·00

(Litho Enschedé)

1960 (3 June). *National Day. W w* **12** (*sideways*). *P* 13½.

No.	Type	Description	Unused	Used
59	**17**	4 c. red, yellow and blue	20	40
60		10 c. red, yellow and grey	40	10

18 Clasped Hands

(Photo Enschedé)

1961 (3 June). *National Day. W w* **12**. *P* 13½.

No.	Type	Description	Unused	Used
61	**18**	4 c. black, brown and pale yellow	20	40
62		10 c. black, deep green and pale yellow	35	10

19 *Arachnis "Maggie Oei"* (orchid)

20 Sea-Horse

21 Six-banded Barb

24 *Vanda "Tan Chay Yan"* (orchid)

26*a* Black-naped Tern

30 White-rumped Shama

(Photo Harrison (orchids, fish and 15 c. bird) D.L.R. (birds, except 15 c.))

1962 (31 Mar)–**66.** *T* **19/21, 24, 26*a*, 30** *and similar designs. W w* **12**. *P* 12½ (i), 14½ × 13½ (ii), 13½ × 14½ (iii), 13½ × 13 (iv) *or* 13 × 13½ (v).

No.	Description	Unused	Used
63	1 c. multicoloured (i) (10.3.63)	10	75
64	2 c. brown and green (ii)	10	75
65	4 c. black and orange-red (iii)	10	30
	a. Black omitted	£120	
66	5 c. red and black (iii)	10	10
	a. Red omitted	£120	
67	6 c. black and greenish yellow (ii)	45	60
68	8 c. multicoloured (i) (10.3.63)	55	2·25
69	10 c. red-orange and black (iii)	15	10
	a. Red-orange omitted	90·00	
70	12 c. multicoloured (i) (10.3.63)	55	2·25
70*a*	15 c. multicoloured (i) (9.11.66)	80	10
	ab. Orange (eye) omitted	10·00	
71	20 c. orange and blue (ii)	30	10
	a. Orange omitted	£150	
72	25 c. black and orange (iii)	35	10
73	30 c. multicoloured (i) (10.3.63)	1·00	10
	a. Yellow (flowers) omitted	30·00	
74	50 c. multicoloured (iv) (10.3.63)	95	10
75	$1 multicoloured (iv) (10.3.63)	10·00	30
76	$2 multicoloured (iv) (10.3.63)	13·00	75
77	$5 multicoloured (v) (10.3.63)	27·00	2·75
63/77	*Set of* 16	48·00	10·00

Designs: *Horiz* (*as T* **21**)—5 c. Clown fish; 10 c. Harlequin; 25 c. Two-spot Gourami. (*As T* **30**)—$1 White-breasted Kingfisher. *Vert* (*as T* **20**)—6 c. Archer fish; 20 c. Butterfly fish. (*As T* **24**)—12 c. *Grammatophyllum speciosum* (orchid); 30 c. *Vanda "Miss Joaquim"* (orchid). (*As T* **26*a***)—$2 Yellow-bellied Sunbird; $5 White-bellied Sea Eagle.

The 15 c., 30 c., $2 and $5 exist with PVA gum as well as gum arabic.

See also Nos. 83/88.

34 "The Role of Labour in Nation-Building"

35 Blocks of Flats, Singapore

(Photo Courvoisier)

1962 (3 June). *National Day. P* 11½ × 12.

No.	Type	Description	Unused	Used
78	**34**	4 c. yellow, rose-carmine and black	15	40
79		10 c. yellow, blue and black	35	10

(Photo Harrison)

1963 (3 June). *National Day. W w* **12**. *P* 12½.

No.	Type	Description	Unused	Used
80	**35**	4 c. orange-red, black, blue & turq-blue	15	40
81		10 c. orange-red, blk, yell-olive & turq-bl	35	10

36 Dancers in National Costume

37 Workers

(Photo Harrison)

1963 (8 Aug). *South East Asia Cultural Festival. W w* **12**. *P* 14 × 14½.

No.	Type	Description	Unused	Used
82	**36**	5 c. multicoloured	15	20

INDEPENDENT REPUBLIC

1966 (1 Mar)–**67.** *As Nos.* 63, 66, 69, 72, 74/5, *but W w* **12** (*sideways*).

No.	Description	Unused	Used
83	1 c. multicoloured (22.2.67)	10	1·50
84	5 c. red and black (30.5.67)	1·25	40
85	10 c. red-orange and black (30.5.67)	65	30
86	25 c. black and orange (9.66*)	70	40
87	50 c. multicoloured (29.1.66*)	3·50	1·75
	a. Imperf (pair)	£300	
88	$1 multicoloured (18.5.67)	7·50	5·00
83/8	*Set of* 6	12·00	8·50

*The 25 and 50 c. values were not released in London until 30.5.67 and 9.6.66. The 25 c. value, however, is known used in September 1966 and the 50 c. on 29.1.66.

The 1 c. and 25 c. exist with PVA gum as well as gum arabic.

(Photo D.L.R.)

1966 (9 Aug). *First Anniv of Republic. W w* **12** (30 *c.*) *or no wmk* (*others*). *P* 12½ × 13.

No.	Type	Description	Unused	Used
89	**37**	15 c. multicoloured	40	30
90		20 c. multicoloured	60	70
91		30 c. multicoloured	80	95
89/91		*Set of* 3	1·60	1·75

38 Flag Procession

(Photo D.L.R.)

1967 (9 Aug). *National Day. P* 14 × 14½.

No.	Type	Description	Unused	Used
92	**38**	6 c. rosine, brown and slate	20	40
93		15 c. reddish purple, brown and slate	40	10
94		50 c. bright blue, brown and slate	75	1·10
92/4		*Set of* 3	1·25	1·40

Nos. 92/4 are respectively inscribed "Build a Vigorous Singapore" in Chinese, Malay and Tamil in addition to the English inscription.

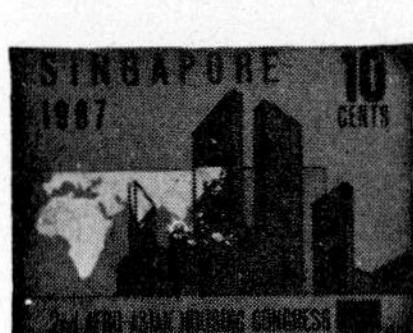

39 Skyscrapers and Afro-Asian Map

40 Symbolical Figure wielding Hammer, and Industrial Outline of Singapore

(Photo D.L.R.)

1967 (7 Oct). *2nd Afro-Asian Housing Congress. P* 14 × 13.

No.	Type	Description	Unused	Used
95	**39**	10 c. multicoloured	25	10
		a. Opt omitted	£180	£180
96		25 c. multicoloured	45	80
97		50 c. multicoloured	70	1·40
95/7		*Set of* 3	1·25	2·10

The above were originally scheduled for release in 1966, and when finally issued were overprinted with the new date and a black oblong obliterating the old date.

(Photo Harrison)

1968 (9 Aug). *National Day. Inscription at top in Chinese* (6 c.), *Malay* (15 c.) *or Tamil* (50 c.). *P* 13½ × 14.

No.	Type	Description	Unused	Used
98	**40**	6 c. orange-red, black and gold	20	20
99		15 c. apple-green, black and gold	25	15
100		50 c. greenish blue, black and gold	65	60
98/100		*Set of* 3	1·00	85

41 Half check Pattern

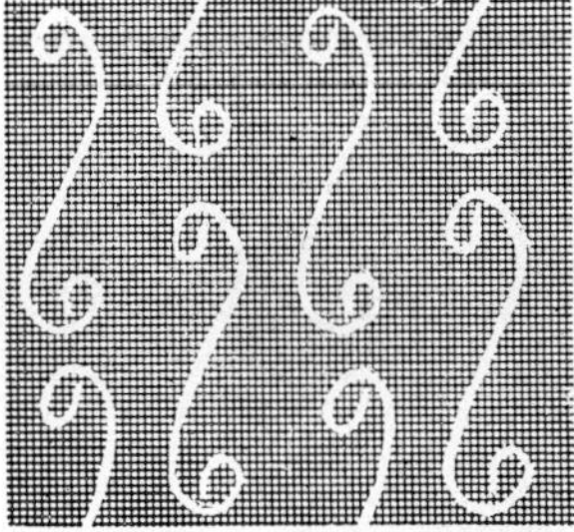

42 Scrolled "S" multiple

43 Mirudhangam

44 Pi Pa

45 Sword Dance

51 Dragon Dance

(Photo D.L.R. (5 c. to $1), Japanese Govt Printing Bureau, Tokyo (others))

1968–73. *T* **43/5**, **51** *and similar designs. 5 c. to $1: Chalk-surfaced paper; W* **41**; *P* 14. *Others: Ordinary paper; W* **42** *upright* (1 c., $5) *or sideways* (4 c., $2, $10); *P* 13½.

No.	Type	Description	Unused	Used
101		1 c. multicoloured (10.11.69)	15	1·50
102		4 c. multicoloured (10.11.69)	30	1·75
103		5 c. multicoloured (29.12.68)	40	40
		a. Glazed unsurfaced paper (16.12.70)	3·25	3·75
		b. Chalky paper. Perf 13 (27.6.73)	3·25	3·75
104		6 c. black, lemon and orange (1.12.68)	15	60
105		10 c. multicoloured (29.12.68)	10	10
		a. Glazed unsurfaced paper (16.12.70)	3·50	3·75
		b. Chalky paper. Perf 13 (14.7.73*)	3·50	3·75
106		15 c. multicoloured (29.12.68)	30	10
107		20 c. multicoloured (1.12.68)	15	20
		a. Perf 13 (12.9.73)	3·75	5·00
108		25 c. multicoloured (29.12.68)	40	40
		a. Perf 13 (27.6.73)	4·25	5·50
109		30 c. multicoloured (1.12.68)	30	40
		a. Perf 13 (12.9.73)	4·25	5·50
110		50 c. blk, orge-red & lt yell-brown (1.12.68)	50	40
		a. Perf 13 (12.9.73)	5·50	9·00
111		75 c. multicoloured (1.12.68)	1·00	70
112		$1 multicoloured (29.12.68)	2·00	70
		a. Perf 13 (12.9.73)	7·00	10·00
113		$2 multicoloured (10.11.69)	3·50	1·00
114		$5 multicoloured (10.11.69)	9·00	2·00
115		$10 multicoloured (6.12.69)	30·00	12·00
101/15		*Set of* 15	42·00	20·00
103b/12a		*Set of* 7	28·00	38·00

Designs: *Vert* (*as T* **45**)—6 c. Lion dance; 10 c. Bharatha Natyam; 15 c. Tari Payong; 20 c. Kathak Kali; 25 c. Lu Chih Shen and Lin Chung; 50 c. Tari Lilin; 75 c. Tarian Kuda Kepang; $1 Yao Chi. (*As T* **44**)—$2, Rebab; $10 Ta Ku. *Horiz* (*as T* **43**)—$5 Vina.

*Earliest known date of use.

58 E.C.A.F.E. Emblem

59 "100000" and Slogan as Block of Flats

(Des Eng Siak Loy. Photo Japanese Govt Ptg Bureau, Tokyo)

1969 (15 Apr). *25th Plenary Session of the U.N. Economic Commission for Asia and the Far East. P* 13.

No.	Type	Description	Unused	Used
116	**58**	15 c. black, silver and pale blue	35	15
117		30 c. black, silver and red	70	80
118		75 c. black, silver and violet-blue	1·25	1·50
116/18		*Set of* 3	2·00	2·25

(Des Tay Siew Chiah. Litho B.W.)

1969 (20 July). *Completion of "100,000 Homes for the People" Project. P* 13½.

No.	Type	Description	Unused	Used
119	**59**	25 c. black and emerald	70	50
120		50 c. black and deep blue	90	1·00

60 Aircraft over Silhouette of Singapore Docks

61 Sea Shells

(Des Eng Siak Loy and Han Kuan Cheng. Litho B.W.)

1969 (9 Aug). *150th Anniv of Founding of Singapore. T* **60** *and similar vert designs. P* 14 × 14½.

No.	Type	Description	Unused	Used
121		15 c. black, vermilion and yellow	1·25	30
122		30 c. black, blue and new blue	1·75	75
123		75 c. multicoloured	3·00	2·00
124		$1 black and vermilion	3·50	3·25
125		$5 vermilion and black	35·00	45·00
126		$10 black and bright green	48·00	48·00
121/6		*Set of* 6	80·00	90·00
MS127		120 × 120 mm. Nos. 121/6. P 13½	£325	£350

Designs:—30 c. U.N. emblem and outline of Singapore; 75 c. Flags and outline of Malaysian Federation; $1 Uplifted hands holding crescent and stars; $5 Tail of Japanese aircraft and searchlight beams; $10 Bust from statue of Sir Stamford Raffles.

(Des Tay Siew Chiah (15 c.), Eng Siak Loy (others). Litho Rosenbaum Bros, Vienna)

1970 (15 Mar). *World Fair, Osaka. T* **61** *and similar vert designs. Multicoloured. P* 13½.

No.	Type	Description	Unused	Used
128		15 c. Type **61**	90	15
129		30 c. Tropical fish	1·75	90
130		75 c. Greater Flamingo and Helmeted Hornbill	4·75	3·75
131		$1 Orchid	4·75	6·00
128/31		*Set of* 4	11·00	9·75
MS132		94 × 154 mm. Nos. 128/31	20·00	21·00

OMNIBUS ISSUES

Details, together with prices for complete sets, of the various Omnibus issues from the 1935 Silver Jubilee series to date are included in a special section following Zimbabwe at the end of Volume 2.

62 "Kindergarten"

63 Soldier charging

(Des Choy Weng Yang. Litho B.W.)

1970 (1 July). *Tenth Anniv of People's Association. T* **62** *and similar square designs. P* 13½.

No.	Type	Description	Unused	Used
133		15 c. agate and bright orange	50	15
134		50 c. ultramarine and yellow-orange	1·40	1·40
135		75 c. bright purple and black	2·25	2·75
133/5		*Set of* 3	3·75	3·75

Designs:—50 c. "Sport"; 75 c. "Culture".

(Des Choy Weng Yang. Litho Rosenbaum Bros, Vienna)

1970 (9 Aug). *National Day. T* **63** *and similar vert designs. Multicoloured. P* 13½.

No.	Type	Description	Unused	Used
136		15 c. Type **63**	70	15
137		50 c. Soldier on assault course	2·75	2·50
138		$1 Soldier jumping	3·75	5·00
136/8		*Set of* 3	6·50	7·00

64 Sprinters

(Des Choy Weng Yang. Photo Japanese Govt Ptg Bureau, Tokyo)

1970 (23 Aug). *Festival of Sports. T* **64** *and similar horiz designs. P* 13 × 13½.

No.	Type	Description	Unused	Used
139		10 c. magenta, black and ultramarine	90	1·25
		a. Horiz strip of 4. Nos. 139/42	4·50	
140		15 c. black, ultramarine and red-orange	1·25	1·60
141		25 c. black, red-orange and bright green	1·40	1·75
142		50 c. black, bright green and magenta	1·50	2·00
139/42		*Set of* 4	4·50	6·00

Designs:—15 c. Swimmers; 25 c. Tennis-players; 50 c. Racing-cars.

Nos. 139/42 were issued together *se-tenant* in horizontal strips of four within the sheet.

65 *Neptune Aquamarine* (freighter)

(Des W. Lee. Litho Rosenbaum Bros, Vienna)

1970 (1 Nov). *Singapore Shipping. T* **65** *and similar horiz designs. P* 12.

No.	Type	Description	Unused	Used
143		15 c. multicoloured	1·10	55
144		30 c. yellow-ochre and ultramarine	3·25	3·75
145		75 c. yellow-ochre and vermilion	5·00	6·00
143/5		*Set of* 3	8·50	8·50

Designs:—30 c. Container berth; 75 c. Ship-building.

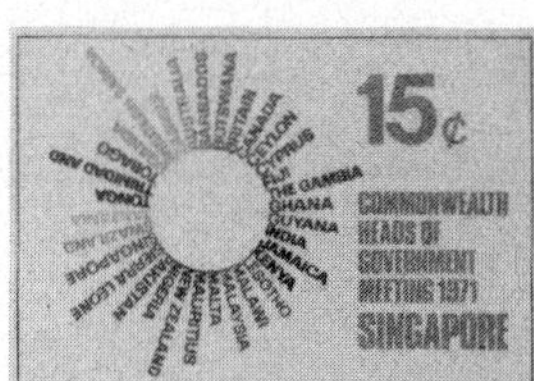

66 Country Names forming Circle

(Des W. Lee. Litho D.L.R.)

1971 (1 Jan). *Commonwealth Heads of Government Meeting, Singapore. T* **66** *and similar horiz designs. Multicoloured. P* 14 ($1) *or* 15 × 14½ (*others*).

No.	Type	Description	Unused	Used
146		15 c. Type **66**	60	15
147		30 c. Flags in circle	1·10	65
148		75 c. Commonwealth flags	2·50	2·75
149		$1 Commonwealth flags linked to Singapore (63 × 61 *mm*)	3·00	3·75
146/9		*Set of* 4	6·50	6·50

Imperforate examples of Nos. 146/7 overprinted "Specimen" are from printer's sample sheets.

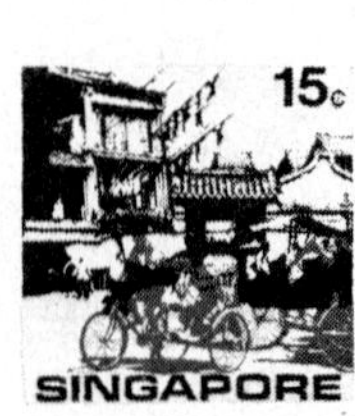

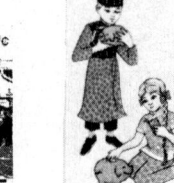

67 Bicycle Rickshaws   68 Chinese New Year

(Des Eng Siak Loy (15, 20 and 30 c.), W. Lee (others). Litho B.W.)

1971 (4 Apr). *Visit A.S.E.A.N. Year (A.S.E.A.N. = Association of South East Asian Nations). T* **67** *and similar designs. P* 13 × 13½ (50, 75 *c.) or* 11½ (*others*).

150	15 c. black, deep bluish violet and orange	40	25
151	20 c. indigo, orange and turquoise-blue	55	40
152	30 c. vermilion and deep maroon	80	1·00
153	50 c. multicoloured	2·75	4·50
154	75 c. multicoloured	3·50	6·00
150/4	*Set of* 5	7·00	11·00

Designs: *As T* **67**—20 c. Houseboat "village" and sampans; 30 c. Bazaar. *Horiz* (68 × 18 *mm*)—50 c. Modern harbour skyline; 75 c. Religious buildings.

(Des W. Lee. Litho Rosenbaum Bros, Vienna)

1971 (9 Aug). *Singapore Festivals. T* **68** *and similar vert designs. Multicoloured. P* 14.

155	15 c. Type **68**	70	15
156	30 c. Hari Raya	2·00	2·00
157	50 c. Deepavali	2·75	4·00
158	75 c. Christmas	3·25	5·00
155/8	*Set of* 4	8·00	10·00
MS159	150 × 125 mm. Nos. 155/8	42·00	35·00

69 "Dish" Aerial

(Des W. Lee. Litho B.W.)

1971 (23 Oct). *Opening of Satellite Earth Station. P* 13½.

160	**69**	15 c. multicoloured	2·75	75
161	–	30 c. multicoloured	8·00	8·00
		a. Block of 4. Nos. 161/4	32·00	
162	–	30 c. multicoloured	8·00	8·00
163	–	30 c. multicoloured	8·00	8·00
164	–	30 c. multicoloured	8·00	8·00
160/4		*Set of* 5	32·00	30·00

Designs:—Nos. 161/4 were printed in *se-tenant* blocks of four throughout the sheet, the four stamps forming a composite design similar to T **69**. They can be identified by the colour of the face value which is: yellow (No. 161), green (No. 162), magenta (No. 163) or orange (No. 164).

70 "Singapore River and Fort Canning, 1843–7" (Lieut. E. A. Porcher)

(Des W. Lee. Litho B.W.)

1971 (5 Dec). *Art. T* **70** *and similar horiz designs. Multicoloured. P* 12½ × 13 (50 *c. and* $1) *or* 13 (*others*).

165	10 c. Type **70**	1·50	1·00
166	15 c. "The Padang, 1851" (J. T. Thomson)	2·25	1·75
167	20 c. "Singapore Waterfront, 1848–9"	2·75	2·50
168	35 c. "View from Fort Canning, 1846" (J. T. Thomson)	5·50	4·75
169	50 c. "View from Mt Wallich, 1857" (P. Carpenter) (69 × 47 *mm*)	8·00	8·00
170	$1 "Singapore Waterfront, 1861" (W. Gray) (69 × 47 *mm*)	11·00	14·00
165/70	*Set of* 6	28·00	29·00

ALTERED CATALOGUE NUMBERS

Any Catalogue numbers altered from the last edition are shown as a list in the introductory pages.

71 One Dollar of 1969

(Des W. Lee. Litho B.W.)

1972 (4 June). *Coins. T* **71** *and similar horiz designs. P* 13½.

171	15 c. orange, black and deep green	45	15
172	35 c. black and vermilion	1·00	1·25
173	$1 yellow, black and bright blue	3·25	4·25
171/3	*Set of* 3	4·25	5·00

Designs:—15 c. One-cent coin of George V; $1 One hundred and fifty dollar gold coin of 1969.

72 "Moon Festival" (Seah Kim Joo)   73 Lanterns and Fish

(Des W. Lee. Litho State Bank Note Printing Works, Helsinki)

1972 (9 July). *Contemporary Art. T* **72** *and similar multicoloured designs. P* 12½.

174	15 c. Type **72**	40	20
175	35 c. "Complimentary Forces" (Thomas Yeo) (36 × 54 *mm*)	1·25	1·50
176	50 c. "Rhythm in Blue" (Yusman Aman) (36 × 54 *mm*)	2·00	2·25
177	$1 "Gibbons" (Chen Wen Hsi)	3·75	4·75
174/7	*Set of* 4	6·75	8·00

(Des Eng Siak Loy. Litho State Bank Note Printing Works, Helsinki)

1972 (9 Aug). *National Day. T* **73** *and similar vert designs symbolising Festivals. Multicoloured. P* 12½.

178	15 c. Type **73**	45	15
179	35 c. Altar and candles	1·00	1·25
180	50 c. Jug, bowl and gifts	1·40	2·50
181	75 c. Candle	2·25	4·00
178/81	*Set of* 4	4·75	7·00

74 Student Welding   75 *Maria Rickmers*

(Des Eng Siak Loy. Photo Kultura, Budapest)

1972 (1 Oct). *Youth. T* **74** *and similar horiz designs. P* 12.

182	15 c. multicoloured	50	10
183	35 c. multicoloured	1·00	1·50
184	$1 red-orange, blue-violet & yellowish grn	3·00	5·50
182/4	*Set of* 3	4·00	6·50

Designs:—35 c. Sport; $1 Dancing.

(Des Choy Weng Yang (Nos. 185/7), Eng Siak Loy (**MS**188). Litho Harrison)

1972 (17 Dec). *Shipping. T* **75** *and similar multicoloured designs. P* 14 × 14½.

185	15 c. *Neptune Ruby* (container ship) (42 × 29 *mm*)	70	40
186	75 c. Type **75**	3·75	4·75
187	$1 Chinese junk	5·00	6·00
185/7	*Set of* 3	8·50	10·00
MS188	152 × 84 mm. Nos. 185/7	17·00	24·00

76 P.Q.R. Slogan   77 Jurong Bird Park

(Des W. Lee. Litho B.W.)

1973 (25 Feb). *"Prosperity through Quality and Reliability" Campaign. T* **76** *and similar vert designs. P* 14.

189	**76**	15 c. multicoloured	40	15
190	–	35 c. multicoloured	85	75
191	–	75 c. multicoloured	1·40	2·50
192	–	$1 multicoloured	1·75	3·25
189/92		*Set of* 4	4·00	6·00

Nos. 190/2 show various P.Q.R. emblems.

(Des Han Kuan Cheng. Litho Harrison)

1973 (29 Apr). *Singapore Landmarks. T* **77** *and similar vert designs. P* 12½.

193	15 c. black and red-orange	55	15
194	35 c. black and myrtle-green	1·00	1·00
195	50 c. black and red-brown	2·00	2·50
196	$1 black and purple	3·25	4·00
193/6	*Set of* 4	6·25	7·00

Designs:—35 c. National Theatre; 50 c. City Hall; $1 Fullerton Building and Singapore River.

78 Aircraft Tail-fins   79 "Culture"

(Des W. Lee. Litho B.W.)

1973 (24 June). *Aviation. T* **78** *and similar horiz designs. Multicoloured. P* 13½ × 13.

197	10 c. Type **78**	25	10
198	35 c. Emblem of Singapore Airlines and destinations	75	75
199	75 c. Emblem on tail-fin	1·40	1·60
200	$1 Emblems encircling the globe	2·00	2·25
197/200	*Set of* 4	4·00	4·25

(Des Eng Siak Loy. Litho Harrison)

1973 (9 Aug). *National Day. T* **79** *and similar vert designs. P* 13½.

201	**79**	10 c. orange and black	1·25	55
		a. Block of 4. Nos. 201/4	6·00	
202	–	35 c. orange and black	1·50	1·25
203	–	50 c. orange and black	1·75	1·50
204	–	75 c. orange and black	2·00	1·75
201/4		*Set of* 4	6·00	4·50

Nos. 201/4 were printed in *se-tenant* blocks of four within the sheet, and form a composite design representing Singapore's culture.

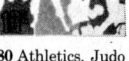

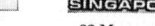

80 Athletics, Judo and Boxing   81 Agave   82 Mangosteen

(Des C. Lim. Photo Heraclio Fournier)

1973 (1 Sept). *Seventh S.E.A.P.* Games. T* **80** *and similar designs. P* 14 (10 *to* 35 *c.*) *or* 13 × 14 (*others*).

205	10 c. gold, silver and indigo	25	20
206	15 c. gold and grey-black	50	30
207	25 c. gold, silver and black	65	65
208	35 c. gold, silver and deep blue	1·10	90
209	50 c. multicoloured	1·75	2·25
210	$1 silver, royal blue and yellow-green	3·25	5·00
205/10	*Set of* 6	7·00	8·50
MS211	130 × 111 mm. Nos. 205/10. P 13 × 14	12·00	15·00

Designs: *As T* **80**—15 c. Cycling, weight-lifting, pistol-shooting and sailing; 25 c. Footballs; 35 c. Table-tennis bat, shuttlecock, tennis ball and hockey stick. *Horiz* (41 × 25 *mm*):—50 c. Swimmers; $1 Stadium.

*S.E.A.P. = South East Asian Peninsula.

(Des W. Lee (1 c. to 75 c.), Eng Siak Loy (others). Photo Heraclio Fournier)

1973. *Various multicoloured designs as T* **81/2**. *With fluorescent security markings.*

(*a*) *Stylized flowers and plants, size as T* **81**. *P* 13 (30.9.73)

212	1 c. Type **81**	20	40
213	5 c. *Coleus blumei*	10	25
	a. Booklet pane. Nos. 213×4, 214×4, 216×2	2·50	
214	10 c. *Vinca rosea*	15	10
215	15 c. *Helianthus angustifolius*	15	10
	a. Green printed double	†	—
216	20 c. *Licuala grandis*	25	40
217	25 c. *Wedelia trilobata*	30	30
218	35 c. *Chrysanthemum frutescens*	50	55
219	50 c. *Costus malortieanus*	75	30
220	75 c. *Gerbera jamesonii*	1·75	70

(*b*) *Fruits, size as T* **82**. *P* 12½ × 13 (1.11.73)

221	$1 Type **82**	1·50	30
222	$2 Jackfruit	3·25	1·25
223	$5 Coconut	6·00	5·00
224	$10 Pineapple	12·00	15·00
212/24	*Set of* 13	24·00	22·00

83 Tiger and Orang-Utans **84** Multicolour Guppy

(Des Eng Siak Loy. Litho B.W.)

1973 (16 Dec). *Singapore Zoo. T* **83** *and similar vert designs. Multicoloured. P* 13.
225 5 c. Type **83** 25 10
226 10 c. Leopard and Waterbuck 45 20
227 35 c. Leopard and Thamin .. .. .. 1·75 1·75
228 75 c. Horse and Lion .. .. 2·75 4·50
225/8 .. .. *Set of* 4 4·50 6·00

(Des Eng Siak Loy. Photo Heraclio Fournier)

1974 (21 Apr). *Tropical Fish. T* **84** *and similar vert designs. Multicoloured. P* 14.
229 5 c. Type **84** 20 10
230 10 c. Half Black Guppy 40 15
231 35 c. Multicolour Guppy (*different*) .. .. 1·10 1·40
232 $1 Black Guppy .. .. 2·75 4·00
229/32 .. .. *Set of* 4 4·00 5·00

85 Scout Badge within "9" **86** U.P.U. Emblem and Multiple "Centenary"

(Des W. Lee. Litho Harrison)

1974 (9 June). *Ninth Asia-Pacific Scout Conference. P* 13½ × 14½.
233 **85** 10 c. multicoloured 40 10
234 75 c. multicoloured .. .. 1·60 1·40

(Des W. Lee. Litho Harrison)

1974 (7 July). *Centenary of Universal Postal Union. T* **86** *and similar vert designs. P* 14 × 13½.
235 10 c. orange-brown, purple-brown and gold .. 20 10
a. Gold (U.P.U. symbol) omitted £160
236 35 c. new blue, deep blue and gold 55 75
237 75 c. multicoloured .. .. 1·25 2·50
235/7 .. .. *Set of* 3 1·75 3·00
Designs:—35 c. U.P.U. emblem and multiple U.N. symbols; 75 c. U.P.U. emblem and multiple peace doves.

87 Family Emblem **88** "Tree and Sun" (Chia Keng San)

(Des Eng Siak Loy. Litho B.W.)

1974 (9 Aug). *World Population Year. T* **87** *and similar horiz designs. Multicoloured. P* 12½ × 13½.
238 10 c. Type **87** 20 10
239 35 c. Male and female symbols .. .. .. 80 1·00
a. Emerald (male symbol) omitted £250
240 75 c. World population map .. .. .. 1·75 3·00
238/40 .. .. *Set of* 3 2·50 3·75

(Des Eng Siak Loy. Photo Heraclio Fournier)

1974 (1 Oct). *Universal Children's Day. T* **88** *and similar vert designs showing children's paintings. Multicoloured. P* 13½.
241 5 c. Type **88** 20 10
242 10 c. "My Daddy and Mummy" (Angeline Ang) 35 10
243 35 c. "A Dump Truck" (Si-Hoe Yeen Joong) .. 1·75 2·25
244 50 c. "My Aunt" (Raymond Teo) .. .. 2·25 3·25
241/4 .. .. *Set of* 4 4·00 5·50
MS245 138 × 100 mm. Nos. 241/4. P 13 .. .. 8·00 9·00

89 Street Scene

(Des Loy Chin. Litho Secura, Singapore)

1975 (26 Jan). *Singapore Views. T* **89** *and similar horiz designs. Multicoloured. P* 14.
246 15 c. Type **89** 45 10
247 20 c. Singapore River 60 70
248 $1 "Kelong" (fish-trap) .. .. .. 2·75 5·50
246/8 .. .. *Set of* 3 3·50 5·75

90 Emblem and Lighters' Prows **91** Satellite Earth Station, Sentosa

(Des Choy Weng Yang. Litho Secura, Singapore)

1975 (10 Mar). *Ninth Biennial Conference of International Association of Ports and Harbours, Singapore. T* **90** *and similar horiz designs. Multicoloured. P* 14.
249 5 c. Type **90** 15 10
250 25 c. Freighter and ship's wheel 70 80
251 50 c. Oil-tanker and flags .. .. .. 1·40 2·00
252 $1 Container-ship and propellers .. .. 2·25 4·25
249/52 .. .. *Set of* 4 4·00 6·50

(Des Sim Tong Khern. Photo Heraclio Fournier)

1975 (29 June). *"Science and Industry". T* **91** *and similar multicoloured designs. P* 13½.
253 10 c. Type **91** 25 10
254 35 c. Oil refineries (*vert*) .. .. .. 75 1·00
255 75 c. "Medical Sciences" .. .. .. 1·50 2·75
253/5 .. .. *Set of* 3 2·25 3·50

92 "Homes and Gardens" **93** South African Crowned Cranes

(Des Tay Siew Chiah. Litho Secura, Singapore)

1975 (9 Aug). *Tenth National Day. T* **92** *and similar square designs. Multicoloured. P* 13½.
256 10 c. Type **92** 20 10
257 35 c. "Shipping and Ship-building" 75 75
258 75 c. "Communications and Technology" .. 1·90 3·00
259 $1 "Trade, Commerce and Industry" .. 2·10 3·50
256/9 .. .. *Set of* 4 4·50 6·50

(Des Eng Siak Loy. Litho Harrison)

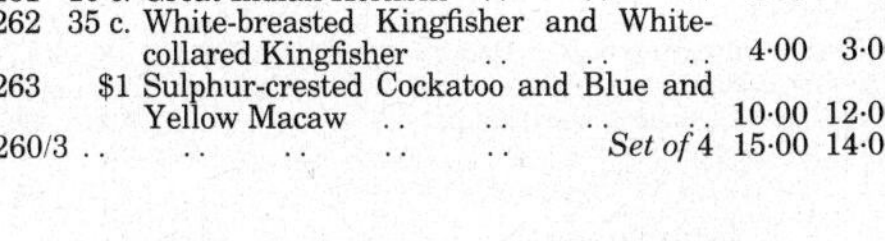

1975 (5 Oct). *Birds. T* **93** *and similar vert designs. Multicoloured. P* 14½ × 13½.
260 5 c. Type **93** .. .. 1·00 20
261 10 c. Great Indian Hornbill .. .. .. 1·50 10
262 35 c. White-breasted Kingfisher and White-collared Kingfisher .. .. 4·00 3·00
263 $1 Sulphur-crested Cockatoo and Blue and Yellow Macaw .. .. 10·00 12·00
260/3 .. .. *Set of* 4 15·00 14·00

94 "Equality" **95** Yellow Flame

(Des Tay Siew Chiah. Litho Secura, Singapore)

1975 (7 Dec). *International Women's Year. T* **94** *and similar square designs. Multicoloured. P* 13½.
264 10 c. Type **94** 25 10
265 35 c. "Development" .. .. 1·50 1·50
266 75 c. "Peace" .. .. 2·75 4·50
264/6 .. .. *Set of* 3 4·00 5·50
MS267 128 × 100 mm. Nos. 264/6 .. .. 6·00 6·50

(Des Tay Siew Chiah. Litho Secura, Singapore)

1976 (18 Apr). *Wayside Trees. T* **95** *and similar vert designs. Multicoloured. P* 14.
268 10 c. Type **95** 50 10
269 35 c. Cabbage Tree .. .. 1·25 1·00
270 50 c. Rose of India .. .. 2·00 2·50
271 75 c. Variegated Coral Tree .. .. .. 2·25 4·00
268/71 .. .. *Set of* 4 5·50 7·00

96 *Arachnis hookeriana* × *Vanda* Hilo Blue **97** Festival Symbol and Band

(Des Eng Siak Loy. Litho Secura, Singapore)

1976 (20 June). *Singapore Orchids. T* **96** *and similar vert designs. Multicoloured. P* 14.
272 10 c. Type **96** 70 10
273 35 c. *Arachnis Maggie Oei* × *Vanda insignis* 1·75 1·10
274 50 c. *Arachnis Maggie Oei* × *Vandu* Rodman 3·00 3·25
275 75 c. *Arachnis hookeriana* × *Vanda* Dawn Nishimura .. .. 3·25 5·50
272/5 .. .. *Set of* 4 8·00 9·00

(Des Han Kuan Cheng. Litho Harrison)

1976 (9 Aug). *Tenth Anniv of Singapore Youth Festival. Horiz designs showing festival symbol as T* **97**. *Multicoloured. P* 12½.
276 10 c. Type **97** 20 10
277 35 c. Athletes 60 60
278 75 c. Dancers .. .. 1·40 1·40
276/8 .. .. *Set of* 3 2·00 1·90

98 "Queen Elizabeth Walk"

(Des H. Weepaul. Litho Secura, Singapore)

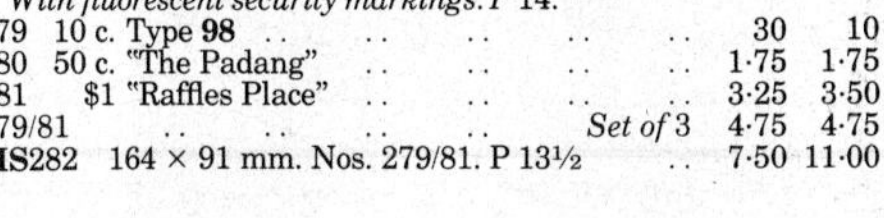

1976 (14 Nov). *Paintings of Old Singapore, circa* 1905–10, *by A. L. Watson. T* **98** *and similar horiz designs. Multicoloured. With fluorescent security markings. P* 14.
279 10 c. Type **98** 30 10
280 50 c. "The Padang" .. .. 1·75 1·75
281 $1 "Raffles Place" .. .. 3·25 3·50
279/81 .. .. *Set of* 3 4·75 4·75
MS282 164 × 91 mm. Nos. 279/81. P 13½ .. 7·50 11·00

99 Chinese Costume **100** Radar, Missile and Soldiers

(Des Margaret Heng. Litho Harrison)

1976 (19 Dec). *Bridal Costumes. T* **99** *and similar vert designs. Multicoloured. P* 14½.
283 10 c. Type **99** 25 10
284 35 c. Indian costume .. .. 1·00 1·00
285 75 c. Malay costume .. .. 1·75 2·00
283/5 .. .. *Set of* 3 2·75 2·75

(Des Eng Siak Loy. Litho Harrison)

1977 (12 Mar). *Tenth Anniv of National Service. T* **100** *and similar vert designs. Multicoloured. P* 14½.
286 10 c. Type **100** 30 10
287 50 c. Tank and soldiers .. .. 1·25 90
288 75 c. Soldiers, wireless operators, pilot and aircraft .. .. 2·00 1·75
286/9 .. .. *Set of* 3 3·25 2·40

101 Lyrate Cockle **102** Spotted Hermit Crab

(Des Tay Siew Chiah. Litho Secura, Singapore)

1977. *Multicoloured designs as T* **101/2**. *With fluorescent security markings. P* 13×13½. (*a*) *Shells as T* **101** (9.4.77).
289 1 c. Type **101** 30 60
290 5 c. Folded Scallop 20 10
a. Booklet pane. Nos. 290 × 4 and 291 × 8 *se-tenant* .. .. 1·75

291	10 c. Marble Cone	20	10
	a. Imperf (pair)	£300	
292	15 c. Scorpion Conch	45	10
293	20 c. Amplustre Bubble	70	10
294	25 c. Spiral Babylon	80	30
295	35 c. Regal Thorny Oyster	1·00	70
296	50 c. Winged Frog Shell	1·25	10
297	75 c. Troschel's Murex	2·00	20
	(b) Fish and Crustaceans as T **102** (4.6.77)		
298	$1 Type **102**	1·75	15
299	$2 Stingray	1·75	50
300	$5 Cuttlefish	4·00	2·25
301	$10 Lionfish	7·50	5·50
289/301	*Set of* 13	20·00	9·50

103 Shipbuilding

104 Keyhole and Banknotes

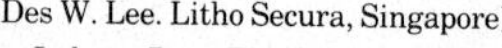

(Des W. Lee. Litho Secura, Singapore)

1977 (1 May). *Labour Day. T* **103** *and similar horiz designs. Multicoloured. P* 13 × 12½.

302	10 c. Type **103**	15	10
303	50 c. Building construction	75	60
304	75 c. Road construction	1·00	1·00
302/4	*Set of* 3	1·75	1·75

(Des Tay Siew Chiah. Litho Secura, Singapore)

1977 (16 July). *Centenary of Post Office Savings Bank. T* **104** *and similar vert designs. Multicoloured. P* 13.

305	10 c. Type **104**	15	10
	a. Perf 14		
306	35 c. On-line banking service	75	50
	a. Perf 14		
307	75 c. GIRO service	1·50	1·25
	a. Perf 14		
305/7	*Set of* 3	2·25	1·60

105 Flags of Member Nations

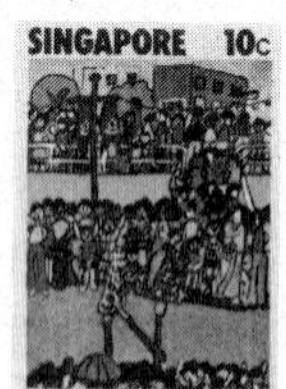

106 "Chingay Procession" (Liang Yik Yin)

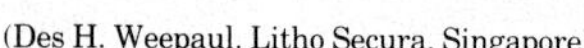

(Des Eng Siak Loy. Litho Secura, Singapore)

1977 (8 Aug). *Tenth Anniv of A.S.E.A.N. (Association of South-East Asian Nations). T* **105** *and similar vert designs. Multi-coloured. P* 14.

308	10 c. Type **105**	15	10
309	35 c. "Agriculture"	60	50
310	75 c. "Industry"	1·25	1·10
308/10	*Set of* 3	1·75	1·50

(Des H. Weepaul. Litho Secura, Singapore)

1977 (1 Oct). *Children's Art. T* **106** *and similar horiz designs. Multicoloured. P* 12½.

311	10 c. Type **106**	20	10
312	35 c. "At the Bus Stop" (Chong Khing Ann)	75	50
313	75 c. "Playground" (Yap Li Hwa)	1·60	1·40
311/13	*Set of* 3	2·25	1·75
MS314	160 × 97 mm. Nos. 311/13	4·50	4·75

107 "Life Sciences"

108 Botanical Gardens and Esplanade, Jurong Bird Park

(Des Tay Siew Chiah. Litho Format)

1977 (10 Dec). *Singapore Science Centre. T* **107** *and similar vert designs. Multicoloured. P* 14½×14.

315	10 c. Type **107**	10	10
316	35 c. "Physical sciences"	45	30
	a. Deep green and brown omitted	£150	
317	75 c. "Science and technology"	1·00	85
318	$1 Singapore Science Centre	1·25	1·00
315/18	*Set of* 4	2·50	2·00

(Des C. Kiat. Litho Harrison)

1978 (22 Apr). *Parks and Gardens. T* **108** *and similar multi-coloured designs. P* 14½.

319	10 c. Type **108**	15	10
320	35 c. Lagoon, East Coast Park (*vert*)	45	35
321	75 c. Botanical Gardens (*vert*)	75	75
319/21	*Set of* 3	1·25	1·10

109 Red-whiskered Bulbul

111 Map of South East Asia showing Cable Network

110 Thian Hock Keng Temple

(Des Eng Siak Loy. Litho Secura, Singapore)

1978 (1 July). *Singing Birds. T* **109** *and similar vert designs. Multicoloured. P* 13½×14.

322	10 c. Type **109**	35	10
323	35 c. Oriental White Eye	85	45
324	50 c. White-rumped Shama	1·10	85
325	75 c. White-crested Laughing Thrush and Huamei	1·50	1·60
322/5	*Set of* 4	3·50	2·75

(Des Eng Siak Loy. Litho Secura, Singapore)

1978 (9 Aug). *National Monuments. T* **110** *and similar horiz designs. Multicoloured. P* 13½.

326	10 c. Type **110**	20	20
327	10 c. Hajjah Fatimah Mosque	20	20
328	10 c. Armenian Church	20	20
329	10 c. Sri Mariamman Temple	20	20
326/9	*Set of* 4	70	70
MS330	173 × 86 mm. 35 c. × 4, as Nos. 326/9	2·75	2·75

Stamps from No. **MS**330 are similar in design to Nos. 326/9 but have no borders and the inscriptions are slightly larger.

(Des J. Heng. Litho Secura, Singapore)

1978 (3 Oct). *A.S.E.A.N. (Association of South East Asian Nations) Submarine Cable Network* (1*st issue*). *Completion of Philippines–Singapore section. P* 14 (*around design as well as stamp*).

331 **111**	10 c. multicoloured	10	10
332	35 c. multicoloured	40	40
333	50 c. multicoloured	50	50
334	75 c. multicoloured	80	1·00
331/4	*Set of* 4	1·60	1·75

See also Nos. 385/8 and 458/62.

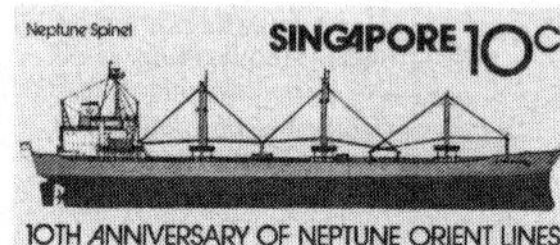

112 *Neptune Spinel* (bulk carrier)

(Des Paul Wee Hui Hong. Litho Secura, Singapore)

1978 (18 Nov). *10th Anniv of Neptune Orient Shipping Lines. T* **112** *and similar horiz designs. Multicoloured. P* 13½×14.

335	10 c. Type **112**	15	10
336	35 c. *Neptune Aries* (tanker)	40	50
337	50 c. *Anro Temasek* (container ship)	45	75
338	75 c. *Neptune Pearl* (container ship)	80	1·40
335/8	*Set of* 4	1·60	2·50

113 "Concorde"

114 10 Kilometre Marker

(Des Paul Wee Hui Hong. Litho Secura, Singapore)

1978 (16 Dec). *Aviation. T* **113** *and similar horiz designs. Multicoloured. P* 13½.

339	10 c. Type **113**	35	15
340	35 c. Boeing "747B"	50	30
341	50 c. Vickers "Vimy"	70	90
342	75 c. Wright Brothers' *Flyer* I	80	1·75
339/42	*Set of* 4	2·10	2·75

(Des W. Lee. Litho Secura, Singapore)

1979 (24 Feb). *Metrication. T* **114** *and similar vert designs. Multi-coloured. P* 13½.

343	10 c. Type **114**	10	10
344	35 c. Tape measure	20	20
345	75 c. Weighing scales	45	45
343/5	*Set of* 3	65	65

115 Vanda Hybrid

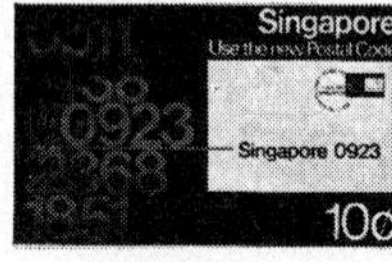

116 Envelope with new Singapore Postcode

(Des Paul Wee Hui Hong. Litho Harrison)

1979 (14 Apr). *Orchids. T* **115** *and similar designs showing different varieties of Vanda Hybrid. P* 15×14 (10, 35 *c.*) *or* 14×15 (*others*).

346	10 c. multicoloured	15	10
347	35 c. multicoloured	35	20
348	50 c. multicoloured (*vert*)	50	30
349	75 c. multicoloured (*vert*)	70	45
346/9	*Set of* 4	1·50	90

(Des Paul Wee Hui Hong. Litho Secura, Singapore)

1979 (1 July). *Postal Code Publicity. P* 13.

350 **116**	10 c. multicoloured	10	10
351 –	50 c. multicoloured	30	35

The 50 c. design is as Type **116**, but the envelope is addressed to the Philatelic Bureau, General Post Office and has the postcode "Singapore 0104".

117 Early Telephone and Overhead Cables

118 "Lantern Festival" (Eng Chun-Ngan)

(Des Eng Siak Loy. Litho J.W.)

1979 (5 Oct). *Centenary of Telephone Service. T* **117** *and similar horiz designs. P* 13½×13.

352	10 c. yellow-brown and new blue	10	10
353	35 c. bright orange, blue and reddish violet	20	25
354	50 c. blue, dp turquoise-grn & yellowish grn	35	40
355	75 c. yellowish green and bright orange	50	80
352/5	*Set of* 4	1·00	1·40

Designs:—35 c. Telephone dial and world map; 50 c. Modern telephone and city scene; 75 c. Latest computerised telephone and circuit diagram.

(Des Han Kuan Cheng. Litho Secura, Singapore)

1979 (10 Nov). *International Year of the Child. Children's Drawings. T* **118** *and similar horiz designs. Multicoloured. P* 13.

356	10 c. Type **118**	10	10
357	35 c. "Singapore Harbour" (Wong Chien Chien)	30	30
358	50 c. "Use Your Hands" (Leong Choy Yeen)	40	45
359	75 c. "Soccer" (Tan Cheong Hin)	60	75
356/9	*Set of* 4	1·25	1·40
MS360	154 × 98 mm. Nos. 356/9	2·25	2·25

119 View of Gardens

120 Hainan Junk

(Des Eng Siak Loy. Litho Secura, Singapore)

1979 (15 Dec). *120th Anniv of Botanic Gardens. T* **119** *and similar horiz designs showing different views of the gardens. P* 13½.

361	10 c. multicoloured	15	10
	a. Imperf (pair)	£375	
362	50 c. multicoloured	60	75
363	$1 multicoloured	1·10	2·00
361/3	*Set of* 3	1·75	2·50

(Des Eng Siak Loy. Litho J.W.)

1980 (5 Apr)–**84**. *Ships. Multicoloured designs as T* **120**. *Ordinary paper* (1 *c.*, 10 *c.*), *phosphorised paper* ($1 *to* $10) *and ordinary or phosphorised paper* (*others*). *P* 14 (1 *to* 75 *c.*) *or* 13½ ($1 *to* $10).

364	1 c. Type **120** (26.4.80)	30	60
365	5 c. Clipper (26.4.80)	10	35
366	10 c. Fujian junk (26.4.80)	10	10
	p. One narrow (4 mm) phosphor band (12.81)	45	20
	pa. One wide (10 mm) phosphor band (2.84)	90	60
367	15 c. Golekkan (26.4.80)	15	15
368	20 c. Palari schooner (26.4.80)	20	30
369	25 c. East Indiaman (26.4.80)	25	30
370	35 c. Galleon (26.4.80)	30	30
371	50 c. Caravel (26.4.80)	50	30
372	75 c. Jiangsu trading junk (26.4.80)	65	65
373	$1 *Kedah* (coaster) (42×25 *mm*)	70	45
	a. Imperf (pair)	£275	
374	$2 *Murex* (oil tanker) (42×25 *mm*)	1·25	90
375	$5 *Chusan* (screw steamer) (42×25 *mm*)	3·00	3·00
376	$10 *Braganza* (paddle-steamer) (42×25 *mm*)	6·00	6·00
364/76	*Set of* 13	12·00	12·00

121 Straits Settlements 1867 1½ c. Stamp and Map of Singapore, 1843
122 C.P.F. Emblem and "Keys to Retirement Benefits"

(Des Paul Wee Hui Hong. Litho Secura, Singapore)

1980 (6 May). *"London 1980" International Stamp Exhibition. T* **121** *and similar vert designs. Multicoloured. P* 13.
377 10 c. Type **121** 20 10
378 35 c. Straits Settlements 1906 $500 stamp and treaty between Johore and British Colony of Singapore . . 35 25
379 $1 1948 $2 stamp and map of Malaysia . . 70 90
380 $2 1969 150th Anniversary of Singapore $10 commemorative and letter to Col. Addenbrooke from Sir Stamford Raffles . . 1·25 2·00
377/80 . . . . *Set of* 4 2·25 3·00
MS381 148 × 104 mm. Nos. 377/80 . . 3·25 4·00

(Des Paul Wee Hui Hong. Litho Secura, Singapore)

1980 (1 July). *25th Anniv of Central Provident Fund Board. T* **122** *and similar vert designs showing C.P.F. emblem. Multicoloured. P* 13.
382 10 c. Type **122** 10 10
383 50 c. "C.P.F. savings for home ownership" . . 40 30
384 $1 "C.P.F. savings for old-age" . . 75 80
382/4 . . . . *Set of* 3 1·10 1·10

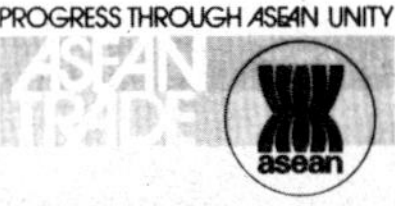

123 Map of South East Asia showing Cable Network
124 A.S.E.A.N. Trade Fair Emblem

(Des J. Heng. Litho Secura, Singapore)

1980 (8 Aug). *A.S.E.A.N. (Association of South East Asian Nations) Submarine Cable Network (2nd issue). Completion of Indonesia–Singapore Section. P* 14 *(around design as well as stamp).*
385 **123** 10 c. multicoloured 10 10
386 35 c. multicoloured 40 25
387 50 c. multicoloured 50 40
388 75 c. multicoloured . . . . 65 1·00
385/8 . . . . *Set of* 4 1·50 1·60

(Des Paul Wee Hui Hong. Litho Secura, Singapore)

1980 (3 Oct). *A.S.E.A.N. (Association of South East Asian Nations) Trade Fair. P* 13.
389 **124** 10 c. multicoloured 10 10
a. Perf 13½×14 . . . .
390 35 c. multicoloured 30 20
a. Perf 13½×14 . . . .
391 75 c. multicoloured 60 80
a. Perf 13½×14 . . . .
389/91 . . . . *Set of* 3 85 1·00

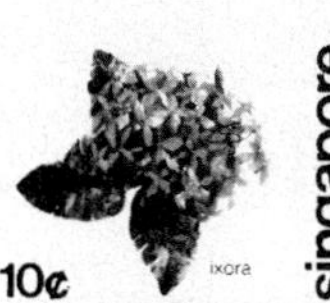

125 Ixora
126 International Currency Symbols

(Des S. Tan and Chua Ban Har. Litho J.W.)

1980 (8 Nov). *National Tree Planting Day. Flowers. T* **125** *and similar horiz designs. Multicoloured. P* 13½ × 13.
392 10 c. Type **125** 10 10
393 35 c. Allamanda 40 25
394 50 c. Sky Vine 50 40
395 75 c. Bougainvillea 60 75
392/5 . . . . *Set of* 4 1·40 1·40

(Des Paul Wee Hui Hong. Litho Secura, Singapore)

1981 (24 Jan). *10th Anniv of Monetary Authority of Singapore. P* 14.
396 **126** 10 c. black, vermilion & greenish yellow 10 10
397 35 c. multicoloured 30 20
398 75 c. multicoloured 55 60
396/8 . . . . *Set of* 3 80 75

(**127**)
128 Woodwork

1981 (4 Mar). *No. 65 surch with T* **127**.
399 **21** 10 c. on 4 c. black and orange-red . . 15 30

(Des Sng Tong Beng. Litho J.W.)

1981 (11 Apr). *Technical Training. T* **128** *and similar vert designs. Multicoloured. P* 13 × 13½.
400 10 c. Type **128** 10 10
401 35 c. Building construction 25 20
402 50 c. Electronics 40 30
403 75 c. Precision machining 50 60
400/3 . . . . *Set of* 4 1·10 1·00

129 Figures representing various Sports
130 "The Rights to Environmental Aids"

(Des Lim Ching San. Litho J.W.)

1981 (25 Aug). *"Sports for All". T* **129** *and similar vert designs showing figures representing various sports. P* 14.
404 10 c. multicoloured 15 10
405 75 c. multicoloured . . . . 1·40 1·60
406 $1 multicoloured . . . . 1·60 2·25
404/6 . . . . *Set of* 3 2·75 3·50

(Des Chua Ban Har. Litho Harrison)

1981 (24 Nov). *International Year for Disabled Persons. T* **130** *and similar vert designs. Multicoloured. One centre phosphor band (10 c.) or phosphorised paper (others). P* 14½.
407 10 c. Type **130** 10 10
408 35 c. "The right to social integration" . . 40 20
409 50 c. "The right to education" . . 60 35
410 75 c. "The right to work" . . 80 70
407/10 . . . . *Set of* 4 1·75 1·10
Nos. 407/10 were printed with phosphor bands or on phosphorised paper similar to that used on contemporary Great Britain issues.

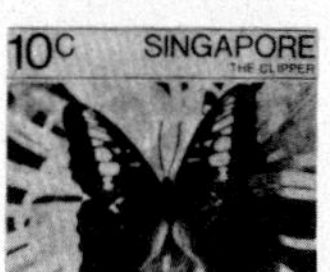

131 Control Tower and Passenger Terminal Building, Changi Airport
132 *Parthenos sylvia*

(Des J. Heng. Litho Secura, Singapore Ltd)

1981 (29 Dec). *Opening of Changi Airport. P* 14 × 13½.
411 **131** 10 c. multicoloured 10 10
412 35 c. multicoloured 35 20
413 50 c. multicoloured 45 30
414 75 c. multicoloured 70 65
415 $1 multicoloured . . . . 80 1·00
411/15 . . . . *Set of* 5 2·25 2·00
MS416 154 × 105 mm. Nos. 411/15 . . 2·25 3·50
The five values show different background emblems representing the Parks and Recreation Dept, Public Works Dept, Telecommunications Authority, Port of Singapore and Dept of Civil Aviation.

(Des Eng Siak Loy. Litho J.W.)

1982 (3 Mar). *Butterflies. T* **132** *and similar horiz designs. Multicoloured. One centre phosphor band (10 c.) or phosphorised paper (others). P* 14.
417 10 c. Type **132** 15 10
418 50 c. *Danaus vulgaris* 60 40
419 $1 *Trogonoptera brookiana* . . 90 1·25
417/19 . . . . *Set of* 3 1·50 1·50

133 A.S.E.A.N. Emblem
134 Football and Stylised Player

(Des Paul Wee Hui Hong. Litho Secura, Singapore)

1982 (14 June). *15th Anniv of A.S.E.A.N. (Association of South East Asian Nations). One centre phosphor band (10 c.) or phosphorised paper (others). P* 14½ × 14.
420 **133** 10 c. multicoloured 10 10
421 35 c. multicoloured 25 30
422 – 50 c. multicoloured 35 40
423 – 75 c. multicoloured 50 75
420/3 . . . . *Set of* 4 1·00 1·40
The 50 and 75 c. values are as Type **133**, but are inscribed "15th ASEAN Ministerial Meeting".

(Des Paul Wee Hui Hong. Litho Secura, Singapore)

1982 (9 July). *World Cup Football Championship, Spain. T* **134** *and similar vert designs. One centre phosphor band (10 c.) or phosphorised paper (others). P* 12.
424 10 c. black, bright blue and greenish blue . . 20 10
425 75 c. multicoloured . . . . 75 1·00
426 $1 multicoloured . . . . 95 1·40
424/6 . . . . *Set of* 3 1·75 2·25
Designs:—75 c. Football and World Cup, Asian Zone Four emblem; $1 Football and globe.

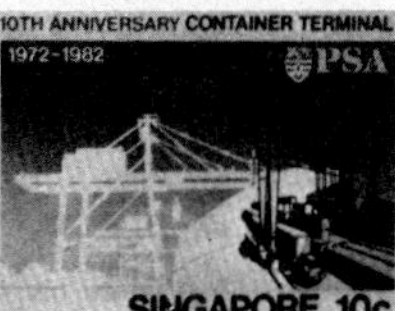

135 Sultan Shoal Lighthouse, 1896
136 Yard Gantry Cranes

(Des Eng Siak Loy. Litho Secura, Singapore)

1982 (7 Aug). *Lighthouses of Singapore. T* **135** *and similar horiz designs. Multicoloured. One centre phosphor band (10 c.) or phosphorised paper (others). P* 12.
427 10 c. Type **135** 10 10
428 75 c. Horsburgh Lighthouse, 1855 . . 55 1·00
429 $1 Raffles Lighthouse, 1855 . . 75 1·40
427/9 . . . . *Set of* 3 1·25 2·25
MS430 148 × 104 mm. Nos. 427/9 . . 2·50 3·25
No. **MS**430 was printed on plain paper without phosphor.

(Des Goh Seng Lim. Litho Secura, Singapore)

1982 (15 Sept). *10th Anniv of Container Terminal. T* **136** *and similar horiz designs. Multicoloured. One centre phosphor band (10 c.) or phosphorised paper (others). P* 13½.
431 10 c. Type **136** 10 10
432 35 c. Computer 20 25
433 50 c. Freightlifter 30 30
434 75 c. Straddle carrier 45 50
431/4 . . . . *Set of* 4 90 1·00

137 Scouts on Parade
138 Productivity Movement Slogans

(Des Poh Siew Wah. Litho Secura, Singapore)

1982 (15 Oct). *75th Anniv of Boy Scout Movement. T* **137** *and similar vert designs. Multicoloured. One centre phosphor band (10 c.) or phosphorised paper (others). P* 14×13½.
435 10 c. Type **137** 15 10
436 35 c. Scouts hiking 45 25
437 50 c. Scouts building tower 65 35
438 75 c. Scouts canoeing 95 80
435/8 . . . . *Set of* 4 2·00 1·25

(Des M. Gan. Litho Secura, Singapore)

1982 (17 Nov). *Productivity Movement. T* **138** *and similar diamond-shaped designs. One centre phosphor band (10 c.) or phosphorised paper (others). P* 13½.
439 10 c. orange and emerald 10 10
440 35 c. yellow-ochre and deep dull blue . . 35 30
441 50 c. maroon, bistre-yellow and brownish grey 55 55
442 75 c. maroon and lemon 75 75
439/42 . . . . *Set of* 4 1·60 1·50
Designs:—35 c. Family and housing ("Benefits of Productivity"); 50 c. Works meeting ("Quality Control Circles"); 75 c. Aspects of Singapore business ("Everybody's Business").

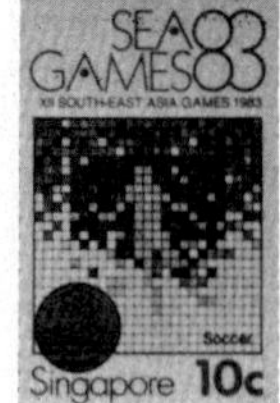

139 Commonwealth Logo and Country Names

140 Soccer

(Des Eng Siak Loy. Litho Secura, Singapore)

1983 (14 Mar). *Commonwealth Day. One centre phosphor band (10 c.) or phosphorised paper (others). P* 13 × 13½.

443 **139** 10 c. multicoloured 10 10
444 35 c. multicoloured 20 25
445 75 c. multicoloured 45 60
446 $1 multicoloured 65 80
443/6 .. .. *Set of* 4 1·25 1·60

(Des Lim Ching San. Litho Secura, Singapore)

1983 (28 May). 12*th South-East Asia Games. T* **140** *and similar vert designs. Multicoloured. One centre phosphor band* (10 c.) *or phosphorised paper (others). P* 13½ × 13.

447 10 c. Type **140** 10 10
448 35 c. Racket games 20 25
449 75 c. Athletics 45 50
450 $1 Swimming 65 70
447/50 .. .. *Set of* 4 1·25 1·40

141 Policeman and Family

142 1977 ASEAN Stamps and Statue of King Chulalongkorn

(Des Lim Ching San. Litho J.W.)

1983 (24 June). *Neighbourhood Watch Scheme. T* **141** *and similar horiz designs. Multicoloured. One wide centre phosphor band (10 c.) or phosphorised paper (others). P* 14.

451 10 c. Type **141** 15 10
452 35 c. Policeman and children 45 30
453 75 c. Policeman and inhabitants with linked arms 80 70
451/3 .. .. *Set of* 3 1·25 95

(Des Sylvia Tan and Ko Hui-Huy. Litho J.W.)

1983 (4 Aug). *Bangkok International Stamp Exhibition. T* **142** *and similar vert designs. Multicoloured. One wide centre phosphor band* (10 c.), *phosphorised paper* (35 c., $1) *or ordinary paper (miniature sheet). P* 14.

454 10 c. Type **142** 10 10
455 35 c. 1980 ASEAN stamps and map of South-East Asia 25 35
456 $1 1982 ASEAN stamps and signatures of Heads of State .. .. 65 1·10
454/6 .. .. *Set of* 3 85 1·40
MS457 147 × 104 mm. Nos. 454/6 .. .. 1·75 2·50

143 Map of South-East Asia showing Cable Network

(Des J. Heng. Litho Secura, Singapore)

1983 (27 Sept). *A.S.E.A.N. (Association of South-East Asian Nations) Submarine Cable Network (3rd issue). Completion of Malaysia-Singapore-Thailand section. One centre phosphor band* (10 c.), *phosphorised paper* (35 c. to 75 c.) *or ordinary paper (miniature sheet). P* 13½ *(around design as well as stamp).*

458 **143** 10 c. multicoloured 10 10
459 35 c. multicoloured 20 25
460 50 c. multicoloured 35 35
461 75 c. multicoloured 45 50
458/61 .. .. *Set of* 4 90 1·00
MS462 146 × 100 mm. Nos. 331, 388, 458/61 .. 1·60 2·50

144 Teletex Service

(Des Sylvia Tan and Ko Hui-Huy. Litho Enschedé)

1983 (10 Nov). *World Communications Year. T* **144** *and similar horiz designs. Phosphorised paper. P* 12½ × 13.

463 10 c. greenish yellow, light emerald and black 10 10
464 35 c. greenish yellow, brt rose-red & chocolate 20 30
465 75 c. bright yellow-green, greenish blue and deep violet-blue 45 65
466 $1 greenish yell, olive-brn & brownish blk 50 85
463/6 .. .. *Set of* 4 1·10 1·75

Designs:—35 c. World telephone numbering plan; 75 c. Satellite transmission; $1 Sea communications.

145 Blue-breasted Banded Rail

146 House of Tan Yeok Nee

(Des Poh Siew Wah. Litho Harrison)

1984 (15 Mar). *Coastal Birds. T* **145** *and similar horiz designs. Multicoloured. One wide centre phosphor band (10 c.) or phosphorised paper (others). P* 14½ × 13½.

467 10 c. Type **145** 30 10
468 35 c. Black Bittern 70 40
469 50 c. Brahminy Kite 85 70
470 75 c. Moorhen .. .. 1·10 1·50
467/70 .. .. *Set of* 4 2·75 2·40

(Des Poh Siew Wah. Litho Secura, Singapore)

1984 (7 June). *National Monuments. T* **146** *and similar vert designs. Multicoloured. One centre phosphor band (10 c.) or phosphorised paper (others). P* 12.

471 10 c. Type **146** 10 10
472 35 c. Thong Chai building 30 35
473 50 c. Telok Ayer market 40 50
474 $1 Nagore Durgha shrine .. .. 80 1·25
471/4 .. .. *Set of* 4 1·40 2·00

147 1970 $1 National Day Stamp

148 Schoolchildren

(Des P. Hong. Litho Secura, Singapore)

1984 (9 Aug–23 Nov). *"25 Years of Nation Building." T* **147** *and similar vert designs showing various Singapore stamps. Multi-coloured. One centre phosphor band (10 c.) or phosphorised paper (others). P* 14 × 14½.

475 10 c. Type **147** 10 10
476 35 c. 1981 $1 "Sports for All" stamp 30 35
477 50 c. 1969 25 c. "100,000 Homes for the People" stamp 40 55
478 75 c. 1976 10 c. Wayside Trees stamp 60 75
479 $1 1981 $1 Opening of Changi Airport stamp 80 1·00
480 $2 1981 10 c. Monetary Authority stamp .. 1·75 2·75
475/80 .. .. *Set of* 6 3·50 5·00
MS481 132 × 106 mm. Nos. 475/80. P 12½ (23 Nov) 4·50 6·00

No. **MS**481 is on ordinary paper without a phosphor band on the 10 c. stamp.

(Des Lim Ching San. Litho Secura, Singapore)

1984 (26 Oct). *"Total Defence". T* **148** *and similar vert designs. One centre phosphor band. P* 12.

482 10 c. brown and orange-vermilion 10 15
a. Horiz strip of 5. Nos. 482/6 45
483 10 c. brown, yellow-olive and new blue 10 15
484 10 c. brown, bright violet and pale salmon .. 10 15
485 10 c. brown, orange-brown and mauve 10 15
486 10 c. brown, yellow and yellow-olive 10 15
482/6 .. .. *Set of* 5 45 65

Designs:—No. 482, Type **148**; 483, People of Singapore; 484, Industrial workers; 485, Civil Defence first aid worker; 486, Anti-aircraft gun crew.

Nos. 482/6 were printed together, *se-tenant*, in horizontal strips of five throughout the sheet.

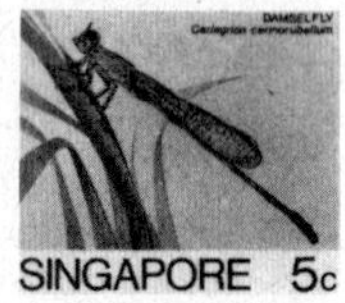

149 Coleman Bridge

150 *Ceriagrion cerinorubellum* (damselfly)

(Des Eng Siak Loy. Recess Harrison)

1985 (15 Mar). *Bridges of Singapore. T* **149** *and similar horiz designs. One phosphor band (10 c.) or phosphorised paper (others). P* 14½ × 14.

487 10 c. black (Type **149**) 15 10
488 35 c. black (Cavenagh Bridge) 30 30
489 75 c. black (Elgin Bridge) 55 55
490 $1 black (Benjamin Sheares Bridge) 70 70
487/90 .. .. *Set of* 4 1·50 1·50

(Des Eng Siak Loy. Litho Japanese Govt Ptg Bureau, Tokyo, to 1987, thereafter Leigh-Mardon Ltd, Melbourne (5 c. to 75 c.). Recess and photo Japanese Govt Ptg Bureau, Tokyo ($1 to $10))

1985 (24 Apr)–**89**. *Insects. T* **150** *and similar horiz designs. Multicoloured. One narrow (5 mm) phosphor band (10 c.) or phosphorised paper (others). P* 13 × 13½.

491 5 c. Type **150** 25 10
a. Leigh-Mardon ptg (13.5.88) .. ..
492 10 c. *Apis javana* (bee) 30 10
a. Leigh-Mardon ptg (on phosphorised paper) (15.10.88) .. .. ..
493 15 c. *Delta arcuata* (wasp) 35 10
a. Leigh-Mardon ptg (2.88) .. ..
494 20 c. *Xylocopa caerulea* (bee) 40 10
a. Leigh-Mardon ptg (8.6.88) .. ..
495 25 c. *Donacia javana* (water beetle) 40 20
a. Leigh-Mardon ptg (8.88) .. ..
496 35 c. *Heteroneda reticulata* (ladybird) 50 25
a. Leigh-Mardon ptg (25.5.88) .. ..
497 50 c. *Catacanthus nigripes* (bug) 70 35
a. Leigh-Mardon ptg (21.1.89) .. ..
498 75 c. *Chremistica pontianaka* (cicada) 80 45
a. Leigh-Mardon ptg (3.7.89) .. ..
499 $1 *Homoexipha lycoides* (cricket) (5.6.85) 1·00 60
500 $2 *Traulia azureipennis* (grasshopper) (5.6.85) .. .. 1·50 1·25
501 $5 *Trithemis aurora* (dragonfly) (5.6.85) 2·75 3·00
502 $10 *Scambophyllum sanguinolentum* (grasshopper) (5.6.85) .. .. 5·75 6·00
491/502 .. .. *Set of* 12 13·00 11·00

Nos. 499/502 are larger, 35×30 mm.

Although the work of the two printers is very similar as far as shade, paper and perforation are concerned Leigh-Mardon used new printing plates taken from the original colour separations and, in consequence, each value does differ from its predecessor printed by the Japanese Government Printing Bureau:

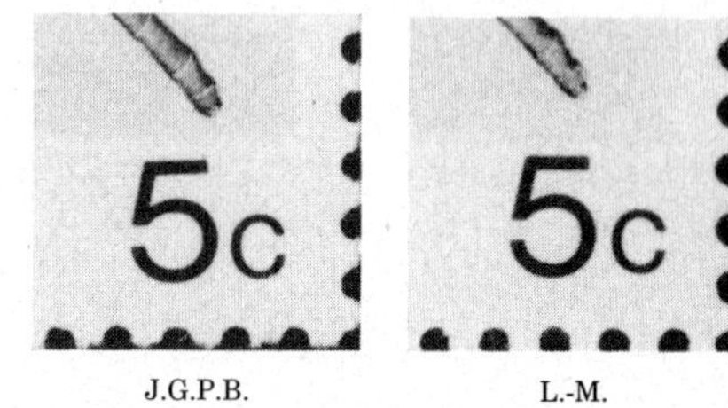

J.G.P.B. L.-M.

5 c. On the J.G.P.B. printing the tail of the insect is ½ mm from the bottom edge of the vignette. On the L.-M. printing the distance is 1 mm.

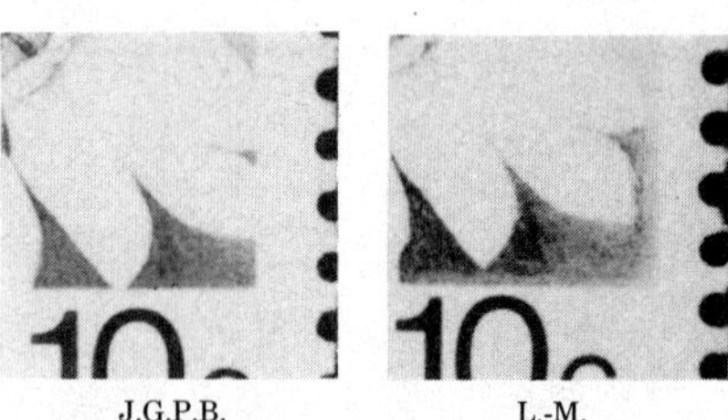

J.G.P.B. L.-M.

10 c. The J.G.P.B. printing shows the petals at bottom right cut by the edge of the design. On the L.-M. printing all three petals are complete.

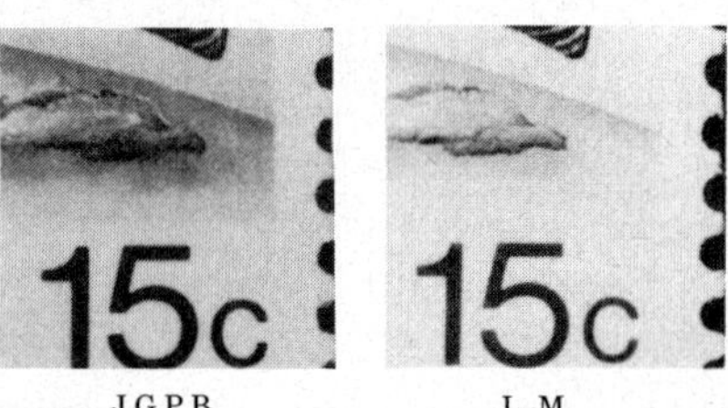

J.G.P.B. L.-M.

15 c. The J.G.P.B. printing shows the rock at bottom right 1½ mm from the right-hand edge. On the L.-M. stamp this distance is 2 mm.

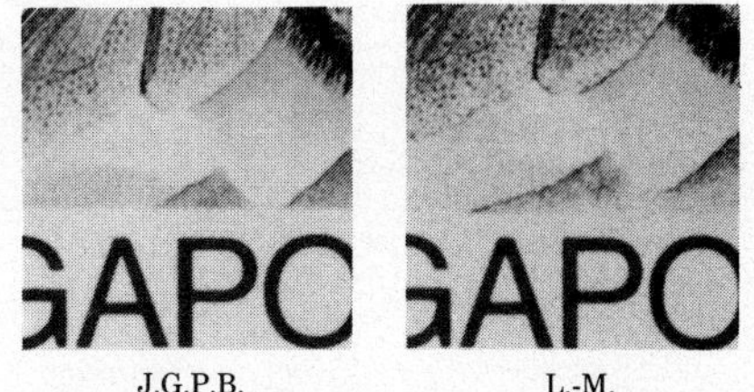

J.G.P.B. L.-M.

20 c. On the J.G.P.B. stamp the pink flowers above "SINGAPORE" touch the edge of the vignette. For the L.-M. printing the right-hand petal is clear of the edge.

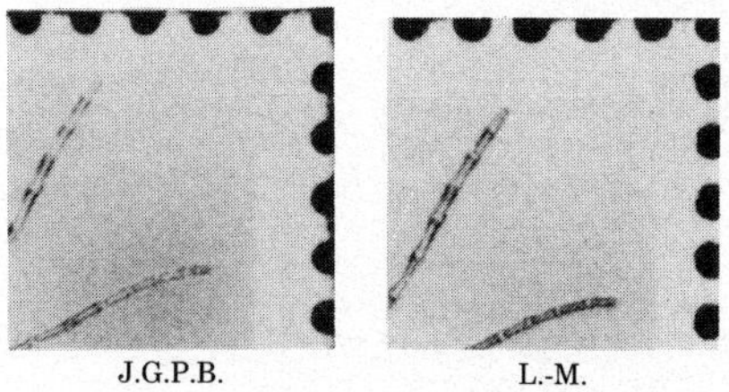

J.G.P.B. L.-M.

25 c. The J.G.P.B. printing shows the uppermost feeler of the water beetle touching the top of the design. On the L.-M. stamp the feeler does not reach the edge of the design.

J.G.P.B. L.-M.

35 c. On the J.G.P.B. printing the vein on the leaf at bottom left stops just short of the corner of the design. The L.-M. stamp shows this vein reaching the left-hand edge of the design above the corner.

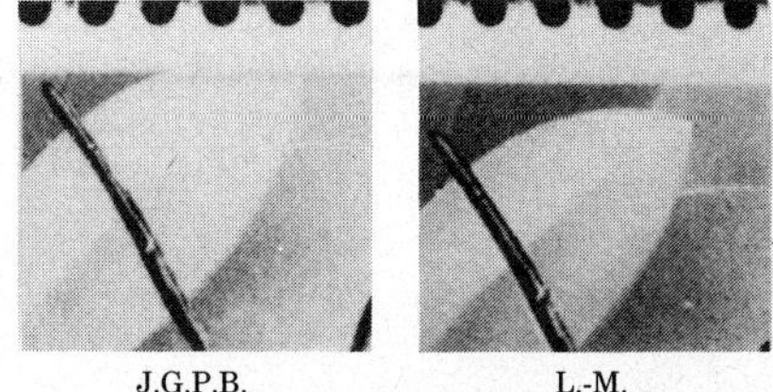

J.G.P.B. L.-M.

50 c. The J.G.P.B. stamp has the uppermost leaf cut by the top edge of the design. On the L.-M. printing the leaf is complete.

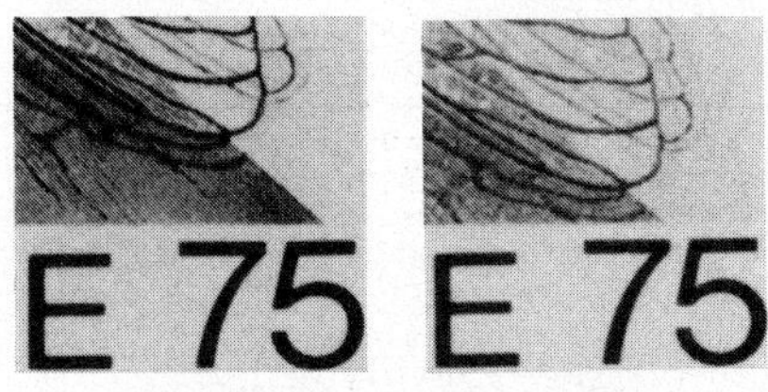

J.G.P.B. L.-M.

75 c. On the J.G.P.B. printing the shadow of the wings is 1½mm above the bottom edge of the vignette. For the L.-M. stamp the shadow touches the bottom edge.

151 Tennis, Canoeing, Judo and Children Playing

(Des M. Chiew. Litho Secura, Singapore)

1985 (1 July). *25th Anniv of the People's Association. T* **151** *and similar horiz designs. Multicoloured. One phosphor band (10 c.) or phosphorised paper (others). P* 13½ × 14.

503 10 c. Type **151**.. .. .. 15 10
504 35 c. Lion dance, martial arts and athletes with flags 30 30
505 50 c. Tae-kwon-do, Indian dance and Dragon dance 40 40
506 75 c. Boxing, table tennis, basketball and dancing 55 55
503/6 .. .. *Set of* 4 1·25 1·25

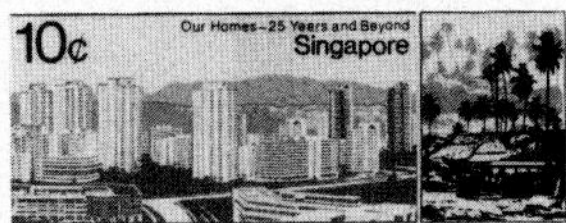

152 Modern Housing Estate and Squatter Settlement

(Des Eng Siak Loy. Litho Secura, Singapore)

1985 (9 Aug). *25th Anniv of Housing and Development Board. Horiz designs as T* **152** *with different aspects of housing shown at left. Multicoloured. One phosphor band (10 c.) or phosphorised paper (others). P* 13½ × 14.

507 10 c. Type **152**.. .. .. 15 10
508 35 c. Singapore family (Home-ownership) .. 30 30
509 50 c. Group of residents (Community development) 40 40
510 75 c. Construction workers (Building technology) 55 55
507/10 .. .. *Set of* 4 1·25 1·25
MS511 126 × 105 mm. Nos. 507/10 .. .. 1·75 2·25

153 Brownies **154** Badges and Emblems of Singapore Youth Organizations

(Des Foo Lye Lin. Litho J.W.)

1985 (6 Nov). *75th Anniv of Girl Guide Movement. T* **153** *and similar vert designs. One phosphor band (10 c.) or phosphorised paper (others). Multicoloured. P* 14.

512 10 c. Type **153**.. .. .. 10 10
513 35 c. Guides practising first aid 30 30
514 50 c. Senior Branch 40 40
515 75 c. Adult leaders and guides 55 55
512/15 .. .. *Set of* 4 1·25 1·25

(Des Eng Siak Loy. Litho Secura, Singapore)

1985 (18 Dec). *International Youth Year. T* **154** *and similar horiz designs. Multicoloured. One phosphor band (10 c.) or phosphorised paper (others). P* 12.

516 10 c. Type **154**.. .. .. 10 10
517 75 c. Hand protecting sapling 50 55
518 $1 Stylised figures and dove 65 70
516/18 .. .. *Set of* 3 1·10 1·25

155 Guava **156** Laboratory Technician and Salesmen with Bar Graph

(Des Poh Siew Wah. Litho J.W.)

1986 (26 Feb). *Singapore Fruits. T* **155** *and similar vert designs. Multicoloured. One centre phosphor band (10 c.) or phosphorised paper (others). P* 14.

519 10 c. Type **155**.. .. .. 10 10
520 35 c. Jambu Air 25 30
521 50 c. Rambutan 30 35
522 75 c. Ciku 50 55
519/22 .. .. *Set of* 4 1·00 1·10

(Des W. Lee. Litho Secura, Singapore)

1986 (1 May). *25th Anniv of National Trades Union Congress. T* **156** *and similar vert designs. Multicoloured. One phosphor band. P* 13½.

523 10 c. Type **156**.. .. .. 20 20
a. Horiz strip of 4. Nos. 523/6 70
524 10 c. Computer operator and welder .. 20 20
525 10 c. Draughtsmen and surveyors 20 20
526 10 c. Group of workers 20 20
523/6 .. .. *Set of* 4 70 70
MS527 148 × 100 mm. As Nos. 523/6, but each stamp with a face value of 35 c. Phosphorised paper .. .. 1·25 1·50

Nos. 523/6 were printed together, *se-tenant*, in horizontal strips of 4 throughout the sheet, forming a composite design.

157 Calligraphy **158** Industrial Automation

(Des Chua Ban Har. Litho (50 c. also die-stamped) Leigh-Mardon Ltd, Melbourne)

1986 (2 May). *"Expo '86" World Fair, Vancouver. T* **157** *and similar horiz designs. Multicoloured. "All-over" phosphor. P* 14 × 14½.

528 50 c. Type **157**.. .. .. 45 55
a. Horiz strip of 3. Nos. 528/30 .. .. 1·60
529 75 c. Garland maker 60 75
530 $1 Batik printer 75 95
528/30 .. .. *Set of* 3 1·60 2·00

Nos. 528/30 were printed together, *se-tenant*, in horizontal strips of 3 throughout the sheet.

(Des Eng Siak Loy. Litho J.W.)

1986 (1 Aug). *25th Anniv of Economic Development Board. T* **158** *and similar vert designs. Multicoloured. Phosphorised paper. P* 15 × 14½.

531 10 c. Type **158**.. .. .. 10 10
532 35 c. Manufacture of aircraft components .. 25 30
533 50 c. Electronics industry 30 40
534 75 c. Biotechnology industry 50 70
531/4 .. .. *Set of* 4 1·00 1·40

159 Map showing Route of Cable and *Vercors* (cable ship)

(Des J. Heng. Litho Secura, Singapore)

1986 (8 Sept). *SEA–ME–WE Submarine Cable Project. Phosphorised paper. P* 13½.

535 **159** 10 c. multicoloured 15 10
536 35 c. multicoloured 35 30
537 50 c. multicoloured 45 45
538 75 c. multicoloured 65 75
535/8 .. .. *Set of* 4 1·40 1·40

160 Stylized Citizens **161** Peace Doves and People of Different Races

(Des W. Lee. Litho Secura, Singapore)

1986 (15 Oct). *21st Anniv of Citizens' Consultative Committees. T* **160** *and similar vert designs showing citizens. Phosphorised paper. P* 12.

539 10 c. multicoloured 20 20
a. Block of 4. Nos. 539/42 .. .. .. 1·40
540 35 c. multicoloured 35 35
541 50 c. multicoloured 40 40
542 75 c. multicoloured 60 60
539/42 .. .. *Set of* 4 1·40 1·40

Nos. 539/42 were printed together, *se-tenant*, in blocks of 4 throughout the sheet, each block forming a composite design.

(Des Eng Siak Loy. Litho Secura, Singapore)

1986 (17 Dec). *International Peace Year. T* **161** *and similar horiz designs. Multicoloured. Phosphorised paper. P* 14 × 13½.

543 10 c. Type **161**.. .. .. 10 10
544 35 c. Doves and map of ASEAN countries .. 25 25
545 $1 Doves and globe 60 60
543/5 .. .. *Set of* 3 85 85

162 Orchard Road **163** Flags of Member Nations and Logo

(Des Chua Ban Har. Litho Secura, Singapore)

1987 (25 Feb). *Singapore Skyline. T* **162** *and similar horiz designs. Multicoloured. Phosphorised paper. P* 12.

546 10 c. Type **162**.. .. .. 15 10
547 50 c. Central Business District 40 30
548 75 c. Marina Centre and Raffles City .. 60 45
546/8 .. .. *Set of* 3 1·00 75

(Des Chua Ban Har. Litho Secura, Singapore)

1987 (15 June). *20th Anniv of Association of South-east Asian Nations. Phosphorised paper. P* 12.

549 **163** 10 c. multicoloured 10 10
550 35 c. multicoloured 25 25
551 50 c. multicoloured 30 30
552 75 c. multicoloured 45 45
549/52 .. .. *Set of* 4 1·00 95

164 Soldier with Rocket Launcher and Tank

165 Singapore River and Dragon Boats

(Des M. Ng Puay Chiew. Litho Questa)

1987 (1 July). *20th Anniv of National Service. T* **164** *and similar vert designs. Multicoloured. Phosphorised paper. P* 15 × 14.

553	10 c. Type **164**	20	25
	a. Horiz strip of 4. Nos. 553/6	70	
554	10 c. Radar operator and patrol boat	20	25
555	10 c. Fighter pilot and aircraft	20	25
556	10 c. Servicemen pledging allegiance	20	25
553/6	*Set of* 4	70	90
MS557	148 × 100 mm. 35 c. × 5. As Nos. 553/6 and Singapore lion symbol (scarlet and black)	1·40	1·25

Nos. 553/6 were printed together, *se-tenant*, in horizontal strips of 4 throughout the sheet.

(Des Ng Keng Seng. Litho Secura, Singapore)

1987 (2 Sept). *River Conservation. T* **165** *and similar square designs. Multicoloured. Phosphorised paper. P* 13½.

558	10 c. Type **165**	10	10
559	50 c. Kallang Basin, canoe and fishing punt	35	30
560	$1 Kranji Reservoir, athletes and cyclist	70	60
558/60	*Set of* 3	1·00	90

166 Majapahit Gold Bracelet and Museum

(Des M. Ng. Litho Secura, Singapore)

1987 (12 Oct). *Centenary of National Museum. T* **166** *and similar horiz designs, each showing different drawings of Museum. Multicoloured. Phosphorised paper. P* 13½ × 14.

561	10 c. Type **166**	10	10
562	75 c. Ming fluted kendi (water vessel)	40	45
563	$1 Patani hulu pekakak keris (sword)	55	60
561/3	*Set of* 3	90	1·00

167 Omni-theatre

(Des Eng Siak Loy. Litho Leigh-Mardon Ltd, Melbourne)

1987 (10 Dec). *10th Anniv of Singapore Science Centre. T* **167** *and similar horiz designs. Multicoloured. Phosphorised paper. P* 14½.

564	10 c. Type **167**	10	10
565	35 c. Omni-planetarium	30	25
566	75 c. Model of body cell	50	45
567	$1 Physical sciences exhibits	70	60
564/7	*Set of* 4	1·40	1·25

168 Modern Anti-aircraft Gun

169 Route Map

(Litho Secura, Singapore)

1988 (22 Feb). *Centenary of Singapore Artillery. T* **168** *and similar horiz designs. Multicoloured. Phosphorised paper. P* 13½ × 14.

568	10 c. Type **168**	25	10
569	35 c. 25-pounder field gun firing salute	55	30
570	50 c. Gunner and 12-pounder gun, c. 1920	80	45
571	$1 Gunner and Maxim gun, 1889	1·25	75
568/71	*Set of* 4	2·50	1·40

(Des Ng Keng Seng. Litho Secura, Singapore)

1988 (12 Mar). *Singapore Mass Rapid Transit System. T* **169** *and similar horiz designs. Multicoloured. Phosphorised paper. P* 13½ × 14.

572	10 c. Type **169**	15	10
573	50 c. Train on elevated section	45	35
574	$1 Train in tunnel	80	60
572/4	*Set of* 3	1·25	95

170 Camera, Film and Outside Broadcast Van

(Des E. Soriano. Litho CPE Australia Ltd, Melbourne)

1988 (4 Apr). *25th Anniv of Television in Singapore. T* **170** *and similar horiz designs. Multicoloured. Phosphorised paper. P* 13½ × 14.

575	10 c. Type **170**	10	10
576	35 c. Camera, studio lights and microphone	20	25
577	75 c. Television set and transmitter	40	45
578	$1 Globe on TV screen and dish aerial	55	60
575/8	*Set of* 4	1·10	1·25

MACHINE LABELS. From 19 April 1988 self-adhesive labels in the above design, with the background printed in orange and grey, were available from machines situated outside a number of Singapore post offices. Face values between 5 c. and $2 could be selected and the location of individual machines is indicated by the code number, from 0001 to 0050, at bottom left.

The design was changed to three lions' heads in red on 5 June 1989, to the Fullerton Building G.P.O. in brown on 8 September 1990 and to Haw Par Villa on 2 October 1991.

Vertical labels inscribed "SINGAPORE POSTAGE" with face values and, in some instances a weight, also exist. These were introduced in January 1983 and come from machines used by P.O. counter clerks to process parcels and registered mail. For a time , during 1986–87, these labels were on self-adhesive paper.

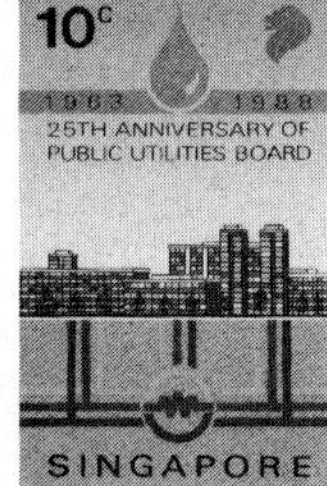

171 Water Droplet and Blocks of Flats

172 Greeting Neighbours

(Des Ng Keng Seng. Litho CPE Australia Ltd, Melbourne)

1988 (4 May). *25th Anniv of Public Utilities Board. T* **171** *and similar vert designs, each showing a different skyline. Multicoloured. Phosphorised paper. P* 13½.

579	10 c. Type **171**	10	10
580	50 c. Electric light bulb and city centre	35	35
581	$1 Gas flame and factories	65	65
579/81	*Set of* 3	1·00	1·00
MS582	116 × 75 mm. Nos. 579/81	1·25	1·40

(Des M. Ng Puay Chiew. Litho Leigh-Mardon Ltd, Melbourne)

1988 (6 July). *10th Anniv of National Courtesy Campaign. T* **172** *and similar horiz designs, each showing campaign mascot "Singa". Multicoloured. Phosphorised paper. P* 14½.

583	10 c. Type **172**	10	10
584	30 c. Queueing at checkout	15	20
585	$1 Helping the elderly	55	60
583/5	*Set of* 3	70	80

173 Modern 30 Metre Turntable Fire Appliance

174 Container Ships and Warehouses

(Des Eng Siak Loy. Litho Secura, Singapore)

1988 (1 Nov). *Centenary of Fire Service. T* **173** *and similar horiz design. Multicoloured. Phosphorised paper. P* 13½.

586	10 c. Type **173**	20	10
587	$1 Steam fire engine, c. 1890	1·25	75

(Des Ng Keng Seng. Litho Secura, Singapore)

1989 (3 Apr). *25th Anniv of Singapore Port Authority. T* **174** *and similar vert designs. Multicoloured. Phosphorised paper. P* 14 × 13½.

588	10 c. Type **174**	15	10
589	30 c. Shipping and oil storage depot	30	30
590	75 c. Container ships and Singapore skyline	70	75
591	$1 Container port at night	80	90
588/91	*Set of* 4	1·75	1·75

175 "Sago Street"

176 North-west Singapore City, 1920

(Litho Questa)

1989 (17 May). *Paintings of Chinatown by Choo Keng Kwang. T* **175** *and similar square designs. Multicoloured. Phosphorised paper. P* 14½.

592	10 c. Type **175**	15	10
593	35 c. "Pagoda Street"	40	40
594	75 c. "Trengganu Street"	90	90
595	$1 "Temple Street"	1·00	1·00
592/5	*Set of* 4	2·25	2·25

(Des Leo Teck Chong. Litho Harrison)

1989 (26 July). *Maps of Singapore. T* **176** *and similar multicoloured designs. Phosphorised paper. P* 14 × 14½ (15 *c.*) *or* 12½ × 13 (*others*).

596	15 c. Type **176** (top left)	20	20
	a. Block of 4. Nos. 596/9	70	
597	15 c. North-east Singapore (top right)	20	20
598	15 c. South-west Singapore (bottom left)	20	20
599	15 c. South-east Singapore (bottom right)	20	20
600	50 c. Singapore Island and Dependencies, 1860s	65	65
601	$1 British Settlement of Singapore, 1820s	1·10	1·10
596/601	*Set of* 6	2·25	2·25

Nos. 596/9 were printed together, *se-tenant*, in blocks of 4 throughout the sheet, each block forming a composite design. Individual stamps can be identified by the position of the lion emblem which is quoted in brackets.

177 Clown Triggerfish

178 "Hari Raya Puasa" (Loke Yoke Yun)

(Des Eng Siak Loy. Litho Harrison)

1989 (6 Sept). *Fishes. T* **177** *and similar horiz designs. Multicoloured. Phosphorised paper. P* 13½.

602	15 c. Type **177**	30	10
603	30 c. Majestic Angelfish	60	40
604	75 c. Emperor Angelfish	1·40	90
605	$1 Royal Empress Angelfish	1·60	1·10
602/5	*Set of* 4	3·50	2·25

(Adapted S. Ang Woon Beng. Litho Harrison)

1989 (25 Oct). *Festivals of Singapore. Children's Drawings. T* **178** *and similar vert designs. Multicoloured. Phosphorised paper. P* 14½.

606	15 c. Type **178**	15	10
607	35 c. "Chinese New Year" (Simon Koh)	30	30
608	75 c. "Thaipusam" (Henry Setiono)	70	70
609	$1 "Christmas" (Wendy Ang Lin Min)	90	1·00
606/9	*Set of* 4	1·90	1·90
MS610	126 × 75 mm. Nos. 606/9. P 14	1·90	2·00

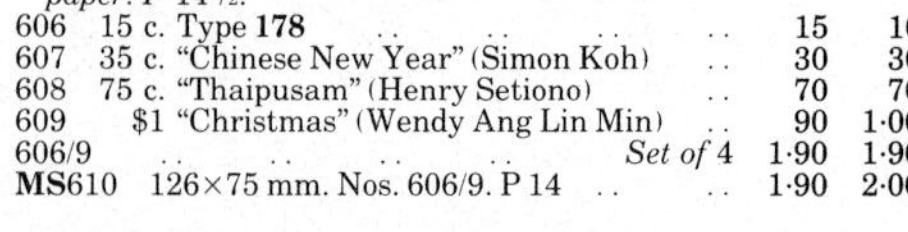

179 North Entrance of Stadium

180 "Singapore River, 1839" (Louis le Breton)

(Des Lim Ching San. Litho Harrison)

1989 (27 Dec). *Opening of Singapore Indoor Stadium. T* **179** *and similar horiz designs. Multicoloured. Phosphorised paper. P* 14.

611	30 c. Type **179**	40	25
612	75 c. Arena	80	65
613	$1 East entrance	1·10	90
611/13	*Set of* 3	2·10	1·60
MS614	104 × 104 mm. Nos. 611/13	2·10	1·90

(Des Choy Weng Yang. Litho Leigh-Mardon Ltd, Melbourne)

1990 (21 Mar). *Lithographs of 19th-century Singapore. T* **180** *and similar horiz designs. Multicoloured. Phosphorised paper. P* 13.

615	15 c. Type **180**	15	10
	a. Booklet pane. No. 615×10	1·40	
616	30 c. "Chinatown, 1837" (Barthelemy Lauvergne)	30	30
617	75 c. "Singapore Harbour, 1837" (Barthelemy Lauvergne)	70	70
618	$1 "View from the French Resident's House, 1824" (Deroy)	85	90
615/18	*Set of* 4	1·75	1·75

The upper and lower edges of booklet pane No. 615a are imperforate.

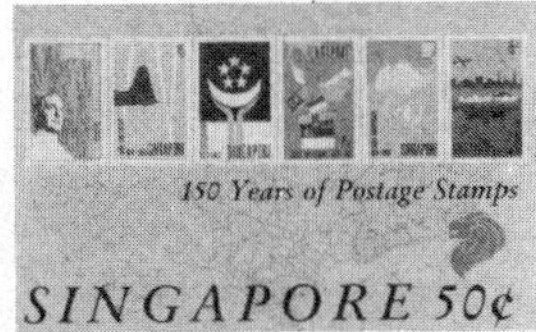

181 1969 150th Anniv of Singapore Stamp Issue

(Des Sylvia Tan. Litho Leigh-Mardon Pty Ltd, Melbourne)

1990 (3 May). *150th Anniv of the Penny Black. T* **181** *and similar horiz designs, each showing a different map in the background. Multicoloured. Phosphorised paper. P* 13½.

619	50 c. Type **181**	55	40
620	75 c. Indian stamps, including bisect, used from Singapore in 1859	80	70
621	$1 Indian stamps used from Singapore in 1854	1·25	90
622	$2 Penny Black and Two Pence Blue	2·00	2·00
619/22	*Set of* 4	4·25	3·50
MS623	134×90 mm. Nos. 619/22	4·25	3·50

No. **MS**623 also commemorates the "Stamp World London 90" international stamp exhibition.

182 Zoological Gardens

183 Chinese Opera Singer and Siong Lim Temple

(Des Ng Keng Seng (5 to 75 c.), Lim Ching San ($1 to $10). Photo (5 to 75 c.) or recess and photo ($1 to $10) Harrison)

1990 (4 July)–**91**. *Tourism. Multicoloured. Phosphorised paper.* (a) *T* **182** *and similar square designs. P* 14½.

624	5 c. Type **182**	10	10
625	15 c. Sentosa Island	10	10
	a. Booklet pane. No. 625×10	1·50	
626	20 c. Singapore River	15	20
	a. Booklet pane. No. 626×10 (6.3.91)	1·40	
627	25 c. Dragon Boat Festival	15	20
628	30 c. Raffles Hotel	20	25
629	35 c. Coffee shop bird singing contest	25	30
630	40 c. Jurong Bird Park	30	35
631	50 c. Chinese New Year boat float	35	40
632	75 c. Peranakan Place	50	55
	(*b*) *T* **183** *and similar horiz designs. P* 15×14 (9.10.90)		
633	$1 Type **183**	70	75
634	$2 Malay dancer and Sultan Mosque	1·40	1·50
635	$5 Indian dancer and Sri Mariamman Temple	3·50	3·75
636	$10 Ballet dancer and Victoria Memorial Hall	7·00	7·25
624/36	*Set of* 13	13·00	14·00

The upper and lower edges of booklet panes Nos. 625a and 626a are imperforate.

184 Armed Forces Personnel

185 Stag's Horn Fern

(Des Chua Ban Har. Litho Harrison)

1990 (16 Aug). *25th Anniv of Independence. T* **184** *and similar horiz designs. Multicoloured. Phosphorised paper. P* 14×15.

637	15 c. Type **184**	20	15
	a. Perf 14	20	20
	ab. Booklet pane. No. 637a×10	1·75	
638	35 c. Inhabitants of Singapore	40	40
639	75 c. Workers and technological achievements	80	80
640	$1 Cultural activities	1·00	1·00
637/40	*Set of* 4	2·25	2·25

Booklet pane No. 637a has margins at the vertical edges of the pane.

(Des Poh Siew Wah. Litho Questa)

1990 (14 Nov). *Ferns. T* **185** *and similar horiz designs. Multicoloured. Phosphorised paper. P* 14.

641	15 c. Type **185**	15	10
642	35 c. Maiden Hair Fern	35	35
643	75 c. Bird's Nest Fern	70	70
644	$1 Rabbit's Foot Fern	90	90
641/4	*Set of* 4	1·90	1·90

186 Carved Dragon Pillar, Hong San See Temple

187 *Vanda* "Miss Joaquim"

(Des Leo Teck Chong. Litho Leigh-Mardon Ltd, Melbourne)

1991 (23 Jan). *National Monuments. T* **186** *and similar multicoloured designs. Phosphorised paper. P* 14½.

645	20 c. Type **186**	25	25
	a. Vert pair. Nos. 645/6	50	50
646	20 c. Hong San See Temple (40×25 *mm*)	25	25
647	50 c. Interior of dome, Abdul Gaffoor Mosque	45	45
	a. Vert pair. Nos. 647/8	90	90
648	50 c. Abdul Gaffoor Mosque (40×25 *mm*)	45	45
649	75 c. Statue of Vishnu, Sri Perumal Hindu Temple	65	65
	a. Vert pair. Nos. 649/50	1·25	1·25
650	75 c. Sri Perumal Temple (40×25 *mm*)	65	65
651	$1 Stained glass window, St Andrew's Cathedral	80	80
	a. Vert pair. Nos. 651/2	1·60	1·60
652	$1 St Andrew's Cathedral (40×25 *mm*)	80	80
645/52	*Set of* 8	3·75	3·75

The two designs for each value were printed together, *se-tenant*, in vertical pairs throughout the sheets.

(Des Chua Ban Har. Litho Leigh-Mardon Ltd, Melbourne)

1991 (24 Apr). *"Singapore '95" International Stamp Exhibition. Orchids (1st issue). T* **187** *and similar horiz design. Multicoloured. Phosphorised paper. P* 14.

653	$2 Type **187**	1·90	1·90
	a. Horiz pair. Nos. 653/4	3·75	3·75
654	$2 *Dendrobium* "Anocha"	1·90	1·90
MS655	123×80 mm. Nos. 653/4	3·75	4·00

Nos. 653/4 were issued together, *se-tenant*, in sheets of 30 (6×5), showing No. 653 in vertical rows 1 and 4, No. 654 in vertical rows 3 and 5, and stamp-size labels with exhibition emblem in vertical rows 2 and 4.

See also Nos. 674/6.

188 Changi Airport Terminal II, 1991, and B747-400

189 *Arachnopsis* "Eric Holttum"

(Des Leo Teck Chong. Recess and litho Harrison)

1991 (1 June). *Singapore Civil Aviation. T* **188** *and similar horiz designs. Multicoloured. Phosphorised paper. P* 13½×14½.

656	20 c. Type **188**	25	20
657	75 c. Changi Airport Terminal I, 1981, and B747-200	75	75
658	$1 Paya Lebar Airport, 1955–1981, and Concorde	95	95
659	$2 Kallang Airport, 1937–1955, and DC-2	1·75	1·90
656/9	*Set of* 4	3·25	3·50

(Des Chua Ban Har. Litho Questa)

1991 (7 Aug). *Orchid Dress Motifs. T* **189** *and similar horiz designs. Multicoloured. Phosphorised paper. P* 14½×14.

660	20 c. Type **189**	25	20
661	30 c. *Cattleya meadii*	35	30
662	$1 *Calanthe vestita*	1·10	1·10
660/2	*Set of* 3	1·50	1·40

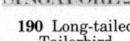

190 Long-tailed Tailorbird

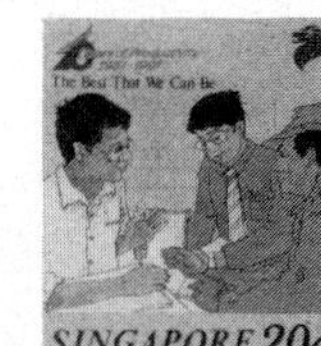

191 Productivity Discussion

(Des M. Ng Puay Chiew. Litho Leigh-Mardon Ltd, Melbourne)

1991 (19 Sept). *Garden Birds. T* **190** *and similar horiz designs. Multicoloured. Phosphorised paper. P* 14.

663	20 c. Type **190**	25	20
	a. Booklet pane. No. 663×10	2·25	
664	35 c. Scarlet-backed Flowerpecker	40	40
665	75 c. Black-naped Oriole	80	80
666	$1 Common Iora	95	95
663/6	*Set of* 4	2·25	2·25

Booklet pane No. 663a has the upper and lower edges imperforate and there are margins at left and right.

(Des Foo Lye Lin. Litho Questa)

1991 (1 Nov). *10th Anniv of Productivity Movement. T* **191** *and similar vert design. Multicoloured. Phosphorised paper. P* 14×14½.

667	20 c. Type **191**	15	20
668	$1 Construction workers	70	75

192 Railway Creeper

193 "Singapore Waterfront" (Georgette Chen Liying)

(Des Eng Siak Loy. Litho Leigh-Mardon Ltd, Melbourne)

1991 (16 Nov). *"Philanippon '91" International Stamp Exhibition, Tokyo. Wild Flowers. T* **192** *and similar vert designs. Multicoloured. Phosphorised paper. P* 14½×14.

669	30 c. Type **192**	20	25
670	75 c. Asystasia	50	55
671	$1 Singapore Rhododendron	70	75
672	$2 Coat Buttons	1·40	1·50
669/72	*Set of* 4	2·50	2·75
MS673	132×90 mm. Nos. 669/72	2·75	3·00

(Des Chua Ban Har. Litho Leigh-Mardon Ltd, Melbourne)

1992 (22 Jan). *"Singapore '95" International Stamp Exhibition. Orchids (2nd issue). Horiz designs as T* **187**. *Multicoloured. Phosphorised paper. P* 14.

674	$2 *Dendrobium* "Sharifah Fatimah"	1·40	1·50
	a. Horiz pair. Nos. 674/5	2·75	3·00
675	$2 *Phalaenopsis* "Shim Beauty"	1·40	1·50
MS676	123×80 mm. Nos. 674/5	2·75	3·00

Nos. 674/5 were printed in the same sheet format as Nos. 653/4.

(Des Lim Ching San. Litho Secura, Singapore)

1992 (11 Mar). *Local Artists. T* **193** *and similar square designs. Multicoloured. Phosphorised paper. P* 14.

677	20 c. Type **193**	15	20
678	75 c. "Kampung Hut" (Lim Cheng Hoe)	50	55
679	$1 "The Bridge" (Poh Siew Wah)	70	75
680	$2 "Singapore River" (Lee Boon Wang)	1·40	1·50
677/80	*Set of* 4	2·50	2·75

POSTAGE DUE STAMPS

The postage due stamps of Malayan Postal Union were in use in Singapore until replaced by the following issues.

D 1

D 2

D 3

(Litho B.W.)

1968 (1 Feb)–**69**. *Toned paper. W w* **12**. *P* 9.

D1	D 1	1 c. green	30	1·50
D2		2 c. red	30	1·75
D3		4 c. yellow-orange	45	2·50
D4		8 c. chocolate	40	90
D5		10 c. magenta	50	90
		a. White paper (16.12.69)	80	1·75
D6		12 c. slate-violet	1·00	1·50
		a. White paper (16.12.69)	2·25	3·50
D7		20 c. new blue	2·00	3·00
		a. White paper (16.12.69)	4·50	7·00
D8		50 c. drab	4·75	4·75
D1/8		*Set of* 8	8·75	15·00

1973. *White paper. W w* **12**. *P* 13 × 13½.

D 9	D 1	10 c. bright magenta (27.4)	75	4·50
D10		50 c. sage-green (24.8)	4·00	12·00

1977–78. *White paper. No wmk. P* 13 × 13½.

D11	D 1	1 c. green	28·00	32·00
D12		4 c. yellow-orange	28·00	32·00
D13		10 c. bright magenta	28·00	32·00
D14		20 c. new blue	38·00	42·00
D15		50 c. sage-green	45·00	48·00
D11/15		*Set of* 5	£150	£170

(Litho Secura, Singapore)

1978 (25 Sept)–**81**. *No wmk. P* 13 × 13½.

D16	D 2	1 c. blue-green	55	1·50
		a. Perf 12 × 11½ (1981)	10	30
D17		4 c. pale orange	65	1·50
		a. Perf 12 × 11½ (1981)	15	40
D18		10 c. cerise	75	1·50
		a. Perf 12 × 11½ (1981)	30	50
D19		20 c. light blue	85	1·60
		a. Perf 12 × 11½ (1981)	40	75
D20		50 c. yellow-green	1·40	2·00
		a. Perf 12 × 11½ (1981)	70	1·25
D16/20		*Set of* 5	3·75	7·25
D16a/20a		*Set of* 5	1·50	3·00

(Litho Secura, Singapore)

1989 (12 July). *P* 13×13½.

D21	D 3	5 c. bright mauve	10	10
D22		10 c. carmine	10	10
D23		20 c. bright greenish blue	15	20
D24		50 c. yellow-green	35	40
D21/4		*Set of* 4	55	65

Solomon Islands

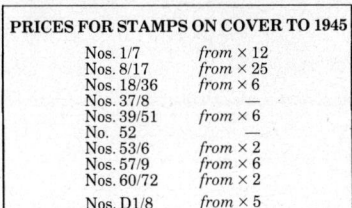

(*formerly* British Solomon Islands)

PRICES FOR STAMPS ON COVER TO 1945	
Nos. 1/7	*from* × 12
Nos. 8/17	*from* × 25
Nos. 18/36	*from* × 6
Nos. 37/8	—
Nos. 39/51	*from* × 6
No. 52	—
Nos. 53/6	*from* × 2
Nos. 57/9	*from* × 6
Nos. 60/72	*from* × 2
Nos. D1/8	*from* × 5

BRITISH PROTECTORATE

1

2

(Des C. M. Woodford. Litho W. E. Smith & Co, Sydney)

1907 (14 Feb). *No wmk. P* 11.

1	**1**	½d. ultramarine	6·50	12·00
2		1d. rose-carmine	20·00	30·00
3		2d. indigo	24·00	30·00
		a. Imperf between (horiz pair)	£9500	
4		2½d. orange-yellow	30·00	35·00
		a. Imperf between (vert pair)	£4000	
		b. Imperf between (horiz pair)	£4000	£4000
5		5d. emerald-green	50·00	65·00
6		6d. chocolate	55·00	60·00
		a. Imperf between (vert pair)	£3250	
7		1s. bright purple	75·00	75·00
1/7		*Set of* 7	£225	£275

Three types exist of the ½d. and 2½d., and six each of the other values, differing in minor details.

Forgeries of Nos. 1/7 show different perforations and have the boat paddle touching the shore. Genuine stamps show a gap between the paddle and the shore.

(Recess D.L.R.)

1908 (1 Nov)–**11**. *Wmk Mult Crown CA (sideways). P* 14.

8	**2**	½d. green	50	80
9		1d. red	1·00	50
10		2d. greyish slate	1·25	1·00
11		2½d. ultramarine	2·00	2·50
11*a*		4d. red/*yellow* (6.3.11)	3·00	11·00
12		5d. olive	8·50	9·00
13		6d. claret	7·00	7·50
14		1s. black/*green*	9·50	12·00
15		2s. purple/*blue* (7.3.10)	27·00	50·00
16		2s. 6d. red/*blue* (7.3.10)	40·00	70·00
17		5s. green/*yellow* (7.3.10)	70·00	£100
8/17		*Set of* 11	£150	£225
8/17 Optd "Specimen"		*Set of* 11	£250	

The ½d. and 1d. were issued in 1913 on rather thinner paper and with brownish gum.

3

4

(T **3** and **4**. Typo D.L.R.)

1913. *Inscribed* "POSTAGE POSTAGE". *Wmk Mult Crown CA. P* 14.

18	**3**	½d. green (1.4)	80	3·50
19		1d. red (1.4)	80	10·00
20		3d. purple/*yellow* (27.2)	80	4·00
		a. On orange-buff	3·25	22·00
21		11d. dull purple and scarlet (27.2)	3·00	14·00
18/21		*Set of* 4	4·75	28·00
18/21 Optd "Specimen"		*Set of* 4	70·00	

1914 (Mar)–**23**. *Inscribed* "POSTAGE REVENUE". *Wmk Mult Crown CA. Chalk-surfaced paper (3d. to £1). P* 14.

22	**4**	½d. green	70	7·00
23		½d. yellow-green (1917)	2·25	11·00
24		1d. carmine-red	70	80
25		1d. scarlet (1917)	3·50	6·50
26		2d. grey (7.14)	1·25	9·00
27		2½d. ultramarine (7.14)	2·00	5·00
28		3d. purple/*pale yellow* (3.23)	18·00	60·00
29		4d. black and red/*yellow* (7.14)	2·00	2·50
30		5d. dull purple and olive-green (7.14)	15·00	26·00
31		5d. brown-purple and olive-green (7.14)	15·00	28·00
32		6d. dull and bright purple (7.14)	6·00	14·00
33		1s. black/*green* (7.14)	3·00	7·00
		a. On blue-green, olive back (1923)	6·50	17·00
34		2s. purple and blue/*blue* (7.14)	6·50	10·00
35		2s. 6d. black and red/*blue* (7.14)	7·50	20·00
36		5s. green and red/*yellow* (7.14)	25·00	38·00
		a. On orange-buff (1920)	42·00	65·00
37	**4**	10s. green and red/*green* (7.14)	75·00	80·00
38		£1 purple and black/*red* (7.14)	£225	£160
22/38		*Set of* 14	£325	£375
22/38 Optd "Specimen"		*Set of* 14	£400	

Variations in the coloured papers are mostly due to climate and do not indicate separate printings.

1922–31. *Wmk Mult Script CA. Chalk-surfaced paper* (4*d. and* 5*d. to* 10*s.*). *P* 14.

39	**4**	½d. green (10.22)	30	1·75
40		1d. scarlet (4.23)	10·00	8·50
41		1d. dull violet (2.27)	1·00	5·00
42	**3**	1½d. bright scarlet (7.24)	1·60	30
43	**4**	2d. slate-grey (4.23)	2·50	8·50
44		3d. pale ultramarine (11.23)	60	2·50
45		4d. black and red/*yellow* (7.27)	3·50	14·00
45*a*		4½d. red-brown (1931)	3·00	14·00
46		5d. dull purple and olive-green (12.27)	2·75	20·00
47		6d. dull and bright purple (12.27)	3·75	15·00
48		1s. black/*emerald* (12.27)	2·75	12·00
49		2s. purple and blue/*blue* (2.27)	7·50	30·00
50		2s. 6d. black and red/*blue* (12.27)	7·50	32·00
51		5s. green and red/*pale yellow* (12.27)	24·00	45·00
52		10s. green and red/*emerald* (1.25)	90·00	£120
39/52		*Set of* 15	£130	£225
39/52 Optd/Perf "Specimen"		*Set of* 15	£300	

1935 (6 May). *Silver Jubilee. As Nos.* 114/17 *of Jamaica, but ptd by D.L.R. P* 13½×14.

53	1½d. deep blue and carmine	75	50
	f. Diagonal line by turret	40·00	
	h. Dot by flagstaff	50·00	
54	3d. brown and deep blue	2·75	4·00
	f. Diagonal line by turret	75·00	
	h. Dot by flagstaff	85·00	
55	6d. light blue and olive-green	6·00	8·50
	a. Frame printed double, one albino	£1000	
	h. Dot by flagstaff	£120	
56	1s. slate and purple	6·00	7·00
	f. Diagonal line by turret	£110	
53/6	*Set of* 4	14·00	18·00
53/6 Perf "Specimen"	*Set of* 4	90·00	

For illustrations of plate varieties see Omnibus section following Zimbabwe.

1937 (13 May). *Coronation. As Nos.* 118/20 *of Jamaica, but ptd by B.W. P* 11×11½.

57	1d. violet	30	40
58	1½d. carmine	30	50
59	3d. blue	40	40
57/9	*Set of* 3	90	1·10
57/9 Perf "Specimen"	*Set of* 3	60·00	

5 Spears and Shield

6 Native Constable and Chief

7 Canoe House

8 Roviana Canoe

(Recess D.L.R. (2d., 3d., 2s. and 2s. 6d.), Waterlow (others))

1939 (1 Feb)–**1951**. *T* **5/8** *and similar designs. Wmk Mult Script CA. P* 13½ (*2d., 3d., 2s. and 2s. 6d.*) *or* 12½ (*others*).

60	½d. blue and blue-green	15	50
61	1d. brown and deep violet	15	30
62	1½d. blue-green and carmine	35	70
63	2d. orange-brown and black	30	85
	a. Perf 12 (7.11.51)	30	1·75
64	2½d. magenta and sage-green	70	55
	a. Imperf horiz (vert pair)	£7000	
65	3d. black and ultramarine	30	60
	a. Perf 12 (29.11.51)	30	1·75
66	4½d. green and chocolate	8·00	13·00
67	6d. deep violet and reddish purple	35	50
68	1s. green and black	50	30
69	2s. black and orange	6·00	3·00
70	2s. 6d. black and violet	23·00	4·50
71	5s. emerald-green and scarlet	22·00	7·50
72	10s. sage-green and magenta (27.4.42)	7·00	8·50
60/72	*Set of* 13	60·00	35·00
60/72 Perf "Specimen"	*Set of* 13	£275	

Designs: *Horiz* (*as T* **8**)—1½d. Artificial Island, Malaita; 1s. Breadfruit; 5s. Malaita canoe. (*As T* **7**)—3d. Roviana canoes; 2s. Tinakula volcano; 2s. 6d. Common Scrub Hen. *Vert* (*as T* **6**)—4½d., 10s. Native house, Reef Islands; 6d. Coconut plantation.

1946 (15 Oct). *Victory. As Nos.* 141/2 *of Jamaica.*

73	1½d. carmine	15	30
74	3d. blue	15	10
73/4 Perf "Specimen"	*Set of* 2	55·00	

OMNIBUS ISSUES

Details, together with prices for complete sets, of the various Omnibus issues from the 1935 Silver Jubilee series to date are included in a special section following Zimbabwe at the end of Volume 2.

Pocket handkerchief flaw (R. 1/6)

1949 (14 Mar). *Royal Silver Wedding. As Nos.* 143/4 *of Jamaica.*

75	2d. black	50	30
	a. Pocket handkerchief flaw	10·00	
76	10s. magenta	11·00	8·00

1949 (10 Oct). *75th Anniv of U.P.U. As Nos.* 145/8 *of Jamaica.*

77	2d. red-brown	75	50
78	3d. deep blue	1·25	70
79	5d. deep blue-green	1·25	75
80	1s. blue-black	1·75	50
77/80	*Set of* 4	4·50	2·25

1953 (2 June). *Coronation. As No.* 153 *of Jamaica.*

81	2d. black and grey-black	30	45

17 Ysabel Canoe

18 Roviana Canoe

24 Native Constable and Chief

25 Arms of the Protectorate

(Des Miss I. R. Stinson (½d.), R. Bailey (2½d.), R. A. Sweet (5d., 1s., 1s. 3d.), Capt. J. Brett Hilder (6d., 8d., 9d., 5s.). Recess B.W. (½d., 2½d., 5d., 6d., 8d., 9d., 1s., 1s. 3d., 5s.), D.L.R. (1d., 2d., 2s.), Waterlow (1½d., 3d., 2s. 6d., 10s., £1), until 1962, then D.L.R.)

1956 (1 Mar)–**63**. *T* **17/18**, **24/5** *and similar horiz designs. Wmk Mult Script CA. P* 12 (*1d., 2d., 2s.*), 13 (*1½d., 3d., 2s 6d., 10s., £1*) *or* 11½ (*others*).

82	½d. orange and purple	15	50
83	1d. yellow-green and red-brown	15	15
84	1½d. slate-green and carmine-red	15	40
	a. Slate-green and brown-red (31.7.63)	40	30
85	2d. deep brown and dull green	20	30
86	2½d. black and blue	25	45
87	3d. blue-green and red	25	15
88	5d. black and blue	30	55
89	6d. black and turquoise-green	50	25
90	8d. bright blue and black	25	15
90*a*	9d. emerald and black (28.1.60)	3·25	80
91	1s. slate and yellow-brown	50	50
	a. Slate and orange-brown (13.6.61)	3·00	2·50
91*b*	1s. 3d. black and blue (28.1.60)	6·00	1·75
	ba. Black and pale ultramarine (11.12.62)	10·00	3·25
92	2s. black and carmine	11·00	90
93	2s. 6d. emerald and bright purple	7·50	45
	a. Emerald and reddish purple (19.2.63)	11·00	1·75
94	5s. red-brown	12·00	1·75
95	10s. sepia	16·00	2·50
96	£1 black and blue (5.11.58)	42·00	35·00
82/96	*Set of* 17	90·00	40·00

Designs: (*As T* **17**)—5d., 1s. 3d. Map; 6d. *Miena* (schooner); 1s. Voyage of H.M.S. *Swallow*, 1767; 2s. 6d. Native house, Reef Islands; 5s. Mendaña and *Todos los Santos*. (*As T* **25**)—1d. Roviana canoe; 1½d. Artificial Island, Malaita; 2d. Canoe house; 3d. Malaita Canoe; 8d., 9d. Henderson airfield, Guadalcanal; 2s. Tinakula volcano.

LEGISLATIVE COUNCIL

32 Great Frigate Bird

(Litho Enschedé)

1961 (19 Jan). *New Constitution*, 1960. *W* w **12** (*sideways*). *P* 13 × 12½.

No.	Type	Description	Unused	Used
97	**32**	2d. black and turquoise-green	10	15
98		3d. black and rose-carmine	10	10
99		9d. black and reddish purple	15	15
97/9		*Set of* 3	30	30

1963 (4 June). *Freedom from Hunger. As No.* 80 *of Lesotho.*

No.	Description	Unused	Used
100	1s. 3d. ultramarine	2·50	35

1963 (2 Sept). *Red Cross Centenary. As Nos.* 203/4 *of Lesotho.*

No.	Description	Unused	Used
101	2d. red and black	60	20
102	9d. red and blue	1·40	70

1963–64. *As Nos.* 83/5, 87, 89, 90*a and* 91*a*/3, *but wmk* w **12**.

No.	Description	Unused	Used
103	1d. yellow-green and red-brown (9.7.64)	25	30
104	1½d. slate-green and red (9.7.64)	25	50
105	2d. deep brown and dull green (9.7.64)	20	20
106	3d. light blue-green and scarlet (16.11.63)	40	15
	a. Yellowish green and red (9.7.64)	90	1·75
107	6d. black and turquoise (7.7.64)	60	40
108	9d. emerald and black (7.7.64)	20	35
109	1s. 3d. black and blue (7.7.64)	60	70
110	2s. black and carmine (9.7.64)	1·00	4·50
111	2s. 6d. emerald & reddish purple (9.7.64)	10·00	10·00
103/11	*Set of* 9	12·00	15·00

33 Makira Food Bowl

2 c

(48)

(Des M. Farrar-Bell. Litho D.L.R.)

1965 (24 May). *Horiz designs as T* **33**. *W* w **12**. *P* 13 × 12½.

No.	Description	Unused	Used
112	½d. black, deep slate-blue and light blue	10	30
113	1d. black, orange and yellow	50	20
114	1½d. black, blue and yellow-green	25	35
115	2d. black, ultramarine and light blue	40	30
116	2½d. black, light brown & pale yellow-brown	10	35
117	3d. black, green and light green	10	10
118	6d. black, magenta and yellow-orange	35	20
119	9d. brownish blk, dp bluish grn & pale yell	40	15
120	1s. black, chocolate and magenta	80	15
121	1s. 3d. black and rose-red	3·50	2·25
122	2s. black, bright purple and lilac	5·50	2·75
123	2s. 6d. black, olive-brown and light brown	1·00	70
124	5s. black, ultramarine and violet	10·00	4·50
125	10s. black, olive-green and yellow	11·00	4·00
126	£1 black, deep reddish violet and pink	11·00	5·00
112/126	*Set of* 15	40·00	18·00

Designs:—1d. *Dendrobium veratrifolium* (orchid); 1½d. Scorpion Shell; 2d. Blyth's Hornbill; 2½d. Ysabel shield; 3d. Rennellese club; 6d. Moorish Idol; 9d. Lesser Frigate Bird; 1s. *Dendrobium macrophyllum* (orchid); 1s. 3d. *Dendrobium spectabilis* (orchid); 2s. Sanford's Sea Eagle; 2s. 6d. Malaita belt; 5s. *Ornithoptera victoreae* (butterfly); 10s. Ducorp's Cockatoo; £1, Western canoe figurehead.

1965 (28 June). *I.T.U. Centenary. As Nos.* 98/9 *of Lesotho.*

No.	Description	Unused	Used
127	2d. orange-red and turquoise-blue	20	10
128	3d. turquoise-blue and olive-brown	20	10

1965 (25 Oct). *International Co-operation Year. As Nos.* 100/1 *of Lesotho.*

No.	Description	Unused	Used
129	1d. reddish purple and turquoise-green	15	10
130	2s. 6d. deep bluish green and lavender	60	15

1966 (24 Jan). *Churchill Commemoration. As Nos.* 102/5 *of Lesotho.*

No.	Description	Unused	Used
131	2d. new blue	15	10
132	9d. deep green	25	10
133	1s. 3d. brown	35	10
134	2s. 6d. bluish violet	40	15
131/4	*Set of* 4	1·00	30

(New Currency. 100 cents = 1 Australian dollar)

8 c.

Normal "8"

8 c.

Inverted "8" (No. 142a) (R. 9/2. Later corrected)

1966–67. *Decimal Currency. Nos.* 112/26 *variously surch as T* **48** *by De La Rue.* A. *Wmk upright.* B. *Wmk sideways.*

No.	Description	A Unused	A Used	B Unused	B Used
135	1 c. on ½d.	10	10	10	10
136	2 c. on 1d.	10	10	10	10
137	3 c. on 1½d.	10	10	15	10
138	4 c. on 2d.	15	10	15	10
139	5 c. on 6d.	15	10	15	10
140	6 c. on 2½d.	15	10	10	10
141	7 c. on 3d.	15	10	10	10
142	8 c. on 9d.	25	10	15	10
	a. Inverted "8"	18·00	14·00	†	
	b. Surch omitted (vert pair)	—	—	†	
143	10 c. on 1s.	30	10	40	10
144	12 c. on 1s. 3d.	†		65	10
145	13 c. on 1s. 3d.	1·50	15	4·50	1·75
146	14 c. on 3d.	†		40	10
147	20 c. on 2s.	75	25	3·25	30
148	25 c. on 2s. 6d.	60	40	2·50	35
149	35 c. on 2d.	†		1·75	25
	a. Surch omitted (horiz pair with normal)	†		—	—
	b. Surch value only omitted	†		—	—
150	50 c. on 5s. (R.)	5·50	2·75	8·50	5·50
151	$1 on 10s.	4·00	3·00	4·00	1·25
152	$2 on £1	3·25	6·50	5·00	3·00
135A/152A	*Set of* 15	15·00	12·00		
135B/152A	*Set of* 18			28·00	11·50

Dates of issue: 1967—1 March, 12 c., 14 c., 35 c. 1966—14 February. All watermark upright. 1966—All other watermark sideways.

The positions of the bars in the surcharge vary considerably from stamp to stamp within the sheets.

The stamps with sideways watermark are all from new printings and in some instances there are marked shade variations from Nos. 112/26 which were used for making Nos. 135A/152A.

No. 142b comes from the bottom left-hand corner of the sheet and was covered by a paper fold. The bottom stamp in the pair is completely without surcharge and the upper has the surcharge value and one bar missing.

1966 (1 July). *World Cup Football Championships. As Nos.* 57/8 *of Pitcairn Islands.*

No.	Description	Unused	Used
153	8 c. violet, yellow-green, lake & yellow-brn	15	10
154	35 c. chocolate, blue-green, lake & yellow-brn	30	10

1966 (20 Sept). *Inauguration of W.H.O. Headquarters, Geneva. As Nos.* 185/6 *of Montserrat.*

No.	Description	Unused	Used
155	3 c. black, yellow-green and light blue	25	10
156	50 c. black, light purple and yellow-brown	1·00	20

1966 (1 Dec). 20*th Anniv of U.N.E.S.C.O. As Nos.* 342/4 *of Mauritius.*

No.	Description	Unused	Used
157	3 c. slate-violet, red, yellow and orange	20	10
158	25 c. orange-yellow, violet and deep olive	55	15
159	$1 black, bright purple and orange	1·50	70
157/9	*Set of* 3	2·00	85

49 Henderson Field

(Des V. Whiteley. Photo Harrison)

1967 (28 Aug). 25*th Anniv of Guadalcanal Campaign* (*Pacific War*). *T* **49** *and similar horiz design. Multicoloured. W* w **12**. *P* 14 × 14½.

No.	Description	Unused	Used
160	8 c. Type **49**	10	10
161	35 c. Red Beach landings	10	10

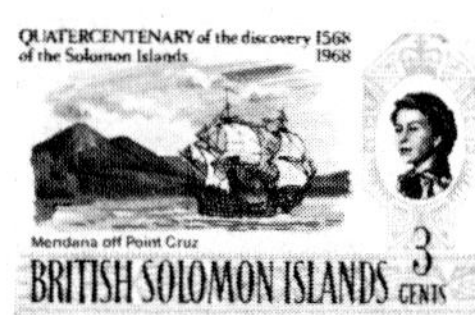

51 Mendaña's *Todos los Santos* off Point Cruz

(Des V. Whiteley. Photo Harrison)

1968 (7 Feb). *Quatercentenary of the Discovery of Solomon Is. T* **51** *and similar horiz designs. Multicoloured. W* w **12**. *P* 14.

No.	Description	Unused	Used
162	3 c. Type **51**	15	10
163	8 c. Arrival of missionaries	15	10
164	35 c. Pacific Campaign, World War II	30	10
165	$1 Proclamation of the Protectorate	50	80
162/5	*Set of* 4	1·00	1·00

55 Vine Fishing

(Des R. Granger Barrett. Photo Harrison)

1968 (20 May)–**71.** *Horiz designs as T* **55**. *Chalk-surfaced paper. W* w **12** (*inverted on No.* 167*a*). *P* 14½.

No.	Description	Unused	Used
166	1 c. turquoise-blue, black and brown	10	10
	a. Glazed, ordinary paper (9.8.71)	90	90
167	2 c. apple-green, black and brown	10	10
	a. Glazed, ordinary paper (9.8.71)	90	90
168	3 c. green, myrtle-green and black	10	10
	a. Glazed, ordinary paper (9.8.71)	90	90
169	4 c. bright purple, black and brown	15	10
	a. Glazed, ordinary paper (9.8.71)	90	90
170	6 c. multicoloured	15	10
171	8 c. multicoloured	25	10
	a. Glazed, ordinary paper (9.8.71)	1·50	1·60
172	12 c. yellow-ochre, brown-red and black	65	40
	a. Glazed, ordinary paper (9.8.71)	2·25	2·50
173	14 c. orange-red, chocolate and black	1·25	90
174	15 c. multicoloured	80	50
	a. Glazed, ordinary paper (9.8.71)	2·50	3·00
175	20 c. bright blue, red and black	2·25	1·00
	a. Glazed, ordinary paper (9.8.71)	4·25	4·50
176	24 c. rose-red, black and yellow	2·00	1·25
177	35 c. multicoloured	1·75	70
178	45 c. multicoloured	1·50	75
179	$1 violet-blue, light green and black	2·50	2·00
180	$2 multicoloured	4·00	5·00
166/80	*Set of* 15	15·00	11·50
166a/75a	*Set of* 8	13·00	14·00

Designs:—2 c. Kite fishing; 3 c. Platform fishing; 4 c. Net fishing; 6 c. Gold Lip shell diving; 8 c. Night fishing; 12 c. Boat building; 14 c. Cocoa; 15 c. Road building; 20 c. Geological survey; 24 c. Hauling timber; 35 c. Copra; 45 c. Harvesting rice; $1, Honiara Port; $2, Internal air service.

The stamps on glazed, ordinary paper exist with PVA gum only. The 1 c. to 12 c. and 20 c. on chalk-surfaced paper exist with PVA gum as well as gum arabic, but the others exist with gum arabic only.

70 Map of Australasia and Diagram 71 Basketball Player

(Des R. Gates. Litho Enschedé)

1969 (10 Feb). *Inaugural Year of the South Pacific University. P* 12½ × 12.

No.	Type	Description	Unused	Used
181	**70**	3 c. multicoloured	10	10
182		12 c. multicoloured	10	10
183		35 c. multicoloured	15	10
181/3		*Set of* 3	20	15

(Des J. Cooter. Photo Harrison)

1969 (13 Aug). *Third South Pacific Games, Port Moresby. T* **71** *and similar vert designs. Multicoloured. W* w **12** (*sideways*). *P* 14½ × 14.

No.	Description	Unused	Used
184	3 c. Type **71**	10	10
185	8 c. Footballer	10	10
186	14 c. Sprinter	10	10
187	45 c. Rugby player	20	15
184/7	*Set of* 4	40	30
MS188	126 × 120 mm. Nos. 184/7	3·50	8·00

Stamps from the miniature sheets differ slightly from those in the ordinary sheets, particularly the 14 c. value, which has a shadow below the feet on the runner. The footballer and rugby player on the 8 c. and 45 c. values also have shadows below their feet, but these are more pronounced than on the stamps from the ordinary sheets.

75 South Sea Island with Star of Bethlehem

76 Southern Cross, "PAX" and Frigatebird (stained glass window)

(Des L. Curtis. Photo Harrison)

1969 (21 Nov). *Christmas. W* w **12** (*sideways*). *P* 14½ × 14.

No.	Type	Description	Unused	Used
189	**75**	8 c. black, violet and turquoise-green	10	10
190	**76**	35 c. multicoloured	20	10

77 "Paid" Stamp, New South Wales 1896–1906 2d. Stamp and 1906–07 Tulagi Postmark

(Des G. Drummond. Litho B.W.)

1970 (15 Apr). *Inauguration of New G.P.O. Honiara. T* **77** *and similar horiz designs. W* w **12** (*sideways*). *P* 13.

No.	Description	Unused	Used
191	7 c. light magenta, deep blue and black	20	15
192	14 c. sage-green, deep blue and black	25	15
193	18 c. multicoloured	25	15
194	23 c. multicoloured	30	20
191/4	*Set of* 4	90	60

Designs:—14 c. 1906–07 2d. stamp and C. M. Woodford; 18 c. 1910–14 5s. stamp and Tulagi postmark, 1913; 23 c. New G.P.O., Honiara.

81 Coat of Arms 83 British Red Cross H.Q., Honiara

(Des V. Whiteley. Photo Harrison)

1970 (15 June). *New Constitution. T* **81** *and similar design. W* w **12** (*sideways on* 18 *c.*). *P* 14½ × 14 (18 *c.*) *or* 14 × 14½ (35 *c.*).

No.	Description	Unused	Used
195	18 c. multicoloured	15	10
196	35 c. pale apple-green, deep blue and ochre	30	20

Design: *Horiz*—35 c. Map.

(Des L. Curtis. Litho Questa)

1970 (17 Aug). *Centenary of British Red Cross. T* **83** *and similar horiz design. W w* **12** *(sideways). P* 14 × 14½.

No.		Description	Unused	Used
197		3 c. multicoloured	10	10
198		35 c. blue, vermilion and black	25	20

Design:—35 c. Wheelchair and map.

86 Reredos (Altar Screen)

(Des L. Curtis. Litho J.W.)

1970 (19 Oct). *Christmas. T* **86** *and similar design. W w* **12** *(sideways on 45 c.). P* 14 × 13½ *(8 c.) or* 13½ × 14 *(45 c.).*

No.		Description	Unused	Used
199		8 c. ochre and bluish violet	10	10
200		45 c. chestnut, yellow-orange & blackish brn	25	20

Design: *Vert*—8 c. Carved angel.

87 La Perouse and *La Boussole*

(Des J.W. Litho Questa)

1971 (28 Jan). *Ships and Navigators (1st series). T* **87** *and similar horiz designs. Multicoloured. W w* **12** *(sideways). P* 14.

No.		Description	Unused	Used
201		3 c. Type **87**	55	20
202		4 c. Astrolabe and Polynesian Reed Map	65	20
203		12 c. Abel Tasman and *Heemskerk*	1·50	45
204		35 c. Te Puki canoe, Santa Cruz	3·00	75
201/4		*Set of* 4	5·00	1·40

See also Nos. 215/18, 236/9, 254/7 and 272/5.

88 J. Atkin, Bishop Patteson and S. Taroaniara

(Des J.W. Litho Questa)

1971 (5 April). *Death Centenary of Bishop Patteson. T* **88** *and similar multicoloured designs. W w* **12** *(sideways on 2 c., 4 c.). P* 14½ × 14 *(2 c., 4 c.) or* 14 × 14½ *(others).*

No.		Description	Unused	Used
205		2 c. Type **88**	10	10
206		4 c. Last Landing at Nukapu	10	10
207		14 c. Memorial Cross and Nukapu *(vert)*	10	10
208		45 c. Knotted Leaf and canoe *(vert)*	20	10
205/8		*Set of* 4	30	30

89 Torch Emblem and Boxers

BRITISH SOLOMON ISLANDS

90 Melanesian Lectern

(Des C. Debenham. Litho Questa)

1971 (9 Aug). *Fourth South Pacific Games, Tahiti. T* **89** *and similar horiz designs. Multicoloured. W w* **12** *(sideways). P* 14.

No.		Description	Unused	Used
209		3 c. Type **89**	10	10
210		8 c. Emblem and footballers	10	10
211		12 c. Emblem and runner	10	10
212		35 c. Emblem and skin-diver	10	10
209/12		*Set of* 4	20	20

(Des C. Abbott. Litho A. & M.)

1971 (15 Nov). *Christmas. T* **90** *and similar vert design. Multicoloured. W w* **12**. *P* 13½.

No.		Description	Unused	Used
213		9 c. Type **90**	10	10
214		45 c. "United we Stand" (Margarita Bara)	15	15

(Des J.W. Litho Questa)

1972 (1 Feb). *Ships and Navigators (2nd series). Horiz designs as T* **87**. *Multicoloured. W w* **12** *(sideways). P* 14.

No.		Description	Unused	Used
215		4 c. Bougainville and *La Boudeuse*	30	10
216		9 c. Horizontal planisphere and ivory backstaff	60	10
217		15 c. Philip Carteret and H.M.S. *Swallow*	85	15
218		45 c. Malaita canoe	3·75	1·25
215/18		*Set of* 4	5·00	1·40

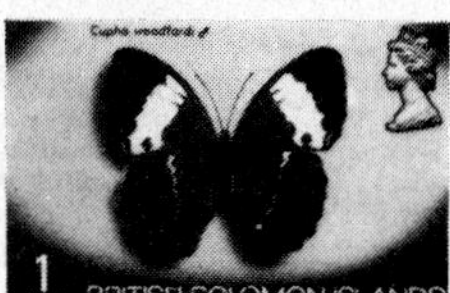

91 *Cupha woodfordi*

(Des R. Granger Barrett. Litho Questa)

1972 (3 July)–**73**. *T* **91** *and similar horiz designs. Multicoloured. Cream paper. W w* **12** *(upright on $5, sideways on others). P* 14.

No.		Description	Unused	Used
219		1 c. Type **91**	15	30
220		2 c. *Ornithoptera priamus*	25	40
221		3 c. *Vindula sapor*	25	40
222		4 c. *Papilio ulysses*	25	40
223		5 c. Great Trevally	25	30
224		8 c. Little Bonito	40	50
225		9 c. Sapphire Demoiselle	50	55
226		12 c. *Costus speciosus*	1·25	80
227		15 c. Orange Anenome Fish	1·25	1·00
228		20 c. *Spathoglottis plicata*	3·25	1·75
229		25 c. *Ephemerantha comata*	3·25	1·50
230		35 c. *Dendrobium cuthbertsonii*	3·50	2·25
231		45 c. *Heliconia salomonica*	3·50	3·00
232		$1 Blue Finned Triggerfish	6·00	4·50
233		$2 *Ornithoptera alottei*	13·00	12·00
233*a*		$5 Great Frigate Bird (2.7.73)	10·00	10·00
219/33*a*		*Set of* 16	42·00	35·00

The 1 to 4 c. and $2 are butterflies; the 5 to 9 c., 15 c. and $1 are fishes; the 12 c. and 20 to 45 c. are flowers and the $5 a bird.

92 Greetings and Message Drum

(Des (from photograph by D. Groves) and photo Harrison)

1972 (20 Nov). *Royal Silver Wedding. Multicoloured; background colour given. W w* **12**. *P* 14 × 14½.

No.		Description	Unused	Used
234	**92**	8 c. rose-carmine	10	10
235		45 c. deep yellow-olive	20	20

(Des J.W. Litho Questa)

1973 (9 Mar). *Ships and Navigators (3rd series). Horiz designs as T* **87**. *Multicoloured. W w* **12**. *P* 14.

No.		Description	Unused	Used
236		4 c. D'Entrecasteaux and *Recherche*	30	15
237		9 c. Ship's hour-glass and chronometer	60	15
238		15 c. Lt. Shortland and H.M.S. *Alexander*	75	20
239		35 c. Tomoko (war canoe)	3·25	1·75
236/9		*Set of* 4	4·50	2·00

93 Pan Pipes

(Des and litho J.W.)

1973 (1 Oct). *Musical Instruments. T* **93** *and similar horiz designs. Multicoloured. W w* **12**. *P* 13½.

No.		Description	Unused	Used
240		4 c. Type **93**	10	10
241		9 c. Castanets	10	10
242		15 c. Bamboo flute	15	10
243		35 c. Bauro gongs	35	25
244		45 c. Bamboo band	35	30
240/4		*Set of* 5	90	65

(Des PAD Studio. Litho Questa)

1973 (14 Nov). *Royal Wedding. As Nos. 322/3 of Montserrat.*

No.		Description	Unused	Used
245		4 c. deep grey-blue	10	10
246		35 c. bright blue	15	10

94 "Adoration of the Kings" (Jan Brueghel)

(Des PAD Studio. Litho Questa)

1973 (26 Nov). *Christmas. T* **94** *and similar designs showing "Adoration of the Kings" by the artists listed. Multicoloured. W w* **12** *(sideways on 22 c.). P* 13½ *(45 c.) or* 14 *(others).*

No.		Description	Unused	Used
247		8 c. Type **94**	10	10
248		22 c. Pieter Brueghel *(vert)*	25	25
249		45 c. Botticelli (48 × 35 *mm*)	50	50
247/9		*Set of* 3	70	70

95 Queen Elizabeth II and Map

96 "Postman"

(Des G. Drummond. Litho Questa)

1974 (18 Feb). *Royal Visit. W w* **12**. *P* 13½.

No.		Description	Unused	Used
250	**95**	4 c. multicoloured	25	10
251		9 c. multicoloured	50	10
252		15 c. multicoloured	60	20
253		35 c. multicoloured	1·10	1·25
250/3		*Set of* 4	2·25	1·40

(Des and litho J.W.)

1974 (15 May). *Ships and Navigators (4th series). Horiz designs as T* **87**. *Multicoloured. W w* **12** *(sideways). P* 14.

No.		Description	Unused	Used
254		4 c. Commissioner landing from S.S. *Titus*	20	10
255		9 c. Radar scanner	25	10
256		15 c. Natives being transported to a "Blackbirder" brig	40	15
257		45 c. Lieut. John F. Kennedy's *P.T. 109*	2·00	1·25
254/7		*Set of* 4	2·50	1·40

(Des Jennifer Toombs. Litho Questa)

1974 (29 Aug). *Centenary of Universal Postal Union. T* **96** *and similar designs showing Origami figures. W w* **12** *(sideways on 9 and 45 c.). P* 14.

No.		Description	Unused	Used
258		4 c. light yellow-green, deep green and black	10	10
259		9 c. light olive-bistre, lake-brown and black	10	10
260		15 c. mauve, purple and black	15	10
261		45 c. cobalt, dull ultramarine and black	35	60
258/61		*Set of* 4	65	70

Designs: *Horiz*—9 c. Carrier-pigeon; 45 c. Pegasus. *Vert*—15 c. St. Gabriel.

97 "New Constitution" Stamp of 1970

(Des R. Granger Barrett. Litho Questa)

1974 (16 Dec). *New Constitution. T* **97** *and similar horiz design. W w* **14** *(sideways). P* 14.

No.		Description	Unused	Used
262	**97**	4 c. multicoloured	10	10
263	–	9 c. dull rose-red, black & lt yell-ochre	10	10
264	–	15 c. dull rose-red, blk & lt greenish yell	15	10
265	**97**	35 c. multicoloured	45	50
262/5		*Set of* 4	70	60
MS266		134 × 84 mm. Nos. 262/5	2·75	3·25

Design:—9 c., 15 c. "New Constitution" stamp of 1961 (inscr "1960").

98 Golden Whistler

(Des G. Drummond. Litho Questa)

1975 (7 Apr). *Birds. T* **98** *and similar horiz designs. Multicoloured. W w* **12**. *P* 14.

No.		Description	Unused	Used
267		1 c. Type **98**	45	45
268		2 c. Common Kingfisher	50	50
269		3 c. Red-bibbed Fruit Dove	55	55
270		4 c. Little Button Quail	55	55
271		$2 Duchess Lorikeet	11·00	9·00
267/71		*Set of* 5	12·00	10·00

See also Nos. 305/20.

(Des and litho J.W.)

1975 (29 May). *Ships and Navigators (5th series). Horiz designs as T* **87**. *Multicoloured. W w* **12**. *P* 13½.

No.		Description	Unused	Used
272		4 c. *Walande* (coaster)	25	10
273		9 c. *Melanesian* (coaster)	30	10
274		15 c. *Marsina* (container ship)	35	15
275		45 c. *Himalaya* (liner)	1·00	1·50
272/5		*Set of* 4	1·75	1·60

99 800-Metres Race

(Des PAD Studio. Litho Walsall)

1975 (4 Aug). *Fifth South Pacific Games, Guam. T* **99** *and similar horiz designs. Multicoloured.* W w **14** (*sideways*). *P* 13½.

No.	Description	Unused	Used
276	4 c. Type **99**	10	10
277	9 c. Long-jump	10	10
278	15 c. Javelin-throwing	15	10
279	45 c. Football	45	45
276/9	*Set of* 4	70	55
MS280	130 × 95 mm. Nos. 276/9	3·75	4·00

100 Christmas Scene and Candles **(101)**

(Des G. Vasarhelyi. Litho Questa)

1975 (13 Oct). *Christmas. T* **100** *and similar horiz designs. Multicoloured.* W w **12** (*sideways*). *P* 14.

No.	Description	Unused	Used
281	15 c. Type **100**	20	10
282	35 c. Shepherds, angels and candles	40	15
283	45 c. The Magi and candles	50	40
281/3	*Set of* 3	1·00	60
MS284	140 × 130 mm. Nos. 281/3	3·75	4·00

1975 (12 Nov). *Nos.* 267/70, 223/32, 271 *and* 233*a with obliterating bar as T* **101** *over* "BRITISH".

No.	Description	Unused	Used
285	1 c. Type **98**	25	45
286	2 c. Common Kingfisher	30	45
287	3 c. Red-bibbed Fruit Dove	30	45
288	4 c. Little Button Quail	35	45
289	5 c. Great Trevally	35	45
290	8 c. Little Bonito	50	60
291	9 c. Sapphire Demoiselle	50	60
292	12 c. *Costus speciosus*	1·50	1·00
293	15 c. Orange Anemone Fish	1·50	1·25
294	20 c. *Spathoglottis plicata*	2·75	1·50
295	25 c. *Ephemerantha comata*	2·75	1·75
296	35 c. *Dendrobium cuthbertsonii*	3·50	1·75
297	45 c. *Heliconia salomonica*	3·50	3·00
298	$1 Blue Finned Triggerfish (*cream paper*)	3·00	2·50
	a. White paper	4·75	4·00
299	$2 Duchess Lorikeet	8·00	10·00
300	$5 Great Frigate Bird (*white paper*)	15·00	18·00
	a. Cream paper	20·00	20·00
285/300	*Set of* 16	38·00	40·00

SELF-GOVERNMENT

102 Ceremonial Food-bowl

(Des J. Cooter. Litho Questa)

1976 (12 Jan). *Artefacts* (1*st series*). *T* **102** *and similar multicoloured designs.* W w **12** (*upright on* 35 *c.; sideways on others*). *P* 14.

No.	Description	Unused	Used
301	4 c. Type **102**	10	10
302	15 c. Chieftains' money	10	10
303	35 c. Nguzu-nguzu (canoe protector spirit) (*vert*)	25	20
304	45 c. Nguzu-nguzu canoe prow	30	25
301/4	*Set of* 4	65	55

See also Nos. 337/40, 353/6 and 376/9.

103 Golden Whistler

(Des G. Drummond. Litho Questa)

1976 (8 Mar–6 Dec). *Nos.* 267/71 *with new country inscr* (*omitting* "BRITISH") *as T* **103**, *and new values. Multicoloured.* W w **14** (*sideways*). *P* 14.

No.	Description	Unused	Used
305	1 c. Type **103**	20	40
306	2 c. Common Kingfisher	25	45
307	3 c. Red-bibbed Fruit Dove	25	40
308	4 c. Little Button Quail	30	40
309	5 c. Willie Wagtail	30	40
310	6 c. Golden Cowrie	60	50
311	10 c. Glory of the Sea Cone	60	50
312	12 c. Rainbow Lory	60	70
313	15 c. Pearly Nautilus	65	40
314	20 c. Venus Comb Murex	1·00	45
315	25 c. Commercial Trochus	85	50
316	35 c. Melon or Baler Shell	1·00	70
317	45 c. Orange Spider Conch	1·50	1·25
318	$1 Pacific Triton	3·25	3·00
319	$2 Duchess Lorikeet	6·50	4·75
320	$5 Great Frigate Bird (6.12)	6·50	6·00
305/20	*Set of* 16	22·00	18·00

104 Coastwatchers, 1942 **105** Alexander Graham Bell

(Des J. Cooter. Litho Walsall)

1976 (24 May). *Bicentenary of American Revolution. T* **104** *and similar horiz designs. Multicoloured.* W w **14** (*sideways*). *P* 14.

No.	Description	Unused	Used
321	6 c. Type **104**	20	10
322	20 c. *Amagiri* ramming *PT109* and Lt. J. F. Kennedy	60	30
323	35 c. Henderson Airfield	1·00	40
324	45 c. Map of Guadalcanal	1·10	70
321/4	*Set of* 4	2·75	1·40
MS325	95 × 115 mm. Nos. 321/4	4·50	6·50

(Des P. Powell. Litho Harrison)

1976 (26 July). *Telephone Centenary. T* **105** *and similar vert designs.* W w **14** (*sideways*). *P* 14½ × 14.

No.	Description	Unused	Used
326	6 c. multicoloured	10	10
327	20 c. multicoloured	15	10
328	35 c. brown-orange, lt orange & lt vermilion	30	15
329	45 c. multicoloured	40	35
326/9	*Set of* 4	85	55

Designs:—20 c. Radio telephone via satellite; 35 c. Ericson's magneto telephone; 45 c. Stick telephone and first telephone.

106 B.A.C. "1–11" **107** The Communion Plate

(Des and litho Walsall)

1976 (13 Sept). *50th Anniv of First Flight to Solomon Islands. T* **106** *and similar horiz designs. Multicoloured.* W w **14** (*sideways*). *P* 14.

No.	Description	Unused	Used
330	6 c. Type **106**	20	10
331	20 c. Britten-Norman "Islander"	35	10
332	35 c. "Dakota DC3"	65	15
333	45 c. De Havilland "DH50A"	75	45
330/3	*Set of* 4	1·75	65

(Des Jennifer Toombs. Litho Questa)

1977 (7 Feb). *Silver Jubilee. T* **107** *and similar vert designs. Multicoloured.* W w **14**. *P* 13½.

No.	Description	Unused	Used
334	6 c. Queen's visit, 1974	10	10
335	35 c. Type **107**	15	20
336	45 c. The Communion	25	45
334/6	*Set of* 3	45	65

108 Carving from New Georgia **109** Spraying Roof and Mosquito

(Des J. Cooter. Litho Questa)

1977 (9 May). *Artefacts* (2*nd series*). *T* **108** *and similar vert designs showing carvings.* W w **14**. *P* 14.

No.	Description	Unused	Used
337	6 c. multicoloured	10	10
338	20 c. multicoloured	10	10
339	35 c. slate-black, grey and rose-red	20	15
340	45 c. multicoloured	25	30
337/40	*Set of* 4	55	50

Designs:—20 c. Sea adaro (spirit); 35 c. Shark-headed man; 45 c. Man from Ulawa or Malaita.

(Des G. Vasarhelyi. Litho Questa)

1977 (27 July). *Malaria Eradication. T* **109** *and similar horiz designs. Multicoloured.* W w **14** (*sideways*). *P* 14.

No.	Description	Unused	Used
341	6 c. Type **109**	10	10
342	20 c. Taking blood samples	20	10
343	35 c. Microscope and map	30	15
344	45 c. Delivering drugs	40	40
341/4	*Set of* 4	90	60

110 The Shepherds **111** Feather Money

(Des M. and G. Shamir. Litho Questa)

1977 (12 Sept). *Christmas. T* **110** *and similar vert designs. Multicoloured.* W w **14**. *P* 14.

No.	Description	Unused	Used
345	6 c. Type **110**	10	10
346	20 c. Mary and Jesus in stable	10	10
347	35 c. The Three Kings	20	15
348	45 c. "The Flight into Egypt"	25	25
345/8	*Set of* 4	50	45

(Des D.L.R. Litho Harrison)

1977 (24 Oct). *Introduction of Solomon Islands Coins and Banknotes. T* **111** *and similar horiz designs. Multicoloured.* W w **14**. *P* 14 × 14½.

No.	Description	Unused	Used
349	6 c. Type **111**	10	10
	a. Horiz pair. Nos. 349/50	20	20
350	6 c. New currency coins	10	10
351	45 c. New currency notes	35	25
	a. Horiz pair. Nos. 351/2	70	50
352	45 c. Shell money	35	25
349/52	*Set of* 4	80	60

The two designs of each value were printed in horizontal *se-tenant* pairs throughout their sheets.

112 Figure from Shortland Island **113** Sandford's Sea Eagle

(Des J. Cooter. Litho Questa)

1978 (11 Jan). *Artefacts* (3*rd series*). *T* **112** *and similar vert designs.* W w **14**. *P* 14.

No.	Description	Unused	Used
353	6 c. multicoloured	10	10
354	20 c. multicoloured	10	10
355	35 c. deep brown, black and orange	20	15
356	45 c. multicoloured	25	30
353/6	*Set of* 4	55	50

Designs:—20 c. Ceremonial shield; 35 c. Santa Cruz ritual figure; 45 c. Decorative combs.

(Des Jennifer Toombs. Litho Questa)

1978 (21 Apr). *25th Anniv of Coronation. T* **113** *and similar vert designs. Multicoloured. P* 15.

No.	Description	Unused	Used
357	45 c. black, vermilion and silver	25	30
	a. Sheetlet. Nos. 357/9 × 2	1·25	
358	45 c. multicoloured	25	30
359	45 c. black, vermilion and silver	25	30
357/9	*Set of* 3	65	80

Designs:—No. 357, King's Dragon; No. 358, Queen Elizabeth II; No. 359, Type **113**.

Nos. 357/9 were printed together in small sheets of 6, containing two *se-tenant* strips of 3, with horizontal gutter margin between.

INDEPENDENT

114 National Flag **115** John

(Des L. Curtis. Litho Questa)

1978 (7 July). *Independence. T* **114** *and similar vert designs. Multicoloured.* W w **14**. *P* 14.

No.	Description	Unused	Used
360	6 c. Type **114**	10	1[illegible]
361	15 c. Governor-General's flag	20	1[illegible]
362	35 c. The Cenotaph, Honiara	35	3[illegible]
363	45 c. National coat of arms	40	5[illegible]
360/3	*Set of* 4	95	8[illegible]

(Des J.W. Litho Questa)

1978 (4 Oct). *450th Death Anniv of Dürer. Details from his Painting "Four Apostles". T* **115** *and similar vert designs. Multicoloured. W* w **14**. *P* 14.

364 6 c. Type **115** 10 10
365 20 c. Peter 10 10
366 35 c. Paul 15 15
367 45 c. Mark 20 30
364/7 .. .. *Set of* 4 45 50

116 Firelighting **117** H.M.S. *Discovery*

(Des K. G. Watkinson; adapted J.W. Litho Questa)

1978 (15 Nov). *50th Anniv of Scouting in Solomon Islands. T* **116** *and similar horiz designs. Multicoloured. W* w **14** (*sideways*). *P* 14.

368 6 c. Type **116** 15 10
369 20 c. Camping 20 20
370 35 c. Solomon Islands Scouts 40 40
371 45 c. Canoeing 50 70
368/71 .. .. *Set of* 4 1·10 1·25

(Des and litho (45 c. also embossed) Walsall)

1979 (16 Jan). *Bicentenary of Captain Cook's Voyages*, 1768–79. *T* **117** *and similar vert designs. P* 11.

372 8 c. multicoloured 30 10
373 18 c. multicoloured 40 15
374 35 c. black, yellowish green and silver 55 25
375 45 c. multicoloured 60 40
372/5 .. .. *Set of* 4 1·75 80

Designs:—18 c. "Captain Cook" (Nathaniel Dance); 35 c. Sextant; 45 c. Flaxman/Wedgwood medallion of Captain Cook.

118 Fish Net Float **119** Running

(Des J. Cooter. Litho Questa)

1979 (21 Mar). *Artefacts* (*4th series*). *T* **118** *and similar designs. W* w **14** (*sideways on* 8 *and* 35 *c.*). *P* 14.

376 8 c. multicoloured 10 10
377 20 c. multicoloured 10 10
378 35 c. black, grey and rose 15 15
379 45 c. black, chestnut and apple-green.. .. .. 20 30
376/9 .. .. *Set of* 4 45 50

Designs: *Vert*—20 c. Armband of shell money; 45 c. Forehead ornament. *Horiz*—35 c. Ceremonial food bowl.

(Des L. Curtis. Litho Format)

1979 (4 June). *South Pacific Games, Fiji. T* **109** *and similar horiz designs. Multicoloured. W* w **14** (*sideways*). *P* 13½.

380 8 c. Type **119** 10 10
381 20 c. Hurdling 10 10
382 35 c. Football 15 15
383 45 c. Swimming 25 35
380/3 .. .. *Set of* 4 55 50

120 1908 6d. Stamp **121** Sea Snake

(Des J.W. Litho Format)

1979 (16 Aug). *Death Centenary of Sir Rowland Hill. T* **120** *and similar vert designs showing stamps. W* w **14**. *P* 14.

384 8 c. carmine and pale rose 10 10
385 20 c. deep mauve and pale mauve 20 30
386 35 c. multicoloured 35 45
384/6 .. .. *Set of* 3 60 75
MS387 121 × 121 mm. 45 c. rosine, deep dull green and pink 45 65

Designs:—20 c. Great Britain 1856 6d.; 35 c. 1978 45 c. Independence commemorative; 45 c. 1922 10s.

(Des L. Curtis. Litho Enschedé)

1979 (18 Sept)–**83.** *Reptiles. Vert designs as T* **121**. *Multicoloured. W* w **14** (*inverted on Nos.* 394B *and* 397B). *P* 13½ × 13.
A. *No imprint*. B. *Imprint date at foot*.

		A		B	
388	1 c. Type **121**	10	15	†	
389	3 c. Red-banded Tree Snake ..	10	15	†	
390	4 c. Whip Snake	10	15	†	
391	6 c. Pacific Boa	10	15	†	
392	8 c. Skink	10	10	†	
393	10 c. Gecko (*Lepidodactylus lugubris*)	10	10	†	
394	12 c. Monitor	50	30	15	30
395	15 c. Anglehead	30	15	†	
396	20 c. Giant Toad	30	20	†	
397	25 c. Marsh Frog	60	40	20	40
398	30 c. Horned Frog	1·50	50	85	85
399	35 c. Tree Frog	30	35	†	
399*a*	40 c. Burrowing Snake	†		35	90
400	45 c. Guppy's Snake	30	60	†	
400*a*	50 c. Tree Gecko	†		40	40
401	$1 Large Skink	1·25	1·50	1·00	70
402	$2 Guppy's Frog	1·25	2·00	†	
403	$5 Estuarine Crocodile ..	3·00	6·00	4·00	4·00
403*a*	$10 Hawksbill Turtle	†		6·50	6·75
388/403	.. .. *Set of* 16	8·50	11·50		
394/403*a*	.. .. *Set of* 8			12·00	13·00

Dates of issue:—18.9.79, Nos. 388A/403A; 25.1.82, Nos. 401B, 403B; 27.8.82, Nos. 394B, 397B; 20.9.82, No. 403*a*; 24.1.83, Nos. 399aB, 400aB; 31.8.83, No. 398B.

122 "Madonna and Child" (Morando) **123** H.M.S. *Curacao*, 1839

(Des BG Studio. Litho Questa)

1979 (15 Nov). *Christmas. International Year of the Child. T* **122** *and similar vert designs showing "Madonna and Child" paintings by various artists. Multicoloured. W* w **14**. *P* 14 × 14½.

404 4 c. Type **122** 10 10
405 20 c. Luini 20 15
406 35 c. Bellini 30 15
407 50 c. Raphael 35 50
404/7 .. .. *Set of* 4 85 80
MS408 92 × 133 mm. Nos. 404/7 .. .. .. 1·00 1·50

(Des L. Curtis. Litho Questa)

1980 (23 Jan). *Ships and Crests* (*1st series*). *T* **123** *and similar horiz designs. Multicoloured. W* w **14** (*sideways*). *P* 14.

409 8 c. Type **123** 20 10
410 20 c. H.M.S. *Herald*, 1854 .. .. 35 15
411 35 c. H.M.S. *Royalist*, 1889 .. .. 55 35
412 45 c. H.M.S. *Beagle*, 1878 .. .. 70 55
409/12 .. .. *Set of* 4 1·60 1·00

See also Nos. 430/3.

124 Steel Fishery Training Vessel

(Des G. Hutchins. Litho Secura, Singapore)

1980 (27 Mar). *Fishing. Ancillary Craft. T* **124** *and similar horiz designs. Multicoloured. W* w **14** (*sideways*). *P* 13½.

413 8 c. Type **124**.. .. .. 15 10
414 20 c. *Solomon Hunter* (fishery training vessel) 20 15
415 45 c. *Ufi Na Tasi* (refrigerated fish transport) 35 35
416 80 c. Research Vessel.. .. .. 60 75
413/16 .. .. *Set of* 4 1·10 1·25

125 *Comliebank* (cargo-liner) and 1935 Tulagi Registered Letter Postmark

(Des A. Theobald. Litho Questa)

1980 (6 May). *"London 1980" International Stamp Exhibition. Mail-carrying Transport. T* **125** *and similar horiz designs. Multicoloured. W* w **14** (*sideways*). *P* 14½ × 14.

417 45 c. Type **125**.. .. .. 35 50
a. Sheetlet. Nos. 417/20 .. .. 1·25
418 45 c. Douglas "C-47" aeroplane (U.S. Army Postal Service, 1943) 35 50
419 45 c. B.A.C. "1-11" airliner and 1979 Honiara postmark 35 50
420 45 c. *Corabank* (container ship) and 1979 Auki postmark 35 50
417/20 .. .. *Set of* 4 1·25 1·75

Nos. 417/20 were printed together as a sheetlet containing a *se-tenant* block of 4.

126 Queen Elizabeth the Queen Mother **127** Angel with Trumpet

(Des Harrison. Litho Questa)

1980 (4 Aug). *80th Birthday of Queen Elizabeth the Queen Mother. W* w **14** (*sideways*). *P* 14.

421 **126** 45 c. multicoloured 40 35

(Des C. Abbott. Litho Walsall)

1980 (2 Sept). *Christmas. T* **127** *and similar vert designs. Multicoloured. W* w **14**. *P* 14½ × 14.

422 8 c. Type **127** 10 10
423 20 c. Angel with fiddle.. .. .. 10 10
424 45 c. Angel with trumpet (*different*) 25 25
425 80 c. Angel with lute 40 45
422/5 .. .. *Set of* 4 70 75

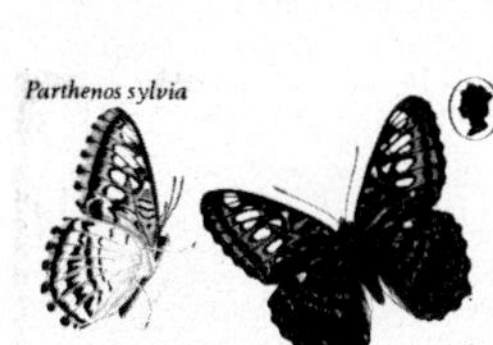

128 *Parthenos sylvia* **129** Francisco Antonio Maurelle

(Des J. Cooter. Litho Secura, Singapore)

1980 (12 Nov). *Butterflies* (1*st series*). *T* **128** *and similar horiz designs. Multicoloured. W* w **14** (*sideways*. *P* 13½.

426 8 c. Type **128** 10 10
427 20 c. *Delias schoenbergi* 25 20
428 45 c. *Jamides cephion* 40 40
429 80 c. *Ornithoptera victoriae* .. .. .. 1·00 1·00
426/9 .. .. *Set of* 4 1·60 1·50

See also Nos. 456/9 and 610/13.

(Des L. Curtis. Litho Questa)

1981 (14 Jan). *Ships and Crests* (*2nd series*). *Horiz designs as T* **123**. *Multicoloured. W* w **14** (*sideways*). *P* 14.

430 8 c. H.M.S. *Mounts Bay* 15 10
431 20 c. H.M.S. *Charybdis* 25 15
432 45 c. H.M.S. *Hydra* 50 35
433 $1 Royal Yacht *Britannia* .. .. .. 1·25 1·00
430/3 .. .. *Set of* 4 1·90 1·40

(Des J. Cooter. Litho Questa)

1981 (23 Mar). *Bicentenary of Maurelle's Visit and Production of Bauche's Chart*, 1791 (*No.* **MS**438). *T* **129** *and similar designs. Wmk CA Diagonal* (*sideways on* 8 *c. and* $1). *P* 13½ × 14 (8 *c.*, $1) *or* 14 × 13½ (*others*).

434 8 c. black, deep brown and greenish yellow .. 15 10
435 10 c. black, vermilion and stone 20 10
436 45 c. multicoloured 60 65
437 $1 multicoloured .. .. 1·00 1·10
434/7 .. .. *Set of* 4 1·75 1·75
MS438 126 × 91 mm. 25 c. × 4, each black, vermilion and stone (wmk sideways). P 14½ .. .. 1·25 1·40

Designs: *Horiz*—10 c. Bellin's map of 1742 showing route of *La Princesa*; 45 c. *La Princesa*. *Vert*—$1 Spanish compass cards, 1745 and 1757. No. **MS**438, "Chart of a part of the South Sea" (*each stamp* 44 × 28 *mm*).

Stamps in No. **MS**438 were printed to form a composite design.

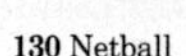

130 Netball **131** Prince Charles as Colonel-in-Chief, Royal Regiment of Wales

(Des R. Granger Barrett. Litho Security Printers (M), Malaysia)

1981 (7 July). *Mini South Pacific Games. T* **130** *and similar vert designs. Multicoloured. W* w **14**. *P* 12.

439 8 c. Type **130** 10 10
440 10 c. Tennis 15 15
441 25 c. Running 25 25
442 30 c. Football 25 25
443 45 c. Boxing 40 40
439/43 .. .. *Set of* 5 1·00 1·00
MS444 102 × 67 mm $1 Stylised athletes (wmk sideways) .. .. 1·00 1·10

(Des and litho J.W.)

1981 (22 July). *Royal Wedding. T* **131** *and similar vert designs. Multicoloured. W* w **14**. *P* 13½ × 13.
445 8 c. Wedding bouquet from Solomon Islands .. 10 10
446 45 c. Type **131** 30 40
447 $1 Prince Charles and Lady Diana Spencer 60 1·00
445/7 .. .. *Set of* 3 90 1·25

132 "Music"

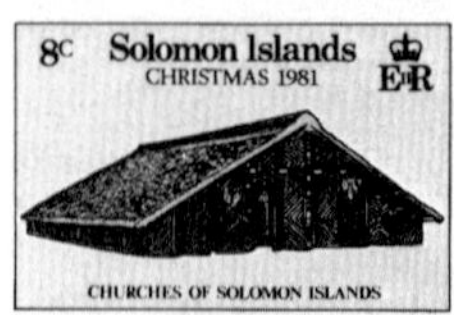

133 Primitive Church

(Des BG Studio. Litho Questa)

1981 (28 Sept). *25th Anniv of Duke of Edinburgh Award Scheme. T* **132** *and similar vert designs. Multicoloured. W* w **14**. *P* 14.
448 8 c. Type **132** 10 10
449 25 c. "Handicrafts" 10 10
450 45 c. "Canoeing" 20 20
451 $1 Duke of Edinburgh 50 70
448/51 .. .. *Set of* 4 75 95

(Des BG Studio. Litho Format)

1981 (12 Oct). *Christmas. Churches. T* **133** *and similar horiz designs. W* w **14** *(sideways). P* 14.
452 8 c. black, buff and cobalt 10 10
453 10 c. multicoloured 10 10
454 25 c. black, buff and dull green 15 10
455 $2 multicoloured .. .. 1·00 1·25
452/5 .. .. *Set of* 4 1·25 1·25

Designs:—10 c. St. Barnabas Anglican Cathedral, Honiara; 25 c. Early church; $2 Holy Cross Cathedral, Honiara.

(Des J. Cooter. Litho Secura, Singapore)

1982 (5 Jan). *Butterflies (2nd series). Horiz designs as T* **128**. *Multicoloured. W* w **14** *(sideways). P* 13½ × 13.
456 10 c. *Doleschallia bisaltide* 15 10
457 25 c. *Papilio bridgei* 35 25
458 35 c. *Taenaris phorcas* 40 30
a. Wmk inverted .. .. .. 50·00
459 $1 *Graphium sarpedon* .. .. .. 1·50 1·50
456/9 .. .. *Set of* 4 2·25 1·90

No. 458a shows a change of watermark position from sideways to inverted.

50 CENTS SURCHARGE
CYCLONE RELIEF FUND
1982

(134)

135 Pair of Sanford's Sea Eagles constructing Nest

5 CENTS SURCHARGE
CYCLONE RELIEF FUND
1982

"0" of "50" omitted from surcharge (R. 4/5)

1982 (3 May). *Cyclone Relief Fund. No. 447 surch with T* **134** *in red.*
460 $1 + 50 c. Prince Charles and Lady Diana Spencer .. .. 2·50 2·75
a. "0" omitted .. .. 10·00

(Des N. Arlott. Litho Walsall)

1982 (15 May). *Sanford's Sea Eagle. T* **135** *and similar vert designs. Multicoloured. W* w **14**. *P* 14.
461 12 c. Type **135** 35 35
a. Horiz strip of 5. Nos. 461/5 .. 1·90
462 12 c. Egg and chick 35 35
463 12 c. Hen feeding chicks 35 35
464 12 c. Fledgelings 35 35
465 12 c. Young bird in flight 35 35
466 12 c. Pair of birds and village dwellings .. 35 35
461/6 .. .. *Set of* 6 1·90 1·90

Nos. 461/6 were printed together, *se-tenant*, in various combinations throughout sheets also including one stamp-size label.

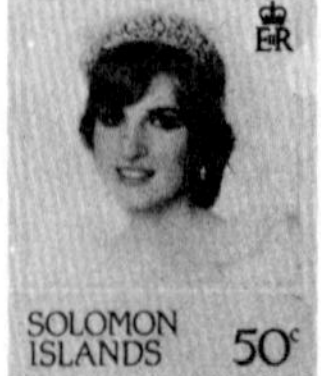

136 Wedding Portrait

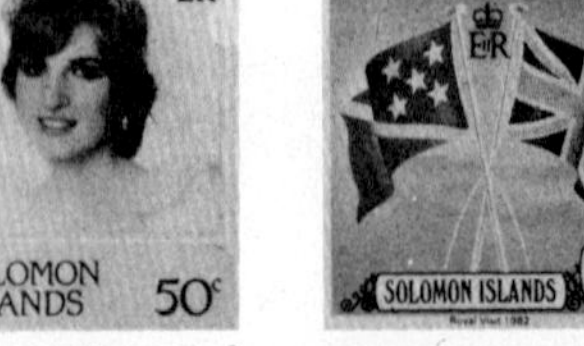

137 Flags of Solomon Islands and United Kingdom

(Des Jennifer Toombs. Litho Walsall)

1982 (1 July). *21st Birthday of Princess of Wales. T* **136** *and similar vert designs. Multicoloured. W* w **14**. *P* 14½ × 14.
467 12 c. Solomon Islands coat of arms 15 10
468 40 c. Lady Diana Spencer at Broadlands, May 1981 .. .. 30 30
469 50 c. Type **136** 35 35
470 $1 Formal portrait 65 65
467/70 .. .. *Set of* 4 1·25 1·25

(Des Studio 53. Litho Questa)

1982 (11 Oct). *Royal Visit (Nos. 471/2,* **MS***475) and Commonwealth Games, Brisbane (Nos. 473/4,* **MS***476). T* **137** *and similar square designs. Multicoloured. W* w **14** *(sideways). P* 14.
471 12 c. Type **137** 15 20
a. Pair. Nos. 471/2 .. .. .. 30 40
472 12 c. Queen and Prince Philip 15 20
473 25 c. Running 30 45
a. Pair. Nos. 473/4 .. .. .. 60 90
474 25 c. Boxing 30 45
471/4 .. .. *Set of* 4 80 1·25
MS475 123 × 123 mm. Nos. 471/2 and $1 Royal Yacht *Britannia* .. .. 1·60 2·25
MS476 123 × 123 mm. Nos. 473/4 and $1 Royal Yacht *Britannia* .. .. 1·60 2·25

Nos. 471/2 and 473/4 were each printed in small sheets of 10, including 2 *se-tenant*, stamp-size, labels, the two stamp designs appearing *se-tenant*, both horizontally and vertically.

138 Boy Scouts

(Des McCombie Skinner. Litho Format)

1982 (4 Nov). *75th Anniv of Boy Scout Movement (Nos. 477, 479, 481, 483) and Centenary of Boys' Brigade (others). T* **138** *and similar horiz designs. Multicoloured. W* w **14** *(sideways). P* 14.
477 12 c. Type **138** 20 15
478 12 c. Boys' Brigade cadets 20 15
479 25 c. Lord Baden-Powell 35 40
480 25 c. Sir William Smith 35 40
481 35 c. Type **138** 40 50
482 35 c. As No. 478 .. .. 40 50
483 50 c. As No. 479 .. .. 60 90
484 50 c. As No. 480 .. .. 60 90
477/84 .. .. *Set of* 8 2·75 3·50

139 Leatherback Turtle

(Des L. Curtis. Litho Format)

1983 (5 Jan). *Turtles. T* **139** *and similar horiz designs. Multicoloured. W* w **14** *(sideways). P* 14½.
485 18 c. Type **139** 25 25
486 35 c. Loggerhead turtle 45 45
487 45 c. Pacific Ridley turtle 60 60
488 50 c. Green turtle 65 65
485/8 .. .. *Set of* 4 1·75 1·75

140 *Oliva vidum, Conus generalis* and *Murex tribulus*

(Des W. Fenton. Litho Questa)

1983 (14 Mar). *Commonwealth Day. Shells. T* **140** *and similar horiz designs. Multicoloured. W* w **14** *(sideways). P* 14.
489 12 c. Type **140** 15 15
490 35 c. Romu, Kurila, Kakadu and money belt .. 35 40
491 45 c. Shells from "Bride-price" necklaces .. 50 60
492 50 c. *Trochus niloticus* polished and in its natural state 55 65
489/92 .. .. *Set of* 4 1·40 1·60

141 Montgolfier Balloon

(Des A. Theobald. Litho Format)

1983 (30 June). *Bicentenary of Manned Flight. T* **141** *and similar horiz designs. Multicoloured. W* w **14** *(sideways). P* 14.
493 30 c. Type **141** 55 40
494 35 c. R.A.A.F. Lockheed "Hercules" 60 45
495 40 c. Wright brothers' *Flyer III* 70 55
496 45 c. Space shuttle *Columbia* 75 60
497 50 c. Beechcraft "Baron-Solair" 80 65
493/7 .. .. *Set of* 5 3·00 2·40

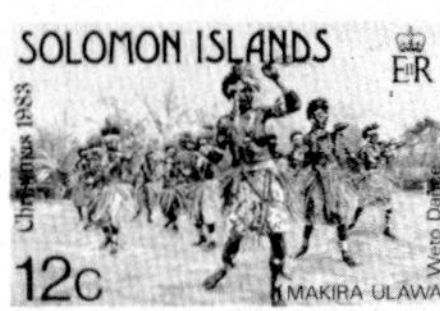

142 Weto Dancers

(Des J.W. Litho Format)

1983 (25 Aug). *Christmas. T* **142** *and similar horiz designs. Multicoloured. W* w **14** *(sideways). P* 14.
498 12 c. Type **142** 15 10
499 15 c. Custom wrestling 20 20
500 18 c. Girl dancers 20 20
501 20 c. Devil dancers 20 20
502 25 c. Bamboo band 30 35
503 35 c. Gilbertese dancers 40 45
504 40 c. Pan pipers 45 55
505 45 c. Girl dancers 50 65
506 50 c. Cross surrounded by flowers 55 70
498/506 .. .. *Set of* 9 2·50 3·00
MS507 153 × 112 mm. Nos. 498/506 .. .. 2·50 3·00

Stamps from No. **MS**507 are without the inscription, "Christmas 1983", shown on Nos. 498/506.

143 Earth Satellite Station

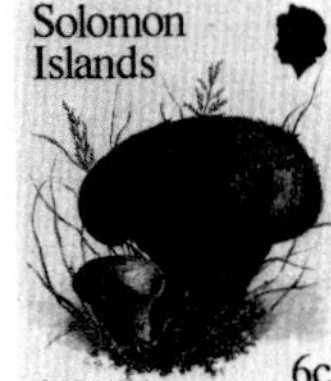

144 *Calvatia gardneri*

(Des Jennifer Toombs. Litho Format)

1983 (19 Dec). *World Communications Year. T* **143** *and similar horiz designs. Multicoloured. W* w **14** *(sideways). P* 14.
508 12 c. Type **143** 20 15
509 18 c. Ham radio operator 25 20
510 25 c. 1908 2½d. Canoe stamp 35 30
511 $1 1908 6d. Canoe stamp .. .. .. 1·25 1·40
508/11 .. .. *Set of* 4 1·90 1·90
MS512 131 × 103 mm. No. 511 .. .. .. 1·40 2·25

(Des Gillian Tomblin. Litho Enschedé)

1984 (30 Jan). *Fungi. T* **144** *and similar vert designs. Multicoloured. W* w **14**. *P* 13½.
513 6 c. Type **144** 10 10
514 18 c. *Marasmiellus inoderma* 20 25
a. Booklet pane of 6 .. .. .. 1·25
515 35 c. *Pycnoporus sanguineus* 35 45
a. Booklet pane of 6 .. .. .. 2·10
516 $2 *Filoboletus manipularis* .. .. .. 2·25 2·50
513/16 .. .. *Set of* 4 2·50 3·00

Booklet panes Nos. 514a and 515a were from special sheets providing blocks of 6 (3 × 2) with vertical margins at both the left and right of each pane.

145 Cross surrounded by Flowers

146 *Olivebank*, 1892

(Des J.W. Litho Format)

1984 (16 Apr). *Visit of Pope John Paul II. W* w **14** *(sideways). P* 14.
517 **145** 12 c. multicoloured 20 1
518 50 c. multicoloured 65 8

(Des Studio 53. Litho Questa)

1984 (21 Apr). *250th Anniv of "Lloyd's List" (newspaper). T* **14** *and similar vert designs. Multicoloured. W* w **14**. *P* 14.
519 12 c. Type **146** 30 1
520 15 c. S.S. *Tinhow*, 1906 .. .. .. 35 3
521 18 c. *Oriana* at Point Cruz, Honiara 40 4
522 $1 Point Cruz, Honiara .. .. .. 1·40 2·2
519/22 .. .. *Set of* 4 2·25 2·7

(Des Jennifer Toombs. Litho Format)

1984 (18 June). *Universal Postal Union Congress, Hamburg. A No.* **MS***512 but with changed sheet inscriptions and U.P.U. log in margin. Multicoloured. W* w **14** *(sideways). P* 14.
MS523 $1 1908 6d. Canoe stamp .. .. .. 1·25 1·4

147 Village Drums

148 Solomon Islands Flag and Torch-bearer

(Des McCombie Skinner Studio. Litho Questa)

1984 (2 July). *20th Anniv of Asia-Pacific Broadcasting Union. T* **147** *and similar horiz designs. Multicoloured.* W w **14** (*sideways*). *P* 13½ × 14.

524 12 c. Type **147** 15 15
525 45 c. Radio City, Guadalcanal . . 60 60
526 60 c. S.I.B.C. studios, Honiara . . 75 80
527 $1 S.I.B.C. Broadcasting House . . 1·25 1·40
524/7 . . *Set of* 4 2·50 2·75

(Des McCombie Skinner Studio. Litho Format)

1984 (4 Aug–22 Sept). *Olympic Games, Los Angeles. T* **148** *and similar multicoloured designs.* W w **14** (*sideways on* 25 *c. to* $1). *P* 14 × 13½ (12 *c.*) *or* 13½ × 14 (*others*).

528 12 c. Type **148** . . 15 20
529 25 c. Lawson Tama Stadium, Honiara (*horiz*) 30 35
a. Booklet pane Nos. 529/30, each × 2 (22.9.84) . . 1·90
530 50 c. Honiara Community Centre (*horiz*) . . 65 70
531 95 c. Alick Wickham inventing crawl stroke, Bronte Baths, New South Wales, 1898 (*horiz*) (22.9.84) . . 1·75 2·00
a. Booklet pane of 1 . . 1·75
532 $1 Olympic Stadium, Los Angeles (*horiz*) . . 1·25 1·40
528/32 . . *Set of* 5 3·75 4·25

No. 531 only exists from $3·95 stamp booklets.

149 Little Pied Cormorant

150 The Queen Mother with Princess Margaret at Badminton Horse Trials

(Des I. Loe. Litho Questa)

1984 (21 Sept). *"Ausipex" International Stamp Exhibition, Melbourne. Birds. T* **149** *and similar vert designs. Multicoloured.* W w **14**. *P* 14½.

533 12 c. Type **149** . . 20 15
534 18 c. Spotbill Duck . . 30 30
535 35 c. Rufous Night Heron . . 50 50
536 $1 Eastern Broad-billed Roller ("Dollar-bird") . . 1·25 2·00
533/6 . . *Set of* 4 2·00 2·75
MS537 130 × 96 mm. Nos. 533/6 . . 2·00 2·75

(Des A. Theobald ($1.50), C. Abbott (others). Litho Questa)

1985 (7 June). *Life and Times of Queen Elizabeth the Queen Mother. T* **150** *and similar vert designs. Multicoloured.* W w **16**. *P* 14½ × 14.

538 12 c. With Winston Churchill at Buckingham Palace, VE Day, 1945 . . 10 10
539 25 c. Type **150** . . 25 30
540 35 c. At a St. Patrick's Day parade . . 30 35
541 $1 With Prince Henry at his christening (from photo by Lord Snowdon) . . 90 95
538/41 . . *Set of* 4 1·40 1·50
MS542 91 × 73 mm. $1.50, In a gondola, Venice, 1985. Wmk sideways . . 1·40 1·50

151 Japanese Memorial Shrine, Mount Austen, Guadalcanal

(Des D. Slater. Litho Questa)

1985 (28 June). *"Expo '85" World Fair, Japan. T* **151** *and similar horiz designs. Multicoloured.* W w **14** (*sideways*). *P* 14.

543 12 c. Type **151** . . 10 10
544 25 c. Digital telephone exchange equipment 25 30
545 45 c. Fishing vessel *Soltai No. 7* . . 40 45
546 85 c. Coastal village scene . . 75 80
543/6 . . *Set of* 4 1·40 1·50

152 Titiana Village

153 Girl Guide Activities

(Des O. Bell. Litho Walsall)

1985 (30 Aug). *Christmas. "Going Home for the Holiday". T* **152** *and similar horiz designs. Multicoloured.* W w **14** (*sideways*). *P* 14½.

547 12 c. Type **152** . . 10 10
548 25 c. Sigana, Santa Isabel . . 25 30
549 35 c. Artificial Island and Langa Lagoon . . 30 35
547/9 . . *Set of* 3 60 70

(Des D. Slater. Litho Walsall)

1985 (30 Sept). *75th Anniv of Girl Guide Movement* (12, 45 *c.*) *and International Youth Year* (*others*). *T* **153** *and similar vert designs. Multicoloured.* W w **16**. *P* 14.

550 12 c. Type **153** . . 35 10
551 15 c. Boys playing and child in wheelchair (Stop Polio) . . 40 20
552 25 c. Runners and Solomon Island scenes . . 60 30
553 35 c. Runners and Australian scenes ("Run Round Australia") . . 75 35
554 45 c. Guide colour party and badges . . 85 45
550/4 . . *Set of* 5 2·75 1·25
MS555 100 × 75 mm. Nos. 552/3 . . 55 60

154 Osprey

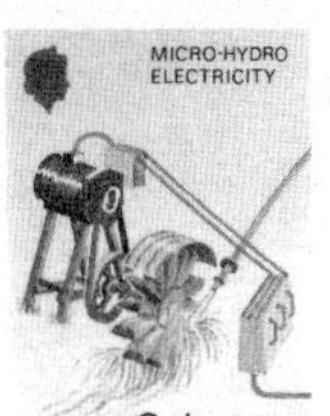

155 Water-powered Generator, Iriri

(Des Annette Robinson and C. Abbott. Litho Format)

1985 (25 Nov). *Birth Bicentenary of John J. Audubon* (*ornithologist*). *Sheet* 121 × 107 *mm containing T* **154** *and similar vert design.* W w **16**. *P* 14.

MS556 45 c. black, gold and deep blue; 50 c. (×2) multicoloured . . 2·50 2·50
Design:—45 c. John J. Audubon.

(Des B. Drake. Litho Walsall)

1986 (24 Jan). *Village Hydro-electric Schemes. Sheet* 109 × 135 *mm. containing T* **155** *and similar vert design. Multicoloured.* W w **16**. *P* 14.

MS557 30 c. Type **155**; 60 c. Domestic lighting . . 75 80

156 Building Red Cross Centre, Gizo

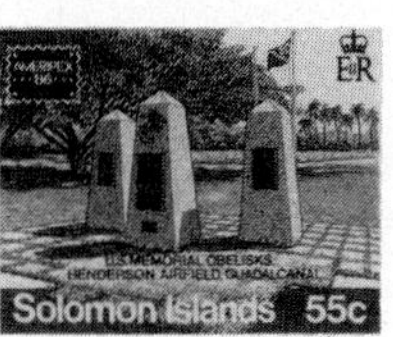

157 U.S. Memorial Obelisks, Henderson Airfield, Guadalcanal

(Des N. Shewring. Litho Walsall)

1986 (27 Mar). *Operation Raleigh* (*volunteer project*). *T* **156** *and similar diamond-shaped designs. Multicoloured.* W w **14**. *P* 14½ × 14.

558 18 c. Type **156** . . 50 20
559 30 c. Exploring rainforest . . 75 30
560 60 c. Observing Halley's Comet . . 1·25 75
561 $1 *Sir Walter Raleigh* and *Zebu* . . 1·75 1·25
558/61 . . *Set of* 4 3·75 2·25

Details of watermark and perforation for the stamps are given with the designs orientated so that the royal cypher appears in the top left corner.

(Des A. Theobald. Litho Questa)

1986 (21 Apr). *60th Birthday of Queen Elizabeth II. Vert designs as T* **230a** *of Jamaica. Multicoloured.* W w **16**. *P* 14½ × 14.

562 5 c. Princess Elizabeth and Duke of Edinburgh at Clydebank Town Hall, 1947 . . 10 10
563 18 c. At St. Paul's Cathedral for Queen Mother's 80th birthday service, 1980 . . 15 20
564 22 c. With children, Solomon Islands, 1982 . . 20 25
565 55 c. At Windsor Castle on her 50th birthday, 1976 . . 40 45
566 $2 At Crown Agents Head Office, London, 1983 . . 1·40 1·50
562/6 . . *Set of* 5 2·00 2·25

(Des D. Miller. Litho Cambec Press, Melbourne)

1986 (22 May). *"Ameripex '86" International Stamp Exhibition, Chicago. International Peace Year. Sheet* 100 × 75 *mm containing T* **157** *and similar horiz design. Multicoloured. P* 13½.

MS567 55 c. Type **157**; $1.65 Peace Corps emblem, President Kennedy and Statue of Liberty (25th anniv of Peace Corps) . . 1·50 1·60

(Des D. Miller. Litho Questa)

1986 (23 July). *Royal Wedding. Square designs as T* **231a** *of Jamaica. Multicoloured.* W w **16**. *P* 14.

568 55 c. Prince Andrew and Miss Sarah Ferguson . . 40 45
569 60 c. Prince Andrew at helm of Yacht *Bluenose II* off Nova Scotia, 1985 . . 45 50

+ 50c Cyclone Relief Fund 1986

158 *Freedom* (winner 1980)

(**159**)

(Des J. Dixon. Litho Leigh-Mardon Ltd, Melbourne)

1986 (22 Aug). *America's Cup Yachting Championship* (1987) (*1st issue*). *T* **158** *and similar vert designs. P* 14½.

570 18 c. multicoloured . . 15 20
a. Sheet of 50 . . 25·00
571 30 c. multicoloured . . 50 70
572 $1 multicoloured . . 75 80
570/2 . . *Set of* 3 1·25 1·50

Nos. 570/2 were issued as a sheet of 50, each horizontal strip of 5 being separated by gutter margins. The sheet contains 20 different designs at 18 c., 10 at 30 c. and 20 at $1. Individual stamps depict yachts, charts, the America's Cup or the emblem of the Royal Perth Yacht Club.

See also No. **MS**575.

1986 (23 Sept). *Cyclone Relief Fund. Nos.* 541 *and* **MS**567 *surch as T* **159** *in red.*

573 $1 + 50 c. Queen Mother with Prince Henry at his christening (from photo by Lord Snowdon) . . 1·10 1·25
MS574 100 × 75 mm. 55 c. + 25 c. Type **157**; $1.65 + 75 c. Peace Corps emblem, President Kennedy and Statue of Liberty (25th anniv of Peace Corps) . . 3·00 3·00

The surcharges on No. **MS**574 are vertical, in smaller type (length 16½ mm) and do not include "1986".

(Des J. Dixon. Litho Leigh-Mardon Ltd, Melbourne)

1987 (4 Feb). *America's Cup Yachting Championship* (*2nd issue*). *Sheet* 111 × 75 *mm, containing vert design as T* **158**. *Multicoloured. P* 14½.

MS575 $5 *Stars and Stripes* (1987 winner) . . 3·25 3·50

No. **MS**575 was also issued printed on gold foil and sold at a premium of $20 over the face value of the stamp.

160 *Dendrophyllia gracilis*

161 *Cassia fistula*

(Des D. Miller. Litho Format)

1987 (11 Feb). *Corals. T* **160** *and similar horiz designs. Multicoloured.* W w **16** (*sideways*). *P* 14.

576 18 c. Type **160** . . 20 15
577 45 c. *Dendronephthya sp* . . 60 50
578 60 c. *Clavularia sp* . . 80 80
579 $1.50, *Melithaea squamata* . . 1·60 1·75
576/9 . . *Set of* 4 3·00 3·00

(Des Gill Tomblin. Litho Walsall)

1987 (12 May)–**88**. *Flowers. T* **161** *and similar vert designs. Multicoloured.* W w **16**. *P* 14½ × 14.

580 1 c. Type **161** . . 10 10
581 5 c. *Allamanda cathartica* . . 10 10
582 10 c. *Catharanthus roseus* . . 10 10
583 18 c. *Mimosa pudica* . . 10 10
584 20 c. *Hibiscus rosa-sinensis* . . 10 10
585 22 c. *Clerodendrum thomsonae* . . 10 10
586 25 c. *Bauhinia variegata* . . 10 15
587 28 c. *Gloriosa rothschildiana* . . 10 15
588 30 c. *Heliconia solomonensis* . . 10 15
589 40 c. *Episcia* hybrid . . 15 20
590 45 c. *Bougainvillea* hybrid . . 20 25
591 50 c. *Alpinia purpurata* . . 20 25
592 55 c. *Plumeria rubra* . . 25 30
593 60 c. *Acacia farnesiana* . . 25 30
594 $1 *Ipomea purpurea* . . 40 45
595 $2 *Dianella ensifolia* . . 85 90
596 $5 *Passiflora foetida* . . 2·10 2·25
597 $10 *Hemigraphis sp* (1.3.88) . . 4·25 4·50
580/97 . . *Set of* 18 8·50 9·25

162 Mangrove Kingfisher on Branch — 163 *Dendrobium conanthum*

(Des Josephine Martin. Litho Format)

1987 (15 July). *Mangrove Kingfisher. T* **162** *and similar vert designs. Multicoloured. W* w **14**. *P* 14.

598 60 c. Type **162**.. .. 1·00 1·25
a. Horiz strip of 4. Nos. 598/601 .. 3·50
599 60 c. Kingfisher diving .. 1·00 1·25
600 60 c. Entering water .. 1·00 1·25
601 60 c. Kingfisher with prey .. 1·00 1·25
598/601 .. *Set of* 4 3·50 4·00

Nos. 598/601 were printed together, *se-tenant*, in horizontal strips of 4 throughout the sheet, forming a composite design.

(Des Sue Wickison. Litho Walsall)

1987 (23 Sept). *Christmas. Orchids* (*1st series*). *T* **163** *and similar vert designs. Multicoloured. W* w **16**. *P* 13½×13.

602 18 c. Type **163**.. 40 10
603 30 c. *Spathoglottis plicata* .. 65 20
604 55 c. *Dendrobium gouldii* .. 85 50
605 $1.50, *Dendrobium goldfinchii* .. 2·00 1·75
602/5 .. *Set of* 4 3·50 2·25

See also Nos. 640/3.

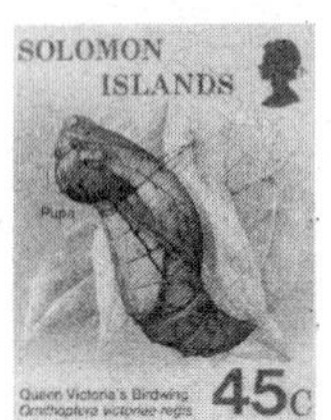

164 Telecommunications Control Room and Satellite — 165 Pupa of *Ornithoptera victoriae*

(Des D. Hartley. Litho CPE Australia Ltd, Melbourne)

1987 (16 Nov). *Asia-Pacific Transport and Communications Decade. T* **164** *and similar horiz designs. Multicoloured. P* 13½.

606 18 c. Type **164**.. 10 15
607 30 c. De Havilland "Twin Otter" mail plane 15 20
608 60 c. Guadalcanal road improvement project 35 40
609 $2 Beechcraft "Queen Air" and Henderson Control Tower .. 1·10 1·25
606/9 .. *Set of* 4 1·50 1·75

(Des R. Lewington. Litho Questa)

1987 (25 Nov). *Butterflies* (*3rd series*). Ornithoptera victoriae (*Queen Victoria's Birdwing*). *T* **165** *and similar vert designs. Multicoloured. W* w **16** (*sideways*). *P* 14½×14.

610 45 c. Type **165**.. 90 90
a. Strip of 4. Nos. 610/13 .. 3·25
611 45 c. Larva .. 90 90
612 45 c. Female butterfly .. 80 90
613 45 c. Male butterfly .. 90 90
610/13 .. *Set of* 4 3·25 3·25

Nos. 610/13 were printed together, *se-tenant*, in horizontal and vertical strips of 4 throughout the sheet of 16.

166 Student and National Agriculture Training Institute — 167 Building a Fishing Boat

(Des D. Miller. Litho Format)

1988 (12 Feb). *10th Anniv of International Fund for Agricultural Development. T* **166** *and similar square designs. Multicoloured. W* w **16**. *P* 14½.

614 50 c. Type **166**.. 30 35
a. Horiz pair. Nos. 614/15.. 60 70
615 50 c. Students working in fields .. 30 35
616 $1 Transport by lorry .. 55 60
a. Horiz pair. Nos. 616/17.. 1·10 1·25
617 $1 Canoe transport.. 55 60
614/17 .. *Set of* 4 1·50 1·75

Nos. 614/15 and 616/17 were printed together, *se-tenant*, in horizontal pairs throughout the sheets, each pair forming a composite design.

(Des N. Shewring. Litho CPE Australia Ltd, Melbourne)

1988 (28 Apr). *"Expo '88" World Fair, Brisbane. T* **167** *and similar horiz designs. Multicoloured. P* 13½×14.

618 22 c. Type **167** .. 15 15
619 80 c. War canoe .. 40 45
620 $1.50, Traditional village .. 80 85
618/20 .. *Set of* 3 1·25 1·25
MS621 130 × 53 mm. Nos. 618/20 .. 1·25 1·40

No. **MS**621 also exists, as a restricted issue, surcharged $3.50 for "New Zealand 1990" International Stamp Exhibition, Auckland.

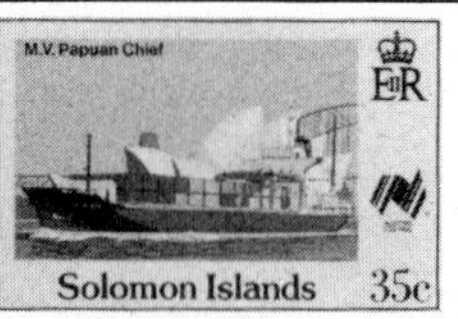

168 *Todos los Santos* in Estrella Bay, 1568 — 169 *Papuan Chief* (container ship)

(Des M. Bradbury and J. Sayer. Litho Walsall)

1988 (6 July). *10th Anniv of Independence. T* **168** *and similar horiz designs. Multicoloured. W* w **14** (*sideways*). *P* 13×13½.

622 22 c. Type **168** .. 25 15
623 55 c. Raising the Union Jack, 1893 .. 50 35
624 80 c. High Court Building .. 70 50
625 $1 Dancers at traditional celebration .. 90 80
622/5 .. *Set of* 4 2·10 1·60

(Des E. Nisbet. Litho Walsall)

1988 (30 July). *Bicentenary of Australian Settlement and "Sydpex '88" National Stamp Exhibition, Sydney. T* **169** *and similar horiz designs. Multicoloured. W* w **16** (*sideways*). *P* 14.

626 35 c. Type **169** .. 20 25
627 60 c. *Nimos* (container ship) .. 30 35
628 70 c. *Malaita* (liner) .. 40 45
629 $1.30, *Makambo* (freighter) .. 70 75
626/9 .. *Set of* 4 1·40 1·60
MS630 140 × 76 mm. Nos. 626/9. W w **14** (sideways) .. 1·60 1·75

170 Archery — 171 *Bulbophyllum dennisii*

(Des Joan Thompson. Litho Walsall)

1988 (5 Aug). *Olympic Games, Seoul. T* **170** *and similar multicoloured designs. W* w **16**. *P* 14½.

631 22 c. Type **170** .. 30 15
632 55 c. Weightlifting .. 50 40
633 70 c. Athletics .. 60 55
634 80 c. Boxing .. 70 60
631/4 .. *Set of* 4 1·90 1·50
MS635 100 × 80 mm. $2 Olympic Stadium (*horiz*). W w **14** (sideways) .. 1·25 1·25

(Des D. Miller (22, 65 c.), O. Bell and D. Miller (50 c.), E. Nisbet and D. Miller ($2). Litho Questa)

1988 (31 Oct). *300th Anniv of Lloyd's of London. Designs as T* **167a** *of Malawi. W* w **16** (*sideways on* 50, 65 *c.*). *P* 14.

636 22 c. brownish black and brown .. 20 15
637 50 c. multicoloured .. 35 30
638 65 c. multicoloured .. 50 45
639 $2 multicoloured .. 1·40 1·50
636/9 .. *Set of* 4 2·25 2·25

Designs: *Vert*—22 c. King George V and Queen Mary laying foundation stone of Leadenhall Street Building, 1925; $2 *Empress of China*, 1911. *Horiz*—50 c. *Forthbank* (container ship); 65 c. Soltel satellite communications station.

(Des Sue Wickison. Litho Walsall)

1989 (20 Jan). *Orchids* (*2nd series*). *T* **171** *and similar vert designs. Multicoloured. W* w **14**. *P* 13½ × 13.

640 22 c. Type **171** .. 35 15
641 35 c. *Calanthe langei* .. 45 30
642 55 c. *Bulbophyllum blumei* .. 65 45
643 $2 *Grammatophyllum speciosum* .. 1·60 1·75
640/3 .. *Set of* 4 2·75 2·40

172 Red Cross Workers with Handicapped Children — 173 *Phyllidia varicosa*

(Des A. Theobald. Litho Questa)

1989 (16 May). *125th Anniv of International Red Cross. T* **172** *and similar horiz designs. Multicoloured. W* w **16** (*sideways*). *P* 14½.

644 35 c. Type **172** .. 15 20
a. Horiz pair. Nos. 644/5 .. 30 40
645 35 c. Handicapped Children Centre minibus 15 20
646 $1.50, Blood donor .. 65 70
a. Horiz pair. Nos. 646/7 .. 1·25 1·40
647 $1.50, Balance test .. 65 70
644/7 .. *Set of* 4 1·40 1·60

Nos. 644/5 and 646/7 were each printed together, *se-tenant*, in horizontal pairs throughout the sheets, each pair forming a composite design.

(Des Sue Wickison. Litho Questa)

1989 (30 June). *Nudibranchs* (*Sea Slugs*). *T* **173** *and similar horiz designs. Multicoloured. W* w **14** (*sideways*). *P* 14×14½.

648 22 c. Type **173** .. 10 10
649 70 c. *Chromodoris bullocki* .. 30 35
650 80 c. *Chromodoris leopardus* .. 35 40
651 $1.50, *Phidiana indica* .. 65 70
648/51 .. *Set of* 4 1·25 1·40

(Des A. Theobald ($4), D. Miller (others). Litho Questa)

1989 (20 July). *20th Anniv of First Manned Landing on Moon. Multicoloured designs as T* **51a** *of Kiribati. W* w **16** (*sideways on* 35, 70 *c.*). *P* 14×13½ (22, 80 *c.*) *or* 14 (*others*).

652 22 c. "Apollo 16" descending by parachute .. 10 10
653 35 c. Launch of "Apollo 16" (30×30 *mm*) .. 15 20
654 70 c. "Apollo 16" emblem (30×30 *mm*) .. 30 35
655 80 c. Ultra-violet colour photograph of Earth 35 40
652/5 .. *Set of* 4 80 90
MS656 100×83 mm. $4 Moon's surface seen from Space. Wmk inverted. P 14×13½ .. 1·75 1·90

174 Five Stones Catch — 175 Fishermen and Butterfly

(Des D. Miller ($3), R. Stewart (others). Litho B.D.T. ($3) or Walsall (others))

1989 (19 Nov). *"World Stamp Expo '89", International Stamp Exhibition, Washington. Children's Games. T* **174** *and similar multicoloured designs. W* w **16** (*sideways on* 67, 73 *c.*). *P* 14.

657 5 c. Type **174** .. 10 10
658 67 c. Blowing soap bubbles (*horiz*) .. 30 35
659 73 c. Coconut shell game (*horiz*) .. 30 35
660 $1 Seed wind sound .. 40 45
657/60 .. *Set of* 4 1·00 1·10
MS661 72×72 mm. $3 Softball. W w 14 .. 2·40 2·40

(Des N. Kohia and C. Vendi, adapted G. Vasarhelyi. Litho Questa)

1989 (30 Nov). *Christmas. T* **175** *and similar horiz designs. Multicoloured. W* w **16** (*sideways*). *P* 14.

662 18 c. Type **175** .. 10 10
663 25 c. The Nativity .. 10 15
664 45 c. Hospital ward at Christmas .. 20 25
665 $1.50, Village tug-of-war .. 65 70
662/5 .. *Set of* 4 95 1·10

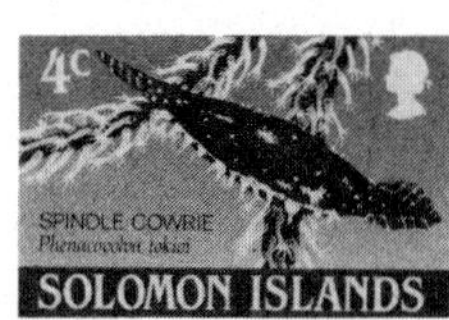

176 Man wearing Headband, Necklace and Sash — 177 Spindle Cowrie

(Des Sue Wickison. Litho Questa)

1990 (14 Mar). *Personal Ornaments. T* **176** *and similar vert designs. Multicoloured. W* w **14**. *P* 14.

666 5 c. Type **176** .. 10 10
667 12 c. Pendant .. 10 10
668 18 c. Man wearing medallion, nose ring and earrings .. 10 10
669 $2 Forehead ornament .. 85 90
666/9 .. *Set of* 4 1·00 1·10

First day covers of Nos. 666/9 were postmarked 26 February 1990, which was the originally intended date of issue, but the stamps were not placed on sale until 14 March.

(Des Lynn Chadwick. Litho Questa)

1990 (23 July). *Cowrie Shells. T* **177** *and similar horiz designs. Multicoloured. W* w **14** (*sideways*). *P* 14.

670 4 c. Type **177** .. 10 10
671 20 c. Map Cowrie .. 10 15
672 35 c. Sieve Cowrie .. 15 20
673 50 c. Egg Cowrie .. 20 25
674 $1 Prince Cowrie .. 40 45
670/4 .. *Set of* 5 85 1·00

(Des D. Miller. Litho Questa)

1990 (4 Aug). *90th Birthday of Queen Elizabeth the Queen Mother. Vert designs as T* **107** (25 *c.*) *or* **108** ($5) *of Kenya. P* 14×15 (25 *c.*) *or* 14½ ($5).

675 25 c. multicoloured .. 10 15
676 $5 black and deep claret .. 2·10 2·25

Designs:—25 c. Queen Mother, 1987; $5 King George VI and Queen Elizabeth inspecting bomb damage to Buckingham Palace, 1940.

178 Postman with Mail Van

(Des N. Shewring. Litho Questa)

1990 (15 Oct). *150th Anniv of the Penny Black. T* **178** *and similar horiz designs. Multicoloured.* W w **14** (*sideways*). *P* 14.

677	35 c. Type **178**	15	20
678	45 c. General Post Office	20	25
679	50 c. 1907 ½d. stamp	20	25
680	55 c. Child collecting stamps	25	30
681	60 c. Penny Black and Solomon Islands 1913 1d. stamp	25	30
677/81	*Set of* 5	95	1·10

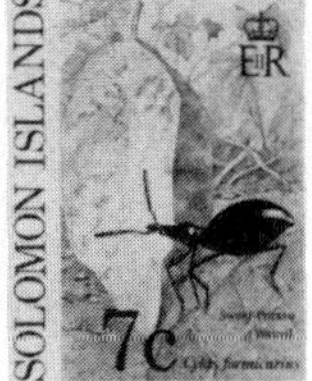

179 Purple Swamphen **180** *Cylas formicarius* (weevil)

(Des N. Arlott. Litho Questa)

1990 (5 Dec). *"Birdpex '90" Stamp Exhibition, Christchurch, New Zealand. T* **179** *and similar horiz designs showing birds. Multicoloured.* W w **14** (*sideways*). *P* 14.

682	10 c. Type **179**	10	10
683	25 c. Mackinlay's Cuckoo Dove ("Rufous Brown Pheasant Dove")	10	10
684	30 c. Superb Fruit Dove	10	15
685	45 c. Cardinal Honeyeater	20	25
686	$2 Finsch's Pygmy Parrot	85	90
682/6	*Set of* 5	1·25	1·40

(Des Josephine Martin. Litho B.D.T.)

1991 (16 Jan). *Crop Pests. T* **180** *and similar vert designs. Multicoloured.* W w **14**. *P* 14.

687	7 c. Type **180**	10	10
688	25 c. *Dacus cucurbitae* (fruit-fly)	10	10
689	40 c. *Papuana uninodis* (beetle)	15	20
690	90 c. *Pantorhytes biplagiastus* (weevil)	35	40
691	$1.50, *Scapanes australis* (beetle)	65	70
687/91	*Set of* 5	1·10	1·40

(Des D. Miller. Litho Questa)

1991 (17 June). *65th Birthday of Queen Elizabeth II and 70th Birthday of Prince Philip. Vert designs as T* **58** *of Kiribati. Multicoloured.* W w **16** (*sideways*). *P* 14½×14.

692	90 c. Prince Philip in evening dress	35	40
	a. Horiz pair. Nos. 692/3 separated by label	1·25	1·25
693	$2 Queen Elizabeth II	85	90

Nos. 692/3 were printed in a similar sheet format to Nos. 366/7 of Kiribati.

181 Child drinking from Coconut **182** Volley Ball

(Des G. Vasarhelyi. Litho Walsall)

1991 (24 June). *Health Campaign. T* **181** *and similar horiz designs. Multicoloured.* W w **14** (*sideways*). *P* 14.

694	5 c. Type **181**	10	10
695	75 c. Mother feeding child	30	35
696	80 c. Breast feeding	35	40
697	90 c. Local produce	35	40
694/7	*Set of* 4	95	1·10

(Des N. Shewring. Litho Questa)

1991 (8 Aug). *9th South Pacific Games. T* **182** *and similar vert designs. Multicoloured.* W w **16**. *P* 14.

698	25 c. Type **182**	10	10
699	40 c. Judo	15	20
700	65 c. Squash	25	30
701	90 c. Bowling	35	40
698/701	*Set of* 4	75	90
MS702	92×112 mm. $2 Games emblem. Wmk sideways	85	90

183 Preparing Food for Christmas **184** Yellowfin Tuna

(Des G. Vasarhelyi. Litho B.D.T.)

1991 (28 Oct). *Christmas. T* **183** *and similar horiz designs. Multicoloured.* W w **14** (*sideways*). *P* 14.

703	10 c. Type **183**	10	10
704	25 c. Christmas Day church service	10	15
705	65 c. Christmas Day feast	25	30
706	$2 Cricket match	85	90
703/6	*Set of* 4	1·10	1·25
MS707	138×110 mm. Nos. 703/6	1·25	1·50

(Des O. Bell. Litho Leigh-Mardon Ltd, Melbourne)

1991 (16 Nov). *"Philanippon '91" International Stamp Exhibition, Tokyo. Tuna Fishing. T* **184** *and similar multicoloured designs.* W w **16** (*sideways*). *P* 14.

708	5 c. Type **184**	10	10
709	30 c. Pole and line tuna fishing boat	10	15
710	80 c. Pole and line fishing	35	40
711	$2 Processing "arabushi" (smoked tuna)	85	90
708/11	*Set of* 4	1·25	1·40
MS712	101×80 mm. 80 c. Plate of "tori nanban" (25×42 *mm*); 80 c. Bowl of "aka miso" (25×42 *mm*). P 14½	65	70

(Des D. Miller. Litho Questa ($5), Leigh-Mardon Ltd, Melbourne (others))

1992 (6 Feb). *40th Anniv of Queen Elizabeth II's Accession. Horiz designs as T* **112** *of Kenya. Multicoloured.* W w **14** (*sideways*) (20 c., 40 c., $5) *or* w **16** (5 c., 60 c.). *P* 14.

713	5 c. Aerial view of Honiara	10	10
714	20 c. Sunset across lagoon	10	10
715	40 c. Honiara harbour	15	20
716	60 c. Three portraits of Queen Elizabeth	25	30
717	$5 Queen Elizabeth II	2·10	2·25
713/17	*Set of* 5	2·50	2·75

185 Mendana's Fleet in Thousand Ships Bay

(Des J. Batchelor. Litho Leigh-Mardon Ltd, Melbourne)

1992 (24 Apr). *"Granada '92" International Stamp Exhibition, Spain. Mendana's Discovery of Solomon Islands. T* **185** *and similar horiz designs.* W w **14** (*sideways*). *P* 15×14½.

718	10 c. Type **185**	10	10
719	65 c. Map of voyage	25	30
720	80 c. Alvaro Mendana de Niera	35	40
721	$1 Settlement at Graciosa Bay	40	45
722	$5 Mendana's fleet at sea	2·10	2·25
718/22	*Set of* 5	2·75	3·00

POSTAGE DUE STAMPS

D 1

(Typo B.W.)

1940 (1 Sept). *Wmk Mult Script CA. P* 12.

D1	D 1	1d. emerald-green	3·75	6·50
D2		2d. scarlet	4·25	6·50
D3		3d. brown	4·50	10·00
D4		4d. blue	7·00	11·00
D5		5d. grey-green	8·00	14·00
D6		6d. purple	8·50	15·00
D7		1s. violet	12·00	26·00
D8		1s. 6d. turquoise-green	22·00	45·00
D1/8		*Set of* 8	65·00	£120
D1/8 Perf "Specimen"		*Set of* 8	£150	

Somaliland Protectorate

Egyptian post offices were opened in Somaliland during 1876 and the stamps of Egypt were used there until the garrisons were withdrawn in 1884.

Cancellations for these offices have been identified as follows (for illustrations of postmark types see after EGYPT):

BARBARA (Berbera). *Open* 1876? *to* 1884. Postmark type D.

ZEILA *Open* 1876 *to* 1884. Postmark types D, or as E without "V. R." (spelt ZEJLA). One example with seal type cancellation is also known.

Stamps of India were used at the two post offices from 1884 until 1903, Berbera usually using a circular datestamp and Zaila a squared circle postmark.

The Protectorate Post Office was established on 1 June 1903, when control of British Somaliland was transferred from the Indian Government to the British Foreign Office.

PRICES FOR STAMPS ON COVER TO 1945

Nos. 1/11	*from* × 25
Nos. 12/13	—
Nos. 18/22	*from* × 12
Nos. 23/4	—
Nos. 25/30	*from* × 30
Nos. 32/59	*from* × 12
Nos. 60/92	*from* × 6
Nos. 93/104	*from* × 3
Nos. 105/16	*from* × 4
Nos. O1/13	*from* × 6
Nos. O14/15	—

BRITISH SOMALILAND

(1)

2

3

SETTINGS OF TYPE 1

In all printings the ½, 1, 2, 2½, 3, 4, 8, 12 a. and 1 r. values were overprinted from a setting of 240 (2 panes 12 × 10, one above the other), covering the entire sheet at one operation.

The 6 a., which was in sheets of 320 (4 panes, each 8 × 10), had a modified setting of 160, applied twice to each sheet.

The high values were overprinted in sheets of 96 (8 panes, each 4 × 3).

The settings for the low value stamps contained two slightly different styles of overprint, identified by the position of "B" of "BRITISH". Type A shows this letter over the "M" of "SOMALILAND" and Type B over the "OM".

For the first printing with the overprint at the top of the design the 240 position setting showed all the stamps in the upper pane and 63 in the lower as Type A, with the remaining 57 as Type B. When the setting was used for the printing with overprint at foot it was amended slightly so that one of the Type A examples in the upper pane became a Type B.

The 6 a. value with overprint at top shows 250 examples of Type A and 70 as Type B in each sheet. This proportion altered in the printing with overprint at foot to 256 as Type A and 64 as Type B.

OVERPRINT VARIETIES

Missing second "I" in "BRITISH"—Occurs on the stamps with overprint at top from R.2/6 of the upper pane and R.5/1 of the lower, although it is believed that the example on the 2½ a. (No. 4a) only occurs from the second position. On the later printing with overprint at foot a similar error can be found on R.7/12 of the upper pane. Some examples of both these errors show traces of the letter remaining, but the prices quoted are for stamps with it completely omitted.

Figure "1" for first "I" in "BRITISH"—Occurs on R.6/4 of the upper pane for all printings of the 240 impression setting. In addition it has been reported from R.7/12 of the Queen Victoria 2½, 12 a. and 1 r. with overprint at foot. Both versions of the 6 a. show the variety on R.6/4 of the upper left and upper right panes.

Curved overprint—Occurs on R.3/4 of the top right-hand pane of the high values.

"SUMALILAND"—Occurs on R.2/9 of the upper pane for all low values with the overprint at foot, except the 6 a. A similar variety occurs on the high values from the same series on R.1/3 of the top left pane.

"SOMAL.LAND"—Occurs on R.7/5 of the lower pane from the 240 impression setting with the overprint at foot. In addition the Edwardian values of this series also have an example on R.6/7. The 6 a. has examples of the flaw on R.6/9 and R.7/5 of both the lower right and left panes. A similar variety occurs on the high values from the same series at R.3/4 of the third pane in the left-hand column.

1903 (1 June). *Stamps of India optd with T* **1**, *at top of stamp, in Calcutta.*

1 **23** ½ a. yellow-green .. 1·25 1·75
a. "BRIT SH" .. £130
2 **25** 1 a. carmine .. 1·25 1·50
a. "BRIT SH" .. £150 £225
b. "BR1TISH" .. £110
3 **27** 2 a. pale violet .. 75 40
a. "BRIT SH" .. £250
b. "BR1TISH" .. £200
c. Opt double .. £600
4 **36** 2½ a. ultramarine .. 2·00 1·75
a. "BRIT SH" .. £325
b. "BR1TISH" .. £225
5 **28** 3 a. brown-orange .. 1·25 1·75
a. "BRIT SH" .. £350
b. "BR1TISH" .. £250
6 **29** 4 a. slate-green .. 1·50 2·75
a. "BR1TISH" .. £250
7 **21** 6 a. olive-bistre .. 3·75 4·50
a. "BR1TISH" .. £180
8 **31** 8 a. dull mauve .. 1·50 5·00
a. "BR1TISH" .. £250
9 **32** 12 a. purple/*red* .. 1·75 7·00
a. "BR1TISH" .. £250
10 **37** 1 r. green and carmine .. 3·25 10·00
a. "BR1TISH" .. £275
11 **38** 2 r. carmine and yellow-brown .. 22·00 32·00
a. Curved opt .. £100
12 3 r. brown and green .. 17·00 35·00
a. Curved opt .. £130
13 5 r. ultramarine and violet .. 20·00 45·00
a. Curved opt .. £150
1/13 .. *Set of* 13 70·00 £130

1903 (1 Sept–2 Nov). *Stamps of India optd with T* **1**, *at bottom of stamp, in Calcutta. (a) On issues of Queen Victoria.*

18 **36** 2½ a. ultramarine (2.11) .. 1·25 4·25
a. "BR1TISH" .. £140
b. "SUMALILAND" .. £180
c. "SOMAL.LAND" .. £180
19 **21** 6 a. olive-bistre (2.11) .. 2·00 4·25
a. "BR1TISH" .. £160
b. "SOMAL.LAND" .. £100
20 **32** 12 a. purple/*red* (2.11) .. 3·50 12·00
a. "BR1TISH" .. £160
b. "SUMALILAND" .. £250
c. "SOMAL.LAND" .. £250
21 **37** 1 r. green and carmine (2.11) .. 2·00 10·00
a. "BR1TISH" .. £180
b. "SUMALILAND" .. £300
c. "SOMAL.LAND" .. £300
22 **38** 2 r. carmine and yellow-brown (2.11) .. 50·00 70·00
a. Curved opt .. £250
b. "SUMALILAND" .. £250
c. "SOMAL.LAND" .. £250
23 3 r. brown and green (2.11) .. 50·00 75·00
a. Opt double, both inverted with one albino .. £475
b. Curved opt .. £250
c. "SUMALILAND" .. £250
d. "SOMAL.LAND" .. £250
24 5 r. ultramarine and violet (2.11) .. 40·00 60·00
a. Curved opt .. £200
b. "SUMALILAND" .. £200
c. "SOMAL.LAND" .. £200

(b) On issues of King Edward VII

25 **42** ½ a. green .. 75 55
a. "BRIT SH" .. £275
b. "BR1TISH" .. 60·00
c. "SUMALILAND" .. 60·00
d. "SOMAL.LAND" .. 20·00
26 **43** 1 a. carmine (8.10) .. 60 30
a. "BRIT SH" .. £180
b. "BR1TISH" .. 65·00 65·00
c. "SUMALILAND" .. 65·00
d. "SOMAL.LAND" .. 22·00 22·00
27 **44** 2 a. violet (2.11) .. 1·00 2·50
a. "BRIT SH" .. £750
b. "BR1TISH" .. £160
c. "SUMALILAND" .. £160
d. "SOMAL.LAND" .. 38·00
28 **46** 3 a. orange-brown (2.11) .. 1·00 2·50
a. "BR1TISH" .. £160
b. "SUMALILAND" .. £160
c. "SOMAL.LAND" .. 38·00
29 **47** 4 a. olive (2.11) .. 1·00 4·00
a. "BR1TISH" .. £180
b. "SUMALILAND" .. £180
c. "SOMAL.LAND" .. 45·00
30 **49** 8 a. mauve (2.11) .. 1·25 2·25
a. "BR1TISH" .. £200
b. "SUMALILAND" .. £200
c. "SOMAL.LAND" .. 55·00
18/30 .. *Set of* 13 £130 £225

(Typo D.L.R.)

1904 (15 Feb–3 Sept). *(a) Wmk Crown CA. P* 14.

32 **2** ½ a. dull green and green .. 30 2·50
33 1 a. grey-black and red (3.9) .. 1·25 1·75
34 2 a. dull and bright purple (3.9) .. 1·50 1·00
35 2½ a. bright blue (3.9) .. 1·75 3·00
36 3 a. chocolate and grey-green (3.9) .. 1·00 2·25
37 4 a. green and black (3.9) .. 1·50 2·75
38 6 a. green and violet (3.9) .. 3·00 8·50
39 8 a. grey-black and pale blue (3.9) .. 2·75 5·50
40 12 a. grey-black and orange-buff (3.9) .. 5·50 11·00

(b) Wmk Crown CC. P 14

41 **3** 1 r. green (3.9) .. 12·00 28·00
42 2 r. dull and bright purple (3.9) .. 28·00 55·00
43 3 r. green and black (3.9) .. 28·00 60·00
44 5 r. grey-black and red (3.9) .. 30·00 60·00
32/44 .. *Set of* 13 £100 £200
32/44 Optd "Specimen" .. *Set of* 13 £180

1905 (July)–**11**. *Wmk Mult Crown CA. Ordinary paper. P* 14.

45 **2** ½ a. dull green and green .. 60 3·50
46 1 a. grey-black and red (10.7.05) .. 2·50 1·60
a. Chalk-surfaced paper (1906) .. 3·50 1·40
47 2 a. dull and bright purple .. 4·50 7·50
a. Chalk-surfaced paper (1909) .. 3·50 8·00
48 2½ a. bright blue .. 3·00 10·00
49 3 a. chocolate and grey-green .. 1·50 7·00
a. Chalk-surfaced paper (1911) .. 3·75 7·00
50 4 a. green and black .. 2·50 10·00
a. Chalk-surfaced paper (1911) .. 4·50 10·00
51 6 a. green and violet .. 2·00 12·00
a. Chalk-surfaced paper (1911) .. 5·00 12·00
52 8 a. grey-black and pale blue .. 2·50 6·50
a. Chalk-surfaced paper. *Black and blue* (27.1.11) .. 38·00 65·00
53 12 a. grey-black and orange-buff .. 2·75 10·00
a. Chalk-surfaced paper. *Black and orange-brown* (9.11.11) .. 16·00 48·00

1909 (30 Apr–May). *Wmk Mult Crown CA. P* 14.

58 **2** ½ a. bluish green (May) .. 8·00 13·00
59 1 a. red (Optd S. £25) .. 2·50 75
45/59 .. *Set of* 11 28·00 75·00

4

5

(Typo D.L.R.)

1912 (Nov)–**19**. *Wmk Mult Crown CA. Chalk-surfaced paper (2 a. and 3 a. to 5 r.). P* 14.

60 **4** ½ a. green (11.13) .. 20 3·50
61 1 a. red .. 90 50
a. Scarlet (1917) .. 3·00 1·25
62 2 a. dull and bright purple (12.13) .. 3·50 8·00
a. Dull purple and violet-purple (4.19) 9·50 17·00
63 2½ a. bright blue (10.13) .. 80 4·50
64 3 a. chocolate and grey-green (10.13) .. 80 3·75
65 4 a. green and black (12.12) .. 80 4·75
66 6 a. green and violet (4.13) .. 80 3·25
67 8 a. grey-black and pale blue (10.13) .. 1·25 7·00
68 12 a. grey-black and orange-buff (10.13) 1·25 13·00
69 **5** 1 r. green .. 4·75 8·00
70 2 r. dull purple and purple (4.19) .. 18·00 45·00
71 3 r. green and black (4.19) .. 48·00 80·00
72 5 r. black and scarlet (4.19) .. 48·00 £100
60/72 .. *Set of* 13 £110 £250
60/72 Optd "Specimen" .. *Set of* 13 £150

1921. *Wmk Mult Script CA. Chalk-surfaced paper (2 a. and 3 a. to 5 r.). P* 14.

73 **4** ½ a. blue-green .. 70 3·00
74 1 a. carmine-red .. 80 30
75 2 a. dull and bright purple .. 1·00 1·00
76 2½ a. bright blue .. 50 3·50
77 3 a. chocolate and green .. 2·50 7·00
78 4 a. green and black .. 2·50 3·75
79 6 a. green and violet .. 1·50 10·00
80 8 a. grey-black and pale blue .. 1·50 5·00
81 12 a. grey-black and orange-buff .. 6·50 15·00
82 **5** 1 r. dull green .. 5·50 27·00
83 2 r. dull purple and purple .. 14·00 32·00
84 3 r. dull green and black .. 26·00 80·00
85 5 r. black and scarlet .. 48·00 £110
73/85 .. *Set of* 13 £100 £275
73/85 Optd "Specimen" .. *Set of* 13 £150

1935 (6 May). *Silver Jubilee. As Nos.* 114/17 *of Jamaica, but ptd by Waterlow. P* 11×12.

86 1 a. deep blue and scarlet .. 1·25 1·50
87 2 a. ultramarine and grey .. 1·25 1·50
j. Kite and vertical log .. 38·00
88 3 a. brown and deep blue .. 2·00 3·50
j. Kite and vertical log .. 60·00
k. Kite and horizontal log .. 55·00
89 1 r. slate and purple .. 5·00 7·00
j. Kite and vertical log .. 90·00
k. Kite and horizontal log .. 80·00
86/9 .. *Set of* 4 8·50 12·00
86/9 Perf "Specimen" .. *Set of* 4 75·00

For illustrations of plate varieties see Omnibus section following Zimbabwe.

1937 (13 May). *Coronation. As Nos.* 118/20 *of Jamaica.*

90 1 a. scarlet .. 10 10
91 2 a. grey-black .. 30 45
92 3 a. bright blue .. 45 50
90/2 .. *Set of* 3 75 95
90/2 Perf "Specimen" .. *Set of* 3 55·00

6 Berbera Blackhead Sheep

7 Lesser Kudu

8 Somaliland Protectorate

(Des H. W. Claxton. Recess Waterlow)

1938 (10 May). *Portrait to left. Wmk Mult Script CA. P* 12½.

93 **6** ½ a. green .. 15 1·25
94 1 a. scarlet .. 15 10
95 2 a. maroon .. 15 15
96 3 a. bright blue .. 3·00 3·50
97 **7** 4 a. sepia .. 1·25 2·25
98 6 a. violet .. 2·50 6·00
99 8 a. grey .. 65 5·00
100 12 a. red-orange .. 65 6·50

101 8 1 r. green .. .. 6·00 20·00
102 2 r. purple .. .. 8·50 20·00
103 3 r. bright blue .. .. 9·00 17·00
104 5 r. black .. .. 13·00 17·00
a. Imperf between (horiz pair) .. £7000
93/104 .. .. .. *Set of* 12 40·00 90·00
93/104 Perf "Specimen" .. .. *Set of* 12 £130

Following the Italian Occupation during 1940–41 the stamps of ADEN were used at Berbera from 1 July 1941 until 26 April 1942.

9 Berbera Blackhead Sheep

5 Cents (10)

1 Shilling (11)

(Recess Waterlow)

1942 (27 Apr). *As T* **6/8** *but with full-face portrait of King George VI, as in T* **9**. *Wmk Mult Script CA. P* 12½.
105 9 ½ a. green 10 10
106 1 a. scarlet 10 10
107 2 a. maroon 40 10
108 3 a. bright blue 50 10
109 7 4 a. sepia 50 10
110 6 a. violet 70 10
111 8 a. grey 45 10
112 12 a. red-orange .. .. 1·00 10
113 8 1 r. green 45 25
114 2 r. purple .. .. 1·00 1·75
115 3 r. bright blue .. .. 1·10 5·50
116 5 r. black .. .. 3·25 4·00
105/16 .. .. .. *Set of* 12 8·50 11·00
105/16 Perf "Specimen" .. .. *Set of* 12 £140

1946 (15 Oct). *Victory. As Nos.* 141/2 *of Jamaica. P* 13½×14.
117 1 a. carmine 10 10
a. Perf 13½ .. .. 4·75 30·00
118 3 a. blue 10 10
117/18 Perf "Specimen" .. .. *Set of* 2 45·00

1949 (28 Jan). *Royal Silver Wedding. As Nos.* 143/4 *of Jamaica.*
119 1 a. scarlet 10 10
120 5 r. black .. .. 3·00 3·25

1949 (10 Oct). *75th Anniv of U.P.U. As Nos.* 145/8 *of Jamaica. Surch with face values in annas.*
121 1 a. on 10 c. carmine 10 10
122 3 a. on 30 c. deep blue (R.) 25 30
123 6 a. on 50 c. purple 25 30
124 12 a. on 1s. red-orange 35 30
121/4 .. .. .. *Set of* 4 90 90

1951 (2 Apr). 1942 *issue surch as T* **10/11**.
125 5 c. on ½ a. green 10 10
126 10 c. on 2 a. maroon 10 10
127 15 c. on 3 a. bright blue 20 10
128 20 c. on 4 a. sepia 30 10
129 30 c. on 6 a. violet 45 10
130 50 c. on 8 a. grey 40 10
131 70 c. on 12 a. red-orange .. .. .. 60 1·25
132 1 s. on 1 r. green 40 10
133 2 s. on 2 r. purple .. .. .. 70 3·25
134 2 s. on 3 r. bright blue .. .. .. 1·25 2·50
135 5 s. on 5 r. black (R.) .. .. .. 2·25 4·00
125/35 .. .. .. *Set of* 11 6·00 10·50
At least one cover is known postmarked 1 April, in error, at Burao.

1953 (2 June). *Coronation. As No.* 153 *of Jamaica.*
136 15 c. black and green 10 15

12 Camel and Gurgi

13 Askari

(Recess B.W.)

1953 (15 Sept)–**58**. *T* **12/13** *and similar horiz designs. Wmk Mult Script CA. P* 12½.
137 12 5 c. slate-black 10 20
138 13 10 c. red-orange 90 20
a. Salmon (20.3.58) .. .. 2·50 90
139 12 15 c. blue-green 40 30
140 20 c. scarlet 40 30
141 13 30 c. reddish brown .. .. .. 1·25 30
142 – 35 c. blue .. .. .. 1·00 60
143 – 50 c. brown and rose-carmine .. .. 1·00 35
144 – 1 s. light blue 50 20
145 – 1 s. 30 c. ultramarine and black (1.9.58) 4·50 3·00
146 – 2 s. brown and bluish violet .. .. 10·00 2·00
147 – 5 s. red-brown and emerald .. .. 10·00 5·50
148 – 10 s. brown and reddish violet .. .. 5·50 11·00
137/48 .. .. .. *Set of* 12 32·00 22·00
Designs:—35 c., 2 s. Somali Stock Dove; 50 c., 5 s. Martial Eagle; 1 s. Berbera Blackhead Sheep; 1 s. 30, Sheikh Isaaq's Tomb; 10 s. Taleh Fort.

OPENING OF THE LEGISLATIVE COUNCIL 1957 (19)

LEGISLATIVE COUNCIL UNOFFICIAL MAJORITY, 1960 (20)

1957 (21 May). *Opening of Legislative Council. Nos.* 140 *and* 144 *optd with T* **19**.
149 20 c. scarlet 10 10
150 1 s. light blue 10 10

1960 (5 Apr). *Legislative Council's Unofficial Majority. Nos.* 140 *and* 145 *optd as T* **20**.
151 20 c. scarlet 10 10
152 1 s. 30, ultramarine and black 10 10

OFFICIAL STAMPS

SERVICE

BRITISH SOMALILAND (O 1)

BRITISH SOMALILAND (O 2)

O.H.M.S. (O 3)

SETTING OF TYPE O 1

The 240 impression setting used for the Official stamps differs considerably from that on the contemporary postage issue with overprint at foot, although the "BR1TISH" error can still be found on R.6/4 of the upper pane. The Official setting is recorded as consisting of 217 overprints as Type A and 23 as Type B.

OVERPRINT VARIETIES

Figure "1" for first "I" in "BRITISH". Occurs on R.6/4 of the upper pane as for the postage issue.
"BRITIS H"—Occurs on R.8, stamps 4 and 10 of the lower pane.

1903 (1 June). *Official stamps of India,* 1883–1900, *optd with Type* O **1** *in Calcutta.*
O1 23 ½ a. yellow-green .. .. .. 3·50 48·00
a. "BR1TISH" £250
b. "BRITIS H" £130
O2 25 1 a. carmine .. .. .. 10·00 7·50
a. "BR1TISH" £275 £225
b. "BRITIS H" £140
O3 27 2 a. pale violet .. .. .. 8·00 48·00
a. "BR1TISH" £300
b. "BRITIS H" £180
O4 31 8 a. dull mauve .. .. .. 10·00 £350
a. "BR1TISH" £600
b. "BRITIS H" £300
O5 37 1 r. green and carmine .. .. 10·00 £475
a. "BR1TISH" £600
b. "BRITIS H" £300
O1/5 .. .. .. *Set of* 5 38·00 £800
The 8 a. is known with the stop omitted after the "M" of "O.H.M.S.".

SETTING OF TYPE O 2

This 240 impression setting of "BRITISH SOMALILAND" also differs from that used to prepare the postage issue with overprint at foot, although many of the errors from the latter still occur in the same positions for the Official stamps. The setting used for Nos. O6/9*f* contained 180 overprints as Type A and 60 as Type B.

OVERPRINT VARIETIES

Missing second "I" in "BRITISH"—Occurs R.7/12 of upper pane as for the postage issue.
Figure "1" for first "I" in "BRITISH"—Occurs R.6/4 of upper pane as for the postage issue.
"SUMALILAND"—Occurs R.2/9 of the upper pane as for the postage issue.
"SOMAL.LAND"—Occurs R.6/7 of the lower pane as for the postage issue.

SERVICE (O 2*a*)

"SERVICE" in wrong fount (Type O **2***a*)—Occurs R.1/7 of lower pane.

1903. *Prepared for use, but not issued. Postage stamps of India, Queen Victoria* 1892 *issue* (1 *r.*) *or King Edward VII* 1902 *issue* (*others*), *optd with Type* O **2** *in Calcutta.*
O6 42 ½ a. green 40
a. "BRIT SH" .. .. 70·00
b. "BR1TISH" .. .. 50·00
c. "SUMALILAND" .. .. .. 50·00
d. "SOMAL.LAND" .. .. .. 30·00
e. "SERVICE" as Type O 2*a* .. .. 40·00
O7 43 1 a. carmine 40
a. "BRIT SH" .. .. 70·00
b. "BR1TISH" .. .. 50·00
c. "SUMALILAND" .. .. .. 50·00
d. "SOMAL.LAND" .. .. .. 30·00
e. "SERVICE" as Type O 2*a* .. .. 40·00
O8 44 2 a. violet 70
a. "BRIT SH" £100
b. "BR1TISH" .. .. 70·00
c. "SUMALILAND" .. .. .. 70·00
d. "SERVICE" as Type O 2*a* .. .. 45·00
O9 49 8 a. mauve .. .. 5·00
a. "BRIT SH" £1400
b. "BR1TISH" £400
c. "SUMALILAND" £400
d. "SERVICE" as Type O 2*a* £400
O9*f* 37 1 r. green and carmine .. .. .. 20·00
fa. "BRIT SH" £1400
fb. "BR1TISH" £400
fc. "SUMALILAND" £400
fd. "SOMAL.LAND" £400
fe. "SERVICE" as Type O 2*a* £400
O6/9*f* .. .. .. *Set of* 5 24·00
Used examples of Nos. O6/9*f* are known, but there is no evidence that such stamps did postal duty.

SETTING OF TYPE O 3

The anna values were overprinted in sheets of 120 (2 panes 6 × 10) from a setting matching the pane size. The full stop after the "M" on the fifth vertical column was either very faint or completely omitted. The prices quoted are for stamps with the stop missing; examples with a partial stop are worth much less.

The 1 r. value was overprinted from a separate setting of 60 which did not show the "missing stop" varieties.

1904 (1 Sept)–**05**. *Stamps of Somaliland Protectorate optd with Type* O **3**. *P* 14. (*a*) *Wmk Crown CA.*
O10 2 ½ a. dull green and green .. .. 3·25 48·00
a. No stop after "M" £400
O11 1 a. grey-black and carmine .. .. 3·25 7·00
a. No stop after "M" £300 £375
O12 2 a. dull and bright purple .. .. £120 48·00
a. No stop after "M" £1400 £650
O13 8 a. grey-black and pale blue .. .. 60·00 £130
a. No stop after "M" £550

(*b*) *Wmk Mult Crown CA*
O14 2 2 a. dull and bright purple, O (7.05?) 75·00 £550
a. No stop after "M" £1200

(*c*) *Wmk Crown CC*
O15 3 1 r. green £150 £450
O10/13, O15 .. .. *Set of* 5 £250 £600
O10/13, O15 Optd "Specimen" .. *Set of* 5 £120

All Somaliland Protectorate stamps were withdrawn from sale on 25 June 1960 and until the unification on 1 July, issues of Italian Somalia together with Nos. 353/5 of Somalia Republic were used. Later issues will be found listed in Part 14 (*Africa since Independence N–Z*) of this catalogue.

South Africa

The South African provinces of Cape of Good Hope (including Griqualand West), Natal (including New Republic and Zululand), Orange Free State and Transvaal produced their own issues before federation on 31 May 1910.

CAPE OF GOOD HOPE

PRICES FOR STAMPS ON COVER

Nos. 1/4	*from* × 4
Nos. 5/14	*from* × 3
Nos. 18/21	*from* × 5
No. 22	—
Nos. 23/6	*from* × 5
Nos. 27/31	*from* × 8
Nos. 32/3	*from* × 10
No. 34	*from* × 25
No. 35	*from* × 20
No. 36	*from* × 10
Nos. 37/8	*from* × 25
Nos. 39/40	*from* × 10
Nos. 41/2	*from* × 12
Nos. 43/54	*from* × 10
Nos. 55/6	*from* × 25
No. 57	*from* × 50
Nos. 58/69	*from* × 10
Nos. 70/8	*from* × 6

PRICES. Our prices for early Cape of Good Hope are for stamps in very fine condition. Exceptional copies are worth more, poorer copies considerably less.

1 Hope

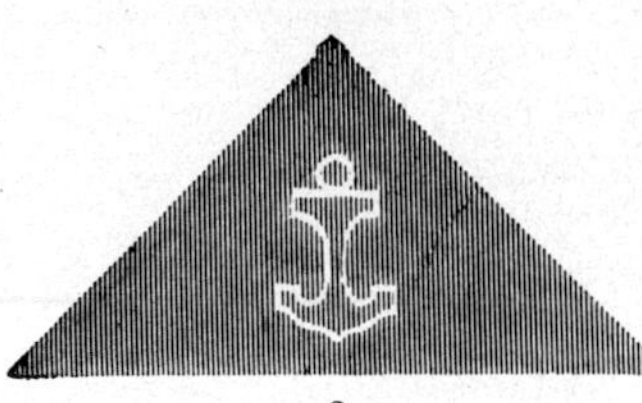

2

(Des Charles Bell, Surveyor-General. Eng W. Humphrys. Recess P.B.)

1853 (1 Sept). *W* **2**. *Imperf.* (*a*) *Paper deeply blued.*
1 1 1d. pale brick-red £3500 £275
a. Deep brick-red £5000 £300
2 4d. deep blue £2000 £160
Plate proofs of the 4d. in a shade similar to the issued stamp exist on ungummed watermarked paper. The blueing on the reverse of these proofs is uneven giving a blotchy appearance.

(b) Paper slightly blued (blueing not so pronounced at back)
3 1 1d. brick-red £3000 £200
a. Brown-red £3250 £225
4 4d. deep blue £1300 £110
a. Blue £1400 £150
Both values are known with wmk sideways.

1855–8. W **2**. *(a) Imperf.*
5 1 1d. brick-red/*cream toned paper* (1857) .. £5000 £900
a. Rose (1858) £450 £200
b. Deep rose-red £600 £225
6 4d. deep blue/*white paper* (1855) .. .. £475 45·00
a. Blue .. .. £275 45·00
7 6d. slate-lilac/*blued paper* (18.2.58) .. £4250 £450
b. Pale rose-lilac/white paper £700 £200
c. Deep rose-lilac/white paper £1700 £300
d. Slate-purple/blued paper £3500 £1000
8 1s. bright yellow-green/*white paper* (18.2.58) £2500 £180
a. Deep dark green £225 £500

The method adopted for producing the plate of the 4d., 6d., and 1s. stamps involved the use of two dies, so that there are two types of each of these values, differing slightly in detail, but produced in equal numbers.

All values of this issue are known with watermark sideways.

The 1d. value in dull rose on ungummed watermarked paper with watermark sideways is a plate proof. The 6d. is known bisected and used with 1d. for 4d. rate.

The paper of No. 5 is similar to that of Nos. 1/4, but is without the blueing. It is much thicker than the white paper used for later printings of the 1d. The evolution of the paper on these Cape of Good Hope stamps is similar to that on the line-engraved issues of Great Britain. Examples of the 6d. slate-lilac apparently on white paper have had the blueing washed out.

The 4d. value is known printed in black on white watermarked paper. Eleven authenticated copies have been recorded, the majority of which show cancellations or, at least, some indication that they have been used.

It was, at one time, believed that these stamps came from a small supply printed in black to mark the death of the Prince Consort, but references to examples can be found in the philatelic press before news of this event reached Cape Town.

It is now thought that these stamps represent proof sheets, possibly pressed into service during a shortage of stamps in 1861. There is, however, no official confirmation of this theory. *(Price £30000 un, £25000 with obliteration).*

(b) Unofficially rouletted
9 1 1d. brick-red .. .. — £2750
10 4d. blue .. .. — £2250
11 6d. rose-lilac .. .. — £1500
12 1s. bright yellow-green .. .. .. — £2750
a. Deep dark green .. .. .. — £3000
These rouletted stamps are best collected on cover.

3 Hope

(Local provisional (so-called "wood-block") issue. Engraved on steel by C. J. Roberts. Printed from stereotyped plates by Saul Solomon & Co, Cape Town)

1861 (Feb–April). *Laid paper. Imperf.*
13 3 1d. vermilion (27 February) £13000 £2000
a. Carmine (7 March) £22000 £3000
b. Brick-red (10 April) £30000 £4250
c. Error. Pale milky blue .. .. — £28000
ca. Pale bright blue .. .. .. — £30000
14 4d. pale milky blue (23 February) £9000 £1500
aa. Retouch or repair to rt-hand corner — £5500
a. Pale grey-blue (March?) .. £10000 £1500
b. Pale bright blue (March?) .. £10000 £1900
ba. Retouch or repair to rt-hand corner — £5500
c. Deep bright blue (12 April) .. £75000 £4500
d. Blue £12000 £3000
e. Error. Vermilion £85000 £40000
ea. Carmine .. .. — £80000
f. Sideways *tête-bêche* (pair) .. † £60000

Nos. 13/14 were each issued in *tête-bêche* pairs normally joined at edges bearing the same inscription ("POSTAGE" against "POSTAGE", etc). No. 14f, of which only one used example is known, comes from the first printing and shows the right-hand stamp misplaced so that "FOUR PENCE" adjoins "POSTAGE".

Both values were officially reprinted in March, 1883, on wove paper. The 1d. is in deep red, and the 4d. in a deeper blue than that of the deepest shade of the issued stamp.

Specimens of the reprints have done postal duty, but their use thus was not intended. There are no reprints of the errors or of the retouched 4d.

Further reprints were made privately but with official permission, in 1940/41, in colours much deeper than those of any of the original printings, and on thick carton paper.

Examples of the 4d. are known unofficially rouletted.

Early in 1863, Perkins Bacon Ltd handed over the four plates used for printing the triangular Cape of Good Hope stamps to De La Rue & Co, Ltd, who made all the subsequent printings.

(Printed from the P.B. plates by D.L.R.)

1863–4. *Imperf. (a)* W **2**.
18 1 1d. deep carmine-red £100 £225
a. Deep brown-red £350 £225
b. Brownish red £350 £225
19 4d. deep blue .. .. £100 42·00
a. Blue .. .. £120 60·00
b. Slate-blue £2000 £500
c. Steel-blue £2000 £300
20 6d. bright mauve £150 £450
21 1s. bright emerald-green £350 £450
a. Pale emerald-green £1100

(b) Wmk Crown CC (sideways)
22 1 1d. deep carmine-red £15000
No. 22 was a trial printing, and is only known unused.

Our prices for the 4d. blue are for stamps which are blue by comparison with the other listed shades. An exceptionally pale shade is recognised by specialists and is rare.

All values of this issue are known with watermark lying sideways.

With the exception of the 4d., these stamps may be easily distinguished from those printed by Perkins Bacon by their colours, which are quite distinct.

The De La Rue stamps of all values are less clearly printed, the figure of Hope and the lettering of the inscriptions standing out less boldly, while the fine lines of the background appear blurred and broken when examined under a glass. The background as a whole often shows irregularity in the apparent depth of colour, due to wear of the plates.

For note regarding the two dies of the 4d., 6d., and 1s. values, see after No. 8.

All the triangular stamps were demonetised as from 1 October 1900.

4 "Hope" seated, with vine and ram. (With outer frame-line)

Four Pence.

(5)

(Des Charles Bell; die engraved on steel and stamps typo by D.L.R.)

1864–77. *With outer frame-line surrounding the design. Wmk Crown CC. P 14.*
23 4 1d. carmine-red (5.65) .. .. .. 75·00 9·00
a. Rose-red .. .. 75·00 9·50
24 4d. pale blue (8.65) .. .. .. 90·00 2·00
a. Blue .. .. £100 2·00
b. Ultramarine .. .. .. £250 50·00
c. Deep blue (1872) .. .. .. £130 2·00
25 6d. pale lilac (before 21.3.64) .. .. £100 14·00
a. Deep lilac .. .. .. £200 6·50
b. Violet (to bright) (1877) .. .. £110 1·50
26 1s. deep green (1.64) .. .. .. £475 13·00
a. Green .. .. 90·00 2·00
b. Blue-green .. .. .. 95·00 3·00

The 1d. rose-red, 6d. lilac, and 1s. blue-green are known imperf, probably from proof sheets.

The 1d. and 4d. stamps of this issue may be found with side and/or top outer frame-lines missing, due to wear of the plates.

(Surch by Saul Solomon & Co, Cape Town)

1868 (17 Nov). *No. 25a surch with T* **5**.
27 4 4d. on 6d. deep lilac (R.) .. .. .. £120 11·00
a. "Peuce" for "Pence" £1800 £700
b. "Fonr" for "Four" .. .. .. — £700

Specimens may also be found with bars omitted or at the top of the stamp, due to misplacement of the sheet.

The space between the words and bars varies from 12½ to 16 mm, stamps with spacing 15½ and 16 mm being rare. There were two printings, one of 120,000 in November 1868 and another of 1,000,000 in December. Stamps showing widest spacings are probably from the earlier printing.

6 (No outer frame-line)

(Die re-engraved. Typo D.L.R.)

1871–6. *Outer frame-line removed. Wmk Crown CC. P 14.*
28 6 ½d. pale grey-black (12.75) .. .. 4·25 3·00
a. Deep grey-black .. .. .. 4·00 2·75
29 1d. pale carmine-red (2.72) .. .. 20·00 35
a. Deep carmine-red .. .. .. 21·00 35
30 4d. dull blue (12.76) .. .. .. 85·00 50
a. Deep blue .. .. .. 85·00 80
b. Ultramarine .. .. .. £190 28·00
31 5s. yellow-orange (25.8.71) .. .. £160 8·00

The ½d., 1d. and 5s. are known imperf, probably from proof sheets.

For the 3d. of this issue see Nos. 36 and 39.

ONE PENNY (7)

THREE PENCE (8)

(Surch by Saul Solomon & Co, Cape Town)

1874–6. *Nos. 25a and 26a surch with T* **7**.
32 4 1d. on 6d. deep lilac (R.) (1.9.74) .. £275 45·00
a. "E" of "PENNY" omitted .. .. — £650
33 1d. on 1s. green (11.76) .. .. 35·00 22·00

These provisionals are found with the bar only, either across the centre of the stamp or at top, with value only; or with value and bar close together, either at top or foot. Such varieties are due to misplacement of sheets during surcharging.

1879 (1 Nov). *No. 30 surch with T* **8**.
34 6 3d. on 4d. blue (R.) .. .. .. 70·00 90
a. "PENCB" for "PENCE" £1300 £275
b. "THE.EE" for "THREE" £1600 £350
c. Surch double £6500 £2750
d. Variety b. double .. .. ..

The double surcharge must also have existed showing variety a. but only variety b. is known.

There are numerous minor varieties, including letters broken or out of alignment, due to defective printing and use of poor type.

The spacing between the bar and the words varies from 16½ to 18 mm.

THREEPENCE (9) 3 (10) 3 (11)

(Surch by D.L.R.)

1880 (Feb). *Special printing of the 4d. in new colour, surch, with T* **9**. *Wmk Crown CC.*
35 6 3d. on 4d. pale dull rose .. .. 38·00 1·50

A minor constant variety exists with foot of "P" in "PENCE" broken off, making the letter appear shorter.

1880 (1 July). *Wmk Crown CC. P 14.*
36 6 3d. pale dull rose .. .. .. £130 11·00

(Surch by Saul Solomon & Co, Cape Town)

1880 (Aug). *No. 36 surch.*
37 10 "3" on 3d. pale dull rose .. .. 32·00 75
a. Surch inverted .. .. .. £650 40·00
b. Vert pair. Nos. 37/8 .. .. £450 £250
38 11 "3" on 3d. pale dull rose .. .. 90·00 3·00
a. Surch inverted £6500 £900

The "3" (T **10**) is sometimes found broken. Vertical pairs are known showing the two types of surcharge *se-tenant*, and vertical strips of three exist, the top stamp having surcharge T **10**, the middle stamp being without surcharge, and the lower stamp having surcharge T **11** *(price for strip of 3 un. £3000).*

1881 (Jan). *Wmk Crown CC. P 14.*
39 6 3d. pale claret .. .. 60·00 1·75
a. Deep claret .. .. 65·00 1·50

This was a definite colour change made at the request of the Postmaster-General owing to the similarity between the colours of the 1d. stamp and the 3d. in pale dull rose. Imperf copies are probably from proof sheets.

Proofs of this value were printed in brown, on unwatermarked wove paper and imperf, but the colour was rejected as unsuitable.

1882 (July). *Wmk Crown CA. P 14.*
40 6 3d. pale claret .. .. 5·50 90
a. Deep claret .. .. 6·50 75

One Half-penny. (12)

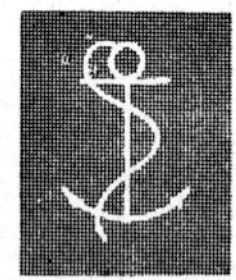
13 "Cabled Anchor"

(Surch by Saul Solomon & Co, Cape Town)

1882 (July). *Nos. 39a and 40a surch with T* **12**.
41 6 ½d. on 3d. deep claret (Wmk CC) .. £1600 £120
a. Hyphen omitted .. .. .. — £3250
42 ½d. on 3d. deep claret (Wmk CA) .. 3·50 2·00
a. "p" in "penny" omitted £2000 £700
b. "y" in "penny" omitted £1000
c. Hyphen omitted £450 £350

Varieties also exist with broken and defective letters, and with the obliterating bar omitted or at the top of the stamp.

1882–83. *Wmk Crown CA. P 14.*
43 6 ½d. black (1.9.82) .. .. .. 7·50 40
a. Grey-black .. .. .. 3·50 15
44 1d. rose-red (7.82) .. .. .. 23·00 15
a. Deep rose-red .. .. .. 22·00 15
45 2d. pale bistre (1.9.82) .. .. .. 55·00 15
a. Deep bistre .. .. .. 60·00 10
46 4 6d. mauve (to bright) (8.82) .. .. 48·00 70
47 6 5s. orange (8.83) £700 £200

Imperf pairs of the ½d., 1d., and 2d. are known, probably from proof sheets.

For the 3d. stamp with this watermark see No. 40.

1884–90. W **13**. *P 14.*
48 6 ½d. black (1.86) .. .. 1·00 10
a. Grey-black .. .. 1·00 10
49 1d. rose-red (12.85) .. .. .. 1·00 10
a. Carmine-red .. .. .. 1·00 10
50 2d. pale bistre (12.84) .. .. .. 8·00 20
a. Deep bistre .. .. .. 2·25 10
51 4d. blue (6.90) .. .. 3·25 15
a. Deep blue .. .. 3·00 15
52 4 6d. reddish purple (12.84) .. .. 50·00 1·60
a. Purple (shades) .. .. .. 2·75 15
b. Bright mauve .. .. .. 9·00 40
53 1s. yellow-green (12.85) .. .. 70·00 3·00
a. Blue-green (1889) .. .. .. 20·00 30
54 6 5s. orange (7.87) .. .. .. 45·00 3·00
48/54 .. .. *Set of 7* 65·00 3·50

All the above stamps are known in imperf pairs, probably from proof sheets.

For later shade and colour changes, etc., see Nos. 59, etc.

2½d (14)

CAPE OF GOOD HOPE 2½ POSTAGE 2½ PENCE
15

ONE PENNY. (16)

(Surch by D.L.R.)

1891 (Mar). *Special printing of the 3d. in new colour, surch with T* **14**.

No.	Type	Description	Unused	Used
55	**6**	2½d. on 3d. pale magenta	2·75	70
		a. Deep magenta	90	20
		b. "1" with horiz serif	42·00	32·00

No. 55b occurs on two stamps (Nos. 8 and 49) of the pane of 60.

Two types of "d" are found in the surcharge, one with square end to serif at top, and the other with pointed serif.

1892 (June). *W* **13**. *P* 14.

No.	Type	Description	Unused	Used
56	**15**	2½d. sage-green	1·50	10
		a. Olive-green	4·00	55

(Surch by W. A. Richards & Sons, Cape Town)

1893 (Mar). *Nos. 50/a surch with T* **16**.

No.	Type	Description	Unused	Used
57	**6**	1d. on 2d. pale bistre	1·75	10
		a. Deep bistre	70	10
		b. No stop after "PENNY"	32·00	11·00
		c. Surch double	—	£400

No. 57b occurs on stamp No. 42 of the upper left-hand pane, and on No. 6 of the lower right-hand pane.

Minor varieties exist showing broken letters and letters out of alignment or widely spaced. Also with obliterating bar omitted, due to misplacement of the sheet during surcharging.

17 "Hope" standing. Table Bay in background

18 Table Mountain and Bay with Arms of the Colony

(Des Mr. Mountford. Typo D.L.R.)

1893 (Oct). *W* **13**. *P* 14.

No.	Type	Description	Unused	Used
58	**17**	1d. rose-red	45	10
		a. Carmine	30	10

The above stamp is known in imperf pairs, probably from proof sheets.

1893–98. *New colours, etc. W* **13**. *P* 14.

No.	Type	Description	Unused	Used
59	**6**	½d. pale yellow-green (12.96)	85	10
		a. Green	2·50	20
60		2d. chocolate-brown (3.97)	1·25	10
61	**15**	2½d. pale ultramarine (3.96)	1·75	15
		a. Ultramarine	1·50	10
62	**6**	3d. bright magenta (9.98)	2·00	40
63		4d. sage-green (3.97)	3·25	45
64		1s. blue-green (12.93)	20·00	50
		a. Deep blue-green	40·00	5·00
65		1s. yellow-ochre (5.96)	5·50	35
66		5s. brown-orange (6.96)	42·00	3·50
59/66		*Set of* 8	70·00	5·00

1898–1902. *W* **13**. *P* 14.

No.	Type	Description	Unused	Used
67	**17**	½d. green (9.98)	30	10
68		3d. magenta (3.02)	3·00	50

(Des E. Sturman. Typo D.L.R.)

1900 (Jan). *W* **13**. *P* 14.

No.	Type	Description	Unused	Used
69	**18**	1d. carmine	35	10

19

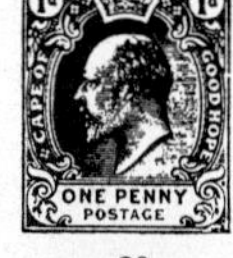

20

21

22

23

24

25

26

27

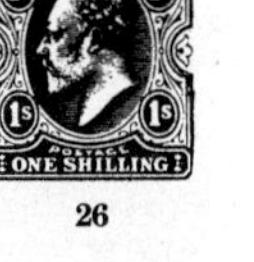

(Typo D.L.R.)

1902 (Dec)–**04**. *W* **13**. *P* 14.

No.	Type	Description	Unused	Used
70	**19**	½d. green	40	10
71	**20**	1d. carmine	40	10
72	**21**	2d. brown (10.04)	2·25	55
73	**22**	2½d. ultramarine (3.04)	2·50	4·50
74	**23**	3d. magenta (4.03)	2·25	30
75	**24**	4d. olive-green (2.03)	3·00	55
76	**25**	6d. bright mauve (3.03)	3·00	30
77	**26**	1s. yellow-ochre	5·50	40
78	**27**	5s. brown-orange (2.03)	35·00	6·50
70/8		*Set of* 9	48·00	12·00

All values exist in imperf pairs, from proof sheets.

Cape of Good Hope became a province of the Union of South Africa on 31 May 1910.

BRITISH KAFFRARIA

The history of the Cape eastern frontier was punctuated by a series of armed conflicts with the native population, known as the Kaffir Wars. After a particularly violent outbreak in 1846 the Governor, Sir Harry Smith, advanced the line of the Cape frontier to the Keikama and Tyumie Rivers. In the area between the new frontier and the Kei River a buffer state, British Kaffraria, was established on 17 December 1847. This area was not annexed to the Cape, but was administered as a separate Crown dependency by the Governor of Cape Colony in his capacity as High Commissioner for South Africa.

The territory, with its administration based on King William's Town, used the stamps of the Cape of Good Hope from 1853 onwards, the mail being sent via Port Elizabeth or overland from the Cape. Covers from British Kaffraria franked with the triangular issues are rare.

The first postal marking known from British Kaffraria is the 1849 type octagonal numeral No. 47 from Port Beaufort. Oval postmarks of the 1853 type were used at Alice, Aliwal North, Bedford, Fort Beaufort, King William's Town and Queenstown. In 1864 numeral cancellations were issued to all post offices within the Cape system and it is known that the following numbers were initially assigned to post towns in Kaffraria: 4 (King William's Town), 7 (Bedford), 11 (Queenstown), 29 (East London), 32 (Fort Beaufort), 38 (Aliwal North) and 104 (Cathcart).

It is believed that post offices may have also existed at Adelaide, Barkly East, Sterkstoom and Stutterheim, but, to date, no examples of handstamps or cancellations are known from them during the British Kaffraria period.

Following the decimation by famine of the Xhosa tribes in 1857 British Kaffraria was annexed to Cape Colony in 1865. The area eventually formed the basis of the Ciskei independent "homeland".

MAFEKING SIEGE STAMPS

PRICES FOR STAMPS ON COVER

Nos. 1/16	*from* × 7
Nos. 17/22	*from* × 8

23 MARCH to 17 MAY 1900

There are numerous forgeries of the Mafeking overprints, many of which were brought home by soldiers returning from the Boer War.

MAFEKING,
3d.
BESIEGED.
(1)

MAFEKING
3d.
BESIEGED.
(2)

(Surcharged by Townsend & Co, Mafeking)

1900 (23 Mar–25 Apr). *Various stamps surch as T* **1** *and* **2**.

(A) *Cape of Good Hope stamps surch as T* **1** (23 Mar)

No.	Type	Description	Unused	Used
1	**6**	1d. on ½d. green	£150	48·00
2	**17**	1d. on ½d. green (24.3)	£180	55·00
3		3d. on 1d. carmine	£150	48·00
4	**6**	6d. on 3d. magenta (24.3)	£6500	£250
5		1s. on 4d. sage-green (24.3)	£3500	£325

A variety in the setting of each value exists without comma after "MAFEKING".

(B) *Nos. 59 and 61/3 of Bechuanaland Protectorate surch as T* **1**

No.	Type	Description	Unused	Used
6		1d. on ½d. vermilion (28.3)	£150	48·00
		a. Surch inverted	†	£3750
		b. Vert pair, surch tête-bêche	†	£7000
7		3d. on 1d. lilac (4.4)	£850	65·00
		a. Surch double	†	£6000
8		6d. on 2d. green and carmine (6.4)	£1000	65·00
9		6d. on 3d. purple/*yellow* (30.3)	£3000	£250
		a. Surch inverted	†	£12000
		b. Surch double		

(C) *Nos. 12 and 35 of British Bechuanaland surch as T* **1**

No.	Type	Description	Unused	Used
10		6d. on 3d. lilac and black (27.3)	£400	60·00
11		1s. on 4d. green and purple-brown (29.3)	£1200	65·00
		a. Surch double	†	£11000
		b. Surch treble	†	£12000
		c. Surch double, one inverted	†	£12000

(D) *Nos. 61/2 and 65 of Bechuanaland Protectorate surch as T* **2** (25 Apr)

No.	Type	Description	Unused	Used
12		3d. on 1d. lilac	£900	55·00
		a. Surch double	†	£6000
13		6d. on 2d. green and carmine	£1100	60·00
14		1s. on 6d. purple/*rose-red*	£2750	80·00

(E) *Nos. 36/7 of British Bechuanaland surch as T* **2**

No.	Type	Description	Unused	Used
15		1s. on 6d. purple/*rose-red* (3.5)	£6000	£600
16		2s. on 1s. green (25.4)	£5500	£300

No. 11a has both surcharges T **1**. Copies exist with normal surcharge T **1** and the second surcharge T **2** but are believed to be trials (*Price* £3750, *unused or used*).

On the stamps overprinted "BECHUANALAND PROTECTORATE" and "BRITISH BECHUANALAND" the local surcharge is so adjusted as not to overlap the original overprint.

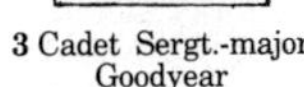

3 Cadet Sergt.-major Goodyear

4 General Baden-Powell

(Des Dr. W. A. Hayes (T **3**), Capt. H. Greener (T **4**))

1900 (7–11 Apr). *Produced photographically by Dr. D. Taylor. Horiz laid paper with sheet wmk* "OCEANA FINE". *P* 12.

(*a*) 18½ *mm wide*. (*b*) 21 *mm wide*

No.	Type	Description	Unused	Used
17	**3**	1d. pale blue/*blue*	£800	£250
18		1d. deep blue/*blue*	£800	£275
19	**4**	3d. pale blue/*blue* (*a*)	£1100	£400
		a. Reversed design	£30000	£20000
20		3d. deep blue/*blue* (*a*)	£1200	£325
		a. Imperf between (horiz pair)	†	£35000
		b. Double print	†	£12000
21		3d. pale blue/*blue* (*b*) (11.4)	£6000	£700
22		3d. deep blue/*blue* (*b*) (11.4)	£6500	£950

These stamps vary a great deal in colour from deep blue to pale grey.

No. 18 in an imperforate pair is now believed to be a proof. The only known example is untrimmed and without gum.

No. 19a comes from a sheet of 12 printed in reverse.

VRYBURG

PRICES FOR STAMPS ON COVER

Nos. 1/4	*from* × 5
Nos. 11/12	*from* × 2

BOER OCCUPATION

Vryburg was occupied by Boer forces on 15 October 1899. Unoverprinted stamps of Transvaal were used initially. Nos. 1/4 were only available from 24 to 29 November. The Boers evacuated the town on 7 May 1900.

½ PENCE
Z.A.R.
(1)

1899 (24 Nov). *Cape stamps surch as T* **1**. *A. Surch* 10 *mm high. B. Surch* 12 *mm high.*

No.	Type	Description	A. Unused	A. Used	B. Unused	B. Used
1	**6**	½ PENCE, green	£200	90·00	£1600	£700
2	**17**	1 PENCE, rose	£250	£110	£1800	£800
3	**4**	2 PENCE on 6d. mauve		†	£2250	£500
4	**15**	2½ pence, blue	£2000	£425	£10000	£4250

Nos. 1A, 2A, 4A and 3B are known with italic "Z" in the surcharge. *Prices from* 6 *times normal.*

BRITISH REOCCUPATION

V. R.
SPECIAL
POST
(2)

1900 (May). *Provisionals issued by the Military Authorities. Stamps of Transvaal handstamped with T* **2**.

No.	Type	Description	Unused	Used
11	**30**	½d. green	—	£1500
12		1d. carmine and green	£6500	£2500
13		2d. deep brown and green		
14		2½d. blue and green		

GRIQUALAND WEST

Griqualand West was situated to the North of Cape Colony, bounded on the north by what became British Bechuanaland and on the east by the Orange Free State.

The area was settled in the early nineteenth century by the Griqua tribal group, although many members of the tribe, including the paramount chief, migrated to Griqualand East (between Basutoland and the east coast of South Africa) in 1861–63. There was little European involvement in Griqualand West before 1866, but in that year the diamond fields along the Vaal River were discovered. Sovereignty was subsequently claimed by the Griqua Chief, the Orange Free State and the South African Republic (Transvaal). In 1871 the British authorities arbitrated in favour of the Griqua Chief who promptly ceded his territory to Great Britain. Griqualand West became a separate Crown Colony in January 1873.

During the initial stages of the prospecting boom mail was passed via the Orange Free State, but a post office connected to the Cape Colony postal system was opened at Klip Drift (subsequently Barkly) in late 1870. Further offices at De Beer's New Rush (subsequently Kimberley), Douglas and Du Toit's Pan (subsequently Beaconsfield) were open by September 1873.

Cape of Good Hope stamps were in use from October 1871, but those originating in Griqualand West can only be identified after the introduction of Barred Oval Diamond Numeral cancellations in 1873. Numbers known to have been issued in the territory are:

1 De Beers N.R. (New Rush) (subsequently Kimberley)
3 Junction R. & M. (Riet and Modder Rivers)
4 Barkly
6 or 9 Du Toit's Pan (subsequently Beaconsfield)
8 Langford (transferred to Douglas)
10 Thornhill

PRICES FOR STAMPS ON COVER

The stamps of Griqualand West are worth from ×10 the price quoted for used stamps, when on cover from the territory.

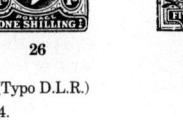

Stamps of the Cape of Good Hope, Crown CC, perf 14, overprinted.

1874 (Sept). *No. 24a of Cape of Good Hope surch "1d." in red manuscript by the Kimberley postmaster.*
1 1d. on 4d. blue £600 £1100

G. W.

1877 (Mar). *T* **6** *optd.* "G.W." *as above. (a) In black.*
2 1d. carmine-red .. .. £400 65·00
a. Overprint double .. .. .. † £1000
(b) In red
3 4d. blue .. .. £300 55·00

G (1) G (2) G (3) G (4) G (5) G (6)
G (7) G (8) G (9) G (10) G (11)
G (12) G (13) G (14)

1877 (Apr)–**78**. *T* **4** *(4d. (Nos. 17/23), 6d. and 1s.) and T* **6** *(others) optd with large capital letter. (a) First printing. Optd in black on 1d. or red (others). Seven principal varieties of opt (T* **1, 2, 3, 4, 5, 6,** *and* **8**).
4 **1** ½d. grey-black .. .. 10·00 11·00
5 **2** ½d. grey-black .. .. 20·00 22·00
6 **3** ½d. grey-black .. .. 13·00 14·00
7 **4** ½d. grey-black .. .. 20·00 22·00
8 **5** ½d. grey-black .. .. 25·00 27·00
9 **6** ½d. grey-black .. .. 13·00 14·00
10 **8** ½d. grey-black .. ..
11 **1** 1d. carmine-red .. .. 10·00 6·50
12 **2** 1d. carmine-red .. .. 21·00 17·00
13 **3** 1d. carmine-red .. .. 13·00 9·50
14 **4** 1d. carmine-red .. .. 21·00 17·00
15 **5** 1d. carmine-red .. .. 35·00 24·00
16 **6** 1d. carmine-red .. .. 12·00 8·50
17 **1** 4d. blue (T **4**) .. .. 90·00 16·00
18 **2** 4d. blue (T **4**) .. .. £200 60·00
19 **3** 4d. blue (T **4**) .. .. £160 26·00
20 **4** 4d. blue (T **4**) .. .. £200 80·00
21 **5** 4d. blue (T **4**) .. .. £275 95·00
22 **6** 4d. blue (T **4**) .. .. £130 26·00
23 **8** 4d. blue (T **4**) .. ..
24 **1** 4d. blue (T **6**) .. .. 70·00 10·00
25 **2** 4d. blue (T **6**) .. .. — 40·00
26 **3** 4d. blue (T **6**) .. .. 95·00 15·00
27 **4** 4d. blue (T **6**) .. .. £150 40·00
28 **5** 4d. blue (T **6**) .. .. £200 55·00
29 **6** 4d. blue (T **6**) .. .. 95·00 15·00
30 **8** 4d. blue (T **6**) £950
31 **1** 6d. dull violet .. .. 48·00 15·00
32 **2** 6d. dull violet .. .. £110 45·00
33 **3** 6d. dull violet .. .. 60·00 18·00
34 **4** 6d. dull violet .. .. £110 45·00
35 **5** 6d. dull violet .. .. £150 60·00
36 **6** 6d. dull violet .. .. 60·00 18·00
37 **8** 6d. dull violet .. ..
38 **1** 1s. green .. .. 60·00 11·00
a. Opt inverted .. .. .. — £250
39 **2** 1s. green .. .. £120 23·00
a. Opt inverted .. .. ..
40 **3** 1s. green .. .. 75·00 13·00
41 **4** 1s. green .. .. £120 23·00
a. Opt inverted .. .. ..
42 **5** 1s. green .. .. £170 30·00
43 **6** 1s. green .. .. 75·00 13·00
a. Opt inverted .. .. ..
44 **8** 1s. green .. ..
45 **1** 5s. orange .. .. £250 10·00
46 **2** 5s. orange .. .. — 25·00
47 **3** 5s. orange .. .. £300 13·00
48 **4** 5s. orange .. .. — 25·00
49 **5** 5s. orange .. .. £550 35·00
50 **6** 5s. orange .. .. £300 13·00
51 **8** 5s. orange £1400

The setting of the above was in two panes of 60. Sub-types of Types **1** and **2** are found. The 1d., Type **8**, of this setting can only be distinguished when *se-tenant* with Type **3**.

(b) Second printing, in black for all values. Nine principal varieties of opt (T **6** *to* **14**) (1878)
52 **7** 1d. carmine-red .. .. 16·00 11·00
53 **8** 1d. carmine-red .. .. 27·00 19·00
54 **9** 1d. carmine-red .. .. 17·00 13·00
55 **10** 1d. carmine-red .. .. 55·00 50·00
56 **11** 1d. carmine-red .. .. 35·00 27·00
57 **12** 1d. carmine-red .. .. 50·00 45·00
58 **13** 1d. carmine-red .. .. 85·00 75·00
59 **14** 1d. carmine-red £350 £300
60 **6** 4d. blue (T **6**) .. .. £160 38·00
61 **7** 4d. blue (T **6**) .. .. 55·00 12·00
62 **8** 4d. blue (T **6**) .. .. £160 38·00
63 **9** 4d. blue (T **6**) .. .. 65·00 14·00
64 **10** 4d. blue (T **6**) .. .. £275 75·00
65 **11** 4d. blue (T **6**) .. .. £180 42·00
66 **12** 4d. blue (T **6**) .. .. £225 55·00
67 **13** 4d. blue (T **6**) £400 £140
68 **14** 4d. blue (T **6**) .. .. — £325
69 **6** 6d. dull violet .. .. £250 90·00
70 **7** 6d. dull violet .. .. £120 50·00
a. Opt double .. ..
71 **8** 6d. dull violet .. .. £250 90·00
72 **9** 6d. dull violet .. .. £160 60·00
a. Opt double .. .. .. — £450
73 **10** 6d. dull violet £325 £130
74 **11** 6d. dull violet .. .. £275 95·00
75 **12** 6d. dull violet £300 £120
76 **13** 6d. dull violet £450 £180
77 **14** 6d. dull violet £1100 £375

The 1d., T **6**, of this printing can only be distinguished from the same variety of the first printing when it is *se-tenant* with another type.

The type without horizontal or vertical serifs, previously illustrated as T 10, is a broken "G" of the type now shown under that number.

Minor varieties may be found of T **7** and **12**.

Red overprints on the 4d., 1s. and 5s. Type **7** and 1s. and 5s. Type **8** exist but there is no evidence as to their status.

G (15) G (16) G (17)

1878 (July)–**79**. *T* **4** *(4d. (Nos. 86/7), 6d. and 1s.) and T* **6** *(others) optd with small capital letter. (a) First printing, in red or in black.*
(i) *Red overprint*
78 **15** ½d. grey-black .. .. 4·50 6·00
a. Opt inverted .. .. 6·00 6·00
b. Opt double .. .. 32·00
c. Opt double, both inverted .. .. 55·00
79 **16** ½d. grey-black .. .. 6·00 6·00
a. Opt inverted .. .. 6·00 7·50
b. Opt double .. .. 55·00 55·00
c. Opt double, both inverted .. ..
80 **15** 4d. blue (T **6**) .. .. £200 75·00
a. Opt inverted .. .. £650 55·00
81 **16** 4d. blue (T **6**) .. .. — 60·00
a. Opt inverted .. .. £200 60·00
(ii) *Black overprint*
82 **15** ½d. grey-black .. .. £140 75·00
a. Opt inverted £140
b. Black opt normal with additional red opt T **15** inverted £275
c. Ditto, but red opt is T **16** .. .. 75·00
83 **16** ½d. grey-black .. .. 25·00 25·00
a. Opt inverted .. .. 25·00 25·00
b. Black opt normal, with additional red opt T **15** inverted .. .. 95·00
84 **15** 1d. carmine-red .. .. 6·00 4·25
a. Opt inverted .. .. 6·00 6·00
b. Ditto, with additional red opt T **15** inverted .. .. 21·00 23·00
c. Ditto, with additional red opt T **16** inverted .. ..
d. Opt double .. .. £130 32·00
e. Opt double, both inverted .. .. £130 48·00
85 **16** 1d. carmine-red .. .. 6·00 6·00
a. Opt inverted .. .. 50·00 20·00
b. Ditto with additional red opt T **16** inverted .. .. 50·00 50·00
c. Opt double .. .. — 60·00
d. Opt double, both inverted .. .. — 75·00
86 **15** 4d. blue (T **4**) .. .. — 90·00
87 **16** 4d. blue (T **4**) .. .. — 95·00
88 **15** 4d. blue (T **6**) .. .. 50·00 14·00
a. Opt inverted .. .. £140 60·00
b. Opt double .. .. — £140
c. Opt double, both inverted .. .. — £190
89 **16** 4d. blue (T **6**) .. .. £100 7·50
a. Opt inverted .. .. £150 20·00
b. Opt double .. .. — £150
c. Opt double, both inverted .. .. — £190
90 **15** 6d. dull violet .. .. 55·00 16·00
91 **16** 6d. dull violet .. .. — 16·00
(b) Second printing, in black only (1879)
92 **17** ½d. grey-black .. .. 6·00 4·75
a. Opt double £225 £225
93 1d. carmine-red .. .. 6·00 3·50
a. Opt inverted .. .. — 75·00
b. Opt double .. .. — £120
c. Opt treble .. .. — £160
94 4d. blue (T **6**) .. .. 10·00 3·50
b. Opt double .. .. — 95·00
95 6d. mauve .. .. 70·00 6·00
a. Opt inverted .. .. — 23·00
b. Opt double £400 £140
96 1s. green .. .. 45·00 3·50
a. Opt double .. .. £190 80·00
97 5s. orange .. .. £225 6·00
a. Opt double .. .. £300 60·00
b. Opt treble .. .. — £250

Besides the type shown above, which is the normal, there are in this printing three or four minor varieties differing in the shape and size of the body of the letter. In this setting are also found at least two varieties very like the upright "antique" of the first printing in small capitals.

Beware of forged overprints.

Griqualand West was merged with Cape Colony in October 1880. The remaining stock of the overprinted stamps was returned from Kimberley to Cape Town and redistributed among various post offices in Cape Colony where they were used as ordinary Cape stamps.

NATAL

PRICES FOR STAMPS ON COVER

Nos. 1/7	*from* × 2
Nos. 9/25	*from* × 3
Nos. 26/56	*from* × 4
Nos. 57/8	—
Nos. 59/65	*from* × 4
Nos. 66/73	*from* × 5
Nos. 76/84	*from* × 4
Nos. 85/93	*from* × 3
Nos. 96/103	*from* × 6
Nos. 104/5	*from* × 5
Nos. 106/25	*from* × 6
Nos. 127/42	*from* × 4
Nos. 143/5a	—
Nos. 146/57	*from* × 4
No. 162	—
Nos. 165/71	*from* × 3
No. F1	—
Nos. O1/6	*from* × 10

1 2 3 4 5

(Embossed in plain relief on coloured wove paper)

1857 (26 May, *the 1d. in* **1858**). *Imperf.*
1 **1** 1d. rose .. .. — £1700
2 1d. buff .. .. — £950
3 1d. blue .. .. — £1100
4 **2** 3d. rose .. .. — £400
a. *Tête-bêche* (pair) .. .. .. — £10000
5 **3** 6d. green .. .. — £1100
6 **4** 9d. blue .. .. — £7000
7 **5** 1s. buff .. .. — £5500

All the above have been reprinted more than once, and the early reprints of some values cannot always be distinguished with certainty from originals.

Stamps on surface-coloured paper, perforated 12½, are fiscals.

NOTE. The value of the above stamps depends on their dimensions, and the clearness of the embossing, but our prices are for fine used.

6

7

(Eng C. H. Jeens. Recess P.B.)

1859–60. *No wmk. P* 14.
9 **6** 1d. rose-red .. .. £120 70·00
10 3d. blue .. .. £100 42·00
a. Imperf between (vert pair) .. .. † £3500

No. 10a is only known from a cover of 1867 franked with two such pairs.

1861. *No wmk. Intermediate perf* 14 *to* 16.
11 **6** 3d. blue .. .. £170 65·00

1862. *No wmk. Rough perf* 14 *to* 16.
12 **6** 3d. blue .. .. 85·00 32·00
a. Imperf between (pair) £1600
b. Imperf (pair) .. .. — £1100
13 6d. grey .. .. £130 45·00

1862. *Wmk Small Star. Rough perf* 14 *to* 16.
15 **6** 1d. rose-red .. .. £100 55·00

The 1d. and 3d. wmk. Star, imperf, are proofs, and are therefore not included. The 3d. wmk Star, perforated, is believed to exist only with forged watermark.

(Recess D.L.R.)

1863. *Thick paper. No wmk. P* 13.
18 **6** 1d. lake .. .. 75·00 27·00
19 1d. carmine-red .. .. 75·00 20·00

1864. *Wmk Crown CC. P* 12½.
20 **6** 1d. brown-red .. .. £110 35·00
21 1d. rose .. .. 80·00 27·00
22 1d. bright-red .. .. 80·00 27·00
23 6d. lilac .. .. 50·00 15·00
24 6d. violet .. .. 38·00 25·00

(Typo D.L.R.)

1867 (April). *Wmk Crown CC. P* 14.
25 **7** 1s. green .. .. £120 26·00

1869 (23 Aug). *Optd horiz in Natal. No wmk* (3d.), *wmk Crown CC* (*others*). *P* 14 *or* 14–16 (3d.), 12½ (1d., 6d) *or* 14 (1s.).

POSTAGE

Tall capitals

26 **6** 1d. rose .. £225 50·00
27 1d. bright red .. £225 50·00
28 3d. blue (No. 10) ..
28*a* 3d. blue (No. 11) .. £350 £190
28*b* 3d. blue (No. 12) .. £225 70·00
29 6d. lilac .. — 55·00
30 6d. violet .. £300 55·00
31 **7** 1s. green .. — £950

Postage.

12¾ mm long

32 **6** 1d. rose .. £225 50·00
33 1d. bright red .. £225 50·00
a. Opt double .. — £475
34 3d. blue (No. 10) .. — £200
34*a* 3d. blue (No. 11) .. £350 £160
34*b* 3d. blue (No. 12) .. £325 65·00
35 6d. lilac .. £300 50·00
36 6d. violet .. £225 50·00
37 **7** 1s. green .. — £375

Postage.

13¾ mm long

38 **6** 1d. rose .. £350 95·00
39 1d. bright red .. — 95·00
40 3d. blue (No. 10) ..
40*a* 3d. blue (No. 11) ..
40*b* 3d. blue (No. 12) .. £800 £250
41 6d. lilac .. — £120
42 6d. violet .. £700 £120
43 **7** 1s. green .. — £1400

Postage.

14½ to 15½ mm long

44 **6** 1d. rose .. £350 £190
45 1d. bright red .. £400 £170
46 3d. blue (No. 10) ..
46*a* 3d. blue (No. 11) .. — £190
46*b* 3d. blue (No. 12) .. — £190
47 6d. lilac .. — 60·00
48 6d. violet .. £800 65·00
49 **7** 1s. green .. — £1400

POSTAGE.

With a stop

50 **6** 1d. rose .. 65·00 25·00
51 1d. bright red .. £120 25·00
52 3d. blue (No. 10) .. £170 50·00
53 3d. blue (No. 11) .. £100 38·00
54 3d. blue (No. 12) .. £130 35·00
a. Opt double .. — £600
54*b* 6d. lilac .. £100 48·00
55 6d. violet .. 95·00 45·00
56 **7** 1s. green .. £100 48·00

All values exist with this overprint at top or bottom of stamp.

POSTAGE

(8)

1870. *No.* 25 *optd with T* **8**.

57 **7** 1s. green (C.) .. £3000
58 1s. green (Blk.) .. £1500 £950
a. Opt double .. £2750 £1000
59 1s. green (G.) .. 45·00 10·00

For 1s. orange, see No. 108.

POSTAGE POSTAGE (9)   POSTAGE (10)   POSTAGE POSTAGE (11)

1870–73. *Optd with T* **9**. *Wmk Crown CC. P* 12½.

60 **6** 1d. bright red .. 55·00 13·00
61 3d. bright blue (R.) .. 55·00 13·00
62 6d. mauve .. £100 25·00

1873 (July). *Optd up centre of stamp with T* **10**. *Wmk Crown CC. P* 14.

63 **7** 1s. purple-brown .. 85·00 16·00

1874 (July). *No.* 21 *optd with T* **11**.

65 **7** 1d. rose .. £120 50·00
a. Opt double

12   13   14

15

16

(Typo D.L.R.)

1874–78. *Wmk Crown CC. P* 14.

66 **12** 1d. dull rose .. 19·00 1·60
67 1d. bright rose .. 19·00 1·60
68 **13** 3d. blue .. 70·00 13·00
a. Perf 14 × 12½ .. £1300 £850
69 **14** 4d. brown (1878) .. 85·00 10·00
a. Perf 12½ .. £300 65·00
70 **15** 6d. lilac .. 29·00 6·00
71 **16** 5s. maroon .. 90·00 28·00
a. Perf 15½ × 15 .. £110 70·00
72 5s. rose .. 65·00 26·00
73 5s. carmine (H/S S. £160) .. 60·00 28·00

The 5s. stamps normally have wmk sideways.

POSTAGE (17)   POSTAGE (18)   ½ HALF (19)

1875. *Wmk Crown CC. P* 14 (1s.) *or* 12½ (*others*). (*a*) *Optd with T* **17**.

76 **6** 1d. rose .. 80·00 35·00
a. Opt double .. £475 £425
77 1d. bright red .. 80·00 48·00

(*b*) *Optd with T* **18** (14½ *mm long, without stop*)

81 **6** 1d. rose .. 70·00 45·00
a. Opt inverted .. £700 £400
82 1d. yellow .. 70·00 65·00
83 6d. violet .. 48·00 5·50
a. Opt double .. — £550
b. Opt inverted .. £650 £150
84 **7** 1s. green .. 70·00 4·50
a. Opt double .. — £325

TYPE 19. There are several varieties of this surcharge, of which T **19** is an example. They may be divided as follows:

(*a*) "½" 4½ mm high, "2" has straight foot.
(*b*) As last but "½" is 4 mm high.
(*c*) As last but "2" has curled foot.
(*d*) "½" 3½ mm. high, "2" has straight foot.
(*e*) As last but "2" has curled foot.
(*f*) As last but "2" smaller.

As the "½" and "HALF" were overprinted separately, they vary in relative position, and are frequently overlapping.

1877 (13 Feb). *No.* 66 *surch as T* **19**.

85 **12** ½d. on 1d. rose (*a*) .. 18·00 60·00
a. "½" double ..
86 ½d. on 1d. rose (*b*) .. 90·00
87 ½d. on 1d. rose (*c*) .. 80·00
88 ½d. on 1d. rose (*d*) .. 42·00
89 ½d. on 1d. rose (*e*) .. 45·00
90 ½d. on 1d. rose (*f*) .. 45·00

POSTAGE Half-penny (21)

23

ONE HALF-PENNY. (24)

1877–79. *T* **6** (*wmk Crown CC, P* 12½) *surch as T* **21**.

91 ½d. on 1d. yellow .. 8·00 11·00
a. Surch inverted .. £200 £200
b. Surch double .. £200 £200
c. Surch omitted (lower stamp, vertical pair) £950 £850
d. "POSTAGE" omitted (in pair with normal) .. £1000
e. "S" of "POSTAGE" omitted .. £180 £170
f. "T" of "POSTAGE" omitted .. £180
92 1d. on 6d. violet .. 40·00 8·00
a. "S" of "POSTAGE" omitted .. £250 £150
93 1d. on 6d. rose .. 85·00 27·00
a. Surch inverted .. — £160
b. Surch double .. — £190
c. Surch double, one inverted .. £250 £250
d. Surch four times .. £325 £160
e. "S" of "POSTAGE" omitted .. £250

No. 93c. is known with one surcharge showing variety "S" of "POSTAGE" omitted.

Other minor varieties exist in these surcharges.

(Typo D.L.R.)

1880 (13 Oct). *Wmk Crown CC. P* 14.

96 **23** ½d. blue-green .. 8·00 10·00
a. Imperf between (vert pair) ..

1882–89. *Wmk Crown CA. P* 14.

97 **23** ½d. blue-green .. 80·00 14·00
a. Dull green .. 50 20
99 **12** 1d. rose (*shades*) .. 65 10
a. Carmine .. 1·90 15
100 **13** 3d. blue .. 85·00 17·00
101 3d. grey (11.89) .. 1·50 95
102 **14** 4d. brown .. 2·50 65
103 **15** 6d. mauve .. 3·00 70
97*a*/103 .. *Set of* 6 85·00 17·00
97*a*, 99*a*, 101/3 H/S "Specimen" .. *Set of* 5 £250

1885 (26 Jan). *No.* 99 *surch with T* **24**.

104 **12** ½d. on 1d. rose .. 16·00 11·00

TWO PENCE (25)

26

TWOPENCE HALFPENNY (27)

1886. *No.* 101 *surch with T* **25** *by D.L.R.*

105 **13** 2d. on 3d. grey .. 18·00 5·50

(Typo D.L.R.)

1887–89. *Wmk Crown CA. P* 14.

106 **26** 2d. olive-green Die I* (Optd S. £60) .. 21·00 75
107 2d. olive-green, Die II (H/S S. £60) .. 1·50 75

*The differences between Dies I and II are shown in the Introduction.

1888 (16 Mar). *As No.* 84, *but colour changed and wmk Crown CA, optd with T* **8** *by D.L.R.*

108 **7** 1s. orange (C.) (H/S S. £90) .. 3·25 85
a. Opt double .. — £1500

1890. *Surch locally with T* **27**.

109 **14** 2½d. on 4d. brown (H/S S. £50) .. 11·00 8·50
a. "TWOPENGE" .. 60·00 60·00
b. "HALFPENN" .. £225 £180
c. Surch double .. £250 £180
d. Surch inverted .. £325 £250

28

POSTAGE. Half-Penny (29)

POSTAGE. Varieties of long-tailed letters

(Typo D.L.R.)

1891 (June). *Wmk Crown CA. P* 14.

113 **28** 2½d. bright blue (H/S S. £60) .. 3·00 50

1895 (12 Mar). *No.* 24 *surch with T* **29** *in carmine.*

114 ½d. on 6d. violet (H/S S. £50) .. 1·00 2·75
a. "Ealf-Penny" .. 18·00 20·00
b. "Half-Penny" and long "P" .. 15·00
ba. "Half Penny" and long "T" and "A" .. 15·00
c. No stop after "POSTAGE" and long "P", "T" and "A" .. 15·00
d. Long "P" .. 2·00 3·50
e. Long "T" .. 2·00 3·50
f. Long "A" .. 3·00 4·25
g. Long "P" and "T" .. 2·00 3·50
h. Long "P" and "A" .. 2·00 3·50
i. Long "T" and "A" .. 2·75 4·00
k. Long "P", "T" and "A" .. 2·75 4·00
ka. Long "P", "T" and "A" with comma after "POSTAGE" .. 6·00 8·50
l. Surcharge double, one vertical .. £250

No. 114 is known with surcharge double and widely spaced, but the second surcharge is extremely faint.

The surcharge was applied as a setting of 60 (12×5) which contained sixteen normals, one each of Nos. 114a, 114b, 114ba, 114c, eight of No. 114d, six of 114e, three of 114f, six of 114g, seven of 114h, four each of Nos. 114i and 114k, and two of No. 114ka.

HALF (30)

31

32

1895 (18 Mar). *No.* 99 *surch with T* **30**.

125 HALF on 1d. rose (*shades*) (H/S S. £50) .. 70 75
a. Surch double .. £325 £325
b. "H" with longer left limb .. 20·00
c. Pair, one without surcharge ..

No. 125b occurs on the second, fourth, sixth etc., stamps of the first vertical row of the righthand pane. It was very soon corrected.

In some printings what appears to be a broken "E" (with the top limb removed) was used instead of "L" in "HALF" on the last stamp in the sheet (*Price* £30)

(Typo D.L.R.)

1902–3. *Inscr* "POSTAGE REVENUE". *Wmk Crown CA. P* 14.
127 31 ½d. blue-green 65 15
128 1d. carmine 80 15
129 1½d. green and black 90 90
130 2d. red and olive-green 80 25
131 2½d. bright blue 90 3·00
132 3d. purple and grey 80 30
133 4d. carmine and cinnamon 2·50 7·00
134 5d. black and orange 1·25 2·25
135 6d. green and brown-purple 1·25 1·10
136 1s. carmine and pale blue 3·50 1·10
137 2s. green and bright violet 42·00 9·00
138 2s. 6d. purple 32·00 12·00
139 4s. deep rose and maize 50·00 40·00
a. Imperf between (horiz pair)
127/139 *Set of* 13 £120 70·00
127/39 Optd "Specimen" *Set of* 13 £150

No. 139a is also imperforate between stamp and left-hand margin.

(Typo D.L.R.)

1902–3. *Wmk Crown CC. P* 14.
140 32 5s. dull blue and rose 16·00 7·50
141 10s. deep rose and chocolate 48·00 23·00
142 £1 black and bright blue £110 42·00
143 £1 10s. green & violet (Optd S. £65) £200 65·00
144 £5 mauve and black (Optd S. £100) £1300 £250
145 £10 green and orange (Optd S. £250) £6000 £2250
145*a* £20 red and green (Optd S. £400) £12000
140/2 Optd "Specimen" *Set of* 3 £110

USED HIGH VALUES. Collectors are warned against fiscally used high value Natal stamps with penmarks cleaned off and forged postmarks added.

1904–8. *Wmk Mult Crown CA. Chalk-surfaced paper* (£1 10s.). *P* 14.
146 31 ½d. blue-green 1·50 15
147 1d. rose-carmine 1·50 15
148 1d. deep carmine 2·50 20
149 2d. red and olive-green 1·75 3·25
152 4d. carmine and cinnamon 1·75 1·00
153 5d. black and orange (1908) 2·50 2·75
155 1s. carmine and pale blue 48·00 6·00
156 2s. dull green and bright violet 38·00 22·00
157 2s. 6d. purple 35·00 25·00
162 32 £1 10s. brown-orange and deep purple (1908) (Optd S. £170) £1100
146/157 *Set of* 9 £110 55·00

1908–9. *Inscr* "POSTAGE POSTAGE". *Wmk Mult Crown CA. P* 14.
165 31 6d. dull and bright purple 4·50 2·00
166 1s. black/*green* 6·00 2·00
167 2s. purple and bright blue/*blue* 15·00 3·00
168 2s. 6d. black and red/*blue* 25·00 3·00
169 32 5s. green and red/*yellow* 18·00 16·00
170 10s. green and red/*green* 48·00 48·00
171 £1 purple and black/*red* £225 £150
165/71 *Set of* 7 £300 £200
165/71 Optd "Specimen" *Set of* 7 £200

FISCALS USED FOR POSTAGE

1869. *Embossed on coloured wove, surfaced paper. P* 12½.
F1 1 1d. yellow 50·00 80·00

Examples of 1d. yellow and 6d. rose values as Type **6**, 1s. purple-brown as Type **7** and various values between 5s. and £10 in the design illustrated above are believed to exist postally used, but, as such use was not authorised, they are not now listed.

OFFICIAL STAMPS

OFFICIAL

(O 1)

1904. *T* **31**, *wmk Mult Crown CA, optd with Type* O **1**. *P* 14.
O1 ½d. blue-green 3·00 35
O2 1d. carmine 1·50 60
O3 2d. red and olive-green 11·00 7·50
O4 3d. purple and grey 7·00 4·00
O5 6d. green and brown-purple 24·00 25·00
O6 1s. carmine and pale blue 60·00 £100
O1/6 *Set of* 6 95·00 £120

The use of stamps overprinted as above was discontinued after 30 May 1907. Stamps perforated with the letters "N.G.R." were for use on Government Railways.

Natal became a province of the Union of South Africa on 31 May 1910.

NEW REPUBLIC

During the unrest following the death of Cetshwayo, the Zulu king, in 1884, a group of Boers from the Transvaal offered their support to his son, Dinizulu. The price for this support was the cession of a sizeable portion of Zulu territory to an independent Boer republic. The New Republic, centred on Vryheid, was proclaimed on 16 August 1884 with the remaining Zulu territory becoming a protectorate of the new administration.

Alarmed by these developments the British authorities annexed the southernmost part of the land grant, around St. Lucia Bay, to prevent access to the Indian Ocean. The remainder of the New Republic was, however, recognised as independent on 22 October 1886. Zululand was annexed by the British on 22 May 1887.

Difficulties beset the New Republic, however, and its Volksraad voted for union with the South African Republic (Transvaal). The two republics united on 21 July 1888. In 1903 the territory of the former New Republic was transferred to Natal.

Mail from Vryheid in 1884–85 was franked with issues of Transvaal (for dispatches made via Utrecht) or Natal (for those sent via Dundee). Issues of the New Republic were never accepted as internationally valid by these administrations so that all external mail continued to show Transvaal or Natal stamps used in combination with those of the republic.

PRICES FOR STAMPS ON COVER
Nos. 1/95 *from* × 10

1

Printed with a rubber handstamp on paper bought in Europe and sent out ready gummed and perforated.

1886 (7 Jan)–**87.** *Various dates indicating date of printing. P* 11½.

A. *Without Arms.* (i) *Yellow paper*
1 1 1d. black (9.1.86) — £2500
2 1d. violet (9.1.86) 10·00 12·00
a. "1d." omitted (in pair with normal) (24.4.86) £1500
3 2d. violet (9.1.86) 10·00 15·00
a. "d" omitted (13.10.86)
4 3d. violet (13.1.86) 23·00
a. "d" omitted (13.10.86)
5 4d. violet (30.8.86) 35·00
6 6d. violet (20.2.86) 30·00
a. "6d." omitted (in pair with normal) (2.7.86)
7 9d. violet (13.1.86) 30·00
8 1s. violet (30.8.86) 65·00
a. "1s." omitted (in pair with normal) (6.9.86)
9 1/s. violet (13.10.86) £500
10 1/6 violet (30.8.86) 65·00
11 1s. 6d. violet (6.9.86) £500
a. "d" omitted (13.10.86) 85·00
12 2s. violet (30.8.86) 38·00
a. *Tête-bêche* (pair) (6.9.86) £475
13 2/6 violet (13.1.86) £150
14 2s. 6d. violet (20.1.86) 95·00
15 4/s. violet (17.1.87) £400
16 5s. violet (1.86) 28·00 30·00
a. "S" omitted (in pair with normal) (7.3.86) £2000
17 5/6 violet (20.2.86) 35·00
18 5s. 6d. violet (13.1.86) £160
19 7/6 violet (13.1.86) £170
20 7s. 6d. violet (24.5.86) 95·00
21 10s. violet (13.1.86) 95·00
22 10s. 6d. violet (7.1.86) £170
a. "d" omitted (1.86) 48·00
23 13s. violet (24.11.86) £400
24 £1 violet (13.1.86) £120
25 30s. violet (13.1.86) 95·00
a. *Tête-bêche* (pair) (24.11.86) £700

(ii) *Blue granite paper*
26 1 1d. violet (20.1.86) 13·00 14·00
a. "d" omitted (24.11.86) £375
b. "1" omitted (in pair with normal) (24.11.86)
27 2d. violet (13.1.86) 13·00 14·00
a. "d" omitted (24.4.86) £750
b. "2d." omitted (in pair with normal) (24.4.86)
28 3d. violet (13.10.86) 16·00 18·00
a. *Tête-bêche* (pair) (13.10.86) £325
29 4d. violet (24.5.86) 13·00 16·00
30 6d. violet (24.5.86) 25·00 21·00
a. "6" omitted (in pair with normal) (24.5.86) £1500
31 9d. violet (6.9.86) 24·00
32 1s. violet (1.86) 28·00 30·00
a. *Tête-bêche* (pair) (21.5.86) £400
b. "1s." omitted (in pair with normal) (29.4.86) £1300
33 1s. 6d. violet (2.7.86) 35·00
a. *Tête-bêche* (pair) (6.9.86) £475
34 1/6 violet (6.9.86) £150
35 2s. violet (21.5.86) £120
a. "2s" omitted (in pair with normal) (24.5.86) £1500
36 2s. 6d. violet (19.8.86) £140
37 2/6 violet (19.8.86) £180
38 4/s. violet (17.1.87) £200
39 5s. 6d. violet (13.1.86) £170
40 1 5/6 violet (13.1.86) £200
a. "/" omitted (13.1.87)
41 7/6 violet (13.1.86) £200
41*a* 7s. 6d. violet (13.1.86)
42 10s. violet (1.86) £200 £200
a. *Tête-bêche* (pair) (2.7.86) £500
b. "s" omitted (13.1.86)
43 10s. 6d. violet (7.1.86) £200
a. *Tête-bêche* (pair) (13.1.86)
b. "d" omitted (2.7.86) £450
44 12s. violet (13.1.86) £300
45 13s. violet (17.1.87) £400
46 £1 violet (13.1.86) £250
47 30s. violet (13.1.86) £250

B. *With embossed Arms of New Republic.* (i) *Yellow paper*
48 1 1d. violet (20.1.86) 13·00 15·00
a. Arms inverted (20.1.86) 25·00 25·00
b. Arms *tête-bêche* (pair) (14.4.86) £100 £120
49 2d. violet (2.12.86) 13·00 15·00
a. Arms inverted (24.11.86) 23·00 28·00
50 4d. violet (2.12.86) 18·00 22·00
a. Arms inverted (12.86) 95·00 60·00
b. Arms *tête-bêche* (pair) (12.86) £250
51 6d. violet (2.12.86) 45·00

(ii) *Blue granite paper*
52 1 1d. violet (20.1.86) 14·00 16·00
a. Arms inverted (10.2.86) 35·00 40·00
b. Arms *tête-bêche* (pair) (3.11.86)
53 2d. violet (30.8.86) 14·00 16·00
a. Arms inverted (30.8.86) 48·00
b. Arms *tête-bêche* (pair) (2.12.86) £500 £500

Stamps as Type **1** were produced as and when stocks were required, each printing including in its design the date on which it was prepared. The dates quoted above for Nos. 1/53 are those on which the various stamps first appeared. Details of the various printing dates are given below. From these dates it can be seen that some values share common printing dates, and, it is believed, that the different values were produced *se-tenant* within the same sheet, at least in some instances. A reported proof sheet in the Pretoria Postal Museum, on yellow paper and embossed, contains 4 examples of the 6d. value and 3 each of the 3d., 4d., 9d., 1s., 1/6, 2/-, 2/6, 3s., 4s., 5s., 5/6, 7/6, 10/-, 10/6, £1 and 30/-.

The significance, if any, of the two coloured papers and the use of the embossing machine have never been satisfactorily explained. Both the different papers and the embossing machine were introduced in January 1886, and occur throughout the period that the stamps with dates were used.

PRINTINGS

Date	*Paper*	*Face value*	*Cat. No.*	*Un.*	*Us.*
Jan 86	*Yellow*	5s.	16	28·00	30·00
		10s. 6d.	22a	80·00	
	Blue	1s.	32		
		10s.	42	£200	£200
7 Jan 86	*Yellow*	10s. 6d.	22	£160	
	Blue	10s.	42		
		10s. 6d.	43	£450	
9 Jan 86	*Yellow*	1d.	1		— £2500
		1d.	2	10·00	12·00
		2d.	3	10·00	15·00
13 Jan 86	*Yellow*	1d.	2	35·00	
		2d.	3	14·00	15·00
		3d.	4	40·00	
		9d.	7	£200	
		2/6	13	£160	
		5s. 6d.	18		
		7/6	19	£170	
		10s.	21		
		£1	24	£130	
		30s	25	95·00	
	Blue	2d.	27		
		5s. 6d.	39	£170	
		5/6	40	£200	
		7/6	41	£200	
		7s. 6d.	41a		
		10s.	42	£400	
		10s.	42b		
		10s. 6d.	43	£200	
		10s. 6d.	43a		
		12s.	44	£300	
		£1	46	£250	
		30s.	47	£250	
20 Jan 86	*Yellow*	1d.	2		
		2s. 6d.	14		
	Blue	1d.	26	£250	
	Yellow, embossed	1d.	48	32·00	
		1d.	48a	48·00	
	Blue, embossed	1d.	52	95·00	
Jan 20 86	*Blue*	1d.	26	23·00	
	Yellow, embossed	1d.	48a		
	Blue, embossed	1d.	52	£100	
24 Jan 86	*Blue*	1d.	26	18·00	
		2d.	27	30·00	
10 Feb 86	*Yellow*	1d.	2		
	Yellow, embossed	1d.	48		
		1d.	48a	48·00	
	Blue, embossed	1d.	52	£130	
		1d.	52a	35·00	
20 Feb 86	*Yellow*	6d.	6		
		2s. 6d.	14	£130	
		5/6	17	£120	
		5s. 6d.	18		
7 Mar 86	*Yellow*	1d.	2	£110	
		2/6	13		
		2s. 6d.	14	95·00	
		5s.	16	£200	85·00
		5s.	16a		
		5/6	17	35·00	
		5s. 6d.	18	£160	
	Blue	2d.	27	95·00	
		1s.	32		
17 Mar 86	*Yellow*	1d.	2	95·00	
	Yellow, embossed	1d.	48	48·00	
	Blue, embossed	1d.	52	95·00	
		1d.	52a	80·00	
26 Mar 86	*Blue, embossed*	1d.	52a	£130	
14 Apr 86	*Yellow*	1d.	2		
	Yellow, embossed	1d.	48	23·00	
		1d.	48a	£120	
		1d.	48b	£100	£120
	Blue, embossed	1d.	52	45·00	
		1d.	52a		

Date	Paper	Face value	Cat. No.	Un.	Us.
24 Apr 86	*Yellow*	1d.	2	£100	
		1d.	2a	£1500	
		5s.	16		
	Blue	2d.	27	28·00	
		2d.	27a	£750	
		2d.	27b		
		1s.	32		
29 Apr 86	*Blue*	1s.	32	£110	
		1s.	32b		
21 May 86	*Yellow*	6d.	6	£130	
	Blue	1d.	26	85·00	
		1s.	32	28·00	30·00
		1s.	32a	£400	
		1s.	32b	£1500	
		2s.	35	£325	
23 May 86	*Yellow, embossed*	1d.	48		
	Blue, embossed	1d.	52a	95·00	
24 May 86	*Yellow*	1d.	2	95·00	
		2d.	3	£120	
		5s.	16	70·00	
		7/6	19	£170	
		7s. 6d.	20	95·00	
	Blue	1d.	26	13·00	14·00
		2d.	27		
		4d.	29	85·00	
		6d.	30	£120	
		6d.	30a		
		1s.	32	£200	
		1s.	32b		
		2s.	35	£120	
		2s.	35a	£1500	
26 May 86	*Yellow*	1d.	2		
	Blue	1d.	26	£110	
	Yellow, embossed	1d.	48	£250	
		1d.	48a	95·00	
	Blue, embossed	1d.	52	£130	
		1d.	52a	48·00	50·00
28 May 86	*Yellow, embossed*	1d.	48	32·00	
30 Jun 86	*Yellow*	1d.	2		
	Blue	1d.	26		
Jun 30 86	*Blue*	1d.	26	15·00	16·00
	Yellow, embossed	1d.	48	14·00	16·00
		1d.	48a	25·00	28·00
		1d.	48b	£200	£225
	Blue, embossed	1d.	52	45·00	40·00
2 Jul 86	*Yellow*	6d.	6		
		6d.	6a		
		9d.	7	95·00	95·00
	Blue	1s.	32		
		1s. 6d.	33	35·00	
		10s.	42	£400	
		10s.	42a	£500	
		10s. 6d.	43		
		10s. 6d.	43b		
7 Jul 86	*Yellow*	1d.	2		
	Blue	1d.	26		
		10s. 6d.	43		
	Yellow, embossed	1d.	48	25·00	
		1d.	48a	95·00	95·00
	Blue, embossed	1d.	52	14·00	16·00
		1d.	52a	55·00	40·00
Jul 7 86	*Blue, embossed*	1d.	52		
		1d.	52a	70·00	
4 Aug 86	*Yellow*	1d.	2		
	Yellow, embossed	1d.	48	55·00	
	Blue, embossed	1d.	52	35·00	
		1d.	52a		
19 Aug 86	*Yellow*	2/6	13		
		2s. 6d.	14	£140	
	Blue	2s. 6d.	36	£140	
		2/6	37	£180	
30 Aug 86	*Yellow*	1d.	2	10·00	12·00
		2d.	3	11·00	
		3d.	4	23·00	
		4d.	5	48·00	
		6d.	6	32·00	
		9d.	7	48·00	
		1s.	8	65·00	
		1/6	10	65·00	
		2s.	12	95·00	
		2/6	13	£150	
	Blue	1d.	26		
		2d.	27	13·00	14·00
	Yellow, embossed	1d.	48		
	Blue, embossed	2d.	53	42·00	
		2d.	53a	£110	
6 Sep 86	*Yellow*	1d.	2	12·00	
		2d.	3	8·50	9·00
		3d.	4	38·00	
		4d.	5	40·00	
		6d.	6	30·00	

Date	Paper	Face value	Cat. No.	Un.	Us.
		9d.	7	30·00	
		1s.	8	95·00	
		1s.	8a		
		1/6	10	70·00	
		1s. 6d.	11	£500	
		2s.	12	£100	
		2s.	12a	£475	
		2/6	13	£150	
		2s. 6d.	14		
		5s.	16	£140	
		7s. 6d.	20	£200	
		10s.	21	95·00	
		£1	24	£120	
	Blue	6d.	30	20·00	21·00
		9d.	31	95·00	
		1s.	32	65·00	
		1s.	32b	£1300	
		1s. 6d.	33	£140	
		1s. 6d.	33a	£475	
		1/6	34		
		2/6	37	£400	
		10s. 6d.	43		
13 Sep 86	*Yellow*	1d.	2		
	Yellow, embossed	1d.	48	48·00	
		1d.	48a	48·00	
	Blue, embossed	1d.	52	85·00	
6 Oct 86	*Yellow*	1d.	2		
	Blue	1d.	26	85·00	
	Yellow, embossed	1d.	48	23·00	18·00
		1d.	48a		
	Blue, embossed	1d.	52	45·00	18·00
		1d.	52a	85·00	
13 Oct 86	*Yellow*	1d.	2	12·00	12·00
		2d.	3	10·00	11·00
		2d.	3a		
		3d.	4	23·00	25·00
		3d.	4a		
		4d.	5	35·00	
		6d.	6	30·00	32·00
		9d.	7	35·00	
		1s.	8	70·00	
		1/s.	9	£500	
		1/6	10	£150	
		1s. 6d.	11a	85·00	
		2s.	12	38·00	
		2/6	13	£160	
		5s.	16	42·00	
		10s.	21	95·00	£100
		10s. 6d.	22a	48·00	
		£1	24	£120	
	Blue	2d.	27	13·00	14·00
		3d.	28	16·00	18·00
		3d.	28a	£325	
		4d.	29	28·00	28·00
		1s.	32	28·00	
		1/6	34	£150	
		2s.	35	£120	
3 Nov 86	*Yellow*	1d.	2	28·00	
		9d.	7		
	Blue	1d.	26		
	Yellow, embossed	1d.	48	13·00	15·00
		1d.	48a	25·00	28·00
		1d.	48b	£100	£120
	Blue, embossed	1d.	52	14·00	
		1d.	52a	35·00	40·00
		1d.	52b		
13 Nov 86	*Yellow*	1d.	2	35·00	
24 Nov 86	*Yellow*	1d.	2	14·00	
		2d.	3	10·00	11·00
		3d.	4	30·00	32·00
		1/6	10		
		10s.	21	£200	
		13s.	23	£400	
		30s.	25	95·00	
		30s.	25a	£700	
	Blue	1d.	26	38·00	17·00
		1d.	26a	£375	
		1d.	26b		
		2d.	27	18·00	
		2d.	27a		
		4d.	29	13·00	16·00
		6d.	30	20·00	21·00
		9d.	31	24·00	
		1s.	32	45·00	48·00
		1/6	34	£160	
		2s.	35	£140	
	Yellow, embossed	2d.	49	£160	
		2d.	49a		
26 Nov 86	*Yellow*	1/6	10	£140	
2 Dec 86	*Yellow*	1d.	2		
		2d.	3		

Date	Paper	Face value	Cat. No.	Un.	Us.
	Yellow, embossed	1d.	48	13·00	15·00
		1d.	48a	£160	
		2d.	49	13·00	15·00
		2d.	49a	23·00	28·00
		4d.	50	80·00	
		6d.	51	45·00	
	Blue, embossed	1d.	52	28·00	
		1d.	52a	£160	
		2d.	53	14·00	16·00
		2d.	53a	48·00	
		2d.	53b	£500	£500
Dec 86	*Yellow*	6d.	6		
	Blue	4d.	29		
		6d.	30		
	Yellow, embossed	4d.	50	18·00	22·00
		4d.	50a	95·00	60·00
		4d.	50b	£250	
		6d.	51	42·00	
4 Jan 87	*Yellow*	1d.	2	35·00	
		2d.	3	32·00	
		13s.	23	£400	
	Blue	1d.	26	13·00	14·00
		2d.	27	16·00	14·00
	Blue, embossed	2d.	53	42·00	
13 Jan 87	*Blue*	5/6	40	£400	
		5/6	40a		
		7/6	41	£400	
17 Jan 87	*Yellow*	1d.	2	38·00	
		2d.	3	30·00	
		3d.	4	45·00	
		4/s.	15	£200	
	Blue	1d.	26	75·00	
		4/s.	38	£200	
		13s.	45	£400	
		30s.	47	£250	
20 Jan 87	*Blue*	2d.	27	32·00	
	Yellow, embossed	2d.	49	50·00	
		2d.	49a	£140	
	Blue, embossed	2d.	53	42·00	
		2d.	53a	95·00	
Jan 20 87	*Yellow, embossed*	1d.	48a	£400	

1887 (Feb–Mar). *As T* **1**, *but without date. With embossed Arms.*

(a) Blue granite paper

72 1d. violet .. .. 14·00 14·00
- a. Imperf between (pair) .. .. ..
- b. Stamps *tête-bêche* (pair) £325
- c. Arms *tête-bêche* (pair) .. .. ..
- d. Arms inverted .. .. 23·00 23·00
- e. Arms omitted £110 £110
- f. Arms sideways .. ..

73 2d. violet .. .. 8·50 8·50
- a. Stamps *tête-bêche* (pair) £325
- b. Arms inverted .. .. 23·00 23·00
- c. Arms omitted .. .. £110 95·00
- d. Arms *tête-bêche* (pair) .. .. ..

74 3d. violet .. .. 13·00 13·00
- a. Stamps *tête-bêche* (pair) £375
- b. Arms *tête-bêche* (pair) .. .. ..
- c. Arms inverted .. .. 48·00 48·00

75 4d. violet .. .. 13·00 13·00
- a. Stamps *tête-bêche* (pair) £325
- b. Arms *tête-bêche* (pair) £275
- c. Arms inverted .. .. 85·00

76 6d. violet .. .. 13·00 13·00
- a. Arms inverted .. .. 85·00

77 1/6 violet .. .. 14·00 14·00
- a. Arms inverted .. .. 80·00

77*b* 2/6d. violet .. .. — £750

(b) Yellow paper (March 1887)

78 2d. violet (*arms omitted*) .. .. .. 13·00 –

79 3d. violet .. .. 13·00 13·00
- a. Imperf between (pair) .. .. ..
- b. Stamps *tête-bêche* (pair) £325 £350
- c. Arms *tête-bêche* (pair) £200
- d. Arms inverted .. .. 23·00 23·00
- da. Double impression .. .. ..

80 4d. violet .. .. 13·00 13·00
- a. Arms inverted .. .. 14·00 14·00

81 6d. violet .. .. 8·00 8·00
- a. Arms *tête-bêche* (pair) £350
- b. Arms inverted .. .. 42·00 42·00
- c. Arms omitted .. .. 80·00
- ca. Double impression .. .. ..

82 9d. violet .. .. 8·50 8·50
- a. Arms inverted £200
- b. Arms *tête-bêche* (pair) £350

83 1s. violet .. .. 8·50 8·50
- a. Arms inverted .. .. 70·00

84 1/6 violet .. 17·00 14·0
85 2s. violet .. 18·00 16·00
a. Arms inverted .. 55·00 50·00
b. Arms omitted .. 70·00
86 2/6 violet .. 23·00 23·00
a. Arms inverted .. 28·00 28·00
87 3s. violet .. 42·00 42·00
a. Arms inverted .. 45·00 45·00
b. Stamps *tête-bêche* (pair) .. £450
88 4s. violet .. 11·00 11·00
a. Arms omitted (4s.) .. £180
b. Arms omitted (4/-) .. £130
89 5s. violet .. 13·00 13·00
a. Imperf between (pair)
b. Arms inverted .. — 80·00
90 5/6 violet .. 12·00 12·00
91 7/6 violet .. 14·00 17·00
a. Arms *tête-bêche* (pair)
a. Arms inverted .. 45·00
92 10s. violet .. 12·00 12·00
a. Imperf between (pair)
b. Arms *tête-bêche* (pair) .. £120
c. Arms inverted .. 23·00
d. Arms omitted .. £110 45·00
93 10/6 violet .. 16·00 16·00
a. Imperf between (pair)
b. Arms inverted
94 £1 violet .. 45·00 45·00
a. Stamps *tête-bêche* (pair) .. £350 £375
b. Arms inverted .. 55·00
95 30s. violet .. £100

New Republic united with the South African Republic (Transvaal) on 21 July 1888. In 1903 the territory of the former New Republic was transferred to Natal.

ORANGE FREE STATE

PRICES FOR STAMPS ON COVER	
Nos. 1/9	*from* × 12
Nos. 10/13	*from* × 10
Nos. 18/19	*from* × 12
No. 20	—
Nos. 21/42	*from* × 10
Nos. 48/51	*from* × 20
Nos. 52/138	*from* × 10
Nos. 139/51	*from* × 7
Nos. F1/17	—
Nos. PF1/3	—
No. M1	—

1

(Typo D.L.R.)

1868 (1 Jan)–**94.** *P* 14.
1 1 1d. pale brown .. 2·25 55
2 1d. red-brown .. 2·25 35
3 1d. deep brown .. 3·50 40
4 6d. pale rose (1868) .. 10·00 3·75
5 6d. rose (1871) .. 3·50 3·25
6 6d. rose-carmine (1891) .. 10·00 12·00
7 6d. bright carmine (1894) .. 3·25 2·00
8 1s. orange-buff .. 50·00 5·00
9 1s. orange-yellow .. 10·00 1·50
a. Double print .. — £2500

4 4 4 4
(2) (*a*) (*b*) (*c*) (*d*)

1877. *No. 6 surcharged T* **2** (*a*) *to* (*d*).
10 1 4d. on 6d. rose (*a*) .. £180 45·00
a. Surch inverted .. — £550
b. Surch double (*a* + *c*)
c. Surch. double. one inverted (*a* + *c* inverted) .. — £1100
d. Surch double, one inverted (*a* inverted + *c*)
11 4d. on 6d. rose (*b*) .. £1100 £160
a. Surch inverted .. — £900
b. Surch double (*b* + *d*)
12 4d. on 6d. rose (*c*) .. 80·00 25·00
a. Surch inverted .. — £325
b. Surch double
13 4d. on 6d. rose (*d*) .. £110 35·00
a. Surch inverted .. £1000 £375

1878 (July). *P* 14.
18 1 4d. pale blue .. 9·00 2·50
19 4d. ultramarine .. 4·00 2·50
20 5s. green .. 8·50 9·00

1d. 1d. 1d. 1d. 1d. 1d.
(3) (*a*) (*b*) (*c*) (*d*) (*e*) (*f*)

Type 3: (*a*) Small "1" and "d." (*b*) Sloping serif. (*c*) Same size as (*b*), but "1" with straighter horizontal serif. (*d*) Taller "1" with horizontal serif and antique "d". (*e*) Same size as (*d*) but with sloping serif and thin line at foot. (*f*) as (*d*) but with Roman "d".

1881 (19 May). *No. 20 surch T* **3** (*a*) *to* (*f*) *with heavy black bar cancelling the old value.*
21 1 1d. on 5s. green (*a*) .. 40·00 10·00
22 1d. on 5s. green (*b*) .. 25·00 10·00
a. Surch inverted .. — £500
b. Surch double .. — £500
23 1d. on 5s. green (*c*) .. 80·00 40·00
a. Surch inverted .. — £600
b. Surch double .. — £700
24 1d. on 5s. green (*d*) .. 35·00 10·00
a. Surch inverted .. £600 £500
b. Surch double .. — £550
25 1d. on 5s. green (*e*) .. £250 £200
a. Surch inverted .. — £1300
b. Surch double .. — £1100
26 1d. on 5s. green (*f*) .. 35·00 10·00
a. Surch inverted .. — £450
b. Surch double .. — £500

No. 21 was the first printing in one type only. Nos. 22 to 25 constitute the second printing about a year later, and are all found on the same sheet; and No. 26 the third printing of which about half have the stop raised.

Owing to defective printing examples of Nos. 22 and 24/5 may be found with the obliterating bar at the top of the stamps or, from the top row, without the bar.

½d
(4)

1882 (Aug). *No. 20 surch with T* **4** *and with a thin black line cancelling old value.*
36 1 ½d. on 5s. green .. 2·50 3·25
a. Surch double .. £350 £300
b. Surch inverted

3d 3d 3d 3d 3d
(5) (*a*) (*b*) (*c*) (*d*) (*e*)

1882. *No. 19 surch with T* **5** (*a*) *to* (*e*) *with thin black line cancelling value.*
38 1 3d. on 4d. ultramarine (*a*) .. 48·00 22·00
a. Surch double .. — £650
39 3d. on 4d. ultramarine (*b*) .. 38·00 16·00
a. Surch double .. — £650
40 3d. on 4d. ultramarine (*c*) .. 25·00 16·00
a. Surch double .. — £650
41 3d. on 4d. ultramarine (*d*) .. 45·00 16·00
a. Surch double .. — £650
42 3d. on 4d. ultramarine (*e*) .. £110 60·00
a. Surch double .. — £750

Examples of Nos. 39 and 41/2 exist without the cancelling bar due to the misplacement of the surcharge.

1883–84. *P* 14.
48 1 ½d. chestnut .. 60 50
49 2d. pale mauve .. 2·75 40
50 2d. bright mauve .. 2·75 30
51 3d. ultramarine .. 1·75 2·00

For 1d. purple, see No. 68.

2d 2d 2d
(6) (*a*) (*b*) (*c*)

1888 (Sept–Oct). *No. 51 surch with T* **6**(*a*), (*b*) *or* (*c*).
(*a*) *Wide "2".* (*b*) *Narrow "2"*
52 1 2d. on 3d. ultramarine (*a*) (Sept) .. 25·00 9·00
a. Surch inverted .. — £700
53 2d. on 3d. ultramarine (*b*) .. 10·00 2·00
a. Surch inverted .. — £300
b. "2" with curved foot (*c*)

1d 1d 1d
(7) (*a*) (*b*) (*c*)

1890 (Dec)–**91.** *Nos. 51 and 19 surch with T* **7** (*a*) *to* (*c*).
54 1 1d. on 3d. ultramarine (*a*) .. 1·10 60
a. Surch double .. 75·00
c. "1" and "d" wide apart .. £140 £110
55 1d. on 3d. ultramarine (*b*) .. 5·00 2·50
a. Surch double .. £140 £160
57 1d. on 4d. ultramarine (*a*) .. 13·00 3·00
a. Surch double .. £120 £110
b. Surch double (*a* + *b*) .. £180
c. Surch triple
58 1d. on 4d. ultramarine (*b*) .. 70·00 48·00
a. Surch double .. £250 £250
59 1d. on 4d. ultramarine (*c*) .. £1000 £450
a. Surch double

The settings of the 1d. on 3d. and on 4d. are not identical. The variety (c) does not exist on the 3d.

2½d.
(8)

1892 (Oct). *No 51 surch with T* **8**.
67 1 2½d. on 3d. ultramarine .. 2·50 70
a. No stop after "d" .. 40·00

1894 (Sept). *Colour changed. P* 14.
68 1 1d. purple .. 60 30

ALTERED CATALOGUE NUMBERS

Any Catalogue numbers altered from the last edition are shown as a list in the introductory pages.

½d ½d ½d
(9) (*a*) (*b*) (*c*)
½d ½d ½d ½d
(*d*) (*e*) (*f*) (*g*)

Types (*a*) and (*e*) differ from types (*b*) and (*f*) respectively, in the serifs of the "1", but owing to faulty overprinting this distinction is not always clearly to be seen.

1896 (Sept). *No. 51 surch with T* **9** (*a*) *to* (*g*).
69 1 ½d. on 3d. ultramarine (*a*) .. 2·00 3·50
70 ½d. on 3d. ultramarine (*b*) .. 4·50 3·50
71 ½d. on 3d. ultramarine (*c*) .. 4·50 2·50
72 ½d. on 3d. ultramarine (*d*) .. 4·50 2·25
73 ½d. on 3d. ultramarine (*e*) .. 3·50 2·25
74 ½d. on 3d. ultramarine (*f*) .. 3·50 4·00
75 ½d. on 3d. ultramarine (*g*) .. 1·75 2·25
a. Surch double .. 12·00 10·00
b. Surch triple

The double and triple surcharges are often different types, but are always type (*g*), or in combination with type (*g*).

Double surcharges in the same type, but without the "d" and bar, also exist, probably from a trial sheet prepared by the printer. Both mint and used examples are known.

Halve
Penny.

2½
(10) (11)

1896. *No. 51 surch with T* **10**.
77 1 ½d. on 3d. ultramarine .. 35 50
(i) *Errors in setting*
78 1 ½d. on 3d. (no stop) .. 8·00 12·00
79 ½d. on 3d. ("Peuny") .. 8·50 12·00
(ii) *Surch inverted*
81 1 ½d. on 3d. .. 50·00
81*a* ½d. on 3d. (no stop)
81*b* ½d. on 3d. ("Peuny")
(iii) *Surch double, one inverted*
81c 1 ½d. on 3d. (Nos. 77 and 81) .. £180 £200
81*d* ½d. on 3d. (Nos. 77 and 81*a*) .. £450
81*e* ½d. on 3d. (Nos. 77 and 81*b*) .. £500
81*f* ½d. on 3d. (Nos. 81 and 78)
82 ½d. on 3d. (Nos. 81 and 79) .. — £425

Examples from the top horizontal row can be found without the bar due to the surcharge being misplaced.

Nos. 69 to 75 also exist surcharged as last but they are considered not to have been issued with authority.

1897 (1 Jan). *No. 51 surch with T* **11**. (*a*) *As in illustration.* (*b*) *With Roman "1" and antique "2" in fraction.*
83 1 2½d. on 3d. ultramarine (*a*) .. 1·25 80
83*a* 2½d. on 3d. ultramarine (*b*) .. £130 90·00

1897. *P* 14.
84 1 ½d. yellow (March) .. 60 35
85 ½d. orange .. 60 35
87 1s. brown (Aug) .. 6·50 1·50

The 6d. blue was prepared for use in the Orange Free State, but had not been brought into use when the stamps were seized in Bloemfontein. A few have been seen without the "V.R.I." overprint, but they were not authorized or available for postage. (*Price* £45.)

BRITISH OCCUPATION

V. R. I. V. R. I. V. R. I.
4d ½d ½d
31 (Level stops) (32) Thin "V" (Raised stops) (33) Thick "V"

V. R I.
Inserted "R"

(Surch by Curling & Co, Bloemfontein)

1900. *T* **1** *surch as T* **31**/**33** (2½d. *on* 3d. *optd "V.R.I." only*).
(*a*) *First printings surch as T* **31** *with stops level* (March)
101 ½d. on ½d. orange .. 1·00 1·00
a. No stop after "V" .. 15·00 15·00
b. No stop after "I" .. £150 £150
c. "½" omitted .. £160 £160
d. "I" omitted
e. "V.R.I." omitted .. £170
f. Value omitted .. £110
g. Small "½" .. 45·00 45·00
h. Surch double .. £130

102 1d. on 1d. purple 80 45
a. Error. Brown £600 £400
b. No stop after "V" 10·00 10·00
c. No stop after "R" £150 £160
d. No stop after "I"
e. "1" omitted £150
f. "I" omitted 55·00 55·00
g. "I" and stop after "R" omitted 65·00 65·00
h. "V.R.I." omitted £170
i. "d" omitted £300
j. Value omitted 90·00
k. Inverted stop after "R" £160
l. Wider space between "1" and "d" £100 £100
m. "V" and "R" close £150
n. Pair, one without surch £400
o. "V" omitted £650
103 2d. on 2d. bright mauve 45 65
a. No stop after "V" 9·00 11·00
b. No stop after "R" £250
c. No stop after "I" £250
d. "V.R.I." omitted £300
e. Value omitted
104 2½d. on 3d. ultramarine (*a*) 4·50 3·50
a. No stop after "V" 55·00 55·00
105 2½d. on 3d. ultramarine (*b*) £160 £160
106 3d. on 3d. ultramarine 90 75
a. No stop after "V" 11·00 11·00
b. Pair, one without surch £325
c. "V.R.I." omitted
d. Value omitted
107 4d. on 4d. ultramarine 3·75 4·75
a. No stop after "V" 45·00 45·00
108 6d. on 6d. bright carmine 35·00 35·00
a. No stop after "V" £250 £275
b. "6" omitted £300 £300
109 6d. on 6d. blue 2·25 3·00
a. No stop after "V" 26·00 26·00
b. "6" omitted 50·00 50·00
c. "V.R.I." omitted
110 1s. on 1s. brown 2·75 3·00
a. Error. Orange-yellow £2750 £2250
b. No stop after "V" 28·00 28·00
c. "1" omitted £100 £100
d. "1" omitted and spaced stop after "s" £110
e. "V.R.I." omitted £150 £150
f. Value omitted £150 £150
g. Raised stop after "s" 9·00 9·50
h. Wider space between "1" and "s" £150 £150
111 5s. on 5s. green 17·00 26·00
a. No stop after "V" £180 £180
b. "5" omitted £750 £750
c. Inverted stop after "R" £550 £550
d. Wider space between "5" and "s" £120 £120
e. Value omitted

All values are found with a rectangular, instead of an oval, stop after "R". Misplaced surcharges (upwards or sideways) occur.

(*b*) *Subsequent printings*. (i) *Surch as T* **32**

112 ½d. on ½d. orange 20 20
a. Raised and level stops mixed 1·40 1·60
b. Pair, one with level stops 8·00 12·00
c. No stop after "V" 2·00 2·00
d. No stop after "I" 24·00 24·00
e. "V" omitted £550
f. Small "½" 11·00 12·00
g. As a, and small "½" 11·00 12·00
i. Space between "V" and "R"
j. Value omitted
113 1d. on 1d. purple 20 20
a. Raised and level stops mixed 1·25 1·40
b. Pair, one with level stops 16·00 16·00
c. No stop after "V" 3·25 4·75
d. No stop after "R" 13·00 13·00
e. No stop after "I" 13·00 13·00
f. No stops after "V" and "I" £325
g. Surch inverted £300
h. Surch double 90·00 80·00
i. Pair, one without surch £180
j. Short figure "1" £100 £100
k. Space between "V" and "R" 70·00 75·00
l. Space between "R" and "I" 90·00
m. Space between "1" and "d" £160
n. Inserted "R" £300
114 2d. on 2d. bright mauve 35 30
a. Raised and level stops mixed 4·00 4·00
b. Pair, one with level stops 6·50 6·50
c. Surch inverted £275 £275
d. "I" raised
e. Pair, one without surch
f. No stop after "V" £1000
115 2½d. on 3d. ultramarine (*a*) £180 £160
a. Raised and level stops mixed
116 2½d. on 3d. ultramarine (*b*) £1200
117 3d. on 3d. ultramarine 30 30
a. Raised and level stops mixed 6·00 6·00
b. Pair, one with level stops 14·00 14·00
c. No stop after "V" £140 £140
d. No stop after "R" — £500
e. "I" omitted £400
f. Surch double £400
g. Surch double, one diagonal £350
h. Ditto, diagonal surch, with mixed stops £6500
n. Inserted "R"
o. Space between "3" and "d"
118 4d. on 4d. ultramarine 1·10 1·50
a. Raised and level stops mixed 6·00
b. Pair, one with level stops 14·00 14·00
119 6d. on 6d. bright carmine 35·00 48·00
a. Raised and level stops mixed £140 £140
b. Pair, one with level stops £200
120 6d. on 6d. blue 70 40
a. Raised and level stops mixed 6·00 6·00
b. Pair, one with level stops 14·00 14·00
c. No stop after "V" £500
d. No stop after "R"
e. Value omitted
121 1s. on 1s. brown 70 45
a. Error. Orange-yellow £1300 £1300
b. Raised and level stops mixed 9·00
c. Pair, one with level stops 20·00 22·00
f. "s" omitted
g. "V.R.I." omitted

122 5s. on 5s. green (H/S S. £50) 4·00 5·50
a. Raised and level stops mixed £300 £300
b. Pair, one with level stops £900
c. Short top to "5" 55·00 55·00

(ii) *Surch as T* **33**

123 ½d. on ½d. orange 85 50
124 1d. on 1d. purple 70 35
a. Inverted "1" for "I" 12·00 14·00
b. No stops after "R" and "I" 85·00 65·00
c. No stop after "R" 35·00 35·00
d. Surch double £300 £300
n. Inserted "R"
125 2d. on 2d. bright mauve 1·75 2·25
a. Inverted "1" for "I" 14·00 14·00
126 2½d. on 3d. ultramarine (*a*) £550 £650
127 2½d. on 3d. ultramarine (*b*)
128 3d. on 3d. ultramarine 2·50 3·25
a. Inverted "1" for "I" 70·00 45·00
b. Surch double
ba. Surch double, one diagonal £400
129 6d. on 6d. bright carmine £425
130 6d. on 6d. blue 4·25 7·50
131 1s. on 1s. brown 6·50 6·50
132 5s. on 5s. green (H/S S. £150) 23·00 32·00

Stamps with thick "V" occur in certain positions in *later* settings of the type with stops above the line (T **32**). *Earlier* settings with stops above the line have all stamps with thin "V".

Some confusion has previously been caused by the listing of certain varieties as though they occurred on stamps with thick "V", in fact they occur on stamps showing the normal thin "V", included in the settings which also contained the thick "V".

As small blocks of unsurcharged Free State stamps could be handed in for surcharging, varieties thus occur which are not found in the complete settings.

The inserted "R" variety occurs on positions 6 (T **32**) and 12 (T **33**) of the forme. The "R." of the original surcharge failed to print and the "R", but not the full stop, was added by the use of a handstamp. Traces of the original letter are often visible. The broken "V" flaw, also shown in the illustration, does not appear on No. 124n.

ORANGE RIVER COLONY

CROWN COLONY

ORANGE RIVER COLONY. (34) 4d (35) E. R. I. 6d (36)

1900 (10 Aug)–**02**. *Nos. 58a, 61a and 67 of Cape of Good Hope (wmk Cabled Anchor. P 14) optd with T* **34** *by W. A. Richards and Sons, Cape Town.*

133 ½d. green (13.10.00) 20 10
a. No stop 7·00 9·50
b. Opt double £550
134 1d. carmine (May 1902) 25 10
a. No stop 9·00 13·00
135 2½d. ultramarine 30 35
a. No stop 40·00 50·00
133/5 *Set of* 3 65 45

In the ½d. and 2½d., the "no stop" after "COLONY" variety was the first stamp in the left lower pane. In the 1d. it is the twelfth stamp in the right lower pane on which the stop was present at the beginning of the printing but became damaged and soon failed to print.

1902 (14 Feb). *Surch with T* **35** *by "Bloemfontein Express".*

136 4d. on 6d. on 6d. blue (No. 120) (R.) 50 60
a. No stop after "R" 30·00 30·00
b. No stop after "I"
c. Surch on No. 130 (Thick "V") 1·75 3·50
ca. Inverted "1" for "I" 4·75 7·00

1902 (Aug). *Surch with T* **36**.

137 1 6d. on 6d. blue 1·75 4·00
a. Surch double, one inverted
b. Wide space between "6" and "d" (R.4/2) 60·00 75·00

One Shilling * (37)

38 King Edward VII, Springbok and Gnu

1902 (Sept). *Surch with T* **37**.

138 1 1s. on 5s. green (O.) 3·50 5·00
a. Thick "V" 9·50 15·00
b. Short top to "5" 65·00 65·00
c. Surch double

(Typo D.L.R.)

1903 (3 Feb)–**04**. *Wmk Crown CA. P* 14.

139 **38** ½d. yellow-green (6.7.03) 3·75 75
140 1d. scarlet 75 10
141 2d. brown (6.7.03) 2·25 70
142 2½d. bright blue (6.7.03) 85 50
143 3d. mauve (6.7.03) 3·25 90
144 4d. scarlet and sage-green (6.7.03) 12·00 2·00
a. "IOSTAGE" for "POSTAGE" £800 £450
145 6d. scarlet and mauve (6.7.03) 4·75 70
146 1s. scarlet and bistre (6.7.03) 13·00 1·75
147 5s. blue and brown (31.10.04) 60·00 20·00
139/47 *Set of* 9 90·00 24·00
139/47 Optd "Specimen" *Set of* 9 £150

No. 144a occurs on R.10/2 of the upper left pane.

Several of the above values are found with the overprint "C.S.A.R.", in black, for use by the Central South African Railways.

1905 (Nov)–**09**. *Wmk Mult Crown CA. P* 14.

148 **38** ½d. yellow-green (28.7.07) 3·25 30
149 1d. scarlet 1·75 20
150 4d. scarlet and sage-green (8.11.07) 4·00 1·75
a. "IOSTAGE" for "POSTAGE" £180 £150
151 1s. scarlet and bistre (2.09) 24·00 7·25
148/51 *Set of* 4 30·00 8·50

POSTCARD STAMPS

From 1889 onwards the Orange Free State Post Office sold postcards franked with adhesives as Type 1, some subsequently surcharged, over which the State Arms had been overprinted.

There are five known dies of the Arms overprint which can be identified as follows:

(a) Shield without flags. Three cows (two lying down, one standing) at left. Point of shield complete.
(b) Shield with flags. Four cows (two lying down, two standing) at left (*illustrated*).
(c) Shield with flags. Three cows (one lying down, two standing) at left.
(d) Shield without flags. Three cows (one lying down, two standing) at left.
(e) Shield without flags. Three cows (two lying down, one standing) at left. Point of shield broken.

There are also other differences between the dies.

PRICES. Those in the left-hand column are for unused examples on complete postcard; those on the right for used examples off card. Examples used on postcard are worth more.

1889 (Feb). *No. 2 (placed sideways on card) optd Shield Type* (a).

P1 1 1d. red-brown 60·00 30·00
a. Optd Shield Type (b) 20·00 5·00

1891 (Aug). *No. 48 optd Shield Type* (b).

P2 1 ½d. chestnut 2·00 1·00
a. Optd Shield Type (c) 6·00 3·00
b. Optd Shield Type (d) 3·00 1·50
c. Optd Shield Type (e) 7·00 3·50

1892 (June). *No. 54 optd Shield Type* (b).

P3 1 1d. on 3d. ultramarine 60·00 35·00
a. Optd Shield Type (c) 7·00 2·00

1½d. (P 1) 1½d. (P 2) 1½d. (P 3)

1892 (Sept)–**95**. *Nos. 50/1 optd Shield Type* (b) *or* (d) (*No.* P6) *and surch with Types* P **1/3**.

P4 1 1½d. on 2d. bright mauve (Type P **1**) (11.92) 5·00 2·50
P5 1½d. on 2d. bright mauve (Type P **2**) (9.93) 2·00 1·00
a. Surch inverted
P6 1½d. on 2d. brt mauve (Type P **3**) (R.) (6.95) 7·00 3·00
P7 1½d. on 3d. ultramarine (Type P **1**) 5·00 1·50

No. P5a shows the stamp affixed to the card upside down with the surcharge correctly positioned in relation to the card.

½d. (P 4)

1895 (Aug). *No. 48 optd Shield Type* (e) *and surch with Type* P **4**.

P8 1 ½d. on ½d. chestnut 6·00 2·00

1897 (Mar). *No. 85 optd Shield Type* (d).

P9 1 ½d. orange 6·00 1·00
a. Optd Shield Type (e) 7·00 2·00

1½d. (P 5) 1½d. (P 6)

1897. *No. 50 optd Shield Type* (e) *and surch with Types* P **5/6**.

P10 1 1½d. on 2d. bright mauve (Type P **5**) (Mar) 3·00 2·00
P11 1½d. on 2d. bright mauve (Type P **6**) (Dec) 3·50 2·50
P12 1½d. on 2d. bright mauve (as Type P **6**, but without stop (Dec) 3·50 2·50

V.R.I. (P 7)

1900. *Nos.* P11/12 *optd as T* **31/2** *or with Type* P **7**.

P13 1 1½d. on 2d. bright mauve (No. P11) (T **31**) 15·00 4·00
P14 1½d. on 2d. bright mauve (No. P12) (T **31**) 15·00 4·00
P15 1½d. on 2d. bright mauve (No. P11) (T **32**) 15·00 4·00
P16 1½d. on 2d. bright mauve (No. P12) (T **32**) 15·00 4·00
P17 1½d. on 2d. brt mve (No. P11) (Type P **7**) 25·00 7·50
P18 1½d. on 2d. brt mve (No. P12) (Type P **7**) 25·00 7·50

NEW INFORMATION

The editor is always interested to correspond with people who have new information that will improve or correct the Catalogue.

POLICE FRANK STAMPS

The following frank stamps were issued to members of the Orange Free State Mounted Police ("Rijdende Dienst Macht") for use on official correspondence.

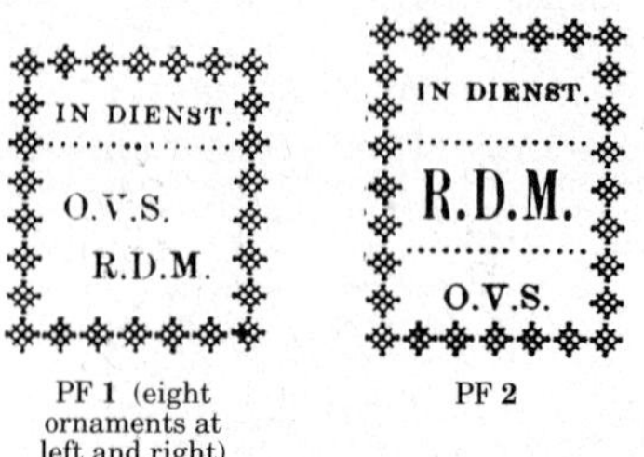

PF 1 (eight ornaments at left and right)   PF 2

1896. *P* 12.
PF1 PF **1** (–) Black .. ..
No. PF1 was printed in horizontal strips of 5 surrounded by wide margins.

1898. *As Type* PF **1**, *but with nine ornaments at left and right. P* 12.
PF2 (–) Black .. ..
No. PF2 was printed in blocks of 4 (2×2) surrounded by wide margins.

1899. *P* 12.
PF3 PF **2** (–) Black/*yellow* .. .. .. — 70·00
No. PF3 was printed in sheets of 24 (6×4) with the edges of the sheet imperforate. It is believed that they were produced from a setting of 8 (2×4) repeated three times.

Examples of No. PF3 are known postmarked as late as 28 April 1900. The O.F.S. Mounted Police were disbanded by the British authorities at the end of the following month.

MILITARY FRANK STAMP

M 1

(Typeset Curling & Co, Bloemfontein)

1899 (15 Oct). *P* 12.
M1 M **1** (–) Black/*bistre-yellow* .. .. .. 10·00 40·00
Supplies of No. M1 were issued to members of the Orange Free State army on active service during the Second Boer War. To pass free through the O.F.S. fieldpost system letters had to be franked with No. M1 or initialled by the appropriate unit commander. The franks were in use between October 1899 and February 1900.
No. M1 was printed in sheets of 20 (5×4) using a setting of five different types in a horizontal row. The colour in the paper runs in water.
Typeset forgeries can be identified by the appearance of 17 pearls, instead of the 16 of the originals, in the top and bottom frames. Forgeries produced by lithography omit the stops after "BRIEF" and "FRANKO".

FISCAL STAMPS USED FOR POSTAGE

The following were issued in 1878 (Nos. F1 and F3 in 1882) and were authorised for postal use between 1882 and 1886.

F 1   F 2

(Typo D.L.R.)

1882–86. *P* 14.
F 1 F **1** 6d. pearl-grey .. .. 2·75 7·00
F 2 6d. purple-brown .. .. — 9·00
F 3 F **2** 1s. purple-brown .. .. 4·00 10·00
F 4 1s. pearl-grey .. .. — 27·00
F 5 1s. 6d. blue .. .. 7·00 5·50
F 6 2s. magenta .. .. 7·00 5·00
F 7 3s. chestnut .. .. 9·00 27·00
F 8 4s. grey .. ..
F 9 5s. rose .. .. 11·00
F10 6s. green .. .. — 27·00
F11 7s. violet .. ..
F12 10s. orange .. .. 22·00 16·00
F13 £1 purple .. .. 30·00 20·00
F14 £2 red-brown .. .. 32·00
F14*a* £4 carmine .. ..
F15 £5 green .. .. 48·00 24·00
A fiscally used example of No. F2 exists showing "ZES PENCE" double, one inverted.
The 8s. yellow was prepared but we have no evidence of its use postally without surcharge Type F **3**.

ZES PENCE.

(F 3)

1886. *Surch with Type* F **3**.
F16 F **2** 6d. on 4s. grey .. ..
F17 6d. on 8s. yellow £110
Postage stamps overprinted for use as Telegraph stamps and used postally are omitted as it is impossible to say with certainty which stamps were genuinely used for postal purposes.

Orange Free State became a province of the Union of South Africa on 31 May 1910.

TRANSVAAL

(*formerly* South African Republic)

PRICES FOR STAMPS ON COVER

Nos. 1/6 are rare used on cover.

Nos. 7/80	*from* × 20
Nos. 86/155	*from* × 3
Nos. 156/62	*from* × 6
Nos. 163/9	*from* × 5
Nos. 170/225	*from* × 10
Nos. 226/34	*from* × 20
Nos. 235/7	—
Nos. 238/43	*from* × 12
Nos. 244/55	*from* × 4
Nos. 256/7	*from* × 6
Nos. 258/9	—
Nos. 260/76	*from* × 20
Nos. D1/7	*from* × 20

The issues for Pietersburg, Lydenburg, Rustenburg, Schweizer Renecke, Volksrust and Wolmaransstad are very rare when on cover.

1 (Eagle with spread wings)   2   3

(Typo Adolph Otto, Gustrow, Mecklenburg-Schwerin)

1869. *Thin paper, clear and distinct impressions.* (*a*) *Imperf.*
1 **1** 1d. brown-lake £350
a. Orange-red £350 £350
2 6d. bright ultramarine £130 £130
a. Pale ultramarine £150 £160
3 1s. deep green £550 £550
a. *Tête-bêche* (pair) .. ..

(*b*) *Fine roulette*, 15½ *to* 16
4 **1** 1d. brown-lake .. .. 85·00
a. Brick-red .. .. 65·00
b. Orange-red .. .. 65·00
c. Vermilion .. .. 65·00
5 6d. bright ultramarine .. .. 60·00 60·00
a. Pale ultramarine .. .. 70·00
6 1s. deep green £130 £130
a. Yellow-green .. .. 90·00 90·00
b. Emerald-green .. .. 75·00 75·00
A *tête-bêche* pair of the 6d. imperforate is also said to exist.

PLATES. The German printings of the 1d., 6d. and 1s. in Type **1** were from two pairs of plates, each pair printing sheets of 80 in two panes of five horizontal rows of eight.
One pair of plates, used for Nos. 4*a*, 4*c*, 5*a* and 6/*a*, produced stamps spaced 1¼ to 1½ mm apart with the rouletting close to the design on all four sides. The 1d. from these "narrow" plates shows a gap in the outer frame line at the bottom right-hand corner. The second pair, used for Nos. 1/3, 4, 4*b*, 5/*a* and 6*b*, had 2½ to 3½ mm between the stamps. These "wide" plates were sent to the Transvaal in 1869 and were used there to produce either single or double pane printings until 1883.
The 6d. and 1s. "wide" plates each had an inverted *cliché*. When printed these occurred on right-hand pane R. 4/1 of the 6d. and right-hand pane R.1/1 of the 1s. These were never corrected and resulted in *tête-bêche* pairs of these values as late as 1883.

REPRINTS AND IMITATIONS. A number of unauthorised printings were made of these stamps by the German printer. Many of these can be identified by differences in the central arms, unusual colours or, in the case of the 1d., by an extra frame around the numeral tablets at top.
Genuine stamps always show the "D" of "EENDRAGT" higher than the remainder of the word, have no break in the border above "DR" and depict the flagstaff at bottom right, behind "MAGT", stopping short of the central shield. They also show the eagle's eye as a clear white circle. On the forgeries the eye is often blurred.
The most difficult of the reprints to detect is the 1s. yellow-green which was once regarded as genuine, but was subsequently identified, by J. N. Luff in *The Philatelic Record* 1911–12, as coming from an unauthorised plate of four. Stamps from this plate show either a white dot between "EEN" and "SHILLING" or a white flaw below the wagon pole.

(Typo M. J. Viljoen, Pretoria)

1870 (4 Apr–4 July).

I. *Thin gummed paper from Germany. Impressions coarse and defective.* (*a*) *Imperf*
8 **1** 1d. dull rose-red .. .. 70·00
a. Reddish pink .. .. 60·00
b. Carmine-red .. .. 55·00 65·00
9 6d. dull ultramarine .. .. £250 60·00
a. *Tête-bêche* (pair) .. ..

(*b*) *Fine roulette*, 15½ *to* 16
10 **1** 1d. carmine-red £700 £200
11 6d. dull ultramarine .. .. .. £180 90·00
a. Imperf between (vert pair) £550

(*c*) *Wide roulette*, 6½
12 **1** 1d. carmine-red .. .. — £850

II. *Thick, hard paper with thin yellow smooth gum* (*No.* 15) *or yellow streaky gum* (*others*). (*a*) *Imperf* (26 Apr)
13 **1** 1d. pale rose-red .. .. 60·00
a. Carmine-red .. .. 60·00 70·00
14 1s. yellow-green .. .. 70·00 70·00
a. *Tête-bêche* (pair) £8000
b. Bisected (6d.) (on cover) .. .. † £1100

(*b*) *Fine roulette*, 15½ *to* 16
15 **1** 1d. carmine-red (24 May) .. .. 80·00
16 6d. ultramarine (10 May) .. .. 80·00 80·00
a. *Tête-bêche* (pair) £14000 £13000
17 1s. yellow-green (26 Apr) £550 £550

III. *Medium paper, blotchy heavy printing and whitish gum. Fine roulette* 15½ *to* 16 (4 July)
18 **1** 1d. rose-red .. .. 60·00 60·00
a. Carmine-red .. .. 38·00 45·00
b. Crimson. From over-inked plate .. £130
19 6d. ultramarine .. .. 65·00 65·00
a. *Tête-bêche* (pair) .. .. ..
b. Deep ultram. From over-inked plate £400 £150
20 1s. deep green .. .. 75·00 65·00
a. From over-inked plate £400 £150
The rouletting machine producing the wide 6½ gauge was not introduced until 1875.
Nos. 18*b*, 19*b* and 20a were printed from badly over-inked plates giving heavy blobby impressions.

(Typo J. P. Borrius, Potchefstroom)

1870 (Sept)–**71**. *Stout paper, but with colour often showing through, whitish gum.* (*a*) *Imperf*
21 **1** 1d. black £120 £120

(*b*) *Fine roulette*, 15½ *to* 16
22 **1** 1d. black .. .. 15·00 20·00
a. Grey-black .. .. 15·00 20·00
23 6d. blackish blue (7.71) .. .. .. £120 50·00
a. Dull blue .. .. 90·00 48·00

(Typo Adolph Otto, Gustrow, Mecklenburg-Schwerin)

1871 (July). *Thin paper, clear and distinct impressions. Fine roulette*, 15½ *to* 16.
24 **2** 3d. pale reddish lilac .. .. .. 80·00 75·00
a. Deep lilac .. .. 85·00 75·00
No. 24 and later printings in the Transvaal were produced from a pair of plates in the same format as the 1869 issue. All genuine stamps have a small dot on the left leg of the eagle.
Imperforate examples in the issued shade, without the dot on eagle's leg, had been previously supplied by the printer, probably as essays, but were not issued for postal purposes. They exist *tête-bêche* (*price for un pair* £3250).
Imperforate and rouletted stamps in other colours are reprints.

(Typo J. P. Borrius, Potchefstroom)

1872–74. *Fine roulette*, 15½ *to* 16. (*a*) *Thin transparent paper*
25 **1** 1d. black £170 £550
26 1d. bright carmine .. .. £140 50·00
27 6d. ultramarine .. .. £100 40·00
28 1s. green .. .. £100 40·00

(*b*) *Thinnish opaque paper, clear printing* (Dec 1872)
29 **1** 1d. reddish pink .. .. 55·00 38·00
a. Carmine-red .. .. 55·00 38·00
30 **2** 3d. grey-lilac .. .. 75·00 38·00
31 **1** 6d. ultramarine .. .. 55·00 27·00
a. Pale ultramarine .. .. 60·00 27·00
32 1s. yellow-green .. .. 60·00 27·00
a. Green .. .. 60·00 29·00
aa. Bisected (6d.) (on cover) .. ..

(*c*) *Thickish wove paper* (1873–74)
33 **1** 1d. dull rose .. .. £400 70·00
a. Brownish rose £475 £110
b. Printed on both sides .. ..
34 6d. milky blue .. .. £140 40·00
a. Deep dull blue .. .. 80·00 35·00
aa. Imperf (pair) £600
ab. Imperf between (horiz pair) £650
ac. Wide roulette 6½ .. .. ..

(*d*) *Very thick dense paper* (1873–74)
35 1d. dull rose £475 £110
a. Brownish rose .. .. £350 85·00
36 6d. dull ultramarine .. .. £170 60·00
a. Bright ultramarine .. .. £180 60·00
37 1s. yellow-green £750 £550

(Typo P. Davis & Son, Pietermaritzburg)

1874 (Sept). *P* 12½. (*a*) *Thin transparent paper.*
38 **1** 1d. pale brick-red .. .. 80·00 35·00
a. Brownish red .. .. 75·00 35·00
39 6d. deep blue .. .. £100 35·00

(*b*) *Thicker opaque paper*
40 **1** 1d. pale red .. .. £130 65·00
41 6d. blue .. .. 95·00 40·00
a. Imperf between (pair) .. ..
b. Deep blue .. .. 90·00 40·00

(Typo Adolph Otto, Gustrow, Mecklenburg-Schwerin)

1874 (Oct). *Thin smooth paper, clearly printed. Fine roulette* 15½ *to* 16.
42 **3** 6d. bright ultramarine .. .. .. 60·00 20·00
a. Bisected (3d.) (on cover) .. ..
Stamps in other shades of blue, brown or red, often on other types of paper, are reprints.

(Typo J. F. Celliers on behalf of Stamp Commission, Pretoria)

1875 (29 Apr)–**77.**

I. *Very thin, soft opaque* (*semi-pelure*) *paper.* (*a*) *Imperf*

43 **1** 1d. orange-red .. .. £120 40·00
a. Pin-perf .. ..
44 **2** 3d. lilac .. .. 80·00 40·00
45 **1** 6d. blue .. .. 75·00 38·00
a. Milky blue .. .. £120 38·00
aa. *Tête-bêche* (pair) £6000
ab. Pin-perf .. .. — £250

(*b*) *Fine roulette,* 15½ *to* 16

46 **1** 1d. orange-red £400 £130
47 **2** 3d. lilac £425 £140
48 **1** 6d. blue £400 £130

(*c*) *Wide roulette,* 6½

49 **1** 1d. orange-red .. .. — £150
50 **2** 3d. lilac £550 £200
51 **1** 6d. blue .. .. — £120
a. Bright blue .. .. — £120
b. Milky blue .. .. — £120

II. *Very thin, hard transparent* (*pelure*) *paper* (1875–76)
(*a*) *Imperf*

52 **1** 1d. brownish red.. .. .. 48·00 24·00
a. Orange-red .. .. 38·00 22·00
b. Dull red.. .. .. 42·00 42·00
ba. Pin-perf.. .. .. £425 £250
53 **2** 3d. lilac .. .. 42·00 38·00
a. Pin-perf .. .. — £225
b. Deep lilac .. .. 55·00 38·00
54 **1** 6d. pale blue .. .. 38·00 38·00
a. Blue .. .. 38·00 20·00
ab. *Tête-bêche* (pair) .. .. .. † £10000
ac. Pin-perf.. .. .. — £200
b. Deep blue .. .. 38·00 20·00

(*b*) *Fine roulette* 15½ *to* 16

55 **1** 1d. orange-red £250 £120
a. Brown-red £250 £120
56 **2** 3d. lilac £325 £110
57 **1** 6d. blue .. .. £150 95·00
a. Deep blue £150 £110

(*c*) *Wide roulette,* 6½

58 **1** 1d. orange-red £700 £150
a. Bright red .. .. — £130
59 **2** 3d. lilac .. .. — £180
60 **1** 6d. deep blue .. .. £700 85·00

III. *Stout hard-surfaced paper with smooth, nearly white, gum* (1876). (*a*) *Imperf*

61 **1** 1d. bright red .. .. 20·00 14·00
62 **2** 3d. lilac .. ..
63 **1** 6d. bright blue .. .. 85·00 20·00
a. *Tête-bêche* (pair) .. .. ..
b. Pale blue .. .. 85·00 20·00
c. Deep blue (deep brown gum) .. .. 50·00 16·00
ca. *Tête-bêche* (pair) .. .. .. — £10000

(*b*) *Fine roulette,* 15½ *to* 16

64 **1** 1d. bright red £400 £150
65 **2** 3d. lilac £275
66 **1** 6d. bright blue .. .. — £100
a. Deep blue (deep brown gum) .. — £250

(*c*) *Wide roulette,* 6½

67 **1** 1d. bright red £450 £140
68 6d. pale blue .. .. — £200
a. Deep blue (deep brown gum) .. £500 £225

IV. *Coarse, soft white paper* (1876–77). (*a*) *Imperf*

69 **1** 1d. brick-red .. .. 85·00 45·00
70 6d. deep blue .. .. £150 45·00
a. Milky blue .. .. £275 85·00
71 1s. yellow-green .. .. £250 85·00
a. Bisected (6d.) (on cover) .. ..

(*b*) *Fine roulette,* 15½ *to* 16

72 **1** 1d. brick-red .. .. — £250
73 6d. deep blue .. .. — £130
74 1s. yellow-green £550 £250

(*c*) *Wide roulette,* 6½

75 **1** 1d. brick-red .. .. — £300
76 6d. deep blue .. ..
77 1s. yellow-green .. .. — £800

(*d*) *Fine × wide roulette*

78 **1** 1d. brick-red £550 £250

V. *Hard, thick, coarse yellowish paper* (1876–77)

79 **1** 1d. brick-red (*imperf*) .. .. .. — £200
80 1d. brick-red (*wide roulette*) .. .. .. — £300

The pin-perforated stamps have various gauges and were probably produced privately or by one or more post offices other than Pretoria.

On Nos. 63c/ca, 66a and 68a the brown gum used was so intense that it caused staining of the paper which is still visible on used examples.

See also Nos. 171/4.

FIRST BRITISH OCCUPATION

By 1876 conditions in the Transvaal had deteriorated and the country was faced by economic collapse, native wars and internal dissension. In early 1877 Sir Theophilus Shepstone, appointed Special Commissioner to the South African Republic by the British Government, arrived in Pretoria and on 12 April annexed the Transvaal with the acquiesence of at least part of the European population.

V. R. TRANSVAAL.
(4)

V. R. TRANSVAAL.
(5)

T 4 is the normal overprint, but in some printings No. 11 (R.2/3) on the pane has a wider-spaced overprint, as T **5**.

1877 (Apr). *Optd with T* **4** *in red.* (*a*) *Imperf.*

86 **2** 3d. lilac (*semi-pelure*) (No. 44) £1100 £225
a. Opt Type **5** .. ..
87 3d. lilac (*pelure*) (No. 53) £1100 £160
a. Opt Type **5** £4750
b. Opt on back £3000
c. Opt double, in red and in black .. £4750
88 **1** 6d. milky blue (No. 70) £1300 £160
a. Opt inverted .. .. — £4250
b. Opt double £3500 £750
c. Opt Type **5** £4250
d. Deep blue .. .. — £225
89 1s. yellow-green (No. 71) £475 £160
a. Bisected (6d.) (on cover) .. .. † £1200
b. Opt inverted .. .. — £3250
c. Opt Type **5** £3000 £750

(*b*) *Fine roulette,* 15½ *to* 16

90 **2** 3d. lilac (*pelure*) (No. 56) .. .. .. — £1100
91 **1** 6d. deep blue (No. 73) .. .. .. — £1100
92 1s. yellow-green (No. 74) £1000 £450
a. Opt Type **5** .. ..

(*c*) *Wide roulette,* 6½

93 **2** 3d. lilac (*pelure*) (No. 59) .. .. .. — £1100
a. Opt Type **5** .. ..
94 **1** 6d. deep blue (No. 76) .. .. .. — £1100
a. Opt Type **5** .. ..
95 1s. yellow-green (No. 77) £2750 £1000
a. Opt inverted .. .. — £3500

Nos. 88a, 89b and 95a occurred on the inverted *cliché* of the basic stamps.

1877 (June). *Optd with T* **4** *in black.*

I. *Very thin, hard transparent* (*pelure*) *paper*

96 **1** 1d. orange-red (*imperf*) (No. 52*a*) .. £170 95·00
97 1d. orange-red (*fine roulette*) (No. 55) .. — £1000

II. *Stout hard-surfaced paper with smooth, nearly white, gum*

98 **1** 1d. bright red (*imperf*) (No. 61) .. .. 20·00 20·00
a. Opt inverted £475 £400
b. Opt Type **5** £550 £600
99 1d. bright red (*fine roulette*) (No. 64) .. £140 45·00
a. Opt inverted .. ..
b. Opt double .. .. — £750
c. Imperf between (horiz pair) £650
100 1d. bright red (*wide roulette*) (No. 67) .. £475 £140

III. *New ptgs on coarse, soft white paper.* (*a*) *Imperf*

101 **1** 1d. brick-red (5.77) .. .. .. 20·00 20·00
a. Opt double .. .. .. — £900
b. Opt Type **5** .. ..
102 **2** 3d. lilac .. .. 70·00 32·00
a. Opt inverted .. ..
b. Deep lilac .. .. £140 80·00
103 **1** 6d. dull blue .. .. 85·00 30·00
a. Opt double £2750
b. Opt inverted £1200 £150
c. *Tête-bêche* (pair) .. .. ..
d. Opt Type **5** .. .. — £750
da. Opt Type **5** inverted .. .. ..
e. Blue (*bright to deep*) .. .. .. £150 22·00
ea. Bright blue, opt inverted .. .. — £475
f. Pin-perf .. .. — £450
104 1s. yellow-green .. .. 80·00 40·00
a. Opt inverted £900 £180
b. *Tête-bêche* (pair) £10000 £10000
c. Opt Type **5** £2750 £900
d. Bisected (6d.) (on cover) .. .. † £900

(*b*) *Fine roulette,* 15½ *to* 16

105 **1** 1d. brick-red .. .. 65·00 65·00
a. Imperf horiz (vert strip of 3) .. ..
b. Imperf between (horiz pair) .. .. † £600
106 **2** 3d. lilac .. .. £140 55·00
107 **1** 6d. dull blue .. .. £160 42·00
a. Opt inverted .. .. — £550
b. Opt Type **5** £3500
108 1s. yellow-green .. .. £150 80·00
a. Opt inverted £800 £375
b. Opt Type **5** .. .. — £2500

(*c*) *Wide roulette,* 6½

109 **1** 1d. brick-red £550 £140
a. Opt Type **5** .. .. — £650
110 **2** 3d. lilac .. .. — £475
111 **1** 6d. dull blue .. .. — £1100
a. Opt inverted .. .. — £3000
112 1s. yellow-green £350 £120
a. Opt inverted £1100 £475

1877 (31 Aug). *Optd with T* **4** *in black.*

113 **1** 6d. blue/*rose* (*imperf*) .. .. .. 65·00 42·00
a. Bisected (3d.) (on cover) .. ..
b. Opt inverted .. .. 85·00 42·00
c. *Tête-bêche* (pair) .. .. ..
d. Opt omitted £2750
114 6d. blue/*rose* (*fine roulette*) .. .. .. £150 60·00
a. Opt inverted .. .. £425 60·00
b. *Tête-bêche* (pair) .. .. ..
c. Opt omitted .. ..
115 6d. blue/*rose* (*wide roulette*) .. .. ..
a. Opt inverted .. ..
b. Opt omitted .. ..

Nos. 113/15 were overprinted from a setting of 40 which was applied upright to one pane in each sheet and inverted on the other.

V. R. Transvaal
(6)

V. R. Transvaal
(7)

1877 (28 Sept)–**79.** *Optd with T* **6** *in black.* (*a*) *Imperf*

116 **1** 1d. red/*blue* .. .. 42·00 22·00
a. "Transvral" (Right pane R. 2/3) .. £4000 £2000
b. Opt double £3000
c. Opt inverted £600 £300
d. Opt omitted .. ..
117 **1** 1d. red/*orange* (6.12.77) .. .. .. 14·00 15·00
a. Pin-perf .. ..
b. Printed both sides .. .. ..
c. Opt double £2500
d. Optd with Type **7** (15.4.78) .. .. 42·00 35·00
118 **2** 3d. mauve/*buff* (24.10.77) .. .. .. 32·00 22·00
a. Opt inverted .. .. — £550
b. Pin-perf .. ..
c. Optd with Type **7** (15.4.78) .. .. 48·00 30·00
ca. Pin-perf £550 £550
119 3d. mauve/*green* (18.4.79) .. .. .. £140 40·00
a. Pin-perf .. ..
b. Opt inverted .. .. — £1500
c. Opt double .. ..
d. Optd with Type **7** .. .. .. 90·00 30·00
da. Opt inverted .. .. — £1500
db. Opt omitted .. .. — £2750
dc. Printed both sides .. .. ..
120 **1** 6d. blue/*green* (27.11.77) .. .. .. 75·00 32·00
a. Deep blue/green .. .. 90·00 35·00
b. Broken "Y" for "V" in "V. R." (Left pane R. 3/7) .. ..
c. Small "v" in "Transvaal" (Left pane R. 5/2) .. ..
d. "V..R" (Right pane R. 3/4) .. .. — £550
e. *Tête-bêche* (pair) .. .. .. — £10000
f. Opt inverted .. .. — £700
g. Pin-perf .. ..
121 6d. blue/*blue* (20.3.78) .. .. .. 48·00 22·00
a. *Tête-bêche* (pair) .. .. ..
b. Opt inverted .. .. — £700
c. Opt omitted .. .. — £1600
d. Opt double .. .. — £2500
e. Pin-perf .. ..
f. Bisected (3d.) (on cover) .. .. † £550
g. Optd with Type **7** .. .. .. 90·00 22·00
ga. *Tête-bêche* (pair) £7500
gb. Opt inverted .. .. — £400

(*b*) *Fine roulette,* 15½ *to* 16

122 **1** 1d. red/*blue* .. .. 70·00 32·00
a. "Transvral" (Right pane R. 2/3) .. — £2250
123 1d. red/*orange* (6.12.77) .. .. .. 28·00 22·00
a. Imperf between (pair) £500
b. Optd with Type **7** (15.4.78) £130 £110
124 **2** 3d. mauve/*buff* (24.10.77) .. .. .. 85·00 22·00
a. Imperf horiz (vert pair) £600
b. Opt inverted .. .. — £2500
c. Optd with Type **7** (15.4.78) .. .. £130 95·00
ca. Imperf between (pair) .. ..
125 3d. mauve/*green* (18.4.79) £550 £150
a. Optd with Type **7** £500 £150
126 6d. blue/*green* (27.11.77) .. .. .. 70·00 22·00
a. "V..R" (Right pane R. 3/4) .. .. — £1000
b. *Tête-bêche* (pair) .. .. ..
c. Opt inverted .. .. — £500
d. Opt omitted .. .. — £3000
e. Bisected (3d.) (on cover) .. .. † £550
127 6d. blue/*blue* (20.3.78) .. .. .. £180 45·00
a. Opt inverted .. .. — £900
b. Opt omitted .. .. — £2500
c. Imperf between (pair) .. ..
d. Bisected (3d.) (on cover) .. .. † £475
e. Optd with Type **7** .. .. .. £300 95·00
ea. Opt inverted .. .. — £800

(*c*) *Wide roulette,* 6¼

128 **1** 1d. red/*orange* (15.4.78) .. .. .. £225 95·00
a. Optd with Type **7** .. .. .. — £225
129 **2** 3d. mauve/*buff* (24.10.77) .. .. .. — 95·00
a. Optd with Type **7** (15.4.78) .. .. — £275
130 3d. mauve/*green* (18.4.79) £350 £250
a. Optd with Type **7** .. .. .. — £275
131 **1** 6d. blue/*green* (27.11.77) .. .. .. — £850
132 6d. blue/*blue* (20.3.78) .. .. .. — £225
a. Opt inverted .. ..
b. Optd with Type **7** .. .. .. — £275
ba. Opt inverted .. ..

Nos. 116/32 were overprinted from various settings covering sheets of 80 or panes of 40 (8 ×5). Initially these settings contained Type **6** only, but the type was reset in March 1878 to contain examples of Type **7** also.

V. R. Transvaal
(8)

V. R. Transvaal
(8*a*)

TRANSVAAL POSTZEGEL SIX PENCE
9

1879 (Aug-Sept). *Optd with T* **8** *in black.* (*a*) *Imperf.*

145 **1** 1d. red/*yellow* .. .. 38·00 32·00
a. Small "T", Type **8***a* £225 £150
b. Red/orange .. .. 32·00 25·00
ba. Small "T", Type **8***a* £160 £150
146 **2** 3d. mauve/*green* .. .. 35·00 20·00
a. Small "T", Type **8***a* .. .. .. £160 85·00
147 3d. mauve/*blue* .. .. 40·00 25·00
a. Small "T", Type **8***a* .. .. .. £170 85·00

(*b*) *Fine roulette,* 15½ *to* 16

148 **1** 1d. red/*yellow* £350 £200
a. Small "T", Type **8***a* £800 £550
b. Red/orange £750 £375
ba. Small "T", Type **8***a* .. .. ..
149 **2** 3d. mauve/*green* £700 £225
a. Small "T", Type **8***a* .. .. ..
150 3d. mauve/*blue* .. .. — £160
a. Small "T", Type **8***a* .. .. .. — £600

(*c*) *Wide roulette,* 6½

151 **1** 1d. red/*yellow* £600 £600
a. Small "T", Type **8***a* .. .. ..
b. Red/orange .. ..
152 **2** 3d. mauve/*green* .. ..
a. Small "T", Type **8***a* .. .. ..
153 3d. mauve/*blue* .. ..

(d) Pin-perf, about 17

154 1 1d. red/*yellow* .. .. — £450
a. Small "T", Type 8*a* .. .. ..
155 2 3d. mauve/*blue* .. .. — £600

The small "T" variety occurs on right pane R. 2/8, 3/8, 4/8 and 5/8 of the 1d. and on the same positions, but from the left pane, for the 3d.

(Recess B.W.)

1878 (26 Aug)–**80**. *P* 14, 14½.

156 9 ½d. vermilion (1880) .. .. .. 16·00 35·00
157 1d. pale red-brown .. .. .. 5·00 3·00
a. Brown-red .. .. .. 4·50 2·25
158 3d. dull rose .. .. .. 6·50 2·50
a. Claret .. .. .. 9·00 4·50
159 4d. sage-green .. .. .. 9·00 4·25
160 6d. olive-black .. .. .. 4·50 3·25
a. Black-brown .. .. .. 6·50 2·75
161 1s. green .. .. .. 90·00 30·00
162 2s. blue .. .. .. £110 65·00

The above prices are for specimens perforated on all four sides. Stamps from margins of sheets, with perforations absent on one or two sides, can be supplied for about 30% less.

1 Penny (10) 1 Penny (11) 1 Penny (12)

1 Penny (13) 1 Penny (14)

1 PENNY (15) 1 Penny (16)

1879 (22 April). *No.* 160*a surch with T* **10** *to* **16**.

A. *In black*. B. *In red*.

				A		B	
163	10	1d. on 6d.	..	65·00	40·00	£180	£120
164	11	1d. on 6d.	..	£160	75·00	£450	£250
165	12	1d. on 6d.	..	£160	75·00	£450	£250
166	13	1d. on 6d.	..	70·00	45·00	£200	£140
167	14	1d. on 6d.	..	£425	£130	—	£1500
168	15	1d. on 6d.	..	35·00	22·00	£110	60·00
169	16	1d. on 6d.	..	£150	70·00	£400	£225

Nos. 163/9 were surcharged from a setting of 60 containing eleven examples of Type **10**, four of Type **11**, four of Type **12**, nine of Type **13**, two of Type **14**, twenty-five of Type **15** and five of Type **16**.

The red surcharges may have been produced first.

SECOND REPUBLIC

Following the first Boer War the independence of the South African Republic was recognised by the Convention of Pretoria from 8 August 1881.

Nos. 156/62 remained valid and some values were available for postage until 1885.

EEN PENNY (17)

1882 (Aug). *No.* 159 *surch with T* **17**.

170 9 1d. on 4d. sage-green .. .. .. 4·75 3·50
a. Surch inverted £300 £200

Used examples of a similar, but larger, surcharge (width 19 mm) are known.

(Typo J. F. Celliers)

1883 (20 Feb). *Re-issue of T* **1** *and* **2**. *P* 12.

171 1 1d. grey (*to* black) (Apr) .. .. .. 1·75 75
a. Imperf vert (horiz pair) £250
172 2 3d. grey-black (*to* black)/*rose* .. .. 9·50 2·25
a. Bisected (1d.) (on cover) .. .. † £475
173 3d. pale red (Mar) .. .. .. 5·00 1·00
a. Bisected (1d.) (on cover) .. ..
b. Chestnut .. .. .. 19·00 2·25
c. Vermilion .. .. .. 17·00 2·50
174 1 1s. green (*to* deep) (July) .. .. 12·00 1·50
a. Bisected (6d.) (on cover) .. .. † £350
b. *Tête-bêche* (pair) £600 £100

Reprints are known of Nos. 172, 173, 173*b* and 173*c*. The paper of the first is *bright rose* in place of *dull rose*, and the impression is brownish black in place of grey-black to deep black. The reprints on white paper have the paper thinner than the originals, and the gum yellowish instead of white. The colour is a dull deep orange-red.

18

PERFORATIONS. Stamps perforated 11½×12 come from the first vertical row of sheets of the initial printing otherwise perforated 12½×12.

REPRINTS. Reprints of the general issues 1885–93, 1894–95, 1895–96 and 1896–97 exist in large quantities. They cannot readily be distinguished from genuine originals except by comparison with used stamps, but the following general characteristics may be noted. The reprints are all perf 12½, large holes; the paper is whiter and thinner than that usually employed for the originals and their colours lack the lustre of those of the genuine stamps.

Forged surcharges have been made on these reprints.

(Des J. Vurtheim. Typo Enschedé)

1885 (13 Mar)–**1893**. *P* 12½.

175 18 ½d. grey (30.3.85) 30 10
a. Perf 13½ .. .. .. 3·50 80
b. Perf 12½×12 .. .. .. 1·50 10
ba. Perf 11½×12 .. .. ..
176 1d. carmine 30 10
a. Perf 12½×12 .. .. .. 70 10
aa. Perf 11½×12 .. .. .. 6·00 2·25
b. Rose 30 10
ba. Perf 12½×12 .. .. .. 30 10
177 2d. brown-purple (*p* 12½×12) (9.85) .. 30 30
178 2d. olive-bistre (14.4.87) 40 10
a. Perf 12½×12 .. .. .. 3·25 10
179 2½d. mauve (*to* bright) (8.93) .. .. 1·00 15
180 3d. mauve (*to* bright) .. .. .. 1·25 50
a. Perf 12½×12 .. .. .. 5·00 65
aa. Perf 11½×12 .. .. .. 19·00 12·00
181 4d. bronze-green .. .. .. 2·00 30
a. Perf 13½ .. .. .. 4·25 65
b. Perf 12½×12 .. .. .. 11·00 65
ba. Perf 11½×12 .. .. .. £140 55·00
182 6d. pale dull blue .. .. .. 1·25 15
a. Perf 13½ .. .. .. 4·00 70
b. Perf 12½×12 .. .. .. 5·00 15
ba. Perf 11½×12 .. .. ..
183 18 1s. yellow-green .. .. .. 2·25 35
a. Perf 13½ .. .. .. 12·00 4·50
b. Perf 12½×12 .. .. .. 6·50 20
184 2s. 6d. orange-buff (*to* buff) (2.12.85) .. 3·50 1·40
a. Perf 12½×12 .. .. .. 6·50 3·25
185 5s. slate (2.12.85) .. .. .. 4·25 1·75
a. Perf 12½×12 .. .. .. 5·00 1·50
186 10s. fawn (2.12.85) .. .. .. 21·00 2·50
187 £5 dp grn (3.92)* (Optd "Monster" £150) £3000 £170

Singles of the 6d. pale dull blue imperforate have been reported used in 1893.

*Most examples of No. 187 on the market are either forgeries or reprints.

HALVE PENNY (19)

1885 (22 May–Aug). *Surch with T* **19**. A. *Reading down*. B. *Reading up*.

				A		B	
188	2	½d. on 3d. (No. 173)	..	1·25	2·00	1·25	2·00
189	1	½d. on 1s. (No. 174) (Aug)		3·75	5·50	3·75	5·50
		a. *Tête-bêche* (pair)	..	†		£500	£250

Nos. 188/9 were surcharged by a setting of 40. After the left pane had been surcharged reading down the sheets were turned so that the right pane had the surcharges reading up.

HALVE PENNY Z.A.R. (20) TWEE PENCE Z. A. R. (21) HALVE PENNY (22)

1885 (1 Sept). *No.* 160*a surch with T* **20/1** *in red*.

190 9 ½d. on 6d. black-brown .. .. .. 7·50 11·00
191 2d. on 6d. black-brown .. .. .. 1·50 1·50

1885 (28 Sept). *No.* 180*a surch with T* **21**.

192 18 ½d. on 3d. mauve .. .. .. 1·00 1·00
a. "PRNNY" (R. 6/6) .. .. .. 22·00
b. 2nd "N" inverted (R. 3/8) .. .. 50·00
c. Perf 11½×12 .. .. .. 3·00

2d (23) 2d (24)

1887 (15 Jan). *No.* 180*a surch with T* **23/4**.

193 18 2d. on 3d. mauve (Type **23**) .. .. 2·75 2·75
a. Surch double .. .. .. — £200
b. Perf 11½×12 .. .. .. 4·50 4·50
194 2d. on 3d. mauve (Type **24**) 55 75
a. Surch double .. .. .. — £160
b. Perf 11½×12 .. .. .. 2·75 2·75

Nos. 193/4 were surcharged from the same setting of 60 (10 × 6) which showed Type **24** on the top five horizontal rows and Type **23** on the sixth horizontal row.

Halve Penny (25) 1 Penny (26)

2½ Pence (27) 2½ Pence (28)

Two types of surcharge:
A. Vertical distance between bars 12½ mm.
B. Distance 13½ mm.

1893. *T* **18** *surch*. *P* 12½. (*a*) *In red*.

195 25 ½d. on 2d. olive-bistre (A) (27 May) .. 50 55
a. Surch inverted .. .. .. 1·10 1·10
b. Surch Type B 90 90
ba. Surch inverted .. .. .. 3·75

(b) In black

196 25 ½d. on 2d. olive-bistre (A) (2 July) .. 50 50
a. Surch inverted .. .. .. 3·00 3·00
b. Extra surch on back inverted .. £120
c. Surch Type B 70 70
ca. Surch inverted .. .. .. — 8·00
cb. Extra surch on back inverted .. £180
197 26 1d. on 6d. blue (A) (26 Jan) 20 20
a. Surch double .. .. .. 38·00 32·00
b. Surch inverted .. .. .. 90 1·00
c. Surch Type B 40 40
ca. Surch inverted .. .. .. 2·75 2·75
cb. Surch double .. .. .. — 50·00
d. Pair with and without surch .. £120
198 27 2½d. on 1s. green (A) (2 Jan) 40 50
a. "2/½" for "2½" (R. 1/10) .. .. 15·00 15·00
b. Surch inverted .. .. .. 1·00 1·10
ba. Surch inverted and "2/½" for "2½" £200 £150
c. Extra surch on back inverted .. £225
d. Surch Type B 75 90
da. Surch inverted .. .. .. 4·50 5·25
199 28 2½d. on 1s. green (A) (24 June) .. .. 1·40 1·40
a. Surch double .. .. .. 23·00 23·00
b. Surch inverted .. .. .. 4·50 4·50
c. Surch Type B .. .. .. 4·00 4·00
ca. Surch double .. .. .. 50·00 50·00
cb. Surch inverted .. .. .. 9·00 9·00

Surcharge Types **25/8** all show a similar setting of the horizontal bars at top and bottom. On horizontal rows 1 to 4 and 6 the bars are 12½ mm apart and on row 5 the distance is 13½ mm.

29 (Wagon with shafts)

30 (Wagon with pole)

1894 (July). *P* 12½.

200 29 ½d. grey 15 10
201 1d. carmine 15 10
202 2d. olive-bistre 15 10
203 6d. pale dull blue 75 40
204 1s. yellow-green .. .. 3·50 4·00

For note *re* reprints, see below T **18**.

1895 (16 Mar)–**96**. *P* 12½.

205 30 ½d. pearl-grey (1895) 15 10
a. Lilac-grey 15 10
206 1d. rose-red 15 10
207 2d. olive-bistre (1895) 15 10
208 3d. mauve (1895) 20 10
209 4d. olive-black (1895) 90 55
210 6d. pale dull blue (1895) 60 30
211 1s. yellow-green (18.3.95) 90 65
212 5s. slate (1896) .. .. .. 3·00 4·00
212*a* 10s. pale chestnut (1896) .. .. .. 4·00 1·25
205/8, 211 Optd "Monster" .. *Set of* 5 £150

For note *re* reprints, see below T **18**.

Halve Penny (31)

1d. (**32**—Round dot) 1d. (**32*a***—Square dot)

1895 (July–August). *Nos.* 211 *and* 179 *surch with T* **31/2**.

213 30 ½d. on 1s. green (R.) 20 10
a. Surch spaced 70 65
b. "Pennij" for "Penny" (R. 6/6) .. 35·00
c. Surch inverted .. .. .. 3·00 2·75
d. Surch double .. .. .. 48·00

214 **18** 1d. on 2½d. bright mauve (G.) .. 20 10
a. Surch inverted .. .. .. 16·00 12·00
b. Surch double .. .. ..
c. Surch on back only .. ..
d. Surch Type **32a** 95 95
da. Surch inverted .. .. .. 42·00

The normal space between "Penny" and the bars is 3 mm. On No. 213a, which comes from the fifth horizontal row of the setting, this is increased to 4 mm. Copies may be found in which one or both of the bars have failed to print.

Type **32a** with square stop occurred on R. 3/3-4, 3/6-8, 4/4-5, 4/7-8, 4/10, 6/3, 6/7-8 and 6/10 of the setting of 60.

33

34

1895 (July). *Fiscal stamp optd* "POSTZEGEL". *P* 11½.
215 **33** 6d. bright rose (G.) 50 65
a. Imperf between (pair) .. ..

(Litho The Press Printing and Publishing Works, Pretoria)

1895 (6 Sept). *Introduction of Penny Postage*. *P* 11.
215*b* **34** 1d. red (pale *to* deep) 50 30
ba. Imperf between (pair) .. .. 50·00 50·00

1896–97. *P* 12½.
216 **30** ½d. green (1896) 15 10
217 1d. rose-red and green (1896) 15 10
218 2d. brown and green (2.97) 15 10
219 2½d. dull blue and green (6.96) 20 10
220 3d. purple and green (3.97) 20 35
221 4d. sage-green and green (3.97) 25 35
222 6d. lilac and green (11.96) 25 35
223 1s. ochre and green (3.96) 35 10
224 2s. 6d. dull violet and green (6.96) .. 75 75

For note *re* reprints, see below T **18**.

SECOND BRITISH OCCUPATION

The Second Boer War began on 11 October 1899 and was concluded by the Peace of Vereeniging on 31 May 1902. Pretoria was occupied by the British on 5 June 1900 and a civilian postal service began operating thirteen days later.

FORGERIES. The forgeries of the "V.R.I." and "E.R.I." overprints most often met with can be recognised by the fact that the type used is perfect and the three stops are always in alignment with the bottom of the letters. In the genuine overprints, which were made from old type, it is impossible to find all three letters perfect and all three stops perfect and in exact alignment with the bottom of the letters.

V. R. I. (35)

E. R. I. (36)

E. R. I. Half Penny (37)

1900 (18 June). *Optd with T* **35**.
226 **30** ½d. green 15 15
a. No stop after "V" .. .. .. 10·00
b. No stop after "R" .. .. .. 7·00
c. No stop after "I" .. .. .. 6·00
d. Opt inverted .. .. .. 7·00
e. Opt double .. .. ..
f. "V.I.R." (R.4/4) £500
227 1d. rose-red and green 15 15
a. No stop after "V" .. .. .. 10·00
b. No stop after "R" .. .. .. 7·00
c. No stop after "I" .. .. .. 4·00
d. Opt inverted .. .. .. 7·00
e. Opt double .. .. .. 42·00
f. No stops after "R" and "I" .. .. 48·00 48·00
g. Opt omitted (in pair with normal) £250
228 2d. brown and green 90 40
a. No stop after "V" .. .. .. 18·00
c. No stop after "I" .. .. .. 22·00
d. Opt inverted .. .. .. 10·00
e. Opt double .. .. ..
f. "V.I.R." (R.4/4) £500
229 2½d. dull blue and green 35 40
a. No stop after "V" .. .. .. 15·00
b. No stop after "R" .. .. .. 35·00
c. No stop after "I" .. .. .. 11·00
d. Opt inverted .. .. .. 7·00
230 3d. purple and green 35 40
a. No stop after "V" .. .. .. 18·00
b. No stop after "R" .. .. .. 30·00
c. No stop after "I" .. .. .. 20·00
d. Opt inverted .. .. .. 42·00
231 4d. sage-green and green 75 20
a. No stop after "V" .. .. .. 26·00
b. No stop after "R" .. .. .. 35·00
c. No stop after "I" .. .. .. 22·00
d. Opt inverted .. .. .. 16·00
f. "V.I.R." (R.4/4) £500
232 6d. lilac and green 75 40
a. No stop after "V" .. .. .. 12·00
b. No stop after "R" .. .. .. 18·00
c. No stop after "I" .. .. .. 16·00
d. Opt inverted .. .. .. 16·00
233 **30** 1s. ochre and green 75 70
a. No stop after "V" .. .. .. 12·00
b. No stop after "R" .. .. ..
c. No stop after "I" .. .. .. 25·00
d. Opt inverted .. .. .. 20·00
e. Opt double .. .. .. 45·00
234 2s. 6d. dull violet and green .. .. 1·50 2·25
a. No stop after "V" .. .. .. 20·00
b. No stop after "R" .. .. .. 40·00
235 5s. slate .. .. 2·50 3·75
a. No stop after "V" .. .. .. 55·00
236 10s. pale chestnut .. .. .. 4·00 4·75
a. No stop after "V" .. .. .. 50·00
c. No stop after "I" .. .. .. 50·00
237 **18** £5 deep green* £1800 £750
a. No stop after "V" .. ..
234/7 Optd "Specimen" .. .. *Set of* 4 £200

*Many examples of No. 237 on the market are forgeries and the stamps should only be purchased if accompanied by a recent expert committee certificate.

The error "V.I.R." occurred on R.4/4 in the first batch of stamps to be overprinted—a few sheets of the ½d., 2d. and 4d. The error was then corrected and stamps showing it are very rare.

A number of different settings were used to apply the overprint to Nos. 226/37. The missing stop varieties listed above developed during overprinting and occur on different positions in the various settings.

1901 (Jan)–**02**. *Optd with T* **36**.
238 **30** ½d. green 15 15
239 1d. rose-red and green (20.3.01) 15 10
a. "E" of opt omitted .. .. .. 50·00
240 3d. purple and green (6.02) .. .. 1·00 1·00
241 4d. sage-green and green (6.02) .. .. 1·00 1·25
242 2s. 6d. dull violet and green (10.02) .. 4·00 4·50

1901 (July). *Surch with T* **37**.
243 **30** ½d. on 2d. brown and green 15 15
a. No stop after "E" (R.4/6) .. .. 38·00

38 (POSTAGE REVENUE) **39** (POSTAGE POSTAGE)

(Typo D.L.R.)

1902 (1 April)–**1903**. *Wmk Crown CA*. *P* 14.
244 **38** ½d. black and bluish green 60 15
245 1d. black and carmine 55 10
246 2d. black and purple .. .. .. 1·00 20
247 2½d. black and blue .. .. .. 1·75 65
248 3d. black and sage-green (1903) .. .. 3·00 30
249 4d. black and brown (1903) .. .. 2·50 50
250 6d. black and orange-brown .. .. 1·25 45
251 1s. black and sage-green .. .. 6·00 2·75
252 2s. black and brown .. .. .. 12·00 13·00
253 **39** 2s. 6d. magenta and black .. .. 8·00 5·50
254 5s. black and purple/*yellow* .. .. 10·00 9·00
255 10s. black and purple/*red* .. .. 25·00 16·00
244/55 .. .. *Set of* 12 65·00 42·00
244/55 Optd "Specimen" .. .. *Set of* 12 £130

The colour of the "black" centres varies from brownish grey or grey to black.

1903. *Wmk Crown CA*. *P* 14.
256 **39** 1s. grey-black and red-brown .. .. 3·25 85
257 2s. grey-black and yellow .. .. 6·00 5·00
258 £1 green and violet .. .. .. 80·00 55·00
259 £5 orange-brown and violet £1200 £400
256/9 Optd "Specimen" .. .. *Set of* 4 £180

1904–9. *Wmk Mult Crown CA*. *Ordinary paper*. *P* 14.
260 **38** ½d. black and bluish green .. .. 1·50 30
261 1d. black and carmine .. .. .. 1·75 10
262 2d. black and purple (*chalk-surfaced paper*) (1906) .. .. 2·25 30
263 2½d. black and blue (1905) .. .. 2·50 1·50
a. Chalk-surfaced paper .. .. 1·50 80
264 3d. black & sage-green (*chalk- surfaced paper*) (1906) .. .. 2·00 15
265 4d. black and brown (*chalk-surfaced paper*) (1906) .. .. 2·00 30
266 6d. black and orange (1905) .. .. 1·90 30
a. Chalk-surfaced paper. *Black and brown-orange* .. .. 1·25 30
267 **39** 1s. black and red-brown (1905) .. .. 1·75 30
268 2s. black and yellow (1906) .. .. 8·00 2·50
269 2s. 6d. magenta and black (1909) .. 17·00 2·00
270 5s. black and purple/*yellow* .. .. 8·50 1·50
271 10s. black and purple/*red* (1907) .. 19·00 2·00
272 £1 green and violet (1908) .. .. 80·00 13·00
a. Chalk-surfaced paper .. .. 80·00 9·50
260/72 .. .. *Set of* 13 £130 18·00

There is considerable variation in the "black" centres as in the previous issue.

1905–9. *Wmk Mult Crown CA*. *P* 14.
273 **38** ½d. yellow-green 70 10
a. Deep green (1908) .. .. .. 1·00 15
274 1d. scarlet 60 10
a. Wmk Cabled Anchor, T **13** of Cape of Good Hope .. .. .. † £325
275 2d. purple (1909) .. .. .. 2·75 15
276 2½d. bright blue (1909) .. .. 6·00 1·75
273/6 .. .. *Set of* 4 9·00 1·75
273/6 Optd "Specimen" .. .. *Set of* 4 50·00

A 2d. grey, T **38**, was prepared for use but not issued. It exists overprinted "Specimen", *price* £120.

The monocoloured ½d. and 1d. are printed from new combined plates. These show a slight alteration in that the frame does not touch the crown.

Many of the King's Head stamps are found overprinted or perforated "C.S.A.R.", for use by the Central South African Railways.

FISCALS WITH POSTAL CANCELLATIONS

Various fiscal stamps are found apparently postally used, but these were used on telegrams not on postal matter.

POSTAGE DUE STAMPS

D 1

(Typo D.L.R.)

1907. *Wmk Mult Crown CA*. *P* 14.
D1 D 1 ½d. black and blue-green .. .. 1·50 1·25
D2 1d. black and scarlet .. .. .. 2·00 70
D3 2d. brown-orange .. .. .. 2·00 1·25
D4 3d. black and blue .. .. .. 2·50 2·00
D5 5d. black and violet .. .. .. 1·50 7·00
D6 6d. black and red-brown .. .. 3·75 8·00
D7 1s. scarlet and black .. .. .. 6·50 5·00
D1/7 .. .. *Set of* 7 18·00 23·00

Transvaal became a province of the Union of South Africa on 31 May 1910.

PIETERSBURG

After the fall of Pretoria to the British in June 1900 the Transvaal government withdrew to the north of the country. Those post offices in areas not occupied by the British continued to function, but by early the following year supplies of stamps were exhausted. The following stamps were then authorised by the State Secretary and remained in use in some towns to early May 1901. Pietersburg itself was taken by British forces on 9 April.

PRICES. Genuinely used examples are very rare. Stamps cancelled by favour exist and are worth the same as the unused prices quoted.

The issued stamps are initialled by the Controller J. T. de V. Smit. All values exist without his signature and these are believed to come from remainders abandoned when the Boers evacuated Pietersburg.

P 1

P 2

P 3

TYPES P 1/3. Each value was printed in sheets of 24 (6×4) of which the first two horizontal rows were as Type P **1**, the third row as Type P **2** and the fourth as Type P **3**. The stamps were issued to post offices in blocks of 12.

(Type-set *De Zoutpansberg Wachter* Press, Pietersburg)

1901 (20 Mar (1*d*.)–3 Apr (*others*)). A. *Imperf*.
(*a*) *Controller's initials in black*
1 P 1 ½d. black/*green* .. .. .. 15·00
e. Controller's initials omitted .. 95·00
2 P 2 ½d. black/*green* .. .. .. 45·00
d. Controller's initials omitted .. 95·00
3 P 3 ½d. black/*green* .. .. .. 45·00
d. Controller's initials omitted .. 95·00
4 P 1 1d. black/*red* .. .. .. 3·50
5 P 2 1d. black/*red* .. .. .. 5·50
6 P 3 1d. black/*red* .. .. .. 7·00
7 P 1 2d. black/*orange* .. .. .. 6·00
8 P 2 2d. black/*orange* .. .. .. 14·00
9 P 3 2d. black/*orange* .. .. .. 22·00
10 P 1 4d. black/*blue* .. .. .. 5·50
11 P 2 4d. black/*blue* .. .. .. 9·50
12 P 3 4d. black/*blue* .. .. .. 32·00
13 P 1 6d. black/*green* .. .. .. 9·50
14 P 2 6d. black/*green* .. .. .. 15·00
15 P 3 6d. black/*green* .. .. .. 40·00
16 P 1 1s. black/*yellow* .. .. .. 8·00
17 P 2 1s. black/*yellow* .. .. .. 14·00
18 P 3 1s. black/*yellow* .. .. .. 25·00
(*b*) *Controller's initials in red*
19 P 1 ½d. black/*green* .. .. .. 15·00
20 P 2 ½d. black/*green* .. .. .. 35·00
21 P 3 ½d. black/*green* .. .. .. 40·00
B. *P* 11½. (*a*) *Controller's initials in red*
22 P 1 ½d. black/*green* .. .. .. 5·50
c. Imperf vert (horiz pair) .. .. 95·00
23 P 2 ½d. black/*green* .. .. .. 17·00
c. Imperf vert (horiz pair) £120
24 P 3 ½d. black/*green* .. .. .. 12·00
b. Imperf vert (horiz pair) £120

(b) Controller's initials in black

25 P 1 1d. black/*red* .. 2·00
m. Imperf vert (horiz pair) .. 55·00
n. Imperf between (vert pair: No. 25 + No. 26)
o. Imperf horiz (vert pair)
26 P 2 1d. black/*red* .. 2·75
f. Imperf vert (horiz pair) .. 80·00
g. Imperf horiz (vert pair: No. 26 + No. 27)
27 P 3 1d. black/*red* .. 4·00
f. Imperf vert (horiz pair) .. 80·00
28 P 1 2d. black/*orange* .. 5·50
29 P 2 2d. black/*orange* .. 8·00
30 P 3 2d. black/*orange* .. 14·00

CONSTANT VARIETIES

Rows 1 and 2 are as Type P 1, *Row 3 as Type* P 2 *and Row 4 as Type* P 3.

½d. value
First printing—Imperf
R.1/2 No stop after left "AFR" (No. 1a) 60·00
R.1/3 "⅓" at top left, no bar over lower right "½" (No. 1b) 60·00
R.1/6 No stop after date (No. 1c) 60·00
R.2/5 "BEP" at left, no stop after date (No. 1d) 60·00
R.3/3 "AFB" at left (No. 2a) 60·00
R.3/4 "POSTZEGEI" (No. 2b) 60·00
R.3/6 No bar over lower right "½" (No. 2c) 60·00
R.4/1 No stop after right "AFR" (No. 3a) 60·00
R.4/4 No stop after left "Z", no bar under top right "½" (No. 3b) 60·00
R.4/5 "POSTZECEL AER" at left (No. 3c) 60·00

Second printing
R.1/4 No stop after right "AFR" .. *Imperf* (No. 19a) 70·00; *Perf* (No. 22a) 40·00
R.2/1 Left side of inner frame too high *Imperf* (No. 19b) 70·00; *Perf* (No. 22b) 40·00
R.3/5 Centre figures "½" level .. *Imperf* (No. 20a) 70·00; *Perf* (No. 23a) 40·00
R.3/6 No stop after right "AFR" .. *Imperf* (No. 20b) 70·00; *Perf* (No. 23b) 40·00
R.4/6 Hyphen between right "AFR" and "REP" .. *Imperf* (No. 21a) 70·00; *Perf* (No. 24a) 40·00

Third printing—Imperf
R.1/1 & 4 Top left "½" inverted, no stop after right "AFR" (No. 19c) 70·00
R.1/2 Top right "½" inverted (No. 19d) 90·00
R.1/3 "⅓" at lower right (No. 19e) 90·00
R.1/5 "POSTZFGEL" (No. 19f) 90·00
R.1/6 Left spray inverted, "AFB" at right (No. 19g) 90·00
R.2/1 "REB" at left, left side of inner frame too high (No. 19h) 90·00
R.2/2 "BEP" at left (No. 19i) 90·00
R.2/3 "POSTZEOEL" (No. 19j) 90·00
R.2/4 "AER" at right (No. 19k) 90·00
R.2/5 No stop after date (No. 19l) 90·00
R.3/1 "⅓" at top left, "PE" of "PENNY" spaced (No. 20c) 90·00
R.3/2 Right spray inverted (No. 20d) 90·00
R.3/3 Top left "½" inverted (No. 20e) 90·00
R.4/3 "⅓" at top right (No. 21b) 90·00
R.4/4 Lower left "½" inverted (No. 21c) 90·00
R.4/5 "¼" at top left (No. 21d) 90·00

1d. value
First printing
R.1/2 Inverted "1" at lower left, first "1" of date dropped .. *Imperf* (No. 4a) 35·00; *Perf* (No. 25a) 22·00
R.1/3 No bar under top left "1" .. *Imperf* (No. 4b) 35·00; *Perf* (No. 25b) 22·00
R.1/4 No bar over lower right "1" .. *Imperf* (No. 4c) 35·00; *Perf* (No. 25c) 22·00
R.1/5 "POSTZFGEL" .. *Imperf* (No. 4d) 35·00; *Perf* (No. 25d) 22·00
R.1/6 "AFB" at right .. *Imperf* (No. 4e) 35·00; *Perf* (No. 25e) 22·00
R.2/1 "REB" at left .. *Imperf* (No. 4f) 35·00; *Perf* (No. 25f) 22·00
R.2/2 "BEP" at left .. *Imperf* (No. 4g) 35·00; *Perf* (No. 25g) 22·00
R.2/3 "POSTZEOEL" .. *Imperf* (No. 4h) 35·00; *Perf* (No. 25h) 22·00
R.2/4 "AER" at right .. *Imperf* (No. 4i) 35·00; *Perf* (No. 25i) 22·00
R.2/5 No stop after date .. *Imperf* (No. 4j) 35·00; *Perf* (No. 25j) 22·00
R.2/6 No stop after "PENNY" .. *Imperf* (No. 4k) 35·00; *Perf* (No. 25k) 22·00
R.3/2 Right spray inverted .. *Imperf* (No. 5a) 35·00; *Perf* (No. 26a) 22·00
R.3/3 No bar over lower left "1" .. *Imperf* (No. 5b) 35·00; *Perf* (No. 26b) 22·00
R.3/4 No stop after left "Z" .. *Imperf* (No. 5c) 35·00; *Perf* (No. 26c) 22·00
R.3/6 "POSTZEGFL", no stop after right "AFR" .. *Imperf* (No. 5d) 35·00; *Perf* (No. 26d) 22·00
R.4/1 No stop after right "AFR" .. *Imperf* (No. 6a) 35·00; *Perf* (No. 27a) 22·00
R.4/2 & 6 Left spray inverted .. *Imperf* (No. 6b) 22·00; *Perf* (No. 27b) 13·00
R.4/3 "POSTZEGEI" .. *Imperf* (No. 6c) 35·00; *Perf* (No. 27c) 22·00
R.4/4 No bar under top right "1" .. *Imperf* (No. 6d) 35·00; *Perf* (No. 27d) 22·00

Second printing
R.1/2 First "1" in date dropped .. *Imperf* (No. 4l) 35·00; *Perf* (No. 25l) 22·00
R.3/6 No stop after right "AFR" .. *Imperf* (No. 5e) 35·00; *Perf* (No. 26e) 22·00
R.4/5 Dropped "P" in "PENNY" .. *Imperf* (No. 6e) 35·00; *Perf* (No. 27e) 22·00

It has been suggested that there may have been a third printing.

2d. value
First printing—Imperf
R.1/1 "1" at lower right (No. 7a) 45·00
R.1/2 No stop after left "AFR" (*on small part of printing*) (No. 7b) 90·00
R.1/3 No bar over lower right "2" (*on small part of printing*) (No. 7c) 90·00
R.1/3 "PENNY" for "PENCE" (No. 7d) 45·00
R.1/5 "POSTZFGEL" (No. 7e) 45·00
R.1/6 "AFB" at right (No. 7f) 45·00
R.2/1 "REB" at left (No. 7g) 45·00
R.2/2 "AFB" at left (No. 7h) 45·00
R.2/3 "POSTZEOEL" (No. 7i) 45·00
R.2/4 "AER" at right (No. 7j) 45·00
R.2/5 No stop after date (No. 7k) 45·00
R.2/6 No stop after date, vertical line after "POSTZEGEL" (No. 7l) 45·00
R.3/2 Right spray inverted (No. 8a) 45·00
R.3/3 No bar over lower left "2" (No. 8b) 45·00
R.3/4 Centre "2" inverted, no stop after left "Z" (No. 8c) 45·00
R.3/6 "POSTZEGFL", no stop after right "AFR" (No. 8d) 45·00
R.4/1 Centre "2" wider, no stop after right "AFR" (*occurs on second printing also*) (No. 9a) 38·00
R.4/2 Centre "2" wider, left spray inverted (No. 9b) 45·00
R.4/3 "POSTZEGEI" (No. 9c) 45·00
R.4/4 No bar under top right "2" (No. 9d) 45·00
R.4/5 "1" at lower left, "P" in "PENCE" dropped (No. 9e) 45·00
R.4/6 Left spray inverted (No. 9f) 45·00

Second printing
R.1/2 First "1" in date dropped .. *Imperf* (No. 7m) 45·00; *Perf* (No. 28a) 30·00
R.2/1 No stop after left "REP" .. *Imperf* (No. 7n) 45·00; *Perf* (No. 28b) 30·00
R.3/4 No stop after left "Z" .. *Imperf* (No. 8e) 45·00
R.3/6 No stop after right "AFR" .. *Imperf* (No. 8f) 45·00; *Perf* (No. 29a) 30·00
R.4/1 Centre 2 wider, no stop after right "AFR" (*occurs on first printing also*) .. *Imperf* (No. 9a) 38·00; *Perf* (No. 30a) 30·00
R.4/2 Centre "2" wider .. *Imperf* (No. 9g) 45·00; *Perf* (No. 30b) 30·00
R.4/5 "P" in "PENCE" dropped .. *Imperf* (No. 9h) 45·00; *Perf* (No. 30c) 30·00

It has been suggested that there was a third printing of this value.

4d. value
First printing
R.1/2 No stop after left "AFR' (No. 10a) 45·00
R.1/3 No bar over lower right "4" (No. 10b) 45·00
R.1/3 "PENNY" for "PENCE" (*on small part of printing*) (No. 10c) 90·00
R.1/5 "POSTZFGEL" (No. 10d) 45·00
R.1/6 "AFB" at right (No. 10e) 45·00
R.2/1 "REB" at left (No. 10f) 45·00
R.2/2 "AFB" at left (No. 10g) 45·00
R.2/3 "POSTZEOEL" (No. 10h) 45·00
R.2/4 "AER" at right (No. 10i) 45·00
R.2/5 No stop after date (No. 10j) 45·00
R.3/2 Right spray inverted (No. 11a) 45·00
R.3/3 No bar over lower left "4" (*on small part of printing*) (No. 11b) 90·00
R.3/4 No stop after left "Z" (No. 11c) 45·00
R.3/6 "POSTZEGFL" (No. 11d) 45·00
R.4/1 Centre "4" wider, no stop after right "AFR" (No. 12a) 45·00
R.4/2 Centre "4" wider, left spray inverted (No. 12b) 45·00
R.4/3 "POSTZEGEI" (No. 12c) 45·00
R.4/4 No bar under top right "4" (No. 12d) 45·00
R.4/5 "AER" at left, "P" in "PENCE" dropped (No. 12e) 45·00
R.4/6 Left spray inverted (No. 12f) 45·00

Second printing
R.2/1 Left inner frame too high (No. 10k) 45·00
R.4/1–2 Centre "4" wider (No. 12g) 35·00
R.4/5 "P" in "PENCE" dropped (No. 12h) 45·00

6d. value
First printing
R.1/2 No stop after left "AFR" (No. 13a) 55·00
R.1/3 No bar over lower right "6" (No. 13b) 55·00
R.1/3 "PENNY" for "PENCE" (*on small part of printing*) (No. 13c) £100
R.1/5 "POSTZFGEL" (No. 13d) 55·00
R.1/6 "AFB" at right (No. 13e) 55·00
R.2/1 "REB" at left (No. 13f) 55·00
R.2/2 "AFB" at left (No. 13g) 55·00
R.2/3 "POSTZEOEL" (No. 13h) 55·00
R.2/4 "AER" at right (No. 13i) 55·00
R.2/5 No stop after date (No. 13j) 55·00
R.3/2 Right spray inverted (No. 14a) 55·00
R.3/4 Centre "6" inverted, no stop after left "Z" (*on small part of printing*) (No. 14b) £100
R.3/4 No stop after left "Z" (No. 14c) 55·00
R.3/6 "POSTZEGFL" (No. 14d) 55·00
R.4/1 Centre "6" wider, no stop after right "AFR" (No. 15a) 55·00
R.4/2 Centre "6" wider, left spray inverted (No. 15b) 55·00
R.4/3 "POSTZEGEI" (No. 15c) 55·00
R.4/4 No bar under top right "6" (No. 15d) 55·00
R.4/5 "AER" at left, "P" in "PENCE" dropped (No. 15e) 55·00
R.4/6 Left spray inverted (No. 15f) 55·00

Second printing
R.2/1 Left inner frame too high, no stop after left "REP" (No. 13k) 55·00
R.4/1–2 Centre "6" wider (No. 15g) 40·00
R.4/5 "P" in "PENCE" dropped (No. 15h) 55·00

1s. value
R.1/2 No stop after left "AFR" (No. 16a) 40·00
R.1/3 No bar over lower right "1" (No. 16b) 40·00
R.2/5 No stop after date (No. 16c) 40·00
R.3/4 "POSTZEGEI", no stop after left "Z" (No. 17a) 40·00
R.4/1 No stop after right "AFR" (No. 18a) 40·00
R.4/4 No bar under top right "1" (No. 18b) 40·00
R.4/5 "AER" at left (No. 18c) 40·00

MINIMUM PRICE

The minimum price quote is 10p which represents a handling charge rather than a basis for valuing common stamps. For further notes about prices see introductory pages.

LOCAL BRITISH OCCUPATION ISSUES DURING THE SOUTH AFRICAN WAR 1900–2

Stamps of the Transvaal Republic, unless otherwise stated, variously overprinted or surcharged.

LYDENBURG

Lydenburg fell to the British on 6 September 1900.

V.R.I.
3d.
(L 1)

1900 (Sept). *No.* 217 *surch with Type* L 1, *others optd* "V.R.I" *only.*

1 30 ½d. green .. 90·00 70·00
2 1d. rose-red and green .. 75·00 70·00
3 2d. brown and green .. £700 £550
4 2½d. blue and green .. £1800 £700
5 3d. on 1d. rose-red and green .. 75·00 60·00
6 3d. purple and green
7 4d. sage-green and green .. £1800 £600
8 6d. lilac and green .. £1800 £500
9 1s. ochre and green .. £3000 £2000

Only one genuine copy of No. 6 (unused) is known.

Type **34** surcharged "V.R.I. 1d." is now considered by experts to be bogus.

The above were cancelled by British Army postal service postmarks. These overprints with Transvaal cancellations are believed to be forgeries.

RUSTENBURG

The British forces in Rustenburg, west of Pretoria, were besieged by the Boers during June 1900. When relieved on the 22 June 1900 no "V.R.I" stamps were available so a local handstamp was applied.

V.R.
(R 1)

1900 (23 June). *Handstamped with Type* R 1 *in violet.*

1 30 ½d. green .. £110 75·00
2 1d. rose-red and green .. 85·00 60·00
3 2d. brown and green .. £190 75·00
4 2½d. blue and green .. £110 65·00
5 3d. purple and green .. £170 75·00
6 6d. lilac and green .. £600 £275
7 1s. ochre and green .. £1400 £700
8 2s. 6d. dull violet and green .. £5000 £3750

SCHWEIZER RENECKE

BESIEGED
(SR 1)

1900 (Aug). *Handstamped with Type* SR 1 *in black, reading vert up or down.* (a) *On stamps of Transvaal.*

1 30 ½d. green .. † £225
2 1d. rose-red and green .. † £225
3 2d. brown and green .. † £300
4 6d. lilac and green .. † £750

(b) On stamps of Cape of Good Hope

5 17 ½d. green .. † £400
6 1d. carmine .. † £400

Schweizer Renecke, near the Bechuanaland border, was under siege from 1 August 1900 to 9 January 1901. The British commander authorised the above stamps shortly after 19 August. All stamps were cancelled with the dated circular town postmark ("Schweizer Renecke, Z.A.R."), usually after having been stuck on paper before use. Unused, without the postmark, do not exist.

VOLKSRUST

1902 (Mar). *Optd with T* 35. *P* 12.

1 33 1d. pale blue .. — 45·00
2 6d. dull carmine .. — 55·00
3 1s. olive-bistre .. — 70·00
4 1s. 6d. brown .. — 80·00
5 2s. 6d. dull purple .. — 80·00

These are the normal Transvaal Revenue stamps of the period, authorised for postal use in Volksrust.

WOLMARANSSTAD

Cancelled
V-R-I.
(L 3)

Cancelled
V-R-I.
(L 4)

1900 (June). *Optd with Type* L 3.

1 30 ½d. green (B.) .. £200 £300
a. Opt inverted .. £600
2 1d. rose-red and green (B.) .. £140 £200
3 2d. brown and green (B.) .. £1300
4 2½d. blue and green (R.) .. £1200
a. Opt in blue .. £2750
5 3d. purple and green (B.) .. £2500 £2750
6 4d. sage-green and green (B.) .. £3000 £3500
7 6d. lilac and green (B.) .. £3000 £3500
8 1s. ochre and green (B.) .. — £6000

1900 (July). *Optd with Type* L 4.

9 34 1d. red (B.) .. £150 £225

ZULULAND

PRICES FOR STAMPS ON COVER

Nos. 1/10	*from* × 20
No. 11	—
Nos. 12/16	*from* × 12
Nos. 20/6	*from* × 20
Nos. 27/9	—
No. F1	*from* × 75

ZULULAND (1) **ZULULAND.** (2)

1888 (1 May)–**93.** *(a) Stamps of Great Britain optd with T* **1.**

1 **71** ½d. vermilion (11.88) .. .. .. 2·00 2·50
2 **57** 1d. deep purple .. .. .. 20·00 4·75
3 **73** 2d. green and carmine .. .. 11·00 16·00
4 **74** 2½d. purple/*blue* (9.91) .. .. .. 14·00 17·00
5 **75** 3d. purple/*yellow* .. .. 22·00 20·00
6 **76** 4d. green and brown .. .. .. 25·00 35·00
7 **78** 5d. dull purple and blue (3.93) .. 70·00 85·00
8 **79** 6d. purple/*rose-red* .. .. .. 11·00 16·00
9 **80** 9d. dull purple and blue (4.92) .. 65·00 65·00
10 **82** 1s. green (4.92) .. .. .. 85·00 95·00
11 **59** 5s. rose (4.92) £500 £600
1/11 .. .. *Set of* 11 £750 £800
1 and 3/11 H/S "Specimen" .. *Set of* 10 £600

(b) No. 97a of Natal optd with T **2.**

12 **23** ½d. green (7.88) .. .. .. 48·00 55·00
a. Opt double £1000 £1100
b. Opt inverted £1300
c. Without stop .. .. .. 18·00 27·00
d. Opt omitted (pair with normal) .. £4500 £4500

1894 (Jan). *No.* 103 *of Natal optd with T* **1.**

16 **15** 6d. mauve .. .. 45·00 45·00

3

4

(Typo D.L.R.)

1894 (18 Apr)–**96.** *Wmk Crown CA. P* 14.

20 **3** ½d. dull mauve and green .. .. 1·50 3·50
21 1d. dull mauve and carmine .. .. 5·00 70
22 2½d. dull mauve and ultramarine .. 12·00 6·00
23 3d. dull mauve and olive-brown .. 8·00 2·75
24 **4** 6d. dull mauve and black .. .. 17·00 16·00
25 1s. green .. .. .. 27·00 32·00
26 2s. 6d. green and black (2.96) .. .. 65·00 65·00
27 4s. green and carmine .. .. 90·00 £110
28 £1 purple/*red* £450 £475
29 £5 purple and black/*red* (Optd S. £375) £3500 £1200
20/8 .. .. *Set of* 9 £550 £600
20/8 Optd "Specimen" .. .. *Set of* 9 £350

Dangerous forgeries exist of the £1 and £5.

FISCAL STAMP USED FOR POSTAGE

1891 (June). *Fiscal stamp of Natal* (*Wmk Crown, CA, P* 14) *optd with T* 1.

F1 1d. dull mauve (Optd S. £60) .. .. 3·00 3·00

Other values, 1s. to £20 as No. F1 exist apparently with postmarks, but, as these were never authorised for postal use, they are no longer listed.

Zululand was annexed to Natal on 31 December 1897 and its stamps were withdrawn from sale on 30 June 1898.

UNION OF SOUTH AFRICA

Although South Africa is now a republic, outside the British Commonwealth, all its stamp issues are listed together here purely as a matter of convenience to collectors.

The province continued to use their existing issues until the introduction of Nos. 3/17. From 19 August 1910 the issues of any province were valid for use throughout the Union until they were demonetised on 31 December 1937.

PRICES FOR STAMPS ON COVER TO 1945

Nos. 1/15	*from* × 4
Nos. 16/17	—
Nos. 18/21	*from* × 6
Nos. 26/32	*from* × 2
No. 33	*from* × 4
Nos. 34/110	*from* × 1
Nos. D1/7	*from* × 4
Nos. D8/33	*from* × 6
Nos. O1/33	*from* × 4

1

(Des H. S. Wilkinson. Recess D.L.R.)

1910 (4 Nov). *Opening of Union Parliament. Inscribed bilingually. Wmk Multiple Rosettes. P* 14.

1 **1** 2½d. deep blue (H/S S. £325) .. .. 3·50 3·00
2 2½d. blue .. .. 2·00 1·25

The deep blue shade is generally accompanied by a blueing of the paper.

The price quoted for the "Specimen" handstamp is for the small italic type with capital and lower case letters.

2

3

4 Springbok's Head

(Typo D.L.R.)

1913 (1 Sept)–**24.** *Inscribed bilingually. W* **4.** *(a) P* 14.

3 **2** ½d. green 60 15
a. Stamp doubly printed £10000
b. Blue-green .. .. .. 1·75 15
c. Yellow-green .. .. .. 2·25 20
d. Booklet pane of 6 .. .. 24·00
4 1d. rose-red (*shades*) 60 10
a. Carmine-red .. .. .. 1·25 10
b. Scarlet (shades) .. .. .. 1·00 15
c. Booklet pane of 6 .. .. 30·00
5 1½d. chestnut (*shades*) (23.8.20) .. 30 10
a. *Tête-bêche* (pair) .. .. 1·75 15·00
b. Booklet pane of 6 (1921) .. 30·00
6 **3** 2d. dull purple .. .. .. 1·25 10
a. Deep purple .. .. .. 2·50 10
b. Booklet pane of 6 (1922) .. 45·00
7 2½d. bright blue .. .. .. 2·50 85
a. Deep blue .. .. .. 5·00 3·00
8 3d. black and orange-red .. .. 6·50 25
a. Black and dull orange-red .. 7·50 70
9 3d. ultramarine (*shades*) (4.10.22) .. 4·50 1·50
10 4d. orange-yellow and olive-green .. 9·00 45
a. Orange-yellow and sage-green .. 7·50 45
11 6d. black and violet .. .. .. 5·50 15
a. Black and bright violet .. .. 7·50 35
12 1s. orange .. .. 15·00 55
a. Orange-yellow .. .. .. 25·00 65
13 1s. 3d. violet (*shades*) (1.9.20) .. 12·00 7·00
14 2s. 6d. purple and green .. .. 55·00 1·00
15 5s. purple and blue .. .. .. £130 5·00
a. Reddish purple and light blue .. £130 8·00
16 10s. deep blue and olive-green .. £225 5·50
17 £1 green and red (7.16) £700 £350
a. Pale olive-green and red (1924) £900 £1200
3/17 .. .. *Set of* 15 £1000 £350
3/8, 10/17 Optd or H/S "Specimen" *Set of* 14 £1300

(b) Coil stamps. P 14 × *imperf*

18 **2** ½d. green .. .. 4·75 1·00
19 1d. rose-red (13.2.14) .. .. .. 6·00 3·75
a. Scarlet .. .. .. 7·00 4·25
20 1½d. chestnut (15.11.20) .. .. .. 5·00 4·25
21 **3** 2d. dull purple (7.10.21) .. .. 7·00 4·25
18/21 .. .. *Set of* 4 20·00 12·00

The 6d. exists with "Z" of "ZUID" wholly or partly missing due to wear of plate (*Price wholly missing, £75 un, £38 us*).

5

(Eng A. J. Cooper. Litho *Cape Times* Ltd)

1925 (26 Feb). *Air. Inscr bilingually. P* 12.

26 **5** 1d. carmine .. .. 3·50 6·00
27 3d. ultramarine .. .. 7·00 8·00
28 6d. magenta .. .. 10·00 13·00
29 9d. green .. .. 18·00 45·00
26/9 .. .. *Set of* 4 35·00 65·00

Beware of forgeries of all values perforated 11, 11½ or 13.

INSCRIPTIONS. From 1926 until 1951 (also Nos. 167 and 262/5), most issues were inscribed in English and Afrikaans alternately throughout the sheets.

As we only stock these in *se-tenant* pairs, unused and used, we no longer quote for single used copies and they must be considered to be worth very much less than half the prices quoted for pairs. Prices are for horizontal pairs, vertical pairs being worth about 50% less.

Similarly, the War Effort bantam stamps (Nos. 96/103), and Nos. 124 and D30/3 are priced for units of two or three as the case may be.

PRICES for Nos. 30/135 are for unused horizontal pairs, used horizontal pairs and used singles (either inscription), *unless otherwise indicated.*

6 Springbok

7 *Dromedaris* (Van Riebeeck's ship)

8 Orange Tree

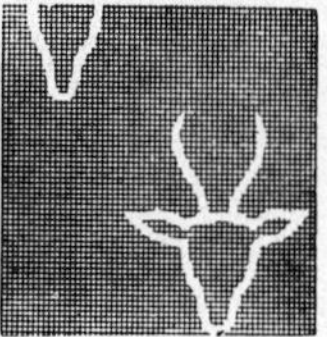
9

(Typo by Waterlow, from 1927 by Govt Printer, Pretoria)

1926 (1 Jan)–**27.** *W* **9.** *P* 14½ × 14.

			Un pair	Used pair	Used single
30	**6**	½d. black and green	2·50	1·75	10
		a. Missing "1" in "½"	£1700		
		b. Booklet pane of 6 ..	60·00		
		c. Perf 13½ × 14 (1927) ..	30·00	30·00	2·25
		ca. *Tête-bêche* (pair) ..	£850		
		cb. Booklet pane of 6 ..	£300		
31	**7**	1d. black and carmine	2·00	45	10
		a. Booklet pane of 6 ..	60·00		
		b. Perf 13½ × 14 (1927) ..	30·00	30·00	2·00
		ba. *Tête-bêche* (pair)	£950		
		bb. Booklet pane of 6 ..	£300		
32	**8**	6d. green and orange (1.5.26) ..	30·00	18·00	1·50
30/2		.. .. .. *Set of* 3	30·00	18·00	1·50

No. 30a exists in Afrikaans only. Nos. 30c and 31b were only issued in booklets.

Nos. 30/1 exist in coils, constructed from normal sheets.

For ½d. with pale grey centre, see No. 126.

For rotogravure printing see Nos. 42, etc.

10 "Hope"

(Recess B.W.)

1926 (1 Jan). *T* **10.** *Inscribed in English* (E) *or Afrikaans* (A). *W* **9.** *Imperf.*

		Single stamps E		A	
33	4d. grey-blue (*shades*)	1·00	60	1·00	60

In this value the English and Afrikaans inscriptions are on separate sheets.

This stamp is known with private perforations or roulettes.

11 Union Buildings, Pretoria

12 Groot Schuur

12*a* A Native Kraal

13 Black and Blue Wildebeest

14 Ox-wagon inspanned

15 Ox-wagon outspanned

16 Cape Town and Table Bay

(Recess B.W.)

1927 (1 Mar)–**28.** *W* **9.** *P* 14 (*early ptgs*) *or* 14 × 13½ (*from* 1930 *onwards*).

			Un pair	Used pair	Used single
34	**11**	2d. grey and maroon	8·00	16·00	50
35	**12**	3d. black and red	18·00	25·00	50
35*a*	**12*a***	4d. brown (23.3.28)	24·00	42·00	85
36	**13**	1s. brown and deep blue ..	30·00	40·00	80
37	**14**	2s. 6d. green and brown ..	£110	£225	14·00
38	**15**	5s. black and green	£225	£450	30·00
39	**16**	10s. bright blue and brown ..	£150	£130	9·00
		a. Centre inverted (*single stamp*)	£9000		
34/9		.. .. .. *Set of* 7	£500	£800	48·00
34/9 H/S "Specimen"		.. *Set of* 7	£850		

17 D.H. "Moth"

(Typo Govt Ptg Wks, Pretoria)

1929 (16 Aug). *Air. Inscribed bilingually. No wmk. P* 14 × 13½.

			Un single	Us single
40	17	4d. green	5·00	2·50
41		1s. orange	9·00	11·00

PRINTER. All the following issues, except *where stated otherwise*, are printed by rotogravure (the design having either plain lines or a dotted screen) by the Government Printer, Pretoria.

I

II

The two types of the 1d. differ in the spacing of the horizontal lines in the side panels:—Type I close; Type II wide. The Afrikaans had the spacing of the words POSSEEL-INKOMSTE close in Type I and more widely spaced in Type II.

Window flaw (R. 20/4 on all ptgs before 1937)

1930–45. *T* **6** *to* **8** *and* **11** *to* **14** *redrawn*, "SUIDAFRIKA" (*in one word*) *on Afrikaans stamps. W* **9.** *P* 15 × 14 (½*d.*, 1*d.*, *and* 6*d.*) *or* 14.

		Un pair	Used pair	Used single
42	½d. black and green (5.30)	1·75	1·50	10
	a. Two English or two Afrikaans stamps *se-tenant* (vert strip of 4)	40·00		
	b. *Tête-bêche*	£850		
	c. Booklet pane of 6	14·00		
43	1d. black and carmine (I) (4.30)	2·75	75	10
	a. *Tête-bêche*	£850		
	b. Frame omitted (*single stamp*)	£450		
	c. Booklet pane of 6	18·00		
43*d*	1d. black and carmine (II) (8.32)	28·00	2·25	10
44	2d. slate-grey and lilac (4.31)	15·00	4·00	20
	a. *Tête-bêche*	£2250		
	b. Frame omitted (*single stamp*)	£1000		
	c. Booklet pane of 6	£120		
44*d*	2d. blue and violet (3.38)	£170	50·00	2·50
45	3d. black and red (11.31)	48·00	55·00	2·50
	a. Window flaw	£110		
45*b*	3d. blue (10.33)	4·50	1·75	10
	ba. Window flaw	25·00		
46	4d. brown (19.11.32)	£140	90·00	8·00
46*a*	4d. brown (*shades*) (*again redrawn*) (1936)	2·75	2·00	10
47	6d. green and orange (5.31)	17·00	2·00	10
48	1s. brown and deep blue (14.9.32)	48·00	18·00	35
49	2s. 6d. green and brown (24.12.32)	90·00	75·00	3·00
49*a*	2s. 6d. blue and brown (1945)	14·00	8·00	20
42/9*a*	*Set of* 13	£500	£275	15·00

For similar designs with "SUID-AFRIKA" hyphenated, see Nos. 54 etc. and Nos. 114 etc.

Nos. 42/3, 43*d*/4 exist in coils.

No. 42a comes from the coil printing on the cylinder for which two horizontal rows were incorrectly etched so that two Afrikaans-inscribed stamps were followed by two English. This variety is normally without a coil join, although some examples do occur showing a repair join.

The 1d. (Type I) exists without watermark from a trial printing (*Price* £80 *un*).

The Rotogravure printings may be distinguished from the preceding Typographed and Recess printed issues by the following tests:—

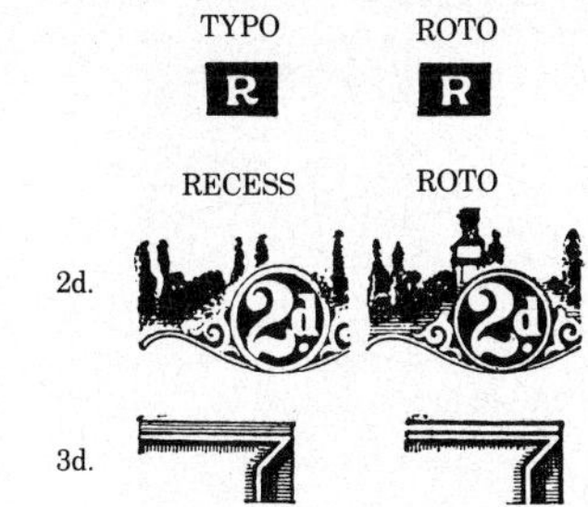

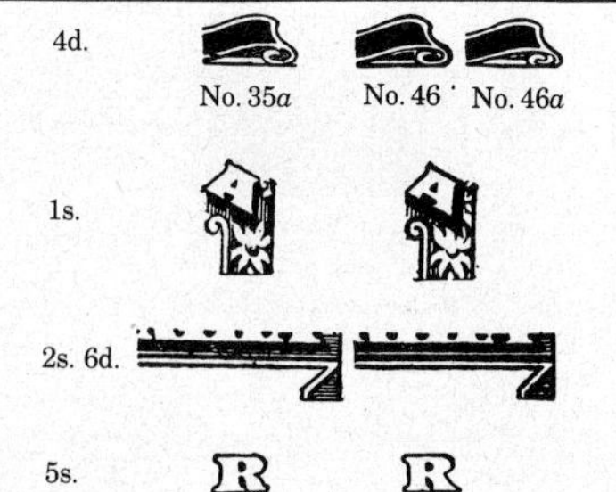

ROTOGRAVURE:

½d., 1d. and 6d. Leg of "R" in "AFR" ends squarely on the bottom line.

2d. The newly built War Memorial appears to the left of the value.

3d. Two fine lines have been removed from the top part of the frame.

4d. No. 46. The scroll is in solid colour.

No. 46*a*. The scroll is white with a crooked line running through it. (No. 35*a*. The scroll is shaded by the diagonal lines.)

1s. The shading of the last "A" partly covers the flower beneath.

2s. 6d. The top line of the centre frame is thick and leaves only one white line through it and the name.

5s. (Nos. 64/*a*). The leg of the "R" is straight.

Rotogravure impressions are generally coarser.

18 Church of the Vow

19 "The Great Trek"

20 A Voortrekker

21 Voortrekker Woman

1933 (3 May)–**36.** *Voortrekker Memorial Fund. W* **9.** *P* 14.

50	18	½d. + ½d. black and green (16.1.36)	3·25	3·50	50
51	19	1d. + ½d. grey-black and pink	3·25	1·50	25
52	20	2d. + 1d. grey-green and purple	4·00	4·00	55
53	21	3d. + 1½d. grey-green and blue	6·00	5·00	70
50/3		*Set of* 4	15·00	12·50	1·75

22 Gold Mine

22*a* Groot Schuur

I

II

III

Dies of 6d.

23 Groot Constantia

1933–49. "SUID-AFRIKA" (*hyphenated*) *on Afrikaans stamps. W* **9.** *P* 15 × 14 (½*d.*, 1*d. and* 6*d.*) *or* 14 (*others*).

54	6	½d. grey and green (9.35)	3·00	80	10
		a. Coil stamp. Perf 13½×14 (1935)	27·00	38·00	1·00
		b. Booklet pane of 6 (with adverts on margins)	18·00		
56	7	1d. grey and carmine (*shades*) (19.4.34)	40	30	10
		a. Imperf (pair)	£130		
		b. Frame omitted (*single stamp*)	£250		
		c. Coil stamp. Perf 13½×14 (1935)	32·00	35·00	90
		d. Booklet pane of 6 (with adverts on margins) (1935)	7·00		
		e. Booklet pane of 6 (with blank margins) (1937)	8·00		
		f. Booklet pane of 2 (1937)	2·00		
		g. Booklet pane of 6 (without margins) (1938)	10·00		
		h. Booklet pane of 6 (with postal slogans on margins) (1948)	4·00		
		i. Grey and bright rose-carmine (7.48)	55	25	10
57	22	1½d. green & brt gold (12.11.36)	1·50	1·00	10
		a. Shading omitted from mine dump (in pair with normal)	90·00		
		b. Blue-grn & dull gold (8.40)	5·50	1·75	10
		c. Booklet pane of 4 (1941)	19·00		
58	11	2d. blue and violet (11.38)	55·00	26·00	1·00
58*a*		2d. grey and dull purple (5.41)	27·00	38·00	1·25
59	22*a*	3d. ultramarine (2.40)	5·00	75	10
61	8	6d. green & verm (I) (10.37)	70·00	18·00	70
61*a*		6d. green & vermilion (II) (6.38)	19·00	1·00	10
61*b*		6d. grn & red-orge (III) (11.46)	12·00	75	10
62	13	1s. brown & chalky blue (2.39)	32·00	4·25	10
		a. Frame omitted (*single stamp*)	£950		
64	15	5s. black and green (10.33)	50·00	40·00	1·50
		a. Black and blue-green (9.49)	32·00	14·00	50
64*b*	23	10s. blue and sepia (8.39)	60·00	14·00	70
		ba. Blue & blackish brn (8.39)	35·00	3·00	30
54/64*ba*		(*only one 6d.*) *Set of* 10	£180	80·00	3·00

The ½d. and 1d. coil stamps may be found in blocks emanating from the residue of the large rolls which were cut into sheets and distributed to Post Offices.

Nos. 54 and 56 also exist in coils.

1d. Is printed from Type II. Frames of different sizes exist due to reductions made from time to time for the purpose of providing more space for the perforations.

3d. In No. 59 the frame is unscreened and composed of solid lines. Centre is diagonally screened. Scrolls above "3d." are clear lined, light in the middle and dark at sides.

6d. Die I. Green background lines faint. "SUID-AFRIKA" 16¼ mm long.

Die II. Green background lines heavy. "SUID-AFRIKA" 17 mm long. "S" near end of tablet. Scroll open.

Die III. Scroll closed up and design smaller (18 × 22 mm).

Single specimens of the 1930 issue inscribed in English may be distinguished from those listed above as follows:—

½d. and 1d. Centres in varying intensities of black instead of grey.

2d. The letters of "SOUTH AFRICA" are wider and thicker.

3d. The trees are shorter and the sky is lined.

6d. The frame is pale orange.

1s. The frame is greenish blue.

For similar designs, but printed in screened rotogravure, see Nos. 114 to 122*a*.

BOOKLET PANES. Booklets issued in 1935 contained ½d. and 1d. stamps in panes with advertisements in the top and bottom margins and no margin at right (Nos. 54b and 56d). These were replaced in 1937 by editions showing blank margins on all four sides (Nos. 56e and 64ca). Following a period when the booklet panes were without margins, a further 3s. booklet was issued in 1948 which had four margins on the panes and postal slogans at top and bottom (Nos. 56h, 87b and 114a).

24

JIPEX
1936
(24*a*)

(Des J. Booysen)

1935 (1 May). *Silver Jubilee. Inscr bilingually. W* **9.** *P* 15×14.

65	24	½d. black and blue-green	2·50	12·00	10
66		1d. black and carmine	2·75	4·00	10
67		3d. blue	23·00	48·00	2·25
68		6d. green and orange	42·00	60·00	3·25
65/8		*Set of* 4	65·00	£110	5·00

In stamps with English at top the ½d., 3d. and 6d. have "SILWER JUBILEUM" to left of portrait, and "POSTAGE REVENUE" or "POSTAGE" (3d. and 6d.) in left value tablet. In the 1d., "SILVER JUBILEE" is to the left of portrait. In alternate stamps the positions of English and Afrikaans inscriptions are reversed.

1936 (2 Nov). *Johannesburg International Philatelic Exhibition. Optd with T* **24a.**

			Un sheet	Us sheet
MS69	6	½d. grey and green (No. 54)	4·00	10·00
MS70	7	1d. grey and carmine (No. 56)	3·00	7·00

Issued each in miniature sheet of six stamps with marginal advertisements.

25

25*a*

(Des J. Prentice)

1937 (12 May). *Coronation. W* **9** (*sideways*). *P* 14.

71	25	½d. grey-black and blue-green	25	40	10
72		1d. grey-black and carmine	35	40	10
73		1½d. orange and greenish blue	50	50	10
74		3d. ultramarine	3·00	1·40	10
75		1s. red-brown & turquoise-blue	5·50	3·25	15
		a. Hyphen on Afrikaans stamp omitted (R. 2/13)	42·00		
71/5		*Set of* 5	8·50	5·50	40

No. 75a shows the hyphen completely omitted and the top of the "K" damaged. A less distinct flaw, on which part of the hyphen is still visible and with no damage to the "K", occurs on R. 4/17.

1937–40. *W* **9.** *P* 15×14.
75*b* **25*a*** ½d. grey and green .. .. 6·50 90 10
ba. Booklet pane of 6 (with blank margins) (1937) .. 35·00
bb. Booklet pane of 2 (1937) .. 13·00
bc. Booklet pane of 6 (without margins) (1938) .. .. 30·00
bd. Grey and blue-green (1940) 3·75 50 10

The lines of shading in T **25*a*** are all horizontal and thicker than in T **6**. In Nos. 75*b* and 75*bd* the design is composed of solid lines. For stamps with designs composed of dotted lines, see No. 114. Later printings of No. 75*bd* have a smaller design.

26 Voortrekker Ploughing

27 Wagon crossing Drakensberg

28 Signing of Dingaan–Retief Treaty

29 Voortrekker Monument

(Des W. Coetzer and J. Prentice)

1938 (14 Dec). *Voortrekker Centenary Memorial Fund. W* **9.** *P* 14 (*Nos.* 76/7) *or* 15 × 14 (*others*).
76 **26** ½d. + ½d. blue and green .. 9·00 4·00 30
77 **27** 1d. + 1d. blue and carmine .. 10·00 5·00 40
78 **28** 1½d. + 1½d. chocolate & blue-grn 12·00 8·50 70
79 **29** 3d. + 3d. bright blue .. .. 13·00 9·50 90
76/9 .. .. .. *Set of* 4 40·00 26·00 2·10

30 Wagon Wheel

31 Voortrekker Family

(Des W. Coetzer and J. Prentice)

1938 (14 Dec). *Voortrekker Commemoration. W* **9.** *P* 15 × 14.
80 **30** 1d. blue and carmine .. .. 2·75 1·25 20
81 **31** 1½d. greenish blue and brown .. 4·25 1·25 20

32 Old Vicarage, Paarl, now a museum

33 Symbol of the Reformation

34 Huguenot Dwelling, Drakenstein Mountain Valley

(Des J. Prentice)

1939 (17 July). *250th Anniv of Huguenot Landing in South Africa and Huguenot Commemoration Fund. W* **9.** *P* 14 (*Nos.* 82/3) *or* 15 × 14 (*No.* 84).
82 **32** ½d. + ½d. brown and green .. 4·50 4·25 30
83 **33** 1d. + 1d. green and carmine .. 8·50 4·50 30
84 **34** 1½d. + 1½d. blue-green and purple 14·00 8·00 70
82/4 .. .. .. *Set of* 3 24·00 15·00 1·10

34*a* Gold Mine

1941 (Aug)–**48.** *W* **9** (*sideways*). *P* 14 × 15.
87 **34*a*** 1½d. blue-grn and yellow-buff (*shades*) 25 15 10
a. Yellow-buff (centre) omitted £950
b. Booklet pane of 6 (with postal slogans on margins) (1948) .. .. .. 3·50

35 Infantry

36 Nurse and Ambulance

37 Airman

38 Sailor, Destroyer and Lifebelts

39 Women's Auxiliary Services

40 Artillery

41 Electric Welding

42 Tank Corps

42*a* Signaller

1941–46. *War Effort. W* **9** (*sideways on* 2*d*., 4*d*., 6*d*.). *P* 14 (2*d*., 4*d*., 6*d*.) *or* 15 × 14 (*others*). (*a*) *Inscr alternately.*
88 **35** ½d. green (19.11.41) 75 65 10
a. Blue-green (7.42) .. .. 2·75 1·60 10
89 **36** 1d. carmine (3.10.41) .. .. 1·25 55 10
90 **37** 1½d. myrtle-green (12.1.42) .. 65 50 10
91 **39** 3d. blue (1.8.41) .. .. .. 11·00 11·00 50
92 **40** 4d. orange-brown (20.8.41) .. 10·00 8·00 10
a. Red-brown (6.42) .. .. 25·00 18·00 1·10
93 **41** 6d. red-orange (3.9.41) .. .. 7·50 5·50 10
94 **42*a*** 1s. 3d. olive-brown (2.1.43) .. 7·50 5·00 15
a. Blackish brown (5.46) .. 5·50 5·00 15

(*b*) *Inscr bilingually*

			Un single	*Us single*
95	**38**	2d. violet (15.9.41)	45	10
96	**42**	1s. brown (27.10.41)	2·50	50
88/96		.. .. .. *Set of 7 pairs and 2 singles*	35·00	28·00

43 Infantry

44 Nurse

45 Airman

46 Sailor

47 Women's Auxiliary Services

48 Electric Welding

49 Heavy Gun in Concrete Turret

50 Tank Corps

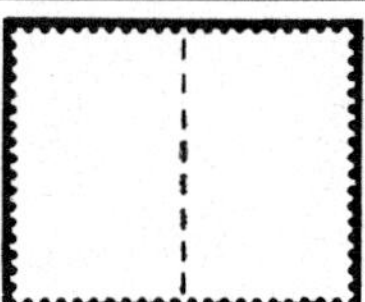

Unit (*pair*)

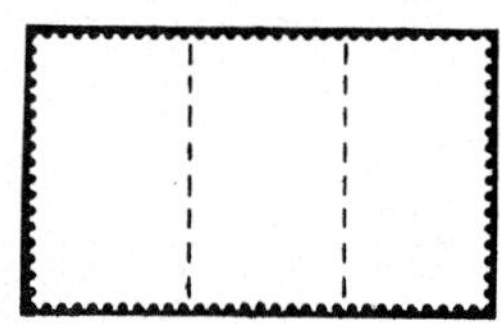

Unit (*triplet*)

1942–44. *War Effort. Reduced sizes. In pairs perf* 14 (P) *or strips of three, perf* 15 × 14 (T), *subdivided by roulette* 6½. *W* **9** (*sideways on 3d., 4d. and 1s.*). (*a*) *Inscr alternately.*

			Un unit	*Us unit*	*Us single*
97	**43**	½d. blue-green (T) (10.42) ..	70	70	10
		a. Green (3.43)	2·50	90	10
		b. Greenish blue (7.44)	2·00	80	10
		c. Roulette omitted	£375		
98	**44**	1d. carmine-red (T) (5.1.43) ..	70	50	10
		a. Bright carmine (3.44) ..	1·00	40	10
		b. Roulette omitted	£375		
99	**45**	1½d. red-brown (P) (9.42) ..	65	40	10
		a. Roulette 13 (8.42)	1·50	2·75	15
		b. Roulette omitted	£225		
100	**46**	2d. violet (P) (2.43)	90	70	10
		a. Reddish violet (6.43) ..	1·50	50	10
		b. Roulette omitted	£300		
101	**47**	3d. blue (T) (10.42)	7·00	8·50	10
102	**48**	6d. red-orange (P) (10.42) ..	2·00	1·40	10
		(*b*) *Inscr bilingually*			
103	**49**	4d. slate-green (T) (10.42) ..	10·00	4·00	10
104	**50**	1s. brown (P) (11.42)	7·00	1·50	10
97/104		.. .. .. *Set of* 8	26·00	16·00	65

52

53

1943. *Coil stamps. Redrawn. In single colours with plain background. W* **9.** *P* 15 × 14.

			Un pair	*Used pair*	*Used single*
105	**52**	½d. blue-green (18.2.43) ..	60	1·40	15
106	**53**	1d. carmine (9.43)	80	1·00	10

Quoted prices are for *vertical* pairs.

54 Union Buildings, Pretoria

1945–46. *Redrawn. W* **9.** *P* 14.
107 **54** 2d. slate and violet (3.45) .. 8·00 2·25 10
a. Slate & brt vio (*shades*) (10.46) 2·00 5·50 15

In Nos. 107 and 107*a* the Union Buildings are shown at a different angle from Nos. 58 and 58*a*. Only the centre is screened i.e., composed of very small square dots of colour arranged in straight diagonal lines. For whole design screened and colours changed, see No. 116. No. 107*a* also shows "2" of "2d." clear of white circle at top.

55 "Victory"

56 "Peace"

57 "Hope"

1945 (3 Dec). *Victory. W* **9.** *P* 14.
108 **55** 1d. brown and carmine 20 65 10
109 **56** 2d. slate-blue and violet .. 20 70 10
110 **57** 3d. deep blue and blue 20 75 10
108/10 .. .. .. *Set of* 3 55 1·75 25

58 King George VI

59 King George VI and Queen Elizabeth

60 Queen Elizabeth II as Princess, and Princess Margaret

(Des J. Prentice)

1947 (17 Feb). *Royal Visit. W* **9.** *P* 15 × 14.

111	**58**	1d. black and carmine	10	10	10
112	**59**	2d. violet	15	15	10
113	**60**	3d. blue	15	15	10
111/13		.. .. .. *Set of* 3	35	35	20

I
II

5s.

1947–54. "SUID-AFRIKA" *hyphenated on Afrikaans stamps. Printed from new cylinders with design in screened rotogravure. W* **9.** *P* 15 × 14 (*½d., 1d. and 6d.*) *or* 14 (*others*).

114	**25*a***	½d. grey and green (frame only screened) (1947)	30	85	10
		a. Booklet pane of 6 (with postal slogans on margins) (1948)	3·00		
		b. Entire design screened (2.49)	50	85	10
		ba. Booklet pane of 6 (with margin at right) (1951) ..	3·50		
115	**7**	1d. grey and carmine (1.9.50)	35	20	10
		a. Booklet pane of 6 (with margin at right) (1951) ..	5·00		
116	**54**	2d. slate-blue and purple (3.50)	30	3·00	10
117	**22*a***	3d. dull blue (4.49)	1·50	2·75	10
117*a*		3d. blue (3.51)	1·25	2·00	10
		b. Deep blue (1954)	60·00	50·00	2·00
118	**12*a***	4d. brown (22.8.52)	80	3·50	10
119	**8**	6d. green & red-orge (III) (1.50)	1·50	40	10
		a. Grn & brn-orge (III) (1951)	1·50	40	10
120	**13**	1s. brown & chalky blue (1.50)	6·00	2·50	10
		a. Blackish brown & ultram (4.52)	16·00	6·50	15
121	**14**	2s. 6d. green and brown (8.49)	8·50	12·00	30
122	**15**	5s. blk & pale blue-grn (I) (9.49)	30·00	19·00	50
122*a*		5s. black and deep yellow-green (II) (1.54)	60·00	50·00	1·25
114/22		.. .. .. *Set of* 9	45·00	40·00	1·25

In screened rotogravure the design is composed of very small squares of colour arranged in straight diagonal lines.

½d. Size 17¾ × 21¾ mm. Early printings have only the frame screened.

1d. Size 18 × 22 mm. For smaller, redrawn design, see No. 135.

2d. For earlier issue with centre only screened, and in different colours, see Nos. 107/*a*.

3d. No. 117. Whole stamp screened with irregular grain. Scrolls above "3d." solid and toneless. Printed from two cylinders.

No. 117*a*/*b*. Whole stamp diagonally screened. Printed from one cylinder. Clouds more pronounced.

4d. Two groups of white leaves below name tablet and a clear white line down left and right sides of stamp.

61 Gold Mine

62 King George VI and Queen Elizabeth

1948 (1 Apr). *W* **9.** *In pair, perf* 14, *sub-divided by roulette* 6½.

			Un unit of 4	*Us unit*	*Used single*
124	**61**	1½d. blue-green and yellow-buff	50	1·50	10

(Des J. Booysen and J. Prentice)

1948 (26 Apr). *Silver Wedding. W* **9.** *P* 14.

			Un pair	*Used pair*	*Used single*
125	**62**	3d. blue and silver	50	30	10

(Typo Government Printer, Pretoria)

1948 (July). *W* **9.** *P* 14½ × 14.

126	**6**	½d. pale grey and blue-green ..	30	2·40	15

This was an economy printing made from the old plates of the 1926 issue for the purpose of using up a stock of cut paper. For the original printing in black and green, see No. 30.

63 *Wanderer* entering Durban

(Des J. Prentice)

1949 (2 May). *Centenary of Arrival of British Settlers in Natal. W* **9.** *P* 15 × 14.

127	**63**	1½d. claret	15	15	10

64 Hermes

65 Wagons approaching Bingham's Berg

"Lake" in East Africa (R. 2/19)

(Des J. Booysen and J. Prentice)

1949 (1 Oct). *75th Anniv of Universal Postal Union. As T* **64** *inscr* "UNIVERSAL POSTAL UNION" *and* "WERELDPOSUNIE" *alternately. W* **9** (*sideways*). *P* 14 × 15.

128	**64**	½d. blue-green	50	50	10
129		1½d. brown-red	60	65	10
130		3d. bright blue	1·25	1·40	10
		a. "Lake" in East Africa ..	15·00		
128/30		.. .. .. *Set of* 3	2·10	2·25	25

(Des W. Coetzer and J. Prentice)

1949 (1 Dec). *Inauguration of Voortrekker Monument, Pretoria. T* **65** *and similar horiz designs. W* **9.** *P* 15 × 14.

		Un single	*Us single*
131	1d. magenta	10	10
132	1½d. blue-green	10	10
133	3d. blue	10	10
131/3	.. .. *Set of* 3	15	15

Designs:—1½d. Voortrekker Monument, Pretoria; 3d. Bible, candle and Voortrekkers.

68 Union Buildings, Pretoria

1950 (Apr)–**51**. *W* **9** (*sideways*). *P* 14 × 15.

			Un pair	*Used pair*	*Used single*
134	**68**	2d. blue and violet	15	20	10
		a. Booklet panes of 6 (with margin at right) (1951)	8·00		

1951 (22 Feb). *As No.* 115, *but redrawn with the horizon clearly defined. Size reduced to* 17¼ × 21¼ *mm.*

135	**7**	1d. grey and carmine	30	30	10

PRICES. All later issues except Nos. 167 and 262/5 are inscribed bilingually and prices are for single copies, unused and used.

69 Seal and Monogram

70 "Maria de la Quellerie" (D. Craey)

(Des Miss R. Reeves and J. Prentice (1d., 4½d.), Mrs T. Campbell and J. Prentice (others))

1952 (14 Mar). *Tercentenary of Landing of Van Riebeeck. T* **69**/**70** *and similar designs. W* **9** (*sideways on* 1d. *and* 4½d.). *P* 14 × 15 (1d. *and* 4½d.) *or* 14 × 15 (*others*).

136	½d. brown-purple and olive-grey	10	10
137	1d. deep blue-green	10	10
138	2d. deep violet	20	10
139	4½d. blue	10	10
140	1s. brown	15	10
136/40	.. .. *Set of* 5	40	30

Designs: *Horiz*—2d. Arrival of Van Riebeeck's ships; 1s. "Landing at the Cape" (C. Davidson Bell). *Vert*—4½d. "Jan van Riebeeck" (D. Craey).

SATISE (74)

SADIPU (75)

76 Queen Elizabeth II

1952 (26 Mar). *South African Tercentenary International Stamp Exhibition, Cape Town. No.* 137 *optd with T* **74** *and No.* 138 *with T* **75**.

141	1d. deep blue-green	15	50
142	2d. deep violet	15	10

(Des H. Kumst)

1953 (3 June). *Coronation. W* **9** (*sideways*). *P* 14 × 15.

143	**76**	2d. deep violet-blue	20	10
		a. Ultramarine	20	10

77 1d. "Cape Triangular" Stamp

(Des H. Kumst)

1953 (1 Sept). *Centenary of First Cape of Good Hope Stamp. T* **77** *and similar horiz design. W* **9.** *P* 15 × 14.

144	1d. sepia and vermilion	10	10
145	4d. deep blue and light blue	10	10

Design:—4d. Four pence "Cape Triangular" stamp.

79 Merino Ram

80 Springbok

81 Aloes

(Des A. Hendriksz and J. Prentice (4½d.))

1953 (1 Oct). *W* **9.** *P* 14.

146	**79**	4½d. slate-purple and yellow	20	10
147	**80**	1s. 3d. chocolate	80	10
148	**81**	1s. 6d. vermilion and deep blue-green	70	25
146/8		.. .. *Set of* 3	1·50	35

82 Arms of Orange Free State and Scroll

(Des H. Kumst)

1954 (23 Feb). *Centenary of Orange Free State. W* **9.** *P* 15 × 14.

149	**82**	2d. sepia and pale vermilion	10	10
150		4½d. purple and slate	10	25

83 Warthog

92 Springbok

93 Gemsbok

(Des H. Kumst)

1954 (14 Oct). *T* **83, 92/3** *and similar designs. W* **9** *(sideways on large vert designs). P* 15 × 14 *(½d. to 2d.), 14 (others).*

151	½d. deep blue-green		10	10
152	1d. brown-lake		10	10
153	1½d. sepia		10	10
154	2d. plum		10	10
155	3d. chocolate and turquoise-blue		15	10
156	4d. indigo and emerald		40	10
157	4½d. blue-black and grey-blue		60	1·25
158	6d. sepia and orange		50	10
159	1s. deep brown and pale chocolate		60	10
160	1s. 3d. brown and bluish green		1·00	10
161	1s. 6d. brown and rose		1·75	60
162	2s. 6d. brown-black and apple-green		3·50	20
163	5s. black-brown and yellow-orange		10·00	90
164	10s. black and cobalt		17·00	4·50
151/64		*Set of* 14	32·00	7·00

Designs: *Vert (as T* **83**)—1d. Black Wildebeest; 1½d. Leopard; 2d. Mountain Zebra. *(As T* **93**)—3d. White Rhinoceros; 4d. African Elephant; 4½d. Hippopotamus; 1s. Greater Kudu; 2s. 6d. Nyala; 5s. Giraffe; 10s. Sable Antelope. *Horiz (as T* **92**)—6d. Lion.

No. 152 exists in coils.

See also Nos. 170/7 and 185/97.

97 President Kruger

98 President M. Pretorius

(Des H. Kumst)

1955 (21 Oct). *Centenary of Pretoria. W* **9** *(sideways). P* 14 × 15.

165	**97**	3d. slate-green	10	10
166	**98**	6d. maroon	10	20

99 A. Pretorius, Church of the Vow and Flag

100 Settlers' Block-wagon and House

(Des H. Kumst)

1955 (1 Dec). *Voortrekker Covenant Celebrations, Pietermaritzburg. W* **9**. *P* 14.

			Un pair	*Us pair*	*Us single*
167	**99**	2d. blue and magenta	45	2·50	10

(Des H. Kumst)

1958 (1 July). *Centenary of Arrival of German Settlers in South Africa. W* **9**. *P* 14.

168	**100**	2d. chocolate and pale purple	10	10

101 Arms of the Academy

(Des H. Kumst)

1959 (1 May). *50th Anniv of the South African Academy of Science and Art, Pretoria. W* **9**. *P* 15 × 14.

169	**101**	3d. deep blue and turquoise-blue	10	10
		a. Deep blue printing omitted	£1200	

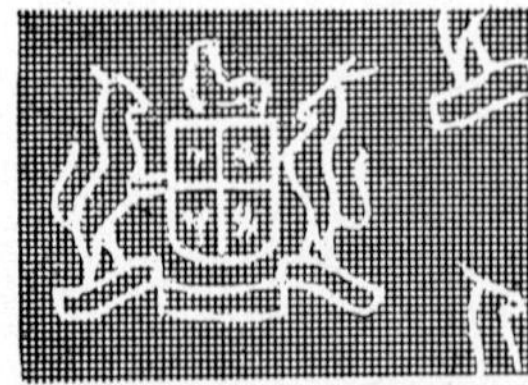

102 Union Coat of Arms

1 S (I) 1 S (II)

1959–60. *As Nos.* 151/2, 155/6, 158/9 *and* 162/3, *but W* **102**.

170	½d. deep greenish blue (12.60)		15	4·00
171	1d. brown-lake (I) (11.59)		10	10
	a. Redrawn. Type II (10.60)		20	10
172	3d. chocolate and turquoise-blue (9.59)		15	10
173	4d. indigo and emerald (1.60)		50	20
174	6d. sepia and orange (2.60)		70	60
175	1s. deep brown and pale chocolate (11.59)		6·00	30
176	2s. 6d. brown-black & apple-green (12.59)		2·75	4·00
177	5s. black-brown & yellow-orange (10.60)		6·00	26·00
170/7		*Set of* 8	14·50	32·00

Nos. 171/a. In Type II "1d. Posgeld Postage" is more to the left in relation to "South Africa", with "1" almost central over "S" instead of to right as in Type I.

No. 171 exists in coils.

103 Globe and Antarctic Scene

(Des H. Kumst)

1959 (16 Nov). *South African National Antarctic Expedition. W* **102**. *P* 14 × 15.

178	**103**	3d. blue-green and orange	15	10

104 Union Flag

106 "Wheel of Progress"

(Des V. Ivanoff and H. Kumst (1s.), H. Kumst (others))

1960 (2 May). *50th Anniv of Union of South Africa. T* **104, 106** *and similar designs. W* **102** *(sideways on 4d. and 6d.). P* 14 × 15 *(4d., 6d.) or* 15 × 14 *(others).*

179	4d. orange-red and blue		25	10
180	6d. red, brown and light green		20	10
181	1s. deep blue and light yellow		20	10
182	1s. 6d. black and light blue		1·00	1·75
179/82		*Set of* 4	1·50	1·75

Designs: *Vert*—6d. Union Arms. *Horiz*—1s. 6d. Union Festival emblem.

See also No. 190, 192/3.

108 Locomotives of 1860 and 1960

(Des V. Ivanoff)

1960 (2 May). *Centenary of South African Railways. W* **102**. *P* 15 × 14.

183	**108**	1s. 3d. deep blue	1·25	30

109 Prime Ministers Botha, Smuts, Hertzog, Malan, Strijdom and Verwoerd

1960 (31 May). *Union Day. W* **102**. *P* 15 × 14.

184	**109**	3d. brown and pale brown	10	10
		a. Pale brown omitted*	£1800	

*This is due to a rectangular piece of paper adhering to the background cylinder, resulting in R.2/1 missing the colour completely and six adjoining stamps having it partially omitted. The item in block of eight is probably unique.

(New Currency. 100 cents=1 rand)

1961 (14 Feb). *As previous issues but with values in cents and rand. W* **102** *(sideways on 3½ c., 7½ c., 20 c., 50 c., 1 r.). P* 15 × 14 *(½ c., to 2½ c., 10 c.),* 14 × 15 *(3½ c., 7½ c.) or* 14 *(others).*

185	½ c. deep bluish green (as 151)		10	10
186	1 c. brown-lake (as 152)		10	10
187	1½ c. sepia (as 153)		10	10
188	2 c. plum (as 154)		10	10
189	2½ c. brown (as 184)		10	10
190	3½ c. orange-red and blue (as 179)		15	80
191	5 c. sepia and orange (as 158)		20	10
192	7½ c. red, brown and light green (as 180)		20	1·00
193	10 c. deep blue and light yellow (as 181)		20	15
194	12½ c. brown and bluish green (as 160)		1·00	1·60
195	20 c. brown and rose (as 161)		2·00	2·75
196	50 c. black-brown & orange-yellow (as 163)		6·00	10·00
197	1 r. black and cobalt (as 164)		17·00	22·00
185/97		*Set of* 13	24·00	35·00

ALTERED CATALOGUE NUMBERS

Any Catalogue numbers altered from the last edition are shown as a list in the introductory pages.

REPUBLIC OF SOUTH AFRICA

110 African Pygmy Kingfisher

111 Kafferboom Flower

112 Afrikander Bull

113 Pouring Gold

114 Groot Constantia

115 Burchell's Gonolek

116 Baobab Tree

117 Maize

118 Cape Town Castle Entrance

119 Protea

120 Secretary Bird

121 Cape Town Harbour

122 Strelitzia

Two types of ½ c.:

I II

Type I from sheets. Spurs of branch indistinct.
Type II from coils. Spurs strengthened.

Three types of 1 c.:

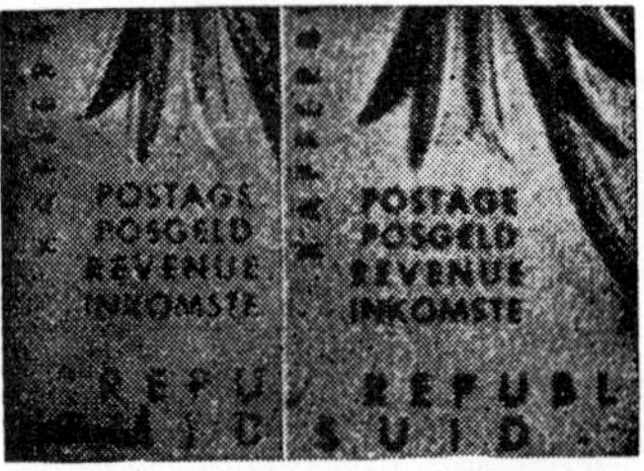

I II

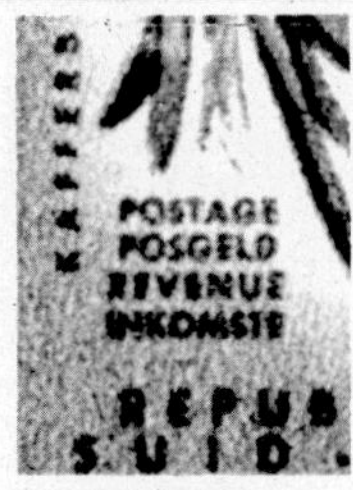

III

Type I. Lowest point of flower between "OS" of "POSTAGE". Right-hand petal over "E".
Type II. Flower has moved fractionally to the right so that lowest point is over "S" of "POSTAGE". Right-hand petal over "E".
Type III. Lowest point directly over "O". Right-hand petal over "G"

Two types of 2½ c.

In Type I the lines of the building are quite faint. In Type II all lines of the building have been strengthened by re-engraving.

(Des Mrs. T. Campbell (½ c., 3 c., 1 r.); Miss N. Desmond (1 c.); De La Rue (2½ c., 5 c., 12½ c.); H. L. Prager (50 c.); Govt. Ptg Dept artist (others))

1961 (31 May)–**63.** *Unsurfaced paper.* W **102** *(sideways on* ½ *c.,* 1½ *c.,* 2½ *c.,* 5 *c. to* 20 *c.). P* 14 × 15 (½ c., 1½ c.), 15 × 14 (1 c.), *or* 14 *(others).*

198 **110** ½ c. bright blue, carmine & brown (I) .. 10 10
 a. Perf 14 (3.63) 10 15
 b. Type II (coils) (18.5.63) 50 30
199 **111** 1 c. red and olive-grey (I) 10 10
 a. Type II (1.62) 10 10
 b. Type III (coils) (5.63) .. .. 1·00 1·00
200 **112** 1½ c. brown-lake and light purple .. 10 10
201 **113** 2 c. ultramarine and yellow .. 35 10
202 **114** 2½ c. violet and green (I) 15 10
 a. Type II. *Dp violet & green* (9.61) 20 10
203 **115** 3 c. red and deep blue 80 10
204 **116** 5 c. yellow and greenish blue .. 30 10
205 **117** 7½ c. yellow-brown and light green .. 60 10
206 **118** 10 c. sepia and green 75 10
207 **119** 12½ c. red, yellow and black-green .. 2·00 20
 a. Yellow omitted £180
 b. Red omitted .. ..
208 **120** 20 c. turquoise-blue, carm & brn-orge 3·50 20
209 **121** 50 c. black and bright blue .. .. 35·00 2·00
210 **122** 1 r. orange, olive-green & light blue 20·00 2·00
198/210 .. .. *Set of* 13 55·00 4·00

1961–74 *Definitives*

Key to designs, perfs, watermarks, papers and phosphors

Value	*Type*	*Perf*	W **102.** *Ordinary*	*No wmk. Ordinary*	W **127.** *Chalky*
½ c. **110**	(I)	14×15	198	—	—
	(I)	14	198a	—	—
	(II)	14×15	198b	—	—
1 c. **111**	(I)	15×14	199	211	—
	(II)		199a	211a	227
	(III)		199b	—	—
1½ c. **112**		14×15	200	—	228
2 c. **113**		14	201	212	229
2½ c. **114**	(I)	14	202	—	—
	(II)		202a	213/*a*	230/*a*
3 c. **115**		14	203	214	—
5 c. **116**		14	204	215	231
7½ c. **117**		14	205	216	232
10 c. **118**		14	206	217/*b*	233/*a*
12½ c. **119**		14	207	—	—
20 c. **120**		14	208	218	234/*a*
50 c. **121**		14	209	219	235
1 r. **122**		14	210	—	236

Redrawn Designs

		W **127** *Upright or Tête-bêche. Plain or phosphorised*	W **127** *Tête-bêche. Phos frame*	*No wmk. Phosphorised Glossy*	*No wmk. Phosphorised Chalky*
½ c. **130*a***	14	238	—	—	—
	14×15	238*b*	—	—	—
	14	238*c*/*d*	—	—	—
1 c. **131**	15×14	239	—	—	—
	13½×14	239a	—	—	—
1½ c. **132**	14×15	240/*b*	284	—	—
	14×13½	240c	—	—	—
2 c. **133**	14	241/*a*	285/*a*	315a	—
	12½	—	—	315	315b
2½ c. **134**	14	242/*a*	286/*a*	—	—
3 c. **135**	14	243/*a*	287	—	—
	12½	—	—	316	316a
4 c. **134**	14	243*b*	288	—	—
5 c. **136**	14	244/*a*	289	318a	—
	12½	—	—	318	318b
6 c. **137**	14	—	290	—	—
	12½	—	—	—	319
7½ c. **137**	14	245	291	—	—
9 c. **139**	14	245*a*	292	—	—
	12½	—	—	320/*a*	—
10 c. **138**	14	246/a	293	321a	—
	12½	—	—	321	321b
12½ c. **139**	14	247/*a*	294	—	—
15 c. **140**	14	248	295	—	—
20 c. **141**	14	249/*a*	296/*a*	—	—
	12½	—	—	323	323a
50 c. **142**	14	250	—	—	—
	12½	—	—	324	324a
1 r. **143**	14	251	—	—	—
	12½	—	—	325	—

New Designs

		W **127** *Tête-bêche. Plain or phosphorised*	W **127** *Tête-bêche. Phos-frame*	*No wmk. Phosphorised Glossy*	*No wmk. Phosphorised Chalky*
½ c. **168**	14 × 13½	276	282	—	—
	14 × 14½	276a	—	313	—
	14 × 15	—	282a	—	—
1 c. **169**	13½ × 14	277	283	—	—
	14	—	—	314	—
4 c. **182**	14	310/*a*	—	—	—
	12½	—	—	317/*b*	317c
15 c. **182*a***	14	311	—	—	—
	12½	—	—	—	322

1961 (Aug)–**63.** *As Nos.* 199, 201/6 *and* 208/9 *but without wmk.*

211 **111** 1 c. red and olive-grey (I) .. 20 30
 a. Type II (9.62) 45 40
212 **113** 2 c. ultramarine and yellow (8.63) 2·75 30
213 **114** 2½ c. deep violet and green (II) .. 30 10
 a. Violet and green (12.61) .. 30 10
214 **115** 3 c. red and deep blue (10.61) .. 45 10
215 **116** 5 c. yellow & greenish blue (12.61) 50 10
216 **117** 7½ c. yellow-brown & lt green (3.62) 80 10
217 **118** 10 c. sepia and green (11.61) .. 1·00 30
 a. Sepia and emerald .. .. 40·00 10·00
 b. Sepia-brown & lt green (7.63) 2·00 35
218 **120** 20 c. turq-bl, carm & brn-orge (4.63) 13·00 1·50
219 **121** 50 c. black and bright blue (8.62) .. 13·50 3·25
211/19 .. .. *Set of* 9 29·00 5·00

123 Blériot Monoplane and Boeing 707 Airliner over Table Mountain

124 Folk-dancers

1961 (1 Dec). *50th Anniv of First South African Aerial Post.* W **102** *(sideways). P* 14 × 15.

220 **123** 3 c. blue and red 20 10

(Des K. Esterhuysen)

1962 (1 Mar). *50th Anniv of Volkspele (folk-dancing) in South Africa.* W **102** *(sideways). P* 14 × 15.

221 **124** 2½ c. orange-red and brown 15 10

125 *The Chapman*

1962 (20 Aug). *Unveiling of Precinct Stone, British Settlers Monument, Grahamstown.* W **102.** *P* 15 × 14.

222 **125** 2½ c. turquoise-green and purple .. 40 10
223 12½ c. blue and deep chocolate .. 2·50 1·75

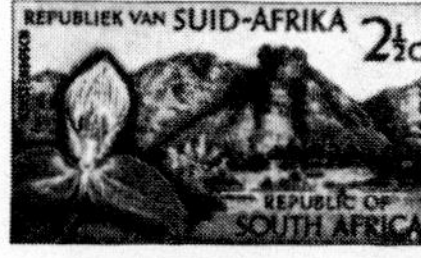

126 Red Disa (orchid), Castle Rock and Gardens

(Des M. F. Stern)

1963 (14 Mar). *50th Anniv of Kirstenbosch Botanic Gardens, Cape Town. P* 13½ × 14.

224 **126** 2½ c. multicoloured 20 10
 a. Red (orchid, etc) omitted .. £950

127 (normal version)

128 Centenary Emblem and Nurse

129 Centenary Emblem and Globe

1963 (30 Aug). *Centenary of Red Cross. Chalk-surfaced paper. Wmk* **127** *(sideways on* 2½ *c.). P* 14 × 13½ (2½ c.) *or* 15 × 14 (12½ c.).

225 **128** 2½ c. red, black and reddish purple .. 20 10
226 **129** 12½ c. red and indigo .. .. .. 4·00 1·00
 a. Red cross omitted.. .. .. £1200

1963–67. *As* 1961–3 *but chalk-surfaced paper and* W **127** *(sideways on* 1½ *c.,* 2½ *c.,* 5 *c.,* 7½ *c.,* 10 *c.,* 20 *c.). P* 15 × 14 (1 c.), 14 × 15 (1½ c.), *or* 14 *(others).*

227 **111** 1 c. red and olive-grey (II) (9.63) .. 10 10
228 **112** 1½ c. brown-lake & lt purple (1.67) 1·75 1·00
229 **113** 2 c. ultramarine and yellow (11.64) 15 15
230 **114** 2½ c. violet and green (II) (10.63) .. 10 10
 a. Bright reddish violet and emerald (II) (3.66) 35 20
231 **116** 5 c. yellow and greenish blue (9.66) 1·25 30
232 **117** 7½ c. yellow-brn & brt grn (23.2.66) 7·00 1·25
233 **118** 10 c. sepia-brown & lt emerald (9.64) 40 10
 a. Sepia-brown and green (1.67) 45 10
234 **120** 20 c. turq-bl, carm & brn-orge (7.64) 1·50 50
 a. Deep turqoise-blue, carmine and flesh (20.7.65) .. 1·75 50
235 **121** 50 c. black and ultramarine (4.66) 30·00 7·50
236 **122** 1 r. orange, lt green & pale bl (7.64) 55·00 27·00
227/36 .. .. *Set of* 10 90·00 35·00

In the 2½ c. (No. 230*a*), 5 c., 7½ c., 10 c. (Jan 1967 printing only) and 50 c. the watermark is indistinct but they can easily be distinguished from the stamps without watermark by their shades and the chalk-surfaced paper which is appreciably thicker and whiter.

130 Assembly Building, Umtata

1963 (11 Dec). *First Meeting of Transkei Legislative Assembly. Chalk-surfaced paper.* W **127.** *P* 15 × 14.

237 **130** 2½ c. sepia and light green 10 10
 a. Light green omitted £1200

130*a* African Pygmy Kingfisher

131 Kafferboom Flower

132 Afrikander Bull

133 Pouring Gold

134 Groot Constantia

135 Burchell's Gonolek

136 Baobab Tree

137 Maize

138 Cape Town Castle Entrance

139 Protea

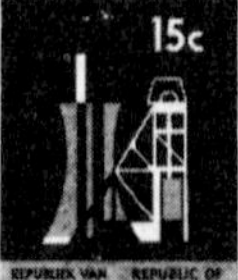

140 Industry

141 Secretary Bird

142 Cape Town Harbour

143 Strelitzia

(15 c. des C. E. F. Skotnes)

Redrawn types.

½ c. "½C" larger and "REPUBLIEK VAN REPUBLIC OF" smaller.

3 c. and 12½ c. Inscriptions and figures of value larger.

Others. "SOUTH AFRICA" and "SUID-AFRIKA" larger and bolder. The differences vary in each design but are easy to see by comparing the position of the letters of the country name with "REPUBLIC OF" and "REPUBLIEK VAN".

1964–72. *As* 1961–63 *but designs redrawn and new values* (4 *c.*, 9 *c. and* 15 *c.*). *Chalk-surfaced paper. W* **127** (*sideways on* ½, 1½, 2½, 4, 5, 7½, 9, 10, 15 *and* 20 *c.*). *P* 14×15 (1½ *c.*), 15×14 (1 *c.*) *or* 14 (*others*).

No.	Type	Value	Description	Un	Us
238	**130*a***	½ c.	brt blue, carm & brn (21.5.64)	10	10
			a. Imperf (pair)	£250	
			b. Perf 14×15. *Brt blue, carmine and yellow-brown* (6.7.67) ..	20	20
			c. Perf 14. *Bright blue, lake and yellow-brown* (3.68)	10	10
			d. Perf 14. *Bright blue, carmine-lake and yellow-brown* (9.68)	30	10
239	**131**	1 c.	red and olive-grey (9.3.67) ..	10	10
			a. Perf 13½×14 (7.68)	30	10
240	**132**	1½ c.	dull red-brn & lt pur (21.9.67)	15	10
			a. Purple-brown & lt pur (1968)	15	10
			b. Brt red-brown & lt pur (5.68)	15	10
			c. Perf 14×13½. *Red-brown and light purple* (14.8.69) ..	35	35
241	**133**	2 c.	ultramarine & yellow (8.1.68)	20	10
			a. Blue and yellow (10.71) ..	25	10
242	**134**	2½ c.	violet and green (19.4.67) ..	20	10
			a. Reddish violet and green (8.67)	20	10
243	**135**	3 c.	red and deep blue (11.64) ..	30	10
			a. Brown-red & deep blue (3.72)	35	10
243*b*	**134**	4 c.	violet and green (10.71) ..	75	30
244	**136**	5 c.	yellow & greenish bl (14.2.68)	40	10
			a. Lemon & dp greenish bl (10.71)	7·50	70
245	**137**	7½ c.	yellow-brn & brt grn (26.7.67)	60	10
245*a*	**139**	9 c.	red, yellow & slate-grn (2.72)	9·00	2·50
246	**138**	10 c.	sepia and green (10.6.68) ..	1·50	10
			a. Brown and pale green (7.68)	4·25	3·25
247	**139**	12½ c.	red, yellow & black-grn (3.64)	1·75	40
			a. Red, pale yell & bl-grn (2.2.66)	2·25	40
248	**140**	15 c.	black, light olive-yellow and red-orange (1.3.67)	2·00	25
249	**141**	20 c.	turquoise-blue, carmine and brown-orange (2.68)	4·50	15
			a. Turquoise-blue, carmine and orange-buff (12.71)	5·00	65
250	**142**	50 c.	black and bright blue (17.6.68)	4·50	40
251	**143**	1 r.	orange, lt green & lt bl (6.65)	5·00	1·00
238/51	..	..	.. .. *Set of* 16	27·00	4·75

WATERMARK. Two forms of the watermark Type **127** exist in the above issue: the normal Type **127** (sometimes indistinct), and a very faint *tête-bêche* watermark, i.e. alternately facing up and down, which was introduced in mid-1967. As it is extremely difficult to distinguish these on single stamps we do not list it.

The ½ (both perfs), 1, 2, 2½, 3, 15 c. and 1 r. are known in both forms, the 1½, 4, 5, 7½, 9, 10, 20 and 50 c. only in the *tête-bêche* form, and the 12½ c. Type **127** only.

GUM. The 2, 3, 5, 20, 50 c. and 1 r. exist with PVA gum as well as gum arabic.

PHOSPHORISED PAPER. From October 1971 onwards phosphor bands (see Nos. 282/96) gave way to phosphorised paper which cannot be distinguished from non-phosphor stamps without the aid of a lamp. For this reason we do not distinguish these printings in the above issue, but some are slightly different shades which are listed in the *Elizabethan Catalogue* and all have PVA gum.

The 4 c. and 9 c. are on phosphorised paper only and differ from Nos. 288 and 292 by the lack of phosphor bands.

145 "Springbok" Badge of Rugby Board

147 Calvin

1964 (8 May). 75*th Anniv of South African Rugby Board. Chalk-surfaced paper. T* **145** *and similar horiz design. W* **127** (*sideways on* 2½ *c.*). *P* 14 × 15 (2½ *c.*) *or* 15 × 14 (12½ *c.*).

No.	Value	Description	Un	Us
252	2½ c.	yellow-brown and deep green.. ..	15	10
253	12½ c.	black and light yellow-green ..	5·50	4·25

Design:—12½ c. Rugby footballer.

1964 (10 July). 400*th Death Anniv of Calvin* (*Protestant reformer*). *Chalk-surfaced paper. W* **127** (*sideways*). *P* 14 × 13½.

No.	Type	Value	Description	Un	Us
254	**147**	2½ c.	cerise, violet and brown	10	10

148 Nurse's Lamp

149 Nurse holding Lamp

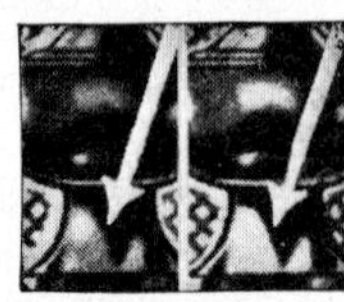
I. Screened base to lamp II. Clear base to lamp

1964 (12 Oct). 50*th Anniv of South African Nursing Association. Chalk-surfaced paper. W* **127** (*sideways on* 2½ *c.*). *P* 14 × 15 (2½ *c.*) *or* 15 × 14 (12½ *c.*).

No.	Type	Value	Description	Un	Us
255	**148**	2½ c.	ultramarine and dull gold (Type I)	10	10
256		2½ c.	brt blue & yellow-gold (Type II) ..	30	10
			a. Ultramarine and dull gold ..	15	10
257	**149**	12½ c.	bright blue and gold	3·25	2·00
			a. Gold omitted	£850	
255/7	..	..	.. .. .. *Set of* 3	3·25	2·00

150 I.T.U. Emblem and Satellites

1965 (17 May). *I.T.U. Centenary. T* **150** *and similar horiz design. Chalk-surfaced paper. W* **127.** *P* 15 × 14.

No.	Value	Description	Un	Us
258	2½ c.	orange and blue	25	10
259	12½ c.	brown-purple and green	3·00	1·75

Design:—12½ c. I.T.U. emblem and symbols.

152 Pulpit in Groote Kerk, Cape Town

153 Church Emblem

1965 (21 Oct). *Tercentenary of Nederduites Gereformeerde Kerk* (*Dutch Reformed Church*) *in South Africa. Chalk-surfaced paper. W* **127** (*sideways on* 2½ *c.*, *inverted on* 12½ *c.*). *P* 14 × 15 (2½ *c.*) *or* 15 × 14 (12½ *c.*).

No.	Type	Value	Description	Un	Us
260	**152**	2½ c.	brown and light yellow	15	10
261	**153**	12½ c.	black, light orange and blue ..	1·75	1·25

154 Diamond

155 Bird in flight

(Des C. E. F. Skotnes)

1966 (31 May). *Fifth Anniv of Republic. T* **154/5** *and similar designs. Chalk-surfaced paper. W* **127** (*sideways on* 1 *c.*, 3 *c.*). *P* 14 × 13½ (1 *c.*), 13½ × 14 (2½ *c.*), 14 × 15 (3 *c.*) *or* 15 × 14 (7½ *c.*).

No.	Value	Description	*Un pair*	*Us pair*	*Us single*
262	1 c.	black, bluish green & olive-yell	45	45	10
263	2½ c.	blue, deep blue & yellow-green	1·25	1·25	10
264	3 c.	red, greenish yellow & red-brn	4·75	4·75	10
265	7½ c.	blue, ultramarine and yellow	5·50	6·00	20
262/5	..	.. .. *Set of* 4	11·00	11·00	40

Designs: *Vert*—3 c. Maize plants. *Horiz*—7½ c. Mountain landscape.

Nos. 262/5 exist on Swiss-made paper with *tête-bêche* watermark from a special printing made for use in presentation albums for delegates to the U.P.U. Congress in Tokyo in 1969, as supplies of the original Harrison paper were by then exhausted (*Set of* 4 *pairs price* £140 *mint*).

158 Verwoerd and Union Buildings, Pretoria

(Des from portrait by Dr. Henkel)

1966 (6 Dec). *Verwoerd Commemoration. T* **158** *and similar designs. Chalk-surfaced paper. W* **127** (*sideways on* 3 *c.*). *P* 14 × 15 (3 *c.*) *or* 15 × 14 (*others*).

No.	Value	Description	Un	Us
266	2½ c.	blackish brown and turquoise ..	10	10
267	3 c.	blackish brown and yellow-green ..	10	10
268	12½ c.	blackish brown and greenish blue ..	70	50
266/8	..	.. .. *Set of* 3	80	50

Designs: *Vert*—3 c. "Dr. H. F. Verwoerd" (I. Henkel). *Horiz*—12½ c. Verwoerd and map of South Africa.

161 "Martin Luther" (Cranach the Elder)

162 Wittenberg Church Door

1967 (31 Oct). 450*th Anniv of Reformation. W* **127** ((*sideways*), *normal on* 2½ *c.*, *tête-bêche on* 12½ *c.*). *P* 14 × 15.

No.	Type	Value	Description	Un	Us
269	**161**	2½ c.	black and rose-red	10	10
270	**162**	12½ c.	black and yellow-orange	1·75	1·75

163 "Profile of Pres. Fouché" (I. Henkel)

164 Portrait of Pres. Fouché

1968 (10 Apr). *Inauguration of President Fouché. W* **127** (*sideways*). *P* 14 × 15.

No.	Type	Value	Description	Un	Us
271	**163**	2½ c.	chocolate and pale chocolate ..	10	10
272	**164**	12½ c.	deep blue and light blue	80	1·25

No. 272 also exists with the watermark *tête-bêche* (*Price un* £1; *used* £1.50).

165 Hertzog in 1902

1968 (21 Sept). *Inauguration of General Hertzog Monument, Bloemfontein. T* **165** *and similar designs. W* **127** (*tête-bêche on* 2½ *c.*, *inverted on* 3 *c.*, *sideways on* 12½ *c.*). *P* 14 × 13½ (12½ *c.*) *or* 13½ × 14 (*others*).

No.	Value	Description	Un	Us
273	2½ c.	black, brown and olive-yellow ..	10	10
274	3 c.	black, red-brown, red-orange and yellow	15	10
275	12½ c.	black, red and yellow-orange ..	2·00	90
273/5	..	.. .. .. *Set of* 3	2·00	90

Designs: *Horiz*—3 c. Hertzog in 1924. *Vert*—12½ c. Hertzog Monument.

168 Natal Kingfisher

169 Kafferboom Flower

1969. *W* **127** (*tête-bêche, sideways on* ½ *c.*). *P* 14 × 13½ (½ *c.*) *or* 13½ × 14 (1 *c.*).

No.	Type	Value	Description	Un	Us
276	**168**	½ c.	new bl, carm-red & yell-ochre (1.69)	10	20
			a. Coil. Perf 14 × 14½ (5.69)	2·00	1·40
277	**169**	1 c.	rose-red and olive-brown (1.69) ..	10	10

See also Nos. 282/3 and 313/14.

170 Springbok and Olympic Torch — 171 Professor Barnard and Groote Schuur Hospital

1969 (15 Mar). *South African Games, Bloemfontein. W* **127** *(tête-bêche, sideways). P* 14 × 13½.
278 **170** 2½ c. black, blue-black, red & sage-grn .. 15 10
279 12½ c. black, blue-blk, red & cinnamon .. 1·00 1·25

1969 (7 July). *World's First Heart Transplant and 47th South African Medical Association Congress. T* **171** *and similar horiz design. W* **127** *(tête-bêche). P* 13½ × 14 (2½ c.) *or* 15 × 14 (12½ c.).
280 2½ c. plum and rose-red 15 10
281 12½ c. carmine-red and royal blue .. .. 1·75 2·25
Design:—12½ c. Hands holding heart.

1969–72. *As 1964–72 issue, Nos. 276/7, and new value (6 c.), but with phosphor bands printed horizontally and vertically between the stamp designs, over the perforations, producing a frame effect. W* **127** *arranged tête-bêche (upright on 1, 2 and 3 c., sideways on others). P* 14×13½ (½, 1½ c.), 13½×14 (1 c.), *or* 14 (*others*).
282 **168** ½ c. new blue, carmine-red and yellow-ochre (1.70) 15 50
a. Coil. Perf 14×15 (2.71) .. 3·25 2·75
283 **169** 1 c. rose-red & olive-brown (12.69) 15 10
284 **132** 1½ c. red-brown & lt purple (12.69) 20 10
285 **133** 2 c. ultramarine and yellow (11.69) 30 10
a. Deep ultramarine & yell (8.70) 70 30
286 **134** 2½ c. violet and green (1.70) .. 25 10
a. Purple and green (24.7.70) .. 50 10
287 **135** 3 c. red and deep blue (30.9.69) .. 70 10
288 **134** 4 c. violet and green (1.3.71) .. 40 30
289 **136** 5 c. yellow & greenish bl (17.11.69) 85 10
290 **137** 6 c. yellow-brn & brt grn (3.5.71) 1·00 30
291 7½ c. yell-brn & brt grn (17.11.69) 3·75 30
292 **139** 9 c. red, yell & black-grn (17.5.71) 1·50 30
293 **138** 10 c. brown and pale green (1.70) .. 2·00 10
294 **139** 12½ c. red, yell & black-grn (2.5.70) 5·50 1·40
295 **140** 15 c. blk, lt ol-yell & red-orge (1.70) 2·75 1·40
296 **141** 20 c. turquoise-blue, carmine and brown-orange (18.2.70) .. 10·00 45
a. Turquoise-blue, carmine and orange-buff (9.72) .. .. 10·00 45
282/96 .. .. *Set of* 15 26·00 5·00
No. 286 exists on normal RSA wmk as well as RSA *tête-bêche* wmk.
The 1, 2, 2½, 3, 10, 15 and 20 c. exist with PVA gum as well as gum arabic, but the 4, 6 and 9 c. exist with PVA gum only.
For stamps without wmk, see Nos. 313, etc.

173 Mail Coach — 174 Transvaal Stamp of 1869

1969 (6 Oct). *Centenary of First Stamps of South African Republic (Transvaal). Phosphor bands on all four sides* (2½ c.). *W* **127** *(tête-bêche, sideways on* 12½ c.). *P* 13½ × 14 (2½ c.) *or* 14 × 13½ (12½ c.).
297 **173** 2½ c. yellow, indigo and yellow-brown 15 10
298 **174** 12½ c. emerald, gold and yellow-brown 3·25 2·50

PHOSPHOR FRAME. Nos. 299/306 have phosphor applied on all four sides as a frame.

175 "Water 70" Emblem — 177 "The Sower"

1970 (14 Feb). *Water 70 Campaign. T* **175** *and similar design. W* **127** *(tête-bêche (sideways on* 2½ c.)). *P* 14 × 13½ (2½ c.) *or* 13½ × 14 (3 c.).
299 2½ c. green, bright blue and chocolate .. 20 10
300 3 c. Prussian blue, royal blue and buff .. 25 10
Design: *Horiz*—3 c. Symbolic waves.

1970 (24 Aug). *150th Anniv of Bible Society of South Africa. T* **177** *and similar horiz design (gold die-stamped on* 12½ c.). *W* **127** *(tête-bêche, sideways on* 2½ c.). *P* 14 × 13½ (2½ c.) *or* 13½ × 14 (12½ c.).
301 2½ c. multicoloured 15 10
302 12½ c. gold, black and blue .. .. .. 2·50 2·50
Design:—12½ c. "Biblia" and open book.

178 J. G. Strijdom and Strijdom Tower — 179 Map and Antarctic Landscape

1971 (22 May). *"Interstex" Stamp Exhibition, Cape Town. P* 14 × 13½.
A. *W* **127** *(sideways tête-bêche)*. B. *W* **102** *(sideways)*.
A B
303 **178** 5 c. light greenish blue, black and pale yellow 20 10 1·75 4·50

1971 (22 May). *Tenth Anniv of Antarctic Treaty. W* **127** *(tête-bêche). P* 13½ × 14.
304 **179** 12½ c. blue-black, greenish bl & orge-red 6·00 5·50

180 "Landing of British Settlers, 1820" (T. Baines)

1971 (31 May). *Tenth Anniv of the Republic of South Africa. T* **180** *and similar design. W* **127** *(tête-bêche sideways on* 4 c.). *P* 13½ × 14 (2 c.) *or* 14 × 13½ (4 c.).
305 2 c. pale flesh and brown-red.. .. .. 15 10
306 4 c. green and black 15 10
Design: *Vert*—4 c. Presidents Steyn and Kruger and Treaty of Vereeniging Monument.
No. 306 exists with PVA gum as well as gum arabic.

PHOSPHORISED PAPER. All issues from here are on phosphorised paper *unless otherwise stated.*

181 View of Dam

(Des C. Bridgeford (4 c.), C. Lindsay (others))

1972 (4 Mar). *Opening of Hendrik Verwoerd Dam. T* **181** *and similar horiz designs. Multicoloured. W* **127** *(tête-bêche). P* 13½ × 14.
307 4 c. Type **181** 20 10
308 5 c. Aerial view of Dam 25 10
309 10 c. Dam and surrounding country (58 × 21 *mm*) .. .. 1·50 2·25
307/9 .. .. *Set of* 3 1·75 2·25

182 Sheep — 182*a* Lamb

(Des K. Esterhuysen (4 c.), H. Botha (15 c.))

1972 (15 May–Oct). *W* **127** *(tête-bêche). P* 14.
310 **182** 4 c. olive-brn, yell, pale bl & slate-bl .. 30 10
a. Grey-olive, yellow, bright blue and slate-blue (10.72) 30 10
311 **182a** 15 c. pale stone, deep blue and dull blue 2·50 20
Other shades exist of the 4 c.
See also Nos. 317 and 322.

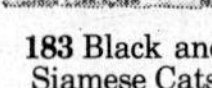

183 Black and Siamese Cats — 184 Transport and Industry

1972 (19 Sept). *Centenary of Societies for the Prevention of Cruelty to Animals. W* **127** *(sideways tête-bêche). P* 14 × 13½.
312 **183** 5 c. multicoloured .. .. .. 1·75 10

1972–74. *As Nos. 310/11 and 282 etc. but no wmk. P* 14 × 14½ (½ c.), 14 (1 c.) *or* 12½ (*others*). *Phosphorised, glossy paper.*
313 **168** ½ c. bright blue, scarlet and yellow-ochre (coil) (6.73) .. .. 15·00 15·00
314 **169** 1 c. rose-red and olive-brown (1.74) 40 10
315 **133** 2 c. blue and orange-yellow (11.72) .. 15 10
a. Perf 14. *Deep ultramarine and orange-yellow* (coil) (7.73) .. 11·00 11·00
b. Chalky paper (17.7.74) 40 50
316 **135** 3 c. scarlet and deep blue (8.5.73) .. 50 15
a. Chalky paper (18.2.74) .. .. 1·00 1·00
317 **182** 4 c. grey-blue, yellow, blue and bluish slate* (1.10.73) 30 30
a. Olive-sepia, yellow, azure and slate-blue (18.2.74) 50 30
*b. Lavender-brown, pale yellow, blue and bluish slate** (26.7.74) .. 30 20
c. Chalky paper* (22.8.74) .. 60 45
318 **136** 5 c. orge-yell & greenish bl (4.10.73) 1·75 70
a. Perf 14. *Yellow and light greenish blue* (coil) (7.73) .. .. 12·00 12·00
b. Chalky paper (5.74) .. .. 2·00 90
319 **137** 6 c. yellow-brown and bright green (*chalky paper*) (22.7.74) .. 2·00 1·50
320 **139** 9 c. red, yellow-green & grn-blk (6.73) 1·75 1·75
a. Red, deep yellowish green and green-black (4.74) .. .. 2·50 1·50
321 **138** 10 c. reddish brown & brt grn (8.5.73) 75 20
a. Perf 14 (coil) (6.73) .. .. 14·00 14·00
b. Chalky paper (17.7.74) .. 1·50 70
322 **182a** 15 c. pale stone, deep blue and dull blue (*chalky paper*) (4.9.74) .. .. 3·25 3·75
323 **141** 20 c. turquoise-blue, rose-carmine and orange-buff (8.5.73) .. .. 3·25 35
a. Chalky paper (5.74) .. .. 5·00 70
324 **142** 50 c. black and bright blue (6.73) .. 4·50 1·00
a. Chalky paper (22.7.74) .. .. 9·00 6·00
325 **143** 1 r. orange, lt green & lt blue (8.10.73) 14·00 2·00
a. Orange omitted £950
313/25 .. .. *Set of* 13 42·00 23·00
*On these stamps the colours are known to vary within the sheet.
No. 314 also differs in that the central design has been moved down about 1 mm.
Nos. 317/c also differ from No. 310 by measuring 26¼ × 21 mm instead of 27¼ × 21¾ mm.

(Des J. Hoekstra (4 c.), M. Barnett (others))

1973 (1 Feb). *50th Anniv of ESCOM (Electricity Supply Commission). T* **184** *and similar vert designs. Multicoloured. P* 12 × 12½ (4 c.) *or* 12½ (*others*).
326 4 c. Type **184** 20 10
327 5 c. Pylon (21 × 28 *mm*) 30 10
328 15 c. Cooling Towers (21 × 28 *mm*) .. .. 3·00 3·25
326/8 .. .. *Set of* 3 3·25 3·25

185 University Coat of arms — 187 C. J. Langenhoven

186 Rescuing Sailors

(Des P. de Wet (15 c.), H. Meiring (others))

1973 (2 Apr). *Centenary of University of South Africa. T* **185** *and similar designs. W* **127** *(tête-bêche)* (5 c.) *or no wmk (others). P* 12 × 12½ (5 c.) *or* 12½ (*others*).
329 4 c. multicoloured 20 10
330 5 c. multicoloured 30 15
331 15 c. black and gold .. .. 3·00 3·00
329/31 .. .. *Set of* 3 3·25 3·00
Designs: *Horiz* (37 × 21 *mm*)—5 c. University Complex, Pretoria. *Vert (As T* **185**)—15 c. Old University Building, Cape Town.

WATERMARK. All issues from this date are on unwatermarked paper, *unless otherwise stated.*

(Des M. Barnett)

1973 (2 June). *Bicentenary of Rescue by Wolraad Woltemade. T* **186** *and similar horiz designs. P* 11½ × 12½.
332 4 c. lt red-brown, lt yellow-green and black .. 25 10
333 5 c. yellow-olive, light yellow-green & black 40 10
334 15 c. red-brown, light yellow-green and black 5·50 5·50
332/4 .. .. *Set of* 3 5·50 5·50
Designs:—5 c. *De Jong Thomas* foundering; 15 c. *De Jong Thomas* breaking up and sailors drowning.

(Des J. Mostert)

1973 (1 Aug). *Birth Centenary of C. J. Langenhoven (politician and composer of national anthem). T* **187** *and similar designs. P* 12½ (4 *and* 5 c.) *or* 11½ × 12½ (15 c.).
335 **187** 4 c. multicoloured 25 10
336 – 5 c. multicoloured 35 10
337 – 15 c. multicoloured .. .. .. 5·00 4·75
335/7 .. .. *Set of* 3 5·00 4·75
Nos. 336/7 are as T **187** but with motifs rearranged. The 5 c. is vert, 21 × 38 mm, and the 15 c. is horiz, 38 × 21 mm.

188 Communications Map

(Des C. Webb)

1973 (1 Oct). *World Communications Day. P* 12½.

(a) No wmk. Glossy paper

338 **188** 15 c. multicoloured .. .. .. 80 1·40

(b) W **127** *(tête-bêche). Chalky paper*

339 **188** 15 c. multicoloured .. .. .. 1·50 4·25

189 Restored Buildings — **190** Burgerspond (obverse and reverse)

(Des W. Jordaan)

1974 (14 Mar). *Restoration of Tulbagh. T* **189** *and similar multicoloured design. P* 12½.

340 4 c. Type **189** 15 10
341 5 c. Restored Church Street (58 × 21 *mm*) .. 40 60

(Des P. de Wet. Litho)

1974 (6 Apr). *Centenary of the Burgerspond (coin). P* 12½ × 12.

342 **190** 9 c. brown, orange-red & pale yell-olive 60 95

191 Dr. Malan — **192** Congress Emblem

(Des I. Henkel)

1974 (22 May). *Birth Centenary of Dr. D. F. Malan (Prime Minister). P* 12½ × 12.

343 **191** 4 c. blue and light blue 15 10

(Des Ingrid Paul)

1974 (13 June). 15*th World Sugar Congress, Durban. P* 12 × 12½.

344 **192** 15 c. deep ultramarine and silver .. 1·00 1·50

193 "50" and Radio Waves

(Des Ingrid Paul)

1974 (13 July). 50*th Anniv of Broadcasting in South Africa. P* 12 × 12½.

345 **193** 4 c. red and black 10 10

194 Monument Building

(Des G. Cunningham)

1974 (13 July). *Inauguration of British Settlers' Monument, Grahamstown. P* 12 × 12½.

346 **194** 5 c. red and black 10 10

COVER PRICES

Cover factors are quoted at the beginning of each country for most issues to 1945. An explanation of the system can be found on page x. The factors quoted do not, however, apply to philatelic covers.

195 Stamps of the South African Provinces

(Des K. Esterhuysen)

1974 (9 Oct). *Centenary of Universal Postal Union. P* 12½.

347 **195** 15 c. multicoloured 80 80

196 Iris — **197** Bokmakierie Shrikes

(Des E. de Jong. Recess and photo)

1974 (20 Nov)–**76**. *Multicoloured. Glossy paper* (2, 3, 4, 6, 7, 30 *c. and* 1 *r.) or chalk-surfaced paper (others). P* 12½ (1 *to* 25 *c.) or* 12×12½ *(others).*

(a) Vert designs as T **196** *showing flowers, or horiz designs showing birds or fish.*

348 1 c. Type **196** 10 10
349 2 c. Wild Heath 15 10
a. Chalk-surfaced paper (2.75) 10 10
350 3 c. Geranium 30 10
a. Chalk-surfaced paper (*deep claret background*) (6.75) 10 10
ab. Imperf (pair) £250
ac. Brown-purple background (6.76) .. 10 10
351 4 c. Arum Lily 30 10
a. Chalk-surfaced paper (2.75) 10 10
ab. Imperf (pair) £160
352 5 c. Cape Gannet 20 10
353 6 c. Galjoen (fish) 25 10
354 7 c. Zebra Fish 25 10
355 9 c. Angel Fish 30 10
356 10 c. Moorish Idol 30 10
357 14 c. Roman (fish) 30 10
358 15 c. Greater Double-collared Sunbird .. 30 10
359 20 c. Yellow-billed Hornbill 45 10
360 25 c. Barberton Daisy 45 10

(b) Horiz designs as T **197**

361 30 c. Type **197** .. .. 7·50 50
362 50 c. Stanley Cranes .. .. .. 2·25 35
363 1 r. Bateleurs .. .. 8·00 2·75
348/63 .. .. *Set of* 16 19·00 3·75

A used block of 4 and a single on cover of No. 351 have been seen with the yellow omitted.

1974 (20 Nov)–**76**. *Coil stamps. As Nos.* 348/9, 352 *and* 356 *but photo, colours changed. Glossy paper. P* 12½.

370 1 c. reddish violet and pink 75 40
a. Perf 14. Chalk-surfaced paper (12.75) .. 55 40
371 2 c. bronze-green and yellow-ochre 80 40
a. Chalk-surfaced paper (7.75) .. .. 1·10 40
b. Perf 14. Chalk-surfaced paper (11.76?) .. 1·40 30
372 5 c. black and light slate-blue .. .. 1·40 60
373 10 c. deep violet-blue and light blue .. 4·25 4·25
a. Perf 14. Chalk-surfaced paper (4.76) .. 3·50 3·50
370/3 .. .. *Set of* 4 5·50 4·25

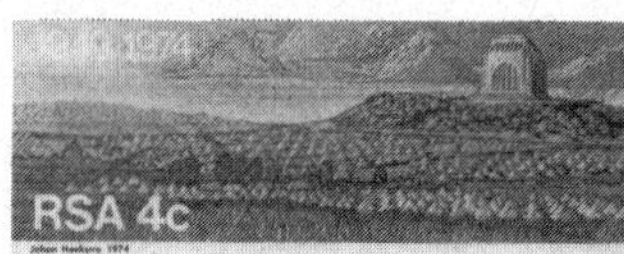

198 Voortrekker Monument and Encampment

(Des J. Hoekstra)

1974 (6 Dec). 25*th Anniv of Voortrekker Monument, Pretoria. P* 12½.

374 **198** 4 c. multicoloured 20 20

199 SASOL Complex — **200** President Diederichs

(Des C. Webb)

1975 (26 Feb). 25*th Anniv of SASOL (South African Coal, Oil and Gas Corporation Ltd). P* 11½ × 12½.

375 **199** 15 c. multicoloured .. .. .. 1·25 1·50

(Des J. L. Booysen. Recess (4 c.) or photo (15 c.))

1975 (19 Apr). *Inauguration of the State President. P* 12½ × 11½.

376 **200** 4 c. agate and gold 10 10
377 15 c. royal blue and gold .. .. .. 70 1·25

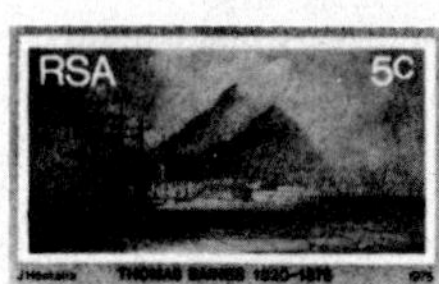

201 Jan Smuts — **202** "Dutch East Indiaman, Table Bay"

(Des J. Hoekstra. Recess and photo)

1975 (24 May). *Jan Smuts Commemoration. P* 12½ × 11½.

378 **201** 4 c. black and olive-black 10 10

(Des J. Hoekstra. Photo (Nos. 379/82) or litho (**MS**383))

1975 (18 June). *Death Centenary of Thomas Baines (painter). T* **202** *and similar horiz designs. Multicoloured. P* 11½ × 12½.

379 5 c. Type **202** 20 10
380 9 c. "Cradock, 1848" 30 20
381 15 c. "Thirsty Flat, 1848" 50 50
382 30 c. "Pretoria, 1874" .. .. 1·00 1·75
379/82 .. .. *Set of* 4 1·75 2·25
MS383 120 × 95 mm. Nos. 379/82 .. .. .. 1·90 4·00

203 Gideon Malherbe's House, Paarl

(Des P. de Wet. Recess and photo)

1975 (14 Aug). *Centenary of Genootskap van Regte Afrikaners (Afrikaner Language Movement). P* 12½.

384 **203** 4 c. multicoloured 10 10

204 "Automatic Sorting" — **205** Title Page of *Die Afrikaanse Patriot*

(Des J. Sampson)

1975 (11 Sept). *Postal Mechanisation. P* 12½ × 11½.

385 **204** 4 c. multicoloured 10 10

(Des K. Esterhuysen. Recess and photo (4 c.). Des P. de Wet. Litho (5 c.))

1975 (10 Oct). *Inauguration of the Language Monument, Paarl. T* **205** *and similar vert design. P* 12½ × 11½.

386 4 c. black, pale stone and bright orange .. 10 10
387 5 c. multicoloured 10 10

Design:—5 c. "Afrikaanse Taalmonument".

206 Table Mountain

(Des P. Bosman and J. Hoekstra. Litho)

1975 (13 Nov). *Tourism. T* **206** *and similar horiz designs. Multicoloured. P* 12½.

388 15 c. Type **206** .. .. 4·50 4·50
a. Block of 4. Nos. 388/91 .. .. 16·00
ab. Yellow-orange and pale lemon ("RSA 15 c") omitted .. .. .. † —
389 15 c. Johannesburg .. .. 4·50 4·50
390 15 c. Cape Vineyards .. .. 4·50 4·50
391 15 c. Lions in Kruger National Park .. 4·50 4·50
388/91 .. .. *Set of* 4 16·00 16·00

Nos. 388/91 were printed together, *se-tenant*, in blocks of 4 throughout the sheet.

Nos. 388/91 were printed in six colours. At least one sheet, subsequently used to prepare official first day covers at Pretoria, had the final two colours, yellow-orange and pale lemon, omitted.

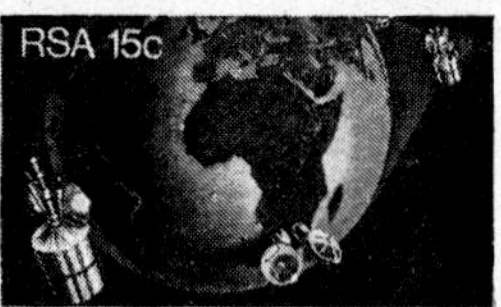

207 Globe and Satellites

(Des J. Hoekstra. Litho)

1975 (3 Dec). *Satellite Communication. P* 12½.
392 **207** 15 c. multicoloured 40 40

208 Bowls **(209)**

(Des J. Maskew. Litho)

1976. *Sporting Commemorations. T* **208** *and similar vert designs. P* 12½ × 11½.
393 15 c. black and light sage-green (18.2) . . 30 70
394 15 c. black and bright yellow-green (15.3) . . 75 1·40
395 15 c. black and pale yellow-olive (16.8) . . 40 60
396 15 c. black and apple-green (2.12) . . 30 55
393/6 . . . . *Set of* 4 1·60 3·00
MS397 161 × 109 mm. Nos. 393/6 (2.12) . . . . 2·75 4·50
Designs:—No. 393, Type **208** (World Bowls Championships. Johannesburg); No. 394, Batsman (Centenary of Organised Cricket in South Africa); No. 395, Polo player; No. 396, Gary Player (golfer).

1976 (6 Apr). *South Africa's Victory in World Bowls Championships. No.* 393 *optd with T* **209** *in gold.*
398 **208** 15 c. black and light sage-green 30 70

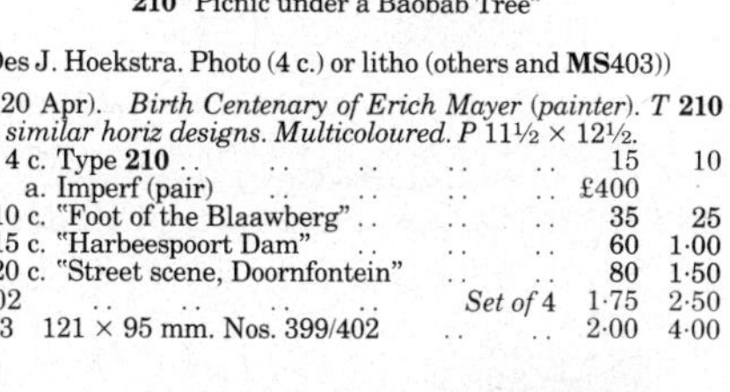

210 "Picnic under a Baobab Tree"

(Des J. Hoekstra. Photo (4 c.) or litho (others and **MS**403))

1976 (20 Apr). *Birth Centenary of Erich Mayer (painter). T* **210** *and similar horiz designs. Multicoloured. P* 11½ × 12½.
399 4 c. Type **210** 15 10
a. Imperf (pair) £400
400 10 c. "Foot of the Blaauwberg" 35 25
401 15 c. "Harbeespoort Dam" . . . . . . 60 1·00
402 20 c. "Street scene, Doornfontein" . . . . 80 1·50
399/402 . . . . *Set of* 4 1·75 2·50
MS403 121 × 95 mm. Nos. 399/402 . . . . 2·00 4·00

211 Cheetah **212** "Emily Hobhouse" (H. Naude)

(Des P. Bosman. Photo (3 c.) or litho (others))

1976 (5 June). *World Environmental Day. T* **211** *and similar horiz designs. Multicoloured. P* 11½ × 12½.
404 3 c. Type **211** 15 10
405 10 c. Black Rhinoceros 70 35
406 15 c. Blesbok . . . . 85 1·10
407 20 c. Mountain Zebra . . . . . . 1·25 1·75
404/7 . . . . *Set of* 4 2·75 3·00

(Des J. Hoekstra)

1976 (8 June). *50th Death Anniv of Emily Hobhouse (welfare worker). P* 12½ × 11½.
408 **212** 4 c. multicoloured 10 10

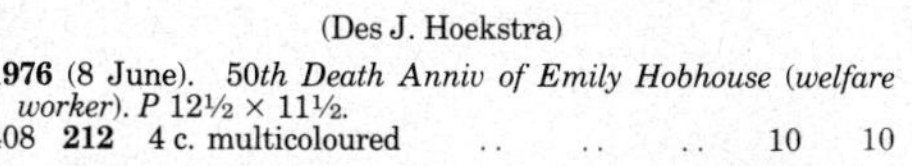

213 Steam Packet, 1876 **214** Family with Globe

(Des K. Esterhuysen. Litho)

1976 (5 Oct). *Ocean Mail Service Centenary. P* 11½ × 12½.
409 **213** 10 c. multicoloured 60 85
a. Imperf (horiz pair) £375

(Des I. Ross)

1976 (6 Nov). *Family Planning and Child Welfare. P* 12½ × 11½.
410 **214** 4 c. chestnut and light salmon 10 10

215 Glasses of Wine **216** Dr. Jacob du Toit

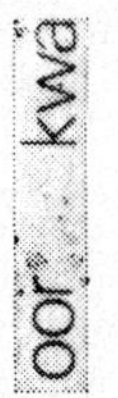

First "die" of Afrikaans inscription at left omitted (R. 1/3 on every third sheet)

(Des H. Botha. Litho)

1977 (14 Feb). *International Wine Symposium, Cape Town. P* 12½ × 11½.
411 **215** 15 c. multicoloured 40 85
a. "die" omitted . . . . . . 15·00

(Des J. Hoekstra)

1977 (21 Feb). *Birth Centenary of J. D. du Toit (theologian and poet). P* 12½ × 11½.
412 **216** 4 c. multicoloured 10 10

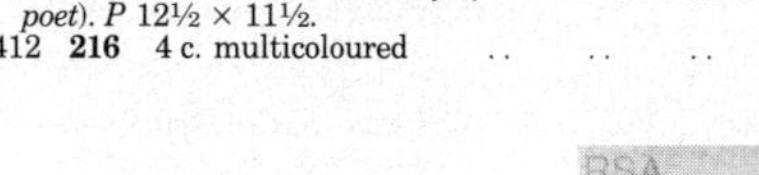

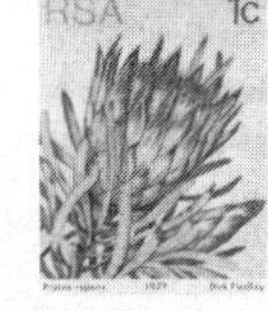

217 Palace of Justice **218** *Protea repens*

(Des H. Meiring)

1977 (18 May). *Centenary of Transvaal Supreme Court. P* 11½ × 12½.
413 **217** 4 c. red-brown 10 10

(Des D. Findlay. Photo (1, 2, 3 c. (No. 416), 4, 5, 8, 10 to 20 c. (Nos. 425/a) and coil stamps) or litho (others))

1977 (27 May)–**82.** *Vert designs as T* **218** *showing Proteas or other Succulents. Multicoloured.* (a) *Sheet stamps. P* 12½.
414 1 c. Type **218** 10 10
415 2 c. *P punctata* 15 20
416 3 c. *P neriifolia (photo) (p* 12½) . . 10 10
416*a* 3 c. *P neriifolia (litho) (p* 14 × 13½) (1.10.79) 10 10
417 4 c. *P longifolia* 10 10
a. Imperf (pair) £100
418 5 c. *P cynaroides* 10 10
a. Perf 14 × 13½ (4.3.81) 10 10
b. Imperf (pair) £130
419 6 c. *P canaliculata* 35 30
a. Black (face value and inscr at foot) omitted £120
b. Perf 14 × 13½ (25.10.79*) 30 30
420 7 c. *P lorea* 25 30
a. Emerald ("RSA") omitted £150
b. Perf 14 × 13½ (19.9.80) 20 30
421 8 c. *P mundii* 20 20
a. Perf 14 × 13½ (10.7.81) 15 10
422 9 c. *P roupelliae* 20 30
a. Perf 14 × 13½ (22.12.78) . . . . 3·75 1·25
423 10 c. *P aristata* 30 10
a. Perf 14 × 13½ (12.1.82) 20 20
424 15 c. *P eximia* 25 10
425 20 c. *P magnifica (photo)* 30 10
a. Perf 14 × 13½ (16.2.78) 60 90
425*b* 20 c. *P magnifica (litho) (p* 14 × 13½) (24.5.82) 85 30
426 25 c. *P grandiceps* 60 30
a. Emerald ("RSA" and leaves) omitted . . £160
b. Perf 14 × 13½ (3.6.80) 40 20
427 30 c. *P amplexicaulis* 45 10
a. Perf 14 × 13½ (19.10.80) 40 30
428 50 c. *Leucospermum cordifolium* 65 15
a. Perf 14 × 13½ (9.10.80) 45 15
429 1 r. *Paranomus reflexus* . . . . 1·00 85
a. Perf 14 × 13½ (30.7.80) 80 60
430 2 r. *Orothamnus zeyheri* . . . . 3·00 2·50
a. Perf 14 × 13½ (22.5.81) . . . . 1·50 1·00

(b) *Coil stamps. Imperf × perf* 14
431 1 c. *Leucadendron argenteum* 35 45
432 2 c. *Mimetes cucullatus* 35 45
433 5 c. *Serruria florida* 35 45
434 10 c. *Leucadendron sessile* 35 55
414/34 . . . . *Set of* 21 6·25 5·00
*Sheets dated 15 August 1979.
There were two emerald plates used for the 7 c.; one for the design and background and a second, common with other values in the issue, used to apply "RSA". No. 420a shows this second emerald plate omitted.
Later printings of the coil stamps come with every fifth stamp numbered on the back.

219 Gymnast **220** Metrication Symbol on Globe

(Des D. Cowie. Litho)

1977 (15 Aug). *Eighth Congress of International Association of Physical Education and Sports for Girls and Women. P* 12½ × 11½.
435 **219** 15 c. black, salmon-red and yellow . . 30 30

(Des L. Wilsenach. Litho)

1977 (15 Sept). *Metrication. P* 12 × 12½.
436 **220** 15 c. multicoloured 30 30

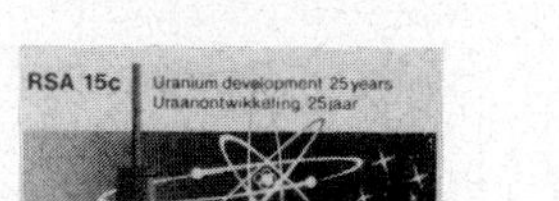

221 Atomic Diagram

(Des R. Sargent. Litho)

1977 (8 Oct). *Uranium Development. P* 12 × 12½.
437 **221** 15 c. multicoloured 30 30

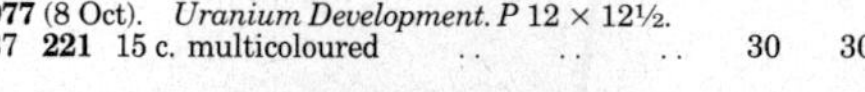

222 National Flag

(Des J. Hoekstra)

1977 (11 Nov). *50th Anniv of National Flag. P* 12 × 12½.
438 **222** 5 c. multicoloured 10 10

223 Walvis Bay, 1878

(Des A. H. Barrett. Litho)

1978 (10 Mar). *Centenary of Annexation of Walvis Bay. P* 12½.
439 **223** 15 c. multicoloured 60 40

224 Dr. Andrew Murray **225** Steel Rail

(Des J. Hoekstra. Litho)

1978 (9 May). *150th Birth Anniv of Dr. Andrew Murray (church statesman). P* 12½ × 12.
440 **224** 4 c. multicoloured 10 10

(Des H. Botha. Litho)

1978 (5 June). *50th Anniv of I.S.C.O.R. (South African Iron and Steel Industrial Corporation). P* 12½.
441 **225** 15 c. multicoloured 30 20

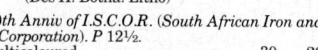

226 Richards Bay

(Des A. H. Barrett. Litho)

1978 (31 July). *Harbours. T* **226** *and similar horiz design. Multicoloured. P* 12½.
442 15 c. Type **226** . . . . 70 1·00
a. Pair. Nos. 442/3 . . . . . . 1·40 2·00
443 15 c. Saldanhabaai . . . . . . 70 1·00
Nos. 442/3 were printed together, *se-tenant*, in horizontal and vertical pairs throughout the sheet.

227 "Shepherd's Lonely Dwelling, Riversdale" **228** Pres. B. J. Vorster

(Des G. Mynhardt. Litho)

1978 (21 Aug). *125th Birth Anniv of J. E. A. Volschenk (painter). T* **227** *and similar horiz designs. Multicoloured. P* 12½.

444 10 c. Type **227** 20 20
445 15 c. "Clouds and Sunshine, Laneberg Range, Riversdale" 50 35
446 20 c. "At the Foot of the Mountain" .. .. .. 70 1·00
447 25 c. "Evening on the Veldt" .. .. .. 80 1·75
444/7 .. .. *Set of* 4 2·00 3·00
MS448 124 × 90 mm. Nos. 444/7 .. .. .. 3·00 4·50

(Des A. H. Barrett. Litho)

1978 (10 Oct). *Inauguration of President Vorster. P* 14 × 13½.

449 **228** 4 c. brown-purple and gold 60 20
a. Perf 12½ × 12 .. .. .. 10 10
450 15 c. dull violet and gold 25 40

229 Golden Gate

(Des A. H. Barrett. Litho)

1978 (13 Nov). *Tourism. T* **229** *and similar horiz designs. Multicoloured. P* 12½.

451 10 c. Type **229** 25 15
452 15 c. Blyde River Canyon 55 40
453 20 c. Amphitheatre, Drakensberg .. .. 75 1·00
454 25 c. Cango Caves .. .. 90 1·60
451/4 .. .. *Set of* 4 2·25 2·75

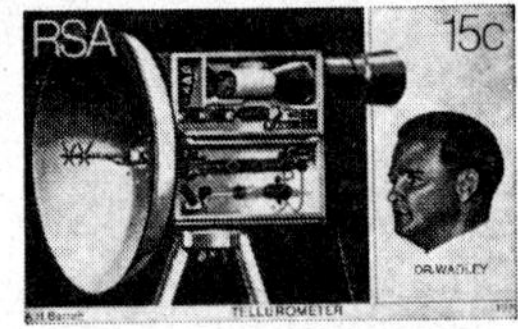

230 Dr. Wadley (inventor) and Tellurometer

(Des A. H. Barrett. Litho)

1979 (12 Feb). *25th Anniv of Tellurometer (radio distance measurer). P* 12½.

455 **230** 15 c. multicoloured 20 20

231 1929 4d. Airmail Stamp

(Des G. Mynhardt. Litho)

1979 (30 Mar). *50th Anniv of Stamp Production in South Africa. P* 14.

456 **231** 15 c. green, cream and slate 20 20

232 "Save Fuel"

(Des A. H. Barrett)

1979 (2 Apr). *Fuel Conservation. P* 12 × 12½.

457 **232** 4 c. black and vermilion 20 35
a. Pair. Nos. 457/8 .. .. .. 40 70
458 – 4 c. black and vermilion 20 35

No. 458 is as T **232** but has face value and country initials in bottom left-hand corner, and Afrikaans inscription above English.

Nos. 457/8 were printed together, *se-tenant*, in horizontal and vertical pairs throughout the sheet.

233 Isandlwana **234** "Health Care"

(Des A. H. Barrett. Litho)

1979 (25 May). *Centenary of Zulu War. T* **233** *and similar horiz designs in black and rose-red, showing drawings. P* 14.

459 4 c. Type **233** 15 10
460 15 c. Ulundi 35 40
461 20 c. Rorke's Drift 40 60
459/61 .. .. *Set of* 3 80 95
MS462 125 × 90 mm. Nos. 459/61. P 12½ .. 2·75 3·50

(Des J. Hoekstra. Litho)

1979 (19 June). *Health Year. P* 12½ × 12.

463 **234** 4 c. multicoloured 10 10
a. Perf 14 × 13½ 30 30

235 Children looking at Candle

(Des G. Mynhardt. Litho)

1979 (13 Sept). *50th Anniv of Christmas Stamp Fund. P* 14.

464 **235** 4 c. multicoloured 10 10

236 University of Cape Town **237** "Gary Player"

(Des G. Mynhardt. Litho)

1979 (1 Oct). *50th Anniv of University of Cape Town. P* 13½ × 14.

465 **236** 4 c. multicoloured 20 30
a. Perf 12 × 12½ 15 15

(Des H. de Klerk. Litho)

1979 (4 Oct). *"Rosafari 1979" World Rose Convention, Pretoria. T* **237** *and similar vert designs. Multicoloured. P* 14 × 13½.

466 4 c. Type **237** 15 10
467 15 c. "Prof. Chris Barnard" 40 40
468 20 c. "Southern Sun" 50 50
469 25 c. "Soaring Wings" 65 65
466/9 .. .. *Set of* 4 1·50 1·40
MS470 100 × 125 mm. Nos. 466/9 .. .. 1·75 2·50

238 University of Stellenbosch **239** F.A.K. Emblem

(Des A. H. Barrett. Litho)

1979 (8 Nov). *300th Anniv of Stellenbosch (oldest town in South Africa). T* **238** *and similar horiz design. Multicoloured. P* 14.

471 4 c. Type **238** 10 10
472 15 c. Rhenish Church on the Braak 20 40

(Des J. Hoekstra)

1979 (18 Dec). *50th Anniv of F.A.K. (Federation of Afrikaans Cultural Societies). P* 12½ × 12.

473 **239** 4 c. multicoloured 10 15

MINIMUM PRICE

The minimum price quote is 10p which represents a handling charge rather than a basis for valuing common stamps. For further notes about prices see introductory pages.

240 "Still-life with Sweet Peas" **241** "Cullinan II"

(Des G. Mynhardt. Litho)

1980 (6 May). *Paintings by Pieter Wenning. T* **240** *and similar multicoloured design. P* 14 × 13½.

474 5 c. Type **240** 10 10
475 25 c. "House in the Suburbs, Cape Town" (44½ × 37 *mm*) 30 60
MS476 94 × 121 mm. Nos. 474/5 .. .. .. 1·25 1·60

(Des A. H. Barrett. Litho)

1980 (12 May). *World Diamond Congresses, Johannesburg. T* **241** *and similar vert design. Multicoloured. P* 14.

477 15 c. Type **241** 60 60
478 20 c. "Cullinan I (Great Star of Africa)" .. 65 65

242 C. L. Leipoldt **243** University of Pretoria

(Des J. Hoekstra. Litho)

1980 (3 Sept). *Birth Centenary of C. L. Leipoldt (poet). P* 14 × 13½.

479 **242** 5 c. multicoloured 10 10

(Des P. de Wet. Litho)

1980 (9 Oct). *50th Anniv of University of Pretoria. P* 14 × 13½.

480 **243** 5 c. multicoloured 10 10

244 "Marine with Shipping" (Willem van de Velde)

(Des G. Mynhardt. Litho)

1980 (3 Nov). *Paintings from South African National Gallery, Cape Town. T* **244** *and similar multicoloured designs. P* 14.

481 5 c. Type **244** 10 1
482 10 c. "Firetail and his Trainer" (George Stubbs) 15 2
483 15 c. "Lavinia" (Thomas Gainsborough) (*vert*) 20 4
484 20 c. "Classical Landscape" (Pieter Post) .. 25 6
481/4 .. .. *Set of* 4 65 1·2
MS485 126 × 90 mm. Nos. 481/4 .. .. .. 1·00 1·7

245 Joubert, Kruger and M. Pretorius (Triumvirate Government) **246** Boers advancing up Amajuba Mountain

(Des A. H. Barrett. Litho)

1980 (15 Dec). *Centenary of Paardekraal Monument (cairn commemorating formation of Boer Triumvirate Government). T* **245** *and similar multicoloured design. P* 14 × 13½ (5 c.) or 13½ × 14 (10 c.).

486 5 c. Type **245** 10 1
487 10 c. Paardekraal Monument (*vert*) 10 3

(Des Diana Arbuthnot. Litho)

1981 (27 Feb). *Centenary of Battle of Amajuba. T* **246** *and similar multicoloured design. P* 13½ × 14 (5 c.) *or* 14 × 13½ (15 c.).
488 5 c. Type **246** 15 10
489 15 c. British troops defending hill (*horiz*) .. 35 35

247 Ballet *Raka*

(Des H. Botha. Litho)

1981 (23 May). *Opening of State Theatre, Pretoria. T* **247** *and similar horiz design. Multicoloured. P* 14.
490 20 c. Type **247** 25 30
491 25 c. Opera *Aida* 30 35
MS492 110 × 90 mm. Nos. 490/1 .. .. .. 60 70

248 Former Presidents C. R. Swart, J. J. Fouché, N. Diederichs and B. J. Vorster

(Des A. H. Barrett. Litho)

1981 (30 May). *20th Anniv of Republic. T* **248** *and similar design. P* 14.
493 5 c. black, grey-olive and bistre 10 10
494 15 c. multicoloured 20 20
Design: (28 × 22 *mm*)—15 c. President Marais Viljoen.

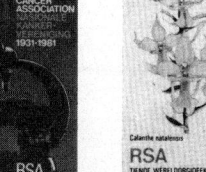

249 Girl with Hearing Aid

250 Microscope

251 *Calanthe natalensis*

(Des Mare Mouton. Litho)

1981 (12 June). *Centenary of Institutes for Deaf and Blind, Worcester. T* **249** *and similar vert design. Multicoloured. P* 13½ × 14.
495 5 c. Type **249** 10 10
496 15 c. Boy reading braille 20 25

(Des N. Hanna. Litho)

1981 (10 July). *50th Anniv of National Cancer Association. P* 13½ × 14.
497 **250** 5 c. multicoloured 10 10

(Des Jeanette Stead. Litho)

1981 (11 Sept). *Tenth World Orchid Conference, Durban. T* **251** *and similar vert designs. Multicoloured. P* 14.
498 5 c. Type **251** 10 10
499 15 c. *Eulophia speciosa* 25 30
500 20 c. *Disperis fanniniae* 30 45
501 25 c. *Disa uniflora* 40 50
498/501 .. .. *Set of* 4 90 1·25
MS502 120 × 91 mm. Nos. 498/501 .. .. 2·25 1·75

252 Voortrekkers in Uniform

253 Lord Baden-Powell

254 Dr. Robert Koch

(Des J. Hoekstra. Litho)

1981 (30 Sept). *50th Anniv of Voortrekker Movement (Afrikaans cultural youth organization). P* 14.
503 **252** 5 c. multicoloured 10 10

(Des J. Meyer. Litho)

1982 (22 Feb). *75th Anniv of Boy Scout Movement. P* 13½ × 14.
504 **253** 15 c. multicoloured 15 15

(Des J. Meyer. Litho)

1982 (24 Mar). *Centenary of Discovery of Tubercle Bacillus by Dr. Robert Koch. P* 13½ × 14.
505 **254** 20 c. multicoloured 15 30

255 *Maria van Riejbeck* (submarine)

256 Old Provost, Grahamstown

(Des A. H. Barrett. Litho)

1982 (2 Apr). *25th Anniv of Simonstown as South African Navy Base. T* **255** *and similar horiz designs. Multicoloured. P* 14.
506 8 c. Type **255** 10 10
507 15 c. Missile patrol vessel 15 30
508 20 c. Minesweeper 25 50
509 25 c. Harbour patrol boats 30 70
506/9 .. .. *Set of* 4 70 1·40
MS510 125 × 90 mm. Nos. 506/9 .. .. .. 1·75 1·75

(Des A. H. Barrett. Recess (Nos. 511, 512*b*, 513, 514, 515*a*, 516*a*, 521, 522*a*, 524, 525 and 526/7), photo (Nos. 528/31) or litho (others))

1982 (15 July)–**87**. *South African Architecture. Designs as T* **256**.

(*a*) *Sheet stamps. P* 14
511 1 c. reddish brown (*recess*) 15 20
511*a* 1 c. reddish brown (*litho*) (2.4.84) .. 30 30
512 2 c. yellow-olive (*litho*) 20 20
512*a* 2 c. deep green (*litho*) (9.5.83) 75 20
512*b* 2 c. bottle green (*recess*) (28.11.83) .. 10 10
512*c* 2 c. bottle green (*litho*) (21.11.85) .. 40 20
513 3 c. violet (*recess*) 30 15
513*a* 3 c. violet (*litho*) (28.11.85) 80 30
514 4 c. brown-olive (*recess*) 20 15
514*a* 4 c. brown-olive (*litho*) (25.3.85) .. 40 15
515 5 c. carmine (*litho*) 30 20
515*a* 5 c. brown-purple (*recess*) (11.11.83) .. 10 10
516 6 c. deep blue-green (*litho*) 45 30
516*a* 6 c. blackish green (*recess*) (9.8.84) .. 45 20
517 7 c. dull yellowish green (*litho*) 20 15
518 8 c. greenish blue (*litho*) 30 30
518*a* 8 c. indigo (*litho*) (3.1.83) 20 10
519 9 c. deep mauve (*litho*) 30 20
520 10 c. Venetian red (*litho*) 40 20
520*a* 10 c. purple-brown (*litho*) (26.1.83) .. 35 10
520*b* 11 c. cerise (*litho*) (2.4.84) 40 15
520*c* 12 c. deep violet-blue (*litho*) (1.4.85) .. 50 10
520*d* 14 c. lake-brown (*litho*) (1.4.86) 65 10
521 15 c. deep violet-blue (*recess*) 30 15
521*a* 16 c. rosine (*litho*) (1.4.87) 80 40
522 20 c. vermilion (*litho*) 65 30
522*a* 20 c. brownish black (*recess*) (15.6.83) .. 80 10
522*b* 20 c. brownish black (*litho*) (14.11.85) .. 1·00 15
523 25 c. bistre (*litho*) 40 30
523*a* 25 c. ochre (*litho*) (3.6.87) .. .. 1·10 30
524 30 c. agate (*recess*) 65 30
524*a* 30 c. reddish brown (*litho*) (12.3.86) .. 75 30
525 50 c. deep turquoise-blue (*recess*) .. 80 30
 a. *Deep slate-blue* (18.3.83) .. .. 1·50 65
525*b* 50 c. turquoise-blue (*litho*) (13.10.86) .. 1·50 20
526 1 r. deep violet (*recess*) .. .. .. 1·00 15
526*a* 1 r. deep violet (*litho*) (17.12.86) .. 1·00 40
527 2 r. deep carmine (*recess*) .. .. 2·00 30
527*a* 2 r. deep carmine (*litho*) (5.12.85) .. 2·00 50
511/27 .. .. *Set of* 21 (*one of each value*) 9·25 3·25

Designs: (28 × 20 *mm*)—2 c. Tuynhuys, Cape Town; 3 c. Appèlhof, Bloemfontein; 4 c. Raadsaal, Pretoria; 5 c. Cape Town Castle; 6 c. Goewermentsgebou, Bloemfontein; 7 c. Drostdy, Graaff-Reinet; 8 c. Leeuwenhof, Cape Town; 9 c. Libertas, Pretoria; 10 c. City Hall, Pietermaritzburg; 11 c. City Hall, Kimberley; 12 c. City Hall, Port Elizabeth; 14 c. City Hall, Johannesburg; 15 c. Matjesfontein; 16 c. City Hall, Durban; 20 c. Post Office, Durban; 25 c. Melrose House, Pretoria. (45 × 28 *mm*)—30 c. Old Legislative Assembly Building, Pietermaritzburg; 50 c. Raadsaal, Bloemfontein; 1 r. Houses of Parliament, Cape Town; 2 r. Uniegebou, Pretoria.

For certain printings of Nos. 511/27*a* the design width of each stamp was reduced by a millimetre. Of the original set of 17 all showed "wide" designs with the exception of the 1 r. Changes in design size occurred in subsequent printings so that Nos. 512*c*, 513, 521 and 524 can be found in both wide and narrow versions. Of the remainder Nos. 511*a*, 512*b*, 513*a*, 514*a*, 515*a*, 516*a*, 520*b*/*d*, 521*a*, 522*a*/*b*, 524*a*, 525*a*/*b*, 526 and 527*a* exist as "narrow" designs only.

(*b*) *Coil stamps. P* 14 × *imperf*
528 1 c. brown 20 30
529 2 c. yellow-green 20 35
530 5 c. lake-brown 20 35
531 10 c. light brown 25 50
528/31 .. .. *Set of* 4 75 1·40

Designs: (28 × 20 *mm*)—1 c. Drostdy, Swellendam; 2 c. City Hall, East London; 5 c. Head Post Office, Johannesburg; 10 c. Morgenster, Somerset West.

257 Bradysaurus

258 Gough Island Base

(Des Sheila Nowers. Litho)

1982 (1 Dec). *Karoo Fossils. T* **257** *and similar horiz designs. Multicoloured. P* 14.
532 8 c. Type **257** 35 10
533 15 c. Lystrosaurus 45 55
534 20 c. Euparkeria 55 65
535 25 c. Thrinaxodon 65 80
532/5 .. .. *Set of* 4 1·75 1·90
MS536 107 × 95 mm. Nos. 532/5 .. .. .. 2·50 2·50

(Des D. Thorpe. Litho)

1983 (19 Jan). *Weather Stations. T* **258** *and similar horiz designs. Multicoloured. P* 13½ × 14.
537 8 c. Type **258** 20 10
538 20 c. Marion Island base 45 45
539 25 c. Taking meteorological readings 45 50
540 40 c. Launching weather balloon, Sanae .. 70 75
537/40 .. .. *Set of* 4 1·60 1·60

259 Class "S2" Light Shunting Locomotive

260 Rugby

(Des H. Botha. Litho)

1983 (27 Apr). *Steam Railway Locomotives. T* **259** *and similar horiz designs. Multicoloured. P* 14.
541 10 c. Type **259** 30 10
542 20 c. Class "16E" express locomotive .. 50 55
543 25 c. Class "6H" locomotive 60 80
544 40 c. Class "15F" main-line locomotive .. 90 1·25
541/4 .. .. *Set of* 4 2·10 2·40

(Des Sheila Nowers. Litho)

1983 (20 July). *Sport in South Africa. T* **260** *and similar multicoloured designs. P* 14.
545 10 c. Type **260** 10 10
546 20 c. Soccer (*horiz*) 25 30
547 25 c. Yachting 30 35
548 40 c. Horse-racing (*horiz*) 50 65
545/8 .. .. *Set of* 4 1·10 1·25

261 Plettenberg Bay

262 Thomas Pringle

(Des A. H. Barrett. Litho)

1983 (12 Oct). *Tourism. Beaches. T* **261** *and similar horiz designs. Multicoloured. P* 14.
549 10 c. Type **261** 10 10
550 20 c. Durban 25 30
551 25 c. West coast 30 35
552 40 c. Clifton 50 65
549/52 .. .. *Set of* 4 1·10 1·25
MS553 128 × 90 mm. Nos. 549/52 .. .. .. 2·00 2·50

(Des J. van Ellinckhuijzen. Litho)

1984 (24 Feb). *South African English Authors. T* **262** *and similar vert designs. P* 14.
554 10 c. olive-brown, yellow-brown and grey .. 10 10
555 20 c. olive-brown, deep bluish green and grey 25 40
556 25 c. olive-brown, deep brown-rose and grey .. 30 50
557 40 c. olive-brown, olive-ochre and grey .. 50 85
554/7 .. .. *Set of* 4 1·10 1·75

Designs:—20 c. Pauline Smith; 25 c. Olive Schreiner; 40 c. Sir Percy Fitzpatrick.

PRICES OF SETS

Set prices are given for many issues, generally those containing three stamps or more. Definitive sets include one of each value or major colour change, but do not cover different perforations, die types or minor shades. Where a choice is possible the set prices are based on the cheapest versions of the stamps included in the listings.

263 Manganese

(Des H. Botha. Litho)

1984 (8 June). *Strategic Minerals. T* **263** *and similar horiz designs. Multicoloured. P* 14.

558	11 c. Type **263**	35	10
559	20 c. Chromium	60	50
560	25 c. Vanadium	80	75
561	30 c. Titanium	90	80
558/61	.. .. *Set of* 4	2·40	1·90

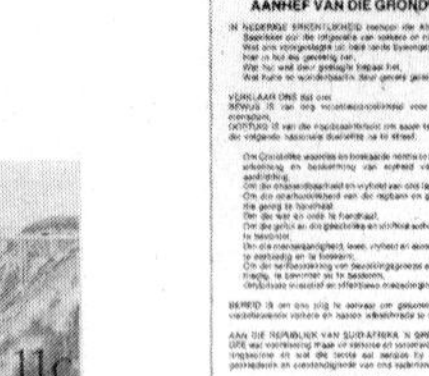

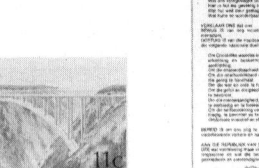

264 Bloukrans River Bridge

265 Preamble to the Constitution in Afrikaans

(Des D. Bagnall. Litho)

1984 (24 Aug). *South African Bridges. T* **264** *and similar horiz designs. Multicoloured. P* 14.

562	11 c. Type **264**	35	10
563	25 c. Durban four level interchange	70	55
564	30 c. Mfolozi rail bridge	75	65
565	45 c. Gouritz River bridge	95	1·25
562/5	.. .. *Set of* 4	2·50	2·25

(Des G. Mynhardt. Litho)

1984 (3 Sept). *New Constitution. T* **265** *and similar vert designs. P* 14.

566	11 c. stone, black and bistre	50	65
	a. Horiz pair. Nos. 566/7	1·00	1·25
567	11 c. stone, black and bistre	50	65
568	25 c. stone, deep claret and bistre	30	35
569	30 c. multicoloured	40	45
566/9	.. .. *Set of* 4	1·50	1·90

Designs:—No. 566, Preamble to the Constitution in English; 568, Last two lines of National Anthem; 569, South African coat of arms.

Nos. 566/7 were printed together, *se-tenant*, in horizontal pairs.

266 Pres. P. W. Botha

267 Pro Patria Medal

1984 (2 Nov). *Inauguration of President Botha. Litho. P* 14.

570 **266**	11 c. multicoloured	20	10
571	25 c. multicoloured	40	30

(Des B. Jackson. Litho)

1984 (9 Nov). *Military Decorations. T* **267** *and similar vert designs. Multicoloured. P* 14.

572	11 c. Type **267**	25	10
573	25 c. De Wet Decoration	55	45
574	30 c. John Chard Decoration	60	65
575	45 c. Honoris Crux (Diamond) Decoration ..	85	1·10
572/5	.. .. *Set of* 4	2·00	2·10
MS576	71 × 116 mm. Nos. 572/5	2·50	2·75

268 "Reflections" (Frans Oerder)

269 Cape Parliament Building

1985 (22 Feb). *Paintings by Frans Oerder. T* **268** *and similar horiz designs. Multicoloured. Litho. P* 14.

577	11 c. Type **268**	30	15
578	25 c. "Ladies in a Garden"	45	35
579	30 c. "Still-life with Lobster"	50	45
580	50 c. "Still-life with Marigolds"	80	70
577/80	.. .. *Set of* 4	1·90	1·50
MS581	129 × 74 mm. Nos. 577/80	2·50	2·75

(Des A. H. Barrett. Litho)

1985 (15 May). *Centenary of Cape Parliament Building. T* **269** *and similar horiz designs. Multicoloured. P* 14.

582	12 c. Type **269**	20	10
583	25 c. Speaker's Chair	30	25
584	30 c. "National Convention 1908–9" (Edward Roworth)	45	40
585	50 c. Republic Parliamentary emblem ..	65	65
	a. Black (inscr and outline) omitted ..	£160	
582/5	.. .. *Set of* 4	1·40	1·25

270 Freesia

271 Sugar Bowl

(Des Sheila Nowers. Litho)

1985 (23 Aug). *Floral Emigrants. T* **270** *and similar vert designs. Multicoloured. P* 14.

586	12 c. Type **270**	20	10
587	25 c. Nerine	35	25
588	30 c. Ixia	45	45
589	50 c. Gladiolus	70	70
586/9	.. .. *Set of* 4	1·50	1·25

(Des H. Botha. Litho)

1985 (5 Nov). *Cape Silverware. T* **271** *and similar multi-coloured designs. P* 14.

590	12 c. Type **271**	20	10
591	25 c. Teapot	40	25
592	30 c. Loving cup (*vert*)	45	45
593	50 c. Coffee pot (*vert*)	70	70
590/3	.. .. *Set of* 4	1·60	1·25

272 Blood Donor Session

273 National Flag

(Des Sheila Nowers. Litho)

1986 (20 Feb). *Blood Donor Campaign. T* **272** *and similar horiz designs. Multicoloured. P* 14.

594	12 c. Type **272**	40	10
595	20 c. Baby receiving blood transfusion ..	65	30
596	25 c. Operation in progress	70	50
597	30 c. Ambulanceman and accident victim ..	85	65
594/7	.. .. *Set of* 4	2·40	1·40

(Des J. Hoekstra. Litho)

1986 (30 May). *25th Anniv of Republic of South Africa. T* **273** *and similar horiz design. Multicoloured. P* 14.

598	14 c. Type **273**	50	70
	a. Horiz pair. Nos. 598/9	1·00	1·40
599	14 c. As Type **273**, but inscr "UNITY IS STRENGTH"	50	70

Nos. 598/9 were printed together, *se-tenant*, in horizontal pairs throughout the sheet.

274 Drostdyhof, Graaff-Reinet

(Des A. H. Barrett. Litho)

1986 (14 Aug). *Restoration of Historic Buildings. T* **274** *and similar horiz designs. Multicoloured. P* 14.

600	14 c. Type **274**	35	10
601	20 c. Pilgrim's Rest mining village	50	35
602	25 c. Strapp's Store, Bethlehem	60	50
603	30 c. Palmdene, Pietermaritzburg	75	60
600/3	.. .. *Set of* 4	2·00	1·40

MACHINE LABELS. From 14 August 1986 gummed labels in the above design, ranging in value from 1 c. to 99 r. 99, were available from an experimental machine at Sunnyside Post Office in Pretoria. The machine was moved to the "Johannesburg 100" exhibition from 6 to 11 October 1986 and was then reinstalled at Sunnyside on 17 October 1986. Further machines were introduced subsequently and each can be identified by a code number, between P.001 and P.034, at right.

275 Von Brandis Square, Johannesburg, *c* 1900

(Des J. van Niekerk. Litho)

1986 (25 Sept). *Centenary of Johannesburg. T* **275** *and similar horiz designs. Multicoloured. P* 14.

604	14 c. Type **275**	35	1
605	20 c. Gold mine (26 × 20 *mm*)	70	4
606	25 c. Johannesburg skyline, 1986	85	6
607	30 c. Gold bars (26 × 20 *mm*)	1·00	7
604/7	.. .. *Set of* 4	2·50	1·6

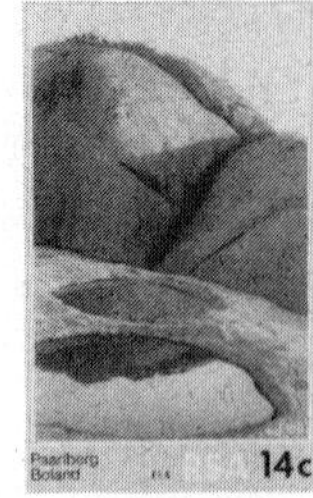

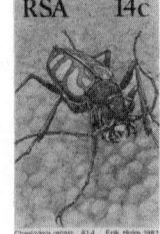

276 Gordon's Rock, Paarlberg

277 *Cicindela regalis*

(Des A. H. Barrett. Litho)

1986 (20 Nov). *Rock Formations. T* **276** *and similar ver[t] designs. Multicoloured. P* 14.

608	14 c. Type **276**	50	1
609	20 c. The Column, Drakensberg	75	6
610	25 c. Maltese Cross, Sederberge	85	8
611	30 c. Bourke's Luck Potholes, Blyde River Gorge	1·10	1·1
608/11	.. .. *Set of* 4	3·00	2·4

(Des E. Holm. Litho)

1987 (6 Mar). *South African Beetles. T* **277** *and similar ver[t] designs. Multicoloured. P* 14.

612	14 c. Type **277**	50	1
613	20 c. *Trichostetha fascicularis*	70	6
614	25 c. *Julodis viridipes*	85	8
615	30 c. *Ceroplesis militaris*	1·10	1·1
612/15	.. .. *Set of* 4	2·75	2·4

278 Eland, Sebaaieni Cave

(Des H. Botha. Litho)

1987 (4 June). *Rock Paintings. T* **278** *and similar horiz designs. Multicoloured. P* 14.

616	16 c. Type **278**	40	1
617	20 c. Leaping lion, Clocolan	60	5
618	25 c. Black Wildebeest, uMhlwazini Valley	80	8
619	30 c. Bushman dance, Floukraal	95	1·0
616/19	.. .. *Set of* 4	2·50	2·2

279 Oude Pastorie, Paarl

(Des A. H. Barrett. Litho)

1987 (3 Sept). *300th Anniv of Paarl. T* **279** *and similar hori[z] designs. Multicoloured. P* 14.

620	16 c. Type **279**	35	1
621	20 c. Grapevines	60	5
622	25 c. Wagon-building	65	6
623	30 c. KWV Cathedral Wine Cellar	80	8
620/3	.. .. *Set of* 4	2·25	1·9

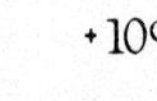

VLOEDRAMP
NATAL

(**280**)

281 "Belshazzar's Feast" (Rembrandt)

1987 (16 Nov). *Natal Flood Relief Fund* (1st issue). *No.* 521*a surch as T* **280** *in Afrikaans or English.*
624 16 c. + 10 c. rosine (surch T **280**) 45 65
a. Pair. Nos. 624/5.. .. .. .. 90 1·25
625 16 c. + 10 c. rosine (surch "NATAL FLOOD DISASTER") 45 65
Nos. 624/5 were surcharged together, *se-tenant*, in horizontal and vertical pairs throughout the sheet.
See also Nos. 629/30 and 635/6.

(Des Sheila Nowers. Litho)

1987 (19 Nov). *The Bible Society of South Africa. T* **281** *and similar multicoloured designs. P* 14.
626 16 c. "The Bible" in 75 languages (54×34 *mm*) 35 10
627 30 c. Type **281**.. .. .. 60 35
628 50 c. "St. Matthew and the Angel" (Rembrandt) (*vert*) 80 50
626/8 .. .. *Set of* 3 1·60 85
A 40 c. value, showing the inscription "The Word of God" in various languages, was prepared, but not issued.

1987 (1 Dec). *Natal Flood Relief Fund* (2nd issue). *No.* 626 *surch as T* **280**, *but larger (Afrikaans version* 32 *mm wide).*
629 16 c. + 10 c. multicoloured (surch "NATAL FLOOD DISASTER") 45 65
a. Pair. Nos. 629/30 .. .. .. 90 1·25
630 16 c. + 10 c. multicoloured (surch as T **280**) .. 45 65
Nos. 629/30 were surcharged together, *se-tenant*, in horizontal and vertical pairs throughout the sheet.
These stamps are known postmarked at Mooirivier on 25 November 1987.

282 Bartolomeu Dias and Cape of Good Hope

283 Huguenot Monument, Franschhoek

(Des Sheila Nowers. Litho)

1988 (3 Feb). *500th Anniv of Discovery of Cape of Good Hope by Bartolomeu Dias. T* **282** *and similar horiz designs. Multicoloured. P* 14.
631 16 c. Type **282**.. .. .. 45 10
632 30 c. Kwaaihoek Monument.. .. .. 65 50
633 40 c. Caravels.. .. .. 80 75
634 50 c. Martellus map, *c.* 1489.. .. .. 1·10 1·10
631/4 .. .. *Set of* 4 2·75 2·25

1988 (1 Mar). *Natal Flood Relief Fund* (3rd issue). *No.* 631 *surch as T* **280**, *but larger (Afrikaans version* 19 *mm wide).*
635 16 c. + 10 c. multicoloured (surch as T **280**) 45 65
a. Pair. Nos. 635/6.. .. .. .. 90 1·25
636 16 c. + 10 c. multicoloured (surch "NATAL FLOOD DISASTER") 45 65
Nos. 635/6 were surcharged together, *se-tenant*, in horizontal and vertical pairs throughout the sheet.

(Des H. Botha. Litho)

1988 (13 Apr). *300th Anniv of Arrival of First French Huguenots at the Cape. T* **283** *and similar vert designs. Multicoloured. P* 14.
637 16 c. Type **283** 25 10
638 30 c. Map of France showing Huguenot areas 45 45
639 40 c. Title page of French/Dutch New Testament of 1672 .. .. 55 55
640 50 c. St. Bartholomew's Day Massacre, Paris, 1572 .. .. 70 80
637/40 .. .. *Set of* 4 1·75 1·60

National Flood Disaster +10c

(**284**)

285 Pelican Point Lighthouse, Walvis Bay

1988 (13 Apr). *National Flood Relief Fund. Nos.* 637/40 *surch as T* **284** *in English* (E) *or in Afrikaans ("Nasionale Vloedramp")* (A).
641 16 c. + 10 c. multicoloured (E) 40 40
a. Pair. Nos. 641/2 .. .. .. 80 80
642 16 c. + 10 c. multicoloured (A) 40 40
643 30 c. + 10 c. multicoloured (A) 55 55
a. Pair. Nos. 643/4 .. .. .. 1·10 1·10
644 30 c. + 10 c. multicoloured (E) 55 55
645 40 c. + 10 c. multicoloured (A) 70 70
a. Pair. Nos. 645/6 .. .. .. 1·40 1·40
646 40 c. + 10 c. multicoloured (E) 70 70
647 50 c. + 10 c. multicoloured (E) 90 90
a. Pair. Nos. 647/8 .. .. .. 1·75 1·75
648 50 c. + 10 c. multicoloured (A) 90 90
641/8 .. .. *Set of* 8 4·50 4·50
The two versions of each surcharge were printed together, *se-tenant*, both horizontally and vertically, throughout the sheets.

(Des Sheila Nowers. Litho)

1988 (9 June). *Lighthouses. T* **285** *and similar horiz designs. Multicoloured. P* 14.
649 16 c. Type **285** 40 10
650 30 c. Green Point, Cape Town 60 45
651 40 c. Cape Agulhas 80 60
652 50 c. Umhlanga Rocks, Durban 95 70
649/52 .. .. *Set of* 4 2·50 1·60
MS653 132 × 112 mm. Nos. 649/52 .. .. 2·50 2·50

286 *Huernia zebrina*

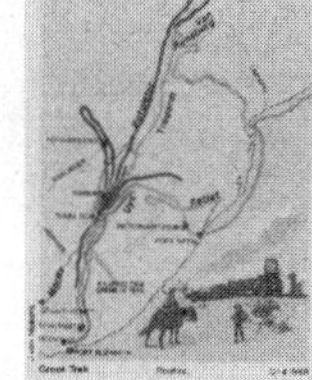

287 Map of Great Trek Routes

(Des H. Botha)

1988 (1 Sept)–**90**. *Succulents. T* **286** *and similar horiz designs. Multicoloured.*

(*a*) *Sheet stamps. Litho. P* 14.
654 1 c. Type **286** 10 10
655 2 c. *Euphorbia symmetrica* 10 10
656 5 c. *Lithops dorotheae* 10 10
657 7 c. *Gibbaeum nebrownii* 10 10
658 10 c. *Didymaotus lapidiformis* 10 10
659 16 c. *Vanheerdea divergens* 10 10
659*a* 18 c. *Faucaria tigrina* (1.4.89) 10 10
660 20 c. *Conophytum mundum* 10 10
660*a* 21 c. *Gasteria armstrongii* (2.4.90) .. 10 10
661 25 c. *Cheiridopsis peculiaris* 10 15
662 30 c. *Tavaresia barklyi* 10 15
663 35 c. *Dinteranthus wilmotianus* 15 20
664 40 c. *Frithia pulchra* 15 20
665 50 c. *Lapidaria margaretae* 20 25
666 90 c. *Dioscorea elephantipes* 35 40
667 1 r. *Trichocaulon cactiforme* 40 45
668 2 r. *Crassula columnaris* 80 85
668*a* 5 r. *Anacampseros albissima* (1.3.90) .. 2·00 2·10
654/68*a* .. .. *Set of* 18 4·25 4·75

(*b*) *Coil stamps. Photo. P* 14 × *imperf.*
669 1 c. *Adromischus marianiae* 10 10
670 2 c. *Titanopsis calcarea* 10 10
671 5 c. *Dactylopsis digitata* 10 10
672 10 c. *Pleiospilos bolusii* 10 10
669/72 .. .. *Set of* 4 20 20

(Des J. van Niekerk (16 c.). Litho)

1988 (21 Nov). *150th Anniv of Great Trek. T* **287** *and similar multicoloured designs. P* 14.
673 16 c. Type **287** 40 10
674 30 c. "Exodus" (tapestry by W. Coetzer) (56 × 20 *mm*) 60 50
675 40 c. "Crossing the Drakensberg" (tapestry by W. Coetzer) (77 × 20 *mm*) 75 80
676 50 c. "After the Service, Church of the Vow" (J. H. Pierneef) (*horiz*) .. .. 90 1·00
673/6 .. .. *Set of* 4 2·40 2·25

288 Coelacanth

289 Man-made Desert

(Des A. McBride. Litho)

1989 (9 Feb). *50th Anniv of Discovery of Coelacanth. T* **288** *and similar horiz designs. Multicoloured. P* 14.
677 16 c. Type **288** 35 10
678 30 c. Prof. J. L. B. Smith and Dr. M. Courtenay-Latimer examining Coelacanth 55 30
679 40 c. J. L. B. Smith Institute of Ichthyology, Grahamstown 70 65
680 50 c. Coelacanth and GEO midget submarine 85 75
677/80 .. .. *Set of* 4 2·25 1·60

(Des D. Murphy. Litho)

1989 (3 May). *National Grazing Strategy. T* **289** *and similar horiz designs. Multicoloured. P* 14.
681 18 c. Type **289** 30 10
682 30 c. Formation of erosion gully 50 40
683 40 c. Concrete barrage in gully 55 55
684 50 c. Reclaimed veldt 65 75
681/4 .. .. *Set of* 4 1·75 1·60

290 South Africa *v* France Match, 1980

291 "Composition in Blue"

(Des B. Jackson. Litho)

1989 (22 June). *Centenary of South African Rugby Board. T* **290** *and similar horiz designs. Multicoloured. P* 14.
685 18 c. Type **290** 20 10
686 30 c. South Africa *v* Australia, 1963 .. 35 30
687 40 c. South Africa *v* New Zealand, 1937 .. 45 40
688 50 c. South Africa *v* British Isles, 1896 .. 55 50
685/8 .. .. *Set of* 4 1·40 1·10

1989 (3 Aug). *Paintings by Jacob Hendrik Pierneef. T* **291** *and similar horiz designs. Multicoloured. Litho. P* 14.
689 18 c. Type **291** 20 10
690 30 c. "Zanzibar" 35 30
691 40 c. "The Bushveld" 45 45
692 50 c. "Cape Homestead" 55 55
689/92 .. .. *Set of* 4 1·40 1·25
MS693 114×86 mm. Nos. 689/92 .. .. 1·40 1·50

292 Pres. F. W. de Klerk

293 Gas-drilling Rig, Mossel Bay

1989 (20 Sept). *Inauguration of President F. W. de Klerk. T* **292** *and similar vert design. Multicoloured. Litho. P* 14.
694 18 c. Type **292** 20 10
695 45 c. F. W. de Klerk (*different*) 40 50

(Des H. Botha. Litho)

1989 (19 Oct). *Energy Sources. T* **293** *and similar horiz designs. Multicoloured. P* 14×14½.
696 18 c. Type **293** 25 10
697 30 c. Coal to oil conversion plant 40 30
698 40 c. Nuclear power station 45 35
699 50 c. Thermal electric power station .. 55 45
696/9 .. .. *Set of* 4 1·50 1·10

294 Electric Goods Train and Map of Railway Routes

295 Great Britain 1840 Penny Black

(Des A. H. Barrett. Litho)

1990 (15 Feb). *Co-operation in Southern Africa. T* **294** *and similar horiz designs. Multicoloured. P* 14½×14.
700 18 c. Cahora Bassa Hydro-electric Scheme, Mozambique, and map of transmission lines (68×26 *mm*) 30 15
701 30 c. Type **294** 40 30
702 40 c. Projected dam on upper Orange River, Lesotho and map of Highlands Water Project (68×26 *mm*) 55 45
703 50 c. Cow, syringe, and outline map of Africa 65 45
700/3 .. .. *Set of* 4 1·75 1·25
MS704 136×78 mm. Nos. 700/3 .. .. 1·75 1·40

1990 (12 May). *National Stamp Day. T* **295** *and similar vert designs showing stamps. Multicoloured. Litho. P* 14.
705 21 c. Type **295** 30 30
a. Horiz strip of 5. Nos. 705/9 .. .. 1·40
706 21 c. Cape of Good Hope 1853 4d. triangular pair 30 30
707 21 c. Natal 1857 1s. 30 30
708 21 c. Orange Free State 1868 1s. 30 30
709 21 c. Transvaal 1869 1s. 30 30
705/9 .. .. *Set of* 5 1·40 1·40
Nos. 705/9 were printed together, *se-tenant*, in horizontal strips of 5 throughout the sheet.

296 Knysna Turaco

297 Karoo Landscape near Britstown

(Des C. Finch-Davies. Litho)

1990 (2 Aug). *Birds. T* **296** *and similar vert designs. Multicoloured. P* 14.
710 21 c. Type **296** 25 10
711 35 c. Red-capped Robin Chat 35 30
712 40 c. Rufus-naped Bush Lark 35 30
713 50 c. Bokmakierie Shrike 45 40
710/13 .. .. *Set of* 4 1·25 1·00

1990 (1 Nov). *Tourism. T* **297** *and similar horiz designs. Multicoloured. Litho. P* 14.
714 50 c. Type **297** 40 40
a. Block of 4. Nos. 714/17 .. .. 1·40
715 50 c. Camps Bay, Cape of Good Hope .. 40 40
716 50 c. Giraffes in Kruger National Park .. 40 40
717 50 c. Boschendal Vineyard, Drakenstein Mts 40 40
714/17 .. .. *Set of* 4 1·40 1·40
Nos. 714/17 were printed together, *se-tenant*, in blocks of 4 throughout the sheet.

298 Woltemade Cross for Bravery

299 Boer Horses

(Des J. Hoekstra. Litho)

1990 (6 Dec). *National Orders. T* **298** *and similar vert designs. Multicoloured. P* 14.
718 21 c. Type **298** 20 20
a. Horiz strip of 5. Nos. 718/22 90
719 21 c. Order of the Southern Cross .. 20 20
720 21 c. Order of the Star of South Africa .. 20 20
721 21 c. Order for Meritorious Service .. 20 20
722 21 c. Order of Good Hope 20 20
718/22 .. .. *Set of* 5 90 90
MS723 143×70 mm. Nos. 718/22 .. .. 1·00 1·00
Nos. 718/22 were printed together, *se-tenant*, in horizontal strips of 5 throughout the sheet.

(Des A. Ainslie. Litho)

1991 (12 Feb). *Animal Breeding in South Africa. T* **299** *and similar horiz designs. Multicoloured. P* 14.
724 21 c. Type **299** 20 20
a. Horiz strip of 5. Nos. 724/8 90
725 21 c. Bonsmara bull 20 20
726 21 c. Dorper sheep 20 20
727 21 c. Ridgeback dogs 20 20
728 21 c. Putterie racing pigeons 20 20
724/8 .. .. *Set of* 5 90 90
Nos. 724/8 were printed together, *se-tenant*, in horizontal strips of five throughout the sheet.

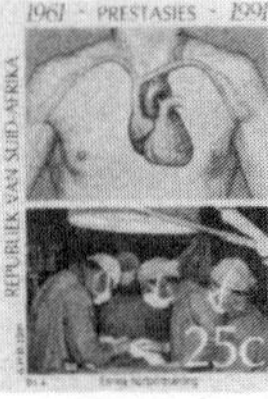
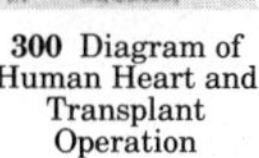
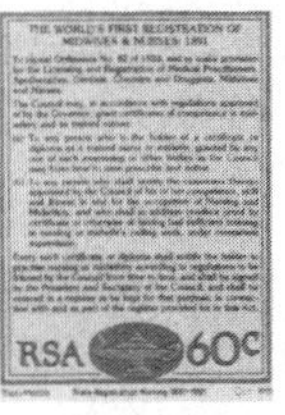

300 Diagram of Human Heart and Transplant Operation

301 State Registration of Nurses Act, 1891

(Des A. H. Barrett. Litho)

1991 (30 May). *30th Anniv of Republic. Scientific and Technological Achievements. T* **300** *and similar multicoloured designs. P* 14.
729 25 c. Type **300** 15 10
730 40 c. Matimba Power Station (*horiz*) .. 25 25
731 50 c. Dolos design breakwater (*horiz*) .. 35 35
732 60 c. Western Deep Levels gold mine .. 45 50
729/32 .. .. *Set of* 4 1·10 1·10

(Des T. Marais. Litho)

1991 (15 Aug). *Centenary of State Registration for Nurses and Midwives. P* 14.
733 **301** 60 c. multicoloured 45 50

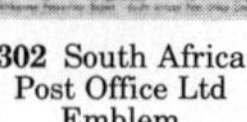

302 South Africa Post Office Ltd Emblem

303 Sir Arnold Theiler (veterinarian)

(Des Liza van der Wal. Litho)

1991 (1 Oct). *Establishment of Post Office Ltd and Telekom Ltd. T* **302** *and similar horiz design. Multicoloured. P* 14×14½.
734 27 c. Type **302** 25 25
a. Vert pair. Nos. 734/5 .. .. 50 50
735 27 c. Telekom SA Ltd emblem 25 25
Nos. 734/5 were printed together, *se-tenant*, in vertical pairs throughout the sheet.

(Des A. H. Barrett. Litho)

1991 (9 Oct). *South African Scientists. T* **303** *and similar horiz designs. Multicoloured. P* 14.
736 27 c. Type **303** 15 15
737 45 c. Sir Basil Schonland (physicist) .. 30 30
738 65 c. Dr. Robert Broom (palaeontologist) .. 40 40
739 85 c. Dr. Alex du Toit (geologist) 50 50
736/9 .. .. *Set of* 4 1·25 1·25

304 *Agulhas* (research ship)

305 Soil Conservation

(Des Liza van der Wal (27 c.), T. Marais (65 c.). Litho)

1991 (5 Dec). *30th Anniv of Antarctic Treaty. T* **304** *and similar horiz design. Multicoloured. P* 14.
740 27 c. Type **304** 20 10
741 65 c. Chart showing South African National Antarctic Expedition base 60 55

(Des J. van Niekerk. Litho)

1992 (6 Feb). *Environmental Conservation. T* **305** *and similar horiz designs. Multicoloured. P* 14×14½.
742 27 c. Type **305** 15 10
743 65 c. Water pollution 45 45
744 85 c. Air pollution 65 70
742/4 .. .. *Set of* 3 1·10 1·10

POSTAGE DUE STAMPS

D 1

UNION OF SOUTH AFRICA (A) UNION OF SOUTH AFRICA (B)

(Typo D.L.R.)

1914–22. *Inscribed bilingually. Lettering as* A. *W* **4.** *P* 14.

			Un single	Used single
D1	D 1	½d. black and green (19.3.15)	1·00	3·50
D2		1d. black and scarlet (19.3.15)	1·25	10
		a. Black ptd double	£1300	
D3		2d. black and reddish violet (12.12.14)	3·75	15
		a. Black and bright violet (1922)	5·00	30
D4		3d. black and bright blue (2.2.15)	2·25	35
D5		5d. black and sepia (19.3.15)	3·50	13·00
D6		6d. black and slate (19.3.15)	6·50	16·00
D7		1s. red and black (19.3.15)	60·00	£110
D1/7		*Set of* 7	70·00	£130

There are interesting minor varieties in some of the above values, e.g. ½d. to 3d., thick downstroke to "d"; 1d., short serif to "1"; raised "d"; 2d., forward point of "2" blunted; 3d., raised "d"; very thick "d".

(Litho Govt Printer, Pretoria)

1922. *Lettering as* A. *No wmk. Rouletted.*

D 8	D 1	½d. black and bright green (6.6.22)	85	5·50
D 9		1d. black and rose-red (3.10.22)	55	75
D10		1½d. black and yellow-brown (3.6.22)	1·00	1·75
D8/10		*Set of* 3	2·25	7·00

(Litho Govt Printer, Pretoria)

1922–26. *Type* D **1** *redrawn. Lettering as* B. *P* 14.

D11	½d. black and green (1.8.22)	30	1·75
D12	1d. black and rose (16.5.23)	35	15
D13	1½d. black and yellow-brown (12.1.24)	50	1·25
D14	2d. black and pale violet (16.5.23)	55	60
	a. Imperf (pair)	£190	£225
	b. Black and deep violet	5·00	3·00
D15	3d. black and blue (3.7.26)	6·50	11·00
D16	6d. black and slate (9.23)	9·00	6·00
D11/16	*Set of* 6	15·00	18·00

The locally printed stamps, perf 14, differ both in border design and in figures of value from the rouletted stamps. All values except the 3d. and 6d. are known with closed "G" in "POSTAGE" usually referred to as the "POSTADE" variety. This was corrected in later printings.

D 2

D 3

D 4

(Typo Pretoria)

1927–28. *Inscribed bilingually. No wmk. P* 13½ × 14.

D17	D 2	½d. black and green	35	2·00
D18		1d. black and carmine	35	30
D19		2d. black and mauve	1·25	30
		a. Black and purple	5·50	80
D20		3d. black and blue	5·50	14·00
D21		6d. black and slate	8·50	6·00
D17/21		*Set of* 5	14·50	20·00

1932–42. *Type* D **2** *redrawn. W* **9.** *P* 15 × 14.

(a) Frame roto, value typo

D22	½d. black and blue-green (1934)	1·00	1·60
D23	2d. black and deep purple (10.4.33)	3·50	1·10

(b) Whole stamp roto

D25	1d. black and carmine (3.34)	80	10
D26	2d. black and deep purple (1940)	6·50	10
	a. Thick (double) "2d." (R. 5/6, R. 18/2)	£130	16·00
D27	3d. black and Prussian blue (3.8.32)	10·00	11·00
D28	3d. deep blue and blue (1935)	4·00	15
	a. Indigo and milky blue (1942)	17·00	1·75
D29	6d. green and brown-ochre (7.6.33)	15·00	4·00
	a. Green and bright orange (1938)	7·00	2·25
D22/9a	*Set of* 7	29·00	14·50

In No. D26 the value, when magnified, has the meshed appearance of a photogravure screen, whereas in No. D23 the black of the value is solid.

1943–44. *Inscr bilingually. Roto. W* **9.** *In units of three, perf* 15 × 14 *subdivided by roulette* 6½.

			Un unit	Us unit	Us single
D30	D 3	½d. blue-green (1944)	4·50	25·00	30
D31		1d. carmine	6·00	3·50	10
D32		2d. dull violet	6·00	8·00	15
		a. Bright violet	13·00	30·00	50
D33		3d. indigo (1943)	35·00	60·00	1·25
D30/3		*Set of* 4	45·00	85·00	1·90

COVER PRICES

Cover factors are quoted at the beginning of each country for most issues to 1945. An explanation of the system can be found on page x. The factors quoted do not, however, apply to philatelic covers.

3D

Split "D" (R. 7/5 on every fourth sheet)

1948–49. *New figure of value and capital "D". Whole stamp roto. W* **9.** *P* 15 × 14.

D34	D 4	½d. black and blue-green	4·25	6·00
D35		1d. black and carmine	4·75	2·50
D36		2d. black and violet (1949)	6·00	3·00
		a. Thick (double) "2D." (R. 15/5–6, R. 16/5–6)	45·00	20·00
D37		3d. deep blue and blue	15·00	10·00
		a. Split "D"	90·00	
D38		6d. green and bright orange (1949)	25·00	8·00
D34/8		*Set of* 5	50·00	27·00

1950–58. *As Type* D 4, *but* "SUID-AFRIKA" *hyphenated. Whole stamp roto. W* **9.** *P* 15 × 14.

D39	1d. black and carmine (5.50)	70	30
D40	2d. black and violet (4.51)	50	20
	a. Thick (double) "2D." (R. 15/5–6, R. 16/5–6)	8·00	6·00
	b. Black and reddish violet (12.52)	50	20
	ba. Thick (double) "2D."	8·00	6·00
D41	3d. deep blue and blue (5.50)	4·00	1·50
	a. Split "D"	45·00	
D42	4d. deep myrtle-green and emerald (2.58)	6·00	6·50
D43	6d. green and bright orange (3.50)	7·00	6·50
D44	1s. black-brown and purple-brown (2.58)	8·00	9·00
D39/44	*Set of* 6	24·00	22·00

D 5

D **6** Afrikaans at top

D **7** English at top

1961 (14 Feb). *Values in cents as Type* D **5.** *Whole stamp roto. W* **102.** *P* 15 × 14.

D45	1 c. black and carmine	20	2·50
D46	2 c. black and violet	35	2·50
D47	4 c. deep myrtle-green and emerald	80	5·50
D48	5 c. deep blue and blue	1·75	5·50
D49	6 c. green and orange-red	4·50	4·75
D50	10 c. sepia and brown-lake	5·50	7·50
D45/50	*Set of* 6	12·00	25·00

1961 (31 May)–**69.** *Roto. W* **102.** *P* 15 × 14.

D51	D **6**	1 c. black and carmine	40	60
D52	D **7**	1 c. black and carmine (6.62)	40	3·25
D53		2 c. black and deep reddish violet	40	55
D54	D **6**	4 c. dp myrtle-green & light emerald	2·00	2·00
D54*a*	D **7**	4 c. dp myrtle-grn & lt emerald (6.69)	6·00	9·00
D55		5 c. deep blue and grey-blue	2·00	3·00
D56		5 c. black and grey-blue (6.62)	1·75	6·50
D57	D **6**	6 c. deep green and red-orange	5·50	4·50
D58	D **7**	10 c. sepia and purple-brown	3·50	2·25
D51/8		*Set of* 9	20·00	28·00

1967 (Dec)–**71.** *Roto. W* **127** *(tête-bêche). P* 15 × 14.

D59	D **6**	1 c. black and carmine	20	55
D60	D **7**	1 c. black and carmine	20	30
D61	D **6**	2 c. black and deep reddish violet	30	85
D62	D **7**	2 c. black and deep reddish violet	30	85
D62*b*		4 c. dp myrtle-green & emerald (6.69)*	13·00	16·00
D62*c*	D **6**	4 c. dp myrtle-green & emerald (6.69)*	£110	90·00
D63		4 c. black and pale green (4.71)	15·00	17·00
D64	D **7**	4 c. black and pale green (4.71)	15·00	17·00
D65	D **6**	5 c. black and deep blue	50	50
D66	D **7**	5 c. black and deep blue	50	50
D67	D **6**	6 c. green and orange-red (1968)	3·50	6·00
D68	D **7**	6 c. green and orange-red (1968)	3·50	6·00
D69	D **6**	10 c. black and purple-brown	1·00	2·75
		a. Black and brown-lake (12.69)	1·00	2·75
D70	D **7**	10 c. black and purple-brown	1·00	2·75
		a. Black and brown-lake (12.69)	1·00	2·75
D59/70*a*		*except* D62*b/c* *Set of* 12	38·00	50·00

Nos. D59/70 were printed in two panes, one with inscriptions as Type D **6** and the other as Type D **7**.

*Nos. D62*b/c* were part of a printing of No. D54*a*. Most were printed on paper with the Arms watermark, but some were printed on RSA paper with the watermark upright and faint. Most of these were spoiled but a few sheets were issued in Types D **7** and D **6**, the latter being very scarce.

1971 *Roto. W* **127** *(tête-bêche). P* 14.

D71	D **6**	2 c. black and deep reddish violet	17·00	7·00
D72	D **7**	2 c. black and deep reddish violet	17·00	7·00
D74		4 c. deep myrtle-green & light emerald	42·00	32·00
D71/4		*Set of* 3	70·00	42·00

Nos. D71/4 were also printed in double panes as Nos. D59/70. Although the 4 c. as Type D **6** must have been printed it has not been possible to confirm that any were actually issued.

D 8

1972 (22 Mar). *English at right* (1, 4 *and* 8 c.) *or at left* (*others*). *W* **127** *(sideways tête-bêche). Chalk-surfaced paper* (4 c. *to* 10 c.). *P* 14×13½.

D75	D **8**	1 c. deep yellowish green	50	1·50
D76		2 c. bright orange	70	1·75
D77		4 c. plum	1·50	2·25
D78		6 c. chrome-yellow	1·75	3·25
D79		8 c. ultramarine	2·00	4·25
D80		10 c. bright scarlet	4·00	5·50
D75/80		*Set of* 6	9·50	17·00

The 6 c. also exists on phosphorised paper.

The use of Postage Due stamps ceased in 1975.

OFFICIAL STAMPS

OFFICIAL. OFFISIEEL. OFFISIEEL OFFICIAL

(O 1) (O 2)

(Approximate measurements between lines of opt are shown in mm in brackets)

1926 (1 Dec). *Optd vertically upwards, with stops, as Type* O 1.

(a) On 1913 issue

O1	3	2d. Nos. 6/6a (12½)	17·00	1·75

(b) On 1926 issue

			Un pair	Us pair	Us single
O2	6	½d. No. 30 (12½)	4·25	10·00	1·50
O3	7	1d. No. 31 (12½)	2·00	3·75	50
O4	8	6d. No. 32 (12½)	£550	75·00	10·00

This overprint is found on the ½d., 1d. and 6d. values of both the London and Pretoria printings. The London printings of the ½d. and 1d. stamps are considerably scarcer than the Pretoria, but the 6d. Pretoria printing is scarcer still.

1928–29. *Optd vertically upwards, as Type* O 1, *but without stops.*

O5	11	2d. No. 34 (17½)	4·50	17·00	2·00
O6		2d. No. 34 (19) (1929)	3·25	10·00	1·50
O7	8	6d. No. 32 (11½)	16·00	24·00	2·75

1929. *Typographed stamps optd with Type* O 2.

O 8	6	½d. No. 30 (13½)	1·75	2·00	30
		a. Stop after "OFFISIEEL" on English stamp	28·00	28·00	3·25
		b. Ditto. On Afrikaans stamp	28·00	28·00	3·25
O 9	7	1d. No. 31 (13½)	3·00	3·75	45
O10	8	6d. No. 32 (13½)	9·00	32·00	3·25
		a. Stop after "OFFISIEEL" on English stamp	55·00	85·00	9·00
		b. Ditto. On Afrikaans stamp	55·00	85·00	9·00
O8/10		*Set of* 3	12·50	35·00	3·50

1930–47. *Rotogravure stamps* ("SUIDAFRIKA" *in one word*) *optd with Type* O 2.

O11	6	½d. No. 42 (9½–12) (1931)	2·00	3·25	35
		a. Stop after "OFFISIEEL" on English stamp	27·00	32·00	3·50
		b. Ditto. On Afrikaans stamp	27·00	32·00	3·50
O12		½d. No. 42 (12½) (1932)	3·25	4·00	50
O13	7	1d. No. 43 (12½ and 13½)	4·25	4·50	55
		a. Stop after "OFFISIEEL" on English stamp	27·00	28·00	3·25
		b. Ditto. On Afrikaans stamp	27·00	28·00	3·25
O14		1d. No. 43*d* (12½) (1932)	9·00	9·00	90
		a. Opt double	£250	£275	
O15	11	2d. No. 44 (21) (1931)	6·00	11·00	1·50
O15*a*		2d. No. 44*d* (20½) (1938)	75·00	90·00	9·00
O16	8	6d. No. 47 (12½) (1931)	7·00	8·50	85
		a. Stop after "OFFISIEEL" on English stamp	45·00	48·00	5·00
		b. Ditto. On Afrikaans stamp	45·00	48·00	5·00
O17	13	1s. No. 48 (19) (1932)	40·00	60·00	7·00
O18		1s. No. 48 (21) (1933)	40·00	60·00	7·00
O19	14	2s. 6d. No. 49 (18) (1933)	60·00	95·00	11·00
O20		2s. 6d. No. 49 (21) (1934)	45·00	65·00	8·00
O20*a*		2s. 6d. No. 49*a* (19½–20) (1947)	24·00	55·00	6·50
		ab. Diaeresis on second "E"	£550	£650	

Nos. O8a/b, O10a/b, O11a/b, O13a/b and O16a/b. The pairs include one stamp with variety and the other normal. Pairs of No. O20ab exist with the variety on either stamp (English or Afrikaans). Pairs with both stamps showing the variety are worth much more.

1931. *Recess-printed stamps opt with Type* O 2.

O21	13	1s. No. 36 (17½, 18 and 20½)	30·00	70·00	8·00
		a. Stop after "OFFICIAL" on Afrikaans stamp	£100	£180	
O22	14	2s. 6d. No. 37 (17½ and 18)	55·00	£120	15·00
		a. Stop after "OFFICIAL" on Afrikaans stamp	£275	£400	

Nos. O21a and O22a. The pairs include one stamp with variety and the other normal.

OFFICIAL OFFISIEEL OFFICIAL OFFISIEEL

(O 3) (O 4)

1935–50. *Rotogravure stamps* ("SUID-AFRIKA" *hyphenated*).

(*a*) *Optd with Type* O 2 ("OFFICIAL" *at right*)

O23 **6** ½d. No. 54 (12½) (1936) .. 3·00 11·00 1·25
O24 **25a** ½d. No. 75*b* (11 and 12½) (1938) .. .. 5·00 6·50 65
O24*a* ½d. No. 75*bd* (12) (1947) .. 90 4·50 45
O24*b* ½d. No. 114 (11) (1949) .. 1·00 4·75 50
O25 **7** 1d. No. 56 (11½–13) .. .. 65 1·00 15
O26 **22** 1½d. No. 57 (20) (1937) .. 12·00 14·00 1·50
O26*a* 1½d. No. 57*b* (20) (1939) .. 23·00 8·50 85
O26*b* **34a** 1½d. No. 87 (14½) (1944) .. 2·50 6·00 60
ba. Diaeresis on second "E" (1946?) £100 £100
O26*c* 1½d. No. 87 (16) (1948) .. 2·00 3·50 35
O27 **11** 2d. No. 58 (20) (1939) .. 45·00 17·00 2·00
O27*a* **54** 2d. No. 107 (20) (1947) .. 2·25 14·00 1·50
ab. Diaeresis on second "E" (1947) £225 £350
O27*b* 2d. No. 107*a* (20) (1949) .. 5·50 13·00 1·40
O28 **8** 6d. No. 61 (12 and 13) (1937) 55·00 30·00 3·50
O28*a* 6d. No. 61*a* (11½–13) (1939) 9·00 10·00 1·25
O28*b* 6d. No. 61*b* (12) (1947) .. 4·00 8·00 85
O29 **13** 1s. No. 62 (20) (1939) .. 32·00 17·00 1·75
aa. Diaeresis on second "E" (1944?) £850 £700
O29*a* 1s. No. 120 (17½–18½) (1950) 9·00 21·00 2·25
O29*b* **15** 5s. No. 64*a* (20) (1948) .. 35·00 80·00 10·00
O29*c* **23** 10s. No. 64*b* (19½) (1948) .. 65·00 £130 17·00

(*b*) *Optd with Type* O 3 ("OFFICIAL" *at left*)

O30 **15** 5s. No. 64*a* (18) (1940) .. 45·00 85·00 11·00
O31 **23** 10s. No. 64*b* (19) (1940) .. £160 £190 25·00

Prices for Nos. O26ba and O27ab are for horizontal pairs with the variety on both stamps. No. O29aa shows the variety on one stamp only, but pairs also exist with it on both.

1944. *Optd with Type* O 4 *reading up and down and with diaeresis over the second* "E" *of* "OFFISIEEL".

O32 **25a** ½d. No. 75*bd* (10) .. .. 8·50 14·00 1·50

OFFISIEEL OFFICIAL
(O 5)

OFFICIAL OFFISIEEL
(O 6)

1944. *Optd with Type* O 5 *reading upwards* ("OFFICIAL" *at right*).

O33 **11** 2d. No. 58*a* (18½) .. .. 3·00 14·00 1·50

1949–50. *Optd with Type* O 6 *reading upwards* ("OFFICIAL" *at left*).

O34 **34a** 1½d. No. 87 (16) .. .. .. 10·00 22·00 2·40
O35 **68** 2d. No. 134 (16) (1950) .. £1000 £1300 £150

OFFISIEEL OFFICIAL
(O 7)

1950–54. *Optd as Type* O 7.

O35*a* **25a** ½d. No. 75*bd* (10) (1951) .. 1·00 6·50 65
O35*b* ½d. No. 114 (10) (1953) .. 70 1·50 15
O36 **7** 1d. No. 56*i* (10) .. 1·00 4·50 45
O36*a* 1d. No. 115 (10) (1951) .. 1·00 1·50 15
O36*b* 1d. No. 135 (10) (1952) .. 90 1·75 20
O37 **34a** 1½d. No. 87 (14½) (1951) .. 1·40 2·50 25
O38 **68** 2d. No. 134 (14½) .. 1·00 2·00 20
a. Opt inverted £1000
O39 **8** 6d. No. 119 (10) .. 1·00 3·50 35
O39*a* 6d. No. 119*a* (10) (1951) .. 1·50 3·50 35
O40 **13** 1s. No. 120 (19) .. 5·50 16·00 1·60
O40*a* 1s. No. 120*a* (19) (1953) .. £100 £140 17·00
O41 **14** 2s. 6d. No. 121 (19) .. 8·50 28·00 3·25
O41*a* **15** 5s. No. 64*a* (19) (1951) .. 95·00 70·00 8·50
O41*b* 5s. No. 122 (19) (1953) .. 22·00 48·00 5·50
O41*c* 5s. No. 122*a* (19) (1954) .. 48·00 70·00 8·50
O42 **23** 10s. No. 64*ba* (19) .. 55·00 £110 16·00

On No. O36*a* the overprint is thicker.

The use of official stamps ceased in January 1955.

South Arabian Federation

ADEN

The first post office in Aden opened during January 1839, situated in what became known as the Crater district. No stamps were initially available, but, after the office was placed under the Bombay Postal Circle, stocks of the 1854 ½ a. and 1 a. stamps were placed on sale in Aden from 10 October 1854. Supplies of the 2 a. and 4 a. values did not arrive until December. Most Indian issues from the 1854 lithographs up to 1935 Silver Jubilee set can be found with Aden postmarks.

During January 1858 a further office, Aden Steamer Point, was opened in the harbour area and much of the business was transferred to it by 1869. The original Aden post office, in Crater, was renamed Aden Cantonment, later to be changed again to Aden Camp.

The first cancellation used with the Indian stamps was a plain diamond of dots. This type was also used elsewhere so that attribution to Aden is only possible when on cover. Aden was assigned "124" in the Indian postal number system and this formed the main feature of marks from 1858, either on its own or as part of a duplex.

1858 "124" Cancellation

1870 Aden Duplex

1872 Aden Steamer Point Duplex

Both post offices used this number until 1871 when Aden Cantonment was assigned "125", only to have this swiftly amended to "124A" in the same year.

1871 Aden Cantonment "125" Cancellation   1871 Aden Cantonment "124A" Cancellation

Cancellations inscribed "Aden Steamer Point" disappear after 1874 and this office was then known simply as Aden. Following this change the office was given number "B-22" under the revised Indian P.O. scheme and this number appears as a major part of the cancellations from 1875 to 1886, either on its own or as part of a duplex, Aden Camp, the alternative name for the Cantonment office, became "B-22/1".

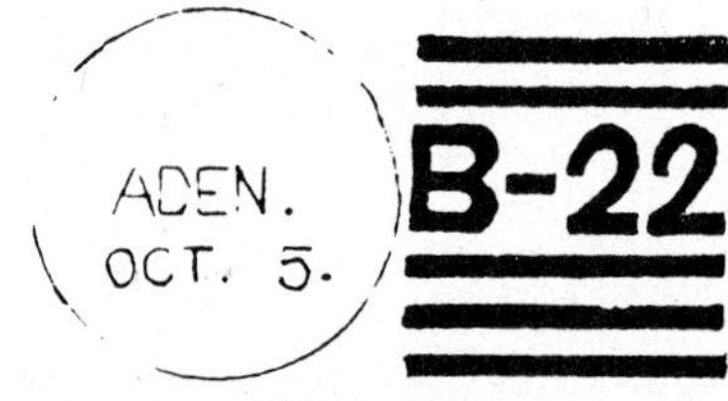

1875 Aden Duplex

Squared-circle types for Aden and Aden Cantonment were introduced in 1884 and 1888 to be in turn replaced by standard Indian double and single circle from 1895 onwards.

A number of other post offices were opened between 1891 and 1937:

Dthali (*opened* 1903, *initially using* "EXPERIMENTAL P.O. B-84" *postmark; closed* 1907)
Kamaran (*opened c* 1915, *but no civilian postmarks known before* 1925)
Khormaksar (*opened* 1892; *closed* 1915; *reopened* 1925)
Maalla (*opened* 1923; *closed* 1931)
Nobat-Dakim (*opened* 1904, *initially using* "EXPERIMENTAL P.O. B-84" *postmark; closed* 1905)
Perim (*opened* 1915; *closed* 1936)
Sheikh Othman (*opened* 1891; *closed* 1915; *reopened* 1922; *closed* 1937)

PRICES FOR STAMPS ON COVER TO 1945

Nos. 1/15 *from* × 5
Nos. 16/27 *from* × 3

1 Dhow

3 Aidrus Mosque, Crater

(Recess D.L.R.)

1937 (1 Apr). *Wmk Mult Script CA sideways. P* 13 × 12.

1 **1** ½ a. yellow-green .. .. 2·75 1·25
2 9 p. deep green .. .. 2·75 1·40
3 1 a. sepia .. .. 2·75 50
4 2 a. scarlet .. .. 2·75 2·00
5 2½ a. bright blue .. .. 2·75 80
6 3 a. carmine .. .. 9·00 6·00
7 3½ a. grey-blue .. .. 3·75 2·00
8 8 a. pale purple .. .. 18·00 5·50
9 1 r. brown .. .. 21·00 7·00
10 2 r. yellow .. .. 45·00 16·00
11 5 r. deep purple .. .. 80·00 60·00
12 10 r. olive-green £150 £140
1/12 .. .. *Set of* 12 £300 £225
1/12 Perf "Specimen" .. .. *Set of* 12 £250

1937 (12 May). *Coronation. As Nos.* 118/20 *of Jamaica. P* 14.

13 1 a. sepia 65 60
14 2½ a. light blue .. .. 90 1·00
15 3½ a. grey-blue .. .. 1·25 1·75
13/15 .. .. *Set of* 3 2·50 3·00

(Recess Waterlow)

1939 (19 Jan)–**48**. *Horiz designs as T* **3**. *Wmk Mult Script CA. P* 12½.

16 ½ a. yellowish green 50 50
a. Bluish green (9.48) .. .. .. 90 2·00
17 ¾ a. red-brown 50 90
18 1 a. pale blue 20 25
19 1½ a. scarlet 45 60
20 2 a. sepia 20 25
21 2½ a. deep ultramarine 30 30
22 3 a. sepia and carmine 50 25
23 8 a. red-orange 35 40
23*a* 14 a. sepia and light blue (15.1.45) .. 1·75 90
24 1 r. emerald-green .. .. .. 1·50 1·25
25 2 r. deep blue and magenta .. .. 4·00 1·75
26 5 r. red-brown and olive-green .. .. 10·00 6·00
27 10 r. sepia and violet .. .. 18·00 10·00
16/27 .. .. .. *Set of* 13 35·00 21·00
16/27 Perf "Specimen" .. *Set of* 13 £160

Designs:—½ a., 2 a., Type **3**; ¾ a., 5 r. Adenese Camel Corps; 1 a., 2 r. The Harbour; 1½ a., 1 r. Adenese Dhow; 2½ a., 8 a. Mukalla; 3 a., 14 a., 10 r. "Capture of Aden, 1839" (Capt. Rundle).

1946 (15 Oct). *Victory. As Nos.* 141/2 *of Jamaica.*

28 1½ a. carmine 15 35
29 2½ a. blue 15 20
28/9 Perf "Specimen" .. .. *Set of* 2 50·00

1949 (7 Jan). *Royal Silver Wedding. As Nos.* 143/4 *of Jamaica.*

30 1½ a. scarlet (*p* 14×15) 40 50
31 10 r. mauve (*p* 11½×11) .. .. 22·00 25·00

1949 (10 Oct). *75th Anniv of U.P.U. As Nos.* 145/8 *of Jamaica, surch with new values by Waterlow.*

32 2½ a. on 20 c. ultramarine 50 90
33 3 a. on 30 c. carmine-red .. .. .. 1·25 90
34 8 a. on 50 c. orange .. .. .. 1·60 1·00
35 1 r. on 1 s. blue .. .. .. 1·90 2·25
32/5 .. .. *Set of* 4 4·75 4·50

(12)

1951 (1 Oct). *Currency changed. Nos.* 18 *and* 20/7 *surch with new values, in cents or shillings, as T* **12**, *or in one line between bars* (30 *c.*) *by Waterlow.*

36 5 c. on 1 a. pale blue 15 40
37 10 c. on 2 a. sepia 15 45
38 15 c. on 2½ a. deep ultramarine 20 85
a. Surch double £550
39 20 c. on 3 a. sepia and carmine 25 40
40 30 c. on 8 a. red-orange (R.) 25 50
41 50 c. on 8 a. red-orange 25 35
42 70 c. on 14 a. sepia and light blue 55 80
43 1 s. on 1 r. emerald-green 35 30
44 2 s. on 2 r. deep blue and magenta .. .. 3·75 2·50
a. Surch albino £225
45 5 s. on 5 r. red-brown and olive-green .. 13·00 3·25
46 10 s. on 10 r. sepia and violet .. .. 17·00 8·00
36/46 .. .. .. *Set of* 11 32·00 16·00

1953 (2 June). *As No.* 153 *of Jamaica.*

47 15 c. black and green 30 95

14 Minaret

25 "Aden in 1572" (F. Hogenberg)

(Recess Waterlow, until 1961, then D.L.R.)

1953 (15 June)–**63**. *T* **14** *and similar designs, and T* **25**. *Wmk Mult Script CA. P* 13½×13 (*No.* 72), 12×13½ (*Nos.* 57, 64, 66, 68) *or* 12 (*others*).

48 5 c. yellowish green 15 10
49 5 c. bluish green (1.6.55) 30 50
a. Perf 12 × 13½ (12.4.56) 10 20
50 10 c. orange 30 10
51 10 c. vermilion (1.2.55) 10 20
52 15 c. blue-green 60 35
53 15 c. greenish grey (26.4.59) .. .. 70 1·25
a. Deep greenish grey (16.1.62) .. .. 2·25 3·00
b. Greenish slate (13.11.62) .. .. 3·00 3·75
54 25 c. carmine-red 30 20
55 25 c. deep rose-red (15.3.56) 50 30
a. Rose-red (13.3.62) .. .. .. 2·00 60

56	35 c. deep ultramarine	1·75	1·25
57	35 c. deep blue (15.10.58)	1·00	1·00
	a. *Violet-blue* (17.2.59)	1·50	1·00
58	50 c. dull blue	15	10
59	50 c. deep blue (1.7.55)	50	70
	a. Perf 12 × 13½ (12.4.56)	45	10
60	70 c. brown-grey	15	10
61	70 c. black (20.9.54)	60	35
	a. Perf 12 × 13½ (12.4.56)	35	10
62	1 s. sepia and reddish violet	30	10
63	1 s. black and violet (1.7.55)	45	10
64	1 s. 25, blue and black (16.7.56)	2·00	40
	a. *Dull blue and black* (16.1.63) ..	4·00	50
65	2 s. sepia and rose-carmine	1·25	40
66	2 s. black and carmine-red (1.3.56) ..	2·75	50
	a. *Black and carmine-rose* (22.1.63) ..	7·00	3·50
67	5 s. sepia and dull blue	1·25	40
68	5 s. black and deep dull blue (11.4.56) ..	2·00	40
	a. *Black and blue* (11.12.62)	14·00	4·50
69	10 s. sepia and olive	1·75	8·00
70	10 s. black and bronze-green (20.9.54) ..	4·25	1·25
71	20 s. chocolate and reddish lilac	6·50	10·00
72	20 s. black and deep lilac (7.1.57)	29·00	13·00
	a. *Deep black and deep lilac* (14.5.58) ..	32·00	13·00
48/72	.. .. *Set of* 25	50·00	35·00

Designs: (*as Type* **14**). *Horiz*—10 c. Camel transport; 15 c. Crater; 25 c. Mosque; 1 s. Dhow building. *Vert*—35 c. Dhow; 50 c. Map; 70 c. Salt works; 1 s. 25 Colony's badge; 2 s. Aden Protectorate levy; 5 s. Crater Pass; 10 s. Tribesman.

On No. 70 the tribesman's skirt is shaded with cross-hatching instead of with mainly diagonal lines as in No. 69.

1954 (27 Apr). *Royal Visit. As No. 62 but inscr* "ROYAL VISIT 1954" *at top.*

73	1 s. sepia and reddish violet	30	30

تعديل الدستور ١٩٥٩

(26)

REVISED CONSTITUTION 1959

(27)

1959 (26 Jan). *Revised Constitution. No. 53 optd with T* **26**, *and No. 64 optd with T* **27**, *in red, by Waterlow.*

74	15 c. slate-green	15	70
75	1 s. 25, blue and black	30	70

1963 (4 June). *Freedom from Hunger. As No. 80 of Lesotho.*

76	1 s. 25, bluish green	1·25	1·40

1964 (5 Feb)–**65**. *As Nos. 48, etc. but wmk* w **12**. *P* 12 (10 *c.*, 15 *c.*, 25 *c.*, 1 *s.*) *or* 12 × 13½ (*others*).

77	5 c. green (16.2.65)	30	60
78	10 c. bright orange	20	30
79	15 c. greenish grey	30	1·25
80	25 c. carmine-red	30	30
81	35 c. indigo-violet	1·00	1·00
82	50 c. indigo-blue	20	15
	a. *Pale indigo-blue* (16.2.65)	30	30
83	70 c. black	25	55
	a. *Brownish grey* (16.2.65)	30	40
84	1 s. black and violet (10.3.64)	4·00	1·00
85	1 s. 25, ultramarine and black (10.3.64) ..	7·50	2·00
86	2 s. black and carmine-rose (16.2.65) ..	2·75	21·00
77/86	.. .. *Set of* 10	15·00	25·00

The stamps of Aden were withdrawn on 31 March 1965 and superseded by those of the South Arabian Federation.

ADEN PROTECTORATE STATES

KATHIRI STATE OF SEIYUN

The stamps of ADEN were used in Kathiri State of Seiyun from 22 May 1937 until 1942. A further office was opened at Tarim on 11 December 1940.

PRICES FOR STAMPS ON COVER TO 1945
Nos. 1/11 *from* × 10

1 Sultan of Seiyun

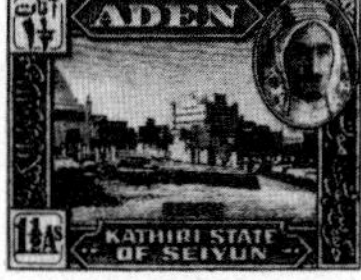

2 Seiyun

(Recess D.L.R.)

1942 (July–Oct). *Designs as T* **1/2**. *Wmk Mult Script CA. T* **1**, *perf* 14; *others, perf* 12 × 13 (*vert*) *or* 13 × 12 (*horiz*).

1	½ a. blue-green	15	35
2	¾ a. brown	15	35
3	1 a. blue	15	35
4	1½ a. carmine	15	40
5	2 a. sepia	15	50
6	2½ a. blue	20	75
7	3 a. sepia and carmine	35	50
8	8 a. red	20	50
9	1 r. green	40	50
10	2 r. blue and purple	5·00	7·50
11	5 r. brown and green	12·00	11·00
1/11	.. .. *Set of* 11	17·00	21·00
1/11 Perf "Specimen"	.. .. *Set of* 11	£110	

Designs:—½ to 1 a. Type **1**. *Vert as T* **2**—2 a. Tarim; 2½ a. Mosque, Seiyun; 1 r. South Gate, Tarim; 5 r. Mosque entrance, Tarim. *Horiz as T* **2**—3 a. Fortress, Tarim; 8 a. Mosque, Seiyun; 2 r. A Kathiri house.

VICTORY
ISSUE
8TH JUNE 1946

(10)

1946 (15 Oct). *Victory. No. 4 optd with T* **10**, *and No. 6 optd similarly but in four lines, by De La Rue.*

12	1½ a. carmine	10	20
13	2½ a. blue (R.)	10	10
	a. Opt inverted	£375	
12/13 Perf "Specimen"	.. *Set of* 2	50·00	

No. 13 is known with surcharge double but the second impression is almost coincident with the first.

1949 (17 Jan). *Royal Silver Wedding. As Nos. 143/4 of Jamaica.*

14	1½ a. scarlet	30	50
15	5 r. green	9·50	8·00

1949 (10 Oct). *75th Anniv of U.P.U. As Nos. 145/8 of Jamaica, surch with new values by Waterlow.*

16	2½ a. on 20 c. ultramarine	25	40
17	3 a. on 30 c. carmine-red	40	55
18	8 a. on 50 c. orange	40	60
19	1 r. on 1 s. blue	60	90
16/19	.. .. *Set of* 4	1·50	2·25

5 CTS (11) 50 CENTS (12) 5/- (13)

1951 (1 Oct). *Currency changed. Nos.* 3 *and* 5/11 *surch as T* **11** (5 *c.*), **12** (10 *c.* ("CTS"), 15 *c.* ("CTS"), 20 *c. and* 50 *c.*) *or* **13** (1*s. to* 5*s.*), *by Waterlow.*

20	5 c. on 1 a. blue (R.)	15	20
21	10 c. on 2 a. sepia	15	20
22	15 c. on 2½ a. blue	15	20
23	20 c. on 3 a. sepia and carmine	15	20
24	50 c. on 8 a. red	15	20
25	1 s. on 1 r. green	20	25
26	2 s. on 2 r. blue and purple	2·00	7·50
27	5 s. on 5 r. brown and green	8·00	20·00
20/27	.. .. *Set of* 8	10·00	26·00

1953 (2 June). *Coronation. As No. 153 of Jamaica.*

28	15 c. black and deep green	30	95

14 Sultan Hussein

15 Tarim

(Des Freya Stark and H. Ingram. Recess D.L.R.)

1954 (15 Jan). *As Nos. 1/11* (*but with portrait of Sultan Hussein as in T* **14/15**). *Wmk Mult Script CA. T* **14**, *perf* 12½; *others, perf* 12 × 13 (*vert*) *or* 13 × 12 (*horiz*).

29	5 c. sepia	10	10
30	10 c. deep blue	15	10
31	15 c. deep bluish green	15	10
32	25 c. carmine-red	15	10
33	35 c. deep blue	15	10
34	50 c. deep brown and carmine-red	15	10
35	1 s. brown-orange	15	10
36	2 s. deep yellow-green	3·25	1·25
37	5 s. deep blue and violet	3·50	3·00
38	10 s. yellow-brown and violet	4·50	6·50
29/38	.. .. *Set of* 10	11·00	10·00

16 Qarn Adh Dhabi

17 Seiyun

(Recess D.L.R.)

1964 (1 July). *Designs as T* **16/17**. *W* w **12**. *P* 12 × 13 (70 *c.*) *or* 13 × 12 (*others*).

39	70 c. black	70	65
40	1 s. 25 c. blue-green	70	3·50
41	1 s. 50 c. deep reddish violet	80	3·50
39/41	.. .. *Set of* 3	2·00	7·00

Design: *Horiz as T* **17**—1 s. 50 c. Gheil Omer.

(New Currency. 1000 fils = 1 dinar)

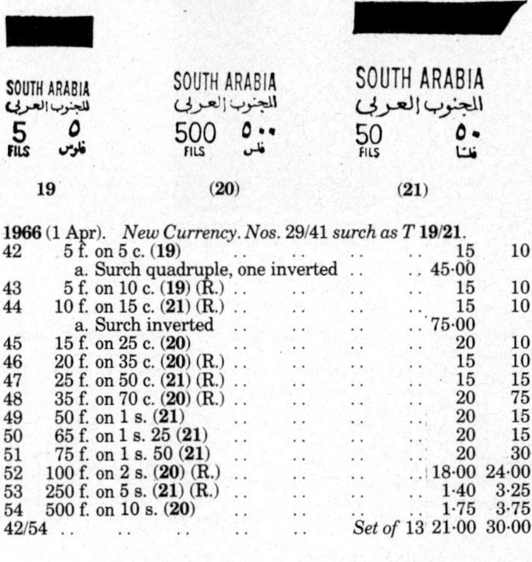

19 (20) (21)

1966 (1 Apr). *New Currency. Nos.* 29/41 *surch as T* **19/21**.

42	5 f. on 5 c. (**19**)	15	10
	a. Surch quadruple, one inverted	45·00	
43	5 f. on 10 c. (**19**) (R.)	15	10
44	10 f. on 15 c. (**21**) (R.)	15	10
	a. Surch inverted	75·00	
45	15 f. on 25 c. (**20**)	20	10
46	20 f. on 35 c. (**20**) (R.)	15	10
47	25 f. on 50 c. (**21**) (R.)	15	15
48	35 f. on 70 c. (**20**) (R.)	20	75
49	50 f. on 1 s. (**21**)	20	15
50	65 f. on 1 s. 25 (**21**)	20	15
51	75 f. on 1 s. 50 (**21**)	20	30
52	100 f. on 2 s. (**20**) (R.)	18·00	24·00
53	250 f. on 5 s. (**21**) (R.)	1·40	3·25
54	500 f. on 10 s. (**20**)	1·75	3·75
42/54	.. .. *Set of* 13	21·00	30·00

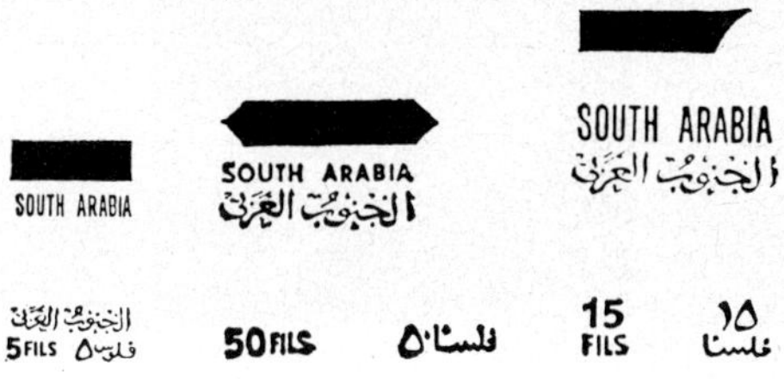

SOUTH ARABIA 5 FILS (22) SOUTH ARABIA 50 FILS (23) SOUTH ARABIA 15 FILS (24)

1966. *Nos.* 29/41 *surch with T* **22/4**.

55	5 f. on 5 c. (**22**) (B.)	30	10
	a. Surch inverted	50·00	
56	5 f. on 10 c. (**22**) (R.)	45	10
57	10 f. on 15 c. (**23**) (Y.)	45	10
	a. Surch inverted	50·00	
58	15 f. on 25 c. (**24**) (B.)	45	10
	a. Surch inverted	50·00	
59	20 f. on 35 c. (**24**) (Y.)	50	10
60	25 f. on 50 c. (**23**) (B.)	50	10
61	35 f. on 70 c. (**24**) (Br.)	50	20
62	50 f. on 1 s. (**23**) (G.)	50	20
	a. Stop after "FILS"	12·00	
63	65 f. on 1 s. 25 (**23**) (Y.)	40	45
64	75 f. on 1 s. 50 (**23**) (G.)	40	50
	a. Surch inverted	50·00	
65	100 f. on 2 s. (**24**) (Y.)	2·00	85
	a. Surch inverted	35·00	
66	250 f. on 5 s. (**23**) (Y.)	2·50	2·75
	a. Surch inverted	60·00	
67	500 f. on 10 s. (**24**) (G.)	2·75	5·00
55/67	.. .. *Set of* 13	10·50	9·00

HELSINKI 1952

(25)

INTERNATIONAL COOPERATION THROUGH OLYMPICS

(26)

1966. *History of Olympic Games. Nos.* 57, 59, 61/7 *Optd as T* **25/6** *in red.*

68	10 f. on 15 c. deep bluish green (**25** ("LOS ANGELES 1932"))	15	10
69	20 f. on 35 c. deep blue (**25** ("BERLIN 1936"))	20	15
70	35 f. on 70 c. black (**26**)	20	15
	a. Opt T **26** inverted	7·00	
71	50 f. on 1 s. brown-orange (**25** ("LONDON 1948"))	25	20
	a. Stop after "FILS"	9·00	
72	65 f. on 1 s. 25, blue-green (**25**)	35	40
73	75 f. on 1 s. 50, deep reddish violet (**25** ("MELBOURNE 1956"))	40	45
74	100 f. on 2 s. deep yellow-green (**25** ("ROME 1960"))	50	55
75	250 f. on 5 s. deep blue and violet (**25** ("TOKYO 1964"))	1·00	1·25
	a. Surch inverted	50·00	
76	500 f. on 10 s. yellow-brown and violet (**25** ("MEXICO CITY 1968"))	1·40	2·50
68/76	.. .. *Set of* 9	4·00	5·25

CHAMPION: ENGLAND

(27)

FOOTBALL 1966

(28)

1966 (19 Sept). *World Cup Football Championships. Nos.* 57, 59, 61/2, 65/7 *optd with T* **27/8**.

77	10 f. on 15 c. deep bluish green (**27**)	40	30
78	20 f. on 35 c. deep blue (**28**)	55	40
79	35 f. on 70 c. black (**28**)	65	40
80	50 f. on 1 s. brown-orange (**27**)	75	40
	a. Stop after "FILS"	14·00	
81	100 f. on 2 s. deep yellow-green (**28**)	3·25	1·75
82	250 f. on 5 s. deep blue and violet (**27**) ..	7·00	4·50
83	500 f. on 10 s. yellow-brown and violet (**28**) ..	9·00	7·00
77/83	.. .. *Set of* 7	19·00	13·50

29 "Telstar"

(Photo State Ptg Wks, Vienna)

1966 (25 Oct). *I.T.U. Centenary* (1965). *T* **29** *and similar vert designs. P* 13½.

No.	Description	Unused	Used
84	5 f. blackish green, black and reddish violet	85	25
85	10 f. maroon, black and bright green	1·00	30
86	15 f. Prussian blue, black and orange	1·40	40
87	25 f. blackish green, black and orange-red	2·00	50
88	35 f. maroon, black and deep olive-yellow	2·50	70
89	50 f. Prussian blue, black and orange-brown	3·00	1·10
90	65 f. blackish green, black and orange-yellow	3·75	1·25
84/90	*Set of* 7	13·00	4·00

Designs:—10, 35 f. "Relay"; 15, 50 f. "Ranger"; others, Type **29**.

32 Churchill at Easel

(Photo State Ptg Wks, Vienna)

1966 (Dec). *Sir Winston Churchill's Paintings. T* **32** *and similar designs in black and gold* (5 *f.*) *or multicoloured* (*others*). *P* 13½.

No.	Description	Unused	Used
91	5 f. Type **32**	1·00	15
92	10 f. "Antibes"	1·25	15
93	15 f. "Flowers" (*vert*)	1·25	20
94	20 f. "Tapestries"	1·40	35
95	25 f. "Village, Lake Lugano"	1·60	35
96	35 f. "Church, Lake Como" (*vert*)	1·75	40
97	50 f. "Flowers at Chartwell" (*vert*)	2·25	65
98	65 f. Type **32**	2·75	90
91/8	*Set of* 8	12·00	2·75

WORLD PEACE
PANDIT NEHRU
(39)

40 "Master Crewe as Henry VIII" (Sir Joshua Reynolds)

1967. *"World Peace". Nos.* 57, 59, 61/7 *optd as T* **39** *in various sizes of type.*

No.	Description	Unused	Used
99	10 f. on 15 c. deep bluish green (Type **39**) (R.)	20	20
100	20 f. on 35 c. deep blue ("WINSTON CHURCHILL") (R.)	3·50	1·25
101	35 f. on 70 c. black ("DAG HAMMARSKJOLD") (B.)	50	50
102	50 f. on 1 s. brown-orange ("JOHN F. KENNEDY") (R.)	60	60
	a. Stop after "FILS"	14·00	
103	65 f. on 1 s. 25, blue-green ("LUDWIG ERHARD") (Pk.)	70	70
104	75 f. on 1 s. 50 dp reddish violet ("LYNDON JOHNSON") (B.)	80	80
105	100 f. on 2 s. deep yellow-green ("ELEANOR ROOSEVELT") (B.)	1·00	1·00
106	250 f. on 5 s. dp blue and violet ("WINSTON CHURCHILL") (R.)	9·00	6·50
107	500 f. on 10 s. yellow-brown & violet ("JOHN F. KENNEDY") (R.)	4·75	6·50
99/107	*Set of* 9	19·00	16·00

(Photo State Ptg Wks, Vienna)

1967. *Paintings. T* **40** *and similar multicoloured designs. P* 13½.

No.	Description	Unused	Used
108	5 f. Type **40**	25	25
109	10 f. "The Dancer" (Degas)	30	30
110	15 f. "The Fifer" (Manet)	35	35
111	20 f. "Stag at Sharkey's" (boxing match, G. Burrows)	40	40
112	25 f. "Don Manuel Osorio" (Goya)	45	45
113	35 f. "St. Martin distributing his Cloak" (A. van Dyck)	65	65
114	50 f. "The Blue Boy" (Gainsborough)	75	75
115	65 f. "The White Horse" (Gauguin)	1·00	1·00
116	75 f. "Mona Lisa" (Da Vinci) (45 × 62 *mm.*)	1·25	1·25
108/16	*Set of* 9	4·75	4·75

SCOTT CARPENTER
(49)

50 Churchill Crown

1967. *American Astronauts. Nos.* 57, 59, 61/2 *and* 65/6 *optd as T* **49** *in various sizes of type, in red.*

No.	Description	Unused	Used
117	10 f. on 15 c. deep bluish green ("ALAN SHEPARD, JR.")	45	60
118	20 f. on 35 c. dp blue ("VIRGIL GRISSOM")	60	70
119	35 f. on 70 c. black ("JOHN GLENN, JR.")	85	1·00
120	50 f. on 1 s. brown-orange (Type **49**)	85	1·00
	a. Stop after "FILS"	15·00	
121	100 f. on 2 s. deep yellow-green ("WALTER SCHIRRA, JR.")	2·00	2·75
122	250 f. on 5 s. deep blue & violet ("GORDON COOPER, JR.")	3·25	4·00
	a. Opt (as T **49**) double	90·00	
117/122	*Set of* 6	7·25	9·00

1967 (Mar). *Churchill Commemoration. Photo. P* 13½.

No.	Description	Unused	Used
123 **50**	75 f. multicoloured	8·50	6·50

Appendix

The following stamps have either been issued in excess of postal needs, or have not been made available to the public in reasonable quantities at face value. Miniature sheets, imperforate stamps etc., are excluded from this section.

1967

Hunting. 20 *f.*
Olympic Games, Grenoble. Postage 10, 25, 35, 50, 75 *f. Air* 100, 200 *f.*
Scout Jamboree, Idaho. Air 150 *f.*
Paintings by Renoir. Postage 10, 35, 50, 65, 75 *f. Air* 100, 200, 250 *f.*
Paintings by Toulouse-Lautrec. Postage 10, 35, 50, 65, 75 *f. Air* 100, 200, 250 *f.*

The National Liberation Front is said to have taken control of Kathiri State of Seiyun on 1 October 1967.

QU'AITI STATE IN HADHRAMAUT

The stamps of ADEN were used in Qu'aiti State in Hadhramaut from 22 April 1937 until 1942. The main post office was at Mukalla. Other offices existed at Du'an (*opened* 1940), Gheil Ba Wazir (*opened* 1942), Haura (*opened* 1940), Shibam (*opened* 1940) and Shihr (*opened* 1939).

PRICES FOR STAMPS ON COVER TO 1945
Nos. 1/11 *from* × 6

I. ISSUES INSCR "SHIHR AND MUKALLA"

1 Sultan of Shihr and Mukalla

2 Mukalla Harbour

VICTORY
ISSUE
8TH JUNE
1946
(10)

(Recess D.L.R.)

1942 (July)–**46**. *Wmk Mult Script CA. Designs as T* **1** (½ *to* 1 *a.*) *or T* **2** (*others*). *P* 14 (½ *to* 1 *a.*), 12 × 13 (1½, 2, 3 *a. and* 1 *r.*) *or* 13 × 12 (*others*).

No.	Description	Unused	Used
1	½ a. blue-green	15	25
	a. Olive-green (12.46)	16·00	23·00
2	¾ a. brown	20	25
3	1 a. blue	30	25
4	1½ a. carmine	35	20
5	2 a. sepia	30	25
6	2½ a. blue	30	20
7	3 a. sepia and carmine	35	25
8	8 a. red	30	40
9	1 r. green	30	50
10	2 r. blue and purple	7·00	6·00
11	5 r. brown and green	9·00	6·50
1/11	*Set of* 11	17·00	13·50
1/11 Perf "Specimen"	*Set of* 11	£110	

Designs: *Vert*—2 a. Gateway of Shihr; 3 a. Outpost of Mukalla; 1 r. Du'an. *Horiz*—2½ a. Shibam; 8 a. 'Einat; 2 r. Mosque in Hureidha; 5 r. Meshhed.

1946 (15 Oct). *Victory. No.* 4 *optd. with T* **10** *and No.* 6 *optd similarly, but in three lines, by De La Rue.*

No.	Description	Unused	Used
12	1½ a. carmine	10	15
13	2½ a. blue (R.)	10	10
12/13 Perf "Specimen"	*Set of* 2	55·00	

1949 (17 Jan). *Royal Silver Wedding. As Nos.* 143/4 *of Jamaica.*

No.	Description	Unused	Used
14	1½ a. scarlet	30	50
15	5 r. green	9·50	8·50

1949 (10 Oct). *75th Anniv of U.P.U. As Nos.* 145/8 *of Jamaica, surch with new values by Waterlow.*

No.	Description	Unused	Used
16	2½ a. on 20 c. ultramarine	20	20
17	3 a. on 30 c. carmine-red	55	50
18	8 a. on 50 c. orange	55	60
19	1 r. on 1s. blue	60	50
	a. Surch omitted	£800	
16/19	*Set of* 4	1·75	1·60

1951 (1 Oct). *Currency changed. Surch with new values in cents or shillings as T* **11** (5 *c.*), **12** (10 *c.* ("CTS"), 15 *c.*, 20 *c. and* 50 *c.*) *or* **13** (1 *s. to* 5 *s.*) *of Seiyun, by Waterlow.*

No.	Description	Unused	Used
20	5 c. on 1 a. blue (R.)	15	15
21	10 c. on 2 a. sepia	15	15
22	15 c. on 2½ a. blue	15	15
23	20 c. on 3 a. sepia and carmine	15	20
	a. Surch double, one albino	£110	
24	50 c. on 8 a. red	15	40
25	1 s. on 1 r. green	30	25
26	2 s. on 2 r. blue and purple	3·50	5·00
27	5 s. on 5 r. brown and green	6·00	8·00
20/27	*Set of* 8	9·50	13·00

1953 (2 June). *Coronation. As No.* 153 *of Jamaica.*

No.	Description	Unused	Used
28	15 c. black and deep blue	30	55

II. ISSUES INSCR "HADHRAMAUT"

11 Metal Work

22 Metal Work

(Des Mme M. de Sturler Raemaekers. Recess D.L.R.)

1955 (1 Sept)–**63**. *T* **11** *and similar designs. Wmk Mult Script CA. P* 11½ × 13–13½ (*vert*) *or* 14 (*horiz*).

No.	Description	Unused	Used
29	5 c. greenish blue	10	10
30	10 c. grey-black	15	10
31	15 c. deep green	15	10
	a. Bronze-green (9.3.63)	15	20
32	25 c. carmine-red	15	10
33	35 c. blue	15	10
34	50 c. orange-red	15	10
	a. Red-orange (9.3.63)	30	30
35	90 c. sepia	15	15
36	1 s. black and deep lilac	20	10
37	1 s. 25, black and red-orange	30	45
38	2 s. black and indigo	2·00	60
39	5 s. black and bluish green	3·25	1·25
40	10 s. black and lake	3·50	2·00
29/40	*Set of* 12	9·00	4·50

Designs: *Vert*—10 c. Mat-making; 15 c. Weaving; 25 c. Pottery; 35 c. Building; 50 c. Date cultivation; 90 c. Agriculture. *Horiz*—1 s. Fisheries; 1 s. 25, 10 s. Lime-burning; 2 s. Dhow building; 5 s. Agriculture.

1963 (20 Oct). *As Nos.* 29/40 *but with inset portrait of Sultan Awadh bin Saleh el-Qu'aiti as in T* **22** *and wmk w* **12**.

No.	Description	Unused	Used
41	5 c. greenish blue	10	10
42	10 c. grey-black	10	10
43	15 c. bronze-green	10	10
44	25 c. carmine-red	10	10
45	35 c. blue	10	10
46	50 c. red-orange	10	10
47	70 c. deep brown (as 90 c.)	15	20
48	1 s. black and deep lilac	20	10
49	1 s. 25, black and red-orange	35	65
50	2 s. black and indigo-blue	1·75	1·00
51	5 s. black and bluish green	6·50	7·00
52	10 s. black and lake	6·50	9·00
41/52	*Set of* 12	14·00	16·00

(New Currency. 1000 fils = 1 dinar)

1966 (1 Apr). *New currency. Nos.* 41/52 *surch as T* **20/21** *of Kathiri State of Seiyun.*

No.	Description	Unused	Used
53	5 f. on 5 c. greenish blue (**20**) (R.)	10	30
54	5 f. on 10 c. grey-black (**20**) (R.)	10	30
55	10 f. on 15 c. bronze-green (**20**) (R.)	10	20
56	15 f. on 25 c. carmine-red (**20**)	10	30
57	20 f. on 35 c. blue (**20**) (R.)	10	40
58	25 f. on 50 c. red-orange (**20**)	10	30
59	35 f. on 70 c. deep brown (**20**) (R.)	10	30
60	50 f. on 1 s. black and deep lilac (**21**) (R.)	10	15
61	65 f. on 1 s. 25, black and red-orange (**21**) (R.)	25	25
62	100 f. on 2 s. black and indigo-blue (**21**) (R.)	45	75
63	250 f. on 5 s. black and bluish green (**21**) (R.)	1·00	1·50
64	500 f. on 10 s. black and lake (**21**) (R.)	12·00	3·00
53/64	*Set of* 12	13·00	7·00

1874-1965
WINSTON CHURCHILL
(23)

1917-1963
JOHN F. KENNEDY
(24)

1966. *Churchill Commemoration. Nos. 54/6 optd with T* **23**.
65 5 f. on 10 c. grey-black (R.) .. .. .. 3·50 4·75
66 10 f. on 15 c. bronze-green (R.) .. .. 4·00 5·50
a. Opt T **23** inverted .. .. .. 75·00
67 15 f. on 25 c. carmine-red (B.). .. .. 6·00 7·50
65/7 .. .. *Set of* 3 12·00 16·00

1966. *President Kennedy Commemoration. Nos. 57/9 optd with T* **24**.
68 20 f. on 35 c. blue (R.) .. .. 1·25 3·00
69 25 f. on 50 c. red-orange (B.) .. .. .. 1·60 3·75
70 35 f. on 70 c. deep brown (B.) .. .. .. 2·25 4·25
68/70 .. .. *Set of* 3 4·50 10·00

25 World Cup Emblem

(Photo State Ptg Wks. Vienna)

1966. *World Cup Football Championship, England. T* **25** *and similar diamond-shaped designs. P* 13½.
71 5 f. maroon and yellow-orange .. .. 1·40 25
72 10 f. slate-violet and light green .. .. 1·75 25
73 15 f. maroon and yellow-orange .. .. 1·90 30
74 20 f. slate-violet and light green .. .. 2·25 40
75 25 f. blackish green and orange-red .. .. 2·50 55
76 35 f. blue and yellow .. .. 3·00 80
77 50 f. blackish green and orange-red .. .. 3·50 1·10
78 65 f. blue and yellow .. .. 4·00 1·40
71/78 .. .. *Set of* 8 18·00 4·50
Designs:—10, 35 f. Wembley Stadium; 15, 50 f. Footballers; 20 f. Jules Rimet Cup and football; 25, 65 f. Type **25**.

29 Mexican Hat and Blanket

(Photo State Ptg Wks, Vienna)

1966 (25 Oct). *Pre-Olympic Games, Mexico* (1968). *P* 13½.
79 **29** 75 f. sepia and light yellow-green .. 1·25 1·25

30 Telecommunications Satellite

(Photo State Ptg Wks, Vienna)

1966 (Dec). *International Co-operation Year* (1965). *T* **30** *and similar horiz designs. P* 13½.
80 5 f. maroon, bright purple and emerald .. 1·75 35
81 10 f. violet, orange, blue-green and new blue 2·00 35
82 15 f. maroon, new blue and red .. .. 2·25 40
83 20 f. Prussian blue, purple and red .. 2·50 45
84 25 f. violet, olive-yellow, red and emerald .. 2·75 50
85 35 f. maroon, rose-red and new blue .. 3·75 80
a. New blue (face values) omitted .. £150
86 50 f. maroon, green and red .. .. 5·00 1·25
87 65 f. chocolate, bluish violet and red .. 5·50 1·75
80/87 .. .. *Set of* 8 23·00 5·25
Designs:—10 f. Olympic runner (inscribed "ROME 1960"); 15 f. Fishes; 25 f. Olympic runner (inscribed "TOKIO 1964"); 50 f. Tobacco plant; others, Type **30**.

NEW INFORMATION

The editor is always interested to correspond with people who have new information that will improve or correct the Catalogue.

Appendix

The following stamps have either been issued in excess of postal needs, or have not been made available to the public in reasonable quantities at face value. Miniature sheets, imperforate stamps etc. are excluded from this section.

1967

Stampex Stamp Exhibition, London. Postage 5, 10, 15, 20, 25 *f. Air* 50, 65 *f.*
Amphilex International Stamp Exhibition, Amsterdam. Air 75 *f.*
Olympic Games, Mexico (1968), 75 *f.*
Paintings. Postage 5, 10, 15, 20, 25 *f. Air* 50, 65 *f.*
Scout Jamboree, Idaho. Air 35 *f.*
Space Research. Postage 10, 25, 35, 50, 75 *f. Air* 100, 250 *f.*

The National Liberation Front is said to have taken control of Qu'aiti State in Hadhramaut on 17 September 1967.

MAHRA SULTANATE OF QISHN AND SOCOTRA

(Currency. 1000 fils = 1 dinar)

1 Mahra Flag

(Des and litho Harrison)

1967 (12 Mar). *Flag in green, black and vermilion; inscriptions in black; background colours given. P* 14 × 14½.
1 **1** 5 f. mauve 95 10
2 10 f. buff 95 15
3 15 f. sage-green 95 15
4 20 f. red-orange 95 20
5 25 f. yellow-brown 95 25
6 35 f. turquoise-green 95 25
7 50 f. new blue 95 25
8 65 f. blackish brown 95 25
9 100 f. violet .. .. 1·00 25
10 250 f. rose-red .. .. 1·25 35
11 500 f. grey-green .. .. 1·50 50
1/11 .. .. *Set of* 11 10·00 2·40

Appendix

The following stamps have either been issued in excess of postal needs, or have not been made available to the public in reasonable quantities at face value. Miniature sheets, imperforate stamps etc., are excluded from this section.

1967

Scout Jamboree, Idaho. 15, 75, 100, 150 *f.*
President Kennedy Commemoration. Postage 10, 15, 25, 50, 75, 100, 150 *f. Air* 250, 500 *f.*
Olympic Games, Mexico (1968). *Postage* 10, 25, 50 *f. Air* 250, 500 *f.*

The National Liberation Front is said to have taken control of Mahra Sultanate of Qishn and Socotra on 1 October 1967.

SOUTH ARABIAN FEDERATION

Comprising Aden and most of the territories of the former Western Aden Protectorate plus one from the Eastern Aden Protectorate.

(Currency. 100 cents=1 shilling)

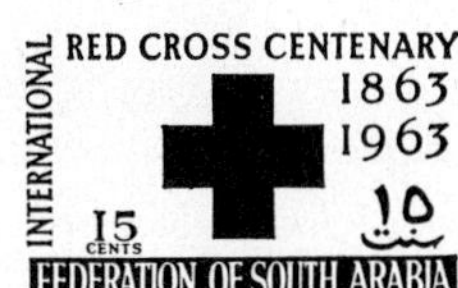

1 Red Cross Emblem

1963 (25 Nov). *Red Cross Centenary. W* w **12.** *P* 13½.
1 **1** 15 c. red and black 20 15
2 1 s. 25, red and blue 40 35

(New Currency. 1000 fils=1 dinar)

2 Federal Crest

3 Federal Flag

(Des V. Whiteley. Photo Harrison)

1965 (1 Apr). *P* 14½ × 14 (*T* **2**) *or* 14½ (*T* **3**).
3 **2** 5 f. blue 10 10
4 10 f. violet-blue 10 10
5 15 f. turquoise-green 10 10
6 20 f. green 10 10
7 25 f. yellow-brown 10 10
8 30 f. yellow-bistre 10 10
9 35 f. chestnut 10 10
10 50 f. red 10 10
11 65 f. yellow-green 30 30
12 75 f. crimson 30 10
13 **3** 100 f. multicoloured 30 10
14 250 f. multicoloured .. .. 1·00 25
15 500 f. multicoloured .. .. 2·50 50
16 1 d. multicoloured .. .. 4·50 2·75
3/16 .. .. *Set of* 14 8·50 4·00

4 I.C.Y. Emblem

(Des V. Whiteley. Litho Harrison)

1965 (24 Oct). *International Co-operation Year. W* w **12.** *P* 14½.
17 **4** 5 f. reddish purple and turquoise-green 20 10
18 65 f. deep bluish green and lavender .. 50 20

5 Sir Winston Churchill and St. Paul's Cathedral in Wartime

(Des Jennifer Toombs. Photo Harrison)

1966 (24 Jan). *Churchill Commemoration. No wmk. P* 14.
19 **5** 5 f. black, cerise, gold and new blue .. 10 10
20 10 f. black, cerise, gold and deep green 25 10
21 65 f. black, cerise, gold and brown .. 65 10
22 125 f. black, cerise, gold and bluish violet 90 75
19/22 .. .. *Set of* 4 1·75 85

6 Footballer's Legs, Ball and Jules Rimet Cup

(Des V. Whiteley. Litho Harrison)

1966 (1 July). *World Cup Football Championship, England. No wmk. P* 14.
23 **6** 10 f. violet, yellow-green, lake & yell-brn 25 10
24 50 f. chocolate, blue-grn, lake & yell-brn 65 20

7 W.H.O. Building

(Des M. Goaman. Litho Harrison)

1966 (20 Sept). *Inauguration of W.H.O. Headquarters, Geneva. No wmk. P* 14.
25 **7** 10 f. black, yellow-green and light blue 25 10
26 75 f. black, light purple and yellow-brown 45 30

8 "Education"

9 "Science"

10 "Culture"

(Des Jennifer Toombs. Litho Harrison)

1966 (15 Dec). *20th Anniv of U.N.E.S.C.O. No wmk. P* 14.

27	**8**	10 f. slate-violet, red, yellow and orange	15	10
28	**9**	65 f. orange-yellow, vio & dp olive ..	60	55
29	**10**	125 f. black, bright purple and orange ..	2·00	1·50
27/9		.. .. *Set of* 3	2·50	1·90

The South Arabian Federation became fully independent on 30 November 1967. Later issues for this area will be found listed in Part 19 (*Middle East*) of this catalogue under Yemen People's Democratic Republic.

South Australia *see* Australia

Southern Cameroons

The following issue, although ordered by the Southern Cameroons authorities, was also on sale in Northern Cameroons, until the latter joined Nigeria. The stamps therefore can be found with Nigerian postmarks.

CAMEROONS
U.K.T.T.
(1)

1960 (1 Oct)–**61**. *Nos.* 69/71, 72 *ca/cc and* 73/80 *of Nigeria optd with T* **1**, *in red.*

1	**18**	½d. black and orange	10	20
2	–	1d. black and bronze-green	10	10
		a. Grey-blk & dull bronze-grn (19.9.61)	40	50
3	–	1½d. blue-green	10	15
4	**21**	2d. grey (Type B)	10	15
		a. Slate-blue (Type A)	†	—
		b. Bluish grey (Type B)	28·00	10·00
		c. Pale grey (Type B) (19.9.61) ..	10	20
5	–	3d. black and deep lilac	15	10
6	–	4d. black and blue	10	40
7	**24**	6d. orange-brown and black (*p* 14) ..	15	10
		a. Perf 13×13½ (19.9.61)	10	45
8	–	1s. black and maroon	15	10
9	**26**	2s. 6d. black and green	80	80
10	–	5s. black and red-orange	90	2·75
11	–	10s. black and red-brown	2·25	3·00
12	**29**	£1 black and violet	6·50	11·00
1/12		.. .. *Set of* 12	10·00	17·00

Nos. 2 and 4/*b* were overprinted on stamps printed by Waterlows' subsidiary, Imprimerie Belge de Securité.

Nos. 2*a*, 4*c* and 7a were from new printings produced by De La Rue instead of Waterlow.

The above stamps were withdrawn on 30 September 1961, when Southern Cameroons became part of the independent republic of Cameroun.

Southern Nigeria *see* Nigeria

Southern Rhodesia *see* Zimbabwe

South Georgia and the South Sandwich Islands

As South Georgia was a dependency of the Falkland Islands between 1963 and 1980 stamps so inscribed are listed under FALKLAND ISLANDS DEPENDENCIES.

Under the new constitution, effective 3 October 1985, South Georgia and South Sandwich Islands ceased to be dependencies of the Falkland Islands.

(Des A. Theobald. Litho Questa)

1986 (21 Apr). *60th Birthday of Queen Elizabeth II. Vert designs as T* **230a** *of Jamaica. Multicoloured. W* w **16.** *P* 14½×14.

153	10p. Four generations of Royal Family at Prince Charles' christening, 1948 ..	25	25
154	24p. With Prince Charles and Lady Diana Spencer, Buckingham Palace, 1981 ..	55	55
155	29p. In robes of Order of the British Empire, St. Paul's Cathedral, London	60	60
156	45p. At banquet, Canada, 1976	95	95
157	58p. At Crown Agents Head Office, London, 1983	1·25	1·25
153/7	.. .. *Set of* 5	3·25	3·25

25a Prince Andrew and Miss Sarah Ferguson at Ascot

26 Southern Black-backed Gull

(Des D. Miller. Litho Questa)

1986 (10 Nov). *Royal Wedding. T* **25a** *and similar vert designs. Multicoloured.* W w **16.** *P* 14½×14.

158	17p. Type **25a**	75	75
159	22p. Wedding photograph	85	85
160	29p. Prince Andrew with Lynx helicopter on board H.M.S. *Brazen*	1·00	1·00
158/60	.. .. *Set of* 3	2·40	2·40

(Des T. Chater. Litho Walsall)

1987 (24 Apr). *Birds. T* **26** *and similar multicoloured designs.* W w **16** (*sideways on horiz designs*). *P* 14½.

161	1p. Type **26**	10	10
162	2p. Blue-eyed Cormorant	10	10
163	3p. Snowy Sheathbill (*vert*)	10	10
164	4p. Great Skua (*vert*)	10	10
165	5p. Pintado Petrel ("Cape Pigeon") ..	10	15
166	6p. Georgian Diving Petrel	10	15
167	7p. South Georgia Pipit (*vert*)	15	20
168	8p. Georgian Teal ("South Georgian Pintail") (*vert*)	15	20
169	9p. Fairy Prion	20	25
170	10p. Chinstrap Penguin	20	25
171	20p. Macaroni Penguin (*vert*)	40	45
172	25p. Light-mantled Sooty Albatross (*vert*) ..	50	55
173	50p. Giant Petrel (*vert*)	1·00	1·10
174	£1 Wandering Albatross	2·00	2·10
175	£3 King Penguin (*vert*)	6·00	6·25
161/75	.. .. *Set of* 15	10·00	10·50

26a I.G.Y. Logo

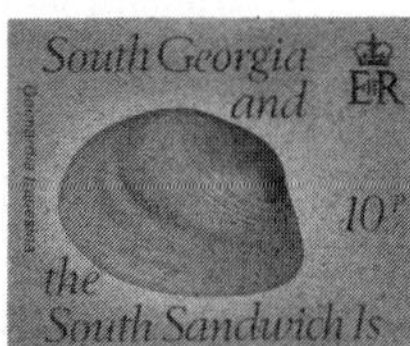

27 *Gaimardia trapesina*

(Des L. Curtis. Litho Questa)

1987 (5 Dec). *30th Anniv of International Geophysical Year. T* **26a** *and similar vert designs.* W w **16.** *P* 14½×14.

176	24p. black and pale turquoise-blue	50	55
177	29p. multicoloured	55	60
178	58p. multicoloured	1·10	1·25
176/8	.. .. *Set of* 3	1·90	2·10

Designs:—29p. Grytviken; 58p. Glaciologist using hand-drill to take core sample.

(Des I. Strange. Litho Questa)

1988 (26 Feb). *Sea Shells. T* **27** *and similar horiz designs. Multicoloured.* W w **16** (*sideways*). *P* 14 × 14½.

179	10p. Type **27**	30	30
180	24p. *Margarella tropidophoroides*	50	60
181	29p. *Trophon scotianus*	55	65
182	58p. *Chlanidota densesculpta*	1·10	1·25
179/82	.. .. *Set of* 4	2·25	2·50

(Des E. Nisbet and D. Miller (24p.), D. Miller (others). Litho Questa)

1988 (17 Sept). *300th Anniv of Lloyd's of London. Designs as T* **167a** *of Malawi.* W w **16** (*sideways on* 24, 29*p.*). *P* 14.

183	10p. brownish black and brown	30	30
184	24p. multicoloured	50	55
185	29p. brownish black and emerald	60	65
186	58p. brownish black and carmine-red ..	1·10	1·25
183/6	.. .. *Set of* 4	2·25	2·50

Designs: *Vert*—10p. Queen Mother at opening of new Lloyd's building, 1957; 58p. *Horatio* (tanker) on fire, 1916. *Horiz*—24p. *Lindblad Explorer* (cruise liner); 29p. Whaling station, Leith Harbour.

28 Glacier Headwall

29 Retracing Shackleton's Trek

(Des I. Loe. Litho Questa)

1989 (31 July). *Glacier Formations. T* **28** *and similar horiz designs. Multicoloured.* W w **16** (*sideways*). *P* 14.

187	10p. Type **28**	35	35
188	24p. Accumulation area	70	70
189	29p. Ablation area	80	80
190	58p. Calving front	1·40	1·40
187/90	.. .. *Set of* 4	3·00	3·00

(Des O. Bell. Litho Questa)

1989 (28 Nov). *25th Anniv of Combined Services Expedition to South Georgia. T* **29** *and similar horiz designs. Multicoloured.* W w **16** (*sideways*). *P* 14×14½.

191	10p. Type **29**	35	35
192	24p. Surveying at Royal Bay	70	70
193	29p. H.M.S. *Protector* (ice patrol ship) ..	80	80
194	58p. Raising Union Jack on Mount Paget ..	1·40	1·40
191/4	.. .. *Set of* 4	3·00	3·00

(Des D. Miller. Litho Questa)

1990 (15 Sept). *90th Birthday of Queen Elizabeth the Queen Mother. Vert designs as T* **107** (26*p.*) *or* **108** (£1) *of Kenya.* W w **16.** *P* 14×15 (26*p.*) *or* 14½ (£1).

195	26p. multicoloured	75	75
196	£1 black and dull ultramarine	2·75	2·75

Designs:—26p. Queen Mother; £1 King George VI and Queen Elizabeth with A.R.P. wardens, 1940.

30 *Brutus*, Prince Olav Harbour

31 Contest between two Bull Elephant Seals

(Des D. Miller. Litho Questa)

1990 (22 Dec). *Wrecks and Hulks. T* **30** *and similar vert designs. Multicoloured.* W w **16.** *P* 14×14½.

197	12p. Type **30**	40	40
198	26p. *Bayard*, Ocean Harbour	80	80
199	31p. *Karrakatta*, Husvik	95	95
200	62p. *Louise*, Grytviken	1·75	1·75
197/200	.. .. *Set of* 4	3·50	3·50

(Des D. Miller. Litho Questa)

1991 (2 July). *65th Birthday of Queen Elizabeth II and 70th Birthday of Prince Philip. Vert designs as T* **58** *of Kiribati. Multicoloured.* W w **16** (*sideways*). *P* 14½×14.

201	31p. Queen Elizabeth II	1·00	1·00
	a. Horiz pair. Nos. 201/2 separated by label	2·00	2·00
202	31p. Prince Philip in Grenadier Guards uniform	1·00	1·00

Nos. 201/2 were printed in a similar sheet format to Nos. 366/7 of Kiribati

(Des D. Miller. Litho Questa)

1991 (2 Nov). *Elephant Seals. T* **31** *and similar horiz designs.* W w **14** (*sideways*). *P* 14.

203	12p. Type **31**	40	40
204	26p. Adult Elephant Seal	85	85
205	29p. Seal throwing sand	95	95
206	31p. Head of Elephant Seal	1·00	1·00
207	34p. Seals on beach	1·10	1·10
208	62p. Cow seal with pup	1·75	1·75
203/8	.. .. *Set of* 6	5·50	5·50

(Des D. Miller. Litho Questa (68p.), Walsall (others))

1992 (6 Feb). *40th Anniv of Queen Elizabeth II's Accession. Horiz designs as T* **112** *of Kenya. Multicoloured.* W w **14** (*sideways*). *P* 14.

209	7p. Ice-covered mountains	30	30
210	14p. Zavodovski Island	55	55
211	29p. Gulbrandsen Lake	95	95
212	34p. Three portraits of Queen Elizabeth ..	1·10	1·10
213	68p. Queen Elizabeth II	1·75	1·75
209/13	.. .. *Set of* 5	4·25	4·25

MINIMUM PRICE

The minimum price quote is 10p which represents a handling charge rather than a basis for valuing common stamps. For further notes about prices see introductory pages.

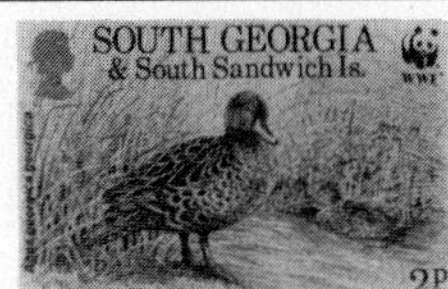

32 Adult Teal and Young Bird

(Des G. Drummond. Litho Questa)

1992 (12 Mar). *Endangered Species. South Georgia Teal. T* **32** *and similar horiz designs. Multicoloured. W w* **16** *(sideways). P* 14.

214	2p. Type **32**	10	10
215	6p. Adult with eggs	10	10
216	12p. Teals swimming	25	30
217	20p. Adult and two chicks	40	45
214/17	*Set of* 4	75	85

South West Africa
see Namibia

Sri Lanka
(*formerly* Ceylon)

CEYLON

PRICES FOR STAMPS ON COVER TO 1945

Nos. 1/4	*from* × 5
Nos. 5/19	*from* × 4
Nos. 23/117	*from* × 8
Nos. 118/20	*from* × 15
Nos. 121/38	*from* × 6
Nos. 139/41	†
Nos. 142/3	*from* × 10
Nos. 146/51	*from* × 6
Nos. 151*a*/2	†
Nos. 153/93	*from* × 8
Nos. 194/201	*from* × 12
Nos. 202/43	*from* × 6
Nos. 245/9	*from* × 4
Nos. 250/5	*from* × 5
Nos. 256/64	*from* × 4
Nos. 265/76	*from* × 3
Nos. 277/88	*from* × 4
Nos. 289/300	*from* × 8
Nos. 301/25	*from* × 2
Nos. 326/9*a*	—
Nos. 330/7*a*	*from* × 4
Nos. 338/52	*from* × 2
Nos. 353/4	—
Nos. 355/9	*from* × 2
No. 360	—
Nos. 360*a*/*g*	*from* × 2
Nos. 361/2	*from* × 5
Nos. 363/71	*from* × 3
Nos. 372/82	*from* × 2
Nos. 383/5	*from* × 3
Nos. 386/97	*from* × 2
Nos. 398/9	*from* × 8
Nos. O1/17	*from* × 30

CROWN COLONY

PRICES. The prices of the imperf stamps of Ceylon vary greatly according to condition. The following prices are for fine copies with four margins.

Poor to medium specimens can be supplied at much lower prices.

1

2

(Recess P.B.)

1857 (1 April). *Blued paper. Wmk Star W w* **1**. *Imperf.*

1	1	6d. purple-brown	£7500	£450

Collectors should beware of proofs with faked watermark, often offered as originals.

(Typo D.L.R.)

1857 (Oct)–**58**. *No wmk. Imperf. (a) Blue glazed paper.*

3	2	½d. lilac	£3250	£450
		(b) White glazed paper		
4	2	½d. lilac (1858)	£160	£140

3

4

NOTE. Beware of stamps of Type **3** which are often offered with corners added.

(Recess P.B.)

1857–9. *White paper. Wmk Star, W w* 1. *(a) Imperf.*

5	1	1d. blue (24.8.57)	£600	19·00
		a. Blued paper	—	£150
6		1d. deep blue	£700	29·00
7		2d. deep green (24.8.57)	£150	50·00
8		2d. yellow-green	£500	90·00
9	3	4d. dull rose (23.4.59)	£50000	£4500
10	1	5d. chestnut (2.7.57)	£1500	£150
11		6d. purple-brown	£1800	£130
12		6d. brown	£6000	£400
12*a*		6d. deep brown	£7000	£1000
13	3	8d. brown (23.4.59)	£19000	£1500
14		9d. purple-brown (23.4.59)	£29000	£900
15	4	10d. orange-vermilion (2.7.57)	£800	£250
16		1s. dull violet (2.7.57)	£4500	£200
17	3	1s. 9d. green (23.4.59)	£700	£800
18		1s. 9d. pale yellow-green	£3000	£2000
19		2s. blue (23.4.59)	£5000	£1100
		(b) "Unofficial" P 7½ (No. 22a) or rouletted (Nos. 20/2)		
20	2	½d. lilac (*No wmk*)	£5000	
21	1	1d. blue (*Wmk Star*)	£5000	
22		2d. deep green (*Wmk Star*)	£1800	£1000
22*a*		1s. 9d. green (*Wmk Star*)	£4000	

These stamps are believed to have been made by a Ceylon firm, or firms, for their own convenience.

(Recess P.B.)

1861. *Wmk Star, W w* **1**. *(a) Clean-cut perf 14 to 15½.*

23	1	1d. deep blue	90·00	13·00
24		1d. pale blue	£300	45·00
25		2d. green	£190	35·00
27		5d. chestnut	75·00	8·00
29	4	1s. dull violet	75·00	26·00
30	3	2s. blue	£1900	£400
		(b) Intermediate perf 14 to 15½		
31	1	1d. deep blue	70·00	12·00
32		1d. blue	70·00	15·00
33		2d. green	75·00	24·00
		a. Imperf between (vert pair)	†	—
34	3	4d. dull rose	£1800	£250
34*a*	1	5d. chestnut	£350	£130
35		6d. brown	£1300	75·00
36		6d. yellowish brown	—	£120
36*a*		6d. olive-brown	—	85·00
37	3	8d. brown	£1300	£350
38		9d. dull purple-brown	£4000	£250
40	4	1s. bright violet	£110	26·00
41		1s. dull violet	65·00	13·00
		(c) Rough perf 14 to 15½		
42	1	1d. blue	60·00	6·00
43		1d. blue (*bleuté paper*)	£325	20·00
44	3	4d. rose-red	£160	42·00
45		4d. deep rose-red	£170	48·00
47	1	6d. yellowish brown	£1200	£100
48		6d. blackish brown	£450	60·00
48*a*		6d. olive-brown	£500	55·00
49	3	8d. brown	£1200	£800
50		8d. yellow-brown	£1000	£250
51		9d. olive-brown	£375	27·00
52		9d. yellowish brown	£500	55·00
53		9d. deep brown	55·00	28·00
53*a*	4	10d. orange-vermilion	£180	20·00
		b. Imperf vert (horiz pair)	†	—
54		1s. dull violet	£225	15·00
55	3	2s. blue	£500	90·00
56		2s. deep blue	£650	£110
		(d) Rough perf 14 to 15½. Prepared for use, but not issued		
57	3	1s. 9d. green	£475	

No. 34 is distinguished from Nos. 44/5 with fraudulently altered perfs by its colour.

(Recess or typo (T **2**). D.L.R.)

1862–64. *No wmk. (a) Smooth paper. P* 13.

58	1	1d. blue	65·00	6·00
59		5d. deep red-brown	£850	£150
60		6d. reddish brown	75·00	22·00
61		6d. deep brown	85·00	22·00
62	3	9d. brown	£900	60·00
63	4	1s. cold violet	£1500	80·00
		(b) Smooth paper. P 11½, 12		
64	1	1d. blue	£600	90·00
		a. Imperf between (horiz pair)	†	£4500
		(c) Glazed paper. P 12½ (1864)		
65	2	½d. pale lilac	£180	£110

The 1s. is known imperf, but not used. The "no wmk" stamps were printed on paper having the papermaker's name and date, "T H SAUNDERS 1862" across the sheets, and one or more of these letters or figures are often found on the stamps.

(Recess P.B., perforated by D.L.R.)

1864 (Sept). *Wmk Star, W w* 1. *P* 12½.

66	4	10d. vermilion (*shades*)	£225	15·00

5

6

T **5**. 23 mm high. "CC" oval.
T **6**. 21½ mm high. "CC" round and smaller.

(Recess or typo (T **2**) D.L.R.)

1863–6. *Paper medium thin and slightly soft. W* **5**. *Wmks arranged in four panes, each of 60, with the words "CROWN COLONIES" between the panes. Portions of these letters often appear on the stamps.*

		(a) P 11½, 12		
68	1	1d. blue	£1600	£180
		(b) P 13		
69	1	6d. brown	£1200	80·00
70	3	9d. brown	£2500	£375
		(c) P 12½		
71	2	½d. mauve	19·00	17·00
72		½d. lilac	23·00	14·00
73		½d. deep lilac	35·00	25·00
74	1	1d. dark blue	55·00	3·00
75		1d. blue	55·00	3·00
76		2d. yellow-green	£6000	£325
77		2d. deep bottle-green	—	£3250
78		2d. grey-green	32·00	6·00
79		2d. emerald-green	90·00	65·00
80		2d. maize	£225	£225
81	3	4d. lake-rose	£375	70·00
82		4d. rose	£170	35·00
83	1	5d. reddish brown	90·00	32·00
84		5d. deep sage-green	£1200	£225
84*a*		5d. pale sage-green	£700	£150
85		6d. brown	60·00	8·00
86		6d. reddish brown	75·00	9·00
87		6d. deep brown	65·00	4·00
88	3	8d. light carmine-brown	70·00	35·00
89		8d. dark carmine-brown	40·00	20·00
90		9d. brown	£190	19·00
91	4	10d. vermilion	£900	32·00
91*a*		10d. orange	£1500	£150
92	3	2s. dark blue	£160	26·00

The ½d. lilac; 1d. blue; 2d. grey-green; 2d. maize; and 5d. deep sage-green and pale sage-green, are known imperf.

1867. *Paper hand-made. Prepared and used only for these Ceylon stamps. W* **6**. *Wmks arranged in one pane of 240 in 20 rows of 12, with the words "CROWN COLONIES" twice in each side margin. P* 12½.

93	1	1d. pale blue	55·00	5·00
94		1d. Prussian blue	50·00	4·00
95		2d. maize	50·00	5·00
96		2d. olive-yellow	27·00	6·00
97		2d. greenish yellow	£130	42·00
98		2d. orange-yellow	26·00	5·00
99	3	4d. pale rose	£100	35·00
100		4d. rose	26·00	8·00
101	1	5d. pale sage-green	32·00	6·00
102		5d. deep olive-green	60·00	7·00
103		5d. deep myrtle-green	16·00	24·00
104		6d. deep brown	35·00	7·00
105		6d. blackish brown	48·00	8·50
106		6d. red-brown	18·00	24·00
107	3	8d. pale carmine-brown	70·00	50·00
108		8d. deep carmine-brown	28·00	40·00
109		9d. bistre-brown	£225	25·00
110		9d. deep brown	20·00	6·00
111	4	10d. vermilion	£1000	£140
111*a*		10d. red-orange	24·00	5·00
112		10d. orange	42·00	7·50
113		1s. lilac	£325	32·00
114		1s. violet	60·00	5·50
115	3	2s. pale blue	£200	45·00
116		2s. blue	85·00	14·00
117		2s. Prussian blue	60·00	11·00

The 1d. pale blue, 1d. Prussian blue, 6d. deep brown, 9d. deep brown and 10d. orange are known imperf but only unused.

PRINTERS. All stamps from No. 118 to 367 were typographed by De La Rue & Co, Ltd, London.

7

8

1866. *Wmk Crown CC. P* 12½.

118	7	3d. rose	£160	55·00

1867–8. *Wmk Crown CC. P* 14.

119	8	1d. blue	9·50	4·50
120	7	3d. pale rose (1867)	42·00	20·00
		a. Deep rose	45·00	24·00

(New Currency. 100 cents = 1 rupee)

9

10

11

12

13

14

15

16

17

18

19

1872–80. *Wmk Crown CC. (a) P* 14.

No.	Type	Description	Unused	Used
121	9	2 c. pale brown (*shades*)	5·00	1·25
122	10	4 c. grey	26·00	90
123		4 c. rosy-mauve (1880)	45·00	1·50
124	11	8 c. orange-yellow	35·00	4·00
		a. Yellow	22·00	4·25
126	12	16 c. pale violet	50·00	2·75
127	13	24 c. green	28·00	2·00
128	14	32 c. slate (1877)	85·00	12·00
129	15	36 c. blue	70·00	13·00
130	16	48 c. rose	60·00	5·00
131	17	64 c. red-brown (1877)	£160	50·00
132	18	96 c. drab	£140	26·00
121/132		*Set of* 11	£600	£100

(b) P 14 × 12½

No.	Type	Description	Unused	Used
133	9	2 c. brown	£350	45·00
134	10	4 c. grey	£400	22·00
135	11	8 c. orange-yellow	£300	32·00

(c) P 12½

No.	Type	Description	Unused	Used
136	9	2 c. brown	£1500	80·00
137	10	4 c. grey	£750	£140

(d) P 12½ × 14

No.	Type	Description	Unused	Used
138	19	2 r. 50 c. dull-rose (1879)	£425	£275

(e) Prepared for use and sent out to Ceylon, but not issued unsurcharged

No.	Type	Description	Unused	Used
139	14	32 c. slate (*p* 14 × 12½)	£700	
140	17	64 c. red-brown (*p* 14 × 12½)	£900	
141	19	2 r. 50, dull rose (*p* 12½)	£900	

FORGERIES.—Beware of forged overprint and surcharge varieties on Victorian issues.

SIXTEEN

16

CENTS

(20)

1882 (Oct). *Nos.* 127 *and* 131 *surch as T* **20** *by Govt Printer.*

No.	Type	Description	Unused	Used
142	13	16 c. on 24 c. green	16·00	6·50
		a. Surch inverted		
143	17	20 c. on 64 c. red-brown	8·50	3·50
		a. Surch double	†	£1100

1883–98. *Wmk Crown CA. (a) P* 14.

No.	Type	Description	Unused	Used
146	9	2 c. pale brown	35·00	1·50
147		2 c. dull green (1884) (Optd S. £140)	1·25	15
148	10	4 c. rosy mauve	1·40	30
149		4 c. rose (1884) (Optd S. £140)	3·00	9·50
150	11	8 c. orange	2·75	6·00
		a. Yellow (1898)	2·75	6·00
151	12	16 c. pale violet	£900	£140

(b) Trial perforation. P 12

No.	Type	Description	Unused	Used
151*a*	9	2 c. dull green	£1600	
151*b*	10	4 c. rose	£1600	
151*c*	13	24 c. brown-purple	£1700	

(c) Prepared for use and sent out to Ceylon, but not issued unsurcharged. P 14

No.	Type	Description	Unused	Used
152	13	24 c. brown-purple (Optd S. £275)	£700	

Postage &

FIVE CENTS

Revenue

(21)

TEN CENTS

(22)

Twenty Cents

(23)

One Rupee Twelve Cents

(24)

1885. *T* **10/19** *surch locally as T* **21/24**.

I. *Wmk Crown CC. (a) P* 14

No.	Type	Description	Unused	Used
153	21	5 c. on 16 c. pale violet		
154		5 c. on 24 c. green	£1000	80·00
155		5 c. on 32 c. slate	45·00	14·00
		a. Surch inverted	†	£700
		b. Dark grey	55·00	18·00
156		5 c. on 36 c. blue	85·00	8·00
		a. Surch inverted	†	£850
157		5 c. on 48 c. rose	£400	26·00
158		5 c. on 64 c. red-brown	45·00	4·50
		a. Surch double	†	£650
159		5 c. on 96 c. drab	£225	45·00
161	22	10 c. on 16 c. pale violet		
162		10 c. on 24 c. green	£275	65·00
163		10 c. on 36 c. blue	£300	£140
164		10 c. on 64 c. red-brown	£200	55·00
165		20 c. on 24 c. green	30·00	12·00
166	23	20 c. on 32 c. slate	24·00	20·00
		a. Dark grey	30·00	20·00
167		25 c. on 32 c. slate	9·50	4·25
		a. Dark grey	13·00	6·50
168		28 c. on 48 c. rose	26·00	4·75
		a. Surch double	†	£750
169	22	30 c. on 36 c. blue	8·00	7·00
		a. Surch inverted	£160	85·00
170		56 c. on 96 c. drab	12·00	9·00

(b) P 14 × 12½

No.	Type	Description	Unused	Used
172	21	5 c. on 32 c. slate	£150	30·00
173		5 c. on 64 c. red-brown	£160	24·00
174	22	10 c. on 64 c. red-brown	35·00	55·00
		a. Imperf between (vert pair)	£1700	
175	24	1 r. 12 c. on 2 r. 50 c. dull rose (*p* 12½)	£225	60·00
176		1 r. 12 c. on 2 r. 50 c. dull rose (*p* 12½ × 14)	50·00	30·00

II. *Wmk Crown CA. P* 14

No.	Type	Description	Unused	Used
177	21	5 c. on 4 c. rosy mauve		
178		5 c. on 4 c. rose	10·00	2·75
		a. Surch inverted	†	£250
179		5 c. on 8 c. orange-yellow	28·00	5·50
		a. Surch double	†	£600
		b. Surch inverted	†	£700
180		5 c. on 16 c. pale violet	40·00	8·50
		a. Surch inverted	†	£140
182		5 c. on 24 c. brown-purple	—	£500
184	22	10 c. on 16 c. pale violet	£2500	£500
185		10 c. on 24 c. brown-purple	8·50	5·00
186		15 c. on 16 c. pale violet	7·00	5·50

Only seven examples, all used, are recorded of No. 153.

The 5 c. on 24 c. green watermarked Crown CA previously catalogued is now regarded as a forgery.

REVENUE AND POSTAGE

5 CENTS

(25)

10 CENTS

(26)

1 R. 12 C.

(27)

1885. *T* **11/15, 18** *and* **19** *surch with T* **25/7** *by D.L.R. P* 14.

(a) Wmk Crown CA

No.	Type	Description	Unused	Used
187	25	5 c. on 8 c. lilac	5·50	70
188	26	10 c. on 24 c. brown-purple	8·50	4·50
189		15 c. on 16 c. orange-yellow	32·00	5·00
190		28 c. on 32 c. slate	11·00	2·50
191		30 c. on 36 c. olive-green	25·00	12·00
192		56 c. on 96 c. drab	30·00	7·00

(b) Wmk Crown CC (sideways)

No.	Type	Description	Unused	Used
193	27	1 r. 12 c. on 2 r. 50, dull rose	26·00	60·00
187/93		*Set of* 7	£120	80·00
187/93 Optd "Specimen"		*Set of* 7	£550	

28

29

1886. *Wmk Crown CA. P* 14.

No.	Type	Description	Unused	Used
195	28	5 c. dull purple	1·10	10
196	29	15 c. sage-green	2·25	75
197		15 c. olive-green	2·50	65
198		25 c. yellow-brown	1·25	1·00
		a. Value in yellow	85·00	60·00
199		28 c. slate	8·50	1·40
195, 197/9 Optd "Specimen"		*Set of* 4	£130	

Six plates were used for the 5 c., No. 195, between 1885 and 1901, each being replaced by its successor as it became worn. Examples from the worn plates show thicker lines in the background and masses of solid colour under the chin, in front of the throat, at the back of the neck and at the base.

30

1887. *Wmk Crown CC (sideways). White or blued paper. P* 14.

No.	Type	Description	Unused	Used
201	30	1 r. 12, dull rose (Optd S. £80)	16·00	14·00
		a. Wmk upright	25·00	35·00

Two CENTS

(31)

Two

(32)

2 Cents

(33)

Two Cents

(34)

2 Cents

(35)

1888–90. *Nos.* 148/9 *surch with T* **31/5**.

No.	Type	Description	Unused	Used
202	31	2 c. on 4 c. rosy mauve	70	30
		a. Surch inverted	10·00	11·00
		b. Surch double, one inverted	—	70·00
203		2 c. on 4 c. rose	60	30
		a. Surch inverted	10·00	11·00
		b. Surch double	—	80·00
204	32	2 (c.) on 4 c. rosy mauve	60	20
		a. Surch inverted	24·00	26·00
		b. Surch double	32·00	32·00
		c. Surch double, one inverted	28·00	26·00
205	32	2 (c.) on 4 c. rose	1·60	20
		a. Surch inverted	75·00	
		b. Surch double	30·00	35·00
		c. Surch double, one inverted	35·00	42·00
206	33	2 c. on 4 c. rosy mauve	30·00	24·00
		a. Surch inverted	—	28·00
		b. Surch double, one inverted	40·00	
207		2 c. on 4 c. rose	1·60	75
		a. Surch inverted	8·00	8·00
		b. Surch double	75·00	75·00
		c. Surch double, one inverted	8·00	8·00
208	34	2 c. on 4 c. rosy mauve	35·00	16·00
		a. Surch inverted	55·00	27·00
209		2 c. on 4 c. rose	1·60	70
		a. Surch inverted	10·00	5·50
		b. Surch double	27·00	32·00
		c. Surch double, one inverted	10·00	5·50
210	35	2 c. on 4 c. rosy mauve	30·00	20·00
		a. Surch inverted	45·00	35·00
		b. Surch double, one inverted	45·00	48·00
		c. Surch double	—	80·00
		d. "s" of "Cents" inverted	—	£170
		e. As d. Whole surch inverted		
211		2 c. on 4 c. rose	3·50	60
		a. Surch inverted	11·00	5·50
		b. Surch double	45·00	38·00
		c. Surch double, one inverted	12·00	7·50
		d. "s" of "Cents" inverted	—	75·00
209, 211 Optd "Specimen"		*Set of* 2	60·00	

The 4 c. rose and the 4 c. rosy mauve are found surcharged "Postal Commission 3 (or "Three") Cents". They denote the extra commission charged by the Post Office on postal orders which had not been cashed within three months of the date of issue. For a short time the Post Office did not object to the use of these stamps on letters.

POSTAGE

Five Cents

REVENUE

(36)

FIFTEEN CENTS

(37)

1890. *No.* 197 *surch with T* **36**.

No.	Type	Description	Unused	Used
233		5 c. on 15 c. olive-green (Optd S. £30)	1·00	1·00
		a. Surch inverted	20·00	22·00
		b. Surch double	80·00	80·00
		c. "Flve" for "Five"	80·00	70·00
		d. Variety as c, inverted	—	£700
		e. "REVENUE" omitted	80·00	70·00
		f. Inverted "s" in "Cents"	20·00	24·00
		g. Variety as f, and whole surch inverted	£700	
		h. "REVENUE" omitted and inverted "s" in "Cents"	£300	
		i. "POSTAGE" spaced between "T" and "A"	38·00	45·00

1891. *Nos.* 198/9 *surch with T* **37**.

No.	Type	Description	Unused	Used
239	29	15 c. on 25 c. yellow-brown	5·50	8·50
240		15 c. on 28 c. slate	5·50	8·50

3 Cents

(38)

39

1892. *Nos.* 148/9 *and* 199 *surch with T* **38**.

No.	Type	Description	Unused	Used
241	10	3 c. on 4 c. rosy mauve	50	1·50
242		3 c. on 4 c. rose (Optd S. £30)	1·00	5·00
243	29	3 c. on 28 c. slate	1·10	1·60
		a. Surch double	55·00	
241/3		*Set of* 3	2·40	7·25

1893–99. *Wmk Crown CA. P* 14.

No.	Type	Description	Unused	Used
245	39	3 c. terracotta and blue-green	1·25	45
246	10	4 c. carmine-rose (1898)	6·50	6·50
247	29	30 c. bright mauve and chestnut	3·75	1·50
		a. Bright violet and chestnut	3·50	1·50
249	19	2 r. 50, purple/*red* (1899)	20·00	40·00
245/9		*Set of* 4	28·00	42·00
245, 247/9 Optd "Specimen"		*Set of* 3	60·00	

Six Cents

(40)

2 R. 25 C.

(41)

1899. (*a*) *No.* 196 *surch with T* **40**.
250 **29** 6 c. on 15 c. sage-green 45 45

(*b*) *As No.* 138 *but colour changed and perf* 14, *surch as T* **41**.
254 **19** 1 r. 50 c. on 2 r. 50, slate .. .. 20·00 35·00
255 2 r. 25 c. on 2 r. 50, yellow .. .. 27·00 60·00
250/5 Optd "Specimen" .. .. *Set of* 3 70·00

43

1899–1900. *Wmk Crown CA* (1 *r.* 50, 2 *r.* 25 *wmk Crown CC*). *P* 14.
256 **9** 2 c. pale orange-brown .. .. .. 1·00 30
257 **39** 3 c. deep green .. .. 1·25 55
258 **10** 4 c. yellow .. .. 1·00 2·00
259 **29** 6 c. rose and black 75 45
260 **39** 12 c. sage-green and rose .. .. 2·50 4·75
261 **29** 15 c. blue .. .. 4·25 1·25
262 **39** 75 c. black and red-brown .. .. 4·25 4·00
263 **43** 1 r. 50, rose .. .. .. 15·00 32·00
264 2 r. 25, dull blue .. .. .. 28·00 32·00
256/64 .. .. .. *Set of* 9 50·00 70·00
256/64 Optd "Specimen" .. .. *Set of* 9 £130

44

45

46

47

48

1903 (29 May)–**05.** *Wmk Crown CA. P* 14.
265 **44** 2 c. red-brown (21.7.03) 70 20
266 **45** 3 c. green (11.6.03) 80 70
267 4 c. orange-yellow and blue .. .. 1·25 2·50
268 **46** 5 c. dull purple (2.7.03) .. .. 1·50 30
269 **47** 6 c. carmine (5.11.03) .. .. 3·75 1·25
270 **45** 12 c. sage-green and rosine (13.8.03) .. 3·75 5·50
271 **48** 15 c. blue (2.7.03) .. .. .. 6·50 1·75
272 25 c. bistre (11.8.03) .. .. .. 4·00 7·00
273 30 c. dull violet and green .. .. 3·25 4·00
274 **45** 75 c. dull blue and orange (31.3.05) .. 2·75 15·00
275 **48** 1 r. 50, greyish slate (7.4.04) .. 50·00 45·00
276 2 r. 25, brown and green (12.4.04) .. 45·00 38·00
265/76 .. .. .. *Set of* 12 £110 £110
265/76 Optd "Specimen" .. .. *Set of* 12 £140

1904 (13 Sept)–**05.** *Wmk Mult Crown CA. Ordinary paper. P* 14.
277 **44** 2 c. red-brown (17.11.04) 55 10
278 **45** 3 c. green (17.11.04) 75 15
279 4 c. orange and ultramarine 35 50
280 **46** 5 c. dull purple (29.11.04) .. .. 1·75 1·00
a. Chalk-surfaced paper (5.10.05) .. 2·00 80
281 **47** 6 c. carmine (11.10.04) .. .. 1·10 15
282 **45** 12 c. sage-green and rosine (29.9.04) .. 1·50 1·75
283 **48** 15 c. blue (1.12.04) 90 50
284 25 c. bistre (5.1.05) .. .. .. 6·00 3·75
285 30 c. violet and green (7.9.05) .. .. 2·50 1·50
286 **45** 75 c. dull blue and orange (25.5.05) .. 5·25 8·00
287 **48** 1 r. 50, grey (5.1.05) .. .. 15·00 10·00
288 2 r. 25, brown and green (22.12.04) .. 18·00 27·00
277/88 .. .. .. *Set of* 12 48·00 48·00

50

51

1908. *Wmk Mult Crown CA. P* 14.
289 **50** 5 c. deep purple (26 May) .. .. 1·50 10
290 5 c. dull purple .. .. .. 2·25 30
291 **51** 6 c. carmine (6 June) 70 10
289, 291 Optd "Specimen" .. *Set of* 2 48·00

1910 (1 Aug)–**11.** *Wmk Mult Crown CA. P* 14.
292 **44** 2 c. brown-orange (20.5.11) .. .. 1·50 1·00
293 **48** 3 c. green (5.7.11) 85 75
294 10 c. sage-green and maroon .. .. 1·50 80
295 25 c. grey .. .. 2·50 70
296 50 c. chocolate .. .. .. 4·00 7·00
297 1 r. purple/*yellow* .. .. .. 7·50 10·00
298 2 r. red/*yellow* .. .. .. 15·00 27·00
299 5 r. black/*green* .. .. .. 35·00 65·00
300 10 r. black/*red* .. .. .. 60·00 £140
292/300 .. .. .. *Set of* 9 £110 £225
292/300 Optd "Specimen" .. .. *Set of* 9 £180

52

53

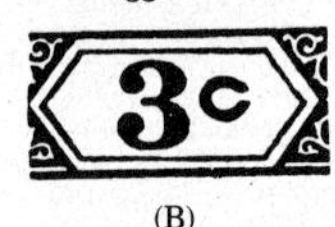

(A) (B)

Most values in Type **52** were produced by two printing operations, using "Key" and "Duty" plates. Differences in the two Dies of the Key plate are described in the introduction to this catalogue.

In the Ceylon series, however, the 1 c. and 5 c. values, together with later printings of the 3 c. and 6 c., were printed from special plates at one operation. These plates can be identified by the large "C" in the value tablet (see illustration A). Examples of these values from Key and Duty plates printing have value tablet as illustration B. The 3 c. and 5 c. stamps from the single plates *resemble* Die I, and the 1 c. and 6 c. Die II, although in the latter case the inner top corners of the side panels are square and not curved.

1912–25. *Wmk Mult Crown CA. Chalk-surfaced paper* (30 *c. to* 1000 *r.*). *P* 14.

(*a*) *Printed from single plates. Value tablet as* A
301 **52** 1 c. brown 40 10
302 3 c. blue-green .. .. 2·00 45
303 5 c. purple .. .. 4·00 2·00
304 5 c. bright magenta 60 40
a. Wmk sideways .. .. .. 55·00
305 6 c. pale scarlet .. .. .. 8·00 85
306 6 c. carmine .. .. 8·50 1·25
a. Wmk sideways .. .. .. 16·00 25·00

(*b*) *Printed from Key and Duty plates at two operations. Die I.* 3 *c. and* 6 *c. have value tablet as* B
307 **52** 2 c. brown-orange 40 20
308 2 c. deep orange-brown 30 20
309 3 c. yellow-green .. .. .. 5·00 2·10
310 3 c. deep green .. .. .. 2·75 90
311 6 c. scarlet .. .. 1·10 50
312 6 c. bright scarlet .. .. .. 1·90 80
313 10 c. sage-green .. .. .. 2·75 1·60
314 10 c. deep sage-green .. .. .. 4·00 2·00
315 15 c. ultramarine .. .. .. 1·50 1·25
316 15 c. deep bright blue .. .. .. 2·50 1·75
317 25 c. yellow and blue .. .. .. 1·75 1·75
318 25 c. orange and blue .. .. .. 5·00 4·00
319 30 c. blue-green and violet .. .. 3·75 2·25
320 30 c. yellow-green and violet .. .. 5·50 3·00
a. Wmk sideways .. .. .. 6·50
321 50 c. black and scarlet .. .. .. 1·25 1·75
322 1 r. purple/*yellow* .. .. .. 1·75 3·00
a. White back (1914) (Optd S. £32) .. 1·25 2·75
b. On lemon (1916) (Optd S. £32) .. 4·00 7·00
c. On orange-buff .. .. .. 20·00 27·00
d. On pale yellow (Optd S. £32) .. 4·00 8·50
323 2 r. black and red/*yellow* .. .. 3·25 8·00
a. White back (1914) (Optd S. £32) .. 2·00 8·00
b. On lemon (1915) (Optd S. £32) .. 17·00 26·00
c. On orange-buff .. .. .. 30·00 32·00
d. On pale yellow .. .. .. 30·00 32·00
324 5 r. black/*green* .. .. .. 14·00 19·00
a. White back (1914) (Optd S. £35) .. 11·00 25·00
b. On blue-green, olive back (1921) (Optd S. £40) .. .. .. 13·00 23·00
c. On emerald back (Die II) (1923) (Optd S. £50) .. .. .. 45·00 75·00
325 10 r. purple and black/*red* .. .. 42·00 50·00
a. Die II (1923) .. .. .. 50·00 80·00
326 20 r. black and red/*blue* .. .. 70·00 60·00
327 **53** 50 r. dull purple (Optd S. £100) .. £300
a. Break in scroll £500
b. Broken crown and scroll £500
328 100 r. grey-black (Optd S. £250) .. £1300
a. Break in scroll £1800
b. Broken crown and scroll £1800
329 500 r. dull green (Optd S. £350) .. £3750
a. Break in scroll £5500
b. Broken crown and scroll £5500
329*c* 1000 r. purple/*red* (1925) (Optd S. £650) £14000
cb. Broken crown and scroll £18000
301/25 .. .. .. *Set of* 14 65·00 80·00
301/26 Optd "Specimen" .. .. *Set of* 15 £200

For illustrations of the varieties on Nos. 327/9c see above No. 58 of Leeward Islands.

WAR
STAMP
(54)

WAR
STAMP
ONE CENT
(55)

1918 (18 Nov). (*a*) *Optd with T* **54**.
330 **52** 2 c. brown-orange 15 40
a. Opt inverted .. .. .. 24·00 27·00
b. Opt double .. .. .. 24·00 27·00
c. Opt omitted in pair with opt inverted £300
331 3 c. blue-green (No. 302) 10 20
332 3 c. yellow-green (No. 309) .. .. 75 2·25
a. Opt double .. .. .. 42·00 45·00
333 5 c. purple 20 30
a. Opt double .. .. .. 24·00 27·00
334 5 c. bright magenta .. .. .. 55 1·00
a. Opt inverted .. .. .. 24·00 27·00
b. Opt double .. .. .. 24·00 29·00

(*b*) *Surch with T* **55**
335 **52** 1 c. on 5 c. purple 30 25
336 1 c. on 5 c. bright magenta 40 20
330/1, 333, 335 Optd "Specimen" .. *Set of* 4 85·00

Collectors are warned against forgeries of the errors in the "WAR STAMP" overprints.

1918. *Surch as T* **55**, *but without* "WAR STAMP".
337 **52** 1 c. on 5 c. purple (Optd S. £30) .. 15 25
337*a* 1 c. on 5 c. bright magenta .. .. 50 1·25
ab. Opt double .. .. .. 90·00

1921–33. *Wmk Mult Script CA. Chalk-surfaced paper* (30 *c. to* 100 r.). *P* 14.

A. **1921–27.** *The original issue.*

(*a*) *Printed from single plates. Value tablet as* A
338 **52** 1 c. brown (1927) 30 35
339 3 c. green (5.5.22) .. .. .. 45 1·00
340 5 c. bright magenta (1927) 10 15
341 6 c. carmine-red (3.8.21) 35 75

(*b*) *Printed from Key and Duty plates at two operations. Die I* (10 *c. to* 30 *c. and* 1 *r.*) *or Die II* (2 *c.*, 50 *c.*, 2 *r. to* 20 *r.*)
342 **52** 2 c. brown-orange (1927) 30 25
343 10 c. sage-green (16.9.21) 60 40
344 15 c. ultramarine (30.5.22) .. .. 2·50 5·00
345 20 c. bright blue (1922) .. .. 2·50 3·75
346 25 c. yellow and blue (17.10.21) .. 80 1·25
347 30 c. yellow-green and violet (15.3.22) 1·40 2·50
348 50 c. black and scarlet (1922) .. .. 1·00 80
349 1 r. purple/*pale yellow* (1923) .. 11·00 17·00
350 2 r. black and red/*pale yellow* (1923) 3·50 6·50
351 5 r. black/*emerald* (1925) .. .. 15·00 30·00
352 20 r. black and red/*blue* (1924) .. 65·00 65·00
353 **53** 50 r. dull purple (1924) (Optd S. £100) £325
a. Break in scroll £550
b. Broken crown and scroll £550
354 100 r. grey-black (1924) (Optd S. £250) £1300
a. Break in scroll £1800
b. Broken crown and scroll £1800
338/51 .. .. .. *Set of* 14 35·00 65·00
338/52 Optd "Specimen" .. .. *Set of* 15 £190

B. **1922–27.** *New values and colour changed.*

(*a*) *Printed from single plates. Value tablet as* A
355 **52** 3 c. slate-grey (1923) 15 20
a. Wmk sideways £350
356 6 c. bright violet 15 15

(*b*) *Printed from Key and Duty plates at two operations. Die I* (12 *c.*, 15 *c.*) *or Die II* (9 *c.*)
357 **52** 9 c. red/*yellow* (1926) 30 35
358 12 c. rose-scarlet (1924) .. .. 2·50 4·00
359 15 c. green/*pale yellow* (1923) .. .. 1·25 1·25
360 **53** 100 r. dull purple and blue (24.10.27) (Optd S. £250) £1200
a. Break in scroll £1700
b. Broken scroll and crown £1700
355/9 Optd "Specimen" .. .. *Set of* 5 £120

C. **1924–25.** *Key and Duty plates. Change to Die II.*
360*c* **52** 10 c. sage-green 45 60
360*d* 12 c. rose-scarlet .. .. .. 80 1·50
360*e* 15 c. green/*pale yellow* .. .. 1·25 1·50
360*f* 20 c. bright blue 55 45
360*g* 25 c. yellow and blue .. .. .. 1·75 1·50
360*h* 30 c. yellow-green and violet .. .. 1·40 1·25
360*i* 1 r. purple/*pale yellow* .. .. 6·00 14·00
360*c/i* .. .. .. *Set of* 7 11·00 19·00

D. **1933** (Dec). *Key and Duty plates. Reappearance of Die I* (*Key Plate* 23).
360*j* **52** 50 c. black and scarlet .. .. 40·00 65·00

For illustrations of the varieties on Nos. 353/4 and 360 see above No. 58 of Leeward Islands.

2 Cents.
(56)

57

(Surch at Ceylon Govt Printing Works)

1926 (27 Nov). *Surch as T* **56**.
361 **52** 2 c. on 3 c. slate-grey .. .. .. 50 1·00
a. Surch double .. .. .. 60·00
b. Bar omitted .. .. .. 50·00 60·00
362 5 c. on 6 c. bright violet 50 40
361/2 Optd "Specimen" .. .. *Set of* 2 50·00

No. 361b comes from the bottom horizontal row of the sheet which was often partially obscured by the selvedge during surcharging.

1927 (27 Nov)–**29.** *Wmk Mult Script CA. Chalk-surfaced paper. P* 14.
363 **57** 1 r. dull and bright purple (1928) .. 1·75 1·25
364 2 r. green and carmine (1929) .. .. 3·75 2·75
365 5 r. green and dull purple (1928) .. 12·00 17·00
366 10 r. green and brown-orange .. .. 28·00 70·00
367 20 r. dull purple and blue .. .. 65·00 £140
363/7 .. .. .. *Set of* 5 £100 £200
363/7 Optd "Specimen" .. .. *Set of* 5 £130

No. 364. Collectors are warned against faked 2 r. stamps, showing what purports to be a double centre.

NEW INFORMATION

The editor is always interested to correspond with people who have new information that will improve or correct the Catalogue.

58 Tapping Rubber **60** Adam's Peak

(Recess D.L.R. (2, 3, 20, 50 c.), B.W. (others))

1935 (1 May)–**36.** *T* **58, 60** *and similar designs. Wmk Mult Script CA (sideways on* 10, 15, 25, 30 *c. and* 1 *r.). Various perfs.*

368 2 c. black and carmine (*p* 12 × 13) 25 25
a. Perf 14 .. .. 6·50 40
369 3 c. blk & ol-green (*p* 13 × 12) (1.10.35) .. 35 30
a. Perf 14 .. .. 18·00 30
370 6 c. black & blue (*p* 11 × 11½) (1.1.36) .. 30 25
371 9 c. green & orange (*p* 11 × 11½) (1.1.36) .. 65 40
372 10 c. black & purple (*p* 11½ × 11) (1.6.35) .. 1·00 90
373 15 c. red-brown and green (*p* 11½ × 11) .. 1·00 50
374 20 c. black & grey-blue (*p* 12 × 13) (1.1.36) .. 1·75 1·60
375 25 c. deep blue & chocolate (*p* 11½ × 11) .. 1·25 75
376 30 c. carm & green (*p* 11½ × 11) (1.8.35) .. 3·00 1·25
377 50 c. black and mauve (*p* 14) (1.1.36) .. .. 3·75 50
378 1 r. vio-bl & chocolate (*p* 11½ × 11) (1.7.35).. 8·00 6·00
368/78 .. .. *Set of* 11 19·00 11·50
368/78 Perf "Specimen" .. .. *Set of* 11 £130

Designs: *Vert*—6 c. Colombo Harbour; 9 c. Plucking tea; 20 c. Coconut Palms. *Horiz*—10 c. Hill paddy (rice); 15 c. River scene; 25 c. Temple of the Tooth, Kandy; 30 c. Ancient irrigation tank; 50 c. Wild elephants; 1 r. Trincomalee.

1935 (6 May). *Silver Jubilee. As Nos.* 114/17 *of Jamaica, but ptd by D.L.R. P* 13½×14.

379 6 c. ultramarine and grey 45 30
g. Dot to left of chapel .. .. .. 25·00
h. Dot by flagstaff .. .. 25·00
i. Dash by turret .. .. 30·00
380 9 c. green and indigo 70 50
g. Dot to left of chapel .. .. .. 40·00
h. Dot by flagstaff .. .. 40·00
381 20 c. brown and deep blue .. .. .. 3·75 1·50
f. Horiz line from turret .. .. .. 80·00
g. Dot to left of chapel .. .. .. 80·00
382 50 c. slate and purple .. .. .. 5·00 3·75
h. Dot by flagstaff £110
379/82 .. .. *Set of* 4 9·00 5·50
379/82 Perf "Specimen" .. .. *Set of* 4 80·00

For illustrations of plate varieties, see Omnibus section following Zimbabwe.

1937 (12 May). *Coronation. As Nos.* 118/20 *of Jamaica, but ptd by B.W. & Co. P* 11×11½.

383 6 c. carmine 55 10
384 9 c. green .. .. 1·50 1·50
385 20 c. blue .. .. 2·50 2·50
383/5 .. .. *Set of* 3 4·00 3·75
383/5 Perf "Specimen" .. .. *Set of* 3 55·00

69 Tapping Rubber **70** Sigiriya (Lion Rock)

71 Ancient Guard-stone, Anuradhapura **72** King George VI

Apostrophe flaw (Frame Pl 1 R. 6/6) (ptg of 1 Jan 1943 only)

(Recess B.W. (stamps perf 11 × 11½ or 11½ × 11), D.L.R. (all others) T **72** typo D.L.R.)

1938–49. *T* **69/72** *and designs as* 1935–36, *but with portrait of King George VI instead of King George V,* "POSTAGE & REVENUE" *omitted and some redrawn. Wmk Mult Script CA (sideways on* 10, 15, 25, 30 *c. and* 1 *r.). Chalk-surfaced paper* (5 *r.). Various perfs.*

386 **69** 2 c. blk & carm (*p* 11½×13) (25.4.38) 5·50 70
a. Perf 13½×13 (1938) .. .. 65·00 1·50
b. Perf 13½ (25.4.38) 30 10
c. Perf 11×11½ (17.2.44) 30 40
d. Perf 12 (22.4.49) .. .. .. 45 1·50
387 **60** 3 c. black & dp blue-green (*p* 13×11½) (21.3.38) .. .. 8·00 30
a. Perf 13×13½ (1938) .. .. £190 4·00
b. Perf 13½ (21.3.38) .. .. 1·50 10
c. Perf 14 (7.41) .. .. .. 70·00 85
d. Perf 11½×11 (14.5.42) 30 10
e. Perf 12 (14.1.46) 20 15
387*f* – 5 c. sage-grn & orge (*p* 13½) (1.1.43) 20 10
fa. Apostrophe flaw .. .. .. 26·00
g. Perf 12 (1947) 40 25
388 – 6 c. black and blue (*p* 11×11½) (1.1.38) 20 10
389 **70** 10 c. blk & light bl (*p* 11½×11) (1.2.38) 60 10
a. Wmk upright (1.6.44) 80 30
390 – 15 c. grn & red-brn (*p* 11½×11) (1.1.38) 50 10
a. Wmk upright (23.7.45) 75 30
391 – 20 c. blk & grey-bl (*p* 11×11½) (15.1.38) 1·75 10
392 – 25 c. dp bl & choc (*p* 11½×11) (15.1.38) 2·00 30
a. Wmk upright (1944) 60 10
393 – 30 c. carm & grn (*p* 11½×11) (1.2.38) 6·00 75
a. Wmk upright (16.4.45) .. .. 5·50 2·00
394 – 50 c. blk & mve (*p* 13×11½) (25.4.38) .. £130 40·00
a. Perf 13×13½ (1938) .. .. £275 2·25
b. Perf 13½ (25.4.38) .. .. 7·00 20
c. Perf 14 (4.42) .. .. .. 75·00 22·00
d. Perf 11½×11 (14.5.42) .. .. 2·00 75
e. Perf 12 (14.1.46) .. .. .. 1·40 15
395 – 1 r. blue-violet & chocolate (*p* 11½×11) (1.2.38) .. .. 6·00 35
a. Wmk upright (1944) .. .. 7·00 80
396 **71** 2 r. blk and carm (*p* 11×11½) (1.2.38) 4·00 1·00
396*a* 2 r. blk & vio (*p* 11×11½) (15.3.47) .. 1·00 75
397 **72** 5 r. green and purple (*p* 14) (10.10.38) 25·00 3·00
a. Ordinary paper. *Green and pale purple* (19.2.43) .. .. .. 11·00 1·25
386/97a (*cheapest*) .. .. *Set of* 14 30·00 4·50
386/97 Perf "Specimen" .. .. *Set of* 14 £275

Designs: *Vert*—5 c. Coconut Palms; 6 c. Colombo Harbour; 20 c. Plucking tea. *Horiz*—15 c. River scene; 25 c. Temple of the Tooth, Kandy; 30 c. Ancient irrigation tank; 50 c. Wild elephants; 1 r. Trincomalee.

3 CENTS
═
(73)

3 CENTS
≡
(74)

1940–41. *Nos.* 388 *and* 391 *surch.*

398 **73** 3 c. on 6 c. (10.5.41) 10 10
399 **74** 3 c. on 20 c. (5.11.40) 50 40

1946 (10 Dec). *Victory. As Nos.* 141/2 *of Jamaica.*

400 6 c. blue 10 10
401 15 c. brown 10 30
400/1 Perf "Specimen" .. .. *Set of* 2 48·00

75 Parliament Building **76** Adam's Peak

(Des R. Tenison and M. S. V. Rodrigo. Recess B.W.)

1947 (25 Nov). *Inauguration of New Constitution. T* **75/6** *and similar designs. Wmk Mult Script CA. P* 11 × 12 (*horiz*) *or* 12 × 11 (*vert*).

402 6 c. black and blue 10 15
403 10 c. black, orange and carmine 10 20
404 15 c. green and purple 10 30
405 25 c. ochre and emerald-green 10 15
402/5 .. .. *Set of* 4 35 70
402/5 Perf "Specimen" .. .. *Set of* 4 80·00

Designs: *Horiz*—15 c. Temple of the Tooth. *Vert*—25 c. Anuradhapura.

DOMINION

79 Lion Flag of Dominion **80** D. S. Senanayake

81 Lotus Flowers and Sinhalese Letters "Sri"

(Recess (flag typo) B.W.)

1949 (4 Feb–5 Apr). *First Anniv of Independence.* (*a*) *Wmk Mult Script CA (sideways on* 4 *c.). P* 12½×12 (4 *c.*) *or* 12×12½ (5 *c.*).

406 **79** 4 c. yellow, carmine and brown .. 10 20
407 **80** 5 c. brown and green 10 10

(*b*) *W* **81** (*sideways on* 15 *c.*). *P* 13 × 12½ (15 *c.*) *or* 12 × 12½ (25 *c.*) (5 April)

408 **79** 15 c. yellow, carmine and vermilion .. 25 15
409 **80** 25 c. brown and blue 15 15
406/9 .. .. *Set of* 4 40 50

The 15 c. is larger, measuring 28 × 12 mm.

82 Globe and Forms of Transport

83 **84**

(Recess D.L.R.)

1949 (10 Oct). *75th Anniv of Universal Postal Union. W* **81.** *P* 13 (25 *c.*) *or* 12 (*others*).

410 **82** 5 c. brown and bluish green 75 10
411 **83** 15 c. black and carmine .. .. .. 1·40 60
412 **84** 25 c. black and ultramarine .. .. 1·40 35
410/12 .. .. *Set of* 3 3·25 95

85 Kandyan Dancer **88** Sigiriya (Lion Rock)

89 Octagon Library, Temple of the Tooth **90** Ruins at Madirigiriya

(Recess B.W.)

1950 (4 Feb). *T* **85, 88/90** *and similar designs. W* **81.** *P* 11 × 11½ (75 *c.*), 11½ × 11 (1 *r.*), 12 × 12½ (*others*).

413 4 c. purple and scarlet 10 10
414 5 c. green 10 10
415 15 c. blue-green and violet .. .. .. 1·25 20
416 30 c. carmine and yellow 30 20
417 75 c. ultramarine and orange 65 10
418 1 r. deep blue and brown .. .. .. 1·25 10
413/18 .. .. *Set of* 6 3·25 55

Designs: *Vert* (*as T* **88**)—5 c. Kiri Vehera, Polonnaruwa; 15 c. Vesak Orchid.

For these values with redrawn inscriptions see Nos. 450/1, 454, 456, 460 and 462.

NEW INFORMATION

The editor is always interested to correspond with people who have new information that will improve or correct the Catalogue.

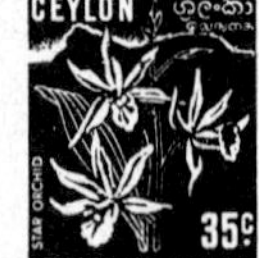

91 Sambars, Ruhuna National Park — **92** Ancient Guard-stone, Anuradhapura — **96** Star Orchid

97 Rubber Plantation — **99** Tea Plantation

I. No. 424 — II. No. 424a (Dot added)

(Photo Courvoisier)

1951 (1 Aug)–**54.** *T* **91/2, 96/7, 99** *and similar designs. No wmk. P* 11½.

419		2 c. brown and blue-green (15.5.54)	10	20
420		3 c. black and slate-violet (15.5.54)	10	30
421		6 c. brown-black & yellow-green (15.5.54)	10	10
422		10 c. green and blue-grey	75	25
423		25 c. orange-brown & bright blue (15.3.54)	10	10
424		35 c. red and deep green (I) (1.2.52)	1·50	60
		a. Type II (1954)	2·75	35
425		40 c. deep brown (15.5.54)	1·25	40
426		50 c. indigo and slate-grey (15.3.54)	30	10
427		85 c. black and deep blue-green (15.5.54)	50	10
428		2 r. blue and deep brown (15.5.54)	4·50	40
429		5 r. brown and orange (15.3.54)	4·75	50
430		10 r. red-brown and buff (15.3.54)	14·00	4·25
419/30		*Set of* 12	25·00	6·25

Designs: *Vert* (*as T* **91**)—6 c. Harvesting rice; 10 c. Coconut trees; 25 c. Sigiriya fresco. (*As T* **99**)—5 r. Bas-relief, Anuradhapura; 10 r. Harvesting rice. *Horiz* (*as T* **97**)—50 c. Outrigger canoe; (*as T* **99**)—2 r. River Gal Dam.

For these values with redrawn inscriptions see Nos. 448, etc.

103 Ceylon Mace and Symbols of Progress

(Photo Harrison)

1952 (23 Feb). *Colombo Plan Exhibition. Chalk-surfaced paper. W* **81** *(sideways). P* 14½ × 14.

431	**103**	5 c. green	10	10
432		15 c. ultramarine	20	15

104 Queen Elizabeth II — **105** Ceremonial Procession

(Recess B.W.)

1953 (2 June). *Coronation. W* **81**. *P* 12 × 13.

433	**104**	5 c. green	40	10

(Recess D.L.R.)

1954 (10 Apr). *Royal Visit. W* **81** *(sideways). P* 13 × 12½.

434	**105**	10 c. deep blue	15	10

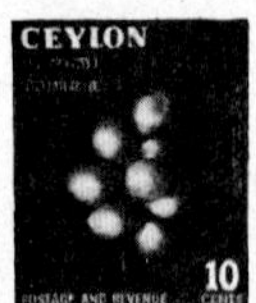

106 King Coconuts — **107** Farm Produce

(Photo Courvoisier)

1954 (1 Dec). *No wmk. P* 11½.

435	**106**	10 c. orange, bistre-brown and buff	10	10

For this design with redrawn inscription see No. 453.

(Photo Harrison)

1955 (10 Dec). *Royal Agricultural and Food Exhibition. W* **81** *(sideways). P* 14 × 14½.

436	**107**	10 c. brown and orange	10	10

108 Sir John Kotelawala and House of Representatives

(Photo Courvoisier)

1956 (26 Mar). *Prime Minister's 25 Years of Public Service. P* 11½.

437	**108**	10 c. deep bluish green	10	10

109 Arrival of Vijaya in Ceylon — **110** Lampstand and Dharmachakra

111 Hand of Peace and Dharmachakra — **112** Dharmachakra encircling the Globe

(Photo Courvoisier)

1956. *Buddha Jayanti. P* 11½.

438	**109**	3 c. blue and brownish grey (23 May)	15	10
439	**110**	4 c. + 2 c. grnish yell & dp bl (10 May)	15	35
440	**111**	10 c. + 5 c. carm, yellow & grey (10 May)	15	30
441	**112**	15 c. bright blue (23 May)	15	10
438/41		*Set of* 4	55	70

113 Mail Transport — **114** Stamp of 1857

(Photo Enschedé (4 c., 10 c.), Courvoisier (others))

1957 (1 Apr). *Centenary of First Ceylon Postage Stamp. P* 12½ × 13 (4 c., 10 c.) *or* 11½ *(others).*

442	**113**	4 c. orange-red and deep bluish green	30	15
443		10 c. vermilion and blue	30	10
444	**114**	35 c. brown, yellow and blue	30	20
445		85 c. brown, yellow and grey-green	70	85
442/5		*Set of* 4	1·40	1·10

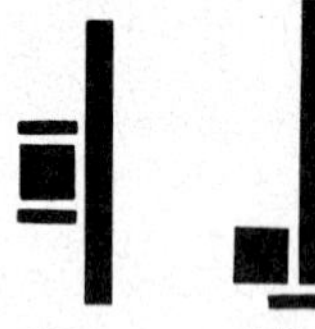

(**115**) — (**116**) — **117** Kandyan Dancer

1958 (15 Jan). *Nos.* 439/40 *with premium obliterated as T* **115** (4 c.) *or T* **116** (10 c.).

446	**110**	4 c. greenish yellow and deep blue	10	10
		a. Opt inverted	8·00	
		b. Opt double	10·00	
447	**111**	10 c. carmine, yellow and grey	10	10
		a. Opt inverted	13·00	15·00

The 4 c. exists with opt misplaced to right so that some stamps show the vertical bar on the left (*Price* £18 *un.*).

(Recess B.W. (4 c., 5 c., 15 c., 30 c., 75 c., 1 r.). Photo Courvoisier (others))

1958 (14 May)–**62.** *As earlier types, but inscriptions redrawn as in T* **117**. *W* **81** (4, 5, 15, 30, 75 c., 1 r.) *or no wmk (others). P* 11×11½ (75 c.), 11½×11 (1 r.), 12×12½ (4, 5, 15 , 30 c.), *or* 11½ *(others).*

448	**91**	2 c. brown and blue-green	10	15
449	**92**	3 c. black and slate-violet	10	35
450	**117**	4 c. purple and scarlet	10	10
451	–	5 c. green (1.10.58)	10	10
		a. Yellow-green (13.6.61)	40	10
		b. Deep green (19.6.62)	30	10
452	–	6 c. brown-black and yellow-green	10	35
453	**106**	10 c. orge, bistre-brown & buff (1.10.58)	10	10
454	–	15 c. blue-green and violet (1.10.58)	2·25	40
455	–	25 c. orange-brown and bright blue	10	10
456	**88**	30 c. carmine and yellow (1.5.59)	15	50
457	**96**	35 c. red and deep green (II) (15.7.58)	3·00	15
459	–	50 c. indigo and slate-grey (15.7.58)	30	10
460	**89**	75 c. ultramarine and orange (1.5.59)	45	40
		a. Ultramarine & brown-orge (3.4.62)	45	30
461	**99**	85 c. black and deep blue-green (1.5.59)	3·75	2·25
462	**90**	1 r. deep blue and brown (1.10.58)	40	10
463	–	2 r. blue and deep brown	75	10
464	–	5 r. brown and orange	1·25	10
465	–	10 r. red-brown and buff	3·50	70
448/65		*Set of* 17	15·00	5·00

Designs: *Vert* (*as T* **117**)—5 c. Kiri Vehera Polonnaruwa; 6 c. Harvesting rice; 15 c. Vesak Orchid; 25 c. Sigiriya fresco. (*as T* **99**)—5 r. Bas-relief, Anuradhapura; 10 r. Harvesting rice. *Horiz* (*as T* **97**)—50 c. Outrigger canoe. (*as T* **99**)—2 r. River Gal Dam.

118 "Human Rights" — **119** Portraits of Founders and University Buildings

(Photo Enschedé)

1958 (10 Dec). *Tenth Anniv of Declaration of Human Rights. P* 13 × 12½.

466	**118**	10 c. vermilion and dull purple	10	10
467		85 c. vermilion and deep blue-green	30	45

(Photo Enschedé)

1959 (31 Dec). *Institution of Pirivena Universities. P* 13 × 12½.

468	**119**	10 c. red-orange and ultramarine	10	10

120 Uprooted Tree — **121** S.W.R.D. Bandaranaike

(Des W. A. Ariyasena. Photo Courvoisier)

1960 (7 Apr). *World Refugee Year. P* 11½.

469	**120**	4 c. red-brown and gold	10	30
470		25 c. blackish violet and gold	10	15

(Photo Courvoisier)

1961 (8 Jan–15 June). *Prime Minister Bandaranaike Commemoration. P* 11½.

471	**121**	10 c. deep blue and greenish blue	10	10
		a. Portrait redrawn (15.6.61)*	10	10

*Earliest known postmark date.

No. 471a can be identified by Mr. Bandaranaike's dark hair at temples.

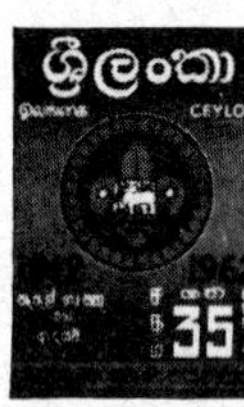

122 Ceylon Scout Badge — **123** Campaign Emblem

(Des W. A. Ariyasena. Photo Courvoisier)

1962 (26 Feb). *Golden Jubilee of Ceylon Boy Scouts Association. P* 11½.

472	**122**	35 c. buff and blue	15	10

(Photo Harrison)

1962 (7 Apr). *Malaria Eradication. W* **81**. *P* 14½ × 14.

473	**123**	25 c. red-orange and sepia	10	10

124 "DH85 Leopard-Moth" and "Comet" Airliner — **125** "Produce" and Campaign Emblem

(Photo Courvoisier)

1963 (28 Feb). *25th Anniv of Airmail. P* 11½.

474	**124**	50 c. black and light blue	15	30

(Photo Courvoisier)

1963 (21 Mar). *Freedom from Hunger. P* 11½.

475	**125**	5 c. vermilion and blue	20	60
476		25 c. brown and yellow-olive	80	30

ශත
2
சதம்

(126)

127 "Rural Life"

1963 (1 June). *No.* 450 *surch with T* **126**.
477 **117** 2 c. on 4 c. purple and scarlet 10 10
a. Surch inverted .. .. .. 16·00
b. Surch double .. .. .. 15·00

(Photo Harrison)

1963 (5 July). *Golden Jubilee of Ceylon Co-operative Movement* (1962). *W* **81**. *P* 14 × 14½.
478 **127** 60 c. rose-red and black 15 30

128 S. W. R. D. Bandaranaike

129 Terrain, Elephant and Tree

(Recess Courvoisier)

1963 (26 Sept). *P* 11½.
479 **128** 10 c. light blue 10 10

(Photo Harrison)

1963 (9 Dec). *National Conservation Week. W* **8**' *(sideways). P* 14×14½.
480 **129** 5 c. sepia and blue 10 20

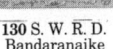

130 S. W. R. D. Bandaranaike

131 Anagarika Dharmapala (Buddhist missionary)

(T **130/1**. Photo Courvoisier)

1964 (1 July). *P* 11½.
481 **130** 10 c. deep violet-blue and greenish grey 10 10

1964 (16 Sept). *Birth Centenary of Anagarika Dharmapala (founder of Maha Bodhi Society). P* 11½.
482 **131** 25 c. sepia and olive-yellow 10 10

134 Southern Grackle

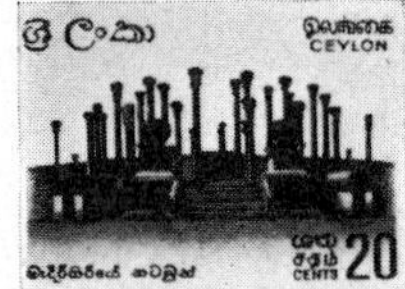
138 Ruins at Madirigiriya

135 D. S. Senanayake 136

146 Tea Plantation

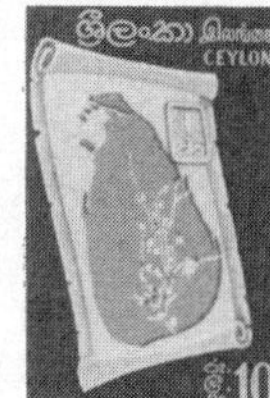
149 Map of Ceylon

(Des A. Dharmasiri (5 r.); P. A. Miththapala (10 r.). Photo Courvoisier (10 c. (486), 20 c.), Harrison (10 c. (487), 60 c., 1 r., 5 r., 10 r.), D.L.R. (others incl sheet))

1964 (1 Oct)–**72**. *T* **134/6, 138, 146, 149** *and similar designs. No wmk (Nos.* 486, 489), *W* **81** *(others; sideways on Nos.* 487, 494, 499). *P* 11½ *(Nos.* 486, 489), 14½ × 14 *(No.* 494) *or* 14 *(others)*.
485 **134** 5 c. multicoloured (5.2.66) 45 60
486 **135** 10 c. myrtle-green (22.3.66) 10 10
487 **136** 10 c. myrtle-green (23.9.68) 10 10
a. Imperf (pair) .. .. .. 40·00
488 – 15 c. multicoloured (5.2.66) 90 30
489 **138** 20 c. brown-purple and buff 10 15
494 – 60 c. multicoloured (5.2.66) .. .. 1·25 50
a. Red omitted .. .. .. 30·00
b. Blue and green omitted* .. .. 30·00
495 – 75 c. multicoloured (5.2.66) .. .. 1·25 50
a. No wmk (8.6.72) .. .. .. 4·50 4·00
497 **146** 1 r. brown and bluish green .. .. 1·00 10
a. Brown omitted £110
b. Bluish green omitted £160
499 – 5 r. multicoloured (15.8.69) .. .. 1·75 1·75
500 **149** 10 r. multicoloured (1.10.69) .. .. 8·50 1·75
485/500 .. .. .. *Set of* 10 14·00 5·25
MS500*a* 148 × 174 mm. As Nos. 485, 488, 494 and 495. Imperf. .. .. 7·00 6·00

Designs: *Horiz (as T* **134**)—15 c. Common Peafowl; 60 c. Ceylon Junglefowl; 75 c. Asian Black-headed Oriole. *(as T* **138**)—5 r. Girls transplanting rice.

The 5 c., 75 c. and 1 r. exist with PVA gum as well as gum arabic.

In the miniature sheet the inscriptions on the 60 c. have been rearranged to conform with the style of the other values.

*Actually only the blue printing is omitted on this sheet, but where this was printed over the yellow to form the leaves it appeared as green.

150 Exhibition Buildings and Cogwheels

151 Trains of 1864 and 1964

(Photo State Printing Works, Budapest)

1964 (1 Dec). *Industrial Exhibition. T* **150** *and similar horiz design. No wmk. P* 11.
501 – 5 c. multicoloured 10 25
a. Pair. Nos. 501/2 .. .. .. 10 1·25
502 **150** 5 c. multicoloured 10 25

No. 501 is inscribed "INDUSTRIAL EXHIBITION" in Sinhala and Tamil, No. 502 in Sinhala and English. The stamps were issued together *se-tenant* in alternate vertical rows, producing horizontal pairs.

(Photo Harrison)

1964 (21 Dec). *Centenary of Ceylon Railways. T* **151** *and similar horiz design. W* **81** *(sideways). P* 14 × 14½.
503 – 60 c. blue, reddish purple & yellow-grn 1·25 20
a. Pair. Nos. 503/4 .. .. .. 2·50 2·50
504 **151** 60 c. blue, reddish purple & yellow-grn 1·25 20

No. 503 is inscribed "RAILWAY CENTENARY" in Sinhala and Tamil, No. 504 in Sinhala and English. The stamps were issued together *se-tenant* in alternate horizontal rows, producing vertical pairs.

152 I.T.U. Emblem and Symbols

153 I.C.Y. Emblem

(Photo Harrison)

1965 (17 May). *I.T.U. Centenary. W* **81** *(sideways). P* 14½.
505 **152** 2 c. bright blue and red 15 65
506 30 c. brown and red .. .. 1·50 45
a. Value omitted £100

No. 506a was caused by the misplacement of the red.

(Photo Courvoisier)

1965 (26 June). *International Co-operation Year. T* **153** *and similar horiz design. P* 11½.
507 3 c. deep blue and rose-carmine 30 50
508 50 c. black, rose-carmine and gold .. .. 1·50 50

No. 508 is similar to T **153** but has the multilingual inscription "CEYLON" rearranged.

154 Town Hall, Colombo

(155)

(Photo Courvoisier)

1965 (29 Oct). *Centenary of Colombo Municipal Council. P* 11 × 11½.
509 **154** 25 c. myrtle-green and sepia 10 10

1965 (18 Dec). *No.* 481 *surch with T* **155**.
510 **130** 5 c. on 10 c. dp vio-bl & greenish grey 10 10

157 Kandy and Council Crest

158 W.H.O. Building

(Photo Harrison)

1966 (15 June). *Kandy Municipal Council Centenary. W* **81**. *P* 14 × 13½.
512 **157** 25 c. multicoloured 10 10

(Litho D.L.R.)

1966 (8 Oct). *Inauguration of W.H.O. Headquarters. Geneva. P* 14.
513 **158** 4 c. multicoloured .. .. .. 75 1·50
514 1 r. multicoloured .. .. .. 3·50 1·50

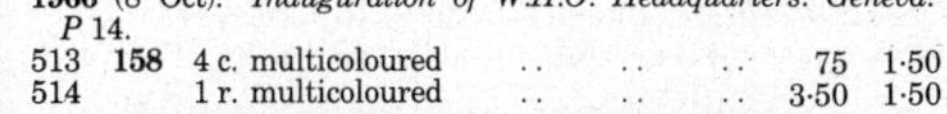

159 Rice Paddy and Map of Ceylon

160 Rice Paddy and Globe

(Photo Courvoisier)

1966 (25 Oct). *International Rice Year. P* 11½.
515 **159** 6 c. multicoloured 20 50
516 **160** 30 c. multicoloured 30 15

161 U.N.E.S.C.O. Emblem

162 Water-resources Map

(Litho State Ptg Wks, Vienna)

1966 (3 Nov). 20*th Anniv of U.N.E.S.C.O. P* 12.
517 **161** 3 c. multicoloured 40 30
518 50 c. multicoloured .. .. .. 2·25 30

(Litho D.L.R.)

1966 (1 Dec). *International Hydrological Decade. P* 14.
519 **162** 2 c. orange-brown, greenish yellow & bl 10 65
520 2 r. orge-brn, grnish yell, bl & yell-grn 60 1·25

163 Devotees at Buddhist Temple

167 Galle Fort and Clock Tower

(Photo State Ptg Wks, Vienna)

1967 (2 Jan). *Poya Holiday System. T* **163** *and similar horiz designs. Multicoloured. P* 12.
521 5 c. Type **163** 10 20
522 20 c. Mihintale 10 10
523 35 c. Sacred Bo-tree, Anuradhapura 10 15
524 60 c. Adam's Peak 10 10
521/4 .. .. *Set of* 4 30 35

(Litho Rosenbaum Brothers, Vienna)

1967 (5 Jan). *Centenary of Galle Municipal Council. P* 13½.
525 **167** 25 c. multicoloured 30 20

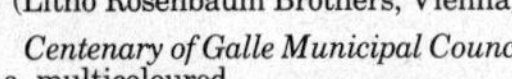

168 Field Research

(Litho Rosenbaum Bros, Vienna)

1967 (1 Aug). *Centenary of Ceylon Tea Industry. T* **168** *and similar horiz designs. Multicoloured. P* 13½.
526 4 c. Type **168** 15 40
527 40 c. Tea-tasting equipment 45 40
528 50 c. Leaves and bud 45 20
529 1 r. Shipping tea 80 10
526/9 .. .. *Set of* 4 1·60 1·00

172 Elephant Ride

173 Ranger, Jubilee Emblem and Flag

(Litho Rosenbaum Bros, Vienna)

1967 (15 Aug). *International Tourist Year. P* 13½.
530 **172** 45 c. multicoloured 80 30

1967 (16 Sept). *1st National Stamp Exhibition. No.* **MS**500*a optd* "FIRST NATIONAL STAMP EXHIBITION 1967".
MS531 148 × 174 mm. Nos. 485, 488, 494/5. Imperf 4·00 4·75

(Litho D.L.R.)

1967 (19 Sept). *Golden Jubilee of Ceylon Girl Guides Association. P* 12½ × 13.
532 **173** 3 c. multicoloured 10 10
533 25 c. multicoloured 25 10

174 Col. Olcott and Buddhist Flag

(Litho Rosenbaum Bros, Vienna)

1967 (8 Dec). *60th Death Anniv of Colonel H. S. Olcott (theosophist). P* 13½.
534 **174** 15 c. multicoloured 15 15

175 Independence Hall

176 Lion Flag and Sceptre

(Photo Harrison)

1968 (2 Feb). *20th Anniv of Independence. W* **81** (*sideways*). *P* 14.
535 **175** 5 c. multicoloured 10 35
536 **176** 1 r. multicoloured 20 10

177 Sir D. B. Jayatilleke

178 Institute of Hygiene

(Litho D.L.R.)

1968 (14 Feb). *Birth Centenary of Sir Baron Jayatilleke (scholar and statesman). P* 14.
537 **177** 25 c. yellow-brown and sepia 10 10

(Litho B.W.)

1968 (7 Apr). *20th Anniv of World Health Organization. W* **81.** *P* 12.
538 **178** 50 c. multicoloured 10 10

179 Aircraft over Terminal Building

181 Open Koran and "1400"

(Des and litho B.W.)

1968 (5 Aug). *Opening of Colombo Airport. W* **81.** *P* 13½.
539 **179** 60 c. grey-blue, chestnut, red and yellow 10 10

(Des M. I. M. Mohideen. Photo Harrison)

1968 (14 Oct). *1400th Anniv of the Holy Koran. W* **81.** *P* 14.
541 **181** 25 c. multicoloured 10 10

COVER PRICES

Cover factors are quoted at the beginning of each country for most issues to 1945. An explanation of the system can be found on page x. The factors quoted do not, however, apply to philatelic covers.

182 Human Rights Emblem

183 All Ceylon Buddhist Congress Headquarters

(Photo Pakistan Security Printing Corp)

1968 (10 Dec). *Human Rights Year. P* 12½ × 13½.
542 **182** 2 c. multicoloured 10 10
543 20 c. multicoloured 10 10
544 40 c. multicoloured 10 10
545 2 r. multicoloured .. .. 45 2·25
542/5 .. .. *Set of* 4 55 2·25

(Des A. Dharmasiri. Litho Rosenbaum Bros, Vienna)

1968 (19 Dec). *Golden Jubilee of All Ceylon Buddhist Congress. P* 13½.
546 **183** 5 c. multicoloured 10 30

A 50 c. value showing a footprint was prepared but its release was stopped the day before it was due for issue. However, some are known to have been released in error at rural offices (*Price* £15 *mint*).

184 E. W. Perera (patriot)

185 Symbols of Strength in Savings

(Photo Harrison)

1969 (17 Feb). *E. W. Perera Commemoration. W* **81.** *P* 14 × 13½.
547 **184** 60 c. brown 10 10

(Des A. Dharmasiri. Photo Harrison)

1969 (20 Mar). *Silver Jubilee of National Savings Movement. W* **81.** *P* 14.
548 **185** 3 c. multicoloured 10 10

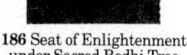

186 Seat of Enlightenment under Sacred Bodhi Tree

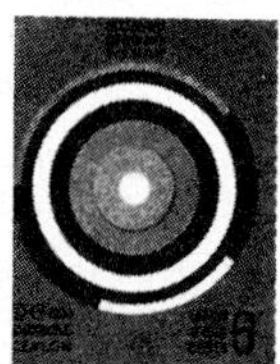
187 Buduresmala (Six fold Buddha-Rays)

(Des L. T. P. Manjusree. Litho D.L.R.)

1969 (10 Apr). *Vesak Day (inscr "Wesak"). W* **81** (*sideways*). *P* 15.
549 **186** 4 c. multicoloured 10 20
550 **187** 6 c. multicoloured 10 20
551 **186** 35 c. multicoloured 10 10
549/51 .. .. *Set of* 3 15 40

No. 549 exists with the gold apparently omitted. Normally the gold appears (without a separate plate number) over an underlay of olive-green on carmine. In one sheet we have seen, the gold only shows as tiny specks under a strong magnifying glass and as there may be intermediate stages of faint printing we do not list this.

188 A. E. Goonesinghe

189 I.L.O. Emblem

(Des and photo Harrison)

1969 (29 Apr). *Commemoration of Goonesinghe (founder of Labour Movement in Ceylon). W* **81.** *P* 14.
552 **188** 15 c. multicoloured 10 10

(Photo Harrison)

1969 (4 May). *50th Anniv of International Labour Organisation. W* **81** (*sideways*). *P* 14.
553 **189** 5 c. black and turquoise-blue 10 10
554 25 c. black and carmine-red 10 10

190 Convocation Hall, University of Ceylon

192 Uranium Atom

(Des Ahangama Edward (35 c.); L. D. P. Jayawardena (50 c.); A. Dharmasiri (60 c.); 4 c. from photograph. Litho Rosenbaum Bros, Vienna)

1969 (1 Aug). *Educational Centenary. T* **190, 192** *and similar multicoloured designs. P* 13½.
555 4 c. Type **190** 10 30
556 35 c. Lamp of Learning, Globe and flags (*horiz*) 10 10
557 50 c. Type **192** 15 10
558 60 c. Symbols of Scientific education 15 10
555/8 .. .. *Set of* 4 40 45

194 Ath Pana (Elephant Lamp)

195 Rock Fortress of Sigiriya

(Des from photographs. Litho Rosenbaum Bros, Vienna)

1969 (1 Aug). *Archaeological Centenary. P* 13½.
559 **194** 6 c. multicoloured 10 40
560 **195** 1 r. multicoloured 25 10

196 Leopard

197 Emblem and Symbols

(Litho Rosenbaum Bros, Vienna)

1970 (11 May). *Wildlife Conservation. T* **196** *and similar horiz designs. Multicoloured. P* 13½.
561 5 c. Water Buffalo 15 60
562 15 c. Slender Loris 50 30
a. Brown-black and orange-brown colours omitted .. .. 50·00
563 50 c. Spotted Deer .. .. 70 1·25
a. Imperf (in vert pair with stamp perf 3 sides) £160
564 1 r. Type **196** .. .. 90 1·75
561/4 .. .. *Set of* 4 2·00 3·50

In No. 562a the sky is blue instead of violet and the animal is in green and yellow only.

(Des A. Dharmasiri. Litho Rosenbaum Bros, Vienna)

1970 (17 June). *Asian Productivity Year. P* 13½.
565 **197** 60 c. multicoloured 10 10

198 New U.P.U. H.Q. Building

199 Oil Lamp and Caduceus

(Litho Rosenbaum Bros, Vienna)

1970 (14 Aug). *New U.P.U. Headquarters Building. P* 13½.
566 **198** 50 c. yellow-orange, black and new blue 10 10
a. New blue (Building) omitted .. 60·00
567 1 r. 10, vermilion, black and new blue 55 30

(Des A. Dharmasiri. Litho Rosenbaum Bros, Vienna)

1970 (1 Sept). *Centenary of Colombo Medical School. P* 13½.
568 **199** 5 c. multicoloured 15 40
a. Vert pair, bottom stamp imperf .. £130
569 45 c. multicoloured 25 40

200 Victory March and S. W. R. D. Bandaranaike

201 U.N. Emblem and Dove of Peace

(Des A. Dharmasiri. Litho D.L.R.)

1970 (25 Sept). *Definitive issue marking establishment of United Front Government. P* 13½.
570 **200** 10 c. multicoloured 10 10

(Des A. Dharmasiri. Photo Pakistan Security Printing Corp)

1970 (24 Oct). *25th Anniv of United Nations. P* 12½ × 13½.
571 **201** 2 r. multicoloured .. .. .. 75 1·40

202 Keppetipola Dissawa

203 Ola Leaf Manuscript

(Des A. Dharmasiri. Litho Harrison)

1970 (26 Nov). *152nd Death Anniv of Keppetipola Dissawa (Kandyan patriot). P* 14 × 14½.
572 **202** 25 c. multicoloured 10 10

(Des A. Dharmasiri. Photo Pakistan Security Printing Corp)

1970 (21 Dec). *International Education Year. P* 13.
573 **203** 15 c. multicoloured 30 40

204 C. H. de Soysa

205 D. E. H. Pedris (patriot)

206 Lenin

(Des L. D. P. Jayawardena. Litho Pakistan Security Printing Corp)

1971 (3 Mar). *135th Birth Anniv of C. H. de Soysa (philanthropist). P* 13½.
574 **204** 20 c. multicoloured 10 30

(Des L. D. P. Jayawardena. Litho Harrison)

1971 (8 July). *D. E. H. Pedris Commemoration. P* 14 × 14½.
575 **205** 25 c. multicoloured 10 35

(Des L. D. P. Jayawardena. Litho Harrison)

1971 (31 Aug). *Lenin Commemoration. P* 14½.
576 **206** 40 c. multicoloured 15 30

207 Ananda Rajakaruna

15 (208)

(Des A. Dharmasiri (Nos. 577 and 579), P. A. Miththapala (Nos. 578 and 580), L. D. P. Jayawardena (No. 581). Litho Harrison)

1971 (29 Oct). *Poets and Philosophers. T* **207** *and similar vert designs. P* 14 × 13½.
577 5 c. royal blue 10 15
578 5 c. lake-brown 10 15
579 5 c. red-orange 10 15
580 5 c. deep slate-blue 10 15
581 5 c. brown 10 15
577/81 .. .. *Set of* 5 30 70

Portraits: No. 577, Type **207**; No. 578, Arumuga Navalar; No. 579, Rev. S. Mahinda; No. 580, Ananda Coomaraswamy; No. 581, Cumaratunga Munidasa.

1971 (26 Nov–2 Dec). *Nos.* 549/50, 555, 559 *and* 570 *surch as T* **208** *(obliterating shape differs).*
582 **186** 5 c. on 4 c. multicoloured .. .. 1·25 1·50
a. Surch inverted .. .. .. 5·50
b. Pair, one with "X" omitted .. 50·00
c. Surch double, one inverted .. 8·50
d. Ditto. Pair, one with "X" omitted 32·00
583 **190** 5 c. on 4 c. multicoloured 10 55
a. Surch inverted .. .. .. 4·25
b. Surch double, one inverted .. 7·50
584 **200** 15 c. on 10 c. multicoloured (2 Dec) .. 10 10
a. Surch inverted .. .. .. 4·00
b. Surch double .. .. .. 7·50
c. Surch and dot transposed ..
d. Surch at right, dot omitted ..
585 **187** 25 c. on 6 c. multicoloured 15 50
a. Surch double, one inverted .. 15·00
b. Surch inverted .. .. .. 12·00
586 **194** 25 c. on 6 c. multicoloured 15 50
a. Surch inverted .. .. .. 4·00
582/6 .. .. *Set of* 5 1·60 2·75

Nos. 584c/d were caused by a misplacement of the surcharge on one sheet.

209 Colombo Plan Emblem and Ceylon

210 Globe and CARE Package

(Des P. A. Miththapala. Litho Harrison)

1971 (28 Dec). *20th Anniv of Colombo Plan. P* 14 × 14½.
587 **209** 20 c. multicoloured 15 20

(Des A. Dharmasiri. Litho Harrison)

1971 (28 Dec). *20th Anniv of CARE (Co-operative for American Relief Everywhere). P* 14 × 13½.
588 **210** 50 c. new blue, lilac and violet 35 30

211 W.H.O. Emblem and Heart

212 Map of Asia and U.N. Emblem

(Des A. Miththapala. Litho D.L.R.)

1972 (2 May). *World Health Day. P* 13 × 13½.
589 **211** 25 c. multicoloured 45 45

(Des L. D. P. Jayawardena. Litho B.W.)

1972 (2 May). *25th Anniv of ECAFE (Economic Commission for Asia and the Far East). P* 13.
590 **212** 85 c. multicoloured .. .. .. 1·75 1·75

SRI LANKA

REPUBLIC

Ceylon became the Republic of Sri Lanka on 22 May 1972.

208 National Flower and Mountain of the Illustrious Foot

209 Map of World with Buddhist Flag

(Des L. D. P. Jayawardena. Litho D.L.R.)

1972 (22 May). *Inauguration of the Republic of Sri Lanka. P* 13.
591 **208** 15 c. multicoloured 15 20

(Des L. D. P. Jayawardena. Litho Harrison)

1972 (26 May). *Tenth Conference of the World Fellowship of Buddhists. P* 14 × 13.
592 **209** 5 c. multicoloured 10 30
a. "1972" ptd double .. .. ..
b. "1972" ptd double, one inverted .. 20·00

This stamp was scheduled for release in May 1971, and when finally released had the year "1972" additionally overprinted in red. Sheets are known without this overprint but their status has not been established.

210 Book Year Emblem

211 Imperial Angelfish

(Des L. D. P. Jayawardena. Photo Pakistan Security Printing Corp)

1972 (8 Sept). *International Book Year. P* 13.
593 **210** 20 c. light yellow-orange and lake-brown 20 30

(Des G. D. Kariyawasam. Litho Rosenbaum Bros, Vienna)

1972 (12 Oct). *T* **211** *and similar horiz designs showing fish. Multicoloured. P* 13 × 13½.
594 2 c. Type **211** 10 40
a. Plum colour omitted .. .. .. 3·00
595 3 c. Green Chromide 10 40
596 30 c. Skipjack 75 15
597 2 r. Black Ruby Barb .. .. .. 1·50 2·00
594/7 .. .. *Set of* 4 2·25 2·75

On No. 594a the stripes of the fish are in green instead of plum.

NEW INFORMATION

The editor is always interested to correspond with people who have new information that will improve or correct the Catalogue.

212 Memorial Hall

(Des R. B. Mawilmada. Litho D.L.R.)

1973 (17 May). *Opening of Bandaranaike Memorial Hall. P* 14.
598 **212** 15 c. light cobalt and deep grey-blue .. 20 15

213 King Vessantara giving away his Children

214 Bandaranaike Memorial Conference Hall

(Des P. Wanigatunga. Litho D.L.R.)

1973 (3 Sept). *Rock and Temple Paintings. T* **213** *and similar vert designs. Multicoloured. P* 13½ × 14.
599 35 c. Type **213** 30 10
600 50 c. The Prince and the Grave-digger .. 35 10
601 90 c. Bearded old man 50 55
602 1 r. 55, Two female figures .. .. 65 1·00
599/602 .. .. *Set of* 4 1·60 1·60
MS603 115 × 141 mm. Nos. 599/602 .. .. 1·60 2·00

(Des and litho Harrison)

1974 (6 Sept). *20th Commonwealth Parliamentary Conference, Colombo. P* 14½.
604 **214** 85 c. multicoloured 20 20

215 Prime Minister Bandaranaike

216 "UPU" and "100"

(Des and photo Harrison)

1974 (25 Sept). *P* 14½.
605 **215** 15 c. multicoloured 15 10
a. Red (face value) omitted .. .. 3·00
b. Pale blue (background) omitted .. 4·00
c. Ultramarine (country inscr) omitted .. .. ..
d. Imperf (pair) .. .. ..

(Des P. Jayatillake. Litho German Bank Note Ptg Co, Leipzig)

1974 (9 Oct). *Centenary of Universal Postal Union. P* 13½ × 13.
606 **216** 50 c. multicoloured 65 65

217 Sri Lanka Parliament Building

218 Sir Ponnambalam Ramanathan (politician)

(Litho Toppan Printing Co, Japan)

1975 (1 Apr). *Inter-Parliamentary Meeting. P* 13.
607 **217** 1 r. multicoloured 30 50

(Des A. Rasiah. Litho Toppan Ptg Co, Japan)

1975 (4 Sep). *Ramanathan Commemoration. P* 13.
608 **218** 75 c. multicoloured 30 50

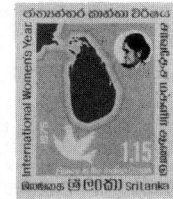

219 D. J. Wimalasurendra (engineer)

220 Mrs. Bandaranaike, Map and Dove

(Des A. Dharmasiri. Litho Toppan Ptg Co, Japan)

1975 (17 Sept). *Wimalasurendra Commemoration*. P 13.
609 **219** 75 c. blue-black and new blue 30 50

(Des B. U. Ananda Somatilaka. Litho Toppan Ptg Co, Japan)

1975 (22 Dec). *International Women's Year*. P 13.
610 **220** 1 r. 15, multicoloured .. .. .. 1·25 1·25

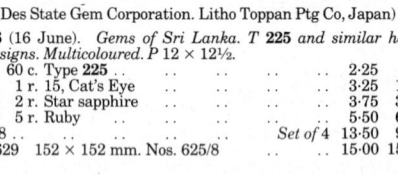

221 Ma-ratmal **222** Mahaweli Dam

(Des and litho Toppan Ptg Co, Japan)

1976 (1 Jan). *Indigenous Flora. T* **221** *and similar vert designs. Multicoloured*. P 13.
611 25 c. Type **221** 10 10
a. Imperf (pair) .. .. 55·00
612 50 c. Binara 10 10
613 75 c. Daffodil orchid 15 15
614 10 r. Diyapara .. .. 3·00 4·00
611/14 .. .. *Set of* 4 3·00 4·00
MS615 153 × 153 mm. Nos. 611/14 .. .. 5·50 6·00
A used example of No. 613 has been seen with the yellow printing apparently omitted. This results in the leaves appearing blue instead of green.

(Des R. B. Mawilmada. Litho German Bank Note Ptg Co, Leipzig)

1976 (8 Jan). *Diversion of the Mahaweli River*. P 13 × 12½.
616 **222** 85 c. turquoise, violet-blue and azure .. 30 50

223 Dish Aerial **224** Conception of the Buddha

(Des P. A. Miththapala. Litho German Bank Note Ptg Co, Leipzig)

1976 (6 May). *Opening of Satellite Earth Station, Padukka*. P 14 × 13½.
617 **223** 1 r. multicoloured 65 75

(Des P. Wanigatunga. Litho Toppan Ptg Co, Japan)

1976 (7 May). *Vesak. T* **224** *and similar horiz designs showing paintings from the Dambava Temple. Multicoloured*. P 13.
618 5 c. Type **224** 10 10
619 10 c. King Suddhodana and the astrologers .. 10 10
620 1 r. 50, The astrologers being entertained .. 20 30
621 2 r. The Queen in a palanquin 25 35
622 2 r. 25, Royal procession 30 70
623 5 r. Birth of the Buddha .. .. .. 70 1·40
618/23 .. .. *Set of* 6 1·40 2·50
MS624 161 × 95 mm. Nos. 618/23 .. .. 6·00 7·50

225 Blue Sapphire **226** Prime Minister Mrs. S. Bandaranaike

(Des State Gem Corporation. Litho Toppan Ptg Co, Japan)

1976 (16 June). *Gems of Sri Lanka. T* **225** *and similar horiz designs. Multicoloured*. P 12 × 12½.
625 60 c. Type **225** .. .. 2·25 30
626 1 r. 15, Cat's Eye .. .. 3·25 1·25
627 2 r. Star sapphire .. .. 3·75 3·25
628 5 r. Ruby .. .. 5·50 6·00
625/8 .. .. *Set of* 4 13·50 9·75
MS629 152 × 152 mm. Nos. 625/8 .. .. 15·00 15·00

(Photo Harrison)

1976 (3 Aug). *Non-aligned Summit Conference, Colombo*. P 14 × 14½.
630 **226** 1 r. 15, multicoloured 25 20
631 2 r. multicoloured 40 35

MINIMUM PRICE

The minimum price quote is 10p which represents a handling charge rather than a basis for valuing common stamps. For further notes about prices see introductory pages.

227 Statue of Liberty **228** Bell, Early Telephone and Telephone Lines

(Des A. Harischandra. Litho German Bank Note Ptg Co, Leipzig)

1976 (29 Nov). *Bicentenary of American Revolution*. P 13½.
632 **227** 2 r. 25, cobalt and indigo 65 75

(Des A. Harischandra. Litho German Bank Note Ptg Co, Leipzig)

1976 (21 Dec). *Telephone Centenary*. P 13.
633 **228** 1 r. multicoloured 30 20

229 Maitreya (pre-carnate Buddha) **230** Kandyan Crown

(Des P. Wanigatunga. Litho German Bank Note Ptg Co, Leipzig)

1977 (1 Jan). *Centenary of Colombo Museum. T* **229** *and similar vert designs showing statues. Multicoloured*. P 12½.
634 50 c. Type **229** 15 15
635 1 r. Sundara Murti Swami (Tamil psalmist) 30 30
636 5 r. Tara (goddess) .. .. 1·10 2·00
634/6 .. .. *Set of* 3 1·40 2·25

(Des R. B. Mawilmada. Litho Toppan Ptg Co, Japan)

1977 (18 Jan). *Regalia of the Kings of Kandy. T* **230** *and similar vert design. Multicoloured*. P 13.
637 1 r. Type **230** 35 40
638 2 r. Throne and footstool .. .. .. 75 2·00

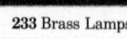

231 Sri Rahula Thero (poet) **232** Sir Ponnambalam Arunachalam (social reformer)

(Des S. Dissanayaka. Litho Toppan Ptg Co, Japan)

1977 (23 Feb). *Sri Rahula Commemoration*. P 13.
639 **231** 1 r. multicoloured 40 55

(Litho Toppan Ptg Co, Japan)

1977 (10 Mar). *Ponnambalam Arunachalam Commemoration*. P 13.
640 **232** 1 r. multicoloured 30 55

233 Brass Lamps

234 Siddi Lebbe (author and educationalist

(Des A. Harischandra. Litho Toppan Ptg Co, Japan)

1977 (7 Apr). *Handicrafts. T* **233** *and similar vert designs. Multicoloured*. P 13.
641 20 c. Type **233** 15 15
642 25 c. Jewellery box 15 15
643 50 c. Caparisoned elephant 30 15
644 5 r. Mask .. .. 1·60 2·75
641/4 .. .. *Set of* 4 2·00 3·00
MS645 205 × 89 mm. Nos. 641/4 .. .. .. 3·25 3·75

(Des Sarasvati Rockwood. Litho Toppan Ptg Co, Japan)

1977 (11 June). *Siddi Lebbe Commemoration*. P 13½.
646 **234** 1 r. multicoloured 30 60

235 Girl Guide **236** Parliament Building and "Wheel of Life"

(Des and litho Asher & Co, Melbourne)

1977 (13 Dec). *60th Anniv of Sri Lanka Girl Guides Association*. P 14½ × 15.
647 **235** 75 c. multicoloured 85 30

(Des R. B. Mawilmada. Photo Enschedé)

1978 (4 Feb). *Election of New President*. P 12 × 12½.
648 **236** 15 c. gold, brt yellow-green & emerald .. 20 10
No. 648 was re-issued on 7 September 1978, additionally dated "1978.09.07" to mark the Promulgation of the Constitution for the Democratic Socialist Republic of Sri Lanka. This re-issue was only available on First Day Covers (*Price on F.D.C.* £2).
See also Nos. 680/c.

237 Youths Running **238** Prince Siddhartha's Renunciation

(Des M. Dissanayake. Litho Asher & Co, Melbourne)

1978 (27 Apr). *National Youth Service Council*. P 15 × 14½.
649 **237** 15 c. multicoloured 20 20

(Des P. Wanigatunga. Litho Metal Box Singapore Ltd)

1978 (16 May). *Vesak. Rock Carvings from Borobudur Temple. T* **238** *and similar horiz design in buff, brown and ultramarine*. P 13.
650 15 c. Type **238** 25 10
651 50 c. Prince Siddhartha shaving his hair .. 45 40

•05

(**239**) **240** Veera Puran Appu

1978 (18 May–20 Nov). *Nos.* 559, 601/2, 605 *and* 648/9 *surch as T* **239**.
652 5 c. on 90 c. Bearded old man (26.6) .. 20 40
a. Surch inverted .. .. .. 12·00
b. Surch double .. ..
653 10 c. on 35 c. Type **213** 20 40
a. Surch inverted .. .. .. 12·00
654 25 c. on 15 c. Type **215** (20.11) .. .. 2·00 1·50
a. Dot after "25" (R.3/4) .. .. 11·00
655 25 c. on 15 c. Type **236** (20.11) .. .. 2·00 1·50
a. Surch inverted .. .. .. 10·00
b. Surch quadruple .. .. ..
656 25 c. on 15 c. Type **237** (Blk & Pink) (20.11) 2·00 1·50
a. Surch and obliterating square inverted 9·00
ab. Surch only inverted .. .. 8·50
657 1 r. on 1 r. 55, Two female figures (17.11) 60 45
a. Surch inverted .. .. ..
652/7 .. .. *Set of* 6 6·25 5·25
No. 656 has the surcharge applied in black on a pink square, previously printed over the original face value.

(Des A. Dharmasiri. Litho Metal Box Singapore Ltd)

1978 (8 Aug). *130th Death Anniv of Veera Puran Appu (revolutionary)*. P 13.
658 **240** 15 c. multicoloured 15 20

241 *Troides helena*

SRI LANKA

15

(**242**)

(Des G. Ratnavira. Litho J.W. or Questa (ptgs of 25 c. from 5 Jan 1990))

1978 (28 Nov). *Butterflies. T* **241** *and similar vert designs. Multicoloured. P* 14.

659 25 c. Type **241** 15 10
660 50 c. *Cethosia nietneri* 40 10
661 5 r. *Kallima horsfieldi* (s sp *philarchus*) .. 1·00 1·00
662 10 r. *Papilio polymnestor* .. .. 1·25 1·50
659/62 .. .. *Set of* 4 2·50 2·40
MS663 203×147 mm. Nos. 659/62 .. .. 5·50 6·00

1979 (22 Mar). *No.* 486 *surch with T* **242** *in black and turquoise-blue.*

664 15 c. on 10 c. myrtle-green 80 55
a. Surch double .. .. 12·00
b. Turq-blue surch omitted .. .. .. 20·00

Type **242** shows only part of the turquoise-blue section of the overprint ("SRI LANKA"), which also includes a rectangle obliterating the original face value. The new value is printed on this rectangle in black.

243 Prince Danta and Princess Hema Mala bringing the Sacred Tooth Relic from Kalinga

244 Piyadasa Sirisena

(Des A. Dharmasiri. Litho J.W.)

1979 (3 May). *Vesak. Kelaniya Temple Paintings. T* **243** *and similar vert designs. Multicoloured. P* 13 × 13½.

665 25 c. Type **243** 10 10
666 1 r. Theri Sanghamitta bringing the Bodhi Tree branch to Sri Lanka 15 15
667 10 r. King Kirti Sri Rajasinghe offering fan of authority to the Sangha Raja .. .. 95 1·10
665/7 .. .. *Set of* 3 1·00 1·10
MS668 120 × 80 mm. Nos. 665/7 .. .. .. 1·40 2·00

(Des P. Jayatillake. Litho Toppan Ptg Co, Japan)

1979 (22 May). *Piyadasa Sirisena (writer) Commemoration. P* 13.

669 **244** 1 r. 25, multicoloured 20 20

245 Wrestlers

246 Dudley Senanayake

(Des R. B. Mawilmada. Litho Metal Box Singapore Ltd)

1979 (28 May). *Wood Carvings from Embekke Temple. T* **245** *and similar vert design. P* 14.

670 20 r. chocolate, ochre and deep green .. 95 1·50
671 50 r. agate, bistre-yellow and deep green .. 2·25 3·00

Design:—50 r. Dancer.

(Photo Heraclio Fournier)

1979 (19 June). *Dudley Senanayake (former Prime Minister) Commemoration. P* 14.

672 **246** 1 r. 25, bottle green 15 20

247 Mother with Child

248 Ceylon 1857 6d. Stamp and Sir Rowland Hill

(Des A. Dharmasiri and R. Mawilmada. Litho Metal Box Singapore Ltd)

1979 (31 July). *International Year of the Child. T* **247** *and similar horiz designs. Multicoloured. P* 12½.

673 5 c. Type **247** 10 10
674 3 r. Superimposed heads of children of different races 30 70
675 5 r. Children playing 40 80
673/5 .. .. *Set of* 3 65 1·40

(Des A. Dharmasiri. Litho Toppan Ptg Co, Japan)

1979 (27 Aug). *Death Centenary of Sir Rowland Hill. P* 13.

676 **248** 3 r. multicoloured 25 45

249 Conference Emblem and Parliament Building

250 Airline Emblem on Aircraft Tail-fin

(Des A. Harischandra. Litho Toppan Ptg Co, Japan)

1979 (28 Aug). *International Conference of Parliamentarians on Population and Development, Colombo. P* 13.

677 **249** 2 r. multicoloured 30 50

(Des S. Saparamadu. Litho Metal Box Singapore Ltd)

1979 (1 Sept). *Inauguration of "Airlanka" Airline. P* 12½.

678 **250** 3 r. black, deep blue-green & vermilion 15 50

251 Coconut Tree

252 Swami Vipulananda

(Des G. Wathuwalagedara. Litho Metal Box Singapore Ltd)

1979 (10 Sept). *10th Anniv of Asian and Pacific Coconut Community. P* 14.

679 **251** 2 r. multicoloured 30 45

1979 (10 Oct)–**87**. *Design as No.* 648 *but smaller,* 20 × 24 *mm. P* 12½ × 13.

680 **236** 25 c. gold, brt yellow-green & emerald 15 20
680*a* 50 c. gold, brt yell-grn & emer (6.6.81) 1·00 10
680*b* 60 c. gold, bright yellow-green and emerald (30.12.83) .. .. 2·00 1·25
680*c* 75 c. gold, bright yellow-green and emerald (1.7.87) 10 10
680/c .. .. *Set of* 4 3·00 1·50

(Des R. B. Mawilmada. Litho Metal Box Singapore Ltd)

1979 (18 Nov). *Swami Vipulananda (philosopher) Commemoration. P* 12½.

681 **252** 1 r. 25, multicoloured 20 30

253 Inscription and Crescent

254 "The Great Teacher" (Institute emblem)

(Des Q. V. Saldin. Litho Metal Box Singapore Ltd)

1979 (22 Nov). *1500th Anniv of the Hegira (Mohammedan religion). P* 12½.

682 **253** 3 r. 75, black, deep green and blue-green 35 1·00

(Des H. P. Rupasinghe. Litho Metal Box Singapore Ltd)

1979 (29 Nov). *50th Anniv of Institute of Ayurveda (school of medicine). P* 13 × 12½.

683 **254** 15 c. multicoloured 20 30

255 Ceylon Blue Magpie

256 Rotary International Emblem and Map of Sri Lanka

(Des G. Ratnavira. Litho German Bank Note Ptg Co, Leipzig)

1979 (13 Dec). *Birds (1st series). T* **255** *and similar vert designs. Multicoloured. P* 13½×14.

684 10 c. Type **255** 10 10
685 15 c. Ceylon Hanging Parrot ("Ceylon Lorikeet") 10 10
686 75 c. Ceylon Whistling Thrush ("Ceylon Arrenga") 15 15
687 1 r. Ceylon Spurfowl 15 15
688 5 r. Yellow-fronted Barbet .. .. .. 60 1·00
689 10 r. Yellow-tufted Bulbul .. .. .. 75 1·75
684/9 .. .. *Set of* 6 1·75 2·75
MS690 151×151 mm. Nos. 684/9 .. .. 3·25 3·75

See also Nos. 827/31 and 985/9.

(Des A. Harischandra. Litho Metal Box Singapore Ltd)

1979 (27 Dec). *50th Anniv of Sri Lanka Rotary Movement and 75th Anniv of Rotary International. P* 14.

691 **256** 1 r. 50, multicoloured 30 45

257 A. Ratnayake

(258)

259 Tank and Stupa (symbols of Buddhist culture)

(Photo Govt Ptg Works, Rome)

1980 (7 Jan). *80th Birth Anniv of A. Ratnayake (politician). P* 13½.

692 **257** 1 r. 25, deep grey-green 20 30

1980 (17 Mar). *No.* 680 *surch with T* **258**.

693 **236** 35 c. on 25 c. gold, brt yell-grn & emer .. 15 15
a. Surch ".33" (R. 6/1) .. .. .. 15·00
b. Dot omitted (R. 7/6) .. .. .. 3·00

(Des R. B. Mawilmada. Photo Govt Ptg Works, Rome)

1980 (25 Mar). *60th Anniv of All Ceylon Buddhist Congress. T* **259** *and similar horiz design showing symbols of Buddhist culture. Multicoloured. P* 13½.

694 10 c. Type **259** 10 20
695 35 c. Bo-leaf wheel and fan 10 20

260 Colonel Olcott

261 Patachara's Journey through Forest

(Des S. Senevirante. Litho J.W.)

1980 (17 May). *Centenary of Arrival of Colonel Olcott (campaigner for Buddhism). P* 14.

696 **260** 2 r. multicoloured 40 50

(Des A. Dharmasiri. Litho Metal Box Singapore Ltd)

1980 (23 May). *Vesak. Details from Temple Paintings, Purvaramaya, Kataluwa. T* **261** *and similar horiz design. Multicoloured. P* 13½.

697 35 c. Type **261** 15 15
698 1 r. 60, Patachara crossing river 40 65

262 George E. de Silva

263 Dalada Maligawa

(Des A. Rasiah. Litho German Bank Note Ptg Co, Leipzig)

1980 (8 June). *George E. de Silva (politician) Commemoration. P* 13.

699 **262** 1 r. 60, multicoloured 15 20

(Des A. Dharmasiri and R. B. Mawilmada. Litho Metal Box Singapore Ltd)

1980 (25 Aug). *U.N.E.S.C.O.—Sri Lanka Cultural Triangle Project. T* **263** *and similar horiz designs. P* 13.

700 35 c. claret 10 15
701 35 c. grey 10 15
702 35 c. rose-carmine 10 15
703 1 r. 60, olive-green 20 40
704 1 r. 60, slate-green 20 40
705 1 r. 60, sepia 20 40
700/5 .. .. *Set of* 6 70 1·50
MS706 215 × 115 mm. Nos. 700/5 .. .. 70 1·50

Designs:—No. 701, Dambulla; No. 702, Alahana Pirivena; No. 703, Jetavanarama; No. 704, Abhayagiri; No. 705, Sigiri.

264 Co-operation Symbols

265 Lanka Mahila Samiti Emblem

(Des R. B. Mawilmada. Litho Metal Box Singapore Ltd)

1980 (1 Oct). *50th Anniv of Co-operative Department. P* 13.
707 **264** 20 c. multicoloured 10 10

(Des R. B. Mawilmada. Photo Govt Ptg Works, Rome)

1980 (7 Nov). *50th Anniv of Lanka Mahila Samiti (Rural Women's Movement). P* 14 × 13.
708 **265** 35 c. violet, rosine and yellow 10 10

266 The Holy Family

267 Colombo Public Library

(Des L. Priyantha Silva. Litho Metal Box Singapore Ltd)

1980 (20 Nov). *Christmas. T* **266** *and similar vert design. Multicoloured. P* 12 × 11½.
709 35 c. Type **266** 10 10
710 3 r. 75, The Three Wise Men 25 40
MS711 125 × 75 mm. Nos. 709/10. P 13½ .. 40 70

(Des P. Jayatillake. Litho Toppan Ptg Co, Japan)

1980 (17 Dec). *Opening of Colombo Public Library. P* 12 × 12½.
712 **267** 35 c. multicoloured 10 10

268 Flag of Walapane Disawa

269 Fishing Cat

(Des Mrs. J. L. M. Fernando. Litho Toppan Ptg Co, Japan)

1980 (18 Dec). *Ancient Flags. T* **268** *and similar horiz designs. P* 13.
713 10 c. black, green and brown-purple 10 10
714 25 c. black, greenish yellow and brown-purple 10 10
715 1 r. 60, black, greenish yellow & brn-purple 15 20
716 20 r. black, greenish yellow and brown-purple 1·25 2·25
713/16 .. .. *Set of* 4 1·40 2·25
MS717 215 × 140 mm. Nos. 713/16 .. .. 1·60 2·25
Designs:—25 c. Flag of the Gajanayaka, Huduhumpola, Kandy; 1 r. 60, Sinhala royal flag; 20 r. Sinhala royal flag, Ratnapura.

(Des L. Ranasinghe. Litho J.W.)

1981 (10 Feb). *Animals. T* **269** *and similar horiz designs. Multicoloured. P* 13½ × 14.
718 2 r. 50 on 1 r. 60, Type **269** 15 15
719 3 r. on 1 r. 50, Golden Palm Civet 15 20
720 4 r. on 2 r. Indian Spotted Chevrotain .. 25 30
721 5 r. on 3 r. 75, Rusty-spotted Cat 35 45
718/21 .. .. *Set of* 4 80 1·00
MS722 165 × 89 mm. Nos. 718/21 .. .. 1·00 2·00
Nos. 718/21 are previously unissued stamps surcharged as in T **269**.
For redrawn designs with revised face values see Nos. 780/3 and No. 1081.

270 Heads and Houses on Map of Sri Lanka

271 Sri Lanka Light Infantry Regimental Badge

(Des D. Hemaratna. Litho Toppan Ptg Co, Japan)

1981 (2 Mar). *Population and Housing Census. P* 12½ × 12.
723 **270** 50 c. multicoloured 15 30

(Des D. Karunaratne. Litho Metal Box Singapore Ltd)

1981 (1 Apr). *Centenary of Sri Lanka Light Infantry. P* 12 × 11½.
724 **271** 2 r. multicoloured 55 30

ALTERED CATALOGUE NUMBERS

Any Catalogue numbers altered from the last edition are shown as a list in the introductory pages.

272 Panel from "The Great Stupa" in Honour of the Buddha, Sanci, India, 1st-century A.D.

273 St. John Baptist de la Salle

(Des P. Jayatillake. Litho German Bank Note Ptg Co, Leipzig)

1981 (5 May). *Vesak. T* **272** *and similar vert designs. P* 13 × 13½.
725 35 c. black, blackish green and sage-green .. 10 10
726 50 c. multicoloured 10 10
727 7 r. black and flesh .. .. 40 1·00
725/7 .. .. *Set of* 3 45 1·10
MS728 147 × 108 mm. Nos. 725/7. P 13 × 14. .. 2·25 1·75
Designs:—50 c. Silk banner representing a Bodhisattva from "Thousand Buddhas", Tun-Huang, Central Asia; 7 r. Bodhisattva from Fondukistan, Afghanistan.

(Des Grant Kenyon and Eckhardt Ltd. Litho State Printing Works, Moscow)

1981 (15 May). *300th Anniv of De La Salle Brothers (Religious Order of the Brothers of the Christian Schools). P* 12½ × 12.
729 **273** 2 r. brt rose, deep violet-blue & new blue 70 50

274 Rev. Polwatte Sri Buddadatta

275 Dr. Al-Haj T. B. Jayah

(Des G. Fernando. Litho Metal Box Singapore Ltd)

1981 (22 May). *National Heroes. T* **274** *and similar vert designs, each showing scholar, writer and Buddhist campaigner. P* 12.
730 50 c. bistre 30 45
731 50 c. brown-rose 30 45
732 50 c. deep mauve 30 45
730/2 .. .. *Set of* 3 80 1·25
Designs:—No. 731, Rev. Mohottiwatte Gunananda; No. 732, Dr. Gnanaprakasar.

(Des P. Jayatillake. Litho Metal Box Singapore Ltd)

1981 (31 May). *Dr. Al-Haj T. B. Jayah (statesman) Commemoration. P* 12.
733 **275** 50 c. grey-green 30 40

276 Dr. N. M. Perera

277 Stylised Disabled Person and Globe

(Des P. Jayatillake. Litho Metal Box Singapore Ltd)

1981 (6 June). *Dr. N. M. Perera (campaigner for social reform) Commemoration. P* 12.
734 **276** 50 c. rose-red 30 40

(Des A. Adhikari. Litho State Printing Works, Moscow)

1981 (19 June). *International Year for Disabled Persons. P* 12 × 12½.
735 **277** 2 r. vermilion, black and grey 40 50

278 Hand placing Vote into Ballot Box

(Des J. Vincent (50 c.), R. Mawilmada (7 r.). Litho State Printing Works, Moscow)

1981 (7 July). *50th Anniv of Universal Franchise. T* **278** *and similar multicoloured design. P* 12½ × 12 *(50 c.) or* 12 × 12½ *(7 r.)*
736 50 c. Type **278** 15 10
737 7 r. Ballot box, and people forming map of Sri Lanka (*vert*) .. .. 1·00 60

279 T. W. Rhys Davids (founder)

280 Federation Emblem and "25"

(Des P. Jayatillake. Litho State Printing Works, Moscow)

1981 (14 July). *Centenary of Pali Text Society. P* 12½ × 12.
738 **279** 35 c. stone, dp brown & orange-brown .. 50 20

(Des R. Mawilmada. Litho Secura, Singapore)

1981 (21 July). *25th Anniv of All Ceylon Buddhist Students' Federation. P* 13½.
739 **280** 2 r. black, greenish yellow & dull verm 60 30

281 "Plan for Happiness"

282 Dove Symbol with Acupuncture Needle and "Yin-Yang" (Chinese universe duality emblem)

(Des D. Wijesinghe. Litho Secura, Singapore)

1981 (25 Sept). *Population and Family Planning. P* 13½ × 13.
740 **281** 50 c. multicoloured 50 30

(Des F. Perera. Litho State Printing Works, Moscow)

1981 (20 Oct). *World Acupuncture Congress. P* 12 × 12½.
741 **282** 2 r. black, yellow and red-orange .. 1·75 2·00

283 Union and Sri Lanka Flags

284 "Conserve our Forests"

(Des and litho J.W.)

1981 (21 Oct). *Royal Visit. P* 14.
742 **283** 50 c. multicoloured 30 20
743 5 r. multicoloured .. .. .. 1·25 1·50
MS744 165 × 90 mm. Nos. 742/3 .. .. .. 1·50 2·00

(Des Ravi Advertising. Litho German Bank Note Co, Leipzig)

1981 (27 Nov). *Forest Conservation. T* **284** *and similar horiz designs. P* 13.
745 35 c. multicoloured 10 10
746 50 c. olive-brown and stone 10 15
747 5 r. multicoloured .. .. 1·25 1·75
745/7 .. .. *Set of* 3 1·25 1·75
MS748 180 × 90 mm. Nos. 745/7. P 14 × 13 .. 1·50 2·00
Designs:—50 c. "Plant a tree"; 5 r. Jak (tree).

285 Sir James Peiris

286 F. R. Senanayaka

(Des P. Jayatillake. Litho Metal Box Singapore Ltd)

1981 (20 Dec). *Birth Centenary of Sir James Peiris (politician). P* 12.
749 **285** 50 c. light brown 45 40

(Des M. Katugampola. Litho J.W.)

1982 (1 Jan). *Birth Centenary of F. R. Senanayaka (national hero). P* 14.
750 **286** 50 c. olive-brown 45 45

287 Philip Gunawardhane 288 Department of Inland Revenue Building, Colombo

(Des P. Jayatillake. Litho J.W.)

1982 (11 Jan). *10th Death Anniv of Philip Gunawardhane (politician). P* 14.
751 **287** 50 c. cerise 45 45

(Des S. Mallikerachchi. Litho J.W.)

1982 (9 Feb). *50th Anniv of Department of Inland Revenue. P* 14.
752 **288** 50 c. black, blue-black & reddish orange 45 45

289 Rupavahini Emblem 290 Cricketer and Ball

(Des G. Arthasad. Litho J.W.)

1982 (15 Feb). *Inauguration of Rupavahini (national television service). P* 14.
753 **289** 2 r. 50, lemon, purple-brown and grey 1·50 1·75

(Des R. Mawilmada. Litho J.W.)

1982 (17 Feb). *First Sri Lanka–England Cricket Test Match, Colombo. P* 14.
754 **290** 2 r. 50, multicoloured .. .. 3·00 3·00

291 *Obsbeckia wightiana* 292 Mother breast-feeding Child

(Des P. Jayatillake. Litho Security Printers (M), Malaysia)

1982 (1 Apr). *Flowers. T* **291** *and similar horiz designs. Multi-coloured. P* 12.
755 35 c. Type **291** 10 10
756 2 r. *Mesua nagassarium* 20 20
757 7 r. *Rhodomyrtus tomentosa* 50 90
758 20 r. *Phaius tancarvilleae* .. .. .. 1·40 2·50
755/8 .. .. *Set of* 4 2·00 3·25
MS759 180 × 110 mm. Nos. 755/8 .. .. 4·50 5·50

(Des A. Ratnapala. Litho Pakistan Security Printing Corp)

1982 (6 Apr). *Food and Nutrition Policy Planning. P* 13.
760 **292** 50 c. multicoloured 60 60

293 Conference Emblem 294 King Vessantara giving away magical, rain-making White Elephant

(Des M. Hussain. Litho J.W.)

1982 (21 Apr). *World Hindu Conference. P* 14.
761 **293** 50 c. multicoloured 60 60

(Des A. Dharmasiri. Litho J.W.)

1982 (23 Apr). *Vesak. Legend of Vessantara Jataka. Details of Cloth Painting from Arattana Rajamaha Vihara (temple), Hanguranketa, District of Nuwara Eliya. T* **294** *and similar horiz designs. Multicoloured. P* 14.
762 35 c. Type **294** 30 10
763 50 c. King Vessantara with family in Vankagiri Forest 40 15
764 2 r. 50, Vessantara giving away his children as slaves .. .. 1·25 1·50
765 5 r. Vessantara and family returning to Jetuttara in royal chariot .. .. 2·00 2·75
762/5 .. .. *Set of* 4 3·50 4·00
MS766 160 × 115 mm. Nos. 762/5 .. .. 4·00 4·00

295 Parliament Buildings, Sri Jayawardanapura 296 Dr. C. W. W. Kannangara

(Des M. Katugampola. Litho J.W.)

1982 (29 Apr). *Opening of Parliament Building Complex, Sri Jayawardanapura, Kotte. P* 14.
767 **295** 50 c. multicoloured 60 60

(Des M. Katugampola. Litho State Printing Works, Moscow)

1982 (22 May). *Dr. C. W. W. Kannangara ("Father of Free Education") Commemoration. P* 12 × 12½.
768 **296** 50 c. yellow-olive 60 60

297 Lord Baden-Powell 298 Dr. G. P. Malalasekara

(Des W. Rohana. Litho State Printing Works, Moscow)

1982 (24 May). *125th Birth Anniv of Lord Baden-Powell. P* 12½ × 12.
769 **297** 50 c. multicoloured 90 60

(Des A. Rasiah. Litho State Printing Works, Moscow)

1982 (26 May). *Dr. G. P. Malalasekara (founder of World Fellowship of Buddhists) Commemoration. P* 12 × 12½.
770 **298** 50 c. deep bluish green 60 60

299 Wheel encircling Globe 300 Wildlife

(Des A. Ratnapala. Litho State Printing Works, Moscow)

1982 (1 June). *World Buddhist Leaders Conference. P* 12½ × 12.
771 **299** 50 c. multicoloured 60 60

(Des U. Karunaratna. Litho State Printing Works, Moscow)

1982 (5 June). *World Environment Day. P* 12½ × 12.
772 **300** 50 c. multicoloured .. .. 1·00 60

301 Sir Waitialingam Duraiswamy

(Des A. Rasiah. Litho State Printing Works, Moscow)

1982 (14 June). *Sir Waitialingam Duraiswamy (statesman and educationalist) Commemoration. P* 12 × 12½.
773 **301** 50 c. blackish brown and brown .. 55 55

302 Y.M.C.A. Emblem

(Des R. Mawilmada. Litho State Printing Works, Moscow)

1982 (24 June). *Centenary of Colombo Y.M.C.A. P* 11½ × 11.
774 **302** 2 r. 50, multicoloured .. .. .. 2·00 2·25

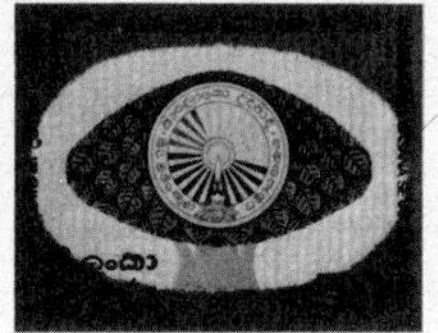

303 Rev. Weliwita Sri Saranankara Sangharaja 304 Maharagama Sasana Sevaka Samithiya Emblem

(Des M. Katugampola. Litho State Printing Works, Moscow)

1982 (5 July). *Rev. Weliwita Sri Saranankara Sangharaja (Buddhist leader) Commemoration. P* 12 × 12½.
775 **303** 50 c. brown and yellow-orange 60 60

(Des A. Ratnapala. Litho Toppan Ptg Co, Japan)

1982 (4 Aug). *Silver Jubilee of Maharagama Sasana Sevaka Samithiya (Buddhist Social Reform Movement). P* 12 × 12½.
776 **304** 50 c. multicoloured 60 60

305 Dr. Robert Koch 306 Sir John Kotelawala

(Des W. Rohana. Litho Toppan Ptg Co, Japan)

1982 (21 Sept). *Centenary of Robert Koch's Discovery of Tubercle Bacillus. P* 12 × 12½.
777 **305** 50 c. multicoloured .. .. .. 1·00 60

(Des A. Rasiah. Litho State Printing Works, Moscow)

1982 (2 Oct). *2nd Death Anniv of Sir John Kotelawala. P* 12 × 12½.
778 **306** 50 c. deep olive 60 60

307 Eye Donation Society and Lions Club Emblems 308 1859 4d. Dull Rose and 1948 15 c. Independence Commemorative

(Des Grant Kenyon and Eckhardt Ltd. Litho State Printing Works, Moscow)

1982 (16 Nov). *World-Wide Sight Conservation Project. P* 12 × 12½.
779 **307** 2 r. 50, multicoloured .. .. .. 1·40 1·60

(Des L. Ranasinghe. Litho Questa (5 r.) or J.W. (others))

1982 (16 Nov)–**89**. *As Nos. 718/21, but without surcharges and showing revised face values. P* 14.
780 2 r. 50, Type **269** (1.6.83) 10 10
781 3 r. Golden Palm Civet (21.6.83) 30 30
782 4 r. Indian Spotted Chevrotain 10 15
783 5 r. Rusty-spotted Cat (1.12.89) 15 20
780/3 .. .. *Set of* 4 55 60
For the 3 r. in similar design, but printed by Questa with imprint date see No. 1081.

(Des D. Karunaratne. Litho Security Printers (M), Malaysia)

1982 (2 Dec). *125th Anniv of First Postage Stamps. T* **308** *and similar horiz design. Multicoloured. P* 13 × 13½.
784 50 c. Type **308** 15 25
785 2 r. 50, 1859 1s. 9d. green and 1981 50 c. "Just Society" stamp 50 85
MS786 59 × 84 mm. Nos. 784/5 (*sold at* 5 r.) .. 65 1·25

309 Sir Oliver Goonetilleke

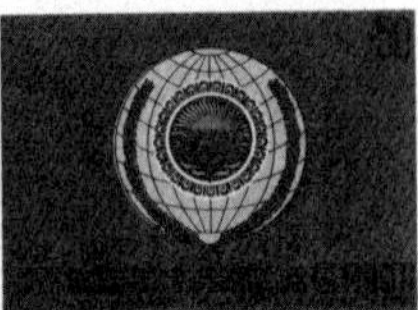

310 Sarvodaya Emblem

(Des A. Ratnapala. Litho State Printing Works, Moscow)

1982 (17 Dec). *4th Death Anniv of Sir Oliver Goonetilleke (statesman). P* 12 × 12½.
787 **309** 50 c. olive-grey, bistre-brown and black .. 30 40

(Des P. Gunasinghe. Litho Secura, Singapore)

1983 (1 Jan). *25th Anniv of Sarvodaya Movement. P* 13 × 13½.
788 **310** 50 c. multicoloured 60 60

311 Morse Key, Radio Aerial and Radio Amateur Society Emblem

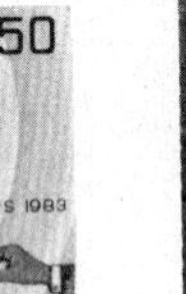

312 Customs Co-operation Council Emblem and Sri Lanka Flag

(Des W. Rohana. Litho Secura, Singapore)

1983 (17 Jan). *Amateur Radio Society. P* 13 × 13½.
789 **311** 2 r. 50, multicoloured .. .. 2·00 2·50

(Des W. Rohana. Litho Secura, Singapore)

1983 (26 Jan). *30th Anniv of International Customs Day. P* 12 × 11½.
790 **312** 50 c. multicoloured 30 30
791 5 r. multicoloured .. .. 2·25 2·50

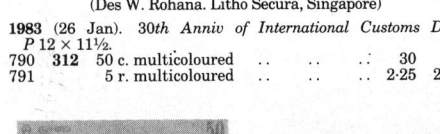

313 Bottle-nosed Dolphin

314 *Lanka Athula* (container ship)

(Des G. Ratnavira. Litho Harrison)

1983 (22 Feb). *Marine Mammals. T* **313** *and similar horiz designs. P* 14½ × 14.
792 50 c. black, new blue and grey-green .. 25 15
793 2 r. multicoloured 40 55
794 2 r. 50, black, dp grey-blue & dp bluish grey 50 55
795 10 r. multicoloured .. .. 1·40 1·75
792/5 .. .. *Set of* 4 2·25 2·75
Designs:—2 r. Dugongs; 2 r. 50, Humpback Whale; 10 r. Sperm Whale.

(Des Vision Ltd. Litho Security Printers (M), Malaysia)

1983 (1 Mar). *Ships of the Ceylon Shipping Corporation. T* **314** *and similar horiz designs. Multicoloured. P* 11½ × 12.
796 50 c. Type **314**.. .. .. 10 10
797 2 r. 50, Map of routes 15 30
798 5 r. *Lanka Kalyani* (freighter) 25 65
799 20 r. *Tammanna* (tanker) .. .. .. 1·10 2·25
796/9 .. .. *Set of* 4 1·40 3·00

315 Woman with I.W.D. Emblem and Sri Lanka Flag

316 Waterfall

(Des R. Mawilmada. Litho Secura, Singapore)

1983 (8 Mar). *International Women's Day. T* **315** *and similar vert design. Multicoloured. P* 13.
800 50 c. Type **315**.. .. .. 10 15
801 5 r. Woman, emblem, map and symbols of progress 25 60

(Des S. Lankatilake. Litho Secura, Singapore)

1983 (14 Mar). *Commonwealth Day. T* **316** *and similar horiz designs. Multicoloured. P* 13.
802 50 c. Type **316**.. .. .. 10 10
803 2 r. 50, Tea plucking 15 25
804 5 r. Harvesting rice 25 40
805 20 r. Decorated elephants .. .. .. 80 2·00
802/5 .. .. *Set of* 4 1·10 2·50

317 Lions Club International Badge

318 "The Dream of Queen Mahamaya"

(Des U. Karunaratna. Litho J.W.)

1983 (7 May). *25th Anniv of Lions Club International in Sri Lanka. P* 14.
806 **317** 2 r. 50, multicoloured .. .. .. 1·25 1·25

(Des G. Keyt and A. Dharmasiri. Litho Toppan Ptg Co, Japan)

1983 (13 May). *Vesak. Life of Prince Siddhartha from temple murals at Gotami Vihara. T* **318** *and similar vert designs. Multicoloured. P* 12½ × 12.
807 35 c. Type **318**.. .. .. 10 10
808 50 c. "Prince Siddhartha given to Maha Brahma".. .. .. 10 10
809 5 r. "Prince Siddhartha and the Sleeping Dancers".. .. .. 25 60
810 10 r. "The Meeting with Mara" .. .. 55 1·50
807/10 .. .. *Set of* 4 80 2·10
MS811 150 × 90 mm. Nos. 807/10 .. .. 90 2·10

319 First Telegraph Transmission Colombo to Galle, 1858

320 Henry Woodward Amarasuriya (philanthropist)

(Des W. Rohana. Litho Toppan Ptg Co, Japan)

1983 (17 May). *125th Anniv of Telecommunications in Sri Lanka (2 r.) and World Communications Year (10 r.). T* **319** *and similar horiz design. Multicoloured. P* 12 × 12½.
812 2 r. Type **319**.. .. .. 10 35
813 10 r. World Communications Year emblem.. 55 1·40

(Litho Security Printers (M), Malaysia (No. 810), Pakistan Security Printing Corp (others))

1983 (22 May). *National Heroes. T* **320** *and similar vert designs. P* 12 × 11½ *(No. 814) or* 13 *(others).*
814 50 c. bright emerald 20 35
815 50 c. new blue.. .. .. 20 35
816 50 c. magenta.. .. .. 20 35
817 50 c. turquoise-green.. .. .. .. 20 35
814/17 .. .. *Set of* 4 70 1·25
Designs:—No. 815, Father Simon Perera (historian); No. 816, Charles Lorenz (lawyer and newspaper editor); No. 817, Noordeen Abdul Cader (first President of All-Ceylon Muslim League).
A fifth design to commemorate C. W. Thamotheram Pillai was prepared for this set, but was withdrawn at the last moment when it was realised that the wrong portrait had been used. It is understood, however, that supplies were sold at some rural post offices where the instruction was not received in time. A corrected version was later issued, see No. 825.

321 Family and Village

322 Caravan of Bulls

(Des K. Gunasiri and U. Karunaratna. Litho Toppan Ptg Co, Japan)

1983 (23 June). *Gam Udawa (Village Re-awakening Movement). T* **321** *and similar horiz design. Multicoloured. P* 12 × 12½.
818 50 c. Type **321**.. .. .. 10 15
819 5 r. Village view 25 65

(Des A. Rasiah (35 c., 2 r.), D. Hemaratna (2 r. 50), U. Karunaratna (5 r.). Litho State Printing Office, Budapest)

1983 (22 Aug). *Transport. T* **322** *and similar horiz designs. Multicoloured. P* 12
820 35 c. Type **322**.. .. .. 10 10
821 2 r. Steam train 50 65
822 2 r. 50, Ox and cart 50 80
823 5 r. Ford motor car .. .. 85 1·60
820/3 .. .. *Set of* 4 1·75 2·75

323 Sir Tikiri Banda Panabokke

324 C. W. Thamotheram Pillai

(Des and litho Harrison)

1983 (2 Sept). *20th Death Anniv of Adigar Sir Tikiri Banda Panabokke. P* 14 × 14½.
824 **323** 50 c. Indian red 60 60

(Des and litho Pakistan Security Printing Corp)

1983 (1 Oct). *C. W. Thamotheram Pillai (Tamil scholar) Commemoration. P* 13.
825 **324** 50 c. orange-brown 60 60
See note below No. 817.

325 Arabi Pasha

326 Sri Lanka Wood Pigeon

(Des and litho Pakistan Security Printing Corp)

1983 (13 Nov). *Centenary of the Exile to Ceylon of Arabi Pasha (Egyptian nationalist). P* 13 × 13½.
826 **325** 50 c. green 60 60

(Des G. Ratnavira. Litho Format)

1983 (22 Nov)–**88**. *Birds (2nd series). T* **326** *and similar horiz designs. Multicoloured. P* 14½.
827 25 c. Type **326** 10 10
828 35 c. Large Sri Lanka White Eye 10 10
829 2 r. Sri Lanka Dusky Blue Flycatcher .. 10 10
829*a* 7 r. As 35 c. (28.9.88) 20 25
830 20 r. Ceylon Coucal 55 60
827/30 .. .. *Set of* 5 80 90
MS831 183 × 93 mm. Nos. 827/9 and 830 .. 4·00 4·50

327 Pelene Siri Vajiragnana

328 Mary praying over Jesus and St. Joseph welcoming Shepherds

(Des and litho Harrison)

1983 (25 Nov). *Pelene Siri Vajiragnana (scholar) Commemoration. P* 14 × 14½.
832 **327** 50 c. red-brown.. .. .. 60 60

(Des P. de Silva. Litho German Bank Note Co, Leipzig)

1983 (30 Nov). *Christmas. P* 12½ × 13.
833 **328** 50 c. multicoloured 10 15
834 5 r. multicoloured 25 60
MS835 85 × 141 mm. Nos. 833/4 .. .. .. 50 1·00

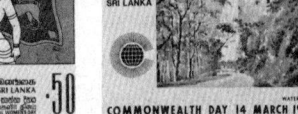

(329) (330)

1983 (1 Dec). *No. 680a surch with T* **329/30** *by Aitken Spence Ptg (Pte) Ltd, Sri Lanka.*
836 **236** 60 c. on 50 c. gold, bright yellow-green and emerald (surch T **329**) .. 40 40
a. Surch inverted .. .. ..
837 60 c. on 50 c. gold, bright yellow-green and emerald (surch T **330**) .. 1·50 1·50

331 Paddy Field, Globe and F.A.O. Emblem

(Des R. Mawilmada. Litho State Ptg Works, Moscow)

1984 (2 Jan). *World Food Day. P* 12½ × 12.
838 **331** 3 r. multicoloured 30 60

332 Modern Tea Factory **333** Students and University

(Des M. Ratnapala. Litho State Ptg Works, Moscow)

1984 (31 Jan). *Centenary of the Colombo Tea Auctions. T* **332** *and similar horiz designs. Multicoloured. P* 12½ × 12.
839 1 r. Type **332** 10 15
840 2 r. Logo 15 35
841 5 r. Girl picking tea 30 80
842 10 r. Auction in progress .. .. .. 65 1·60
839/42 .. .. *Set of* 4 1·00 2·75

(Des R. Mawilmada. Litho Security Printers (M), Malaysia)

1984 (10 Feb). *4th Anniv of Mahapola Scheme for Development and Education. T* **333** *and similar vert designs. Multicoloured. P* 12.
843 60 c. Type **333** 10 15
844 1 r. Teacher with Gnana Darsana class .. 10 15
845 5 r. 50, Student with books and microscope 35 1·00
846 6 r. Mahapola lamp symbol .. .. 40 1·25
843/6 .. .. *Set of* 4 75 2·25

334 King Daham Sonda instructing Angels **335** Development Programme Logo

(Des A. Dharmasiri. Litho D.L.R)

1984 (27 Apr). *Vesak. The Story of King Daham Sonda from ancient casket paintings. T* **334** *and similar horiz designs. Multicoloured. A. P* 14. *B. P* 13 × 13½.

		A		B	
847	35 c. Type **334**	10	10	25	20
848	60 c. Elephant paraded with gift of gold	10	25	20	30
849	5 r. King Daham Sonda leaps into mouth of God Sakra ..	30	85	45	1·25
850	10 r. God Sakra carrying King Daham Sonda	65	1·50	65	2·00
847/50	.. .. .. *Set of* 4	95	2·40	1·40	3·25
MS851	154 × 109 mm. Nos. 847/50. P 13			1·00	2·00

(Des R. Mawilmada. Litho Harrison)

1984 (5 May). *Sri Lanka Lions Clubs' Development Programme. P* 14 × 14½.
852 **335** 60 c. multicoloured 60 60

336 Dodanduwe Siri Piyaratana Tissa Mahanayake Thero (Buddhist scholar) **337** Association Emblem

(Litho State Ptg Works, Moscow)

1984 (22 May). *National Heroes. T* **336** *and similar vert designs. P* 12 × 12½.
853 60 c. yellow-bistre 10 20
854 60 c. yellow-green 10 20
855 60 c. emerald-green 10 20
856 60 c. red 10 20
857 60 c. deep yellow-brown 10 20
853/7 .. .. *Set of* 5 30 90

Designs:—No. 853, Type **336**; 854, G. P. Wickremarachchi (physician); 855, Sir Mohamed Macan Markar (politician); 856, Dr. W. Arthur de Silva (philanthropist), 857, K. Balasingham (lawyer).

(Des A. Harischandra. Litho Govt Printing Bureau, Tokyo)

1984 (16 June). *Centenary of Public Service Mutual Provident Association. P* 13 × 13½.
858 **337** 4 r. 60, multicoloured 30 90

338 Sri Lanka Village **339** World Map showing A.P.B.U. Countries

(Des S. Herath. Litho State Ptg Wks, Moscow)

1984 (23 June). *6th Anniv of "Gam Udawa" (Village Reawakening Movement). P* 12 × 12½.
859 **338** 60 c. multicoloured 20 30

(Des G. Arthasad. Litho State Ptg Wks, Moscow)

1984 (30 June). *20th Anniv of Asia-Pacific Broadcasting Union. P* 12½ × 12.
860 **339** 7 r. multicoloured .. .. .. 1·10 1·50

340 Drummers and Elephant carrying Royal Instructions **341** *Vanda memoria* Ernest Soysa (orchid)

(Des R. Mawilmada. Litho State Ptg Wks, Moscow)

1984 (11 Aug). *Esala Perahera (Procession of the Tooth), Kandy. T* **340** *and similar horiz designs. Multicoloured. P* 12½ × 12.
861 4 r. 60, Type **340** 70 90
a. Horiz strip of 4. Nos. 861/4 .. .. 2·50
862 4 r. 60, Dancers and elephants 70 90
863 4 r. 60, Elephant carrying Tooth Relic .. 70 90
864 4 r. 60, Custodian of the Sacred Tooth and attendants 70 90
861/4 .. .. *Set of* 4 2·50 3·25
MS865 223 × 108 mm. Nos. 861/4 .. .. 2·50 3·50

Nos. 861/4 were printed together, *se-tenant*, in horizontal strips of 4 throughout the sheet, forming a composite design.

(Des G. Ratnavira. Litho D.L.R.)

1984 (22 Aug). *50th Anniv of Ceylon Orchid Circle. T* **341** *and similar vert designs, showing orchids. Multicoloured. A. P* 14. *B. P* 13½ × 13.

		A		B	
866	60 c. Type **341**	50	20	25	40
867	4 r. 60, *Acanthephippium bicolor*	1·25	1·75	65	1·75
868	5 r. *Vanda tessellata var. rufescens*	1·75	2·00	45	1·75
869	10 r. *Anoectochilus setaceus* ..	1·75	2·75	†	
866/9	.. .. .. *Set of* 4	4·75	6·00	†	
MS870	155 × 110 mm. Nos. 866/9. P 13			4·25	5·00

342 Symbolic Athletes and Stadium **343** D. S. Senanayake, Temple and Fields

(Des M. Heenkenda. Litho Govt Printing Bureau, Tokyo)

1984 (5 Oct). *1st National School Games. P* 13½ × 13.
871 **342** 60 c. black, grey and bright new blue .. 50 50

(Des L. Jayawardena (35 c.), G. Fernando (60 c.), N. Lasantha (4 r. 60), R. Mawilmada (6 r.). Litho J.W.)

1984 (20 Oct). *Birth Centenary of D. S. Senanayake (former Prime Minister). T* **343** *and similar horiz designs. Multicoloured. P* 14.
872 35 c. Type **343** 10 10
873 60 c. Senanayake and statue 10 10
874 4 r. 60, Senanayake and irrigation project .. 25 50
875 6 r. Senanayake and House of Representatives 30 60
872/5 .. .. *Set of* 4 55 1·10

344 Lake House **345** Agricultural Workers and Globe

(Des Grant Kenyon and Eckhardt Ltd. Litho State Printing Office, Budapest)

1984 (19 Nov). *150th Anniv of the "Observer" Newspaper. P* 13 × 13½.
876 **344** 4 r. 60, multicoloured .. .. .. 50 1·10

(Des M. Ratnapala. Litho German Bank Note Ptg Co, Leipzig)

1984 (10 Dec). *20th Anniv of World Food Programme. P* 13 × 13½.
877 **345** 7 r. multicoloured 70 75

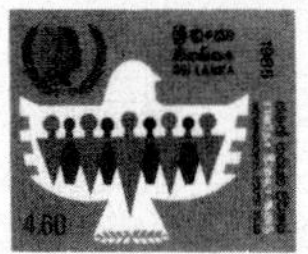

346 College Emblem **347** Dove and Stylized Figures

(Des S. Herath. Litho J.W.)

1984 (24 Dec). *Centenary of Baari Arabic College, Weligama. P* 13 × 12½.
878 **346** 4 r. 60, blackish olive, turquoise-green and turquoise-blue .. .. 70 1·00

(Des S. Chandrajeewa (4 r. 60), O. Weerakkody (20 r.). Litho J.W.)

1985 (1 Jan). *International Youth Year. T* **347** *and similar horiz design. Multicoloured. P* 12½ × 13.
879 4 r. 60, Type **347** 30 50
880 20 r. Dove, stylized figures and flower .. 1·25 2·00

348 Religious Symbols **349** College Crest

(Des R. Mawilmada. Litho Security Printers (M), Malaysia)

1985 (20 Jan). *World Religion Day. P* 12.
881 **348** 4 r. 60, multicoloured 35 60

(Des G. Arthasad. Litho J.W.)

1985 (29 Jan). *150th Anniv of Royal College, Colombo. T* **349** *and similar vert design. P* 13 × 12½.
882 60 c. bright yellow and deep ultramarine .. 10 20
883 7 r. multicoloured .. .. 50 1·40

Design:—7 r. Royal College.

350 Banknotes, Buildings, Ship and "Wheel of Life" **351** Wariyapola Sri Sumangala Thero

(Des R. Mawilmada. Litho J.W.)

1985 (7 Feb). *5th Anniv of Mahapola Scheme. P* 14.
884 **350** 60 c. multicoloured 40 55

(Des G. Fernando. Litho State Printing Office, Budapest)

1985 (2 Mar). *Wariyapola Sri Sumangala Thero (Buddhist priest and patriot) Commemoration. P* 13 × 13½.
885 **351** 60 c. blk, reddish brn & greenish yell 40 55

352 Victoria Dam **353** Cover of 50th Edition of International Buddhist Annual, *Vesak Sirisara*

(Des G. Arthasad. Litho State Ptg Wks, Moscow)

1985 (12 Apr). *Inauguration of Victoria Hydro-electric Project. T* **352** *and similar multicoloured design. P* 12½ × 12 (60 *c.*) *or* 12 × 12½ (7 *r.*).
886 60 c. Type **352** 40 40
887 7 r. Map of Sri Lanka enclosing dam and power station (*vert*) .. .. .. 1·75 2·25

(Des B. Harischandra (35 c.), R. Mawilmada (others). Litho J.W.)

1985 (26 Apr). *Centenary of Vesak Poya Holiday. T* **353** *and similar vert designs. Multicoloured. P* 13 × 12½.
888 35 c. Type **353** 10 10
889 60 c. Buddhists worshipping at temple .. 10 10
890 6 r. Buddhist Theosophical Society Headquarters, Colombo 30 35
891 9 r. Buddhist flag 50 55
888/91 .. .. *Set of* 4 80 90
MS892 180 × 110 mm. Nos. 888/91 .. .. 3·50 4·00

354 Ven. Waskaduwe Sri Subhuthi (priest and scholar) **355** Stylised Village and People

(Des S. Silva. Litho J.W.)

1985 (22 May). *Personalities. T* **354** *and similar vert designs. P* 13 × 12½.
893 60 c. black, yellow-orange and lake-brown .. 15 20
894 60 c. black, yellow-orange and deep mauve .. 15 20
895 60 c. black, yellow-orange and light brown .. 15 20
896 60 c. black, yellow-orange and emerald .. 15 20
893/6 .. .. *Set of* 4 55 70

Designs:— No. 893, Type **354**; 894, Revd. Fr. Peter A. Pillai (educationist and social reformer); 895, Dr. Senarath Paranavitane (scholar); 896, A. M. Wapche Marikar (architect and educationist).

(Des S. Herath. Litho German Bank Note Co, Leipzig)

1985 (23 June). *Gam Udawa '85 (Village Re-awakening Movement). P* 13½ × 13.
897 **355** 60 c. multicoloured 60 60

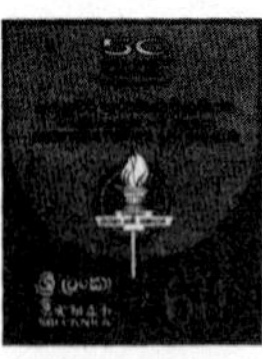

356 Emblem **357** Kothmale Dam and Reservoir

(Des B. Harischandra. Litho German Bank Note Co, Leipzig)

1985 (25 June). *50th Anniv of Colombo Young Poets' Association. P* 14.
898 **356** 60 c. multicoloured 20 30

(Des R. Mawilmada. Litho J.W.)

1985 (24 Aug). *Inauguration of Kothmale Hydro-electric Project. T* **357** *and similar horiz design. Multicoloured. P* 14.
899 60 c. Type **357** 10 15
900 6 r. Kothmale Power Station 35 60

358 Federation Logo **359** Breast Feeding

(Des R. Mawilmada. Litho J.W.)

1985 (2 Sept). *10th Asian and Oceanic Congress of Obstetrics and Gynaecology. P* 14.
901 **358** 7 r. multicoloured .. .. .. 2·00 1·75

(Des B. Harischandra. Litho Cartor, France)

1985 (5 Sept). *U.N.I.C.E.F. Child Survival and Development Programme. T* **359** *and similar vert designs. Multicoloured. W* w **17**. *P* 13½.
902 35 c. Type **359** 10 10
903 60 c. Child and oral rehydration salts .. 15 20
904 6 r. Weighing child (growth monitoring) .. 1·00 1·25
905 9 r. Immunization .. .. 1·40 1·75
902/5 .. .. *Set of* 4 2·40 3·00
MS906 99 × 180 mm. Nos. 902/5. P 12½ .. 2·40 3·25

ALTERED CATALOGUE NUMBERS

Any Catalogue numbers altered from the last edition are shown as a list in the introductory pages.

360 Blowing Conch Shell **361** Casket containing Land Grant Deed

(Des G. Malaviachi. Litho Heraclio Fournier, Spain)

1985 (27 Sept). *10th Anniv of World Tourism Organization. T* **360** *and similar horiz designs. Multicoloured. P* 14.
907 1 r. Type **360** 10 10
908 6 r. Parliamentary Complex, Jayawardhanapura, Kotte 30 50
909 7 r. Tea plantation 40 65
910 10 r. Ruwanveliseya (Buddhist shrine), Anuradhapura 60 85
907/10 .. .. *Set of* 4 1·25 1·90
MS911 179 × 89 mm. Nos. 907/10. P 13½ .. 1·40 2·00

(Des B. Harischandra. Litho Harrison)

1985 (15 Oct). *50th Anniv of Land Development Ordinance. P* 14 × 15.
912 **361** 4 r. 60, multicoloured 50 95

362 Koran and Map of Sri Lanka **363** "Our Lady of Matara" Statue

(Des R. Mawilmada. Litho Cartor, France)

1985 (17 Oct). *Translation of The Koran into Sinhala. W* w **17**. *P* 13½.
913 **362** 60 c. gold and bright violet 30 50

(Des S. Silva. Litho Security Printers (M), Malaysia)

1985 (5 Nov). *Christmas. T* **363** *and similar vert design. Multicoloured. P* 12.
914 60 c. Type **363** 10 10
915 9 r. "Our Lady of Madhu" statue 50 60
MS916 180 × 100 mm. Nos. 914/15 .. .. 2·75 3·50

(**364**) **365** Linked Arms and Map of S.A.A.R.C. Countries

1985 (1 Dec)–**86**. *Nos.* 680*b*, 780, 823, 860 *and* 879 *surch as T* **364** *by Aitken Spence Ptg (Pte) Ltd, Sri Lanka.*
917 **236** 75 c. on 60 c. gold, bright yellow-green and emerald (G.) 10 10
a. Surch double .. .. .. † —
918 **347** 1 r. on 4 r. 60, mult (29.4.86) .. 60 50
919 **339** 1 r. on 7 r. multicoloured (20.1.86) .. 90 50
920 **269** 5 r. 75 on 2 r. 50, multicoloured (Br) .. 1·00 35
a. Surch double .. .. ..
921 – 7 r. on 35 c. mult (No. 828) (10.3.86) 1·40 65
a. Surch inverted .. .. ..
b. Surch double .. .. ..
c. Surch triple .. .. ..
917/21 .. .. *Set of* 5 3·50 1·90

(Des B. Harischandra. Litho J.W.)

1985 (8 Dec). *1st Summit Meeting of South Asian Association for Regional Co-operation, Dhaka, Bangladesh. T* **365** *and similar horiz design. Multicoloured. P* 14.
922 60 c. Type **365** .. .. 75 2·00
923 5 r. 50, Logo and flags of member countries .. .. 75 1·00

No 922 was, reportedly, withdrawn on 11 December after Pakistan objected to the boundaries shown on the map.

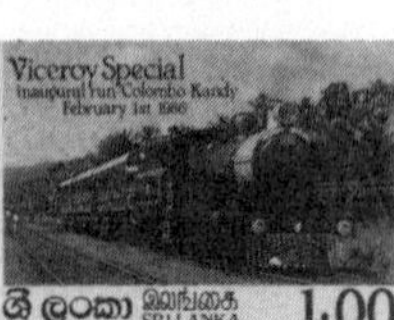

366 "Viceroy Special" Train

(Des G. Malaviachi. Litho Format)

1986 (2 Feb). *Inaugural Run of "Viceroy Special" Train from Colombo to Kandy. P* 12½.
924 **366** 1 r. multicoloured .. .. .. 1·50 80

367 Girl and Boy Students **368** D. R. Wijewardena

(Des S. Silva. Litho Heraclio Fournier, Spain)

1986 (14 Feb). *6th Anniv of Mahapola Scheme. P* 14.
925 **367** 75 c. multicoloured 20 40

(Des S. Silva. Litho J.W.)

1986 (23 Feb). *Birth Centenary of D. R. Wijewardena (newspaper publisher). P* 14 × 14½.
926 **368** 75 c. orange-brown and deep olive .. 20 40

369 Ven Welitara Gnanatillake Maha Nayake Thero **370** Red Cross Flag and Personnel

(Des S. Silva. Litho Cartor, France)

1986 (26 Feb). *Ven. Welitara Gnanatillake Maha Nayake Thero (scholar) Commemoration. W* w **17**. *P* 13½.
927 **369** 75 c. multicoloured 50 50

(Des W. Rohana. Litho Format)

1986 (31 Mar). *50th Anniv of Sri Lanka Red Cross Society. P* 12½.
928 **370** 75 c. multicoloured 75 50

371 Comet depicted as Goddess visiting Sun-god **372** Woman lighting Lamp

(Des W. Rohana. Litho Format)

1986 (5 Apr). *Appearance of Halley's Comet. T* **371** *and similar horiz designs. Multicoloured. P* 12½.
929 50 c. Type **371** 10 10
930 75 c. Comet and constellations of Scorpius and Sagittarius 10 20
931 6 r. 50, Comet's orbit 45 80
932 8 r. 50, Edmond Halley .. .. 60 1·25
929/32 .. .. *Set of* 4 1·10 2·10
MS933 180 × 115 mm. Nos. 929/32 .. .. 4·00 4·50

(Des B. Harischandra. Litho Format)

1986 (10 Apr). *Sinhalese and Tamil New Year. T* **372** *and similar vert designs. Multicoloured. P* 12½.
934 50 c. Type **372** 10 10
935 75 c. Woman and festive foods 15 15
936 6 r. 50, Women playing drum .. .. 55 1·00
937 8 r. 50, Anointing and making offerings at temple .. .. 75 1·40
934/7 .. .. *Set of* 4 1·40 2·40
MS938 178 × 108 mm. Nos. 934/7 .. .. 2·75 3·25

373 The King donating Elephant to the Brahmin **374** Ven. Kalukondayave Sri Prajnasekhara Maha Nayake Thero (Buddhist leader and social reformer

(Des N. Bulathsinhala. Litho Format)

1986 (16 May). *Vesak. Wall paintings from Samudragiri Temple, Mirissa. T* **373** *and similar horiz designs. Multicoloured. P* 12½.

939	50 c. Type **373**	10	10
940	75 c. The Bodhisattva in the Vasavarthi heaven	10	15
941	5 r. The offering of milk rice by Sujatha	35	75
942	10 r. The offering of parched corn and honey by Thapassu and Bhalluka	60	1·25
939/42	*Set of* 4	90	2·00

(Des S. Silva. Litho Format)

1986 (22 May). *National Heroes. T* **374** *and similar vert designs. Multicoloured. P* 12½.

943	75 c. Type **374**	15	25
944	75 c. Brahmachari Walisinghe Harischandra (social reformer) (birth centenary)	15	25
945	75 c. Martin Wickramasinghe (author and scholar)	15	25
946	75 c. G. G. Ponnambalam (politician)	15	25
947	75 c. A. M. A. Azeez (Islamic scholar) (75th birth anniv)	15	25
943/7	*Set of* 5	65	1·10

375 Stylised Village and People **376** Co-op Flag and Emblem

(Des S. Herath. Litho German Bank Note Co, Leipzig)

1986 (23 June). *Gam Udawa '86 (Village Re-awakening Movement). P* 13½×13.

948	**375**	75 c. multicoloured	45	30

(Des A. Harischandra. Litho Format)

1986 (5 July). *75th Anniv of Sri Lanka Co-operative Movement. P* 12½.

949	**376**	1 r. multicoloured	80	80

377 Arthur V. Dias **378** Bull Elephant

(Des S. Silva. Litho Harrison)

1986 (31 July). *Birth Centenary of Arthur V. Dias (philanthropist). P* 14×15.

950	**377**	1 r. chestnut and dull violet-blue	55	55

(Des G. Ratnavira. Litho Harrison)

1986 (5 Aug). *Sri Lanka Wild Elephants. T* **378** *and similar horiz designs. Multicoloured. P* 15×14.

951	5 r. Type **378**	1·00	1·25
	a. Horiz strip of 4. Nos. 951/4	3·50	
952	5 r. Cow elephant and calf	1·00	1·25
953	5 r. Cow elephant	1·00	1·25
954	5 r. Elephants bathing	1·00	1·25
951/4	*Set of* 4	3·50	4·50

Nos. 951/4 were printed, together, *se-tenant*, in horizontal strips of four throughout the sheet.

379 Congress Logo **380** Map showing Route of Cable and Telephone Receiver

(Des S. Silva. Litho Govt Printing Bureau, Tokyo)

1986 (14 Aug). *2nd Indo-Pacific Congress on Legal Medicine and Forensic Sciences. P* 13½×13.

955	**379**	8 r. 50, multicoloured	70	1·00

(Des R. Mawilmada. Litho Security Printers (M), Malaysia)

1986 (8 Sept). *SEA-ME-WE Submarine Cable Project. P* 13½×14.

956	**380**	5 r. 75, multicoloured	50	85

381 Anniversary Logo **382** Logo on Flag

(Des R. Mawilmada. Litho Format)

1986 (20 Sept). *25th Anniv of Dag Hammarskjöld Award. P* 12½.

957	**381**	2 r. multicoloured	60	40

(Des A. Harischandra. Litho Security Printers (M), Malaysia)

1986 (22 Sept). *2nd National School Games. P* 12.

958	**382**	1 r. multicoloured	60	40

383 Logo **384** College Building and Crest

(Des W. Rohana. Litho Govt Printing Bureau, Tokyo)

1986 (27 Sept). *60th Anniv of Surveyors' Institute of Sri Lanka. P* 13½×13.

959	**383**	75 c. red-brown and cinnamon	20	30

(Des W. Rohana. Litho Security Printers (M), Malaysia)

1986 (1 Nov). *Centenary of Ananda College, Colombo. T* **384** *and similar horiz designs. P* 12.

960	75 c. multicoloured	10	10
961	5 r. multicoloured	25	30
962	5 r. 75, multicoloured	25	30
963	6 r. carmine-red, gold and rose-lilac	25	30
960/3	*Set of* 4	75	90

Designs:—5 r. Sports field and college crest; 5 r. 75, Col. H. S. Olcott (founder), Ven. Migettuwatte Gunananda, Ven. Hikkaduwe Sri Sumangala (Buddhist leaders) and Buddhist flag; 6 r. College flag.

385 Mangrove Swamp **386** Family and Housing Estate

(Des G. Ratnavira. Litho Security Printers (M), Malaysia)

1986 (11 Nov). *Mangrove Conservation. T* **385** *and similar horiz designs. Multicoloured. P* 12.

964	35 c. Type **385**	10	10
965	50 c. Mangrove tree	15	10
966	75 c. Germinating mangrove flower	20	15
967	6 r. Fiddler Crab	95	1·00
964/7	*Set of* 4	1·25	1·25

(Des R. Mawilmada. Litho Govt Printing Bureau, Tokyo)

1987 (1 Jan). *International Year of Shelter for the Homeless. P* 13×13½.

968	**386**	75 c. multicoloured	60	30

387 Ven. Ambagahawatte Indasabhawaragnanasamy Thero **388** Proctor John de Silva

(Des S. Silva. Litho Security Printers (M), Malaysia)

1987 (29 Jan). *Ven. Ambagahawatte Indasabhawaragnanasamy Thero (Buddhist monk) Commemoration. P* 12.

969	**387**	5 r. 75, multicoloured	40	30

(Des S. Silva. Litho Security Printers (M), Malaysia)

1987 (31 Jan). *Proctor John de Silva (playwright) Commemoration. P* 12.

970	**388**	5 r. 75, multicoloured	30	30

389 Mahapola Logo and Aspects of Communication **390** Dr. R. L. Brohier

(Des R. Mawilmada. Litho Security Printers (M), Malaysia)

1987 (6 Feb). *7th Anniv of Mahapola Scheme. P* 12.

971	**389**	75 c. multicoloured	20	30

(Des S. Silva. Litho Security Printers (M), Malaysia)

1987 (10 Feb). *Dr. Richard L. Brohier (historian and surveyor) Commemoration. P* 12.

972	**390**	5 r. 75, multicoloured	40	30

391 Tyre Corporation Building, Kelaniya, and Logo

(Des A. Harischandra. Litho Questa)

1987 (23 Mar). *25th Anniv of Sri Lanka Tyre Corporation. P* 14.

973	**391**	5 r. 75, black, lake and bright orange	30	30

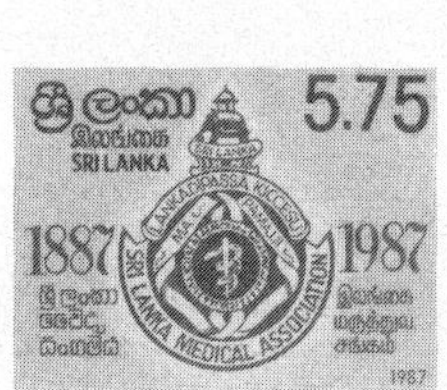

392 Logo **393** Clasped Hands, Farmer and Paddy Field

(Des A. Harischandra. Litho Govt Printing Bureau, Tokyo)

1987 (24 Mar). *Centenary of Sri Lanka Medical Association. P* 13×13½.

974	**392**	5 r. 75, lake-brown, greenish yellow & blk	30	30

(Des B. Harischandra. Litho Questa)

1987 (29 Mar). *Inauguration of Farmers' Pension and Social Security Benefit Scheme. P* 14.

975	**393**	75 c. multicoloured	15	15

394 Exhibition Logo **395** Young Children with W.H.O. and Immunization Logos

(Des W. Rohana. Litho Security Printers (M), Malaysia)

1987 (2 Apr). *Mahaweli Maha Goviya Contest and Agro Mahaweli Exhibition. P* 12.

976	**394**	75 c. multicoloured	15	15

(Des B. Harischandra. Litho Questa)

1987 (7 Apr). *World Health Day. P* 14.

977	**395**	1 r. multicoloured	75	30

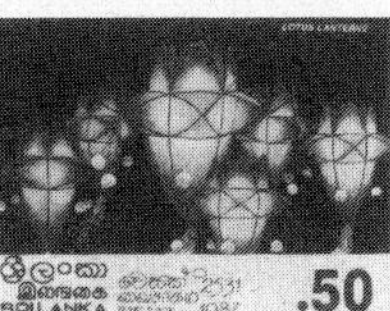

396 Girls playing on Swing **397** Lotus Lanterns

(Des G. Fernando. Litho Security Printers (M), Malaysia)

1987 (9 Apr). *Sinhalese and Tamil New Year. T* **396** *and similar vert design. Multicoloured. P* 12.

978	75 c. Type **396**	10	10
979	5 r. Girls with oil lamp and sun symbol	30	40

(Des W. Rohana. Litho Security Printers (M), Malaysia)

1987 (4 May). *Vesak. T* **397** *and similar horiz designs. Multicoloured. P* 12.

980	50 c. Type **397**	10	10
981	75 c. Octagonal lanterns	10	10
982	5 r. Star lanterns	30	30
983	10 r. Gok lanterns	45	55
980/3	*Set of* 4	80	90
MS984	150×90 mm. Nos. 980/3	80	1·00

398 Emerald-collared Parakeet

399 Ven. Heenatiyana Sri Dhammaloka Maha Nayake Thero (Buddhist monk)

(Des G. Ratnavira. Litho Questa)

1987 (18 May). *Birds (3rd series). T* **398** *and similar horiz designs. Multicoloured. P* 14.

985	50 c. Type **398**	10	10
986	1 r. Legge's Flowerpecker	10	10
987	5 r. Ceylon White-headed Starling	15	20
988	10 r. Ceylon Jungle Babbler (*Turdoides rufescens*)	30	35
985/8	*Set of* 4	50	60
MS989	140×80 mm. Nos. 985/8	2·50	2·00

Nos. 986 and 988 exist with different imprint dates beneath the designs.

(Des S. Silva. Litho Security Printers (M), Malaysia)

1987 (22 May). *National Heroes. T* **399** *and similar vert designs. Multicoloured. P* 12.

990	75 c. Type **399**	15	15
991	75 c. P. de S. Kularatne (educationist)	15	15
992	75 c. M. C. Abdul Rahuman (legislator)	15	15
990/2	*Set of* 3	40	40

400 Peasant Family and Village

401 *Mesua nagassarium*

(Des J. Semage. Litho Security Printers (M), Malaysia)

1987 (23 June). *Gam Udawa '87 (Village Re-awakening Movement). P* 12.

993 **400** 75 c. multicoloured 15 15

(Des P. Hewabettage (75 c.), B. Harischandra (5 r.). Litho Security Printers (M), Malaysia)

1987 (25 June). *Forest Conservation. T* **401** *and similar horiz design. Multicoloured. P* 12.

994	75 c. Type **401**	10	10
995	5 r. Elephants in forest	50	30

402 Dharmaraja College, Crest and Col. H. Olcott (founder)

403 Youth Services Logo

(Des C. Kandewela. Litho Security Printers (M), Malaysia)

1987 (30 June). *Centenary of Dharmaraja College, Kandy. P* 12.

996 **402** 75 c. multicoloured 50 20

(Des H. Dayaratne. Litho Security Printers (M), Malaysia)

1987 (15 July). *20th Anniv of National Youth Services. P* 12.

997 **403** 75 c. multicoloured 15 15

404 Arm holding Torch and Mahaweli Logo

405 Open Bible and Logo

(Des W. Rohana. Litho Security Printers (M), Malaysia)

1987 (5 Sept). *Mahaweli Games. P* 12.

998 **404** 75 c. multicoloured 55 55

(Des C. Beling. Litho Security Printers (M), Malaysia)

1987 (2 Oct). *175th Anniv of Ceylon Bible Society. P* 12.

999 **405** 5 r. 75, multicoloured 30 30

406 Hurdler and Committee Symbol

407 Madonna and Child, Flowers and Oil Lamp

(Des R. Mawilmada. Litho Heraclio Fournier, Spain)

1987 (8 Oct). *50th Anniv of National Olympic Committee. P* 13.

1000 **406** 10 r. multicoloured 60 60

(Des B. Mendis. Litho Security Printers (M), Malaysia)

1987 (17 Nov). *Christmas. T* **407** *and similar vert design. Multicoloured. P* 12 (75 *c.*) *or* 12½×13 (10 *r.*).

1001	75 c. Type **407**	10	10
1002	10 r. Christ Child in manger, star and dove	35	40
MS1003	145×82 mm. Nos. 1001/2. P 12	60	70

408 Sir Ernest de Silva

409 Society Logo

(Des P. Gunasinghe. Litho German Bank Note Co, Leipzig)

1987 (25 Nov). *Birth Centenary of Sir Ernest de Silva (philanthropist and philatelist). P* 13×13½.

1004 **408** 75 c. multicoloured 15 15

(Des W. Rohana. Litho German Bank Note Co, Leipzig)

1987 (28 Nov). *150th Anniv of Kandy Friend-in-Need Society. P* 13½×13.

1005 **409** 75 c. multicoloured 15 15

410 University Flag and Graduates

411 Father Joseph Vaz

(Des R. Samarasinghe. Litho Security Printers (M), Malaysia)

1987 (14 Dec). *First Convocation of Buddhist and Pali University. P* 12.

1006 **410** 75 c. multicoloured 15 15

(Des S. Silva. Litho Security Printers (M), Malaysia)

1987 (15 Dec). *300th Anniv of Arrival of Father Joseph Vaz in Kandy. P* 12.

1007 **411** 75 c. multicoloured 15 15

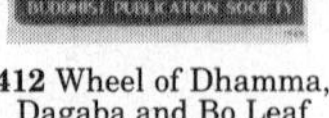

412 Wheel of Dhamma, Dagaba and Bo Leaf

413 Dharmayatra Lorry

(Des W. Rohana. Litho Security Printers (M), Malaysia)

1988 (1 Jan). *30th Anniv of Buddhist Publication Society, Kandy. P* 12.

1008 **412** 75 c. multicoloured 15 15

(Des B. Harischandra. Litho German Bank Note Co, Leipzig)

1988 (4 Jan). *5th Anniv of Mahapola Dharmayatra Service. P* 13½×13.

1009 **413** 75 c. multicoloured 15 15

414 Society Logo

415 National Youth Centre, Maharagama

(Des R. Samarasinghe. Litho Security Printers (M), Malaysia)

1988 (8 Jan). *Centenary of Ceylon Society of Arts. P* 12.

1010 **414** 75 c. multicoloured 15 15

(Des R. Chandrajeewa. Litho Security Printers (M), Malaysia)

1988 (31 Jan). *Opening of National Youth Centre, Maharagama. P* 13½×13.

1011 **415** 1 r. multicoloured 50 20

416 Citizens with National Flag and Map of Sri Lanka

417 Graduates, Clay Lamp and Open Book

(Des R. Samarasinghe. Litho Security Printers (M), Malaysia)

1988 (4 Feb). *40th Anniv of Independence. T* **416** *and similar vert design. Multicoloured. P* 12.

1012	75 c. Type **416**	10	10
1013	8 r. 50, "40" in figures and lion emblem	50	50

(Des R. Samarasinghe. Litho Security Printers (M), Malaysia)

1988 (11 Feb). *8th Anniv of Mahapola Scheme. P* 12.

1014 **417** 75 c. multicoloured 15 15

418 Bus and Logo

419 Ven. Weligama Sri Sumangala Maha Nayake Thero

(Des W. Rohana. Litho Security Printers (M), Malaysia)

1988 (19 Feb). *30th Anniv of Sri Lanka Transport Board. P* 12.

1015 **418** 5 r. 75, multicoloured 30 30

(Des S. Silva. Litho Security Printers (M), Malaysia)

1988 (13 Mar). *Ven. Weligama Sri Sumangala Maha Nayake Thero (Buddhist monk) Commemoration. P* 12.

1016 **419** 75 c. multicoloured 15 15

420 Regimental Colour

421 Chevalier I. X. Pereira

(Des W. Rohana. Litho Security Printers (M), Malaysia)

1988 (20 Apr). *Centenary of Regiment of Artillery. P* 12.

1017 **420** 5 r. 75, multicoloured 40 30

(Des S. Silva. Litho Security Printers (M), Malaysia)

1988 (26 Apr). *Birth Centenary of Chevalier I. X. Pereira (politician). P* 12.

1018 **421** 5 r. 75, multicoloured 30 30

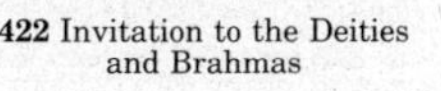

422 Invitation to the Deities and Brahmas

423 Father Ferdinand Bonnel (educationist)

(Des N. Bulathsinhala. Litho State Ptg Wks, Moscow)

1988 (13 May). *Vesak. Paintings from Narendrarama Rajamaha Temple, Suriyagoda. T* **422** *and similar horiz design. Multicoloured. P* 12½ × 12.

1019 50 c. Type **422** 15 15
1020 75 c. Bodhisathva at the Seventh Step .. 15 15
MS1021 150 × 92 mm. Nos. 1019/20 .. .. 50 50

(Des S. Silva. Litho State Ptg Wks, Moscow)

1988 (22 May). *National Heroes. T* **423** *and similar vert designs. Multicoloured. P* 12 × 12½.

1022 75 c. Type **423** 15 15
1023 75 c. Sir Razik Fareed (politician) .. 15 15
1024 75 c. W. F. Gunawardhana (scholar) .. 15 15
1025 75 c. Edward Nugawela (politician) .. 15 15
1026 75 c. Chief Justice Sir Arthur Wijeyewardene 15 15
1022/6 .. .. *Set of* 5 60 60

424 Stylized Figures and Reawakened Village

425 Maliyadeva College, Kurunegala, and Crest

(Des P. Gunasinghe. Litho Security Printers (M), Malaysia)

1988 (23 June). *10th Anniv of Gam Udawa (Village Re-awakening Movement). P* 12.

1027 **424** 75 c. multicoloured 15 15

(Des W. Rohana. Litho German Bank Note Co, Leipzig)

1988 (30 June). *Centenary of Maliyadeva College, Kurunegala. P* 13½ × 13.

1028 **425** 75 c. multicoloured 15 15

426 M.J.M. Lafir, Billiard Game and Trophy

427 Flags of Australia and Sri Lanka, Handclasp and Map of Australia

(Des S. Silva. Litho State Ptg Wks, Moscow)

1988 (5 July). *Mohamed Junaid Mohamed Lafir (World Amateur Billiards Champion,* 1973) *Commemoration. P* 12½ × 12.

1029 **426** 5 r. 75, multicoloured 30 30

(Des R. Samarasinghe. Litho Security Printers (M), Malaysia)

1988 (19 July). *Bicentenary of Australian Settlement. P* 12.

1030 **427** 8 r. 50, multicoloured 30 35

428 Ven. Kataluwe Sri Gunaratana Maha Nayake Thero

429 Athlete, Rice and Hydro-electric Dam

(Des S. Silva. Litho State Ptg Wks, Moscow)

1988 (11 Aug). *Ven. Kataluwe Sri Gunaratana Maha Nayake Thero (Buddhist monk) Commemoration. P* 12 × 12½.

1031 **428** 75 c. multicoloured 15 15

(Des P. Gunasinghe. Litho Security Printers (M), Malaysia)

1988 (3 Sept). *Mahaweli Games. P* 12.

1032 **429** 75 c. multicoloured 15 15

430 Athletics

431 Outline Map of Sri Lanka and Anniversary Logo

(Des P. Gunasinghe. Litho State Ptg Wks, Moscow)

1988 (6 Sept). *Olympic Games, Seoul. T* **430** *and similar vert designs. Multicoloured. P* 12 × 12½.

1033 75 c. Type **430** 10 10
1034 1 r. Swimming 10 10
1035 5 r. 75, Boxing 20 25
1036 8 r. 50, Map of Sri Lanka and logos of Olympic Committee and Seoul Games 30 35
1033/6 .. .. *Set of* 4 55 65
MS1037 181 × 101 mm. Nos. 1033/6 .. .. 75 85

(Des S. Silva. Litho Security Printers (M), Malaysia)

1988 (12 Sept). *40th Anniv of World Health Organization. P* 12.

1038 **431** 75 c. multicoloured 15 15

432 Games Logo

433 Mahatma Gandhi

(Des A. Harischandra. Litho Security Printers (M), Malaysia)

1988 (20 Sept). *3rd National School Games. P* 12.

1039 **432** 1 r. black, gold and mauve 50 15

(Des S. Silva. Litho Security Printers (M), Malaysia)

1988 (2 Oct). *40th Death Anniv of Mahatma Gandhi. P* 12.

1040 **433** 75 c. multicoloured 30 15

434 Globe with Forms of Transport and Communications

435 Woman with Rice Sheaf and Hydro-electric Project

(Des R. Samarasinghe. Litho State Ptg Wks, Moscow)

1988 (28 Oct). *Asia–Pacific Transport and Communications Decade. T* **434** *and similar horiz design. P* 12½ × 12.

1041 75 c. multicoloured 10 10
1042 5 r. 75, magenta, royal blue and black .. 40 30

Design:—5 r. 75, Antenna tower with dish aerials and forms of transport.

(Des B. Harischandra. Litho Security Printers (M), Malaysia)

1988 (31 Oct). *Commissioning of Randenigala Project. T* **435** *and similar horiz design. Multicoloured. P* 12.

1043 75 c. Type **435** 10 10
1044 5 r. 75, Randenigala Dam and reservoir 20 25

436 Handicrafts and Centre Logo in Cupped Hands

437 Angel, Dove, Olive Branch and Globe

(Des R. Samarasinghe. Litho Secura, Singapore)

1988 (17 Nov). *Opening of Gramodaya Folk Art Centre, Colombo. P* 13½.

1045 **436** 75 c. multicoloured 15 15

(Des B. Mendis. Litho State Ptg Wks, Moscow)

1988 (21 Nov). *Christmas. T* **437** *and similar vert design. Multicoloured. P* 12×12½.

1046 75 c. Type **437** 10 10
1047 8 r. 50, Shepherds and Star of Bethlehem 30 35
MS1048 175×100 mm. Nos. 1046/7 .. .. 60 60

438 Dr. E. W. Adikaram

439 Open Book in Tree and Children reading

(Des S. Silva. Litho Security Printers (M), Malaysia)

1988 (28 Dec). *Dr. E. W. Adikaram (educationist) Commemoration. P* 12.

1049 **438** 75 c. multicoloured 15 15

(Des Lakmini Amararatne. Litho German Bank Note Co, Leipzig)

1989 (23 Jan). *10th Anniv of Free Distribution of School Text Books. P* 13½×13.

1050 **439** 75 c. multicoloured 15 15

440 Wimalaratne Kumaragama

441 Logo and New Chamber of Commerce Building

(Des S. Silva. Litho German Bank Note Co, Leipzig)

1989 (27 Jan). *Poets of Sri Lanka. T* **440** *and similar vert designs. Multicoloured. P* 13×13½.

1051 75 c. Type **440** 10 10
1052 75 c. G. H. Perera 10 10
1053 75 c. Sagara Palansuriya 10 10
1054 75 c. P. B. Alwis Perera 10 10
1051/4 .. .. *Set of* 4 20 20

(Des Mel Ads Ltd. Litho Security Printers (M), Malaysia)

1989 (25 Mar). *150th Anniv of Ceylon Chamber of Commerce. P* 12.

1055 **441** 75 c. multicoloured 15 15

442 Bodhisatva at Lunch and Funeral Pyre

443 Parawahera Vajiragnana Thero (Buddhist monk)

(Des N. Bulathsinhala. Litho State Ptg Wks, Moscow)

1989 (15 May). *Vesak. Wall Paintings from Medawala Monastery, Harispattuwa. T* **442** *and similar horiz designs. Multicoloured. P* 12½×12.

1056 50 c. Type **442** 10 10
1057 75 c. Rescue of King Vessantara's children by god Sakra 10 10
1058 5 r. Bodhisatva ploughing and his son attacked by snake 20 25
1059 5 r. 75, King Vessantara giving away his children 20 25
1056/9 .. .. *Set of* 4 55 65
MS1060 150×90 mm. Nos. 1056/9 .. .. 75 75

(Des S. Silva. Litho Security Printers (M), Malaysia)

1989 (22 May). *National Heroes. T* **443** *and similar multicoloured designs. P* 12.

1061 75 c. Type **443** 15 15
1062 75 c. Father Maurice Jacques Le Goc (educationist) 15 15
1063 75 c. Hemapala Munidasa (author) .. 15 15
1064 75 c. Ananda Samarakoon (composer) .. 15 15
1065 75 c. Simon Casie Chitty (scholar) (*horiz*) 15 15
1061/5 .. .. *Set of* 5 65 65

444 College Crest

445 Dramachakra, Lamp, Buddhist Flag and Map

(Des K. Wickramanayake. Litho Security Printers (M), Malaysia)

1989 (5 June). *150th Anniv of Hartley College, Point-Pedro* (1988). *P* 12.
1066 **444** 75 c. multicoloured 15 15

(Des P. Gunasinghe. Litho State Ptg Wks, Moscow)

1989 (18 June). *Establishment of Ministry of Buddha Sasana. P* $12^1/_2$×12.
1067 **445** 75 c. multicoloured 15 15

446 Hands holding Brick and Trowel, House and Family

447 Two Families and Hand turning Cogwheel

(Des P. Gunasinghe. Litho State Ptg Wks, Moscow)

1989 (23 June). *Gam Udawa '89 (Village Re-awakening Movement). P* $12^1/_2$×12.
1068 **446** 75 c. multicoloured 15 15

(Des P. Gunasinghe. Photo State Ptg Works, Moscow)

1989 (23 June)–**90**. *Janasaviya Development Programme. P* 12×$11^1/_2$.
1069 **447** 75 c. multicoloured 15 15
1070 1 r. multicoloured (31.1.90) 15 15

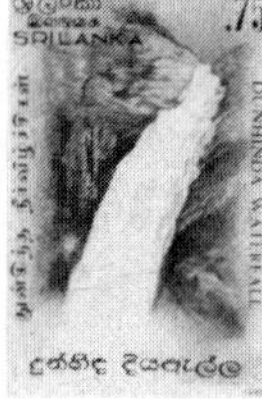

448 Dunhinda Falls

449 Rev. James Chater (missionary) and Baptist Church

(Des S. Silva. Litho State Ptg Works, Moscow)

1989 (11 Aug). *Waterfalls. T* **448** *and similar vert designs. Multicoloured. P* 12.
1071 75 c. Type **448** 10 10
1072 1 r. Rawana Falls 15 10
1073 5 r. 75, Laxapana Falls 25 25
1074 8 r. 50, Diyaluma Falls 35 35
1071/4 . . . . . . *Set of* 4 75 70

(Des S. Silva. Litho State Ptg Works, Moscow)

1989 (19 Aug). *177th Anniv of Baptist Church in Sri Lanka. P* $12^1/_2$×12.
1075 **449** 5 r. 75, multicoloured 15 20

450 Bicentenary Logo

451 Old and New Bank Buildings and Logo

(Des R. Samarasinghe. Litho German Bank Note Co, Leipzig)

1989 (26 Aug). *Bicentenary of French Revolution. P* $13^1/_2$×13.
1076 **450** 8 r. 50, black, deep blue & brt carmine 20 25

(Des W. Rohana. Litho German Bank Note Co, Leipzig)

1989 (31 Aug). *50th Anniv of Bank of Ceylon. T* **451** *and similar horiz design. Multicoloured. P* $13^1/_2$×13.
1077 75 c. Type **451** 10 10
1078 5 r. "Bank of Ceylon" orchid and logo . . 20 20

452 Water Lily, Dharma Chakra and Books

453 Wilhelm Geiger

(Des P. Gunasinghe. Litho Security Printers (M), Malaysia)

1989 (22 Sept). *State Literary Festival. P* 12.
1079 **452** 75 c. multicoloured 15 15

(Des S. Silva. Litho German Bank Note Co, Leipzig)

1989 (30 Sept). *Wilhelm Geiger (linguistic scholar) Commemoration. P* 13×$13^1/_2$.
1080 **453** 75 c. multicoloured 15 15

(Litho Questa)

1989 (11 Oct). *As No.* 781, *but different printer. Face value and inscriptions in black. With imprint date. P* 14.
1081 3 r. Golden Palm Civet 10 10
No. 781 has face value and inscriptions in red-brown and is without imprint date.

454 H. V. Perera, Q.C.

455 Sir Cyril de Zoysa

(Des S. Silva. Litho Security Printers (M), Malaysia)

1989 (16 Oct). *Constitutional Pioneers. T* **454** *and similar vert design. Multicoloured. P* 12.
1082 75 c. Type **454** 15 15
1083 75 c. Prof. Ivor Jennings 15 15

(Des S. Silva. Litho German Bank Note Co, Leipzig)

1989 (26 Oct). *Sir Cyril de Zoysa (Buddhist philanthropist) Commemoration. P* 13×$13^1/_2$.
1084 **455** 75 c. multicoloured 15 15

456 Map of South-east Asia and Telecommunications Equipment

457 Members with Offerings and Water Lily on Map of Sri Lanka

(Des W. Rohana. Litho State Ptg Works, Moscow)

1989 (1 Nov). *10th Anniv of Asia-Pacific Telecommunity. P* 12×$12^1/_2$.
1085 **456** 5 r. 75, multicoloured 20 20

(Des P. Gunasinghe. Litho Security Printers (M), Malaysia)

1989 (9 Nov). *50th Anniv of Sri Sucharitha Welfare Movement. P* 13.
1086 **457** 75 c. multicoloured 15 15

458 "Apollo 11" Blast-off and Astronauts

459 Shepherds

(Des W. Rohana. Litho State Ptg Works, Moscow)

1989 (10 Nov). *20th Anniv of First Manned Landing on Moon. T* **458** *and similar vert designs. Multicoloured. P* 12×$12^1/_2$.
1087 75 c. Type **458** 10 10
1088 1 r. Armstrong leaving lunar module *Eagle* 10 10
1089 2 r. Astronaut on Moon 10 10
1090 5 r. 75, Lunar surface and Earth from Moon 15 20
1087/90 . . . . . . *Set of* 4 30 30
MS1091 100×160 mm. Nos. 1087/90 . . . . 70 70

(Des Father P. Silva. Litho Secura, Singapore)

1989 (21 Nov). *Christmas. T* **459** *and similar vert design. Multicoloured. P* $13^1/_2$.
1092 75 c. Type **459** 10 10
1093 8 r. 50, Magi with gifts 20 40
MS1094 160×100 mm. Nos. 1092/3 . . . . 50 60

460 Ven. Sri Devananda Nayake Thero

461 College Building, Crest and Revd. William Ault (founder)

(Des S. Silva. Litho Security Printers (M), Malaysia)

1989 (25 Nov). *Ven. Sri Devananda Nayake Thero (Buddhist monk) Commemoration. P* 12.
1095 **460** 75 c. multicoloured 10 10

(Des W. Rohana. Litho Security Printers (M), Malaysia)

1989 (29 Nov). *175th Anniv of Methodist Central College, Batticaloa. P* 12.
1096 **461** 75 c. multicoloured 10 10

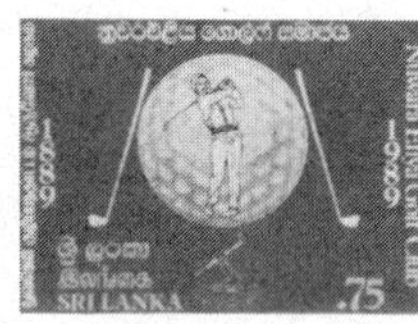

462 Golf Ball, Clubs and Logo

463 "Raja"

(Des G. Bozell. Litho Pakistan Security Ptg Corp, Karachi)

1989 (8 Dec). *Centenary of Nuwara Eliya Golf Club. T* **462** *and similar horiz design. Multicoloured. P* $13^1/_2$.
1097 75 c. Type **462** 15 10
1098 8 r. 50, Course and club house 40 40

(Litho German Bank Note Co, Leipzig)

1989 (12 Dec). *"Raja" Royal Ceremonial Elephant, Kandy, Commemoration. P* 13×$13^1/_2$.
1099 **463** 75 c. multicoloured 10 10

464 College Building and G. Wickremarachchi (founder)

465 Ven. Udunuwara Sri Sarananda Thero

(Des S. Silva. Litho German Bank Note Co, Leipzig)

1989 (14 Dec). *60th Anniv of Gampaha Wickremarachchi Institute of Ayurveda Medicine. P* $13^1/_2$×13.
1100 **464** 75 c. multicoloured 10 10

(Des S. Silva. Litho State Ptg Wks, Moscow)

1989 (20 Dec). *Ven. Udunuwara Sri Sarananda Thero (Buddhist monk) Commemoration. P* 12×$12^1/_2$.
1101 **465** 75 c. multicoloured 10 10

NEW INFORMATION

The editor is always interested to correspond with people who have new information that will improve or correct the Catalogue.

466 Diesel Train on Viaduct, Ella-Demodara

467 Cardinal Thomas Cooray

(Des R. Mawilmada. Litho Security Printers (M), Malaysia)

1989 (27 Dec). *125 Years of Sri Lanka Railways. T* **466** *and similar horiz designs. Multicoloured. P* 12 (75 *c.,* 7 *r.*) *or* 13 (*others*).
1102 75 c. Type **466** 10 10
1103 2 r. Diesel train at Maradana Station .. 15 15
1104 3 r. Steam train 20 20
1105 7 r. Steam train, 1864 .. .. 40 40
1102/5 .. .. *Set of* 4 75 75

(Des S. Silva. Litho German Bank Note Co, Leipzig)

1989 (28 Dec). *Cardinal Thomas Cooray Commemoration. P* 13×13½.
1106 **467** 75 c. multicoloured 30 15

468 Farmer and Wife with Dagaba and Dam

469 Justin Wijayawardena

(Des P. Gunasinghe. Litho Security Printers (M), Malaysia)

1989 (29 Dec). *Agro Mahaweli Development Programme. P* 12.
1107 **468** 75 c. multicoloured 10 10

(Des S. Silva. Litho State Ptg Wks, Moscow)

1990 (14 Jan). *Justin Wijayawardena (scholar) Commemoration. P* 12×12½.
1108 **469** 1 r. multicoloured 40 20

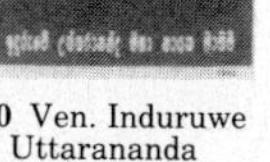

470 Ven. Induruwe Uttarananda Mahanayake Thero

471 Two Graduates, Lamp and Open Book

(Des S. Silva. Litho Security Printers (M), Malaysia)

1990 (15 Mar). *4th Death Anniv of Ven. Induruwe Uttarananda Mahanayake Thero (Buddhist theologian). P* 12.
1109 **470** 1 r. multicoloured 15 20

(Des P. Gunasinghe. Litho Secura, Singapore)

990 (25 Mar). *9th Anniv of Mahapola Scheme. P* 13½.
110 **471** 75 c. multicoloured 10 10

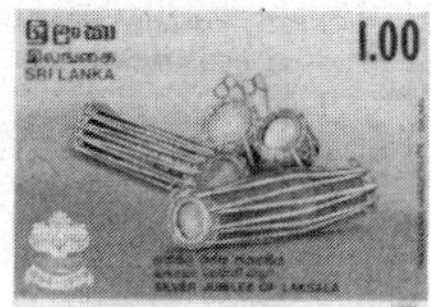

472 Traditional Drums

Des R. Samarasinha. Litho Security Printers (M), Malaysia)

990 (2 Apr). *25th Anniv of Laksala Traditional Handicrafts Organization. T* **472** *and similar horiz designs. Multicoloured. P* 12.
111 1 r. Type **472** 10 10
112 2 r. Silverware 15 15
113 3 r. Lacquerware 15 20
114 8 r. Dumbara mats 35 40
111/14 .. .. *Set of* 4 65 75

473 King Maha Prathapa visiting Queen Chandra

474 Father T. Long (educationist)

(Des N. Bulathsinhala. Litho State Ptg Wks, Moscow)

1990 (2 May). *Vesak. Wall Paintings from Buduraja Maha Viharaya, Wewurukannala. T* **473** *and similar horiz designs. Multicoloured. P* 12½×12.
1115 75 c. Type **473** 10 10
1116 1 r. Execution of Prince Dharmapala .. 10 10
1117 2 r. Prince Mahinsasaka with the Water Demon 15 15
1118 8 r. King Dahamsonda with the God Sakra disguised as a demon .. 35 35
1115/18 .. .. *Set of* 4 55 55
MS1119 160×99 mm. Nos. 1115/18 .. .. 80 80

(Des S. Silva. Litho Security Printers (M), Malaysia (No. 1120), State Ptg Wks, Moscow (others))

1990 (22 May). *National Heroes. T* **474** *and similar vert designs. Multicoloured. P* 12 (*No.* 1120) *or* 12×12½ (*others*).
1120 1 r. Type **474** 10 10
1121 1 r. Prof. M. Ratnasuriya (37×25 *mm*) .. 10 10
1122 1 r. D. Wijewardene (patriot) (37×25 *mm*) 10 10
1123 1 r. L. Manjusri (artist) (37×25 *mm*) .. 10 10
1120/3 .. .. *Set of* 4 20 20

475 Janasaviya Workers

476 Gold Reliquary

(Des P. Dissanayake. Litho State Ptg Wks, Moscow)

1990 (23 June). *12th Anniv of Gam Udawa and Opening of Janasaviya Centre, Pallekele. P* 12½×12.
1124 **475** 1 r. multicoloured 10 10

(Des N. Bulathsinhala. Litho Security Printers (M), Malaysia)

1990 (7 July). *Centenary of Department of Archaeology. T* **476** *and similar vert designs. P* 12.
1125 1 r. black and orange-yellow 10 10
1126 2 r. black and greenish grey 15 15
1127 3 r. black, apple-green and ochre .. 15 20
1128 8 r. black and ochre 30 35
1125/8 .. .. *Set of* 4 60 65
Designs:—2 r. Statuette of Ganesh; 3 r. Terrace of the Bodhi-tree, Isurumuniya Vihara; 8 r. Inscription of King Nissankamalla.

477 Male Tennis Player at Left

478 Spotted Loach

(Des S. Rohana. Litho Pakistan Security Ptg Corp, Karachi)

1990 (14 Aug). *75th Anniv of Sri Lanka Tennis Association. T* **477** *and similar horiz designs. Multicoloured. P* 13½.
1129 1 r. Type **477** 15 15
a. Horiz pair. Nos. 1129/30 .. .. 30 30
1130 1 r. Male tennis player at right 15 15
1131 8 r. Male tennis players 40 40
a. Horiz pair. Nos. 1131/2 .. .. 80 80
1132 8 r. Female tennis players 40 40
1129/32 .. .. *Set of* 4 1·00 1·00
Nos. 1129/30 and 1131/2 were each printed together, *se-tenant*, in horizontal pairs throughout the sheets, each pair forming a composite design of a singles (1 r.) or doubles (8 r.) match.

(Des R. Samarasinghe. Litho State Ptg Wks, Moscow)

1990 (14 Sept). *Endemic Fishes. T* **478** *and similar horiz designs. Multicoloured. P* 11½.
1133 25 c. Type **478** 10 10
1134 2 r. Ornate Paradise Fish 10 10
1135 8 r. Mountain Labeo 20 25
1136 20 r. Cherry Barb 55 60
1133/6 .. .. *Set of* 4 75 85
MS1137 150×90 mm. Nos. 1133/6 .. .. 80 90

479 Rukmani Devi

480 Innkeeper turning away Mary and Joseph

(Litho Security Printers (M), Malaysia)

1990 (28 Oct). *12th Death Anniv of Rukmani Devi (actress and singer). P* 12.
1138 **479** 1 r. multicoloured 30 20

(Des P. Silva. Litho Security Printers (M), Malaysia)

1990 (28 Nov). *Christmas. T* **480** *and similar vert design. Multicoloured. P* 13.
1139 1 r. Type **480** 10 10
1140 10 r. Adoration of the Magi 35 40
MS1141 190×114 mm. Nos. 1139/40. P 12 .. 50 60

481 Health Worker talking to Villagers

482 Main College Building and Flag

(Des S. Rohana. Litho Security Printers (M), Malaysia)

1990 (30 Nov). *World Aids Day. T* **481** *and similar horiz design. Multicoloured. P* 12.
1142 1 r. Type **481** 10 10
1143 8 r. Emblem and Aids virus 35 45

(Des P. Gunasinghe. Litho Security Printers (M), Malaysia)

1990 (8 Dec). *50th Anniv of Dharmapala College, Pannipitiya. P* 12.
1144 **482** 1 r. multicoloured 20 20

483 Peri Sundaram

484 Letter Box, Galle, 1904

(Litho S. Rohana. Litho Security Printers (M), Malaysia)

1990 (14 Dec). *Birth Centenary of Peri Sundaram (lawyer and politician). P* 12.
1145 **483** 1 r. red-brown and yellow-green .. 20 20

(Des S. Rohana. Litho Security Printers (M), Malaysia)

1990 (26 Dec). *175th Anniv of Sri Lanka Postal Service. T* **484** *and similar vert designs. Multicoloured. P* 12.
1146 1 r. Type **484** 10 10
1147 2 r. Mail runner, 1815 .. .. .. 10 10
1148 5 r. Mail coach, 1832 .. .. .. 20 25
1149 10 r. Nuwara-Eliya Post Office, 1894 .. 35 40
1146/9 .. .. *Set of* 4 60 70

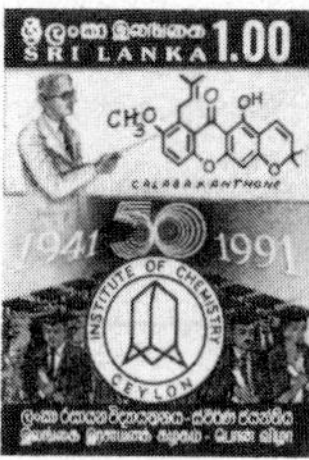

485 Chemical Structure Diagram, Graduating Students and Emblem

486 Kastavahana on Royal Elephant

(Des S. Rohana. Litho Security Printers (M), Malaysia)

1991 (25 Jan). *50th Anniv of Institute of Chemistry. P* 12.
1150 **485** 1 r. multicoloured 20 20

(Des U. Karunaratne. Litho Security Printers (M), Malaysia)

1991 (17 May). *Vesak. Temple Paintings from Karagampitiya Subodarama. T* **486** *and similar horiz designs. Multicoloured. P* 12

1151	75 c. Type **486**	10	10
1152	1 r. Polo Janaka in prison	10	10
1153	2 r. Two merchants offering food to Buddha	15	15
1154	11 r. Escape of Queen	50	50
1151/4	.. .. .. *Set of* 4	75	75
MS1155	150×90 mm. Nos. 1151/4	80	90

487 Narada Thero (Buddhist missionary)

488 Society Building

(Des S. Silva. Litho State Ptg Works, Moscow)

1991 (22 May). *National Heroes. T* **487** *and similar vert designs. Multicoloured. P* 12×12½.

1156	1 r. Type **487**	10	10
1157	1 r. Wallewatta Silva (novelist)	10	10
1158	1 r. Sir Muttu Coomaraswamy (lawyer and politician)	10	10
1159	1 r. Dr. Andreas Nell (opthalmic surgeon)	10	10
1156/9	.. .. *Set of* 4	20	20

(Des R. de Silva. Litho Security Printers (M), Malaysia)

1991 (31 May). *Centenary of Maha Bodhi Society. P* 12.

1160 **488** 1 r. multicoloured 10 10

489 Women working at Home

490 Globe and Plan Symbol

(Des T. Kariyawasam. Litho Security Printers (M), Malaysia)

1991 (23 June). *13th Anniv of Gum Udawa Movement. P* 12½.

1161 **489** 1 r. multicoloured 10 10

(Des R. Mawilmada. Litho Security Printers (M), Malaysia)

1991 (1 July). *40th Anniv of Colombo Plan. P* 12.

1162 **490** 1 r. bright violet and new blue 10 10

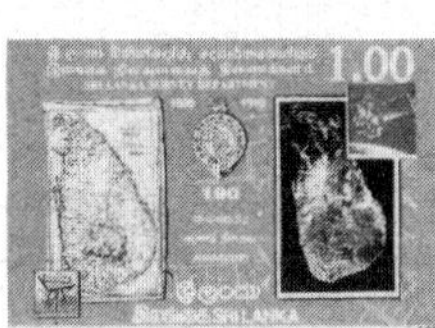
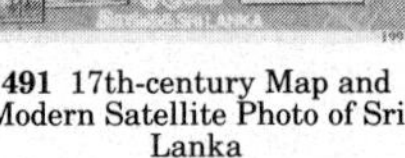

491 17th-century Map and Modern Satellite Photo of Sri Lanka

492 Ven. Henpitagedera Gnanaseeha Nayake Thero

(Des P. Mittapala. Litho Security Printers (M), Malaysia)

1991 (1 Aug). *190th Anniv of Sri Lanka Survey Department. P* 12½.

1163 **491** 1 r. multicoloured 10 10

(Des S. Silva. Litho Security Printers (M), Malaysia)

1991 (1 Aug). *10th Death Anniv of Ven. Nayak Henpitagedera Gnanaseeha Nayake Thero (Buddhist theologian). P* 12½.

1164 **492** 1 r. multicoloured 10 10

PRICES OF SETS

Set prices are given for many issues, generally those containing three stamps or more. Definitive sets include one of each value or major colour change, but do not cover different perforations, die types or minor shades. Where a choice is possible the set prices are based on the cheapest versions of the stamps included in the listings.

OFFICIAL STAMPS

1869. *Issues of 1867–68 overprinted "SERVICE" in block letters.*

Although these stamps were prepared for use and sent out to the colony, they were never issued.

Prices:

Narrow "SERVICE"		Wide "SERVICE"	
No. 98. 2d. ..	50·00	No. 119. 1d. ..	48·00
104. 6d. ..	60·00	120. 3d. ..	75·00
108. 8d. ..	70·00		
113. 1s. ..	85·00		
116. 2s. ..	95·00		
116. 2s. *imp.* ..	£600		

Until 1 October 1895 all Official mail was carried free. After that date postage was paid on Official letters to the general public, on certain interdepartmental mail and on all packets over 1lb in weight. Nos. O1/17 were provided for ths purpose.

On
Service
(O 3)

1895. *Optd with Type* O **3** *by the Govt Printer, Colombo.*

O1	**9**	2 c. green (No. 147)	5·50	25
O2	**39**	3 c. terracotta and blue-green (No. 245)	8·00	40
O3	**28**	5 c. dull purple (No. 195)	1·25	20
O4	**29**	15 c. sage-green (No. 196)	8·50	30
O5		25 c. yellow-brown (No. 198)	10·00	80
O6		30 c. bright mauve and chestnut (No. 247)	11·00	30
O7	**30**	1 r. 12, dull rose (*wmk sideways*) (No. 201)	50·00	45·00
		a. Opt double, one albino	£150	
		b. Wmk upright	65·00	55·00
O1/7		.. .. *Set of* 7	85·00	45·00

1899 (June)–**1900.** *Nos.* 256/7 *and* 261/2 *optd with Type* O **3**.

O 8	**9**	2 c. pale orange-brown (3.00)	2·25	60
O 9	**39**	3 c. deep green (9.00)	7·50	60
O10	**29**	15 c. blue (9.00)	12·00	60
O11	**39**	75 c. black and red-brown (R.)	5·50	4·00
O8/11		.. .. *Set of* 4	24·00	5·25

1903 (26 Nov)–**04.** *Nos.* 265/6, 268 *and* 271/3 *optd with Type* O **3**.

O12	**44**	2 c. red-brown (4.1.04)	5·00	70
O13	**45**	3 c. green	3·00	2·00
O14	**46**	5 c. dull purple	7·50	80
O15	**48**	15 c. blue	18·00	2·50
O16		25 c. bistre (15.7.04)	19·00	15·00
O17		30 c. dull violet and green (14.3.04) ..	6·50	1·50
O12/17		.. .. *Set of* 6	55·00	20·00

Stamps overprinted "On Service" were withdrawn on 1 October 1904.

POSTAL FISCALS

1952 (1 Dec). *As T* **72** *but inscr* "REVENUE" *at sides. Chalk-surfaced paper.*

F1 10 r. dull green and yellow-orange .. .. 50·00 28·00

This revenue stamp was on sale for postal use from 1 December 1952, until 14 March 1954.

F 1 Republic Crest

(Recess Harrison)

1979 (28 May)–**83.** *As Type* F **1**, *but with additional Sinhala and Tamil inscrs on either side of crest. W* **4** *of Maldive Islands. P* 13×12.

F2	20 r. blackish green	4·00	2·50
F3	50 r. deep slate-violet	8·50	5·50
F4	100 r. deep carmine-red (14.10.83) ..	17·00	16·00

The above, together with 500 and 1000 r. values, were originally released for fiscal purposes on 24 June 1974. The dates quoted are those on which they were validated for postal use. All three were withdrawn on 6 August 1984.

(Litho Harrison)

1984 (15 Aug). *W* **77** *of Brunei. P* 14½×14.

F5	F **1**	50 r. orange	15·00	10·00
F6		100 r. dull chocolate	30·00	30·00

A 500 r. value also exists, but was not valid for postal purposes.

(Recess Harrison)

1984 (21 Sept). *W* **77** *of Brunei. P* 14½×14.

F7	F **1**	50 r. orange-vermilion	1·40	1·50
F8		100 r. deep reddish purple	2·75	3·00

Stamps in this series with face values of 500 or 1000 r. were not valid for postal purposes.

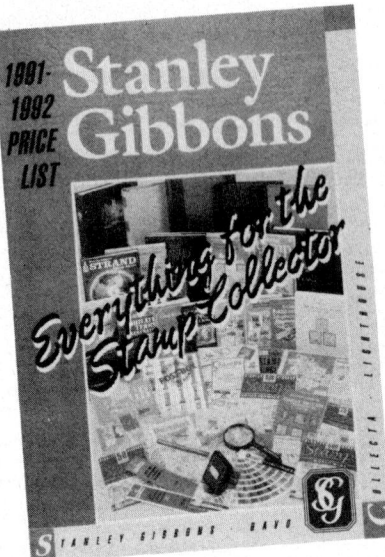

Sudan

ANGLO-EGYPTIAN CONDOMINIUM

An Egyptian post office was opened at Suakin in 1867 and the stamps of Egypt, including postage dues and the official (No. O64), were used in the Sudan until replaced by the overprinted "SOUDAN" issue of 1897.

Cancellations have been identified from eleven post offices, using the following postmark types:

A

B

C

D

E

F

G

H

I

J

K

L

BERBER (*spelt* BARBAR). *Open* 1873 *to* 1884. *Postmark type* G.
DABROUSSA. *Open* 1889? *onwards. Postmark as type* J *but with* 11 *bars in arcs.*
DONGOLA. *Open* 1873 *to* 1885 *and* 1896 *onwards. Postmark types* F, G, K, L.
GEDAREF. *Open* ? *Postmark type* H.
KASSALA. *Open* 1875 *to* 1885. *Postmark type* G.
KHARTOUM. *Open* 1873 *to* 1884. *Postmark types* E (*spelt* KARTUM), G (*spelt* HARTUM), I (*with or without line of Arabic above date*).
KORTI. *Open* 1884/5 *and* 1897. *Postmark type* K.
SUAKIN. *Open* 1867 *onwards. Postmark types* A, B, C (*spelt* SUAKIM), D (*spelt* SUAKIM *and also with year replaced by concentric arcs*), I (*spelt* SOUAKIN), J (*spelt* SAWAKIN, *number of bars differs*).
TANI. *Open* 1885. *Postmark type* K.
TOKAR. *Open* 1891 *onwards. Postmark type* J (7 *bars in arcs*).
WADI HALFA. *Open* 1873 *onwards. Postmark types* F (*spelt* WADI HALFE), G (*spelt* WADI HALFE), I, J (*number of bars differs*).
WADI HALFA CAMP. *Open* 1896 *onwards. Postmark type* I.

Official records also list post offices at the following locations, but no genuine postal markings from them have yet been reported: Chaka, Dara, Debeira, El Abiad, El Fasher, El Kalabat, Faras, Fashoda, Fazogl, Ishkeit, Kalkal, Karkok, Mesellemia, Sara, Sennar and Taoufikia (not to be confused with the town of the same name in Egypt.

M

The post office at Kassala was operated by Italy from 1894 until 1896, using stamps of Eritrea cancelled with postmark type M.

From the last years of the nineteenth century that part of Sudan lying south of the 5 degree North latitude line was administered by Uganda (the area to the east of the Nile) (until 1912) or by Belgium (the area to the west of the Nile, known as the Lado Enclave) (until 1910).

Stamps of Uganda or East Africa and Uganda were used at Gondokoro and Nimuli between 1901 and 1911, usually cancelled with circular date stamps or, probably in transit at Khartoum, by a lozenge-shaped grid of 18 × 17 dots.

Stamps of Belgian Congo were used from the Lado Enclave between 1897 and 1910, as were those of Uganda (1901–10) and Sudan (1902–10), although no local postmarks were supplied, examples being initially cancelled in manuscript.

Stamps of Sudan were used at Gambeila (Ethiopia) between 1910 and 10 June 1940 and from 22 March 1941 until 15 October 1956. Sudan stamps were also used at Sabderat (Eritrea) between March 1910 and 1940.

PRICES FOR STAMPS ON COVER TO 1945

Nos. 1/9	*from* × 20
Nos. 10/17	*from* × 6
Nos. 18/29	*from* × 5
Nos. 30/95	*from* × 2
Nos. D1/11	*from* × 30
Nos. O1/3	—
Nos. O4/22	*from* × 15
Nos. A1/16	*from* × 6

السودان
SOUDAN
(1)

1897 (1 Mar). *Nos.* 54*b*, 55*a*, 57/*a*, 58*a*, 59, 60, 62*a and* 63 *of Egypt optd as T* 1 *by Govt Ptg Wks, Bûlâq, Cairo.*

No.	Description	Unused	Used
1	1 m. pale brown	1·25	2·00
	a. Opt inverted	£250	
	b. Opt omitted (in vert pair with normal)	£900	
	c. *Deep brown*	1·50	2·25
3	2 m. green	1·25	1·75
	a. Opt omitted (in vert pair with normal)	£3000	
4	3 m. orange-yellow	1·40	1·50
	a. Opt omitted (in vert pair with normal)	£3000	
5	5 m. rose-carmine	2·00	70
	a. Opt inverted	£300	
	b. Opt omitted (in vert pair with normal)	£900	
6	1 p. ultramarine	7·00	2·00
7	2 p. orange-brown	40·00	12·00
8	5 p. slate	40·00	12·00
	a. Opt double	£2000	
	b. Opt omitted (in vert pair with normal)	£2750	
9	10 p. mauve	30·00	40·00
1/9	*Set of* 8	£110	65·00

Numerous forgeries exist including some which show the characteristics of the varieties mentioned below.

There are six varieties of the overprint on each value most of which can be supplied in vertical strips at double the catalogue price.

In some printings the large dot is omitted from the left-hand Arabic character on one stamp in the pane of 60.

Only two examples, one unused and the other used (in the Royal Collection), are known of No. 8a. In both instances one impression is partially albino.

PRINTERS. All stamps of Sudan were printed by De La Rue & Co, Ltd, London, *except where otherwise stated.*

2 Arab Postman

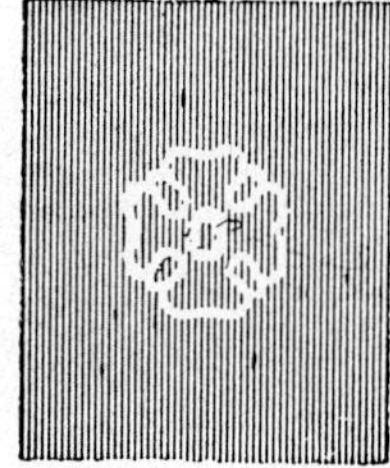
3

(Des E. A. Stanton. Typo)

1898 (1 Mar). *W* 3. *P* 14.

No.	Type	Description	Unused	Used
10	2	1 m. brown and pink	30	40
11		2 m. green and brown	1·00	1·00
12		3 m. mauve and green	1·50	2·00
13		5 m. carmine and black	75	30
14		1 p. blue and brown	4·00	3·00
15		2 p. black and blue	12·00	6·50
16		5 p. brown and green	20·00	7·50
17		10 p. black and mauve	20·00	2·25
10/17		*Set of* 8	55·00	21·00

4

5 Milliemes
(5)

1902–21. *W* 4. *Ordinary paper. P* 14.

No.	Type	Description	Unused	Used
18	2	1 m. brown and carmine (5.05)	30	10
19		2 m. green and brown (11.02)	1·00	10
20		3 m. mauve and green (7.03)	1·25	25
21		4 m. blue and bistre (20.1.07)	1·50	2·50
22		4 m. vermilion and brown (10.07)	1·50	75
23		5 m. scarlet and black (12.03)	2·00	10
24		1 p. blue and brown (12.03)	1·60	15
25		2 p. black and blue (2.08)	22·00	1·75
26		2 p. purple & orge-yellow (*chalk-surfaced paper*) (22.12.21)	3·25	6·00
27		5 p. brown and green (2.08)	22·00	30
		a. Chalk-surfaced paper	22·00	70
28		10 p. black and mauve (2.11)	22·00	1·75
		a. Chalk-surfaced paper	22·00	3·25
18/28		*Set of* 11	70·00	12·50

1903 (Sept). *No.* 16 *surch at Khartoum with T* 5, *in blocks of* 30.

No.	Description	Unused	Used
29	5 m. on 5 pi. brown and green	6·50	9·00
	a. Surch inverted	£300	£275

6

7

1921–23. *Chalk-surfaced paper. Typo. W* 4. *P* 14.

No.	Type	Description	Unused	Used
30	6	1 m. black and orange (4.2.22)	80	1·75
31		2 m. yellow-orange and chocolate (1922)	5·50	6·00
		a. *Yellow and chocolate* (1923)	6·00	6·50
32		3 m. mauve and green (25.1.22)	2·50	4·00
33		4 m. green and chocolate (21.3.22)	3·25	1·25
34		5 m. olive-brown and black (4.2.22)	1·75	10
35		10 m. carmine and black (1922)	1·50	10
36		15 m. bright blue and chestnut (14.12.21)	2·75	1·00
30/36		*Set of* 7	16·00	12·50

1927–41. *W* 7. *Chalk-surfaced paper. P* 14.

No.	Type	Description	Unused	Used
37	6	1 m. black and orange	20	10
		a. Ordinary paper (1941)	20	10
38		2 m. orange and chocolate	20	10
		a. Ordinary paper (1941)	30	10
39		3 m. mauve and green	20	10
		a. Ordinary paper (1941)	40	10

40 6 4 m. green and chocolate 30 10
a. Ordinary paper (1941) 50 10
41 5 m. olive-brown and black 30 10
a. Ordinary paper (1941) 50 10
42 10 m. carmine and black 30 10
a. Ordinary paper (1941) 60 10
43 15 m. bright blue and chestnut 30 10
a. Ordinary paper (1941) 50 10
44 2 2 p. purple and orange-yellow 30 10
a. Ordinary paper (1941) 50 10
44*b* 3 p. red-brown and blue (1.1.40) .. 2·00 10
ba. Ordinary paper (1941) .. .. 3·25 10
44*c* 4 p. ultramarine and black (2.11.36) .. 1·60 10
45 5 p. chestnut and green 80 10
a. Ordinary paper (1941) .. .. 1·00 10
45*b* 6 p. greenish blue and black (2.11.36) 2·00 20
ba. Ordinary paper (1941) .. .. 3·50 50
45*c* 8 p. emerald and black (2.11.36) .. 2·50 90
ca. Ordinary paper (1941) .. .. 4·50 90
46 10 p. black and reddish purple 90 10
a. Ordinary paper. *Black and bright mauve* (1941) .. .. 8·00 70
46*b* 20 p. pale blue and blue (17.10.35) .. 2·00 10
ba. Ordinary paper (1941) .. .. 1·75 10
37/46*b* .. .. *Set of* 15 12·00 1·50

The ordinary paper of this issue is thick, smooth and opaque and was a wartime substitute for chalk-surfaced paper.

For similar stamps, but with different Arabic inscriptions, see Nos. 96/111.

AIR MAIL (8) — AIR MAIL (9) — AIR Extended foot to "R" (R.5/12)

1931 (15 Feb–Mar). *Air. Stamps of* 1927 *optd with T* **8** *or* **9** (2 *p.*).
47 5 m. olive-brown and black (Mar) 35 70
48 10 m. carmine and black .. .. .. 85 3·25
49 2 p. purple and orange-yellow .. .. 85 3·25
a. Extended foot to "R" .. .. .. 18·00
47/9 .. .. *Set of* 3 1·90 6·50

2½ 2½

10 Statue of Gen. Gordon — AIR MAIL (11)

1931 (1 Sept)–**37**. *Air. Recess. W* **7** (*sideways*). *P* 14.
49*b* 10 3 m. green and sepia (1.1.33) .. .. 2·50 5·50
50 5 m. black and green .. .. 1·00 20
51 10 m. black and carmine .. .. 1·00 35
52 15 m. red-brown and sepia 40 10
a. Perf 11½ × 12½ (1937) .. 3·00 10
53 2 p. black and orange 30 10
a. Perf 11½ × 12½ (1937) .. 4·50 13·00
53*b* 2½ p. magenta and blue (1.1.33) .. 3·25 10
c. Perf 11½ × 12½ (1936) .. 1·50 15
ca. Aniline magenta and blue .. 4·50 3·25
54 3 p. black and grey 60 15
a. Perf 11½ × 12½ (1937) .. 85 55
55 3½ p. black and violet .. .. 1·25 80
a. Perf 11½ × 12½ (1937) .. 2·50 10·00
56 4½ p. red-brown and grey .. .. 9·00 15·00
57 5 p. black and ultramarine .. .. 1·00 40
a. Perf 11½ × 12½ (1937) .. 2·00 35
57*b* 7½ p. green and emerald (17.10.35) .. 4·75 3·50
c. Perf 11½ × 12½ (1937) .. 3·00 5·50
57*d* 10 p. brown and greenish blue (17.10.35) 8·00 40
e. Perf 11½ × 12½ (1937) .. 2·25 10·00
49*b*/57*d* .. .. *Set of* 12 (*p* 14) 28·00 24·00
52a/7e .. .. *Set of* 8 (*p* 11½×12½) 16·00 35·00

1932 (18 July). *Air. No.* 44 *surch with T* **11**.
58 2½ p. on 2 p. purple and orange-yellow .. 2·00 3·50

12 Gen. Gordon (after C. Ouless)

13 Gordon Memorial College, Khartoum

14 Gordon Memorial Service, Khartoum (after R. C. Woodville)

1935 (1 Jan). *50th Death Anniv of General Gordon, Recess. W* **7**. *P* 14.
59 12 5 m. green 35 10
60 10 m. yellow-brown 55 25
61 13 m. ultramarine .. .. .. 85 5·00
62 15 m. scarlet .. .. .. 1·25 25
63 13 2 p. blue .. .. 1·25 20
64 5 p. orange-vermilion .. .. .. 1·25 40
65 10 p. purple .. .. 6·50 6·00
66 14 20 p. black .. .. 22·00 45·00
67 50 p. red-brown .. .. .. 65·00 80·00
59/67 .. .. *Set of* 9 90·00 £120

7½ PIASTRES (15) — 5 MILLIEMES (16)

1935. *Air. Surch as T* **15**.
68 10 15 m. on 10 m. black and carmine (Apr) .. 40 10
a. Surch double £600 £700
69 2½ p. on 3 m. green and sepia (Apr) .. 85 4·75
a. Second arabic letter from left missing 65·00 £100
b. Small "½" .. .. .. 2·75 15·00
70 2½ p. on 5 m. black and green (Apr) .. 40 2·00
a. Second Arabic letter from left missing 35·00 55·00
b. Small "½" .. .. .. 1·75 9·00
c. Surch inverted £600 £700
d. Ditto with variety a. £2750
e. Ditto with variety b. £1100
71 3 p. on 4½ p. red-brown and grey (Apr) 1·75 9·00
72 7½ p. on 4½ p. red-brown and grey (Mar) 6·00 32·00
73 10 p. on 4½ p. red-brown and grey (Mar) 5·00 32·00
68/73 .. .. *Set of* 6 13·00 70·00

Nos. 69a and 70a occur in position 49 of the sheet of 50; the small "½" variety occurs in positions 17, 27, 32, 36, 41, 42 and 46.

The 15 m. on 10 m. and the 7½ p. on 4½ p. surcharged in red and the 2½ p. on 3 m. and 2½ p. on 5 m. in green are from proof sheets; the latter two items being known cancelled. A 7¼ p. on 4½ p. also exists from a proof sheet.

1938 (1 July). *Air. Surch as T* **16**.
74 10 5 m. on 2½ p. (*p* 11½ × 12½) .. .. 1·75 10
75 3 p. on 3½ p. (*p* 14) .. .. 22·00 25·00
a. Perf 11½ × 12½ £350 £475
76 3 p. on 7½ p. (*p* 14) .. .. 5·00 6·00
a. Perf 11½ × 12½ £350 £475
77 5 p. on 10 p. (*p* 14) .. .. 1·50 4·25
a. Perf 11½ × 12½ £350 £475
74/7 .. .. *Set of* 4 27·00 32·00

A 5 p. on 2½ p., perf 11½×12½, exists either mint or cancelled from a trial printing (*Price* £350 *unused*).

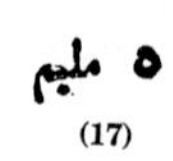

(17)

Normal ("Malime")

"Malmime" (Left-hand pane R. 5/1) — Short "mim" (Right-hand pane R. 3/1) — Broken "lam" (Right-hand pane R. 6/2)

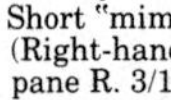

5 M

Inserted "5" (Bottom right-hand pane R. 4/5)

1940 (25 Feb). *Surch with T* **17** *by McCorquodale (Sudan) Ltd, Khartoum.*
78 6 5 m. on 10 m. carmine and black 50 30
a. "Malmime" .. .. .. 30·00 35·00
b. Two dots omitted (Right-hand pane R. 8/6) .. .. .. 30·00 35·00
c. Short "mim" .. .. .. 30·00 35·00
d. Broken "lam" .. .. .. 30·00 35·00
e. Inserted "5" .. .. .. 95·00

4½ PIASTRES (18) — 4½ Piastres (19)

1940–1. *Surch as T* **18** *or* **19** *at Khartoum.*
79 6 4½ p. on 5 m. olive-brown & blk (9.2.41) .. 35·00 2·00
80 2 4½ p. on 8 p. emerald and black (12.12.40) 23·00 4·50

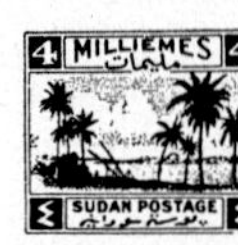

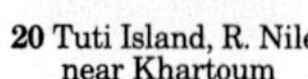

20 Tuti Island, R. Nile, near Khartoum

21 Tuti Island, R. Nile near Khartoum

(Des Miss H. M. Hebbert. Litho Security Printing Press, Nasik, India)

1941 (25 Mar–10 Aug). *P* 14 × 13½ (*T* **20**) *or P* 13½ × 14 (*T* **21**).
81 20 1 m. slate and orange (10.8) .. .. 10 1·00
82 2 m. orange and chocolate (10.8) 30 75
83 3 m. mauve and green (10.8) 30 10
84 4 m. green and chocolate (10.8) 15 20
85 5 m. olive-brown and black (10.8) 15 10
86 10 m. carmine and black (10.8) .. .. 6·00 1·75
87 15 m. bright blue and chestnut 20 10
88 21 2 p. purple and orange-yellow (10.8) .. 3·25 60
89 3 p. red-brown and blue 70 10
90 4 p. ultramarine and black 60 10
91 5 p. chestnut and green (10.8) .. .. 4·50 5·00
92 6 p. greenish blue and black (10.8) .. 14·00 40
93 8 p. emerald and black (10.8) .. .. 11·00 45
94 10 p. slate and purple (10.8) .. .. 40·00 75
95 20 p. pale blue and blue (10.8) .. .. 40·00 22·00
81/95 .. .. *Set of* 15 £110 30·00

22

23

1948 (1 Jan–June). *Arabic inscriptions below camel altered. Typo. W* **7**. *Ordinary paper* (8, 10, 20 *p.*) *or chalk-surfaced paper* (*others*). *P* 14.
96 22 1 m. black and orange 35 75
97 2 m. orange and chocolate 80 90
98 3 m. mauve and green 30 40
99 4 m. deep green and chocolate 30 10
100 5 m. olive-brown and black 75 40
101 10 m. rose-red and black .. .. 1·50 10
a. Centre inverted .. .. † —
102 15 m. ultramarine and chestnut 75 10
103 23 2 p. purple and orange-yellow .. .. 3·00 10
104 3 p. red-brown and deep blue .. .. 2·00 10
105 4 p. ultramarine and black .. .. 2·25 65
106 5 p. brown-orange and deep green .. .. 2·25 35
107 6 p. greenish blue and black .. .. 2·00 90
108 8 p. bluish green and black .. .. 2·25 1·25
109 10 p. black and mauve .. .. 4·00 90
a. Chalk-surfaced paper (June) .. 6·00 1·50
110 20 p. pale blue and deep blue .. .. 2·75 10
a. Perf 13. Chalk-surfaced paper (June) .. .. 38·00 70·00
111 50 p. carmine and ultramarine .. .. 5·00 40
96/111 .. .. *Set of* 16 27·00 6·50

A single used example is known of No. 101a.

For similar stamps, but with different Arabic inscriptions, see Nos. 37/46*b*.

24

25

1948 (1 Oct). *Golden Jubilee of "Camel Postman" design. Chalk-surfaced paper. Typo. W* **7**. *P* 13.
112 24 2 p. black and light blue 10 10

1948 (23 Dec). *Opening of Legislative Assembly, Chalk-surfaced paper. Typo. W* **7**. *P* 13.
113 25 10 m. rose-red and black 10 10
114 5 p. brown-orange and deep green .. 10 30

26 Blue Nile Bridge, Khartoum

(Des Col. W. L. Atkinson (2½ p., 6 p.), G. R. Wilson (3 p.), others from photographs. Recess)

1950 (1 July). *Air. T* **26** *and similar horiz designs. W* **7**. *P* 12.
115 2 p. black and blue-green .. .. 3·00 2[illegible]
116 2½ p. light blue and red-orange .. .. 50 4[illegible]
117 3 p. reddish purple and blue .. .. 2·00 1[illegible]
118 3½ p. purple-brown and yellow-brown .. 75 2·0[illegible]
119 4 p. brown and light blue .. .. 70 7[illegible]
120 4½ p. black and ultramarine .. .. 2·00 2·7[illegible]
a. Black and steel-blue .. .. 2·25 3·0[illegible]
121 6 p. black and carmine .. .. 60 5[illegible]
122 20 p. black and purple .. .. 1·75 2·2[illegible]
115/122 .. .. *Set of* 8 10·00 8·0[illegible]

Designs:—2½ p. Kassala Jebel; 3 p. Sagia (water wheel); 3½ p. Port Sudan; 4 p. Gordon Memorial College; 4½ p. Gordon Pasha (Nile mail boat); 6 p. Suakin; 20 p. G.P.O., Khartoum.

34 Ibex 35 Cotton Picking

(Des Col. W. L. Atkinson (1 m., 2 m., 4 m., 5 m., 10 m., 3 p., 3½ p., 20 p.), Col. E. A. Stanton (50 p.) others from photographs. Typo)

1951 (1 Sept)–**62**? *Designs as T* **34/5**. *Chalk-surfaced paper.* **W 7**. *P* 14 (*millieme values*) *or* 13 (*piastre values*).

123 1 m. black and orange 10 80
124 2 m. black and bright blue 40 15
125 3 m. black and green 1·75 1·75
126 4 m. black and yellow-green 30 70
127 5 m. black and purple 30 10
a. *Black and reddish purple* (1962?) 60 10
128 10 m. black and pale blue 15 10
129 15 m. black and chestnut 40 10
a. *Black and brown-orange* (1962?) 40 10
130 2 p. deep blue and pale blue 15 10
a. *Deep blue and very pale blue* (1962?) 60 10
131 3 p. brown and deep ultramarine 1·00 10
a. *Brown and deep blue* (1962?) 1·75 20
132 3½ p. bright green and red-brown 30 10
133 4 p. ultramarine and black 30 10
a. *Deep blue and black* (1962?) 1·25 10
134 5 p. orange-brown and yellow-green 30 10
135 6 p. blue and black 2·25 65
a. *Deep blue and black* (1962?) 3·50 1·50
136 8 p. blue and brown 3·25 70
a. *Deep blue and brown* (1962?) 4·00 40
137 10 p. black and green 1·00 10
138 20 p. blue-green and black 3·00 50
139 50 p. carmine and black 7·00 55
123/139 *Set of* 17 20·00 5·00

Designs: *Vert as T* **34**—2 m. Whale-headed Stork; 3 m. Giraffe; 4 m. Baggara girl; 5 m. Shilluk warrior; 10 m. Hadendowa; 15 m. Policeman. *Horiz as T* **35**—3 p. Ambatch reed canoe; 3½ p. Nuba wrestlers; 4 p. Weaving; 5 p. Saluka farming; 6 p. Gum tapping; 8 p. Darfur chief; 10 p. Stack Laboratory; 20 p. Nile Lechwe. *Vert as T* **35**—50 p. Camel postman.

SELF-GOVERNMENT

51 Camel Postman

1954 (9 Jan). *Self-Government. Chalk-surfaced paper. Typo.* **W 7**. *P* 13.

140 **51** 15 m. orange-brown and bright green 40 40
141 3 p. blue and indigo 40 60
142 5 p. black and reddish purple 40 30
140/2 *Set of* 3 1·10 1·10

Stamps as Type **51**, but dated "1953" were released in error at the Sudan Agency in London. They had no postal validity (*Price per set* £14 *un*).

Later issues of Sudan as an independent republic will be found in Part 14 (*Africa since Independence N–Z*) of this catalogue.

POSTAGE DUE STAMPS

1897 (1 Mar). *Type* D **3** *of Egypt, optd with* T **1** *at Bûlâq*.

D1 2 m. green 1·75 8·00
a. Opt omitted (in horiz pair with normal) £2250
D2 4 m. maroon 1·75 8·00
a. Bisected (2 m.) (on cover) † —
D3 1 p. ultramarine 6·00 5·00
D4 2 p. orange 7·50 11·00
a. Bisected (1 p.) (on cover) † £1200
D1/4 *Set of* 4 15·00 29·00

In some printings the large dot is omitted from the left-hand Arabic character on one stamp in the pane.

No. D1 has been recorded used as a bisect.

D 1 Gunboat *Zafir* D 2

1901 (1 Jan)–**12**. *Typo.* **W 4** (*sideways*). *Ordinary paper. P* 14.

D5 D **1** 2 m. black and brown 55 60
a. Wmk upright
b. Chalk-surfaced paper (1912) 55 1·25
D6 4 m. brown and green 2·00 90
a. Chalk-surfaced paper (1912) 2·25 1·40
D7 10 m. green and mauve 3·75 3·75
a. Wmk upright † —
b. Chalk-surfaced paper (1912) 6·00 4·25
D8 20 m. ultramarine and carmine 3·25 3·25
a. Chalk-surfaced paper (1912) 7·00 7·50
D5/8 *Set of* 4 8·00 7·50

Nos. D6 and D8 exist used as bisects.

1927–30. **W 7**. *Chalk-surfaced paper. P* 14.

D 9 D **1** 2 m. black and brown (1930) 1·75 2·00
D10 4 m. brown and green 90 80
D11 10 m. green and mauve 1·25 1·60
a. Ordinary paper
D9/11 *Set of* 3 3·50 4·00

1948 (1 Jan). *Arabic inscriptions at foot altered. Chalk-surfaced paper. Typo.* **W 7**. *P* 14.

D12 D **2** 2 m. black and brown-orange 80 13·00
D13 4 m. brown and green 2·00 16·00
D14 10 m. green and mauve 6·50 10·00
D15 20 m. ultramarine and carmine 11·00 16·00
D12/15 *Set of* 4 18·00 50·00

The 10 and 20 m. were reissued in 1980 on Sudan arms watermarked paper.

OFFICIAL STAMPS

1900 (8 Feb). *5 mils of* 1897 *punctured* "S G" *by hand. The* "S" *has* 14 *and the* "G" 12 *holes*.

O1 5 m. rose-carmine 45·00 20·00

1901 (Jan). *1 m. wmk Quatrefoil, punctured as No.* O1.

O2 1 m. brown and pink 42·00 30·00

Nos. O1/2 are found with the punctured "SG" inverted, reversed or inverted and reversed.

O.S.G.S. **O.S.G.S.**

(O 1) ("On Sudan Government Service") (O 2)

1902. *No.* 10 *optd at Khartoum as Type* O **1** *in groups of* 30 *stamps*.

O3 **2** 1 m. brown and pink 2·00 7·50
a. Oval "O" (No. 19) 65·00 £110
b. Round stops. (Nos. 25 to 30) 7·50 30·00
c. Opt inverted £275 £350
d. Ditto and oval "O" £2000
e. Ditto and round stops £600 £750
f. Opt double £350
g. Ditto and round stops £800
h. Ditto and oval "O"

1903–12. *T* **2** *optd as Type* O **2**, *by D.L.R. in sheets of* 120 *stamps*.

(i) *Wmk Quatrefoil* (3.06)

O 4 10 p. black and mauve 13·00 15·00
a. Malformed "O" £120

(ii) *Wmk Mult Star and Crescent*

O 5 1 m. brown and carmine (9.04) 40 10
a. Opt double
b. Malformed "O" 19·00
O 6 3 m. mauve and green (2.04) 1·50 15
a. Opt double £850 £850
b. Malformed "O" 35·00
O 7 5 m. scarlet and black (1.1.03) 1·75 10
a. Malformed "O" 40·00
O 8 1 p. blue and brown (1.1.03) 1·75 10
a. Malformed "O" 40·00
O 9 2 p. black and blue (1.1.03) 11·00 20
a. Malformed "O" £110
O10 5 p. brown and green (1.1.03) 2·00 30
a. Malformed "O" 45·00
O11 10 p. black and mauve (9.12) 4·00 35·00
a. Malformed "O" 65·00
O4/11 *Set of* 8 32·00 45·00

The malformed "O" is slightly flattened on the left-hand side and occurs on position 7 of the lower pane.

1913 (Jan)–**22**. *Nos.* 18/20 *and* 23/8 *punctured* "SG" *by machine. The* "S" *has* 12 *holes and the* "G" 13.

O12 **2** 1 m. brown and carmine 2·25 25
O13 2 m. green and brown (1915) 4·75 2·00
O14 3 m. mauve and green 3·25 70
O15 5 m. scarlet and black 1·40 15
O16 1 p. blue and brown 2·25 35
O17 2 p. black and blue 3·00 65
O18 2 p. purple and orange-yellow (*chalk-surfaced paper*) (1922) 3·75 2·75
O19 5 p. brown and green 6·50 1·50
a. Chalk-surfaced paper 6·50 1·50
O20 10 p. black and mauve (1914) 9·00 9·00
a. Chalk-surfaced paper 9·00 9·00
O12/20 *Set of* 9 32·00 16·00

1922. *Nos.* 32/5 *punctured* "SG" *by machine. The* "S" *has* 9 *holes and the* "G" 10.

O21 **6** 3 m. mauve and green 10·00 5·50
O22 4 m. green and chocolate 10·00 5·00
O23 5 m. olive-brown and black 1·00 55
O24 10 m. carmine and black 2·00 60
O21/4 *Set of* 4 21·00 10·50

1927–30. *Nos.* 39/42, 44, 45 *and* 46 *punctured* "SG" *by machine. Nos.* O25/8 *have* 9 *holes in the* "S" *and* 10 *in the* "G"; *Nos.* O29/31 12 *holes in the* "S" *and* 13 *in the* "G".

O25 **6** 3 m. mauve and green (1928) 6·00 2·25
O26 4 m. green and chocolate (1930) 50·00 30·00
O27 5 m. olive-green and black 1·50 10
O28 10 m. carmine and black 2·50 35
O29 **2** 2 p. purple and orange-yellow 5·50 75
O30 5 p. chestnut and green 11·00 3·50
O31 10 p. black and reddish purple 19·00 10·00
O25/31 *Set of* 7 85·00 42·00

The use of Nos. O25/31 on internal official mail ceased in 1932, but they continued to be required for official mail to foreign destinations until replaced by Nos. O32/46 in 1936.

S.G. **S.G.** **S.G.**

(O 3) (O 4) (O 4*a*)

1936 (19 Sept)–**46**. *Nos.* 37a, 38a, 39/43 *optd with Type* O **3**, *and* 44, 44ba, 44c, 45, 45ba, 45c, 46 *and* 46ba *with Type* O **4**. **W 7**. *P* 14.

O32 **6** 1 m. black and orange (22.11.46) 35 5·00
a. Opt double † —
O33 2 m. orange and chocolate (4.45) 30 2·00
O34 3 m. mauve and green (1.37) 1·00 10
O35 4 m. green and chocolate 1·25 2·25
O36 5 m. olive-brown and black (3.40) 40 10
a. Ordinary paper 5·00 40
O37 10 m. carmine and black (6.46) 35 10
O38 15 m. bright blue and chestnut (21.6.37) 1·50 10
a. Ordinary paper 6·00 40
O39 **2** 2 p. purple and orange-yellow (4.37) 3·00 10
a. Ordinary paper 9·50 2·50
O39*b* 3 p. red-brown and blue (4.46) 75 50
O39*c* 4 p. ultramarine and black (4.46) 3·00 15
ca. Ordinary paper 15·00 4·00
O40 5 p. chestnut and green 4·50 10
a. Ordinary paper 15·00 4·00
O40*b* 6 p. greenish blue and black (4.46) 3·00 1·00
O40*c* 8 p. emerald and black (4.46) 3·25 10·00
O41 10 p. black and reddish purple (10.37) 9·00 3·50
a. Ordinary paper. *Black and bright mauve* (1941) 16·00 2·25
O42 20 p. pale blue and blue (6.46) 9·50 13·00
O32/42 *Set of* 15 35·00 32·00

1948 (1 Jan). *Nos.* 96/102 *optd with Type* O **3**, *and* 103/111 *with Type* O **4**.

O43 **22** 1 m. black and orange 10 1·00
O44 2 m. orange and chocolate 30 10
O45 3 m. mauve and green 40 1·75
O46 4 m. deep green and chocolate 40 10
O47 5 m. olive-brown and black 30 10
O48 10 m. rose-red and black 30 15
O49 15 m. ultramarine and chestnut 30 10
O50 **23** 2 p. purple and orange-yellow 35 10
O51 3 p. red-brown and deep blue 35 10
O52 4 p. ultramarine and black 50 10
a. Perf 13 (optd Type O 4*a*) 12·00 14·00
O53 5 p. brown-orange and deep green 50 10
O54 6 p. greenish blue and black 50 10
O55 8 p. bluish green and black 50 30
O56 10 p. black and mauve 60 20
O57 20 p. pale blue and deep blue 2·25 25
O58 50 p. carmine and ultramarine 35·00 15·00
O43/58 *Set of* 16 38·00 17·00

1950 (1 July). *Air. Optd with Type* O **4***a*.

O59 2 p. black and blue-green (R.) 7·50 1·25
O60 2½ p. light blue and red-orange 1·25 80
O61 3 p. reddish purple and blue 80 70
O62 3½ p. purple-brown and yellow-brown 80 3·50
O63 4 p. brown and light blue 80 2·75
O64 4½ p. black and ultramarine (R.) 2·50 7·50
a. *Black and steel-blue* 3·75 8·50
O65 6 p. black and carmine (R.) 1·00 3·50
O66 20 p. black and purple (R.) 5·00 10·00
O59/66 *Set of* 8 18·00 27·00

1951 (1 Sept)–**62**? *Nos.* 123/9 *optd with Type* O **3**, *and* 130/9 *with Type* O **4***a*.

O67 1 m. black and orange (R.) 30 2·00
O68 2 m. black and bright blue (R.) 30 10
O69 3 m. black and green (R.) 1·50 7·50
O70 4 m. black and yellow-green (R.) 10 1·40
O71 5 m. black and purple (R.) 10 10
O72 10 m. black and pale blue (R.) 10 10
O73 15 m. black and chestnut (R.) 10 10
O74 2 p. deep blue and pale blue 10 10
a. Opt inverted £375
b. *Deep blue and very pale blue* (1962?) 20 10
O75 3 p. brown and pale ultramarine 75 10
a. *Brown and deep blue* (1962?) 1·75 20
O76 3½ p. bright green and red-brown 25 10
a. *Light emerald & red-brown* (1962?) 1·00 20
O77 4 p. ultramarine and black 25 10
a. *Deep blue and black* (1962?) 30 10
O78 5 p. orange-brown and yellow-green 25 10
O79 6 p. blue and black 30 95
a. *Deep blue and black* (1962?) 1·50 1·75
O80 8 p. blue and brown 45 10
a. *Deep blue and brown* (1962?) 80 25
O81 10 p. black and green (R.) 50 10
O81*a* 10 p. black and green (Blk.) (1958) 6·50 15
O82 20 p. blue-green and black 1·25 25
a. Opt inverted — £550
O83 50 p. carmine and black 3·50 1·25
O67/83 *Set of* 18 14·00 13·00

The 5, 10 and 15 m. values were later reissued with a thinner overprint.

ARMY SERVICE STAMPS

ARMY OFFICIAL ARMY OFFICIAL **Army Service**

(A 1) (A 2) (A 3)

1905 (Jan). *T* **2** *optd at Khartoum as Types* A **1** *or* A **2**. *Wmk Mult Star and Crescent*. (i) "ARMY" *reading up*.

A1 1 m. brown and carmine (A 1) 2·50 2·00
a. "!" for "I" 45·00 24·00
b. Opt Type A **2** 32·00 16·00

(ii) *Overprint horizontal*

A2 1 m. brown and carmine (A 1) £325
a. "!" for "I" £3500
b. Opt Type A **2** £2000

The horizontal overprint exists with either "ARMY" or "OFFICIAL" reading the right way up. It did not fit the stamps, resulting in misplacements where more than one whole overprint appears, or when the two words are transposed.

(iii) "ARMY" *reading down*

A3 1 m. brown and carmine (A 1) .. .. 65·00 55·00
a. "!" for "I".. .. .. £700 £700
b. Opt Type A **2** £600 £425

1905 (Nov). *As No* A 1, *but wmk Quatrefoil, W* **3**.

A4 1 m. brown and pink (A 1) £100 £110
a. "!" for "I".. .. .. £2500 £1600
b. Opt Type A **2** £1100 £1100

The 29th stamp in each setting of 30 (Nos. A1–A4) has an exclamation mark for first "I" in "OFFICIAL" while the 6th and 12th stamps are Type A **2**.

Two varieties of the 1 millieme

A. 1st Ptg. 14 mm between lines of opt.
B. Later Ptgs. 12 mm between lines.
All other values are Type B.

1906 (Jan)–**11**. *T* **2** *optd as Type* A **3**.

(i) *Wmk Mult Star and Crescent, W* 4

A 5 1 m. brown and carmine (Type A) £225 £180
A 6 1 m. brown and carmine (Type B) .. .. 1·50 20
a. Opt double, one diagonal .. .. † £650
b. Opt inverted £325 £325
c. Pair, one without opt .. .. ..
d. "Service" omitted .. .. .. † £3250
e. "A" for "A" in "Army" £150 £150
A 7 2 m. green and brown .. .. .. 5·00 1·00
a. Pair, one without opt £1600
b. "Army" omitted £2500
A 8 3 m. mauve and green .. .. .. 16·00 40
a. Opt inverted £1700
A 9 5 m. scarlet and black .. .. .. 1·25 10
a. Opt. double £190 £190
ab. Opt double, one diagonal £200
b. Opt inverted .. .. † £200
c. "Amry" .. .. † £2250
d. "A" for "A" in "Army" .. .. .. — £250
e. Opt double, one inverted £700 £350
A10 1 p. blue and brown.. .. .. .. 8·50 15
a. "Army" omitted .. .. † £2000
A11 2 p. black and blue (1.09) .. .. .. 22·00 11·00
a. Opt double .. .. † £2250
A12 5 p. brown and green (5.08) .. .. 75·00 42·00
A13 10 p. black and mauve (5.11) £450 £550
A6/10 Optd "Specimen" .. .. *Set of* 5 £150

There were a number of printings of these Army Service stamps; the earlier are as Type A **3**; the 1908 printing has a narrower "A" in "Army" and the 1910–11 printings have the tail of the "y" in "Army" much shorter.

(ii) *Wmk Quatrefoil, W* 3

A14 2 p. black and blue .. .. 40·00 9·00
A15 5 p. brown and green .. .. .. 90·00 £100
A16 10 p. black and mauve £120 £150
A14/16 .. .. *Set of* 3 £225 £225
A14/16 Optd "Specimen" .. .. *Set of* 3 £120

1912 (1 Jan)–**22**. *Nos.* 18/20 *and* 23/8 *punctured* "AS" *by machine. The* "A" *has* 12 *holes and the* "S" 11.

A17 **2** 1 m. brown and carmine .. .. 12·00 1·50
A18 2 m. green and brown .. .. .. 2·50 70
A19 3 m. mauve and green .. .. .. 17·00 1·50
A20 5 m. scarlet and black .. .. .. 2·00 35
a. On No. 13 .. ..
A21 1 p. blue and brown .. .. .. 5·50 50
A22 2 p. black and blue .. .. .. 13·00 2·25
A23 2 p. purple and orange-yellow (*chalk-surfaced paper*) (1922) .. .. 23·00 13·00
A24 5 p. brown and green .. .. .. 18·00 10·00
a. Chalk-surfaced paper .. .. 18·00 10·00
A25 10 p. black and mauve (1914) £400 £225
A17/25 .. .. *Set of* 9 £450 £225

1922–24. *Nos.* 31*a and* 34/5 *punctured* "AS" *by machine. The* "A" *has* 8 *holes and the* "S" 9.

A26 **6** 2 m. yellow and chocolate (1924) .. 28·00 16·00
A27 5 m. olive-brown and black (4.2.22) .. 3·00 75
A28 10 m. carmine and black.. .. .. 4·00 1·25
A26/8.. .. .. *Set of* 3 32·00 16·00

The use of Nos. A17/28 on internal Army mail ceased when the Egyptian units were withdrawn at the end of 1924, but existing stocks continued to be used on Army mail to foreign destinations until supplies were exhausted.

Swaziland

PRICES FOR STAMPS ON COVER TO 1945

Nos. 1/10	*from* × 40
Nos. 11/20	*from* × 4
Nos. 21/4	*from* × 5
Nos. 25/7	*from* × 10
Nos. 28/38	*from* × 4
Nos. 39/41	*from* × 5
Nos. D1/2	*from* × 30

TRIPARTITE GOVERNMENT

Following internal unrest and problems caused by the multitude of commercial concessions granted by the Swazi king the British and Transvaal governments intervened during 1889 to establish a tripartite administration under which the country was controlled by their representatives, acting with the agent of the Swazi king.

The Pretoria government had previously purchased the concession to run the postal service and, on the establishment of the tripartite administration, provided overprinted Transvaal stamps for use from the post offices opened at Bremersdorp, Darkton and Embekelweni.

Swazieland
(1)

1889 (18–20 Oct). *Stamps of Transvaal (South African Republic) optd with T* **1**, *in black*. (*a*) *P* 12½ × 12.

1 **18** 1d. carmine .. .. 14·00 15·00
a. Opt inverted.. .. .. .. £425 £500
2 2d. olive-bistre .. .. 70·00 15·00
a. Opt inverted.. .. .. .. — £900
b. "Swazielan" £900 £650
3 1s. green .. .. 10·00 13·00
a. Opt inverted.. .. .. .. £475 £450

(*b*) *P* 12½

4 **18** ½d. grey .. .. 8·50 16·00
a. Opt inverted.. .. .. .. £425 £475
b. "Swazielan" £750 £650
c. "Swazielan" inverted .. .. — £2250
5 2d. olive-bistre .. .. 12·00 14·00
a. Opt inverted.. .. .. .. £425 £450
b. "Swazielan" £425 £450
c. "Swazielan" inverted £1600 £1600
d. Opt double £1800
6 6d. blue .. .. 15·00 30·00
7 2s. 6d. buff (20 Oct) £110 £150
8 5s. slate-blue (20 Oct) £110 £150
a. Opt inverted.. .. .. .. £1600 £1600
b. "Swazielan" £4000
c. "Swazielan" inverted .. ..
9 10s. fawn (20 Oct) £4500 £2750

The variety without "d" occurs on the left-hand bottom corner stamp in each sheet of certain printings.

1892 (Aug). *Optd in carmine. P* 12½.

10 **18** ½d. grey.. .. .. 7·00 13·00
a. Opt inverted £475
b. Opt double £400 £400
c. Pair, one without opt .. .. — £600

A printing of the above with stop after "Swazieland" was made in July 1894 but these were not issued.

After further negotiations in 1894 the British and Transvaal governments agreed that Swaziland would become a protectorate of the Transvaal in February 1895. The overprinted stamps were withdrawn on 7 November 1894 and replaced by ordinary issues of the Transvaal.

Shortly after the outbreak of the Boer War in 1899 the Transvaal administration withdrew from Swaziland and there was no postal service from the area until the country became a British Protectorate in March 1902. From that date, until the introduction of the 1933 definitives, the post offices listed below used Transvaal or South Africa stamps.

The following post offices or postal agencies existed in Swaziland before 1933. Dates given are those on which it is generally accepted that the offices were first opened. Some were subsequently closed before the end of the period.

Bremersdorp (1889)	Mankaiana (1913)
Darkton (1889)	Mbabane (*previously* Embabaan) (1905)
Dwaleni (1918)	M'dimba (1898)
Embabaan (1895)	Mhlotsheni (1910)
Embekelweni (1889)	Mooihoek (1918)
Ezulweni (1910)	Motshane (1929)
Forbes Reef (1906)	Nomahasha (1904)
Goedgegun (1925)	Nsoko (1927)
Hlatikulu (1903)	Piggs Peak (1899)
Hluti (1912)	Sandhlan (1903)
Ivy (1912)	Sicunusa (1913)
Kubuta (1926)	Stegi (1910)
Mahamba (1899)	Umkwakweni (1898)
Malkerns (1914)	White Umbuluzi (1925)
Malomba (1928)	

BRITISH PROTECTORATE

2 King George V

3 King George VI

(Des Rev. C. C. Tugman. Recess D.L.R.)

1933 (2 Jan). *Wmk Mult Script CA. P* 14.

11 **2** ½d. green 25 30
12 1d. carmine 25 10
13 2d. brown 30 45
14 3d. blue 45 50
15 4d. orange .. .. 1·00 1·40
16 6d. bright purple .. .. 1·00 80
17 1s. olive .. .. 1·50 2·75
18 2s. 6d. bright violet .. .. .. 15·00 28·00
19 5s. grey .. .. 35·00 50·00
20 10s. sepia £100 £120
11/20 .. .. *Set of* 10 £140 £180
11/20 Perf "Specimen" .. .. *Set of* 10 £225

The ½d., 1d., 2d. and 6d. values exist overprinted "OFFICIAL", but authority for their use was withdrawn before any were actually used. However, some stamps had already been issued to the Secretariat staff before instructions were received to invalidate their use (*Price £10000 per set un*).

1935 (4 May). *Silver Jubilee. As Nos.* 114/17 *of Jamaica. P* 11×12.

21 1d. deep blue and scarlet 30 20
a. Extra flagstaff .. .. 85·00
b. Short extra flagstaff .. .. .. 55·00
c. Lightning conductor .. .. .. 60·00
d. Flagstaff on right-hand turret .. .. 50·00
e. Double flagstaff .. .. 50·00
22 2d. ultramarine and grey-black 30 30
a. Extra flagstaff .. .. 80·00
b. Short extra flagstaff .. .. .. 60·00
c. Lightning conductor .. .. .. 55·00
23 3d. brown and deep blue .. .. .. 45 1·25
a. Extra flagstaff .. .. 65·00
b. Short extra flagstaff .. .. .. 55·00
c. Lightning conductor .. .. .. 50·00
24 6d. slate and purple .. .. 60 1·00
a. Extra flagstaff .. .. 75·00
b. Short extra flagstaff .. .. .. 60·00
c. Lightning conductor .. .. .. 60·00
21/4 .. .. *Set of* 4 1·50 2·50
21/4 Perf "Specimen" .. .. *Set of* 4 75·00

For illustrations of plate varieties see Omnibus section following Zimbabwe.

1937 (12 May). *Coronation. As Nos.* 118/20 *of Jamaica, but ptd by B.W. P* 11×11½.

25 1d. carmine 65 20
26 2d. yellow-brown 65 10
27 3d. blue 65 30
25/7 .. .. *Set of* 3 1·75 55
25/7 Perf "Specimen" .. .. *Set of* 3 60·00

(Recess D.L.R.)

1938 (1 Apr)–**54**. *Wmk Mult Script CA. P* 13½ × 13.

28 **3** ½d. green 70 35
a. Perf 13½ × 14 (1.43) 15 80
b. Perf 13½ × 14. *Bronze-green* (2.50) .. 30 1·50
29 1d. rose-red 65 20
a. Perf 13½ × 14 (1.43) 30 35
30 1½d. light blue .. .. 2·50 40
a. Perf 14 (1941) 75 80
b. Perf 13½ × 14 (1.43) 15 35
31 2d. yellow-brown .. .. 2·00 50
a. Perf 13½ × 14 (1.43) 15 15
32 3d. ultramarine .. .. 3·50 80
a. *Deep blue* (10.38) .. .. .. 3·50 80
b. Perf 13½ × 14. *Ultramarine* (1.43) .. 60 1·40
c. Perf 13½ × 14. *Light ultram* (10.46) 2·50 2·75
d. Perf 13½ × 14. *Deep blue* (10.47) .. 2·50 2·75
33 4d. orange .. .. 1·50 75
a. Perf 13½ × 14 (1.43) .. .. .. 30 1·00
34 6d. deep magenta .. .. 3·25 80
a. Perf 13½ × 14 (1.43) .. .. .. 1·25 2·00
b. Perf 13½ × 14. *Reddish purple (shades)* (7.44) .. .. 1·25 55
c. Perf 13½ × 14. *Claret* (13.10.54) .. 1·50 55
35 1s. brown-olive .. .. 5·50 50
a. Perf 13½ × 14 (1.43) 30 20
36 2s. 6d. bright violet .. .. .. 15·00 4·00
a. Perf 13½ × 14. *Violet* (1.43) .. .. 3·75 1·50
b. Perf 13½ × 14. *Reddish violet* (10.47) .. .. 3·25 2·75
37 5s. grey .. .. 32·00 5·50
a. Perf 13½ × 14. *Slate* (1.43) .. .. 45·00 40·00
b. Perf 13½ × 14. *Grey* (5.44).. .. 11·00 8·00
38 10s. sepia .. .. 35·00 4·75
a. Perf 13½ × 14 (1.43) .. .. .. 5·00 4·50
28/38a .. .. *Set of* 11 20·00 13·50
28/38 Perf "Specimen" .. .. *Set of* 11 £190

The above perforations vary slightly from stamp to stamp, but the average measurements are respectively: 13.3 × 13.2 comb (13½ × 13), 14.2 line (14) and 13.3 × 13.8 comb (13½ × 14).

Swaziland
(4)

1945 (3 Dec). *Victory. Nos.* 108/10 *of South Africa optd with T* **4**.

			Un pair	*Us pair*
39	1d. brown and carmine	.. .. ..	30	30
40	2d. slate-blue and violet	.. .. ..	30	30
41	3d. deep blue and blue	.. .. ..	35	1·00
39/41	.. ..	*Set of* 3 *pairs*	85	1·40

1947 (17 Feb). *Royal Visit. As Nos.* 32/5 *of Lesotho.*

			Un	*Us*
42	1d. scarlet	.. ..	10	10
43	2d. green	.. ..	10	10
44	3d. ultramarine	.. ..	10	10
45	1s. mauve	.. ..	10	10
42/5	.. ..	*Set of* 4	15	20
42/5 Perf "Specimen"	.. ..	*Set of* 4	80·00	

1948 (1 Dec). *Royal Silver Wedding. As Nos.* 143/4 *of Jamaica.*

46 1½d. ultramarine 30 10
47 10s. purple-brown .. .. 17·00 12·00

1949 (10 Oct). *75th Anniv of U.P.U. As Nos. 145/8 of Jamaica.*

48	1½d. blue	10	10
49	3d. deep blue	40	30
50	6d. magenta	50	40
51	1s. olive	50	40
48/51	*Set of* 4	1·40	1·10

1953 (3 June). *Coronation. As No. 153 of Jamaica.*

52	2d. black and yellow-brown	10	15

5 Havelock Asbestos Mine

7 Swazi Married Woman

(Recess B.W.)

1956 (2 July). *T* **5, 7** *and similar designs. Wmk Mult Script CA. P* 13 × 13½ (*horiz*) *or* 13½ × 13 (*vert*).

53	**5**	½d. black and orange	10	10
54	–	1d. black and emerald	10	10
55	**7**	2d. black and brown	10	10
56	–	3d. black and rose-red	10	10
57	–	4½d. black and deep bright blue	40	10
58	–	6d. black and magenta	20	10
59	**5**	1s. black and deep olive	15	10
60	–	1s. 3d. black and sepia	80	45
61	–	2s. 6d. emerald and carmine-red	1·00	70
62	–	5s. deep lilac and slate-black	3·50	85
63	**7**	10s. black and deep lilac	9·00	4·00
64	–	£1 black and turquoise-blue	25·00	24·00
53/64		*Set of* 12	35·00	27·00

Designs: *Horiz*—1d., 2s. 6d. A Highveld view; *Vert*—3d., 1s. 3d. Swazi courting couple; 4½d., 5s. Swazi warrior; 6d., £1. Greater Kudu.

(New Currency. 100 cents = 1 rand)

½c (11) 1c (12) 2c (13) 3½c (14)

2½c (I) 2½c (II) 4c (I) 4c (II)

5c (I) 5c (II) 25c (I) 25c (II)

50c (I) 50c (II) 50c (III)

R1 (I) R1 (II) R1 (III) R2 (I) R2 (II)

1961 (14 Feb–May). *Nos. 53/64 surch as T* **11** *to* **14**.

65	½c. on ½d.	2·00	2·00
	a. Surch inverted	£225	
66	1 c. on 1d.	10	15
	a. Surch double*	£300	
67	2 c. on 2d.	10	15
68	2½ c. on 2d.	10	10
69	2½ c. on 3d. (Type I)	10	10
	a. Type II	10	15
70	3½ c. on 2d. (May)	10	10
71	4 c. on 4½d. (Type I)	10	10
	a. Type II	20	10
72	5 c. on 6d. (Type I)	10	10
	a. Type II	10	10
73	10 c. on 1s.	10·00	3·00
	a. Surch double*	£250	
74	25 c. on 2s. 6d. (Type I)	30	65
	a. Type II (central)	75	60
	b. Type II (bottom left)	£120	£160
75	50 c. on 5s. (Type I)	30	60
	a. Type II	4·00	2·25
	b. Type III	£250	£375
76	1 r. on 10s. (Type I)	1·25	60
	a. Type II	2·75	2·75
	b. Type III	38·00	45·00
77	2 r. on £1 (Type I)	9·00	9·00
	a. Type II (middle left)	4·50	5·50
	b. Type II (bottom)	38·00	70·00
65/77a	*Set of* 13	17·00	11·50

*On both Nos. 66a and 73a the second surcharge falls across the horizontal perforations.

No. 74b has the thin Type II surcharge at bottom left, in similar position to the thicker Type I, No. 74, with which it should not be confused.

No. 77b has the surcharge centrally placed at bottom. No. 77a has it at middle left, above "KUDU".

No. 66 with surcharge central (instead of bottom left) and No. 75a bottom left (instead of middle left) are believed to be from trial sheets released with the normal stocks. They do not represent separate printings. (No. 66 *price* £35 *un*).

(Recess B.W.)

1961. *As 1956 issue, but with values in cents and rands. Wmk Mult Script CA. P* 13 × 13½ (*horiz*) *or* 13½ × 13 (*vert*).

78	½ c. black and orange (as ½d.) (14.2)	10	15
79	1 c. black and emerald (as 1d.) (14.2)	10	10
80	2 c. black and brown (as 2d.) (10.9)	10	40
81	2½ c. black and rose-red (as 3d.) (14.2)	15	10
82	4 c. black & dp bright bl (as 4½d) (10.9)	15	40
83	5 c. black and magenta (as 6d.) (10.9)	30	15
84	10 c. black and deep olive (as 1s.) (14.2)	15	10
85	12½ c. black and sepia (as 1s 3d.) (14.2)	90	40
86	25 c. emerald and carmine-red (as 2s 6d.) (1.8)	1·25	1·25
87	50 c. deep lilac & slate-blk (as 5s.) (10.9)	2·00	1·40
88	1 r. black and deep lilac (as 10s.) (10.9)	3·00	3·75
89	2 r. black and turquoise-blue (as £1) (1.8)	9·00	11·00
78/89	*Set of* 12	16·00	17·00

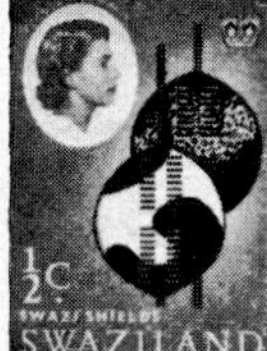

15 Swazi Shields

16 Battle Axe

(Des Mrs. C. Hughes. Photo Enschedé)

1962 (24 Apr)–**66**. *Various designs as T* **15/16**. *W w* **12**. *P* 14×13 (*horiz*) *or* 13×14 (*vert*).

90	½ c. black, brown and yellow-brown	10	10
91	1 c. yellow-orange and black	10	10
92	2 c. dp bluish green, black & yellow-olive	10	10
93	2½ c. black and vermilion	10	10
	a. Black and dull red (5.66)	10	10
94	3½ c. yellow-green and deep grey	10	10
95	4 c. black and turquoise-green	10	10
	a. Black & deep turquoise-green (5.66)	10	10
96	5 c. black, red and orange-red	30	10
97	7½ c. deep brown and buff	30	15
	a. Blackish brn & yellowish buff (5.66)	30	20
98	10 c. black and light blue	70	10
99	12½ c. carmine and grey-olive	50	70
100	15 c. black and bright purple	75	50
101	20 c. black and green	30	70
102	25 c. black and bright blue	30	60
103	50 c. black and rose-red	5·50	2·50
104	1 r. emerald and ochre	2·50	2·25
105	2 r. carmine-red and ultramarine	8·50	5·50
90/105	*Set of* 16	18·00	12·00

Designs: *Vert*—2 c. Forestry; 2½ c. Ceremonial headdress; 3½ c. Musical instrument; 4 c. Irrigation; 5 c. Long-tailed Whydah; 7½ c. Rock paintings; 10 c. Secretary Bird; 12½ c. Pink Arum; 15 c. Swazi married woman; 20 c. Malaria control; 25 c. Swazi warrior; 1 r. Aloes. *Horiz*—50 c. Southern Ground Hornbill; 2 r. Msinsi in flower.

1963 (4 June). *Freedom from Hunger. As No. 80 of Lesotho.*

106	15 c. reddish violet	40	15

1963 (2 Sept). *Red Cross Centenary. As Nos. 203/4 of Jamaica.*

107	2½ c. red and black	10	10
108	15 c. red and blue	40	20

31 Train and Map

(Des R. A. H. Street. Recess B.W.)

1964 (5 Nov). *Opening of Swaziland Railway. W w* **12**. *P* 11½.

109	**31**	2½ c. emerald-green and purple	20	10
110		3½ c. turquoise-blue & deep yellow-ol	20	10
111		15 c. red-orange and deep chocolate	30	20
112		25 c. olive-yellow and deep ultram	45	25
109/12		*Set of* 4	1·00	50

1965 (17 May). *I.T.U. Centenary. As Nos. 98/9 of Lesotho.*

113	2½ c. light blue and bistre	10	10
114	15 c. bright purple and rose	25	20

1965 (25 Oct). *International Co-operation Year. As Nos. 100/1 of Lesotho.*

115	½ c. reddish purple and turquoise-green	10	10
116	15 c. deep bluish green and lavender	40	20

1966 (24 Jan). *Churchill Commemoration. As Nos. 102/5 of Lesotho.*

117	½ c. new blue	10	10
118	2½ c. deep green	20	10
119	15 c. brown	35	15
120	25 c. bluish violet	50	35
117/20	*Set of* 4	1·00	55

1966 (1 Dec). *20th Anniv of U.N.E.S.C.O. As Nos. 342/4 of Mauritius.*

121	2½ c. slate-violet, red, yellow and orange	10	10
122	7½ c. orange-yellow, violet and deep olive	20	10
123	15 c. black, bright purple and orange	35	20
121/3	*Set of* 3	60	30

PROTECTED STATE

32 King Sobhuza II and Map

33 King Sobhuza II

(Des and photo Harrison)

1967 (25 Apr). *Protected State. W w* **12** (*sideways on horiz designs*). *P* 14½.

124	**32**	2½ c. multicoloured	10	10
125	**33**	7½ c. multicoloured	10	10
126	**32**	15 c. multicoloured	10	10
127	**33**	25 c. multicoloured	15	10
124/7		*Set of* 4	35	30

34 Students and University

(Des V. Whiteley. Photo Harrison)

1967 (7 Sept). *First Conferment of University Degrees. P* 14 × 14½.

128	**34**	2½ c. sepia, ultramarine & lt yellow-orge	10	10
129		7½ c. sepia, ultramarine & lt greenish bl	10	10
130		15 c. sepia, ultramarine and rose	10	10
131		25 c. sepia, ultramarine and light violet	10	10
128/31		*Set of* 4	30	20

35 Inclawa Ceremony

36 Reed Dance

(Des Mrs. G. Ellison. Photo Harrison)

1968 (5 Jan). *Traditional Customs. P* 14.

132	**35**	3 c. silver, vermilion and black	10	10
133	**36**	10 c. silver, light brown, orange and black	10	10
134	**35**	15 c. gold, vermilion and black	10	10
135	**36**	25 c. gold, light brown, orange and black	10	10
132/5		*Set of* 4	30	20

(37)

38 Cattle Ploughing

1968 (1 May). *No. 96 surch with T* **37**.

136	3 c. on 5 c. black, red and orange-red	15	10

INDEPENDENT

(Des Mrs. G. Ellison. Photo Enschedé)

1968 (6 Sept). *Independence. T* **38** *and similar horiz designs. W w* **12** (*sideways*). *P* 14 × 12½.

137	3 c. multicoloured	10	10
	a. Imperf (pair)	£120	
138	4½ c. multicoloured	10	10
	a. Imperf (pair)	£120	
139	17½ c. yellow, green, black and gold	15	10
140	25 c. slate, black and gold	45	45
137/40	*Set of* 4	65	65
MS141	180 × 162 mm. Nos. 137/40 each × 5	14·00	17·00
	a. Error. Imperf	£1300	

Designs:—4½ c. Overhead cable carrying asbestos; 17½ c. Cutting sugar cane; 25 c. Iron ore mining and railway map.

Nos. 137/40 were printed in sheets of 50, but also in miniature sheets of 20 (4 × 5) containing *se-tenant* strips of each value.

INDEPENDENCE 1968

(42)

43 Cape Porcupine

1968 (6 Sept). *Nos. 90/105 optd as T 42, and No. 93 additionally surch 3 c., by Enschedé. (a) Wmk upright.*
142 ½ c. black, brown and yellow-brown 10 10
a. Brown omitted £170
b. Albino opt .. .. 40·00
143 1 c. yellow-orange and black 10 10
144 2 c. dp bluish green, black & yellow-olive 10 10
145 2½ c. black and vermilion 30 10
a. Black and dull red 30 10
146 3 c. on 2½ c. black and vermilion .. 10 10
a. Black and dull red 10 10
147 3½ c. yellow-green and deep grey .. 15 10
148 4 c. black and turquoise-green 10 10
a. Black and deep turquoise-green .. 25 15
b. Black and pale turquoise-green .. 20 30
149 5 c. black, red and orange-red .. .. 1·25 10
150 7½ c. deep brown and buff 20 10
151 10 c. black and light blue .. .. 1·25 10
152 12½ c. carmine and grey-olive 25 30
153 15 c. black and bright purple 25 30
154 20 c. black and green .. .. .. 75 1·00
155 25 c. black and bright blue 35 40
156 50 c. black and rose-red .. .. .. 4·25 2·50
157 1 r. emerald and ochre .. .. .. 2·50 3·00
158 2 r. carmine-red and ultramarine .. 5·50 7·50
(b) *Wmk sideways*
159 50 c. black and rose-red .. .. .. 2·25 2·00
160 2 r. carmine-red and ultramarine .. 5·50 5·00
142/60 .. .. *Set of* 19 22·00 20·00

The 2½ c., 3½ c., 5 c., 12½ c., 50 c. (No. 156) and 2 r. (No. 158) exist with gum arabic only, the 1 c., 2 c., 3 c., 4 c., and 15 c. with both gum arabic and PVA gum and the remainder with PVA gum only.

(Des and litho D.L.R.)

1969 (1 Aug)–**75**. *T 43 and similar designs showing animals. Multicoloured. W w 12 (sideways on 3 c., 3½ c., 1 r., 2 r.). P 13 × 13½ (3 c., 3½ c.), 12½ × 13 (1 r., 2 r.) or 13 × 12½ (others).*
161 ½ c. Caracal 10 10
162 1 c. Type **43** 10 10
163 2 c. Crocodile 20 10
a. Perf 12½ × 12 (29.9.75) .. .. 3·00 1·50
164 3 c. Lion 60 10
165 3½ c. African Elephant 60 10
166 5 c. Bush Pig 30 10
167 7½ c. Impala 35 10
168 10 c. Chacma Baboon 45 10
169 12½ c. Ratel .. .. 70 1·25
170 15 c. Leopard .. .. 1·25 70
171 20 c. Blue Wildebeest 95 60
172 25 c. White Rhinoceros .. .. .. 1·40 1·00
173 50 c. Common Zebra .. .. .. 1·50 2·25
174 1 r. Waterbuck (*vert*) .. .. .. 3·00 4·25
175 2 r. Giraffe (*vert*) .. .. .. 6·00 8·50
161/75 .. .. *Set of* 15 15·00 17·00

Nos. 161/73 are horizontal as Type **43** but the 3 c. and 3½ c. are larger, 35 × 24½ mm.
No. 163a was printed by the D.L.R. works in Bogotá, Colombia.
See also Nos. 219/20 and 229.

44 King Sobhuza II and Flags

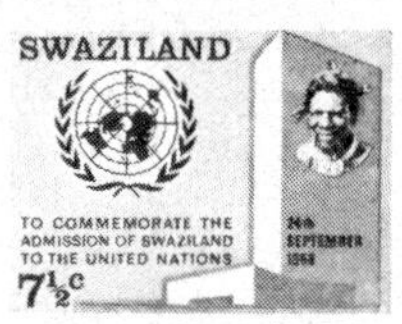

45 King Sobhuza II, U.N. Building and Emblem

(Des D.L.R. Litho P.B.)

1969 (24 Sept). *Admission of Swaziland to the United Nations. W w 12 (sideways). P 13½.*
176 **44** 3 c. multicoloured 10 10
177 **45** 7½ c. multicoloured 15 10
178 **44** 12½ c. multicoloured 20 10
179 **45** 25 c. multicoloured 30 30
176/9 .. .. *Set of* 4 60 45

46 Athlete, Shield and Spears

47 *Bauhinia galpinii*

(Des L. Curtis. Litho Format)

1970 (16 July). *Ninth Commonwealth Games, Edinburgh. T 46 and similar vert designs. Multicoloured. W w 12. P 14.*
180 3 c. Type **46** 10 10
181 7½ c. Runner 15 10
182 12½ c. Hurdler 20 10
183 25 c. Procession of Swaziland competitors .. 30 30
180/3 .. .. *Set of* 4 60 45

(Des L. Curtis from "Wild Flowers of Natal" by Dr. W. G. Wright. Litho Questa)

1971 (1 Feb). *Flowers. T 47 and similar vert designs. Multicoloured. W w 12. P 14½.*
184 3 c. Type **47** 20 10
185 10 c. *Crocosmia aurea* 35 10
186 15 c. *Gloriosa superba* 50 15
187 25 c. *Watsonia densiflora* 70 35
184/7 .. .. *Set of* 4 1·60 60

48 King Sobhuza II in Ceremonial Dress

49 UNICEF emblem

(Des L. Curtis. Litho Format)

1971 (22 Dec). *Golden Jubilee of Accession of King Sobhuza II. T 48 and similar vert designs. Multicoloured. W w 12. P 14.*
188 3 c. Type **48** 10 10
189 3½ c. Sobhuza II in medallion 10 10
190 7½ c. Sobhuza II attending Incwala ceremony 10 10
191 25 c. Sobhuza II and aides at opening of Parliament 20 35
188/91 .. .. *Set of* 4 30 40

(Des Sylvia Goaman. Litho J.W.)

1972 (17 Apr). *25th Anniv of UNICEF. W w 12 (sideways). P 13½.*
192 **49** 15 c. black and bright lilac 15 10
193 – 25 c. black and yellow-olive 20 20
The 25 c. value is as T **49**, but the inscription is rearranged.

50 Local Dancers

(Des G. Drummond. Litho Questa)

1972 (11 Sept). *Tourism. T 50 and similar horiz designs. Multicoloured. W w 12. P 13½ × 14.*
194 3½ c. Type **50** 10 10
195 7½ c. Swazi beehive hut 15 10
196 15 c. Ezulwini Valley 30 20
197 25 c. Fishing, Usutu River 80 40
194/7 .. .. *Set of* 4 1·25 65

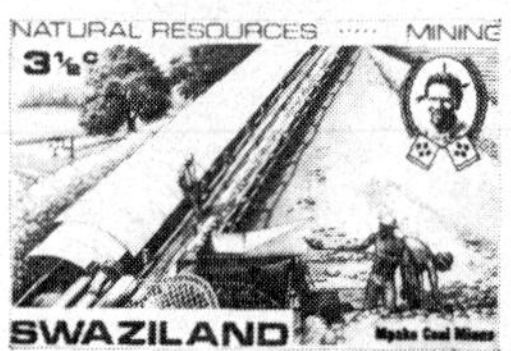

51 Spraying Mosquitoes

(Des PAD Studio. Litho Questa)

1973 (21 May). *25th Anniv of W.H.O. T 51 and similar horiz design. Multicoloured. W w 12. P 14.*
198 3½ c. Type **51** 15 10
199 7½ c. Anti-malaria vaccination 25 20

52 Mining

(Des G. Drummond. Litho Questa)

1973 (21 June). *Natural Resources. T 52 and similar horiz designs. Multicoloured. W w 12. P 13½.*
200 3½ c. Type **52** 20 10
201 7½ c. Cattle 25 10
202 15 c. Water 30 15
203 25 c. Rice 35 30
200/3 .. .. *Set of* 4 1·00 55

53 Coat of Arms

54 Flags and Mortar-board

(Des J.W. Litho Walsall)

1973 (7 Sept). *Fifth Anniv of Independence. T 53 and similar horiz designs. Multicoloured (except 3 c.). W w 12. P 14.*
204 3 c. Type **53** (salmon and black) 10 10
205 10 c. King Sobhuza II saluting 20 10
206 15 c. Parliament Buildings 35 30
207 25 c. National Somhlolo Stadium 40 40
204/7 .. .. *Set of* 4 95 75

(Des P. Powell. Litho Format)

1974 (29 Mar). *Tenth Anniv of University of Botswana, Lesotho and Swaziland. T 54 and similar vert designs. Multicoloured. W w 12 (sideways). P 14.*
208 7½ c. Type **54** 15 10
209 12½ c. University campus 20 10
210 15 c. Map of Southern Africa 25 20
211 25 c. University badge 35 35
208/11 .. .. *Set of* 4 85 60

55 King Sobhuza as College Student

56 New Post Office, Lobamba

(Des Mary Nelson; adapted PAD Studio. Litho Enschedé)

1974 (22 July). *75th Birthday of King Sobhuza II. T 55 and similar vert designs. Multicoloured. W w 12. P 13 × 10½.*
212 3 c. Type **55** 10 10
213 9 c. King Sobhuza in middle-age 10 10
214 50 c. King Sobhuza at 75 years of age .. 50 60
212/14 .. .. *Set of* 3 60 60

(Des R. Granger Barrett. Litho Questa)

1974 (9 Oct). *Centenary of Universal Postal Union. T 56 and similar horiz designs. Multicoloured. W w 12 (sideways). P 14.*
215 4 c. Type **56** 10 10
216 10 c. Mbabane Temporary Post Office, 1902 .. 25 15
217 15 c. Carrying mail by cableway 45 50
218 25 c. Mule-drawn mail-coach 55 70
215/18 .. .. *Set of* 4 1·25 1·25

(New Currency. 100 cents = 1 lilangeni (*plural* emalangeni))

1975 (2 Jan). *New currency. As Nos. 174/5 but inscr in emalangeni. W w 12 (upright). P 12½ × 13.*
219 1 e. Waterbuck .. .. 2·00 2·50
220 2 e. Giraffe .. .. 4·00 4·50

57 Umcwasho Ceremony

58 Control Tower, Matsapa Airport

(Des PAD Studio. Litho Kynoch Press)

1975 (20 Mar). *Swazi Youth. T 57 and similar multicoloured designs. W w 12 (sideways on 3, 10 and 25 c.). P 14.*
221 3 c. Type **57** 10 10
222 10 c. Butimba (hunting party) 15 10
223 15 c. Lusekwane (sacred shrub) (*horiz*) .. 25 15
224 25 c. Goina Regiment 30 30
221/4 .. .. *Set of* 4 70 45

(Des V. Whiteley Studio. Litho Questa)

1975 (18 Aug). *Tenth Anniv of Internal Air Service. T 58 and similar horiz designs. Multicoloured. W w 14 (sideways). P 14.*
225 4 c. Type **58** 30 10
226 5 c. Fire engine 40 10
227 15 c. Douglas "Dakota" .. .. .. 1·60 80
228 25 c. Hawker Siddeley "748" .. .. 1·90 1·25
225/8 .. .. *Set of* 4 3·75 2·00

(Litho De La Rue, Bogotá, Colombia)

1975 (29 Sept). *As No. 164 but W w 12 upright.*
229 3 c. Lion .. .. 3·00 2·75

NEW INFORMATION

The editor is always interested to correspond with people who have new information that will improve or correct the Catalogue.

3c

(59)

1975 (15 Nov). *Nos.* 167 *and* 169 *surch as T* **59**.

230	3 c. on 7½ c. Impala	1·25	70
231	6 c. on 12½ c. Ratel	1·75	80

60 Elephant Symbol

(Des Mary-Jane Rostami. Litho Questa)

1975 (22 Dec). *International Women's Year. T* **60** *and similar designs. W* w **14** (*sideways on* 4 *and* 5 *c.*). *P* 14.

232	4 c. light bluish grey, black & light brt blue	15	10
233	5 c. multicoloured	15	10
234	15 c. multicoloured	40	35
235	25 c. multicoloured	60	50
232/5	.. .. *Set of* 4	1·10	90

Designs: *Horiz*—5 c. Queen Labotsibeni. *Vert*—15 c. Craftswoman; 25 c. "Women in Service".

61 African Black-headed Oriole

(Des C. Abbott. Litho Questa)

1976 (2 Jan)–**78**. *Birds. T* **61** *and similar multicoloured designs. W* w **14** (*sideways on* 1 *c.*, 3 *c.*, 2 *e.*). *Chalk-surfaced paper. P* 14.

236	1 c. Type **61**	60	35
237	2 c. African Green Pigeon (*vert*)	65	30
238	3 c. Green-winged Pytilia	80	35
239	4 c. Violet Starling (*vert*)	80	15
	a. Ordinary paper (31.7.78)	60	40
240	5 c. Black-headed Heron (*vert*)	90	30
241	6 c. Stonechat (*vert*)	1·25	30
242	7 c. Chorister Robin Chat (*vert*)	90	30
243	10 c. Four-coloured Bush-shrike (*vert*) ..	1·00	30
244	15 c. Black-collared Barbet (*vert*)	1·25	55
245	20 c. Grey Heron (*vert*)	1·75	75
246	25 c. Giant Kingfisher (*vert*)	1·75	75
247	30 c. Verreaux's Eagle (*vert*)	1·75	95
248	50 c. Red Bishop (*vert*)	1·50	1·25
	a. Ordinary paper (31.7.78)	90	1·00
249	1 e. Pin-tailed Whydah (*vert*)	2·25	2·75
	a. Ordinary paper (31.7.78)	1·75	2·50
250	2 e. Lilac-breasted Roller	4·00	5·00
	a. Ordinary paper (31.7.78)	3·00	4·50
236/50a	.. .. *Set of* 15	17·00	12·00

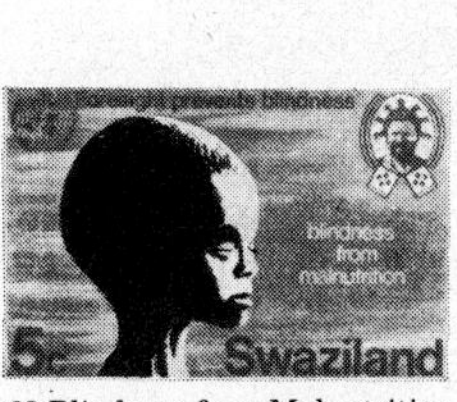

62 Blindness from Malnutrition

63 Marathon

(Des Jennifer Toombs. Litho Questa)

1976 (15 June). *Prevention of Blindness. T* **62** *and similar horiz designs. Multicoloured. W* w **14** (*sideways*). *P* 14.

251	5 c. Type **62**	15	10
252	10 c. Infected retina	25	10
253	20 c. Blindness from trachoma	40	35
254	25 c. Medicines	50	40
251/4	.. .. *Set of* 4	1·10	80

(Des PAD Studio. Litho Walsall)

1976 (17 July). *Olympic Games, Montreal. T* **63** *and similar vert designs. Multicoloured. W* w **14** (*inverted*). *P* 14.

255	5 c. Type **63**	10	10
256	6 c. Boxing	15	10
257	20 c. Football	35	25
258	25 c. Olympic torch and flame	40	35
255/8	.. .. *Set of* 4	90	65

MINIMUM PRICE

The minimum price quote is 10p which represents a handling charge rather than a basis for valuing common stamps. For further notes about prices see introductory pages.

64 Footballer Shooting

65 Alexander Graham Bell and Telephone

(Des J.W. Litho Questa)

1976 (13 Sept). *F.I.F.A. Membership. T* **64** *and similar vert designs. Multicoloured. W* w **14**. *P* 14.

259	4 c. Type **64**	15	10
260	6 c. Heading	15	10
261	20 c. Goalkeeping	40	25
262	25 c. Player about to shoot	45	30
259/62	.. .. *Set of* 4	1·00	60

(Des J.W. Litho Walsall)

1976 (22 Nov). *Telephone Centenary. T* **65** *and similar horiz designs. W* w **14** (*sideways*). *P* 14.

263	4 c. multicoloured	10	10
264	5 c. multicoloured	10	10
265	10 c. multicoloured	15	10
266	15 c. multicoloured	30	20
267	20 c. multicoloured	40	30
263/7	.. .. *Set of* 5	95	55

Nos. 264/7 are as T **65**, but show different telephones.

66 Queen Elizabeth II and King Sobhuza II

(Des Walsall. Litho Questa)

1977 (7 Feb). *Silver Jubilee. T* **66** *and similar horiz designs. Multicoloured. W* w **14** (*sideways*). *P* 13½.

268	20 c. Type **66**	20	20
269	25 c. Coronation Coach at Admiralty Arch ..	20	20
270	50 c. Queen in coach	30	45
268/70	.. .. *Set of* 3	65	75

67 Matsapa College

(Des J. Cooter. Litho Questa)

1977 (2 May). 50*th Anniv of Police Training. T* **67** *and similar multicoloured designs. W* w **14** (*upright on* 20 *c., sideways on others*). *P* 14.

271	5 c. Type **67**	10	10
272	10 c. Uniformed police and land rover ..	30	10
273	20 c. Police badge (*vert*)	45	25
274	25 c. Dog handling	50	35
271/4	.. .. *Set of* 4	1·25	65

68 Animals and Hunters

(Des BG Studio. Litho Questa)

1977 (8 Aug). *Rock Paintings. T* **68** *and similar horiz designs. Multicoloured. W* w **14** (*sideways*). *P* 14.

275	5 c. Type **68**	25	10
276	10 c. Four dancers in a procession	30	10
277	15 c. Man with cattle	40	20
278	20 c. Four dancers	45	30
275/8	.. .. *Set of* 4	1·25	55
MS279	103 × 124 mm. Nos. 275/8	1·75	2·50

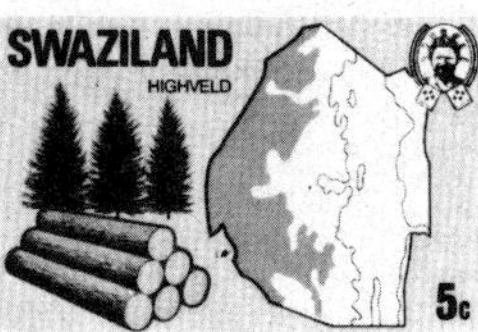

69 Timber, Highveld Region

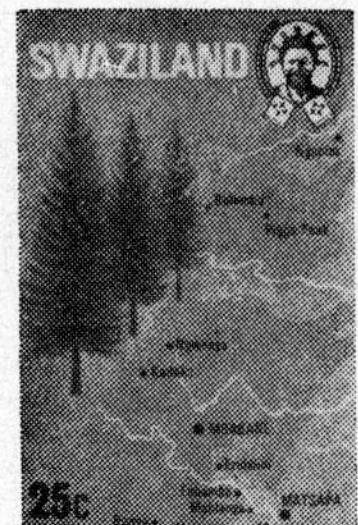

70 Timber, Highveld Region

(Des L. Curtis. Litho D.L.R.)

1977 (17 Oct). *Maps of the Regions. T* **69** *and similar horiz designs. Multicoloured. W* w **14** (*sideways*). *P* 13½.

280	5 c. Type **69**	10	10
281	10 c. Pineapple, Middleveld	20	10
282	15 c. Orange and Lemon, Lowveld	30	20
283	20 c. Cattle, Lubombo region	40	30
280/3	.. .. *Set of* 4	90	55
MS284	87 × 103 mm. Four 25 c. designs as T **70**, together forming a composite map of Swaziland ..	1·40	1·60

71 Cabbage Tree

(Des Jennifer Toombs. Litho Walsall)

1978 (12 Jan). *Trees of Swaziland. T* **71** *and similar horiz designs. Multicoloured* (*except* 5 *c.*). *W* w **14** (*sideways*). *P* 13½.

285	5 c. Type **71** (apple-green, ochre and black) ..	15	10
286	10 c. Marula	35	10
287	20 c. Kiaat	55	40
288	25 c. Lucky bean-tree	60	50
285/8	.. .. *Set of* 4	1·50	90

72 Rural Electrification at Lobamba

73 Elephant

(Des G. Drummond. Litho Questa)

1978 (6 Mar). *Hydro-electric Power. T* **72** *and similar horiz designs. W* w **14** (*sideways*). *P* 13½.

289	5 c. black and buff	10	10
290	10 c. black and light green	15	10
291	20 c. black and pale blue	25	30
292	25 c. black and magenta	30	35
289/92	.. .. *Set of* 4	70	65

Designs:—10 c. Edwaleni Power Station; 20 c. Switchgear, Magudza Power Station; 25 c. Turbine Hall, Edwaleni.

(Des C. Abbott. Litho Questa)

1978 (2 June). 25*th Anniv of Coronation. T* **73** *and similar vert designs. P* 15.

293	25 c. chalky blue, black and sage-green ..	20	30
	a. Sheetlet. Nos. 293/5 × 2	1·10	
294	25 c. multicoloured	20	30
295	25 c. chalky blue, black and sage-green ..	20	30
293/5	.. .. *Set of* 3	55	80

Designs:—No. 293, Queen's Lion; No. 294, Queen Elizabeth II; No. 295, Type **73**.

Nos. 293/5 were printed together in small sheets of 6, containing two *se-tenant* strips of 3, with horizontal gutter margin between.

74 Clay Pots

(Des C. Abbott. Litho Questa)

1978 (24 July). *Handicrafts* (1*st series*). *T* **74** *and similar horiz designs. Multicoloured. W* w **14** (*sideways*). *P* 13½ × 14.

296	5 c. Type **74**	10	10
297	10 c. Basketwork	10	10
298	20 c. Wooden utensils	15	15
299	30 c. Wooden pot	25	30
296/9	.. .. *Set of* 4	50	50

See also Nos. 310/13.

75 Defence Force

(Des BG Studio. Litho Questa)

1978 (6 Sept). *10th Anniv of Independence. T* **75** *and similar horiz designs. Multicoloured. W* w **14** *(sideways). P* 14.

300	4 c. Type **75**	10	10
301	6 c. The King's Regiment	10	10
302	10 c. Tinkabi tractor (agricultural development)	15	10
303	15 c. Water-pipe laying (self-help scheme) ..	20	10
304	25 c. Sebenta adult literacy scheme	25	25
305	50 c. Fire emergency service	40	50
300/5	.. .. *Set of* 6	1·00	85

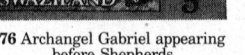

76 Archangel Gabriel appearing before Shepherds

77 Prospecting at Phophonyane

(Des V. Whiteley Studio. Litho Harrison)

1978 (12 Dec). *Christmas. T* **76** *and similar horiz designs. Multicoloured. W* w **14**. *P* 14½ × 14.

306	5 c. Type **76**	10	10
307	10 c. Three Wise Men paying homage to infant Jesus	10	10
308	15 c. Archangel Gabriel warning Joseph ..	10	10
309	25 c. Flight into Egypt	20	20
306/9	.. .. *Set of* 4	30	35

(Des C. Abbott. Litho Walsall)

1979 (10 Jan). *Handicrafts (2nd series). Horiz designs as T* **74**. *Multicoloured. W* w **14** *(sideways). P* 13½.

310	5 c. Sisal bowls	10	10
311	15 c. Pottery	10	10
312	20 c. Basket work	15	15
313	30 c. Hide shield	20	20
310/13	.. .. *Set of* 4	45	45

(Des L. Curtis. Litho Questa)

1979 (27 Mar). *Centenary of Discovery of Gold in Swaziland. T* **77** *and similar vert designs. W* w **14**. *P* 14.

314	5 c. gold and deep ultramarine	15	10
315	15 c. gold and deep brown	30	20
316	25 c. gold and deep green	45	30
317	50 c. gold and carmine-red	70	90
314/17	.. .. *Set of* 4	1·40	1·25

Designs:—15 c. Early 3-stamp battery mill; 25 c. Cyanide tanks at Piggs Peak; 50 c. Pouring off molten gold.

78 "Girls at the Piano"

(Des BG Studio. Litho Questa)

1979 (8 May). *International Year of the Child. Paintings by Renoir. T* **78** *and similar horiz designs. Multicoloured. W* w **14** *(sideways). P* 13½.

318	5 c. Type **78**	10	10
319	15 c. "Madame Charpentier and her Children"	25	10
320	25 c. "Girls picking Flowers"	35	15
321	50 c. "Girl with Watering Can"	70	55
318/21	.. .. *Set of* 4	1·25	70
MS322	123 × 135 mm. Nos. 318/21	1·25	1·25

79 1933 1d. Carmine Stamp and Sir Rowland Hill

(Des J.W. Litho Walsall)

1979 (17 July). *Death Centenary of Sir Rowland Hill. T* **79** *and similar horiz designs showing stamps and portrait of Sir Rowland Hill. Multicoloured. W* w **14** *(sideways). P* 14½ × 14.

323	10 c. 1945 3d. Victory commemorative ..	15	10
324	20 c. Type **79**	25	25
325	25 c. 1968 25 c. Independence commemorative	25	30
323/5	.. .. *Set of* 3	60	60
MS326	115 × 90 mm. 50 c. 1956 6d. Great Kudu Antelope definitive	65	85

80 Obverse and Reverse of 5 Cents

(Des G. Hutchins. Litho Walsall)

1979 (6 Sept). *Coins. T* **80** *and similar horiz designs. W* w **14** *(sideways). P* 13½.

327	5 c. black and light brown	10	10
328	10 c. black and new blue	15	10
329	20 c. black and yellowish green	25	20
330	50 c. black and yellow-orange	45	45
331	1 e. black and cerise	75	80
327/31	.. .. *Set of* 5	1·50	1·50

Designs:—10 c. Obverse and reverse of 10 cents; 20 c. Obverse and reverse of 20 cents; 50 c. Reverse of 50 cents; 1 e. Reverse of 1 lilangeni.

81 Big Bend Post Office

(Des J. Cooter. Litho Questa)

1979 (22 Nov). *Post Office Anniversaries. T* **81** *and similar designs. W* w **14** *(sideways on* 5, 20 *and* 50 c.). *P* 13½.

332	5 c. multicoloured	10	10
333	15 c. multicoloured	15	10
334	20 c. black, sage-green and magenta	20	15
335	50 c. multicoloured	40	60
332/5	.. .. *Set of* 4	70	80

Designs and commemorations: *Horiz*—5 c. Type **81** (25th anniversary of Posts and Telecommunications Services); 20 c. 1949 75th anniversary of U.P.U. 1s. commemorative stamp (10th anniversary of U.P.U. membership); 50 c. 1974 centenary of U.P.U. 25 c. commemorative stamp (10th anniversary of U.P.U. membership). *Vert*—15 c. Microwave antenna. Mount Ntondozi (25th anniversary of Posts and Telecommunications Services).

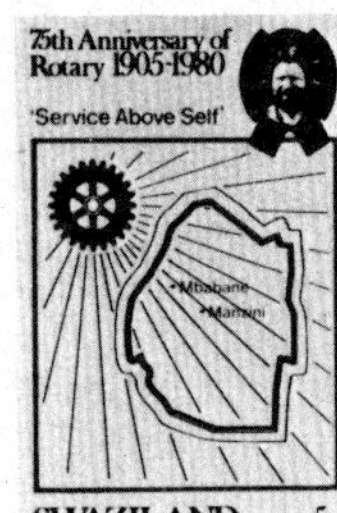

82 Map of Swaziland

83 *Brunsvigia radulosa*

(Des BG Studio. Litho Walsall)

1980 (23 Feb). *75th Anniv of Rotary International. T* **82** *and similar vert designs in gold and bright blue. W* w **14**. *P* 13½.

336	5 c. Type **82**	10	10
337	15 c. Vitreous cutter and optical illuminator ..	15	10
338	50 c. Scroll	40	55
339	1 e. Rotary Headquarters, Evanston, U.S.A.	80	1·25
336/9	.. .. *Set of* 4	1·40	1·75

(Des BG Studio. Litho Secura, Singapore)

1980 (28 Apr)–**83**. *Flowers. Multicoloured designs as T* **83**.

A. *Without imprint date below design. P* 13½.

340A	1 c. Type **83**	15	10
341A	2 c. *Aloe suprafoliata*	15	10
342A	3 c. *Haemanthus magnificus*	15	10
	c. Perf 12..	1·25	1·00
343A	4 c. *Aloe marlothii*..	20	10
	c. Perf 12..	2·50	1·50
344A	5 c. *Dicoma zeyheri*	15	10
	c. Perf 12..	1·75	1·25
345A	6 c. *Aloe kniphofioides*	20	20
346A	7 c. *Cyrtanthus bicolor*	15	10
347A	10 c. *Eucomis autumnalis*	25	10
348A	15 c. *Leucospermum gerrardii*	15	10
	c. Perf 12..		
349A	20 c. *Haemanthus multiflorus*	40	25
350A	30 c. *Acridocarpus natalitius*	20	20
351A	50 c. *Adenium swazicum*	30	30
352A	1 e. *Protea simplex*..	55	60
353A	2 e. *Calodendrum capense*	1·10	1·25
354A	5 e. *Gladiolus ecklonii*	2·75	3·00
340A/54A	.. .. .. *Set of* 15	6·00	5·50

B. *With imprint date. P* 12 (12.83)

340B	1 c. Type **83**	45	30
341B	2 c. *Aloe suprafoliata*	45	30
343B	4 c. *Aloe marlothii*..	60	30
345B	6 c. *Aloe kniphofioides*	70	35
347B	10 c. *Eucomis autumnalis*	70	30
349B	20 c. *Haemanthus multiflorus*	1·10	50
340B/9B	.. .. .. *Set of* 6	3·50	1·90

Nos. 347/51 are horizontal, 42 × 25 mm, and Nos. 352/4 vertical, 28 × 38 mm.

84 Mail Runner

(Des A. Theobald. Litho Walsall)

1980 (6 May). *"London 1980" International Stamp Exhibition. T* **84** *and similar horiz designs. Multicoloured. W* w **14** *(sideways). P* 14.

355	10 c. Type **84**	15	10
356	20 c. Post Office mail truck	25	15
357	25 c. Mail sorting office	30	20
358	50 c. Ropeway conveying mail at Bulembu ..	70	70
355/8	.. .. *Set of* 4	1·25	1·00

85 Yellow Fish

(Des and litho Walsall)

1980 (25 Aug). *River Fishes. T* **85** *and similar horiz designs. Multicoloured. W* w **14** *(sideways). P* 13½.

359	5 c. Type **85**	10	10
360	10 c. Silver Barbel	15	10
361	15 c. Tiger Fish	20	15
362	30 c. Squeaker Fish	40	30
363	1 e. Bream	1·10	1·40
359/63	.. .. *Set of* 5	1·75	1·75

86 Oribi

(Des G. Drummond. Litho Harrison)

1980 (1 Oct). *Wildlife Conservation. T* **86** *and similar multicoloured designs. W* w **14** *(sideways on* 5 *and* 50 c.). *P* 14.

364	5 c. Type **86**	10	10
365	10 c. Nile Crocodile (*vert*)	15	10
366	50 c. Temminck's Ground Pangolin.. ..	70	70
367	1 e. Leopard (*vert*)	1·25	1·50
364/7	.. .. *Set of* 4	1·90	2·00

87 Public Bus Service

(Des G. Hutchins. Litho Format)

1981 (5 Jan). *Transport. T* **87** *and similar horiz designs. Multicoloured. W* w **14** *(sideways). P* 14½.

368	5 c. Type **87**	10	10
369	25 c. Royal Swazi National Airways	25	15
370	30 c. Swaziland United Transport	30	20
371	1 e. Swaziland Railway	1·75	1·75
368/71	.. .. *Set of* 4	2·10	2·00

88 Mantenga Falls

89 Prince Charles on Hike

(Des L. Curtis. Litho Format)

1981 (16 Mar). *Tourism. T* **88** *and similar horiz designs. Multicoloured. W* w **14** *(sideways). P* 14.

372	5 c. Type **88**	10	10
373	15 c. Mananga Yacht Club	15	10
374	30 c. White Rhinoceros in Mlilwane Game Sanctuary	40	30
375	1 e. Roulette wheel, playing cards and dice ("casinos")	1·40	1·60
372/5	.. .. *Set of* 4	1·75	1·90

(Des J.W. Litho Walsall)

1981 (21 July). *Royal Wedding. T* **89** *and similar vert designs. Multicoloured. W* w **14**. *P* 14.

376	10 c. Wedding bouquet from Swaziland	15	10
377	25 c. Type **89**	15	10
378	1 e. Prince Charles and Lady Diana Spencer	60	70
376/8	*Set of* 3	80	75

90 Installation of King Sobhuza II, 22 December 1921 **91** "Physical Recreation"

(Des J.W. Litho Harrison)

1981 (24 Aug). *Diamond Jubilee of King Sobhuza II. T* **90** *and similar horiz designs. Multicoloured. W* w **14** (*sideways*). *P* 14½.

379	5 c. Type **90**	10	10
380	10 c. Royal visit, 1947	15	10
381	15 c. King Sobhuza II and Coronation of Queen Elizabeth II, 1953	20	15
382	25 c. King Sobhuza taking Royal Salute, Independence, 1968	25	25
383	30 c. King Sobhuza in youth	30	30
384	1 e. King Sobhuza and Parliament Buildings	90	1·25
379/84	*Set of* 6	1·60	1·90

(Des BG Studio. Litho Questa)

1981 (5 Nov). *25th Anniv of Duke of Edinburgh Award Scheme. T* **91** *and similar vert designs. Multicoloured. W* w **14**. *P* 14.

385	5 c. Type **91**	10	10
386	20 c. "Expeditions"	15	10
387	50 c. "Skills"	40	25
388	1 e. Duke of Edinburgh in ceremonial dress	80	80
385/8	*Set of* 4	1·25	1·00

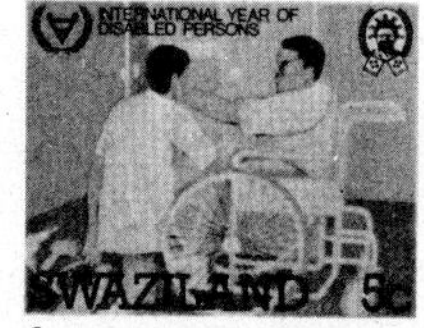

92 Disabled Person in Wheelchair

(Des and litho Walsall)

1981 (16 Dec). *International Year for the Disabled. T* **92** *and similar multicoloured designs. W* w **14** (*sideways on* 5 c. *and* 1 e.). *P* 14 × 14½ (5 c., 1 e.) *or* 14½ × 14 (*others*).

389	5 c. Type **92**	15	10
390	15 c. Teacher with disabled child (*vert*)	30	15
391	25 c. Disabled craftsman (*vert*)	50	20
392	1 e. Disabled driver in invalid carriage	1·75	1·40
389/92	*Set of* 4	2·40	1·60

93 *Papilio demodocus* **94** Man holding a Flower, after discarding Cigarettes

(Des I. Loe. Litho Rosenbaum Bros, Vienna)

1982 (6 Jan). *Butterflies. T* **93** *and similar horiz designs. Multicoloured. W* w **14** (*sideways*). *P* 14.

393	5 c. Type **93**	40	10
394	10 c. *Charaxes candiope*	50	10
395	50 c. *Papilio nireus*	1·50	85
396	1 e. *Terias desjardinsii*	2·00	2·00
393/6	*Set of* 4	4·00	2·75

(Des PAD Studio. Litho Format)

1982 (27 Apr). *Pan-African Conference on Smoking and Health. T* **94** *and similar vert design. Multicoloured. W* w **14**. *P* 14.

397	5 c. Type **94**	30	30
398	10 c. Smoker and non-smoker climbing stairs	40	40

95 Male Fishing Owl **96** Swaziland Coat of Arms

(Des G. Drummond. Litho J.W.)

1982 (16 June). *Wildlife Conservation (1st series). Pel's Fishing Owl. T* **95** *and similar vert designs. Multicoloured. W* w **14**. *P* 13½ × 13.

399	35 c. Type **95**	1·10	1·25
	a. Horiz strip of 5. Nos. 399/403	5·00	
400	35 c. Female Fishing Owl at nest	1·10	1·25
401	35 c. Pair of Fishing Owls	1·10	1·25
402	35 c. Fishing Owl, nest and egg	1·10	1·25
403	35 c. Adult Fishing Owl with youngster	1·10	1·25
399/403	*Set of* 5	5·00	5·75

Nos. 399/403 were printed together, *se-tenant*, in horizontal and vertical strips of 5 throughout the sheet.

See also Nos. 425/9 and Nos. 448/52.

(Des C. Abbott. Litho W. S. Cowells Ltd)

1982 (1 July). *21st Birthday of Princess of Wales. T* **96** *and similar vert designs. Multicoloured. W* w **14**. *P* 14½.

404	5 c. Type **96**	10	10
405	20 c. Princess leaving Eastleigh Airport, Southampton, August 1981	15	10
406	50 c. Bride at Buckingham Palace	35	35
407	1 e. Formal portrait	80	80
404/7	*Set of* 4	1·25	1·25

97 Irrigation

(Des G. Hutchins. Litho Walsall)

1982 (1 Sept). *Sugar Industry. T* **97** *and similar horiz designs. Multicoloured. W* w **14** (*sideways*). *P* 14 × 14½.

408	5 c. Type **97**	10	10
409	20 c. Harvesting	25	15
410	30 c. Mhlume mills	35	25
411	1 e. Sugar transportation by train	1·00	1·40
408/11	*Set of* 4	1·50	1·75

98 Nurse with Child

(Des L. Curtis. Litho Questa)

1982 (9 Nov). *Swaziland Red Cross Society (Baphaladi). T* **98** *and similar horiz designs. Multicoloured. W* w **14** (*sideways*). *P* 14.

412	5 c. Type **98**	10	10
413	20 c. Juniors carrying stretcher	25	15
414	50 c. Disaster relief	55	60
415	1 e. Henri Dunant (founder of Red Cross)	1·25	1·40
412/15	*Set of* 4	1·90	2·00

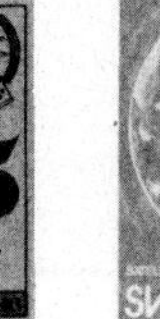

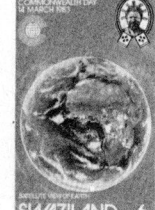

99 Taking the Oath **100** Satellite View of Earth

(Des B. Melton. Litho Format)

1982 (6 Dec). *75th Anniv of Boy Scout Movement. T* **99** *and similar horiz designs. Multicoloured. W* w **14** (*sideways*). *P* 14 × 13½.

416	5 c. Type **99**	10	10
417	10 c. Hiking and exploration	15	10
418	25 c. Community development	30	20
419	75 c. Lord Baden-Powell	1·00	1·00
416/19	*Set of* 4	1·40	1·25
MS420	107 × 109 mm. 1 e. World Scout badge	1·25	1·40

(Des A. Theobald. Litho Harrison)

1983 (14 Mar). *Commonwealth Day. T* **100** *and similar multicoloured designs. W* w **14** (*sideways on* 50 c., 1 e.). *P* 14.

421	6 c. Type **100**	10	10
422	10 c. King Sobhuza II	10	10
423	50 c. Swazi woman and beehive huts (*horiz*)	35	55
424	1 e. Spraying sugar crops (*horiz*)	70	1·00
421/4	*Set of* 4	1·10	1·50

(Des G. Drummond. Litho J.W.)

1983 (16 May). *Wildlife Conservation (2nd series). Lammergeier. Vert designs as T* **95**. *Multicoloured. W* w **14**. *P* 13½ × 13.

425	35 c. Adult male	1·00	1·00
	a. Horiz strip of 5. Nos. 425/9	4·50	
426	35 c. Pair	1·00	1·00
427	35 c. Nest and egg	1·00	1·00
428	35 c. Female at nest	1·00	1·00
429	35 c. Adult bird with fledgling	1·00	1·00
425/9	*Set of* 5	4·50	4·50

Nos. 425/9 were printed together, *se-tenant*, in horizontal strips of 5 throughout the sheet.

101 Swaziland National Football Team **102** Montgolfier Balloon

(Des G. Vasarhelyi. Litho Format)

1983 (20 Aug). *Tour of Swaziland by English Football Clubs. Three sheets,* 101 × 72 *mm, each containing one* 75 c. *stamp as T* **101**. *Multicoloured. W* w **14** (*sideways*). *P* 13½.

MS430	75 c. Type **101**; 75 c. Tottenham Hotspur; 75 c. Manchester United *Set of* 3 *sheets*	2·25	3·00

(Des. D. Hartley-Marjoram. Litho Format)

1983 (22 Aug). *Bicentenary of Manned Flight. T* **102** *and similar multicoloured designs. W* w **14** (*sideways on* 10 c. *to* 50 c.). *P* 14.

431	5 c. Type **102**	10	10
432	10 c. Wright brothers' *Flyer* (*horiz*)	15	10
433	25 c. Fokker "Fellowship" (*horiz*)	30	35
434	50 c. Bell "X-1" (*horiz*)	60	65
431/4	*Set of* 4	95	1·00
MS435	73 × 73 mm. 1 e. Space shuttle *Columbia*	1·25	1·40

103 Dr. Albert Schweitzer (Peace Prize, 1952)

(Des G. Vasarhelyi. Litho Harrison)

1983 (21 Oct). *150th Birth Anniv of Alfred Nobel. T* **103** *and similar horiz designs. Multicoloured. W* w **14** (*sideways*). *P* 14.

436	6 c. Type **103**	25	10
437	10 c. Dag Hammarskjöld (Peace Prize, 1961)	25	10
438	50 c. Albert Einstein (Physics Prize, 1921)	1·25	70
439	1 e. Alfred Nobel	1·75	1·50
436/9	*Set of* 4	3·25	2·10

104 Maize

(Des Jennifer Toombs. Litho Harrison)

1983 (29 Nov). *World Food Day. T* **104** *and similar horiz designs. Multicoloured. W* w **14** (*sideways*). *P* 14.

440	6 c. Type **104**	10	10
441	10 c. Rice	10	10
442	50 c. Cattle herding	55	65
443	1 e. Ploughing	1·10	1·40
440/3	*Set of* 4	1·60	2·00

105 Women's College **106** Male on Ledge

(Des C. Abbott. Litho Format)

1984 (12 Mar). *Education. T* **105** *and similar horiz designs. Multicoloured.* W w **14** *(sideways). P* 14.
444 5 c. Type **105** 10 10
445 15 c. Technical Training School 15 15
446 50 c. University 45 60
447 1 e. Primary school .. .. 90 1·10
444/7 .. .. *Set of* 4 1·40 1·75

(Des G. Drummond. Litho J.W.)

1984 (18 May). *Wildlife Conservation. (3rd series) Bald Ibis. T* **106** *and similar vert designs. Multicoloured.* W w **14**. *P* 13½ × 13.
448 35 c. Type **106** .. .. 1·40 1·40
a. Horiz strip of 5. Nos. 448/52 .. .. 6·25
449 35 c. Male and female .. .. 1·40 1·40
450 35 c. Bird and egg .. .. 1·40 1·40
451 35 c. Female on nest of eggs .. .. .. 1·40 1·40
452 35 c. Adult and fledgling .. .. .. 1·40 1·40
448/52 .. .. *Set of* 5 6·25 6·25
Nos. 448/52 were printed together, *se-tenant*, in horizontal strips of 5 throughout the sheet.

107 Mule-drawn Passenger Coach

(Des A. Theobald. Litho Walsall)

1984 (15 June). *Universal Postal Union Congress, Hamburg. T* **107** *and similar horiz designs. Multicoloured.* W w **14** *(sideways). P* 14½.
453 7 c. Type **107** 20 10
454 15 c. Ox-drawn post wagon 25 15
455 50 c. Mule-drawn mail coach 65 60
456 1 e. Bristol to London mail coach .. .. 1·10 1·10
453/6 .. .. *Set of* 4 2·00 1·75

108 Running

(Des Harrison. Litho Walsall)

1984 (27 July). *Olympic Games, Los Angeles. T* **108** *and similar horiz designs. Multicoloured.* W w **14** *(sideways). P* 14.
457 7 c. Type **108** 10 10
458 10 c. Swimming 10 10
459 50 c. Shooting 45 50
460 1 e. Boxing 90 95
457/60 .. .. *Set of* 4 1·40 1·40
MS461 100 × 70 mm. Nos. 457/60 .. .. 1·50 2·00

109 *Suillus bovinus*

(Des J. Spencer. Litho Format)

1984 (19 Sept). *Fungi. T* **109** *and similar multicoloured designs.* W w **14** *(sideways on* 10 c., 1 e.). *P* 14.
462 10 c. Type **109** 40 10
463 15 c. *Langermannia gigantea (vert)* 65 15
464 50 c. *Coriolus versicolor (vert)* .. .. .. 1·25 55
465 1 e. *Boletus edulis* .. .. 1·75 1·40
462/5 .. .. *Set of* 4 3·50 2·00

110 King Sobhuza opening Railway, 1964

(**111**)

(Des W. Fenton. Litho Walsall)

1984 (5 Nov). *20th Anniv of Swaziland Railways. T* **110** *and similar horiz designs. Multicoloured.* W w **14** *(sideways). P* 14.
466 10 c. Type **110** 25 10
467 25 c. Type "15A" locomotive at Siweni Yard .. 55 30
468 30 c. Container loading, Matsapha Station .. 55 30
469 1 e. Locomotive No. 268 leaving Alto Tunnel 1·50 95
466/9 .. .. *Set of* 4 2·50 1·50
MS470 144 × 74 mm. Nos. 466/9 .. .. .. 3·50 4·00

1984 (15 Dec). *Nos.* 340B, 341A, 342A, 343A, 345B *and* 346A *surch as T* **111**.
471 10 c. on 4 c. *Aloe marlothii* .. ..
a. Surch on No. 343Ac 20 10
b. Surch on No. 343B .. .. .. 1·75 1·75
472 15 c. on 7 c. *Cyrtanthus bicolor* 30 10
473 20 c. on 3 c. *Haemanthus magnificus* 40 15
a. Surch on No. 342Ac .. .. .. 1·75 1·75
474 25 c. on 6 c. *Aloe kniphofioides* 40 20
a. Surch triple .. .. † —
b. Surch double .. ..
475 30 c. on 1 c. Type **83** 50 20
a. Surch omitted (horiz pair with normal)
476 30 c. on 2 c. *Aloe suprafoliata* 55 60
a. Surch on No. 341B .. .. .. 1·75 1·75
471a/6 .. .. *Set of* 6 2·10 1·25

112 Rotary International Logo and Map of World

113 Male Ground Hornbill

(Des G. Vasarhelyi. Litho Questa)

1985 (23 Feb). *80th Anniv of Rotary International. T* **112** *and similar horiz designs. Multicoloured.* W w **14** *(sideways). P* 14.
477 10 c. Type **112** 25 10
478 15 c. Teacher and handicapped children .. 35 20
479 50 c. Youth exchange 80 55
480 1 e. Nurse and children .. .. .. 1·40 1·10
477/80 .. .. *Set of* 4 2·50 1·75

(Des G. Drummond. Litho Harrison)

1985 (15 May). *Birth Bicentenary of John J. Audubon (ornithologist). Southern Ground Hornbills. T* **113** *and similar vert designs. Multicoloured.* W w **14**. *P* 14.
481 25 c. Type **113** 85 85
a. Horiz strip of 5. Nos. 481/5 .. .. 3·75
482 25 c. Male and female Ground Hornbills .. 85 85
483 25 c. Female at nest 85 85
484 25 c. Ground Hornbill in nest, and egg .. 85 85
485 25 c. Adult and fledgeling 85 85
481/5 .. .. *Set of* 5 3·75 3·75
Nos. 481/5 were printed together, *se-tenant*, in horizontal strips of 5 throughout the sheet.

114 The Queen Mother in 1975

115 Buick "Tourer"

(Des A. Theobald (2 e.), C. Abbott (others). Litho Questa)

1985 (7 June). *Life and Times of Queen Elizabeth the Queen Mother. T* **114** *and similar vert designs. Multicoloured.* W w **16**. *P* 14½ × 14.
486 10 c. The Queen Mother in South Africa, 1947 .. .. 10 10
487 15 c. With the Queen and Princess Margaret, 1985 (from photo by Norman Parkinson) 10 10
488 50 c. Type **114** 30 35
489 1 e. With Prince Henry at his christening (from photo by Lord Snowdon) .. 65 70
486/9 .. .. *Set of* 4 1·00 1·10
MS490 91×73 mm. 2 e. Greeting Prince Andrew. Wmk sideways .. .. 1·25 1·40

(Des D. Hartley. Litho Walsall)

1985 (16 Sept). *Century of Motoring. T* **115** *and similar horiz designs. Multicoloured.* W w **14** *(sideways). P* 14.
491 10 c. Type **115** 30 10
492 15 c. Four cylinder Rover 45 15
493 50 c. De Dion Bouton .. .. 1·00 75
494 1 e. "Model T" Ford .. .. 1·60 2·00
491/4 .. .. *Set of* 4 3·00 2·75

116 Youths building Bridge over Ravine

(Des Vrein Barlocher. Litho Format)

1985 (2 Dec). *International Youth Year* (10, 50 c.), *and 75th Anniv of Girl Guide Movement (others). T* **116** *and similar horiz designs. Multicoloured.* W w **16** *(sideways). P* 14.
495 10 c. Type **116** 15 10
496 20 c. Girl Guides in camp 20 15
497 50 c. Youth making model from sticks .. 45 60
498 1 e. Guides collecting brushwood .. .. 80 1·25
495/8 .. .. *Set of* 4 1·40 1·90

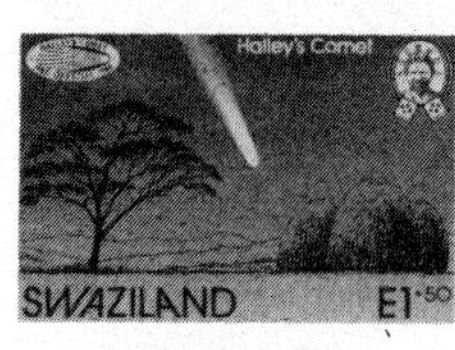

117 Halley's Comet over Swaziland

118 King Mswati III

(Des Jennifer Toombs. Litho B.D.T.)

1986 (27 Feb). *Appearance of Halley's Comet.* W w **14** *(sideways). P* 14.
499 **117** 1 e. 50, multicoloured .. .. .. 2·25 2·25

(Des A. Theobald. Litho Format)

1986 (21 Apr). *60th Birthday of Queen Elizabeth II. Vert designs as T* **230a** *of Jamaica. Multicoloured.* W w **16**. *P* 14×14½.
500 10 c. Christening of Princess Anne, 1950 .. 10 10
501 30 c. On Palace balcony after wedding of Prince and Princess of Wales, 1981 .. 20 25
502 45 c. Royal visit to Swaziland, 1947 .. 25 30
503 1 e. At Windsor Polo Ground, 1984 .. 55 60
504 2 e. At Crown Agents Head Office, London, 1983 .. .. 1·10 1·25
500/4 .. .. *Set of* 5 1·90 2·25

(Des L. Curtis. Litho Walsall)

1986 (25 Apr). *Coronation of King Mswati III. T* **118** *and similar designs.* W w **16** *(sideways on* 20 c. *to* 2 e.). *P* 14½×14 (10 c.) *or* 14×14½ *(others).*
505 10 c. black and gold 30 10
506 20 c. multicoloured 50 30
507 25 c. multicoloured 55 35
508 30 c. multicoloured 60 40
509 40 c. multicoloured 65 65
510 2 e. multicoloured .. .. 2·50 3·50
505/10 .. .. *Set of* 6 4·50 4·75
Designs: *Horiz*—20 c. Prince with King Sobhuza II at Incwala ceremony; 25 c. At primary school; 30 c. At school in England; 40 c. Inspecting guard of honour at Matsapha Airport; 2 e. Dancing the Simemo.

119 Emblems of Round Table and Project Orbis (eye disease campaign)

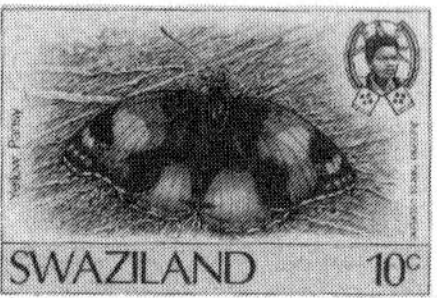

120 *Precis hierta*

(Des M. Kesson, adapted G. Vasarhelyi. Litho Walsall)

1986 (6 Oct). *50th Anniv of Round Table Organization. T* **119** *and similar vert designs showing branch emblems. Multicoloured.* W w **16**. *P* 14.
511 15 c. Type **119** 10 10
512 25 c. Ehlanzeni 51 .. .. 15 20
513 55 c. Mbabane 30 .. .. 35 40
514 70 c. Bulembu 54 .. .. 45 50
515 2 e. Manzini 44 .. .. 1·25 1·40
511/15 .. .. *Set of* 5 2·10 2·40

(Des I. Loe. Litho Questa)

1987 (17 Mar). *Butterflies. T* **120** *and similar horiz designs. Multicoloured. P* 14.
516 10 c. Type **120** 10 10
517 15 c. *Hamanumida daedalus* 10 10
518 20 c. *Charaxes boueti* 10 10
519 25 c. *Abantis paradisea* 10 10
520 30 c. *Acraea anemosa* 10 15
521 35 c. *Graphium leonidas* 15 20
522 45 c. *Graphium antheus* 20 25
523 50 c. *Precis orithya* 20 25
524 55 c. *Pinacopteryx eriphia* 20 25
525 70 c. *Precis octavia* 30 35
526 1 e. *Mylothris chloris* 40 45
527 5 e. *Colotis regina* .. .. 2·00 2·10
528 10 e. *Spindasis natalensis* .. .. .. 4·00 4·25
516/28 .. .. *Set of* 13 7·00 7·75

NEW INFORMATION

The minimum price quote is 10p which represents a handling charge rather than a basis for valuing common stamps. For further notes about prices see introductory pages.

121 Two White Rhinoceroses

122 Hybrid Tea Rose "Blue Moon"

(Des Doreen McGuinness. Litho Questa)

1987 (1 July). *White Rhinoceros. T* **121** *and similar horiz designs. Multicoloured. W w* **16** *(sideways). P* 14½.

529 15 c. Type **121** 45 15
530 25 c. Female and calf 70 55
531 45 c. Rhinoceros charging 1·25 1·25
532 70 c. Rhinoceros wallowing 1·75 2·00
529/32 *Set of* 4 3·75 3·50

(Des Josephine Martin. Litho Questa)

1987 (19 Oct). *Garden Flowers. T* **122** *and similar vert designs. Multicoloured. W w* **16**. *P* 14½.

533 15 c. Type **122** 45 15
534 35 c. Rambler Rose "Danse du feu" 75 55
535 55 c. Pompon Dahlia "Odin" 1·25 90
536 2 e. *Lilium davidii var. willmottiae* 3·00 3·50
533/6 *Set of* 4 5·00 4·50

1987 (9 Dec). *Royal Ruby Wedding. Nos.* 501/4 *optd with T* **45a** *of Kiribati in silver.*

537 30 c. On Palace balcony after wedding of Prince and Princess of Wales, 1981 20 20
538 45 c. Royal visit to Swaziland, 1947 30 30
539 1 e. At Windsor Polo Ground, 1984 80 85
540 2 e. At Crown Agents Head Office, London, 1983 1·50 1·75
537/40 *Set of* 4 2·50 2·75

123 *Zabalius aridus* (grasshopper)

(Des I. Loe. Litho Questa)

1988 (14 Mar). *Insects. T* **123** *and similar horiz designs. Multicoloured. W w* **16** *(sideways). P* 14.

541 15 c. Type **123** 45 15
542 55 c. *Callidea bohemani* (shieldbug) 1·25 85
543 1 e. *Phymateus viridipes* (grasshopper) 1·90 2·00
544 2 e. *Nomadacris septemfasciata* (locust) 3·25 3·50
541/4 *Set of* 4 6·25 6·00

124 Athlete with Swazi Flag and Olympic Stadium

(Des C. Abbott. Litho Format)

1988 (22 Aug). *Olympic Games, Seoul. T* **124** *and similar horiz designs. Multicoloured. W w* **16** *(sideways). P* 14.

545 15 c. Type **124** 25 10
546 35 c. Taekwondo 55 35
547 1 e. Boxing 1·25 1·25
548 2 e. Tennis 2·25 2·50
545/8 *Set of* 4 4·00 3·75

125 Savanna Monkey ("Green Monkey")

126 Dr. David Hynd (founder of Swazi Red Cross)

(Des I. Loe. Litho Questa)

1989 (16 Jan). *Small Mammals. T* **125** *and similar horiz designs. Multicoloured. W w* **16** *(sideways). P* 14.

549 35 c. Type **125** 55 25
550 55 c. Large-toothed Rock Hyrax ("Rock Dassie") 75 55
551 1 e. Zorilla 1·40 1·40
552 2 e. African Wild Cat 2·50 2·75
549/52 *Set of* 4 4·75 4·50

(Des T. Chance. Litho Security Printers (M), Malaysia)

1989 (21 Sept). *125th Anniv of International Red Cross. T* **126** *and similar horiz designs. Multicoloured. W w* **14** *(sideways). P* 12.

553 15 c. Type **126** 20 15
554 60 c. First aid training 55 40
555 1 e. Sigombeni Clinic 90 80
556 2 e. Refugee camp 1·40 1·40
553/6 *Set of* 4 2·75 2·50

127 King Mswati III with Prince of Wales, 1987

128 Manzini to Mahamba Road

(Des L. Curtis. Litho Harrison)

1989 (15 Nov). *21st Birthday of King Mswati III. T* **127** *and similar horiz designs. Multicoloured. P* 14×14½.

557 15 c. Type **127** 10 10
558 60 c. King with Pope John Paul II, 1988 30 35
559 1 e. Introduction of Crown Prince to people, 1983 50 55
560 2 e. King Mswati III and Queen Mother 95 1·00
557/60 *Set of* 4 1·60 1·75

(Des A. Theobald. Litho Questa)

1989 (18 Dec). *25th Anniv of African Development Bank. T* **128** *and similar horiz designs. Multicoloured. W w* **16** *(sideways). P* 14×14½.

561 15 c. Type **128** 10 10
562 60 c. Microwave Radio Receiver, Mbabane 30 35
563 1 e. Mbabane Government Hospital 50 65
564 2 e. Ezulwini Power Station switchyard 95 1·25
561/4 *Set of* 4 1·60 2·10

129 International Priority Mail Van

(Des G. Vasarhelyi. Litho Security Printers (M), Malaysia)

1990 (3 May). *"Stamp World London 90" International Stamp Exhibition. T* **129** *and similar horiz designs. Multicoloured. W w* **14** *(sideways). P* 12½.

565 15 c. Type **129** 15 10
566 60 c. Facsimile Service operators 40 40
567 1 e. Rural post office 75 75
568 2 e. Ezulwini Earth Station 1·40 1·40
565/8 *Set of* 4 2·40 2·40
MS569 105×85 mm. 2 e. Mail runner. Wmk upright 1·50 2·00

No. **MS**569 also commemorates the 150th anniversary of the Penny Black.

(Des D. Miller. Litho Questa)

1990 (4 Aug). *90th Birthday of Queen Elizabeth the Queen Mother. Vert designs as T* **107** *(75 c.) or* **108** *(4 e.) of Kenya. W w* **16**. *P* 14×15 *(75 c.) or* 14½ *(4 e.).*

570 75 c. multicoloured 50 50
571 4 e. brownish black & dp turquoise-green 2·25 2·25

Designs:—75 c. Queen Mother; 4 e. King George VI and Queen Elizabeth visiting Civil Resettlement Unit, Hatfield House.

130 Pictorial Teaching

131 Rural Water Supply

(Des D. Aryeequaye. Litho Questa)

1990 (21 Sept). *International Literacy Year. T* **130** *and similar horiz designs. Multicoloured. W w* **14** *(sideways). P* 14.

572 15 c. Type **130** 10 10
573 75 c. Rural class 45 45
574 1 e. Modern teaching methods 60 60
575 2 e. Presentation of certificates 1·10 1·10
572/5 *Set of* 4 2·00 2·00

(Des D. Aryeequaye. Litho Cartor, France)

1990 (10 Dec). *40th Anniv of United Nations Development Programme. "Helping People to Help Themselves". T* **131** *and similar vert designs. Multicoloured. W w* **14**. *P* 13½×14.

576 60 c. Type **131** 35 35
577 1 e. Seed multiplication project 60 60
578 2 e. Low-cost housing project 1·25 1·25
576/8 *Set of* 3 2·00 2·00

10c ■

(**132**)

133 Lobamba Hot Spring

1990 (17 Dec). *Nos.* 519/20, 522 *and* 524 *surch as T* **132**.

579 10 c. on 25 c. *Abantis paradisea* 10 10
580 15 c. on 30 c. *Acraea anemosa* 10 10
581 20 c. on 45 c. *Graphium antheus* 10 10
582 40 c. on 55 c. *Pinacopteryx eriphia* 15 10
579/82 *Set of* 4 30 35

(Des D. Aryeequaye. Litho Harrison)

1991 (11 Feb). *National Heritage. T* **133** *and similar horiz designs. Multicoloured. W* **77** *of Brunei (sideways). P* 14½.

583 15 c. Type **133** 15 10
584 60 c. Sibebe Rock 40 40
585 1 e. Jolobela Falls 70 70
586 2 e. Mantjolo Sacred Pool 1·25 1·40
583/6 *Set of* 4 2·25 2·40
MS587 80×60 mm. 2 e. Usushwana River. P 14 1·25 1·50

134 King Mswati III making Speech

135 *Xerophyta retinervis*

(Des D. Aryeequaye. Litho Cartor)

1991 (24 Apr). *5th Anniv of King Mswati III's Coronation. T* **134** *and similar horiz designs. Multicoloured. W w* **14** *(sideways). P* 14×13½.

588 15 c. Type **134** 15 10
589 75 c. Butimba Royal Hunt 50 50
590 1 e. King and visiting school friends from Sherborne, 1986 70 70
591 2 e. King opening Parliament 1·25 1·40
588/91 *Set of* 4 2·40 2·40

(Des D. Miller. Litho Questa)

1991 (17 June). *65th Birthday of Queen Elizabeth II and 70th Birthday of Prince Philip. Vert designs as T* **58** *of Kiribati. Multicoloured. W w* **16** *(sideways). P* 14½×14.

592 1 e. Prince Philip 70 70
a. Horiz pair. Nos. 592/3 separated by label 1·90 2·10
593 2 e. Queen Elizabeth II 1·25 1·40

Nos. 592/3 were printed in a similar sheet format to Nos. 366/7 of Kiribati

(Des D. Aryeequaye. Litho Questa)

1991 (30 Sept). *Indigenous Flowers. T* **135** *and similar vert designs. Multicoloured. W w* **14** *(sideways). P* 14.

594 15 c. Type **135** 15 10
595 75 c. *Bauhinia galpinii* 50 50
596 1 e. *Dombeya rotundifolia* 70 70
597 2 e. *Kigelia africana* 1·40 1·50
594/7 *Set of* 4 2·50 2·50

136 Father Christmas arriving with Gifts

137 Lubombo Flat Lizard

(Des D. Aryeequaye. Litho Cartor)

1991 (18 Dec). *Christmas. T* **136** *and similar vert designs. Multicoloured. W w* **14**. *P* 13½.

598 20 c. Type **136** 15 10
599 70 c. Singing carols 45 45
600 1 e. Priest reading from Bible 60 60
601 2 e. The Nativity 1·25 1·40
598/601 *Set of* 4 2·25 2·25

(Des D. Aryeequaye. Litho Cartor)

1992 (25 Feb). *Reptiles. T* **137** *and similar horiz designs. Multicoloured. W w* **14** *(sideways). P* 13½.

602 20 c. Type **137** 15 10
603 70 c. Natal Hinged Tortoise 45 45
604 1 e. Swazi Thick-toed Gecko 70 70
605 2 e. Nile Monitor 1·25 1·25
602/5 *Set of* 4 2·25 2·40

POSTAGE DUE STAMPS

D 1

Postage Due
2d

(D 2)

D 3

(Typo D.L.R.)

1933 (2 Jan)–**57**. *Wmk Mult Script CA. P* 14.

D1	D 1	1d. carmine	20	4·25
		a. Chalk-surfaced paper. *Deep carmine* (24.10.51)	20	6·00
		ac. Error. St Edward's Crown, W **9***b* ..	70·00	
D2		2d. pale violet	1·00	12·00
		a. Chalk-surfaced paper (22.2.57) ..	3·00	17·00
D1/2 Perf "Specimen"		.. .. *Set of* 2	40·00	

1961 (8 Feb). *No.* 55 *surch with Type* D **2**.

D3	**7**	2d. on 2d.	3·00	5·50

Another 2d. on 2d. Postage Due, with small surcharge as Type D **5**, was produced *after the currency change*, to meet the philatelic demand (*Price* 15*p unused*).

(Typo D.L.R.)

1961 (14 Feb). *Chalk-surfaced paper. Wmk Mult Script CA. P* 14.

D4	D **3**	1 c. carmine	15	75
D5		2 c. violet	15	1·10
D6		5 c. green	20	1·10
D4/6 ..		.. .. *Set of* 3	45	2·75

Postage Due
1c

(D 4)

Postage Due
1c

(D 5)

1961. *No.* 55 *surcharged*. A. *As Type* D **4**. (14 Feb).

D 7	**7**	1 c. on 2d..	1·25	2·25
D 8		2 c. on 2d.	1·25	2·25
D 9		5 c. on 2d.	1·50	2·25
D7/9 ..		.. .. *Set of* 3	3·50	6·00

B. *As Type* D **5**. (Date?)

D10	**7**	1 c. on 2d.	80	2·25
D11		2 c. on 2d.	55	1·75
D12		5 c. on 2d.	1·00	2·25
D10/12		.. .. *Set of* 3	2·10	5·75

D **6**

(Des and litho B.W.)

1971 (1 Feb). *W* w **12**. *P* 11½.

D13	D **6**	1 c. bright rose-red	55	2·00
D14		2 c. purple	75	2·25
D15		5 c. dull green	1·00	2·50
D13/15		.. .. *Set of* 3	2·10	6·00

1977 (17 Jan). *W* w **14** (*sideways*). *P* 11½.

D16	D **6**	1 c. rose-red	55	2·00
D17		2 c. purple	75	2·50
D18		5 c. dull green	1·25	2·75
D16/18		.. .. *Set of* 3	2·25	6·50

(Litho Harrison)

1978 (20 Apr)–**85**. *W* w **14**. *P* 15×14.

D19	D **6**	1 c. carmine	20	30
D19*a*		1 c. brown-red (13.3.85)	20	40
D20		2 c. purple	20	30
D21		5 c. blue-green	20	30
D19/21		.. .. *Set of* 4	70	1·10

(Litho Harrison)

1991 (17 July). *With imprint date. W* w **14** (*sideways*). *P* 15×14.

D23	D **6**	2 c. purple	10	10
D24		5 c. bright blue-green	10	10
D25		10 c. pale greenish blue	10	10
D26		25 c. red-brown	10	15
D23/6		.. .. *Set of* 4	25	30

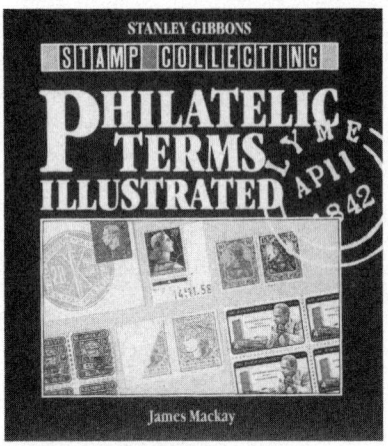

Tanzania
(*formerly* Tanganyika)

TANGANYIKA

The stamps of GERMANY were used in the colony between October 1890 and July 1893 when issues for GERMAN EAST AFRICA were provided.

PRICES FOR STAMPS ON COVER TO 1945

The Mafia Island provisionals (No. M1/52) are very rare used on cover.

Nos. N1/5	*from* × 8
Nos. 45/59	*from* × 6
Nos. 60/2	—
Nos. 63/73	*from* × 6
Nos. 74/86	*from* × 8
Nos. 87/8	—
Nos. 89/92	*from* × 6
Nos. 93/106	*from* × 3
No. 107	—

MAFIA ISLAND
BRITISH OCCUPATION

Mafia Island was captured by the British from the Germans in January 1915. Letters were first sent out unstamped, then with stamps handstamped with Type M 1. Later the military were supplied with handstamps by the post office in Zanzibar. These were used to produce Nos. M11/52.

(M 1)

(M 3)

1915 (Jan). *German East Africa Yacht types, handstamped with Type* M 1. *Wmk Lozenges, or no wmk* (1 *r.*, 2 *r.*). A. *In black* (2½ *h. in blackish lilac*). B. *In deep purple*. C. *In reddish violet.*

		A	B	C
M 1	2½ h. brown	£350	†	£200
	a. Pair, one without handstamp	†		£1100
M 2	4 h. green	£350	£300	£180
	a. Pair, one without handstamp	†		£1000
M 3	7½ h. carmine	£350	£300	£100
	a. Pair, one without handstamp	£1700		† £1000
M 4	15 h. ultramarine	£475	£400	£130
	a. Pair, one without handstamp	†		£1000
M 5	20 h. black and red/*yellow*	£475	£400	£225
	a. Pair, one without handstamp		† £1700	£1100
M 6	30 h. black and carmine	£550	£450	£275
	a. Pair, one without handstamp	£1700		† £1100
M 7	45 h. black and mauve	£600	£500	£325
	a. Pair, one without handstamp	£1700		† £1200
M 8	1 r. carmine	£3250		† £3000
M 9	2 r. green	£3750		† £3500
M10	3 r. blue-black and red	£4500		† £3750

Prices are for unused examples.

A few contemporary Zanzibar stamps (1, 3, 6 and 15 c.) are known with the above handstamp.

1915 (May). *German East Africa Yacht types with handstamped four-line surcharge* "G.R.—POST—6 CENTS—MAFIA" *in black, green or violet. Wmk Lozenges or no wmk* (1 *r.*, 2 *r.*).

M11	6 c. on 2½ h. brown	£550	£750
	a. Pair, one without handstamp	†	—
M12	6 c. on 4 h. green	£550	£750
	a. Pair, one without handstamp		
M13	6 c. on 7½ h. carmine	£550	£750
	a. Pair, one without handstamp		
M14	6 c. on 15 h. ultramarine	£550	£750
M15	6 c. on 20 h. black and red/*yellow*	£550	£750
M16	6 c. on 30 h. black and carmine	£750	£850
M17	6 c. on 45 h. black and mauve	£750	£850
	a. Pair, one without handstamp		
M18	6 c. on 1 r. carmine	£4500	
M19	6 c. on 2 r. green	£5500	
M20	6 c. on 3 r. blue-black and red	£6500	

The 5, 20 and 40 pesa values of the 1901 Yacht issue are also known with the above surcharge as are the contemporary 1 c. and 6 c. Zanzibar stamps.

1915 (Sept). (*a*) *German East African fiscal stamps.* "Statistik des Waaren-Verkehrs" (*Trade Statistical Charge*) *handstamped in bluish green or violet,* "O.H.B.M.S. Mafia" *in a circle, as Type* M 3.

M21	24 pesa, vermilion/*buff*	£350	£475
M22	12½ heller, drab	£350	£475
	a. Pair, one without handstamp	£1300	
M23	25 heller, dull green	£350	£475
M24	50 heller, slate	£350	£475
	a. Pair, one without handstamp	£1300	
M25	1 rupee, lilac	£350	£475

(*b*) *German East African* "Ubersetzungs- Gebühren" (*Translation Fee*) *stamp, overprinted as before*

M26	25 heller, grey	£450	£600

G. R / POST / MAFIA (M 4) G. R. / Post / MAFIA. (M 5)

(*c*) *Stamps as above, but with further opt as Type* M 4, *in bluish green or violet*

M27	24 pesa, vermilion/*buff*	£475
M28	12½ heller, drab	£475
M29	25 heller, dull green	£475
M30	50 heller, slate	£475
M31	1 rupee, lilac	£475
M32	25 heller, grey (No. M26)	£600
	a. Pair, one without handstamp Type M 4	£1900

Type M 3 is also known handstamped on the 7½ h., 20 h. and 30 h. values of German East Africa 1905 Yacht issue and also on contemporary 1, 3, 6 and 25 c. Zanzibar stamps.

1915 (Sept). *Stamps of Indian Expeditionary Forces* (*India optd* "I.E.F.") *with a further opt Type* M 4 *handstruck in green, greenish black or dull blue.*

M33	**55**	3 p. grey	17·00	35·00
		a. Pair, one stamp without opt	—	£375
M34	**56**	½ a. green	27·00	38·00
		a. Pair, one stamp without opt	—	£425
M35	**57**	1 a. carmine	30·00	38·00
M36	**59**	2 a. mauve	42·00	65·00
M37	**61**	2½ a. ultramarine	55·00	80·00
M38	**62**	3 a. orange-brown	55·00	80·00
		a. Pair, one stamp without opt	—	£500
M39	**63**	4 a. olive	75·00	£100
M40	**65**	8 a. purple	£130	£180
		a. Pair, one stamp without opt	—	£650
M41	**66**	12 a. dull claret	£200	£275
M42	**67**	1 r. brown and green	£225	£300
M33/42		*Set of* 10	£750	£1000

All values exist with the overprint inverted, and several are known with overprint double or sideways.

1916 (Oct). *Stamps of Indian Expeditionary Forces* (*India optd* "I.E.F.") *with further opt Type* M 5 *handstruck in green, greenish black or dull blue.*

M43	**55**	3 p. grey	80·00	95·00
M44	**56**	½ a. green	80·00	95·00
M45	**57**	1 a. carmine	75·00	85·00
M46	**59**	2 a. mauve	£100	£120
M47	**61**	2½ a. ultramarine	£110	£140
M48	**62**	3 a. orange-brown	£110	£140
M49	**63**	4 a. olive	£130	£150
M50	**65**	8 a. purple	£170	£225
M51	**66**	12 a. dull claret	£225	£300
M52	**67**	1 r. brown and green	£225	£300
M43/52		*Set of* 10	£1100	£1500

Stamps with handstamp inverted are known.

NYASALAND-RHODESIAN FORCE

This issue was sanctioned for use by the Nyasaland-Rhodesian Force during operations in German East Africa, Mozambique and Nyasaland. Unoverprinted Nyasaland stamps were used by the Force prior to the introduction of Nos. N1/5 and, again, in 1918.

N. F.
(N 1)

1916 (7 Aug–18 Sept*). *T* 15 *of Nyasaland optd with Type* N 1 *by Govt Printer, Zomba.*

N1	**15**	½d. green	80	4·50
N2		1d. scarlet	70	2·50
N3		3d. purple/*yellow* (15 Sept*)	5·00	14·00
		a. Opt double	†	£7000
N4		4d. black and red/*yellow* (13 Sept*)	20·00	30·00
N5		1s. black/*green* (18 Sept*)	21·00	32·00
N1/5		*Set of* 5	42·00	70·00
N1/5 Optd "Specimen"		*Set of* 5	£250	

* Earliest known dates of use.

Of No. N3a only six copies were printed, these being the bottom row on one pane issued at M'bamba Bay F.P.O., German East Africa in March 1918.

This overprint was applied in a setting of 60 (10 rows of 6) and the following minor varieties occur on all values: small stop after "N" (R. 1/1); broken "F" (R. 4/3); very small stop after "F" (R. 6/5); no serifs at top left and bottom of "N" (R. 10/1).

TANGANYIKA
BRITISH OCCUPATION OF GERMAN EAST AFRICA

Following the invasion of German East Africa by Allied forces civilian mail was accepted by the Indian Army postal service, using Indian stamps overprinted "I.E.F.". Some offices reverted to civilian control on 1 June 1917 and these used stamps of East Africa and Uganda until the "G.E.A." overprints were ready. The last field post offices, in the southern part of the country, did not come under civilian control until 15 March 1919.

G.E.A. (1) G.E.A. (2) G.E.A. (3)

1917 (Oct)–**21**. *Stamps of Kenya, Uganda and Tanganyika optd with T* 1 *and* 2. *Wmk Mult Crown CA. Ordinary paper* (1 *c. to* 15 *c.*) *or chalk-surfaced paper* (*others*).

45	**3**	1 c. black (R.)	15	70
46		1 c. black (Verm)	13·00	15·00
47		3 c. green	15	15
48		6 c. scarlet	15	10
		a. Wmk sideways	†	£1500
49		10 c. orange	15	30
50		12 c. slate-grey	15	1·25
51		15 c. bright blue	15	1·75
52	**3**	25 c. black and red/*yellow*	30	2·25
		a. On pale yellow (1921) (Optd S. £35)	1·40	7·50
53		50 c. black and lilac	50	2·75
54		75 c. black/*blue-green, olive back* (R.)	65	3·00
		a. On emerald back (Optd S. £42)	2·00	20·00
55	**4**	1 r. black/*green* (R.)	1·00	5·50
		a. On emerald back	2·50	20·00
56		2 r. red and black/*blue*	4·50	19·00
57		3 r. violet and green	6·50	32·00
58		4 r. red and green/*yellow*	15·00	48·00
59		5 r. blue and dull purple	26·00	50·00
60		10 r. red and green/*green*	45·00	£110
		a. On emerald back	55·00	£140
61		20 r. black and purple/*red*	£150	£200
62		50 r. carmine and green (S. £150)	£500	£700
45/61		*Set of* 16	£225	£425
45/61 Optd "Specimen"		*Set of* 16	£375	

Early printings of the rupee values exist with very large stop after the "E" in "G.E.A." (R.5/3). There are round stops after "E" varieties, which in one position of later printings became a small stop.

The only known example of No. 48a was used at Tanga in August 1918.

1921. *As* 1917–21 *but wmk Mult Script CA. Chalk-surfaced paper* (50 *c. to* 5 *r.*).

63	**3**	12 c. slate-grey	3·00	35·00
64		15 c. bright blue	30	2·75
65		50 c. black and dull purple	7·50	40·00
66	**4**	2 r. red and black/*blue*	32·00	80·00
67		3 r. violet and green	45·00	95·00
68		5 r. blue and dull purple	55·00	£100
63/8		*Set of* 6	£130	£300
63/8 Optd "Specimen"		*Set of* 6	£200	

1922. *T* 3 *of Kenya optd by the Government printer at Dar-es-Salaam with T* 3. *Wmk Mult Script CA.*

72		1 c. black (R.)	30	8·00
73		10 c. orange-yellow	45	12·00

BRITISH MANDATED TERRITORY

4

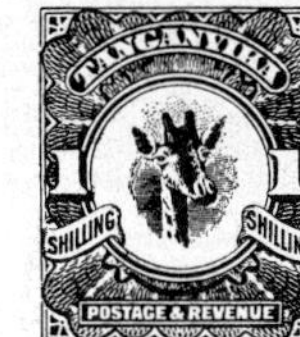
5

Giraffe

(Recess B.W.)

1922. *Head in black. Wmk Mult Script CA.* (*a*) *P* 15 × 14.

74	**4**	5 c. slate-purple	65	20
75		10 c. green	30	20
76		15 c. carmine-red	55	10
77		20 c. orange	45	10
78		25 c. black	3·00	5·50
79		30 c. blue	3·00	2·50
80		40 c. yellow-brown	1·50	3·00
81		50 c. slate-grey	1·25	1·50
82		75 c. yellow-bistre	2·75	11·00

(*b*) *P* 14. A. *Wmk sideways.* B. *Wmk upright*

			A		B	
83	**5**	1 s. green	1·75	8·50	1·25	6·00
84		2 s. purple	4·25	9·50	2·50	14·00
85		3 s. black	6·50	20·00	†	
86		5 s. scarlet	11·00	48·00	7·50	45·00
87		10 s. deep blue	55·00	£110	35·00	70·00
88		£1 yellow-orange	£100	£180	95·00	£180
74/88		*Set of* 15 (*incl* 85A)			£140	£325
74/88 Optd "Specimen"		*Set of* 15			£425	

In the £1 stamp the words of value are on a curved scroll running across the stamp above the words "POSTAGE AND REVENUE".

1925. *As* 1922. *Frame colours changed.*

89	**4**	5 c. green	30	90
90		10 c. orange-yellow	1·75	1·00
91		25 c. blue	2·00	12·00
92		30 c. purple	75	6·50
89/92		*Set of* 4	4·25	18·00
89/92 Optd "Specimen"		*Set of* 4	70·00	

6

7

(Typo D.L.R.)

1927–31. *Head in black. Wmk Mult Script CA. Chalk-surfaced paper* (5 *s.*, 10 *s.*, £1). *P* 14.

93	**6**	5 c. green	20	10
94		10 c. yellow	30	10
95		15 c. carmine-red	20	10
96		20 c. orange-buff	50	10
97		25 c. bright blue	75	75
98		30 c. dull purple	90	2·50
98*a*		30 c. bright blue (1931)	14·00	30
99		40 c. yellow-brown	1·00	2·75
100		50 c. grey	75	30
101		75 c. olive-green	1·75	8·50
102	**7**	1 s. green	2·25	90
103		2 s. deep purple	5·00	2·25
104		3 s. black	8·00	30·00
105		5 s. carmine-red	9·00	14·00

106 **7** 10 s. deep blue .. .. 38·00 70·00
107 £1 brown-orange .. .. .. 85·00 £120
93/107 .. .. *Set of* 16 £140 £225
93/107 Optd/Perf "Specimen" .. *Set of* 16 £250

Tanganyika became part of the joint East African postal administration on 1 January 1933 and subsequently used the stamps of KENYA, UGANDA AND TANGANYIKA.

INDEPENDENT REPUBLIC

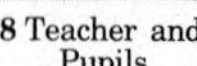
8 Teacher and Pupils

9 District Nurse and Child

14 "Maternity"

15 Freedom Torch over Mt Kilimanjaro

(Des V. Whiteley. Photo Harrison)

1961 (9 Dec)–**64**. *Independence. T* **8/9**, **14/15** *and similar designs. P* 14×15 (5 *c.*, 30 *c.*), 15×14 (10 *c.*, 15 *c.*, 20 *c.*, 50 *c.*) *or* 14½ (*others*).
108 5 c. sepia and light apple-green 10 10
109 10 c. deep bluish green 10 10
110 15 c. sepia and blue 10 10
a. Blue omitted £225
111 20 c. orange-brown 10 10
112 30 c. black, emerald and yellow 10 10
a. Inscr "UHURU 196" £375 £140
b. "1" inserted after "196" .. .. 10·00
113 50 c. black and yellow 10 10
114 1 s. brown, blue and olive-yellow 15 10
115 1 s. 30, red, yellow, black, brown and blue 1·00 10
a. Red, yellow, blk, brn & dp bl (10.3.64) 1·50 10
116 2 s. blue, yellow, green and brown .. 40 10
117 5 s. deep bluish green and orange-red .. 50 40
118 10 s. black, reddish purple and light blue .. 10·00 2·75
a. Reddish purple (diamond) omitted .. £150
119 20 s. red, yellow, black, brown and green .. 3·00 7·00
108/19 .. .. *Set of* 12 14·00 9·50

Designs: *Vert* (*as T* **9**)—15 c. Coffee-picking; 20 c. Harvesting maize; 50 c. Serengeti lions. *Horiz* (*as T* **8**)—30 c. Tanganyikan flag. (*As T* **14**)—2 s. Dar-es-Salaam waterfront; 5 s. Land tillage; 10 s. Diamond and mine. *Vert*—20 s. Type **15**.

No. 112a. The missing "1" in "1961" occurs on emerald Plate 1C, R. 10/10. The "1" was later inserted but it is, however, very slightly shorter and the figure is more solid than normal.

19 Pres. Nyerere inaugurating Self-help Project

20 Hoisting Flag on Mt Kilimanjaro

(Photo Harrison)

1962 (9 Dec). *Inauguration of Republic. Vert designs as T* **19/20**. *P* 14½.
120 30 c. emerald 10 10
121 50 c. yellow, black, green, red and blue .. 10 10
122 1 s. 30, multicoloured 10 10
123 2 s. 50, black, red and blue 15 30
120/3 .. .. *Set of* 4 30 35

Designs:—1 s. 30, Presidential emblem; 2 s. 50, Independence Monument.

23 Map of Republic

24 Torch and Spear Emblem

(Des M. Goaman. Photo Harrison)

1964 (7 July). *United Republic of Tanganyika and Zanzibar Commemoration. P* 14 × 14½.
124 **23** 20 c. yellow-green and light blue .. 10 10
125 **24** 30 c. blue and sepia 10 10
126 1 s. 30, orange-brown and ultramarine 10 10
127 **23** 2 s. 50, purple and ultramarine .. 35 30
124/7 .. .. *Set of* 4 50 35

Despite the inscription on the stamps the above issue was only on sale in Tanganyika and had no validity in Zanzibar.

OFFICIAL STAMPS

OFFICIAL (O 1)   **OFFICIAL** (O 2) (3½ mm tall)

1961 (9 Dec). *Nos.* 108/14 *and* 117 *optd with Type* O **1** (10, 15, 20, 50 *c. or larger* (17 *mm*) 5, 30 *c.*) *or with Type* O **2** (1 *s. or larger* (22 *mm*) 5 *s.*).
O1 5 c. sepia and light apple-green 10 10
O2 10 c. deep bluish green 10 10
O3 15 c. sepia and blue 10 10
O4 20 c. orange-brown 10 10
O5 30 c. black, emerald and yellow 10 10
O6 50 c. black and yellow 10 10
O7 1 s. brown, blue and olive-yellow 10 10
O8 5 s. deep bluish green and orange-red .. 65 75
O1/8 .. .. *Set of* 8 90 90

ZANZIBAR

Stamps of INDIA were used in Zanzibar from 1 October 1875 until 10 November 1895, when the administration of the postal service was transferred from India to British East Africa.

A French post office was opened on the island in January 1889 and this service used the stamps of FRANCE until 1894 when specific stamps for this office were provided. The French postal service on the island closed on 31 July 1904 and it is known that French stamps were again utilised during the final month.

A German postal agency operated in Zanzibar between 27 August 1890 and 31 July 1891, using the stamps of GERMANY.

PRICES FOR STAMPS ON COVER TO 1945

Nos. 1/2	—
Nos. 3/18	*from* × 30
Nos. 19/21	—
Nos. 22/174	*from* × 12
Nos. 175/7	—
Nos. 178/87	*from* × 15
Nos. 188/204	*from* × 10
Nos. 205/9	*from* × 15
Nos. 210/38	*from* × 10
Nos. 239/45	—
Nos. 246/59	*from* × 8
Nos. 260/*f*	—
Nos. 261/330	*from* × 4
Nos. D1/17	*from* × 12
Nos. D18/30	*from* × 15

PROTECTORATE

Zanzibar
(1)

1895 (10 Nov)–**96**. *Contemporary stamps of India optd with T* **1** *by Zanzibar Gazette.*

(*a*) *In blue*
1 **23** ½ a. blue-green £7500 £2250
2 **25** 1 a. plum £1800 £475
j. "Zanzidar" .. .. .. — £8500

(*b*) *In black*
3 **23** ½ a. blue-green .. .. .. 3·00 2·50
j. "Zanzidar" £650 £475
k. "Zanibar" £700 £800
l. Diaeresis over last "a" £500
4 **25** 1 a. plum .. .. .. 3·25 3·00
j. "Zanzidar" £1800 £1200
k. "Zanibar" £800 £900
l. Diaeresis over last "a" £600
5 **26** 1 a. 6 p. sepia .. .. .. 3·75 3·00
j. "Zanzidar" £1800 £750
k. "Zanibar" £800 £900
l. "Zanizbar" .. .. ..
m. Diaeresis over last "a" £550
6 **27** 2 a. pale blue .. .. .. 3·50 3·50
7 2 a. blue .. .. .. 3·75 3·75
j. "Zanzidar" £1600 £1100
k. "Zanibar" £1600 £1000
l. Diaeresis over last "a" £550
m. Opt double £190
8 **36** 2½ a. yellow-green .. .. .. 4·25 4·25
j. "Zanzidar" £1600 £850
k. "Zanibar" £375 £600
l. "Zapzibar" .. .. ..
m. "Zanzipar" .. .. ..
n. Diaeresis over last "a" £550 £550
o. Second "z" italic £150 £225
9 **28** 3 a. orange .. .. .. 6·50 8·50
10 3 a. brown-orange .. .. .. 6·50 8·50
j. Zanzidar" £425 £750
k. "Zanizbar" £1600 £1700
11 **29** 4 a. olive-green .. .. .. 12·00 12·00
j. "Zanzidar" £2250 £1300
12 4 a. slate-green .. .. .. 8·00 9·50
l. Diaeresis over last "a" £750
13 **21** 6 a. pale brown .. .. .. 9·00 10·00
j. "Zanzidar" £2500 £1400
k. "Zanibar" £550 £850
l. "Zanzibarr" £1700 £1700
m. Opt double .. .. ..
14 **31** 8 a. dull mauve .. .. .. 15·00 16·00
j. "Zanzidar" £2750 £2750
15 8 a. magenta (7.96) .. .. .. 9·00 15·00
16 **32** 12 a. purple/*red* .. .. .. 14·00 10·00
j. "Zanzidar" £3250 £2000
17 **33** 1 r. slate .. .. .. 65·00 65·00
j. "Zanzidar" £3000 £2750
18 **37** 1 r. green and carmine (7.96) .. 10·00 14·00
j. Opt vert downwards £375
19 **38** 2 r. carmine and yellow-brown .. 28·00 42·00
j. "r" omitted £4250
k. "r" inverted £2500 £2500
20 3 r. brown and green .. .. .. 30·00 42·00
j. "r" omitted £4250
k. "r" inverted £2500 £2500
21 5 r. ultramarine and violet .. .. 30·00 45·00
j. "r" omitted £4250
k. "r" inverted £1900
l. Opt double, one inverted £700
3/21 .. .. *Set of* 15 £200 £250

Many forgeries of this overprint exist and also bogus errors.

MINOR VARIETIES. The following minor varieties of type exist on Nos. 1/21:

A. First "Z" antique (all values)
B. Broken "p" for "n" (all values to 1 r.)
C. Tall second "z" (all values)
D. Small second "z" (all values)
E. Small second "z" and inverted "q" for "b" (all values)
F. Second "z" Gothic (½ a. to 12 a. and 1 r.) (No. 18) (black opts only)
G. No dot over "i" (all values to 1 r.)
H. Inverted "q" for "b" (all values to 1 r.)
I. Arabic "2" for "r" (all values to 1 r.) (black opts only)

The scarcity of these varieties varies from normal catalogue value (D. and E.) to 4 times catalogue value (B.).

1895–98. *Provisionals.* I *Stamps used for postal purposes.*

2½ (2)   2½ (3)   2½ (4)   2½ (5)

1895 (Dec.) *No.* 5 *surch with T* **2** *in red.*
22 2½ on 1½ a. sepia .. .. .. 24·00 27·00
j. "Zanzidar" £950 £900
k. "Zanizbar" £2000 £1400
l. Inverted "1" in "½" £800 £700

1896 (11 May). *No.* 4 *surch in black.*
23 **3** 2½ on 1 a. plum £120 £100
24 **4** 2½ on 1 a. plum £300 £225
j. Inverted "1" in "½" £1600
25 **5** 2½ on 1 a. plum £120 £100

2½ (6)   2½ (7)   2½ (8)

1896 (15 Aug). *No.* 6 *surch in red.*
26 **6** 2½ on 2 a. pale blue .. .. .. 30·00 20·00
j. Inverted "1" in "½" £325 £225
k. Roman "I" in "½" £200 £150
27 **7** 2½ on 2 a. pale blue .. .. .. £110 75·00
j. "2" of "½" omitted £2250
k. "22" for "2½" £3000
l. "1" of "½" omitted £2250 £2250
m. Inverted "1" in "½" £1000
28 **8** 2½ on 2 a. pale blue £1800 £900

No. 28 only exists with small "z".

1896 (15 Nov). *No* 5 *surch in red.*
29 **6** 2½ on 1½ a. sepia .. .. .. £110 90·00
j. Inverted "1" in "½" £900 £800
k. Roman "I" in "½" £650 £600
30 **7** 2½ on 1½ a. sepia £325 £275
31 **8** 2½ on 1½ a. sepia £5000 £3500

No. 31 only exists with small "z".

II. *Stamps prepared for official purposes*

1898 (Jan). *Nos.* 4, 5 *and* 7 *surch as before in red.*
32 **3** 2½ on 1 a. plum £225 £375
33 **4** 2½ on 1 a. plum £400 £550
34 **5** 2½ on 1a. plum £250 £400
35 **3** 2½ on 1½ a. sepia .. .. .. 65·00 £110
j. Diaeresis over last "a" £1800
36 **4** 2½ on 1½ a. sepia £140 £250
37 **5** 2½ on 1½ a. sepia .. .. .. 90·00 £150
38 **3** 2½ on 2 a. dull blue .. .. .. 75·00 £130
39 **4** 2½ on 2 a. dull blue £140 £250
40 **5** 2½ on 2 a. dull blue .. .. .. 90·00 £160

It is doubtful whether Nos. 32/40 were issued to the public.

1896. *Stamps of British East Africa, T* **11**, *optd with T* **1**.
41 ½ a. yellow-green (1 June) .. .. 21·00 15·00
42 1 a. carmine-rose (1 June) .. .. 21·00 15·00
j. Opt double £425 £450
43 2½ a. deep blue (R.) (24 May) .. .. 75·00 40·00
44 4½ a. orange-yellow (12 Aug) .. .. 30·00 42·00
45 5 a. olive-bistre (12 Aug) .. .. 35·00 18·00
j. "r" omitted .. .. .. — £1400
46 7½ a. mauve (12 Aug) .. .. .. 24·00 32·00
41/6 .. .. *Set of* 6 £190 £150

MINOR VARIETIES. The various minor varieties of type detailed in the note below No. 21 also occur on Nos. 22 to 46 as indicated below:

A. Nos. 23, 25, 27, 30, 35, 38, 41/6
B. Nos. 22, 26, 29/30, 32/3, 36, 39, 44/6
C. Nos. 22, 25/6, 32, 36, 38, 40/6
D. Nos. 22/46
E. Nos. 22/46
F. Nos. 22, 25/6, 29, 41/6
G. Nos. 25/6, 29, 35, 37/8, 40/6
H. Nos. 22, 41/6 (on the British East Africa stamps this variety occurs in the same position as variety C.)
I. Nos. 26, 29, 35, 38, 41/6

The scarcity of these varieties on the surcharges (Nos. 22/40) is similar to those on the basic stamps, but examples on the British East Africa values (Nos. 41/6) are more common.

PRINTERS. All Zanzibar stamps up to Type **37** were printed by De La Rue & Co.

12

13

14 Sultan Seyyid Hamed-bin-Thwain

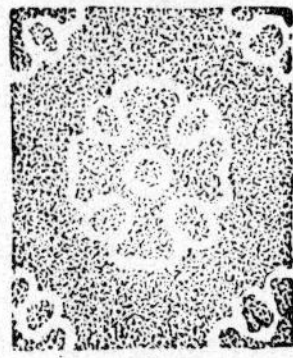
18

1896 (Dec.). *Recess. Flags in red on all values. W* **12**. *P* 14.

No.	Type	Description	Unused	Used
156	**13**	½ a. yellow-green	1·25	60
157		1 a. indigo	1·00	1·00
158		1 a. violet-blue	2·75	2·75
159		2 a. red-brown	1·00	65
160		2½ a. bright blue	4·00	50
161		2½ a. pale blue	4·50	60
162		3 a. grey	2·75	3·25
163		3 a. bluish grey	3·25	3·75
164		4 a. myrtle-green	2·75	2·75
165		4½ a. orange	2·50	2·75
166		5 a. bistre	2·25	2·25
		a. Bisected (2½ a.) (on cover)	†	£1700
167		7½ a. mauve	2·25	2·25
168		8 a. grey-olive	5·00	4·25
169	**14**	1 r. blue	9·00	9·00
170		1 r. deep blue	15·00	12·00
171		2 r. green	13·00	9·50
172		3 r. dull purple	19·00	9·50
173		4 r. lake	14·00	13·00
174		5 r. sepia	18·00	13·00
156/74		*Set of* 15	85·00	65·00
156/74 Optd "Specimen"		*Set of* 15	£180	

The ½, 1, 2, 2½, 3 and 8 a. are known without wmk, these being from edges of the sheets.

1897 (5 Jan). *No.* 164 *surch as before, in red.*

No.	Type	Description	Unused	Used
175	**3**	2½ on 4 a. myrtle-green	48·00	28·00
176	**4**	2½ on 4 a. myrtle-green	£130	£100
177	**5**	2½ on 4 a. myrtle-green	60·00	42·00
175/7		*Set of* 3	£200	£150

1898 (May). *Recess. W* **18**. *P* 14.

No.	Type	Description	Unused	Used
178	**13**	½ a. yellow-green	50	35
179		1 a. indigo	60	45
		a. Greenish black	2·25	90
180		2 a. red-brown	1·00	75
		a. Deep brown	2·50	1·50
181		2½ a. bright blue	85	30
182		3 a. grey	2·25	60
183		4 a. myrtle-green	1·50	1·00
184		4½ a. orange	2·50	70
185		5 a. bistre	6·00	1·50
		a. Pale bistre	6·50	2·00
186		7½ a. mauve	2·25	2·75
187		8 a. grey-olive	3·75	2·25
178/87		*Set of* 10	19·00	9·50

19

20 Sultan Seyyid Hamoud-bin-Mohammed bin Said

1899 (June)–**1901**. *Recess. Flags in red. W* **18** (*Nos.* 188/99) *or W* **12** (*others*). *P* 14.

No.	Type	Description	Unused	Used
188	**19**	½ a. yellow-green	55	25
		a. Wmk sideways	3·50	2·25
189		1 a. indigo	1·25	20
		a. Wmk sideways	6·50	70
190		1 a. carmine (1901)	65	10
191		2 a. red-brown	75	30
192		2½ a. bright blue	1·00	50
193		3 a. grey	1·25	1·40
194		4 a. myrtle-green	1·25	1·00
195		4½ a. orange	3·50	2·25
196		4½ a. blue-black (1901)	4·75	4·75
197		5 a. bistre	1·50	1·25
198		7½ a. mauve	2·25	3·25
199		8 a. grey-olive	2·25	3·50
200	**20**	1 r. blue	15·00	12·00
201		2 r. green	15·00	14·00
202		3 r. dull purple	15·00	22·00
203		4 r. lake	24·00	35·00
204		5 r. sepia	35·00	42·00
188/204		*Set of* 17	£110	£130
188/204 Optd "Specimen"		*Set of* 17	£180	

One	Two & Half	Two & Half	Two & Half
(21)	(22)	(22*a*) Thin open "w"	(22*b*) Serif to foot of "f"

1904. *Stamps of* 1899/1901 *surch as T* **21** *and* **22**, *in black or lake* (L.) *by Zanzibar Gazette.*

No.	Type	Description	Unused	Used
205	**19**	1 on 4½ a. orange	1·40	3·00
206		1 on 4½ a. blue-black (L.)	4·25	11·00
207		2 on 4 a. myrtle-green (L.)	11·00	16·00
208		2½ on 7½ a. mauve	12·00	16·00
		a. Opt Type **22*a***	60·00	80·00
		b. Opt Type **22*b***	90·00	£120
		c. "Hlaf" for "Half"	£7500	
209		2½ on 8 a. grey-olive	13·00	26·00
		a. Opt Type **22*a***	80·00	£120
		b. Opt Type **22*b***	£110	£140
		c. "Hlaf" for "Half"	£7000	£4000
205/9		*Set of* 5	35·00	65·00

23

24

Monogram of Sultan Seyyid Ali bin Hamoud bin Naherud

1904 (8 June). *Typo. Background of centre in second colour. W* **18**. *P* 14.

No.	Type	Description	Unused	Used
210	**23**	½ a. green	65	15
211		1 a. rose-red	65	10
212		2 a. brown	1·25	45
213		2½ a. blue	1·60	35
214		3 a. grey	1·50	1·25
215		4 a. deep green	1·75	1·25
216		4½ a. black	3·00	2·50
217		5 a. yellow-brown	3·25	1·25
218		7½ a. purple	3·50	4·50
219		8 a. olive-green	3·50	2·50
220	**24**	1 r. blue and red	14·00	8·50
		a. Wmk sideways	45·00	35·00
221		2 r. green and red	12·00	24·00
		a. Wmk sideways	70·00	85·00
222		3 r. violet and red	32·00	55·00
223		4 r. claret and red	38·00	70·00
224		5 r. olive-brown and red	42·00	75·00
210/24		*Set of* 15	£140	£225
210/24 Optd "Specimen"		*Set of* 15	£130	

25

26

27 Sultan Ali bin Hamoud

28 View of Port

1908 (May)–**09**. *Recess. W* **18** (*sideways on* 10 *r. to* 30 *r.*). *P* 14.

No.	Type	Description	Unused	Used
225	**25**	1 c. pearl-grey (10.09)	25	25
226		3 c. yellow-green	1·25	10
		a. Wmk sideways	1·25	60
227		6 c. rose-carmine	3·00	10
		a. Wmk sideways	3·00	90
228		10 c. brown (10.09)	1·50	1·75
229		12 c. violet	3·75	55
		a. Wmk sideways	3·75	40
230	**26**	15 c. ultramarine	3·25	40
		a. Wmk sideways	3·50	2·00
231		25 c. sepia	2·50	80
232		50 c. blue-green	3·25	3·50
233		75 c. grey-black (10.09)	6·00	8·00
234	**27**	1 r. yellow-green	12·00	5·00
		a. Wmk sideways	20·00	7·00
235		2 r. violet	11·00	14·00
		a. Wmk sideways	50·00	35·00
236		3 r. orange-bistre	16·00	35·00
237		4 r. vermilion	27·00	60·00
238		5 r. steel-blue	32·00	48·00
239	**28**	10 r. blue-green and brown (S. £22)	65·00	£110
240		20 r. black and yellow-green (S. £30)	£160	£275
241		30 r. black and sepia (S. £40)	£250	£400
242		40 r. black and orange-brown (S. £50)	£400	
243		50 r. black and mauve (S. £60)	£350	
244		100 r. black and steel-blue (S. £100)	£650	
245		200 r. brown and greenish black (S. £150)	£950	
225/38		*Set of* 14	£110	£160
225/38 Optd "Specimen"		*Set of* 14	£140	

Specimen copies of Nos. 239/45 are all overprinted.

29 Sultan Kalif bin Harub

30 Sailing Canoe

31 Dhow

1913. *Recess. W* **18** (*sideways on* 75 *c. and T* **31**). *P* 14.

No.	Type	Description	Unused	Used
246	**29**	1 c. grey	15	20
247		3 c. yellow-green	35	20
248		6 c. rose-carmine	70	10
249		10 c. brown	80	75
250		12 c. violet	70	15
251		15 c. blue	1·00	30
252		25 c. sepia	80	45
253		50 c. blue-green	2·00	2·50
254		75 c. grey-black	1·50	1·75
255	**30**	1 r. yellow-green	3·00	3·50
256		2 r. violet	8·00	16·00
257		3 r. orange-bistre	10·00	24·00
258		4 r. scarlet	16·00	42·00
259		5 r. steel-blue	20·00	24·00
260	**31**	10 r. green and brown	60·00	90·00
260*a*		20 r. black and green (S. £20)	85·00	£160
260*b*		30 r. black and brown (S. £30)	£110	£200
260*c*		40 r. black and vermilion (S. £50)	£225	£350
260*d*		50 r. black and purple (S. £55)	£225	£350
260*e*		100 r. black and blue (S. £80)	£300	
260*f*		200 r. brown and black (S. £110)	£600	
246/60		*Set of* 15	£110	£180
246/60 Optd "Specimen"		*Set of* 15	£130	

Specimen copies of Nos. 260*a*/*f* are all overprinted.

1914–22. *Wmk Mult Crown CA* (*sideways on* 10 *r.*). *P* 14.

No.	Type	Description	Unused	Used
261	**29**	1 c. grey	20	25
262		3 c. yellow-green	45	10
		a. Dull green	1·40	15
263		6 c. deep carmine	75	10
		a. Bright rose-carmine	75	10
264		8 c. purple/*pale yellow* (1922)	60	2·50
265		10 c. myrtle/*pale yellow* (1922)	60	35
266		15 c. deep ultramarine	90	2·00
268		50 c. blue-green	3·50	4·00
269		75 c. grey-black	2·75	13·00
270	**30**	1 r. yellow-green	4·00	2·75
271		2 r. violet	4·25	8·00
272		3 r. orange-bistre	11·00	24·00
273		4 r. scarlet	14·00	48·00
274		5 r. steel-blue	16·00	42·00
275	**31**	10 r. green and brown	55·00	£150
261/75		*Set of* 14	£100	£250
261/75 Optd "Specimen"		*Set of* 14	£130	

1921–29. *Wmk Mult Script CA* (*sideways on* 10 *r. to* 30 *r.*). *P* 14.

No.	Type	Description	Unused	Used
276	**29**	1 c. slate-grey	10	4·00
277		3 c. yellow-green	15	1·25
278		3 c. yellow (1922)	15	10
279		4 c. green (1922)	50	60
280		6 c. carmine-red	30	50
281		6 c. purple/*blue* (1922)	35	10
282		10 c. brown	70	4·00
283		12 c. violet	30	30
284		12 c. carmine-red (1922)	40	35
285		15 c. blue	55	3·75
286		20 c. indigo (1922)	1·00	30
287		25 c. sepia	60	4·50
288		50 c. myrtle-green	1·25	2·00
289		75 c. slate	2·50	22·00
290	**30**	1 r. yellow-green	1·40	1·60
291		2 r. deep violet	2·50	4·50
292		3 r. orange-bistre	3·75	6·00
293		4 r. scarlet	9·50	22·00
294		5 r. Prussian blue	12·00	42·00
295	**31**	10 r. green and brown	40·00	95·00
296		20 r. black and green (Optd S. £55)	95·00	£200
297		30 r. black and brown (1929) (Perf S. £65)	£150	£300
276/95		*Set of* 20	70·00	£190
276/95 Optd "Specimen"		*Set of* 20	£160	

32 Sultan Kalif bin Harub **33**

1926–27. *T* **32** ("CENTS" *in serifed capitals*). *Recess. Wmk Mult Script CA. P* 14.

No.	Type	Description	Unused	Used
299	**32**	1 c. brown	15	10
300		3 c. yellow-orange	15	15
301		4 c. deep dull green	20	30
302		6 c. violet	15	10
303		8 c. slate	90	2·00
304		10 c. olive-green	75	40
305		12 c. carmine-red	1·50	10
306		20 c. bright blue	40	30
307		25 c. purple/*yellow* (1927)	3·00	2·50
308		50 c. claret	90	35
309		75 c. sepia (1927)	2·50	7·00
299/309		*Set of* 11	9·50	12·00
299/309 Optd "Specimen"		*Set of* 11	85·00	

(New Currency. 100 cents = 1 shilling)

1936 (1 Jan). *T* **33** *("CENTS" in sans-serif capitals), and T* **30/1**, *but values in shillings. Recess. Wmk Mult Script CA. P* 14×13½–14.

310 **33** 5 c. green 10 10
311 10 c. black 10 10
312 15 c. carmine-red 10 15
313 20 c. orange 10 10
314 25 c. purple/*yellow* 10 10
315 30 c. ultramarine 10 10
316 40 c. sepia 15 10
317 50 c. claret 15 10
318 **30** 1 s. yellow-green 45 10
319 2 s. slate-violet 55 30
320 5 s. scarlet 2·25 3·25
321 7 s. 50, light blue 7·00 8·00
322 **31** 10 s. green and brown 4·50 4·75
310/22 *Set of* 13 14·00 15·00
310/22 Perf "Specimen" *Set of* 13 £100

36 Sultan Kalif bin Harub

1936 (9 Dec). *Silver Jubilee of Sultan. Recess. Wmk Mult Script CA. P* 14.

323 **36** 10 c. black and olive-green 70 30
324 20 c. black and bright purple 70 30
325 30 c. black and deep ultramarine 1·50 35
326 50 c. black and orange-vermilion 1·75 45
323/6 *Set of* 4 4·25 1·25
323/6 Perf "Specimen" *Set of* 4 60·00

37 *Sham Alam* (Sultan's dhow)

VICTORY ISSUE
8TH JUNE 1946
(**38**)

1944 (20 Nov). *Bicentenary of Al Busaid Dynasty. Recess. Wmk Mult Script CA. P* 14.

327 **37** 10 c. ultramarine 15 40
328 20 c. red 15 50
329 50 c. blue-green 15 30
330 1 s. dull purple 15 45
327/30 *Set of* 4 55 1·50
327/30 Perf "Specimen" *Set of* 4 70·00

1946 (11 Nov). *Victory. Optd with T* **38**.

331 **33** 10 c. black (R.) 20 20
332 30 c. ultramarine (R.) 20 40
331/2 Perf "Specimen" *Set of* 2 45·00

1949 (10 Jan). *Royal Silver Wedding. As Nos.* 143/4 *of Jamaica.*

333 20 c. orange 25 40
334 10 s. brown 10·00 16·00

1949 (10 Oct). *75th Anniv of U.P.U. As Nos.* 145/8 *of Jamaica.*

335 20 c. red-orange 30 35
336 30 c. deep blue 90 50
337 50 c. magenta 1·10 65
338 1 s. blue-green 1·10 1·25
335/8 *Set of* 4 3·00 2·50

39 Sultan Kalif bin Harub

40 Seyyid Khalifa Schools, Beit-el-Ras

1952 (26 Aug)–**55**. *Wmk Mult Script CA. P* 12½ *(cent values) or* 13 *(shilling values).*

339 **39** 5 c. black 10 10
340 10 c. red-orange 10 10
341 15 c. green 30 20
a. *Yellow-green* (12.11.53) 45 20
342 20 c. carmine-red 20 20
343 25 c. reddish purple 35 10
344 30 c. deep bluish green 15 10
a. *Deep green* (29.3.55) 1·50 1·75
345 35 c. bright blue 20 60
346 40 c. deep brown 25 40
a. *Sepia* (12.11.53) 30 50
347 50 c. violet 25 10
a. *Deep violet* (29.3.55) 45 30
348 **40** 1 s. deep green and deep brown 25 10
349 2 s. bright blue and deep purple 85 30
350 5 s. black and carmine-red 1·50 1·50
351 7 s. 50, grey-black and emerald 12·00 20·00
352 10 s. carmine-red and black 6·00 3·25
339/52 *Set of* 14 20·00 24·00

41 Sultan Kalif bin Harub

(Photo Harrison)

1954 (26 Aug). *Sultan's 75th Birthday. Wmk Mult Script CA. Chalk-surfaced paper. P* 13 × 12.

353 **41** 15 c. deep green 10 10
354 20 c. rose-red 10 10
355 30 c. bright blue 10 10
356 50 c. purple 10 10
357 1 s. 25, orange-red 15 40
353/7 *Set of* 5 30 55

42 Cloves

43 Dhows

44 Sultan's Barge

45 Map of East African Coast

46 Minaret Mosque

47 Dimbani Mosque

48 Kibweni Palace

(Des W. J. Jennings (T **42**), A. Farhan (T **43**), Mrs. M. Broadbent (T **44, 46**), R. A. Sweet (T **45**), A. S. B. New (T **47**), B. J. Woolley (T **48**). Recess B.W.)

1957 (26 Aug). *W* w **12**. *P* 11½ (5 *c.*, 10 *c.*), 11 × 11½ (15 *c.*, 30 *c.*, 1 *s.* 25), 14 × 13½ (20 *c.*, 25 *c.*, 35 *c.*, 50 *c.*,), 13½ × 14 (40 *c.*, 1 *s.*, 2 *s.*) *or* 13 × 13½ (5 *s.*, 7 *s.* 50, 10 *s.*).

358 **42** 5 c. orange and deep green 10 10
359 10 c. emerald and carmine-red 10 10
360 **43** 15 c. green and sepia 10 30
361 **44** 20 c. ultramarine 10 10
362 **45** 25 c. orange-brown and black 10 10
363 **43** 30 c. carmine-red and black 15 10
364 **45** 35 c. slate and emerald 15 15
365 **46** 40 c. brown and black 15 10
366 **45** 50 c. blue and grey-green 15 10
367 **47** 1 s. carmine and black 20 10
368 **43** 1 s. 25, slate and carmine 55 10
369 **47** 2 s. orange and deep green 60 30
370 **48** 5 s. deep bright blue 3·00 1·75
371 7 s. 50, green 3·00 4·00
372 10 s. carmine 3·00 2·50
358/72 *Set of* 15 10·00 8·50

49 Sultan Seyyid Sir Abdulla bin Khalifa

50 "Protein Foods"

(Recess B.W.)

1961 (17 Oct). *As T* **42/8**, *but with portrait of Sultan Sir Abdulla as in T* **49**, *W* w **12**. *P* 13 × 13½ (20 *s.*), *others as before.*

373 **49** 5 c. orange and deep green 10 10
374 10 c. emerald and carmine-red 10 10
375 **43** 15 c. green and sepia 20 40
376 **44** 20 c. ultramarine 15 10
377 **45** 25 c. orange-brown and black 15 10
378 **43** 30 c. carmine-red and black 60 10
379 **45** 35 c. slate and emerald 80 30
380 **46** 40 c. brown and black 30 10
381 **45** 50 c. blue and grey-green 30 10
382 **47** 1 s. carmine and black 40 10
383 **43** 1 s. 25, slate and carmine 80 35
384 **47** 2 s. orange and deep green 40 40
385 **48** 5 s. deep bright blue 90 1·00
386 7 s. 50, green 2·25 9·00
387 10 s. carmine 2·25 5·50
388 20 s. sepia 12·00 21·00
373/88 *Set of* 16 20·00 35·00

(Des M. Goaman. Photo Harrison)

1963 (4 June). *Freedom from Hunger. W* w **12**. *P* 14 × 14½.

389 **50** 1 s. 30, sepia 55 30

INDEPENDENT

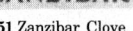

51 Zanzibar Clove

53 "Religious Tolerance" (mosques and churches)

(Photo Harrison)

1963 (10 Dec). *Independence. Portrait of Sultan Seyyid Jamshid bin Abdulla. T* **51, 53** *and similar vert designs. P* 12½.

390 30 c. multicoloured 10 20
391 50 c. multicoloured 10 25
392 1 s. 30, multicoloured 10 1·25
393 2 s. 50, multicoloured 15 2·25
390/3 *Set of* 4 40 3·50

Designs:—50 c. "To Prosperity" (Zanzibar doorway); 2 s. 50, "Towards the Light" (Mangapwani Cave).

REPUBLIC

When the Post Office opened on 14 January 1964, after the revolution deposing the Sultan, the stamps on sale had the portrait cancelled by a manuscript cross. Stamps thus cancelled on cover or piece used between January 14 and 17 are therefore of interest.

JAMHURI 1964

(**55**= "Republic")

1964 (17 Jan). *Locally handstamped as T* **55** *in black.*

(i) *Nos.* 373/88.

394 **49** 5 c. orange and deep green 30 10
395 10 c. emerald and carmine-red 30 10
396 **43** 15 c. green and sepia 30 30
397 **44** 20 c. ultramarine 30 10
398 **45** 25 c. orange-brown and black 30 10
399 **43** 30 c. carmine-red and black 30 10
400 **45** 35 c. slate and emerald 30 20
401 **46** 40 c. brown and black 30 30
402 **45** 50 c. blue and grey-green 30 10
403 **47** 1 s. carmine and black 30 30
404 **43** 1 s. 25, slate and carmine 30 40
405 **47** 2 s. orange and deep green 1·50 45
406 **48** 5 s. deep bright blue 1·50 55
407 7 s. 50, green 2·00 1·00
408 10 s. carmine 2·00 90
409 20 s. sepia 2·50 3·00

(ii) *Nos.* 390/3 *(Independence)*

410 30 c. multicoloured 10 10
411 50 c. multicoloured 15 10
412 1 s. 30, multicoloured 25 10
413 2 s. 50, multicoloured 40 30
a. Green omitted £100
394/413 *Set of* 20 12·00 7·50

T **55** occurs in various positions—diagonally, horizontally or vertically.

NOTE. Nos. 394 to 413 are the only stamps officially authorised to receive the handstamp but it has also been seen on Nos. 353/7, 389 and the Postage Dues. There are numerous errors but it is impossible to distinguish between cases of genuine oversight and those made deliberately at the request of purchasers.

JAMHURI 1964
(**56**)

JAMHURI
1964
(**57**)

1964 (28 Feb). *Optd by Bradbury, Wilkinson.*

(i) *As T* **56** *on Nos.* 373/88

414 **49** 5 c. orange and deep green 10 10
415 10 c. emerald and carmine-red 10 10
416 **43** 15 c. green and sepia 10 10
417 **44** 20 c. ultramarine 10 10
418 **45** 25 c. orange-brown and black 10 10
419 **43** 30 c. carmine-red and black 10 10
420 **45** 35 c. slate and emerald 10 10
421 **46** 40 c. brown and black 10 10
422 **45** 50 c. blue and grey-green 10 10
423 **47** 1 s. carmine and black 10 10
424 **43** 1 s. 25, slate and carmine 35 10
425 **47** 2 s. orange and deep green 25 10
426 **48** 5 s. deep bright blue 50 35
427 7 s. 50, green 65 1·00
428 10 s. carmine 75 1·00
429 20 s. sepia 1·50 1·75

The opt T **56** is set in two lines on Types **46/8**.

(ii) *As T* **57** *on Nos.* 390/3 *(Independence)*

430 30 c. multicoloured 10 10
431 50 c. multicoloured 10 10
432 1 s. 30, multicoloured 10 10
433 2 s. 50, multicoloured 15 10
a. Green omitted 42·00
414/33 *Set of* 20 4·25 4·50

The opt T **57** is set in one line on No. 432.

For the set inscribed "UNITED REPUBLIC OF TANGANYIKA AND ZANZIBAR" see Nos. 124/7 of Tanganyika.

58 Axe, Spear and Dagger

59 Zanzibari with Rifle

(Litho German Bank Note Ptg Co, Leipzig)

1964 (21 June). *T* **58/9** *and similar designs inscr.* "JAMHURI ZANZIBAR 1964". *Multicoloured. P* 13 × 13½ (*vert*) *or* 13½ × 13 (*horiz*).

434	5 c. Type **58**	10	10
435	10 c. Bow and arrow breaking chains	10	10
436	15 c. Type **58**	10	10
437	20 c. As 10 c.	10	10
438	25 c. Type **59**	10	10
439	30 c. Zanzibari breaking manacles	10	10
440	40 c. Type **59**	10	10
441	50 c. As 30 c.	10	10
442	1 s. Zanzibari, flag and Sun	10	10
443	1 s. 30, Hands breaking chains (*horiz*)	15	10
444	2 s. Hand waving flag (*horiz*)	20	10
445	5 s. Map of Zanzibar and Pemba on flag (*horiz*)	55	20
446	10 s. Flag on Map	1·75	90
447	20 s. National flag (*horiz*)	2·25	7·00
434/47	*Set of* 14	4·75	8·00

68 Soldier and Maps

69 Building Construction

(Litho German Bank Note Ptg Co, Leipzig)

1965 (12 Jan). *First Anniv of Revolution. P* 13 × 13½ (*vert*) *or* 13½ × 13 (*horiz*).

448	**68**	20 c. apple-green and deep green	10	10
449	**69**	30 c. chocolate and yellow-orange	10	10
450	**68**	1 s. 30, light blue and ultramarine	10	10
451	**69**	2 s. 50, reddish violet and rose	10	15
448/51		*Set of* 4	30	30

70 Planting Rice

(Litho German Bank Note Ptg Co, Leipzig)

1965 (17 Oct). *Agricultural Development. T* **70** *and similar horiz design. P* 13 × 12½.

452	**70**	20 c. sepia and blue	10	30
453	–	30 c. sepia and magenta	10	30
454	–	1 s. 30, sepia and yellow-orange	30	70
455	**70**	2 s. 50, sepia and emerald	50	2·00
452/5		*Set of* 4	85	3·00

Design:—30 c., 1 s. 30, Hands holding rice.

72 Freighter, Tractor, Factory, and Open Book and Torch

73 Soldier

(Litho German Bank Note Ptg Co, Leipzig)

1966 (12 Jan). *2nd Anniv of Revolution. P* 12½ × 13.

456	**72**	20 c. multicoloured	10	10
457	**73**	50 c. multicoloured	10	10
458	**72**	1 s. 30, multicoloured	10	10
459	**73**	2 s. 50, multicoloured	15	30
456/9		*Set of* 4	40	45

For stamps with similar inscription or inscribed "TANZANIA" only, and with commemorative date 26th April 1966, see Nos. Z142/5 of TANZANIA.

74 Tree-felling

75 Zanzibar Street

(Litho German Bank Note Ptg Co, Leipzig)

1966 (5 June). *Horiz designs as T* **74**, *and T* **75**. *P* 12½ × 13 (50 c., 10 s.) *or* 13 × 12½ (*others*).

460	5 c. maroon and yellow-olive	15	30
461	10 c. brown-purple and bright emerald	15	30
462	15 c. brown-purple and light blue	15	30
463	20 c. ultramarine and light orange	15	10
464	25 c. maroon and orange-yellow	15	10
465	30 c. maroon and ochre-yellow	15	10
466	40 c. purple-brown and rose-pink	30	10
467	50 c. green and pale greenish yellow	30	10
468	1 s. maroon and bright blue	30	10
469	1 s. 30, maroon and turquoise	30	40
470	2 s. brown-purple and light blue-green	30	15
471	5 s. rose-red and pale blue	80	3·50
472	10 s. crimson and pale yellow	2·25	9·50
473	20 s. deep purple-brown and magenta	4·25	17·00
460/473	*Set of* 14	8·50	28·00

Designs:—5 c., 20 s. Type **74**; 10 c., 1 s. Clove cultivation; 15, 40 c. Chair-making; 20 c., 5 s. Lumumba College; 25 c., 1 s. 30, Agriculture; 30 c., 2 s. Agricultural workers; 50 c., 10 s. Type **75**.

81 "Education"

(Litho D.L.R.)

1966 (25 Sept). *Introduction of Free Education. P* 13½ × 13.

474	**81**	50 c. black, light blue and orange	10	20
475		1 s. 30, black, lt blue and yellow-green	15	30
476		2 s. 50, black, light blue and pink	30	2·75
474/6		*Set of* 3	50	3·00

82 A.S.P. Flag

(Litho D.L.R.)

1967 (5 Feb). *Tenth Anniv of Afro-Shirazi Party* (*A.S.P.*). *T* **82** *and similar multicoloured design. P* 14.

477	30 c. Type **82**	10	20
478	50 c. Vice-President M. A. Karume of Tanzania, flag and crowd (*vert*)	10	20
479	1 s. 30, As 50 c.	10	40
480	2 s. 50, Type **82**	15	1·00
477/80	*Set of* 4	30	1·60

84 Voluntary Workers

(Photo Delrieu)

1967 (20 Aug). *Voluntary Workers Brigade. P* 12½ × 12.

481	**84**	1 s. 30, multicoloured	15	30
482		2 s. 50, multicoloured	30	3·00

POSTAGE DUE STAMPS

Insufficiently prepaid.
Postage due.

1 cent.

D 1

Insufficiently prepaid
Postage due.

6 cents.

D 2

(Types D **1** and D **2** typo by the Government Printer)

1929–30. *Rouletted* 10, *with imperf sheet edges. No gum.*

D 1	D 1	1 c. black/*orange*	10·00	48·00
D 2		2 c. black/*orange*	3·75	22·00
D 3		3 c. black/*orange*	3·75	22·00
		a. "cent.s" for "cents."	75·00	
D 4		6 c. black/*orange*		
		a. "cent.s" for "cents."		
D 5		9 c. black/*orange*	2·25	12·00
		a. "cent.s" for "cents."	13·00	40·00
D 6		12 c. black/*orange*	£4250	
		a. "cent.s" for "cents."		
D 7		12 c. black/*green*	£900	£475
		a. "cent.s" for "cents."	£2250	£1300
D 8		15 c. black/*orange*	2·50	12·00
		a. "cent.s" for "cents."	14·00	40·00
D 9		18 c. black/*salmon*	3·00	20·00
		a. "cent.s" for "cents."	24·00	65·00
D10		18 c. black/*orange*	9·50	28·00
		a. "cent.s" for "cents."	42·00	85·00
D11		20 c. black/*orange*	3·75	17·00
		a. "cent.s" for "cents."	24·00	65·00
D12		21 c. black/*orange*	3·25	14·00
		a. "cent.s" for "cents."	20·00	60·00
D13		25 c. black/*magenta*	£1700	£1000
		a. "cent.s" for "cents."	—	£3000
D14		25 c. black/*orange*	£4000	
D15		31 c. black/*orange*	8·00	35·00
		a. "cent.s" for "cents."	42·00	
D16		50 c. black/*orange*	20·00	75·00
		a. "cent.s" for "cents."	80·00	
D17		75 c. black/*orange*	65·00	£150
		a. "cent.s" for "cents."	£190	

Sheets of the first printings of all values except the 1 c. and 2 c. contained one stamp showing the error "cent.s" for "cents."

1930–33. *Rouletted* 5. *No gum.*

D18	D **2**	2 c. black/*salmon*	4·50	16·00
D19		3 c. black/*rose*	3·00	26·00
D21		6 c. black/*yellow*	3·00	17·00
D22		12 c. black/*blue*	4·00	13·00
D23		25 c. black/*rose*	9·00	32·00
D24		25 c. black/*lilac*	7·00	25·00
D18/24		*Set of* 6	27·00	£110

D 3

(Typo D.L.R.)

1936 (1 Jan)–**62**. *Wmk Mult Script CA. P* 14.

D25	D **3**	5 c. violet	55	2·75
		a. Chalk-surfaced paper (18.7.56)	20	4·75
D26		10 c. scarlet	45	1·00
		a. Chalk-surfaced paper (6.3.62)	25	2·25
D27		20 c. green	65	2·50
		a. Chalk-surfaced paper (6.3.62)	20	4·75
D28		30 c. brown	2·75	6·50
		a. Chalk-surfaced paper (18.7.56)	30	4·50
D29		40 c. ultramarine	2·75	12·00
		a. Chalk-surfaced paper (18.7.56)	40	7·50
D30		1 s. grey	2·75	16·00
		a. Chalk-surfaced paper (18.7.56)	1·00	7·50
D25/30		*Set of* 6	9·00	38·00
D25a/30a		*Set of* 6	2·10	28·00
D25/30 Perf "Specimen"		*Set of* 6	60·00	

See footnote after No. 413.

All Zanzibar issues were withdrawn on 1 January 1968 and replaced by Tanzania issues. Zanzibar stamps remained valid for postage in Zanzibar for a limited period.

TANZANIA

The United Republic of Tanganyika and Zanzibar, formed 26 April 1964, was renamed the United Republic of Tanzania on 29 October 1964.

Issues to No. 176, except Nos. Z142/5, were also valid in Kenya and Uganda.

25 Hale Hydro-Electric Scheme

26 Tanzanian Flag

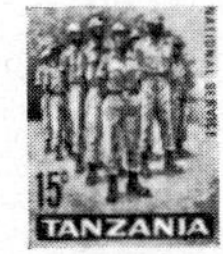

27 National Servicemen

33 Dar-es-Salaam Harbour

38 Arms of Tanzania

(Des V. Whiteley. Photo Harrison)

1965 (9 Dec). *T* **25/7, 33, 38** *and similar designs. P* 14 × 14½ (5 *c.*, 10 *c.*, 20 *c.*, 50 *c.*, 65 *c.*), 14½ × 14 (15 *c.*, 30 *c.*, 40 *c.*), *or* 14 (*others*).

128	5 c. ultramarine and yellow-orange	10	10
129	10 c. black, greenish yellow, green & blue	10	10
130	15 c. multicoloured	10	10
131	20 c. sepia, grey-green and greenish blue	10	10
132	30 c. black and red-brown	10	10
133	40 c. multicoloured	30	20
134	50 c. multicoloured	30	10
135	65 c. green, red-brown and blue	1·75	1·25
136	1 s. multicoloured	50	10
137	1 s. 30, multicoloured	4·00	60
138	2 s. 50, blue and orange-brown	2·75	90
139	5 s. lake-brown, yellow-green and blue	80	20
140	10 s. olive-yellow, olive-green and blue	1·00	1·75
141	20 s. multicoloured	3·75	10·00
128/41	*Set of* 14	14·00	13·50

Designs: *Horiz* (*as T* **25**)—20 c. Road-building; 50 c. Common Zebras, Manyara National Park; 65 c. Mt Kilimanjaro. *Vert* (*as T* **27**)—30 c. Drum, spear, shield and stool; 40 c. Giraffes, Mikumi National Park. *Horiz* (*As T* **33**)—1 s. 30, Skull of *Zinjanthropus* and excavations, Olduvai Gorge, 2 s. 50, Fishing; 5 s. Sisal industry; 10 s. State House, Dar-es-Salaam.

Z **39** Pres. Nyerere and First Vice-Pres. Karume within Bowl of Flame

Z **40** Hands supporting Bowl of Flame

(Des J. Ahmed (Type Z **39**), G. Vasarhelyi (Type Z **40**). Photo Enschedé)

1966 (26 April). *2nd Anniv of United Republic. P* 14 × 13.

Z142	Z **39**	30 c. multicoloured	15	10
Z143	Z **40**	50 c. multicoloured	15	10
Z144		1 s. 30, multicoloured	15	15
Z145	Z **39**	2 s. 50, multicoloured	30	90
Z142/5		*Set of* 4	65	1·00

Nos. Z142/5 were on sale in Zanzibar only.

39 Cardinal

40 Mud Skipper

41 Scorpion Fish

(Des Rena Fennessy. Photo Harrison)

1967 (9 Dec)–**73**. *Designs as T* **39/41**. *Chalk-surfaced paper. P* 14 × 15 (5 *c. to* 70 *c.*) *or* 14½ (*others*).

142	5 c. magenta, yellow-olive and black	10	30
	a. Glazed, ordinary paper (22.1.71)	30	55
143	10 c. brown and bistre	10	10
	a. Glazed, ordinary paper (27.9.72)	30	55
144	15 c. grey, turquoise-blue and black	10	30
	a. Glazed, ordinary paper (22.1.71)	30	70
145	20 c. brown and turquoise-green	10	10
	a. Glazed, ordinary paper (16.7.73)	30	60
146	30 c. sage-green and black	10	10
	a. Glazed, ordinary paper (3.5.71)	1·25	60
147	40 c. yellow, chocolate and bright green	15	10
	a. Glazed, ordinary paper (10.2.71)	35	30
148	50 c. multicoloured	15	10
	a. Glazed, ordinary paper (10.2.71)	30	55
149	65 c. orange-yellow, bronze-green and black	3·50	4·00
150	70 c. multicoloured (15.9.69)	1·00	2·50
	a. Glazed, ordinary paper (22.1.71)	4·25	6·00
151	1 s. orange-brown, slate-blue and maroon	30	10
	a. Glazed, ordinary paper (3.2.71)	50	10
152	1 s. 30, multicoloured	4·00	10
153	1 s. 50, multicoloured (15.9.69)	2·25	50
	a. Glazed, ordinary paper (27.9.72)	2·00	10
154	2 s. 50, multicoloured	3·00	60
	a. Glazed, ordinary paper (27.9.72)	6·00	10
155	5 s. greenish yellow, black & turquoise-grn	4·00	90
	a. Glazed, ordinary paper (3.2.71)	3·25	10
156	10 s. multicoloured	2·00	1·40
	a. Glazed, ordinary paper (*dull blue-green background*) (3.2.71)	2·50	10
	ab. Deep dull green background (12.9.73)	3·00	50
157	20 s. multicoloured	4·00	4·00
	a. Glazed, ordinary paper (3.2.71)	8·00	15
142/57	*Set of* 16	21·00	13·00
142a/57a	*Set of* 14	26·00	9·00

Designs: *Horiz as T* **39/40**—15 c. White Spotted Puffer; 20 c. Sea Horses; 30 c. Bat Fish; 40 c. Sweetlips; 50 c. Blue Club-nosed Wrasse; 65 c. Bennett's Butterfly; 70 c. Striped Grouper. *Horiz as T* **41**—1 s. 30, Powder Blue Surgeon; 1 s. 50, Fusilier; 2 s. 50, Red Snapper; 5 s. Moorish Idol; 10 s. Picasso Fish; 20 s. Squirrel Fish.

On chalk-surfaced paper all values except the 30 c., exist with PVA gum as well as gum arabic, but the 70 c. and 1 s. 50 exist with PVA gum only. Stamps on glazed, ordinary paper come only with PVA gum.

53 *Papilio hornimani*

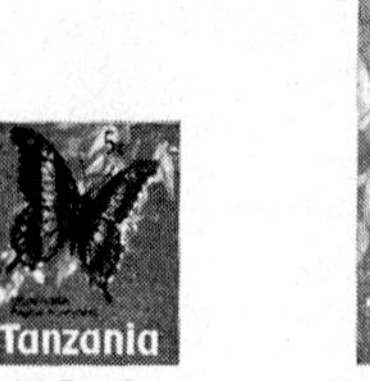

54 *Euphaedra neophron*

80c

(55)

(Des Rena Fennessy. Photo Harrison)

1973 (10 Dec)–**78**. *Various vert designs as T* **53/4**.

(a) Size as T **53**. *P* 14½×14

158	5 c. light yellow-olive, lt violet-blue & black	30	20
159	10 c. multicoloured	40	15
160	15 c. light violet-blue and black	40	15
161	20 c. reddish cinnamon, orange-yellow & blk	50	15
162	30 c. yellow, orange and black	50	10
	a. Bistre-yellow, orange & black (20.4.78)	60	10
163	40 c. multicoloured	60	15
164	50 c. multicoloured	70	15
165	60 c. lt grey-brown, lemon & reddish brown	1·00	20
166	70 c. turquoise-green, pale orange and black	1·00	20

(b) Size as T **54**. *P* 14

167	1 s. multicoloured	1·00	15
168	1 s. 50, multicoloured	2·00	45
169	2 s. 50, multicoloured	2·50	80
170	5 s. multicoloured (*brt green background*)	2·75	85
	a. Apple-green background (20.4.78)	2·50	60
171	10 s. multicoloured	3·75	3·50
172	20 s. multicoloured	5·50	8·00
158/72	*Set of* 15	21·00	13·50

Butterflies:—10 c. *Colotis ione*; 15 c. *Amauris hyalites* (s sp *makuyuensis*); 20 c. *Libythea labdaca* (s sp *laius*); 30 c. *Danaus chrysippus;* 40 c. *Asterope rosa*; 50 c. *Axiocerses styx*; 60 c. *Terias hecabe*; 70 c. *Acraea insignis;* 1 s. 50, *Precis octavia*; 2 s. 50, *Charaxes eupale*; 5 s. *Charaxes pollux*; 10 s. *Salamis parhassus;* 20 s. *Papilio ophidicephalus.*

Nos. 159 and 164 exist in coils, constructed from normal sheets.

A used example of No. 167 has been seen apparently showing the yellow colour omitted.

1975 (17 Nov). *Nos.* 165, 168/9 *and* 172 *surch as T* **55**.

173	80 c. on 60 c. *Terias hecabe*	1·75	1·00
174	2 s. on 1 s. 50, *Precis octavia*	3·25	3·25
175	3 s. on 2 s. 50, *Charaxes eupale*	13·00	19·00
176	40 s. on 20 s. *Papilio ophidicephalus*	6·00	8·50
173/6	*Set of* 4	22·00	28·00

1976 (15 Apr). *Telecommunications Development. As Nos.* 56/60 *of Kenya but inscr* "TANZANIA".

177	50 c. Microwave Tower	10	10
178	1 s. Cordless switchboard	15	10
179	2 s. Telephones	25	30
180	3 s. Message Switching Centre	30	40
177/80	*Set of* 4	70	70
MS181	120 × 120 mm. Nos. 177/80	1·25	1·50

Nos. 177/8 and 180 exist imperforate from stock dispersed by the liquidator of Format International Security Printers Ltd.

1976 (5 July). *Olympic Games, Montreal. As Nos* 61/5 *of Kenya but inscr* "TANZANIA".

182	50 c. Akii Bua, Ugandan hurdler	15	10
183	1 s. Filbert Bayi, Tanzanian runner	15	10
184	2 s. Steve Muchoki, Kenyan boxer	35	40
185	3 s. Olympic flame and East Africa flags	45	55
182/5	*Set of* 4	1·00	1·00
MS186	129 × 154 mm. Nos. 182/5	5·50	4·00

Nos. 182/4 exist imperforate from stock dispersed by the liquidator of Format International Security Printers Ltd.

1976 (4 Oct). *Railway Transport. As Nos.* 66/70 *of Kenya but inscr* "TANZANIA".

187	50 c. Tanzania-Zambia Railway	20	10
188	1 s. Nile Bridge, Uganda	30	10
189	2 s. Nakuru Station, Kenya	75	40
190	3 s. Class "A" locomotive, 1896	90	65
187/90	*Set of* 4	1·90	1·00
MS191	154 × 103 mm. Nos. 187/90	5·00	3·50

Nos. 187/8 exist imperforate from stock dispersed by the liquidator of Format International Security Printers Ltd.

1977 (10 Jan). *Game Fish of East Africa. As Nos.* 71/5 *of Kenya but inscr* "TANZANIA".

192	50 c. Nile Perch	30	10
193	1 s. Tilapia	40	10
194	3 s. Sailfish	1·60	60
195	5 s. Black Marlin	1·75	80
192/5	*Set of* 4	3·50	1·40
MS196	153 × 129 mm. Nos. 192/5	3·75	2·25

1977 (15 Jan). *Second World Black and African Festival of Arts and Culture, Nigeria. As Nos* 76/80 *of Kenya but inscr* "TANZANIA".

197	50 c. Maasai Manyatta (village), Kenya	15	10
198	1 s. "Heartbeat of Africa" (Ugandan dancers)	20	10
199	2 s. Makonde sculpture	45	60
200	3 s. "Early Man and Technology" (skinning hippopotamus)	55	85
197/200	*Set of* 4	1·25	1·50
MS201	132 × 190 mm. Nos. 197/200	2·50	3·50

1977 (5 Apr). *25th Anniv of Safari Rally. As Nos* 81/5 *of Kenya but inscr* "TANZANIA".

202	50 c. Rally-car and villagers	15	10
203	1 s. Pres. Kenyatta starting rally	20	10
204	2 s. Car fording river	50	60
205	5 s. Car and elephants	1·25	1·75
202/5	*Set of* 4	1·90	2·25
MS206	126 × 93 mm. Nos. 202/5	3·50	3·25

1977 (30 June). *Centenary of Ugandan Church. As Nos.* 86/90 *of Kenya but inscr* "TANZANIA".

207	50 c. Canon Kivebulaya	10	10
208	1 s. Modern Namirembe Cathedral	15	10
209	2 s. The first Cathedral	30	40
210	5 s. Early congregation, Kigezi	60	90
207/10	*Set of* 4	1·00	1·25
MS211	126 × 89 mm. Nos. 207/10	1·50	2·00

1977 (26 Sept). *Endangered Species. As Nos.* 96/101 *of Kenya but inscr* "TANZANIA".

212	50 c. Pancake Tortoise	20	10
213	1 s. Nile Crocodile	25	10
214	2 s. Hunter's Hartebeest	1·00	55
215	3 s. Red Colobus monkey	1·75	1·00
216	5 s. Dugong	2·00	2·00
212/16	*Set of* 5	4·75	3·25
MS217	127 × 101 mm. Nos. 213/16	5·00	5·50

56 Prince Philip and President Nyerere

(Des G. Vasarhelyi. Litho Questa)

1977 (23 Nov). *Silver Jubilee. T* **56** *and similar horiz designs. Multicoloured. P* 14 × 13½.

218	50 c. Type **56**	15	10
219	5 s. Pres. Nyerere with Queen and Prince Philip	35	35
220	10 s. Jubilee emblem and Commonwealth flags	60	60
221	20 s. The Crowning	1·00	1·00
218/21	*Set of* 4	1·90	1·90
MS222	128 × 102 mm. Nos. 218/21	1·90	2·75

57 Improvements in Rural Living Standards

(Des P. Ndembo. Litho J.W.)

1978 (5 Feb). *First Anniv of Chama Cha Mapinduzi* (*New Revolutionary Party*). *T* **57** *and similar horiz designs. P* 13½ × 14.

223	50 c. multicoloured	10	10
224	1 s. multicoloured	10	10
225	3 s. multicoloured	35	60
226	5 s. black, light green and greenish yellow	55	85
223/6	*Set of* 4	1·00	1·40
MS227	142 × 106 mm. Nos. 223/6	1·00	1·40

Designs:—1 s. Flag raising ceremony, Zanzibar; 3 s. Handing over of TANU headquarters, Dodoma; 5 s. Chairman Julius Nyerere.

1978 (17 Apr). *World Cup Football Championship, Argentina. As Nos.* 122/6 *of Kenya but inscr* "TANZANIA".

228	50 c. Joe Kadenge and forwards	15	10
229	1 s. Mohamed Chuma and cup presentation	15	10
230	2 s. Omari Kidevu and goalmouth scene	40	60
231	3 s. Polly Ouma and forwards	50	75
228/31	*Set of* 4	1·10	1·25
MS232	136 × 81 mm. Nos. 228/31	2·00	1·75

25th ANNIVERSARY CORONATION

2nd JUNE 1953

(58)

25th ANNIVERSARY CORONATION

2nd JUNE 1953

(59)

1978 (2 June). *25th Anniv of Coronation. Nos.* 218/22. A. *Optd as T* **58**. *P* 14 × 13½. B. *Optd as T* **59**. *P* 12 × 11½.

No.	Description	A		B	
233	50 c. Type **56**	10	10	10	10
234	5 s. Pres. Nyerere with Queen and Prince Philip	35	45	35	50
235	10 s. Jubilee emblem and Commonwealth flags	50	65	50	65
236	20 s. The Crowning	80	1·25	80	1·25
233/6	*Set of* 4	1·60	2·25	1·60	2·25
MS237	128 × 102 mm. Nos. 233/6	1·60	2·50	1·60	2·50

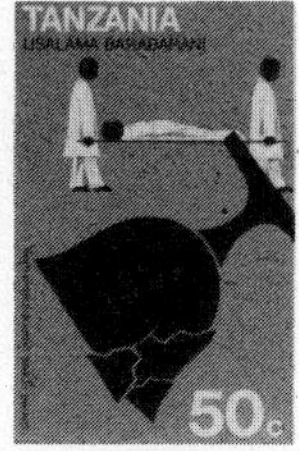

60 "Do not Drink and Drive"   **61** Lake Manyara Hotel

(Des and litho J.W.)

1978 (1 July). *Road Safety. T* **60** *and similar vert designs. P* 13½ × 13.
238 50 c. multicoloured 15 10
239 1 s. multicoloured 20 10
240 3 s. orange-red, black and light brown .. 70 60
241 5 s. multicoloured .. .. 1·00 90
238/41 .. .. *Set of* 4 1·90 1·40
MS242 92 × 129 mm. Nos. 238/41. P 14 .. .. 2·00 2·00
Designs:—1 s. "Show courtesy to young, old and crippled"; 3 s. "Observe the Highway Code"; 5 s. "Do not drive a faulty vehicle".

(Des M. Raza. Litho J.W.)

1978 (11 Sept). *Game Lodges. T* **61** *and similar horiz designs. Multicoloured. P* 13½ × 13.
243 50 c. Type **61** 10 10
244 1 s. Lobo Wildlife Lodge 20 10
245 3 s. Ngorongoro Crater Lodge 40 35
246 5 s. Ngorongoro Wildlife Lodge 55 55
247 10 s. Mafia Island Lodge .. .. .. 1·00 1·25
248 20 s. Mikumi Wildlife Lodge .. .. .. 2·00 3·00
243/8 .. .. *Set of* 6 3·75 4·75
MS249 118 × 112 mm. Nos. 243/8 .. .. 6·00 7·50

62 "Racial Suppression"   **63** Fokker "Friendship"

(Des local artist; adapted G. Hutchins. Litho Harrison)

1978 (24 Oct). *International Anti-Apartheid Year. T* **62** *and similar vert designs. P* 14½ × 14.
250 50 c. multicoloured 10 10
251 1 s. black, yellowish green and yellow .. 15 10
252 2 s. 50, multicoloured 40 40
253 5 s. multicoloured 70 85
250/3 .. .. *Set of* 4 1·25 1·25
MS254 127 × 132 mm. Nos. 250/3 .. .. 1·75 2·25
Designs:—1 s. "Racial division"; 2 s. 50, "Racial harmony"; 5 s. "Fall of suppression and rise of freedom".

(Des J. Mzinga; adapted J.W. Litho Walsall)

1978 (28 Dec). *75th Anniv of Powered Flight. T* **63** *and similar horiz designs. Multicoloured. P* 13½.
255 50 c. Type **63** 20 10
256 1 s. "Dragon" on Zanzibar Island, 1930's .. 25 10
257 2 s. "Concorde" .. .. 1·00 45
258 5 s. Wright brothers' *Flyer*, 1903 .. .. 1·25 85
255/8 .. .. *Set of* 4 2·40 1·25
MS259 133 × 97 mm. Nos. 255/8 .. .. .. 2·75 3·00

64 Corporation Emblem

(Des local artists; adapted BG Studio. Litho Harrison)

1979 (3 Feb). *1st Anniv of Tanzania Posts and Telecommunications Corporation. T* **64** *and similar horiz design. Multicoloured. P* 14½ × 14.
260 50 c. Type **64** 10 10
261 5 s. Headquarters buildings 50 70
MS262 82 × 97 mm. Nos. 260/1 .. .. .. 1·00 1·50

65 Pres. Nyerere (patron of National I.Y.C. Committee) with Children

30c

(66)

(Des J. Mzinga. Litho B.W.)

1979 (25 June). *International Year of the Child. T* **65** *and similar horiz designs. Multicoloured. P* 14½.
263 50 c. Type **65** 10 10
264 1 s. Day care centre 15 10
265 2 s. "Immunisation" (child being vaccinated) 25 45
266 5 s. National I.Y.C. Committee emblem .. 40 80
263/6 .. .. *Set of* 4 80 1·25
MS267 127 × 91 mm. Nos. 263/6 .. .. .. 1·75 1·50

1979 (Aug–Sept*). *Nos.* 159 *and* 166 *surch as T* **66** *(No. 269 has horiz bar through original value).*
268 10 c. + 30 c. multicoloured 50 60
a. Surch inverted .. .. † —
269 50 c. on 70 c. turquoise-green, pale orge & bl. 1·25 1·40
* The earliest known postmark date for No. 268 is 15 September and for No. 269 30 August.
The face value of No. 268 was 40 c.; the 30 c. surcharge being added to the original 10 c., which was not obliterated. This method was adopted because of difficulties during the actual surcharging. On No. 269 the 70 c. face value is obliterated by a bar.
Examples of No. 268a were used at Singida in December 1979.

67 Planting Young Trees   **68** Mwenge Satellite Earth Station

(Des J. Mzinga. Litho J.W.)

1979 (24 Sept). *Forest Preservation. T* **67** *and similar vert designs. Multicoloured. P* 14 × 14½.
270 50 c. Type **67** 10 10
271 1 s. Replacing dead trees with saplings .. 20 10
272 2 s. Rainfall cycle 50 50
273 5 s. Forest fire warning .. .. .. 80 1·50
270/3 .. .. *Set of* 4 1·40 2·00

(Des and litho J.W.)

1979 (14 Dec). *Opening of Mwenge Satellite Earth Station. P* 13½.
274 **68** 10 c. multicoloured 10 10
275 40 c. multicoloured 10 10
276 50 c. multicoloured 10 10
277 1 s. multicoloured 20 20
274/7 .. .. *Set of* 4 40 40

69 Tabata Dispensary, Dar-es-Salaam

(Litho J.W.)

1980 (10 Apr). *75th Anniv of Rotary International. T* **69** *and similar horiz designs. Multicoloured. P* 13.
278 50 c. Type **69** 10 10
279 1 s. Ngomvu Village water project 15 10
280 5 s. Flying Doctor service (plane donation) 55 70
281 20 s. Torch and 75th Anniversary emblem .. 1·75 2·50
278/81 .. .. *Set of* 4 2·25 3·00
MS282 120 × 101 mm. Nos. 278/81. P 14 .. .. 2·50 3·00

70 Zanzibar 1896 2 r. Stamp and 1964 25 c. Definitive

'LONDON 1980'
PHILATELIC EXHIBITION

(71)

(Des J.W. Litho Questa)

1980 (21 Apr). *Death Centenary of Sir Rowland Hill* (1979). *T* **70** *and similar multicoloured designs. P* 14.
283 40 c. Type **70** 10 10
284 50 c. Tanganyika 1962 Independence 50 c. commemorative and man attaching stamp to letter (*vert*) 10 10
285 10 s. Tanganyika 1922 25 c. stamp and 1961 1 s. 30, definitive .. .. .. 1·00 1·25
286 20 s. Penny Black and Sir Rowland Hill (*vert*) 1·50 2·00
283/6 .. .. *Set of* 4 2·25 3·00
MS287 158 × 120 mm. Nos. 283/6 .. .. 2·25 3·50

1980 (5 May). *"London 1980" International Stamp Exhibition. Nos.* 283/7 *optd with T* **71**.
288 40 c. Type **71** 10 10
289 50 c. Tanganyika 1962 Independence 50 c. commemorative and man attaching stamp to letter 10 10
290 10 s. Tanganyika 1922 25 c. stamp and 1961 1 s. 30, definitive .. .. .. 75 1·25
291 20 s. Penny Black and Sir Rowland Hill .. 1·10 1·75
288/91 .. .. *Set of* 4 1·75 2·75
MS292 158 × 120 mm. Nos. 288/91 .. .. 3·00 3·50

District 920 - 55th Annual Conference, Arusha, Tanzania

(72)

1980 (23 June). *Annual Conference of District 920, Rotary International, Arusha. Nos.* 278/82 *optd as T* **72**.
293 50 c. Type **69** 20 10
294 1 s. Ngomvu Village water project 25 10
295 5 s. Flying Doctor service (plane donation) 70 70
296 20 s. Torch and 75th Anniversary of Rotary International Emblem .. .. .. 2·25 2·50
293/6 .. .. *Set of* 4 3·00 3·00
MS297 120 × 101 mm. Nos. 293/6 .. .. 3·00 3·50

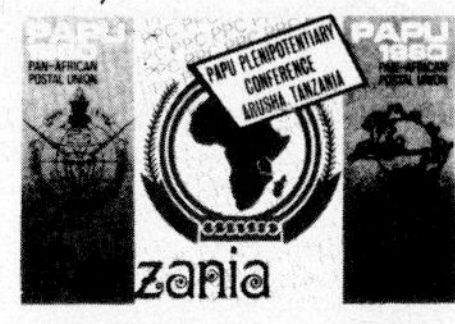

73 Conference, Tanzanian Posts and Telecommunications Corporation and U.P.U. Emblems

(Des and litho J.W.)

1980 (1 July). *P.A.P.U. (Pan-African Postal Union) Plenipotentiary Conference, Arusha. P* 13.
298 **73** 50 c. black and bright violet 10 10
299 1 s. black and ultramarine 15 10
300 5 s. black and orange-red 65 65
301 10 s. black and blue-green .. .. 1·25 1·40
298/301 .. .. *Set of* 4 2·00 2·00

74 Gidamis Shahanga (marathon)

(Litho J.W.)

1980 (18 Aug). *Olympic Games, Moscow. T* **74** *and similar horiz designs. Multicoloured. P* 13.
302 50 c. Type **74** 10 15
a. Horiz strip of 4. Nos. 302/5 .. .. 2·25
303 1 s. Nzael Kyomo (sprints) 15 15
304 10 s. Zakayo Malekwa (javelin) .. .. 80 1·25
305 20 s. William Lyimo (boxing) .. .. .. 1·50 2·00
302/5 .. .. *Set of* 4 2·25 3·25
MS306 172 × 117 mm. Nos. 302/305. P 14 .. 2·25 3·25
Nos. 302/305 were printed either in separate sheets or together, *se-tenant*, in horizontal strips of 4 throughout the sheet.

75 Spring Hare   **76** Impala

(Des Rena Fennessy. Litho B.W.)

1980 (1 Oct). *Wildlife. Multicoloured designs. P* 14.

(a) Horiz as T **75**
307 10 c. Type **75** 10 15
308 20 c. Large-spotted Genet 10 15
309 40 c. Banded Mongoose 15 10
310 50 c. Ratel 15 10
311 75 c. Large-toothed Rock Hyrax 15 15
312 80 c. Leopard 20 15

(b) Horiz as T **76**
313 1 s. Type **76** 15 10
314 1 s. 50, Giraffe 20 15
315 2 s. Common Zebra 20 15
316 3 s. Buffalo 25 15
317 5 s. Lion 50 25
318 10 s. Black Rhinoceros 85 70
319 20 s. African Elephant .. .. .. 1·50 1·10
320 40 s. Cheetah .. .. 2·25 2·50
307/20 .. .. *Set of* 14 6·00 5·50

1980 (2 Dec)–**81**. *Nos.* O41 *and* O43 *with* "OFFICIAL" *opt Type* O 1 *obliterated by horizontal line.*
320*a* 10 c. multicoloured .. ..
320*b* 40 c. multicoloured (21.2.81) .. ..
Nos. 320*a/b* exist on commercial mail from Morogoro. The dates given are those of the earliest postmarks reported.

77 Ngorongoro Conservation Area Authority Emblem

ROYAL WEDDING
H.R.H. PRINCE CHARLES
29th JULY 1981

(78)

(Des D. Kyungu. Litho J.W.)

1981 (2 Feb). *60th Anniv of Ngorongoro and Serengeti National Parks. T* **77** *and similar horiz designs. P* 13.

321 50 c. multicoloured 10 10
322 1 s. black, gold and deep blue-green 10 10
323 5 s. multicoloured 55 60
324 20 s. multicoloured 2·10 2·25
321/4 *Set of* 4 2·50 2·75

Designs:—1 s. Tanzania National Parks emblem; 5 s. Friends of the Serengeti emblem; 20 s. Friends of Ngorongoro emblem.

Nos. 321/4 exist overprinted "75th ANNIVERSARY GIRL GUIDES 1910 1985" or "CONGRATULATIONS TO THE DUKE & DUCHESS OF YORK ON THE OCCASION OF THEIR MARRIAGE", but there is no evidence that these overprints were available from post offices in Tanzania.

1981 (29 July). *Royal Wedding. Nos.* 220/1 *optd with T* **78**.

325 10 s. Jubilee emblem and Commonwealth flags 1·25 1·00
326 20 s. Crowning 1·75 1·25
MS327 88×97 mm. Nos. 325/6 8·00 5·00

79 Mail Runner

(Des D. Kyungu. Litho State Printing Works, Moscow)

1981 (21 Oct). *Commonwealth Postal Administrations Conference, Arusha. T* **79** *and similar horiz designs. Multicoloured. P* 12½ × 12.

328 50 c. Type **79** 10 10
329 1 s. Letter sorting 15 15
330 5 s. Letter Post symbols 65 1·00
331 10 s. Flags of Commonwealth nations 1·25 2·00
328/31 *Set of* 4 1·90 3·00
MS332 130×100 mm. Nos. 328/31 1·90 3·00

80 Morris Nyunyusa (blind drummer)

(Des and litho Harrison)

1981 (30 Nov). *International Year for Disabled Persons. T* **80** *and similar horiz designs. Multicoloured. P* 14.

333 50 c. Type **80** 20 10
334 1 s. Mgulani Rehabilitation Centre, Dar-es-Salaam 25 10
335 5 s. Aids for disabled persons 1·75 2·00
336 10 s. Disabled children cleaning school compound 2·50 3·00
333/6 *Set of* 4 4·25 4·75

81 President Mwalimu Julius K. Nyerere **82** Ostrich

(Litho J.W.)

1982 (13 Jan). *20th Anniv of Independence. T* **81** *and similar horiz designs. Multicoloured. P* 13 × 13½.

337 50 c. Type **81** 10 10
338 1 s. Electricity plant, Mtoni 15 10
339 3 s. Sisal industry 45 80
340 10 s. "Universal primary education" 1·10 2·00
337/40 *Set of* 4 1·60 2·75
MS341 120×85 mm. Nos. 337/40 2·00 2·75

(Des and litho J.W.)

1982 (25 Jan). *Birds. T* **82** *and similar vert designs. Multicoloured. P* 13½ × 13.

342 50 c. Type **82** 40 10
343 1 s. Secretary Bird 55 10
344 5 s. Kori Bustard 2·00 2·50
345 10 s. Saddle-bill Stork 3·00 3·50
342/5 *Set of* 4 5·50 5·50

83 Jella Mtaga

(Des P. Ndembo. Litho J.W.)

1982 (2 June). *World Cup Football Championship, Spain. T* **83** *and similar horiz designs. Multicoloured. P* 14.

346 50 c. Type **83** 30 10
347 1 s. Football stadium 35 10
348 10 s. Diego Maradona 2·25 2·75
349 20 s. FIFA emblem 4·00 4·50
346/9 *Set of* 4 6·25 6·50
MS350 130×100 mm. Nos. 346/9 6·50 6·50

Nos. 346/9 exist overprinted "CONGRATULATIONS TO THE DUKE & DUCHESS OF YORK ON THE OCCASION OF THEIR MARRIAGE", but there is no evidence that these overprints were available from post offices in Tanzania.

84 "Jade" of Seronera (cheetah) with Cubs

(Des and litho Harrison)

1982 (15 July). *Animal Personalities. T* **84** *and similar horiz designs. Multicoloured. P* 14.

351 50 c. Type **84** 20 10
352 1 s. Female Golden Jackal and cubs (incorrectly inscr "Wild dog") 30 10
353 5 s. "Fifi" and two sons of "Gombe" (chimpanzees) 1·00 2·00
354 10 s. "Bahati" of Lake Manyara with twins, "Rashidi" and "Ramadhani" (elephants) 1·90 3·00
351/4 *Set of* 4 3·00 4·75
MS355 120×89 mm. Nos. 351/4. P 14½ 3·50 5·00

85 Brick-laying

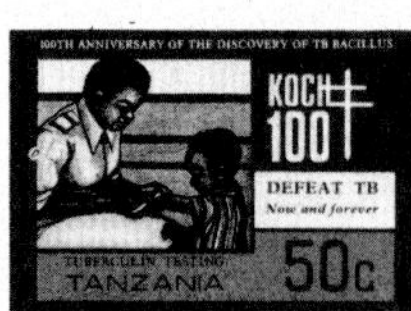

86 Ploughing Field

(Des P. Ndembo. Litho J.W.)

1982 (25 Aug). *75th Anniv of Boy Scout Movement. T* **85** *and similar horiz designs. Multicoloured. P* 14.

356 50 c. Type **85** 15 10
357 1 s. Camping 20 10
358 10 s. Tracing signs 1·50 2·25
359 20 s. Lord Baden-Powell 2·50 3·75
356/9 *Set of* 4 4·00 5·50
MS360 130×100 mm. Nos. 356/9 5·00 6·00

No. **MS**360 exists overprinted "75th ANNIVERSARY GIRL GUIDES 1910–1985", but there is no evidence that this overprint was available from post offices in Tanzania.

(Des P. Ndembo. Litho J.W.)

1982 (16 Oct). *World Food Day. T* **86** *and similar horiz designs. Multicoloured. P* 14.

361 50 c. Type **86** 10 10
362 1 s. Dairy farming 15 10
363 5 s. Maize farming 60 75
364 10 s. Grain storage 1·00 1·60
361/4 *Set of* 4 1·60 2·25
MS365 129×99 mm. Nos. 361/4 2·00 2·50

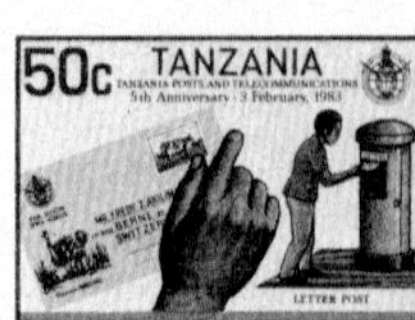

87 Immunization

(Des P. Ndembo. Litho State Printing Works, Moscow)

1982 (1 Dec). *Centenary of Robert Koch's Discovery of Tubercle Bacillus. T* **87** *and similar horiz designs. Multicoloured. P* 12½ × 12.

366 50 c. Type **87** 15 10
367 1 s. Dr. Robert Koch 20 10
368 5 s. International Union Against TB emblem 65 1·25
369 10 s. World Health Organization emblem 1·25 2·25
366/9 *Set of* 4 2·00 3·25

88 Letter Post

(Litho State Printing Works, Moscow)

1983 (3 Feb). *5th Anniv of Posts and Telecommunications Corporation. T* **88** *and similar horiz designs. Multicoloured. P* 12.

370 50 c. Type **88** 10 10
371 1 s. Training institute 10 10
372 5 s. Satellite communications 55 90
373 10 s. U.P.U., I.T.U. and T.P.T.C.C. (Tanzania Posts and Telecommunications Corporation) emblems 1·10 2·00
370/3 *Set of* 4 1·75 2·75
MS374 126×96 mm. Nos. 370/3 1·75 3·00

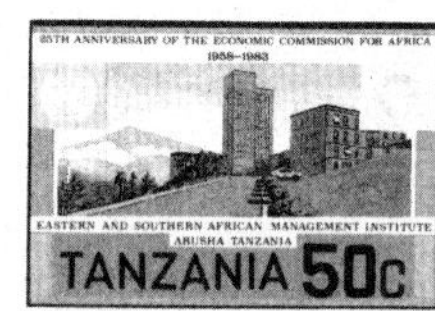

89 Pres. Mwalimu Julius Nyerere

(Litho J.W.)

1983 (14 Mar). *Commonwealth Day. T* **89** *and similar horiz designs. Multicoloured. P* 14.

375 50 c. Type **89** 10 10
376 1 s. Athletics and boxing 15 10
377 5 s. Flags of Commonwealth countries 60 80
378 10 s. Pres. Nyerere and members of British Royal Family 1·25 1·75
375/8 *Set of* 4 1·90 2·40
MS379 121×100 mm. Nos. 375/8 1·75 2·75

Nos. 375/8 exist overprinted "CONGRATULATIONS TO THE DUKE & DUCHESS OF YORK ON THE OCCASION OF THEIR MARRIAGE", but there is no evidence that these overprints were available from post offices in Tanzania.

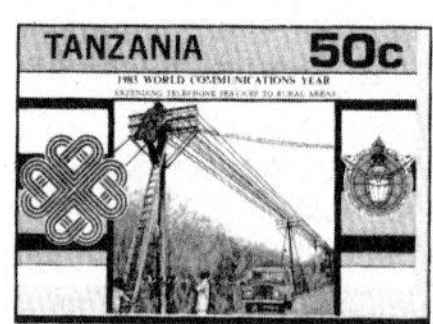

90 Eastern and Southern African Management Institute, Arusha, Tanzania

(Des P. Ndembo. Litho State Ptg Wks, Moscow)

1983 (12 Sept). *25th Anniv of the Economic Commission for Africa. T* **90** *and similar horiz designs. Multicoloured. P* 12½ × 12.

380 50 c. Type **90** 15 10
381 1 s. 25th Anniversary inscription and U.N. logo 20 10
382 5 s. Mineral collections 2·00 2·00
383 10 s. E.C.A. Silver Jubilee logo and O.A.U. flag 2·00 3·00
380/3 *Set of* 4 4·00 4·75
MS384 132×102 mm. Nos. 380/3 4·00 4·75

91 Telephone Cables

(Des P. Ndembo. Litho J.W.)

1983 (17 Oct). *World Communications Year. T* **91** *and similar horiz designs. Multicoloured. P* 14.

385 50 c. Type **91** 15 10
386 1 s. W.C.Y. logo 20 10
387 5 s. Postal service 1·00 1·40
388 10 s. Microwave tower 1·75 2·25
385/8 *Set of* 4 2·75 3·50
MS389 102×92 mm. Nos. 385/88 2·75 3·50

92 Bagamoyo Boma

(Des J. de Silva and P. Ndembo. Litho State Ptg Wks, Moscow)

1983 (12 Dec). *Historical Buildings. T* **92** *and similar horiz designs. Multicoloured. P* 12½ × 12.

390 1 s. Type **92** 10 10
391 1 s. 50, Beit el Ajaib, Zanzibar 15 25
392 5 s. Anglican Cathedral, Zanzibar 55 1·00
393 10 s. Original German Government House and present State House, Dar-es-Salaam 1·10 2·00
390/3 *Set of* 4 1·75 3·00
MS394 130×100 mm. Nos. 390/3 1·90 3·00

93 Sheikh Abeid Amani Karume (founder of Afro-Shirazi Party)

(Des P. Ndembo. Litho J.W.)

1984 (18 June). *20th Anniv of Zanzibar Revolution. T* **93** *and similar horiz designs. Multicoloured. P* 14.

395	1 s. Type **93**	10	10
396	1 s. 50, Clove farming	15	25
397	5 s. Symbol of Industrial Development	55	1·00
398	10 s. New housing schemes	1·10	2·00
395/8	*Set of* 4	1·75	3·00
MS399	130 × 100 mm. 15 s. *Mapinduzi* (ferry) and map	1·50	3·00

94 Boxing

(Des P. Ndembo. Litho State Ptg Wks, Moscow)

1984 (6 Aug). *Olympic Games, Los Angeles. T* **94** *and similar horiz designs. Multicoloured. P* 12½ × 12.

400	1 s. Type **94**	10	10
401	1 s. 50, Running	15	10
402	5 s. Basketball	45	60
403	20 s. Football	1·50	2·25
400/3	*Set of* 4	2·00	2·75
MS404	130 × 100 mm. Nos. 400/3	2·00	2·75

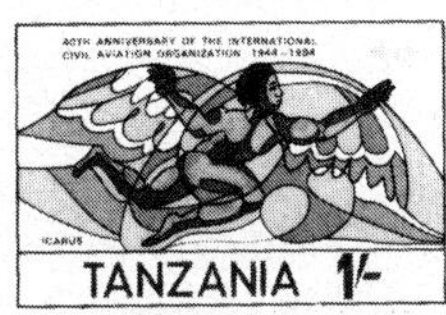

95 Icarus in Flight

(Des P. Ndembo. Litho J.W.)

1984 (15 Nov). *40th Anniv of International Civil Aviation Organization. T* **95** *and similar horiz designs. Multicoloured. P* 13 × 12½.

405	1 s. Type **95**	10	10
406	1 s. 50, Aircraft and air traffic controller	15	20
407	5 s. Aircraft undergoing maintenance	55	1·25
408	10 s. I.C.A.O. badge	1·10	2·00
405/8	*Set of* 4	1·75	3·25
MS409	130 × 100 mm. Nos. 405/8	1·90	3·00

96 Sochi – Conical House

(Des P. Ndembo. Litho State Ptg Wks, Moscow)

1984 (20 Dec). *Traditional Houses. T* **96** *and similar horiz designs. Multicoloured. P* 12½ × 12.

410	1 s. Type **96**	10	10
411	1 s. 50, Isyenga – circular type	15	20
412	5 s. Tembe – flatroofed type	45	1·25
413	10 s. Banda – coastal type	90	2·00
410/13	*Set of* 4	1·40	3·25
MS414	129 × 99 mm. Nos. 410/13	1·50	3·00

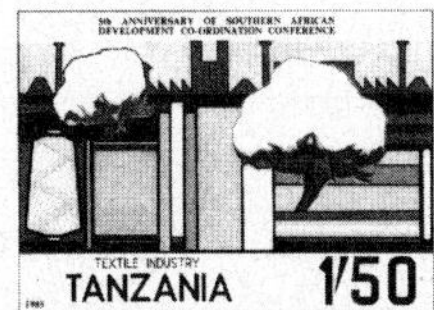

97 Production of Cotton Textiles

(Des P. Ndembo. Litho J.W.)

1985 (1 Apr). *5th Anniv of Southern African Development Co-ordination Conference. T* **97** *and similar horiz designs. Multicoloured. P* 14.

415	1 s. 50, Type **97**	30	15
416	4 s. Diamond mining	1·75	1·25
417	5 s. Map of member countries and means of communication	1·75	1·25
418	20 s. Flags and signatures of member countries	2·50	3·00
415/18	*Set of* 4	5·75	5·00
MS419	110 × 104 mm. Nos. 415/18	5·75	5·00

98 Tortoise

(Des P. Ndembo (15s., 20s.), J. de Silva (others). Litho J.W.)

1985 (8 May). *Rare Animals of Zanzibar. T* **98** *and similar multicoloured designs. P* 12½ × 13 (17 *s.* 50) *or* 13 × 12½ (*others*).

420	1 s. Type **98**	15	10
421	4 s. Leopard	60	80
422	10 s. Civet Cat	1·25	2·25
423	17 s. 50, Red Colobus Monkey (*vert*)	2·00	2·75
420/3	*Set of* 4	3·50	5·50
MS424	110 × 93 mm. 15 s. Black Rhinoceros; 20 s. Giant Ground Pangolin	1·75	2·75

Nos. 420/4 exist imperforate from a restricted printing.

99 The Queen Mother

(Litho Holders Press)

1985 (30 Sept). *Life and Times of Queen Elizabeth the Queen Mother. T* **99** *and similar horiz designs. Multicoloured. P* 14.

425	20 s. Type **99**	20	35
426	20 s. Queen Mother waving to crowd	20	35
427	100 s. Oval portrait with flowers	90	1·40
428	100 s. Head and shoulders portrait	90	1·40
425/8	*Set of* 4	2·00	3·25
MS429	Two sheets, each 125 × 63 mm. (a) Nos. 425 and 427; (b) Nos. 426 and 428. *Set of* 2 *sheets*	2·00	2·75

Nos. 425/9 exist imperforate from a restricted printing.

100 Locomotive No. 3022

GOLD MEDAL
HENRY TILLMAN
USA
(**101**)

(Litho Holders Press)

1985 (7 Oct). *Tanzanian Railway Locomotives* (1*st series*). *T* **100** *and similar horiz designs. Multicoloured. P* 14.

430	5 s. Type **100**	20	25
431	10 s. Locomotive No. 3107	35	50
432	20 s. Locomotive No. 6004	60	80
433	30 s. Locomotive No. 3129	80	1·10
430/3	*Set of* 4	1·75	2·40
MS434	125 × 93 mm. Nos. 430/3	2·00	3·00

See also Nos. 445/50.

1985 (22 Oct). *Olympic Games Gold Medal Winners, Los Angeles. Nos.* 400/4 *optd as T* **101**.

435	1 s. Type **94** (optd with T **101**)	10	10
436	1 s. 50, Running (optd "GOLD MEDAL USA")	15	20
437	5 s. Basketball (optd "GOLD MEDAL USA")	45	1·00
438	20 s. Football (optd "GOLD MEDAL FRANCE")	1·75	2·75
435/8	*Set of* 4	2·25	3·50
MS439	130 × 100 mm. Nos. 435/8	6·50	8·00

102 Cooking and Water Pots **103** Class "64" Locomotive

(Des J. Mzinga. Litho State Ptg Wks, Moscow)

1985 (4 Nov). *Pottery. T* **102** *and similar horiz designs. Multicoloured. P* 12½ × 12.

440	1 s. 50, Type **102**	15	10
441	2 s. Large pot and frying pot with cover	20	10
442	5 s. Trader selling pots	50	30
443	40 s. Beer pot	2·00	2·25
440/3	*Set of* 4	2·50	2·50
MS444	129 × 98 mm. 30 s. Water pots	2·50	2·50

(Des P. Ndembo. Litho State Ptg Wks, Moscow)

1985 (25 Nov). *Tanzanian Railway Locomotives* (2*nd series*). *T* **103** *and similar horiz designs. P* 12½ × 12.

445	1 s. 50, multicoloured	20	10
446	2 s. multicoloured	30	20
447	5 s. multicoloured	50	50
448	10 s. multicoloured	85	90
449	30 s. black, brownish black and red	2·25	2·50
445/9	*Set of* 5	3·75	3·75
MS450	130 × 100 mm. 15 s. black, blackish brown and rose-pink; 20 s. black, blackish brown and rose-pink	4·00	4·00

Designs:—2 s. Class "36" locomotive; 5 s. "DFH1013" shunting locomotive; 10 s. "DE 1001" diesel-electric locomotive; 15 s. Class "30" steam locomotive; 20 s. Class "11" steam locomotive; 30 s. Steam locomotive, Zanzibar, 1906.

Nos. 445/50 exist imperforate from a restricted printing.

Nos. 445/6 and 448/9 exist overprinted "CONGRATULATIONS TO THE DUKE & DUCHESS OF YORK ON THE OCCASION OF THEIR MARRIAGE", but there is no evidence that these overprints were available from post offices in Tanzania.

104 Young Pioneers

(Des P. Ndembo. Litho J.W.)

1986 (20 Jan). *International Youth Year. T* **104** *and similar horiz designs. P* 14.

451	1 s. 50, multicoloured	15	15
452	4 s. reddish brown, pale brown and black	30	45
453	10 s. multicoloured	70	1·10
454	20 s. reddish brown, pale brown and black	1·40	2·00
451/4	*Set of* 4	2·25	3·25
MS455	130 × 100 mm. 30 s. reddish brown, pale brown and black	2·25	3·25

Designs:—4 s. Child health care; 10 s. Uhuru Torch Race; 20 s. Young workers and globe; 30 s. Young people farming.

105 Rolls-Royce "20/25" (1936)

(Litho Holders Press)

1986 (10 Mar). *Centenary of Motoring. T* **105** *and similar horiz designs. Multicoloured. P* 14.

456	1 s. 50, Type **105**	10	10
457	5 s. Rolls-Royce "Phantom II" (1933)	20	25
458	10 s. Rolls-Royce "Phantom I" (1926)	35	50
459	30 s. Rolls-Royce "Silver Ghost" (1907)	80	1·10
456/9	*Set of* 4	1·40	1·75
MS460	125 × 93 mm. Nos. 456/9	1·40	2·25

Nos. 456/60 exist imperforate from a restricted printing.

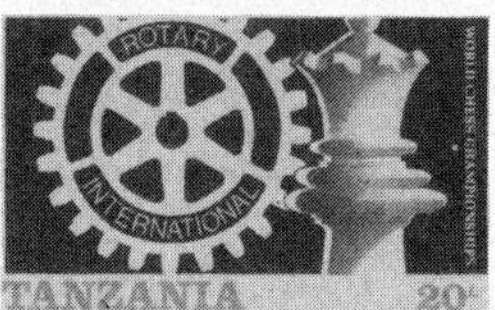

106 Rotary Logo and Queen Chess Piece

(Litho Holders Press)

1986 (17 Mar). *World Chess Championships, Moscow. T* **106** *and similar horiz design. P* 14.

461	20 s. new blue and magenta	50	50
462	100 s. multicoloured	1·50	2·25
MS463	124 × 64 mm. Nos. 461/2	2·50	3·25

Design:—100 s. Hand moving chess piece.

No. 461 also commemorates Rotary International.

Slightly different versions of Nos. 461/2, incorporating the Tanzania emblem and with "TANZANIA" and face value at top on the 100 s., were not issued.

107 Mallard

(Litho Holders Press)

1986 (22 May). *Birth Bicentenary of John J. Audubon* (*ornithologist*) (1985). *T* **107** *and similar horiz designs. Multicoloured. P* 14.

464	5 s. Type **107**	30	25
465	10 s. Eider	55	50
466	20 s. Scarlet Ibis	80	1·25
467	30 s. Roseate Spoonbill	1·00	1·50
464/7	*Set of* 4	2·40	3·25
MS468	122 × 91 mm. Nos. 464/7	2·40	3·50

Nos. 464/8 exist imperforate from a restricted printing.

108 Pearls

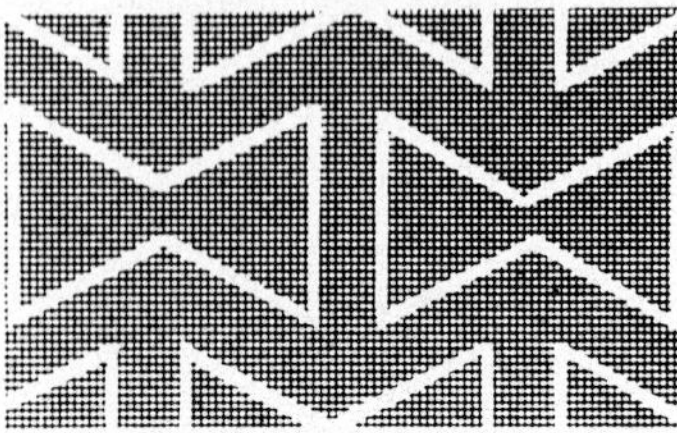

109

(Litho J.W.)

1986 (27 May). *Tanzanian Minerals. T* **108** *and similar horiz designs. Multicoloured. Phosphorised paper* (*Nos.* 469/72). *P* 14.

469 1 s. 50, Type **108** .. 40 15
470 2 s. Sapphire .. 55 40
471 5 s. Tanzanite .. 85 75
472 40 s. Diamonds .. 4·25 4·50
469/72 .. *Set of* 4 5·50 5·25
MS473 130×100 mm. 30 s. Rubies. W **109** .. 4·50 4·75

110 *Hibiscus calyphyllus* **111** Oryx

(Litho Holders Press)

1986 (25 June). *Flowers of Tanzania. T* **110** *and similar vert designs. Multicoloured. P* 14.

474 1 s. 50, Type **110** .. 10 10
475 5 s. *Aloe graminicola* .. 15 15
476 10 s. *Nersium oleander* .. 25 25
477 30 s. *Nymphaea caerulea* .. 65 65
474/7 .. *Set of* 4 1·00 1·00
MS478 90×119 mm. Nos. 474/7 .. 1·60 1·90

Nos. 474/8 exist imperforate from a restricted printing.

(Litho Holders Press)

1986 (30 June). *Endangered Animals of Tanzania. T* **111** *and similar vert designs. Multicoloured. P* 14.

479 5 s. Type **111** .. 30 15
480 10 s. Giraffe .. 55 45
481 20 s. Rhinoceros .. 1·00 1·00
482 30 s. Cheetah .. 1·10 1·50
479/82 .. *Set of* 4 2·75 2·75
MS483 91×121 mm. Nos. 479/82 .. 2·75 3·50

112 Immunization **113** Butterfly Fish

(Des P. Ndembo. Litho State Ptg Wks, Moscow)

1986 (29 July). *U.N.I.C.E.F. Child Survival Campaign. T* **112** *and similar horiz designs. Multicoloured. P* 12½×12.

484 1 s. 50, Type **112** .. 10 10
485 2 s. Growth monitoring .. 10 10
486 5 s. Oral rehydration therapy .. 15 15
487 40 s. Breast feeding .. 1·00 1·25
484/7 .. *Set of* 4 1·25 1·40
MS488 110×101 mm. 30 s. Healthy baby .. 60 1·00

(Des P. Ndembo. Litho State Ptg Wks, Moscow)

1986 (28 Aug). *Marine Life. T* **113** *and similar horiz designs. Multicoloured. P* 12½×12

489 1 s. 50, Type **113** .. 20 10
490 4 s. Parrot Fish .. 35 30
491 10 s. Turtle .. 70 70
492 20 s. Octopus .. 1·25 1·25
489/92 .. *Set of* 4 2·25 2·00
MS493 131×101 mm. 30 s. Corals .. 75 1·00

NEW INFORMATION

The editor is always interested to correspond with people who have new information that will improve or correct the Catalogue.

114 Team Captains shaking Hands **115** Pres. Nyerere receiving Beyond War Award

(Litho Questa)

1986 (30 Oct). *World Cup Football Championship, Mexico. T* **114** *and similar horiz designs. Multicoloured. P* 14.

494 1 s. 50, Type **114** .. 15 10
495 2 s. Referee sending player off .. 15 10
496 10 s. Goalkeeper and ball in net .. 60 60
497 20 s. Goalkeeper saving ball .. 1·00 1·40
494/7 .. *Set of* 4 1·75 2·00
MS498 95×72 mm. 30 s. Winning Argentine team .. 60 70

(Des P. Ndembo. Litho Mardon Printers Ltd, Zimbabwe)

1986 (20 Dec). *International Peace Year. T* **115** *and similar horiz designs. Multicoloured. P* 14½.

499 1 s. 50, Type **115** .. 25 10
500 2 s. Children of many races .. 40 10
501 10 s. African cosmonaut and rocket launch 80 90
502 20 s. United Nations Headquarters, New York .. 1·25 1·40
499/502 .. *Set of* 4 2·40 2·25
MS503 109×86 mm. 30 s. International Peace Year symbols .. 70 80

116 Mobile Bank Service

(Des P. Ndembo. Litho Questa)

1987 (7 Feb). *20th Anniv of National Bank of Commerce. T* **116** *and similar horiz designs. Multicoloured. P* 14.

504 1 s. 50, Type **116** .. 20 10
505 2 s. National Bank of Commerce Head Office .. 30 15
506 5 s. Pres. Mwinyi laying foundation stone 45 45
507 20 s. Cotton harvesting .. 1·25 1·50
504/7 .. *Set of* 4 2·00 2·00

117 Parade of Young Party Members

(Litho Holders Press)

1987 (10 Mar). *10th Anniv of Chama Cha Mapinduzi Party and 20th Anniv of Arusha Declaration. T* **117** *and similar horiz designs. Multicoloured. P* 14.

508 2 s. Type **117** .. 15 10
509 3 s. Harvesting coffee .. 20 10
510 10 s. Pres. Nyerere addressing Second Peace Initiative Reunion .. 30 20
511 30 s. Presidents Julius Nyerere and Ali Hassan Mwinyi .. 50 60
508/11 .. *Set of* 4 1·10 90

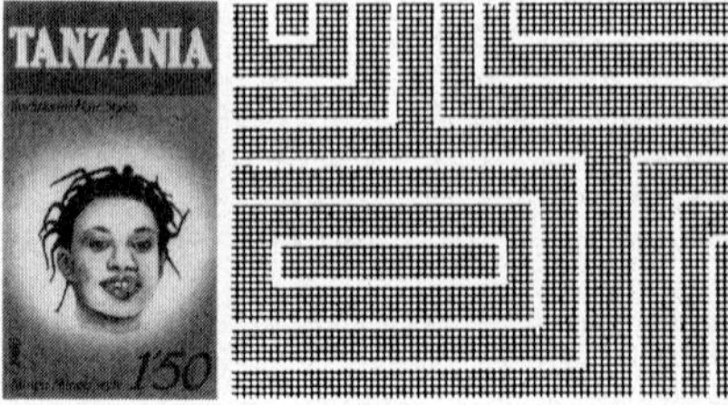

118 Nungu Nungu Hair Style **119**

(Litho Leigh-Mardon Ltd, Melbourne)

1987 (16 Mar). *Traditional Hair Styles. T* **118** *and similar vert designs. Multicoloured. W* **119**. *P* 14½.

512 1 s. 50, Type **118** .. 25 10
513 2 s. Upanga wa jogoo style .. 35 20
514 10 s. Morani style .. 60 60
515 20 s. Twende kilioni style .. 1·25 1·40
512/15 .. *Set of* 4 2·25 2·10
MS516 110×99 mm. 30 s. Hair plaiting .. 1·50 1·75

120 Royal Family on Buckingham Palace Balcony after Trooping the Colour

(Litho Holders Press)

1987 (24 Mar). *60th Birthday of Queen Elizabeth II* (1986). *T* **120** *and similar horiz designs. Multicoloured. P* 14.

517 5 s. Type **120** .. 15 10
518 10 s. Queen and Prince Philip at Royal Ascot 25 20
519 40 s. Queen Elizabeth II .. 80 80
520 60 s. Queen Elizabeth with crowd .. 1·10 1·25
517/20 .. *Set of* 4 2·10 2·10
MS521 125×90 mm. Nos. 517/20 .. 2·25 2·40

Nos. 517/21 exist imperforate from a restricted printing.

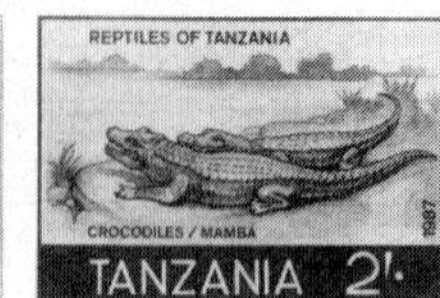

121 *Apis mellifera* (bee) **122** Crocodile

(Litho State Ptg Wks, Moscow)

1987 (22 Apr). *Insects. T* **121** *and similar horiz designs. Multicoloured. P* 12½×12.

522 1 s. 50, Type **121** .. 30 10
523 2 s. *Prostephanus truncatus* (grain borer) 40 20
524 10 s. *Glossina palpalis* (tsetse fly) .. 75 75
525 20 s. *Polistes* sp (wasp) .. 1·25 1·40
522/5 .. *Set of* 4 2·40 2·25
MS526 110×101 mm. 30 s. *Anopheles* sp (mosquito) .. 1·25 1·50

(Des J. Mzinga (3 s., 30 s.), P. Ndembo (others). Litho State Ptg Wks, Moscow)

1987 (2 July). *Reptiles. T* **122** *and similar horiz designs. Multicoloured. P* 12½×12.

527 2 s. Type **122** .. 15 10
528 3 s. Black-striped Grass-snake .. 20 15
529 10 s. Adder .. 35 30
530 20 s. Green Mamba .. 65 70
527/30 .. *Set of* 4 1·25 1·10
MS531 101×101 mm. 30 s. Tortoise .. 85 90

123 Emblems of Posts/ Telecommunications and Railways **124** Basketry

(Des and litho Questa)

1987 (27 July). *10th Anniv of Tanzania Communications and Transport Corporations. T* **123** *and similar horiz designs. Multicoloured. P* 14.

532 2 s. Type **123** .. 10 10
533 8 s. Emblems of Air Tanzania and Harbours Authority .. 20 20
MS534 100×66 mm. 20 s. Methods of transport and communication .. 30 35

(Des P. Ndembo. Litho State Ptg Wks, Moscow)

1987 (15 Dec). *Traditional Handicrafts. T* **124** *and similar horiz designs. Multicoloured. P* 12½×12.

535 2 s. Type **124** .. 15 10
536 3 s. Decorated gourds .. 15 15
537 10 s. Stools .. 25 20
538 20 s. Makonde carvings .. 40 45
535/8 .. *Set of* 4 85 80
MS539 89×89 mm. 40 s. Makonde carver at work .. 65 75

10th Anniversary of TANZANIA ZAMBIA RAILWAY AUTHORITY 1976-1986

(**125**)

1987 (30 Dec). *10th Anniv of Tanzania–Zambia Railway* (1986). *Nos.* 445/9 *optd with T* **125**.

540 **103** 1 s. 50, multicoloured .. 10 10
541 – 2 s. multicoloured .. 15 15
542 – 5 s. multicoloured .. 20 20
543 – 10 s. multicoloured .. 30 30
544 – 30 s. black, brownish black and red .. 50 50
540/4 .. *Set of* 5 1·10 1·10

126 Mdako (pebble game)

(Des P. Ndembo. Litho State Ptg Wks, Moscow)

1988 (15 Feb). *Traditional Pastimes. T* **126** *and similar horiz designs. Multicoloured. P* 12½×12.
545 2 s. Type **126** .. 10 10
546 3 s. Wrestling .. 10 10
547 8 s. Bullfighting, Zanzibar .. 15 15
548 20 s. Bao (board game) .. 35 35
545/8 .. *Set of* 4 65 65
MS549 100×90 mm. 30 s. Archery .. 50 60

127 Plateosaurus

(Des G. Vasarhelyi. Litho Format)

1988 (22 Apr). *Prehistoric and Modern Animals. T* **127** *and similar trapezium-shaped designs. Multicoloured. P* 12½.
550 2 s. Type **127** .. 15 10
a. *Tête-bêche* (horiz pair) .. 30 20
551 3 s. Pteranodon .. 15 10
a. *Tête-bêche* (horiz pair) .. 30 20
552 5 s. Jurassic Brontosaurus .. 15 10
a. *Tête-bêche* (horiz pair) .. 30 20
553 7 s. Lion .. 20 15
a. *Tête-bêche* (horiz pair) .. 40 30
554 8 s. Tiger .. 20 15
a. *Tête-bêche* (horiz pair) .. 40 30
555 12 s. Orang-utan .. 25 15
a. *Tête-bêche* (horiz pair) .. 50 30
556 20 s. Elephant .. 50 35
a. *Tête-bêche* (horiz pair) .. 1·00 70
557 100 s. Stegosaurus .. 1·50 1·25
a. *Tête-bêche* (horiz pair) .. 3·00 2·50
550/7 .. *Set of* 8 2·75 2·00

Nos. 550/7 were issued in sheets which had the second and fourth stamps *tête-bêche* in each horizontal row of five.

128 Marchers with Party Flag

129 Population Symbols on Map

(Des P. Ndembo. Litho Questa)

1988 (1 July). *National Solidarity Walk. T* **128** *and similar horiz designs. Multicoloured. P* 14×14½.
558 2 s. + 1 s. Type **128** .. 15 15
559 3 s. + 1 s. Pres. Mwinyi leading Walk .. 15 15
MS560 121×121 mm. 50 s. + 1 s. Pres. Ali Hassan Mwinyi (35×25 *mm*). P 14½ .. 75 85

(Des P. Ndembo. Litho Questa)

1988 (8 Aug). *Third National Population Census. T* **129** *and similar horiz designs. Multicoloured. P* 14.
561 2 s. Type **129** .. 10 10
562 3 s. Census official at work .. 10 10
563 10 s. Community health care .. 15 15
564 20 s. Population growth 1967–1988 .. 30 30
561/4 .. *Set of* 4 55 55
MS565 96×91 mm. 40 s. Development of modern Tanzania .. 55 60

130 Javelin

131 Football

(Litho State Ptg Wks, Moscow)

1988 (5 Sept). *Olympic Games, Seoul (1st issue). T* **130** *and similar horiz designs. Multicoloured. P* 12½×12.
566 2 s. Type **130** .. 10 10
567 3 s. Hurdling .. 10 10
568 7 s. Long distance running .. 15 15
569 12 s. Relay racing .. 25 25
566/9 .. *Set of* 4 50 50
MS570 100×70 mm. 40 s. Badminton .. 70 70

(Des D. Miller. Litho Questa)

1988 (5 Sept). *Olympic Games, Seoul (2nd issue). T* **131** *and similar vert designs. Multicoloured. P* 14.
571 10 s. Type **131** .. 10 10
572 20 s. Cycling .. 20 25
573 50 s. Fencing .. 45 50
574 70 s. Volleyball .. 60 65
571/4 .. *Set of* 4 1·25 1·40
MS575 77×92 mm. 100 s. Gymnastics .. 90 95

(Des D. Miller. Litho Questa)

1988 (5 Sept). *Winter Olympic Games, Calgary. Vert designs as T* **131**. *Multicoloured. P* 14.
576 5 s. Cross-country skiing .. 10 10
577 25 s. Figure skating .. 20 25
578 50 s. Downhill skiing .. 45 50
579 75 s. Bobsleighing .. 65 70
576/9 .. *Set of* 4 1·25 1·40
MS580 77×92 mm. 100 s. Ice hockey sticks wrapped in Olympic and Canadian colours .. 90 95

132 Goat

133 "Love You, Dad" (Pinocchio)

(Litho Questa)

1988 (9 Sept). *Domestic Animals. T* **132** *and similar multicoloured designs. P* 14.
581 4 s. Type **132** .. 10 10
582 5 s. Rabbit (*horiz*) .. 10 10
583 8 s. Cows (*horiz*) .. 15 15
584 10 s. Kitten (*horiz*) .. 20 20
585 12 s. Pony .. 25 25
586 20 s. Puppy .. 45 45
581/6 .. *Set of* 6 1·10 1·10
MS587 102×73 mm. 100 s. Chicken (*horiz*) .. 1·50 1·50

(Des Walt Disney Company. Litho Questa)

1988 (9 Sept). *Greetings Stamps. T* **133** *and similar horiz designs showing Walt Disney cartoon characters. Multicoloured. P* 14×13½.
588 4 s. Type **133** .. 10 10
589 5 s. "Happy Birthday" (Brer Rabbit and Chip n'Dale) .. 10 10
590 10 s. "Trick or Treat" (Daisy and Donald Duck) .. 10 10
591 12 s. "Be kind to Animals" (Ferdie and Mordie with Pluto) .. 10 10
592 15 s. "Love" (Daisy and Donald Duck) .. 15 15
593 20 s. "Let's Celebrate" (Mickey Mouse and Goofy) .. 25 25
594 30 s. "Keep in Touch" (Daisy and Donald Duck) .. 35 35
595 50 s. "Love you, Mom" (Minnie Mouse with Ferdie and Mordie) .. 60 60
588/95 .. *Set of* 8 1·50 1·50
MS596 Two sheets, each 127×101 mm. (a) 150 s. "Let's work together" (Goofy dressed as a fireman). (b) 150 s. "Have a super Sunday" (Goofy dressed as American footballer) *Set of* 2 *sheets* 3·75 4·00

134 *Charaxes varanes*

135 Independence Torch and Mt Kilimanjaro

(Des Jennifer Toombs. Litho Questa)

1988 (17 Oct). *Butterflies. T* **134** *and similar horiz designs. Multicoloured. P* 14½.
597 8 s. Type **134** .. 30 10
598 30 s. *Neptis melicerta* .. 65 30
599 40 s. *Mylothris chloris* .. 75 40
600 50 s. *Charaxes bohemani* .. 90 50
601 60 s. *Myrina silenus* (s sp *ficedula*) .. 1·00 70
602 75 s. *Papilio phorcas* .. 1·50 90
603 90 s. *Cyrestis camillus* .. 1·75 1·10
604 100 s. *Salamis temora* .. 2·00 1·25
597/604 .. *Set of* 8 8·00 4·75
MS605 Two sheets, each 80×50 mm. (a) 200 s. *Asterope rosa*. (b) 250 s. *Kallima rumia* *Set of* 2 *sheets* 7·00 6·00

(Des R. Vigurs. Litho Questa)

1988 (1 Nov). *National Monuments. T* **135** *and similar vert designs. Multicoloured. P* 14.
606 5 s. Type **135** .. 10 10
607 12 s. Arusha Declaration Monument .. 10 10
608 30 s. Askari Monument .. 25 30
609 60 s. Independence Monument .. 55 60
606/9 .. *Set of* 4 80 90
MS610 100×89 mm. 100 s. Askari Monument statue .. 1·25 1·40

136 Eye Clinic

137 Loading Patient into Ambulance

(Des P. Ndembo. Litho National Printing & Packaging, Zimbabwe)

1988 (19 Dec). *25th Anniv of Dar-es-Salaam Lions Club. T* **136** *and similar horiz designs. Multicoloured. P* 14½.
611 2 s. Type **136** .. 10 10
612 3 s. Family at shallow water well .. 10 10
613 7 s. Rhinoceros and map of Tanzania .. 15 15
614 12 s. Club presenting school desks .. 15 15
611/14 .. *Set of* 4 35 35
MS615 100×65 mm. 40 s. Lions International logo .. 60 65

(Des P. Ndembo. Litho State Ptg Wks, Moscow)

1988 (30 Dec). *125th Anniv of International Red Cross and Red Crescent. T* **137** *and similar horiz designs. Multicoloured. P* 12½×12.
616 2 s. Type **137** .. 10 10
617 3 s. Mother and baby health clinic .. 10 10
618 7 s. Red Cross flag .. 10 10
619 12 s. Henri Dunant (founder) .. 15 15
616/19 .. *Set of* 4 30 30
MS620 90×90 mm. 40 s. Members of Red Cross International Committee, 1863 .. 50 55

138 Paradise Whydah

139 Bushbaby

(Des S. Barlowe. Litho B.D.T.)

1989 (15 Mar). *Birds. T* **138** *and similar vert designs. Multicoloured. P* 13½.
621 20 s. Type **138** .. 10 15
a. Sheetlet. Nos. 621/40 .. 1·75
622 20 s. Black-collared Barbet .. 10 15
623 20 s. Bateleur .. 10 15
624 20 s. Lilac-breasted Roller and Openbill Storks in flight .. 10 15
625 20 s. Red-tufted Malachite Sunbird and Openbill Stork in flight .. 10 15
626 20 s. Dark Chanting Goshawk .. 10 15
627 20 s. White-fronted Bee Eater, Carmine Bee Eater and Little Bee Eaters .. 10 15
628 20 s. Narina Trogon and Marabou Stork in flight .. 10 15
629 20 s. Grey Parrot .. 10 15
630 20 s. Hoopoe .. 10 15
631 20 s. Masked Lovebird ("Yellow-collared Lovebird") .. 10 15
632 20 s. Yellow-billed Hornbill .. 10 15
633 20 s. Hammerkop .. 10 15
634 20 s. Violet-crested Turaco and flamingos in flight .. 10 15
635 20 s. Malachite Kingfisher .. 10 15
636 20 s. Greater Flamingos .. 10 15
637 20 s. Yellow-billed Storks .. 10 15
638 20 s. Whale-headed Stork ("Shoebill Stork") .. 10 15
639 20 s. Saddle-bill Stork and Blacksmith Plover .. 10 15
640 20 s. Crowned Crane .. 10 15
621/40 .. *Set of* 20 1·75 2·75
MS641 Two sheets, each 105×75 mm. (a) 350 s. Helmet Guineafowl (28×42 *mm*). (b) 350 s. Ostrich (28×42 *mm*). P 14 .. *Set of* 2 *sheets* 3·50 3·75

Nos. 622/41 were printed together, *se-tenant*, in a sheetlet of 20 forming a composite design of birds at a waterhole.

(Des J. Barbaris (Nos. 642/4, 648, **MS**650a), S. Barlowe (others). Litho Questa)

1989 (20 Mar). *Fauna and Flora. T* **139** *and similar multicoloured designs. P* 14.
642 5 s. Type **139** .. 10 10
643 10 s. Bushbaby holding insect (*horiz*) .. 10 10
644 20 s. Bushbaby on forked branch .. 10 15
645 30 s. Black Cobra on Umbrella Acacia .. 15 20
646 45 s. Bushbaby at night (*horiz*) .. 20 25
647 70 s. Red-billed Tropic Bird and Tree Ferns 35 40
648 100 s. African Tree Frog on Cocoa Tree .. 50 55
649 150 s. Black-headed Heron and Egyptian Papyrus .. 75 80
642/9 .. *Set of* 8 1·90 2·25
MS650 Two sheets. (a) 115×85 mm. 350 s. African Palm Civet (*horiz*). (b) 65×65 mm. 350 s. Pink-backed Pelican and Baobab Tree (*horiz*) *Set of* 2 *sheets* 3·50 3·75

Nos. 645, 647/9 and **MS**650 are without the World Wildlife Fund logo.

140 Juma Ikangaa (marathon runner)

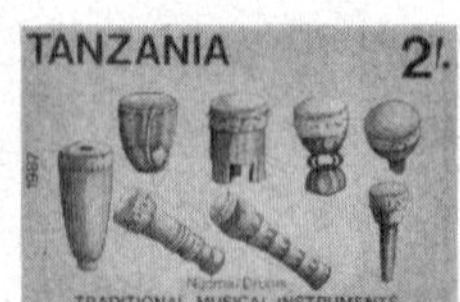

141 Drums

(Des W. Storozuk. Litho Questa)

1989 (10 Apr). *International Sporting Personalities. T* **140** *and similar vert designs. Multicoloured. P* 14.

651 4 s. Type **140** 10 10
652 8 s. 50, Steffi Graf (tennis player) .. 10 10
653 12 s. Yannick Noah (tennis player) .. 10 10
654 40 s. Pelé (footballer) 20 25
655 100 s. Erhard Keller (speed skater) .. 50 55
656 125 s. Sadanoyama (sumo wrestler) .. 60 65
657 200 s. Taino (sumo wrestler) .. .. 1·00 1·10
658 250 s. T. Nakajima (golfer) .. .. 1·25 1·40
651/8 .. .. *Set of* 8 3·25 3·75
MS659 Two sheets. (a) 100×71 mm. 350 s. Joe Louis (boxer). (b) 100×76 mm. 350 s. I. Aoki (golfer) .. .. .. *Set of* 2 *sheets* 3·50 3·75

The captions on Nos. 658 and MS659b are transposed.

(Des P. Ndembo. Litho Harrison)

1989 (29 June). *Musical Instruments. T* **141** *and similar horiz designs. Multicoloured. P* 14.

660 2 s. Type **141** 10 10
661 3 s. Xylophones 10 10
662 10 s. Thumbpiano 15 20
663 20 s. Fiddles 30 40
660/3 .. .. *Set of* 4 50 70
MS664 91×80 mm. 40 s. Violins with calabash resonators 55 55

142 Chama Cha Mapinduzi Party Flag

143 Class "P36" Locomotive, U.S.S.R.

(Des P. Ndembo. Litho Questa)

1989 (1 July). *National Solidarity Walk. T* **142** *and similar multicoloured designs. P* 14½.

665 5 s. + 1 s. Type **142** 10 10
666 10 s. + 1 s. Marchers with party flag and President Mwinyi 10 10
MS667 122×122 mm. 50 s. + 1 s. President Mwinyi (*vert*) 25 30

(Des W. Wright. Litho B.D.T.)

1989 (22 Aug). *Steam Locomotives. T* **143** *and similar multicoloured designs. P* 14.

668 10 s. Type **143** 10 10
669 25 s. Class "12", Belgium 10 15
670 60 s. Class "C62", Japan 30 35
671 75 s. Pennsylvania Railroad Class "T1", U.S.A. 35 40
672 80 s. Class "WP", India 40 45
673 90 s. East African Railways Class "59" .. 45 50
674 150 s. Class "People", China 75 80
675 200 s. Southern Pacific "Daylight Express" U.S.A. .. .. 1·00 1·10
668/75 .. .. *Set of* 8 3·00 3·50
MS676 Two sheets, each 114×85 mm. (a) 350 s. Stephenson's *Planet*, Great Britain (*vert*). (b) 350 s. "Coronation Scot", Great Britain (*vert*) *Set of* 2 *sheets* 3·50 3·75

(Des Design Element. Litho Questa)

1989 (17 Nov). *"World Stamp Expo '89" International Stamp Exhibition, Washington. Landmarks of Washington. Sheet 78×62 mm containing horiz design as T* **193a** *of Lesotho. Multicoloured. P* 14.

MS677 500 s. Union Station .. .. .. 2·50 2·75

144 "Luna 3" Satellite orbiting Moon, 1959

Gold-USSR
Silver-Brazil
Bronze-W.Germany

(145)

(Des G. Vasarhelyi. Litho Questa)

1989 (22 Nov). *History of Space Exploration and 20th Anniv of First Manned Landing on Moon. T* **144** *and similar horiz designs. Multicoloured. P* 14.

678 20 s. Type **144** 10 15
679 30 s. "Gemini 6" and "7", 1965 .. .. 15 20
680 40 s. Astronaut Edward White in space, 1965 .. .. 20 25
681 60 s. Astronaut Aldrin on Moon, 1969 .. 30 35
682 70 s. Aldrin performing experiment, 1969 35 40
683 100 s. "Apollo 15" astronaut and lunar rover, 1971 .. .. 50 55
684 150 s. "Apollo 18" and "Soyuz 19" docking in space, 1975 .. .. 75 80
685 200 s. Spacelab, 1983 .. .. .. 1·00 1·10
678/85 .. .. *Set of* 8 3·00 3·50
MS686 Two sheets, each 110×90 mm. (a) 250 s. Lunar module *Eagle* and "Apollo 11" emblem. (b) 250 s. Projected U.S. space station *Set of* 2 *sheets* 2·50 2·75

1989 (11 Dec). *Olympic Medal Winners, Calgary and Seoul. Optd as T* **145**. (a) *On Nos.* 571/5

687 10 s. Type **131** (optd with T **145**) 10 10
688 20 s. Cycling (optd "Men's Match Sprint, Lutz Hesslich, DDR") 10 15
689 50 s. Fencing (optd "Epee, Schmitt, W. Germany") 25 30
690 70 s. Volleyball (optd "Men's Team, USA") 35 40
687/90 .. .. *Set of* 4 70 80
MS691 77×92 mm. 100 s. Gymnastics ("Women's Team, Gold – USSR") 50 55

(*b*) *On Nos.* 576/80

692 5 s. Cross-country skiing (optd "Biathlon, Peter-Roetsch, DDR") 10 10
693 25 s. Figure skating (optd "Pairs, Gordeeva & Grinkov, USSR") 10 15
694 50 s. Downhill skiing (optd "Zurbriggen, Switzerland") 25 30
695 75 s. Bobsleighing (optd "Gold – USSR Silver – DDR Bronze – DDR") 35 40
692/5 .. .. *Set of* 4 70 80
MS696 77×92 mm. 100 s. Ice hockey sticks wrapped in Olympic and Canadian colours (optd "Ice Hockey: Gold – USSR") 50 55

146 Tiger Tilapia

(Des W. Hanson Studio. Litho Questa)

1989 (14 Dec). *Reef and Freshwater Fishes of Tanzania. T* **146** *and similar multicoloured designs. P* 14.

697 9 s. Type **146** 10 10
698 13 s. Picasso Fish 10 10
699 20 s. Powder-blue Surgeonfish 10 15
700 40 s. Butterflyfish 20 25
701 70 s. Guenther's Notho 35 40
702 100 s. Ansorge's Neolebias 50 55
703 150 s. Lyretail Panchax 75 80
704 200 s. Regal Angelfish .. .. .. 1·00 1·10
697/704 .. .. *Set of* 8 2·75 3·00
MS705 Two sheets, each 112×83 mm. (a) 350 s. Jewel Cichlid (50×38 *mm*). P 14×13½. (b) 350 s. Batfish (38×50 *mm*). P 13½×14 *Set of* 2 *sheets* 3·50 3·75

147 Rural Polling Station

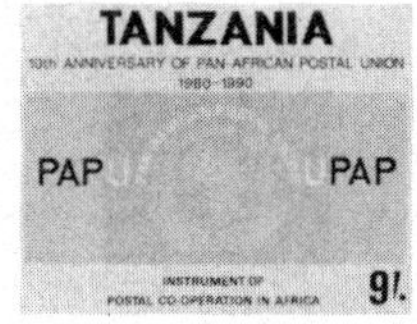

148 Logo

(Des P. Ndembo. Litho State Ptg Wks, Moscow)

1989 (22 Dec). *Centenary of Inter-Parliamentary Union. T* **147** *and similar horiz designs. P* 12½×12.

706 9 s. multicoloured 10 10
707 13 s. multicoloured 10 10
708 80 s. multicoloured 40 45
709 100 s. black, dull ultramarine and pale blue 50 55
706/9 .. .. *Set of* 4 90 1·00
MS710 90×90 mm. 40 s. multicoloured .. 20 25

Designs:—13 s. Parliament Building, Dar-es-Salaam; 40 s. Sir William Randal Cremer and Frederic Passy (founders); 80 s. Tanzania Parliament in session; 100 s. Logo.

(Des P. Ndembo. Litho Cartor, France)

1990 (10 Jan). *10th Anniv of Pan-African Postal Union. T* **148** *and similar horiz designs. P* 13½.

711 9 s. greenish yellow, dull green and black 10 10
712 13 s. multicoloured 10 10
713 70 s. multicoloured 35 40
714 100 s. multicoloured 50 55
711/14 .. .. *Set of* 4 85 95
MS715 90×90 mm. 40 s. multicoloured. P 12½ 20 25

Designs:—13 s. Collecting mail from post office box; 40 s. Logos of Tanzania Posts and Telecommunications Corporation, P.A.P.U. and U.P.U.; 70 s. Taking mail to post office; 100 s. Mail transport.

149 Admiral's Flag and *Nina*

(Des T. Agans. Litho Questa)

1990 (12 Feb). *500th Anniv of Discovery of America by Columbus* (1992) (50, 60, 75, 200 *s.*) *and Modern Scientific Discoveries* (*others*). *T* **149** *and similar horiz designs. Multicoloured. P* 14.

716 9 s. Bell X-1 aircraft (first supersonic flight, 1947) 10 10
717 13 s. *Trieste* (bathyscaph) (first dive to depth of 35,000 ft, 1960) 10 10
718 50 s. Type **149** 25 30
719 60 s. Fleet flag and *Pinta* 30 35
720 75 s. Standard of Castile and León and *Santa Maria* 35 40
721 150 s. Transistor technology 75 80
722 200 s. Arms of Columbus and map of First Voyage .. .. 1·00 1·10
723 250 s. DNA molecule .. .. .. 1·25 1·40
716/23 .. .. *Set of* 8 3·50 4·00
MS724 Two sheets, each 106×78 mm. (a) 350 s. Caravels in the Caribbean. (b) 350 s. *Voyager II* and Neptune .. .. .. *Set of* 2 *sheets* 3·50 3·75

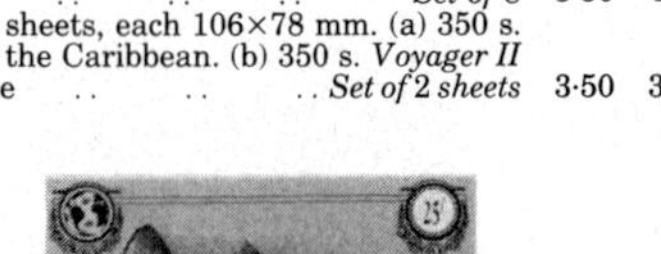

150 Tecopa Pupfish

(Des J. Genzo. Litho Questa)

1990 (20 Feb). *Extinct Species. T* **150** *and similar multicoloured designs. P* 14.

725 25 s. Type **150** 10 15
726 40 s. Thylacine 20 25
727 50 s. Quagga 25 30
728 60 s. Passenger Pigeon 30 35
729 75 s. Rodriguez Saddleback Tortoise .. 35 40
730 100 s. Toolache Wallaby 50 55
731 150 s. Texas Red Wolf 75 80
732 200 s. Utah Lake Sculpin .. .. .. 1·00 1·10
725/32 .. .. *Set of* 8 3·00 3·50
MS733 Two sheets (a) 102×74 mm. 350 s. South Island Whekau. (b) 71×99 mm. 350 s. Hawaiian O-O (*vert*) .. .. .. *Set of* 2 *sheets* 3·50 3·75

151 Camping

(Des P. Ndembo. Litho State Ptg Wks, Moscow)

1990 (22 Feb). *60th Anniv of Girl Guides Movement in Tanzania. T* **151** *and similar multicoloured designs.* P 12½×12.

734 9 s. Type **151** 10 10
735 13 s. Guides planting sapling 10 10
736 50 s. Guide teaching woman to write .. 25 30
737 100 s. Guide helping at child-care clinic .. 50 55
734/7 .. .. *Set of* 4 75 85
MS738 89×89 mm. 40 s. Guide teaching child to read (*vert*). P 12×12½ 20 25

152 Fishing

153 Footballer

(Des P. Ndembo. Litho State Ptg Wks, Moscow)

1990 (25 Apr). *25th Anniv of Union of Tanganyika and Zanzibar. T* **152** *and similar multicoloured designs.* P 12½×12 (*horiz*) *or* 12×12½ (*vert*).

739 9 s. Type **152** 10 10
740 13 s. Vineyard 10 10
741 50 s. Cloves 25 30
742 100 s. Presidents Nyerere and Karume exchanging Union instruments (*vert*) 55 60
739/42 .. .. *Set of* 4 80 90
MS743 90×90 mm. 40 s. Arms (*vert*) 20 25

(Litho B.D.T.)

1990 (1 June). *World Cup Football Championship, Italy* (1*st issue*). *T* **153** *and similar vert designs. Multicoloured. P* 14.

744 25 s. Type **153** 10 15
745 60 s. Player passing ball 30 35
746 75 s. Player turning 35 40
747 200 s. Player kicking ball .. .. .. 1·00 1·25
744/7 .. .. *Set of* 4 1·60 1·90
MS748 Two sheets, each 105×76 mm. (a) 350 s. Two players fighting for possession. (b) 350 s. Player kicking ball .. .. *Set of* 2 *sheets* 3·50 3·75

See also Nos. 789/93 and 794/8.

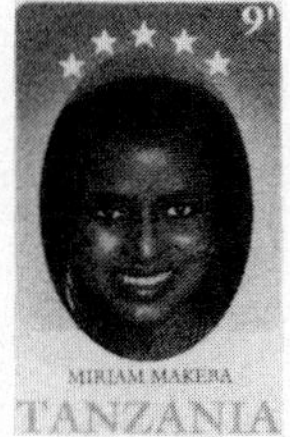

154 Miriam Makeba

155 Ring of People round Party Flag

(Des A. Fagbohun. Litho Questa)

1990 (29 June). *Famous Black Entertainers. T* **154** *and similar vert designs. Multicoloured. P* 14.

749 9 s. Type **154** 10 10
750 13 s. Manu Dibango 10 10
751 25 s. Fela 10 15
752 70 s. Smokey Robinson 35 40
753 100 s. Gladys Knight 50 55
754 150 s. Eddie Murphy 75 80
755 200 s. Sammy Davis Jnr. .. .. .. 1·00 1·10
756 250 f. Stevie Wonder .. .. .. 1·25 1·40
749/56 .. .. *Set of* 8 3·75 4·00
MS757 Two sheets, each 69×88 mm. (a) 350 s. Bill Cosby (30×39 *mm*). (b) 350 s. Michael Jackson (30×39 *mm*). P 14½ .. *Set of* 2 *sheets* 3·50 3·75

(Litho Cartor)

1990 (6 July). *Solidarity Walk,* 1990. *T* **155** *and similar multicoloured designs. P* 13½.

758 9 s. + 1 s. Type **155** 10 10
759 13 s. + 1 s. President Mwinyi 10 10
MS760 90×90 mm. 50 s. + 1 s. Handclasp on map (*vert*). P 12½ 25 30

156 Passenger Train

157 Pope John Paul II

(Des P. Ndembo. Litho Cartor)

1990 (8 Aug). *10th Anniv of Southern African Development Co-ordination Conference. T* **156** *and similar horiz designs. Multicoloured. P* 13½.

761 8 s. Type **156** 10 10
762 11 s. 50, Paper-making plant 10 10
763 25 s. Tractor factory and ploughing .. 10 15
764 100 s. Map and national flags 50 55
761/4 .. .. *Set of* 4 65 70
MS765 89×89 mm. 50 s. Map of Southern Africa. P 12½ 25 30

(Des P. Ndembo. Litho Questa)

1990 (1 Sept). *Papal Visit to Tanzania. T* **157** *and similar multicoloured designs. P* 14.

766 10 s. Type **157** 10 10
767 15 s. Pope in ceremonial robes 10 10
768 20 s. Pope giving blessing 10 10
769 100 s. Papal coat of arms 50 55
766/9 .. .. *Set of* 4 65 70
MS770 172×143 mm. 50 s. Pope John Paul II (*horiz*); 50 s. St. Joseph's Cathedral, Dar-es-Salaam (*horiz*); 50 s. Christ the King Cathedral, Moshi (*horiz*); 50 s. Saint Theresa's Cathedral, Tabora (*horiz*); 50 s. Cathedral of the Epiphany, Bugando Mwanza (*horiz*); 50 s. St. Mathias Mulumba Kalemba Cathedral, Songea (*horiz*) .. .. 1·50 1·60

158 Mickey and Minnie Mouse in Herby the Love Bug

(Des Walt Disney Co. Litho Questa)

1990 (7 Nov). *Motor Cars from Disney Films. T* **158** *and similar horiz designs. Multicoloured. P* 14×13½.

771 20 s. Type **158** 10 15
772 30 s. The Absent-minded Professor's car .. 15 20
773 45 s. Chitty-Chitty Bang-Bang 20 25
774 60 s. Mr. Toad's car 30 35
775 75 s. Scrooge's limousine 35 40
776 100 s. The Shaggy Dog's car 50 55
777 150 s. Donald Duck's nephews cleaning car 75 80
778 200 s. Fire engine from *Dumbo* .. .. 1·00 1·10
771/8 .. .. *Set of* 8 3·00 3·00
MS779 Two sheets, each 127×112, (a) 350 s. The Mickeymobile. (b) 350 s. Cruella De Vil and dog wagon from *101 Dalmations* .. *Set of* 2 *sheets* 3·50 3·75

159 "St. Mary Magdalen in Penitence" (detail)

160 Klinsmann of West Germany

(Litho Questa)

1990 (7 Nov). *Paintings by Titian. T* **159** *and similar vert designs. Multicoloured. P* 13½×14.

780 5 s. Type **159** 10 10
781 10 s. "Averoldi Polyptych" (detail) .. 10 10
782 15 s. "Saint Margaret" (detail) 10 10
783 50 s. "Venus and Adonis" (detail) .. 25 30
784 75 s. "Venus and the Lutenist" (detail) .. 35 40
785 100 s. "Tarquin and Lucretia" (detail) .. 50 55
786 125 s. "Saint Jerome" (detail) 60 65
787 150 s. "Madonna and Child in Glory with Saints" (detail) 75 80
780/7 .. .. *Set of* 8 2·40 2·50
MS788 Three sheets. (a) 95×110 mm. 300 s. "Adoration of the Holy Trinity" (detail). (b) 95×110 mm. 300 s. "St. Catherine of Alexandria at Prayer" (detail). (c) 110×95 mm. 300 s. "The Supper at Emmaus" (detail) .. *Set of* 3 *sheets* 4·50 4·75

(Des Young Phillips Studio. Litho Questa)

1990 (17 Nov). *World Cup Football Championship, Italy* (2nd *issue*). *T* **160** *and similar vert designs. Multicoloured. P* 14.

789 10 s. Type **160** 10 10
790 60 s. Serena of Italy 30 35
791 100 s. Nicol of Scotland 50 55
792 300 s. Susic of Yugoslavia .. .. .. 1·50 1·60
789/92 .. .. *Set of* 4 2·10 2·25
MS793 Two sheets, each 85×95 mm. (a) 400 s. Montero of Costa Rica. (b) 400 s. Seifo of Belgium *Set of* 2 *sheets* 4·00 4·25

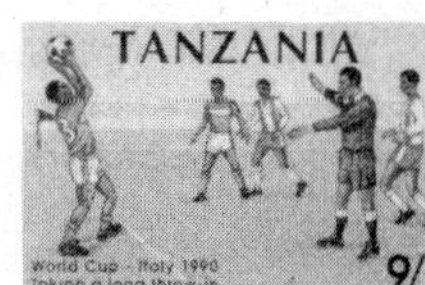

161 Throw-in

(Litho Questa)

1990 (17 Nov). *World Cup Football Championship, Italy* (3rd *issue*). *T* **161** *and similar horiz designs. Multicoloured. P* 14.

794 9 s. Type **161** 10 10
795 13 s. Penalty kick 10 10
796 25 s. Dribbling 10 10
797 100 s. Corner kick 50 55
794/7 .. .. *Set of* 4 65 70
MS798 82×82 mm. 50 s. World Cup and world map 25 30

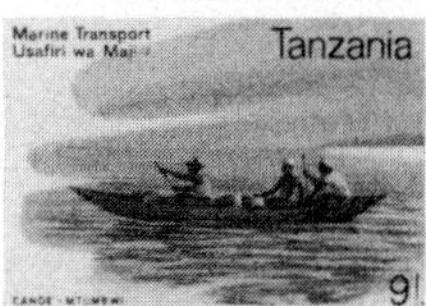

162 Dugout Canoe

(Des M. Raza. Litho State Ptg Works, Moscow)

1990 (24 Nov). *Marine Transport. T* **162** *and similar horiz designs. Multicoloured. P* 12½×12.

799 9 s. Type **162** 10 10
800 13 s. Sailing canoe 10 10
801 25 s. Dhow 10 15
802 100 s. Freighter 50 55
799/802 .. .. *Set of* 4 65 70
MS803 90×90 mm. 40 s. Mashua dhow .. 20 25

ALTERED CATALOGUE NUMBERS

Any Catalogue numbers altered from the last edition are shown as a list in the introductory pages.

163 Lesser Masked Weaver

164 Lesser Flamingo

(Litho Questa)

1990 (15 Dec). *Birds. Horiz designs as T* **163** (5 *s. to* 25 *s.*) *or* **164** (40 *s. to* 500 *s.*). *Multicoloured. P* 14.

804 5 s. Type **163** 10 10
a. Booklet pane. Nos. 804/9 each × 2 with margins all round 80
805 9 s. African Emerald Cuckoo 10 10
806 13 s. Little Bee Eater 10 10
807 15 s. Red Bishop 10 10
808 20 s. Bateleur 10 15
809 25 s. Scarlet-chested Sunbird 10 15
810 40 s. Type **164** 20 25
811 70 s. Helmet Guineafowl 35 40
812 100 s. Eastern White Pelican 50 55
813 170 s. Saddle-bill Stork 85 90
814 200 s. South African Crowned Crane .. 1·00 1·10
815 500 s. Ostrich .. .. 2·50 2·75
804/15 .. .. *Set of* 12 5·25 5·75
MS816 100×102 mm. 40 s. Superb Starling; 60 s. Lilac-breasted Roller 50 55

165 Athletics

(Des P. Ndembo. Litho Questa)

1990 (29 Dec). *14th Commonwealth Games, Auckland, New Zealand. T* **165** *and similar multicoloured designs. P* 14.

817 9 s. Type **165** 10 10
818 13 s. Netball (*vert*) 10 10
819 25 s. Pole vaulting 10 15
820 100 s. Long jumping (*vert*) 50 55
817/20 .. .. *Set of* 4 65 70
MS821 100×100 mm. 40 s. Boxing (*vert*) .. 20 25

OFFICIAL STAMPS

(Opt photo Harrison)

1965 (9 Dec). *Nos.* 128/32, 134, 136, 139 *optd as Types* O 1 (15 c., 30 c. *or larger* (17 *mm*) 5 c., 10 c., 20 c., 50 c.), *or with* O **2** *of Tanganyika* (1 *s*., 5 *s*.).

No.	Description	Mint	Used
O 9	5 c. ultramarine and yellow-orange	10	10
O10	10 c. black, greenish yellow, green & blue	10	10
O11	15 c. multicoloured	10	10
O12	20 c. sepia, grey-green and greenish blue	10	10
O13	30 c. black and red-brown	10	10
O14	50 c. multicoloured	15	10
O15	1 s. multicoloured	30	10
O16	5 s. lake-brown, yellow-green and blue	1·50	2·25
O9/16	*Set of* 8	2·00	2·50

OFFICIAL

(O 3) (3 mm tall)

(Opt litho Govt Printer, Dar-es-Salaam)

1967 (10–18 Nov). *Nos.* 134, 136 *and* 139 *optd as No.* O14 (50 *c.*) *or with Type* O **3** (*others*).

No.	Description	Mint	Used
O17	50 c. multicoloured (18.11)		
O18	1 s. multicoloured (18.11)	13·00	3·00
O19	5 s. lake-brown, yellow-green and blue	9·00	5·50

The issue dates given are for the earliest known postmarked copies.

Nos. O9/16 were overprinted by Harrison in photogravure and Nos. O17/19 have litho overprints by the Government Printer, Dar-es-Salaam. On No. O17 the overprint is the same size (17 mm long) as on No. O14.

1967 (9 Dec)–**71**. *Nos.* 142/6, 148, 151 *and* 155 *optd as Type* O **1**, *but larger* (*measuring* 17 *mm*) (5 *c. to* 50 *c.*) *or as Type* O **2** *of Tanganyika* (1 *s. and* 5 *s.*). *Chalk-surfaced paper.*

No.	Description	Mint	Used
O20	5 c. magenta, yellow-olive and black	10	40
	a. Glazed, ordinary paper (22.1.71)	1·25	1·25
O21	10 c. brown and bistre	10	15
O22	15 c. grey, turquoise-blue and black	10	30
	a. Glazed, ordinary paper (22.1.71)	1·25	1·75
O23	20 c. brown and turquoise-green	10	10
O24	30 c. sage-green and black	10	10
O25	50 c. multicoloured	15	20
	a. Glazed, ordinary paper (22.1.71)	1·50	1·00
O26	1 s. orange-brown, slate-blue and maroon	30	40
	a. Glazed, ordinary paper (3.2.71)	2·00	1·00
O27	5 s. greenish yellow, black & turquoise-grn.	2·25	3·50
	a. Glazed, ordinary paper (3.2.71)	4·50	6·00
O20/7	*Set of* 8	2·75	4·50

The chalk-surfaced paper exists with both PVA gum and gum arabic, but the glazed, ordinary paper exists PVA gum only.

OFFICIAL (O 4) **OFFICIAL** (O 5)

1970 (10 Dec)–**73**. *Nos.* 142/8, 151 *and* 155 *optd locally by letterpress as Type* O 4 (5 *to* 50 *c.*) *or as Type* O **2** *of Tanganyika, but measuring* 28 *mm* (1 *s. and* 5 *s.*).

(*a*) *Chalk-surfaced paper*

No.	Description	Mint	Used
O28	5 c. magenta, yellow-olive and black	10	50
	a. "OFFCIAL" (R.7/6)		
O29	10 c. brown and bistre	10	15
	a. "OFFCIAL" (R.7/6)		
O30	20 c. brown and turquoise-green	20	40
O31	30 c. sage-green and black	25	40
O28/31	*Set of* 4	55	1·25

(*b*) *Glazed, ordinary paper* (1973)

No.	Description	Mint	Used
O32	5 c. magenta, yellow-olive and black	—	1·25
	a. "OFFCIAL" (R.7/6)	—	22·00
	b. "OFFICIA" (R.10/9)	—	22·00
O33	10 c. brown and bistre		
	a. "OFFCIAL" (R.7/6)		
O34	15 c. grey, turquoise-blue and black		
	a. "OFFCIAL" (R.7/6)		
O35	20 c. brown and turquoise-green		
O36	40 c. yellow, chocolate and bright green	—	2·25
	a. Opt double		
	b. "OFFICIA" (R.10/9)	—	45·00
O37	50 c. multicoloured	—	1·75
	a. "OFFCIAL" (R.7/6)	—	35·00
O38	1 s. orange-brown, slate-blue and maroon		
	a. Opt double		
O39	5 s. greenish yellow, black & turquoise-grn		

The letterpress overprint can be distinguished from the photogravure by its absence of screening dots and the overprint showing through to the reverse, apart from the difference in length.

1973 (10 Dec). *Nos.* 158/9, 161, 163/4 *and* 166/70 *optd with Type* O 1 *of Tanganyika* (5 *to* 70 *c.*) *or Type* O 5 (*others*).

No.	Description	Mint	Used
O40	5 c. light yellow-olive, lt violet-blue & black	30	40
O41	10 c. multicoloured	40	10
O42	20 c. reddish cinnamon, orange-yellow & blk	50	10
O43	40 c. multicoloured	70	20
O44	50 c. multicoloured	75	20
O45	70 c. turquoise-green, pale orange and black	1·00	50
O46	1 s. multicoloured	1·00	20
O47	1 s. 50, multicoloured	2·00	1·25
	a. Pair, one without opt	†	—
O48	2 s. 50, multicoloured	2·25	2·25
O49	5 s. multicoloured	3·00	3·25
O40/9	*Set of* 10	11·00	7·50

No. O47a is due to a paper fold and comes from a sheet used at Kigoma in 1974.

1977 (Feb). *Nos.* 159, 161 *and* 163/4 *optd locally by letterpress as Type* O **4**.

No.	Description	Mint	Used
O50	10 c. multicoloured	—	1·75
	a. "OFFCIAL" (R. 7/6)	—	35·00
O51	20 c. multicoloured	—	1·75
	a. "OFFCIAL" (R. 7/6)	—	35·00
	b. Opt inverted		
	c. Opt double		
O52	40 c. multicoloured	—	2·25
	a. "OFFCIAL" (R. 7/6)	—	45·00
O53	50 c. multicoloured	—	2·25
	a. "OFFCIAL" (R. 7/6)	—	45·00
	b. Opt inverted		

OFFICIAL (O 6) OFFICIAL (O 7)

1980 (Nov)–**85**. *Nos.* 307/12 *optd with Type* O **6**, *and Nos.* 313/17 *optd with Type* O **7**.

No.	Description	Mint	Used
O54	10 c. Type **75**	15	10
O55	20 c. Large-spotted Genet	20	15
O56	40 c. Banded Mongoose	20	15
O57	50 c. Ratel	20	15
O58	75 c. Large-toothed Rock Hyrax	30	30
O59	80 c. Leopard	35	35
O60	1 s. Type **76**	35	15
O61	1 s. 50, Giraffe (29.8.85)*	1·50	1·75
O62	2 s. Common Zebra	55	55
O63	3 s. African Buffalo	65	70
O64	5 s. Lion	85	95
O54/64	*Set of* 11	4·75	4·75

*Earliest known postmark date.

On the stamps overprinted with Types O **6** and O **7** the overprint reads downwards on the 10 c., 50 c., 2 s. and 5 s. and upwards on the others.

OFFICIAL (O 8) **OFFICIAL** (O 9)

1990 (15 Dec). *Nos.* 804/12 *optd with Type* O **8** (5 *s. to* 25 *s.*) *or Type* O **9** (40 *s. to* 100 *s.*).

No.	Description	Mint	Used
O65	5 s. Type **163**	10	10
O66	9 s. African Emerald Cuckoo	10	10
O67	13 s. Little Bee Eater	10	10
O68	15 s. Red Bishop	10	10
O69	20 s. Bateleur	10	15
O70	25 s. Scarlet-chested Sunbird	10	15
O71	40 s. Type **164**	20	25
O72	70 s. Helmet Guineafowl	35	40
O73	100 s. Eastern White Pelican	50	55
O65/73	*Set of* 9	1·25	1·50

POSTAGE DUE STAMPS

Postage Due stamps of Kenya and Uganda were issued for provisional use as such in Tanganyika on 1 July 1933. The postmark is the only means of identification.

The Postage Due stamps of Kenya, Uganda and Tanganyika were used in Tanganyika until 2 January 1967.

D 1

D 2

(Litho D.L.R.)

1967 (3 Jan). *P* 14 × 13½.

No.	Type	Description	Mint	Used
D1	D 1	5 c. scarlet	35	3·75
D2		10 c. green	45	4·00
D3		20 c. deep blue	70	5·00
D4		30 c. red-brown	70	5·50
D5		40 c. bright purple	70	7·00
D6		1 s. orange	1·25	9·00
D1/6		*Set of* 6	3·75	30·00

1969–71. *As Nos.* D1/6, *but perf* 14 × 15.

A. *Chalk-surfaced paper* (19.12.69).

B. *Glazed, ordinary paper* (13.7.71).

No.	Type	Description	A Mint	A Used	B Mint	B Used
D 7	D 1	5 c. scarlet	25	3·50	2·50	4·75
D 8		10 c. green	40	3·50	75	3·25
D 9		20 c. deep blue	40	4·25	1·75	5·50
D10		30 c. red-brown	50	7·50	85	4·00
D11		40 c. bright purple	1·00	8·00	4·50	13·00
D12		1 s. orange	†		4·50	16·00
D7/11A		*Set of* 5	2·25	24·00		
D7B/12B		*Set of* 6			13·50	42·00

The stamps on chalk-surfaced paper exist only with gum arabic, but the stamps on glazed paper exist only with PVA gum.

1973 (12 Dec). *As Nos.* D1/6, *but glazed ordinary paper. P* 15.

No.	Type	Description	Mint	Used
D13	D 1	5 c. scarlet	50	4·25
D14		10 c. emerald	50	4·25
D15		20 c. deep blue	70	5·00
D16		30 c. red-brown	75	5·50
D17		40 c. bright mauve	75	7·50
D18		1 s. bright orange	1·25	9·50
D13/18		*Set of* 6	4·00	32·00

(Litho Questa)

1978 (31 July). *Chalky paper. P* 13½ × 14.

No.	Type	Description	Mint	Used
D19	D 1	5 c. brown-red	10	70
D20		10 c. emerald	10	70
D21		20 c. steel-blue	15	90
D22		30 c. red-brown	20	1·25
D23		40 c. bright purple	25	1·40
D24		1 s. bright orange	35	1·75
D19/24		*Set of* 6	1·00	6·00

(Litho Questa)

1990 (15 Dec). *P* 14½×14.

No.	Type	Description	Mint	Used
D25	D 2	50 c. myrtle-green	10	10
D26		80 c. ultramarine	10	10
D27		1 s. orange-brown	10	10
D28		2 s. yellow-olive	10	10
D29		3 s. purple	10	10
D30		5 s. grey-brown	10	10
D31		10 s. reddish brown	10	10
D32		20 s. brown-ochre	10	15
D25/32		*Set of* 8	40	45

Appendix

The following stamps have either been issued in excess of postal needs, or have not been made available to the public in reasonable quantities at face value. Miniature sheets, imperforate stamps, etc., are excluded from this section.

1986

Caribbean Royal Visit. Optd on previous issues. (*a*) *On Nos.* 425/8 20 *s.* × 2, 100 *s.* × 2. (*b*) *On Nos.* 430/3 5, 10, 20, 30 *s.* *"Ameripex" International Stamp Exhibition, Chicago. Optd on Nos.* 425/8. 20 *s.* × 2, 100 *s.* × 2.

1988

Centenary of Statue of Liberty (1986). 1, 2, 3, 4, 5, 6, 7, 8, 10, 12, 15, 18, 20, 25, 30, 35, 40, 45, 50, 60 *s.*

Royal Ruby Wedding. Optd on No. 378. 10 *s.*

125*th Anniv of Red Cross. Optd on Nos.* 486/7. 5, 40 *s.*

63*rd Anniv of Rotary International in Africa. Optd on Nos.* 422/3. 10 *s.*, 17 *s.* 50.

Tasmania
see Australia

Togo

The stamps of GERMANY were used in the colony from March 1888 until June 1897 when issues for TOGO were provided.

PRICES FOR STAMPS ON COVER

Nos. H1/22	*from* × 6
Nos. H23/33	—
Nos. H34/58	*from* × 6

ANGLO-FRENCH OCCUPATION

British and French forces invaded Togo on 12 August 1914 and the German administration surrendered on 26 August 1914.

***Stamps of German Colonial issue Types* A *and* B 1900 *and* 1909–14 (5 *pf. and* 10 *pf.*)**

TOGO
Anglo-French
Occupation
(1)

Half penny
(2)

SETTINGS. Nos. H1/33 were all overprinted or surcharged by the Catholic Mission, Lome.

The initial setting for the 3 pf. to 80 pf. was of 50 (10×5), repeated twice on each sheet of 100. Overprints from this setting, used for Nos. H1/9, had the lines of type 3 mm apart.

Nos. H1/2 were subsequently surcharged, also from a setting of 50, to form Nos. H12/13. The surcharge setting showed a thin dropped "y" with small serifs on R. 1/1–2, 2/1, 3/1, 4/1 and 5/1–2.

The type from the overprint and surcharge was then amalgamated in a new setting of 50 on which the lines of the overprint were only 2 mm apart. On this amalgamated setting, used for Nos. H27/8, the thin "y" varieties were still present and R. 4/7 showed the second "O" of "TOGO" omitted.

The surcharge was subsequently removed from this "2 mm" setting which was then used to produce Nos. H17/19. The missing "O" was spotted and corrected before any of the 30 pf. stamps were overprinted.

The remaining low values of the second issue, Nos. H14/16 and H20/2, were overprinted from settings of 25 (5×5), either taken from the last setting of 50 or from an amended version on which there was no space either side of the hyphen. This slightly narrower overprint was subsequently used for Nos. H29/33. It shows the top of the second "O" broken so that it resembles a "U" on R. 1/5.

The mark values were overprinted from settings of 20 (5×4), showing the same differences in the spacing of the lines as on the low values.

It is believed that odd examples of some German colonial values were overprinted from individual settings in either spacing.

1914 (24 Sept). *Optd with T* **1** *by Catholic Mission, Lome. Wide setting. Lines 3 mm apart.*

H 1	3 pf. brown	£110	95·00
H 2	5 pf. green	£100	90·00
H 3	10 pf. carmine (Wmk Lozenges)	£120	£100
	a. Opt inverted	£7500	£4000
	b. Opt *tête-bêche* in vert pair	†	£6500
	c. No wmk	†	£5500
H 4	20 pf. ultramarine	28·00	25·00
H 5	25 pf. black and red/*yellow*	28·00	23·00
H 6	30 pf. black and orange/*buff*	30·00	32·00
H 7	40 pf. black and carmine	£225	£250
H 8	50 pf. black and purple/*buff*	£9000	£7000
H 9	80 pf. black and carmine/*rose*	£250	£275
H10	1 m. carmine	£5000	£2500
H11	2 m. blue	£7500	£8000
	a. "Occupation" double	£12000	£10000
	b. Opt inverted	£9500	

The *tête-bêche* overprint on the 10 pf. is due to the sheet being turned round after the upper 50 stamps had been overprinted so that vertical pairs from the two middle rows have the overprint *tête-bêche*.

1914 (1 Oct). *Nos.* H1 *and* H2 *surch as T* **2**.

H12	½d. on 3 pf. brown	£200	£200
	a. Thin "y" in "penny"	£500	£475
H13	1d. on 5 pf. green	£200	£200
	a. Thin "y" in "penny"	£500	£475

TOGO
Anglo-French
Occupation
(3)

TOGO
Anglo-French
Occupation
Half penny
(4)

1914 (Oct). (*a*) *Optd with T* **3**. *Narrow Setting. Lines 2 mm apart.*

H14	3 pf. brown	£4000	£700
H15	5 pf. green	£850	£550
H16	10 pf. carmine	†	£1400
H17	20 pf. ultramarine	14·00	12·00
	a. "TOG"	£4000	£4000
	b. Nos. H4 and H17 *se-tenant* (vert pair)	£6500	
H18	25 pf. black and red/*yellow*	19·00	27·00
	a. "TOG"	£12000	
H19	30 pf. black and orange/*buff*	19·00	27·00
H20	40 pf. black and carmine	£4000	£1200
H21	50 pf. black and purple/*buff*	†	£5500
H22	80 pf. black and carmine/*rose*	£1700	£1700
H23	1 m. carmine	£7000	£3750
H24	2 m. blue	†	£7500
H25	3 m. violet-black	†	£30000
H26	5 m. lake and black	†	£30000

(*b*) *Narrow setting, but including value, as T* **4**

H27	½d. on 3 pf. brown	26·00	26·00
	a. "TOG"	£425	£300
	b. Thin "y" in "penny"	55·00	55·00
H28	1d. on 5 pf. green	4·00	4·25
	a. "TOG"	£130	£110
	b. Thin "y" in "penny"	12·00	15·00

In the 20 pf. one half of a sheet was overprinted with the wide setting (3 mm), and the other half with the narrow setting (2 mm), so that vertical pairs from the middle of the sheet show the two varieties of the overprint.

TOGO
Anglo-French
Occupation
(6)

TOGO
ANGLO-FRENCH
OCCUPATION
(7)

TOGO
ANGLO-FRENCH
OCCUPATION
(8)

1915 (7 Jan). *Optd as T* **6**. *The words* "Anglo-French" *measure* 15 *mm instead of* 16 *mm as in T* **3**.

H29	3 pf. brown	£6000	£2500
H30	5 pf. green	£200	£130
	a. "Occupation" omitted	£6000	
H31	10 pf. carmine	£200	£130
	a. No wmk	†	£7000
H32	20 pf. ultramarine	£1400	£475
H32*a*	40 pf. black and carmine	†	£7500
H33	50 pf. black and purple/*buff*	£9500	£6500

This printing was made on another batch of German Togo stamps, found at Sansane-Mangu.

Stamps of Gold Coast overprinted

1915 (May). *Stamps of Gold Coast, optd locally with T* **7** ("OCCUPATION" 14½ *mm long*).

H34	**9**	½d. green	25	60
		g. Opt double	£300	£400
H35	**10**	1d. red	25	30
		g. Opt double	£250	£350
		h. Opt inverted	£130	£180
		ha. Ditto. "TOGO" omitted		
H36	**11**	2d. greyish slate	30	40
H37	**9**	2½d. bright blue	40	60
H38	**11**	3d. purple/*yellow*	65	80
		a. White back	3·50	7·00
H40		6d. dull and bright purple	65	1·75
H41	**9**	1s. black/*green*	1·25	3·00
		g. Opt double	£450	
H42		2s. purple and blue/*blue*	5·50	7·00
H43	**11**	2s. 6d. black and red/*blue*	4·50	9·50
H44	**9**	5s. green and red/*yellow* (*white back*)	8·00	12·00
H45		10s. green and red/*green*	32·00	45·00
H46		20s. purple and black/*red*	£120	£120
H34/46		*Set of* 12	£150	£170

Varieties (Nos. indicate positions in pane).
A. *Small* "F" *in* "FRENCH" (25, 58 *and* 59).
B. *Thin* "G" *in* "TOGO" (24).
C. *No hyphen after* "ANGLO" (5).
D. *Two hyphens after* "ANGLO" (5).
E. "CUPATION" *for* "OCCUPATION" (33).
F. "CCUPATION" *for* "OCCUPATION" (57).

Varieties C and E also occur together on position 28 of the ½d. value only.

Prices are for unused. Used are worth more

		A	B	C	D	E	F
H34	½d.	1·50	3·00	3·00	†	80·00	42·00
H35	1d.	1·75	4·25	4·25	†	†	£100
	h. Inverted	£600	£1200	£1200	†	†	†
H36	2d.	1·75	5·50	48·00	25·00	†	£100
H37	2½d.	2·50	6·00	24·00	30·00	†	90·00
H38	3d.	2·50	6·00	30·00	†	†	£100
	a. White back	14·00	40·00	†	†	†	†
H40	6d.	4·25	8·00	†	†	†	£150
H41	1s.	4·25	9·00	†	†	†	80·00
H42	2s.	18·00	30·00	80·00	†	†	£200
H43	2s. 6d.	18·00	30·00	85·00	†	†	£375
H44	5s.	25·00	42·00	£110	†	†	£200
H45	10s.	70·00	£120	†	†	†	£350
H46	20s.	£225	£325	†	†	†	£500

1916 (Apr). *London opt T* **8** ("OCCUPATION" 15 *mm long*). *Heavy type and thicker letters showing through on back.*

H47	**9**	½d. green	15	60
H48	**10**	1d. red	15	40
H49	**11**	2d. greyish slate	35	45
H50	**9**	2½d. bright blue	45	90
H51	**11**	3d. purple/*yellow*	55	70
H52		6d. dull and bright purple	55	1·00
H53	**9**	1s. black/*green*	1·25	1·50
		a. On blue-green, olive back	3·25	4·50
		b. On emerald back	£180	£275
H54		2s. purple and blue/*blue*	4·50	5·50
H55	**11**	2s. 6d. black and red/*blue*	4·50	6·00
H56	**9**	5s. green and red/*yellow*	8·00	18·00
		a. On orange-buff	8·00	22·00
H57		10s. green and red/*green*	24·00	50·00
		a. On blue-green, olive back	16·00	40·00
H58		20s. purple and black/*red*	£120	£120
H47/58		*Set of* 12	£140	£160
H47/58 Optd "Specimen"		*Set of* 12	£300	

Tokelau
see after New Zealand

Tonga

The Tongan Post Office was established in 1885 and FIJI 2d. and 6d. stamps are recorded in use until the arrival of Nos. 1/4.

PRICES FOR STAMPS ON COVER TO 1945

Nos. 1/4	*from* × 20
Nos. 5/9	*from* × 10
Nos. 10/28	*from* × 5
Nos. 29/32	*from* × 4
Nos. 33/7	*from* × 5
Nos. 38/54	*from* × 4
Nos. 55/63	*from* × 6
Nos. 64/70	*from* × 3
Nos. 71/87	*from* × 2

The Official stamps, Nos. O1/10, are very rare used on cover.

PROTECTORATE KINGDOM
King George I, 1845–93

1 King George I

2

(Eng Bock and Cousins. Plates made and typo Govt Ptg Office, Wellington)

1886–88. *W* **2**. *P* 12½ (*line*) *or* 12 × 11½ (*comb*)*.

1	**1**	1d. carmine (*p* 12½) (27.8.86)	£200	6·00
		a. Perf 12½ × 10		
		b. Perf 12 × 11½ (15.7.87)	10·00	3·25
		ba. Pale carmine (*p* 12 × 11½)	16·00	8·00
2		2d. pale violet (*p* 12½) (27.8.86)	35·00	10·00
		a. Bright violet	55·00	3·50
		b. Perf 12 × 11½ (15.7.87)	24·00	2·75
		ba. Bright violet (*p* 12 × 11½)	24·00	3·00
3		6d. blue (*p* 12½) (9.10.86)	38·00	2·25
		a. Perf 12 × 11½ (15.10.88)	32·00	2·25
		ab. Dull blue (*p* 12 × 11½)	16·00	2·25
4		1s. pale green (*p* 12½) (9.10.86)	75·00	4·00
		a. Deep green (*p* 12½)	80·00	2·25
		b. Perf 12 × 11½ (15.10.88)	40·00	6·00
		ba. Deep green (*p* 12 × 11½)	40·00	3·25

*See note after New Zealand, No. 186.

FOUR
PENCE.
(3)

EIGHT
PENCE.
(4)

(Surch Messrs Wilson & Horton, Auckland, N.Z.)

1891 (10 Nov). *Nos.* 1b *and* 2b *surch.*

5	**3**	4d. on 1d. carmine	2·00	10·00
		a. No stop after "PENCE"	38·00	70·00
6	**4**	8d. on 2d. violet	35·00	70·00
		a. Short "T" in "EIGHT"	£110	£160

No. 5a occurred on R. 6/8 and 9, R. 10/11, all from the righthand pane.

1891 (23 Nov). *Optd with stars in upper right and lower left corners. P* 12½.

7	**1**	1d. carmine	35·00	45·00
		a. Three stars	£180	
		b. Four stars	£250	
		c. Five stars	£400	
		d. Perf 12 × 11½	£170	
		da. Three stars	£325	
		db. Four stars	£375	
		dc. Five stars	£600	
8		2d. violet	42·00	38·00
		a. Perf 12 × 11½	£180	

1892 (15 Aug). *W* **2**. *P* 12 × 11½.

9	**1**	6d. yellow-orange	11·00	22·00

5 Arms of Tonga

6 King George I

(Dies eng A. E. Cousins. Typo at Govt Printing Office, Wellington, N.Z.)

1892 (10 Nov). *W* **2**. *P* 12 × 11½.

No.	Type	Description	Unused	Used
10	**5**	1d. pale rose	12·00	16·00
		a. Bright rose	12·00	16·00
		b. Bisected diag (½d.) (1893) (on cover)	†	£650
11	**6**	2d. olive	11·00	15·00
12	**5**	4d. chestnut	32·00	48·00
13	**6**	8d. bright mauve	48·00	80·00
14		1s. brown	60·00	80·00
10/14		*Set of* 5	£150	£225

No. 10b was used from 31 May 1893 to provide a 2½d. rate before the arrival of No. 15, and on subsequent occasions up to 1895.

½ d. (7) 2½d. (8) FIVE PENCE. (9) 7½d. (10)

1893. *Printed in new colours and surch with T* **7/10** *by Govt Printing Office, Wellington. (a) In carmine. P* 12½ (21 Aug).

No.	Type	Description	Unused	Used
15	**5**	½d. on 1d. bright ultramarine	23·00	23·00
		a. Surch omitted		
16	**6**	2½d. on 2d. green	14·00	12·00
17	**5**	5d. on 4d. orange	4·00	6·50
18	**6**	7½d. on 8d. carmine	24·00	65·00

(*b*) *In black. P* 12 × 11½ (Nov)

No.	Type	Description	Unused	Used
19	**5**	½d. on 1d. dull blue	45·00	48·00
20	**6**	2½d. on 2d. green	17·00	17·00
		a. Surch double	—	£950

SURCHARGE. HALF-PENNY (11) SURCHARGE, 2½d. (12)

(Surch at the *Star* Office, Auckland, N.Z.)

1894. *Surch with T* **11** *or* **12**.

No.	Type	Description	Unused	Used
21	**5**	½d. on 4d. chestnut (B.)	1·50	7·00
		a. "SURCHARCE"	7·50	16·00
22	**6**	½d. on 1s. brown (June)	1·50	11·00
		a. "SURCHARCE"	10·00	35·00
		b. Surch double	£300	
		c. Surch double with "SURCHARCE"	£900	
23		2½d. on 8d. bright mauve	5·00	9·50
		a. No stop after "SURCHARGE"	32·00	50·00
		b. "2½d." omitted		
24		2½d. on 1s. green (No. 4*a*) (June)	27·00	20·00
		a. No stop after "SURCHARGE"	85·00	
		b. Perf 12×11½	15·00	28·00
		ba. No stop after "SURCHARGE"	55·00	

Nos. 21/4 were surcharged in panes of 60 (6 × 10) with Nos. 21a and 22a occurring on R. 1/6, 3/6, 5/6, 8/6, and 10/6, 23a on R. 3/1–3 and 24a and 24ba on R. 6/3 and R. 7/3 or R. 7/1–2.

(Design resembling No. 11 litho and surch at *Star* Office, Auckland, N.Z.)

1895 (June). *As T* **6** *surch as T* **11** *and* **12**. *No wmk. P* 12.

No.	Type	Description	Unused	Used
25	**11**	1d. on 2d. pale blue (C.)	29·00	22·00
26	**12**	1½d. on 2d. pale blue (C.)	40·00	27·00
		a. Perf 12 × 11	35·00	27·00
27		2½d. on 2d. pale blue (C.)*	40·00	45·00
		a. No stop after "SURCHARGE"	£225	£225
28		7½d. on 2d. pale blue (C.)	£225	
		a. Perf 12 × 11	55·00	45·00

*The 2½d. on 2d. is the only value which normally has a stop after the word "SURCHARGE".

No. 27a occurs on R. 1/3 of the right-hand pane.

King George II, 1893–1918

13 King George II

Half Penny VAEUA OE PENI (14)

(Litho *Star* Office, Auckland, N.Z.)

1895 (16 Aug). *No wmk. P* 12.

No.	Type	Description	Unused	Used
29	**13**	1d. olive-green	15·00	20·00
		a. Bisected diagonally (½d.) (on cover)	†	£650
		b. Imperf between (horiz pair)	—	£5500
30		2½d. rose	20·00	20·00
		a. Stop (flaw) after "POSTAGE"	60·00	60·00
31		5d. blue	13·00	35·00
		a. Perf 12×11	15·00	35·00
		b. Perf 11	£325	
32		7½d. orange-yellow	20·00	35·00
		a. Yellow	20·00	35·00

1895 (Sept). *T* **13** *redrawn and surch. No wmk. P* 12.

No.	Type	Description	Unused	Used
33	**11**	½d. on 2½d. vermilion	30·00	32·00
		a. "SURCHARCE"	70·00	
		b. Stop after "POSTAGE"	75·00	
34		1d. on 2½d. vermilion	35·00	28·00
		a. Stop after "POSTAGE"	75·00	
35	**12**	7½d. on 2½d. vermilion	48·00	48·00
		a. Stop after "POSTAGE"	90·00	

In the ½d. surcharge there is a stop after "SURCHARGE" and not after "PENNY". In the 1d. and 7½d. the stop is after the value only.

1896 (May). *Nos.* 26a *and* 28a *with typewritten surcharge* "Half-Penny-", *in violet, and Tongan surcharge, in black, as T* **14**.

A. *Tongan surch reading downwards (right panes)*
B. *Tongan surch reading upwards (left panes)*

No.	Type	Description	A Unused	A Used	B Unused	B Used
36	**6**	½d. on 1½d. on 2d.	£250	—	£250	—
		a. Perf 12	£200	£200	£225	£225
		ab. "Haalf" (*p* 12)	†		£850	—
		c. "H" double	†		—	—
		d. Tongan surch omitted	†		£2250	—
37		½d. on 7½d. on 2d.	50·00	70·00	50·00	70·00
		a. "Hafl" for "Half"	£650	£700	†	
		b. "Hafl" ("Penny" omitted)	£950	—	†	
		c. "PPenny"	£350	—	†	
		d. Stops instead of hyphens	£325	—	£425	—
		e. "Halyf"	—	—	†	
		f. "Half-Penny-" inverted	£1100	—	£1500	—
		g. No hyphen after "Penny"	—	—	†	
		h. "Hwlf"	†		—	—
		j. "Penny" double	†		—	—
		k. "Penny" twice, with "Half" on top of upper "Penny"	†		£1100	—
		l. Capital "P" over small "p"	—	—	†	
		m. Perf 12	£350	—	£400	—
		ma. No hyphen after "Half" (*p* 12)	—	—	†	
		mb. Tongan surch double	†		£1200	—

Nos. 26a and 28a were in sheets of 48 (2 panes 6×4). The panes were separated before the surcharges were applied.

There are variations in the relative positions of the words "Half" and "Penny", both vertically and horizontally.

15 Arms

16 Ovava Tree, Kana-Kubolu

17 King George II

18 Prehistoric Trilith at Haamonga

19 Bread Fruit

20 Coral

21 View of Haapai

22 Red Shining Parrot

23 View of Vavau Harbour

I No sword hilt

II Top of hilt showing

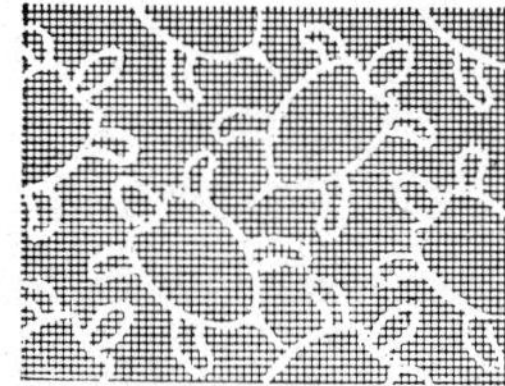

24 Tortoises (*upright*)

WATERMARKS. Stamps with W **24** upright show all the tortoise heads pointing upwards, or downwards if inverted. On stamps with sideways watermark the heads point upwards or downwards alternately.

(Recess D.L.R.)

1897 (1 June). *W* **24**. *P* 14.

No.	Type	Description	Unused	Used
38	**15**	½d. indigo	1·50	1·75
		a. Wmk sideways	70	90
39	**16**	1d. black and scarlet	80	50
		a. Wmk sideways	3·25	1·75
40	**17**	2d. sepia and bistre (I)	6·50	2·50
		a. Wmk sideways	6·50	2·50
41		2d. sepia and bistre (II)	50·00	6·50
		a. Wmk sideways	35·00	5·50
42		2d. grey and bistre (II)	10·00	1·75
		a. Wmk sideways	4·50	70
43		2½d. black and blue	3·50	70
		a. No fraction bar in "½"	85·00	85·00
		b. Wmk sideways	2·00	1·00
		ba. No fraction bar in "½"	60·00	60·00
44	**18**	3d. black and yellow-green	2·25	3·00
		a. Wmk sideways	2·50	3·25
45	**19**	4d. green and purple	3·75	4·00
		a. Wmk sideways	3·75	4·00
46	**17**	5d. black and orange	18·00	9·50
		a. Wmk sideways		
47	**20**	6d. red	7·00	3·25
		a. Wmk sideways	6·50	3·00
48	**17**	7½d. black and green	8·00	17·00
		a. Centre inverted	£3250	
49		10d. black and lake	19·00	26·00
		a. Wmk sideways		
50		1s. black and red-brown	9·50	6·00
		a. No hyphen before "TAHA"	£140	£140
		b. Wmk sideways		
51	**21**	2s. black and ultramarine	45·00	50·00
		a. Wmk sideways	18·00	20·00
52	**22**	2s. 6d. deep purple	40·00	26·00
		a. Wmk sideways	55·00	35·00
53	**23**	5s. black and brown-red	40·00	38·00
		a. Wmk sideways	24·00	25·00
38/52		*Set of* 14	£140	£130

The 1d., 3d. and 4d. are known bisected and used for half their value.

T – L 1 June, 1899. (25)

26 Queen Salote

1899 (1 June). *Royal Wedding. No.* 39a *optd with T* **25** *at* "Star" *Office, Auckland, N.Z.*

No.	Type	Description	Unused	Used
54	**16**	1d. black and scarlet	24·00	48·00
		a. "1889" for "1899" (R. 8/1, 8/4)	£200	£275
		b. Wmk upright	32·00	60·00

The Letters "T L" stand for Taufa'ahau, the King's family name, and Lavinia, the bride.

No. 54 was overprinted from a setting of 30 (3×10) applied twice to the sheets of 60.

Queen Salote, 1918–65

Die I

Die II

(Recess D.L.R.)

1920–37. *W* **24** (*sideways*). *P* 14.

No.	Type	Description	Unused	Used
55	**15**	½d. yellow-green (1934)	20	80
		a. Wmk upright	5·50	6·50
56	**26**	1½d. grey-black (1935)	20	1·50
57		2d. slate-purple and violet	3·00	12·00
		a. Wmk upright	7·00	18·00
57*b*		2d. black and dull purple (Die I) (1924)	4·00	65
		ba. Wmk upright		
		c. Die II (1937)	2·50	2·00

58 **26** 2½d. black and blue .. .. .. 2·75 18·00
59 2½d. bright ultramarine (1934) .. 50 40
60 5d. black and orange-vermilion .. 3·25 3·25
61 7½d. black and yellow-green .. .. 1·75 1·75
62 10d. black and lake .. .. .. 1·25 4·50
63 1s. black and red-brown .. .. 1·25 1·50
a. Wmk upright .. .. .. 9·00 10·00
55/63 .. .. *Set of* 10 15·00 40·00
55/63 Optd/Perf "Specimen" .. *Set of* 9 £170

In Die II the ball of the "2" is larger and the word "PENI-E-UA" is re-engraved and slightly shorter; the "U" has a spur on the left side.

TWO PENCE

PENI-E-UA
(27)

TWO PENCE

PENI-E-UA
(28)

1923 (20 Oct)–**24**. *Nos.* 46, 48/9, 50, 51/2 *and* 53a *surch as T* **27** (*vert stamps*) *or* **28** (*horiz stamps*).
64 **17** 2d. on 5d. black and orange (B.) 65 85
a. Wmk sideways .. .. .. 1·50 1·75
65 2d. on 7½d. black and green (B.) .. .. 12·00 20·00
a. Wmk sideways .. .. .. 20·00 30·00
66 2d. on 10d. black and lake (B.) .. .. 4·75 24·00
a. Wmk sideways .. .. .. 10·00 35·00
67 2d. on 1s. black and red-brown (B.) .. 24·00 22·00
a. No hyphen before "TAHA" £275
b. Wmk sideways .. .. .. 32·00 32·00
68 **21** 2d. on 2s. black and ultramarine (R.) .. 6·50 9·00
a. Wmk sideways .. .. .. 3·50 4·50
69 **22** 2d. on 2s. 6d. deep purple (R.) .. .. 17·00 6·50
a. Wmk sideways .. .. .. 55·00 25·00
70 **23** 2d. on 5s. black and brown-red (R.) .. 3·00 3·50
a. Wmk sideways .. .. .. 2·00 2·50
64/70 .. .. *Set of* 7 55·00 70·00

29 Queen Salote

(Recess D.L.R.)

1938 (12 Oct). 20*th Anniv of Queen Salote's Accession. Tablet at foot dated* "1918–1938". *W* **24**. *P* 14.
71 **29** 1d. black and scarlet .. .. .. 55 2·00
72 2d. black and purple .. .. .. 4·25 1·50
73 2½d. black and ultramarine .. .. 4·25 2·00
71/3 .. .. *Set of* 3 8·00 5·00
71/3 Perf "Specimen" .. .. *Set of* 3 65·00

For Silver Jubilee issue in a similar design, see Nos. 83/87.

Die III

(Recess D.L.R.)

1942–49. *Wmk Mult Script CA (sideways on 5s.). P* 14.
74 **15** ½d. yellow-green 15 75
75 **16** 1d. black and scarlet 25 65
76 **26** 2d. black and purple (Die II) 30 35
a. Die III (4.49) .. .. .. 3·50 5·50
77 2½d. bright ultramarine 15 30
78 **18** 3d. black and yellow-green 15 30
79 **20** 6d. red 30 50
80 **26** 1s. black and red-brown .. .. 20 1·00
81 **22** 2s. 6d. deep purple .. .. .. 12·00 16·00
82 **23** 5s. black and brown-red .. .. 14·00 27·00
74/82 .. ..*Set of* 9 25·00 42·00
74/82 Perf "Specimen" .. .. ..*Set of* 9 £170

In Die III the foot of the "2" is longer than in Die II and extends towards the right beyond the curve of the loop; the letters of "PENI-E-UA" are taller and differently shaped.

UANIMA TAU 'OE PULE 'A 'ENE 'AFIO 1918-1943

30

(Recess D.L.R.)

1944 (25 Jan). *Silver Jubilee of Queen Salote's Accession. As T* **29**, *but inscr* "1918–1943" *at foot, as T* **30**. *Wmk Mult Script CA. P* 14.
83 1d. black and carmine 15 15
84 2d. black and purple 15 15
85 3d. black and green 15 15
86 6d. black and orange 15 45
87 1s. black and brown 15 45
83/7 .. .. *Set of* 5 65 1·25
83/7 Perf "Specimen" .. .. *Set of* 5 70·00

1949 (10 Oct). 75*th Anniv of U.P.U. As Nos.* 145/8 *of Jamaica.*
88 2½d. ultramarine 30 10
89 3d. olive 40 90
90 6d. carmine-red 40 20
91 1s. red-brown 40 35
88/91 .. .. *Set of* 4 1·40 1·40

31 Queen Salote **33**

32 Queen Salote

(Photo Waterlow)

1950 (1 Nov). *Queen Salote's Fiftieth Birthday. Wmk Mult Script CA. P* 12½.
92 **31** 1d. carmine 30 30
93 **32** 5d. green 30 30
94 **33** 1s. violet 30 75
92/4 .. .. *Set of* 3 80 1·25

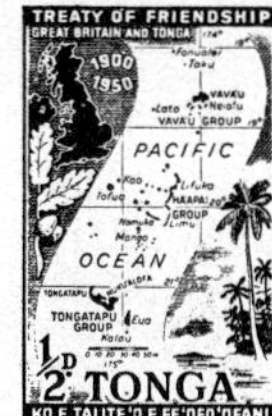

34 Map **35** Palace, Nuku'alofa

(Recess Waterlow)

1951 (2 July). 50*th Anniv of Treaty of Friendship between Great Britain and Tonga. T* **34/5** *and similar designs. Wmk Mult Script CA. P* 12½ (3*d.*), 13 × 13½ (½*d.*), 13½ × 13 (*others*).
95 ½d. green 20 50
96 1d. black and carmine 10 30
97 2½d. green and brown 30 50
98 3d. yellow and bright blue 35 50
99 5d. carmine and green 30 30
100 1s. yellow-orange and violet 30 30
95/100 .. .. *Set of* 6 1·40 2·25

Designs: *Horiz*—2½d. Beach scene; 5d. Flag; 1s. Arms of Tonga and G.B. *Vert*—3d. H.M.N.Z.S. *Bellona*.

40 Royal Palace, Nuku'alofa **43** Swallows' Cave, Vava'u

52 Queen Salote **53** Arms of Tonga

(Des J. Berry. Centre litho, frame recess (£1), recess (others) B.W.)

1953 (1 July). *T* **40**, **43**, **52/3** *and similar designs. W* **24**. *P* 11 × 11½ (*vert*) *or* 11½ × 11 (*horiz*).
101 1d. black and red-brown 10 10
102 1½d. blue and emerald 10 10
103 2d. deep turquoise-green and black .. 40 10
104 3d. blue and deep bluish green 20 10
105 3½d. yellow and carmine-red 30 40
106 4d. yellow and deep rose-carmine 45 10
107 5d. blue and red-brown 30 10
108 6d. black and deep blue 30 20
109 8d. emerald and deep reddish violet .. 40 30
110 1s. blue and black 40 10
111 2s. sage-green and brown 45 60
112 5s. orange-yellow and slate-lilac .. .. 12·00 4·50
113 10s. yellow and black .. .. .. 5·50 4·50
114 £1 yellow, scarlet, ultramarine & dp brt bl 8·00 6·50
101/14 .. .. *Set of* 14 26·00 16·00

Designs: *Horiz (as T* **40**)—1½d. Shore fishing with throw-net; 2d. *Hifofua* and *Aoniu* (ketches); 3½d. Map of Tongatapu; 4d. Vava'u Harbour; 5d. Post Office, Nuku'alofa; 6d. Aerodrome, Fua'amotu; 8d. Nuku'alofa wharf; 2s. Lifuka, Ha'apai; 5s. Mutiny of the *Bounty*. *Vert (as T* **43**)—1s. Map of Tonga Islands.

54 Stamp of 1886 **55** Whaling Ship and Whaleboat

(Des D. M. Bakeley. Photo Harrison)

1961 (1 Dec). 75*th Anniv of Tongan Postal Service. T* **54/5** *and similar horiz designs. W* **24**. *P* 14½ × 13½.
115 1d. carmine and brown-orange 10 10
116 2d. ultramarine 20 10
117 4d. blue-green 10 10
118 5d. violet 25 10
119 1s. red-brown 25 10
115/19 .. .. *Set of* 5 80 30

Designs:—4d. Queen Salote and Post Office, Nuku'alofa; 5d. *Aoniu II* (inter-island freighter); 1s. Mailplane over Tongatapu.

1862
TAU'ATAINA

(59)

60 "Protein Foods"

1962 (7 Feb). *Centenary of Emancipation. Nos.* 101, 104, 107/10, 112, 117 *optd with T* **59** (*No.* 126 *surch also*), *in red, by R. S. Wallbank, Govt Printer.*
120 1d. black and red-brown 10 10
121 4d. blue-green 10 15
122 5d. blue and red-brown 15 15
123 6d. black and deep blue 15 20
124 8d. emerald and deep reddish violet .. 30 25
125 1s. blue and black 15 20
a. Opt inverted £350 £190
126 2s. on 3d. blue and deep bluish green .. 40 55
a. Missing fraction-bar in surch .. .. 10·00
127 5s. orange-yellow and slate-lilac 50 85
a. Opt inverted £180 £250
120/127 .. ..*Set of* 8 1·75 2·25

(Des M. Goaman. Photo Harrison)

1963 (4 June). *Freedom from Hunger. W* **24**. *P* 14 × 14½.
128 **60** 11d. ultramarine 20 15

61 Coat of Arms

62 Queen Salote

63 Queen Salote

(Des Ida West. Die-cut Walsall)

1963 (17 June). *First Polynesian Gold Coinage Commemoration. Circular designs. Embossed on gold foil, backed with paper, inscr overall* "TONGA THE FRIENDLY ISLANDS". *Imperf.*

(a) Postage. $\frac{1}{4}$ *koula coin. Diameter* $1\frac{5}{8}$ *in.*

129	**61**	1d. carmine	10	10
130	**62**	2d. deep blue	10	10
131	**61**	6d. blue-green	15	15
132	**62**	9d. bright purple	15	15
133	**61**	1s. 6d. violet	20	25
134	**62**	2s. light emerald	25	30
		(b) Air. (i) $\frac{1}{2}$ *koula coin. Diam* $2\frac{1}{8}$ *in.*		
135	**63**	10d. carmine	20	20
136	**61**	11d. blue-green	20	20
137	**63**	1s. 1d. deep blue	20	20
		(ii) 1 koula coin. Diam $3\frac{1}{8}$ *in.*		
138	**63**	2s. 1d. bright purple	30	30
139	**61**	2s. 4d. light emerald	35	35
140	**63**	2s. 9d. violet	35	40
129/140 *and* O17		*Set of* 13	5·50	6·50

Examples of a 9d. Postage value in the design of the 1s. 6d. exists, but these have been identified as proofs.

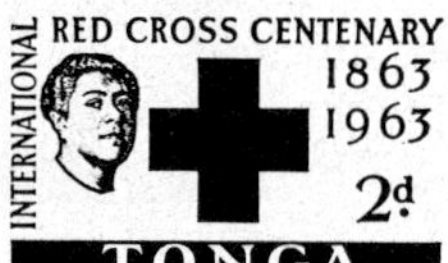

64 Red Cross Emblem

(Des V. Whiteley. Litho B.W.)

1963 (7 Oct). *Red Cross Centenary. W* **24**. *P* $13\frac{1}{2}$.

141	**64**	2d. red and black	10	10
142		11d. red and blue	20	20

65 Queen Salote

66 Map of Tongatapu

(Des M. Meers. Die-cut Walsall)

1964 (19 Oct). *Pan-Pacific South-East Asia Woman's Association Meeting, Nuku'alofa. Embossed on gold foil, backed with paper inscr overall* "TONGA THE FRIENDLY ISLANDS". *Imperf.*

		(a) Postage		
143	**65**	3d. pink	10	10
144		9d. light blue	10	10
145		2s. yellow-green	15	20
146		5s. lilac	30	40
		(b) Air		
147	**66**	10d. blue-green	10	10
148		1s. 2d. black	15	15
149		3s. 6d. cerise	20	25
150		6s. 6d. violet	35	50
143/150		*Set of* 8	1·25	1·60

(67)

1965 (18 Mar). *"Gold Coin" stamps of* 1963 *surch as T* **67** *by Walsall Lithographic Co. New figures of value in gold; obliterating colours shown in brackets. (a) Postage.*

151	**61**	1s. 3d. on 1s. 6d. violet (R.)	15	15
152	**62**	1s. 9d. on 9d. bright purple (W.)	15	20
153	**61**	2s. 6d. on 6d. blue-green (R.)	20	35
154		5s. on 1d. carmine	14·00	16·00
155	**62**	5s. on 2d. deep blue	2·50	3·00
156		5s. on 2s. light emerald	60	75
		(b) Air		
157	**63**	2s. 3d. on 10d. carmine	15	25
158	**61**	2s. 9d. on 11d. blue-green (W.)	20	35
159	**63**	4s. 6d. on 2s. 1d. bright purple (R.)	10·00	12·00
160	**61**	4s. 6d. on 2s. 4d. light emerald (R.)	10·00	12·00
161	**63**	4s. 6d. on 2s. 9d. violet (R.)	7·00	7·00
151/161 *and* O18		*Set of* 12	42·00	48·00

King Taufa'ahau IV, 16 December 1965

1866-1966
TUPOU COLLEGE
& SECONDARY
EDUCATION

(68)

AIRMAIL
1866 CENTENARY 1966
TUPOU COLLEGE
&
SECONDARY EDUCATION
10d XX

(69)

1966 (18 June). *Centenary of Tupou College and Secondary Education. Nos.* 115/16 *and* 118/19 *optd or surch. (a) Postage. As T* **68**.

162	1d. carmine and brown-orange (P.)	10	10
163	3d. on 1d. carmine and brown-orange (P.)	10	10
	a. Misplaced "3d" (R. 2/5)	2·00	
164	6d. on 2d. ultramarine (R.)	10	10
165	1s. 2d. on 2d. ultramarine (R.)	10	10
166	2s. on 2d. ultramarine (R.)	15	10
167	3s. on 2d. ultramarine (R.)	15	15
	(b) Air. As T **69**		
168	5d. violet	10	10
169	10d. on 1d. carmine and brown-orange	10	10
170	1s. red-brown	10	10
171	2s. 9d. on 2d. ultramarine	15	15
	a. Sideways second "X" (R. 3/4)	7·00	
172	3s. 6d. on 5d. violet	15	15
	a. Sideways second "X" (R. 3/4)	7·00	
173	4s. 6d. on 1s. red-brown	20	15
	a. Sideways second "X" (R. 3/4)	7·00	
162/173 and O19/20	*Set of* 14	2·00	1·75

On No. 163a the "d" is 20 mm from the "X" instead of the normal 22 mm.

(70)

(71)

1966 (16 Dec). *Queen Salote Commemoration. "Women's Association" stamps of* 1964 *optd as T* **70/1**, *or surch also, by Walsall Lithographic Co. Inscriptions and new figures of value in first colour and obliterating shapes in second colour given.*

		(a) Postage. Optd as T **70**		
174	**65**	3d. (silver and ultramarine)	10	10
175		5d. on 9d. (silver and black)	10	10
176		9d. (silver and black)	15	10
177		1s. 7d. on 3d. (silver and ultramarine)	20	15
178		3s. 6d. on 9d. (silver and black)	35	20
179		6s. 6d. on 3d. (silver and ultramarine)	60	30
		(b) Air. Optd as T **71**		
180	**66**	10d. (silver and black)	10	10
181		1s. 2d. (black and gold)	15	10
182		4s. on 10d. (silver and black)	40	20
183		5s. 6d. on 1s. 2d. (black and gold)	55	30
184		10s. 6d. on 1s. 2d. (gold and black)	75	45
174/184		*Set of* 11	3·00	1·75

(New Currency. 100 seniti = 1 pa'anga)

1 SENITI 1

(72)

10
Seniti
10

(73)

1967 (25 Mar). *Decimal currency. Various stamps surch as T* **72/3**.

185	1 s. on 1d. (No. 101)	10	10
186	2 s. on 4d. (No. 106)	10	10
187	3 s. on 5d. (No. 107)	10	10
188	4 s. on 5d. (No. 107)	30	30
189	5 s. on $3\frac{1}{2}$d. (No. 105)	10	10
190	6 s. on 8d. (No. 109)	10	10
191	7 s. on $1\frac{1}{2}$d. (No. 102)	10	10
192	8 s. on 6d. (No. 108)	10	10
193	9 s. on 3d. (No. 104)	15	15
194	10 s. on 1s. (No. 110)	15	15
195	11 s. on 3d. on 1d. (No. 163)	15	20
	a. Misplaced "3d" (R. 2/5)	2·50	
196	21 s. on 3s. on 2d. (No. 167)	25	35
197	23 s. on 1d. (No. 101)	25	35
198	30 s. on 2s. (No. 111)* (R.)	1·25	1·75
199	30 s. on 2s. (No. 111)* (R.)	1·50	2·00
200	50 s. on 6d. (No. 108) (R.)	85	1·25
201	60 s. on 2d. (No. 103) (R.)	1·25	1·75
185/201 and O21	*Set of* 18	7·50	10·00

The above surcharges come in a variety of types and sizes.
*No. 198 has the surcharged value expressed horizontally; No. 199 has the figures "30" above and below "SENITI".

74 Coat of Arms (reverse)

75 King Taufa'ahau IV (obverse)

(Die-cut Walsall)

1967 (4 July). *Coronation of King Taufa'ahau IV. Circular designs. Embossed on palladium foil, backed with paper inscr overall* "The Friendly Islands Tonga", *etc. Imperf.*

Sizes

(*a*) *Diameter* $1\frac{1}{2}$ *in.* (*d*) *Diameter* $2\frac{3}{10}$ *in.*
(*b*) *Diameter* $1\frac{7}{10}$ *in.* (*e*) *Diameter* $2\frac{7}{10}$ *in.*
(*c*) *Diameter* 2 *in.* (*f*) *Diameter* $2\frac{9}{10}$ *in.*

		(a) Postage		
202	**74**	1 s. orange and greenish blue (*b*)	10	10
203	**75**	2 s. greenish blue and deep magenta (*c*)	10	10
204	**74**	4 s. emerald and bright purple (*d*)	10	10
205	**75**	15 s. turquoise and violet (*e*)	25	25
206	**74**	28 s. black and bright purple (*a*)	50	40
207	**75**	50 s. carmine-red and ultramarine (*c*)	85	65
208	**74**	1 p. blue and carmine (*f*)	1·50	1·10
		(b) Air		
209	**75**	7 s. carmine-red and black (*b*)	10	10
210	**74**	9 s. brown-purple and emerald (*c*)	10	10
211	**75**	11 s. greenish blue and orange (*d*)	15	15
212	**74**	21 s. black and emerald (*e*)	30	30
213	**75**	23 s. bright purple and light emerald (*a*)	40	35
214	**74**	29 s. ultramarine and emerald (*c*)	50	40
215	**75**	2 p. bright purple and orange (*f*)	2·00	1·25
202/15		*Set of* 14	6·00	4·50

The commemorative coins depicted in reverse (Type **74**) are inscribed in various denominations as follows: 1 s.—"20 SENITI"; 4 s.—"PA'ANGA"; 9 s.—"50 SENITI"; 21 s.—"TWO PA'ANGA"; 28 s.—"QUARTER HAU"; 29 s.—"HALF HAU"; 1 p. "HAU".

The
Friendly Islands
welcome the
United States
Peace Corps

S

(76)

1967 (15 Dec). *Arrival of U.S. Peace Corps in Tonga. As Nos. 101/14, but imperf in different colours and surch as T* **76**.

(a) Postage.

216	1 s. on 1d. black and orange-yellow	10	10
217	2 s. on 2d. ultramarine and carmine-red	10	10
218	3 s. on 3d. chestnut and yellow	10	10
219	4 s. on 4d. reddish violet and yellow	10	10
220	5 s. on 5d. green and yellow	10	10
221	10 s. on 1s. carmine-red and yellow	10	10
222	20 s. on 2s. claret and new blue	15	15
223	50 s. on 5s. sepia and orange-yellow	30	35
224	1 p. on 10s. orange-yellow	50	55

(b) Air

225	11 s. on 3½d. ultramarine (R.)	10	10
226	21 s. on 1½d. emerald	20	20
227	23 s. on 3½d. ultramarine	20	20
216/27 *and* O26/8	*Set of* 15	2·75	3·00

On Nos. 219 and 224 the opt is smaller, and in four lines instead of five. On Nos. 216/20 the surcharge takes the form of an alteration to the currency name as in T **76**.

10 SENITI 10

2 SENITI 2

(77) (78)

1968 (6 Apr). *Various stamps surch as T* **77/8**.

(a) Postage

228	1 s. on 1d. (No. 101) (R.)	10	10
229	2 s. on 4d. (No. 106)	10	10
230	3 s. on 3d. (No. 104) (B.)	10	10
231	4 s. on 5d. (No. 107) (R.)	10	10
232	5 s. on 2d. (No. 103) (R.)	10	10
233	6 s. on 6d. (No. 108) (R.)	10	10
234	7 s. on 1½d. (No. 102) (R.)	10	10
235	8 s. on 8d. (No. 109) (R.)	10	10
236	9 s. on 3½d. (No. 105)	20	20
237	10 s. on 1s. (No. 110) (R.)	20	20
238	20 s. on 5s. (No. 112) (R.)	40	40
239	2 p. on 2s. (No. 111) (R.)	1·50	1·50

(b) Air. Surch as T **78** *with* "AIRMAIL" *added*

240	11 s. on 10s. (No. 113) (R.)	25	25
241	21 s. on 10s. (No. 113) (R.)	40	40
242	23 s. on 10s. (No. 113) (R.)	40	40
228/42 *and* O22/5	*Set of* 19	6·50	6·50

H M'S BIRTHDAY 4 JULY 1968

(79)

Friendly Islands
Field & Track Trials
South Pacific Games
Port Moresby
1969

s

(80)

1968 (4 July). *50th Birthday of King Taufa'ahua IV. Nos. 202/15 optd as T* **79**. *(a) Postage.*

243	**74**	1 s. orange and greenish blue *(b)* (R.)	10	10
244	**75**	2 s. greenish blue & dp magenta *(b)* (B.)	10	10
245	**74**	4 s. emerald and bright purple *(d)* (R.)	10	10
246	**75**	15 s. turquoise and violet *(e)* (B.)	25	15
247	**74**	28 s. black and bright purple *(a)* (R.)	55	30
248	**75**	50 s. carmine-red and ultramarine *(c)* (B.)	1·00	60
249	**74**	1 p. blue and carmine *(f)* (R.)	2·25	1·25

(b) Air

250	**75**	7 s. carmine-red and black *(b)* (B.)	10	10
251	**74**	9 s. brown-purple and emerald *(c)* (R.)	15	10
252	**75**	11 s. greenish blue and orange *(d)* (B.)	15	10
253	**74**	21 s. black and emerald *(e)* (R.)	40	25
		a. Opt (gold only) double	£275	
254	**75**	23 s. bright purple & lt emerald *(a)* (B.)	40	25
255	**74**	29 s. ultramarine and emerald *(c)* (R.)	65	35
256	**75**	2 p. bright purple and orange *(f)* (B.)	4·50	2·50
243/56 *and* O29/32		*Set of* 18	17·00	10·00

The overprints vary in size, but are all crescent-shaped as Type **79** and inscribed "H.M'S BIRTHDAY 4 JULY 1968" (Type **79**) or "HIS MAJESTY'S 50th BIRTHDAY" (others).

1968 (19 Dec). *South Pacific Games Field and Track Trials, Port Moresby, New Guinea. Nos. 101/14, but imperf, in different colours and surch as T* **80**. *(a) Postage.*

257	5 s. on 5d. green and yellow (R.)	10	10
258	10 s. on 1s. carmine-red and yellow	10	10
259	15 s. on 2s. claret and new blue	15	15
260	25 s. on 2d. ultramarine and carmine-red	15	15
261	50 s. on 1d. black and orange-yellow	30	30
262	75 s. on 10s. orange-yellow (G.)	45	45

(b) Air

263	6 s. on 6d. black and yellow*	10	10
264	7 s. on 4d. reddish violet and yellow	10	10
265	8 s. on 8d. black and greenish yellow	10	10
	a. Surch 11½ mm as on 6d.	†	90·00
266	9 s. on 1½d. emerald	10	10
267	11 s. on 3d. chestnut and yellow	10	10
268	21 s. on 3½d. ultramarine	15	15
269	38 s. on 5s. sepia and orange-yellow	20	20
270	1 p. on 10s. orange-yellow	50	50
257/70 *and* O33/4	*Set of* 16	2·75	2·75

*On No. 263 the surcharge is smaller (11½ mm wide).

1s 1s

(81) (82)

1969. *Emergency Provisionals. Various stamps (Nos. 273/6 are imperf and in different colours) surch as T* **81** *or* **82**. *(a) Postage.*

271	1 s. on 1s. 2d. on 2d. ultramarine (No. 165)	1·00	65
272	1 s. on 2s. on 2d. ultramarine (No. 166)	1·00	65
273	1 s. on 6d. black and yellow (as No. 108)	40	25
274	2 s. on 3½d. ultramarine (as No. 105)	45	30
275	3 s. on 1½d. emerald (as No. 102)	45	30
276	4 s. on 8d. black & greenish yell (as No. 109)	70	50

(b) Air. Nos. 171/3 surch with T **82**

277	1 s. on 2s. 9d. on 2d. ultramarine	1·00	65
	a. Sideways second "X" (R. 3/4)	6·00	
278	1 s. on 3s. 6d. on 5d. violet	1·00	65
	a. Sideways second "X" (R. 3/4)	6·00	
279	1 s. on 4s. 6d. on 1s. red-brown	1·00	65
	a. Sideways second "X" (R. 3/4)	6·00	
271/9	*Set of* 9	6·25	4·25

SELF-ADHESIVE ISSUES. From No. 280 until No. 922 all stamps were manufactured by Walsall Security Printers Ltd and are self-adhesive. The backing paper is separated by roulette or perforations (from No. 780 onwards), and shows on its reverse the words *"TONGA where time begins"*, or, from No. 568 onwards, various texts or illustrations. This also applies to the Official stamps.

83 Banana

1969 (21 Apr). *Coil stamps.*

280	**83**	1 s. scarlet, black and greenish yellow	30	35
281		2 s. brt green, black & greenish yellow	40	45
282		3 s. violet, black and greenish yellow	45	50
283		4 s. ultramarine, black & greenish yell	55	60
284		5 s. bronze-green, black & greenish yell	75	80
280/4		*Set of* 5	2·25	2·40

Nos. 280/4 were produced in rolls of 200, each even stamp having a number applied to the front of the backing paper, with the usual inscription on the reverse.

See also Nos. 325/9, 413/17 and 675/89.

84 Putting the Shot **86** Oil Derrick and Map

1969 (13 Aug). *Third South Pacific Games, Port Moresby. T* **84** *and similar design. (a) Postage.*

285	**84**	1 s. black, red and buff	10	10
286		3 s. bright green, red and buff	10	10
287		6 s. blue, red and buff	10	10
288		10 s. bluish violet, red and buff	10	10
289		30 s. blue, red and buff	15	20

(b) Air

290	–	9 s. black, violet and orange	10	10
291	–	11 s. black, ultramarine and orange	10	10
292	–	20 s. black, bright green and orange	15	15
293	–	60 s. black, cerise and orange	45	55
294	–	1 p. black, blue-green and orange	70	80
285/94 *and* O35/6		*Set of* 12	2·75	3·25

Design:—9, 11, 20, 60 s., 1 p. Boxing.

1969 (23 Dec). *First Oil Search in Tonga. T* **86** *and similar vert design.*

(a) Postage

295	**86**	3 s. multicoloured	10	10
296		7 s. multicoloured	15	15
297		20 s. multicoloured	40	40
298		25 s. multicoloured	45	45
299		35 s. multicoloured	70	70

(b) Air

300	–	9 s. multicoloured	20	20
301	–	10 s. multicoloured	20	20
302	–	24 s. multicoloured	45	45
303	–	29 s. multicoloured	50	50
304	–	38 s. multicoloured	70	70
295/304 *and* O37/8		*Set of* 12	7·50	7·00

Design:—Nos. 300/4, Oil derrick and island of Tongatapu.

87 Members of the British and Tongan Royal Families

1970 (7 Mar). *Royal Visit. T* **87** *and similar design. Multicoloured.*

(a) Postage

305	**87**	3 s. multicoloured	20	10
306		5 s. multicoloured	25	10
307		10 s. multicoloured	40	20
308		25 s. multicoloured	1·00	55
309		50 s. multicoloured	1·75	90

(b) Air

310	–	7 s. multicoloured	35	15
311	–	9 s. multicoloured	40	20
312	–	24 s. multicoloured	1·00	55
313	–	29 s. multicoloured	1·25	60
314	–	38 s. multicoloured	1·50	80
305/14 *and* O39/41		*Set of* 13	17·00	9·00

Design:—Nos. 310/14, Queen Elizabeth II and King Taufa'ahau Tupou IV.

89 Book, Tongan Rulers and Flag

1970 (4 June). *Entry into British Commonwealth. T* **89** *and similar design. (a) Postage.*

315	**89**	3 s. multicoloured	10	10
316		7 s. multicoloured	15	15
317		15 s. multicoloured	25	20
318		25 s. multicoloured	35	25
319		50 s. multicoloured	60	50

(b) Air

320	–	9 s. turquoise-blue, gold and scarlet	15	15
321	–	10 s. bright purple, gold and greenish blue	15	15
322	–	24 s. olive-yellow, gold and green	35	30
323	–	29 s. new blue, gold and orange-red	40	30
324	–	38 s. deep orange-yellow, gold & brt emer	50	40
315/24 *and* O42/4		*Set of* 13	5·00	4·50

Design: *"Star" shaped* (44 × 51 *mm*)—Nos. 320/4, King Taufa'ahau Tupou IV.

90 Coconut

1970 (9 June). *Coil stamps. (a) As T* **83** *but colours changed.*

325	**83**	1 s. greenish yellow, bright purple & blk	15	20
326		2 s. greenish yellow, ultramarine & black	20	30
327		3 s. greenish yellow, chocolate and black	25	30
328		4 s. greenish yellow, emerald and black	25	30
329		5 s. greenish yellow, orge-red & bl	30	35

(b) T **90**. *Multicoloured; colour of face value given*

330	**90**	6 s. rose-carmine	35	40
331		7 s. bright purple	40	45
332		8 s. bluish violet	45	55
333		9 s. turquoise	55	65
334		10 s. pale orange	55	65
325/34		*Set of* 10	3·00	3·75

Nos. 325/34 and O45/54 were produced in rolls of 200, each even stamp having a number applied to the front of the backing paper, with the usual inscription on the reverse.

MINIMUM PRICE

The minimum price quote is 10p which represents a handling charge rather than a basis for valuing common stamps. For further notes about prices see introductory pages.

91 "Red Cross"

(Litho (postage) or litho and die-stamped (air))

1970 (17 Oct). *Centenary of British Red Cross. T* **91** *and similar "cross" shaped design. (a) Postage.*

No.	Type	Description	Unused	Used
335	**91**	3 s. vermilion, black and light green ..	10	10
336		7 s. vermilion, black and ultramarine ..	15	15
337		15 s. vermilion and bright purple ..	30	30
338		25 s. vermilion, black and turquoise-blue	50	50
339		75 s. vermilion and deep red-brown ..	3·00	3·00
		(b) Air		
340	–	9 s. vermilion and silver..	20	20
341	–	10 s. vermilion and bright purple ..	20	20
342	–	18 s. vermilion and green..	35	35
343	–	38 s. vermilion and ultramarine	1·50	1·50
344	–	1 p. vermilion and turquoise-blue ..	4·00	4·00
335/44 *and* O55/7		.. .. .. *Set of* 13	15·00	15·00

Design: *As T* **91**—Nos. 340/4 as Nos. 335/9 but with inscription rearranged and coat of arms omitted.

On Nos. 335/6 and 338 the black colour is produced as a composite of the other two colours used.

(92)

(93)

1971 (30 Jan). *Fifth Death Anniv of Queen Salote. Nos. 174/84 surch as T* **92/3**. *Obliterating shapes in black; inscriptions and figures of value in colour given. (a) Postage. Surch as T* **92**.

No.	Type	Description	Unused	Used
345	**65**	2 s. on 5d. on 9d. (silver)..	10	10
346		3 s. on 9d. (orange-red)	10	10
347		5 s. on 3d. (bright green)..	15	15
348		15 s. on 3s. 6d. on 9d. (orange-brown) ..	45	35
		a. Surch double	—	30·00
349		25 s. on 6s. 6d. on 3d. (purple) ..	80	65
350		50 s. on 1s. 7d. on 3d. (gold)	1·75	1·25
		(b) Air. Surch as T **93**		
351	**66**	9 s. on 10d. (silver)	30	20
352		24 s. on 4s. on 10d. (orange-brown) ..	80	60
353		29 s. on 5s. 6d. on 1s. 2d. (orange-red) ..	90	80
354		38 s. on 10s. 6d. on 1s. 2d. (bright green)	1·40	1·00
345/54 *and* O58/61		.. .. .. *Set of* 14	15·00	11·50

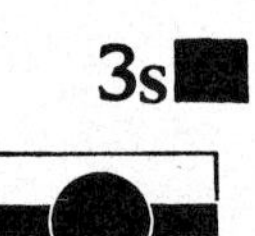

(94)

HONOURING JAPANESE POSTAL CENTENARY 1871-1971

15s

(95)

1971 (17 Apr). *"Philatokyo 1971" Stamp Exhibition. As Nos. 101/2, 106 and 109/11, but imperf, colours changed and surch as T* **94** *(Nos. 355/6, 358/61 and 363), as T* **95** *(Nos. 357, 362) or with similar surcharge in four lines (No. 364). (a) Postage.*

No.	Type	Description	Unused	Used
355		3 s. on 8d. blk & greenish yellow (Blk. & R.)	10	10
356		7 s. on 4d. reddish violet & yellow (Blk. & R.)	10	10
357		15 s. on 1s. carmine, red and yellow ..	20	20
358		25 s. on 1d. black & orange-yellow (Blk. & R.)	30	30
359		75 s. on 2s. claret & new blue (Blk. & R.) ..	85	85
		(b) Air. Additionally surch "AIRMAIL"		
360		9 s. on 1½d. emerald (Blk. and R.) ..	10	10
361		10 s. on 4d. reddish violet & yellow (Blk. & R.)	10	10
362		18 s. on 1s. carmine-red and yellow (V.) ..	20	20
363		38 s. on 1d. black & orange-yellow (Blk. & R.)	40	40
364		1 p. on 2s. claret and new blue	1·00	1·00
355/64 *and* O62/4		.. .. .. *Set of* 13	5·50	5·50

96 Wristwatch

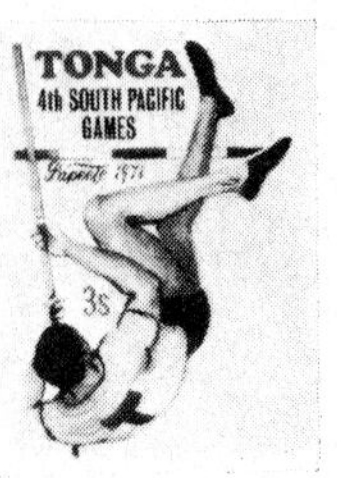

97 Pole-vaulter

1971 (20 July)–**72**. *Air. Backed with paper bearing advertisements.*

No.	Type	Description	Unused	Used
365	**96**	14 s. multicoloured	55	55
365*a*		17 s. multicoloured (20.7.72)	65	65
366		21 s. multicoloured	75	75
366*a*		38 s. multicoloured (20.7.72)	1·10	1·10
365/6*a and* O65/6*a*		.. .. .. *Set of* 8	5·50	5·50

1971 (20 July). *Fourth South Pacific Games, Tahiti. T* **97** *and similar design. (a) Postage.*

No.	Type	Description	Unused	Used
367	**97**	3 s. multicoloured	10	10
368		7 s. multicoloured	10	10
369		15 s. multicoloured	15	15
370		25 s. multicoloured	25	30
371		50 s. multicoloured	40	60
		(b) Air		
372	–	9 s. multicoloured	10	10
373	–	10 s. multicoloured	10	10
374	–	24 s. multicoloured	25	30
375	–	29 s. multicoloured	30	40
376	–	38 s. multicoloured	35	50
367/76 *and* O67/9		.. .. .. *Set of* 13	3·50	5·00

Design: *Horiz*—Nos. 372/6, High-jumper.

98 Medal of Merit (reverse)

99 Child

1971 (30 Oct). *Investiture of Royal Tongan Medal of Merit. T* **98** *and similar "medal" shaped design. Multicoloured; colour of medal given.*

No.	Type	Description	Unused	Used
		(a) Postage		
377	**98**	3 s. gold	10	10
378		24 s. silver..	20	20
379	–	38 s. brown	30	30
		(b) Air		
380	–	10 s. gold	15	15
381	–	75 s. silver..	65	65
382	**98**	1 p. brown	75	75
377/82 *and* O70/2		.. .. .. *Set of* 9	3·75	3·75

Design: *As T* **98**—Nos. 379/81, Obverse of the Medal of Merit.

1971 (31 Dec). *25th Anniv of UNICEF. T* **99** *and similar design.*

No.	Type	Description	Unused	Used
		(a) Postage		
383	**99**	2 s. multicoloured	10	10
384		4 s. multicoloured	10	10
385		8 s. multicoloured	10	10
386		16 s. multicoloured	20	20
387		30 s. multicoloured	30	30
		(b) Air		
388	–	10 s. multicoloured	15	15
389	–	15 s. multicoloured	20	20
390	–	25 s. multicoloured	30	30
391	–	50 s. multicoloured	60	60
392	–	1 p. multicoloured	1·25	1·25
383/92 *and* O73/5		.. .. .. *Set of* 13	5·50	5·50

Design: *Vert (21 x 42 mm)*—Nos. 388/92, Woman.

PRICES OF SETS

Set prices are given for many issues, generally those containing three stamps or more. Definitive sets include one of each value or major colour change, but do not cover different perforations, die types or minor shades. Where a choice is possible the set prices are based on the cheapest versions of the stamps included in the listings.

100 Map of South Pacific, and *Olovaha*

1972 (14 Apr). *Merchant Marine Routes. T* **100** *and similar design.*

No.	Type	Description	Unused	Used
		(a) Postage		
393	**100**	2 s. multicoloured	10	10
394		10 s. multicoloured	20	10
395		17 s. multicoloured	40	20
396		21 s. multicoloured	50	25
397		60 s. multicoloured	2·00	1·25
		(b) Air		
398	–	9 s. multicoloured	20	10
399	–	12 s. multicoloured	25	15
400	–	14 s. multicoloured	30	15
401	–	75 s. multicoloured	2·25	1·50
402	–	90 s. multicoloured	2·75	2·00
393/402 *and* O76/8		.. .. .. *Set of* 13	13·00	8·50

Design:—Nos. 398/402, Map of South Pacific and *Niuvakai*.

101 ¼ Hau Coronation Coin

1972 (15 July). *Fifth Anniv of Coronation. T* **101** *and similar design.*

No.	Type	Description	Unused	Used
		(a) Postage		
403	**101**	5 s. multicoloured	10	10
404		7 s. multicoloured	10	10
405		10 s. multicoloured	15	10
406		17 s. multicoloured	25	15
407		60 s. multicoloured	85	40
		(b) Air		
408	–	9 s. multicoloured	15	10
409	–	12 s. multicoloured	20	10
410	–	14 s. multicoloured	25	1
411	–	21 s. multicoloured	30	1
412	–	75 s. multicoloured	1·10	4
403/12 *and* O79/81		.. .. .. *Set of* 13	7·00	3·5

Design (47 × 41 *mm*):—Nos. 408/12, as T **101**, but with coins above inscription instead of beneath it.

102 Water Melon

1972 (30 Sept). *Coil stamps. (a) As T* **83**, *but inscription altered omitting "Best in the Pacific", and colours changed.*

No.	Type	Description	Unused	Used
413	**83**	1 s. light yellow, scarlet and black ..	15	1
414		2 s. light yellow, ultramarine and black	20	1
415		3 s. light yellow, yellow-green and black	25	2
416		4 s. light yellow, royal blue and black ..	25	2
417		5 s. light yellow, reddish brn & bl ..	25	2
		(b) As T **90** *but colours changed. Colour of face value given*		
418	**90**	6 s. dull orange	25	2
419		7 s. ultramarine	30	2
420		8 s. bright magenta	30	2
421		9 s. brown-orange	30	2
422		10 s. bright new blue	35	3
		(c) T **102**. *Colour of face value given*		
423	**102**	15 s. new blue	55	4
424		20 s. reddish orange	70	6
425		25 s. chocolate	80	7
426		40 s. yellow-orange	1·75	1·5
427		50 s. lemon	2·00	1·7
413/27		.. .. *Set of* 15	7·50	6·5

Nos. 413/27 and O82/96 were produced in rolls, each even stam having a number applied to the front of the backing paper, with th usual inscription on the reverse.

7s

NOVEMBER 1972
INAUGURAL
Internal Airmail
Nuku'alofa — Vava'u

(103)

1972 (2 Nov). *Inaugural Internal Airmail. No.* 398 *surch with T* **103**.

428		7 s. on 9 s. multicoloured	1·10	1·50

104 Hoisting Tongan Flag

1972 (9 Dec). *Proclamation of Sovereignty over Minerva Reefs. T* **104** *and similar design. (a) Postage.*

429	**104**	5 s. multicoloured	10	10
430		7 s. multicoloured	10	10
431		10 s. multicoloured	15	10
432		15 s. multicoloured	25	15
433		40 s. multicoloured	80	40
		(b) Air		
434	–	9 s. multicoloured	15	10
435	–	12 s. multicoloured	20	10
436	–	14 s. multicoloured	25	15
437	–	38 s. multicoloured	75	35
438	–	1 p. multicoloured	2·00	1·00
429/38 *and* O97/9		*Set of* 13	8·00	4·25

Design: *Spherical* (52 *mm diameter*)—Nos. 434/8, Proclamation in Govt Gazette.

105 Coins around Bank

1973 (30 Mar). *Foundation of Bank of Tonga. T* **105** *and similar design. (a) Postage.*

439	**105**	5 s. multicoloured	10	10
440		7 s. multicoloured	10	10
441		10 s. multicoloured	15	10
442		20 s. multicoloured	25	15
443		30 s. multicoloured	35	25
		(b) Air		
444	–	9 s. multicoloured	20	10
445	–	12 s. multicoloured	20	10
446	–	17 s. multicoloured	25	15
447	–	50 s. multicoloured	80	40
448	–	90 s. multicoloured	1·50	90
439/48 *and* O100/2		*Set of* 13	7·50	4·25

Design: *Horiz* (64 × 52 *mm*)—Nos. 444/8, Bank and banknotes.

106 Handshake and Scout in Outrigger Canoe

973 (29 June). *Silver Jubilee of Scouting in Tonga. T* **106** *and similar design. (a) Postage.*

49	**106**	5 s. multicoloured	20	10
50		7 s. multicoloured	30	15
51		15 s. multicoloured	95	40
52		21 s. multicoloured	1·25	50
53		50 s. multicoloured	4·50	1·75
		(b) Air		
454	–	9 s. multicoloured	50	25
455	–	12 s. multicoloured	60	30
456	–	14 s. multicoloured	85	50
457	–	17 s. multicoloured	95	60
458	–	1 p. multicoloured	15·00	5·50
449/58 *and* O103/5		*Set of* 13	£110	42·00

Design: *Square* (53 × 53 *mm*)—Nos. 454/8, Scout badge.

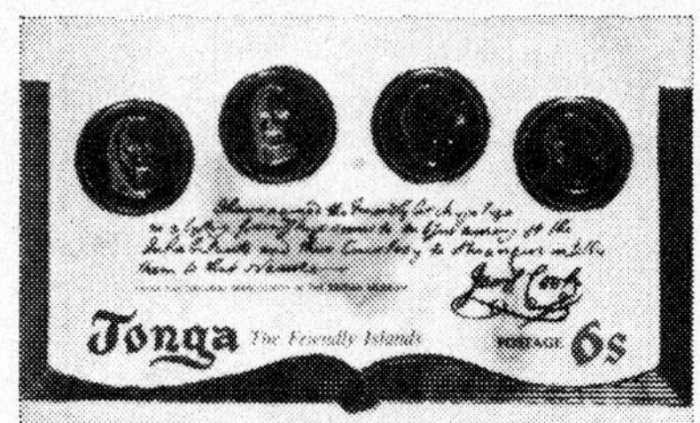

107 Excerpt from Cook's Log-book

1973 (2 Oct). *Bicentenary of Capt. Cook's Visit to Tonga. T* **107** *and similar design. (a) Postage.*

459	**107**	6 s. multicoloured	20	15
460		8 s. multicoloured	25	20
461		11 s. multicoloured	40	25
462		35 s. multicoloured	3·00	1·40
463		40 s. multicoloured	3·00	1·40
		(b) Air		
464	–	9 s. multicoloured	45	20
465	–	14 s. multicoloured	75	30
466	–	29 s. multicoloured	2·75	1·25
467	–	38 s. multicoloured	3·00	1·50
468	–	75 s. multicoloured	6·00	2·75
459/68 *and* O106/8		*Set of* 13	32·00	15·00

Design: *Vert*—Nos. 464/8, H.M.S. *Resolution*.

(108)

109 Red Shining Parrot

1973 (19 Dec). *Commonwealth Games, Christchurch, New Zealand. Various stamps optd as T* **108** *(No.* 474 *optd* "AIRMAIL" *in addition). (a) Postage.*

469		5 s. on 50 s. (No. 371) (Blk. and Gold)	15	10
470		12 s. on 38 s. (No. 379) (R. and Silver)	30	15
471		14 s. on 75 s. (No. 381) (R. and Gold)	30	15
472		20 s. on 1 p. (No. 382) (Blk. and Gold)	50	25
473		50 s. on 24 s. (No. 378) (Blk. and Silver)	1·25	65
		(b) Air		
474		7 s. on 25 s. (No. 370) (Blk. and Silver)	15	10
475		9 s. on 38 s. (No. 376) (V.)	20	10
476		24 s. (No. 374)	60	25
477		29 s. on 9 s. (No. 454) (B.)	70	35
478		40 s. on 14 s. (No. 456)	1·00	60
469/78 *and* O109/11		*Set of* 13	9·00	5·50

1974 (20 Mar). *Air.*

479	**109**	7 s. multicoloured	30	20
480		9 s. multicoloured	35	25
481		12 s. multicoloured	40	30
482		14 s. multicoloured	45	35
483		17 s. multicoloured	55	50
484		29 s. multicoloured	95	80
485		38 s. multicoloured	1·25	1·00
486		50 s. multicoloured	1·75	1·50
487		75 s. multicoloured	2·25	2·00
479/87		*Set of* 9	7·50	6·25

Nos. 479/87 and O112/20 were produced in rolls, each stamp having a number applied to the front of the backing paper, with the usual inscription on the reverse.

110 "Stamped Letter"

1974 (20 June). *Centenary of Universal Postal Union. T* **110** *and similar design. (a) Postage.*

488	**110**	5 s. multicoloured	10	10
489		10 s. multicoloured	15	10
490		15 s. multicoloured	25	15
491		20 s. multicoloured	30	25
492		50 s. multicoloured	1·25	75
		(b) Air		
493	–	14 s. multicoloured	25	15
494	–	21 s. multicoloured	35	30
495	–	60 s. multicoloured	1·40	75
496	–	75 s. multicoloured	1·60	85
497	–	1 p. multicoloured	1·90	1·10
488/97 *and* O121/3		*Set of* 13	9·50	5·75

Design: *Horiz*—Nos. 493/7, Carrier pigeon scattering letters over Tonga.

111 Girl Guide Badges

1974 (11 Sept). *Tongan Girl Guides. T* **111** *and similar design.*

		(a) Postage		
498	**111**	5 s. multicoloured	40	10
499		10 s. multicoloured	60	20
500		20 s. multicoloured	1·50	55
501		40 s. multicoloured	3·25	1·25
502		60 s. multicoloured	4·00	2·00
		(b) Air		
503	–	14 s. multicoloured	1·00	35
504	–	16 s. multicoloured	1·00	35
505	–	29 s. multicoloured	2·00	80
506	–	31 s. multicoloured	2·25	90
507	–	75 s. multicoloured	5·50	2·50
498/507 *and* O124/6		*Set of* 13	32·00	15·00

Design: *Vert*—Nos. 503/7, Girl Guide leaders.

112 H.M.S. *Resolution*

1974 (11 Dec). *Establishment of Royal Marine Institute. T* **112** *and similar design. (a) Postage.*

508	**112**	5 s. multicoloured	55	10
509		10 s. multicoloured	75	20
510		25 s. multicoloured	1·25	45
511		50 s. multicoloured	2·25	1·25
512		75 s. multicoloured	3·25	2·00
		(b) Air		
513	–	9 s. multicoloured	90	20
514	–	14 s. multicoloured	1·25	35
515	–	17 s. multicoloured	1·40	40
516	–	60 s. multicoloured	3·25	1·75
517	–	90 s. multicoloured	4·50	2·75
508/17 *and* O127/9		*Set of* 13	24·00	12·50

Design: *Horiz* (51 × 46 *mm*)—Nos. 513/17, *James Cook* (bulk carrier).

113 Dateline Hotel, Nuku'alofa

1975 (11 Mar). *South Pacific Forum and Tourism. T* **113** *and similar vert designs. (a) Postage.*

518 **113** 5 s. multicoloured 10 10
519 10 s. multicoloured 10 10
520 15 s. multicoloured 20 20
521 30 s. multicoloured 45 45
522 1 p. multicoloured .. .. .. 1·60 1·50

(b) Air

523 – 9 s. multicoloured 10 10
524 – 12 s. multicoloured 15 15
525 – 14 s. multicoloured 20 20
526 – 17 s. multicoloured 20 20
527 – 38 s. multicoloured 55 55
518/27 *and* O130/2 .. .. .. *Set of* 13 8·00 7·00

Designs (46 × 60 *mm*):—9, 12, 14 s. Beach; 17, 38 s. Surf and sea.

114 Boxing

1975 (11 June). *Fifth South Pacific Games, Guam. T* **114** *and similar "star"-shaped design. (a) Postage.*

528 **114** 5 s. multicoloured 10 10
529 10 s. multicoloured 15 10
530 20 s. multicoloured 25 20
531 25 s. multicoloured 30 25
532 65 s. multicoloured 70 55

(b) Air

533 – 9 s. multicoloured 15 10
534 – 12 s. multicoloured 20 15
535 – 14 s. multicoloured 20 15
536 – 17 s. multicoloured 25 20
537 – 90 s. multicoloured 90 80
528/37 *and* O133/5 .. .. .. *Set of* 13 5·25 4·00

Design (37 × 43 *mm*):—Nos. 533/7, Throwing the Discus.

115 Commemorative Coin

1975 (3 Sept). *F.A.O. Commemoration. T* **115** *and similar designs.*

(a) Postage

538 5 s. multicoloured 10 10
539 20 s. multicoloured 30 15
540 50 s. new blue, black and silver 65 35
541 1 p. ultramarine, black and silver .. .. 1·25 75
542 2 p. black and silver .. .. 2·25 1·75

(b) Air

543 12 s. multicoloured 25 15
544 14 s. multicoloured 25 15
545 25 s. vermilion, black and silver 35 20
546 50 s. bright magenta, black and silver .. 60 40
547 1 p. black and silver .. .. 1·25 75
538/47 .. .. *Set of* 10 6·50 4·25

Nos. 539/47 are as T **115** but show different coins. Nos. 542 and 544 are horiz, size 75 × 42 mm.

116 Commemorative Coin

1975 (4 Nov). *Centenary of Tongan Constitution. T* **116** *and similar designs showing coinage. Multicoloured. (a) Postage.*

548 5 s. Type **116** 10 10
549 10 s. King George I 15 10
550 20 s. King Taufa'ahau IV 30 20
551 50 s. King George II 60 35
552 75 s. Tongan arms .. .. 1·00 70

(b) Air

553 9 s. King Taufa'ahau IV 15 10
554 12 s. Queen Salote 20 10
555 14 s. Tongan arms 20 10
556 38 s. King Taufa'ahau IV 40 25
557 1 p. Four monarchs .. .. 1·25 70
548/57 *and* O136/8 .. .. .. *Set of* 13 6·00 3·75

Sizes:—60 × 40 mm, Nos. 549 and 551; 76 × 76 mm, Nos. 552 and 557; 57 × 56 mm, others.

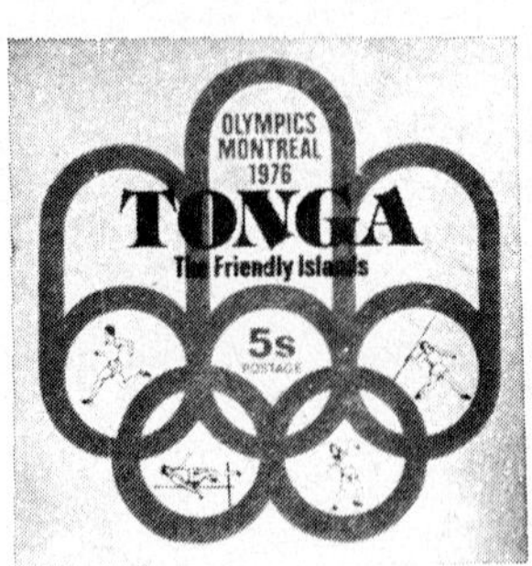

117 Montreal Logo

1976 (24 Feb). *First Participation in Olympic Games. (a) Postage.*

558 **117** 5 s. vermilion, black and blue 15 10
559 10 s. vermilion, black and emerald .. 25 10
560 25 s. vermilion, black and bistre .. 65 35
561 35 s. vermilion, black and mauve .. 75 40
562 70 s. vermilion, black and olive-yellow .. 2·00 90

(b) Air. Montreal logo optd on Girl Guide stamps (Nos. 500 *etc*)

563 **111** 12 s. on 20 s. multicoloured 30 15
564 – 14 s. on 16 s. multicoloured 30 15
565 – 16 s. multicoloured 35 15
566 **111** 38 s. on 40 s. multicoloured .. .. 1·00 45
567 – 75 s. multicoloured .. .. .. 2·25 95
558/67 *and* O139/41 .. .. .. *Set of* 13 13·00 6·50

118 Signatories of Declaration of Independence

1976 (26 May). *Bicentenary of American Revolution. T* **118** *and similar horiz designs showing signatories to the Declaration of Independence. (a) Postage.*

568 **118** 9 s. multicoloured 40 15
569 – 10 s. multicoloured 40 15
570 – 15 s. multicoloured 70 35
571 – 25 s. multicoloured .. .. .. 1·25 60
572 – 75 s. multicoloured .. .. .. 3·75 1·75

(b) Air

573 – 12 s. multicoloured 50 15
574 – 14 s. multicoloured 60 20
575 – 17 s. multicoloured 80 35
576 – 38 s. multicoloured .. .. .. 1·90 75
577 – 1 p. multicoloured .. .. .. 4·50 2·00
568/77 *and* O142/4 .. .. .. *Set of* 13 20·00 9·00

119 Nathaniel Turner and John Thomas (Methodist missionaries)

1976 (25 Aug). *150th Anniv of Christianity in Tonga. T* **119** *and similar design. (a) Postage.*

578 **119** 5 s. multicoloured 20 15
579 10 s. multicoloured 30 25
580 20 s. multicoloured 50 40
581 25 s. multicoloured 55 45
582 85 s. multicoloured .. .. .. 2·25 1·90

(b) Air. Design showing Missionary Ship "Triton" (45 × 59 *mm*)

583 – 9 s. multicoloured 30 25
584 – 12 s. multicoloured 35 30
585 – 14 s. multicoloured 40 35
586 – 17 s. multicoloured 50 40
587 – 38 s. multicoloured .. .. .. 1·25 1·00
578/87 *and* O145/7 .. .. .. *Set of* 13 12·00 10·00

120 Emperor Wilhelm I and King George Tupou I

1976 (1 Nov). *Centenary of Treaty of Friendship with Germany.*

(a) Postage

588 **120** 9 s. multicoloured 20 20
589 15 s. multicoloured 30 30
590 22 s. multicoloured 40 40
591 50 s. multicoloured 90 90
592 73 s. multicoloured .. .. .. 1·40 1·40

(b) Air. Circular design (52 mm diameter) showing Treaty Signing

593 – 11 s. multicoloured 25 25
594 – 17 s. multicoloured 40 40
595 – 18 s. multicoloured 40 40
596 – 31 s. multicoloured 60 60
597 – 39 s. multicoloured 70 70
588/97 *and* O148/50 .. .. *Set of* 13 9·50 9·50

121 Queen Salote and Coronation Procession

1977 (7 Feb). *Silver Jubilee. (a) Postage.*

598 **121** 11 s. multicoloured .. .. .. 1·50 3
599 20 s. multicoloured 75 3
600 30 s. multicoloured .. .. .. 1·00 3
601 50 s. multicoloured .. .. .. 1·75 6
602 75 s. multicoloured .. .. .. 2·25 8

(b) Air. Square design (59 × 59 *mm*) *showing Queen Elizabeth an King Taufa'ahau*

603 – 15 s. multicoloured 80 2
604 – 17 s. multicoloured 90 3
605 – 22 s. multicoloured .. .. .. 12·00 1·7
a. Horiz roul omitted (vert pair) ..
606 – 31 s. multicoloured 90 4
607 – 39 s. multicoloured 95 4
598/607 *and* O151/3 .. .. *Set of* 13 25·00 6·2

122 Tongan Coins

1977 (4 July). *Tenth Anniv of King's Coronation. (a) Postage.*

608 **122** 10 s. multicoloured 20 2
609 15 s. multicoloured 25 2
610 25 s. multicoloured 35 3
611 50 s. multicoloured 75 7
612 75 s. multicoloured .. .. .. 1·00 1·0

(b) Air. Oval design (64 × 46 *mm*) *showing* 1967 *Coronation Coi*

613 – 11 s. multicoloured 25 2
614 – 17 s. multicoloured 30 3
615 – 18 s. multicoloured 30 3
616 – 39 s. multicoloured 45 4
617 – 1 p. multicoloured .. .. .. 1·50 1·5
608/17 *and* O154/6 .. .. .. *Set of* 13 7·50 7·5

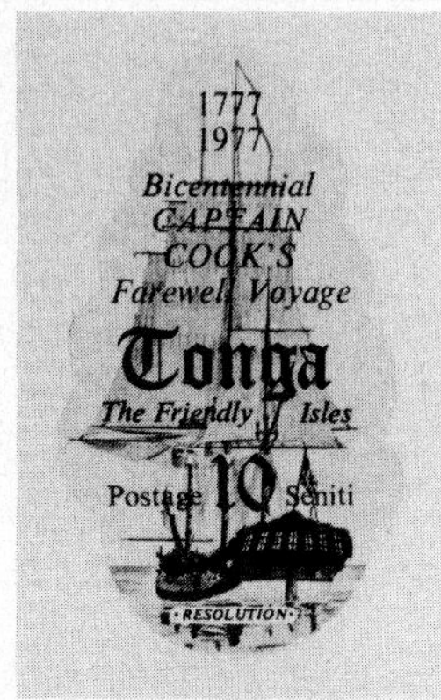

123 H.M.S. *Resolution*

1977 (28 Sept). *Bicentenary of Capt. Cook's Last Voyage.*

(a) Postage.

618 **123** 10 s. multicoloured .. .. .. 1·40 60
619 17 s. multicoloured .. .. .. 1·75 95
620 25 s. multicoloured .. .. .. 3·00 1·75
621 30 s. multicoloured .. .. .. 3·00 2·00
622 40 s. multicoloured .. .. .. 3·75 2·50

(b) Air. Horiz design (52 × 46 mm) showing coin and extract from Cook's journal

623 – 15 s. multicoloured .. .. .. 1·50 90
624 – 22 s. multicoloured .. .. .. 2·50 1·60
625 – 31 s. multicoloured .. .. .. 3·00 2·00
626 – 50 s. multicoloured .. .. .. 4·00 3·00
627 – 1 p. multicoloured .. .. .. 7·50 6·00
618/27 *and* O157/9 .. .. .. *Set of* 13 42·00 29·00

124 Humpback Whale (**125**)

1977 (16 Dec). *Whale Conservation. (a) Postage.*

628 **124** 15 s. black, grey and bright blue .. 1·00 40
629 22 s. black, grey and dull green.. .. 1·25 55
630 31 s. black, grey and orange .. 1·50 70
631 38 s. black, grey and bright lilac .. 2·00 95
632 64 s. black, grey and red-brown.. .. 3·25 1·50

(b) Air. Hexagonal design (66 × 51 mm) showing Sei and Fin Whales

633 – 11 s. multicoloured .. .. .. 1·00 35
634 – 17 s. multicoloured .. .. .. 1·25 50
635 – 18 s. multicoloured .. .. .. 1·25 50
636 – 39 s. multicoloured .. .. .. 2·00 1·00
637 – 50 s. multicoloured .. .. .. 2·75 1·40
628/37 *and* O160/2 .. .. .. *Set of* 13 24·00 12·00

1978 (17 Feb). *Various stamps surch as T* **125**. *(a) Postage.*

638 **115** 15 s. on 5 s. multicoloured .. .. 1·00 1·40
639 **119** 15 s. on 5 s. multicoloured (Br.).. .. 1·00 1·40
640 **117** 15 s. on 10 s. verm, blk & emerald (G.) .. 1·00 1·40
641 **119** 15 s. on 10 s. multicoloured .. .. 1·00 1·40
642 **121** 15 s. on 11 s. multicoloured (Blk. & Sil.) 3·00 3·25
643 **114** 15 s. on 20 s. multicoloured .. .. 1·00 1·40
644 – 15 s. on 38 s. mult (No. O133) (V.) .. 1·00 1·40

(b) Air

645 – 17 s. on 9 s. multicoloured (No. 533) .. 1·00 1·40
646 – 17 s. on 9 s. multicoloured (583) (V.) .. 1·00 1·40
647 – 17 s. on 12 s. multicoloured (534) (V.) .. 1·00 1·40
648 – 17 s. on 12 s. mult (573) (R. & Gold) .. 1·00 1·40
649 – 17 s. on 18 s. mult (595) (Olive & Br.) .. 1·00 1·40
650 – 17 s. on 38 s. multicoloured (527) (G.) .. 1·00 1·40
651 – 17 s. on 38 s. multicoloured (556) .. 1·00 1·40
652 – 1 p. on 35 s. mult (O151) (Silver & B.) .. 24·00 24·00
653 – 1 p. on 38 s. mult (576) (V. & Gold) .. 6·50 8·00
654 – 1 p. on 75 s. mult (572) (G. & Sil.) .. 6·50 8·00
638/54 .. .. *Set of* 17 48·00 55·00

The surcharges on Nos. 638/9 are formed by adding a figure "1" to the existing face value.

The surcharge on No. 644 includes the word "POSTAGE".

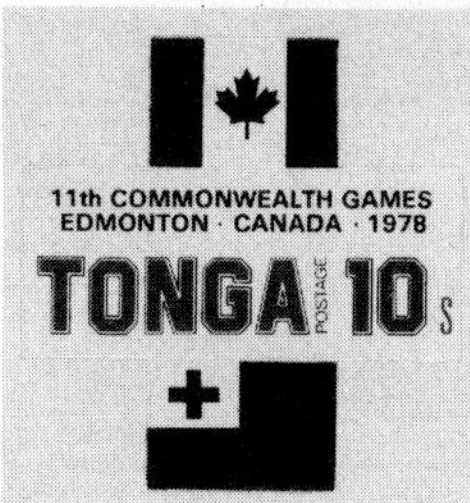

126 Flags of Canada and Tonga

1978 (5 May). *Commonwealth Games, Edmonton. (a) Postage.*

655 **126** 10 s. blue, red and black 15 15
656 15 s. multicoloured 25 25
657 20 s. turquoise-green, black and red .. 35 35
658 25 s. red, blue and black 40 40
659 45 s. black and red 90 90

(b) Air. Leaf-shaped design (39 × 40 mm) showing Maple Leaf

660 – 17 s. black and red 30 30
661 – 35 s. black, red and blue 60 60
662 – 38 s. black, red and turquoise-green .. 75 75
663 – 40 s. black, red and green 80 80
664 – 65 s. black, red and chestnut .. .. 1·40 1·40
655/64 *and* O163/5 .. .. .. *Set of* 13 8·00 8·00

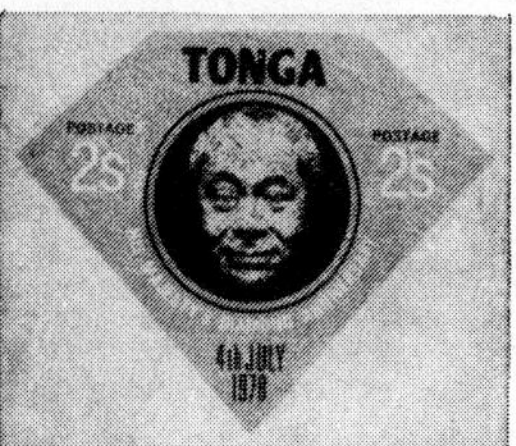

127 King Taufa'ahau Tupou IV

1978 (4 July). *60th Birthday of King Taufa'ahau Tupou IV.*

(a) Postage

665 **127** 2 s. black, deep blue and cobalt .. 10 10
666 5 s. black, deep blue and rose-pink .. 10 10
667 10 s. black, deep blue and mauve .. 20 20
668 25 s. black, deep blue and brownish grey 45 35
669 75 s. black, deep blue and yellow-ochre .. 1·10 1·00

(b) Air. Star-shaped design (44 × 51 mm) showing portrait of King

670 – 11 s. black, dp blue & greenish yellow .. 20 20
671 – 15 s. black, deep blue and cinnamon .. 30 25
672 – 17 s. black, deep blue and bright lilac .. 35 25
673 – 39 s. black, dp blue & turquoise-green .. 60 55
674 – 1 p. black, deep blue and pink .. .. 1·75 1·40
665/74 *and* O166/8 .. .. .. *Set of* 13 7·00 6·00

128 Banana

1978 (29 Sept)–**82.** *(a) Coil stamps. Designs as T* **128** *showing bananas (the number coinciding with the face value).*

675 1 s. black and greenish yellow 10 10
676 2 s. deep blue and greenish yellow 10 10
677 3 s. purple-brown, yellow and greenish yellow 15 15
678 4 s. deep blue, yellow and greenish yellow .. 15 15
679 5 s. vermilion, yellow and greenish yellow .. 15 15

(b) Coil stamps. Coconut-shaped design (18 × 26 mm)

680 6 s. purple, emerald and bistre-brown .. 20 20
681 7 s. greenish blue, emerald and light brown .. 30 30
682 8 s. vermilion, emerald and light brown .. 30 30
683 9 s. deep mauve, emerald and light brown .. 30 30
684 10 s. emerald and light brown 30 30

(c) Coil stamps. Pineapple-shaped design (17 × 30 mm)

684*a* 13 s. deep mauve, emerald and cinnamon (17.12.82).. .. .. .. 2·75 2·75
685 15 s. blue-green, orange-brown and emerald .. 50 50
686 20 s. brown, orange-brown and emerald .. 60 60
687 30 s. magenta, orange-brown and emerald .. 70 70
688 50 s. black, orange-brown and emerald .. 1·10 1·10
689 1 p. purple, orange-brown and emerald .. 1·90 1·90

(d) Mixed fruit oval design (55 × 29 mm)

689*a* 2 p. multicoloured (17.12.82).. .. .. 6·50 6·50
689*b* 3 p. multicoloured (17.12.82).. .. .. 8·50 8·50
675/89*b* .. .. *Set of* 18 22·00 22·00

Nos. 675/89 and O169/83 were produced in rolls, each even stamp having a number applied to the backing paper, with the usual inscription on the reverse.

129 Humpback Whale

1978 (15 Dec). *Endangered Wildlife Conservation. T* **129** *and similarly shaped designs. Multicoloured. (a) Postage.*

690 15 s. Type **129** 70 30
691 18 s. Insular Flying Fox 70 35
692 25 s. Turtle 80 40
693 28 s. Red Shining Parrot 90 50
694 60 s. Type **129** .. .. 1·75 1·40

(b) Air

695 17 s. Type **129** 70 35
696 22 s. As 18 s. 70 45
697 31 s. As 25 s. 85 55
698 39 s. As 28 s. .. .. 1·25 70
699 45 s. Type **129** .. .. 1·50 95
690/9 *and* O184/6 .. .. .. *Set of* 13 14·00 8·00

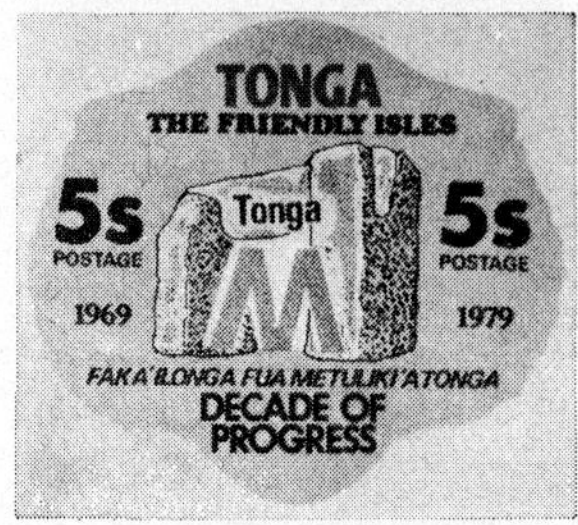

130 Metrication Symbol

1979 (16 Feb). *Decade of Progress. T* **130** *and other multi-angular designs in ultramarine and gold (31 s.) or multicoloured (others).*

(a) Postage

700 5 s. Type **130** 10 10
701 11 s. Map of South Pacific Islands 15 15
702 18 s. "Building wall of progress" with the assistance of the United States Peace Corps 25 20
703 22 s. New churches 35 25
704 50 s. Map showing air routes 70 50

(b) Air

705 15 s. As 50 s. 20 20
706 17 s. As 11 s. 25 20
707 31 s. Rotary International emblem 40 35
708 39 s. Government offices 55 40
709 1 p. "Communications" .. .. .. 1·40 1·25
700/9 *and* O187/9 .. .. .. *Set of* 13 6·50 5·00

131 Various Envelopes bearing Self-adhesive Stamps

1979 (1 June). *Death Centenary of Sir Rowland Hill and 10th Anniv of Tongan Self-adhesive Stamps. (a) Postage.*

710 **131** 5 s. multicoloured 10 10
711 10 s. multicoloured 20 15
712 25 s. multicoloured 55 35
713 50 s. multicoloured .. .. .. 1·00 60
714 1 p. multicoloured .. .. .. 2·00 1·25
a. Horiz roul omitted (vert pair) ..

(b) Air. Multi-angular design (53 × 53 mm) showing various self-adhesive stamps

715 – 15 s. multicoloured 30 20
716 – 17 s. multicoloured 35 25
717 – 18 s. multicoloured 35 25
718 – 31 s. multicoloured 60 40
719 – 39 s. multicoloured 75 45
710/19 *and* O190/2 .. .. .. *Set of* 13 9·00 6·00

132

(Des R. Edge and K. Jones)

1979 (17 Aug)–**82.** *Air. Coil stamps.*

720 **132** 5 s. black and cobalt 15 15
721 11 s. black and bright blue 25 25
722 14 s. black and violet 25 25
723 15 s. black and mauve 30 30
724 17 s. black and bright magenta 30 30
725 18 s. black and bright rose-red 30 30
726 22 s. black and orange-vermilion 35 35
726*a* 29 s. black and rose (17.12.82) .. .. 3·50 3·75
727 31 s. black and orange-yellow 55 55
727*a* 32 s. black and yellow-ochre (17.12.82) .. 4·00 4·50
728 39 s. black and bright yellow-green .. 70 70
728*a* 47 s. black and light brown (17.12.82) .. 5·00 5·50
729 75 s. black and bright blue-green .. 1·25 1·50
730 1 p. black and emerald .. .. .. 1·75 2·00
720/30 .. .. *Set of* 14 17·00 18·00

Nos. 720/30 and O193/203 were produced in rolls, each even stamp having a number applied to the backing paper, with the usual inscription on the reverse.

133 Rain Forest, Island of 'Eua

1979 (23 Nov). *Views as seen through the Lens of a Camera.*

(a) Postage

731 **133** 10 s. multicoloured 20 15
732 18 s. multicoloured 25 25
733 31 s. multicoloured 35 35
734 50 s. multicoloured 60 45
735 60 s. multicoloured 70 60

(b) Air. Design as T **133** *but showing Isle of Kao*

736 – 5 s. multicoloured 10 10
737 – 15 s. multicoloured 25 20
738 – 17 s. multicoloured 25 25
739 – 39 s. multicoloured 50 40
740 – 75 s. multicoloured 80 75
731/40 *and* O204/6 .. .. .. *Set of* 13 5·50 4·50

134 King George Tupou I, Admiral Du Bouzet and Map of Tonga

(135)

1980 (9 Jan). *125th Anniv of France–Tonga Treaty of Friendship.*

(a) Postage

741 **134** 7 s. multicoloured 10 15
742 10 s. multicoloured 15 20
743 14 s. multicoloured 20 25
744 50 s. multicoloured 70 75
745 75 s. multicoloured .. .. 1·00 1·10

(b) Air. Design as T **134** *but showing King George Tupou I, Napoleon III and "L'Aventure" (French warship)*

746 – 15 s. multicoloured 20 25
747 – 17 s. multicoloured 25 30
748 – 22 s. multicoloured 35 40
749 – 31 s. multicoloured 40 45
750 – 39 s. multicoloured 55 60
741/50 *and* O207/9 .. .. .. *Set of* 13 6·50 7·00

1980 (30 Apr). *Olympic Games, Moscow. Nos.* 710/19 *surch or optd only (No.* 755) *as T* **135** *in black on silver background.*

(a) Postage

751 **131** 13 s. on 5 s. multicoloured 30 30
752 20 s. on 10 s. multicoloured 40 40
753 25 s. multicoloured 45 45
754 33 s. on 50 s. multicoloured 55 55
755 1 p. multicoloured .. .. 2·00 2·00

(b) Air

756 – 9 s. on 15 s. multicoloured 25 25
757 – 16 s. on 17 s. multicoloured 40 40
758 – 29 s. on 18 s. multicoloured 60 60
759 – 32 s. on 31 s. multicoloured 65 65
760 – 47 s. on 39 s. multicoloured 85 85
751/60 *and* O210/12 .. .. .. *Set of* 13 9·00 9·00

136 Scout at Camp-fire

1980 (30 Sept). *South Pacific Scout Jamboree, Tonga and 75th Anniv of Rotary International. (a) Postage.*

761 **136** 9 s. multicoloured 30 15
762 13 s. multicoloured 40 20
763 15 s. multicoloured 40 20
764 30 s. multicoloured 75 40

(b) Air. Design as T **136** *showing Scout activities and Rotary emblem*

765 – 29 s. multicoloured 75 45
766 – 32 s. multicoloured 80 45
767 – 47 s. multicoloured .. .. 1·10 70
768 – 1 p. multicoloured .. .. 2·00 1·25
761/8 *and* O214/15 .. .. *Set of* 10 9·50 6·50

9

(137)

138 Red Cross and Tongan Flags, with Map of Tonga

1980 (3 Dec)–**82.** *Various stamps surch as T* **137**. *(a) Postage.*

769 **117** 9 s. on 35 s. vermilion, black and mauve 30 30
770 **119** 13 s. on 20 s. multicoloured 45 45
771 13 s. on 25 s. multicoloured 45 45
772 – 19 s. on 25 s. multicoloured (No. 571) .. 65 65
773 **114** 1 p. on 65 s. multicoloured .. .. 2·75 2·75
773*a* – 5 p. on 25 s. multicoloured (No. O214) (B.) (4.1.82) .. .. 9·50 9·50
773*b* – 5 p. on 2 p. multicoloured (No. O215) (B.) (4.1.82) .. .. 9·50 9·50
ba. Stamp omitted (centre stamp of strip of 3) .. ..

(b) Air

774 – 29 s. on 14 s. multicoloured (No. 585) .. 80 80
775 – 29 s. on 39 s. multicoloured (No. 597) .. 80 80
776 – 32 s. on 12 s. multicoloured (No. 554) .. 95 95
777 – 32 s. on 14 s. multicoloured (No. 574) .. 95 95
778 – 47 s. on 12 s. multicoloured (No. 524) .. 1·40 1·40
779 – 47 s. on 12 s. multicoloured (No. 584) .. 1·40 1·40
769/79 *and* O216 .. .. .. *Set of* 14 30·00 30·00

On No. 773ba the centre stamp in a vertical strip of 3 became detached so that the surcharge was applied to the white backing paper.

1981 (9 Sept). *International Year for Disabled Persons.*

(a) Postage. P 14½ × 14.

780 **138** 2 p. multicoloured .. .. .. 1·50 1·00
781 3 p. multicoloured .. .. .. 1·75 1·25

(b) Air. Vert design (25 × 33 mm) showing Red Cross flag and map depicting Tongatapu and Eua. P 13½

782 – 29 s. multicoloured 30 20
783 – 32 s. multicoloured 35 25
784 – 47 s. multicoloured 45 30
780/4 .. .. *Set of* 5 4·00 2·75

139 Prince Charles and King Taufa'ahau Tupou IV

1981 (21 Oct). *Royal Wedding and Centenary of Treaty of Friendship between Tonga and Great Britain. T* **139** *and similar vert designs. Multicoloured. P* 13½.

785 13 s. Type **139** 30 20
786 47 s. Prince Charles and Lady Diana Spencer 45 30
787 1 p. 50, Prince Charles and Lady Diana (*different*) .. .. 1·10 90
a. Imperf backing paper (pair) .. ..
788 3 p. Prince and Princess of Wales after wedding ceremony .. .. 2·00 1·40
785/8 .. .. *Set of* 4 3·50 2·50

140 Report of Printing in *Missionary Notices*

1981 (25 Nov). *Christmas. 150th Anniv of first Books Printed in Tonga. T* **140** *and similar horiz designs. Multicoloured. P* 13½.

789 9 s. Type **140** 25 15
790 13 s. *Missionary Notices* report (*different*) .. 30 20
791 32 s. Type in chase 75 40
792 47 s. Bible class .. .. 1·25 70
789/92 .. .. *Set of* 4 2·25 1·25

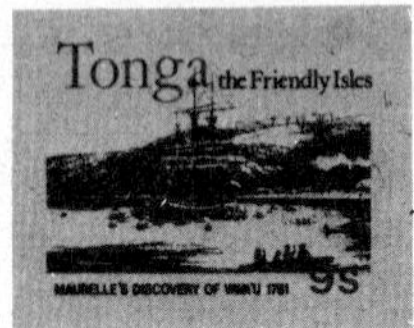

141 Landing Scene

1981 (25 Nov). *Bicentenary of Maurelle's Discovery of Vava'u. T* **141** *and similar horiz designs. Multicoloured. P* 14 × 14½.

793 9 s. Type **141** 30 20
794 13 s. Map of Vava'u 50 25
795 47 s. *La Princesa* .. .. 2·00 1·25
796 1 p. *La Princesa* (*different*) .. .. .. 4·50 3·00
793/6 .. .. *Set of* 4 6·50 4·25
MS797 100 × 78 mm. As No. 796. Imperf. .. 6·50 6·50

The stamp from No. **MS**797 is as No. 796 but without inscription at foot of design.

142 Battle Scene

1981 (16 Dec). *175th Anniv of Capture of "Port au Prince" (ship). T* **142** *and similar horiz designs in black and new blue. P* 13½.

798 29 s. Type **142** 45 2
799 32 s. Battle scene (*different*) 50 3
800 47 s. Map of Ha'apai Group 60 5
801 47 s. Native canoes preparing to attack .. 60 5
802 1 p. *Port au Prince* .. .. 1·25 7
798/802 .. .. *Set of* 5 3·00 2·1

The 47 s. values were printed together, *se-tenant*, in horizontal and vertical pairs throughout the sheet.

143 Baden-Powell at Brownsea Island, 1907

CYCLONE RELIEF

T$1+50s

POSTAGE & RELIEF

(144)

1982 (22 Feb). *75th Anniv of Boy Scout Movement and 125th Birth Anniv of Lord Baden-Powell. T* **143** *and similar vert designs. P* 13½.

803 29 s. Type **143** 45 3
804 32 s. Baden-Powell on his charger "Black Prince" 55 3
805 47 s. Baden-Powell at Imperial Jamboree, 1924 75 4
806 1 p. 50, Cover of first *Scouting for Boys* journal 1·90 1·2
807 2 p. 50, Newsboy, 1900 and Mafeking Siege 3d. stamp .. .. 3·75 2·7
803/7 .. .. *Set of* 5 6·75 4·5

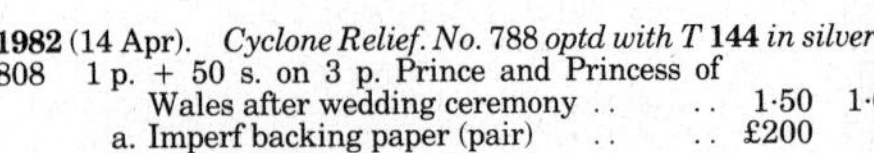

1982 (14 Apr). *Cyclone Relief. No.* 788 *optd with T* **144** *in silver.*

808 1 p. + 50 s. on 3 p. Prince and Princess of Wales after wedding ceremony .. .. 1·50 1·6
a. Imperf backing paper (pair) £200

145 Ball Control

146 M.V. *Olovaha II*

1982 (7 July). *World Cup Football Championship, Spain. T* 14 *and similar vert designs. Multicoloured. P* 13½.

809 32 s. Type **145** 45 4
810 47 s. Goalkeeping 60 6
811 75 s. Heading .. .. 1·00 9
812 1 p. 50, Shooting .. .. 1·75 1·7
809/12 .. .. *Set of* 4 3·50 3·2

1982 (11 Aug). *Inter-Island Transport. T* **146** *and similar horiz design. Multicoloured. P* 14 × 14½.
813 9 s. Type **146** 10 10
814 13 s. Type **146** 15 15
815 47 s. SPIA "Twin Otter" 55 60
816 1 p. As 47 s. 1·25 1·40
813/16 *Set of* 4 1·90 2·00

147 Mail Canoe

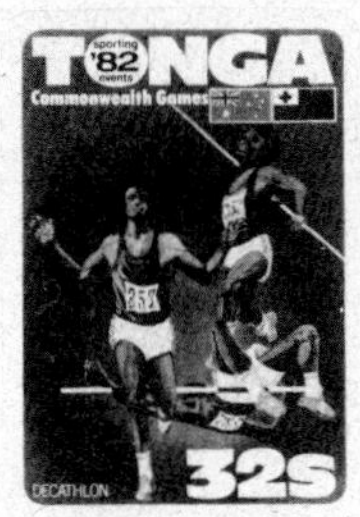

148 Decathlon

1982 (29 Sept). *Tin Can Mail Centenary. T* **147** *and similar vert designs. P* 13½ × 14.
817 13 s. multicoloured 15 15
818 32 s. multicoloured 25 25
819 47 s. multicoloured 35 35
820 2 p. black and pale turquoise-green 1·40 1·40
817/20 *Set of* 4 2·00 2·00
MS821 135 × 90 mm. Nos. 817/19. Imperf 1·25 1·50
MS822 135 × 89 mm. As No. 820 but with gold inscriptions. Imperf 2·75 3·25
Designs:—32 s. Mail canoe and ship; 47 s. Collecting Tin Can mail; 2 p. Map of Niuafo'ou.

1982 (25 Oct). *Commonwealth Games, Brisbane. T* **148** *and similar multicoloured design. P* 13½.
823 32 s. Type **148** 50 30
824 1 p. 50, Tongan Police band at opening ceremony (*horiz*) 2·75 1·50

149 Pupils

Christmas
Greetings
1982

(150)

1982 (25 Oct). *Tonga College Centenary. T* **149** *and similar multicoloured designs. P* 13½ (*Nos.* 825/6) *or* 14 × 14½ (*others*).
825 5 s. Type **149** (Tongan inscription) 25 10
826 5 s. Type **149** (English inscription) 25 10
827 29 s. School crest and monument (Tongan inscr) (29 × 22 *mm*) 85 65
828 29 s. As No. 827, but inscr in English 85 65
829 29 s. King George Tupou I (founder) and school (Tongan inscr) (29 × 22 *mm*) 85 65
830 29 s. As No. 829, but inscr in English 85 65
825/30 *Set of* 6 3·50 2·50
Nos. 825/6 were printed together, *se-tenant*, in pairs and Nos. 827/30 in blocks of four throughout the sheets.

1982 (17 Nov). *Christmas. Nos.* 817/19 *optd as T* **150** *in bright carmine* (13 *s.*) *or silver* (*others*).
831 13 s. Type **147** 15 15
a. Bright purple opt
832 32 s. Mail boat and ship 35 35
833 47 s. Collecting Tin Can mail 40 50
831/3 *Set of* 3 80 90

151 H.M.S. *Resolution*, and S. S. *Canberra*

1983 (22 Feb). *Sea and Air Transport. T* **151** *and similar horiz designs. Multicoloured. P* 14.
834 29 s. Type **151** (sage-green background) 75 75
835 32 s. Type **151** (buff background) 85 85
836 47 s. Montgolfier's balloon and "Concorde" (pale blue background) 1·50 1·50
837 1 p. 50, As No. 836 (lilac background) 2·75 2·75
834/7 *Set of* 4 5·25 5·25
MS838 120 × 165 mm. 2 p. 50, S.S. *Canberra* and "Concorde" 3·50 3·50

152 Globe and Inset of Tonga

153 SPIA DH "Twin Otter"

1983 (14 Mar). *Commonwealth Day. T* **152** *and similar horiz designs. Multicoloured. P* 14.
839 29 s. Type **152** 35 30
840 32 s. Tongan dancers 6·00 2·00
841 47 s. Trawler 50 50
842 1 p. 50, King Taufa'ahau Tupou IV and flag 1·75 1·75
839/42 *Set of* 4 7·75 4·00

1983 (11 May). *Inauguration of Niuafo'ou Airport. T* **153** *and similar horiz design. Multicoloured. P* 14 × 14½.
843 32 s. Type **153** 20 20
844 47 s. Type **153** 25 25
845 1 p. SPIA Boeing "707" 60 70
846 1 p. 50, As 1 p. 80 1·25
843/6 *Set of* 4 1·75 2·25

154 "Intelsat IV" Satellite

155 Obverse and Reverse of Pa'anga Banknote

1983 (22 June). *World Communications Year. T* **154** *and similar multicoloured designs. P* 11 (2 *p.*) *or* 14 × 14½ (*others*).
847 29 s. Type **154** 20 20
848 32 s. "Intelsat IVA" satellite 25 25
849 75 s. "Intelsat V" satellite 50 50
850 2 p. Moon post cover (45 × 32 *mm*) 1·10 1·40
847/50 *Set of* 4 1·90 2·10

1983 (3 Aug). *10th Anniv of Bank of Tonga. P* 14.
851 **155** 1 p. multicoloured 60 65
852 2 p. multicoloured 1·10 1·25

156 Early Printing Press

157 Yacht off Coast

(Des A. Benjamin and R. Edge)

1983 (22 Sept). *Printing in Tonga. T* **156** *and similar vert designs. Multicoloured. P* 14.
853 13 s. Type **156** 15 15
854 32 s. Arrival of W. Woon 25 25
855 1 p. Early Tongan print 50 60
856 2 p. *The Tonga Chronicle* 90 1·25
853/6 *Set of* 4 1·60 2·00

1983 (17 Nov). *Christmas. Yachting off Vava'u. T* **157** *and similar vert designs. Multicoloured. P* 11.
857 29 s. Type **157** 25 25
858 32 s. View of yacht from cave 25 25
859 1 p. 50, Anchored yacht 80 1·00
860 2 p. 50, Yacht off coast (*different*) 1·25 1·50
857/60 *Set of* 4 2·25 2·75

158 Abel Tasman and *Zeehan*

159 *Swainsonia casta*

(Des R. Edge)

1984 (12 Mar). *Navigators and Explorers of the Pacific* (1*st series*). *T* **158** *and similar horiz designs. P* 14.
861 32 s. deep dull green and black 80 80
862 47 s. reddish violet and black 1·25 1·25
863 90 s. light brown and black 2·00 2·00
864 1 p. 50, royal blue and black 3·00 3·00
861/4 *Set of* 4 6·25 6·25
Designs:—47 s. Samuel Wallis and H.M.S. *Dolphin*; 90 s. William Bligh and H.M.S. *Bounty*; 1 p. 50, James Cook and H.M.S. *Resolution*.
See also Nos. 896/9.

STAMPS DIE-CUT OR PERFORATED. During 1985 developments took place in the production of Tonga and Niuafo'ou self-adhesive stamps. Since 1981 these had been produced in traditional formats on backing paper perforated in the usual way. The individual stamps were, however, separated by the removal of the margins between them by the die-cutting process.

As an experiment some supplies of Tonga Nos. 870, 896, **MS**904, 905/9, 915/18, O225 and Niuafo'ou Nos. 56/60, together with the entire printing of Tonga Nos. 910/14, were produced with the margins intact so that both stamps and backing paper were perforated through.

Such issues are usually inscribed "Bend forward and peel off backing paper" on the reverse.

1984 (10 Apr)–**85**. *Marine Life. T* **159** *and similar multicoloured designs. Stamps die-cut and backing paper perf* 14 (1, 2, 3, 5 *p.*) *or* 14½ (*others*).
865 1 s. Type **159** 15 15
866 2 s. *Porites sp* (26.6.84) 25 25
867 3 s. *Holocentrus ruber* (18.5.84) 30 30
868 5 s. *Cyprae mappa viridis* 30 30
869 6 s. *Dardanus megistos* (crab) (17.9.84) 35 35
870 9 s. *Stegostoma fasciatum* (18.5.84) 35 35
b. Stamp perforated (28.5.85) 35 35
871 10 s. *Conus bullatus* 45 45
872 13 s. *Pterois volitans* (18.5.84) 45 45
873 15 s. *Conus textile* 50 50
874 20 s. *Dascyllus aruanus* (18.5.84) 60 60
875 29 s. *Conus aulicus* 70 70
876 32 s. *Acanthurus leucosternon* (18.5.84) 80 80
877 47 s. *Lambis truncata* 1·10 1·10
878 1 p. *Millepora dichotoma* (26.6.84) 2·50 2·50
879 2 p. *Birgus latro* (crab) (17.9.84) 4·00 4·00
880 3 p. *Chicoreus palma-rosae* 5·00 5·00
881 5 p. *Thunnus albacares* (18.5.84) 7·50 7·50
865/81 *Set of* 17 23·00 23·00
Nos. 878/81 are horizontal, 38 × 23 mm.
For 1, 2, 5, 6, 10, 15, 20, 32 s. and 3 p. with normal gum and perforations see Nos. 976*a*/*b*, 999/1017 and 1087/95.

160 Printer checking Newspaper

161 U.S.A. Flag and Running

1984 (26 June). *20th Anniv of* Tonga Chronicle (*newspaper*). *Die-cut.*
882 **160** 3 s. grey-brown and bright blue 10 10
a. Sheetlet of 12 50
883 32 s. grey-brown and vermilion 40 45
a. Sheetlet of 12 4·75
Nos. 882/3 were each printed in sheetlets of 12, the designs being superimposed on a reproduction of the front page from the first edition. This was printed in grey and is in Tongan for the 3 s. and English for the 32 s.

(Des R. Edge)

1984 (23 July). *Olympic Games, Los Angeles. T* **161** *and similar horiz designs, each showing U.S. flag. Each printed in black, scarlet-vermilion and bright new blue. P* 14 × 14½.
884 29 s. Type **161** 25 25
885 47 s. Javelin-throwing 30 30
886 1 p. 50, Shot-putting 85 85
887 3 p. Olympic torch 1·60 1·60
884/7 *Set of* 4 2·75 2·75

162 Sir George Airy and Dateline on World Map

163 Australia 1914 Kookaburra 6d. Stamp

(Des R. Edge)

1984 (20 Aug). *Centenary of International Dateline. T* **162** *and similar horiz design. Multicoloured. P* 14.
888 47 s. Type **162** 75 75
889 2 p. Sir Sandford Fleming and Map of Pacific time zones 3·00 3·25

1984 (17 Sept). *"Ausipex" International Stamp Exhibition, Melbourne. T* **163** *and similar vert design. Multicoloured. P* 14.
890 32 s. Type **163** 60 60
891 1 p. 50, Tonga 1897 Parrot 2s. 6d. stamp 2·25 2·25
MS892 90 × 100 mm. As Nos. 890/1, but without exhibition logo and with "TONGA" and face values in gold. Die-cut 1·90 2·25
Examples of No. **MS**892 without face values are Exhibition Banquet souvenirs without postal validity.

MINIMUM PRICE

The minimum price quote is 10p which represents a handling charge rather than a basis for valuing common stamps. For further notes about prices see introductory pages.

164 Beach at Sunset ("Silent Night")

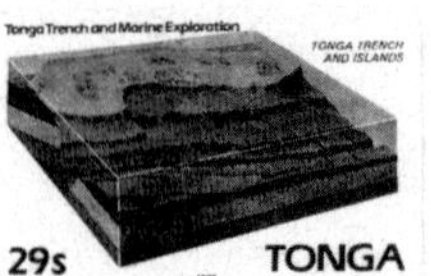

165 Section of Tonga Trench

(Des R. Edge)

1984 (12 Nov). *Christmas. Carols. T* **164** *and similar vert designs. Multicoloured. P* 14.

893 32 s. Type **164** 40 45
894 47 s. Hut and palm trees ("Away in a Manger") 60 65
895 1 p. Sailing boats ("I Saw Three Ships") .. 1·25 1·40
893/5 .. .. *Set of* 3 1·90 2·25

Nos. 893/5 were each issued in sheets of 20 stamps with 5 labels, in the central vertical row, showing progressive stages of the design.

(Des R. Edge)

1985 (27 Feb). *Navigators and Explorers of the Pacific* (2*nd series*). *Horiz designs as T* **158**. *Stamps die-cut and backing paper perf* 14.

896 32 s. black and turquoise-blue 90 55
b. Stamp perforated .. .. .. 25·00 25·00
897 47 s. black and blue-green .. .. .. 1·25 75
898 90 s. black and scarlet .. .. .. 2·25 1·75
899 1 p. 50, black and buff .. .. .. 3·25 2·50
896/9 .. .. *Set of* 4 7·00 5·00

Designs:—32 s. Willem Schouten and *Eendracht*; 47 s. Jacob Le Maire and *Hoorn*; 90 s. Fletcher Christian and *Bounty*; 1 p. 50, Francisco Maurelle and *La Princessa*.

No. 896b has no inscription on the reverse.

1985 (10 Apr). *Geological Survey of the Tonga Trench. T* **165** *and similar multicoloured designs. Stamps die-cut and backing paper perf* 14.

900 29 s. Type **165** .. .. 1·00 1·00
901 32 s. Diagram of marine seismic survey .. 1·00 1·00
902 47 s. Diagram of aerial oil survey (*vert*) .. 1·25 1·25
903 1 p. 50, Diagram of sea bed survey (*vert*) .. 3·00 3·00
900/3 .. .. *Set of* 4 5·75 5·75
MS904 100 × 100 mm. 1 p. 50, Angler Fish. Die-cut .. .. 1·75 2·00
b. Stamp perforated .. .. .. 5·00

166 *Port au Prince* at Gravesend, 1805

167 Quintal (Byron Russell) and Capt. Bligh (Charles Laughton)

1985 (18 June). *175th Anniv of Will Mariner's Departure for England. T* **166** *and similar horiz designs. Multicoloured. A. Stamp die-cut and backing paper perf* 14. *B. Both stamp and backing paper perf* 14.

		A		B	
905	29 s. Type **166**	30	35	30	35
906	32 s. Capture of *Port au Prince*, Tonga, 1806	30	35	30	35
907	47 s. Will Mariner on Tongan canoe, 1807	45	50	45	50
908	1 p. 50, Mariner boarding brig *Favourite*, 1810	1·40	1·50	1·40	1·50
909	2 p. 50, *Cuffnells* in English Channel, 1811	2·40	2·50	2·40	2·50
905/9	.. .. .. *Set of* 5	4·25	4·50	4·25	4·50

1985 (16 July). *50th Anniv of Film "Mutiny on the Bounty". T* **167** *and similar horiz designs showing film stills. Multicoloured. Both stamp and backing paper perf* 14.

910 47 s. Type **167** .. .. 1·75 1·75
a. Horiz strip of 5. Nos. 910/14 .. .. 8·00
911 47 s. Captain Bligh and prisoners .. .. 1·75 1·75
912 47 s. Fletcher Christian (Clark Gable) .. 1·75 1·75
913 47 s. Mutineers threatening Bligh .. .. 1·75 1·75
914 47 s. Bligh and Roger Byam (Franchot Tone) in boat .. .. 1·75 1·75
910/14 .. .. *Set of* 5 8·00 8·00

Nos. 910/14 were printed together, *se-tenant*, in horizontal strips of 5 throughout the sheet.

168 Lady Elizabeth Bowes-Lyon, 1910

169 Mary and Joseph arriving at Inn

1985 (20 Aug). *Life and Times of Queen Elizabeth the Queen Mother and 75th Anniv of Girl Guide Movement. T* **168** *and similar horiz designs. A. Stamp die-cut and backing paper perf* 14. *B. Both stamp and backing paper perf* 14.

		A		B	
915	32 s. black, salmon-pink and reddish brown	30	35	60	65
916	47 s. black, pale rose-lilac and reddish brown	45	50	90	1·00
917	1 p. 50, black, olive-yellow and reddish brown	1·40	1·50	2·75	3·00
918	2 p. 50, multicoloured	2·40	2·50	4·75	5·00
915/18	.. .. *Set of* 4	4·00	4·25	8·00	8·50

Designs:—47 s. Duchess of York at Hadfield Girl Guides' Rally, 1931; 1 p. 50, Duchess of York in Girl Guide uniform; 2 p. 50, Queen Mother in 1985 (from photo by Norman Parkinson).

1985 (12 Nov). *Christmas. T* **169** *and similar vert designs. Multicoloured. P* 14.

919 32 s. Type **169** 25 30
920 42 s. The shepherds 35 40
921 1 p. 50, The Three Wise Men .. .. 1·25 1·40
922 2 p. 50, The Holy Family .. .. .. 2·10 2·25
919/22 .. .. *Set of* 4 3·50 4·00

NOTE. Unless stated otherwise Tonga issues from No. 922 had the normal form of gum and were not self-adhesive.

170 Comet and Slogan "Maybe Twice in a Lifetime"

4s ■ 4s

(171)

(Litho Walsall)

1986 (26 Mar). *Appearance of Halley's Comet. T* **170** *and similar horiz designs. Multicoloured. P* 14.

923 42 s. Type **170** 80 80
a. Horiz strip of 5. Nos. 923/7 .. .. 3·50
924 42 s. Edmond Halley 80 80
925 42 s. Solar System 80 80
926 42 s. Telescope 80 80
927 42 s. *Giotto* spacecraft 80 80
928 57 s. Type **170** 90 90
a. Horiz strip of 5. Nos. 928/32 .. .. 4·00
929 57 s. As No. 924 .. .. 90 90
930 57 s. As No. 925 .. .. 90 90
931 57 s. As No. 926 .. .. 90 90
932 57 s. As No. 927 .. .. 90 90
923/32 .. .. *Set of* 10 7·50 7·50

Nos. 923/7 and 928/32 were each printed together, *se-tenant*, in horizontal strips of five, forming composite designs, throughout the sheets.

1986 (16 Apr). *Nos.* 866/7, 869/70, 872, 874, 879 *and* 881 *surch as T* **171**.

933 4 s. on 2 s. *Porites sp.* 10 10
934 4 s. on 13 s. *Pterois volitans* 10 10
935 42 s. on 3 s. *Holocentrus ruber* 30 35
936 42 s. on 9 s. *Stegostoma fasciatum* 30 35
937 57 s. on 6 s. *Dardanus megistos* 40 45
938 57 s. on 20 s. *Dascyllus aruanus* 40 45
939 2 p. 50 on 2 p. *Birgus latro* .. .. .. 2·10 2·25
940 2 p. 50 on 5 p. *Thunnus albacares* .. .. 2·10 2·25
933/40 .. .. *Set of* 8 5·00 5·50

172 King Taufa'ahau Tupou IV of Tonga

(Litho Walsall)

1986 (22 May). *Royal Links with Great Britain and 60th Birthday of Queen Elizabeth II. T* **172** *and similar designs. P* 14.

941 **172** 57 s. multicoloured 65 65
a. Horiz pair. Nos. 941/2 .. .. 1·25 1·25
942 – 57 s. multicoloured 65 65
943 – 2 p. 50, reddish brown, blk & pale new bl 2·25 2·50
941/3 .. .. *Set of* 3 3·50 3·75

Designs: *Horiz* (*as T* **172**)—No. 942, Queen Elizabeth II. *Square* (40 × 40 *mm*)—No. 943, Queen Elizabeth II and King Taufa'ahau Tupou IV, Tonga, 1970.

Nos. 941/2 were printed together, *se-tenant*, in horizontal pairs throughout the sheet, and No. 943 in sheetlets of five stamps and one stamp-size label.

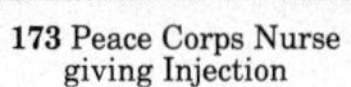

173 Peace Corps Nurse giving Injection

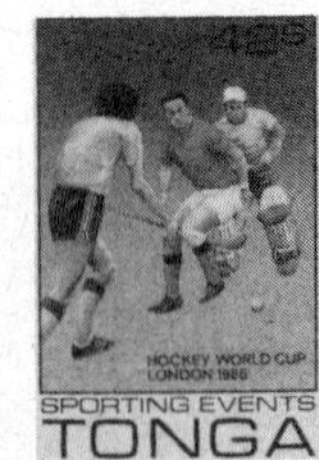

174 Hockey (World Hockey Cup for Men, London)

(Litho Walsall)

1986 (22 May). *"Ameripex '86" International Stamp Exhibition, Chicago. 25th Anniv of United States Peace Corps. T* **173** *and similar horiz design. Multicoloured. P* 14.

944 57 s. Type **173** 45 50
945 1 p. 50, Peace Corps teacher and pupil .. 1·25 1·40
MS946 90 × 90 mm. Nos. 944/5, magnifying glass and tweezers. Imperf .. .. 1·75 2·00

(Litho Walsall)

1986 (23 July). *Sporting Events. T* **174** *and similar vert designs. Multicoloured. P* 14.

947 42 s. Type **174** 65 65
948 57 s. Handball (13th Commonwealth Games, Edinburgh) 75 75
949 1 p. Boxing (13th Commonwealth Games, Edinburgh) .. .. 1·40 1·40
950 2 p. 50, Football (World Cup Football Championship, Mexico) .. .. 3·50 3·50
947/50 .. .. *Set of* 4 5·75 5·75

175 1886 1d. King George I Definitive

(Des A. Benjamin. Litho Walsall)

1986 (27 Aug). *Centenary of First Tonga Stamps. T* **175** *and similar multicoloured designs. P* 14.

951 32 s. Type **175** 65 65
952 42 s. 1897 7½d. King George II inverted centre error 80 80
953 57 s. 1950 Queen Salote's 50th Birthday 1d. 1·00 1·00
954 2 p. 50, 1986 Royal Links with Great Britain 2 p. 50 .. .. 3·00 3·00
951/4 .. .. *Set of* 4 5·00 5·00
MS955 132 × 104 mm. 50 s. × 8 Vert designs forming montage of Tonga stamps .. .. .. 6·00 6·50

Nos. 951/5 were printed with an overall pattern similar to watermark W **24**.

176 Girls wearing Shell Jewellery

(177)

(Litho Walsall)

1986 (12 Nov). *Christmas. T* **176** *and similar multicoloured designs. P* 14.

956 32 s. Type **176** 50 45
957 42 s. Boy with wood carvings (*vert*) 70 60
958 57 s. Children performing traditional dance (*vert*) 85 75
959 2 p. Children in dugout canoe .. .. 2·75 3·00
956/9 .. .. *Set of* 4 4·25 4·25

1986 (2 Dec). *Scout Jamboree, Tongatapu. Nos.* 957/8 *optd with T* **177** *in silver.*

960 42 s. Boy with wood carvings (*vert*) .. .. 1·25 1·25
961 57 s. Children performing traditional dance (*vert*) .. .. 1·75 1·75

178 Dumont D'Urville and *L'Astrolabe*

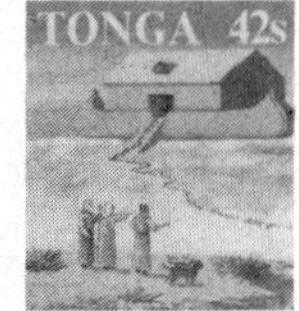

179 Noah's Ark

(Litho Walsall)

1987 (24 Feb). *150th Anniv of Dumont D'Urville's Second Voyage. T* **178** *and similar horiz designs. Multicoloured. P* 14.

962 32 s. Type **178** .. .. 1·10 1·1
963 42 s. Tongan girls (from *Voyage au Pole et dans l'Oceanie*) .. .. 1·40 1·4
964 1 p. Contemporary chart .. .. .. 2·75 2·7
965 2 p. 50, Wreck of *L'Astrolabe* .. .. 5·00 5·0
962/5 .. .. *Set of* 4 8·50 8·5

(Des and litho Walsall)

1987 (6 May). *World Wildlife Fund. Sheet* 115 × 110 *mm containing T* **179** *and similar vert designs. Multicoloured. P* 13½.

MS966 42 s. Type **179**; 42 s. Eagles; 42 s. Giraffes and birds; 42 s. Gulls; 42 s. Ostriches and elephants; 42 s. Elephant; 42 s. Lions, zebras, antelopes and giraffes; 42 s. Chimpanzees; 42 s. Frogs and antelopes; 42 s. Lizard and tigers; 42 s. Snake and tiger; 42 s. *Papilio machaon* (butterfly) .. .. 6·00 6·5

The stamps within No. **MS**966 show a composite design of animals entering Noah's Ark.

180 Two Paddlers in Canoe **181** King Taufa'ahau Tupou IV

(Des C. Abbott. Litho Questa)

1987 (1 July). *"Siv'a'alo" (Tonga-Fiji-Samoa) Canoe Race. T* **180** *and similar square designs. Multicoloured. P* 14.
967 32 s. Type **180**.. .. .. 25 30
968 42 s. Five paddlers 35 40
969 57 s. Paddlers and canoe bow 45 50
a. Value omitted (R. 3/2) £500
970 1 p. 50, Two paddlers (different) .. .. 1·10 1·25
967/70 .. .. *Set of* 4 1·90 2·25
MS971 153×59 mm. Nos. 967/70 .. .. 2·10 2·50

The stamps within No. **MS**971 show a composite design of two canoes racing.

No. 969a occurred on a batch of fifty sheets distributed to local post offices in Tonga. The remainder of the first printing was withdrawn and replaced, later in the month, by sheets showing the error corrected.

(Des and litho Walsall)

1987 (1 July)–**88**. *20th Anniv of Coronation of King Taufa'ahau Tupou IV. Self-adhesive. Stamps die-cut.*
972 **181** 1 s. black and olive-green 10 10
a. Booklet pane. Nos. 972×2, 974×4, 975×2 and 976×4 .. .. 1·60
b. Booklet pane. Nos. 972, 972*d*×2, 973×2, 974×4 and 975×3 (4.7.88) 95
c. Booklet pane. Nos. 972×4, 972*d*×2 and 976×6 (4.7.88) .. .. 1·90
972*d* 2 s. black and pale orange (4.7.88) .. 10 10
973 5 s. black and pale magenta 10 10
a. Booklet pane. Nos. 973×7, 974×2 and 975×3.. 80
974 10 s. black and reddish lilac 10 10
975 15 s. black and rose-red.. .. .. 15 20
976 32 s. black and turquoise-blue.. .. 30 35
972/6 .. .. *Set of* 6 55 70

Nos. 972/6 were only available from stamp booklets. These are self-adhesive stamps and the backing card forms the booklet cover.

(Litho Walsall)

1987 (Sept). *As Nos.* 871 *and* 876 *(previously self-adhesive), but printed with normal gum and perforations. Multicoloured. P* 14½.
976*a* 10 s. *Conus bullatus* .. .. .. 4·00 4·00
976*b* 32 s. *Acanthurus leucosternon* .. .. 11·00 11·00

Nos. 976*a/b* were printed from the same plates as the self-adhesive issue. They are without imprint date at foot and show a space of 23 mm between the two horizontal lines across each design.

For redrawn versions of these stamps with imprint date see Nos. 1005 and 1008.

182 Arms and Tongan Citizens **183** Father Christmas Octopus and Rat with Sack of Presents

(Des and litho Walsall)

1987 (23 Sept). *125th Anniv of First Parliament. P* 14½×14.
977 **182** 32 s. multicoloured 25 30
978 42 s. multicoloured 35 40
979 75 s. multicoloured 60 65
980 2 p. multicoloured .. .. .. 1·60 1·75
977/80 .. .. *Set of* 4 2·50 2·75

(Des and litho Walsall)

1987 (25 Nov). *Christmas. T* **183** *and similar horiz designs showing cartoons. Multicoloured. P* 13½×14.
981 42 s. Type **183** 40 45
982 57 s. Delivering presents by outrigger canoe 60 65
983 1 p. Delivering presents by motorised tricycle .. .. 95 1·00
984 3 p. Drinking cocktails .. .. .. 2·75 3·00
981/4 .. .. *Set of* 4 4·00 4·50

PRICES OF SETS

Set prices are given for many issues, generally those containing three stamps or more. Definitive sets include one of each value or major colour change, but do not cover different perforations, die types or minor shades. Where a choice is possible the set prices are based on the cheapest versions of the stamps included in the listings.

184 King Taufa'ahau Tupou IV, *Olovaha* (inter-island ferry), Oil Rig and Pole Vaulting

(Des and litho Walsall)

1988 (4 July). *70th Birthday of King Taufa'ahau Tupou IV. T* **184** *and similar horiz designs, each showing portrait. Multicoloured. P* 11½.
985 32 s. Type **184** 30 35
986 42 s. Banknote, coins, Ha'amonga Trilithon and woodcarver 40 45
987 57 s. Rowing, communications satellite and Red Cross worker 60 65
988 2 p. 50, Scout emblem, 1982 47 s. Scout stamp and Friendly Island Airways aircraft .. .. 2·40 2·50
985/8 .. .. *Set of* 4 3·25 3·50

For similar designs issued in 1990 for the King's Silver Jubilee see Nos. 1082/5.

185 Capt. Cook and Journal **186** Athletics

(Des and litho Walsall)

1988 (11 July). *Bicentenary of Australian Settlement. Sheet* 115 × 110 *mm containing T* **185** *and similar vert designs. Multicoloured. P* 13½.
MS989 42 s. Type **185**; 42 s. Ships in Sydney Harbour and Governor Philip; 42 s. Australia 1952 2s. 6d. aborigine definitive and early settlement; 42 s. Burke and Wills (explorers); 42 s. Emu, opals and gold prospector's licence; 42 s. ANZAC cap badge and soldier; 42 s. Cover from first overland mail by Trans Continental; 42 s. Ross Smith, England–Australia flown cover and G.B. 1969 1s. 9d. commemorative stamp; 42 s. Don Bradman and Harold Larwood (cricketers); 42 s. World War II campaign medals; 42 s. Australia 1978 18 c. Flying Doctor Service stamp and sheep station; 42 s. Sydney Opera House .. .. 6·00 6·50

(Des and litho Walsall)

1988 (11 Aug). *Olympic Games, Seoul. T* **186** *and similar vert designs. Multicoloured. P* 14.
990 57 s. Type **186** 60 65
991 75 s. Yachting 70 75
992 2 p. Cycling .. .. 1·90 2·00
993 3 p. Tennis .. .. 2·75 3·00
990/3 .. .. *Set of* 4 5·25 5·75

187 Traditional Tongan Fale

(Des and litho Walsall)

1988 (9 Sept). *Music in Tonga. T* **187** *and similar horiz designs. Multicoloured. P* 14.
994 32 s. Type **187** 30 35
995 42 s. Church choir 40 45
996 57 s. Tonga Police Band outside Royal Palace 55 60
997 2 p. 50, "The Jets" pop group .. .. 2·40 2·50
994/7 .. .. *Set of* 4 3·25 3·50

188 Olympic Flame

(Des and litho Walsall)

1988 (9 Sept). *"Sport Aid '88". Sheet* 105 × 75 *mm, containing T* **188** *and design as No.* 997. *Multicoloured. P* 14.
MS998 57 s. Type **188**; 57 s. As No. 997 .. 1·10 1·40

Two types of 42 s.:

Type I. Background shading in bright blue extending to the perforation margin. Plumage is light brown.
Type II. Background shading in oval of new blue bleeding off at edges. Plumage is sepia.

(Litho Walsall)

1988 (4 Oct)–**92**. *Redrawn designs as Nos.* 865/6, 868/9, 871/6, 879/81 *(previously self-adhesive) and new values* (7, 35, 42, 57 *s.*, 1 *p.*, 1 *p.* 50, 10 *p.*), *all with normal gum, perforations and imprint date at foot. Multicoloured. Chalk-surfaced paper* (4, 7, 35, 42, 50, 57 *s.*, 1 *p.*, 1 *p.* 50., 2 *p.*, 5 *p.*, 10 *p.*). *P* 14 (1 *p.* to 10 *p.*) *or* 14½×14 *(others).*
999 1 s. Type **159** 10 10
1000 2 s. *Porites* sp (18.10.88) 10 10
a. Chalk-surfaced paper (4.90) .. 15 15
1001 4 s. *Pterois volitans* (2.3.89) 10 10
1002 5 s. *Cypraea mappa viridis* 10 10
a. Chalk-surfaced paper (4.90) .. 15 15
1003 6 s. *Dardanus megistos* (crab) (18.10.88) 10 10
1004 7 s. Wandering Albatross (2.3.89) .. 10 10
1005 10 s. *Conus bullatus* 10 10
a. Chalk-surfaced paper (4.90) .. 15 15
1006 15 s. *Conus textile* (18.10.88) 15 20
1007 20 s. *Dascyllus aruanus* 20 25
1008 32 s. *Acanthurus leucosternon* 35 30
a. Chalk-surfaced paper (4.90) .. 35 30
1009 35 s. Sea Horse (2.3.89) 35 40
1010 42 s. Lesser Frigate Bird (I) (18.10.88) .. 40 45
a. Type II .. .. 7·00
1011 50 s. *Conus aulicus* (2.3.89) 45 50
1012 57 s. Brown Booby (18.10.88) 50 55
1013 1 p. *Chelonia mydas* (turtle) (2.3.89) .. 90 95
1014 1 p. 50, Humpback Whale (2.3.89) .. 1·40 1·50
1015 2 p. *Birgus latro* (crab) (19.1.89) .. 1·90 2·00
1016 3 p. *Chicoreus palma-rosae* (18.10.88) .. 2·75 3·00
1017 5 p. *Thunnus albacares* (19.1.89) .. 4·50 4·75
1017*a* 10 p. *Stegostoma fasciatum* (12.5.92) .. 9·25 9·50
999/1017*a* .. .. .. *Set of* 20 22·00 23·00

Nos. 1013/17 are horizontal, 41×26 mm and No. 1017*a* vertical, 26×41 mm.

On the redrawn designs there is a larger gap between the two horizontal lines on each design. For Nos. 1005 and 1008 this measures 25 mm. For these two values with a gap of 23 mm and no imprint date see Nos. 916*a/b*.

For 2, 5, 10, 15 and 32 s. values in a smaller format see Nos. 1087/95

189 Capt. Cook's H.M.S. *Resolution* **190** Girl in Hospital Bed

(Des and litho Walsall)

1988 (20 Oct). *Centenary of Tonga–U.S.A. Treaty of Friendship. T* **189** *and similar horiz designs. Multicoloured. P* 14.
1018 42 s. Type **189** 40 45
1019 57 s. *Santa Maria*.. .. .. .. 55 60
1020 2 p. Cook and Christopher Columbus .. 1·90 2·00
1018/20 .. .. *Set of* 3 2·50 2·75
MS1021 140 × 115 mm. Nos. 1018/20 .. .. 2·75 3·25

(Des and litho Walsall)

1988 (17 Nov). *Christmas. 125th Anniv of International Red Cross and 25th Anniv of Tongan Red Cross. T* **123** *and similar horiz designs. Multicoloured. P* 14½.
1022 15 s. Type **190** (A) 15 20
a. Horiz pair. Nos. 1022/3 .. .. 30 40
1023 15 s. Type **190** (B).. .. .. .. 15 20
1024 32 s. Red Cross nurse reading to boy (A) .. 30 35
a. Horiz pair. Nos. 1024/5 .. .. 60 70
1025 32 s. Red Cross nurse reading to boy (B) .. 30 35
1026 42 s. Red Cross nurse taking pulse (A) .. 40 45
a. Horiz pair. Nos. 1026/7 .. .. 80 85
1027 42 s. Red Cross nurse taking pulse (B) .. 40 45
1028 57 s. Red Cross nurse with sleeping child (A) 55 60
a. Horiz pair. Nos. 1028/9 .. .. 1·10 1·25
1029 57 s. Red Cross nurse with sleeping child (B) 55 60
1030 1 p. 50, Boy in wheelchair (A) .. .. 1·40 1·50
a. Horiz pair. Nos. 1030/1 .. .. 2·75 3·00
1031 1 p. 50, Boy in wheelchair (B) .. .. 1·40 1·50
1022/31 .. .. *Set of* 10 5·00 5·50

Nos. 1022/3, 1024/5, 1026/7, 1028/9 and 1030/1 were printed together, *se-tenant*, in horizontal pairs throughout the sheets with the first stamp in each pair inscribed "INTERNATIONAL RED CROSS 125th ANNIVERSARY" (A) and the second "SILVER JUBILEE OF TONGAN RED CROSS" (B).

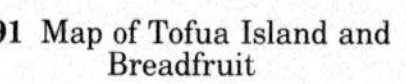

191 Map of Tofua Island and Breadfruit **192** *Hypolimnas bolina*

(Des and litho Walsall)

1989 (28 Apr). *Bicentenary of Mutiny on the* Bounty. *T* **191** *and similar multicoloured designs. P* 13½×14.

1032 32 s. Type **191** 60 60
1033 42 s. H.M.S. *Bounty* and chronometer .. 80 80
1034 57 s. Captain Bligh and *Bounty's* launch cast adrift .. .. 1·25 1·25
1032/4 .. .. *Set of* 3 2·40 2·40
MS1035 106×80 mm. 2 p. Fletcher Christian on H.M.S. *Bounty* (*vert*); 3 p. Bligh cast adrift. P 14×13½ (2 p.) or 13½×14×13½×13½ (3 p.) 6·00 7·00

(Litho Walsall)

1989 (18 May). *Butterflies. T* **192** *and similar vert designs. Multicoloured. P* 14½×14.

1036 42 s. Type **192** 70 70
1037 57 s. *Jamides bochus* 90 90
1038 1 p. 20, *Melanitis leda* .. .. .. 1·50 1·50
1039 2 p. 50, *Danaus plexippus* .. .. .. 3·50 3·50
1036/9 .. .. *Set of* 4 6·00 6·00

193 Football at Rugby School, 1870

194 Short "S30" Flying Boat, 1939 (50th anniv of first flight)

(Litho Walsall)

1989 (22 Aug). *Inauguration of National Sports Stadium and South Pacific Mini Games, Tonga. T* **193** *and similar horiz designs showing development of rugby, tennis and cricket. Multicoloured. P* 14.

1040 32 s. Type **193** 30 35
a. Sheetlet. Nos. 1040/4×2 .. .. 3·00
1041 32 s. D. Gallaher (All Black's captain, 1905) and Springboks rugby match, 1906 30 35
1042 32 s. King George V with Cambridge team, 1922 and W. Wakefield (England captain, 1926) 30 35
1043 32 s. E. Crawford (Ireland captain, 1926) and players on cigarette cards .. 30 35
1044 32 s. S. Mafi (Tonga captain, 1970s) and modern rugby match 30 35
1045 42 s. Royal tennis, 1659 .. .. .. 40 45
a. Sheetlet. Nos. 1045/9×2 .. .. 4·00
1046 42 s. Major Wingfield and lawn tennis, 1873 .. .. 40 45
1047 42 s. Oxford and Cambridge tennis teams, 1884 .. .. 40 45
1048 42 s. Bunny Ryan, 1910, and players on cigarette cards 40 45
1049 42 s. Boris Becker and modern tennis match 40 45
1050 57 s. Cricket match, 1743, and F. Pilch memorial 55 60
a. Sheetlet. Nos. 1050/4×2 .. .. 5·50
1051 57 s. W. G. Grace (19th-century cricketer) 55 60
1052 57 s. *Boys Own Paper* cricket article, 1909 55 60
1053 57 s. Australian cricket team, 1909, and players on cigarette cards 55 60
1054 57 s. The Ashes urn, and modern cricket match 55 60
1040/54 .. .. *Set of* 15 5·50 6·25

Nos. 1040/4, 1045/9 and 1050/4 were each issued in sheetlets of ten containing two horizontal strips of five separated by a central inscribed gutter.

(Litho Walsall)

1989 (23 Oct). *Aviation in Tonga. T* **194** *and similar horiz designs. Multicoloured. P* 14½×14.

1055 42 s. Type **194** 80 80
1056 57 s. Vought "F4U Corsair", 1943 .. 1·25 1·25
1057 90 s. Boeing "737" at Fua'amotu Airport 1·75 1·75
1058 3 p. Montgolfier balloon, Wright biplane, "Concorde" and space shuttle (97×26 *mm*) .. .. 5·50 5·50
1055/8 .. .. *Set of* 4 8·50 8·50

195 Aircraft landing

196 Rowland Hill, Mulready Cover and Penny Blacks

(Litho Walsall)

1989 (9 Nov). *Christmas. "Flying Home". T* **195** *and similar vert designs. P* 14×13½.

1059 32 s. blue-green, deep brown & dull orange 50 50
1060 42 s. blue-green, deep brown and emerald 60 60
1061 57 s. blue-green, deep brown and vermilion 80 80
1062 3 p. blue-green, deep brown & deep mauve 3·75 3·75
1059/62 .. .. *Set of* 4 5·00 5·00

Designs:—42 s. Villagers waving to aircraft; 57 s. Outrigger canoe and aircraft; 3 p. Aircraft over headland.

(Litho Walsall)

1989 (17 Nov). *20th Universal Postal Union Congress, Washington. Sheet* 115×110 *mm containing T* **196** *and similar vert designs. Multicoloured. P* 13½.

MS1063 57 s. Type **196**; 57 s. Early train and steam ship; 57 s. Stage coach, Pony Express poster and rider; 57 s. French hot-air balloon and flown cover; 57 s. Samuel Morse and telegraph key; 57 s. Early British mail van and pillar box; 57 s. Unloading early mail plane; 57 s. *Queen Mary* and *Graf Zeppelin* flown cover; 57 s. Helicopter and mail van; 57 s. Computer and fax machine; 57 s. "Apollo 11" emblem and space cover; 57 s. U.P.U. Monument and space shuttle 7·50 8·50

197 1989 U.P.U. Congress Stamps

198 Boxing

(Litho Walsall)

1989 (17 Nov). *"World Stamp Expo '89" International Stamp Exhibition, Washington. P* 14.

1064 **197** 57 s. multicoloured 85 85

(Litho Walsall)

1990 (14 Feb). *14th Commonwealth Games, Auckland. T* **198** *and similar vert designs. Multicoloured. P* 14.

1065 42 s. Type **198** 70 70
1066 57 s. Archery 85 85
1067 1 p. Bowls .. .. 1·40 1·40
1068 2 p. Swimming .. .. 2·50 2·50
1065/8 .. .. *Set of* 4 5·00 5·00

199 Wave Power Installation

200 Penny Black

(Litho Walsall)

1990 (11 Apr). *Alternative Sources of Electricity. T* **199** *and similar vert designs. Multicoloured. P* 14.

1069 32 s. Type **199** 50 50
1070 57 s. Wind farm 85 85
1071 1 p. 20, Experimental solar cell vehicle .. 2·00 2·00
1069/71 .. .. *Set of* 3 3·00 3·00
MS1072 110×90 mm. 2 p. 50, Planet Earth .. 4·50 4·75

(Litho Walsall)

1990 (1 May). *150th Anniv of the Penny Black. T* **200** *and similar horiz designs showing stamps. P* 14.

1073 42 s. multicoloured 70 70
a. Horiz pair. Nos. 1073/4 .. .. 1·40 1·40
1074 42 s. multicoloured 70 70
1075 57 s. scarlet and black 85 85
1076 1 p. 50, multicoloured .. .. .. 2·00 2·00
1077 2 p. 50, multicoloured .. .. .. 3·50 3·50
1073/7 .. .. *Set of* 5 7·00 7·00

Designs:—42 s. (No. 1074) Great Britain 1840 Twopence Blue; 57 s. Tonga 1886 1d.; 1 p. 50, 1980 South Pacific Scout Jamboree and Rotary 75th anniv 2 p. official stamp; 2 p. 50, 1990 Alternative Sources of Electricity 57 s.

Nos. 1073/4 were printed together, *se-tenant*, in horizontal pairs throughout the sheet.

Nos. 1073/7 show a faint grey pattern similar to W **24** in the background.

201 Departure of Canoe

202 Iguana searching for Food

(Des G. Bennett. Litho Walsall)

1990 (6 June). *Polynesian Voyages of Discovery. T* **201** *and similar vert designs. P* 14½.

1078 32 s. deep blue-green 55 55
1079 42 s. deep dull blue 80 80
1080 1 p. 20, reddish brown .. .. .. 2·25 2·25
1081 3 p. deep reddish violet .. .. .. 4·75 4·75
1078/81 .. .. *Set of* 4 7·50 7·50

Designs:—42 s. Navigating by night; 1 p. 20, Canoe and sea birds; 3 p. Landfall.

(Des and litho Walsal)

1990 (4 July). *Silver Jubilee of King Taufa'ahau Tupou IV. Designs as Nos.* 985/8, *but inscribed* "Silver Jubilee of His Majesty King Taufa'ahau Tupou IV. 1965–1990" *and with* "TONGA" *and values in silver. P* 11½.

1082 32 s. As Type **184** 30 30
1083 42 s. Banknote, coins, Ha'amonga Trilithon and woodcarver 40 40
1084 57 s. Rowing, communications satellite and Red Cross worker 55 55
1085 2 p. 50, Scout emblem, 1982 47 s. Scout stamp and Friendly Island Airways aircraft .. .. 2·50 2·50
1082/5 .. .. *Set of* 4 3·50 3·50

(Litho Walsall)

1990 (6 July)–**92**. *Designs as Nos.* 1000, 1002, 1003 (*value changed*), 1005 *and* 1008 *redrawn smaller,* 19×22 *mm. Multicoloured. Chalk-surfaced paper. P* 14.

1087 2 s. *Porites* sp 10 10
a. Booklet pane. No. 1087×10 (4.9.90) 20
1089 5 s. *Cypraea mappa viridis* 10 10
a. Booklet pane. No. 1089×10 (4.9.90) 45
1092 10 s. *Conus bullatus* 10 10
a. Booklet pane. No. 1092×10 (4.9.90) 90
1093 15 s. *Dardanus megistos* (crab) (as No. 1003) (12.5.92) 15 20
1095 32 s. *Acanthurus leucosternon* 30 35
a. Booklet pane. No. 1095×10 (4.9.90) 3·00
1087/95 .. .. *Set of* 5 55 65

The outer edges of booklet panes Nos. 1087a, 1089a, 1092a, 1095a are imperforate so that stamps from them have one or two adjacent sides imperforate.

Nos. 1087, 1089 and 1092 exist with different imprint dates below the designs.

(Des G. Drummond. Litho Questa)

1990 (12 Sept). *Endangered Species. Banded Iguana. T* **202** *and similar horiz designs. Multicoloured. P* 14.

1105 32 s. Type **202** 35 35
1106 42 s. Head of male 45 45
1107 57 s. Pair of iguanas during courtship .. 60 60
1108 1 p. 20, Iguana basking .. .. .. 1·40 1·40
1105/8 .. .. *Set of* 4 2·50 2·50

203 Tourism

204 Boy

(Des A. Benjamin and R. Edge. Litho Walsall)

1990 (25 Oct). *40th Anniv of United Nations Development Programme. T* **203** *and similar horiz designs. Multicoloured. P* 13½×14.

1109 57 s. Type **203** 70 70
a. Pair. Nos. 1109/10 .. .. .. 1·40 1·40
1110 57 s. Agriculture and Fisheries 70 70
1111 3 p. Education .. .. 3·25 3·25
a. Pair. Nos. 1111/12 .. .. .. 6·50 6·50
1112 3 p. Healthcare .. .. 3·25 3·25
1109/12 .. .. *Set of* 4 7·25 7·25

The two designs for each value were printed together, *se-tenant*, in horizontal and vertical pairs throughout the sheets.

(Des and litho Walsall)

1990 (28 Nov). *Christmas. Rotary International Interact Project. T* **204** *and similar vert designs. Multicoloured. P* 14.

1113 32 s. Type **204** 40 40
1114 42 s. Young boys 55 55
1115 2 p. Girls in western clothes .. .. .. 2·25 2·25
1116 3 p. Girls in traditional costumes .. .. 3·50 3·50
1113/16 .. .. *Set of* 4 6·00 6·00

205 Safety at Work

206 Yacht at Dawn

(Des C. Abbott. Litho Walsall)

1991 (10 Apr). *Accident Prevention. T* **205** *and similar vert designs. Multicoloured. P* 14½×14.

1117	32 s. Type **205** (English inscription)	30	35
	a. Horiz pair. Nos. 1117/18	60	70
1118	32 s. Safety at home (English inscription)	30	35
1119	32 s. As No. 1118 (Tongan inscription)	30	35
	a. Horiz pair. Nos. 1119/20	60	70
1120	32 s. As Type **205** (Tongan inscription)	30	35
1121	42 s. Safety in cars (English inscription)	40	45
	a. Horiz pair. Nos. 1121/2	80	90
1122	42 s. Safety on bikes (English inscription)	40	45
1123	42 s. As No. 1122 (Tongan inscription)	40	45
	a. Horiz pair. Nos. 1123/4	80	90
1124	42 s. As No. 1121 (Tongan inscription)	40	45
1125	57 s. Safety at sea (English inscription)	50	55
	a. Horiz pair. Nos. 1125/6	1·00	1·10
1126	57 s. Safety on the beach (English inscription)	50	55
1127	57 s. As No. 1126 (Tongan inscription)	50	55
	a. Horiz pair. Nos. 1127/8	1·00	1·10
1128	57 s. As No. 1125 (Tongan inscription)	50	55
1117/28	*Set of* 12	4·25	4·75

Nos. 1117/28 were printed in sheets of 20, two panes (2×5) separated by a vertical gutter, for each value with the left-hand panes containing *se-tenant* horizontal pairs of the designs with English inscriptions and the right-hand panes similar pairs inscribed in Tongan.

(Des D. Miller. Litho Walsall)

1991 (2 July). *Around the World Yacht Race. Sheet* 120×103 *mm containing T* **206** *and similar vert designs. Multicoloured. P* 14½×14.

MS1129 1 p. Type **206**; 1 p. Yacht in the morning; 1 p. Yacht at midday; 1 p. Yacht in the evening; 1 p. Yacht at night . . 4·50 4·75

207 Fishes in the Sea

208 Tonga Temple

(Des D. Miller. Litho Walsall)

1991 (2 July). *Heilala Week. T* **207** *and similar vert designs. Multicoloured. P* 14½×14.

1130	42 s. Type **207**	40	45
1131	57 s. Island and yacht	50	55
1132	2 p. Pile of fruit	1·90	2·00
1133	3 p. Turtle on beach	2·75	3·00
1130/3	*Set of* 4	5·00	5·50

(Des R. Edge. Litho Walsall)

1991 (19 Aug). *Centenary of Church of Latter Day Saints in Tonga. T* **208** *and similar vert design. Multicoloured. P* 14½.

1134	42 s. Type **208**	40	45
1135	57 s. Temple at night	50	55

209 Making T.V. Childcare Programme

(Des R. Edge. Litho Walsall)

1991 (15 Oct). *Telecommunications in Tonga. T* **209** *and similar horiz designs. Multicoloured. P* 14½.

1136	15 s. Type **209**	15	20
	a. Horiz strip of 3. Nos. 1136/8	45	
1137	15 s. T.V. satellite	15	20
1138	15 s. Mothers watching programme	15	20
1139	32 s. Man on telephone and woman with computer	30	35
	a. Horiz strip of 3. Nos. 1139/41	90	
1140	32 s. Telecommunications satellite	30	35
1141	32 s. Overseas customer on telephone	30	35
1142	42 s. Sinking ship	40	45
	a. Horiz strip of 3. Nos. 1142/4	1·25	
1143	42 s. Coastguard controller	40	45
1144	42 s. Maritime rescue	40	45
1145	57 s. Weather satellite above Southern Hemisphere	50	55
	a. Horiz strip of 3. Nos. 1145/7	1·50	
1146	57 s. Meteorologists collecting data	50	55
1147	57 s. T.V. weather map and storm	50	55
1136/47	*Set of* 12	3·75	4·25

The three designs for each value were printed together, *se-tenant*, in horizontal strips of three throughout the sheets.

210 Women's Rowing Eight

(Des D. Miller. Litho Walsall)

1991 (29 Oct). *"Siu'a'alo" Rowing Festival. T* **210** *and similar horiz designs. Multicoloured. P* 14.

1148	42 s. Type **210**	40	45
1149	57 s. Longboat	50	55
1150	1 p. Outrigger canoe	90	95
1151	2 p. Stern of fautasi (large canoe)	1·90	2·00
	a. Horiz pair. No. 1152/3	3·75	4·00
1152	2 p. Bow of fautasi	1·90	2·00
1148/52	*Set of* 5	5·00	5·25

Nos. 1151/2 were printed together, *se-tenant*, in horizontal pairs throughout the sheet, forming a composite design

211 Turtles pulling Santa's Sledge

212 *Pangai* (patrol boat)

(Litho Walsall)

1991 (11 Nov). *Christmas. T* **211** *and similar horiz designs. Multicoloured. P* 14.

1153	32 s. Type **211**	30	35
1154	42 s. Santa Claus on roof of fala (Tongan house)	40	45
1155	57 s. Family opening presents	50	55
1156	3 p. 50, Family waving goodbye to Santa	3·25	3·50
1153/6	*Set of* 4	4·00	4·25

(Des R. Edge. Litho Walsall)

1991 (15 Dec). *Royal Tongan Defence Force. T* **212** *and similar multicoloured designs. P* 14.

1157	42 s. Type **212**	40	45
	a. Horiz pair. Nos. 1157/8	80	
1158	42 s. Marine in battle dress	40	45
1159	57 s. Tonga Royal Guards	50	55
	a. Horiz pair. Nos. 1159/60	1·00	
1160	57 s. Raising the ensign on *Neiafu*	50	55
1161	2 p. *Savea* (patrol boat) (*horiz*)	1·90	2·00
	a. Horiz pair. Nos. 1161/2	3·75	
1162	2 p. King Taufa'ahau Tupou IV inspecting parade (*horiz*)	1·90	2·00
1157/62	*Set of* 6	5·00	5·50

The two designs for each value were printed together, *se-tenant*, in horizontal pairs throughout the sheets.

XXX

1s

(**213**)

214 Columbus and Signature

1992 (19 Mar). *No.* 1007 *surch with T* **213.**

1163	1 s. on 20 s. *Dascyllus aruanus*	10	10

(Des R. Edge. Litho Walsall)

1992 (28 Apr). *500th Anniv of Discovery of America by Columbus. Sheet* 119×109 *mm containing T* **214** *and similar vert designs. Multicoloured. P* 13½.

MS1164 57 s. Type **214**; 57 s. Monastery of Santa Maria de la Chevas; 57 s. Obverse and reverse of coin of Ferdinand and Isabella; 57 s. Spain commemorative stamps of 1930; 57 s. Compass and astrolabe; 57 s. Model of *Santa Maria*; 57 s. Sketch map and signature; 57 s. 15th-century woodcut of Columbus arriving in New World; 57 s. Lucayan artefacts and parrot; 57 s. Pineapple, bird pendant and Indian nose ring; 57 s. Columbus reporting to Spanish Court; 57 s. Medal showing Columbus and signature . . 6·25 6·50

EXPRESS STAMP

E 1 Owl in Flight

(Litho Walsall)

1990 (21 Feb). *Air. P* 11½.

E1	E 1 10 p. black, vermilion and ultramarine	9·25	9·50

OFFICIAL STAMPS

G.F.B.

(O 1) (O 2)

(G.F.B. = Gaue Faka Buleaga = On Government Service)

1893 (13 Feb). *Optd with Type* O 1 *by Govt Printing Office, Wellington, N.Z.* W **2**. *P* 12 × 11½.

O1 **5** 1d. ultramarine (C.) .. .. .. 9·00 32·00
a. Bisected diagonally (½d.) (on cover)
O2 **6** 2d. ultramarine (C.) .. .. .. 22·00 40·00
O3 **5** 4d. ultramarine (C.) .. .. .. 38·00 80·00
O4 **6** 8d. ultramarine (C.) .. .. .. 80·00 £140
O5 1s. ultramarine (C.) .. .. .. 90·00 £160
O1/5 .. .. *Set of* 5 £200 £400

Above prices are for stamps in good condition and colour. Faded and stained stamps from the remainders are worth much less.

1893 (Dec). *Nos* O1 *to* O5 *variously surch with new value, sideways as Type* O **2**.

O 6 **5** ½d. on 1d. ultramarine .. .. 13·00 38·00
O 7 **6** 2½d. on 2d. ultramarine .. .. 18·00 32·00
O 8 **5** 5d. on 4d. ultramarine .. .. 18·00 32·00
O 9 **6** 7½d. on 8d. ultramarine .. .. 18·00 50·00
a. "D" of "7½D." omitted £750
b. Surch double £1200
O10 10d. on 1s. ultramarine .. .. 22·00 55·00
O6/10 .. .. *Set of* 5 80·00 £180

OFFICIAL AIR MAIL
1862
TAU'ATĀINA
EMANCIPATION
1962

OFFICIAL
AIRMAIL
40
SENITI

(O 3) (O 4)

1962 (7 Feb). *Air. Centenary of Emancipation. Nos.* 112/14, 116 *and* 118/19 *optd with Type* O **3** *in red by R. S. Wallbank, Govt Printer.*

O11 – 2d. ultramarine .. .. .. 11·00 6·00
a. "OFFICIAI" .. .. .. 20·00 11·00
b. "MAII" .. .. .. 20·00 11·00
O12 – 5d. violet .. .. .. 12·00 6·50
a. "OFFICIAI" .. .. .. 22·00 12·00
b. "MAII" .. .. .. 22·00 12·00
O13 – 1s. red-brown .. .. .. 7·50 3·75
a. "OFFICIAI" .. .. .. 25·00 11·00
b. "MAII" .. .. .. 25·00 11·00
c. Opt double .. .. ..
ca. "OFFICIAI" .. .. ..
cb. "MAII" .. .. ..
O14 – 5s. orange-yellow and slate-lilac .. 90·00 55·00
a. "MAII" .. .. .. £200 75·00
O15 **52** 10s. yellow and black .. .. 42·00 22·00
a. "MAII" £100
O16 **53** £1 yellow, scar, ultram & dp brt blue .. 70·00 35·00
a. "MAII" £150
O11/O16 .. .. .. *Set of* 6 £200 £120

SET PRICES. Official Stamps from here onwards are included in the complete set prices given with any corresponding Postage issues.

1963 (15 July). *Air. First Polynesian Gold Coinage Commemoration. As T* **63** *but inscr* "OFFICIAL AIRMAIL". 1 *koula coin (diam* 3⅛ *in.). Imperf.*

O17 **63** 15s. black .. .. 3·50 4·50

1965 (18 Mar). *No.* O17 *surch as T* **67**.

O18 **63** 30s. on 15s. black .. .. .. 3·00 3·50

1966 (18 June). *Air. Centenary of Tupou College and Secondary Education. No.* 117 *surch with* "OFFICIAL AIRMAIL" *and new value, with commemorative inscription as in T* **69** *but in italic capital letters.*

O19 10s. on 4d. blue-green 40 35
a. Surch inverted £350 £150
O20 20s. on 4d. blue-green 60 50

1967 (25 Mar). *Air. Decimal currency. No.* 112 *surch* "OFFICIAL AIRMAIL ONE PA'ANGA" *in three lines, in red.*

O21 1 p. on 5s. .. .. 1·75 2·25
a. "AIRMAIL" above "OFFICIAL" .. £130

No. O21a occurred once in a number of sheets until it was corrected.

1967 (4 July). *Air. No.* 114 *surch in various denominations as Type* O **4**.

O22 **53** 40 s. on £1 .. .. 50 50
O23 60 s. on £1 .. .. 70 70
O24 1 p. on £1 .. .. 90 90
O25 2 p. on £1 .. .. 1·50 1·50

Nos. O22/5 were first used on 4 July 1967, but supplies of unused stamps were not made available until April 1968.

The Friendly Islands welcome the United States Peace Corps Official Airmail 30s

Friendly Islands Trials Field & Track South Pacific Games Port Moresby 1969 T$1·00 OFFICIAL AIRMAIL

(O 5) (O 6)

1967 (15 Dec). *Air. Arrival of U.S. Peace Corps in Tonga. As No.* 114, *but imperf, and background colour changed, and surch as Type* O **5**.

O26 **53** 30 s. on £1 yellow, scarlet, ultramarine and emerald-green 20 25
O27 70 s. on £1 yellow, scarlet, ultramarine and emerald-green 40 45
O28 1 p. 50, on £1 yellow, scarlet, ultramarine and emerald-green 70 85

1968 (4 July). 50*th Birthday of King Taufa'ahua IV. No.* 207 *surch.* "HIS MAJESTY'S 50th BIRTHDAY" *(as T* **79**), "OFFICIAL AIRMAIL" *and new value.*

O29 **75** 40 s. on 50 s. (Turq.) .. .. .. 1·00 60
O30 60 s. on 50 s. (G.) .. .. 1·50 90
O31 1 p. on 50 s. (V.) .. .. 2·25 1·50
O32 2 p. on 50 s. (P.) .. .. 4·00 2·25

1968 (19 Dec). *Air. South Pacific Games Field and Track Trials, Port Moresby, New Guinea. As No.* 114, *but imperf, background colour changed and surch as Type* O **6**.

O33 **53** 20 s. on £1 yellow, scarlet, ultramarine and emerald-green 15 15
O34 1 p. on £1 yellow, scarlet, ultramarine and emerald-green 40 40

1969 (13 Aug). *Air. Third South Pacific Games, Port Moresby. Design as Nos.* 290/4.

O35 70 s. carmine-red, bright green and turquoise 45 60
O36 80 s. carmine-red, orange and turquoise .. 55 70

OFFICIAL AIRMAIL
1969 OIL SEARCH 90s

Royal Visit
MARCH
1970
OFFICIAL
AIRMAIL
T$1·25

(O 7) (O 8)

1969 (23 Dec). *Air. First Oil Search in Tonga. As No.* 114 *but imperf, background colour changed to emerald-green, and surch as Type* O **7**.

O37 **53** 90 s. on £1 multicoloured .. .. 2·25 2·00
a. "1966" for "1969" .. ..
O38 1 p. 10 on £1 multicoloured (R.) .. 2·25 2·00
a. "1966" for "1969" .. .. ..

No. O38 is surch as Type O **7**, but without "OFFICIAL AIRMAIL".

1970 (7 Mar). *Royal Visit. As No.* 110 *but imperf, colours changed, and surch as Type* O **8**.

O39 75 s. on 1s. carmine-red and yellow .. 3·00 1·50
O40 1 p. on 1s. carmine-red and yellow (B.) .. 3·50 2·00
O41 1 p. 25 on 1s. carmine-red & yellow (G.) .. 4·25 2·50

OFFICIAL
Commonwealth
Member
JUNE 1970
50s
AIRMAIL

(O 9)

1970 (4 June). *Entry into British Commonwealth. As No.* 112 *but imperf, background colour changed, and surch as Type* O **9**.

O42 50 s. on 5s. orange-yellow and sepia .. 60 50
O43 90 s. on 5s. orange-yellow and sepia (R.) .. 80 70
O44 1 p. 50 on 5s. orange-yellow & sepia (G.) .. 1·50 1·25

1970 (4 June). *As Nos.* 325/34, *but inscr.* "OFFICIAL POST". *Colour of* "TONGA" *given for* 6 *to* 10 *s.*

O45 **83** 1 s. greenish yellow, brt purple & blk .. 15 15
O46 2 s. greenish yellow, ultram & black .. 20 20
O47 3 s. greenish yellow, chocolate & blk .. 25 25
O48 4 s. greenish yellow, emerald and black 25 25
O49 5 s. greenish yellow, orange-red & blk .. 30 30
O50 **90** 6 s. ultramarine 35 35
O51 7 s. deep mauve 40 40
O52 8 s. gold 45 45
O53 9 s. bright carmine 55 55
O54 10 s. silver 55 55
O45/54 .. .. .. *Set of* 10 3·00 3·00

The note after No. 334 also applies here.
See also Nos. O82/91.

Centenary
British Red Cross
1870-1970

OFFICIAL AIRMAIL 30s

(O 10)

1970 (17 Oct). *Centenary of British Red Cross. As Nos.* 102 *and* 112 *but imperf, colours changed and surch as Type* O **10**.

O55 30 s. on 1½d. emerald (Blk. and R.) .. 1·00 1·00
O56 80 s. on 5s. orange-yellow & sepia (B. & R.) .. 3·00 3·00
O57 90 s. on 5s. orange-yellow & sepia (B. & R.) .. 3·00 3·00

1965 IN MEMORIAM 1970

(O 11) (O 12)

1971 (30 Jan). *Air. Fifth Death Anniv of Queen Salote. As No.* 113, *but imperf, colours changed and surch as Type* O **11**.

O58 **52** 20 s. on 10s. orange-yellow 70 60
O59 30 s. on 10s. orange-yellow (V.) .. 90 80
O60 50 s. on 10s. orange-yellow (B.) .. 1·75 1·25
O61 2 p. on 10s. orange-yellow (G.) .. 6·50 5·00

1971 (17 Apr). *Air.* "*Philatokyo 1971*" *Stamp Exhibition. Unissued Red Cross surcharges on No.* 107, *but imperf, colours changed and additionally surch as Type* O **12**.

O62 30 s. on 5d. green and yellow (B. & R.) .. 40 40
O63 80 s. on 5d. green and yellow (Blk. & R.) .. 1·00 1·00
O64 90 s. on 5d. green and yellow (P. & R.) .. 1·25 1·25

1971 (20 July)–**72**. *Air. As Nos.* 365/6a, *but inscr* "OFFICIAL AIRMAIL".

O65 **96** 14 s. multicoloured 55 55
O65*a* 17 s. multicoloured (20.7.72) 65 65
O66 21 s. multicoloured 75 75
O66*a* 38 s. multicoloured (20.7.72) .. .. 1·10 1·10

O **13** Football

1971 (20 July). *Air. Fourth South Pacific Games, Tahiti.*

O67 O **13** 50 s. multicoloured 40 55
O68 90 s. multicoloured 60 95
O69 1 p. 50, multicoloured .. .. .. 80 1·25

INVESTITURE 1971
OFFICIAL 60s AIRMAIL

(O 14)

(*Illustration reduced. Actual size* 61 × 13 *mm*)

1971 (30 Oct). *Air. Investiture of Royal Tongan Medal of Merit. Nos.* 315, 318 *and* 316 *surch as Type* O **14**.

O70 **89** 60 s. on 3 s. multicoloured 50 50
O71 80 s. on 25 s. multicoloured 70 70
O72 1 p. 10 on 7 s. multicoloured 80 80

O **15** "UNICEF" and Emblem

1971 (31 Dec). *Air.* 25*th Anniv of UNICEF.*

O73 O **15** 70 s. multicoloured 90 90
O74 80 s. multicoloured .. .. .. 1·00 1·00
O75 90 s. multicoloured .. .. .. 1·10 1·10

1972 (14 Apr). *Air. Merchant Marine Routes. Design similar to T* **100**, *but inscr* "OFFICIAL AIRMAIL".

O76 20 s. multicoloured 50 40
O77 50 s. multicoloured .. .. 1·75 1·10
O78 1 p. 20, multicoloured .. .. .. 3·25 2·25

Design:—Nos. O76/8, Map of South Pacific, and *Aoniu*.

1972 (15 July). *Air. Fifth Anniv of Coronation. Design similar to T* **101**, *but inscr* "OFFICIAL AIRMAIL".

O79 50 s. multicoloured 80 45
O80 70 s. multicoloured .. .. 1·10 60
O81 1 p. 50, multicoloured .. .. .. 2·40 1·00

Design (47 × 57 *mm*):—Nos. O79/81, As T **101**, but with different background.

1972 (30 Sept). *As Nos. 413/27, but inscr "OFFICIAL POST".*

(a) As Nos. 413/17

O82 **83** 1 s. light yellow, scarlet and black .. 15 10
O83 2 s. light yellow, dp blue-green & black 20 15
O84 3 s. light yellow, yellow-green and black 25 20
O85 4 s. light yellow and black 25 20
O86 5 s. light yellow and black 25 20

(b) As Nos. O50/4, but colours changed. Colour of "TONGA" given

O87 **90** 6 s. light green 25 20
O88 7 s. light green 30 25
O89 8 s. light green 30 25
O90 9 s. light green 30 25
O91 10 s. light green 35 30

(c) As Nos. 423/7. Colour of face value given

O92 **102** 15 s. new blue 55 45
O93 20 s. reddish orange 70 60
O94 25 s. chocolate 80 70
O95 40 s. yellow-orange .. .. .. 1·75 1·50
O96 50 s. royal blue .. .. 2·00 1·75
O82/96 .. .. *Set of* 15 7·50 6·50

The note after No. 427 also applies here.

1972 (9 Dec). *Air. Proclamation of Sovereignty over Minerva Reefs. Design similar to T* **104**, *but inscr "OFFICIAL AIRMAIL".*

O97 25 s. multicoloured 40 25
O98 75 s. multicoloured .. .. 1·25 70
O99 1 p. 50, multicoloured .. .. .. 2·50 1·25

Design: *Horiz* (64 × 39 *mm*)—Nos. O97/9, Flags and map.

ESTABLISHMENT
BANK OF TONGA
40s
OFFICIAL AIRMAIL

(O 16)

1973 (30 Mar). *Air. Foundation of Bank of Tonga. No. 396 surch as Type* O 16.

O100 **100** 40 s. on 21 s. mult (Blk. & G.) .. 85 50
O101 85 s. on 21 s. multicoloured (B. & G.) 1·75 90
O102 1 p. 25 on 21 s. multicoloured (Br.) .. 2·00 1·10

SILVER JUBILEE
TONGAN SCOUTING
1948 - 1973

(O 17)

1973 (29 June). *Silver Jubilee of Scouting in Tonga. Nos. O76, O74 and 319 variously optd or surch as Type* O 17 *in silver (Nos. O103/4) or silver and blue (No. O105).*

O103 – 30 s. on 20 s. multicoloured .. .. 15·00 3·50
O104 **O 15** 80 s. multicoloured .. .. .. 32·00 11·00
O105 **89** 1 p. 40 on 50 s. multicoloured .. 48·00 24·00

1973 (2 Oct). *Air. Bicentenary of Capt. Cook's Visit. Design similar to T* **107**, *but inscr "OFFICIAL AIRMAIL".*

O106 25 s. multicoloured .. .. 2·25 1·00
O107 80 s. multicoloured .. .. 6·00 2·75
O108 1 p. 30, multicoloured .. .. .. 7·50 4·00

Design: *Horiz* (52 × 45 *mm*)—Nos. O106/8, *James Cook* (bulk carrier).

1974

(O 18)

1973 (19 Dec). *Air. Commonwealth Games. Nos. O67/9 optd with Type* O 18.

O109 **O 13** 50 s. multicoloured (B.) .. .. 1·00 60
O110 90 s. multicoloured (Blk.) .. .. 1·75 1·00
O111 1 p. 50, multicoloured (G.) .. 2·50 1·75
a. Opt double £150

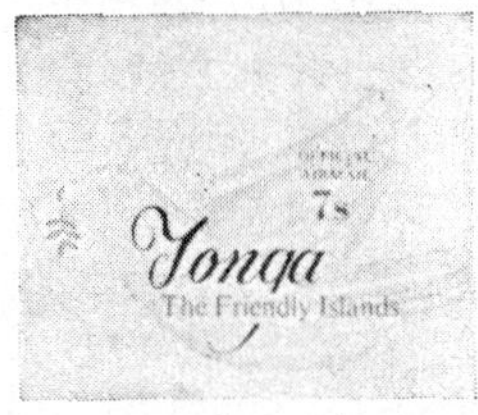

O 19 Dove of Peace

1974 (20 Mar). *Air.*

O112 **O 19** 7 s. turq-grn, reddish vio & orge-red 25 20
O113 9 s. turq-grn, reddish vio & red-brn 30 25
O114 12 s. turq-grn, reddish vio & yell-orge 35 30
O115 14 s. turquoise-green, reddish violet and bistre-yellow 40 35
O116 17 s. multicoloured 50 45
O117 29 s. multicoloured 80 70
O118 38 s. multicoloured .. .. .. 1·00 90
O119 50 s. multicoloured .. .. .. 1·50 1·25
O120 75 s. multicoloured .. .. .. 2·00 1·75
O112/120 .. .. *Set of* 9 6·50 5·50

1974 (20 June). *Air. Centenary of Universal Postal Union. Design similar to T* **110**, *but inscr "OFFICIAL AIRMAIL".*

O121 25 s. dp red-orange, lt yellow-green & black 60 35
O122 35 s. lemon, magenta and black 75 45
O123 70 s. deep orange, bright blue and black .. 1·75 1·00

Design: *Square* (40 × 40 *mm*)—Letters "UPU".

1974 (11 Sept). *Air. Tongan Girl Guides. Design similar to T* **111**, *but inscr "OFFICIAL AIRMAIL".*

O124 45 s. multicoloured .. .. 4·00 1·75
O125 55 s. multicoloured .. .. 4·25 2·00
O126 1 p. multicoloured .. .. 7·50 3·75

Design: *Oval* (35 × 52 *mm*)—Lady Baden-Powell.

(O 20)

1974 (11 Dec). *Air. Establishment of Royal Marine Institute. Nos. 446 and 451 surch as Type* O 20, *each obliterating the centre part of the original design.*

O127 30 s. on 15 s. multicoloured (Gold, B. & P.) 2·00 85
O128 35 s. on 15 s. multicoloured (Sil., B. & Blk.) 2·25 1·00
a. Black ("TONGA TONGA") omitted .. £200
O129 80 s. on 17 s. multicoloured (Blk. & R.) .. 3·75 2·50

1975 (11 Mar). *Air. South Pacific Forum and Tourism. Designs similar to T* **113** *but inscr "OFFICIAL AIRMAIL".*

O130 50 s. multicoloured .. .. 1·10 80
O131 75 s. multicoloured .. .. 1·75 1·25
O132 1 p. 25, multicoloured .. .. .. 2·50 1·75

Designs: (49 × 43 *mm*)—50 s. Jungle arch; others, Sunset scene.

1975 (11 June). *Air. Fifth South Pacific Games. Design similar to T* **114** *but inscr "OFFICIAL AIRMAIL".*

O133 38 s. multicoloured 45 30
O134 75 s. multicoloured 80 60
O135 1 p. 20, multicoloured .. .. .. 1·40 1·25

Design: *Oval* (51 × 27 *mm*):—Runners on track.

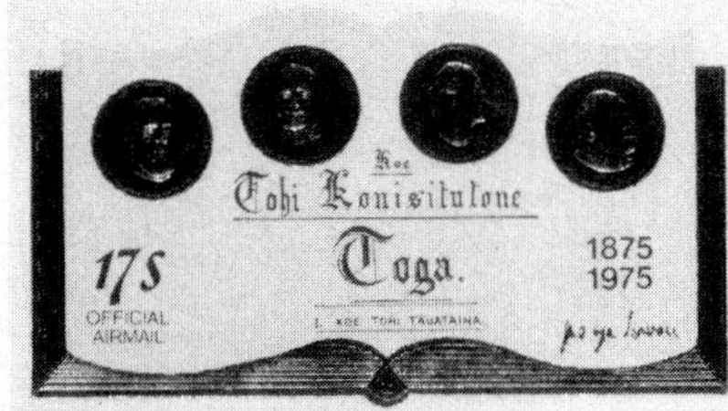

O 21 Tongan Monarchs

1975 (4 Nov). *Air. Centenary of Tongan Constitution.*

O136 **O 21** 17 s. multicoloured 30 25
O137 60 s. multicoloured 80 55
O138 90 s. multicoloured .. .. .. 1·25 75

1976 (24 Feb). *Air. First Participation in Olympic Games. Design similar to T* **117** *but inscr "OFFICIAL AIRMAIL".*

O139 45 s. multicoloured .. .. 1·75 85
O140 55 s. multicoloured .. .. 2·00 1·00
O141 1 p. multicoloured .. .. 3·25 1·90

Design: *Oval* (36 × 53 *mm*)—Montreal logo.

1976 (26 May). *Air. Bicentenary of American Revolution. Designs as T* **118** *showing signatories to the Declaration of Independence. Inscr "OFFICIAL AIRMAIL".*

O142 20 s. multicoloured .. .. 1·00 40
O143 50 s. multicoloured .. .. 2·25 1·00
O144 1 p. 15, multicoloured .. .. .. 4·75 2·50

1976 (25 Aug). *Air. 150th Anniv of Christianity in Tonga. Hexagonal design* (65 × 52 *mm*) *showing Lifuka Chapel.*

O145 65 s. multicoloured .. .. 1·75 1·40
O146 85 s. multicoloured .. .. 2·00 1·75
O147 1 p. 15, multicoloured .. .. .. 2·75 2·50

1976 (1 Nov). *Air. Centenary of Treaty of Friendship with Germany. Rectangular design* (51 × 47 *mm*) *showing text.*

O148 30 s. multicoloured 60 60
O149 60 s. multicoloured .. .. 1·40 1·40
O150 1 p. 25, multicoloured .. .. .. 2·75 2·75

1977 (7 Feb). *Air. Silver Jubilee. Vert design* (57 × 66 *mm*) *showing flags of Tonga and the U.K.*

O151 35 s. multicoloured .. .. 3·00 50
O152 45 s. multicoloured 80 30
O153 1 p. 10, multicoloured .. .. .. 1·10 50

1977 (4 July). *Air. Tenth Anniv of King's Coronation. Square design* (50 × 50 *mm*) *showing 1967 Coronation Coin.*

O154 20 s. multicoloured 40 40
O155 40 s. multicoloured 80 80
O156 80 s. multicoloured .. .. 1·75 1·75

1977 (28 Sept). *Air. Bicentenary of Capt. Cook's Last Voyage. Rectangular design* (52 × 46 *mm*) *showing text.*

O157 20 s. multicoloured .. .. 2·50 1·60
O158 55 s. on 20 s. multicoloured .. .. 5·50 3·50
O159 85 s. on 20 s. multicoloured (V. and Blk.) .. 8·00 5·50

The face values of Nos. O158/9 are surcharged on the stamps, the original face value being incorrect.

1977 (16 Dec). *Air. Whale Conservation. Hexagonal design* (66 × 51 *mm*) *showing Blue Whale.*

O160 45 s. multicoloured .. .. 2·25 1·25
O161 65 s. multicoloured .. .. 3·25 1·90
O162 85 s. multicoloured .. .. 3·75 2·25

1978 (5 May). *Air. Commonwealth Games, Edmonton. "Teardrop" design* (35 × 52 *mm*) *showing Games Emblem.*

O163 30 s. black, blue and red 45 45
O164 60 s. black, red and blue .. .. .. 1·00 1·00
O165 1 p. black, red and blue .. .. .. 1·60 1·60

1978 (4 July). *Air. 60th Birthday of King Taufa'ahau Tupou IV. Medal-shaped design* (21 × 45 *mm*) *showing portrait of King.*

O166 26 s. black, vermilion and yellow 35 30
O167 85 s. black, light brown and yellow .. .. 1·10 1·00
O168 90 s. black, bright violet and yellow .. .. 1·25 1·10

1978 (29 Sept). *Coil stamps. (a) Designs similar to Nos. 675/9 but inscr "OFFICIAL POST".*

O169 1 s. purple and greenish yellow 10 10
O170 2 s. brown and greenish yellow 10 10
O171 3 s. carmine, yellow and greenish yellow .. 10 10
O172 4 s. brown, yellow and greenish yellow .. 10 10
O173 5 s. blue-green, yellow and greenish yellow 10 10

(b) Designs similar to Nos. 680/4 but inscr "OFFICIAL POST"

O174 6 s. yellow-brown, emerald and light brown 15 15
O175 7 s. blue-black, emerald and light brown .. 20 20
O176 8 s. magenta, emerald and light brown .. 20 20
O177 9 s. red-brown, emerald and light brown .. 25 25
O178 10 s. deep green, emerald and light brown .. 25 25

(c) Designs similar to Nos. 685/9 but inscr "OFFICIAL POST"

O179 15 s. grey-black, orange-brown and emerald 35 35
O180 20 s. vermilion, orange-brown and emerald 40 40
O181 30 s. emerald and orange-brown 50 50
O182 50 s. new blue, orange-brown and emerald .. 90 90
O183 1 p. reddish violet, orange-brown & emer .. 1·75 1·75
O169/83 .. .. .. *Set of* 15 4·75 4·75

1978 (15 Dec). *Air. Endangered Wildlife Conservation. Designs as Nos. 690/2 but inscr "OFFICIAL AIRMAIL".*

O184 40 s. Type **129** .. .. 1·50 75
O185 50 s. Insular Flying Fox .. .. .. 1·50 85
O186 1 p. 10, Turtle .. .. 2·75 2·00

1979 (16 Feb). *Air. Decade of Progress. Designs similar to Nos. 700/9 but inscr "OFFICIAL AIRMAIL".*

O187 38 s. Tonga Red Cross emblem 55 40
O188 74 s. As No. 702 .. .. 1·00 75
O189 80 s. As No. 701 .. .. 1·10 80

1979 (1 June). *Air. Death Centenary of Sir Rowland Hill and 10th Anniv of Tongan Self-adhesive Stamps. Hand-shaped design* (45 × 53 *mm*) *showing self-adhesive stamps being removed from backing paper.*

O190 45 s. multicoloured 90 60
O191 65 s. multicoloured .. .. 1·25 85
O192 80 s. multicoloured .. .. 1·60 1·10

O 22 Blue-crowned Lory with foliage

O 23 Blue-crowned Lory without foliage

1979 (17 Aug). *Air. Coil stamps.*

O193 **O 22** 5 s. mult (face value in black) .. 15 15
O194 11 s. multicoloured 25 25
O195 14 s. multicoloured 25 25
O196 15 s. multicoloured 30 30
O197 17 s. multicoloured 30 30
O198 18 s. multicoloured 30 30
O199 22 s. multicoloured 35 35
O200 31 s. multicoloured 55 55
O201 39 s. multicoloured 70 70
O202 75 s. multicoloured .. .. .. 1·25 1·50
O203 1 p. multicoloured .. .. .. 1·75 2·00
O193/203 .. .. .. *Set of* 11 5·50 6·00

See also No. O213.

1979 (23 Nov). *Air. Views as seen through the Lens of a Camera. Design as T* **133** *but showing Niuatoputapu and Tafahi.*

O204 35 s. multicoloured 45 35
O205 45 s. multicoloured 55 40
O206 1 p. multicoloured .. .. 1·10 1·00

1980 (9 Jan). *Air. 125th Anniv of France-Tonga Treaty of Friendship. Design as T* **134** *but showing the Establishment of the Principle of Religious Freedom in the Pacific Islands.*

O207 40 s. multicoloured 55 60
O208 55 s. multicoloured 80 85
O209 1 p. 25, multicoloured .. .. .. 1·75 1·90

1980 (30 Apr). *Air. Olympic Games, Moscow. Nos. O190/2 surch as T* **135** *in black on silver background.*

O210 26 s. on 45 s. multicoloured 45 45
O211 40 s. on 65 s. multicoloured 75 75
O212 1 p. 10, on 1 p. multicoloured .. .. 2·25 2·25

1980 (May). *No.* O193 *redrawn without foliage as Type* O **23**.
O213 O **23** 5 s. mult (face value in magenta) .. £100

1980 (30 Sept). *Air. South Pacific Scout Jamboree, Tonga and 75th Anniv of Rotary International. Design showing Scout camp and Rotary emblem.*
O214 25 s. multicoloured 70 40
O215 2 p. multicoloured .. .. 3·50 3·00

T$2 **OFFICIAL** OFFICIAL

(O **24**) (O **25**) (O **26**)

1980 (3 Dec). *Air. No.* O145 *surch with Type* O **24**.
O216 2 p. on 65 s. multicoloured .. .. .. 4·00 4·50

1983 (22 Feb–Mar). *Nos.* 834/6 *handstamped with Type* O **25** (29 *s.*, 32 *s.*) *or optd with Type* O **26** (47 *s.*).
O217 29 s. Type **151** .. .. 2·75 2·75
O218 32 s. Type **151** .. .. 3·50 3·50
O219 47 s. Montgolfier's balloon and "Concorde" (Mar) .. .. 5·00 5·00
O217/19 .. .. *Set of* 3 10·00 10·00

OFFICIAL ***OFFICIAL*** *OFFICIAL*

(O **27**) (O **28**) (O **29**)

1984 (10 Apr)–**85**. *Nos.* 865/79 *and* 881 *optd with Type* O **27** (1, 5, 10, 15, 29, 47 *s.*) *or with Type* O **28** (*others*).
O220 1 s. Type **159** 10 10
O221 2 s. *Porites sp* (26.6.84) 15 15
O222 3 s. *Holocentrus ruber* (18.5.84) 15 15
O223 5 s. *Cypraea mappa viridis* 15 15
O224 6 s. *Dardanus megistos* (17.9.84) 15 15
O225 9 s. *Stegostoma fasciatum* (18.5.84) .. 55 55
b. Optd on No. 870b (28.5.85) 30 30
O226 10 s. *Conus bullatus* 15 15
O227 13 s. *Pterois volitans* (18.5.84) 20 20
O228 15 s. *Conus textile* 25 25
O229 20 s. *Dascyllus aruanus* (18.5.84) 30 30
O230 29 s. *Conus aulicus* 35 35
O231 32 s. *Acanthurus leucosternon* (18.5.84) .. 40 40
O232 47 s. *Lambis truncata* 55 55
O233 1 p. *Millepora dichotama* (26.6.84) .. 1·25 1·25
O234 2 p. *Birgus latro* (17.9.84) .. .. .. 2·00 2·00
O235 5 p. *Thunnus albacares* (28.5.85) .. .. 4·75 4·75
O220/35 .. .. *Set of* 16 10·00 10·00

1986 (16 Apr). *Nos.* 933/9 *optd with Type* O **29**.
O236 4 s. on 2 s. *Porites sp.* 15 15
O237 4 s. on 13 s. *Pterois volitans* 15 15
O238 42 s. on 3 s. *Holocentrus ruber* 70 70
O239 42 s. on 9 s. *Stegostoma fasciatum* .. 70 70
O240 57 s. on 6 s. *Dardanus megistos* 85 85
O241 57 s. on 20 s. *Dascyllus aruanus* 85 85
O242 2 p. 50 on 2 p. *Birgus latro* .. .. 3·00 3·00
O236/42 .. .. *Set of* 7 5·75 5·75

NIUAFO'OU

The following stamps were provided for the remote island of Niuafo'ou and were not valid for postage in the remainder of Tonga.

SELF-ADHESIVE ISSUES. Nos. 1/63 were manufactured by Walsall Security Printers using the self-adhesive system as described above Tonga No. 280.

T$1

1 Map of Niuafo'ou

NIUAFO'OU
KINGDOM OF TONGA

(2)

1983 (11 May). *(a) P* 14.
1 **1** 1 s. pale stone, black and rosine .. 10 10
2 2 s. pale stone, black and light emerald 10 10
3 3 s. pale stone, black & dull ultram .. 10 10
4 3 s. pale stone, black and chestnut .. 10 10
5 5 s. pale stone, black and deep magenta 10 10
6 6 s. pale stone, black and greenish blue 10 10
7 9 s. pale stone, black & dull yell-grn .. 10 10
8 10 s. pale stone, black & dull ultram .. 15 15
9 13 s. pale stone, black and light emerald 30 30
10 15 s. pale stone, black and chestnut .. 30 30
11 20 s. pale stone, black and greenish blue 35 35
12 29 s. pale stone, black and deep magenta 50 50
13 32 s. pale stone, black & dull yellow-green 60 60
14 47 s. pale stone, black and rosine .. 75 75

(b) No. 820 of Tonga surch (No. 15) with T **2** *by lithography or optd only (No. 16) by typography. P* 13½
15 1 p. on 2 p. pale turquoise-green & black (V.) 1·75 2·00
a. Deep mauve surch in typography .. 11·00 11·00
16 2 p. pale turquoise-green (Gold) .. .. 2·75 3·00
1/16 .. .. *Set of* 16 7·00 7·50

Most examples of No. 15 have the surcharge printed by lithography. A small quantity did, however, receive a typography surcharge in a different shade to form No. 15a. In addition to the colour the typography printing can be identified by the white rims to the letters and figures. All examples of No. 16 were printed by typography.

1983 (11 May). *Inauguration of Niuafo'ou Airport. As T* **153** *of Tonga. P* 14 × 14½.
17 29 s. multicoloured .. .. 80 1·00
18 1 p. multicoloured .. .. 2·50 3·25

3s

(3)

4 Eruption of Niuafo'ou

1983 (30 May). *As T* **1**, *but without value, surch with T* **3** *by Tonga Government Printer.*
19 3 s. pale stone, black and royal blue .. 10 10
20 5 s. pale stone, black and royal blue .. 10 10
21 32 s. pale stone, black and royal blue .. 65 65
a. Surch inverted £600
22 2 p. pale stone, black and royal blue .. .. 3·00 3·25
a. Surch inverted .. .. 90·00
b. Surch double .. .. ..
19/22 .. .. *Set of* 4 3·50 3·75

(Des R. Edge)

1983 (29 Sept). *25th Anniv of Re-settlement. T* **4** *and similar horiz designs. Multicoloured. P* 14.
23 5 s. Type **4** 30 20
24 29 s. Lava flow 80 70
25 32 s. Islanders fleeing to safety 90 80
26 1 p. 50, Evacuation by canoe .. .. 3·00 3·25
23/6 .. .. *Set of* 4 4·50 4·50

5 Purple Swamphen

6 Green Turtle

(Des N. Arlott)

983 (15 Nov). *Birds of Niuafo'ou. T* **5** *and similar designs. P* 11 (1 *p.*, 2 *p.*), 14 (20 *s. to* 47 *s.*) *or* 14½ *(others).*
7 1 s. black and deep mauve 20 20
8 2 s. black and bright blue 20 20
9 3 s. black and blue-green 20 20
30 5 s. black and yellow 20 20
31 6 s. black and red-orange 20 20
32 9 s. multicoloured 20 20
33 10 s. multicoloured 30 30
34 13 s. multicoloured 35 35
35 15 s. multicoloured 35 35
36 20 s. multicoloured 50 50
37 29 s. multicoloured 80 80
38 32 s. multicoloured 90 90
39 47 s. multicoloured .. .. 1·40 1·40
40 1 p. multicoloured .. .. 3·00 3·00
41 2 p. multicoloured .. .. 4·50 4·50
27/41 .. .. *Set of* 15 12·00 12·00

Designs: *Vert* (22 × 29 *mm*)—2 s. White-collared Kingfisher; 3 s. Red-headed Parrot Finch; 5 s. Banded Rail; 6 s. Polynesian Scrub Hen ("Niuafo'ou Megapode"); 9 s. Green Honeyeater; 10 s. Purple Swamphen *(different)*; (22 × 36 *mm*)—29 s. Red-headed Parrot Finch *(different)*; 32 s. White-collared Kingfisher *(different)*; (29 × 42 *mm*)—1 p. As 10 s. *Horiz* (29 × 22 *mm*)—13 s. Banded Rail *(different)*; 15 s. Polynesian Scrub Hen ("Niuafo'ou Megapode") *(different)*; (36 × 22 *mm*)—20 s. As 13 s.; 47 s. As 15 s.; (42 × 29 *mm*)—2 p. As 15 s.

(Des R. Edge)

1984 (7 Mar). *Wildlife and Nature Reserve. T* **6** *and similar multi-coloured designs. P* 14.
42 29 s. Type **6** 50 50
43 32 s. Insular Flying Fox *(vert)* 50 50
44 47 s. Humpback Whale 80 80
45 1 p. 50, Polynesian Scrub Hen ("Niuafo-ou Megapode") *(vert)* .. .. .. 2·75 2·75
42/5 .. .. *Set of* 4 4·00 4·00

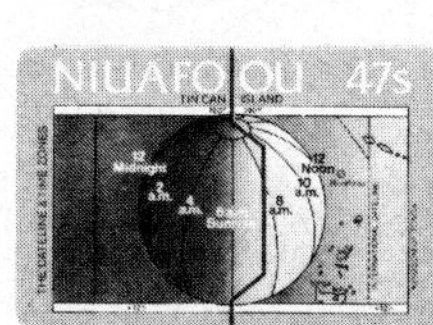

7 Diagram of Time Zones

8 Australia 1913 £2 Kangaroo Definitive

(Des R. Edge)

1984 (20 Aug). *Centenary of International Dateline. T* **7** *and similar horiz design. Multicoloured. P* 14.
46 47 s. Type **7** 40 50
47 2 p. Location map showing Niuafo'ou .. 1·50 1·75

1984 (17 Sept). *"Ausipex" International Stamp Exhibition, Melbourne. T* **8** *and similar vert design. Multicoloured. P* 14.
48 32 s. Type **8** 40 45
49 1 p. 50, Niuafo'ou 1983 10 s. map definitive .. 1·50 2·00
MS50 90 × 100 mm. As Nos. 48/9, but without exhibition logo and with face value at foot. Die cut. .. 1·75 2·25

Examples of No. **MS**50 without face values are Exhibition Banquet souvenirs without postal validity.

9 Dutch Brass Band entertaining Tongans

10 *Ysabel*, 1902

(Des R. Edge)

1985 (20 Feb). *400th Birth Anniv of Jacob Le Maire (discoverer of Niuafo'ou). T* **9** *and similar vert designs. P* 14.
51 13 s. purple-brown, pale cinnamon & brt orge 20 20
52 32 s. purple-brn, pale cinnamon & brt new bl 50 50
53 47 s. purple-brn, pale cinnamon & brt green 65 65
54 1 p. 50, purple-brn, pale cinnamon & lemon 2·00 2·00
51/4 .. .. *Set of* 4 3·00 3·00
MS55 90 × 90 mm. 1 p. 50, purple-brown, pale cinnamon and new blue. Imperf .. .. 1·50 1·75

Designs:—No. 52, Tongans preparing kava; No. 53, Tongan canoes and outriggers; Nos. 54/5, *Eendracht* at anchor off Tafahi Island.

1985 (22 May). *Mail Ships. T* **10** *and similar horiz designs. Multicoloured. A. Stamp die-cut and backing paper perf* 14. *B. Both stamp and backing paper perf* 14.

		A		B	
56	9 s. Type **10**	15	15	30	30
57	13 s. *Tofua I*, 1908	20	20	40	40
58	47 s. *Mariposa*, 1934	55	55	85	85
59	1 p. *Matua*, 1936	1·60	1·60	2·25	2·25
56/9	.. .. .. *Set of* 4	2·25	2·25	3·50	3·50

For description of the two forms of perforation see after Tonga No. 864.

11 Preparing to fire Rocket

12 Halley's Comet, 684 A.D.

1985 (5 Nov). *Niuafo'ou Rocket Mails. T* **11** *and similar horiz designs. Multicoloured. P* 14.
60 32 s. Type **11** 60 60
61 42 s. Rocket in flight 80 80
62 57 s. Ship's crew watching rocket's descent .. 1·00 1·00
63 1 p. 50, Islanders reading mail .. .. 2·50 2·50
60/3 .. .. *Set of* 4 4·50 4·50

(Des and litho Walsall)

1986 (26 Mar). *Appearance of Halley's Comet. T* **12** *and similar vert designs. Multicoloured. P* 14.
64 42 s. Type **12** 80 80
a. Horiz strip of 5. Nos. 64/8 .. .. 3·50
65 42 s. Halley's Comet, 1066, from Bayeux Tapestry 80 80
66 42 s. Edmond Halley 80 80
67 42 s. Halley's Comet, 1910 .. .. .. 80 80
68 42 s. Halley's Comet, 1986 .. .. .. 80 80
69 57 s. Type **12** .. .. 1·10 1·10
a. Horiz strip of 5. Nos. 69/73 .. .. 5·00
70 57 s. As No. 65 .. .. 1·10 1·10
71 57 s. As No. 66 .. .. 1·10 1·10
72 57 s. As No. 67 .. .. 1·10 1·10
73 57 s. As No. 68 .. .. 1·10 1·10
64/73 .. .. *Set of* 10 8·50 8·50

Nos. 64/8 and 69/73 were each printed together, *se-tenant*, in horizontal strips of five, forming composite designs, throughout the sheets.

X X

(13)

14 Swimmers with Mail

1986 (16 Apr). *Nos. 32/9 surch as T* **13** *in blue.*
74 4 s. on 9 s. Green Honeyeater 20 20
75 4 s. on 10 s. Purple Swamphen 20 20
76 42 s. on 13 s. Banded Rail 80 80
77 42 s. on 15 s. Polynesian Scrub Hen 80 80
78 57 s. on 29 s. Red-headed Parrot Finch .. 1·10 1·10
79 57 s. on 32 s. White-collared Kingfisher .. 1·10 1·10
80 2 p. 50 on 20 s. Banded Rail .. .. .. 3·50 3·50
81 2 p. 50 on 47 s. Polynesian Scrub Hen .. 3·50 3·50
74/81 .. .. *Set of* 8 10·00 10·00

(Des and litho Walsall)

1986 (22 May). *"Ameripex '86" International Stamp Exhibition, Chicago. 25th Anniv of United States Peace Corps. Horiz designs as T* **173** *of Tonga. Multicoloured. P* 14.
82 57 s. Peace Corps surveyor and pipeline .. 1·00 1·00
83 1 p. 50, Inspecting crops .. .. .. 2·00 2·00
MS84 90 × 90 mm. Nos. 82/3, magnifying glass and tweezers. Imperf .. .. 3·50 4·00

(Des Walsall. Litho Questa)

1986 (27 Aug). *Centenary of First Tonga Stamps. T* **14** *and similar horiz designs showing Niuafo'ou mail transport. Multicoloured. P* 14.
85 42 s. Type **13** 80 80
86 57 s. Collecting tin can mail .. .. .. 1·00 1·00
87 1 p. Ship firing mail rocket .. .. .. 1·75 1·75
88 2 p. 50, "Collecting the Mails" (detail) (C. Mayger) .. .. 3·25 3·25
85/8 .. .. *Set of* 4 6·25 6·25
MS89 135 × 80 mm. No. 88 .. .. .. 4·50 5·00

Nos. 85/8 were issued in sheets of twenty stamps and five *se-tenant* labels, in the central vertical column, showing the colour separations of the designs.

PRINTERS AND PROCESS. The following issues were lithographed by Walsall Security Printers, *unless otherwise stated*.

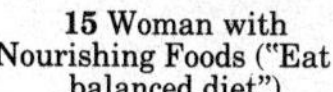

15 Woman with Nourishing Foods ("Eat a balanced diet")

16 Hammerhead Shark

(Des C. Abbott)

1987 (11 Mar). *Red Cross. Preventive Medicine. T* **15** *and similar horiz designs. Multicoloured. P* 14×14½.

90 15 s. Type **15** 55 55
91 42 s. Nurse with baby ("Give them post-natal care") .. .. 1·40 1·40
92 1 p. Man with insecticide ("Insects spread disease") .. .. 2·25 2·25
93 2 p. 50, Boxer ("Say no to alcohol, drugs, tobacco") .. .. 3·75 3·75
90/3 .. .. *Set of* 4 7·25 7·25

1987 (29 Apr). *Sharks. T* **16** *and similar horiz designs. Multicoloured. P* 14.

94 29 s. Type **16** 80 80
95 32 s. Tiger Shark 85 85
96 47 s. Grey Nurse Shark .. .. 1·25 1·25
97 1 p. Great White Shark .. .. 2·25 2·25
94/7 .. .. *Set of* 4 4·50 4·50
MS98 90×90 mm. 2 p. Shark and fishes .. 4·50 5·00

17 Capt. E. C. Musick and Sikorsky "S-42" Flying Boat

1987 (2 Sept). *Air Pioneers of the South Pacific. T* **17** *and similar horiz designs. Multicoloured. P* 14.

99 42 s. Type **17** 85 85
100 57 s. Capt. J. W. Burgess and Shorts "S-30" flying boat .. .. 1·25 1·25
101 1 p. 50, Sir Charles Kingsford Smith and Fokker "F.VIIb-3m" *Southern Cross* .. 2·00 2·00
102 2 p. Amelia Earhart and Lockheed "Electra 10A" .. .. 2·50 2·50
99/102 .. .. *Set of* 4 6·00 6·00

18 Polynesian Scrub Hen and 1983 1 s. Map Definitive

19 Sailing Ship and Ship's Boat

1988 (18 May). *5th Anniversaries of First Niuafo'ou Postage Stamp (42, 57 s.) or Niuafo'ou Airport Inauguration (1, 2 p.). T* **18** *and similar horiz designs. Multicoloured. P* 14.

103 42 s. Type **18** 65 65
104 57 s. As Type **18**, but with stamp at left .. 85 85
105 1 p. "Concorde" and 1983 Airport Inauguration 29 s. stamp .. .. .. 1·75 1·75
106 2 p. As 1 p., but with stamp at left .. 2·75 2·75
103/6 .. .. *Set of* 4 5·50 5·50

1988 (11 July). *Bicentenary of Australian Settlement. Sheet 115 × 110 mm containing T* **19** *and similar vert designs. Multicoloured. P* 13½.

MS107 42 s. Type **19**; 42 s. Aborigines; 42 s. Early settlement; 42 s. Marine and convicts; 42 s. Sheep station; 42 s. Mounted stockman; 42 s. Kangaroos and early Trans Continental locomotive; 42 s. Kangaroos and train carriages; 42 s. Flying Doctor aircraft; 42 s. Cricket match; 42 s. Wicket and Sydney skyline; 42 s. Fielders and Sydney Harbour Bridge .. .. .. 8·00 8·50

Each horizontal strip of 4 within No. **MS**107 shows a composite design.

20 Audubon's Shearwaters and Blowholes, Houma, Tonga

21 Sextant

1988 (18 Aug). *Islands of Polynesia. T* **20** *and similar vert designs. Multicoloured. P* 14.

108 42 s. Type **20** 85 85
109 57 s. Kiwi at Akaroa Harbour, New Zealand 1·25 1·25
110 90 s. Red-tailed Tropic Birds at Rainmaker Mountain, Samoa .. .. 1·75 1·75
111 2 p. 50, Laysan Albatross at Kapoho Volcano, Hawaii .. .. 3·75 3·75
108/11 .. .. *Set of* 4 7·00 7·00

1989 (28 Apr). *Bicentenary of Mutiny on the* Bounty. *Sheet 115×110 mm containing T* **21** *and similar vert designs. Multicoloured. P* 13½.

MS112 42 s. Type **21**; 42 s. Capt. Bligh; 42 s. Lieutenant, 1787; 42 s. Midshipman, 1787; 42 s. Tahitian woman and contemporary newspaper; 42 s. Breadfruit plant; 42 s. Pistol and extract from *Mutiny on the Bounty*; 42 s. Book illustration of Bligh cast adrift; 42 s. Profile of Tahitian woman and extract from contemporary newspaper; 42 s. Signatures of *Bounty* officers; 42 s. Fletcher Christian; 42 s. Tombstone of John Adams, Pitcairn Island .. .. .. 8·50 9·00

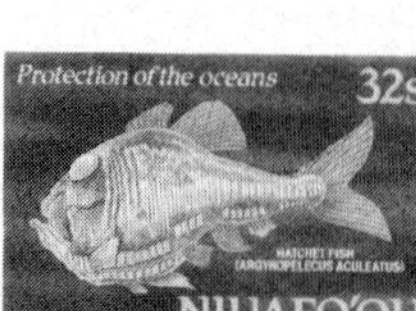

22 Hatchet Fish

23 Formation of Earth's Surface

1989 (2 June). *Fishes of the Deep. T* **22** *and similar horiz designs. Multicoloured. P* 14.

113 32 s. Type **22** 50 50
114 42 s. Snipe Eel 65 65
115 57 s. Viper Fish 80 80
116 1 p. 50, Football Fish .. .. 1·75 1·75
113/16 .. .. *Set of* 4 3·25 3·25

1989 (6 June–1 Aug). *The Evolution of the Earth. T* **23** *and similar vert designs. Multicoloured.*

(*a*) *Size* 27×35½ *mm. P* 14½

117 1 s. Type **23** 10 10
118 2 s. Cross-section of Earth's crust .. 10 10
119 5 s. Volcano 10 10
120 10 s. Cross-section of Earth during cooling 10 10
121 15 s. Sea 15 20
122 20 s. Mountains 20 25
123 32 s. River gorge 30 35
124 42 s. Early plant life, Silurian era .. 40 45
125 50 s. Fossils and Cambrian lifeforms .. 45 50
126 57 s. Carboniferous forest and coal seams 50 55

(*b*) *Size* 25½×40 *mm. P* 14 (1 Aug)

127 1 p. Dragonfly and amphibians, Carboniferous era 90 95
128 1 p. 50, Dinosaurs, Jurassic era .. .. 1·40 1·50
129 2 p. Early bird and mammals, Jurassic era 1·90 2·00
130 5 p. Human family and domesticated dog, Pleistocene era .. .. 4·50 4·75
117/30 .. .. *Set of* 14 9·75 10·50

24 Astronaut on Moon and Newspaper Headline

25 Lake Vai Lahi

1989 (17 Nov). *"World Stamp Expo '89" International Stamp Exhibition, Washington. P* 14.

131 **24** 57 s. multicoloured 85 85

1989 (17 Nov). *20th Universal Postal Union Congress, Washington. Miniature sheet, 185 × 150 mm, containing designs as Nos. 117/31, but with U.P.U. emblem at top right and some new values. P* 14½×14 (*top two rows*) *or* 14 (*bottom row*).

MS132 32 s. × 5 (as Nos. 117/21); 42 s. × 5 (as Nos. 122/6); 57 s. × 5 (as Nos. 127/31) .. 8·00 8·00

On No. **MS**132 the row of five 57 s. values are at the foot of the sheet and are perforated in a different gauge from the top two rows.

1990 (4 Apr). *Niuafo'ou Crater Lake. T* **25** *and similar horiz designs. Multicoloured. P* 14.

133 42 s. Type **25** 55 55
a. Sheetlet. Nos. 133/8 .. .. .. 5·00
134 42 s. Islands in centre of lake 55 55
135 42 s. South-west end of lake and islet .. 55 55
136 1 p. Type **25** .. .. 1·25 1·25
137 1 p. As No. 134 .. .. 1·25 1·25
138 1 p. As No. 135 .. .. 1·25 1·25
133/8 .. .. *Set of* 6 5·00 5·00

Nos. 133/8 were printed together, *se-tenant*, as a sheetlet of six containing horizontal strips of three of each value forming composite designs and separated by an inscribed horizontal gutter.

COVER PRICES

Cover factors are quoted at the beginning of each country for most issues to 1945. An explanation of the system can be found on page x. The factors quoted do not, however, apply to philatelic covers.

26 Penny Black and Tin Can Mail Service

1990 (1 May). *150th Anniv of the Penny Black. T* **26** *and similar horiz designs, each showing stamp and Tin Can Mail. Multicoloured. P* 14.

139 42 s. Type **26** 70 70
140 57 s. U.S.A. 1847 10 c. 85 85
141 75 s. Western Australia 1854 1d. .. .. 1·00 1·00
142 2 p. 50, Mafeking Siege 1900 1d. .. .. 3·50 3·50
139/42 .. .. *Set of* 4 5·50 5·50

27 Humpback Whale surfacing

(Des G. Bennett)

1990 (6 June–4 Sept). *Polynesian Whaling. T* **27** *and similar horiz designs. Multicoloured. P* 11½.

143 15 s. Type **27** 45 45
144 42 s. Whale diving under canoe 80 80
145 57 s. Tail of Blue Whale .. .. .. 1·00 1·00
146 2 p. Old man and pair of whales .. .. 2·75 2·75
143/6 .. .. *Set of* 4 4·50 4·50
MS147 120×93 mm. 1 p. Pair of whales (38×30 *mm*). P 14×14½ (4 Sept) .. .. .. 1·50 1·75

No. **MS**147 shows "1990A" as an imprint on the 1p. stamp. Examples of this miniature sheet with "1990" as the imprint were mainly used for the surcharge, No. **MS**156, although a few unsurcharged examples with this imprint were used on Niuafo'ou in 1991.

(Des A. Benjamin and R. Edge)

1990 (25 Oct). *40th Anniv of United Nations Development Programme. Horiz designs as T* **203** *of Tonga. Multicoloured. P* 13½×14.

148 57 s. Agriculture and Fisheries 75 75
a. Pair. Nos. 148/9 .. .. .. 1·50 1·50
149 57 s. Education 75 75
150 2 p. 50, Healthcare .. .. 3·00 3·00
a. Pair. Nos. 150/1 .. .. .. 6·00 6·00
151 2 p. 50, Communications .. .. .. 3·00 3·00
148/51 .. .. *Set of* 4 6·75 6·75

The two designs for each value were printed together, *se-tenant*, in horizontal and vertical pairs throughout the sheets.

28 H.M.S. *Bounty*

XX
1991 ORNITHOLOGICAL AND
SCIENTIFIC EXPEDITION.
T$1

(29)

(Des D. Miller)

1991 (25 July). *Bicentenary of Charting of Niuafo'ou. T* **28** *and similar vert designs. Multicoloured. P* 14½×14.

152 32 s. Type **28** 55 55
a. Horiz strip of 3. Nos. 152/4 .. .. 1·90
153 42 s. Chart of *Pandora's* course 70 70
154 57 s. H.M.S. *Pandora* 85 85
152/4 .. .. *Set of* 3 1·90 1·90
MS155 120×93 mm. 2 p. Capt. Edwards of the *Pandora*; 3 p. Capt. Bligh of the *Bounty* .. 6·50 7·00

Nos. 152/4 were printed together, *se-tenant*, in horizontal strips of three throughout the sheet.

1991 (31 July). *Ornithological and Scientific Expedition to Niuafo'ou. No.* **MS**147 *surch with T* **29** *in blue by Govt. Printer, Tonga.*

MS156 120×93 mm. 1 p. on 1 p. multicoloured .. 1·25 1·40

No. **MS**156 shows "1990" as the imprint date.

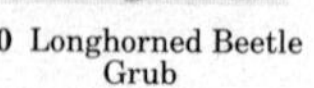

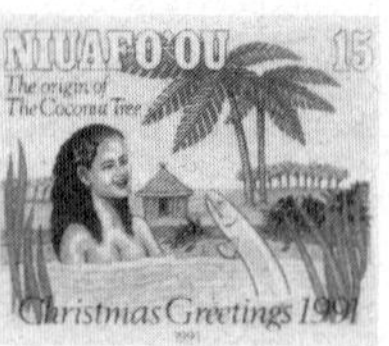

30 Longhorned Beetle Grub

31 Heina meeting the Eel

(Des G. Bennett)

1991 (11 Sept). *Longhorned Beetle. T* **30** *and similar vert designs. Multicoloured. P* 14½×14.

157	42 s. Type **30**	60	60
158	57 s. Adult beetle	80	80
159	1 p. 50, Grub burrowing	2·00	2·00
160	2 p. 50, Adult on treetrunk	3·00	3·00
157/60	.. .. *Set of* 4	5·75	5·75

(Des D. Miller)

1991 (12 Nov). *The Legend of the Coconut Tree. T* **31** *and similar horiz designs. Multicoloured. P* 14×14½.

161	15 s. Type **31**	25	25
162	42 s. Heina crying over the eel's grave ..	60	60
MS163	96×113 mm. 15 s. Type **31**; 42 s. No. 162; 1 p. 50, Heina's son collecting coconuts; 3 p. Milk flowing from coconut	5·50	6·00

(Des R. Edge)

1992 (28 Apr). 500*th Anniv of Discovery of America by Columbus. Sheet* 119×109 *mm. containing vert designs as T* **214** *of Tonga. Multicoloured. P* 13½.

MS164	57 s. Columbus; 57 s. Queen Isabella and King Ferdinand; 57 s. Columbus being blessed by Abbot of Palos; 57 s. 15th-century compass; 57 s. Wooden traverse, windrose and the *Nina*; 57 s. Bow of *Santa Maria*; 57 s. Stern of *Santa Maria*; 57 s. The *Pinta*; 57 s. Crew erecting cross; 57 s. Sailors and Indians; 57 s. Columbus reporting to King and Queen; 57 s. Coat of Arms	6·00	6·25

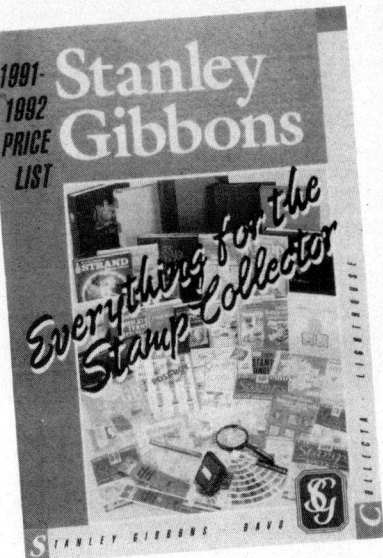

Transjordan

PRICES FOR STAMPS ON COVER

Nos. 1/88*a*	*from* × 10
Nos. 89/142	*from* × 5
Nos. 143/243	*from* × 3
Nos. D112/24	*from* × 5
Nos. D159/248	*from* × 3
No. O117	*from* × 5

Transjordan was part of the Turkish Empire from 1516 to 1918. The area was overrun by British and Arab forces, organised by Colonel T. E. Lawrence, in September 1918, and as Occupied Enemy Territory (East), became part of the Syrian state under the Emir Faisal, who was king of Syria from 11 March to 24 July 1920. On 25 April 1920 the Supreme Council of the Allies assigned to the United Kingdom a mandate to administer both Palestine and Transjordan, as the area to the east of the Jordan was called. The mandate came into operation on 29 September 1923. During 1920 the stamps of the Arab Kingdom of Syria were in use.

BRITISH MANDATED TERRITORY

(1000 milliemes = 100 piastres = £1 Egyptian)

"EAST". Where the word "East" appears in the Arabic overprints it is not used in its widest sense but as implying the land or government "East of Jordan".

شرقي الاردن

("East of Jordan")
(1)

(1*a*)

(Optd at Greek Orthodox Convent, Jerusalem)

1920 (Nov). *T* 3 *of Palestine optd with T* 1. (*a*) *P* 15 × 14.

1 1 1 m. sepia — 40 80
a. Opt inverted — £120
2 2 m. blue-green — 4·50 6·00
a. Silver opt — £180 £200
3 3 m. yellow-brown — 50 80
a. Opt Type 1*a* — £1100
4 4 m. scarlet — 60 80
5 5 m. yellow-orange — 70 1·00
5*a* 1 p. deep indigo (Silver) — £2000
6 2 p. olive — 2·00 4·00
a. Opt Type 1*a* — £1100
7 5 p. deep purple — 17·00 22·00
a. Opt Type 1*a* — £1200
8 9 p. ochre — £1000 £1200
1/7 (*ex* 5*a*) — *Set of* 7 23·00 32·00

(*b*) *P* 14

9 1 1 m. sepia — 40 60
a. Opt inverted — £150
10 2 m. blue-green — 30 60
a. Silver opt — £200
11 3 m. yellow-brown — 7·00 7·50
12 4 m. scarlet — 13·00 15·00
13 5 m. orange — 1·00 80
14 1 p. deep indigo (Silver) — 90 1·75
15 2 p. deep olive — 1·40 2·50
16 5 p. purple — 2·00 5·00
17 9 p. ochre — 3·50 15·00
18 10 p. ultramarine — 4·00 15·00
19 20 p. pale grey — 8·00 24·00
9/19 — *Set of* 11 38·00 80·00

Emir Abdullah, 1 April 1921–22 May 1946

Abdullah, a son of the King of the Hejaz, was made Emir of Transjordan in 1921. On 26 May 1923 Transjordan was recognised as an autonomous state and on 20 February 1928 it was accorded a degree of independence.

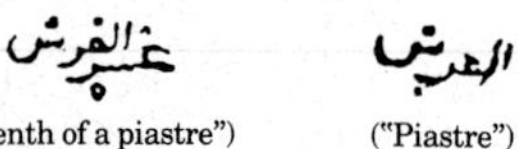

("Tenth of a piastre") (2) ("Piastre") (3)

1922 (Nov). *Nos.* 1/19 *additionally handstamped with steel dies at Amman as T* 2 *or* 3. (*a*) *P* 15 × 14.

20 2 1/10 p. on 1 m. sepia — 25·00 45·00
a. Red surch — 70·00 70·00
b. Violet surch — 70·00 70·00
21 2/10 p. on 2 m. blue-green — 28·00 28·00
a. Error. Surch "3/10" for "2/10" — £110 £110
b. Red surch — 80·00 80·00
c. Violet surch — £100 £100
22 3/10 p. on 3 m. yellow-brown — 10·00 10·00
a. Pair, one without surch — £750
b. Opt Type 1*a* — £1500
c. Violet surch — £150 £150
23 4/10 p. on 4 m. scarlet — 50·00 50·00
24 5/10 p. on 5 m. yellow-orange — £180 £100
a. Violet surch — £350 £300
25 3 2 p. on 2 p. olive — £250 75·00
aa. Opt Type 1*a* — £1500
a. Red surch — £275 80·00
b. Violet surch — £300 90·00
26 5 p. on 5 p. deep purple — 50·00 70·00
a. Opt Type 1*a* — £1500
27 9 p. on 9 p. ochre — £300 £350
a. Red surch — £130 £140

(*b*) *P* 14

28 2 1/10 p. on 1 m. sepia — 20·00 25·00
a. Red surch — 60·00 60·00
b. Violet surch — £250 £300
29 2/10 p. on 2 m. blue-green — 25·00 25·00
a. Error. Surch "3/10" for "2/10" — £100 £100
b. Red surch — 80·00 80·00
c. Violet surch — 80·00 80·00
30 2 5/10 p. on 5 m. orange — £250 £100
a. Violet surch — £275
31 3 1 p. on 1 p. deep indigo (R.) — £200 60·00
a. Violet surch — £400
32 9 p. on 9 p. ochre (R.) — £500 £500
33 10 p. on 10 p. ultramarine — £950 £1000
34 20 p. on 20 p. pale grey — £800 £850
a. Violet surch — £900 £950

T 3 *of Palestine (perf* 15×14) *similarly surch*

35 3 10 p. on 10 p. ultramarine — £2000 £2500
36 20 p. on 20 p. pale grey — £2500 £3000

T 2 reads "tenths of a piastre". T 3 reads "the piastre", both with Arabic figures below. These surcharges were supplied in order to translate the Egyptian face values of the stamps into terms intelligible to the local population, *i.e.* tenths of a piastre (= milliemes) and piastres of the Turkish gold pound; but the actual face value of the stamps remained unchanged.

Being handstamped the surcharge may be found either at the top or bottom of the stamp, and exists double on most values.

("Arab Government of the East, April 1921")
(4)

1922 (Dec). *Stamps of* 1920, *handstamped with a steel die as T* 4 *in red-purple, violet or black.** (*a*) *P* 15 × 14.

37 4 1 m. sepia (R.P.) — 25·00 25·00
a. Violet opt — 28·00 28·00
b. Black opt — 22·00 22·00
38 2 m. blue-green (R.P.) — 22·00 22·00
a. Violet opt — 20·00 20·00
b. Black opt — 18·00 18·00
39 3 m. yellow-brown (R.P.) — 25·00 25·00
a. Opt Type 1*a* — £1600
b. Violet opt — 7·00 7·00
ba. Pair, one without opt — £1000
c. Black opt — 8·00 8·00
40 4 m. scarlet (R.P.) — 45·00 50·00
a. Violet opt — 45·00 50·00
b. Black opt — 45·00 50·00
41 5 m. yellow-orange (R.P.) — 35·00 10·00
a. Violet opt — 15·00 10·00
42 2 p. olive (No. 6) (R.P.) — 55·00 40·00
a. Violet opt — 20·00 15·00
b. Black opt — 12·00 10·00
c. On No. 6a (R.P.) — £1500
d. On No. 6a (V.) — £1500 £1300
43 5 p. deep purple (R.P.) — 80·00 £100
aa. Pair, one without opt — £1500
a. Violet opt — 60·00 80·00
44 9 p. ochre (R.P.) — £400 £450
a. Violet opt — £200 £250
ab. Opt Type 1*a* — £2000
b. Black opt — 65·00 80·00

(*b*) *P* 14

45 4 1 m. sepia (R.P.) — 12·00 15·00
a. Pair, one without opt — £1000
b. Violet opt — 22·00 20·00
c. Black opt — 18·00 18·00
46 2 m. blue-green (R.P.) — 25·00 25·00
a. Violet opt — 8·00 8·00
b. Black opt — 10·00 10·00
46*c* 3 m. yellow-brown (V.) — £750 £350
47 5 m. orange (R.P.) — £300 75·00
a. Violet opt — 25·00 20·00
48 1 p. deep indigo (R.P.) — 25·00 15·00
a. Violet opt — 15·00 9·00
49 2 p. olive (V.) — 75·00 80·00
50 5 p. purple (R.P.) — 90·00 £100
a. Violet opt — £100 £110
51 9 p. ochre (V.) — £900 £1000
52 10 p. ultramarine (R.P.) — £1800 £1900
a. Violet opt — £1500 £1600
53 20 p. pale grey (R.P.) — £1900 £2000
a. Violet opt — £1600 £1700

*The ink of the "black" overprint is not a true black, but is caused by a mixture of inks from different ink-pads. The colour is, however, very distinct from either of the others. Other values may exist with "black" overprint.

Most values are known with inverted and/or double overprints.

حكومة الشرق
العربية
نيسان سنة ١٩٢١

("Arab Government of the East, April 1921")
(5)

1923 (1 Mar). *Stamps of* 1920, *with typographed overprint, T* 5.

(*a*) *P* 15 × 14

54 5 1 m. sepia (Gold) — £1800 £2000
55 2 m. blue-green (Gold) — 20·00 22·00
56 3 m. yellow-brown (Gold) — 12·00 15·00
a. Opt double — £250
b. Opt inverted — £275
c. Black opt — 75·00 85·00
57 4 m. scarlet — 10·00 12·00
58 5 m. yellow-orange — 50·00 45·00
59 2 p. olive (No. 6) (Gold) — 15·00 15·00
a. Black opt — £300
b. On No. 6a (Gold) — £1200 £1000
60 5 p. deep purple (No. 7) (Gold) — 60·00 80·00
a. Opt inverted — £300
b. On No. 7a — £1500
ba. Ditto. Gold opt inverted — £2000

(*b*) *P* 14

62 5 1 m. sepia (Gold) — 18·00 24·00
a. Opt inverted — £300
63 5 2 m. blue-green (Gold) — 15·00 18·00
a. Opt inverted — £350
b. Opt double — £275
64 5 m. orange — 12·00 12·00
65 1 p. deep indigo (Gold) — 12·00 14·00
a. Opt double — £450 £475
b. Black opt — £800 £850
66 9 p. ochre — 75·00 £100
67 10 p. ultramarine (Gold) — 75·00 £100
68 20 p. pale grey (Gold) — 75·00 £100
a. Opt inverted — £350
b. Opt double — £425
c. Opt double, one inverted — £425
e. Opt double, one gold, one black, latter inverted — £650
f. Black opt — £800
fa. Black opt inverted — £1000
fb. Black opt double, one inverted — £1200

There are numerous constant minor varieties in this overprint in all values.

The 20 p. exists with top line of overprint only or with the lines transposed, both due to misplacement.

Same overprint on stamp of Palestine, T 3

69 5 5 m. orange — £1200 £1400

In this variety the overprint, T 1 of Jordan, has been applied to the stamp, but is not inked, so that it is hardly perceptible.

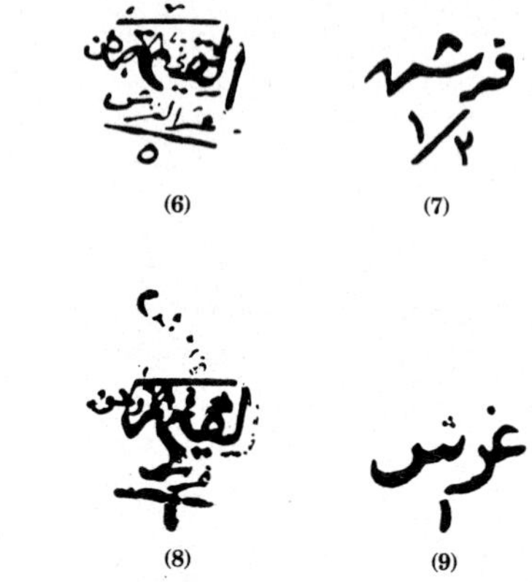

(6) (7)

(8) (9)

1923 (April–Oct). *Stamps of the preceding issues further surch by means of handstamps.* (*a*) *Issue of Nov* 1920.

70 – 2½/10ths p. on 5 m. (13) (B.–Blk.) — £160 £160
a. Black surch — £160 £160
b. Violet surch — £160 £160

(*b*) *Stamp of Palestine*

71 6 5/10 p. on 3 m. (7) — £7500

(*c*) *Issue of Nov* 1922

72 6 5/10 p. on 3 m. (22) — £7000
73 5/10 p. on 5 p. (26) (V.) — 70·00 80·00
73*b* 5/10 p. on 9 p. (27a) — £350 £375
74 7 ½ p. on 5 p. (26) — 70·00 80·00
75 ½ p. on 9 p. (27) — £7500
a. On No. 27a — £350 £400
76 ½ p. on 9 p. (32) — — £8000
77 8 1 p. on 5 p. (26) — 80·00 £100

(*d*) *Issue of Dec* 1922

78 6 5/10 p. on 3 m. (39) — 85·00 £100
a. On No. 39a — £750
ab. Pair, one without surch — £1400
b. On No. 39b — 40·00 50·00
c. Without numeral of value — £150
79 5/10 p. on 5 p. (43a) — 8·00 14·00
c. Pair, one without surch — £500
79*d* 5/10 p. on 9 p. (44b) — — £1200
e. Surch on No. 44a — — £1300
80 7 ½ p. on 2 p. (42) — £100 £120
b. On No. 42a — 80·00 £110
c. On No. 42b — 60·00 £110
e. On No. 42b. Pair, one without surch — £1000
f. On No. 42c — £2000
81 ½ p. on 5 p. (43a) — £3000
82 ½ p. on 5 p. (50) — £1800
83 8 1 p. on 5 p. (43) — £3750
b. On No. 43a — £2000 £2250

(*e*) *Issue of* 1 *March* 1923

84 6 5/10 p. on 3 m. (56) — 25·00 30·00
85 7 ½ p. on 9 p. (*p* 15×14) — 90·00 £150
86 ½ p. on 9 p. (66) — £150
87 9 1 p. on 10 p. (67) — £2250 £2500
a. Violet surch — £2750
88 2 p. on 20 p. (68) — 60·00 80·00
88*a* 2 p. on 20 p. (68f) — £2000

The handstamp on No. 88 has an Arabic "2" in place of the "1" shown in the illustration of Type **9**.

Being handstamped many of the above exist inverted or double.

TYPES OF SAUDI ARABIA. The following illustrations are repeated here for convenience from Saudi Arabia.

11

20

21

22

حكومة

الشرق العربية

٩ شعبان ١٣٤١

("Arab Government of the East, 9 Sha'ban 1341") (10)

("Arab Government of the East. Commemoration of Independence, 25 May 1923") (11)

It should be noted that as Arabic is read from right to left, the overprint described as reading downwards appears to the English reader as though reading upwards. Our illustration of Type **11** shows the overprint reading downwards.

1923 (April). *Stamps of Saudi Arabia. T* **11**, *with typographed opt, T* **10**.

No.	Type	Description	Unused	Used
89	10	1/8 p. chestnut	2·00	1·75
		a. Opt double	£200	
		b. Opt inverted	£150	
90		1/2 p. scarlet	2·00	1·75
91		1 p. blue	1·25	80
		a. Opt inverted	£160	£180
92		1 1/2 p. lilac	1·50	1·75
		a. Opt double	£225	
		b. Top line omitted	—	£225
		c. Pair, one without opt	£300	
93		2 p. orange	2·00	5·00
94		3 p. brown	3·00	7·00
		a. Opt inverted	£300	
		b. Opt double	£300	
		c. Pair, one without opt	£500	
95		5 p. olive	5·00	8·00
89/95		*Set of* 7	15·00	23·00

On same stamps, surcharged with new values (Saudi Arabia, Nos. 47 and 49)

No.	Type	Description	Unused	Used
96	10	1/4 p. on 1/8 p. chestnut	4·00	5·00
		a. Opt and surch inverted	£200	
		b. Ditto. but 2nd and 3rd lines of opt omitted	£250	
97		10 p. on 5 p. olive	15·00	20·00

In this setting, the first line of the overprint measures 9 mm, the second 18½–19½ mm, and the third, 19–21 mm. On 35 stamps out of the setting of 36 the Arabic "9" (right-hand character in bottom line) is widely spaced from the rest of the inscription. Minor varieties of this setting exist on all values.

For later setting, varying from the above, see Nos. 121/4.

٩٢٣ ٩٣٣

Normal. "923" Error. "933"

An error reading "933" instead of "923" occurs as No. 2 in the setting of 24 on all values. As only 24 stamps were overprinted for each of Nos. 103A, 105B, 107B and 108A only one example of the error can exist for each. No such examples have so far been recorded.

1923 (25 May). *T* **3** *of Palestine optd with T* **11**, *reading up or down, in black or gold.* A. *Reading downwards.* B. *Reading upwards.*

No.	Description	A		B	
98	1 m. (Blk.)	17·00	17·00	90·00	£100
	a. Opt double, one inverted (Blk.)	£750	£750	†	
	b. Gold opt	£150	£160	£150	£160
	c. Opt double, one inverted (Gold)	£900	—	†	
	d. Opt double (Blk. + Gold)	£900	£900	†	
	e. Arabic "933"	85·00	—	£250	—
99	2 m. (Blk.)	28·00	35·00	45·00	50·00
	a. Arabic "933"	£140	—	£200	—
100	3 m. (Blk.)	10·00	12·00	90·00	£100
	a. Arabic "933"	70·00	—	£250	—
101	4 m. (Blk.)	10·00	12·00	25·00	32·00
	a. Arabic "933"	70·00	—	£130	—
102	5 m. (Blk.)	50·00	60·00	†	
	a. Arabic "933"	£250	—	—	—
103	1 p. (Gold)	£750	—	50·00	60·00
	a. Opt double	£900	£900	—	—
	b. Black opt	†		—	—
	c. Arabic "933"	—	—	£250	—
104	2 p. (Blk.)	50·00	70·00	—	—
	a. Arabic "933"	£250	—	—	—
105	5 p. (Gold)	60·00	70·00	£750	£550
	a. Opt double	£650	—	†	
	b. Arabic "933"	£275	—	—	—
106	9 p. (Blk.)	70·00	90·00	50·00	60·00
	a. Arabic "933"	£300	—	£250	—
107	10 p. (Blk.)	60·00	80·00	£600	—
	a. Arabic "933"	£275	—	—	—
108	20 p. (Blk.)	£700	—	70·00	90·00
	a. Arabic "933"	—	—	£300	—

The 9 and 10 p. are perf 14, all the other values being perf 15×14.

No. 107A *surch with T* **9**

No.	Description	Unused	Used
109	1 p. on 10 p. ultramarine	£6000	

نصف قرش

(12)

1923 (Sept). *No.* 92 *surch with T* **12**. (*a*) *Handstamped.*

No.	Type	Description	Unused	Used
110	12	1/2 p. on 1 1/2 p. lilac	6·00	6·00
		a. Surch and opt inverted	75·00	
		b. Opt double	75·00	
		c. Opt double, one inverted	90·00	£100
		d. Pair, one without opt	£180	

This handstamp is known inverted, double and double, one inverted.

(*b*) *Typographed*

No.	Type	Description	Unused	Used
111	12	1/2 p. on 1 1/2 p. lilac	50·00	50·00
		a. Surch inverted	£250	
		b. Surch double	£200	
		c. Pair, one without surch	£500	

حكومة حكومة

الشرق العربية الشرق العربية

٩ شبان ١٣٤١ ٩ شعان ١٣٤١

(13*a*) (13*b*)

("Arab Government of the East, 9 Sha'ban, 1341")

These two types differ in the spacing of the characters and in the position of the bottom line which is to the left of the middle line in T **13***a* and centrally placed in T **13***b*.

1923 (Oct). *T* **11** *of Saudi Arabia handstamped as T* **13***a or* **13***b*.

No.	Type	Description	Unused	Used
112	13*a*	1/2 p. scarlet	6·00	7·00
113	13*b*	1/2 p. scarlet	6·00	7·00

د · ق · ج

ملك العرب

ا ج ٣٤٢

(15 "Arab Government of the East") ("Commemorating the coming of His Majesty the King of the Arabs" and date) (16)

1924 (Jan). *T* **11** *of Saudi Arabia with typographed opt T* **15**.

No.	Type	Description	Unused	Used
114	15	1/2 p. scarlet	6·00	8·00
		a. Opt inverted	£250	
115		1 p. blue	£300	£200
116		1 1/2 p. lilac	£350	

The ½ p. exists with thick, brown gum, which tints the paper, and with white gum and paper.

1924 (18 Jan). *Visit of King Hussein of Hejaz. T* **11** *of Saudi Arabia optd with T* **15** *and with further typographed opt T* **16**.

A. *In Black.* B. *In Gold*

No.	Type	Description	A		B	
117	16	1/2 p. scarlet	1·00	1·00	2·00	2·00
		a. Type **15** omitted	£150	—	†	
		b. Type **16** inverted	£200	—	†	
		c. Imperf between (pr)	£110	—	—	—
118		1 p. blue	1·25	1·25	2·00	2·00
		a. Type **15** omitted	£150	—	†	
		b. Both opts inverted	£200	—	£300	—
		d. Imperf between (pr)	†		—	—
119		1 1/2 p. lilac	2·00	2·00	3·00	3·00
		a. Type **15** inverted	£130	—	£150	—
120		2 p. orange	4·00	4·00	6·00	6·00

The spacing of the lines of the overprint varies considerably, and a variety dated "432" for "342" occurs on the twelfth stamp in each sheet.

1924 (Mar–May). *T* **11** *of Saudi Arabia optd as T* **10** (*new setting*).*

No.	Description	Unused	Used
121	1/2 p. scarlet	3·00	3·00
	a. Opt inverted	£120	
122	1/2 p. maroon	10·00	8·00
	a. Opt inverted	£120	
123	1 p. blue	5·00	2·00
	a. Opt double	£150	
124	1 1/2 p. lilac	7·50	8·50

*This setting is from fresh type, the first line measuring 8¾ mm, the second nearly 20 mm and third 18¼ mm.

On all stamps in this setting (except Nos. 1, 9, 32 and 33) the Arabic "9" is close to the rest of the inscription.

The dots on the character "Y" (the second character from the left in the second line) are on many stamps vertical (:) instead of horizontal (..).

There are many errors. In the third line, No. 24 of the setting reads "Shabál", and No. 27 reads "Shabn" (instead of "Shab'an").

On some sheets of the ½ p. (both colours), the right hand character, "H", in the first line, was omitted from the second stamp in the first row of the sheet.

NEW INFORMATION

The editor is always interested to correspond with people who have new information that will improve or correct the Catalogue.

حكومة الشرق

العربي

١٣٤٢

("Government of the Arab East, 1342") (17)

حكومة

الشرق العربي

سنة ١٣٤٣

("Government of the Arab East, 1343") (18)

1924 (Sept–Nov). *T* **11** *of Saudi Arabia with type-set opt as T* **17**.

No.	Type	Description	Unused	Used
125	17	1/8 p. chestnut	35	25
		a. Opt inverted	£130	
126		1/4 p. green	30	30
		a. *Tête-bêche* (pair)	7·50	10·00
		b. Opt inverted	£100	
127		1/2 p. scarlet	30	30
128		1/2 p. maroon	1·50	60
129		1 p. blue	2·50	1·50
		a. Imperf between (horiz pair)	£130	
		b. Opt inverted		
130		1 1/2 p. lilac	2·50	2·50
131		2 p. orange	2·00	2·00
132		3 p. brown-red	1·50	1·50
		a. Opt inverted	£100	
		b. Opt double	£100	
133		5 p. olive	2·00	2·50
134		10 p. brown-purple and mauve (R.)	4·00	5·00
		a. Centre inverted		
		b. Black opt	£140	
125/34		*Set of* 10	15·00	15·00

Varieties may be found with dates "1242" or "1343", with "1" or "2" inverted, and other errors exist.

1925 (Aug). *T* **20**/**22** *of Saudi Arabia with lithographed opt T* **18**.

No.	Type	Description	Unused	Used
135	18	1/8 p. chocolate	30	60
		a. Imperf between (horiz pair)	£110	£130
136		1/4 p. ultramarine	30	60
137		1/2 p. carmine	40	35
138		1 p. green	40	35
139		1 1/2 p. orange	75	1·50
140		2 p. blue	1·00	1·75
		a. Opt treble	£150	£200
141		3 p. sage-green (R.)	1·25	2·50
		a. Imperf between (horiz pair)	£110	£160
		b. Black opt	£120	£150
142		5 p. chestnut	2·00	5·00
135/42		*Set of* 8	5·75	11·50

The whole series exists imperforate and (except the 1 and 2 p.) with inverted overprint, both perf and imperf.

("East of the Jordan") (19)

22 Emir Abdullah

23 Emir Abdullah

(Opt typo by Waterlow)

1925 (1 Nov). *Stamps of Palestine, 1922* (*without the three-line Palestine opt*), *optd with T* **19**. *Wmk Mult Script CA.* (*a*) *P* 14.

No.	Type	Description	Unused	Used
143	19	1 m. deep brown	10	15
144		2 m. yellow	10	15
145		3 m. greenish blue	10	15
146		4 m. carmine-pink	10	15
147		5 m. orange	10	15
		a. Yellow-orange	35·00	20·00
148		6 m. blue-green	15	20
149		7 m. yellow-brown	15	20
150		8 m. scarlet	20	30
151		13 m. ultramarine	40	60
152		1 p. grey	40	40
153		2 p. olive	60	70
		a. Olive-green	£100	25·00
154		5 p. deep purple	2·50	3·00
155		9 p. ochre	4·00	4·50
156		10 p. light blue	7·00	8·00
		a. Error. "E.F.F." in bottom panel	£900	£800
157		20 p. bright violet	14·00	15·00
143/57		*Set of* 15	27·00	30·00
143/57 Optd "Specimen"		*Set of* 15	£120	

(*b*) *P* 15 × 14

No.	Type	Description	Unused	Used
157*a*	19	9 p. ochre	£1000	£1100
158		10 p. blue	75·00	85·00
158*a*		20 p. bright violet	£1000	£1000

(New Currency. 1000 milliemes = £1 Palestinian)

(Recess Perkins, Bacon & Co)

1927 (1 Nov)–**29**. *New Currency. Wmk Mult Script CA. P* 14.

No.	Type	Description	Unused	Used
159	22	2 m. greenish blue	15	15
160		3 m. carmine-pink	20	20
161		4 m. green	50	70
162		5 m. orange	25	20
163		10 m. scarlet	50	45
164		15 m. ultramarine	60	25
165		20 m. olive-green	80	85
166	23	50 m. purple	2·50	2·75
167		90 m. bistre	5·00	7·00
168		100 m. blue	6·50	5·50
169		200 m. violet	16·00	18·00
170		500 m. brown (1929)	60·00	75·00
171		1000 m. slate-grey (1929)	£100	£130
159/71		*Set of* 13	£180	£225
159/71 Optd/perf "Specimen"		*Set of* 13	£180	

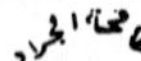

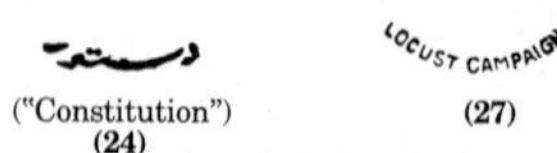

("Constitution")
(24)

(27)

(Optd at Cairo)

1928 (1 Sept). *New Constitution of 20 February 1928. Optd with T* **24**.

172 **22** 2 m. greenish blue .. .. 50 1·00
173 3 m. carmine-pink .. .. 60 1·50
174 4 m. green .. .. 60 1·75
175 5 m. orange 60 75
176 10 m. scarlet .. .. 1·00 2·25
177 15 m. ultramarine .. .. 1·00 1·25
178 20 m. olive-green .. .. 3·00 5·00
179 **23** 50 m. purple .. .. 5·00 5·50
180 90 m. bistre .. .. 13·00 24·00
181 100 m. blue .. .. 22·00 30·00
182 200 m. violet .. .. 60·00 85·00
172/82 .. .. *Set of* 11 95·00 £140

(Optd at Alexandria by Whitehead, Morris & Co)

1930 (1 Apr). *Locust Campaign. Optd as T* **27**.

183 **22** 2 m. greenish blue .. .. 75 2·00
a. Opt inverted £250
184 3 m. carmine-pink .. .. 80 2·00
185 4 m. green .. .. 60 2·50
186 5 m. orange .. .. 8·50 10·00
a. Opt double £400 £550
b. Pair, one without bottom line .. £500
187 10 m. scarlet .. .. 55 2·00
188 15 m. ultramarine .. .. 80 1·75
a. Opt inverted £225 £350
189 20 m. olive-green .. .. 1·00 2·50
190 **23** 50 m. purple .. .. 5·00 8·00
191 90 m. bistre .. .. 10·00 26·00
192 100 m. blue .. .. 12·00 26·00
193 200 m. violet .. .. 30·00 65·00
194 500 m. brown .. .. 75·00 £110
a. "C" of "LOCUST" omitted (R. 5/3) £700 £700
183/94 .. .. *Set of* 12 £130 £225

28 29

(Re-engraved with figures of value at left only. Recess Perkins, Bacon)

1930 (1 June)–**39**. *Wmk Mult Script CA. P* 14.

194*b* **28** 1 m. red-brown (6.2.34) 15 35
c. Perf 13½ × 13 (1939) .. .. 1·50 1·50
195 2 m. greenish blue 20 40
a. Perf 13½ × 13. *Bluish green* (1939) .. .. .. 3·50 1·50
196 3 m. carmine-pink 30 40
196*a* 3 m. green (6.2.34) 50 50
b. Perf 13½ × 13 (1939) .. .. 7·00 3·50
197 4 m. green 60 80
197*a* 4 m. carmine-pink (6.2.34) .. .. 1·50 80
b. Perf 13½ × 13 (1939) .. .. 35·00 9·00
198 5 m. orange 40 20
a. Coil stamp. P 13½ × 14 (1936) .. 14·00 4·50
b. Perf 13½ × 13 (1939) .. .. 32·00 2·25
199 10 m. scarlet 50 15
a. Perf 13½ × 13 (1939) .. .. 55·00 3·75
200 15 m. ultramarine 55 20
a. Coil stamp. P 13½ × 14 (1936) .. 14·00 4·75
b. Perf 13½ × 13 (1939) .. .. 17·00 3·50
201 20 m. olive-green .. .. 1·25 35
a. Perf 13½ × 13 (1939) .. .. 35·00 10·00
202 **29** 50 m. purple .. .. 1·50 1·00
203 90 m. bistre .. .. 2·50 3·75
204 100 m. blue .. .. 3·50 3·75
205 200 m. violet .. .. 8·50 11·00
206 500 m. brown .. .. 20·00 30·00
207 £P1 slate-grey .. .. 45·00 70·00
194*b*/207 .. .. .. *Set of* 16 75·00 £110
194*b*/207 Perf "Specimen" .. *Set of* 16 £130

For stamps perf 12 see Nos. 230/43, and for T **28** lithographed, perf 13½, see Nos. 222/9.

30 Mushetta

31 Threshing Scene

32 The Khazneh at Petra

33 Emir Abdullah

(Vignettes from photographs; frames des Yacoub Sukker. Recess Bradbury, Wilkinson)

1933 (1 Feb). *As T* **30** (*various designs*) *and T* **31/3**. *Wmk Mult Script CA. P* 12.

208 1 m. black and maroon 40 75
209 2 m. black and claret 40 55
210 3 m. blue-green 50 85
211 4 m. black and brown .. .. .. 75 1·50
212 5 m. black and orange 80 90
213 10 m. carmine .. .. 1·50 2·25
214 15 m. blue .. .. 2·50 1·25
215 20 m. black and sage-green .. .. 3·25 3·75
216 50 m. black and purple .. .. 6·50 8·00
217 90 m. black and yellow .. .. 10·00 17·00
218 100 m. black and blue .. .. .. 12·00 17·00
219 200 m. black and violet .. .. 40·00 48·00
220 500 m. scarlet and red-brown £130 £170
221 £P1 black and yellow-green £425 £650
208/21 .. .. *Set of* 14 £600 £800
208/21 Perf "Specimen" .. *Set of* 14 £500

Designs: *As T* **30**—2 m. Nymphaeum, Jerash; 3 m. Kasr Kharana; 4 m. Kerak Castle; 5 m. Temple of Artemis, Jerash; 10 m. Ajlun Castle; 20 m. Allenby Bridge over the Jordan.

The 90 m., 100 m. and 200 m. are similar to the 3 m., 5 m. and 10m. respectively, but are larger (33½ × 23½ mm). The 500 m. is similar to T **32**, but larger (23½ × 33½ mm).

34

(Litho Survey Dept, Cairo)

1942 (18 May). *T* **28**, *but with Arabic characters above portrait and in top left circle modified as in T* **34**. *No wmk. P* 13½.

222 **34** 1 m. red-brown 40 80
223 2 m. green 60 70
224 3 m. yellow-green .. .. .. 75 1·25
225 4 m. carmine-pink .. .. .. 90 1·25
226 5 m. yellow-orange .. .. .. 1·40 30
227 10 m. scarlet .. .. 1·50 1·25
228 15 m. blue .. .. 2·00 1·60
229 20 m. olive-green .. .. .. 4·50 4·00
222/9 .. .. *Set of* 8 11·00 10·00

(Recess Bradbury, Wilkinson)

1943 (1 Jan)–**44**. *Wmk Mult Script CA. P* 12.

230 **28** 1 m. red-brown 10 40
231 2 m. bluish green 20 40
232 3 m. green 20 50
233 4 m. carmine-pink 20 30
234 5 m. orange 30 10
235 10 m. red 60 20
236 15 m. blue 70 20
237 20 m. olive-green (5.44) 75 45
238 **29** 50 m. purple (5.44) .. .. .. 1·40 65
239 90 m. bistre (5.44) .. .. .. 3·50 2·00
240 100 m. blue (5.44) .. .. .. 4·00 1·00
241 200 m. violet (5.44) .. .. .. 7·50 4·50
242 500 m. brown (5.44) .. .. .. 13·00 10·00
243 £P1 slate-grey (5.44) .. .. 24·00 18·00
230/43 .. .. *Set of* 14 50·00 35·00

Nos. 237/43 were released in London by the Crown Agents about May 1944 but were not put on sale in Transjordan until 26 August 1946.

Printings of the 3, 4, 10, 12, 15 and 20 m. in changed colours were released on 12 May 1947.

POSTAGE DUE STAMPS

حكومة
مستحق
الشرق العربية
٩ شعبان ١٣٤١ مستحق

(D 1 "Due") (D 2)

1923 (Sept). *Issue of April, 1923, with opt T* **10**, *with further typographed opt Type* D **1** (*the 3 p. with handstamped surch as T* **12** *at top*).

D112 ½ p. on 3 p. brown .. .. .. 12·00 15·00
a. "Due" inverted .. .. .. 50·00 55·00
b. "Due" double .. .. .. 50·00 60·00
ba. "Due" double, one inverted .. £150
c. Arabic "t" & "h" transposed .. £100
ca. As c, inverted £250
d. Surch at foot of stamp .. .. 25·00
da. Ditto, but with var. c £120
e. Surch omitted £200
D113 1 p. blue .. .. 8·00 9·00
a. Type **10** inverted .. .. 80·00
b. "Due" inverted .. .. .. 45·00 40·00
c. "Due" double .. .. .. 50·00
d. "Due" double, one inverted .. £150
e. Arabic "t" & "h" transposed .. 70·00
f. "Due" omitted (in vertical pair) £200
D114 1½ p. lilac .. .. 8·00 9·00
a. "Due" inverted .. .. .. 45·00 45·00
b. "Due" double .. .. .. 50·00
ba. "Due" double, one diagonal .. 75·00
c. Arabic "t" & "h" transposed .. 70·00
ca. As c, inverted £200
d. "Due" omitted (in pair) £200
D115 2 p. orange .. .. 9·00 10·00
a. "Due" inverted .. .. .. 60·00 60·00
b. "Due" double .. .. .. 65·00
ba. "Due" double, one diagonal .. £100
c. "Due" treble £150
d. Arabic "t" & "h" transposed .. 70·00
e. Arabic "h" omitted .. .. 90·00

The variety, Arabic "t" and "h" transposed, occurred on No. 2 in the first row of all values in the first batch of sheets printed. The variety, Arabic "h" omitted, occurred on every stamp in the first three rows of at least three sheets of the 2 p.

Handstamped in four lines as Type D **2** *and surch as on No.* D112

D116 ½ p. on 3 p. brown .. .. .. 40·00 50·00
a. Opt and surch inverted £200
b. Opt double £200
c. Surch omitted £225
d. Opt inverted. Surch normal, but at foot of stamp £150
e. Opt omitted and opt inverted (pair) £300
f. "Due" double, one inverted £160
g. "Due" double, one larger £180
h. Surch double £250

حكومة
الشرق العربية
مستحق
٩ شعبان ١٣٤١

مستحق
شرق الاردن

(D 3) ("Due. East of the Jordan")
(D 4)

1923 (Oct). *T* **11** *of Saudi Arabia handstamped with Type* D **3**.

D117 ½ p. scarlet .. .. 1·00 1·75
D118 1 p. blue .. .. 1·50 2·00
D119 1½ p. lilac .. .. 1·75 2·75
D120 2 p. orange .. .. 2·25 3·25
D121 3 p. brown .. .. 3·75 6·50
a. Pair, one without handstamp .. £200
D122 5 p. olive .. .. 6·50 9·00
D117/22 .. .. *Set of* 6 15·00 22·00

There are three types of this handstamp, differing in some of the Arabic characters. They occur inverted, double etc.

1923 (Nov). *T* **11** *of Saudi Arabia with opt similar to Type* D **3** *but first three lines typo and fourth handstruck.*

D123 1 p. blue .. .. 50·00
D124 5 p. olive .. .. 6·00

(Opt typo by Waterlow)

1925 (Nov). *Stamps of Palestine 1922* (*without the three-line Palestine opt*), *optd with Type* D **4**. *P* 14.

D159 1 m. deep brown .. .. .. 1·40 3·00
D160 2 m. yellow .. .. 1·75 2·25
D161 4 m. carmine-pink .. .. .. 2·75 3·50
D162 8 m. scarlet .. .. 3·75 5·50
D163 13 m. ultramarine .. .. .. 4·50 5·50
D164 5 p. deep purple .. .. .. 5·00 7·00
a. Perf 15 × 14 .. .. .. 40·00 55·00
D159/64 .. .. *Set of* 6 17·00 24·00
D159/64 Optd "Specimen" .. *Set of* 6 60·00

مستحق

١ مليم (1 m.) (D 5) ٢ مليم (2 m.) ٤ مليم (4 m.)

٨ مليم (8 m.) ١٣ مليم (13 m.) ٥ قروش (5 p.)

(Surch typo at Jerusalem)

1926. *Postage stamps of* 1 *November* 1925, *surch "Due" and new value as Type* D **5**. *Bottom line of surcharge differs for each value as illustrated.*

D165 1 m. on 1 m. deep brown .. .. 2·00 3·25
D166 2 m. on 1 m. deep brown .. .. 2·25 3·25
D167 4 m. on 3 m. greenish blue .. .. 2·50 4·00
D168 8 m. on 3 m. greenish blue .. .. 2·50 4·50
D169 13 m. on 13 m. ultramarine .. .. 2·50 5·00
D170 5 p. on 13 m. ultramarine .. .. 3·50 6·00
D165/70 .. .. *Set of* 6 14·00 23·00

1 1

(D 6 "Due")

D 7

D 8

(Surch at Cairo)

1929 (1 Jan). *Nos. 159 etc. optd only or surch in addition as Type* D **6**.

D183 **22** 1 m. on 3 m. carmine-pink .. .. 60 1·50
D184 2 m. greenish blue .. .. .. 70 1·50
a. Pair, one without surch .. £250
D185 4 m. on 15 m. ultramarine .. .. 1·00 1·75
a. Surch inverted £100 £150
D186 10 m. scarlet .. .. 1·00 1·75
D187 **23** 20 m. on 100 m. blue .. .. .. 3·50 5·50
a. Vert pair, one without surch .. £250
D188 50 m. purple .. .. 4·50 7·50
a. Pair, one without surch .. £300
D183/8 .. .. *Set of* 6 10·00 18·00

(Recess Perkins, Bacon)

1929 (1 Apr)–**39.** *Wmk Mult Script CA. P* 14.

D189	D 7	1 m. red-brown	30	1·00
		a. Perf 13½ × 13 (1939)	80·00	50·00
D190		2 m. orange-yellow	30	1·25
D191		4 m. green	30	1·40
D192		10 m. scarlet	75	1·50
D193		20 m. olive-green	2·50	5·50
D194		50 m. blue	3·00	6·50
D189/94		*Set of* 6	6·50	15·00
D189/94 Perf "Specimen"		*Set of* 6	50·00	

(Litho Survey Dept, Cairo)

1942 (22 Dec). *Redrawn. Top line of Arabic in taller lettering. No wmk. P* 13½.

D230	D 8	1 m. red-brown	50	3·00
D231		2 m. orange-yellow	2·00	3·00
D232		10 m. scarlet	2·00	2·00
D230/2		*Set of* 3	4·00	7·25

(Recess Bradbury, Wilkinson)

1944. *Wmk Mult Script CA. P* 12.

D244	D 7	1 m. red-brown	10	75
D245		2 m. orange-yellow	10	90
D246		4 m. green	20	1·40
D247		10 m. carmine	50	1·60
D248		20 m. olive-green	7·50	11·00
D244/8		*Set of* 5	7·50	14·00

OFFICIAL STAMP

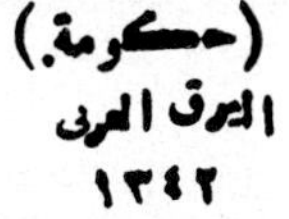

("Arab Government of the East, 1342" = 1924)
(O 1)

1924. *T* **11** *of Saudi Arabia with typographed opt, Type* O **1**.

O117	½ p. scarlet	25·00	£100

By treaty of 22 March 1946 with the United Kingdom, Transjordan was proclaimed an independent kingdom on 25 May 1946.

Later issues are listed under JORDAN in Part 19 (*Middle East*) of this catalogue.

Transvaal
see South Africa

Trinidad and Tobago

TRINIDAD

CROWN COLONY

The first post office was established at Port of Spain in 1800 to deal with overseas mail. Before 1851 there was no post office inland service, although a privately-operated one along the coast did exist, for which rates were officially fixed (see No. 1). During 1851 the colonial authorities established an inland postal system which commenced operation on 14 August. Responsibility for the overseas mails passed to the local post authorities in 1858.

No. CC1 is recorded in the G.P.O. Record Book on 21 March 1852 and most examples are found used with the early Britannia 1d. stamps to indicate prepayment of the additional overseas rate in cash or, later, to show that letters were fully franked with adhesive stamps. This is the normal usage of the handstamp and commands little, if any premium over the cover price quoted below for the stamps involved. The use of the handstamp without an adhesive is rare.

PORT OF SPAIN

CROWNED-CIRCLE HANDSTAMPS

CC 1

CC1 CC **1** TRINIDAD (R.) (*without additional adhesive stamp*) (21.3.52) *Price on cover* £500

PRICES FOR STAMPS ON COVER

No. 1	*from* × 2
Nos. 2/12	*from* × 5
No. 13	—
Nos. 14/20	*from* × 2
Nos. 25/30	—
Nos. 31/44	*from* × 3
No. 45	—
Nos. 46/59	*from* × 3
Nos. 60/3	*from* × 4
Nos. 64/8	*from* × 3
Nos. 69/85	*from* × 12
No. 87	—
Nos. 88/90	*from* × 15
Nos. 91/7	*from* × 10
Nos. 98/102	*from* × 5
No. 103	—
Nos. 104/5	*from* × 15
Nos. 106/12	*from* × 8
No. 113	—
Nos. 114/21	*from* × 4
Nos. 122/4	—
No. 125	*from* × 10
Nos. 126/30	*from* × 5
No. 131	—
Nos. 132/43	*from* × 3
Nos. 144/5	—
Nos. 146/8	*from* × 3
Nos. D1/17	*from* × 12

1

2 Britannia

1847 (24 Apr). *Litho. Imperf.*

1	**1**	(5 c.) blue	£13000	£7000

The "LADY McLEOD" stamps were issued in April 1847, by David Bryce, owner of the S.S. *Lady McLeod*, and sold at five cents each for the prepayment of the carriage of letters by his vessel between Port of Spain and San Fernando.

The price quoted for used examples of No. 1 is for pen-cancelled. Stamps cancelled by having a corner skimmed-off are worth less.

(Recess P.B.)

1851 (14 Aug)–**1856.** *No value expressed. Imperf. Blued paper.*

2	**2**	(1d.) purple-brown (1851)	4·75	55·00
3		(1d.) blue *to* deep blue (1851)	4·25	35·00
4		(1d.) deep blue (1853)*	£150	70·00
5		(1d.) grey (1851)	26·00	45·00
6		(1d.) brownish grey (1853)	24·00	55·00
7		(1d.) brownish red (1853)	£300	45·00
8		(1d.) brick-red (1856)	£120	50·00

*No. 4 shows the paper deeply and evenly blued, especially on the back. It has more the appearance of having been printed on blue paper rather than on white paper that has become blued.

1854–57. *Imperf. White paper.*

9	**2**	(1d.) deep purple (1854)	10·00	55·00
10		(1d.) dark grey (1854)	20·00	65·00
11		(1d.) blue (? date)		
12		(1d.) rose-red (1857)	£1500	50·00

PRICES. Prices quoted for the unused of most of the above issues and Nos. 25 and 29 are for "remainders" with original gum, found in London. Old colours that have been out to Trinidad are of much greater value.

3 Britannia 4

The following provisional issues were lithographed in the Colony (from die engraved by Charles Petit), and brought into use to meet shortages of the Perkins Bacon stamps during the following periods:

(1) Sept 1852–May 1853; (2) March 1855–June 1855; (3) Dec 1856–Jan 1857; (4) Oct 1858–Jan 1859; (5) March 1860–June 1860.

1852–60. *No value expressed. Imperf.*

A. *First Issue* (Sept 1852). *Fine impression; lines of background clear and distinct.* (i) *Yellowish paper*

13	**3**	(1d.) blue	£8500	£2000

(ii) *Bluish cartridge paper* (Feb 1853)

14	**3**	(1d.) blue	—	£2250

B. *Second issue* (March 1855). *Thinner paper. Impression less distinct than before*

15	**3**	(1d.) pale blue *to* greenish blue	—	£900

C. *Third issue* (December 1856). *Background often of solid colour, but with clear lines in places*

16	**3**	(1d.) bright blue *to* deep blue	£4500	£1200

D. *Fourth issue* (October 1858). *Impression less distinct, and rarely showing more than traces of background lines*

17	**3**	(1d.) very deep greenish blue	—	£650
18		(1d.) slate-blue	£4000	£650

E. *Fifth issue* (March 1860). *Impression shows no (or hardly any) background lines*

19	**3**	(1d.) grey *to* bluish grey	£4000	£450
20		(1d.) red (*shades*)	11·00	£450

In the worn impression of the fourth and fifth issues, the impression varies according to the position on the stone. Generally speaking, stamps of the fifth issue have a flatter appearance and cancellations are often less well defined. The paper of both these issues is thin or very thin. In all issues except 1853 (Feb) the gum tends to give the paper a toned appearance.

Stamps in the slate-blue shade (No. 18) also occur in the fifth issue, but are not readily distinguishable.

(Recess P.B.)

1859 (9 May). *Imperf.*

25	**4**	4d. grey-lilac	55·00	£275
28		6d. deep-green	—	£425
29		1s. indigo	60·00	£275
30		1s. purple-slate		

No. 30 may be of unissued status.

1859 (Sept). (*a*) *Pin-perf* 12½.

31	**2**	(1d.) rose-red	£500	42·00
32		(1d.) carmine-lake	£500	42·00
33	**4**	4d. dull lilac	—	£700
34		4d. dull purple	—	£700
35		6d. yellow-green	£1800	£150
36		6d. deep green	£1800	£130
37		1s. purple-slate	£2750	£850

(*b*) *Pin-perf* 13½–14

38	**2**	(1d.) rose-red	65·00	19·00
39		(1d.) carmine-lake	£110	17·00
40	**4**	4d. dull lilac	£650	65·00
40*a*		4d. brownish purple	60·00	85·00
41		4d. dull purple	£200	85·00
42		6d. yellow-green	£300	60·00
43		6d. deep green	£250	55·00
43*a*		6d. bright yellow-green	60·00	70·00
		b. Imperf between (vert pair)	£3500	
44		1s. purple-slate	—	£550

(*c*) *Compound pin-perf* 13½–14 × 12½

45	**2**	(1d.) carmine-lake		
45*a*	**4**	4d. dull purple	†	—

PRICES. The Pin-perf stamps are very scarce with perforations on all sides and the prices quoted above are for good average specimens.

The note after No. 12 also applies to Nos. 38, 40*a*, 43*a*, 46, 47 and 50.

1860 (Aug). *Clean-cut perf* 14–16½.

46	**2**	(1d.) rose-red	70·00	38·00
		a. Imperf vert (horiz pair)	£1100	
47	**4**	4d. brownish lilac	85·00	65·00
48		4d. lilac	—	£225
49		6d. bright yellow-green	£200	75·00
50		6d. deep green	£150	£120

1861 (June). *Rough perf* 14–16½.

52	**2**	(1d.) rose-red	65·00	20·00
53		(1d.) rose	65·00	17·00
54	**4**	4d. brownish lilac	£160	42·00
55		4d. lilac	£350	42·00
		a. Imperf		
56		6d. yellow-green	£150	55·00
57		6d. deep green	£350	55·00
58		1s. indigo	£600	£130
59		1s. deep bluish purple	£750	£225

(Recess D.L.R.)

1862–63. *Thick paper.* (*a*) *P* 11½, 12.

60	**2**	(1d.) crimson-lake	70·00	10·00
61	**4**	4d. deep purple	70·00	45·00
62		6d. deep green	£500	50·00
63		1s. bluish slate	£650	65·00

(*b*) *P* 11½, 12, *compound with* 11

63*a*	**2**	(1d.) crimson-lake	—	£350
63*b*	**4**	6d. deep green	—	£5000

(*c*) *P* 13 (1863)

64	**2**	(1d.) lake	25·00	15·00
65	**4**	6d. emerald-green	£275	45·00
67		1s. bright mauve	£2750	£225

(*d*) *P* 12½ (1863)

68	**2**	(1d.) lake	22·00	16·00

1863–75. *Wmk Crown CC. P* 12½.

69	**2**	(1d.) lake	26·00	3·25
		a. Wmk sideways	75·00	7·00
70		(1d.) rose	26·00	1·40
		a. Imperf (pair)		
71		(1d.) scarlet	26·00	90
72		(1d.) carmine	26·00	1·50
73	**4**	4d. bright violet	70·00	8·00
74		4d. pale mauve	£120	9·00
75		4d. dull lilac	65·00	9·50
77		6d. emerald-green	50·00	10·00
78		6d. deep green	£200	7·50
80		6d. yellow-green	38·00	3·00
81		6d. apple-green	38·00	4·50
82		6d. blue-green	65·00	4·75
83		1s. bright deep mauve	90·00	6·00
84		1s. lilac-rose	75·00	5·00
85		1s. mauve (aniline)	65·00	4·25

The 1s. in a purple-slate shade is a colour changeling.

5

(Typo D.L.R.)

1869. *Wmk Crown CC. P* 12½.

87	**5**	5s. rose-lake	£110	60·00

1872. *Colours changed. Wmk Crown CC. P 12½.*
88 4 4d. grey .. .. 75·00 3·25
89 4d. bluish grey .. .. 75·00 4·00
90 1s. chrome-yellow .. .. .. 90·00 1·00

1876. *Wmk Crown CC. (a) P 14.*
91 2 (1d.) lake .. .. 9·00 50
a. Bisected (½d.) (on cover) .. .. † £450
92 (1d.) rose-carmine .. .. .. 9·00 1·00
93 (1d.) scarlet .. .. 25·00 75
94 4 4d. bluish grey .. .. 65·00 70
95 6d. bright yellow-green .. .. .. 55·00 1·25
96 6d. deep yellow-green .. .. .. 60·00 1·00
97 1s. chrome-yellow .. .. .. 65·00 2·50
(b) P 14 × 12½
97*a* 4 6d. yellow-green .. .. .. — £4500

(6) (7)

1879–82. *Surch with T* **6** *or* **7**. *P 14.*
(a) Wmk Crown CC (June 1879)
98 2 ½d. lilac .. .. 7·00 4·75
99 ½d. mauve .. .. 7·00 4·75
a. Wmk sideways .. .. .. 45·00 45·00
(b) Wmk Crown CA (1882)
100 2 ½d. lilac .. .. £200 60·00
101 1d. rosy carmine .. .. .. 15·00 30
a. Bisected (½d.) (on cover) .. .. † £375

1882. *Wmk Crown CA. P 14.*
102 4 4d. bluish grey .. .. .. £110 5·00

1d 1d 1d

(8) Various styles

1882 (9 May). *Surch by hand in various styles as T* **8** *in red or black ink and the original value obliterated by a thick or thin bar or bars, of the same colour.*
103 1d. on 6d. (No. 95) (Bk.) .. .. .. — £1500
104 1d. on 6d. (No. 95) (R.) .. .. .. 3·00 3·25
105 1d. on 6d. (No. 96) (R.) .. .. .. 3·25 3·25
a. Bisected (½d.) (on cover) .. .. † £300

10 11 Britannia 12 Britannia

(Typo D.L.R.)

1883–94. *P 14. (a) Wmk Crown CA.*
106 10 ½d. dull green 30 15
107 1d. carmine .. .. 1·75 10
a. Bisected (½d.) (on cover) .. .. † £425
108 2½d. bright blue .. .. .. 4·00 15
110 4d. grey .. .. 2·25 20
111 6d. olive-black (1884) .. .. .. 2·00 1·50
112 1s. orange-brown (1884) .. .. 2·00 1·50
(b) Wmk Crown CC
113 5 5s. maroon (1894) .. .. .. 20·00 40·00
106/13 .. .. *Set of 7* 29·00 40·00
106/12 Optd "Specimen" .. .. *Set of 6* £400

Two types of 1d. value:

ONE PENNY **ONE PENNY**
(I) (round "o") (II) (oval "o")

(Typo D.L.R.)

1896 (17 Aug)–**1900**. *P 14. (a) Wmk Crown CA.*
114 11 ½d. dull purple and green 50 15
115 1d. dull purple and rose (I) .. .. 2·50 10
116 1d. dull purple and rose (II) (1900) .. 75·00 2·00
117 2½d. dull purple and blue .. .. 2·00 15
118 4d. dull purple and orange .. .. 3·75 6·50
119 5d. dull purple and mauve .. .. 5·00 6·00
120 6d. dull purple and black .. .. 3·50 4·50
121 1s. green and brown .. .. .. 4·50 5·00
(b) Wmk CA over Crown. Ordinary paper
122 12 5s. green and brown .. .. .. 28·00 55·00
123 10s. green and ultramarine £100 £120
124 £1 green and carmine .. .. 85·00 £110
a. Chalk-surfaced paper .. ..
114/24 .. .. *Set of 10* £200 £275
114/24 Optd "Specimen" .. .. *Set of 10* £150

No. 119, surcharged "3d." was prepared for use but not issued (*Price £2750 unused*). It also exists overprinted "Specimen" (*Price £75*).

Collectors are warned against apparently postally used copies of this issue which bear "REGISTRAR-GENERAL" obliterations and are of very little value.

13 Landing of Columbus

(Recess D.L.R.)

1898. *Discovery of Trinidad Commemoration. Wmk Crown CC. P 14.*
125 13 2d. brown and dull violet .. .. 1·50 50
125 Optd "Specimen" .. .. 50·00

1901–06. *Colours changed. Wmk Crown CA or CA over Crown (5s.). Ordinary paper. P 14.*
126 11 ½d. grey-green (1902) 35 55
127 1d. black/*red* (II) 80 10
a. Value omitted £10000
128 2½d. purple and blue/*blue* (1902) .. 4·50 25
129 4d. green and blue/*buff* (1902) .. 1·50 5·00
a. Chalk-surfaced paper .. .. 1·75 5·00
130 1s. black and blue/*yellow* (1903) .. 13·00 4·00
131 12 5s. lilac and mauve .. .. .. 25·00 42·00
a. Deep purple and mauve (1906) .. 38·00 60·00
ab. Chalk-surfaced paper .. .. 45·00 65·00
126/31 .. .. *Set of* 6 40·00 48·00
126/31 Optd "Specimen" .. .. *Set of* 6 £100

A pane of sixty of No. 127a was found in a post office in Trinidad but not more than nine copies are believed to have been sold, and the rest withdrawn.

1904–09. *Wmk Mult Crown CA. Ordinary paper* (½d., 1d., 2½d. (No. 137)) *or chalk-surfaced paper (others). P 14.*
132 11 ½d. grey-green .. .. .. 1·00 30
a. Chalk-surfaced paper .. .. 1·00 40
133 ½d. blue-green (1906) .. .. 3·25 1·00
134 1d. black/*red* (II) .. .. .. 1·10 10
a. Chalk-surfaced paper .. .. 1·10 10
135 1d. rose-red (1907) 80 10
136 2½d. purple and blue/*blue* .. .. 10·00 90
137 2½d. blue (1906) .. .. .. 1·50 15
138 4d. grey and red/*yellow* (1906) .. 1·00 4·75
a. Black and red/yellow .. .. 8·00 16·00
139 6d. dull purple and black (1905) .. 8·50 14·00
140 6d. dull and bright purple (1906) .. 3·50 5·50
141 1s. black and blue/*yellow* .. .. 12·00 7·50
142 1s. purple and blue/*golden yellow* .. 7·50 9·50
143 1s. black/*green* (1906) .. .. 1·00 1·25
144 12 5s. deep purple and mauve (1907) .. 35·00 60·00
145 £1 green and carmine (1907) .. 90·00 £110
132/45 .. .. *Set of 14* £150 £180
135, 137/8, 140, 142/3 Optd "Specimen" .. *Set of 6* £100

No. 135 is from a new die, the letters of "ONE PENNY" being short and thick, while the point of Britannia's spear breaks the uppermost horizontal line of shading in the background.

14 15 16

(Typo D.L.R.)

1909. *Wmk Mult Crown CA. P 14.*
146 14 ½d. green 80 10
147 15 1d. rose-red 35 10
148 16 2½d. blue .. .. 4·50 1·25
146/8 .. .. *Set of 3* 5·00 1·25
146/8 Optd "Specimen" .. .. *Set of 3* 50·00

TOBAGO

Although early postal markings are recorded from 1772 onwards it was not until 1841 that the British G.P.O. established a branch office at Scarborough, the island capital, to handle the overseas mail.

The stamps of Great Britain were in use from May 1858 to the end of March 1860 when the control of the postal service passed to the local authorities.

From 1 April 1860 Nos. CC1/2 were again used on overseas mail, pending the introduction of Tobago stamps in 1879.

SCARBOROUGH

CROWNED-CIRCLE HANDSTAMPS

CC 1 CC 2

CC1 CC 1 TOBAGO (R.) (31.10.1851) *Price on cover* £600
CC2 CC 2 TOBAGO (R.) (1875) *Price on cover* £850

Stamps of GREAT BRITAIN *cancelled* "A 14" *as Type* Z 1 *of Jamaica.*

1858 *to* **1860**.
Z 1 1d. rose-red (1857), *perf* 14 .. .. £650
Z 2 4d. rose (1857) £225
Z 3 6d. lilac (1856) £200
Z 4 1s. green (1856) £700

PRICES FOR STAMPS ON COVER	
Nos. 1/4	*from* × 25
Nos. 5/7	—
Nos. 8/12	*from* × 10
Nos. 13/19	*from* × 6
Nos. 20/4	*from* × 40
Nos. 26/33	*from* × 25

CANCELLATIONS. Beware of early stamps of Tobago with fiscal endorsements removed and forged wide "A 14" postmarks added.

2½ PENCE

1 2 (3)

(T 1 and 2. Typo D.L.R.)

1879 (1 Aug). *Fiscal stamps issued provisionally pending the arrival of stamps inscr "POSTAGE". Wmk Crown CC. P 14.*
1 1 1d. rose .. .. 65·00 50·00
2 3d. blue .. .. 55·00 35·00
3 6d. orange .. .. 24·00 38·00
4 1s. green .. .. £350 60·00
a. Bisected (6d.) (on cover) .. ..
5 5s. slate £550 £500
6 £1 mauve £5000

The stamps were introduced for fiscal purposes on 1 July 1879.

Stamps of T **1**, watermark Crown CA, are fiscals which were never admitted to postal use.

1880 (Nov). *No. 3 bisected vertically and surch with pen and ink.*
7 1 1d. on half of 6d. orange £4500 £600

1880 (20 Dec). *Wmk Crown CC. P 14.*
8 2 ½d. purple-brown .. .. .. 18·00 28·00
9 1d. Venetian red .. .. .. 60·00 32·00
a. Bisected (½d.) (on cover) .. .. † £1400
10 4d. yellow-green .. .. .. £180 23·00
a. Bisected (2d.) (on cover) .. .. † £1400
b. Malformed "CE" in "PENCE" .. £1100 £400
11 6d. stone .. .. £250 90·00
12 1s. yellow-ochre .. .. .. 45·00 42·00

For illustration of Nos. 10b, 18a, 22b, 30a, 31a and 33b see above No. 4 of Dominica.

1883 (Apr). *No. 11 surch with T* **3**.
13 2 2½d. on 6d. stone .. .. .. 22·00 20·00
a. Surch double £2500 £1200
b. Large "2" with long tail £100 £110

"SLASH" FLAW. Stamps as Type **2** were produced from Key and Duty plates. On the Key plate used for consignments between 2 October 1892 and 16 December 1896, damage in the form of a large cut or "slash" shows after the "E" of "POSTAGE" on R.1/4.

After 1896 an attempt was made to repair the "slash". This resulted in its disappearance, but left an incomplete edge to the circular frame at right.

1882–84. *Wmk Crown CA. P 14.*
14 2 ½d. purple-brown (1882) .. .. 1·00 11·00
15 1d. Venetian red (1882) .. .. 1·00 1·25
a. Bisected diag (½d.) (on cover) ..
16 2½d. dull blue (1883) .. .. .. 7·00 80
a. Bright blue .. .. .. 1·75 75
b. Ultramarine .. .. .. 1·75 75
c. "Slash" flaw .. .. .. 14·00 22·00
ca. "Slash" flaw repaired .. .. 60·00
18 4d. yellow-green (1882) .. .. £170 90·00
a. Malformed "CE" in "PENCE" .. £950 £400
19 6d. stone (1884) £550 £475

1885–96. *Colours changed and new value. Wmk Crown CA. P 14.*
20 2 ½d. dull green (1886) 20 35
a. "Slash" flaw .. .. .. 9·00 20·00
ab. "Slash" flaw repaired .. .. 18·00
21 1d. carmine (1889) 45 20
a. "Slash" flaw .. .. .. 7·00 10·00
ab. "Slash" flaw repaired .. .. 25·00

22 2 4d. grey (1885) .. 50 55
a. Imperf (pair) .. £1700
b. Malformed "CE" in "PENCE" .. 50·00 80·00
c. "Slash" flaw .. 50·00 85·00
ca. "Slash" flaw repaired .. 75·00
23 6d. orange-brown (1886) .. 60 2·50
a. "Slash" flaw .. 50·00 85·00
ab. "Slash" flaw repaired .. 75·00
24 1s. olive-yellow (1894) .. 70 6·50
a. *Pale olive-yellow* .. 6·50
b. "Slash" flaw .. 60·00 £120
ba. "Slash" flaw repaired .. 85·00
24*c* 1s. orange-brown (1896) .. 3·25
ca. "Slash" flaw .. 75·00
20, 21 and 23 Optd "Specimen" .. *Set of* 3 £170

No. 24*c* was printed in the colour of the 6d. by mistake.

½ PENNY (4) 2½ PENCE (5) ½d POSTAGE (6)

1886–89. *Nos. 16, 19 and 23 surch as T* **4**.
26 ½d. on 2½d. dull blue (4.86) .. 2·25 6·00
a. Figure further from word .. 14·00 32·00
b. Surch double .. £1300 £1100
c. Surch omitted. Vert pair with No. 26 .. £8000
d. Ditto with No. 26a .. £15000
27 ½d. on 6d. stone (1.86) .. 1·50 13·00
a. Figure further from word .. 35·00 85·00
b. Surch inverted .. £1300
c. Surch double .. £1500
28 ½d. on 6d. orange-brown (8.87) .. 60·00 80·00
a. Figure further from word .. £225 £250
b. Surch double .. — £1000
29 1d. on 2½d. dull blue (7.89) .. 23·00 14·00
a. Figure further from word .. 70·00 75·00

The surcharge is in a setting of 12 (two rows of 6) repeated five times in the pane. Nos. 7, 9 and 10 in the setting have a raised "P" in "PENNY", and No. 10 also shows the wider spacing between figure and word.

1891–92. *No. 22 surch with T* **4** *or* **5**.
30 ½d. on 4d. grey (3.92) .. 8·50 26·00
a. Malformed "CE" in "PENCE" .. £275 £400
b. Surch double .. £1800
31 2½d. on 4d. grey (8.91) .. 3·00 6·50
a. Malformed "CE" in "PENCE" .. £200 £275
b. Surch double .. £1800 £1800

1896. *Fiscal stamp* (*T* **1**, *value in second colour, wmk Crown CA, P* 14), *surch with T* **6**.
33 ½d. on 4d. lilac and carmine .. 22·00 23·00
a. Space between "½" and "d" .. 50·00 55·00
b. Malformed "CE" in "PENCE" .. £375 £400

From 1896 until 1913 Trinidad stamps were used in Tobago.

TRINIDAD AND TOBAGO

PRICES FOR STAMPS ON COVER	
Nos. 149/55	*from* × 3
Nos. 156/7	—
Nos. 174/89	*from* × 10
Nos. 206/56	*from* × 2
Nos. D18/25	*from* × 12

17

18

(Typo D.L.R.)

1913–23. *Wmk Mult Crown CA. Ordinary paper* (½d. *to* 4d. *and* 1s.) *or chalk-surfaced paper* (*others*). *P* 14.
149 17 ½d. green .. 75 10
a. Yellow-green (1915) .. 1·25 15
b. Blue-green (*thick paper*) (1917) .. 2·00 40
c. Blue-green/bluish (3.18) .. 9·50 9·50
150 1d. bright red .. 40 15
a. Red (*thick paper*) (1916) .. 40 10
b. Pink (1918) .. 6·50 80
c. Carmine-red (5.18) .. 45 10
151 2½d. ultramarine .. 3·25 30
a. Bright blue (*thick paper*) (1916) .. 1·50 30
b. Bright blue (*thin paper*) (1918) .. 3·50 40
152 4d. black and red/*yellow* ..
a. Chalk-surfaced paper .. 50 3·00
b. White back (12.13) (Optd S. £16) .. 1·75 6·50
c. On lemon (1917) .. 10·00
d. On pale yellow (1923) (Optd S. £20) 2·75 7·00
153 6d. dull and reddish purple .. 3·25 3·25
a. Dull and deep purple (1918) .. 1·75 3·75
b. Dull purple and mauve (2.18) .. 5·50 6·00
154 1s. black/*green* .. 75 2·50
a. White back (Optd S. £16) .. 65 3·25
b. On blue-green, olive back .. 2·00 4·50
c. On emerald back (Optd S. £20) .. 1·00 2·50
155 18 5s. dull purple and mauve (1914) .. 28·00 60·00
a. Deep purple and mauve (1918) .. 28·00 60·00
b. Lilac and violet .. 55·00 75·00
c. Dull purple and violet .. 60·00 80·00
d. Brown-purple and violet .. 26·00 60·00
156 £1 grey-green and carmine (1914) .. 90·00 £110
a. Deep yellow-green and carmine (1918) .. 90·00 £110
149/56 .. *Set of* 8 £110 £140
149/56 Optd "Specimen" .. *Set of* 8 £140

No. 156*a* is from a plate showing background lines very worn.

18*a*

1914 (18 Sept). *Red Cross Label authorised for use as ½d. stamp. Typo. P* 11–12.
157 18*a* (½d.) Red .. 9·00 £190

The above was authorised for internal use on one day only, to raise funds for the Red Cross. The used price is for stamp on cover.

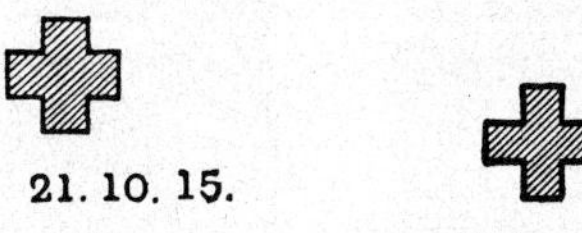

(19) (19*a*)

1915 (21 Oct). *Optd with T* **19**. *Cross in red with outline and date in black.*
174 17 1d. red .. 40 40
a. Cross 2 mm to right .. 12·00 12·00
b. "1" of "15" forked foot .. 5·00 7·50
c. Broken "0" in "10" .. 9·00 9·50

The varieties occur in the following positions on the *pane* of 60: a. No. 11. b. No. 42. c. No. 45. Variety a. is only found on the right-hand pane.

1916 (19 Oct). *Optd with T* **19***a*. *Cross in red with outline and date in black.*
175 17 1d. scarlet .. 10 30
a. No stop after "16" .. 6·50 14·00
b. "19.10.16" omitted ..

No. 175a appears on stamp No. 36 on the right-hand pane only.

FORGERIES. Beware of forgeries of the "War Tax" errors listed below. There are also other unlisted errors which are purely fakes.

WAR TAX (19*b*) WAR TAX (20) WAR TAX (21) WAR TAX (22)

1917 (2 Apr). *Optd with T* **19***b*.
176 17 1d. red .. 15 70
a. Opt inverted .. £140
b. Scarlet .. 15 80

1917 (May). *Optd with T* **20**.
177 17 ½d. green .. 10 10
a. Pair, one without opt .. £170
178 1d. red .. 15 30
a. Pair, one without opt .. £170
b. Scarlet .. 45 15
ba. Opt double .. 80·00

The varieties without overprint were caused by the type being shifted over towards the left so that one stamp in the lowest row of each pane escaped.

1917 (21 June). *Optd with T* **21**.
179 17 ½d. yellow-green .. 75 2·00
a. Pale green .. 10 1·50
b. Deep green .. 60 2·00
180 1d. red .. 10 10
a. Pair, one without opt ..

No. 180a was caused by a shifting of the type to the left-hand side, but only a few stamps on the right-hand vertical row escaped the overprint and such pairs are very rare.

1917 (21 July–Sept). *Optd with T* **22**.
181 17 ½d. yellow-green .. 2·25 3·50
a. Deep green .. 10 70
182 1d. red (Sept) .. 30 15

WAR TAX (23) WAR TAX (24) WAR TAX (25)

1917 (1 Sept). *Optd with T* **23** (*closer spacing between lines of opt*).
183 17 ½d. deep green .. 10 1·00
a. Pale yellow-green ..
184 1d. red .. 9·50 15·00

1917 (31 Oct). *Optd with T* **24**.
185 17 1d. scarlet .. 10 60
a. Opt inverted .. 70·00

1918 (7 Jan). *Optd with T* **25**.
186 17 1d. scarlet .. 10 10
a. Opt double .. £130
b. Opt inverted .. 80·00

War Tax (26) War Tax (26a)

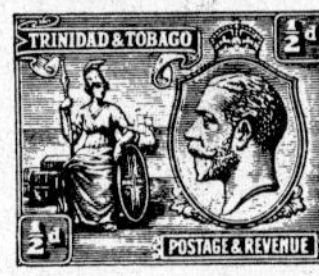

27

1918 (13 Feb–May). *Optd with T* **26**.
187 17 ½d. bluish green .. 10 40
a. Pair, one without opt .. £400
b. "TAX" omitted ..
188 1d. scarlet .. 10 40
a. Opt double .. 80·00
b. Rose-red (1.5.18) .. 10 30

No. 187b occurs on R. 10/1 and was caused by a paper fold.

1918 (14 Sept). *New printing as T* **26**, *but 19 stamps on each sheet have the letters of the word "Tax" wider spaced, the "x" being to the right of "r" of "War" as T* **26***a*. *Thick bluish paper.*
189 17 1d. scarlet ("Tax" spaced) .. 35 2·00
a. Opt double .. £140

1921–22. *Wmk Mult Script CA. Chalk-surfaced paper* (6d. *to* £1). *P* 14.
206 17 ½d. green .. 35 60
207 1d. scarlet .. 20 20
208 1d. brown (17.2.22) .. 20 30
209 2d. grey (17.2.22) .. 1·00 1·25
210 2½d. bright blue .. 70 5·50
211 3d. bright blue (17.2.22) .. 1·75 1·75
212 6d. dull and bright purple .. 1·50 9·00
213 18 5s. dull purple and purple (1921) .. 30·00 80·00
214 5s. deep purple and purple (1922) .. 30·00 80·00
215 £1 green and carmine .. 75·00 £170
206/15 .. *Set of* 9 £100 £250
206/15 Optd "Specimen" .. *Set of* 9 £200

(Typo D.L.R.)

1922–28. *P* 14. *Chalk-surfaced paper* (4d. *to* £1).

(*a*) *Wmk Mult Crown CA*
216 27 4d. black and red/*pale yellow* .. 55 90
217 1s. black/*emerald* .. 1·50 4·25

(*b*) *Wmk Mult Script CA*
218 27 ½d. green .. 10 10
219 1d. brown .. 15 10
220 1½d. bright rose .. 50 10
a. Scarlet .. 20 10
222 2d. grey .. 20 30
223 3d. blue .. 40 30
224 4d. black and red/*pale yellow* (1928) .. 2·50 2·00
225 6d. dull purple and bright magenta .. 2·00 12·00
226 6d. green and red/*emerald* (1924) .. 80 30
227 1s. black/*emerald* .. 90 90
228 5s. dull purple and mauve .. 12·00 18·00
229 £1 green and bright rose .. 85·00 £170
216/29 .. *Set of* 13 95·00 £190
216/29 Optd "Specimen" .. *Set of* 13 £225

(New Currency. 100 cents = 1 dollar)

28 First Boca

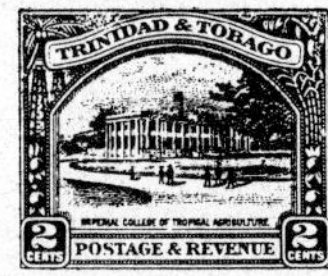

29 Imperial College of Tropical Agriculture

(Recess B.W.)

1935 (1 Feb)–**37.** *T* **28/9** *and similar horiz designs. Wmk Mult Script CA* (*sideways*). *P* 12.
230 1 c. blue and green .. 30 10
a. Perf 13 × 12½ (1936) .. 10 10
231 2 c. ultramarine and yellow-brown .. 30 10
a. Perf 13 × 12½ (1936) .. 35 10
232 3 c. black and scarlet .. 20 10
a. Perf 13 × 12½ (1936) .. 50 10
233 6 c. sepia and blue .. 1·00 30
a. Perf 13 × 12½ (1937) .. 1·25 80
234 8 c. sage-green and vermilion .. 60 80
235 12 c. black and violet .. 1·00 45
a. Perf 13 × 12½ (1937) .. 1·25 1·25
236 24 c. black and olive-green .. 35 40
a. Perf 13 × 12½ (1937) .. 5·00 2·75
237 48 c. deep green .. 4·00 11·00
238 72 c. myrtle-green and carmine .. 16·00 18·00
230/8 .. *Set of* 9 21·00 28·00
230/8 Perf "Specimen" .. *Set of* 9 90·00

Designs:—3 c. Mt Irvine Bay, Tobago; 6 c. Discovery of Lake Asphalt; 8 c. Queen's Park, Savannah; 12 c. Town Hall, San Fernando; 24 c. Government House; 48 c. Memorial Park; 72 c. Blue Basin.

1935 (6 May). *Silver Jubilee. As Nos. 114/17 of Jamaica. P* 11 × 12.
239 2 c. ultramarine and grey-black .. 30 20
a. Extra flagstaff .. 32·00
b. Short extra flagstaff .. 27·00
c. Lightning conductor .. 24·00
d. Flagstaff on right-hand turret .. 32·00
240 3 c. deep blue and scarlet .. 30 30
a. Extra flagstaff .. 50·00
c. Lightning conductor .. 35·00

241	6 c. brown and deep blue	80	1·75
	a. Extra flagstaff	85·00	
	b. Short extra flagstaff	70·00	
	c. Lightning conductor	55·00	
242	24 c. slate and purple	3·50	3·75
	a. Extra flagstaff	£110	
	c. Lightning conductor	70·00	
	d. Flagstaff on right-hand turret	95·00	
239/42	*Set of* 4	4·50	5·50
239/42 Perf "Specimen"	*Set of* 4	75·00	

For illustrations of plate varieties see Omnibus section following Zimbabwe.

1937 (12 May). *Coronation. As Nos.* 118/20 *of Jamaica.*

243	1 c. green	15	10
244	2 c. yellow-brown	35	10
245	8 c. orange	85	20
243/5	*Set of* 3	1·25	35
243/5 Perf "Specimen"	*Set of* 3	55·00	

37 First Boca

47 King George VI

1938 (2 May)–**44**. *T* **37** *and similar horiz designs, and T* **47**. *Wmk Mult Script CA* (*sideways on* 1 *c. to* 60 *c.*)

(*a*) *P* 11½ × 11

246	1 c. blue and green	15	10
247	2 c. blue and yellow-brown	15	10
248	3 c. black and scarlet	10·00	50
248*a*	3 c. green and purple-brown (1941)	15	10
249	4 c. chocolate	23·00	1·00
249*a*	4 c. scarlet (1941)	40	40
249*b*	5 c. magenta (1.5.41)	15	10
250	6 c. sepia and blue	20	15
251	8 c. sage-green and vermilion	50	15
252	12 c. black and purple	8·00	95
	a. Black and slate-purple (1944)	2·00	10
253	24 c. black and olive-green	35	10
254	60 c. myrtle-green and carmine	7·00	40

(*b*) *T* **47**. *P* 12

255	$1.20, blue-green (1.40)	3·75	25
256	$4.80, rose-carmine (1.40)	18·00	12·00
246/56	*Set of* 14	60·00	13·50
246/56 *exc* 249*b* Perf "Specimen"	*Set of* 13	£190	

Designs:—2 c. Imperial College of Tropical Agriculture; 3 c. Mt Irvine Bay, Tobago; 4 c. Memorial Park; 5 c. G.P.O. and Treasury; 6 c. Discovery of Lake Asphalt; 8 c. Queen's Park, Savannah; 12 c. Town Hall, San Fernando; 24 c. Government House; 60 c. Blue Basin.

1946 (1 Oct). *Victory. As Nos.* 141/2 *of Jamaica.*

257	3 c. chocolate	10	10
258	6 c. blue	10	15
257/8 Perf "Specimen"	*Set of* 2	45·00	

1948 (22 Nov). *Royal Silver Wedding. As Nos.* 143/4 *of Jamaica, but* $4.80 *in recess.*

259	3 c. red-brown	10	10
260	$4.80, carmine	14·00	13·00

1949 (10 Oct). 75*th Anniv of U.P.U. As Nos.* 145/8 *of Jamaica.*

261	5 c. bright reddish purple	30	10
262	6 c. deep blue	30	20
263	12 c. violet	30	30
264	24 c. olive	30	20
261/4	*Set of* 4	1·10	70

1951 (16 Feb). *University College of B.W.I. As Nos.* 149/50 *of Jamaica.*

265	3 c. green and red-brown	15	10
266	12 c. black and reddish violet	20	10

48 First Boca

49 Mt Irvine Bay, Tobago

(Recess B.W.)

1953 (20 Apr)–**59**. *Designs previously used for King George VI issue, but with portrait of Queen Elizabeth II as in T* **48** (1 *c.*, 2 *c.*, 12 *c.*) *or* **49** (*other values*). *Wmk Mult Script CA. P* 12 (*dollar values*) *or* 11½×11 (*others*).

267	1 c. blue and green	15	10
	a. Blue and bluish green (10.6.59)	1·25	1·25
268	2 c. indigo and orange-brown	15	10
269	3 c. deep emerald and purple-brown	15	10
270	4 c. scarlet	20	10
271	5 c. magenta	30	10
272	6 c. brown and greenish blue	30	10
273	8 c. deep yellow-green and orange-red	60	10
274	12 c. black and purple	30	10
275	24 c. black and yellow-olive	40	10
	a. Black and olive (16.11.55)	50	10
	b. Black and greenish olive (12.12.56)	1·00	30
276	60 c. blackish green and carmine	8·00	40
277	$1.20, bluish green	90	75
	a. Perf 11½ (19.1.55)	1·00	15
278	$4.80, cerise	5·00	12·00
	a. Perf 11½ (16.12.55)	5·50	7·50
267/78a	*Set of* 12	15·00	7·50

Designs: *Horiz*—2 c. Imperial College of Tropical Agriculture; 4 c. Memorial Park; 5 c. G.P.O. and Treasury; 6 c. Discovery of Lake Asphalt; 8 c. Queen's Park, Savannah; 12 c. Town Hall, San Fernando; 24 c. Government House; 60 c. Blue Basin. *Vert* (18 × 21 *mm*)—$1.20, $4.80, Queen Elizabeth II.

1953 (3 June). *Coronation. As No.* 153 *of Jamaica.*

279	3 c. black and green	10	10

ONE CENT

(**50**)

1956 (20 Dec). *No.* 268 *surch with T* **50**.

280	1 c. on 2 c. indigo and orange-brown	20	40

1958 (22 Apr). *Inauguration of British Caribbean Federation. As Nos.* 175/7 *of Jamaica.*

281	5 c. deep green	20	10
282	6 c. blue	25	15
283	12 c. scarlet	25	10
281/3	*Set of* 3	65	30

PRINTERS. Nos. 284 to 354 were printed in photogravure by Harrison & Sons, *unless otherwise stated.*

51 Cipriani Memorial

52 Queen's Hall

53 Copper-rumped Hummingbird

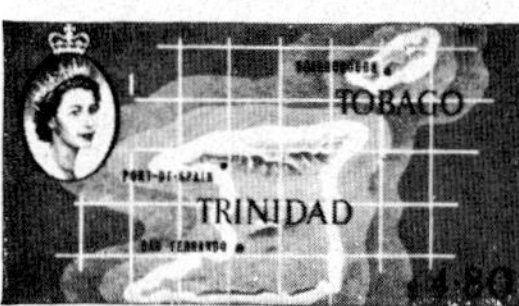

54 Map of Trinidad and Tobago

(Des V. Whiteley (1, 2, 12, 35, 60 c., $4.80), J. Matthews (5 c.), H. Baxter (6, 8, 10, 15 c.), M. Goaman (25 c., 50 c., $1.20))

1960 (24 Sept)–**67**. *Designs as T* **51**/**4**. *W w* **12** (*upright*). *P* 13½×14½ (1 *c.*, 60 *c.*, $1.20, $4.80) *or* 14½×13½ (*others*).

284	1 c. stone and black	10	10
285	2 c. bright blue	10	10
	a. Blue (23.6.64)	60	10
	b. New blue (18.4.67)	60	10
286	5 c. chalky blue	10	10
287	6 c. red-brown	10	10
	a. Pale chestnut (13.4.67)	60	10
288	8 c. yellow-green	10	10
289	10 c. deep lilac	10	10
290	12 c. vermilion	10	10
291	15 c. orange	90	45
291*a*	15 c. orange (15.9.64)	1·00	10
292	25 c. rose-carmine and deep blue	35	10
293	35 c. emerald and black	1·00	10
294	50 c. yellow, grey and blue	35	10
295	60 c. vermilion, yellow-green and indigo	45	20
	a. Perf 14½ (1.10.65)*	£100	40·00
296	$1.20, multicoloured	6·00	1·25
297	$4.80, apple-green and pale blue	4·50	4·50
284/97	*Set of* 15	13·50	6·50

Designs: *Vert as T* **51**—60 c. Anthurium Lilies. *Horiz as T* **52**–5 c. Whitehall; 6 c. Treasury Building; 8 c. Governor-General's House; 10 c. General Hospital, San Fernando; 12 c. Oil refinery; 15 c. (No. 291), Crest; 15 c. (No. 291*a*), Coat of arms; 25 c. Scarlet Ibis; 35 c. Pitch Lake; 50 c. Mohammed Jinnah Mosque.

*This is the earliest date reported to us. It comes from an unannounced printing which was despatched to Trinidad on 3 December 1964.

The 2, 5, 6, 12 and 25 c. exist with PVA gum as well as gum arabic.

See also No. 317.

65 Scouts and Gold Wolf Badge

1961 (4 Apr). *Second Caribbean Scout Jamboree. Design multi-coloured; background colours below. W w* **12**. *P* 13½ × 14½.

298	**65**	8 c. light green	15	10
299		25 c. light blue	15	10

INDEPENDENT

66 "Buccoo Reef" (painting by Carlisle Chang)

71 "Protein Foods"

1962 (31 Aug). *Independence. T* **66** *and similar horiz designs. W w* **12**. *P* 14½.

300	5 c. bluish green	10	10
301	8 c. grey	10	10
302	25 c. reddish violet	10	10
303	35 c. brown, yellow, green and black	60	10
304	60 c. red, black and blue	80	40
300/4	*Set of* 5	1·50	60

Designs:—8 c. Piarco Air Terminal; 25 c. Hilton Hotel, Port-of-Spain; 35 c. Greater Bird of Paradise and map; 60 c. Scarlet Ibis and map.

(Des M. Goaman)

1963 (4 June). *Freedom from Hunger. W w* **12**. *P* 14 × 13½.

305	**71**	5 c. brown-red	10	10
306		8 c. yellow-bistre	10	10
307		25 c. violet-blue	20	10
305/7		*Set of* 3	35	15

72 Jubilee Emblem

1964 (15 Sept). *Golden Jubilee of Trinidad and Tobago Girl Guides' Association. W w* **12**. *P* 14½ × 14.

308	**72**	6 c. yellow, ultramarine and rose-red	10	10
309		25 c. yellow, ultramarine and bright blue	15	10
310		35 c. yellow, ultramarine & emerald-grn	15	10
308/10		*Set of* 3	30	15

73 I.C.Y. Emblem

(Litho State Ptg Wks, Vienna)

1965 (15 Nov). *International Co-operation Year. P* 12.

311	**73**	35 c. red-brown, dp green & ochre-yell	25	10

74 Eleanor Roosevelt, Flag and U.N. Emblem

1965 (10 Dec). *Eleanor Roosevelt Memorial Foundation. W w* **12**. *P* 13½ × 14.

312	**74**	25 c. black, red and ultramarine	10	10

75 Parliament Building

FIFTH YEAR OF INDEPENDENCE 31st AUGUST 1967

(**79**)

1966 (8 Feb). *Royal Visit. T* **75** *and similar horiz designs. Multi-coloured. W w* **12** (*sideways*). *P* 13½ × 14½.

313	5 c. Type **75**	15	10
314	8 c. Map, Royal Yacht *Britannia* and Arms	1·00	70
315	25 c. Map and flag	1·10	55
316	35 c. Flag and panorama	1·25	70
313/16	*Set of* 4	3·25	1·75

1966 (15 Nov). *As No.* 284 *but W w* **12** (*sideways*).

317	1 c. stone and black	10	10

No. 317 exists with PVA gum as well as gum arabic.

1967 (31 Aug). *Fifth Year of Independence. Nos.* 288/9, 291*a and* 295 *optd as T* **79**.

318	8 c. yellow-green	10	10
319	10 c. deep lilac	10	10
320	15 c. orange	10	10
321	60 c. vermilion, yellow-green and indigo	25	10
318/21	*Set of* 4	30	15

On No. 321 the overprint is in five lines.

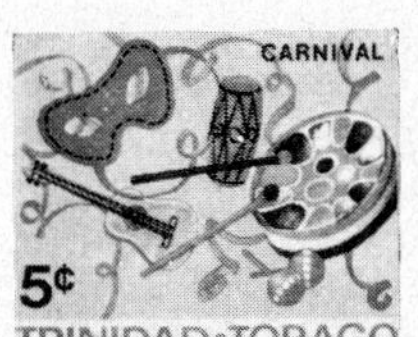

80 Musical Instruments

81 Calypso King

1968 (17 Feb). *Trinidad Carnival. Horiz designs as T* **80** (15 *and* 25 c.), *or vert designs as T* **81** (35 *and* 60 c.). *Multicoloured. P* 12.

322	5 c. Type **80**	10	10
323	10 c. Type **81**	10	10
324	15 c. Steel band	10	10
325	25 c. Carnival procession	10	10
326	35 c. Carnival King	10	10
327	60 c. Carnival Queen	20	15
322/7	.. .. *Set of* 6	35	30

86 Doctor giving Eye-Test

87 Peoples of the World and Emblem

1968 (7 May). *20th Anniv of World Health Organization.* W w **12** (*sideways*). *P* 14.

328	**86**	5 c. red, blackish brown and gold ..	10	10
329		25 c. orange, blackish brown and gold ..	15	10
330		35 c. bright blue, black and gold	20	10
328/30		.. .. *Set of* 3	40	20

1968 (5 Aug). *Human Rights Year.* W w **12** (*sideways*). *P* 13½ × 14.

331	**87**	5 c. cerise, black and greenish yellow ..	10	10
332		10 c. new blue, black and greenish yellow	10	10
333		25 c. apple-green, black & greenish yell ..	10	10
331/3		.. .. *Set of* 3	15	15

88 Cycling

(Des G. Vasarhelyi. Islands additionally die-stamped in gold (5 c. to 35 c.))

1968 (14 Oct). *Olympic Games, Mexico. T* **88** *and similar horiz designs. Multicoloured.* W w **12**. *P* 14.

334	5 c. Type **88**	10	10
335	15 c. Weightlifting	10	10
336	25 c. Relay-racing	10	10
337	35 c. Sprinting	15	10
338	$1.20, Maps of Mexico and Trinidad ..	45	30
334/8	.. .. *Set of* 5	65	50

93 Cocoa Beans

94 Green Hermit

(Des G. Vasarhelyi. Queen's profile die-stamped in gold (G.) or silver (S.), also the Islands on 20, 25 c.)

1969–72. *Designs as T* **93/4**. *W* w **12** (*sideways on* 1 *to* 8 *c.*, 40 *c.*, 50 *c.*). *P* 14 × 14½ ($2.50, $5) *or* 14 (*others*).

A. *Chalk-surfaced paper* (1.4.69)
B. *Glazed, ordinary paper* (24.3.72*)

		A		B	
339	1 c. multicoloured (S.) ..	10	10	10	10
	a. Queen's head omitted ..	75·00	—	†	
340	3 c. multicoloured (G.) ..	10	10	10	10
341	5 c. multicoloured (G.) ..	40	10	40	10
	a. Queen's head omitted ..	†		—	—
	b. Imperf (pair)	†		£200	—
	ba. Ditto and Queen's head omitted	†		£325	—
342	6 c. multicoloured (G.) ..	10	10	75	75
	a. Queen's head omitted ..	£100	—	†	
	b. Imperf (pair)	£250	—	†	
343	8 c. multicoloured (S.) ..	10	10	†	
344	10 c. multicoloured (G.) ..	40	10	40	10
345	12 c. mult (blue-grn leaves) (S.)	15	30	30	70
	a. Myrtle-green leaves ..	3·25	2·00	†	
346	15 c. multicoloured (S.) ..	10	10	20	10
	a. Queen's head omitted ..	£350	—	†	
347	20 c. scarlet, black & grey (G.)	15	10	30	20
348	25 c. scarlet, blk & new bl (S.)	15	15	1·25	40
	a. Silver (Queen's head and island) omitted	†		85·00	—
349	30 c. multicoloured (S.) ..	25	10	50	25
350	40 c. multicoloured (G.) ..	2·00	10	3·50	60
351	50 c. multicoloured (S.) ..	25	40	1·50	2·25
352	$1 multicoloured (G.) ..	60	15	1·50	2·25
	a. Gold (Queen's head) omitted	£120	—	—	—
353	$2.50, multicoloured (G.) ..	80	2·50	†	
	a. Perf 14 (1972)	15·00	17·00	†	
354	$5 multicoloured (G.) ..	1·50	3·00	†	
	a. Gold (Queen's head) omitted	£300	—	†	
	b. Perf 14 (1972)	35·00	38·00	†	
339A/54A	.. .. *Set of* 16	6·00	6·50	†	
339B/52B	.. .. *Set of* 13	†		9·75	7·00

Designs: *Horiz as T* **93**—3 c. Sugar refinery; 5 c. Rufous-vented Chachalaca; 6 c. Oil refinery; 8 c. Fertilizer plant; 40 c. Scarlet Ibis; 50 c. Maracas Bay; $2.50, Fishing; $5, Red House. *Vert as T* **94**—12 c. Citrus fruit; 15 c. Arms of Trinidad and Tobago; 20, 25 c. Flag and outline of Trinidad and Tobago; 30 c. Chaconia plant; $1, Poui tree.

*This was the date of receipt at the G.P.O.; the dates of issue are not known.

The listed missing die-stamped heads have the heads completely omitted and, except for No. 352a which results from a shift, show a blind impression of the die. They should not be confused with stamps from sheets containing a row of partially missing heads progressing down to mere specks of foil. The 20 c. value also exists with the gold omitted from the map only. We have also seen stamps with an additional "blind" profile cutting into the rear of the head but without a second die-stamped impression. Varieties of this nature are outside the scope of this catalogue.

See also Nos. 432/4 and 473.

108 Captain A. A. Cipriani (labour leader) and Entrance to Woodford Square

(Photo State Ptg Works, Vienna)

1969 (1 May). *50th Anniv of International Labour Organization. T* **108** *and similar horiz design. P* 12.

355	6 c. black, gold and carmine-red	10	10
356	15 c. black, gold and new blue	10	10

Design:—15 c. Arms of Industrial Court and entrance to Woodford Square.

110 Cornucopia and Fruit

111 Map showing "CARIFTA" Countries

(Des and photo State Ptg Works, Vienna)

1969 (1 Aug). *First Anniv of CARIFTA (Caribbean Free Trade Area). T* **110/11** *and similar multicoloured designs. P* 13½.

357	6 c. Type **110**	10	10
358	10 c. British and member nations' flags (*horiz*)	10	10
359	30 c. Type **111**	15	10
360	40 c. Boeing "727" in flight (*horiz*)	20	15
357/60	.. .. *Set of* 4	45	30

114 Space Module landing on Moon

(Des G. Vasarhelyi. Litho D.L.R.)

1969 (2 Sept). *First Man on the Moon. T* **114** *and similar multicoloured designs. P* 14.

361	6 c. Type **114**	10	10
362	40 c. Space module and astronauts on Moon (*vert*)	15	10
363	$1 Astronauts seen from inside space module	35	20
361/3	.. .. *Set of* 3	55	30

The above were released by the Philatelic Agency in the U.S.A. on 1 September, but not sold locally until 2 September.

COVER PRICES

Cover factors are quoted at the beginning of each country for most issues to 1945. An explanation of the system can be found on page x. The factors quoted do not, however, apply to philatelic covers.

117 Parliamentary Chamber, Flags and Emblems

(Photo Harrison)

1969 (23 Oct*). *15th Commonwealth Parliamentary Association Conference, Port-of-Spain. T* **117** *and similar horiz designs. Multicoloured.* W w **12**. *P* 14½ × 13½.

364	10 c. Type **117**	10	10
365	15 c. J.F. Kennedy College	10	10
366	30 c. Parliamentary maces	25	15
367	40 c. Cannon and emblem	25	15
364/7	.. .. *Set of* 4	60	30

*This was the local release date; the Philatelic Agency in New York released the stamps ten days earlier.

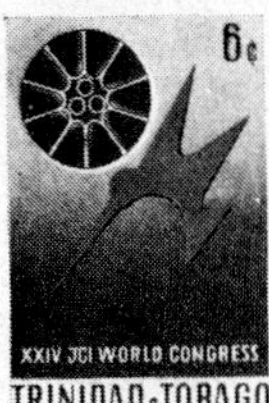

121 Congress Emblem

122 Emblem and Islands at Daybreak

(Photo Rosenbaum Bros, Vienna)

1969 (3 Nov). *International Congress of the Junior Chamber of Commerce. T* **121/2** *and similar vert design. P* 13½.

368	6 c. black, red and gold	10	10
369	30 c. gold, lake and light blue	15	15
370	40 c. black, gold and ultramarine	15	15
368/70	.. .. *Set of* 3	30	30

Design:—40 c. Emblem, palm-trees and ruin.

The above were released by the Philatelic Agency in the U.S.A. on 2 November, but not sold locally until 3 November.

124 "Man in the Moon"

129 Statue of Gandhi

(Des V. Whiteley. Litho Questa)

1970 (6 Feb). *Carnival Winners. T* **124** *and similar multicoloured designs.* W w **12** (*sideways on* 40 *c.*). *P* 14.

371	5 c. Type **124**	10	10
372	6 c. "City beneath the Sea"	10	10
373	15 c. "Antelope" God Bamibara	15	10
374	30 c. "Chanticleer" Pheasant Queen of Malaya	25	10
375	40 c. Steel Band of the Year (*horiz*)	25	15
371/5	.. .. *Set of* 5	70	30

The above were released by the Philatelic Agency in the U.S.A. on 2 February, but not sold locally until 6 February.

(Photo State Printing Works, Vienna)

1970 (2 Mar). *Gandhi Centenary Year* (1969). *T* **129** *and similar multicoloured design. P* 12.

376	10 c. Type **129**	20	10
377	30 c. Head of Gandhi and Indian flag (*horiz*) ..	40	20

131 Symbols of Culture, Science, Arts and Technology

132 New U.P.U. H.Q. Building

(Des G. Lee. Photo State Printing Works, Vienna)

1970 (26 June). *25th Anniv of United Nations. T* **131/2** *and similar designs. Multicoloured. P* 12 (30 c.), 13½ × 14 (10 c.) *or* 13½ (*others*).

378 5 c. Type **131** 10 10
379 10 c. Children of different races, map and flag (34 × 25 *mm*) 15 10
380 20 c. Noah's Ark, rainbow and dove (35 × 24 *mm*) 30 15
381 30 c. Type **132** 30 15
378/81 .. .. *Set of* 4 75 30

NATIONAL
COMMERCIAL
BANK
ESTABLISHED
1.7.70

(133) **134** "East Indian Immigrants" (J. Cazabon)

1970 (1 July). *Inauguration of National Commercial Bank. No.* 341A *optd with T* **133**.

382 5 c. multicoloured 10 10

(Des from paintings by Cazabon. Litho Questa)

1970 (Oct). *125th Anniv of San Fernando. T* **134** *and similar designs. W w* **12** (*sideways on* 5 c. *and* 40 c.). *P* 13½.

383 3 c. multicoloured 10 15
384 5 c. black, blue and yellow-ochre 10 10
385 40 c. black, blue and yellow-ochre 45 15
383/5 .. .. *Set of* 3 55 30

Designs: *Horiz*—5 c. "San Fernando Town Hall"; 40 c. "San Fernando Harbour, 1860".

135 "The Adoration of the Shepherds" (detail, School of Seville)

(Des G. Drummond. Litho Format)

1970 (8 Dec). *Christmas. Paintings. T* **135** *and similar vert designs. Multicoloured. P* 13½.

386 3 c. Type **135** 10 10
387 5 c. "Madonna and Child with Saints" (detail, Titian) 10 10
388 30 c. "The Adoration of the Shepherds" (detail, Le Nain) 20 15
389 40 c. "The Virgin and Child, St. John and an Angel" (Morando) 20 10
390 $1 "The Adoration of the Kings" (detail, Veronese) 75 85
386/90 .. .. *Set of* 5 1·10 1·00
MS391 114 × 153 mm. Nos. 386/9 .. .. 2·00 2·50

136 Red Brocket

(Des State Printing Works, Vienna. Litho Questa)

1971 (9 Aug). *Trinidad Wildlife. T* **136** *and similar horiz designs. Multicoloured. W w* **12** (*sideways*). *P* 13½.

392 3 c. Type **136** 20 15
393 5 c. Collared Peccary ("Quenk") 25 15
394 6 c. Paca ("Lappe") 30 30
395 30 c. Brazilian Agouti .. .. .. 1·50 3·00
396 40 c. Ocelot .. .. 1·75 2·75
392/6 .. .. *Set of* 5 3·50 5·50

ALTERED CATALOGUE NUMBERS

Any Catalogue numbers altered from the last edition are shown as a list in the introductory pages.

137 A. A. Cipriani **138** "Virgin and Child with St. John" (detail, Bartolommeo)

(Litho D.L.R.)

1971 (30 Aug*). *Ninth Anniv of Independence. T* **137** *and similar vert design. Multicoloured. W w* **12**. *P* 14.

397 5 c. Type **137** 10 10
398 30 c. Chaconia medal 20 30

*This was the local release date, but the New York agency issued the stamps on 25 August.

(Litho Harrison)

1971 (25 Oct). *Christmas. T* **138** *and similar vert designs. Multicoloured. W w* **12** (*sideways on* 10 *and* 15 c.). *P* 14 × 14½.

399 3 c. Type **138** 10 10
400 5 c. Local crèche 10 10
401 10 c. "Virgin and Child with Saints Jerome and Dominic" (detail, Lippi) 15 10
402 15 c. "Virgin and Child with St. Anne" (detail, Gerolamo dai Libri) 20 15
399/402 .. .. *Set of* 4 50 30

139 Satellite Earth Station, Matura

(Litho Harrison)

1971 (18 Nov). *Satellite Earth Station. T* **139** *and similar vert designs. Multicoloured. W w* **12** (*sideways on* 10 c.). *P* 14 (10 c.) *or* 14 × 13½ (*others*).

403 10 c. Type **139** 10 10
404 30 c. Dish antennae 20 20
405 40 c. Satellite and the earth 30 30
403/5 .. .. *Set of* 3 55 55
MS406 140 × 76 mm. Nos. 403/5 (wmk sideways). Imperf .. .. 1·25 2·00
a. Yellow and pale blue omitted .. ..

140 *Morpho peleides* × *achilleana*

(Des G. Drummond. Photo Harrison)

1972 (18 Feb). *Butterflies. T* **140** *and similar horiz designs. Multicoloured. W w* **12** (*sideways on* 5 c.). *P* 14.

407 3 c. Type **140** 40 10
408 5 c. *Eryphanis polyxena* 50 10
409 6 c. *Phoebis philea* 55 10
410 10 c. *Prepona laertes* 80 15
411 20 c. *Eurytides telesilaus* .. .. .. 1·25 1·40
412 30 c. *Eurema proterpia* .. .. .. 1·75 2·25
407/12 .. .. *Set of* 6 4·75 3·50

141 *Lady McLeod* (paddle-steamer) and McLeod Stamp **142** Trinity Cross

(Des J. Cooter. Litho Harrison)

1972 (24 Apr*). *125th Anniv. of First Trinidad Postage Stamp. T* **141** *and similar horiz designs. W w* **12**. *P* 14.

413 5 c. multicoloured 15 10
414 10 c. multicoloured 25 10
415 30 c. greenish blue, reddish chestnut and black 70 45
413/15 .. .. *Set of* 3 1·00 55
MS416 83 × 140 mm. Nos. 413/15 .. .. 1·00 1·25
a. Wmk sideways .. .. 20·00 25·00

Designs:—10 c. Map and Lady McLeod stamp; 30 c. Lady McLeod stamp and inscription.

*This was the local release date, but the New York Agency issued the stamps on 12 April.

(Des G. Drummond. Photo Enschedé)

1972 (28 Aug). *Tenth Anniv of Independence. T* **142** *and similar vert designs. Multicoloured. W w* **12**. *P* 13½ × 13.

417 5 c. Type **142** 10 10
418 10 c. Chaconia Medal 10 10
419 20 c. Hummingbird Medal 15 15
420 30 c. Medal of Merit 15 20
417/20 .. .. *Set of* 4 40 40
MS421 93 × 121 mm. Nos. 417/20 .. .. .. 60 1·00

One example of MS421 has been seen with the blue (background and frame) omitted from the 10 c. Another example has been seen with carmine (background and frame) omitted from the 30 c.

See also Nos. 440/4.

143 Bronze Medal, 1964 Relay

(Des G. Drummond. Litho Questa)

1972 (7 Sept). *Olympic Games, Munich. T* **143** *and similar horiz designs. Multicoloured. W w* **12**. *P* 14.

422 10 c. Type **143** 10 10
423 20 c. Bronze, 1964 200 metres 30 10
424 30 c. Silver, 1952 weightlifting 40 15
425 40 c. Silver, 1964 400 metres 40 20
426 50 c. Silver, 1948 weightlifting 40 50
422/6 .. .. *Set of* 5 1·40 90
MS427 153 × 82 mm. Nos. 422/6 .. .. .. 1·40 1·75

144 "Adoration of the Kings" (detail, Dosso)

(Des G. Drummond. Photo J.W.)

1972 (9 Nov). *Christmas. T* **144** *and similar horiz design. Multicoloured. W w* **12**. *P* 14.

428 3 c. Type **144** 10 10
429 5 c. "The Holy Family and a Shepherd" (Titian) 10 10
430 30 c. As 5 c. 70 55
428/30 .. .. *Set of* 3 80 60
MS431 73 × 99 mm. Nos. 428/30 .. .. .. 85 1·50

1973–74. *Nos.* 340/2, *but W w* **12** (*upright*). *Glazed, ordinary paper*.

432 3 c. multicoloured (9.74?) .. .. .. 4·50 6·50
433 5 c. multicolourex (1973) .. .. .. 7·50 1·75
a. Yellow (background) omitted £130
434 6 c. multicoloured (1974) .. .. .. 2·50 1·50
432/4 .. .. *Set of* 3 13·00 8·75

145 E.C.L.A. Building, Chile

(Des G. Drummond. Litho Questa)

1973 (15 Aug). *Anniversaries. Events described on stamps. T* **145** *and similar horiz designs. Multicoloured. W w* **12**. *P* 14.

435 10 c. Type **145** 10 10
436 20 c. Interpol emblem 45 20
437 30 c. W.M.O. emblem 45 20
438 40 c. University of the West Indies 45 20
435/8 .. .. *Set of* 4 1·25 60
MS439 155 × 92 mm. Nos. 435/8 .. .. .. 1·25 1·25

(Des J. Cooter. Litho Harrison)

1973 (30 Aug). *Eleventh Anniv of Independence. Vert designs as T* **142**. *Multicoloured. W w* **12**. *P* 14½ × 14.

440 10 c. Trinity Cross 10 10
441 20 c. Medal of Merit 20 15
442 30 c. Chaconia Medal 20 20
443 40 c. Hummingbird Medal 30 30
440/3 .. .. *Set of* 4 70 65
MS444 75 × 122 mm. Nos. 440/3. P 14 .. .. 70 1·25

146 G.P.O., Port-of-Spain **147** "Madonna with Child" (Murillo)

(Des J. Cooter. Photo J.W.)

1973 (8 Oct). *Second Commonwealth Conference of Postal Administrations, Trinidad. T* **146** *and similar horiz design. Multicoloured. W* w **12** *(sideways). P* 14.

445 30 c. Type **146** 20 20
446 40 c. Conference Hall, Chaguaramas* 30 30
MS447 115 × 115 mm. Nos. 445/6 .. .. 90 90
*Wrongly inscr "CHAGARAMAS" on stamp.

(Des PAD Studio. Photo Harrison)

1973 (22 Oct). *Christmas. W* w **12** *(sideways on* **MS**450). *P* 14½ × 14.

448 **147** 5 c. multicoloured 10 10
449 $1 multicoloured 75 60
MS450 94 × 88 mm. Nos. 448/9. P 14 .. .. 85 1·40

148 Berne H.Q. within U.P.U. Emblem

(Des PAD Studio. Photo Harrison)

1974 (18 Nov). *Centenary of Universal Postal Union. T* **148** *and similar horiz design. Multicoloured. W* w **12** *(sideways). P* 13 × 14.

451 40 c. Type **148** 35 25
452 50 c. Map within emblem 35 50
MS453 117 × 104 mm. Nos. 451/2. P 13 × 14½ 16·00 18·00

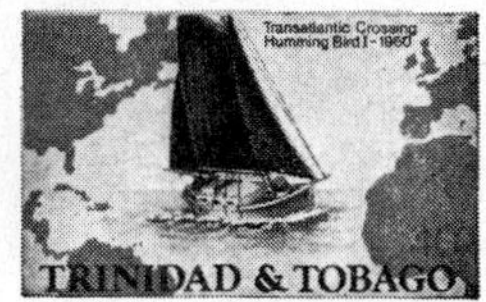

149 *Humming Bird I* crossing Atlantic Ocean (1960)

(Des and photo Harrison)

1974 (2 Dec). *First Anniv of World Voyage by H. and K. La Borde. T* **149** *and similar horiz design. Multicoloured. W* w **12** *(sideways). P* 14.

454 40 c. Type **149** 45 15
455 50 c. *Humming Bird II* crossing globe .. 55 35
MS456 109 × 84 mm. Nos. 454/5 (wmk upright) .. 2·00 4·00

150 "Sex Equality"

(Des Hetty J. Mejias de Grannes; adapted V. Whiteley. Litho Harrison)

1975 (23 June). *International Women's Year. W* w **14** *(sideways). P* 14.

457 **150** 15 c. multicoloured 15 10
458 30 c. multicoloured 35 40

151 Common Vampire Bat, Microscope and Syringe

(Des PAD Studio. Photo Harrison)

1975 (23 Sept). *Isolation of Rabies Virus. T* **151** *and similar horiz design. Multicoloured. W* w **14**. *P* 14 × 14½.

459 25 c. Type **151** 40 30
460 30 c. Dr. Pawan, instruments and book .. 50 35

152 Route-map and Tail of Boeing "707"

(Des C. Abbott. Litho Walsall)

1975 (27 Nov). *35th Anniv of British West Indian Airways. T* **152** *and similar horiz designs. W* w **14** *(sideways). P* 14.

461 20 c. Type **152** 20 10
462 30 c. "707" on ground 30 30
463 40 c. "707" in flight 40 50
461/3 .. .. *Set of* 3 80 80
MS464 119 × 110 mm. Nos. 461/3 .. .. 1·25 1·75

153 "From the Land of the Humming Bird"

(Des and photo Harrison)

1976 (12 Jan). *Carnival. 1974 Prizewinning Costumes. T* **153** *and similar horiz design. Multicoloured. W* w **14** *(sideways). P* 14.

465 30 c. Type **153** 10 10
466 $1 "The Little Carib" 40 50
MS467 83 × 108 mm. Nos. 465/6 .. .. .. 90 90

154 Angostura Building, Port-of-Spain

(Des Jennifer Toombs. Litho J.W.)

1976 (14 July). *150th Anniv. of Angostura Bitters. T* **154** *and similar horiz designs. Multicoloured. W* w **14** *(sideways). P* 13.

468 5 c. Type **154** 10 10
469 35 c. Medal, New Orleans 1885/6 .. .. 20 25
470 45 c. Medal, Sydney 1879 .. .. .. 25 40
471 50 c. Medal, Brussels 1897 .. .. .. 25 50
468/71 .. .. *Set of* 4 65 1·10
MS472 119 × 112 mm. Nos. 468/71. P 14 .. .. 90 1·25

REPUBLIC

1976 (2 Aug). *As No.* 344B *but W* w **14**.

473 10 c. multicoloured 75 75

1976 (4 Oct). *West Indian Victory in World Cricket Cup. As Nos.* 419/20 *of Jamaica.*

474 35 c. Caribbean map 45 30
475 45 c. Prudential Cup 55 40
MS476 80 × 80 mm. Nos. 474/5 .. .. .. 1·75 2·50

155 "Columbus sailing through the Bocas" (Campins)

(Des J.W. Litho Questa)

1976 (1 Nov)–**78**. *Paintings, Hotels and Orchids. Horiz designs as T* **155**. *Multicoloured. W* w **14**. *P* 14.

479 5 c. Type **155** 60 10
480 6 c. Robinson Crusoe Hotel, Tobago (17.1.78) 10 30
482 10 c. "San Fernando Hill" (J. Cazabon) .. 10 10
483 12 c. *Paphinia cristata* (7.6.78) .. .. 1·25 30
484 15 c. Turtle Beach Hotel (17.1.78) 40 40
485 20 c. "East Indians in a Landscape" (J. Cazabon) 40 10
486 25 c. Mt Irvine Hotel (17.1.78) 40 10
487 30 c. *Caularthon bicornutum* (7.6.78) .. 1·25 30
488 35 c. "Los Gallos Point" (J. Cazabon) .. 70 10
489 40 c. *Miltassia* (7.6.78) .. .. .. 1·25 10
490 45 c. "Corbeaux Town" (J. Cazabon) 80 10
491 50 c. *Oncidium ampliatum* (7.6.78) .. .. 1·50 20
492 70 c. Beach facilities, Mt Irvine Hotel (17.1.78) 50 80
494 $2.50, *Oncidium papilio* (7.6.78) .. .. 2·00 1·00
495 $5 Trinidad Holiday Inn (17.1.78) .. .. 1·75 4·50
479/95 .. .. *Set of* 15 11·50 7·50
MS497 171 × 100 mm. Nos. 479, 482, 485, 488 and 490. Wmk sideways .. .. 2·00 1·50
MS498 171 × 88 mm. Nos. 480, 484, 486, 492 and 495. Wmk sideways (17.1.78) .. .. .. 3·00 4·00
MS499 170 × 90 mm. Nos. 483, 487, 489, 491 and 494. Wmk sideways (7.6.78) .. .. .. 3·75 4·00

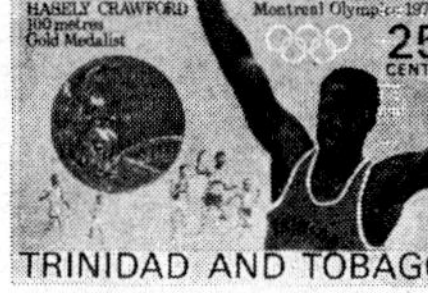

156 Hasely Crawford and Olympic Gold Medal

(Des J.W. Litho D. L. R.)

1977 (4 Jan). *Hasely Crawford Commemoration. W* w **14** *(sideways). P* 12 × 12½.

501 **156** 25 c. multicoloured 20 30
MS502 93 × 70 mm. No. 501 .. .. .. 30 50

OMNIBUS ISSUES

Details, together with prices for complete sets, of the various Omnibus issues from the 1935 Silver Jubilee series to date are included in a special section following Zimbabwe at the end of Volume 2.

157 Lindbergh's Sikorsky "S-38", 1929

158 National Flag

(Des and litho J.W.)

1977 (4 Apr). *50th Anniv of Airmail Service. T* **157** *and similar horiz designs. Multicoloured. W* w **14** *(sideways). P* 13.

503 20 c. Type **157** 25 20
504 35 c. Arrival of Charles and Anne Lindbergh 35 35
505 45 c. Boeing "707", c. 1960 .. .. .. 45 50
506 50 c. Boeing "747", 1969 .. .. .. 1·10 2·25
503/6 .. .. *Set of* 4 1·90 3·00
MS507 130 × 100 mm. Nos. 503/6. P 14 .. .. 3·50 3·50

(Des and litho J.W.)

1977 (26 July). *Inauguration of the Republic. T* **158** *and similar vert designs. Multicoloured. W* w **14**. *P* 13.

508 20 c. Type **158** 15 10
509 35 c. Coat of Arms 25 25
510 45 c. Government House 35 35
508/10 .. .. *Set of* 3 65 60
MS511 125 × 84 mm. Nos. 508/10. P 14 .. .. 60 1·25

159 White Poinsettia

160 Miss Janelle (Penny) Commissiong with Trophy

(Des J.W. Litho Walsall)

1977 (11 Oct). *Christmas. T* **159** *and similar vert design. Multicoloured. W* w **14**. *P* 14 × 14½.

512 10 c. Type **159** 15 10
513 35 c. Type **159** 25 10
514 45 c. Red Poinsettia 35 25
515 50 c. As 45 c. 45 60
512/15 .. .. *Set of* 4 1·10 90
MS516 112 × 142 mm. Nos. 512/15 .. .. 1·10 1·50

(Des BG Studio. Litho Questa)

1978 (2 Aug). *Miss Janelle (Penny) Commissiong ("Miss Universe 1977") Commemoration. T* **160** *and similar vert designs showing Miss Commissiong. Multicoloured. W* w **14**. *P* 14½.

517 10 c. Type **160** 15 10
518 35 c. Portrait 40 40
519 45 c. In evening dress 55 65
517/19 .. .. *Set of* 3 1·00 1·00
MS520 186 × 120 mm. Nos. 517/19 .. .. 90 1·25
a. 45c. value imperf on three sides £500

161 Tayra

162 "Burst of Beauty"

(Des G. Drummond. Litho Walsall)

1978 (7 Nov). *Wildlife. T* **161** *and similar horiz designs. Multicoloured. W* w **14** *(sideways). P* 13½.

521 15 c. Type **161** 20 10
522 25 c. Ocelot 30 20
523 40 c. Brazilian Tree Porcupine 50 30
524 70 c. Tamandua .. .. 65 1·00
521/4 .. .. *Set of* 4 1·50 1·40
MS525 128 × 101 mm. Nos. 521/4 .. .. 1·75 2·50

(Des C. Abbott. Litho Format)

1979 (1 Feb). *Carnival* 1978. *T* **162** *and similar vert designs. P* 13½.

526 5 c. multicoloured 10 10
527 10 c. multicoloured 10 10
528 35 c. multicoloured 10 10
529 45 c. multicoloured 10 10
530 50 c. yellow-brown, rosine and deep lilac .. 10 15
531 $1 multicoloured 20 40
526/31 .. .. *Set of* 6 50 60

Designs:—10 c. Rain worshipper; 35 c. "Zodiac"; 45 c. Praying mantis; 50 c. "Eye of the Hurricane"; $1 Steel orchestra.

163 Day Care

164 Geothermal Exploration

(Des BG Studio. Litho J.W.)

1979 (5 June). *International Year of the Child.* T **163** *and similar vert designs. Multicoloured.* P 13.

532 5 c. Type **163** 10 10
533 10 c. School feeding programme 10 10
534 35 c. Dental care 25 15
535 45 c. Nursery school 25 20
536 50 c. Free bus transport 25 30
537 $1 Medical care 55 80
532/7 .. .. *Set of* 6 1·25 1·50
MS538 114 × 132 mm. Nos. 532/7. P 14 × 13½ .. 1·25 1·75

(Des local artist; adapted L. Curtis. Litho Format)

1979 (3 July). *4th Latin American Geological Congress.* T **164** *and similar horiz designs. Multicoloured.* W w **14** (*sideways*). P 13½.

539 10 c. Type **164** 15 10
540 35 c. Hydrogeology 25 25
541 45 c. Petroleum exploration 30 30
542 70 c. Environmental preservation .. .. 40 1·00
539/42 .. .. *Set of* 4 1·00 1·50
MS543 185 × 89 mm. Nos. 539/42 .. .. 1·25 1·60

165 1879 1d. rose and Map of Tobago

(Des J. Cooter. Litho Format)

1979 (1 Aug). *Tobago Stamp Centenary.* T **165** *and similar horiz designs in black, rose-lilac and dull orange* ($1) *or multicoloured* (*others*). W w **14** (*sideways*). P 13½ × 14.

544 10 c. Type **165** 10 10
545 15 c. 1879 3d. and 1880 ½d. surcharged on half of 6d. 10 10
546 35 c. 1879 6d. and 1886 ½d. surcharged on 6d. 35 30
547 45 c. 1879 1s. and 1886 ½d. surcharged on 2½d. 40 30
548 70 c. 1879 5s. and Great Britain 1856 1s. with "A14" (Scarborough, Tobago) postmark 55 1·00
549 $1 1879 £1 and General Post Office, Scarborough, Tobago .. .. 75 1·50
544/9 .. .. *Set of* 6 2·00 3·00
MS550 165 × 155 mm. Nos. 544/9 .. .. 2·25 3·00

166 1962 60 c. Independence Commemorative and Sir Rowland Hill

(Des and litho J.W.)

1979 (4 Oct). *Death Centenary of Sir Rowland Hill.* T **166** *and similar horiz designs showing stamps and Sir Rowland Hill. Multicoloured.* W w **14** (*sideways*). P 13.

551 25 c. Type **166** 30 15
552 45 c. 1977 35 c. Inauguration of Republic commemorative 40 20
553 $1 1879 Trinidad ½d. surcharge and Tobago 1880 4d. .. .. 65 1·00
551/3 .. .. *Set of* 3 1·25 1·25
MS554 115 × 125 mm. No. 551/3. P 13½ × 14 .. 1·25 1·50

1844–
1980
POPULATION
CENSUS
12th MAY 1980

167 Poui Tree in Churchyard (**168**)

(Des G. Hutchins. Litho Format)

1980 (21 Jan). *Centenary of Princes Town.* T **167** *and similar horiz designs. Multicoloured.* W w **14** (*sideways*). P 14½ × 14.

555 5 c. Type **167** 10 10
556 10 c. Princes Town Court House 10 10
557 50 c. Locomotive of the Royal Train, 1880 .. 60 90
558 $1.50, H.M.S. *Bacchante* (corvette) .. 1·00 1·60
555/8 .. .. *Set of* 4 1·60 2·40
MS559 177 × 102 mm. Nos. 555/8 .. .. 1·90 2·50

1980 (8 Apr). *Population Census. Nos.* 479/80 *and* 482 *optd with* T **168**.

560 5 c. Type **155** 10 20
561 6 c. Robinson Crusoe Hotel, Tobago 10 30
562 10 c. "Old View" (Cazabon) 15 20
560/2 .. .. *Set of* 3 30 60

169 Scarlet Ibis (male)

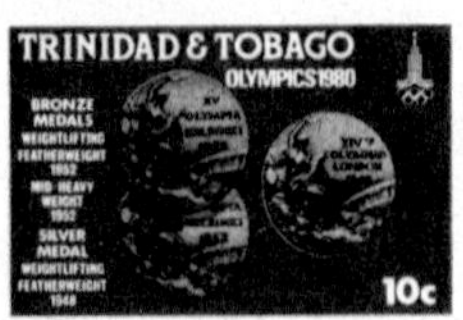

170 Silver and Bronze Medals for Weightlifting, 1948 and 1952

(Des G. Drummond. Litho Questa)

1980 (6 May). *Scarlet Ibis.* T **169** *and similar vert designs. Multicoloured.* W w **14**. P 14.

563 50 c. Type **169** 80 80
a. Strip of 5. Nos. 563/7 .. .. .. 3·50
564 50 c. Male and female 80 80
565 50 c. Hen and nest 80 80
566 50 c. Nest and eggs 80 80
567 50 c. Chick in nest 80 80
563/7 .. .. *Set of* 5 3·50 3·50

Nos. 563/7 were printed together, *se-tenant*, in horizontal and vertical strips of 5 throughout.

(Des G. Hutchins. Litho Walsall)

1980 (22 July). *Olympic Games, Moscow.* T **170** *and similar designs.* W w **14** (*sideways*). P 14.

568 10 c. multicoloured 10 10
569 15 c. multicoloured 10 10
570 70 c. multicoloured 30 45
568/70 .. .. *Set of* 3 30 50
MS571 110 × 149 mm. $2.50, black, silver and orange-vermilion (wmk upright) .. .. 1·25 1·75

Designs: *Horiz*—15 c. Hasely Crawford (100 metres sprint winner, 1976) and gold medal; 70 c. Silver medal for 400 metres and bronze medals for 4 × 400 metres relay, 1964. *Vert*—$2.50, Olympic Games emblems for Moscow, 1980, Olympia, 776 B.C. and Athens, 1896.

171 Charcoal Production

(Des J. Cooter. Litho Walsall)

1980 (8 Sept). *11th Commonwealth Forestry Conference.* T **171** *and similar horiz designs. Multicoloured.* W w **14** (*sideways*). P 14.

572 10 c. Type **171** 10 10
573 55 c. Logging 45 25
574 70 c. Teak plantation 55 40
575 $2.50, Watershed management .. .. 1·40 1·50
572/5 .. .. *Set of* 4 2·25 2·00
MS576 135 × 87 mm. Nos. 572/5 .. .. 2·50 2·75

172 Beryl McBurnie (dance and culture) and Audrey Jeffers (social worker)

(Des BG Studio. Litho Questa)

1980 (29 Sept). *Decade for Women* (*1st issue*). T **172** *and similar horiz designs. Multicoloured.* W w **14** (*sideways*). P 14.

577 $1 Type **172** 55 55
578 $1 Elizabeth Bourne (judiciary) and Isabella Teshier (government) 55 55
579 $1 Dr. Stella Abidh (public health) and Louise Horne (nutrition) 55 55
577/9 .. .. *Set of* 3 1·50 1·50

See also Nos. 680/2.

173 Netball Stadium

(Des BG Studio. Litho Format)

1980 (21 Oct). *World Netball Tournament.* W w **14** (*sideways*). P 13½ × 14.

580 **173** 70 c. multicoloured 30 45

174 I.Y.D.P. Emblem, Athlete and Disabled Person

175 "Our Land Must Live"

(Des BG Studio. Litho Format)

1981 (23 Mar). *International Year for Disabled Persons.* T **174** *and similar horiz designs.* W w **14**. P 14½.

581 10 c. black, vermilion and dull yellowish green 15 10
582 70 c. black, vermilion and buff 50 70
583 $1.50, black, vermilion and cobalt .. .. 90 1·40
584 $2 black, vermilion and flesh .. .. 1·25 1·75
581/4 .. .. *Set of* 4 2·50 3·50

Designs:—70 c. I.Y.D.P. emblem and doctor with disabled person; $1.50, Emblem, and blind man and woman; $2 Emblem and inscription.

(Des Debbie Galt; adapted G. Vasarhelyi. Litho J.W.)

1981 (7 July). *Environmental Preservation.* T **175** *and similar horiz designs. Multicoloured.* W w **14** (*sideways*). P 13 × 13½.

585 10 c. Type **175** 10 10
586 55 c. "Our seas must live" 30 30
587 $3 "Our skies must live" .. .. .. 1·50 1·60
585/7 .. .. *Set of* 3 1·75 1·75
MS588 142 × 89 mm. Nos. 585/7 .. .. .. 4·00 4·25

176 "Food or Famine"

177 "First Aid Skills"

(Des and litho Harrison)

1981 (16 Oct). *World Food Day.* T **176** *and similar horiz designs. Multicoloured.* W w **14** (*sideways*). P 14½ × 14.

589 10 c. Type **176** 10 10
590 15 c. "Produce more" (threshing and milling rice) 10 10
591 45 c. "Fish for food" (Bigeye) 30 20
592 55 c. "Prevent hunger" 35 25
593 $1.50, "Fight malnutrition" 85 90
594 $2 "Fish for food" (Smallmouth Grunt) .. 1·10 1·25
589/94 .. .. *Set of* 6 2·40 2·40
MS595 164 × 98 mm. Nos. 589/94 .. .. 2·75 3·50

(Des L. Curtis. Litho Format)

1981 (17 Nov). *President's Award Scheme.* T **177** *and similar vert designs. Multicoloured.* W w **14**. P 14.

596 10 c. Type **177** 20 10
597 70 c. "Motor mechanics" 70 45
598 $1 "Expedition" 85 55
599 $2 Presenting an award .. .. .. 1·40 1·40
596/9 .. .. *Set of* 4 2·75 2·25

178 Pharmacist at Work

179 "Production"

(Des C. Abbott. Litho Questa)

1982 (12 Feb). *Commonwealth Pharmaceutical Conference.* T **178** *and similar vert designs.* W w **14**. P 14½ × 14.

600 10 c. Type **178** 10 10
601 $1 Gerritoute (plant) .. .. 1·25 1·25
602 $2 Rachette (plant) .. .. 2·00 2·25
600/2 .. .. *Set of* 3 3·00 3·25

(Des Debbie Galt; adapted G. Vasarhelyi. Litho Questa)

1982 (28 June). *75th Anniv of Boy Scout Movement.* T **179** *and similar vert designs. Multicoloured.* W w **14**. P 14.

603 15 c. Type **179** 45 10
604 55 c. "Tolerance" 90 25
605 $5 "Discipline" .. .. 4·50 3·75
603/5 .. .. *Set of* 3 5·25 3·75

MINIMUM PRICE

The minimum price quote is 10p which represents a handling charge rather than a basis for valuing common stamps. For further notes about prices see introductory pages.

180 Charlotteville

181 "Pa Pa Bois"

(Des Harrison. Litho Format)

1982 (18 Oct). *25th Anniv of Tourist Board. T* **180** *and similar vert designs. Multicoloured.* W w **14**. *P* 13½ × 14.

606 55 c. Type **180** 35 25
607 $1 Boating 55 55
608 $3 Fort George . . . . 1·75 1·90
606/8 . . . . *Set of* 3 2·40 2·40

(Des D. Louison. Litho Harrison)

1982 (8 Nov). *Folklore. Local Spirits and Demons. T* **181** *and similar horiz designs. Multicoloured.* W w **14** (*sideways*). *P* 14.

609 10 c. Type **181** 10 10
610 15 c. "La Diablesse" 10 10
611 65 c. "Lugarhoo", "Phantom" and "Soucouyant" 35 30
612 $5 "Bois de Soleil", "Davens" and "Mamma de l'Eau" . . . . 2·50 3·25
609/12 . . . . *Set of* 4 2·75 3·25
MS613 133 × 100 mm. Nos. 609/12 . . . . 3·50 4·00

182 Cane Harvesting

((Des W. Fenton. Litho Harrison)

1982 (13 Dec). *Canefarmers' Association Centenary. T* **182** *and similar horiz designs. Multicoloured.* W w **14** (*sideways*). *P* 14.

614 30 c. Type **182** 15 15
615 70 c. Farmers loading bullock cart 40 40
616 $1.50, Cane field in bloom 85 95
614/16 . . . . *Set of* 3 1·25 1·40
MS617 72 × 117 mm. Nos. 614/16. P 14½. . . 1·40 1·50

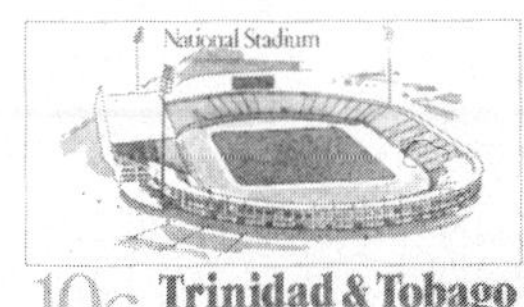

183 National Stadium

(Des McCombie Skinner. Litho Harrison)

1982 (28 Dec). *20th Anniv of Independence. T* **183** *and similar horiz designs. Multicoloured.* W w **14** (*sideways*). *P* 13 × 14.

618 10 c. Type **183** 10 10
619 35 c. Caroni water treatment plant 20 15
620 50 c. Mount Hope Maternity Hospital 30 25
621 $2 National Insurance Board Mall, Tobago 80 1·25
618/21 . . . . *Set of* 4 1·25 1·50

184 Commonwealth Flags

(Des C. Abbott. Litho Harrison)

1983 (14 Mar). *Commonwealth Day. T* **184** *and similar multi-coloured designs.* W w **14** (*sideways on* 10, 55 *c.*). *P* 14.

622 10 c. Type **184** 10 10
623 55 c. Satellite view of Trinidad and Tobago . . 25 20
624 $1 "Nodding donkey" oil pump (*vert*) . . 40 50
625 $2 Map of Trinidad and Tobago (*vert*) . . 85 1·00
622/5 . . . . *Set of* 4 1·40 1·60

185 BW1A "Tristar"

(Des D. Miller. Litho Format)

1983 (11 July). *10th Anniv of CARICOM.* W w **14** (*sideways*). *P* 14.

626 **185** 35 c. multicoloured 80 60

186 V.D.U. Operator

(Des G. Vasarhelyi. Litho Harrison)

1983 (5 Aug). *World Communications Year. T* **186** *and similar horiz designs. Multicoloured.* W w **14** (*sideways*). *P* 14.

627 15 c. Type **186** 15 10
628 55 c. Scarborough Post Office, Tobago . . 60 20
629 $1 Textel building 95 60
630 $3 Morne Blue E.C.M.S. station . . . . 2·40 1·90
627/30 . . . . *Set of* 4 3·75 2·50

187 Financial Complex

(Des D. Miller. Litho Format)

1983 (19 Sept). *Conference of Commonwealth Finance Ministers.* W w **14** (*sideways*). *P* 14.

631 **187** $2 multicoloured . . . . . . 1·50 1·00

188 Kingfish

189 Bois Pois

(Des N. Weaver. Litho Format)

1983 (17 Oct). *World Food Day. T* **188** *and similar horiz designs. Multicoloured.* W w **14** (*sideways*). *P* 14 × 13½ (10 *c.*, 55 *c.*) *or* 13½ (*others*).

632 10 c. Type **188** 20 10
633 55 c. Flying Fish . . . . 1·00 40
634 70 c. Queen Conch . . . . 1·25 1·00
635 $4 Red Shrimp . . . . 4·50 6·00
632/5 . . . . *Set of* 4 6·25 6·75

(Des I. Loe. Litho Questa)

1983 (14 Dec)–**84**. *Flowers. T* **189** *and similar multicoloured designs.* W w **14** (*sideways on* 5 *c. to* $1.50). *P* 14. *A. Without imprint date. B. With imprint date* (10.84).

		A		B	
636	5 c. Type **189**	30	15	45	30
637	10 c. Maraval Lily	30	15	40	20
638	15 c. Star Grass	35	15	20	20
639	20 c. Bois Caco	10	10	†	
640	25 c. Strangling Fig	35	35	45	45
641	30 c. *Cassia moschata*	30	15	†	
642	50 c. Chalice Flower	15	15	†	
643	65 c. Black Stick	40	25	†	
644	80 c. *Columnea scandens*	50	35	†	
645	95 c. Cat's Claw	65	40	†	
646	$1 Bois L'agli	75	40	†	
647	$1.50, *Eustoma exaltatum*	1·00	75	†	
648	$2 Chaconia	1·25	1·00	†	
649	$2.50, *Chrysothemis pulchella*	75	1·00	†	
650	$5 *Centratherum punctatum*	3·00	3·50	†	
651	$10 Savanna Flower	4·25	5·50	†	
636A/51A	*Set of* 16	13·00	13·00	†	
636B/40B	*Set of* 4			1·40	1·10

Nos. 648/51 are horizontal, 39 × 29 mm.
No. 637B exists with different imprint dates at foot.
For these designs watermarked w **16** see Nos. 686/701.

190 Castle Chess Pieces in Staunton and 17th-century Styles

191 Swimming

(Des L. Curtis. Litho Questa)

1984 (14 Sept). *60th Anniv of World Chess Federation. T* **190** *and similar vert designs. Multicoloured.* W w **14**. *P* 14.

652 50 c. Type **190** . . . . 1·50 35
653 70 c. Staunton and 12th-century Bishops . . 1·75 75
654 $1.50, Staunton and 13th-century Queens . . 2·50 2·50
655 $2 Staunton and 19th-century Kings . . 3·00 3·50
652/5 . . . . *Set of* 4 8·00 6·50

(Des Garden Studio. Litho Harrison)

1984 (21 Sept). *Olympic Games, Los Angeles. T* **191** *and similar vert designs. Multicoloured.* W w **14**. *P* 14 × 14½.

656 15 c. Type **191** 10 10
657 55 c. Track and field events 30 20
658 $1.50, Sailing 70 80
659 $4 Cycling . . . . 2·00 2·50
656/9 . . . . *Set of* 4 2·75 3·25
MS660 132 × 85 mm. Nos. 656/9 . . . . . . 4·00 6·00

192 Slave Schooner and Shackles

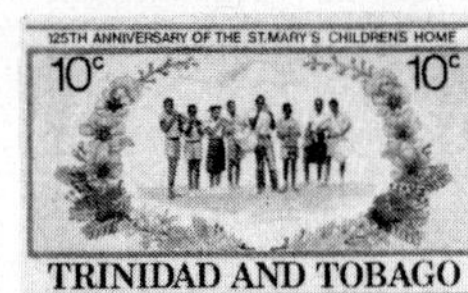

193 Children's Band

(Des O. Bell. Litho Walsall)

1984 (22 Oct). *150th Anniv of Abolition of Slavery. T* **192** *and similar vert designs. Multicoloured.* W w **14**. *P* 13½ × 13.

661 35 c. Type **192** 75 20
662 55 c. Slave and "Slave Triangle" map . . . . 1·00 30
663 $1 *Capitalism and Slavery* (book by Dr. Eric Williams) . . . . 1·75 75
664 $2 Toussaint l'Ouverture (Haitian revolutionary) . . . . 2·25 1·90
661/4 . . . . *Set of* 4 5·25 2·75
MS665 95 × 100 mm. Nos. 661/4 . . . . . . 5·25 5·75

(Des G. Vasarhelyi. Litho J.W.)

1984 (13 Nov). *125th Anniv of St. Mary's Children's Home. T* **193** *and similar horiz designs. Multicoloured.* W w **14** (*sideways*). *P* 13½.

666 10 c. Type **193** 10 10
667 70 c. St. Mary's Children's Home 40 40
668 $3 Group of children . . . . 2·00 2·25
666/8 . . . . *Set of* 3 2·25 2·40

194 Parang Band

195 Capt. A. A. Cipriani and T. U. B. Butler

(Des D. Miller. Litho Questa)

1984 (26 Nov). *Parang Festival. T* **194** *and similar horiz designs. Multicoloured.* W w **14** (*sideways*). *P* 14 × 14½.

669 10 c. Type **194** 10 10
670 30 c. Music and poinsettia 20 15
671 $1 Bandola, bandolin and cuatro (musical instruments) 70 65
672 $3 Double bass, fiddle and guitar (musical instruments) . . . . 2·00 2·00
669/72 . . . . *Set of* 4 2·75 2·50

(Des G. Vasarhelyi. Litho Questa)

1985 (17 June). *Labour Day. Labour Leaders. T* **195** *and similar horiz designs.* W w **14**. *P* 14.

673 55 c. black and bright rose 45 45
674 55 c. black and orange-yellow 45 45
675 55 c. black and emerald 45 45
673/5 . . . . *Set of* 3 1·25 1·25

Designs:—No. 674, C. P. Alexander and Q. O'Connor; 675, A. Cola Rienzi and C. T. W. E. Worrell.

196 *Lady Nelson* (1928)

(Des E. Nisbet. Litho Format)

1985 (20 Aug). *Ships. T* **196** *and similar horiz designs. Multicoloured.* W w **14**. *P* 14½ × 14.

676 30 c. Type **196** 70 15
677 95 c. *Lady Drake* (1928) . . . . . . 1·25 50
678 $1.50, *Federal Palm* (1961) . . . . . . 1·75 2·00
679 $2 *Federal Maple* (1961) . . . . . . 2·25 2·50
676/9 . . . . *Set of* 4 5·50 4·75

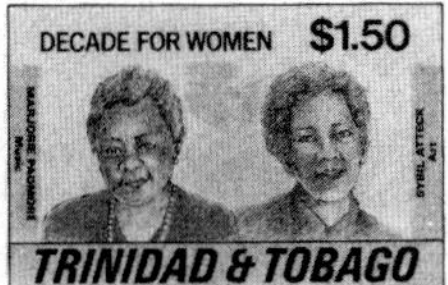

197 Marjorie Padmore (music) and Sybil Atteck (art)

(Des Julijana Zappin. Litho Walsall)

1985 (11 Nov). *Decade for Women (2nd issue). T* **197** *and similar horiz designs. Multicoloured. W* w **16** *(sideways). P* 14.

680 $1.50, Type **197** .. .. 90 1·00
681 $1.50, May Cherrie (medical social worker) and Evelyn Tracey (social worker) .. 90 1·00
682 $1.50, Umilta McShine (education) and Jessica Smith-Phillips (public service) .. 90 1·00
680/2 .. .. *Set of* 3 2·50 2·75

198 Badge of Trinidad and Tobago Cadet Force (75th Anniv) **199** Anne-Marie Javouhey (foundress)

(Des D. Slater. Litho Harrison)

1985 (9 Dec). *International Youth Year. T* **198** *and similar horiz designs. Multicoloured. W* w **16** *(sideways). P* 14 × 14½.

683 10 c. Type **198**.. .. .. 15 10
684 65 c. Guide badges (75th anniv of Girl Guide movement) 65 75
685 95 c. Young people of Trinidad .. .. 90 1·00
683/5 .. .. *Set of* 3 1·50 1·60

1985 (Dec)–**89**. *As Nos.* 636/7, 639/41 *and* 643/51, *but W* w **16** *(sideways on* 5, 10, 20, 25, 30, 65, 80, 95 *c.,* $1, $1.50). *With imprint date. P* 14.

686 5 c. Type **189** 15 10
687 10 c. Maraval Lily (4.8.86) 15 10
689 20 c. Bois Caco (8.88) 40 30
690 25 c. Strangling Fig (8.88) 40 30
691 30 c. *Cassia moschata* (5.87) 40 30
693 65 c. Black Stick (5.87) 45 45
694 80 c. *Columnea scandens* (5.87) 55 55
695 95 c. Cat's Claw 40 40
696 $1 Bois L'agli 45 30
697 $1.50, *Eustoma exaltatum* (5.87) .. 75 75
698 $2 Chaconia (39×29 *mm*) (5.87) .. 95 95
699 $2.50, *Chrysothemis pulchella* (39×29 *mm*) (5.89) .. .. .. 1·25 1·25
700 $5 *Centratherum punctatum* (39×29 *mm*) 1·50 1·50
701 $10 Savanna Flower (39×29 *mm*) .. 2·75 3·00
686/701 .. .. *Set of* 14 9·50 9·25

Nos. 687, 689/91, 693/8 and 700/1 exist with different imprint dates at foot.

(Des Joan Thompson. Litho Format)

1986 (19 Mar). *150th Anniv of Arrival of Sisters of St. Joseph de Cluny. T* **199** *and similar vert designs. Multicoloured. W* w **16** *(sideways). P* 14×14½.

702 10 c. Type **199** 10 10
703 65 c. St. Joseph's Convent, Port-of-Spain .. 35 50
704 95 c. Children and statue of Anne-Marie Javouhey 45 75
702/4 .. .. *Set of* 3 80 1·25

200 Tank Locomotive *Arima* **201** Scout Camp

(Des J.W. Litho Format)

1986 (26 May). *"Ameripex '86" International Stamp Exhibition, Chicago. Trinidad Railway Locomotives. T* **200** *and similar horiz designs. W* w **16**. *P* 14½×14.

705 65 c. Type **200**.. .. .. 25 30
706 95 c. Canadian-built locomotive No. 22 .. 35 40
707 $1.10, Tender engine 40 65
708 $1.50, Saddle tank.. .. .. .. 60 90
705/8 .. .. *Set of* 4 1·40 2·00
MS709 105×80 mm. Nos. 705/8 .. .. .. 1·75 2·50

(Des N. Shewring. Litho Questa)

1986 (21 July). *75th Anniv of Trinidad and Tobago Boy Scouts. T* **201** *and similar horiz design. Multicoloured. W* w **16** *(sideways). P* 14.

710 $1.70, Type **201** .. .. 1·00 1·25
711 $2 Scouts of 1911 and 1986 .. .. .. 1·25 1·50

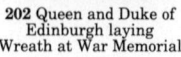

202 Queen and Duke of Edinburgh laying Wreath at War Memorial **203** Eric Williams at Graduation, 1935

(Des C. Abbott. Litho Walsall)

1986 (16 Sept). *60th Birthday of Queen Elizabeth II. T* **202** *and similar vert designs. Multicoloured. W* w **16**. *P* 14½×14.

712 10 c. Type **202**.. .. .. .. 10 10
713 15 c. Queen with Trinidadian dignitaries aboard *Britannia* 20 10
714 30 c. With President Ellis Clarke 30 15
715 $5 Receiving bouquet .. .. .. 2·50 3·00
712/15 .. .. *Set of* 4 2·75 3·00

(Des D. Miller. Litho Format)

1986 (25 Sept). *75th Birth Anniv of Dr. Eric Williams. T* **203** *and similar multicoloured designs. W* w **14** *(sideways on* 95 *c.,* $5). *P* 14.

716 10 c. Type **203**.. .. .. 15 10
717 30 c. Premier Eric Williams (wearing red tie) 30 15
718 30 c. As No. 717, but wearing black and orange tie 30 15
719 95 c. Arms of University of West Indies and Dr. Williams as Pro-Chancellor (*horiz*) 60 40
720 $5 Prime Minister Williams and Whitehall (*horiz*) .. .. 2·00 2·00
716/20 .. .. *Set of* 5 3·00 2·50
MS721 105×100 mm. Nos. 716/17 and 719/20. Wmk sideways .. .. 4·50 4·50

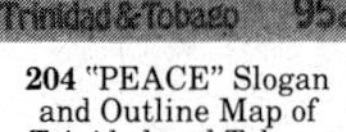

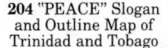

204 "PEACE" Slogan and Outline Map of Trinidad and Tobago **205** Miss Giselle La Ronde and BWIA Airliner

(Adapted L. Curtis. Litho Questa)

1986 (3 Nov). *International Peace Year. T* **204** *and similar horiz design. Multicoloured. W* w **16** *(sideways). P* 14.

722 95 c. Type **204**.. .. .. 40 50
723 $3 Peace dove with olive branch .. .. 1·25 1·75

(Des D. Miller. Litho Walsall)

1987 (27 July). *Miss World* 1986. *T* **205** *and similar vert designs. Multicoloured. W* w **16**. *P* 14.

724 10 c. Type **205**.. .. .. 20 10
725 30 c. In swimsuit on beach 45 15
726 95 c. Miss Giselle La Ronde 80 65
727 $1.65, Wearing Miss World sash .. .. 1·25 1·50
724/7 .. .. *Set of* 4 2·40 2·25

206 Colonial Bank, Port of Spain **207** Sergeant in Parade Order and Soldiers in Work Dress and Battle Dress

(Des J.W. Litho Walsall)

1987 (21 Dec). *150th Anniv of Republic Bank. T* **206** *and similar horiz designs. Multicoloured. W* w **14** *(sideways). P* 14.

728 10 c. Type **206**.. .. .. 10 10
729 65 c. Cocoa plantation 40 40
730 95 c. Oil field 75 75
731 $1.10, Belmont Tramway Company tramcar .. .. 1·00 1·00
728/31 .. .. *Set of* 4 2·00 2·00

(Des C. Abbott. Litho Questa)

1988 (29 Feb). *25th Anniv of Defence Force. T* **207** *and similar vert designs. Multicoloured. W* w **16** *(sideways). P* 14.

732 10 c. Type **207**.. .. .. 20 10
733 30 c. Women soldiers.. .. .. .. 60 20
734 $1.10, Defence Force officers .. .. 1·25 1·00
735 $1.50, Naval ratings and patrol boat .. 1·50 1·25
732/5 .. .. *Set of* 4 3·25 2·25

(Des D. Hartley and L. Curtis. Litho Walsall)

1988 (6 June). *West Indian Cricket. Horiz designs as T* **243a** *of Jamaica, each showing portrait, cricket equipment and early belt buckle. Multicoloured. W* w **14** *(sideways). P* 14.

736 30 c. George John 55 20
737 65 c. Learie Constantine 85 55
738 95 c. Sonny Ramadhin .. .. .. 1·00 85
739 $1.50, Gerry Gomez .. .. .. 1·75 1·75
740 $2.50, Jeffrey Stollmeyer .. .. .. 2·00 2·50
736/40 .. .. *Set of* 5 5·50 5·25

208 Uriah Butler (labour leader) **209** Mary Werges and Santa Rosa Church

(Des G. Vasarhelyi. Litho Walsall)

1988 (11 July). *50th Anniv of Oilfield Workers Trade Union* (1987). *T* **208** *and similar vert designs. Multicoloured. W* w **16**. *P* 14½ × 14.

741 10 c. Type **208** 10 10
742 30 c. Adrian Rienzi (O.W.T.U. president, 1937-42) 10 10
743 65 c. John Rojas (O.W.T.U. president, 1943-62) 15 20
744 $5 George Weekes (O.W.T.U. president, 1962-87) .. .. 1·25 1·40
741/4 .. .. *Set of* 4 1·40 1·60

(Des O. Bell. Litho Walsall)

1988 (22 Aug). *Centenary of Borough of Arima. T* **209** *and similar horiz designs. Multicoloured. W* w **16** *(sideways). P* 14 × 14½.

745 20 c. Type **209** 10 10
746 30 c. Governor W. Robinson and Royal Charter 10 10
747 $1.10, Arrival of Governor Robinson .. 45 45
748 $1.50, Mayor J. F. Wallen and Centenary logo 65 65
745/8 .. .. *Set of* 4 1·10 1·10

(Des D. Miller (30 c.), S. Noon and D. Miller (others). Litho Questa)

1988 (21 Nov). *300th Anniv of Lloyd's of London. Multicoloured designs as T* **167a** *of Malawi. W* w **16** *(sideways on* $1.10, $1.55). *P* 14.

749 30 c. Queen Mother at Topping-out Ceremony of new building, 1984 .. .. 15 10
750 $1.10, BWIA Tristar "500" airliner (*horiz*) 60 35
751 $1.55, Steel works, Trinidad (*horiz*) .. 75 45
752 $2 *Atlantic Empress* on fire off Tobago, 1979 .. .. 90 55
749/52 .. .. *Set of* 4 2·25 1·25

210 Colonial Arms of Trinidad & Tobago and 1913 1d. Stamp

(Des W. Carr, adapted D. Miller. Litho Questa)

1989 (20 Mar). *Centenary of Union of Trinidad and Tobago. T* **210** *and similar horiz designs. Multicoloured. W* w **16** *(sideways). P* 14½.

753 40 c. Type **210** 15 10
754 $1 Pre-1889 Tobago emblem and Tobago 1896 ½d. on 4d. stamp 50 30
755 $1.50, Pre-1889 Trinidad emblem and Trinidad 1883 4d. stamp 70 55
756 $2.25, Current Arms of Trinidad and Tobago and 1977 45 c. Republic stamp 95 85
753/6 .. .. *Set of* 4 2·10 1·60

211 Common Piping Guan **212** Blind Welfare (75th Anniversary)

(Des Doreen McGuinness. Litho Walsall)

1989 (31 July). *Rare Fauna of Trinidad and Tobago. T* **211** *and similar horiz designs. Multicoloured. W* w **14** *(sideways). P* 14×14½.

757 $1 Type **211** 90 90
a. Vert strip of 5. Nos. 757/61 .. .. 4·00
758 $1 *Phyllodytes auratus* (frog) 90 90
759 $1 *Cebus albifrons trinitatis* (monkey) .. 90 90
760 $1 Tamandua 90 90
761 $1 *Lutra longicaudis* (otter) 90 90
757/61 .. .. *Set of* 5 4·00 4·00

Nos. 757/61 were printed together, *se-tenant*, in vertical strips of 5 throughout the sheet, forming a composite background design.

(Des S. Noon. Litho Walsall)

1989 (2 Oct). *Anniversaries. T* **212** *and similar vert designs. Multicoloured. W* w **14**. *P* 14½×14.

762 10 c. Type **212** 10 10
763 40 c. Port-of-Spain City Hall (75th anniv) .. 25 15
764 $1 Guides and Brownies (75th anniv) .. 75 40
765 $2.25, Red Cross members (50th anniv) .. 1·50 1·40
762/5 .. .. *Set of* 4 2·40 1·75

213 Tenor Pan

214 *Xeromphalina tenuipes*

(Des T. Mussio, adapted D. Miller. Litho Questa)

1989 (30 Nov). *Steel Pans* (1*st series*). *T* **213** *and similar vert designs. Multicoloured. W* w **16**. *P* 14½×14.

766 10 c. Type **213** 10 10
767 40 c. Guitar pans 15 15
768 $1 Cello pans 45 45
769 $2.25, Bass pans 85 85
766/9 .. .. *Set of* 4 1·40 1·40

(Des McCombie Skinner. Litho Questa)

1990 (3 May). *"Stamp World London 90" International Stamp Exhibition, London. Fungi. T* **214** *and similar horiz designs. Multicoloured. W* w **16** (*sideways*). *P* 14×13½.

770 10 c. Type **214** 10 10
771 40 c. *Dictyophora indusiata* 20 20
772 $1 *Leucocoprinus birnbaumii* 70 50
773 $2.25, *Crinipellis perniciosa* .. .. 1·50 1·75
770/3 .. .. *Set of* 4 2·25 2·25

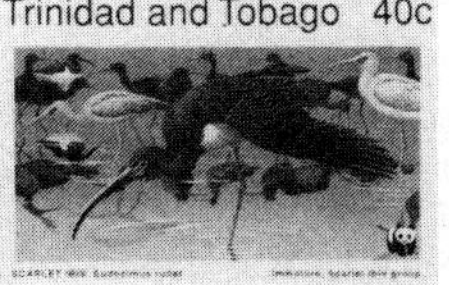

215 Scarlet Ibis in Immature Plumage

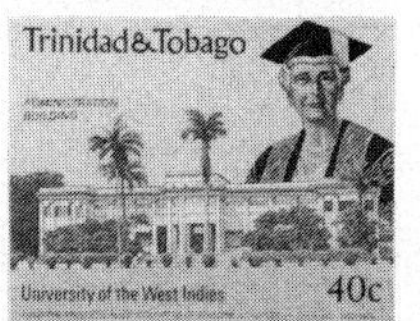

216 Princess Alice and Administration Building

(Litho Questa)

1990 (7 Sept). *Scarlet Ibis. T* **215** *and similar horiz designs. Multicoloured. W* w **16** (*sideways*). *P* 14.

774 40 c. Type **215** 30 20
775 80 c. Pair in pre-nuptial display 55 50
776 $1 Male in breeding plumage 55 55
777 $2.25, Adult on nest with chick .. .. 1·60 1·75
774/7 .. .. *Set of* 4 2·75 2·75

(Des L. Curtis. Litho B.D.T.)

1990 (15 Oct). *40th Anniv of University of West Indies. T* **216** *and similar horiz designs. Multicoloured. W* w **14** (*sideways*). *P* 13½×14.

778 40 c. Type **216** 20 15
779 80 c. Sir Hugh Wooding and Library 35 30
780 $1 Sir Allen Lewis and Faculty of Engineering 45 35
781 $2.25, Sir Shridath Ramphal and Faculty of Medical Sciences .. .. .. 1·00 1·25
778/81 .. .. *Set of* 4 1·75 1·90

217 Lockheed Lodestar

218 Yellow Oriole

(Des E. Nisbet. Litho B.D.T)

1990 (27 Nov). *50th Anniv of British West Indies Airways. T* **217** *and similar horiz designs. Multicoloured. W* w **14** (*sideways*). *P* 14.

782 40 c. Type **217** 20 15
783 80 c. Vickers Viking 1A 35 30
784 $1 Vickers Viscount 702 .. .. .. 45 30
785 $2.25, Boeing 707 .. .. 1·00 1·25
782/5 .. .. *Set of* 4 1·75 1·75
MS786 77×52 mm. $5 Lockheed Tristar 500 .. 1·90 2·25

(Des D. Miller. Litho Questa)

1990 (17 Dec). *Birds. T* **218** *and similar vert designs. Multicoloured. W* w **16** (*sideways*). *P* 14.

787 20 c. Type **218** 10 10
788 25 c. Green-rumped Parrotlet 10 10
789 40 c. Fork-tailed Flycatcher 10 15
790 50 c. Copper-rumped Hummingbird 15 20
791 $1 Bananaquit 30 35
792 $2 Violaceous Euphonia 55 60
793 $2.25, Channel-billed Toucan 65 70
794 $2.50, Bay-headed Tanager 70 75
795 $5 Green Honeycreeper .. .. 1·40 1·50
796 $10 Cattle Egret .. .. 2·75 3·00
797 $20 Golden Olive Woodpecker .. .. .. 5·50 5·75
798 $50 Peregrine Falcon .. .. 14·00 14·50
787/98 .. .. *Set of* 12 22·00 23·00

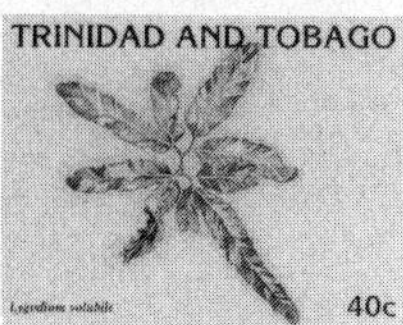

219 *Lygodium volubile*

(Des T. Musio. Litho B.D.T)

1991 (1 July). *Ferns. T* **219** *and similar horiz designs. Multicoloured. W* w **14** (*sideways*). *P* 13½×14.

799 40 c. Type **219** 20 15
800 80 c. *Blechnum occidentale* 35 30
801 $1 *Gleichenia bifida* 45 35
802 $2.25, *Polypodium lycopodioides* .. .. 1·25 1·40
799/802 .. .. *Set of* 4 2·00 2·00

220 Trinidad and Tobago Regiment Anti-aircraft Battery

(Des A. Theobald. Litho Questa)

1991 (7 Dec). *50th Anniv of Second World War. T* **220** *and similar horiz designs. Multicoloured. W* w **16** (*sideways*). *P* 13½×14.

803 40 c. Type **220** 15 10
804 80 c. Fairey Barracuda attacking U-boat .. 30 30
805 $1 Avro Lancaster 40 35
806 $2.25, River class frigate escorting convoy 90 1·00
803/06 .. .. *Set of* 4 1·60 1·60
MS807 117×85 mm. $2.50, Presentation Spitfire; $2.50, Presentation Wellington bomber 1·75 2·00

POSTAGE DUE STAMPS

D 1

D 2

(Typo D.L.R.)

1885 (1 Jan). *Wmk Crown CA. P* 14.

D1 D 1 ½d. slate-black .. .. 22·00 35·00
D2 1d. slate-black .. .. 1·60 15
D3 2d. slate-black .. .. 12·00 15
D4 3d. slate-black .. .. 29·00 40
D5 4d. slate-black .. .. 18·00 3·75
D6 5d. slate-black .. .. 18·00 60
D7 6d. slate-black .. .. 29·00 5·00
D8 8d. slate-black .. .. 32·00 3·75
D9 1s. slate-black .. .. 38·00 7·00
D1/9 .. .. *Set of* 9 £180 48·00

1905–6. *Wmk Mult Crown CA. P* 14.

D10 D 1 1d. slate-black .. .. 1·50 15
D11 2d. slate-black .. .. 4·75 15
D12 3d. slate-black .. .. 2·75 75
D13 4d. slate-black .. .. 7·00 7·00
D14 5d. slate-black .. .. 6·50 8·50
D15 6d. slate-black .. .. 6·00 9·50
D16 8d. slate-black .. .. 12·00 14·00
D17 1s. slate-black .. .. 12·00 23·00
D10/17 .. .. *Set of* 8 48·00 55·00

1923–45. *Wmk Mult Script CA. P* 14.

D18 D 1 1d. black (1923) 30 80
D19 2d. black (1923) 30 75
D20 3d. black (1925) .. .. 30 1·25
D21 4d. black (1929) .. .. 1·50 7·00
D22 5d. black (1944) .. .. 22·00 38·00
D23 6d. black (1945) .. .. 26·00 16·00
D24 8d. black (1945) .. .. 32·00 65·00
D25 1s. black (1945) .. .. 50·00 70·00
D18/25 .. .. *Set of* 8 £120 £180
D18/25 Optd/Perf "Specimen" .. *Set of* 8 £140

1947 (1 Sept)–**61**. *Values in cents. Wmk Mult Script CA. Ordinary paper. P* 14.

D26 D 1 2 c. black .. .. 95 2·25
a. Chalk-surfaced paper (20.1.53) .. 20 1·50
ab. Error. Crown missing. W **9***a* .. 50·00
ac. Error. St. Edward's Crown. W **9***b* 22·00
D27 4 c. black .. .. 85 3·00
a. Chalk-surfaced paper (10.8.55) .. 65 2·75
D28 6 c. black .. .. 85 6·00
a. Chalk-surfaced paper (20.1.53) .. 25 3·75
ab. Error. Crown missing. W **9***a* .. £100
ac. Error. St. Edward's Crown. W **9***b* 48·00
D29 8 c. black .. .. 90 13·00
a. Chalk-surfaced paper (10.9.58) .. 35 5·50
D30 10 c. black .. .. 85 2·75
a. Chalk-surfaced paper (10.8.55) .. 1·00 4·50
D31 12 c. black .. .. 90 9·00
a. Chalk-surfaced paper (20.1.53) .. 40 6·00
ab. Error. Crown missing. W **9***a* .. £140
ac. Error. St. Edward's Crown. W **9***b* 75·00
D32 16 c. black .. .. 2·00 18·00
a. Chalk-surfaced paper (22.8.61) .. 3·50 18·00
D33 24 c. black .. .. 3·75 7·50
a. Chalk-surfaced paper (10.8.55) .. 2·75 16·00
D26/33 .. .. *Set of* 8 9·75 55·00
D26/33a .. .. *Set of* 8 8·00 50·00
D26/33 Perf "Specimen" .. .. *Set of* 8 £140

(Litho B.W.)

1969 (25 Nov)–**70**. *Size* 19 × 24 *mm. P* 14 × 13½.

D34 D 2 2 c. pale blue-green .. .. .. 15 1·75
D35 4 c. magenta (1970) .. .. .. 25 2·50
D36 6 c. brown (1970) .. .. .. 50 3·50
D37 8 c. slate-lilac (1970) .. .. .. 65 4·00
D38 10 c. dull red (1970) .. .. .. 65 4·00
D39 12 c. pale orange (1970) .. .. .. 70 4·50
D40 16 c. bright apple-green (1970) .. .. 15 1·50
D41 24 c. grey (1970) .. .. 20 1·75
D42 50 c. grey-blue (1970) .. .. .. 35 2·25
D43 60 c. sage-green (1970) .. .. .. 45 2·25
D34/43 .. .. *Set of* 10 3·50 25·00

(Litho Questa)

1976 (3 May)*–**77**. *Redrawn in smaller size* (17 × 21 *mm*). *P* 13½ × 14.

D44 D 2 2 c. pale blue-green (31.3.77) 10 65
D45 4 c. light claret 10 65
D46 6 c. brown (31.3.77) 15 75
D47 8 c. bright lilac (31.3.77) 15 75
D48 10 c. dull red (31.3.77) 15 75
D49 12 c. pale orange .. .. 20 1·00
D44/9 .. .. *Set of* 6 75 4·00

*The date for the 4 and 12 c. is the local date; the Crown Agents released the stamps on 19 March.

"TOO LATE" STAMPS

A handstamp with the words "TOO LATE" was used upon letters on which a too-late fee had been paid, and was sometimes used for cancelling the stamps on such letters.

OFFICIAL STAMPS

O S (O 1) OFFICIAL (O 2) OFFICIAL (O 3)

1894. *Optd with Type* O 1 (*a*) *Wmk Crown CA. P* 14.

O1 10 ½d. dull green .. .. 28·00 42·00
O2 1d. carmine .. .. 32·00 45·00
O3 2½d. ultramarine .. .. 40·00 65·00
O4 4d. grey .. .. 40·00 70·00
O5 6d. olive-black .. .. 40·00 70·00
O6 1s. orange-brown .. .. 50·00 85·00

(*b*) *Wmk Crown CC. P* 12½.

O7 5 5s. rose-lake £110 £190

1909. *Optd with Type* O **2**. *Wmk Mult Crown CA. P* 14.

O8 11 ½d. green .. .. 30 2·50
O9 1d. rose-red .. .. 30 2·50
a. Opt double .. .. — £200
b. Opt vertical .. .. 45·00
c. Opt inverted .. .. — £150

1910. *Optd with Type* O **2**. *Wmk Mult Crown CA. P* 14.

O10 14 ½d. green .. .. 1·00 1·75

1913. *Optd with Type* O **3**.

O11 17 ½d. green .. .. 30 1·25
a. Opt vertical .. ..

OFFICIAL (O 4) OFFICIAL (O 5) OFFICIAL (O 6)

1914. *Optd with Type* O **4**.

O12 17 ½d. green .. .. 1·10 4·00

1914–17. *Optd with Type* O **5** (*without stop*).

O13 17 ½d. green .. .. 75 5·00
a. Blue-green (*thick paper*) (1917) .. 40 4·00

1916. *Optd with Type* O **5** (*with stop*).

O14 17 ½d. yellow-green 30 50
a. Opt double .. .. 20·00

1917 (22 Aug). *Optd with Type* O **6**.

O15 17 ½d. green .. .. 85 5·50
a. Yellow-green .. .. 1·25 7·50
b. Blue-green (*thick paper*) .. .. 30 5·50

Tristan Da Cunha

Although first settled in 1817 no surviving mail is known from Tristan da Cunha until two whaler's letters written in 1836 and 1843, these being carried home in other whaling ships. Then there is a long gap until the late 1800's when other letters are known—surprisingly only some seven in number, up to 1908 when the first of the island cachet handstamps came into use.

The collecting of postal history material from 1908 to 1952, when Tristan's first stamps were issued, revolves around the numerous cachets of origin which were struck on mail from the island during these 44 years. The handstamps producing these cachets were supplied over the years by various people particularly interested in the island and the islanders, and were mostly used by the clergymen who volunteered to go and serve as the community's ministers.

The postal cachets are illustrated below. The use of the different cachets on mail frequently overlapped, at one period in 1930 there were five different types of handstamp in use. As there was no official source for providing them they appeared on the island from various donors; then disappeared without trace once they became worn out. Only one of these early rubber handstamps has apparently survived, Cachet Va.

Covers bearing the cachets are recognised collector's items, but are difficult to value in general terms. As elsewhere the value is discounted by poor condition of the cover, and may be increased by use on a scarce date or with additional postal markings.

Cachet Types V and VII on cover are the commonest, Type Va, used only for three months, and Type IVa are the scarcest, equalling the scarcest use of Type I examples. All cacheted covers, particularly if non-philatelic, are desirable forerunner items. Even a philatelic cover of Type V is, at present, worth in the region of £35.

Dates given are of the first recorded use.

Cachet I   Cachet II

Cat. No.			*Value on cover*
C1	**1908** (May).	Cachet I	*from* £4000
C2	**1919** (31 July).	Cachet II	*from* £400

Cachet III

C3	**1921** (8 Feb).	Cachet III	*from* £225

Cachet IVa

C4	**1927** (1 Oct).	Cachet IV (*as* IVa, *but without centre label*)	*from* £800
C5	**1928** (28 Oct).	Cachet IVa	*from* £5500

Cachet V   Cachet VI

C6	**1929** (24 Feb).	Cachet V	*from* 35·00
C7	**1929** (15 May).	Cachet Va (*as* V, *but without break in inner ring. Shows* "T" "C" *and* "N" *damaged*)	*from* £6500
C8	**1936** (Aug).	Cachet VI	*from* 55·00

Cachet VII

C9	**1936** (1 Feb).	Cachet VII	*from* 20·00

During World War II there was little mail from the island as its function as a meteorological station was cloaked by security. Such covers as are known are generally struck with the "tombstone" naval censor mark and postmarked "maritime mail" or have South African postal markings. A few philatelic items from early in the war bearing cachets exist, but this usage was soon stopped by the military commander and the handstamps were put away until peace returned. Covers from the period would be worth from £75 to, at least, £350.

Cachet VIII

C10	**1946** (8 May).	Cachet VIII	*from* 70·00

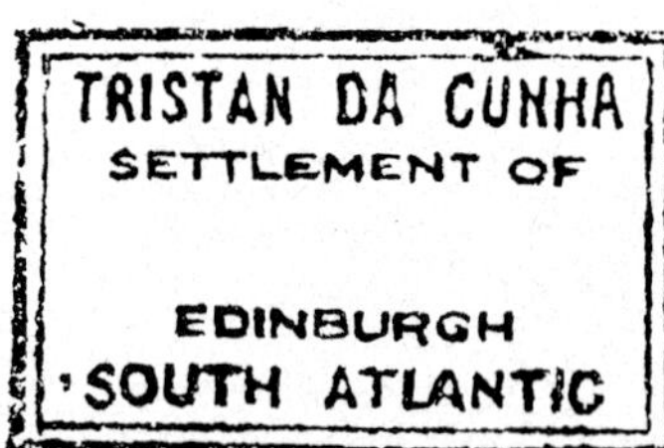

Cachet IX

C11	**1948** (29 Feb).	Cachet IX	*from* 45·00

Cachet X

C12	**1948** (6 Mar).	Cachet X	*from* 35·00

Cachet XI

Cachet XII

RESETTLEMENT
SURVEY - 1962

Cachet XIII

Cachets XI to XIII from the 1961/63 "volcano eruption" and "return to the island" period vary in value from £30 to £120, due to philatelic usage on the one hand and scarce mailings from the small survey parties on shore during this period on the other.

TRISTAN
DA CUNHA
(1)

1952 (1 Jan). *Stamps of St. Helena, optd with T* **1**.

1	**33** ½d. violet		15	85
2		1d. black and green	30	1·25
3		1½d. black and carmine	30	1·25
4		2d. black and scarlet	30	1·50
5		3d. grey	40	1·25
6		4d. ultramarine	1·25	2·00
7		6d. light blue	3·00	2·50
8		8d. sage-green	2·50	3·00
9		1s. sepia	2·75	2·00
10		2s. 6d. maroon	19·00	14·00
11		5s. chocolate	26·00	27·00
12		10s. purple	48·00	55·00
1/12		*Set of* 12	95·00	£100

1953 (2 June). *Coronation. As No.* 153 *of Jamaica.*

13	3d. black and grey-green	90	1·50

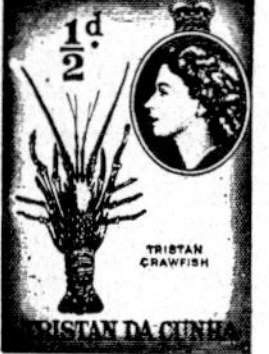

2 Tristan Crawfish   **3** Carting Flax for Thatching

(Recess D.L.R.)

1954 (2 Jan). *T* **2/3** *and similar designs. Wmk Mult Script CA. P* 12½ × 13 (*horiz*) *or* 13 × 12½ (*vert*).

14	½d. red and deep brown	10	10
15	1d. sepia and bluish green	10	15
16	1½d. black and reddish purple	2·50	30
17	2d. grey-violet and brown-orange	30	15
18	2½d. black and carmine-red	2·00	50
19	3d. ultramarine and olive-green	80	20
20	4d. turquoise-blue and deep blue	1·25	40
21	5d. emerald and black	1·25	40
22	6d. deep green and violet	1·25	45
23	9d. reddish violet and Venetian red	1·25	45
24	1s. deep yellow-green and sepia	1·25	45
25	2s. 6d. deep brown and light blue	26·00	10·00
26	5s. black and red-orange	48·00	16·00
27	10s. brown-orange and purple	32·00	20·00
14/27	*Set of* 14	£110	45·00

Designs: *Vert*—1½d. Rockhopper Penguin; 3d. Island longboat. *Horiz*—2d. Big Beach factory; 2½d. Yellow-nosed Albatross; 4d. Tristan from the south-west; 5d. Girls on donkeys; 6d. Inaccessible Island from Tristan; 9d. Nightingale Island; 1s. St. Mary's Church; 2s. 6d. Southern Elephant-Seal at Gough Island; 5s. Inaccessible Island Rail; 10s. Island spinning wheel.

16 Starfish   **17** Concha Fish

(Des Mr. and Mrs. G. F. Harris. Recess Waterlow)

1960 (1 Feb). *Marine Life. Vert designs as T* **16/17**. *W* w **12**. *P* 13.

28	½d. black and orange	15	30
29	1d. black and bright purple	15	15
30	1½d. black and light turquoise-blue	15	25
31	2d. black and bluish green	20	20
32	2½d. black and sepia	25	20
33	3d. black and brown-red	25	15
34	4d. black and yellow-olive	30	20
35	5d. black and orange-yellow	45	30
36	6d. black and blue	50	25
37	9d. black and rose-carmine	55	30
38	1s. black and light brown	75	25
39	2s. 6d. black and ultramarine	11·00	15·00
40	5s. black and light emerald	28·00	22·00
41	10s. black and violet	48·00	40·00
28/41	*Set of* 14	80·00	70·00

Designs:—1½d. Klip Fish; 2d. Heron Fish; 2½d. Swordfish; 3d. Tristan Crawfish; 4d. Soldier Fish; 5d. "Five Finger" Fish; 6d. Mackerel; 9d. Stumpnose Fish; 1s. Blue Fish; 2s. 6d. Snoek; 5s. Shark; 10s. Black Right Whale.

NEW INFORMATION

The editor is always interested to correspond with people who have new information that will improve or correct the Catalogue.

961 (15 Apr). *As Nos. 28/30 and 32/41 but values in South African decimal currency.*
2 ½ c. black and orange (as ½d.) 10 15
3 1 c. black and bright purple (as 1d.) .. 15 15
4 1½ c. black and light turquoise-blue (as 1½d.) 35 20
5 2 c. black and sepia (as 2½d.) 40 20
6 2½ c. black and brown-red (as 3d.) 50 20
7 3 c. black and yellow-olive (as 4d.) .. 65 20
8 4 c. black and orange-yellow (as 5d.) .. 80 20
9 5 c. black and blue (as 6d) 85 20
0 7½ c. black and rose-carmine (as 9d.) .. 90 20
1 10 c. black and light brown (as 1s.) .. 1·00 20
2 25 c. black and ultramarine (as 2s. 6d.) .. 6·00 11·00
3 50 c. black and light emerald (as 5s.) .. 28·00 22·00
4 1 r. black and violet (as 10s.) .. .. 48·00 42·00
2/54 .. .. *Set of* 13 80·00 70·00

Following a volcanic eruption the island was evacuated on 10 October 1961, but resettled in 1963.

TRISTAN DA CUNHA RESETTLEMENT 1963

(30)

963 (12 Apr). *Tristan Resettlement. As Nos. 176/88 of St. Helena, but Wmk Mult Script CA (sideways on 1d., 2d., 7d., 10d., 2s. 6d., 10s), optd with T* **30**.
5 1d. bright blue, dull violet, yellow & carmine 15 15
6 1½d. yellow, green, black and light drab .. 20 15
7 2d. scarlet and grey 25 15
8 3d. light blue, black, pink and deep blue .. 30 20
a. Black printed double* £350
9 4½d. yellow-green, green, brown and grey .. 50 30
0 6d. red, sepia and light yellow-olive.. .. 75 15
1 7d. red-brown, black and violet 50 20
2 10d. brown-purple and light blue 50 15
3 1s. greenish yellow, bluish green & brown .. 50 15
4 1s. 6d. grey, black and slate-blue .. .. 1·50 60
5 2s. 6d. red, pale yellow and turquoise .. 1·00 45
6 5s. yellow, brown and green.. .. .. 5·00 1·25
7 10s. orange-red, black and blue .. .. 6·50 1·25
5/67 .. .. *Set of* 13 15·00 4·50
*No. 58a shows the outline round the Queen's head printed double.

963 (1 Oct). *Freedom from Hunger. As No. 80 of Lesotho.*
8 1s. 6d. carmine 90 30

964 (1 Feb). *Red Cross Centenary. As Nos. 203/4 of Jamaica.*
9 3d. red and black 35 15
0 1s. 6d. red and blue 65 20

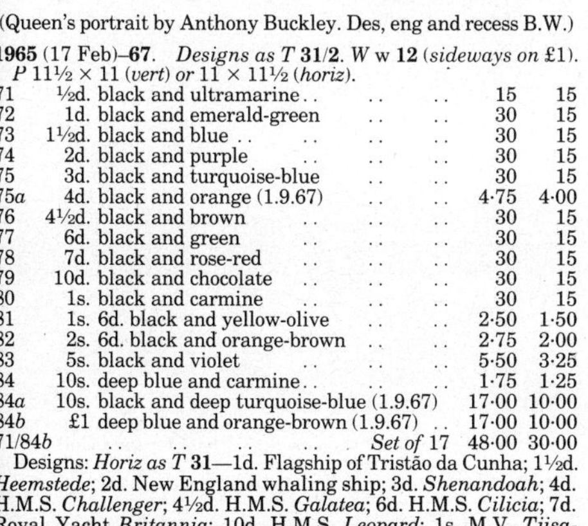

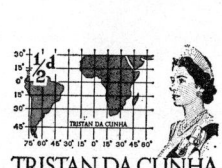

31 South Atlantic Map **32** Queen Elizabeth II

(Queen's portrait by Anthony Buckley. Des, eng and recess B.W.)

1965 (17 Feb)–**67**. *Designs as T* **31/2**. *W* w **12** (*sideways on* £1). *P* 11½ × 11 (*vert*) *or* 11 × 11½ (*horiz*).
1 ½d. black and ultramarine.. .. .. 15 15
2 1d. black and emerald-green 30 15
3 1½d. black and blue 30 15
4 2d. black and purple 30 15
5 3d. black and turquoise-blue 30 15
5*a* 4d. black and orange (1.9.67) .. .. 4·75 4·00
6 4½d. black and brown 30 15
7 6d. black and green 30 15
8 7d. black and rose-red 30 15
9 10d. black and chocolate 30 15
0 1s. black and carmine 30 15
1 1s. 6d. black and yellow-olive .. .. 2·50 1·50
2 2s. 6d. black and orange-brown .. .. 2·75 2·00
3 5s. black and violet .. .. .. 5·50 3·25
4 10s. deep blue and carmine.. .. .. 1·75 1·25
4*a* 10s. black and deep turquoise-blue (1.9.67) 17·00 10·00
4*b* £1 deep blue and orange-brown (1.9.67) .. 17·00 10·00
1/84*b* .. .. *Set of* 17 48·00 30·00
Designs: *Horiz as T* **31**—1d. Flagship of Tristão da Cunha; 1½d. *Heemstede*; 2d. New England whaling ship; 3d. *Shenandoah*; 4d. H.M.S. *Challenger*; 4½d. H.M.S. *Galatea*; 6d. H.M.S. *Cilicia*; 7d. Royal Yacht *Britannia*; 10d. H.M.S. *Leopard*; 1s. M.V. *Tjisadane*; 1s. 6d. M.V. *Tristania*; 2s. 6d. M.V. *Boissevain*; 5s. M.S. *Bornholm*; 10s. (No. 84*a*), Research Vessel *R.S.A. Vert*—10s. (No. 84), £1, Type **32**.

965 (11 May*). *I.T.U. Centenary. As Nos. 98/9 of Lesotho.*
5 3d. orange-red and grey 50 15
6 6d. reddish violet and yellow-orange .. 60 15
*This is the local date of issue; the stamps were not released in London until 17 May.

965 (25 Oct). *International Co-operation Year. As Nos. 100/1 of Lesotho.*
7 1d. reddish purple and turquoise-green .. 40 15
8 6d. deep bluish green and lavender .. .. 1·50 25

966 (24 Jan). *Churchill Commemoration. As Nos. 102/5 of Lesotho.*
9 1d. new blue 50 25
a. Value omitted £350
0 3d. deep green .. .. 2·50 40
1 6d. brown .. .. 3·50 45
2 1s. 6d. bluish violet .. .. 4·00 60
9/92 .. .. *Set of* 4 9·50 1·50
No. 89a was caused by misplacement of the gold and also shows the country inscription moved to the right.

45 H.M.S. *Falmouth* at Tristan and Soldier of 1816

(Des V. Whiteley. Litho Harrison)

1966 (15 Aug). *150th Anniv of Tristan Garrison. W* w **12** (*sideways*). *P* 14½.
93 **45** 3d. multicoloured 20 10
94 6d. multicoloured 20 10
95 1s. 6d. multicoloured 20 10
96 2s. 6d. multicoloured 30 10
93/6 .. .. *Set of* 4 80 35

1966 (1 Oct*). *World Cup Football Championships. As Nos. 57/8 of Pitcairn Islands.*
97 3d. violet, yellow-grn, lake & yell-brn .. 25 10
98 2s. 6d. chocolate, blue-grn, lake & yellow-brn 65 20
*Released in St. Helena on 1 July in error.

1966 (1 Oct). *Inauguration of W.H.O. Headquarters, Geneva. As Nos. 185/6 of Montserrat.*
99 6d. black, yellow-green and light blue .. 1·00 30
100 5s. black, light purple and yellow-brown .. 1·25 70

1966 (1 Dec). *20th Anniv of U.N.E.S.C.O. As Nos. 342/4 of Mauritius.*
101 10d. slate-violet, red, yellow and orange .. 60 15
102 1s. 6d. orange-yellow, violet and deep olive 65 15
103 2s. 6d. black, bright purple and orange .. 80 20
101/3 .. .. *Set of* 3 1·90 45

46 Calshot Harbour

(Des V. Whiteley. Litho D.L.R.)

1967 (2 Jan). *Opening of Calshot Harbour. P* 14 × 14½.
104 **46** 6d. multicoloured 10 10
105 10d. multicoloured 10 10
106 1s. 6d. multicoloured 10 10
107 2s. 6d. multicoloured 15 15
104/7 .. .. *Set of* 4 30 30

(47)

48 Prince Alfred, First Duke of Edinburgh

1967 (10 May). *No. 76 surch with T* **47**.
108 4d. on 4½d. black and brown 10 10

(Des M. Goaman. Litho Harrison)

1967 (10 July). *Centenary of First Duke of Edinburgh's Visit to Tristan. W* w **12**. *P* 14½.
109 **48** 3d. multicoloured 10 10
110 6d. multicoloured 10 10
111 1s. 6d. multicoloured 10 10
112 2s. 6d. multicoloured 15 10
109/12 .. .. *Set of* 4 30 20

49 Wandering Albatross

(Des V. Whiteley. Photo Harrison)

1968 (15 May). *Birds. T* **49** *and similar horiz designs. Multicoloured. W* w **12**. *P* 14 × 14½.
113 4d. Type **49** 40 10
114 1s. Wilkin's Finch 45 10
115 1s. 6d. Tristan Thrush 50 15
116 2s. 6d. Greater Shearwater 90 20
113/16 .. .. *Set of* 4 2·00 45

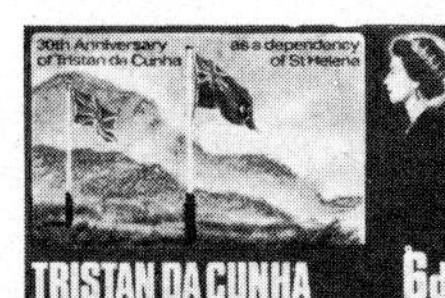

53 Union Jack and Dependency Flag

(Des Jennifer Toombs. Litho D.L.R.)

1968 (1 Nov). *30th Anniv of Tristan da Cunha as a Dependency of St. Helena. T* **53** *and similar horiz design. W* w **12** (*sideways*). *P* 14.
117 **53** 6d. multicoloured 10 10
118 – 9d. sepia, blue and turquoise-blue .. 10 10
119 **53** 1s. 6d. multicoloured 10 10
120 – 2s. 6d. carmine, blue and turquoise-blue 15 10
117/20 .. .. *Set of* 4 40 35
Design:—9d., 2s. 6d. St. Helena and Tristan on chart.

55 Frigate

(Des and recess B.W.)

1969 (1 June). *Clipper Ships. T* **55** *and similar horiz designs. W* w **12**. *P* 11 × 11½.
121 4d. new blue 40 10
122 1s. carmine (full-rigged ship) 40 15
123 1s. 6d. blue-green (barque) 45 20
124 2s. 6d. chocolate (full-rigged clipper) .. 50 25
121/4 .. .. *Set of* 4 1·60 60

59 Sailing Ship off Tristan da Cunha

(Des Jennifer Toombs. Litho Format)

1969 (1 Nov). *United Society for the Propagation of the Gospel. T* **59** *and similar horiz designs. Multicoloured. W* w **12** (*sideways*). *P* 14½ × 14.
125 4d. Type **59** 10 10
126 9d. Islanders going to first Gospel service .. 10 10
127 1s. 6d. Landing of the first minister .. 10 15
128 2s. 6d. Procession outside St. Mary's Church 15 20
125/8 .. .. *Set of* 4 40 50

63 Globe and Red Cross Emblem

(Des and litho B.W.)

1970 (1 June). *Centenary of British Red Cross. T* **63** *and similar designs. W* w **12** (*sideways on vert designs*). *P* 13.
129 **63** 4d. lt emerald, scarlet & dp bluish green 10 10
130 9d. bistre, scarlet and deep bluish green 10 10
131 – 1s. 9d. light drab, scarlet & ultramarine 20 15
132 – 2s. 6d. reddish purple, scarlet & ultram 25 30
129/32 .. .. *Set of* 4 60 60
Design: *Vert*—1s. 9d., 2s. 6d., Union Jack and Red Cross Flag.

64 Crawfish and Longboat

(65)

(Des Harrison. Litho Enschedé)

1970 (1 Nov). *Crawfish Industry. T* **64** *and similar horiz design. Multicoloured. W* w **12**. *P* 12½ × 13.
133 4d. Type **64** 20 10
134 10d. Packing and storing Crawfish 25 10
135 1s. 6d. Type **64** 35 25
136 2s. 6d. As 10d. 40 30
133/6 .. .. *Set of* 4 1·10 70

1971 (14 Feb).* *Decimal Currency. As Nos. 72/4, 75a, 77/83 and 84a surch as T* **65**, *by B.W. in typo. Glazed paper.*
137 ½p. on 1d. black and emerald-green .. 15 15
138 1p. on 2d. black and purple 15 15
139 1½p. on 4d. black and orange 30 15
140 2½p. on 6d. black and green 30 15
141 3p. on 7d. black and rose-red 30 15
142 4p. on 10d. black and chocolate 30 20
143 5p. on 1s. black and carmine 30 20
144 7½p. on 1s. 6d. black and yellow-olive .. 1·75 95
145 12½p. on 2s. 6d. black and orange-brown .. 2·00 2·50
146 15p. on 1½d. black and blue .. .. 3·50 3·00
147 25p. on 5s. black and violet .. .. 3·50 5·00
148 50p. on 10s. black and deep turquoise-blue 8·00 11·00
137/48 .. .. *Set of* 12 18·00 21·00
*This was the local release date, but the Crown Agents issued the stamps one day later.

66 *Quest*

(Des V. Whiteley. Litho J.W.)

1971 (1 June). *50th Anniv of Shackleton–Rowett Expedition. T* **66** *and similar horiz designs. W* w **12** *(sideways). P* 13½ × 14.

149 1½p. multicoloured 90 30
150 4p. sepia, pale green and apple-green .. 1·00 40
151 7½p. black, bright purple and pale green .. 1·00 40
152 12½p. multicoloured .. .. 1·40 45
149/52 .. .. *Set of* 4 4·00 1·40

Designs:—4p. Presentation of Scout Troop flag; 7½p. Cachet on pair of 6d. G.B. stamps; 12½p. Shackleton, postmarks and longboat taking mail to the *Quest*.

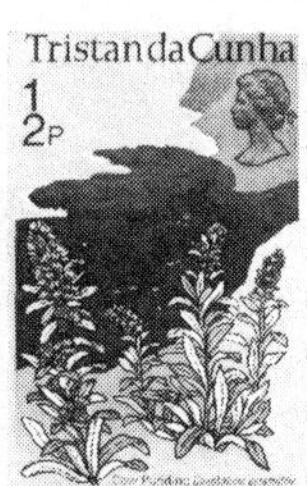

67 H.M.S. *Victory* at Trafalgar and Thomas Swain catching Nelson

68 Cow Pudding

(Des R. Granger Barrett. Litho Questa)

1971 (1 Nov). *Island Families. T* **67** *and similar horiz designs showing ships and the names of families associated with them. Multicoloured. W* w **12** *(sideways). P* 13½.

153 1½p. Type **67** 25 30
154 2½p. *Emily of Stonington* (P. W. Green) .. 35 40
155 4p. *Italia* (Lavarello and Repetto) .. 40 50
156 7½p. H.M.S. *Falmouth* (William Glass) .. 55 65
157 12½p. American whaling ship (Rogers and Hagan) 65 80
153/7 .. .. *Set of* 5 2·00 2·40

(Des M. and Sylvia Goaman. Recess and litho B.W. (50p., £1); Litho A. & M. (others))

1972 (29 Feb). *T* **68** *and similar multicoloured designs showing flowering plants. W* w **12** *(sideways on horiz designs). P* 13.

158 ½p. Type **68** 20 10
159 1p. Peak Berry 40 10
160 1½p. Sand Flower (*horiz*) 40 15
161 2½p. N.Z. Flax (*horiz*) 40 15
162 3p. Island Tree 40 15
163 4p. Bog Fern 40 15
164 5p. Dog Catcher 40 15
165 7½p. Celery .. .. 2·00 30
166 12½p. Pepper Tree .. .. 1·50 60
167 25p. Foul Berry (*horiz*) .. .. .. 1·75 1·50
168 50p. Tussock .. .. 5·00 1·75
169 £1 Tussac (*horiz*) .. .. 5·00 3·00
158/69 .. .. *Set of* 12 16·00 7·00

69 Launching

(Des R. Svensson. Litho Walsall)

1972 (1 June). *Tristan Longboats. T* **69** *and similar multicoloured designs. W* w **12** *(sideways on* 2½*p. and* 4*p.). P* 14.

170 2½p. Type **69** 15 10
171 4p. Under oars 20 10
172 7½p. Coxswain Arthur Repetto (*vert*) .. 25 15
173 12½p. Under sail for Nightingale Island (*vert*) 30 20
170/73 .. .. *Set of* 4 80 50

70 Tristan Thrushes and Wandering Albatrosses

(Des (from photographs by D. Groves) and photo Harrison)

1972 (20 Nov). *Royal Silver Wedding. Multicoloured; background colours given. W* w **12**. *P* 14 × 14½.

174 **70** 2½p. red-brown 35 40
175 7½p. dull ultramarine 15 40

71 Church Altar

(Des J. Cooter. Litho Questa)

1973 (8 July). *Golden Jubilee of St. Mary's Church. W* w **12**. *P* 13½.

176 **71** 25p. multicoloured 60 50

72 H.M.S. *Challenger's* Laboratory

(Des V. Whiteley Studio. Litho Questa)

1973 (15 Oct). *Centenary of H.M.S. Challenger's Visit. T* **72** *and similar horiz designs. Multicoloured. W* w **12**. *P* 13½.

177 4p. Type **72** 30 25
178 5p. H.M.S. *Challenger* off Tristan .. 30 25
179 7½p. *Challenger's* pinnace off Nightingale Is 30 30
180 12½p. Survey route 40 40
177/80 .. .. *Set of* 4 1·10 1·10
MS181 145 × 96 mm. Nos. 177/80 .. .. .. 1·10 3·50

73 Approaching English Port

(Des Jennifer Toombs. Litho Questa)

1973 (10 Nov). *Tenth Anniv of Return to Tristan da Cunha. T* **73** *and similar horiz designs. Multicoloured (except* 4*p.). W* w **12**. *P* 14.

182 4p. Type **73** (reddish brn, lemon & gold) 25 25
183 5p. Survey party 25 25
184 7½p. Embarking on *Bornholm* 35 35
185 12½p. Approaching Tristan 45 45
182/5 .. .. *Set of* 4 1·10 1·10

1973 (14 Nov). *Royal Wedding. As Nos.* 322/3 *of Montserrat.*

186 7½p. bright blue 15 10
187 12½p. light turquoise-green 15 10

74 Rockhopper Penguin and Egg

(Des R. Granger Barrett. Litho Questa)

1974 (1 May). *Rockhopper Penguins. T* **74** *and similar horiz designs. W* w **12**. *P* 14.

188 2½p. Type **74** .. .. 3·00 75
189 5p. Rockhopper Colony, Inaccessible Island 3·50 1·00
190 7½p. Penguin fishing .. .. 4·00 1·25
191 25p. Adult and fledgling .. .. .. 4·50 1·50
188/91 .. .. *Set of* 4 13·50 4·00

75 Map with Rockhopper Penguin and Wandering Albatross

(Des J.W. Litho Questa)

1974 (1 Oct). *"The Lonely Island". Sheet* 154 × 104 *mm. W* w **12** *(sideways). P* 13½.

MS192 **75** 35p. multicoloured .. .. .. 2·50 2·75

76 Blenheim Palace

(Des Sylvia Goaman. Litho Questa)

1974 (30 Nov). *Birth Centenary of Sir Winston Churchill. T* **76** *and similar horiz design. W* w **14** *(sideways). P* 14.

193 7½p. pale yellow and black 15 10
194 25p. black, sepia and grey 40 25
MS195 93 × 93 mm. Nos. 193/4. *W* w **12** (sideways) 75 1·60

Design:—25p. Churchill with Queen Elizabeth II.

77 *Plocamium fuscorubrum*

(Des Sylvia Goaman. Litho Harrison)

1975 (16 Apr). *Sea Plants. T* **77** *and similar horiz designs. W* w **12** *(sideways). P* 13 × 13½.

196 4p. rose-carmine, light lilac and black .. 15 1
197 5p. apple-green, light violet-blue and deep bluish green 15 1
198 10p. red-orange, stone and brown-purple .. 20 1
199 20p. multicoloured 30 2
196/9 .. .. *Set of* 4 70 6

Designs:—5p. *Ulva lactua;* 10p. *Epymenia flabellata;* 20p *Macrocystis pyrifera*.

78 Killer Whale

(Des G. Drummond. Litho Walsall)

1975 (1 Nov). *Whales. T* **78** *and similar horiz designs. Multicoloured. W* w **12** *(sideways). P* 13½.

200 2p. Type **78** 40 2
201 3p. Rough-toothed Dolphin 40 2
202 5p. Black Right Whale 45 3
203 20p. Fin Whale .. .. 1·00 7
200/3 .. .. *Set of* 4 2·00 1·4

79 ½d. Stamp of 1952

80 Island Cottage

(Des C. Abbott. Litho J.W.)

1976 (27* May). *Festival of Stamps, London. T* **79** *and simila designs. W* w **14** *(sideways on* 5 *and* 25*p). P* 13½.

204 5p. black, violet and light lilac 15 2
205 9p. black, deep green and turquoise 15 2
206 25p. multicoloured 40 5
204/6 .. .. *Set of* 3 65 8

Designs: *Vert*—9p. 1953 Coronation stamp. *Horiz*—25p. Ma carrier *Tristania II*.

*This is the local date of issue. The stamps were released by th Crown Agents on 4 May.

For miniature sheet containing No. 206 see No. **MS**218 o Ascension.

(Des C. Abbott. Litho Questa)

1976 (4 Oct). *Paintings by Roland Svensson (1st series). T* **80** *an similar multicoloured designs. W* w **14** *(sideways on* 5*p.,* 10*p. an* **MS**211*). P* 14.

207 3p. Type **80** 15 1
208 5p. The potato patches (*horiz*) 15 2
209 10p. Edinburgh from the sea (*horiz*) 20 2
210 20p. Huts, Nightingale Island 30 3
207/10 .. .. *Set of* 4 70 8
MS211 125 × 112 mm. Nos. 207/10 .. .. 80 1·7

See also Nos. 234/8 and 272/6.

81 The Royal Standard

(Des and litho J.W.)

1977 (7 Feb). *Silver Jubilee. T* **81** *and similar horiz designs. Multicoloured. W* w **14** (*sideways*). *P* 13.

212	10p. Royal Yacht *Britannia*	25	30
213	15p. Type **81**	15	20
214	25p. Royal family	25	25
212/14	.. .. *Set of* 3	60	65

For Nos. 213/14 surcharged, see Nos. 232/3.

82 H.M.S. *Eskimo*

(Des L. Curtis. Litho Walsall)

1977 (1 Oct). *Ships' Crests. T* **82** *and similar horiz designs. Multicoloured. W* w **14** (*sideways*). *P* 14.

215	5p. Type **82**	20	15
216	10p. H.M.S. *Naiad*	30	15
217	15p. H.M.S. *Jaguar*	40	25
218	20p. H.M.S. *London*	45	30
215/18	.. .. *Set of* 4	1·25	75
MS219	142 × 140 mm. Nos. 215/18	1·75	2·50

83 Great-winged Petrel

(Des BG Studio. Litho Walsall)

1977 (1 Dec). *Multicoloured designs as T* **83** *showing birds. W* w **14** (*sideways on* 1 *and* 2p.). *P* 13½.

220	1p. Type **83**	10	10
221	2p. White-faced Storm Petrel	15	15
222	3p. Hall's Giant Petrel	15	15
223	4p. Soft-plumaged Petrel	50	20
224	5p. Wandering Albatross	50	20
225	10p. Kerguelen Petrel	50	30
226	15p. Swallow-tailed Tern	50	50
227	20p. Greater Shearwater	85	55
228	25p. Broad-billed Prion	95	65
229	50p. Great Skua	1·50	1·00
230	£1 Common Diving Petrel	2·00	1·75
231	£2 Yellow-nosed Albatross	4·25	3·25
220/31	.. .. *Set of* 12	11·00	8·00

The 3p. to £2 are vertical designs.

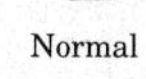

(**84**)

½ Normal

½ Straight top to serif in "½" (Pl 1C R. 5/1–5)

1978 (19 Jan*). *Provisional definitives. Nos.* 213/14 *surch as T* **84**.

232	4p. on 15p. Type **81**	2·25	6·50
233	7½p. on 25p. Royal family	2·25	6·50
	a. Straight top to serif	21·00	

*This is the local date of issue. Covers dated 26 November 1977 are philatelic mail forwarded to the island for cancellation, the stamps having been released in London on 31 October 1977. Supplies for the island population did not arrive until 19 January.

(Des C. Abbott. Litho Questa)

1978 (1 Mar). *Paintings by Roland Svensson (2nd series). Horiz designs as T* **80**. *Multicoloured. W* w **14** (*sideways*). *P* 14.

234	5p. St. Mary's Church	15	15
235	10p. Longboats	20	25
236	15p. A Tristan home	25	30
237	20p. The harbour, 1970	30	40
234/7	.. .. *Set of* 4	80	1·00
MS238	115 × 128 mm. Nos. 234/7	1·60	2·40

ALTERED CATALOGUE NUMBERS

Any Catalogue numbers altered from the last edition are shown as a list in the introductory pages.

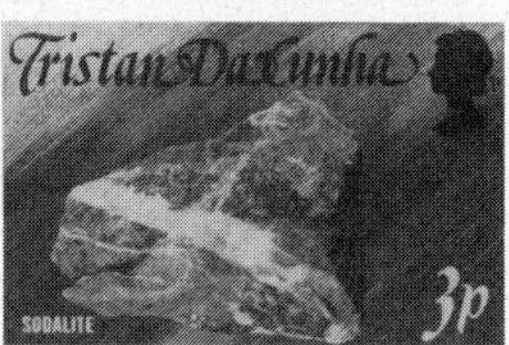

85 King's Bull **86** Sodalite

(Des Jennifer Toombs. Litho Questa)

1978 (21 Apr). *25th Anniv of Coronation. T* **85** *and similar vert designs. W* w **14**. *P* 15.

239	25p. bistre, bright violet and silver	35	35
	a. Sheetlet Nos. 239/41 × 2	1·90	
240	25p. multicoloured	35	35
241	25p. bistre, bright violet and silver	35	35
239/41	.. .. *Set of* 3	95	95

Designs:—No. 239, Type **85**; No. 240, Queen Elizabeth II; No. 241, Tristan crawfish.

Nos. 239/41 were printed together in small sheets of 6, containing two *se-tenant* strips of 3, with horizontal gutter margin between.

(Des J.W. Litho Questa)

1978 (9 June). *Local Minerals. T* **86** *and similar horiz designs. Multicoloured. W* w **14** (*sideways*). *P* 13½.

242	3p. Type **86**	25	10
243	5p. Aragonite	30	15
244	10p. Sulphur	45	25
245	20p. Lava containing pyroxene crystal ..	65	35
242/5	.. .. *Set of* 4	1·50	75

87 Klipfish

(Des R. Granger Barrett. Litho Harrison)

1978 (29 Sept). *Fish. T* **87** *and similar horiz designs. W* w **14** (*sideways*). *P* 14.

246	5p. black, yellow-brown and yellow-green ..	10	10
247	10p. black, yellow-brown and emerald ..	15	15
248	15p. multicoloured	20	20
249	20p. multicoloured	30	25
246/9	.. .. *Set of* 4	65	60

Designs:—10p. Fivefinger; 15p. Concha; 20p. Soldier.

TRISTAN da CUNHA 5p

88 R.F.A. *Orangeleaf* **89** Southern Elephant Seal

(Des R. Granger Barrett. Litho Cartor S.A., France)

1978 (24 Nov). *Royal Fleet Auxiliary Vessels. T* **88** *and similar horiz designs. Multicoloured. W* w **14** (*sideways*). *P* 12½ × 12.

250	5p. Type **88**	15	10
251	10p. R.F.A. *Tarbatness*	20	10
252	20p. R.F.A. *Tideréach*	35	25
253	25p. R.F.A. *Reliant*	45	30
250/3	.. .. *Set of* 4	1·10	65
MS254	136 × 140 mm. Nos. 250/3 (Wmk inverted)	2·00	3·00

(Des J.W. Litho Questa)

1979 (3 Jan). *Wildlife Conservation. T* **89** *and similar vert designs. Multicoloured. W* w **14**. *P* 14.

255	5p. Type **89**	15	10
256	10p. Afro-Australian Fur Seal	25	15
257	15p. Tristan Thrush	40	20
258	20p. Nightingale Finch	50	25
255/8	.. .. *Set of* 4	1·10	60

90 Tristan Longboat

(Des R. Granger Barrett. Litho Questa)

1979 (8 Feb). *Visit of R.M.S. "Queen Elizabeth 2". T* **90** *and similar horiz designs. Multicoloured. W* w **14** (*sideways*). *P* 14½.

259	5p. Type **90**	20	20
260	10p. R.M.S. *Queen Mary*	25	30
261	15p. R.M.S. *Queen Elizabeth*	30	35
262	20p. R.M.S. *Queen Elizabeth 2*	30	40
259/62	.. .. *Set of* 4	95	1·10
MS263	148×96 mm. 25p. R.M.S. *Queen Elizabeth 2* (131×27 *mm*)	1·00	2·25

91 1952 "TRISTAN DA CUNHA" overprinted St. Helena 10s. Definitive

(Des J.W. Litho Questa)

1979 (27 Aug). *Death Centenary of Sir Rowland Hill. T* **91** *and similar designs showing stamps. W* w **14** (*sideways on* 5 *and* 10p.). *P* 14.

264	5p. black, lilac and bistre-yellow	15	15
265	10p. black, red and apple-green	20	20
266	25p. multicoloured	30	30
264/6	.. .. *Set of* 3	60	60
MS267	83 × 103 mm. 50p. black and vermilion ..	60	70

Designs: *Horiz*—10p. 1954 5s. definitive. *Vert*—25p. 1963 3d. Tristan da Cunha Resettlement commemorative; 50p. 1946 1d. 4 Potatoes local label.

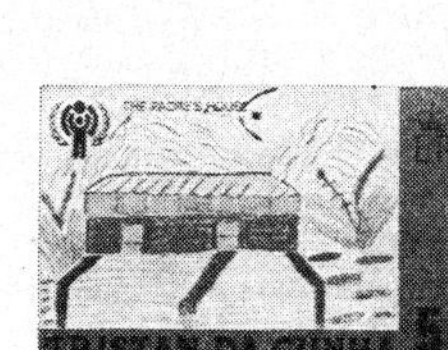

92 "The Padre's House" **93** *Tristania II* (mail ship)

(Des G. Hutchins. Litho Questa)

1979 (26 Nov). *International Year of the Child. Children's Drawings. T* **92** *and similar horiz designs. Multicoloured. W* w **14** (*sideways*). *P* 14.

268	5p. Type **92**	10	10
269	10p. "Houses in the Village"	15	15
270	15p. "St. Mary's Church"	15	15
271	20p. "Rockhopper Penguins"	25	25
268/71	.. .. *Set of* 4	60	60

(Des C. Abbott. Litho Questa)

1980 (29 Feb). *Paintings by Roland Svensson (3rd series). Landscapes. Multicoloured designs as T* **80**. *W* w **14** (*sideways on* 5 *and* 10p.). *P* 14.

272	5p. "Stoltenhoff Island" (*horiz*)	10	10
273	10p. "Nightingale from the East" (*horiz*) ..	15	20
274	15p. "The Administrator's Abode"	20	25
275	20p. "Ridge where the Goat jump off" ..	25	30
272/5	.. .. *Set of* 4	60	75
MS276	126 × 109 mm. Nos. 272/5 (wmk sideways)	70	1·00

(Des C. Abbott. Litho Walsall)

1980 (6 May). *"London 1980" International Stamp Exhibition. T* **93** *and similar vert designs. Multicoloured. W* w **14**. *P* 14.

277	5p. Type **93**	15	15
278	10p. Unloading mail at Calshot Harbour ..	15	15
279	15p. Tractor transporting mail to Post Office	25	25
280	20p. Ringing the "dong" to summons people to Post Office	30	30
281	25p. Distributing mail	30	30
277/81	.. .. *Set of* 5	1·00	1·00

94 Queen Elizabeth the Queen Mother at Royal Opera House, 1976 **95** *Golden Hind*

(Des Harrison. Litho Questa)

1980 (11 Aug*). *80th Birthday of Queen Elizabeth the Queen Mother. W* w **14** (*sideways*). *P* 14.

282 **94**	14p. multicoloured	25	25

*This is the local date of issue. The Crown Agents released this stamp in London on 4 August.

(Des G. Vasarhelyi. Litho Walsall)

1980 (6 Sept). *400th Anniv of Sir Francis Drake's Circumnavigation of the World. T* **95** *and similar vert designs. Multicoloured. W* w **14**. *P* 14½ × 14.

283	5p. Type **95**	20	10
284	10p. Drake's route	25	15
285	20p. Sir Francis Drake	30	20
286	25p. Queen Elizabeth I	40	25
283/6	.. .. *Set of* 4	1·00	65

96 "Humpty Dumpty"

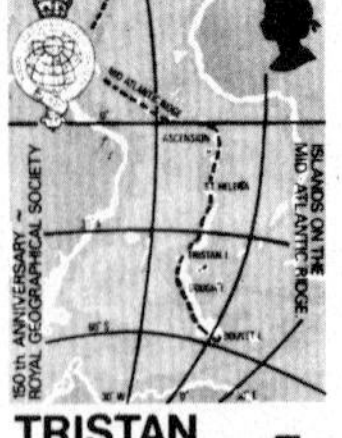

97 South Atlantic Ocean showing Islands on Mid-Atlantic Ridge

(Des G. Vasarhelyi. Litho J.W.)

1980 (31 Oct). *Christmas. Scenes from Nursery Rhymes. T* **96** *and similar horiz designs. Multicoloured.* W w **14** (*sideways*). *P* 13.

287	15p. Type **96**	20	25
	a. Sheetlet Nos. 287/95	1·60	
288	15p. "Mary had a little Lamb"	20	25
289	15p. "Little Jack Horner"	20	25
290	15p. "Hey Diddle Diddle"	20	25
291	15p. "London Bridge"	20	25
292	15p. "Old King Cole"	20	25
293	15p. "Sing a Song of Sixpence"	20	25
294	15p. "Tom, Tom the Piper's Son"	20	25
295	15p. "The Owl and the Pussy Cat"	20	25
287/95	*Set of* 9	1·60	1·75

Nos. 287/95 were printed together, *se-tenant*, within a small sheet of 9 stamps.

(Des A. Crawford, adapted BG Studio. Litho Rosenbaum Bros, Vienna)

1980 (15 Dec). *150th Anniv of Royal Geographical Society. Maps. T* **97** *and similar vert designs. Multicoloured.* W w **14**. *P* 13½.

296	5p. Type **97**	15	15
297	10p. Tristan da Cunha group (Beauforts Survey, 1806)	20	20
298	15p. Tristan Island (Crawford, 1937–38)	30	30
299	20p. Gough Island (1955–56)	35	40
296/9	*Set of* 4	90	95

98 Revd. Edwin Dodgson as Young Man

99 Detail from Captain Denham's Plan, 1853

(Des Jennifer Toombs. Litho Questa)

1981 (23 Mar). *Centenary of Revd. Edwin Dodgson's Arrival on Tristan da Cunha. T* **98** *and similar multicoloured designs.* W w **14** (*sideways on* 20p.). *P* 14.

300	10p. Type **98**	20	15
301	20p. Dodgson and view of Tristan da Cunha (*horiz*)	30	30
302	30p. Dodgson with people of Tristan da Cunha	45	45
300/2	*Set of* 3	85	80
MS303	140 × 134 mm. Nos. 300/2 (wmk sideways)	1·00	1·50

(Des L. McCombie. Litho Questa)

1981 (22 May). *Early Maps. T* **99** *and similar horiz designs. Multicoloured.* W w **14** (*sideways*). *P* 13½ × 14.

304	5p. Type **99**	15	10
305	14p. Detail from map by A. Dalrymple, 17 March 1781	25	20
306	21p. Detail from Captain Denham's plan, 1853 (*different*)	35	30
304/6	*Set of* 3	65	55
MS307	110 × 70 mm. 35p. Detail from map by J. van Keulen, *circa* 1700	50	60

100 Wedding Bouquet from Tristan da Cunha

101 Explorer with Rucksack

(Des J.W. Litho Walsall)

1981 (22 July). *Royal Wedding. T* **100** *and similar vert designs. Multicoloured.* W w **14**. *P* 14.

308	5p. Type **100**	10	10
309	20p. Prince of Wales at Investiture	25	25
310	50p. Prince Charles and Lady Diana Spencer	65	65
308/10	*Set of* 3	90	90

(Des BG Studio. Litho Questa)

1981 (14 Sept). *25th Anniv of Duke of Edinburgh Award Scheme. T* **101** *and similar vert designs. Multicoloured.* W w **14**. *P* 14.

311	5p. Type **101**	10	10
312	10p. Explorer at campsite	15	15
313	20p. Explorer map reading	25	25
314	25p. Duke of Edinburgh	30	30
311/14	*Set of* 4	70	70

102 Inaccessible Island Rail on Nest

(Des R. Granger Barrett. Litho Walsall)

1981 (1 Nov). *Inaccessible Island Rail. T* **102** *and similar horiz designs. Multicoloured.* W w **14** (*sideways*). *P* 13½ × 14.

315	10p. Type **102**	30	30
	a. Strip of 4. Nos. 315/18	1·10	
316	10p. Inaccessible Island Rail eggs	30	30
317	10p. Rail chicks	30	30
318	10p. Adult Rail	30	30
315/18	*Set of* 4	1·10	1·10

Nos. 315/18 were printed together, *se-tenant*, in horizontal and vertical strips of 4 throughout the sheet.

103 Six-gilled Shark

(Des I. Loe. Litho Enschedé)

1982 (8 Feb). *Sharks. T* **103** *and similar horiz designs. Multicoloured.* W w **14** (*sideways*). *P* 13½.

319	5p. Type **103**	20	10
320	14p. Porbeagle Shark	35	20
321	21p. Blue Shark	50	35
322	35p. Hammerhead Shark	60	50
319/22	*Set of* 4	1·50	1·00

104 *Marcella*

105 Lady Diana Spencer at Windsor, July 1981

(Des J. Cooter. Litho Questa)

1982 (5 Apr). *Sailing Ships* (*1st series*). *T* **104** *and similar horiz designs. Multicoloured.* W w **14** (*sideways*). *P* 13½.

323	5p. Type **104**	30	35
324	15p. *Eliza Adams*	35	50
325	30p. *Corinthian*	60	80
326	50p. *Samuel and Thomas*	1·00	1·10
323/6	*Set of* 4	2·00	2·50

See also Nos. 341/4.

(Des Jennifer Toombs. Litho Walsall)

1982 (1 July). *21st Birthday of Princess of Wales. T* **105** *and similar vert designs. Multicoloured.* W w **14**. *P* 14½ × 14.

327	5p. Tristan da Cunha coat of arms	15	15
328	15p. Type **105**	25	25
329	30p. Prince and Princess of Wales in wedding portrait	45	45
330	50p. Formal portrait	75	75
327/30	*Set of* 4	1·40	1·40

106 Lord Baden-Powell

1ST PARTICIPATION
COMMONWEALTH
GAMES 1982

(**107**)

(Des C. Abbott. Litho J.W.)

1982 (20 Sept). *75th Anniv of Boy Scout Movement. T* **106** *and similar multicoloured designs.* W w **14** (*sideways on No.* 333). *P* 13 × 13½ (50p.) *or* 13½ × 13 (*others*).

331	5p. Type **106**	20	15
332	20p. First Scout camp, Brownsea, 1907	40	35
333	50p. Local Scouts on parade (*horiz*)	80	75
331/3	*Set of* 3	1·25	1·10
MS334	88 × 104 mm. 50p. Moral of the Acorn and the Oak. P 14	1·10	1·10

1982 (28 Sept). *Commonwealth Games, Brisbane. Nos.* 224 *and* 228 *optd with T* **107**.

335	5p. Wandering Albatross	10	10
336	25p. Broad-billed Prion	35	30

108 Formation of Island

109 Tractor pulling Trailer

(Des J.W. Litho Questa)

1982 (1 Nov). *Volcanoes. T* **108** *and similar horiz designs. Multicoloured.* W w **14** (*sideways*). *P* 14 × 14½.

337	5p. Type **108**	15	15
338	15p. Plan of surface cinder cones and cross-section of volcano showing feeders	30	35
339	25p. Eruption	45	50
340	35p. 1961 Tristan eruption	65	70
337/40	*Set of* 4	1·40	1·50

(Des J. Cooter. Litho Questa)

1983 (1 Feb). *Sailing Ships* (*2nd series*). *Multicoloured designs as T* **104**. W w **14** (*sideways on* 20p., 35p.). *P* 13½.

341	5p. *Islander* (*vert*)	25	15
342	20p. *Roscoe*	45	35
343	35p. *Columbia*	60	55
344	50p. *Emeline* (*vert*)	80	80
341/4	*Set of* 4	1·90	1·75

(Des C. Abbott. Litho Format)

1983 (2 May). *Land Transport. T* **109** *and similar horiz designs. Multicoloured.* W w 14 (*sideways*). *P* 14.

345	5p. Type **109**	15	15
346	15p. Pack donkeys	25	25
347	30p. Bullock cart	50	50
348	50p. Landrover	75	75
345/8	*Set of* 4	1·50	1·50

110 Early Chart of South Atlantic

111 "Christ's Charge to St. Peter" (detail) (Raphael)

(Des L. Curtis. Litho Questa)

1983 (1 Aug). *Island History. T* **110** *and similar horiz designs. Multicoloured* (*except* 50p. *black, bright scarlet and buff*). W w **14** (*sideways*). *P* 14.

349	1p. Type **110**	30	20
350	3p. Tristao da Cunha's caravel	30	20
351	4p. Notice left by Dutch on first landing, 1643	30	20
352	5p. 17th-century views of the island	30	20
353	10p. British army landing party, 1815	35	30
354	15p. 19th-century view of the settlement	45	40
355	18p. Governor Glass's house	45	40
356	20p. The Revd. W. F. Taylor and Peter Green	50	50
357	25p. *John and Elizabeth* (American whaling ship)	75	60
358	50p. Letters Patent declaring Tristan da Cunha a dependency of St. Helena	1·40	1·25
359	£1 Commissioning H.M.S. *Atlantic Isle*, 1944	2·50	2·50
360	£2 Evacuation, 1961	3·75	4·00
349/60	*Set of* 12	10·00	9·75

(Des and litho Walsall)

1983 (27 Oct). *500th Birth Anniv of Raphael. T* **111** *and similar designs, showing different details of "Christ's Charge to St. Peter".* W w **14**. *P* 14½.

361	10p. multicoloured	20	20
362	25p. multicoloured	35	35
363	40p. multicoloured	60	60
361/3	*Set of* 3	1·00	1·00
MS364	115 × 90 mm. 50p. multicoloured (*horiz*). Wmk sideways	70	80

On No. **MS**364 the Queen's head has been replaced by the Royal Cypher.

ALTERED CATALOGUE NUMBERS

Any Catalogue numbers altered from the last edition are shown as a list in the introductory pages.

112 1952 6d. Stamp

113 *Agrocybe praecox var. cutefracta*

(Des C. Abbott. Litho Questa)

1984 (3 Jan). *150th Anniv of St. Helena as a British Colony. T* **112** *and similar horiz designs showing 1952 overprints on St. Helena stamps. Multicoloured.* W w **14** (*sideways*). P 14.

365 10p. Type **112** 15 15
366 15p. 1952 1s. stamp 25 25
367 25p. 1952 2s. stamp 35 35
368 60p. 1952 10s. stamp 85 85
365/8 .. .. *Set of* 4 1·40 1·40

(Des McCombie Skinner Studio. Litho Questa)

1984 (25 Mar). *Fungi. T* **113** *and similar multicoloured designs.* W w **14** (*sideways on* 30 *p.*, 50 *p.*). P 14.

369 10p. Type **113** 40 40
370 20p. *Laccaria tetraspora* 60 60
371 30p. *Agrocybe cylindracea* (*horiz*) 70 70
372 50p. *Sacoscypha coccinea* (*horiz*) .. .. 1·10 1·10
369/72 .. .. *Set of* 4 2·50 2·50

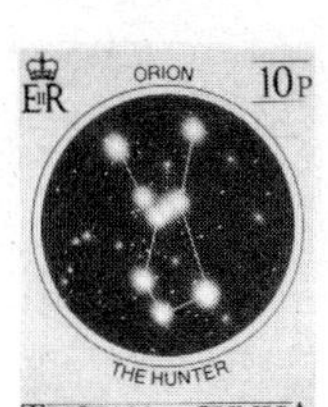

114 Constellation of "Orion"

115 Sheep-shearing

(Des Harrison. Litho Questa)

1984 (30 July). *The Night Sky. T* **114** *and similar vert designs. Multicoloured.* W w **14**. P 14½ × 14.

373 10p. Type **114** 45 40
374 20p. "Scorpius" 65 50
375 25p. "Canis Major" 75 60
376 50p. "Crux" .. .. 1·10 1·00
373/6 .. .. *Set of* 4 2·75 2·25

(Des G. Wilby. Litho Walsall)

1984 (1 Oct). *Tristan Woollens Industry. T* **115** *and similar vert designs. Multicoloured.* W w **14**. P 14½.

377 9p. Type **115** 20 20
378 17p. Carding wool 30 30
379 29p. Spinning 50 50
380 45p. Knitting 75 75
377/80 .. .. *Set of* 4 1·60 1·60
MS381 120 × 85 mm. As Nos. 377/80, but without white borders around the designs.. .. .. 1·60 2·25

116 "Christmas Dinner-table"

117 "H.M.S. *Julia* Ashore, 1817" (Midshipman C. W. Browne)

(Des G. Vasarhelyi. Litho Questa)

1984 (3 Dec). *Christmas. Children's Drawings. T* **116** *and similar horiz designs. Multicoloured.* W w **14** (*sideways*). P 14.

382 10p. Type **116** 20 20
383 20p. "Santa Claus in ox cart" 30 30
384 30p. "Santa Claus in longboat" 50 50
385 50p. "The Nativity" 85 85
382/5 .. .. *Set of* 4 1·75 1·75

(Des A. Crawford, adapted G. Vasarhelyi. Litho Questa)

1985 (4 Feb). *Shipwrecks* (1*st series*). *T* **117** *and similar designs.* W w **14** (*sideways on* 35*p.*). P 14 × 13½ (10, 25*p.*) *or* 13½ × 14 (35, 60*p.*).

386 10p. royal blue and light grey-blue 50 50
387 25p. red-brown and emerald .. .. .. 1·00 1·00
388 35p. yellow-brown and orange-yellow .. .. 1·25 1·25
386/8 .. .. *Set of* 3 2·50 2·50
MS389 142 × 101 mm. 60p. multicoloured. Wmk sideways .. .. 1·60 1·60

Designs: *Vert*—25p. *Mabel Clark's* Bell, St. Mary's Church. *Horiz*—35p. "Barque *Glenhuntley* foundering, 1898" (John Hagan); 60p. Map of Tristan da Cunha showing sites of shipwrecks.

See also Nos. 411/14 and 426/9.

118 The Queen Mother at Ascot with Princess Margaret

119 Jonathan Lambert and "Isles of Refreshment" Flag, 1811

(Des A. Theobald (80p.), C. Abbott (others). Litho Questa)

1985 (7 June). *Life and Times of Queen Elizabeth the Queen Mother. T* **118** *and similar vert designs. Multicoloured.* W w **16**. P 14½ × 14.

390 10p. The Queen Mother and Prince Charles, 1954 .. .. 20 30
391 20p. Type **118** 40 55
392 30p. Queen Elizabeth the Queen Mother .. 60 75
393 50p. With Prince Henry at his christening 1·00 1·25
390/3 .. .. *Set of* 4 2·00 2·50
MS394 91 × 73 mm. 80p. The Queen Mother and the young Princess Anne at Trooping the Colour. Wmk sideways .. .. 2·00 2·00

(Des D. Slater. Litho J.W.)

1985 (30 Sept). *Flags. T* **119** *and similar multicoloured designs.* W w **16** (*sideways on* 10*p.*, *inverted on others*). P 14.

395 10p. Type **119** 50 50
396 15p. 21st Light Dragoons guidon and cannon from Fort Malcolm (1816–17) (*vert*) .. 70 70
397 25p. White Ensign and H.M.S. *Falmouth* offshore, 1816 (*vert*) .. .. .. 90 1·00
398 60p. Union Jack and Tristan da Cunha (*vert*) 2·00 2·25
395/8 .. .. *Set of* 4 3·75 4·00

120 Lifeboat heading for Barque *West Riding*

121 Halley's Comet, 1066, from Bayeux Tapestry

(Des D. Miller. Litho Format)

1985 (28 Nov). *Centenary of Loss of Island Lifeboat. T* **120** *and similar vert designs. Multicoloured.* W w **14**. P 14 × 13½.

399 10p. Type **120** 35 55
400 30p. Map of Tristan da Cunha .. .. .. 80 1·25
401 50p. Memorial plaque to lifeboat crew .. 1·25 1·50
399/401 .. .. *Set of* 3 2·25 3·00

(Des D. Miller. Litho Walsall)

1986 (3 Mar). *Appearance of Halley's Comet. T* **121** *and similar horiz designs. Multicoloured.* W w **16** (*sideways*). P 14.

402 10p. Type **121** 40 45
403 20p. Path of Comet 65 70
404 30p. Comet over Inaccessible Island .. .. 85 1·00
405 50p. H.M.S. *Paramour* and map of South Atlantic .. .. 1·40 1·75
402/5 .. .. *Set of* 4 3·00 3·50

(Des A. Theobald. Litho Questa)

1986 (21 Apr). *60th Birthday of Queen Elizabeth II. Vert designs as T* **230a** *of Jamaica. Multicoloured.* W w **16**. P 14½ × 14.

406 10p. With Prince Charles, 1950 .. .. .. 20 25
407 15p. Queen at Trooping the Colour 30 35
408 25p. In robes of Order of the Bath, Westminster Abbey, 1972 .. .. 50 55
a. Silver (cypher and logo) omitted £275
409 45p. In Canada, 1977 .. .. 90 95
410 65p. At Crown Agents Head Office, London, 1983 .. .. 1·25 1·40
406/10 .. .. *Set of* 5 2·75 3·25

122 "*Allanshaw* wrecked on East Beach, 1893" (drawing by John Hagan)

123 Wandering Albatross

(Des A. Crawford, adapted G. Vasarhelyi. Litho J.W.)

1986 (2 June). *Shipwrecks* (2*nd series*). *T* **122** *and similar designs.* W w **16** (*sideways on* 9*p.*). P 13½ × 13 (9*p.*) *or* 13 × 13½ (*others*).

411 9p. dp turquoise-blue, dp grey-blue & black 25 25
412 20p. grey-olive, olive-yellow and black .. 45 45
413 40p. bright blue, bright violet and black .. 85 85
411/13 .. .. *Set of* 3 1·75 1·75
MS414 142 × 80 mm. 65p. orange-brown and black. Wmk sideways. P 13½ × 13 .. .. 1·75 2·50

Designs: *Vert*—20p. Church font from wreck of *Edward Vittery*, 1881; 40p. Ship's figurehead. *Horiz*—65p. Gaetano Lavarello and Andrea Repetto, survivors from *Italia*, 1892.

(Des D. Miller. Litho Questa)

1986 (23 July). *Royal Wedding. Square designs as T* **231a** *of Jamaica. Multicoloured.* W w **16**. P 14.

415 10p. Prince Andrew and Miss Sarah Ferguson 20 30
416 40p. Prince Andrew piloting helicopter, Digby, Canada, 1985 .. .. 80 1·10

(Des A. Theobald. Litho Questa)

1986 (30 Sept). *Flora and Fauna of Inaccessible Island. T* **123** *and similar vert designs. Multicoloured.* W w **16**. P 14.

417 5p. Type **123** 20 30
418 10p. *Lagenophora nudicaulis* (daisy) 30 40
419 20p. *Cynthia virginiensis* (butterfly) 65 75
420 25p. Wilkin's Finch 75 85
421 50p. White-chinned Petrel .. .. 1·25 1·25
417/21 .. .. *Set of* 5 2·75 3·25

124 *Dimorphinoctua cunhaensis* (flightless moth) and Edinburgh

125 Castaways from *Blenden Hall* attacking Sea Elephant, 1821

(Des C. Abbott. Litho Walsall)

1987 (23 Jan). *Island Flightless Insects and Birds. T* **124** *and similar vert designs. Multicoloured.* W w **14**. P 14½.

422 10p. Type **124** 25 35
423 25p. *Tristanomyia frustilifera* (fly) and Crater Lake 55 65
424 35p. Inaccessible Island Rail and Inaccessible Island .. .. 1·00 1·25
425 50p. Gough Island Coot and Gough Island .. 1·50 1·50
422/5 .. .. *Set of* 4 3·00 3·25

(Des A. Crawford, adapted G. Vasarhelyi. Litho Walsall)

1987 (2 Apr*). *Shipwrecks* (3*rd series*). *T* **125** *and similar designs.* W w **16** (*sideways on* 17*p.*). P 13½ × 14 (17*p.*) *or* 14 × 13½ (*others*).

426 11p. black and olive-brown 30 30
427 17p. black and bright lilac 45 45
428 45p. black and deep blue-green .. .. .. 1·00 1·00
426/8 .. .. *Set of* 3 1·60 1·60
MS429 131 × 70 mm. 70p. royal blue, bright green and pale blue. Wmk sideways. P 13½ × 14 .. .. 2·00 2·25

Designs: *Horiz*—17p. Barquentine *Henry A. Paull* stranded at Sandy Point, 1879; 70p. Map of Inaccessible Island showing sites of shipwrecks. *Vert*—45p. Gustav Stoltenhoff, 1871, and Stoltenhoff Island.

*This is the local date of issue. The Crown Agents placed the stamps on sale from 2 February 1987.

126 Rockhopper Penguin swimming

127 Microscope and Published Report

(Des I. Strange. Litho Questa)

1987 (22 June). *Rockhopper Penguins. T* **126** *and similar horiz designs. Multicoloured.* W w **16** (*sideways*). P 14½.

430 10p. Type **126** 35 30
431 20p. Adult with egg 55 50
432 30p. Adult with juvenile 75 70
433 50p. Head of Rockhopper Penguin .. .. 1·25 1·10
430/3 .. .. *Set of* 4 2·75 2·40

(Des N. Shewring. Litho Questa)

1987 (7 Dec). *50th Anniv of Norwegian Scientific Expedition. T* **127** *and similar square designs. Multicoloured.* W w **16** (10*p.*, 20*p.*) *or* w **14** (30*p.*, 50*p.*) (*all sideways*). P 14.

434 10p. Type **127** 50 50
435 20p. Scientists ringing Yellow-nosed Albatross .. .. 1·00 1·00
436 30p. Expedition hut, Little Beach Point .. 1·40 1·40
437 50p. S.S. *Thorshammer* (whale factory ship) 2·00 2·00
434/7 .. .. *Set of* 4 4·50 4·50

1988 (9 Mar). *Royal Ruby Wedding. Nos.* 406/10 *optd with T* **45***a of Kiribati in silver.*

438	10p. Princess Elizabeth with Prince Charles, 1950	20	25
439	15p. Queen Elizabeth II at Trooping the Colour	30	35
440	25p. In robes of Order of the Bath, Westminster Abbey, 1972	50	55
441	45p. In Canada, 1977	90	95
442	65p. At Crown Agents Head Office, London, 1983	1·25	1·40
438/42	*Set of* 5	2·75	3·25

128 Nightingale Finch ("Tristan Bunting")

129 Painted Penguin Eggs

(Des A. Theobald. Litho Questa)

1988 (21 Mar). *Fauna of Nightingale Island. T* **128** *and similar vert designs. Multicoloured. W w* **16**. *P* 14.

443	5p. Type **128**	20	15
444	10p. Tristan Thrush (immature)	30	25
445	20p. Yellow-nosed Albatross (chick)	50	45
446	25p. Greater Shearwater	60	55
447	50p. Elephant Seal	1·10	1·10
443/7	*Set of* 5	2·40	2·25

(Des O. Bell. Litho Questa)

1988 (30 May). *Tristan da Cunha Handicrafts. T* **129** *and similar horiz designs. Multicoloured. W w* **16** *(sideways). P* 14 × 14½.

448	10p. Type **129**	25	25
449	15p. Moccasins	35	35
450	35p. Knitwear	75	75
451	50p. Model longboat	1·10	1·10
448/51	*Set of* 4	2·25	2·25

130 Processing Blubber

(Des N. Shewring. Litho Questa)

1988 (6 Oct). *19th-century Whaling. T* **130** *and similar horiz designs. Multicoloured. W w* **16** *(sideways). P* 14 × 14½.

452	10p. Type **130**	25	25
453	20p. Harpoon guns	45	45
454	30p. Scrimshaw (carved whale bone)	65	65
455	50p. Whaling ships	1·10	1·10
452/5	*Set of* 4	2·25	2·25
MS456	76 × 56 mm. £1 Right Whale	2·10	2·10

(Des E. Nisbet and D. Miller (25, 35p.), D. Miller (others). Litho Harrison)

1988 (7 Nov). *300th Anniv of Lloyd's of London. Designs as T* **167***a of Malawi. W w* **16** *(sideways on* 25, 35*p.). P* 14.

457	10p. multicoloured	25	25
458	25p. multicoloured	55	55
459	35p. brownish black and emerald	80	80
460	50p. brownish black and carmine-red	1·25	1·25
457/60	*Set of* 4	2·50	2·50

Designs: *Vert*—10p. New Lloyd's Building, 1988; 50p. *Kobenhavn* (barque), 1928. *Horiz*—25p. *Tristania II* (crawfish trawler); 35p. *St. Helena* (mail ship).

131 "Government House"

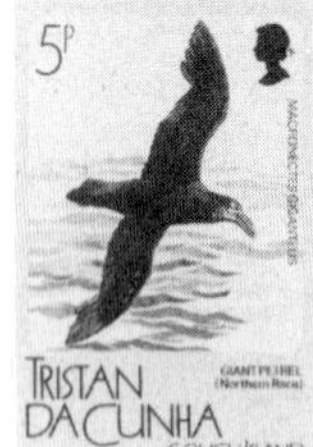

132 Giant Petrel

(Des N. Harvey. Litho Walsall)

1988 (10 Dec). *Augustus Earle's Paintings,* 1824. *T* **131** *and similar horiz designs. Multicoloured. W w* **16** *(sideways). P* 14.

461	1p. Type **131**	10	10
462	3p. "Squall off Tristan"	10	10
463	4p. "Rafting Blubber"	10	10
464	5p. "View near Little Beach"	10	15
465	10p. "Man killing Albatross"	20	25
466	15p. "View on The Summit"	30	35
467	20p. "Nightingale Island"	40	45
468	25p. "Earle on Tristan"	50	55
469	35p. "Solitude–Watching the Horizon"	70	75
470	50p. "Northeaster"	1·00	1·10
471	£1 "Tristan Village"	2·00	2·10
472	£2 "Governor Glass at Dinner"	4·00	4·25
461/72	*Set of* 12	8·50	9·25

Examples of Nos. 461/72 showing Earle's dates as "1793–1835" were sold by the U.S.A. agents, and by the authorities on Ascension, in error. Supplies sent to Tristan da Cunha show the correct dates "1793–1838".

(Des A. Theobald. Litho Walsall)

1989 (6 Feb). *Fauna of Gough Island. T* **132** *and similar vert designs. Multicoloured. W w* **16**. *P* 14.

473	5p. Type **132**	15	15
474	10p. Gough Island Coot ("Gough Moorhen")	20	25
475	20p. Gough Island Finch ("Gough Bunting")	40	45
476	25p. Sooty Albatross	50	55
477	50p. Amsterdam Fur Seal	1·00	1·10
473/7	*Set of* 5	2·00	2·25

133 *Eriosorus cheilanthoides*

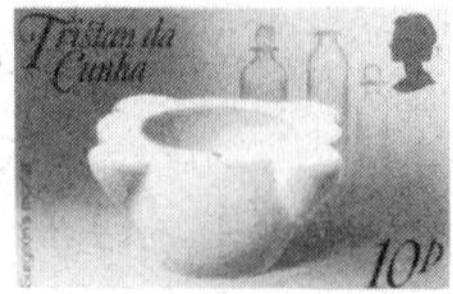

134 Surgeon's Mortar

(Des Jane Fern. Litho Walsall)

1989 (22 May). *Ferns. T* **133** *and similar vert designs. Multicoloured. W w* **14**. *P* 14×13½.

478	10p. Type **133**	35	35
479	25p. *Asplenium alvarezense*	75	75
480	35p. *Elaphoglossum hybridum*	85	85
481	50p. *Ophioglossum opacum*	1·40	1·40
478/81	*Set of* 4	3·00	3·00

(Des Jennifer Toombs. Litho Questa)

1989 (25 Sept). *Nautical Museum Exhibits. T* **134** *and similar horiz designs. Multicoloured. W w* **16** *(sideways). P* 14.

482	10p. Type **134**	35	35
483	20p. Parts of darting-gun harpoon	60	60
484	30p. Ship's compass with binnacle-hood	80	80
485	60p. Rope-twisting device	1·60	1·60
482/5	*Set of* 4	3·00	3·00

135 Cattle Egret

136 *Peridroma saucia*

(Des Josephine Martin and Sally Hynard. Litho Questa)

1989 (20 Nov). *Vagrant Birds. T* **135** *and similar vert designs. Multicoloured. W w* **16**. *P* 14.

486	10p. Type **135**	45	35
487	25p. Spotted Sandpiper	80	70
488	35p. Purple Gallinule	1·00	90
489	50p. Barn Swallow	1·40	1·40
486/9	*Set of* 4	3·25	3·00

(Des I. Loe. Litho Questa)

1990 (1 Feb). *Moths. T* **136** *and similar horiz designs. Multicoloured. W w* **14** *(sideways). P* 14.

490	10p. Type **136**	30	35
491	15p. *Ascalapha odorata*	40	45
492	35p. *Agrius cingulata*	80	90
493	60p. *Eumorpha labruscae*	1·50	1·60
490/3	*Set of* 4	2·75	3·00

137 Sea Urchin

138 H.M.S. *Pyramus* (frigate), 1829

(Des Anna Hecht. Litho Questa)

1990 (12 June). *Echinoderms. T* **137** *and similar vert designs showing starfishes. W w* **14**. *P* 13½×14.

494	10p. multicoloured	40	30
495	20p. multicoloured	60	50
496	30p. multicoloured	85	75
497	60p. multicoloured	1·50	1·50
494/7	*Set of* 4	3·00	2·75

(Des D. Miller. Litho Questa)

1990 (4 Aug). *90th Birthday of Queen Elizabeth the Queen Mother. Vert designs as T* **107** *(25p.) or* **108** *(£1) of Kenya. W w* **16**. *P* 14×15 *(25p.) or* 14½ *(£1).*

498	25p. multicoloured	75	60
499	£1 agate and Prussian blue	2·50	2·40

Designs:—25p. Queen Mother at the London Coliseum; £1 Queen Elizabeth broadcasting to women of the Empire, 1939.

(Des L. Curtis. Litho Walsall)

1990 (13 Sept). *Maiden Voyage of* St. Helena II. *Horiz designs as T* **162** *of St. Helena. Multicoloured. W w* **14** *(sideways). P* 14×14½.

500	10p. *Dunnottar Castle* (mail ship), 1942	35	35
501	15p. *St. Helena I* at Tristan	50	50
502	35p. Launch of *St. Helena II*	1·00	1·00
503	60p. Duke of York launching *St. Helena II*	1·75	1·75
500/3	*Set of* 4	3·25	3·25
MS504	100×100 mm. £1 *St Helena II* and outline map of Tristan da Cunha	2·50	3·00

No. **MS**504 also contains two imperforate designs of similar stamps from Ascension and St. Helena without face values.

(Des E. Nisbet. Litho Questa)

1990 (30 Nov). *Ships of the Royal Navy (1st series). T* **138** *and similar horiz designs. Multicoloured. W w* **14** *(sideways). P* 14.

505	10p. Type **138**	35	35
506	25p. H.M.S. *Penguin* (sloop), 1815	80	80
507	35p. H.M.S. *Thalia* (screw corvette), 1886	1·00	1·00
508	50p. H.M.S. *Sidon* (paddle frigate), 1858	1·60	1·60
505/8	*Set of* 4	3·25	3·25

(Des E. Nisbet. Litho Questa)

1991 (4 Feb). *Ships of the Royal Navy (2nd series). Horiz designs as T* **138**. *Multicoloured. W w* **14** *(sideways). P* 14.

509	10p. H.M.S. *Milford* (sloop), 1938	35	35
510	25p. H.M.S. *Dublin* (cruiser), 1923	80	80
511	35p. H.M.S. *Yarmouth* (cruiser), 1919	1·00	1·00
512	50p. H.M.S. *Carlisle* (cruiser), 1937	1·60	1·60
509/12	*Set of* 4	3·25	3·25

No. 512 is inscribed "1938" in error.

139 *Royal Viking Sun* (cruise liner)

(Des L. Curtis. Litho B.D.T.)

1991 (1 Apr). *Visit of* Royal Viking Sun. *Sheet* 62×47 *mm. W w* **16** *(sideways). P* 14.

MS513	**139** £1 multicoloured	2·50	3·00

140 Prince Alfred and H.M.S. *Galatea*, 1867

(Des D. Miller. Litho Questa)

1991 (10 June). *70th Birthday of Prince Philip, Duke of Edinburgh. T* **140** *and similar horiz designs. W w* **16** *(sideways). P* 14.

514	10p. brownish black, pale blue & dp dull bl	40	40
515	25p. brownish black, pale blue-green and myrtle-green	80	80
516	30p. black, deep brown & pale bistre-yellow	90	90
517	50p. multicoloured	1·40	1·40
514/17	*Set of* 4	3·25	3·25

Designs:—25p. Prince Philip meeting local inhabitants, 1957; 30p. Prince Philip and Royal Yacht *Britannia*, 1957; 50p. Prince Philip and Edinburgh settlement.

141 Pair of Gough Island Coots

(Des G. Vasarhelyi. Litho Questa)

1991 (1 Oct). *Endangered Species. Birds. T* **141** *and similar horiz designs. Multicoloured. W w* **14** *(sideways). P* 14.

518	8p. Type **141**	30	30
519	10p. Gough Island Finch	35	35
520	12p. Gough Island Coot on nest	40	40
521	15p. Gough Island Finch feeding chicks	50	50
518/21	*Set of* 4	1·40	1·40

(Des R. Watton. Litho Walsall)

1992 (23 Jan). *500th Anniv of Discovery of America by Columbus and Re-enactment Voyages. Horiz designs as T* **168** *of St. Helena. Multicoloured. W w* **14** *(sideways). P* 13½×14.

No.	Description	Unused	Used
522	10p. Map of re-enactment voyages and *Eye of the Wind* (cadet ship)	35	35
523	15p. Compass rose and *Soren Larsen* (cadet ship)	55	55
524	35p. Ships of Columbus	95	95
525	60p. Columbus and *Santa Maria*	1·50	1·50
522/5	.. .. *Set of* 4	3·00	3·00

(Des D. Miller. Litho Questa (65p.), Walsall (others))

1992 (6 Feb). *40th Anniv of Queen Elizabeth II's Accession. Horiz designs as T* **112** *of Kenya. Multicoloured. W w* **14** *(sideways). P* 14.

No.	Description	Unused	Used
526	10p. Tristan from the sea	35	35
527	20p. Longboat under sail	60	60
528	25p. Aerial view of Edinburgh	70	70
529	35p. Three portraits of Queen Elizabeth ..	90	90
530	65p. Queen Elizabeth II	1·75	1·75
526/30	.. .. *Set of* 5	4·00	4·00

POSTAGE DUE STAMPS

D 1

3d. Normal

3d. Lower serif at left of "3" missing (R. 9/1)

(Typo D.L.R.)

1957 (1 Feb). *Chalk-surfaced paper. Wmk Mult Script CA. P* 14.

No.	Type	Description	Unused	Used
D1	D 1	1d. scarlet	1·75	5·00
D2		2d. orange-yellow	2·25	4·50
D3		3d. green	3·50	5·50
		a. Missing serif	35·00	
D4		4d. ultramarine	6·00	7·00
D5		5d. lake	5·00	16·00
D1/5		.. .. .. *Set of* 5	17·00	35·00

D 2

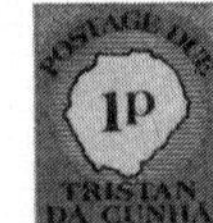

D 3 Outline Map of Tristan da Cunha

(Des J.W. Litho Questa)

1976 (27 May*). *W w* **12** *(sideways). P* 13½ × 14.

No.	Type	Description	Unused	Used
D 6	D 2	1p. magenta	25	60
D 7		2p. dull emerald	25	70
D 8		4p. bluish violet	25	70
D 9		5p. new blue	25	70
D10		10p. chestnut	40	1·10
D6/10		.. .. .. *Set of* 5	1·25	3·50

*This is the local date of issue; the Crown Agents released the stamps four days later.

1976 (3 Sept). *W w* **14** *(sideways). P* 13½ × 14.

No.	Type	Description	Unused	Used
D11	D 2	1p. magenta	10	30
D12		2p. dull emerald	10	35
D13		4p. bluish violet	15	45
D14		5p. new blue	15	50
D15		10p. chestnut	15	70
D11/15		.. .. .. *Set of* 5	50	2·10

(Des L. Curtis. Litho Questa)

1986 (20 Nov). *W w* **16**. *P* 14½×14.

No.	Type	Description	Unused	Used
D16	D 3	1p. deep brown and cinnamon ..	10	10
D17		2p. deep brown and bright orange ..	10	10
D18		5p. deep brown and orange-vermilion	10	15
D19		7p. black and bright reddish violet ..	15	20
D20		10p. black and violet-blue	20	25
D21		25p. black and pale emerald	50	55
D16/21		.. .. *Set of* 6	95	1·10

POSTAL FISCAL STAMPS

NATIONAL
SAVINGS

(F 1)

(F 2)

1970 (15 May). *No. 77 optd with Type* F **1** *in red.*

No.	Description	Unused	Used
F1	6d. black and green	10	15

No. F1 was originally intended as a National Savings Stamp, but also retained postal validity.

(Handstamped locally by rubber handstamp)

1971 (Feb). *Decimal currency. No.* F 1 *handstamped with Type* F **2**, *in violet.*

No.	Description	Unused	Used
F2	2½p. on 6d. black and green	4·75	8·00
	a. Pair, one without handstamp ..	£375	£375

Beware of forgeries of this handstamp.

Trucial States

The Trucial States consisted of Abu Dhabi, Ajman (with Manama), Dubai, Fujeira, Ras al Khaima, Sharjah and Umm al Qiwain. However the following issue of stamps was only put into use in Dubai, despite the inscription "TRUCIAL STATES".

The first organised postal service in Dubai commenced on 19 August 1909 when an Indian Branch Office, administered from Karachi, was opened, using the unoverprinted stamps of India, principally the ½ a. and 1 a. values.

The initial cancellation was a single-ring type inscribed "DUBAI B.O. PERSIAN GULF", which remained in use until 1933.

1909 Cancellation

Its replacement was of the Indian double-circle type showing a similar inscription.

Dubai was upgraded to Sub-Post Office status on 1 April 1942 and this change was reflected in a new double-ring mark inscribed "DUBAI" only. At the same time the office was provided with a single-ring handstamp which also incorporated a cancelling device of seven wavy lines.

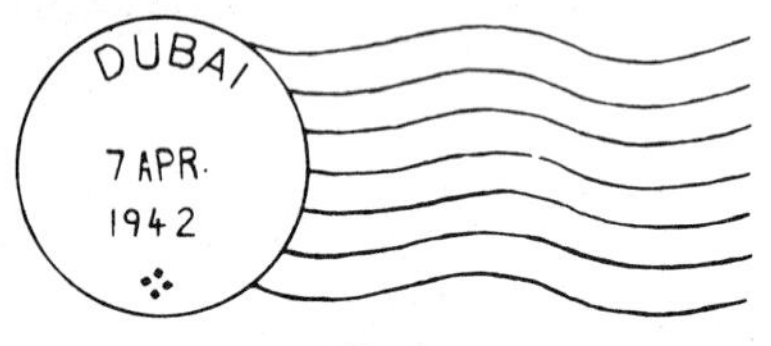

1942 Handstamp

(illustration reduced: actual size 65 × 27 mm)

A further version of the double-ring type appeared in 1946, showing the "PERSIAN GULF" inscription restored to the lower segment of the postmark.

In October 1947 control of the Dubai Post Office passed to Pakistan whose stamps were used there until the end of March 1948.

On 1 April 1948 the post office was transferred, yet again, to British control and Great Britain stamps surcharged for use in the British Postal Agencies in Eastern Arabia were then sold in Dubai until 6 January 1961, being cancelled with British style single and double-ring postmarks.

1 Palms

2 Dhow

(Des M. Goaman. Photo Harrison (T **1**). Des M. Farrar-Bell. Recess D.L.R. (T **2**))

1961 (7 Jan). *P* 15 × 14 (*T* **1**) *or* 13 × 12½ (*T* **2**).

1	**1**	5 n.p. green	30	10
2		15 n.p. red-brown	30	10
3		20 n.p. bright blue	40	10
4		30 n.p. orange-red	40	10
5		40 n.p. reddish violet	40	10
6		50 n.p. bistre	40	10
7		75 n.p. grey	60	10
8	**2**	1 r. green	3·00	40
9		2 r. black	3·00	5·50
10		5 r. carmine-red	4·50	10·00
11		10 r. deep ultramarine	12·00	19·00
1/11		*Set of* 11	22·00	32·00

The Dubai Post Department took over the postal services on 14 June 1963. Later issues for Dubai will be found in Part 19 (*Middle East*) of this catalogue.

Turks and Caicos Islands

TURKS ISLANDS

DEPENDENCY OF JAMAICA

A branch of the British Post Office opened at Grand Turk on 11 December 1854 replacing an earlier arrangement under which mail for the islands was sorted by local R.M.S.P. agents.

No. CC1 is known used between 22 October 1857 and 20 April 1862.

GRAND TURK

CROWNED-CIRCLE HANDSTAMPS

CC 1

CC1 CC 1 TURKS-ISLANDS (1857) *Price on cover* £4250

PRICES FOR STAMPS ON COVER TO 1945	
Nos. 1/5	*from* × 25
No. 6	—
Nos. 7/20	*from* × 25
Nos. 20*a*/48	—
Nos. 49/52	*from* × 4
Nos. 53/7	*from* × 5
Nos. 58/65	*from* × 15
Nos. 66/9	*from* × 5
Nos. 70/2	*from* × 10
Nos. 101/9	*from* × 8
Nos. 110/26	*from* × 6
Nos. 129/39	*from* × 4
Nos. 140/53	*from* × 12
Nos. 154/90	*from* × 3
Nos. 191/3	*from* × 10
Nos. 194/205	*from* × 2

1

(Recess P.B.)

1867 (4 April). *No wmk. P* 11–12.

1	**1**	1d. dull rose	32·00	40·00
2		6d. black	70·00	80·00
3		1s. dull blue	65·00	55·00

1873–79. *Wmk Small Star. W* w **2** (*sideways on Nos.* 5 *and* 6). *P* 11–12 × 14½–15½.

4	**1**	1d. dull rose-lake (7.73)	40·00	40·00
		a. Wmk sideways	75·00	75·00
5		1d. dull red (1.79)	48·00	50·00
		a. Imperf between (horiz pair)	£9000	
		c. Wmk upright		
6		1s. lilac (1.79)	£5000	£2000

1881 (1 Jan). *Stamps of the preceding issues surcharged locally, in black.*

There are twelve different settings of the ½d., nine settings of the 2½d., and six settings of the 4d.

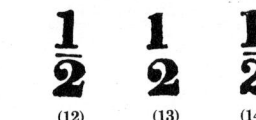

(2) (3)

Setting 1. *T* **2**. *Long fraction bar. Two varieties repeated fifteen times in the sheet.*

7	½ on 6d. black	55·00	70·00

Setting 2. *T* **3**. *Short fraction bar. Three varieties in a vertical strip repeated ten times in sheet.*

Setting 3. *Similar to setting* 2, *but the middle stamp of the three varieties has a longer bar.*

8	½ on 6d. black (*setting* 2 *only*)	55·00	
9	½ on 1s. dull blue	70·00	95·00
	a. Surch double	£3750	

(4) (5) (6)

Three varieties in a vertical strip repeated ten times in sheet.
Section 4. *Types* **4, 5, 6**.
Setting 5. *Types* **4** (*without bar*), **5, 6**.
Setting 6. *Types* **4, 5, 6** (*without bar*).
Setting 7. *Types* **4** (*shorter thick bar*), **6, 6**.

10	½ on 1d. dull red (*setting* 7 *only*) (T **6**)	£1000	
	a. Type **4** (shorter thick bar)	£1700	
11	½ on 1s. dull blue (*setting* 6 *and* 7) (T **4**)	£475	
	a. Type **4** (shorter thick bar)	£475	
	b. Type **5**	£475	
	c. Type **6**	£300	
	d. Type **6** (without bar)	£475	
	e. Surch double (T **6** without bar)		
12	½ on 1s. lilac (T **4**)	£275	£325
	a. Without bar	£450	
	b. With short thick bar	£450	
	c. Surch double		
13	½ on 1s. lilac (T **5**)	£110	£140
	a. Surch double	£1500	
14	½ on 1s. lilac (T **6**)	90·00	
	a. Without bar	£475	

(7) (8) (9) (10)

Setting 8. *T* **7**. *Three varieties in a vertical strip. All have a very short bar.*

15	½ on 1d. dull red	50·00	

Setting 9. *T* **8**. *Three varieties in a vertical strip. Bars long and thick and "1" leaning a little to left.*

16	½ on 1d. dull red	£140	
	a. Surch double		

Setting 10. *T* **9** *and* **10**. *Fifteen varieties repeated twice on a sheet. Ten are of T* **9**, *five of T* **10**.

17	½ on 1d. dull red (T **9**)	50·00	55·00
	a. Surch double	£2000	
18	½ on 1d. dull red (T **10**)	60·00	70·00
19	½ on 1s. lilac (T **9**)	75·00	95·00
20	½ on 1s. lilac (T **10**)	£140	£180
20*a*	½ on 1s. dull blue (T **9**)	£6000	

Types **9** *and* **11**. The difference is in the position of the "2" in relation to the "1". In setting 10 the "2" is to the left of the "1" except on No. 10 and in setting 11 it is to the right except on No. 2

(11) (12) (13) (14)

Setting 11. *T* **11** *to* **14**. *Fifteen varieties repeated twice in a sheet. Ten of T* **11**, *three of T* **12**, *and one each of T* **13** *and* **14**.

Setting 12. *Similar to last, but T* **13** *replaced by another T* **12**.

21	½ on 1d. dull red (T **11**)	55·00	
22	½ on 1d. dull red (T **12**)	£110	
23	½ on 1d. dull red (T **13**)	£1000	
24	½ on 1d. dull red (T **14**)	£325	
24*a*	½ on 1s. dull blue (T **11**)	£8000	

(15) (16)

Setting 1. *T* **15**. *Fraction in very small type.*

25	2½ on 6d. black	£6500	

Setting 2. *T* **16**. *Two varieties repeated fifteen times in a sheet. Large "2" on level with top of the "1", long thin bar.*

26	2½ on 6d. black	£225	
	a. Imperf between (pair)		
	b. Surch double	£4250	

(17) (18) (19)

Setting 3. *T* **17**. *As T* **16**, *but large "2" not so high up.*

27	2½ on 1s. lilac	£1400	

Setting 4. *T* **18**. *Three varieties in a vertical strip repeated ten times in sheet. Large "2" placed lower and small bar.*

28	2½ on 6d. black	£110	£140
	a. Surch double		

Setting 5. *T* **19**. *Three varieties in a vertical strip repeated ten times in sheet "2" further from "½", small fraction bar.*

29	2½ on 1s. lilac	£550	£650

(20) (21)

Setting 6. *T* **20** *and* **21**. *Fifteen varieties. Ten of T* **20** *and five of T* **21**, *repeated twice in a sheet.*

30	2½ on 1s. lilac (T **20**)	£5500	
31	2½ on 1s. lilac (T **21**)	£8000	

(22) (23) (24)

Setting 7. T **22**. *Three varieties in a vertical strip, repeated ten times in a sheet.*
32 2½ on 6d. black £7000
33 2½ on 1s. dull blue £7000

Setting 8. T **23** *and* **24**. *Fifteen varieties. Ten of T* **23** *and five of T* **24**, *repeated twice in a sheet.*
34 2½ on 1d. dull red (T **23**) £425
35 2½ on 1d. dull red (T **24** £750
36 2½ on 1s. lilac (T **23**) £475
  a. Surch "½" double £2250
37 2½ on 1s. lilac (T **24**) £1200
  a. Surch "½" double £3750

2½ 2½ 2½
(25) (26) (27)

Setting 9. T **25, 26,** *and* **27**. *Fifteen varieties. Ten of T* **25**, *three of T* **26**, *one of T* **26** *without bar, and one of T* **27**, *repeated twice in a sheet.*
38 2½ on 1s. dull blue (T **25**) £450
39 2½ on 1s. dull blue (T **26**) £1400
40 2½ on 1s. dull blue (T **26**) (without bar) .. £6000
41 2½ on 1s. dull blue (T **27**) £6000

4 4 4
(28) (29) (30)

Setting 1. *T* **28**. *"4" 8 mm high, pointed top.*
42 4 on 6d. black £250 £300

Settings 2–6. *T* **29** *and* **30**.
43 4 on 6d. black (T **29**) .. .. .. 45·00
44 4 on 6d. black (T **30**) £325 £375
45 4 on 1s. lilac (T **29**) £375
  a. Surch double .. ..
46 4 on 1s. lilac (T **30**) £2000
  a. Surch double .. ..
47 4 on 1d. dull red (T **29**) £500 £450
48 4 on 1d. dull red (T **28**) £500 £450

The components of these settings can only be distinguished when in blocks. Details are given in the handbook by John J. Challis.

TURKS ISLANDS HALF PENNY
31

One Penny
(32)

(Typo D.L.R.)

1881. *Wmk Crown CC (sideways; upright on 4d.). P* 14.
49 **1** 1d. brown-red (Oct) .. .. .. 42·00 50·00
50 **31** 4d. ultramarine (Die I) (Aug) .. .. 75·00 60·00
51 **1** 6d. olive-black (Oct) .. .. .. 75·00 90·00
52 1s. slate-green (Oct) £100 £100

1882–85. *Wmk Crown CA. P* 14.
53 **31** ½d. blue-green (Die I) (2.82) .. .. 5·50 16·00
  a. Pale green (12.85) .. .. .. 60 3·50
55 **1** 1d. orange-brown (10.83) .. .. 40·00 30·00
  a. Bisected (½d.) (on cover) .. .. † £1600
56 **31** 2½d. red-brown (Die I) (2.82) .. .. 11·00 13·00
57 4d. grey (Die I) (10.84) .. .. .. 5·50 2·00
  a. Bisected (2d.) (on cover) .. .. † £1400

1887 (July)–**89**. *Wmk Crown CA. (a) P* 12.
58 **1** 1d. crimson-lake .. .. 7·00 2·50
  a. Imperf between (horiz pair) £7500

(b) P 14
59 **1** 6d. yellow-brown (2.89) (Optd S. £60) .. 2·00 2·75
60 1s. sepia .. .. 2·25 2·75

During a shortage of 1d. stamps a supply of JAMAICA No. 27 was sent to the Turks and Caicos Islands in April 1889 and used until replaced by No. 61.

1889 (May). *Surch at Grand Turk with T* **32**.
61 **31** 1d. on 2½d. red-brown .. .. .. 4·50 9·50
  a. "ONE" omitted .. .. ..
  b. Bisected (½d.) (on cover) .. .. † —

No. 61a was caused by misplacement of the surcharge. Stamps from the same sheet can be found with the surcharge reading "Penny One".

1889–93. *Wmk Crown CA. P* 14.
62 **1** 1d. crimson-lake (7.89) .. .. .. 2·25 3·50
  a. Bisected (½d.) (on cover) .. .. † —
63 1d. lake .. .. 1·25 2·25
  a. Bisected (½d.) (on cover) .. .. † —
64 1d. pale rosy lake .. .. 65 3·75
65 **31** 2½d. ultram (Die II) (4.93) (Optd S. £55) 1·00 75

NEW INFORMATION

The editor is always interested to correspond with people who have new information that will improve or correct the Catalogue.

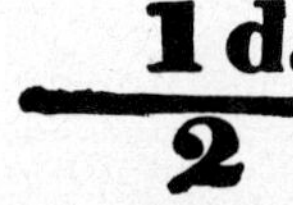
(33)

34

1893 (July). *No. 57 surch at Grand Turk with T* **33**.

Setting 1. *Bars between "1d." and "2" separate, instead of continuous across the rows of stamps.*
66 ½d. on 4d. grey £250 £160

Setting 2. *Continuous bars. Thin and thick bar 10¾ mm apart. "2" under the "1".*
67 ½d. on 4d. grey £110 £110

Setting 3. *As last, but bars 11¾ mm apart.*
68 ½d. on 4d. grey £100 £100

Setting 4. *Bars 11 mm apart. Five out of the six varieties in the strip have the "2" below the space between the "1" and "d".*
69 ½d. on 4d. grey £100

There is a fifth setting, but the variation is slight.

(Typo D.L.R.)

1894–95. *Wmk Crown CA. P* 14.
70 **31** ½d. dull green (Die II) (1894) 30 75
71 4d. dull purple & ultram (Die II) (5.95) 5·50 11·00
72 **34** 5d. olive-green and carmine (6.94) .. 2·25 10·00
  a. Bisected (2½d.) (on cover) .. .. † £2750
70/2 .. .. *Set of* 3 7·25 20·00
71/2 Optd "Specimen" .. .. *Set of* 2 £100

TURKS AND CAICOS ISLANDS

35 Salt raking 36

The dates on the stamps have reference to the political separation from Bahamas.

(Recess D.L.R.)

1900 (10 Nov)–**04**. *Wmk Crown CA (½d. to 1s.) or Wmk Crown CC (2s., 3s.). P* 14.
101 **35** ½d. green .. .. 2·50 3·75
102 1d. red .. .. 2·75 75
103 2d. sepia .. .. 75 1·25
104 2½d. blue .. .. 3·75 8·50
  a. Greyish blue (1904) .. .. .. 90 1·00
105 4d. orange .. .. 3·50 7·00
106 6d. dull mauve .. .. 1·25 5·50
107 1s. purple-brown .. .. 1·75 9·50
108 **36** 2s. purple .. .. 38·00 55·00
109 3s. lake .. .. 48·00 70·00
101/9 .. .. *Set of* 9 90·00 £140
101/9 Optd "Specimen" .. .. *Set of* 9 £225

1905–08. *Wmk Mult Crown CA. P* 14.
110 **35** ½d. green 40 15
111 1d. red .. .. 7·50 50
112 3d. purple/*yellow* (1908) (Optd S. £50) .. 90 5·00
110/12 .. .. *Set of* 3 8·00 5·00

37 Turk's-head Cactus 38

(Recess D.L.R.)

1909 (2 Sept)–**11**. *Wmk Mult Crown CA. P* 14.
115 **37** ¼d. rosy mauve (1910) .. .. .. 30 1·00
116 ¼d. red (1911) 20 25
117 **38** ½d. yellow-green 20 25
118 1d. red 20 30
119 2d. greyish slate .. .. 90 1·40
120 2½d. blue .. .. 1·25 3·75
121 3d. purple/*yellow* .. .. 1·75 2·00
122 4d. red/*yellow* .. .. 3·00 7·00
123 6d. purple .. .. 6·00 7·00
124 1s. black/*green* .. .. 2·50 8·50
125 2s. red/*green* .. .. 20·00 35·00
126 3s. black/*red* .. .. 20·00 35·00
115/26 .. .. *Set of* 12 50·00 90·00
115/26 Optd "Specimen" .. .. *Set of* 12 £225

See also Nos. 154 and 162.

39

WAR TAX
(40)

1913 (1 Apr)–**21**. *Wmk Mult Crown CA. P* 14.
129 **39** ½d. green .. .. 30 1·00
130 1d. red .. .. 75 1·10
  a. Bright scarlet .. .. 1·10 1·75
  b. Rose-carmine (1918) .. .. .. 1·00 2·25
131 2d. greyish slate .. .. 1·10 1·25
132 2½d. ultramarine .. .. 1·90 2·50
  a. Bright blue (1918) .. .. .. 3·00 2·50
133 3d. purple/*yellow* .. .. 2·25 5·50
  a. On lemon .. .. 13·00
  b. On yellow-buff .. .. 2·50 5·50
  c. On orange-buff 70
  d. On pale yellow .. .. 1·50 4·00
134 4d. red/*yellow* .. .. 80 6·00
  a. On orange-buff (Optd S. £48) .. .. 1·00 6·50
  b. Carmine on pale yellow .. .. .. 3·25 9·50
135 5d. pale olive-green (18.5.16) .. .. 3·50 8·50
136 6d. dull purple .. .. 2·25 3·25
137 1s. brown-orange .. .. 1·50 4·00
138 2s. red/*blue-green* .. .. 6·00 14·00
  a. On greenish white (1919) .. .. 18·00 55·00
  b. On emerald (3.21) (Optd S. £48) .. 27·00 55·00
139 3s. black/*red* .. .. 15·00 25·00
129/39 .. .. *Set of* 11 30·00 60·00
129/39 Optd "Specimen" .. .. *Set of* 11 £180

1917 (3 Jan). *Optd with T* **40** *at bottom of stamp.*
140 **39** 1d. red 10 60
  a. Overprint double £150
  b. "TAX" omitted .. .. ..
  c. "WAR TAX" omitted in vert pair with normal .. .. ..
  d. Opt inverted at top .. .. .. 85·00
  e. Opt double, one inverted* £100
  f. Opt inverted only, in pair with No. 140e* £400
141 3d. purple/*yellow-buff* .. .. .. 45 2·25
  a. Opt double .. .. 42·00
142 3d. purple/*lemon* .. .. 1·25 3·50
  a. Opt double .. .. 38·00
  b. Opt double, one inverted £250

*In Nos. 140e/f the inverted overprint is at foot and reads "TAX WAR" owing to displacement. No. 140e also exists with "WAR" omitted from the inverted overprint.

In both values of the first printings the stamp in the bottom left-hand corner of the sheet has a long "T" in "TAX", and on the first stamp of the sixth row the "X" is damaged and looks like a reversed "K".

1917 (Oct). *Second printing with overprint at top or in middle of stamp.*
143 **39** 1d. red 10 50
  a. Inverted opt at bottom or centre .. 25·00
  c. Overprint omitted, in pair with normal £160
  d. Double overprint, one at top, one at bottom .. .. 38·00
  e. As d., but additional overprint in top margin .. .. 90·00
  f. Vertical pair, one as d., the other normal £180
  g. Pair, one overprint inverted, one normal £225
  h. Double overprint at top (in pair with normal £180
  i. Overprint double .. .. .. 35·00 35·00
144 3d. purple/*yellow* .. .. 35 1·50
  a. Opt double .. .. 21·00
  b. Opt double, one inverted £200
144*c* 3d. purple/*lemon* 80

1918. *Overprinted with T* **40**.
145 **39** 3d. purple/*yellow* (R.) .. .. .. 5·00 15·00
  a. Opt double .. ..

WAR TAX
(41)

WAR TAX
(42)

WAR TAX
(43)

1918. *Optd with T* **41** *in London by D.L.R.*
146 **39** 1d. rose-carmine .. .. 20 1·00
  a. Bright rose-scarlet 15 90
147 3d. purple/*yellow* .. .. 15 1·00
146/7 Optd. "Specimen" .. .. *Set of* 2 80·00

1919. *Optd with T* **41** *in London by D.L.R.*
148 **39** 3d. purple/*orange-buff* (R.) .. .. 10 1·10
148 Optd "Specimen" .. .. 40·00

1919. *Local overprint. T* **40**, *in violet.*
149 **39** 1d. bright rose-scarlet .. .. .. 10 1·00
  a. "WAR" omitted £100
  b. Opt double .. .. 17·00
  c. Opt double in pair with normal .. £100
  d. Opt double, one inverted .. ..
  e. Rose-carmine .. .. 5·00 8·00
  ea. Opt double .. ..

1919. *Optd with T* **42**.
150 **39** 1d. scarlet 10 60
  a. Opt double £100 £100
  b. Opt double, one albino and reversed ..
151 3d. purple/*orange-buff* .. .. .. 30 1·75

1919 (17 Dec). *Optd with T* **43**.
152 **39** 1d. scarlet 10 75
  a. Opt inverted .. ..
153 3d. purple/*orange-buff* 10 80

The two bottom rows of this setting have the words "WAR" and "TAX" about 1 mm further apart.

1921 (23 April). *Wmk Mult Script CA. P 14.*
154 **37** ¼d. rose-red 60 4·50
155 **39** ½d. green 80 4·50
156 1d. carmine-red 45 3·00
157 2d. slate-grey 80 12·00
158 2½d. bright blue 1·40 5·00
159 5d. sage-green 5·50 24·00
160 6d. purple 5·50 26·00
161 1s. brown-orange 6·00 20·00
154/161 *Set of* 8 19·00 90·00
154/61 Optd "Specimen" *Set of* 8 £140

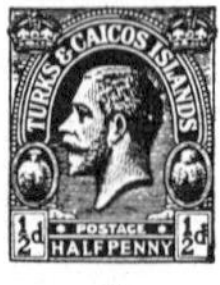

44

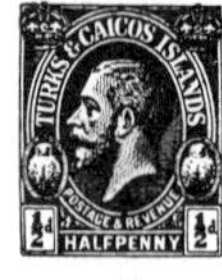

45

(Recess D.L.R.)

1922 (20 Nov)–**26**. *P 14. (a) Wmk Mult Script CA.*
162 **37** ¼d. black (11.10.26) 15 50
163 **44** ½d. yellow-green 30 90
a. Bright green 35 85
b. Apple-green 2·75 6·00
164 1d. brown 40 2·75
165 1½d. scarlet (24.11.25) 2·50 4·50
166 2d. slate 40 2·00
167 2½d. purple/*pale yellow* 30 60
168 3d. bright blue 40 1·50
169 4d. red/*pale yellow* 75 4·00
a. Carmine/pale yellow 2·75 8·00
170 5d. sage-green 65 7·50
171 6d. purple 60 2·75
172 1s. brown-orange 70 5·00
173 2s. red/*emerald* 2·00 4·75

(b) Wmk Mult Crown CA
174 **44** 2s. red/*emerald* (24.11.25) 16·00 45·00
175 3s. black/*red* (24.11.25) 5·00 13·00
162/75 *Set of* 14 27·00 85·00
162/75 Optd "Specimen" *Set of* 14 £200

1928 (1 Mar). *Inscr* "POSTAGE & REVENUE". *Wmk Mult Script CA. P 14.*
176 **45** ½d. green 40 40
177 1d. brown 40 70
178 1½d. scarlet 40 1·25
179 2d. grey 35 30
180 2½d. purple/*yellow* 35 1·00
181 3d. bright blue 35 1·75
182 6d. purple 40 2·75
183 1s. brown-orange 2·50 3·50
184 2s. red/*emerald* 3·25 18·00
185 5s. green/*yellow* 11·00 30·00
186 10s. purple/*blue* 38·00 75·00
176/86 *Set of* 11 50·00 £120
176/86 Optd "Specimen" *Set of* 11 £160

1935 (6 May). *Silver Jubilee. As Nos. 114/17 of Jamaica, but ptd by Waterlow. P 11×12.*
187 ½d. black and green 15 40
j. Kite and vertical log 20·00
k. Kite and horizontal log 20·00
188 3d. brown and deep blue 1·50 1·75
j. Kite and vertical log 50·00
189 6d. light blue and olive-green 1·50 2·25
j. Kite and vertical log 50·00
190 1s. slate and purple 1·50 3·25
j. Kite and vertical log 50·00
187/90 *Set of* 4 4·25 7·00
187/90 Perf "Specimen" *Set of* 4 75·00

For illustrations of plate varieties see Omnibus section following Zimbabwe.

1937 (12 May). *Coronation. As Nos. 118/20 of Jamaica.*
191 ½d. myrtle-green 10 10
a. Deep green
192 2d. grey-black 40 15
193 3d. bright blue 60 20
191/3 *Set of* 3 1·00 35
191/3 Perf "Specimen" *Set of* 3 55·00

46 Raking Salt

47 Salt Industry

(Recess Waterlow)

1938 (18 June)–**45**. *Wmk Mult Script CA. P 12½.*
194 **46** ¼d. black 10 10
195 ½d. yellowish green 1·25 15
a. Deep green (6.11.44) 15 50
196 1d. red-brown 15 10
197 1½d. scarlet 30 15
198 2d. grey 40 30
199 2½d. yellow-orange 1·75 30
a. Orange (6.11.44) 1·00 55
200 3d. bright blue 20 20
201 6d. mauve 6·00 1·25
201*a* 6d. sepia (9.2.45) 15 15
202 1s. yellow-bistre 2·25 5·50
202*a* 1s. grey-olive (9.2.45) 15 15
203 **47** 2s. deep rose-carmine 25·00 6·50
a. Bright rose-carmine (6.11.44) 14·00 8·50
204 5s. yellowish green 35·00 12·00
a. Deep green (6.11.44) 23·00 12·00
205 10s. bright violet 4·75 5·00
194/205 *Set of* 14 48·00 28·00
194/205 Perf "Specimen" *Set of* 14 £200

1946 (4 Nov). *Victory. As Nos. 141/2 of Jamaica.*
206 2d. black 10 10
207 3d. blue 15 10
206/7 Perf "Specimen" *Set of* 2 50·00

1948 (13 Sept). *Royal Silver Wedding. As Nos. 143/4 of Jamaica.*
208 1d. red-brown 15 10
209 10s. mauve 5·00 5·50

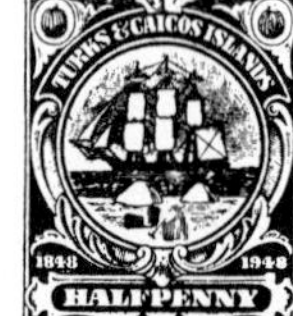

50 Badge of the Islands

53 Queen Victoria and King George VI

(Recess Waterlow)

1948 (14 Dec). *Centenary of Separation from Bahamas. T* **50**, **53** *and similar designs. Wmk Mult Script CA. P 12½.*
210 **50** ½d. blue-green 15 15
211 2d. carmine 30 15
212 – 3d. blue 35 15
213 – 6d. violet 30 20
214 **53** 2s. black and bright blue 35 35
215 5s. black and green 80 60
216 10s. black and brown 80 3·00
210/16 *Set of* 7 2·75 4·25

Designs: *Horiz*—3d. Flag of Turks and Caicos Islands; 6d. Map of islands.

1949 (10 Oct). *75th Anniv of U.P.U. As Nos. 145/8 of Jamaica.*
217 2½d. red-orange 30 30
218 3d. deep blue 40 40
219 6d. brown 40 40
220 1s. olive 40 30
217/20 *Set of* 4 1·40 1·25

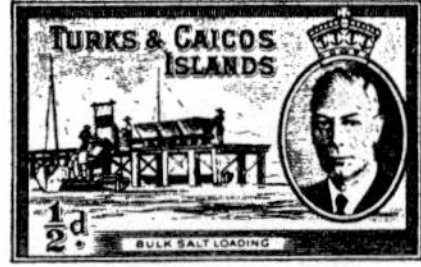

65 Bulk Salt Loading

66 Dependency's Badge

(Recess Waterlow)

1950 (1 Aug). *T* **65** *and similar horiz designs, and T* **66**. *Wmk Mult Script CA. P 12½.*
221 ½d. green 15 40
222 1d. red-brown 15 65
223 1½d. deep carmine 20 55
224 2d. red-orange 15 40
225 2½d. grey-olive 20 50
226 3d. bright blue 20 40
227 4d. black and rose 1·50 70
228 6d. black and blue 1·00 50
229 1s. black and blue-green 55 40
230 1s. 6d. black and scarlet 2·00 3·25
231 2s. emerald and ultramarine 1·25 3·50
232 5s. blue and black 6·00 3·75
233 10s. black and violet 13·00 13·00
221/33 *Set of* 13 24·00 25·00

Designs:—1d. Salt Cay; 1½d. Caicos mail; 2d. Grand Turk; 2½d. Sponge diving; 3d. South Creek; 4d. Map; 6d. Grand Turk Light; 1s. Government House; 1s. 6d. Cockburn Harbour; 2s. Government Offices; 5s. Loading salt.

1953 (2 June). *Coronation. As No. 153 of Jamaica, but ptd by B.W. & Co.*
234 2d. black and orange-red 15 80

67 M.V. *Kirksons*

(Recess Waterlow)

1955 (1 Feb). *T* **67** *and similar horiz design. Wmk Mult Script CA. P 12½.*
235 5d. black and bright green 30 30
236 8d. black and brown 70 20

Design:—8d. Greater Flamingoes in flight.

69 Queen Elizabeth II (after Annigoni)

70 Bonefish

82 Dependency's Badge

(Recess B.W.)

1957 (25 Nov). *T* **69/70**, **82** *and similar horiz design as T* **70**. *W w* **12**. *P 13½ × 14 (1d.), 14 (10s.) or 13½ (others).*
237 1d. deep blue and carmine 15 20
238 1½d. grey-green and orange 15 30
239 2d. red-brown and olive 15 15
240 2½d. carmine and green 15 15
241 3d. turquoise-blue and purple 15 15
242 4d. lake and black 20 15
243 5d. slate-green and brown 30 40
244 6d. carmine-rose and blue 75 20
245 8d. vermilion and black 2·25 10
246 1s. deep blue and black 20 10
247 1s. 6d. sepia and deep ultramarine 1·25 50
248 2s. deep ultramarine and brown 3·00 2·25
249 5s. black and carmine 75 2·00
250 10s. black and purple 7·00 8·00
237/250 *and* 253 *Set of* 15 42·00 27·00

Designs:—2d. Red Grouper; 2½d. Spiny Lobster; 3d. Albacore; 4d. Muttonfish Snapper; 5d. Permit; 6d. Conch; 8d. Greater Flamingoes; 1s. Spanish Mackerel; 1s. 6d. Salt Cay; 2s. *Uakon* (Caicos sloop); 5s. Cable Office.

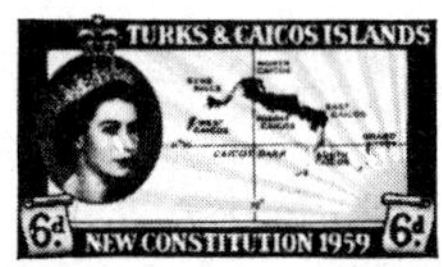

83 Map of the Turks and Caicos Islands

(Photo D.L.R.)

1959 (4 July). *New Constitution. Wmk Mult Script CA. P 13½ × 14.*
251 **83** 6d. deep olive and light orange 15 10
252 8d. violet and light orange 15 10

84 Brown Pelican

(Des Mrs. S. Hurd. Photo Harrison)

1960 (1 Nov). *W w 12. P 14 × 14½.*
253 **84** £1 sepia and deep red 30·00 16·00

CROWN COLONY

1963 (4 June). *Freedom from Hunger. As No. 80 of Lesotho.*
254 8d. carmine 20 10

1963 (2 Sept). *Red Cross Centenary. As Nos. 203/4 of Jamaica.*
255 2d. red and black 15 15
256 8d. red and blue 30 25

1964 (23 Apr). *400th Birth Anniv of William Shakespeare. As No. 156 of Montserrat.*
257 8d. green 10 10

1965 (17 May). *I.T.U. Centenary. As Nos. 98/9 of Lesotho.*
258 1d. vermilion and brown 10 10
259 2s. light emerald and turquoise-blue 20 20

1965 (25 Oct). *International Co-operation Year. As Nos. 100/1 of Lesotho.*
260 1d. reddish purple and turquoise-green 10 10
261 8d. deep bluish green and lavender 20 10

1966 (24 Jan). *Churchill Commemoration. As Nos. 102/5 of Lesotho.*
262 1d. new blue 10 10
263 2d. deep green 15 10
264 8d. brown 15 10
a. Gold ptg double £130
265 1s. 6d. bluish violet 25 25
262/5 *Set of* 4 50 35

1966 (4 Feb). *Royal Visit. As Nos. 183/4 of Montserrat.*
266 8d. black and ultramarine 25 10
267 1s. 6d. black and magenta 45 20

85 Andrew Symmer going ashore

(Des V. Whiteley. Photo D.L.R.)

1966 (1 Oct). *Bicentenary of "Ties with Britain" T* **85** *and similar horiz designs. P* 13½.

No.	Description		Unused	Used
268	1d. deep blue and orange		10	10
269	8d. red, blue and orange-yellow		10	10
270	1s. 6d. multicoloured		15	10
268/70		*Set of* 3	30	15

Designs:—8d. Andrew Symmer and Royal Warrant; 1s. 6d. Arms and Royal Cypher.

1966 (1 Dec). *20th Anniv of U.N.E.S.C.O. As Nos.* 342/4 *of Mauritius.*

No.	Description		Unused	Used
271	1d. slate-violet, red, yellow and orange		10	10
272	8d. orange-yellow, violet and deep olive		15	10
273	1s. 6d. black, bright purple and orange		20	40
271/3		*Set of* 3	35	50

88 Turk's-head Cactus

89 Boat-building

90 Arms of Turks and Caicos Islands

91 Queen Elizabeth II

(Des V. Whiteley. Photo Harrison)

1967 (1 Feb). *Designs as T* **88/91**. *W w* **12**. *P* 14½ × 14 (*vert*) *or* 14 × 14½ (*horiz*).

No.	Description		Unused	Used
274	1d. olive-yellow, vermilion & brt bluish vio		10	10
275	1½d. brown and orange-yellow		10	10
276	2d. deep slate and deep orange-yellow		15	10
277	3d. agate and dull green		20	10
278	4d. bright mauve, black and turquoise		30	10
279	6d. sepia and new blue		30	10
280	8d. yellow, turquoise-blue and deep blue		20	10
281	1s. maroon and turquoise		20	10
282	1s. 6d. orange-yellow, lake-brn & dp turq-bl		50	20
283	2s. multicoloured		60	85
284	3s. maroon and turquoise-blue		55	30
285	5s. ochre, blue and new blue		1·25	1·75
286	10s. multicoloured		1·75	2·25
287	£1 Prussian blue, silver and crimson		3·25	4·75
274/287		*Set of* 14	8·25	9·50

Designs: *Vert as T* **88**—2d. Donkey; 3d. Sisal industry; 6d. Salt industry; 8d. Skin-diving; 1s. 6d. Water-skiing. *Horiz as T* **89**—4d. Conch industry; 1s. Fishing; 2s. Crawfish industry; 3s. Maps of Turks and Caicos Islands and West Indies; 5s. Fishing industry.

102 Turks Islands 1d. Stamp of 1867

(Des R. Granger Barrett. Photo Harrison)

1967 (1 May). *Stamp Centenary. T* **102** *and similar horiz designs. W w* **12**. *P* 14½.

No.	Description		Unused	Used
288	1d. black and light magenta		10	10
289	6d. black and bluish grey		10	10
290	1s. black and turquoise-blue		10	10
288/90		*Set of* 3	15	10

Designs:—6d. Queen Elizabeth "stamp" and Turks Islands 6d. stamp of 1867; 1s. Turks Islands 1s. stamp of 1867.

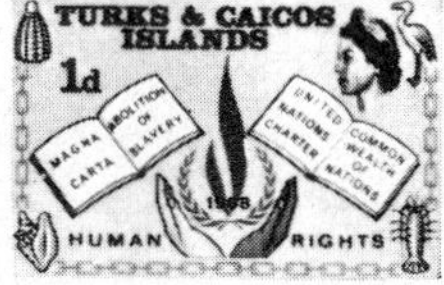

104 Human Rights Emblem and Charter

(Des R. Granger Barrett. Photo Harrison)

1968 (1 Apr). *Human Rights Year. W w* **12**. *P* 14 × 14½.

No.	Type	Description		Unused	Used
291	104	1d. multicoloured		10	10
292		8d. multicoloured		10	10
293		1s. 6d. multicoloured		10	10
291/3			*Set of* 3	15	15

105 Dr Martin Luther King and "Freedom March"

(Des V. Whiteley. Photo Harrison)

1968 (1 Oct). *Martin Luther King Commemoration. W w* **12**. *P* 14 × 14½.

No.	Type	Description		Unused	Used
294	105	2d. yellow-brown, blackish brn & dp bl		10	10
295		8d. yellow-brown, blackish brn & lake		10	10
296		1s. 6d. yellow-brn, blackish brn & vio		10	10
294/6			*Set of* 3	15	15

(New Currency. 100 cents=1 dollar)

1c

(106)

107 "The Nativity with John the Baptist"

1969 (8 Sept)–**71**. *Decimal currency. Nos.* 274/87 *surch as T* **106** *by Harrison & Sons, and new value* (¼ *c.*) *as T* **90**.

No.	Description		Unused	Used
297	¼ c. pale greenish grey and multicoloured		10	10
	a. Bronze-green & multicoloured (2.2.71)		30	10
298	1 c. on 1d. olive-yell, verm & brt bluish vio		10	10
	a. Wmk sideways		10	10
299	2 c. on 2d. deep slate & deep orange-yellow		10	10
	a. Wmk sideways		10	10
300	3 c. on 3d. agate and dull green		10	10
	a. Wmk sideways		10	10
301	4 c. on 4d. bright mauve, black & turquoise		10	10
302	5 c. on 6d. sepia and new blue		10	10
	a. Wmk sideways		10	10
303	7 c. on 8d. yellow, turquoise-blue & dp blue		10	10
	a. Wmk sideways		10	10
304	8 c. on 1½d. brown and orange-yellow		10	10
305	10 c. on 1s. maroon and turquoise		20	10
306	15 c. on 1s. 6d. orange-yellow, lake-brown and deep turquoise-blue		25	10
	a. Wmk sideways		20	25
307	20 c. on 2s. multicoloured		30	25
308	30 c. on 3s. maroon and turquoise-blue		55	35
309	50 c. on 5s. ochre, blue and new blue		1·00	45
310	$1 on 10s. multicoloured		1·50	1·00
311	$2 on £1 Prussian blue, silver and crimson		4·00	10·00
	a. Wmk sideways		1·50	3·00
297/311a		*Set of* 15	5·00	4·75

The 4, 8, 10, 20, 30, 50 c., and $1 exist with PVA gum as well as gum arabic.

No. 311 was only on sale through the Crown Agents.

(Des adapted by V. Whiteley. Litho D.L.R.)

1969 (20 Oct). *Christmas. Scenes from* 16*th-cent Book of Hours. T* **107** *and similar vert design. Multicoloured. W w* **12**. *P* 13 × 12½.

No.	Description		Unused	Used
312	1 c. Type **107**		10	10
313	3 c. "The Flight into Egypt"		10	10
314	15 c. Type **107**		15	10
315	30 c. As 3 c.		25	10
312/15		*Set of* 4	40	30

109 Coat of Arms

110 "Christ bearing the Cross"

(Des L. Curtis. Litho B.W.)

1970 (2 Feb). *New Constitution. Multicoloured; background colours given. W w* **12** (*sideways*). *P* 13 × 12½.

No.	Type	Description		Unused	Used
316	109	7 c. brown		20	10
317		35 c. deep violet-blue		35	20

(Des, recess and litho Enschedé)

1970 (17 Mar). *Easter. Details from the "Small Engraved Passion" by Dürer. T* **110** *and similar vert designs. W w* **12** (*sideways*). *P* 13 × 13½.

No.	Description		Unused	Used
318	5 c. olive-grey and blue		10	10
319	7 c. olive-grey and vermilion		10	10
320	50 c. olive-grey and red-brown		30	30
318/20		*Set of* 3	40	40

Designs:—7 c. "Christ on the Cross"; 50 c. "The Lamentation of Christ".

113 Dickens and Scene from *Oliver Twist*

(Des Sylvia Goaman. Recess and litho D.L.R.)

1970 (17 June). *Death Centenary of Charles Dickens. T* **113** *and similar horiz designs. W w* **12** (*sideways*). *P* 13.

No.	Description		Unused	Used
321	1 c. black and yellow-brown/*yellow*		10	10
322	3 c. black and Prussian blue/*flesh*		10	10
323	15 c. black and grey-blue/*flesh*		15	10
324	30 c. black and drab/*blue*		30	10
321/4		*Set of* 4	45	30

Designs (each incorporating portrait of Dickens as in T **113**, and a scene from one of his novels):—3 c. *A Christmas Carol*; 15 c. *Pickwick Papers*; 30 c. *The Old Curiosity Shop*.

114 Ambulance—1870

(Des Harrison. Litho B.W.)

1970 (4 Aug). *Centenary of British Red Cross. T* **114** *and similar horiz design. Multicoloured. W w* **12**. *P* 13½ × 14.

No.	Description		Unused	Used
325	1 c. Type **114**		10	10
326	5 c. Ambulance—1970		10	10
	a. Wmk sideways		15	10
	ab. Grey omitted		£250	
327	15 c. Type **114**		20	10
	a. Wmk sideways		30	10
328	30 c. As 5 c.		30	10
	a. Wmk sideways		45	40
325/8		*Set of* 4	55	30

115 Duke of Albermarle and Coat of Arms

(Des V. Whiteley. Litho Enschedé)

1970 (1 Dec). *Tercentenary of Issue of Letters Patent. T* **115** *and similar horiz design. Multicoloured. W w* **12**. *P* 12½ × 13½.

No.	Description		Unused	Used
329	1 c. Type **115**		10	10
330	8 c. Arms of Charles II and Elizabeth II		20	20
331	10 c. Type **115**		20	15
332	35 c. As 8 c.		40	65
329/32		*Set of* 4	75	1·00

116 Boat-building

117 Seahorse

1971 (2 Feb). *Designs as T* **88/91** *etc., but inscr in decimal currency as in T* **116**. *W w* **12** (*sideways on* 1 *c.*, 2 *c.*, 3 *c.*, 5 *c.*, 7 *c.*, 15 *c. and* $2).

No.	Description		Unused	Used
333	1 c. olive-yell, verm & brt bluish vio (as 1d.)		10	10
334	2 c. deep slate & deep orange-yell (as 2d.)		10	10
335	3 c. agate and dull green (as 3d.)		15	10
336	4 c. bright mauve, black & turquoise (as 4d.)		40	10
337	5 c. sepia and new blue (as 6d.)		20	10
338	7 c. yellow, turquoise-blue & dp blue (as 8d.)		25	10
339	8 c. brown and orange-yellow		50	10
340	10 c. maroon and turquoise (as 1s.)		50	10
341	15 c. orange-yellow, lake-brown and deep turquoise-blue (as 1s. 6d.)		1·00	40
342	20 c. multicoloured (as 2s.)		1·25	1·25
343	30 c. maroon and turquoise-blue (as 3s.)		1·75	80

344 50 c. ochre, blue and new blue (as 5s.) .. 2·50 2·00
345 $1 multicoloured (as 10s.) .. .. .. 2·75 3·00
a. Green omitted .. ..
346 $2 Prussian blue, silver and crimson (as £1) 4·00 7·50
333/46 .. .. *Set of* 14 14·00 14·00

The ¼ c. value was also re-issued, but it can only be distinguished from No. 297 by its revised sheet format of 25 instead of 60.

(Des G. Vasarhelyi. Litho J.W.)

1971 (4 May). *Tourist Development. T* **117** *and similar multi-coloured designs. W* w **12** *(sideways on Nos.* 348/50). *P* 14 × 14½ (1 c.) *or* 14½ × 14 *(others).*

347 1 c. Type **117** 10 10
348 3 c. Queen Conch Shell *(horiz)* 10 10
349 15 c. Oystercatcher *(horiz)* 30 10
350 30 c. Blue Marlin *(horiz)* 30 15
347/50 .. .. *Set of* 4 60 30

118 Pirate Sloop

119 The Wilton Diptych (Left Wing)

(Des and litho J.W.)

1971 (27 July). *Pirates. T* **118** *and similar horiz designs. Multi-coloured. W* w **12** *(sideways). P* 14.

351 2 c. Type **118** 10 10
352 3 c. Pirate treasure 10 10
353 15 c. Marooned sailor 45 15
354 30 c. Buccaneers 70 45
351/4 .. .. *Set of* 4 1·25 70

(Des J.W. Litho Questa)

1971 (12 Oct). *Christmas. T* **119** *and similar vert design. Multi-coloured. W* w **12**. *P* 13½.

355 2 c. Type **119** 10 10
a. Horiz pair. Nos. 355/6 .. .. 10 10
356 2 c. The Wilton Diptych (Right Wing) .. 10 10
357 8 c. Type **119** 10 10
a. Horiz pair. Nos. 357/8 .. .. 20 10
358 8 c. As No. 356 .. .. 10 10
359 15 c. Type **119** 20 10
a. Horiz pair. Nos. 359/60 .. .. 40 20
360 15 c. As No. 356 .. .. 20 10
355/60 .. .. *Set of* 6 65 35

The two stamps of each denomination were printed in horizontal *se-tenant* pairs throughout the sheet.

120 Cape Kennedy Launching Area

121 "Christ before Pilate" (Rembrandt)

(Des V. Whiteley. Litho A. & M.)

1972 (21 Feb). *Tenth Anniv of Colonel Glenn's Splashdown. T* **120** *and similar multicoloured designs. W* w **12** *(sideways on* 5, 10 *and* 15 *c.). P* 13½.

361 5 c. Type **120** 10 10
362 10 c. "Friendship 7" space capsule 10 10
363 15 c. Map of Islands and splashdown 15 10
364 20 c. N.A.S.A. Space Medal *(vert)* 15 10
361/4 .. .. *Set of* 4 40 30

(Des and litho J.W.)

1972 (21 Mar). *Easter. T* **121** *and similar designs. W* w **12** *(sideways on* 15 *c.). P* 13½.

365 2 c. black and lilac 10 10
366 15 c. black and rose-pink 15 10
367 30 c. black and greenish yellow 25 15
365/7 .. .. *Set of* 3 40 30

Designs: *Horiz*—15 c. "The Three Crosses" (Rembrandt). *Vert*—30 c. "The Descent from the Cross" (Rembrandt).

122 Christopher Columbus

123 Turk's-head Cactus and Spiny Lobster

(Des P. Powell. Litho J.W.)

1972 (28 July*). *Discoverers and Explorers. T* **122** *and similar multicoloured designs. W* w **12** *(sideways on* 8 *and* 30 *c.). P* 13½.

368 ¼ c. Type **122** 10 10
369 8 c. Sir Richard Grenville *(horiz)* 30 10
370 10 c. Capt. John Smith 35 10
371 30 c. Juan Ponce de Leon *(horiz)* 85 75
368/71 .. .. *Set of* 4 1·40 75

*This was the local date of issue; the Crown Agents released the stamps on 4 July.

(Des (from photograph by D. Groves) and photo Harrison)

1972 (20 Nov). *Royal Silver Wedding. Multicoloured; background colour given. W* w **12**. *P* 14 × 14½.

372 **123** 10 c. dull ultramarine 10 10
373 20 c. myrtle-green 15 10

124 Treasure Hunting, *circa* 1700

125 Arms of Jamaica and Turks & Caicos Islands

(Des C. Abbott. Litho Questa)

1973 (18 Jan). *Treasure. T* **124** *and similar vert designs. W* w **12** *(sideways). P* 14 × 14½.

374 3 c. multicoloured 10 10
375 5 c. reddish purple, silver and black 10 10
376 10 c. magenta, silver and black 20 10
377 30 c. multicoloured 60 30
374/7 .. .. *Set of* 4 85 35
MS378 127 × 108 mm. Nos. 374/7 .. .. 1·50 2·00

Designs:—5 c. Silver Bank medallion (obverse); 10 c. Silver Bank medallion (reverse); 30 c. Treasure hunting, 1973.

(Des PAD Studio. Litho Walsall)

1973 (16 Apr). *Centenary of Annexation to Jamaica. W* w **12** *(sideways). P* 13½ × 14.

379 **125** 15 c. multicoloured 30 10
380 35 c. multicoloured 60 20

126 Sooty Tern

127 Bermuda Sloop

(Des R. Granger Barrett. Litho Questa)

1973 (1 Aug). *T* **126** *and similar vert designs. W* w **12** *(sideways). P* 14.

381 ¼ c. Type **126** 10 15
382 1 c. Magnificent Frigate Bird 20 30
383 2 c. Common Noddy 30 30
384 3 c. Blue-grey Gnatcatcher 85 40
385 4 c. Little Blue Heron 35 50
386 5 c. Catbird 30 20
387 7 c. Black-whiskered Vireo .. .. 2·25 20
388 8 c. Osprey .. .. 3·00 55
389 10 c. Greater Flamingo 70 40
390 15 c. Brown Pelican .. .. .. 1·25 50
391 20 c. Parula Warbler .. .. .. 3·50 1·25
392 30 c. Northern Mockingbird .. .. 1·75 90
393 50 c. Ruby-throated Hummingbird .. .. 3·25 3·00
394 $1 Bananaquit .. .. .. 3·50 4·00
395 $2 Cedar Waxwing .. .. .. 5·50 5·50
381/95 .. .. .. *Set of* 15 24·00 16·00

See also Nos. 411/14 and 451/64.

(Des R. Granger Barrett. Litho Questa)

1973 (14 Aug). *Vessels. T* **127** *and similar horiz designs. Multi-coloured. W* w **12**. *P* 13½.

396 2 c. Type **127** 15 10
397 5 c. H.M.S. *Blanche* 25 10
398 8 c. U.S. privateer *Grand Turk* and P.O. packet *Hinchinbrooke* 30 15
399 10 c. H.M.S. *Endymion* 30 15
400 15 c. R.M.S. *Medina* 35 70
401 20 c. H.M.S. *Daring* 45 75
396/401 .. .. .. *Set of* 6 1·60 1·75
MS402 198 × 101 mm. Nos. 396/401 .. .. 1·60 2·75

1973 (14 Nov). *Royal Wedding. As Nos.* 322/3 *of Montserrat.*

403 12 c. light turquoise-blue 10 10
404 18 c. dull indigo 10 10

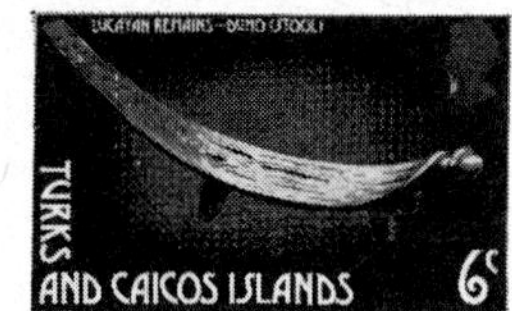

128 Duho (stool)

(Des Jennifer Toombs. Litho Questa)

1974 (17 July). *Lucayan Remains. T* **128** *and similar horiz designs. Multicoloured. W* w **12** *(sideways). P* 14½ × 14.

405 6 c. Type **128** 10 10
406 10 c. Broken wood bowl 15 10
407 12 c. Greenstone axe 15 10
408 18 c. Wood bowl 15 10
409 35 c. Fragment of duho 20 20
405/9 .. .. *Set of* 5 65 40
MS410 240 × 90 mm. Nos. 405/9 .. .. 75 1·25

1974–75. *As Nos.* 381 *etc, but W* w **12** *(upright).*

411 1 c. Magnificent Frigate Bird (11.6.75) .. 75 1·00
412 2 c. Common Noddy (27.9.74) .. .. 1·00 70
413 3 c. Blue-grey Gnatcatcher (19.3.75) .. 2·75 1·00
414 20 c. Parula Warbler (11.6.75) .. .. 2·75 3·50
411/14 .. .. *Set of* 4 6·50 5·50

Nos. 415/25 vacant.

129 G.P.O., Grand Turk

(Des G. Drummond. Litho Questa)

1974 (9 Oct). *Centenary of Universal Postal Union. T* **129** *and similar horiz designs. Multicoloured. W* w **12**. *P* 14.

426 4 c. Type **129** 10 10
427 12 c. Sloop and island map 20 10
428 18 c. "U.P.U." and globe 20 10
429 55 c. Posthorn and emblem 35 35
426/9 .. .. *Set of* 4 75 55

130 Churchill and Roosevelt

131 Spanish Captain, *circa* 1492

(Des V. Whiteley. Litho Questa)

1974 (30 Nov). *Birth Centenary of Sir Winston Churchill. T* **130** *and similar horiz design. Multicoloured. W* w **14** *(sideways). P* 14.

430 12 c. Type **130** 15 15
431 18 c. Churchill and vapour-trails 15 15
MS432 85 × 85 mm. Nos. 430/1 .. .. 40 55

(Des J.W. Litho Questa)

1975 (26 Mar). *Military Uniforms. T* **131** *and similar vert designs. Multicoloured. W* w **14**. *P* 14.

433 5 c. Type **131** 10 10
434 20 c. Officer, Royal Artillery, 1783 .. .. 30 15
435 25 c. Officer, 67th Foot, 1798 .. .. 35 15
436 35 c. Private, 1st West India Regt, 1833 .. 45 25
433/6 .. .. *Set of* 4 1·10 50
MS437 145 × 88 mm. Nos. 433/6 .. .. 1·25 2·00

132 Ancient Windmill, Salt Cay

133 Star Coral

(Des P. Powell. Litho Questa)

1975 (16 Oct). *Salt-raking Industry. T* **132** *and similar multi-coloured designs. W w* **12** *(sideways on* 10 *and* 20 *c.). P* 14.

438	6 c. Type **132**	15	10
439	10 c. Salt pans drying in sun (*horiz*)	15	10
440	20 c. Salt-raking (*horiz*)	20	15
441	25 c. Unprocessed salt heaps	25	20
438/41	*Set of* 4	65	40

(Des C. Abbott. Litho Questa)

1975 (4 Dec). *Island Coral. T* **133** *and similar horiz designs. Multicoloured. W w* **14** *(sideways). P* 14.

442	6 c. Type **133**	15	10
443	10 c. Elkhorn Coral	20	10
444	20 c. Brain Coral	35	15
445	25 c. Staghorn Coral	40	20
442/5	*Set of* 4	1·00	40

134 American Schooner

135 1s. 6d. Royal Visit Stamp of 1966

(Des J.W. Litho Questa)

1976 (28 May). *Bicentenary of American Revolution. T* **134** *and similar vert designs. Multicoloured. W w* **14.** *P* 13½.

446	6 c. Type **134**	30	10
447	20 c. British ship of the line	70	15
448	25 c. American privateer *Grand Turk*	70	20
449	55 c. British ketch	1·25	60
446/9	*Set of* 4	2·75	95
MS450	95 × 151 mm. Nos. 446/9	2·75	4·50

Each value depicts, at the top, the engagement between the *Grand Turk* and the P.O. Packet *Hinchinbrooke*, as in T **134**.

1976–77. *As Nos.* 381/95, *and new value* ($5), *but W w* **14** *(upright).*

451	¼ c. Type **126** (12.77)	40	1·25
452	1 c. Magnificent Frigate Bird (12.77)	45	60
453	2 c. Common Noddy (12.77)	45	1·00
454	3 c. Blue-grey Gnatcatcher (14.6.76)	90	40
455	4 c. Little Blue Heron (12.77)	1·00	90
456	5 c. Catbird (12.77)	1·00	1·00
457	10 c. Greater Flamingo (12.77)	1·25	1·25
458	15 c. Brown Pelican (12.77)	1·25	1·75
459	20 c. Parula Warbler (30.11.76)	1·50	75
460	30 c. Northern Mockingbird (12.77)	1·25	2·00
461	50 c. Ruby-throated Hummingbird (12.77)	1·50	2·00
462	$1 Bananaquit (12.77)	2·25	2·75
463	$2 Cedar Waxwing (12.77)	3·75	4·50
464	$5 Painted Bunting (24.11.76)	3·50	4·00
451/64	*Set of* 14	18·00	22·00

No. 465 vacant.

(Des V. Whiteley Studio. Litho Walsall)

1976 (14 July). *Tenth Anniv of Royal Visit. T* **135** *and similar horiz design. Multicoloured. W w* **14** *(sideways). P* 14½ × 14.

466	20 c. Type **135**	50	30
467	25 c. 8d. Royal Visit stamp	60	30

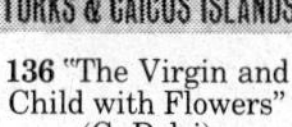

136 "The Virgin and Child with Flowers" (C. Dolci)

137 Balcony Scene, Buckingham Palace

(Des G. Drummond. Litho Questa)

1976 (10 Nov). *Christmas. T* **136** *and similar vert designs. Multicoloured. W w* **14.** *P* 13½.

468	6 c. Type **136**	10	10
469	10 c. "Virgin and Child with St. John and an Angel" (Studio of Botticelli)	10	10
470	20 c. "Adoration of the Magi" (Master of Paraiso)	30	15
471	25 c. "Adoration of the Magi" (French miniature)	30	20
468/71	*Set of* 4	65	35

(Des J.W. (**MS**475), C. Abbott (others) Litho Questa)

1977 (7 Feb–6 Dec). *Silver Jubilee. T* **137** *and similar vert designs. Multicoloured. W w* **14.** *P* 14 × 13½ (**MS**475) *or* 13½ *(others).*

472	6 c. Queen presenting O.B.E. to E. T. Wood	10	10
473	25 c. The Queen with regalia	20	25
474	55 c. Type **137**	40	55
472/4	*Set of* 3	60	75
MS475	120 × 97 mm. $5 Queen Elizabeth II (6.12.77)	1·00	1·40

138 Col. Glenn's "Mercury" Capsule

139 "Flight of the Holy Family" (Rubens)

(Des and litho J.W.)

1977 (20 June). *25th Anniv of U.S. Tracking Station. T* **138** *and similar multicoloured designs. W w* **14** *(sideways on horiz designs). P* 13½.

476	1 c. Type **138**	10	10
477	3 c. Moon buggy "Rover" (*vert*)	10	10
478	6 c. Tracking Station, Grand Turk	10	10
479	20 c. Moon landing craft (*vert*)	15	15
480	25 c. Col. Glenn's rocket launch (*vert*)	20	20
481	50 c. "Telstar 1" satellite	30	40
476/81	*Set of* 6	70	80

(Des J.W. Litho Questa)

1977 (23 Dec). *Christmas and 400th Birth Anniv of Rubens. T* **139** *and similar vert designs. Multicoloured. P* 14.

482	¼ c. Type **139**	10	10
483	½ c. "Adoration of the Magi" (1634)	10	10
484	1 c. "Adoration of the Magi" (1624)	10	10
485	6 c. "Virgin within Garland"	10	10
486	20 c. "Madonna and Child Adored by Angels"	15	10
487	$2 "Adoration of the Magi" (1618)	1·25	1·25
482/7	*Set of* 6	1·40	1·25
MS488	100 × 81 mm. $1 detail of 20 c.	60	1·00

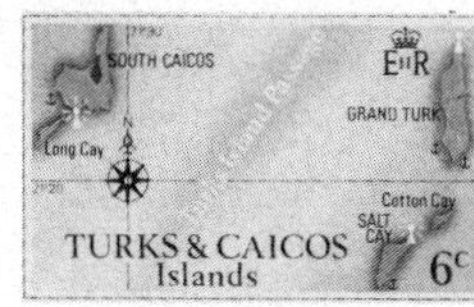

140 Map of Passage

(Des R. Granger Barrett. Litho J.W.)

1978 (2 Feb). *Turks Islands Passage. T* **140** *and similar horiz designs. Multicoloured. P* 13½. *A. No wmk. B. W w* **14** *(sideways).*

No.	Description	A		B	
489	6 c. Type **140**	10	10	10	10
490	20 c. Caicos sloop passing Grand Turk Lighthouse	35	55	35	55
491	25 c. Motor cruiser	40	65	40	65
492	55 c. *Jamaica Planter* (freighter)	85	1·60	85	1·60
489/92	*Set of* 4	1·50	2·50	1·50	2·50
MS493	136 × 88 mm. Nos. 489/92. P 14½	1·50	2·25	55·00	—

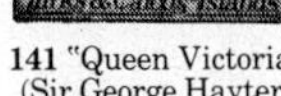

141 "Queen Victoria" (Sir George Hayter)

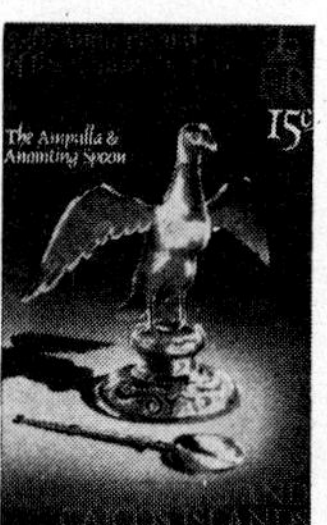

142 Ampulla and Anointing Spoon

(Manufactured by Walsall (Nos. 499/501). Des PAD Studio. Litho Questa (others))

1978 (2 June–July). *25th Anniv of Coronation. Multicoloured.*

(*a*) *Sheet stamps. Vert designs as T* **141** *showing British monarchs in coronation robes. P* 14

494	6 c. Type **141**	10	10
495	10 c. "King Edward VII" (Sir Samuel Fildes)	10	15
496	25 c. King George V	20	15
497	$2 King George VI	1·00	1·00
494/7	*Set of* 4	1·25	1·10
MS498	161 × 113 mm. $2.50, Queen Elizabeth II	1·00	1·00

(*b*) *Booklet stamps. Vert designs as T* **142.** *Imperf × roul* 5*. *Self-adhesive* (July)

499	15 c. Type **142**	15	30
	a. Booklet pane. Nos. 499/501	1·90	
	b. Booklet pane. Nos. 499/500, each × 3	1·25	
500	25 c. St. Edward's Crown	15	30
501	$2 Queen Elizabeth II in coronation robes	1·75	2·75
499/501	*Set of* 3	1·90	3·00

Nos. 494/7 also exist perf 12 (*Price for set of* 4 £1.25 *mint or used*) from additional sheetlets of 3 stamps and 1 label. Stamps perforated 14 are from normal sheets of 50.

*Nos. 499/501 are separated by various combinations of rotary-knife (giving a straight edge) and roulette.

143 Wilbur Wright and *Flyer III*

(Des Curtis Design. Litho Format)

1978 (July). *75th Anniv of Powered Flight. T* **143** *and similar horiz designs. Multicoloured. P* 14½.

502	1 c. Type **143**	10	10
503	6 c. Wright brothers and Cessna "337"	10	10
504	10 c. Orville Wright and "Electra"	10	10
505	15 c. Wilbur Wright and "C-47"	15	15
506	35 c. Wilbur Wright and "Islander"	35	35
507	$2 Wilbur Wright and Wright biplane	1·25	1·50
502/7	*Set of* 6	1·75	2·00
MS508	111 × 84 mm. $1 Orville Wright and Wright glider	75	1·40

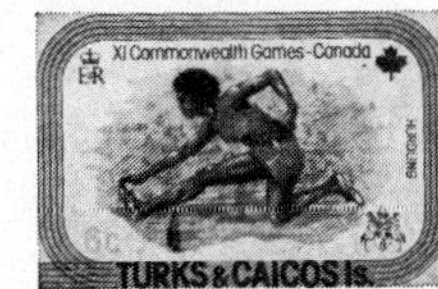

144 Hurdling

(Des J.W. Litho Format)

1978 (3 Aug). *Commonwealth Games, Edmonton. T* **144** *and similar horiz designs. Multicoloured. P* 14½.

509	6 c. Type **144**	10	10
510	20 c. Weightlifting	15	15
511	55 c. Boxing	30	30
512	$2 Cycling	1·00	1·00
509/12	*Set of* 4	1·25	1·25
MS513	105 × 79 mm. $1 Sprinting	75	1·25

145 Indigo Hamlet

146 "Madonna of the Siskin"

(Des G. Drummond. Litho Questa)

1978 (17 Nov)–**83.** *Fishes. Horiz designs as T* **145.** *Multicoloured.*

A. *No imprint date. P* 14

514A	1 c. Type **145**	10	25
515A	2 c. Tobacco fish (19.1.79)	40	10
516A	3 c. Passing Jack	15	10
517A	4 c. Porkfish (19.1.79)	40	20
518A	5 c. Spanish Grunt	20	20
519A	7 c. Yellowtail Snapper (19.1.79)	50	15
520A	8 c. Foureye Butterflyfish (19.1.79)	60	10
521A	10 c. Yellowfin Grouper	30	15
522A	15 c. Beau Gregory	50	30
523A	20 c. Queen Angelfish	30	30
524A	30 c. Hogfish (19.1.79)	1·00	40
525A	50 c. Fairy Basslet (19.1.79)	1·00	65
526A	$1 Clown Wrasse (19.1.79)	1·75	1·60
527A	$2 Stoplight Parrotfish (19.1.79)	3·25	2·50
528A	$5 Queen Triggerfish (19.1.79)	3·25	6·50
514A/28A	*Set of* 15	12·00	11·50

B. *With imprint date at foot of design. P* 14 (15 *c.*) *or* 12 *(others).*

514B	1 c. Type **145** (15.12.81)	50	45
518B	5 c. Spanish Grunt (15.12.81)	65	35
521B	10 c. Yellowfin Grouper (15.12.81)	75	45
522B	15 c. Beau Gregory (25.1.83)	1·25	80
523B	20 c. Queen Angelfish (15.12.81)	1·25	1·00
	a. Perf 14 (25.1.83)	85	90
525B	50 c. Fairy Basslet (15.12.81)	1·75	1·50
526B	$1 Clown Wrasse (15.12.81)	3·25	3·00
	a. Perf 14 (25.1.83)	2·00	2·75
527B	$2 Stoplight Parrotfish (15.12.81)	5·50	5·00
	a. Perf 14 (25.1.83)	3·00	4·00
528B	$5 Queen Triggerfish (15.12.81)	9·50	11·00
	a. Perf 14 (25.1.83)	7·50	9·00
514B/28B	*Set of* 9	22·00	21·00

(Des BG Studio. Litho Questa)

1978 (11 Dec). *Christmas. Paintings by Dürer. T* **146** *and similar multicoloured designs. P* 14.

529	6 c. Type **146**	10	10
530	20 c. "The Virgin and Child with St. Anne"	15	10
531	35 c. "Paumgärtner Nativity" (*horiz*)	20	15
532	$2 "Praying Hands"	85	1·00
529/32	*Set of* 4	1·10	1·10
MS533	137 × 124 mm. $1 "Adoration of the Magi" (*horiz*)	60	1·00

MINIMUM PRICE

The minimum price quote is 10p which represents a handling charge rather than a basis for valuing common stamps. For further notes about prices see introductory pages.

147 Osprey

(Des G. Drummond. Litho Questa)

1979 (29 May). *Endangered Wildlife. T* **147** *and similar horiz designs. Multicoloured. P* 14.

534 6 c. Type **147** 40 10
535 20 c. Green Turtle 45 20
536 25 c. Queen Conch 50 25
537 55 c. Rough-toothed Dolphin 90 50
538 $1 Humpback Whale .. .. .. 1·50 1·25
534/8 .. .. *Set of* 5 3·25 2·10
MS539 117 × 85 mm. $2 Iguana .. .. .. 2·25 3·00

148 "The Beloved" (painting by D. G. Rossetti)

(Des G. Vasarhelyi. Litho Questa)

1979 (2 July). *International Year of the Child. T* **148** *and similar horiz designs showing paintings and I.Y.C. emblem. Multicoloured. P* 14.

540 6 c. Type **148** 10 10
541 25 c. "Tahitian Girl" (P. Gauguin) 15 10
542 55 c. "Calmady Children" (Sir Thomas Lawrence) 25 20
543 $1 "Mother and Daughter" (detail, P. Gauguin) 45 45
540/3 .. .. *Set of* 4 80 70
MS544 112 × 85 mm. $2 "Marchesa Elena Grimaldi" (A. van Dyck) .. .. 55 1·25

149 R.M.S.P. *Medina* and Handstamped Cover

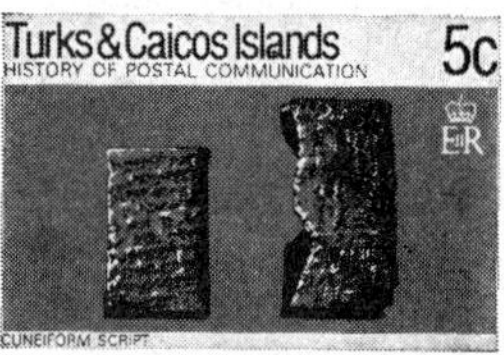

150 Cuneiform Script

(Des J.W. Litho Questa (Nos. 545/51). Des and litho Walsall (Nos. 552/64))

1979 (27 Aug)–**80**. *Death Centenary of Sir Rowland Hill.*

(*a*) *Sheet stamps. Horiz designs as T* **149**. *Multicoloured. P* 12 ($2) *or* 14 (*others*)

545 6 c. Type **149** 10 10
546 20 c. Sir Rowland Hill and map of Caribbean 15 15
547 45 c. R.M.S. *Orinoco* and cover bearing Penny Black stamp 25 25
548 75 c. R.M.S. *Shannon* and letter to Grand Turk 40 40
549 $1 R.M.S.P. *Trent* and map of Caribbean .. 55 55
550 $2 Turks Islands 1867 and Turks and Caicos Islands 1900 1d. stamps (6.5.80) .. 90 90
545/50 .. .. *Set of* 6 2·10 2·10
MS551 170 × 113 mm. As No. 550. P 12 .. .. 1·00 1·75

Nos. 545/9 also exist perf 12 (*Price for set of* 5 £1·75 *mint or used*) from additional sheetlets of 5 stamps and 1 label. No. 550 only exists in this format and has the inscription "International Stamp Exhibition Earls Court—London 6–14 May 1980. LONDON 1980" overprinted on the sheet margin. The individual stamps are not overprinted. Stamps perforated 14 are from normal sheets of 40.

(*b*) *Booklet stamps. Designs as T* **150**. *Imperf* × *roul* 5*. *Self-adhesive* (27.9.79)

552 5 c. black and bright emerald 10 10
a. Booklet pane. Nos. 552/7 80
553 5 c. black and bright emerald 10 10
554 5 c. black and bright emerald 10 10
555 15 c. black and light blue 20 20
556 15 c. black and light blue 20 20
557 15 c. black and light blue 20 20
558 25 c. black and light blue 30 30
a. Booklet pane. Nos. 558/63 .. .. 2·25
559 25 c. black and light blue 60 45
560 25 c. black and light blue 30 30
561 40 c. black and bright rosine 45 45
562 40 c. black and bright rosine 45 45
563 40 c. black and bright rosine 45 45
564 $1 black and lemon .. .. 1·10 1·25
a. Booklet pane of 1 .. .. .. 1·10

Designs: *Horiz*—No. 552, Type **150**; No. 553, Egyptian papyrus; No. 554, Chinese paper; No. 555, Greek runner; No. 556, Roman post horse; No. 557, Roman post ship; No. 558, Pigeon post; No. 559, Railway post; No. 560, Packet paddle-steamer; No. 561, Balloon post; No. 562, First airmail; No. 563, Supersonic airmail. *Vert*—No. 564, Original stamp press.

*Nos. 552/63 are separated by various combinations of rotary knife (giving a straight edge) and roulette. No. 564 exists only with straight edges.

BRASILIANA 79

(**151**)

152 "St. Nicholas", Prikra, Ukraine

1979 (10 Sept). *"Brasiliana 79" International Stamp Exhibition, Rio de Janeiro. No.* **MS**551 *optd with T* **151**.

MS565 170 × 113 mm. $2 Turks Islands 1867 and Turks and Caicos Islands 1900 1d. stamps .. 55 1·25

Stamps from Nos. **MS**551 and **MS**565 are identical as the overprint on **MS**565 appears on the margin of the sheet.

(Des M. Diamond. Litho Questa)

1979 (19 Oct). *Christmas. Art. T* **152** *and similar vert designs. Multicoloured. P* 13½ × 14.

566 1 c. Type **152** 10 10
567 3 c. "Emperor Otto II with Symbols of Empire" (Master of the Registrum Gregorii) .. 10 10
568 6 c. "Portrait of St. John" (Book of Lindisfarne) 10 10
569 15 c. "Adoration of the Majestas Domini" (Prayer Book of Otto II) 10 10
570 20 c. "Christ attended by Angels" (Book of Kells) 15 15
571 25 c. "St. John the Evangelist" (Gospels of St. Medard of Soissons), Charlemagne .. 20 15
572 65 c. "Christ Pantocrator", Trocany, Ukraine 30 25
573 $1 "Portrait of St. John" (Canterbury Codex Aureus) 45 45
566/73 .. .. *Set of* 8 1·10 1·10
MS574 106 × 133 mm. $2 "Portrait of St. Matthew" (Book of Lindisfarne) .. .. 70 1·50

153 Pluto and Starfish

(Litho Format)

1979 (2 Nov). *International Year of the Child. Walt Disney Cartoon Characters. T* **153** *and similar vert designs showing characters at the seaside. Multicoloured. P* 11.

575 ¼ c. Type **153** 10 10
576 ½ c. Minnie Mouse in summer outfit 10 10
577 1 c. Mickey Mouse underwater 10 10
578 2 c. Goofy and turtle 10 10
579 3 c. Donald Duck and dolphin 10 10
580 4 c. Mickey Mouse fishing 10 10
581 5 c. Goofy surfing 10 10
582 25 c. Pluto and crab 45 20
583 $1 Daisy water-skiing .. .. .. 2·00 1·10
575/83 .. .. *Set of* 9 2·50 1·25
MS584 126 × 96 mm. $1.50, Goofy after water-skiing accident. P 13½ .. .. .. 1·25 1·40
a. Error. Imperf £180

154 "Christina's World" (painting by Andrew Wyeth)

(Des J.W. Litho Format)

1979 (19 Dec). *Works of Art. T* **154** *and similar multicoloured designs. P* 13½.

585 6 c. Type **154** 10 10
586 10 c. Ivory Leopards, Benin (19th-cent) .. 10 10
587 20 c. "The Kiss" (painting by Gustav Klimt) (*vert*) 15 15
588 25 c. "Portrait of a Lady" (painting by R. van der Weyden) (*vert*) 15 15
589 80 c. Bull's head harp, Sumer, *c.* 2600 B.C. (*vert*) 30 30
590 $1 "The Wave" (painting by Hokusai) .. 45 45
585/90 .. .. *Set of* 6 95 95
MS591 110 × 140 mm. $2 "Holy Family" (painting by Rembrandt) (*vert*) .. .. 70 1·25

155 Pied-billed Grebe

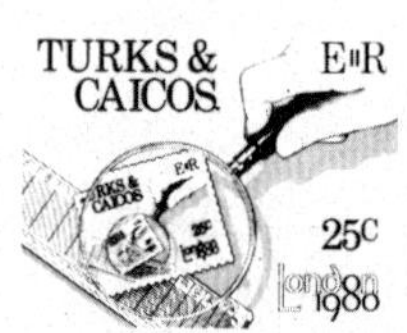

156 Stamp, Magnifying Glass and Perforation Gauge

(Des G. Drummond. Litho Questa)

1980 (20 Feb). *Birds. T* **155** *and similar horiz designs. Multicoloured. P* 14.

592 20 c. Type **155** 60 15
593 25 c. Ovenbirds at nest 65 20
594 35 c. Hen Harrier 90 30
595 55 c. Yellow-bellied Sapsucker .. .. 1·10 35
596 $1 Blue-winged Teal .. .. .. 1·40 80
592/6 .. .. *Set of* 5 4·25 1·60
MS597 107 × 81 mm. $2 Glossy Ibis .. .. 2·75 2·50

(Des BG Studio. Litho Questa)

1980 (6 May). *"London 1980" International Stamp Exhibition. T* **156** *and similar horiz designs. P* 14.

598 25 c. black and chrome-yellow 15 15
599 40 c. black and bright green 25 25
MS600 76 × 97 mm. $2 vermilion, black and blue 70 1·10

Designs:—40 c. Stamp, tweezers and perforation gauge; $2, Earls Court Exhibition Centre.

157 Trumpet Triton

158 Queen Elizabeth the Queen Mother

(Des G. Drummond. Litho Questa)

1980 (26 June). *Shells. T* **157** *and similar horiz designs. Multicoloured. P* 14.

601 15 c. Type **157** 20 20
602 20 c. Measled Cowry 25 25
603 30 c. True Tulip 35 35
604 45 c. Lion's Paw 45 45
605 55 c. Sunrise Tellin 55 55
606 70 c. Crown Cone 70 70
601/6 .. .. *Set of* 6 2·25 2·25

(Des G. Vasarhelyi. Litho Questa)

1980 (4 Aug). *80th Birthday of Queen Elizabeth the Queen Mother. P* 14.

607 **158** 80 c. multicoloured .. .. .. 1·60 1·25
MS608 57 × 80 mm. **158** $1.50, multicoloured. P 12. 2·25 2·50

159 Doctor examining Child and Lions International Emblem

(Des Design Images. Litho Questa)

1980 (29 Aug). *"Serving the Community". T* **159** *and similar horiz designs. Multicoloured. P* 14.

609 10 c. Type **159** 15 10
610 15 c. Students receiving scholarships and Kiwanis International emblem 20 10
611 45 c. Teacher with students and Soroptimist emblem 50 35
612 $1 Lobster trawler and Rotary International emblem .. .. 1·00 80
609/12 .. .. *Set of* 4 1·75 1·25
MS613 101 × 74 mm. $2 School receiving funds and Rotary International emblem .. .. 1·50 2·00

No. **MS**613 also commemorates the 75th anniversary of Rotary International.

(Litho Walsall)

1980 (30 Sept). *Christmas. Scenes from Walt Disney's Cartoon Film "Pinocchio". Horiz designs as T* **153**. *Multicoloured. P* 11.

614 ¼ c. Scene from *Pinocchio* 10 10
615 ½ c. As puppet 10 10
616 1 c. Pinocchio changed into a boy 10 10
617 2 c. Captured by fox 10 10
618 3 c. Pinocchio and puppeteer 10 10
619 4 c. Pinocchio and bird's nest nose 10 10
620 5 c. Pinocchio eating 10 10
621 75 c. Pinocchio with ass ears 60 70
622 $1 Pinocchio underwater 80 95
614/22 .. .. *Set of* 9 1·50 1·75
MS623 127 × 102 mm. $2 Pinocchio dancing (*vert*) 2·50 2·00

160 Martin Luther King Jr

(Des Design Images. Litho Questa)

1980 (22 Dec). *Human Rights. Personalities. T* 160 *and similar horiz designs. Multicoloured. P* 14 × 13½.
624 20 c. Type 160 .. .. 15 10
625 30 c. John F. Kennedy 30 25
626 45 c. Roberto Clemente (baseball player) .. 45 35
627 70 c. Sir Frank Worrel (cricketer) 90 80
628 $1 Harriet Tubman .. .. 1·10 1·00
624/8 .. .. *Set of* 5 2·50 2·25
MS629 103 × 80 mm. $2 Marcus Garvey .. 1·10 1·25

161 Yachts

162 Night Queen Cactus

(Litho Questa)

1981 (29 Jan). *South Caicos Regatta. T* 161 *and similar horiz designs. Multicoloured. P* 14.
630 6 c. Type 161 .. .. 10 10
631 15 c. Trophy and yachts 15 15
632 35 c. Spectators watching speedboat race .. 25 20
633 $1 Caicos sloops 60 50
630/3 .. .. *Set of* 4 90 80
MS634 113 × 85 mm. $2 Queen Elizabeth II and map of South Caicos (*vert*) .. .. .. 1·10 1·75

(Des J. Cooter. Litho Questa)

1981 (10 Feb). *Flowering Cacti. T* 162 *and similar vert designs. Multicoloured. P* 13½ × 14.
635 25 c. Type 162 .. .. 25 25
636 35 c. Ripsaw Cactus 35 35
637 55 c. Royal Strawberry Cactus 40 50
638 80 c. Caicos Cactus 60 75
635/8 .. .. *Set of* 4 1·40 1·75
MS639 72 × 86 mm. $2 Turks Head Cactus. P 14½ 1·25 2·00

(Litho Format)

1981 (16 Feb). *50th Anniv of Walt Disney's Cartoon Character, Pluto. Vert designs as T* 153. *Multicoloured. P* 13½.
640 10 c. Pluto playing on beach with shell .. 10 10
641 75 c. Pluto on raft, and porpoise 75 75
MS642 127 × 101 mm. $1.50 Pluto in scene from film *Simple Things* .. .. 1·60 1·75

(Litho Format)

1981 (20 Mar). *Easter. Walt Disney Cartoon Characters. Vert designs as T* 153. *Multicoloured. P* 11.
643 10 c. Donald Duck and Louie 20 20
644 25 c. Goofy and Donald Duck 40 40
645 60 c. Chip and Dale 85 85
646 80 c. Scrooge McDuck and Huey .. .. 1·25 1·25
643/6 .. .. *Set of* 4 2·40 2·40
MS647 126 × 101 mm. $4 Chip (or Dale). P 13½ 4·00 3·00

163 "Woman with Fan"

164 Kensington Palace

(Des J.W. Litho Questa)

1981 (28 May). *Birth Centenary of Picasso. T* 163 *and similar vert designs. Multicoloured. P* 13½ × 14.
648 20 c. Type 163 .. .. 20 15
649 45 c. "Woman with Pears" 35 30
650 80 c. "The Accordionist" 60 50
651 $1 "The Aficionado" 80 80
648/51 .. .. *Set of* 4 1·75 1·60
MS652 102 × 127 mm. $2 "Girl with a Mandolin" 1·10 1·25

(Des J.W. Litho Questa)

1981 (23 June). *Royal Wedding. T* 164 *and similar vert designs. Multicoloured. P* 14.
653 35 c. Prince Charles and Lady Diana Spencer 20 15
654 65 c. Type 164 .. .. 35 30
655 90 c. Prince Charles as Colonel of the Welsh Guards 45 45
653/5 .. .. *Set of* 3 90 80
MS656 96 × 82 mm. $2 Glass Coach .. .. 90 1·00

Nos. 653/5 also exist perforated 12 (*price for set of* 3 £1 *mint or used*) from additional sheetlets of five stamps and one label. These stamps have changed background colours.

165 Lady Diana Spencer

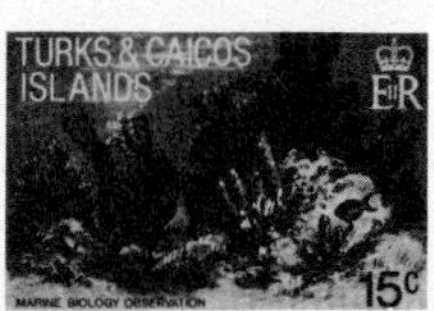

166 Marine Biology Observation

(Manufactured by Walsall)

1981 (7 July). *Royal Wedding. Booklet stamps. T* 165 *and similar vert designs. Multicoloured. Roul* 5 × *imperf**. *Self-adhesive.*
657 20 c. Type 165 .. .. 25 30
a. Booklet pane. Nos. 657/8, each × 3 .. 2·25
658 $1 Prince Charles .. .. 50 1·00
659 $2 Prince Charles and Lady Diana Spencer 2·00 2·50
a. Booklet pane of 1 .. .. 2·00
657/9 .. .. *Set of* 3 2·50 3·50

*The 20 c. and $1 values were each separated by various combinations of rotary knife (giving a straight edge) and roulette. The $2 value exists only with straight edges.

(Des G. Drummond. Litho Questa)

1981 (21 Aug). *Diving. T* 166 *and similar horiz designs. Multicoloured. P* 14.
660 15 c. Type 166 .. .. 20 15
661 40 c. Underwater photography 50 35
662 75 c. Wreck diving 90 70
663 $1 Diving with dolphins .. .. .. 1·25 1·00
660/3 .. .. *Set of* 4 2·50 2·00
MS664 91 × 75 mm. $2 Diving flag .. .. 1·75 2·25

(Litho Questa)

1981 (2 Nov). *Christmas. Horiz designs as T* 153 *showing scenes from Walt Disney's cartoon film "Uncle Remus". P* 13½.
665 ¼ c. multicoloured 10 10
666 ½ c. multicoloured 10 10
667 1 c. multicoloured 10 10
668 2 c. multicoloured 10 10
669 3 c. multicoloured 10 10
670 4 c. multicoloured 10 10
671 5 c. multicoloured 10 10
672 75 c. multicoloured 60 60
673 $1 multicoloured 80 80
665/73 .. .. *Set of* 9 1·40 1·40
MS674 128 × 103 mm. $2 multicoloured .. .. 1·75 1·90

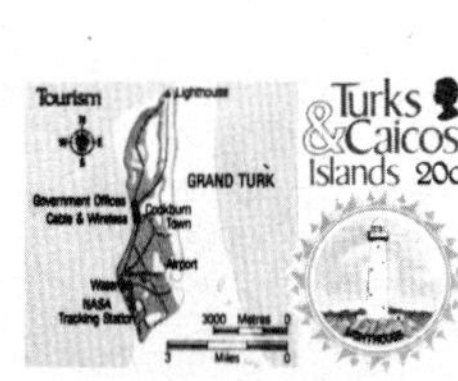

167 Map of Grand Turk, and Lighthouse

168 *Junonia evarete*

(Des J.W. Litho Questa)

1981 (1 Dec). *Tourism. T* 167 *and similar horiz designs. Multicoloured. P* 14.
675 20 c. Type 167 .. .. 35 35
a. Vert strip of 10. Nos. 675/84 .. .. 3·25
676 20 c. Map of Salt Cay, and "industrial archaeology" 35 35
677 20 c. Map of South Caicos, and "island flying" 35 35
678 20 c. Map of East Caicos, and "beach combing" 35 35
679 20 c. Map of Grand Caicos (middle), and cave exploring 35 35
680 20 c. Map of North Caicos, and camping and hiking 35 35
681 20 c. Map of North Caicos, Parrot Cay, Dellis Cay, Fort George Cay, Pine Cay and Water Cay, and "environmental studies" 35 35
682 20 c. Map of Providenciales, and scuba diving 35 35
683 20 c. Map of West Caicos, and "cruising and bird sanctuary" 35 35
684 20 c. Turks and Caicos Islands flag 35 35
675/84 .. .. *Set of* 10 3·25 3·25

Nos. 675/84 were printed together, *se-tenant*, in vertical strips of 10 throughout the sheet of 40, the two panes (2 × 10), separated by a gutter margin, being *tête-bêche*.

(Des J. Cooter. Litho Questa)

1982 (21 Jan). *Butterflies. T* 168 *and similar vert designs. Multicoloured. P* 14.
685 20 c. Type 168 .. .. 30 30
686 35 c. *Strymon maesites* 50 55
687 65 c. *Agraulis vanillae* .. .. 90 1·00
688 $1 *Eurema dina* .. .. 1·40 2·00
685/8 .. .. *Set of* 4 2·75 3·50
MS689 72×56 mm. $2 *Anaea intermedia* .. 2·75 3·50

OMNIBUS ISSUES

Details, together with prices for complete sets, of the various Omnibus issues from the 1935 Silver Jubilee series to date are included in a special section following Zimbabwe at the end of Volume 2.

169 Flag Salute on Queen's Birthday

170 Footballer

(Litho Questa)

1982 (17 Feb). *75th Anniv of Boy Scout Movement. T* 169 *and similar vert designs. Multicoloured. P* 14.
690 40 c. Type 169 .. .. 50 50
691 50 c. Raft building 60 60
692 75 c. Sea scout cricket match .. .. .. 1·10 1·40
693 $1 Nature study .. .. 1·50 1·60
690/3 .. .. *Set of* 4 3·25 3·75
MS694 100 × 70 mm. $2 Lord Baden-Powell and scout salute .. .. 2·50 2·75

(Des G. Vasarhelyi. Litho Questa)

1982 (30 Apr). *World Cup Football Championship, Spain. T* 170 *and similar designs showing footballers. P* 14.
695 10 c. multicoloured 15 15
696 25 c. multicoloured 20 20
697 45 c. multicoloured 25 25
698 $1 multicoloured 80 80
695/8 .. .. *Set of* 4 1·25 1·25
MS699 117 × 83 mm. $2 multicoloured (*horiz*) .. 1·25 2·00

171 Washington crossing the Delaware and Phillis Wheatley (poetess)

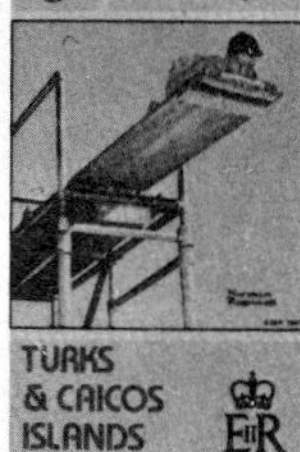

172 "Second Thoughts"

(Des Design Images. Litho Questa)

1982 (3 May). *250th Birth Anniv of George Washington* (20, 35 c.) *and Birth Centenary of Franklin D. Roosevelt* (65, 80 c.). *T* 171 *and similar horiz designs. Multicoloured. P* 14.
700 20 c. Type 171 .. .. 30 30
701 35 c. George Washington and Benjamin Banneker (surveyor) 45 45
702 65 c. Franklin D. Roosevelt meeting George Washington Carver (agricultural researcher) 80 80
703 80 c. Roosevelt as stamp collector .. .. 1·00 1·00
700/3 .. .. *Set of* 4 2·25 2·25
MS704 100 × 70 mm. $2 Roosevelt with stamp showing profile of Washington .. .. .. 2·00 2·50

(Litho Questa)

1982 (23 June). *Norman Rockwell (painter) Commemoration. T* 172 *and similar vert designs. Multicoloured. P* 14 × 13½.
705 8 c. Type 172 .. .. 15 10
706 15 c. "The Proper Gratuity" 20 20
707 20 c. "Before the Shot" 25 25
708 25 c. "The Three Umpires" 25 25
705/8 .. .. *Set of* 4 75 70

173 Princess of Wales

174 "Skymaster" over Caicos Cays

(Des PAD Studio. Litho Questa)

1982 (1 July–18 Nov). *21st Birthday of Princess of Wales. T* 173 *and similar vert designs. Multicoloured. P* 14½ × 14.

(*a*) *Sheet stamps. Pale green frames*
709 55 c. Sandringham 70 55
710 70 c. Prince and Princess of Wales 85 70
711 $1 Type 173 .. .. 1·25 1·25
709/11 .. .. *Set of* 3 2·50 2·25
MS712 102 × 76 mm. $2 Princess Diana (*different*) 2·00 2·25

(*b*) *Booklet stamps. As Nos.* 709/11 *but printed with new values and blue frame* (18.11.82)
713 8 c. Sandringham 35 55
714 35 c. Prince and Princess of Wales .. .. 70 1·25
715 $1.10, Type 173 .. .. 1·75 2·25
713/15 .. .. *Set of* 3 2·50 3·50

Nos. 713/15 also exist from sheets printed in horizontal *tête-bêche* pairs throughout.

(Des MBI Studios. Litho Questa)

1982 (23 Aug). *Aircraft. T* **174** *and similar horiz designs. Multicoloured. P* 14.

716	8 c. Type **174**	15	15
717	15 c. "Jetstar" over Grand Turk	20	25
718	65 c. Helicopter over South Caicos	65	80
719	$1.10, Seaplane over Providenciales	1·10	1·25
716/19	*Set of* 4	1·90	2·25
MS720	99 × 69 mm. $2 Boeing "727" over Turks and Caicos Islands	2·00	2·50

(Litho Questa)

1982 (1 Dec). *Christmas. Scenes from Walt Disney's Cartoon Film "Mickey's Christmas Carol". Horiz designs as T* **153**. *Multicoloured. P* 13½.

721	1 c. Donald Duck, Mickey Mouse and Scrooge	10	10
722	1 c. Goofy (Marley's ghost) and Scrooge	10	10
723	2 c. Jiminy Cricket and Scrooge	10	10
724	2 c. Huey, Dewey and Louie	10	10
725	3 c. Daisy Duck and youthful Scrooge	10	10
726	3 c. Giant and Scrooge	10	10
727	4 c. Two bad wolves, a wise pig and a reformed Scrooge	10	10
728	65 c. Donald Duck and Scrooge	1·00	65
729	$1.10, Mortie and Scrooge	1·60	1·10
721/9	*Set of* 9	2·50	1·75
MS730	126 × 101 mm. $2 Mickey and Minnie Mouse with Mortie	2·75	2·00

175 West Caicos Trolley Tram

(Des N. Waldman. Litho Questa)

1983 (18 Jan). *Trams and Locomotives. T* **175** *and similar horiz designs. Multicoloured. P* 14

731	15 c. Type **175**	20	25
732	55 c. West Caicos steam locomotive	65	70
733	90 c. East Caicos sisal locomotive	90	1·00
734	$1.60, East Caicos steam locomotive	1·75	1·90
731/4	*Set of* 4	3·25	3·50
MS735	99 × 69 mm. $2.50, Steam engine pulling cars of sisal	2·25	2·25

176 Policewoman on Traffic Duty

177 "St. John and the Virgin Mary" (detail)

(Des N. Waldman. Litho Questa)

1983 (14 Mar). *Commonwealth Day. T* **176** *and similar horiz designs. Multicoloured. P* 14

736	1 c. Type **176**	15	20
	a. Vert strip of 4. Nos. 736/9	2·40	
737	8 c. Stylised sun and weather vane	15	20
738	65 c. Yacht	85	90
739	$1 Cricket	1·50	1·60
736/9	*Set of* 4	2·40	2·50

Nos. 736/9 were printed together, *se-tenant*, in vertical strips of four throughout the sheet.

(Des Design Images. Litho Questa)

1983 (7 Apr). *Easter. T* **177** *and similar vert designs showing details from the "Mond Crucifixion" by Raphael. Multicoloured. P* 13½ × 14.

740	35 c. Type **177**	20	25
741	50 c. "Two Women"	30	35
742	95 c. "Angel with two jars"	50	60
743	$1.10, "Angel with one jar"	60	80
740/3	*Set of* 4	1·40	2·00
MS744	100 × 130 mm. $2.50, "Christ on the Cross"	1·60	2·00

178 Minke Whale

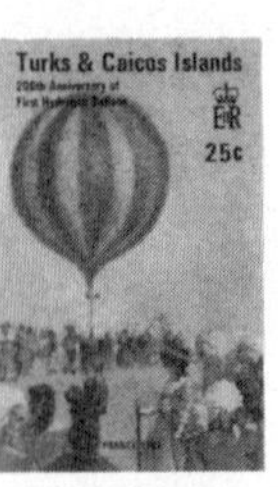

179 First Hydrogen Balloon, 1783

(Des D. Hamilton. Litho Questa)

1983 (16 May–11 July). *Whales. T* **178** *and similar horiz designs. Multicoloured. P* 13½.

745	50 c. Type **178**	1·00	1·00
746	65 c. Black Right Whale (11.7.83)	1·25	1·25
747	70 c. Killer Whale (13.6.83)	1·50	1·50
748	95 c. Sperm Whale (13.6.83)	1·75	1·75
749	$1.10, Cuvier's Beaked Whale (11.7.83)	2·00	2·00
750	$2 Blue Whale (13.6.83)	3·50	3·50
751	$2.20, Humpback Whale	3·75	3·75
752	$3 Long-finned Pilot Whale	4·75	4·75
745/52	*Set of* 8	18·00	18·00
MS753	112 × 82 mm. $3 Fin Whale (11.7.83)	4·50	5·00

Nos. 745/52 were each issued in sheetlets of four.

(Des BG Studio. Litho Questa)

1983 (30 Aug). *Bicentenary of Manned Flight. T* **179** *and similar vert designs. Multicoloured. P* 14.

754	25 c. Type **179**	25	25
755	35 c. *Friendship 7*	35	35
756	70 c. First hot air balloon, 1783	70	70
757	95 c. Space shuttle *Columbia*	90	90
754/7	*Set of* 4	2·00	2·00
MS758	112 × 76 mm. $2 Montgolfier balloon and Space shuttle	1·50	2·00

180 Fiddler Pig

181 Bermuda Sloop

(Litho Format)

1983 (4 Oct). *Christmas. Walt Disney Cartoon Characters. T* **180** *and similar vert designs. Multicoloured. P* 11.

759	1 c. Type **180**	10	10
760	1 c. Fifer Pig	10	10
761	2 c. Practical Pig	10	10
762	2 c. Pluto	10	10
763	3 c. Goofy	10	10
764	3 c. Mickey Mouse	10	10
765	35 c. Gyro Gearloose	35	35
766	50 c. Ludwig von Drake	50	50
767	$1.10, Huey, Dewey and Louie	1·00	1·00
759/67	*Set of* 9	1·75	1·75
MS768	127 × 102 mm. $2.50, Mickey and Minnie Mouse with Huey, Dewey and Louie. P 13½	3·25	3·00

(Des G. Drummond. Litho Questa)

1983 (5 Oct)–**85**. *Ships. T* **181** *and similar horiz designs. Multicoloured. A. P* 14. *B. P* 12½ × 12.

		A		B	
769	4 c. Arawak dug-out canoe	40	30	40	40
770	5 c. *Santa Maria*	50	30	40	40
771	8 c. British and Spanish ships in battle	1·50	30	50	40
772	10 c. Type **181**	1·50	35	40	40
773	20 c. U.S. privateer *Grand Turk*	60	45	50	40
774	25 c. H.M.S. *Boreas*	2·50	45	50	40
775	30 c. H.M.S. *Endymion* attacking French ship, 1790s	2·50	60	75	50
776	35 c. *Caesar* (barque)	1·00	60	60	50
777	50 c. *Grapeshot* (schooner)	3·00	75	60	60
778	65 c. H.M.S. *Invincible* (battle cruiser)	4·00	1·50	1·00	1·00
779	95 c. H.M.S. *Magicienne*	4·00	1·40	1·50	1·50
780	$1.10, H.M.S. *Durban*	4·75	2·40	2·25	2·25
781	$2 *Sentinel* (cable ship)	6·00	2·75	2·25	2·50
782	$3 H.M.S. *Minerva*	7·00	4·00	5·00	6·00
783	$5 Caicos sloop	7·50	8·00	8·00	9·00
769/83	*Set of* 15	42·00	21·00	22·00	23·00

Dates of issue:—5.10.83, Nos. 772A, 775A, 778A, 780A/2A; 16.12.83, Nos. 771A, 774A, 777A, 779A; 9.1.84, Nos. 769A/70A, 773A, 776A, 783A; 3.85, Nos. 769B, 771B/2B, 775B, 778B, 780B, 783B; 12.8.85, Nos. 770B, 773B/4B, 776B/7B, 779B, 781B; 12.85, No. 782B.

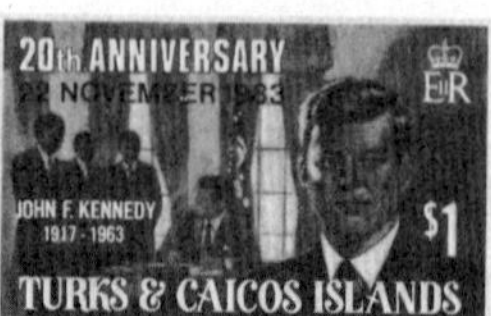

182 President Kennedy and Signing of Civil Rights Legislation

(Des Design Images. Litho Questa)

1983 (22 Dec). *20th Death Anniv of President J. F. Kennedy. P* 14.

784	**182**	20 c. multicoloured	20	15
785		$1 multicoloured	1·10	1·25

183 Clarabelle Cow Diving

(Litho Questa)

1984 (21 Feb–Apr). *Olympic Games, Los Angeles. T* **183** *and similar horiz designs showing Disney cartoon characters in Olympic events. Multicoloured. A. Inscr* "1984 LOS ANGELES". *P* 14 × 13½. *B. Inscr* "1984 OLYMPICS LOS ANGELES" *and Olympic emblem. P* 14 × 13½ (**MS** 795B) *or* 12 (*others*) (4.84).

		A		B	
786	1 c. Type **183**	10	10	10	10
787	1 c. Donald Duck in 500m kayak race	10	10	10	10
788	2 c. Huey, Dewey and Louie in 1000m kayak race	10	10	10	10
789	2 c. Mickey Mouse in single kayak	10	10	10	10
790	3 c. Donald Duck highboard diving	10	10	10	10
791	3 c. Minnie Mouse in kayak slalom	10	10	10	10
792	25 c. Mickey Mouse freestyle swimming	40	45	40	45
793	75 c. Donald Duck playing water-polo	1·25	1·40	1·25	1·40
794	$1 Uncle Scrooge and Donald Duck yachting	1·60	1·75	1·60	1·75
786/94	*Set of* 9	3·25	3·50	3·25	3·50
MS795	117 × 90 mm. $2 Pluto platform diving	2·75	3·00	2·75	3·00

184 "Cadillac V–16", 1933

185 "Rest during the Flight to Egypt, with St. Francis"

(Des N. Waldman. Litho Questa)

1984 (15 Mar). *Classic Cars and 125th Anniv of first Commercial Oil Well. T* **184** *and similar horiz designs. Multicoloured. P* 14.

796	4 c. Type **184**	10	10
797	8 c. Rolls-Royce "Phantom III", 1937	15	15
798	10 c. Saab "99", 1969	15	15
799	25 c. Maserati "Bora", 1973	40	40
800	40 c. Datsun "260Z", 1970	65	65
801	55 c. Porsche "917", 1971	80	80
802	80 c. Lincoln "Continental", 1939	90	90
803	$1 Triumph "TR3A", 1957	1·25	1·25
796/803	*Set of* 8	4·00	4·00
MS804	70 × 100 mm. $2 Daimler, 1886	2·00	2·50

(Des S. Karp. Litho Walsall)

1984 (9 Apr). *Easter. 450th Death Anniv of Correggio (painter). T* **185** *and similar vert designs. Multicoloured. P* 14.

805	15 c. Type **185**	20	15
806	40 c. "St. Luke and St. Ambrose"	45	40
807	60 c. "Diana and her Chariot"	65	65
808	95 c. "The Deposition of Christ"	80	80
805/8	*Set of* 4	1·90	1·75
MS809	100 × 79 mm. $2 "The Nativity with Saints Elizabeth and John the younger" (*horiz*)	1·50	2·25

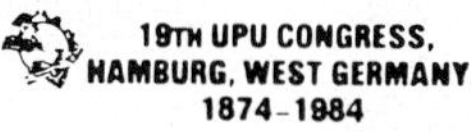

(**186**)

1984 (19 June). *Universal Postal Union Congress, Hamburg. Nos.* 748/9 *and* **MS**753 *optd with T* **186**.

810	95 c. Sperm Whale	2·00	1·50
811	$1.10, Cuvier's Beaked Whale	2·00	1·60
MS812	112 × 82 mm. $3 Fin Whale	4·00	4·25

187 "The Adventure of the Second Stain"

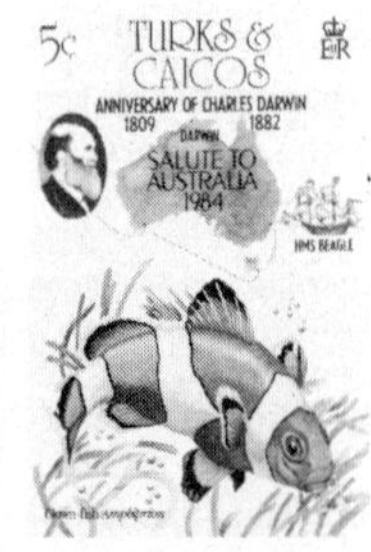

188 Clown-Fish

(Des S. Karp. Litho Walsall)

1984 (16 July). *125th Birth Anniv of Sir Arthur Conan Doyle (author). T* **187** *and similar horiz designs showing scenes from Sherlock Holmes stories. Multicoloured. P* 14.

813 25 c. Type **187** .. .. 1·75 1·25
814 45 c. "The Adventure of the Final Problem" .. 2·50 2·00
815 70 c. "The Adventure of the Empty House" .. 4·00 3·25
816 85 c. "The Adventure of the Greek Interpreter" 4·50 3·50
813/16 .. .. *Set of* 4 11·50 9·00
MS817 100 × 70 mm. $2 Sir Arthur Conan Doyle 7·50 4·00

(Des Susan David. Litho Walsall)

1984 (22 Aug). *"Ausipex" International Stamp Exhibition, Melbourne. 175th Birth Anniv of Charles Darwin. T* **188** *and similar vert designs. Multicoloured. P* 14 × 13½.

818 5 c. Type **188** 40 30
819 35 c. Monitor Lizard .. .. 1·75 1·75
820 50 c. Rainbow Lory .. .. 2·50 2·50
821 $1.10, Koalas .. .. 3·25 3·25
818/21 .. .. *Set of* 4 7·00 7·00
MS822 100×70 mm. $2 Eastern Grey Kangaroo .. .. 3·50 4·25

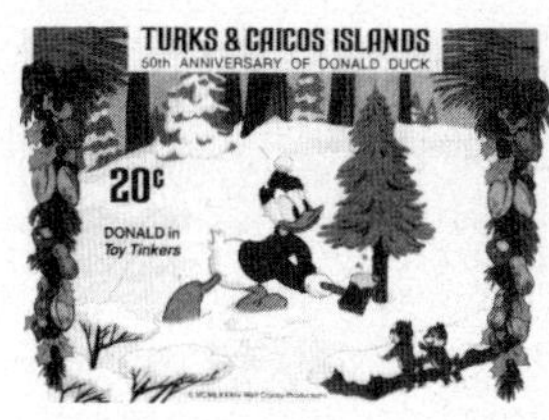

189 Donald Duck cutting down Christmas Tree

(Litho Questa)

1984 (8 Oct–26 Nov). *Christmas. Walt Disney Cartoon Characters. T* **189** *and similar horiz designs showing scenes from "Toy Tinkers". Multicoloured. P* 12 (75 *c.*) *or* 14 × 13½ (*others*).

823 20 c. Type **189** 85 45
824 35 c. Donald Duck and Chip n'Dale playing with train set .. .. 1·10 65
825 50 c. Donald Duck and Chip n'Dale playing with catapult .. .. 1·60 85
826 75 c. Donald Duck, Chip n'Dale and Christmas tree (26.11) .. .. 2·25 1·40
827 $1.10, Donald Duck, toy soldier and Chip n'Dale .. .. 2·50 1·90
823/7 .. .. *Set of* 5 7·50 4·75
MS828 126 × 102 mm. $2 Donald Duck as Father Christmas .. .. 3·00 3·25

No. 826 was printed in sheetlets of 8 stamps.

190 Magnolia Warbler

191 Leonardo da Vinci and Illustration of Glider Wing (15th century)

(Des Susan David. Litho Walsall)

1985 (28 Jan). *Birth Bicentenary of John J. Audubon (ornithologist). T* **190** *and similar vert designs. Multicoloured. P* 14.

829 25 c. Type **190** .. .. 1·50 45
830 45 c. Short-eared Owl .. .. 2·25 80
831 70 c. Mourning Dove and eggs .. .. .. 2·50 1·50
832 85 c. Caribbean Martin .. .. 2·75 1·75
829/32 .. .. *Set of* 4 8·00 4·00
MS833 100×70 mm. $2 Oystercatcher and chicks .. .. 3·75 4·00

(Des K. Gromol. Litho Walsall)

1985 (22 Feb). *40th Anniv of International Civil Aviation Organization. Aviation Pioneers. T* **191** *and similar horiz designs. Multicoloured. P* 14.

834 8 c. Type **191** 40 15
835 25 c. Sir Alliott Verdon Roe and "C.102" jetliner (1949) 75 40
836 65 c. Robert H. Goddard and first liquid fuel rocket (1926) .. .. 1·75 95
837 $1 Igor Sikorsky and Sikorsky "VS300" helicopter (1939) .. .. 2·25 1·50
834/7 .. .. *Set of* 4 4·50 2·75
MS838 100 × 70 mm. $2 Amelia Earhart's Lockheed "10E Electra" (1937) .. .. .. 2·75 3·00

192 Benjamin Franklin and Marquis de Lafayette

(Des Susan David. Litho Walsall)

1985 (28 Mar). *Centenary of the Statue of Liberty's Arrival in New York. T* **192** *and similar horiz designs. Multicoloured. P* 14.

839 20 c. Type **192** 80 50
840 30 c. Frederic Bartholdi (designer) and Gustave Eiffel (engineer) 90 60
841 65 c. Sailing ship *Isere* arriving in New York with statue, 1885 .. .. 2·25 1·50
842 $1.10, United States fund raisers Louis Agassiz, Charles Sumner, H. W. Longfellow and Joseph Pulitzer .. .. 2·50 1·75
839/42 .. .. *Set of* 4 5·75 4·00
MS843 99×69 mm. $2 Dedication ceremony, 1886 .. .. 3·00 3·50

193 Sir Edward Hawke and H.M.S. *Royal George*

(Des Susan David. Litho Walsall)

1985 (17 Apr). *Salute to the Royal Navy. T* **193** *and similar multicoloured designs. P* 14.

844 20 c. Type **193** .. .. 1·50 1·25
845 30 c. Lord Nelson and H.M.S. *Victory* .. 2·00 1·75
846 65 c. Admiral Sir George Cockburn and H.M.S. *Albion* .. .. 2·75 2·25
847 95 c. Admiral Sir David Beatty and H.M.S. *Indefatigable* .. .. 3·75 3·00
844/7 .. .. *Set of* 4 9·00 7·50
MS848 99×69 mm. $2 18th-century sailor and cannon (*vert*) .. .. 3·25 3·50

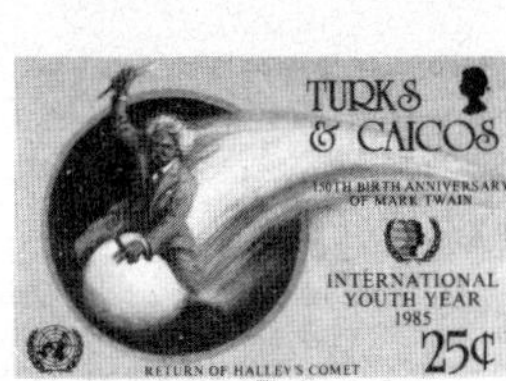

194 Mark Twain riding on Halley's Comet

195 The Queen Mother outside Clarence House

(Des J. Iskowitz. Litho Walsall)

1985 (17 May). *International Youth Year. Birth Annivs of Mark Twain (150th) and Jakob Grimm (Bicentenary). T* **194** *and similar multicoloured designs. P* 13½ × 14 (25, 35 *c.*, $2) *or* 14 × 13½ (50, 95 *c.*).

849 25 c. Type **194** 85 40
850 35 c. *Grand Turk* (Mississippi river steamer) .. .. 1·25 55
851 50 c. Hansel and Gretel and gingerbread house (*vert*) .. .. 1·50 75
852 95 c. Rumpelstiltskin (*vert*) .. .. .. 2·25 1·50
849/52 .. .. *Set of* 4 5·25 3·00
MS853 99×68 mm. $2 Mark Twain and the Brothers Grimm .. .. 2·75 3·00

(Des J.W. Litho Questa)

1985 (15 July). *Life and Times of Queen Elizabeth the Queen Mother. T* **195** *and similar multicoloured designs. P* 14.

854 30 c. Type **195** 45 45
855 50 c. Visiting Biggin Hill airfield (*horiz*) .. 75 75
856 $1.10, 80th birthday portrait .. .. .. 1·90 1·90
854/6 .. .. *Set of* 3 2·75 2·75
MS857 56×85 mm. $2 With Prince Charles at Garter ceremony, Windsor Castle, 1968 .. 2·75 3·00

196 King George II and Score of "Zadok the Priest" (1727)

197 Harley-Davidson Dual Cylinder (1915) on Middle Caicos

(Des Susan David. Litho Format)

1985 (17 July). *300th Birth Anniv of George Frederick Handel (composer). T* **196** *and similar vert designs. P* 15.

858 4 c. multicoloured 65 40
859 10 c. multicoloured .. .. 1·00 50
860 50 c. multicoloured .. .. 2·75 1·50
861 $1.10, multicoloured .. .. 4·75 3·75
858/61 .. .. *Set of* 4 8·25 5·50
MS862 101×76 mm. $2 black, deep dull purple and dull violet-blue .. .. 5·50 4·50

Designs:—10 c. Queen Caroline and score of "Funeral Anthem" (1737); 50 c. King George I and score of "Water Music" (1714); Queen Anne and score of "Or la Tromba" from *Rinaldo* (1711); $2 George Frederick Handel.

(Des Susan David. Litho Format)

1985 (17 July). *300th Birth Anniv of Johann Sebastian Bach (composer). Vert designs as T* **204a** *of Maldive Islands. Multicoloured. P* 15.

863 15 c. Bassoon .. .. 1·00 40
864 40 c. Natural Horn .. .. 1·75 85
865 60 c. Viola D'Amore .. .. 2·25 1·25
866 95 c. Clavichord .. .. 2·75 2·25
863/6 .. .. *Set of* 4 7·00 4·25
MS867 102×76 mm. $2 Johann Sebastian Bach .. .. 4·00 3·50

(Des Mary Walters. Litho Questa)

1985 (4 Sept). *Centenary of the Motor Cycle. T* **197** *and similar multicoloured designs. P* 14.

868 8 c. Type **197** 40 30
869 25 c. Triumph "Thunderbird" (1950) on Grand Turk 90 70
870 55 c. BMW "K100RS" (1985) on North Caicos .. .. 1·75 1·50
871 $1.20, Honda "1100 Shadow" (1985) on South Caicos .. .. 3·00 2·50
868/71 .. .. *Set of* 4 5·50 4·50
MS872 106×77 mm. $2 Daimler single track (1885) (*vert*) .. .. 2·75 3·00

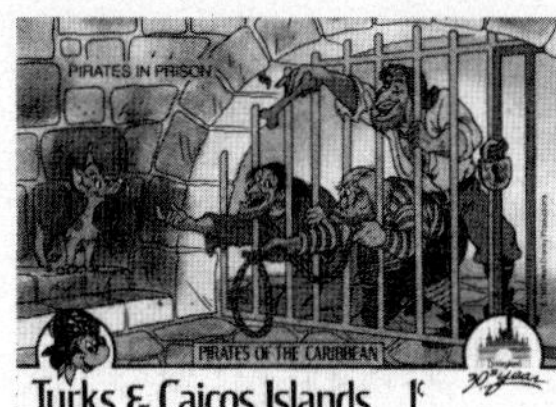

198 Pirates in Prison

(Des Walt Disney Productions. Litho Questa)

1985 (4 Oct). *30th Anniv of Disneyland, U.S.A. T* **198** *and similar horiz designs showing scenes from "Pirates of the Caribbean" exhibition. Multicoloured. P* 14 × 13½.

873 1 c. Type **198** 10 10
874 1 c. The fate of Captain William Kidd .. 10 10
875 2 c. Bartholomew Roberts 10 10
876 2 c. Two buccaneers 10 10
877 3 c. Privateers looting 10 10
878 3 c. Auction of captives 10 10
879 35 c. Singing pirates .. .. 1·25 55
880 75 c. Edward Teach—"Blackbeard" .. .. 2·50 1·25
881 $1.10, Sir Henry Morgan .. .. .. 2·75 1·60
873/81 .. .. *Set of* 9 6·00 3·25
MS882 123 × 86 mm. $2.50, Mary Read and Anne Bonney .. .. 3·50 3·75

199 Brownies from China, Turks and Caicos and Papua New Guinea

(Des Mary Walters. Litho Questa)

1985 (4 Nov). *75th Anniv of Girl Guide Movement and 35th Anniv of Grand Turk Company. T* **199** *and similar horiz designs. Multicoloured. P* 14.

883 10 c. Type **199** 75 30
884 40 c. Brownies from Surinam, Turks and Caicos and Korea .. .. 1·75 1·25
885 70 c. Guides from Australia, Turks and Caicos and Canada .. .. 2·50 2·00
886 80 c. Guides from West Germany, Turks and Caicos and Israel .. .. 2·75 2·25
883/6 .. .. *Set of* 4 7·00 5·25
MS887 107×76 mm. $2 75th anniversary emblem .. .. 3·00 3·50

200 Iguana and Log

201 Duke and Duchess of York after Wedding

(Des I. MacLaury. Litho Questa)

1986 (20 Nov). *Turks and Caicos Ground Iguana. T* **200** *and similar horiz designs. Multicoloured. P* 14.

888 8 c. Type **200** .. .. 1·00 70
889 10 c. Iguana on beach .. .. 1·25 85
890 20 c. Iguana at nest .. .. 1·75 1·75
891 35 c. Iguana eating flowers .. .. .. 3·00 3·00
888/91 .. .. *Set of* 4 6·25 5·75
MS892 105×76 mm. $2 Map showing habitat .. 7·50 8·00

(Litho Questa)

1986 (19 Dec). *Royal Wedding. T* **201** *and similar vert designs. Multicoloured. P* 14.
893 35 c. Type **201** 65 55
894 65 c. Miss Sarah Ferguson in wedding carriage . . . . 1·10 1·10
895 $1.10, Duke and Duchess of York on Palace balcony after wedding . . 1·75 2·00
893/5 . . . . *Set of* 3 3·25 3·25
MS896 85×85 mm. $2 Duke and Duchess of York leaving Westminster Abbey . . . . 2·50 3·00

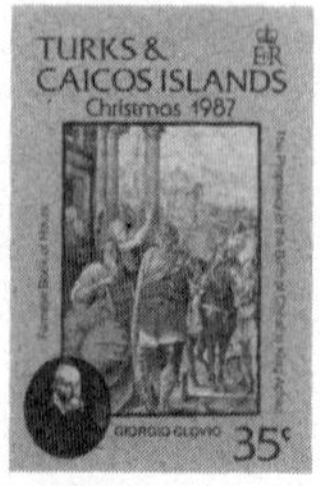

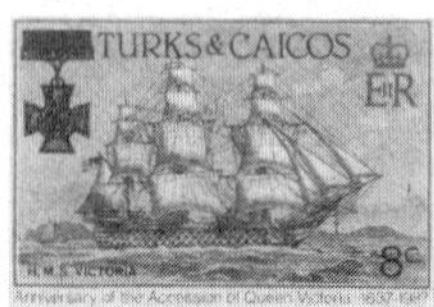

202 "The Prophecy of the Birth of Christ to King Achaz"
203 H.M.S. *Victoria*, 1859, and Victoria Cross

(Litho Questa)

1987 (9 Dec). *Christmas. T* **202** *and similar vert designs, each showing illuminated illustration by Giorgio Clovio from "Farnese Book of Hours". Multicoloured. P* 14.
897 35 c. Type **202** . . . . 1·00 75
898 50 c. "The Annunciation" . . . . 1·40 1·25
899 65 c. "The Circumcision" . . . . 2·00 1·75
900 95 c. "Adoration of the Kings" . . . . 3·00 3·50
897/900 . . . . *Set of* 4 6·75 6·50
MS901 76×106 mm. $2 "The Nativity" . . . . 4·00 4·50

(Litho Questa)

1987 (24 Dec). *150th Anniv of Accession of Queen Victoria. T* **203** *and similar horiz designs. Multicoloured. P* 14.
902 8 c. Type **203** 55 35
903 35 c. *Victoria* (paddle-steamer) and gold sovereign . . . . 1·50 1·25
904 55 c. Royal Yacht *Victoria and Albert I* and 1840 Penny Black stamp . . . . 1·75 1·75
905 95 c. Royal Yacht *Victoria and Albert II* and Victoria Public Library . . . . 2·50 2·75
902/5 . . . . *Set of* 4 5·75 5·50
MS906 129×76 mm. $2 *Victoria* (barque) . . 3·75 4·50

(Des and litho Questa)

1987 (31 Dec). *Bicentenary of U.S. Constitution. Multicoloured designs as T* **210***a of Sierra Leone. P* 14.
907 10 c. State Seal, New Jersey 20 15
908 35 c. 18th-century family going to church ("Freedom of Worship") (*vert*) 55 55
909 65 c. U.S. Supreme Court, Judicial Branch, Washington (*vert*) . . . . 1·00 1·00
910 80 c. John Adams (statesman) (*vert*) . . 1·25 1·40
907/10 . . . . *Set of* 4 2·75 2·75
MS911 105×75 mm. $2 George Mason (Virginia delegate) (*vert*) . . . . 2·40 3·00
Nos. 907/10 were each printed in sheetlets of five stamps and one stamp-size label, which appears in the centre of the bottom row.

204 *Santa Maria*
205 Arawak Artifact and Scouts in Cave, Middle Caicos

(Litho Questa)

1988 (20 Jan). *500th Anniv of Discovery of America by Columbus* (1992) (*1st issue*). *T* **204** *and similar horiz designs. Multicoloured. P* 14.
912 4 c. Type **204** 15 15
913 25 c. Columbus meeting Tainos Indians . . 65 50
914 70 c. *Santa Maria* anchored off Indian village . . . . 1·75 1·75
915 $1 Columbus in field of grain . . . . 2·25 2·25
912/15 . . . . *Set of* 4 4·25 4·25
MS916 105 × 76 mm. $2 *Santa Maria, Pinta* and *Nina* . . . . 3·25 4·00
See also Nos. 947/51.

(Litho Questa)

1988 (12 Feb). *World Scout Jamboree, Australia. T* **205** *and similar multicoloured designs. P* 14.
917 8 c. Type **205** 20 15
918 35 c. *Santa Maria*, scouts and Hawks Nest Island (*horiz*) 55 55
919 65 c. Scouts diving to wreck of galleon . . 95 95
920 95 c. Visiting ruins of 19th-century sisal plantation (*horiz*) . . . . 1·40 1·40
917/20 . . . . *Set of* 4 2·75 2·75
MS921 118 × 82 mm. $2 Splashdown of John Glenn's "Mercury" capsule, 1962 . . . . 3·50 4·00
No. **MS**921 is inscribed "Sight" in error.

40TH WEDDING ANNIVERSARY
H.M. QUEEN ELIZABETH II
H.R.H. THE DUKE OF EDINBURGH

(**206**)

207 Football

1988 (14 Mar). *Royal Ruby Wedding. Nos.* 772A, 774A *and* 781A *optd with T* **206**.
922 10 c. Type **181** 30 30
923 25 c. H.M.S. *Boreas* 55 55
924 $2 *Sentinel* (cable ship) . . . . 3·25 3·25
922/4 . . . . *Set of* 3 3·75 3·75

(Des L. Fried. Litho B.D.T.)

1988 (29 Aug). *Olympic Games, Seoul. T* **207** *and similar vert designs. Multicoloured. P* 14.
925 8 c. Type **207** 15 15
926 30 c. Yachting 35 40
927 70 c. Cycling 85 90
928 $1 Athletics . . . . 1·25 1·40
925/8 . . . . *Set of* 4 2·25 2·50
MS929 102 × 71 mm. $2 Swimming . . . . 2·40 2·50

208 Game-fishing Launch and Swordfish
209 Princess Alexandra and Government House

(Des L. Birmingham. Litho Questa)

1988 (5 Sept). *Billfish Tournament. T* **208** *and similar multicoloured designs. P* 14.
930 8 c. Type **208** 20 15
931 10 c. Competitors with swordfish catch . . 30 15
932 70 c. Game-fishing launch . . . . 1·40 1·40
933 $1 Blue Marlin . . . . 1·90 2·10
930/3 . . . . *Set of* 4 3·50 3·50
MS934 119 × 85 mm. $2 Stylized Sailfish (*horiz*) 3·00 3·50

(Litho Questa)

1988 (24 Oct). *Christmas. 500th Birth Anniv of Titian (artist). Vert designs as T* **186***a of Lesotho inscr* "CHRISTMAS 1988" *and with royal cypher at top right. Multicoloured. P* 13½×14.
935 15 c. "Madonna and Child with Saint Catherine" 30 30
936 25 c. "Madonna with a Rabbit" 40 40
937 35 c. "Virgin and Child with Saints" . . 50 50
938 40 c. "The Gypsy Madonna" 60 60
939 50 c. "The Holy Family and a Shepherd" . . 70 70
940 65 c. "Madonna and Child" 85 85
941 $3 "Madonna and Child with Saints" . . 3·75 3·75
935/41 . . . . *Set of* 7 6·50 6·50
MS942 Two sheets, each 110 × 95 mm. (a) $2 "Adoration of the Magi" (detail). (b) $2 "The Annunciation" (detail) . . . . *Set of* 2 *sheets* 5·50 6·50

(Des and litho Questa)

1988 (14 Nov). *Visit of Princess Alexandra. T* **209** *and similar multicoloured designs. P* 14.
943 70 c. Type **209** . . . . 1·50 1·50
944 $1.40, Princess Alexandra and map of islands . . . . 2·50 2·50
MS945 92 × 72 mm. $2 Princess Alexandra (*vert*) 3·75 4·00

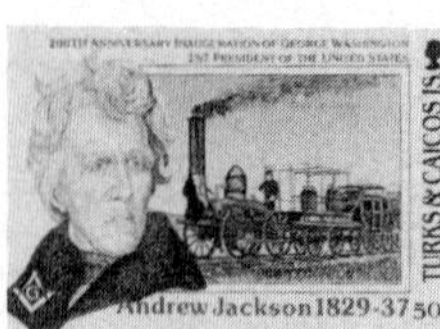

210 Coat of Arms
210*a* Andrew Jackson and *De Witt Clinton* Railway Locomotive

(Des and litho Questa)

1988 (15 Dec). *P* 14½ × 15.
946 **210** $10 multicoloured . . . . 10·50 11·00

(Des D. Miller. Litho Questa)

1989 (15 May). *500th Anniv of Discovery of America by Columbus* (1992) (*2nd issue*). *Pre-Columbian Carib Society. Multicoloured designs as T* **69** *of St. Vincent Grenadines. P* 14.
947 10 c. Cutting tree bark for canoe 15 15
948 50 c. Body painting (*horiz*) 80 80
949 65 c. Religious ceremony (*horiz*) 95 95
950 $1 Canoeing . . . . 1·50 1·50
947/50 . . . . *Set of* 4 3·00 3·00
MS951 84×70 mm. $2 Cave pictograph (*horiz*) 3·50 4·00

(Des Design Element. Litho Questa)

1989 (17 Nov). *"World Stamp Expo '89" International Stamp Exhibition, Washington (1st issue). Sheet 77×62 mm containing horiz design as T* **193***a of Lesotho. Multicoloured. P* 14.
MS952 $1.50, Lincoln Memorial . . . . 2·50 2·75

(Des W. Hanson Studio. Litho Questa)

1989 (19 Nov). *"World Stamp Expo '89" International Stamp Exhibition, Washington (2nd issue). Bicentenary of the U.S. Presidency. T* **210***a and similar horiz designs. Multicoloured. P* 14.
953 50 c. Type **210***a* 60 65
a. Sheetlet. Nos. 953/8 . . . . 3·50
954 50 c. Martin van Buren, Moses Walker and early baseball game 60 65
955 50 c. William H. Harrison and campaign parade 60 65
956 50 c. John Tyler, Davy Crockett and the Alamo, Texas 60 65
957 50 c. James K. Polk, California gold miner and first U.S. postage stamp . . 60 65
958 50 c. Zachary Taylor and Battle of Buena Vista, 1846 . . . . 60 65
959 50 c. Rutherford B. Hayes and end of Confederate Reconstruction 60 65
a. Sheetlet. Nos. 959/64 . . . . 3·50
960 50 c. James A. Garfield and Battle of Shiloh 60 65
961 50 c. Chester A. Arthur and opening of Brooklyn Bridge, 1883 . . . . 60 65
962 50 c. Grover Cleveland, Columbian Exposition, Chicago, 1893, and commemorative stamp 60 65
963 50 c. Benjamin Harrison, Pan-American Union Building and map of Americas 60 65
964 50 c. William McKinley and Rough Rider Monument 60 65
965 50 c. Herbert Hoover, Sonya Heine (skater) and Ralph Metcalf (athlete) . . 60 65
a. Sheetlet. Nos. 965/70 . . . . 3·50
966 50 c. Franklin D. Roosevelt with dog and in wheelchair 60 65
967 50 c. Statue of Washington by Frazer and New York World's Fair, 1939 . . 60 65
968 50 c. Harry S. Truman, Veterans Memorial Building, San Francisco, and U.N. emblem 60 65
969 50 c. Dwight D. Eisenhower and U.S. troops landing in Normandy, 1944 . . 60 65
970 50 c. John F. Kennedy and "Apollo 11" astronauts on Moon, 1969 . . . . 60 65
953/70 . . . . *Set of* 18 9·75 10·50
Nos. 953/8, 959/64 and 965/70 were each printed together, *se-tenant*, in sheetlets of six stamps.

(Litho Questa)

1989 (18 Dec). *Christmas. Paintings by Bellini. Vert designs as T* **193***b of Lesotho. Multicoloured. P* 14.
971 15 c. "Madonna and Child" 25 25
972 25 c. "The Madonna of the Shrubs" . . 35 35
973 35 c. "The Virgin and Child" 45 45
974 40 c. "The Virgin and Child with a Greek Inscription" 55 55
975 50 c. "The Madonna of the Meadow" . . 65 65
976 65 c. "The Madonna of the Pear" 80 80
977 70 c. "The Virgin and Child" (*different*) . . 90 90
978 $1 "Madonna and Child" (*different*) . . 1·40 1·40
971/8 . . . . *Set of* 8 4·75 4·75
MS979 Two sheets, each 96 × 72 mm. (a) $2 "The Virgin and Child enthroned". (b) $2 "The Madonna with John the Baptist and another Saint" . . . . *Set of* 2 *sheets* 6·00 6·50

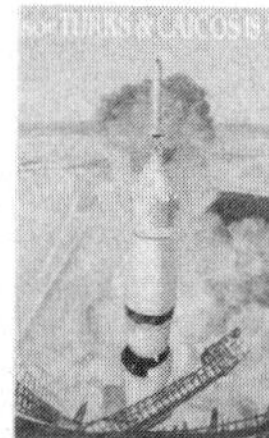

211 Lift-off of "Apollo 11"
212 *Zephyranthes rosea*

(Des W. Hanson Studio. Litho Questa)

1990 (8 Jan). *20th Anniv of First Manned Landing on Moon. T* **211** *and similar vert designs. Multicoloured. P* 14.
980 50 c. Type **211** 60 65
a. Sheetlet. Nos. 980/4 and 5 labels 2·75
981 50 c. Lunar module *Eagle* on Moon . . 60 65
982 50 c. Aldrin gathering dust sample . . 60 65
983 50 c. Neil Armstrong with camera . . 60 65
984 50 c. *Eagle* re-united with command module *Columbia* 60 65
980/4 . . . . *Set of* 5 2·75 3·00
Nos. 980/4 were printed together, *se-tenant*, in sheetlets of five stamps, and five stamp-size labels, with Nos. 981/3 forming a composite design.

(Des C. Abbott. Litho Questa)

1990 (11 Jan–21 May). *Island Flowers. T* **212** *and similar vert designs. Multicoloured. P* 14.

985 8 c. Type **212** 10 10
986 10 c. *Sophora tomentosa* 10 15
987 15 c. *Coccoloba uvifera* 15 20
988 20 c. *Encyclia gracilis* 25 30
989 25 c. *Tillandsia streptophylla* 30 35
990 30 c. *Maurandella antirrhiniflora* .. 35 40
991 35 c. *Tillandsia balbisiana* 40 45
992 50 c. *Encyclia rufa* 60 65
993 65 c. *Aechmea lingulata* 75 80
994 80 c. *Asclepias curassavica* .. .. 95 1·00
995 $1 *Caesalpinia bahamensis* .. .. 1·10 1·25
996 $1.10, *Capparis cynophallophora* .. 1·25 1·40
997 $1.25, *Stachytarpheta jamaicensis* .. 1·40 1·50
998 $2 *Cassia biflora* .. .. .. 2·25 2·40
1000 $10 *Opuntia bahamana* (21 May) .. 11·50 12·00
985/1000 .. .. *Set of* 15 18·00 19·00

213 Queen Parrotfish

(Des J. Barbaris. Litho B.D.T.)

1990 (12 Feb). *Fishes. T* **213** *and similar horiz designs. Multicoloured. P* 14.

1001 8 c. Type **213** 10 10
1002 10 c. Queen Triggerfish 10 15
1003 25 c. Sergeant Major 30 35
1004 40 c. Spotted Goatfish 45 50
1005 50 c. Neon Goby 60 65
1006 75 c. Nassau Grouper 85 90
1007 80 c. Jawfish .. .. 95 1·00
1008 $1 Blue Tang .. .. 1·10 1·25
1001/8 .. .. *Set of* 8 4·00 4·50
MS1009 Two sheets, each 115×80 mm. (a) $2 Butter Hamlet. (b) $2 Queen Angelfish *Set of* 2 *sheets* 4·75 5·00

214 Yellow-billed Cuckoo

215 *Anartia jatrophae*

(Des W. Wright. Litho B.D.T.)

1990 (19 Feb). *Birds* (1*st series*). *T* **214** *and similar horiz designs. Multicoloured. P* 14.

1010 10 c. Type **214** 10 15
1011 15 c. White-tailed Tropic Bird 15 20
1012 20 c. Kirtland's Warbler 25 30
1013 30 c. Yellow-crowned Night Heron .. 35 40
1014 50 c. Black-billed Whistling Duck ("West Indian Tree Duck") 60 65
1015 80 c. Yellow-bellied Sapsucker .. .. 95 1·00
1016 $1 American Kestrel .. .. .. 1·10 1·25
1017 $1.40, Northern Mockingbird .. .. 1·60 1·75
1010/17 .. .. *Set of* 8 4·50 5·25
MS1018 Two sheets, each 104×78 mm. (a) $2 Yellow Warbler. (b) $2 Osprey .. *Set of* 2 *sheets* 4·75 5·00
See also Nos. 1050/8.

(Des Linda Vorovik. Litho Questa)

1990 (19 Mar). *Butterflies* (1*st series*). *T* **215** *and similar multicoloured designs. P* 14.

1019 15 c. Type **215** 15 20
1020 25 c. *Phoebis sennae* (*horiz*) 30 35
1021 35 c. *Euptoieta hegesia* (*horiz*) 40 45
1022 40 c. *Hylephila phylaeus* (*horiz*) 45 50
1023 50 c. *Eurema chamberlaini* (*horiz*) .. 60 65
1024 60 c. *Brephidium exilis* 70 75
1025 90 c. *Papilio aristodemus* (*horiz*) .. .. 1·00 1·10
1026 $1 *Marpesia eleuchea* .. .. .. 1·10 1·25
1019/26 .. .. *Set of* 8 4·25 4·75
MS1027 Two sheets, each 106×76 mm. (a) $2 *Hemiargus thomasi* (*horiz*). (b) $2 *Danaus gilippus* (*horiz*) .. .. .. *Set of* 2 *sheets* 4·75 5·00
See also Nos. 1081/9.

(Des Mary Walters. Litho Questa)

1990 (2 Apr). 500*th Anniv of Discovery of America by Columbus* (1992) (3*rd issue*). *New World Natural History – Fishes. Horiz designs as T* **60** *of Nevis* (*St. Kitts-Nevis*). *Multicoloured. P* 14.

1028 10 c. Rock Beauty 10 15
1029 15 c. Coney 15 20
1030 25 c. Red Hind 30 35
1031 50 c. Banded Butterflyfish 60 65
1032 60 c. French Angelfish 70 75
1033 75 c. Blackbar Soldierfish 85 90
1034 90 c. Stoplight Parrotfish .. .. .. 1·00 1·10
1035 $1 French Grunt .. .. .. 1·10 1·25
1028/35 .. .. *Set of* 8 4·25 4·75
MS1036 Two sheets, each 109×75 mm. (a) $2 Blue Chromis. (b) $2 Grey Angelfish *Set of* 2 *sheets* 4·75 5·00

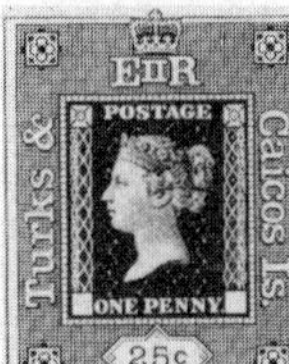

216 Penny "Rainbow Trial" in Blue

217 Pillar Box No. 1, 1855

(Des M. Pollard. Litho B.D.T.)

1990 (3 May). 150*th Anniv of the Penny Black. T* **216** *and similar vert designs. P* 14.

1037 25 c. deep violet-blue 30 35
1038 75 c. lake-brown 85 90
1039 $1 blue .. .. 1·10 1·25
1037/9 .. .. *Set of* 3 2·00 2·25
MS1040 144×111 mm. $2 brownish black .. 2·25 2·50
Designs:—75 c. 1d. red-brown colour trial of December, 1840; $1 2d. blue of 1840; $2 Penny Black.

(Des M. Pollard. Litho B.D.T.)

1990 (3 May). *"Stamp World London 90" International Stamp Exhibition. British Pillar Boxes. T* **217** *and similar vert designs. P* 14.

1041 35 c. purple-brown and brownish grey .. 40 45
1042 50 c. deep violet-blue and brownish grey .. 60 65
1043 $1.25, dull ultramarine & brownish grey 1·40 1·50
1041/3 .. .. *Set of* 3 2·10 2·40
MS1044 143×111 mm. $2 brown-lake and black 2·25 2·40
Designs:—50 c. Penfold box, 1866; $1.25, Air mail box, 1935; $2 "K" type box, 1979.

218 Queen Elizabeth the Queen Mother

219 Stripe-headed Tanager

(Des D. Miller. Litho Questa)

1990 (20 Aug). 90*th Birthday of Queen Elizabeth the Queen Mother. T* **218** *and similar vert designs showing recent photographs of the Queen Mother. P* 14.

1045 10 c. multicoloured 10 15
1046 25 c. multicoloured 30 35
1047 75 c. multicoloured 85 90
1048 $1.25, multicoloured .. .. .. 1·40 1·50
1045/8 .. .. *Set of* 4 2·40 2·50
MS1049 70×73 mm. $2 multicoloured .. .. 2·25 2·40

(Des Tracy Pedersen. Litho Questa)

1990 (24 Sept). *Birds* (2*nd series*). *T* **219** *and similar multicoloured designs. P* 14.

1050 8 c. Type **219** 10 10
1051 10 c. Black-whiskered Vireo (*horiz*) .. 10 15
1052 25 c. Blue-grey Gnatcatcher (*horiz*) .. 30 35
1053 40 c. Lesser Scaup (*horiz*) 45 50
1054 50 c. White-cheeked Pintail (*horiz*) .. 60 65
1055 75 c. Black-winged Stilt (wrongly inscr "Common Stilt") (*horiz*) 85 90
1056 80 c. Common Oystercatcher .. .. 95 1·00
1057 $1 Tricoloured Heron (*horiz*) .. .. 1·10 1·25
1050/7 .. .. *Set of* 8 4·00 4·50
MS1058 Two sheets, each 98×69 mm. (a) $2 American Coot (*horiz*). (b) $2 Bahama Woodstar (*horiz*) .. .. *Set of* 2 *sheets* 4·75 5·00

220 "Triumph of Christ over Sin and Death" (detail, Rubens)

221 Canoeing

(Litho Questa)

1990 (17 Dec). *Christmas. 350th Death Anniv of Rubens. T* **220** *and similar vert designs. Multicoloured. P* 13½×14.

1059 10 c. Type **220** 10 15
1060 35 c. "St. Theresa Praying" (detail) .. 40 45
1061 45 c. "St. Theresa Praying" (different detail) 50 55
1062 50 c. "Triumph of Christ over Sin and Death" (different detail) 60 65
1063 65 c. "St. Theresa Praying" (different detail) 75 80
1064 75 c. "Triumph of Christ over Sin and Death" (different detail) 85 90
1065 $1.25, "St. Theresa Praying" (different detail) .. .. 1·40 1·50
1059/65 .. .. *Set of* 7 4·25 4·50
MS1066 Two sheets, each 70×100 mm. (a) $2 "Triumph of Christ over Sin and Death" (different detail). (b) $2 "St. Theresa Praying" (different detail) .. .. *Set of* 2 *sheets* 4·75 5·00

(Des D. Miller. Litho Questa)

1991 (7 Jan). *Olympic Games, Barcelona* (1992). *T* **221** *and similar vert designs. Multicoloured. P* 14.

1067 10 c. Type **221** 10 15
1068 25 c. 100 metre sprint 30 35
1069 75 c. Pole vaulting 85 90
1070 $1.25, Javelin .. .. 1·40 1·50
1067/70 .. .. *Set of* 4 2·40 2·50
MS1071 109×70 mm. $2 Baseball .. .. 2·25 2·40

(Des T. Agans. Litho Questa)

1991 (15 Apr). 500*th Anniv of Discovery of America by Columbus* (1992) (4*th issue*). *History of Exploration. Multicoloured designs as T* **64** *of Nevis* (*St. Kitts-Nevis*). *P* 14.

1072 5 c. Henry Hudson in Hudson's Bay, 1611 10 10
1073 10 c. Roald Amundsen's airship *Norge*, 1926 .. .. 10 15
1074 15 c. Amundsen's *Gjoa* in the Northwest Passage, 1906 .. .. .. 15 20
1075 50 c. Submarine U.S.S. *Nautilus* under North Pole, 1958 .. .. 60 65
1076 75 c. Robert Scott's *Terra Nova*, 1911 .. 85 90
1077 $1 Byrd and Bennett's Fokker aircraft over North Pole, 1926 .. .. 1·10 1·25
1078 $1.25, Lincoln Ellsworth's *Polar Star* on trans-Antarctic flight, 1935 .. .. 1·40 1·50
1079 $1.50, Capt. James Cook in the Antarctic, 1772–1775 .. .. 1·75 1·90
1072/9 .. .. *Set of* 8 5·50 6·00
MS1080 Two sheets, each 116×76 mm. (a) $2 The *Santa Maria* (*vert*). (b) $2 Bow of *Nina* (*vert*) *Set of* 2 *sheets* 4·75 5·00

222 *Anartia jatrophae*

(Des D. Miller. Litho Questa)

1991 (13 May). *Butterflies* (2*nd series*). *T* **222** *and similar horiz designs. Multicoloured. P* 14.

1081 5 c. Type **222** 10 10
1082 25 c. *Historis osius* 30 35
1083 35 c. *Agraulis vanillae* 40 45
1084 45 c. *Junonia evarete* 50 55
1085 55 c. *Dryas julia* 65 70
1086 65 c. *Siproeta stelenes* 75 80
1087 70 c. *Appias drusilla* 80 85
1088 $1 *Ascia monuste* .. .. .. 1·10 1·25
1081/8 .. .. *Set of* 8 4·25 4·50
MS1089 Two sheets, each 114×72 mm. (a) $2 *Phoebis philea*. (b) $2 *Pseudolycaena marsyas* *Set of* 2 *sheets* 4·75 5·00

223 Protohydrochoerus

(Des R. Frank. Litho Questa)

1991 (3 June). *Extinct Species of Fauna. T* **223** *and similar horiz designs. Multicoloured. P* 14.

1090 5 c. Type **223** 10 10
1091 10 c. Phororhacos 10 10
1092 15 c. Prothylacynus 15 20
1093 50 c. Borhyaena 60 65
1094 75 c. Smilodon 85 90
1095 $1 Thoatherium .. .. .. 1·10 1·25
1096 $1.25, Cuvieronius .. .. .. 1·40 1·50
1097 $1.50, Toxodon .. .. 1·75 1·90
1090/7 .. .. *Set of* 8 5·50 6·00
MS1098 Two sheets, each 79×59 mm. (a) $2 Astrapotherium. (b) $2 Mesosaurus *Set of* 2 *sheets* 4·75 5·00

(Des D. Miller. Litho Walsall)

1991 (8 June). 65*th Birthday of Queen Elizabeth II. Horiz designs as T* **210** *of Lesotho. Multicoloured. P* 14.

1099 25 c. Queen and Prince Philip at St. Paul's Cathedral, 1988 .. .. .. 30 35
1100 35 c. Queen and Prince Philip 40 45
1101 65 c. Queen and Prince Philip at Garter Ceremony, 1988 .. .. .. 75 80
1102 80 c. Queen at Windsor, May 1988 .. 95 1·00
1099/1102 .. .. *Set of* 4 2·25 2·50
MS1103 68×90 mm. $2 Separate photographs of Queen and Prince Philip .. .. .. 2·25 2·50

224 *Pluteus chrysophlebius*

(Des Wendy Smith-Griswold. Litho Questa)

1991 (24 June). *Fungi. T* **224** *and similar multicoloured designs. P* 14.

1104	10 c. Type **224**	10	10
1105	15 c. *Leucopaxillus gracillimus*	15	20
1106	20 c. *Marasmius haematocephalus*	25	30
1107	35 c. *Collybia subpruinosa*	40	45
1108	50 c. *Marasmius atrorubens* (*vert*)	60	65
1109	65 c. *Leucocoprinus birnbaumii* (*vert*)	75	80
1110	$1.10, *Trogia cantharelloides* (*vert*)	1·25	1·40
1111	$1.25, *Boletellus cubensis* (*vert*)	1·40	1·50
1104/11	*Set of* 8	4·50	4·75
MS1112	Two sheets, each 85×59 mm. (a) $2 *Pyrrhoglossum pyrrhum* (*vert*). (b) $2 *Gerronema citrinum* .. *Set of* 2 *sheets*	4·75	5·00

(Des D. Miller. Litho Walsall)

1991 (29 July). 10*th Wedding Anniv of Prince and Princess of Wales. Horiz designs as T* **210** *of Lesotho. Multicoloured. P* 14.

1113	10 c. Prince and Princess of Wales, 1987	10	10
1114	45 c. Separate photographs of Prince, Princess and sons	50	55
1115	50 c. Prince Henry in fire engine and Prince William applauding	60	65
1116	$1 Princess Diana in Derbyshire, 1990, and Prince Charles	1·10	1·25
1113/16	*Set of* 4	2·25	2·50
MS1117	68×90 mm. $2 Prince, Princess and family, Majorca, 1990	2·25	2·50

(Litho B.D.T.)

1992 (26 Aug). *Death Centenary of Vincent van Gogh* (*artist*) (1990). *Multicoloured designs as T* **255** *of Maldive Islands. P* 13.

1118	15 c. "Weaver with Spinning Wheel" (*horiz*)	15	20
1119	25 c. "Head of a Young Peasant with Pipe"	30	35
1120	35 c. "Old Cemetery Tower at Nuenen"	40	45
1121	45 c. "Cottage at Nightfall" (*horiz*)	50	55
1122	50 c. "Still Life with Open Bible" (*horiz*)	60	65
1123	65 c. "Lane, Jardin du Luxembourg" (*horiz*)	75	80
1124	80 c. "Pont du Carrousel and Louvre, Paris" (*horiz*)	95	1·00
1125	$1 "Vase with Poppies, Cornflowers, Peonies and Chrysanthemums"	1·10	1·25
1118/25	*Set of* 8	4·25	4·75
MS1126	Two sheets, each 117×80 mm. (a) $2 "Ploughed Field" (*horiz*). (b) $2 "Entrance to the Public Park" (*horiz*). Imperf .. *Set of* 2 *sheets*	4·75	5·00

225 Series "8550" Steam Locomotive

(Litho Questa)

1991 (4 Nov). *"Philanippon '91" International Stamp Exhibition, Tokyo. Japanese Steam Locomotives. T* **225** *and similar horiz designs. Multicoloured. P* 14.

1127	8 c. Type **225**	10	10
1128	10 c. Class "C 57"	10	10
1129	45 c. Series "4110"	50	55
1130	50 c. Class "C 55"	60	65
1131	65 c. Series "6250"	75	80
1132	80 c. Class "E 10"	95	1·00
1133	$1 Series "4500"	1·10	1·25
1134	$1.25, Class "C 11"	1·40	1·50
1127/34	*Set of* 4	5·00	5·50
MS1135	Two sheets, each 112×80 mm. (a) $2 Class "C 58". (b) $2 Class "C 62" .. *Set of* 2 *sheets*	4·75	5·00

(Litho Walsall)

1991 (23 Dec). *Christmas. Religious Paintings by Gerard David. Vert designs as T* **211** *of Lesotho. Multicoloured. P* 12.

1136	8 c. "Adoration of the Shepherds" (detail)	10	10
1137	15 c. "Virgin and Child Enthroned with Two Angels"	15	20
1138	35 c. "The Annunciation" (outer wings)	40	45
1139	45 c. "The Rest on the Flight to Egypt"	50	55
1140	50 c. "The Rest on the Flight to Egypt" (*different*)	60	65
1141	65 c. "Virgin and Child with Angels"	75	80
1142	80 c. "Adoration of the Shepherds"	95	1·00
1143	$1.25, "Perussis Altarpiece" (detail)	1·40	1·50
1136/43	*Set of* 8	4·25	4·75
MS1144	Two sheets, each 102×127 mm. (a) $2 "The Nativity". (b) $2 "Adoration of the Kings". P 14 .. *Set of* 2 *sheets*	4·75	5·00

NEW INFORMATION

The editor is always interested to correspond with people who have new information that will improve or correct the Catalogue.

226 Garden overlooking Sea

(Des D. Miller. Litho Questa)

1992 (6 Feb). 40*th Anniv of Queen Elizabeth II's Accession. T* **226** *and similar horiz designs. Multicoloured. P* 14.

1145	10 c. Type **226**	10	10
1146	20 c. Jetty	25	30
1147	25 c. Small bay	30	35
1148	35 c. Island road	40	45
1149	50 c. Grand Turk	60	65
1150	65 c. Beach	75	80
1151	80 c. Marina	95	1·00
1152	$1.10, Grand Turk (*different*)	1·25	1·40
1145/52	*Set of* 8	4·00	4·50
MS1153	Two sheets, each 75×97 mm. (a) $2 Beach (*different*). (b) $2 Foreshore, Grand Turk *Set of* 2 *sheets*	4·75	5·00

CAICOS ISLANDS

CAICOS ISLANDS

(1)

1981 (24 July). *Nos.* 514A, 518A, 520A, 523A *and* 525A/7A *of Turks and Caicos Islands optd with T* **1**.

1	1 c. Indigo Hamlet	10	10
2	5 c. Spanish Grunt	10	10
3	8 c. Foureye Butterflyfish	10	10
4	20 c. Queen Angelfish	25	30
5	50 c. Fairy Basslet	65	70
6	$1 Clown Wrasse	1·00	1·25
7	$2 Stoplight Parrotfish	2·50	2·75
1/7	*Set of* 7	4·25	4·75

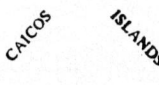

Caicos Islands CAICOS ISLANDS

(2) (3)

1981 (24 July). *Royal Wedding. Nos.* 653/6 *of Turks and Caicos Islands optd. A. With T* **2** *in London. B. With T* **3** *in New York.*

		A		B	
8	35 c. Prince Charles and Lady Diana Spencer	25	25	1·25	1·25
	a. Opt inverted		†	£130	—
9	65 c. Kensington Palace	40	40	2·00	2·00
	a. Opt inverted		†	95·00	—
10	90 c. Prince Charles as Colonel of the Welsh Guards	50	50	2·25	2·25
	a. Opt inverted		†	£110	—
	b. Opt double		†	£110	—
8/10	*Set of* 3	1·00	1·00	5·00	5·00
MS11	96 × 82 mm. $2 Glass Coach	3·00	3·00	4·50	4·50
	a. Opt inverted		†	—	—

Nos. 8B/10 come either in sheets of 40 (2 panes 4 × 5) or in sheetlets of 5 stamps and one label. Examples of Nos. 8Ba, 9Ba and 10Ba are known from both formats, but No. 10Bb only exists from sheetlets.

Nos. 8/10 also exist perforated 12 (*Price for set of* 3 *with London opt* £4 *or with New York opt* £9, *mint or used*) from additional sheetlets of five stamps and one label. These stamps have changed background colours.

1981 (29 Oct). *Royal Wedding. Booklet stamps. As Nos.* 657/9 *of Turks and Caicos Islands, but each inscr* "Caicos Islands". *Multicoloured. Roul* 5 × *imperf**. *Self-adhesive.*

12	20 c. Lady Diana Spencer	80	60
	a. Booklet pane. Nos. 12/13, each × 3	4·00	
13	$1 Prince Charles	3·75	2·75
14	$2 Prince Charles and Lady Diana Spencer	10·00	6·00
	a. Booklet pane of 1	10·00	
12/14	*Set of* 3	13·00	8·50

*The 20 c. and $1 values were each separated by various combinations of rotary knife (giving a straight edge) and roulette. The $2 value exists only with straight edges.

4 Conch and Lobster Fishing, South Caicos

(Des J. Cooter (8 c. to 21 c.). Litho)

1983 (6 June)–**84**. *T* **4** *and similar horiz designs. Multicoloured. P* 14.

15	8 c. Type **4**	15	15
16	10 c. Hawksbill Turtle, East Caicos	20	20
17	20 c. Arawak Indians and idol, Middle Caicos	30	40
18	35 c. Boat-building, North Caicos	55	60
19	50 c. Marine biologist at work, Pine Cay	75	75
20	95 c. Boeing "707" airliner at new airport, Providenciales	1·50	1·60
21	$1.10, Columbus' *Pinta*, West Caicos	2·00	1·75
22	$2 Fort George Cay (18.5.84)	3·50	3·00
23	$3 Pirates Anne Bonny and Calico Jack at Parrot Cay (18.5.84)	6·00	4·75
15/23	*Set of* 9	13·50	12·00

5 Goofy and Patch

6 "Leda and the Swan"

(Litho Walsall)

1983 (7 Nov). *Christmas. T* **5** *and similar vert designs showing Disney cartoon characters. Multicoloured. P* 11.

30	1 c. Type **5**	10	10
31	1 c. Chip and Dale	10	10
32	2 c. Morty	10	10
33	2 c. Morty and Ferdie	10	10
34	3 c. Goofy and Louie	10	10
35	3 c. Donald Duck, Huey, Dewey and Louie	10	10
36	50 c. Uncle Scrooge	1·50	90
37	70 c. Mickey Mouse and Ferdie	2·00	1·25
38	$1.10, Pinocchio, Jiminy Cricket and Figaro	2·50	1·90
30/8	*Set of* 9	6·00	3·75
MS39	126 × 101 mm. $2 Morty and Ferdie. P 13½ × 14	3·50	3·50

(Des and litho Questa)

1983 (15 Dec). *500th Birth Anniv of Raphael. T* **6** *and similar vert designs. Multicoloured. P* 14.

40	35 c. Type **6**	70	50
41	50 c. "Study of Apollo for Parnassus"	90	70
42	95 c. "Study of two figures for the battle of Ostia"	1·75	1·25
43	$1.10, "Study for the Madonna of the Goldfinch"	2·00	1·50
40/3	*Set of* 4	4·75	3·50
MS44	71 × 100 mm. $2.50, "The Garvagh Madonna"	3·00	3·25

7 High Jumping

8 Horace Horsecollar and Clarabelle Cow

(Litho Questa)

1984 (1 Mar). *Olympic Games, Los Angeles. T* **7** *and similar designs. P* 14.

45	4 c. multicoloured	10	10
46	25 c. multicoloured	20	20
47	65 c. black, deep grey-blue and new blue	50	50
48	$1.10, multicoloured	85	85
45/8	*Set of* 4	1·50	1·50
MS49	105 × 75 mm. $2 multicoloured	2·25	3·00

Designs: *Vert*—25 c. Archery; 65 c. Cycling; $1.10, Football. *Horiz*—$2 Show jumping.

(Des Walt Disney Productions. Litho Questa)

1984 (23 Apr). *Easter. Walt Disney Cartoon Characters. T* **8** *and similar horiz designs. Multicoloured. P* 14 × 13½.

50	35 c. Type **8**	60	60
51	45 c. Mickey and Minnie Mouse, and Chip	75	75
52	75 c. Gyro Gearloose, Chip 'n Dale	1·25	1·25
53	85 c. Mickey Mouse, Chip 'n Dale	1·40	1·40
50/3	*Set of* 4	3·50	3·50
MS54	127 × 101 mm. $2.20, Donald Duck	3·50	3·75

UNIVERSAL POSTAL UNION 1874-1984  **AUSIPEX 1984**

(9) (10)

1984 (19 June). *Universal Postal Union Congress, Hamburg. Nos.* 20/1 *optd with T* **9**.

55	95 c. Boeing "707" airliner at new airport, Providenciales	1·00	1·25
56	$1.10, Columbus' *Pinta*, West Caicos	1·25	1·50

1984 (22 Aug). *"Ausipex" International Stamp Exhibition, Melbourne. No.* 22 *optd with T* **10**.

57	$2 Fort George Cay	2·40	2·50

11 Seamen sighting American Manatees

(Des L. Lightbourne. Litho Walsall)

1984 (12 Sept). *492nd Anniv of Columbus' First Landfall. T* **11** *and similar horiz designs. Multicoloured. P* 14.

58	10 c. Type **11**	30	15
59	70 c. Fleet of Columbus	1·75	1·10
60	$1 First landing in West Indies	2·25	1·60
58/60	*Set of* 3	4·00	2·50
MS61	99 × 69 mm. $2 Fleet of Columbus (*different*)	2·75	3·00

NEW INFORMATION

The editor is always interested to correspond with people who have new information that will improve or correct the Catalogue.

12 Donald Duck and Mickey Mouse with Father Christmas

(Litho Questa)

1984 (26 Nov). *Christmas. Walt Disney Cartoon Characters. T* **12** *and similar vert designs. Multicoloured. P* 12 ($2) *or* 13½ × 14 (*others*).

62	20 c. Type **12**	70	40
63	35 c. Donald Duck opening refrigerator	1·00	65
64	50 c. Mickey Mouse, Donald Duck and toy train	1·25	90
65	75 c. Donald Duck and parcels	1·75	1·25
66	$1.10, Donald Duck and carol singers	2·25	1·75
62/6	*Set of* 5	6·25	4·50
MS67	127 × 102 mm. $2 Donald Duck as Christmas tree	3·00	3·50

No. 65 was printed in sheetlets of 8 stamps.

13 Thick-billed Vireo

14 Two Children learning to Read and Write (Education)

(Des Susan David. Litho Walsall)

1985 (12 Feb). *Birth Bicentenary of John J. Audubon (ornithologist). T* **13** *and similar horiz designs. Multicoloured. P* 14.

68	20 c. Type **13**	1·00	40
69	35 c. Black-faced Grassquit	1·40	65
70	50 c. Pearly-eyed Thrasher	1·75	90
71	$1 Greater Antillean Bullfinch	2·25	1·75
68/71	*Set of* 4	5·75	3·25
MS72	100 × 70 mm. $2 Stripe-headed Tanager	3·25	3·50

(Des C. Walters. Litho Walsall)

1985 (8 May). *International Youth Year and 40th Anniv of United Nations. T* **14** *and similar vert designs. Multicoloured. P* 14.

73	16 c. Type **14**	20	25
74	35 c. Two children on playground swings (Health)	50	55
75	70 c. Boy and girl (Love)	1·00	1·10
76	90 c. Three children (Peace)	1·25	1·40
73/6	*Set of* 4	2·75	3·00
MS77	101 × 71 mm. $2 Child, dove carrying ears of wheat and map of the Americas	2·75	3·00

15 Air Caicos "DC-3" on Ground

16 The Queen Mother visiting Foundation for the Disabled, Leatherhead

(Des K. Gromol. Litho Walsall)

1985 (23 May). *40th Anniv of International Civil Aviation Organization. T* **15** *and similar horiz designs. Multicoloured. P* 14.

78	35 c. Type **15**	75	55
79	75 c. Air Caicos Convair "440"	1·50	1·25
80	90 c. TCNA "Islander"	1·75	1·40
78/80	*Set of* 3	3·50	3·00
MS81	100 × 70 mm. $2.20, Hang-gliding over the Caicos Islands	3·00	3·25

(Des J.W. Litho Questa)

1985 (8 July). *Life and Times of Queen Elizabeth the Queen Mother. T* **16** *and similar multicoloured designs. P* 14.

82	35 c. Type **16**	50	55
83	65 c. With Princess Anne (*horiz*)	90	95
84	95 c. At Epsom, 1961	1·40	1·60
82/4	*Set of* 3	2·50	2·75
MS85	56 × 85 mm. $2 visiting Royal Hospital, Chelsea	2·75	3·00

(Des Walt Disney Productions. Litho Questa)

1985 (5 Dec). *150th Birth Anniv of Mark Twain (author). Multicoloured designs as T* **160a** *of Lesotho, but horiz, showing Walt Disney cartoon characters in scenes from "Tom Sawyer, Detective". P* 14×13½.

86 8 c. Huckleberry Finn (Goofy) and Tom Sawyer (Mickey Mouse) reading reward notice 30 10
87 35 c. Huck and Tom meeting Jake Dunlap 1·00 55
88 95 c. Huck and Tom spying on Jubiter Dunlap 2·00 1·40
89 $1.10, Huck and Tom with hound (Pluto) 2·25 1·60
86/9 *Set of* 4 5·00 3·25
MS90 127 × 101 mm. $2 Tom unmasking Jubiter Dunlap 2·75 3·00

(Des Walt Disney Productions. Litho Questa)

1985 (5 Dec). *Birth Bicentenaries of Grimm Brothers (folklorists). Multicoloured designs as T* **160b** *of Lesotho, but horiz, showing Walt Disney cartoon characters in scenes from "Six Soldiers of Fortune". P* 14×13½.

91 16 c. The Soldier (Donald Duck) with his meagre pay 20 25
92 25 c. The Soldier meeting the Strong Man (Horace Horsecollar) 30 35
93 65 c. The Soldier meeting the Marksman (Mickey Mouse) 85 90
94 $1.35, The Fast Runner (Goofy) winning the race against the Princess (Daisy Duck) 1·75 1·90
91/4 *Set of* 4 2·75 3·00
MS95 126 × 101 mm. $2 The Soldier and the Strong Man with sack of gold 2·50 2·75

Tuvalu

Formerly known as the Ellice Islands when they shared a joint administration with the Gilbert group. On 1 January 1976 the two island-groups separated and the Ellice Islands were renamed Tuvalu.

CROWN COLONY

1 Gilbertese and Tuvaluan

(Des Iakopo Nivatui; adapted J. Cooter. Litho Questa)

1976 (1 Jan). *Separation of the Islands. T* **1** *and similar multicoloured designs. W w* **14** *(sideways on 4 and 35 c.). P* 13½.

1 4 c. Type **1** 45 80
2 10 c. Map of the islands (*vert*) 55 1·00
3 35 c. Canoes 75 1·50
1/3 *Set of* 3 1·60 3·00

TUVALU

(2)

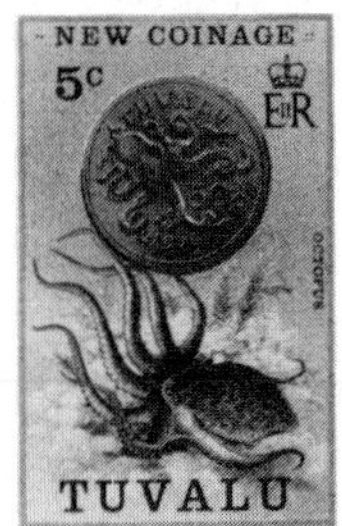

3 50 c. Coin and Octopus

1976 (1 Jan). *Nos. 173 etc. of Gilbert & Ellice Is optd as T* **2** *in silver (35 c.) or blue (others). (a) W w* **12** *(upright).*

4 2 c. Lagoon fishing £750 £140
5 5 c. Gilbertese canoe 80 60
6 8 c. Weaving pandanus fronds 95 60
7 10 c. Weaving a basket 1·50 80
8 50 c. Local handicrafts 27·00 18·00
9 $1 Weaving coconut screen 65·00 70·00

(b) W w **12** *(sideways)*

10 2 c. Lagoon fishing £140 30·00
11 3 c. Cleaning pandanus leaves 85 60
12 5 c. Gilbertese canoe 2·25 1·50
13 25 c. Loading copra 4·00 3·50

(c) W w **14** *(inverted)*

14 1 c. Cutting toddy 30 30
15 6 c. De-husking coconuts 90 40
16 15 c. Tiger shark 1·00 65
17 50 c. Local handicrafts 1·75 80
18 $1 Weaving coconut screen 3·00 1·25
19 $2 Coat of arms 3·00 1·25

(d) W w **14** *(sideways)*

20 2 c. Lagoon fishing 80 40
21 3 c. Cleaning pandanus leaves 90 30
22 4 c. Casting nets 1·00 45
23 20 c. Beating a rolled pandanus leaf 1·00 1·00
24 25 c. Loading copra 1·25 75
25 35 c. Fishing at night 2·25 1·75
5/7 *and* 14/25 *Set of* 15 17·00 9·50

(Des G. Drummond. Litho Walsall)

1976 (21 Apr). *New Coinage. Vert designs, each showing coin as in T* **3**. *Multicoloured. W w* **14** *(inverted). P* 13½.

26 5 c. Type **3** 25 15
27 10 c. Red-eyed Crab 35 20
28 15 c. Flying Fish 45 25
29 35 c. Green Turtle 60 45
26/9 *Set of* 4 1·50 95

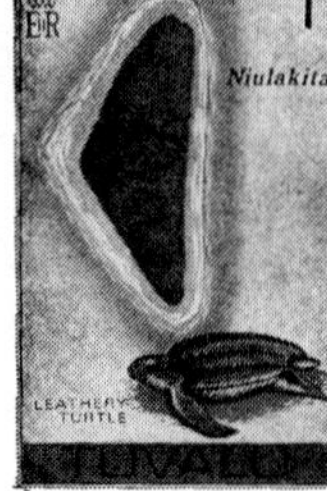

4 Niulakita and Seven-ridged Leathery Turtle

5 Title page of New Testament

(Des J. Cooter. Litho Questa)

1976 (1 July–1 Sept). *Vert designs showing maps (1 to 25 c.) or horiz designs showing scenes (others). Multicoloured. W w* **14** *(sideways on 35 c. to $5). P* 13½.

30 1 c. Type **4** 85 60
31 2 c. Nukulaelae and sleeping mat 40 35
32 4 c. Nui and talo (vegetable) 40 20
33 5 c. Nanumanga and grass skirt 1·25 20
34 6 c. Nukufetau and Coconut Crab 70 30
35 8 c. Funafuti and Banana tree 75 50
36 10 c. Map of Tuvalu 75 20
37 15 c. Niutao and Flying fish 1·00 20
38 20 c. Vaitupu and Maneapa (house) 70 20
39 25 c. Nanumea and fish-hook 4·00 90
40 35 c. Te Ano (game) 60 20
41 50 c. Canoe pole fishing 75 30
42 $1 Reef fishing by flare 80 40
43 $2 Living house 1·50 60
44 $5 M.V. *Nivanga* (1.9.76) 38·00 14·00
30/44 *Set of* 15 45·00 16·00

See also Nos. 58/69.

(Des G. Drummond. Litho Harrison)

1976 (6 Oct). *Christmas. T* **5** *and similar horiz designs. Multicoloured. W w* **14**. *P* 14 × 14½.

45 5 c. Type **5** 70 40
46 20 c. Lotolelei Church 70 40
47 25 c. Kelupi Church 70 40
48 30 c. Mataloa o Tuvalu Church 80 40
49 35 c. Palatasio o Keliso Church 80 40
45/9 *Set of* 5 3·25 1·75

6 Queen Elizabeth and Prince Philip

(Des G. Vasarhelyi. Litho Format)

1977 (9 Feb). *Silver Jubilee. T* **6** *and similar horiz designs. Multicoloured. P* 13½.

50 15 c. Type **6** 75 30
51 35 c. Prince Philip carried ashore at Vaitupu 1·00 40
52 50 c. Queen and attendants 1·00 50
50/2 *Set of* 3 2·50 1·10
MS53 98 × 144 mm. Nos. 50/2. P 15 6·00 6·00

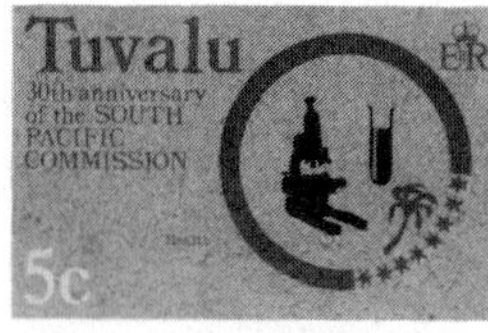

7 "Health"

(Des I. Oliver. Litho Format)

1977 (4 May). *30th Anniv of South Pacific Commission. T* **7** *and similar horiz designs. Multicoloured. P* 13½.

54 5 c. Type **7** 20 20
55 20 c. "Education" 25 20
56 30 c. "Fruit-growing" 25 20
57 35 c. Map of S.P.C. area 30 25
54/7 *Set of* 4 90 75

1977 (13 June)–**78**. *As Nos. 30/6, 38/9 and 44, but no wmk, or new values and designs. (30, 40 c.).*

58 1 c. Type **4** (9.77) 20 15
59 2 c. Nukulaelae and sleeping mat (3.78) 20 25
60 4 c. Nui and talo (vegetable) (3.78) 20 15
61 5 c. Nanumanga and grass skirt (9.77) 25 15
62 6 c. Nukufetau and Coconut Crab (3.78) 20 35
63 8 c. Funafuti and Banana tree (9.77) 20 25
64 10 c. Map of Tuvalu (9.77) 20 20
65 20 c. Vaitupu and Maneapa (house) (10.78) 90 1·50
66 25 c. Nanumea and fish-hook (9.77) 1·25 20
67 30 c. Fatele (local dancing) (19.4.78) 30 20
68 40 c. Screw Pine (19.4.78) 30 15
69 $5 M.V. *Nivanga* 8·00 5·00
58/69 *Set of* 12 11·00 7·00

No. 70/2 vacant.

8 Scout Promise

(Des I. Oliver. Litho Format)

1977 (10 Aug). *50th Anniv of Scouting in the Central Pacific. T* **8** *and similar horiz designs. Multicoloured. P* 13½.

73 5 c. Type **8** 30 25
74 20 c. Canoeing 30 25
75 30 c. Scout shelter 40 30
76 35 c. Lord Baden-Powell 40 30
73/6 *Set of* 4 1·25 1·00

9 Hurricane Beach (Expedition photo)

(Des I. Oliver. Litho Format)

1977 (2 Nov). *Royal Society Expeditions, 1896/7. T* **9** *and similar designs. P* 13½ × 14 *(5 and 35 c.) or* 14 × 13½ *(others).*

77 5 c. multicoloured 25 15
78 20 c. black and light blue 40 20
79 30 c. black and light blue 40 20
80 35 c. multicoloured 40 20
77/80 *Set of* 4 1·25 65

Designs: *Vert*—20 c. Boring apparatus on H.M.S. *Porpoise*; 30 c. Dredging chart. *Horiz*—35 c. Charles Darwin and H.M.S. *Beagle*.

10 Pacific Pigeon

11 *Lawedua* (coaster)

(Des G. Drummond. Litho Format)

1978 (25 Jan). *Wild Birds. T* **10** *and similar vert designs. Multicoloured. P* 14 × 13½.

81 8 c. Type **10** 1·00 35
82 20 c. Eastern Reef Heron 1·25 50
83 30 c. White Tern 1·75 60
84 40 c. Lesser Frigate Bird 1·75 65
81/4 *Set of* 4 5·25 1·90

(Des I. Oliver. Litho Format)

1978 (5 Apr). *Ships. T* **11** *and similar horiz designs. Multicoloured. P* 13½ × 14.

85 8 c. Type **11** 15 15
86 10 c. *Wallacia* (tug) 15 15
87 30 c. *Cenpac Rounder* (freighter) 20 20
88 40 c. *Pacific Explorer* (freighter) 25 20
85/8 *Set of* 4 65 65

(Des G. Drummond. Litho Format)

1978 (2 June). *25th Anniv of Coronation. Horiz designs as Nos. 422/5 of Montserrat. Multicoloured. P* 13½ × 14.

89 8 c. Canterbury Cathedral 10 10
90 30 c. Salisbury Cathedral 10 10
91 40 c. Wells Cathedral 15 10
92 $1 Hereford Cathedral 40 30
89/92 *Set of* 4 60 40
MS93 137 × 108 mm. Nos. 89/92. P 15 80 90

Nos. 89/92 were each printed in sheets containing 2 *se-tenant* stamp-size labels.

INDEPENDENT

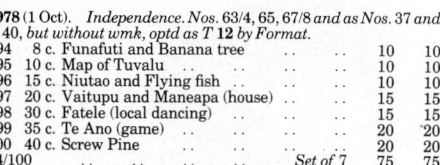

INDEPENDENCE 1ST OCTOBER 1978

(12)

13 White Frangipani

1978 (1 Oct). *Independence. Nos.* 63/4, 65, 67/8 *and as Nos.* 37 *and* 40, *but without wmk, optd as T* **12** *by Format.*
94 8 c. Funafuti and Banana tree 10 10
95 10 c. Map of Tuvalu 10 10
96 15 c. Niutao and Flying fish 10 10
97 20 c. Vaitupu and Maneapa (house) 15 15
98 30 c. Fatele (local dancing) 15 15
99 35 c. Te Ano (game) 20 20
100 40 c. Screw Pine 20 20
94/100 .. .. *Set of* 7 75 75

(Des J. Cooter. Litho Format)

1978 (4 Oct). *Wild Flowers. T* **13** *and similar vert designs. Multicoloured. P* 14.
101 8 c. Type **13** 15 10
102 20 c. Susana 15 10
103 30 c. Tiale 20 15
104 40 c. Inato 25 25
101/4 .. .. *Set of* 4 65 55

14 Squirrelfish

(Des G. Drummond. Litho Format)

1979 (24 Jan)–**81**. *Fishes. Multicoloured designs as T* **14**. *P* 14.
105 1 c. Type **14** 10 10
106 2 c. Yellow-banded Goatfish 10 10
107 4 c. Imperial Angelfish 10 10
108 5 c. Rainbow Butterfly 15 10
109 6 c. Blue Angelfish 15 10
110 8 c. Blue Striped Snapper 15 10
111 10 c. Orange Clownfish 25 10
112 15 c. Chevroned Coralfish 25 10
113 20 c. Fairy Cod 35 15
114 25 c. Clown Triggerfish 35 20
115 30 c. Long-nosed Butterfly 35 10
116 35 c. Yellowfin Tuna 40 20
117 40 c. Spotted Eagle Ray 40 10
117*b* 45 c. Black-tipped Rock Cod (16.6.81) .. 1·50 2·00
118 50 c. Hammerhead Shark 50 20
119 70 c. Lionfish (*vert*) 65 30
120 $1 White-barred Triggerfish (*vert*).. .. 70 55
121 $2 Beaked Coralfish (*vert*) .. .. .. 1·50 60
122 $5 Tiger Shark (*vert*) .. .. .. 2·75 1·25
105/22 .. .. *Set of* 19 9·00 5·50

Nos. 105/22 were each printed in sheets containing 2 *se-tenant* stamp-size printed labels.

Both fine (300 lines of dots per linear inch) and coarse (175 lines of dots per linear inch) screens were used to produce plates for this issue. The 1, 5, 8, 10, 30 and 40 c. values can be found with either screen. The 15, 25, 35, 45 and 50 c. only exist with coarse screen and the remainder only with fine screen.

15 "Explorer of the Pacific"

(Des J. Cooter. Litho Format)

1979 (14 Feb). *Death Bicentenary of Captain Cook. T* **15** *and similar horiz designs. Multicoloured. P* 14 × 14½.
123 8 c. Type **15** 30 20
a. Horiz strip of 4. Nos. 123/6 .. .. 1·40
ab. Imperf. Horiz strip of 4 ..
124 30 c. "A new island is discovered" 40 25
125 40 c. "Transit of Venus, Tahiti, 3 June, 1769" 40 25
126 $1 Death of Captain Cook, Hawaii, 14 February, 1779 .. .. 50 35
123/6 .. .. *Set of* 4 1·40 95

Nos. 123/6 were printed together, *se-tenant*, in horizontal strips of 4 throughout the sheet.

16 Grumman "Goose G21A" and Nukulaelae Island

(Des J. Cooter. Litho Format)

1979 (16 May). *Internal Air Service. T* **16** *and similar horiz designs. Multicoloured. P* 13½.
127 8 c. Type **16** 15 15
128 20 c. "Goose" and Vaitupu 20 20
129 30 c. "Goose" and Nui 30 30
130 40 c. "Goose" and Funafuti 35 35
127/30 .. .. *Set of* 4 90 90

17 Sir Rowland Hill, 1976 4 c. Separation Commemorative and London's First Pillar Box, 1855

18 Child's Face

(Des J. Cooter. Litho Format)

1979 (27 Aug). *Death Centenary of Sir Rowland Hill. T* **17** *and similar horiz designs. Multicoloured. P* 13½ × 14.
131 30 c. Type **17** 25 15
132 40 c. Sir Rowland Hill, 1976 10 c. Separation commemorative and Penny Black .. 25 15
133 $1 Sir Rowland Hill, 1976 35 c. Separation commemorative and mail coach.. .. 50 30
131/3 .. .. *Set of* 3 90 55
MS134 148 × 140 mm. Nos. 131/3. P 15 .. .. 1·00 1·25

(Des G. Vasarhelyi. Litho Format)

1979 (20 Oct). *International Year of the Child. T* **18** *and similar vert designs showing children's faces. P* 14 × 13½.
135 8 c. multicoloured 10 10
136 20 c. multicoloured 15 10
137 30 c. multicoloured 15 15
138 40 c. multicoloured 20 25
135/8 .. .. *Set of* 4 55 55

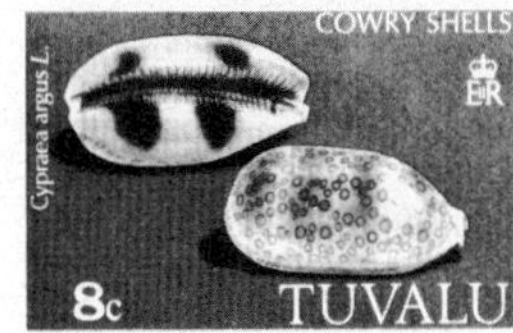

19 *Cypraea argus*

(Des J. Cooter. Litho Format)

1980 (20 Feb). *Cowrie Shells. T* **19** *and similar horiz designs. Multicoloured. P* 13½ × 14.
139 8 c. Type **19** 15 10
140 20 c. *Cypraea scurra* 15 10
141 30 c. *Cypraea carneola*.. .. .. .. 20 15
142 40 c. *Cypraea aurantium* 30 20
139/42 .. .. *Set of* 4 70 45

20 Philatelic Bureau, Funafuti, and 1976 8 c. Definitive

21 Queen Elizabeth the Queen Mother at Royal Variety Performance, 1978

(Des J. Cooter. Litho Questa)

1980 (30 Apr). *"London 1980" International Stamp Exhibition. T* **20** *and similar horiz designs. Multicoloured. P* 13½ × 14.
143 10 c. Type **20** 15 15
144 20 c. Gilbert and Ellice Islands stamp with Nukulaelae postmark of 1946 and 1976 2 c. definitive 25 20
145 30 c. Fleet Post Office, U.S. Navy, airmail letter of 1943 .. .. 25 25
146 $1 Tuvalu coat of arms and map 50 45
143/6 .. .. *Set of* 4 1·00 95
MS147 160 × 136 mm. Nos. 143/6 .. .. 1·00 1·40

(Des G. Drummond. Litho Format)

1980 (14 Aug). *80th Birthday of Queen Elizabeth the Queen Mother. P* 13½.
148 **21** 50 c. multicoloured 35 25

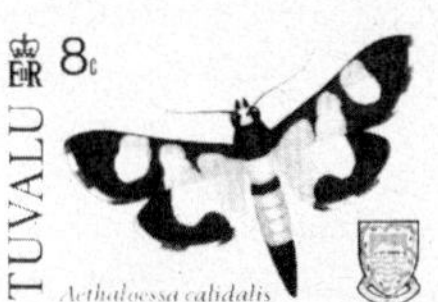

22 *Aethaloessa calidalis*

(Des J. Cooter. Litho Format)

1980 (20 Aug). *Moths. T* **22** *and similar horiz designs. Multicoloured. P* 14.
149 8 c. Type **22** 10 10
150 20 c. *Parotis suralis* 15 10
151 30 c. *Dudua aprobola* 20 15
152 40 c. *Decadarchis simulans* 20 15
149/52 .. .. *Set of* 4 60 45

23 Air Pacific "Heron"

(24)

(Des G. Drummond. Litho Format)

1980 (5 Nov). *Aviation Commemorations. T* **23** *and similar horiz designs. Multicoloured. P* 13½ × 14.
153 8 c. Type **23** 10 10
154 20 c. Hawker Siddeley "748" 15 10
155 30 c. "Sunderland" flying boat 15 15
156 40 c. Orville Wright and *Flyer* 20 15
153/6 .. .. *Set of* 4 55 45

Commemorations:—8 c. 1st regular air service to Tuvalu, 1964; 20 c. Air service to Tuvalu; 30 c. War time R.N.Z.A.F. flying boat service to Funafuti, 1945; 40 c. Wright Brothers' 1st flight, 17 December 1903.

TWO TYPES OF SURCHARGE FOR NO. 157

Type I

Type II

Type I. Applied by lithography. Clean lines with an even distribution of the ink.

Type II. Applied by typography. Ragged lines with an uneven distribution of the ink, especially at the edges of the figures and bars. On some stamps the impression of the surcharge is visible on the back.

1981 (19 Jan). *No.* 118 *surch with T* **24**.
157 45 c. on 50 c. Hammerhead Shark (I).. .. 25 40
a. Type II (typo) surch .. .. .. 4·00 2·25

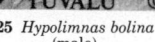

25 *Hypolimnas bolina* (male)

26 Brig *Elizabeth*, 1809

(Des J. Cooter. Litho Questa)

1981 (3 Feb). *Butterflies. T* **25** *and similar horiz designs. Multicoloured. P* 14 × 14½.

158 8 c. Type **25** 15 10
159 20 c. *Hypolimnas bolina* (female) 20 15
160 30 c. *Hypolimnas bolina* (female) (*different*) 20 20
161 40 c. *Precis villida* 25 20
158/61 .. .. *Set of* 4 70 60

(Des R. Granger Barrett. Litho Format)

1981 (13 May). *Ships* (1*st series*). *T* **26** *and similar horiz designs. Multicoloured. W* w **15** (*sideways*). *P* 14.

162 10 c. Type **26** 20 20
163 25 c. Brigantine *Rebecca*, 1819 .. .. 25 30
164 35 c. Whaling ship *Independence II*, 1821 .. 30 35
165 40 c. H.M.S. *Basilisk*, 1872 .. .. .. 35 40
166 45 c. H.M.S. *Royalist*, 1890 .. .. .. 40 50
167 50 c. Barque *Olivebank*, 1920 .. .. 40 50
162/7 .. .. *Set of* 6 1·75 2·00

Nos. 162/7 were each produced in sheets of six stamps and two labels, these occurring in the second horizontal row.

See also Nos. 235/40 and 377/80.

(Des D. Shults. Litho Questa)

1981 (10 July–26 Nov). *Royal Wedding. Horiz designs as T* **26/27** *of Kiribati. Multicoloured.* (*a*) *W* w **15**. *P* 14.

168 10 c. *Carolina* 10 15
a. Sheetlet. No. 168 × 6 and No. 169 .. 90
169 10 c. Prince Charles and Lady Diana Spencer 35 35
170 45 c. *Victoria and Albert III* 20 20
a. Sheetlet. No. 170 × 6 and No. 171 .. 1·40
171 45 c. As No. 169 .. .. 30 30
172 $2 *Britannia* 50 50
a. Sheetlet No. 172 × 6 and No. 173 .. 4·25
173 $2 As No. 169 .. .. 1·75 1·75
168/73 .. .. *Set of* 6 2·75 2·75
MS174 120 × 109 mm. $1.50, As No. 169. Wmk sideways. P 12 (26 Nov) .. .. .. 1·50 1·00

(*b*) *Booklet stamps. No wmk. P* 12 (26 Nov)

175 10 c. As No. 168 .. .. 15 15
a. Booklet pane. No. 175 × 4 55
176 45 c. As No. 171 .. .. 75 80
a. Booklet pane. No. 176 × 2 .. .. 1·50

Nos. 168/73 were printed in sheetlets of seven stamps of the same face value, each containing six of the "Royal Yacht" design and one of the larger design showing Prince Charles and Lady Diana.

Nos. 175/6 come from $1.70 stamp booklets.

27 U.P.U. Emblem

28 Map of Funafuti and Anchor

(Des, eng and recess Harrison)

1981 (19 Nov). *U.P.U. Membership. W* **4** *of Maldive Islands. P* 14½ × 14.

177 **27** 70 c. deep ultramarine 30 30
178 $1 red-brown 50 60
MS179 86 × 71 mm. Nos. 177/8. No wmk .. 2·25 2·50

(Des J. Cooter. Litho Questa)

1982 (17 Feb). *Amatuku Maritime School. T* **28** *and similar horiz designs. Multicoloured. W* w **15** (*sideways*). *P* 13½ × 14.

180 10 c. Type **28** 10 10
181 25 c. Motor launch 25 25
182 35 c. School buildings and jetty 35 35
183 45 c. School flag and freighters 40 40
180/3 .. .. *Set of* 4 1·00 1·00

29 Caroline of Brandenburg–Ansbach, Princess of Wales, 1714

TONGA CYCLONE
RELIEF
1982 +20c

(30)

(Des D. Shults and J. Cooter. Litho Format)

1982 (19 May). *21st Birthday of Princess of Wales. T* **29** *and similar vert designs. Multicoloured. W* w **15**. *P* 13½ × 14.

184 10 c. Type **29** 10 10
185 45 c. Coat of arms of Caroline of Brandenburg-Ansbach 20 15
186 $1.50, Diana, Princess of Wales 60 60
184/6 .. .. *Set of* 3 75 75

1982 (20 May). *Tonga Cyclone Relief. Nos.* 170/1 *surch as T* **30** (*words in one line on No.* 188).

187 45 c. + 20 c. *Victoria and Albert III* 30 50
a. Sheetlet. No. 187 × 6 and No. 188 .. 3·75
b. Surch inverted .. .. 15·00
c. Surch inverted (horiz pair) .. .. 25·00
d. Surch double .. .. 8·00
188 45 c. + 20 c. Prince Charles and Lady Diana Spencer 50 75
a. Surch inverted .. .. 30·00
b. Surch double .. .. 28·00

No. 187c shows the long surcharge, intended for No. 188, inverted and struck across a horizontal pair of No. 187. No. 188a shows two examples of Type **30** inverted on the same stamp.

1982 (14 July). *Birth of Prince William of Wales. Nos.* 184/6 *optd with T* **19** *of St. Kitts.*

189 10 c. Type **29** 10 10
190 45 c. Coat of Arms of Caroline of Brandenburg-Ansbach 20 15
a. Opt inverted .. .. 32·00
191 $1.50, Diana, Princess of Wales 60 60
189/91 .. .. *Set of* 3 75 75

31 Tuvalu and World Scout Badges

32 Tuvalu Crest and Duke of Edinburgh's Standard

(Des J. Cooter. Litho Walsall)

1982 (18 Aug). *75th Anniv of Boy Scout Movement. T* **31** *and similar horiz designs. Multicoloured. W* w **15** (*sideways*). *P* 13½ × 14.

192 10 c. Type **31** 15 15
193 25 c. Camp-fire 40 40
194 35 c. Parade 45 45
195 45 c. Boy Scout 55 55
192/5 .. .. *Set of* 4 1·40 1·40

(Des J. Cooter. Litho Format)

1982 (26 Oct). *Royal Visit. T* **32** *and similar vert designs. Multicoloured. W* w **15**. *P* 14.

196 25 c. Type **32** 25 25
197 45 c. Tuvalu flag and Royal Standard .. 40 40
198 50 c. Portrait of Queen Elizabeth II 40 40
196/8 .. .. *Set of* 3 95 95
MS199 104 × 85 mm. Nos. 196/8. Wmk inverted .. .. 1·00 1·50

33 Fisherman's Hat and Equipment

(Des G. Drummond. Litho Walsall)

1983 (14 Mar)–**84**. *Handicrafts. T* **33** *and similar multicoloured designs. W* w **15** (*sideways on* 1 c. *to* 45 c.). *P* 14.

200 1 c. Type **33** 30 10
201 2 c. Cowrie shell handbags 30 10
202 5 c. Wedding and babyfood baskets 30 10
203 10 c. Model canoe 30 10
203*a* 15 c. Ladies' sun hats (30.4.84) .. .. 1·25 80
204 20 c. Palm climbing rope and platform with toddy pot 30 20
205 25 c. Pandanus baskets 30 20
205*a* 30 c. Basket tray and coconut stands (18.4.84) 1·50 85
206 35 c. Pandanus pillows and shell necklaces .. 30 30
207 40 c. Round baskets and fans 30 35
208 45 c. Reef sandals and fish trap 35 40
209 50 c. Rat trap (*vert*) 40 45
209*a* 60 c. Fisherman's waterproof boxes (*vert*) (18.4.84) .. .. 2·25 90
210 $1 Pump drill and adze (*vert*) 75 70
211 $2 Fisherman's hat and canoe bailers (*vert*) 1·50 1·25
212 $5 Fishing rod, lures and scoop nets (*vert*) .. 3·50 2·50
200/12 .. .. *Set of* 16 12·50 8·00

34 *Te Tautai* (trawler)

(Des G. Drummond. Litho Format)

1983 (14 Mar). *Commonwealth Day. T* **34** *and similar horiz designs. Multicoloured. W* w **15**. *P* 14.

213 20 c. Type **34** 15 15
214 35 c. Traditional dancing, Motufoua School .. 25 25
215 45 c. Satellite view of Pacific 30 30
216 50 c. *Morning Star* (container ship) 40 40
213/16 .. .. *Set of* 4 1·00 1·00

No. 214 is incorrectly inscribed "MOTOFOUA SCHOOL".

35 *Pantala flavescens*

(Des J. Cooter. Litho Format)

1983 (25 May). *Dragonflies. T* **35** *and similar horiz designs. Multicoloured. W* w **15** (*sideways*). *P* 14.

217 10 c. Type **35** 20 10
218 35 c. *Anax guttatus* 55 40
219 40 c. *Tholymis tillarga* 60 45
220 50 c. *Diplacodes bipunctata* 75 60
217/20 .. .. *Set of* 4 1·90 1·40

36 Brigade Members Racing

60c

(37)

(Des J. Cooter. Litho Format)

1983 (10 Aug). *Centenary of Boys' Brigade. T* **36** *and similar multicoloured designs. W* w **15** (*sideways on* 10 c., 35 c.). *P* 13½.

221 10 c. Type **36** 15 15
222 35 c. B. B. members in outrigger canoe .. 40 45
223 $1 On parade (*vert*) .. .. .. 1·25 1·75
221/3 .. .. *Set of* 3 1·60 2·10

1983 (26 Aug). *No.* 210 *surch with T* **37**.

224 60 c. on $1 Pump drill and adze 70 70

38 Montgolfier Balloon, 1783 **39** Early Communications

(Des A. Theobald. Litho Format)

1983 (21 Sept). *Bicentenary of Manned Flight. T* **38** *and similar multicoloured designs. W* w **15** (*sideways on* 35 c., 45 c.). *P* 14.

225 25 c. Type **38** 30 30
226 35 c. McKinnon (Grumman) "Turbo-goose" (*horiz*) 40 40
a. No wmk .. ..
227 45 c. Beechcraft "Super King Air 200" (*horiz*) 50 50
228 50 c. *Double Eagle II* balloon 60 60
225/8 .. .. *Set of* 4 1·60 1·60
MS229 114 × 145 mm. Nos. 225/8. Wmk sideways 1·75 1·90

(Des J.W. Litho Questa)

1983 (18 Nov). *World Communications Year. T* **39** *and similar horiz designs. Multicoloured. W* w **15**. *P* 14.

230 25 c. Type **39** 25 25
231 35 c. Radio operator 30 30
232 45 c. Modern telephone 35 35
233 50 c. Funafuti transmitting station 40 40
230/3 .. .. *Set of* 4 1·10 1·10

30c

(40)

1984 (1 Feb). *No.* 208 *surch with T* **40**.

234 30 c. on 45 c. Reef sandals and fish trap .. 35 40

(Des R. Granger Barrett. Litho Format)

1984 (16 Feb). *Ships* (2*nd series*). *Horiz designs as T* **26**. *Multicoloured. W* w **15** (*sideways*). *P* 14.

235 10 c. S.S. *Titus*, 1897 .. .. 15 15
236 20 c. S.S. *Malaita*, 1905 .. .. .. 20 20
237 25 c. S.S. *Aymeric*, 1906 .. .. .. 20 20
238 35 c. S.S. *Anshun*, 1965 .. .. .. 25 25
239 45 c. M.V. *Beaverbank*, 1970 .. .. .. 35 35
240 50 c. M.V. *Benjamin Bowring*, 1981 .. .. 35 35
235/40 .. .. *Set of* 6 1·40 1·40

Nos. 235/40 were each produced in sheets of six stamps and two labels, these occurring in the second horizontal row.

41 Class "GS-4"

(Des J.W. Litho Format)

1984 (29 Feb). *Leaders of the World. Railway Locomotives (1st series). T* **41** *and similar horiz designs, the first in each pair showing technical drawings and the second the locomotive at work. P* 12½.

241 1 c. multicoloured 10 10
a. Vert pair. Nos. 241/2 .. .. 10 10
242 1 c. multicoloured 10 10
243 15 c. multicoloured 20 25
a. Vert pair. Nos. 243/4 .. .. 40 50
244 15 c. multicoloured 20 25
245 40 c. multicoloured 25 35
a. Vert pair. Nos. 245/6 .. .. 50 70
246 40 c. multicoloured 25 35
247 60 c. multicoloured 35 45
a. Vert pair. Nos. 247/8 .. .. 70 90
248 60 c. multicoloured 35 45
241/8 .. .. *Set of* 8 1·40 2·00

Designs:—Nos. 241/2, Class "GS-4", U.S.A. (1941); 243/4, Class "AD 60", Australia (1952); 245/6, Class "C 38", Australia (1943); 247/8, *Lord of the Isles*, Great Britain (1892).

See also Nos. 253/68, 273/80, 313/20 and 348/55.

42 *Ipomoea pes-caprae*

(Des Michael and Sylvia Goaman. Litho Questa)

1984 (30 May). *Beach Flowers. T* **42** *and similar horiz designs. Multicoloured.* W w **15**. *P* 14.

249 25 c. Type **42** 25 25
250 45 c. *Ipomoea macrantha* 40 40
251 50 c. *Triumfetta procumbens* 45 45
252 60 c. *Portulaca quadrifida* 50 50
249/52 .. .. *Set of* 4 1·40 1·40

(Des J.W. Litho Format)

1984 (27 June). *Leaders of the World, Railway Locomotives (2nd series). Designs as T* **41**, *the first in each pair showing technical drawings and the second the locomotive at work. P* 12½.

253 10 c. multicoloured 15 15
a. Vert pair. Nos. 253/4 .. .. 25 30
254 10 c. multicoloured 15 15
255 15 c. multicoloured 15 20
a. Vert pair. Nos. 255/6 .. .. 30 40
256 15 c. multicoloured 15 20
257 20 c. multicoloured 20 30
a. Vert pair. Nos. 257/8 .. .. 40 60
258 20 c. multicoloured 20 30
259 25 c. multicoloured 20 30
a. Vert pair. Nos. 259/60 .. .. 40 60
260 25 c. multicoloured 20 30
261 40 c. multicoloured 20 30
a. Vert pair. Nos. 261/2 .. .. 40 60
262 40 c. multicoloured 20 30
263 50 c. multicoloured 20 40
a. Vert pair. Nos. 263/4 .. .. 40 80
264 50 c. multicoloured 20 40
265 60 c. multicoloured 25 45
a. Vert pair. Nos. 265/6 .. .. 50 90
266 60 c. multicoloured 25 45
267 $1 multicoloured 30 55
a. Vert pair. Nos. 267/8 .. .. 60 1·10
268 $1 multicoloured 30 55
253/68 .. .. *Set of* 16 3·00 4·75

Designs:—Nos. 253/4, "Casey Jones" type engine, U.S.A. (1896); 255/6, Triplex type, U.S.A. (1914); 257/8, Class "370" Advanced Passenger Train, Great Britain (1981); 259/60, Class "4F", Great Britain (1924); 261/2, Class "Tornado Rover", Great Britain (1888); 263/4, *Broadlands*, Great Britain (1967); 265/6, *Locomotion No.* 1, Great Britain (1825); 267/8, Class "C57", Japan, (1937).

Nos. 253/68 were issued in a similar sheet format to Nos. 241/8.

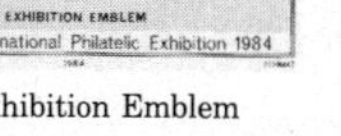

43 Exhibition Emblem **44** A. Shrewsbury

(Des G. Drummond. Litho Format)

1984 (21 Aug). *"Ausipex" International Stamp Exhibition, Melbourne (Nos. 269/70) and 15th South Pacific Forum (others). T* **43** *and similar horiz designs. Multicoloured,* W w **15** *(sideways). P* 14.

269 60 c. Type **43** 30 40
270 60 c. Royal Exhibition Building, Melbourne .. 30 40
271 60 c. Arms of Tuvalu 30 40
272 60 c. Tuvalu flag 30 40
269/72 .. .. *Set of* 4 1·10 1·40

IMPERFORATES AND MISSING COLOURS. Various issues between Nos. 273 and 529 exist either imperforate or with colours omitted. Such items are not listed as there is no evidence that they fulfil the criteria outlined on page xi of this catalogue.

(Des J.W. Litho Format)

1984 (4 Oct). *Leaders of the World. Railway Locomotives (3rd series). Horiz designs as T* **41**, *the first in each pair showing technical drawings and the second the locomotive at work. P* 12½.

273 1 c. multicoloured 10 10
a. Vert pair. Nos. 273/4 .. .. 10 10
b. Error. Wmk w **15** .. .. 6·00
ba. Vert pair. Nos. 273b/4b .. .. .. 12·00
274 1 c. multicoloured 10 10
b. Error. Wmk w **15** .. .. 6·00
275 15 c. multicoloured 15 20
a. Vert pair. Nos. 275/6 .. .. 30 40
276 15 c. multicoloured 15 20
277 30 c. multicoloured 35 40
a. Vert pair. Nos. 277/8 .. .. 70 80
b. Error. Wmk w **15** .. .. 6·00
ba. Vert pair. Nos. 277b/8b .. .. .. 12·00
278 30 c. multicoloured 35 40
b. Error. Wmk w **15** .. .. 6·00
279 $1 multicoloured .. .. 70 1·00
a. Vert pair. Nos. 279/80 .. .. 1·40 2·00
b. Error. Wmk w **15** .. .. 11·00
ba. Vert pair. Nos. 279b/80b .. .. .. 22·00
280 $1 multicoloured .. .. 70 1·00
b. Error. Wmk w **15** .. .. 11·00
273/80 .. .. *Set of* 8 2·25 3·00

Designs:—Nos. 273/4, Class "9700", Japan (1897); 275/6, Class "231" C/K, France (1909); 277/8, Class "640", Italy (1907); 279/80, Class "4500", France (1906).

Nos. 273/80 were issued in a similar sheet format to Nos. 241/8.

(Des Court House Studio. Litho Format)

1984 (5 Nov). *Leaders of the World. Cricketers. T* **44** *and similar vert designs, the first listed in each pair showing the cricketer in action and the second a head portrait. P* 12½.

281 5 c. multicoloured 10 10
a. Horiz pair. Nos. 281/2 .. .. 20 20
282 5 c. multicoloured 10 10
283 30 c. multicoloured 35 40
a. Horiz pair. Nos. 283/4 .. .. 70 80
284 30 c. multicoloured 35 40
285 50 c. multicoloured 55 60
a. Horiz pair. Nos. 285/6 .. .. 1·10 1·25
286 50 c. multicoloured 55 60
287 60 c. multicoloured 65 70
a. Horiz pair. Nos. 287/8 .. .. 1·25 1·40
288 60 c. multicoloured 65 70
281/8 .. .. *Set of* 8 3·00 3·25

Designs:—Nos. 281/2, A. Shrewsbury; 283/4, H. Verity; 285/6, E. H. Hendren; 287/8, J. Briggs.

Nos. 281/2, 283/4, 285/6 and 287/8 were printed together, *se-tenant*, in horizontal pairs throughout the sheets.

Similar stamps showing Close (5 c.), (Boycott (15 c.), Bairstow (30 c.), and Evans ($1) were prepared, but not issued. They exist imperforate from stock dispersed by the liquidator of Format International Security Printers Ltd.

45 Trees and Stars

(Des Jennifer Toombs. Litho Format)

1984 (14 Nov). *Christmas. Children's Drawings. T* **45** *and similar horiz designs. Multicoloured.* W w **15** *(sideways). P* 14½ × 14.

289 15 c. Type **45** 10 10
290 40 c. Fishing from outrigger canoes 20 20
291 50 c. Three Wise Men bearing gifts 25 25
292 60 c. The Holy Family 35 35
289/92 .. .. *Set of* 4 75 75

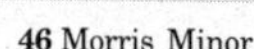

46 Morris Minor **47** Common Flicker

(Des J.W. ($1), Artists International (others). Litho Format)

1984 (7 Dec). *Leaders of the World. Automobiles (1st series). T* **46** *and similar horiz designs, the first in each pair showing technical drawings and the second paintings. P* 12½.

293 1 c. black, pale cinnamon and yellow-ochre .. 10 10
a. Vert pair. Nos. 293/4 .. .. 10 10
294 1 c. multicoloured 10 10
295 15 c. black, pale flesh and brown-lilac .. 15 20
a. Vert pair. Nos. 295/6 .. .. 30 40
296 15 c. multicoloured 15 20
297 50 c. black, pale cinnamon and dull mauve .. 40 45
a. Vert pair. Nos. 297/8 .. .. 80 90
298 50 c. multicoloured 40 45
299 $1 black, pale green and cobalt 60 80
a. Vert pair. Nos. 299/300 .. .. 1·10 1·60
300 $1 multicoloured 60 80
293/300 .. .. *Set of* 8 2·00 2·75

Designs:—Nos. 293/4, Morris "Minor"; 295/6, Studebaker "Avanti"; 297/8, Chevrolet "International Six"; 299/300, Allard "J2".

Nos. 293/4, 295/6, 297/8 and 299/300 were printed together, *se-tenant*, in vertical pairs throughout the sheets.

See also Nos. 321/8, 356/71, 421/32 and 446/70.

(Des R. Vigurs. Litho Format)

1985 (12 Feb). *Leaders of the World. Birth Bicentenary of John J. Audubon (ornithologist). T* **47** *and similar vert designs. Multicoloured. P* 12½.

301 1 c. Type **47** 10 10
a. Horiz pair. Nos. 301/2 .. .. 10 10
302 1 c. Say's Phoebe 10 10
303 25 c. Townsend's Warbler 30 35
a. Horiz pair. Nos. 303/4 .. .. 60 70
304 25 c. Bohemian Waxwing 30 35
305 50 c. Prothonotary Warbler 55 60
a. Horiz pair. Nos. 305/6 .. .. 1·10 1·25
306 50 c. Worm-eating Warbler 55 60
307 70 c. Broad-winged Hawk 80 85
a. Horiz pair. Nos. 307/8 .. .. 1·60 1·75
308 70 c. Hen Harrier 80 85
301/8 .. .. *Set of* 8 3·00 3·25

Nos. 301/2, 303/4, 305/6 and 307/8 were printed together, *se-tenant*, in horizontal pairs throughout the sheets.

48 Black-naped Tern

(Des G. Drummond. Litho Format)

1985 (27 Feb). *Birds and their Eggs. T* **48** *and similar horiz designs. Multicoloured.* W w **15** *(sideways). P* 14.

309 15 c. Type **48** 35 20
310 40 c. White-capped Noddy 75 50
311 50 c. White-tailed Tropicbird 85 60
312 60 c. Sooty Tern .. .. 1·00 70
309/12 .. .. *Set of* 4 2·75 1·75

(Des J.W. (5 c., $1), T. Hadler (others). Litho Format)

1985 (19 Mar). *Leaders of the World. Railway Locomotives (4th series). Horiz designs as T* **41** *the first in each pair showing technical drawings and the second the locomotive at work. P* 12½.

313 5 c. multicoloured 10 10
a. Vert pair. Nos. 313/14 .. .. 10 10
314 5 c. multicoloured 10 10
315 10 c. multicoloured 10 10
a. Vert pair. Nos. 315/16 .. .. 20 20
316 10 c. multicoloured 10 10
317 30 c. multicoloured 30 35
a. Vert pair. Nos. 317/18 .. .. 60 70
318 30 c. multicoloured 30 35
319 $1 multicoloured .. .. 75 1·00
a. Vert pair. Nos. 319/20 .. .. 1·50 2·00
320 $1 multicoloured .. .. 75 1·00
313/20 .. .. *Set of* 8 2·25 2·75

Designs:—Nos. 313/14, "Churchward 28XX", Great Britain (1905); 315/16, Class "KF", China (1935); 317/18, Class "99.77", East Germany (1952); 319/20, Pearson type, Great Britain (1853).

Nos. 313/20 were issued in a similar sheet format to Nos. 241/8.

(Des Artists International. Litho Format)

1985 (3 Apr). *Leaders of the World. Automobiles (2nd series). Horiz designs as T* **46**, *the first in each pair showing technical drawings and the second paintings. P* 12½.

321 1 c. black, apple green and deep dull green 10 10
a. Vert pair. Nos. 321/2 .. .. 10 10
322 1 c. multicoloured 10 10
323 20 c. black, pink and rose-red 15 20
a. Vert pair. Nos. 323/4 .. .. 30 40
324 20 c. multicoloured 15 20
325 50 c. black, dull violet-blue & brt reddish vio 30 45
a. Vert pair. Nos. 325/6 .. .. 60 90
326 50 c. multicoloured 30 45
327 70 c. black, dull pink and grey-brown .. 30 60
a. Vert pair. Nos. 327/8 .. .. 60 1·10
328 70 c. multicoloured 30 60
321/8 .. .. *Set of* 8 1·40 2·25

Designs:—Nos. 321/2, Rickenbacker (1923); 323/4, Detroit-Electric Two Door Brougham (1914); 325/6, Packard "Clipper" (1941); 327/8, Audi "Quattro" (1982).

Nos. 321/8 were issued in a similar sheet format to Nos. 293/300.

49 Curtiss "P-40N" **50** Queen Elizabeth the Queen Mother

(Des A. Theobald. Litho Questa)

1985 (29 May). *World War II Aircraft. T* **49** *and similar horiz designs. Multicoloured.* W w **15**. *P* 14.
329 15 c. Type **49** 60 20
330 40 c. Consolidated "B-24 Liberator" .. .. 1·00 45
331 50 c. Lockheed "PV-1 Ventura" .. .. 1·10 55
332 60 c. Douglas "C-54 Skymaster" .. .. 1·10 65
329/32 .. .. *Set of* 4 3·50 1·60
MS333 110×108 mm. Nos. 329/32. Wmk sideways .. .. 3·50 2·25

(Des D. Ewart ($1.20), Maxine Marsh (others). Litho Format)

1985 (4 July). *Leaders of the World. Life and Times of Queen Elizabeth the Queen Mother. Various vertical portraits as T* **50**. *P* 12½.
334 5 c. multicoloured 10 10
a. Horiz pair. Nos. 334/5 .. .. .. 10 10
335 5 c. multicoloured 10 10
336 30 c. multicoloured 15 20
a. Horiz pair. Nos. 336/7 .. .. .. 30 40
337 30 c. multicoloured 15 20
338 60 c. multicoloured 25 35
a. Horiz pair. Nos. 338/9 .. .. .. 50 70
339 60 c. multicoloured 25 35
340 $1 multicoloured 40 55
a. Horiz pair. Nos. 340/1 .. .. .. 80 1·10
341 $1 multicoloured 40 55
334/41 .. .. *Set of* 8 1·40 2·00
MS342 85×114 mm. $1.20, multicoloured; $1.20, multicoloured .. .. 1·10 2·00

The two designs of each value were issued, *se-tenant*, in horizontal pairs within the sheets.

Each *se-tenant* pair shows a floral pattern across the bottom of the portraits which stops short of the left-hand edge on the left-hand stamp and of the right-hand edge on the right-hand stamp.

Designs as Nos. 336/7 and 338/9, but with face values of $2×2 and $3×2, also exist in additional miniature sheets from a restricted printing issued 10 January 1986.

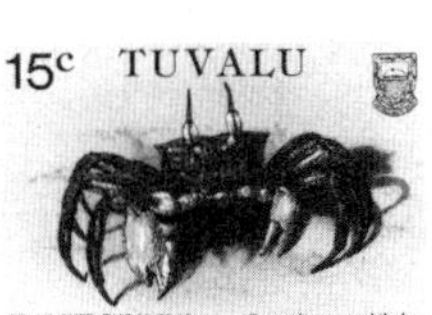

51 Guide playing Guitar **52** Stalk-eyed Ghost Crab

(Des Jennifer Toombs. Litho Format)

1985 (28 Aug). *75th Anniv of Girl Guide Movement. T* **51** *and similar vert designs. Multicoloured.* W w **15** (*sideways*). *P* 15.
343 15 c. Type **51** 15 20
344 40 c. Building camp-fire 40 45
345 50 c. Patrol Leader with Guide flag 50 55
346 60 c. Guide saluting 60 65
343/6 .. .. *Set of* 4 1·50 1·60
MS347 141×77 mm. Nos. 343/6. Wmk upright .. 1·75 2·00

(Des J.W. (10 c.), T. Hadler (others). Litho Format)

1985 (18 Sept). *Leaders of the World. Railway Locomotives* (*5th series*). *Horiz designs as T* **41**, *the first in each pair showing technical drawings and the second the locomotive at work. P* 12½.
348 10 c. multicoloured 10 15
a. Vert pair. Nos. 348/9 .. .. .. 20 30
349 10 c. multicoloured 10 15
350 40 c. multicoloured 40 45
a. Vert pair. Nos. 350/1 .. .. .. 80 90
351 40 c. multicoloured 40 45
352 65 c. multicoloured 70 75
a. Vert pair. Nos. 352/3 .. .. .. 1·40 1·50
353 65 c. multicoloured 70 75
354 $1 multicoloured .. .. 1·10 1·25
a. Vert pair. Nos. 354/5 .. .. .. 2·25 2·50
355 $1 multicoloured .. .. 1·10 1·25
348/55 .. .. *Set of* 8 4·00 4·50

Designs:—Nos. 348/9, *Green Arrow*, Great Britain (1936); 350/1, Class "SD-50" diesel, U.S.A. (1982); 352/3, D.R.G. *Flying Hamburger*, Germany (1932); 354/5, Class "1070", Japan (1908).

Nos. 348/55 were issued in a similar sheet format to Nos. 241/8.

(Des Artists International. Litho Format)

1985 (8 Oct). *Leaders of the World. Automobiles* (*3rd series*). *Horiz designs as T* **46**, *the first in each pair showing technical drawings and the second paintings. P* 12½.
356 5 c. black, grey and bright mauve 10 10
a. Vert pair. Nos. 356/7 .. .. .. 10 15
357 5 c. multicoloured 10 10
358 10 c. black, pale salmon-pink and Indian red 10 15
a. Vert pair. Nos. 358/9 .. .. .. 20 30
359 10 c. multicoloured 10 15
360 15 c. black, light brown and Indian red .. 15 20
a. Vert pair. Nos. 360/1 .. .. .. 30 40
361 15 c. multicoloured 15 20
362 35 c. black, brown-red & light turq-blue .. 30 40
a. Vert pair. Nos. 362/3 .. .. .. 60 80
363 35 c. multicoloured 30 40
364 40 c. black, dull yellow-grn & yellowish grn 30 40
a. Vert pair. Nos. 364/5 .. .. .. 60 80
365 40 c. multicoloured 30 40
366 55 c. black, pale stone and brown-olive .. 35 40
a. Vert pair. Nos. 366/7 .. .. .. 70 80
367 55 c. multicoloured 35 40
368 $1 black, brown and lake-brown 55 70
a. Vert pair. Nos. 368/9 .. .. .. 1·10 1·40
369 $1 multicoloured 55 70
370 $1.50, black, flesh and dull scarlet .. 60 80
a. Vert pair. Nos. 370/1 .. .. .. 1·10 1·40
371 $1.50, multicoloured 60 80
356/71 .. .. *Set of* 16 4·25 5·50

Designs:—Nos. 356/7, Cord "L-29" (1929); 358/9, Horch "670 V-12" (1932); 360/1, Lanchester (1901); 362/3, Citroen "2 CV" (1950); 364/5, MGA (1957); 366/7, Ferrari "250 GTO" (1962); 368/9, Ford "V-8" (1932); 370/1, Aston Martin "Lagonda" (1977).

Nos. 356/71 were issued in a similar sheet format to Nos. 293/300.

(Des G. Drummond. Litho Format)

1986 (7 Jan). *Crabs. T* **52** *and similar horiz designs. Multicoloured. P* 15.
372 15 c. Type **52** 20 25
373 40 c. Red and White Painted Crab 45 55
374 50 c. Red-spotted Crab 55 70
375 60 c. Red Hermit Crab 70 90
372/5 .. .. *Set of* 4 1·75 2·25

53 Chess Knight on Board and Flags of U.S. and U.S.S.R. (World Chess Championships) **54** Peace Dove carrying Wreath and Rainbow

(Des Court House Studio. Litho Format)

1986 (19 Mar). *International Events. Sheet* 148×127 *mm, containing T* **53** *and similar vert design. Multicoloured. P* 12½.
MS376 $3 Type **53**: $3 Emblem (80th anniv of Rotary .. .. 7·50 7·50

No. **MS**376 exists with plain or decorative margins.

Overprints on this miniature sheet commemorating "Capex 87" International Stamp Exhibition, Toronto, or the World Scout Jamboree, were not authorised by the Tuvalu administration.

(Des R. Granger Barrett. Litho Format)

1986 (14 Apr). *Ships* (*3rd series*). *Missionary Vessels. Horiz designs as T* **26**. *Multicoloured.* W w **15**. *P* 15.
377 15 c. *Messenger of Peace* 15 15
378 40 c. *John Wesley* 35 40
379 50 c. *Duff* 40 45
380 60 c. *Triton* 50 55
377/80 .. .. *Set of* 4 1·25 1·40

(Des Court House Studio. Litho Format)

1986 (21 Apr–14 June). *60th Birthday of Queen Elizabeth II. Multicoloured designs as T* **117a** *of Montserrat. P* 12½.
381 10 c. Queen wearing ceremonial cloak, New Zealand, 1977 .. .. 15 10
382 90 c. Before visit to France, 1957 .. .. 55 75
383 $1.50, Queen in 1982 .. .. .. 70 1·00
384 $3 In Canberra, 1982 (*vert*) .. .. 1·40 2·00
381/4 .. .. *Set of* 4 2·50 3·50
MS385 85×115 mm. $4 Queen carrying bouquet (14.6) .. .. 3·25 4·00

The 10 c., 90 c. and $1.50 values exist with PVA gum as well as gum arabic.

(Des Gloria McConnaghy. Litho Questa)

1986 (22 May). *25th Anniv of United States Peace Corps.* W w **15**. *P* 14.
386 **54** 50 c. multicoloured 80 80

55 Island and Flags of Tuvalu and U.S.A. **56** South Korean Player

(Des Court House Studio. Litho Questa)

1986 (22 May). *"Ameripex" International Stamp Exhibition, Chicago.* W w **15**. *P* 14×13½.
387 **55** 60 c. multicoloured 85 85

(Des Court House Studio. Litho Format)

1986 (30 June). *World Cup Football Championship, Mexico. T* **56** *and similar multicoloured designs. P* 15 (1 *c. to* 40 *c.*) *or* 12½ (*others*).
388 1 c. Type **56** 10 10
389 5 c. French player 10 10
390 10 c. West German captain with World Cup trophy, 1974 .. .. 10 10
391 40 c. Italian player 50 40
392 60 c. World Cup final, 1974 (59×39 *mm*) .. 65 55
393 $1 Canadian team (59×39 *mm*) .. .. 1·00 1·00
394 $2 Northern Irish team (59×39 *mm*) .. 2·00 2·00
395 $3 English team (59×39 *mm*) .. .. 3·00 3·00
388/95 .. .. *Set of* 8 6·50 6·50
MS396 Two sheets, each 85×114 mm. (a) $1.50, As No. 393; (b) $2·50, As No. 394 *Set of* 2 *sheets* 4·50 5·00

(Litho Format)

1986 (18 July–15 Oct). *Royal Wedding. Multicoloured designs as T* **118a** *of Montserrat. P* 12½.
397 60 c. Prince Andrew and Miss Sarah Ferguson 35 45
a. Pair. Nos. 397/8 .. .. 70 90
398 60 c. Prince Andrew with prizewinning bull 35 45
399 $1 Prince Andrew at horse trials (*horiz*) .. 60 75
a. Pair. Nos. 399/400 .. .. .. 1·10 1·50
400 $1 Miss Sarah Ferguson and Princess Diana (*horiz*) 60 75
397/400 .. .. *Set of* 4 1·60 2·25
MS401 85×115 mm. $6 Duke and Duchess of York after wedding (*horiz*) (15.10) .. .. 4·50 5·50

Nos. 397/8 and 399/400 were printed together, *se-tenant*, in horizontal and vertical pairs throughout the sheets.

57 Mourning Gecko (**58**)

(Des Jennifer Toombs. Litho Questa)

1986 (30 July). *Lizards. T* **57** *and similar horiz designs. Multicoloured.* W w **15**. *P* 14.
402 15 c. Type **57** 55 55
403 40 c. Oceanic Stump-toed Gecko .. .. 1·00 1·00
404 50 c. Azure-tailed Skink .. .. .. 1·25 1·25
405 60 c. Moth Skink .. .. 1·50 1·50
402/5 .. .. *Set of* 4 4·00 4·00

1986 (4 Aug). *"Stampex '86" Stamp Exhibition, Adelaide. No.* 386 *optd with T* **58**.
406 **54** 50 c. multicoloured 40 45

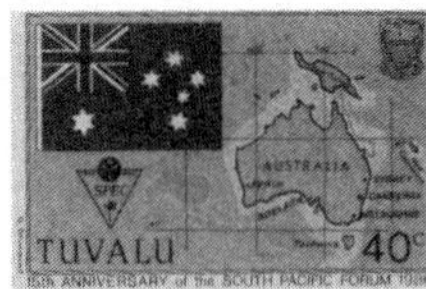

59 Map and Flag of Australia

(Des G. Drummond. Litho Format)

1986 (4 Aug). *15th Anniv of South Pacific Forum. T* **59** *and similar horiz designs showing maps and national flags. Multicoloured.* W w **15**. *P* 15.
407 40 c. Type **59** 45 45
a. Sheetlet. Nos. 407/20 .. .. .. 5·50
408 40 c. Cook Islands 45 45
409 40 c. Micronesia 45 45
410 40 c. Fiji 45 45
411 40 c. Kiribati 45 45
412 40 c. Western Samoa 45 45
413 40 c. Nauru 45 45
414 40 c. Vanuatu 45 45
415 40 c. New Zealand 45 45
416 40 c. Tuvalu 45 45
417 40 c. Tonga 45 45
418 40 c. Solomon Islands 45 45
419 40 c. Papua New Guinea 45 45
420 40 c. Niue 45 45
407/20 .. .. *Set of* 14 5·50 5·50

Nos. 407/20 were printed together, *se-tenant*, as a sheetlet of fourteen stamps arranged round a central label.

(Des Court House Studio. Litho Format)

1986 (13 Oct). *Automobiles* (*4th series*). *Horiz designs as T* **46**, *the first in each pair showing technical drawings and the second paintings. P* 12½.
421 15 c. multicoloured 15 15
a. Vert pair. Nos. 421/2 .. .. .. 30 30
422 15 c. multicoloured 15 15
423 40 c. multicoloured 35 40
a. Vert pair. Nos. 423/4 .. .. .. 70 80
424 40 c. multicoloured 35 40
425 50 c. multicoloured 45 50
a. Vert pair. Nos. 425/6 .. .. .. 90 1·00
426 50 c. multicoloured 45 50
427 60 c. multicoloured 45 60
a. Vert pair. Nos. 427/8 .. .. .. 90 1·25
428 60 c. multicoloured 45 60
429 90 c. multicoloured 65 75
a. Vert pair. Nos. 429/30 .. .. .. 1·25 1·50
430 90 c. multicoloured 65 75
431 $1.50, multicoloured .. .. .. 75 1·10
a. Vert pair. Nos. 431/2 .. .. .. 1·50 2·10
432 $1.50, multicoloured .. .. .. 75 1·10
421/32 .. .. *Set of* 12 5·00 6·25

Designs:—Nos. 421/2, Cooper "500" (1953); 423/4, Rover "2000" (1964); 425/6, Ruxton (1930); 427/8, Jowett "Jupiter" (1950); 429/30, Cobra "Daytona Coupe" (1964); 431/2, Packard Model F "Old Pacific" (1903).

Nos. 421/32 were issued in a similar sheet format to Nos. 293/300.

1986 (28 Oct). *Royal Wedding* (2*nd issue*). *Nos.* 397/400 *optd as T* **121** *of Montserrat in silver.*

433 60 c. Prince Andrew and Miss Sarah Ferguson 70 70
 a. Pair. Nos. 433/4.. .. .. 1·40 1·40
434 60 c. Prince Andrew with prizewinning bull 70 70
435 $1 Prince Andrew at horse trials (*horiz*) .. 1·00 1·00
 a. Pair. Nos. 435/6.. .. .. 2·00 2·00
436 $1 Miss Sarah Ferguson and Princess Diana (*horiz*) .. .. 1·00 1·00
433/6 .. .. *Set of* 4 3·00 3·00

60 Sea Star

61 *Nephrolepis saligna*

(Des G. Drummond. Litho Questa)

1986 (5 Nov). *Coral Reef Life* (1*st series*). *T* **60** *and similar horiz designs. Multicoloured. P* 14.

437 15 c. Type **60** 45 45
438 40 c. Pencil Urchin .. .. 1·00 1·00
439 50 c. Fragile Coral .. .. 1·10 1·10
440 60 c. Pink Coral .. .. 1·25 1·25
437/40 .. .. *Set of* 4 3·50 3·50
See also Nos. 498/501 and 558/62.

(Des Court House Studio. Litho Format)

1986 (24 Nov). *Centenary of Statue of Liberty. Vert views of Statue as T* **121a** *of Montserrat in separate miniature sheets. Multicoloured. P* 14×13½.

MS441 Nine sheets, each 85×115 mm. $1.25; $1.50; $1.80; $2; $2.25; $2.50; $3; $3.25; $3.50 .. .. .. *Set of* 9 *sheets* 10·00 15·00

(Des R. Granger Barrett. Litho Questa)

1987 (4 Feb). *Ships* (4*th series*). *Missionary Steamers. Horiz designs as T* **26**. *Multicoloured. P* 14.

442 15 c. *Southern Cross IV* 50 50
443 40 c. *John Williams VI* .. .. .. 1·00 1·00
444 50 c. *John Williams IV* .. .. .. 1·25 1·25
445 60 c. *M.S. Southern Cross* .. .. .. 1·40 1·40
442/5 .. .. *Set of* 4 3·75 3·75

(Litho Format)

1987 (7 May–6 June). *Automobiles* (5*th series*). *Horiz designs as T* **46**, *the first in each pair showing technical drawings and the second paintings. P* 12½.

446 1 c. multicoloured 10 10
 a. Vert pair. Nos. 446/7 .. .. .. 10 10
447 1 c. multicoloured 10 10
448 2 c. multicoloured 10 10
 a. Vert pair. Nos. 448/9 .. .. .. 10 10
449 2 c. multicoloured 10 10
450 5 c. multicoloured 10 10
 a. Vert pair. Nos. 450/1 .. .. .. 10 15
451 5 c. multicoloured 10 10
452 10 c. multicoloured 10 15
 a. Vert pair. Nos. 452/3 .. .. .. 20 30
453 10 c. multicoloured 10 15
454 20 c. multicoloured 20 25
 a. Vert pair. Nos. 454/5 .. .. .. 40 50
455 20 c. multicoloured 20 25
456 30 c. multicoloured 25 30
 a. Vert pair. Nos. 456/7 .. .. .. 50 60
457 30 c. multicoloured 25 30
458 40 c. multicoloured 35 40
 a. Vert pair. Nos. 458/9 .. .. .. 70 80
459 40 c. multicoloured 35 40
460 50 c. multicoloured 45 50
 a. Vert pair. Nos. 460/1 .. .. .. 90 1·00
461 50 c. multicoloured 45 50
462 60 c. multicoloured 45 50
 a. Vert pair. Nos. 462/3 .. .. .. 90 1·00
463 60 c. multicoloured 45 50
464 70 c. multicoloured 50 60
 a. Vert pair. Nos. 464/5 .. .. .. 1·00 1·10
465 70 c. multicoloured 50 60
466 75 c. multicoloured 50 60
 a. Vert pair. Nos. 466/7 .. .. .. 1·00 1·10
467 75 c. multicoloured 50 60
468 $1 multicoloured 70 80
 a. Vert pair. Nos. 468/9 .. .. .. 1·40 1·60
469 $1 multicoloured 70 80
446/9 .. .. *Set of* 24 6·50 7·50
MS470 100×85 mm. Nos. 468/9 (6.6) .. .. 1·75 2·25

Designs:—Nos. 446/7, Talbot-Lago (1938); 448/9, Du Pont "Model G" (1930); 450/1, Riley "RM" (1950); 452/3, Chevrolet "Baby Grand" (1915); 454/5, Shelby "Mustang GT 500 KR" (1968); 456/7, Ferrari "212 Export Barchetta" (1952); 458/9, Peerless "Model 48-Six" (1912); 460/1, Sunbeam "Alpine" (1954); 462/3, Matra-Ford "MS 80" (1969); 464/5, Squire 1½ Litre (1934); 466/7, Talbot "105" (1931); 468/9, Plymouth "Model Q" (1928).

Nos. 446/69 were issued in a similar sheet format to Nos. 293/300.

(Des J. Cooter. Litho Questa)

1987 (7 July). *Ferns. T* **61** *and similar vert designs. Multicoloured. W w* **15** (*sideways*). *P* 14.

471 15 c. Type **61** 40 40
472 40 c. *Asplenium nidus* 70 70
473 50 c. *Microsorum scolopendria* 85 85
474 60 c. *Pteris tripartita* 95 95
471/4 .. .. *Set of* 4 2·50 2·50
MS475 62×62 mm. $1.50, *Psilotum nudum*. Wmk upright .. .. 2·25 2·75

62 Floral Arrangement

63 Queen Victoria, 1897 (photo by Downey)

(Des Jennifer Toombs. Litho Questa)

1987 (12 Aug). *Flowers and "Fous". T* **62** *and similar vert designs showing either floral arrangements or "fous" (women's headdresses). Multicoloured. W w* **15** (*sideways*). *P* 14.

476 15 c. Type **62** 15 15
 a. Horiz pair. Nos. 476/7 .. .. .. 30 30
477 15 c. "Fou" 15 15
478 40 c. "Fou" 35 40
 a. Horiz pair. Nos. 478/9 .. .. .. 70 80
479 40 c. Floral arrangement 35 40
480 50 c. Floral arrangement 45 50
 a. Horiz pair. Nos. 480/1 .. .. .. 90 1·00
481 50 c. "Fou" 45 50
482 60 c. "Fou" 55 60
 a. Horiz pair. Nos. 482/3 .. .. .. 1·10 1·25
483 60 c. Floral arrangement 55 60
476/83 .. .. *Set of* 8 2·75 3·00

The two designs of each value were printed together, *se-tenant*, in horizontal pairs throughout the sheets.

(Litho Format)

1987 (15 Oct). *Royal Ruby Wedding and 150th Anniv of Queen Victoria's Accession. T* **63** *and similar square designs. P* 15.

484 40 c. brownish black, black and deep olive .. 35 40
485 60 c. purple-black, black and deep blue-green 55 60
486 80 c. brownish black, black and deep dull blue 70 75
487 $1 brownish black, black and deep claret .. 90 95
488 $2 multicoloured .. .. 1·75 1·90
484/8 .. .. *Set of* 5 3·75 4·25
MS489 86×101 mm. $3 brownish black .. 2·75 3·25

Designs:—60 c. Wedding of Princess Elizabeth and Duke of Edinburgh, 1947; 80 c. Queen, Duke of Edinburgh and Prince Charles, *c.* 1950; $1 Queen with Princess Anne, 1950; $2 Queen Elizabeth II, 1970; $3 Queen and Prince Charles at Princess Anne's christening, 1950.

64 Coconut Crab

(Des M. Pollard. Litho Questa)

1987 (11 Nov). *Crustaceans. T* **64** *and similar diamond-shaped designs. Multicoloured. W w* **15**. *P* 14.

490 40 c. Type **64** 55 55
491 50 c. Painted Crayfish 70 70
492 60 c. Ocean Crayfish 80 80
490/2 .. .. *Set of* 3 1·90 1·90

65 Aborigine and Ayers Rock

(Des Young Philips. Litho Format)

1987 (2 Dec). *World Scout Jamboree, Australia. T* **65** *and similar horiz designs. Multicoloured. P* 12½.

493 40 c. Type **65** 40 40
494 60 c. Capt. Cook and H.M.S. *Endeavour* .. 80 80
495 $1 Scout saluting and Scout Park entrance 1·10 1·10
496 $1.50, Koala and kangaroo .. .. .. 1·40 1·40
493/6 .. .. *Set of* 4 3·25 3·25
MS497 115×85 mm. $2.50, Lord and Lady Baden-Powell .. .. 2·50 3·00

(Des G. Drummond. Litho Format)

1988 (29 Feb). *Coral Reef Life* (2*nd series*). *Horiz designs as T* **60**. *Multicoloured. P* 15.

498 15 c. Spanish Dancer 50 50
499 40 c. Hard corals 90 90
500 50 c. Feather Stars .. .. 1·00 1·00
501 60 c. Staghorn corals .. .. 1·10 1·10
498/501 .. .. *Set of* 4 3·25 3·25

66 Red Junglefowl

67 Henri Dunant (founder)

(Des Jennifer Toombs. Litho Format)

1988 (2 Mar). *Birds. T* **66** *and similar horiz designs. Multicoloured. P* 15.

502 5 c. Type **66** 10 10
503 10 c. White Tern 10 15
504 15 c. Common Noddy 15 20
505 20 c. Phoenix Petrel 20 25
506 25 c. American Golden Plover 25 30
507 30 c. Crested Tern 30 35
508 35 c. Sooty Tern 30 35
509 40 c. Bristle-thighed Curlew 35 40
510 45 c. Bar-tailed Godwit 40 45
511 50 c. Eastern Reef Heron 45 50
512 55 c. Great Frigate Bird 50 55
513 60 c. Red-footed Booby 55 60
514 70 c. Rufous-necked Sandpiper ("Red-necked Stint") 65 70
515 $1 Long-tailed Koel ("Long-tailed Cuckoo") 90 95
516 $2 Red-tailed Tropic Bird .. .. .. 1·90 2·00
517 $5 Banded Rail .. .. 4·50 4·75
502/17 .. .. *Set of* 16 10·50 11·50

(Des M. Pollard. Litho Format)

1988 (9 May). *125th Anniv of International Red Cross. T* **67** *and similar horiz designs. P* 12½.

518 15 c. vermilion and pale reddish brown .. 25 25
519 40 c. vermilion and ultramarine 60 60
520 50 c. vermilion and turquoise-green .. 75 75
521 60 c. vermilion and purple 85 85
518/21 .. .. *Set of* 4 2·25 2·25
MS522 96 × 66 mm. $1.50, vermilion & emerald 1·60 2·00

Designs:—40 c. Junior Red Cross members on parade; 50 c. Red Cross worker with boy in wheelchair; 60 c. First aid training; $1.50, Lecture.

68 H.M.S. *Endeavour*

(Litho Format)

1988 (15 June). *Voyages of Captain Cook. T* **68** *and similar horiz designs. Multicoloured. P* 12½.

523 20 c. Type **68** 55 55
524 40 c. Stern of H.M.S. *Endeavour* 80 80
525 50 c. Cook preparing to land at Tahiti (*vert*) 90 90
526 60 c. Maori chief (*vert*) .. .. .. 1·00 1·00
527 80 c. H.M.S. *Resolution* and Hawaiian canoe 1·25 1·25
528 $1 "Captain Cook" (after Nathaniel Dance) (*vert*) .. .. 1·50 1·50
523/8 .. .. *Set of* 6 5·50 5·50
MS529 115 × 85 mm. $2.50, H.M.S. *Resolution* in Antarctica .. .. 4·50 4·50

69 *Ganoderma applanatum*

(Des J. Cooter. Litho Format)

1988 (25 July). *Fungi* (1*st series*). *T* **69** *and similar vert designs. Multicoloured. P* 15.

530 40 c. Type **69** 75 65
531 50 c. *Pseudoepicoccum cocos* (brown leaf spot) 80 70
532 60 c. *Rigidoporus zonalis* 90 80
533 90 c. *Rigidoporus microporus* .. .. 1·40 1·10
530/3 .. .. *Set of* 4 3·50 3·00
See also Nos. 554/7.

COVER PRICES

Cover factors are quoted at the beginning of each country for most issues to 1945. An explanation of the system can be found on page x. The factors quoted do not, however, apply to philatelic covers.

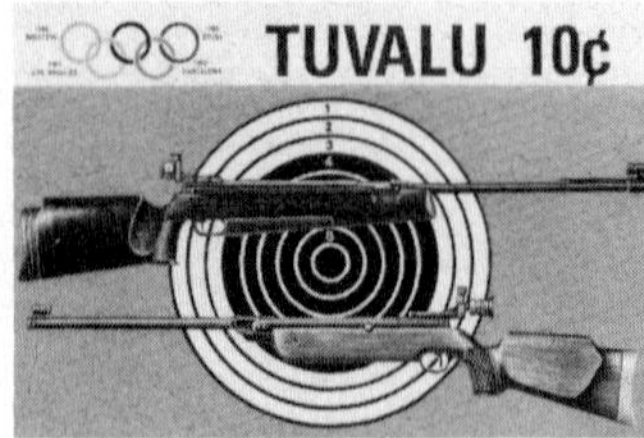

70 Rifle-shooting

(Litho Format)

1988 (19 Aug). *Olympic Games, Seoul. T* **70** *and similar horiz designs. Multicoloured. P* 12½.

534 10 c. Type **70** 10 15
535 20 c. Judo 20 25
536 40 c. Canoeing 40 45
537 60 c. Swimming 55 60
538 80 c. Yachting 75 80
539 $1 Gymnastics 95 1·00
534/9 *Set of* 6 2·75 3·00

71 Queen Elizabeth II in Ceremonial Canoe

72 Virgin Mary

(Des and litho Questa)

1988 (28 Sept). *10th Anniv of Independence. T* **71** *and similar designs showing scenes from Royal Visit of* 1982. *W* w **15** *(sideways on* 60, 90 *c.,* $1.20). *P* 14.

540 60 c. multicoloured 60 60
541 90 c. multicoloured 90 90
542 $1 multicoloured (*horiz*) 1·00 1·00
543 $1.20, multicoloured 1·25 1·25
540/3 *Set of* 4 3·50 3·50
MS544 Designs as Nos. 540/3 in separate miniature sheets, each 85 × 85 mm *Set of* 4 *sheets* 3·50 4·00

(Des M. Pollard. Litho Questa)

1988 (5 Dec). *Christmas. T* **72** *and similar diamond-shaped designs. Multicoloured. P* 14.

545 15 c. Type **72** 15 20
546 40 c. Christ Child 40 45
547 60 c. Joseph 55 60
545/7 *Set of* 3 1·00 2·00
MS548 73 × 99 mm. $1.50, Angel 1·40 1·75

73 Dancing Skirt and Dancer

(Des Jennifer Toombs. Litho Questa)

1989 (31 Mar). *Traditional Dancing Skirts. T* **73** *and similar designs showing skirts and dancer silhouettes. P* 14½.

549 40 c. multicoloured 60 60
550 50 c. multicoloured 70 70
551 60 c. multicoloured 80 80
552 90 c. multicoloured 1·25 1·25
549/52 *Set of* 4 3·00 3·00
MS553 110×75 mm. $1.50, multicoloured (dancer) (*vert*) 2·50 2·75

(Litho Questa)

1989 (24 May). *Fungi* (2*nd series*). *Vert designs as T* **69**. *Multicoloured. P* 14.

554 40 c. *Trametes muelleri* 90 90
555 50 c. *Pestalotiopsis palmarum* (grey leaf spot) 1·10 1·10
556 60 c. *Trametes cingulata* 1·10 1·10
557 90 c. *Schizophyllum commune* 1·50 1·50
554/7 *Set of* 4 4·25 4·25

(Des G. Drummond. Litho Questa)

1989 (31 July). *Coral Reef Life* (3*rd series*). *Horiz designs as T* **60**. *Multicoloured. P* 14.

558 40 c. Pennant Coralfish 75 75
559 50 c. Anemone Fish 90 90
560 60 c. Batfish 1·00 1·00
561 90 c. Threadfin Coralfish 1·50 1·50
558/61 *Set of* 4 3·75 3·75
MS562 110×85 mm. Nos. 558/61 4·75 5·00

74 *Nivaga II*

75 Conch Shell

(Des M. Pollard. Litho Questa)

1989 (9 Oct). *Delivery of* Nivaga II (*new inter-island ship*). *Sheet* 116×85 *mm. P* 14.

MS563 **74** $1.50, multicoloured 2·40 2·40

(Des Jennifer Toombs. Litho Questa)

1989 (29 Nov). *Christmas. T* **75** *and similar vert designs. Multicoloured. P* 14.

564 40 c. Type **75** 55 55
565 50 c. Posy of flowers 70 70
566 60 c. Germinating coconut 75 75
567 90 c. Jewellery 1·25 1·25
564/7 *Set of* 4 3·00 3·00

76 *Cocus nucifera*

77 Penny Black with "Stamp World London 90" Emblem

(Des M. Pollard. Litho Questa)

1990 (28 Feb). *Tropical Trees. T* **76** *and similar vert designs. Multicoloured. P* 14½.

568 15 c. Type **76** 30 30
569 30 c. *Rhizophora samoensis* 50 50
570 40 c. *Messerschmidia argentea* 65 65
571 50 c. *Pandanus tectorius* 75 75
572 60 c. *Hernandia nymphaeifolia* 85 85
573 90 c. *Pisonia grandis* 1·25 1·25
568/73 *Set of* 6 3·75 3·75

(Des M. Pollard. Litho Questa)

1990 (3 May). *150th Anniv of the Penny Black, and "Stamp World London 90" International Stamp Exhibition. P* 14.

574 **77** 15 c. multicoloured 35 35
575 40 c. multicoloured 80 80
576 90 c. multicoloured 1·75 1·75
574/6 *Set of* 3 2·50 2·50
MS577 115×85 mm. **77** $2 multicoloured 3·25 3·50

78 Japanese Camouflaged Freighter

79 *Erythrina fusca*

(Litho Questa)

1990 (25 July). *50th Anniv of Second World War. Ships. T* **78** *and similar horiz designs. Multicoloured. P* 14.

578 15 c. Type **78** 35 35
579 30 c. U.S.S *Unimack* (seaplane tender) 60 60
580 40 c. *Amagari* (Japanese destroyer) 70 70
581 50 c. U.S.S *Platte* (transport) 85 85
582 60 c. Japanese Shumushu Class escort 95 95
583 90 c. U.S.S *Independence* (aircraft carrier) 1·50 1·50
578/83 *Set of* 6 4·50 4·50

(Des Jennifer Toombs. Litho Questa)

1990 (21 Sept). *Flowers. T* **79** *and similar vert designs. Multicoloured. P* 14½×14.

584 15 c. Type **79** 25 25
585 30 c. *Capparis cordifolia* 45 45
586 40 c. *Portulaca pilosa* 55 55
587 50 c. *Cordia subcordata* 70 70
588 60 c. *Scaevola taccada* 80 80
589 90 c. *Suriana maritima* 1·25 1·25
584/9 *Set of* 6 3·50 3·50

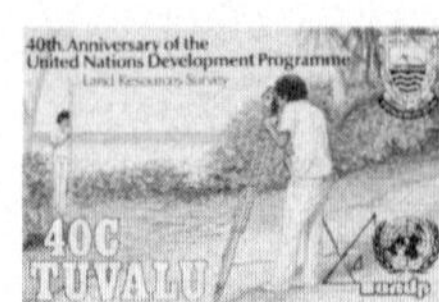

80 Land Resources Survey

81 Mary and Joseph travelling to Bethlehem

(Litho Questa)

1990 (20 Nov). *40th Anniv of United Nations Development Programme. T* **80** *and similar horiz designs. P* 14.

590 40 c. Type **80** 55 55
591 60 c. Satellite earth station 75 75
592 $1.20, *Te Tautai* (trawler) 1·40 1·40
590/2 *Set of* 3 2·40 2·40

(Des M. Pollard. Litho Questa)

1990 (20 Nov). *Christmas. T* **81** *and similar square designs. Multicoloured. P* 14.

593 15 c. Type **81** 25 25
594 40 c. The Nativity 55 55
595 60 c. Shepherds with flock 80 80
596 90 c. Wise Men bearing gifts 1·25 1·25
593/6 *Set of* 4 2·50 2·50

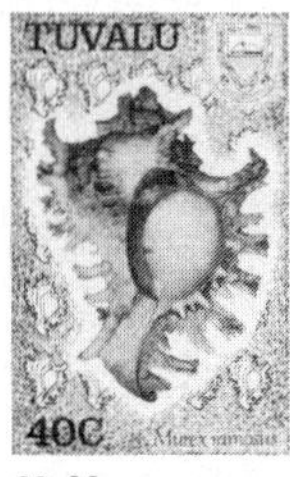

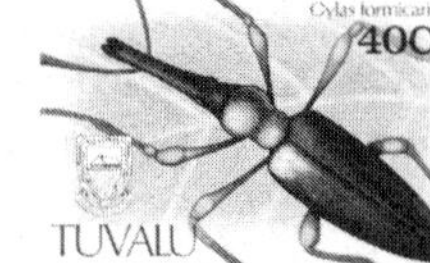

82 *Murex ramosus*

83 *Cylas formicarius* (beetle)

(Des D. Miller. Litho Questa)

1991 (18 Jan). *Sea Shells. T* **82** *and similar vert designs. Multicoloured. P* 14.

597 40 c. Type **82** 55 55
598 50 c. *Conus marmoreus* 65 65
599 60 c. *Trochus niloticus* 75 75
600 $1.50, *Cypraea mappa* 1·90 1·90
597/600 *Set of* 4 3·50 3·50

(Des D. Miller. Litho Questa)

1991 (22 Mar). *Insects. T* **83** *and similar horiz designs. Multicoloured. P* 14.

601 40 c. Type **83** 60 60
602 50 c. *Heliothis armiger* (moth) 75 75
603 60 c. *Spodoptera litura* (moth) 90 90
604 $1.50, *Agrius convolvuli* (moth) 2·25 2·25
601/4 *Set of* 4 4·00 4·00

84 Green Turtle

85 Football

(Des D. Miller. Litho Questa)

1991 (31 May). *Endangered Marine Life. T* **84** *and similar vert designs. Multicoloured. P* 14.

605 40 c. Type **84** 55 55
606 50 c. Humpback Whale 65 65
607 60 c. Hawksbill Turtle 75 75
608 $1.50, Sperm Whale 2·00 2·00
605/8 *Set of* 4 3·50 3·50

(Des D. Miller. Litho Questa)

1991 (31 July). *9th South Pacific Games. T* **85** *and similar vert designs. Multicoloured. P* 14.

609 40 c. Type **85** 60 60
610 50 c. Volleyball 80 80
611 60 c. Lawn tennis 95 95
612 $1.50, Cricket 2·40 2·40
609/12 *Set of* 4 4·25 4·25

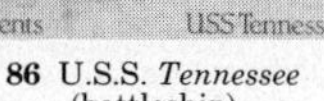

86 U.S.S. *Tennessee* (battleship) — 87 Traditional Dancers

(Des D. Miller. Litho Questa)

1991 (15 Oct). *Second World Warships. T* **86** *and similar horiz designs. Multicoloured. P* 14.

613	40 c. Type **86**	60	60
614	50 c. *Haguro* (Japanese cruiser)	80	80
615	60 c. H.M.N.Z.S. *Achilles* (cruiser)	95	95
616	$1.50, U.S.S. *North Carolina* (battleship)	2·40	2·40
613/16	*Set of* 4	4·25	4·25

(Des. D. Miller. Litho Questa)

1991 (13 Dec). *Christmas. T* **87** *and similar vert designs. Multicoloured. P* 14.

617	40 c. Type **87**	60	60
618	50 c. Solo dancer	75	75
619	60 c. Dancers in green costumes	85	85
620	$1.50, Dancers in multicoloured costumes	2·00	2·00
617/20	*Set of* 4	3·75	3·75

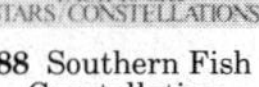

88 Southern Fish Constellation — 89 King George VI and Cargo Liner

(Des D. Miller. Litho Questa)

1992 (29 Jan). *Pacific Star Constellations. T* **88** *and similar vert designs. Multicoloured. P* 14.

621	40 c. Type **88**	50	50
622	50 c. Scorpion	65	65
623	60 c. Archer	80	80
624	$1.50, Southern Cross	2·25	2·25
621/4	*Set of* 4	3·75	3·75

(Des D. Miller. Litho Questa)

1992 (23 Mar). *Centenary of British Occupation of Tuvalu. T* **89** *and similar horiz designs. P* 14.

625	40 c. Type **89**	35	40
626	50 c. King George V and freighter with barges at wharf	45	50
627	60 c. King Edward VII and freighter	55	60
628	$1.50, Queen Victoria and warship	1·40	1·50
625/8	*Set of* 4	2·50	2·75

It is probable that the ship shown on No. 628 is intended to be H.M.S. *Royalist* (corvette) launched 1883, but the vessel depicted appears to be H.M.S. *Royalist* (cruiser) launched 1915.

POSTAGE DUE STAMPS

D 1 Tuvalu Crest

(Des G. Drummond. Litho Questa)

1981 (3 May). *P* 13½ × 14.

D1	D 1	1 c. black and bright purple	10	10
D2		2 c. black and greenish blue	10	10
D3		5 c. black and ochre	10	10
D4		10 c. black and blue-green	20	20
D5		20 c. black and purple-brown	35	35
D6		30 c. black and bright orange	40	40
D7		40 c. black and blue	50	50
D8		50 c. black and yellow-green	60	60
D9		$1 black and deep mauve	1·10	1·10
D1/9		*Set of* 9	3·00	3·00

1982 (25 Nov)–**83.** *As Nos.* D1/9 *but P* 14½ × 15 *and with imprint date at foot.*

D10	D 1	1 c. black and bright purple	10	10
D11		2 c. black and greenish blue	10	10
D12		5 c. black and ochre	10	10
D13		10 c. black and blue-green	10	10
D14		20 c. black and purple-brown	15	20
D15		30 c. black and bright orange (25.5.83)	20	25
D16		40 c. black and blue (25.5.83)	30	35
D17		50 c. black and yellow-green (25.5.83)	40	45
D18		$1 black and deep mauve (25.5.83)	75	80
D10/18		*Set of* 9	1·90	2·10

The imprint date on Nos. D10/14 is "1982" and on Nos. D15/18 "1983".

OFFICIAL STAMPS

For the use of the Philatelic Bureau.

OFFICIAL (O 1) — OFFICIAL (O 2)

TWO TYPES OF OVERPRINT FOR NOS. O1/19

This issue was overprinted using two different processes.

All values, except for the 35, 45 and 50 c., come with the overprint applied by typography. This process results in ragged lines, uneven distribution of the ink, especially at the edges of the letters, and often has the impression of the letters visible from the reverse.

In addition nine of these values have been found with overprints applied by lithography. These show clean lines and an even distribution of the ink.

The 35, 45 and 50 c. values have only been seen with overprints applied by lithography.

1981 (2 July). *Nos.* 105/22 *optd with Type* O **1**.

O 1	1 c. Type **14**	10	10
	a. Litho opt		
O 2	2 c. Yellow-banded Goatfish	10	10
O 3	4 c. Imperial Angelfish	10	10
O 4	5 c. Rainbow Butterfly	10	10
O 5	6 c. Blue Angelfish	10	10
	a. Litho opt	30	30
O 6	8 c. Blue Striped Snapper	10	10
O 7	10 c. Orange Clownfish	15	15
	a. Litho opt	30	25
O 8	15 c. Chevroned Coralfish	20	20
O 9	20 c. Fairy Cod	25	25
O10	25 c. Clown Triggerfish	25·00	
	a. Litho opt	30	30
O11	30 c. Long-nosed Butterfly	30	30
	a. Litho opt		
O12	35 c. Yellowfin Tuna (*litho opt*)	35	35
O13	40 c. Spotted Eagle Ray	40	40
O14	45 c. Black-tipped Rock Cod (*litho opt*)	45	45
O15	50 c. Hammerhead Shark (*litho opt*)	50	50
O16	70 c. Lionfish	75	75
	a. Litho opt	4·00	3·00
O17	$1 White-barred Triggerfish	1·10	1·10
	a. Litho opt	2·50	2·50
O18	$2 Beaked Coralfish	3·25	3·00
	a. Litho opt	2·25	2·25
O19	$5 Tiger Shark	5·50	6·00
	a. Litho opt	15·00	12·00
O1/19	*Set of* 19	11·00	11·00

1983 (26 Aug)–**85.** *Nos.* 202/3a, 205/12, 224 *and* 234 *optd as Type* O **1**, *but* 20½ × 4 *mm.* (5 c.), *or as Type* O **2** (*others*).

O20	5 c. Wedding and baby food baskets (1.2.84)	10	15
	a. Optd as Type O **2** (5.85)	15	15
O21	10 c. Hand-carved model of canoe (1.2.84)	10	15
O22	15 c. Ladies' sun hats (30.4.84)	15	20
O23	25 c. Pandanus baskets (1.2.84)	25	30
O24	30 c. on 45 c. Reef sandals and fish trap (1.2.84)	50	60
O25	30 c. Basket tray and coconut stand (30.4.84)	30	40
O26	35 c. Pandanus pillows and shell necklaces (1.2.84)	40	45
O27	40 c. Round baskets and fans (1.2.84)	45	50
O28	45 c. Reef sandals and fish trap (1.2.84)	45	50
O29	50 c. Rat trap (1.2.84)	50	60
O30	60 c. on $1 Pump drill and adze	75	85
O31	60 c. Fisherman's waterproof boxes (30.4.84)	60	80
O32	$1 Pump drill and adze (1.2.84)	1·00	1·00
O33	$2 Fisherman's hat and canoe bailers (1.2.84)	1·75	2·00
O34	$5 Fishing rod, lures and scoop nets (1.2.84)	4·25	4·75
O20/34	*Set of* 15	10·50	12·00

OFFICIAL

(O 3)

1989 (22 Feb). *Nos.* 502/17 *optd with Type* O **3**.

O35	5 c. Type **66**	10	10
O36	10 c. White Tern	10	15
O37	15 c. Common Noddy	15	20
O38	20 c. Phoenix Petrel	20	25
O39	25 c. American Golden Plover	25	30
O40	30 c. Crested Tern	30	35
O41	35 c. Sooty Tern	30	35
O42	40 c. Bristle-thighed Curlew	35	40
O43	45 c. Bar-tailed Godwit	40	45
O44	50 c. Eastern Reef Heron	45	50
O45	55 c. Great Frigate Bird	50	55
O46	60 c. Red-footed Booby	55	60
O47	70 c. Rufous-necked Sandpiper ("Red-necked Stint")	65	70
O48	$1 Long-tailed Koel ("Long-tailed Cuckoo")	90	95
O49	$2 Red-tailed Tropic Bird	1·90	2·00
O50	$5 Banded Rail	4·50	4·75
O35/50	*Set of* 16	10·50	11·50

Appendix

The following issues for individual islands of Tuvalu fall outside the criteria for full listing as detailed on page xi of this edition.

FUNAFUTI

1984

Leaders of the World. Railway Locomotives (1st series). *Two designs for each value, the first showing technical drawings and the second the locomotive at work.* 15, 20, 30, 40, 50, 60 c., *each* × 2

Leaders of the World. Automobiles (1st series). *Two designs for each value, the first showing technical drawings and the second the car in action.* 1, 10, 40 c., $1, *each* × 2

Leaders of the World. Railway Locomotives (2nd series). *Two designs for each value, the first showing technical drawings and the second the locomotive at work.* 5, 15, 25, 35, 40, 55, 60 c., $1, *each* × 2

1985

Leaders of the World. Automobiles (2nd series). *Two designs for each value, the first showing technical drawings and the second the car in action.* 1, 30, 55, 60 c., *each* × 2

Leaders of the World. Railway Locomotives (3rd series). *Two designs for each value, the first showing technical drawings and the second the locomotive at work.* 5, 15, 35, 40, 50 c., $1, *each* × 2

Leaders of the World. Life and Times of Queen Elizabeth the Queen Mother. Two designs for each value, showing different portraits. 5, 25, 80 c., $1.05, *each* × 2

1986

60th Birthday of Queen Elizabeth II. 10, 50 c., $1.50, $3.50

Royal Wedding (1st issue). 60 c., $1, *each* × 2

Royal Wedding (2nd issue). *Previous Royal Wedding stamps optd* "Congratulations T.R.H. The Duke & Duchess of York". 60 c., $1, *each* × 2

Railway Locomotives (4th series). *Two designs for each value, the first showing technical drawings and the second the locomotive at work.* 20, 40, 60 c., $1.50, *each* × 2

1987

Automobiles (3rd series). *Two designs for each value, the first showing technical drawings and the second the car in action.* 10, 20, 40, 60, 75, 80 c., $1, $1.50, *each* × 2

Royal Ruby Wedding. 20, 50, 75 c., $1.20, $1.75

1988

Olympic Games, Seoul. 10, 20, 40, 50, 80, 90 c.

NANUMAGA

1984

Leaders of the World. Automobiles (1st series). *Two designs for each value, the first showing technical drawings and the second the car in action.* 5, 10, 25, 30, 40 c., $1, *each* × 2

Leaders of the World. British Monarchs. Two designs for each value, forming a composite picture. 10, 20, 30, 40, 50 c., $1, *each* × 2

Leaders of the World. Automobiles (2nd series). *Two designs for each value, the first showing technical drawings and the second the car in action.* 5, 10, 50 c., $1, *each* × 2

1985

Leaders of the World. Railway Locomotives. Two designs for each value, the first showing technical drawings and the second the locomotive at work. 10, 25, 50, 60 c., *each* × 2

Leaders of the World. Flowers. 25, 30, 40, 50 c., *each* × 2

Leaders of the World. Automobiles (3rd series). *Two designs for each value, the first showing technical drawings and the second the car in action.* 10, 25, 75 c., $1, *each* × 2

Leaders of the World. Life and Times of Queen Elizabeth the Queen Mother. Two designs for each value, showing different portraits. 15, 55, 65, 90 c., *each* × 2

1986

60th Birthday of Queen Elizabeth II. 5 c., $1, $1.75, $2.50

World Cup Football Championship, Mexico. 1, 5, 5, 10, 20, 35, 50, 60, 75 c., $1, $2, $4

Royal Wedding (1st issue). 60 c., $1, *each* × 2

Royal Wedding (2nd issue). *Previous Royal Wedding stamps optd as for Funafuti.* 60 c., $1, *each* × 2

1987

Automobiles (4th series). *Two designs for each value, the first showing technical drawings and the second the car in action.* 5, 10, 15, 20, 25, 40, 60 c., $1, *each* × 2

Royal Ruby Wedding. 15, 35, 60 c., $1.50, $1.75

NANUMEA

1984

Leaders of the World. Railway Locomotives (1st series). *Two designs for each value, the first showing technical drawings and the second the locomotive at work.* 15, 20, 30, 40, 50, 60 c., *each* × 2

Leaders of the World. Famous Cricketers. Two designs for each value, the first showing a portrait and the second the cricketer in action. 1, 10, 40 c., $1, *each* × 2

1985

Leaders of the World. Automobiles (1st series). *Two designs for each value, the first showing technical drawings and the second the car in action.* 5, 40, 50, 60 c., *each* × 2

Leaders of the World. Railway Locomotives (2nd series). *Two designs for each value, the first showing technical drawings and the second the locomotive at work.* 1, 35, 50, 60 c., *each* × 2

Leaders of the World. Automobiles (2nd series). *Two designs for each value, the first showing technical drawings and the second the car in action.* 15, 20, 50, 60 c., *each* × 2

Leaders of the World. Cats. 5, 30, 50 c., $1, *each* × 2

Leaders of the World. Life and Times of Queen Elizabeth the Queen Mother. Two designs for each value, showing different portraits. 5, 30, 75 c., $1.05, *each* × 2

1986

60th Birthday of Queen Elizabeth II. 10, 80 c., $1.75, $3

World Cup Football Championship, Mexico. 1, 2, 5, 10, 25, 40, 50, 75, 90 c., $1, $2.50, $4

Royal Wedding (1st issue). 60 c., $1, *each* × 2

Royal Wedding (2nd issue). *Previous Royal Wedding stamps optd as for Funafuti.* 60 c., $1, *each* × 2

Automobiles (3rd series). *Two designs for each value, the first showing technical drawings and the second the car in action.* 10, 20, 35, 50, 75 c., $2, *each* × 2

1987

Royal Ruby Wedding. 40, 60, 80 c., $1, $2

NIUTAO

1984

Leaders of the World. Automobiles (1st series). *Two designs for each value, the first showing technical drawings and the second the car in action.* 15, 30, 40, 50 c., *each* × 2

Leaders of the World. Railway Locomotives (1st series). *Two designs for each value, the first showing technical drawings and the second the locomotive at work.* 5, 10, 20, 40, 50 c., $1, *each* × 2

1985

Leaders of the World. Famous Cricketers. Two designs for each value, the first showing a portrait and the second the cricketer in action. 1, 15, 50 c., $1, *each* × 2

Leaders of the World. Birth Bicent of John J. Audubon (ornithologist). *Birds.* 5, 15, 25 c., $1, *each* × 2

Leaders of the World. Automobiles (2nd series). *Two designs for each value, the first showing technical drawings and the second the car in action.* 20, 25, 40, 60 c., *each* × 2

Leaders of the World. Railway Locomotives (2nd series). *Two designs for each value, the first showing technical drawings and the second the locomotive at work.* 10, 30, 45, 60, 75 c., $1.20, *each* × 2

Leaders of the World. Life and Times of Queen Elizabeth the Queen Mother. Two designs for each value, showing different portraits. 15, 35, 70, 95 c., *each* × 2

1986

60th Birthday of Queen Elizabeth II. 5, 60 c., $1.50, $3.50

Royal Wedding (1st issue). 60 c., $1, *each* × 2

Royal Wedding (2nd issue). *Previous Royal Wedding stamps optd as for Funafuti.* 60 c., $1, *each* × 2

1987

Royal Ruby Wedding. 60th Birthday of Queen Elizabeth II issue of 1986 optd "40th WEDDING ANNIVERSARY OF H.M. QUEEN ELIZABETH II". 5, 60 c., $1.50, $3.50

NUI

1984

Leaders of the World. Railway Locomotives (1st series). *Two designs for each value, the first showing technical drawings and the second the locomotive at work.* 15, 25, 30, 50 c., *each* × 2

Leaders of the World. British Monarchs. Two designs for each value, forming a composite picture. 1, 5, 15, 40, 50 c., $1, *each* × 2

1985

Leaders of the World. Railway Locomotives (2nd series). *Two designs for each value, the first showing technical drawings and the second the locomotive at work.* 5, 15, 25 c., $1, *each* × 2

Leaders of the World. Automobiles (1st series). *Two designs for each value, the first showing technical drawings and the second the car in action.* 25, 30, 40, 50 c., *each* × 2

Leaders of the World. Famous Cricketers. Two designs for each value, the first showing a portrait and the second the cricketer in action. 1, 40, 60, 70 c., *each* × 2

Leaders of the World. Life and Times of Queen Elizabeth the Queen Mother. Two designs for each value, showing different portraits. 5, 50, 75, 85 c., *each* × 2

Leaders of the World. Automobiles (2nd series). *Two designs for each value, the first showing technical drawings and the second the car in action.* 5, 15, 40, 60, 90 c., $1.10, *each* × 2

1986

60th Birthday of Queen Elizabeth II. 10, 80 c., $1.75, $3

Royal Wedding (1st issue). 60 c., $1, *each* × 2

Royal Wedding (2nd issue). *Previous Royal Wedding stamps optd as for Funafuti.* 60 c., $1, *each* × 2

1987

Railway Locomotives (3rd series). *Two designs for each value, the first showing technical drawings and the second the locomotive at work.* 10, 25, 35, 40, 60, 75 c., $1, $1.25, *each* × 2

Royal Ruby Wedding. 20, 50, 75 c., $1.20, $1.75

1988

Railway Locomotives (4th series). *Two designs for each value, the first showing technical drawings and the second the locomotive at work.* 5, 10, 20, 25, 40, 50, 60, 75 c., *each* × 2

NUKUFETAU

1984

Leaders of the World. Automobiles (1st series). *Two designs for each value, the first showing technical drawings and the second the car in action.* 10, 25, 30, 50, 60 c., *each* × 2

Leaders of the World. British Monarchs. Two designs for each value forming a composite picture. 1, 10, 30, 50, 60 c., $1, *each* × 2

1985

Leaders of the World. Famous Cricketers. Two designs for each value, the first showing a portrait and the second the cricketer in action. 1, 10, 55 c., $1, *each* × 2

Leaders of the World. Railway Locomotives (1st series). *Two designs for each value, the first showing technical drawings and the second the locomotive at work.* 1, 10, 60, 70 c., *each* × 2

Leaders of the World. Automobiles (2nd series). *Two designs for each value, the first showing technical drawings and the second the car in action.* 5, 10, 15, 20, 50, 60, 75 c., $1.50, *each* × 2

Leaders of the World. Life and Times of Queen Elizabeth the Queen Mother. Two designs for each value, showing different portraits. 10, 45, 65 c., $1, *each* × 2

1986

Leaders of the World. Railway Locomotives (2nd series). *Two designs for each value, the first showing technical drawings and the second the locomotive at work.* 20, 40, 60 c., $1.50, *each* × 2

60th Birthday of Queen Elizabeth II. 5, 40 c., $2, $4

Royal Wedding (1st issue). 60 c., $1, *each* × 2

Royal Wedding (2nd issue). *Previous Royal Wedding stamps optd as for Funafuti.* 60 c., $1, *each* × 2

1987

Railway Locomotives (3rd series). *Two designs for each value, the first showing technical drawings and the second the locomotive at work.* 5, 10, 15, 25, 30, 50, 60 c., $1, *each* × 2

Royal Ruby Wedding. 60th Birthday of Queen Elizabeth II issue of 1986 optd as for Niutao. 5, 40 c., $2, $4

NUKULAELAE

1984

Leaders of the World. Railway Locomotives (1st series). *Two designs for each value, the first showing technical drawings and the second the locomotive at work.* 5, 15, 40 c., $1, *each* × 2

Leaders of the World. Famous Cricketers. Two designs for each value, the first showing a portrait and the second the cricketer in action. 5, 15, 30 c., $1, *each* × 2

Leaders of the World. Railway Locomotives (2nd series). *Two designs for each value, the first showing technical drawings and the second the locomotive at work.* 5, 20, 40 c., $1, *each* × 2

1985

Leaders of the World. Automobiles. Two designs for each value, the first showing technical drawings and the second the car in action. 5, 35, 50, 70 c., *each* × 2

Leaders of the World. Dogs. 5, 20, 50, 70 c., *each* × 2

Leaders of the World. Railway Locomotives (3rd series). *Two designs for each value, the first showing technical drawings and the second the locomotive at work.* 10, 25, 50 c., $1, *each* × 2

Leaders of the World. Automobiles (2nd series). *Two designs for each value, the first showing technical drawings and the second the car in action.* 10, 25, 35, 50, 75 c., $1, *each* × 2

Leaders of the World. Life and Times of Queen Elizabeth the Queen Mother. Two designs for each value, showing different portraits. 5, 25, 85 c., $1, *each* × 2

1986

60th Birthday of Queen Elizabeth II. 10 c., $1, $1.50, $3

Railway Locomotives (4th series). *Two designs for each value, the first showing technical drawings and the second the locomotive at work.* 10, 15, 25, 40, 50, 80 c., $1, $1.50, *each* × 2

Royal Wedding (1st issue). 60 c., $1, *each* × 2

Royal Wedding (2nd issue). *Previous Royal Wedding stamps optd as for Funafuti.* 60 c., $1, *each* × 2

1987

Royal Ruby Wedding. 15, 35, 60 c., $1.50, $1.75

VAITUPU

1984

Leaders of the World. Automobiles (1st series). *Two designs for each value, the first showing technical drawings and the second the car in action.* 15, 25, 30, 50 c., *each* × 2

Leaders of the World. British Monarchs. Two designs for each value, forming a composite picture. 1, 5, 15, 40, 50 c., $1, *each* × 2

Leaders of the World. Automobiles (2nd series). *Two designs for each value, the first showing technical drawings and the second the car in action.* 5, 15, 25, 30, 40, 50, 60 c., $1, *each* × 2

1985

Leaders of the World. Railway Locomotives (1st series). *Two designs for each value, the first showing technical drawings and the second the locomotive at work.* 10, 25, 50, 60 c., *each* × 2

Leaders of the World, Butterflies. 5, 15, 50, 75 c., *each* × 2

Leaders of the World. Automobiles (3rd series). Two designs for each value, the first showing technical drawings and the second the car in action. 15, 30, 40, 60 c., *each* × 2

Leaders of the World. Life and Times of Queen Elizabeth the Queen Mother. Two designs for each value, showing different portraits. 15, 40, 65, 95 c., *each* × 2

1986

Leaders of the World. Railway Locomotives (2nd series). Two designs for each value, the first showing technical drawings and the second the locomotive at work. 5, 25, 80 c., $1, *each* × 2

60th Birthday of Queen Elizabeth II. 5, 60 c., $2, $3.50

Royal Wedding (1st issue). 60 c., $1, *each* × 2

Royal Wedding (2nd issue). Previous Royal Wedding stamps optd as for Funafuti. 60 c., $1, *each* × 2

1987

Railway Locomotives (3rd series). Two designs for each value, the first showing technical drawings and the second the locomotive at work. 10, 15, 25, 35, 45, 65, 85 c., $1, *each* × 2

Royal Ruby Wedding. 60th Birthday of Queen Elizabeth II issue of 1986 optd as for Niutao. 5, 60 c., $2, $3.50

Uganda

PRICES FOR STAMPS ON COVER TO 1945

The type-written stamps of Uganda, Nos. 1/53, are very rare used on cover.

Nos. 54/60	*from* × 20
No. 61	—
Nos. 70/5	*from* × 12
No. 76	—
Nos. 84/90	*from* × 20
No. 91	—
Nos. 92/3	*from* × 40

PROTECTORATE

U G
50

1

U G
20

2

TYPE-WRITTEN STAMPS. Nos. 2/53 were type-written by the Revd. E. Millar at Mengo. For all "printings" a thin laid paper was used, and all issues were imperforate.

The original typewriter used had wide letters, but in late April, 1895 Millar obtained a new machine on which the type face was in a narrower fount.

Each sheet was made up of whatever values were required at the time, so that different values can be found *se-tenant* or *tête-bêche*. These last were caused by the paper being inverted in the machine so that space at the foot could be utilised.

For the first issue the sheets were of 117 (9 × 13), but with the introduction of the narrower width (Nos. 17 onwards) a larger number of stamps per sheet, 143 (11 × 13), was adopted.

The manuscript provisionals, Nos. 9*a*/16, come from the Mission at Ngogwe, most of the manuscript surcharges including the initials of the Revd. G. R. Blackledge stationed there.

1895 (20 Mar). *Wide letters. Wide stamps, 20 to 26 mm wide.*

2	**1**	10 (cowries), black	£1800	£1000
4		20 (cowries), black	£2500	£1000
6		30 (cowries), black	£1100	£1100
7		40 (cowries), black	£1800	£1100
8		50 (cowries), black	£1000	£950
9		60 (cowries), black	£1300	£1300

It is now believed that the 5, 10 and 25 cowries values in this width, previously Nos. 1, 3 and 5, do not exist.

A strip of three of No. 2 is known on cover of which one copy has the value "10" altered to "5" in manuscript and initialled "E.M.".

1895 (May). *Wide stamps with pen-written surcharges, in black.*

9*a*	**1**	10 on 30 (c.) black	†	£26000
10		10 on 50 (c.) black	†	£20000
11		15 on 10 (c.) black	†	£20000
12		15 on 20 (c.) black	†	£24000
13		15 on 40 (c.) black	†	£20000
14		15 on 50 (c.) black	†	£26000
15		25 on 50 (c.) black	†	£26000
16		50 on 60 (c.) black	†	£26000

1895 (April). *Wide letters. Narrow stamps, 16 to 18 mm wide.*

17	**1**	5 (c.) black	£1100	£850
18		10 (c.) black	£1100	£950
19		15 (c.) black	£800	£850
20		20 (c.) black	£900	£600
21		25 (c.) black	£750	£800
22		30 (c.) black	£5500	£5500
23		40 (c.) black	£5000	£5000
24		50 (c.) black	£2500	
25		60 (c.) black	£3250	

1895 (May). *Narrow letters. Narrow stamps 16 to 18 mm wide.*

26	**2**	5 (c.) black	£475
27		10 (c.) black	£450
28		15 (c.) black	£450
29		20 (c.) black	£375
30		25 (c.) black	£450
31		30 (c.) black	£475
32		40 (c.) black	£550
33		50 (c.) black	£450
34		60 (c.) black	£1100

1895 (Nov). *Narrow letters. Narrow stamps, 16–18 mm wide. Change of colour.*

35	**2**	5 (c.) violet	£350	£400
36		10 (c.) violet	£325	£350
37		15 (c.) violet	£375	£325
38		20 (c.) violet	£300	£275
		a. "G U" for "U G"		
39		25 (c.) violet	£450	£450
40		30 (c.) violet	£550	£450
41		40 (c.) violet	£450	£450
42		50 (c.) violet	£450	£500
43		100 (c.) violet	£2250	£2250

Stamps of 35 (c.) and 45 (c.) have been chronicled in both colours. They were never prepared for postal use, and did not represent a postal rate, but were type-written to oblige a local official.

V.96.R
25
Uganda

3

1896 (June).

44	**3**	5 (c.) violet	£300	£375
45		10 (c.) violet	£300	£300
46		15 (c.) violet	£300	£350
47		20 (c.) violet	£250	£190
48		25 (c.) violet	£325	
49		30 (c.) violet	£350	£475
50		40 (c.) violet	£350	£475
51		50 (c.) violet	£425	£475
52		60 (c.) violet	£1200	
53		100 (c.) violet	£1200	£1200

UGANDA
POSTAGE
V†R
1 ANNA
PROTECTORATE

4 (Thin "1")

UGANDA
POSTAGE
V†R
1 ANNA
PROTECTORATE

5 (Thick "1")

UGANDA
POSTAGE
V†R
4 ANNAS
PROTECTORATE

6

UGANDA
POSTAGE
L
4 ANNAS
PROTECTORATE

7

In the 2 a. and 3 a. the dagger points upwards; the stars in the 2 a. are level with the top of "VR". The 8 a. is as T **6** but with left star at top and right star at foot. The 1 r. has three stars at foot. The 5 r. has central star raised and the others at foot.

(Type-set by the Revd. F. Rowling at Lubwa's, in Usoga)

1896 (7 Nov). (*a*) *Types* **4/6**.

A. *Normal.* B. *Small* "o" *in* "POSTAGE"

			A		B	
54	**4**	1 a. black	55·00	55·00	£200	£200
55	**5**	1 a. black	7·50	8·50	28·00	30·00
56	**6**	2 a. black	8·50	9·00	30·00	32·00
57		3 a. black	9·50	11·00	35·00	38·00
58		4 a. black	9·50	11·00	35·00	38·00
59		8 a. black	15·00	18·00	50·00	55·00
60		1 r. black	40·00	45·00	£170	£190
61		5 r. black	£130	£170	£350	£425

(*b*) *Optd* "L", *in black as in T* **7** *for local use, by a postal official, R. R. Racey, at Kampala*

			A		B	
70	**4**	1 a. black	90·00	80·00	£500	—
71	**6**	2 a. black	35·00	60·00	£110	£160
72		3 a. black	90·00	£100	£500	—
73		4 a. black	50·00	85·00	£170	—
74		8 a. black	90·00	£110	£450	—
75		1 r. black	£180	£225	£550	—
76		5 r. black	£4500	£4500	—	—

Tête-bêche pairs of all values may be found owing to the settings of 16 (4 × 4) being printed side by side or above one another. They are worth a premium. The variety with small "O" occurs on R. 3/1.

8

9

UGANDA

(10)

(Recess D.L.R.)

1898–1902. *P* 14. (*a*) *Wmk Crown CA.*

84	**8**	1 a. scarlet	75	35
		a. Carmine-rose (1902)	30	35
86		2 a. red-brown	40	2·25
87		3 a. pale grey	3·50	7·00
		a. Bluish grey	3·50	6·00
88		4 a. deep green	1·75	4·50
89		8 a. pale olive	2·75	14·00
		a. Grey-green	3·50	15·00
		(*b*) *Wmk Crown CC*		
90	**9**	1 r. dull blue	18·00	20·00
		a. Bright blue	24·00	27·00
91		5 r. brown	48·00	55·00
84/91		*Set of* 7	65·00	90·00
84/91 Optd "Specimen"		*Set of* 7	£150	

1902. *T* **11** *of British East Africa (Kenya, Uganda and Tanganyika) optd with T* **10.**

92	½ a. yellow-green	50	35
	a. Opt omitted (in pair with normal) ..	£1800	
	b. Opt inverted (at foot)	£850	
	c. Opt double	£950	
93	2½ a. deep blue (R.)	50	1·40
	a. Opt double	£600	
	b. Inverted "S" (R. 1/1)		

For issues between 1903 and 1976 see KENYA, UGANDA AND TANGANYIKA.

SELF-GOVERNMENT

11 Ripon Falls and Speke Memorial

(Des S. Scott. Recess B.W.)

1962 (28 July). *Centenary of Speke's Discovery of Source of the Nile. W* w **12.** *P* 14.

95	**11**	30 c. black and red	10	10
96		50 c. black and slate-violet	10	10
97		1 s. 30, black and green	15	10
98		2 s. 50, black and blue	40	55
95/8		.. .. *Set of* 4	55	60

INDEPENDENT

12 Murchison Falls **13** Tobacco-growing

14 Mulago Hospital

(Des V. Whiteley. Photo Harrison)

1962 (9 Oct)–**64.** *Independence. Various designs as T* **12/14.** *P* 15×14 (5 *c. to* 50 *c.*) *or* 14½ (*others*).

99	5 c. deep bluish green	10	10
100	10 c. reddish brown	10	10
	a. Brown (coil)	10	10
	b. Deep yellow-brown (17.10.64) ..	10	10
101	15 c. black, red and green	10	10
102	20 c. plum and buff	10	10
103	30 c. blue	10	10
104	50 c. black and turquoise-green ..	10	10
105	1 s. sepia, red and turquoise-green ..	15	10
106	1 s. 30, yellow-orange and violet ..	20	10
107	2 s. black, carmine and light blue ..	40	30
108	5 s. vermilion and deep green ..	2·50	75
109	10 s. slate and chestnut	1·75	1·50
110	20 s. brown and blue	4·50	11·00
99/110	.. .. *Set of* 12	9·00	12·50

Designs: *As T* **12/13**—10 c. Tobacco growing; 15 c. Coffee growing; 20 c. Ankole cattle; 30 c. Cotton; 50 c. Mountains of the Moon. *As T* **14**—1 s. 30, Cathedrals and Mosque; 2 s. Makerere College; 5 s. Copper mining; 10 s. Cement industry; 20 s. Parliament Buildings.

15 South African Crowned Crane

(Photo Harrison)

1965 (20 Feb). *International Trade Fair, Kampala. P* 14½ × 14.

111	**15**	30 c. multicoloured	10	10
112		1 s. 30, multicoloured	20	10

16 Black Bee Eater **17** African Jacana

18 Ruwenzori Turaco

(Des Mrs. R. Fennessy. Photo Harrison)

1965 (9 Oct). *Birds. Various designs as T* **16/18.** *P* 15 × 14 (5 *c.*, 15 *c.*, 20 *c.*, 40 *c.*, 50 *c.*), 14 × 15 (10 *c.*, 30 *c.*, 65 *c.*) *or* 14½ (*others*).

113	5 c. multicoloured	10	10
114	10 c. chestnut, black and light blue ..	10	10
115	15 c. yellow and sepia	15	10
116	20 c. multicoloured	15	10
117	30 c. black and brown-red	1·25	10
118	40 c. multicoloured	80	30
119	50 c. grey-blue and reddish violet ..	25	10
	a. White bird (grey-blue omitted) ..	£100	
120	65 c. orange-red, black and light grey ..	2·25	95
121	1 s. multicoloured	50	10
122	1 s. 30, chestnut, black and yellow ..	4·50	30
123	2 s. 50, multicoloured	4·25	65
124	5 s. multicoloured	7·00	2·00
125	10 s. multicoloured	9·50	6·50
126	20 s. multicoloured	21·00	24·00
113/26	.. .. .. *Set of* 14	45·00	32·00

Designs: *Vert as T* **16**—15 c. Orange Weaver; 20 c. Narina Trogon; 40 c. Blue-breasted Kingfisher; 50 c. Whale-headed Stork. *Horiz as T* **17**—30 c. Sacred Ibis; 65 c. Red-crowned Bishop. *As T* **18.** *Vert*—1 s. 30, African Fish Eagle; 5 s. Lilac-breasted Roller. *Horiz*—2 s. 50, Great Blue Turaco; 10 s. Black-collared Lovebird; 20 s. South African Crowned Crane.

The 15 c., 40 c., 65 c., and 1s. exist with PVA gum as well as gum arabic.

19 Carved Screen

(Des Mrs. R. Fennessy. Photo Harrison)

1967 (26 Oct). *13th Commonwealth Parliamentary Association Conference. T* **19** *and similar horiz designs. Multicoloured. P* 14.

127	30 c. Type **19**	10	10
128	50 c. Arms of Uganda	10	10
129	1 s. 30, Parliamentary Building ..	10	10
130	2 s. 50, Conference Chamber	15	70
127/30	.. .. *Set of* 4	30	70

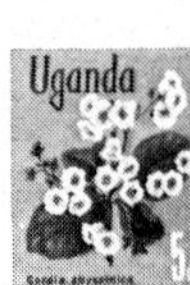

20 *Cordia abyssinica* **21** *Acacia drepanolobium*

(Des Mrs. R. Fennessy. Photo Harrison)

1969 (9 Oct)–**74.** *Flowers. Various designs as T* **20/1.** *Chalk-surfaced paper. P* 14½×14 (5 *c. to* 70 *c.*) *or* 14 (*others*).

131	5 c. brown, green and light olive-yellow ..	10	40
	a. Glazed, ordinary paper (11.4.73) ..	40	10
132	10 c. multicoloured	10	10
	a. Glazed, ordinary paper (27.9.72) ..	40	10
133	15 c. multicoloured	30	10
134	20 c. bluish violet, yellow-ol & pale sage-grn	15	10
	a. Glazed, ordinary paper (27.9.72) ..	40	10
135	30 c. multicoloured	20	10
136	40 c. reddish violet, yell-grn & pale ol-grey	20	10
137	50 c. multicoloured	20	10
138	60 c. multicoloured	45	90
	a. Glazed, ordinary paper (9.5.73) ..	3·75	40
139	70 c. multicoloured	35	30
	a. Glazed, ordinary paper (27.9.72) ..	90	45
140	1 s. multicoloured	20	10
	a. Glazed, ordinary paper (22.1.71) ..	80	10
141	1 s. 50, multicoloured (cobalt background)	35	10
	a. Glazed, ordinary paper (3.2.71) ..	50	10
	b. Azure background (chalk-surfaced paper) (21.1.74)	55	20
142	2 s. 50, multicoloured	70	60
	a. Glazed, ordinary paper (3.2.71) ..	1·25	10
143	5 s. multicoloured	1·50	90
	a. Glazed, ordinary paper (3.2.71) ..	1·75	10
144	10 s. multicoloured	3·50	2·50
	a. Glazed, ordinary paper (3.2.71) ..	3·75	10
145	20 s. multicoloured	6·50	3·50
	a. Glazed, ordinary paper (22.1.71) ..	11·00	15
131/45	.. .. .. *Set of* 15	13·00	8·50
131a/45a	.. .. .. *Set of* 11	23·00	1·40

Designs: *As T* **20**—10 c. *Grewia similis*; 15 c. *Cassia didymobotrya*; 20 c. *Coleus barbatus*; 30 c. *Ockna ovata*; 40 c. *Ipomoea spathulata*; 50 c. *Spathodea nilotica*; 60 c. *Oncoba spinosa*; 70 c. *Carissa edulis*. *As T* **21**—1 s. 50, *Clerodendrum myricoides*; 2 s. 50, *Acanthus arboreus*; 5 s. *Kigelia aethiopium*; 10 s. *Erythrina abyssinica*; 20 s. *Monodora myristica*.

(22)

1975 (29 Sept). *Nos.* 141/2 *and* 145a *surch as T* **22.**

146	2 s. on 1 s. 50, multicoloured	2·00	1·50
147	3 s. on 2 s. 50, multicoloured	20·00	35·00
148	40 s. on 20 s. multicoloured	5·50	3·50
	a. Surch on No. 145	—	3·50
146/8	.. .. *Set of* 3	25·00	35·00

23 Millet **24** Maize

(Des Mrs. R. Fennessy. Photo Harrison)

1975 (9 Oct). *Ugandan Crops. T* **23/4** *and similar horiz designs. P* 14 × 14½ (10 *to* 80 *c.*) *or* 14 (*others*).

149	10 c. black, apple-green and yellow-brown ..	10	10
150	20 c. multicoloured	10	10
151	30 c. multicoloured	10	10
152	40 c. multicoloured	10	10
153	50 c. multicoloured	10	10
154	70 c. black, apple-green and light blue-green	15	15
155	80 c. multicoloured	15	15
156	1 s. multicoloured	15	15
157	2 s. multicoloured	30	30
158	3 s. multicoloured	50	45
159	5 s. multicoloured	90	75
160	10 s. multicoloured	1·50	1·25
161	20 s. apple-green, black and bright purple ..	2·50	2·50
162	40 s. apple-green, black and yellow-orange ..	5·00	4·75
149/62	.. .. .. *Set of* 14	10·00	9·50

Designs: *As T* **23**—20 c. Sugar; 30 c. Tobacco; 40 c. Onions; 50 c. Tomatoes; 70 c. Tea; 80 c. Bananas. *As T* **24**—2 s. Pineapples; 3 s. Coffee; 5 s. Oranges; 10 s. Groundnuts; 20 s. Cotton; 40 s. Runner Beans.

Face value colours: 5 s. green; 10 s. brown; 20 s. bright purple; 40 s. yellow-orange. For 5 s. to 40 s. with colours changed see Nos. 220/3.

Nos. 149 and 153 exist in coils constructed from normal sheets.

1976 (15 Apr). *Telecommunications Development. As Nos.* 56/60 *of Kenya, but inscr* "UGANDA".

163	50 c. Microwave tower	10	10
164	1 s. Cordless switchboard	10	10
165	2 s. Telephone	20	25
166	3 s. Message Switching Centre	30	45
163/6	.. .. *Set of* 4	60	70
MS167	120 × 120 mm. Nos. 163/6	90	1·25

Nos. 164 and 166 exist imperforate from stock dispersed by the liquidator of Format International Security Printers Ltd.

1976 (5 July). *Olympic Games, Montreal. As Nos.* 61/5 *of Kenya but inscr* "UGANDA".

168	50 c. Akii Bua, hurdler	15	10
169	1 s. Filbert Bayi, runner	20	10
170	2 s. Steve Muchoki, boxer	40	30
171	3 s. East African flags	55	45
168/71	.. .. *Set of* 4	1·10	75
MS172	129 × 154 mm. Nos. 168/71	4·50	4·50

Nos. 168/70 exist imperforate from stock dispersed by the liquidator of Format International Security Printers Ltd.

1976 (4 Oct). *Railway Transport. As Nos.* 66/70 *of Kenya, but inscr* "UGANDA".

173	50 c. Tanzania–Zambia railway	20	10
174	1 s. Nile Bridge, Uganda	35	10
175	2 s. Nakuru Station, Kenya	75	45
176	3 s. Class A loco, 1896	95	55
173/6	.. .. *Set of* 4	2·00	1·00
MS177	154 × 103 mm. Nos. 173/6	3·25	2·50

Nos. 173/4 exist imperforate from stock dispersed by the liquidator of Format International Security Printers Ltd.

1977 (10 Jan). *Game Fish of East Africa. As Nos.* 71/5 *of Kenya, but inscr* "UGANDA".

178	50 c. Nile Perch	15	10
179	1 s. Tilapia	20	10
180	3 s. Sailfish	70	40
181	5 s. Black Marlin	1·00	60
178/81	.. .. *Set of* 4	1·90	1·00
MS182	153 × 129 mm. Nos. 178/81	3·75	2·00

1977 (15 Jan). *Second World Black and African Festival of Arts and Culture, Nigeria. As Nos.* 76/80 *of Kenya, but inscr* "UGANDA".

183	50 c. Maasai Manyatta (village)	15	10
184	1 s. "Heartbeat of Africa" (Ugandan dancers)	20	10
185	2 s. Makonde sculpture	45	45
186	3 s. "Early Man and Technology" (skinning hippopotamus)	60	80
183/6	.. .. *Set of* 4	1·25	1·25
MS187	132 × 109 mm. Nos. 183/6	2·00	2·25

1977 (5 Apr). *25th Anniv of Safari Rally. As Nos.* 81/5 *of Kenya but inscr* "UGANDA".

188	50 c. Rally-car and villagers	15	10
189	1 s. Starting-line	15	10
190	2 s. Car fording river	35	35
191	5 s. Car and elephants	90	1·00
188/91	.. .. *Set of* 4	1·40	1·40
MS192	126 × 93 mm. Nos. 188/91	1·75	2·50

1977 (30 June). *Centenary of Ugandan Church. As Nos. 86/90 of Kenya, but inscr* "UGANDA".
193 50 c. Canon Kivebulaya 10 10
194 1 s. Modern Namirembe Cathedral 15 10
195 2 s. Old Namirembe Cathedral 30 40
196 5 s. Early congregation, Kigezi 60 90
193/6 .. .. *Set of* 4 1·00 1·25
MS197 126 × 89 mm. Nos. 193/6 .. .. .. 1·00 1·75

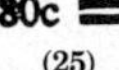

(25)

26 Shot Putting

1977 (22 Aug). *Design as No. 155 surch with T* **25** *in mauve by Harrison.*
198 80 c. on 60 c. multicoloured 25 20
a. Surch omitted £180
A 60 c. stamp was to have been added to Nos. 149/62 using the design of the 80 c. (bananas), but it was cancelled and those already printed were surcharged to make No. 198.

1977 (26 Sept). *Endangered Species. As Nos. 96/101 of Kenya, but inscr* "UGANDA".
199 50 c. Pancake Tortoise 30 10
200 1 s. Nile Crocodile 45 10
201 2 s. Hunter's Hartebeest .. .. .. 1·75 40
202 3 s. Red Colobus monkey .. .. .. 2·00 75
203 5 s. Dugong .. .. 2·25 1·40
199/203 .. .. *Set of* 5 6·00 2·50
MS204 127 × 101 mm. Nos. 200/3 .. .. 6·50 4·00

1978 (10 Apr). *World Cup Football Championship, Argentina* (1st *issue*). *As Nos.* 122/6 *of Kenya but inscr* "UGANDA".
205 50 c. Joe Kadenge and forwards 15 10
206 1 s. Mohamed Chuma and cup presentation 15 10
207 2 s. Omari Kidevu and goalmouth scene .. 40 35
208 5 s. Polly Ouma and forwards 70 85
205/8 .. .. *Set of* 4 1·25 1·10
MS209 136 × 81 mm. Nos. 205/8 .. .. .. 2·50 2·75

(Litho Questa)

1978 (28 Aug). *Commonwealth Games, Edmonton. T* **26** *and similar horiz designs. Multicoloured. P* 14.
210 50 c. Type **26** 15 10
211 1 s. Long jumping 15 10
212 2 s. Running 30 30
213 5 s. Boxing 55 70
210/13 .. .. *Set of* 4 1·00 1·00
MS214 114×85 mm. Nos. 210/13. P 12½×12 .. 1·75 3·00

1978 (11 Sept). *World Cup Football Championship, Argentina* (2nd *issue*). *Designs as Nos.* 205/8 *but additionally inscr* "WORLD CUP 1978".
215 50 c. Polly Ouma and forwards 15 10
216 2 s. Omari Kidevu and goalmouth scene .. 45 40
217 5 s. Joe Kadenge and forwards .. .. 1·00 90
218 10 s. Mohamed Chuma and cup presentation 1·75 1·60
215/18 .. .. *Set of* 4 3·00 2·75
MS219 140×87 mm. Nos. 215/18. P 12×11½ .. 3·00 3·25

(Litho Questa)

1978. *As Nos.* 159/62 *but printing process and colours changed.*
220 5 s. multicoloured (face value in blue) .. 70 70
221 10 s. multicoloured (face value in magenta) .. 1·00 1·25
222 20 s. multicoloured (face value in brown) .. 1·50 2·00
223 40 s. multicoloured (face value in red) .. 2·75 3·50
220/3 .. .. *Set of* 4 5·50 6·50

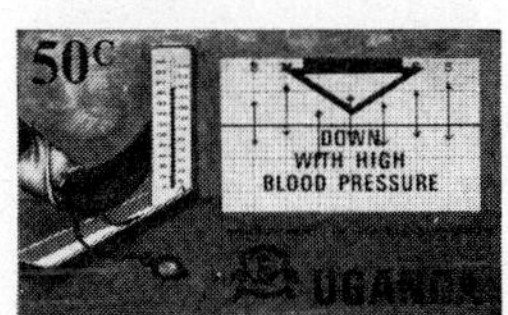

27 Measurements of High Blood Pressure

(Litho Questa)

1978 (25 Sept). *"Down with High Blood Pressure". T* **27** *and similar horiz designs. Multicoloured. P* 14 × 13½.
224 50 c. Type **27** 20 10
225 1 s. Hypertension and the heart 30 10
226 2 s. Fundus of the eye in hypertension .. 70 35
227 5 s. Kidney and high blood pressure.. .. 1·25 80
224/7 .. .. *Set of* 4 2·25 1·10
MS228 180 × 115 mm. Nos. 224/7 .. .. 2·50 2·75

28 Off Loading Cattle

(Litho Questa)

1978 (16 Dec). *75th Anniv of Powered Flight. T* **28** *and similar horiz designs. Multicoloured. P* 14.
229 1 s. Type **28** 15 10
230 1 s. 50, "Domestic services" (passengers boarding "Islander" light aircraft) .. 20 15
231 2 s. 70, Export of Uganda coffee 40 35
232 10 s. "Time machines in the air" (Wright *Flyer* and "Concorde") .. .. 1·50 1·25
229/32 .. .. *Set of* 4 2·00 1·60
MS233 166 × 110 mm. Nos. 229/32 .. .. 2·25 2·75

29 Queen Elizabeth II leaving Owen Falls Dam

(Des BG Studio. Litho Ashton-Potter)

1979 (15 Feb). *25th Anniv of Coronation* (1978). *T* **29** *and similar horiz designs. Multicoloured. P* 12½ × 12.
234 1 s. Type **29** 15 10
235 1 s. 50, Regalia 20 10
236 2 s. 70, Coronation ceremony 45 20
237 10 s. Royal family on balcony of Buckingham Palace .. .. 1·00 60
234/7 .. .. *Set of* 4 1·60 80
MS238 150 × 102 mm. Nos. 234/7 .. .. 1·75 1·75

30 Dr. Joseph Kiwanuka (first Ugandan bishop)

(Des G. Vasarhelyi. Litho Questa)

1979 (15 Feb). *Centenary of Catholic Church in Uganda. T* **30** *and similar horiz designs. Multicoloured. P* 14.
239 1 s. Type **30** 15 10
240 1 s. 50, Lubaga Cathedral 15 10
241 2 s. 70, Ugandan pilgrimage to Rome, Holy Year, 1975 .. .. 20 25
242 10 s. Friar Lourdel-Mapeera (early missionary) 60 80
239/42 .. .. *Set of* 4 1·00 1·10
MS243 128 × 91 mm. Nos. 239/42 .. .. 1·40 1·75

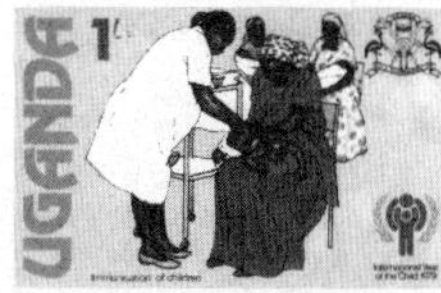

31 Immunisation of Children

(Des J.W. Litho Questa)

1979 (28 June). *International Year of the Child. T* **31** *and similar horiz designs. Multicoloured. P* 14.
244 1 s. Type **31** 15 10
245 1 s. 50, Handicapped children at play .. 20 20
246 2 s. 70, Ugandan I.Y.C. emblem 35 35
247 10 s. Children in class.. .. .. .. 80 90
244/7 .. .. *Set of* 4 1·40 1·40
MS248 136 × 113 mm. Nos. 244/7 .. .. 1·40 2·00

UGANDA LIBERATED 1979 (32)   UGANDA LIBERATED 1979 (33)   UGANDA LIBERATED 1979 (34)

1979 (12 July–16 Aug?). *Liberation.*
(*a*) *Nos.* 149/55 *optd with T* **32** *and* 156/62 *with T* **33** (12 July)
249 10 c. black, apple-green and yellow-brown .. 10 10
250 20 c. multicoloured 10 10
251 30 c. multicoloured 10 10
252 40 c. multicoloured 10 10
253 50 c. multicoloured 10 10
254 70 c. black, apple-green and light blue-green 10 10
255 80 c. multicoloured 10 10
a. Opt double £110
256 1 s. multicoloured 15 15
257 2 s. multicoloured 20 25
258 3 s. multicoloured 35 40
259 5 s. multicoloured 55 60
260 10 s. multicoloured .. .. 1·10 1·25
261 20 s. apple-green, black and bright purple .. 2·25 2·40
262 40 s. apple-green, black and yellow-orange .. 4·50 4·75
a. Opt double £130

(*b*) *Nos.* 210/13 (*Commonwealth Games*) *optd with T* **34** (1 Aug)
263 50 c. Type **26** 10 10
264 1 s. Long jumping 15 20
265 2 s. Running 25 30
266 5 s. Boxing 60 65

(*c*) *Nos.* 207, 215 *and* 217/18 (*World Cup Football Championships*) *optd with T* **34** (1 Aug)
267 50 c. Polly Ouma and forwards 10 10
268 2 s. Omari Kidevu and goal-mouth scene .. 25 30
a. Optd on No. 216 .. .. 14·00 23·00
269 5 s. Joe Kadenge and forwards 60 65
270 10 s. Mohamed Chuma and cup presentation 1·25 1·40

(*d*) *Nos.* 220/3 *optd with T* **33** (1979)
271 5 s. multicoloured 55 60
272 10 s. multicoloured .. .. 1·10 1·25
273 20 s. multicoloured .. .. 2·25 2·40
274 40 s. multicoloured .. .. 4·50 4·75

(*e*) *Nos.* 229/32 (*75th Anniv of Powered Flight*) *optd with T* **34** (1 Aug)
275 1 s. Type **28** 15 20
276 1 s. 50, "Domestic services" (passengers boarding "Islander" light aircraft) .. 20 25
277 2 s. 70, Export of Uganda coffee 40 45
278 10 s. "Time machines in the air" (Wright *Flyer* and "Concorde") .. .. 1·25 1·40

(*f*) *Nos.* 234/7 (*25th Anniv of Coronation*) *optd as T* **33** *or surch also and No.* **MS**238 *additionally inscr* "Diplomatic Relations Normalised" *with Ugandan and British flags replacing portrait of Amin* (12 July)
279 1 s. Type **29** 15 20
280 1 s. 50, Regalia 20 25
281 2 s. 70, Coronation ceremony 40 45
282 15 s. on 10 s. Royal family on balcony of Buckingham Palace .. .. .. 1·75 1·90
MS283 150×102 mm. Nos. 234/6 and 15 s. as No. 237* .. ..
* The sheet contains unoverprinted stamps; the additional inscriptions and changes in design appear only on the sheet margin.

(*g*) *Nos.* 239/42 (*Centenary of Catholic Church in Uganda*) *optd with T* **34** *and No.* **MS**243 *with additional inscr* "FREEDOM OF WORSHIP DECLARED" *replacing part of the margin decoration* (1 Aug)
284 1 s. Type **30** 15 20
285 1 s. 50, Lubaga Cathedral 20 25
286 2 s. 70, Ugandan pilgrimage to Rome, Holy Year, 1975 .. .. 40 45
287 10 s. Friar Lourdel-Mapeera (early missionary) .. .. 1·25 1·40
MS288 128×91 mm. Nos. 239/42*. P 12½×12 (1979) .. .. 2·25 2·75
* The sheet contains the original unoverprinted stamps; the additional inscription appears on the sheet margin.

(*h*) *Nos.* 244/8 (*International Year of the Child*) *optd with T* **34** (16 Aug)
289 1 s. Type **31** 15 20
290 1 s. 50, Handicapped children at play .. 20 25
291 2 s. 70, Ugandan I.Y.C. emblem 40 45
292 10 s. Children in class .. .. 1·25 1·40
MS293 136 × 113 mm. Nos. 289/92 .. .. 2·25 2·75
249/82, 284/7 *and* 289/92 .. .. *Set of* 42 26·00 29·00

35 Radio Wave Symbol

(Des G. Vasarhelyi. Litho Questa)

1979 (11 Sept). *50th Anniv of International Consultative Radio Committee and International Telecommunications Union. P* 14.
294 **35** 1 s. multicoloured 15 10
295 1 s. 50, multicoloured 20 10
296 2 s. 70, multicoloured 35 35
297 10 s. multicoloured 80 90
294/7 .. .. *Set of* 4 1·40 1·25

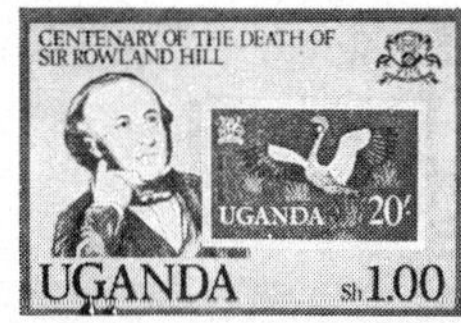

36 20s. Definitive Stamp of 1965 and Sir Rowland Hill

(Des BG Studio. Litho Questa)

1979 (Oct). *Death Centenary of Sir Rowland Hill. T* **36** *and similar horiz designs showing stamps and Sir Rowland Hill. Multicoloured. P* 14.
298 1 s. Type **36** 15 10
299 1 s. 50, 1967 13th Commonwealth Parliamentary Association Conference 50 c. commemorative 25 10
300 2 s. 70, 1962 Independence 20 s. commemorative 45 40
301 10 s. Uganda Protectorate 1898 1 a. .. .. 1·00 1·50
298/301 .. .. *Set of* 4 1·75 1·75
MS302 154×98 mm. Nos. 298/301 .. .. 1·75 2·00

37 Impala **38** Lions with Cub

(Des G. Drummond. Litho Questa)

1979 (3 Dec)–**82**. *Wildlife. Horiz designs as T* **37** (10 *to* 80 *c.*) *or T* **38** (1 *to* 40 *s.*). *Multicoloured. P* 14 × 13½ (10 *to* 80 *c.*) *or* 14 (1 *to* 40 *s.*). A. *No imprint date.* B. *With imprint date* ("1982") *at foot of design* (1982).

		A		B	
303	10 c. Type **37**	10	10	†	
304	20 c. Large-spotted Genet	10	10	†	
305	30 c. Thomson's Gazelle	15	10	†	
306	50 c. Lesser Bushbaby	15	10	†	
307	80 c. Hunting Dog	20	10	†	
308	1 s. Type **38**	30	10	15	10
309	1 s. 50, Gorilla	45	10	†	
310	2 s. Common Zebra	45	15	25	20
311	2 s. 70, Leopard with cub	60	15	†	
312	3 s. 50, Black Rhinoceros	70	20	†	
313	5 s. Waterbuck	70	30	40	40
314	10 s. African Buffalo	70	60	†	
315	20 s. Hippopotamus	80	1·25	†	
316	40 s. African Elephant	1·50	2·50	†	
303/16	*Set of* 14	6·00	5·00		

For designs as Nos. 308/12 and 315/16, but with face values in revalued currency, see Nos. 433/9.

LONDON 1980

(**39**) **40** Rotary Emblem

1980 (6 May). *"London 1980" International Stamp Exhibition. Nos.* 298/302 *optd as T* **39**.

317	1 s. Type **36**	15	10
318	1 s. 50, 1967 13th Commonwealth Parliamentary Association Conference 50 c. commemorative	20	10
319	2 s. 70, 1962 Independence 20s. commemorative	35	25
320	10 s. Uganda Protectorate 1898 1a.	80	80
317/20	*Set of* 4	1·40	1·10
MS321	154 × 99 mm. Nos. 317/20	1·40	1·75

(Des BG Studio. Litho Questa)

1980 (25 Aug). *75th Anniv of Rotary International. T* **40** *and similar multicoloured design. P* 14.

322	1 s. Type **40**	10	10
323	20 s. Paul Harris (founder) with wheel-barrow containing "Rotary projects" (*horiz*)	1·50	1·50
MS324	100 × 76 mm. Nos. 322/3. Imperf.	2·10	2·50

FOOTBALL
GOLD MEDALISTS, C.S.S.R.

41 Football (**42**)

(Des G. Vasarhelyi. Litho Questa)

1980 (29 Dec). *Olympic Games, Moscow. T* **41** *and similar horiz designs. Multicoloured. P* 14.

325	1 s. Type **41**	10	10
326	2 s. Relay	10	10
327	10 s. Hurdles	40	60
328	20 s. Boxing	80	1·25
325/8	*Set of* 4	1·25	1·75
MS329	118×90 mm. 2 s. 70, 3 s., 5 s., 25 s. As Nos. 325/8	1·75	2·75

1980 (29 Dec). *Olympic Games, Moscow. Medal Winners. Nos.* 325/9 *optd as T* **42**.

330	1 s. Type **41**	10	10
331	2 s. Relay	10	15
332	10 s. Hurdles	40	50
333	20 s. Boxing	80	1·00
330/3	*Set of* 4	1·25	1·50
MS334	118×90 mm. 2 s. 70, 3 s., 5 s., 25 s. As Nos. 330/3	1·50	3·00

Overprints:—2s. "RELAY GOLD MEDALIST U.S.S.R."; 10s. "HURDLES 110 m. GOLD MEDALIST THOMAS MUNKLET, D.D.R."; 20s. "BOXING WELTERWEIGHT SILVER MEDALIST JOHN MUGABI, UGANDA".

NEW INFORMATION

The editor is always interested to correspond with people who have new information that will improve or correct the Catalogue.

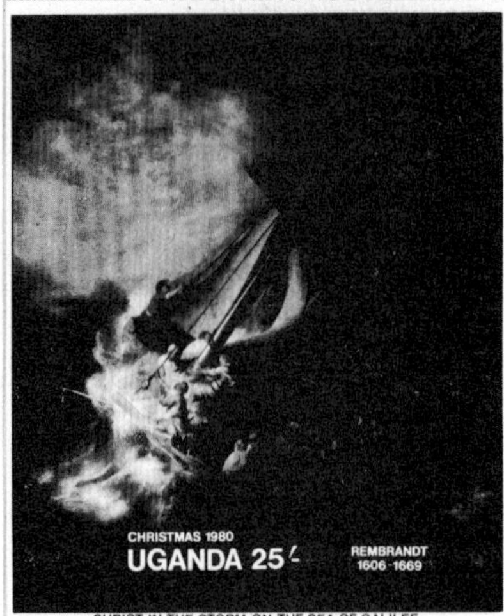

43 "Christ in the Storm on the Sea of Galilee" (painting, Rembrandt)

1980 (31 Dec). *Christmas. Sheet* 79 × 101 *mm. Litho. Imperf.*

MS335	**43**	25 s. multicoloured	3·25	4·00

44 Heinrich von Stephan and U.P.U. Emblem **45** Tower of London

(Des BG Studio. Litho Questa)

1981 (2 June). *150th Birth Anniv of Heinrich von Stephan (founder of U.P.U.). T* **44** *and similar horiz designs. Multicoloured. P* 14.

336	1 s. Type **44**	10	10
337	2 s. U.P.U. Headquarters	15	15
338	2 s. 70, Air mail, 1935	20	20
339	10 s. Mail transport by train, 1927	80	80
336/9	*Set of* 4	1·10	1·10
MS340	112 × 95 mm. Nos. 336/9	2·50	1·90

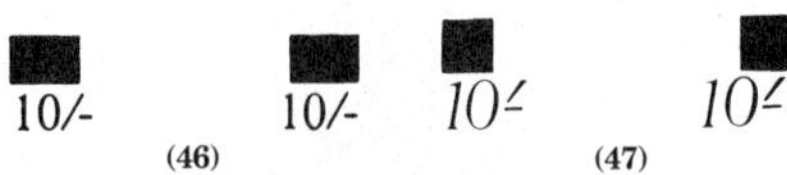

(**46**) (**47**)

(Des J.W. Litho Questa)

1981 (July). *Royal Wedding. T* **45** *and similar vert designs. Multicoloured. P* 14. (*a*) *Unissued stamps surcharged* (13 July). A. *As T* **46**. B. *As T* **47**.

		A		B	
341	10 s. on 1 s. Prince Charles and Lady Diana Spencer	65	65	25	20
	a. Surch on 5 s. value	50·00	—	†	
	b. Surch on 20 s. value	45·00	—	†	
	c. Surch omitted	90·00	—	†	
342	50 s. on 5 s. Type **45**	1·00	1·00	40	30
	a. Surch omitted	85·00	—	†	
343	200 s. on 20 s. Prince Charles at Balmoral	3·00	3·00	1·50	1·25
	a. Surch omitted	£130	—	†	
	b. Surch inverted	50·00	—	†	
	c. Surch inverted on 1 s. value	50·00	—	†	
	d. Surch inverted on 5 s. value	50·00	—	†	
341/3	*Set of* 3	4·25	4·25	2·00	1·60
MS344	95×80 mm. 250 s. on 25 s. Royal Mews	12·00	12·00	2·75	2·00
	a. Surch omitted	—	—	†	

(*b*) *Redrawn with new face values. Background colours changed* (29 July)

345	10 s. As No. 341	15	15
346	50 s. Type **45**	20	20
347	200 s. As No. 343	50	50
345/7	*Set of* 3	75	75
MS348	95×80 mm. 250 s. As No. **MS**344	90	1·25

Nos. 345/7 also exist perforated 12 (*price for set of* 3 75*p mint or used*) from additional sheetlets of 5 stamps and one label. These stamps have changed background colours.

The issue was originally printed with face values of 1, 5 and 20 s. and 25 s. for the miniature sheet. Before it could be placed on sale the Uganda currency was devalued and the stamps were surcharged, and later reprinted with corrected face values.

48 "Sleeping Woman before Green Shutters"

(Des J.W. Litho Questa)

1981 (21 Sept). *Birth Centenary of Picasso. T* **48** *and similar multicoloured designs. P* 14 × 13½.

349	10 s. Type **48**	10	10
350	20 s. "Bullfight"	20	20
351	30 s. "Detail of a Nude asleep in a Landscape"	25	25
352	200 s. "Interior with a Girl Drawing"	2·25	2·25
349/52	*Set of* 4	2·50	2·50
MS353	120×146 mm. 250 s. "Minotaure" (112×139 *mm*). Imperf	3·00	3·00

49 Deaf People using Sign Language

(Des Design Images. Litho Format)

1981 (28 Dec). *International Year for Disabled Persons. T* **49** *and similar horiz designs. Multicoloured. P* 15.

354	1 s. Type **49**	10	10
355	10 s. Disabled teacher in classroom	15	10
356	50 s. Teacher and disabled children	70	50
357	200 s. Blind person with guide dog	2·00	2·00
354/7	*Set of* 4	2·50	2·25
MS358	122 × 93 mm. Nos. 354/7	4·50	4·00

50 Footballers

(Des G. Vasarhelyi. Litho Questa)

1982 (11 Jan). *World Cup Football Championship, Spain. T* **50** *and similar horiz designs showing World Cup* (250 *s.*) *or footballers* (*others*). *P* 14.

359	1 s. multicoloured	10	10
360	10 s. multicoloured	15	10
361	50 s. multicoloured	70	50
362	200 s. multicoloured	2·00	2·00
359/62	*Set of* 4	2·50	2·25
MS363	116×77 mm. 250 s. multicoloured	2·75	3·00

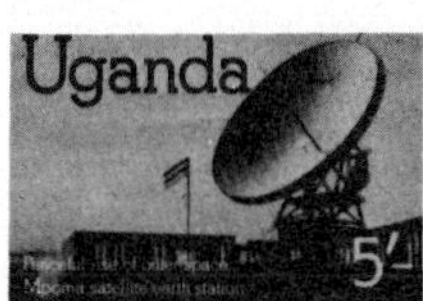

51 Mpoma Satellite Earth Station

(Des Artists International. Lithò Format)

1982 (10 May). *"Peaceful Use of Outer Space". T* **51** *and similar horiz designs. Multicoloured. P* 15.

364	5 s. Type **51**	20	15
365	10 s. *Pioneer II* (satellite)	30	25
366	50 s. Space Shuttle	1·40	1·50
367	100 s. *Voyager* 2 (satellite)	2·50	2·75
364/7	*Set of* 4	4·00	4·25
MS368	118×89 mm. 150 s. Space Shuttle (*different*)	3·25	2·00

No. 364 exists imperforate from stock dispersed by the liquidator of Format International Security Printers Ltd.

21st BIRTHDAY
HRH Princess of Wales
JULY 1 1982

52 Dr. Robert Koch (**53**)

(Des R. Vigurs. Litho Questa)

1982 (14 June). *Centenary of Robert Koch's Discovery of Tubercle Bacillus. T* **52** *and similar multicoloured designs. P* 14.
369 1 s. Type **52** 30 10
370 10 s. Microscope .. .. 1·00 40
371 50 s. Ugandans receiving vaccinations .. 2·50 2·25
372 100 s. Tubercle virus .. .. 3·75 3·25
369/72 .. .. *Set of* 4 6·75 5·50
MS373 85 × 64 mm. 150 s. Medical College class-room scene (*horiz*).. .. .. 5·00 3·25

1982 (7 July). *21st Birthday of Princess of Wales. Nos.* 345/8 *optd with T* **53.** *P* 14.
374 10 s. Prince Charles and Lady Diana Spencer 20 15
375 50 s. Type **45** 75 50
376 200 s. Prince Charles at Balmoral .. .. 2·50 2·00
374/6 .. .. *Set of* 3 3·00 2·40
MS377 95 × 82 mm. 250 s. Royal Mews .. .. 2·75 2·25
Nos. 374/6 also exist perforated 12 (*price for set of* 3 £1·75 *mint or used*) from additional sheetlets of 5 stamps and one label. These stamps have changed background colours.
Nos. 374/7, and the sheetlets, also exist with the top line of the overprint shown as "21st Birthday" instead of "21st BIRTHDAY" as in Type **53**. (*Price for set of* 3 *and miniature sheet* £8 *mint*).

Examples of an unissued 150 s. miniature sheet for the 20th Anniversary of Independence exist from stock dispersed by the liquidator of Format International Security Printers Ltd.

54 Yellow-billed Hornbill **55** Scout Band

(Des Artists International. Litho Questa)

1982 (12 July). *Birds. T* **54** *and similar vert designs. Multicoloured. P* 14.
378 1 s. Type **54** 15 10
379 20 s. Superb Starling.. .. .. 60 35
380 50 s. Bateleur.. .. .. 1·25 1·50
381 100 s. Saddle-bill Stork .. .. 2·00 2·50
378/81 .. .. *Set of* 4 3·50 4·00
MS382 115 × 85 mm. 200 s. Laughing Dove .. 6·00 6·00

(Des G. Vasarhelyi. Litho Questa)

1982 (23 Aug). *75th Anniv of Boy Scout Movement. T* **55** *and similar horiz designs. Multicoloured. P* 14.
383 5 s. Type **55** 40 10
384 20 s. Scout receiving Bata Shoe trophy .. 90 45
385 50 s. Scouts with wheelchair patient.. .. 2·00 1·50
386 100 s. First aid instruction .. .. .. 2·75 2·75
383/6 .. .. *Set of* 4 5·50 4·25
MS387 112 × 85 mm. 150 s. Lord Baden-Powell .. .. 3·75 3·00

56 Swearing-in of Roosevelt

(Des Design Images. Litho Format)

1982 (8 Nov). *250th Birth Anniv of George Washington (Nos.* 389/90) *and Birth Centenary of Franklin D. Roosevelt (others). T* **56** *and similar horiz designs. Multicoloured. P* 15.
388 50 s. Type **56** 30 30
389 200 s. Swearing-in of Washington .. .. 1·25 1·25
MS390 100 × 69 mm. 150 s. Washington at Mt Vernon .. .. 1·40 1·60
MS391 100 × 70 mm. 150 s. Roosevelt at Hyde Park Mansion .. .. 1·40 1·60

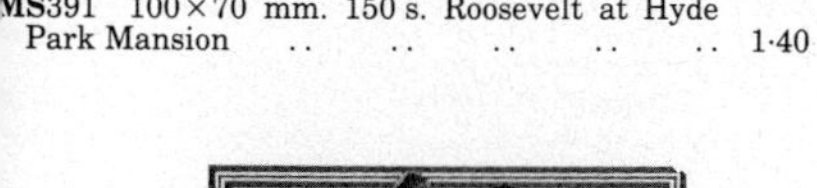

57 Italy v West Germany

(Des D. Miller. Litho)

1982 (30 Dec). *World Cup Football Championship Winners. T* **57** *and similar horiz designs. Multicoloured. P* 14½.
392 10 s. Type **57** 50 25
393 200 s. Victorious Italian team.. .. .. 2·50 2·75
MS394 97 × 117 mm. 250 s. Espana '82 emblem with Spanish and Italian flags .. .. .. 1·90 2·40

500th ANNIVERSARY BIRTH OF RAPHAEL
UGANDA 5/-

58 Dancers **59** "St. George and the Dragon" (Raphael)

(Des and litho Questa)

1983 (14 Mar). *Commonwealth Day. Cultural Art. T* **58** *and similar horiz designs. Multicoloured. P* 14.
395 5 s. Type **58** 10 10
396 20 s. Traditional currency 20 20
397 50 s. Homestead 45 45
398 100 s. Drums 85 85
395/8 .. .. *Set of* 4 1·40 1·40

(Des Design Images. Litho Questa)

1983 (16 Apr). *500th Birth Anniv of Raphael (painter). T* **59** *and similar vert designs. Multicoloured. P* 13½.
399 5 s. Type **59** 10 10
400 20 s. "St. George and the Dragon" (*different*) 30 30
401 50 s. "Crossing the Red Sea" (*detail*).. .. 70 70
402 200 s. "The Expulsion of Heliodorus" (*detail*) .. 2·25 2·50
399/402 .. .. *Set of* 4 3·00 3·25
MS403 126 × 101 mm. 250 s. "The Meeting of Pope Leo the Great and Attila the Hun" (*detail*) .. .. 1·50 1·75

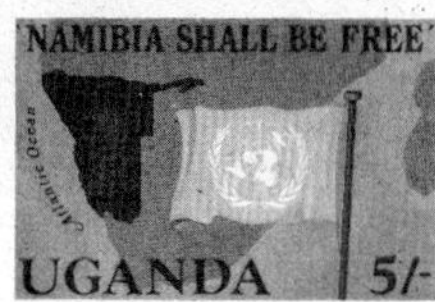

60 Map showing Namibia and U.N. Flag

(Des R. Vigurs. Litho Format)

1983 (15 Aug). *Commemorations. T* **60** *and similar horiz design. Multicoloured. P* 15.
404 5 s. Type **60** 10 10
405 200 s. 7th Non-aligned Summit Conference logo 1·25 1·75

BOYS BRIGADE CENTENARY 1883-1983

61 Elephants in Grassland **(62)**

(Des J. Iskowitz. Litho Format)

1983 (22 Aug). *Endangered Species (1st series). T* **61** *and similar multicoloured designs. P* 15.
406 5 s. Elephants in "Elephants' Graveyard" 60 20
407 10 s. Type **61** 90 35
408 30 s. Elephants at waterhole .. .. 2·00 1·50
409 70 s. Elephants having dust bath .. .. 3·25 2·75
406/9 .. .. *Set of* 4 6·00 4·25
MS410 87 × 64 mm. 300 s. Grevy's Zebra drinking (*vert*) .. .. 2·50 3·00
See also Nos. 642 and 970/4.

1983 (19 Sept). *Centenary of Boys' Brigade. Nos.* 383/7 *optd with T* **62** *or surch also.*
411 5 s. Type **55** 10 10
412 20 s. Scout receiving Bata Shoe trophy .. 15 15
413 50 s. Scouts with wheelchair patient .. 25 30
414 400 s. on 100 s. First aid instruction .. 2·40 2·75
411/14 .. .. *Set of* 4 2·50 3·00
MS415 112 × 85 mm. 150 s. Lord Baden-Powell .. 90 1·25

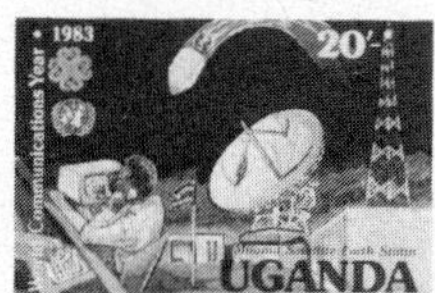

100/-

63 Mpoma Satellite Earth Station **(64)**

(Des D. Dorfman. Litho Format)

1983 (3 Oct). *World Communications Year. T* **63** *and similar horiz designs. Multicoloured. P* 15.
416 20 s. Type **63** 20 15
417 50 s. Railroad computer and operator .. 55 55
418 70 s. Cameraman filming lions 65 70
419 100 s. Aircraft cockpit .. .. 85 1·00
416/19 .. .. *Set of* 4 2·00 2·25
MS420 128 × 103 mm. 300 s. Communications satellite .. .. 1·60 2·00
No. 416 has the "o" omitted from "Station".

1983 (7 Oct). *Nos.* 303, 305/7, 308A, 309 *and* 313A *surch as T* **64**.
421 100 s. on 10 c. Type **37** 45 45
422 135 s. on 1 s. Type **38** 60 60
423 175 s. on 30 c. Thomson's Gazelle 75 75
424 200 s. on 50 c. Lesser Bushbaby 85 85
425 400 s. on 80 c. Hunting Dog .. .. 1·60 1·60
426 700 s. on 5 s. Waterbuck .. .. .. 2·75 3·00
427 1000 s. on 1 s. 50, Gorilla .. .. .. 4·00 4·00
421/7 .. .. *Set of* 7 10·00 10·00

65 The Nativity

(Des PAD Studio. Litho Questa)

1983 (12 Dec). *Christmas. T* **65** *and similar horiz designs. Multicoloured. P* 14.
428 10 s. Type **65**.. .. .. 10 10
429 50 s. Shepherds and Angels 25 30
430 175 s. Flight into Egypt .. .. .. 80 1·00
431 400 s. Angels blowing trumpets .. .. 1·90 2·25
428/31 .. .. *Set of* 4 2·75 3·25
MS432 85 × 57 mm. 300 s. The Three Kings .. 1·40 1·50

1983 (19 Dec). *Designs as Nos.* 308/12 *and* 315/16 *but with face values in revalued currency.*
433 100 s. Type **38** 65 35
434 135 s. Gorilla 75 50
435 175 s. Common Zebra 95 70
436 200 s. Leopard with cub .. .. 1·25 80
437 400 s. Black Rhinoceros .. .. 2·00 2·00
438 700 s. African Elephant .. .. 3·50 3·75
439 1000 s. Hippopotamus .. .. 4·25 4·75
433/9 .. .. *Set of* 7 12·00 11·50

66 Ploughing with Oxen

(Des J.W. Litho Questa)

1984 (16 Jan). *World Food Day. T* **66** *and similar horiz design. Multicoloured. P* 14.
440 10 s. Type **66**.. .. .. 10 10
441 300 s. Harvesting bananas .. .. .. 3·00 3·00

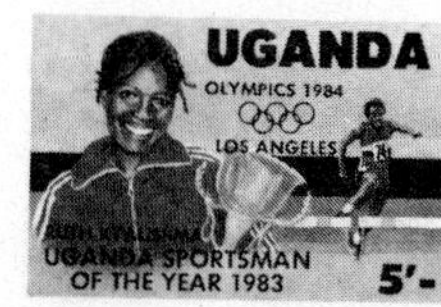

67 Ruth Kyalisiima, Sportsman of the Year 1983

(Des J. Iskowitz. Litho Format)

1984 (1 Oct). *Olympic Games, Los Angeles. T* **67** *and similar multicoloured designs. P* 15.
442 5 s. Type **67**.. .. .. 10 10
443 115 s. Javelin-throwing 40 45
444 155 s. Wrestling 50 55
445 175 s. Rowing 60 65
442/5 .. .. *Set of* 4 1·40 1·50
MS446 108 × 79 mm. 500 s. Fund-raising walk (*vert*) .. .. 1·50 1·60

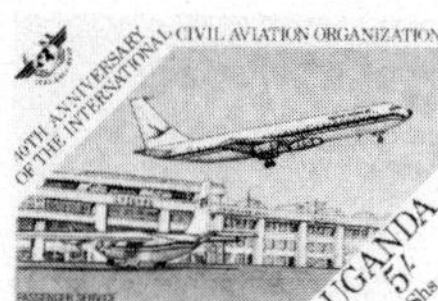

68 Entebbe Airport

(Des BG Studio. Litho Format)

1984 (29 Oct). *40th Anniv of International Civil Aviation Organization. T* **68** *and similar horiz designs. Multicoloured. P* 15.
447 5 s. Type **68**.. .. .. 15 10
448 115 s. Loading cargo plane .. .. .. 1·50 1·50
449 155 s. Uganda police helicopter .. .. 2·25 2·25
450 175 s. East African Civil Flying School, Soroti 2·50 2·50
447/50 .. .. *Set of* 4 5·75 5·50
MS451 100 × 70 mm. 250 s. Balloon race .. 2·25 1·75

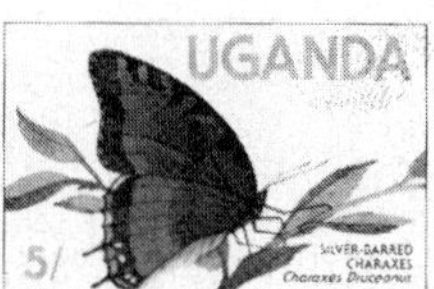

69 *Charaxes druceanus*

(Des J. Johnson. Litho Questa)

1984 (19 Nov). *Butterflies. T* **69** *and similar horiz designs. Multi-coloured. P* 14.

452 5 s. Type **69** 25 10
453 115 s. *Papilio lormieri* .. .. .. 1·60 1·25
454 155 s. *Druryia antimachus* .. .. .. 2·00 1·50
455 175 s. *Salamis temora* .. .. .. 2·75 1·75
452/5 .. .. *Set of* 4 6·00 4·25
MS456 127×90 mm. 250 s. *Colotis protomedia* 1·50 1·50

70 *Nothobranchius taeniopygus*

(Des Associated Creative Designers. Litho Format)

1985 (1 Apr–10 June). *Lake Fishes. T* **70** *and similar horiz designs. Multicoloured. P* 15.

457 5 s. Type **70** 10 10
458 10 s. *Bagrus dogmac* 15 10
459 50 s. *Polypterus senegalus* 45 15
460 100 s. *Clarias* 45 20
461 135 s. *Mormyrus kannume* (10 June) .. 50 35
462 175 s. *Synodontis victoriae* 50 50
463 205 s. *Haplochromis brownae* 60 60
464 400 s. *Lates niloticus* 80 80
465 700 s. *Protopterus aethiopicus* .. .. 1·00 1·00
466 1000 s. *Barbus radcliffii* .. .. .. 1·25 1·25
467 2500 s. *Malapterus electricus* (10 June) .. 1·25 1·25
457/67 .. .. *Set of* 11 6·25 5·75

71 The Last Supper

(Des Associated Creative Designers. Litho Questa)

1985 (13 May). *Easter. T* **71** *and similar horiz designs. Multicoloured. P* 14.

468 5 s. Type **71** 10 10
469 115 s. Christ showing the nail marks to Thomas 70 40
470 155 s. The raising of the Cross 80 50
471 175 s. Pentecost 95 60
468/71 .. .. *Set of* 4 2·25 1·40
MS472 99×70 mm. 250 s. The last prayer in the Garden .. .. 80 1·00

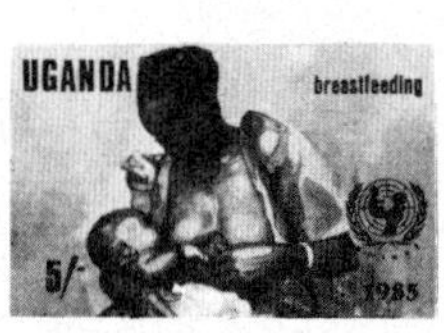

72 Breast Feeding

73 Queen Elizabeth the Queen Mother

(Des Associated Creative Designers. Litho Questa)

1985 (29 July). *U.N.I.C.E.F. Child Survival Campaign. T* **72** *and similar horiz designs. Multicoloured. P* 14.

473 5 s. Type **72** 10 10
474 115 s. Growth monitoring .. .. .. 1·00 1·00
475 155 s. Immunisation .. .. 1·40 1·40
476 175 s. Oral re-hydration therapy .. .. 1·60 1·60
473/6 .. .. *Set of* 4 3·50 3·50
MS477 75×55 mm. 500 s. Pregnant woman preparing nourishing food .. .. 3·00 3·00

(Des J.W. Litho Questa)

1985 (21 Aug). *Life and Times of Queen Elizabeth the Queen Mother and Decade for Women. T* **73** *and similar vert design. Multicoloured. P* 14.

478 1000 s. Type **73** .. .. 2·00 2·10
MS479 57×81 mm. 1500 s. The Queen Mother inspecting Kings African Rifles, Kampala .. 3·25 3·50

74 Sedge Warbler

GOLD MEDALIST
BENITA BROWN-FITZGERALD
USA

(**75**)

(Des S. Heinmann. Litho Questa)

1985 (21 Aug). *Birth Bicentenary of John J. Audubon (ornithologist) (1st issue). T* **74** *and similar vert designs. Multi-coloured. P* 14.

480 115 s. Type **74** .. .. 1·00 1·00
481 155 s. Cattle Egret .. .. 1·25 1·25
482 175 s. Crested Lark .. .. 1·50 1·50
483 500 s. Tufted Duck .. .. 2·00 2·00
480/3 .. .. *Set of* 4 5·25 5·25
MS484 99×69 mm. 1000 s. Tawny Owl .. .. 7·00 5·00

See also Nos. 494/8.

1985 (21 Aug). *Olympic Gold Medal Winners, Los Angeles. Nos. 442/6 optd or surch as T* **75** *in gold.*

485 5 s. Type **67** (optd T **75**) 10 10
486 115 s. Javelin-throwing (optd "GOLD MEDALIST ARTO HÄERKOENEN FINLAND") 25 30
487 155 s. Wrestling (optd "GOLD MEDALIST ATSUJI MIYAHARA JAPAN") .. 30 35
488 1000 s. on 175 s. Rowing (surch "GOLD MEDALIST WEST GERMANY") .. 1·90 2·00
485/8 .. .. *Set of* 4 2·25 2·00
MS489 108×79 mm. 1200 s. on 500 s. Fund-raising walk (surch "MEN'S HURDLES EDWIN MOSES USA") .. .. 2·25 2·50

On No. **MS**489 only the new value appears on the stamp, the remainder of the surcharge is on the sheet margin.

76 Women carrying National Women's Day Banner

77 Man beneath Tree laden with Produce (F.A.O.)

(Des and litho Questa)

1985 (1 Nov). *Decade for Women. T* **76** *and similar multicoloured designs. P* 14.

490 5 s. Type **76** 10 10
491 115 s. Girl Guides (*horiz*) .. .. .. 1·25 1·25
492 155 s. Mother Teresa (Nobel Peace Prize winner, 1979) .. .. 2·00 2·00
490/2 .. .. *Set of* 3 3·00 3·00
MS493 85×59 mm. 1500 s. As 115 s. .. .. 3·50 3·50

Nos. 491 and **MS**493 also commemorate the 75th anniversary of the Girl Guide movement.

(Litho Questa)

1985 (23 Dec). *Birth Bicentenary of John J. Audubon (ornithologist) (2nd issue). Multicoloured designs as T* **201** *of Maldive Islands, but horiz, showing original paintings. P* 12.

494 5 s. Rock Ptarmigan 45 10
495 155 s. Sage Grouse .. .. 1·50 1·25
496 175 s. Lesser Yellowlegs .. .. .. 1·75 1·75
497 500 s. Brown-headed Cowbird .. .. 2·75 2·75
494/7 .. .. *Set of* 4 5·75 5·25
MS498 72×102 mm. 1000 s. Whooping Crane. P 14 .. .. 7·00 6·00

Nos. 494/7 were each printed in sheetlets of 5 stamps and one stamp-size label which appears in the centre of the bottom row.

(Des BG Studio. Litho Format)

1986 (1 Apr). *40th Anniv of United Nations Organization. T* **77** *and similar designs. P* 15.

499 10 s. multicoloured 10 10
500 180 s. multicoloured 60 30
501 200 s. new blue, agate and bright green .. 65 35
502 250 s. new blue, brownish blk & scar-verm 70 40
503 2000 s. multicoloured .. .. 3·00 3·50
499/503 .. .. *Set of* 5 4·50 4·25
MS504 69×69 mm. 2500 s. multicoloured .. 2·50 2·75

Designs: *Horiz*—180 s. Soldier of U.N. Peace-Keeping Force; 250 s. Hands releasing peace dove. *Vert*—200 s. U.N. emblem; 2000 s. Flags of U.N. and Uganda; 2500 s. U.N. Building, New York, and flags of member nations.

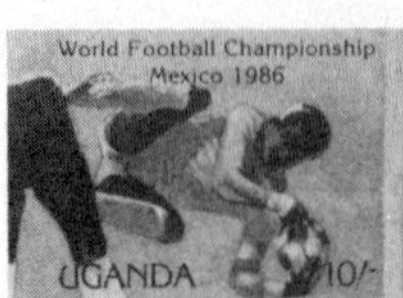

78 Goalkeeper catching Ball

NRA LIBERATION
1986

(**79**)

(Des Shelley Haas. Litho Questa)

1986 (17 Apr). *World Cup Football Championship, Mexico. T* **78** *and similar multicoloured designs. P* 14.

505 10 s. Type **78** 10 10
506 180 s. Player with ball 75 45
507 250 s. Two players competing for ball .. 85 55
508 2500 s. Player running with ball .. .. 4·00 4·50
505/8 .. .. *Set of* 4 5·00 5·00
MS509 87×66 mm. 3000 s. Player kicking ball (*vert*) .. .. 4·25 3·50

1986 (30 Apr). *Liberation by National Resistance Army. Nos. 462, 464/7 and* **MS**493 *optd with T* **79** *or larger* (22×8 *mm*) (*No.* **MS**493).

510 175 s. *Synodontis victoriae* (Sil.) 50 50
511 400 s. *Lates niloticus* 80 80
512 700 s. *Protopteris aethiopicus* (Sil.) .. 1·40 1·40
513 1000 s. *Barbus radcliffii* .. .. .. 1·75 2·00
514 2500 s. *Malapterus electricus* .. .. 3·25 3·50
510/14 .. .. *Set of* 5 7·00 7·25
MS514*a* 85×59 mm. 1500 s. Girl Guides .. 3·00 2·50

Nos. 510/14 also exist with the overprint colours transposed.

(Des W. Hanson. Litho Questa)

1986 (30 Apr). *Appearance of Halley's Comet* (1*st issue*). *Horiz designs as T* **162***a of Lesotho. Multicoloured. P* 14.

515 50 s. Tycho Brahe and Arecibo Radio Telescope, Puerto Rico 20 1
516 100 s. Recovery of astronaut John Glenn from sea, 1962 .. .. .. 35 1
517 140 s. "The Star in the East" (painting by (Giotto) 50 3
518 2500 s. Death of Davy Crockett at the Alamo, 1835 .. .. 3·50 4·0
515/18 .. .. *Set of* 4 4·00 4·0
MS519 102×70 mm. 3000 s. Halley's Comet over Uganda .. .. 5·00 4·0

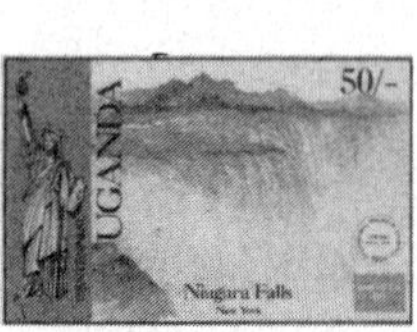

80 Niagara Falls

81 *Gloria* (Colombia)

(Des Mary Walters. Litho Format)

1986 (22 May). *"Ameripex '86" International Stamp Exhibition Chicago. American Landmarks. T* **80** *and similar hori designs. Multicoloured. P* 15.

520 50 s. Type **80** 15 1
521 100 s. Jefferson Memorial, Washington D.C. 25 1
522 250 s. Liberty Bell, Philadelphia 50 3
523 1000 s. The Alamo, San Antonio, Texas .. 1·75 1·6
524 2500 s. George Washington Bridge, New York–New Jersey .. .. .. 3·25 3·2
520/4 .. .. *Set of* 5 5·50 4·7
MS525 87×64 mm. 3000 s. Grand Canyon .. 3·00 3·2

(Litho Questa)

1986 (24 May). *60th Birthday of Queen Elizabeth II. Ver designs as T* **163***a of Lesotho. P* 14.

526 100 s. black and yellow 25 1
527 140 s. multicoloured 30 2
528 2500 s. multicoloured .. .. .. 3·00 3·0
526/8 .. .. *Set of* 3 3·25 3·0
MS529 120×85 mm. 3000 s. black & grey-brown 3·25 3·5

Designs:—100 s. Princess Elizabeth at London Zoo; 140 s Queen Elizabeth at race meeting, 1970; 2500 s. With Princ Philip at Sandringham, 1982; 3000 s. Engagement photograph 1947.

(Des J. Iskowitz. Litho Questa)

1986 (2 July). *Centenary of Statue of Liberty. T* **81** *and simila multicoloured designs showing cadet sailing ships. P* 14.

530 50 s. Type **81** 35 1
531 100 s. *Mircea* (Rumania) 65 3
532 140 s. *Sagres II* (Portugal) (*horiz*) .. .. 1·00 8
533 2500 s. *Gazela Primiero* (U.S.A.) (*horiz*) .. 5·50 6·5
530/3 .. .. *Set of* 4 6·75 7·0
MS534 113×82 mm. 3000 s. Statue of Liberty .. 3·25 3·5

(Des and litho Questa)

1986 (23 July). *Royal Wedding. Multicoloured designs as T* **170***a of Lesotho. P* 14.

535 50 s. Prince Andrew and Miss Sarah Ferguson (*horiz*) 10 1
536 140 s. Prince Andrew with Princess Anne at shooting match (*horiz*) 20 2
537 2500 s. Prince Andrew and Miss Sarah Ferguson at Ascot (*horiz*) .. .. 2·75 3·0
535/7 .. .. *Set of* 3 2·75 3·0
MS538 88×88 mm. 3000 s. Prince Andrew and Miss Sarah Ferguson (*different*) .. .. .. 3·50 3·2

WINNERS

Argentina 3 W.Germany 2

(**82**)

1986 (15 Sept). *World Cup Football Championship Winners Mexico. Nos. 505/9 optd as T* **82**, *or surch also, in gold.*

539 50 s. on 10 s. Type **78** 10 1
540 180 s. Player with ball 25 2
541 250 s. Two players competing for ball .. 35 3
542 2500 s. Player running with ball .. .. 2·75 3·2
539/42 .. .. *Set of* 4 3·00 3·5
MS543 87×66 mm. 3000 s. Player kicking ball (*vert*) .. .. 3·50 3·2

986 (15 Oct). *Appearance of Halley's Comet* (*2nd issue*). *Nos.* 515/19 *optd with T* **213b** *of Maldive Islands* (*in silver on* 3000 *s.*).
544 50 s. Tycho Brahe and Arecibo Radio Telescope, Puerto Rico 20 15
545 100 s. Recovery of astronaut John Glenn from sea, 1962 .. .. 35 20
546 140 s. "The Star in the East" (painting by Giotto) 55 40
547 2500 s. Death of Davy Crockett at the Alamo, 1835 .. .. 4·25 4·25
544/7 .. .. *Set of* 4 4·75 4·50
MS548 102 × 70 mm. 3000 s. Halley's Comet over Uganda .. .. 3·00 3·50

83 St. Kizito

(Des Associated Creative Designers. Litho Questa)

1986 (15 Oct). *Christian Martyrs of Uganda. T* **83** *and similar horiz designs. Multicoloured. P* 14.
549 50 s. Type **83** 10 10
550 150 s. St. Kizito instructing converts .. 15 20
551 200 s. Martyrdom of Bishop James Hannington, 1885.. .. .. 20 25
552 1000 s. Burning of Bugandan Christians, 1886 .. .. 1·00 1·50
549/52 .. .. *Set of* 4 1·25 1·75
MS553 89 × 59 mm. 1500 s. King Mwanga of Buganda passing sentence on Christians .. 1·50 2·00

84 "Madonna of the Cherries" (Titian)

(Litho Questa)

1986 (26 Nov). *Christmas. Religious Paintings. T* **84** *and similar multicoloured designs. P* 14.
554 50 s. Type **84** 20 15
555 150 s. "Madonna and Child" (Dürer) (*vert*).. 50 30
556 200 s. "Assumption of the Virgin" (Titian) (*vert*) 60 35
557 2500 s. "Praying Hands" (Dürer) (*vert*) .. 4·00 4·50
554/7 .. .. *Set of* 4 4·75 4·75
MS558 Two sheets, each 102 × 76 mm. (a) 3000 s. "Presentation of the Virgin in the Temple" (Titian). (b) 3000 s. "Adoration of the Magi" (Dürer) .. .. .. *Set of 2 sheets* 5·00 5·50

85 Red-billed Firefinch and Glory Lily

(Litho Format)

1987 (22 July). *Flora and Fauna. T* **85** *and similar horiz designs. Multicoloured. P* 15.
559 2 s. Type **85**.. .. .. 10 10
560 5 s. African Pygmy Kingfisher and Nandi Flame 15 15
561 10 s. Scarlet-chested Sunbird and Crown of Thorns 20 25
562 25 s. White Rhinoceros and Yellow-billed Oxpecker 50 55
563 35 s. Lion and Elephant Grass 70 75
564 45 s. Cheetahs and Doum Palm 90 95
565 50 s. Cordon Bleu and Desert Rose .. 1·00 1·10
566 100 s. Giant Eland and Acacia .. .. 2·00 2·10
559/66 .. .. *Set of* 8 5·00 5·25
MS567 98 × 67 mm. (a) 150 s. Carmine Bee Eaters and Sausage Tree. (b) 150 s. Cattle Egret and Zebras .. .. .. *Set of 2 sheets* 6·00 7·00

86 Tremml's *Eagle* (longest man-powered flight), 1987

(Des W. Hanson. Litho Format)

1987 (14 Aug). *Milestones of Transportation. T* **86** *and similar horiz designs. Multicoloured. P* 15.
568 2 s. Type **86**.. .. .. 10 10
569 3 s. Junkers "W-33L" *Bremen* (first east-west transatlantic flight), 1928 .. 10 10
570 5 s. Lockheed *Winnie Mae* (Post's first solo round-the-world flight), 1933.. .. 20 20
571 10 s. *Voyager* (first non-stop round-the-world flight), 1986 .. .. 40 40
572 15 s. Chanute biplane glider, 1896 .. 60 60
573 25 s. Airship *Norge* and Polar Bear (first transpolar flight), 1926 .. .. 90 90
574 35 s. Curtis biplane and U.S.S. *Pennsylvania* (first take-off and landing from ship), 1911 .. .. 1·25 1·25
575 45 s. Shepard and "Freedom 7" spacecraft (first American in space), 1961 .. 1·40 1·40
576 100 s. "Concorde" (first supersonic passenger flight), 1976 .. .. 3·50 3·50
568/76 .. .. *Set of* 9 7·50 7·50

87 Olympic Torch-bearer

(Litho Questa)

1987 (5 Oct). *Olympic Games, Seoul* (1988) (*1st issue*). *T* **87** *and similar horiz designs. Multicoloured. P* 14.
577 5 s. Type **87**.. .. .. 10 10
578 10 s. Swimming 20 25
579 50 s. Cycling.. .. .. 1·00 1·10
580 100 s. Gymnastics .. .. 2·00 2·10
577/80 .. .. *Set of* 4 3·00 3·25
MS581 100 × 75 mm. 150 s. Boxing .. .. 3·00 4·00
See also Nos. 628/32.

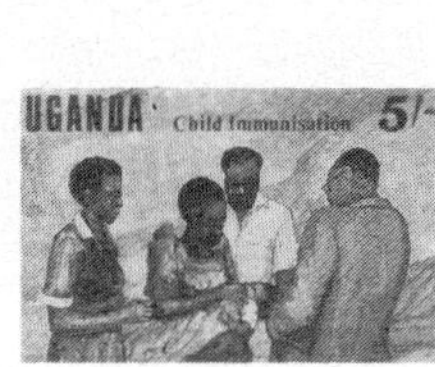

88 Child Immunization **89** Golden-backed Weaver

(Des Associated Creative Designers. Litho Questa)

1987 (8 Oct) *25th Anniv of Independence. T* **88** *and similar horiz designs. P* 14.
582 5 s. multicoloured 10 10
583 10 s. multicoloured 20 25
584 25 s. multicoloured 50 55
585 50 s. multicoloured .. .. 1·00 1·10
582/5 .. .. *Set of* 4 1·60 1·75
MS586 90 × 70 mm. 100 s. black, bright scarlet and greenish yellow .. .. 2·00 2·75
Designs:—10 s. Mulago Hospital, Kampala; 25 s. Independence Monument, Kampala City Park; 50 s. High Court, Kampala; 100 s. Stylized head of Crested Crane, "25" and Ugandan flag.

(Des Jennifer Toombs. Litho Questa)

1987 (19 Oct). *Birds of Uganda. T* **89** *and similar multicoloured designs. P* 14.
587 5 s. Type **89**.. .. .. 25 25
588 10 s. Hoopoe 40 40
589 15 s. Red-throated Bee Eater 50 50
590 25 s. Lilac-breasted Roller 75 75
591 35 s. Pygmy Goose .. .. 1·10 1·10
592 45 s. Scarlet-chested Sunbird .. .. 1·40 1·40
593 50 s. Crowned Crane .. .. 1·50 1·50
594 100 s. Long-tailed Fiscal Shrike .. .. 2·50 2·50
587/94 .. .. *Set of* 8 7·75 7·75
MS595 80 × 60 mm. (a) 150 s. African Fish Eagle. (b) 150 s. African Barn Owl *Set of 2 sheets* 6·00 7·00

90 Hippocrates (physician) and Surgeons performing Operation

(Des L. Nelson. Litho Questa)

1987 (2 Nov). *Great Scientific Discoveries. T* **90** *and similar multicoloured designs. P* 14.
596 5 s. Type **90** 30 30
597 25 s. Einstein and Deep Space (Theory of Relativity) .. .. 1·25 1·25
598 35 s. Isaac Newton and diagram from *Opticks* (Theory of Colour and Light) .. 1·50 1·50
599 45 s. Karl Benz, early Benz and modern Mercedes cars .. .. 2·00 2·00
596/9 .. .. *Set of* 4 4·50 4·50
MS600 97 × 70 mm. 150 s. *Challenger* (space shuttle) (*vert*) .. .. 3·00 3·75

COVER PRICES

Cover factors are quoted at the beginning of each country for most issues to 1945. An explanation of the system can be found on page x. The factors quoted do not, however, apply to philatelic covers.

91 Scout with Album and Uganda Stamps

(Des Mary Walters. Litho Questa)

1987 (20 Nov). *World Scout Jamboree, Australia. T* **91** *and similar horiz designs. Multicoloured. P* 14.
601 5 s. Type **91** 10 10
602 25 s. Scouts planting tree 50 55
603 35 s. Canoeing on Lake Victoria 70 75
604 45 s. Hiking 90 95
601/4 .. .. *Set of* 4 2·00 2·25
MS605 95 × 65 mm. 150 s. Jamboree and Uganda scout emblems .. .. 3·00 3·75

92 "The Annunciation"

(Litho Questa)

1987 (18 Dec). *Christmas. T* **92** *and similar multicoloured designs showing scenes from French diptych, c.* 1250. *P* 14.
606 5 s. Type **92**.. .. .. 10 10
607 10 s. "The Nativity".. .. .. 20 25
608 50 s. "Flight into Egypt" .. .. .. 1·00 1·10
609 100 s. "The Adoration of the Magi" .. .. 2·00 2·10
606/9 .. .. *Set of* 4 3·00 3·25
MS610 76 × 105 mm. 150 s. "Mystic Wine" (tapestry detail) (*vert*) .. .. 3·00 3·50

93 Class "12" Light Shunter Locomotive **94** Columbite-Tantalite

(Des BG Studio. Litho Questa)

1988 (18 Jan). *Locomotives of East Africa Railways. T* **93** *and similar horiz designs. Multicoloured. P* 14.
611 5 s. Type **93** 30 30
612 10 s. Class "92" diesel-electric 30 30
613 15 s. Locomotive No. 2506 .. .. .. 35 35
614 25 s. Tank locomotive No. 126 .. .. 55 55
615 35 s. Class "31" locomotive 70 70
616 45 s. Class "31" locomotive (*different*) .. 85 85
617 50 s. Class "59" Double Garratt locomotive 95 95
618 100 s. Class "87" diesel-electric shunter .. 1·75 1·75
611/18 .. .. *Set of* 8 5·25 5·25
MS619 Two sheets, each 100 × 74 mm. (a) 150 s. Class "31". (b) 150 s. Class "59" Double Garratt *Set of 2 sheets* 4·00 4·50

(Des Mary Walters. Litho Questa)

1988 (18 Jan). *Minerals. T* **94** *and similar vert designs. Multicoloured. P* 14.
620 1 s. Type **94** 10 10
621 2 s. Galena 15 15
622 5 s. Malachite 20 20
623 10 s. Cassiterite 35 35
624 35 s. Ferberite .. .. 1·00 1·00
625 50 s. Emerald .. .. 1·40 1·40
626 100 s. Monazite .. .. 2·25 2·25
627 150 s. Microcline .. .. 3·25 3·25
620/7 .. .. *Set of* 8 7·75 7·75

95 Hurdling

(Des BG Studio. Litho Questa)

1988 (16 May). *Olympic Games, Seoul* (*2nd issue*). *T* **95** *and similar horiz designs. Multicoloured. P* 14.
628 5 s. Type **95** 10 10
629 25 s. High jumping 20 25
630 35 s. Javelin throwing 25 30
631 45 s. Long jumping 30 35
628/31 .. .. *Set of* 4 70 90
MS632 85 × 114 mm. 150 s. Olympic medals .. 1·00 1·50

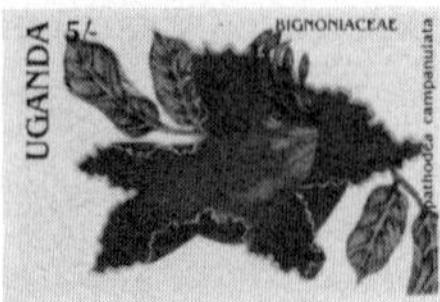

96 *Spathodea campanulata*

(Des L. Nelson. Litho Format)

1988 (29 July). *Flowers. T* **96** *and similar multicoloured designs. P* 15.
633 5 s. Type **96** 10 10
634 10 s. *Gloriosa simplex* 10 10
635 20 s. *Thevetica peruviana (vert)* 15 15
636 25 s. *Hibiscus schizopetalus* 20 25
637 35 s. *Aframomum sceptrum* 25 30
638 45 s. *Adenium obesum* 30 35
639 50 s. *Kigelia africana (vert)* 35 40
640 100 s. *Clappertonia ficifolia* 70 75
633/40 .. .. *Set of* 8 1·90 2·10
MS641 Two sheets, each 109 × 79 mm. (a) 150 s. *Costus spectabilis.* (b) 150 s. *Canarina abyssinica (vert)* .. .. *Set of* 2 *sheets* 2·00 2·50

97 Elephants in Grassland (Type **61** redrawn)

(Litho Questa)

1988 (29 July). *Endangered Species* (2*nd series*). *P* 14.
642 **97** 10 s. multicoloured .. .. ..

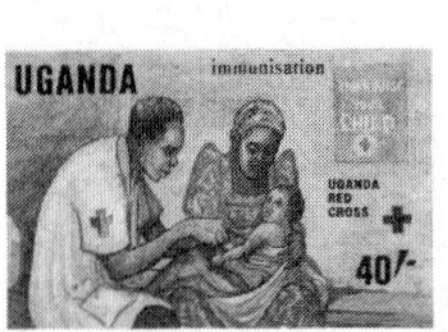

98 Red Cross Worker vaccinating Baby

99 Giraffes, Kidepo Valley National Park

(Des Associated Creative Art Designers. Litho Questa)

1988 (28 Oct). *125th Anniv of International Red Cross. T* **98** *and similar designs. P* 14.
643 10 s. bright scarlet, pale yellow and black 20 15
644 40 s. multicoloured 50 50
645 70 s. multicoloured 90 90
646 90 s. multicoloured .. .. .. 1·25 1·25
643/6 .. .. *Set of* 4 2·50 2·50
MS647 110 × 78 mm. 150 s. multicoloured .. 1·00 1·40
Designs: *Horiz*—10 s. "AIDS" with test tube as "I"; 70 s. Distributing food to refugees; 90 s. Red Cross volunteers with accident victim. *Vert*—150 s. Henri Dunant (founder).

(Litho Questa)

1988 (31 Oct). *500th Birth Anniv of Titian (artist). Vert designs as T* **186a** *of Lesotho. Multicoloured. P* 13½×14.
648 10 s. "Portrait of a Lady" 10 10
649 20 s. "Portrait of a Man" 15 15
650 40 s. "Isabella d'Este" 25 30
651 50 s. "Vincenzo Mosti" 35 40
652 70 s. "Pope Paul III Farnese" 45 50
653 90 s. "Violante" 60 65
654 100 s. "Titian's Daughter Lavinia" 70 75
655 250 s. "Dr. Parma" .. .. 1·75 1·90
648/55 .. .. *Set of* 8 3·75 4·25
MS656 Two sheets, each 110 × 95 mm. (a) 350 s. "The Speech of Alfonso D'Avalos" (detail). (b) 350 s. "Cain and Abel" (detail) .. *Set of* 2 *sheets* 5·00 6·00

(Des Mary Walters. Litho Questa)

1988 (18 Nov). *National Parks of Uganda. T* **99** *and similar vert designs. Multicoloured. P* 14.
657 10 s. Type **99** 30 15
658 25 s. Zebras, Lake Mburo National Park 55 30
659 100 s. African Buffalo, Murchison Falls National Park .. .. .. 1·50 1·50
660 250 s. Pelicans, Queen Elizabeth National Park .. .. 3·50 3·75
657/60 .. .. *Set of* 4 5·25 5·25
MS661 97 × 68 mm. 350 s. Roan Antelopes, Lake Mburo National Park .. .. 2·50 3·00

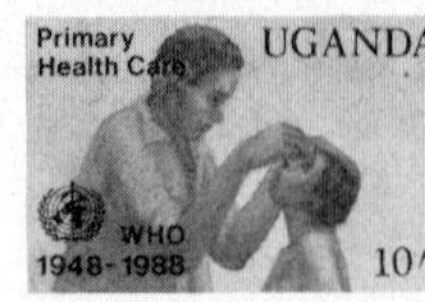

100 Doctor examining Child's Eyes

(Des L. Watkins. Litho Questa)

1988 (1 Dec). *40th Anniv of World Health Organization. T* **100** *and similar horiz designs. Multicoloured. P* 14.
662 10 s. Type **100** 10 10
663 25 s. Mental health therapist with patient 20 25
664 45 s. Surgeon performing operation .. 30 35
665 100 s. Dentist treating girl 70 75
666 200 s. Doctor examining child .. .. 1·40 1·50
662/6 .. .. *Set of* 5 2·40 2·75
MS667 107 × 88 mm. 350 s. Delegates approving Declaration of Alma-Ata, 1978 .. .. 2·50 3·00

100a Father Christmas with List

110 M HURDLES
R. KINGDOM
USA

(**101**)

(Des Walt Disney Co. Litho Questa)

1988 (2 Dec). *Christmas. "Santa's Helpers". T* **100a** *and similar vert designs showing Walt Disney cartoon characters. Multicoloured. P* 13½×14.
668 50 c. Type **100a** 50 50
a. Sheetlet. Nos. 668/75 .. .. 3·50
669 50 c. Goofy carrying presents 50 50
670 50 c. Mickey Mouse on toy train .. 50 50
671 50 c. Reindeer at window 50 50
672 50 c. Donald Duck's nephew with building blocks 50 50
673 50 c. Donald Duck holding sack 50 50
674 50 c. Chip n'Dale on conveyor belt .. 50 50
675 50 c. Donald Duck's nephew operating conveyor belt 50 50
668/75 .. .. *Set of* 8 3·50 3·50
MS676 Two sheets, each 127×102 mm. (a) 350 s. Mickey Mouse loading sack of toys on sleigh (*horiz*). P 14×13½. (b) 350 s. Mickey Mouse and Chip n'Dale grooming reindeer. P 13½×14 *Set of* 2 *sheets* 5·00 6·00
Nos. 668/75 were printed together, *se-tenant* as a composite design, in sheetlets of eight.

1989 (30 Jan). *Olympic Gold Medal Winners, Seoul. Nos.* 628/32 *optd as T* **101** *or surch also.*
677 5 s. Type **95** (optd with T **101**) 10 10
678 25 s. High jumping (optd "HIGH JUMP G. AVDEENKO USSR") 20 25
679 35 s. Javelin throwing (optd "JAVELIN T. KORJUS FINLAND") 25 30
680 300 s. on 45 s. Long jumping (optd "LONG JUMP C. LEWIS USA") .. .. 2·25 2·40
677/80 .. .. *Set of* 4 2·50 2·75
MS681 85×114 mm. 350 s. on 150 s. Olympic medals with medal table optd on sheet margin 3·00 3·00

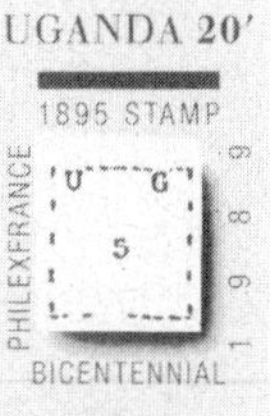

102 Goalkeeper with Ball

103 1895 5 Cowries Stamp

(Des J. Genzo. Litho Questa)

1989 (24 Apr). *World Cup Football Championship, Italy* (1990) (1*st issue*). *T* **102** *and similar multicoloured designs. P* 14.
682 10 s. Type **102** 10 10
683 25 s. Player kicking ball (*horiz*) 10 10
684 75 s. Heading ball towards net (*horiz*) .. 10 15
685 200 s. Tackling 25 30
682/5 .. .. *Set of* 4 40 50
MS686 118×87 mm. 300 s. Football and World Cup trophy (*horiz*) 35 40
See also Nos. 849/53.

(Litho Questa)

1989 (15 May). *Japanese Art. Paintings by Hokusai. Horiz designs as T* **187a** *of Lesotho. Multicoloured. P* 14×13½.
687 10 s. "Fuji and the Great Wave off Kanagawa" 10 10
688 15 s. "Fuji from Lake Suwa" 10 10
689 20 s. "Fuji from Kajikazawa" 10 10
690 60 s. "Fuji from Shichirigahama" 10 10
691 90 s. "Fuji from Ejiri in Sunshu" 10 15
692 120 s. "Fuji above Lightning" 15 20
693 200 s. "Fuji from Lower Meguro in Edo" 25 30
694 250 s. "Fuji from Edo" 30 35
687/94 .. .. *Set of* 8 90 1·10
MS695 Two sheets, each 102×76 mm. (a) 500 s. "The Red Fuji from the Foot". (b) 500 s. "Fuji from Umezawa" .. .. .. *Set of* 2 *sheets* 1·25 1·40
Nos. 687/94 were each printed in sheetlets of 10 containing two horizontal strips of 5 stamps separated by printed labels commemorating Emperor Hirohito.

(Des U. Purins. Litho B.D.T.)

1989 (7 July). *"Philexfrance 89" International Stamp Exhibition, Paris. T* **103** *and similar vert designs. P* 14.
696 20 s. black, brt scarlet & pale grey-brown 10 10
697 70 s. black, yellowish green and azure .. 10 10
698 100 s. black, dull violet and pale brown-rose 10 15
699 250 s. black, orange-yell & pale greenish yell 30 35
696/9 .. .. *Set of* 4 50 60
MS700 176×131 mm. Nos. 696/9 (*sold at* 500 *s.*) 60 65
Designs:—70 s. 1895 10 on 50 cowries stamp; 100 s. 1896 25 cowries stamp; 250 s. 1896 1 rupee stamp.

104 Scout advising on Immunization

105 *Suillus granulatus*

(Des Associated Creative Designers. Litho Questa)

1989 (3 Aug). *2nd All African Scout Jamboree, Uganda, and 75th Anniv of Ugandan Scout Movement. T* **104** *and similar multicoloured designs. P* 14.
701 10 s. Type **104** 10 1
702 70 s. Poultry keeping 10 1
703 90 s. Scout on crutches leading family to immunization centre 10 15
704 100 s. Scouts making bricks 10 15
701/4 .. .. *Set of* 4 30 40
MS705 99×67 mm. 500 s. Ugandan Scout logo (*vert*) 60 65

(Des Mary Walters. Litho B.D.T.)

1989 (14 Aug). *Fungi. T* **105** *and similar vert designs Multicoloured. P* 14.
706 10 s. Type **105** 10 1
707 15 s. *Omphalotus olearius* 10 1
708 45 s. *Oudemansiella radicata* 10 1
709 50 s. *Clitocybe nebularis* 10 1
710 60 s. *Macrolepiota rhacodes* 10 1
711 75 s. *Lepista nuda* 10 1
712 150 s. *Suillus luteus* 20 2
713 200 s. *Agaricus campestris* 25 3
706/13 .. .. *Set of* 8 70 8
MS714 Two sheets, each 100×68 mm. (a) 350 s. *Bolbitius vitellinus.* (b) 350 s. *Schizophyllum commune* .. .. .. *Set of* 2 *sheets* 85 9

106 Saddle-bill Stork

107 Rocket on Launch Pad

(Des S. Barlowe. Litho Questa)

1989 (12 Sept). *Wildlife at Waterhole. T* **106** *and similar vert designs. Multicoloured. P* 14½×14.
715 30 s. Type **106** 10 1
a. Sheetlet. Nos. 715/34 90
716 30 s. Eastern White Pelican 10 1
717 30 s. Marabou Stork 10 1
718 30 s. Egyptian Vulture 10 1
719 30 s. Bateleur 10 1
720 30 s. African Elephant 10 1
721 30 s. Giraffe 10 1
722 30 s. Goliath Heron 10 1
723 30 s. Black Rhinoceros 10 1
724 30 s. Common Zebra and Oribi 10 1
725 30 s. African Fish Eagle 10 1
726 30 s. Hippopotamus 10 1
727 30 s. Black-backed Jackal and Eastern White Pelican 10 1
728 30 s. African Buffalo 10 1
729 30 s. Olive Baboon 10 1
730 30 s. Bohar Reedbuck 10 1
731 30 s. Lesser Flamingo and Serval 10 1
732 30 s. Whale-headed Stork ("Shoebill Stork") 10 1
733 30 s. Crowned Crane 10 1
734 30 s. Impala 10 1
715/34 .. .. *Set of* 20 90 9
MS735 Two sheets, each 99×68 mm. (a) 500 s. Lion. (b) 500 s. Long-crested Eagle *Set of* 2 *sheets* 1·25 1·4
Nos. 715/34 were printed together, *se-tenant*, in a sheetlet of 20 stamps, forming a composite design showing wildlife at a waterhole.

(Des T. Agans. Litho Questa)

1989 (20 Oct). *20th Anniv of First Manned Landing on Moon. T* **107** *and similar multicoloured designs. P* 14.
736 10 s. Type **107** 10 1
737 20 s. Lunar module *Eagle* on Moon .. 10 1
738 30 s. "Apollo 11" command module .. 10 1
739 50 s. *Eagle* landing on Moon 10 1
740 70 s. Astronaut Aldrin on Moon 10 1
741 250 s. Neil Armstrong alighting from *Eagle* (*vert*) 30 3

742 300 s. *Eagle* over Moon 35 40
743 350 s. Astronaut Aldrin on Moon (*vert*) 40 45
736/43 .. .. *Set of* 8 1·25 1·40
MS744 Two sheets, each 77×104 mm. (a) 500 s. "Saturn" rocket (*vert*). (b) 500 s. "Apollo 11" capsule on parachutes (*vert*) .. *Set of* 2 *sheets* 1·25 1·40

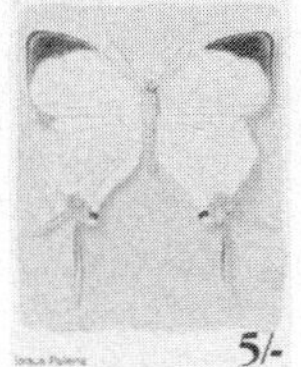

108 *Aphniolaus pallene*

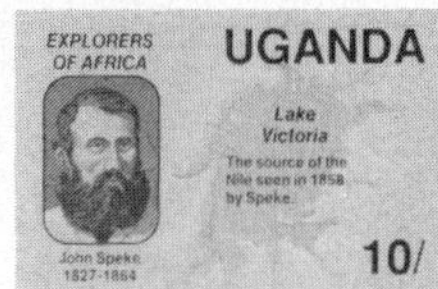

109 John Hanning Speke and Map of Lake Victoria

(Des S. Heimann. Litho Questa)

1989 (13 Nov)–**92.** *Butterflies. T* **108** *and similar vert designs. Multicoloured. P* 14.
745 5 s. Type **108** 10 10
746 10 s. *Hewitsonia boisduvali* 10 10
747 20 s. *Euxanthe wakefieldi* 10 10
748 30 s. *Papilio echerioides* 10 10
749 40 s. *Acraea semivitrea* 10 10
750 50 s. *Colotis antevippe* 10 10
751 70 s. *Acraea perenna* 10 10
752 90 s. *Charaxes cynthia* 10 15
753 100 s. *Euphaedra neophron* 10 15
754 150 s. *Cymothoe beckeri* 20 25
755 200 s. *Vanessula milca* 35 30
756 400 s. *Mimacraea marshalli* 50 55
757 500 s. *Axiocerses amanga* 60 65
758 1000 s. *Precis hierta* .. .. .. 1·25 1·40
759 2000 s. As 1000 s. (1.11.90) .. .. 2·40 2·75
759*a* 3000 s. *Euphaedra eusemoides* (2.1.92) .. 3·75 4·00
759*b* 4000 s. *Acraea natalica* (2.1.92) .. .. 4·75 5·00
745/759*b* .. .. *Set of* 17 13·00 14·00

(Des A. Granberg. Litho Questa)

1989 (15 Nov). *Exploration of Africa. T* **109** *and similar horiz designs. Multicoloured. P* 14.
760 10 s. Type **109** 10 10
761 25 s. Sir Richard Burton and map of Lake Tanganyika 10 10
762 40 s. Richard Lander and Bakota bronze .. 10 10
763 90 s. René Caillié and mosque, Timbuktu 10 10
764 125 s. Sir Samuel Baker and Dorcas Gazelle 10 15
765 150 s. Pharaoh Necho and ancient Phoenician merchant ship 20 25
766 250 s. Vasco da Gama and 15th-century caravel 30 35
767 300 s. Sir Henry Morton Stanley and *Lady Alice* (sectional boat) 35 40
760/7 .. .. *Set of* 8 1·10 1·40
MS768 Two sheets, each 73×103 mm. (a) 500 s. Dr. David Livingstone and steam launch *Ma Robert;* (b) 500 s. Mary Kingsley and map of Ogooué River .. .. .. *Set of* 2 *sheets* 1·25 1·40

110 Logo (25th anniv of African Development Bank)

111 *Aerangis kotschyana*

(Des D. Miller. Litho Questa)

1989 (12 Dec). *Anniversaries. T* **110** *and similar horiz designs. Multicoloured. P* 14.
769 10 s. Type **110** 10 10
770 20 s. Arrows and dish aerials (World Telecommunication Day) 10 10
771 75 s. Nehru and Gandhi (birth centenary of Nehru) 10 15
772 90 s. Pan Am *Dixie Clipper* flying boat (50th anniv of first scheduled trans-Atlantic airmail flight) 10 15
773 100 s. George Stephenson and *Locomotion*, 1825 (175th anniv of first practical steam locomotive) 10 15
774 150 s. "Concorde" cockpit (20th anniv of first test flight) 20 25
775 250 s. *Wapen von Hamburg* and *Leopoldus Primus* (galleons) (800th anniv of Port of Hamburg) 30 35
776 300 s. "Concorde" and cockpit interior (20th anniv of first test flight) 35 40
769/76 .. .. *Set of* 8 1·10 1·40
MS777 Two sheets (a) 91×87 mm. 500 s. Revolutionary with musket and Bastille, Paris (bicentenary of French Revolution). (b) 110×82 mm. 500 s. Emperor Frederick I Barbarossa and Hamburg charter (800th anniv of Port of Hamburg) .. .. .. *Set of* 2 *sheets* 1·25 1·40

(Des W. Wright. Litho Questa)

1989 (18 Dec). *Orchids. T* **111** *and similar vert designs. Multicoloured. P* 14.
778 10 s. Type **111** 10 10
779 15 s. *Angraecum infundibulare* 10 10
780 45 s. *Cyrtorchis chailluana* 10 10
781 50 s. *Aerangis rhodosticta* 10 10
782 100 s. *Eulophia speciosa* 10 15
783 200 s. *Calanthe sylvatica* 25 30
784 250 s. *Vanilla imperialis* 30 35
785 350 s. *Polystachya vulcanica* 40 45
778/85 .. .. *Set of* 8 1·10 1·25
MS786 Two sheets, each 110×82 mm. (a) 500 s. *Ansellia africana.* (b) 500 s. *Ancistrochilus rothschildianus* .. .. .. *Set of* 2 *sheets* 1·25 1·40

(Litho Questa)

1989 (21 Dec). *Christmas. Paintings by Fra Angelico Vert designs as T* **193***b of Lesotho. Multicoloured. P* 14.
787 10 s. "Madonna and Child" 10 10
788 20 s. "Adoration of the Magi" 10 10
789 40 s. "Virgin and Child enthroned with Saints" 10 10
790 75 s. "The Annunciation" 10 15
791 100 s. "Virgin and Child" (detail, "St. Peter Martyr" triptych) 10 15
792 150 s. "Virgin and Child enthroned with Saints" (*different*) 20 25
793 250 s. "Virgin and Child enthroned" .. 30 35
794 350 s. "Virgin and Child" (from Annalena altarpiece) 40 45
787/94 .. .. *Set of* 8 1·10 1·40
MS795 Two sheets, each 72×96 mm. (a) 500 s. "Virgin and Child" (from Bosco ai Frati altarpiece). (b) 500 s. "Madonna and Child with Twelve Angels" .. .. *Set of* 2 *sheets* 1·25 1·40

112 *Thevetia peruviana*

(113)

(Des Jennifer Toombs. Litho B.D.T.)

1990 (17 Apr). *"EXPO '90" International Garden and Greenery Exhibition, Osaka (1st issue). Flowering Trees. T* **112** *and similar vert designs. Multicoloured. P* 14.
796 10 s. Type **112** 10 10
797 20 s. *Acanthus eminens* 10 10
798 90 s. *Gnidia glauca* 10 15
799 150 s. *Oncoba spinosa* 20 25
800 175 s. *Hibiscus rosa-sinensis* 20 25
801 400 s. *Jacaranda mimosifolia* 45 50
802 500 s. *Erythrina abyssinica* 60 65
803 700 s. *Bauhinia purpurea* 90 95
796/803 .. .. *Set of* 8 2·25 2·50
MS804 Two sheets, each 93×85 mm. (a) 1000 s. *Delonix regia.* (b) 1000 s. *Cassia didymobotrya* *Set of* 2 *sheets* 2·40 2·50
See also Nos. 820/8.

(Des W. Wright. Litho Questa)

1990 (8 June). *50th Anniv of Second World War. Multicoloured designs as T* **242** *of Maldive Islands. P* 14.
805 5 s. Allied penetration of German West Wall, 1944 .. .. .. 10 10
806 10 s. Flags of the Allies, VE Day, 1945 .. 10 10
807 20 s. Capture of Okinawa, 1945 .. .. 10 10
808 75 s. Appointment of Gen. De Gaulle to command all Free French forces, 1944 10 15
809 100 s. Invasion of Saipan, 1944 .. .. 10 15
810 150 s. Airborne landing, Operation Market Garden, 1944 .. .. .. 20 25
811 200 s. MacArthur's return to Philippines, 1944 .. .. 25 30
812 300 s. Japanese attack on U.S. carrier, Coral Sea, 1942 .. .. 35 40
813 350 s. First Battle of El Alamein, 1942 .. 40 45
814 500 s. Naval Battle of Guadalcanal, 1942 .. 60 65
805/14 .. .. *Set of* 10 1·90 2·25
MS815 112×83 mm. 1000 s. Battle of Britain, 1940 (*vert*) .. .. 1·25 1·40

(Des Young Phillips Studio. Litho Questa)

1990 (5 July). *90th Birthday of Queen Elizabeth the Queen Mother. Vert designs as T* **198***a of Lesotho, showing portraits, 1940–49. P* 14.
816 250 s. black, deep magenta and new blue .. 30 35
a. Strip of 3. Nos. 816/18 80
817 250 s. black, deep magenta and new blue .. 30 35
818 250 s. black, deep magenta and new blue .. 30 35
816/18 .. .. *Set of* 3 80 95
MS819 90×75 mm. 1000 s. multicoloured .. 1·25 1·40
Designs:—No. 816, Queen Elizabeth with corgi; Nos. 817, **MS**819, Queen Elizabeth wearing feathered hat; No. 818, Queen Elizabeth at wartime inspection.
Nos. 816/18 were printed together, horizontally and vertically *se-tenant*, in sheetlets of 9 (3×3).

1990 (30 July). *"EXPO 90" International Garden and Greenery Exhibition, Osaka (2nd issue). Nos. 778/86 optd as T* **113** *in silver.*
820 10 s. Type **111** 10 10
821 15 s. *Angraecum infundibulare* 10 10
822 45 s. *Cyrtorchis chailluana* 10 10
823 50 s. *Aerangis rhodosticta* 10 10
824 100 s. *Eulophia speciosa* 10 15
825 200 s. *Calanthe sylvatica* 25 30
826 250 s. *Vanilla imperialis* 30 35
827 350 s. *Polystachya vulcanica* 40 45
820/7 .. .. *Set of* 8 1·10 1·25
MS828 Two sheets, each 110×82 mm. (a) 500 s. *Ansellia africana.* (b) 500 s. *Ancistrochilus rothschildianus* .. .. .. *Set of* 2 *sheets* 1·25 1·40
The overprint on No. **MS**828 occurs on the sheet margin and includes an additional inscription.

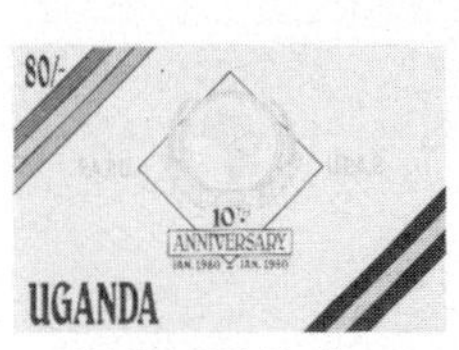

114 P.A.P.U. Emblem

115 Unissued G. B. "V R" Penny Black

(Des L. Fried. Litho B.D.T.)

1990 (3 Aug). *Tenth Anniv of Pan-African Postal Union (80 s.) and Second United Nations Conference on Least Developed Countries, Paris (750 s.). T* **114** *and similar horiz design. P* 14.
829 80 s. multicoloured 10 15
MS830 97×67 mm. 750 s. black and new blue 90 95
Design:—750 s. Clasped hands.

(Des and litho B.D.T.)

1990 (6 Aug). *150th Anniv of the Penny Black. T* **115** *and similar vert designs. P* 14.
831 25 s. multicoloured 10 10
832 50 s. brown-lake, blk & pale turquoise-grn 10 10
833 100 s. multicoloured 10 15
834 150 s. multicoloured 20 25
835 200 s. multicoloured 25 30
836 300 s. multicoloured 35 40
837 500 s. multicoloured 60 65
838 600 s. multicoloured 70 75
831/8 .. .. *Set of* 8 2·10 2·40
MS839 Two sheets (a) 107×77 mm. 1000 s. multicoloured. (b) 119×85 mm. 1000 s. black and rosine .. .. .. *Set of* 2 *sheets* 2·40 2·50
Designs:—50 s. Canada 1858-59 3d. Beaver; 100 s. Baden 1851 9 k. on green error; 150 s. Basel 1845 2½ r. Dove; 200 s. U.S.A. 1918 24 c. Inverted "Jenny" error; 300 s. Western Australia 1854 1d. Black Swan; 500 s. Uganda 1895 20 c. "narrow" typewritten stamp; 600 s. Great Britain Twopenny blue; 1000 s. (No. **MS**839a), Uganda 1895 20 c. "wide" typewritten stamp; 1000 s. (No. **MS**839b), Sir Rowland Hill.
No. **MS**839 also commemorates "Stamp World London 90" International Stamp Exhibition.

116 African Jacana

(Des P. Gonzalez. Litho Questa)

1990 (3 Sept). *Wild Birds of Uganda. T* **116** *and similar multicoloured designs. P* 14.
840 10 s. Type **116** 10 10
841 15 s. Ground Hornbill 10 10
842 45 s. Kori Bustard (*vert*) 10 10
843 50 s. Secretary Bird 10 10
844 100 s. Egyptian Geese 10 15
845 300 s. Goliath Heron (*vert*) 35 40
846 500 s. Ostrich with chicks (*vert*) 60 65
847 650 s. Saddlebill Stork (*vert*) 80 85
840/7 .. .. *Set of* 8 1·90 2·00
MS848 Two sheets, each 98×69 mm. (a) 1000 s. Lesser Flamingo (*vert*). (b) 1000 s. Vulturine Guineafowl (*vert*) .. .. *Set of* 2 *sheets* 2·40 2·50

117 Roger Milla of Cameroun

(Des Young Phillips Studio. Litho Questa)

1990 (21 Sept). *World Cup Football Championship, Italy (2nd issue). T* **117** *and similar horiz designs. Multicoloured. P* 14.
849 50 s. Type **117** 10 10
850 100 s. Ramzy of Egypt 10 15
851 250 s. David O'Leary of Ireland 30 35
852 600 s. Littbarsky of West Germany .. 70 75
849/52 .. .. *Set of* 4 1·00 1·10
MS853 Two sheets, each 75×90 mm. (a) 1000 s. Ali McCoist of Scotland. (b) 1000 s. Ekstrom of Sweden .. .. .. *Set of* 2 *sheets* 2·40 2·50

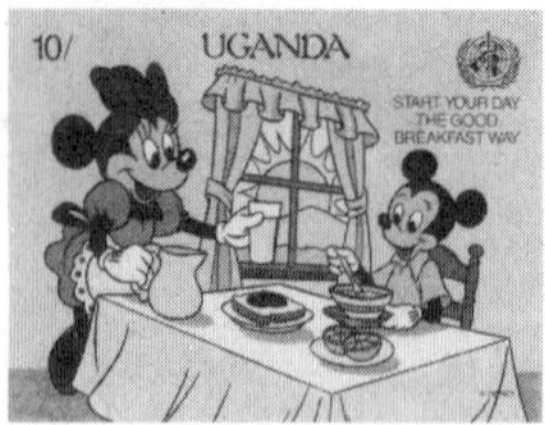

118 Mickey and Minnie Mouse at Breakfast

(Des Walt Disney Co. Litho B.D.T.)

1990 (19 Oct). *Health and Safety Campaign. T* **118** *and similar multicoloured designs showing Walt Disney cartoon characters. P* 13.
854 10 s. Type **118** 10 10
855 20 s. Donald Duck's nephews doing kerb drill 10 10
856 50 s. Donald and Mickey stopping Big Pete smoking 10 10
857 90 s. Mickey stopping Donald choking .. 10 15
858 100 s. Mickey and Goofy using seat belts .. 10 15
859 250 s. Mickey and Minnie dancing .. 30 35
860 500 s. Donald Duck's fitness class 60 65
861 600 s. Mickey's nephews showing lights at night 70 75
854/61 .. .. *Set of* 8 1·75 2·00
MS862 Two sheets, each 135×115 mm. (a) 1000 s. Mickey weighing nephew (*vert*). (b) 1000 s. Mickey and Pluto walking (*vert*) *Set of* 2 *sheets* 2·40 2·50

(Litho Questa)

1990 (17 Dec). *Christmas. 350th Death Anniv of Rubens. Multicoloured designs as T* **250** *of Maldive Islands, but inscr* "CHRISTMAS 1990". *P* 13½×14.
863 10 s. "Baptism of Christ" (detail) (*vert*) .. 10 10
864 20 s. "St. Gregory the Great and other Saints" (detail) (*vert*) 10 10
865 100 s. "Saints Nereus, Domitilla and Achilleus" (detail) (*vert*) 10 15
866 150 s. "St. Gregory the Great and other Saints" (different detail) (*vert*) .. 20 25
867 300 s. "Saint Augustine" (detail) (*vert*) .. 35 40
868 400 s. "St. Gregory the Great and other Saints" (different detail) (*vert*) .. 50 55
869 500 s. "Baptism of Christ" (different detail) (*vert*) 60 65
870 600 s. "St. Gregory the Great and other Saints (different detail) (*vert*) .. 70 75
863/70 .. .. *Set of* 8 2·25 2·50
MS871 Two sheets, each 110×71 mm. (a) 1000 s. "The Triumph of Faith" (detail). (b) 1000 s. "The Victory of Eucharistic Truth over Heresy" (detail). P 14×13½ .. .. *Set of* 2 *sheets* 2·40 2·50

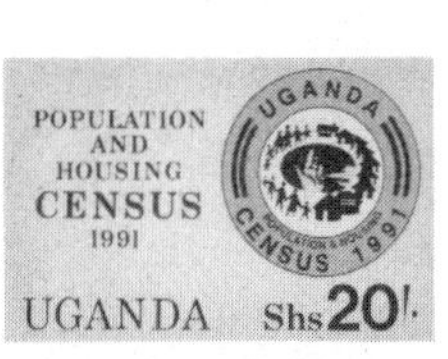

119 Census Emblem

120 Damselfly

(Litho Questa)

1990 (28 Dec). *National Population and Housing Census. T* **119** *and similar horiz design. Multicoloured. P* 14.
872 20 s. Type **119** 10 10
MS873 105×73 mm. 1000 s. Symbolic people and dwellings .. .. 1·25 1·40

(Des I. Maclaury. Litho B.D.T.)

1991 (8 Jan). *Fauna of Uganda's Wetlands. T* **120** *and similar multicoloured designs. P* 14.
874 70 s. Type **120** 10 10
a. Sheetlet of 16. Nos. 874/89 .. .. 1·25
875 70 s. Purple Gallinule 10 10
876 70 s. Sitatunga 10 10
877 70 s. Purple Heron 10 10
878 70 s. Bushpig 10 10
879 70 s. Vervet Monkey 10 10
880 70 s. Long Reed Frog 10 10
881 70 s. Malachite Kingfisher 10 10
882 70 s. Marsh Mongoose 10 10
883 70 s. Painted Reed Frog 10 10
884 70 s. Jacana 10 10
885 70 s. Charaxes butterfly 10 10
886 70 s. Nile Crocodile 10 10
887 70 s. Herald Snake 10 10
888 70 s. Dragonfly 10 10
889 70 s. Lungfish 10 10
874/89 .. .. *Set of* 16 1·25 1·40
MS890 118×78 mm. 1000 s. Nile Monitor (*horiz*) 1·25 1·40
Nos. 874/89 were printed together, *se-tenant*, in sheetlets of 16 forming a composite design.

121 *Haplochromis limax*

(Des Susan Fuller. Litho B.D.T.)

1991 (18 Jan). *Fishes of Uganda. T* **121** *and similar horiz designs. Multicoloured. P* 14.
891 10 s. Type **121** 10 10
892 20 s. *Nothobranchius palmqvisti* 10 10
893 40 s. *Distichodus affinis* 10 10
894 90 s. *Haplochromis sauvagei* 10 15
895 100 s. *Aphyosemion calliurum* 10 15
896 350 s. *Haplochromis johnstoni* 40 45
897 600 s. *Haplochromis dichrourus* 70 75
898 800 s. *Hemichromis bimaculatus* .. .. 95 1·00
891/8 .. .. *Set of* 8 2·10 2·40
MS899 Two sheets, 100×74 mm. (a) 1000 s. *Haplochromis* sp. (b) 1000 s. *Aphyosemion striatum* .. .. .. *Set of* 2 *sheets* 2·40 2·50

(Des B. Grout. Litho Questa)

1991 (25 Feb). *Olympic Games, Barcelona* (1992). *Multicoloured designs as T* **202** *of Lesotho. P* 14.
900 20 s. Women's 100 metres hurdles .. 10 10
901 40 s. Long jump 10 10
902 125 s. Table tennis 15 20
903 250 s. Football 30 35
904 500 s. Men's 800 metres 60 65
900/4 .. .. *Set of* 5 1·00 1·10
MS905 Two sheets, each 110×71 mm. (a) 1200 s. Opening Ceremony at Seoul Games (*horiz*). (b) 1200 s. Women's 4 × 100 metres relay (*horiz*) *Set of* 2 *sheets* 3·00 3·25

122 Class "10" Steam Locomotive, Zimbabwe

(Des O. Fernandez. Litho Walsall)

1991 (2 Apr). *African Railway Locomotives. T* **122** *and similar horiz designs. Multicoloured. P* 14.
906 10 s. Type **122** 10 10
907 20 s. Class "12" steam locomotive, Zimbabwe 10 10
908 80 s. Class "Tribal" steam locomotive, Tazara Railway 10 10
909 200 s. 4-6-0 type steam locomotive, Egypt 25 30
910 300 s. Mikado type steam locomotive, Sudan 35 40
911 400 s. Class "Mountain" Garrat steam locomotive, Uganda 50 55
912 500 s. Mallet type steam locomotive, Uganda 60 65
913 1000 s. 5 F 1 electric locomotive, South Africa .. .. 1·25 1·40
906/13 .. .. *Set of* 8 2·75 3·25
MS914 Two sheets, each 100×70 mm. (a) 1200 s. Atlantic type, steam locomotive, Egypt. (b) 1200 s. 4-8-2 type steam locomotive, Zimbabwe *Set of* 2 *sheets* 3·00 3·25

123 Lord Baden-Powell and Scout Emblem

124 General Charles de Gaulle

(Des W. Hanson Studio. Litho Questa)

1991 (27 May). *World Scout Jamboree Mount Sorak, Korea. T* **123** *and similar horiz designs. P* 14.
915 20 s. multicoloured 10 10
916 80 s. multicoloured 10 15
917 100 s. multicoloured 10 15
918 150 s. black and pale yellow-olive .. 20 25
919 300 s. multicoloured 35 40
920 400 s. multicoloured 50 55
921 500 s. multicoloured 60 65
922 1000 s. multicoloured .. .. .. 1·25 1·40
915/22 .. .. *Set of* 8 2·75 3·25
MS923 Two sheets. (a) 76×115 mm. 1200 s. black and stone. (b) 115×76 mm. 1200 s. black and dull violet-blue .. .. *Set of* 2 *sheets* 3·00 3·25
Designs:—80 s. Scouts and Uganda 1982 100 s. anniversary stamp; 100 s. Scout encampment, New York World's Fair, 1939; 150 s. Cover and illustration from *Scouting for Boys*; 300 s. Cooking on camp fire; 400 s. Aldrin and Armstrong on Moon; 500 s. Scout salutes; 1000 s. Statue to the Unknown Scout, Gillwell Park; 1200 s. (**MS**923a) Jamboree emblem; 1200 s. (**MS**923b) Lord Baden-Powell, W. Boyce and Revd. L. Hadley.

(Des Walt Disney Co. Litho Questa)

1991 (29 May). *"Philanippon '91" International Stamp Exhibition, Tokyo. Multicoloured designs as T* **204** *of Lesotho showing Walt Disney cartoon characters and Japanese traditions. P* 14×13½.
924 10 s. Uncle Scrooge celebrating Ga-No-Iwai 10 10
925 20 s. Mickey Mouse removing shoes .. 10 10
926 70 s. Goofy leading cart-horse 10 10
927 80 s. Daisy Duck and Minnie Mouse exchanging gifts 10 15
928 300 s. Minnie kneeling at doorway .. 35 40
929 400 s. Donald Duck and Mickey taking a hot volcanic sand bath 45 50
930 500 s. Clarabelle Cow burning incense .. 60 65
931 1000 s. Mickey and Minnie writing New Year cards .. .. 1·25 1·40
924/31 .. .. *Set of* 8 2·75 3·00
MS932 Two sheets, each 127×112 mm. (a) 1200 s. Mickey conducting (*vert*). (b) 1200 s. Mickey in public bath (*vert*). P 13½×14 *Set of* 2 *sheets* 3·00 3·25

(Litho Walsall)

1991 (26 June). *Death Centenary of Vincent van Gogh (artist)* (1990). *Multicoloured designs as T* **255** *of Maldive Islands. P* 13½.
933 10 s. "Snowy Landscape with Arles" (*horiz*) 10 10
934 20 s. "Peasant Woman binding Sheaves" 10 10
935 60 s. "The Drinkers" (*horiz*) 10 10
936 80 s. "View of Auvers" (*horiz*) 10 10
937 200 s. "Mourning Man" 25 30
938 400 s. "Still Life: Vase with Roses" (*horiz*) 45 50
939 800 s. "The Raising of Lazarus" (*horiz*) .. 90 95
940 1000 s. "The Good Samaritan" .. .. 1·25 1·50
933/40 .. .. *Set of* 8 2·75 3·00
MS941 Two sheets, each 102×76 mm. (a) 1200 s. "First Steps" (95×71 *mm*). (b) 1200 s. "Village Street and Steps in Auvers" (95×71 *mm*). Imperf *Set of* 2 *sheets* 5·75 6·00

(Des D. Miller. Litho Walsall)

1991 (5 July). *65th Birthday of Queen Elizabeth II. Horiz designs as T* **210** *of Lesotho. Multicoloured. P* 14.
942 70 s. Queen and Prince Charles after polo match 10 10
943 90 s. Queen at Balmoral, 1976 .. .. 10 10
944 500 s. Queen with Princess Margaret, August 1980 .. .. 60 65
945 600 s. Queen and Queen Mother leaving St. George's Chapel, Windsor 70 75
942/5 .. .. *Set of* 4 2·75 3·00
MS946 68×90 mm. 1200 s. Separate photographs of Queen and Prince Philip .. 1·50 1·75

(Des D. Miller. Litho Walsall)

1991 (5 July). *10th Wedding Anniv of Prince and Princess of Wales. Horiz designs as T* **210** *of Lesotho. Multicoloured. P* 14.
947 20 s. Prince and Princess of Wales in July 1986 .. .. 10 10
948 100 s. Separate photographs of Prince, Princess and sons 10 10
949 200 s. Prince Henry and Prince William .. 25 30
950 1000 s. Separate photographs of Prince and Princess in 1988 .. .. .. 1·25 1·50
947/50 .. .. *Set of* 4 1·50 1·75
MS951 68×90 mm. 1200 s. Princes William and Henry on Majorca and Prince and Princess of Wales in Cameroun .. .. 1·50 1·75

(Litho Questa)

1991 (15 July). *Birth Centenary of Charles de Gaulle (French statesman)* (1990). *T* **124** *and similar multicoloured designs. P* 14.
952 20 s. Type **124** 10 10
953 70 s. Liberation of Paris, 1944 .. .. 10 10
954 90 s. De Gaulle with King George VI, 1940 .. .. 10 10
955 100 s. Reviewing Free French troops, 1940 (*horiz*) 10 10
956 200 s. Broadcasting to France, 1940 (*horiz*) 25 30
957 500 s. De Gaulle in Normandy, 1944 (*horiz*) 60 65
958 600 s. De Gaulle at Albert Hall, 1940 (*horiz*) 70 75
959 1000 s. Inauguration as President, 1959 .. 1·25 1·40
952/9 .. .. *Set of* 8 2·50 3·00
MS960 Two sheets. (a) 104×76 mm. 1200 s. De Gaulle entering Paris, 1944. (b) 107×76 mm. 1200 s. De Gaulle with Eisenhower, 1942 (*horiz*) *Set of* 2 *sheets* 2·75 3·00

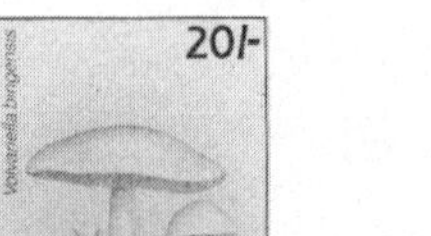

125 *Volvariella bingensis*

(Des K. Botis. Litho Questa)

1991 (19 July). *Fungi. T* **125** *and similar multicoloured designs. P* 14.
961 20 s. Type **125** 10 10
962 70 s. *Agrocybe broadwayi* 10 10
963 90 s. *Camarophyllus olidus* 10 10

964	140 s. *Marasmius arborescens*	15	20
965	180 s. *Marasmiellus subcinereus*	20	25
966	200 s. *Agaricus campestris*	25	30
967	500 s. *Chlorophyllum molybdites*	60	65
968	1000 s. *Agaricus bingensis*	1·25	1·50
961/8	*Set of* 8	2·50	3·00
MS969	Two sheets, each 96×65 mm. (a) 1200 s. *Leucocoprinus cepaestipes (horiz)*. (b) 1200 s. *Laccaria lateritia (horiz)* .. *Set of* 2 *sheets*	2·75	3·00

Des J. Iskowitz (Nos. 970/3), O. Fernandez (No. **MS**974). Litho Questa (Nos. 970/3) or Cartor (No. **MS**974))

1991 (1 Aug). *Endangered Species (3rd series). As Nos.* 406/9, *but with changed face values, and additional horiz designs as T* **61**. *Multicoloured. P* 14.

970	100 s. Elephants in "Elephants' Graveyard"	10	10
971	140 s. Type **61**	15	20
972	200 s. Elephants at waterhole	25	30
973	600 s. Elephants having dust bath	70	75
970/3	*Set of* 4	1·10	1·25
MS974	Two sheets, each 102×74 mm. (a) 1200 s. Giraffe. (b) 1200 s. Rhinoceros and tick birds. P 13×12 .. *Set of* 2 *sheets*	2·75	3·00

POSTAGE DUE STAMPS

The Postage Due stamps of Kenya, Uganda and Tanganyika were used in Uganda until 2 January 1967.

D 1

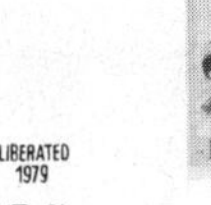

(D **2**)

D **3** Lion

(Litho D.L.R.)

1967 (3 Jan). *Chalk-surfaced paper. P* 14 × 13½.

D1	D 1	5 c. scarlet	20	2·75
D2		10 c. green	20	2·75
D3		20 c. deep blue	35	3·25
D4		30 c. red-brown	40	4·00
D5		40 c. bright purple	60	6·00
D6		1 s. orange	1·50	9·50
D1/6		*Set of* 6	3·00	26·00

1970 (31 Mar). *As Nos.* D1/6, *but on glazed ordinary paper. P* 14 × 15.

D 7	D 1	5 c. scarlet	15	1·50
D 8		10 c. green	15	1·50
D 9		20 c. deep blue	25	2·00
D10		30 c. red-brown	35	2·50
D11		40 c. bright purple	55	3·00
D7/11		*Set of* 5	1·25	9·50

1973 (12 Dec). *Glazed, ordinary paper. P* 15.

D12	D 1	5 c. scarlet	70	3·50
D13		10 c. emerald	70	3·50
D14		20 c. deep blue	1·00	4·00
D15		30 c. red-brown	1·25	4·75
D16		40 c. bright mauve	1·75	7·00
D17		1 s. bright orange	2·50	8·00
D12/17		*Set of* 6	7·25	28·00

"UGANDA LIBERATED" OVERPRINTS. Nos. D1/17 were overprinted "UGANDA LIBERATED 1979", in very limited quantities, using a style of overprint similar to Type **32** (*Prices: Nos.* D1/6 *set of* 6 £275; D7/11 *set of* 5 £125; D12, 14/17 *set of* 5 £100; D13 £90, *all mint*).

(Litho Questa)

1979 (Dec). *Liberation. As Nos.* D1/6 *optd with Type* D **2**. *Chalk-surfaced paper. P* 13½ × 14.

D18	D 1	5 c. scarlet	15	30
D19		10 c. green	15	30
D20		20 c. dull ultramarine	20	30
D21		30 c. red-brown	20	40
D22		40 c. bright purple	25	40
D23		1 s. orange	25	40
D18/23		*Set of* 6	1·10	1·90

(Litho Questa)

1985 (11 Mar). *Animals. Type* D **3** *and similar vert designs. P* 14½ × 14.

D24	5 s. black and bright turquoise-green	10	10
D25	10 s. black and dull rose-lilac	10	10
D26	20 s. black and dull orange	10	10
D27	40 s. black and bright lilac	15	20
D28	50 s. black and pale greenish blue	30	35
D29	100 s. black and mauve	60	65
D24/9	*Set of* 6	1·10	1·25

Designs:—10 s. African Buffalo; 20 s. Kob; 40 s. African Elephant; 50 s. Common Zebra; 100 s. Black Rhinoceros.

Vanuatu
(*formerly* New Hebrides)

NEW HEBRIDES

Stamps of NEW SOUTH WALES were used by various Postal Agencies in the New Hebrides from 1891 onwards. Similar Postal Agencies supplying the stamps of NEW CALEDONIA were opened from 1903 onwards.

PRICES FOR STAMPS ON COVER TO 1945

Nos. 1/8 (F1/5)	*from* × 10
No. 9	*from* × 2
Nos. 10/16 (F6/10)	*from* × 8
Nos. 18/28 (F11/32)	*from* × 6
Nos. 30/4 (F33/7)	*from* × 4
No. 35 (F32*a*)	—
Nos. 36/9	*from* × 3
Nos. 40/2 (F38/41)	*from* × 4
Nos. 43/51 (F42/52)	*from* × 5
Nos. 52/63 (F53/64)	*from* × 3
Nos. D1/10 (FD53/69)	*from* × 8

ANGLO-FRENCH CONDOMINIUM

The New Hebrides, an island group in the south-west Pacific, were recognised as an area of joint Anglo-French influence in 1878. The position was regularised by the Convention of 20 October 1906 which created a Condominium, the two nations having equal rights and shares in the administration of the islands.

Stamps inscribed in English or French were issued concurrently and had equal validity throughout the islands. A common currency was reflected in the face values from 1938.

Where common designs were used the main differences between stamps inscribed in English and those in French are as follows:
- (a) Inscriptions in English or French.
- (b) Position of cyphers. French issues normally have "RF" to the right or above the British royal cypher.
- (c) French issues are without watermark, *unless otherwise stated.*

Inscriptions in English

Inscriptions in French

I. STAMPS INSCRIBED IN ENGLISH

NEW HEBRIDES.

CONDOMINIUM.

(1)

NEW HEBRIDES

CONDOMINIUM

(2)

1908 (29 Oct). *T 23 and 24 of Fiji optd with T 1 by Govt Printing Establishment, Suva. On the bicoloured stamps the word "FIJI" obliterated by a bar in the colour of the word. P 14.*

(a) Wmk Multiple Crown CA. Ordinary paper (½d., 1d.) or chalk-surfaced paper (1s.)

1	½d. green and pale green (No. 115)	1·50	9·50
1*a*	½d. green (No. 118)	40	6·00
2	1d. red	45	40
	a. Opt omitted (in vert pair with normal)	£5000	
3	1s. green and carmine	16·00	12·00

(b) Wmk Crown CA

4	½d. green and grey-green	50·00	80·00
5	2d. dull purple and orange	60	70
6	2½d. dull purple and blue/*blue*	60	70
7	5d. dull purple and green	80	2·00
8	6d. dull purple and carmine	70	1·25
9	1s. green and carmine	£150	£200
1/9	*Set of* 9	£180	£250

1910 (15 Dec). *Types as last optd with T 2 by D.L.R. Wmk Multiple Crown CA. Ordinary paper (½d. to 2½d.) or chalk-surfaced paper (5d., 6d., 1s.). P 14.*

10	½d. green	3·50	23·00
11	1d. red	10·00	8·50
12	2d. grey	60	3·00
13	2½d. bright blue	65	3·75
14	5d. dull purple and olive-green	65	5·00
15	6d. dull and deep purple	85	5·00
16	1s. black/*green* (R.)	85	7·00
10/16	*Set of* 7	15·00	50·00
10/16 Optd "Specimen"	*Set of* 7	£250	

3 Weapons and Idols

1d.

(4)

(Des J. Giraud. Recess D.L.R.)

1911 (25 July). *Wmk Mult Crown CA. P 14.*

18	3	½d. green	85	1·60
19		1d. red	2·50	2·00
20		2d. grey	3·50	3·75
21		2½d. ultramarine	1·60	4·25
24		5d. sage-green	2·00	4·25
25		6d. purple	1·50	4·75
26		1s. black/*green*	1·50	7·50
27		2s. purple/*blue*	13·00	18·00
28		5s. green/*yellow*	26·00	48·00
18/28		*Set of* 9	45·00	85·00
18/28 Optd "Specimen"		*Set of* 9	£160	

1920 (June)–**21**. *Surch with T 4 at Govt Printing Establishment, Suva.*

(a) On Nos. 24 and 26/8

30	3	1d. on 5d. sage-green (10.3.21)	7·00	60·00
		a. Surch inverted	£1200	
31		1d. on 1s. black/*green*	1·00	11·00
32		1d. on 2s. purple/*blue*	1·00	10·00
33		1d. on 5s. green/*yellow*	1·00	10·00

(b) On No. F16

34	3	2d. on 40 c. red/*yellow*	1·00	13·00

(c) On No. F27

35	3	2d. on 40 c. red/*yellow*	£120	£300

1921 (Sept–Oct). *Wmk Mult Script CA. P 14.*

36	3	1d. scarlet	2·00	12·00
37		2d. slate-grey	3·25	21·00
39		6d. purple	11·00	48·00
36/9		*Set of* 3	15·00	75·00
36/9 Optd "Specimen"		*Set of* 3	65·00	

1924 (1 May). *Surch as T 4, at Suva.*

40	3	1d. on ½d. green (No. 18)	2·50	17·00
41		3d. on 1d. scarlet (No. 36)	2·25	11·00
42		5d. on 2½d. ultramarine. (No. 21)	4·75	18·00
		a. Surch inverted	£1000	
40/2		*Set of* 3	8·50	42·00

5

(Recess D.L.R.)

1925 (June). *Wmk Mult Script CA. P 14.*

43	5	½d. (5 c.) black	60	5·00
44		1d. (10 c.) green	90	5·00
45		2d. (20 c.) slate-grey	1·75	2·25
46		2½d. (25 c.) brown	1·00	4·75
47		5d. (50 c.) ultramarine	1·50	2·50
48		6d. (60 c.) purple	2·75	7·50
49		1s. (1.25 fr.) black/*emerald*	3·00	12·00
50		2s. (2.50 fr.) purple/*blue*	6·00	18·00
51		5s. (6.25 fr.) green/*yellow*	6·00	21·00
43/51		*Set of* 9	21·00	70·00
43/51 Optd "Specimen"		*Set of* 9	£180	

CURRENCY. The currency used for the face values of issues to 1977 was an artificial, rather than an actual, monetary unit. The actual currencies in use being Australian dollars and the local franc.

6 Lopevi Is and Copra Canoe

(Des J. Kerhor. Recess B.W.)

1938 (1 June). *Gold Currency. Wmk Mult Script CA. P 12.*

52	6	5 c. blue-green	2·50	1·90
53		10 c. orange	1·25	50
54		15 c. bright violet	2·00	1·50
55		20 c. scarlet	1·60	80
56		25 c. reddish brown	1·60	1·00
57		30 c. blue	1·60	1·00
58		40 c. grey-olive	4·25	2·00
59		50 c. purple	1·60	50
60		1 f. red/*green*	4·00	6·50
61		2 f. blue/*green*	26·00	16·00
62		5 f. red/*yellow*	65·00	48·00
63		10 f. violet/*blue*	£170	70·00
52/63		*Set of* 12	£250	£130
52/63 Perf "Specimen"		*Set of* 12	£225	

(Recess Waterlow)

1949 (10 Oct). *75th Anniv of U.P.U. As Nos. 145/8 of Jamaica. Wmk Mult Script CA. P 13½×14.*

64	10 c. red-orange	30	15
65	15 c. violet	30	15
66	30 c. ultramarine	30	15
67	50 c. purple	40	20
64/7	*Set of* 4	1·10	60

MINIMUM PRICE

The minimum price quote is 10p which represents a handling charge rather than a basis for valuing common stamps. For further notes about prices see introductory pages.

7 Outrigger Sailing Canoes

(Des C. Hertenberger (1 f. to 5 f.), R. Serres (others). Recess Waterlow)

1953 (30 Apr). *T 7 and similar horiz designs. Wmk Mult Script CA. P 12½.*

68	5 c. green	40	10
69	10 c. scarlet	40	10
70	15 c. yellow-ochre	40	10
71	20 c. ultramarine	40	10
72	25 c. olive	40	10
73	30 c. brown	40	10
74	40 c. blackish brown	40	10
75	50 c. violet	60	10
76	1 f. orange	5·50	70
77	2 f. reddish purple	6·50	8·50
78	5 f. scarlet	12·00	30·00
68/78	*Set of* 11	25·00	35·00

Designs:—5 to 20 c. Type 7; 25 to 50 c. Native carving; 1 to 5 f. Two natives outside hut.

1953 (2 June). *Coronation. As No. 153 of Jamaica.*

79	10 c. black and carmine	30	25

10 Quirós Galleon and Map

(Photo Harrison)

1956 (20 Oct). *50th Anniv of Condominium. T 10 and similar horiz design. Wmk Mult Script CA. P 14½ × 14.*

80	5 c. emerald	10	10
81	10 c. scarlet	10	10
82	20 c. deep bright blue	10	10
83	50 c. deep lilac	15	15
80/3	*Set of* 4	35	30

Designs:—5, 10 c. Type 10; 20, 50 c. "Marianne", "Talking Drum" and "Britannia".

12 Port Vila: Iririki Islet

13 River Scene and Spear Fisherman

(Des H. Cheffer (T 12), P Gandon (others). Recess Waterlow)

1957 (3 Sept). *Wmk Mult Script CA. T 12/13 and similar horiz design. P 13½.*

84	12	5 c. green	40	10
85		10 c. scarlet	30	10
86		15 c. yellow-ochre	50	20
87		20 c. ultramarine	40	10
88	13	25 c. olive	45	10
89		30 c. brown	45	10
90		40 c. sepia	45	10
91		50 c. violet	45	10
92	–	1 f. orange	1·00	80
93	–	2 f. mauve	6·00	4·00
94	–	5 f. black	15·00	6·00
84/94		*Set of* 11	23·00	10·00

Design:—1 to 5 f. Woman drinking from coconut.

1963 (2 Sept). *Freedom from Hunger. As No. 80 of Lesotho.*

95	60 c. green	50	15

15 Red Cross Emblem

(Des V. Whiteley. Litho B.W.)

1963 (2 Sept). *Red Cross Centenary. W w 12. P 13½.*

96	15	15 c. red and black	35	10
97		45 c. red and blue	45	10

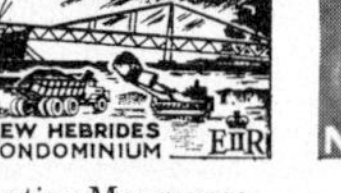

16 Exporting Manganese, Forari

17 Cocoa Beans

Des V. Whiteley, from drawings by J. White (10 c., 20 c.), K. Penny (40 c.), C. Robin (3 f.). Photo Harrison. Des C. Robin (5 c., 1 f.), J. White (15 c.), G. Vasarhelyi (25 c., 5 f.), A. Larkins, Turrell and Thomas (30 c., 50 c., 2 f.). Recess Govt Printing Works, Paris)

1963 (25 Nov)–**72.** *T* **16/17** *and similar horiz designs. W w* **12** *(10 c., 20 c., 40 c., 3 f.) or no wmk (others). P 14 (3 f.), 12½ (10 c., 20 c., 40 c.) or 13 (others).*

98 5 c. lake, purple-brown and greenish blue (15.8.66) .. 35 30
a. *Lake and greenish blue** (29.2.72) .. 35·00 35·00
99 10 c. light brown, buff & emerald (16.8.65) .. 15 10
100 15 c. yellow-bistre, red-brown & deep violet .. 15 10
101 20 c. black, olive-grn & greenish bl (16.8.65) .. 45 10
102 25 c. reddish violet, orange-brown and crimson (15.8.66) .. 50 70
103 30 c. chestnut, bistre and violet .. 75 10
104 40 c. vermilion and deep blue (16.8.65) .. 80 1·40
105 50 c. green, yellow and greenish blue .. 60 10
106 1 f. red, black & deep bluish green (15.8.66) .. 2·50 2·50
107 2 f. black, brown-purple & yellow-olive .. 2·50 1·75
108 3 f. deep violet, orange-brown, emerald and black (16.8.65) .. 13·00 8·00
109 5 f. blue, deep blue and black (24.1.67) .. 18·00 15·00
98/109 .. *Set of* 12 35·00 27·00

Designs:—15 c. Copra; 20 c. Fishing from Palikulo Point; 25 c. Picasso Fish; 30 c. Nautilus shell; 40 c. Stingfish; 50 c. Blue-lined Surgeon (fish); 1 f. Cardinal Honeyeater; 2 f. Buff-bellied Flycatcher; 3 f. Thicket Warbler; 5 f. White-collared Kingfisher.

*In No. 98*a* the globe is printed in the same colour as the centre, instead of in purple-brown.

See also No. 129.

28 I.T.U. Emblem

(Des M. Goaman. Litho Enschedé)

1965 (17 May). *I.T.U. Centenary. W w* **12.** *P* 11 × 11½.

110 **28** 15 c. scarlet and drab .. 20 10
111 60 c. blue and light red .. 35 20

29 I.C.Y. Emblem

(Des V. Whiteley. Litho Harrison)

1965 (24 Oct). *International Co-operation Year. W w* **12.** *P* 14½.

112 **29** 5 c. reddish purple and turquoise-green 15 10
113 55 c. deep bluish green and lavender .. 20 20

30 Sir Winston Churchill and St. Paul's Cathedral in Wartime

(Des Jennifer Toombs. Photo Harrison)

1966 (24 Jan). *Churchill Commemoration. W w* **12.** *P* 14.

114 **30** 5 c. black, cerise, gold and new blue .. 20 10
115 15 c. black, cerise, gold and deep green .. 40 10
116 25 c. black, cerise, gold and brown .. 50 10
117 30 c. black, cerise, gold and bluish violet 50 10
114/17 .. *Set of* 4 1·40 35

31 Footballer's Legs, Ball and Jules Rimet Cup

(Des V. Whiteley. Litho Harrison)

1966 (1 July). *World Cup Football Championships. W w* **12** *(sideways). P* 14.

118 **31** 20 c. violet, yellow-green, lake & yell-brn 20 15
119 40 c. chocolate, blue-grn, lake & yell-brn 30 15

32 W.H.O. Building

(Des M. Goaman. Litho Harrison)

1966 (20 Sept). *Inauguration of W.H.O. Headquarters, Geneva. W w* **12** *(sideways). P* 14.

120 **32** 25 c. black, yellow-green and light blue .. 20 10
121 60 c. black, light purple and yellow-brown 55 20

33 "Education"

(Des Jennifer Toombs. Litho Harrison)

1966 (1 Dec). *20th Anniv of U.N.E.S.C.O. W w* **12** *(sideways). T* **33** *and similar horiz designs. P* 14.

122 15 c. slate-violet, red, yellow and orange .. 20 10
123 30 c. orange-yellow, violet and deep olive .. 65 10
124 45 c. black, bright purple and orange .. 70 15
122/4 .. *Set of* 3 1·40 30

Designs:—30 c. "Science"; 45 c. "Culture".

36 The Coast Watchers

(Des R. Granger Barrett. Photo Enschedé)

1967 (26 Sept). *25th Anniv of the Pacific War. T* **36** *and similar horiz designs. Multicoloured. W w* **12.** *P* 14 × 13.

125 15 c. Type **36** .. 10 10
126 25 c. Map of war zone, U.S. marine and Australian soldier .. 10 15
127 60 c. H.M.A.S. *Canberra* .. 15 15
128 1 f. "Flying Fortress" .. 20 15
125/8 .. *Set of* 4 50 40

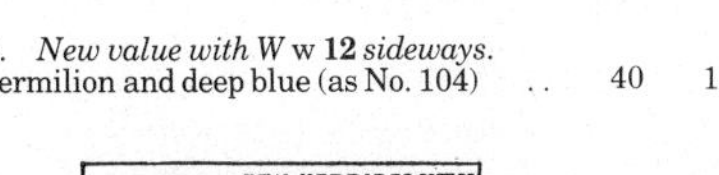

1967 (5 Dec). *New value with W w* **12** *sideways.*

129 60 c. vermilion and deep blue (as No. 104) .. 40 15

40 Globe and Hemispheres

(Des and eng J. Combet. Recess Govt Printing Works, Paris)

1968 (23 May). *Bicentenary of Bougainville's World Voyage. T* **40** *and similar horiz designs. P* 13.

130 15 c. emerald, slate-violet and red .. 10 10
131 25 c. deep olive, maroon and ultramarine .. 15 10
132 60 c. bistre-brown, brown-pur & myrtle-grn .. 15 15
130/2 .. *Set of* 3 35 30

Designs:—25 c. Ships *La Boudeuse* and *L'Etoile*, and map; 60 c. Bougainville, ship's figure-head and bougainvillea flowers.

43 "Concorde" and Vapour Trails **45** Kauri Pine

(Des S. W. Moss (25 c.), R. Granger Barrett (60 c.). Litho D.L.R.)

1968 (9 Oct). *Anglo-French "Concorde" Project. T* **43** *and similar horiz design. W w* **12** *(sideways). P* 14.

133 25 c. lt blue, orange-red & deep violet-blue .. 50 20
134 60 c. red, black and bright blue .. 60 25

Design:—60 c. "Concorde" in flight.

(Des V. Whiteley. Litho Format)

1969 (30 June). *Timber Industry. W w* **12.** *P* 14½.

135 **45** 20 c. multicoloured (*shades*) .. 10 10

No. 135 was issued in small sheets of 9 (3 × 3) printed on a simulated wood-grain background and with a decorative border showing various stages of the local timber industry. There is a wide range of shades on the printing.

ALTERED CATALOGUE NUMBERS

Any Catalogue numbers altered from the last edition are shown as a list in the introductory pages.

46 Cyphers, Flags and Relay Runner receiving Baton **48** Diver on Platform

(Des C. Haley. Photo Delrieu)

1969 (13 Aug). *Third South Pacific Games, Port Moresby. T* **46** *and similar horiz design. Multicoloured. P* 12½.

136 25 c. Type **46** .. 10 10
137 1 f. Cyphers, flags and relay runner passing baton .. 20 20

(Des V. Whiteley. Litho P.B.)

1969 (15 Oct). *Pentecost Island Land Divers. T* **48** *and similar vert designs. Multicoloured. W w* **12** *(sideways). P* 12½.

138 15 c. Type **48** .. 10 10
139 25 c. Diver jumping .. 10 10
140 1 f. Diver at end of fall .. 20 20
138/40 .. *Set of* 3 30 30

51 U.P.U. Emblem and New Headquarters Building **52** General Charles de Gaulle

(Des and eng J. Gauthier. Recess Govt Ptg Wks, Paris)

1970 (20 May). *Inauguration of New U.P.U. Headquarters Building. P* 13.

141 **51** 1 f. 05, slate, red-orange & bright purple 15 15

(Des V. Whiteley. Photo Govt Ptg Wks, Paris)

1970 (20 July). *30th Anniv of New Hebrides' Declaration for the Free French Government. P* 13.

142 **52** 65 c. multicoloured .. 35 15
143 1 f. 10, multicoloured .. 45 15

(**53**) **54** "The Virgin and Child" (Bellini)

1970 (15 Oct). *As No. 101, but W w* **12** *(sideways) and surch with T* **53.**

144 35 c. on 20 c. black, ol-grn & greenish black .. 30 30

(Des V. Whiteley. Litho Harrison)

1970 (30 Nov). *Christmas. T* **54** *and similar vert design. Multicoloured. W w* **12** *(sideways). P* 14½ × 14.

145 15 c. Type **54** .. 10 10
146 50 c. "The Virgin and Child" (Cima) .. 10 10

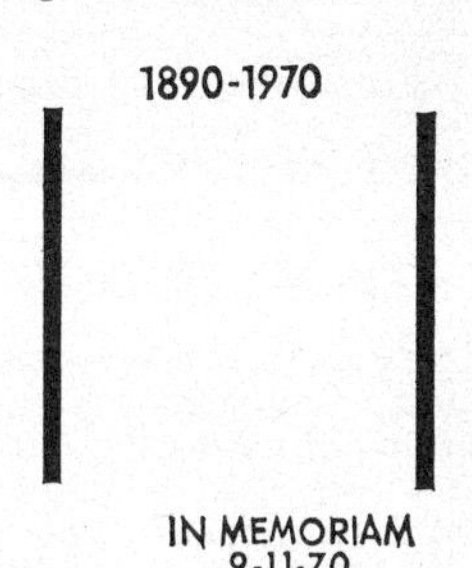

(**55**)

1971 (19 Jan). *Death of General Charles de Gaulle. Nos.* 142/3 *optd with T* **55**, *vertical bars in black, inscriptions in gold.*
147 **52** 65 c. multicoloured 15 10
148 1 f. 10, multicoloured 15 20

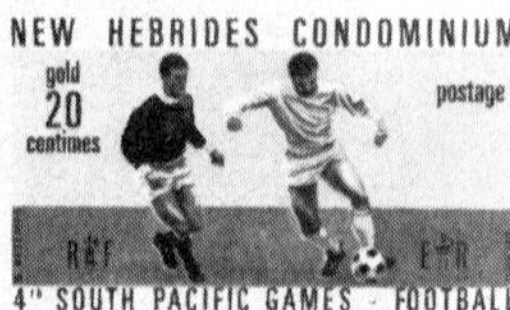

56 Football

(Des G. Bétemps. Photo Delrieu)

1971 (13 July). *Fourth South Pacific Games, Papeete, French Polynesia. T* **56** *and similar multicoloured design. P* 12½.
149 20 c. Type **56** 10 10
150 65 c. Basketball (*vert*) 30 20

57 Kauri Pine, Cone and Arms of Royal Society
58 "The Adoration of the Shepherds" (detail, Louis le Nain)

(Des P. Powell. Litho Harrison)

1971 (7 Sept). *Royal Society Expedition to New Hebrides,* 1971. *W* w **12** (*sideways*). *P* 14½ × 14.
151 **57** 65 c. multicoloured 20 10

(Des G. Drummond. Litho Questa)

1971 (23 Nov). *Christmas. T* **58** *and similar vert design. Multicoloured. W* w **12**. *P* 14 × 13½.
152 25 c. Type **58** 10 10
153 50 c. "The Adoration of the Shepherds" (detail, Tintoretto) 20 20

59 "Drover" Mk III
60 Ceremonial Headdress, South Malekula

(Des M. Goaman. Photo Delrieu)

1972 (29 Feb). *Aircraft. T* **59** *and similar horiz designs. Multicoloured. P* 13.
154 20 c. Type **59** 35 15
155 25 c. "Sandringham" flying-boat 45 15
156 30 c. D.H. "Dragon Rapide" 45 15
157 65 c. "Caravelle" .. .. 1·25 1·25
154/7 .. .. *Set of* 4 2·25 1·50

(Des Odette Baillais (bird designs), Pierrette Lambert (others). Photo Govt Printing Works, Paris)

1972 (24 July). *T* **60** *and similar vert designs. Multicoloured. P* 12½ × 13.
158 5 c. Type **60** 10 10
159 10 c. Baker's Pigeon 25 10
160 15 c. Gong and carving, North Ambrym .. 15 15
161 20 c. Red-headed Parrot Finch 40 25
162 25 c. *Cribraria fischeri* (shell) 40 25
163 30 c. *Oliva rubrolabiata* (shell) 50 30
164 35 c. Chestnut-bellied Kingfisher 65 40
165 65 c. *Strombus plicatus* (shell) 75 60
166 1 f. Gong (North Malekula) and carving (North Ambrym) .. .. 1·25 1·00
167 2 f. Palm Lorikeet .. .. 4·00 4·50
168 3 f. Ceremonial headdress, South Malekula (*different*) .. .. 3·75 6·00
169 5 f. Green snail shell .. .. 7·50 13·00
158/69 *and* 199 .. .. .. *Set of* 13 27·00 40·00

PRICES OF SETS

Set prices are given for many issues, generally those containing three stamps or more. Definitive sets include one of each value or major colour change, but do not cover different perforations, die types or minor shades. Where a choice is possible the set prices are based on the cheapest versions of the stamps included in the listings.

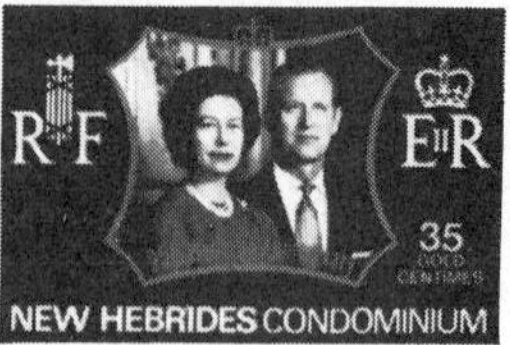

61 "Adoration of the Kings" (Spranger)
62 Royal and French Cyphers

(Des G. Drummond. Litho J.W.)

1972 (25 Sept). *Christmas. T* **61** *and similar vert design. Multicoloured. W* w **12**. *P* 14.
170 25 c. Type **61** 10 10
171 70 c. "The Virgin and Child in a Landscape" (Provoost) 20 20

(Des (from photographs by D. Groves) and photo Harrison)

1972 (20 Nov). *Royal Silver Wedding. Multicoloured; background colour given. W* w **12**. *P* 14 × 14½.
172 **62** 35 c. violet-black 15 10
173 65 c. yellow-olive 20 10

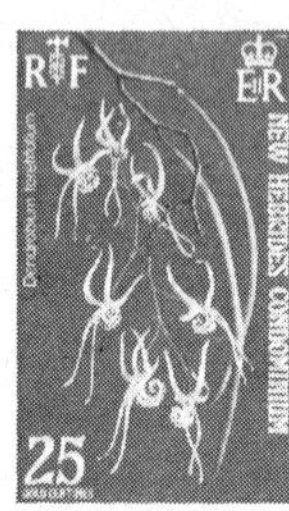

63 *Dendrobium teretifolium*
64 New Wharf at Vila

(Des Jennifer Toombs. Litho Questa)

1973 (26 Feb). *Orchids. T* **63** *and similar vert designs. Multicoloured. W* w **12** (*sideways*). *P* 14 × 14½.
174 25 c. Type **63** 25 10
175 30 c. *Ephemerantha comata* 30 10
176 35 c. *Spathoglottis petri* 35 10
177 65 c. *Dendrobium mohlianum* 60 55
174/7 .. .. *Set of* 4 1·40 70

(Des PAD Studio. Litho Questa)

1973 (14 May). *Opening of New Wharf at Vila. P* 14 × 14½ (25 *c.*) *or* 14½ × 14 (70 *c.*).
178 **64** 25 c. multicoloured 20 10
179 – 70 c. multicoloured 40 30
The 70 c. is as T **64**, but in a horizontal format.

65 Wild Horses
66 Mother and Child

(Des Pierrette Lambert. Photo Govt Printing Works, Paris)

1973 (13 Aug). *Tanna Island. T* **65** *and similar horiz design. Multicoloured. P* 13 × 12½.
180 35 c. Type **65** 30 15
181 70 c. Yasur Volcano 55 20

(Des Moutouh (35 c.), Tatin d'Avesnières (70 c.); adapted PAD Studio. Litho Questa)

1973 (19 Nov). *Christmas. T* **66** *and similar vert design. Multicoloured. W* w **12** (*sideways*). *P* 13½.
182 35 c. Type **66** 10 10
183 70 c. Lagoon scene 20 20

67 Pacific Pigeon

ROYAL VISIT 1974

(68)

(Des J. and H. Bregulla. Photo Govt Printing Works, Paris)

1974 (11 Feb). *Wild Life. T* **67** *and similar horiz designs. Multicoloured. P* 13 × 12½.
184 25 c. Type **67** 95 35
185 35 c. *Lyssa curvata* (moth) .. .. .. 1·25 60
186 70 c. Green Sea Turtle .. .. 1·50 70
187 1 f. 15, Grey-headed Flying Fox .. .. 1·75 1·50
184/7 .. .. *Set of* 4 5·00 2·75

1974 (11 Feb). *Royal Visit of Queen Elizabeth II. Nos.* 164 *and* 167 *optd with T* **68**.
188 35 c. Chestnut-bellied Kingfisher (R.) 15 10
189 2 f. Palm Lorikeet 30 40

69 Old Post Office

(Des Odette Baillais. Photo Govt Printing Works, Paris)

1974 (6 May). *Inauguration of New Post Office, Vila. T* **69** *and similar triangular design. Multicoloured. P* 12.
190 35 c. Type **69** 15 40
a. *Tête-bêche* (pair). Nos. 190/1 .. .. 30 85
191 70 c. New Post Office 15 45
Nos. 190/1 were printed together, in *tête-bêche* pairs throughout the sheet.

70 Capt. Cook and Map

(Des J. Cooter. Litho J.W.)

1974 (1 Aug). *Bicentenary of Discovery. T* **70** *and similar horiz designs. Multicoloured. W* w **12** (*sideways on* 1 *f.* 15). *P* 11 (1 *f.* 15) *or* 13 (*others*).
192 35 c. Type **70** .. .. 1·75 1·75
a. Horiz strip of 3. Nos. 192/4 .. .. 5·00
193 35 c. William Wales and beach landing .. 1·75 1·75
194 35 c. William Hodges and island scene .. 1·75 1·75
195 1 f. 15, Capt Cook, map and H.M.S. *Resolution* (59 × 34 *mm*) .. .. .. 4·00 4·00
192/5 .. .. *Set of* 4 8·00 8·00
Nos. 192/4 were printed together, *se-tenant*, in horizontal strips of 3 throughout the sheet forming a composite design.

71 U.P.U. Emblem and Letters
72 "Adoration of the Magi" (Velazquez)

(Des Pierrette Lambert. Photo Govt Printing Works, Paris)

1974 (9 Oct). *Centenary of Universal Postal Union. P* 13 × 12½.
196 **71** 70 c. multicoloured 30 50

(Des J. Cooter. Litho Questa)

1974 (14 Nov). *Christmas. T* **72** *and similar multicoloured design. W* w **12** (*sideways on* 70 *c.*). *P* 14 × 13½ (35 *c.*) *or* 13½ × 14 (70 *c.*).
197 35 c. Type **72** 10 10
198 70 c. "The Nativity" (Gerard van Honthorst) (*horiz*) 20 20

73 Charolais Bull
74 Canoeing

(Des and eng J. Pheulpin. Recess Govt Printing Works, Paris)

1975 (29 Apr). *P* 13 × 12½.
199 **73** 10 f. bistre-brown, green & dull ultram 11·00 18·00

(Des J. Cooter. Litho Questa)

1975 (5 Aug). *World Scout Jamboree, Norway. T* **74** *and similar vert designs. Multicoloured. P* 13½.

200 25 c. Type **74** 30 10
201 35 c. Preparing meal 30 10
202 1 f. Map-reading 70 15
203 5 f. Fishing . . . . 3·00 2·50
200/3 . . . . *Set of* 4 4·00 2·50

75 "Pitti Madonna" (Michelangelo)

(Des PAD Studio. Litho Harrison)

1975 (11 Nov). *Christmas. Michelangelo's Sculptures. T* **75** *and similar vert designs. Multicoloured. W w* **12** (*sideways*). *P* 14½ × 14.

204 35 c. Type **75** 10 10
205 70 c. "Bruges Madonna" 15 10
206 2 f. 50, "Taddei Madonna" 70 50
204/6 . . . . *Set of* 3 85 55

76 "Concorde"

(Des J. B. F. Chesnot. Typo Edila)

1976 (30 Jan). *First Commercial Flight of "Concorde". P* 13.

207 **76** 5 f. multicoloured . . . . 15·00 6·00

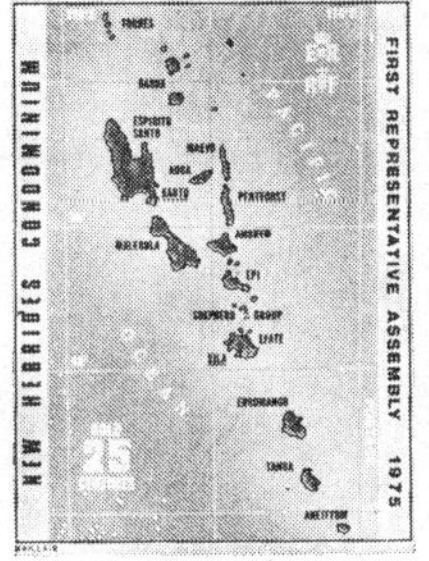

77 Telephones of 1876 and 1976 **78** Map of the Islands

(Des J. Gauthier. Photo Delrieu)

1976 (31 Mar). *Telephone Centenary. T* **77** *and similar vert designs. Multicoloured. P* 13½.

208 25 c. Type **77** 15 10
209 70 c. Alexander Graham Bell 30 10
210 1 f. 15, Satellite and Nouméa Earth Station 50 50
208/10 . . . . *Set of* 3 85 60

(Des Odette Baillais. Photo Govt Printing Works, Paris)

1976 (29 June). *Constitutional Changes. T* **78** *and similar multicoloured designs. P* 13 (25 c.) *or* 13 × 12½ (*others*).

211 25 c. Type **78** 20 15
212 1 f. View of Santo (36×27 *mm*) 45 60
213 2 f. View of Vila (36×27 *mm*) . . . . 65 1·25
211/13 . . . . *Set of* 3 1·10 1·75

No. 211 shows the incorrect longitude, 116°E instead of 166°E.

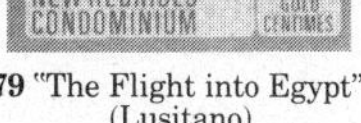

79 "The Flight into Egypt" (Lusitano) **80** Royal Visit, 1974

(Des J. Cooter. Litho Walsall)

1976 (8 Nov). *Christmas. T* **79** *and similar vert designs. Multicoloured. W w* **14**. *P* 13½.

214 35 c. Type **79** 10 10
215 70 c. "Adoration of the Shepherds" 15 10
216 2 f. 50, "Adoration of the Magi" 45 50
214/16 . . . . *Set of* 3 60 55

Nos. 215/16 show retables by the Master of Santos-o-Novo.

(Des BG Studio. Litho Walsall)

1977 (7 Feb). *Silver Jubilee. T* **80** *and similar vert designs. Multicoloured. W w* **14**. *P* 13½.

217 35 c. Type **80** 15 10
218 70 c. Imperial State Crown 20 10
219 2 f. The Blessing 40 65
217/19 . . . . *Set of* 3 65 70

(New Currency: 100 centimes=1 New Hebrides franc)

FNH FNH FNH 25 FNH

(**81**) (5 f.) (**82**) (10 f., 20 f.) (**83**) (15 f.) (**84**)

1977 (1 July). *Currency change. Surch by Govt. Ptg Works, Paris. Nos.* 220/3 *as T* **81/3**, *others as T* **84**.

220 5 f. on 5 c. Type **60** 40 30
221 10 f. on 10 c. Baker's Pigeon 80 35
222 15 f. on 15 c. Gong and carving 60 60
223 20 f. on 20 c. Red-headed Parrot Finch . . 1·25 55
224 25 f. on 25 c. *Cribraria fischeri* (shell) . . 1·00 1·00
225 30 f. on 30 c. *Oliva rubrolabiata* (shell) . . 1·25 50
226 35 f. on 35 c. Chestnut-bellied Kingfisher . . 1·50 1·25
227 40 f. on 65 c. *Strombus plicatus* (shell) . . 1·25 1·50
228 50 f. on 1 f. Gong and carving . . . . 1·50 1·50
229 70 f. on 2 f. Palm Lorikeet . . . . 3·00 1·00
230 100 f. on 3 f. Ceremonial headdress . . . . 3·00 4·25
231 200 f. on 5 f. Green snail shell . . . . 7·00 14·00
232 500 f. on 10 f. Type **73** . . . . 17·00 24·00
220/32 . . . . *Set of* 13 35·00 45·00

FNH FNH FNH

(**85**) (5 f.) (**86**) (10 f.) (**87**) (15 f.)

Two settings of 35 f. and 200 f. surcharges:
Setting I. Space of 1.4 mm between figures and "FNH".
Setting II. Space of 2.1 mm between figures and "FNH".

1977 (18 July)–**78**. *Nos.* 158/60, 162/5 *and* 169 *surch by I.P.V., Port Vila, in typography with T* **85/7** *or similar surcharges.*

233 5 f. on 5 c. Type **60** (10.8.77) 50 15
 a. Surch double
234 10 f. on 10 c. Baker's Pigeon (10.7.77) . . 50 15
235 15 f. on 15 c. Gong and carving (18.7.77) . . 2·50 1·25
 b. Short bar in surcharge (5.8.77) . . 1·50 90
 ba. Surch inverted
236 25 f. on 25 c. *Cribraria fischeri* (shell) (10.9.77) . . . . 50·00 20·00
 a. "FHN" for "FNH" (R. 5/1) . . £400
237 30 f. on 30 c. *Oliva rubrolabiata* (shell) (Setting I) (10.9.77) . . . . £190 65·00
 a. "FHN" for "FNH" (R. 5/1) . . £1200
 b. Setting II (6.1.78)
238 35 f. on 35 c. Chestnut-bellied Kingfisher (10.9.77) . . . . 2·00 55
239 40 f. on 65 c. *Strombus plicatus* (shell) (12.9.77) . . . . 1·50 55
240 200 f. on 5 f. Green snail shell (Setting I) (22.8.77) . . . . 17·00 17·00
 a. Setting II (13.1.78)
241 500 f. on 10 f. Type **73** (14.9.77) . . 18·00 17·00
233/41 . . . . *Set of* 9 £250 £110

50 f. and 100 f. local surcharges were also prepared but these were not put on general sale, being available from the Philatelic Bureau only (*Price for set of* 2 £40 *mint*, £40 *used*).

Dates are those on which the various values were surcharged.

Surcharges on Nos. 236/41 are similar to Type **84**, but with new currency inscription as Type **86**.

89 Island of Erromango and Kauri Pine **90** "Tempi Madonna" (Raphael)

(Des L. Curtis. Litho J.W. (15, 30, 40 f.), Walsall (10, 35, 70, 500 f.), Questa (others))

1977 (6 Sept)–**78**. *Maps of the Islands. T* **89** *and similar vert designs. Multicoloured. W w* **14**. *P* 13½ × 13 (15, 30, 40 *f.*) *or* 14 (*others*).

242 5 f. Type **89** 30 10
243 10 f. Territory map and copra-making (9.5.78) 40 30
244 15 f. Espiritu Santo and cattle (23.11.77) . . 30 30
245 20 f. Efate and Vila P.O. 30 25
246 25 f. Malekula and headdresses (23.11.77) 40 40
247 30 f. Aoba, Maewo and pigs' tusks (23.11.77) 45 50
248 35 f. Pentecost and land diver (9.5.78) . . 50 65
249 40 f. Tanna and John Frum cross (23.11.77) 70 60
250 50 f. Shepherd Island and canoe 70 40
251 70 f. Banks Island and dancers (9.5.78) . . 1·75 1·40
252 100 f. Ambrym and idols . . . . 1·75 90
253 200 f. Aneityum and baskets . . . . 2·75 2·50
254 500 f. Torres Islands and archer fisherman (9.5.78) . . . . 6·00 7·50
242/54 . . . . *Set of* 13 14·00 14·00

(Des J.W. Litho Cartor S.A., France)

1977 (8 Dec). *Christmas. T* **90** *and similar vert designs. Multicoloured. W w* **14**. *P* 12.

255 10 f. Type **90** 10 10
256 15 f. "The Flight into Egypt" (Gerard David) 15 15
257 30 f. "Virgin and Child" (Batoni) 20 40
255/7 . . . . *Set of* 3 40 60

91 "Concorde" over New York **92** White Horse of Hanover

(Des BG Studio. Litho Rosenbaum Bros, Vienna)

1978 (9 May). *"Concorde" Commemoration. T* **91** *and similar horiz designs. Multicoloured. W w* **14** (*sideways*). *P* 13½.

258 10 f. Type **91** 65 65
259 20 f. "Concorde" over London 85 85
260 30 f. "Concorde" over Washington . . 1·10 1·10
261 40 f. "Concorde" over Paris . . . . 1·40 1·40
258/61 . . . . *Set of* 4 3·50 3·50

(Des Jennifer Toombs. Litho Questa)

1978 (2 June). *25th Anniv of Coronation. T* **92** *and similar vert designs. P* 15.

262 40 f. sepia, turquoise-blue and silver . . 35 55
 a. Sheetlet. Nos. 262/4, each × 2 . . 1·90
263 40 f. multicoloured 35 55
264 40 f. sepia, turquoise-blue and silver . . 35 55
262/4 . . . . *Set of* 3 95 1·50

Designs:—No. 262, Type **92**. No. 263, Queen Elizabeth II; No. 264, Gallic Cock.

Nos. 262/4 were printed together in small sheets of 6, containing two *se-tenant* strips of 3 with horizontal gutter margin between.

93 "Madonna and Child" (**94**)

(Des C. Abbott. Litho Questa)

1978 (1 Dec). *Christmas. Paintings by Dürer. T* **93** *and similar vert designs. Multicoloured. W w* **14**. *P* 14 × 13½.

265 10 f. Type **93** 10 10
266 15 f. "The Virgin and Child with St. Anne" . . 10 10
267 30 f. "Madonna of the Siskin" 10 10
268 40 f. "The Madonna of the Pear" 15 15
265/8 . . . . *Set of* 4 40 30

1979 (11 Jan). *1st Anniv of Internal Self-Government. As No.* 211 *surch as T* **94**.

269 **78** 10 f. on 25 c. multicoloured (blue background) 10 10
270 40 f. on 25 c. multicoloured (pale blue-green background) 20 20

95 1938 5 c. Stamp and Sir Rowland Hill

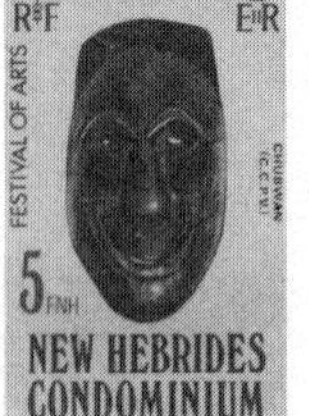

96 Chubwan Mask

(Des J.W. Litho Questa)

1979 (10 Sept). *Death Centenary of Sir Rowland Hill.* T **95** *and similar horiz designs showing stamps and Sir Rowland Hill. Multicoloured.* W w **14** (*sideways*). P 14.

No.	Description		Unused	Used
271	10 f. Type **95**		10	10
272	20 f. 1969 25 c. Pentecost Island Land Divers commemorative		15	10
273	40 f. 1925 2d. (20 c.)		20	20
271/3		*Set of* 3	35	30
MS274	143 × 94 mm. No. 272 and as No. F286, but W w **14** (sideways)		75	90

(Des BG Studio. Litho Format)

1979 (16 Nov). *Festival of Arts.* T **96** *and similar vert designs. Multicoloured.* W w **14**. P 14.

No.	Description		Unused	Used
275	5 f. Type **96**		10	10
276	10 f. Nal-Nal clubs and spears		10	10
277	20 f. Ritual puppet		15	10
278	40 f. Neqatmalow headdress		25	15
275/8		*Set of* 4	55	30

97 "Native Church" (Metas Masongo)

(Litho Delrieu)

1979 (4 Dec). *Christmas and International Year of the Child. Children's Drawings.* T **97** *and similar multicoloured designs. No wmk.* P 13×13½ (*horiz*) *or* 13½×13 (*vert*).

No.	Description		Unused	Used
279	5 f. Type **97**		10	10
280	10 f. "Priest and Candles" (Herve Rutu)		10	10
281	20 f. "Cross and Bible" (Mark Deards) (*vert*)		10	10
282	40 f. "Green Candle and Santa Claus" (Dev Raj) (*vert*)		15	15
279/82		*Set of* 4	30	30

98 White-bellied Honeyeater

(Des G. Drummond. Litho Walsall)

1980 (27 Feb). *Birds.* T **98** *and similar horiz designs. Multicoloured.* W w **14** (*sideways*). P 14.

No.	Description		Unused	Used
283	10 f. Type **98**		50	10
284	20 f. Scarlet Robin		70	10
285	30 f. Yellow-fronted White Eye		90	35
286	40 f. Fan-tailed Cuckoo		1·00	55
283/6		*Set of* 4	2·75	1·00

POSTAGE DUE STAMPS

POSTAGE DUE (D 1) — **POSTAGE DUE** (D 2) — **POSTAGE DUE** (D 3)

1925 (June). *Optd with Type* D **1**, *by D.L.R.*

No.	Type	Description		Unused	Used
D1	**5**	1d. (10 c.) green		38·00	1·00
D2		2d. (20 c.) slate-grey		45·00	1·00
D3		3d. (30 c.) red		50·00	2·50
D4		5d. (50 c.) ultramarine		55·00	4·50
D5		10d. (1 f.) carmine/*blue*		60·00	5·50
D1/5			*Set of* 5	£225	13·00
D1/5 Optd "Specimen"			*Set of* 5	£225	

1938 (1 June). *Optd with Type* D **2**, *by B.W.*

No.	Type	Description		Unused	Used
D 6	**6**	5 c. blue-green		14·00	20·00
D 7		10 c. orange		14·00	20·00
D 8		20 c. scarlet		21·00	25·00
D 9		40 c. grey-olive		30·00	40·00
D10		1 f. red/*green*		45·00	55·00
D6/10			*Set of* 5	£110	£140
D6/10 Perf "Specimen"			*Set of* 5	£120	

1953 (30 Apr). *Nos.* 68/9, 71, 74 *and* 76 *optd with Type* D **3**, *by Waterlow.*

No.	Description		Unused	Used
D11	5 c. green		5·00	6·50
D12	10 c. scarlet		1·75	4·50
D13	20 c. ultramarine		5·50	11·00
D14	40 c. blackish brown		8·50	20·00
D15	1 f. orange		6·00	20·00
D11/15		*Set of* 5	24·00	55·00

1957 (3 Sept). *Nos.* 84/5, 87, 90 *and* 92 *optd with Type* D **3**, *by Waterlow.*

No.	Type	Description		Unused	Used
D16	**12**	5 c. green		30	1·25
D17		10 c. scarlet		30	1·25
D18		20 c. ultramarine		1·25	1·75
D19	**13**	40 c. sepia		2·50	3·50
D20	–	1 f. orange		4·00	6·50
D16/20			*Set of* 5	7·50	12·50

II. STAMPS INSCRIBED IN FRENCH

NOUVELLES HEBRIDES (F 1) — NOUVELLES-HEBRIDES (F 2)

1908 (21 Nov). T **15/17** *of New Caledonia optd with Types* F **1** *or* F **2** (1 *f.*), *by Govt Ptg Wks, Paris.*

No.	Description		Unused	Used
F1	5 c. green		1·00	1·60
F2	10 c. carmine		80	80
F3	25 c. blue/*greenish* (R.)		3·50	2·75
F4	50 c. red/*orange*		6·00	5·50
F5	1 f. blue/*green* (R.)		8·00	6·50
F1/5		*Set of* 5	17·00	15·00

CONDOMINIUM (F 3) — 10c. (F 4)

1910 (Aug)–**11**. *Nos.* F1/5 *further optd with Type* F **3**, *or larger* (1 *f.*), *by Govt Ptg Wks, Paris.*

No.	Description		Unused	Used
F 6	5 c. green		1·25	1·50
F 7	10 c. carmine		1·25	60
F 8	25 c. blue/*greenish* (R.) (1911)		2·00	3·25
F 9	50 c. red/*orange* (1911)		4·50	5·50
F10	1 f. blue/*green* (R.)		12·00	13·00
F6/10		*Set of* 5	19·00	21·00

All the above were released in Paris on 16 March 1910. The 5 c., 10 c. and 1 f. were issued in New Hebrides in August but the 25 c. and 50 c. were not received until 1911 after the issue of the definitive stamps and they were placed in reserve, although some may have been issued on request.

1911 (12 July). *Wmk Mult Crown CA.* P 14.

No.	Type	Description		Unused	Used
F11	**3**	5 c. green		1·00	1·75
F12		10 c. carmine		45	60
F13		20 c. greyish slate		1·00	1·50
F14		25 c. ultramarine		3·00	4·00
F15		30 c. brown/*yellow*		5·00	3·00
F16		40 c. red/*yellow*		1·40	2·75
F17		50 c. sage-green		2·00	2·75
F18		75 c. orange		6·50	11·00
F19		1 f. red/*blue*		2·00	2·25
F20		2 f. violet		8·00	13·00
F21		5 f. red/*green*		11·00	18·00
F11/21			*Set of* 11	35·00	55·00

1913. *As last but wmk* "R F" *in sheet or without wmk.*

No.	Type	Description		Unused	Used
F22	**3**	5 c. green		75	2·25
F23		10 c. carmine		75	1·50
F24		20 c. greyish slate		80	2·25
F25		25 c. ultramarine		75	2·75
F26		30 c. brown/*yellow*		1·50	5·00
F27		40 c. red/*yellow*		22·00	38·00
F28		50 c. sage-green		11·00	13·00
F29		75 c. orange		11·00	21·00
F30		1 f. red/*blue*		4·25	5·00
F31		2 f. violet		8·50	17·00
F32		5 f. red/*green*		12·00	23·00
F22/32			*Set of* 11	65·00	£120

The above were placed on sale in Paris on 29 April 1912.

1920–21. *Surch as Type* F **4**, *at Govt Printing Establishment, Suva, Fiji.* (*a*) *On stamps of* 1908–11 (June 1920).

No.	Type	Description	Unused	Used
F32*a*		5 c. on 50 c. red/*orange* (F4)	£375	£375
F33		5 c. on 50 c. red/*orange* (F9)	2·00	4·00
F33*a*		10 c. on 25 c. blue/*greenish* (F8)	30	1·25
		(*b*) *On stamps of* 1911–13 (10.3.21)		
F34	**3**	5 c. on 40 c. red/*yellow* (F27)	24·00	50·00
F35		20 c. on 30 c. brown/*yellow* (F15)	8·00	32·00
F36		20 c. on 30 c. brown/*yellow* (F26)	12·00	35·00
		(*c*) *On Inscr in English* (10.3.21)		
F37	**3**	10 c. on 5d. sage-green (24)	14·00	23·00

1924 (1 May). *Stamps of* 1911–13 *surch as Type* F **4**, *at Suva.*

No.	Type	Description		Unused	Used
F38	**3**	10 c. on 5 c. green (F22)		1·50	2·00
F39		30 c. on 10 c. carmine (F23)		1·25	1·50
F40		50 c. on 25 c. ultramarine (F14)		25·00	45·00
F41		50 c. on 25 c. ultramarine (F25)		2·50	14·00
F38/41			*Set of* 4	27·00	55·00

F 5

France Libre (F 6)

(Recess D.L.R.)

1925 (June). *Wmk* "R F" *in sheet or without wmk.* P 14.

No.	Type	Description		Unused	Used
F42	F **5**	5 c. (½d.) black		60	5·00
F43		10 c. (1d.) green		50	4·00
F44		20 c. (2d.) greyish slate		50	1·60
F45		25 c. (2½d.) brown		50	3·00
F46		30 c. (3d.) red		50	2·75
F47		40 c. (4d.) red/*yellow*		70	2·75
F48		50 c. (5d.) ultramarine		80	2·50
F49	F **5**	75 c. (7½d.) yellow-brown		1·50	5·00
F50		1 f. (10d.) carmine/*blue*		2·00	3·00
F51		2 f. (1/8) violet		4·00	14·00
F52		5 f. (4s.) carmine/*green*		5·50	18·00
F42/52			*Set of* 11	15·00	55·00
F42/52 Optd "Specimen"			*Set of* 11	£250	

In July 1929 a batch of mail was carried by aircraft from Port Vila to the French cruiser *Tourville* for sorting and forwarding at Nouméa, New Caledonia. Stamps of the above issue (including those with English inscriptions) were affixed to covers and hand-stamped "PAR AVION" before cancellation.

1938 (1 June). *Gold Currency. Wmk* "R F" *in sheet or without wmk.* P 12.

No.	Type	Description		Unused	Used
F53	**6**	5 c. blue-green		1·50	1·50
F54		10 c. orange		1·50	75
F55		15 c. bright violet		1·25	1·25
F56		20 c. scarlet		1·25	1·00
F57		25 c. reddish brown		2·75	1·40
F58		30 c. blue		2·75	1·40
F59		40 c. grey-olive		1·25	2·75
F60		50 c. purple		1·25	1·00
F61		1 f. lake/*pale green* (*shades*)		1·50	2·25
F62		2 f. blue/*pale green* (*shades*)		16·00	15·00
F63		5 f. red/*yellow*		28·00	25·00
F64		10 f. violet/*blue*		75·00	55·00
F53/64			*Set of* 12	£120	95·00
F53/64 Optd "Specimen"			*Set of* 12	£275	

1941 (15 Apr). *Adherence to General de Gaulle. Optd with Type* F **6**, *at Nouméa, New Caledonia.*

No.	Type	Description		Unused	Used
F65	**6**	5 c. blue-green		3·25	11·00
F66		10 c. orange		3·75	8·50
F67		15 c. bright violet		4·75	14·00
F68		20 c. scarlet		8·50	14·00
F69		25 c. reddish brown		11·00	15·00
F70		30 c. blue		11·00	15·00
F71		40 c. grey-olive		11·00	16·00
F72		50 c. purple		11·00	14·00
F73		1 f. lake/*pale green*		11·00	15·00
F74		2 f. blue/*pale green*		11·00	17·00
F75		5 f. red/*yellow*		11·00	17·00
F76		10 f. violet/*blue*		13·00	18·00
F65/76			*Set of* 12	£100	£160

1949 (10 Oct). *75th Anniv of U.P.U. As Nos.* 64/7. *Wmk* "R F" *in sheet or without wmk.* P 13½.

No.	Description		Unused	Used
F77	10 c. red-orange		2·25	2·50
F78	15 c. violet		4·25	4·00
F79	30 c. ultramarine		5·50	6·50
F80	50 c. purple		6·50	7·00
F77/80		*Set of* 4	17·00	18·00

1953 (30 Apr). *As Nos.* 68/78. *Wmk* "R F" *in sheet or without wmk.* P 12½.

No.	Type	Description		Unused	Used
F81	**7**	5 c. green		30	30
F82		10 c. scarlet		50	30
F83		15 c. yellow-ochre		50	40
F84		20 c. ultramarine		60	40
F85	–	25 c. olive		50	40
F86	–	30 c. brown		50	40
F87	–	40 c. blackish brown		50	50
F88	–	50 c. violet		50	40
F89	–	1 f. orange		11·00	3·50
F90	–	2 f. reddish purple		16·00	24·00
F91	–	5 f. scarlet		26·00	48·00
F81/91			*Set of* 11	50·00	70·00

1956 (20 Oct). *Fiftieth Anniv of Condominium. As Nos.* 80/3. *Wmk* "R F" *in sheet or without wmk.* P 14½ × 14.

No.	Type	Description		Unused	Used
F92	**10**	5 c. emerald		1·00	70
F93		10 c. scarlet		1·00	70
F94	–	20 c. deep bright blue		1·00	80
F95	–	50 c. deep lilac		1·40	1·60
F92/5			*Set of* 4	4·00	3·50

1957 (3 Sept). *As Nos.* 84/94. *Wmk* "R F" *in sheet or without wmk.* P 13½.

No.	Type	Description		Unused	Used
F 96	**12**	5 c. green		65	40
F 97		10 c. scarlet		65	30
F 98		15 c. orange-yellow		1·00	40
F 99		20 c. ultramarine		1·00	40
F100	**13**	25 c. yellow-olive		1·00	40
F101		30 c. brown		1·10	50
F102		40 c. sepia		1·10	50
F103		50 c. reddish violet		1·10	40
F104	–	1 f. red-orange		7·00	2·50
F105	–	2 f. mauve		18·00	22·00
F106	–	5 f. black		28·00	32·00
F96/106			*Set of* 11	55·00	55·00

F 7 Emblem and Globe

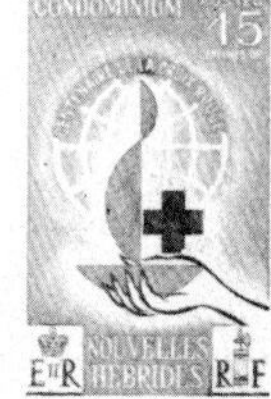

F 8 Centenary Emblem

(Des and eng J. Derrey. Recess Govt Ptg Wks, Paris)

1963 (2 Sept). *Freedom from Hunger.* P 13.

No.	Type	Description	Unused	Used
F107	F **7**	60 c. deep bluish green and chestnut	13·00	9·00

(Des and eng J. Combet. Recess Govt Ptg Wks, Paris)

1963 (2 Sept). *Red Cross Centenary.* P 13.

No.	Type	Description	Unused	Used
F108	F **8**	15 c. red, grey and orange	7·50	5·00
F109		45 c. red, grey and yellow-bistre	13·50	16·00

1963 (25 Nov)–**72**. *As Nos.* 98/109 *and* 129. *No wmk.* *P* 12½ (10, 20, 40, 60 *c.*), 14 (3 *f.*) *or* 13 (*others*).
F110 5 c. lake, purple-brown and greenish blue (15.8.66) . . 40 30
a. *Lake and greenish blue* (29.2.72) . . 50·00 45·00
F111 10 c. lt brown, buff & emerald* (16.8.65) . . 80 80
F112 10 c. lt brown, buff and emerald (5.8.68) . . 30 15
F113 15 c. yellow-bistre, red-brown & dp violet . . 4·50 40
F114 20 c. black, ol-green & grnsh bl* (16.8.65) . . 2·25 2·75
F115 20 c. black, ol-green & grnsh bl (5.8.68) . . 60 25
F116 25 c. reddish violet, orange-brown and crimson (15.8.66) . . 60 60
F117 30 c. chestnut, bistre and violet . . 5·50 60
F118 40 c. vermilion and deep blue* (16.8.65) . . 3·50 5·00
F119 50 c. green, yellow and greenish blue . . 5·50 60
F120 60 c. vermilion and deep blue (5.12.67) . . 1·50 80
F121 1 f. red, black & dp bluish grn (15.8.66) . . 2·00 2·50
F122 2 f. black, brown-purple & yellow-olive . . 18·00 7·00
F123 3 f. multicoloured* (16.8.65) . . 11·00 18·00
F124 3 f. multicoloured (5.8.68) . . 5·50 7·50
F125 5 f. blue, deep blue and black (24.1.67) . . 18·00 22·00
F110/25 . . *Set of* 16 70·00 60·00

*Normally all French New Hebrides issues have the "RF" inscription on the right to distinguish them from the British New Hebrides stamps which have it on the left. The stamps indicated by an asterisk have "RF" wrongly placed on the left.

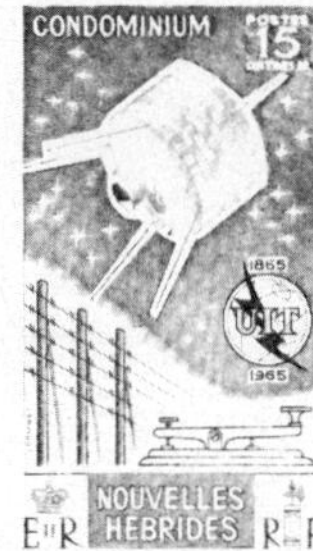

F 9 "Syncom" Communications Satellite, Telegraph Poles and Morse Key

(Des and eng J. Combet. Recess Govt Ptg Wks, Paris)

1965 (17 May). *Air. I.T.U. Centenary. P* 13.
F126 **F 9** 15 c. blue, emerald and red-brown . . 6·00 5·00
F127 60 c. cerise, slate and deep bluish green 16·00 17·00

1965 (24 Oct). *International Co-operation Year. As Nos.* 112/13. *P* 14½.
F128 **29** 5 c. dp reddish purple & turquoise-grn 3·00 2·25
F129 55 c. deep bluish green and lavender . . 9·00 7·75

1966 (24 Jan). *Churchill Commemoration. As Nos.* 114/17. *P* 14.
F130 **30** 5 c. black, cerise, gold and new blue . . 1·00 55
F131 15 c. black, cerise, gold and deep green . . 2·75 70
F132 25 c. black, cerise, gold and brown . . 3·25 3·25
F133 30 c. black, cerise, gold and bluish violet 4·00 3·50
F130/3 . . *Set of* 4 10·00 7·25

1966 (1 July). *World Cup Football Championships. As Nos.* 118/19. *P* 14.
F134 **31** 20 c. violet, yellow-grn, lake & yell-brn 2·50 2·25
F135 40 c. chocolate, bl-grn, lake & yell-brn 4·00 3·75

1966 (20 Sept). *Inauguration of W.H.O. Headquarters, Geneva. As Nos.* 120/1. *P* 14.
F136 **32** 25 c. black, yellow-green and light blue 3·00 1·50
F137 60 c. black, mauve and yellow-ochre . . 4·50 4·00

1966 (1 Dec). *20th Anniv of U.N.E.S.C.O. As Nos.* 122/4. *P* 14.
F138 **33** 15 c. slate-violet, red, yellow and orange 1·25 75
F139 – 30 c. orange-yellow, violet & dp olive . . 2·25 2·00
F140 – 45 c. black, bright purple and orange . . 2·50 2·50
F138/40 . . *Set of* 3 5·50 4·75

1967 (26 Sept). *25th Anniv of the Pacific War. As Nos.* 125/8. *P* 14 × 13.
F141 15 c. Type **36** . . 40 30
F142 25 c. War Zone map, U.S. marine and Australian soldier . . 65 40
F143 60 c. H.M.A.S. *Canberra* . . 95 1·00
F144 1 f. "Flying Fortress" . . 1·50 1·75
F141/4 . . *Set of* 4 3·25 3·00

1968 (23 May). *Bicentenary of Bougainville's World Voyage. As Nos.* 130/2. *P* 13.
F145 **40** 15 c. emerald, slate-violet and red . . 20 20
F146 – 25 c. dp olive, maroon & ultramarine . . 40 40
F147 – 60 c. bistre-brn, brn-pur & myrtle-grn . . 90 90
F145/7 . . *Set of* 3 1·40 1·40

1968 (9 Oct). *Anglo-French "Concorde" Project. As Nos.* 133/4. *P* 14.
F148 **43** 25 c. lt blue, orange-red & dp violet-bl . . 2·00 1·50
F149 – 60 c. red, black and bright blue . . 3·50 3·00

1969 (30 June). *Timber Industry. As No.* 135. *P* 14½.
F150 **45** 20 c. multicoloured (*shades*) . . 20 30

1969 (13 Aug). *3rd South Pacific Games, Port Moresby, Papua New Guinea. As Nos.* 136/7. *Multicoloured. P* 12½.
F151 25 c. Type **46** . . 30 30
F152 1 f. Runner passing baton, and flags . . 1·50 1·75

1969 (15 Oct). *Pentecost Island Land Divers. As Nos.* 138/40. *Multicoloured. P* 12½.
F153 15 c. Type **48** . . 30 30
F154 25 c. Diver jumping . . 40 40
F155 1 f. Diver at end of fall . . 1·40 1·40
F153/5 . . *Set of* 3 1·90 1·90

1970 (20 May). *Inauguration of New U.P.U. Headquarters Building, Berne. As No.* 141. *P* 13.
F156 **51** 1 f. 05, slate, red-orange & brt purple . . 50 70

1970 (20 July). *30th Anniv of New Hebrides' Declaration for the Free French Government. As Nos.* 142/3. *P* 13.
F157 **52** 65 c. multicoloured . . 55 55
F158 1 f. 10, multicoloured . . 1·10 1·10

1970 (15 Oct). *No.* F115 *surch with T* **53**.
F159 35 c. on 20 c. black, ol-green & greenish blue 60 50

1970 (30 Nov). *Christmas. As Nos.* 145/6. *Multicoloured. P* 14½ × 14.
F160 15 c. Type **54** . . 15 15
F161 50 c. "The Virgin and Child" (G. Cima) . . 25 40

1971 (19 Jan). *Death of General Charles de Gaulle. Nos.* F157/8 *optd with T* **55**, *the vertical bars in black and inscriptions in gold.*
F162 **52** 65 c. multicoloured . . 75 55
a. Gold opt omitted . .
F163 1 f. 10, multicoloured . . 1·50 1·25
On No. F162a the vertical black bars are still present.

1971 (13 July). *4th South Pacific Games, Papeete, French Polynesia. As Nos.* 149/50. *Multicoloured. P* 12½.
F164 20 c. Type **56** . . 35 20
F165 65 c. Basketball (*vert*) . . 95 80

1971 (7 Sept). *Royal Society's Expedition to New Hebrides. As No.* 151. *P* 14½ × 14.
F166 **57** 65 c. multicoloured . . 50 50

1971 (23 Nov). *Christmas. As Nos.* 152/3. *Multicoloured. P* 14 × 13½.
F167 25 c. Type **58** . . 15 20
F168 50 c. "Adoration of the Shepherds" (J. Tintoretto) . . 30 35

1972 (29 Feb). *Aircraft. As Nos.* 154/7. *Multicoloured. P* 13.
F169 20 c. Type **59** . . 1·00 60
F170 25 c. "Sandringham" flying-boat . . 1·00 70
F171 30 c. DH "Dragon Rapide" . . 1·10 75
F172 65 c. "Caravelle" . . 3·00 4·00
F169/72 . . *Set of* 4 5·50 5·50

1972 (24 July). *As Nos.* 158/69. *Multicoloured. P* 12½ × 13.
F173 5 c. Type **60** . . 40 10
F174 10 c. Baker's Pigeon . . 1·40 50
F175 15 c. Gong and carving, North Ambrym . . 50 15
F176 20 c. Red-headed Parrot Finch . . 2·00 30
F177 25 c. *Cribraria fischeri* (shell) . . 1·50 30
F178 30 c. *Oliva rubrolabiata* (shell) . . 1·50 30
F179 35 c. Chestnut-bellied Kingfisher . . 2·75 40
F180 65 c. *Strombus plicatus* (shell) . . 2·50 60
F181 1 f. Gong, North Malekula and carving, North Ambrym . . 2·50 1·75
F182 2 f. Palm Lorikeet . . 13·00 9·00
F183 3 f. Ceremonial headdress, South Malekula (*different*) . . 9·00 12·00
F184 5 f. Green snail shell . . 15·00 20·00
F173/84 *and* F213 . . *Set of* 13 70·00 70·00

1972 (25 Sept). *Christmas. As Nos.* 170/1. *Multicoloured. P* 14.
F185 25 c. Type **61** . . 25 20
F186 70 c. "Virgin and Child" (Provoost) . . 50 45

1972 (20 Nov). *Royal Silver Wedding. As Nos.* 172/3. *W w* **12**. *P* 14 × 14½.
F187 **62** 35 c. multicoloured . . 75 50
F188 65 c. multicoloured . . 1·25 1·25

1973 (26 Feb). *Orchids. As Nos.* 174/7. *Multicoloured. P* 14 × 14½.
F189 25 c. Type **63** . . 85 30
F190 30 c. *Ephemerantha comata* . . 90 50
F191 35 c. *Spathoglottis petri* . . 1·00 65
F192 65 c. *Dendrobium mohlianum* . . 2·75 3·25
F189/92 . . *Set of* 4 5·00 4·25

1973 (14 May). *Opening of New Wharf, Vila. As Nos.* 178/9. *Multicoloured. P* 14 × 14½ (25 *c.*) *or* 14½ × 14 (70 *c.*).
F193 25 c. Type **64** . . 75 50
F194 70 c. View of wharf (*horiz*) . . 1·50 1·75

1973 (13 Aug). *Tanna Island. As Nos.* 180/1. *Multicoloured. P* 13 × 12½.
F195 35 c. Type **65** . . 2·00 1·00
F196 70 c. Yasur Volcano . . 3·00 2·25

1973 (19 Nov). *Christmas. As Nos.* 182/3. *Multicoloured. P* 14 × 13½.
F197 35 c. Type **66** . . 45 35
F198 70 c. Lagoon scene . . 1·00 75

1974 (11 Feb). *Wild Life. As Nos.* 184/7. *Multicoloured. P* 13 × 12½.
F199 25 c. Type **67** . . 3·75 1·25
F200 35 c. *Lyssa curvata* . . 5·50 1·50
F201 70 c. Green Sea Turtle . . 5·50 3·25
F202 1 f. 15, Grey-headed Flying Fox . . 6·00 7·50
F199/202 . . *Set of* 4 19·00 12·00

VISITE ROYALE
1974
(F 10)

1974 (11 Feb). *Royal Visit of Queen Elizabeth II. Nos.* F179 *and* F182 *optd with Type* F **10**.
F203 35 c. Chestnut-bellied Kingfisher (R.) . . 1·50 40
F204 2 f. Palm Lorikeet . . 4·50 4·75

1974 (6 May). *Inauguration of New Post Office, Vila. As Nos.* 190/1. *Multicoloured. P* 12.
F205 35 c. Type **69** . . 50 65
a. *Tête-bêche* (pair). Nos. F205/6 . . 1·10 1·50
F206 70 c. New Post Office . . 60 85

1974 (1 Aug). *Bicentenary of Discovery. As Nos.* 192/5. *Multicoloured. P* 11 (1 *f.* 15) *or* 13 × 13½ (*others*).
F207 35 c. Type **70** . . 4·00 3·25
a. Horiz strip of 3. Nos. F207/9 . . 11·00
F208 35 c. William Wales and beach landing . . 4·00 3·25
F209 35 c. William Hodges and island scene . . 4·00 3·25
F210 1 f. 15, Capt. Cook, *Resolution* and map of islands (64 × 39 *mm*) . . 9·00 7·50
F207/10 . . *Set of* 4 18·00 15·00

1974 (9 Oct). *Centenary of Universal Postal Union. As No.* 196. *P* 13 × 12½.
F210*a* **71** 70 c. dp turquoise-blue, rosine & black 1·00 1·00

1974 (4 Nov). *Christmas. As Nos.* 197/8. *Multicoloured. P* 14 × 13½ (35 *c.*) *or* 13½ × 14 (70 *c.*).
F211 35 c. Type **72** . . 25 20
F212 70 c. "The Nativity" (G. van Honthorst) (*horiz*) . . 55 45

1975 (29 Apr). *As No.* 199. *P* 13 × 12½.
F213 **73** 10 f. bistre-brown, yellow-green & blue 25·00 32·00

1975 (5 Aug). *World Scout Jamboree, Norway. As Nos.* 200/3. *Multicoloured. P* 14 × 13½.
F214 25 c. Type **74** . . 55 20
F215 35 c. Preparing meal . . 75 30
F216 1 f. Map-reading . . 1·90 1·10
F217 5 f. Fishing . . 10·00 9·00
F214/17 . . *Set of* 4 12·00 9·50

1975 (11 Nov). *Christmas. As Nos.* 204/6. *Multicoloured. P* 14½ × 14.
F218 35 c. Type **75** . . 25 15
F219 70 c. "Bruges Madonna" . . 40 25
F220 2 f. 50, "Taddei Madonna" . . 2·25 2·75
F218/20 . . *Set of* 3 2·75 2·75

1976 (30 Jan). *First Commercial Flight of "Concorde". As No.* 207. *P* 13.
F221 **76** 5 f. multicoloured . . 18·00 13·00

1976 (31 Mar). *Telephone Centenary. As Nos.* 208/10. *Multicoloured. P* 13½.
F222 25 c. Type **77** . . 45 35
F223 70 c. Alexander Graham Bell . . 1·25 90
F224 1 f. 15, Satellite and Earth Station, Nouméa 1·60 2·00
F222/4 . . *Set of* 3 3·00 3·00

1976 (29 June). *Constitutional Changes. As Nos.* 211/13. *Multicoloured. P* 13 (25 *c.*) *or* 13 × 12½ (*others*).
F225 25 c. Type **78** . . 50 30
F226 1 f. Luganville (36 × 27 *mm*) . . 1·50 1·00
F227 2 f. Vila (36 × 27 *mm*) . . 2·50 1·90
F225/7 . . *Set of* 3 4·00 2·75
No. F225 shows the incorrect longitude, 116°E, instead of 166°E.
Nos. F226/7 exist with the inscription "PREMIERE ASSEMBLEE REPRESENTATIVE 1975" and the name of the city. These stamps were not available in the New Hebrides.

1976 (8 Nov). *Christmas. As Nos.* 214/16. *Multicoloured. P* 13½.
F228 35 c. Type **79** . . 25 15
F229 70 c. "Adoration of the Shepherds" . . 40 25
F230 2 f. 50, "Adoration of the Magi" . . 2·25 2·75
F228/30 . . *Set of* 3 2·75 2·75

1977 (7 Feb). *Silver Jubilee. As Nos.* 217/19. *Multicoloured. P* 13½.
F231 35 c. Type **80** . . 50 20
F232 70 c. Imperial State Crown . . 75 50
F233 2 f. The Blessing . . 1·00 1·25
F231/3 . . *Set of* 3 2·00 1·75

1977 (1 July). *Currency Change. Nos.* F173/84 *and* F214 *surch as T* **81/3** (*Nos.* F234/7) *or as T* **84** (*others*) *by Govt Ptg Wks, Paris.*
F234 5 f. on 5 c. Type **60** . . 40 40
F235 10 f. on 10 c. Baker's Pigeon . . 85 40
F236 15 f. on 15 c. Gong and carving, North Ambrym . . 70 60
F237 20 f. on 20 c. Red-headed Parrot Finch . . 1·50 85
F238 25 f. on 25 c. *Cribraria fischeri* (shell) . . 1·50 1·00
F239 30 f. on 30 c. *Oliva rubrolablata* (shell) . . 1·75 1·50
F240 35 f. on 35 c. Chestnut-bellied Kingfisher . . 2·50 1·50
F241 40 f. on 65 c. *Strombus plicatus* (shell) . . 2·50 2·00
F242 50 f. on 1 f. Gong, North Malekula, and carving, North Ambrym . . 2·50 2·00
F243 70 f. on 2 f. Palm Lorikeet . . 4·25 2·75
a. Surch double . .
F244 100 f. on 3 f. Ceremonial headdress, South Malekula . . 4·50 4·50
F245 200 f. on 5 f. Green snail shell . . 14·00 19·00
F246 500 f. on 10 f. Type **73** . . 26·00 35·00
F234/46 . . *Set of* 13 55·00 65·00

1977 (18 July)–**78**. *Nos.* F173/5, F177/180, F184 *and* F213 *surch by I.P.V., Port Vila, in typography with T* **85/7** *or similar surcharges.*
F247 5 f. on 5 c. Type **60** (10.8.77) . . 1·00 1·00
F248 10 f. on 10 c. Baker's Pigeon (20.7.77) . . 1·75 55
F249 15 f. on 15 c. Gong and carving (18.7.77) 2·25 1·25
a. Short bar in surcharge (5.8.77) . . 2·50 2·25
F250 25 f. on 25 c. *Cribraria fischeri* (shell) (10.9.77) . . £120 60·00
a. "FHN" for "FNH" (R. 5/1) . . £750
F251 30 f. on 30 c. *Oliva rubrolabiata* (shell) (10.9.77) . . £225 60·00
a. "FHN" for "FNH" (R. 5/1) . . £1300
F252 35 f. on 35 c. Chestnut-bellied Kingfisher (Setting I) (10.9.77) . . 4·00 4·25
a. "NH" for "FNH" (R. 4/2) . .
b. Setting II (6.1.78) . . 20·00 13·00
F253 40 f. on 65 c. *Strombus plicatus* (shell) (12.9.77) . . 4·50 4·50
F254 200 f. on 5 f. Green snail shell (Setting I) (22.8.77) . . 35·00 45·00
a. Setting II (13.1.78) . .
F255 500 f. on 10 f. Type **73** (14.9.77) . . 40·00 48·00
F247/55 . . *Set of* 9 £375 £200
Dates are those on which the various values were surcharged.
50 f., 70 f. and 100 f. local surcharges were also prepared, but were not put on general sale, being available from the Philatelic Bureau only.

1977 (7 Sept)–**78.** *Maps of the Islands. As Nos.* 242/54. *Multicoloured. P* 13½ × 13 (15, 30, 40 *f.*) *or* 14 (*others*).

F256	5 f. Type **89**	40	20
F257	10 f. Territory map and copra-making (9.5.78)	60	20
F258	15 f. Espiritu Santo and cattle (23.11.77) ..	60	20
F259	20 f. Efate and Vila Post Office	65	30
F260	25 f. Malekula and headdresses (23.11.77)	70	40
F261	30 f. Aoba, Maewo and pigs' tusks (23.11.77)	70	45
F262	35 f. Pentecost and land diver (9.5.78) ..	1·25	60
F263	40 f. Tanna and John Frum cross (23.11.77)	1·25	75
F264	50 f. Shepherd Island and canoe	2·00	75
F265	70 f. Banks Island and dancers (9.5.78) ..	3·25	1·50
F266	100 f. Ambrym and idols	3·00	2·25
F267	200 f. Aneityum and baskets	4·75	7·00
F268	500 f. Torres Islands and archer fisherman (9.5.78)	10·00	12·00
F256/68	.. .. *Set of* 13	26·00	24·00

1977 (8 Dec). *Christmas. As Nos.* 255/7. *Multicoloured. P* 12.

F269	10 f. Type **90**	20	20
F270	15 f. "The Flight into Egypt" (G. David) ..	35	35
F271	30 f. "Virgin and Child" (Pompeo Batoni) ..	85	85
F269/71	.. .. *Set of* 3	1·25	1·25

1978 (9 May). *"Concorde". As Nos.* 258/61. *Multicoloured. P* 13½.

F272	10 f. Type **91**	2·00	1·00
F273	20 f. "Concorde" over London	2·25	1·50
F274	30 f. "Concorde" over Washington	2·75	2·00
F275	40 f. "Concorde" over Paris	3·50	3·25
F272/5	.. .. *Set of* 4	9·50	7·00

1978 (2 June). *25th Anniv of Coronation. As Nos.* 262/4. *P* 15.

F276 **92**	40 f. sepia, turquoise-blue and silver ..	50	85
	a. Sheetlet. Nos. F276/8 × 2	2·75	
F277 –	40 f. multicoloured	50	85
F278 –	40 f. sepia, turquoise-blue and silver ..	50	85
F276/8	.. .. *Set of* 3	1·40	2·25

Nos. F276/278 were printed together in small sheets of 6, containing two *se-tenant* strips of 3, with horizontal gutter margin between.

1978 (1 Dec). *Christmas. As Nos.* 265/8. *Multicoloured. P* 14 × 13½.

F279	10 f. Type **93**	20	20
F280	15 f. "The Virgin and Child with St. Anne" ..	25	30
F281	30 f. "The Madonna with the Goldfinch" ..	40	60
F282	40 f. "The Madonna with the Child"	50	70
F279/82	.. .. *Set of* 4	1·25	1·60

166°E

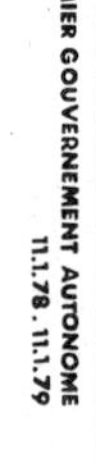

(F 11)

1979 (11 Jan). *1st Anniv of Internal Self-Government. As No.* F225 *surch as Type* F **11**.

F283 **78**	10 f. on 25 c. multicoloured (blue background)	35	25
F284	40 f. on 25 c. multicoloured (pale blue-green background)	90	1·00

1979 (10 Sept). *Death Centenary of Sir Rowland Hill. As Nos.* 271/3. *Multicoloured. P* 14.

F285	10 f. Type **95**	30	35
F286	20 f. 1969 Land Divers 25 c. commemorative	45	55
F287	40 f. 1925 20 c. (2d.)	65	75
F285/7	.. .. *Set of* 3	1·25	1·50

For miniature sheet containing No. F286, see No. **MS**274.

1979 (16 Nov). *Festival of Arts. As Nos.* 275/8. *Multicoloured. P* 14.

F288	5 f. Type **96**	20	10
F289	10 f. Nal-Nal clubs and spears	25	15
F290	20 f. Ritual puppet	45	40
F291	40 f. Neqatmalow headdress	75	1·00
F288/91	.. .. *Set of* 4	1·50	1·50

1979 (4 Dec). *Christmas and International Year of the Child. As Nos.* 279/82. *Multicoloured. P* 13 × 13½ (*horiz*) *or* 13½ × 13 (*vert*).

F292	5 f. Type **97**	55	35
F293	10 f. "Priest and Candles" (Herve Rutu) ..	75	35
F294	20 f. "Cross and Bible" (Mark Deards) (*vert*)	1·00	1·00
F295	40 f. "Green Candle and Santa Claus" (Dev Raj) (*vert*)	1·90	2·00
F292/5	.. .. *Set of* 4	3·75	3·25

1980 (27 Feb). *Birds. As Nos.* 283/6. *Multicoloured. P* 14.

F296	10 f. Type **98**	1·00	35
F297	20 f. Scarlet Robin	1·25	80
F298	30 f. Yellow-fronted White Eye	1·75	1·50
F299	40 f. Fan-tailed Cuckoo	2·00	2·00
F296/9	.. .. *Set of* 4	5·50	4·25

POSTAGE DUE STAMPS

CHIFFRE TAXE (FD 1) — **CHIFFRE TAXE** (FD 2) — **TIMBRE-TAXE** (FD 3)

1925 (June). *Optd with Type* FD **1**, *by D.L.R.*

FD53 **F 5**	10 c. (1d.) green	40·00	2·25
FD54	20 c. (2d.) greyish slate	40·00	2·25
FD55	30 c. (3d.) red	40·00	2·25
FD56	50 c. (5d.) ultramarine	40·00	2·25
FD57	1 f. (10d.) carmine/*blue*	40·00	2·25
FD53/7	.. .. *Set of* 5	£180	10·00
FD53/7 Optd "Specimen"	.. .. *Set of* 5	£200	

Although on sale in Paris, the Postmaster would not issue any in unused condition for about a year and most copies are cancelled-to-order.

1938 (1 June). *Optd with Type* FD **2**, *by Bradbury, Wilkinson.*

FD65 **6**	5 c. blue-green	11·00	20·00
FD66	10 c. orange	14·00	20·00
FD67	20 c. scarlet	18·00	26·00
FD68	40 c. grey-olive	35·00	45·00
FD69	1 f. lake/*pale green*	40·00	55·00
FD65/9	.. .. *Set of* 5	£110	£150
FD65/9 Optd "Specimen"	.. .. *Set of* 5	£200	

1941 (15 Apr). *Nos.* FD65/9 *optd with Type* F **6** *at Nouméa, New Caledonia.*

FD77 **6**	5 c. blue-green	8·00	18·00
FD78	10 c. orange	8·00	18·00
FD79	20 c. scarlet	8·00	18·00
FD80	40 c. grey-olive	8·00	18·00
FD81	1 f. lake/*pale green*	12·00	18·00
FD77/81	.. .. *Set of* 5	40·00	80·00

1953 (30 Apr). *Optd with Type* FD **3**, *by Waterlow.*

FD92 **7**	5 c. green	3·25	7·50
FD93	10 c. scarlet	3·25	7·50
FD94	20 c. ultramarine	8·50	13·00
FD95 –	40 c. blackish brown	13·00	25·00
FD96 –	1 f. orange	19·00	30·00
FD92/6	.. .. *Set of* 5	42·00	75·00

1957 (3 Sept). *Optd with Type* FD **3**, *by Waterlow.*

FD107 **12**	5 c. green	1·75	4·00
FD108	10 c. scarlet	1·75	4·00
FD109	20 c. ultramarine	4·00	6·00
FD110 **13**	40 c. sepia	8·50	12·00
FD111 –	1 f. red-orange	10·00	15·00
FD107/11	.. .. *Set of* 5	23·00	38·00

VANUATU

The former Condominium of the New Hebrides became the Republic of Vanuatu on 30 July 1980 and was admitted as a member of the Commonwealth.

99 Island of Erromángo and Kauri Pine

100 Rotary International

(Des L. Curtis. Litho J.W. (15, 30, 40 f.), Walsall (10, 35, 70, 500 f.), Questa (others))

1980 (30 July). *As Nos.* 242/54 *of New Hebrides but inscr "VANUATU" and without cyphers as in T* **99**. *P* 13 (15, 30, 40 *f.*) *or* 14 (*others*).
E. *Inscr in English. W* w **14.** F. *Inscr in French. No wmk.*

		E		F	
287	5 f. Type **99**	15	15	35	15
288	10 f. Territory map and copra making	15	15	40	15
289	15 f. Espiritu Santo and cattle	25	25	45	25
290	20 f. Efate and Vila P.O. ..	30	30	50	30
291	25 f. Malakula and head-dresses	35	35	55	35
292	30 f. Aoba, Maewo and pigs' tusks	45	45	55	45
293	35 f. Pentecost and land diver	50	50	60	50
294	40 f. Tanna and John Frum cross	60	60	90	60
295	50 f. Shepherd Island and out-rigger canoe	65	70	1·00	70
296	70 f. Banks Island and custom dancers	1·00	1·00	1·40	1·00
297	100 f. Ambrym and idols ..	1·25	80	1·50	1·10
298	200 f. Aneityum and baskets ..	1·40	1·40	1·75	1·75
299	500 f. Torres Island and archer fisherman	2·50	3·00	4·00	3·50
287/99	.. .. .. *Set of* 13	8·50	8·50	12·50	9·50

(Des L. Curtis. Litho Walsall)

1980 (16 Sept). *75th Anniv of Rotary International. T* **100** *and similar multicoloured design. P* 14. E. *Inscr in English. W* w **14** (*sideways on* 10 *f.*). F. *Inscr in French. No wmk.*

		E		F	
300	10 f. Type **100**	10	10	10	10
301	40 f. Rotary emblem (*vert*) ..	30	20	30	20

MINIMUM PRICE

The minimum price quote is 10p which represents a handling charge rather than a basis for valuing common stamps. For further notes about prices see introductory pages.

101 Kiwanis Emblem and Globe

102 "The Virgin and Child enthroned with Saints and Angels" (Umkreis Michael Pacher)

(Des L. Curtis. Litho Walsall)

1980 (16 Sept). *Kiwanis International (service club), New Zealand District Convention, Port Vila. T* **101** *and similar design. P* 14. E. *Inscr in English. W* w **14** (*sideways on* 40 *f.*). F. *Inscr in French. No wmk.*

		E		F	
302	10 f. gold, ultram & chestnut ..	10	10	20	10
303	40 f. gold, blue-grn & brt bl ..	30	20	50	25

Design: *Horiz*—40 f. Kiwanis and Convention emblems.

(Des BG Studio. Litho Questa)

1980 (12 Nov). *Christmas. Details from Paintings. T* **102** *and similar vert designs. Multicoloured. W* w **14.** *P* 14 × 13½.

304	10 f. Type **102**	10	10
305	15 f. "The Virgin and Child with Saints, Angels and Donors" (Hans Memling) ..	10	10
306	30 f. "The Rest on the Flight to Egypt" (Adriaen van der Werff)	20	20
304/6	.. .. *Set of* 3	35	35

103 Blue-faced Parrot Finch

104 Tribesman with Portrait of Prince Philip

(Des G. Drummond. Litho Questa)

1981 (18 Feb). *Birds (1st series). T* **103** *and similar vert designs. Multicoloured. W* w **14.** *P* 14.

307	10 f. Type **103**	40	20
308	20 f. Emerald Dove	60	40
309	30 f. Golden Whistler	80	60
310	40 f. Silver-shouldered Fruit Dove	90	75
307/10	.. .. *Set of* 4	2·50	1·75

See also Nos. 327/30.

(New Currency. Vatus)

(Des A. Theobald. Litho Format)

1981 (10 June). *60th Birthday of Prince Philip, Duke of Edinburgh. T* **104** *and similar vert designs. Multicoloured W* w **14.** *P* 14 × 14½.

311	15 v. Type **104**	20	15
312	25 v. Prince Philip in casual dress	30	20
313	35 v. Queen and Prince Philip with Princess Anne and Master Peter Phillips ..	40	25
314	45 v. Prince Philip in ceremonial dress ..	50	35
311/14	.. .. *Set of* 4	1·25	85

105 Prince Charles with his Dog, Harvey

106 National Flag and Map of Vanuatu

(Des J.W. Litho Walsall)

1981 (22 July). *Royal Wedding. T* **105** *and similar vert designs. Multicoloured. W* w **14.** *P* 14.

315	15 v. Wedding bouquet from Vanuatu ..	15	15
316	45 v. Type **105**	25	25
317	75 v. Prince Charles and Lady Diana Spencer	45	45
315/17	.. .. *Set of* 3	75	75

(Des C. Abbott. Litho Format)

1981 (30 July). *First Anniv of Independence. T* **106** *and similar designs. W w* **14** *(sideways on 25 and 45 v.). P* 14.

318 15 v. multicoloured 20 15
319 25 v. multicoloured 25 20
320 45 v. greenish yellow and brown-lake .. 35 30
321 75 v. multicoloured 60 70
318/21 .. .. *Set of* 4 1·25 1·25

Designs: *Horiz*—25 v. Vanuatu emblem; 45 v. Vanuatu national anthem. *Vert*—75 v. Vanuatu coat of arms.

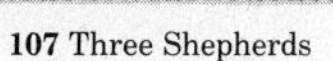

107 Three Shepherds

108 New Caledonian Myiagra Flycatcher

(Adapted G. Vasarhelyi. Litho Questa)

1981 (11 Nov). *Christmas. Children's Paintings. T* **107** *and similar multicoloured designs. W w* **14** *(sideways on 25 and 45 v.). P* 14.

322 15 v. Type **107** 10 10
323 25 v. Vanuatu girl with lamb *(vert)* 15 15
324 35 v. Angel as butterfly 15 20
325 45 v. Boy carrying torch and gifts *(vert)* .. 25 30
322/5 .. .. *Set of* 4 60 65
MS326 133 × 94 mm. Nos. 322/5 (wmk sideways) 80 1·25

(Des G. Drummond. Litho Questa)

1982 (8 Feb). *Birds (2nd series). T* **108** *and similar vert designs. Multicoloured. W w* **14**. *P* 14½ × 14.

327 15 v. Type **108** 45 20
328 20 v. Rainbow Lorys 50 30
329 25 v. Buff-bellied Flycatchers 55 35
330 45 v. Collared Grey Fantails 80 65
327/30 .. .. *Set of* 4 2·10 1·40

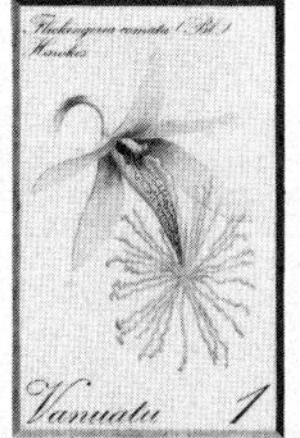

109 *Flickingeria comata*

110 Scouts round Camp-fire

(Des Jennifer Toombs. Litho Enschedé)

1982 (15 June). *Orchids. Multicoloured designs as T* **109**. *W w* **14** *(sideways on 35, 45, 50 and 75 v.). P* 13½.

331 1 v. Type **109** 10 30
332 2 v. *Calanthe triplicata* 10 30
333 10 v. *Dendrobium sladei* 15 20
334 15 v. *Dendrobium mohlianum* 20 20
335 20 v. *Dendrobium macrophyllum* 25 30
336 25 v. *Dendrobium purpureum* 30 35
337 30 v. *Robiquetia mimus* 35 40
338 35 v. *Dendrobium mooreanum (horiz)* .. 40 50
339 45 v. *Spathoglottis plicata (horiz)* 55 70
340 50 v. *Dendrobium seemannii (horiz)* 60 80
341 75 v. *Dendrobium conanthum (horiz)* .. .. 95 1·50
342 100 v. *Dendrobium macranthum* .. .. 1·25 1·50
343 200 v. *Coelogyne lamellata* .. .. .. 2·25 2·50
344 500 v. *Bulbophyllum longioscapum* .. .. 5·00 6·00
331/44 .. .. *Set of* 14 11·00 14·00

(Des L. Curtis. Litho Questa)

1982 (1 Sept). *75th Anniv of Boy Scout Movement. T* **110** *and similar horiz designs. Multicoloured. W w* **14** *(sideways). P* 14.

345 15 v. Type **110** 45 20
346 20 v. First aid 50 25
347 25 v. Constructing tower 55 40
348 45 v. Constructing raft 80 70
349 75 v. Scout saluting .. .. 1·25 1·25
345/9 .. .. *Set of* 5 3·25 2·50

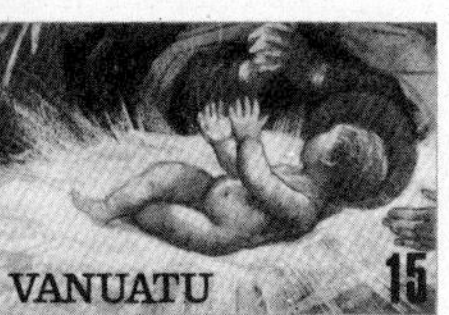

111 Baby Jesus

112 *Euploea sylvester*

(Des G. Vasarhelyi. Litho Questa)

1982 (1 Nov). *Christmas. Nativity Scenes. T* **111** *and similar multicoloured designs. W w* **14** *(sideways on 15, 25 v.). P* 14.

350 15 v. Type **111** 30 15
351 25 v. Mary and Joseph 45 35
352 35 v. Shepherds *(vert)* 55 60
353 45 v. Kings bearing gifts *(vert)* 70 90
350/3 .. .. *Set of* 4 1·75 1·75
MS354 132 × 92 mm. As Nos. 350/3 but without yellow borders .. .. 2·00 2·50

(Des J. Cooter. Litho Questa)

1983 (17 Jan). *Butterflies. T* **112** *and similar horiz designs. Multicoloured. W w* **14** *(sideways). P* 14 × 14½.

355 15 v. Type **112** 30 25
a. Pair. Nos. 355/6 .. .. 60 50
356 15 v. *Hypolimnas octocula* 30 25
357 20 v. *Papilio canopus* 45 35
a. Pair. Nos. 357/8 .. .. 90 70
358 20 v. *Polyura sacco* 45 35
359 25 v. *Luthrodes cleotas* 50 40
a. Pair. Nos. 359/60 .. .. 1·00 80
360 25 v. *Danaus pumila* 50 40
355/60 .. .. *Set of* 6 2·25 1·75

Nos. 355/6, 357/8 and 359/60 were each printed in *se-tenant* pairs, horizontally and vertically throughout the sheets.

113 President Afi George Sokomanu

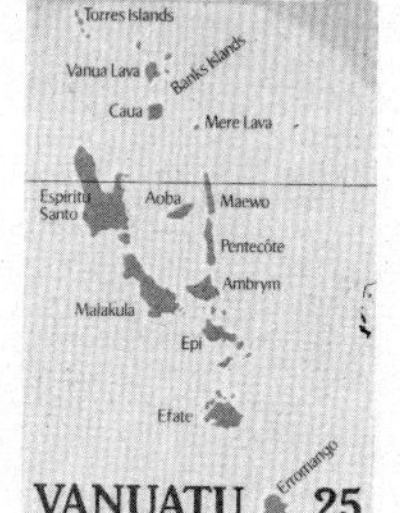

114 Map of Northern Vanuatu

(Des L. Curtis. Litho Enschedé)

1983 (14 Mar). *Commonwealth Day. T* **113** *and similar horiz designs. Multicoloured. W w* **14** *(sideways). P* 13½ × 14.

361 15 v. Type **113** 15 10
362 20 v. Fisherman and liner *Oriana* 20 15
363 25 v. Herdsman and cattle 25 15
364 75 v. World map showing position of Vanuatu with Commonwealth and Vanuatu flags 50 70
361/4 .. .. *Set of* 4 1·00 1·00

(Des A. Theobald. Litho Harrison)

1983 (23 May). *Economic Zone. Sheet* 120 × 120 *mm containing T* **114** *and similar vert designs. Multicoloured. W w* **14**. *P* 13½ × 13.

MS365 25 v. × 6 Yellowfin Tuna; Type **114**; Map of Matthew Island; Map of Hunter Island; Grouper; Oceanic Bonito .. .. 1·75 1·90

115 Montgolfier Balloon of De Rozier and D'Arlandes, 1783

116 Mail at Bauerfield Airport

(Des A. Theobald. Litho Questa)

1983 (4 Aug). *Bicentenary of Manned Flight. T* **115** *and similar multicoloured designs, each with manned flight logo. W w* **14** *(sideways on 35, 40 and 45 v.). P* 13½.

366 15 v. Type **115** 15 15
367 20 v. J. A. C. Charles balloon (first use of hydrogen), 1783 .. .. 25 25
368 25 v. Blanchard and Jeffries crossing English Channel, 1785 .. .. 30 30
369 35 v. Giffard's airship, 1852 *(horiz)* 40 40
370 40 v. *La France* (airship of Renard and Krebs), 1884 *(horiz)* 45 45
371 45 v. *Graf Zeppelin* (first aerial circumnavigation), 1929 *(horiz)* 55 55
366/71 .. .. *Set of* 6 1·90 1·90

(Des L. McCombie. Litho Questa)

1983 (10 Sept). *World Communications Year. T* **116** *and similar horiz designs. Multicoloured. W w* **14** *(sideways). P* 14.

372 15 v. Type **116** 20 25
373 20 v. Switchboard operator 30 35
374 25 v. Telex operator 35 40
375 45 v. Satellite Earth station 65 70
372/5 .. .. *Set of* 4 1·40 1·50
MS376 138 × 95 mm. Nos. 372/5 .. .. .. 1·50 1·75

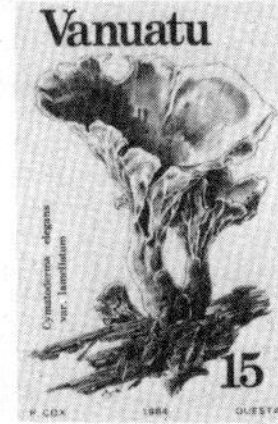

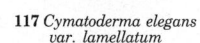

117 *Cymatoderma elegans var. lamellatum*

118 Port Vila

(Des P. Cox. Litho Questa)

1984 (9 Jan). *Fungi. T* **117** *and similar multicoloured designs. W w* **14** *(sideways on 35 v., inverted on 45 v.). P* 14.

377 15 v. Type **117** 40 25
378 25 v. *Lignosus rhinoceros* 55 40
379 35 v. *Stereum ostreu (horiz)* 70 50
380 45 v. *Ganoderma boninense* .. .. .. 1·10 70
377/80 .. .. *Set of* 4 2·50 1·75

(Des D. Miller. Litho Questa)

1984 (30 Apr). *250th Anniv of "Lloyd's List" (newspaper). T* **118** *and similar vert designs. Multicoloured. W w* **14**. *P* 14½ × 14.

381 15 v. Type **118** 20 25
382 20 v. *Induna* (container ship) 30 35
383 25 v. Air Vanuatu aircraft 35 40
384 45 v. *Brahman Express* (container ship) .. 65 70
381/4 .. .. *Set of* 4 1·40 1·50

(Des A. Theobald. Litho Questa)

1984 (11 June). *Universal Postal Union Congress, Hamburg. As No.* 371 *but inscribed "UPU CONGRESS HAMBURG" and with U.P.U. logo. W w* **14** *(sideways). P* 13½ × 14.

385 45 v. multicoloured 65 70

119 Charolais

(Des Doreen McGuinness. Litho J.W.)

1984 (24 July). *Cattle. T* **119** *and similar horiz designs. Multicoloured. W w* **14** *(sideways). P* 14.

386 15 v. Type **119** 20 25
387 25 v. Charolais-afrikander 35 40
388 45 v. Friesian 65 70
389 75 v. Charolais-brahman .. .. .. 1·10 1·25
386/9 .. .. *Set of* 4 2·10 2·40

120 *Makambo*

(Des L. Dunn. Litho Walsall)

1984 (7 Sept). *"Ausipex" International Stamp Exhibition, Melbourne. T* **120** *and similar horiz designs showing ships. Multicoloured. W w* **14** *(sideways). P* 14.

390 25 v. Type **120** 60 50
391 45 v. *Rockton* .. .. 1·00 90
392 100 v. *Waroonga* .. .. 1·90 2·50
390/2 .. .. *Set of* 3 3·25 3·50
MS393 140 × 70 mm. Nos. 390/2 .. .. .. 3·25 3·50

5

121 Father Christmas in Children's Ward

=

(122)

(Des D. Slater. Litho Questa)

1984 (19 Nov). *Christmas. T* **121** *and similar horiz designs. Multicoloured. W w* **14** *(sideways). P* 14.

394 25 v. Type **121** 40 40
395 45 v. Nativity play 70 70
396 75 v. Father Christmas distributing presents 1·25 1·25
394/6 .. .. *Set of* 3 2·10 2·10

1985 (16 Jan). *No.* 331 *surch with T* **122**.

397 5 v. on 1 v. Type **109** 30 30

PRICES OF SETS

Set prices are given for many issues, generally those containing three stamps or more. Definitive sets include one of each value or major colour change, but do not cover different perforations, die types or minor shades. Where a choice is possible the set prices are based on the cheapest versions of the stamps included in the listings.

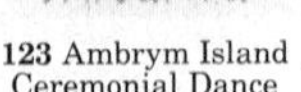

123 Ambrym Island Ceremonial Dance

124 Peregrine Falcon diving

(Des D. Slater. Litho Questa)

1985 (22 Jan). *Traditional Costumes. T* **123** *and similar vert designs. Multicoloured.* W w **14**. *P* 14.

398	20 v. Type **123**	30	35
399	25 v. Pentecost Island marriage ceremony ..	35	40
400	45 v. Women's grade ceremony, South West Malakula	65	70
401	75 v. Ceremonial dance, South West Malakula	1·10	1·25
398/401	.. .. *Set of* 4	2·10	2·40

(Des N. Arlott. Litho Questa)

1985 (26 Mar). *Birth Bicentenary of John J. Audubon (ornithologist). Peregrine Falcon. T* **124** *and similar vert designs. Multicoloured.* W w **14**. *P* 14.

402	20 v. Type **124**	60	35
403	35 v. Peregrine Falcon in flight	75	50
404	45 v. Peregrine Falcon perched on branch	90	80
405	100 v. "Peregrine Falcon" (John J. Audubon)	1·60	1·75
402/5	.. .. *Set of* 4	3·50	3·00

125 The Queen Mother on her 80th Birthday

126 *Mala* (patrol boat)

(Des A. Theobald (100 v.), C. Abbott (others). Litho Questa)

1985 (7 June). *Life and Times of Queen Elizabeth the Queen Mother. T* **125** *and similar vert designs. Multicoloured.* W w **16**. *P* 14½×14.

406	5 v. Duke and Duchess of York on wedding day, 1923	10	10
407	20 v. Type **125**	35	35
408	35 v. At Ancona, Italy	55	50
409	55 v. With Prince Henry at his christening (from photo by Lord Snowdon) ..	85	80
406/9	.. .. *Set of* 4	1·60	1·50
MS410	91×73 mm. 100 v. At Royal Opera House, Covent Garden. Wmk sideways ..	1·40	1·50

(Des A. Theobald. Litho Format)

1985 (26 July). *5th Anniv of Independence and "Expo '85" World Fair, Japan. T* **126** *and similar horiz designs. Multicoloured.* W w **16** (*sideways*). *P* 14.

411	35 v. Type **126**	45	50
412	45 v. Japanese fishing fleet..	65	70
413	55 v. Vanuatu Mobile Force Band	75	80
414	100 v. Prime Minister Fr. Walter H. Lini ..	1·40	1·50
411/14	.. .. *Set of* 4	3·00	3·25
MS415	116×102 mm. Nos. 411/14	3·25	3·75

127 "Youth Activities" (Alain Lagaliu)

(Des D. Miller. Litho Questa)

1985 (16 Sept). *International Youth Year. Children's Paintings. T* **127** *and similar horiz designs. Multicoloured.* W w **14** (*sideways*). *P* 14.

416	20 v. Type **127**	40	35
417	30 v. "Village" (Peter Obed)	50	45
418	50 v. "Beach and "PEACE" Slogan" (Mary Estelle)	85	75
419	100 v. "Youth Activities" (*different*) (Abel Merani)	1·50	1·50
416/19	.. .. *Set of* 4	3·00	2·75

NEW INFORMATION

The editor is always interested to correspond with people who have new information that will improve or correct the Catalogue.

128 Map of Vanuatu with National and U.N. Flags

129 *Chromodoris elisabethina*

(Des D. Hartley. Litho Questa)

1985 (24 Sept). *4th Anniv of United Nations Membership.* W w **14** (*sideways*). *P* 14.

420	**128** 45 v. multicoloured	70	70

(Des A. Riley. Litho Questa)

1985 (11 Nov). *Marine Life (1st series). Sea Slugs. T* **129** *and similar multicoloured designs.* W w **14** (*sideways on* 35, 55 *v.*). *P* 14½×14 (20, 100 *v.*) *or* 14×14½ (*others*).

421	20 v. Type **129**	30	35
422	35 v. *Halgerda aurantiomaculata* (*horiz*) ..	45	50
423	55 v. *Chromodoris kuniei* (*horiz*) ..	75	80
424	100 v. *Notodoris minor*	1·40	1·50
421/4	.. .. *Set of* 4	2·50	2·75

See also Nos. 442/5 and 519/22.

130 Scuba Diving

131 Liner S.S. *President Coolidge* leaving San Francisco

(Des O. Bell. Litho Walsall)

1986 (22 Jan). *Tourism. T* **130** *and similar vert designs. Multicoloured.* W w **16**. *P* 14.

425	30 v. Type **130**	70	40
426	35 v. Yasur volcano, Tanna	80	45
427	55 v. Land diving, Pentecost Island ..	1·00	70
428	100 v. Windsurfing	1·40	1·25
425/8	.. .. *Set of* 4	3·50	2·50

(Des A. Theobald. Litho Format)

1986 (21 Apr). *60th Birthday of Queen Elizabeth II. Vert designs as T* **230a** *of Jamaica. Multicoloured.* W w **16**. *P* 14×14½.

429	20 v. With Prince Charles and Princess Anne, 1951	25	30
430	35 v. Prince William's Christening, 1982 ..	40	45
431	45 v. In New Hebrides, 1974 ..	55	60
432	55 v. On board Royal Yacht *Britannia*, Mexico, 1974	65	70
433	100 v. At Crown Agents Head Office, London, 1983	1·10	1·25
429/33	.. .. *Set of* 5	2·75	3·00

(Des L. Curtis. Litho Walsall)

1986 (19 May). *"Ameripex '86" International Stamp Exhibition, Chicago. Sinking of S.S.* President Coolidge. *T* **131** *and similar horiz designs. Multicoloured.* W w **16** (*sideways*). *P* 14.

434	45 v. Type **131**	55	60
435	55 v. S.S. *President Coolidge* as troopship, 1942	65	70
436	135 v. Map of Espiritu Santo showing site of sinking, 1942	1·50	1·60
434/6	.. .. *Set of* 3	2·40	2·50
MS437	80×105 mm. Nos. 434/6	3·50	3·00

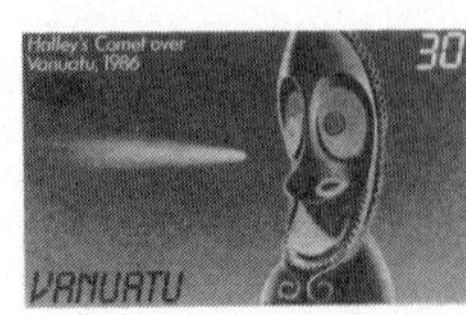

132 Halley's Comet and Vanuatu Statue

(Des Jennifer Toombs. Litho Questa)

1986 (23 June). *Appearance of Halley's Comet. T* **132** *and similar horiz designs. Multicoloured.* W w **16** (*sideways*). *P* 14½.

438	30 v. Type **132**	75	50
439	45 v. Family watching Comet	95	80
440	55 v. Comet passing Earth	1·10	1·25
441	100 v. Edmond Halley	1·75	2·00
438/41	.. .. *Set of* 4	4·00	4·00

133 Daisy Coral

(Des I. Loe. Litho Walsall)

1986 (27 Oct). *Marine Life (2nd series). Corals. T* **133** *and similar horiz designs. Multicoloured.* W w **16** (*sideways*). *P* 14.

442	20 v. Type **133**	50	30
443	45 v. Organ Pipe Coral	80	70
444	55 v. Sea Fan	90	90
445	135 v. Soft Coral	2·00	2·50
442/5	.. .. *Set of* 4	3·75	4·00

134 Children of Different Races

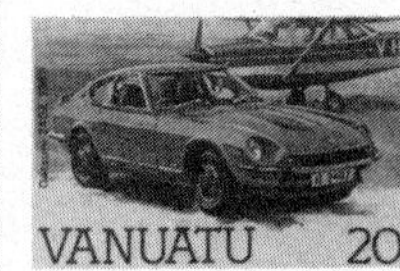

135 Datsun "240Z" (1969)

(Des C. Austin. Litho Harrison)

1986 (3 Nov). *Christmas. International Peace Year. T* **134** *and similar horiz designs. Multicoloured.* W w **14** (*sideways*). *P* 14.

446	30 v. Type **134**	75	50
447	45 v. Church and boy praying	95	85
448	55 v. U.N. discussion and Headquarters Building, New York	1·10	1·25
449	135 v. People of different races at work ..	2·25	3·00
446/9	.. .. *Set of* 4	4·50	5·00

(Des J.W. Litho Questa)

1987 (22 Jan). *Motor Vehicles. T* **135** *and similar horiz designs. Multicoloured.* W w **14** (*sideways*). *P* 14.

450	20 v. Type **135**	30	30
451	45 v. Ford "Model A" (1927)	60	60
452	55 v. Unic lorry (1924–5)	70	70
453	135 v. Citroen "DS19" (1975)	1·60	1·90
450/3	.. .. *Set of* 4	3·00	3·25

Hurricane Relief Fund +10

(136)

137 Young Coconut Plants

1987 (12 May). *Hurricane Relief Fund. No. 332, already surc as T* **122**, *and Nos. 429/33, all surch as T* **136**.

454	20 v. + 10 v. on 2 v. *Calanthe triplicata* ..	35	4
455	20 v. + 10 v. Princess Elizabeth with Prince Charles and Princess Anne, 1951 ..	35	4
456	35 v. + 15 v. Prince William's Christening, 1982	60	6
457	45 v. + 20 v. Queen in New Hebrides, 1974	75	8
458	55 v. + 25 v. Queen on board Royal Yacht *Britannia*, Mexico, 1974	95	1·0
459	100 v. + 50 v. Queen at Crown Agents Head Office, London, 1983	1·75	1·9
454/9	.. .. .. *Set of* 6	4·25	4·7

The surcharge as T **136** on No. 454 includes the word "Surcharge" in addition to the inscription illustrated.

(Des R. Corringe. Litho Format)

1987 (13 May). *25th Anniv of I.R.H.O. Coconut Researc Station. T* **137** *and similar horiz designs. Multicoloure* W w **16** (*sideways*). *P* 14.

460	35 v. Type **137**	40	4
461	45 v. Coconut flower and fronds	55	6
462	100 v. Coconuts	1·10	1·2
463	135 v. Research Station	1·60	1·7
460/3	.. .. *Set of* 4	3·25	3·7

The inscriptions on Nos. 462/3 are in French.

138 Spotted Hawkfish

139 *Xylotrupes gideon* (beetle)

(Des N. Harvey. Litho Questa)

1987 (15 July). *Fishes. T* **138** *and similar horiz designs Multicoloured.* W w **16** (*sideways*). *P* 14×14½.

464	1 v. Type **138**	10	1
465	5 v. Moorish Idol	10	1
466	10 v. Black-saddled Puffer	10	1
467	15 v. Anemone Fish..	15	2
468	20 v. Striped Surgeon	20	2
469	30 v. Six-barred Wrasse	30	3
470	35 v. Purple Queenfish	35	4
471	40 v. Long-jawed Squirrelfish	40	4

472 45 v. Clown Triggerfish 45 50
473 50 v. Scribed Wrasse 50 55
474 55 v. Regal Angelfish 55 60
475 65 v. Lionfish 65 70
476 100 v. Fosters Hawkfish .. .. .. 1·00 1·10
477 300 v. Vermiculated Triggerfish .. .. 3·00 3·25
478 500 v. Saddled Butterfly Fish .. .. 5·00 5·25
464/78 .. .. *Set of* 15 11·50 12·50

(Des I. Loe. Litho Questa)

1987 (22 Sept). *Insects. T* **139** *and similar horiz designs. Multicoloured.* W w **16** *(sideways).* P 14.
479 45 v. Type **139** 55 60
480 55 v. *Phyllodes imperialis* (moth) .. 65 70
481 65 v. *Cyphogastra* sp (beetle) 75 80
482 100 v. *Othreis fullonia* (moth) .. .. 1·10 1·25
479/82 .. .. *Set of* 4 2·75 3·00

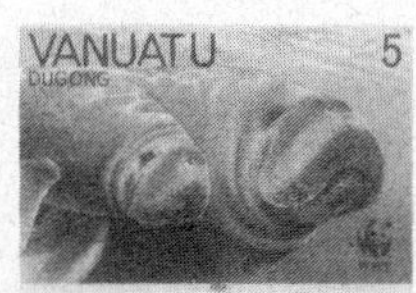

140 Away in a Manger" **141** Dugong Cow and Calf

(Des Josephine Martin. Litho Security Printers (M), Malaysia)

1987 (10 Nov). *Christmas. Christmas Carols. T* **140** *and similar vert designs. Multicoloured.* W w **14**. P 13½ × 14.
483 20 v. Type **140** 25 30
484 45 v. "Once in Royal David's City" 55 60
485 55 v. "While Shepherds watched their Flocks" 65 70
486 65 v. "We Three Kings of Orient Are" .. 75 80
483/6 .. .. *Set of* 4 2·00 2·10

1987 (9 Dec). *Royal Ruby Wedding. Nos. 429/33 optd with T* **45a** *of Kiribati in silver.*
487 20 v. Princess Elizabeth with Prince Charles and Princess Anne, 1951 .. 25 30
488 35 v. Prince William's Christening, 1982 .. 40 45
489 45 v. Queen in New Hebrides, 1974 .. 55 60
490 55 v. Queen on board Royal Yacht *Britannia*, Mexico, 1974 .. .. .. 65 70
491 100 v. Queen at Crown Agents Head Office, London, 1983 .. .. 1·10 1·25
487/91 .. .. *Set of* 5 2·75 3·00

(Des Doreen McGuinness. Litho Walsall)

1988 (29 Feb). *Dugong. T* **141** *and similar horiz designs. Multicoloured.* W w **16** *(sideways).* P 13 × 13½.
492 5 v. Type **141** 30 15
493 10 v. Dugong underwater 45 15
494 20 v. Two dugongs surfacing to breathe .. 70 50
495 45 v. Four dugongs swimming .. .. 1·10 1·40
492/5 .. .. *Set of* 4 2·25 2·00

142 S.S. *Tambo* **143** Captain James Cook

(Des E. Nisbet. Litho Security Printers (M), Malaysia)

1988 (18 May). *Bicentenary of Australian Settlement. Ships. T* **142** *and similar horiz designs. Multicoloured.* W w **14** *(sideways).* P 12.
496 20 v. Type **142** 20 25
497 45 v. S.S. *Induna* 50 55
498 55 v. S.S. *Morinda* 60 65
499 65 v. S.S. *Marsina* 70 75
496/9 .. .. *Set of* 4 1·75 2·00

(Des A. Theobald. Litho Format)

1988 (29 July). *"Sydpex '88" National Stamp Exhibition, Sydney.* W w **16**. P 14.
500 **143** 45 v. black and rosine 50 55
No. 500 was printed in small sheets of 10 (5 × 2), the two strips separated by a horizontal gutter of five illustrated stamp-size labels. The outer edges of the sheet are imperforate so that the stamps have one or two adjacent sides imperforate.

(Des O. Bell, adapted D. Miller. Litho Walsall)

1988 (24 Aug). *"Expo '88" World Fair, Brisbane. Sheet 100 × 80 mm. containing designs as Nos. 427/8, but with addition of Australian Bicentenary symbol and imprint date. Multicoloured.* W w **14**. P 14.
MS501 55 v. Land diving, Pentecost Island; 100 v. Windsurfing .. .. 1·90 1·90

ALTERED CATALOGUE NUMBERS

Any Catalogue numbers altered from the last edition are shown as a list in the introductory pages.

144 Boxer in training **145** Agricultural Crops

(Des S. Noon. Litho Security Printers (M), Malaysia)

1988 (19 Sept). *Olympic Games, Seoul. T* **144** *and similar vert designs. Multicoloured.* W w **14**. P 13½ × 14.
502 20 v. Type **144** 20 25
503 45 v. Athletics 50 55
504 55 v. Signing Olympic agreement .. 60 65
505 65 v. Soccer 70 75
502/5 .. .. *Set of* 4 1·75 2·00
MS506 54 × 66 mm. 150 v. Tennis. P 13½ .. 1·75 1·90

(Des O. Bell and D. Miller (55, 65 v.), D. Miller (20, 145 v.). Litho Questa)

1988 (25 Oct). *300th Anniv of Lloyd's of London. Multicoloured designs as T* **167a** *of Malawi.* W w **16** *(sideways on 55, 65 v.).* P 14.
507 20 v. Interior of new Lloyd's Building, 1988 25 25
508 55 v. *Shirrabank* (freighter) *(horiz)* .. 65 65
509 65 v. *Adela* (ferry) *(horiz)* 75 75
510 145 v. *General Slocum* (excursion steamer) on fire, New York, 1904 .. .. 1·75 1·75
507/10 .. .. *Set of* 4 3·00 3·00

(Des A. Edmonston. Litho Format)

1988 (14 Nov). *Food and Agriculture Organization. T* **145** *and similar multicoloured designs.* W w **16** *(sideways on 45, 120 v.).* P 14½ × 14 *(horiz)* or 14 × 14½ *(vert).*
511 45 v. Type **145** 50 55
512 55 v. Fisherman with catch *(vert)* .. 60 65
513 65 v. Livestock on smallholding *(vert)* .. 70 75
514 120 v. Market women with produce .. 1·25 1·40
511/14 .. .. *Set of* 4 2·75 3·00

146 Virgin and Child ("Silent Night") **147** *Periclimenes brevicarpalis*

(Des Josephine Martin. Litho Format)

1988 (1 Dec). *Christmas. Carols. T* **146** *and similar horiz designs. Multicoloured.* W w **16** *(sideways).* P 14½ × 14.
515 20 v. Type **146** 20 25
516 45 v. Angels ("Angels from the Realms of Glory") 50 55
517 65 v. Shepherd boy with lamb ("O Come all ye Faithful") 70 75
518 155 v. Baby ("In that Poor Stable how Charming Jesus Lies") .. .. 1·75 1·90
515/18 .. .. *Set of* 4 2·75 3·00

(Des A. Riley. Litho Questa)

1989 (1 Feb). *Marine Life (3rd series). Shrimps. T* **147** *and similar horiz designs. Multicoloured.* W w **16** *(sideways).* P 14.
519 20 v. Type **147** 20 25
520 45 v. *Lysmata grabhami* 50 55
521 65 v. *Rhynchocinetes* sp 70 75
522 150 v. *Stenopus hispidus* .. .. .. 1·75 1·90
519/22 .. .. *Set of* 4 2·75 3·00

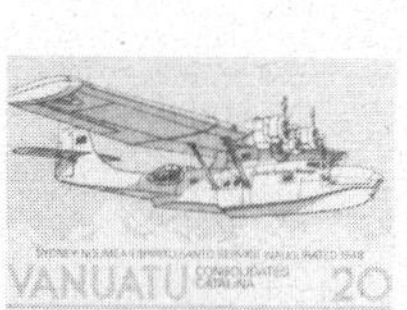

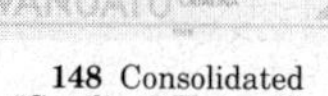

148 Consolidated "Catalina" Flying Boat **149** Porte de Versailles Hall No. 1

(Des A. Theobald. Litho Security Printers (M), Malaysia)

1989 (5 Apr). *Economic and Social Commission for Asia and the Pacific. Aircraft. T* **148** *and similar horiz designs.* W w **14** *(sideways).* P 12.
523 20 v. black and cobalt 30 30
524 45 v. black and turquoise-green 65 65
525 55 v. black and orange-yellow 80 80
526 200 v. black and orange-red .. .. 2·75 3·00
523/6 .. .. *Set of* 4 4·00 4·25
Designs:—45 v. Douglas "DC-3"; 55 v. Embraer "EMB110 Bandeirante"; 200 v. Boeing "737-300".

(Des O. Bell (Nos. 527/8), D. Miller (No. **MS**529). Litho Security Printers, Malaysia (Nos. 527/8), B.D.T. (No. **MS**529))

1989 (5 July). *"Philexfrance '89" International Stamp Exhibition, Paris. T* **149** *and similar horiz designs.* W w **14**. P 12.
527 **149** 100 v. multicoloured .. .. 1·40 1·40
a. Horiz pair. Nos. 527/8 .. 2·75 2·75
528 – 100 v. multicoloured (Eiffel Tower) 1·40 1·40
MS529 115×101 mm. 100 v. black, grey and scarlet (Revolt of French troops, Nancy, 1790 (42×28 *mm*)). W w **16** (sideways). P 14 .. 1·40 1·50
Nos. 527/8 were printed together, *se-tenant*, in horizontal pairs throughout the sheet, each pair forming a composite design.

(Des A. Theobald (100 v.), D. Miller (others). Litho Questa)

1989 (20 July). *20th Anniv of First Manned Landing on Moon. Multicoloured designs as T* **51a** *of Kiribati.* W w **16** *(sideways on 55, 65 v.).* P 14×13½ (45, 120 *v.*) or 14 (*others*).
530 45 v. Command module seen from lunar module 70 70
531 55 v. Crew of "Apollo 17" (30×30 *mm*) .. 80 80
532 65 v. "Apollo 17" emblem (30×30 *mm*) 90 90
533 120 v. Launch of "Apollo 17" .. .. 1·60 1·60
530/3 .. .. *Set of* 4 3·50 3·50
MS534 99×82 mm. 100 v. Recovery of "Apollo 11". Wmk inverted. P 14×13½ .. .. 1·40 1·50

100

(150) **151** New Hebrides 1978 "Concorde" 30 f. (French inscr) Stamp

1989 (18 Oct). *"Melbourne Stampshow '89". No.* 332 *surch with T* **150**.
535 100 v. on 2 v. *Calanthe triplicata* .. .. 2·00 2·00

(Des A. Theobald. Litho Leigh-Mardon Ltd, Melbourne)

1989 (6 Nov). *"World Stamp Expo '89", International Stamp Exhibition, Washington. T* **151** *and similar horiz designs. Multicoloured.* W w **16** *(inverted).* P 13½.
536 65 v. Type **151** 90 90
MS537 105×100 mm. 65 v. New Hebrides 1978 "Concorde" 10 f. (English inscr) stamp; 100 v. White House, Washington .. .. .. 3·25 3·50

152 *Alocasia macrorrhiza* **153** Kava (National plant)

(Des Jennifer Toombs. Litho Security Printers (M), Malaysia)

1990 (5 Jan). *Flora. T* **152** *and similar vert designs. Multicoloured.* W w **14**. P 12.
538 45 v. Type **152** 65 65
539 55 v. *Acacia spirorbis* 75 75
540 65 v. *Metrosideros collina* 85 85
541 145 v. *Hoya australis* .. .. .. 2·00 2·25
538/41 .. .. *Set of* 4 3·75 4·00

(Des O. Bell. Litho Security Printers (M), Malaysia)

1990 (30 Apr). *"Stamp World London 90" International Stamp Exhibition. T* **153** *and similar vert designs. Multicoloured.* W w **14** *(sideways).* P 13½.
542 45 v. Type **153** 75 75
543 65 v. Luganville Post Office .. .. 1·00 1·00
544 100 v. Mail plane and sailing packet .. 1·75 1·75
545 200 v. Penny Black and Vanuatu 1980 10 f. definitive .. .. 2·75 2·75
542/5 .. .. *Set of* 4 5·75 5·75
MS546 110×70 mm. 150 v. New Hebrides 1974 New Post Office *tête-bêche* pair with first day postmark. Wmk upright .. .. .. 3·25 3·50

154 National Council of Women Logo

(Des D. Ashby. Litho Security Printers (M), Malaysia)

1990 (30 July). *10th Anniv of Independence. T* **154** *and similar horiz designs. W w* **14** *(sideways). P* 14×13½.

547 25 v. black and pale blue 40 40
548 50 v. multicoloured 75 75
549 55 v. bright purple, black and buff .. 75 75
550 65 v. multicoloured 90 90
551 80 v. multicoloured .. .. .. 1·40 1·40
547/51 .. .. *Set of* 5 3·75 3·75
MS552 109×82 mm. 150 v. multicoloured. Wmk upright.. .. .. 3·25 3·50

Designs:—50 v. President Frederick Kalomuana Timakata; 55 v. Preamble to the Constitution; 65 v. Vanuaaku Pati party flag; 80 v. Reserve Bank of Vanuatu; 150 v. Prime Minister Fr. Walter Lini taking oath.

No. **MS**552 also commemorates the South Pacific Forum, Port Vila, 1990.

155 General De Gaulle at Bayeux, 1944

156 Angel facing Right

(Des G. Vasarhelyi. Litho B.D.T)

1990 (22 Nov). *Birth Centenary of General Charles de Gaulle (French statesman). T* **155** *and similar horiz designs. Multicoloured. W w* **14** *(sideways). P* 14.

553 20 v. Type **155** 55 55
a. Sheetlet. Nos. 553/4, and 555/8 each × 2 .. .. 8·50
554 25 v. Generals De Lattre de Tassigny, De Gaulle, Devers and Patch in Alsace, 1945 .. .. 65 65
555 30 v. De Gaulle as President of the French Republic 75 75
556 45 v. De Gaulle at Biggin Hill, 1942 .. 90 90
557 55 v. Roosevelt, De Gaulle and Churchill, Casablanca, 1943 .. .. .. 1·00 1·00
558 65 v. General De Gaulle and Liberation of Paris, 1944 .. .. 1·00 1·00
553/8 .. .. *Set of* 6 4·25 4·25

Nos. 553/8 were printed together, *se-tenant*, in sheetlets of 12 (4×3) containing one each of the 20 c. and 25 c. values and two each of the others plus two labels, showing the Cross of Lorraine, at each end of the centre row.

(Des Jennifer Toombs. Litho Cartor, France)

1990 (5 Dec). *Christmas. T* **156** *and similar vert designs. Multicoloured. W w* **14** *(sideways). P* 13.

559 25 v. Type **156** 45 45
a. Horiz strip of 5. Nos. 559/63 .. .. 3·50
560 50 v. Shepherds 75 75
561 65 v. Nativity 85 85
562 70 v. Three Kings 90 90
563 80 v. Angel facing left .. .. .. 1·00 1·00
559/63 .. .. *Set of* 5 3·50 3·50

Nos. 559/63 were printed together, *se-tenant*, in horizontal strips of 5 throughout the sheet, forming a composite design.

157 *Parthenos sylvia*

158 Dance Troupe from South-west Malakula

(Des I. Loe. Litho Questa)

1991 (9 Jan). *Butterflies. T* **157** *and similar horiz designs. Multicoloured. W w* **16**. *P* 14×14½.

564 25 v. Type **157** 40 30
565 55 v. *Euploea leucostictus* 80 60
566 80 v. *Lampides boeticus* .. .. .. 1·10 1·25
567 150 v. *Danaus plexippus* .. .. .. 2·40 2·75
564/7 .. .. *Set of* 4 4·25 4·50

Nos. 564/7 were each printed in sheets of 10 with the two horizontal rows of five being separated by a row of labels illustrating the butterfly's life cycle.

(Des Sue Wickison. Litho Cartor)

1991 (2 May). *Second National Art Festival, Luganville. T* **158** *and similar vert designs. Multicoloured. W w* **14**. *P* 13½×14.

568 25 v. Type **158** 45 35
569 65 v. Women weavers and baskets .. 1·00 1·00
570 80 v. Woodcarver and carved animals, masks, dish and ceremonial figures 1·40 1·50
571 150 v. Musicians playing bamboo flute, youtatau and pan pipes .. .. 2·75 3·00
568/71 .. .. *Set of* 4 5·00 5·25

(**159**)

160 White-collared Kingfisher

1991 (12 June). *Nos.* 332/4 *and* 337 *surch as T* **159** *by Mercury-Walch Pty, Hobart.*

572 20 v. on 2 v. *Calanthe triplicata* 30 30
573 60 v. on 10 v. *Dendrobium sladei* 80 80
574 70 v. on 15 v. *Dendrobium mohlianum* .. 90 90
575 80 v. on 30 v. *Robiquetia mimus* .. .. 1·00 1·00
572/5 .. .. *Set of* 4 2·75 2·75

(Des D. Miller. Litho Questa)

1991 (17 June). *65th Birthday of Queen Elizabeth II and 70th Birthday of Prince Philip. Vert designs as T* **58** *of Kiribati. Multicoloured. W w* **16** *(sideways). P* 14½×14.

576 65 v. Queen Elizabeth II .. .. .. 1·00 1·00
a. Horiz pair. Nos. 576/7 separated by label .. .. 2·00 2·00
577 70 v. Prince Philip .. .. 1·00 1·00

Nos. 576/7 were printed in a similar sheet format as Nos. 366/7 of Kiribati.

(Des N. Arlott. Litho Questa)

1991 (15 Nov). *"Philanippon '91" International Stamp Exhibition, Tokyo. Birds. T* **160** *and similar vert designs. Multicoloured. W w* **14**. *P* 14½×14.

578 50 v. Type **160** 75 75
579 55 v. Palm Lorikeet 80 80
580 80 v. Scarlet Robin .. .. .. 1·25 1·25
581 100 v. Pacific Swallow .. .. .. 1·40 1·40
578/81 .. .. *Set of* 4 3·75 3·75
MS582 75×56 mm. 150 v. Eastern Reef Heron 2·25 2·25

161 Group of Islanders

(Des C. Bulewal and Sue Wickison (80 v.), Sue Wickison (others). Litho Questa)

1991 (29 Nov). *World AIDS Day. T* **161** *and similar horiz designs. Multicoloured. W w* **16** *(sideways). P* 14.

583 25 v. Type **161** 40 30
584 65 v. Caring for AIDS victim 85 85
585 80 v. AIDS Shark .. .. 1·25 1·25
586 150 v. Children's playground .. .. 2·50 2·75
583/6 .. .. *Set of* 4 4·50 4·75

(Des D. Miller. Litho Questa (70 v.), Leigh-Mardon Ltd, Melbourne (others))

1992 (6 Feb). *40th Anniv of Queen Elizabeth II's Accession. Horiz designs as T* **112** *of Kenya. Multicoloured. W w* **14** *(sideways) (70 v.) or w* **16** *(sideways) (others). P* 14.

587 20 v. Reserve Bank of Vanuatu building, Port Vila 35 30
588 25 v. Port Vila 40 40
589 60 v. Mural, Parliament House 85 85
590 65 v. Three portraits of Queen Elizabeth .. 90 90
591 70 v. Queen Elizabeth II .. .. .. 1·25 1·40
587/91 .. .. *Set of* 5 3·25 3·50

Victoria
see Australia

Virgin Islands
see British Virgin Islands

Western Australia
see Australia

Western Samoa
see Samoa

Zambia
(*formerly* Northern Rhodesia)

NORTHERN RHODESIA

The north-eastern and north-western provinces of Rhodesia, previously administered by the British South Africa Company, were annexed by the British Government on 12 September 1923.

PRICES FOR STAMPS ON COVER TO 1945
Nos. 1/21 *from* × 2
Nos. 22/4 *from* × 5
Nos. 25/45 *from* × 2
Nos. D1/4 *from* × 15

1

2

(Eng W. G. Fairweather. Recess Waterlow)

1925 (1 April)–**29**. *Wmk Mult Script CA. P* 12½.
1 1 ½d. green .. 40 10
2 1d. brown .. 40 10
3 1½d. carmine-red .. 40 20
4 2d. yellow-brown .. 45 10
5 3d. ultramarine .. 75 30
6 4d. violet .. 90 35
7 6d. slate-grey .. 90 30
8 8d. rose-purple .. 3·75 13·00
9 10d. olive-green .. 3·75 12·00
10 2 1s. yellow-brown and black .. 1·00 75
11 2s. brown and ultramarine .. 5·50 10·00
12 2s. 6d. black and green .. 6·00 4·50
13 3s. violet and blue (1929) .. 15·00 9·00
14 5s. slate-grey and violet .. 10·00 8·50
15 7s. 6d. rose-purple and black .. 85·00 £120
16 10s. green and black .. 42·00 48·00
17 20s. carmine-red and rose-purple .. £150 £160
1/17 .. *Set of* 17 £300 £350
1/17 Optd/Perf "Specimen" .. *Set of* 17 £850

1935 (6 May). *Silver Jubilee. As Nos.* 114/17 *of Jamaica, but ptd by D.L.R. P* 13½×14.
18 1d. light blue and olive-green .. 50 20
f. Diagonal line by turret .. 30·00
h. Dot by flagstaff .. 32·00
i. Dash by turret .. 32·00
19 2d. green and indigo .. 50 40
f. Diagonal line by turret .. 38·00
g. Dot to left of chapel .. 38·00
20 3d. brown and deep blue .. 2·00 2·50
g. Dot to left of chapel .. 65·00
21 6d. slate and purple .. 2·00 1·00
a. Frame printed double, one albino .. £1500
h. Dot by flagstaff .. 65·00
18/21 .. *Set of* 4 4·50 3·75
18/21 Perf "Specimen" .. *Set of* 4 80·00

For illustrations of plate varieties see Omnibus section following Zimbabwe.

THERN-RHODE

Hyphen between "NORTHERN" AND "RHODESIA" (R. 9/6)

1937 (12 May). *Coronation. As Nos.* 118/20 *of Jamaica, but ptd by B.W. P* 11×11½.
22 1½d. carmine .. 40 35
23 2d. buff .. 70 35
24 3d. blue .. 1·25 1·75
a. Hyphen flaw .. 60·00
22/4 .. *Set of* 3 2·10 2·25
22/4 Perf "Specimen" .. *Set of* 3 60·00

3

4

"Tick bird" flaw (R. 7/1)

(Recess Waterlow)

1938 (1 Mar)–**52**. *Wmk Mult Script CA. P* 12½.
25 3 ½d. green .. 10 10
26 ½d. chocolate (15.11.51) .. 10 70
a. Perf 12½×14 (22.10.52) .. 70 3·00
27 1d. brown .. 10 10
a. Chocolate (1948) .. 55 50
28 1d. green (15.11.51) .. 60 60
29 1½d. carmine-red .. 24·00 25
a. Imperf between (horiz pair) .. £9000
b. "Tick bird" flaw .. £650 32·00
30 1½d. yellow-brown (10.1.41) .. 10 10
b. "Tick bird" flaw .. 25·00 12·00
31 2d. yellow-brown .. 65·00 70
32 2d. carmine-red (10.1.41) .. 20 10
33 2d. purple (1.12.51) .. 45 30
34 3d. ultramarine .. 20 10
35 3d. scarlet (1.12.51) .. 50 50
36 4d. dull violet .. 20 10
37 4½d. blue (5.5.52) .. 40 2·25
38 6d. grey .. 20 10
39 9d. violet (5.5.52) .. 40 2·00
40 4 1s. yellow-brown and black .. 50 10
41 2s. 6d. black and green .. 4·75 1·25
42 3s. violet and blue .. 9·00 4·00
43 5s. grey and dull violet .. 6·00 3·00
44 10s. green and black .. 5·00 8·50
45 20s. carmine-red and rose-purple .. 24·00 38·00
25/45 .. *Set of* 21 £130 55·00
25/45 Perf "Specimen" .. *Set of* 15 £275

Nos. 26a and 28 exist in coils, constructed from normal sheets.

1946 (26 Nov). *Victory. As Nos.* 141/2 *of Jamaica. P* 13½×14.
46 1½d. red-orange .. 10 10
a. Perf 14×13½ .. 1·75 2·00
47 2d. carmine .. 10 10
46/7 Perf "Specimen" .. *Set of* 2 48·00

1948 (1 Dec). *Royal Silver Wedding. As Nos.* 143/4 *of Jamaica, but* 20s. *ptd in recess.*
48 1½d. orange .. 30 10
49 20s. brown-lake .. 38·00 38·00

1949 (10 Oct). *75th Anniv of U.P.U. As Nos.* 145/8 *of Jamaica.*
50 2d. carmine .. 30 30
51 3d. deep blue .. 85 1·00
52 6d. grey .. 85 1·00
53 1s. red-orange .. 85 1·00
50/3 .. *Set of* 4 2·50 3·00

5 Cecil Rhodes and Victoria Falls

(Recess D.L.R.)

1953 (30 May). *Birth Centenary of Cecil Rhodes. Wmk Mult Script CA. P* 12 × 11½.
54 5 ½d. brown .. 30 30
55 1d. green .. 30 40
56 2d. mauve .. 30 15
57 4½d. blue .. 40 3·25
58 1s. orange and black .. 45 2·00
54/8 .. *Set of* 5 1·60 5·50

6 Arms of the Rhodesias and Nyasaland

(Recess Waterlow)

1953 (30 May). *Rhodes Centenary Exhibition. Wmk Mult Script CA. P* 14 × 13½.
59 6 6d. violet .. 20 30

1953 (2 June). *Coronation. As No.* 153 *of Jamaica.*
60 1½d. black and yellow-orange .. 15 10

7

8

(Recess Waterlow)

1953 (15 Sept). *Wmk Mult Script CA. P* 12½ × 14 (*pence values*) *or* 12½ × 13½ (*shilling values*).
61 7 ½d. deep brown .. 65 10
62 1d. bluish green .. 65 10
63 1½d. orange-brown .. 60 10
64 2d. reddish purple .. 75 10
65 3d. scarlet .. 60 10
66 4d. slate-lilac .. 1·25 50
67 4½d. deep blue .. 60 75
68 6d. grey-black .. 1·25 10
69 9d. violet .. 60 60
70 8 1s. orange-brown and black .. 60 10
71 2s. 6d. black and green .. 5·00 2·75
72 5s. grey and dull purple .. 5·50 12·00
73 10s. green and black .. 5·50 14·00
74 20s. rose-red and rose-purple .. 16·00 23·00
61/74 .. *Set of* 14 35·00 48·00

For issues from 1954 to 1963, see RHODESIA AND NYASALAND.

9

10

Arms

(Photo Harrison)

1963 (10 Dec). *Arms black, orange and blue; portrait and inscriptions black; background colours below. P* 14½ (*T* **9**) *or* 13½ × 13 (*T* **10**).
75 9 ½d. bright violet .. 20 35
a. Value omitted .. £375
76 1d. light blue .. 30 10
a. Value omitted .. 7·00
77 2d. brown .. 20 10
78 3d. yellow .. 15 10
a. Value omitted .. 60·00
b. Value and orange (eagle) omitted .. 85·00
c. Eagle printed double .. £300
79 4d. green .. 20 10
a. Value omitted .. 75·00
80 6d. light olive-green .. 20 10
a. Value omitted .. £190
81 9d. yellow-brown .. 20 20
a. Value omitted .. £150
b. Value and orange (eagle) omitted .. £225
82 1s. slate-purple .. 20 10
83 1s. 3d. bright purple .. 70 10
84 10 2s. orange .. 70 60
85 2s. 6d. lake-brown .. 80 80
86 5s. magenta .. 3·00 3·50
a. Value omitted .. £850
87 10s. mauve .. 3·00 4·50
88 20s. blue .. 5·00 14·00
a. Value omitted .. £600
75/88 .. *Set of* 14 13·00 21·00

Nos. 75/6 exist in coils, constructed from normal sheets.

A used example of the 3d. has been seen on which only the orange (eagle) has been omitted.

The stamps of Northern Rhodesia were withdrawn on 23 October 1964 when the territory attained independence as the Republic of Zambia.

ZAMBIA

INDEPENDENT

11 Pres. Kaunda and Victoria Falls

12 College of Further Education, Lusaka

(Des M. Goaman (3d., 6d.), Mrs. G. Ellison (1s. 3d.). Photo Harrison)

1964 (24 Oct). *Independence. T* **11/12** *and similar vert design. P* 13½ × 14½ *(6d.) or* 14½ × 13½ *(others).*

91 3d. sepia, yellow-green and blue 10 10
92 6d. deep violet and yellow 15 10
93 1s. 3d. red, black, sepia and orange .. 20 15
91/3 .. .. *Set of* 3 40 30
Design:—1s. 3d. Barotse dancer.

14 Maize-Farmer and Silo

15 Health—Radiographer

21 Fishing at Mpulungu

22 Tobacco Worker

(Des Mrs. G. Ellison. Photo Harrison)

1964 (24 Oct). *T* **14/15, 21/2** *and similar designs. P* 14½ *(½d. to 4d.),* 14½ × 13½ *(1s. 3d., 2s. and £1) or* 13½ × 14½ *(others).*

94 ½d. red, black and yellow-green 10 20
95 1d. brown, black and bright blue 10 10
96 2d. red, deep brown and orange 10 10
97 3d. black and red 10 10
98 4d. black, brown and orange 15 10
99 6d. orange, deep brown & deep bluish green 15 10
100 9d. carmine, black and bright blue 15 10
101 1s. black, yellow-bistre and blue 15 10
102 1s. 3d. light red, yellow, black and blue .. 20 10
103 2s. bright blue, black, deep brown & orange 25 10
104 2s. 6d. black and orange-yellow 60 35
105 5s. black, yellow and green .. .. .. 1·25 45
106 10s. black and orange .. .. .. 3·25 3·25
107 £1 black, brown, yellow and red .. .. 3·25 4·25
94/107 .. .. *Set of* 14 8·50 8·00

Designs: *Vert (as T* **15**)—2d. Chinyau dancer; 3d. Cotton-picking. *(As T* **22**)—2s. Tonga basket-making; £1 Makishi dancer. *Horiz (as T* **14**)—4d. Angoni bull. *(As T* **21**)—6d. Communications, old and new; 9d. Zambezi sawmills and Redwood flower; 2s. 6d. Luangwa Game Reserve; 5s. Education—student; 10s. Copper mining.

Nos. 94/5 and 97 exist in coils, constructed from normal sheets.

28 I.T.U. Emblem and Symbols

29 I.C.Y. Emblem

(Photo Harrison)

1965 (26 July). *I.T.U. Centenary. P* 14 × 14½.

108 **28** 6d. light reddish violet and gold 15 10
109 2s. 6d. brownish grey and gold 70 90

(Photo Harrison)

1965 (26 July). *International Co-operation Year. P* 14½.

110 **29** 3d. turquoise and gold 10 10
111 1s. 3d. ultramarine and gold 35 45

30 State House, Lusaka

34 W.H.O. Building and U.N. Flag

(Des Mrs. G. Ellison. Photo Harrison)

1965 (18 Oct). *First Anniv of Independence. T* **30** *and similar multicoloured designs. No wmk. P* 13½ × 14½ *(3d.),* 14 × 13½ *(6d.) or* 13½ × 14 *(others).*

112 3d. Type **30** 10 10
113 6d. Fireworks, Independence Stadium .. 10 10
a. Bright purple (fireworks) omitted .. 50·00
114 1s. 3d. Clematopsis *(vert)* 10 10
115 2s. 6d. *Tithonia diversifolia (vert)* 25 60
112/15 .. .. *Set of* 4 40 70

(Des M. Goaman. Photo Harrison)

1966 (18 May). *Inauguration of W.H.O. Headquarters, Geneva. P* 14½.

116 **34** 3d. lake-brown, gold and new blue .. 15 10
a. Gold omitted .. .. 70·00
117 1s. 3d. gold, new blue & deep bluish vio 30 30

35 University Building

36 National Assembly Building

(Des Mrs. G. Ellison. Photo Harrison)

1966 (12 July). *Opening of Zambia University. P* 14½.

118 **35** 3d. blue-green and copper-bronze .. 10 10
119 1s. 3d. reddish violet and copper-bronze 10 10

(Des Mrs. G. Ellison. Photo Harrison)

1967 (2 May). *Inauguration of National Assembly Building. P* 14½.

120 **36** 3d. black and copper-bronze 10 10
121 6d. olive-green and copper-bronze .. 10 10

37 Airport Scene

(Des Mrs. G. Ellison. Photo Harrison)

1967 (2 Oct). *Opening of Lusaka International Airport. P* 13½ × 14½.

122 **37** 6d. violet-blue and copper-bronze .. 10 10
123 2s. 6d. brown and copper-bronze .. 30 60

38 Youth Service Badge

39 "Co-operative Farming"

(Des Mrs. G. Ellison. Photo Harrison)

1967 (23 Oct). *National Development. T* **38/9** *and similar designs. P* 13½ × 14½ *(6d., 1s. 6d.) or* 14½ × 13½ *(others).*

124 4d. black, red and gold 10 10
125 6d. black, gold and violet-blue 10 10
126 9d. black, grey-blue and silver 15 20
127 1s. multicoloured 30 10
128 1s. 6d. multicoloured .. .. .. 40 1·00
124/8 .. .. *Set of* 5 90 1·40

Designs: *Vert*—9d "Communications"; 1s. Coalfields. *Horiz*—1s. 6d. Road link with Tanzania.

(New Currency. 100 ngwee=1 kwacha)

43 Lusaka Cathedral

44 Baobab Tree

52 Chokwe Dancer

53 Kafue Railway Bridge

(Des Mrs. G. Ellison. Photo Harrison)

1968 (16 Jan). *Decimal Currency. T* **43/4, 52/3** *and similar designs. P* 13½ × 14½ *(1, 3, 15, 50 n.) or* 14½ × 13½ *(others).*

129 1 n. multicoloured 10 10
a. Copper-bronze (including value) omitted 65·00
b. Ultramarine (windows) omitted .. 65·00
130 2 n. multicoloured 10 10
131 3 n. multicoloured 10 10
132 5 n. bistre-brown and copper-bronze .. 10 10
133 8 n. multicoloured 15 10
a. Copper-bronze (background) omitted ..
b. Blue (of costumes) omitted .. .. 50·00
134 10 n. multicoloured 25 10
135 15 n. multicoloured .. .. 2·75 10
136 20 n. multicoloured .. .. 2·00 10
137 25 n. multicoloured 25 10
138 50 n. chocolate, red-orange & copper-bronze .. 30 15
139 1 k. royal blue and copper-bronze .. .. 3·25 20
140 2 k. black and copper-bronze .. .. 2·25 1·25
129/40 .. .. *Set of* 12 10·50 1·75

Designs: *Horiz (as T* **43**)—3 n. Zambia Airways jetliner. *(As T* **53**)—15 n. *Imbrasia zambesina* (moth); 2 k. Eland. *Vert (as T* **44**)—5 n. National Museum, Livingstone; 8 n. Vimbuza dancer; 10 n. Tobacco picking. *(As T* **52**)—20 n. South African Crowned Cranes; 25 n. Angoni warrior.

All values exist with PVA gum as well as gum arabic.

Nos. 129/30 and 132 exist in coils, constructed from normal sheets.

55 Ndola on Outline of Zambia

56 Human Rights Emblem and Heads

(Des Mrs G. Ellison. Photo Harrison)

1968 (29 June). *Trade Fair, Ndola. P* 14.

141 **55** 15 n. green and gold 10 10

(Des Mrs. G. Ellison. Photo and die-stamped (gold emblem) Harrison)

1968 (23 Oct). *Human Rights Year. P* 14.

142 **56** 3 n. deep blue, pale violet and gold .. 10 10

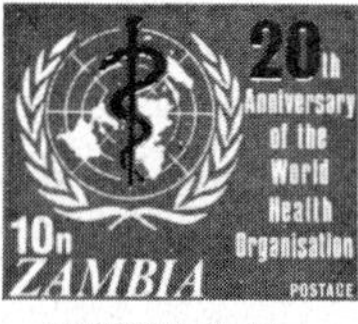

57 W.H.O. Emblem

58 Group of Children

(Des Mrs. G. Ellison. Photo and die-stamped (gold staff and "20") Harrison)

1968 (23 Oct). *20th Anniv of World Health Organization. P* 14.

143 **57** 10 n. gold and bluish violet 10 10

(Des Mrs. G. Ellison. Photo and die-stamped (gold children) Harrison)

1968 (23 Oct). *22nd Anniv. of U.N.I.C.E.F. P* 14.

144 **58** 25 n. black, gold and ultramarine .. 15 70

59 Copper Miner

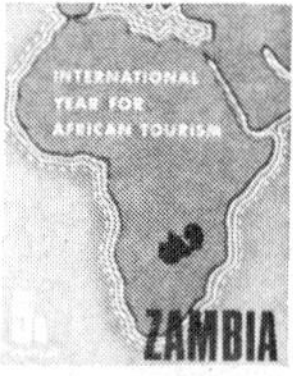

61 Zambia outlined on Map of Africa

(Des Mrs. G. Ellison. Photo Harrison)

1969 (18 June). *50th Anniv of International Labour Organization. T* **59** *and similar design. P* 14½ × 13½ *(3 n.) or* 13½ × 14½ *(25 n.).*

145 3 n. copper-bronze and deep violet 10 10
146 25 n. pale yell, copper-bronze & blackish brn 60 70

Design: *Horiz*—25 n. Poling a furnace.

A used example of No. 145 exists with the copper-bronze omitted.

(Des Mrs. G. Ellison. Photo Harrison)

1969 (23 Oct). *International African Tourist Year. T* **61** *and similar multicoloured designs. P* 14 × 14½ *(5 n., 25 n.) or* 14½ × 14 *(others).*

147 5 n. Type **61** 10 10
148 10 n. Waterbuck *(horiz)* 15 10
149 15 n. Golden Perch *(horiz)* 35 40
150 25 n. Carmine Bee Eater .. .. .. 1·00 1·00
147/50 .. .. *Set of* 4 1·40 1·40

PREVENTIVE MEDICINE

65 Satellite "Nimbus 3" orbiting the Earth

66 Woman collecting Water from Well

(Des Mrs. G. Ellison. Litho Enschedé)

1970 (23 Mar). *World Meteorological Day. P* 13 × 10½.
151 **65** 15 n. multicoloured 15 40

(Des V. Whiteley (from local designs). Litho B.W.)

1970 (4 July). *Preventive Medicine. T* **66** *and similar vert designs. P* 13½ × 12.
152 3 n. multicoloured 10 10
153 15 n. multicoloured 15 15
154 25 n. greenish blue, rosine and sepia 30 30
152/4 . . . . *Set of* 3 45 45
Designs:—15 n. Child on scales; 25 n. Child being immunized.

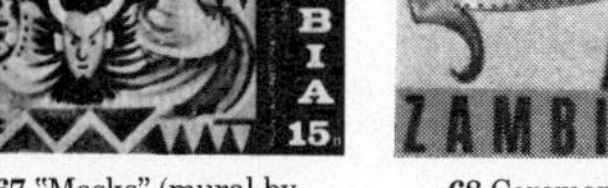

67 "Masks" (mural by Gabriel Ellison

68 Ceremonial Axe

(Des Mrs. G. Ellison. Litho Harrison)

1970 (8 Sept). *Conference of Non-Aligned Nations. P* 14 × 14½.
155 **67** 15 n. multicoloured 30 20

(Des Mrs. G. Ellison. Litho D.L.R.)

1970 (30 Nov). *Traditional Crafts. T* **68** *and similar multicoloured designs. P* 13½ (15 *n.*), 12½ (25 *n.*) *or* 14 (*others*).
156 3 n. Type **68** 10 10
157 5 n. Clay Smoking-Pipe Bowl 15 10
158 15 n. Makishi Mask (30 × 47 *mm*) 35 40
159 25 n. Kuomboka Ceremony (72 × 19 *mm*) . . 70 1·00
156/9 . . . . *Set of* 4 1·10 1·60
MS160 133 × 83 mm. Nos. 156/9. Imperf. . . . . 9·00 13·00

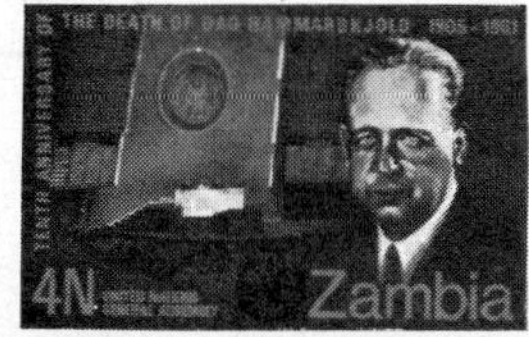

69 Dag Hammarskjöld and U.N. General Assembly

(Des J.W. Litho Questa)

1971 (18 Sept). *Tenth Death Anniv of Dag Hammarskjöld. T* **69** *and similar horiz designs, each with portrait of Hammarskjöld. Multicoloured. P* 13½.
161 4 n. Type **69** 10 10
162 10 n. Tail of aircraft 10 10
163 15 n. Dove of Peace 15 25
164 25 n. Memorial tablet . . . . 35 1·50
161/4 . . . . *Set of* 4 55 1·75

70 Red-breasted Bream

71 North African Crested Porcupine

(Des G. Drummond. Litho J.W.)

1971 (10 Dec). *Fish. T* **70** *and similar horiz designs. Multicoloured. P* 13½.
165 4 n. Type **70** 20 10
166 10 n. Green-headed Bream 35 30
167 15 n. Tiger fish . . . . 70 1·75
165/7 . . . . *Set of* 3 1·10 2·00

(Des and litho J.W.)

1972 (15 Mar). *Conservation Year* (1*st issue*). *T* **71** *and similar multicoloured designs. P* 13½.
168 4 n. Cheetah (58 × 21 *mm*) 20 25
169 10 n. Lechwe (58 × 21 *mm*) 50 60
170 15 n. Type **71** 80 85
171 25 n. African Elephant . . . . 2·00 2·25
168/71 . . . . *Set of* 4 3·25 3·50

(Des and litho J.W.)

1972 (30 June). *Conservation Year* (2*nd issue*). *Designs similar to T* **71**. *Multicoloured. P* 13½.
172 4 n. Soil conservation 20 20
173 10 n. Forestry 40 45
174 15 n. Water (58 × 21 *mm*) 60 70
175 25 n. Maize (58 × 21 *mm*) . . . . . . 1·25 1·40
172/5 . . . . *Set of* 4 2·25 2·50

72 Giraffe and Common Zebra

(Des and litho J.W.)

1972 (30 June). *National Parks. Sheet* 114 × 140 *mm containing T* **72** *and similar vert designs. Multicoloured. P* 13½.
MS176 10 n. (× 4). Type **72**; Black Rhinoceros; Hippopotamus and Common Panther; Lion . . 8·00 14·00
Each design includes part of a map showing Zambian National Parks, the four forming a composite design.

73 Zambian Flowers

(Des and litho J.W.)

1972 (22 Sept). *Conservation Year* (3*rd issue*). *T* **73** *and similar horiz designs. Multicoloured. P* 13½.
177 4 n. Type **73** 30 30
178 10 n. *Papilio demodocus* (butterfly) 70 70
179 15 n. *Apis mellifera* (bees) . . . . . . 1·25 1·25
180 25 n. *Nomadacris septemfasciata* (locusts) 2·00 2·00
177/80 . . . . *Set of* 4 3·75 3·75

74 Mary and Joseph

75 *Oudenodon* and *Rubidgea*

(Des V. Whiteley. Litho Questa)

1972 (1 Dec). *Christmas. T* **74** *and similar horiz designs. Multicoloured. P* 14.
181 4 n. Type **74** 10 10
182 9 n. Mary, Joseph and Jesus 10 10
183 15 n. Mary, Jesus and the shepherds 10 10
184 25 n. The Three Wise Men 20 40
181/4 . . . . *Set of* 4 35 50

(Des Mrs. G. Ellison; adapted J.W. Litho Questa)

1973 (1 Feb). *Zambian Prehistoric Animals. T* **75** *and similar horiz designs. Multicoloured. P* 14 × 13½ (4 *n.*) *or* 13½ × 14 (*others*).
185 4 n. Type **75** 85 85
186 9 n. Broken Hill Man 90 90
187 10 n. *Zambiasaurus* . . . . 1·00 1·50
188 15 n. *Luangwa drysdalli* . . . . . . 1·10 2·00
189 25 n. *Glossopteris* . . . . 1·25 3·00
185/9 . . . . *Set of* 5 4·50 7·50

76 "Dr. Livingstone, I Presume"

(Des J.W. Litho Format)

1973 (1 May). *Death Centenary of Dr. Livingstone. T* **76** *and similar horiz designs. Multicoloured. P* 13½.
190 3 n. Type **76** 35 15
191 4 n. Scripture Lesson 35 15
192 9 n. Victoria Falls 70 40
193 10 n. Scattering slavers 70 45
194 15 n. Healing the sick . . . . 1·00 1·50
195 25 n. Burial place of Livingstone's heart . . 1·40 2·25
190/5 . . . . *Set of* 6 4·00 4·50

77 Parliamentary Mace

(Des Mrs. G. Ellison. Litho Questa)

1973 (24 Sept). *Third Commonwealth Conference of Speakers and Presiding Officers, Lusaka. P* 13½.
196 **77** 9 n. multicoloured 80 65
197 15 n. multicoloured . . . . . . 1·00 1·75
198 25 n. multicoloured . . . . . . 1·50 2·50
196/8 . . . . *Set of* 3 3·00 4·50

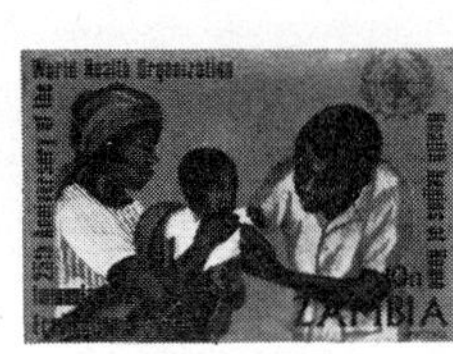

78 Inoculation

79 U.N.I.P. Flag

(Des Mrs. G. Ellison. Litho Questa)

1973 (16 Oct). *25th Anniv of W.H.O. T* **78** *and similar multicoloured designs. P* 14.
199 4 n. Mother washing baby (*vert*) . . . . 48·00 23·00
200 9 n. Nurse weighing baby (*vert*) . . . . 45 1·50
201 10 n. Type **78** . . . . 50 2·00
202 15 n. Child eating meal . . . . 90 3·50
199/202 . . . . *Set of* 4 48·00 27·00
Only a small quantity of No. 199 was produced, and most examples were issued to post offices for local use.

(Des Mrs. G. Ellison. Litho Questa)

1973 (13 Dec). *1st Anniv of Second Republic. T* **79** *and similar vert designs. Multicoloured. P* 14 × 13½.
203 4 n. Type **79** . . . . 10·00 8·00
204 9 n. Freedom House . . . . 40 1·50
205 10 n. Army band . . . . 40 2·00
206 15 n. "Celebrations" (dancers) . . . . . . 70 3·50
207 25 n. Presidential chair . . . . 1·40 5·00
203/7 . . . . *Set of* 5 11·50 18·00

80 President Kaunda at Mulungushi

81 Nakambala Sugar Estate

(Des Mrs. G. Ellison. Litho Harrison)

1974 (28 Apr). *President Kaunda's 50th Birthday. T* **80** *and similar horiz designs. Multicoloured. P* 14½ × 14 (4 *n.*) *or* 14 × 14½ (*others*).
208 4 n. Type **80** . . . . 1·00 1·00
209 9 n. President's former residence 50 50
210 15 n. President holding Independence flame . . 1·40 2·50
208/10 . . . . *Set of* 3 2·50 3·50

(Des G. Vasarhelyi. Litho Questa)

1974 (23 Oct). *Tenth Anniv of Independence. T* **81** *and similar horiz designs. Multicoloured. P* 13½.
211 3 n. Type **81** 20 15
212 4 n. Local market 20 15
213 9 n. Kapiri glass factory 35 45
214 10 n. Kafue hydro-electric scheme 40 50
215 15 n. Kafue Railway Bridge . . . . . . 70 1·50
216 25 n. Non-aligned Conference, Lusaka, 1970 1·10 1·75
211/16 . . . . *Set of* 6 2·75 4·00
MS217 141 × 105 mm. 15 n. (× 4) Academic Education; Teacher Training College; Technical Education; Zambia University . . . . . . 7·50 8·50

82 Mobile Post-van

(Des Mrs. G. Ellison. Litho Format)

1974 (15 Nov). *Centenary of Universal Postal Union. T* **82** *and similar horiz designs. Multicoloured. P* 13½.

218	4 n. Type **82**	20	15
219	9 n. Aeroplane on tarmac	40	30
220	10 n. Chipata Post Office	40	40
221	15 n. Modern training centre	65	1·75
218/21	*Set of* 4	1·50	2·40

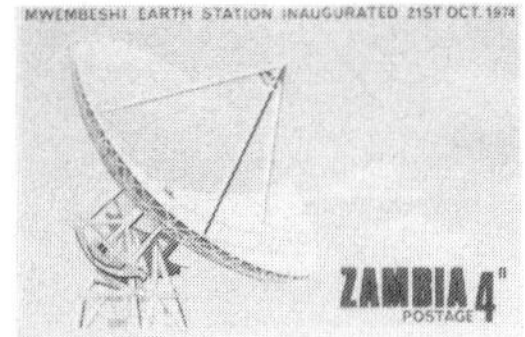

83 Dish Aerial

(Des Mrs. G. Ellison. Litho Questa)

1974 (16 Dec). *Opening of Mwembeshi Earth Station* (21 *October*). *T* **83** *and similar horiz designs. Multicoloured. P* 13½.

222	4 n. Type **83**	30	20
223	9 n. View at dawn	65	50
224	15 n. View at dusk	1·00	1·25
225	25 n. Aerial view	1·50	2·25
222/5	*Set of* 4	3·00	3·75

84 Black Rhinoceros and Calf

85 Independence Monument

(Des Mrs. G. Ellison. Litho J.W.)

1975 (3 Jan). *T* **84/5** *and similar horiz designs. Multicoloured.*

(*a*) *Size as T* **84**. *P* 13½ × 14

226	1 n. Type **84**	30	15
227	2 n. Helmet Guineafowl	30	15
228	3 n. National Dancing Troupe	15	10
229	4 n. African Fish Eagle	40	10
230	5 n. Knife-edge Bridge	45	15
231	8 n. Sitatunga (antelope)	45	15
232	9 n. African Elephant, Kasaba Bay	75	15
233	10 n. Temminck's Ground Pangolin	20	10

(*b*) *Size as T* **85**. *P* 13

234	15 n. Type **85**	30	10
	a. Magenta omitted		
235	20 n. Harvesting groundnuts	65	65
236	25 n. Tobacco-growing	70	30
237	50 n. Flying-Doctor service	90	1·40
238	1 k. Lady Ross's Turaco	2·50	1·50
239	2 k. Village scene	2·75	4·25
226/39	*Set of* 14	9·75	8·25

No. 234a shows much of the design in yellow-green due to the omission of the magenta which was used as an overlay on other colours.

Nos. 226/7 exist in coils, constructed from normal sheets.

86 Map of Namibia

87 Erection of Sprinkler Irrigation

(Des PAD Studio. Litho Questa)

1975 (26 Aug). *Namibia Day. P* 13½.

240	**86**	4 n. green and light yellow-green	20	20
241		9 n. steel-blue and light turquoise-green	30	30
242		15 n. orange-yellow and greenish yellow	65	75
243		25 n. orange and light orange	85	1·25
240/3		*Set of* 4	1·75	2·25

(Des and litho J.W.)

1975 (16 Dec). *Silver Jubilee of the International Commission on Irrigation and Drainage. T* **87** *and similar horiz designs. Multicoloured. P* 13.

244	4 n. Type **87**	15	15
245	9 n. Sprinkler irrigation (*different*)	30	40
246	15 n. Furrow irrigation	65	1·25
244/6	*Set of* 3	1·00	1·60

88 Mutondo

(Des A. Chimfwembe. Litho J.W.)

1976 (22 Mar). *World Forestry Day. T* **88** *and similar horiz designs showing trees. Multicoloured. P* 13.

247	3 n. Type **88**	25	10
248	4 n. Mukunyu	25	10
249	9 n. Mukusi	45	25
250	10 n. Mopane	45	25
251	15 n. Musuku	70	1·40
252	25 n. Mukwa	85	1·75
247/52	*Set of* 6	2·75	3·50

89 Passenger Train

(Des A. Chimfwembe. Litho J.W.)

1976 (10 Dec). *Opening of Tanzania-Zambia Railway. T* **89** *and similar horiz designs. Multicoloured. P* 13½ (**MS**257) *or* 13 (*others*).

253	4 n. Type **89**	30	30
254	9 n. Copper exports	55	55
255	15 n. Machinery imports	90	95
256	25 n. Goods train	1·40	1·75
253/6	*Set of* 4	2·75	3·25
MS257	140 × 106 mm. 10 n. Clearing bush; 15 n. Laying track; 20 n. Railway workers; 25 n. Completed track	3·50	4·00

90 Kayowe Dance

91 Grimwood's Longclaw

(Des BG Studio. Litho Questa)

1977 (18 Jan). *Second World Black and African Festival of Arts and Culture, Nigeria. T* **90** *and similar horiz designs. Multicoloured. P* 13½.

258	4 n. Type **90**	15	10
259	9 n. Lilombola dance	25	25
260	15 n. Initiation ceremony	45	50
261	25 n. Munkhwele dance	75	1·25
258/61	*Set of* 4	1·40	1·90

(Des Mrs. G. Ellison. Litho Questa)

1977 (1 July). *Birds of Zambia. T* **91** *and similar vert designs. Multicoloured. P* 14½.

262	4 n. Type **91**	40	10
263	9 n. Shelley's Sunbird	70	60
264	10 n. Black-cheeked Lovebird	70	60
265	15 n. Locust Finch	1·40	2·00
266	20 n. Black-chinned Tinkerbird	1·60	2·25
267	25 n. Chaplin's Barbet	2·00	2·75
262/7	*Set of* 6	6·00	7·50

92 Girls with Building Blocks

(Des Mrs. G. Ellison. Litho Questa)

1977 (20 Oct). *Decade for Action to Combat Racism and Racial Discrimination. T* **92** *and similar horiz designs. Multicoloured. P* 14 × 14½.

268	4 n. Type **92**	10	10
269	9 n. Women dancing	15	20
270	15 n. Girls with dove	25	60
268/70	*Set of* 3	45	80

93 Angels and Shepherds

(Des Mrs. G. Ellison. Litho J.W.)

1977 (20 Dec). *Christmas. T* **93** *and similar horiz designs. Multicoloured. P* 14.

271	4 n. Type **93**	10	10
272	9 n. The Holy Family	10	10
273	10 n. The Magi	10	15
274	15 n. Jesus presented to Simeon	20	60
271/4	*Set of* 4	40	85

94 African Elephant and Road Check

8n

(95)

(Des Mrs. G. Ellison. Litho Questa)

1978 (1 Aug). *Anti-Poaching Campaign. T* **94** *and similar horiz designs. Multicoloured. P* 14 × 14½.

275	8 n. Type **94**	25	10
276	18 n. Lechwe and canoe patrol	40	55
277	28 n. Warthog and helicopter	60	85
278	32 n. Cheetah and game guard patrol	75	1·10
275/8	*Set of* 4	1·75	2·40

1979 (15 Mar). *Nos.* 228, 232, 234 *and* 236 *surch as T* **95**.

279	8 n. on 9 n. African Elephant, Kasaba Bay	30	10
	a. Surch inverted		
280	10 n. on 3 n. National Dancing Troupe	10	10
	a. Surch inverted		
	b. Surch omitted (in pair with normal)		
281	18 n. on 25 n. Tobacco-growing	15	15
	a. Surch inverted		
282	28 n. on 15 n. Type **85**	20	25
	a. Surch inverted	8·00	
	b. Albino surch		
279/82	*Set of* 4	65	55

No. 280b was caused by a corner paper fold.

96 Kayowe Dance

97 "Kalulu and the Tug of War"

(Des Mrs. G. Ellison. Litho Questa)

1979 (1 Aug). *Commonwealth Summit Conference, Lusaka. T* **96** *and similar horiz designs. Multicoloured. P* 14.

283	18 n. Type **96**	15	25
284	32 n. Kutambala dance	25	40
285	42 n. Chitwansombo drummers	35	60
286	58 n. Lilombola dance	50	80
283/6	*Set of* 4	1·10	1·90

(Des Mrs. G. Ellison. Litho Questa)

1979 (21 Sept). *International Year of the Child. Illustrations from Children's Books. T* **97** *and similar vert designs. Multicoloured. P* 14.

287	18 n. Type **97**	40	30
288	32 n. "Why the Zebra has no Horns"	55	55
289	42 n. "How the Tortoise got his Shell"	60	85
290	58 n. "Kalulu and the Lion"	80	1·10
287/90	*Set of* 4	2·10	2·50
MS291	90 × 120 mm. Nos. 287/90	2·25	2·75

98 Children of Different Races holding Anti-Apartheid Emblem

(Des Mrs. G. Ellison. Litho Questa)

1979 (13 Nov). *International Anti-Apartheid Year. T* **98** *and similar horiz designs showing children of different races together. Multicoloured. P* 14½.

292	18 n. Type **98**	15	25
293	32 n. Children with toy car	25	40
294	42 n. Young children with butterfly	35	60
295	58 n. Children with microscope	50	80
292/5	*Set of* 4	1·10	1·90

LONDON 1980

99 Sir Rowland Hill and 2s. Definitive Stamp of 1964 (**100**)

(Des Mrs. G. Ellison. Litho Format)

1979 (20 Dec). *Death Centenary of Sir Rowland Hill. T* **99** *and similar horiz designs. Multicoloured. P* 14½.

296 18 n. Type **99** 20 25
297 32 n. Sir Rowland Hill and mailman 40 55
298 42 n. Sir Rowland Hill and Northern Rhodesia 1963 ½d. definitive stamp 50 70
299 58 n. Sir Rowland Hill and mail-carrying oxwaggon .. .. 65 1·10
296/9 .. .. *Set of* 4 1·60 2·40
MS300 112 × 89 mm. Nos. 296/9 .. .. 2·00 2·75

1980 (16 May). *"London 1980" International Stamp Exhibition. Nos. 296/300 optd with T* **100**.

301 18 n. Type **99** 35 40
302 32 n. Sir Rowland Hill and mailman 55 70
303 42 n. Sir Rowland Hill and Northern Rhodesia 1963 ½d. definitive stamp 70 90
304 58 n. Sir Rowland Hill and mail-carrying oxwaggon .. .. 90 1·10
301/4 .. .. *Set of* 4 2·25 2·75
MS305 112 × 89 mm. Nos. 301/4 .. .. 3·00 3·75

101 Rotary Anniversary Emblem

(Des J.W. Litho Questa)

1980 (18 June). *75th Anniv of Rotary International. P* 14.

306 **101** 8 n. multicoloured 10 10
307 32 n. multicoloured 40 55
308 42 n. multicoloured 45 80
309 58 n. multicoloured .. .. 70 1·00
306/9 .. .. *Set of* 4 1·50 2·25
MS310 115 × 89 mm. Nos. 306/9 .. .. 2·00 2·50

102 Running

(Des Mrs. G. Ellison. Litho J.W.)

1980 (19 July). *Olympic Games, Moscow. T* **102** *and similar horiz designs. Multicoloured. P* 13.

311 18 n. Type **102** 25 25
312 32 n. Boxing 35 45
313 42 n. Football 40 80
314 58 n. Swimming .. .. 70 1·25
311/14 .. .. *Set of* 4 1·50 2·50
MS315 142 × 144 mm. Nos. 311/14. P 14 .. .. 1·50 2·50

103 *Euphaedra zaddachi* **104** Zambia Coat of Arms

(Des Mrs. G. Ellison. Litho Questa)

1980 (27 Aug). *Butterflies. T* **103** *and similar horiz designs. Multicoloured. P* 14.

316 18 n. Type **103** 15 15
317 32 n. *Aphnaeus questiauxi* 25 40
318 42 n. *Abantis zambesiaca* 40 80
319 58 n. *Spindasis modesta* .. .. 60 1·10
316/19 .. .. *Set of* 4 1·25 2·25
MS320 114×86 mm. Nos. 316/19 .. .. 2·75 3·00

(Des Mrs. G. Ellison. Litho Format)

1980 (27 Sept). *26th Commonwealth Parliamentary Association Conference, Lusaka. P* 14.

321 **104** 18 n. multicoloured 15 25
322 32 n. multicoloured 25 45
323 42 n. multicoloured 30 65
324 58 n. multicoloured 40 90
321/4 .. .. *Set of* 4 1·00 2·00

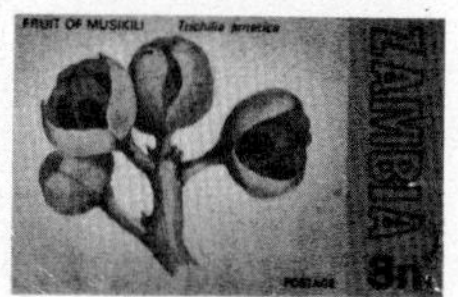

105 Nativity and St. Francis of Assisi (stained glass window, Ndola Church) **106** Musikili

(Des Mrs. G. Ellison. Litho Questa)

1980 (3 Nov). *50th Anniv of Catholic Church on the Copperbelt. P* 13½.

325 **105** 8 n. multicoloured 10 10
326 28 n. multicoloured 30 50
327 32 n. multicoloured 30 50
328 42 n. multicoloured 35 65
325/8 .. .. *Set of* 4 95 1·60

(Des Mrs. G. Ellison. Litho Questa)

1981 (21 Mar). *World Forestry Day. Seedpods. T* **106** *and similar horiz designs. Multicoloured. P* 14.

329 8 n. Type **106** 10 10
330 18 n. Mupapa 30 45
331 28 n. Mulunguti 40 80
332 32 n. Mulama .. .. 45 1·25
329/32 .. .. *Set of* 4 1·10 2·00

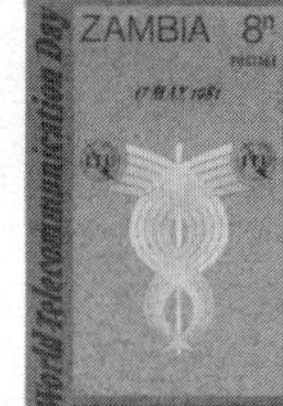

107 I.T.U. Emblem **108** Mask Maker

(Des J.W. Litho Format)

1981 (15 May). *World Telecommunications and Health Day. T* **107** *and similar vert design. Multicoloured. P* 14½.

333 8 n. Type **107** 20 10
334 18 n. W.H.O. emblems 45 35
335 28 n. Type **107** 80 60
336 32 n. As 18 n. 95 75
333/6 .. .. *Set of* 4 2·25 1·60

(Des Mrs. G. Ellison. Litho Harrison)

1981 (2 June)–**83**. *Multicoloured designs as T* **108**. *P* 14 × 13½ (50 *n*., 75 *n*., 1 *k*., 2 *k*.) *or* 14½ (*others*).

337 1 n. Type **108** 10 10
338 2 n. Blacksmith 10 10
339 5 n. Pottery making 10 10
340 8 n. Straw-basket fishing 10 10
341 10 n. Thatching 10 10
342 12 n. Mushroom picking (17.2.83) .. .. 1·25 65
343 18 n. Millet grinding on stone 20 10
344 28 n. Royal Barge paddler (11.11.81) 40 10
345 30 n. Makishi tightrope dancer (11.11.81) .. 40 10
346 35 n. Tonga Ila granary and house (11.11.81) .. 45 10
347 42 n. Cattle herding (11.11.81) 45 40
348 50 n. Traditional healer (38 × 26 *mm*) (11.11.81) 45 10
349 75 n. Women carrying water (38 × 26 *mm*) (17.2.83) 45 50
350 1 k. Pounding maize (38 × 26 *mm*) (17.2.83) 45 50
351 2 k. Pipe-smoking, Gwembe Valley Belle (38 × 26 *mm*) 45 50
337/48 .. .. *Set of* 15 4·50 2·75

Nos. 338/9 and 341 exist in coils, constructed from normal sheets.

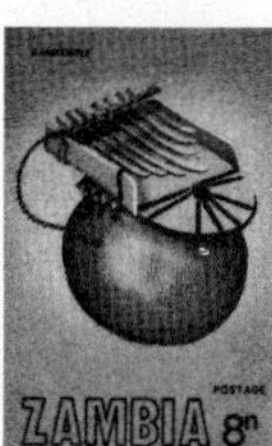

109 Kankobele **110** Banded Ironstone

(Des Mrs. G. Ellison. Litho Format)

1981 (30 Sept*). *Traditional Musical Instruments. T* **109** *and similar vert designs. Multicoloured. P* 15.

356 8 n. Type **109** 25 10
357 18 n. Inshingili 55 35
358 28 n. Ilimba 80 80
359 32 n. Bango .. .. 90 1·10
356/9 .. .. *Set of* 4 2·25 2·10

*It has been reported that the Ndola Philatelic Bureau inadvertently sold some of these stamps some days earlier, and that cancelled-to-order examples exist postmarked 14 or 15 September.

(Des Mrs. G. Ellison. Litho Questa)

1982 (5 Jan). *Minerals* (*1st series*). *T* **110** *and similar vert designs. Multicoloured. P* 14.

360 8 n. Type **110** 40 10
361 18 n. Cobaltocalcite .. .. 1·00 70
362 28 n. Amazonite .. .. 1·25 1·00
363 32 n. Tourmaline .. .. 1·40 1·60
364 42 n. Uranium ore .. .. 1·75 2·00
360/4 .. .. *Set of* 5 5·25 4·75

See also Nos. 370/4.

111 Zambian Scouts

(Des Mrs. G. Ellison. Litho Questa)

1982 (30 Mar). *75th Anniv of Boy Scout Movement. T* **111** *and similar horiz designs. Multicoloured. P* 14.

365 8 n. Type **111** 30 10
366 18 n. Lord Baden-Powell and Victoria Falls 70 40
367 28 n. African Buffalo and Zambian Scout patrol pennant 70 50
368 1 k. African Fish Eagle and Zambian Conservation badge .. .. 2·00 3·00
365/8 .. .. *Set of* 4 3·25 3·50
MS369 105×78 mm. Nos. 365/8 .. .. 3·25 4·00

(Des Mrs. G. Ellison. Litho Questa)

1982 (1 July). *Minerals* (*2nd series*). *Vert designs as T* **110**. *Multicoloured. P* 14.

370 8 n. Bornite 60 10
371 18 n. Chalcopyrite .. .. 1·50 75
372 28 n. Malachite .. .. 2·00 2·00
373 32 n. Azurite .. .. 2·00 2·00
374 42 n. Vanadinite .. .. 2·50 3·00
370/4 .. .. *Set of* 5 7·75 7·00

112 Drilling Rig, 1926

(Des Mrs G. Ellison. Litho Harrison)

1983 (26 Jan). *Early Steam Engines. T* **112** *and similar horiz designs. Multicoloured. P* 14 × 14½.

375 8 n. Type **112** 40 10
376 18 n. Fowler road locomotive, 1900 .. .. 60 60
377 28 n. Borsig ploughing engine, 1925 .. .. 90 1·50
378 32 n. Class "7" railway locomotive, 1900 .. 1·10 1·75
375/8 .. .. *Set of* 4 2·75 3·50

113 Cotton Picking **114** *Eulophia cucullata*

(Des Mrs G. Ellison. Litho Harrison)

1983 (10 Mar). *Commonwealth Day. T* **113** *and similar horiz designs. Multicoloured. P* 14 × 13½.

379 12 n. Type **113** 15 10
380 18 n. Mining 30 30
381 28 n. Ritual pot and traditional dances .. 30 50
382 1 k. Violet-crested Turaco and Victoria Falls 2·25 3·50
379/82 .. .. *Set of* 4 2·75 4·00

(Des Mrs G. Ellison. Litho Questa)

1983 (26 May). *Wild Flowers. T* **114** *and similar vert designs. Multicoloured. P* 14.

383 12 n. Type **114** 20 10
384 28 n. *Kigelia africana* 35 40
385 35 n. *Protea gaguedi* 45 70
386 50 n. *Leonotis nepetifolia* .. .. 65 1·40
383/6 .. .. *Set of* 4 1·50 2·40
MS387 141 × 71 mm. Nos. 383/6. P 12 .. .. 1·50 2·75

115 Giraffe

(Des Mrs. G. Ellison. Litho Harrison)

1983 (21 July). *Zambia Wildlife. T* **115** *and similar horiz designs. Multicoloured. P* 14 × 13½.
388 12 n. Type **115** 60 10
a. Orange-brown and brown (inscr and face value) omitted .. .. ..
389 28 n. Blue Wildebeest 80 60
390 35 n. Lechwe 95 80
391 1 k. Yellow-backed Duiker .. .. .. 2·00 3·00
388/91 .. .. *Set of* 4 4·00 4·00

116 Tiger Fish

117 The Annunciation

(Des Mrs. G. Ellison. Litho J.W.)

1983 (29 Sept). *Zambia Fishes. T* **116** *and similar horiz designs. Multicoloured. P* 14.
392 12 n. Type **116** 15 10
393 28 n. Silver Barbel 30 50
394 35 n. Spotted Squeaker 35 90
395 38 n. Red-breasted Bream 35 90
392/5 .. .. *Set of* 4 1·10 2·25

(Des Mrs. G. Ellison. Litho J.W.)

1983 (12 Dec). *Christmas. T* **117** *and similar vert designs. Multicoloured. P* 14.
396 12 n. Type **117** 10 10
397 28 n. The Shepherds 25 40
398 35 n. Three Kings 30 90
399 38 n. Flight into Egypt .. .. .. 35 1·25
396/9 .. .. *Set of* 4 90 2·40

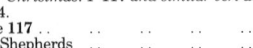

118 Boeing "737"

(Des Mrs. G. Ellison. Litho Harrison)

1984 (26 Jan). *Air Transport. T* **118** *and similar horiz designs. Multicoloured. P* 14 × 13½.
400 12 n. Type **118** 15 10
401 28 n. "Beaver" 30 40
402 35 n. Short "Solent" flying boat 35 70
403 1 k. "D.H.66 Hercules" .. .. .. 85 2·25
400/3 .. .. *Set of* 4 1·50 3·00

119 Receiving Flowers

120 Football

(Des and litho J.W.)

1984 (28 Apr). *60th Birthday of President Kaunda. T* **119** *and similar multicoloured designs. P* 14½ × 14 (12 *n.*, 60 *n.*) *or* 14 × 14½ (*others*).
404 12 n. Type **119** 40 10
405 28 n. Swearing-in ceremony (*vert*) 55 40
406 60 n. Planting cherry tree .. .. .. 1·25 1·50
407 1 k. Opening of 5th National Assembly (*vert*) 1·75 2·25
404/7 .. .. *Set of* 4 3·50 3·75

(Des Mrs. G. Ellison. Litho Format)

1984 (18 July). *Olympic Games, Los Angeles. T* **120** *and similar vert designs. Multicoloured. P* 14½ × 14.
408 12 n. Type **120** 20 10
409 28 n. Running 30 45
410 35 n. Hurdling 40 60
411 50 n. Boxing 50 80
408/11 .. .. *Set of* 4 1·25 1·75

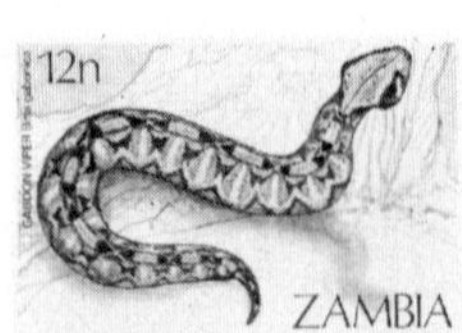

121 Gaboon Viper

(Des Mrs. G. Ellison. Litho Harrison)

1984 (5 Sept). *Reptiles. T* **121** *and similar horiz designs. Multicoloured. P* 14.
412 12 n. Type **121** 15 10
413 28 n. Chameleon 30 40
414 35 n. Nile Crocodile 40 60
415 1 k. Blue-headed Agama .. .. .. 85 2·25
412/15 .. .. *Set of* 4 1·50 3·00
MS416 120 × 101 mm. Nos. 412/15 .. .. 2·00 3·50

122 Pres. Kaunda and Mulungushi Rock

123 *Amanita flammeola*

(Des Mrs. G. Ellison. Litho Harrison)

1984 (22 Oct). *26th Anniv of United National Independence Party* (12 *n.*) *and 20th Anniv of Independence* (*others*) (1*st issue*). *T* **122** *and similar horiz designs. Multicoloured. P* 14.
417 12 n. Type **122** 30 10
418 28 n. Freedom Statue 45 45
419 1 k. Pres. Kaunda and agricultural produce ("Lima Programme") .. .. .. 1·25 2·00
417/19 .. .. *Set of* 3 1·75 2·25
See also Nos. 438/40.

(Des Mrs. G. Ellison. Litho J.W.)

1984 (12 Dec). *Fungi. T* **123** *and similar vert designs. Multicoloured. P* 14 × 14½.
420 12 n. Type **123** 55 15
421 28 n. *Amanita zambiana* 75 55
422 32 n. *Termitomyces letestui* .. .. .. 1·00 85
423 75 n. *Cantharellus miniatescens* .. .. 1·75 2·00
420/3 .. .. *Set of* 4 3·50 3·25

(**124**)

125 Chacma Baboon

1985 (5 Mar). *No.* 237 *surch with T* **124**.
424 5 k. on 50 n. Flying-doctor service .. .. 1·00 1·60

(Des Mrs. G. Ellison. Litho Harrison)

1985 (25 Apr). *Zambian Primates. T* **125** *and similar horiz designs. Multicoloured. P* 14.
425 12 n. Type **125** 25 10
426 20 n. Diademed Monkey 40 20
427 45 n. Diademed Monkey (*different*) 70 70
428 1 k. Savanna Monkey .. .. .. 1·00 1·10
425/8 .. .. *Set of* 4 2·10 1·90

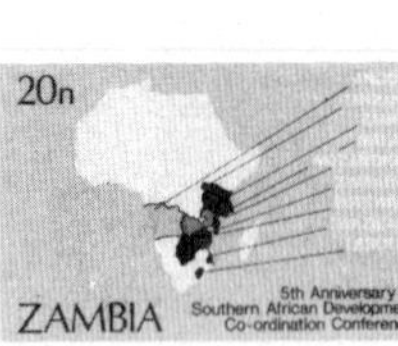

126 Map showing S.A.D.C.C. Member States

127 The Queen Mother in 1980

(Des Mrs. G. Ellison. Litho Harrison)

1985 (9 July). *5th Anniv of Southern African Development Co-ordination Conference. T* **126** *and similar horiz designs. P* 14.
429 20 n. multicoloured 40 15
430 45 n. black, new blue and pale blue .. .. 1·00 75
431 1 k. multicoloured .. .. 1·50 2·00
429/31 .. .. *Set of* 3 2·75 2·75
Designs:—45 n. Mining; 1 k. Flags of member states and Mulungushi Hall.

(Des and litho Harrison)

1985 (2 Aug). *Life and Times of Queen Elizabeth the Queen Mother. T* **127** *and similar designs. P* 14.
432 25 n. multicoloured 10 10
433 45 n. deep violet-blue and gold 10 15
434 55 n. deep violet-blue and gold 15 20
435 5 k. multicoloured .. .. 1·25 2·00
432/5 .. .. *Set of* 4 1·40 2·25
Designs: *Vert*—45 n. The Queen Mother at Clarence House, 1963. *Horiz*—55 n. With the Queen and Princess Margaret, 1980; 5 k. At Prince Henry's christening, 1984.

(**128**)

129 Postman and Lusaka Post Office, 1958

1985 (12 Sept–25 Nov). *Nos.* 340 *and* 342 *surch as T* **128** *in chestnut* (20 *n.*) *or greenish blue* (25 *n.*).
436 20 n. on 12 n. Mushroom picking .. .. 1·25 20
437 25 n. on 8 n. Straw-basket fishing (25.11) .. 50 30

1985 (23 Oct). *26th Anniv of United National Independence Party* (*No.* 438) *and 20th Anniv of Independence* (*others*) (2*nd issue*). *Designs as Nos.* 417/19 *but larger,* 55 × 34 *mm, embossed on gold foil. P* 10.
438 5 k. Type **122** .. .. 1·60 2·50
439 5 k. Freedom Statue .. .. 1·60 2·50
440 5 k. Pres. Kaunda and agricultural produce ("Lima Programme") .. .. .. 1·60 2·50
438/40 .. .. *Set of* 3 4·25 6·75

(Des Mrs. G. Ellison. Litho J.W.)

1985 (12 Dec). *10th Anniv of Posts and Telecommunication Corporation. T* **129** *and similar horiz designs. Multicoloured. P* 13 × 12½.
441 20 n. Type **129** 25 10
442 45 n. Postman and Livingstone Post Office, 1950 .. .. 45 20
443 55 n. Postman and Kalomo Post Office, 1902 .. .. 55 40
444 5 k. Africa Trans-Continental Telegraph Line under construction, 1900 .. 2·00 3·00
441/4 .. .. *Set of* 4 3·00 3·25

130 Boy in Maize Field

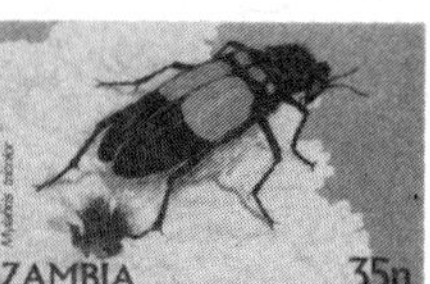

131 *Mylabris tricolor*

(Des Mrs. G. Ellison. Litho Harrison)

1985 (19 Dec). *40th Anniv of United Nations Organization. T* **130** *and similar vert designs. P* 14.
445 20 n. multicoloured 30 10
446 45 n. black, new blue and brownish black .. 40 20
447 1 k. multicoloured 70 90
448 2 k. multicoloured .. .. 1·25 1·60
445/8 .. .. *Set of* 4 2·40 2·50
Designs:—45 n. Logo and "40"; 1 k. President Kaunda addressing U.N. General Assembly, 1970; 2 k. Signing of U.N. Charter, San Francisco, 1945.

(Des Mrs. G. Ellison. Litho Harrison)

1986 (20 Mar). *Beetles. T* **131** *and similar horiz designs. Multicoloured. P* 14.
449 35 n. Type **131** 10 10
450 1 k. *Phasgonocnema melanianthe* 15 20
451 1 k. 70, *Amaurodes passerinii* 25 40
452 5 k. *Ranzania petersiana* .. .. .. 70 1·50
449/52 .. .. *Set of* 4 1·10 2·00

(Des A. Theobald. Litho Format)

1986 (21 Apr). *60th Birthday of Queen Elizabeth II. Vert designs as T* **230***a of Jamaica. Multicoloured. W* w **16.** *P* 14 × 14½ (1 *k.* 95) *or* 14 × 13½ (*others*).
453 35 n. Princess Elizabeth at Flower Ball, Savoy Hotel, 1951 .. .. 10 10
a. Perf 14 × 14½ .. .. 1·00
454 1 k. 25, With Prince Andrew, Lusaka Airport, 1979 .. .. 15 20
a. Perf 14 × 14½ .. .. 15·00
455 1 k. 70, With President Kaunda 20 25
a. Perf 14 × 14½ .. .. 12·00
456 1 k. 95, In Luxembourg, 1976 .. .. 25 30
457 5 k. At Crown Agents Head Office, London, 1983 .. .. 60 85
453/7 .. .. *Set of* 5 1·10 1·50

(Des D. Miller. Litho Questa)

1986 (23 July). *Royal Wedding. Square designs as T* **231***a of Jamaica. Multicoloured. W* w **16.** *P* 14.
458 1 k. 70, Prince Andrew and Miss Sarah Ferguson 30 30
459 5 k. Prince Andrew in Zambia, 1979 .. 80 1·25

ALTERED CATALOGUE NUMBERS

Any Catalogue numbers altered from the last edition are shown as a list in the introductory pages.

132 Goalkeeper saving Goal **133** Sculpture of Edmond Halley by Henry Pegram

(Des Mrs. G. Ellison. Litho Mardon Printers Ltd, Zimbabwe)

1986 (30 July). *World Cup Football Championship, Mexico. T* **132** *and similar vert designs. Multicoloured. P* 14½.
460 35 n. Type **132** 50 15
461 1 k. 25, Player kicking ball .. .. .. 1·25 1·00
462 1 k. 70, Two players competing for ball .. 1·40 1·40
463 5 k. Player scoring goal .. .. .. 3·00 3·50
460/3 .. .. *Set of* 4 5·50 5·50

(Des Jennifer Toombs. Litho Mardon Printers Ltd, Zimbabwe)

1986 (6 Aug). *Appearance of Halley's Comet. T* **133** *and similar horiz designs. P* 14½.
464 1 k. 25, multicoloured 55 35
465 1 k. 70, multicoloured 70 55
466 2 k. multicoloured 90 80
467 5 k. light blue and blue-black .. .. 2·50 2·75
464/7 .. .. *Set of* 4 4·25 4·00

Designs:—1 k. 70, *Giotto* spacecraft approaching nucleus of Comet; 2 k. Studying Halley's Comet in 1682 and 1986; 5 k. Part of Halley's chart of southern sky.

134 The Nativity

(Des and litho Harrison)

1986 (15 Dec). *Christmas. Children's Paintings. T* **134** *and similar horiz designs. Multicoloured. P* 14.
468 35 n. Type **134** 20 10
469 1 k. 25, The Visit of the Three Kings .. 75 50
470 1 k. 60, The Holy Family with Shepherd and King 85 70
471 5 k. Angel and Christmas Tree .. .. 2·50 3·00
468/71 .. .. *Set of* 4 4·00 3·75

135 Train in Kasama Cutting

(Des G. Vasarhelyi. Litho Questa)

1986 (22 Dec). *10th Anniv of Tanzania-Zambia Railway. T* **135** *and similar horiz designs. Multicoloured. P* 14.
472 35 n. Type **135** 20 10
473 1 k. 25, Train leaving Tunnel No. 21 .. 35 40
474 1 k. 70, Train between Tunnels No. 6 and 7 .. .. 40 60
475 5 k. Trains at Mpika Station .. .. 1·00 1·75
472/5 .. .. *Set of* 4 1·75 2·50

136 President Kaunda and Graduate **137** Arms of Kitwe

(Litho Harrison)

1987 (27 Jan). *20th Anniv of University of Zambia. T* **136** *and similar multicoloured designs. P* 14.
476 35 n. Type **136** 20 10
477 1 k. 25, University Badge (*vert*) 50 40
478 1 k. 60, University Statue 60 55
479 5 k. President Kaunda laying foundation stone (*vert*) .. .. 2·00 2·75
476/9 .. .. *Set of* 4 3·00 3·50

(Litho Harrison)

1987 (26 Mar). *Arms of Zambian Towns. T* **137** *and similar vert designs. Multicoloured. P* 14.
480 35 n. Type **137** 10 10
481 1 k. 25, Ndola 15 20
482 1 k. 70, Lusaka 20 25
483 20 k. Livingstone .. .. 2·40 3·25
480/3 .. .. *Set of* 4 2·50 3·50

138 Chestnut-headed Crake **139** Look-out Tree, Livingstone

Two types of surcharge for 20 n., 75 n.:

20n 20n 75n 75n
I II I II

I Surch by Format in Great Britain
II Surch in Zambia

(Des Mrs. G. Ellison. Litho Questa)

1987 (16 Apr)–**88**. *Birds* (*1st series*). *T* **138** *and similar vert designs, some additionally surch as T* **128**. *Multicoloured. P* 11×13. (5 *n. to* 40 *n.,* 75 *n.,* 1 *k.* 65) *or* 14 (*others*).
484 5 n. Cloud-scraping Cisticola (8.10.87) .. 10 10
485 10 n. White-winged Starling (8.10.87) .. 10 10
486 20 n. on 1 n. Yellow Swamp Warbler (I) (10.3.88) 30 10
a. Surch Type II 20 10
487 25 n. Type **138** 20 10
488 30 n. Miombo Pied Barbet (8.10.87) .. 10 10
489 35 n. Black and Rufous Swallow 30 20
490 40 n. Wattled Crane (8.10.87) 10 10
491 50 n. Slaty Egret (8.10.87) 10 10
492 75 n. on 2 n. Olive-flanked Robin (I) (10.3.88) 30 30
a. Surch Type II 30 30
493 1 k. Bradfield's Hornbill 30 15
494 1 k. 25, Boulton's Puff-back Flycatcher ("Margaret's Batis") 30 30
495 1 k. 60, Anchieta's Sunbird 35 35
496 1 k. 65 on 30 n. Miombo Pied Barbet (10.3.88) 30 40
497 1 k. 70, Boehm's Bee Eater 45 45
498 1 k. 95, Gorgeous Bush Shrike 45 45
499 2 k. Whale-headed Stork ("Shoebill") (8.10.87) 35 35
500 5 k. Taita Falcon 75 55
501 10 k. on 50 n. Slaty Egret (10.3.88) .. 1·10 1·40
502 20 k. on 2 k. Whale-headed Stork (10.3.88) 2·10 2·50
484/502 .. .. *Set of* 19 7·00 7·00

Nos. 491, 493/5 and 497/502 are larger, size 24×39 mm.

The 1 n. and 2 n. values were not officialy issued without surcharge, but examples with c-t-o cancellations of 10 March 1988 are known.

No. 502 is surcharged "K 20" only. For "K 20·00" surcharge see No. 594.

For further surcharges see Nos. 587/95, and for different designs see Nos. 625/8.

(Litho Questa)

1987 (30 June). *Tourism. T* **139** *and similar horiz designs. Multicoloured. P* 14.
503 35 n. Type **139** 30 15
504 1 k. 25, Rafting on Zambezi 60 40
505 1 k. 70, Tourists photographing lions, Luangwa Valley 90 60
506 10 k. White Pelicans .. .. 4·00 4·00
503/6 .. .. *Set of* 4 5·25 4·75

K3

(**140**)

141 De Havilland "Beaver"

1987 (14 Sept). *Various stamps surch as T* **140**.

(*a*) *On Nos.* 432/5 *in gold*
507 **127** 3 k. on 25 n. multicoloured 40 45
508 – 6 k. on 45 n. deep violet-blue and gold 85 90
509 – 10 k. on 55 n. deep violet-blue and gold 1·40 1·50
510 – 20 k. on 5 k. multicoloured .. .. 2·75 3·00

(*b*) *On Nos.* 453/7
511 3 k. on 35 n. Princess Elizabeth at Flower Ball, Savoy Hotel, 1951 .. .. 40 45
512 4 k. on 1 k. 25, With Prince Andrew, Lusaka Airport, 1979 .. .. .. 55 60
513 6 k. on 1 k. 70, With President Kaunda .. 85 90
514 10 k. on 1 k. 95, In Luxembourg, 1976 .. 1·40 1·50
515 20 k. on 5 k. At Crown Agents Head Office, London, 1983 .. .. 2·75 3·00

(*c*) *On Nos.* 460/3
516 3 k. on 35 n. Type **132** 40 45
517 6 k. on 1 k. 25, Player kicking ball .. 85 90
518 10 k. on 1 k. 70, Two players competing for ball .. .. 1·40 1·50
519 20 k. on 5 k. Player scoring goal .. .. 2·75 3·00

(*d*) *On Nos.* 464/7 *in gold*
520 **133** 3 k. on 1 k. 25, multicoloured 40 45
a. Surch omitted (in horiz pair with normal) .. .. 80·00
521 – 6 k. on 1 k. 70, multicoloured 85 90
522 – 10 k. on 2 k. multicoloured .. .. 1·40 1·50
523 – 20 k. on 15 k. light blue and blue-black 2·75 3·00
507/23 .. .. *Set of* 17 20·00 22·00

(Des and litho Questa)

1987 (21 Sept). *20th Anniv of Zambia Airways. T* **141** *and similar horiz designs showing aircraft. Multicoloured. P* 14.
524 35 n. Type **141** 25 10
525 1 k. 70, Douglas "DC-10" 75 35
526 5 k. Douglas "DC-3 Dakota" .. .. 1·75 1·50
527 10 k. Boeing "707" .. .. 2·75 3·00
524/7 .. .. *Set of* 4 5·00 4·50

142 Friesian/Holstein Cow **143** Mpoloto Ne Mikobango

(Des Mrs. G. Ellison. Litho Format)

1987 (1 Oct). *40th Anniv of Food and Agriculture Organization. T* **142** *and similar horiz designs. Multicoloured. P* 14½×15.
528 35 n. Type **142** 10 10
529 1 k. 25, Simmental bull 20 25
530 1 k. 70, Sussex bull 25 30
531 20 k. Brahman bull .. .. 2·75 3·00
528/31 .. .. *Set of* 4 3·00 3·25

(Litho Format)

1987 (3 Nov). *People of Zambia. T* **143** *and similar vert designs. Multicoloured. P* 12½.
532 35 n. Type **143** 10 10
533 1 k. 25, Zintaka 20 25
534 1 k. 70, Mufuluhi 25 30
535 10 k. Ntebwe .. .. 1·40 1·50
536 20 k. Kubangwa Aa Mbulunga .. .. 2·75 3·00
532/6 .. .. *Set of* 5 4·25 4·50

144 Black Lechwe at Waterhole **145** Cassava Roots

(Des Mrs. G. Ellison. Litho Questa)

1987 (21 Dec). *Black Lechwe. T* **144** *and similar multicoloured designs. P* 14.
537 50 n. Type **144** 30 10
538 2 k. Black Lechwe resting by pool (*horiz*) 75 40
539 2 k. 50, Running through water (*horiz*) 85 50
540 10 k. Watching for danger .. .. .. 2·25 2·50
537/40 .. .. *Set of* 4 3·75 3·25
MS541 Two sheets, each 105×74 mm. (a) 20 k. Caracal (predator). (b) 20 k. Cheetah (predator) *Set of* 2 *sheets* 5·50 6·00

(Des Mrs. G. Ellison. Litho Questa)

1988 (20 May). *International Fund for Agricultural Development. T* **145** *and similar horiz designs. Multicoloured. P* 14.
542 50 n. Type **145** 10 10
543 2 k. 50, Fishing 30 35
544 2 k. 85, Farmer and cattle 35 40
545 10 k. Picking coffee beans .. .. .. 1·25 1·40
542/5 .. .. *Set of* 4 1·75 2·00

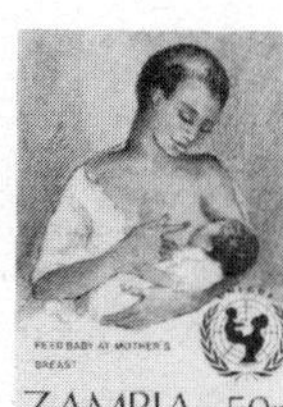

146 Breast feeding **147** Asbestos Cement

(Des Mrs. G. Ellison. Litho Format)

1988 (12 Sept). *U.N.I.C.E.F. Child Survival Campaign. T* **146** *and similar vert designs. Multicoloured. P* 12½.
546 50 n. Type **146** 10 10
547 2 k. Growth monitoring 25 30
548 2 k. 85, Immunization 35 40
549 10 k. Oral rehydration .. .. 1·25 2·00
546/9 .. .. *Set of* 4 1·75 2·50

(Des Mrs. G. Ellison. Litho Format)

1988 (10 Oct). *Preferential Trade Area Fair. T* **147** *and similar vert designs. Multicoloured. P* 12½.
550 50 n. Type **147** 10 10
551 2 k. 35, Textiles 25 30
552 2 k. 50, Tea 30 40
553 10 k. Poultry .. .. 1·25 2·25
550/3 .. .. *Set of* 4 1·60 2·75

148 Emergency Food Distribution

(Des Mrs. G. Ellison. Litho Questa)

1988 (20 Oct). *125th Anniv of International Red Cross. T* **148** *and similar horiz designs. Multicoloured. P* 14.
554 50 n. Type **148** .. 10 10
555 2 k. 50, Giving first aid .. 30 40
556 2 k. 85, Practising bandaging .. 35 50
557 10 k. Henri Dunant (founder) .. 1·25 2·00
554/7 .. *Set of* 4 1·75 2·75

149 Aardvark

(Des Mrs. G. Ellison. Litho Questa)

1988 (5 Dec). *Endangered Species of Zambia. T* **149** *and similar horiz designs. Multicoloured. P* 14.
558 50 n. Type **149** .. 15 10
559 2 k. Temminck's Ground Pangolin .. 30 35
560 2 k. 85, Hunting Dog .. 40 50
561 20 k. Black Rhinoceros and calf .. 2·75 4·00
558/61 .. *Set of* 4 3·25 4·50

150 Boxing

151 Red Toad

(Des Mrs. G. Ellison. Litho Questa)

1988 (30 Dec). *Olympic Games, Seoul. T* **150** *and similar horiz designs. Multicoloured. P* 14.
562 50 n. Type **150** .. 15 10
563 2 k. Athletics .. 30 35
564 2 k. 50, Hurdling .. 35 45
565 20 k. Football .. 2·75 4·00
562/5 .. *Set of* 4 3·25 4·50
MS566 Two sheets, each 97×72 mm. (a) 30 k. Tennis. (b) 30 k. Karate .. *Set of* 2 *sheets* 8·00 9·00

(Des Mrs. G. Ellison. Litho Format)

1989 (25 Jan). *Frogs and Toads. T* **151** *and similar horiz designs. Multicoloured. P* 12½.
567 50 n. Type **151** .. 15 10
568 2 k. 50, Puddle Frog .. 40 40
569 2 k. 85, Marbled Reed Frog .. 45 55
570 10 k. Young Reed Frogs .. 1·40 2·25
567/70 .. *Set of* 4 2·25 3·00

152 Common Slit-faced Bat

153 Pope John Paul II and Map of Zambia

(Des Mrs. G. Ellison. Litho Format)

1989 (22 Mar). *Bats. T* **152** *and similar horiz designs. Multicoloured. P* 12½.
571 50 n. Type **152** .. 15 10
572 2 k. 50, Little Free-tailed Bat .. 45 55
573 2 k. 85, Hildebrandt's Horseshoe Bat .. 55 65
574 10 k. Peters' Epauletted Fruit Bat .. 1·50 2·25
571/4 .. *Set of* 4 2·40 3·25

(Des and litho Harrison)

1989 (2 May). *Visit of Pope John Paul II. T* **153** *and similar vert designs each with inset portrait. Multicoloured. P* 12½.
575 50 n. Type **153** .. 40 15
576 6 k. 85, Peace dove with olive branch .. 1·75 2·00
577 7 k. 85, Papal arms .. 2·00 2·25
578 10 k. Victoria Falls .. 2·50 3·00
575/8 .. *Set of* 4 6·00 6·50

K19.50 =   (**154**)

K20.00 =   (**155**)

1989 (1 July–1 Nov). *Various stamps surch.*

(*a*) *Nos.* 339, 341/3, 345/6, 349 *and* 351 *surch as T* **154** (1 *k.* 20, 19 *k.* 50, 20 *k.* 50) *or as T* **155** (*others*)
579 1 k. 20 on 35 n. Tonga Ila granary and house (Br.) (1 Nov) .. 10 10
580 3 k. 75 on 5 n. Pottery making .. 15 15
581 8 k. 11 on 10 n. Thatching .. 30 30
582 9 k. on 30 n. Makishi tightrope dancer .. 30 30
583 10 k. on 75 n. Women carrying water (38×26 *mm*) .. 30 30
584 18 k. 50 on 2 k. Pipe-smoking, Gwembe Valley Belle (38×26 *mm*) .. 70 70
585 19 k. 50 on 12 n. Mushroom picking (Br.) (1 Nov) .. 70 70
586 20 k. 50 on 18 n. Millet grinding on stone (V.) (1 Nov) .. 70 70

(*b*) *Nos.* 484, 489, 493/5 *and* 497/500 *surch as T* **158**.
587 70 n. on 35 n. Black and Rufous Swallow .. 10 10
588 3 k. on 5 n. Cloud-scraping Cisticola .. 15 15
589 8 k. on 1 k. 25, Boulton's Puff-back Flycatcher ("Margaret's Batis") .. 30 30
590 9 k. 90 on 1 k. 70, Boehm's Bee Eater .. 40 40
591 10 k. 40 on 1 k. 60, Anchieta's Sunbird .. 40 40
592 12 k. 50 on 1 k. Bradfield's Hornbill .. 50 50
593 15 k. on 1 k. 95, Gorgeous Bush Shrike .. 60 60
594 20 k. on 2 k. Whale-headed Stork ("Shoebill") .. 70 70
595 20 k. 35 on 5 k. Taita Falcon .. 70 70
579/95 .. *Set of* 17 6·50 6·50
No. 594 shows the surcharge as "K20·00". The previously listed 20 k. on 2 k., No. 502, is surcharged "K20" only.

156 *Parinari curatellifolia*

157 *Lamarckiana* sp

1989 (26 July). *Edible Fruits. T* **156** *and similar vert designs. Multicoloured. P* 14½.
596 50 n. Type **156** .. 15 10
597 6 k. 50, *Uapaca kirkiana* .. 1·25 1·50
598 6 k. 85, Wild Fig .. 1·25 1·75
599 10 k. Bottle Palm .. 2·25 2·50
596/9 .. *Set of* 4 4·50 5·25

(Des Mrs. G. Ellison. Litho Cartor, France)

1989 (8 Nov). *Grasshoppers. T* **157** *and similar horiz designs. Multicoloured. P* 14×13½.
600 70 n. Type **157** .. 15 10
601 10 k. 40, *Dictyophorus* sp .. 1·25 1·25
602 12 k. 50, *Cymatomera* sp .. 1·50 1·50
603 15 k. *Phymateus iris* .. 2·00 2·00
600/3 .. *Set of* 4 4·50 4·25

158 Fireball

159 Postvan, Postman on Bicycle and Main Post Office, Lusaka

(Des Mrs. G. Ellison. Litho National Printing & Packing, Zimbabwe)

1989 (6 Dec). *Christmas. Flowers. T* **158** *and similar vert designs. Multicoloured. P* 14½.
604 70 n. Type **158** .. 15 10
605 10 k. 40, Flame Lily .. 1·00 1·00
606 12 k. 50, Foxglove Lily .. 1·40 1·40
607 20 k. Vlei Lily .. 2·40 2·40
604/7 .. *Set of* 4 4·50 4·50

(Des D. Miller. Litho Questa)

1990 (2 May). *"Stamp World London 90" International Stamp Exhibition. T* **159** *and similar horiz designs. Multicoloured. P* 14.
608 1 k. 20, Type **159** .. 10 10
609 19 k. 50, Zambia 1980 18 n. butterflies stamp .. 1·25 1·25
610 20 k. 50, Rhodesia and Nyasaland 1962 9d. and Northern Rhodesia 1925 ½d. stamps .. 1·25 1·25
611 50 k. 1840 Penny Black and Maltese Cross cancellation .. 3·00 3·00
608/11 .. *Set of* 4 5·00 5·00

160 Footballer and Ball

161 Road Tanker

(Des R. Vigurs. Litho Questa)

1990 (7 July). *World Cup Football Championship, Italy. T* **160** *and similar vert designs showing football scenes. P* 14.
612 1 k. 20, multicoloured .. 10 10
613 18 k. 50, multicoloured .. 1·00 1·00
614 19 k. 50, multicoloured .. 1·00 1·00
615 20 k. 50, multicoloured .. 1·00 1·00
612/15 .. *Set of* 4 2·75 2·75
MS616 100×73 mm. 50 k. multicoloured .. 3·75 4·00
No. **MS**616 also exists imperforate.

(Litho Harrison)

1990 (23 July). *10th Anniv of Southern African Development Co-ordination Conference. T* **161** *and similar horiz designs, each showing map of Southern Africa. Multicoloured. P* 12½.
617 1 k. 20, Type **161** .. 10 10
618 19 k. 50, Telecommunications .. 1·00 1·00
619 20 k. 50, "Regional Co-operation" .. 1·00 1·00
620 50 k. Transporting coal by cable .. 3·00 3·00
617/20 .. *Set of* 4 4·50 4·50

162 Irrigation

163 The Bird and the Snake

(Des Mrs. G. Ellison. Litho Questa)

1990 (23 Oct). *26th Anniv of Independence. T* **162** *and similar horiz designs. Multicoloured. P* 14.
621 1 k. 20, Type **162** .. 10 10
622 19 k. 50, Shoe factory .. 70 70
623 20 k. 50, Mwembeshi II satellite earth station .. 70 70
624 50 k. "Mother and Child" (statue) .. 1·75 2·00
621/4 .. *Set of* 4 2·75 3·25

(Des Mrs. G. Ellison. Litho Questa)

1990 (30 Oct)–**91**. *Birds* (2*nd series*). *Vert designs as T* **138**. *Multicoloured. P* 11×13 (10, 15, 30, 50 *n.*, 1 *k.*, 1 *k.* 20, 2 *k.*, 3 *k.*, 5 *k.*) *or* 14 (*others*).
625 10 n. Livingstone's Flycatcher .. 10 10
626 15 n. Bar-winged Weaver .. 10 10
627 30 n. Purple-throated Cuckoo Shrike .. 10 10
628 50 n. Red-billed Helmet Shrike .. 10 10
629 50 n. As 10 n. (7.5.91) .. 10 10
630 1 k. As 15 n. (7.5.91) .. 10 10
631 1 k. 20, Western Bronze-naped Pigeon .. 10 10
632 2 k. As 30 n. (7.5.91) .. 10 10
633 3 k. As 50 n. (No. 628) (7.5.91) .. 10 10
634 5 k. As 1 k. 20 (7.5.91) .. 10 10
635 15 k. Corncrake .. 25 30
636 20 k. Dickinson's Grey Kestrel (7.5.91) .. 30 35
637 20 k. 50, As 20 k. .. 30 35
638 50 k. Denham's Bustard .. 75 80
625/38 .. *Set of* 14 1·90 2·10
Nos. 635/8 are larger, size 23×39 mm.

(Des Mrs. G. Ellison. Litho Questa)

1991 (11 Jan). *International Literacy Year. Folklore. T* **163** *and similar vert designs. Multicoloured. P* 14.
639 1 k. 20, Type **163** .. 15 10
640 18 k. 50, Kalulu and the Leopard .. 1·00 1·00
641 19 k. 50, The Mouse and the Lion .. 1·00 1·00
642 20 k. 50, Kalulu and the Hippopotamus .. 1·00 1·00
639/42 .. *Set of* 4 2·75 2·75

164 Genet

K2 =   (**165**)

(Des Mrs. G. Ellison. Litho Questa)

1991 (25 Jan). *Small Carnivores. T* **164** *and similar horiz designs. Multicoloured. P* 14.
643 1 k. 20, Type **164** .. 15 10
644 18 k. 50, Civet .. 1·00 1·00
645 19 k. 50, Serval .. 1·00 1·00
646 20 k. 50, African Wild Cat .. 1·00 1·00
643/6 .. *Set of* 4 2·75 2·75

1991 (4 Mar). *Nos.* 441/4 *surch with T* **165**.
647 2 k. on 20 n. Type **129** .. 30 15
648 2 k. on 45 n. Postman and Livingstone Post Office, 1950 .. 30 15
649 2 k. on 55 n. Postman and Kalomo Post Office, 1902 .. 30 15
650 2 k. on 5 k. African Trans-Continental Telegraph Line under construction, 1900 .. 30 15
647/50 .. *Set of* 4 1·10 55

166 Woman Cooking   **167** Chilubula Church near Kasama

(Des A. Mwansa and Daniela Schepp. Litho Cartor)

1991 (28 June). *Soya Promotion Campaign. T* **166** *and similar vert designs. Multicoloured. P* 13½.

651	1 k. Type **166**	10	10
652	2 k. Soya bean and field	10	10
653	5 k. Mother feeding child	15	15
654	20 k. Healthy and malnourished children	50	50
655	50 k. President Kaunda holding child	95	95
651/5	*Set of* 5	1·50	1·50

(Des Mrs. G. Ellison. Litho Cartor)

1991 (18 July). 500*th Birth Anniv of St. Ignatius Loyola. T* **167** *and similar vert designs. Multicoloured. P* 13½.

656	1 k. Type **167**	10	10
657	2 k. Chikuni Church near Monze	10	10
658	20 k. Bishop Joseph du Pont	50	50
659	50 k. Saint Ignatius Loyola	95	95
656/9	*Set of* 4	1·40	1·40

168 *Adansonia digitata*   **169** *Disa hamatopetala*

(Des Mrs G. Ellison. Litho Cartor)

1991 (28 Nov). *Flowering Trees. T* **168** *and similar horiz designs. Multicoloured. P* 13½.

660	1 k. Type **168**	10	10
661	2 k. *Dichrostachys cinerea*	10	10
662	10 k. *Sterospernum kunthianum*	25	25
663	30 k. *Azana garckeana*	70	70
660/3	*Set of* 4	1·00	1·00

(Des D. Miller. Litho Cartor)

1992 (6 Feb). 40*th Anniv of Queen Elizabeth II's Accession. Horiz designs as T* **112** *of Kenya. Multicoloured. W w* **14** *(sideways). P* 13½.

664	4 k. Queen's House	10	10
665	32 k. Traditional village	50	55
666	35 k. Fishermen hauling nets	55	60
667	38 k. Three portraits of Queen Elizabeth	60	65
668	50 k. Queen Elizabeth II	75	80
664/8	*Set of* 5	2·25	2·50

(Des Mrs G. Ellison. Litho Cartor)

1992 (28 Feb). *Orchids. T* **169** *and similar vert designs. Multicoloured. P* 13½.

669	1 k. Type **169**	10	10
670	2 k. *Eulophia paivaeana*	10	10
671	5 k. *Eulophia quartiniana*	10	10
672	20 k. *Aerangis verdickii*	30	35
669/72	*Set of* 4	55	60

170 Kasinja Mask

(Des Mrs. G. Ellison. Litho Cartor)

1992 (10 Mar). *Tribal Masks. T* **170** *and similar vert designs. Multicoloured. P* 13½.

673	1 k. Type **170**	10	10
674	2 k. Chizaluke	10	10
675	10 k. Mwanapweu	15	20
676	30 k. Maliya	55	60
673/6	*Set of* 4	80	90

POSTAGE DUE STAMPS

D 1   D 2

(Typo D.L.R.)

1929–52. *Wmk Mult Script CA. Ordinary paper. P* 14.

D1	D 1	1d. grey-black	2·50	2·50
		a. Chalk-surfaced paper. *Blk* (22.1.52)	5·00	8·50
		ab. Error. St. Edward's Crown, W9*b*	£450	
D2		2d. grey-black	3·00	3·00
D3		3d. grey-black	3·00	21·00
		a. Chalk-surfaced paper. *Blk* (22.1.52)	7·50	32·00
		ab. Error. Crown missing, W9*a*	£150	
		ac. Error. St. Edward's Crown, W9*b*	£120	
D4		4d. grey-black	5·00	26·00
D1/4		*Set of* 4	12·00	48·00
D1/4 Perf "Specimen"		*Set of* 4	80·00	

The 2d. is known bisected and used as a 1d. at Nkana on various dates between 1937 and 1951 and on understamped letters from South Africa at Chingola in May 1950 (*Price on cover from* £225).

Following the increase in the internal letter rate from 1½d. to 2d. on 1 July 1953 stocks of postage due stamps at Mkushi became exhausted. As an emergency measure the sub-postmaster was authorised to surcharge examples of Nos. 28 and 55 "POSTAGE DUE 1d." in red by typewriter. Examples properly used on cover between 6 July and 15 September 1953 are of considerable scarcity (*Price on cover* £1100). No unused examples exist.

(Des D. Smith. Litho Govt Ptr, Lusaka)

1963 (10 Dec). *P* 12½.

D 5	D **2**	1d. orange	30	1·75
D 6		2d. deep blue	30	2·00
D 7		3d. lake	35	2·50
D 8		4d. ultramarine	50	3·50
D 9		6d. purple	1·25	4·00
D10		1s. light emerald	3·50	10·00
		a. Imperf (vert pair)	£160	
		b. Block of four imperf horiz and imp between vert	£475	
D5/10		*Set of* 6	5·50	21·00

In all values the stamps in the right-hand vertical row of the sheet are imperforate on the right.

D 3

(Des D. Smith. Litho Govt Printer, Lusaka)

1964 (24 Oct). *P* 12½.

D11	D **3**	1d. orange	30	85
D12		2d. deep blue	35	1·10
D13		3d. lake	45	1·40
D14		4d. ultramarine	45	1·75
D15		6d. purple	45	2·00
D16		1s. light emerald	55	4·00
D11/16		*Set of* 6	2·25	10·00

In all values the left-hand vertical row of the sheet is imperf at left and the bottom horizontal row is imperf at bottom. The above were crudely perforated, resulting in variations in the sizes of the stamps.

The above were withdrawn on 15 January 1968 and thereafter decimal currency postage stamps were used for postage due purposes with appropriate cancellations.

Appendix

The following stamps have either been issued in excess of postal needs, or have not been made available to the public in reasonable quantities at face value. Miniature sheets, imperforate stamps etc., are excluded from this section.

1984

Olympic Games, Los Angeles. 90 *n.* × 5, *each embossed on gold foil.*

1986

Classic Cars. 1 *k.* 50 × 25, *each embossed on gold foil.*

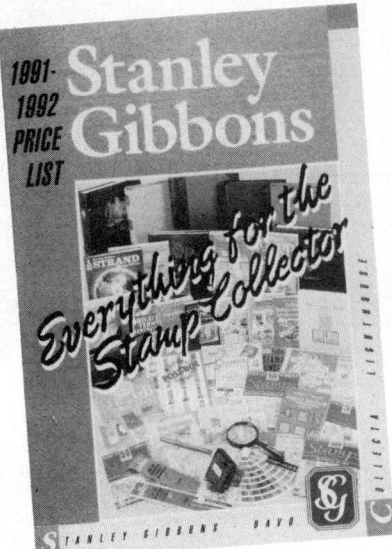

Zanzibar *see* Tanzania

Zimbabwe
(formerly Rhodesia)

SOUTHERN RHODESIA

PRICES FOR STAMPS ON COVER TO 1945
Nos. 1/61 *from* × 2

SELF-GOVERNMENT

The southern part of Rhodesia, previously administered by the British South Africa Company, was annexed by the British Government on 12 September 1923 and granted the status of a self-governing colony.

1

2 King George V

3 Victoria Falls

(Recess Waterlow)

1924 (1 Apr)–**29**. *P* 14.
1 **1** ½d. blue-green 70 10
a. Imperf between (horiz pair) .. £500 £500
b. Imperf between (vert pair) .. £600 £600
c. Imperf vert (horiz pair) £650
2 1d. bright rose 90 10
a. Imperf between (horiz pair) .. £600 £550
b. Imperf between (vert pair) .. £650
c. Perf 12½ (coil) (1929) .. .. 2·75 55·00
3 1½d. bistre-brown 70 30
a. Imperf between (horiz pair) .. £7000
b. Imperf between (vert pair) .. £3500
c. Printed double, once albino .. 90·00
4 2d. black and purple-grey 55 30
a. Imperf between (horiz pair) .. £6000
5 3d. blue .. .. 1·50 2·00
6 4d. black and orange-red .. .. 1·10 2·75
7 6d. black and mauve .. .. .. 1·10 2·25
a. Imperf between (horiz pair) .. £8500
8 8d. purple and pale green .. .. 10·00 32·00
9 10d. blue and rose .. .. .. 11·00 35·00
10 1s. black and light blue .. .. 3·25 3·00
11 1s. 6d. black and yellow .. .. 18·00 27·00
12 2s. black and brown .. .. .. 17·00 17·00
13 2s. 6d. blue and sepia .. .. .. 32·00 48·00
14 5s. blue and blue-green .. .. .. 55·00 85·00
1/14 .. .. *Set of* 14 £140 £225

Prices for "imperf between" varieties are for adjacent stamps from the same pane and not for those separated by wide gutter margins between vertical or horizontal pairs, which come from the junction of two panes.

(T **2** recess by B.W.; T **3** typo by Waterlow)

1931 (1 April)–**37**. *T* **2** (*line perf* 12 *unless otherwise stated*) *and* **3** (*comb perf* 15 × 14). (*The* 11½ *perf is comb.*).
15 **2** ½d. green 20 20
a. Perf 11½ (1933) 20 10
b. Perf 14 (1935) 50 10
16 1d. scarlet 20 10
a. Perf 11½ (1933) 50 10
b. Perf 14 (1935) 35 10
16*c* 1½d. chocolate (1933) .. .. .. 50·00 30·00
d. Perf 11½ (1.4.32) .. .. .. 1·25 45
17 **3** 2d. black and sepia .. .. .. 3·25 70
18 3d. deep ultramarine .. .. .. 8·50 11·00
19 **2** 4d. black and vermilion .. .. 1·10 70
a. Perf 11½ (1935) .. .. .. 15·00 5·00
b. Perf 14 (10.37) .. .. .. 32·00 40·00
20 6d. black and magenta .. .. .. 2·00 75
a. Perf 11½ (1933) .. .. .. 12·00 55
b. Perf 14 (1936) .. .. .. 20·00 60
21 8d. violet and olive-green .. .. 1·75 3·25
a. Perf 11½ (1934) .. .. .. 15·00 25·00
21*b* 9d. vermilion and olive-green (1.9.34) .. 6·00 7·50
22 10d. blue and scarlet .. .. .. 6·00 3·00
a. Perf 11½ (1933) .. .. .. 6·00 13·00
23 1s. black and greenish blue .. .. 1·75 2·00
a. Perf 11½ (1935) .. .. .. 65·00 40·00
b. Perf 14 (10.37) £170 £130
24 1s. 6d. black and orange-yellow .. .. 10·00 16·00
a. Perf 11½ (1936) .. .. .. 48·00 55·00
25 2s. black and brown .. .. .. 13·00 4·50
a. Perf 11½ (1933) .. .. .. 35·00 30·00
26 2s. 6d. blue and drab .. .. .. 30·00 35·00
a. Perf 11½ (1933) .. .. .. 28·00 30·00
27 5s. blue and blue-green .. .. .. 48·00 48·00
a. Printed on gummed side £3000
15/27 .. .. *Set of* 15 £120 £110

No. 16c was issued in booklets only.

PRINTERS. All stamps from Types **4** to **29** were recess-printed by Waterlow and Sons, Ltd, London, except where otherwise stated.

4

1932 (1 May). *P* 12½.
29 **4** 2d. green and chocolate .. .. .. 2·50 30
30 3d. deep ultramarine .. .. .. 3·25 1·75
a. Imperf horiz (vert pair) £6000 £6500
b. Imperf between (vert pair) £8500

5 Victoria Falls

1935 (6 May). *Silver Jubilee. P* 11 × 12.
31 **5** 1d. olive and rose-carmine .. .. 1·50 60
32 2d. emerald and sepia .. .. .. 3·00 2·75
33 3d. violet and deep blue .. .. .. 5·00 10·00
34 6d. black and purple .. .. .. 7·00 8·50
31/4 .. .. *Set of* 4 15·00 20·00

1935–41. *Inscr* "POSTAGE AND REVENUE".
35 **4** 2d. green and chocolate (*p* 12½) .. .. 1·40 3·75
a. Perf 14 (1941) 30 10
35*b* 3d. deep blue (*p* 14) (1938) 75 10

6 Victoria Falls and Railway Bridge

7 King George VI

1937 (12 May). *Coronation. P* 12½.
36 **6** 1d. olive and rose-carmine 65 30
37 2d. emerald and sepia 65 60
38 3d. violet and blue .. .. .. 3·25 4·00
39 6d. black and purple .. .. .. 2·25 1·75
36/9 .. .. *Set of* 4 6·00 6·00

1937 (25 Nov). *P* 14.
40 **7** ½d. green 30 10
41 1d. scarlet 20 10
42 1½d. red-brown 45 10
43 4d. red-orange 75 10
44 6d. grey-black 80 10
45 8d. emerald-green .. .. .. 1·60 80
46 9d. pale blue .. .. 1·00 20
47 10d. purple .. .. 1·10 1·75
48 1s. black and blue-green 75 10
a. Double print of frame £650
49 1s. 6d. black and orange-yellow .. .. 6·00 1·25
50 2s. black and brown .. .. .. 8·00 55
51 2s. 6d. ultramarine and purple .. .. 6·00 2·00
52 5s. blue and blue-green .. .. .. 24·00 2·00
40/52 .. .. *Set of* 13 45·00 8·00

Nos. 40/1 exist in coils, constructed from normal sheets.

8 British South Africa Co's Arms

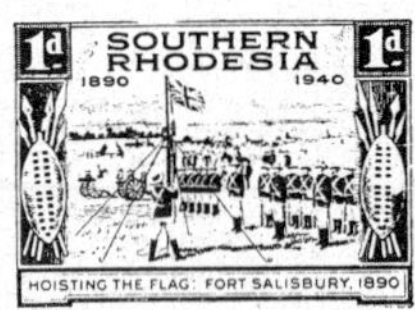

9 Fort Salisbury, 1890

10 Cecil John Rhodes (after S. P. Kendrick)

15 Lobengula's Kraal and Govt House, Salisbury

Recess shirt collar (R. 6/1)

(Des Mrs. L. E. Curtis (½d., 1d., 1½d., 3d.), Mrs I. Mount (others))

1940 (3 June). *British South Africa Company's Golden Jubilee. T* **8/10**, **15** *and similar designs. P* 14.
53 ½d. slate-violet and green 10 10
54 1d. violet-blue and scarlet 10 10
55 1½d. black and red-brown 10 10
a. Recut shirt collar .. .. .. 6·00
56 2d. green and bright violet 30 20
57 3d. black and blue 30 30
58 4d. green and brown 95 80
59 6d. chocolate and green 30 70
60 1s. blue and green .. .. 35 1·25
53/60 .. .. *Set of* 8 2·25 3·00

Designs: *Horiz* (*as T* **8**)—2d. Fort Victoria; 3d. Rhodes makes peace. *Vert* (*as T* **10**)—4d. Victoria Falls Bridge; 6d. Statue of Sir Charles Coghlan.

16 Mounted Pioneer

Hat brim retouch (Pl 1B R. 1/8)

(Roto South African Govt Printer, Pretoria)

1943 (1 Nov). *50th Anniv of Occupation of Matabeleland. W* **9** *of South Africa* (*Mult Springbok*) *sideways. P* 14.
61 **16** 2d. brown and green 10 15
a. Hat brim retouch .. .. .. 10·00

17 Queen Elizabeth II when Princess and Princess Margaret

1947 (1 Apr). *Royal Visit. T* **17** *and similar horiz design. P* 14.
62 ½d. black and green 10 15
63 1d. black and scarlet 10 15

Design:—1d. King George VI and Queen Elizabeth.

19 Queen Elizabeth

20 King George VI

21 Queen Elizabeth II when Princess

22 Princess Margaret

1947 (8 May). *Victory. P* 14.
64 **19** 1d. carmine 10 10
65 **20** 2d. slate 10 10
a. Double print £850
66 **21** 3d. blue 15 15
67 **22** 6d. orange 15 15
64/7 .. .. *Set of* 4 40 40

(Recess B.W.)

1949 (10 Oct). *75th Anniv of U.P.U. As Nos.* 145/8 *of Jamaica.*
68 2d. slate-green 65 20
69 3d. blue .. .. 1·10 2·50

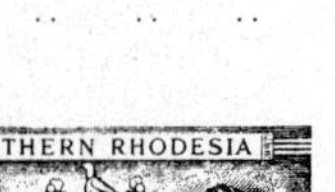

23 Queen Victoria, Arms and King George VI

1950 (12 Sept). *Diamond Jubilee of Southern Rhodesia. P* 14.
70 **23** 2d. green and brown 15 20

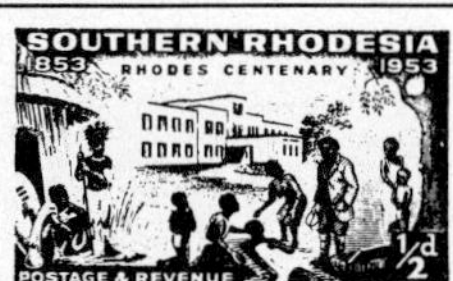

24 "Medical Services"

(Des A. R. Winter (2d.), Mrs. J. M. Enalim (others))

1953 (15 Apr). *Birth Centenary of Cecil Rhodes. T* **24** *and similar horiz designs. P* 14.

71 ½d. pale blue and sepia 15 50
72 1d. chestnut and blue-green 15 10
73 2d. grey-green and violet 15 10
74 4½d. deep blue-green & deep ultramarine .. 75 1·75
75 1s. black and red-brown .. .. .. 3·00 60
71/5 .. .. *Set of* 5 3·75 2·75

Designs:—1d. "Agriculture"; 2d. "Building"; 4½d. "Water Supplies"; 1s. "Transport".

No. 74 also commemorates the Diamond Jubilee of Matabeleland.

1953 (30 May). *Rhodes Centenary Exhibition, Bulawayo. As No. 59 of Zambia, but without watermark.*

76 6d. violet 15 15

30 Queen Elizabeth II

(Recess D.L.R.)

1953 (1 June). *Coronation. P* 12 × 12½.

77 **30** 2s. 6d. carmine .. .. 5·50 5·00

31 Sable Antelope

33 Rhodes's Grave

34 Farm Worker

42 Basket Maker

43 Balancing Rocks

44 Coat of Arms

(Recess, centre typo (4d.), B.W.)

1953 (31 Aug). *T* **31, 33/4, 42/4** *and similar designs. P* 13½ × 14 *(2d., 6d., 5s.), 14 (10s., £1) or* 14 × 13½ *(others).*

78 ½d. grey-green and claret 15 30
79 1d. green and brown 15 10
80 2d. deep chestnut and reddish violet .. 15 10
81 3d. chocolate and rose-red 45 50
82 4d. red, green and indigo .. .. .. 1·50 10
83 4½d. black and deep bright blue .. .. 1·25 1·25
84 6d. brown-olive & deep turquoise-green .. 2·00 20
85 9d. deep blue and reddish brown .. .. 3·25 1·50
86 1s. reddish violet and light blue 75 10
87 2s. purple and scarlet .. .. .. 6·50 3·25
88 2s. 6d. yellow-olive and orange-brown .. 5·50 3·75
89 5s. yellow-brown and deep green .. .. 14·00 7·50
90 10s. red-brown and olive .. .. .. 16·00 35·00
91 £1 rose-red and black .. .. .. 25·00 35·00
78/91 .. .. *Set of* 14 70·00 80·00

Designs: *Vert (as T* **31**)—1d. Tobacco planter. *(As T* **33**)—6d. Baobab tree. *Horiz (as T* **34**)—4d. Flame Lily; 4½d. Victoria Falls; 9d. Lion; 1s. Zimbabwe Ruins; 2s. Birchenough Bridge; 2s. 6d. Kariba Gorge.

For issues from 1954 to 1963 see under RHODESIA AND NYASALAND.

45 Maize

50 Flame Lily

56 Cattle

58 Coat of Arms

(Des V. Whiteley. Photo Harrison)

1964 (19 Feb). *T* **45, 50, 56, 58** *and similar horiz designs. P* 14½ *(½d. to 4d.),* 13½ × 13 *(6d. to 2s. 6d.) or* 14½ × 14 *(others).*

92 ½d. yellow, yellow-green and light blue .. 15 40
93 1d. reddish violet and yellow-ochre .. 15 10
  a. Reddish violet omitted £750
94 2d. yellow and deep violet 15 10
95 3d. chocolate and pale blue 15 10
96 4d. yellow-orange and deep green 30 10
97 6d. carmine-red, yellow and deep dull green 40 10
98 9d. red-brown, yellow and olive-green .. 2·00 80
99 1s. blue-green and ochre .. .. .. 2·25 10
  a. blue-green (Queen and emeralds) omitted £1000
100 1s. 3d. red, violet and yellow-green .. 3·00 10
101 2s. blue and ochre .. .. 2·25 85
102 2s. 6d. ultramarine and vermilion .. 2·75 70
  a. Vermilion omitted £700
  b. Ultramarine omitted £1000
103 5s. light brown, bistre-yellow & light blue 4·50 2·00
104 10s. black, yell-ochre, lt blue & carmine-red 11·00 6·50
105 £1 brown, yellow-green, buff & salmon-pink 7·00 13·00
92/105 .. .. *Set of* 14 32·00 21·00

Designs: *(As T* **45**)—1d. African Buffalo; 2d. Tobacco; 3d. Greater Kudu; 4d. Citrus. *(As T* **50**)—9d. Ansellia Orchid; 1s. Emeralds; 1s. 3d. Aloe; 2s. Lake Kyle; 2s. 6d. Tiger Fish. *(As T* **56**)—10s. Helmet Guineafowl.

Nos. 92 and 93 exist in coils constructed from normal sheets.

Nos. 102a and 102b each occurred on one vertical row of stamps from separate sheets. They were caused by the printing press being stopped and then restarted.

See also Nos. 359/72 of Rhodesia.

In October 1964 Southern Rhodesia was renamed Rhodesia.

RHODESIA

59 "Telecommunications"

60 Bangala Dam

(Des V. Whiteley. Photo Harrison)

1965 (17 May). *I.T.U. Centenary. P* 14½.

351 **59** 6d. violet and light yellow-olive .. 1·00 25
352 1s. 3d. violet and lilac .. .. 1·00 35
353 2s. 6d. violet and light brown .. .. 2·00 3·00
351/3 .. .. *Set of* 3 3·50 3·25

(Des V. Whiteley. Photo Harrison)

1965 (19 July). *Water Conservation. T* **60** *and similar vert designs. Multicoloured. P* 14.

354 3d. Type **60** 20 10
355 4d. Irrigation canal 75 60
356 2s. 6d. Cutting sugar cane .. .. .. 1·50 1·75
354/6 .. .. *Set of* 3 2·25 2·25

63 Sir Winston Churchill, Quill, Sword and Houses of Parliament

(Des H. Baxter. Photo Harrison)

1965 (16 Aug). *Churchill Commemoration. P* 14½.

357 **63** 1s. 3d. black and bright blue 50 35

UNILATERAL DECLARATION OF INDEPENDENCE

Independence was declared by Rhodesia on 11 November 1965 but this was not recognised by the British Government. Following a conference in London during 1979 it was agreed that the British Government should resume control, pending elections to be held in February 1980.

After the elections Rhodesia became an independent republic within the Commonwealth on 18 April 1980, as ZIMBABWE.

64 Coat of Arms

(Des Col. C. R. Dickenson. Litho Mardon Printers, Salisbury)

1965 (8 Dec). *"Independence". P* 11.

358 **64** 2s. 6d. multicoloured 15 15
  a. Imperf (pair) £500

INDEPENDENCE
11th November
1965

INDEPENDENCE
11th November 1965 = 5/-

(**65**) (**66**)

1966 (17 Jan). *(a) Nos. 92/105 optd with T* **65** *or larger (5s. to £1).*

359 ½d. yellow, yellow-green and light blue .. 10 10
  a. Pair, one stamp without opt. £1600
360 1d. reddish violet and yellow-ochre .. 10 10
361 2d. yellow and deep violet 10 10
362 3d. chocolate and pale blue 10 10
363 4d. yellow-orange and deep green .. 15 10
364 6d. carmine-red, yellow & dp dull green .. 15 10
365 9d. red-brown, yellow and olive-green .. 20 10
  a. Opt double £170
366 1s. blue-green and ochre 25 10
  a. Opt double £170
367 1s. 3d. red, violet and yellow-green .. 80 10
368 2s. blue and ochre .. .. 90 2·25
369 2s. 6d. ultramarine and vermilion .. 60 25
370 5s. light brown, bistre-yellow & lt blue .. 8·00 5·00
  a. Opt double £250
371 10s. black, yellow-ochre, lt bl & carm-red .. 3·25 1·25
372 £1 brown, yell-green, buff & salmon-pink 1·50 1·50

(b) No. 357 surch with T **66**

373 5s. on 1s. 3d. black and bright blue (R.) 20·00 35·00
  a. "5/-" omitted .. ..
359/73 .. .. *Set of* 15 32·00 40·00

Owing to the existence of forgeries, No. 370a should only be purchased when accompanied by a certificate of genuineness.

67 Emeralds

68 Zeederberg Coach, *circa* 1895

(Des V. Whiteley. Photo Harrison)

1966 (9 Feb). *As Nos. 92/105, but inscr "RHODESIA" as T* **67.** *Some designs and colours changed. P* 14½ *(1d. to 4d.),* 13½×13 *(6d. to 2s. 6d) or* 14½×14 *(5s. to £1).*

374 – 1d. reddish violet and yellow-ochre .. 10 10
375 – 2d. yell-orge and dp grn (as No. 96) .. 10 10
  a. Yellow-orange omitted £600
376 – 3d. chocolate and pale blue 10 10
  a. Chocolate omitted £800
  b. Pale blue omitted £650
377 **67** 4d. emerald and sepia 30 10
378 **50** 6d. carmine-red, yellow & dp dull grn .. 15 10
379 – 9d. yellow and deep violet (as No. 94) .. 15 20
380 **45** 1s. yellow, yellow-green and light blue 15 10
381 – 1s. 3d. blue and ochre (as No. 101) .. 25 15
382 – 1s. 6d. red-brn, yell & olive-grn (as No. 98) 75 25
383 – 2s. red, violet and yell-grn (as No. 100) 40 80
384 – 2s. 6d. blue, vermilion & turquoise-bl 40 20
385 **56** 5s. light brown, bistre-yellow & lt blue 40 90
386 – 10s. black, yell-ochre, lt bl & carm-red .. 2·50 4·00
387 **58** £1 brown, yell-green, buff & salmon-pk 17·00 10·00
374/87 .. .. *Set of* 14 20·00 15·00

Nos. 379/80 are in larger format, as T **50**.

No. 374 exists in coils constructed from normal sheets. Coil-vending machines were withdrawn from service in 1967.

No. 376a occurred in the bottom row of a sheet and No. 376b in the top two rows of a sheet.

For stamps printed by lithography, see Nos. 397/407.

PRINTERS. All the following stamps were printed by lithography by Mardon Printers, Salisbury.

(Des V. Whiteley (Nos. 388/90))

1966 (2 May). *28th Congress of Southern Africa Philatelic Federation ("Rhopex"). T* **68** *and similar horiz designs. P* 14½.

388 3d. multicoloured 30 10
389 9d. grey-buff, sepia and grey-green 40 35
390 1s. 6d. pale blue and black 60 50
391 2s. 6d. salmon-pink, pale dull grn & blk 70 80
388/91 .. .. *Set of* 4 1·75 1·50
MS392 126×84 mm. Nos. 388/91 *(toned paper)* 22·00 30·00
  a. White paper .. .. 30·00 32·00

Designs:—9d. Sir Rowland Hill; 1s. 6d. The Penny Black; 2s. 6d. Rhodesian stamp of 1892 (No. 12).

69 De Havilland "Rapide" (1946)

70 Kudu

1966 (1 June). *20th Anniv of Central African Airways. T* **69** *and similar horiz designs. P* 14½ × 14.

No.	Description	Unused	Used
393	6d. black, blue, yellow and green	1·00	35
394	1s. 3d. blue, yellow-orange, black and green	1·25	55
395	2s. 6d. black, blue, yellow and green ..	3·50	1·75
396	5s. black and blue	6·00	3·50
393/6	.. .. *Set of* 4	10·50	5·50

Aircraft:—1s. 3d. Douglas "DC3." (1953); 2s. 6d. Vickers "Viscount" (1956); 5s. Modern jet.

1966–69. *As Nos.* 374/87 *but litho. P* 14½ (1*d. to* 2*s.*) *or* 14½ × 14 (*others*).

No.	Description	Unused	Used
397	1d. reddish violet and yellow-ochre (*shades*) (2.6.66)	15	10
398	2d. orange and green (1.11.67)	85	40
399	3d. chocolate-brn & pale grnsh bl (29.1.68) ..	75	10
400	4d. emerald, bistre-brown & drab (21.9.66)	65	10
401	6d. carmine-red, yell & ol-grey (1.11.66) ..	60	40
402	9d. yellow and light violet (20.11.67) ..	30	10
403	1s. 3d. blue and ochre (1.11.66)	4·50	30
404	2s. dull red, violet & sage-green (18.7.66) ..	3·75	5·00
405	5s. yellow-brown, deep bistre-yellow and light blue (25.6.66)	10·00	4·50
406	10s. black, buff, lt bl & carm-red (10.8.66) ..	40·00	48·00
407	£1 pale brown, yellow-green, brown-ochre and salmon (10.8.66)	45·00	55·00
397/407	.. .. *Set of* 11	90·00	£100

In addition to the change in printing process from photogravure to lithography and the difference in perforation in the 6d. to 2s. values (14½ instead of 13½ × 13) and shade variations, the oval portrait frame is larger (and in some values thicker) in the 1d. to 2s., and in the 1s. 3d. the Queen's head is also larger.

Trial printings, made in June 1966, exist of the 5s., 10s., and £1 values on a slightly thinner paper. These are rare.

1967–68. *Dual Currency Issue. As Nos.* 376, 380 *and* 382/4 *but value in decimal currency in addition as in T* **70**. *P* 14½. *White gum* (*No.* 408) *or cream gum* (*others*).

No.	Description	Unused	Used
408	3d./2½ c. chocolate-brown and pale greenish blue (15.3.67)	60	20
409	1s./10 c. yell, grn & greenish bl (1.11.67) ..	70	45
410	1s. 6d./15 c. red-brown, yellow and yellow-green (11.3.68)	4·75	90
411	2s./20 c. dull red, viol and sage-grn (11.3.68)	10·00	9·00
412	2s. 6d./25 c. ultramarine-blue, vermilion and bright turquoise-blue (9.12.68)	50·00	60·00
408/12	.. .. *Set of* 5	60·00	65·00

71 Dr. Jameson (administrator)

(Des from painting by F. M. Bennett)

1967 (17 May). *Famous Rhodesians (1st issue) and 50th Death Anniv of Dr. Jameson. P* 14½.

No.	Type	Description	Unused	Used
413	**71**	1s. 6d. multicoloured	30	35

See also Nos. 426, 430, 457, 458, 469, 480, 488 and 513.

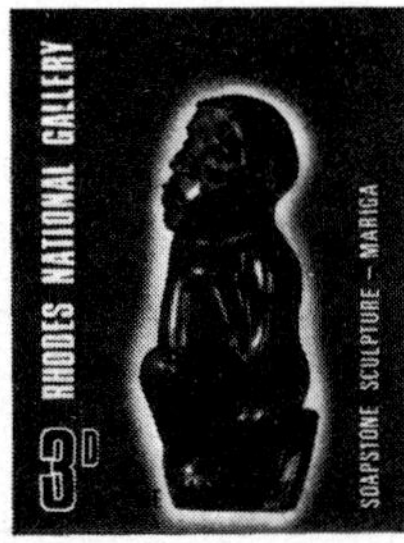

72 Soapstone Sculpture (Joram Mariga)

1967 (12 July). *Tenth Anniv of Opening of Rhodes National Gallery. T* **72** *and similar vert designs. P* 14½ × 14 (3*d.*, 9*d.*) *or* 14 (*others*).

No.	Description	Unused	Used
414	3d. reddish chestnut, yellow-olive and black	10	10
415	9d. lt greenish blue, dp olive-brown & black	20	20
	a. Perf 13½	7·50	18·00
416	1s. 3d. multicoloured	20	25
417	2s. 6d. multicoloured	25	35
414/17	.. .. *Set of* 4	65	75

Designs:—9d. "The Burgher of Calais" (detail, Rodin); 1s. 3d. "The Knight" (stamp design wrongly inscr) (Roberto Crippa); 2s. 6d. "John the Baptist" (M. Tossini).

73 Baobab Tree

1967 (6 Sept). *Nature Conservation. T* **73** *and similar designs. P* 14½.

No.	Description	Unused	Used
418	4d. light brown and black	20	25
419	4d. yellow-olive and black	20	25
420	4d. deep grey and black	20	25
421	4d. yellow-orange and black	20	25
418/21	.. .. *Set of* 4	70	90

Designs: *Horiz*—No. 418, Type **73**; No. 419, White Rhinoceros; No. 420, African Elephants. *Vert*—No. 421, Wild Gladiolus.

74 Wooden Hand Plough

(Des Rose Martin)

1968 (26 Apr). *15th World Ploughing Contest, Norton, Rhodesia. T* **74** *and similar horiz designs. P* 14½.

No.	Description	Unused	Used
422	3d. pale orange, orange-verm & lake-brown	10	10
423	9d. multicoloured	20	20
424	1s. 6d. multicoloured	30	45
425	2s. 6d. multicoloured	35	70
422/5	.. .. *Set of* 4	85	1·40

Designs:—9d. Early wheel plough; 1s. 6d. Steam powered tractor, and ploughs; 2s. 6d. Modern tractor, and plough.

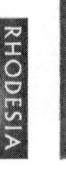

75 Alfred Beit (national benefactor)

76 Raising the Flag, Bulawayo, 1893

(Des from painting by A. Haywood)

1968 (15 July). *Famous Rhodesians (2nd issue). P* 14½.

No.	Type	Description	Unused	Used
426	**75**	1s. 6d. pale orange, black and brown ..	30	30

(Des Rose Martin)

1968 (4 Nov). *75th Anniv of Matabeleland. T* **76** *and similar vert designs. P* 14½.

No.	Description	Unused	Used
427	3d. pale orange, red-orange and black ..	10	10
428	9d. multicoloured	15	20
429	1s. 6d. pale turquoise-green, deep emerald and blackish green	20	35
427/9	.. .. *Set of* 3	40	55

Designs:—9d. View and coat of arms of Bulawayo; 1s. 6d. Allan Wilson (combatant in the Matabele War).

77 Sir William Henry Milton (administrator)

(Des from painting by S. Kendrick)

1969 (15 Jan). *Famous Rhodesians (3rd issue). P* 14½.

No.	Type	Description	Unused	Used
430	**77**	1s. 6d. multicoloured	20	45

78 2 ft Gauge Steam Locomotive, Beira-Salisbury Line, 1899

(Des Rose Martin)

1969 (22 May). *70th Anniv of Opening of Beira-Salisbury Railway. T* **78** *and similar horiz designs showing locomotives. Multicoloured. P* 14½.

No.	Description	Unused	Used
431	3d. Type **78**	1·00	10
432	9d. Steam locomotive, 1904	2·00	75
433	1s. 6d. Articulated steam locomotive, 1950 ..	6·50	3·25
434	2s. 6d. Diesel locomotive, 1955	8·50	6·50
431/4	.. .. *Set of* 4	16·00	9·50

79 Low Level Bridge

(Des Rose Martin)

1969 (18 Sept). *Bridges of Rhodesia. T* **79** *and similar horiz designs. Multicoloured. P* 14½.

No.	Description	Unused	Used
435	3d. Type **79**	75	10
436	9d. Mpudzi bridge	1·25	25
437	1s. 6d. Umniati bridge	3·50	1·00
438	2s. 6d. Birchenough bridge	4·50	1·50
435/8	.. .. *Set of* 4	9·00	2·50

(New Currency. 100 cents = 1 dollar)

80 Harvesting Wheat

81 Devil's Cataract, Victoria Falls

(Des from colour-transparencies (3, 6 c.), Rose Martin (others))

1970 (17 Feb)–**73.** *Decimal Currency. T* **80/1** *and similar horiz designs. P* 14½.

No.	Description	Unused	Used
439	1 c. multicoloured	10	10
	a. Booklet pane of 4	20	
440	2 c. multicoloured	10	10
441	2½ c. multicoloured	10	10
	a. Booklet pane of 4	20	
441*c*	3 c. multicoloured (1.1.73)	1·25	10
	ca. Booklet pane of 4	4·50	
442	3½ c. multicoloured	10	10
	a. Booklet pane of 4	40	
442*b*	4 c. multicoloured (1.1.73)	1·50	30
	ba. Booklet pane of 4	5·50	
443	5 c. multicoloured	15	10
443*b*	6 c. multicoloured (1.1.73)	4·50	3·00
443*c*	7½ c. multicoloured (1.1.73)	9·00	1·25
444	8 c. multicoloured	1·75	20
445	10 c. multicoloured	60	10
446	12½ c. multicoloured	1·25	10
446*a*	14 c. multicoloured (1.1.73)	16·00	1·50
447	15 c. multicoloured	3·50	15
448	20 c. multicoloured	2·50	15
449	25 c. multicoloured	3·75	65
450	50 c. turquoise and ultramarine	2·75	70
451	$1 multicoloured	4·00	4·00
452	$2 multicoloured	15·00	25·00
439/52	.. .. *Set of* 19	55·00	32·00

Designs: *Size as T* **80**—2 c. Pouring molten metal; 2½ c. Zimbabwe Ruins; 3 c. Articulated lorry; 3½ c. and 4 c. Statute of Cecil Rhodes; 5 c. Mine headgear. *Size as T* **81**—6 c. Hydrofoil *Seaflight*; 7½ c. As 8 c.; 10 c. Yachting on Lake McIlwaine; 12½ c. Hippopotamus in river; 14 c. and 15 c. Kariba Dam; 20 c. Irrigation canal. *As T* **80/1** *but larger* (31 × 26 *mm*)—25 c. Bateleur Eagles; 50 c. Radar antenna and Vickers "Viscount"; $1 "Air Rescue"; $2 Rhodesian flag.

82 Despatch Rider, *circa* 1890

(Des Rose Martin)

1970 (1 July). *Inauguration of Posts and Telecommunications Corporation. T* **82** *and similar horiz designs. Multicoloured. P* 14½.

No.	Description	Unused	Used
453	2½ c. Type **82**	25	10
454	3½ c. Loading mail at Salisbury airport ..	40	25
455	15 c. Constructing telegraph line, *circa* 1890	1·25	2·00
456	25 c. Telephone and modern telecommunications equipment	2·00	3·50
453/6	.. .. *Set of* 4	3·50	5·25

83 Mother Patrick (Dominican nurse and teacher)

(Des Rose Martin from photograph)

1970 (16 Nov). *Famous Rhodesians (4th issue). P* 14½.

No.	Type	Description	Unused	Used
457	**83**	15 c. multicoloured	40	40

84 Frederick Courteney Selous (big-game hunter, explorer and pioneer)

(Des from painting by L. C. Dickinson)

1971 (1 Mar). *Famous Rhodesians (5th issue). P* 14½.

No.	Type	Description	Unused	Used
458	**84**	15 c. multicoloured	40	40

85 Hoopoe

86 Porphyritic Granite

(Des from photographs by Peter Ginn)

1971 (1 June). *Birds of Rhodesia (1st series). T* **85** *and similar multicoloured designs. P* 14½.
459 2 c. Type **85** . . 1·25 20
460 2½ c. Half-collared Kingfisher (*horiz*) 1·25 20
461 5 c. Golden-breasted Bunting 3·50 60
462 7½ c. Carmine Bee Eater 4·00 1·00
463 8 c. Red-eyed Bulbul 4·00 1·25
464 25 c. Senegal Wattled Plover (*horiz*) 8·50 2·75
459/64 *Set of* 6 20·00 5·50
See also Nos. 537/42.

Des from photographs by University of Rhodesia and Dept of Geological Survey)

1971 (30 Aug). *"Granite 71" Geological Symposium. T* **86** *and similar vert designs. Multicoloured. P* 14.
465 2½ c. Type **86** . . 75 10
466 7½ c. Muscovite mica seen through microscope 1·75 80
467 15 c. Granite seen through microscope 2·50 3·25
468 25 c. Geological map of Rhodesia 3·25 4·75
465/8 *Set of* 4 7·50 8·00

87 Dr. Robert Moffat (missionary)

1972 (14 Feb). *Famous Rhodesians (6th issue). P* 14½.
469 **87** 13 c. multicoloured 1·00 90

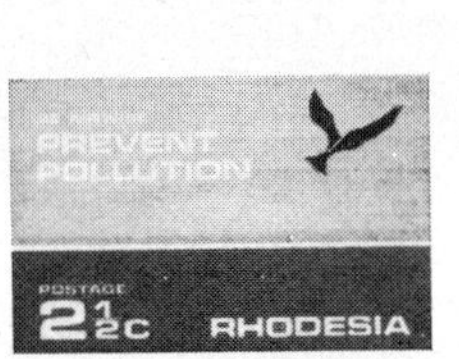

88 Bird ("Be Airwise") **89** "The Three Kings"

(Des C. Lawton)

1972 (17 July). *"Prevent Pollution". T* **88** *and similar horiz designs. Multicoloured. P* 14½.
470 2½ c. Type **88** . . 20 10
471 3½ c. Antelope ("Be Countrywise") 20 10
472 7 c. Fish ("Be Waterwise") 30 45
473 13 c. City ("Be Citywise") 45 70
470/3 *Set of* 4 1·00 1·25

1972 (28 Aug). *"Rhophil '72". As Nos.* 439a, 441a *and* 442a *with commemorative inscr in margins. Each* 66 × 78 *mm.*
MS474 1 c. multicoloured 2·50 3·50
MS475 2½ c. multicoloured 2·50 3·50
MS476 3½ c. multicoloured 2·50 3·50
MS474/6 *Set of* 3 *sheets* 6·75 9·50

(Des Rose Martin)

1972 (18 Oct). *Christmas. P* 14.
477 **89** 2 c. multicoloured 10 10
478 5 c. multicoloured 20 15
479 13 c. multicoloured 50 45
477/9 *Set of* 3 70 60

90 Dr. David Livingstone **91** W.M.O. Emblem

1973 (2 Apr). *Famous Rhodesians (7th issue). P* 14.
480 **90** 14 c. multicoloured 70 75

(Des S. J. Ivey)

1973 (2 July). *I.M.O./W.M.O. Centenary. P* 14.
481 **91** 3 c. multicoloured 15 10
482 14 c. multicoloured 50 60
483 25 c. multicoloured 1·00 1·50
481/3 *Set of* 3 1·50 2·00

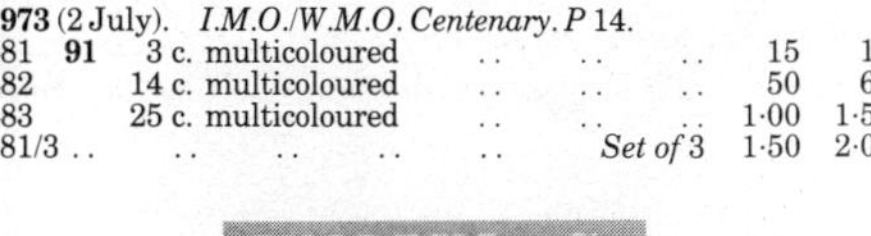

92 Arms of Rhodesia

1973 (10 Oct). *50th Anniv of Responsible Government. P* 14.
484 **92** 2½ c. multicoloured 15 10
485 4 c. multicoloured 20 20
486 7½ c. multicoloured 35 70
487 14 c. multicoloured 60 1·75
484/7 *Set of* 4 1·10 2·40

93 George Pauling (construction engineer)

(Des P. Birch)

1974 (15 May). *Famous Rhodesians (8th issue). P* 14.
488 **93** 14 c. multicoloured 1·00 1·50

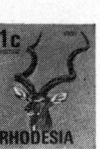

94 Greater Kudu **95** Thunbergia **96** *Charaxes varanes*

(Des J. Huntly)

1974 (14 Aug)–**76**. *Various vert designs as T* **94/6**. *Multicoloured. P* 14½ *(1 to 14 c.) or* 14 *(others). (a) Antelopes. Size as T* **94**.
489 1 c. Type **94** . . 10 10
490 2½ c. Eland 75 10
a. Booklet pane of 4 2·75
491 3 c. Roan Antelope 10 10
a. Booklet pane of 4 70
492 4 c. Reedbuck 10 10
a. Booklet pane of 4 70
493 5 c. Bushbuck 30 10

(b) Wild Flowers. Size as T **95**
494 6 c. Type **95** 40 10
495 7½ c. Flame Lily 3·00 35
496 8 c. As 7½ c. (1.7.76) 40 10
497 10 c. Devil Thorn 30 10
498 12 c. Hibiscus (1.7.76) 70 60
499 12½ c. Pink Sabi Star 4·50 50
500 14 c. Wild Pimpernel 7·50 70
501 15 c. As 12½ c. (1.7.76) 70 60
502 16 c. As 14 c. (1.7.76) 70 45

(c) Butterflies. Size as T **96**
503 20 c. Type **96** 1·50 35
504 24 c. *Precis hierta* (s sp *cebrene*) (1.7.76) 1·50 40
505 25 c. As 24 c. 8·50 3·00
506 50 c. *Colotis regina* 70 90
507 $1 *Graphium antheus* 70 1·25
508 $2 *Hamanumida daedalus* 80 1·50
489/508 *Set of* 20 28·00 11·00

97 Collecting Mail **98** Thomas Baines (artist)

(Des M. Chase)

1974 (20 Nov). *Centenary of Universal Postal Union. T* **97** *and similar horiz designs. Multicoloured. P* 14.
509 3 c. Type **97** . . 15 10
510 4 c. Sorting mail 20 10
511 7½ c. Mail delivery 50 65
512 14 c. Weighing parcel 1·00 1·75
509/12 *Set of* 4 1·75 2·25

(Des from self-portrait)

1975 (12 Feb). *Famous Rhodesians (9th issue). P* 14.
513 **98** 14 c. multicoloured 80 1·25

99 *Euphorbia confinalis* **100** Prevention of Head Injuries

(Des Nancy Abrey)

1975 (16 July). *International Succulent Congress, Salisbury ("Aloe '75"). T* **99** *and similar vert designs. Multicoloured. P* 14½.
514 2½ c. Type **99** . . 20 10
515 3 c. *Aloe excelsa* 20 10
516 4 c. *Hoodia lugardii* 30 15
517 7½ c. *Aloe orthopolpha* 55 55
518 14 c. *Aloe musapana* 1·50 1·25
519 25 c. *Aloe saponaria* 2·00 2·00
514/19 *Set of* 6 4·25 3·50

(Des Val Bond)

1975 (15 Oct). *Occupational Safety. T* **100** *and similar horiz designs. Multicoloured. P* 14.
520 2½ c. Type **100** 15 10
521 4 c. Bandaged hand and gloved hand 20 10
522 7½ c. Broken glass and eye 35 20
523 14 c. Blind man and welder with protective mask 50 60
520/3 *Set of* 4 1·10 80

101 Telephones, 1876 and 1976

8c

(102)

(Des M. Chase)

1976 (10 Mar). *Telephone Centenary. T* **101** *and similar vert design. P* 14.
524 3 c. grey-black and pale blue 10 10
525 14 c. brownish black and light stone 20 35
Design:—14 c. Alexander Graham Bell.

1976 (1 July). *Nos.* 495, 500 *and* 505 *surch as T* **102**.
526 8 c. on 7½ c. Flame Lily 15 15
a. Surch double, one albino
527 16 c. on 14 c. Wild Pimpernel 20 25
528 24 c. on 25 c. *Precis hierta* (s sp *cebrene*) 30 50
526/8 *Set of* 3 60 80

103 Roan Antelope **104** Msasa

(Des N. Pedersen)

1976 (21 July). *Vulnerable Wildlife. T* **103** *and similar horiz designs. Multicoloured. P* 14.
529 4 c. Type **103** . . 20 10
530 6 c. Brown Hyena 25 10
531 8 c. Hunting Dog 35 25
532 16 c. Cheetah 45 45
529/32 *Set of* 4 1·10 75

(Des Nancy Abrey)

1976 (17 Nov). *Trees of Rhodesia. T* **104** *and similar vert designs. Multicoloured. P* 14.
533 4 c. Type **104** . . 15 10
534 6 c. Red Mahogany 15 10
535 8 c. Mukwa 20 30
536 16 c. Rhodesian Teak 25 50
533/6 *Set of* 4 65 75

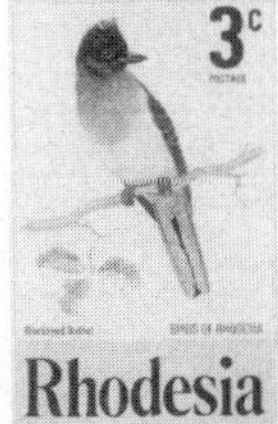

105 Common Bulbul **106** "Lake Kyle" (Joan Evans)

(Des B. Finch)

1977 (16 Mar). *Birds of Rhodesia (2nd series). T* **105** *and similar vert designs. Multicoloured. P* 14.
537 3 c. Type **105** . . 20 10
538 4 c. Yellow-mantled Whydah 20 10
539 6 c. Cape Longclaw 25 35
540 8 c. Eastern Long-tailed Shrike 45 50
541 16 c. Lesser Blue-eared Glossy Starling 75 1·00
542 24 c. Green Wood Hoopoe 95 1·25
537/42 *Set of* 6 2·50 3·00

1977 (20 July). *Landscape Paintings. T* **106** *and similar horiz designs. Multicoloured. P* 14.
543 3 c. Type **106** . . 15 10
544 4 c. "Chimanimani Mountains" (Joan Evans) 15 10
545 6 c. "Rocks near Bonsor Reef", (Alice Balfour) 15 10
546 8 c. "A Dwala near Devil's Pass" (Alice Balfour) 25 10
547 16 c. "Zimbabwe" (Alice Balfour) 35 50
548 24 c. "Victoria Falls" (Thomas Baines) 40 60
543/8 *Set of* 6 1·25 1·25

107 Virgin and Child

108 Fair Spire

(Des Dianne Deudney)

1977 (16 Nov). *Christmas. P* 14.

549 **107** 3 c. multicoloured 10 10
550 6 c. multicoloured 10 10
551 8 c. multicoloured 15 10
552 16 c. multicoloured 30 50
549/52 .. .. *Set of* 4 75 65

1978 (15 Mar). *Trade Fair Rhodesia, Bulawayo. T* **108** *and similar vert design. Multicoloured. P* 14.

553 4 c. Type **108** 15 10
554 8 c. Fair Spire (*different*) 20 25

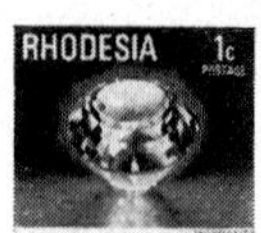

109 Morganite

110 White Rhinoceros

111 Odzani Falls

(Des N. Pedersen (1 to 17 c.), D. Myles (21 c. to $2))

1978 (16 Aug). *Multicoloured.*

(*a*) *Horiz designs as T* **109** *showing gemstones. P* 14½

555 1 c. Type **109** 20 10
556 3 c. Amethyst 30 10
557 4 c. Garnet 30 10
558 5 c. Citrine 30 10
559 7 c. Blue Topaz 30 10

(*b*) *Horiz designs as T* **110** *showing wild animals. P* 14½

560 9 c. Type **110** 20 10
561 11 c. Lion 20 15
562 13 c. Warthog 20 15
563 15 c. Giraffe 20 15
564 17 c. Common Zebra 20 10

(*c*) *Horiz designs as T* **111** *showing waterfalls. P* 14

565 21 c. Type **111** 20 30
566 25 c. Goba Falls 20 40
567 30 c. Inyangombi Falls 25 30
568 $1 Bridal Veil Falls 50 80
569 $2 Victoria Falls .. .. 75 1·00
555/69 .. .. *Set of* 15 3·50 3·00

112 Wright *Flyer*

(Des C. Herbert)

1978 (18 Oct). *75th Anniv of Powered Flight. T* **112** *and similar horiz designs. Multicoloured. P* 14.

570 4 c. Type **112** 10 10
571 5 c. Blériot "XI" 10 10
572 7 c. Vickers "Vimy" *Silver Queen* II 10 10
573 9 c. "A.W. 15 Atalanta" 10 10
574 17 c. Vickers "Viking 1B" 15 15
575 25 c. Boeing "720B" 20 30
570/5 .. .. *Set of* 6 65 65

ZIMBABWE

REPUBLIC

Rhodesia became independent under majority rule on 18 April 1980 and was renamed Zimbabwe.

PRINTERS. All stamps of Zimbabwe were printed in lithography by Mardon Printers (Pvt) Ltd, subsequently (from Nos. 724/7) National Printing and Packaging, Harare, *unless otherwise stated.*

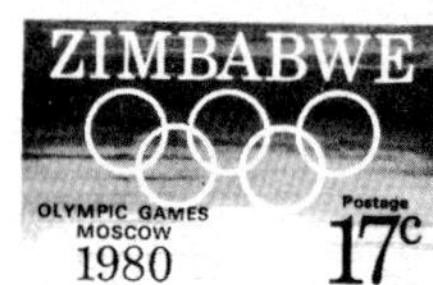

113 Morganite

114 Rotary Anniversary Emblem

1980 (18 Apr)–**83.** *As Nos.* 555/69 *and new value* (40 c.), *all inscr* "ZIMBABWE" *as in T* **113.**

576 1 c. Type **113** 20 10
577 3 c. Amethyst 30 10
578 4 c. Garnet 30 10
579 5 c. Citrine 35 10
580 7 c. Blue Topaz 35 10
581 9 c. White Rhinoceros 15 10
582 11 c. Lion 15 15
583 13 c. Warthog 15 15
584 15 c. Giraffe 15 20
585 17 c. Common Zebra 15 20
586 21 c. Odzani Falls 20 25
587 25 c. Goba Falls 25 30
588 30 c. Inyangombi Falls 30 50
588*a* 40 c. Bundi Falls (14.3.83) .. .. .. 3·50 3·25
589 $1 Bridal Veil Falls .. .. 1·10 2·00
590 $2 Victoria Falls .. .. 2·25 3·75
576/90 .. .. *Set of* 16 9·00 10·00

1980 (18 June). *75th Anniv of Rotary International. P* 14½.

591 **114** 4 c. multicoloured 10 10
592 13 c. multicoloured 20 30
593 21 c. multicoloured 35 55
594 25 c. multicoloured 45 80
591/4 .. .. *Set of* 4 95 1·60
MS595 140 × 84 mm. Nos. 591/4 .. .. .. 1·25 1·60

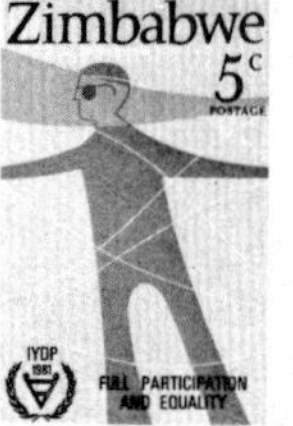

115 Olympic Rings

(Des Nancy Abrey)

1980 (19 July). *Olympic Games, Moscow. P* 14½.

596 **115** 17 c. multicoloured 30 40

116 Gatooma Post Office, 1912

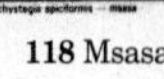

117 Stylised Blind Person

(Des Mortimer Tiley and Partners Ltd)

1980 (17 Oct). *75th Anniv of Post Office Savings Bank. T* **116** *and similar horiz designs. P* 14.

597 5 c. black and yellow-brown 10 10
598 7 c. black and red-orange 10 10
599 9 c. black and olive-yellow 10 10
600 17 c. black and light blue 25 25
597/600 .. .. *Set of* 4 40 40
MS601 125 × 84 mm. Nos. 597/600 .. .. 1·00 1·25

Designs:—7 c. Salisbury Post Office, 1912; 9 c. Umtali Post Office, 1901; 17 c. Bulawayo Post Office, 1895.

(Des Rose Martin)

1981 (23 Sept). *International Year for Disabled Persons. T* **117** *and similar vert designs showing stylised figures. Multicoloured. P* 14.

602 5 c. Type **117** 10 10
603 7 c. Deaf person 15 10
604 11 c. Person with one leg 25 15
605 17 c. Person with one arm 35 35
602/5 .. .. *Set of* 4 75 60

118 Msasa

119 Painting from Gwamgwadza Cave, Mtoko Area

(Des Nancy Abrey)

1981 (4 Dec). *National Tree Day. T* **118** *and similar vert designs. Multicoloured. P* 14½.

606 5 c. Type **118** 10 10
607 7 c. Mopane 15 15
608 21 c. Flat-crowned Acacia 55 60
609 30 c. Pod Mahogany 60 90
606/9 .. .. *Set of* 4 1·25 1·60

1982 (17 Mar). *Rock Paintings. T* **119** *and similar horiz designs showing paintings from various locations. Multicoloured. P* 14½.

610 9 c. Type **119** 65 20
611 11 c. Epworth Mission, near Harare 85 20
612 17 c. Diana's Vow, near Harare 85 50
613 21 c. Gwamgwadza Cave, Mtoko Area (*different*) .. .. 1·25 1·00
614 25 c. Mucheka Cave, Msana Communal Land 1·50 1·75
615 30 c. Chinzwini Shelter, Chiredzi Area .. 1·75 2·00
610/15 .. .. *Set of* 6 6·00 5·00

120 Scout Emblem

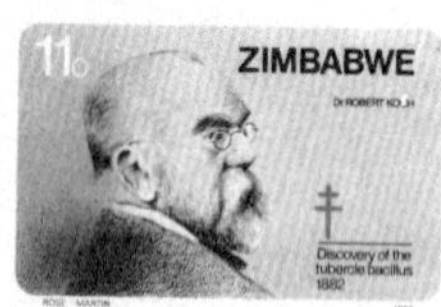

121 Dr. Robert Koch

(Des Rose Martin)

1982 (21 July). *75th Anniv of Boy Scout Movement. T* **120** *and similar vert designs. Multicoloured. P* 14½ × 14.

616 9 c. Type **120** 35 15
617 11 c. Scouts around campfire 35 15
618 21 c. Scouts map-reading 50 75
619 30 c. Lord Baden-Powell .. .. 65 1·40
616/19 .. .. *Set of* 4 1·75 2·25

(Des Rose Martin)

1982 (17 Nov). *Centenary of Dr. Robert Koch's Discovery of Tubercle Bacillus. T* **121** *and similar horiz design. P* 14.

620 11 c. salmon, black and greenish grey .. 75 25
621 30 c. multicoloured .. .. 1·75 2·00

Design:—30 c. Man looking through microscope.

122 "Wing Woman" (Henry Mudzengerere)

123 Traditional Ploughing Team (moving right)

1983 (14 Mar). *Commonwealth Day. Sculptures. T* **122** *and similar multicoloured designs. P* 14.

622 9 c. Type **122** 10 10
623 11 c. "Telling Secrets" (Joseph Ndandarika) (*horiz*) 15 10
624 30 c. "Hornbill Man" (John Takawira) (*horiz*) 35 45
625 $1 "The Chief" (Nicholas Mukomberanwa) 1·00 1·75
622/5 .. .. *Set of* 4 1·40 2·10

(Des Rose Martin)

1983 (13 May). *30th World Ploughing Contest, Zimbabwe. T* **123** *and similar horiz designs. Multicoloured. P* 14.

626 21 c. Type **123** 25 35
a. Horiz pair. Nos. 626/7 .. .. .. 50 70
627 21 c. Traditional ploughing team (moving left) 25 35
628 30 c. Tractor ploughing 40 65
a. Horiz pair. Nos. 628/9 .. .. .. 80 1·25
629 30 c. Modern plough 40 65
626/9 .. .. *Set of* 4 1·25 1·75

The two designs of each value were issued in horizontal *se-tenant* pairs, forming composite designs, throughout the sheets.

124 Postman on Cycle

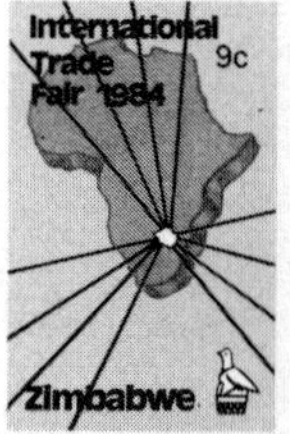

125 Map of Africa showing Zimbabwe

(Des R. Phillips)

1983 (12 Oct). *World Communications Year. T* **124** *and similar multicoloured designs. P* 14.

630	9 c. Type **124**	15	10
631	11 c. Aircraft controller directing aircraft	20	10
632	15 c. Switchboard operator	25	30
633	17 c. Printing works	30	30
634	21 c. Road transport (*horiz*)	40	60
635	30 c. Rail transport (*horiz*)	60	90
630/5	*Set of* 6	1·75	2·00

(Des Bunty Woods and Nancy Abrey)

1984 (11 Apr). *Zimbabwe International Trade Fair. T* **125** *and similar vert designs. Multicoloured. P* 14½.

636	9 c. Type **125**	10	10
637	11 c. Globe	15	10
638	30 c. Zimbabwe flag and Trade Fair logo	45	35
636/8	*Set of* 3	65	50

126 Cycling

(Des Vivienne Fick (11 c.), Joanna Hogg (21 c.), Blessing Chikoore (30 c.), Wayne Gubb (40 c.))

1984 (18 July). *Olympic Games, Los Angeles. Children's Pictures. T* **126** *and similar horiz designs. Multicoloured. P* 14½.

639	11 c. Type **126**	30	15
640	21 c. Swimming	40	40
641	30 c. Running	55	65
642	40 c. Hurdling	70	80
639/42	*Set of* 4	1·75	1·75

127 Liberation Heroes

128 African Fish Eagle

(Des N. Pearce (11 c.), J. Akester (others))

1984 (8 Aug). *Heroes' Days. T* **127** *and similar multicoloured designs showing various aspects of Heroes' Acre. P* 14½.

643	9 c. Type **127**	30	10
644	11 c. Symbolic tower and flame (*vert*)	30	10
645	17 c. Bronze sculpture (*vert*)	50	20
646	30 c. Section of bronze mural	70	35
643/6	*Set of* 4	1·60	65

(Des B. Finch)

1984 (10 Oct). *Birds of Prey. T* **128** *and similar vert designs. Multicoloured. P* 14½.

647	9 c. Type **128**	50	20
648	11 c. Long-crested Eagle	50	20
649	13 c. Bateleur	65	45
650	17 c. Verreaux's Eagle	80	45
651	21 c. Martial Eagle	90	1·25
652	30 c. Bonelli's Eagle	1·25	2·00
647/52	*Set of* 6	4·25	4·00

129 Class "9" Locomotive No. 86

130 "Intelsat V" Telecommunications Satellite

(Des G. Cameron)

1985 (15 May). *"Zimbabwe Steam Safaris". Railway Locomotives. T* **129** *and similar horiz designs. Multicoloured. P* 14½.

653	9 c. Type **129**	75	20
654	11 c. Class "12" No. 190	75	20
655	17 c. Class "Garratt 15A" *Isilwane*	1·25	85
656	30 c. Class "Garratt 20A" *Gwaai*	2·00	2·25
653/6	*Set of* 4	4·25	3·25

1985 (8 July). *Earth Satellite Station, Mazowe. T* **130** *and similar multicoloured design. P* 14½ × 14 (26 c.) *or* 14½ (57 c.).

657	26 c. Type **130**	1·50	50
658	57 c. Earth Satellite Station, Mazowe (65 × 25 *mm*)	2·75	3·50

131 Tobacco

132 Chief Mutapa Gatsi Rusere and 17th-century Seal

(Des Rose Rigden)

1985 (21 Aug). *National Infrastructure. T* **131** *and similar horiz designs. Multicoloured. P* 14½.

659	1 c. Type **131**	10	10
660	3 c. Maize	10	10
661	4 c. Cotton	10	10
662	5 c. Tea	10	10
663	10 c. Cattle	10	10
664	11 c. Birchenough Bridge	20	10
665	12 c. Ore stamp mill	50	10
666	13 c. Gold pouring	50	15
667	15 c. Dragline coal mining	50	15
668	17 c. Uncut amethyst	50	15
669	18 c. Electric locomotive	50	20
670	20 c. Kariba Dam	50	15
671	23 c. Elephants at water hole	50	15
672	25 c. Sunset over Zambezi	40	20
673	26 c. Baobab tree	40	20
674	30 c. Ruins of Great Zimbabwe	45	20
675	35 c. Traditional dancing	45	30
676	45 c. Village women crushing maize	50	40
677	57 c. Woodcarving	60	45
678	$1 Playing Mbira (musical instrument)	1·00	65
679	$2 Mule-drawn Scotch cart	1·75	2·00
680	$5 Zimbabwe coat-of-arms	3·50	4·00
659/80	*Set of* 22	12·00	9·00

(Des C. Herbert)

1985 (18 Sept). *50th Anniv of National Archives. T* **132** *and similar horiz designs. Multicoloured. P* 14½.

681	12 c. Type **132**	15	15
682	18 c. Chief Lobengula, seal and 1888 Treaty	20	35
683	26 c. Exhibition gallery	25	40
684	35 c. National Archives building	30	60
681/4	*Set of* 4	80	1·40

MACHINE LABELS. From 24 October 1985 gummed labels in the above design varying in value from 1 c. to $99.99, were available from four automatic machines located at the Philatelic Bureau and at the main post offices in Bulawayo, Gwelo and Harare.

133 Computer Operator

(Des C. Herbert)

1985 (13 Nov). *United Nations Decade for Women. T* **133** *and similar horiz designs. Multicoloured. P* 14½.

685	10 c. Type **133**	45	10
686	17 c. Nurse giving injection	75	45
687	26 c. Woman student	1·40	1·75
685/7	*Set of* 3	2·40	2·00

134 Harare Conference Centre

(Des C. Herbert)

1986 (29 Jan). *Harare International Conference Centre. T* **134** *and similar horiz design. Multicoloured. P* 14½.

688	26 c. Type **134**	60	30
689	35 c. Interior of conference hall	1·00	1·10

135 Grain Storage Silo

136 *Bunaeopsis jacksoni*

(Des C. Herbert)

1986 (1 Apr). *6th Anniv of Southern African Development Co-ordination Conference. T* **135** *and similar horiz designs. Multicoloured. P* 14½.

690	12 c. Type **135**	40	15
691	18 c. Rhinoceros and hawk at sunset	1·50	1·00
692	26 c. Map showing S.A.D.C.C. member states, and Boeing "737"	1·75	1·40
693	35 c. Map and national flags of S.A.D.C.C. members	2·00	1·60
690/3	*Set of* 4	5·00	3·75

1986 (18 June). *Moths of Zimbabwe. T* **136** *and similar horiz designs. Multicoloured. P* 14½ × 14.

694	12 c. Type **136**	90	20
695	18 c. *Deilephila nerii*	1·40	60
696	26 c. *Bunaeopsis zaddachi*	1·75	1·00
697	35 c. *Heniocha apollonia*	2·10	2·40
694/7	*Set of* 4	5·50	3·75

137 Victoria Falls

138 Sopwith Motorcycle (1921)

(Des C. Herbert)

1986 (26 Aug). *8th Non-Aligned Summit Conference. T* **137** *and similar horiz design. Multicoloured. P* 14½ × 14 (26 c.) *or* 14½ ($1).

698	26 c. Type **137**	1·00	30
699	$1 Ruins of Great Zimbabwe (62 × 24 *mm*)	3·50	4·00

(Des G. Cameron)

1986 (8 Oct). *Centenary of Motoring. T* **138** *and similar horiz designs. Multicoloured. P* 14½.

700	10 c. Type **138**	55	10
701	12 c. Gladiator motor car (1902)	55	30
702	17 c. Douglas motorcycle (1920)	90	35
703	26 c. Ford "Model A" (1930)	1·25	70
704	35 c. Schacht motor car (1909)	1·40	1·60
705	40 c. Benz three-wheeled car (1886)	1·40	1·60
700/5	*Set of* 6	5·50	4·25

139 Growth Monitoring

140 Barred Owlet

(Des Barbara Chalk)

1987 (11 Feb). *Child Survival Campaign. T* **139** *and similar vert designs. Multicoloured. P* 14 × 14½.

706	12 c. Type **139**	90	1·00
	a. Block of 4. Nos. 706/9	3·25	
707	12 c. Breast-feeding	90	1·00
708	12 c. Oral rehydration therapy	90	1·00
709	12 c. Immunization	90	1·00
706/9	*Set of* 4	3·25	3·50

Nos. 706/9 were printed together, *se-tenant*, in blocks of four throughout the sheet.

(Des B. Finch)

1987 (15 Apr). *Owls. T* **140** *and similar vert designs. Multicoloured. P* 14½.

710	12 c. Type **140**	1·00	15
711	18 c. Pearl-spotted Owlet	1·50	70
712	26 c. White-faced Scops Owl	2·00	1·10
713	35 c. African Scops Owl	2·75	3·00
710/13	*Set of* 4	6·50	4·50

141 Brownie, Guide and Ranger saluting ("Commitment")

142 Common Grey Duiker

(Des Barbara Connelly)

1987 (24 June). *75th Anniv of Girl Guides' Association of Zimbabwe. T* **141** *and similar horiz designs. Multicoloured. P* 14½.

714	15 c. Type **141**	30	15
715	23 c. Guides preparing meal over campfire ("Adventure")	45	30
716	35 c. Guide teaching villagers to read ("Service")	55	35
717	$1 Handshake and globe ("International Friendship")	1·40	80
714/17	*Set of* 4	2·40	1·40

(Des Patricia Wilson)

1987 (7 Oct). *Duikers of Africa Survey. T* **142** *and similar horiz designs, each showing duiker and distribution map. Multicoloured. P* 14½ × 14.

718 15 c. Type **142** 30 15
719 23 c. Zebra Duiker 35 20
720 25 c. Yellow-backed Duiker 35 30
721 30 c. Blue Duiker 45 35
722 35 c. Jentink's Duiker 45 35
723 38 c. Red Duiker 55 40
718/23 .. .. *Set of* 6 2·25 1·60

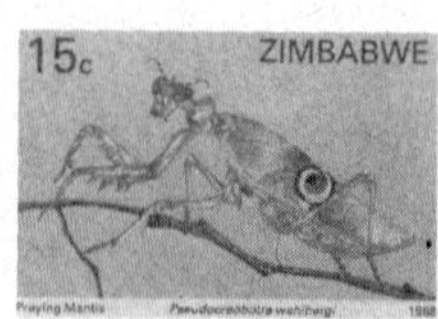

143 *Pseudocreobotra wahlberghi* (mantid)

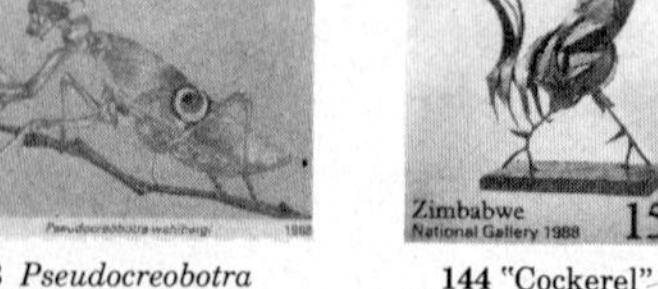

144 "Cockerel" (Arthur Azevedo)

(Des Janet Duff)

1988 (12 Jan). *Insects. T* **143** *and similar horiz designs. Multicoloured. P* 14½.

724 15 c. Type **143** 30 15
725 23 c. *Dicranorrhina derbyana* (beetle) .. 40 20
726 35 c. *Dictyophorus spumans* (grasshopper) 50 25
727 45 c. *Chalcocoris rutilus* (bug) 75 35
724/7 .. .. *Set of* 4 1·75 85

1988 (14 Apr). *30th Anniv of National Gallery of Zimbabwe. T* **144** *and similar multicoloured designs showing painting (38 c.) or sculptures (others). P* 14 × 14½ *(vert) or* 14½ × 14 *(horiz).*

728 15 c. Type **144** 15 10
729 23 c. "Man into Hippo" (Bernard Matemera) 25 20
730 30 c. "Spirit Python" (Henry Munyaradzi) .. 30 25
731 35 c. "Spirit Bird carrying People" (Thomas Mukarobgwa) *(horiz)* 30 25
732 38 c. "The Song of the Herd Boy" (George Nene) *(horiz)* 30 30
733 45 c. "War Victim" (Joseph Muzondo) *(horiz)* 35 40
728/33 .. .. *Set of* 6 1·50 1·40

145 *Aloe cameronii var. bondana*

146 White-faced Whistling Duck

(Des Nancy Abrey)

1988 (14 July). *Aloes. T* **145** *and similar vert designs. Multicoloured. P* 14½.

734 15 c. Type **145** 20 10
735 23 c. *Orbeopsis caudata* 35 20
736 25 c. *Euphorbia wildii* 35 20
737 30 c. *Euphorbia fortissima* 40 30
738 35 c. *Aloe aculeata* 40 35
739 38 c. *Huernia zebrina* 45 35
734/9 .. .. *Set of* 6 2·00 1·40

(Des B. Finch and C. Herbert)

1988 (6 Oct). *Wild Ducks and Geese of Zimbabwe. T* **146** *and similar horiz designs. Multicoloured. P* 14½ × 14.

740 15 c. Type **146** 15 10
741 23 c. African Pygmy Goose 25 20
742 30 c. Hottentot Teal 30 25
743 35 c. Comb Duck ("Knob billed Duck") .. 35 25
744 38 c. White-backed Duck 35 25
745 45 c. Maccoa Duck 45 30
740/5 .. .. *Set of* 6 1·75 1·25

147 O'Shaughnessy's Banded Gecko

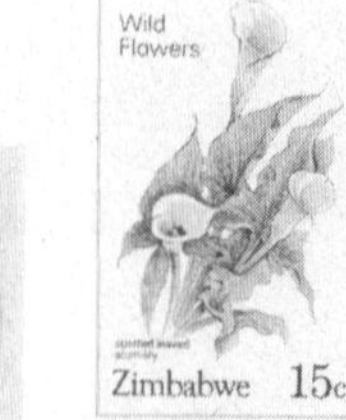

148 Spotted Leaved Arum-Lily

1989 (10 Jan). *Geckos. T* **147** *and similar horiz designs. Multicoloured. P* 14½.

746 15 c. Type **147** 20 10
747 23 c. Tiger Rock Gecko 30 20
748 35 c. Tasman's Gecko 40 30
749 45 c. Bibron's Gecko 50 35
746/9 .. .. *Set of* 4 1·25 85

1989 (12 Apr). *Wild Flowers. T* **148** *and similar vert designs. Multicoloured. P* 14½.

750 15 c. Type **148** 20 10
751 23 c. Grassland Vlei-lily 25 20
752 30 c. Manica Protea 30 30
753 35 c. Flame Lily 30 30
754 38 c. Poppy Hibiscus 40 35
755 45 c. Blue Sesbania 45 40
750/5 .. .. *Set of* 6 1·75 1·50

149 Red-breasted Bream

150 Black Rhinoceros

(Des C. Herbert)

1989 (12 July). *Fishes. T* **149** *and similar horiz designs. Multicoloured. P* 14½.

756 15 c. Type **149** 20 10
757 23 c. Chessa 30 20
758 30 c. Eastern Bottle-nose 35 30
759 35 c. Vundu 35 30
760 38 c. Largemouth Black Bass 40 35
761 45 c. Tiger Fish 50 40
756/61 .. .. *Set of* 6 1·90 1·50

1989 (10 Oct). *Endangered Species. T* **150** *and similar horiz designs. Multicoloured. P* 14½×14.

762 15 c. Type **150** 30 10
763 23 c. Cheetah 40 30
764 30 c. Wild Dog 50 50
765 35 c. Pangolin 50 50
766 38 c. Brown Hyena 55 60
767 45 c. Roan Antelope 70 85
762/7 .. .. *Set of* 6 2·75 2·50

151 Tiger Fish

152 Headrest

153 Bicycles

(Des Janet Duff (1 to 9 c.), Rose Rigden (15 to 30 c.), Nancy Abrey (33 c. to $2))

1990 (2 Jan). *Multicoloured.*

(a) Horiz designs as T **151** *showing wildlife. P* 14

768 1 c. Type **151** 10 10
769 2 c. Helmet Guineafowl 10 10
770 3 c. Scrub Hare 10 10
771 4 c. Temminck's Ground Pangolin 10 10
772 5 c. Greater Kudu 10 10
773 9 c. Black Rhinoceros 10 10

(b) Horiz designs as T **152** *showing cultural artifacts. P* 14½×14

774 15 c. Type **152** 10 10
775 20 c. Hand axe and adze 10 10
776 23 c. Gourd and water pot 10 10
777 25 c. Snuff container 10 10
778 26 c. Winnowing tray and basket 10 10
779 30 c. Grinding stone 10 10

(c) Horiz designs as T **153** *showing transport. P* 14½

780 33 c. Type **153** 10 10
781 35 c. Buses 10 10
782 38 c. Passenger train 10 15
783 45 c. Mail motorcycle and trailer 10 15
784 $1 Air Zimbabwe Boeing airliner 25 30
785 $2 Lorry 50 55
768/85 .. .. *Set of* 18 1·60 1·75

154 Pres. Mugabe and Joshua Nkomo at Signing of Unity Accord, 1987

155 Runhare House, 1986

(Adapted Nancy Abrey)

1990 (17 Apr). *10th Anniv of Independence. T* **154** *and similar horiz designs. Multicoloured. P* 14½×14.

786 15 c. Type **154** 15 10
787 23 c. Conference Centre, Harare 20 15
788 30 c. Children in class 25 20
789 35 c. Intelsat aerial, Mazowe Earth Satellite Station 30 30
790 38 c. National Sports Stadium 30 40
791 45 c. Maize field 50 55
786/91 .. .. *Set of* 6 1·50 1·50

1990 (11 July). *Centenary of the City of Harare. T* **155** *and similar horiz designs. Multicoloured. P* 14½.

792 15 c. Type **155** 15 10
793 23 c. Market Hall, 1894 .. .. .. 20 20
794 30 c. Charter House, 1959 .. .. .. 25 25
795 35 c. Supreme Court, 1927 .. .. .. 30 30
796 38 c. Standard Chartered Bank, 1911 .. 30 30
797 45 c. The Town House, 1933 .. .. 45 50
792/7 .. .. *Set of* 6 1·50 1·50

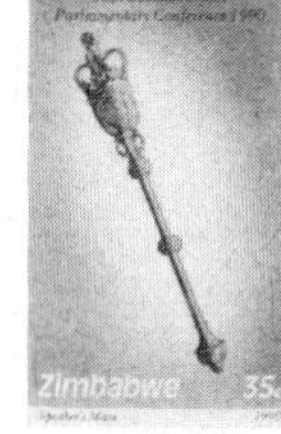

156 Speaker's Mace

157 Small-spotted Genet

1990 (17 Sept). *36th Commonwealth Parliamentary Conference, Harare. T* **156** *and similar vert design. Multicoloured. P* 14½.

798 35 c. Type **156** 30 25
799 $1 Speaker's chair 70 75

(Des Barbara Chalk)

1991 (15 Jan). *Small Mammals. T* **157** *and similar horiz designs. Multicoloured. P* 14½×14.

800 15 c. Type **157** 20 10
801 23 c. Red Squirrel 20 15
802 35 c. Night-ape 35 35
803 45 c. Bat-eared Fox 45 50
800/3 .. .. *Set of* 4 1·10 1·00

158 Hosho (rattles)

159 Snot-apple

(Des R. Pletts)

1991 (16 Apr). *Traditional Musical Instruments. T* **158** *and similar vert designs. Multicoloured. P* 14½.

804 15 c. Type **158** 15 10
805 23 c. Mbira (thumb piano) 15 10
806 30 c. Ngororombe (pan pipes) 15 10
807 35 c. Chipendani (mouth bow) 20 20
808 38 c. Marimba (xylophone) 20 20
809 45 c. Ngoma (drum) 20 20
804/9 .. .. *Set of* 6 95 75

(Des Barbara Chalk)

1991 (17 July). *Wild Fruits. T* **159** *and similar vert designs. Multicoloured. P* 14×14½.

810 20 c. Type **159** 15 10
811 39 c. Marula 15 15
812 51 c. Mobola Plum 20 20
813 60 c. Water Berry 20 25
814 65 c. Northern Dwaba Berry 20 25
815 77 c. Mahobohobo 30 35
810/15 .. .. *Set of* 6 1·10 1·10

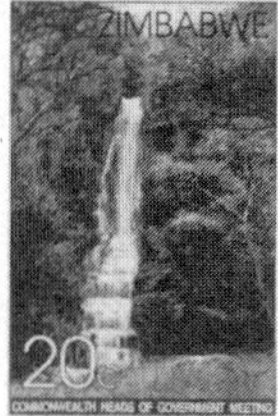

160 Bridal Veil Falls

161 Lion

(Des R. Jeffrey)

1991 (16 Oct). *Commonwealth Heads of Government Meeting, Harare. T* **160** *and similar vert designs. Multicoloured. P* 14½.

16	20 c. Type **160**	15	10
17	39 c. Meeting logo	15	10
18	51 c. Chinhoyi Caves	20	20
19	60 c. Kariba Dam	25	25
20	65 c. Victoria Falls	25	25
21	77 c. Balancing rocks	30	30
16/21	*Set of* 6	1·10	1·10

(Des R. Pletts)

1992 (8 Jan). *Wildlife Conservation. Big Cats. T* **161** *and similar horiz designs. Multicoloured. P* 14½×14.

22	20 c. Type **161**	10	10
23	39 c. Leopard	15	15
24	60 c. Cheetah	25	25
25	77 c. Serval	25	25
22/5	*Set of* 4	65	65

POSTAGE DUE STAMPS

SOUTHERN

RHODESIA

(D 1)

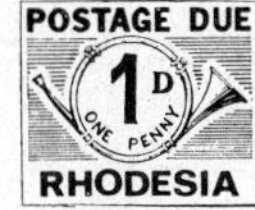

D 2

1951 (1 Oct). *Postage Due stamps of Great Britain optd with Type* D 1.

D1	D 1	½d. emerald (No. D27)	3·25	9·00
D2		1d. violet-blue (No. D36)	1·75	65
D3		2d. agate (No. D29)	4·00	1·75
D4		3d. violet (No. D30)	2·75	1·25
D5		4d. blue (No. D38)	1·50	2·25
D6		4d. dull grey-green (No. D31)	£130	£250
D7		1s. deep blue (No. D33)	3·00	1·75
D1/5, 7		*Set of* 6	14·50	15·00

(Typo Printing and Stationery Dept, Salisbury)

1965 (17 June). *Roul* 9.

D 8	D 2	1d. orange-red (*roul* 5)	70	9·50
		a. Roul 9	1·25	4·00
D 9		2d. deep blue	50	8·00
D10		4d. green	60	8·00
D11		6d. plum	60	6·00
D8a/11		*Set of* 4	2·25	23·00

The 2d. has a stop below the "D".

D 3 Zimbabwe Bird (soapstone sculpture)

D 4 Zimbabwe Bird (soapstone sculpture)

(Litho Mardon Printers, Salisbury)

1966 (15 Dec). *P* 14½.

D12	D 3	1d. red	1·25	2·50
D13		2d. bluish violet	1·50	2·75
D14		4d. pale green	1·75	4·50
D15		6d. reddish violet	1·75	2·75
D16		1s. red-brown	2·00	3·00
D17		2s. black	3·00	6·50
D12/17		*Set of* 6	10·00	20·00

1970 (17 Feb)–**73.** *Decimal Currency. As Type* D 3, *but larger* (26 × 22½ *mm*). *P* 14½.

D18	D 3	1 c. bright green	1·00	1·40
D19		2 c. ultramarine	1·00	80
D20		5 c. bright reddish violet	2·50	2·00
D21		6 c. pale lemon (7.5.73)	3·75	2·75
D22		10 c. cerise	2·50	3·50
D18/22		*Set of* 5	9·75	9·50

1980. *P* 14½.

D23	D 4	1 c. bright green	30	80
D24		2 c. ultramarine	40	90
D25		5 c. bright reddish violet	50	90
		a. Imperf (pair)	85·00	
D26		6 c. pale lemon	70	1·60
D27		10 c. cerise	90	2·00
D23/7		*Set of* 5	2·50	5·75

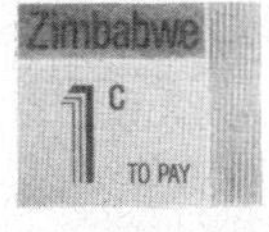

D 5

(D 6)

1985 (21 Aug). *P* 14½.

D28	D 5	1 c. yellow-orange	10	10
D29		2 c. magenta	10	10
D30		6 c. blue-green	10	10
D31		10 c. orange-brown	10	10
D32		13 c. new blue	10	10
D28/32		*Set of* 5	25	30

1990 (2 Jan). *No.* D27 *surch with Type* D **6**.

D33	D 4	25 c. on 10 c. cerise	6·00	6·00

No. D33 is reported to have been issued to the main post offices at Bulawayo, Gweru, Harare and Mutare.

Zululand
see South Africa

Note. The first Supplement recording new stamps not in this Catalogue appeared in the September 1992 number of *Gibbons Stamp Monthly*.

Set Prices for British Commonwealth Omnibus Issues

The composition of these sets is in accordance with the tables on the following pages. Only such items considered basic stamps are included; varieties such as shades, perforation changes and watermark changes are excluded. Great Britain issues which come on both ordinary paper and on paper with phosphor bands are however covered.

Stamps issued in connection with any of the events by countries which are no longer in the British Commonwealth and which are not listed in the Part 1 Catalogue are omitted.

		Price Un	Used
1935. Silver Jubilee.	*Complete set of* 250 *stamps*	£750	£850

The concept initiated by the 1935 Silver Jubilee omnibus issue has provided a pattern for a series of Royal commemoratives over the past 50 years which have introduced countless collectors to the hobby.

The Crown Colony Windsor Castle design by Harold Fleury is, surely, one of the most impressive produced in the 20th-century and its reproduction in the recess process by three of the leading stamp-printing firms of the era has provided a subject for philatelic research which has yet to be exhausted.

Each of the three, Bradbury, Wilkinson & Co. and Waterlow and Sons, who both produced fifteen issues, together with De La Rue & Co. who printed fourteen, used a series of vignette (centre) plates coupled with individual frame plates for each value. All were taken from dies made by Waterlow. Several worthwhile varieties exist on the frame plates, but most interest has been concentrated on the centre plates, each of which was used to print a considerable number of different stamps.

Sheets printed by Bradbury, Wilkinson were without printed plate numbers, but research has now identified eleven centre plates which were probably used in permanent pairings. A twelfth plate awaits confirmation. Stamps from some of these centre plates have revealed a number of prominent plate flaws, the most famous of which, the extra flagstaff, has been eagerly sought by collectors for many years.

Extra flagstaff (Plate "1" R.9/1)

Short extra flagstaff (Plate "2" R.2/1)

Lightning conductor (Plate "3" R.2/5)

Flagstaff on right-hand turret (Plate "5" R.7/1)

Double flagstaff (Plate "6" R.5/2)

De La Rue sheets were initially printed with plate numbers, but in many instances these were subsequently trimmed off. Surviving examples do, however, enable a positive identification of six centre plates, 2A, 2B, (2A), (2B), 4 and 4/ to be made. The evidence of sheet markings and plate flaws clearly demonstrates that there were two different pairs of plates numbered 2A 2B. The second pair is designated (2A) (2B) by specialist collectors to avoid further confusion. The number of major plate flaws is not so great as on the Bradbury, Wilkinson sheets, but four examples are included in the catalogue.

Diagonal line by turret (Plate 2A R. 10/2)

Dot to left of chapel (Plate 2B R.8/3)

Dot by flagstaff (Plate 4 R.8/4)

Dash by turret (Plate 4/ R.3/6)

Much less is known concerning the Waterlow centre plate system as the sheets did not show plate numbers. Ten individual plates have, so far, been identified and it is believed that these were used in pairs. The two versions of the kite and log flaw from plate "2" show that this plate exists in two states.

Kite and vertical log (Plate "2A" R.10/6)

Kite and horizontal log (Plate "2B" R.10/6)

1937. Coronation.	*Complete set of* 202 *stamps*	£100	70·00

1945–46. Victory.	*Complete set of* 164 *stamps*	30·00	26·00

1948–49. Royal Silver Wedding.	*Complete set of* 138 *stamps*	£1400	£1300

1949. U.P.U. 75th Anniversary	*Complete set of* 310 *stamps*	£275	£22

1951. B.W.I. University College	*Complete set of* 28 *stamps*	6·50	4·2

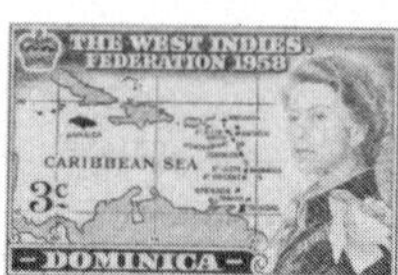

1953. Coronation.	*Complete set of* 106 *stamps*	90·00	60·0

1953–54. Royal Visit.	*Complete set of* 13 *stamps*	2·50	2·40

1958. Caribbean Federation.	*Complete set of* 30 *stamps*	10·00	7·00

1963. Freedom from Hunger.	*Complete set of* 77 *stamps*	£150	75·00

1963. Red Cross Centenary.	*Complete set of* 108 *stamps and* 2 *miniature sheets*	£200	£150

1964. Shakespeare. 400th Birth Anniversary.
Complete set of 25 stamps 21·00 19·00

1965. I.T.U. Centenary.
Complete set of 112 *stamps and* 1 *miniature sheet* £140 75·00

1965. I.C.Y.
Complete set of 107 *stamps and* 2 *miniature sheets* £110 55·00

1965–67. Churchill. *Complete set of* 182 *stamps* £200 90·00

1966. Royal Visit to the Caribbean.
Complete set of 34 *stamps* 26·00 11·00

1966. World Cup Football Championship.
Complete set of 68 *stamps and* 1 *miniature sheet* 80·00 55·00

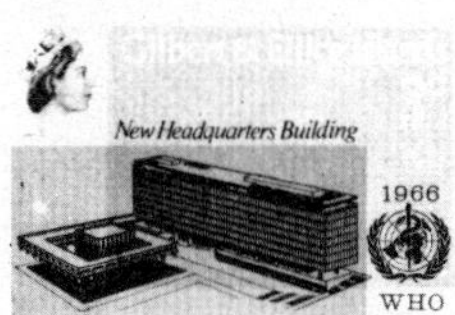

1966. W.H.O. New Headquarters.
Complete set of 58 *stamps and* 1 *miniature sheet* 70·00 40·00

1966–67. U.N.E.S.C.O. 20th Anniversary.
Complete set of 110 *stamps and* 1 *miniature sheet* £120 75·00

1972. Royal Silver Wedding.
Complete set of 78 *stamps* 35·00 27·00

1973. Royal Wedding.
Complete set of 72 *stamps and* 6 *miniature sheets* 35·00 20·00

1977. Silver Jubilee. *Set of* 220 *basic stamps* £100 80·00
Set of 24 *miniature sheets* 45·00 55·00

1977. Royal Visit. *Set of* 46 *basic stamps* 13·00 10·00
Set of 8 *miniature sheets* 11·00 15·00

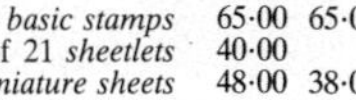

1978. Coronation. 25th Anniversary.
Set of 195 *basic stamps* 65·00 65·00
Set of 21 *sheetlets* 40·00
Set of 27 *miniature sheets* 48·00 38·00

1980. Queen Mother's Birthday.
Set of 41 *stamps* 30·00 25·00
Set of 12 *miniature sheets* 27·00 27·00

1981. Royal Wedding. *Set of* 244 *basic stamps* £130 £120
Set of 35 *miniature sheets* 70·00 65·00

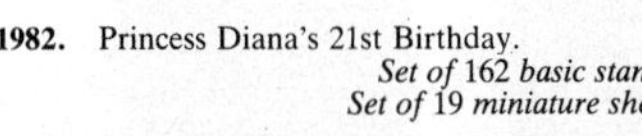

1982. Princess Diana's 21st Birthday.
Set of 162 *basic stamps* 90·00 90·00
Set of 19 *miniature sheets* 45·00 48·00

1982. Birth of Prince William.

Set of 124 basic stamps	£120	95·00
Set of 22 miniature sheets	70·00	65·00

The Life and Times of
Her Majesty Queen Elizabeth The Queen Mother

(*Illustration reduced*)

1985. Life and Times of Queen Elizabeth the Queen Mother.

Set of 226 stamps	£120	£130
Set of 47 miniature sheets	£100	£110

1986. 60th Birthday of Queen Elizabeth II.

Set of 233 stamps	£150	£110
Set of 28 miniature sheets	90·00	£100

1986. Royal Wedding.

Set of 142 stamps	£100	£110
Set of 24 miniature sheets	75·00	85·00

1987. Royal Ruby Wedding.

Set of 117 stamps	90·00	95·00
Set of 14 miniature sheets	35·00	40·00

1990. 90th Birthday of Queen Elizabeth the Queen Mother.

Set of 119 stamps	£100	£100
Set of 19 miniature sheets	65·00	70·00

1991. 65th Birthday of Queen Elizabeth II and 70th Birthday of Prince Philip.

Set of 69 stamps	65·00	70·00
Set of 7 miniature sheets	15·50	15·00

1992. 40th Anniversary of Queen Elizabeth II's Accession.

Set of 127 stamps	65·00	65·00
Set of 2 miniature sheets	4·25	5·00

1935 SILVER JUBILEE TO 1973 ROYAL WEDDING

Issuing Countries	1935 *Silver Jubilee*	1937 *Coronation*	1945–46 *Victory*	1948 *Silver Wedding*	1949 *U.P.U.*	1951 *B.W.I. Univ*	1953 *Coronation*	1953–54 *Royal Visit*	1958 *Caribbean Fed.*	1963 *F.F.H.*	1963 *Red Cross*	1964 *Shakespeare*	1965 *I.T.U.*	1965 *I.C.Y.*	1965–66 *Churchill*	1966 *Royal Visit*	1966 *Football Cup*	1966 *W.H.O.*	1966–67 *UNESCO*	1972 *Silver Wedding*	1973 *Royal Wedding*
Great Britain	4	1	2	2	4	—	4	—	—	2+2	3+3	5+4	2+2	2+2	2+2	—	3+3	—	—	2	2
Guernsey	—	—	—	—	—	—	—	—	—	—	—	—	—	—	—	—	—	—	—	4	1
Isle of Man	—	—	—	—	—	—	—	—	—	—	—	—	—	—	—	—	—	—	—	—	1
Jersey	—	—	—	—	—	—	—	—	—	—	—	—	—	—	—	—	—	—	—	4	2
Anguilla	—	—	—	—	—	—	—	—	—	—	—	—	—	—	—	—	—	—	—	2	2
Antigua	4	3	2	2	4	2	1	—	3	1	2	1	2	2	4	2	2	2	3	2	2+MS
Barbuda	—	—	—	—	—	—	—	—	—	—	—	—	—	—	—	—	—	—	—	—	2
Ascension	4	3	2	2	4	—	1	—	—	1	2	—	2	2	4	—	2	2	3	2	2
Australia	3	—	3	—	1	—	3	3	—	—	1	—	1	1	1	—	—	—	—	—	—
Bahamas	4	3	2	2	4	—	1	—	—	1	2	1	2	2	4	2	2	2	3	2	—
Bahrain	—	—	—	2	4	—	4	—	—	—	—	—	—	—	—	—	—	—	—	—	—
Barbados	4	3	2	2	4	2	1	—	3	—	—	—	2	—	4	2	—	—	3	—	—
Belize/British Honduras ..	4	3	2	2	4	2	1	—	—	1	2	—	2	2	4	—	—	—	—	2	2
Bermuda	4	3	2	2	4	—	1	1	—	1	2	—	2	2	4	—	2	—	3	2	2
Botswana/Bechuanaland ..	4	3	3×2	2	4	—	1	—	—	1	2	1	2	2	4	—	—	—	—	—	—
British Antarctic Territory ..	—	—	—	—	—	—	—	—	—	—	—	—	—	—	4	—	—	—	—	2	2
British Indian Ocean Terr. ..	—	—	—	—	—	—	—	—	—	—	—	—	—	—	—	—	—	—	—	2	—
British P.A's in Eastern Arabia	—	—	—	2	4	—	4	—	—	—	—	—	—	—	—	—	—	—	—	—	—
British Virgin Islands	4	3	2	2	4	2	1	—	—	1	2	1	2	2	4	2	—	—	3	2	2
Brunei	—	—	—	—	4	—	—	—	—	1	—	—	2	2	4	—	2	2	3	2	2
Burma	—	—	4	—	—	—	—	—	—	—	—	—	—	—	—	—	—	—	—	—	—
Canada	6	1	—	—	—	—	1	—	—	—	—	—	—	1	1	—	—	—	—	—	—
Newfoundland	4	14	—	—	—	—	—	—	—	—	—	—	—	—	—	—	—	—	—	—	—
Cayman Islands	4	3	2	2	4	—	1	—	—	1	2	1	2	2	4	2	2	2	3	2	2
Cook Islands	3	3	4	—	—	—	2	—	—	—	—	—	—	—	6	—	—	—	—	4	3+MS
Aitutaki	—	—	—	—	—	—	—	—	—	—	—	—	—	—	—	—	—	—	—	2	2+MS
Penrhyn	—	—	—	—	—	—	—	—	—	—	—	—	—	—	—	—	—	—	—	—	3
Cyprus	4	3	2	2	4	—	1	—	—	2	2	4	3	2	—	—	—	—	1	—	—
Dominica	4	3	2	2	4	2	1	—	3	1	2	1	2	2	4	2	2	2	3	2	2+MS
Egypt/British Forces in Egypt ..	1	—	—	—	—	—	—	—	—	—	—	—	—	—	—	—	—	—	—	—	—
Falkland Islands	4	3	2	2	4	—	1	—	—	1	2	1	2	2	4	—	—	—	—	2	2
Falkland Islands Dependencies	—	—	2	2	4	—	1	—	—	—	—	—	—	—	—	—	—	—	—	—	—
South Georgia	—	—	—	—	—	—	—	—	—	—	—	—	—	—	—	—	—	—	—	2	2
Fiji	4	3	2	2	4	—	1	1	—	1	2	—	2	2	4	—	2	2	—	2	—
Gambia	4	3	2	2	4	—	1	—	—	1	2	1	2	—	3	—	—	—	—	—	—
Ghana/Gold Coast	4	3	2	2	4	—	1	—	—	3	4+MS	—	4+MS	4+MS	—	—	5+MS	4+MS	5+MS	—	—
Gibraltar	4	3	2	2	4	—	1	1	—	1	2	1	2	2	4	—	2	2	3	2	2
Gilbert and Ellice Islands ..	4	3	2	2	4	—	1	—	—	1	2	—	2	2	4	—	2	2	3	2	2
Grenada	4	3	2	2	4	2	1	—	3	1	2	—	2	2	4	2	2	2	3	2	2+MS
Grenadines	—	—	—	—	—	—	—	—	—	—	—	—	—	—	—	—	—	—	—	—	2+MS
Guyana/British Guiana ..	4	3	2	2	4	2	1	—	—	1	2	—	2	2	2	2	—	—	—	—	—
Hong Kong	4	3	2	2	4	—	1	—	—	1	2	—	2	2	4	—	—	2	3	2	2
India	7	—	4	—	4	—	—	—	—	1	1	—	1	1	—	—	—	—	—	—	—
Hyderabad	—	—	1	—	—	—	—	—	—	—	—	—	—	—	—	—	—	—	—	—	—
Ireland	—	—	—	—	—	—	—	—	—	2	2	—	2	2	—	—	—	—	—	—	—
Jamaica	4	3	2	2	4	2	1	1	3	2	2	—	1	—	2	4	—	—	—	—	—
K.U.T./East Africa	4	3	2	2	4	—	1	1	—	4	2	—	4	4	—	—	—	—	4	—	—
Kuwait	—	—	—	2	4	—	4	—	—	—	—	—	—	—	—	—	—	—	—	—	—
Leeward Islands	4	3	2	2	4	2	1	—	—	—	—	—	—	—	—	—	—	—	—	—	—
Lesotho/Basutoland	4	3	3×2	2	4	—	1	—	—	1	2	—	2	2	4	—	—	—	4	—	—
Malawi/Nyasaland	4	3	2	2	4	—	1	—	—	—	—	—	—	—	—	—	—	—	—	—	—
Malayan States, etc.	4	3	—	22	44	—	11	—	—	3	—	—	3	—	—	—	—	—	—	—	—
North Borneo	—	—	—	2	4	—	1	—	—	1	—	—	—	—	—	—	—	—	—	—	—
Sarawak	—	—	—	2	4	—	1	—	—	1	—	—	—	—	—	—	—	—	—	—	—
Maldive Islands	—	—	—	—	—	—	—	—	—	7	5	—	—	5+MS	6	—	—	—	6	—	—
Malta	4	3	2	2	4	—	1	1	—	1	2	—	—	—	4	—	—	—	—	—	—
Mauritius	4	3	2	2	4	—	1	—	—	1	2	—	2	2	4	—	—	—	3	—	—
Montserrat	4	3	2	2	4	2	1	—	3	1	2	1	2	2	4	2	—	2	3	2	2
Morocco Agencies/Tangier ..	15	3	2	4	4	—	4	—	—	—	—	—	—	—	—	—	—	—	—	—	—
Namibia/South West Africa ..	4	8×2	3×2	1×2	3×2	—	5	—	—	—	2	—	—	—	—	—	—	—	—	—	—
Nauru	4	4	—	—	—	—	—	—	—	—	—	—	—	—	—	—	—	—	—	—	—
New Zealand	3	3	11	—	—	—	5	2	—	—	—	—	1	1	1	—	—	—	—	—	—
Tokelau Islands	—	—	—	—	—	—	1	—	—	—	—	—	—	—	—	—	—	—	—	—	—
Nigeria	4	3	2	2	4	—	1	—	—	2	3+MS	—	3	3	—	—	—	—	3	—	—
Niue	3	3	4	—	—	—	2	—	—	—	—	—	—	—	—	—	—	—	—	—	—
Pakistan	—	—	—	—	—	—	—	—	—	2	1	—	1	2	—	—	—	—	1	—	—
Bahawalpur Postage and Officials	—	—	1	—	4+4	—	—	—	—	—	—	—	—	—	—	—	—	—	—	—	—
P.N.G./Papua	4	4	—	—	—	—	—	—	—	—	1	—	—	—	—	—	—	—	—	—	—
New Guinea	2	4	—	—	—	—	—	—	—	—	—	—	—	—	—	—	—	—	—	—	—
Pitcairn Islands	—	—	2	2	4	—	1	—	—	1	2	—	2	2	4	—	2	2	3	2	2
Rhodesia and Nyasaland ..	—	—	—	—	—	—	—	—	—	—	1	—	—	—	—	—	—	—	—	—	—
St. Helena	4	3	2	2	4	—	1	—	—	1	2	—	2	2	4	—	2	2	3	2	2
St. Kitts-Nevis	4	3	2	2	4	2	1	—	3	—	2	—	2	2	4	2	2	2	3	2	2
St. Lucia	4	3	2	2	4	2	1	—	3	1	2	1	2	2	4	2	2	2	3	2	2
St. Vincent	4	3	2	2	4	2	1	—	3	1	2	—	2	—	4	2	—	2	3	2	2
Grenadines	—	—	—	—	—	—	—	—	—	—	—	—	—	—	—	—	—	—	—	—	2
Samoa	3	—	4	—	—	—	2	—	—	—	—	—	—	—	—	—	—	4	—	—	—
Seychelles	4	3	2	2	4	—	1	—	—	1	2	—	2	2	4	—	2	2	3	2	2
Sierra Leone	4	3	2	2	4	—	1	—	—	2	3	—	—	—	11	—	—	—	—	—	—
Singapore	—	—	—	2	4	—	1	—	—	—	—	—	—	—	—	—	—	—	—	—	—
Solomon Islands	4	3	2	2	4	—	1	—	—	1	2	—	2	2	4	—	2	2	3	2	2
Somaliland Protectorate ..	4	3	2	2	4	—	1	—	—	—	—	—	—	—	—	—	—	—	—	—	—
South Africa	4×2	5×2	3×2	1×2	3×2	—	1	—	—	—	2	—	2	—	—	—	—	—	—	—	—
South Arabian Fed./Aden ..	—	3	2	2	4	—	1	1	—	1	2	—	—	2	4	—	2	2	3	—	—
Seiyun	—	—	2	2	4	—	1	—	—	—	—	—	7	—	1	—	7	—	—	—	—
Shihr and Mukalla ..	—	—	2	2	4	—	1	—	—	—	—	—	—	8	3	—	8	—	—	—	—
Sri Lanka/Ceylon	4	3	2	—	3	—	1	1	—	2	—	—	2	2	—	—	—	2	2	—	—
Swaziland	4	3	3×2	2	4	—	1	—	—	1	2	—	2	2	4	—	—	—	3	—	—
Tanzania/Zanzibar	—	—	2	2	4	—	—	—	—	1	—	—	—	—	—	—	—	—	—	—	—
Tonga	—	—	—	—	4	—	—	—	—	1	2	—	—	—	—	—	—	—	—	—	—
Trinidad and Tobago	4	3	2	2	4	2	1	—	3	3	—	—	—	1	—	4	—	—	—	—	—
Tristan da Cunha	—	—	—	—	—	—	1	—	—	1	2	—	2	2	4	—	2	2	3	2	2
Turks and Caicos Islands ..	4	3	2	2	4	—	1	—	—	1	2	1	2	2	4	2	—	—	3	2	2
Vanuatu/New Hebrides (English & French inscr)	—	—	—	—	4+4	—	1	—	—	1+1	2+2	—	2+2	2+2	4+4	—	2+2	2+2	3+3	2+2	—
Zambia/Northern Rhodesia ..	4	3	2	2	4	—	1	—	—	—	—	—	2	2	—	—	—	2	—	—	—
Zimbabwe/Southern Rhodesia ..	4	4	4	—	2	—	1	—	—	—	—	—	3	—	1	—	—	—	—	—	—
Total number of stamps ..	250	202	164	138	310	28	106	13	30	77	108 +2 MS	25	112 +MS	107 +2 MS	182	34	68 + MS	58 + MS	110 + MS	78	72 +6 MS

BRITISH COMMONWEALTH OMNIBUS ISSUES

NOTE Countries marked with an asterisk are those which comprise the Crown Agents Omnibus issue.

1977 SILVER JUBILEE

Country	*Catalogue Nos.*	*Stamps*	*MS*
Great Britain	1033/7	5	—
Guernsey	149/50	2	—
Isle of Man	94/6	3	—
Jersey	168/70	3	—
Anguilla	269/73	4	1
Antigua	526/31	5	1
Barbuda	298/304, 323/28	11	2
Ascension*	222/4	3	—
Australia	645/6	2	—
Bahamas	488/92	4	1
Bangladesh	93/6	3	1
Barbados*	574/6	3	—
Belize*	449/51	3	—
Bermuda*	371/3	3	—
Botswana*	391/3	3	—
British Antarctic Territory*	83/5	3	—
British Virgin Islands*	364/6	3	—
Brunei	264/6	3	—
Canada	855	1	—
Cayman Islands*	427/9	3	—
Christmas Island	83	1	—
Cook Islands	564/70	6	1
Aitutaki	225/9	4	1
Penrhyn	100/3	3	1
Cyprus	485	1	—
Dominica	562/7	5	1
Falkland Islands*	325/7	3	—
South Georgia*	50/2	3	—
Fiji*	536/8	3	—
Gambia*	365/7	3	—
Gibraltar	371/3	2	1
Grenada	857/62	5	1
Grenadines of Grenada	215/18	3	1
Hong Kong*	361/3	3	—
Kenya	91/5	4	2
Kiribati / Gilbert Islands*	48/50	3	—
Maldive Islands	673/9	6	1
Mauritius*	516/18	3	—
Montserrat	396/8	3	—
New Zealand	**MS**1137	—	1
Niue	213/15	2	1
Norfolk Island	196	1	—
Papua New Guinea	330/2	3	—
Pitcairn Islands*	171/3	3	—
St. Helena*	332/4	3	—
St. Kitts-Nevis*	367/9	3	—
St. Lucia	443/7	4	1
St. Vincent	502/14	12	1
Grenadines of St. Vincent	93/5	3	—
Samoa	479/82	4	—
Seychelles	393/401	8	1
Sierra Leone	597/8	2	—
Solomon Islands*	334/6	3	—
Swaziland*	268/70	3	—
Tanzania	218/22	4	1
Tonga	598/607, O151/3	13	—
Tristan da Cunha*	212/14	3	—
Turks and Caicos Islands*	472/5	3	1
Tuvalu	50/3	3	1
Vanuatu/New Hebrides* (English & French inscr)	217/19 F231/3	3+3	—
Total number of items		220	24

The Turks and Caicos Islands miniature sheet, **MS**475, did not form part of the Crown Agents Omnibus issue.

1977 ROYAL VISIT

Country	*Catalogue Nos.*	*Stamps*	*MS*
Anguilla	298/302	4	1
Antigua	548/53	5	1
Barbuda	345/54	8	2
Bahamas	500/4	4	1
Barbados	590/2	3	—
British Virgin Islands	371/3	3	—
Dominica	591/6	5	1
Grenada	894/9	5	1
Grenadines of Grenada	239/42	3	1
Montserrat	409/11	3	—
St. Vincent	540	1	—
Grenadines of St. Vincent	104/5	2	—
Total number of items		46	8

1978 CORONATION ANNIVERSARY

Country	*Catalogue Nos.*	*Stamps*	*Sheetlets*	*MS*
Great Britain	1059/62	4	—	—
Guernsey	167	1	—	—
Isle of Man	132	1	—	—
Jersey	195/6	2	—	—
Anguilla	320/4	4	—	1
Antigua	581/6	5	—	1
Barbuda	408/20, 445/6	12	—	3
Ascension*	233/5	3	1	—
Bahamas	515/17	2	—	1
Bangladesh	116/20	4	—	1
Barbados*	597/9	3	1	—
Belize*	464/6, 495/503	11	1	2
Bermuda	384/6	3	—	—
British Antarctic Territory*	86/8	3	1	—
British Virgin Islands*	384/6	3	1	—
Brunei	267/9	3	—	—
Cayman Islands*	468/70	3	1	—
Christmas Island*	96/8	3	1	—
Cook Islands	593/601	8	—	1
Aitutaki	257/60	3	—	1
Penrhyn	121/4	3	—	1
Dominica	612/15	3	—	1
Falkland Islands*	348/50	3	1	—
South Georgia*	67/9	3	1	—
Fiji*	549/51	3	1	—
Gambia*	397/9	3	1	—
Gibraltar	400/3	4	—	—
Grenada	946/9	3	—	1
Grenadines of Grenada	272/5	3	—	1
Hong Kong	373/4	2	—	—
Kiribati/Gilbert Islands*	68/70	3	1	—
Maldive Islands	755/61	6	—	1
Mauritius*	549/51	3	1	—
Montserrat	422/6	4	—	1
New Zealand Dependency of Tokelau	61/4	4	—	—
Niue	245/8	3	—	1
Norfolk Island	207/8	2	—	—
Pitcairn Islands	**MS**189	—	—	1
St. Helena*	338/40	3	1	—
St. Kitts-Nevis*	389/91	3	1	—
St. Lucia	468/72	4	—	1
St. Vincent	556/60	4	—	1
Grenadines of St. Vincent	130/4	4	—	1
Samoa*	508/10	3	1	—
Seychelles	428/32	4	—	1
Sierra Leone	601/3	3	—	—
Solomon Islands*	357/9	3	1	—
Swaziland	293/5	3	1	—
Tanzania	233/7	4	—	1
Tristan da Cunha*	239/41	3	1	—
Turks and Caicos Islands	494/8	4	—	1
Tuvalu	89/93	4	—	1
Uganda	234/8	4	—	1
Vanuatu/New Hebrides* (English & French inscr)	262/4, F276/8	3+3	1+1	—
Total number of items		195	21	27

The Crown Agents Omnibus issue was printed in matching sheetlets, each containing two *se-tenant* strips of the three designs.
Barbuda Nos. 445/6 form part of a general anniversaries issue.
Belize Nos. 495/503 were not part of the Crown Agents Omnibus issue.

1980 QUEEN MOTHER's 80th BIRTHDAY

Country	*Catalogue Nos.*	*Stamps*	*MS*
Great Britain	1129	1	—
Anguilla	411/15	4	1
Antigua	663/5	2	1
Barbuda	533/5	2	1
Ascension*	269	1	—
Bangladesh	172/4	2	1
Belize	592/3	1	1
Bermuda*	425	1	—
Cayman Islands*	506	1	—
Cook Islands	701/2	1	1
Penrhyn	150/1	1	1
Dominica	732/4	2	1
Falkland Islands*	383	1	—
Gambia*	440	1	—
Gibraltar*	436	1	—
Hong Kong*	390	1	—
Lesotho	423/5	3	—
Maldive Islands	886/7	1	1
Niue	364/5	1	1
Norfolk Island	252/3	2	—
Pitcairn Islands*	206	1	—
St. Helena*	366	1	—
St. Kitts-Nevis			
St. Kitts	48	1	—
Nevis	50	1	—
St. Lucia	534/6	2	1
Samoa*	572	1	—
Solomon Islands*	421	1	—
Tristan da Cunha*	282	1	—
Turks and Caicos Islands	607/8	1	1
Tuvalu	148	1	—
Total number of items		41	12

1981 ROYAL WEDDING

Country	*Catalogue Nos.*	*Stamps*	*MS*
Great Britain	1160/1	2	—
Guernsey	232/9	7	1
Isle of Man	202/4	2	1
Jersey	284/5	2	—
Anguilla	464/7	3	1
Antigua	702/5	3	1
Barbuda	565/75	9	2
Ascension*	302/4	3	—
Australia	821/2	2	—
Bahamas	586/8	2	1
Barbados*	674/6	3	—
Belize	614/20	6	1
Bermuda*	436/8	3	—
British Virgin Islands*	463/5	3	—
Brunei*	304/6	3	—
Cayman Islands*	534/6	3	—
Cocos (Keeling) Islands	70/1	2	—
Cook Islands	812/14	2	1
Aitutaki	391/3	3	—
Penrhyn	223/8	5	1
Cyprus	580	1	—
Turkish Cypriot Posts	121	1	—
Dominica	747/50	3	1
Falkland Islands*	402/4	3	—
Dependencies*	95/7	3	—
Fiji*	612/14	3	—
Gambia*	454/6	3	—
Ghana	948/54	6	1
Gibraltar	450	1	—
Grenada	1130/5	5	1
Grenadines of Grenada	444/9	5	1
Guyana	769/70, 841/3, 930/6	12	—
Hong Kong*	399/401	3	—
Jamaica	516/20	4	
Kenya	207/11	4	
Kiribati	149/55	6	
Lesotho*	451/4	3	
Maldive Islands	918/21	3	
Mauritius*	615/17	3	—
Montserrat	510/15	6	
New Zealand	1247/8	2	—
Niue	430/3	3	
Norfolk Island*	262/4	3	—
Pitcairn Islands*	219/21	3	—
St. Helena*	378/80	3	—
St. Kitts-Nevis			
St. Kitts	75/81	6	
Nevis	72/8	6	
St. Lucia	576/9	3	
St. Vincent	668/74	6	
Grenadines of St. Vincent	195/201	6	
Samoa*	599/601	3	—
Seychelles	505/11	6	
Zil Elwagne Sesel	23/9	6	
Sierra Leone*	668/74	6	
Solomon Islands*	445/7	3	—
Swaziland*	376/8	3	—
Tanzania	325/7	2	1
Tonga	785/8	4	—
Tristan da Cunha*	308/10	3	—
Turks and Caicos Islands	653/6	3	
Caicos Islands	8/11	3	
Tuvalu	168/74	6	
Uganda	341/8	6	
Vanuatu*	315/17	3	—
Total number of items		244	3

The Lesotho miniature sheet, No. **MS**454, and Sierra Leone Nos 671/3 do not form part of the Crown Agents Omnibus issue.

1982 PRINCESS DIANA'S 21st BIRTHDAY

Country	*Catalogue Nos.*	*Stamps*	*MS*
Anguilla	507/14	6	
Antigua	748/51	3	
Barbuda	624/30	6	
Ascension*	322/5	4	—
Bahamas*	622/5	4	—
Barbados*	705/8	4	—
Belize	680/6	6	
British Antarctic Territory*	109/12	4	—
British Virgin Islands*	488/91	4	—
Cayman Islands*	549/52	4	—
Cook Islands	833/7	4	1
Aitutaki	411/14	3	1
Penrhyn	250/5	5	1
Dominica	821/4	3	1
Falkland Islands*	426/9	4	—
Dependencies*	108/11	4	—
Fiji*	640/3	4	—
Gambia*	476/9	4	—
Grenada	1188/94	6	1
Grenadines of Grenada	493/9	6	1
Guyana	979/81	3	—
Jamaica	551/7	6	1
Kiribati	183/5	3	—
Lesotho*	514/17	4	—
Maldive Islands	964/7	3	1
Mauritius*	643/6	4	—
Montserrat	542/4	3	—
Niue	454/7	3	1
Pitcairn Islands*	226/9	4	—
St. Helena*	397/400	4	—
St. Kitts-Nevis			
St. Kitts	95/7	3	—
Nevis	85/7	3	—
St. Lucia	625/8	3	1
St. Vincent	694/6	3	—
Grenadines of St. Vincent	229/31	3	—
Sierra Leone	707/10	3	1
Solomon Islands*	467/70	4	—
Swaziland*	404/7	4	—
Tristan da Cunha*	327/30	4	—
Turks and Caicos Islands	709/12	3	1
Tuvalu	184/6	3	—
Uganda	374/7	1	1
Total number of items		162	19

1982 BIRTH OF PRINCE WILLIAM

Country	*Catalogue Nos.*	*Stamps*	*MS*
Great Britain			
Isle of Man	**MS**227	—	1
Antigua	757/60	3	1
Barbuda	613/16, 632/5	6	2
Belize	707/20	12	2
Cook Islands	838/47, 856/61	13	3
Aitutaki	415/24	9	1
Penrhyn	256/72	15	2
Dominica	830/3	3	1
Grenada	1200/6	6	1
Grenadines of Grenada	505/11	6	1
Guyana	982/7	6	—
Jamaica	558/64	6	1
Kiribati	186/8	3	—
Lesotho	521/2	2	—
Maldive Islands	968/72	4	1
Mauritius	647	1	—
Niue	458/74	13	4
St. Kitts-Nevis			
St. Kitts	98/100	3	—
Nevis	88/90	3	—
St. Vincent	699/701	3	—
Grenadines of St. Vincent	234/6	3	—
Sierra Leone	711/14	3	1
Tuvalu	189/91	3	—
Total number of items		124	22

1985 LIFE AND TIMES OF QUEEN ELIZABETH THE QUEEN MOTHER

Country	Catalogue Nos.	Stamps	MS
nguilla	655/8	3	1
ntigua	946/9	3	1
Barbuda	776/82, 809/15 826/9	17	1
scension*	376/80	4	1
ahamas*	712/16	4	1
arbados*	779/83	4	1
elize	827/31	4	1
ermuda*	494/8	4	1
ritish Virgin Islands	579/87	8	1
ook Islands	1035/9	4	1
Aitutaki	523/7	4	1
Penrhyn	378/82	4	1
ominica	949/52	3	1
alkland Islands*	505/9	4	1
Dependencies*	129/33	4	1
iji*	701/5	4	1
ambia	586/9	3	1
hana	1140/3	3	1
renada	1426/9	3	1
Grenadines of Grenada	689/92	3	1
uyana	1536/9	3	1
ong Kong*	493/6	4	—
amaica*	625/9	4	1
esotho	635/9	4	1
aldive Islands	1099/102	4	1
auritius*	699/703	4	1
ontserrat	636/44	8	1
iue	587/90	3	1
orfolk Island*	364/8	4	1
itcairn Islands*	268/72	4	1
t. Helena*	454/8	4	1
t. Kitts-Nevis			
Nevis	309/17	8	1
t. Lucia	832/40	8	1
t. Vincent	910/18	8	1
Grenadines of St. Vincent	403/11	8	1
amoa*	700/4	4	1
eychelles*	614/18	4	1
Zil Elwannyen Sesel*	115/19	4	1
ierra Leone	872/5	3	1
olomon Islands*	538/42	4	1
waziland*	486/90	4	1
anzania	425/9	4	1
onga	915/18	4	—
ristan da Cunha*	390/4	4	1
urks and Caicos Islands	854/7	3	1
Caicos Islands	82/5	3	1
uvalu	334/42	8	1
ganda	478/9	1	1
anuatu*	406/10	4	1
ambia	432/5	4	—
otal number of items		226	47

1986 QUEEN ELIZABETH II's 60th BIRTHDAY

Country	Catalogue Nos.	Stamps	MS
reat Britain	1316/19	4	—
Guernsey	365	1	—
Isle of Man	328/30	3	—
Jersey	389	1	—
nguilla	711/14	3	1
ntigua	1005/8	3	1
Barbuda	861/4, 872/5	6	2
scension*	397/401	5	—
ustralia	1009	1	—
ahamas*	741/5	5	—
arbados*	810/14	5	—
elize	905/9	4	1
ermuda*	524/8	5	—
ritish Virgin Islands	600/4	4	1
ayman Islands*	621/5	5	—
ook Islands	1065/8	3	1
Aitutaki	542/3	1	1
Penrhyn	394/6	3	—
yprus—Turkish Cypriot Posts	201	1	—
ominica	998/1001	3	1
alkland Islands*	522/6	5	—
iji*	714/18	5	—
ambia	641/4	3	1
ibraltar	540	1	—
renada	1499/502	3	1
Grenadines of Grenada	753/6	3	1
uyana	1684/5	1	1
ong Kong*	512/16	5	—
amaica*	646/50	5	—
iribati*	251/5	5	—
esotho	701/4	3	1
aldive Islands	1170/3	3	1
auritius*	724/8	5	—
ontserrat	677/81	4	1
iue	615/19	3	2
orfolk Island	389/92	4	—
apua New Guinea*	520/4	5	—
itcairn Islands*	285/9	5	—
t. Helena*	477/81	5	—
t. Kitts—Nevis			
St. Kitts	185/8	4	—
Nevis	384/8	4	1
t. Lucia	876/85	8	2
t. Vincent	978/82, 996/1000	8	2
Grenadines of St. Vincent	459/63	4	1
amoa*	726/30	5	—
eychelles*	639/43	5	—
Zil Elwannyen Sesel*	128/32	5	—
ierra Leone	937/40	3	1
olomon Islands*	562/6	5	—
outh Georgia and Sandwich Islands*	153/7	5	—
waziland*	500/4	5	—
anzania	517/21	4	1
onga	941/3	3	—
rinidad and Tobago	712/15	4	—
ristan da Cunha*	406/10	5	—
Tuvalu	381/5	4	1
Uganda	526/9	3	1
Vanuatu*	429/33	5	—
Zambia*	453/7	5	—
Total number of items		233	28

1986 ROYAL WEDDING

Country	Catalogue Nos.	Stamps	MS
Great Britain	1333/4	2	—
Guernsey	369/70	2	—
Isle of Man	326/7	2	—
Jersey	395/6	2	—
Anguilla	720/4	4	1
Antigua	1019/22	3	1
Barbuda	891/4	3	1
Ascension*	407/8	2	—
Bahamas*	756/7	2	—
Barbados*	822/3	2	—
Belize	941/4	3	1
British Virgin Islands	605/9	4	1
Cayman Islands*	633/4	2	—
Christmas Island*	220/1	2	—
Cook Islands	1075/7	3	—
Aitutaki	547/8	1	1
Penrhyn	400/1	2	—
Cyprus—Turkish Cypriot Posts	200	1	—
Dominica	1018/21	3	1
Falkland Islands	536/8	3	1
Gambia	664/7	3	1
Gibraltar	**MS**545	—	1
Grenada	1512/15	3	1
Grenadines of Grenada	762/5	3	1
Jamaica*	656/7	2	—
Lesotho	736/9	3	1
Maldive Islands	1179/82	3	1
Montserrat	691/5, 705/8	8	1
Niue	625/6	1	1
Pitcairn Islands*	290/1	2	—
St. Helena*	486/7	2	—
St. Kitts—Nevis			
St. Kitts*	189/90	2	—
Nevis	406/10, 454/7	8	1
St. Lucia	890/3, 897/901	8	1
St. Vincent	1009/13, 1022/5	8	1
Grenadines of St. Vincent	481/5, 486/9	8	1
Seychelles*	651/2	2	—
Zil Elwannyen Sesel*	133/4	2	—
Sierra Leone	946/9	3	1
Solomon Islands*	568/9	2	—
South Georgia and Sandwich Islands	158/60	3	—
Tristan da Cunha*	415/16	2	—
Turks and Caicos Islands	893/6	3	1
Tuvalu	397/401, 433/6	8	1
Uganda	535/8	3	1
Zambia*	458/9	2	—
Total number of items		142	24

1987 ROYAL RUBY WEDDING

Country	Catalogue Nos.	Stamps	MS
Anguilla	788/91	4	—
Antigua	1149/53	4	1
Barbuda	1029/33	4	1
Ascension*	447/51	5	—
Belize	980/4	4	1
Cook Islands	1193/4	2	—
Aitutaki	572/4	3	—
Penrhyn	413/14	2	—
Dominica	1109/13	4	1
Gambia	765/9	4	1
Grenada	1737/41	4	1
Grenadines of Grenada	928/32	4	1
Guyana	2233/4	1	1
Kiribati*	279/83	5	—
Lesotho	806/9	3	1
Maldive Islands	1282/5	3	1
Montserrat	739/42	8	—
Niue	657/8	2	—
St. Helena*	514/18	5	—
St. Vincent	1079/84	5	1
Grenadines of St. Vincent	536/41	5	1
Seychelles*	674/8	5	—
Zil Elwannyen Sesel*	157/61	5	—
Sierra Leone	1116/20	4	1
Swaziland*	537/40	4	—
Tristan da Cunha*	438/42	5	—
Turks and Caicos Islands	922/4	3	—
Tuvalu	484/9	5	1
Vanuatu*	487/91	5	—
Total number of items		117	14

1990 QUEEN MOTHER'S 90TH BIRTHDAY

Country	Catalogue Nos.	Stamps	MS
Great Britain	1507/10	4	–
Isle of Man	448	1	–
Anguilla	859	1	–
Antigua	1415/19	4	1
Barbuda	1206/10	4	1
Ascension*	525/6	2	–
Bahamas*	880/1	2	–
Barbados*	919/20	2	–
British Antarctic Territory*	186/7	2	–
British Indian Ocean Territory*	106/7	2	–
British Virgin Islands	746/50	4	1
Cayman Islands*	711/12	2	–
Cook Islands	1245/6	1	1
Aitutaki	**MS**614	–	1
Penrhyn	445/6	1	1
Dominica	1373/7	4	1
Falkland Islands*	606/7	2	–
Gambia	1060/3	3	1
Grenada	2131/4	3	1
Grenadines of Grenada	1262/5	3	1
Kenya*	545/6	2	—
Kiribati*	341/2	2	–
Lesotho	967/70	3	1
Maldive Islands	1396/9	3	1
Niue	689/90	1	1
Pitcairn Islands*	378/9	2	–
St. Helena*	570/1	2	–
St. Kitts-Nevis			
Nevis	555/8	3	1
St. Lucia*	1053/4	2	–
St. Vincent	1536/9	3	1
Grenadines of St. Vincent	705/32	27	1
Seychelles*	782/3	2	—
Zil Elwannyen Sesel*	212/13	2	—
Sierra Leone	1493/6	3	1
Solomon Islands*	675/6	2	–
South Georgia and South Sandwich Islands*	195/6	2	–
Swaziland*	570/1	2	–
Tristan da Cunha*	498/9	2	–
Turks and Caicos Islands	1045/9	4	1
Uganda	816/19	3	1
Total number of items		119	19

65TH BIRTHDAY OF QUEEN ELIZABETH II AND 70TH BIRTHDAY OF PRINCE PHILIP

Country	Catalogue Nos.	Stamps	MS
Ascension*	539/40	2	—
Australia	1286	1	—
Bahamas*	913/14	2	—
Belize*	1104/5	2	—
Bermuda*	634/5	2	—
Cook Islands	1255	1	—
Aitutaki	622	1	—
Penryhn	456	1	—
Grenada Grenadines	1385/9	4	1
Kiribati*	366/7	2	—
Maldive Islands	1506/10	4	1
Mauritius*	849/50	2	—
Niue	706	1	—
Pitcairn Islands*	399/400	2	—
St. Helena*	591/2	2	—
St. Kitts-Nevis			
St. Kitts*	336/7	2	—
Nevis	622/6	4	1
St. Vincent	1686/90	4	1
Grenadines of St. Vincent	750/4	4	1
Samoa*	861/2	2	—
Seychelles*	799/800	2	—
Zil Elwannyen Sesel*	234/5	2	—
Solomon Islands*	692/5	2	—
South Georgia and South Sandwich Islands*	201/2	2	—
Swaziland*	592/3	2	—
Tristan da Cunha	514/17	4	—
Turks and Caicos Islands	1099/1103	4	1
Uganda	942/6	4	1
Vanuatu*	576/7	2	—
Total number of items		69	7

40TH ANNIV OF QUEEN ELIZABETH II'S ACCESSION

Country	Catalogue Nos.	Stamps	MS
Great Britain	1602/6	5	—
Guernsey	552/5	4	—
Isle of Man	508/12	5	—
Ascension*	569/73	5	—
Bahamas*	928/32	5	—
Bermuda*	640/4	5	—
British Indian Ocean Territory*	119/23	5	—
Cayman Islands*	737/41	5	—
Falkland Islands*	647/51	5	—
Gibraltar*	673/7	5	—
Hong Kong*	691/5	5	—
Kenya*	561/5	5	—
Kiribati*	377/81	5	—
Pitcairn Islands*	409/13	5	—
St. Helena*	607/11	5	—
St. Kitts-Nevis			
St. Kitts*	350/4	5	—
Samoa*	876/80	5	—
Seychelles*	810/14	5	—
Zil Elwannyen Sesel*	240/4	5	—
Solomon Islands*	713/7	5	—
South Georgia and South Sandwich Islands*	209/13	5	—
Tristan da Cunha*	526/30	5	—
Turks and Caicos Islands	1145/53	8	2
Vanuatu*	587/91	5	—
Zambia*	664/8	5	—
Total number of items		127	2

Index

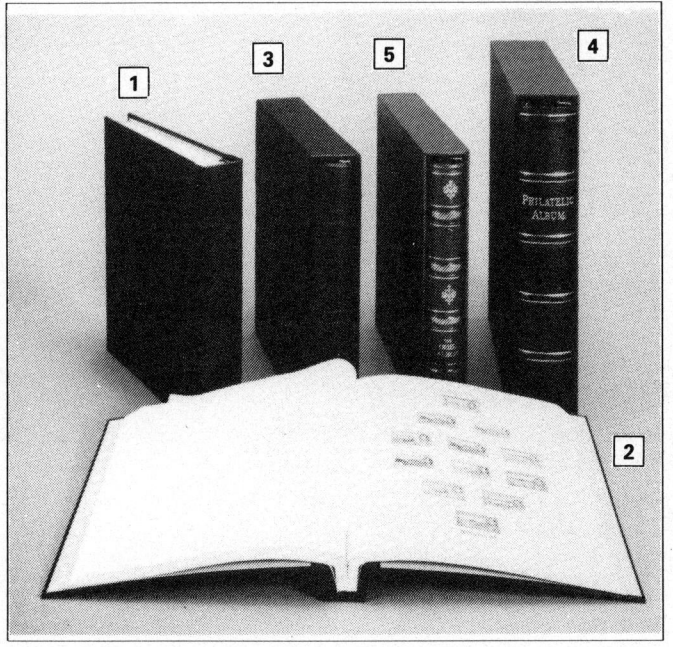